1974 Edition

THE WORLD ALMANAC®

and BOOK OF FACTS

The Authority Since 1868

Executive Editor

George E. Delury

Associate Editors

Albert C. Aumuller • Vincent P. Bannan • Kenneth C. Johnston

Senior Assistants

Thomas J. McGuire • Florence Byrnes • Clive D. Louden

Hana Umlauf

Senior Editor, Canada

Dr. Paul W. Fox

Glenda M. Patrick, Asst. Ed.

Publisher

Edward R. Kennedy

The World Almanac, 230 Park Avenue, New York, N.Y. 10017

Published Annually by

NEWSPAPER ENTERPRISE ASSOCIATION

Hard Cover Edition: Doubleday and Co., Inc.
Microform Editions since 1868: Bell and Howell Co.
Library of Congress Card Number 4-3781
California State Adoption Code No. 50/3657
ISSN 0084-1382
Copyright© Newspaper Enterprise Association, Inc. 1973
Printed in the United States of America

NEWSPAPER ENTERPRISE ASSOCIATION, INC., 230 Park Avenue, New York, N.Y. 10017, 1200 West Third Street, Cleveland, Ohio 44113. Robert Roy Metz, president; Earl H. Anderson, vice president and general manager; Edward R. Kennedy, vice president-publications.

QUICK REFERENCE INDEX

First Class Postal Rates in Brief

(As of Oct. 30, 1973; for detailed postal information on all classes of mail, see pages 1033-1039.)

United States Domestic

Letters—8¢ per ounce or fraction thereof, limit 12 ounces.
Air Mail Letters—11¢ an ounce or fraction thereof; limit 8 ounces. Includes mail to Armed Forces outside U.S. when addressed APO or FPO, New York, N.Y., San Francisco, Calif., or Seattle, Wash.
Postal Cards—6¢ each (up to 4½ x 6 in.) Double cards, 12¢. Private cards, 12¢.
Air mail post cards—9¢ each.

United States International

Letters—(1) Canada and Mexico, 8¢ per ounce to 12 ounces; over 12 ounces to 1 pound, $1.00; over 1 pound to 1½ pounds, $1.50; over 1½ to 2 pounds, $1.77; over 2 to 2½ pounds, $2.16; over 2½ to 3 pounds, $2.54; over 3 to 3½ pounds, $2.93; and over 3½ to 4 pounds, $3.31. TO CANADA ONLY: Over 4 to 4½ pounds, $3.70; over 4½ to 5 pounds, $4.08; over 5 pounds, 80¢ each pound or fraction.
(2) Countries other than Canada and Mexico, 1 ounce, 15¢; over 1 to 2 ounces, 26¢; over 2 to 4 ounces, 34¢; over 4 to 8 ounces, 76¢; over 8 ounces to 1 pound, $1.44; over 1 to 2 pounds, $2.40; and over 2 to 4 pounds, $3.84.
Air Mail Letters—(1) Canada and Mexico, 11¢ per ounce. (2) Cen. America, S. America, the Caribbean Is., Bahamas, Bermuda and St. Pierre and Miquelon, 17¢ per half ounce. (3) All other countries, 21¢ per half ounce.
Aerogrammes—To all countries, 15¢ each.
Postal cards—To Canada and Mexico 6¢ each. To all other countries, 10¢ each.
Air mail post cards—To Canada and Mexico 9¢ each, to other countries 15¢ each.

Canada

Domestic—1 oz., 8¢; 1-2 oz., 14¢; 2-4 oz., 20¢; 4-8 oz., 32¢; 8-12 oz., 44¢; 12 oz.-1 lb., 54¢. **Postcards** 10¢.
International—Letters to U.S.: by air, 10¢ each oz.; surface—same as domestic first class, except: 8 oz.-1 lb., 54¢; 1-2 lb., $1.50; 2-4 lb., $3.00. **Letters other than to U.S.:** 1 oz., 15¢; 1-2 oz., 30¢; 2-4 oz., 40¢; 4-8 oz., 90¢. **Postcards** 10¢.
Aerogrammes 15¢.

531
W92w
1974

General Index

Late News, Addenda, Changes

U.S. ADMINISTRATION (Pp 818-821)

Vice President: Spiro T. Agnew resigned Oct. 10; Gerald R. Ford, House minority leader, was nominated by Pres. Nixon, Oct. 12.

Secy. of State: Henry A. Kissinger was confirmed by the Senate Sept. 21.

Attorney General: Sen. William B. Saxbe (R., Ohio) was named by President Nixon Nov. 1 to succeed Elliot L. Richardson.

Secy. of Commerce: The correct spelling should be Frederick B. Dent.

Secy. of Health, Education and Welfare: Caspar W. Weinberger.

Secy. of Housing and Urban Development: James T. Lynn.

Secy. of Transportation: Claude S. Brinegar.

Deletions: Where the names Elliot L. Richardson, Richard G. Kleindienst and William D.

Ruckelshaus appear they should be deleted.

Department of State

Ambassador at Large—Ellsworth Bunker, confirmed.

Asst. Secy. for Public Affairs—Carol C. Laise, confirmed.

Treasury Department

Under Secretary—Helmut Sonnenfeldt, nominated.

Deputy Under Secy.—William L. Gifford, confirmed.

U.S. Secret Service—James J. Rowley, retired.

Department of Defense

Asst. Secy. for Manpower & Reserve—William K. Brehm, confirmed.

(Continued on page 34)

(Continued from page 33)

Army Under Secretary—Herman R. Staudt, confirmed.

Navy Under Secretary—J. William Middendorf 2nd, confirmed.

Secy. of the Air Force—John L. McLucas, confirmed.

Department of Justice

Asst. Attorney Gen., Administrative—Glen E. Pommerening, confirmed.

Federal Bureau of Investigation—Clarence M. Kelley, confirmed.

Department of the Interior

Bureau of Land Management—Curtis J. Berklund, confirmed.

Department of Agriculture

Foreign Agriculture Service—David L. Hume, confirmed.

Department of Commerce

Under Secretary of Commerce—John K. Tabor, confirmed.

General Counsel—Karl B. Bakke, confirmed.

Office of Foreign Direct Investments—Robert H. Enslow, confirmed.

Department of Health, Education, and Welfare

Assistant Secretaries: Planning and Evaluation—William Morrill, confirmed; Education—Charles Saunders, acting; Comptroller—John D. Young, confirmed.

General Counsel—John B. Rhinelander, confirmed.

Social and Rehabilitation Service—James Dwight, confirmed.

Commissioner of Social Security—James B. Cardwell, nominated.

Commissioner of Food & Drug Admin.—Dr. Alexander Schmidt, confirmed.

Surgeon General, Public Health Service—Dr. Paul Ehrlich, acting.

U.S. GOVERNMENT AGENCIES (P 840)

Russell E. Train was confirmed Aug. 2 as administrator of the Environmental Protection Agency, succeeding Robert F. Fri.

William Colby was confirmed as director of the Central Intelligence Agency.

Alvin J. Arnett became director of the Office of Economic Opportunity.

GOVERNORS (P 835)

In the election for governor of Virginia, between Lt. Gov. Henry Howell, independent, and ex-Gov. Mills Godwin, Republican, the latter was the winner. (P 839)

In the election for governor of New Jersey, between Charles W. Sandman, Jr., Republican, and Brendan T. Byrne, Democrat, the latter was the winner. (P 838)

HEADS OF STATE (Pp 626-7)

Argentina: Juan D. Peron was sworn in as President Oct. 12, 18 years after his overthrow and exile; his 3d wife Isabel became Vice President,

1st woman to hold that post in the Western Hemisphere.

Canada: Jules Leger of Quebec was appointed Governor-General Oct. 5 to succeed Roland Michener who will retire in Jan. 1974.

East Germany: Willi Stoph was named State Council Chairman, or President, and was succeeded as Premier by Horst Sindermann, Oct. 3.

Norway: Labor party leader Trygve M. Bratteli became Premier Oct. 16.

Thailand: Sanva Dharmasakti became Premier Oct. 14 after violence between troops and students.

U.S. CONGRESS (Pp 831-4)

Robert O. Bauman, a Republican, was elected Aug. 21, to fill the 1st Maryland District seat in the House of Representatives which became vacant upon the death of William O. Mills. (P 832)

Rep. John P. Saylor, Republican, Pennsylvania 12th District, died Oct. 28. (P 833)

AMBASSADORS (Pp 821-2)

New ambassadors, named by the President and confirmed by the Senate, included:

Afghanistan: Theodore L. Eliot, Jr.
Bahamas: Ronald I. Spiers.
Central African Rep.: William N. Dale.
Denmark: Philip K. Crowe.
Dominican Republic: Robert A. Hurwitch.
Ecuador: Robert C. Brewster.
Morocco: Robert G. Neumann.
Nepal: William I. Cargo.
Netherlands: Kingdon Gould, Jr.
Norway: Thomas R. Byrne.
Pakistan: Henry A. Byroade.
Saudi Arabia: James E. Akins.
Somali Democratic Rep.: Roger Kirk.
Thailand: William R. Kintner.

Ambassador Emory Swank ended his tour in Cambodia, placing Thomas O. Enders in charge.

Vincent W. de Roulet resigned as ambassador to Jamaica.

Robert F. Corrigan resigned as ambassador to Rwanda.

New envoys to the U.S. included:

Australia: Sir Patrick Shaw.
Bahamas: Sen. Livingston Basil Johnson.
Ireland: John G. Molloy.

SPORTS (Pp 884-978)

Baseball: Gene Mauch of the Montreal Expos was named National League manager of the year (his 3rd win); Earl Weaver of the Baltimore Orioles was named in the American League.

Baseball: Tom Seaver of the N.Y. Mets won the National League Cy Young Award as outstanding pitcher, with a 19-10 record, most strike-outs (251) and lowest ERA (2.07). It was his 2d win.

Pro Football: O. J. Simpson of the Buffalo Bills became the first National Football League player ever to gain over 1,000 yds. in 7 games, actually 1,025, and broke a 39-year-old record with 39 rushes in one game, helping defeat the Kansas City Chiefs, 23-14, Oct. 29. The old record for rushes was 38, set by Harry Newman in 1934 and Jim Nance in 1966. Jim Brown set the old yards-gained record, 971, with the Cleveland Browns in 1963.

(Continued on page 46)

106th ANNIVERSARY EDITION

The World Almanac

and Book of Facts for 1974

The 198th anniversary of the adoption of the Declaration of Independence, 1776, falls on July 4, 1974. The 187th anniversary of the signing of the Constitution of the United States, 1787, falls on September 17, 1974. The Government declared the Constitution in effect March 4, 1798.

The first edition of the WORLD ALMANAC, a 120-page hand-set volume containing 12 pages of advertisements, was published by the NEW YORK WORLD 106 years ago, in 1868. Annual publication was suspended in 1876. Joseph Pulitzer, publisher of the New York World, revived the WORLD ALMANAC in 1886 with the goal of making it a "compendium of universal knowledge." It has been published annually since. In 1931, it was acquired by Scripps-Howard; until 1951 it bore the imprint of the New York World-Telegram, thereafter until 1967 that of the New York World-Telegram and Sun. It is now published in paper and cloth-bound editions by Newspaper Enterprise Association, Inc.

The origin of the word "almanac" is obscure. In modern Arabic, "al-manakh" means climate or weather. The word came to Western Europe from Spanish Arabic, where it meant calendar. However, the word does not appear to have been used in classical Arabic and its origins cannot be traced, with any certainty, beyond early medieval times.

Henry Adams (1838-1918) grandson of Presidents and noted American historian and essayist, wrote in his auto-biographical The Education of Henry Adams (1907): "Nothing in education is so astonishing as the amount of ignorance it accumulates in the form of inert facts."

☞ The Editor acknowledges with thanks the many letters, whether of helpful comment or criticism, that attest the usefulness of the WORLD ALMANAC, and invites suggestions for improvement of its services to readers. Because of the vast volume of the mail directed to the WORLD ALMANAC by its readers, it is not possible to send a personal reply to each writer. However, every communication will be read by the Editor, and all comments and suggestions will receive careful attention. Address: 230 Park Avenue, New York, N.Y. 10017.
The WORLD ALMANAC does not decide wagers.

Some Major Events and Trends of 1973
See Chronology and consult Index for More Complete Reports

Alarms of impeachment sounded on Capitol Hill as President Nixon fired Watergate special prosecutor Archibald Cox and momentarily defied a court order to surrender evidence in the Watergate case. A year of turmoil over the case reached a preliminary crisis when public outrage persuaded the President to turn the evidence over to the courts. Initial steps toward impeachment continued, however, placing greater burdens on an Administration handicapped by the accumulated weight of public distrust.

Untouched by the Watergate scandal, Vice President Spiro T. Agnew resigned and pleaded guilty to tax evasion on payments to him by Maryland contractors. Agnew was sentenced to 3-years probation and fined $10,000. In the first use of 25th Amendment procedures, President Nixon nominated Gerald Rudolph Ford, 60-year-old House minority leader from Michigan, to become the 40th Vice President.

Middle East tensions burst into war for the 4th time in 25 years. Egypt and Syria, in coordinated attacks on the Jewish holy day of Yom Kippur, attempted to retake territories lost in 1967. After 3 weeks of war with heavy casualties and materiel losses on both sides, the combatants accepted a ceasefire with international supervision.

Unprecedented peacetime price increases and sudden shortages of commonplace food items marked the American economic year, as the dollar was devalued for the 2d time in 14 months and price controls were reinstated.

Light at the end of the tunnel became reality with the signing of a Vietnam ceasefire agreement in January. Fighting continued between the Vietnamese, but all American troops were withdrawn and U.S. prisoners of war were repatriated by March 29.

Long-threatened energy shortages became reality when service stations began to ration gasoline and government controls were slapped on the allocation of heating fuels.

Ending nearly 3 years of proto-Marxist rule in Chile, military leaders overthrew the Government of Salvador Allende. Allende was found shot to death, reportedly a suicide.

Relatively important news stories appeared less significant during the turbulent year. Among these were the struggle between President Nixon and Congress over the bombing of Cambodia; the long face-off between Indian militants and federal officers at Wounded Knee, S.D.; and Soviet leader Brezhnev's visit to the U.S.; and the return of Juan Peron to power in Argentina.

Middle East: The Yom Kippur War

On the afternoon of Yom Kippur, the Jewish Holy Day of Atonement, the 4th and biggest Arab-Israeli War in 25 years erupted, **Oct. 6,** along the 103-mile-long Suez Canal and on the Golan Heights. Marked by heavy troop and material losses on both sides, the bitter conflict culminated, by month's end, in a tenuous cessation of hostilities, but not before the international arena had faced the danger of confrontation between the United States and the Soviet Union.

Although both sides accused the other of initiating hostilities, United Nations Observers in the Middle East reported that Egyptian forces had crossed the Suez Canal at 5 points and that Syrian forces had attacked at 2 points on the Golan Heights.

Insisting that Israeli forces had been massing for months, Syrian Pres. Hafez al-Assad said, "We did not allow the enemy to take us by surprise and our forces struck to repel this aggression at the right moment." Israeli Defense Minister Moshe Dayan claimed Israel had decided against a preventative assault to gain the political advantage of the nation under attack. He predicted Israel might lose some ground before completion of mobilization allowed a successful counterattack. The Israeli Government said its war aims were to inflict heavy casualties on the Arabs and thwart any Arab effort to alter the 1967 cease-fire lines.

During the early days of the war, Israeli strategy was characterized by an all-out effort to quickly regain the Golan Heights while maintaining a holding position in the Sinai. By **Oct. 10,** the Israeli command claimed they had driven the Syrian army back to the 1967 cease-fire line. Despite the introduction of Iraqi forces, Israel claimed, **Oct. 12,** that its forces had pushed to within 18 miles of Damascus. Advancement of a detachment of Jordan's best military formations to the Syrian front, **Oct. 13,** did not stem the Israeli threat.

A steady stream of Egyptian troops and armor crossed to the East bank of the Suez Canal to paint a very different picture for Israel in the Sinai. In a major setback, Israel, **Oct. 9,** was forced to abandon the Bar Lev line, a defense system of bunkers along the eastern bank of the Canal. As Egyptian Sam-6's stymied the Israeli air offensive, the Egyptians, by **Oct. 11,** established a bridgehead of about 60,000 men in the Sinai. However, Israel, **Oct. 14,** stemmed Egyptian attempts to breakout of its bridgehead.

Soviet Airlift

U.S. officials reported, **Oct. 10,** evidence the Soviets were airlifting military equipment to both fronts, an action which put a "new face" on the Middle East conflict. On **Oct. 15,** as the USSR pledged to "assist in every way" the Arab effort to recapture territory seized by Israel in 1967, the U.S. announced it had begun to supply military equipment to Israel to counter the Soviet airlift to the Arabs.

On **Oct. 16,** Israel announced it had sent a task force across the Suez Canal to attack Egyptian tanks, artillery and missile sites on the west bank. Egyptian Pres. Anwar el-Sadat called for a cease-fire based on immediate withdrawal of Israeli forces from territories occupied in 1967.

Heavy tank battles in the Sinai, **Oct. 17,** signalled the beginning of a climactic struggle for the area. While Israel refused to release information about its task force on the west bank, the Egyptian command denied the presence of any Israeli force on the west bank.

On the diplomatic front, the Soviet Union, **Oct. 17,** initiated high-level efforts to convince Egypt and Syria to use their successes to settle the Middle East conflict by diplomatic means. In Washington, D.C., 4 Arab foreign ministers meeting with President Richard M. Nixon, asked the U.S. to participate directly in mediation of the Arab-Israeli conflict.

In a heavy armored battle with Egyptian units on the Egyptian side of the Suez Canal, Israelis claimed, **Oct. 18,** they had driven a wedge several miles wide through Egyptian positions. Also on **Oct. 18,** Egypt announced that Soviet Premier Aleksi N. Kosygin had been in Cairo for 3 lengthy meetings with Pres. Sadat.

The Egyptians conceded, **Oct. 21,** that Israeli forces had established 2 beachheads on the west bank of the Suez but said the Israelis were "completely besieged." The Israeli command described their expanded west bank beachhead as 19 miles deep along a 25-mile front.

Meanwhile, on the international level, U.S. Secretary of State Henry A. Kissinger, **Oct. 20,** discussed the Middle East conflict with Soviet party leader Leonid A. Brezhnev in Moscow. In New York, meeting at the special request of the U.S. and USSR, the UN Security Council in the early morning hours of **Oct. 22,** passed, 14-0, a U.S.-USSR sponsored resolution calling for a cease-fire in place. The U.S. announced that the resolution had arisen directly from the Kissinger-Brezhnev talks in Moscow. Israeli representative Yosef Tekoah said Israel would participate if negotiations for a permanent peace were begun concurrently with the cease-fire. He also demanded a complete exchange of prisoners. Egypt announced it would accept the cease-fire if Israeli forces withdrew from all territories occupied since the 1967 Arab-Israeli war.

Cease Fire

In the Middle East, before the cease-fire went into effect, fighting was heavy, **Oct. 22,** along both the Suez and Syrian fronts. Twelve hours after the cease-fire began, fighting erupted again on the west bank of the Canal and each side accused the other of violating the truce. One Egyptian correspondent described the hostilities as "the most vicious fighting since the outbreak of the war."

Israel announced, **Oct. 24,** that through the office of the UN Truce Supervision Organization, she and Egypt had agreed on a new cease-fire. Despite sporadic shooting, the Syrian and Suez fronts were reported calm after the 2d cease-fire went into effect. Israel also announced that in the 1½ days between the 2 cease-fires, her forces, advancing 11 miles south of the city of Suez on the southern tip of the Suez Canal, had trapped and cut-off about 200 tanks and some 20,000 men of Egypt's Third Army.

In New York the Security Council met again, **Oct. 24,** to consider an Egyptian proposal that the U.S. and USSR send troops to the Middle East to supervise the cease-fire they had sponsored. The U.S. adamantly rejected the proposal. Soviet representative Yakov A. Malik avoided Soviet commitment but said the U.S. "should use its weight to bring Israel to order."

On **Oct. 25,** the U.S. startled the international community by suddenly placing its military forces on a worldwide "precautionary alert." Later in the day, Secretary of State Kissinger asserted that the U.S. was not seeking a confrontation with the USSR, but that "ambiguous" signs the USSR might intervene militarily in the Middle East had necessitated the alert. The sudden crisis abated abruptly when the USSR and U.S. joined in a Security Council vote barring the superpowers from participation in a Middle East peacekeeping force. Two hours later, Waldheim announced he was transferring 900 UN military officers currently on Cyprus to Egypt.

Pres. Nixon, in a press conference **Oct. 26,** described the events leading to the precautionary military alert as "the most difficult crisis" since the 1962 Cuban missile crisis. He said his close relationship with Brezhnev had enabled their 2 countries to ease the crisis. The next day, the USSR dismissed as "absurd" Nixon's justification for the alert.

On **Oct. 27,** as the cease-fire appeared to be holding, the UN Security Council approved arrangements for a 7,000-man UN peace-keeping force for an initial period of 6 months at a cost of $30 million to be shared by all UN members.

According to U.S. estimates, the toll in casualties and destruction of material during the 18 days of ferocious fighting was staggering. Israel had 4,100 men killed or wounded, Egypt 7,500 and Syria 7,300. Aircraft losses were put at 107 for Israel, 242 for Egypt and 179 for Syria. Israel lost 840 tanks, Egypt 895 and Syria 880.

The Watergate Crisis

It began with quiet meetings in the U.S. Attorney General's office to discuss a plot to plant listening devices in Democratic headquarters in the Watergate office complex in Washington, D.C. Less than 2 years later, the ramifications of the plot, its bungled execution and the subsequent cover-up of White House involvement ,had brought the nation to the brink of the gravest constitutional crisis since the Civil War.

Several of the cloak-and-dagger men arrested in the Democrats' headquarters were found to be connected to such varied activities as receiving illegal campaign contributions, burglarizing a psychiatrist's office, sending out scurrilous letters in the name of some Democrats to the detriment of others, hiding important witnesses in obscure hospitals, abusing CIA connections and other major indiscretions.

These crimes pointed toward potential major scandals: the alleged fixing of an anti-trust case against ITT in exchange for $400,000 worth of campaign assistance, the alleged quashing of a securities fraud case in exchange for another $200,000, the alleged granting of milk price increases and import quotas in exchange for promises of up to $2,000,000 in campaign contributions and acceptance of illegal corporate contributions from several major companies.

Beyond these irregularities, the President was beset by suspicion over his personal finances. What were the financial details of his purchase of the San Clemente estate? Was public money unjustifiably spent on his properties in Key Biscayne and San Clemente? Could he legally claim tax deductions for gifts of his papers to the National Archives? And what was the meaning of the $100,000 contribution from billionaire Howard Hughes, returned to the donor after it was left untouched for 3 years in the safe-deposit box of Nixon's closest personal friend?

Seldom, if ever, had so many allegations surrounded a President at one time, and in the midst of such major crises as the resignation of the Vice President in face of criminal charges and the outbreak of a war in the Middle East.

At the center of the storm, the hearings of the Senate Select Committee on Campaign Practices, during the summer and autumn of 1973, drew one of the largest daytime TV audiences in history. At issue was whether President Nixon knew of either the Watergate break-in or its cover-up.

The testimony, complex and often contradictory, did not provide an answer. But with the testimony unraveled and reassembled in chronological order, below, it is possible to see who did what, when, and according to whom. Where versions of events are in conflict or unverified, the source of each version is indicated in parentheses, e.g. (Dean) or (Hald).

--------------- WHO ---------------

Anderson, Jack — syndicated news columnist
Baldwin, A. C. — tape monitor for Watergate gang
Barker, B. L. — a leader of Watergate gang
Beard, Dita — lobbyist for ITT
Buchanan, P. J. — consultant to President
Bull, S. — assistant to President
Butterfield, A. P. — former secretary to President
Buzhardt, J. F. — counsel to President
Caulfield, J. J. — former employee of CRP
Chapin, D. L. — former secretary to President
CIA — Central Intelligence Agency
Colson, C. W. — former counsel to President
Cox, A. — former special Watergate prosecutor
CRP — Committee to Re-elect the President
Cushman, Gen. R. E. — former CIA dep. director
Dean, J. W. — former counsel to President
DNC — Democratic National Committee
Ehrlichman, J. D. (Ehrl) — former chief domestic advisor to President
Ellsberg, D. J. — released Pentagon Papers to the press.
Fielding, F. — assistant to Dean
Fielding, Dr. L. — Ellsberg's psychiatrist
Geneen, H. S. — ITT president.
Gonzales, V. R. — member of Watergate gang
Gray, P. L. — former FBI acting director
Haldeman, H. R. (Hald) — former chief of White House staff
Helms, R. M. — former CIA director
Higby, L. M. — assistant to Haldeman
Hunt, E. H. — a leader of Watergate gang, and a "plumber"
Huston, T. C. — White House aide, deviser of domestic intelligence plan in 1970.

ITT — International Telephone and Telegraph
Kalmbach, H. W. (Kalm) — Nixon's personal lawyer
Kleindienst, R. G. (Klein) — Attorney General, 3-1-72 to 4-30-73
Krogh, E. — assistant to Ehrlichman, head of "plumbers"
LaRue, F. C. (LaR) — aide to Mitchell at CRP
Liddy, G. G. — leader of Watergate gang, and a "plumber"
MacGregor, C. — chairman of CRP after 7-1-72
Magruder, J. S. (Mag) — former CRP asst. chairman
Mardian, R. C. (Mar) — former deputy manager of CRP
Martinez, E. R. — member of Watergate gang
McCord, J. W. (McC) — member of Watergate gang
Mitchell, J. N. (Mitch) — former Attorney General; chairman of CRP, 3-1-72 to 7-1-72
Moore, R. A. — counsel to President
O'Brien, L. F. — chairman of DNC
O'Brien, P. L. — a CRP attorney
Odle, R. C. — administrator of CRP
Peterson, H. E. (Pete) — assistant Attorney General
Porter, H. L. — former assistant at CRP
Reisner, R. (Reis) — assistant to Magruder
Segretti, D. H. — campaign saboteur
Sloan, H. W. — treasurer of CRP
Stans, M. H. — chairman of finance section of CRP
Strachan, G. C.(Strach) — assistant to Haldeman
Sturgis, F, A. — member of Watergate gang
Ulasewicz, A. T. — aide to Caulfield
Walters, Gen. V. A. (Walt) — dep. director of CIA
Young, D. R. — White House aide, a leader of the "plumbers"
Ziegler, R. L. — White House press secretary

--------------- WHAT, WHEN ---------------

1972

Jan 27 — Liddy presents $1-million espionage plan against Democrats to Mitchell, Magruder and Dean in the Attorney General's office. Plan rejected.

Feb 4 — Liddy presents $500,000 plan, same people, same place. Dean objects to discussing subject in Attorney General's office (Mitch). Targets for bugging discussed (Dean, Mag); not discussed (Mitch).

Feb 29 — Jack Anderson publishes alleged ITT memo (dated 6-25-71) by Dita Beard, describing success of

plan for settling an anti-trust problem in exchange for heavy ITT underwriting of costs of GOP 1972 convention.

Mar 1 — Mitchell becomes chairman of CRP.

Mar 2 — Liddy secretly conducts Dita Beard to seclusion in a Denver hospital, where she is subsequently questioned by Hunt as to the authenticity of the ITT memo.

Mar 10 — Last date for which campaign finance reports are required under old 1925 Corrupt Practices Act; no reports required for dates between March 11 and April 6.

37

Mar 17—Dita Beard says alleged ITT memo is a forgery.
Mar 24—FBI says alleged memo seems to be genuine.
Mar 30—At Key Biscayne, Mitchell, Magruder and LaRue discuss a $250,000 Liddy plan to bug the DNC, Democratic convention headquarters in Miami Beach, and Democratic candidates' offices. Plan rejected (Mitch); decision deferred (LaR); plan approved (Mag).
—Memo from Colson to Haldeman about the Kleindienst nomination hearings: "... there is the possibility of serious additional exposure ... Ehrlichman assured Geneen that the President had 'instructed' the Justice Department with respect to the bigness policy. It is, of course, appropriate for the President to instruct the Justice Department on policy, but in the context of these hearings, that revelation would lay this case on the President's doorstep ... There is a Kleindienst to Haldeman memo dated June 30, 1971, which of course precedes the date of the ITT settlement, setting forth the $400,000 arrangement with ITT."
—About this time, Colson in a phone call to Magruder urges approval of Liddy plan budget (Mag; Colson confirms, but denies knowledge of plan details).
Mar 31 or later—Strachan is informed by Magruder of approval of "sophisticated intelligence plan" and he informs Haldeman (Strach).

Apr 3—U.S. company routes $100,000 contribution to CRP through Ogarrio, a Mexican lawyer.
Apr 6—Mexican money arrives at CRP in 4 bank drafts totalling $89,000 and $11,000 cash. Bank drafts are given to Liddy to turn into cash.
Apr 7—New campaign spending law becomes effective.
Apr 7(?)—Liddy tells Sloan he will soon need $83,000; Sloan checks with Magruder and Stans (Sloan). Stans checks with Mitchell (Sloan, Stans). Mitchell checks with Magruder who tells him the money is to buy equipment to initiate the Liddy plan (Mag). Mitchell instructs Stans that Magruder is authorized to disburse money to Liddy. (Stans).
Apr 10—Dahlberg converts a $25,000 contribution into a cashier's check in his name.
Apr 11—Dahlberg, a CRP fund raiser gives check to Stans; Stans to Sloan; Sloan to Liddy; Liddy to Barker.
Apr 12—Liddy gives McCord $65,000 in $100 bills to buy equipment and tells McCord Mitchell has approved the plan and wants it in operation within 30 days (McC).
Apr 19-20—Barker deposits Mexican bank drafts and Dahlberg check in his Miami bank account.

May 2—J. Edgar Hoover dies; Gray named acting FBI director on May 3.
May 28—First Watergate break-in; bugs are planted in DNC phones, DNC documents are photographed.

June 8—Kleindienst confirmed as Attorney General.
June 9—Magruder shows transcripts of bugs (called Gemstone file) and photographs of DNC documents to Mitchell; Mitchell subsequently complains they are no good and Liddy promises to correct problem (Mag; Mitchell denies all of above).
—At about same time, Gemstone material goes to Strachan (Mag, Reis).
June 17—McCord, Barker, Sturgis, Gonzales and Martinez arrested in DNC offices in early morning with photo and bugging equipment and large number of $100 bills in sequence.
—Liddy informs Magruder in California of arrests; LaRue, Mitchell and Magruder discuss problem (Mag).
—Magruder, by phone, instructs Reisner and Odle to remove certain files from his office (Odle).
June 19—Strachan tells Dean that Haldeman ordered him to destroy documents and that Haldeman's files are now clean (Dean, Strach; Haldeman denies requesting destruction of documents).
—Liddy tells Dean that Magruder pushed him into making the 2d break-in (Dean).
—Ehrlichman calls Dean and tells him to tell Liddy to tell Hunt to flee the country; order is rescinded when Colson protests (Dean).
—Colson tells Dean that Hunt's safe must be cleaned out; Dean instructs aide to take care of it (Dean).
—Mitchell, Dean, Magruder, Mardian and LaRue meet in Mitchell's apartment. Mitchell suggests that incrim-

inating files be destroyed (Mag, LaR); no such suggestion made (Dean, Mar, Mitch).
June 19 or 20—Dean expresses concern to Kleindienst that Watergate matter might lead to the President; Dean tells Peterson the White House might not be able to stand a wide-open investigation (Dean).
June 20—Mitchell-Nixon phone conversation. Mitchell apologizes to President for not knowing what was happening and for not having more control of the staff of CRP (Mitch). **Tape ordered by Cox; nonexistent.**
—President meets in Executive Office Building with Ehrlichman and Haldeman; they discuss government wire-tapping and perhaps Watergate (Ehrl). **Tape ordered by Cox.** About this time, Nixon instructs Ehrlichman and Haldeman to be sure the FBI investigation does not expose either any unrelated CIA operation or the work of the White House investigations unit (Nixon).
—DNC announces it will sue CRP for $1 million in civil damages; increased to $6.4 million in 1973.
—Dean gets contents of Hunt's safe; finds forged cables and files on Pentagon Papers and Ellsberg (Dean). Safe also contained a notebook of names, addresses, aliases and phone numbers of everyone Hunt dealt with in the anti-Democratic espionage operation (Hunt). Ehrlichman tells Dean to shred documents and "deep six" Hunt's brief case (Dean; Ehrlichman denies this).
—Liddy, Mardian and LaRue meet in LaRue's apartment. Liddy tells them of espionage operation, Ellsberg investigation and other activities (LaR; Mardian says meeting occurred on June 21).
June 21—Ehrlichman tells Gray to deal directly with Dean on Watergate matters (Ehrl).
—Gray tells Dean that Ogarrio and Dahlberg checks have been traced and raises possibility of CIA involvement in the break-in (Gray).
June 21 or 22—Mardian briefs Mitchell on Liddy's role in Watergate and other "White House horrors".
About June 21—Magruder suggests that Sloan lie to FBI about amount of money given to Liddy (Sloan).
June 22—Gray tells Dean evidence links Watergate break-in with CRP, and informs the prosecutors that money found on burglars and in Barker's bank is CRP money (Gray).
June 23—Haldeman, Ehrlichman, Helms and Walters meet at President's request. Haldeman makes vague references to Mexico and the CIA and tells Walters to speak to Gray about danger of FBI investigation into Mexican funds; Helms goes along with this because the President often knew things nobody else did (Helms). Helms repeatedly reassures Haldeman that no CIA operation in Mexico would be compromised (Walt). Meeting was held because Dean had said the FBI sought guidance on investigation aspects that might concern the CIA (Hald).
—Walters informs Gray that the FBI investigation is "likely" to expose a CIA operation (Gray, Walt).
—Walters later informs White House that no CIA operation is endangered, but Nixon doesn't believe him (Ehrl).
—Dean tells Gray to go slow investigating Ogarrio (Gray).
June 24—Mitchell, Stans and Magruder meet to discuss problem of amount of money given to Liddy, and Stans is asked to try to get Sloan to be "more cooperative" (Mag; Stans denies this).
June 26—Dean asks Walters for help with bail and salaries of jailed men; Walters refuses.
June 27—Dean tells Gray not to interview Dahlberg because of a CIA interest in him (Gray).
—Gray calls Helms to ask about Dahlberg and Ogarrio; Helms calls back to say that CIA has no interest in them (Gray).
June 28—Gray asks Ehrlichman who is to decide who the FBI will interview; Ehrlichman replies, "You do" (Gray).
—Mitchell fires Liddy from CRP job.
—Dean requests Walters' help to restrict FBI investigation (Walters memo of June 29).
—Gray, Dean and Ehrlichman meet in latter's office,

and Dean gives Gray 2 files from Hunt's safe. Ehrlichman and Dean suggest he destroy them (Gray). Gray is told they are "political dynamite" and "should never see the light of day" (Dean). Sensitivity of documents and need for secrecy is emphasized (Ehrl).

—Mitchell, LaRue, Mardian and Dean meet in Mitchell's office to discuss "the need for support money in exchange for the silence of" Liddy, Hunt and the jailed men; Dean is told to ask Ehrlichman and Haldeman for permission to contact Kalmbach to have him raise the money (Dean). Mitchell does not attend this meeting and subsequently goes along with support payments, not with money for silence (Mitch). Haldeman not informed of use of Kalmbach (Hald).

June 29 — Kalmbach and Dean meet in park in Washington and Kalmbach agrees to raise money secretly. Kalmbach immediately gets $75,000 from Stans at CRP.
June 30 — Kalmbach gives Ulasewicz $75,000 to pass on to the defendants.
—Nixon, Haldeman and Mitchell meet in President's EOB office. **Tape ordered by Cox.**
Late June — Kleindienst denies Dean access to raw FBI data.
July 1 — Mitchell resigns as CRP chairman, citing family problems.
July 6 — Walters and Gray meet; Walters tells Gray that he can't say or write that a full investigation would threaten CIA operations. Gray and Walters discuss their White House problems and Walters says he'll resign rather than give in (Gray; Walters memo of July 6).
—Nixon calls Gray to congratulate him on foiling an airplane hijack. Gray, on the strength of his earlier conversation with Walters, informs Nixon that men around him are attempting to "mortally wound" him by confusing the issue with the CIA (Gray, Walters). Gray suggests the Watergate investigation might lead higher, and Nixon tells him to press on (Nixon, 5-22-73). Nixon thinks Gray is suggesting that White House people weren't cooperating because they were reluctant to expose the CIA; he asks Gray if he had talked with Walters about that, urging him to press on when Gray said he had (Nixon, 8-22-73).
July 7 — Hunt's attorneys inform FBI their client will come in voluntarily.
July 8 (?) — Ulasewicz makes first payoff — to Bittman, Hunt's attorney.
Early July — Dean asks Gray for FBI reports on urging of Mitchell, Haldeman and Ehrlichman (Dean).
July 13 — LaRue suggests that Sloan take the 5th amendment or perjure himself; Sloan refuses and LaRue suggests he resign (Sloan). He does.
July 20 — Gray's legal advisor informs him that FBI records may not be released to anyone without the consent of the Attorney General.
July 21 — Gray begins sending FBI reports to Dean without Kleindienst's knowledge (Gray, Dean). The first report charges CRP attorneys are hampering the investigation. Mardian subsequently tells Dean to tell Gray to slow down the investigation (Dean; Mardian denies seeing reports).
July 26 — Kalmbach receives assurance from Ehrlichman that fund-raising for the Watergate defendants is legal and proper (Kalmbach).
Aug. 16 — After coaching by Dean and LaRue, Magruder commits perjury before the Watergate grand jury. Mardian was also present during coaching (Mag); not present (Mar).
Mid-Aug. — Kalmbach refuses to collect more money for the Watergate defendants.
Aug. 22 — Nixon nominated as Republican presidential candidate.
Aug. 26 — Government Accounting Office (GAO) report on CRP finances cites 11 possible violations involving up to $350,000, including $114,000 that ended up in Barker's bank account.
Aug. 29 — Nixon (at a press conference in San Clemente): "…under my direction, counsel to the President, Mr. Dean, has conducted a complete investigation of all leads which might involve any present members of the White House staff or anybody in the Government. I

can say categorically that his investigation indicates that no one in the White House staff, no one in this Administration, presently employed, was envolved in this very bizarre incident…we are doing everything we can to take this incident and investigate it and not to cover it up.…What really hurts is if you try to cover it up. I would say that here we are, with control of the agencies of the Government and presumably with control of the investigatory agencies of the Government with the exception of the GAO, which is independent. We have cooperated completely."
—Dean has never made such an investigation or report and fears he may be "set up" to take the blame (Dean).
—Ehrlichman: "….we kept informed through John Dean and other sources on the assumption that he was giving us complete and accurate reports."
—Haldeman: "Dean kept Ehrlichman and me posted from time to time on developments and, through us, the President."
Sept 15 — Federal grand jury indicts Liddy, Hunt, Barket, McCord, Sturgis, Martinez, and Gonzales for conspiracy and for the break-in.
—Dean meets with Nixon and Haldeman in White House. Discussion centers on DNC civil suit; Dean says nothing harmful will come out of further investigation and the President congratulates him on his handling of the whole Watergate matter — the indictments confirmed what Dean had been saying all along (Hald). Nixon congratulates Dean and expresses pleasure that indictments went no further than Liddy; Dean tells the President the case is not closed and the matter might still unravel; the conversation goes on to problems with the press and the use of the IRS against enemies (Dean). Dean gives Nixon "at that meeting no reason to believe that any others were involved" (Nixon). **Tape ordered by Cox.**
Sept 19 — Ulasewicz quits as payoff bagman; replaced by LaRue on Sept 21.
Nov 7 — Nixon is re-elected in a landslide.
Nov 24 — Hunt calls Colson; Colson tapes call: Colson tells Hunt not to give him any details of his involvement in the Watergate break-in. Hunt says, "We're protecting the guys who are really responsible.…(But) this is a two-way street," and asks for money. Colson replies: "I'm reading you, You don't need to be more specific."
Nov 30 — Hunt's wife Dorothy tells McCord he will get no money unless he pleads guilty, stays silent, and accepts executive clemency (McC).
Late Nov — Dean tells Haldeman that Watergate matter is likely to go back to the grand jury and that the jury would get into questions of obstruction of justice which would lead right to them; Haldeman says that Nixon wants to get the whole story out now that the election is over, but that Dean's information makes that approach look unlikely (Dean).
Early Dec — Mitchell tells Dean that a special fund of $350,000 controlled by Haldeman could be used to pay the Watergate defendants. Dean contacts Haldeman who approves (Dean; Mitchell says the suggestion was made to LaRue). The $350,000 is transfered to the CRP when it needs money to pay legal fees and family support of Watergate defendants (Hald). The funds were left over from the 1968 primary campaign (Hald).
Dec 2 — Colson resigns.
Dec 7 — A White House secretary, Dorothy Chenow, names Krogh, Young, Hunt and Liddy as members of a White House "plumbers" unit assigned to investigate leaks to the news media. Their reports were sent to Ehrlichman; their telephone bills to her house.
Dec 8 — Washington Post reports that Chenow says the "plumbers'" telephone was used mostly by Hunt to call Barker and that she forwarded the bills to Ehrlichman's office.
—Airplane crash in Chicago kills Dorothy Hunt; authorities recover her purse containing $10,000 in $100 bills.
Dec 12 — White House confirms existence of "plumbers" unit, but denies that Liddy and Hunt were members and that calls were made to Barker.
After Dec 25 — Gray burns Hunt files in the furnace of his Connecticut home.

1973

Jan 3 – Hunt repeats demand for more money and executive clemency (Dean; Hunt says he never asked for clemency).
Jan 4 – Dean learns from Ehrlichman that he has given Colson the go-ahead to offer clemency to Hunt (Dean).
Jan 8 – Ulasewicz, on instructions from Caulfield who is acting for Dean, calls McCord with a cryptic message suggesting clemency after one year.
Jan 10 – With jurors chosen, the Watergate criminal trial begins before Judge Sirica.
– Mitchell and P. O'Brien tell Dean that Caulfield should offer clemency to McCord (Dean; Mitchell says this is a complete fabrication).
Jan 11 – Hunt pleads guilty in the criminal trial.
Jan 12 – First McCord-Caulfield meeting: Caulfield offers clemency "from the highest levels of the White House."
Jan 14 – Second McCord-Caulfield meeting: Caulfield says everyone is "on track" except McCord.
Jan 15 – Barker, Gonzalez, Martinez and Sturgis plead guilty to the Watergate break-in.
Jan 18 – Ellsberg trial opens, in Los Angeles before Judge Byrne.
Jan 19 – Mitchell, Dean and LaRue ask Kalmbach to collect more money, but he refuses (Kalmbach).
Jan 20 – Richard M. Nixon is inaugurated for 2nd term as President of the United States.
Jan 25 – Third Caulfield-McCord meeting: Caulfield tells McCord he is "fouling up the game plan."
Jan 30 – Watergate jury finds Liddy and McCord guilty.

Early Feb – Colson tells Haldeman there may have been perjury and obstruction of justice at Watergate trial, and that payments to defendants could be seen as hush money; Haldeman says he knows about the payments and isn't worried (Colson).
Feb 7 – Senate votes 70-0 to establish Select Committee to investigate Watergate affair and other campaign practices.
Feb 10-11 – La Costa, near San Clemente, is site of strategy meeting of Dean, Ehrlichman, Haldeman and Moore to discuss executive privilege and/or Watergate hearings. The need for more money for Watergate burglars is discussed (Dean, Moore).
Feb 27 – Dean begins a series of nearly daily meetings with Nixon; this is their first meeting since Sept. 15. Nixon tells Dean to report to him directly on Watergate since Ehrlichman and Haldeman are "principals" in the matter (Dean).
– Nixon tells Ehrlichman and Haldeman to remove themselves from the Watergate problem and concentrate on more important things, while Dean concentrates on Watergate (Ehrl.).
Feb 14 – Colson tells Nixon he should force Mitchell to reveal his role in planning the Watergate bugging, but Nixon does not believe Mitchell or other top aides were involved (Colson).
Mid-Feb – P. O'Brien tells Dean that Magruder has just told him that final authorization for the Liddy plan came from Strachan, who said Haldeman had cleared the plan with the President; Dean tells this to Haldeman, who shows concern over the statement (Dean).
Feb 28 – Dean tells Nixon of his own role in the Watergate cover-up; Nixon tells him not to worry and not to go into any further detail beyond what was just said (Dean).
– Confirmation hearings on Gray's appointment as FBI director open. Gray reveals that he has been providing Dean with FBI files.
Mar 13 – Dean tells Nixon of money demands of Watergate burglars; Haldeman enters meeting and says there is no money to meet their demands; Nixon asks how much, Dean says $1 million, and Nixon says that is "no problem" (Dean). Nixon mentions that he discussed Hunt's clemency with Ehrlichman and Colson (Dean; Haldeman, after hearing the tapes of the Mar 21 meeting, said the items mentioned here by Dean were discussed Mar 21; Haldeman denies any memory of Mar 13 meeting)- **Tape ordered by Cox.**

Mar 15 – Dean, Nixon and Moore hold a meeting on routine matters (Dean).
Mar 17 – Nixon first learns of the burglary of Ellsberg's psychiatrist's office (Nixon).
Mar 20 – After Dean and Moore meet with Nixon, Moore tells Dean he thinks Nixon is unaware of the problems that worry Dean (Moore).
– Dean calls Nixon and says he thinks the President doesn't have all the facts or recognize their implications (Dean); a meeting is arranged for the following morning.
– Dean calls Haldeman to inform him that he is going to inform Nixon of the details; Haldeman agrees that is the best course (Dean).
Mar 21 – Dean tells Nixon of a cancer growing on the Presidency; that Mitchell had probably got records of the DNC bugs; that Haldeman probably got the same records through Strachan; that Kalmbach collected money for the Watergate burglars with the approval of Ehrlichman, Haldeman and Mitchell; that Dean coached Magruder on his perjury before the grand jury; and that White House cash was used for hush money. Nixon suggests Dean give the Cabinet a briefing on these matters (Dean). Dean says there was a cancer on the presidency, but that no White House people are involved in the break-in; that Magruder and perhaps Mitchell know of the Liddy operation; that the Colson call to Magruder about Liddy's plans could be misconstrued; that Haldeman might have gotten some bugging records through Strachan; and that there had been payoffs in response to pressure from Hunt. Nixon responds that payoffs would be wrong, that there could be no clemency, and that perhaps everyone should go to the grand jury and tell the truth (Haldeman, after hearing a tape of the conversation). **Two tapes ordered by Cox.**
– Dean, Haldeman and Ehrlichman discuss the need to get Mitchell to clarify his role in the Watergate affair (Dean). Meeting concentrated on question of executive privilege (Ehrl).
– Dean, Haldeman and Ehrlichman meet with Nixon; Dean, believing they mean to continue the cover-up, says that he, Haldeman and Ehrlichman are indictable (Dean).
– Dean tells Moore that he told the President everything and that the President was surprised (Moore).
– Nixon begins "extensive new inquiries" into the Watergate affair (Nixon).
Mar 22 – At Nixon's suggestion, Haldeman, Ehrlichman, Mitchell and Dean meet. Mitchell is not disturbed by the Watergate problem (Dean). Later, with Nixon, the 4 discuss the approaching Senate hearings and possible White House responses (Dean); they discuss problems of executive privilege (Ehrl). Mitchell suggests they all testify to the Senate Committee in executive session (Nixon). **Tape ordered by Cox.**
Mar 23 – Nixon tells Dean to go to Camp David, relax, and analyze the situation; later, Haldeman calls Dean at Camp David and tells him to write a report on all he knows about Watergate (Dean); written report requested by Nixon (Ehrl).
– Judge Sirica reads a letter from McCord which declares that others have escaped trial, that there was perjury during the trial, and that there was political pressure to plead guilty and remain silent.
– Sirica imposes provisional maximum sentences on Watergate burglars.
– McCord sees Senate Committee counsel accompanied by a new lawyer.
Mar 27 – Nixon "had a contact made with the Attorney General himself and...told him...to report to me directly anything he found" (Nixon).
Mar 28 – Ehrlichman-to-Kleindienst phone call is taped by Ehrlichman. Ehrlichman: "Now, the President said for me to say this to you: that the best information he had and has is that neither Dean nor Haldeman nor Colson nor I nor anybody in the White House had any prior knowledge of this burglary. He said that he's counting on you to provide him with any information to the contrary if it ever turns up and you just contact him direct. Now as far as the CRP is concerned, he said that serious questions are being raised

with regard to Mitchell and he would likewise want you to communicate to him any evidence…on that subject…" (Transcript provided to Senate Committee, source not known to editor.)

— Krogh tells Dean that the orders to break into the office of Ellsberg's psychiatrist came "from the Oval Office" of the President and that Ehrlichman did not know about it until after it was done (Dean; Krogh later states that it was done without the knowledge of "any superior").

Mar 30 — Nixon asks Ehrlichman to conduct the Watergate inquiry (Nixon), because Dean has failed to turn in a written report (Ehrl).

Apr 2 — Dean's lawyers inform federal prosecutors that Dean will give evidence freely.

Apr 5 — From P. O'Brien, Ehrlichman learns about the Liddy plan, that Magruder has named Mitchell as the approver of the plan, that Hunt was the leader of a group of agents planted in Democratic candidates' headquarters, and that Kalmbach was making payoffs (Ehrl).

— Ehrlichman, at San Clemente, tells Judge Byrne, who is presiding over the Ellsberg trial, that he is being considered for the post of FBI director; Nixon shakes hands with Byrne.

— Gray's nomination as FBI director is withdrawn.

Apr 8 — Dean talks with Watergate prosecutors.

Early Apr — Haldeman listens to the tape of the March 21 Nixon-Dean meeting at Nixon's request.

Apr 7 — Ehrlichman and Byrne meet again in Santa Monica.

Apr 8 — Dean, Haldeman and Ehrlichman meet. Dean tells them they are not indictable but that they are in an awkward situation, and Haldeman suggests that the problem stems from trying to cover-up for Mitchell (Ehrl).

Apr 12 — Magruder tells prosecutors he committed perjury.

Apr 14 — Ehrlichman gives his report to Nixon, implicating Mitchell, Dean and Magruder; he is directed to relay this to Kleindienst (Ehrl).

— Magruder tells an aide "it is all over," that Nixon has directed everyone to tell the truth.

— Dean talks to prosecutors, implicating Haldeman, Ehrlichman, Mitchell, Magruder.

— Magruder talks to prosecutors, implicating Dean and Mitchell.

— Prosecutors inform Kleindienst and Peterson of what Magruder and Dean have said. Kleindienst and Peterson meet with Nixon. Peterson recommends that Haldeman and Ehrlichman be fired but that Dean be retained because he is speaking freely. The president is "dumbfounded" (Klein); "calm" (Pete).

Apr 15 — Dean and Nixon meet. Nixon is cordial, asks leading questions — "which made me think that the conversation was being taped and that a record was being made to protect himself" (Dean). Nixon says that the statement about a $1 million being no problem was a joke; he also says, very quietly in a corner of the room, that he was probably foolish to discuss clemency with Colson (Dean). **Tape ordered by Cox; nonexistent.**

— Nixon orders all Administration members to tell the truth (Nixon).

— Haldeman, Ehrlichman and Gray meet. Gray tells them he has destroyed Hunt's files (Hald).

Apr 16 — Nixon requests Dean's resignation, presenting him with a letter to sign which Dean later calls a virtual confession. Dean refuses to resign unless Haldeman and Ehrlichman also resign (Dean).

Apr 17 — Nixon says that since March 21, as the result of serious charges which came to his attention, he has launched new inquiries which have resulted in major developments in the case.

Apr 18 — Peterson tells Nixon the Justice Department has learned that the office of Ellsberg's psychiatrist was burglarized. Nixon tells him to "stay out of that" because "this is a national security matter" (Nixon).

Apr 19 — CRP offers $525,000 to DNC to settle a $6.4-million civil damage suit out of court; offer rejected.

— Ehrlichman tapes a phone call with Kalmbach. Ehrlichman says that Dean is telling the prosecutors that he, Dean, was a "mere agent." Ehrlichman affirms

he assured Kalmbach about the propriety of collecting money, but maintains it was for a defense fund." Ehrlichman says Dean was told by the prosecutors that unless he implicates Ehrlichman and Haldeman he will get no consideration for his own problems. Ehrlichman advises Kalmbach not to "haul the President into it if you can help it." Ehrlichman emphasizes, several times, that he, Ehrlichman, acted only on the basis of what Dean told him. Ehrlichman suggests that Kalmbach say that he talked with Ehrlichman most recently in California and try to obscure the fact of the present phone call, without lying. (Transcript provided to Senate Committee by Ehrlichman.)

Apr 25 — Peterson and Kleindienst meet with Nixon to discuss the break-in at the office of Ellsberg's psychiatrist. Nixon agrees to make the break-in known to Judge Byrne at the Ellsberg trial.

Apr 27 — Gray resigns as acting director of the FBI after he reveals that he destroyed Hunt's files.

— Ehrlichman admits that he ordered a secret investigation of Ellsberg at Nixon's request.

— Nixon is informed by the Watergate prosecutors that Dean's demands for immunity do not justify his retention on the White House staff (from the White House account of June 27, later repudiated).

Apr 30 — White House announces the resignations of Haldeman, Ehrlichman and Dean. Kleindienst resigns the same day. Nixon concedes there has been a cover-up, but denies any personal knowledge of the cover-up or the break-in.

May 9 — FBI informs Byrne that Ellsberg was overheard in a tap on someone else's phone in 1969 or 1970, but says the tapes have been lost.

May 10 — Mitchell and Stans are indicted for conspiracy and perjury. They are alleged to have participated in quashing an investigation of a securities fraud in exchange for a $200,000 campaign contribution.

— Mardian tells the FBI that records of overheard Ellsberg calls may be in the White House.

May 11 — Judge Byrne dismisses the Ellsberg case, charging Government misconduct, especially in the loss of records of the overheard Ellsberg conversations.

— Wiretap records of Ellsberg's conversations are found in Ehrlichman's outer office.

— Ehrlichman says the wiretap files containing Ellsberg's conversations were in his safe for more than a year, but that he was unaware that they contained material on Ellsberg.

May 16 — Ziegler confirms that Nixon did not directly order Dean to investigate the Watergate break-in. He states that Ehrlichman received only one informal oral report from Dean.

May 17 — Senate Watergate hearings open.

May 18 — Cox is named special Watergate prosecutor.

May 19 — GAO charges that $460,000 of CRP money was used to pay off the Watergate burglars.

June 4 — Nixon listens to tapes of White House conversations (Ziegler says later that Nixon listened to more than 2 tapes; Bull says later that it was 8 to 10 tapes).

— Bull listens to the tape of the Nixon-Dean Moore meeting on March 15 and reports to Nixon on its contents (Ziegler later confirmed this in testimony to an executive session of the Senate Committee).

June 9 — Colson, in an extensive interview with the New York Times, states that he had withheld his story until the present because he feared Haldeman and Ehrlichman would try to frame him.

June 27 — LaRue pleads guilty to one count of conspiracy to obstruct justice; he confesses also to conveying over $300,000 to the Watergate burglars and their lawyers, and to destroying incriminating documents.

— Buzhardt, at Nixon's request listens to some tapes, including that of the 3-20-73 Nixon-Dean conversation, and reports to Nixon on contents (Buzhardt).

July 9 — Haldeman listens to the tape of the Nixon-Dean meeting of Sept. 15, 1972, at Nixon's request.

July 16 — Butterfield reveals that Nixon has been taping all phone calls and conversations in his offices in the White House, the Executive Building and Camp David since mid-1970.

(For further events, see Chronology.)

1973 Off-Year Elections

Americans voted decisively on issues and personalities in the "off-year" Nov. 6, 1973, elections but produced no clear patterns, despite several landslide Democratic victories. On the question of Watergate reaction and tax-and-spend issues, there were split decisions.

A smashing 2-to-1 victory was scored in New Jersey's battle for governor by Democrat Brendan T. Byrne, a judge and former prosecutor, over conservative Republican Congressman Charles W. Sandman, Jr. The Democrats also seized control of both legislative houses for only the third time in this century.

But in Virginia, Mills Godwin, a one-time Democratic governor who became a Republican, won a return to the gubernatorial mansion by narrowly defeating Lt. Gov. Henry Howell, another former Democrat running as an independent populist.

In New York City, soft-spoken Comptroller Abraham D. Beame, Democrat, won a smashing victory in a 4-way race for Mayor, polling more votes than the combined total of his opponents, who included a Republican and 2 other Democrats running under other banners. Beame will succeed retiring Mayor John V. Lindsay, a former Republican turned Democrat.

Voters resoundingly rejected attempts to give Texas legislators 300% pay raises and Washington state lawmakers 193% boosts.

Spending and Saving

Two perennial Republican Presidential hopefuls suffered sharp rebuffs on pet proposals: California Gov. Ronald Reagan's plan to put strict curbs on the legislature's revenue raising and spending powers, accompanied by an immediate 7.5% cut in state income taxes, was defeated.

New York Gov. Nelson A. Rockefeller's $3.5-billion transportation bond issue proposal likewise was turned down. It would have aided both mass transit and highways, but there was debate over how each would fare. N.Y. City voters gave it narrow approval but upstate it was soundly trounced.

The votes on opposite coasts thus saw New Yorkers turn down a huge spending plan while Californians in contrast rejected a wide-scale economy measure.

Blacks captured the mayoralty races in 2 cities, Detroit and Raleigh, N.C. The former was the 3d major city to elect a black mayor in 1973; earlier in the year, blacks had won in Los Angeles and Atlanta. But in Youngstown, Ohio, and Louisville, Ky., black candidates who ran as independents trailed well behind the major party white candidate in the November elections.

The Democratic victory in New Jersey, where the retiring governor was a Republican, and the GOP win in Virginia, where the retiring governor also was a Republican, increased the total number of Democratic governors to 32 as against 18 Republicans.

It was an exact reversal of the 1968 situation and the biggest lead in governorships for the Democrats since 1964 when they held 33.

States: Yes and No

In other state results:

Maine: Voters approved a state lottery by about 151,000 to 88,000. They turned down a proposal for a public power authority, strongly opposed by private utilities, by about 148,000 to 93,000.

Ohio: Voters approved 4 constitutional amendments providing a maximum $500 Vietnam War era veterans bonus, a real estate tax break for farmers, authority to the General Assembly to give large families more personal income tax exemptions than the current $3,000 ceiling, and a court reorganization plan.

Washington: Voters defeated a proposal to establish the state's first income tax by a 3-1 margin. They approved, by a similarly overwhelming margin, an initiative (a referendum put on the ballot by petition of citizens) to override a law passed by the legislature raising legislators' salaries by 193% and salaries of other state officials by somewhat lesser percentages. By the terms of the initiative which the voters approved the raises will be limited to 5.5%, in accord with the guideline set by the U.S. Cost of Living Council.

Beame's whopping win in the 4-way N.Y. City mayoralty race, in which he took over 56% of the vote, was accompanied by even larger percentage victories for 2 running-mates, Paul O'Dwyer for City Council president and Harrison J. Goldin for Beame's old job as comptroller. But O'Dwyer, brother of the late Mayor William O'Dwyer, and Goldin only had 2 opponents each.

City Reports

Results in other cities:

Buffalo: Democratic Mayor Stanley M. Makowski defeated Republican Stewart M. Levy in N.Y. State's 2d largest city.

Dearborn, Mich.: Orval Hubbard, 72, the nation's longest-serving mayor, won reelection to his 15th term; he had won every election since Nov. 4, 1941.

Cleveland: Republican Mayor Ralph J. Perk easily won a 2d term by a 2-1 margin over a last-minute Democratic challenger, Mercedes Cotner, in what was officially a nonpartisan race. She was a substitute for another Democrat who dropped out of the campaign.

Detroit: State Sen. Coleman A. Young, Democrat, became the city's first black mayor-elect by narrowly defeating John F. Nichols, a former police commissioner, white. Both candidates had sought to keep racism out of the campaign.

Grand Rapids, Mich.: Lyman S. Parks, a pastor of the African Methodist Church, became the city's first elected black mayor by narrowly defeating former mayor Robert Boelens.

Louisville, Ky.: Millionaire physician Harvey Sloane, Democrat, overwhelmingly defeated former police chief C.J. Hyde, Republican, for the job of mayor, Walter (Pete) Cosby, a black independent, ran 3d.

Miami: Maurice Ferre, millionaire industrialist who was born in Puerto Rico, garnered the needed majority of votes from a field of 7 to win the nonpartisan race for mayor.

Minneapolis: Alfred J. Hofstede, running with the endorsement of a rejuvenated Democratic-Farmer-Labor party, defeated independent incumbent Mayor Charles Stenvig in a close race.

Raleigh, N.C.: Clarence Lightner, a black city councilman, staged an upset victory over Wesley Williams, executive of the Raleigh Merchants Bureau, in the mayoralty race.

Seattle: Mayor Wes Uhlman, Democrat, won reelection despite a strong effort by his opponent, City Council President Liem Eng Tuai, son of a Chinese immigrant cook. Tuai had quit his council post to make the race.

Houston: Conservative Dick Gottlieb and liberal Fred Hofheinz far outpaced 5 other candidates in the campaign for mayor and were headed for a Dec. 4 runoff election.

Mayors and City Managers of Larger North American Cities

AS OF NOVEMBER 6 ELECTIONS, 1973

* Asterisk before name denotes city manager. All others are mayors. For mayors, dates are those of expiration of term, for city managers, they are dates of appointment.

D., Democrat; R., Republican; N-P, Non-Partisan.

City	Name	Term
Abilene, Tex......	*H. P. Clifton	1963, July
Abington, Pa......	*Fred Schaefer	1958, June
Akron, Ohio	John S. Ballard, R.	1975, Dec.
Alameda, Calif. ..	*H. D. Weller	1957, Oct.
Albany, Ga.......	*S. A. Roos	1961, Aug.
Albany, N.Y.	Erastus Corning, 2nd, D.	1975, Dec.
Albuquerque N.M.	*Herbert H. Smith	1972, July
Alexandria, La....	John K. Snyder, D.	1977, June
Alexandria, Va...	*Wayne F. Anderson	1970, Dec.
Alhambra, Calif...	*Harry S. Scott	1968, Sept.
Allen Park, Mich...	Frank J. Lada, N-P	1975, Nov.
Allentown, Pa. ...	Joseph Daddona, D. ...	1978, Jan.
Alton, Ill.	Paul A. Lenz, N-P	1977, Apr.
Altoona, Pa......	William C. Stouffer, R...	1976, Jan.
Amarillo, Tex.....	*John S. Stiff	1963, Sept.
Ames, Iowa	*J. R. Castner........	1964, Oct.
Anaheim, Calif. ..	*Keith A. Murdoch	1950, Dec.
Anchorage, Alas...	*Robert E. Sharp	1968, Apr.
Anderson, Ind....	Robert Rock, D.	1976, Jan.
Anderson, S.C....	*Charles B. Martin	1973, Mar.
Ann Arbor, Mich..	*G. C. Larcom, Jr.	1956, Apr.
Appleton, Wis. ..	Jas. P. Sutherland, N-P .	1976, Apr.
Ardmore, Calif	*Lyman H. Cozad	1966, Aug.
Arlington, Mass. .	*John H. McinNie	1966, Nov.
Arlington, Tex....	*Herman J. Vesclla	1976, Dec.
Arlington, Va. ...	*Bert Johnson	1962, Dec.
Arlington Hts., Ill.	*L. A. Hanson	1958, Oct.
Arvada, Colo.....	*Vacant	
Asheville, N.C. ...	*Ernest J. Ward	1972, Sept.
Athens, Ga.......	Julius Bishop, D.	1975, Nov.
Atlanta, Ga......	Maynard Jackson, D. ..	1977, Oct.
Atlantic City, N.J.	Joseph Bradway, Jr., N-P	1976, May
Auburn, N.Y......	*Bruce L. Clifford	1966, Aug.
Augusta, Ga.....	Lewis A. Newman	1975, Dec.
Aurora, Colo.....	*W. Robert Semple	1972, Feb.
Aurora, Ill.	Albert D. McCoy, N-P ..	1977, Apr.
Austin, Tex.......	*Dan H. Davidson	1972, Sept.
Bakersfield, Cal. .	*Harold E. Bergen	1966, July
Baldwin Park, Cal.	*James S. Mocalis	1971, Dec.
Baltimore, Md.....	William Schaefer, D.....	1975, Dec.
Bangor, Me......	*Merle F. Goff	1966, Dec.
Baton Rouge, La..	W. W. Dumas, D.	1976, Dec.
Battle Creek, Mich.	*Aaron Marsh	1971, Sept.
Bay City, Mich. ..	*E. J. Redmond	1973, July
Baytown, Tex.....	*Fritz Lanham	1972, May
Beaumont, Tex. ..	*Charles Hill	1970, Sept.
Belleville, Ill.	Chas. E. Nichols, N-P ..	1977, Apr.
Belleville, N.J....	Joseph F. McGreevy, N-P	1975, May
Bellevue, Wash...	*L. Joe Miller	1961, Jan.
Bellflower, Calif. .	*Peter B. Feenstra	1968, Oct.
Bellingham, Wash.	Reginald Williams, N-P .	1976, Jan.
Beloit, Wisc.	*H. Herbert Holt	1971, Jan.
Berkeley, Calif. ..	*Paul H. Williamson, Act.	1972, Feb.
Berwyn, Ill.	Emil Vacin, D.	1977, Apr.
Bessemer, Ala....	Jess Lanier, D.	1974, Sept.
Bethlehem, Pa. ..	Gordon Mowrer, D.....	1977, Dec.
Beverly, Mass. ...	James Vitale	1975, Dec.
Billings, Mont. ...	Joseph Leone, D.	1977, May
Biloxi, Miss.	Jerry O'Keefe, D.	1977, July
Binghamton, N.Y.	Alfred J. Libous, R.	1977, Dec.
Birmingham, Ala.	George Seibels, R.	1975, Nov.
Bloomfield, N.J...	*H. Joseph North	1967, Oct.
Bloomington, Ill. .	*Richard Blodgett	1970, June
Bloomington, Ind.	Francis X. McCloskey, D.	1975, Dec.
Bloomington, Minn.	*John Pidgeon	1967, Dec.
Boise, Idaho	Dick Eardlay, N-P	1977, Dec.
Bossier City, La..	James Cathey, D.	1977, June
Boston, Mass. ...	Kevin White, D.	1975, Dec.
Boulder, Colo. ...	*Archie J. Twitchell ...	1973, June
Bowie, Md.	*A. Louis Hayward	1968, July
Bowling Green, Ky.	*Paul McCauley	1973, Jan.
Braintree, Mass. .	Board of Selectmen ...	
Bridgeport, Ct.....	Nicholas A. Panuzio, R..	1975, Nov.
Bristol, Conn. ...	Frank Longo, D.	1975, Nov.
Brockton, Mass. ..	David L. Crosby	1975, Dec.
Brookfield, Wisc. .	Franklin Wirth, N-P ...	1974, Apr.
Brookline, Mass. .	Board of Selectmen ...	
Brooklyn Center, Minn.	*Donald G. Poss	1966, June
Brownsville, Tex. .	*Kirby Lilljedahl	1970, Mar.
Bryan, Texas	*Fred C. Sandlin	1958, Sept.
Buffalo, N.Y......	Stanley M. Makowsky, D.	1977, Dec.
Burbank, Calif ...	*Robert R. Daniels	1968, Feb.
Burlington, Vt. ...	Gordon H. Paquette, D..	1975, Apr.
Calumet City, Ill. .	Robert C. Stefaniak, D. .	1977, Apr.
Cambridge, Mass.	*James L. Sullivan	1968, July
Camden, N.J.	Angelo Errichetti.....	1975, July
Canton, Ohio	Stanley A. Cmich, R....	1975, Dec.

City	Name	Term
Cape Girardeau, Mo.	*W. G. Lawley	1970, July
Carson, Calif.	*E. Frederick Bien	1968, Apr.
Casper, Wyo......	*Kenneth Erickson	1969, Oct.
Cedar Rapids	Donald J. Canney, N-P .	1975, Dec.
Champaign, Ill....	*Warren B. Browning ...	1962, Oct.
Charleston, S.C...	J. Palmer Gailliard, D. ..	1975, Dec.
Charleston, W. Va..	*H. Hugh Bosely	1973, Apr.
Charlotte, N.C....	*David A. Burkhalter ...	1971, May
Charlottesville, Va.	*Cole Hendrix	1971, Jan.
Chattanooga	Robert Kirk Walker, D...	1975, Apr.
Chesapeake, Va...	*Durwood S. Curling ...	1971, Jan.
Chester, Pa.	John Nacrelli, R.	1976, Jan.
Cheyenne, Wyo...	Bill Nation, N-P	1976, Dec.
Chicago, Ill.	Richard J. Daley, D. ...	1975, Apr.
Chicopee, Mass. .	Edward Ziemba	1976, Jan.
Chula Vista, Calif.	*John R. Thomson	1971, Feb.
Cicero, Ill.	John Karner, R.	1974, Apr.
Cincinnati, Ohio .	*E. Robert Turner	1972, June
Clarksville, Tenn..	Charles W. Crow, D. ...	1975, Jan.
Clearwater, Fla. ..	*Merrett R. Stierheim ..	1967, Nov.
Cleveland, Ohio ..	Ralph J. Perk, R.	1975, Nov.
Cleveland Heights	*William C. Lahman ...	1964, Oct.
Clifton, N.J.......	*William Holster	1957, Mar.
Coffeyville, Kan. .	*George H. Fellows	1966, July
Columbia, Mo....	*Don R. Allard	1962, Mar.
Columbia, S.C....	*Graydon V. Olive, Jr. ..	1971, Mar.
Columbus, Ga....	*Franklin Lambert	1971, Jan.
Columbus, Ohio ..	Tom Moody, R.	1976, Jan.
Commerce, Calif..	*Robert Hinderliter ...	1973, Sept.
Compton, Calif...	*Vacant	
Concord, Calif. ...	*F. A. Stewart	1960, Apr.
Concord, N.H. ...	*James E. Henchey	1968, Jan.
Coon Rapids, Minn.	*John K. Cottingham ..	1969, July
Coral Gables, Fla.	*L. W. Robinson, Jr. ...	1959, Jan.
Corpus Christi ...	*R. Marvin Townsend ..	1968, Nov.
Corvallis, Ore. ...	*C. Dean Smith	1968, Jan.
Costa Mesa, Calif.	*Fred Sorsabel	1970, Nov.
Council Bluffs, Ia.	*M. Don Harmon	1968, Feb.
Covington, Ky.....	Bernard A. Grimm, D...	1975, Dec.
Cranston, R.I.....	James L. Taft, Jr., R....	1975, Jan.
Crystal, Minn.....	*John Irving	1963, Sept.
Culver City, Cal. ..	*H. Dale Jones	1969, Aug.
Cuyahoga Falls, O.	Robert Quirk, D.......	1977, Dec.
Dallas, Tex.......	*George R. Schrader ...	1972, Nov.
Daly City, Calif. ..	*David R. Rowe	1969, Aug.
Danbury, Conn....	Charles A. Ducibella, D.	1975, Dec.
Danville, Ill.	Rolland Craig, R.	1975, Apr.
Danville, Va......	*James W. Lord	1971, Nov.
Davenport, Ia	Kathryn Kirschbaum, D.	1975, Dec.
Dayton, Ohio	*Whitney Shartzer, (act.)	1973, Sept.
Daytona Bch., Fla.	*Charles E. Jackson ...	1966, Aug.
Dearborn, Mich...	Orville L. Hubbard, N-P.	1978, Jan.
Decatur, Ala.....	Russell Bolding, N-P ...	1976, Oct.
Decatur, Ill.	*Leslie T. Allen	1972, Sept.
Denton, Tex......	*Jim White	1968, May
Denver, Colo.	William H. McNichols, D.	1975, July
Des Moines, Ia. ..	*Richard Wilkey (act.) ..	1973, Oct.
Des Plaines, Ill. ..	Herbert Behrel, R.	1977, Apr.
Detroit, Mich.....	Coleman A. Young, N-P.	1978, Jan.
Dotham, Ala......	James W. Grant	1977, Oct.
Downers Grove, Ill.	*James R. Griesemer ..	1972, Sept.
Dubuque, Ia	*Gilbert D. Chavenelle ..	1960, July
Duluth, Minn.....	Ben Boo, R.	1976, Jan.
Durham, N.C.....	*I Harding Hughes, Jr...	1063, Feb
E. Chicago, Ind. ..	Robert A. Pastrick, D. ..	1975, Dec.
E. Cleveland, O. ..	*Gladstone L. Chandler, Jr.	1970, Oct.
E. Detroit, Mich. ..	*Chas. H. Beaubien ...	1951, July
E. Hartford, Conn.	Richard H. Blackstone, D.	1975, Nov.
E. Lansing, Mich..	*John Patriarche	1948, Jan.
E. Orange, N.J....	William S. Hart, D.	1977, Dec.
E. Point, Ga.	Bruce Bannister, N-P ..	1974, Dec.
E. Providence, R.I.	*Paul A. Flynn	1972, July
E. St. Louis, Ill...	James E. Williams, N-P .	1975, Apr.
Eau Claire, Wis. ..	*Ray E. Wachs	1970, June
Edina, Minn......	*Warren Hyde	1955, May
Edison, N.J.......	*John Delesandro	1965, Feb.
El Cajon, Calif. ...	*Robert M. Applegate ..	1958, Sept.
Elgin, Ill.	*Leo Nelson	1972, Dec.
Elizabeth, N.J....	Thomas G. Dunn, D. ...	1976, Dec.
Elkhart, Ind.	Daniel Hayes, D.	1975, Dec.
Elmhurst, Ill.	*Robert T. Palmer	1953, Aug.
Elmira, N.Y.......	*Joseph E. Sartori	1972, June
El Monte, Calif. ..	*Kenneth Botts	1969, Aug.
El Paso, Tex......	Fred Hervey, R.	1975, Apr.
Elyria, O.	L. P. Reichlin, D.	1975, Dec.
Enfield, Conn. ...	*C. Samuel Kissinger ..	1968, June
Enid, Okla	*Tom Sailors, Jr.	1969, Oct.
Erie, Pa..........	Louis J. Tullio, D.	1977, Dec.

City	Name	Term
Escondido, Calif.	*George Patterson	1970, May
Euclid, Ohio	Harry Knuth, R.	1975, Dec.
Eugene, Ore.	*Hugh McKinley	1960, Oct.
Evanston, Ill.	*Edward A. Martin	1971, Mar.
Evansville, Ind.	Russell Lloyd, R.	1976, Jan.
Everett, Mass.	George R. McCarthy, D.	1975, Dec.
Everett, Wash.	Robert C. Anderson, N-P	1978, Jan.
Fairborn, Ohio	*Claude Malone, Jr.	1970, July
Fairfield, Calif.	*B. Gale Wilson	1956, Mar.
Fairfield, Conn.	John J. Sullivan, D.	1975, Nov.
Fair Lawn, N.J.	*George Pellack	1960, June
Fall River, Mass.	Wilfred C. Driscoll, D.	1975, Dec.
Fayetteville, Ark.	*Donald Grimes	1972, Apr.
Fayet'ville, N.C.	*J. Guy Smith	1971, Jan.
Fitchburg, Mass.	Hedley Bray	1976, Jan.
Flagstaff, Ariz.	*Leland C. McPherson	1970, May
Flint, Mich.	*Brian W. Rapp	1971, Dec.
Florissant, Mo.	James J. Eagen, D.	1975, Apr.
Fond du Lac, Wisc.	*Myron J. Medin, Jr.	1967, Nov.
Ft. Collins, Colo.	*Robert L. Brunton	1972, Oct.
Ft. Lauderdale	*Robert H. Bubier	1962, Dec.
Ft. Lee, N.J.	*James J. Mulcare	1973, Jan.
Ft. Smith, Ark.	*Ray A. Riley	1972, Dec.
Ft. Wayne, Ind.	Ivan Lebamoff, D.	1975, Dec.
Ft. Worth, Tex.	*Roger Line	1971, Apr.
Fremont, Calif.	*Don Driggs	1967, Jan.
Fresno, Calif.	*Ralph W. Hanley	1973, Sept.
Fullerton, Calif.	*W. F. Cornett, Jr.	1966, Oct.
Gadsden, Ala.	L. L. Gilliland, D.	1974, Oct.
Gainesville, Fla.	*B. Harold Farmer	1968, Nov.
Galesburg, Ill.	*Thomas B. Herring	1960, Nov.
Galveston, Tex.	*John Unverfert	1967, July
Gardena, Calif.	*Harvey Hurlburt	1973, Mar.
Garden Grove, Calif.	*Richard R. Powers	1972, Apr.
Garfield Hts., Ohio	Raymond Stachewicz, D.	1975, Dec.
Garland, Tex.	*C. E. Duckworth	1965, Jan.
Gary, Ind.	R. G. Hatcher, D.	1975, Nov.
Gastonia, N.C.	*J. E. Robinette, Act.	1973, June
Glendale, Ariz.	*S. F. Van de Putte	1960, Sept.
Glendale, Calif.	*C. E. Perkins	1952, Apr.
Gr. Forks, N.D.	Cyril P. O'Neill, D.	1976, Apr.
Gr. Island, Nebr.	*John M. Carpenter	1964, Aug.
Gr. Prairie, Tex.	*Clifford A. Johnson	1962, Sept.
Gr. Rapids, Mich.	*Joseph R. Grassie	1970, June
Granite City, Ill.	Paul Schuler, D.	1977, Apr.
Great Falls, Mont.	*Richard D. Thomas	1973, Apr.
Green Bay, Wis.	Thomas Atkinson, N-P	1975, Apr.
Greensboro, N.C.	*Thomas Z. Osborne	1973, Jan.
Greenville, Miss.	Patrick Dunne, D.	1976, Jan.
Greenville, S.C.	*John J. Dullea	1971, Oct.
Greenwich, Ct.	William B. Lewis, R.	1975, Dec.
Gulfport, Miss.	C. L. Bullock, D.	1977, July
Hackensack, N.J.	*Joseph J. Squillace	1964, Oct.
Hagerstown, Md.	Varner L. Paddack, R.	1977, Mar.
Hamden, Conn.	Lucien A. DiMeo, R.	1975, Nov.
Hamilton, Ohio	*Edward C. Smith	1971, June
Hammond, Ind.	Joseph E. Klen, D.	1975, Dec.
Hampton, Va.	*C. E. Johnson	1956, May
Harlingen, Tex.	*George Adkins	1972, Aug.
Harrisburg, Pa.	Harold Swenson, D.	1978, Jan.
Hartford, Conn.	*Edward Curtin	1971, June
Harvey, Ill.	James A. Haines	1975, Apr.
Hattiesburg, Miss.	A. L. Gerrard, Jr., D.	1977, July
Haverhill, Mass.	William Ryan	1975, Dec.
Hawthorne, Calif.	*Donald W. Mansfield	1972, Jan.
Hayward, Calif.	*William C. Hanley	1972, Feb.
Hempstead, N.Y.	Dalton R. Miller, R.	1977, Apr.
Hialeah, Fla.	Henry A. Milander, N-P	1975, Nov.
High Point, N.C.	*Harold R. Cheek	1960, Mar.
Highland Pk., Ill.	*Stan Kennedy	1965, Feb.
Hoboken, N.J.	Steve Cappiello, N-P	1977, July
Holyoke, Mass.	William Taupier, D.	1976, Jan.
Hollywood, Fla.	*F. T. Kain	1971, July
Honolulu, Hawaii	Frank F. Fasi	1976, Dec.
Hot Springs, Ark.	Tom Ellsworth, N-P	1974, Dec.
Houston, Tex.	Louie Welch, N-P	1974, Jan.
Huntington, W. Va.	*Barry R. Evans	1973, Mar.
Huntington Beach Calif.	*David D. Rowlands	1972, Feb.
Huntsville, Ala.	Joe W. Davis, N-P	1976, Oct.
Hutchinson, Kan.	*George W. Pyle	1967, Sept.
Independence, Mo.	*Lyle Alberg	1968, Sept.
Indianapolis, Ind.	Richard Lugar, R.	1975, Dec.
Inglewood, Calif.	*Douglas W. Ayres	1968, Apr.
Inkster, Mich.	*David S. Williams	1973, Oct.
Iowa City, Iowa	*Ray S. Wells	1972, May
Irving, Tex.	*Darwin McGill	1973, June
Irvington, N.J.	Harry Stevenson, N-P	1974, June
Jackson, Mich.	*James E. Malone	1970, Jan.
Jackson, Miss.	Russell C. Davis, D.	1977, July
Jackson, Tenn.	Bob Conger, D.	1975, July
Jacksonville, Fla.	Hans Tanzler, Jr., D.	1975, June
Jamestown, N.Y.	Stanley Lundine, D.	1975, Dec.
Janesville, Wis.	*Robert O. Bailey	1971, Jan.
Jefferson City, Mo.	John G. Christy, D.	1975, Apr.
Jersey City, N.J.	Paul Jordan, D.	1977, July
Johnson City, Tenn.	Kyle Chinouth, R.	1975, May
Johnstown, Pa.	Herbert Pfuhl, R.	1978, Jan.
Joliet, Ill.	*Lynn Neuhart	1972, Feb.
Joplin, Mo.	*Robert E. Metzinger	1968, Mar.
Kalamazoo, Mich.	*James Caplinger	1968, July
Kan. City, Kan.	Richard F. Walsh, R.	1975, Apr.
Kan. City, Mo.	*John L. Taylor	1968, Feb.
Kearny, N.J.	David C. Rowlands, R.	1975, Dec.
Kenosha, Wis.	Wallace E. Burkee, N-P	1976, Apr.
Kettering, O.	*Ervin L. Welch	1954, Dec.
Key West, Fla.	*Charles P. Aguero, Act.	1973, Apr.
Killeen, Tex.	*Robert Brockman	1972, Jan.
Knoxville, Tenn.	Kyle C. Testerman, N-P	1976, Dec.
Kokomo, Ind.	John Peacock, D.	1976, Jan.
LaCrosse, Wis.	Peter Gilberton, N-P	1975, Apr.
Lafayette, Ind.	James Riehle, D.	1975, Dec.
Lafayette, La.	Kenneth Bowen, D.	1976, June
La Habra, Calif.	*Lee Risner	1971, Nov.
La Mesa, Calif.	*Donald P. Wolfer	1972, July
La Mirada, Calif.	*Claude J. Klug	1971, Aug.
Lake Chas., La.	James Sudduth, D.	1977, June
Lakeland, Fla.	*Robert V. Youkey	1960, Jan.
Lakewood, Calif.	*Milton R. Farrell	1972, Dec.
Lakewood, Colo.	*Walter Kane	1970, Mar.
Lakewood, Ohio	Robert M. Lawther, R.	1975, Dec.
Lancaster, Pa.	Richard M. Scott, R.	1978, Jan.
Lansing, Mich.	Gerald Graves, N-P.	1977, Dec.
Laredo, Tex.	J. C. Martin, Jr., N-P	1974, May
Las Cruces, N.M.	*A. J. Vasilakis	1965, Sept.
Las Vegas, Nev.	*Arthur R. Trelease	1965, Jan.
Lawrence, Kan.	*Buford M. Watson, Jr.	1970, Jan.
Lawrence, Mass.	John J. Buckley, N-P	1975, Dec.
Lawton, Okla.	*Henry B. Nabers	1970, Nov.
Lewiston, Ma.	John C. Orestis, D.	1976, Jan.
Lexington, Ky.	*Edgar E. Maroney	1971, Mar.
Lima, Ohio	Harry Moyer, R.	1977, Nov.
Lincoln, Nebr.	Sam Schwartzkop, D.	1975, May
Lincoln Pk., Mich.	Max S. Schiebold, N-P	1975, Dec.
Linden, N.J.	John Gregorio, D.	1974, Dec.
Little Rock, Ark.	*Carleton E. McMullin	1973, Nov.
Livermore, Calif.	*William H. Parness	1957, Oct.
Livonia, Mich.	E. H. McNamara, N-P	1976, Jan.
Lombard, Ill.	*Paul L. White	1969, June
Long Beach, Cal.	*John R. Mansell	1961, Mar.
Long Beach, N.Y.	*James Nagourney	1972, Jan.
Longview, Tex.	*Harry G. Mosley	1952, July
Lorain, Ohio	Joseph J. Zahorec, D.	1975, Dec.
Los Angeles, Cal.	Thomas Bradley, D.	1977, June
Louisville, Ky.	Dr. Harvey Sloane, D.	1977, Dec.
Lowell, Mass.	*James L. Sullivan	1970, Sept.
L. Merion, Pa.	*Thomas B. Fulweiler	1968, Jan.
Lubbock, Tex.	*N. B. McCullough	1971, Oct.
Lynchburg, Va.	*David B. Norman	1970, Dec.
Lynn, Mass.	Donald Phillips	1976, Jan.
Lynwood, Calif.	*Stephen Wright	1972, Dec.
Macon, Ga.	Ronnie Thompson, R.	1976, Jan.
Madison, Wisc.	Paul Soglin, N-P	1975, Mar.
Malden, Mass.	Walter J. Kelliher, D.	1976, Jan.
Manchester, Ct.	*Robt. B. Weiss	1971, Nov.
Manchester, N.H.	Silvio Dupuis, D.	1976, Jan.
Manitowoc, Wisc.	Anthony V. Dufek, D.	1975, Apr.
Mansfield, Ohio	Richard A. Porter, R.	1975, Dec.
Maple Hts., Ohio	Emil J. Lisy, Jr., N-P	1975, Dec.
Marion, Ind.	W. Ray Burns, D.	1977, Jan.
Marion, Ohio	Don Quaintance, R.	1975, Dec.
McKeesport, Pa.	John E. Pribanic, D.	1977, Dec.
Medford, Mass.	*James Nicholson	1970, Oct.
Melbourne, Fla.	*Earnest E. Watkins	1969, Nov.
Memphis, Tenn.	Wyeth Chandler, N-P	1975, Dec.
Mentor, Ohio	*Arthur V. Dickard	1969, Apr.
Meridian, Miss.	*Joel W. Forrester	1973, July
Mesa, Ariz.	*J. A. Petrie	1952, June
Mesquite, Tex.	*Billy G. York	1969, Oct.
Miami, Fla.	*P. W. Andrews	1973, Aug.
Miami Bch., Fla.	*Frank Spence	1972, Nov.
Michigan City, Ind.	Randall C. Miller, R.	1975, Dec.
Middletown, O.	*Dale F. Helsel	1970, Oct.
Midland, Tex.	*James W. Brown	1964, Nov.
Midwest City, Okla.	*W. D. Baker	1966, June
Milford, Conn.	Joel Baldwin, D.	1975, Nov.
Milwaukee, Wis.	Henry W. Maier, D.	1974, Apr.
Minneapolis	Albert J. Hofstede, D.	1976, Jan.
Minnetonka, Minn.	*Carsten D. Leikvold	1972, Dec.
Minot, N.D.	*John Arnold	1972, Oct.
Mishawaka, Ind.	Margaret H. Prickett, R.	1975, Dec.
Mobile, Ala.	Gary A. Greenough	1975, Feb.
Modesto, Calif.	*John C. Keefe	1963, May
Moline, Ill.	Earl Wendt, R.	1977, May
Monroe, La.	Ralph T. Troy, D.	1976, June
Montebello, Cal.	*Roy Pederson	1969, Jan.
Monterey Park, Calif.	*Gerald C. Weeks	1970, Aug.
Montgomery, Ala.	Jim Robinson, N-P	1975, Oct.
Mt. Prospect, Ill.	*Robert J. Eppley	1971, Aug.
Mt. Vernon, N.Y.	August Petrillo, R	1975, Dec.
Mt. View, Cal.	*Richard De Long	1973, Oct.
Munice, Ind.	Paul Cooley, D	1975, Dec.
Mundelein, Ill.	Maurice A. Noll, N-P	1977, Apr.
Muskegon, Mich.	*Paul F. Frederick	1970, June
Muskogee, Okla.	*W. T. Smith	1971, Oct.

City	Name	Term
Napa, Calif.	*Lee M. Roberts	1953, Aug.
Nashua, N.H.	Dennis Sullivan, D	1975, Dec.
Nashville, Tenn.	C. Beverly Briley, D	1975, Sept.
National City, Cal.	*Cleo Osburn	1965, July
New Albany, Ind.	Warren V. Nash, D	1975, Dec.
New Bedford, Mass.	John Markey, D.	1976, Jan.
New Britain, Conn.	Stanley J. Pac, D.	1975, Nov.
New Brunswick, N.J.	Patricia O. Sheehan, D	1975, Jan.
New Castle, Pa.	Francis J. Rogan, D.	1975, Dec.
New Haven, Ct.	Bartholomew Guida, D.	1976, Jan.
N. Kensington, Pa.	Verle N. Bevan, D.	1977, Dec.
New Orleans, La.	Moon Landrieu, D	1974, May
New Rochelle, N.Y.	*Murray Fuerst	1965, Feb.
New York, N.Y.	Abraham Beame, D.	1977, Dec.
Newark, N.J.	Kenneth Gibson, N-P	1974, July
Newark, Ohio	Richard Baker, R	1975, Dec.
Newport, R.I.	*B. Cowles Mallory	1968, Feb.
Newport Beach, Calif.	*Harvey L. Hurlburt	1965, Mar.
Newport News	*W. E. Lawson, Jr.	1965, Sept.
Newton, Mass.	Theodore Mann	1977, Dec.
Niagara Falls	*Morton Abramowitz	1970, Jan.
Niles, Ill.	*Kenneth Scheel	1973, May
Niles, Ohio	W. A. Thorp, R	1975, Dec.
Norfolk, Va.	*G. Robert House	1971, Jan.
Norman, Okla.	*Richard Gray	1972, Nov.
North Chicago, Ill.	Leo F. Kukla, D	1977, Apr.
No. Little Rock, Ark.	Robert L. (Bob) Rosamond	1976, Dec.
No. Olmstead, Ohio	Ralph Christman, R.	1975, Dec.
Norristown, Pa.	[illegible]	1971, May
Norwalk, Calif.	*William H. Kraus	[illegible]
Norwalk, Conn.	Donald J. Irwin, D.	1975, Nov.
Norwich, Conn.	*Thomas H. Hissom	1967, July
Novato, Calif.	*Charles A. Brown	1968, Dec.
Oak Lawn, Ill.	*Robert H. Oldland	1972, Apr.
Oak Park, Ill.	*Lee A. Ellis	1971, Sept.
Oak Pk., Mich.	*James B. Thompson	1970, Sept.
Oakland, Calif.	*Cecil S. Riley	1972, Sept.
Oak Ridge, Tenn.	*William N. Haddock (act.)	1973, Oct.
Oceanside, Calif.	*Lawrence M. Bagley	1970, July
Odessa, Tex.	*Ronald J. Neighbors	1968, Nov.
Ogden, Utah	*R. L. Larsen	1972, Feb.
Okla. City, Okla.	*Pat Painter (act.)	1973, July
Omaha, Nebr.	Edward Zorinsky, R	1977, May
Ontario, Calif.	*H. K. Hun	1966, Jan.
Orange, Calif.	*Gifford Miller	1968, Dec.
Orange, N.J.	Joel Shain, D	1974, June
Orlando, Fla.	Carl Langford, D	1976, Oct.
Oshkosh, Wis.	*Gordon Jaeger	1970, Dec.
Owensboro, Ky.	*Max N. Rhoads	1959, Sept.
Oxnard, Calif.	*Paul E. Wolven	1953, Feb.
Pacifica, Calif.	*David J. Thompson	1972, Nov.
Palo Alto, Cal.	*George Sipel	1972, Feb.
Parkersburg, W.Va.	John Nicely, R.	1973, Dec.
Parma, Ohio	John Petruska, D.	1975, Dec.
Pasadena, Calif.	*Donald F. McIntyre	1973, June
Pasadena, Tex.	John Ray Harrison, D	1977, Apr.
Passaic, N.J.	Gerald Goldman, R	1977, June
Paterson, N.J.	Thomas J. Rooney, Con.	1975, Dec.
Pawtucket, R.I.	Dennis Lynch, D.	1976, Jan.
Pekin, Ill.	William L. Waldmeier	1975, May
Pensacola, Fla.	*Frank A. Faison	1971, Apr.
Peoria, Ill.	*Robert O. Wright	1970, Oct.
Perth Amboy, N.J.	*Robert J. Cabana	1973, July
Petersburg, Va.	*Roy F. Ash	1950, Jan.
Philadelphia, Pa.	Frank L. Rizzo, D	1976, Jan.
Phoenix, Ariz.	*John B. Wentz	1970, July
Pico Rivera, Cal.	*Howard Schroyer	1970, July
Pittsburgh, Pa.	Peter Flaherty, D.	1977, Dec.
Pittsfield, Mass.	Evan S. Dobelle	1976, Jan.
Plainfield, N.J.	*Kennedy Shaw	1969, Feb.
Pocatello, Idaho	*Charles W. Moss	1970, Sept.
Pompona, Calif.	*Jerrold R. Gonce	1973, Oct.
Pompano Bch., Fla.	*John Cartwright	1972,
Pontiac, Mich.	*Frank Smiley	1972, Jan.
Portage, Mich.	*David E. Firestone	1966, Aug.
Port Arthur, Tex.	*George E. Dibrell	1962, Oct.
Port Huron, Mich.	*Gerald R. Bouchard	1965, June
Portland, Me.	*John Menario	1967, June
Portland, Ore.	Neil Goldschmidt, N-P	1976, Jan.
Portsmouth, O.	*Huxley Kennedy	1967, Feb.
Portsmouth, Va.	*A. P. Johnson, Jr.	1958, Sept.
Poughkeepsie	*Donald J. O'Hara	1972, June
Providence, R.I.	J. A. Doorley, Jr., D	1975, Jan.
Provo, Utah	Russell D. Grange, N-P	1977, Dec.
Pueblo, Colo.	*Fred E. Weisbrod	1967, Feb.
Quincy, Ill.	Don Nicholson, D	1977, May
Quincy, Mass.	Walter Hannon, R.	1974, Jan.
Racine, Wis.	Stephen Olson, N-P	1975, Apr.
Raleigh, N.C.	*William H. Carper	1950, Sept.
Rapid City, S.D.	Don Barnett, N-P	1975, May
Raytown, Mo.	Willard H. Ross, R.	1975, Apr.
Reading, Pa.	Eugene L. Shirk, R	1976, Jan.
Redlands, Calif.	*R. P. Merritt, Jr.	1964, Mar.
Redondo Beach	*Joseph P. Leach	1973, Feb.
Redwood City	*James M. Fales, Jr.	1971, June
Reno, Nev.	*Joe Latimore	1960, Oct.

City	Name	Term
Revere, Mass.	William Reinstein	1976, Jan.
Richardson, Tex.	*R. B. Sherrill, Jr.	1956, Nov.
Richfield, Minn.	*Wayne Burggraaff	1968, Dec.
Richmond, Calif.	*Kenneth Smith	1967, Sept.
Richmond, Ind.	Byron E. Klute, D.	1975, Dec.
Richmond, Va.	*William J. Leidinger	1972, June
Riverside, Calif.	*Daniel E. Stone	1970, July
Roanoke, Va.	*Byron E. Haner	1973, Jan.
Rochester, Minn.	*James F. Andre	1966, Mar.
Rochester, N.Y.	*Thomas T. Mooney	1973, Aug.
Rock Hill, S.C.	*Max Holland	1965, Mar.
Rock Island, Ill.	*Raymond P. Botch	1961, Feb.
Rockford, Ill.	Robert McGaw, D	1977, Apr.
Rockville, Md.	*Larry N. Blick	1971, Nov.
Rome, N.Y.	Wm. A. Valentine, R	1975, Dec.
Rosemead, Calif.	*Lee Gunn	1969,
Roseville, Mich.	*James D. Bottomley	1972, Apr.
Roseville, Minn.	*Burke Raymond	1969, Apr.
Roswell, N.M.	*Robert J. Owen	1973, Oct.
Royal Oak, Mich.	*Bruce W. Love	1961, June
Sacramento, Cal.	*R. L. Rathfon	1969, Jan.
Saginaw, Mich.	*E. H. Potthoff, Jr.	1961, July
St. Clair Shores, Mi.	*Donald J. Harm	1962, Jan.
St. Joseph, Mo.	William Bennett, N-P	1974, Apr.
St. Louis, Mo.	John Poelker, D	1977, Apr.
St. Louis, Pk. Minn.	*Chris Cherches	1968, Oct.
St. Paul, Minn.	*Frank Marzitelli	1972, Dec.
St. Petersburg, Fla.	*R. E. Harbaugh	1970, May
Salem, Mass.	Gene Levesque	1976, Jan.
Salem, Ore.	*Robert S. Moore	1968, Aug.
Salina, Kan.	*Norris D. Olson	1963, May
Salinas, Calif.	*Robert Christofferson	1972, Dec.
Salt Lake City	Jake Garn, N-P	1976, Jan.
San Angelo, Tex.	*[illegible]	[illegible], July
San Antonio, Tex.	*Sam Granata, Jr.	1973, May
San. Bernardino	*Marshall Julian	1971, Nov.
San Diego, Calif.	*Kimball H. Moore	1971, Dec.
San Francisco	Joseph Alioto, D	1976, Jan.
San Jose, Calif.	*Ted Tedesco	1973, Feb.
San Leandro	*Wesley McCure	1948, May
San Mateo, Calif.	*Donald E. Mueller	1970, Jan.
San Rafael, Cal.	*William J. Bielser	1973, Jan.
Sandusky, Ohio	*Frank Link	1972, Jan.
Santa Ana, Calif.	*Bruce C. Spragg	1972, Sept.
Santa Barbara	*John L. Scott	1973, Mar.
Santa Cruz, Calif.	*David C. Koester	1962, Oct.
Santa Fe, N.M.	*Philip Baca	1972, Aug.
Santa Maria, Cal.	*Robert Grogan	1960, Jan.
Santa Monica	*James D. Williams	1973, Oct.
Santa Rosa, Calif.	*Kenneth R. Blackman	1970, July
Sarasota, Fla.	*Kenneth Thompson	1950, Feb.
Savannah, Ga.	*Arthur A. Mendonsa	1971, Sept.
Schenectady, N.Y.	*Peter Caputo	1973, Oct.
Scottsdale, Ariz.	*Dale Carter	1971, Apr.
Scranton, Pa.	Eugene J. Peters, R.	1977, Dec.
Seattle, Wash.	Wesley C. Uhlman, N-P	1977, Dec.
Shaker Hghts., O.	Walter C. Kelley	1975, Dec.
Sheboygan, Wis.	Richard Suscha, R	1977, Apr.
Shreveport, La.	L. Calhoun Allen, Jr., D	1974, Nov.
Simi Valley, Calif.	*Bruce A. Altman	1970, Jan.
Sioux City, Ia.	*Samuel McAllister, Jr.	1970, Apr.
Sioux Falls, S.D.	M. E. Schirmer, N-P	1974, May
Skokie, Ill.	*John N. Matzer, Jr.	1970, Jan.
Somerville, Mass.	S. Lester Ralph	1976, Jan.
South Bend, Ind.	Jerry Miller, D.	1975, Dec.
So. Gate, Calif.	Don Sawyer, R	1974, Apr.
So. S.F., Calif.	*Edward G. Alario (act.)	1973, July
Southfield, Mich.	*Peter Cristiano	1968, July
Southgate, Mich.	*William Valusek	1972, Feb.
Spartanb'g, S.C.	*Lott T. Rogers	1958, Oct.
Spokane, Wash.	*F. Sylvin Fulwiler	1963, Aug.
Springfield, Ill.	William C. Telford, N-P	1975, Apr.
Springfield, Mass.	William Sullivan	1976, Jan.
Springfield, Mo.	*Don G. Busch	1971, Oct.
Springfield, Ohio	*Alfred Strozdas	1968, Nov.
Stamford, Conn.	Frederick P. Lenz, D.	1975, Nov.
Sterling Hts., Mich.	*Leonard Hendricks	1968, Aug.
Stillwater, Okla.	*Lawrence Gish	1966,
Stockton, Calif.	*Elder Gunter	1969, July
Stratford, Conn.	*Joseph W. Venables	1970, Apr.
Sunnyvale, Cal.	*John E. Dever	1967, Aug.
Syracuse, N.Y.	Lee Alexander, D.	1977, Dec.
Tacoma, Wash.	*William V. Donaldson	1971, Apr.
Tallahassee, Fla.	*Arvah B. Hopkins	1952, Feb.
Tampa, Fla.	Dick Greco, Jr., D	1975, Sept.
Taunton, Mass.	Theodore Aleixo	1975, Dec.
Taylor, Mich.	S. Richard Marshall, N-P	1975, Dec.
Teaneck, N.J.	*Werner H. Schmid	1959, Mar.
Tempe, Ariz.	*Kenneth A. McDonald	1968, June
Terre Haute, Ind.	William Brighton, D	1975, Dec.
Thousand Oaks, Cal.	*Glenn Kendall	1966,
Titusville, Gla.	*Lee Ayres	1969, Apr.
Toledo, Ohio	*James B. Daken	1971, Mar.
Topeka, Kan.	William McCormick, N-P	1975, Apr.
Torrance, Calif.	*Edward J. Ferraro	1964, Mar.
Trenton, N.J.	Arthur Holland, D	1974, July
Troy, Mich.	*Frank Gerstenecker	1970, Feb.
Troy, N.Y.	*John P. Buckley	1972, June

City	Name	Term
Tuscon, Ariz.	*Clifford W. O'Key	1972, Dec.
Tulsa, Okla.	Robert La Fortune, R.	1974, May
Tuscaloosa, Ala.	C. Snow Hinton, D	1977, Oct.
Tyler, Tex.	*Ed Wagoner	1972, Nov.
Univ. City, Mo.	*Charles T. Henry	1958, Dec.
Upland, Calif.	*Edwin Alder	1955, Feb.
U. Arlington, O.	*H. W. Hyrne	1968, May
Urbana, Ill.	Hiram Paley, D	1977, May
Utica, N.Y.	Edward Hanna, N-P	1975, Dec.
Vallejo, Calif.	*Gerald R. Davis	1973, Aug.
Vancouver, Wash.	*Alan Harvey	1969, May
Ventura, Calif.	*Edward E. McCombs	1970, Mar.
Victoria, Tex.	*John Lee	1959, Sept.
Vineland, N.J.	Joseph D'Ippolito, R	1976, June
Virginia Beach, Va.	*Roger Scott	1968, July
Waco, Tex.	*David F. Smith, Jr.	1971, Sept.
Walnut Creek, Cal.	*Thomas G. Dunne	1972, May
Waltham, Mass.	Arthur J. Clark	1976, Jan.
Warren, Mich.	Ted Bates, N-P	1975, Apr.
Wash. D.C.	Walter Washington	
Waterbury, Ct.	Victor A. Mambruno, D.	1975, Dec.
Waterloo, Ia.	Leo Rooff, N-P	1976, Jan.
Waukegan, Ill.	Robert Sabonjian, R	1977, Apr.
Waukesha, Wisc.	Paul Vrakas, N-P	1974, Apr.
Wauwatosa, Wis.	*J. William Little	1972, Mar.
West Allis, Wis.	Urban E. Ganser, N-P	1974, Apr.
W. Covina, Cal.	*George Aiassa	1958, May
W. Hartford, Ct.	*Richard H. Custer	1962, Sept.
W. Haven, Conn.	Robert A. Johnson, D.	1975, Dec.
W. New York, N.J.	Anthony De Fino, D.	1975, May
W. Orange, N.J.	Louis P. Falcone, D	1974, June
W. Palm Beach	*Richard Simmons	1969, Sept.
Westland, Mich.	Eugene McKinney, N-P	1975, Dec.
Westminster, Cal.	*Robert J. Huntley	1967, July
Weymouth, Mass.	Board of Selectmen	
Wheeling, W. Va.	*Charles Steele	1973, Jan.
White Plains, N.Y.	Carl Delfino, R.	1975, Dec.
Wichita, Kan.	*Ralph Wulz	1968, Sept.
Wichita Falls, Tex.	*Gerald G. Fox	1969, Feb.
Wheaton, Ill.	*William E. Kirchhoff	1973, May

City	Name	Term
Wilkes-Barre, Pa.	*Bernard J. Gallagher	1972, June
Williamsport, Pa.	John R. Coder, R	1976, Jan.
Wilmington, Del.	Thomas Maloney, D	1977, Jan.
Wilmington, N.C.	*John A. Jones.	1971, Sept.
Winston-Salem	*Orville W. Powell	1972, Nov.
Woodbridge, N.J.	*David Miller (act.)	1972, Oct.
Woodbridge, N.J.	John J. Cassidy, R	1975, Dec.
Woonsocket, R.I.	John A. Cummings, D	1975, Nov.
Worcester, Mass.	*Francis J. McGrath	1951, Apr.
Wyandotte, Mich.	William Sullivan, N-P	1975, Apr.
Wyoming, Mich.	*William P. Von Houten	1972, May
Yakima, Wash.	*Craig McMicken	1967, Sept.
Yonkers, N.Y.	*Seymour Scher	1970, Jan.
Youngstown, O.	Jack Hunter, R.	1975, Dec.
York, Pa.	John D. Krout, R.	1978, Jan.
Zanesville, Ohio	*Samuel Grey	1962, Aug.

Canadian Cities

City	Name	Term
Calgary, Alta.	Rod Sykes	1974, Oct.
Halifax, N.S.	Walter R. Fitzgerald	1974, Nov.
Hamilton, Ont.	Victor K. Copps	1976, Dec.
Hull, Que.	Jean-Marie Seguin	1974, Nov.
Kingston, Ont.	George N. Speal	1974, Dec.
Kitchener, Ont.	Sid McLennan	1973. Dec.
London, Ont.	Mrs. Jane Bigelow	1973, Dec.
Moncton, N.B.	Leonard Jones	1974, June
Montreal, Que	Jean Drapeau	1974, Oct.
Ottawa, Ont.	Pierre Benoit	1973, Dec.
Regina, Sask.	*Bruce Smith	1960, Jan.
St. John, N.B.	Robert Lockhart	1974, June
Saskatoon, Sask.	Herbert S. Sears	1973, Dec.
Sherbrooke, Que,	Marc Bureau	1974, Nov.
Sudbury, Ont.	Joseph J. Fabbro	1974, Dec.
Toronto, Ont.	David Crombie	1974, Dec.
Vancouver, B.C.	Art Phillips	1974. Dec.
Victoria, B.C.	*James H. Bramley	1973, June
Waterloo, Ont.	Donovan Meston	1974, Dec.
Windsor, Ont.	*John Steel	1969, July
Winnipeg, Man.	Stephen Juba	1974, Oct.

(Continued from page 34)

CAPE CANAVERAL

The name Cape Canaveral was restored to what had been, since 1963, Cape Kennedy, by action of the State of Florida, May 28, and by the U.S. Dep't of the Interior, Oct. 9. (Map Pp 518, 520, 528). The name of the John F. Kennedy Space Center was not affected by the change.

1973 AWARDS, PRIZES (Pp 403-411)

Nobel Prize for Peace: Henry Kissinger, U.S., and Le Duc Tho, North Vietnam, for negotiating the Vietnam cease-fire. Tho rejected it.

Nobel Memorial Prize for Economics: Wassily Leontief, U.S., for input-output analysis system.

Nobel Prize for Literature: Patrick White, Australia, for his novels.

Nobel Prize for Physiology-Medicine: Dr. Karl von Frisch and Dr. Konrad Lorenz, both W. Germany, and Nikolaas Tinbergen, Netherlands-Great Britain, for work in ethology (comparative behavior studies).

Nobel Prize for Physics: Dr. Ivar Giaever, U.S., Dr. Leo Esaki, Japan-U.S., and Dr. Brian D. Josephson, Great Britain, for theories on miniature electronics.

Nobel Prize for Chemistry: Dr. Ernst Otto Fischer, W. Germany, and Geoffrey Wilkinson, Great Britain, for independent work on merging of organic and metallic atoms.

SPRINGFIELD, MASS. (P 681)

Donald R. Newhouse, 54, general manager of The Springfield Union, Springfield Sunday Republican and Springfield Daily News, died Oct. 18 during heart surgery.

RELIGION

William Cardinal Heard died Sept. 16 (P 353).

Rufino Cardinal Santos, Archbishop of Manilla, died Sept. 3. (P 354)

Claire Randall, 54, was elected to become general secretary of the National Council of Churches, to take office Dec. 31, 1973. (P 346)

The Senior Bishop of the African Methodist Episcopal Church is Bishop Decatur Ward Nichols, 2522 Barhamville Rd., Columbia, S.C. 29204. (P 346)

The Right Rev. John M. Allin was confirmed Oct. 4 as Presiding Bishop of the Protestant Episcopal Church. (Pp. 344, 346, 350)

Dr. Kenneth L. Teegarden was elected General Minister and President of the Christian Church (Disciples of Christ). (Pp. 343, 345)

BEVERAGE PURCHASE AGE (P 135)

The minimum legal age for purchase of beer and wine in Illinois was reduced to 19 on Oct. 1.

U.S. POPULATION (P 146)

Vincent P. Barabba, whose by-line appears on the population article, has since become Director of the Census Bureau.

TALL BUILDINGS (P 703)

The height of Vancouver Square, Vancouver, B.C., should be 586 ft. The B.C. Tel Tower should be deleted.

AEROSPACE (P. 485)

New "duration of manned space flight" and "distance covered" records were set by Capt. Alan L. Bean, Dr. Owen K. Garriott and Maj. Jack R. Lousma in the Skylab 2 mission. Duration was 59 days, 11 hours and 9 minutes; distance covered was 24.5 million miles. Capt. Bean has spent more time in space than any other human—69 days, 15 hours and 46 minutes.

Spiro T. Agnew, 20th Century Icarus
By Kenneth C. Johnston

On a black, almost unbelievable day, Oct. 10, 1973, Vice President of the United States Spiro T. Agnew resigned his lofty post and confessed to falsifying his federal income tax return. He was fined $10,000 and put on probation for 3 years.

It was a sudden, precipitous fall, the like of which had not been seen in American history. Agnew was the second Vice President to resign, but the first to do so under a cloud.

He stood straight and tall, as was his style, in Baltimore Federal Court, hands trembling slightly, and read from a statement which referred only to one year when he had been Maryland Governor:

"I admit that I did receive payments during the year 1967 which were not expended for political purposes and that, therefore, those payments were income taxable to me in that year and that I so knew.

"I further acknowledge that contracts were awarded by state agencies in 1967 and other years to those who made such payments, and that I was aware of such awards."

Nolo Contendere

He also denied in his statement to the stilled courtroom that the 1967 payments "in any way influenced my official actions" and he gave as his reason for pleading *nolo contendere* (no contest) that "protracted proceedings before the grand jury, the Congress and the courts, with the speculation and controversy surrounding them, would seriously prejudice the national interest."

Federal Judge Walter E. Hoffman noted that Agnew had waived indictment, pleading to a Justice Department charge instead, and pointed out that the plea was "the full equivalent of a plea of guilty."

To the man whose resignation as Vice President had been handed minutes earlier to Secretary of State Henry Kissinger in Washington, Judge Hoffman said he normally imposed prison sentences in tax evasion cases. But, the judge said, he was "making an exception" because of Attorney General Elliot L. Richardson's recommendation for leniency.

Plea Bargaining

Richardson, in a statement he read into the court record, revealed an agreement had been reached between Agnew's lawyers and the Justice Department in what had been protracted plea bargaining. The agreement included Agnew's resignation, his plea, the "no-jail" recommendation, and entry of a 40-page record of the evidence against Agnew in the court record.

That statement, or criminal information, denied by Agnew, alleged he had received cash totaling over $100,000 while Baltimore County executive, Maryland Governor and Vice President.

Among details, it said Allen Green, head of an engineering company, stated he gave Agnew about $50,000 from 1966 to Dec. 1972. It also said Lester Matz, head of another engineering firm, claimed he gave more than $47,000, including an envelope containing $10,000 which, he said, he delivered to Agnew, then newly Vice President, in the Executive Office Building in Washington, and that he later told a friend he was "shaken" at having just made a "payoff" to the Vice President of the United States.

In the end, the man who had been the Administration's Mr. Law and Order himself was in disgrace. Many thought, and some said, he had been let off lightly, that less-favored folk have been sent for a long time to jail for less.

Agnew's rise to power and affluence had seemed a true American success story, Horatio Alger style.

Son of a Greek immigrant, he was elected Baltimore County executive and then Governor of Maryland. Next, although his name was admittedly "not exactly a household word," he was chosen by Richard M. Nixon in 1968 to be his Presidential running-mate.

He was twice elected Vice President, only a step from the Presidency, and he appeared a likely Republican candidate for that great office in 1976.

Alliterative Attacks

Handsome, impressive, convincing, Agnew made his mark as a speaker given to eloquent flights of alliterative prose (often composed by a staff of pro speechwriters). He was at his most pressing his long vendetta against the news media, liberals and intellectuals, labeling them, among other things, "nattering nabobs of negativism" or "effete, impudent snobs" or "pusillanimous pussy-footers."

Golfing companion of millionaires Bob Hope and Frank Sinatra, he retained the human touch with a boyish awkwardness when a wayward golf or tennis ball beaned an innocent bystander.

Many Americans thought he was wonderful, but some did not. Many enjoyed his attacks on the news media, but he failed to shake the mass of Americans' belief in freedom of the press. He made it clear, however, that there is nothing sacrosanct about the news industry and that he, for one, was not afraid to challenge it.

He Lived Well

He lived well, although, as the event showed, not entirely wisely. Airborne coast to coast for speeches and golf games, a goodwill ambassador on round-world trips, a VP among the VIPs, he was sought after by the rich and powerful and, his prosecutors charged in court, by those who wanted to make fortunes through his favors.

The downfall of the 39th Vice President began quietly in late 1972 when George Beall, U.S. attorney for the Maryland district, set out to investigate rumors about some government contractors, modestly expecting, he later said, to maybe catch "a couple of building inspectors." He soon found leads to bigger game and higher drama.

Two days after Agnew's downfall, President Nixon named Congressman Gerald R. Ford, 60, of Grand Rapids, Mich., House minority leader, to succeed Agnew.

The announcement of Ford's appointment was made at a fairly festive White House evening affair. Forgotten already, it seemed, was the son of a Greek immigrant (the father's name was originally Anagnostopoulos); a son who in 1972 was named Father of the Year, and, among other honors, made the Gallup Poll's 1969 list of "Men Most Admired by Americans," topped only by Richard Nixon and the Rev. Billy Graham.

War in Southeast Asia Ends for U.S.

Participation by American military forces in the Vietnam and related Southeast Asia wars ended, not with a bang but with a lond-drawn-out withdrawal. In 1973, at last, the U.S. closed out the longest war in its history.

The cease-fire agreement, which took effect Jan. 27 (EST), Jan. 28 (Vietnam Time), was complicated by a 60-day timetable for withdrawal of the last U.S. troops and return of U.S. prisoners, mostly from North Vietnam.

But the original war, between South Vietnam's government on one side and the rebel Vietcong and invading North Vietnamese on the other, continued, though at a slackened pace.

So did the fighting in Cambodia between the rebel Khmer Rouge, aided by North Vietnam, and Cambodia's new government, helped for a while by heavy U.S. bombings.

In Laos, fighting diminished. The government, which had been bolstered by U.S.-trained forces, and the rebel Pathet Lao, long aided by North Vietnamese troops, signed an agreement Sept. 14 to create a coalition government.

U.S. President Nixon made good his oft-questioned 1968 election campaign promise to get the U.S. out of the war by "Vietnamizing" the struggles of the Vietnamese. In a compromise with Congressional forces, he ended U.S. bombings in Cambodia on Aug. 15.

Hopefully, he called it "peace with honor." But there was no peace in South Vietnam and Cambodia where the governments and the North Vietnam-supported rebels resisted proposals for coalition rule.

The U.S. continued helping the South Vietnam and Cambodia governments with economic aid

and military supplies but also offered to help rebuild bomb-shattered parts of North Vietnam.

For their long negotiations which led to the cease-fire, America's Henry A. Kissinger and North Vietnam's Le Duc Tho were awarded the 1973 Nobel Peace Prize, to share. But Tho, blaming the continued fighting solely on South Vietnam and U.S. aid, rejected the prize.

The war was a sequel to an earlier one begun in 1946 after withdrawal of Japanese troops and attempts by France to reestablish colonial rule, opposed by nationalist forces of Ho Chi Minh (later President of North Vietnam). France helped set up a separate South Vietnam state in 1949 but withdrew its forces in 1954 after defeat at Dien Bien Phu in North Vietnam.

U.S. involvement began, by various reckonings, in 1950 when President Truman set up a 35-man Military Assistance Group; in 1955 when President Eisenhower agreed to U.S. training for the South's troops; in 1961 when President Kennedy offered to help preserve South Vietnam's independence, or in 1964-65 as President Johnson pressed escalation of U.S. forces. They reached a high of 543,400 in Apr. 1969.

President Nixon began withdrawing troops in mid-1969; at the cease-fire 23,000 were left.

U.S. prisoners of war released totaled 590, including 2 held in China; 24 of them were civilians. U.S. "Missing in Action" totalled 1,300 as of mid-1973. Displaced war refugees totaled over 6,500,000 in South Vietnam, over 2,000,000 in Cambodia, over 1,000,000 in Laos. Combat deaths included U.S. 46,079; South Vietnam 184,089; other free world forces 5,225, estimated enemy forces in South Vietnam 925,692.

U.S. Military Casualties in Southeast Asia

Source: Defense Department, as of Jan. 25, 1973; See Footnotes for Some Later Figures

U.S. Casualties Resulting from Action by Hostile Forces Since Jan. 1, 1961

	Army	Navy[2]	Marines	Air Force	Total
1. Killed	25,371	1,092	11,477	494	38,434
2. Wounded or injured					
a. Died of wounds	3,516	146	1,451	48	5,161
b. Nonfatal wounds					
Hospital care required	96,800	4,178	51,391	931	153,300[5]
Hospital care not required	104,718	5,897	37,202	2,505	150,322[6]
3. Missing					
a. Died while missing	1,689	187	5	440	2,321
b. Returned to control	54	5	2	35	96
c. Current missing	258	140	96	722	1,216
4. Captured or interned					
a. Died while captured or interned	15	1	3	2	21
b. Returned to control	57	7	12	8	84
c. Current captured or interned	87	169	26	309	591
5. Deaths					
a. From aircraft accidents/incidents					
Fixed wing	90	166	144	761	1,161
Helicopter	2,388	66	432	75	2,961
b. From ground action	28,113	1,194	12,360	148	41,815
Total Deaths[1]	30,591	1,426	12,936	984	45,937[7]

U.S. Casualties Not the Result of Hostile Action – Since Jan. 1, 1961

	Army	Navy[2]	Marines	Air Force	Total
6. Current Missing	103	1	14	–	118
7. Deaths					
a. From aircraft accidents/incidents					
Fixed wing	276	184	46	290	796
Helicopter	1,875	55	242	19	2,191
b. From other causes	4,995	636	1,392	290	7,313
Total Deaths	7,146	875	1,680	599	10,300

Combat Deaths for Other Forces in Vietnam – Since Jan. 1, 1961

	RVNAF[3][4]	Other Free World Forces	Enemy[4]
Total Deaths	184,089	5,225	925,692

(1) Sum of Lines 1, 2a, 3a, and 4a. (2) Navy figures include Coast Guard. (3) Does not include para-military losses. (4) Includes adjustments from previous periods and is subject to later adjustment in turn. (5) 153,312 as of Aug. 25, 1973. (6) 150,357 as of Aug. 25. (7) 46,079 as of Aug. 25.

Off-Beat News Stories of 1973

It was the grimmest of years, it was the silliest of years. In 1973, much of the news was grave, but there was also light, off-beat news. Take these tales from 2 cities, with their "signs of the crimes":

The Des Moines, Ia., zoo was prey to vandals who came by night and killed or maimed small animals. So the zoo people let some big animals out of their cages—one night a tiger, the next a leopard—but on chains, of course. A sign was erected: "Trespassers Will Be Eaten." No more vandals were reported.

Meanwhile, an Ottawa, Can., supermarket was plagued by food pilferers. It put up a sign: "Shoplifters Will Be Prosecuted." Someone stole the sign. So the store put up a new one—and also hired security guards. At last report both the store sign and the zoo sign remained inviolate.

The National Geodetic Survey revealed that the Washington Monument, which weighs 81,120 tons, is sinking into the ground at the rate of .0047 ft. a year, or .47 ft. per century, roughly one foot every 200 years. At that rate, the NGS figured, the 555.5-ft monument, finished in 1884, won't disappear completely into the ground until 112,072 A.D. give or take a bit. "Despite its weight, its subsidence is minimal," was the official but reassuring pronouncement.

The Mr. vs. Ms. Battle

In the endless war of the sexes, a quiet protest against rules that newspaper classified ads must be sexless was entered by an advertiser in the Salt Lake City Deseret News. His ads: "Man or woman to work in advertising agency making razor blade commercials. Must have heavy beard." And: "Pregnant man or woman to model maternity clothes."

One of the freed POWs made his first call home to his wife when he reached the U.S. base in the Philippines. He walked away groaning "Oh, no. She did it, she did it!" Asked what she did, he replied "She bought a motorcycle."

The Fort Erie, Ont., annual beauty contest was canceled. No entrants.

It's hard to say who won this fray: In N.Y. a mugger slugged a girl and seized her purse. A woman bar manager felled him with 2 punches and sat on him. Another thief grabbed *her* purse and ran while she held the first man. Police arrived and as they led him off to the pokey he was so angry he plucked out his glass eye and threw it at them.

National Affairs

Nations and leaders dealt with serious affairs in 1973, but also with some unusual matters. Spain's Generalissimo Francisco Franco, 80, kept his post as Chief of State but resigned as Premier in favor of a younger man. He chose Admiral Carerro Blanco, 70.

President Jose Figueres of Costa Rica, temporarily without his car, waited for a bus to take him from his home to his office in San Jose. None came, so he tried to thumb a ride. Cars whizzed by. Finally, according to a San Jose newspaper, a woman driver recognized him and gave him a lift.

N.Y. Gov. Nelson Rockefeller was lauding the work of his $70,000-a-year, oft-criticized chairman of the Metropolitan Transportation Authority. Declared the Governor: "William Ronan has done an absolutely horrendous job!" An aide rushed to whisper in his ear and Rockefeller hastened to say he hadn't thought horrendous was "a dirty word."

(Dictionaries agree it means frightful or horrible.) The Governor delivered some alternative adjectives, ranging from "fabulous" to "terrific." (Purists might say "Ooops" again: dictionaries agree the prime meaning of-terrific is causing great fear, terrible or appalling.)

The Egyptian government announced that divorces in that country are now twice as numerous as marriages, 700,000 divorces and 325,000 marriages in one year. It would seem things can't go on long at that rate or no one would be left married, especially since Egyptian Moslem men may divorce a wife by simply declaring 3 times "I divorce thee." Actually, it could continue quite some time since the men are permitted to have 4 wives.

Congressman Bertram Podell, Democrat from Brooklyn, rose on the House floor to point out it was National Procrastination Week. "So," he added as he sat down, "I will put off my remarks on the subject until a later time."

Israel's Premier Golda Meir digressed during a dinner speech to remark: "Let me tell you something we Israelis have against Moses. He took us 40 years through the desert in order to bring us to the one spot in the Middle East that has no oil."

Justice had its usual (or unusual?) quirks. The Soviet newspaper Trud reported a tractor driver paid 1,400 rubles, plus a lot of flour, rice, cloth, etc., for his bride. A few days later she complained about him to the police. He counter-claimed that he had been cheated. The police pointed out that wife-buying is illegal in the first place and both were sent off to a work camp.

A Twist in Crime

Con men and other criminals devised some new tricks. One left the city government of Kearny, N.J., $5,625.27 poorer. A U.S. Treasury check in that amount, made out to "Kearny, N.J.," disappeared. It turned up in a New York bank where an obliging teller had cashed it for an enterprising fellow who endorsed it with the signature "Nathan J. Kearny."

Robbers took $7,000 from a bank in Granby, Quebec, then raced safely away on snowmobiles.

The U.S. director of the International Monetary Fund was stopped on a street in Nairobi, Kenya, where he was attending a meeting of international money experts. Two men who said they were Kenya detectives told him the money he had in his wallet was foreign currency and had to be "registered." They took his $150, walked into a building and disappeared. The director returned to the conference, joining his colleagues in further deliberations on international finance.

People had trouble, too, with buildings. One fellow built his home in the Latonia section of Covington, Ky. Soon a railroad built a spur line with the tracks making a curve that came about 10 yards from our homeowner's front door. One day, a train jumped the track and smacked into the house. It was repaired and another train smashed into it. The railroad offered to move the house for him, out of the danger zone. The moving date was set for May 29, 1973. That morning, before the movers arrived, another train did. Hit the house again. But the railroad promised to fix it up and move it anyway.

Scientists studying the effects of wind found out the hard way. They set up a research station in Cranfield, England. Next morning they found the roof had been blown off.

Deaths, Nov. 1, 1972—Nov. 1, 1973

A

Adrian, Max, 69; British stage, screen actor; London, Jan. 19.

Aiken, Conrad, 84; poet won Pulitzer Prize and National Book Award; Savannah, Ga., Aug. 17.

Allen, George Edward, 77; intimate friend of Presidents Roosevelt, Truman and Eisenhower; Palm Desert, Calif., Apr. 23.

Allende Gossens, Salvador, 65; Marxist President of Chile; reported suicide during successful military coup; Santiago, Sept. 11.

Alvarez, Joseph, 58; manager of editorial services for WNBC-TV in New York; Waldwick, N.J., Aug. 3.

Ancerl, Karel, 65; conductor of the Czech. Philharmonic and Toronto Symphony Orchestras; Toronto, July 3.

Armstrong, Hamilton Fish, 80; international political expert and editor of Foreign Affairs for 44 years; New York, N.Y., Apr. 24.

Armstrong, Robert, 82; actor appeared in over 100 movies in a career that spanned 50 years; Santa Monica, Calif., Apr. 20.

Atlas, Charles, 79; built a business empire on muscle-building correspondence course; Long Beach, N.Y., Dec. 24.

Auden, W.H., 66; major poet, won Pulitzer Prize in 1948; Vienna, Sept. 28.

B

Baker, John, 79; conservationist and naturalist, former president of the Audubon Society; Bedford, Mass., Sept. 21.

Banner, John, 63; Sgt. Schultz of TVs "Hogan's Heroes"; Vienna, Jan. 28.

Barker, Lex, 53; actor played Tarzan in the movies; New York, May 11.

Batista, Fulgencio, 72; Cuban dictator overthrown in 1959; Guadalmina, Spain, Aug. 6.

Behrman, S. N., 80; Broadway playwright wrote 2 dozen comedies; New York, Sept. 9.

Bemis, Samuel Flagg, 81; historian won 2 Pulitzer Prizes; leading authority on the diplomatic history of U.S.; Bridgeport, Conn., Sept. 26.

Bentley, Doug, 56; hockey star, member of Hockey Hall of Fame; Saskatoon, Sask., Nov. 24.

Benton, William, 72; former Senator from Conn. and Asst. Secy. State; publisher of the Encyclopaedia Britannica; New York, Mar. 18.

Bertrand, Jean-Jacques, 56; former Premier of Quebec; Montreal, Feb. 22.

Bickel, Karl A., 90; former president of United Press; Sarasota, Fla., Dec. 11.

Bikila, Abebe, 46; Ethiopian runner was the only man to win 2 Olympic marathons, 1960-64; Addis Ababa, Ethiopia, Oct. 25.

Blackmer, Sidney, 78; actor appeared in some 200 films, 40 Broadway plays and numerous TV dramas; won Tony Award in 1950 "Come Back Little Sheba"; New York, Oct. 5.

Bonlieu, Francois, 36; French skier won gold medal at 1964 Olympics; Nice, France, Aug. 18.

Bonnet, Georges, 83; French Foreign Minister in 1938, signer of the Munich agreement; Paris, June 18.

Bow, Frank T., Rep., 71; congressman from Ohio since 1950; Bethesda, Md., Nov. 13.

Bowen, Elizabeth, 73; Irish born novelist "The Death of the Heart"; London, Feb. 22.

Bowles, Jane, 56; dramatist and novelist; Malaga, Spain, May 4.

Brazle, Alpha, 59; former St. Louis Cardinals pitcher won 133 games; Grand Junction, Colo., Oct. 24.

Brian, Havergal, 96; British composer wrote 32 symphonies, 5 operas and many choral works; Shoreham, Eng., Nov. 28.

Brookeborough, Lord (Sir Basil Brooke), 85; Prime Minister of Northern Ireland, 1943-63; opposed reconciliation with the Irish Republic; Colebrook, No. Ireland, Aug. 18.

Browder, Earl, 82; head of the American Communist Party 1930-1945; Princeton, N.J., June 27.

Brown, Joe E., 80; rubber-mouthed comedian of movies and stage; Brentwood, Calif., July 6.

Buck, Pearl S., 80; author of over 85 books and winner of the Pulitzer and Nobel Prizes in literature; best known work "The Good Earth"; Danby, Vt., Mar. 6.

Budenny, Marshal Semyon, 90; Cossack leader was last surviving military commander of the Bolshevik Revolution; Oct. 27.

C

Carey, James B., 62; labor leader founded International Union of Electrical Workers; Silver Springs, Md., Sept. 11.

Casals, Pablo, 96; world renowned cellist and conductor; Puerto Rico, Oct. 22.

Castle, Peggy, 45; film and television actress; Hollywood, Aug. 10.

Chandler, Norman, 74; former publisher of the Los Angeles Times and a builder of one of the great American publishing empires; Los Angeles, Oct. 20.

Chaney, Jr., Lon, 67; actor starred in many monster films; played "The Wolf Man"; San Clemente, Calif., July 12.

Charriere, Henri, 66; former French convict wrote "Papillon"; Madrid, July 29.

Chasen, Dave, 74; famed Hollywood restaurateur; Los Angeles, June 16.

Chehab, Fuad, 70; former President and first commander of Lebanese Army; Beirut, Apr. 25.

Chow, Bacon Field, 63; biochemist helped to isolate first pure antibody; Baltimore, Sept. 27.

Clemente, Roberto, 38; star outfielder of the Pittsburgh Pirates set dozens of baseball records; in plane crash off San Juan, Dec. 31.

Cobham, Sir Alan, 79; pioneer in commercial aviation, developed systems for refueling aircraft in flight; Bournemouth, Eng., Oct. 21.

Condon, Eddie, 67; jazz guitarist; New York, N.Y., Aug. 4.

Connor, Eugene "Bull", 75; Birmingham police commissioner who used dogs and fire hoses on civil rights demonstrators in the 1960's; Birmingham, Mar. 10.

Cooper, Melville, 76; character actor known for his butler roles; Woodland Hills, Calif., Mar. 29.

Copley, James S., 57; chairman of Copley Press, Inc., and publisher of the San Diego Union and Evening Tribune; San Diego, Oct. 6.

Costello, Frank, 82; underworld leader; New York, Feb. 18.

Coward, Noel, 73; playwright, actor, songwriter, composer and director; famed as master of sophisticated comedy; Jamaica, Mar. 26.

Cox, Wally, 48; actor and comic won fame for his portrayal of TV's "Mr. Peepers"; Bel Air, Calif., Feb. 15.

Creasey, John, 64; wrote 560 mystery and detective novels under 28 pen names, (J.J. Marric, Jeremy York); one of the most prolific writers in publishing history; Wiltshire, Eng., June 9.

Croce, Jim, 30; entertainer wrote and sang "You Don't Mess Around With Jim" "Bad, Bad, Leroy Brown" in a plane crash; Sept. 20.

D

Daniels, Charles M., 88; swimming champion held four Olympic gold medals; Carmel Valley, Calif., Aug. 9.

Despres, Emile, 63; economist; Portola Valley, Calif., Apr. 23.

Dies, Martin, Jr., 72; former Texas congressman organized House Un-American Activities Committee in 1938; Lufkin, Tex., Nov. 13.

Dieterle, William, 79; screen, stage director "The Life of Emile Zola", "Pasteur", "The Hunchback of Notre Dame"; Ottobruenn, West Germany, Dec. 10.

Dodd, Dr. Charles, 89; leading expert on the New Testament, directed a panel of scholars who translated "The New English Bible"; Sept. 22, Goring, England.

Drew, George A., 78; former Premier of Ontario; Toronto Jan. 4.

Duckwitz, Georg Ferdinand, 68; German diplomat who in 1943 defied Nazi orders and allowed over 5,000 Danish Jews to escape to Sweden; Bonn, Feb. 16.

Durham, Yancey (Yank), 52; boxing manager of Joe Frazier, Bob Foster; Philadelphia, Aug. 30.

Dunn, Michael, 39; 3-ft. 10-in. actor appeared on TV, stage, and in films "Ship of Fools"; London, Aug. 29.

F

Farber, Dr. Sidney, 69; pioneer in children's cancer research; Boston, Mar. 30.

Field, Betty, 55; actress starred in theater, television and movies "Of Mice and Men"; Hyannis, Mass. Sept. 13.

Firestone, Harvey S., Jr., 75; president and board chairman of Firestone Tire & Rubber Co.; Akron, Ohio, June 1.

Fleming, James, 91; president and publisher of the Ft. Wayne Journal-Gazette; Ft. Wayne, Indiana, June 11.

Fletcher, Adm. Frank Jack, 87; task force commander in the battles of the Coral Sea and Midway; Bethesda, Md., Apr. 25.

Ford, John, 78; film director won 4 Oscars "The Informer", "The Grapes of Wrath", "How Green Was My Valley", "The Quiet Man"; Palm Desert, Calif., Aug. 31.

Freed, Arthur, 78; producer of many film musicals; won Oscars for "An American in Paris" and "Gigi"; Hollywood, Apr. 12.

Friml, Rudolf, 92; composer of 13 operettas including "Rose Marie" and "The Vagabond King"; Hollywood, Calif., Nov. 12.

Frisch, Frankie, 74; in baseball hall of fame, the "Fordham Flash" was regarded as one of the game's greatest second basemen; Wilmington, Del., Mar. 12.

Frost, Leslie M., 77; former Conservative Premier of Ontario; Lindsay, Ontario, May 4.

G

Gibbon, John H. Jr., Dr., 69; performed the first successful open-heart operation; Philadelphia, Feb. 5.

Gilette, Guy M., 94; former congressman from Iowa; Cherokee, Iowa, Mar. 3.

Grable, Betty, 56; star of numerous Hollywood musicals of 1940's was famed for her legs; favorite pin-up girl of G.I.'s during World War 2; Santa Monica, Calif., July 2.

Graff, George, 86; wrote lyrics to "When Irish Eyes Are Smiling"; Stroudsburg, Pa., Jan. 24.

Green, Abel, 72; editor of the show-business weekly "Variety"; New York, May 10.

Gross, Milton, 61; nationally syndicated sports columnist of the N.Y. Post; New York, May 9.

Grossinger, Jennie, 80; co-founder and hostess of famous Grossinger's resort in Catskills, N.Y.; Grossinger's, Nov. 20.

King Gustaf VI Adolf of Sweden, 90; scholarly monarch reigned for nearly 23 years; Halsingborg, Sweden, Sept. 15.

H

Hafey, Chick, 69; star outfielder for St. Louis Cardinals and member of baseball's Hall of Fame; Napa, Calif., July 2.

Halliday, Richard, 67; theatrical producer; Brazil, Mar. 3.

Hamilton, John, 81; GOP strategist, national chairman, 1936-40; Clearwater, Fla., Sept. 24.

Hammond, Laurens, 78; inventor of the electric organ; Cornwall, Conn., July 1.

Hartley, L.P., 76; English short-story writer, novelist "The Go-Between"; London, Dec. 13.

Hartnett, Gabby (Charles Leo), 72; former Chicago Cubs star catcher managed the team to National League pennant in 1938; Park Ridge, Ill., Dec. 20.

Hatch, Eric, 71; author wrote over 25 novels "My Man Godfrey"; Torrington, Conn., July 4.

Hawkins, Jack, 62; British stage and screen actor whose career spanned 4 decades; London, July 18.

Heiskell, John N., 100; editor of Arkansas Gazette for 70 years and oldest active newspaper editor in U.S.; Little Rock, Dec. 28.

Heschel, Rabbi Abraham Joshua, 65; Jewish theologian was first rabbi named to faculty of the Protestant Union Theological Seminary; New York, Dec. 23.

Hirshberg, Al, 63; former Boston sportswriter and author of some 33 books; Sarasota, Fla., Apr. 11.

Holden, Fay, 70; actress was best known as Andy Hardy's mother in series of 15 films; Los Angeles, June 23.

Holt, Tim, 54; western film star made 149 pictures; Shawnee, Okla., Feb. 15.

Horenstein, Jascha, 74; conductor; London, Apr. 2.

Horowitz, Al, 65; former chess columnist for N.Y. Times won U.S. Open Chess Championship 3 times; New York, N.Y., Jan. 18.

Howes, Royce, 72; won the 1955 Pulitzer Prize for editorial writing as editorial director of the Detroit Free Press; Royal Oak, Mich., Mar. 18.

Hume, Dr. David M., 55; helped develop the technique of human organ transplants; in plane crash at Van Nuys Airport; May 19.

Huntington, Anna Hyatt, 97; sculptor known for heroic statuary; Redding, Conn., Oct. 4.

Inge, William, 60; Pulitzer Prize winning playwright, wrote "Come Back Little Sheba", "Picnic", "Bus Stop"; Hollywood Hills, Calif., June 10.

J

Jacobs, Arthur P., 51; film producer "Planet of the Apes", "Tom Sawyer"; Hollywood, June 27.

Jenks, C. Wilfred, 64; director general of the International Labor Organization; Rome, Oct. 9.

Johnson, Lyndon Baines, 64; 36th President of the United States; San Antonio, Texas, Jan. 22.

Jones, Dr. E. Stanley, 89; Methodist evangelist wrote 29 books on faith; Bareilly, India, Jan. 25.

K

Kellaway, Cecil, 79; veteran character actor in over 75 feature films; Hollywood, Feb. 28.

Kelly, Walt, 60; cartoonist created the nationally syndicated strip "Pogo"; Hollywood, Oct. 18.

Kinkaid, Adm. (Ret.) Thomas C., 84; one of Navy's top combat commanders in Pacific during World War 2; Washington, D.C., Nov. 17.

Klemperer, Otto, 88; conductor was one of the century's great masters of the German musical repertory; Zurich, July 6.

Knight, Frank, 79; radio & TV announcer, "Longine Symphonette"; New York, Oct. 18.

Knutson, Kent S., 48; president of the American Lutheran Church; Rochester, Minn., Mar. 12.

Konev, Marshall Ivan S., 75; Soviet military leader; masterly tactician and commander of mechanized troops in World War 2; USSR, reported May 21.

Krupa, Gene, 64; drummer, one of the major jazz figures, known for his flamboyant performances; Yonkers, N.Y., Oct. 16.

L

Lake, Veronica, 53; box-office favorite of the 1940's with peekaboo hair style; Burlington, Vt., July 7.

Lefevre, Theo, 59; Premier of Belgium, 1961-65; Brussels, Sept. 18.

Lawrence, David, 84; syndicated columnist and founder and editor of "U.S. News & World Report" magazine; Sarasota, Fla., Feb. 11.

Layden, Elmer, 70; fullback of Notre Dame's 1924 famed "Four Horsemen" backfield; Chicago, June 30.

Leahy, Frank, 64; coach of many of Notre Dame's greatest football teams; Portland, Oregon, June 21.

Lee, Bruce, 32; American-born Chinese actor starred in Kung-Fu films; Hong Kong, July 20.

Leonard, Jack E., 62; comedian whose trademark was the one-line insult; New York, May 10.

Lienart, Achille Cardinal, 89; champion of progressive Roman Catholic Church movements; Lille, France, Feb. 15.

Limon, Jose Arcadia, 64; pioneer of modern dance, choreographer "The Moor's Pavane"; his dance company was first to tour for the State Dept.; Flemington, N.J., Dec. 2.

Lipschitz, Jacques, 81; one of the foremost sculptors of the 20th century; Capri, May 26.

Litton, Charles, 69; founder of Litton Industries, Carson City, Nev., Nov. 14.

Long, Edward V., 64; U.S. Sen., D., Mo., 1960-68; Eolia, Mo., Nov. 6.

Lurie, Harry L., 81; social worker, author, and a founder and executive director of the Council of Federations and Welfare Funds; Ogunquit, Maine, June 25.

Lytell, Jimmy, 67; Original Memphis Five jazz bandleader and radio star; Kings Point, N.Y., Nov. 26.

M

Mackenzie, Sir Compton, 89; author of nearly 100 books and dean of British literature "Whiskey Galore"; Edinburgh, Scotland, Nov. 29.

Macready, George, 63; character actor often portrayed a villain in over 70 films; Santa Monica, Calif., July 2.

Malipiero, Gian Francesco, 91; Italian composer of 40 operas; Treviso, Italy, Aug. 1.

Magnani, Anna, 65; Italian actress won Oscar as best actress for "The Rose Tattoo"; Rome, Sept. 26.

Manstein, Field Marshall Erich von, 85; strategist in armored warfare played key role in German victories and defeats in Poland, France and Russia; W. Germany, June 10.

Marcel Gabriel, 83; philosopher founded the French school of Roman Catholic existentialism; Paris, Oct. 8.

Maritain, Jacques, 91; French Roman Catholic philosopher and educator, wrote over 50 books; Toulouse, France, Apr. 28.

Maynard, Ken, 77; white-hatted cowboy hero of some 300 westerns; Hollywood, Mar. 23.

Melchior, Lauritz, 83; Wagnerian tenor; Santa Monica, Calif., Mar. 18.

Millionshchikov, Mikhail D., 60; Soviet scientist and principal spokesman for scientific contacts with the West. Moscow, May 27.

Mitford, Nancy, 68; British essayist, novelist and historian; Versailles, France, June 30.

Moberg, Vilholm, 74; Swedish novelist wrote "The Emigrants" and "The Immigrants"; Vaeddoe, Sweden, Aug. 8.

Mooney, Ria, 69; veteran actress with Ireland's Abbey Theater in its golden years; Dublin, Jan. 3.

Monroe, Vaughn, 62; singer and band-leader best known for "Ghost Riders in the Sky", and "Racing With the Moon". Stuart, Fla., May 21.

Moreland, Mantan, 72; actor-comedian made over 300 movies; Birmingham Brown in the Charlie Chan films; Hollywood, Sept. 28.

Morin, Relman (Pat), 65; AP correspondent won 2 Pulitzer Prizes; New York, July 16.

Mott, Charles Stewart, 97; philanthropist and automobile industry pioneer; Flint, Mich., Feb. 18.

MacGowran, Jack, 54; Irish actor; New York, Jan. 30.

MacMillan, Sir Ernest, 79; composer-conductor directed the Toronto Symphony Orchestra, 1931-1956; Ottawa, May 6.

McBride, Arthur (Mickey), 85; founder of Cleveland Browns football team; Cleveland, Nov. 10.

McElroy, Neil, 69; Defense Secretary in Eisenhower Administration; Cincinnati, Nov. 30.

McKernan, Ron, 27; member of the rock band The Grateful Dead, better known as "Pig Pen"; Corte Madera, Calif., March.

N

Naish, J. Carrol, 73; actor appeared in over 250 movies and starred in radio's "Life With Luigi"; La Jolla, Calif., Jan. 24.

Neill, A. S., 89; founder of the Summer-hill School which allowed children to develop in their own way; Suffolk, England, Sept. 23.

Neruda, Pablo, 69; Nobel Prize winning poet (1971), lifelong leftist political activist; Santiago, Chile, Sept. 23.

Nichols, Roy F., 76; won 1949 Pulitzer

Prize in history; Philadelphia, Jan. 11.

Nover, Barnet, 74; syndicated columnist and editor known as foreign affairs expert; Boston, Apr. 15.

Nurmi, Paavo, 76; Finnish track immortal won 9 gold medals in 3 Olympics; Helsinki, Oct. 2.

O

Offenhauser, Fred, 85; built racing engine that won the Indianapolis 500 28 times; Los Angeles, Aug. 17.

Onassis, Alexander, 24; only son of multimillionaire Aristotle Onassis; in plane crash at Athens airport, Jan. 23.

Orbach, Nathan M., 87; founder of "a profit in pennies" store chain; New York, Nov. 19.

Ory, Edward (Kid), 86; Dixieland jazz trombonist wrote "Muskrat Ramble"; Honolulu, Jan. 23.

Owen, Reginald, 85; British-born star of stage and screen; Boise, Idaho, Nov. 5.

P

Pack, Warren, 52; sports writer and harness racing handicapper; New York, Sept. 8.

Parsons, Louella, 91; Hollywood; gossip columnist was syndicated in 407

Parsons, Louella, 91; Hollywood gossip columnist was syndicated in 407 newspapers; Santa Monica, Calif., Dec. 9.

Paxinou, Katina, 73; Greek actress won Oscar in 1943 for "For Whom the Bell Tolls"; Athens, Feb. 22.

Pearson, Lester Bowles, 75; Canada's 14th Prime Minister (1963-68) won Nobel Peace prize for role in resolving 1956 Suez crisis; Ottawa, Dec. 27.

Perryman, Rufus (Speckled Red), 80; blues pianist and songwriter ("Highway 61 Blues," "Goin Down Slow"); St. Louis, Jan. 2.

Phillips, Stephen, 86; inventor of the mobile starting gate that revolutionized harness racing; Xenia, Ohio, Sept. 26.

Picasso, Pablo, 91; the greatest artist of the 20th century; Mougins, France, April 8.

Podell, Jules, 74; owner of the Copacabana, famed New York nightclub; New York, Sept. 27.

Post, Marjorie Merriweather, 86; businesswoman and philanthropist, was one of the world's wealthiest women; Washington, D.C., Sept. 12.

Pound, Ezra, 87; ex-patriate American poet and influential 20th Century literary figure; Venice, Nov. 1.

R

Radford, Adm. Arthur, 77; Pacific task force commander in World War 2, first Navy man to be chairman of Joint Chiefs of Staff; Bethesda, Md., Aug. 17.

Rankin, Jeannette, 92; women's rights leader was first woman to serve in Congress; voted against entry into World War 1, sole member of Congress to vote against entry into World War 2. Carmel, Calif., May 18.

Razaf, Andy, 77; composer and lyricist contributed to over 1,000 songs; No. Hollywood, Feb. 3.

Richman, Harry, 77; popular Broadway band leader in 1920s and 1930s; Hollywood, Nov. 3.

Rickenbacker, Edward, 82; World War 1 flyer ace and retired chairman of Eastern Air Lines; Zurich, July 23.

Robbins, Rear Adm. (Ret.) Thomas H., Jr., naval aviation leader and former head of Naval War College; New London, Conn., Dec. 12.

Robinson, Edward G., 79; actor appeared in 40 Broadway plays and over 100 movies; gained fame as "Little Caesar" and other gangster roles in the 30s; Hollywood, Jan. 26.

Robinson, Dr. Preston, 70; scientist and inventor who designed the energy storage capacitators that triggered the first atomic bomb. Williamstown, Mass., May 21.

Rockefeller, Winthrop, 60; former governor of Arkansas, Palm Springs, Calif., Feb. 22.

Rodriguez, Tito, 50; Puerto Rican singer and band leader; New York, Mar. 7.

Rosenman, Samuel I., 77; advisor to Presidents Roosevelt and Truman; coined the historic phrase "New Deal" and assembled the original "Brain Trust"; New York, N.Y., June 24.

Ryan, Irene, 70; veteran actress greatest fame as "Granny" on TV's "Beverly Hillbillies" series; Santa Monica, Calif., Apr. 26.

Ryan, Robert, 63; actor appeares in over 90 films; New York, July 11.

S

St. Laurent, Louis, 91; Prime Minister of Canada, 1948-1957; Quebec City, July 25.

Sanderson, Ivan, 62; author and naturalist; Columbia, N.J., Feb. 19.

Sands, Diana, 39; actress appeared in television, movies and the theater; acclaimed for "Raisin in the Sun"; New York, Sept. 21.

Saylor, Rep. John, 65; Rep. from Pennsylvania for 25 years was widely known as a conservationist; Houston, Oct. 28.

Segni, Antonio, 81; former premier and president of Italy; Rome, Dec. 1.

Senanayake, Dudley, 57; three times Prime Minister of Ceylon; Colombo, Sri Lanka, Apr. 12.

Sherman, Al, 76; songwriter wrote over 500 songs, "Potatoes Are Cheaper", "For Sentimental Reasons"; Los Angeles, Sept. 15.

Siodmak, Robert, 72; film director and producer; Switzerland, Mar. 10.

Sisler, George, 80; baseball hall of famer who twice batted over 400. St. Louis; Mar. 26.

Smith, Delos, 68; science editor of United Press International; New York, May 31.

Strauss, Leo, 74; political philosopher and interpreter of classical political theory; Annapolis, Md., Oct. 18.

Steichen, Edward, 93; photographer hailed as a craftsman of genius who transformed his medium into an art; West Redding, Conn., Mar. 25.

Stern, G. B., 83; British novelist and playwright; Berkshire, England, Sept. 19.

Stone, Walker, 68; retired editor in chief of Scripps-Howard Newspapers; Woodville, Va., Mar. 18.

Stossel, Ludwig, 89; TV's "Little Old Winemaker"; Hollywood, Jan. 29.

Swados, Harvey, 52; novelist, social critic "Standing Fast," "False Coin"; Holyoke, Mass., Dec. 11.

Szigeti, Joseph, 80; world renowned violinist; Lucerne, Switzerland, Feb. 19.

T

Thompson, Lawrence R., 67; biographer won 1971 Pulitzer Prize for "Robert Frost: The Years of Triumph, 1915-1938"; Princeton, N.J., Apr. 15.

Thorndike, Russell, 87; British actor, author of "Dr. Syn" novels; London, Nov. 7.

Tolkien, J.R.R., 81; author of the fantasy trilogy "The Lord of the Rings"; Bournemouth, England, Sept. 2.

Trammell, Niles, 78; former president and board chairman of NBC; North Miami, Fla., Mar. 28.

Tregaskis, Richard, 56; war correspondent and author of "Guadalcanal Diary"; Honolulu, Aug. 15.

Truex, Ernest, 83; actor made hundreds of appearances in theater, movies and television; Fallbrook, Calif., June 26.

Truman, Harry S, 88, 33rd President of the United States; Independence, Mo., Dec. 26.

Tupolev, Andrei N., 84; pioneer aircraft designer; Moscow, Dec. 23.

U

Ulbricht, Walter, 80; East Germany head of state built the Berlin Wall in 1961; E. Berlin, Aug. 1.

V

Van Doren, Mark, 78; poet, novelist, critic and retired professor taught many who became noted writers in 4 decades at Columbia U; Torrington, Conn., Dec. 10.

Van Rooten, Luis, 66; character actor and master of dialect participated in over 9,000 radio broadcasts, several hundred TV shows and 30 films; Chatham, Mass., June 17.

Vandergrift, Alexander A., 86; former Marine Corps commandant led Marines at Guadalcanal; Bethesda, Md., May 8.

Vernadsky, George, 85; an authority on Russian history; New Haven, Conn., June 12.

W

Waksman, Dr. Selman A., 85; principal discoverer of Streptomycin, coined the word "antibiotic"; Hyannis, Mass., Aug. 16.

Walker, Ralph T., 83; hailed by A.I.A. in 1957 as "Architect of the Century"; Chappaqua, N.Y., Jan. 17.

Wallington, Jimmy, 64; radio announcer in the 1930s and 1940s (Eddie Cantor, Fred Allen shows); Arlington, Va., Dec. 21.

Watkins, Arthur V., 86; Utah Senator presided over special committee that censured Sen. Joseph R. McCarthy in 1954; Orem., Utah, Sept. 1.

Wheeler, John N., 87; former chairman of the North American Newspaper Alliance; Norwalk, Conn., Oct. 13.

White, Dr. Paul Dudley, 87; international authority on heart disease, advocated exercise as prevention and therapy; Boston, Oct. 31.

White, William L., 73; editor and publisher of Emporia (Kansas) Gazette; author of "They Were Expendable"; Emporia, Kansas, July 26.

Wiley, George, 42; civil rights leader, former head of National Welfare Rights Org., drowned in Chesapeake Bay, Md., Aug. 8.

Wilson, Marie, 56; comedienne played radio and TV versions of "My Friend Irma;" Hollywood, Nov. 23.

Winterhalter, Hugo, 64; pop music arranger of the 50's; Greenwich, Conn., Sept. 17.

Y

Young, Chic, 72; creator of the comic strip "Blondie"; St. Petersburg, Mar. 14.

Z

Zerbe, Karl L., 69; expressionist painter revived ancient medium of encaustic, a hot wax painting technique; Tallahassee, Nov. 28.

Laws Passed by 93d Congress, 1st Session (1973)

The 93d Congress, First Session, convened Jan. 3, 1973. Major bills passed by Congress and signed into law by President Nixon, as well as other Congressional actions, follow:

Aid to Elderly. This extended for 3 years a series of programs to aid elderly persons, but at a possibly lower cost than provided in a bill vetoed by the President in late 1972; the new bill was signed by the President May 3.

Old-Age Benefits. This provided for a 5.6% increase in Social Security pension benefits, effective July 1, 1974. The bill originally provided for a Jan. 1, 1974, effective date; the July 1 date was a compromise with the Administration; signed by the President July 11.

Disaster Relief. This revived a disaster relief loan program, killed by the White House the previous December, for victims of the 1972 tropical storm Agnes and South Dakota floods; signed by the President Apr. 28.

Wage-Price Controls. A compromise bill, this extended for another year the President's power to regulate wages and prices, but raised requirements on profit disclosures by large corporations seeking price increases; signed Apr. 30.

Health, Economics, Bombs

Health Programs. The bill extended for the fiscal year hospital construction, medical and mental health programs the President had planned to eliminate, totaling $1.2 billion; in signing it June 19, the President urged Congress to hold down actual appropriations.

Cambodia Bombing Cutoff. A compromise, this set Aug. 15 as the deadline for a cutoff of all funds for U.S. military actions in Cambodia, Laos, North Vietnam and South Vietnam; Congress had wanted to set July 1; the President agreed not to veto the bill and pledged to seek Congressional approval if U.S. military action was needed after Aug. 15; he signed the bill July 1.

Supplemental Funds. Part of the war funds cutoff compromise were 2 bills, one a resolution allowing federal agencies to continue spending until Sept. 30 in the absence of regular appropriations bills, the other a $3.3 billion supplemental funding bill; the President signed both July 1.

Change in Farm Aid

New Farm Aid Program. The old farm subsidy system with acreage restrictions and government purchases to keep prices up was ended; the new program set "target prices" for wheat, feed grains and cotton and, if the farmer's average sales prices should fall below the target, the government would pay him the difference; it was felt farmers would plant more to meet food shortages, have an assured income and, with current high prices, the program would cost the government and taxpayers nothing; the President signed the bill Aug. 10.

Mass Transit Aid from Highway Funds. A 3-year bill, this provided that starting July 1, 1974, $200,000,000 would be released for city bus aid, and $800,000,000 starting July 1, 1975, for buses, rail systems and subways; but communities could get immediate aid for mass transit by giving up highway projects and using the money for bus or rail projects; the President signed it Aug. 13.

REA Loans. This revived the low-cost loan program of the Rural Electrification Administration for electric and telephone projects which the Administration had ended Jan. 1; a compromise,

the bill revived 2% loans for sparsely settled areas, but required 5% loans elsewhere; signed May 11.

Law Enforcement Aid. Extending the Law Enforcement Assistance Administration program for states and communities for 3 years, this bill was signed by the President Aug. 6.

Ecology and TV

Ecology Acts. Bills approving a one-year extension of funding authority at $474,000,000 for administration of the clean air law and $238,500,000 for the solid waste disposal law were signed by the President Apr. 10.

Sports Broadcasts. Prohibited TV blackouts of professional sports home games that are sold out 72 hours in advance; signed by the President Sept. 14.

OK for "Action". A bill formally consolidating the government's major volunteer service programs under the Action agency was signed by the President Oct. 1; included were Vista, the Peace Corps, the Service Corps of Retired Executives and Foster Grandparents.

Vocational Rehabilitation. The President signed Sept. 26 a bill authorizing $1.54 billion in grants to states, local governments and private agencies to run programs to rehabilitate the handicapped for jobs; in Oct. 1972 and Mar. 1973 he had vetoed similar but more costly bills.

Government Pay Raises. An attempt by the President to postpone pay increases for federal workers and military personnel, due Oct. 1, until Dec. 1, was disapproved by the Senate, legally nullifying the proposed delay.

Confirmations by Senate

The Senate, which acts alone on confirmations of Presidential appointments, appeared likely to kill the nomination of L. Patrick Gray, 3d, to be FBI director; at Gray's request the President withdrew his name Apr. 5. The Senate confirmed Elliott L. Richardson as Attorney General May 23, after receiving a written agreement that he would appoint an independent prosecutor in the Watergate affair. A Senate committee killed the nomination of G. McMurtrie Godley, former Ambassador to Laos, to be Ass't. Secretary of State for East Asian Affairs, July 12, recommending he be nominated for a post not connected with Southeast Asia. Most Presidential appointments were confirmed without controversy.

Vetoes

Congress, through Oct. 22, failed to override any of the President's vetoes, but did pass several compromise bills, partly meeting Administration objections, which the President then signed.

Among those vetoed were bills to require Senate confirmation of the director and deputy director of the Office of Management and Budget; to raise the minimum wage to $2.20 an hour by July 1, 1974; to provide improved emergency medical services; to supply vocational aid to the handicapped; to annul Administration impoundment of funds for rural water and sewer programs and to continue the programs for another year; to liberalize the disaster loan program; to force the President to obtain Congressional approval before attempting to cut back a federal spending program; to cut off all funds for bombing Cambodia after July 1.

The President on Sept. 10 told Congress he would veto any further bills which would raise the cost of domestic programs above his budget or cut defense spending below it.

Major Decisions of the U.S. Supreme Court, 1973

The court ruled, 6-3, that while the one-man, one-vote principle controls most executive and legislative elections, justices of the state courts may be elected from districts of widely varying populations (Jan. 8).

The court also:

Declared, 5-4, that no matter how poor a person may be, he must pay the legal $50 fee before he may go into bankruptcy (Jan. 10).

Unanimously held, in a South Carolina case, that black defendants in state criminal trials are entitled to have prospective jurors questioned as to whether they are prejudiced against Negroes. But the court held, 7-2, a defendant does not have a right to questions as to prejudice against beards (Jan. 17).

Decided, 7-2, that illegitimate children have the same right to financial support from their fathers as do legitimate children. The decision affected only Texas, Wyoming and Idaho, the only states without laws to that effect (Jan. 17).

Abortions Legal

Declared unconstitutional, 7-2, all state laws restricting a woman's right to have an abortion during the first 3 months of pregnancy, adding that during the remaining 6 months states may regulate abortion procedures "in ways that are reasonably related to maternal health," and that in the final 10 weeks states may prohibit abortions, if they wish, except where they may be necessary to preserve the life or health of the mother (Jan. 22).

Ruled, 7-2, that the self-incrimination ban does not protect a grand jury witness from making a voice recording for identification purposes, and ruled, 6-3, that the ban on search and seizure does not permit a grand jury witness to refuse to give a handwriting sample (Jan. 22).

Turned down, 7-0, an appeal by Sirhan Sirhan from his conviction and life sentence for the assassination of Sen. Robert F. Kennedy (Feb. 20).

Decided in a Virginia case, 5-3, that the one-man, one-vote rule need not be followed so strictly in laying out state legislative districts as in Congressional districts (Feb. 21).

Pool Club Desegregated

Unanimously held that a suburban swimming club in Maryland, which gave preference to residents of the neighborhood, could not refuse to accept blacks living in that neighborhood (Feb. 27).

Ruled, 7-1, that Petersburg, Va., could not annex a mostly white area, changing the percentage of whites in the city from 45% to 54%, unless it changed the way it elected city councilmen, which was by the "at large" system, under which a white majority could theoretically prevent any black representation (Mar. 5).

Upheld an Oregon law requiring poor persons to pay a $25 fee to appeal an adverse welfare decision (Mar. 5).

Refused to review the contempt conviction of Peter Bridge, a New Jersey reporter, for refusing to testify to a grand jury about confidential information given him by a Newark, N.J., official (Mar. 19).

Upheld, 6-3, Arizona and Georgia laws requiring voters be residents and registered 50 days before state and local elections. A 1972 decision by the court in a Texas case had suggested that 30 days should be a sufficient limit (Mar. 19).

Unanimously upheld the constitutionality of state and local laws giving preference to veterans in obtaining civil service jobs and promotions (Mar. 19).

Held, 5-4, that states could finance public school systems with property taxes, which tend to provide more money and better school facilities for students living in wealthy districts than for those in poor districts (Mar. 21).

Upheld, 5-4, N.Y. State's requirement that a voter must register in a political party 8 to 11 months in advance to vote in the party primary (Mar. 21).

Refused, 8-1, to review the contempt citation of Harvard Prof. Samuel L. Popkin who refused to answer grand jury questions involving the Pentagon papers (Mar. 26).

Alaska Pipeline

Declined to review a lower court decision barring the Secretary of the Interior from issuing permits for construction of the proposed Alaska oil pipeline (Apr. 2).

Let stand a lower court decision that the firing of a Rochester, N.Y., teacher for refusing to recite the Pledge of Allegiance with pupils was an unconstitutional violation of freedom of speech (Apr. 16).

Dismissed, 6-3, an appeal by 15 Elks lodges in Maine from a state ruling denying liquor licenses to organizations discriminating against blacks (Apr. 16).

Ruled, 6-3, in Mississippi and Tennessee cases, that challenges against grand juries from which blacks are excluded must be raised before, not after conviction (Apr. 17).

Oil Spillage

Unanimously upheld a Florida law making shippers, off-shore oil drillers and oil terminals liable for damage caused to the state and property owners by oil spillages (Apr. 18).

Held, 5-4, a criminal defendant connot claim he was unfairly trapped by government agents if they helped him commit a crime but did not give him the idea of committing the crime (Apr. 24).

Ruled, 8-1, unconstitutional a New Jersey law prohibiting "working poor" benefits to families with one or more illegitimate children (May 7).

By 4-4 vote affirmed a lower court decision calling unconstitutional a Richmond, Va., desegregation plan to merge the mostly black city schools with mostly white suburban schools into a single school system (May 21).

Ruled, 8-1, that females in the armed forces are entitled to the same dependency benefits for their husbands as service men receive for their wives (June 21).

In a series of 5-4 decisions ruled that states may ban books, magazines, movies and plays that are offensive to local standards (June 21).

Upheld, 5-4, a Pittsburgh ordinance prohibiting newspapers from carrying sex-designated employment ads such as "Help Wanted—Male" (June 21).

Held, 7-2, in a New York case, that states may require able-bodied welfare recipients to seek and accept employment or be put to work on public works projects (June 21).

Overruled, 8-1, a decision by Supreme Court Justice William O. Douglas overruling a stay of execution of a lower court ban against continued bombing of Cambodia (Aug. 4).

PERSONAL FINANCE
The Inflationary Way of Life

by Jerome Shuchter, Editor, Jeremiad
Box 36496, Los Angeles, Calif. 90036

In May of 1973, the price index prepared by the U.S. Department of Labor stood at 131.5 index points. Such numbers are known as "relatives." They have no intrinsic value except as they are compared to other indexes of the same form. An index of 131.5 for the Consumer Price Index (CPI) means that the typical product or service purchased by city workers had gone up from 100% in 1967, the base or reference year, to 131.5% in May. Every month the Bureau of Labor Statistics rechecks the prices for the same "market basket" of products and services at the point of sale, then compares these prices to the prices of the same products in 1967, and an index number is calculated to represent the entire aggregation of products and services.

Measuring Inflation

To define inflation, a common method is to calculate the percentage change from one year to the next. The 1973 record of such comparisons shows inflation on the rise all year, from +3.7% in January to +5.9% in June, then declining slightly to +5.7% in July as prices were frozen, and expanding to +7.5% when the freeze ended in August.

year-to-year measure. With regard to the CPI it suffers from a distortion. As published, the CPI is not corrected for ordinary seasonal changes in prices, so that part of any month-to-month movement may be a normal seasonal regularity, rather than inflation. Although the index itself is not published with seasonal adjustment, a "seasonally adjusted percent change" is announced each month. In August 1973 the rise was 1.8% before seasonal adjustment and 1.9% after such adjustment. In annual terms, the 1.9% increase would come to 25%.

The CPI considers 2 main categories of consumer spending, commodities and services. Services other than rent, such as medical care, shave been on a sharp climb for decades, much sharper than other prices. Among the commodities, the year 1973 featured a spectacular rise in food costs, far outrunning other consumer prices.

Another important breakdown furnished by the Bureau of Labor Statistics is the CPI for major cities. The figures take in also the entire urban portion of the cities' Standard Metropolitan Statistical Area, as defined by the Census Bureau.

Average Consumer Price Indexes

Source: Bureau of Labor Statistics, United States Department of Labor

The Consumer Price Index measures the average change in prices of goods and services purchased by urban wage-earner and clerical-worker families and single workers living alone. Data for 56 large, medium size, and small cities are combined for the all-city average.

(1967 = 100)

Year and month	All items	Food	Housing Total	Rent	Gas and electricity	Fuel and Utilities	Household furnishings & operation	Apparel and Upkeep	Transportation	Medical care	Personal care	Reading and recreation	Other goods and services
1965....	94.5	94.4	94.9	96.9	99.4	98.3	95.3	93.7	95.9	89.5	95.2	95.9	94.2
1970....	116.3	114.9	118.9	110.1	107.3	107.6	113.4	116.1	112.7	120.6	113.2	113.4	116.0
1971....	121.3	118.4	124.3	115.2	114.7	115.1	118.1	119.8	118.6	128.4	116.8	119.3	120.9
1972....	125.3	123.5	129.2	119.2	120.5	120.1	121.0	122.3	119.9	132.5	119.8	122.8	125.5
1973 Jan.	127.7	128.6	131.4	121.5	124.1	122.8	122.2	123.0	121.0	134.9	121.8	124.1	126.7
Feb.	128.6	131.1	132.0	122.1	124.5	124.1	122.6	123.6	121.1	135.3	122.4	124.3	127.1
Mar.	129.8	134.5	132.3	122.6	125.0	124.6	123.0	124.8	121.5	135.8	123.1	124.5	127.6
Apr.	130.7	136.5	132.8	123.0	125.5	125.1	123.6	125.8	122.6	136.2	123.8	125.2	128.2
May	131.5	137.9	133.3	123.5	125.7	125.4	123.9	126.7	123.5	136.6	124.4	125.6	128.5
June	132.4	139.8	133.9	123.9	125.4	125.6	124.7	126.8	124.6	137.0	124.9	125.9	129.0
July	132.7	140.9	134.2	124.3	125.5	125.7	125.0	125.8	124.8	137.3	125.3	126.2	129.5

Indexes of Retail Prices of Foods

Source: Bureau of Labor Statistics, United States Department of Labor (1967 = 100)

Year and month	Total food	Food at home	Cereals, bakery products	Meats, poultry, fish	Dairy products	Fruits, vegetables	Other foods
1968..............	103.6	103.2	100.4	102.2	103.3	107.9	102.6
1969..............	108.9	108.2	103.3	110.8	106.7	109.3	107.9
1970..............	114.9	113.7	108.9	116.5	111.8	113.4	114.1
1971..............	118.4	116.4	113.9	116.9	115.3	119.1	115.9
1972..............	123.5	121.6	114.7	128.0	117.1	125.0	116.7
1973 Jan.	128.6	127.2	116.3	136.1	119.1	130.5	123.8
May	137.9	137.6	122.1	155.6	123.2	144.6	125.4
July	140.9	140.9	123.5	157.8	124.1	153.7	128.5

Year-to-year change is but one way of measuring inflation. Another is to calculate the percentage change in the indexes from month to month, then explode the one-month increase for the full year equivalent. From April to May 1973, for example, prices rose by .61%, which (compounded) is equivalent to an annual rate of 7.6%. Obviously such a measure is more sensitive and volatile than the

The Bureau publishes also 2 series measuring the purchasing power of the dollar, one in terms of consumer prices, the other in terms of wholesale prices. The series are just the inverse of their parents. The CPI tells us what a dollar's worth of 1967 goods and services would cost today. The CPI version of the purchasing power of the dollar series tells us what the 1967 dollar itself is worth

Indexes By Cities, All Items and Food (1967 = 100)

City	Annual Average All Items 1971	1972	Food 1971	1972	City	Annual Average All Items 1971	1972	Food 1971	1972
U.S. City Average	121.3	125.3	118.4	123.5	Los Angeles, Calif. ...	118.5	122.3	114.9	120.4
Atlanta, Ga...........	121.7	125.5	118.1	124.4	Milwaukee, Wis.......	120.1	123.7	115.7	120.6
Baltimore, Md.......	123.4	126.3	121.0	124.7	Minneapolis, Minn....	121.7	125.5	119.2	124.4
Boston, Mass.	122.8	127.1	118.5	123.7	New York, N.Y........	125.9	131.4	123.1	128.6
Buffalo, N.Y.........	121.8	126.6	119.7	123.5	Philadelphia, Pa......	123.5	127.0	120.1	124.4
Chicago, Ill.....,.....	120.8	124.3	118.5	123.9	Pittsburgh, Pa.......	121.5	125.3	118.9	122.8
Cincinnati, Ohio......	120.7	124.7	118.4	124.5	Portland, Ore........	116.1	119.5	113.4	118.0
Cleveland, Ohio	122.8	126.5	118.9	123.3	St. Louis, Mo.........	119.6	122.3	118.0	122.5
Dallas, Texas	121.3	124.9	117.8	123.0	San Diego, Calif.	119.9	124.4	117.3	123.3
Detroit, Mich.........	121.7	126.2	117.3	122.9	San Francisco, Calif. .	120.2	124.3	116.1	121.4
Honolulu, Hawaii.....	118.9	122.8	118.1	123.2	Scranton, Pa.........	121.4	125.9	120.1	123.4
Houston, Tex.........	120.9	125.2	118.8	125.0	Seattle, Wash.	116.4	119.7	115.9	120.7
Kansas City, Mo.	120.5	124.0	118.6	123.6	Washington, D.C......	122.7	126.9	120.2	125.8

Purchasing Power of the Dollar

Source: U.S. Department of Labor, Bureau of Labor Statistics

1967 = $1.00

Beginning 1961, wholesale prices include data for Alaska and Hawaii; and, beginning 1964 consumer prices include them. Obtained by dividing the average price index for 1967 base period (100.0) by the price index for given period and expressing the result in dollars and cents.

Year	Monthly average as measured by— Wholesale prices	Con- sumer prices	Year	Monthly average as measured by— Wholesale prices	Con- sumer prices
1940..............	$2.469	$2.381	1962.............	$1.055	$1.104
1950..............	1.222	1.387	1963.............	1.058	1.091
1953..............	1.144	1.248	1964.............	1.056	1.076
1954..............	1.142	1.242	1965.............	1.035	1.058
1955..............	1.139	1.247	1966.............	1.002	1.029
1956..............	1.103	1.229	1967.............	1.000	1.000
1957.......'......	1.072	1.186	1968.............	.976	.960
1958.....,.......	1.057	1.155	1969.............	.939	.911
1959..............	1.055	1.145	1970.............	.906	.860
1960..............	1.054	1.127	1971.............	.878	.824
1961..............	1.058	1.116	1972.............	.840	N.A.

today to the consumer.

Putting CPI To Work—Real Income

Statistics expressed in dollars are converted to real terms to state what the figure would have been if the inflationary content were stripped away. The average wage of U.S. workers is commonly expressed in dollars of the sliding value we all know. Divide the wage by the CPI for the same period, and you have the real wage, expressed in terms of dollars with the buying power of 1967. Such a calculation of Real Earnings is made in the report below by the Bureau of Labor Statistics. In addition to skimming inflation from the wage, the series goes on to express the earnings on a take-home basis, that is, after deductions for social security and for federal withholding taxes. Such deductions vary, so the calculation is made twice, once for workers without dependents and once for a worker with three dependents. When seasonal adjustments are added, the July 1973 report showed that real take-home earnings for all nonagricultural workers with three dependents reached a peak of $97.49 per week in October 1972, and has dropped steadily since to a low of $95.51 in June 1973. In July's freeze, there was a small recovery, to $96.17.

Other Indexes

The construction of index numbers, such as the CPI, is a highly technical task by which thousands of readings are reduced to a single index number. Although the CPI is the most widely known measure of inflation, there are a number of competing indexes in the U.S. statistical arsenal.

The Wholesales Price Index (WPI), also published by the Bureau of Labor Statistics, measures the prices businessmen charge each other for products as they move through trade channels. Since these transactions precede the sale of products at retail, price changes in the WPI

are sure to surface in the CPI at a later date. The WPI falls short on several counts of being a good direct measure of inflation. The reporting system which gives rise to the WPI has been strongly criticized, not least by its constructors, for including book prices of products instead of the prices at which transactions actually take place. There are also important industries not adequately represented—there is a negligible wholesale market for automobiles.

The Department of Commerce publishes a quarterly series of Implicit Price Deflators in conjunction with its work on the Gross National Product. GNP is calculated in common dollar terms, then in real terms, the ratio of the two giving rise to the implicit deflator. The deflator series is broader than the others, including along with consumer items the prices of business transactions, foreign commerce and government operations. Thus, if inflation is being considered as a broad general phenomenon at the national level, the deflators provide a valid measure. If inflation is considered in terms of impact on consumers—or if monthly readings are needed—the CPI is preferable.

Living With Inflation

This inflation is an upheaval in economic affairs shaped by remote military adventures, superimposed on the prevailing mild inflationary drift, spanning the world through the channels of international commerce and finance, exacerbated by a variety of chancy events—hardly the subject for instant cure. Some analysts consider a 5-year run to be plausible, a pleasant outlook which figures the rate of inflation will dwindle slowly until it flickers into extinction. By this reckoning, the present outbreak is but an erratic incident on the high road to economic plenty.

Unfortunately inflation has never been like that. Inflation below 10% has considerable discomfort for some, but the real threat lies in what it forebodes. History provides 2 possible courses: either the inflation breaks out into a virulent form or it ends up in a bust. Wars have not only inflation in their van, but a recession right behind. In the transition from tonic to toxic, only the details differ. Here, after Vietnam, we have an inflation rather more obstreperous than most, and it hardly seems possible that it will leave like a pussycat.

Inflation Survival Kit

Having discovered that inflation is pervasive and universal, what can we do about it?

The national policy is wage and price control, with the stated expectation that controls will be jettisoned the moment inflationary pressures relax. Unfortunately, inflation tends to entrench itself; it sets up trends that persist into the future. Interest rates on loans and deposits are based on the present inflated costs of money. Wage increases are negotiated for years ahead. In every section of the business world decisions are made which appear to be judicious but which tend to extend the inflationary life span. So the problem tends to linger.

National programs can only follow a well-worn groove. Government spending right now to be balanced, and the expansion of money supply kept within modest limits. Hopefully, with the military infections reduced, with the chain of unhappy mishaps (shortages, weather, etc.) halted, with the rampaging dollar's wings clipped abroad, we should find the inflationary impulse receding, more subject to management.

How can individuals survive? In approaching this problem the individual's goals will vary according to his role: citizen, breadwinner, householder.

As **citizen**, the individual ought to be aware that reforms requiring monetary outlays should have counterpart tax reforms to raise the required funds, so the inflationary impulse is not stirred to life. There is no plausible reason for budget deficits or exaggerated monetary policies on the one hand; on the other, the threat of inflation is too often used as an excuse for stifling progress.

As **breadwinner**, the consumer often faces a self-serving cry for restraint from those making hay from the inflationary boom. It is plain that inflation sprouted while the real wage was declining. It is plain that other income earners have been making strong progress while labor's wage languished.

As **householder**, the consumer should not be deceived by the money illusion. Dollars are just not the same money they were a year ago. During inflation you should take stock from time to time to see how your status measures up against the averages, and, if need be, to make appropriate changes. Here are some suggestions:

In handling money and investments do not keep idle dollars at home or in checking accounts which earn no interest. There is an inflationary penalty for idle funds. Moderate sums should be kept in interest-bearing accounts. Larger sums can be invested for increasing returns on your money: bonds, certificates, term accounts, mortgages—all paying rates of interest above bank accounts. Invest cautiously at all events; do not assume investment you do not fully understand; consider the risk of losing part of your capital; consider time restrictions in terms of when you are likely to need the funds.

See your situation realistically. If inflation has found you with a fixed or declining income, your way of life should respond to the fact that you have lost ground. Prices are unlikely ever to revert to the old level, so some part of your budget—food, rent, clothing, savings—has to be reduced. Sometimes judicious shifts in spending—other foods, a different apartment, etc.—can take up the slack. While accommodating to the realities, seek redress in legitimate ways from your employer and by supporting suitable government policies.

Buy ahead, but judiciously. It may be wise to replace your car now at lower prices, instead of waiting. You might invest in scarce items such as jewels, silver, real estate, antiques, art objects. There is room for judicious steps in such directions, but stay within sensible and responsible bounds. Avoid speculations outside your ken (unless you are a dashing cocoa futures trader). Don't play the hoarding game: buying up common food or household products in anticipation of rising prices simply guarantees high prices for everyone.

Average Weekly Earnings of Production Workers[1]

Source: Bureau of Labor Statistics

	Private nonagricultural workers				Manufacturing workers			
	Spendable average weekly earnings[2]				Spendable average weekly earnings[2]			
	Workers with no dependents		Worker with 3 dependents		Worker with no dependents		Worker with 3 dependents	
	Current dollars	1967 dollars	Current dollars	1967 dollars	Current dollars	1967 dollars	Current dollars	1967 dollars
1965	78.99	83.59	86.30	91.32	89.08	94.26	96.78	102.41
1966	81.29	83.63	88.66	91.21	91.57	94.21	99.45	102.31
1967	83.38	83.38	90.86	90.86	93.28	93.28	101.26	101.26
1968	86.71	83.21	95.28	91.44	97.70	93.76	106.75	102.45
1969	90.96	82.84	99.99	91.07	101.90	92.81	111.14	101.49
1970	95.94	82.49	104.61	89.95	106.62	91.68	115.90	99.66
1971	103.51	85.33	112.12	92.43	114.68	94.54	123.93	102.17
1972	111.37	88.88	120.79	96.40	125.32	100.02	135.56	108.19
1973: January	112.09	87.78	121.63	95.25	127.48	99.83	138.03	108.09
February	112.91	87.80	122.51	95.26	128.87	100.21	139.54	108.51
March	113.73	87.62	123.38	95.05	129.71	99.93	140.44	108.20
April	114.54	87.64	124.25	95.07	130.29	99.69	141.06	107.93
May	115.36	87.73	125.11	95.14	130.57	99.29	141.36	107.50
June (p)	117.32	88.61	127.18	96.06	131.72	99.49	142.59	107.70
July (p)	118.43	89.25	128.35	96.72	131.44	99.05	142.29	107.23

[1] Data relate to production workers in mining and manufacturing; to construction workers in contract construction; and to non-supervisory workers in transportation and public utilities; wholesale and retail trade; finance, insurance, and real estate; and services.

[2] Spendable average weekly earnings are based on gross average weekly earnings less the estimated amount of the worker's Federal social security and income taxes. (p)—preliminary

TAXATION
Federal Individual Income Tax
Source: Tax Foundation: Internal Revenue Service, Treasury Dept.

Who Must File
Every individual under 65 years of age who resided in the United States and had a gross income of $2,050 or more during the year, must file a Federal income tax return. Anyone 65 or older on the last day of the tax year is not required to file a return unless he had gross income of $2,800 or more during the year. A married couple both 65 or older, need not file unless their gross income exceeds $4,300.

A taxpayer with gross income of less than $2,050 (or less than $2,800 if 65 or older) should file a return to claim the refund of any taxes withheld, even if he is listed as a dependent by another taxpayer.

Forms to Use
A taxpayer may, at his election, file Form 1040 and let IRS compute his tax if his income is $20,000 or less and consists only of wages or salaries and tips, dividends, interest, pensions and annuities and he chooses the standard deductions.

However, a taxpayer may generally use short Form 1040A if all his income is from wages, tips, and interest income and he is taking the standard deduction.

Deductions
A taxpayer may either itemize deductions or choose one of the two types of standard deduction—the percentage standard deduction or the low-income allowance. For taxpayers with adjusted gross income of $10,000 or more, the percentage standard deduction is 15% of adjusted gross income up to a maximum of $2,000 ($1,000 for married persons filing separate returns). The low-income allowance of up to $1,300 is built into the tax tables; it is available only to taxpayers with adjusted gross incomes below $10,000.

Dates For Filing Returns
For individuals using the calendar year, Apr. 15 is final date (unless it falls on a Saturday, Sunday or a legal holiday) for filing income tax returns and for payment of any tax due, and the first quarterly installment of the estimated tax. Other installments of estimated tax to be paid June 15, Sept. 15 and Jan. 15.

Apr. 15 is final date for filing declaration of estimated tax. Amended declarations may be filed June 15, Sept. 15, and Jan. 15.

Instead of paying the 4th installment a final income return may be filed Jan. 31. Farmers may file a final return Mar. 1 to satisfy estimated tax requirements.

Joint Return
A husband and wife may make a return jointly, even if one has no income personally. Their tax will be twice the tax imposed if the income were cut in half and taxed at the married filing separate rate.

One provision stipulates that if one spouse dies, the survivor may compute his tax using joint return rates for the first two taxable years following, provided he or she also was entitled to file a joint return the year of the death, and furnishes over half the cost of maintaining in his household a home for a dependent child or stepchild. If the taxpayer remarries before the end of the taxable year these privileges are lost but he is permitted to file a joint return with his new spouse. An individual legally separated or divorced is not considered married.

Estimated Tax
If total tax exceeds withheld tax by at least $100, declarations of estimated tax are required from (1) single individuals, heads of a household or surviving spouses, or a married person entitled to file a joint return whose spouse does not receive wages, who expects a gross income over $20,000; (2) married individuals with over $10,000 where both spouses receive wages; (3) married individuals with over $5,000 not entitled to file a joint return; and (4) individuals whose gross income can reasonably be expected to include more than $500 from sources other than wages subject to withholdings.

Exemptions
Personal exemption is $750.

Every individual has an exemption of $750, to be deducted from gross income. A husband and a wife are each entitled to a $750 exemption. A taxpayer 65 or over on the last day of the year, gets another exemption of $750. A person blind on the last day of the year, gets another exemption of $750.

Exemption for dependents, over one-half of whose total support comes from the taxpayer and for whom the other dependency tests have been met is $750. This applies to a child, stepchild or adopted child as well as certain other relatives with less than $750 gross income; also to a child, stepchild, or adopted child of the taxpayer who is under 19 at the end of the year or was a full-time student during 5 months of the year even if he makes $750 or more. A dependent can be a non-relative if a member of the taxpayer's household and living there all year.

Taxpayer gets the exemption for his child who is a student regardless of the student's age or earnings, provided the taxpayer provides over half of the student's total support. If the student gets a scholarship, this is not counted as support.

Child and Disabled Dependent Care
Taxpayers with adjusted gross income of $18,000 or less may be able to deduct up to $400 per month for household and dependent care expenses.

To qualify, a taxpayer must be employed and provide over one-half the cost of maintaining a household for a dependent child under 15, a disabled dependent of any age, or a disabled spouse.

Household expenses incurred to permit a taxpayer to be gainfully employed may be deducted. Expenses incurred outside the home for the care of a child under 15 also qualify but the deduction for these expenses is limited to $200 per month for one child, $300 for two children and $400 for three or more children.

Life Insurance
Life insurance paid to survivors is not taxed as income. Interest on life insurance left with the insurance company and paid to survivors at intervals is taxable when available. Surviving spouse has an exclusion of the prorata amount of principal payable at death plus up to $1,000 per year of interest earned when life insurance proceeds are payable in installments.

Regular payments under the Railroad Retirement Act, and those received as social security are exempt.

Dividends
The first $100 in dividends can be excluded from income. If husband and wife both receive $100 on their joint return they can exclude $200.

The exclusion does not apply to dividends from tax-exempt corporations, mutual savings banks, building and loan associations and several others.

Dividends paid in stock or in stock rights are generally exempt from tax, except when paid in place of preferred stock dividends of the current or preceding year, or when the stockholder has an option to take stock or property or when the stock distribution is disproportionate.

Deductible Medical Expenses
Expenses for medical care, not compensated for by insurance or other payment for taxpayer, spouse, and dependents, in excess of 3% of adjusted gross income are deductible. This rule also applies to taxpayers 65 or over and dependent parents 65 or over. Previously these persons were not subject to the percentage limitations. There is no limit to the maximum amount of medical expense that can be deducted.

Medical care includes diagnosis, treatment and prevention of disease or for the purpose of affecting any structure or function of the body, and amounts paid for insurance to reimburse for hospitalization, surgical fees and other medical expenses.

Only medicine and drugs in excess of 1% of adjusted

1973 Income Tax Rate Schedules*

(A.) Married Individuals Filing Joint Returns and Certain Surviving Spouses.

If taxable income is: — The tax is:
Not over $1,000 .... 14% of the taxable income.

Over	But not over			Of excess over
$1,000—	$2,000	$140,	plus 15%	$1,000
$2,000—	$3,000	$290,	plus 16%	$2,000
$3,000—	$4,000	$450,	plus 17%	$3,000
$4,000—	$8,000	$620,	plus 19%	$4,000
$8,000—	$12,000	$1,380,	plus 22%	$8,000
$12,000—	$16,000	$2,260,	plus 25%	$12,000
$16,000—	$20,000	$3,260,	plus 28%	$16,000
$20,000—	$24,000	$4,380,	plus 32%	$20,000
$24,000—	$28,000	$5,660,	plus 36%	$24,000
$28,000—	$32,000	$7,100,	plus 39%	$28,000
$32,000—	$36,000	$8,660,	plus 42%	$32,000
$36,000—	$40,000	$10,340,	plus 45%	$36,000
$40,000—	$44,000	$12,140,	plus 48%	$40,000
$44,000—	$52,000	$14,060,	plus 50%	$44,000
$52,000—	$64,000	$18,060,	plus 53%	$52,000
$64,000—	$76,000	$24,420,	plus 55%	$64,000
$76,000—	$88,000	$31,020,	plus 58%	$76,000
$88,000—$100,000		$37,980,	plus 60%	$88,000
$100,000—$120,000		$45,180,	plus 62%	$100,000
$120,000—$140,000		$57,580,	plus 64%	$120,000
$140,000—$160,000		$70,380,	plus 66%	$140,000
$160,000—$180,000		$83,580,	plus 68%	$160,000
$180,000—$200,000		$97,180,	plus 69%	$180,000
$200,000			plus 70%	$200,000

(B.) Certain Heads of Households

Not over $1,000 .... 14% of the taxable income.

Over	But not over			Of Excess over
$1,000—	$2,000	$140,	plus 16%	$1,000
$2,000—	$4,000	$300,	plus 18%	$2,000
$4,000—	$6,000	$660,	plus 19%	$4,000
$6,000—	$8,000	$1,040,	plus 22%	$6,000
$8,000—	$10,000	$1,480,	plus 23%	$8,000
$10,000—	$12,000	$1,940,	plus 25%	$10,000
$12,000—	$14,000	$2,440,	plus 27%	$12,000
$14,000—	$16,000	$2,980,	plus 28%	$14,000
$16,000—	$18,000	$3,540,	plus 31%	$16,000
$18,000—	$20,000	$4,160,	plus 32%	$18,000
$20,000—	$22,000	$4,800,	plus 35%	$20,000
$22,000—	$24,000	$5,500,	plus 36%	$22,000
$24,000—	$26,000	$6,220,	plus 38%	$24,000
$26,000—	$28,000	$6,980,	plus 41%	$26,000
$28,000—	$32,000	$7,800,	plus 42%	$28,000
$32,000—	$36,000	$9,480,	plus 45%	$32,000
$36,000—	$38,000	$11,280,	plus 48%	$36,000
$38,000—	$40,000	$12,240,	plus 51%	$38,000
$40,000—	$44,000	$13,260,	plus 52%	$40,000
$44,000—	$50,000	$15,340,	plus 55%	$44,000
$50,000—	$52,000	$18,640,	plus 56%	$50,000
$52,000—	$64,000	$19,760,	plus 58%	$52,000
$64,000—	$70,000	$26,720,	plus 59%	$64,000
$70,000—	$76,000	$30,260,	plus 61%	$70,000
$76,000—	$80,000	$33,920,	plus 62%	$76,000
$80,000—	$88,000	$36,400,	plus 63%	$80,000
$88,000—$100,000		$41,440,	plus 64%	$88,000
$100,000—$120,000		$49,120,	plus 66%	$100,000
$120,000—$140,000		$62,320,	plus 67%	$120,000
$140,000—$160,000		$75,720,	plus 68%	$140,000
$160,000—$180,000		$89,320,	plus 69%	$160,000
$180,000		$103,120,	plus 70%	$180,000

(C.) Married Individuals Filing Separate Returns

If Taxable income is: — The tax is:
Not over $500 .... 14% of the taxable income

Over	But not over			Of excess over
$500—	$1,000	$70,	plus 15%	$500
$1,000—	$1,500	$145,	plus 16%	$1,000
$1,500—	$2,000	$225,	plus 17%	$1,500
$2,000—	$4,000	$310,	plus 19%	$2,000
$4,000—	$6,000	$690,	plus 22%	$4,000
$6,000—	$8,000	$1,130,	plus 25%	$6,000
$8,000—	$10,000	$1,630,	plus 28%	$8,000
$10,000—	$12,000	$2,190,	plus 32%	$10,000
$12,000—	$14,000	$2,830,	plus 36%	$12,000
$14,000—	$16,000	$3,550,	plus 39%	$14,000
$16,000—	$18,000	$4,330,	plus 42%	$16,000
$18,000—	$20,000	$5,170,	plus 45%	$18,000
$20,000—	$22,000	$6,070,	plus 48%	$20,000
$22,000—	$26,000	$7,030,	plus 50%	$22,000
$26,000—	$32,000	$9,030,	plus 53%	$26,000
$32,000—	$38,000	$12,210,	plus 55%	$32,000
$38,000—	$44,000	$15,510,	plus 58%	$38,000
$44,000—	$50,000	$18,990,	plus 60%	$44,000
$50,000—	$60,000	$22,590,	plus 62%	$50,000
$60,000—	$70,000	$28,790,	plus 64%	$60,000
$70,000—	$80,000	$35,190,	plus 66%	$70,000
$80,000—	$90,000	$41,790,	plus 68%	$80,000
$90,000—	$100,000	$48,590,	plus 69%	$90,000
$100,000		$55,490,	plus 70%	$100,000

(D.) Unmarried Individuals (Other Than Certain Surviving Spouse and Heads of Households).

Not over $500 .... 14% of the taxable income

Over	But not over			Of excess over
$500—	$1,000	$70,	plus 15%	$500
$1,000—	$1,500	$145,	plus 16%	$1,000
$1,500—	$2,000	$225,	plus 17%	$1,500
$2,000—	$4,000	$310,	plus 19%	$2,000
$4,000—	$6,000	$690,	plus 21%	$4,000
$6,000—	$8,000	$1,110,	plus 24%	$6,000
$8,000—	$10,000	$1,590,	plus 25%	$8,000
$10,000—	$12,000	$2,090,	plus 27%	$10,000
$12,000—	$14,000	$2,630,	plus 29%	$12,000
$14,000—	$16,000	$3,210,	plus 31%	$14,000
$16,000—	$18,000	$3,830,	plus 34%	$16,000
$18,000—	$20,000	$4,510,	plus 36%	$18,000
$20,000—	$22,000	$5,230,	plus 38%	$20,000
$22,000—	$26,000	$5,990,	plus 40%	$22,000
$26,000—	$32,000	$7,590,	plus 45%	$26,000
$32,000—	$38,000	$10,290,	plus 50%	$32,000
$38,000—	$44,000	$13,290,	plus 55%	$38,000
$44,000—	$50,000	$16,590,	plus 60%	$44,000
$50,000—	$60,000	$20,190,	plus 62%	$50,000
$60,000—	$70,000	$26,390,	plus 64%	$60,000
$70,000—	$80,000	$32,790,	plus 66%	$70,000
$80,000—	$90,000	$39,390,	plus 68%	$80,000
$90,000—$100,000		$46,190,	plus 69%	$90,000
$100,000		$53,090,	plus 70%	$100,000

*Under the tax reform act of 1969 the maximum rate of earned income is 50% for single taxpayers earning taxable income in excess of $50,000 and for married persons filing jointly with taxable income in excess of $100,000.

gross income may be included in medical expenses.

One-half the cost of medical care insurance premiums up to $150 can be deducted without regard to the 3% limitation. The other half plus any excess over $150 is included with other medical expenses subject to the 3% limit.

Medical expenses for a decedent paid by his estate within one year after his death may be treated as expenses of the decedent taxpayer.

Medical and hospital benefits provided by the employer may be exempt from individual income tax. Wages paid as "sick pay" are exempt up to $100 a week after a certain waiting period.

Deductions For Contributions

Deductions up to 50% of taxpayers' adjusted gross income may be taken for contribution to most publicly supported charitable organizations, including churches or associations of churches, tax-exempt educational institutions, tax-exempt hospitals, and medical research organizations associated with a hospital, and nonprofit cemeteries. The deduction is generally limited to 20% for such organizations as private foundations.

Taxpayers also are permitted to carry over for five years certain contributions, generally to publicly supported organizations, which exceed the 50% allowable deduction the year the contribution was made.

Also permissible is the deduction as a charitable contribution of unreimbursed amounts up to $50 a month spent to maintain an elementary or high school student, other than a dependent or relative, in taxpayer's home.

Deductions For Interest Paid

Interest paid by the taxpayer is deductible.

If personal property is bought under a contract providing for payment by installments, and in which carrying charges are stated but interest is not ascertainable, then subject to limitation payments are held to include interest equal to 6% on average unpaid balance.

However, the amount charged to a customer's revolving charge account is solely for the privilege of deferring payment and is interest.

Prizes and Awards

All prizes and awards must be reported in gross income, except when received without action by the recipient. To be exempt, awards must be received primarily in recognition of religious, charitable, scientific, educational, artistic, literary, or civic achievement. (Nobel and Pulitzer prizes exempt.)

Deductions For Employees

An employee may take the standard deduction and deduct as well the following if in connection with his employment: transportation, except commuting; automobile expense, including gas, oil and depreciation; however, meals and lodging are deductible as traveling expense only if the employee is away from home overnight.

An outside salesman—a salesman who works full-time outside the office, using the latter only for incidentals--may deduct both the standard deduction and all his business expenses.

An employee who is reimbursed and is required to account to his employer for his business expenses will not be required to report either the reimbursement or the expenses on his tax return. Any allowance to the employee in excess of his expenses must be included in gross income. If he claims a deduction for an excess of expenses over reimbursement he will have to report the reimbursement and claim actual expenses.

An employee who is not required to account to his employer must report on his return the total amounts of reimbursements and expenses for travel, transportation, entertainment, etc., that he incurs under a reimbursement arrangement with his employer.

The expense of moving to a new place of employment may be deducted under certain circumstances regardless of whether the taxpayer is a new or continuing employee, or whether he pays his own expenses or is reimbursed by his employer. Reimbursement must be reported as income.

Retirement Income Credit

A credit against the tax otherwise due, of 15% of retirement income up to $1,524 included in gross income, is allowed to persons 65 and over. Persons under 65 and retired under a public retirement system (firemen, policemen, teachers, Federal employees) are allowed the same credit on income from pensions and annuities paid under the system, but not on dividends, interest and rent. Included in public systems are funds for members of the Armed Forces for 1955 and subsequent years. Any pension or annuity received under the Social Security Act or the Railroad Retirement Act reduces the $1,524. Compensation in excess of $900 received by an individual under 62 and compensation in excess of $1,200 for one over 62 but under 72 will reduce the $1,524 by varying amounts. No reduction if the individual is 72 or older.

Net Capital Losses

An individual taxpayer may deduct capital losses up to $1,000 against his ordinary income. However, it takes $2 of net long-term capital loss to get $1 of offset against other income. He may carry the rest over to subsequent years at the same rate, no legal limit on the number of years.

Income Averaging

Individuals with large fluctuations in their annual income may be able to take advantage of averaging provisions available to taxpayers whose income for a particular year exceeds 120% of their average income for the prior 4 years, if the excess is more than $3,000.

Individual Income Tax Returns (1971)

Source: Internal Revenue Service

(* Money amounts in thousands of dollars)

Size of Adjusted Gross Incomes	All Returns	Number	Taxable Returns Adjusted Gross Income*	Taxable Income*	Tax After Credit*	Average Tax
Total	74,601,327	59,921,538	$651,436,631	$413,572,198	$85,310,122	$ 1,426
No adjusted gross income	416,986					
$1 under $600	2,972,587	—				
$600 under $1,000	2,465,049					
$1,000 under $2,000	5,960,147	1,083,641	1,982,861	168,609	23,992	23
$2,000 under $3,000	5,365,424	3,731,800	9,313,359	2,496,343	359,628	96
$3,000 under $4,000	5,054,232	3,970,263	13,944,737	5,372,734	802,470	202
$4,000 under $5,000	4,927,472	4,348,663	19,600,645	8,750,036	1,367,528	315
$5,000 under $6,000	4,588,404	4,294,370	23,591,069	11,768,469	1,891,596	441
$6,000 under $7,000	4,251,416	4,091,701	26,592,559	14,151,823	2,312,603	565
$7,000 under $8,000	4,402,168	4,319,301	32,333,536	17,868,691	2,962,587	686
$8,000 under $9,000	4,188,795	4,147,746	35,251,970	20,258,766	3,420,682	825
$9,000 under $10,000	4,015,229	3,991,586	37,902,766	22,563,392	3,874,405	971
$10,000 under $11,000	3,698,415	3,679,330	38,624,379	23,282,317	4,026,784	1,094
$11,000 under $12,000	3,282,354	3,274,950	37,643,994	23,111,240	4,045,228	1,235
$12,000 under $13,000	2,901,662	2,895,797	36,154,748	22,857,070	4,049,698	1,399
$13,000 under $14,000	2,545,424	2,542,221	34,303,971	22,172,145	3,996,437	1,572
$14,000 under $15,000	2,185,765	2,182,952	31,633,607	20,839,150	3,812,789	1,747
$15,000 under $20,000	6,455,678	6,447,857	110,212,947	75,551,485	14,413,516	2,236
$20,000 under $25,000	2,383,423	2,379,478	52,562,559	37,887,338	7,805,897	3,281
$25,000 under $30,000	968,176	966,620	26,263,533	19,440,387	4,304,204	4,455
$30,000 under $50,000	1,075,772	1,073,213	39,995,647	30,694,991	7,886,256	7,356
$50,000 under $100,000	405,463	404,453	26,675,777	21,171,635	7,314,538	18,136
$100,000 under $200,000	73,025	72,821	9,524,009	7,554,749	3,399,363	47,066
$200,000 under $500,000	15,208	15,149	4,289,994	3,281,586	1,779,338	119,666
$500,000 under $1,000,000	2,189	2,178	1,460,158	1,099,185	665,806	314,628
$1,000,000 or more	864	862	1,692,991	1,229,531	794,702	962,973

Excise Taxes On Selected Items

Source: Tax Foundation (As of Nov. 1, 1973)

Gasoline, diesel fuel, benzol, naphtha, for vehicle propulsion are taxed at 4¢ a gallon scheduled through Sept. 30, 1977, and at 1.5¢ thereafter.

Liquor taxes:
Distilled spirits . . . . $10.50 per proof gallon
Perfumed, imported (containing distilled spirits) . . . . $10.50 per wine gallon
Still wines (including vermouth and artificial or imitation wines)
   Not over 14% alcohol . . . . 17¢ per wine gallon
   Not over 21% alcohol . . . . 67¢ per wine gallon
   Not over 24% alcohol . . . . $2.25 per wine gallon

Beer and fermented liquors:
(Beer, ale, porter, etc., containing 1% or more of alcohol) . . . . $9.00 per barrel

Champagnes, sparkling wines, liqueurs and cordials:
   Champagne or sparkling wine . . $3.40 per wine gallon
   Artificially carbonated wine . . . . $2.40 per wine gallon
Liqueurs and cordials
   (containing wine) . . . . $1.92 per wine gallon
Tires and tubes (per lb.) . . . . 10¢
Pistols, revolvers (Mfg's sales) 10%
Slot machines, $250 a year each. This applies to all gaming devices.
Sugar (per lb.) . . . . 0.53¢
Fishing equipment (Mfg's sales) 10%
Tobacco-small cigarettes weighing less than 3 lbs. per thousand, $4.00 per thousand.
Air travel tickets (domestic) 8%
Telephone: Local and toll service 10%, to be reduced to 9% in 1973; and by 1% annually until rate reaches 1% in 1981.

Canada: Taxable Returns by Income
Source: Taxation Statistics

Total Income $, 1971	Number	%	Total income (millions)	%	Taxed income (millions)	Fed. Tax[1] (millions)	%
0-1,100	12,201	.17	$ 8.3	.02	$ 5.0	1.1	.02
1,100-2,000	267,950	3.63	479.4	.89	184.2	13.5	.18
2,000-3,000	767,941	10.42	1,926.3	3.61	940.2	100.5	1.51
3,000-4,000	872,520	11.83	3,057.6	5.73	1,756.8	227.9	3.41
4,000-6,000	1,676,446	22.74	8,333.7	15.62	5,376.3	795.6	11.89
6,000-8,000 . . . . . . ,	1,396,723	16.94	9,743.1	18.26	6,741.2	1,105.3	16.53
8,000-10,000	1,020,036	13.74	9,103.6	17.07	6,574.3	1,131.5	16.91
10,000-12,000	583,331	7.91	6,355.9	11.91	4,725.5	829.0	12.40
12,000-15,000	391,734	5.32	5,195.4	9.74	3,983.8	723.8	10.82
15,000-20,000	219,288	2.97	3,719.8	6.97	2,936.4	577.4	8.63
20,000-50,000	145,856	1.98	4,057.5	7.60	3,379.7	801.2	11.98
50,000-100,000 . . .	16,400	.22	1,072.2	2.01	961.7	287.7	4.30
100,000-200,000 . . .	1,953	.03	247.3	.47	224.2	75.6	1.13
200,000 & over	192	–	56.0	.10	50.4	18.5	.28
Total	7,372,571	100.00	53,356.2	100.00	37,839.7	6,688.8	100.00

(1) Federal taxes include income tax, social development tax and old age security tax.

Effective Federal Taxes Rates

Selected Total Incomes, 1971	Rate on Total Income	Rate on Taxed Income	Selected Total Incomes, 1971	Rate on Total Income	Rate on Taxed Income
1,600 to 1,700	1.70	5.36	9,000 to 9,500	12.57	17.27
2,000 to 2,100	3.81	8.72	10,000 to 11,000	12.89	17.46
2,500 to 2,600	5.37	10.73	13,000 to 14,000	13.53	18.70
3,000 to 3,100	6.52	12.01	15,000 to 16,000	14.91	19.06
3,500 to 3,600	7.25	12.77	18,000 to 19,000	16.04	20.16
4,000 to 4,500	8.69	14.04	20,000 to 25,000	17.62	21.73
5,000 to 5,500	9.78	14.97	25,000 to 50,000	21.06	24.87
6,000 to 6,500	10.71	15.79	50,000 to 100,000	26.84	29.92
7,000 to 7,500	11.60	16.66	100,000 to 200,000	30.57	33.72
8,000 to 8,500	12.14	17.04	200,000 & over	32.99	36.68

City Income Tax in Cities Over 50,000

Compiled by Tax Foundation from Commerce Clearing House data and other sources.

City	Rates% 1973	Orig.	Year start	City	Rates% 1973	Orig.	Year start
Cities with 500,000 or more inhabitants				**Cities with 50,000 to 99,000 inhabitants**			
Baltimore, Md. . . . . (50% of state tax)	1.0	1966		Toledo, Ohio	1.5	1.0	1946
Cleveland, Ohio	1.0	.5	1967	Youngstown, Ohio	1.5	.3	1948
Columbus, Ohio	1.5	.5	1947	Altoona, Pa.	1.0	1.0	1948
Detroit, Mich.	2.0	1.0	1964	Bethlehem, Pa.	1.0	1.0	1957
Kansas City, Mo.	1.0	.5	1964	Chester, Pa.	1.0	1.0	1956
New York, N.Y.	.7-3.5	.4-2.0	1966	Covington, Ky.	2.5	1.0	1956
Philadelphia, Pa.	3.125	1.5	1939	Euclid, Ohio	1.0	.5	1967
St. Louis, Mo.	1.0	.25	1948	Gadsden, Ala.	2.0	1.0	1956
Cities with 100,000 to 499,000 inhabitants				Hamilton, Ohio	1.5	.8	1960
Akron, Ohio	1.5	1.0	1963	Harrisburg, Pa.	1.0	1.0	1966
Allentown, Pa.	1.0	1.0	1958	Johnstown, Pa.	1.0	1.0	1948
Birmingham, Ala.	1.0	1.0	1970	Kettering, Ohio	1.0	1.0	1968
Canton, Ohio	1.5	.6	1954	Lakewood, Ohio	1.0	1.0	1968
Cincinnati, Ohio	2.0	1.0	1954	Lancaster, Pa.	1.0	.5	1959
Dayton, Ohio	1.0	.5	1949	Lima, Ohio	1.0	.75	1959
Erie, Pa.	1.0	1.0	1948	Lorain, Ohio	1.0	.5	1967
Flint, Mich.	1.0	1.0	1965	Pontiac, Mich.	1.0	1.0	1968
Grand Rapids, Mich.	1.0	1.0	1967	Saginaw, Mich.	1.0	1.0	1965
Lansing, Mich.	1.0	1.0	1968	Springfield, Ohio	1.5	1.0	1948
Lexington, Ky.	1.5	1.0	1952	Warren, Ohio	1.0	.5	1952
Louisville, Ky.	2.0	1.0	1940	Wilkes-Barre, Pa.	0.5	1.0	1966
Parma, Ohio	1.0	.5	1967	York, Pa.	1.0	1.0	1965
Scranton, Pa.	1.0	1.0	1948	Wilmington, Del.	.25-1.5	.5	1970

Tax Loopholes and Tax Losses

There are numerous sections of the income tax law through which individuals and corporations are able to lower their income taxes. Among them are the following, shown with the estimated 1972 loss to U.S. government revenues.

	Billions
Capital gains, lower tax (excl. Farming)	$7.6
State-local sales and income taxes, deduction	5.3
Pension plans—company contributions and annual investment earnings	4.2
Investment tax credit	3.8
Special benefits for aged, blind and disabled	3.6
Interest on home mortgages, deduction	3.5
Company insurance and other employee benefits	3.3
Property taxes on homes	3.3
Charitable contributions, deduction	3.4
Interest on state-local bonds, exemption	2.9
Corporate profits, lower rate of first $25,000	2.5
Medical expenses, deduction	1.9
Depletion allowances (excess over cost)	1.7
Interest on life insurance, exclusion	1.7
Interest on consumer credit, deduction	1.2
Excess of standard over minimum deduction	1.1

State Inheritance Tax Rates and Exemptions

Source: Compiled by Tax Foundation from Commerce Clearing House data
As of Sept. 1, 1973

State (a)	Rates (per cent)(b)			Max. Rate applies above ($1,000)	Exemptions (c) ($1,000)			
	Spouse Child or parent	Brother or sister	Other than relative		Spouse	Child or parent	Brother or sister	Other than relative
California	3-14	6-20	10-24	$400	$5 (d)	$5 (e)	$2	$.3
Colorado (f)	2-8	3-10	10-19	500	30	10(e)	2	.5 (h)
Connecticut (i)	2-8	4-10	8-14	1,000	50	10	3	.5
Delaware	1-6	5-10	10-16	200	20	3	1	None
Dist. of Col.	1-8	5-23	5-23	1,000	5	5	1	1
Hawaii	1.5-7.5	3.5-9	3.5-9	250	20	5	.5	.5
Idaho	2-15	4-20	8-30	500	10 (d, g)	4 (e)	1	None
Illinois	2-14	6-16	10-30	500	20	20	10	.1
Indiana	1-10	5-15	7-20	1,500	15	2 (e)	.5	.1
Iowa	1-8	5-10	10-15	150	40	10 (e)	None	None
Kansas	1-5	3-12.5	10-15	500	75	15	5	.2 (h)
Kentucky	2-10	4-16	6-16	500	10 (g)	5 (e)	1	.5
Louisiana	2-3	5-7	5-10	25	5	5	1	.5
Maine	2-6	8-12	12-18	250	15	10	.5	.5
Maryland (k)	1	7.5	7.5	(l)	.15 (h)	.15 (h)	.15 (h)	.15 (h)
Massachusetts (m)	1.8-11.8	5.5-19.3	8-19.3	1,000	30 (h)	15 (n)	5 (n)	5 (n)
Michigan	2-8(o)	2-8 (o)	10-15 (o)	750	30 (e)	5	5	None
Minnesota	1.5-10	6-25	8-30	1,000	30 (s)	6 (e)	1.5	.5
Missouri	1-6	3-18	5-30	400	20 (p)	5 (e)	.5	.1 (h)
Montana	2-8	4-16	8-32	100	20	2 (e)	.5	None
Nebraska	1	6-9	16-18	60	10	10	10*	.5
New Hampshire	(q)	15	15	(l)	(q)	(q)	None	None
New Jersey	1-16	11-16	15-16	3,200	5	5	.5 (h)	.5 (h)
New Mexico	1	5	5	(l)	(r)	(r)	(r)	(r)
North Carolina	1-12	4-16	8-17	3,000	10 (q)	2 (e)	None	None
Oregon (a)	2-10	2-10 (s)	2-10 (s)	500	(s)	(s)	3	.5
Pennsylvania	6	15	15	(l)	None (t)	None (t)	None	None
Rhode Island	2-9	3-10	8-15	1,000	10	10	5	1
South Dakota (a)	(u)	4-16	6-24	100	15	.3 (e)	.5	.1
Tennessee	5.5-9.5	6.5-20	6.5-20	500	60	60	1	1
Texas	1-6	3-10	5-20	1,000	25 (d)	25	10	.5
Virginia	1-5	2-10	5-15	1,000	5	5	2	1
Washington	1-10	3-20	10-25	500	10 (d)	10	1	None
West Virginia (a)	3-13	4-18	10-30	1,000	15	5	None	None
Wisconsin	2.5-12.5	5-25	10-30	500	50	4	1	.5
Wyoming	2	2	6	(l)	10	10	10	None

(a) In addition to an inheritance tax, all states listed also levy an estate tax, generally to assure full absorption of the Federal credit. Exceptions are Ore., S. D., and W. V. See page 103 for taxes not listed here.

(b) Rates generally apply to excess above graduated absolute amounts.

(c) Generally, transfers to governments or to solely charitable, educational, scientific, religious, literary, public, and other similar organizations in the U.S. are wholly exempt. Some states grant additional exemptions either for insurance, homestead, joint deposits, support allowance, disinherited minor children, orphaned, incompetent or blind children, and for previously or later transfers. In many states, exemptions are deducted from the first bracket only. Adopted children generally receive the same consideration as natural children.

(d) Community property state in which, in general, either all community property to the surviving spouse is exempt, or only one-half of the community property is taxable on the death of either spouse.

(e) Exemption for child (in thousands): $15 in Iowa; and $10 in S. D. Exemption for minor child is (in thousands): $12 in Calif.; $10 in Idaho; $5 in Ind.; $10 in Ky.; $15 in Minn.; $5 in Mont.; $5 in N. C.; and $5 in Colo. In Mo. the exemption for an insane, blind or otherwise incapacitated lineal descendant is (thousands) $15. In Mich. a widow receives $5,000 for every minor child to whom no property is transferred in addition to the normal exception for a spouse.

(f) Colo. imposes an additional tax of 10% upon the amount of tax computed at above rates.

(g) Exemption for widower differs in the following states (thousands): Idaho, $4; Ky., $5; Minn., $6; N. C., $2; Wis., $5.

(h) No exemption if share exceeds amount stated.

(i) On estates an additional inheritance tax equal to 30% of the basic tax is imposed.

(j) Estates over $3,000,000 are not subject to the inheritance tax but are subject to an estate tax equal to the amount of the Federal credit.

(k) Where property of a decedent subject to administration in Md. is $2,000 or less, no inheritance taxes are due.

(l) Rate applies to entire share.

(m) Mass. imposes a 14% surtax in addition to the inheritance tax on all property or interests passing or accruing upon the death of persons who die on or after July 18, 1969.

(n) No exemption if share exceeds amount stated except that the tax shall not reduce the share below the amount of the exemption. In addition there are certain exemptions for the spouse's home.

(o) Transfers of real estate are taxable at 75% of specified rates. There is no tax on the share of any beneficiary if the value of the share is less than $100.

(p) In addition, an exemption of one-half of the decedent's estate, or one-third if decedent is survived by lineal descendants.

(q) Spouses, minor children and minor adopted children in the decedent's line of succession are entirely exempt. Parents have no exemption and are taxable at the flat rate of 15%.

(r) Only one exemption is allowed upon aggregate of property passing to each class of beneficiaries: $10,000 for parents, spouse, lineal descendants, brothers, and sisters; $500 for all others. Amount of exemption for each class is proportionate to the respective shares of the estate and shared proportionately by the beneficiaries within the class.

(s) An additional tax of 2-20% is levied on all beneficiaries other than grandparents, parents, spouse, children, stepchildren or lineal descendants. These categories of beneficiaries are exempt from the additional taxes.

(t) However, the $1,500 family exemption is specifically allowed as a deduction.

(u) The rates range from 1.5-6% for a spouse or a child and from 3-12% for parents.

Federal Estate Tax

Source: Tax Foundation

An estate tax return must be filed for every citizen or resident of the United States whose gross estate exceeds $60,000 in value at the time of his death. In general, the tax must be paid within 15 mos. from the date of death. Extensions may be granted in hardship cases. A return must be filed for a non-resident, not a citizen, if his gross estate in the U. S. exceeds $30,000 in value.

An estate gets credit for state death taxes, according to a graduated table; also deductions for funeral expenses, administration, claims, and bequests to religious, charitable and fraternal organizations or government welfare agencies.

Life insurance payable to named beneficiaries is not to be included in the gross estate if the insured retained no incidents of ownership in the policy. A reversionary interest which exceeds 5 per cent of the value of the policy is considered an incident of ownership in the policy.

The marital deduction provides that the value of the taxable estate "shall be determined by deducting from the value of the gross estate an amount equal to the value of any interest in property which passes or has passed from the decedent to his surviving spouse." Thus the deduction applies when the surviving spouse has a right to the income for life from all or only a part of the property, as well as power to appoint all, or the part in which the survivor has income rights, whether or not the property is held in trust. If the spouse has control only over part, the deduction is limited proportionally. The deduction is limited, however, to the value of one-half of the adjusted gross estate.

ESTATE TAX RATE

The tax is computed under the rates listed below on the net taxable estate of the decedent, citizen or resident of the United States after allowing for the specific exemption of $60,000 and deduction for debts, expenses, charitable, marital deductions. There is a credit allowance for state death taxes.

If the taxable estate is:			The tax shall be:	
Not over $5,000			3% of the taxable estate	
Over	$5,000 but not over	$10,000	$150, plus 7% of excess over	$5,000
Over	$10,000 but not over	$20,000	$500, plus 11% of excess over	$10,000
Over	$20,000 but not over	$30,000	$1,600, plus 14% of excess over	$20,000
Over	$30,000 but not over	$40,000	$3,000, plus 18% of excess over	$30,000
Over	$40,000 but not over	$50,000	$4,800, plus 22% of excess over	$40,000
Over	$50,000 but not over	$60,000	$7,000, plus 25% of excess over	$50,000
Over	$60,000 but not over	$100,000	$9,500, plus 28% of excess over	$60,000
Over	$100,000 but not over	$250,000	$20,700, plus 30% of excess over	$100,000
Over	$250,000 but not over	$500,000	$65,700, plus 32% of excess over	$250,000
Over	$500,000 but not over	$750,000	$145,700, plus 35% of excess over	$500,000
Over	$750,000 but not over	$1,000,000	$233,200, plus 37% of excess over	$750,000
Over	$1,000,000 but not over	$1,250,000	$325,700, plus 39% of excess over	$1,000,000
Over	$1,250,000 but not over	$1,500,000	$423,200, plus 42% of excess over	$1,250,000
Over	$1,500,000 but not over	$2,000,000	$528,200, plus 45% of excess over	$1,500,000
Over	$2,000,000 but not over	$2,500,000	$753,200, plus 49% of excess over	$2,000,000
Over	$2,500,000 but not over	$3,000,000	$998,200, plus 53% of excess over	$2,500,000
Over	$3,000,000 but not over	$3,500,000	$1,263,200, plus 56% of excess over	$3,000,000
Over	$3,500,000 but not over	$4,000,000	$1,543,200, plus 59% of excess over	$3,500,000
Over	$4,000,000 but not over	$5,000,000	$1,838,200, plus 63% of excess over	$4,000,000
Over	$5,000,000 but not over	$6,000,000	$2,468,200, plus 67% of excess over	$5,000,000
Over	$6,000,000 but not over	$7,000,000	$3,138,200, plus 70% of excess over	$6,000,000
Over	$7,000,000 but not over	$8,000,000	$3,838,200, plus 73% of excess over	$7,000,000
Over	$8,000,000 but not over	$10,000,000	$4,568,200, plus 76% of excess over	$8,000,000
Over $10,000,000			$6,088,200, plus 77% of excess over	$10,000,000

State Estate Tax Rates and Exemptions*

Source: Compiled by Tax Foundation from Commerce Clearing House Data
As of Sept. 1, 1973.*See Index for state inheritance tax rates and exemptions.

State (a)	Rates (on net estate after exemptions) (b)	Maximum rate applies above	Exemption
Alabama	Maximum Federal Credit (c, d)	$10,040,000	$60,000
Alaska	Maximum Federal Credit (c, d)	10,040,000	60,000
Arizona	0.8% on first $50,000 to 16% (c)	10,000,000	100,000 (f, g)
Arkansas	Maximum Federal Credit (c, d)	10,040,000	60,000 (g)
Florida	Maximum Federal Credit (c, d)	10,040,000	60,000
Georgia	Maximum Federal Credit (c, d)	10,040,000	60,000
Mississippi	1% on first $60,000 to 16%	10,000,000	60,000 (f, g)
New York	2% on first $50,000 to 21% (e, h)	10,100,000	(f, g, i)
North Dakota	2% on first $25,000 to 23%	1,500,000	20,000 (g, j)
Ohio	2% on first $40,000 to 7% (e)	500,000	5,000 (g, k)
Oklahoma	1% on first $10,000 to 10% (e)	10,000,000	15,000 (g, l)
South Carolina	4% on first $40,000 to 6%	100,000	60,000 (g)
Utah	5% of first $35,000 to 10% (e)	85,000	40,000 (g)

(a) Excludes states shown in table on page 62 which levy an estate tax, in addition to their inheritance taxes, to assure a full absorption of the Federal credit.

(b) The rates generally are in addition to graduated absolute amounts.

(c) Maximum Federal credit allowed under the 1954 code for state estate taxes paid is expressed as a percentage of the taxable estate (after $60,000 exemption) in excess of $40,000, plus a graduated absolute amount.

(d) A tax on nonresident estates is imposed on the proportionate share of the net estate which the property located in the state bears to the entire estate wherever situated.

(e) An additional estate tax is imposed to assure full absorption of the Federal credit.

(f) Insurance receives special treatment.

(g) Transfers to religious, charitable, educational, and municipal corporations are fully exempt. Limited in Mississippi to those located in U.S.; does not extend to governmental (municipal) corporations in North Dakota.

(h) On net estate before consumption.

(i) The specific exemptions ($20,000 of the net estate transferred to spouse and $5,000 to lineal ancestors and descendants and certain other named relatives) are taken out of the first bracket which is fixed at $50,000. Net estates which do not exceed $2,000, after deducting the applicable exemptions, are not taxed.

(j) A marital deduction of 50% of adjusted gross estate is allowed instead, if larger. Exemption for a lineal descendant, if a minor, is $5,000; for other lineal descendants and ancestors, $2,000.

(k) Property is exempt to the extent transferred to surviving spouse not exceeding $20,000; for a child under 21, $7,000 and for each child over 21, $3,000.

(l) An estate valued at $100 or less is exempt.

State Individual Income Taxes: Rates, Exemptions

Source: Analysis Staff, Tax Division, Treasury Dept. Data as of July 1, 1973

State	Net income after pers'l. exemption	Percentage rates	Net income after pers'l. exemption	Percentage rates	Personal Exemp. Single	Married family head	Credit. Depends.
Alabama[1]	First $1,000 1,001- 3,000	1.5 3	$3,001-$5,000 Over 5,000	4.5 5	$1,500	$3,000	$300
Alaska	16% of Federal income tax				750	1,500	750
Arizona[1 2]	First 1,000 1,001- 2,000 2,001- 3,000	2 3 4	3,001- 4,000 4,001- 5,000 5,001- 6,000	5 6 7	1,000 Over	2,000 6,000	600 8
Arkansas[3]	First 3,000 3,001- 6,000 6,001- 9,000	1 2.5 3.5	9,001-15,000 15,001-25,000 Over 25,000	4.5 6 7	17.50	35	6
California[1 2]	First 2,000 2,001- 3,500 3,501- 5,000 5,001- 6,500 6,501- 8,000	1 2 3 4 5	8,001- 9,500 9,501-11,000 11,001-12,500 12,501-14,000 14,001-15,500 Over 15,500	6 7 8 9 10 11	25 Heads of households have slightly less tax rates.	50	8
Colorado[1 4]	First 1,000 1,001- 2,000 2,001- 3,000 3,001- 4,000 4,001- 5,000 5,001- 6,000	3 3.5 4 4.5 5 5.5	6,001- 7,000 7,001- 8,000 8,001- 9,000 9,001-10,000 Over 10,000	6 6.5 7 7.5 8	750 Surtax on intangible income over $5,000, 2%. A credit equal to ½ of 1% of net taxation is allowed for income under $9,000.	1,500	750
Connecticut	Capital gains	6					
Delaware[3]	First 1,000 1,001- 2,000 2,001- 3,000 3,001- 4,000 4,001- 5,000 5,001- 6,000	1.5 2 3 6 5 6	6,001- 8,000 8,001-20,000 20,001-25,000 25,001-30,000 30,001-40,000 40,001-50,000	7 8 8.5 9 11 12	600 50,001-75,000 14 75,001-100,000 15 Over 100,000 18	1,200	600
Dist. of Col.[1 4]	First 1,000 1,001- 2,000 2,001- 3,000 3,001- 5,000 5,001- 8,000	2 3 4 5 6	8,001-12,000 12,001-17,000 17,001-25,000 Over 25,000	7 8 9 10	1,000	2,000	500
					A tax credit is provided for low-income taxpayers (adjusted gross not over $6,000) for increased sales tax on food ($2 to $6 credit per exemption). A refund is allowed if the tax exceeds tax liability.		
Georgia[3 5]	First 750 751- 2,250 2,251- 3,750 3,751- 5,250	1 2 3 4	5,251- 7,000 Over 7,000	5 6	1,500	3,000	700
					Students above high school level and handicapped or retarded children under 21 are allowed a $1,400 exemption.		
Hawaii[1 4]	First 500 501- 1,000 1,001- 1,500 1,501- 2,000 2,001- 3,000 3,001- 5,000	2.25 3.25 4.5 5 6.5 7.5	5,001-10,000 10,001-14,000 14,001-20,000 20,001-30,000 Over 30,000	8.5 9.5 10 10.5 11	750 Special tax rates for heads of households.	1,500	750
Idaho[2 3 4]	First 1,000 1,001- 2,000 2,001- 3,000	2 4 4.5	3,001- 4,000 4,001- 5,000 Over 5,000	5.5 6.5 7.5	750	1,500	750
Illinois	Net taxable income			2.5	1,000	2,000	1,000
Indiana[4]	Adjusted gross	2			1,000	*2,000	500
*Lesser of $1,000 or adjusted gross income of each spouse, but not less than $500.							
Iowa[1]	First 1,000 1,001- 2,000 2,001- 3,000	.75 1.5 3	3,001- 4,000 4,001- 7,000 7,001- 9,000	4 5 6	15 Incomes $3,000 or less are exempt. Over	30 9,000	10 7
Kansas[1 4]	First 2,000 2,001- 3,000 3,001- 5,000	2 3.5 4	5,001- 7,000 Over 7,000	5 6.5	600	1,200	600
Kentucky[1]	First 3,000 3,001- 4,000	2 3	4,001- 5,000 5,001- 8,000	4 5	20 Over	40 8,000	20 6

State	Net Income after pers'l. exemption	Percentage rates	Net income after pers'l. exemption	Percentage rates	Personal Exemp. Single	Married family head	Credit Depends.
Louisiana[2][3]	First 10,000 10,001-50,000	2 4	Over 50,000	6	2,500	5,000	400

Credits are allowed against new income which is taxed at 2%; additional $1,000 exemp. for blindness allowed for dependents.

| Maine .... | First 2,000
2,001- 5,000
5,001-10,000 | 1
2
3 | 10,001-25,000
25,000-50,000
Over 50,000 | 4
5
6 | 1,000 | 2,000 | 1,000 |

| Maryland[1][4]...... | First 1,000
1,001- 2,000 | 2
3 | 2,001- 3,000
Over 3,000 | 4
5 | 800 | 1,600 | 800 |

An additional exemption of $800 is allowed for each dependent 65 or over.

| Massachusetts[4] | Earned and business income: 5
Interest, divs., capital gains on intangibles: 9 | | | | 2,000 | 2,600-
4,600 | 600 |

The exemptions shown are those allowed against business income, including salaries and wages. A specific exemption of $2,000 is allowed for each taxpayer. In addition, a dependency exemption of $600 is allowed for a dependent spouse who has income from all sources of less than $2,000. In the case of a joint return, the exemption is the smaller of (1) $4,600 or (2) $2,600 plus the income of the spouse having the smaller income. The exemption allowed against annuity income is the amount of any unused business income exemptions. Married persons must file a joint return in order to obtain any non-business income exemption.

| Michigan[4] .... | All taxable income | | | 3.9 | 1,500 | 3,000 | 1,500 |

| Minnesota ....| First 500
501- 1,000
1,001- 2,000
2,001- 3,000
3,001- 4,000
4,001- 5,000 | 1.6
2.2
3.5
5.8
7.3
8.8 | 5,001- 7,000
7,001- 9,000
9,001-12,500
12,501-20,000
Over 20,000 | 10.2
11.5
12.8
14
15 | 21
An additional tax credit of $21 is allowed for each taxpayer 65 years old. | 42 | 21 |

| Mississippi[3] .... | First 5,000 | 3 | Over 5,000 | 4 | 4,500 | 6,500 | 750 |

| Missouri[1] .... | First 1,000
1,001- 2,000
2,001- 3,000
3,001- 4,000
4,001- 5,000 | 1.5
2
2.5
3
3.5 | 5,001- 6,000
6,001- 7,000
7,001- 8,000
8,001- 9,000
Over 9,000 | 4
4.5
5
5.5
6 | 1,200 | 2,400 | 400 |

| Montana[3] .... | First 1,000
1,001-2,000
2,001-4,000
4,001-6,000
6,001-8,000 | 2
3
4
5
6 | 8,001-10,000
10,001-14,000
14,001-20,000
20,001-35,000
Over 35,000 | 7
8
9
10
11 | 600 | 1,200 | 600 |

Nebraska[4].......   Federal exemptions
The tax is imposed as a % of the taxpayer's Fed. income tax liability (not including surtax) before credits, with limited adjustments. For the year 1973 the rate was set at 13% by State Board of Equalization and Assessment.

| New Hampshire.. | Interest and dividends (except interest on savings accounts). | 4.25 | 4% commuter tax | | 600 | 600-
1,200 | |

Joint returns are not permitted; each spouse with taxable income is allowed a $600 exemption.

| New Jersey[3] ..... | First 1,000
1,001- 3,000
3,001- 5,000
5,001- 7,000
7,001- 9,000
9,001-11,000
11,001-13,000 | 2
3
4
5
6
7
8 | 13,001-15,000
15,001-17,000
17,001-19,000
19,001-21,000
21,001-23,000
23,001-25,000
Over 25,000 | 9
10
11
12
13
14
15 | 650 | 1,300 | 650 |

The Tax is imposed on the net income derived from New York sources by New Jersey residents. The rates are the same as those in effect in New York. A surtax of 2.5% is imposed on both the regular income tax and minimum tax on tax preference items. The surtax is computed before the allowance of any applicable credits and is effective through the 1976 calendar year. The rate of tax on minimum taxable income is 6%.

| New Mexico[2][3] ... | First 500
501- 1,000
1,001- 1,500
1,501- 2,000
2,001- 3,000
3,001- 4,000
4,001- 5,000
5,001- 6,000
6,001- 7,000 | 1
1.5
1.5
2
2.5
3
3.5
4
4.5 | 7,001- 8,000
8,001-10,000
10,001-12,000
12,001-20,000
20,001-50,000
50,001-100,000
Over 100,000 | 5
6
7
7.5
8
8.5
9 | 750 | 1,500 | 750 |

The income classes reported are for individuals. For joint returns and heads of households, a separate rate schedule is provided. A credit is allowed for state and local taxes for gross income of less than $6,000.

| New York[1] .... | First 1,000
1,001- 3,000
3,001- 5,000
5,001- 7,000
7,001- 9,000
9,001-11,000
11,001-13,000 | 2
3
4
5
6
7
8 | 13,001-15,000
15,001-17,000
17,001-19,000
19,001-21,000
21,001-23,000
23,001-25,000
Over 25,000 | 9
10
11
12
13
14
15 | 650 | 1,300 | 650 |

Tax credits of $12.50 for single persons, $12.50 for married persons filing separately, and $25 for married persons filing jointly and heads of households are allowed.

Income from unincorporated business is taxed at 5½%. The following credit is allowed: $100 or less-full amount: $100-200-difference between $200 and amount of tax; $200 or more, no credit. A 2.5% surtax is imposed.

State	Net Income after pers'l. exemption	Percentage rates	Net income after pers'l. exemption	Percentage rates	Personal Exemp. Single	Married family head	Credit Depends.
North Carolina[3]	First 2,000 2,001- 4,000 4,001- 6,000	3 4 5	6,001-10,000 Over 10,000	6 7	1,000	2,000 3,000	600

An additional exemption of $1,000 is allowed a married woman with a separate income; joint returns not permitted.

North Dakota[3]	First 1,000 1,001-3,000 3,001- 5,000 5,001- 6,000	1 2 3 5	6,001- 8,000 Over 8,000	7.5 10	750	1,500	750

An additional 1% tax is imposed on net incomes of individuals, estates, trusts and corporations (minimum $2.50; maximum $12.50).

Ohio[4]	First 5,000 5,001-10,000 10,001-15,000	0.5 1 2 ·	15,001-20,000 20,001-40,000 Over 40,000	2.5 3 3.5	500	1,000	500

Maximum personal exemption is $3,000 per return. Taxpayers age 65 or older are allowed a $25 credit, or if they have received a lump sum distribution from a pension, retirement or profit sharing plan during the tax year, they are allowed a credit equal to $25 times the taxpayer's expected remaining life. Credit may not exceed tax otherwise due. Credit is also allowed for an amount paid during the school year for elementary and secondary education or instruction or training of dependents who do not have a high school diploma.

Oklahoma[1]	First 1,000 1,001- 2,500 2,501- 3,750 3,751- 5,000	0.5 1 2 3	5,001- 6,250 6,251- 7,500 Over 7,500	4 5 6	750	1,500	750

For joint returns the rates shown apply to income classes twice as large. Rates of heads of households range from ½% on the first $1,500 to 6% on taxable income over $11,250. Non-residents are taxed at a flat rate of 6% of Oklahoma taxable income.

Oregon[1]	First $500 501- 1,000 1,001- 2,000 2,001- 3,000	4 5 6 7	3,001- 4,000 4,001- 5,000 Over 5,000	8 9 10	750	1,500	750

A credit is provided in an amount and equal to 25% of the Federal retirement income tax credit to the extent that such a credit is based on Oregon taxable income.

Pennsylvania	Modified Federal taxable income	2.3					

Pennsylvania residents working in New Jersey are subject to a flat 2.3% commuter's tax on their New Jersey income.

Rhode Island	Federal income tax liability	15			750	1,500	750

South Carolina[1]	First 2,000 2,001- 4,000 4,001- 6,000	2 3 4	6,001- 8,000 8,001-10,000 Over 10,000	5 6 7	800	1,600	800

Tennessee	Interest and dividends	6					

Dividends from corporations, 75% of whose property is taxable in Tenn., are taxed at 4%.

Utah[3]	First 750 751- 1,500 1,501- 2,250	2 3 4	2,251- 3,000 3,001- 3,750 Over 3,750	5 6 7.25	Federal exemptions		

Vermont					750	1,500	750

The tax is imposed at a rate of 25% of the Fed. income tax liability of the taxpayer for the taxable year after certain credits (retirement income, investment, foreign tax and tax-free covenant bonds) but before any surtax on Fed. liability, reduced by a % equal to the % of the taxpayer's adjusted gross income for the taxable year which is not Vermont income. A 15% surcharge will be reduced to 12% from Jan. 1, 1973 to Dec. 31, 1973, and 9% on Jan. 1, 1974, and thereafter.

Virginia[3]	First 3,000 3,001- 5,000	2 3	5,001-12,000 Over 12,000	5 5.75	600	1,200	600

West Virginia[1]	First 2,000 2,001- 4,000 4,001- 6,000 6,001- 8,000 8,001-10,000 10,001-12,000 12,001-14,000 14,001-16,000 16,001-18,000 18,001-20,000 20,001-22,000 22,001-26,000	2.1 2.3 2.8 3.2 3.5 4 4.6 4.9 5.3 5.4 6 6.1	26,001-32,000 32,001-38,000 38,001-44,000 44,001-50,000 50,001-60,000 60,001-70,000 70,001-80,000 80,001-90,000 90,001-100,000 100,001-150,000 150,001-200,000 Over 200,000	6.5 6.8 7.2 7.5 7.9 8.2 8.6 8.8 9.1 9.3 9.5 9.6	600	1,200	600

For joint returns and a return of a surviving spouse, a separate rate schedule is provided.

Wisconsin[1][4]	First 1,000 1,001- 2,000 2,001- 3,000 3,001- 4,000 4,001- 5,000 5,001- 6,000 6,001- 7,000 7,001- 8,000	3.1 3.4 3.6 4.8 5.4 5.9 6.5 7.6	8,001- 9,000 9,001-10,000 10,001-11,000 11,001-12,000 12,001-13,000 13,001-14,000 Over 14,000	8.2 8.8 9.3 9.9 10.5 11.1 11.4	15	30	15

(1) A standard deduction and optional tax table are provided.

(2) Community property State in which, in general, one-half of the community income is taxable to each spouse.

(3) A standard deduction is allowed.

(4) A limited tax credit is allowed for sales taxes in Colorado, the District of Columbia, Hawaii, Idaho, Indiana, Massachusetts, Nebraska, and Vermont; for property taxes on homesteads of the elderly in Colorado, Kansas, Michigan, Minnesota, Vermont, and Wisconsin; for property taxes and city income taxes in Michigan; and for personal property taxes in Maryland.

(5) Tax credits are allowed: $15 for single person or married person filing separately if AGI is $3,000 or less. (For each dollar by which the Federal AGI exceeds $3,000, the credit is reduced by $1 until no credit is allowed if Federal AGI is $3,015 or more.) $30 for heads of households or married persons filing jointly with $6,000 or less AGI. (For each dollar by which Federal AGI exceeds $6,000, credit is reduced by $1 until no credit is allowed if Federal AGI is $6,030 or more).

State Retail Sales Taxes; Types and Rates

Source: Analysis Staff, Tax Division, Treasury Dept. Data as of July 1, 1973

State	Tangible Personal Property	Admissions	Rest. Meals	Selected Service Transient Lodging	Public Utilities	Rates on other services and nonretail business
Alabama[2]	4%[3]	4%	4%	4%	...	Gross rcpts of amus't operators,
4%; agric., mining and mfg. mach., 1.5%.						
Arizona[2]	3	3	3	3	3	Timbering, 1.5%; storage, apt.,
office rental, 3%; meat pkg. and wholesale sales of feed to poultrymen and stockmen, ⅜%.						
Arkansas[2]	3	3	3	3	3	Printing, photographic services;
rcpts. from coin-operated dev.; repair services incl. auto and elect., 3%.						
California[2]	4.75[5]	...	4.75	...	...	Renting, leasing, producing,
fabricating, processing, printing 4.75%						
Colorado[2]	3	...	3	3	3	
Connecticut	6.5	12	6.5[7]	6.5[10]	6.5[14]	Storing for use or consumption of personal property items, 6.5%
D. of C.	5[3]	5	6	6	5	Duplicating, mailing, addressing and public stenographic services, 5%; sales of food for off-premise consumption, nonprescription medicines, 2%.
Florida	4	4	4	4	...	Rental income of amus't. mach., 4%
Georgia	3	3	3	3	3	Levies on amus't dev., 3%.
Hawaii[1]	4	4	4	4	...	Sugar processors, pineapple farmers and selected businesses, ½%; insur. solicitors, 2%; contractors, sales rep., professions, radio stations, 4%.[6]
Idaho[6]	3	3	3	3	...	Closed circuit tv boxing, wrestling, 5%.
Illinois[2][9]	4	...	4	...	...	Property sold in connection with a sale of service, 4%; remodeling, repairing and reconditioning of tangible personal property, 4%.
Indiana	4	...	4	4	4	
Iowa	3	3	3	3	3	Laundry, dry cleaning, automobile and cold storage, photography, printing, repairs, barber and beauty parlor services, advt., dry cleaning equip. rentals and gross rcpts. from amus't dev., 3%.
Kansas[2]	3	3	3	3	3	Gross rcpts. from operation of coin-operated devices; commer. amus't; 3%.
Kentucky	5	5	5	5	5	Storage, sewer services, photog. and photo fin., 5%; ticket sales to boxing or wrestling on closed circuit tv 5% of gross rcpts.; tax also applies to pay'ts for right to broadcast matches.
Louisiana[2]	3	3	3	3	...	Food and prescpt'n. drugs, 2%.
Maine	5	...	5	5	5	Proceeds from closed circuit tv, 5%.
Maryland	4[3]	12	4[7]	4	4	Farm equip., 2%; mfg. equip., including that used in generation of electricity or in R. & S. sold to mfrs., 2%; watercraft, 3%.
Mass.	3	...	7	5[10]	...	
Michigan	4	...	4	4	4	
Minnesota[2]	4	4	4	4	4	Food, medicines and clothing are exempt; coin-operated vending mach., 3% of gross sales.
Mississippi[1]	5[3]	...	5	5	5	Wholesaling, ⅛% (one-half of 1% on sales of meat for human consumption; 5% on beer, alc. bevs., soft drinks and motor fuel); extracting or mining of minerals, specified miscellaneous bus. incl. bowling, pool halls, warehouses, laundry and dry cleaning, pest control services, specified repair services, 5%; cotton ginning, 15¢ per bale; sales of materials to railroads for use in track structures, 3%; tractors, indust. fuel and mfg. mach. sales over $500, 1%.
Missouri[2]	3	3	3	3	3	
Nebraska[2]	2.5	2.5	2.5	2.5	2.5	
Nevada[2]	3[11]	...	3	...	...	

State	Tangible Personal Property	Admissions	Rest. Meals	Selected Service Transient Lodging	Public Utilities	Rates on other services and nonretail business
New Jersey[1]	5	5[12]	5	5[10]	...	
N.M.[1-2]	4[3]	4	4	4	4	
N.Y.[2]	4	4[12]	4[7]	4[10]	4	Safe deposit rentals, 4%.
N.C.[2]	3[3]	...	3	3	...	Farm and industrial machinery, 1% ($80 max.); airplanes, boats and locomotives, 2% ($120 max.); sales of horses and mules, 1%.
N.D.	4	4	4	4	4	Severance of sand or gravel from the soil, 4%.
Ohio[2]	4	...	4	4	...	
Okla.[2]	2[3]	2	2	2	2	Advert. (exclusive of newspapers, periodicals, billboards), printing, auto storage, gross proceeds from amusement dev., 2%.
Penn.[2]	6	...	6[7]	6	6	Cleaning, polishing, lubr. and insp. motor vehicles, rental income of coin-operated amuse. dev., 6%.
R.I.	5	...	5	5	5	
S.C.	4	...	4	4	4	
S.D.[1-2]	4[3]	3	4	3	3	Farm mach. and agric. irrigation equip., 2%; gross rcpts. from professions (other than medical), 4%.
Tenn.[2-9]	3.5	...	3.5	3.5	3.5	Vending machines, 1.5% (except tobacco products, 2.5%); industrial, farm equipment and machinery, 1%.
Texas[2]	4[3]	...	4	...	4	
Utah[2]	4	4	4	4	4	
Vt.	3	3	[13]	[13]	3	
Va.[2]	3[3]	...	3	3	...	Closed cir. tv., 5% of gross.
Wash.[1-2]	4.5	4.5	4.5	4.5	...	Rentals, auto. parking, other specified services, amusements, recreations, 4.5% (unless subject to county or city adm. taxes, when they remain taxable under the state business, occupation levy, 1%).
W. Va.[1]	3[3]	3	3	3	...	All services except public util. and pers., prof., 3%.
Wis.	4	4[12]	4	4	4	
Wyo.	3	3	3	3	3	

(1) All but a few States levy sales taxes of the single-stage retail type. Hi. and Miss. levy multiple-stage sales taxes. The N.M. and S.D. taxes have broad bases with respect to taxable services but they are not multiple-stage taxes. Wash. and W.Va. levy gross receipts taxes on all business, distinct from their sales taxes. Alaska also levies a gross receipts tax on businesses. The rates applicable to retailers, with exceptions, under these gross receipts taxes are as follows: Alaska, 1/2% on gross receipts of $20,000-$100,000 and 1/4% on gross receipts in excess of $100,000; Wash., 44/100%; and W. Va., 55/100%. N.J. imposes a tax of 1/20 of 1% on retail stores with income in excess of $150,000, and an unincorporated business tax at the rate of 1% if gross receipts exceed $5,000.

(2) In addition to the State tax, sales taxes are also levied by certain cities and/or countries.

(3) Motor vehicles are taxed at the general sales tax rates with the following exceptions: Ala., 1 1/2%; Miss., 3%; and N.C., 2% ($120 maximum) Motor vehicles are exempt from the general sales and use taxes but are taxed under motor vehicle tax laws in Md., 4%; Minn., 4%; N.M., 2%; N.D., 4%; Okla., 2%; S.D. and W.V., 3%; Tex., 4%; Va., 2%; and the D.C., 4%.

(4) Ariz. and Miss. also tax the transportation of oil and gas by pipeline. Ga., Mo., Okla. and Utah do not tax transportation of property. Miss. taxes taxicab transportation at the rate of 2%. Okla. does not tax fares of 15¢ or less on local transportation. Utah does not tax street railway fares.

(5) "Lease" excludes the use of tangible personal property for a period of less than one day for a charge of less than $10 where the privilege of using the property is restricted to use on the premises or at a business location of the grantor.

(6) A limited credit (or refund) in the form of a flat dollar amount per personal exemption is allowed against the personal income tax to compensate for (1) sales taxes paid on food in Colo., D.C. and Neb.; and (2) all sales taxes paid in Hi., Idaho, Mass. and Vt. Low-income taxpayers (adjusted gross income not over $6,000) are allowed a credit against D.C. tax liability ranging from $2 to $6 per personal exemption, depending on taxpayer's income bracket. A refund is allowed if credit exceeds tax liability.

(7) Restaurant meals below a specified price are exempt: Conn. and Md. less than $1; N.Y. less than $1 (when alcoholic beverages are sold, meals are taxable regardless of price); and Penn., 50¢ or less. In Mass., restaurant meals ($1 or more) which are taxed at 5% under the meals excise tax are exempt.

(8) Conn., exempts clothing for children under 10 years of age. Penn. and Wisc. exempt clothing with certain exceptions.

(9) In Ill., the rate will revert to 3.5% on 1/1/74 if approved by the Governor. In Tenn., the 3 1/2% rate is effective 6/1/71 to 6/30/74, thereafter reverting to 3%.

(10) In Del. a 6% hotel occupancy tax is imposed. In Colo. and Conn., the first 30 consecutive days of rental or occupancy of rooms is taxable. Over 30 days is exempt. In Mass., transient lodging (in excess of $2 a day) is subject to a 5.7% (5% plus 14% surtax) room occupancy excise tax. In N.J. and N.Y., rooms which rent for $2 a day or less are exempt.

(11) Includes a statewide mandatory 1% county sales tax collected by the state and paid to the counties for support of local school districts.

(12) Conn. imposes an admissions tax of 10% of charges for admissions to places of amusement, entertainment or recreation. The tax also applies to charges to cabarets and to dues. Md. taxes at 1/2 of 1% gross receipts derived from charges for rentals of sporting or recreational equipment, and admissions, cover charges for tables, services or merchandise at any roof garden or cabaret. In N.J., admissions to a place of amusement are taxable if the charge is in excess of 75¢. N.Y. taxes admissions when the charge is over 10¢; exempt are participating sports (such as bowling and swimming), motion picture theaters, race tracks, boxing, wrestling, and live dramatic or musical performances. In Wisc., sales of admissions to motion picture theaters costing 75¢ or less are exempt.

(13) Meals and rooms are exempt from sales tax, but are subject to a special excise tax of 5%.

(14) Gas, water, electricity, telephone and telegraph services provided to consumers through mains, lines or pipes are exempt to the extent of $10 per month. Gas and electric energy used for domestic heating are exempt. Interstate telephone calls are exempt, as are calls from coin-operated telephones.

Savings by Individuals in the United States

Source: Federal Reserve System
(Billions of Dollars)* Indicates less than $50 million

	1969	1970	1971	1972	1973¹	
Incr. in financial assets	63.3	80.2	100.9	124.9	114.4	124.9
Currency and demand deposits	2.6	9.1	11.0	12.9	-4.7	14.0
Savings accounts	6.0	44.4	70.8	75.5	96.1	68.3
Securities	30.7	-1.2	-14.0	5.4	-8.7	7.3
U.S. Savings bonds	-.4	.3	2.4	3.3	3.9	3.6
Other U.S. Treasury Sec.	12.8	-11.7	-10.9	1.7	-11.4	-8.0
U.S.G. agency securities	2.8	2.7	-3.6	-.4	6.8	8.1
State & local obligations	9.6	-.5	-.9	1.3	2.1	7.5
Corporation & foreign bonds	7.4	10.1	8.2	4.9	-.7	1.2
Commercial paper	2.7	.6	-3.9	.4	-2.7	3.1
Investment company shares	4.8	2.6	1.2	-.6	-2.3	-2.2
Other corporate stock	-9.0	-5.2	-6.6	-5.2	-4.4	-6.0
Private life insurance reserves	4.9	5.1	6.1	7.2	7.7	7.7
Private insured pension reserves	2.9	3.3	5.2	4.6	5.2	5.0
Private noninsured pension reserves	6.3	7.1	7.3	5.7	8.0	7.8
Government ins. & pension reserves	6.6	8.8	9.7	10.5	9.2	11.7
Miscellaneous financial assets	3.1	3.6	4.9	3.1	1.5	3.1
Gross investment in tangible assets	143.0	140.2	165.8	190.5	215.2	216.0
Nonfarm homes	22.0	19.6	26.8	34.3	38.1	40.7
Noncorporate business construction & equipment	29.2	30.4	34.3	39.5	43.2	41.5
Consumer durables	90.8	91.3	103.5	117.4	132.2	133.1
Inventories	1.1	-1.1	1.1	-.8	1.8	.6
Capital consumption allowances	104.5	112.4	121.3	130.6	137.5	140.7
Nonfarm homes	8.7	9.0	9.4	10.2	10.3	10.4
Noncorporate business plant and equipment	21.3	22.6	24.4	26.7	27.8	28.5
Consumer durables	74.6	80.7	87.5	93.8	99.4	101.7
Net investment in tangible assets	38.5	27.8	44.5	59.8	77.8	75.3
Nonfarm homes	13.3	10.6	17.4	24.1	27.9	30.3
Noncorporate business construction and equipment	7.9	7.7	9.9	12.8	15.3	13.0
Consumer durables	16.2	10.6	16.0	23.6	32.8	31.4
Inventories	1.1	-1.1	1.1	-.8	1.8	.6
Increase in debt	39.8	30.6	54.6	84.1	84.6	86.3
Mortage debt on nonfarm homes	16.1	12.5	24.1	38.4	39.2	42.5
Noncorporate business mortgage debt	7.0	8.0	11.2	13.2	14.3	14.9
Consumer credit	10.4	6.0	11.2	19.2	25.3	24.1
Security credit	-3.4	-1.8	2.6	4.7	-4.0	-6.5
Policy loans	2.6	2.3	1.0	.9	1.2	1.8
Other debt	7.1	3.6	4.4	7.7	8.6	9.4
Individual saving	62.0	77.4	90.8	100.6	107.6	113.9
Less-Govt. Ins & Pen Reserves	6.6	8.8	9.7	10.5	9.2	11.7
Net inv. in cons. dur.	16.2	10.6	16.0	23.6	32.8	31.4
Capital gains dividends from invest. cos.	2.5	.9	.8	1.4	1.0	2.0
Net savings by farm corps.	*	-.1	*	*	-.1	-.1
Equals pers saving, F/F basis	36.6	57.2	64.3	65.1	64.6	68.8
Personal saving, NIA basis	38.2	56.2	60.2	49.7	50.0	52.4
Difference	-1.6	1.0	4.2	15.4	14.6	16.5

(1.) First and second quarter of 1973.

FEDERAL GIFT TAX

Any citizen or resident who within the calendar year makes gifts in excess of $3,000 to any one individual, or any gift of a future interest regardless of value, must file a gift tax return on or before April 15 of the following year. In addition to the annual $3,000 exclusion for each person to whom gifts are made, each donor also has a specific lifetime excemption of $30,000, and this may be taken all at one time of spread over years.

When a husband or wife transfers by gift an interest in property to his or her spouse a deduction in computing gift tax will be allowed to the extent of one-half of the value of the gift. Also gifts to a third party by either husband or wife may be treated as made one-half by each. *Tax Foundation*

If the taxable gifts are:			The tax will be:	
Not over $5,000			2¼% of the taxable gifts	
Over	$5,000 but not over	$10,000	$112.50, plus 5¼% of excess over	$5,000
Over	$10,000 but not over	$20,000	$375, plus 8¼% of excess over	$10,000
Over	$20,000 but not over	$30,000	$1,200, plus 10½% of excess over	$20,000
Over	$30,000 but not over	$40,000	$2,250, plus 13½% of excess over	$30,000
Over	$40,000 but not over	$50,000	$3,600, plus 16½% of excess over	$40,000
Over	$50,000 but not over	$60,000	$5,250, plus 18¾% of excess over	$50,000
Over	$60,000 but not over	$100,000	$7,125, plus 21 % of excess over	$60,000
Over	$100,000 but not over	$250,000	$15,525, plus 22½% of excess over	$100,000
Over	$250,000 but not over	$500,000	$49,275, plus 24 % of excess over	$250,000
Over	$500,000 but not over	$750,000	$109,275, plus 26¼% of excess over	$500,000
Over	$750,000 but not over	$1,000,000	$174,900, plus 27¾% of excess over	$750,000
Over	$1,000,000 but not over	$1,250,000	$244,275, plus 29¼% of excess over	$1,000,000
Over	$1,250,000 but not over	$1,500,000	$317,400, plus 31½% of excess over	$1,250,000
Over	$1,500,000 but not over	$2,000,000	$396,150, plus 33¾% of excess over	$1,500,000
Over	$2,000,000 but not over	$2,500,000	$564,900, plus 36¾% of excess over	$2,000,000
Over	$2,500,000 but not over	$3,000,000	$748,650, plus 39¾% of excess over	$2,500,000
Over	$3,000,000 but not over	$3,500,000	$947,400, plus 42 % of excess over	$3,000,000
Over	$3,500,000 but not over	$4,000,000	$1,157,400 plus 44¼% of excess over	$3,500,000
Over	$4,000,000 but not over	$5,000,000	$1,378,650, plus 47¼% of excess over	$4,000,000
Over	$5,000,000 but not over	$6,000,000	$1,851,150, plus 50¼% of excess over	$5,000,000
Over	$6,000,000 but not over	$7,000,000	$2,353,650, plus 52½% of excess over	$6,000,000
Over	$7,000,000 but not over	$8,000,000	$2,878,650, plus 54¾% of excess over	$7,000,000
Over	$8,000,000 but not over	$10,000,000	$3,426,150, plus 57 % of excess over	$8,000,000
Over	$10,000,000		$4,566,150, plus 57¾% of excess over	$10,000,000

Social Security Programs

Source: Office of Research and Statistics, Social Security Administration,
Dept. of Health, Education and Welfare

Medicare; Old-Age, Survivors and Disability Insurance

Amendments to the Social Security Act, signed by the President on July 9, 1973, make changes in cash benefit provisions, in the new supplementary security income (SSI) program, and in Medicaid. The law provides for a cost-of-living increase of 5.9 percent in the regular monthly cash benefits and in the special age-72 payments, effective for June 1974. The maximum amount of earnings taxable and creditable for benefit purposes is raised to $12,600 in 1974, rather than to $12,000 as under the previous law. The annual exempt amount of earnings is increased from $2,100 to $2,400, effective January 1, 1974. The amount of wages a beneficiary may earn in a month and still receive full benefits for the month is raised from $175 to $200. Effective for July 1974 the new legislation provides for an increase in the income payment levels under the SSI program—from $130 to $140 per month for an individual and from $195 to $210 for a couple. The new legislation also protects the Medicaid eligibility of the medically indigent who were disabled or blind under State definitions in December 1973 but who do not meet the SSI definitions of disability or blindness.

The Commissioner of Social Security is James B. Cardwell. There are 636 district offices, with 384 branches and 129 metropolitan branch offices, where the public may obtain information about benefit rights.

Medicare
Health Insurance for Aged

Beginning July 1966, most Americans aged 65 and over became eligible for hospital insurance and, if they choose to take it, for voluntary medical insurance in addition. The 1972 amendments extend Medicare protection to persons entitled for not less than 24 months to social security cash benefits because of disability and to women getting mother's benefits who for 2 years previous would have been entitled to disability benefits but had not filed an application. Medicare benefits are also extended to persons under age 65 who have chronic kidney disease and need hemodialysis or renal transplantation.

Persons eligible for both hospital and medical insurance or for medical insurance only may choose to have their covered services provided through a Health Maintenance Organization (a prepaid group health or other capitation plan that meets prescribed standards).

Hospital insurance.—In the seventh year of operation (July 1972-June 1973) about $6.6 billion was withdrawn from the hospital insurance trust fund for hospital and related benefits. About 21,000,000 persons were enrolled as of January 1972.

The hospital insurance program pays the cost of covered services for hospital and posthospital care as follows:

• Up to 90 days of hospital care during a benefit period (spell of illness, starting on the 1st day of care as a bed-patient is received in a hospital or skilled nursing facility and ending when the individual has not been a bed-patient for 60 consecutive days). For the first 60 days, the hospital insurance pays for all but the first $72 of expenses; for the 61st to 90th day, the program pays all but $18 a day for covered services. In addition, each

person has a 60-day lifetime reserve that can be used after the 90 days of hospital care in a benefit period are exhausted, and all but $36 a day of expenses during the reserve days are paid. Once used the reserve days are not replaced. (Payment for care in a mental hospital is limited to 190 days.)

• Up to 100 days' care in a skilled nursing facility (skilled nursing home) in each benefit period. Hospital insurance pays for all covered services for the first 20 days and all but $9 daily for the next 80 days. At least 3 day's hospital stay must precede these services, and the skilled nursing facility must be entered within 14 days after leaving the hospital. (The 1972 law permits more than 14 days in certain circumstances.)

• Up to 100 visits by nurses or other health workers (not doctors) from a home health agency in the 365 days after release from a hospital or extended-care facility.

Money to pay these benefits comes from special contributions paid by workers, their employers, and the self-employed. The 1974 rate is 1.0% on earnings up to $12,600 (the maximum taxable for that year). Beginning July 1, 1973, persons reaching 65 who are ineligible for hospital insurance may enroll voluntarily for hospital benefits, on the same conditions as enrollments for medical insurance, and pay the full cost of the protection, ($33 a month at the start).

Medical insurance—Aged persons can receive benefits under this supplementary program **only** if they sign up for them and agree to pay a monthly premium ($6.30 from Aug. 13, 1973 to June 30, 1974). The Federal Government pays a matching amount. In December of each year the Secretary of Health, Education, and Welfare announces the amount of the premium payable starting in July of the following year. The 1972 amendments provide that the premiums be increased only when there is a general benefit increase in the year and it will rise no more than the percent by which the cash benefits have been increased since the last premium increase.

Benefit payments under the medical insurance program from July 1972 through June 1973 totaled $2.4 billion. As of Jan. 1, 1972, 20,100,000 persons were enrolled.

The medical insurance program pays 80% of the reasonable charges (after the first $60 in each calendar year) for the following services:

• Physicians' surgeons' services, whether in the doctor's office, a clinic, or hospital or at home (but physician's charges for X-ray or clinical laboratory services for hospital bed-patients are paid in full and without meeting the deductible).

• Other medical and health services, such as diagnostic tests, surgical dressings and splints, and rental or purchase of medical equipment. Beginning July 1, 1973, services of a physical therapist in independent practice, furnished in his office or the patient's home. Beginning Jan. 1, 1973, a hospital or extended-care facility may provide covered outpatient physical therapy services under the medical insurance program to its patients who have exhausted their hospital insurance coverage.

• Physical therapy services furnished under the supervision of a participating hospital, clinic, skilled nursing facility, or agency.

• Certain services by podiatrists.

- All outpatient services of a participating hospital (including diagnostic tests).
- Beginning Jan. 1, 1973, under the 1972 amendments, outpatient speech pathology services, under the same requirements as physical therapy.
- Services of licensed chiropractors who meet uniform standards, but only for treatment by means of manual manipulation of the spine and treatment of subluxation of the spine demonstrated by X-ray.
- Supplies related to colostomies are considered prosthetic devices and payable under the program. Home health services even without a hospital stay (up to 100 visits a year) are paid up to 100%.

To get medical insurance protection, persons approaching age 65 may enroll in the 7-month period that includes 3 months before the 65th birthday, the month of the birthday, and 3 months after the birthday, but if they wish coverage to begin in the month they reach 65 they must enroll in the 3 months **before** their birthday. Persons not enrolling within their first enrollment period may enroll later, during the first 3 months of each year but their premium is 10% higher for each 12-month period elapsed since they first could have enrolled.

The monthly premium is deducted from the cash benefit for persons receiving social security, railroad retirement, or civil service retirement benefits. Income from the medical premiums and the Federal matching payments are put in a Supplementary Medical Insurance Trust Fund, from which benefits and administrative expenses are paid.

Persons qualifying for hospital insurance under social security receive a health insurance card similar to the cards now used by Blue Cross and other health agencies. The card indicates whether the individual has taken out medical insurance protection. It is to be shown to the hospital, skilled nursing facility, home health agency, doctor, or whoever provides the covered services. The part of the bill for which payment can be made is taken care of by the program. Payments are made only in the 50 States, Puerto Rico, the Virgin Islands, Guam, and American Samoa, **except that** hospital services may be provided in border areas immediately outside the U.S. if comparable services are not accessible in the U.S. for a beneficiary who becomes ill or is injured in the U.S.

Old-Age, Survivors, and Disability Insurance

Retired and disabled workers and their families and the survivors of deceased workers received $47.3 billion in social security cash benefits in the 12 months ended in June 1973. In that month the average benefit being received by a retired worker was about $165; for retired workers just coming on the rolls, the average benefit award was about $167. For a disabled worker, the average June check was $156 and new disabled-worker beneficiaries were awarded $197, on the average.

Old-age, survivors, and disability insurance covers almost all jobs in which people work for wages or salaries, as well as most work of self-employed persons, whether in a city job, or in business, or on a farm.

Old-age, survivors, and disability insurance is paid for by a tax on earnings (for 1974 up to $12,600). The employed worker and his employer share the tax equally. (Beginning 1966, cash tips count as covered wages if they amount to $20 or more from one place of employment. The worker reports them to his employer, who includes them in his social security tax reports, but only the worker pays contributions on the amount of the tips.)

The employer deducts the tax each payday and sends it, with an equal amount as his own share, to the District Director of Internal Revenue. The collected taxes are deposited in the Federal Old-Age and Survivors Insurance Trust Fund and the Federal Disability Insurance Trust Fund; they can be used only to pay benefits, the costs of rehabilitation services, and administrative expenses.

Amount of Work Required

To qualify for benefits for himself and his family, the worker must have been in covered employment long enough to become insured. Just how long depends on his date of birth (or if he dies or becomes disabled, the date of his death or disability).

A person is fully covered if he has one quarter of coverage for every year after 1950 up to but not including the year in which he reaches age 62. (The 1972 law permits 62 to be used for men as it is for women, except that the shift to age 62 will take until 1975 to be complete.)

Certain provisions in the law permit special monthly payments under the social security program to persons aged 72 and over who are not eligible for regular social security benefits since they had little or no opportunity to earn social security work credits during their working lifetime.

To get disability benefits, the worker must also have credit for 5 out of 10 years before he becomes disabled. Persons disabled before age 31 can qualify with a briefer period of coverage.

Work Years Required

The following table shows the number of work years required to be fully insured for old-age or survivors benefits, according to the year worker reaches retirement age or dies.

Work credit for retirement benefits:

If you reach 62 in	Years men need	Years women need
1971	5¾	5
1972	6	5¼
1973	6	5½
1974	6	5¾
1975	6	6
1977	6½	6½
1979	7	7
1981	7½	7½
1983	8	8
1987	9	9
1991 or later	10	10

Work credit for survivors checks

Born after 1929, die at	Born before 1930, die before age 62	Years you need
28 or younger		1½
30		2
32		2½
34		3
36		3½
38		4
40		4½
42		5
44	1973	5½
46	1975	6
48	1977	6½
50	1979	7
52	1981	7½
54	1983	8
56	1985	8½
58	1987	9
60	1989	9½
62 or older	1991 or later	10

Self-Employed

A self-employed person who has earnings of $400 or more in a year must report his earnings for income-tax and social security tax purposes. If he is not a farmer he reports only net returns from his business. He need not add income from real estate, savings, dividends, loans, pensions or insurance policies if these are not part of his business.

A self-employed person who has net earnings of $400 or more in a year gets 4 quarters of coverage for that year. If his earnings are less than $400 in a year they do not count toward social security credits.

Under a 1966 law, the nonfarm self-employed person must make estimated payments of his social security taxes, on a quarterly basis, for taxable years after Dec. 31, 1966, if combined estimated income tax and social security tax amount to at least $40.

New 1972 amendments permit the self-employed to have the option, comparable to that for farm workers, of reporting their earnings as $2/3$ of their gross income from self-employment but not more than $1,600 a year. This option can be used only if actual net earnings from self-employment income is less than $1,600 and less than $2/3$ of gross income. and may be used only 5 times.

When a person has both taxable wages and earnings from self-employment, only as much of the self-employment income as will bring total earnings up to the current taxable maximum is subject to tax for social security purposes. A self-employed person pays the tax at a lower rate than the combined rate for an employee and his employer — about $1 1/2$ times what the employee alone pays.

Farm Owners and Hands

Self-employed farmers whose gross annual earnings from farming are under $2,400 may report $2/3$ of their gross earnings instead of net earnings for social security purposes. Cash or crop shares received from a tenant or share farmer count if the owner participated materially in production or management. The self-employed farmer pays contributions at the same rate as other self-employed, but he may make his tax returns annually.

Farm Workers. Earnings from farm work count toward benefits (1) if the employer pays $150 or more in cash during the year; (2) if the employee works on 20 or more days for cash pay figured on a time basis. Under these rules a person gets credit for one calendar quarter for each $100 in cash pay in a year but no more than four quarters in any one year.

Foreign farm workers admitted to the United States on a temporary basis will not be covered.

Household Workers

Anyone working as maid, cook, laundress, nursemaid, baby-sitter, chauffeur, gardener and at other household tasks in the house of another, is covered by social security if he or she earns $50 or more in cash in three months from any one employer. Room and board do not count, but carfare counts if paid cash. The job does not have to be regular or fulltime. The employee should get a card at the social security office and show it to the employer.

The employer deducts the amount of the social security tax from the worker's pay, adds an identical amount as his own tax and sends the total amount to the Federal Government, with the number of the employee's social security card.

What Aged Workers Get

When a person has enough work in covered employment and reaches retirement age (65 for full benefit, 62 for reduced benefit), he may retire and get monthly old-age benefits. If he continues to work and has earnings of more than $2,400, $1 in benefits will be withheld for every $2 above $2,400. The amount that can be earned in a month without loss of any benefits has been raised from $175 to $200. The annual exempt amount and the monthly test will be raised automatically in the future, according to the rise in general earnings levels. The eligible worker who is 72 receives the full amount of benefit, regardless of earnings.

A worker's benefit will be raised by 1% for each year after 1970 for which the worker between 65 and 72 did not receive benefits because of earnings from work. No increases are to be paid to the worker's dependents or survivors under this provision.

The 1972 amendments provided for a special minimum benefit payable to persons who worked 20 or more years under social security. This is paid as an alternative to the regular minimum of $84.50 when a higher amount results. The highest minimum under this provision would be $170 a month for a person ($255 for a couple) with 30 or more years of coverage.

When a person receives old-age benefits, payments can also be made to certain of his dependents including a wife 62 or over, dependent children under 18 or who became totally disabled before age 22 or who are full-time students not yet aged 22, a wife (regardless of age) if caring for an eligible child, and a dependent husband 62 or over.

The special benefit for persons aged 72 or over who do not meet the regular coverage requirements is $58 a month ($87 for a couple if both members are eligible). It is not paid to persons on the public assistance rolls.

Social Security benefits are not subject to income taxes.

A woman worker is eligible for a full old-age benefit at age 65, but she may retire at 62 and get 80% of her full benefit for the rest of her life; the nearer she is to 65 when she begins collecting her benefit, the larger it will be. (Benefits for men retiring before 65 are reduced at the same rate as benefits for women retiring before 65.)

A child can get benefits based on his mother's earnings on the same conditions as those entitling a child to benefits based on his father's earnings record.

Benefits for Worker's Wife (or Husband)

The wife of a man who is getting social security retirement or disability payments may become entitled to wife's insurance benefits in a reduced amount when she reaches 62, or she may wait until she reaches 65 and get the entire amount of the wife's benefit, which is one-half of the husband's benefits. Benefits are also payable to the divorced wife of an insured worker if she was married to him for at least 20 years and he was contributing to or was ordered by a court to contribute to her support.

If a woman worker entitled to old-age benefit has a dependent husband aged 65 or over, he may draw a benefit similar to a wife's benefit at 65 (or a reduced benefit at age 62).

Benefits for Children of Retired or Disabled Workers

If a worker has children under 18 when he retires for age or disability they will get a benefit that is half his benefit, and so will his wife, even if she is under 62. Total benefits paid on a worker's earnings record are subject to a maximum and if the total paid to a family exceeds that maximum, the individual dependents' benefits are adjusted downward. (Total benefits paid to the family of a worker who retired in 1973 at age 62 with average yearly earnings of $5,838 could be no higher than $488.)

When his children reach 18, their benefits will stop, except that a child permanently and totally disabled before 22 may get a benefit as long as his disability meets the definition in the law. In addition, child's benefits are payable until the child reaches his 22nd birthday if he is attending school as a full-time student. Benefits may now be paid to a grandchild or step grandchild of a worker or of his spouse, in special circumstances.

What Disabled Worker Gets

If a worker becomes so severely disabled that he is unable to work, he may be eligible to receive a monthly disability benefit that is the same amount he would receive as an old-age benefit if he were 65 at the start of his disability. When he reaches 65, his disability benefit becomes an old-age benefit.

Benefits like those provided for dependents of retired-worker beneficiaries may be paid to dependents of disabled beneficiaries.

Survivor Benefits

If a worker should die while insured, one or more types of benefits would be payable to survivors.

1. A cash payment to cover burial expenses that amounts to 3 times the basic benefit but not more than $255, paid at the death of every insured worker.

2. A benefit for each child until the child reaches 18 (or up to age 22, if he is attending school). The monthly benefit of each child of a worker who has died is three-quarters of the amount the worker would have received if he had lived and drawn retirement benefits. A child with a permanent disability that began before age 22 may receive his benefit after that age.

3. A mother's benefit for the widow, if children under 18 are left in her care. Her benefit is 75% of the basic benefit and she draws it until the youngest child reaches 18. Payments stop then even if the child's benefit continues because he is attending school. They will start again when she is 62 (or 60), unless she marries. If she marries and the marriage is ended, she regains benefit rights. If she has a disabled child beneficiary aged 18 or over in her care, her benefits also continue.

The 1967 amendments provide that disabled widows and widowers will be eligible for benefits at age 50 at reduced rates depending on the age at entitlement. The widow or widower must have become totally disabled before or within 7 years after the spouse's death.

4. If there are no children entitled to receive benefits, the widow will get a benefit at 62 that is 82½% of the basic benefit amount. She may choose to start getting benefits at age 60; if she makes this choice, her benefit is reduced by 5/9 of 1% for each month she receives a benefit before she is 62. A widow (or widower) who first becomes entitled to benefits at age 65 will receive a benefit that is 100% of what her husband would be receiving if he were alive. Dependent widowers aged 60 or over are entitled to survivor benefits on same basis as widows.

5. Dependent parents may be eligible for benefits, if they have been receiving at least half their support from the worker before his death, have reached retirement age (62) and are not eligible for an old-age benefit based on their own earnings. Each parent receives 75% of the basic benefit except that, if there is only one surviving parent, the benefit is 82% of the basic benefit.

The survivors of a woman worker receive benefits on the same basis as those of men workers.

Maximum Benefits Payable

The illustrative table below shows a column heading for average earnings of $9,000, but the benefit amounts shown in the column are not in general payable yet, since it will be some time before workers can have an average that high (years when the maximum creditable amount of earnings was lower than $9,000—the 1972 maximum—must currently be included when the average is figured). Benefit amounts larger than those shown in the table will eventually be payable to persons who raise their average yearly earnings for social security purposes by earning, for a sufficient period, the highest creditable amount in years with the higher maximums specified in the law—$10,800 in 1973, $12,000 in 1974, and possible automatic increases in the maximum thereafter. The table does not reflect the 5.9% increase that becomes effective in June 1974.

Examples of Monthly OASDI Cash Payments

$923 (Effective through May 1974)

	$923 or less	$1,800	$3,000	$4,200	$5,400	$6,600	$7,800	$9,000
Average yearly earnings after 1950*								
Retired Worker 65 or older Disabled Worker under 65 }	$ 84.50	$134.30	$174.80	$213.30	$250.60	$288.40	$331.00	$354.50
Wife 65 or older	42.30	67.20	87.40	106.70	125.30	144.20	165.50	177.30
Retired worker at 62	67.60	107.50	139.90	170.70	200.50	230.80	264.80	283.60
Wife at 62, no child	31.80	50.40	65.60	80.10	94.00	108.20	124.20	133.00
Widow at 60	73.30	96.10	125.10	152.60	179.30	206.30	236.70	253.50
Widow or widower at 62	84.50	110.80	144.30	176.00	206.80	238.00	273.10	292.50
Disabled worker at 50	51.30	67.30	87.50	106.80	125.50	144.30	165.60	177.30
Wife under 65 and one child	42.30	67.20	92.50	157.40	217.30	233.90	248.30	265.90
Widowed mother and one child	126.80	201.50	262.20	320.00	376.60	432.60	496.60	531.80
Widowed mother and two children	126.80	201.50	267.30	370.70	467.90	522.30	579.30	620.40
One child of retired or disabled worker	42.30	67.20	87.40	106.70	125.30	144.20	165.50	177.30
One surviving child	84.50	100.80	131.10	160.00	188.00	216.30	248.30	265.90
Maximum family payment	126.80	201.50	267.30	370.70	467.90	522.30	579.30	620.40

*Generally, average earnings are figured over the period from 1951 until the worker reaches retirement age, becomes disabled, or dies. Up to 5 years of low earnings or no earnings can be excluded. The maximum earnings creditable for social security are $3,600 for 1951-1954; $4,200 for 1955-1958; $4,800 for 1959-65; $6,600 for 1966-67; $7,800 for 1968-71; $9,000 for 1972; $10,800 for 1973; and $12,600 for 1974. As the text under the heading "Maximum Benefits Payable" explains, amounts shown in the last column will generally not be payable until later. When a person is entitled to more than one benefit, the amount actually payable is limited to the larger of the benefits.

Contribution Rate for Employees, Employers, and Self-Employed

Percent of Covered Earnings

Years	Employees and employers			Self-employed		
	OASDI Benefits	Hospital Insurance	Total	OASDI Benefits	Hospital Insurance	Total
1973-77	4.85	1.00	5.85	7.00	1.00	8.00
1978-80	4.80	1.25	6.05	7.00	1.25	8.25
1981-85	4.80	1.35	6.15	7.00	1.35	8.35
1986-97	4.80	1.45	6.25	7.00	1.45	8.45
1998-2010*	4.80	(1.45)	(6.25)	7.00	(1.45)	(8.45)
2011 & after*	5.85	(1.45)	(7.30)	7.00	(1.45)	(8.45)

*Costs of hospital insurance estimated only through 1997.

Social Security Trust Funds
Old-Age and Survivors and Disability Insurance Trust Funds, 1936-1973
[In thousands]

Period and fiscal year	Receipts		Interchange with railroad account	Expenditures		Total asset at period end
	Net contribution income and transfers	Net interest received		Benefit[1] payments	Administrative expenses	
1936-37	$265,000	$2,262		$27		$267,235
1940-41	688,141	55,958		64,342	$26,840	2,397,615
1945-46	1,238,218	147,766		320,510	37,427	7,641,428
1950-51	3,124,098	287,392		1,498,088	70,447	14,735,567
1955-56	6,442,370	487,450	−$7,439	5,360,813	124,339	22,593,109
1960-61	12,314,678	591,713	336,882	11,888,527	272,188	23,404,734
1965-66	19,422,599	648,635	468,782	19,794,079	437,159	21,558,397
1966-67	24,910,399	792,741	538,680	20,753,134	432,735	25,536,995
1967-68	25,455,798	984,310	458,044	22,841,115	559,645	28,118,300
1968-69	29,898,716	1,154,940	512,810	26,175,447	598,523	31,868,478
1969-70	34,554,182	1,572,375	589,257	29,045,046	623,055	37,719,951
1970-71	36,949,617	1,943,206	626,266	34,482,466	741,764	40,739,117
1971-72	41,101,267	2,106,805	748,531	38,615,706	793,594	43,789,335
1972-73[3]	47,310,833	2,281,098	802,457	47,372,752	966,537	44,259,519
Cumulative* to June 1973[3]	4,088,914,569	20,680,143	7,439,341	369,355,951	8,559,901	44,259,519

(1.)Beginning 1966, includes amounts for rehabilitative services, authorized by 1965 amendments (a total of $110,404,000 from 1965-66 to 1971-72).
(2.)Preliminary.
*Cumulative totals are not totals of columns since several years are omitted.

Hospital Insurance Trust Fund: Status, 1966-73
[In thousands]

Period	Receipts					Expenditures	Total assets
	Net contribution income[1]	Transfers from general revenues[2]	Transfers from railroad retirement account[3]	Net interest[4]	Net hospital and related service benefits[5]	Administrative expenses[6]	
Jan. 1966-June 1973[7]	$34,100,497	$3,875,326	$363,155	$919,426	$33,902,644	$992,543	$4,363,218
Fiscal year:							
1965-66	908,797			5,970		63,564	851,204
1966-67	2,688,684	337,850	16,200	45,903	2,507,773	88,848	1,343,221
1967-68	3,514,049	283,631	43,613	61,091	3,736,322	78,647	1,430,636
1968-69	4,423,236	770,968	53,776	96,063	4,653,976	104,182	2,016,521
1969-70	4,784,789	628,262	61,307	139,423	4,804,242	148,660	2,677,401
1970-71	4,897,979	873,849	63,255	183,027	5,442,971	149,434	3,103,106
1971-72	5,225,891	551,351	63,782	190,105	6,109,139	166,370	2,858,725
1972-73[7]	7,657,072	429,415	61,222	197,844	6,648,221	192,839	4,363,218

(1.)Represents amounts appropriated (estimated tax collections with suitable subsequent adjustments), after deductions for refund of estimated amount of employee-tax overpayment.
(2.)Represents Federal Government transfers from general funds appropriations to meet costs of benefits for persons not insured for cash benefits under OASDHI or railroad retirement and for costs of benefits arising from military wage credits.
(3.)Represents receipts under the financial interchange with railroad retirement account with respect to contributions for hospital insurance coverage of railroad workers.
(4.)Represents interest and profit on investments after transfers of interest on administrative expenses reimbursed to the OASI trust fund and on amounts transferred from railroad accounts.
(5.)Represents (1) payment vouchers on letters of credit issued to fiscal intermediaries under sec. 1816 and (2) direct payments to providers of services under sec. 1815 of the Social Security Act.
(6.)Subject to subsequent adjustment among all 4 social security trust funds, for allocated cost of each operation.
(7.)Preliminary.

Supplementary Medical Insurance Trust Fund: Status, 1966-73
[In thousands]

Period	Receipts			Expenditures		Total assets
	Premium income[1]	Transfers from general Revenues[2]	Net Interest[3]	Net medical service benefits[4]	Administrative expenses[5]	
Jan. 1966-June 1973[6]	$7,203,431	$7,210,466	$161,041	$12,539,136	$1,470,034	$745,768
Fiscal year:						
1966-67	646,682	623,000	14,052	664,261	133,682	485,791
1967-68	698,465	634,000	20,677	1,389,622	142,608	306,703
1968-69	902,821	984,287	23,466	1,644,842	194,660	377,774
1969-70	936,000	928,151	11,536	1,979,287	216,993	57,181
1971-72	1,340,052	1,365,295	28,993	2,255,069	288,619	480,709
1972-73[6]	1,426,476	1,430,451	45,049	2,391,056	245,861	745,768

(1.)Represents voluntary premium payments from and in behalf of insured persons.
(2.)Represents Federal Government transfers from general funds appropriations to match aggregate premiums paid.
(3.)Represents interest and profit on investments after transfers of interest on administrative expenses reimbursed to the OASI trust fund (see footnote 5).
(4.)Represents payment vouchers on letters of credit issued to carriers under section 1842 of the Social Security Act.
(5.)Subject to subsequent adjustment among all 4 social security trust funds for allocated cost of each operation.
(6.)Preliminary.

Employment Services and Unemployment Insurance

Source: Manpower Administration, U.S. Department of Labor

Training and Employment Services

The Federal-State Employment Service consists of the U.S. Employment Service and affiliated state employment services with their network of about 2,400 local offices. During the fiscal year 1973, these offices recorded over 4,500,000 placements in nonagricultural jobs. Vietnam-era veterans accounted for 382,000 of the individuals placed in nonfarm jobs, an increase of almost 9% over the previous year. Use of computers was extended, with statewide job bank systems operating in 34 states and covering nearly 75% of the nation's population at year's end.

The employment service is concerned with full utilization of the nation's human resources; it works to refer employable applicants to job openings that use their highest skills and assists the unemployed to arrange for the services or training needed to make them employable. Special attention is devoted to the needs of veterans, especially disabled veterans, older workers, youth, minority group members, migrants, the handicapped, and the disadvantaged In addition, services are offered to workers who lost their jobs because of foreign trade competition.

The employment service assists employers in meeting their labor needs and offers employment-related personnel services. Other functions include assisting in developing and using civilian manpower capacity to meet national emergency and disaster needs and enforcing applicable standards relating to housing, transportation, and other conditions for farm and woods workers recruited for jobs in other states. The employment service continued experiments bringing manpower services to remote rural areas.

Special Veterans Service

Service to veterans was emphasized during the year. The Vietnam Era Veterans Readjustment Assistance Act of 1972 requires certain firms and subcontractors with Federal contracts to list their openings with employment service offices. All local offices offer special veterans services and carry out the Manpower Administration's policy of absolute preference for veterans in job and training placements. All enlisted personnel about to be discharged are contacted to help them find jobs rapidly or obtain benefits while in school or training.

Work Incentive Program

The Manpower Administration continued to offer training and other services to prepare workers for jobs. Particular attention was devoted to the needs of welfare recipients, minority members, and others with special problems in finding and holding a job. At the beginning of fiscal 1973, the Work Incentive Program, which provides job information, needed services such as child care, and training to people on Aid to Families with Dependent Children (AFDC), started operating as WIN II, a redirected program authorized by the 1971 amendments to the Social Security Act. Under the amendments, all adults applying for or receiving AFDC not exempt by law must register for WIN II, which stresses activities that help them move quickly into appropriate work. During the year the program registered about 1,280,000, appraised 525,000 to determine their job potential, and placed 142,000 in unsubsidized jobs. To increase the opportunities for WIN participants, the Revenue Act of 1971 gives employers who hire and retain them for 2 years a tax credit equal to 20% of their first year's wages.

The manpower needs of blacks, Spanish-speaking workers, and Indians received special attention. In addition, activities to assist ex-offenders were continued.

Other Manpower Programs

Other manpower programs provided jobs, training, and work experience for jobless and underemployed workers. They include the Job Opportunities in the Business Sector (JOBS) and JOBS-Optional programs, which support training jobs in private industry; Manpower Development and Training Act programs for residents of redevelopment areas and regular institutional training; the Neighborhood Youth Corps, providing paid work, summer jobs, and training for youth; and Operation Mainstream, offering paid work experience and training to low-income people, a large share of them older rural workers.

The Public Employment Program continued to subsidize jobs in state and local government for unemployed workers, including sizable proportions of veterans, the disadvantaged, and minorities. With expiration of the Emergency Employment Act of 1971, which authorized the program, it started to phase out its operations at year's end and looked to easing the transition of its workers to regular jobs. The Job Corps, which trains disadvantaged youth, largely in a residential setting, planned to expand labor union programs of training and placement for its enrollees.

Unemployment Insurance

Unlike old-age and survivors insurance, entirely a Federal program, the unemployment insurance program is a Federal-State system which provides insured wage earners with partial replacement of wages lost during involuntary unemployment. The program protects most workers in the industry, but few in agriculture. Some 60,807,000 jobs in commerce, industry, and government, including the Armed Forces, were covered under the Federal-State system during calendar year 1972. In addition, 588,000 railroad workers were insured against unemployment under a system administered by the Railroad Retirement Board.

Each state, as well as the District of Columbia and Puerto Rico, has its own law and operates its own program. The amount and duration of the weekly benefits are determined by state laws, based on prior wages and length of employment. States are required to extend the duration of benefits when unemployment rises to and remains above specified state or national levels; costs of these extended benefits are shared equally by the state and Federal governments.

Under the Federal Unemployment Tax Act, as amended in 1970, the tax rate is 3.2% (3.2% for 1973) on the first $4,200 paid to each employee of employers with one or more employees in 20 weeks of the year. A credit of up to 2.7% is allowed for taxes paid under state unemployment insurance laws that meet certain criteria, leaving the Federal share at 0.5% (0.58% for 1973) of taxable wages, from which the Federal government pays its share of the cost of extended benefits and makes grants to the states to cover the administrative costs of the unemployment insurance and employment service programs. Grants from this source for employment service administrative costs are limited to that proportion of total employment service costs that is attributable to the covered work force.

Social Security Requirement

The Social Security Act requires, as a condition of such grants, prompt payment of due benefits. The Federal Unemployment Tax Act provides safeguards for workers' rights to benefits if they refuse jobs that fail to meet certain labor standards. Through the Unemployment Insurance Service of the Manpower Administration, the Secretary of Labor determines whether states qualify for grants for unemployment insurance administration and for tax offset credit for employers.

Benefits are financed solely by employer contributions, except in Alaska, Alabama, and New Jersey, where employees also contribute. Benefits are paid through the public employment offices, at which unemployed workers must register for work and to which they must report regularly for referral to a possible job during the time when they are drawing weekly benefit payments. During the 1972 calendar year, $4.47 billion in benefits were paid under the state unemployment insurance programs to 5,818,953 beneficiaries, representing compensation for 81,805,243 weeks of unemployment. They received an average weekly payment of $55.82 for

Employment Security

Source: Manpower Administration, U.S. Dept. of Labor
Selected Unemployment Insurance Data by State
Fiscal year 1972-73, State Program Only

State	Insured Claimants[1]	Benefici-aries[2]	Exhaus-tions[3]	Initial Claims[4]	Benefit payments Total[5] ($1,000)	Avg. weekly benefit for total unemploy. (dollars)	Funds available for benefits June 30, 1972[6] (1,000)	Employers subject to State law March 31, 1972
Alabama	80,484	65,600	19,553	143,342	34,421	46.25	115,147	25,096
Alaska	18,429	18,042	5,335	32,467	16,463	53.13	38,313	5,912
Arizona	41,133	30,483	8,410	87,345	18,919	52.97	144,404	21,890
Arkansas	55,401	39,687	10,637	100,400	20,240	46.87	54,988	35,131
California	979,187p	753,049	234,085	1,916,000	602,970	58.41	1,090,000	358,034
Colorado	38,068	26,911	4,736	69,655	15,141	65.46	113,409	21,583
Connecticut	160,654	149,895	42,575	295,826	128,576	68.50	40,709	60,617
Delaware	23,960	20,715	3,218	41,472	9,533	53.74	33,964	10,489
Dist. of Col.	23,725	20,107	6,484	32,415	25,102	76.16	56,255	16,333
Florida	97,520	69,371	27,518	202,271	38,085	47.17	328,703	66,627
Georgia	90,654	48,392	21,398	118,632	30,042	47.81	422,875	38,477
Hawaii	36,005	26,415	8,828	53,949	25,943	66.99	25,594	14,706
Idaho	25,191	21,516	4,915	55,134	11,350	53.54	50,202	15,297
Illinois	296,571p	238,983	74,407	530,515	194,663	59.78	332,170	97,473
Indiana	137,568	110,618	34,991	235,407	46,349	44.68	348,783	40,093
Iowa	49,109	37,116	10,781	90,072	26,675	58.35	111,963	27,913
Kansas	40,975	37,499	8,523	66,908	20,199	53.24	97,310	22,641
Kentucky	85,747	78,572	15,616	135,415	42,299	55.03	185,058	28,012
Louisiana	103,251	82,338	26,691	192,447	59,859	52.94	113,915	30,484
Maine	47,420	42,289	13,544	99,176	22,795	50.17	22,105	9,645
Maryland	109,138	85,381	21,166	191,813	64,874	60.22	137,480	57,627
Massachusetts	273,824	223,295	84,372	475,117	236,584	62.81	207,102	104,480
Michigan	491,109	303,369	98,008	672,283	214,791	60.20	487,995	129,264
Minnesota	108,704	92,086	31,672	172,555	64,309	53.43	79,427	47,069
Mississippi	34,609	23,970	5,219	58,615	10,311	40.83	100,825	16,137
Missouri	154,576	117,889	29,651	336,305	71,982	53.15	228,420	42,266
Montana	22,779	18,468	6,017	42,993	11,410	44.12	21,782	16,671
Nebraska	32,946	24,728	7,651	43,536	14,999	51.46	55,285	15,291
Nevada	28,266p	27,191	9,365	86,150	22,387	62.35	28,899	11,627
New Hampshire	26,323	20,354	743	50,422	7,809	53,42	53,880	8,743
New Jersey	413,636p	7	114,768	606,559	307,015	7	153,115	130,669
New Mexico	21,383	19,226	4,995	63,497	13,388	48.24	40,463	18,681
New York	809,760	657,483	177,455	1,588,969	593,293	60.22	1,271,747	374,016
North Carolina	118,639	80,100	13,119	215,076	29,415	40.03	481,345	46,379
North Dakota	12,540	9,074p	2,363p	20,943p	7,922	51.23p	14,651	6,711
Ohio	220,822	176,746	38,240	427,461	119,224	57.39	692,165	104,053
Oklahoma	57,297	41,913	18,442	101,645	26,768	44.18	48,180	21,584
Oregon	89,447	66,880	15,291	216,074	41,902	47.68	115,817	43,057
Pennsylvania	481,244	400,502	78,270	988,583	364,946	67.83	575,898	182,460
Puerto Rico	101,506p	102,911	55,674	232,228	57,318	34.80	26,402	29,541
Rhode Island	62,875p	45,068	15,590	117,779	33,710	60.83	37,163	21,790
South Carolina	58,107	34,154	13,164	89,212	18,674	44.32	198,043	18,776
South Dakota	8,641	7,221	1,752	14,911	3,445	45.27	21,491	7,246
Tennessee	97,700	76,990	19,501	159,440	38,101	45.46	267,079	28,789
Texas	155,924	108,793	43,430	280,106	69,111	51.24	308,660	102,653
Utah	31,474	26,440	6,797	54,543	17,878	57.20	49,615	20,102
Vermont	18,465	15,206	3,566	33,502	13,013	60.69	2,699	6,350
Virginia	54,823	33,300	7,744	84,803	16,341	50.90	234,699	36,358
Washington	155,403	146,977	58,142	448,641	124,348	60.35	4,093	67,076
West Virginia	59,483p	50,991	8,930	104,208	25,239	44.09	108,869	13,129
Wisconsin	116,278	93,580	24,218	209,676	80,599	65.93	278,993	42,599
Wyoming	6,233p	5,403	932	9,671	2,813	52.60	22,406	9,502
Total	6,865,006p	5,053,287p	1,598,492p	12,696,164p	4,113,542	$57.60p	$10,080,557	2,727,149

(1) Claimants whose base-period earnings or whose employment — covered by the unemployment insurance program — was sufficient to make them eligible for unemployment insurance benefits as provided by State law.
(2) Based on number of first payments.
(3) Based on final payments. Some claimants shown, therefore, actually experienced their final week of compensable unemployment toward the end of the previous fiscal year but received their final payments in the current fiscal year. Similarly, some claimants who served their last week of compensable unemployment toward the end of the current fiscal year did not receive their final payment in this fiscal year and hence are not shown. A final week of compensable unemployment in a benefit year results in the exhaustion of benefit rights for the benefit year. Claimants who exhaust their benefit rights in one benefit year may be entitled to further benefits in the following benefit year.
(4) Excludes intrastate transitional claims to reflect more nearly instances of new unemployment. Includes claims filed by interstate claimants in the Virgin Islands.
(5) Adjusted for voided benefit checks and transfers under interstate combined wage plan.
(6) Sum of balance in State clearing accounts, benefit-payment accounts, and unemployment trust fund accounts maintained in the U.S. Treasury. (7) Excludes New Jersey. (8) Includes Virgin Islands. (p' Preliminary).

(cont'd. from page 75)

total unemployment for an average of 14.3 weeks. See table above for data by states for fiscal year 1973.

Federal Worker Benefits

Title 5, chapter 85 of the U.S. Code provided unemployment insurance protection during calendar year 1972 to about 2,832,004 Federal civilian employees and about 2,348,000 members of the Armed Forces. Benefits for unemployed Federal workers and ex-servicemen are financed through direct Federal appropri-ations but are paid by the state employment security agencies as agents of the Federal government.

During calendar year 1972 a total of $98,783,000 was paid to 97,400 unemployed Federal civilian workers for a total of 1,722,000 weeks of unemployment. The average weekly payment was $57.37 and was paid for an average of 17.7 weeks. A total of $315,518,000 was paid to 346,900 unemployed ex-servicemen for 5,336,000 weeks of unemployment. The average weekly benefit was $59.13 and was paid for an average of 15.4 weeks.

How and Where to Get Help on Consumer Complaints
by Kenneth C. Johnston

Some of the nation's largest corporations, facing up to a storm of consumer complaints about faulty merchandise and incompetent or grudging repair services, have created new pathways to provide personal attention to customers' grievances.

Government agencies, particularly state and local, have also improved and expanded their agencies which aid the consumer.

What big businesses have done is to provide phone numbers (often offering free calls) and addresses through which customers can complain, receive courteous consideration and have some hope of action.

The business programs are aimed at overcoming public frustration, anger and resultant sales resistance.

They are reportedly performing well. Where they aren't, or for firms that couldn't care less, there are other ways of bringing a balky dealer, salesman, serviceman or manufacturer to heel: Better Business Bureaus, government prosecutors, small claims courts and consumer affairs agencies. There are also industry or trade associations and those newspapers and radio stations which offer to intercede for readers or listeners who need a champion.

What Corporations Provide

Here's what some big companies suggest you do if you can't get satisfaction from your local dealer:

General Motors: Phone or write GM zone office nearest you (listed in your owner's manual). If still unsatisfied, phone or write Divisional Owner Relations Office (also in your manual).

Ford: Phone or write Ford Motor Co., Ford Customer Service Div., district office (get phone no. or address from phone book or local Ford dealer); or phone 800 648-4848 (free call) for all vehicles made by Ford.

Chrysler: Phone or write Chrysler Corp., Customer Service (get phone or address from dealer or phone book); or write to: Consumer Affairs, Chrysler Corp., P.O. Box 1086, Detroit, Mich. 48231; include your own phone no.

General Electric: Write to Manager of Customer Relations, General Electric Co., 570 Lexington Ave., New York, N.Y. 10022. But, on appliances, the warranty tells customer where to write.

Westinghouse: Phone 800 245-0600 (free call) and ask for Betty Wade, national consumer service manager.

RCA: On any RCA product, phone 212 598-4921 or write Customer Relations, RCA Corp., 30 Rockefeller Plaza, New York, N.Y. 10020.

Union Carbide: The product or the guarantee has address to write to; or write Union Carbide Corp., Consumer Information, 270 Park Ave., New York, N.Y. 10017.

American Motors: Phone 800 521-7500 (free call) or phone or write nearest AM zone customer relations department.

Exxon: Write to John B. Boatwright, Marketing Department, Exxon, Box 2180, Houston, Tex. 77001, on product, service or credit card complaints.

Gulf Oil: See phone book or dealer for nearest Gulf Oil district office or write Gulf Oil Corp., 1290 Ave. of the Americas, New York, N.Y. 10019, on products or service; for credit card troubles, see address on bill.

Mobil Oil: See dealer or phone book for regional Customer Relations Department, Mobil Oil Corp., in Chicago, Los Angeles, Philadelphia or Scarsdale, N.Y. For credit card troubles, write Mobil Oil, Credit Card Customer Relations Department, 150 E. 42d St., New York, N.Y. 10017.

Texaco: See dealer or phone book for Texaco, Inc., district office; if not satisfied, write Texaco, Inc., Retail Sales Office, 135 E. 42d St., New York, N.Y. 10017.

ARCO: See phone book or dealer for Atlantic Richfield district office or write to Atlantic Richfield Co., Marketing Manager, P.O. Box 2679 T.A., Los Angeles, Cal. 96051. On credit cards, use free "800" phone no. shown on bill.

Goodyear: See dealer or phone book for Goodyear Tire & Rubber Co. customer service representative at district office, or write Director of Consumer Affairs, Goodyear Tire & Rubber Co., 1144 E. Market St., Akron, Ohio 44316.

Sears, Roebuck: Ask for Customer Service at the store; then, the store manager; finally, write Sears, Roebuck & Co., Customer Relations, 925 S. Homan Ave., Chicago, Ill. 60607.

J. C. Penney: See department manager or, in large stores, Customer Service manager; then store manager; finally, write Patricia Ludorf, Customer Relations Department, J. C. Penney Co., 1301 Avenue of the Americas, New York, N.Y. 10019.

Kresge's: See section supervisor; then, store manager; finally, get from manager address of S.S. Kresge Co. regional office, write to Customer Relations there.

Kodak: See phone book under Eastman Kodak Co. for Kodak Consumer Center (in some 35 cities) for free minor adjustments and advice; or for Customer Equipment Services Division (in 8 cities) for service and repairs; or write Consumer Photo Information Department, Eastman Kodak Co., 343 State St., Rochester, N.Y. 14650.

A & P: See store manager or phone book under A & P Food Stores or Great Atlantic & Pacific Tea Co. for Customer Relations Department (in 32 cities); finally, write Executive Office, A & P Food Stores, 420 Lexington Ave., New York, N.Y. 10017.

Firestone: See dealer or phone book, under Firestone Tire & Rubber Co., for district office, contact consumer affairs representative there (in some 50 cities); write Consumer Affairs Director, Firestone Tire & Rubber Co., 1200 Firestone Parkway, Akron, Ohio 44317.

DuPont: See dealer or phone book under du Pont de Nemours, Product Information (in 8 major cities), or write du Pont Co., Wilmington, Del. 19898.

General Foods: Write to General Foods Corp., 250 North St., White Plains, N.Y. 10625.

Woolworth's: See store manager for address of Regional Vice President, F.W. Woolworth Co., or write Vice President Public Affairs, Executive Office, F. W. Woolworth Co., 233 Broadway, New York, N.Y. 10007.

Panasonic: Write nearest regional office listed on card accompanying product.

Procter & Gamble: Write Consumer Services, P.O. Box 599, Cincinnati, Ohio 45201. If possible, include your phone number, times you can be reached and name and serial number from the product package.

Government Agencies

There are numerous government agencies

which can be helpful, though in varying degrees.

Some cities have Offices of Consumer Complaints or Departments of Consumer Affairs (see phone book). In New York City, for example, the department will investigate the complaint, then may try to work out a settlement; it may sue on behalf of a consumer, issue violation notices, hold hearings and fine a company or revoke or suspend a company's license to operate in the city.

Many towns and counties also have consumer protection agencies.

States likewise offer aid to the unhappy consumer. Usually, it is a part of the Attorney General's office. Write or phone the Attorney General, Attention Consumer Protection Office, in your state.

Nationally, one may write to the Bureau of Consumer Protection, Federal Trade Commission, Washington, D.C. 20580, or the nearest FTC regional office. If you complain to the Office of Consumer Affairs, Department of Health, Education and Welfare, Washington, D.C. 20201, your complaint will generally be referred to "the proper agency for action," federal, state or local, or the office will write the manufacturer or seller, but its spokesman says it has no powers beyond that of persuasion.

Bills to create a full-fledged federal consumer protection agency were still awaiting action in Congress in Sept. 1973.

In **Canada,** one may write the Director, Trade Practices Branch, Department of Consumer and Corporate Affairs, 219 Laurier Ave. West, Ottawa, Ontario.

Other Industry Aids

Within industry groups there are industry and trade associations which may be helpful. One which claims an excellent record in handling a large number of complaints is MACAP, the **Major Appliance Consumer Action Panel,** 20 North Wacker Drive, Chicago, Ill. 60606. You may write or make a free, collect phone call to 312 236-3165, if you don't get satisfaction from a manufacturer of home laundry equipment, range, refrigerator, freezer, room air conditioner, water heater, dehumidifier, dishwasher, disposer, gas incinerator or humidifier. Give full details.

A similar organization is CRICAP, the **Carpet and Rug Industry Consumer Action Panel,** Box 1568, Dalton, Ga. 30720. Write them, if the dealer and maker won't cooperate, giving full details and your phone number. They will recommend appropriate action to the company involved; they claim good results, especially among firms that are members of the Carpet & Rug Institute.

A similar group is planned by the furniture industry.

Don't Forget

The complaining consumer will find it helpful to provide whatever agency you appeal to with copies of receipts and guarantees (not the actual receipts). You should be as specific as possible about the dealer's name and address, purchase date, price, name and serial number (if any) of the product, places you may already have sought relief, with dates. Don't forget your name, address and phone number (some companies or agencies may want to serve you as rapidly as possible and may need further information).

The consumer may even return the favor in some cases and help the manufacturer: as a Procter & Gamble spokesman points out, some manufacturers will want the consumer to hold on to the offending product so that the maker can analyze it, find out what went wrong and try to prevent its happening again.

Consumers' Association of Canada

Consumers' Association of Canada is a voluntary, non-profit organization, founded in 1947.

CAC's aims are:

(a) to unite the strength of consumers to improve the standards of living in Canadian homes;

(b) to study Consumer problems and make recommendations for their solution;

(c) to bring the views of consumers to the attention of governments, trade and industry, and provide a channel from these two to the consumer;

(d) to obtain and provide for consumers information and council on consumer goods and services and to conduct research and tests

for the better accomplishment of the objects of the corporation.

CAC publishes a bi-monthly magazine, CANADIAN CONSUMER which provides test results on consumer products and information on legislation and other consumer concerns.

There are seventy-seven local associations across Canada, and eight provincial representatives.

CAC's achievements in the areas of textile labelling, hazardous products, packaging, selling practices, and food and drug regulations.

National Office is located at 100 Gloucester Street, Ottawa, Ontario, K2P 2E5.

Consumer Credit Statistics

Source: Federal Reserve System (Estimated amounts outstanding. In millions of dollars)

End of year or month	Total	Instalment credit						Noninstalment credit				
		Total	Automobile paper[1]	Other consumer goods paper[1]	Repair and modernization loans[2]	Personal loans	Total	Single payment loans	Charge accounts	Service credit
1960.......	56,141	42,968	17,658	11,545	3,148	10,617	13,173	4,507	5,329	3,337
1965.......	89,883	70,893	28,437	18,483	3,736	20,237	18,990	7,671	6,430	4,889
1970.......	127,163	102,064	35,184	31,465	5,070	30,345	25,099	9,675	7,968	7,456
1971.......	138,394	111,295	38,664	34,353	5,413	32,865	27,099	10,585	8,350	8,164
1972.......	157,564	127,332	44,129	40,080	6,201	36,922	30,232	12,256	9,002	8,974
1973 June..	167,083	136,018	48,549	41,853	6,688	38,928	31,065	12,990	8,555	9,520

(1.) Includes all consumer installment credit extended for the purpose of purchasing automobiles and other consumer goods, whether held by retail outlets or financial institutions. Includes credit on purchases by individuals of automobiles or other consumer goods that may be used in part for business.

(2.) Includes only repair and modernization loans held by financial institutions; such loans held by retail outlets are included in "other consumer goods paper."

Interest Laws and Consumer Finance Loan Rates

Source: Revised by Roger S. Barrett of Chicago, Editor Consumer Finance Law Bulletin

Most states have laws regulating interest rates. These laws fix a legal or conventional rate which applies when there is no contract for interest. They also fix a general maximum contract rate, but in many states there are so many exceptions that the general contract maximum actually applies only to exceptional cases.

1. Legal rate of interest. The legal or conventional rate of interest applies to money obligations when no interest rate is contracted for and also to judgments. The rate is usually 6% a year; 5% or 7% in some states.

2. General maximum contract rates. The most common general maximum rate is 8% a year but many states permit 9%, 10%, or 12%. Rhode Island permits 21%. The general maximum is fixed by the State Constitution rather than by statute at 10% per year in Arkansas, California, Tennessee, and Texas. Loans to corporations are frequently exempted or subject to a higher maximum. Courts generally hold that installment sale charges are not interest, but installment sale charges are limited by laws in many states.

3. Specific enabling acts. In many states special statutes permit industrial loan companies and banks to charge interest and fees without regard to installment payments which yield 1½% a month or more. Laws regulating charge accounts and credit cards generally limit charges to 1½% per month. Credit unions may generally charge 1% a month. Pawnbrokers' rates vary widely. Building and loan associations, and loans insured by the F.H.A., are also specially regulated.

4. Consumer finance loan statutes. Most consumer finance loan statutes are based on early models drafted by the Russell Sage Foundation (1916-42) to provide small loans to wage earners under license and other protective regulations. Since 1969, however, the model has frequently been the Uniform Consumer Credit Code which applies to credit sales and loans for consumer purposes up to $25,000. In general, licensed lenders may charge 2½% or 3% a month for $300 or less and reduced rates for additional amounts up to $2,000 or more. A number of states permit add-on rates of 17% to 20% ($17 to $20 per $100) a year of the original principal for $300 and lower rates for additional amounts. An add-on of 17% ($17 per $100) per year yields about 2½% per month when the loan is paid in equal monthly installments. In the table below unless otherwise stated, monthly and annual rates are based on reducing principal balances, annual add-on rates are based on the original principal for the full term, and two or more rates apply to different portions of balance or original principal.

The states with consumer finance loan laws and the rates of charge as of October 1, 1973, are as follows:

Maximum rate — Monthly unless otherwise stated — Maximum rate

Ala... Annual add-on: 15% to $500, 10% to $1,000, 8% to $2,000. Over $2,000, 8% add-on on entire balance. Higher rates for loans up to $300.

Ak... 3% to $400, 2% to $800, 1% to $1,500; 5% for loans up to $50.

Ariz.. 3% to $300. 2% to $600. 1½% to $1,500. 1% to $2,500.

Calif.. 2½% to $200. 2% to $500, 1½% to $1,500, 1% to $10,000 (1½% min.).

Colo.. 36% per annum to $300. 21% to $1,000, 15% to $25,000 (18% min.).

Conn. Annual Add-on: 17% to $300. 11% to $1,800.

Dela.. Annual Discount: 9% for 1st 36 mos., 6% for remaining months; plus 2% fee.

Fla... 30% per annum to $300, 24% to $600, 16% to $2,500.

Haw. 3½% to $100, 2½% to $300.

Idaho. 36% per annum to $360, 21% to $1,200, 15% to $30,000 (18% min.).

Ill.... 3% to $150, 2% to $300, 1% to $800.

Ind... 36% per annum to $300, 21% to $1,000 and 15% to $27,500 (18% min.).

Ia.... 3% to $250, 2% to $400, 1½% to $1,000.

Kan.. 3% to $300, ⅚% to $25,000; or 18% per annum to $1,000, 14.45% to $25,000 (eff. 1/1/74).

Ky.... 3% to $300, 2% to $1,000, 1% to $1,200; or annual add-on of 20% to $300; 16% to $800, 13% to $1,200.

La.... 36% per annum to $800, 27% to $2,000, 21% to $3,500, 15% to $25,000 (18% min.).

Me... 2½% to $300, 1½% to $2,000; 25¢ minimum.

Md... 3% to $300, 2% to $500.

Mass. 2½% to $200, 2% to $600; 1¾% to $1,000, ¾% to $3,000.

Mich. 2½% to $400, 1¼% to $1,500.

Minn. 2¾% to $300, 1½% to $600, 1¼% to $900.

Miss.. Interest and service charges combined not to exceed 2% per month add-on.

Mo... 2.218% to $500, 8% per annum on any remainder.

Mont. Annual Add-on; 20% to $300, 16% to $500, 12% to $1,000, 10% to $2,500. Special rate to $90.

Neb.. 30% per annum to $300, 24% to $500, 18% to $1,000, 12% to $3,000.

Nev.. Annual Add-on: 9% to $1,000, 8% to $2,500; monthly fee of 1% on first $200 and ½% on next $200; over $2,500 to $10,000 annual interest is 17.74%.

N.H.. 2% to $600, 1½% to $1,500, 1½% on larger loans to $5,000.

N.J... 24% per annum to $500, 22% to $1,000.

N.M.. 3% to $150, 2½% to $300, 1% to $2,500 (1½% min.).

N.Y... 2½% to $100, 2% to $300, 1½% to $900, 1¼% to $2,500.

N.C... Annual Add-on: 18% to $300, 10% to $600, 8% to $900. Special rate up to $95.

N.D.. 2½% to $250, 2% to $500, 1¾% to $750, 1½% to $1,000.

Ohio. Annual Add-on: 16% to $500, 9% $1,000, 7% to $2,000; or equivalent simple interest rate.

Okla.. 30% per annum to $300, 21% to $1,000, 15% to $25,000. Special rates to $100 (18% min.).

Ore... 3% to $300, 1¾% to $1,000, 1¼% to $5,000. Over $5,000, 1½%.

Pa.... 3% to $150, 2% to $300, 1% to $600.

P.R... Annual Add-on: 20% to $300, 7% to $600.

R.I... 3% to $300, 2½% for loans between $300 and $800; 2% for larger loans to $2,500.

S.C... Annual Add-on: 20% to $100, 18% to $300, 9% to $1,000; 7% for larger loans to $7,500, plus service fee. Special rate to $150.

S.D... 2½% to $300, 2% to $600, 1½% to $1,200, 1% to $2,500; $2 minimum.

Tenn. 7½% per annum discount plus fees; no size limit.

Texas Annual Add-on: 18% to $300, 8% to $2,500. Special rates to $100.

Utah. 36% per annum to $360, 21% to $1,200, 15% to $30,000 (18% min.).

Vt.... Annual add-on of 14% to $1,500.

Va.... 2½% to $300, 1½% to $1,000; or annual add-on of 17% to $300, 12% to $1,000.

Wash. 3% to $300, 1½% to $500, 1% to $1,000; $1 minimum.

W. Va. 3% to $200, 2% to $600, 1½% to $800; or annual add-on of 19% to $200, 16% to $600, 12% to $800.

Wis... Annual Discount: 9½% on first $1,000, 8% to $3,000 up to 36 months; 18% per annum for larger loans.

Wyo.. 36% per annum to $300, 21% to $1,000, 15% to $25,000 (18% min.).

Economics

Why Inflation?

by Jerome Shuchter, Editor, Jeremiad
Box 36496, Los Angeles, Calif. 90036

Modern statecraft—like every householder—is mystified by inflation. No nation's history shows it immune from the price fever or capable of stemming it short of disastrous recession. In particular, all nations know the war-related variety. The puzzle now is the peacetime inflation that besets half the world: the half which prides itself still on its open and competitive markets, for the entire community has contracted the virus. In Japan and half a dozen nations of Europe prices rise faster than 10% per year. In the United States the rate runs a few percentage points lower, headed to the 6%-7% range in 1973.

A Global Problem

Inflation in the U.S. is the main concern of the people. A remarkable 80%, according to Gallup, clamor for price controls to replace the creaky system of free market prices. Overseas, the feelings are similar as each nation's prices make the run up, threatening to impede progress toward international agreements on trade and currency and placing roadblocks in the path of European union. In Chile we have seen the extreme tragedy—a 300% inflation which embittered the middle class, a factor in the overthrow of the Socialist Allende government.

Is inflation all bad? One scarcely praises rising prices for bread and milk—yet inflation is hardly a devil. A case can be made for the notion that, sprinkled thinly, inflation is a kind of faery dust which makes modern economies dance. It arises in peace and war from the pursuit of policies which have popular acclaim. Thus, World War II, the war on poverty, the lavish outlay for space travel, the rebuilding of cities, the ecological movement, all have an inflationary thrust. Behind the heightened spending one finds a government zealous to pursue popular causes, but without troubling to tap the public's purse to pay the bill. Like as not, if not paid for at once by taxes, the costs will be sweated from the public by inflation.

Winners and Losers

The practical difference between taxation and inflation is that taxes may be shaped to reach specific groups while inflation emerges without discipline, its impact unplanned and accidental. A second difference we have already alluded to, the political one: popular policies may be pursued by a regime without unpopular taxes to cover their costs, piling up political credit on both counts. From this follows the commonplace that the **ins** know nothing about abating the price fever while the **outs** know it all.

Some people are favored by inflation and some are losers. The most favored are the debtors. Anyone who mortgaged a home 10 years ago is now repaying that loan with cheaper dollars, 45% cheaper, and probably out of a dollar income grown much larger. Indeed, the history of the nation shows a knowledgeable debtor class advancing a greenback or free silver program designed purposely to cheapen the dollar to relieve the debt burden.

A large section of the nation finds immunity from inflation's ravages by keeping its income ahead of prices. Strong labor unions can win wage increases to offset price increases, along with escalator clauses to guard against slippage of real wages during the contract years. Strong companies also keep prices soaring to match the increase in costs.

At the other end of the scale, those most harmed by inflation are those with hoards of cash which decline in value as the dollar's value shrinks. Some of the wealthy may be hurt, but inflation attacks the cash savings of even the poorest among us and devastates those who have retired on fixed income plans or a nest egg. "You can feel the raw emotions, especially of the retirees and the elderly," says Representative Edward I. Koch of New York. "They are near tears and some are in tears."

So inflation breeds everywhere; it has the power to ravage a nation; it appears to be built into the modern economic system; its impact can be violent and uncertain. How does such a monstrosity arise?

Inflation and Prosperity

Inflation, it turns out, is also the handmaiden of prosperity. The very overspending for war or peace which sends prices skyrocketing is also the spending which spawns prosperity.

The deficit spending policy of the Keynesian economic school has now become the conventional means of keeping economies booming. Not that the policy aims at inflation. Keynesians hold that there is small danger of an inflationary takeoff if the timing of policy is adept. Deficit spending works well only to the point where unemployment is eliminated and idled factories set to hum again; then it should cease forthwith. But such a careful orchestration of boom, inflation, and unemployment is a rarity, and no Keynesian system exists without at least a small persistent inflation.

The danger does not stop there. Mild Keynesian inflation has a penchant to take more virulent form as policies waver, time lags grow uncertain, and exceptions intrude on the fine tuning. Finally, in the course of decades, the accumulated miscalculations of an age of Keynes, operating in a score of nations, may well take the form of an overriding and pervasive inflationary way of life, providing fertile soil for the universal inflation prevailing today.

The Military Jolt

The inflationary bias of Keynesian policy was a mere matter of 1% or 2% a year, but now we explore ranges of price increases on the order of 10%. Did some massive jolt displace the price system from its modest instability into the present extravaganza? The curious are led back to Lyndon Johnson launching his Great Society program of the mid-1960s to solve such problems as poverty, health, education, and housing. Measures were installed with a free Keynesian hand, involving only a modest inflation. Then came war.

In 1966 the President escalated the U.S. war effort in Vietnam, boosting the armed forces by 900,000 men during the next few years. The military budget climbed from $50 billion in 1965 to $61 billion in 1966 and to $72 billion in 1967. No effort was made to finance the conflict through taxation —in fact every effort was made at first to depreciate the need for financing at all. Years later, Dr. Arthur Okun, an economic adviser to the President, would propose that military spending ought rightly be on a pay-as-you-go basis, the taxpayer dunned every year for a military tax levy. Had some such tax law been in effect back in 1966 perhaps there would have been second thoughts about the escalation itself. Or, had we paid the tax bill in the prosperous years of 1966 and 1967 there would have been no inflationary fuse to ignite. The record shows that, without such financing, inflation shook free from pre-escalation rates below 2% and increased year-by-year to the 6% zone in 1970.

The general inflation, by this account, is the logical aftermath of Vietnam, bringing a flare-up in the bland inflation of the Keynesians.

Spreading Inflation Abroad

During the 1960s the 21 nations (U.S. included) which make up the OECD (Organization for Economic Corporation and Development) sailed along with an inflation averaging 3.4%, up to 1971 the average was up to 5.3%. In 1972, a reprieve: the rate fell to 4.7%. Then, in early 1973 it raced along at 8.5%. In every period the rate of inflation for the United States was somewhat less than the average.

It is understandable that all these nations are on an inflationary course together, following as they do the same Keynesian track. But there is a puzzle here too: the other nations have gone for many years without war, the notorious breeding ground for inflation. Nor are there any particularly profligate governments among them, many being in the hands of the most arrant conservatives. Furthermore, as the OECD notes, not only do we share inflation, but the major nations have harmonized their cycles—they enjoy booms and endure price surges in concert.

Two major developments in particular seem to account for the heft and thrust of the inflationary surge abroad and its simultaneous outbreak everywhere. One was the emergence of the giant multinational corporation whose production and distribution facilities intertwine in the economies of all nations. Through the multinational's operations, inflation begun in the U.S. would show up abroad as costlier parts and materials shipped from a U.S. plant to its overseas counterpart, to be assembled into some final product with the higher cost added to the selling price—transmitting the U.S. infla-

tion.

The multinational also played a role in the second major cause of inflation's internationalization: the export of dollars. The dollar, at least prior to devaluation, had foraged freely abroad, purchasing goods, paying military bills, making investments until a gigantic float of some $200 billion remains abroad, around $80 billion in national treasuries, the balance in private hands. As the dollars were deposited in foreign banks, the funds became part of bank reserves, expanding each nation's credit and money supply. Pure inflation. Measures taken by foreign powers to stem the tide proved fruitless. In 1970, $10 billion passed into foreign reserves; in 1971, $30 billion; in 1972, $10 billion; and in the first quarter of 1973, another $10 billion.

In early 1973, in final defense against the flood of dollars, foreign nations shifted en masse to a system of floating exchange rates and currency prices were freed to find their own levels in the marketplace.

Accidents And Shortages

Inflation is fed by shortages, and in 1973 an unusual outcropping of accidents and shortages threw fuel on the fire. The boom which accompanied inflation had raised the demand for many goods to such a pitch that many a ceiling on supplies was revealed where none had been thought to exist. Commodity prices, by **The Economist's** calculations, had almost doubled in a year.

Abetting the problem, the world was suddenly plagued by a rash of crop failures. Major nations fell victim to drought and were suddenly desperately in the market for enormous quantities of feed, fiber and grain. For the first time in modern history world wheat production actually declined. A spectacular deal between the United States and the Soviet Union threw domestic prices out of kilter and strained domestic facilities for storage and transit. The deal eliminated the set-aside supplies in our granaries and brought a revolution in farm policy, taking the lid off planting restrictions. As wheat prices rose we found shortages also in meat, in forest products, in soybeans, in gasoline. Habituated to overproduction, the nation suddenly found itself stripped of important products. Prices surged.

So another period of uncertainty began. The inflationary burden, partly welcomed as an alternative to recession and unemployment, partly detested for its blind and destructive impact on our fortunes, seemed to have become a way of life.

Net Public and Private Debt
Source: Office of Economic Analysis, U.S. Dept. of Commerce
(In billions of dollars)

End of year	Public and private total	Public				Total private	Private Individual and noncorporate						
		Total public	Federal[1]	State and Local			Corporate	Farm		Nonfarm Mortgage		Other nonfarm	
								Production	Mortgage	1-4 family residential	Multifamily residential & commercial	Commercial	Financial	Consumer
1965..	1,243.0	373.7	266.4	98.3	870.0	454.3	18.1	21.2	208.7	28.1	27.0	22.7	89.9
1967..	1,438.7	408.8	286.5	113.4	1,029.9	553.7	22.8	25.5	232.0	34.9	31.1	29.1	100.8
1968..	1,582.5	437.1	291.9	123.9	1,145.4	631.5	24.3	27.5	246.5	38.4	33.4	33.0	110.8
1969..	1,735.0	452.4	289.3	132.6	1,282.6	734.2	26.0	29.5	261.5	42.4	35.6	32.3	121.1
1970..	1,854.1	484.7	301.1	144.8	1,369.4	793.5	27.5	31.2	274.6	46.3	35.8	33.3	127.2
1971..	2,018.3	528.7	325.9	163.0	1,489.6	858.6	30.3	32.9	299.7	52.9	39.6	37.3	138.4
1972..	2,227.3	560.2	341.2	176.5	1,667.0	952.3	32.4	35.4	336.4	61.4	44.5	47.0	157.6

(1.) Net Federal Government debt is the outstanding debt held by the public, as defined in the Budget of the U.S. Govt., Fiscal Year 1974.

United States Budget Receipts and Outlays—1972-1973

Source: Treasury Department; each fiscal year ends June 30 (data preliminary)

Classification	Fiscal 1972	Fiscal 1973
RECEIPTS	(in thousands)	
Individual income taxes	$108,879,186	$125,127,670
Corporate income taxes	34,925,546	38,988,895
Social insurance taxes and contributions:		
Federal old-age and survivors insurance	35,480,381	41,085,731
Federal disability insurance	4,822,357	5,428,269
Federal hospital insurance	5,255,988	7,652,338
Railroad Retirement Tax Act	1,008,994	1,183,234
Total employment taxes and contributions	46,567,719	55,349,572
Other insurance and retirement:		
Unemployment	4,369,871	6,082,213
Federal supplementary medical insurance	1,340,052	1,426,476
Federal employees retirement	2,058,437	2,144,752
Civil service retirement and disability	38,833	41,033
Total other insurance and retirement	3,437,322	3,612,261
Total social insurance taxes and contributions	54,374,912	65,044,045
Excise taxes	16,847,036	16,583,919
Estate and gift taxes	5,489,969	4,957,282
Customs duties	3,394,299	3,294,992
Deposits of earnings-Federal Reserve Banks	3,252,197	3,495,069
All other miscellaneous receipts	3,632,735	3,944,620
TOTAL BUDGET RECEIPTS	$227,543,683	$257,941,424
Refunds	18,895,124	25,749,582
Net Budget Receipts	208,648,559	232,191,842
OUTLAYS		
Legislative Branch	501,438	555,372
The Judiciary	174,816	190,232
Executive Office of the President	54,147	60,464
Funds appropriated to the President:		
Appalachian regional development	241,638	264,050
Disaster relief	92,169	358,447
Economic stabilization activities	13,402	26,405
Emergency fund for the President	455	14
Expansion of defense production	1,542	103,875
Expenses of management improvement	655	548
Foreign assistance-security	2,822,619	3,118,445
Foreign assistance-development	1,596,462	1,557,418
Foreign assistance-contingency fund	43,270	10,532
Office of Economic Opportunity	1,052,699	800,377
Miscellaneous	1,571	40
Total funds appropriated to the President	5,866,482	6,240,151
Agriculture Department	20,461,595	21,707,069
Commerce Department	1,333,661	1,455,477
Defense Department:		
Military personnel	23,035,793	23,283,526
Retired military personnel	3,884,688	4,390,384
Operation and maintenance	21,674,910	21,073,090
Procurement	17,131,395	15,659,952
Research and development	7,881,208	8,155,708
Military construction	1,108,005	1,116,916
Family housing	692,478	731,130
Civil Defense	74,524	73,954
Special foreign currency program	2,645	3,799
Revolving and Management funds	−201,649	−1,031,459
Corps of Engineers	1,512,270	1,705,265
Total Defense Department	77,113,099	75,486,031
Health, Education and Welfare Department	71,842,591	82,070,480
Housing and Urban Development Department	7,353,346	9,273,596
Interior Department	2,299,481	2,540,619
Justice Department	1,187,060	1,538,859
Labor Department	10,034,409	8,637,934
State Department	541,335	597,234
Transportation Department	7,600,562	8,248,327
Treasury Department-Internal Revenue Service	1,374,610	1,430,481
Interest on the public debt	21,848,807	24,167,493
Total Treasury Department	22,729,995	31,732,734
Atomic Energy Commission	2,392,374	2,393,484
Environmental Protection Agency	763,331	1,113,408
General Services Administration	742,504	941,817
National Aeronautics and Space Administration	3,434,842	3,329,082
Veterans Administration	12,458,584	13,779,663
Other independent agencies:		
Action	129,225	151,310
Administrative Conference of the U.S.	418	364
American Battle Monuments Commission	3,369	3,226
Arms Control and Disarmament Agency	9,006	8,686
Civil Aeronautics Board	76,192	86,548
Civil Service Commission	5,570,251	6,516,773
Commission of Fine Arts	128	143
Commission on Civil Rights	3,637	4,620
Consumer Product Safety	−	20
Corporation for Public Broadcasting	35,000	35,000
District of Columbia federal payment	177,740	185,574
Equal Employment Opportunity Commission	20,796	28,148

Classification	Fiscal 1972	Fiscal 1973
NET EXPENDITURES (cont'd.)	(in thousands)	
Export-Import Bank of the U.S.	153,074	–
Farm Credit Administration	4,840	5,513
Federal Communications Commission	28,515	33,888
Federal Deposit Insurance Corporation	118,377	97,142
Federal Home Loan Bank Board	66,476	-30,490
Federal Maritime Commission	5,162	5,385
Federal Mediation and Concilation Service	10,011	10,641
Federal Power Commission	21,362	22,473
Federal Trade Commission	24,556	26,628
Foreign Claims Settlement Commission	632	768
Historical and Memorial Commission	1,861	7,066
Indian Claims Commission	1,044	1,060
Intergovernmental Agencies	85,637	80,336
Interstate Commerce Commission	60,099	44,915
National Capital Planning Commission	1,161	1,302
National Council on Indian Opportunity	300	219
National Credit Union Administration	9,744	11,759
National Foundation-Arts and Humanities	44,022	65,668
National Labor Relations Board	47,467	48,414
National Mediation Board	2,440	2,814
National Science Foundation	566,620	582,665
Occupational Safety Commission	837	3,933
President's Council on Youth Opportunity	81	6
Railroad Retirement Board	2,123,490	2,437,047
Renegotiation Board	4,678	4,721
Securities and Exchange Commission	25,889	29,865
Selective Service System	74,867	78,988
Small Business Administration	837,383	1,764,422
Smithsonian Institution	57,931	70,464
Subversive Activities Control Board	421	338
Tariff Commission	9,180	5,579
Temporary Study Commissions	10,831	10,725
Tennessee Valley Authority	1,086,152	1,130,472
United States Information Agency	198,314	206,474
Water Resources Council	5,429	6,855
Total-Other independent agencies	24,685,115	25,451,394
Undistributed intrabudgetary transactions	-7,857,514	-8,372,951
TOTAL BUDGET OUTLAYS	265,713,255	288,970,475
Applicable receipts	33,837,401	42,367,116
Net Budget Outlays	231,875,854	246,603,359
Less net receipts	208,648,559	232,191,842
Deficit	-23,227,295	-14,411,517

United States Net Receipts and Outlays

Source: Treasury Department; annual statements for year ending June 30

Yearly average	Re-ceipts	Expend-itures	Yearly average	Re-ceipts	Expend-itures	Yearly average	Re-ceipts	Expen-ditures
	$1,000	$1,000		$1,000	$1,000		$1,000	$1,000
1789-1800[1]	5,717	5,776	1871-1875	336,830	287,460	1911-1915	710,227	720,252
1801-1810[2]	13,056	9,086	1876-1880	288,124	255,598	1916-1920[6]	3,483,652	8,065,333
1811-1820[2]	21,032	23,943	1881-1885	366,961	257,691	1921-1925	4,306,673	3,578,989
1821-1830[2]	21,923	16,162	1886-1890	375,448	279,134	1926-1930	4,069,138	3,182,807
1831-1840[2]	30,461	24,495	1891-1895	352,891	363,599	1931-1935[4]	2,770,973	5,214,874
1841-1850[2]	28,545	34,097	1896-1900	434,877	457,451	1936-1940[4]	4,960,614	10,192,367
1851-1860	60,237	60,163	1901-1905	559,481	535,559	1941-1945[4]	25,951,137	66,037,928
1861-1865	160,907	683,785	1906-1910	628,507	639,178	1946-1950[578]	39,047,243	42,334,534
1866-1870	447,301	377,642						

Fiscal Year	Receipts	Expenditures	Fiscal Year	Receipts	Expenditures
1954	64,655,386,989	67,772,353,245	1964	89,458,664,071	97,684,374,794
1955	60,389,743,895	64,569,972,817	1965	93,071,796,891	96,506,904,210
1956	68,165,329,582	69,539,776,178	1966	106,978,344,155	104,727,263,667
1957	71,028,649,978	69,433,078,427	1967	149,554,815,000	153,184,886,000
1958	69,116,717,311	71,936,171,353	1968	153,675,705,000	172,803,186,000
1959	67,915,348,624	80,342,335,375	1969	187,792,337,000	183,079,841,000
1960	77,763,460,220	76,539,412,798	1970	193,843,791,000	194,968,258,000
1961	77,659,424,905	81,515,167,453	1971	188,332,129,000	210,652,667,000
1962	81,409,092,072	87,786,766,580	1972[9]	215,262,638,670	238,285,906,846
1963	86,357,020,251	92,589,764,029	1973	232,191,842,000	246,603,359,000

(1) Average for period March 4, 1789, to Dec. 31, 1800.
(2) Years ended Dec. 31, 1801, to 1842; average for 1841-1850 is for the period Jan. 1, 1841, to June 30, 1850.
(3) Receipts from 1937 on have deducted appropriations to Federal old-age and survivors insurance trust fund.
(4) Expenditures for years 1932 through 1946 have been revised to include Government Corps. (wholly owned) etc. (net).
(5) Effective January 3, 1949, amounts refunded by the Government, principally for the overpayment of taxes, are being reported as deductions from total receipts rather than as expenditures. Also, effective July 1, 1948, payments to the Treasury, principally by wholly owned Government corporations for retirement of capital stock and for disposition of earnings, are excluded in reporting both budget receipts and expenditures. Neither of these changes affects the size of the budget surplus or deficit. Beginning 1931 figures in each case have been adjusted accordingly for comparative purposes.
(6) Figures for 1918 through 1946 are revised to exclude statutory debt retirement (sinking fund, etc.).
(7) Excludes $3 billion transferred to Foreign Economics Corporation Trust Fund.
(8) Includes $3 billion representing expenditures made from the FEC Trust Fund.
(9) Effective fiscal year 1972 loan repayments and loan disbursements will be netted against expenditures and known as outlays.

Summary of U.S. Receipts by Source and Outlays by Function

Source: U.S. Treasury Department (June 30, 1973 preliminary)

Net Receipts Fiscal Year	(in thousands) 1973	1972	1971
Individual income taxes	$103,260,527	$ 94,736,616	$ 86,230,010
Corporation income taxes	36,096,144	32,165,916	26,784,575
Social Insurance taxes and contributions:			
Employment taxes and contributions	54,870,061	46,119,776	41,699,329
Unemployment insurance	6,063,441	4,356,671	3,673,955
Contributions for other insurance and retirement	3,612,261	3,437,322	3,205,057
Excise taxes	16,271,536	15,476,901	16,614,237
Estate and gift taxes	4,898,489	5,435,862	3,735,078
Customs	3,175,268	3,286,906	2,591,407
Miscellaneous	3,944,115	3,632,589	3,858,214
Total	**232,191,842**	**208,648,559**	**188,391,860**
Outlays			
National defense	76,055,667	78,336,072	77,662,721
International affairs and finance	3,185,343	3,785,746	2,883,729
Space research and technology	3,315,699	3,421,763	3,380,620
Agriculture and rural development	6,180,602	7,061,398	5,311,732
Natural resources	610,604	3,759,276	2,713,470
Commerce and transportation	12,392,883	11,196,707	11,282,562
Community development and housing	4,166,696	4,215,694	3,382,478
Education and manpower	10,820,501	10,198,471	8,650,255
Health	18,359,453	16,980,431	14,464,208
Income security	72,834,876	64,557,519	55,703,992
Veterans benefits and services	12,003,592	10,747,366	9,786,918
Interest	22,796,433	20,584,295	19,608,153
General government	5,617,593	4,888,631	3,970,547
General revenue sharing	6,636,369	....	....
Undistributed intrabudgetary transactions	−8,372,951	7,857,514	−7,376,357
Total	**246,603,359**	**231,875,854**	**211,425,028**

United States Customs and Internal Revenue Receipts

Source: Treasury Department

Gross. Not reduced by appropriations to Federal old-age and survivors insurance trust fund or refunds or receipts. Data are for fiscal years.

Year	Customs	Internal Revenue	Year	Customs	Internal Revenue	Year	Customs	Internal Revenue
1930	$587,000,903	$3,039,295,014	1958	799,504,808	$79,978,476,483	1966	$1,811,170,211	$128,842,531,268
1935	343,353,034	3,277,690,028	1959	948,412,215	79,797,972,808	1967	1,971,799,790	147,899,815,000
1940	348,590,635	5,303,133,988	1960	1,123,037,579	91,774,802,823	1968	2,113,474,950	153,675,705,000
1945	354,775,542	43,902,001,929	1961	1,007,755,214	94,401,086,397	1969	2,318,962,000	187,792,337,000
1950	422,650,329	39,448,607,109	1962	1,171,205,973	99,440,839,244	1970	2,429,799,000	193,743,251,000
1955	606,396,634	66,288,691,586	1963	1,240,537,884	105,925,395,281	1971	2,589,973,339	188,332,129,000
1956	704,897,516	75,109,083,197	1964	1,284,176,379	112,206,115,000	1972	3,284,922,000	208,595,814,000
1957	754,461,446	80,171,970,804	1965	1,477,548,820	114,428,991,753	1973	3,175,268,000	232,191,842,000

U.S. Direct Investments Abroad, Countries and Industries

Source: Bureau of Economic Analysis, U.S. Dept. of Commerce

(Millions of Dollars)

	Book Value at Year-End		Net Capital Outflows		Reinvested Earnings		Earnings		Int. Div. Branch Earnings	
	1970	1971	1970	1971	1970	1971	1970	1971	1970	1971
Total	78,178	86,001	4,400	4,765	2,948	3,116	8,789	10,228	6,001	7,286
By area										
Developed countries	53,145	58,346	3,218	2,824	2,075	2,375	4,652	5,324	2,733	3,114
Canada	22,790	24,030	908	226	787	1,046	1,586	1,913	944	1,000
Europe	24,516	27,621	1,914	2,083	988	1,009	2,384	2,652	1,390	1,659
Japan	1,483	1,818	128	211	115	125	220	284	100	151
Australia, New Zealand, and South Africa	4,356	4,876	288	304	184	196	462	474	299	304
Developing countries	21,448	23,337	935	1,397	601	546	3,699	4,294	3,093	3,740
Latin American Rep. and other West. Hemisphere	14,760	15,763	568	668	442	373	1,482	1,467	1,057	1,124
Other Africa	2,614	2,869	327	174	99	98	707	577	610	481
Middle East	1,617	1,657	−166	54	−21	−9	1,193	1,876	1,218	1,888
Other Asia and Pacific	2,457	3,048	206	501	80	85	317	374	208	247
International, unallocated	3,586	4,318	227	543	273	195	438	610	176	433
By industry										
Mining and smelting	6,168	6,720	383	519	111	26	675	504	553	484
Petroleum	21,714	24,258	1,460	1,940	425	616	2,935	3,982	2,608	3,459
Manufacturing	32,261	35,475	1,295	1,468	1,534	1,785	3,416	3,759	1,859	1,941
Other Industries	18,035	19,549	1,262	837	877	689	1,764	1,983	981	1,402

Public Debt of The United States

Source: Treasury Department (p preliminary subject to revision. r revised)

Fiscal Year	Gross Debt Dollars	Per Cap. Dollars	Fiscal Year	Gross Debt Dollars	Per Cap. Dollars	Fiscal Year	Gross Debt Dollars	Per Cap. Dollars
1870.	2,436,453,269	61.06	1930.	16,185,309,831	131.51	1968.	347,578,406,426(r)	1,727.72
1880.	2,090,908,872	41.60	1940.	42,967,531,038	367.48	1969.	353,720,253,841(r)	1,740.631
1890.	1,132,396,584	17.80	1950.	257,357,352,351	1,696.67	1970.	370,918,706,950(r)	1,811.12
1900.	1,263,416,913	16.60	1960.	286,330,760,848	1,584.70	1971.	398,129,744,455(r)	1,923.12
1910.	1,146,939,969	12.41	1965.	317,273,898,984	1,630.46	1972.	427,260,460,940(p)	2,046.00
1920.	24,299,321,467	228.23	1966.	319,907,087,795(r)	1,624.66	1973.	458,141,605,312(p)	2,177.30

Appropriations by the Federal Government

Source: Treasury Department (Fiscal Year)

Year	Appropriations	Year	Appropriations	Year	Appropriations	Year	Appropriations
1890...	395,430,284.26	1940...	13,349,202,681.73	1953...	94,916,821,231.67	1963...	102,149,886,566.52
1895...	492,477,759.97	1944...	118,411,173,965.24	1954...	74,744,844,304.88	1964...	101,978,886,034.43
1900...	698,912,982.83	1945...	73,067,712,071.39	1955...	54,761,172,461.58	1965...	107,555,087,622.62
1905...	781,288,215.95	1946...	76,597,999,662.67	1956...	63,857,731,203.86	1966...	125,998,173,095.19
1910...	1,044,433,622.64	1947...	40,823,734,061.18	1957...	70,717,305,080.55	1967...	140,861,235,376.56
1915...	1,122,471,919.12	1948...	42,098,608,820.42	1958...	77,145,934,082.25	1968 [1]	195,908,743,535.65
1920...	6,454,596,649.56	1949...	47,357,993,957.59	1959...	82,055,863,758.58	1969...	203,049,351,090.91
1925...	3,748,651,750.35	1950...	52,867,672,466.21	1960...	80,169,728,902.87	1970...	222,200,021,901.52
1930...	4,665,236,678.04	1951...	67,966,083,088.46	1961...	89,229,575,129.94	1971...	247,623,820,964.75
1935...	7,527,559,327.66	1952...	127,788,153,262.97	1962...	91,447,827,731.00	1972...	247,638,104,722.57

(1) The appropriation for 1968 incorporates for the first time the changes in the President's Budget for 1969, in consonance with those recommendations of the President's Commission on Budget Concepts which were adopted and implemented during fiscal year 1968.

Gross National Product, National Income, and Personal Income

Source: Department of Commerce. Office of Economic Analysis
(In millions of dollars) Includes Alaska and Hawaii beginning in 1960 (1.) revised

	1950	1960	1968	1969	1970	1971	1972
Gross national product	284,769	503,734	864,202	930,284	977,080	1,055,450	1,155,155
Less: Capital consumption allowances	18,342	43,408	74,504	81,563	87,254	93,834	102,357
Equals: Net national product	266,427	460,326	789,698	848,721	889,826	961,616	1,052,798
Less: Indirect business tax and nontax liability..	23,334	45,200	78,583	85,929	93,461	102,438	109,541
Business transfer payments	778	1,878	3,445	3,837	3,989	4,319	4,610
Statistical discrepancy	1,488	-1,031	-2,735	-6,050	-6,392	-3,363	-1,481
Plus: Subsidies minus current surplus of government enterprises	247	243	735	1,044	1,694	1,227	1,664
Equals: National income.	241,074	414,522	711,140	766,049	800,462	859,449	941,792
Less: Corporate profits and inventory valuation adjustment	37,669	49,904	84,301	79,779	69,240	80,133	91,120
Contributions for social insurance	6,870	20,672	47,102	54,173	57,708	64,598	73,729
Wage accruals less disbursement	24	0	0	0	0	582	-511
Plus: Government transfer payments to persons.	14,294	26,609	56,111	61,931	75,119	88,889	98,343
Net Interest paid by gov't and consumers..	7,198	15,083	26,079	28,725	30,988	31,029	32,713
Dividends.	8,838	13,437	23,552	24,331	24,680	25,142	26,041
Business transfer payments	778	1,878	3,445	3,837	3,989	4,319	4,610
Equals: Personal income	227,619	400,953	688,924	750,921	808,290	863,575	939,161

National Income by Type of Income

(Millions of dollars) (1.) Revised

	1900	1965	1967	1968	1969	1970	1971	1972
Compensation of employees	294,226	393,844	467,240	511,596	565,988	603,869	644,103	707,052
Wage and salaries	270,844	358,885	423,075	464,862	509,690	541,970	573,832	627,004
Private	222,108	289,621	337,322	369,168	405,568	426,875	449,711	493,276
Military	9,894	12,143	16,210	17,934	19,048	19,561	19,419	20,276
Government, civilian	38,842	57,121	69,543	77,760	85,074	95,540	104,702	113,782
Supplements to wages, sal.	23,382	34,959	44,165	49,734	56,298	61,893	70,271	79,718
Empl. contrib. soc. ins.	11,380	16,217	21,869	24,338	27,849	29,717	33,702	39,002
Other labor income	12,002	18,742	22,296	25,396	28,449	32,176	36,569	40,716
Empl. contrib. priv. pen	9,684	15,623	18,531	21,351	23,913	27,214	31,104	34,672
Other	2,318	3,119	3,765	4,045	4,536	4,962	5,465	6,044
Proprietors' income	46,209	57,253	62,147	64,214	67,191	66,919	68,724	74,227
Business and professional	34,244	42,416	47,315	49,534	50,450	50,017	51,893	53,987
Income unic. enterprises	34,263	42,796	47,603	50,268	51,228	50,723	52,552	55,104
Inventory valuation adj.	-19	-380	-288	-734	-778	-706	-659	-1,117
Farm	11,965	14,837	14,832	14,680	16,741	16,902	16,831	20,240
Rental income of persons	15,822	18,952	21,091	21,160	22,551	23,938	24,530	24,148
Corp. prof., inv. adjust.	49,904	76,070	78,686	84,301	79,779	69,240	80,133	91,120
Corp. profits before tax	49,712	77,787	79,815	87,636	84,904	74,041	85,053	98,037
Corp. profits tax liability	23,032	31,326	33,177	39,858	40,060	34,789	37,444	42,687
Corp. profits after tax	26,680	46,461	46,638	47,778	44,844	39,252	47,609	55,350
Dividends	13,437	19,808	21,385	23,552	24,331	24,680	25,142	26,041
Undistributed profits	13,243	26,653	25,253	24,226	20,513	14,572	22,467	29,309
Inventory valuation adj	192	-1,717	-1,129	-3,335	-5,125	-4,801	-4,920	-6,917
Net interest	8,361	18,217	24,416	26,869	30,540	36,496	41,959	45,245
National income	414,522	564,336	653,580	711,140	766,049	800,462	859,449	941,792

National Income by Industry

Source: Department of Commerce, Bureau of Economic Analysis
(Millions of dollars)

	1960	1965	1967	1968	1969	1970	1971	1972
Agricul., forestry, fisheries............	16,852	21,017	21,646	22,080	24,819	25,582	26,218	30,395
Farms.............................	15,857	19,630	20,084	20,425	22,918	23,639	24,028	27,967
Agri. Services, forestry, fisheries ...	995	1,417	1,562	1,655	1,901	1,943	2,190	2,428
Mining	5,732	6,116	6,345	6,702	6,775	7,682	7,012	8,246
Metal mining	817	908	667	888	975	1,177	970	1,035
Coal mining......................	1,253	1,332	1,453	1,429	1,494	2,157	2,052	2,375
Crude petroleum, natural gas	2,734	2,754	2,995	3,153	3,055	3,048	2,571	3,279
Nonmetallic min. & quar.	928	1,122	1,230	1,232	1,251	1,300	1,419	1,557
Contract construction................	20,810	29,116	33,223	36,270	40,862	42,791	46,692	51,694
Manufacturing	125,822	172,572	195,192	212,672	222,270	217,505	226,363	252,589
Nondurable goods	52,208	66,482	75,492	82,069	85,801	88,902	91,828	99,881
Food, kindred products..........	12,225	14,495	16,315	17,130	17,821	19,530	19,866	20,774
Tobacco Manufacturers	1,017	1,111	1,270	1,359	1,480	1,738	1,770	1,805
Textile mill products	4,488	5,837	6,234	7,123	7,440	7,419	7,379	8,237
Appa'l, other fabric prod.	4,953	6,556	7,543	8,307	8,670	8,634	8,950	9,564
Paper, allied products	4,707	5,929	6,735	7,338	7,918	7,970	8,041	9,318
Ptg., pub., allied indust.	6,655	8,746	9,944	10,766	11,720	11,929	12,401	13,622
Chemicals, allied products.......	9,159	12,648	14,068	15,614	16,143	16,342	16,827	18,236
Petroleum refining, related ind. ..	4,586	5,381	6,494	6,680	6,329	7,342	7,917	8,634
Rubber, misc. plastic products ...	2,809	3,949	4,725	5,477	6,030	5,776	6,482	7,497
Leather, leather products.......	1,609	1,830	2,164	2,275	2,250	2,222	2,195	2,194
Durable goods....................	73,614	106,090	119,700	130,603	136,469	128,603	134,535	152,708
Lumber, wood, except furn.......	3,255	4,212	4,238	5,035	5,623	5,135	5,705	7,109
Furniture and fixtures	2,092	2,870	3,218	3,485	3,867	3,657	3,735	4,543
Stone, clay, glass products.......	4,640	5,713	5,785	6,329	6,978	6,894	7,517	8,533
Primary metal industries.........	11,103	14,735	15,348	15,871	16,377	15,961	15,325	17,404
Fabricated metal products.......	8,113	11,518	13,385	14,354	15,204	14,635	15,082	17,543
Machinery, except electrical	11,861	18,357	21,814	22,891	24,416	24,296	23,596	26,585
Electrical machinery	10,469	14,850	18,595	19,772	20,896	20,327	20,614	22,539
Trans. equip. exc. autos	8,270	11,361	15,282	16,435	15,869	14,347	13,750	15,066
Motor vehicles equipment	8,532	15,432	13,599	17,156	17,312	13,801	19,454	22,555
Instruments	2,954	4,170	5,165	5,742	6,185	5,843	5,843	6,477
Misc. manufacturing	2,325	2,872	3,271	3,533	3,742	3,707	3,914	4,354
Transportation	18,177	23,150	25,223	26,909	28,739	29,824	32,819	36,008
Railroad.........................	6,718	7,047	6,821	6,992	7,351	7,358	8,083	8,464
Local suburban highway pass.....	1,639	1,897	2,049	2,210	2,163	2,285	2,373	2,349
Motor freight trans., warehous'g..	5,840	8,317	9,178	10,326	11,211	11,632	13,295	14,924
Water transportation	1,654	1,990	2,320	2,476	2,392	2,502	2,341	2,551
Air transportation	1,400	2,697	3,456	3,556	4,120	4,374	5,030	5,863
Pipeline transportation	355	401	423	414	447	518	524	555
Transportation service	571	801	976	935	1,055	1,155	1,173	1,302
Communication	8,237	11,241	13,092	14,131	15,786	16,787	17,826	19,966
Telephone and telegraph	7,304	9,991	11,727	12,594	14,139	15,074	16,026	17,907
Radio broadcasting, television	933	1,250	1,365	1,537	1,647	1,713	1,800	2,059
Electric, gas, sanitary services........	8,934	11,447	12,604	13,391	14,215	14,718	16,462	18,167
Wholesale and retail trade	64,396	84,302	97,518	106,069	114,811	121,274	130,900	139,682
Wholesale trade.................	23,126	30,341	35,238	38,394	41,872	44,430	46,951	50,531
Retail trade.....................	41,270	53,961	62,280	67,675	72,939	76,844	83,949	89,151
Finance, ins. and real estate	45,940	61,857	71,897	77,755	84,451	89,948	100,139	107,865
Banking..........................	7,276	8,989	10,738	12,258	15,009	16,437	16,855	18,671
Credit agencies, holding, other								
investment co...................	−435	−505	−1,041	−1,209	−1,680	−1,873	−1,480	−2,448
Security, commodity brokers.......	1,243	1,903	3,107	4,023	3,426	2,675	3,864	4,259
Insurance carriers	4,641	5,186	6,400	6,520	6,789	8,544	10,484	11,801
Insurance agents, brokers, service..	1,948	2,671	3,010	3,299	3,509	3,871	4,334	4,700
Real estate	31,267	43,613	49,683	52,864	57,398	60,294	66,082	70,882
Services..........................	44,371	64,076	78,540	85,721	94,706	102,876	109,824	120,137
Hotels, other lodging places........	2,111	2,788	3,435	3,744	4,051	4,236	4,490	5,029
Personal services	4,608	5,993	6,955	7,265	7,384	7,433	7,370	7,420
Misc. business services...........	5,093	8,413	10,600	11,490	12,980	13,984	14,508	15,965
Automobile repair, serv., garages ...	1,762	2,450	2,879	3,106	3,449	3,628	4,059	4,473
Misc. repair services	1,105	1,501	1,735	1,866	2,092	2,117	2,283	2,503
Motion pictures	894	1,205	1,350	1,535	1,465	1,565	1,542	1,624
Amusement, recreation services ...	1,661	2,221	2,512	2,783	2,863	3,244	3,389	3,870
Medical, other health services......	10,724	16,256	20,640	23,250	26,604	29,942	32,822	36,378
Legal services	2,636	4,069	4,820	5,114	5,631	6,443	7,242	8,230
Education services................	2,402	4,191	5,394	5,975	6,648	7,231	7,818	8,678
Nonprofit membership org.	3,815	5,306	6,346	6,955	7,762	8,376	9,024	9,791
Misc. professional services	3,761	5,719	7,397	8,009	9,092	9,847	10,318	11,195
Private households...............	3,799	3,964	4,477	4,629	4,685	4,830	4,959	5,021
Govt., govt. enterprises................	52,891	75,233	93,790	104,704	114,325	126,850	138,242	149,507
Federal	21,868	33,458	41,751	46,058	49,291	53,414	56,497	59,677
General Govt......................	25,524	28,450	35,865	39,496	42,177	45,164	47,563	50,281
Govt. Enterprises.................	3,656	5,008	5,886	6,562	7,114	8,250	8,934	9,396
State & local.....................	25,615	41,775	52,039	58,646	65,034	73,436	81,745	89,830
General Govt.....................	27,367	39,345	49,222	55,434	61,644	69,553	77,562	85,145
Government enterprises	1,752	2,430	2,817	3,212	3,390	3,883	4,183	4,685
Rest of the world.....................	2,360	4,179	4,510	4,736	4,290	4,625	6,952	7,536
All industries, total.................	414,522	564,336	653,580	711,140	766,049	800,462	859,449	941,792

State Finances
Revenues, Expenditures, Debts, Taxes, U.S. Aid, Military Contracts

For fiscal 1972 (year ending June 30, 1972, except: Alabama, Sept. 30; New York, Mar. 31; Texas, Aug. 31).
All figures are in dollars.

Sources: Census Bureau, Treasury and Defense Depts. * Military prime contracts.

State	Receipts (add 000)	Outlays (add 000)	Total Debt (add 000)	Per Cap Debt	Per Cap Taxes	Per Cap U.S. Aid	*Mltry Cntrcts (add 000)
Ala.	1,707,167	1,666,890	838,477	238.88	232.95	194	295,369
Alaska	457,770	594,198	373,854	1,150.32	314.10	570	107,079
Ariz.	1,075,768	1,004,858	89,248	45.89	306.12	154	431,669
Ark.	869,930	786,973	111,152	56.19	232.45	200	60,433
Cal.	13,729,653	12,569,221	6,132,166	299.60	329.31	200	6,015,505
Col.	1,294,652	1,193,122	121,131	51.39	255.49	183	163,654
Conn.	1,639,182	1,820,174	2,351,967	763.13	320.75	144	1,270,983
Del.	410,491	423,513	488,645	864.86	454.39	170	21,131
Fla.	3,149,195	2,862,509	1,121,757	154.53	274.14	114	1,156,668
Ga.	2,178,284	2,031,973	984,360	208.55	253.82	177	738,239
Hawaii	754,124	826,673	789,647	976.08	480.67	202	95,847
Idaho	419,175	390,716	37,929	50.17	264.63	180	7,746
Ill.	5,858,705	5,495,894	1,769,876	157.31	302.00	157	580,186
Ind.	2,069,129	2,016,631	605,691	114.48	224.39	102	795,032
Iowa	1,393,345	1,391,065	117,756	40.84	263.41	112	166,073
Kan.	961,706	932,251	214,641	95.06	233.75	131	327,497
Ky.	1,007,103	1,663,653	1,810,228	548.72	260.97	181	74,936
La.	2,136,504	2,086,437	1,120,278	292.30	297.07	195	243,426
Me.	580,638	570,303	273,369	265.66	268.67	186	48,904
Md.	2,092,937	2,240,446	1,425,117	351.36	313.71	134	721,908
Mass.	3,174,665	3,296,909	2,323,606	401.52	312.03	190	1,440,605
Mich.	5,472,906	5,151,735	1,351,183	148.78	337.19	147	468,316
Minn.	2,336,233	2,278,780	633,786	162.68	339.95	163	479,030
Miss.	1,192,143	1,137,368	534,364	236.13	259.94	256	571,741
Mo.	1,885,446	1,791,610	139,210	29.29	220.99	151	1,743,813
Mont.	465,413	424,304	94,955	132.07	254.27	252	214,274
Neb.	602,396	575,479	83,176	54.54	209.50	134	76,934
Nev.	366,739	340,562	55,085	104.53	343.21	179	14,749
N.H.	387,661	398,215	182,705	236.97	180.51	123	146,648
N.J.	3,501,578	3,572,230	2,567,558	348.52	220.75	141	1,120,466
N.M.	747,012	665,087	140,110	131.56	334.62	277	112,401
N.Y.	12,794,733	13,593,727	10,259,823	558.63	382.15	239	3,523,648
N.C.	2,496,897	2,287,430	538,267	103.23	280.18	141	498,629
N.D.	366,759	346,741	55,998	88.60	249.69	201	61,012
Ohio	4,798,358	4,380,118	1,965,302	182.26	203.04	112	1,009,439
Okla.	1,331,461	1,317,488	753,944	286.24	246.54	190	144,257
Ore.	1,290,596	1,244,709	923,503	423.24	232.77	202	42,936
Pa.	6,645,178	6,694,330	4,264,717	357.60	323.91	135	1,121,817
R.I.	559,469	560,225	390,234	403.13	310.85	184	103,655
S.C.	1,210,225	1,125,160	531,791	199.55	256.25	153	104,362
S.D.	310,818	306,871	39,629	58.36	196.39	194	36,522
Tenn.	1,636,377	1,522,748	592,383	146.96	220.16	174	396,821
Tex.	4,684,211	4,330,004	1,341,263	115.14	220.79	142	2,491,742
Utah.	694,850	670,413	97,016	86.16	273.46	196	138,961
Vt.	347,892	367,615	331,479	717.49	342.54	234	37,090
Va.	2,245,232	2,112,753	350,094	73.49	249.53	130	1,021,718
Wash.	2,370,022	2,292,901	981,560	285.09	341.15	184	988,629
W. Va.	1,108,140	1,119,286	685,771	385.05	297.24	251	41,604
Wis.	2,634,918	2,515,176	800,691	177.14	360.19	117	379,914
Wyo.	265,655	255,216	38,180	110.67	281.58	369	18,742
Total or Average	**112,309,441**	**109,242,690**	**53,832,669**	**259.45**	**288.55**	**—**	**—**

U.S. Money in Circulation, by Denominations
Source: Federal Reserve System
Outside Treasury and Federal Reserve Banks. (In millions of dollars)

End of year	Total in circulation	Coin and small denomination							Large denomination currency							Unassorted
		Total	Coin	$1	$2	$5	$10	$20	Total	$50	$100	$500	$1,000	$5,000	$10,000	
1950	27,741	19,305	1,554	1,113	64	2,049	5,998	8,529	8,438	2,422	5,043	368	588	4	12	2
1955	31,158	22,021	1,927	1,312	75	2,151	6,617	9,940	9,136	2,736	5,641	307	438	3	12	....
1960	32,869	23,521	2,427	1,533	88	2,246	6,691	10,536	9,348	2,815	5,954	249	316	3	10	....
1965	42,056	29,842	4,027	1,908	127	2,618	7,794	13,369	12,214	3,540	8,135	245	288	3	4	....
1970	57,093	39,639	6,281	2,310	136	3,161	9,170	18,581	17,454	4,896	12,084	215	252	3	4	....
1971	61,068	41,831	6,775	2,408	135	3,273	9,348	19,893	19,237	5,377	13,414	203	237	2	4	....
1972	66,516	45,105	7,287	2,523	135	3,449	9,827	21,883	21,411	5,868	15,118	193	225	2	4	....

Bureau of the Mint
Source: Bureau of the Mint

The first United States Mint was established in Philadelphia, Pa., then the nation's capital, by the Act of April 2, 1792 which provided for gold, silver and copper coinage. Originally, supervision of the Mint was a function of the Secretary of State, but it became (1799) an independent agency reporting directly to the President. When the Coinage Act of 1873 was passed, all mint and assay office activities were placed under a newly organized Bureau of the Mint in the Department of the Treasury.

The Bureau of the Mint manufactures all U.S. coins and distributes them through the Federal Reserve banks and branches. The Mint also maintains physical custody of the Treasury's monetary stocks of gold and silver; and refines and processes silver bullion. Functions performed by the Mint on a reimbursable basis include: the manufacture and sale of medals of a national character; the production and sale of numismatic coins and coin sets; and, as scheduling permits, the manufacture of foreign coins.

Amendments to the Coinage Act of 1965 (Public Law 91-607, Dec. 31, 1970) authorized the production of dollar coins and provided that the dollar and half dollar coins for general circulation be of the same nonsilver clad composition as the quarter dollars and dimes. The cladding is an alloy of 75 percent copper and 25 percent nickel, bonded to a core of pure copper. The legislation authorized the Secretary of the Treasury to mint and issue not more than 150 million one dollar pieces containing 40-percent silver, for sale to the public at premium prices. The new dollar coins bear the likeness of the late President of the United States, Dwight David Eisenhower, and a design emblematic of the symbolic eagle of the Apollo 11 landing on the moon. The silver-clad and cupronickel dollars and the cupronickel half dollars were first minted and issued during the calendar year 1971. The composition of the five cent and one cent coins remains unchanged. The five cent pieces are 75 percent copper, 25 percent nickel, while the one cent pieces are 95 percent copper and 5 percent zinc.

Calendar year 1972 coinage production for general circulation follows:

Domestic Coinage Executed During Calendar Year 1972

Denomination	Philadelphia	Denver	San Francisco	Total Value	Total Pieces
Dollars—non-silver	$75,890,000.00	$92,548,511.00	-0-	$168,438,511.00	168,438,511
Half dollars	76,590,000.00	70,945,000.00	-0-	147,535,000.00	295,070,000
Quarter dollars	53,762,000.00	77,766,933.00	-0-	131,528,933.00	526,115,732
Dimes	43,154,000.00	33,029,000.00	-0-	76,183,000.00	761,830,000
Five-cent pieces	10,101,800.00	17,584,730.00	-0-	27,686,530.00	553,730,600
Once-cent pieces	29,332,550.00	26,650,714.00	3,802,001.04	59,785,265.04	5,978,526,504
Total	288,830,350.00	318,524,888.00	3,802,001.04	611,157,239.04	8,283,711,347

Large Denominations of U.S. Currency Discontinued

The largest denomination of United States currency now being issued is the $100 bill. Issuance of currency in denominations of $500, $1,000, $5,000 and $10,000 has been discontinued because their use has declined sharply over the past two decades. Issuance of $2 bills has also been discontinued because of a lack of public interest.

As large denomination bills reach the Federal Reserve Bank they are removed from circulation. Existing stocks of $2 bills in condition fit for circulation will be circulated as long as the supply lasts.

Because some of the discontinued currency is expected to be in the hands of holders for many years, the descriptions of the various denominations below is continued:

Portraits on U.S. Currency

Amt.	Portrait	Embellishment on Back	Amt.	Portrait	Embellishment on Back
$1	Washington	Great Seal of U. S.	$100	Franklin	Independence Hall
2	Jefferson	Monticello	*500	McKinley	Ornate denominational marking
5	Lincoln	Lincoln Memorial	*1,000	Cleveland	Ornate denominational marking
10	Hamilton	U. S. Treasury	*5,000	Madison	Ornate denominational marking
20	Jackson	White House	*10,000	Chase	Ornate Denominational marking
50	Grant	U. S. Capitol	*100,000	Wilson	Ornate denominational marking

*For use only in transactions between Federal Reserve System and Treasury Department.

Portraits on U.S. Treasury Bills, Bonds, Notes and Savings Bonds

Denomination	Savings bonds	Treas. bills	Treas. bonds	Treas. notes
25	Washington			
50	Jefferson		Jefferson	
75	Kennedy			
100	Cleveland		Jackson	
200	F. D. Roosevelt			
500	Wilson		Washington	
1,000	Lincoln	H. McCulloch	Lincoln	Lincoln
5,000		J. G. Carlisle	Monroe	Monroe
10,000	T. Roosevelt	J. Sherman	Cleveland	Cleveland
50,000		C. Glass		
100,000		A. Gallatin	Grant	Grant
1,000,000		O. Wolcott	T. Roosevelt	T. Roosevelt
100,000,000				Madison
500,000,000				McKinley

How to Determine the Value of Silver in Coins
Source: Treasury Department

To figure the value of the silver contained in the silver coins issued by the U. S. Treasury prior to the clad or copper sandwiched coins it is necessary to find the value of pure silver. This may be accomplished by taking the market price as listed and dividing by .999 (the fineness of commercial grade silver) to arrive at the price for silver 1,000 fine. Then multiply by the fraction shown under the table beneath. This will give you the value of the silver content in each coin.

	Fine Troy Weight			Fine Troy Weight	
	Oz.	Grain		Oz.	Grain
Dollar	.7734375	371.25	Quarter	.18084375	86.805
Half-Dollar	.3616875	173.61	Dime	.0723375	34.722

For example: The market price on July 8, 1973 was $2.72 per fine troy ounce. Divide $2.72 by .999 the fineness of commercial grade silver = $2.7227 per troy ounce fine. The value of the silver in the dollar is .7734375 x $2.7227, or $2.11.

The silver content of the new silver-copper half dollar is .14789341504 of a fine troy ounce, and this multiplied by the selling price of $2.7227 gives a value for the silver content of 40.3 cents.

U.S. Currency and Coin—June 30, 1973

Source: Treasury Department
Amounts Outstanding and In Circulation

| | Currencies Presently Being Issued[c] | | | | Coin[a] | |
	Total	Federal Reserve Notes[d]	United States Notes	Total	Dollars	Fractional Coin
Outstanding.....	$64,265.460,343	$63,653,442,103	$322,539.016	$7,919.146,898	[b]$767,404,898	$7,151,742,000
Held by:						
The Treasury...	145,155.841	142.408,144	2,584,555	116,730.927	21.719,291	95,011,636
Fed. Res. Banks	3,847,105,976	3,846,769.889	162.872	304,386,702	40,804,999	263.581,703
In circulation....	60,273,198,526	59,664,264,070	319,791,589	7,498,029,269	704,880,608	6,793,148,661

| | Currencies No Longer Issued | | | | | |
	Total	Federal Reserve Notes	Fed. Res. Bank Notes	National Bank Notes	Certificates Gold	Certificates Silver	Treas. Notes of 1890
Outstanding.....	$289,479,224	$766,090	$51,704,801	$19,860.570	$3,633.519	$213,503,710	$10,534
Held by:							
The Treasury...	163,142	11.545	50,509	9.096	87,580	4.412	.....
Fed. Res. Banks	173,215	.....	121.800	8 425	.....	42.990	.....
In circulation....	289,142,867	754,545	51,532,492	19,843,049	3,545,939	213,456.308	10,534

| Currency by Denomination and Coin In Circulation | | | | |
Denomination	Federal Reserve[d]	U.S. Notes	No Longer Issued	Total
One dollar	$2,274,303,000	$144.503	$158.029,917	$2,432,703,415
Two dollars............		135,365,370	13.070	135,378,850
Five dollars............	3,145.392,785	120,244,270	43,666,955	3,309,304,010
Ten dollars............	9,620.805,500	10.745	27,258.045	9,648,074,290
Twenty dollars........	22,383,755,940	4.070	20,859,314	22.404.619,324
Fifty dollars	6,011.453,950	25	13,032.825	6,024.486.800
One hundred dollars.....	15,813,857,400	64,020.600	25.600.850	15,903,478,850
Five hundred dollars.....	188.443,500	2.000	224,000	188,669.500
One thousand dollars.......	219.861.000	....	262,000	220,123,000
Five thousand dollars........	2,175.000	....	65,000	2,240.000
Ten thousand dollars..........	3.990,000	....	130,000	4.120,000
Fractional parts	....	....	487	487
Total currency	59,664,264,070	319,791,589	289,142,867	60,273,198,526
Total coin				7,498,029,269
Total currency and coin				67,771,227,795

| Comparative Totals of Money in Circulation (selected Dates) | | | | | |
Date	Amounts (in millions)	Per Capita[g]	Date	Amounts (in millions)	Per Capita[e]
June 30. 1973...............	[f]$67.771.2	$322.08	June 30, 1945..............	26.746.4	191.14
May 31. 1973...............	67.161.1	319.38	June 30, 1940..............	7.847.5	59.40
June 30. 1972...............	62.200.7	297.84	June 30, 1935..............	5.567.1	43.75
June 30. 1970...............	54.351.0	265.39	June 30. 1930..............	4.522.0	36.74
June 30, 1965...............	39.719.8	204.14	June 30, 1925..............	4,815.2	41.56
June 30, 1960...............	32.064.6	177.47	June 30, 1920..............	5,467.6	51.36
June 30, 1955...............	30.229.3	182.90	June 30, 1915..............	3,319.6	33.01
June 30. 1950...............	27.156.3	179.03	June 30, 1910..............	3,148.7	34.07

(a) Excludes coin sold to collectors at premium prices. (b) Includes $481,781,898 in standard silver dollars. (c) Excludes gold certificates, Series of 1934, which are issued only to Federal Reserve banks and do not appear in circulation. (d) Issued on and after July 1, 1929. (e) Based on Bureau of the Census estimates of population. (f) Highest amount to date. (g) Revised.

The requirement for a gold reserve against U.S. notes was repealed by Public Law 90-269 approved Mar. 18, 1968. Silver certificates issued on and after July 1, 1929 became redeemable from the general fund on June 24, 1968. The amount of security after those dates has been reduced accordingly.

---

*Seigniorage on Coin and Silver Bullion

Source: Fiscal Service, Dept. of Treasury
(Jan. 1, 1935 to June 30, 1973)

	Total	Potential[1]
Fiscal Year Jan. 1, 1935-June 30, 1965. cumulative	$2,525,927,763.84	[2]$ 6,560,393.72
1967..	r836,734,039.35	980,037,560.91
1968..	r383,141,339.00	759,844,047.56
1969..	250,170,276.34	700,000,000.00
1970..	274,217,884.01	....
1971..	399,652,811.18	....
1972..	p580,586,683.00	....
1973..	p399,799,682.00	....
Jan. 1, 1935-June 30, 1973, cumulative	p6,299,034,805.51	....

*Seigniorage is the profit from coining money; it is the difference between the monetary value of coins and their cost; including the manufacturing expense.
(r.) Revised to include seigniorage on clad coins. (p.) Preliminary.
(1.) Not cumulative, as coinage metals held by the Treasurer of the United States changes, the potential seigniorage changes. Potential seigniorage also changes depending on the denomination of the coins manufactured.
(2.) Represents potential seigniorage as of June 30, 1965.

World Gold Production

Source: Federal Reserve System. In millions of dollars at $35 per fine troy ounce.

Year or month	estimated world prod.	Africa			North and South America					Other				
		South Africa	Ghana	Zaire	United States	Canada	Mexico	Nicaragua	Colombia	Australia	India	Japan	Phil-ippines	All other
1960......	1,175.0	748.4	30.8	11.1	58.8	162.0	10.5	7.0	15.2	38.0	5.6	11.8	14.4	61.4
1964......	1,405.0	1,018.9	30.3	7.8	51.4	133.0	7.4	6.9	12.8	33.7	5.2	16.1	14.9	66.6
1965......	1,440.0	1,069.4	26.4	2.3	58.6	125.6	7.6	5.4	11.2	30.7	4.6	18.1	15.3	64.8
1966......	1,445.0	1,080.8	24.0	5.6	63.1	114.6	7.5	5.2	9.8	32.1	4.2	19.4	15.8	62.9
1967......	1,410.0	1,068.7	26.7	5.4	53.4	103.7	5.8	5.2	9.0	28.4	3.4	23.7	17.2	59.4
1968......	1,420.0	1,088.0	25.4	5.9	53.9	94.1	6.2	4.9	8.4	27.6	4.0	21.5	18.5	61.6
1969......	1,420.0	1,090.7	24.8	6.0	60.1	89.1	6.3	3.7	7.7	24.5	3.4	23.7	20.0	60.0
1970	1,450.0	1,128.0	24.8	6.2	63.5	84.3	6.9	4.0	7.1	21.7	3.7	24.8	21.1	54.1
1971p		1,098.7	24.4	6.0	52.3	79.1	5.3	3.7	6.6	23.5	4.1	27.0	22.2	
1972p		1,109.8			54.3	77.2			7.1		4.0	32.2	23.0	

(p) Preliminary.

Gold Reserves of Central Banks and Governments

Source: Federal Reserve Board

Millions of dollars; valued at $35 per ounce through 1971 and at $38 for 1972.

Dec.	(Est.) total world[1]	Int'l Mone-tary Fund	United States	Canada	(Est.) rest of world	Bel-gium	France	Ger-many Fed. Rep. of	Italy	Neth-er-lands	Swit-zer-land	United King dom
1960......	40,540	2,439	17,804	885.3	20,295	1,170	1,641	2,971	2,203	1,451	2,185	2,800
1965......	43,230	1,869	13,806	1,150.8	27,285	1,558	4,706	4,410	2,404	1,756	3,042	2,265
1968......	40,905	2,288	10,892	863.1	27,725	1,524	3,877	4,539	2,923	1,697	2,624	1,471
1969......	41,015	2,310	11,859	872.3	26,845	1,520	3,547	4,079	2,956	1,720	2,642	1,411
1970......	41,275	4,339	11,072	790.7	25,865	1,470	3,532	3,980	2,887	1,787	2,732	1,349
1971.....	41,175	4,732	10,206	791.8	26,235	1,544	3,523	4,077	2,884	1,909	2,909	775
1972.....	44,925	5,830	10,487	834.0	28,610	1,638	3,826	4,459	3,130	2,059	3,158	800

(1.) Excludes USSR, other Eastern European countries, and China Mainland.
Argentina 152, Australia 281, Austria 792, Brazil 50, Chile 51, Colombia 16, Denmark 69, Dominican Rep. 3, Ecuador 14, El Salvador 19, Finland 53, Greece 133, Guatemala 19, India 264, Iran 142, Iraq 156, Ireland 17, Israel 43, Japan 801, Lebanon 350, Mexico 188, Norway 37, Pakistan 60, Peru 41, Philippines 71, Portugal 1,021, South Africa 681, Spain 541, Sweden 217, Thailand 89, Turkey 136, Egypt 92, Uruguay 169, Venezuela 425, Yugoslavia 56, B.I.S. (net) 218, European Fund 49.

U.S. and World Silver Production

Source: Bureau of Mines

Largest production of silver in the United States in 1915 – 74,961,075 fine ounces. (r) revised (p) preliminary

Year (Cal.)	United States Fine ozs.	Value	World Fine ozs.	Year (Cal.)	United States Fine ozs.	Value	World Fine ozs.
1925...	66,155,424	$45,911,000	245,213,993	1960...	36,000,000	$33,305,858	241,300,000
1930...	50,748,127	19,538,000	248,708,426	1965r...	39,806,033	51,469,201	257,415,000
1935...	45,924,454	33,008,000	220,704,231	1968r...	32,729,000	70,190,613	275,264,000
1940...	69,585,734	49,483,000	275,387,000	1969r...	41,906,000	75,039,817	295,718,000
1945...	29,063,255	20,667,200	162,000,000	1970r	45,006,000	79,697,000	310,891,000
1950...	42,308,739	38,291,545	203,300,000	1971...	41,564,000	64,258,000	298,783,000
1955...	36,469,610	33,006,839	224,000,000	1972..	37,233,000	62,737,000	286,750,000

Bank Rates on Short-Term Business Loans

Source: Reserve System

% per annum. Estimates based on reports from banks in 35 centers. Short-term loans: loans maturing within one year.

	Ave. 35 Cities	7 N.Y. C.	8 Other N.E.	7 No. Cent.	8 S. E.	4 S. W.	West	$1-9	$10-99	$100 to 499	$500 to 999	$1,000 and over
1967 Aug. 1-15	5.95	5.66	6.29	5.92	5.92	6.01	6.02	6.58	6.46	6.16	5.89	5.72
Nov. 1-15	5.96	5.71	6.29	5.91	5.94	6.03	6.03	6.60	6.48	6.17	5.90	5.73
1968 Aug. 1-15	6.89	6.67	7.16	6.96	6.74	6.86	6.86	7.35	7.27	7.07	6.90	6.70
Nov. 1-15	6.61	6.40	6.95	6.69	6.44	6.48	6.62	7.27	7.14	6.80	6.57	6.40
1969 Aug. 1-15	8.82	8.65	9.14	8.85	8.46	8.85	8.75	8.99	9.14	8.96	8.84	8.67
Nov. 1-15	8.83	8.66	9.21	8.83	8.58	8.79	8.81	9.05	9.20	9.00	8.84	8.66
1970 Aug. 1-15	8.50	8.24	8.89	8.47	8.49	8.53	8.54	9.15	9.07	8.75	8.46	8.25
Nov. 1-15	8.07	7.74	8.47	8.05	8.15	8.08	8.16	8.89	8.79	8.34	8.09	7.74
1971 Aug.	6.51	6.25	6.77	6.46	6.77	6.64	6.54	7.68	7.27	6.88	6.58	6.27
Nov.	6.18	5.86	6.40	6.13	6.47	6.43	6.21	7.51	7.05	6.51	6.26	5.93
1972 Aug.	5.84	5.55	6.14	5.79	6.06	6.07	5.82	7.27	6.72	6.20	5.91	5.59
Nov.	6.33	6.09	6.61	6.27	6.56	6.36	6.41	7.52	7.10	6.60	6.24	6.14
1973 Feb.	6.52	6.22	6.89	6.45	6.76	6.63	6.50	7.63	7.29	6.83	6.52	6.30
May	7.35	7.04	7.71	7.45	7.37	7.33	7.25	8.05	7.85	7.61	7.34	7.19

NOTE:—The Quarterly Survey of Interest Rates Charged by Banks on Business Loans has been revised beginning with the survey period of February 1971. The revision incorporates a number of technical changes in coverage, sampling, and interest rate calculations. These include elimination of accounts receivable loans from the survey, shortening the sample period for respondent banks in most districts, and calculation of effective annual interest rates on discounted loans using a revised formula based on annual rather than quarterly compounding of interest. As a result of the above changes, new weights derived from this Survey have been used to calculate the weighted average rates.

U.S. Commercial Banks With Deposits Over One Billion

A compilation of the 300 largest commercial banks in the United States is made twice a year by the American Banker, daily banking newspaper, 525 W. 42 St., New York, N.Y. 10036. Of these the first 75 banks had deposits of more than $1 billion on June 30, 1973. They are listed below. (Copyright 1973, by American Banker.)

1st 75 Largest Commercial Banks In Order of Deposits 6/30/73

Rank 6/30/73	June 30, 1973 Deposits	Rank 6/30/73	June 30, 1973 Deposits
1 Bank of America NT&SA, S. F.	$ 36,861,723,000	41 Fidelity Bank, Philadelphia	1,847,530,579
2 First National City Bank, N.Y.	29,551,669,000	42 First City Nat'l. Bank, Houston, Tex.	1,801,824,281
3 Chase Manhattan Bank NA, N.Y.	26,175,776,664	43 Pittsburgh National Bank, Pa.	1,756,142,095
4 Manufacturers Hanover Trust, N.Y.	15,072,333,225	44 Marine Midl'd. Bk. — West'n, Buffalo, N.Y.	1,743,350,275
5 Morgan Guaranty Trust Co., N.Y.	13,140,262,197	45 Bank of New York	1,690,926,691
6 Chemical Bank, N.Y.	12,868,844,000	46 Nat'l. Bank of Commerce, Seattle	1,687,580,297
7 Bankers Trust Co., N.Y.	12,212,133,000	47 Security Nat'l. Bank, Hempstead, N.Y.	1,595,517,000
8 Security Pacific NB, L.A.	11,304,686,261	48 First Nat'l. Bank of Ariz., Phoenix	1,492,758,065
9 Continental Illinois NB&T Co., Chi.	11,203,108,131	49 National City Bank, Cleveland	1,411,005,000
10 First National Bank, Chi.	10,725,514,219	50 Texas Commerce Bank NA, Houston	1,380,982,915
11 Wells Fargo Bank NA, S. F.	8,317,071,000	51 Conn. Bank & Trust Co., Hartford	1,356,173,200
12 Irving Trust Co., New York	6,637,579,751	52 Ind. NB of R. I., Providence	1,346,712,000
13 Mellon Bank NA, Pitts.	6,553,202,000	53 Hartford Nat'l. B&T Co., Conn.	1,337,482,000
14 Crocker National Bank, S. F.	6,532,087,124	54 Maryland Nat'l. Bank, Baltimore	1,326,090,555
15 United California Bank, L. A.	6,386,378,836	55 Central Nat'l. Bank, Cleveland	1,317,226,861
16 Marine Midland Bank — N. Y.	5,871,799,000	56 American Fletcher NB&T Co., Ind'polis.	1,315,927,425
17 National Bank of Detroit	5,397,184,003	57 First Union NB, Charlotte, N. C.	1,311,921,278
18 First National Bank, Boston	5,221,311,400	58 Michigan Nat'l. Bank, Lansing	1,294,085,855
19 First Pennsylvania Bkg. & Tr., Phila.	3,428,869,000	59 Virginia Nat'l. Bank, Norfolk	1,248,460,421
20 Franklin National Bank, N. Y.	3,408,244,319	60 American National B&T Co., Chi.	1,242,595,741
21 Harris Trust & Savings Bank, Chi.	2,959,843,974	61 Western Pennsylvania NB, Pitts.	1,238,380,581
22 Union Bank, Los Angeles	2,930,064,000	62 National Shawmut Bank, Boston	1,171,151,000
23 Seattle-First National Bank	2,625,612,048	63 ...	...
24 Republic National Bank, Dallas	2,596,078,738	64 Trust Co. of Georgia, Atlanta	1,142,767,897
25 ...	2,560,088,799	65 First Western B&T Co., L. A.	1,138,666,000
26 N. C. National Bank, Charlotte	2,516,535,691	66 Provident National Bank, Phila.	1,128,242,993
27 Cleveland Trust Co.	2,512,604,715	67 Manufact. & Traders Trust, Buffalo, N. Y.	1,106,763,648
28 Girard Trust Bank, Phila.	2,470,295,107	68 Riggs Nat'l. Bank, Washington, D. C.	1,077,285,238
29 First National Bank, Dallas	2,441,369,000	69 First Nat'l. Bank, Memphis, Tenn.	1,059,957,432
30 Wachovia B&T NA, Winston-Salem, N. C.	2,400,145,457	70 Northwestern NB, Minneapolis	1,043,783,294
31 Detroit Bank & Trust Co.	2,293,842,031	71 First Nat'l. Bank, Atlanta, Ga.	1,039,124,008
32 Northern Trust Co., Chicago	2,265,367,774	72 State Street Bank & Trust Co., Boston	1,037,115,941
33 Nat'l. Bank of North America, N. Y.	2,256,196,983	73 Union Commerce Bank, Cleveland	1,023,229,555
34 Valley Nat'l. Bank, Phoenix, Ariz.	2,249,002,538	74 First Nat'l. Bank, Miami, Fla.	1,019,125,196
35 Manufacturers Nat'l. Bank, Detroit	2,207,487,000	75 First Nat'l. Bank, Minneapolis, Minn.	1,011,452,432
36 Citizens & Southern NB, Atlanta, Ga.	2,152,400,039		
37 Bank of California NA, S. F.	2,108,302,000		
38 First Nat'l. Bank of Ore., Portland	2,106,061,575		
39 U. S. Nat'l. Bank of Ore., Portland	1,942,619,259		
40 First Wisc. Nat'l. Bank, Milw'kee.	1,853,694,836		

Largest Bank in Each of 39 Foreign Countries

Source: 500 Largest Banks in the Free World, compiled by the American Banker, New York. (Copyright 1973) Based on deposits Jan. 1, 1973, or nearest fiscal year-end.

Banks and Country	Deposits in U.S. $	Banks and Country	Deposits in U.S. $
Argentina, Banco de la Nacion	$ 795,406,000	Korea, Korea Exchange Bank	740,298,000
Australia, Commonwealth Banking Corp.	6,902,398,000	Kuwait, National Bank of	863,642,000
Austria, Creditanstalt-Bankverein	2,688,721,000	Luxembourg, Cie. Luxembourgeoise	1,392,693,000
Belgium, Societe Generale de Banque	6,382,183,000	Mexico, Banco de Comercio	1,373,746,000
Brazil, Banco do Brasil	5,495,978,000	Netherlands, Cooperatieve Centrale Raiffeisen-Boerenleenbank	7,945,526,000
Chile, Banco del Estado	931,113,000	New Zealand, Bank of	1,211,703,000
Denmark, Copenhagen Handelsbank	1,418,969,000	No. Ireland, Northern Bank Ltd.	545,682,000
Egypt, National Bank of Egypt	1,553,190,000	Norway, Norske Creditbank	910,695,000
England, National Westminster Bank	18,889,725,000	Pakistan, Habib Bank Ltd.	572,766,000
Finland, Kansallis-Osake Pankki	1,434,033,000	Peru, Banco de la Nacion	1,285,184,000
France, Banque Nationale de Paris	20,762,595,000	Portugal, Banco Portugues do Atlantico	1,367,123,000
Germany, Deutsche Bank	17,055,574,000	Scotland, Royal Bank of	1,988,212,000
Grocco, National Bank of Greece	2,947,150,000	South Africa, Standard Bank of	2,001,190,000
Hong Kong, Hongkong & Shanghai	4,988,379,000	Spain, Banco Espanol de Credito	4,398,307,000
India, State Bank of India	3,370,000,000	Sweden, Skandinaviska Enskilda Banken	4,253,815,000
Iran, Bank Melli Iran	2,017,918,000	Switzerland, Union Bank of	10,066,162,000
Ireland, Bank of Ireland	2,063,256,000	Taiwan, Bank of	825,629,000
Israel, Bank of Leumi le-Israel	3,702,832,000	Thailand, Bangkok Bank Ltd.	784,463,000
Italy, Banca Nazionale del Lavoro	16,723,829,000	Turkey, Cumhuriyeti Ziraat Bankasi	1,207,752,000
Japan, Dai-Ichi Kangyo Bank Ltd.	20,465,195,000		

Federal Deposit Insurance Corporation (FDIC)

The primary purpose of the Federal Deposit Insurance Corporation (FDIC) is to insure the deposits of all banks entitled to insurance benefits under the Federal Deposit Insurance Act. The main functions of the FDIC are to pay off depositors of insured banks closed without adequate provision having been made to pay depositors' claims, to act as receiver for all national banks placed in receivership and for state banks placed in receivership when appointed receiver by state authorities, and to prevent the continuance or development of unsafe and unsound banking practices. The FDIC's entire income consists of assessments on insured banks and income from investments; it receives no appropriations from Congress. It may borrow from the U.S. Treasury not to exceed $3 billion outstanding at any one time, but has made no such borrowings since it was organized in 1933. The FDIC surplus (Deposit Insurance Fund) as of June 30, 1973, was $5,393,006,000.

CORPORATION TAXES

Corporations are taxed under a separate body of law with technical and complex provisions. For information contact your District Director, Internal Revenue Service.

Assets and Liabilities of Insured Commercial Banks

As of December 31, 1972
(In thousands of dollars)

State	Loans and Securities	Total Assets	Total Deposits	Total Liabilities	Reserves and Cap. Accts.	State	Loans and Securities	Total Assets	Total Deposits	Total Liabilities	Reserves and Cap. Accts.
Alabama.	6,561,342	7,804,035	6,791,991	7,159,714	644,300	Neb.....	4,515,530	5,369,174	4,657,217	4,921,299	447,875
Alaska..	697,770	833,585	741,538	769,234	64,351	Nev.....	1,479,690	1,753,898	1,545,068	1,626,710	127,188
Arizona..	5,313,581	6,216,946	5,248,277	5,793,232	423,714	N.H.	1,283,897	1,487,886	1,288,344	1,350,646	137,240
Arkansas	3,945,530	4,829,140	4,230,118	4,434,737	394,403	N.J.....	18,729,517	21,746,166	19,299,144	19,976,917	1,769,249
Calif. ...	61,484,298	77,030,436	64,068,070	71,713,432	5,316,951	N.M.....	2,059,749	2,508,286	2,200,622	2,317,395	190,891
Colorado.	5,677,080	6,943,627	5,976,933	6,422,269	521,312	New York	99,277,798	136,029,223	106,274,852	124,379,314	11,649,909
Conn. ...	5,989,387	7,441,557	6,446,554	6,850,198	591,359	N.C.	9,641,450	11,916,449	10,075,609	10,969,452	946,974
Delaware.	1,668,615	2,011,925	1,674,400	1,849,243	162,682	N.D.	1,773,000	1,995,055	1,790,093	1,832,228	162,827
D.C.	3,037,925	3,719,703	3,204,862	3,383,552	336,151	Ohio	26,523,200	31,344,684	26,678,839	28,598,258	2,746,284
Florida..	18,438,652	22,392,577	19,713,837	20,674,550	1,718,027	Okla	7,084,769	8,610,818	7,408,064	7,901,280	709,489
Georgia.	9,788,033	12,172,948	9,924,902	11,110,793	1,062,155	Oregon..	4,979,359	6,016,490	5,169,436	5,536,321	480,169
Hawaii..	2,018,522	2,377,941	2,107,647	2,185,239	192,702	Penn.....	36,755,779	43,596,122	35,792,904	39,795,015	3,798,075
Idaho...	1,744,091	2,100,072	1,867,344	1,952,533	147,406	R.I.	2,191,538	2,522,927	2,144,627	2,319,992	202,935
Illinois..	46,255,796	54,633,507	45,431,781	50,176,133	4,457,334	S.C......	3,083,563	3,733,848	3,208,453	3,413,562	320,286
Indiana..	13,335,604	15,776,649	13,485,881	14,614,890	1,161,758	S.D......	1,961,237	2,250,632	2,016,819	2,069,344	181,288
Iowa	8,193,860	9,567,474	8,369,324	8,775,372	791,976	Tenn. ...	9,916,344	12,102,692	10,328,621	11,169,803	932,453
Kansas..	6,287,651	7,439,308	6,433,887	6,783,233	655,855	Texas ...	32,888,789	41,188,672	34,681,551	38,041,151	3,147,102
Kentucky	6,656,043	8,047,340	7,036,624	7,389,947	657,393	Utah	2,353,217	2,855,728	2,460,313	2,630,658	224,982
La.....	8,485,551	10,343,281	8,813,932	9,489,187	854,082	Vermont .	1,129,643	1,257,938	1,128,509	1,155,451	102,487
Maine...	1,537,685	1,802,969	1,576,548	1,646,835	156,134	Virginia .	10,626,950	12,438,710	10,753,060	11,482,324	955,806
Md......	6,698,765	7,858,283	6,847,964	7,184,372	673,911	Wash....	6,833,303	8,372,583	6,997,505	7,760,968	611,590
Mass....	12,686,140	16,069,781	12,783,430	14,705,886	1,363,895	W. Va....	1,137,577	1,258,531	3,868,734	4,098,834	403,218
Mich....	24,624,694	29,077,520	25,434,932	26,809,495	2,267,967	Wis.....	11,986,242	13,970,505	12,101,322	12,898,074	1,072,411
Minn. ...	11,610,449	13,554,552	11,449,343	12,493,622	1,060,882	Wyoming	1,043,461	1,244,046	1,108,675	1,144,186	99,860
Miss. ...	3,982,041	4,831,956	4,252,125	4,447,154	384,781	*Other ..	3,580,703	4,936,823	3,886,115	4,720,216	216,607
Missouri.	13,845,326	16,628,788	13,973,493	15,232,285	1,396,502	Total ...	595,516,420	734,455,864	616,907,567	678,416,789	59,277,002
Montana.	2,115,684	2,442,078	2,157,335	2,260,254	181,824						

*Includes Guam, Puerto Rico, and Virgin Islands.

Bank Suspensions

Source: Federal Reserve System. The figures for bank suspensions represent banks which during the periods shown, closed temporarily or permanently on account of financial difficulties; does not include banks whose deposit liabilities were assumed by other banks at the time of closing (in some instances with Federal Deposit Insurance Corp. loans).

Year	Suspensions	Deposits	Year	Suspensions	Deposits	Year	Suspensions	Deposits	Year	Suspensions	Deposits
1929..	659	230,643,000	1939..	42	34,998,000	1952..	3	1,414,000	1962..	2	1,201,000
1930..	1,352	853,363,000	1940..	22	5,943,000	1953..	4	44,412,000	1963..	2	23,256,000
1931..	2,294	1,690,669,000	1941..	8	3,726,000	1954..	3	2,880,000	1964..	8	22,022,000
1932..	1,456	715,626,000	1942..	9	1,702,000	1955..	4	6,498,000	1965..	7	44,857,000
1933*	4,004	3,598,975,000	1943..	4	6,223,000	1956..	3	11,881,000	1967..	4	10,802,000
1934..	57	36,937,000	1944(a)		405,000	1957..	3	12,869,000	1969..	4	8,910,000
1935..	34	10,015,000	1947..	1	167,000	1958..	8	6,287,000	1970..	1	149,500
1936..	44	11,306,000	1949..	4	2,443,000	1959..	3	2,048,000	1971..	1	516,000
1937..	59	19,723,000	1950..	1	42,000	1960..	1	7,987,000	1972..	1	20,579
1938..	55	13,012,000	1951..	3	3,113,000	1961..	9	7,527,000	1973..	2	8,836,000

*Figures for 1933 comprise 628 banks with deposits of $360,413,000 suspended before or after the banking holiday (the holiday began March 6 and closed March 15) or placed in receivership during the holiday; 2,124 banks with deposits of $2,520,391,000 which were not licensed following the banking holiday and were placed in liquidation or receivership; and 1,252 banks with deposits of $718,171,000 which had not been licensed by June 30, 1933. (a) No suspensions in years 1945, 1946, 1948 and 1968.

Federal Reserve System

The Federal Reserve System, central banking system of the United States, was established Dec. 23, 1913, by an Act of Congress to give the country an elastic currency, to provide facilities for discounting commercial paper, and to improve supervision of banking. Today it is generally recognized that the primary function of the System is to foster a flow of credit and money that will facilitate orderly economic growth, a stable dollar, and a long-run balance in international payments.

The Federal Reserve System consists of the (1) Board of Governors of the Federal Reserve System; (2) Federal Open Market Committee; (3) 12 Fed. Reserve Banks and 24 branches; (4) member banks; and (5) Fed. Advisory Council.

The 7 members of the Board of Governors in Washington are appointed by the President with the advice and consent of the Senate; Dr. Arthur F. Burns is chairman. One of the Board's principal functions is in the area of monetary policy. The Board has authority to approve changes in discount rates, to change member bank reserve requirements within specified limits, to set margin requirements for certain kinds of stock transactions, and to set maximum interest rates payable on member banks' savings and time deposits. Another important duty of the Board relates to supervision of Federal Reserve Banks, member banks and bank holding companies. Expenses of the Board of Governors are paid out of assessments upon the Reserve Banks.

The Federal Open Market Committee is composed of the 7 members of the Board of Governors and 5 Federal

Reserve Bank representatives elected annually. The Committee establishes System open market policy for the purchases and sales of securities and for operations in foreign currencies.

Rather than having one central bank in the political capital, as in central banking systems of most countries, the Federal Reserve System is divided into 12 districts, each with a Federal Reserve Bank—in Boston, New York, Philadelphia, Cleveland, Richmond, Atlanta, Chicago, St. Louis, Minneapolis, Kansas City, Dallas, and San Francisco. Reserve Banks are operated for public service. By statute, their stock is held entirely by member banks, which include all national and such state banks and trust companies as have been admitted to membership. Ownership of Reserve Bank stock is in the nature of an obligation incident to membership in the System and does not carry with it the attributes of control and financial interest ordinarily attached to stock ownership in corporations that are operated for profit. The amount of stock that member banks own is specified by law and dividends are limited to 6% per annum. In case of the liquidation of any Reserve Bank, its surplus would be paid entirely to the United States. Each Reserve Bank has 9 directors, 6 of whom are chosen by member banks and 3 by the Board of Governors.

The 12-member Federal Advisory Council is composed of one member selected annually by the directors of each Federal Reserve Bank. The Council meets in Washington at least 4 times a year and advises the Board of Governors on matters within the Board's jurisdiction.

U.S. Balance of International Payments

Source: Bureau of Economic Analysis, Dept. of Commerce
(In millions of dollars. Excludes military transfers under grants. Revised. Credits +; debits −)

	1955	1960	1965	1968	1969	1970	1971	1972
Exports of goods and services	19,948	27,490	39,407	50,623	55,501	62,874	66,136	73,462
Merchandise adjusted	14,424	19,650	26,438	33,588	36,417	41,963	42,770	48,769
Transfers under U.S. military agency sales contracts	200	335	830	1,395	1,512	1,479	1,923	1,166
Receipts of income on U.S. investments abroad	2,602	3,939	7,092	9,233	10,539	11,428	12,900	13,925
Other services	2,722	3,567	5,047	6,407	7,033	8,004	8,543	9,602
Imports of goods and services	−17,795	−23,364	−32,277	−48,134	−53,594	−59,308	−65,410	−78,071
Merchandise, adjusted	−11,527	−14,744	−21,496	−32,964	−35,796	−39,799	−45,459	−55,681
Direct defense expenditures	−2,901	−3,087	−2,952	−4,535	−4,856	−4,852	−4,817	−4,724
Payments of income on foreign investments in U.S.	−511	−1,098	−1,798	−3,013	−4,564	−5,167	−4,905	−6,063
Other services	2,856	−4,435	−6,033	−7,621	−8,377	−9,490	−10,229	−11,603
Unilateral transfers, net	−2,498	−2,292	−2,835	−2,875	−2,947	−3,208	−3,575	−3,744
U.S. Government capital flows, net	−310	−1,104	−1,598	−2,268	−2,193	−1,584	−1,892	−1,576
U.S. Private capital flows, net	−1,255	−3,878	−3,794	−5,383	−5,424	−6,886	−9,781	−8,534
Foreign capital flows, net	1,357	2,120	383	9,411	12,309	5,945	22,381	20,833
Transaction in U.S. official reserve assets, net	182	2,145	1,222	−880	−1,187	2,477	2,348	32
Allocation of special drawing rights (SDR)	—	—	—	—	—	867	717	710
Errors and omissions, net	371	−1,116	−507	−493	−2,876	−1,075	−10,928	−3,112
Balance on goods and services	2,153	4,126	7,130	2,489	1,907	3,563	727	−4,609
Balance on goods, services, and remittances	1,556	3,498	6,102	1,321	610	2,089	−802	−6,179
Balance on current account	−345	1,834	4,295	−386	−899	355	−2,847	−8,353
Balance on current account and long-term capital	n.a.	−1,155	−1,814	−1,349	−3,118	−3,061	−9,374	−9,842
Net liquidity balance	n.a.	−3,655	−2,493	−1,610	−6,128	−3,851	−21,965	−13,882
Official reserve transactions balance	n.a.	−3,403	−1,289	1,641	2,700	9,839	29,765	10,340
Liquidity balance, excluding SDR	−1,242	−3,711	−1,335	172	−6,963	−4,721	−23,994	−10,828

Details may not add to total because of rounding. N.S.S.-not shown separately. N.A.-Not available.

All Banks in United States — Number, Deposits

Source: Federal Reserve System

Comprises all national banks in the United States and all state commercial banks, trust companies, mutual and stock savings banks, private and industrial banks and special types of institutions that are treated as banks by the Fed. bank supervisory agencies.

Date June 30	Number of Banks						Total Deposits (in millions of dollars)				
	Total all banks	Member banks			Nonmember banks		Total all banks	Member banks			Nonmember banks	
		Total	National	State	Mutual savings	Other		Total	National	State	Mutual savings	Other
1925	28,479	9,538	8,066	1,472	621	18,320	51,641	32,457	19,912	12,546	7,089	12,095
1930	23,855	8,315	7,247	1,068	604	14,936	59,828	38,069	23,235	14,834	9,117	12,642
1935	16,047	6,410	5,425	985	569	9,068	51,149	34,938	22,477	12,461	9,830	6,381
1940	14,955	6,398	5,164	1,234	551	8,008	70,770	51,729	33,014	18,715	10,631	8,410
1945	14,542	6,840	5,015	1,825	539	7,163	151,033	118,378	76,534	41,844	14,413	18,242
1950	14,674	6,885	4,971	1,914	527	7,262	163,770	122,707	82,430	40,277	19,927	21,137
1955	14,309	6,611	4,744	1,867	525	7,173	208,850	154,670	98,636	56,034	27,310	26,870
1960	14,006	6,217	4,542	1,675	513	7,276	249,163	179,519	116,178	63,341	35,316	34,328
1965	14,295	6,235	4,803	1,432	504	7,556	362,611	259,743	171,528	88,215	50,980	51,889
1970	14,167	5,803	4,637	1,166	496	7,868	502,658	346,229	254,261	91,967	69,285	87,145
1971	14,219	5,736	4,598	1,138	490	7,993	582,081	401,509	294,025	107,484	78,318	102,254
1972	14,363	5,714	4,606	1,108	488	8,161	640,951	433,993	322,288	111,705	87,813	119,145
1973*	14,412	5,704	4,612	1,092	485	8,223	708,815	482,505	359,319	123,186	92,219	134,091

*First 6 months of fiscal year — to DEC. 31, 1972.

Bank Clearings In Chief United States Cities

Year (Cal.)	New York $1,000	Chicago $1,000	Phila. $1,000	Los Ang. $1,000	Boston $1,000	San Fran. $1,000	Detroit $1,000	Dallas $1,000
1935	181,551,008	13,194,988	16,909,000	5,852,244	10,645,822	6,478,835	4,523,167	1,969,290
1940	160,878,038	16,684,672	21,455,000	7,543,880	11,943,665	6,773,877	6,312,233	2,986,774
1945	334,432,654	27,279,588	34,710,000	17,144,078	19,589,725	15,743,086	16,472,971	6,634,514
1950	399,308,634	40,674,983	51,102,000	26,504,731	25,348,336	21,982,689	22,855,273	14,451,332
1955	530,883,498	52,818,527	59,962,000	42,818,633	32,472,726	31,492,157	36,364,754	21,678,567
1960	738,604,276	66,651,600	56,716,000	53,635,826	40,759,040	39,787,147	39,101,854	27,811,939
1965	1,280,402,568	82,507,560	69,116,728	111,587,481	60,318,717	87,095,481	56,068,833	42,414,327
1970	3,752,515,518	110,219,418	94,003,896	174,153,125	125,033,163	122,929,389	136,965,556	51,886,403
1971	4,208,890,740	118,508,177	98,275,037	196,698,129	134,930,871	140,478,781	172,079,317	57,320,551
1972	6,897,248,349	126,959,884	104,819,843	222,499,794	113,515,212	155,684,868	175,620,419	63,336,639

Year (Cal.)	Kan. City $1,000	Houston $1,000	Pittsb'rgh $1,000	Cleveland $1,000	St. Louis $1,000	Minneap. $1,000	Baltimore $1,000	Atlanta $1,000
1935	4,348,113	1,420,404	5,245,718	3,417,055	3,940,654	3,044,735	2,910,637	2,204,500
1940	4,997,593	2,568,518	7,074,775	5,734,407	4,822,016	3,787,088	4,201,985	3,430,900
1945	10,856,497	5,982,318	12,978,668	11,529,428	9,723,815	8,196,279	8,315,468	8,263,900
1950	16,707,120	11,922,307	16,782,419	17,683,829	14,896,444	14,113,814	12,154,904	12,910,100
1955	20,057,800	19,199,929	21,142,527	26,426,614	18,481,105	18,496,868	17,071,914	18,597,100
1960	24,967,583	21,887,839	23,913,706	32,364,009	21,138,861	25,219,318	20,423,684	22,993,200
1965	33,936,377	33,938,170	29,070,474	44,600,090	28,399,392	34,029,120	25,893,740	34,371,000
1970	53,509,523	39,855,427	42,418,973	52,690,067	33,611,932	43,112,445	29,964,761	53,784,237
1971	52,040,273	43,761,645	40,791,361	54,307,281	39,218,274	46,940,376	31,025,066	66,327,913
1972	56,063,129	58,312,671	48,606,390	57,634,920	40,485,176	52,798,284	32,179,679	73,475,516

Corporations and Stocks

Over 31,700,000 Persons Own Shares in U.S. Corporations

Some 31,700,000 persons owned shares in American corporations in 1973, compared to 32,500,000 in 1972 and 8,630,000 in 1956.

The N.Y. Stock Exchange listed 2,044 issues of 1,544 companies for a total of 20.5 billion shares, valued as of Aug. 31, 1973, at $765.76 billion. Average daily trading was 14,892,046 shares through Aug. 31, compared to 16,612,417 in 1972.

The American Stock Exchange listed 1,419 issues of 1,321 companies, totaling 3.36 billion shares, valued Jan. 2, 1973, at $55.6 billion. Average daily volume through Sept. 25, 1973, was 2,870,000 shares, compared to 4,640,000 a year earlier.

The N.Y. Stock Exchange reported 72 of its listed companies had sales or revenues of over $2 billion in 1972. There were 61 in 1971, 46 in 1968. (See list below.)

U.S. Companies with Largest Annual Sales or Revenues

Top listed firms of N.Y. Stock Exchange for 1972 as shown by its Research Dep't.

Company	Sales or revenues (in millions)	Net profit (*deficit) (in millions)	Company	Sales or revenues (in millions)	Net profit (*deficit) (in millions)
General Motors Corp	$30,435.2	$2,162.8	Atlantic Richfield	3,831.3	192.5
Exxon Corp.	22,070.6	1,531.8	Kroger Co.	3,790.5	23.2
American Tel & Tel	20,904.1	2,532.1	Continental Oil Co.	3,649.6	170.2
Ford Motor	20,194.4	870.0	Procter & Gamble	3,514.4	276.3
Sears, Roebuck	10,991.0	614.4	International Harvester	3,493.3	86.6
General Electric	10,239.5	530.0	Eastman Kodak	3,477.8	546.3
Mobil Oil	10,189.8	574.2	LTV Corp.	3,442.3	8.0
Chrysler Corp	9,759.1	220.5	Marcor Inc.	3,369.3	72.7
IBM	9,532.6	1,279.3	Tenneco Inc.	3,275.4	203.0
Texaco Inc.	8,693.0	889.0	Union Carbide Corp.	3,261.3	207.4
International Tel & Tel	8,556.8	476.6	Esmark Inc (Swift)	3,240.9	37.0
Gulf Oil Corp.	7,624.0	447.0	Kraftco Corp.	3,196.8	100.6
Standard Oil Calif.	6,476.7	547.1	Woolworth (F.W.) Co.	3,148.1	79.2
Great A & P Tea Co.	6,368.9	*51.3	Bethlehem Steel	3,113.6	134.6
Safeway Stores	6,057.6	91.1	American Brands	2,998.9	123.3
Penney (J.C.) Co.	5,529.6	162.6	Reynolds Industries	2,857.6	237.5
U.S. Steel Corp.	5,428.9	157.0	Greyhound Corp.	2,912.6	70.1
Standard Oil (Ind.)	5,400.7	374.7	Beatrice Foods Co.	2,787.0	90.4
Westinghouse	5,086.6	198.7	McDonnell Douglas Corp.	2,725.7	111.7
Shell Oil Co.	4,817.5	260.5	Occidental Petroleum	2,720.8	19.7
duPont de Nemours	4,365.9	414.5	Firestone Tire	2,691.0	135.8
General Tel & Elec.	4,326.7	301.3	Rockwell Int.	2,683.1	94.3
Goodyear Tire	4,071.5	193.2	Federated Stores	2,665.1	108.6
RCA Corp.	3,838.2	158.1	General Foods Corp.	2,632.3	110.4
Kresge (S.S.) Co.	3,836.8	114.7	Caterpillar Tractor	2,602.2	206.4

Largest Industrial Companies Outside the U.S.

Reprinted by special permission from the Fortune Directory, as listed for 1972; ©1973, Time Inc.

Company	Sales (add 000)	Net profit (or *loss) (add 000)	Company	Sales (add 000)	Net profit (or *loss) (add 000)
Royal Dutch Shell N-B	$14,060,307	$704,566	BASF (Badische Anilin) G	$3,719,942	$128,106
Unilever B-N	8,864,440	331,869	Fiat I	3,644,732	27,147
Philips' Gloeilampenfab N	6,207,009	223,427	British Steel B	3,630,264	7,369
British Petroleum B	5,711,555	175,813	Montedison I	3,597,628	*779,506
Nippon Steel J	5,364,332	68,155	Renault F	3,536,805	14,800
Volkswagenwerk G	5,016,949	59,952	Matsushita Elec Ind J	3,433,771	229,140
Siemens G	4,712,910	124,694	Bayer G	3,314,578	118,297
Hitachi J	4,353,643	210,913	British Leyland Motor B	3,247,877	59,715
ICI (Imperial Chem Ind) B	4,236,275	229,082	AEG-Telefunken G	3,151,424	10,928
Toyota Motor J	4,187,549	197,986	August Thyssen-Hutte G	3,060,170	15,002
Daimler-Benz G	4,156,667	85,993	Tokyo Shibaura Electric J	2,921,555	57,288
Nestle S	4,130,163	170,759	Cie Fr. Des Petroles F	2,806,126	114,623
Farbwerke Hoechst G	4,075,712	99,423	ENI I	2,747,973	17,646
Mitsubishi Heavy Inds J	3,980,559	59,271	Dunlop Pirelli Union B-I	2,745,988	9,153
Nissan Motors J	3,957,557	181,977	Pechiney Ugine Kuhlmann F	2,661,565	54,202

Nation of Hqs: N Netherlands; B Britain; G Germany; S Switzerland; I Italy; F France; J Japan

Stocks Most Widely Held by Investment Cos., Insurance Cos., Trust Funds

As listed in 1973 in Growth Leaders on the Big Board, published by the N.Y. Stock Exchange (In order of number of institutions, etc., which held shares, 1973)

Intnatl Bus Machs	Sears Roebuck	duPont (E.I.)	Merck & Co	Warner Lambert
General Motors	Ford Motor	Standard Oil (Ind)	Texas Utilities	Southern Co
Exxon Corp	Mobil Oil	Int Tel & Tel	Phillips Petroleum	Avon Products
Amer Tel & Tel	General Tel & Elec	Goodyear Tire & R	Standard Oil (Cal)	Honeywell Inc
General Electric	Minn Mining & Mfg	Atlantic Richfield	Pfizer Inc	Continental Oil
Eastman Kodak	Gulf Oil	Union Carbide	Int Nickel of Can	Int Paper
Texaco Inc	First Natl City Corp	Dow Chemical	Caterpillar Tractor	Penney (JC) Co
Xerox Corp	Westinghouse Elec	Burroughs Corp	Amer Home Prods	So Calif Edison

Highest-Paid Executives of U.S. Companies
Data for 1972: Reprinted by permission of Forbes magazine

Company	Number of Employees (000)	Chief Executive	Remuneration (000)	Company	Number of Employees (000)	Chief Executive	Remuneration (000)
General Motors	759.5	Richard C. Gerstenberg	$875	White Consolidated	21.5	Edward S. Reddig	$399
Ford Motor	442.6	Henry Ford II	875	Clark Equipment	28.3	Walter E. Schirmer	399
Johnson & Johnson	43.3	Philip B. Hofmann	874	Fruehauf	16.9	William E. Grace	396
Int. Tel. & Tel.	428.0	Harold S. Geneen	813	International Paper	51.2	Paul A. Gorman	392
Chrysler	244.8	Lynn Townsend	639	Avon Products	25.1	Fred G. Fusee	387
Goodyear Tire & Rub.	145.2	Russell De Young	570	Deere	45.1	William A. Hewitt	387
J.C. Penney	175.0	William M. Batten	551	Alcoa	44.5	John D. Harper	386
Exxon	141.0	John K. Jamieson	539	Norton Simon	27.0	David J. Mahoney	380
American Brands	49.0	Robert B. Walker	501	Burroughs	41.6	Ray W. Macdonald	380
Am. Home Products	43.8	William F. Laporte	500	First Chicago Corp.	6.0	Gaylord Freeman	378
Procter & Gamble	45.0	Howard J. Morgens	486	American Express	27.6	Howard L. Clark	370
Xerox	75.9	C. Peter McColough	480	Continental Oil	38.1	John G. McLean	355
Sears, Roebuck	380.0	Gordon M. Metcalf	478	IU International	40.0	John M. Seabrook	355
RCA Corp.	122.0	Robert W. Sarnoff	475	W.T. Grant	75.0	Richard W. Mayer	354
Rapid-American	99.0	Meshulam Riklis	473	B.F. Goodrich	50.8	O. Pendleton Thomas	350
City Investing	33.8	George T. Scharffenberger	461	Anheuser-Busch	11.6	August A. Busch, Jr.	350
Mobil Oil	75.4	Rawleigh Warner, Jr.	455	Gulf Oil	57.5	B. R. Dorsey	345
Monroe Auto Equip.	3.8	Charles S. McIntyre	435	Standard Oil (Ohio)	21.1	Charles E. Spahr	342
Int. Business Mach.	262.2	T. Vincent Learson	434	Phillips Petroleum	35.3	William W. Keeler	342
Standard Oil (Ind.)	46.6	John E. Swearingen	428	Champion Int'l.	48.5	Karl R. Bendetsen	342
Am. Broadcasting Cos.	14.5	Leonard H. Goldenson	420	Minn. Mining & M'f'g.	71.7	Harry Heltzer	341
U.S. Industries	50.1	I. John Billera	419	GAF Corp	22.8	Jesse Werner	340
Westinghouse Elec.	183.8	Donald C. Burnham	416	Eli Lilly	23.8	Eugene N. Beesley	336
Chubb	6.7	William M. Rees	403	R.J. Reynolds Inds.	30.0	Alexander H. Galloway	334
CBS	27.8	William S. Paley	400	Borden	46.7	Augustine R. Marusi	329

N.Y. Stock Exchange Transactions and Seat Prices
Source: New York Stock Exchange

Year (Cal.)	Stocks Shares No.	Bonds Par Value Dollars	Seats High Dollars	Seats Low Dollars	Year (Cal.)	Stocks Shares No.	Bonds Par Value Dollars	Seats High Dollars	Seats Low Dollars
1900	138,981,000	579,293,000	47,500	37,500	1935	381,635,752	3,339,458,000	140,000	65,000
1905	260,569,000	1,026,254,000	85,000	72,000	1940	207,599,749	1,669,438,000	60,000	33,000
1910	163,705,000	634,863,000	94,000	65,000	1945	377,563,575	2,261,985,100	95,000	49,000
1915	172,497,000	961,700,000	74,000	38,000	1950	524,799,621	1,112,425,170	54,000	46,000
1920	227,636,000	3,868,422,000	115,000	85,000	1955	649,602,291	1,045,949,100	90,000	80,000
1925	459,717,623	3,427,042,210	150,000	99,000	1960	766,693,818	1,346,419,750	162,000	135,000
1929	1,124,800,410	2,996,398,000	625,000	550,000	1970	2,937,359,448	4,494,864,600	320,000	130,000
1930	810,632,546	2,720,301,800	480,000	205,000	1971	3,891,317,731	*6,563,822,400	300,000	145,000
					1972	*4,138,187,706	5,444,117,100	250,000	150,000

*Record high for trading in stocks and bonds.

American Stock Exchange Transactions and Seat Prices
Source: American Stock Exchange

Date	Yearly volumes Stocks	Bonds Par Values	Seat price High	Seat price Low	Date	Yearly volumes Stocks	Bonds Par Values	Seat price High	Seat price Low
1929	476,140,375	$513,551,000	$254,000	$150,000	1960	286,039,982	$32,670,000	$60,000	$51,000
1930	222,270,065	863,541,000	225,000	70,000	1965	534,221,999	146,927,000	80,000	55,000
1940	42,928,377	303,902,000	7,250	6,900	1969	1,240,742,012	913,940,000	350,000	150,000
1945	143,309,392	167,333,000	32,000	12,000	1970	843,116,260	641,270,000	180,000	70,000
1950	107,792,340	47,549,000	11,000	6,500	1971	1,070,924,002	867,046,000	150,000	65,000
1955	228,955,915	35,330,000	22,000	17,500	1972	1,117,989,153	728,524,000	145,000	70,000

U.S. Business Indexes
Source: Federal Reserve System

Year	Industrial production (Physical volume) 1967 = 100 Manufacturers Total	Total	Durable	Non-Durable	Mining	Utilities	Construct'n contracts (value)[1] 1967 = 100 Total	Residential	All other	Employment[2] 1967 = 100 Manuf. production workers Non-agricultural	Employment	Payrolls	Prices 1967 100 Consumer	Wholesale commodity
1960	66.2	65.4	63.3	68.6	82.7	61.8	69	77	64	82.4	88.0	78.1	88.7	94.9
1964	81.7	81.2	79.0	84.4	91.1	81.9	89	105	80	88.6	89.3	89.6	92.9	94.7
1965	89.2	89.1	88.5	90.0	93.9	86.9	93	109	84	92.3	93.9	93.6	94.5	96.6
1966	97.9	98.3	99.0	97.3	98.4	93.6	95	91	97	97.1	99.9	99.7	97.2	99.8
1967	100.0	100.0	100.0	100.0	100.0	100.0	100	100	100	100.0	100.0	100.0	100.0	100.0
1968	105.7	105.7	105.5	106.0	103.9	109.4	113	117	111	103.1	101.4	106.6	104.2	102.5
1969	110.7	110.5	110.0	111.1	107.2	19.5	124	119	126	106.7	103.2	112.7	109.8	106.5
1970	106.6	105.2	101.4	110.6	109.7	128.3	123	115	130	107.2	98.0	114.1	116.3	110.4
1971	106.8	105.2	99.4	113.5	107.0	133.7	145	163	134	107.3	93.9	116.3	121.3	113.9
1972	115.2	114.0	108.4	122.1	108.8	143.4	N.A.	N.A.	N.A.	110.5	96.7	130.2	N.A.	N.A.

(1.) Indexes beginning 1960 are based on data from 48 states. (2.) Revisions have been made in some figures.

Per Capita Personal Income, by States and Regions

Source: Department of Commerce, Bureau of Economic Analysis. r Revised

State and Region	1969ʳ	1970ʳ	1971ʳ	1972ʳ	State and Region	1969ʳ	1970ʳ	1971ʳ	1972ʳ
	Per Capita Income (dollars)					Per Capita Income (dollars)			
United States	3,708	3,943	4,164	4,492	Southeast	2,979	3,223	3,458	3,801
New England	4,015	4,278	4,454	4,756	Virginia	3,348	3,653	3,918	4,298
Maine	3,030	3,272	3,366	3,610	West Virginia	2,755	3,047	3,272	3,594
New Hampshire	3,492	3,745	3,935	4,241	Kentucky	2,886	3,104	3,310	3,609
Vermont	3,139	3,311	3,528	3,686	Tennessee	2,883	3,082	3,329	3,671
Massachusetts	4,045	4,340	4,535	4,855	North Carolina	2,988	3,218	3,433	3,799
Rhode Island	3,711	3,941	4,170	4,483	South Carolina	2,741	2,963	3,157	3,477
Connecticut	4,634	4,871	5,013	5,328	Georgia	3,120	3,318	3,566	3,909
Mideast	4,181	4,454	4,699	5,008 ·	Florida	3,393	3,692	3,992	4,378
New York	4,447	4,714	4,957	5,242	Alabama	2,690	2,913	3,137	3,420
New Jersey	4,331	4,635	4,904	5,232	Mississippi	2,378	2,596	2,790	3,137
Pennsylvania	3,693	3,943	4,166	4,465	Louisiana	2,865	3,068	3,264	3,543
Delaware	4,331	4,483	4,800	5,188	Arkansas	2,614	2,869	3,030	3,365
Maryland	3,986	4,281	4,512	4,882	Southwest	3,257	3,519	3,672	3,965
District of Columbia	4,879	5,333	5,763	6,265	Oklahoma	3,106	3,350	3,503	3,795
Great Lakes	3,955	4,113	4,373	4,725	Texas	3,318	3,576	3,706	3,991
Michigan	4,090	4,156	4,455	4,881	New Mexico	2,874	3,117	3,273	3,564
Ohio	3,825	3,992	4,207	4,534	Arizona	3,312	3,631	3,926	4,263
Indiana	3,674	3,752	4,031	4,366	Rocky Mountain	3,279	3,580	3,810	4,187
Illinois	4,271	4,492	4,789	5,140	Montana	3,170	3,498	3,562	3,999
Wisconsin	3,531	3,794	3,965	4,255	Idaho	3,046	3,280	3,444	3,780
Plains	3,506	3,745	3,936	4,278	Wyoming	3,399	3,796	3,857	4,330
Minnesota	3,578	3,818	4,020	4,298	Colorado	3,516	3,839	4,173	4,574
Iowa	3,523	3,749	3,847	4,300	Utah	2,979	3,228	3,447	3,728
Missouri	3,523	3,768	4,004	4,293	Far West	4,122	4,346	4,535	4,866
North Dakota	3,017	3,120	3,474	3,738	Washington	3,938	4,022	4,169	4,472
South Dakota	2,972	3,124	3,298	3,699	Oregon	3,498	3,694	3,949	4,287
Nebraska	3,597	3,794	3,961	4,355	Nevada	4,163	4,452	4,753	5,078
Kansas	3,565	3,841	4,070	4,455	California	4,218	4,467	4,654	4,988
					Alaska	4,219	4,603	4,907	5,141
					Hawaii	4,098	4,562	4,749	5,031

(1.) Per capita personal income for each state is derived by the division of total personal income by total population. Personal income is a measure of the income received from all sources during the calendar year by the residents of each state. It comprises income received by persons in the form of wages and salaries, net income of proprietors (including farmers) dividends, interest, net rents, and other items such as social insurance benefits, relief, veterans pensions and benefits, and allotment payments to dependents of military personnel.

Average Percent Increase in Earnings

Source: Bureau of Labor Statistics, United States Department of Labor

Period and area May 1971 to May 1972	All industries				Manufacturing			
	Office Clerical	Indus- trial nurses	Skilled main- tenance	Un- skilled plant	Office Clerical	Indus- trial nurses	Skilled main- tenance	Un- skilled plant
United States	5.6	6.6	7.4	7.9	5.7	6.5	7.0	7.3
Northeast	5.9	7.3	7.8	8.2	6.6	7.3	7.5	7.8
South	5.3	6.3	7.2	7.0	5.4	5.7	7.0	6.5
North Central	5.4	6.4	7.3	7.8	5.4	6.4	6.9	7.5
West	5.8	5.9	7.5	8.6	4.8	5.7	6.5	6.1

Output and Labor Costs, Industrial Nations

Source: U.S. Bureau of Labor Statistics

Output per Man-Hour

Country	1960	1965	1966	1967	1968	1969	1970	1971[1]
United States	80.5	98.7	99.9	100.0	104.7	106.2	107.8	111.5
Ten industrial nations	69.1	90.0	94.8	100.0	108.3	116.4	123.2	130.1
Canada	76.0	94.5	97.4	100.0	[1]107.5	[1]113.1	[1]114.6	118.3
Japan	52.6	79.0	87.3	100.0	114.8	133.3	[1]152.2	162.9
Belgium	68.1	86.7	93.1	100.0	107.7	[1]116.5	[1]122.0	126.8
France	69.6	88.7	94.8	100.0	106.6	112.7	119.0	125.7
Germany	66.4	90.4	94.1	100.0	107.6	113.8	116.8	123.7
Italy	65.1	91.7	96.0	100.0	108.4	112.6	118.3	121.8
Netherlands	67.2	87.6	93.7	100.0	111.2	123.4	133.7	142.9
Sweden[2]	62.5	87.9	92.8	100.0	110.9	[1]119.4	[1]125.6	133.6
Switzerland (wage earners only)	80.5	90.6	95.2	100.0	105.3	116.1	125.5	129.8
United Kingdom	77.7	93.4	96.4	100.0	106.3	108.7	111.5	116.5
Eight European Countries	69.7	90.5	95.0	100.0	107.3	113.1	118.1	124.4
EEC	67.2	89.8	94.7	100.0	107.5	113.7	118.7	125.3

Unit Labor Costs in U.S. Dollars

Country	1960	1965	1966	1967	1968	1969	1970	1971[1]
United States	95.2	92.4	95.4	100.0	102.3	107.4	112.8	115.8
Ten industrial nations	83.6	97.8	100.1	100.0	98.3	100.9	110.4	121.8
Canada	104.1	91.4	95.7	100.0	100.2	105.4	[1]115.7	125.7
Japan	82.8	102.7	101.8	100.0	101.9	104.5	[1]109.4	121.9
Belgium	80.1	96.1	97.3	100.0	97.4	[1]96.5	[1]104.1	[1]115.5
France	81.4	98.0	[1]97.3	[1]100.0	[1]105.2	[1]102.4	[1]99.4	[1]104.9
Germany	78.1	95.6	100.1	100.0	98.5	103.5	126.2	143.5
Italy	76.3	97.1	95.1	100.0	99.0	103.6	118.6	132.0
Netherlands	65.2	91.0	95.6	100.0	98.4	[1]101.2	[1]106.8	118.2
Sweden[2]	84.2	94.2	97.4	100.0	98.3	[1]102.0	[1]108.5	115.6
Switzerland (wage earners only)	75.8	96.5	99.1	100.0	100.2	97.1	99.6	114.2
United Kingdom	85.3	98.1	104.4	100.0	89.0	93.9	104.9	115.3
Eight European Countries	80.5	96.8	99.7	100.0	97.8	100.4	111.6	123.2
EEC	78.1	96.3	98.1	100.0	100.6	102.9	114.8	126.9

[1]Estimates derived from preliminary or partial year data or current data from other series.   [2]Mining and manufacturing.

U.S. Labor Force, Employment and Unemployment

Source: Bureau of the Census, U.S. Dept of Commerce; Bureau of Labor Statistics, U.S. Dept. of Labor
(Unemployment by sex, age, color and other characteristics)

	1970	1971	1972	Jan.	Feb.	Mar.	Apr.	May	June	July
							1973			
				(Numbers in thousands)						
U.S. Pop. (incl. armed forces overseas)	¹204,879	¹207,045	¹208,842	209,717	209,826	209,915	210,036	210,157	N.A.	N.A.
Labor Force²										
Labor force, persons 16 years of age and over	85,903	86,929	88,991	88,122	89,075	89,686	89,823	89,891	92,729	93,227
Civilian labor force	82,715	84,113	86,542	85,718	86,683	87,325	87,473	87,557	90,414	90,917
Employed, total	78,627	79,120	81,702	81,043	81,838	82,814	83,299	83,758	85,567	86,367
Agriculture	3,462	3,387	3,472	2,955	2,956	3,131	3,295	3,467	4,053	4,165
Nonagricultural industries	75,165	75,732	78,230	78,088	78,882	79,683	80,004	80,291	81,514	82,201
Unemployed	4,088	4,993	4,840	4,675	4,845	4,512	4,174	3,799	4,847	4,550
Long-term, 15 weeks and over	662	1,181	1,158	942	979	1,121	1,022	904	775	750
Seasonally adjusted										
Civilian labor force	......	......	......	86,921	87,569	88,268	88,350	88,405	88,932	88,810
Employed total	......	......	......	82,555	83,127	83,889	83,917	84,024	84,674	84,614
Agriculture	......	......	......	3,501	3,424	3,480	3,311	3,275	3,403	3,516
Nonagricultural industries	......	......	......	79,054	79,703	80,409	80,606	80,749	81,271	81,098
Unemployed	......	......	......	4,366	4,442	4,379	4,433	4,381	4,258	4,196
Long-term, 15 weeks and over	......	......	......	919	895	859	763	802	775	678
Rates (unemployed in each group as percent of total in the group):										
All civilian workers	4.9	5.9	5.6	5.0	5.1	5.0	5.0	5.0	4.8	4.7
Men, 20 years and over	3.5	4.4	4.0	3.3	3.4	3.4	3.4	3.4	3.2	3.0
Women, 20 years and over	4.8	5.7	5.4	5.3	4.9	4.9	4.7	4.6	4.9	4.9
Both sexes, 16-19 years	15.3	16.9	16.2	14.3	15.8	14.2	15.4	15.4	13.3	14.4
White	4.5	8.1	8.0	4.6	4.6	4.4	4.5	4.4	4.3	4.1
Negro and other races	8.2	9.9	10.0	8.9	9.0	9.0	9.1	9.4	8.0	9.0
Household heads	2.9	3.6	3.3	2.9	3.0	3.0	3.0	2.9	2.9	2.7
Married men	2.6	3.2	2.8	2.4	2.4	2.5	2.4	2.3	2.3	2.1
Occupation:										
White-collar workers	2.8	3.5	3.4	3.2	3.0	2.9	3.1	2.8	2.8	2.9
Blue-collar workers	6.2	7.4	6.5	5.6	5.7	5.4	5.4	5.4	5.3	5.3
Industry of last job (nonagricultural):										
Private wage and salary workers	5.2	6.2	5.7	5.1	5.1	4.9	4.9	4.9	4.7	4.7
Construction	9.7	10.4	10.3	9.0	8.7	8.5	9.4	9.0	7.9	9.6
Manufacturing	5.6	6.8	5.6	5.0	4.5	4.6	4.3	4.5	4.4	3.8
Durable goods	5.7	7.0	5.4	4.6	4.3	4.5	3.8	4.1	3.7	3.3

(1) As of July 1. (2) Effective January 1972, data reflect adjustment to the 1970 Census of Population. For example the civilian labor force and employment totals were increased by a little more than 300,000; unemployment levels and rates were essentially unchanged. A subsequent census adjustment, primarily affecting whites and Negroes and other race groups, was introduced into the survey for March 1973. As a result, the white labor force and employment levels were lowered by about 150,000, while Negro levels were raised by 210,000. Consequently, the overall labor force and employment showed a net increase of about 60,000. Unemployment levels and rates were not affected significantly. Comparisons with data prior to these two dates should take these adjustments into account. N.A. — Not available.

Employed Persons by Major Occupational Groups and Sex
Source: Bureau of Labor Statistics
Annual Averages 1972

	Thousands of persons			Percent Distribution		
OCCUPATIONAL GROUP	Both sexes	Males	Females	Both sexes	Males	Females
Total Employed	81,702	50,630	31,072	100.0	100.0	100.0
White-collar workers	39,092	20,176	18,915	47.8	39.9	60.9
Professional and technical	11,459	6,957	4,502	14.0	13.7	14.5
Managers and administrators, except farm	8,032	6,621	1,410	9.8	13.1	4.5
Sales workers	5,354	3,127	2,226	6.6	6.2	7.2
Clerical workers	14,247	3,470	10,777	17.4	6.9	34.7
Blue-collar workers	28,576	23,800	4,776	35.0	47.0	15.3
Craftsmen and kindred workers	10,810	10,424	386	13.2	20.6	1.2
Operatives, except transport	10,340	6,351	3,989	12.7	12.5	12.8
Transport equipment operatives	3,209	3,075	134	3.9	6.1	.4
Nonfarm laborers	4,217	3,950	267	5.2	7.8	.9
Service workers	10,966	4,128	6,838	13.4	8.2	22.0
Private household workers	1,437	34	1,403	1.8	.1	4.5
Other service workers	9,529	4,094	5,435	11.7	8.1	17.5
Farm workers	3,069	2,526	543	3.8	5.0	1.7
Farmers and farm managers	1,688	1,588	100	2.1	3.1	.3
Farm laborers and foremen	1,381	938	443	1.7	1.9	1.4

Employment and Unemployment in the United States
Civilian Labor Force, Persons 16 Years of Age and Over

Year	Civilian Labor Force	Employed	Unemployed	Year	Civilian Labor Force	Employed	Unemployed
					First Half Average		
1965	74,455,000	71,088,000	3,366,000	1967	76,292,000	73,284,000	3,008,000
1966	75,770,000	72,895,000	2,875,000	1968	77,992,000	75,042,000	2,950,000
1967	77,347,000	74,372,000	2,975,000	1969	79,691,000	76,893,000	2,798,000
1968	78,737,000	75,920,000	2,817,000	1970	81,907,000	78,151,000	3,756,000
1969	80,733,000	77,902,000	2,831,000	1971	83,165,000	78,064,000	5,101,000
1970	82,715,000	78,627,000	4,088,000	1972	85,615,000	80,524,000	5,090,000
1971	84,113,000	79,120,000	4,993,000	1973	87,529,000	83,053,000	4,476,000
1972	86,542,000	81,702,000	4,840,000				

Canadian Labor Force

Source: Statistics Canada

(June, 1973, seasonally adjusted)

(thousands of workers)

	Can.	Nfld.	P.E.I.	N.S.	N.B.	Que.	Ont.	Man.	Sask.	Alta.	B.C.
Labor Force	9,327	181	44	283	243	2,569	3,532	410	350	721	1,005
Employed	8,836	159	40	263	219	2,378	3,404	395	339	695	944
Unemployed..............	491	22	n.a.	20	24	191	128	15	11	26	61
Percent unemployed	5.3	12.2	n.a.	7.1	9.9	7.4	3.6	3.7	3.1	3.6	6.1

Canada: Labor Force Characteristics

Source: Statistics Canada

	Labor force (000)	Employed (thousands)					Unem- ployed (000)	Unem- ployed %
			All workers			Paid workers		
		Total	Agri- culture	Non-Agri- culture	Total	Non-agri- culture		
1950.....	5,163	4,976	1,018	3,958	3,522	3,411	186	3.6
1955.....	5,610	5,364	819	4,546	4,133	4,027	245	4.4
1960.....	6,411	5,965	683	5,282	4,843	4,732	446	7.0
1965.....	7,141	6,862	594	6,268	5,760	5,655	280	3.9
1968.....	7,919	7,537	546	6,992	6,490	6,391	382	4.8
1969.....	8,162	7,780	535	7,245	6,720	6,625	382	4.7
1970.....	8,374	7,879	511	7,368	6,839	6,740	495	5.9
1971.....	8,631	8,079	510	7,569	7,029	6,927	552	6.4
1972.....	8,891	8,329	481	7,848	7,310	7,211	562	6.3

Average Weekly Canadian Wages and Salaries, by Province (C$)

Source: Canadian Statistical Review, June 1973 (p) Preliminary

Year & Month	Canada	Nfld.	P.E.I.	N.S.	N.B.	Que.	Ont.	Man.	Sask.	Alta.	B.C.
1960	117.63	106.00	80.87	94.51	96.80	114.24	121.55	107.67	107.90	117.95	129.35
1970	126.82	117.70	83.82	104.21	104.01	122.38	131.52	115.88	114.87	128.15	137.97
1971	137.64	123.79	89.96	112.82	113.36	132.04	143.02	123.84	121.71	138.78	152.50
1972	149.21	135.30	101.04	123.40	125.07	142.87	154.90	135.59	133.26	149.97	164.75
Jan.	143.68	130.20	98.76	119.82	123.40	136.84	149.81	129.54	127.03	142.70	158.10
Feb.	144.64	133.81	97.91	119.67	124.91	137.00	150.70	130.43	128.95	145.64	159.64
1973 Jan (p)...	155.39	144.21	108.70	132.24	133.12	148.53	161.51	139.45	136.53	155.87	170.00
Feb (p)...	156.94	144.45	110.34	133.06	134.17	150.50	163.09	139.37	137.82	157.51	171.44

Canada: Regional Unemployment Rates, 1972

Source: Statistics Canada

Region	Jan.	March	May	July	Sept.	Dec.	Region	Jan.	March	May	July	Sept.	Dec.
Vancouver—Victoria	6.9	6.8	6.9	7.1	7.3	7.7	Hamilton—Toronto..	5.1	5.0	4.8	4.8	4.7	4.7
Alberta	4.5	4.3	4.2	4.2	4.3	4.4	Montreal	7.5	7.4	7.5	7.5	7.5	7.5
Saskatchewan	3.8	4.0	4.1	4.1	4.3	4.4	New Brunswick, P.E.I.	7.7	8.0	8.1	8.3	8.5	8.8
Manitoba...........	4.9	5.0	4.9	4.7	4.6	4.7	Nova Scotia	7.7	7.7	7.7	7.8	7.7	7.5
London—Windsor...	5.2	5.0	4.5	4.2	4.0	4.0	Canada	6.4	6.3	6.2	6.2	6.3	6.3

Activities of the Unemployment Insurance Commission—Canada

Source: Canadian Statistical Review

Year and Month	Claims Data		(000)	Weeks Paid (thousands)	Total paid[3,4]	Benefits Paid (thousand dollars)				
	Claimants[1,2]	Claims received	Claims received			Regular	Sickness	Maternity	Retirement	Fishing
1971......	603	2,371		22,634	890,594	–	–	–	–	–
1972......	804	2,469		30,462	1,871,802	1,764,040	50,855	36,431	2,440	20,402
1973										
Jan......	1,056	270		3,634	244,437	227,883	6,521	5,289	378	5,875
Feb.	1,055	155		3,268	222,661	206,339	6,769	5,049	264	5,366
Mar.	1,003	158		3,148	214,380	198,759	7,474	5,294	273	4,381

(1) Persons who have applied for or are in receipt of unemployment insurance benefit at end of month.
(2) Annual figures are annual averages.
(3) Prior to July 1971, total includes ordinary, seasonal and fishing benefits.
(4) Includes adjustments for cancellation of warrants and collection of overpayments.

Overseas Direct Investment in the United States

Source: U.S. Dept of Commerce

The value of overseas direct investments in the United States increased $708,000,000 in 1972 to $14.363 billion at year-end. The increase resulted from reinvested earnings of $548 million and net capital inflows of $160 million. *Interest, dividends, and branch profits account for most of the income received by foreign owners from direct investments in the U.S.

(Millions of dollars)	Book Value	Net Cap. inflows	Total	Earnings		
				Int.*	div.	Reinv'd.
1971	13,655	-115	1,110	621		498
1972 Total (prelim.)	14,363	160	1,233	719		548
By country						
Canada	3,612	123	264	115		150
United Kingdom	4,581	4	415	274		139
Netherlands ...	2,331	19	193	108		87
Switzerland ...	1,595	29	118	70		29
Other	2,244	-15	120	2		143

Civilian Employment of the Federal Government

Source: United States Civil Service Commission, Manpower Statistics Division, data as of June 30, 1973

Includes all paid employees of agencies listed; excludes employees of Central Intelligence Agency, National Security Agency (not reported to Civil Service Commission) and uncompensated employees.
Excludes 56,707 Youth Programs appointees and 1,873 Public Service Career employees.

Agency	All Areas	United States			Outside United States		
		Total	Full-Time a/	Part-Time a/	Total	Territories	Foreign Countries
Total, all agencies	2,765,662	2,630,665	2,406,198	191,595	134,997	35,218	99,779
Percent distribution	100	95	90	—	5	—	—
Legislative Branch	34,793	34,692	31,407	710	101	......	101
Congress	14,863	14,863	14,863	......	......	......	......
Architect of the Capitol	1,824	1,824	......	......	......	......	......
Botanic Garden	55	55	......	......	......	......	......
General Accounting Office	4,968	4,879	4,833	46	89	......	89
Government Printing Office	8,521	8,521	7,495	517	......	......	......
Library of Congress	4,375	4,363	4,216	147	12	......	12
United States Tax Court	187	187	......	......	......	......	......
Judicial Branch	8,740	8,659	8,117	542	81	81	......
Executive Branch	2,722,129	2,587,314	2,366,674	190,343	134,815	35,815	99,678
Executive Office of the President	4,744	4,744	......	......	......	......	......
White House Office	542	542	......	......	......	......	......
Office of the Vice President	29	29	......	......	......	......	......
Office of Management and Budget	637	637	......	......	......	......	......
Council of Economic Advisers	53	53	......	......	......	......	......
Citizens' Advisory Committee on Environmental Quality	1	1	......	......	......	......	......
Cost of Living Council	938	938	......	......	......	......	......
Council on Environmental Quality	70	70	......	......	......	!!!!!!	......
Council on International Economic Policy	36	36	......	......	......	......	......
Domestic Council	33	33	......	......	......	......	......
Executive Mansion and Grounds	71	71	......	......	......	......	......
National Aeronautics and Space Council	7	7	......	......	......	......	......
National Security Council	82	82	......	......	......	......	......
Office of Economic Opportunity	1,636	1,636	......	......	......	......	......
Office of Emergency Preparedness	475	475	......	......	......	......	......
Office of Special Representative for Trade Negotiations	41	41	......	......	......	......	......
Office of Telecommunications Policy	70	70	......	......	......	......	......
Special Action Office for Drug Abuse Prevention	133	133	......	......	......	......	......
Executive Departments	1,662,584	1,554,527	1,516,565	37,962	108,057	15,566	92,491
State b/	34,421	10,390	9,843	547	24,031	......	24,031
Treasury	106,555	105,766	104,326	1,440	789	519	270
Defense	1,030,965	952,097	946,695	5,402	78,868	12,259	66,609
Office of the Secretary	1,967	1,922	1,843	79	45	......	45
Department of the Army	366,163	335,696	334,086	1,610	30,467	4,199	26,268
Department of the Navy	321,765	292,609	290,007	2,602	29,156	5,292	23,864
Department of the Air Force	270,488	252,119	251,114	1,005	18,369	2,646	15,723
Other Defense Activities	70,582	69,751	69,645	106	831	122	709
Justice	47,214	46,527	45,556	971	687	302	385
Interior	71,414	70,950	66,895	4,055	464	376	88
Agriculture	111,285	110,010	93,196	16,814	1,275	657	618
Commerce	34,260	33,936	30,653	3,283	324	135	189
Labor	13,611	13,530	13,113	417	81	67	14
Health, Education and Welfare	125,152	124,667	120,660	4,007	485	407	78
Housing and Urban Development	17,950	17,757	17,587	170	193	192	1
Transportation	69,957	68,897	68,041	856	860	652	208
Independent agencies	1,054,801	1,028,043	850,109	152,381	26,758	19,571	7,187
ACTION	1,746	1,201	......	......	545	27	518
Atomic Energy Commission	7,396	7,378	7,247	131	18	3	15
Board of Governors, Federal Reserve System	1,240	1,240	......	......	......	......	......
Canal Zone Government	3,316	......	......	......	3,316	3,316	......
Civil Aeronautics Board	684	684	......	......	......	......	......
Civil Service Commission	6,751	6,742	6,193	549	9	9	......
Environmental Protection Agency	9,404	9,390	9,117	273	14	7	7
Federal Communications Commission	1,772	1,767	......	......	5	5	......
Federal Power Commission	1,251	1,251	......	......	......	......	......
Federal Trade Commission	1,530	1,530	......	......	......	......	......
General Services Administration	37,671	37,597	36,791	806	74	62	12
Information Agency	9,195	3,276	3,246	29	5,919	......	5,919
Interstate Commerce Commission	1,814	1,814	......	......	......	......	......
National Aeronautics and Space Administration	26,777	26,757	26,675	82	20	1	19
National Labor Relations Board	2,409	2,385	......	......	24	24	......
Panama Canal Company	11,654	91	4	......	11,563	11,563	......
Securities and Exchange Commission	1,632	1,632	......	......	......	......	......
Selective Service Commission	5,480	5,385	4,529	856	95	95	......
Small Business Administration	4,926	4,851	4,799	52	75	75	......
Tennessee Valley Authority	23,446	23,442	23,177	265	4	......	......
U.S. Postal Service	682,120	679,479	546,909	132,570	2,641	2,641	......
Veterans Administration	194,362	192,429	175,887	16,542	1,933	1,635	298
Miscellaneous	18,225	17,722	17,496	226	503	108	395

a/ Data not collected from agencies with fewer than 2,500 employees. b/ Includes 10,417 employees in Agency for International Development (3,088 in Wash., D.C.); employees in foreign countries include 3,302 paid from local currency trust funds established by foreign governments. c/ Civilian employment of Federal Govt. June 30(1930) 601,319; (1940) 1,042,420; (1950) 1,960,708; (1960) 2,398,704; (1965) 2,527,915; (1970) 2,921,909; (1971) 2,862,894; (1972) 2,811,779; (1973) 2,765,662.

Wholesale Price Indexes

Source: Bureau of Labor Statistics, United States Department of Labor

The Wholesale Primary Market Price Index is designed to show the rate and direction of the composite of price movements, and to measure price changes not influenced by quality, quantity, terms of sale, etc. Wholesale refers to sales in quantities, not to prices received or paid by wholesalers.

Commodity group (1967 = 100)	1973 June	1973 Jan.	1972 Avg.
All commodities	136.7	124.5	119.1
Farm products, and processed foods, and feeds	163.6	137.0	122.4
Farm products	182.3	144.2	125.0
Processed foods and feeds	151.8	132.4	120.8
All commodities except farm products	131.4	122.2	118.4
Industrial commodities	126.9	120.0	117.9
Textile products and apparel	123.7	116.6	113.6
Hides, skins, leather, and related products	140.9	143.9	131.3
Fuels and related products and power	142.8	122.2	118.6
Chemicals and allied products	110.4	105.1	104.2
Rubber and plastic products	112.6	110.0	109.3
Lumber and wood products	183.1	151.0	144.3
Pulp, paper, and allied products	122.0	115.8	113.4
Metals and metal products	132.5	125.6	123.5
Machinery and equipment	121.9	118.9	117.9
Furniture and household durables	115.2	112.6	111.4
Nonmetallic mineral products	131.1	128.2	126.1
Transportation equipment (Dec. 1968 = 100)	115.0	114.1	113.7
Miscellaneous products	120.2	115.8	114.6

Commercial and Industrial Failures in the United States (in $1,000)

Source: Dun & Bradstreet, Inc.; data do not include banks *Data exclude Alaska and Hawaii.

Year*	Number	Liabilities	Year*	Number	Liabilities	Year*	Number	Liabilities
1940	13,619	$166,684	1960	15,445	$ 938,630	1967	12,364	$1,265,227
1945	809	30,225	1961	17,075	1,090,123	1968	9,636	940,996
1950	9,162	248,283	1962	15,782	1,213,601	1969	9,154	1,142,113
1955	10,969	449,380	1963	14,374	1,352,593	1970	10,748	1,887,754
1959	14,053	682,808	1964	13,501	1,329,223	1971	10,326	1,916,929
			1965	13,514	1,321,666	1972	9,566	2,000,244

A business failure, as defined for this record, occurs when a commercial or industrial enterprise is involved in a court proceeding or a voluntary action which is likely to end in loss to creditors. Specifically, the Dun and Bradstreet record of failure includes discontinuances following assignment, voluntary or involuntary petition in bankruptcy, attachment, execution, foreclosure, etc.; voluntary withdrawals from business with known loss to creditors; also enterprises involved in court action, such as receivership, and since June, 1943, reorganization, or arrangement, which may or may not lead to disturbances; as well as businesses making voluntary compromises with creditors out of court. Comparison of this series with the bankruptcy reports of the Attorney General of the United States is not possible. The latter give complete coverage of all types of cases, including farmers, employees, professional men and others not in business, all which are excluded from the Dun & Bradstreet statistics.

U.S. Savings Bonds Series A to K*

Source: Treasury Department (in millions as of December 31)

Year	Amounts outstanding	Funds rec. from sale	Accrued discounts	Redemption[2]	Year	Amounts outstanding[1]	Funds rec. from sale	Accrued discounts	Redemption[2]
1935-41	6,140	6,486	201	547	1965	50,324	4,486	1,527	5,441
1945	48,183	12,937	484	5,558	1969	51,549	4,393	1,832	6,639
1950	58,019	6,074	1,104	5,840	1970	51,842	4,665	1,909	6,295
1955	57,924	6,276	1,216	7,301	1971	54,275	5,477	2,192	5,244
1960	47,159	4,350	1,262	6,732	1972	57,579	6,236	2,426	5,365

(1.) Interest-bearing debt only. (2.) Comprises both matured and unmatured bonds. *Series E and H are the only series currently on sale.

Pulpwood, Wood Pulp and Newsprint—Canada

(thousand tons)
Source: Canadian Statistical Review, June 1973

Year and Month	Pulpwood Production (thousand units[1])	Wood Pulp Production[2] Total	Mechanical	Chemical	Wood Pulp Exports[3]	News-Print Production	Newsprint Shipments Total	Domestic	Export[4]
1971	15,563	17,588.6	7,213.7	10,336.2	6,545.8	8,297.0	8,209.8	719.7	7,489.9
1972	15,805	18,440.8	7,413.4	10,984.3	6,071.2	8,660.8	8,739.4	779.7	7,959.8
1973									
Jan.	1,287	1,614.2	677.7	933.3	539.7	767.4	729.2	65.5	663.8
Feb.	1,504	1,577.6	631.7	942.8	525.6	721.9	739.4	59.8	670.6
Mar.	1,340	1,771.9	708.2	1,060.6	543.5	811.3	788.1	71.6	716.6

(1) 100 cu. ft. of solid wood; pulpwood produced for domestic use and excluding exports, but including receipts of purchased roundwood.
(2) Total pulp production covers "screenings" which are already included in exports. "Screenings" are excluded throughout from mechanical and chemical pulp.
(3) Customs exports.
(4) Mill shipments destined for export.

Total Value of Construction Work Performed in Canada by Province (1970-72)*

Source: Statistic Canada

Province	1970			1971			1972		
	New	Repair	Total	New	Repair	Total	New	Repair	Total
Newfoundland	368,101	46,998	415,099	496,491	42,724	539,215	548,678	45,998	594,676
Prince Edward Island	34,247	11,414	45,661	47,897	9,491	57,388	56,827	10,289	67,116
Nova Scotia	402,916	81,793	484,709	376,673	89,338	466,011	437,240	89,224	526,464
New Brunswick	273,743	66,155	339,898	281,001	68,847	349,848	317,377	73,482	390,859
Quebec	2,192,704	595,829	2,788,533	2,670,416	582,173	3,252,589	2,913,614	603,774	3,517,388
Ontario.	4,127,041	857,824	4,984,865	4,707,969	915,630	5,623,599	4,798,918	959,914	5,758,832
Manitoba.	574,766	120,344	695,110	577,475	119,987	697,462	637,479	126,416	763,895
Saskatchewan	345,794	129,869	475,663	388,645	135,241	523,886	404,839	138,531	543,370
Alberta.	1,431,735	278,215	1,709,950	1,481,631	282,564	1,764,195	1,529,902	298,117	1,828,019
British Columbia . . .	1,568,982	272,748	1,841,730	2,084,000	289,173	2,373,173	2,040,697	309,598	2,350,295

*Includes residential, industrial, commercial, institutions, and engineering construction.

Valuation of U.S. Private Permit-Authorized Construction

Authorized by building permits in 13,000 selected permit issuing places

	1971 Total	1972 Total (P)
All private construction	$48,198,000,000	$56,378,000,000
Private residential construction	28,306,000,000	34,275,000,000
(P) Preliminary		

Canadu Produation of Eloatrio Fnergy

Source: Statistics Canada

Year	Fuel Used[1]				Hydro[2] (billion kwh)	Total[2] (billion kwh)
	Coal (short tons)	Petroleum (Imp Gallons)	Gas (000 cu. ft.)	Other (000 cu. ft.)		
1960 . .	1,846,149	71,707,376	37,940,728	–	1,058.8	1,144.6
1965 . .	7,721,714	190,536,082	59,601,324	14,897	1,170.6	1,442.7
1968 . .	11,098,800	434,312,353	74,736,686	34,929	1,349.7	1,763.8
1969 . .	11,873,750	421,561,985	58,853,928	12,852	1,492.5	1,911.0
1970 . .	15,199,471	408,911,792	70,725,852	13,373	1,567.1	2,047.2
1971 . .	17,213,408	430,444,085	70,332,525	14,906	1,609.8	2,164.7

(1) Utilities only. (2) Industry and utilities.

Telephones in North American Cities With Over 100,000 Telephones (1973)

Source: American Telephone and Telegraph Co., and Trans-Canada Telephone Systems

City	Number	City	Number	City	Number	City	Number
Akron	313,879	Eugene, Springfield,		Miami	798,558	St. Louis	565,837
Albany, N.Y.	158,150	Ore.	103,220	Milwaukee	716,084	St. Petersburg . . .	215,767
Albuquerque, ...	207,974	Evansville	105,618	Minn.-St. Paul . . .	1,306,300	Salt Lake City	329,909
Alexandria, Va.	189,905	Flint	185,395	Mobile	163,688	San Antonio	355,439
Allentown, Pa.	121,467	Ft. Lauderdale	237,050	Monterrey	101,714	San Diego (Area) . . .	761,417
Amarillo	102,312	Fort Wayne	149,982	Montgomery	109,867	San Francisco	716,821
Anaheim, Calif.	166,915	Fort Worth	273,886	Montreal	1,030,481	San Jose	415,724
Ann Arbor, Mich. . . .	100,372	Fresno	189,711	Mt. Vernon, N.Y. . . .	114,487	Santa Ana	254,401
Atlanta, Ga.	727,303	Gary	112,075	Nashville	298,615	Santa Barbara	107,915
Augusta, Ga.	103,444	Grand Rapids	240,441	New Haven	244,164	Savannah	108,210
Austin, Tex.	210,898	Greensboro	141,628	New Orleans	553,731	Schenectady	119,212
Bakersfield, Calif. . . .	126,479	Greenville, N.C.	122,616	New York	5,825,460	Seattle	528,754
Baltimore	1,104,806	Halifax	107,407	Newark	307,371	Shreveport	156,151
Baton Rouge	190,617	Hamilton	163,165	Newport News	171,245	Skokie, Ill.	132,579
Birmingham	328,712	Harrisburg	174,466	Norfolk	351,766	South Bend	118,500
Boston	496,960	Hartford	290,170	Oklahoma City	247,316	Spokane	167,241
Bridgeport	163,835	Hayward, Calif.	114,369	Omaha	345,100	Springfield, Ill.	113,156
Buffalo	440,123	Hollywood, Fla.	150,394	Orlando	181,628	Springfield, Mass. . .	138,603
Calgary	259,937	Honolulu	297,676	Ottawa	289,867	Stockton, Calif. . . .	107,668
Cambridge	103,157	Houston	1,009,193	Palo Alto	127,931	Syracuse	250,042
Canton	113,725	Huntsville, Ala. . . .	120,343	Passaic	127,031	Tacoma	181,644
Charleston, S.C.	144,428	Indianapolis	564,966	Paterson	108,542	Tampa	259,228
Charlotte	253,878	Jackson, Miss.	140,447	Pensacola	111,473	Toledo	276,449
Chattanooga	186,174	Jacksonville	324,352	Peoria	149,234	Toronto	708,073
Chicago	2,358,668	Jersey City	165,358	Philadelphia	1,545,192	Tucson	212,686
Cincinnati	632,491	Kalamazoo	118,634	Phoenix	622,161	Tulsa	269,924
Cleveland	863,851	Kansas City, Kans. . .	145,499	Pittsburgh	727,141	Union City, N.J. . . .	106,995
Colorado Springs . .	156,939	Kansas City, Mo. . . .	326,608	Pomona	132,840	Vancouver	351,506
Columbia, S.C.	181,813	Knoxville	156,352	Portland, Ore.	416,576	Victoria	102,087
Columbus, Ga.	129,870	Lansing	180,131	Providence	231,359	Warren, Mich.	253,978
Columbus, Ohio . . .	435,922	Las Vegas	198,856	Quebec City	200,308	Washington, D.C. . . .	911,125
Corpus Christi	118,736	Lexington	121,207	Raleigh	129,882	Weston	168,982
Dallas	651,657	Lincoln	114,100	Reading, Pa.	140,156	West Palm Beach . .	191,293
Dayton	344,672	Little Rock	162,342	Richmond, Va.	308,714	Wichita	179,349
Denver	875,722	Livonia, Mich.	143,284	Riverside, Calif. . . .	119,587	Willowdale	150,984
Des Moines	224,800	London	129,329	Roanoke, Va.	100,465	Wilmington, Del. . .	180,603
Detroit	1,384,820	Los Angeles (Area) .	4,942,510	Rochester, N.Y. . . .	353,219	Windsor	104,950
East Orange, N.J. . .	118,839	Louisville	426,560	Rockford, Ill.	148,314	Winnipeg	299,348
Edmonton	229,641	Lubbock, Tex.	118,163	Royal Oak, Mich. . .	181,611	Winston-Salem . . .	127,435
El Paso	192,950	Madison, Wisc.	154,827	Sacramento	380,734	Worcester.	123,455
Erie	120,493	Memphis	437,658	Saginaw, Mich. . . .	104,216	Youngstown	163,313
		Mexico City	897,789				

Manufactures and Minerals
General Statistics for Major Industry Groups
Source: Bureau of the Census

The estimates for 1971 in the following table are based upon reports from a representative sample of about 65,000 manufacturing establishments.

Industry	All employees		Production workers			Value added by mf'r adj. (Millions)
	Number (1,000)	Payroll (Millions)	Number (1,000)	Man-hours (Millions)	Wages (Millions)	
Food and kindred products	1,574.1	12,179.9	1,072.7	2,145.4	7,437.5	34,109.8
Tobacco manufactures	67.1	470.5	58.5	109.2	376.3	2,559.9
Textile mill products	906.8	5,330.1	794.4	1,605.2	4,212.1	9,995.2
Apparel and other textile products	1,318.8	6,499.8	1,148.9	2,054.4	4,942.7	12,448.4
Lumber and wood products	530.1	3,461.8	465.2	909.3	2,781.9	6,760.9
Furniture and fixtures	435.5	2,820.9	360.1	710.5	2,034.0	5,226.9
Paper and allied products	631.9	5,536.8	494.7	1,024.7	3,950.6	11,682.1
Printing and publishing	1,049.1	8,975.9	626.3	1,192.0	5,010.1	18,086.4
Chemicals and allied products	848.9	8,259.9	528.6	1,060.5	4,451.2	29,431.5
Petroleum and coal products	141.3	1,564.1	97.1	197.6	993.5	5,616.8
Rubber and plastics products, n.e.c.	543.5	4,285.7	422.2	844.4	2,968.4	9,521.2
Leather and leather products	273.8	1,500.6	240.4	441.8	1,155.0	2,760.8
Stone, clay, and glass products	582.6	4,801.6	462.4	927.8	3,503.4	10,757.8
Primary metal industries	1,169.3	11,204.6	931.4	1,831.8	8,300.6	21,133.1
Fabricated metal products	1,279.2	11,022.1	980.9	1,971.4	7,577.5	21,966.3
Machinery, except electrical	1,743.5	16,235.0	1,187.2	2,334.8	9,740.0	30,680.9
Electrical equipment and supplies	1,659.0	14,436.7	1,119.4	2,182.7	8,140.0	27,874.2
Transportation equipment	1,620.8	16,697.8	1,186.0	2,370.8	11,047.9	34,845.0
Instruments and related products	381.7	3,345.7	244.9	465.1	1,732.9	8,385.9
Miscellaneous manufacturing industries	411.3	2,739.9	319.1	604.4	1,773.2	5,707.3
Ordnance and accessories[1]	258.0	2,876.9	134.5	282.1	934.4	4,601.3
Administrative and auxiliary[2]	936.8	11,956.5	—	—	—	—
All industries total	18,363.1	156,202.8	12,874.9	25,265.9	93,063.2	314,151.7

(1.) Includes data for privately owned or operated establishments. Gov. owned and operated establishments are excluded.
(2.) In addition to the employment and payroll for operating manufacturing establishments, manufacturing concerns reported separately for central administrative offices or auxiliary units (e.g., research laboratories, storage warehouses, power plants, garages, repair shops, etc.) which serve the manufacturing establishments of a company rather than the public.

Manufacturing Production Worker Statistics
Source: Bureau of Labor Statistics, U.S. Dept. of Labor[P] Preliminary

Year	All Employees	Production Workers	Payroll Index 1967 = 100	Average Earnings	Avg. Hourly Earnings	Avg. Hrs. Weekly
1955	16,882,000	13,288,000	61.1	75.70	1.86	40.7
1960	16,796,000	12,586,000	68.9	89.72	2.26	39.7
1965	18,062,000	13,434,000	88.1	107.53	2.61	41.2
1967	19,447,000	14,308,000	100.0	114.90	2.83	40.6
1968	19,781,000	14,514,000	108.3	122.51	3.01	40.7
1969	20,167,000	14,767,000	116.6	129.51	3.19	40.6
1970	19,349,000	14,020,000	114.1	133.73	3.36	39.8
1971	18,529,000	13,434,000	116.3	142.04	3.56	39.9
1972	18,933,000	13,838,000	130.2	154.69	3.81	40.6
1973 Jan.	19,279,000	14,130,000	137.1	159.20	3.98	40.0
Feb.	19,420,000	14,258,000	140.2	161.18	3.97	40.6
Mar.	19,521,000	14,345,000	141.7	162.38	3.98	40.8
Apr.	19,586,000	14,394,000	143.2	163.21	4.01	40.7
May	19,667,000	14,457,000	144.4	163.61	4.02	40.7
June	20,002,000	14,739,000	148.3	165.24	4.04	40.9
July[P]	19,724,000	14,460,000	145.3	165.24	4.07	40.6

Hourly Earnings in Manufacturing Industries
Source: Bureau of Labor Statistics, U.S. Dept. of Labor[P] Preliminary

Year and month (annual average)	Manufacturing		Durable goods		Nondurable goods	
	Gross	Excluding overtime	Gross	Excluding overtime	Gross	Excluding overtime
1950	$1.440	$1.39	$1.519	$1.46	$1.347	$1.31
1955	1.86	1.79	1.99	1.91	1.67	1.62
1960	2.26	2.20	2.43	2.36	2.05	1.99
1965	2.61	2.51	2.79	2.67	2.36	2.27
1967	2.83	2.72	3.00	2.88	2.57	2.47
1968	3.01	2.88	3.19	3.05	2.74	2.63
1969	3.19	3.06	3.38	3.24	2.91	2.79
1970	3.36	3.24	3.55	3.43	3.08	2.97
1971	3.56	3.44	3.79	3.66	3.26	3.14
1972	3.81	3.65	4.05	3.88	3.47	3.33
1973 Jan.	3.98	3.81	4.23	4.04	3.61	3.47
Feb.	3.97	3.80	4.23	4.03	3.59	3.45
Mar.	3.98	3.81	4.23	4.03	3.61	3.46
Apr.	4.01	3.83	4.26	4.06	3.63	3.48
May	4.02	3.85	4.28	4.08	3.64	3.50
June	4.04	3.86	4.30	4.09	3.66	3.51
July[P]	4.07	3.89	4.32	4.12	3.70	3.54

General Manufacturing Statistics for States

Source: Bureau of the Census, Census of Manufacturers 1971 preliminary report

Divisions, Regions and States	All employees		Production workers			Value added by mfr.	Mate-rials	Capital expend.
	Number (1,000)	Payroll (millions)	Number (1,000)	Man-hrs. (millions)	Wages (millions)	(millions)	(millions)	(millions)
New England Division	1,348.9	$10,968.3	917.4	1,788.2	$6,156.8	$19,871.9	$16,823.8	$1,109.2
Maine	95.4	615.6	78.5	151.6	448.7	1,208.3	1,303.3	120.8
New Hampshire	81.9	576.4	60.0	117.4	356.2	1,088.7	926.3	79.7
Vermont	37.4	296.2	25.6	51.9	161.3	562.1	540.4	49.7
Massachusetts	616.5	5,109.3	407.8	784.0	2,755.1	9,494.6	7,572.3	454.3
Rhode Island	110.6	757.8	84.5	162.5	486.9	1,468.9	1,248.4	80.0
Connecticut	407.0	3,613.0	261.0	520.7	1,948.5	6,049.3	5,233.2	324.7
Middle Atlantic Division ...	3,924.8	34,346.2	2,607.4	5,031.8	18,720.3	65,220.0	63,241.2	3,718.2
New York	1,701.9	15,263.4	1,076.1	2,066.3	7,648.0	28,862.2	25,961.4	1,431.7
New Jersey	796.5	7,258.2	517.4	1,023.5	3,880.9	14,393.8	14,540.0	798.4
Pennsylvania	1,426.4	11,824.6	1,013.9	1,941.5	7,191.4	21,964.0	22,739.8	1,487.9
East North Central Division	4,793.0	45,573.3	3,355.3	6,619.3	28,277.0	87,602.4	101,441.1	5,242.3
Ohio	1,331.5	12,512.9	922.3	1,819.3	7,796.1	23,991.7	25,920.7	1,310.2
Indiana	665.1	6,003.1	491.0	957.4	3,957.9	12,073.9	13,281.1	847.1
Illinois	1,282.2	11,701.6	871.2	1,708.9	6,875.9	22,789.8	25,109.0	1,476.3
Michigan	1,034.4	11,128.6	728.6	1,463.5	6,965.4	20,270.6	26,787.3	1,202.3
Wisconsin	479.8	4,227.1	342.2	670.2	2,681.7	8,476.4	10,343.0	406.4
West North Central Division	1,145.0	9,696.5	783.0	1,528.2	5,811.1	20,863.4	30,565.2	1,140.8
Minnesota	277.5	2,467.6	177.3	347.2	1,352.2	4,827.2	6,454.6	271.1
Iowa	200.8	1,729.3	143.2	279.8	1,122.3	3,941.1	6,317.0	262.6
Missouri	436.5	3,673.2	296.0	569.5	2,135.0	7,525.1	9,699.9	363.3
North Dakota	10.1	70.3	6.9	14.5	42.9	189.0	349.8	11.3
South Dakota	16.1	118.8	11.3	22.5	78.4	226.2	516.8	13.5
Nebraska	80.2	618.0	58.7	119.2	411.2	1,594.1	3,234.6	86.5
Kansas	123.8	1,019.3	89.6	175.5	669.2	2,560.6	3,992.5	132.5
South Atlantic Division	2,580.2	18,041.1	1,963.2	3,890.9	11,615.3	38,914.7	45,409.7	3,329.8
Delaware	69.6	734.8	34.5	71.5	282.2	1,281.0	1,951.8	78.2
Maryland	254.4	2,183.7	176.0	1,346.9	1,311.2	4,279.4	4,812.2	311.5
District of Columbia	21.8	215.2	10.2	18.1	95.6	380.1	269.7	27.7
Virginia	350.6	2,448.1	269.5	528.3	1,610.1	5,172.8	5,737.5	435.3
West Virginia	118.3	1,017.7	89.4	175.1	701.4	2,387.7	2,188.6	241.3
North Carolina	699.0	4,267.3	566.3	1,118.8	2,949.5	9,824.2	11,104.2	810.4
South Carolina	324.4	2,026.6	264.5	535.8	1,448.7	4,234.5	4,801.3	499.3
Georgia	433.7	2,865.5	340.3	674.8	1,920.3	6,533.2	9,372.4	508.4
Florida	308.5	2,282.2	211.6	422.0	1,296.4	4,821.8	5,172.1	417.0
East South Central Division	1,167.7	7,920.5	927.3	1,814.0	5,527.3	18,665.2	21,105.8	1,358.2
Kentucky	242.8	1,854.9	187.1	358.0	1,247.4	5,168.2	5,600.9	284.0
Tennessee	444.2	2,955.3	346.9	679.8	2,006.5	6,728.9	7,409.8	529.7
Alabama	299.0	2,040.1	243.1	479.8	1,485.6	4,530.9	5,041.2	355.5
Mississippi	181.7	1,070.2	150.2	296.4	787.8	2,237.2	3,053.9	189.0
West South Central Division	1,152.3	9,040.8	822.3	1,644.3	5,481.2	21,552.8	31,111.0	2,372.9
Arkansas	165.1	979.9	134.9	268.7	714.9	2,420.0	3,261.7	171.7
Louisiana	161.0	1,347.0	119.4	246.6	898.4	3,504.5	5,840.5	536.5
Oklahoma	132.2	1,024.0	88.2	173.5	567.4	1,834.4	2,719.0	158.4
Texas	694.0	5,689.8	480.3	955.5	3,300.5	13,793.9	19,289.8	1,506.3
Mountain Division	349.2	2,916.3	240.2	469.1	1,750.9	5,874.9	8,542.6	628.8
Montana	19.9	158.5	15.4	30.9	118.8	330.4	882.2	50.4
Idaho	43.7	316.4	33.3	64.1	208.8	669.0	1,001.6	54.2
Wyoming	6.4	51.1	4.8	9.8	37.8	119.4	244.2	6.3
Colorado	116.9	1,071.6	78.4	155.4	646.0	2,088.5	2,590.9	238.3
New Mexico	22.7	141.7	17.0	32.8	88.8	272.9	496.6	43.9
Arizona	82.6	721.1	52.4	102.3	387.3	1,384.6	1,775.7	142.2
Utah	49.5	391.4	33.5	63.3	223.0	864.2	1,388.1	71.9
Nevada	7.5	64.6	5.3	10.5	40.3	145.9	163.3	21.7
Pacific Division	1,869.6	17,524.5	1,240.9	2,418.8	9,764.5	35,124.5	37,196.0	2,060.2
Washington	220.7	2,061.8	148.2	276.5	1,205.6	4,117.0	5,560.8	364.5
Oregon	169.4	1,406.8	131.9	252.8	1,011.7	2,806.6	3,390.0	232.3
California	1,447.3	13,799.1	739.2	1,843.5	7,382.3	27,568.2	27,541.7	1,416.9
Alaska	7.7	80.1	6.0	11.6	59.0	197.7	237.6	18.5
Hawaii	24.4	176.6	17.5	34.3	105.7	435.0	465.9	28.0
Total	18,330.7	$156,027.5	12,857.0	25,204.6	$93,104.4	$313,689.8	$355,436.4	$20,960.4

Employees in Non-Agricultural Establishments

Source: Bureau of Labor Statistics, U.S. Dept. of Labor[P] Preliminary

ANNUAL AVERAGE BY INDUSTRY DIVISION
(In thousands)

Year	Total	Mining	Contract construc-tion	Manu-factur-ing	Trans. and public utilities	Whole., retail trade	Finance, insur., real estate	Service, miscel-laneous	Govern-ment
1955	50,675	792	2,802	16,882	4,141	10,535	2,335	6,274	6,914
1960	54,234	712	2,885	16,796	4,004	11,391	2,669	7,423	8,353
1965	60,815	632	3,186	18,062	4,036	12,716	3,023	9,087	10,074
1967	65,857	613	3,208	19,447	4,261	13,606	3,225	10,099	11,398
1968	67,915	606	3,285	19,781	4,310	14,084	3,382	10,623	11,845
1969	70,284	619	3,435	20,167	4,429	14,639	3,564	11,229	12,202
1970	70,593	623	3,381	19,349	4,493	14,914	3,688	11,612	12,535
1971	70,645	602	3,411	18,529	4,442	15,142	3,796	11,869	12,856
1972	72,764	607	3,521	18,933	4,495	15,683	3,927	12,309	13,290
1973 (July)[P]	75,404	644	3,933	19,724	4,654	16,241	4,112	12,985	13,111

Profits of Manufacturing Corporations by Industry Groups

Source: Federal Trade Commission and the Securities and Exchange Commission

Industry Group (Amounts estimated in millions of dollars)	Before Income Taxes 1972	Pct. of sales 1972	Pct. of sales 1971	Profits After Taxes 1972	Pct. of sales 1972	Pct. of sales 1971
Durable goods	33,602	7.7	6.9	18,448	4.2	3.8
Transportation equipment	8,331	7.5	7.1	4,419	4.0	3.8
Motor vehicles and equipment	6,905	8.9	8.7	3,639	4.7	4.6
Electrical machinery, equipment and supplies	5,571	7.2	6.4	2,999	3.9	3.5
Other machinery	6,614	9.2	8.3	3,481	4.8	4.2
Other fabricated metal products	2,944	6.5	5.7	1,569	3.4	2.9
Primary iron and steel	1,650	5.0	4.1	1,022	3.0	2.6
Primary nonferrous metals	1,050	5.6	4.7	687	3.7	3.3
Stone, clay, and glass products	1,810	7.9	7.8	1,060	4.6	4.5
Furniture and fixtures	690	7.0	5.9	369	3.7	3.0
Other lumber and wood products	1,606	8.0	6.8	1,012	5.0	4.4
Instruments and related products	2,736	14.8	13.3	1,514	8.2	7.2
Miscellaneous manufacturing	598	6.2	6.2	314	3.2	3.2
Nondurable goods	29,649	7.2	7.2	18,019	4.4	4.5
Food and kindred products	5,508	4.6	4.9	3,021	2.5	2.6
Tobacco manufactures	1,246	11.1	11.5	676	6.0	6.1
Textile mill products	1,212	4.7	4.6	659	2.6	2.4
Apparel and other finished products	1,237	4.3	4.3	679	2.3	2.4
Paper and allied products	1,584	6.8	4.3	941	4.0	2.3
Printing and publishing	2,498	8.6	7.8	1,335	4.6	4.1
Chemicals and allied products	7,904	11.2	10.8	4,499	6.4	6.1
Petroleum refining and related products	6,549	8.4	9.5	5,201	6.7	8.2
Petroleum refining[1]	6,455	8.4	9.6	5,151	6.6	8.3
Rubber and miscellaneous plastic products	1,599	7.4	6.6	859	4.0	3.6
Leather and leather products	314	5.1	4.8	148	2.4	2.2
All Manufacturing Corps.	63,249	7.4	7.0	36,467	4.3	4.1

[1] Included in major industry above.

Occupational Earnings in Selected Cities

Source: Bureau of Labor Statistics, Dept. Labor

(Average earnings (1) for selected occupations studied in 6 broad industry divisions: Manufacturing; transportation, communication, and other public utilities; wholesale; retail; finance, insurance, and real estate; and services, March-May 1973)

Occupations	Albany-Schenectady-Troy, N.Y.	Worcester, Mass.	Atlanta, Ga.	Houston, Tex.	Milwaukee, Wis.	Albuquerque, N.Mex.	San Francisco-Oakland, Calif.
Office workers – Men		Average weekly earnings, straight-time					
Accounting clerks[2]	$169.00	$163.00	$166.00	$178.00	$178.00	–	$182.00
Draftsmen[2]	–	217.50	206.50	211.50	214.00	–	232.00
Messengers (office boys)	108.00	90.50	108.00	100.00	113.00	$84.50	110.50
Office workers – Women							
Accounting clerks[2]	146.00	148.00	145.50	141.50	145.50	127.00	162.50
Billers (billing machine)	–	114.50	130.50	105.50	–	–	136.00
Bookkeeping-machine operators[2]	–	–	132.50	122.00	135.50	124.00	153.00
Keypunch operators[2]	133.00	130.00	147.00	124.50	127.50	110.50	151.00
Nurses, industrial (registered)	177.50	165.50	190.00	174.50	183.50	–	196.00
Messengers (office girls)	110.00	90.50	104.00	92.00	101.00	–	108.50
Payroll clerks	117.00	127.00	129.00	135.50	135.50	113.00	163.00
Secretaries	152.00	144.50	150.00	149.50	153.00	136.00	162.00
Stenographers (general)	127.00	125.50	131.50	127.50	122.00	106.00	129.00
Switchboard operators[2]	134.00	129.00	148.50	129.50	130.00	–	144.50
Typists[2]	131.00	115.00	126.00	117.00	121.50	102.50	125.50
Maintenace, custodial, and material movement workers – Men		Average hourly earnings, straight-time					
Carpenters	4.78	4.28	5.53	5.00	5.19	–	6.05
Electricians	4.98	4.92	5.46	5.27	5.89	4.81	5.89
Engineers, stationary	4.32	4.56	5.05	4.45	5.03	3.34	6.18
Helpers, trades	–	–	3.47	3.77	4.61	–	4.77
Machinists	5.03	4.59	5.24	5.35	5.77	–	5.92
Mechanics, automotive	5.25	4.54	5.08	5.03	5.61	5.43	6.60
Painters	4.60	–	5.23	4.76	5.62	–	6.27
Guards and watchmen	2.65	2.61	2.30	2.27	2.49	2.77	2.92
Janitors, porters, cleaners	3.18	3.02	2.29	2.18	2.92	2.38	3.77
Laborers, material handling	4.03	3.56	3.09	2.90	4.14	2.85	5.09
Packers, shipping	3.00	3.77	3.08	2.89	4.07	–	4.57
Shipping clerks	3.82	3.62	3.93	3.49	4.39	–	4.91
Truckdrivers, local	5.21	4.53	4.37	3.86	5.49	4.08	6.02

(1) Weekly earnings relate to regular straight-time salaries that are paid for standard workweeks. Hourly earnings exclude premium pay for overtime, weekends, holidays, or late shifts.

(2) More than one skill level surveyed. Earnings are for highest level surveyed.

NOTE: Maintenance plumbers are no longer surveyed by the Bureau.

Annual Rates of Profit on Stockholders' Equity

Source: Federal Trade Commission

(Each rate is the arithmetic mean of four quarterly rates, each on an annual basis.)

By industry after taxes: by percent	1950	1960	1965	1968	1969[1]	1970	1971	1972
All manufacturing corporations, except newspapers	15.4	9.2	13.0	12.1	11.5	9.3	9.7	10.6
Durable goods industries	16.8	8.6	13.8	12.2	11.4	8.3	9.1	10.8
Metals and metal fabricating industries	16.9	8.6	14.2	12.0	11.2	*	*	*
Transportation equipment	21.5	11.7	18.5	14.7	12.0	6.3	11.2	12.5
Motor vehicles and equipment	25.2	13.5	19.5	15.1	12.6	6.1	13.0	14.6
Aircraft and parts	*	7.4	15.1	14.2	10.6	6.8	5.8	7.9
Electrical machinery, equipment and supplies	20.8	9.5	13.5	12.2	11.1	9.1	9.5	10.8
Machinery, except electrical	14.0	7.6	14.1	12.3	12.2	9.9	8.7	10.6
Metalworking machinery and equipment	*	5.3	14.4	12.4	11.6	8.3	3.8	6.5
Other fabricated metal products	15.9	5.6	13.2	11.7	11.3	8.6	8.3	10.8
Primary metal industries	14.5	7.2	10.6	8.9	9.5	7.0	4.8	6.0
Blast furnaces, steel works and foundries	14.3	7.2	9.8	7.6	7.6	4.3	4.5	6.0
Nonferrous metals	15.0	7.1	11.9	10.7	12.2	10.7	5.1	5.9
Other durable goods industries	16.3	8.6	12.2	12.8	12.4	*	*	*
Lumber and wood products, except furniture	17.4	3.6	10.0	14.6	13.2	5.9	11.3	16.2
Furniture and fixtures	15.1	6.5	13.3	12.2	12.6	7.9	9.5	13.3
Stone, clay and glass products	17.6	9.9	10.2	9.2	9.2	6.9	9.1	10.1
Instruments and related products	16.7	11.6	17.5	16.5	15.6	14.2	13.5	14.8
Miscellaneous manufacturing and ordnance	12.2	9.2	10.7	12.4	11.6	10.0	9.0	10.7
Nondurable goods industries	14.0	9.8	12.2	11.9	11.5	10.3	10.3	10.5
Chemicals; petroleum, rubber and plastics	15.4	10.8	13.0	12.6	12.0	*	*	*
Chemicals and allied products	17.8	12.2	15.2	13.3	12.8	11.5	11.8	12.8
Basic chemicals and related products	*	11.1	14.3	11.0	10.5	8.5	8.7	10.0
Drugs	*	16.0	20.0	19.2	19.4	17.0	17.0	18.0
Petroleum refining and related industries	13.8	10.1	11.8	12.2	11.7	11.0	10.3	8.7
Petroleum refining	*	10.1	11.8	12.3	11.7	11.0	10.3	8.7
Rubber and miscellaneous plastics products	16.7	9.1	11.7	12.2	10.4	7.1	9.6	10.8
Other nondurable goods industries	12.8	8.5	11.1	10.9	10.8	*	*	*
Food and kindred products	12.3	8.7	10.7	10.7	10.9	10.8	11.0	11.0
Dairy products	*	*	10.6	9.8	10.1	10.2	11.1	10.1
Bakery products	*	*	9.3	11.7	8.6	8.8	10.7	10.6
Alcoholic beverages	*	7.1	9.3	10.1	10.3	10.5	10.6	10.7
Tobacco manufacturers	11.5	13.4	13.5	14.4	14.4	15.7	15.7	15.4
Textile mill products	12.6	5.8	10.8	8.8	7.9	5.1	6.6	7.5
Apparel and other fabricated textile products	10.1	7.7	12.6	12.9	11.9	9.3	11.0	11.9
Paper and allied products	16.1	8.5	9.4	9.7	10.1	7.0	4.8	9.0
Printing and publishing, except newspapers	11.5	10.6	14.1	12.6	12.6	11.2	10.7	12.0
Leather and leather products	10.9	6.3	11.6	13.0	9.3	9.4	8.2	9.1

* — Not available. (1). Includes newspapers for the first time.

Personal Consumption Expenditures for the U.S.

Source: Bureau of Economic Analysis, U.S. Department of Commerce

(In millions of dollars)

	1950	1955	1960	1965	1969	1970	1971	1972
Food and tobacco	58,120	72,236	87,510	107,183	130,707	111,181	148,344	157,892
Clothing, accessories and jewelry	23,709	27,982	33,032	43,318	59,924	62,834	66,961	72,676
Personal care	2,438	3,461	5,324	7,578	9,760	10,420	10,600	11,119
Housing	21,286	33,738	46,305	63,509	84,141	90,926	98,477	105,517
Household operation	29,461	37,322	46,906	61,789	82,294	87,360	93,836	104,830
Medical care	8,788	12,755	19,116	28,082	42,814	47,401	52,015	57,431
Personal business	6,858	10,049	14,974	21,879	33,277	35,314	38,641	41,226
Transportation	24,672	35,574	43,134	58,154	77,772	77,776	90,441	100,159
Recreation	11,147	14,078	18,295	26,298	36,901	40,653	42,652	47,826
Private education and research	1,618	2,339	3,718	5,927	9,536	10,363	10,849	12,008
Religious and welfare activities	2,282	3,257	4,748	5,072	8,084	8,601	9,134	10,096
Foreign travel and remittances—net	630	1,590	2,179	3,150	4,247	4,815	5,201	5,726
Total personal consumption Expenditures	191,009	254,381	325,241	432,839	579,457	617,644	667,151	726,506

Work Stoppages (Strikes) in the United States

Source: Bureau of Labor Statistics, U.S. Department of Labor

Year	Number stoppages	Workers involved	Man days idle	Year	Number stoppages	Workers involved	Man days idle
Average 1935 to 1939	2,862	1,130,000	16,900,000	1967	4,595	2,870,000	42,100,000
				1968	5,045	2,649,000	49,018,000
War Period Dec. 8, 1941- Aug. 14, 1945	14,371	6,744,000	36,300,000	1969	5,700	2,481,000	42,869,000
				1970	5,716	3,305,000	66,414,000
				1971	5,138	3,280,000	47,589,000
				1972[1]	5,100	1,700,000	26,000,000
Average 1947-49	3,573	2,380,000	39,700,000	1973 Jan.	310	118,000	1,433,000
				Feb.	380	141,000	1,281,000
1950	4,843	2,410,000	38,800,000	Mar.	410	110,000	1,330,000
1955	4,320	2,650,000	28,200,000	Apr.	470	146,000	1,890,000
1960	3,333	1,320,000	19,100,000	May	580	155,000	2,483,000
1965	3,963	1,550,000	23,300,000	June	520	238,000	2,173,000

[1] Preliminary

Retail Store Sales, by Kind of Business

Source: Bureau of the Census, U.S. Dept. of Commerce. In millions of dollars

Kinds of business	1972	1971	Kinds of business	1972	1971
All retail stores[1]	448,379	408,850			
Durable goods store[1]	149,659	131,814	Apparel group	21,993	20,804
Automotive group	88,612	78,916	Men's and boys' wear stores	5,198	4,727
Motor vehicle, other			Women's apparel, accessory		
automotive dealers	81,521	72,538	stores	8,386	8,193
Tire, battery, accessory			Shoe stores	3,774	3,532
dealers	7,091	6,378	Food group[1]	95,020	89,239
Furniture and appliance group	21,315	18,560	Grocery stores	88,340	82,793
Furniture, home furnishings			General merchandise group		
stores	12,550	11,004	with non stores	74,903	68,134
Household appliance, radio			Department stores, excl.		
T.V. stores	7,029	6,221	mail order	46,302	42,027
Lumber, building, hardware			Mail order (catalog sales)	4,997	4,301
group	20,238	17,378	Variety stores	7,756	6,972
Lumber, building materials			Eating and drinking places	33,891	31,131
dealers	15,973	13,733	Gasoline service stations	31,044	29,163
Hardware stores	4,265	3,645	Drug and proprietary stores	14,523	13,736
Nondurable goods stores	298,720	277,036	Liquor stores	9,215	8,773

(1) Sales by jewelry stores, other durable goods stores, other general merchandise stores, and other nondurable goods stores are not shown separately but are included in totals.

Total Retail Stores Sales (In millions of dollars)—(1955) 183,851; (1956) 189,729; (1957) 200,002; (1958) 200,353; (1959) 215,413; (1960) 219,529; (1961) 218,992; (1962) 235,563; (1963) 246,666; (1964) 261,870; (1965) 284,128; (1966) 303,956; (1967) 313,809; (1968) 341,876; (1969) 357,885; (1970) 375,527; (1971) 408,850.

Cotton, Wool, Silk, and Man-Made Fibers Production

Source: Economic Research Service, U.S. Dept. of Agriculture

Cotton and wool from reports of the Dept. of Agriculture; silk, rayon and non-cellulosic man-made fibers from Textile Organon, a publication of the Textile Economics Bureau, Inc.

Year	Cotton[1] U.S.	Cotton[1] World	Wool[2] U.S.	Wool[2] World	Silk World	Rayon & Acetate U.S.	Rayon & Acetate World	Non-Cellulosic[4] U.S.	Non-Cellulosic[4] World
	Mil. bales[5]	Mil. bales[5]	Mil. lb.	Mil. lb.	Mil. lb.	Mil. lb.	Mil.	Mil.	Mil.
1940	12.6	31.2	434.0	4,180	130	471.2	2,485.3	4.6	4.6
1950	10.0	30.6	249.3	4,000	42	1,259.4	3,552.8	145.9	177.4
1960	14.2	46.2	298.9	5,615	68	1,028.5	5,749.1	854.2	1,779.1
1964	15.1	52.8	237.4	5,766	71	1,431.8	7,245.4	1,646.2	4,067.3
1965	15.0	54.6	224.8	5,836	72	1,527.0	7,359.4	2,062.4	4,928.9
1966	9.6	49.8	219.2	5,958	72	1,519.0	7,364.8	2,415.2	5,965.7
1967	7.4	48.9	211.4	6,040	75	1,388.1	7,306.4	2,662.1	6,828.5
1968	10.9	54.2	197.9	6,295	82	1,594.3	7,778.4	3,632.1	8,978.7
1969	10.0	52.5	182.8	6,248	86	1,576.2	7,837.2	4,029.3	10,506.6
1970	10.2	52.4	176.8	6,155	90	1,373.2	7,568.9	4,053.5	11,942.9
1971	10.5	57.3	172.2	6,006	88	1,392.4	7,587.7	4,761.0	14,157.5
1972[6]	13.7	56.7	167.6	5,846	88	1,394.3	7,787.4	5,927.3	16,212.0

(1.) Year beginning Aug. 1. (2.) Grease basis. (3.) Includes filament yarn and staple and tow fiber. (4.) Includes textile glass fiber. (5.) 480-pound net weight bales, U.S. beginning 1960 and World beginning 1965. (6.) Preliminary.

World Production of Natural Rubber

Source: Business and Defense Services Administration, U. S. Dept. of Commerce

Long Tons—Estimated

Year	Far East	Tropical America	Africa	Total	Year	Far East	Tropical America	Africa	Total
1940	1,357,000	26,000	16,000	1,399,000	1966	2,195,038	30,962	174,000	2,400,000
1945	170,500	48,000	53,500	272,000	1967	2,261,417	27,833	163,250	2,452,500
1950	1,760,500	27,000	55,000	1,842,500	1968	2,396,000	29,958	167,022	2,593,000
1955	1,787,000	27,500	98,000	1,912,500	1969	2,630,000	30,500	178,100	2,838,600
1960	1,813,267	29,733	147,000	1,990,000	1970	2,811,500	31,500	209,600	3,052,600
1964	2,041,374	34,876	158,750	2,235,000	1971	2,788,400	30,700	191,600	3,010,700
1965	2,149,673	35,827	157,000	2,342,500	1972	2,831,400	32,900	184,000	3,048,300

Distilled Spirits and Beer Production

Source: Internal Revenue Service. (Figures show thousands of tax gallons or barrels)

Year fiscal	Whky.	Rm.	Bdy.	Alcoh.	Total*	Beer Total	Year fiscal	Whky.	Rm.	Bdy.	Alcoh.	Total*	Beer Total
	Gals.	Gals.	Gals.	Gals.	Gals.	Bbls.		Gals.	Gals.	Gals.	Gals.	Gals.	Bbls.
1945	41,562	2,888	26,596	1,101,286	1,174,391	86,608	1965	117,930	2,274	11,522	695,332	865,240	108,015
1950	118,760	1,781	5,364	391,129	521,770	88,807	1970	160,039	1,029	14,785	691,767	917,457	134,654
1955	103,927	2,005	4,008	465,069	593,982	89,791	1971	127,220	1,011	13,662	569,971	759,251	134,092
1960	149,545	1,866	10,114	613,924	803,751	94,541	1972	126,274	1,313	15,210	569,034	764,351	140,327

*Includes gin, vodka and Okelehao.

Full-time and Part-time Status of Civilian Labor Force (Seasonally adjusted)

Source: Bureau of Labor Statistics, U.S. Dept. of Labor (in thousands)

Employment Status	July	Aug.	Sept.	Oct.	Nov.	Dec.	Jan.	Feb.	Mar.	April	May	June	July
			1972							1973			
Total, 16 years and over													
Full Time Civilian Labor Force	74,143	74,261	74,275	74,688	74,402	74,715	74,935	75,244	75,557	75,604	75,818	76,181	75,963
Employed	70,384	70,482	70,572	70,947	70,969	71,224	71,491	71,755	72,136	72,213	72,487	72,984	72,847
Unemployed	3,759	3,779	3,703	3,741	3,433	3,491	3,444	3,489	3,421	3,391	3,329	3,197	3,116
Unemployment rate	5.1	5.1	5.0	5.0	4.6	4.7	4.6	4.6	4.5	4.5	4.4	4.2	4.1
Part Time Civilian Labor Force	12,275	12,738	12,931	12,559	12,679	12,705	12,220	12,589	12,708	12,873	12,787	12,456	12,538
Employed	11,277	11,616	11,811	11,495	11,616	11,640	11,249	11,600	11,754	11,792	11,690	11,386	11,489
Unemployed	998	1,122	1,120	1,064	1,063	1,065	971	989	954	1,081	1,097	1,070	1,049
Unemployment rate	8.1	8.8	8.7	8.5	8.4	8.4	7.9	7.9	7.5	8.4	8.6	8.6	8.4

Labor-Union Memberships

Source: AFL-CIO and World Almanac Questionnaire
UNIONS WITH A MEMBERSHIP OF 25,000 OR OVER (As of June 1973)

AFL-CIO UNIONS	MEMBERS
Actors and Artistes of America, Associated	76,000
Air Line Pilots Association	41,000
Aluminum Workers International Union	26,000
Bakery and Confectionery Workers International Union of America	131,000
Barbers, Hairdressers and Cosmetologists' International Union of America, the Journeymen	49,000
Boilermakers, Iron Ship Builders, Blacksmiths, Forgers and Helpers, International Brotherhood of	116,000
Boot and Shoe Workers' Union	36,000
Brewery, Flour, Cereal, Soft Drink and Distillery Workers, International Union of United	40,000
Bricklayers, Masons and Plasterers International Union of America	139,000
Carpenters and Joiners of America, United Brotherhood of	700,000
Cement, Lime and Gypsum Workers International Union, United	30,000
Chemical Workers Union, Intl.	70,000
Clothing Workers of America, Amalgamated	252,000
Communications Workers of America	467,000
Electrical, Radio and Machine Workers, International Union of	200,000
Electrical Workers, International Brotherhood of	778,000
Engineers, International Union of Operating	300,000
Farm Workers, United	(A)
Fire Fighters, International Association of	105,000
Firemen and Oilers, International Brotherhood of	40,000
Furniture Workers of America, United	30,000
Garment Workers of America, United	32,000
Garment Workers Union, International Ladies'	363,000
Glass and Ceramic Workers of North America, United	30,000
Glass Bottle Blowers' Association of the United States and Canada	74,000
Glass Workers Union, American Flint	35,000
Government Employees, American Federation of	260,000
Grain Millers, American Federation of	26,000
Graphic Arts Intl. Union	97,000
Hotel and Restaurant Employees' and Bartenders' International Union	332,000
Industrial Workers of America, International Union, Allied	90,000
Iron Workers, International Association of Bridge and Structural	160,000
Laborers' International Union of North America	475,000
Leather Goods, Plastics and Novelty Workers Union, International	40,000
Letter Carriers, National Association of	151,000
Longshoremen's Association AFL-CIO, International	59,000
Machinists and Aerospace Workers, International Association of	627,000
Maintenance of Way Employees, Brotherhood of	72,000
Maritime Union of America, National	43,000
Meat Cutters and Butcher Workmen of North America, Amalgamated	471,000
Mechanics Educational Society of America	25,000
Molders and Allied Workers Union AFL-CIO, International	50,000
Musicians, American Federation of	206,000
Newspaper Guild, American	26,000
Office and Professional Employees International Union	68,000
Oil, Chemical and Atomic Workers International Union	145,000
Painters and Allied Trades of the United States and Canada, International Brotherhood of	160,000
Paperworkers International Union, United	242,000
Plasters' and Cement Masons' International Association of the United States and Canada, Operative	68,000
Plumbing and Pipe Fitting Industry of the United States and Canada, United Association of Journeymen and Apprentices of the	228,000
Postal Workers Union, American	239,000

AFL-CIO UNIONS	MEMBERS
Printing Pressmen's and Assistants' Union of North America, International	103,000
Railway Carmen of the United States and Canada, Brotherhood	62,000
Railway, Airline and Steamship Clerks, Freight Handlers, Express and Station Employees, Brotherhood of	152,000
Retail Clerks International Association	586,000
Retail, Wholesale and Department Store Union	96,000
Roofers, Damp and Waterproof Workers Association, United Slate, Tile and Composition	26,000
Rubber, Cork, Linoleum and Plastic Workers of America, United	171,000
Seafarers International Union of North America	80,000
Service Employees International Union, AFL-CIO	437,000
Sheet Metal Workers International Association	120,000
Shoe Workers of America, United	33,000
Stage Employees and Moving Picture Machine Operators of the United States and Canada, International Alliance of Theatrical	50,000
State, County and Municipal Employees, American Federation of	565,000
Stonecutters of America, United	891,000
Teachers, American Federation of	229,000
Textile Workers of America, United	38,000
Textile Workers Union of America	115,000
Tobacco Workers International Union	25,000
Transit Union, Amalgamated	88,000
Transport Workers Union of America	95,000
Transportation Union, United	134,000
Typographical Union, International	80,000
Upholsters' International Union of North America	50,000
Utility Workers Union of America	59,000
Woodworkers of America, International	56,000

INDEPENDENT UNIONS

INDEPENDENT UNIONS	MEMBERS
Automobile, Aerospace and Agricultural Implement Workers of America, Intl. Union, United	1,400,000
Chemical Workers Union, Int.	86,000
Civil Service Association of Ontario, The	30,499
Distributive Workers of America, Natl. Council of	40,000
Electrical, Radio and Machine Workers of America, United	165,000
Federal Employees, Nat'l. Federation of	100,000
Government Employees, Nat'l. Assn. of	200,000
Internal Revenue Employees, Nat'l. Assn.	26,360
Letter Carriers Ass'n. Nat'l. Rural	41,192
Locomotive Engineers, Brotherhood of	39,000
Longshoremen's and Warehousemen's Union Int'l.	60,000
Mine Workers of America, United	450,000
Postal Union, National	80,000
Postal and Federal Employees, Nat'l. Alliance of	45,000
Postal Supervisors, Nat'. Assn. of	33,000
Postmasters, Nat'l Assn. of	28,273
Teamsters, Chauffeurs, Warehousemen and Helpers of America, Int'l. Brotherhood of	2,000,000
Telephone Unions, Alliance of Independent	53,098

CLC UNIONS

CLC UNIONS	MEMBERS
Automobile, Aerospace and Agricultural Implement Workers of America, International Union, United	111,219
Public Employees, Canadian Union of	138,088
Public Service Alliance of Canada — Union of National Defense Employees	28,450
Railway, Transport and General Workers, Canadian Brotherhood of	33,037

CNTU UNIONS

CNTU UNIONS	MEMBERS
Government Employees' Union, Quebec	30,000
Public Service Employees Inc., Federation of	28,149
Services, Inc., National Federation of	52,307
Steel, Mine and Chemical Workers, Federation of	30,641

(A) United Farm Workers claims 60,000 membership during peak dues paying periods.

Mineral Production in United States[1]

Source: Bureau of Mines

MINERAL FUELS	1971 Quantity	1971 Value (thousands)	1972 Quantity	1972 Value (thousands)
Asphalt and related bitumens (native):				
Bituminous limestone & sandstone & gilsonite...short tons	1,668,928	$8,291	1,995,374	$10,303
Carbon dioxide, natural (e)........... thousand cubic feet	1,271,995	216	1,228,741	165
Coal:Bituminous and lignite[2]........ thousand short tons	552,192	3,901,496	595,386	4,561,983
Pennsylvania anthracite........ thousand short tons	8,727	103,469	7,100	85,251
Helium: Crude........................ million cubic feet	3,988	47,856	3,462	41,544
Grade A........................ million cubic feet	577	14,539	627	15,603
Natural gas.......................... million cubic feet	22,493,012	(r)4,085,482	22,531,698	4,185,869
Natural gas liquids:Gasoline products . thousand 42-gal. bbls.	200,181	616,657	193,480	604,423
LP gases.........thousand 42-gal. bbls.	417,634	769,397	444,736	847,810
Peat................... thousand short tons	600	7,011	607	7,112
Petroleum (crude)................,........ thousand 42-gal. bbls.	3,453,914	11,692,998	3,455,368	11,706,510
Total mineral fuels...................................	XX	(r)21,247,000	XX	22,067,000
NON METALS (except fuels)				
Abrasive stones[3]............................. short tons	2,349	563	3,241	670
Asbestos.................................... short tons	130,882	12,174	131,663	13,408
Barite................,.......... thousand short tons	825	13,491	906	14,883
Boron minerals .... thousand short tons	1,047	89,856	1,121	95,882
Bromine............................... thousand pounds	355,946	61,750	386,864	63,689
Calcium-magnesium chloride.................. short tons	W	W	W	W
Cement: Portland .... thousand short tons	75,881	1,421,388	77,973	1,588,290
Masonry.............. thousand short tons	3,341	84,556	3,777	100,269
Natural and slag .... thousand short tons	W	W	W	W
Clays.............................. thousand short tons	56,666	274,431	59,456	303,022
Diatomite .... short tons	535,318	34,392	576,089	37,554
Feldspar .... short tons	742,810	9,969	732,439	10,372
Fluorspar .... short tons	272,071	17,263	250,347	17,315
Garnet (abrasive) .... short tons	18,984	1,934	18,916	1,957
Gem stones (e)...................................	NA	2,589	NA	2,728
Gypsum .... thousand short tons	10,418	39,057	12,328	48,504
Lime .... thousand short tons	19,591	308,100	20,290	339,304
Magnesium compounds from sea water and brine				
(except for metals) .... short tons, MgO equivalent	668,649	62,322	729,472	63,915
Mica: Scrap......................... thousand short tons	127	2,917	160	4,354
Sheet .... pounds	17,005	7	14,280	7
Perlite .... short tons	432,208	4,941	544,594	6,231
Phosphate rock .... thousand short tons	38,886	203,828	40,831	207,910
Potassium salts ...... thousand short tons, K2O equivalent	2,587	100,527	2,659	106,680
Pumice .... thousand short tons	(r)3,391	(r)5,214	3,813	6,539
Pyrites .... thousand long tons	808	7,137	741	6,652
Salt .... thousand short tons	44,077	303,687	45,022	296,772
Sand and gravel...................... thousand short tons	919,593	1,148,969	913,375	1,199,520
Sodium carbonate (natural)........... thousand short tons	2,878	60,774	3,218	71,689
Sodium sulfate (natural)............. thousand short tons	688	11,008	701	11,396
Stone[4] .... thousand short tons	(r)876,123	(r)1,594,065	923,852	1,683,332
Sulfur: Frasch process mines .... thousand long tons	(r)6,738	(r)117,894	7,613	132,385
Other mines .... thousand long tons	....	....	....	....
Talc, soapstone, and pyrophyllite.............. short tons	1,037,297	7,634	1,107,404	7,835
Tripoli.................................... short tons	75,134	569	87,864	797
Vermiculite.......................... thousand short tons	301	7,198	337	8,092
Value of items that cannot be disclosed: Aplite, brucite, emery, graphite, iodine, kyanite, lithium, minerals, magnesite, greensand marl, olivine, staurolite, wollastonite, and values of nonmetal items indicated by symbol W	XX	(r)47,358	XX	(r)39,730
Total nonmetals	XX	(r)6,058,000	XX	(r)6,492,000
METALS				
Antimony ore & concentrate, short tons, antimony content	1,025	933	489	386
Bauxite .... thousand long tons, dried equivalent	1,988	28,543	1,812	23,238
Beryllium concentrate............. short tons, gross weight	W	W	W	W
Copper (recoverable content of ores, etc.)...... short tons	1,522,183	1,583,071	1,664,840	1,704,796
Gold (recoverable content of ores, etc.) .... troy ounces	1,495,108	61,673	1,449,943	84,967
Iron ore, (excluding iron sinter) thousand long tons, gr. wgt.	77,106	891,002	77,883	950,395
Lead (recoverable content of ores, etc.) .... short tons	578,550	159,679	618,915	186,046
Manganese ore (35% or more Mn).. short tons, gross weight	142	W	578	W
Manganiferous ore (5 to 35% Mn) .. short tons, gross weight	198,334	W	147,161	W
Mercury................................ 76-pound flasks	(r)17,883	(r)5,229	7,286	1,590
Molybdenum (content of concentrate) ... thousand pounds	97,882	164,917	102,197	170,530
Nickel (content of ore and concentrate)........ short tons	17,036	W	16,864	W
Rare-earth metal concentrates................. short tons	17,194	7,538	19,520	8,479
Silver (recoverable content of ores, etc.) thousand troy ozs.	41,564	64,258	37,233	62,737
Titanium concentrate, ilmenite... short tons, gross weight	(r)713,610	(r)15,936	725,728	16,265
Tungsten ore and concentrate... short tons, 60% WO3 basis	7,173	20,184	7,401	18,104
Uranium (recoverable content U3O8) ..... thousand pounds	(r)24,515	(r)151,996	25,758	162,272
Vanadium (recoverable in ore and concentrate) .. short tons	5,252	37,690	4,887	30,867
Zinc (recoverable content of ores, etc.)......... short tons	491,407	158,234	478,318	169,803
Value of items that cannot be disclosed: symbol W	XX	51,690	XX	50,664
Total metals	XX	(r)3,641,000	XX	3,641,000
Grand total mineral production	XX	(r)30,708,000	XX	32,199,000

(e) Estimate. (r) Revised. NA Not available. (W) Withheld to avoid disclosing individual company confidential data; included with "Value of items that cannot be disclosed." (XX) Not applicable.
(1) Production as measured by mine shipments, sales, or marketable production (including consumption by producers).
(2) Includes a small quantity of anthracite mined in States other than Pennsylvania. In 1971 value excluded that of Arizona, to avoid disclosing confidential data; value included with "Nonmetal items that cannot be disclosed."
(3) Grindstones, pulpstones, grinding pebbles, sharpening stones, and tube mill liners.
(4) Excludes abrasive stone, bituminous limestone, bituminous sandstone, and soapstone, all included elsewhere.

Mineral Production in U.S.—Leading States

Source: Bureau of Mines (1971)

STATE	VALUE (thousands)	RANK	Percent of U.S. total	PRINCIPAL MINERALS, in order of value
Texas..............	$6,807,955	1	22.15	Petroleum, natural gas, natural gas liquids, cement.
Louisiana..........	5,530,009	2	18.07	Petroleum, natural gas, natural gas liquids, sulfur.
California.........	1,920,648	3	6.25	Petroleum, natural gas, cement, sand and gravel.
West Virginia......	1,273,960	4	4.15	Coal, natural gas, stone, sand and gravel.
Oklahoma..........	1,189,516	5	3.87	Petroleum, natural gas, natural gas liquids, stone.
Pennsylvania......	1,149,107	6	3.74	Coal, cement, stone, sand and gravel.
New Mexico........	1,046,484	7	3.41	Petroleum, natural gas, copper, potassium salts.
Arizona............	981,020	8	3.19	Copper, molybdenum, cement, sand and gravel.
Kentucky..........	925,884	9	3.01	Coal, stone, petroleum, natural gas.
Wyoming...........	717,864	10	2.34	Petroleum, natural gas, sodium carbonate, uranium.

Value of Mineral Production in the United States[2]

Source: Bureau of Mines (r-Revised)
(In millions of dollars)

Year[1]	Fuels	Nonme-tallic	Metals	Total[3]	Year[1]	Fuels	Nonme-tallic	Metals	Total[3]
1930....	2,500	973	501	3,980	1966.....	15,088	5,176	2,703	22,968
1940....	2,662	784	752	4,198	1967.....	16,195	5,200	2,327	r23,723
1950....	8,689	1,882	1,351	11,862	1968.....	16,820	5,449	2,698	r24,966
1960....	12,142	3,868	2,022	18,032	1969.....	17,965	5,624	3,333	26,921
1963....	13,317	4,316	2,002	19,635	1970.....	20,152	r5,712	3,928	r29,792
1964....	13,623	4,623	2,366	20,612	1971.....	21,247	6,058	3,403	30,708
1965....	14,047	4,933	2,544	21,524	1972.....	22,067	6,492	3,641	32,199

(1.) Excludes Alaska and Hawaii, 1930-53. (2.) Production as measured by mine shipments sales or marketable production. (3.) Data may not add to total because of rounding figures. (P.) Preliminary.

United States Pig Iron and Steel Output

Source: American Iron and Steel Institute; figures show net tons

Year	Total pig iron	Pig iron and ferro-alloys	Raw steel	Year	Total pig iron	Pig iron and ferro-alloys	Raw Steel
1940.......	46,071,666	47,398,529	66,982,686	1967.......	86,984,000	89,472,000	127,213,000
1945.......	53,223,169	54,919,029	79,701,648	1968.......	88,780,000	91,362,000	131,462,000
1950.......	64,586,907	66,400,311	96,836,075	1969.......	95,017,000	97,593,000	141,262,000
1955.......	76,857,417	79,263,865	117,036,085	1970.......	91,435,000	93,851,000	131,514,000
1960.......	66,480,648	68,566,384	99,281,601	1971.......	81,299,000	83,468,000	120,443,000
1965.......	88,184,901	90,918,040	131,461,601	1972.......	88,942,000	91,338,000	133,241,000

Steel figures include only that portion of the capacity and production of steel for castings used by foundries which were operated by companies producing steel ingots.

Raw Steel Production
(Thousands of Net Tons)

State	1972
New York...........................	4,114
Pennsylvania.......................	30,416
R. I., Conn, N. J., Del., Md........	6,224
Va., W. Va., Ga., Fla., N. C., S. C.	5,562
Kentucky...........................	2,463
Ala., Tenn., Miss..................	4,812
Ohio...............................	23,851
Indiana............................	21,268
Illinois...........................	12,152
Michigan...........................	9,380
Minn., Mo., Okla., Texas...........	4,843
Ariz., Colo., Utah, Wash., Ore., Hawaii.	4,594
California.........................	3,562
Total..............................	133,241

1972 Scrap Iron Production and Export

Source: Institute of Scrap Iron & Steel
(net tons 2,000 pounds each)

The United States generated an estimated 95,552,828 tons of ferrous scrap. Of this total, 31,851,000 tons is attributed to "prompt industrial" scrap, the leftovers from the fabrication of new iron and steel products.

Consumption of mill revert and purchased scrap......................	90,404,308
Consumption of purchased scrap only....................	41,766,790 n.t. (est.)
Value of exports........................	$233,395,596
Sales of scrap amounted to............	$3,154,000,000
Exports of iron and steel scrap............	7,176,222 n.t.
Imports of iron and steel scrap..............	312,000 n.t.

(Export and import figures are from Minerals Yearbook, Dept. or Interior)

U.S. Primary Aluminum Production

Source: The Aluminum Association

Year	Short tons	Year	Short tons	Year	Short tons	Year	Short tons
1883-1902 ..	13,981	1930......	114,518	1964......	2,552,747	1968......	3,255,042
1903-1912 ..	108,412	1940......	206,280	1965......	2,754,478	1969	3,793,062
1913-1923 ..	282,722	1950......	718,622	1966......	2,968,366	1970......	3,976,148
1924-1925 ...	145,340	1960......	2,014,498	1967......	3,269,259	1971......	3,925,224
						1972......	4,122,392

Estimated Markets For Total U.S. Aluminum Shipments (Data for 1972)

Market	Thousands of Lbs.	Percent	Market	Thousands of Lbs.	Percent
Building & Construction .	3,168,000	26.5%	Containers & Packaging .	1,816,000	15.2%
Transportation..........	2,214,000	18.5%	Exports	562,000	4.7%
Consumer Durables	1,107,000	9.2%	Other	854,000	7.1%
Electrical..............	1,523,000	12.7%			
Machinery & Equipment .	736,000	6.1%	Total Industry	11,980,000	100.0%

Copper, Lead and Zinc Production in the U.S.

Source: Bureau of Mines

Year	Copper Mil. lbs.	Copper $1,000	Lead[1] Short Tons	Lead $1,000	Zinc Short tons	Zinc Mil. dol.	Year	Copper Mil. lbs.	Copper $1,000	Lead[1] Short Tons	Lead $1,000	Zinc Short tons	Zinc Mil. dol.
1950	1,823	379,122	418,809	113,078	591,454	167	1968	2,445	1,008,195	359,156	94,903	529,446	143
1960	2,286	733,708	228,899	53,562	334,101	87	1969	3,089	1,468,400	509,013	151,635	553,124	162
1965	2,703	957,028	301,147	93,959	611,153	178	1970	3,439	1,984,484	571,767	178,609	534,136	164
1966	2,858	1,033,850	327,368	98,964	572,558	166	1971	3,044	1,583,071	578,550	159,679	491,407	158
1967	1,908	729,401	316,931	88,741	549,413	151	1972	3,330	1,704,796	618,915	186,046	478,318	170

(1.) Production from domestic ores.

Energy

Energy: Get A Horse?

by Hana Umlauf

President Nixon's energy adviser John A. Love announced, Oct. 2, the immediate institution of a system of mandatory allocations of propane gas under a priority program. He also said detailed regulations affecting heating oil would be announced and placed into effect shortly. The controls were being instituted, Love said, because it was clear the nation "will experience some fuel shortages this winter and perhaps over the next few years."

The announcement confirmed the gloomy predictions that winter fuel shortages were impending. Added to the summer's short supply of gasoline—which had forced many gas stations to close—the priority rationing program supported the widely-argued conviction that the United States was in the midst of a severe energy crisis.

Nixon Energy Policy

On April 19, President Richard M. Nixon outlined his energy policy for Congress. There was no alarm in the President's message, although he did recognize that "if present trends go unchecked we could face a genuine energy crisis." And he conceded that "in years immediately ahead, we must face up to the possibility of occasional energy shortages and some increases in energy prices."

His policy emerged basically as a call for the production of more fuel and power to meet America's growing energy appetite. To facilitate production, the President ended, May 1, the controversial oil import quota system imposed in 1959. He recommended that the oil industry be given an additional tax subsidy in the form of a tax credit for discovering new sources of oil. The President also urged Congress to end federal regulation of natural gas prices to create an incentive for exploration for new natural gas resources. He asked the states to encourage the use of coal, which he described as America's most abundant fuel. To facilitate the use of coal, Nixon urged states to take their time about putting into effect secondary air-pollution controls.

Lastly, the President urged Americans to save energy—to turn out lights, tune up their cars and use less air-conditioning and heating. He recommended that industry make more efficient electrical products and said that the Government will develop "a voluntary system of energy efficiency labels" for major home appliances.

"A Serious Problem"

On June 29, Pres. Nixon came back to Congress with his plan to meet the nation's energy needs. This time, his tone was more urgent: "America faces a serious energy problem. While we have 6% of the world's population, we consume one-third of the world's energy output. The supply of domestic energy resources available to us is not keeping pace with our ever-growing demand, and unless we act swiftly and effectively, we could face a genuine energy crisis in the foreseeable future."

The President's plan called for a voluntary conservation drive. While he asked that personal consumption be cut by 5% during the next 12 months, he stated that the Government would reduce its anticipated consumption by 7% during the same period. And finally, Nixon asked for the expansion of research aimed toward developing new energy sources.

To give highest priority to energy matters, Nixon announced that he had appointed Colorado Gov. John A. Love to head a White House energy office. Love would be responsible for coordinating energy policies throughout the executive branch.

Crunch or Crisis?

Oil industry executives, utilities men, bankers, engineers, geologists and some independent economists approved of the President's policy. They believe that the "energy crisis" is, in fact, an "energy crunch"—a short-term problem of supply and demand. Therefore, freeing natural gas prices, removing oil import quotas and encouraging offshore drilling for oil and gas will ease the supply crunch. This group tends to blame the current fuel shortages on environmentalists who have tried to block potential sources of fuel, such as the Alaska pipeline, offshore oil drilling and the construction of nuclear power plants.

Columnist Joseph Alsop, on the other hand, called the President's energy message a "poultice to cure a cancer." "It muffled the hard realities," he continued. "It did not insist on any of the hard measures needed to meet the crisis."

Environmentalist Ann Roosevelt of the Friends of the Earth criticized the President's policy message because it put "economics over ecology." While the President advocated more energy development, ecology proponents argue that the environment is being destroyed by the demand for energy and that this is too high a price to pay for an economy of perpetual growth.

Vast Energy Appetite

The United States has developed a vast appetite for energy in the past 2 decades. U.S. consumption of energy doubled between 1950 and 1970 and is expected to double once again between 1970 and 1985.

National Petroleum Council Chairman John G. McLean says the U.S. has the "basic energy materials to meet our needs for at least 200 years at present levels of consumption," but the U.S. does not, at present, have means to make those resources available. The United States is currently consuming energy faster than the rate of expansion of proven energy reserves.

Time, money, technological capability, and political and environmental considerations currently stand in the way of further expansion of proven reserves and the discovery of new resources.

Ford Foundation's S. David Freeman believes that the basic cause of this situation is that Government policy hasn't changed since the 1930's when it aimed at keeping energy costs down in order to stimulate ever-expanding use for the good of the people. Says Freeman, "This was right for the times but times have changed and policy hasn't."

Short-sighted Policies

The effects of short-sighted policies can be seen clearly in the case of natural gas, the cleanest and environmentally most desirable fuel. In 1975, natural gas production in the U.S. is expected to peak at 24.7-trillion cubic feet. Since the 1938 Natural Gas Act, the Government has had the right to set wellhead prices for natural gas. The

How The U.S. Uses Its Energy

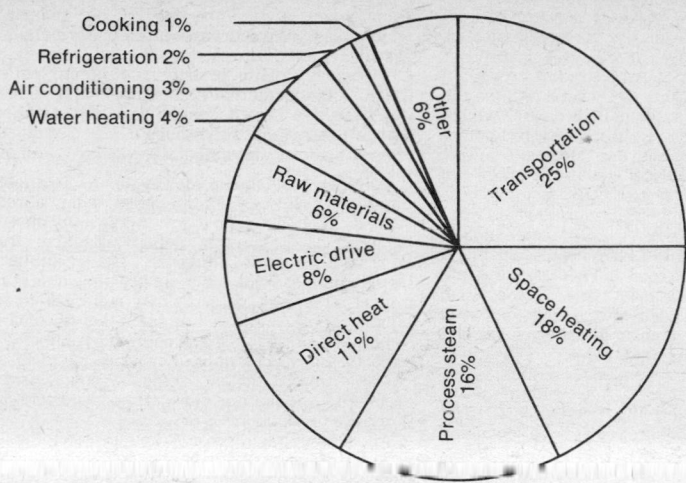

Cooking 1%
Refrigeration 2%
Air conditioning 3%
Water heating 4%
Other 6%
Transportation 25%
Raw materials 6%
Electric drive 8%
Direct heat 11%
Process steam 16%
Space heating 18%

price of America's premium fuel was kept low, with the result that industries and utilities turned to it, instead of coal or oil. The financial incentive to find new sources was nonexistent, and exploration came to a virtual standstill.

The U.S. is also on the threshold of a coal shortage, but for different reasons. As far as reserves go, the total potential resources base is nearly 800 billion tons or enough to last 1,500 years at current consumption levels. However, because of a severe loss of market due to the conversion of railroads to diesel fuel and electricity and to the availability of gas at low prices, the industry was not able to generate sufficient capital to develop additional productive capacity.

Today, besides needing extensive capital to re-develop coal production, the industry faces severe environmental problems: some 80% of supplies is high in sulphur content and emits harmful pollutants when burned. The cost of removing the sulphur is substantial. Coal is also unwieldy and expensive to transport. Strip mining, on which the coal industry will have to depend more and more, carries with it the high cost of land reclamation.

Nation Runs On Oil

The crunch in natural gas and coal reserves has made oil the primary energy source. Its advantages are numerous — it can run both huge electric generators as well as the family car. It's easily transported. Unless other energy sources are found, oil will be carrying more than 50% of the U.S. energy burden by 1980.

A large portion of that oil will have to be imported. The United States exhausted its reserve production capacity in 1970 and will never again be able to meet its oil demands with domestic petroleum. According to the State Department, while demand in 1973 is running at about 17-million barrels per day, domestic supply consists of a little more than 11-million barrels per day. By 1980, demand daily will be 24-million and supply only 12-million barrels.

Oil industry critics don't believe that gasoline shortages are a case of capacity shortages. They charge shortages are part of a conspiracy by the major oil companies to force up prices and drive out competition.

Development of potential offshore and Alaskan reserves has been delayed by environmental considerations: the danger of oil spills and the possible destruction of the Arctic tundra. Even if these projects get the go-ahead, it will be years before the oil begins to flow; and it is unlikely these sources will be able to fulfill the escalating demand for oil. The National Petroleum Council estimates that in 1985, the Alaskan North Slope will supply between 7% and 13% of U.S. oil demand, a modest contribution to national energy needs.

Insufficient Refining Capacity

A major barrier to the availability of petroleum products has been insufficient refining capacity. Oil industry leaders argue that low profits and high costs, along with environmental opposition have brought the building of refineries to a standstill. It is estimated that 7 new refineries will be needed on the east coast of the U.S. by 1975; they will not be there. A new refinery has not been built on the east coast since 1959. Even if construction were to begin shortly, it would take at least 6 years to build a refinery. This July, the Federal Trade Commission charged that oil companies have conspired to monopolize refining of petroleum products.

"Crisis" or "crunch", one thing is clear — the U.S. faces a drastic shortage of fossil fuels for the next several years. In the meanwhile, the U.S. must rely on existing energy sources, most of them outside of the continental United States.

In the past, we have imported increasing amounts of oil — 20% in 1965, 23% in 1971, 27% in 1972 — mostly from Canada and Venezuela. However, Venezuela, which is already worried about conservation of its oil resources, cannot begin to fulfill escalating demands for oil. Canada, which does have potentially great reserves of oil, has already clamped down on the export of oil and natural gas.

Middle East Oil

The U.S. is left with one alternative. The Middle East and North Africa are oil rich. Although not limitless by any means, their reserves are monumental. Of the 500-billion proven oil reserves in the non-communist world, 300-billion barrels lie in the Middle East and North Africa. And when it comes to probable reserves, most will also be found in the Middle East.

James Akins, U.S. Ambassador to Saudi Arabia, feels that world need for oil has given the Middle East a unique position: "It's an area which, inherently, has little power. But now it has potentially enormous economic and strategic power, because there's no replacement in the short run for oil as the basic energy fuel."

Through the vehicle of the Organization of Petroleum Exporting Countries (OPEC), formed in 1960, the oil-producing countries have begun to demand higher payments for their oil and to dictate the rate at which it will be extracted. "We are in a position to dictate prices, and we are going to be very rich," said the Saudi Arabian Minister of Petroleum Affairs Ahmad Zaki Yamani.

The impending U.S. dependence on Middle East oil is fraught with difficulties. According to the International Institute for Strategic Studies, "The threat of the burgeoning power and changing tactics of the Middle East oil-producing countries seemed to overshadow almost all military threats to North America, Europe and Japan."

Oil Boycott Threat

Until recently, Saudi Arabia has declined to use oil for political purposes. But on Sept. 4 King Faisal said that Saudi Arabia will not increase its output of oil as long as U.S. policy favors Israel at the expense of the Arabs.

Akins believes that an oil boycott would be an effective weapon and that the Arabs will be willing to use it. He argues that the Arabs would not boycott everyone. Western Europe and Japan are also large importers of Middle East oil and would insure the Arab nations a continued income of considerable proportions. Akins says that unless the U.S. could persuade Europe and Japan to join in joint action against the Arabs, the U.S. will be left with few alternatives: war with the Arabs, acceding to their demands, or accepting severe damage to the American economy.

Maury Adelman of the Massachusetts Institute of Technology argues that the strength of the OPEC cartel is fostered in part by the State Department and supported by oil companies which pass price increases on to consumers. The first order of business, he says, is to crush the OPEC cartel. He suggests that consuming nations must get together — to auction quotas for oil imports on a sealed competitive bid basis and, thereby, strain the unity of OPEC.

Oil vs. The Dollar

Political problems aside, as the U.S. imports more oil, it will be spending more money abroad. Already in 1972, $4 billion of the $6.5-billion U.S. balance of payments deficit resulted from increased energy imports. The Commerce Department estimates that by 1980 the value of net imports of energy materials may reach $18- to $24-billion annually. Akins estimates that it could be $40 billion, or about 66% of the total value of U.S. exports today. The only alternative to an insupportable international payments deficit is, he argues, to reduce our consumption and increase domestic production.

According to the Nixon Administration, the fast breeder reactor is "our best hope for meeting the nation's growing demand for economical clean energy." However, technical and construction difficulties and the opposition of environmentalists have pushed extensive nuclear power development further and further into the future. There are now only 29 conventional nuclear power plants operating in the U.S. The Atomic Energy Commission just recently ordered the first demonstrator breeder plant to be built near Oak Ridge, Tenn. The cost will run more than $700 million, and it will not be in operation before the 1980's.

Nuclear Energy Doubts

The problems are considerable. To begin with, contrary to much public opinion, nuclear power can never satisfy all energy needs — it is virtually limited to the production of electricity by electric utilities. The public and environmentalists have consistently opposed the building of nuclear power plants because of fear of radiation dangers. Although nuclear engineers claim stations are so

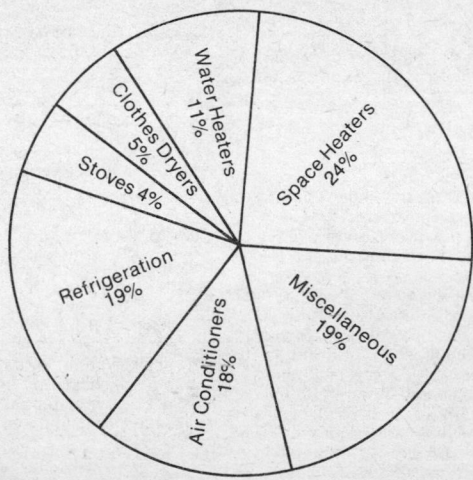

Electricity In The Home — Share Of The 1960-70 Increase In Demand

well designed that chance of accident is minimal, that chance still exists and the consequences could be monumental.

The breeder reactor carries with it problems that go beyond the radiation hazards associated with early nuclear power generation. Breeder reactors create plutonium as a "waste" product. Plutonium is extremely lethal and remains dangerous to humans for more than 200,000 years. Proponents argue that the inherent problems, waste storage among them, can be managed, but at present the costs are prohibitive.

Solar Power

Solar power is yet another potentially large source of energy. Already, spacecraft are converting sunlight into energy and solar water heaters are in use in Australia, Israel and Japan. The National Science Foundation estimates that the potential solar energy falling on the surface of Lake Erie in one day is greater than the nation's annual energy consumption.

Last December, a joint NASA-National Science Foundation panel recommended that the U.S. launch a huge solar energy research effort. According to their predictions, by 2020, the sun could provide 35% of heating and cooling in buildings and 20% of the nation's electricity.

Again, however, the inherent problems are considerable. Current technology calls for much development and sophistication, as well as money. Nevertheless, NASA contends the initial expense will pay off in the long run: "The cost of converting solar energy is now higher than conventional fuels, but due to increasing constraints on their use it will be competitive in the near future."

Geothermal Power

Returning to the practicable, geothermal energy, or heat from the interior of the earth, is hailed by many as a significant energy source in the long run. Reserves of subterranean hot water, mostly in the western states, are almost limitless. In December, 1972, a National Science Foundation panel headed by Walter Hickel recommended that the Federal Government put into operation a $684.7-million program on geothermal energy. NSF estimates that by the year 2000 such an effort could lead to a geothermal electricity generating capacity that would exceed the current total U.S. electricity generating capacity.

Another plus factor is that the technology exists to utilize geothermal energy. Until the current "energy crisis", geothermal development was held back by the availability of cheaper hydrocarbon fuels and a consequent lack of venture capital; now there are many signs of activity in this field.

Coal Gasification

The President has urged the nation to turn to its abundant supply of coal as a major energy source. One approach suggested is the development of synthetic gas from coal. In the process, an additional chemical reaction eliminates the polluting sulfur, opening up the availability of low-grade coal as an energy resource. Unfortunately, synthetic gas, in most cases, does not burn as hot as natural gas.

Nevertheless, MIT Professor Carroll Wilson who drew up a "Decade Program" for energy independence in the July 1973 issue of Foreign Affairs, cites the adaptability and transportability inherent in pipeline-quality coal gas as the basis for a massive crash program and capital investment in coal gasification plants. At the same time, he recognizes the environmental issues involved:

the need for federal standards covering strip mining, including provision for land restoration, and provision of pollution controls on coal gasification plants. "It is a big job," Wilson admits, "but no bigger than the Manhattan or Apollo projects — in fact substantially less in proportion to the scale of the American economy in the 1970s and 1980s."

In the search for alternative energy sources, some groups, including the National Petroleum Council, have looked enthusiastically toward refining extensive shale deposits in Colorado, Utah and Wyoming into a burnable oil. The President has already urged the leasing of shale lands. Many industry engineers prefer shale oil to synthetic gas because chemically it is more like petroleum.

However, the National Petroleum Council foresees that by 1985, shale refineries would only supply, at maximum feasible capacity, between $2\frac{1}{2}\%$ and $3\frac{1}{2}\%$ of the national demand for oil, and would require a $4-billion capital investment. The proponents of shale oil also face a stiff environmental problem: how to dispose of the leftover shale (80% of the original ore) after extraction.

The refinement of any one or more of these potential energy sources may well insure a secure energy supply in the future. But that doesn't mean the U.S. should be distracted from the serious issues of the current energy situation. Many argue that the time has come to consider the meaning of the ever-increasing U.S. need for and dependence on electrical and combustion energy. ARCO President Thornton Bradshaw said recently, ". . . the important thing is that the American people come to the realization . . . that the profligate use of energy is not a good way to live . . . Because it just leads to a way of life that in the long run is not acceptable."

A Stitch In Time . . .

Dr. Barry Commoner argues that the solution to the "energy crisis" requires conservation practices that can bring about a 23% reduction in energy usage without reducing the amount of goods produced. Obviously, such a reduction would entail major changes in the nation's industrial structure as well as in lifestyles, including a 75% reduction in automobile traffic.

Eric Hirst, a researcher at the Oak Ridge National Laboratory, and Robert Herendeen, a research associate at the University of Illinois Center for Advanced Computation have detailed some ways to reduce energy usage. More energy-efficient transportation could cut almost 8% from the U.S. energy budget. Proper insulation would require 40% less heating energy; if all homes met proper insulation standards, total energy use would decrease by almost 5%. Improvement of air-conditioning efficiency would also decrease energy usage. In the commercial sector, which accounts for 15% of total energy usage, space heating and air-conditioning account for more than half of commercial consumption. Savings could be made in this area. Industry accounts for more than 40% of the U.S. energy budget, much of it for the production of a few basic materials: primary metals, chemicals and paper. Increased recycling would reduce energy consumption as well as conserve natual resources and alleviate solid waste problems.

Considering that escalating energy demands are likely to damage the environment, devalue the dollar and distort U.S. foreign policy, a thorough revaluation of the American "energy-oriented" lifestyle is probably the first and best basis for a U.S. energy policy.

Coal: Strip Mining Increase

Source: U.S. Dept. of Interior, Nat'l. Coal Assoc.

Strip Mining by State 1972 (millions of tons)

Alabama	13.2	Kansas	1.2	Oklahoma	2.5
Alaska	.7	Kentucky	55.8	Penn.	26.3
Arizona	2.9	Maryland	1.4	Tenn.	5.1
Arkansas	.4	Missouri	4.6	Utah	.03
Colorado	2.5	Montana	8.2	Virginia	7.9
Illinois	33.3	No. Dakota	6.6	Wash.	2.6
Indiana	24.5	New Mexico	7.2	W. Virginia	19.1
Iowa	.5	Ohio	34.1	Wyoming	10.5

1964 Total soft coal, 487,000,000 tons; Strip mined 152,000,000 tons; 31%.
1968 Total soft coal, 545,000,000 tons; Strip mined 186,000,000 tons; 34%.
1972 Total soft coal, 595,386,000 tons; Strip mined 275,730,000 tons; 46%.

Coal and Coke Production in the United States

Source: Bureau of Mines

Year	Penn. Anthracite Production 1,000 net tons	Value $1,000	Bituminous Production 1,000 net tons	Value $1,000	Year	Penn. Anthracite Production 1,000 net tons	Value $1,000	Bituminous Produc tion 1,000 net tons	Value $1,000
1945	54,934	323,944	577,617	1,768,204	1965	14,866	122,021	512,088	2,276,022
1950	44,077	392,398	516,311	2,500,374	1966	12,941	100,663	533,881	2,421,293
1955	26,205	206,097	464,633	2,092,383	1967	12,256	96,160	552,026	2,555,377
1960	18,817	147,116	415,512	1,950,421	1968	11,461	97,245	545,245	2,546,340
1961	17,446	140,338	402,977	1,844,567	1969	10,473	100,769	560,505	2,795,509
1962	16,894	134,094	422,149	1,891,555	1970	9,729	105,341	602,932	3,772,662
1963	18,267	153,503	458,928	2,013,390	1971	8,727	103,469	552,192	3,901,496
1964	17,184	148,648	486,998	2,165,582	1972	7,100	85,251	595,386	4,561,983

Coke production (1,000 net tons — Value in $1,000) — (1967) 64,580; $1,123,173; (1968) 63,653, $1,157,359; (1969) 64,757,$1,355,260; (1970) 66,525, $1,849,160; (1971) 57,436, $1,745,693; (1972) 60,507, $2,012,486.
Coke Exports (1,000 short tons) — (1967) 710,380; (1968) 791,909; (1969) 1,629,000; (1970) 2,478,338 (1971) 1,508,639; (1972) 1,231,633; Imports — (1967) 92,001; (1968) 94,085; (1969) 173,052 (1970) 152,879; (1971) 173,914; (1972) 185,023
Anthracite exports (net tons) — (1965) 850,630; (1966) 766,025; (1967) 594,797; (1968) 518,159; (1969) 627,492; (1970) 789,499; (1971) 671,024; (1972) 743,451

U.S. Petroleum and Natural Gas Production

Source: Bureau of Mines

Year	Crude oil Production 1,000 bbls.	Value $1,000	Natural gas liquids Production 1,000 bbls.	Value $1,000	Total 42 gal. bbls.	Natural gas Marketed Mil. cu. ft.	Value $1,000
1945	1,713,655	2,094,250	112,004	187,564	1,828,539,000	3,944,021	191,006
1950	1,973,574	4,963,380	181,961	419,605	2,155,693,000	6,282,060	408,521
1955	2,484,428	6,870,380	281,371	619,006	2,766,325,000	9,405,351	978,357
1960	2,574,933	7,420,181	340,157	808,385	2,915,365,000	12,771,038	1,789,970
1965	2,848,514	8,158,298	441,556	911,603	3,290,083,000	16,042,753	2,494,542
1968	3,329,042	9,794,826	550,311	1,124,014	3,879,353,000	19,322,400	3,168,688
1969	3,371,751	10,426,680	580,241	1,102,011	3,951,992,000	20,698,240	3,455,615
1970	3,517,450	11,173,726	605,916	1,275,112	4,123,366,000	21,920,642	3,745,680
1971	3,453,914	11,692,998	617,815	1,386,054	4,071,729,000	22,493,012	4,085,482
1972	3,455,368	11,706,510	638,216	1,452,233	4,093,584,000	22,531,698	4,185,869

U.S. Total Fuel Supply and Demand[1]

In thousands of 42-gallon barrels. *Includes special naphtha production. *Includes kerosene type jet fuel.

Year	Gasoline* Production	Total Demand	Kerosene* Production	Total Demand	Distillate fuel oil Production	Total Demand	Residual fuel oil Production	Total Demand
1950	1,024,181	1,019,011	118,512	119,922	398,912	75,435	425,217	570,021
1960[2]	1,522,497	1,525,126	136,842	133,188	667,050	695,165	332,147	577,934
1965	1,733,258	1,756,419	201,788	219,932	765,071	779,644	268,567	601,893
1969	2,057,041	2,076,612	319,811	353,582	848,404	900,262	265,906	721,924
1970	2,135,838	2,165,395	313,544	358,025	897,097	927,211	257,510	804,288
1971 (rev.)	2,231,157	2,242,921	306,847	364,908	912,097	971,316	274,684	838,045
1972	2,352,310	2,382,293	313,554	379,849	963,625	1,066,049	292,519	925,647

(1) Demand in some cases exceeds the production; in these cases the difference is made up by dipping into stocks or by imports. (2) In the years prior to 1960 figures are on a 48-state basis.

U.S. Motor Fuel Supply[1] and Demand

Source: Bureau of Mines (Figures in 42-gallon barrels)

Year	Supply Production (1,000)	Daily average (1,000)	Demand Domestic (1,000)	Export (1,000)	Year	Supply Production (1,000)	Daily average (1,000)	Demand Domestic (1,000)	Export (1,000)
1945	793,431	2,174	696,333	88,059	1965	1,733,258	4,749	1,750,028	6,391
1950	1,024,181	2,806	994,290	24,721	1969	2,057,041	5,636	2,072,144	4,468
1955	1,373,950	3,764	1,329,788	34,521	1970	2,135,838	5,852	2,162,439	2,956
1959*	1,488,860	4,079	1,485,277	16,743	1971(rev)	2,231,157	6,113	2,242,921	3,104
1960	1,522,497	4,160	1,511,670	13,456	1972	2,352,310	6,427	2,382,293	2,441

*Beginning with 1959 Alaska and Hawaii are included. (1.) Includes special naphtha.

World Production of Crude Petroleum[1]

Source: Bureau of Mines; in thousands of 42-gallon barrels

Country	1971	1972 p
North America:		
Canada	495,743	560,693
Cuba(e)	785	775
Mexico[1]	155,912	185,011
Trinidad and Tobago	47,148	51,719
United States[1]	3,453,914	3,455,368
South America:		
Argentina	154,514	158,464
Bolivia	13,446	15,967
Brazil	63,617	61,088
Chile	12,883	12,527
Colombia	78,635	71,674
Ecuador	1,354	28,579
Peru	22,588	23,635
Venezuela	1,295,406	1,178,487
Europe:		
Albania	8,674	10,508
Austria	17,549	17,284
Bulgaria	2,336	1,825
Czechoslovakia	1,356	1,322
Denmark		1,281
France	13,651	10,811
Germany, East	435	1,806
Germany, West	53,597	51,271
Hungary	14,879	15,084
Italy	8,952	7,850
Netherlands	11,727	10,885
Norway		12,078
Poland	2,116	2,574
Romania	102,479	105,296
Spain	1,874	1,020
U.S.S.R.	2,778,300	2,895,900
United Kingdom	1,499	607
Yugoslavia	21,932	23,709
Africa:		
Algeria	279,627	384,858
Angola	41,228	43,161
Congo (Brazzaville)	(e)130	(e)2,146
Egypt, Arab Republic of	106,993	78,800
Gabon	41,911	45,671
Libya	1,007,687	819,619
Morocco	172	216
Nigeria	558,375	665,282
Tunisia	31,542	31,607
Asia:		
Bahrain	27,346	25,547
Brunei	47,482	67,008
Burma	6,652	7,466
China, People's Rep. of(e)	167,900	216,080
India	52,091	56,965
Indonesia	325,673	395,581
Iran	1,661,901	1,843,869
Iraq	624,312	529,419
Israel[2]	44,618	43,920
Japan	5,529	5,242
Kuwait[3]	1,167,329	1,201,346
Malaysia	25,017	33,867
Mongolia(e)	90	90
Oman	107,430	103,131
Pakistan	3,650	3,294
Qatar	156,882	176,545
Saudi Arabia[3]	1,741,149	2,202,049
Syrian Arab Republic	36,462	39,879
Taiwan	803	732
Thailand	95	(e)112
Trucial States:		
Abu Dhabi	341,007	384,190
Dubai	45,648	50,942
Turkey	24,723	24,416
Oceania:		
Australia	112,914	119,516
New Zealand[1]	804	1,119
Total	17,634,608	18,583,783

(e)Estimate. (p)Preliminary. (r)Revised. [1]Includes field condensate. [2]Estimates of Israeli production from Sinai peninsula oilfields included with Israel rather than with United Arab Republic. [3]Date for both Kuwait and Saudi Arabia include those countries' share of production from former Kuwait-Saudi Arabia Neutral Zone.

U.S. Crude Petroleum Production By Chief States

(Figures represent thousands of 42-gallon barrels)

Year	Ark.	Calif.	Ill.	Kans.	La.	Miss.	N.M.	N.D.	Okla.	Texas	Wyo.
1950	31,108	327,607	62,028	107,586	208,965	38,236	47,367	....	164,599	829,874	61,631
1960	30,117	305,352	77,341	113,453	400,832	51,673	107,380	21,992	192,913	927,479	133,910
1965	25,930	316,428	63,708	104,733	594,853	56,183	119,166	26,350	203,441	1,000,749	138,314
1968	19,464	375,496	56,391	94,505	817,603	58,708	128,550	25,040	223,623	1,133,380	144,250
1969	18,049	375,291	50,724	88,716	884,603	64,283	129,227	22,703	224,729	1,151,775	154,945
1970	18,035	372,191	43,747	84,853	906,907	65,119	128,184	21,998	223,574	1,249,697	160,345
1971	18,263	358,484	39,084	78,532	935,243	64,066	118,412	21,653	213,313	1,222,926	148,114
1972	18,519	347,022	34,874	73,744	891,827	61,100	110,525	20,624	207,633	1,301,685	140,011

World's Largest Hydroelectric Generating Plants

Source: Bureau of Reclamation

Ultimate capacity of 1,000,000 kilowatts or more. UC - Under construction. NA - Not available. Year - Initial operation.

Name	Present Megawatts	Ultimate Megawatts	Year
Itaipu, Brazil-Paraguay		10,710	U.C.
Grand Coulee, U.S.A.	2,161	9,780	1941
Guri, Venezuela	524	6,500	1967
Sayansk, U.S.S.R.		6,400	U.C.
Krasnoyarsk, U.S.S.R.	6,096	6,096	1968
Paulo Afonso, Brazil	1,030	5,942	1955
Churchill Falls, Canada	1,900	5,225	1971
Bratsk, U.S.S.R.	4,500	4,600	1964
Sukhovo, U.S.S.R.		4,500	U.C.
Ust-Ilimsk, U.S.S.R.	720	4,300	U.C.
Cabora Basa, Portugal (Mozambique)		4,000	U.C.
Inga, Zaire	350	3,700	U.C.
Chief Joseph, U.S.A.	1,024	3,642	1956
Ilha Solteira, Brazil		3,200	U.C.
John Day, U.S.A.	2,160	2,700	1968
Nurek, U.S.S.R.		2,700	U.C.
Volga - 22nd Congress, U.S.S.R.	2,543	2,560	1958
Volga - V.I. Lenin, U.S.S.R.	2,100	2,300	1955
W.A.C. Bennett, Canada	1,816	2,270	1969
Iron Gate, Romania-Yugo.	500	2,160	U.C.
Saad-El-Aali (High Aswan), Egypt	1,750	2,100	1967
Robert Moses-Niagara, U.S.A.	1,950	1,950	1961
St. Lawrence Power Dam, U.S.A./Canada	1,824	1,824	1958
The Dalles, U.S.A.	1,291	1,807	1957
Mica, Canada		1,740	U.C.
Kemano, Canada	813	1,670	1954
Beauharnois, Canada	1,021	1,670	1950
Cheboksary, U.S.S.R.		1,632	U.C.
Inguri, U.S.S.R.		1,600	U.C.
Kariba, Rhodesia	600	1,500	1959
Liukiahsia, China		1,500	1963
Tumut-3, Australia	750	1,500	1972
McNary, U.S.A.	980	1,406	1953
Jupia, Brazil	600	1,400	1966
Marimbondo, Brazil		1,400	U.C.
Saratov, U.S.S.R.		1,359	1967
Daniel Johnson, Canada	165	1,353	1970
Hoover, U.S.A.	1,345	1,345	1936
Wanapum, U.S.A.	831	1,330	1964
Zeya, U.S.S.R.		1,290	U.C.
Priest Rapids, U.S.A.	789	1,262	1959
Castaic, U.S.A.		1,250	U.C.
Keban, Turkey	620	1,240	1955
Kettle Rapids, Canada	612	1,224	1970
Sir Adam Beck (#2), Canada	1,224	1,224	1954
Rocky Reach, U.S.A.	775	1,215	1961
Furnas, Brazil	900	1,200	1963
Toktogul, U.S.S.R.		1,200	U.C.
El Chocon, Argentina		1,200	U.C.
Manicouagan No. 3, Canada		1,176	U.C.

Name	Pres. Mega.	Ult. Mega.	Year	Name	Pres. Mega.	Ulti. Mega.	Year
Sanmen Hsia, China	...	1,100		Manicouagan No. 2, Canada	...	1,015	1965
Nizhne-Kamskaya, U.S.S.R.	...	1,090	U.C.	Votkinsk, U.S.S.R.	...	1,000	1961
Dworshak, U.S.A.	90	1,060	U.C.	Mangla, Pakistan	300	1,000	U.C.
Bersimis No. 1, Canada	912	1,050	1956	Chirkey, U.S.S.R.	...	1,000	U.C.
Bhakra, India	450	1,050	1963	Kaniji, Nigeria	...	1,000	U.C.
Estreito, Brazil	1,050	1,050	1969	Northfield Mountain, U.S.A.	...	1,000	U.C.
Salto Osorio, Brazil	...	1,050	U.C.	Chivor, Colombia	...	1,000	U.C.
Lago Delio, Italy	...	1,016	U.C.	Blenheim-Gilboa, U.S.A.	...	1,000	U.C.

Non-Federal Hydroelectric Plants in U.S.
CAPACITIES OF 100,000 KILOWATTS OR MORE AS OF JANUARY 1, 1973
Auxiliary and Pumped Storage Units are not included in Hydroelectric Capacities
Source: Federal Power Commission, Bureau of Power

Plant	State	Owner	Kilowatts
Robert Moses Niagara	N. Y.	Power Authority State of N. Y.	1,953,900
Robert Moses (Massena)	N. Y.	Power Authority State of N. Y.	912,000
Wanapum	Wash.	Grant County Dist. No. 2.	831,250
Priest Rapids	Wash.	Grant County Dist. No 2	788,500
Wells	Wash.	Douglas County PUD No. 1	774,300
Rocky Reach	Wash.	Chelan County Dist. No. 1	711,550
Boundary	Wash.	Seattle Dept. of Lighting	551,000
Conowingo	Md.	Philadelphia Electric Co.	474,480
Hells Canyon	Ore.	Idaho Power Co.	391,500
Brownlee	Idaho	Idaho Power Co	360,400
Ross	Wash.	Seattle Dept. of Lighting Co	360,000
Edward Hyatt	Calif.	Calif. dept. of Water Resources	351,000
Cowans Ford	N. C.	Duke Power Co	350,000
Upper Smith Mt	Va.	Appalachian Power Co	300,200
Mossyrock	Wash.	City of Tacoma	300,000
New Colgate	Calif.	Yuba County Water Agency	284,400
Noxon Rapids	Mont	The Washington Water Power Co	282,880
Round Butte	Ore.	Portland Gen. Elec. Co.	247,050
Safe Harbor	Pa.	Safe Harbor Water Power Corp	228,000
Walter Bouldin	Ala	Alabama Power Co	225,000
Rock Island	Wash.	Chelan County Dist. No. 1	212,100
Swift No. 1	Wash.	Pacific Power and Light Co.	204,000
Cabinet Gorge	Idaho	The Washington Water Power Co	200,000
Saluda	S.C.	So. Carolina Electric and Gas Co.	197,500
Oxbow	Oreg.	Idaho Power Co	190,000
White Rock	Calif.	Sacramento Mun. Utility Dist.	190,000
Caribou No. 1 & 2	Calif.	Pacific Gas and Electric Co.	184,800
Gaston	N. C.	Virginia Electric and Power Co	177,920
Lay Dam	Ala.	Alabama Power Co	177,000
Osage	Mo	Union Electric Co. of Mo	172,000
Kerr	Mont	The Montana Power Co	168,000
Lewis Smith	Ala	Alabama Power Co	157,500
James B. Black	Calif.	Pacific Gas and Electric Co	154,800
Martin Dam	Ala	Alabama Power Co	154,200
Camino	Calif.	Sacramento Mun. Utility Dist.	142,500
Pit No. 5	Calif.	Pacific Gas and Electric Co.	140,560
Comerford	N. H.	New England Power Co	140,400
S. C. Moore	N. H.	New England Power Co	140,400
Keowee	S.C.	Duke Power Co.	140,000
Gorge	Wash.	Seattle Department of Lighting Co.	137,700
New Don Pedro	Calif.	Turlock Modesto Irr. Dist.	136,515
Merwin	Wash.	Pacific Power and Light Co.	135,000
D. R. Holm	Calif.	San Francisco Utilities Commission	135,000
Haas	Calif.	Pacific Gas and Electric Co.	135,000
Jaybird	Calif.	Sacramento Mun. Util. Dist.	133,000
Pinopolis	S. C	So. Carolina Public Service Authority	132,615
Mammoth Pool	Calif.	Southern California Edison Co	129,360
Logan-Martin	Ala	Alabama Power Co	128,250
Balch No. 1 & 2	Calif.	Pacific Gas and Electric	128,200
Keokuk	Iowa	Union Electric Co	124,800
Poe	Calif.	Pacific Gas and Electric Co.	124,200
Mayfield	Wash.	City of Tacoma	121,500
Calderwood	Tenn	Tapoco Inc	121,500
Diablo	Wash.	Seattle Department of Lighting Co	120,000
Belden	Calif.	Pacific Gas and Electric Co.	117,900
Rock Creek	Calif.	Pacific Gas and Electric Co.	113,400
Cheoah	N. C.	Tapoco Inc	110,000
Middle Fork American	Calif.	Placer County Water Agency	109,800
Markham Ferry	Okla	Grand River Dam Auth.	108,000
Walters	N. C.	Carolina Power and Light Co	108,000
Yale	Wash.	Pacific Power and Light Co.	108,000
Pelton	Oreg.	Portland General Electric Co	108,000
Holtwood	Pa.	Pennsylvania Power and Light Co	107,200
Big Creek No. 3	Calif.	Southern California Edison Co	106,500
Pit No. 7	Calif.	Pacific Gas and Electric Co.	104,400
Hawks Nest	W. Va	Union Carbide Corp	102,000
Roanoke Rapids	N. C.	Virginia Electric and Power Co	100,080
Jordan No. 1	Ala	Alabama Power Co	100,000

World Electric Power
Source: Federal Power Commission
Electric generating capacity as of Jan. 1, 1970; electric energy production in 1969[1]
Kilowatts in thousands, Kilowatt hours in millions.

Country	Kw	Kwhrs.	Country	Kw	Kwhrs.
United States	332,606	1,552,757	France	36,326	131,583
USSR	153,790	659,210	Italy	31,034	106,329
United Kingdom	61,372	222,295	China (Mainland)	17,000	50,000
Japan[3]	59,482	305,917	India[3]	15,493	55,247
Germany (West)	48,812	210,985	**Subtotal**	**795,753**	**3,484,742**
Canada	39,838	190,419	**World Total**	**1,046,230**	**4,443,247**

(1) Year end except as noted (2) Including Alaska and Hawaii (3) Year beginning April 1, 1969.

Nuclear Power Reactors in U.S.

Source: U.S. Atomic Energy Commission (June 30, 1972)

State	Site	Plant Name	Capacity (kilowatts)	Utility	Commercial Operation
Alabama	Decatur	Browns Ferry Unit 1	1,065,000	Tennessee Valley Authority	1973
	Decatur	Browns Ferry Unit 2	1,065,000	Tennessee Valley Authority	1974
	Decatur	Browns Ferry Unit 3	1,065,000	Tennessee Valley Authority	1974
	Dothan	Joseph M. Farley	829,000	Alabama Power Co.	1975
	Dothan	Joseph M. Farley, Unit 2	829,000	Alabama Power Co.	1977
Arkansas	Russellville	Arkansas Unit 1	820,000	Ark. Power & Light Co.	1973
	Russellville	Arkansas Unit 2	902,000	Ark. Power & Light Co.	1976
California	Humboldt Bay	Humboldt Bay Power Unit 3	68,500	Pacific Gas & Electric Co.	1963
	San Clemente	San Onofre Unit 1	430,000	So. Calif. Ed. & San Diego Gas & El. Co.	1968
	San Clemente	San Onofre Unit 2	1,140,000	So. Calif. Ed. & San Diego Gas & El. Co.	1978
	San Clemente	San Onofre Unit 3	1,140,000	So. Calif. Ed. & San Diego Gas & El. Co.	1979
	Diablo Canyon	Diablo Canyon Unit 1	1,060,000	Pacific Gas & Electric Co.	1975
	Diablo Canyon	Diablo Canyon Unit 2	1,060,000	Pacific Gas & Electric Co.	1976
	Clay Station	Rancho Seco Station	804,000	Sacramento Mun. Utility District	1974
	Pt. Arena	Mendocino Unit 1	1,128,000	Pacific Gas & Electric Co.	1981
	Pt. Arena	Mendocino Unit 2	1,128,000	Pacific Gas & Electric Co.	1982
		Eastern Desert Plant: Unit 1	770,000	Southern California Edison Co.	1981
		Eastern Desert Plant: Unit 2	770,000	Southern California Edison Co.	1982
Colorado	Platteville	Ft. St. Vrain Station	330,000	Public Service Co. of Colo.	1973
Connecticut	Haddam Neck	Haddam Neck	575,000	Conn. Yankee Atomic Power Co.	1968
	Waterford	Millstone Station: Unit 1	652,100	Northeast Utilities	1971
	Waterford	Millstone Station: Unit 2	828,000	Northeast Utilities	1974
Delaware	Middletown	Delmarva Unit 1	770,000	Delmarva Power & Light Co.	1979
	Middletown	Delmarva Unit 2	770,000	Delmarva Power & Light Co.	1982
Florida	Florida City	Turkey Point Unit 3	693,000	Fla. Power & Light Co.	1972
	Florida City	Turkey Point Unit 4	693,000	Fla. Power & Light Co.	1973
	Red Level	Crystal River Unit 3	825,000	Fla. Power Corp.	1973
	Ft. Pierce	St. Lucie Plant: Unit 2	801,000	Fla. Power & Light Co.	1978
Georgia	Baxley	Edwin I. Hatch Unit 1	786,000	Georgia Power Co.	1974
	Baxley	Edwin I. Hatch Unit 2	795,000	Georgia Power Co.	1978
	Waynesboro	Alvin W. Vogtle, Jr. Plant: Unit 1	1,121,000	Georgia Power Co.	1980
	Waynesboro	Alvin W. Vogtle, Jr. Plant: Unit 2	1,121,000	Georgia Power Co.	1981
Illinois	Morris	Dresden Station: Unit 1	200,000	Commonwealth Edison Co.	1960
	Morris	Dresden Station: Unit 2	809,000	Commonwealth Edison Co.	1970
	Morris	Dresden Station: Unit 3	809,000	Commonwealth Edison Co.	1971
	Zion	Zion: Unit 1	1,050,000	Commonwealth Edison Co.	1973
	Zion	Zion: Unit 2	1,050,000	Commonwealth Edison Co.	1974
	Cordova	Quad-Cities Station: Unit 1	800,000	Comm. Ed. Co.-Ia.-Ill. Gas & Elec. Co.	1972
	Cordova	Quad-Cities Station: Unit 2	800,000	Comm. Ed. Co.-Ia.-Ill. Gas & Elec. Co.	1972
	Seneca	LaSalle Co. Station: Unit 1	1,078,000	Comm. Ed. Co.-Ia.-Ill. Gas & Elec. Co.	1977
	Seneca	LaSalle Co. Station: Unit 2	1,078,000	Comm. Ed. Co.-Ia.-Ill. Gas & Elec. Co.	1978
	Byron	Byron Station: Unit 1	1,120,000	Comm. Edison Co.	1979
	Byron	Byron Station: Unit 2	1,120,000	Comm. Edison Co.	1980
	Braidwood	Braidwood: Unit 1	1,100,000	Comm. Edison Co.	1979
	Braidwood	Braidwood: Unit 2	1,100,000	Comm. Edison Co.	1980
	Clinton	Clinton Plant: Unit 1	950,000	Illinois Power Co.	1980
	Clinton	Clinton Plant: Unit 2	950,000	Illinois Power Co.	1982
Indiana	Dune Acres	Bailly Station	660,000	Northern Ind. Public Service Co.	1977
Iowa	Palo	Duane Arnold Unit 1	529,700	Iowa Electric Light and Power Co.	1974
Louisiana	Taft	Waterford Sta.	1,113,000	La. Power & Light Co.	1977
	St. Francisville	River Bend Station	934,000	Gulf States Utilities Co.	1979
Maine	Wiscasset	Maine Yankee Atomic Power	790,000	Me. Yankee Atomic Power Co.	1972
Maryland	Lusby	Calvert Cliffs Unit 1	845,000	Baltimore Gas and Electric Co.	1974
	Lusby	Calvert Cliffs Unit 2	845,000	Baltimore Gas and Electric Co.	1975
	Douglas Point	Douglas Pt. Proj.: Unit 1	1,178,000	Potomac Electric Power Co.	1980
	Douglas Point	Douglas Pt. Proj.: Unit 2	1,178,000	Potomac Electric Power Co.	1981
Massachusetts	Rowe	Yankee Station	175,000	Yankee Atomic Electric Co.	1961
	Plymouth	Pilgrim Station: Unit 1	664,000	Boston Edison Co.	1972
	Plymouth	Pilgrim Station: Unit 2	1,180,000	Boston Edison Co.	1978
Michigan	Big Rock Point	Big Rock Point	70,300	Consumers Power Co.	1965
	South Haven	Palisades Station	700,000	Consumers Power Co.	1971
	Lagoona Beach	Enrico Fermi Unit 2	1,123,000	Detroit Edison Co.	1976
	Lagoona Beach	Enrico Fermi Unit 3	1,125,000	Detroit Edison Co.	1979
	Bridgman	Donald C. Cook Unit 1	1,060,000	Ind. & Michigan Electric Co.	1974
	Bridgman	Donald C. Cook Unit 2	1,060,000	Ind. & Michigan Electric Co.	1975
	Midland	Midland Unit 1	492,000	Consumers Power Co.	1979
	Midland	Midland Unit 2	818,000	Consumers Power Co.	1980
	St. Clair Cty.	Greenwood: Unit 2	1,240,000	Detroit Edison Co.	1980
	St. Clair Cty.	Greenwood: Unit 3	1,240,000	Detroit Edison Co.	1981
	Quanicassee	Quanicassee: Unit 1	1,150,000	Consumers Power Co.	1981
	Quanicassee	Quanicassee: Unit 2	1,150,000	Consumers Power Co.	1982
Minnesota	Monticello	Monticello	545,000	Northern States Power Co.	1971
	Red Wing	Prairie Island Unit 1	530,000	Northern States Power Co.	1973
	Red Wing	Prairie Island Unit 2	530,000	Northern States Power Co.	1974
Mississippi	Port Gibson	Grand Gulf Nuclear Stn.	1,290,000	Mississippi Power & Light Co.	1979
Nebraska	Fort Calhoun	Ft. Calhoun Unit 1	457,400	Omaha Public Power District	1973
	Brownville	Cooper Station	778,000	Pub. Power Dist. Ia. Power	1973
N. Hampshire	Seabrook		1,100,000	Public Service of N.H.	1979
	Seabrook		1,100,000	Public Service of N.H.	1981
New Jersey	Toms River	Oyster Creek Unit 1	640,000	Jersey Central Power Co.	1969
	Forked River	Forked River Unit 1	1,070,000	Jersey Central Power Co.	1978
	Salem	Salem Nuclear Unit 1	1,090,000	Pub. Service Elec. and Gas	1975
	Salem	Salem Nuclear Unit 2	1,115,000	Pub. Service Elec. and Gas	1976
	Bordentown	Newbold Unit 1	1,067,000	Pub. Service Elec. and Gas	1979
	Bordentown	Newbold Unit 2	1,067,000	Pub. Service Elec. and Gas	1980
	Little Egg Inlet	Atlantic Gen. Sta.: Unit 1	1,150,000	Pub. Service Elec. and Gas	1980
	Little Egg Inlet	Atlantic Gen. Sta.: Unit 2	1,150,000	Pub. Service Elec and Gas	1981
New York	Indian Point	Indian Point Unit 1	265,000	Consolidated Edison Co.	1962
	Indian Point	Indian Point Unit 2	873,000	Consolidated Edison Co.	1973
	Indian Point	Indian Point Unit 3	965,000	Consolidated Edison Co.	1974

State	Site	Plant Name	Capacity (kilowatts)	Utility	Commercial Operation
	Scriba	Nine Mile Point: Unit 1	625,000	Niagara Mohawk Power Co.	1969
	Scriba	Nine Mile Point: Unit 2	1,080,000	Niagara Mohawk Power Co.	1978
	Ontario	R. E. Ginna Unit 1	420,000	Rochester Gas & Electric Co.	1970
	Brookhaven	Shoreham	819,000	Long Island Lighting Co.	1977
	Scriba	James A. Fitzpatrick	821,000	Power Authority of State of N.Y.	1973
	(*)		1,150,000	Long Island Lighting Co.	1981
North Carolina	Southport	Brunswick Steam Unit 1	821,000	Carolina Power and Light Co.	1975
	Southport	Brunswick Steam Unit 2	821,000	Carolina Power and Light Co.	1974
	Cowans Ford	Wm. B. McGuire Unit 1	1,180,000	Duke Power Co.	1976
	Cowans Ford	Wm. B. McGuire Unit 2	1,180,000	Duke Power Co.	1977
	Bonsal	Shearon Harris Unit 1	915,000	Carolina Power & Light	1978
	Bonsal	Shearon Harris Unit 2	915,000	Carolina Power & Light	1979
	Bonsal	Shearon Harris Unit 3	915,000	Carolina Power & Light	1980
	Bonsal	Shearon Harris Unit 4	915,000	Carolina Power & Light	1981
	(*)		1,200,000	Duke Power Co.	1981
	(*)		1,200,000	Duke Power Co.	1982
	(*)		1,200,000	Duke Power Co.	1983
	(*)		1,200,000	Duke Power Co.	1984
	(*)		1,200,000	Duke Power Co.	1985
	(*)		1,200,000	Duke Power Co.	1986
Ohio	Oak Harbor	Davis-Besse	906,000	Toledo-Cleveland Elec. Co.	1975
	Painesville	Perry Nuclear: Unit 1	1,205,000	Cleveland Electric Illuminating Co.	1979
	Painesville	Perry Nuclear: Unit 2	1,205,000	Cleveland Electric Illuminating Co.	1980
	Moscow	Wm. H. Zimmer Unit 1	810,000	Cincinnati Gas & Electric Co.	1977
	Prescott	Trojan Nuclear: Unit 1	1,130,000	Portland General Electric Co.	1975
	Boardman		1,200,000	Portland General Electric Co.	1980
Pennsylvania	Peach Bottom	Peach Bottom Unit 1	40,000	Philadelphia Electric Co.	1967
	Peach Bottom	Peach Bottom Unit 2	1,065,000	Philadelphia Electric Co.	1973
	Peach Bottom	Peach Bottom Unit 3	1,065,000	Philadelphia Electric Co.	1974
	Pottstown	Limerick Unit 1	1,065,000	Philadelphia Electric Co.	1978
	Pottstown	Limerick Unit 2	1,065,000	Philadelphia Electric Co.	1980
	Shippingport	Shippingport Unit 1	90,000	Duquesne Light Co.	1957
	Shippingport	Beaver Valley: Unit 1	852,000	Duquesne Light Co.-Ohio Edison Co.	1974
	Shippingport	Beaver Valley: Unit 2	852,000	Duquesne Light Co.-Ohio Edison Co.	1978
	Goldsboro	Three Mile Island: Unit 1	819,000	Metropolitan Edison Co.	1974
	Goldsboro	Three Mile Island: Unit 2	905,000	Jersey Central Power & Light Co.	1976
	Berwick	Susquehanna Steam: Unit 1	1,052,000	Pennsylvania Power and Light	1979
	Berwick	Susquehanna Steam: Unit 2	1,052,000	Pennsylvania Power and Light	1981
	Fulton Township	Phila. El. Co.: HTGR No. 1	1,140,000	Philadelphia Electric Co.	1981
	Fulton Township	Phila. El. Co.: HTGR No. 2	1,140,000	Philadelphia Electric Co.	1983
South Carolina	Hartsville	H. B. Robinson Unit 2	700,000	Carolina Power & Light Co.	1971
	Seneca	Oconee Unit 1	841,000	Duke Power Co.	1973
	Seneca	Oconee Unit 2	886,000	Duke Power Co.	1973
	Seneca	Oconee Unit 3	886,000	Duke Power Co.	1974
	Broad River	Virgil C. Summer Unit 1	900,000	S.C. Electric & Gas Co.	1977
	Lake Wylie	Catawba Nuclear: Unit 1	1,180,000	Duke Power Co.	1979
	Lake Wylie	Catawba Nuclear: Unit 2	1,180,000	Duke Power Co.	1980
Tennessee	Daisy	Sequoyah Unit 1	1,140,000	Tennessee Valley Authority	1975
	Daisy	Sequoyah Unit 2	1,140,000	Tennessee Valley Authority	1975
	Spring City	Watts Bar Unit 1	1,169,000	Tennessee Valley Authority	1977
	Spring City	Watts Bar Unit 2	1,169,000	Tennessee Valley Authority	1978
	Oak Ridge	Fast Breeder Demo Plant	400,000	Tennessee Valley Authority	1980
Texas	Glen Rose	Comanche Peak: Unit 1	1,150,000	Texas Utilities Services, Inc.	1980
	Glen Rose	Comanche Peak: Unit 2	1,150,000	Texas Utilities Services, Inc.	1982
	Newton County	Blue Hills: Unit 1	918,000	Gulf States Util	1980
Vermont	Vernon	Vermont Yankee	513,900	Vt. Yankee Nu. Power Corp.	1972
Virginia	Gravel Neck	Surry Power Unit 1	788,000	Va. Electric & Power Co.	1972
	Gravel Neck	Surry Power Unit 2	788,000	Va. Electric & Power Co.	1973
	Mineral	North Anna Unit 1	898,000	Va. Electric & Power Co.	1974
	Mineral	North Anna Unit 2	898,000	Va. Electric & Power Co.	1975
	Mineral	North Anna Unit 3	907,000	Va. Electric & Power Co.	1977
	Mineral	North Anna Unit 4	907,000	Va. Electric & Power Co.	1978
	Gravel Neck	Surry Power: Unit 3	882,000	Virginia Electric & Power Co.	1980
	Gravel Neck	Surry Power: Unit 4	882,000	Virginia Electric & Power Co.	1981
Washington	Richland	N-Rector/WPPSS Steam	800,000	Atomic Energy Commission	1966
	Richland	WPPSS No. 1	1,120,000	Wash. Pub. Power Supply	1980
	Richland	WPPSS No. 2	1,103,000	Wash. Pub. Power Supply	1977
Wisconsin	Genoa	Genoa Station	53,200	Dairyland Power Corporation	1971
	Two Creeks	Point Beach Unit 1	497,000	Wis. Mich. Power Co.	1970
	Two Creeks	Point Beach Unit 2	497,000	Wis. Mich. Power Co.	1972
	Carlton	Kewaunee Unit 1	541,000	Wis. Mich. Power Co.	1973
Puerto Rico	Puerto De Jobas	Aguirre	583,000	P.R. Water Resources Auth	1979

Nuclear plant capacity (kilowatts): In operation 19,005,000, being built 51,076,100; planned (reactors ordered) 86,382,000; total 156,463,100. *Site not selected.

Production of Electric Energy in the U. S.

Source: The Federal Power Commission

These amounts include both the privately owned and publicly-owned utilities.

Calendar Year	Total 1,000 Kw. hrs.	Hydro 1,000 Kw. hrs.	Steam 1,000 Kw. hrs.	Gas Turbine(a) 1,000 Kw. hrs.	Internal Comb'n(n) 1,000 Kw. hrs.	Coal Short tons	Oil 42 Gal. Barrels	Gas 1,000 Cu. ft.
						Fuel Consumed in the Year		
1935	95,287,390	38,372,154	56,144,412		770,824	32,714,761	11,256,565	124,117,769
1940	141,837,010	47,321,278	93,001,735		1,513,997	51,473,881	16,325,122	180,096,185
1945	222,486,283	79,970,312	140,435,268		2,080,703	74,724,956	20,228,215	326,211,969
1950	329,141,343	95,938,317	229,543,366		3,659,660	91,870,770	75,420,490	628,918,834
1955	547,037,985	112,975,069	430,119,086		3,943,830	143,759,195	75,273,862	1,153,279,586
1960	753,350,271	145,516,253	603,341,840		4,492,178	176,633,789	85,340,108	1,724,762,376
1965	1,055,251,929	193,850,603	856,312,128		5,089,198	244,788,119	115,202,583	2,321,100,937
1968	1,329,443,027	222,490,584	1,101,767,366		5,185,000	297,779,069	188,641,862	3,147,908,961
1969	1,442,182,474	250,192,655	1,178,182,761	8,227,148	5,579,910	310,316,640	250,937,800	3,487,642,263
1970	1,531,608,921	247,456,119	1,262,358,866	15,732,082	6,061,854	320,818,141	335,503,752	3,931,996,247
1971 (Prelim.)	1,613,935,744	266,320,232	1,319,291,654	22,072,221	6,251,637	327,926,249	396,237,967	3,992,980,610
1972 (Prelim.)	1,747,322,933	272,733,504	1,438,420,059	29,493,248		351,050,000	493,930,000	3,978,700,000

(a.)Data prior to 1969 included under steam.

TRADE AND TRANSPORTATION
Notable Steamships and Motorships

Source: Lloyd's Register of Shipping as of May 1, 1973
Gross tonnage is a measurement of enclosed space (1 gross ton = 100 cu.ft.)

WORLD'S LARGEST PASSENGER SHIPS
30,000 gross tons and over

Name-registry	Gross ton.	Lgth. Ft.	Bdth. Ft.
France, Fr.	66,348	1035	110
Queen Elizabeth 2, Br.	65,863	963	105
Raffaello, It.	45,933	904	101
Michelangelo, It.	45,911	904	101
Canberra, Br.	44,807	818	102
Oriana, Br.	41,910	804	97
*United States, U.S.	38,216	990	101
Rotterdam, Neth.	37,783	748	94
Nieuw Amsterdam, Neth.	36,982	758	88
Windsor Castle, Br.	36,277	783	92
Leonardo Da Vinci, It.	33,340	767	92
Eugenio C., It.	30,567	713	96
S. A. Vaal, S. Af. (1)	30,213	760	90

*Remeasured 1972

CONTAINER, LIQUEFIED GAS, MISC. SHIPS
27,000 gross tons and over

Name-registry	Gross ton.	Lgth. Ft.	Bdth. Ft.
Abel Tasman, Neth.	27,614	740	100
Arcadia Forest, Nor.	36,862	857	106
Antilla Bay, Neth.	34,015	710	106
Arctic Toykyo, Lib.	44,089	798	111
Asialighter, Br.	30,303		
Asialiner, Br.	30,909	798	101
Atlantic Forest, Br.	36,870	857	106
Benalder, Br.	57,887	950	106
Benavon, Br.	57,887	946	105
Bilderdyk, Neth	36,974	859	105
Bremen Express, Ger.	57,535	941	106
Bridgestone Maru V, Jap.	40,934	690	106
Cardigan Bay, Br.	58,899	950	106
City of Edinburgh, Br.	58,900	950	106
Dart America, Br.	31,036	759	100
Dart Atlantic, Br.	31,036	759	100
Dart Europe, Bel.	31,611	759	100
Delta Mar, U.S.	30,500	843	100
Descartes, Fr.	32,702	721	104
Dorsetown, Br.	32,000	710	106
Elbe Maru, Jap.	51,623	882	105
Esso Brega, It.	30,445	681	96
Esso Fuji, Pan.	55,897	807	131
Esso Liguria, It.	30,445	681	96
Esso Portovenere, It.	30,445	681	96
Eurofreighter, Br.	30,909	798	100
Euroliner, Br.	30,909	798	100
Gadila, Br.	48,662	852	114
Gadinia, Br.	48,662	852	114
Gari, Br.	48,662	852	114
Garmula, Br.	32,211	678	103
Gay Lussac, Pan.	27,725	648	95
Hamburg Express, Ger.	58,088	943	105
Hassi R' Mel, Alg.	31,420	656	96
Hoegh Multina, Nor.	31,918	679	103
HongKong Express, Ger.	57,535	941	106
Izumisan Maru, Jap.	38,872	705	105
Japan Ambrose, Jap.	33,287	748	106
Jovama Maru, Jap.	29,489	649	95
Jutlandia, Den.	49,961	900	105
Kamakura Maru, Jap.	51,139	856	105
Kanayama Maru, Jap.	41,939	734	113
Kazutama Maru, Jap.	34,529	656	103
Kiso Maru, Jap.	38,540	n.r.	105
Kitano Maru, Jap.	51,159	856	105
Korrigan, Fr.	54,000	946	105
Kosmonaut Gagarin, USSR	32,291	757	101
Kowloon Bay, Br.	58,889	950	106
Kurama Maru, Jap.	51,139	856	105
Kurobe Maru, Jap.	37,845	846	105
Laieta, Sp.	30,394	682	96
Liverpool Bay, Br.	58,889	950	105
Lloydiana, It.	28,500	740	100
Munchen, Ger.	37,134	857	105
Nedlloyd Dejima, Neth	57,500	941	106
Nedlloyd Delft, Neth.	57,500	941	106
New Jersey Maru, Jap.	37,800	810	105
New York Maru, Jap.	38,825	862	105
Nihon, Sw.	50,805	902	105
Ogden Bridgestone, Pan.	36,125	690	106
Osaka Bay, Br.	58,889	949	105
Pacific Arrow, Jap.	30,500	718	102
Polar Alaska, Lib.	44,089	798	111
Remuera, Br.	42,000	826	105
Rhine Maru, Jap.	51,085	856	105
Sea-Land Commerce, U.S.	41,100	946	105
Sea-Land Exchange, U.S.	41,100	946	105
Sea-Land Galloway, U.S.	41,127	946	105
Sea-Land McLean, U.S.	41,127	946	105
Sea-Land Trade, U.S.	41,100	946	105
Selandia, Den.	49,890	900	105
Silver Arrow, Jap.	30,135	739	100
Sovietskaya Rossia, USSR.	33,154	713	94
Sovietskaya Ukraina, USSR	32,024	713	94
Sydney Express, Ger.	27,407	743	100
Tatsuno Maru, Jap.	31,083	663	98
Tohbei Maru, Jap.	35,492	806	105
Tokio Express, Ger.	58,100	941	106
Tokyo Bay, Br.	58,889	900	105
Toyama, Nor.	52,196	902	105
World Bridgestone, Pan.	36,556	690	106
World Rainbow, Pan.	36,917	734	113
Yusho Maru, Jap.	47,783	744	114

NUCLEAR POWERED MERCHANT SHIPS

Name-registry	Gross ton.	Lgth. Ft.	Bdth. Ft.
Lenin, USSR.	14,067	439	90
Mutsu, Jap.	8,350	426	62
Otto Hahn, Ger.	16,871	564	76
Savannah, U.S.	15,585	595	78

OIL TANKERS
275,000 tons deadweight and over

Deadweight tonnage is the weight (long tons) of cargo, fuel etc., which a vessel is designed to carry safely.

Name-registry	Dwght ton.	Lgth. Ft.	Bdth. Ft.
Globtik Tokyo, Br.	483,664	1243	203
Nisseki Maru, Jap.	366,813	1138	179
Universe Iran, Lib.	326,933	1132	175
Universe Kuwait, Lib.	326,848	1132	175
Universe Korea, Lib	326,676	1132	175
Universe Portugal, Lib.	326,676	1132	175
Universe Ireland, Lib.	326,585	1132	175
Universe Japan, Lib.	326,562	1132	175
Venoil, Lib.	325,728	1056	175
Venpet, Lib.	325,720	1056	175
Arteaga, Sp.	318,061	1139	175
Arietta Livanos, Lib.	285,050	1140	170
Eugenie Livanos, Lib.	285,075	1140	170
Richard Maersk, Den.	284,600	1140	170
Rosa Maersk, Den.	284,600	1140	170
Romo Maersk, Den.	284,600	1140	170
Rasmine Maersk, Den.	284,500	1140	170
Regina Maersk, Den.	284,500	1140	170
Roy Maersk, Den.	284,500	1140	170
Fabian, Nor.	283,000	1140	169
Berge Queen, Nor.	280,476	1125	170
Berge King, Nor.	280,420	1125	170
Berge Princess, Nor.	280,015	1125	170
Berge Prince, Nor.	280,000	1125	170
Thorsholm, Nor.	279,310	1125	170

BULK, ORE, BULK/OIL & OIL/ORE CARRIERS
160,000 tons deadweight and over

Name-registry	Dwght ton.	Lgth. Ft.	Bdth. Ft.
Usa Maru, Jap.	264,523	1108	178
Lauderdale, Br.	260,424	1101	176
Naess Ambassador, Br.	260,308	1049	175
La Loma, Br.	245,288	1069	170
Hoegh Hill, Nor.	241,447	1069	170
Berge Istra, Lib.	223,963	1030	164
Berge Adria, Lib.	223,960	1030	164
Sysla, Nor.	223,500	1096	149
Andros Aries, Gr.	220,900	1061	158
Andros Atlas, Gr.	220,534	1007	158
Tantalus, Br.	215,680	1074	164
Tarter, Nor.	215,621	1075	164
Jarl Malmros, Sw.	215,500	1075	164

Name-registry	Gross ton.	Lgth. Ft.	Bdth. Ft.	Name-registry	Gross ton.	Lgth. Ft.	Bdth. Ft.
Tsurumi Maru, Jap.	215,000	1075	164	Cypress King, Sing.	164,200	967	155
Adria Maru, Jap.	183,572	1023	156	Yamazuru Maru, Jap.	163,600	948	157
Arafura Maru, Jap.	183,526	1023	156	Niizuru Maru, Jap.	162,586	1028	145
Larina, Lib.	175,935	984	167	Shinryu Maru, Jap.	162,415	959	146
Romantic, Lib.	174,107	995	151	Eastern Spirit, Lib.	162,141	964	155
Rhetoric, Lib.	173,668	995	151	Chidorisan Maru, Jap.	162,043	959	146
Cedros, Lib. (2)	170,418	995	142	Golden Clover, Lib.	162,039	967	155
Cetra, Centaurus, Fr.	170,414	981	143	World Splendour, Lib.	162,039	967	155
English Bridge, Br.	168,700	965	145	World Guard, Lib.	162,018	1030	145
Bristol Maru, Jap.	168,100	964	155	Golden Tulip, Lib.	161,918	967	155
Tyne Bridge, Br.	166,753	965	145	Polysaga, Nor.	160,400	1009	144
Hampton Maru, Jap.	166,191	974	155	Universe Aztec, Lib.	160,242	990	142
Furness Bridge, Br.	166,064	965	145	Kohjusan Maru, Jap.	160,000	967	154
Pacific Maru, Jap.	165,400	974	155				
Wakazuru Maru, Jap.	165,087	984	158	(1) Former name. Transvaal Castle, (2) Salt/oil carrier,			
Laura, Lib.	165,000	935	155	operates as an oil carrier. n.r.-not recorded.			

U.S. Exports and Imports of Leading Commodities

Source: Bureau of International Commerce, Dept. of Commerce,

(Value in millions of dollars)

Commodity	Exports 1971	Exports 1972	Imports 1971	Imports 1972
Total	$43,492	$48,968	$45,563	$55,555
Food and live animals	4,367	5,665	5,529	6,362
Meat	192	252	1,050	1,223
Dairy products and eggs	185	143	...	...
Cheese	...	...	76	111
Fish	114	135	879	1,205
Grains and preparations	2,449	3,505	72	92
Wheat and wheat flour	1,090	1,456	...	...
Rice	257	389	...	...
Corn	746	1,241	...	...
Fruit and nuts	430	526	460	496
Vegetables	182	209	287	350
Sugar	...	...	764	824
Coffee, green	...	...	1,167	1,182
Beverages and Tobaccos	709	908	876	1,010
Alcoholic Beverages	...	...	766	824
Tobacco, unmanufactured	462	639	89	157
Crude materials, inedible other than fuels	4,329	5,029	3,382	3,860
Synthetic rubber	173	161	...	...
Ores and metal scrap	486	508	1,044	1,022
Coal	902	984	...	...
Petroleum and products	479	445	3,323	4,300
Animal and vegetable oils and fats	615	507	172	180
Chemicals	3,836	4,134	1,612	2,015
Medicinal and Pharmaceutical	396	474	119	149
Machinery and transport equipment	19,460	21,514	13,873	17,400
Automotive engines	404	485	719	846
Agricultural machinery	180	249	181	237
Tractors and parts	186	249	151	211
Metalworking machinery	405	410	107	140
Textile and leather machinery	253	272	501	638
Other nonelectrical machinery	908	1,039	618	798
Electrical apparatus	3,067	3,699	2,555	3,375
Transport equipment	7,621	7,944	7,814	9,484
New motor vehicles	1,824	2,061	5,085	5,704
Aircraft and parts	3,387	3,011	338	415
Other manufactured goods	7,147	8,094	14,929	18,332
Rubber manufactures	205	231	...	...
Paper and manufactures	685	726	1,157	1,261
Diamonds excluding industrial	125	172	473	637
Metals and manufactures	754	828	5,114	6,004
Iron and steel-mill products	760	800	2,615	2,743
Nonferrous base metals	597	567	1,431	1,754
Textiles other than clothing	632	779	1,391	1,528
Clothing	55	215	1,521	1,883
Other transactions	1,531	1,563	1,476	1,598

U.S. Merchandise Exports and Imports, by Continent

Source: International Trade Analysis Division, Dept. of Commerce

Value in millions of dollars

Year	Exports Western Hemisp.	Exports Europe	Exports Asia & Oceania	Exports Africa	General imports Western Hemisp.	General imports Europe	General imports Asia & Oceania	General imports Africa
1965	9,932	9,397	7,129	1,071	9,257	6,292	4,999	867
1966	11,447	10,089	7,734	1,159	10,889	7,857	5,891	974
1967	11,890	10,382	8,233	1,116	13,802	8,229	4,078	901
1968	13,411	11,347	8,656	1,221	14,148	10,338	7,640	1,090
1969	14,713	12,642	9,327	1,324	15,547	10,334	9,141	1,008
1970	15,611	14,817	11,294	1,502	16,928	11,395	10,515	1,090
1971	16,850	14,574	11,082	1,631	18,801	12,846	12,697	1,218
1972	19,694	16,160	12,411	1,501	21,912	15,740	16,273	1,578

United States Foreign Trade with Leading Countries

Source: Bureau of International Commerce, Dept. of Commerce

(Value in millions of dollars)

Exports from the U.S. to the following areas and countries and imports into the U. S. from those areas and countries:	Exports		Imports	
	1971	1972	1971	1972
Total (incl. special category) see *	$44,130	$49,768	$45,563	$55,555
Western Hemisphere	16,849	19,694	18,730	21,912
Canada	10,365	12,415	12,692	14,909
19 American Republics	5,666	6,471	4,881	5,772
Central American Common Market	408	439	447	485
Latin American Free Trade Ass'n	4,849	5,580	4,153	4,949
Domican Republic	164	183	175	232
Panama	209	216	66	55
Bahamas	141	144	229	247
Bermuda	91	48	3	3
Jamaica	216	221	170	181
Netherlands Antilles	119	122	386	400
Surinam	36	37	68	69
Trinidad and Tobago	117	122	215	251
Europe	14,562	16,160	12,881	15,740
OECD Countries [2]	13,986	15,154	12,559	15,264
Western Europe	14,178	15,342	12,658	15,420
European Economic Community	11,141	11,881	10,432	12,485
Belgium and Luxembourg	1,077	1,138	844	968
France	1,373	1,610	1,088	1,369
Germany, Federal Republic of	2,831	2,811	3,650	4,249
Italy	1,314	1,430	1,406	1,756
Netherlands	1,786	1,851	534	639
United Kingdom	2,369	2,658	2,499	2,986
Denmark	233	200	222	357
Ireland	138	125	125	152
European Free Trade Association	1,635	1,775	1,545	1,984
Austria	101	96	128	173
Finland	90	91	123	142
Iceland	19	20	60	59
Norway	185	213	175	241
Portugal	142	212	113	150
Sweden	470	472	454	601
Switzerland	627	672	493	619
Greece	275	250	57	90
Spain	627	930	458	600
Turkey	307	317	67	106
Yugoslavia	174	169	96	150
Eastern Europe	384	819	223	321
Asia	9,918	11,376	11,799	15,128
Near East	1,816	1,975	593	773
Egypt	63	76	19	17
Iraq	32	23	9	10
Iran	482	559	136	199
Israel	707	558	173	222
Jordan	78	65	—	—
Kuwait	84	111	36	49
Lebanon	93	130	13	21
Saudi Arabia	164	314	99	194
Japan	4,055	4,965	7,259	9,064
East and South Asia	4,047	4,375	3,941	5,258
China, Republic of (Taiwan)	510	631	817	1,294
Hong Kong	424	489	991	1,249
India*	648	350	329	427
Indonesia	263	308	207	278
Korea, Republic of	681	735	462	708
Malaysia [3]	72	128	269	301
Singapore	315	385	136	265
Pakistan*	211	183	77	40
Philippines	340	366	496	484
Thailand*	144	170	97	116
Vietnam, Republic of*	297	318	2	2
Oceania	1,168	1,035	895	1,145
Australia	1,004	843	619	807
New Zealand and Western Samoa	111	137	230	277
Africa	1,631	1,501	1,217	1,578
North Africa excluding Egypt	340	345	156	309
Algeria	82	98	20	104
Ethiopia	26	24	61	58
Libya	78	85	51	116
Morocco	102	58	7	11
Tunisia	42	55	5	8
Western and Equatorial Africa	442	399	542	675
Angola	36	26	89	90
Ghana	55	44	106	80
Ivory Coast	22	22	83	92
Liberia	43	41	49	53
Nigeria	168	114	130	271
Central and Southern Africa	849	756	520	595
Kenya	41	26	26	27
South Africa, Republic of	622	602	287	325
Tanzania	13	12	20	21
Uganda	7	3	43	49
Zaire	84	37	45	43

*Where the asterisk appears the "special category shipments" are excluded.
(1.)Includes Paraguay and Uruguay. (2.)Excludes dependencies and Yugoslavia. (3.)Includes Sarawak and Sabah.

Important Waterways and Canals

The St. Lawrence & Great Lakes Waterway, the largest inland navigation system on the continent, extends from the Atlantic Ocean to Duluth at the western end of Lake Superior, a distance of 2,342 miles. With the deepening of channels and locks to 27 ft., ocean carriers are able to penetrate to ports in the Canadian interior and the American midwest.

The major canals are those of the St. Lawrence-Great Lakes waterway—the 3 new canals of the St. Lawrence Seaway, with their 7 locks, providing navigation for vessels of 26 foot draught from Montreal to Lake Ontario; the Welland Ship Canal by-passing the Niagara River between Lake Ontario and Lake Erie with its 8 locks, and the Sault Ste. Marie Canal and lock between Lake Huron and Lake Superior. These 16 locks overcome a drop of 580 ft. from the head of the lakes to Montreal. From Montreal to Lake Ontario the former bottleneck of narrow, shallow canals and of slow passage through 22 locks has been overcome, giving faster and safer movement for larger vessels. The new locks and linking channels now accommodate all but the largest ocean-going vessels and the upper St. Lawrence and Great Lakes are open to 80% of the world's saltwater fleet.

Subsidiary Canadian canals or branches include the St. Peters Canal between Bras d'Or Lakes and the Atlantic Ocean in Nova Scotia; the St. Ours and Chambly Canals on the Richelieu River, Quebec; the Ste. Anne and Carillon Canals on the Ottawa River; the Rideau Canal between the Ottawa River and Lake Ontario, the Trent and Murray Canals between Lake Ontario and Georgian Bay in Ontario and the St. Andrew's Canal on the Red River. The commerical value of these canals is not great but they are maintained to control water levels and permit the passage of small vessels and pleasure craft. The Canso Canal, completed 1957, permits shipping to pass through the causeway connecting Cape Breton Island with the Nova Scotia mainland.

St Lawrence Seaway traffic reached a new record level during the 1972 navigation season. Total cargo traffic of 53,700,000 tons exceeded the 1971 record by 669,000 tons. Bulk cargo of 45,800,000 tons combined with general cargo of 7,900,000 tons set the record. Grain shipments increased 4%; container traffic increased 32% over 1971.

St. Lawrence Seaway provides a navigational channel with a minimum water depth of 27 ft. to link the Great Lakes to the Atlantic Ocean. A vessel entering the Great Lakes from the Atlantic ascends 20 ft. above sea level in the 1,000-mile long reach up the Gulf of St. Lawrence and St. Lawrence River to Montreal, Quebec. At Montreal, the vessel enters the first of 7 new locks, 5 of which are in Canadian waters and 2 within United States waters, which raise or lower shipping a total of 226 ft. in the 182-mile stretch of the St. Lawrence River between Montreal and Lake Ontario. Crossing Lake Ontario, the vessel enters Canada's 28-mile-long Welland Canal, with 8 locks to compensate for the difference in elevation of 326 ft. between Lake Ontario and Lake Erie.

The signing of the Merchant Marine Bill of 1970 removed the major obstacles to the future development of the St. Lawrence Seaway. The bill eliminated interest payments on the Seaway's debt, gave official "fourth seacoast" identity to the Great Lakes-St. Lawrence Waterway, and enabled lake shipbuilders to qualify for federal shipbuilding subsidies.

Richard M. Nixon, President of the U.S. and Pierre E. Trudeau, Prime Minister of Canada, signed the Great Lakes Water Quality Agreement in 1971. Both nations agreed to roll back the present level of pollution in the Great Lakes and to protect this vital waterway against future pollution.

Saint Lawrence Seaway Development Corporation (U.S.), Seaway Circle, Massena, New York, David W. Oberlin, Administrator.

St. Lawrence Seaway Authority (Canada), Ottawa, Ontario, Dr. Pierre Camu, president.

The Welland Canal overcomes the 326-ft. drop of Niagara Falls and the rapids of the Niagara River. It has 8 locks, each 859 ft. long, 80 ft. wide and 30 ft. deep. Regulations permit ships of 730-ft. length and 75-ft. beam to transit with special handling, while largest size for regular handling is 715-ft. length and 72-ft. beam.

In 1971 the Welland Canal carried 62,900,000 cargo tons.

Sault Ste. Marie Canal reported 95,812,826 short tons passing through the American locks and 1,120,567 short tons passing through the Canadian canal for a total of 96,933,393 tons for the season of 1972.

Panama Canal

The Panama Canal is a lock and lake canal, crossing the Isthmus of Panama from the Caribbean Sea in a southeasterly direction to the Bay of Panama of the Pacific Ocean. It is 50 mi. long from deep water to deep water, at least 500 ft. wide at the bottom of excavated channels, 110 ft. wide in lock chambers, which have a usable length of 1,000 ft. Depth varies, but is not less than 40 ft. Average time in transit is 12 hours.

Gatun Dam blocks the Chagres river near its Atlantic mouth, creating Gatun lake, 23¾ mi. long, 85 ft. above sea level, about 45 ft. deep. Ships ascend to the lake by locks and then pass through Gaillard (formerly Culebra) Cut, 8 mi. long.

Cargo tonnage on the Panama Canal in fiscal 1973 amounted to 126,500,000 compared with 111,100,000 tons in 1972. Transit of oceangoing ships in fiscal 1973 totaled 14,238 compared with 14,238 in fiscal 1972 (same figure). Toll collections in fiscal 1973 were 113,400,000 compared with 101,500,000 in 1972.

Improvements have included the widening of the eight-mile long channel through Gaillard Cut from 300 to 500 feet, costing $60,000,000; illumination of Gaillard Cut and installation of new towing locomotives at the locks costing $8,000,000.

Thatcher Ferry Bridge, opened 1962, spans Panama Canal 201 ft. above the water level near Balboa. It is a steel-arch bridge, about 1 mi. long, with 3 spans and 4 lanes. It cost $20,000,000 authorized by the U. S. Congress in 1956.

Other Foreign Canals

One of the busiest canals in Europe is the Gota, in Sweden, 115 mi. long. Others: Kiel Canal, Germany, connecting the Baltic with the North Sea, 61 mi.; Elbe, Germany, 41 mi.; Amsterdam, Netherlands, 16 mi. Also the Manchester Ship Canal, England, 35.5 mi.

United States Foreign Trade, by Economic Classes

Source: International Trade Analysis Div., Dept. of Commerce. (Value in Millions of dollars)

Year (cal.)	Value of domestic exports					Value of imports				
	Crude Mater'ls	Crude Foods	Manu'd Foods	Semi-Manuf's	Finish. Manuf's	Crude Mater'ls	Crude Foods	Manu'd Foods	Semi-Manuf's	Finish. Manuf's
1965..	2,887	2,587	1,590	4,114	16,008	3,709	2,008	1,877	4,964	8,871
1970..	4,492	2,748	1,921	6,866	26,563	4,126	2,579	3,519	7,263	22,464
1971..	4,563	2,677	2,021	5,678	28,553	4,374	2,614	3,695	8,558	26,322
1972..	5,242	3,738	2,325	6,163	31,500	5,354	2,868	4,320	10,262	32,751

Total agricultural exports were valued as follows (in millions of dollars): 1965—1,942; 1968—2,177; 1969—2,057; 1970—2,524; 1971—2,884; 1972—3,325. Agricultural imports for consumption were valued as follows (in millions of dollars): 1965—864; 1968—834; 1969—909; 1970—797; 1971—685; 1972—801.

Shortest Navigable Distances Between Ports

Source: Distances Between Ports, 1965. Defense Mapping Agency Hydrographic Center.

Distances shown are in nautical miles (1,852 meters or about 6,076.115 feet).

To get statute miles, multiply by 1.151 (one statute mile equals 5,280 feet).

TO	FROM New York	Montreal	Colon[1]	TO	FROM San Fran.	Vancouver	Panama[1]
Algiers, Algeria	3,617	3,600	4,745	Acapulco, Mexico	1,833	2,613	1,426
Amsterdam, Netherlands	3,438	3,162	4,825	Anchorage, Alas.	1,872	1,444	5,077
Baltimore, Md.	417	1,769	1,901	Bombay, India	9,794	9,578	12,962
Barcelona, Spain	3,714	3,697	4,842	Calcutta, India	8,991	8,728	12,154
Boston, Mass.	386	1,308	2,157	Colon, Panama[1]	3,298	4,076	44
Buenos Aires, Argentina	5,817	6,455	5,472	Djakarta, Indonesia	7,641	7,360	10,637
Cape Town, So. Africa[2]	6,786	7,118	6,494	Haiphong, No. Vietnam	6,496	6,231	9,673
Cherbourg, France	3,154	2,878	4,541	Hong Kong	6,044	5,777	9,195
Cobh, Ireland	2,901	2,603	4,308	Honolulu, Hawaii	2,091	2,423	4,685
Copenhagen, Denmark	3,846	3,570	5,233	Los Angeles, Calif.	371	1,161	2,913
Dakar, Senegal	3,335	3,566	3,694	Manila, Philippines	6,221	5,976	9,347
Galveston, Texas	1,882	3,165	1,492	Melbourne, Australia	6,970	7,343	7,928
Gibraltar[3]	3,204	3,187	4,332	Pusan, So. Korea	4,914	4,623	8,074
Glasgow, Scotland	3,086	2,691	4,508	Saigon, So. Vietnam	6,878	6,664	10,017
Halifax, N.S.	600	895	2,295	San Francisco, Calif.		812	3,245
Hamburg, W. Germany	3,674	3,398	5,061	Seattle, Wash.	807	126	4,020
Hamilton, Bermuda	697	1,572	1,659	Shanghai, China	5,396	5,110	8,566
Havana, Cuba	1,186	2,473	998	Singapore	7,353	7,078	10,505
Helsinki, Finland	4,309	4,033	5,696	Suva, Fiji	4,749	5,183	6,325
Istanbul, Turkey	5,001	4,984	6,129	Valparaiso, Chile	5,140	5,915	2,616
Kingston, Jamaica	1,474	2,690	551	Vancouver, B.C.	812		4,032
Lagos, Nigeria	4,883	5,130	5,049	Vladivostok, Sov. Union	4,563	4,378	7,741
Lisbon, Portugal	3,372	3,010	1,100	Yokohama, Japan	4,536	4,060	7,690
Marseille, France	3,891	3,874	5,019				
Montreal, Quebec	1,460		3,126		Port	Cape	
Naples, Italy	4,181	4,164	5,309	TO FROM	Said	Town[2]	Singapore
Nassau, Bahamas	962	2,274	1,166	Bombay, India	3,049	4,616	2,441
New Orleans, La.	1,708	2,991	1,389	Calcutta, India	4,695	5,638	1,649
New York, N.Y.		1,460	1,974	Dar es Salaam, Tanzania	3,238	2,365	4,042
Norfolk, Va.	294	1,700	1,779	Djakarta, Indonesia	5,293	5,276	525
Oslo, Norway	3,827	3,165	5,053	Hong Kong	6,462	7,006	1,454
Piraeus, Greece	4,688	4,671	5,816	Kuwait	3,360	5,176	3,833
Port Said, Egypt	5,123	5,106	6,251	Manila, Philippines	6,348	6,777	1,330
Rio de Janeiro, Brazil	4,770	5,354	4,367	Melbourne, Australia	7,842	5,963	3,844
St. John's, Nfld.	1,093	1,043	2,695	Saigon, So. Vietnam	5,667	6,263	649
San Juan, Puerto Rico	1,399	2,445	993	Singapore	5,018	5,614	
Southampton, England	3,189	2,913	4,576	Yokohama	7,907	8,503	2,889

(1)Colon on the Atlantic is 44 nautical miles from Panama (port) on the Pacific. (2)Cape Town is 35 nautical miles northwest of the Cape of Good Hope. (3)Gibraltar (port) is 24 nautical miles east of the Straits of Gibraltar.

Mississippi River System and Gulf Intracoastal Waterway
Source: Dept. of the Army, Corps of Engineers

(Note—The Mississippi River System comprises main channels and all tributaries of the Mississippi, Illinois, Missouri and Ohio Rivers. The Gulf Intracoastal Waterway, 1,137 miles long, extends from Apalachee Bay, Florida, to the Mexican border).

Port	1962 Tonnage	1971 Tonnage	1972 Tonnage	Port	1962 Tonnage	1971 Tonnage	1972 Tonnage
Minneapolis	569,610	1,303,132	1,671,323	Lake Providence	Not Compiled	439,196	366,387
St. Paul	3,910,305	4,827,607	5,059,621	Vicksburg	1,138,073	2,370,389	2,571,546
Metropolitan St. Louis*	9,971,897	11,215,807	22,008,151	Natchez	656,180	646,174	898,682
Memphis	6,903,281	10,404,823	10,612,101	Baton Rouge	31,095,502	47,018,527	52,903,352
Helena	1,802,162	2,377,060	2,672,209	New Orleans	71,569,913	120,066,944	125,719,378
Greenville	1,198,891	1,793,974	2,278,634				

Reach

Mississippi R. System	257,961,556	395,600,891	419,805,850				
Minneapolis to the Gulf	149,897,602	255,239,767	271,980,414	Baton Rouge to N. Orleans	66,755,381	136,685,284	163,345,088
Minneapolis to St. Louis	30,524,460	52,773,097	60,746,385	New Orleans to the Gulf	93,752,682	162,168,551	171,370,861
St. Louis to Cairo	35,183,709	58,518,767	67,545,404	Gulf Intracoastal			
Cairo to Baton Rouge	46,273,601	90,328,619	102,698,573	Waterway	60,424,304	105,975,450	108,999,010

*Port limits expanded in 1972.

Ton-Mileage of Freight Carried on Inland Waterways
Source: Corps of Engineers, Department of the Army, Calendar Years

System	1971	1970	1969
Atlantic coast waterways	28,619,707,000	28,571,788,000	26,602,679,000
Gulf coast waterways	30,473,095,000	28,582,418,000	27,807,696,000
Pacific coast waterways	8,525,013,000	8,397,133,000	8,060,940,000
Mississippi River system, including Ohio River and tributaries	142,385,476,000	138,533,627,000	125,195,008,000
Great Lakes system. Includes Alaskan waterways	105,027,016,000	114,475,222,000	115,234,685,000
Total	**315,030,307,000**	**318,560,188,000**	**302,901,008,000**

Commerce at Principal North American Ports
EXCLUDING GREAT LAKES SHIPPING
Source: Corps of Engineers, U.S. Army
Calendar Year 1971. In tons of 2,000 pounds.

PORTS HANDLING OVER 7,500,000 TONS

Port	Tons
Port of New York, N.Y. and N.J.	181,024,686
New Orleans, La.	120,066,944
Houston, Texas	68,423,829
Philadelphia Harbor, Pa.	51,133,893
Norfolk Harbor, Va.	47,120,158
Baltimore Harbor and Channels, Md.	44,002,785
Baton Rouge, La.	47,016,527
Beaumont, Texas	30,979,877
Tampa Harbor, Fla.	34,975,145
Los Angeles Harbor, Calif.	23,491,008
Corpus Christi, Texas	21,776,171
Port Arthur, Texas	23,296,357
Portland Harbor, Me.	31,679,119
Paulsboro, N.J. and vicinity	25,926,099
Mobile Harbor, Ala.	24,919,228
Boston, Mass.	26,156,517
Marcus Hook, Pa. and vicinity	21,033,381
Huntington, W. Va.	23,099,982
Lake Charles, La.	19,218,439
Texas City, Tex.	17,952,004
Richmond Harbor, Calif.	13,084,609
Portland, Ore.	15,485,979
Clairton-Elizabeth, Pa.	10,659,618
Seattle Harbor, Wash.	14,557,965
Port of Newport News, Va.	12,901,985
Long Beach, Calif.	20,697,508
Pascagoula Harbor, Miss.	10,098,503
Penn Manor, Pa. and vicinity	9,918,239
New Castle, Del. and vicinity	10,916,617
New Haven Harbor, Conn.	11,854,626
St. Louis, Mo.	11,215,807
Jacksonville Harbor, Fla.	12,448,895
Cincinnati, Ohio	9,769,357
Providence River and Harbor, R.I.	8,762,293
Pittsburgh, Pa.	8,343,964
Port of Albany, N.Y.	10,209,438
Louisville, Ky.	9,690,213
Memphis, Tenn.	10,404,823
Port Everglades Harbor, Fla.	10,065,815
Vancouver, B.C.	*26,517,891
Sept-Iles, P.Q.	*24,240,914
Montreal, P.Q.	*22,376,281
Thunder Bay, Ont.	*20,754,165
Port Cartier, P.Q.	*16,017,407
Hamilton, Ont.	*2,881,123
Halifax, N.S.	*11,072,468
Quebec, P.Q.	*8,552,289
Baie Comeau, P.Q.	*7,695,715

OTHER PORTS MAINE TO WASHINGTON

Port	Tons
Searsport Harbor, Maine	1,013,537
Portsmouth Harbor, N.H.	2,174,425
Burlington Harbor, Vt.	546,643
Beverley Harbor, Mass.	250,385
Fall River Harbor, Mass.	3,970,302
Gloucester Harbor, Mass.	260,206
New Bedford, Fairhaven Harbor, Mass.	486,349
Salem Harbor, Mass.	1,047,989
Bridgeport Harbor, Conn.	3,548,554
New London Harbor, Conn.	3,883,247
Norwalk Harbor, Conn.	919,446
Stamford Harbor, Conn.	1,086,747
Hempstead Harbor, N.Y.	4,328,107
Huntington Harbor, N.Y.	282,288
Peekskill Harbor, N.Y.	227,859
Plattsburg, N.Y.	486,871
Port Chester Harbor, N.Y.	500,702
Port Jefferson Harbor, N.Y.	4,249,598
Rondout Harbor, N.Y.	610,536
Tarrytown Harbor, N.Y.	608,437
Camden-Gloucester, N.J.	10,042,102
Trenton Harbor, N.J.	1,385,806
Aliquippa-Rochester, Pa.	5,969,305
Chester, Pa.	786,692
Wilmington Harbor, Del.	2,967,223
Washington Harbor, D.C.	2,615,242
Alexandria, Va.	634,286
Port of Hopewell, Va.	1,224,630
Port of Richmond, Va.	2,414,056
Morehead City Harbor, N.C.	1,289,768
Port of Wilmington, N.C.	6,050,538
Charleston Harbor, S.C.	6,945,951
Georgetown Harbor, S.C.	1,190,637
Brunswick Harbor, Ga.	1,059,104
Savannah Harbor, Ga.	7,231,944
Canaveral Harbor, Fla.	1,998,560
Charlotte Harbor, Fla.	2,406,828
Fernandina Harbor, Fla.	318,596
Miami Harbor, Fla.	2,643,596
Palm Beach Harbor, Fla.	954,921
Panama City Harbor, Fla.	1,677,227
Pensacola Harbor, Fla.	1,081,729
Port St. Joe Harbor, Fla.	689,180
St. Petersburg Harbor, Fla.	345,977
Weedon Island, Fla.	1,293,864

*1970.

Port	Tons
Guntersville, Ala.	1,765,930
Greenville, Miss.	1,793,974
Gulfport Harbor, Miss.	1,315,431
Natchez, Miss.	646,174
Vicksburg, Miss.	2,370,389
Brownsville, Texas	4,573,292
Freeport Harbor, Texas	5,723,061
Galveston, Texas	3,952,969
Harbor Island, Texas	4,978,297
Orange, Texas	1,483,455
Port Isabel, Texas	440,334
Matagorda Ship Channel, Port Lavaca, Tex.	4,689,767
Sabine Pass Harbor, Texas	203,478
Victoria, Texas	2,686,164
Helena, Ark.	2,377,060
Chattanooga, Tenn.	2,208,295
Knoxville, Tenn.	552,984
Nashville, Tenn.	3,618,973
Kansas City, Mo.	1,655,914
Mount Vernon, Ind.	3,497,132
Minneapolis, Minn.	1,303,132
St. Paul, Minn.	4,827,607
Carpinteria, Calif.	490,054
Crescent City Harbor, Calif.	264,405
El Segundo, Calif.	4,696,069
Ellwood, Calif.	109,742
Gaviota, Santa Barbara County, Calif.	186,495
Humboldt Harbor and Bay, Calif.	1,113,955
Moss Landing Harbor, Calif.	259,932
Oakland Harbor, Calif.	5,339,859
Redwood City Harbor, Calif.	919,538
San Diego Harbor, Calif.	1,809,371
San Francisco Harbor, Calif.	2,099,729
San Luis Obispo Harbor, Calif.	1,287,307
Stockton, Calif.	3,590,006
Ventura Harbor, Calif.	3,607,418
Astoria, Ore.	1,540,977
Coos Bay, Ore.	6,747,507
Oregon Slough (No. Portland Hbr.), Ore.	229,842
Port of St. Helens, Ore.	35,077
Anacortes Harbor, Wash.	3,833,991
Bellingham Bay and Harbor, Wash.	2,078,573
Everett Harbor, Wash.	4,767,379
Grays Harbor and Chehalis River, Wash.	2,753,320
Hammersley Inlet, Wash. (Shelton Hbr.)	1,130,201
Longview, Wash.	4,362,251
Olympia Harbor, Wash.	1,090,610
Port Angeles Harbor, Wash.	2,580,864
Port Gamble Harbor, Wash.	376,041
Port Townsend Harbor, Wash.	1,132,289
Tacoma Harbor, Wash.	7,109,860
Vancouver, Wash.	2,705,168
Willapa Riv. & Hbr., Naselle Riv., Wash.	426,574

ALASKA, HAWAII, PUERTO RICO

Port	Tons
Anchorage, Alaska	1,782,064
Iliuliuk Harbor, Alaska	245,163
Juneau Harbor, Alaska	146,833
Ketchikan Harbor, Alaska	1,606,637
Sitka Harbor, Alaska	1,039,017
Skagway Harbor, Alaska	1,451,202
Whittier Harbor, Alaska	713,290
Wrangell Harbor, Alaska	922,439
Barbers Point, Oahu, Hawaii	2,677,542
Hilo Harbor, Hawaii, Hawaii	1,064,384
Honolulu Harbor, Oahu, Hawaii	7,390,015
Kahului Harbor, Maui, Hawaii	1,067,941
Kaumalapau Harbor, Lanai, Hawaii	320,213
Kaunakakai Harbor, Molokai, Hawaii	172,647
Kawaihae Harbor, Hawaii, Hawaii	355,546
Nawiliwili Harbor, Kauai, Hawaii	460,259
Pearl Harbor, Oahu, Hawaii	1,013,263
Wake Island Harbor	174,330
Guanica Harbor, P.R.	136,018
Mayaguez Harbor, P.R.	209,616
Ponce Harbor, P.R.	353,429
San Juan Harbor, P.R.	9,353,699
St. Thomas Harbor, V.I.	488,800
Guam Island, Pacific Ocean	275,853
Corner Brook, Nfld.	*1,225,372
St. John's, Nfld.	*794,494
Charlottetown, P.E.I.	*554,399
Hantsport, N.S.	*1,648,191
Sydney, N.S.	*1,966,105
Saint John, N.B.	*6,400,885
Port Alfred, Que.	*4,973,666
Sorel, Que.	*6,813,817
Trois Rivieres, Que.	*4,954,649
Port Colborne, Ont.	*2,259,345
Sarnia, Ont.	*7,331,360
Sault Ste. Marie, Ont.	*5,753,245
Toronto, Ont.	*5,162,904
Windsor, Ont.	*3,550,556
Nanaimo, B.C.	*2,492,110
New Westminster, B.C.	*4,564,477
Powell River, B.C.	*1,783,686
Victoria, B.C.	*2,071,342

Commerce at Great Lakes Ports
Source: Corps of Engineers, U.S. Army
Calendar Year 1971. In tons of 2,000 pounds.

Port	Tons	Port	Tons
Duluth-Superior Hbr., Minn. & Wis.	37,050,852	Port Dolomite, Mich.	2,708,619
Silver Bay, Minn.	10,616,338	Port Gypsum, Mich.	339,226
Taconite Harbor, Minn.	10,668,395	Port Huron, Mich.	886,739
Ashland Harbor, Wis.	355,299	Port Inland, Mich.	4,519,314
Green Bay Harbor, Wis.	2,763,287	Port of Detroit, Mich.	30,051,909
Kewaunee Harbor, Wis.	1,258,120	Presque Isle Harbor, Mich.	3,549,274
Manitowoc Harbor, Wis.	1,932,495	St. Clair, Mich.	3,994,987
Milwaukee Harbor, Wis.	5,660,299	St. Ignace, Mich.	120,652
Oak Creek, Wis.	874,120	St. Joseph Harbor, Mich.	626,871
Port Washington Harbor, Wis.	903,773	Sault Ste. Marie, Mich.	116,564
Racine Harbor, Wis.	124,533	Stoneport, Mich.	7,049,105
Sheboygan Harbor, Wis.	228,280	Traverse City Harbor, Mich.	308,475
Two Rivers Harbor, Wis.	94,299	Wells, Mich.	123,992
Alabaster, Mich.	513,020	Port of Chicago, Ill.	47,430,340
Alpena Harbor, Mich.	3,637,720	Waukegan Harbor, Ill.	588,866
Calcite, Mich.	12,321,454	Buffington Harbor, Ind.	1,456,002
Cheboygan Harbor, Mich.	135,202	Gary Harbor, Ind.	8,240,139
Detour, Mich.	213,454	Indiana Harbor, Ind.	15,914,661
Drummond Island, Mich.	2,045,120	Michigan City Harbor, Ind.	154
Escanaba, Mich.	9,381,838	Ashtabula Harbor, Ohio	11,261,010
Frankfort Harbor, Mich.	1,563,448	Cleveland Harbor, Ohio	20,551,928
Gladstone Harbor, Mich.	320,779	Conneaut Harbor, Ohio	15,851,802
Gd. Haven Harbor & Gd. River, Mich.	3,134,058	Fairport Harbor, Ohio	2,679,385
Holland Harbor, Mich.	276,872	Huron Harbor, Ohio	3,332,027
Lime Island, Mich.	86,832	Lorain Harbor, Ohio	7,483,789
Ludington Harbor, Mich.	4,258,442	Marblehead, Ohio	1,585,587
Mackinaw City, Mich.	56,588	Sandusky Harbor, Ohio	4,883,103
Manistee Harbor, Mich.	503,734	Toledo Harbor, Ohio	27,310,667
Manistique Harbor, Mich.	301	Erie Harbor, Pa.	1,249,218
Marine City, Mich.	835,359	Ogdensburg Harbor, N.Y.	237,557
Marysville, Mich.	678,524	Oswego Harbor, N.Y.	491,100
Menominee Harbor, Mich. & Wis.	279,372	Port of Buffalo, N.Y.	11,067,491
Muskegon Harbor, Mich.	3,541,910	Rochester (Charlotte) Harbor, N.Y.	307,249
Petoskey Penn Dixie Harbor, Mich.	542,011		

Net Total Water-Borne Commerce of the United States
Source: Corps of Engineers, Department of the Army, Calendar Years. In tons of 2,000 pounds

Type of traffic	1970	1971	Type of traffic	1970	1971
Net total water-borne commerce of the U.S.	1,531,696,507	1,512,583,690	Foreign		
			Imports	339,339,772	359,745,840
			Coastal ports	312,933,583	333,776,713
Domestic			Gt. Lakes, Canada	21,820,193	19,104,708
Coastwise	238,440,385	242,916,056	Gt. Lakes, overseas	4,585,996	6,864,419
Lakewise	157,058,867	140,954,956	Exports	241,629,361	206,239,744
Internal	472,123,417	479,217,765	Coastal ports	205,697,712	172,758,807
Local	81,474,805	81,252,652	Gt. Lakes to Canada	29,146,465	24,757,317
Intraterritory	1,629,900	2,256,677	Gt. Lakes to overseas	6,785,184	8,723,620
Total domestic	950,727,374	946,598,106	Total foreign	580,969,133	565,985,584

Value of U.S. Merchandise Exports and Imports
Source: International Trade Analysis Division, Dept. of Commerce
Value in Millions of dollars (Revised)

Year	U.S. exports					U.S. imports		Gross merchandise balance[1]
	Domestic and foreign							
	Total	Military aid	Excl. military aid	Domestic merchandise	Foreign merchandise	General	For consumption	
1950	10,279	282	9,997	10,146	133	8,954	8,844	1,043
1955	15,554	1,256	14,298	15,426	128	11,566	11,519	2,732
1960	20,608	949	19,659	20,408	201	15,073	15,069	4,586
1965	27,521	779	26,742	27,178	343	21,427	21,345	5,315
1970	43,224	565	42,659	42,590	634	39,952	39,756	2,707
1971	44,137	581	43,555	43,497	639	45,602	45,546	−2,047
1972	49,768	560	49,208	48,968	799	55,282	55,555	−6,347

(1.) Balance represents exports excluding military grant-aid valued f.a.s. less imports which are valued generally at the market value in the foreign country. Export values include both commercially-financed shipments and shipments under government-financed programs. (2.) Includes data from April when shipments under the program began.

Total Exports and Exports Financed by Foreign Aid
Source: Bureau of International Commerce, Dept. of Commerce

(In millions of dollars)	1965	1967	1968	1969	1970	1971	1972
Exports, total	27,530	31,622	34,636	38,006	43,224	44,137	49,768
Agricultural commodities	6,306	6,448	6,300	6,004	7,349	7,783	9,508
Nonagricultural commodities	20,445	24,582	27,763	31,328	35,310	35,772	39,700
Manufactured goods (domestic)	17,439	20,844	23,818	26,785	29,343	30,449	33,742
Military grant–aid	779	592	573	674	565	581	560
Export financed under P.L. 480	1,323	1,237	1,178	1,019	1,021	971	1,064
Sales for foreign currency	899	736	539	337	276	171	70
Donations, including disaster relief	253	287	251	256	255	291	376
Barter for strategic goods	19	13	3	—	—	—	—
Long-term dollar credit sales	152	201	384	426	490	509	618

Merchant Fleets of the World

Source: Maritime Administration, U.S. Dept. of Commerce

Excludes ships operating exclusively on the Great Lakes and inland waterways and special types such as channel ships, icebreakers, cable ships etc., and merchant ships owned by any military force.

Gross Tons: Volume, not weight; each gross ton represents 100 cubic ft. of enclosed space. **Deadweight Tons:** Number of long tons (2,240 lbs. ea.) of cargo, fuel, etc., a ship can carry at maximum draft.

Registry Jan. 1, 1973 (Tonnage in 1,000)	Total No.	Gross tons	Dwt. tons	Psgr.-Cargo No.	Dwt.	Freighters No.	Dwt.	Tankers No.	Dwt.
Total-All Countries	21,009	250,543	399,552	830	3,754	11,087	88,970	4,581	192,894
United States¹	1,150	13,111	17,949	149	920	666	7,990	280	8,193
Privately owned	651	9,300	13,638	8	72	361	5,063	246	7,764
Government owned ...	499	3,811	4,311	141	848	305	2,927	34	429
United Kingdom	1,627	27,214	43,495	38	280	700	6,610	437	24,447
Australia	91	928	1,326	3	7	36	251	15	302
British Colonies	100	1,289	2,080	5	17	48	342	18	1,136
Canada	66	260	313	15	17	25	102	19	139
Cyprus	401	2,284	3,271	8	55	325	2,350	29	474
Ghana	16	118	154	–	–	16	154	–	–
India	253	2,672	4,125	12	69	183	1,924	13	510
Malaysia	19	176	219	1	1	13	139	2	8
New Zealand	40	120	155	–	–	26	111	–	–
Nigeria	14	92	134	–	–	14	134	–	–
Pakistan	63	527	708	7	61	54	616	–	–
Singapore	176	1,025	1,425	18	90	135	950	14	129
*Albania	10	50	68	–	–	7	56	–	–
Algeria	14	125	158	–	–	7	40	4	82
Argentina	155	1,224	1,687	10	47	61	533	57	830
Belgium	76	1,086	1,629	2	25	36	437	15	501
Brazil	233	1,722	2,436	6	16	148	1,024	44	808
*Bulgaria	110	705	1,011	4	8	60	376	17	308
Burma	10	58	73	2	3	8	70	–	–
Chile	47	388	577	3	5	30	274	6	163
China (Taiwan)	162	1,423	2,166	5	17	101	823	15	627
*China (Communist)	272	1,500	2,033	20	41	198	1,582	30	300
Colombia	40	224	289	–	–	38	271	1	16
*Cuba	57	345	465	–	–	40	361	7	77
*Czechoslovakia	12	113	162	–	–	9	67	–	–
Denmark	297	3,718	6,084	7	16	178	1,454	58	3,624
Ecuador	9	50	59	–	–	5	43	2	3
Ethiopia	7	43	64	–	–	4	26	2	36
Finland	213	1,455	2,166	5	5	137	732	49	1,212
France	427	7,337	11,733	11	57	182	1,657	132	8,152
Germany (West)	797	7,612	11,536	6	25	591	4,701	70	3,184
*Germany (East)	140	1,009	1,381	5	33	103	760	9	290
Greece	1,549	16,227	25,926	59	259	903	8,123	256	9,848
Honduras	13	60	57	–	–	–	–	–	–
*Hungary	17	41	55	–	–	17	55	–	–
Iceland	25	51	70	1	2	15	43	–	–
Indonesia	139	443	529	29	82	87	328	16	96
Iran	16	160	225	–	–	11	141	4	80
Ireland	14	120	179	–	–	7	50	2	3
Israel	71	626	853	–	–	50	350	–	–
Italy	625	7,762	11,688	57	240	201	1,356	208	5,613
Ivory Coast	11	79	112	–	–	10	109	–	–
Japan	2,210	31,804	52,267	32	80	1,148	9,210	436	23,281
Korea (South)	119	874	1,361	1	11	74	424	24	582
*Korea (North)²	8	30	33	1	2	5	26	–	–
Kuwait	34	655	1,095	–	–	27	304	6	790
Lebanon	38	103	147	1	4	31	125	–	–
Liberia	2,139	45,695	83,208	26	186	513	5,144	809	50,273
Malagasy	15	74	115	–	–	11	68	4	47
Maldives	25	69	88	–	–	22	83	–	–
Mexico	41	351	535	–	–	16	116	21	354
Morocco	14	40	55	–	–	10	45	–	–
Netherlands	436	4,442	6,495	11	88	288	2,423	82	3,200
Norway	1,188	22,665	38,211	29	64	390	3,210	376	20,280
Panama	887	7,767	12,348	32	184	528	3,151	198	7,313
Peru	35	257	367	1	12	25	234	5	69
Philippines	170	870	1,253	21	37	102	724	29	296
Poland	253	1,793	2,499	2	7	176	1,447	4	79
Portugal	114	912	1,191	19	124	65	485	22	452
*Romania	56	394	571	1	2	37	179	4	110
Saudi Arabia	11	47	64	2	4	6	28	1	28
Somalia	148	1,034	1,510	2	8	122	998	11	231
South Africa	53	403	494	–	–	40	320	2	32
Spain	423	3,706	5,911	38	149	210	1,015	109	3,515
Sudan	7	32	39	–	–	6	34	–	–
Sweden	337	5,217	8,309	5	16	148	1,264	78	3,795
Switzerland	27	219	312	–	–	22	236	–	–
Thailand	21	74	109	–	–	11	63	9	44
Tunisia	10	25	34	–	–	7	15	2	15
Turkey	93	628	851	16	34	59	468	14	263
United Arab Republic	44	199	256	7	40	28	115	9	101
Uruguay	16	154	238	1	10	7	45	7	180
*USSR²	2,140	12,116	15,413	78	202	1,250	7,747	444	5,437
Venezuela	40	360	523	–	–	20	114	16	390
Yugoslavia	187	1,516	2,191	11	60	136	1,225	17	382

*Source material limited. (1.) Excludes 73 non-merchant type ships which are currently in the National Defense Reserve Fleet. (2.) Includes the following U.S. Government-owned ships transferred to USSR under lend-lease agreements, 42 of which are still under that registry and 2 under North Korean registry.

Notable Ocean Passages by Ships

Time	From	To	Distance Naut. mi.	Date	Ship
ONE HUNDRED YEARS OF SAILING VESSELS					
16d	Liverpool	New York	3,150	Nov., 1846	Yorkshire
76d 6h	San Francisco	Boston		1853	Northern Light
12d 6h	Boston Light	Light Rock		1854	James Baines
89d	New York	San Francisco	15,091	1854	Flying Cloud
89d 20h	New York	San Francisco	13,700	1860	Andrew Jackson
63d 18h 15m	Liverpool	Melbourne		1868-69	Thermopylae
13d 1h 25m	New York	Liverpool	3,150		Red Jacket
36d	50 S. Lat	Golden Gate			Starr King
12d 12h	Equator	San Francisco			Golden Fleece
12d 4h 1m	Sandy Hook	England	3,013	1905	Atlantic
23d	England	Sandy Hook	3,013	1928	Atlantic
22d 6h 7m	Bishop's Rock	Boston Light		1936	Yankee
ATLANTIC CROSSINGS BY POWER VESSELS					
29d 4h	Savannah	Liverpool		May 22, 1819	Savannah (Amer.) (a)
15d	Bristol	New York		Apr., 1838	Great Western (Br.)
14d 8h	Liverpool	New York	3,150	July, 1840	Britannia (Br.) (b)
9d 19h 25m	Atlantic			May, 1851	Pacific
9d 13h	Liverpool	New York	3,054	Aug., 1852	Baltic (Amer.)
8d 1h 45m	Queenstown	New York	2,780	1856	Persia
8d 2h 48m	Queenstown	New York	2,780	1866	Scotia
7d 4h 1m	Queenstown	New York		1867	City of Paris (Br.)
7d 22h 3m	Queenstown	New York	2,780	1869	City of Brussels (Br.)
7d 20h 9m	Queenstown	New York	2,780	1873	Baltic (Br.)
7d 15h 48m	Queenstown	New York	2,780	1875	City of Berlin (Br.)
7d 11h 37m	Queenstown	New York	2,780	1876	Germanic (Br.)
7d 10h 53m	Queenstown	New York	2,780	1877	Britannic (Br.)
7d 8h 0m	New York	Queenstown	2,790	1879	Arizona (Br.)
6d 7h 23m	Queenstown	New York	2,790	1880	Arizona (Br.)
6d 18h 37m	New York	Queenstown	2,780	1882	Alaska (Br.)
6d 21h 40m	New York	Queenstown	2,780	1883	Alaska (Br.)
6d 10h 40m	New York	Queenstown	2,780	1884	Oregon (Br.)
6d 4h 34m	Queenstown	New York	2,780	1887	Umbria (Br.)
6d 1h 55m	Queenstown	New York	2,780	1888	Etruria (Br.)
5d 22h 50m	New York	Queenstown	2,780	1889	City of Paris (Br.)
5d 16h 31m	Queenstown	New York	2,780	1891	Teutonic (Br.)
5d 14h 24m	Queenstown	New York	2,780	1892	City of Paris (Br.)
5d 9h 6m	Queenstown	New York	2,780	1893	Campania (Br.)
5d 7h 23m	Queenstown	New York	2,780	1894	Lucania (Br.)
5d 15h 20m	Southampton	New York	3,189	1898	Kaiser Wilhelm Der Grosse (Ger.)
5d 7h 38m	Sandy Hook	Plymouth	3,082	Sept., 1900	Deutschland (Ger.)
4d 11h 42m	Queenstown	New York	2,780	1909	Lusitania (Br.)
4d 10h 41m	Queenstown	New York	2,780	1910	Mauretania (Br.)
5d 6h 21m	New York	Cherbourg	3,227	Oct., 1924	Leviathan (Amer.)
6d 5h 30m	Cherbourg	Cape Henry	3,320	June, 1927	U.S.S. Memphis (c)
4d 17h 42m	Cherbourg	Ambrose Lt	3,164	July, 1929	Bremen (Ger.)*
4d 14h 30m	New York	Plymouth	3,082	July, 1929	Bremen (Ger.)*
4d 19h 57m	Ambrose Lt	Cherbourg	3,196	June, 1933	Europa (Ger.)
4d 16h 48m	Cherbourg	New York	3,149	July, 1933	Europa (Ger.)
4d 13h 58m	Gibraltar	Ambrose Lt	3,181	Aug., 1933	Rex (Ital.)
4d 14h 27m	Cherbourg	Ambrose Lt	3,092	Nov., 1934	Bremen (Ger.)
4d 12h 24m	Cherbourg	Ambrose Lt	3,158	May-June, '36	Queen Mary (Br.)*
3d 23h 02m	Bishop's Rock	Ambrose Lt	2,906	July-Aug., '37	Normandie (Fr.)
3d 22h 07m	New York	Southampton	2,936	Aug., 1937	Normandie (Fr.)
3d 20h 42m	Ambrose Lt	Bishop's Rock	3,120	Aug., 10-14, '38	Queen Mary (Br.)
3d 21h 48m	Bishop's Rock	Ambrose Lt	3,120	Aug., 1948	Queen Mary (Br.)
3d 10h 40m	Ambrose Lt	Bishop's Rock	2,942	July, 3-7, 1952	United States (U. S.)* (e)
3d 12h 12m	Bishop's Rock	Ambrose Lt	2,902	July, 11-14, '52	United States (U. S.) (e)
3d 20h 30m	Ambrose Lt	Bishop's Rock	3,053	May 10, 1973	Sea-Land McLean (j)
OTHER OCEAN PASSAGES					
3d 00h 36m	San Pedro	Honolulu	2,226	June, 1928	U.S.S. Lexington
3d 2h 30m	San Francisco	Oahu, Hawaii	2,091	July, 16-19 '45	U.S.S. Indianapolis (d)
4d 8h 51m	Gibraltar	Newp't News	3,360	Nov., 26, 1945	U.S.S. Lake Champlain
7d 18h 36m	Japan	San Francisco	5,000	July-Aug. 4, '50	U.S.S. Boxer
7d 13h	Yokosuka	Alameda	5,000	June 1-9, 1951	U.S.S. Philippine Sea
8d 11h	Nantucket	Portland, Eng	3,161	Feb. 25-Mar. 4, '58	U.S.S. Skate (f)
7d 5h	Lizard Head	Nantucket		Mar. 23-29, '58	U.S.S. Skate (f)
15d	Pearl Harbor	Iceland (via N. Pole)		July 23-Aug. 7,'58	U.S.S. Nautilus (g)
84d	New London	Rehoboth, Del	41,500	Feb. 16-May 10, '60	S.S. Triton (h)
6d	Baffin Bay	N.W. Passage, Pac.		Aug. 15-20, '60	U.S.S. Seadragon (i)
12d 16h 22m	New York	Cape Town	6,786	Oct. 30-Nov. 11,'62	African Comet*

*Maiden voyage. (a) The Savannah, a fully rigged sailing vessel with steam auxiliary (over 300 tons, 98.5 ft. long, beam 25.8 ft., depth 12.9 ft.), was launched in the East River in 1818. It was the first ship to use steam in crossing any ocean. It was supplied with engines and detachable iron paddle wheels. On its famous voyage it used steam 105 hours during parts of 12 days. The world's first nuclear-powered merchant ship, the N.S. Savannah, was named for the old steamship. (b) First Cunard liner. (c) Carried Charles A. Lindbergh back to the United States after his flight from New York to Paris. (d) Carried Hiroshima atomic bomb in World War II. (e) Set world speed record; average speed eastbound on maiden voyage 35.59 knots (about 41 m.p.h.); westbound, 34.51 knots. (f) First atomic submarine to cross Atlantic both ways submerged. (g) World's first atomic submarine also first to make undersea voyage under polar ice cap, 1,830 mi. from Point Barrow, Alaska, to Atlantic Ocean, Aug. 1-4, 1958, reaching North Pole Aug. 3. Second undersea transit of the North Pole made by submarine USS Skate Aug. 11, 1958, during trip from New London, Conn., and return. (h) World's largest submarine. Nuclear-powered Triton was submerged during nearly all its voyage around the globe. It duplicated the route of Ferdinand Magellan's circuit (1519-1522), 30,708 mi., starting from St. Paul Rocks off the NE coast of Brazil, Feb. 24-Apr. 25, 1960, then sailed to Cadiz, Spain, before returning home. (i) First underwater transit of Northwest Passage. (j) Fastest freighter crossing of Atlantic.

Distances Between Great Lakes Ports

Source: Lake Survey Center, 630 Federal Bldg. Detroit, Mich.

In Statute Miles	St. Lawrence				Erie					St. Clair and Huron				
	Quebec	Montreal	Ogdensburg	Kingston	Buffalo	Prt. Colborne	Erie	Cleveland	Toledo	Detroit	Port Huron	Bay City	Alpena	Collingwood
Quebec, Canada		157	283	346	553	531	596	691	768	775	837	999	994	1095
Montreal, Canada	157		126	189	396	374	439	534	611	618	680	842	837	938
Ogdensburg, New York	283	126		63	270	248	313	408	485	492	554	716	711	812
Kingston, Canada	346	189	63		208	186	251	346	423	430	492	654	649	750
Buffalo, New York	553	396	270	208		22	78	176	254	261	322	484	479	580
Port Colborne, Canada	531	374	248	186	22		65	160	237	244	306	468	463	564
Erie, Pennsylvania	596	439	313	251	78	65		102	185	191	253	415	410	511
Cleveland, Ohio	691	534	408	346	176	160	102		96	108	170	331	326	427
Toledo, Ohio	768	611	485	423	254	237	185	96		54	116	278	273	374
Detroit, Michigan	775	618	492	430	261	244	191	108	54		62	224	219	320
Port Huron, Michigan	837	680	554	492	322	306	253	170	116	62		162	157	258
Bay City, Michigan	999	842	716	654	484	468	415	331	278	224	162		116	257
Alpena, Michigan	994	837	711	649	479	463	410	326	273	219	157	116		185
Collingwood, Canada	1095	938	812	750	580	564	511	427	374	320	258	257	185	
Oswego, New York	391	234	108	55	190	168	233	328	405	412	474	636	631	732
Rochester, New York	432	275	149	89	139	117	182	277	354	361	423	585	580	681
Toronto, Canada	506	349	223	161	77	55	120	215	292	299	361	523	518	619
Sault Ste. Marie	1106	949	823	761	592	575	522	438	385	331	269	232	137	259
Marquette, Michigan	1266	1109	983	921	751	735	682	598	545	491	429	391	297	418
Houghton, Michigan	1327	1170	1044	982	813	796	743	659	606	552	490	453	358	480
Ashland, Wisconsin	1455	1298	1172	1110	941	924	871	788	734	680	618	581	486	608
Duluth, Minnesota	1501	1344	1218	1156	986	970	917	833	781	726	664	627	532	653
Thunder Bay, Canada	1379	1222	1096	1034	864	848	795	711	658	604	542	505	410	531
Escanaba, Michigan	1213	1056	930	868	699	682	629	545	492	438	376	339	244	376
Green Bay, Wisconsin	1282	1125	999	937	767	751	698	614	561	507	445	407	313	444
Muskegon, Michigan	1308	1151	1025	963	794	777	724	640	587	533	471	434	339	471
Milwaukee, Wisconsin	1343	1186	1060	998	828	812	759	675	622	568	506	468	374	505
Chicago, Illinois	1408	1251	1125	1063	893	877	824	740	688	633	571	534	439	570

In Statute Miles	Ontario			Superior						Michigan				
	Oswego	Rochester	Toronto	Sault Ste. Marie	Marquette	Houghton	Ashland	Duluth	Thunder Bay	Escanaba	Green Bay	Muskegon	Milwaukee	Chicago
Quebec, Canada	391	432	506	1106	1266	1327	1455	1501	1379	1213	1282	1308	1343	1408
Montreal, Canada	234	275	349	949	1109	1170	1298	1344	1222	1056	1125	1151	1186	1251
Ogdensburg, New York	108	149	223	823	983	1044	1172	1218	1096	930	999	1025	1060	1125
Kingston, Canada	55	89	161	761	921	982	1110	1156	1034	868	937	963	998	1063
Buffalo, New York	190	139	77	575	751	813	941	986	864	699	767	794	828	893
Port Colborne, Canada	168	117	55	575	735	796	924	970	848	682	751	777	812	877
Erie, Pennsylvania	233	182	120	522	682	743	871	917	795	629	698	724	759	824
Cleveland, Ohio	328	277	215	438	598	659	788	833	711	545	614	640	675	740
Toledo, Ohio	405	354	292	385	545	606	734	781	658	492	561	587	622	688
Detroit, Michigan	412	361	299	331	491	552	680	726	604	438	507	533	568	633
Port Huron, Michigan	474	423	361	269	429	490	618	664	542	376	445	471	506	571
Bay City, Michigan	636	585	523	232	391	453	581	627	505	339	407	434	468	534
Alpena, Michigan	631	580	518	137	297	358	486	532	410	244	313	339	374	439
Collingwood, Canada	732	681	619	259	418	480	608	653	531	376	444	471	505	570
Oswego, New York		59	145	743	903	964	1092	1138	1016	850	919	945	980	1045
Rochester, New York	59		95	692	852	913	1041	1087	965	799	868	894	929	994
Toronto, Canada	145	95		630	790	851	979	1025	903	737	806	832	867	932
Sault Ste. Marie	743	692	630		159	221	349	394	273	219	288	314	349	414
Marquette, Michigan	903	852	790	159		84	213	261	171	378	447	474	508	573
Houghton, Michigan	964	913	851	221	84		131	179	116	440	509	535	570	635
Ashland, Wisconsin	1092	1041	979	349	213	131		93	164	568	637	663	698	763
Duluth, Minnesota	1138	1087	1025	394	261	179	93		195	614	682	709	743	808
Port Arthur, Canada	1016	965	903	273	171	116	164	195		492	560	587	621	686
Escanaba, Michigan	850	799	737	219	378	440	568	614	492		101	181	201	274
Green Bay, Wisconsin	919	868	806	288	447	509	637	682	560	101		171	180	255
Muskegon, Michigan	945	894	832	314	474	535	663	709	587	181	171		80	114
Milwaukee, Wisconsin	980	929	867	349	508	570	698	743	621	201	180	80		85
Chicago, Illinois	1045	994	932	414	573	635	763	808	686	274	255	114	85	

Canadian Urban Transit by Provinces 1972

	Fis. yr.	Atlantic	Quebec	Ontario	Man. & Sas.	Alb. & B.C.
Passenger fares						
Motor bus	63,271,069[1]	1,830,107	18,875,629	23,352,754	6,292,813	12,919,766[1]
Trolley coach	3,078,672	–	–	2,905,514	173,158	–
Street car	5,372,125	–	–	5,372,125	–	–
Subway	15,795,383	–	6,339,834	9,455,549	–	–
Chartered[2]	804,501	629	223,578	524,955	–	55,339
Total	88,321,750	1,830,736	25,439,041	41,610,897	6,465,971	12,975,105

[1]Includes initial revenue passenger fares for trolley coaches of the Edmonton Transit System, the Calgary Transit System and the British Columbia Hydro and Power Authority for which no breakdown is available.
[2]The number of revenue passenger fares reported for chartered service is only approximate, as exact counts are not made for all trips.

Fastest Scheduled Train Runs in United States and Canada

Source: Donald M. Steffee and Trains Magazine; figures are based on 1972 timetables

Electric Traction-Passenger-(80 m.p.h. and over)

Railroad	Train	From	To	Dis.	Time	Speed
Penn-Central	Metroliners (13)	Baltimore	Wilmington	68.4	44	93.3
Penn-Central	Metroliners (12)	Wilmington	Baltimore	68.4	45	91.2
Penn-Central	Metroliner	Wilmington	Baltimore	68.4	46	89.2
Penn-Central	Metroliner	Newark	Philadelphia	80.5	56	86.2
Penn-Central	Metroliner	Newark	Trenton	48.1	34	84.9
Penn-Central	Metroliner	Metro Park	Trenton	33.9	24	84.7
Penn-Central	Metroliner	No. Philadelphia	Newark	76.0	54	84.4
Penn-Central	Metroliner	Trenton	No. Philadelphia	27.9	20	83.7
Penn-Central	Metroliners (3)	Newark	Philadelphia	80.5	58	83.3
Penn-Central	Metroliner	Baltimore	Philadelphia	94.0	68	82.9
Penn-Central	Metroliner	Philadelphia	Baltimore	94.0	68	82.9
Penn-Central	Metroliners (2)	Metro Park	Philadelphia	66.3	48	82.9
Penn-Central	Metroliner	Baltimore	Capital Beltway	30.3	22	82.6
Penn-Central	Metroliner	Trenton	Newark	48.1	35	82.4
Penn-Central	Metroliners (5)	Philadelphia	Newark	80.5	59	81.9
Penn-Central	Metroliner	Newark	Philadelphia	80.5	59	81.9
Penn-Central	Metroliners (2)	Trenton	Metro Park	33.9	25	81.2
Penn-Central	Metroliners (4)	Philadelphia	Metro Park	66.3	49	81.2
Penn-Central	Metroliner	New York	Trenton	58.1	43	81.1

Diesel Traction-Passenger—(75 m.p.h. and over)

Railroad	Train	From	To	Dis.	Time	Speed
Canadian National	Turbotrain	Guildwood	Dorval	310.9	207	90.1
Canadian National	Turbotrain	Dorval	Guildwood	310.9	210	88.8
Canadian National	Rapido	Guildwood	Belleville	100.5	72	83.7
Canadian National	Rapido	Dorval	Brockville	115.3	86	80.4
Santa Fe	Super Chief-El Capitan	Croton City	Lamar	111.0	76	78.9
Illinois Central Gulf	Panama Limited; Shawnee	Champaign	Mattoon	44.0	34	78.4
Santa Fe	Texas Chief	Marceline	Carrollton	39.1	30	78.2
Burlington Northern	Illinois Zephyr	Mendota	Plano	31.2	24	78.0
Canadian National	Ontarian	Trenton	Cobourg	31.2	24	78.0
Illinois Central Gulf	City of New Orleans; Shawnee	Centralia	Effingham	53.2	41	77.9
Santa Fe	Super Chief-El Capitan	Dodge City	Hutchinson	120.1	93	77.6
Santa Fe	Super Chief-El Capitan	Lamar	Garden City	99.9	78	76.8
Burlington Northern	Illinois Zephyr	Princeton	Kewanee	26.8	21	76.6
Canadian National	Bonaventure	Cobourg	Belleville	43.3	34	76.3
Canadian National	Lakeshore	Prescott	Cornwall	45.8	36	76.3
Burlington Northern	Denver Zephyr	Akron	McCook	143.0	114	75.3
Canadian National	Bonaventure	Brockville	Cornwall	57.6	46	75.1
Canadian National	Bonaventure	Cornwall	Brockville	57.6	46	75.1

Diesel Traction-Freight-(64 m.p.h. and over)

Railroad	Train	From	To	Dis.	Time	Speed
Santa Fe	Super C	Waynoka	Amarillo	205.2	175	70.3
Santa Fe	Super C	Winslow	Gallup	127.2	110	69.4
Santa Fe	Super C	Gallup	Winslow	127.2	110	69.4
Santa Fe	Super C	Vaughn	Clovis	130.8	115	68.3
Santa Fe	Super C	Wellington	Waynoka	106.6	95	67.2
Union Pacific	Overland Mail East	Green River	Rawlins	134.2	120	67.1
Santa Fe	Super C	Amarillo	Waynoka	205.2	185	66.6
Santa Fe	Super C	Clovis	Vaughn	130.8	120	65.4
Southern Pacific	Blue Streak Merchandise	East Yard	Del Rio	171.2	159	64.6
Santa Fe	Super C	Gallup	Belen	144.4	135	64.2
Santa Fe	Super C	Emporia	Kansas City	112.1	105	64.1
Santa Fe	Super C	Kansas City	Emporia	112.1	105	64.1
Santa Fe	Super C	Waynoka	Wellington	106.6	100	64.0

Some Fast Railway Runs in the United States and Canada

Date	Railroad	Run	Miles	H.	M.	S.	M.P.H.
Aug., 1894	Atlantic Coast Line Route	Jacksonville-Washington	780.9	15	49		49.4
May, 1905	Atlantic City	Camden—Atlantic City	55.5		42	33	78.3
July, 1905	Atchison, Topeka & Santa Fe	Los Angeles-Chicago	2244.5	44	54		50.0
April, 1911	Lake Shore & Michigan Southern	Toledo—Elkhart	133.0	1	46		75.28
May, 1923	Canadian National	Montreal-Toronto	335	6	45	0	49.6
Nov., 1925	Canadian National	Montreal-Vancouver	2937.5	67	0	0	43.8
June, 1927	Pennsylvania	Washington—New York	224.6	3	7		72.1
May, 1934	Chicago, Burlington & Quincy	Denver—Chicago	1015.31	13	5	44	77.6
July, 1934	Chicago, Milwaukee, St. Paul & Pacific	Chicago—Milwaukee	85.0	1	7	35	75.46
Oct., 1934	Union Pacific	Cheyenne—Omaha	506.7	6	11	0	81.95
Oct., 1934	Union Pacific, Chicago & North-western, New York Central	Los Angeles—New York	3257.6	56	55		57.2
Jan., 1935	Pennsylvania	Philadelphia—Washington	134.2	1	50		73.2
April, 1935	New York, New Haven & Hartford	Providence—Boston	43.8		32	35	80.6
Oct., 1936	Chicago, Burlington & Quincy	Chicago—Denver	1017.23	12	12	27	83.3
May, 1937	Atchison, Topeka & Santa Fe	Los Angeles—Chicago	2228.6	36	49		60.5
May, 1955	Baltimore & Ohio	Washington—Chicago (Train consisted of 3 Budd Rail Diesel cars)	768.0	12	29	30	61.5
July, 1966	New York Central	Bryan, Ohio (MP 350-345)	5.0		1	39¾	181.0*
May, 1967	Pennsylvania	County Tower—Milheim Tower	21.2		11†		115.66†
Jan., 1968	Atchison, Topeka & Santa Fe	Corwith—Hobart Yards (Super C Frgt.)	2202.1	34	35	40	63.6

*The official speed measured by ground instruments was 183.85 mph on passing mile post 347 + 13 over an accurately measured 300 feet of track. This is the highest speed on rails ever recorded in the United States. The run was made by a single Budd Rail Diesel car fitted with two turbo-jet J-47 aircraft engines mounted on forward end. †Time and speed calculated from standing start at County to passing Milheim Tower (end of test track) at 80-mph, after which the train was gradually braked down on regular track to a stop in Trenton passenger station. Between mileposts 46 and 51, speed was 150 mph. or over, a momentary peak of 156 mph. was reached in the vicinity of milepost 47.

72 Japanese Trains Average Over 100 Miles per Hour

Service between Tokyo and Osaka via the standard-gauged New Tokaido Line is headed by 36 "Hikari" superexpress trains daily in each direction which make the 320.1-mile run, inclusive of stops at Nagoya and Kyoto, in 3 hrs. 10 mins.-at average overall speed of 101.1 mph.

With opening of the new Sanyo Line on Mar. 15, 1972, westward from Osaka to Okayama, the runs of most of the "Hikari" trains were extended to provide service over the new line. Four trains in each direction cover the 99.9 miles between the two cities in 58 minutes nonstop—at 103.3 mph. Best time between Tokyo and Okayama, 420 miles, is 4 hrs. 10 mins.—100.8 mph including stops at Nagoya, Kyoto and Osaka.

French Achieve 90-100 Miles Per Hour Speeds On Regular Schedules.

Having upgraded about 80% of its Paris to Bordeaux mainline to a 125-mile an hour standard, French National Railways has quickened the times of a number of trains between the two cities. Below are shown the fastest point-to-point timings in current French timetables.

Train	From	To	Dis.	Time	Speed
L'Etendard	St. Pierre des Corps.	Poitiers	62.93	37	102.0
L'Etendard	Paris	St. Pierre des Corps.	143.4	92	93.5
L'Etendard	Angouleme	Paris	276.3	178	93.1
L'Aquitaine	Angouleme	Poitiers	70.0	46	91.3

American Railway Statistics

Source: Interstate Commerce Commission

Year	Mileage Owned	Miles Built	Loco-mo'es in use	Freight Cars in use	Pass. Cars in use	Passengers	Freight Carried	Em-ployees	Employees Wages
	Miles	Miles	No.	No.	No.	No.	Tons	No.	Dollars
1960 ...	217,552	21	31,178	1,690,396	25,746	327,171,745	2,409,039,608	793,071	4,956,902,360
1965 ...	211,384	59	30,061	1,515,169	20,022	305,825,407	2,741,706,964	654,670	4,886,739,954
1970 ...	205,782	80	29,122	1,453,708	11,378	289,468,947	2,798,324,161	577,435	5,646,480,859
1971 ...	204,696	21	29,185	1,440,873	8,869	275,534,319	2,626,280,490	555,139	5,990,314,000

PASSENGER AND FREIGHT DATA

Year	Passenger Revenue	Freight Revenue	Miles Traveled by Passenger	Rev. per Pas. Mile	Ave. Trip per Pas.	Fre. Rev. a ton Mile	Miles Traveled by Pas. Trains	Miles Traveled by Freight Trains	Casualties Kill'd	Inj.
	Dollars	Dollars	Thousands	Cts.	Miles	Cts.	Miles	Miles	No.	No.
1960 ...	641,495,655	8,151,706,391	21,284,084	3.01	65.05	1.42	209,676,995	411,173,556	2,248	19,577
1965 ...	555,985,653	9,036,540,448	17,453,919	3.19	57.07	1.28	173,579,220	430,716,900	2,399	25,789
1970 ...	423,190,535	11,124,128,498	10,785,746	3.92	37.26	1.44	93,575,236	434,584,544	2,225	21,327
1971 ...	384,116,475	11,995,673,685	8,862,819	4.33	32.17	1.61	69,928,752	436,563,277	2,010	18,972

REVENUES, EXPENSES AND DIVIDENDS

Year	Total Operating Revenues	Operating Expenses	Tax Accruals	Net Railway Operating Income	Net Income	Dividends Declared	Ratio Oper. Exp. to Oper. Rev.
	Dollars	Dollars	Dollars	Dollars	Dollars	Dollars	Pct.
1960	9,641,592,812	7,657,328,712	1,020,471,011	594,618,250	473,174,842	411,649,958	79.42
1965	10,425,052,359	8,002,684,949	949,215,638	980,065,623	865,898,537	532,649,374	76.76
1969	11,658,525,466	9,209,136,766	1,065,134,402	667,156,801	*517,066,302	534,848,548	78.99
1970	12,209,237,323	9,805,555,323	1,103,988,230	505,669,405	*126,429,274	486,132,169	80.31
1971	13,017,853,817	10,387,692,423	1,138,011,752	629,364,586	*337,893,849	804,344,547	79.80

VALUES, STOCKS, BONDS, AND CAPITAL

Year	Investment In Road and Equipment	Common Stock Outstand.[1]	Preferred Stock Outstand.[1]	Funded Debt Outstand.[1]	Tot. Railway Capital Outstand.[1]	Amount of Stock Pay Dividends
	Dollars	Dollars	Dollars	Dollars	Dollars	Dollars
1960	35,513,350,796	6,185,117,735	1,218,060,497	8,730,551,088	16,133,729,320	5,617,239,155
1965	35,489,328,198	5,579,833,608	1,115,727,381	8,161,792,077	14,857,353,066	4,845,089,946
1970	37,918,381,770	5,604,882,147	718,205,376	8,015,822,800	14,338,910,323	3,594,834,452
1971	38,022,034,488	5,656,310,057	727,529,963	7,204,216,451	13,588,056,471	3,598,324,243

(1.) Data for years prior to 1965 have been revised to represent amounts actually outstanding in order that they may be comparable to those shown for the year 1965.   *After extraordinary and prior period time.

Tracks All Over the U.S.

Source: Assn. of American Railroads

On Jan. 1, 1973, there was an aggregate of 204,000 miles of railroad tracks in the United States, not including yard tracks or sidings. Although separation by states is not yet available, the data will change only slightly from the yearend 1971 data below showing Texas first with 13,563 miles; Rhode Island last with 146. Mileage shared by two or more railroads is not duplicated, nor is that of parallel trackage.

Ala.	4,567	Ill.	10,822	Mont.	4,981	R.I.	146
Alaska	544	Ind.	6,405	Neb.	5,420	S.C.	3,059
Arizona	2,052	Iowa	7,903	Nev.	1,574	S.D.	3,505
Ark.	3,582	Kan.	7,776	N.H.	817	Tenn.	3,214
Calif	7,385	Ky.	3,504	N.J.	1,742	Texas	13,563
Colo.	3,572	La.	3,753	N.M.	2,120	Utah	1,750
Conn.	664	Me.	1,666	N.Y.	5,595	Vt.	766
Del.	291	Md.	1,110	N.C.	4,144	Va.	3,895
D. of C.	30	Mass.	1,430	N.D.	5,108	Wash.	4,887
Fla.	4,157	Mich.	6,159	Ohio	7,804	W. Va.	3,569
Ga.	5,402	Minn.	7,700	Okla.	5,332	Wisc.	5,926
Idaho	2,668	Miss.	3,653	Ore.	3,068	Wyo.	1,812
		Mo.	6,337	Pa.	8,273	**Total U.S.**	**205,202**

State Automobile Speed Limits

(Except as otherwise posted)

Source: American Automobile Assn. Digest of Motor Laws 1973

Alabama: Interstate highways, 70 mph. daytime, 60 mph. nighttime; open highways, 60 mph. daytime, 50 mph. nighttime; residential districts, 25 mph.; business districts, school zones, etc., 15 mph.

Alaska: Divided highways, 70 mph; state highways, surfaced, 60 mph; unsurfaced, 50 mph; city streets, 30 mph.

Arizona: All highways, 65 mph. or as posted; residential areas, business districts, 25 mph. or as posted; school zones, 15 mph.

Arkansas: Interstate and controlled access roads, 75 mph; urban districts, 30 mph.

California: Statewide limit, 65 mph. (except freeways posted for 70 mph.); residential and business districts, school zones, 25 mph.

Colorado: 4-lane highways, 70 mph; open highways, 60 mph.; residential districts, 30 mph.; business districts, 25 mph.; open mountain highway, 40 mph.; winding mountain highway, 20 mph.

Connecticut: Reasonable and proper for conditions. Posted limits prima facie evidence of reasonable speed; residential and business districts posted locally.

Delaware: Open highways, 4-lane, 60 mph., 2-lane, 50 mph.; residential and business districts, 25 mph.

District of Columbia: Highways, 30 mph; school and playground areas, 15 mph.; other roads, 25 mph.

Florida: Interstate highways, 70 mph. day, 65 mph. night; open highway, 65 mph. day, 60 mph. night; residential & business districts, 30 mph.

Georgia: Interstate highways, 70 mph. daytime, 65 mph. nighttime; open highway, 60 mph. daytime, 50 mph. nighttime; residential, business and school areas, 25 mph.

Hawaii: Open highways, 45 mph.; or as posted. Residential and business districts, local ordinances govern.

Idaho: Interstate highways, 70 mph.; open highway, 60 mph. daytime, 55 mph. nighttime; urban and business districts, 35 mph.

Illinois: Expressways, 70 mph.; open highways, 65 mph.; urban areas, 30 mph.; school zones, 20 mph.

Indiana: Interstate highways, 70 mph.; Open highways, 65 mph.; residential district, 30 mph.; school zones as posted.

Iowa: Interstate limited access roads, 75 mph. daytime, 65 mph. nighttime; open highways, 70 mph. daytime, 60 mph. nighttime; suburban, 45 mph.; residential and school districts, 25 mph.; business districts, 20 mph.; secondary roads, 60 mph. daytime, 50 mph. nighttime.

Kansas: Interstate highways 75 mph. daytime, 70 nighttime; open highways, 70 mph. daytime, 60 mph. nighttime; residential districts, 30 mph.; business districts, 20 mph.; Kansas Turnpike, 75 mph.; 40 mph. minimum.

Kentucky: Interstate highways, 70 mph.; open highways, 60 mph. daytime, 50 mph. nighttime; residential and business districts, 35 mph.

Louisiana: Open highways 4-lane, 70 mph.; other open highways, 60 mph.

Maine: Turnpikes, 70 mph. daytime, 65 mph. nighttime; open highways, 45 mph ; residential and business districts, 25 mph.

Maryland: Interstate highways 70 mph.; Open country, expressways, 60 mph.; dual lane highways, 55 mph.; other highways, 50 mph.; residential and business districts, 30 mph.; thinly settled areas, 35 mph., other highways 30 mph.

Massachusetts: Turnpike, 65 mph.; divided highway, 50 mph.; other highways, 40 mph.; residential and business districts, 30 mph.; school zones, 20 mph.

Michigan: Freeways, 70 mph.; open highways, 65 mph. daytime, 55 mph. nighttime; residential, 25 mph.

Minnesota: Open highways, 65 mph. daytime, 55 mph. nighttime; all speeds in urban districts, 30 mph.

Mississippi: Interstate highways 70 mph.; Open highways, 65 mph.; residential districts, 25 mph.; business districts, 20 mph.; school zones, 15 mph.

Missouri: Dual lane U. S. routes, 70 mph.; undivided U.S. routes, 70 mph. daytime, 65 mph. nighttime; other open highways, 65 mph. daytime, 60 mph. nighttime; municipalities, 45 mph.

Montana: Open highways, day, reasonable and prudent unless posted, 55 mph. night, except Interstate highways 65 mph. nights; residential and business districts, 25 mph.

Nebraska: Interstate highways, 75 mph.; open highways, 65 mph., residential districts, 25 mph.; business districts, 20 mph.; on non-hard surfaced roads, 50 mph.

Nevada: Careful and prudent; residential and business, as posted.

New Hampshire: Turnpike, 70 mph.; open highways, 60 mph.; rural residential districts, 35 mph.; urban and business districts, 30 mph.; school zones, 20 mph.

New Jersey: Turnpike, 60 mph.; open highways, 50 mph.; residential and business districts, 25 mph.

New Mexico: Open highways, 70 mph. daytime, 60 mph. nighttime; other highways, 60 mph. daytime, 50 mph. nighttime; residential and business districts, 25 mph.; school zones, 15 mph.

New York: New York State Thruway, 65 mph.; open highways, 55 mph.; school zones when children going to and from school as posted.

North Carolina: Interstate, 70 mph., open highways, 65 or 60 mph. permitted as posted, otherwise 55 mph.; residential districts, 35 mph; business, 20 mph.

Ohio: Ohio Turnpike and expressways, 70 mph.; open highways, 60 mph. daytime, 50 mph. nighttime; within municipal corporations, 25 mph; school zones, 20 mph.

Oklahoma: Turnpikes and Interstate highways, 70 mph.; open highways, 65 mph. daytime, 55 mph. nighttime; school zones, 25 mph.

Oregon: Open highways, 55 mph.; freeways up to 75 mph; residential districts, 25 mph.; business and school zones, 20 mph.

Pennsylvania: Turnpike, 65 mph.; open highways 55 mph; residential and business districts, 15 to 40 mph.; school zones, 15 mph.

Rhode Island: Residential and business districts, 25 mph.; elsewhere, 50 mph. daytime, 45 mph. nighttime.

South Carolina: Interstate System 70 mph. daytime, 65 mph. night; State highways 60 mph. daytime, 55 mph. night; urban districts 30 mph.

South Dakota: Interstate highways, 75 mph. daytime, 70 mph. nighttime; open highways, 70 mph. daytime, 60 mph. nighttime; residential and business districts, 30 mph.; school zones, 15 mph.

Tennessee: Open highways, 65 mph. day, 55 mph. night; school zones, 15 mph; Interstate highways 75 mph.

Texas: Federal or State roads, 70 mph. daytime, 65 mph. nighttime; other rural roads, 60 mph. daytime, 55 mph. nighttime; in urban districts, 30 mph.

Utah: Open highways, as posted; residential and business districts, 25 mph; school zones, 20 mph.

Vermont: Interstate highways, 65 mph.; open highways, 50 mph.

Virginia: Interstate 70 mph., all others, 55 mph. or as posted; residential, business and school areas, 25 mph.

Washington: County roads, 50 mph.; cities and towns, 25 mph.; school zones, 20 mph; Interstate highways 70 mph.; in other locations, 60 mph.

West Virginia: Interstate highways, 70 mph.; Turnpike 60 mph.; open highways, 55 mph.; residential districts, 25 mph.; school zones, 15 mph.

Wisconsin: Interstate highways, 70 mph. daytime, 60 mph. nighttime; open highways, 65 mph. daytime, 55 mph. nighttime; residential and business districts, 25 mph.; school zone, 15 mph.

Wyoming: Open highways 4-lane divided, 75 mph; open highways, 65 mph.; residential districts, 30 mph.; business and school districts, 20 mph.

Canal Zone: Outside town limits, 40 mph.; within town limits, 25 mph.

Guam: Roads, 45 mph.; school zones when children at recess or going to and from school, 10 mph.

Puerto Rico: Open highways, 45 mph.; urban districts and school zones, 25 mph.

Passenger Car License Plates by States (1973-74)

Source: Federal Highway Adm., U.S. Dept. of Transportation

	Color							Must be
	Numerals	Background	Type[1]	Num-ber	Car[2] Sold	Slogan	Special[3]	on by:[4]
Alabama	Red	White	A	1	V	Heart of Dixie	...	11/16
Alaska	Blue	Gold	S	2	V	North to the Future	$20	6/1
Arizona	Green	Copper	P	2	V	Grand Canyon State	...	3/1
Arkansas	Red	White	P	1	O	......	10	Stag. Mo.
California	Ch. Yellow	Blue	P	2	V	......	25/10	1st Fri. Feb.
Colorado	Green	White	A	2	O	Colorful	...	3/1
Connecticut	White	Blue	P	2	O	......	15/0	Stag. Mo.
Delaware	Gold	Blue	P	1	V	The First State	25	Stag. Mo.
Florida	Green	White	A	1	V	Sunshine State	12	8/21
Georgia	Blue	White	S	1	V	(County name)	10	4/2
Hawaii	Black	Lemon Yel.	P	2	V	Aloha State	100	4/1
Idaho	Green	White	S	2	O	Famous Potatoes	25	Stag. Mo.
Illinois	Green	White	A	2	O	Land of Lincoln	...	12/31
Indiana	Red	White	A	1	O	......	...	Stag. Mo.
Iowa	Black	Yellow	S	2	V	.	...	3/15
Kansas	White	Red	A	1	O	(State outline)	...	Stag. Mo.
Kentucky	White	Blue	A	1	V	(County name)	...	3/2
Louisiana	Blue	White	S	1	V	Sportsman's Paradise	...	2/7
Maine	Black	Yellow	S	2	O	Vacationland	5	3/1
Maryland	White	Blue	S	2	O	......	25	4/1
Massachusetts	Red	Silver	S	2	O	......	9	Stag. Mo.
Michigan	White	Blue	S	2	O	Great Lake State	...	4/1
Minnesota	Green	White	S	2	V	10,000 Lakes	...	3/2
Mississippi	Red	White	A	1	V	(County name)	...	11/1
Missouri	Black	White	A	2	O	......	...	Stag. Mo.
Montana	White	Green	S	2	O	Big Sky Country	...	2/16
Nebraska	Scarlet	Cream	S	2	O	Cornhusker State	50/25	3/1
Nevada	Silver	Blue	P	2	O	......	25/15	Stag. Mo.
New Hampshire	Green	White	A	2	O	Live Free or Die	5	4/1
New Jersey	Black	Straw	P	2	O	Garden State	10	Stag. Mo.
New Mexico	Red	White	S	1	O	Land of Enchantment	15	3/3
New York	Blue	Gold-Orange	P	2	O	......	5	Stag. Mo.
North Carolina	Red	White	A	1	O	......	10	12/31
North Dakota	Blue	Silver-Gray	S	2	V	Peace Garden State	100	5/2
Ohio	White	Green	A	2	O	Seat Belts Fastened	5	4/16
Oklahoma	Red	White	A	1	V	Oklahoma is OK	10	3/2
Oregon	Yellow	Blue	P	2	V	......	25	Stag. Mo.
Pennsylvania	Yellow	Blue	S	1	O	Bicentennial State '76	14	4/1
Rhode Island	Black	White	S	2	O	Ocean State	10	4/1
South Carolina	White	Blue	A	2	V	......	15	11/16
South Dakota	Red	White	A	2	V	(Mt. Rushmore Memorial)	...	4/1
Tennessee	Black	White	A	2	O	(State Outline)	...	4/16
Texas	Black	White	A	2	O	(Star)	10	4/2
Utah	Black	Silver	S	2	O	......	...	3/1
Vermont	White	Green	S	2	O	See Vermont	5	3/1
Virginia	Blue	White	S	2	O	......	10	4/15
Washington	Green	White	S	2	O	......	30	2/4
West Viriginia	Blue	Yellow Gold	S	1	O	Mountain State	5	Stag. Mo.
Wisconsin	Red	White	S	2	O	America's Dairyland	3	Stag. Mo.
Wyoming	Black	White	A	2	O	(Bucking Bronco)	15	3/1
Dist. of Col.	Black	Silver-White	S	2	O	Nation's Capital	5	4/1

(1) Type of plate—A annual, P permanent, S semipermanent. (2) Disposition of license plate when car is sold, O stays with owner, V stays with vehicle. (3) Special or personalized plates fees shown are paid annually and are in addition to the regular registration fees. Where two numbers are shown: first is original cost; second, annual cost. (4) Indicates date when law will be enforced. Many states have a staggered month of issue, these states have no period of grace; plates must be on the vehicle by expiration date for previous plates.

The 1973 American Motorist Drove One Trillion Miles

The mileage traveled by the over 96,000,000 passenger cars registered in the United States in 1973 was estimated at one trillion miles. In addition, more than 275 billion miles were driven by the more than 22,000,000 trucks and buses.

It is estimated that private passenger cars are used for 90% of all vacation and recreation trips in the U.S. During 1973, some 110,000,000 Americans took to the highways within their own country for at least one vacation or pleasure trip by automobile, setting a new record. They spent $45 billion and traveled an estimated 350 billion miles.

Mobile Homes and Recreational Vehicles Sales

Source: Construction Review, U.S. Dept. of Commerce and Recreational Vehicle Institute

A mobile home, or housing-type trailer is a vehicular portable structure built on a chassis and designed to be used without a permanent foundation as a year-round dwelling when connected to utilities. Mobile homes are defined as units 29 feet or longer and weighing over 4,500 pounds. Travel trailers are vehicular structures mounted on wheels (2 or 4 wheel units depending on weight), do not require special highway movement permits when towed. Motor homes are self-powered and self-contained units built directly on a truck or bus chassis. Truck campers are portable structures that are loaded onto or affixed to the bed or chassis of a truck; in most states they do not require special state licenses.

Camping trailers are mounted on wheels with collapsible side walls of fabric, plastic or other pliable material. They unfold into large tent-top structures that will sleep 4 to 8 people. Pickup covers are shells which resemble truck campers without the overcab section. They are mostly utilitarian and offer no built-in sleeping or cooking.

Year	Travel Trailers	Motor Homes	Truck Campers	Camping Trailers	Pickup Covers
1969	144,000	23,100	92,500	141,000	113,500
1970	138,000	30,300	95,900	116,100	91,700
1971	190,800	57,200	107,200	95,800	98,400
1972	250,800	105,500	105,100	110,200	164,600

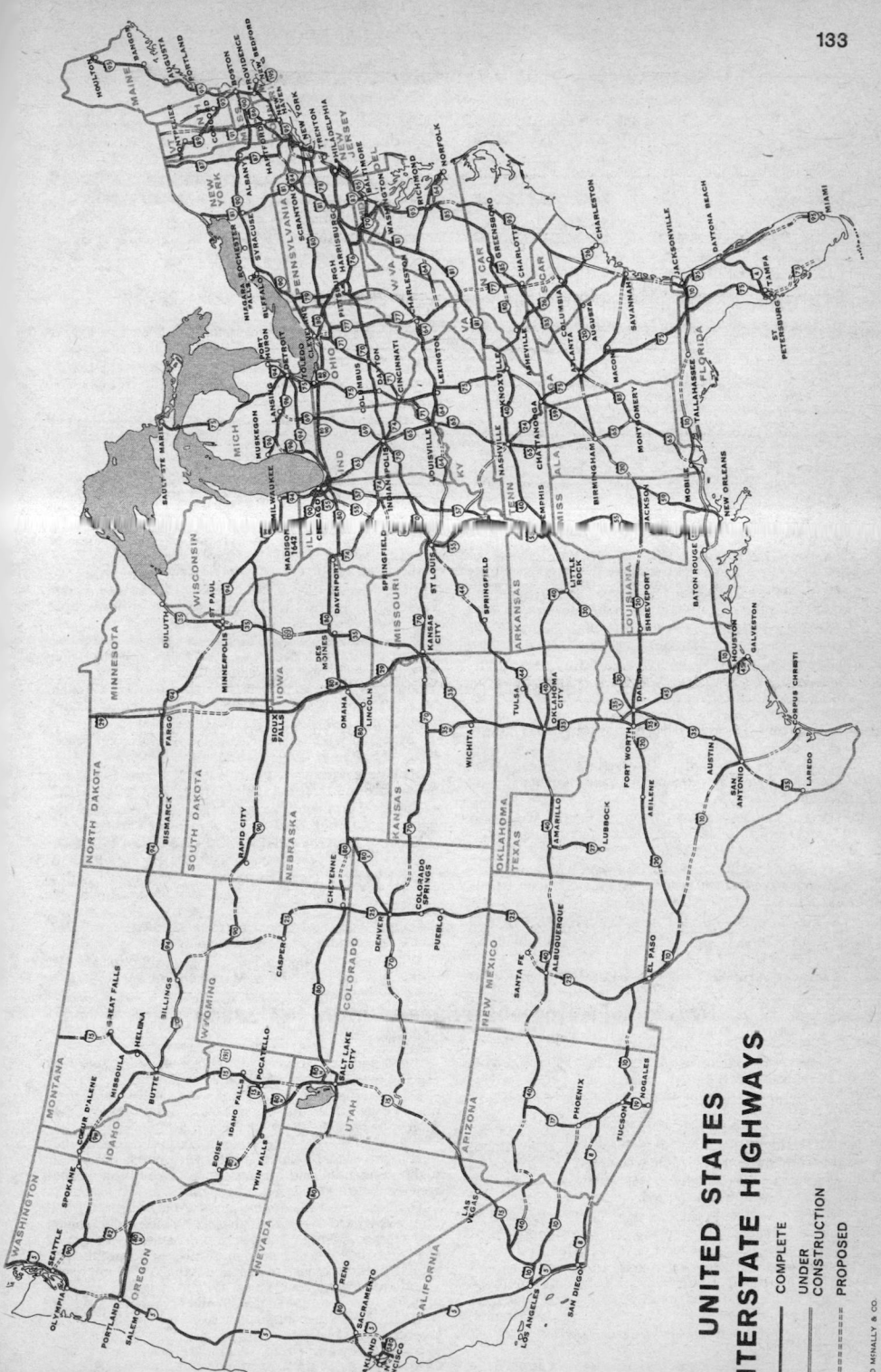

UNITED STATES
INTERSTATE HIGHWAYS

———— COMPLETE

———— UNDER
CONSTRUCTION

┄┄┄┄ PROPOSED

©RAND McNALLY & CO.

Major North American Turnpikes; Tolls and Speed Limits
Source: American Automobile Association, Washington, D.C. 20006

Airport Expressway: Miami International Airport to North—South Expressway interchange, 4.4 miles. Speed limit 60 mph. Toll 5¢ per axle.

Atlantic City Expressway: N.J. Freeway at Turnersville to Atlantic City, N.J. 44 miles. Speed limit 70 mph. Maximum toll $1.25.

Bluegrass Parkway: Fort Springs to Elizabethtown, Ky. 72 miles. Speed limit 70 mph. max. Maximum toll $1.30.

Connecticut Turnpike: N. Y. State line near Greenwich, Conn. to R.I. State line at Killingly, Conn., 129 miles. Speed limit 60 mph. Maximum toll $2.

Dallas-Ft. Worth Turnpike: Dallas to Ft. Worth 30 miles. Speed limit 70 mph. Maximum toll 60¢.

Dallas North tollway 9.8 miles long, speed limit 55 mph. Maximum toll 20¢.

Eastern Townships Autoroute: Montreal to Sherbrooke, Quebec. 75 miles. Speed limit 70 mph. (50 minimum) car and passengers 25¢ at each toll gate.

Ensenada-Tijuana Tollway: Ensenada to Tijuana, Mexico, 63 miles. Speed limit 62 mph. Maximum toll $2.40.

Everett Turnpike: Mass.-N. H. state line to Concord, N. H. 40 miles. Speed limit 70 mph. Toll maximum 50¢.

Florida Turnpike: Miami, Fla., to Wildwood, Fla., 265 miles. Speed limit 70 mph. (40 mph. minimum). Maximum toll $4.80.

Garden State Parkway: Montvale, N. J. to Cape May, N. J. 173 miles. Speed limit 60-65 mph. Max. toll $2.75.

H. E. Bailey Turnpike: Oklahoma City to Randlett, Okla., 86.4 miles. Speed limit 70 mph. Toll max. $1.70.

Hutchinson River Parkway: N.Y.C. to Conn. state line, 15 miles. Speed limit 50 mph. Toll 25¢.

Illinois Tollway: Includes Tri-State Tollway from Indiana state line to Deerfield; Northwest Tollway from the Tri-State to Wisconsin state line at So. Beloit, Ill., and East-West Tollway between Chicago and Aurora. 187 miles. Maximum tolls, Tri-State $1.80, Northwest $1.50 and East-West 50¢.

Indian Nation Turnpike: Henryetta to Hugo, Okla. 105.2 miles. Speed limit 70 mph. (40 mph. minimum) Maximum toll $2.25.

Indiana Toll Road: Eastpoint (Ohio line) to Westpoint (Illinois line), 157 miles. Speed limit 70 mph. (45 mph. minimum). Maximum toll $2.80.

John F. Kennedy Memorial Highway: Baltimore, Md., to Wilmington, Del., 60 miles. Speed limit 60 mph. Maximum toll 90¢ Md., 30¢ Del. portion.

Kansas Turnpike: Kansas City to South Haven, Kan. 236 miles. Speed limit 75 mph (70 mph at night). 40 mph minimum. Maximum toll $5.25.

Kentucky Turnpike: Louisville to Elizabethtown, Ky. 40 miles. Speed limit 70 mph. 40 minimum. Max. toll 60¢.

Maine Turnpike: York, Me., to Augusta, Me., 100 miles. Speed limit 70 mph. (65 at night). Max. toll $2.15.

Massachusetts Turnpike: Downtown Boston to state line, Mass., (N. Y. border), 135 miles. Speed limit 65 mph. (40 mph. minimum). Maximum toll $3.30.

Merritt Parkway: New York-Conn. state line to Housatonic River, Stratford, Conn., 37½ miles. Speed limit 60 mph. Toll 20¢.

Montreal-Laurentian Autoroute: Montreal to Ste. Adele. 45 miles. Speed limit 70 mph. Toll: 25¢ at each gate.

Mountain Parkway: Winchester to Salyersville, Ky., 76 miles. Speed limit 70 mph. Maximum toll $1.60.

New Hampshire Turnpike: Mass.-N. H. state line to Portsmouth, N. H., 14.7 miles. Speed limit 70 mph. Toll 15¢ to 25¢.

New Jersey Turnpike: Deepwater, N. J. to Ridgefield Park, N. J., 141 miles including extensions. Speed limit 60 mph. (50 mph. on Hudson County extension). Maximum toll $1.75.

New York Thruway (Thomas E. Dewey Thruway): Pennsylvania border near Erie to New York City, 559 miles including extensions. Speed limit 65 mph. Max. toll $8.20.

Ohio Turnpike: Ohio-Pennsylvania line to Ohio-Indiana line, 241 miles. Speed limit 70 mph. Maximum toll $3.50.

Pennsylvania Turnpike: Gateway (state line near Youngstown, Ohio) to New Jersey line at Levittown, Pa., then to Scranton, 470 miles. Speed limit 65 mph. Maximum toll $7.10.

Richmond-Petersburg Turnpike: North of Richmond, Va., to south of Petersburg, Va., 34.7 miles, speed 65 mph. (minimum 40 mph.) Maximum toll 95¢.

Saw Mill River Parkway: New York City to Katonah, N. Y. 30 miles. Speed limit 50 mph. Maximum toll 25¢. Trailers not permitted.

Seventeen-Mile Drive: Pacific Grove through Pebble Beach, Monterey, Calif. Maximum toll $3.00.

Spaulding Turnpike: Portsmouth, N. H. to Rochester, N. H., 22.8 miles. Speed limit 70 mph. Max. toll 10-15¢.

Turner Turnpike: Oklahoma City to Tulsa, Okla., 86 miles. Speed limit 70 mph. Maximum toll $1.60.

Western Kentucky Parkway: Elizabethtown to Princeton, 135 miles. Speed limit 70 mph. Maximum toll $2.20.

West Virginia Turnpike: Princeton, W. Va., to Charleston, W. Va., 88 miles. Speed limit 60 mph. Maximum toll $2.75.

Wilbur Cross Parkway: Milford to Meriden, Conn. 29.5 miles. Speed limit 60 mph. Maximum toll 35¢.

Will Rogers Turnpike: Tulsa, Okla., to Joplin, Mo., 88 miles. Speed limit 70 mph. Maximum toll $1.60.

Provincial Automobile Speed Limits in Canada
Source: Digest of Motor Laws. 1973

Alberta: Open highway, 60 mph, day, 50 mph, night; 4-lane highway, 70 mph day, 60 mph night, or as posted; urban areas, 30 mph or as posted; school zone, urban 20 mph, rural, 25 mph.

British Columbia: Open highway, 50 mph or as posted; residential and business districts, 30 mph; school and playground zones, 20 mph, when posted.

Manitoba: Open highway, 60 mph or as posted; urban areas 30 mph or as posted.

New Brunswick: Fixed maximum limits: residential or business districts, 30 mph; open highway, 60 mph where posted; cities and towns, local laws as posted.

Newfoundland: Reasonable and prudent not to exceed 60 mph on paved portions of trans-Canada highway, 50 mph on other paved highways; unpaved roads, 40 mph under all conditions except through settlements, 30 mph; municipalities, school zones and places of public assembly, as posted.

Nova Scotia: Reasonable and prudent with prima facie limits; residential and business districts, curves, inter-

sections and school zones, 30 mph. Maximum speed on any highway, 60 mph or 65 mph when posted.

Ontario: Fixed maximum limits: open highway, 50 mph or as posted; cities, towns, villages and built-up areas, 30 mph or as posted; railway crossings, 20 mph.

Prince Edward Island: Reasonable and proper within maximum limits: open highway, 60 mph day, 55 mph night; residential and business districts, 30 mph; school zones, curves and intersections, 20 mph.

Quebec: Fixed maximum limits. Auto routes 70 mph; numbered hard-surfaced highways outside cities, towns and villages, 60 mph; hard-surfaced highways or gravel roads, outside cities, towns and villages, 50 mph; earth roads, outside cities, towns and villages, 40 mph; all speeds reduced at least 5 mph at night or in bad weather; in cities, towns, and villages, 30 mph or as posted; school zones at times when pupils enter or leave school, and at level crossing, 30 mph.

Saskatchewan: Fixed maximum limits as posted. Open highway 50 mph, or as posted. Local speeds set by municipalities.

Highway Mileage Between Selected Canadian and U.S. Cities

	CALGARY	EDMONTON	HALIFAX	LONDON	MONCTON	MONTREAL	OTTAWA	QUEBEC	REGINA	ST. JOHN	SAULT STE. MARIE	THUNDER BAY	TORONTO	VANCOUVER	WINNIPEG
BANGOR, ME.	2592	2595	450	762	287	310	436	241	2115	188	936	1331	651	3250	1760
BOSTON, MASS.	2620	2639	683	675	520	333	458	390	2142	421	958	1403	564	3168	1812
BUFFALO, N.Y.	2106	2125	1141	142	978	383	350	533	1628	879	532	977	102	2878	1377
BUTTE, MONT.	378	561	2950	1859	2787	2309	2033	2470	629	2739	1533	1303	1972	764	875
CALGARY, ALB.		183	3073	2246	2910	2282	2202	2432	478	2862	1601	1271	2142	659	832
DETROIT, MICH.	1915	1934	1336	122	1204	576	475	738	1437	1156	246	691	235	2505	1149
DULUTH, MINN.	1240	1243	1842	777	1679	1051	925	1199	763	1631	425	195	865	1898	408
EDMONTON, ALB.	183		3076	2249	2913	2285	2205	2435	497	2865	1632	1274	2145	842	835
FARGO, N.D.	989	1172	2092	1048	1929	1502	1175	1764	511	1881	675	445	1161	1654	233
HALIFAX, N.S.	3073	3076		1243	163	791	917	657	2596	262	1417	1812	1132	3731	2241
LONDON, ONTARIO	2246	2249	1243		1080	452	359	602	1769	1032	403	985	111	2904	1414
MONCTON, N.B.	2910	2913	163	1080		628	754	494	2433	99	1254	1649	969	3568	2078
MONTREAL, QUE.	2282	2285	791	452	628		126	150	1805	580	626	1021	341	2940	1450
OTTAWA, ONT.	2202	2205	917	359	754	126		274	1725	706	500	941	248	2860	1370
QUEBEC, QUE.	2432	2435	657	602	494	150	274		1955	446	774	1171	491	3090	1600
REGINA, SASK.	478	497	2596	1769	2433	1805	1725	1955		2385	1146	794	1665	1136	355
ST. JOHN, N.B.	2862	2865	262	1032	99	580	706	446	2385		1206	1601	921	3520	2030
SAULT STE. MARIE	1601	1632	1417	403	1254	626	500	774	1146	1206		445	440	2201	797
SEATTLE, WASH.	762	945	3494	2489	3331	2693	2577	2934	1092	3283	2077	1883	2600	146	1444
THUNDER BAY, ONT.	1271	1274	1812	985	1649	1021	941	1171	794	1601	445		881	1929	439
TORONTO, ONT.	2142	2145	1132	111	969	341	248	491	1665	921	440	881		2800	1310
VANCOUVER, B.C.	659	842	3731	2904	3568	2940	2860	3090	1136	3520	2201	1929	2800		1490
WINNIPEG, MAN.	832	835	2241	1414	2078	1450	1370	1600	355	2030	797	439	1310	1490	

Motor Bus Passenger Operations, Intercity Class I Carriers

Source: Interstate Commerce Commission

Year ended December 31	1968	1969	1970	1971	1972
Number of carriers reporting	159	70	71	72	72
Miles of line, regular route	216,668	190,270	192,130	193,948	NA
Regular route intercity service revenue (dollars)	484,709,405	483,357,563	509,753,126	540,809,039	534,611,714
Local and suburban revenue (dollars)	16,092,699	13,422,071	13,894,726	13,268,731	11,652,843
Charter or special service bus (dollars)	83,463,349	73,981,338	80,473,873	86,236,590	93,953,690
Total operating revenue (dollars)	685,662,405	676,353,629	722,174,070	760,911,530	768,055,522
Total expenses (dollars)	604,808,045	593,645,109	638,435,771	666,541,446	682,458,001
Net operating revenue (dollars)	80,854,360	82,708,610	83,738,299	94,370,084	85,597,521
Bus-miles in intercity line service	814,587,544	739,828,202	745,691,295	729,206,679	698,920,436
Bus-miles in local and suburban service	23,644,551	17,734,597	17,869,121	17,014,044	14,499,911
Bus-miles in charter or special service	125,941,786	106,836,538	111,236,118	114,015,821	121,363,601
Intercity revenue passengers carried	160,692,862	135,687,849	132,041,325	128,329,446	120,899,734
Local and suburban revenue passengers carried	28,871,544	22,693,335	21,782,439	19,479,449	15,500,788
Charter or special revenue passengers carried	27,806,221	16,574,017	19,683,951	19,502,788	20,389,118

Intercity Bus Operations

Source: National Association of Motor Bus Owners

	1969	1970	1971	1972
Operating Companies	1,050	1,000	1,000	1,000
Buses	22,700	23,100	23,000	22,700
Miles of highway served (Dec. 31)[1]	266,000	267,000	267,000	267,000
Employees (Dec. 31)[2]	48,100	49,500	50,200	48,600
Total bus miles	1,195,000,000	1,209,000,000	1,202,000,000	1,181,000,000
Revenue passengers	396,000,000	401,000,000	395,000,000	387,000,000
Revenue passenger-miles	24,900,000,000	25,300,000,000	25,500,000,000	25,600,000,000
Operating revenue, all services	$845,700,000	$901,400,000	$953,200,000	$971,600,000
Operating expenses	$751,900,000	$812,200,000	$851,800,000	$879,900,000
Net operating rev. before inc. taxes	$93,800,000	$89,200,000	$101,400,000	$91,700,000
Taxes assignable to operations[3]	$70,100,000	$75,500,000	$79,500,000	$92,900,000

(1.)Includes duplication between carriers. (2.)Operating companies only. (3.)Excludes income taxes.

Minimum Legal Age for Purchase of Alcoholic Beverages

In the United States and Canada

State/Province	Years	State/Province	Years	State/Province	Years	State/Province	Years
Alabama	21	Indiana	21	New Brunswick	21	Quebec	18
Alaska	19	Iowa	18	Newfoundland	21	Rhode Island	18
Alberta	18	Kansas (c)	21	New Hampshire	18	Saskatchewan	18
Arizona	19	Kentucky	21	New Jersey	18	South Carolina (e)	21
Arkansas	21	Louisiana	18	New Mexico	21	South Dakota (g)	21
British Columbia	19	Maine	18	New York	18	Tennessee	18
California	21	Manitoba	18	North Carolina (b)	21	Texas	18
Colorado (c)	21	Maryland	21	North Dakota	21	Utah	21
Connecticut	18	Massachusetts	18	Northwest Territories	19	Vermont	18
Delaware	20	Michigan	18	Nova Scotia	19	Virginia (c)	21
Dist. of Col. (b)	21	Minnesota	21	Ohio (c)	21	Washington	21
Florida	21	Mississippi (h)	21	Oklahoma (d)	21	West Virginia	18
Georgia	18	Missouri	21	Oregon	21	Wisconsin	18
Hawaii	18	Montana	18	Ontario	18	Wyoming	19
Idaho	19	Nebraska	19	Pennsylvania	21	Yukon Territory	19
Illinois	21	Nevada	21	Prince Edward Island	18		

(b) Light wine, beer 18. (c) 3.2 beer 18. (d) 3.2 beer; male 21; female 18 (e) Beer and wine 18. (g) 3.2 beer (h) Beer not over 4% by wt. 18.

Highway Mileage Between Selected Cities

Cities In The East*

	ALBANY, N.Y.	ATLANTA, GA.	BALTIMORE, MD.	BANGOR, ME.	BIRMINGHAM, ALA.	BOSTON, MASS.	BUFFALO, N.Y.	CHARLESTON, W. VA.	CHICAGO, ILL.	CINCINNATI, OHIO	CLEVELAND, OHIO	DETROIT, MICH.	INDIANAPOLIS, IND.	JACKSON, MISS.	JACKSONVILLE, FLA.
ALBANY		988	321	366	1091	170	283	712	807	707	466	536	766	1379	1117
ATLANTA	988		671	1315	155	1070	876	519	707	467	692	726	539	400	315
BALTIMORE	321	671		632	800	400	366	391	690	497	348	510	565	998	794
BANGOR	366	1315	632		1407	233	652	1018	1174	1094	827	892	1136	1635	1426
BIRMINGHAM	1091	155	800	1407		1210	932	589	661	499	742	743	492	243	427
BOSTON	170	1070	400	233	1210		458	781	974	861	640	707	931	1446	1201
BUFFALO	283	876	366	652	932	458		439	520	428	186	249	486	1115	1080
CHARLESTON	712	519	391	1018	589	781	439		483	202	268	357	301	786	671
CHICAGO	807	707	690	1174	661	974	520	483		294	345	269	188	747	1017
CINCINNATI	707	467	497	1094	499	861	428	202	294		244	251	104	678	783
CLEVELAND	466	692	348	827	742	640	186	268	345	244		168	300	924	971
DETROIT	536	726	510	892	743	707	249	357	269	251	168		277	931	1039
INDIANAPOLIS	766	539	565	1136	492	931	486	301	188	104	300	277		631	852
JACKSON	1379	400	998	1635	243	1446	1115	786	747	678	924	931	631		597
JACKSONVILLE	1117	315	794	1426	427	1201	1080	671	1017	783	971	1039	852	597	
LOUISVILLE	827	428	602	1198	362	964	537	266	304	108	351	363	114	573	766
MEMPHIS	1217	366	951	1594	247	1340	924	615	548	487	737	726	444	210	672
MIAMI	1468	665	1143	1773	765	1539	1431	1043	1377	1133	1322	1387	1197	920	345
NASHVILLE	1090	251	732	736	201	1126	717	409	452	289	532	544	293	375	577
NEW ORLEANS	1476	517	1153	1747	359	1556	1248	936	929	820	1060	1077	839	182	568
NEW YORK	147	863	192	450	988	211	367	566	828	635	486	626	716	1232	979
NORFOLK	560	592	249	881	753	543	561	397	874	600	531	699	698	996	661
PHILADELPHIA	233	771	99	541	897	303	360	481	758	571	425	578	639	1153	889
PITTSBURGH	457	737	230	819	763	576	220	233	459	278	127	287	355	972	893
PORTLAND, ME.	275	1185	513	128	1325	106	574	895	1089	967	752	817	1037	1552	1293
RICHMOND	472	545	144	773	697	543	473	309	786	512	443	611	620	944	646
ST. LOUIS	1016	553	804	1379	503	1188	723	538	291	338	540	513	239	505	881
TAMPA	1331	464	986	1620	552	1383	1263	884	1187	948	1166	1201	1005	678	194
TRENTON	223	783	128	520	915	289	358	513	780	590	435	594	660	1163	921
WASHINGTON	367	640	39	673	767	440	372	355	687	497	362	516	567	1000	754

	LOUISVILLE, KY.	MEMPHIS, TENN.	MIAMI, FLA.	NASHVILLE, TENN.	NEW ORLEANS, LA.	NEW YORK, N.Y.	NORFOLK, VA.	PHILADELPHIA, PA.	PITTSBURGH, PA.	PORTLAND, ME.	RICHMOND, VA.	ST. LOUIS, MO.	TAMPA, FLA.	TRENTON, N.J.	WASHINGTON, D.C.
ALBANY	827	1217	1468	1090	1476	147	560	233	457	275	472	1016	1331	223	367
ATLANTA	428	366	665	251	517	863	592	771	737	1185	545	553	464	783	640
BALTIMORE	602	951	1143	732	1153	192	249	99	230	513	144	804	986	128	39
BANGOR	1198	1594	1773	736	1747	450	881	541	819	128	773	1379	1620	520	673
BIRMINGHAM	362	247	765	201	359	988	753	897	763	1325	697	503	552	915	767
BOSTON	964	1340	1539	1126	1556	211	543	303	576	106	543	1188	1383	289	440
BUFFALO	537	924	1431	717	1248	367	561	360	220	574	473	723	1263	358	372
CHARLESTON	266	615	1043	409	936	566	397	481	233	895	309	538	884	513	355
CHICAGO	304	548	1377	452	929	828	874	758	459	1089	786	291	1187	780	687
CINCINNATI	108	487	1133	289	820	635	600	571	278	967	512	338	948	590	497
CLEVELAND	351	737	1322	532	1060	486	531	425	127	752	443	540	1166	435	362
DETROIT	363	726	1387	544	1077	626	699	578	287	817	611	513	1201	594	516
INDIANAPOLIS	114	444	1197	293	839	716	698	639	355	1037	620	239	1005	660	567
JACKSON	573	210	920	375	182	1232	996	1153	972	1552	944	505	678	1163	1000
JACKSONVILLE	766	672	345	577	568	979	661	889	893	1293	646	881	194	921	754
LOUISVILLE		365	1078	180	719	759	693	682	398	1070	575	267	865	705	605
MEMPHIS	365		1017	220	399	1142	958	1057	786	1446	845	294	782	1064	917
MIAMI	1078	1017		916	878	1327	1013	1230	1237	1649	994	1222	248	1276	1105
NASHVILLE	180	220	916		536	929	713	838	568	1232	625	295	908	853	697
NEW ORLEANS	719	399	878	536		1353	1101	1239	1113	1655	1057	699	644	1270	1150
NEW YORK	759	1142	1327	929	1353		441	91	363	317	330	961	1176	70	226
NORFOLK	693	958	1013	713	1101	441		348	400	649	88	930	859	359	195
PHILADELPHIA	682	1057	1230	838	1239	91	348		294	409	240	881	1083	32	136
PITTSBURGH	398	786	1237	568	1113	363	400	294		682	312	599	1045	205	229
PORTLAND, ME.	1070	1446	1649	1232	1655	317	649	409	682		649	1294	1488	395	549
RICHMOND	575	845	994	625	1057	330	88	240	312	649		842	842	277	107
ST. LOUIS	267	294	1222	295	699	961	930	881	599	1294	842		1030	897	804
TAMPA	865	782	248	908	644	1176	859	1083	1045	1488	842	1030		1109	947
TRENTON	705	1064	1276	853	1270	70	359	32	205	395	277	897	1109		169
WASHINGTON	605	917	1105	150	1226	226	195	136	229	549	107	804	947	169	

* Directions for Use of Mileage Charts

To measure mileage between the east and west charts there are 5 key cities: Chicago, Jackson (Miss.), Memphis, New Orleans and St. Louis.

Plot your course between the city listed nearest your home town and whichever of the 5 key cities you desire to pass through to the city of your destination. Add the mileage shown and this will give you the approximate total mileage.

For example: The mileage between Cheyenne and Philadelphia through St. Louis: Philadelphia to St. Louis = 881 miles, St. Louis to Cheyenne = 910; the total is 1,791 miles.

Highway Mileage Between Selected Cities

Cities In The West

	ALBUQUERQUE, N.M.	BOISE, IDAHO	CHEYENNE, WYO.	CHICAGO, ILL.	DALLAS, TEXAS	DENVER, COLO.	DES MOINES, IOWA	FARGO, N.D.	HELENA, MONT.	HOUSTON, TEXAS	JACKSON, MISS.	KANSAS CITY, MO.	LITTLE ROCK, ARK.	LOS ANGELES, CALIF.	MEMPHIS, TENN.
ALBUQUERQUE		980	545	1285	650	432	1032	1310	1111	844	1062	791	901	805	1032
BOISE	980		766	1726	1637	867	1397	1228	494	1825	2063	1446	1833	887	1913
CHEYENNE	545	766		967	880	101	632	823	700	1143	1282	657	1053	1182	1127
CHICAGO	1285	1726	967		936	1018	330	657	1478	1092	747	505	652	2106	548
DALLAS	650	1637	880	936		784	704	1110	1571	245	411	498	330	1410	468
DENVER	432	867	101	1018	784		674	901	792	1028	1219	613	962	1162	1058
DES MOINES	1032	1397	632	330	704	674		491	1162	948	828	207	581	1788	608
FARGO, N.D.	1310	1228	823	657	1110	901	491		822	1364	1271	636	1054	1935	1061
HELENA	1111	494	700	1478	1571	792	1162	822		1813	1922	1261	1666	1234	1720
HOUSTON	844	1825	1143	1092	245	1028	948	1364	1813		433	744	439	1554	572
JACKSON	1062	2063	1282	747	411	1219	828	1271	1922	433		613	257	1864	210
KANSAS CITY	791	1446	657	505	498	613	207	636	1261	744	613		409	1620	467
LITTLE ROCK	901	1833	1053	652	330	962	581	1045	1666	439	257	409		1698	139
LOS ANGELES	805	887	1182	2106	1410	1162	1788	1935	1234	1554	1864	1620	1698		1823
MEMPHIS	1032	1913	1127	548	468	1058	627	1061	1720	572	210	467	139	1823	
MILWAUKEE	1200	1762	1010	97	1063	1039	358	573	1392	1163	826	564	727	2145	632
MINNEAPOLIS	1223	1446	821	418	964	845	254	239	1056	1211	1062	461	833	1996	851
NEW ORLEANS	1145	2140	1376	929	500	1284	1028	1479	2070	358	182	846	434	1916	399
OKLAHOMA CITY	545	1489	702	826	212	616	566	900	1392	458	587	357	350	1353	482
OMAHA	892	1267	491	465	672	537	139	436	1056	917	882	208	623	1698	671
PHOENIX	449	1020	924	1753	1021	826	1449	1726	1147	1158	1456	1238	1337	389	1470
PORTLAND, ORE.	1461	435	1211	2131	2057	1285	1819	1590	657	2282	2506	1901	2284	994	2367
RENO	1036	427	995	1970	1695	1040	1638	1639	905	1888	2104	1665	2030	476	2083
ST. LOUIS	1057	1701	910	291	651	863	349	812	1498	801	505	254	357	1862	294
SALT LAKE CITY	612	363	457	1443	1262	512	1089	1215	500	1453	1685	1118	1444	730	1570
SAN FRANCISCO	1132	654	1209	2183	1773	1267	1851	1873	1134	1955	2203	1893	2032	403	2162
SEATTLE	1511	529	1279	2031	2136	1377	1766	1505	611	2354	2601	1904	2273	1177	2362
SIOUX FALLS	1082	1295	654	525	844	655	282	230	960	1110	1013	390	799	1817	858
TUCSON	454	1191	999	1739	951	845	1462	1746	1270	1070	1362	1255	1278	512	1417
WICHITA	620	1663	590	711	386	512	403	731	1241	629	733	202	472	1384	549

	MILWAUKEE, WIS.	MINNEAPOLIS, MINN.	NEW ORLEANS, LA.	OKLAHOMA CITY, OKLA.	OMAHA, NEB.	PHOENIX, ARIZ.	PORTLAND, ORE.	RENO, NEV.	ST. LOUIS, MO.	SALT LAKE CITY, UTAH	SAN FRANCISCO, CALIF.	SEATTLE, WASH.	SIOUX FALLS, S.D.	TUCSON, ARIZ.	WICHITA, KAN.
ALBUQUERQUE	1390	1223	1145	545	892	449	1461	1036	1057	612	1132	1511	1082	454	620
BOISE	1763	1446	2140	1489	1267	1020	435	427	1701	363	654	525	1295	1191	1663
CHEYENNE	1019	821	1376	702	491	924	1211	995	910	457	1209	1279	654	999	590
CHICAGO	87	418	929	826	465	1753	2131	1970	291	1443	2183	2031	525	1739	711
DALLAS	1063	964	500	212	672	1021	2057	1695	651	1262	1773	2136	844	951	386
DENVER	1039	845	1284	616	537	826	1285	1040	863	512	1267	1377	655	845	512
DES MOINES	358	254	1028	566	139	1449	1819	1638	349	1089	1851	1766	282	1462	403
FARGO, N.D.	573	239	1479	900	436	1726	1590	1639	812	1215	1873	1505	230	1746	731
HELENA	1392	1056	2070	1392	1056	1147	657	905	1498	500	1134	611	960	1270	1241
HOUSTON	1163	1211	358	458	917	1158	2282	1888	801	1453	1955	2354	1110	1070	629
JACKSON	826	1062	182	587	882	1456	2506	2104	505	1685	2203	2601	1013	1362	733
KANSAS CITY	564	461	846	357	208	1238	1901	1665	254	1118	1893	1904	390	1255	202
LITTLE ROCK	727	833	434	350	623	1337	2284	2030	357	1444	2032	2273	799	1278	472
LOS ANGELES	2145	1996	1916	1353	1698	389	994	476	1862	730	403	1177	1817	512	1384
MEMPHIS	632	852	399	482	671	1470	2367	2083	294	1570	2162	2362	858	1417	549
MILWAUKEE		334	1034	905	501	1833	2069	2003	371	1502	2203	2045	507	1819	792
MINNEAPOLIS	334		1251	818	364	1671	1721	1797	553	1246	2001	1673	221	1677	650
NEW ORLEANS	1034	1251		684	1065	1527	2591	2199	699	1773	2278	2645	1265	1436	840
OKLAHOMA CITY	905	818	648		477	989	1926	1529	523	1112	1692	1975	644	941	168
OMAHA	1501	364	1065	477		1325	1700	1500	453	955	1720	1657	187	1341	309
PHOENIX	1833	1671	1527	989	1325		1273	762	1492	688	794	1510	1481	123	1040
PORTLAND, ORE.	2069	1721	2591	1926	1700	1273		566	2113	807	669	173	1580	1396	1854
RENO	2003	1797	2199	1529	1500	762	566		1906	531	227	760	1472	912	1542
ST. LOUIS	371	553	699	523	453	1492	2113	1879		1381	2133	2102	632	1457	460
SALT LAKE CITY	1502	1246	1773	1112	953	688	807	531	1381		755	869	941	820	1020
SAN FRANCISCO	2203	2001	2278	1692	1720	794	669	227	2133	755		858	1696	921	1730
SEATTLE	2045	1673	2645	1975	1657	1510	173	760	2102	869	858		1526	1666	1842
SIOUX FALLS	507	221	1265	644	187	1481	1580	1472	632	941	1696	1526		1536	493
TUCSON	1819	1677	1436	941	1341	123	1396	912	1457	820	921	1666	1536		1074
WICHITA	792	650	840	168	309	1040	1854	1542	460	1020	1730	1842	493	1074	

Trucking: Fewer Workers, Bigger Payroll

Source: American Trucking Assns.; Dept. of Transportation

1971	Employees	Annual Payroll	Truck Registration New	Total	1971	Employees	Annual Payroll	Truck Registration New	Total
Ala..	161,200	$1,129,690,000	35,779	428,556	Nebr..	91,100	$ 632,143,000	22,592	282,186
Alaska	14,400	174,168,000	4,690	48,326	Nev..	41,900	345,172,000	9,396	93,343
Ariz..	114,000	892,506,000	30,813	289,797	N.H..	28,100	199,229,000	10,126	60,291
Ark..	134,700	806,045,000	33,247	319,616	N.J..	211,400	1,801,551,000	38,765	368,222
Calif..	1,182,800	11,721,214,000	197,087	2,111,817	N.M.	66,200	467,372,000	17,881	192,665
Colo..	145,600	1,135,680,000	37,057	366,624	N.Y..	407,700	3,664,408,000	89,474	697,557
Conn..	126,800	1,064,613,000	3,228	157,683	N.C..	310,400	1,987,802,000	51,671	615,609
Del..	29,700	249,599,000	5,635	51,147	N.D..	37,000	246,716,000	9,071	164,214
D. of C..	15,100	153,265,000	2,140	18,711	Ohio	330,200	2,828,823,000	77,651	680,256
Fla..	269,000	1,983,875,000	70,643	608,281	Okla..	167,100	1,239,548,000	NA	517,176
Ga..	215,000	1,523,060,000	56,022	548,337	Ore..	119,500	918,836,000	37,293	259,416
Hawaii	21,000	168,252,000	5,579	49,585	Penn..	451,100	3,524,444,000	85,699	776,688
Idaho	49,000	334,474,000	15,272	153,194	R.I..	35,600	254,433,000	4,077	56,590
Ill..	340,200	2,989,678,000	73,427	681,738	S.C..	143,700	918,806,000	24,649	255,239
Ind..	321,500	2,599,016,000	55,748	551,832	S.D..	37,500	234,600,000	9,609	140,181
Iowa	164,000	1,190,968,000	32,062	410,585	Tenn..	142,200	974,212,000	45,166	424,352
Kans..	148,000	1,051,984,000	30,221	438,933	Texas	676,000	5,088,252,000	151,878	1,624,858
Ky..	153,100	1,109,516,000	32,983	407,513	Utah..	59,400	424,057,000	17,515	196,411
La..	166,400	1,254,989,000	39,351	386,559	Vt..	18,500	134,921,000	6,901	42,374
Me..	54,800	361,680,000	12,526	103,208	Va..	180,000	1,319,940,000	44,931	387,464
Md..	121,900	957,159,000	30,032	262,884	Wash..	192,800	1,639,764,000	35,210	497,585
Mass..	165,100	1,290,091,000	30,336	260,795	W.Va..	87,300	691,940,000	23,712	199,828
Mich..	314,900	2,894,246,000	92,725	673,908	Wisc..	154,700	1,219,191,000	35,612	349,647
Minn..	189,700	1,479,660,000	42,142	466,813	Wyo..	30,000	205,410,000	9,380	91,686
Miss..	105,700	656,714,000	26,413	302,185	Total..	9,034,000	$72,405,973,000	1,981,294	*19,802,490
Mo..	240,600	1,925,965,000	51,335	539,232	1970 Totals..	8,894,000	$61,355,349,000	1,790,177	18,747,781
Mont..	50,400	347,306,000	15,806	180,993	*Incl. 34,876 Fed. Govt. trucks, 25,860 motor homes.				

653,742,494 Tons of Intercity Freight Moved

Source: American Trucking Associations
Based on operations of 2,224 Class I & II intercity motor carriers. In tons.

Region	1971	1972	Commodity Class	1971	1972
New England	22,167,859	22,991,667	General Freight	221,130,486	237,809,618
Middle Atlantic	132,387,958	141,819,248	Household Goods	2,902,424	3,207,646
Central	155,766,998	166,727,657	Heavy Machinery	6,532,367	7,542,849
Southern	102,452,463	112,285,412	Liquid Petroleum	155,280,168	167,059,159
Northwestern	41,329,230	42,778,779	Refrig. Solids & Liquids	11,705,898	12,742,943
Midwestern	36,890,364	41,582,730	Agric. Commodities	9,471,945	10,509,936
Southwestern	49,479,619	54,474,260	Motor Vehicles	22,079,087	23,966,001
Rocky Mountain	17,017,465	19,783,061	Building Materials	28,300,359	28,410,999
Pacific	50,118,274	51,299,680	All Other Classes	150,207,496	162,493,343
United States	607,610,230	653,742,494	All Commodities	607,610,230	653,742,494

Automobile Factory Sales

Source: Motor Vehicle Manufacturers Association, Detroit, Mich.-Values, Wholesale

Year	Passenger Cars Number	Value	Motor Trucks, Buses Number	Value	Total Number	Value
1900	4,192	$4,899,443			4,192	$4,899,443
1905	24,250	38,670,000	750	$1,330,000	25,000	40,000,000
1910	181,000	215,340,000	6,000	9,660,000	187,000	225,000,000
1915	895,930	575,978,000	74,000	125,800,000	969,930	701,778,000
1920	1,905,560	1,809,170,963	321,789	423,249,410	2,227,349	2,232,420,373
1925	3,735,171	2,458,370,026	530,659	458,400,277	4,265,830	2,916,770,303
1930	2,787,456	1,644,083,152	575,364	390,752,061	3,362,820	2,034,835,213
1935	3,273,874	1,707,836,325	697,367	380,997,330	3,971,241	2,088,833,655
1940	3,717,385	2,370,654,083	754,901	567,820,414	4,472,286	2,938,474,497
1945	69,532	57,254,655	655,683	1,181,955,532	725,215	1,239,210,187
1950	6,665,863	8,468,137,000	1,337,193	1,707,748,000	8,003,056	10,175,885,000
1955	7,920,186	12,452,871,000	1,249,106	2,020,973,000	9,169,292	14,473,844,000
1960	6,674,796	12,164,234,000	1,194,475	2,350,680,000	7,869,271	14,514,914,000
1965	9,305,561	18,330,036,000	1,751,805	3,733,664,000	11,057,366	22,113,700,000
1970	6,546,817	14,630,217,000	1,692,440	4,819,752,000	8,239,257	19,449,969,000
1971	8,584,592	21,300,000,000	2,053,146	5,800,000,000	10,637,738	27,100,000,000
1972	8,823,938	23,133,051,000	2,446,807	7,654,180,000	11,270,745	30,787,231,000

After July 1, 1964 all tactical vehicles are excluded. Federal excise taxes are excluded in all years. *Preliminary.

Automotive Exports from United States

Source: Bureau of Economic Analysis, Dept. of Commerce
(in millions)

	Total Value Vehicles	Automotive*		Total Value Vehicles	Automotive*		Total Value Vehicles	Automotive*
1940	$147	$259	1965	739	1,929	1969	1,553	3,887
1950	406	746	1966	942	2,354	1970	1,397	3,652
1955	747	1,276	1967	1,236	2,784	1971	1,784	4,397
1960	634	1,266	1968	1,415	3,453	1972	2,008	5,125

*Includes used passenger cars and trucks, trailers, parts for assembly, and garage equipment.

How Hungry Is Your Car For Gas?

To no one's surprise, small imported cars get better mileage than their American competitors, according to a study by the Environmental Protection Agency. The tests cover a representative cross-section of all engines certified as meeting 1973 air pollution standards. EPA points out that the tests aren't exact yardsticks but are a valid means of comparison nonetheless.

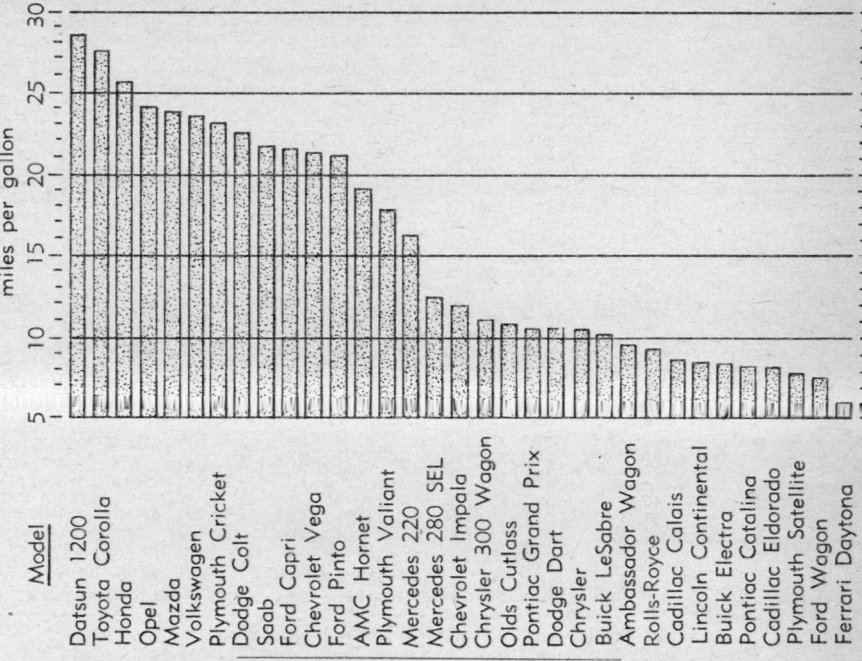

Motor Vehicle Safety Recalls Hit Record High

Manufacturers' recalls of motor vehicles for correction of safety defects reached a new high of 12,081,803 in 1972, the most in any year since the 1966 National Traffic and Motor Vehicle Safety Act required makers to notify owners about suspected hazards.

The pace continued high in 1973 as over 4,233,900 recalls were issued in the first 2 months of the year. Recalls included autos, campers, trailers, trucks and motorcycles.

Foreign-made cars accounted for a disproportionately high share of the 1972 total — which consisted of 7,813,613 vehicles manufactured by U.S. companies and 4,268,190 made abroad and sold to Americans. Foreign vehicles, while totaling 15% of total sales in the U.S., were responsible for 30% of those recalled for defects.

Even Rolls-Royces did not escape unscathed, although only 194 of them had to be called back.

The U.S. Department of Transportation, to which manufacturers must report all recalls, announced the 1972 figures.

Ford Motor Co. vehicles of numerous makes and models led the parade back to the service station with a total of 5,775,514 in 18 separate recall campaigns. Over 4,000,000 were for possibly defective shoulder safety belts. General Motors had been tops in 1971 when one of its campaigns involved some 6,600,000 Chevrolets for possibly defective engine mounts.

Volkswagen was second in '72 with 3,727,994 cars, most of them for possible window wiper troubles. Next came General Motors, with 1,346,390 of many makes and models, but almost half Chevrolet

Vegas with possible rear axle problems.

Fourth place went to American Motors with 332,972 recalls, including 270,000 Hornets, Matadors, Gremlins, Javelins and Ambassadors with possible loss of braking action. Nissan Motor Corp. was next with 209,861 Datsuns in 3 campaigns involving possible hood latch, brake hose or gas pedal problems.

Sixth was Chrysler Motors with 200,920, among them 56,371 Plymouth Furys with possible bumper jacking problems and 42,000 Plymouth Crickets for possible stearing gear trouble. Next came 162,520 Toyotas, including 110,614 Corolla 1200s and 1600s with possible high-speed engine stalls and 51,906 Mark IIs with possibly defective outside rearview mirrors.

Eighth in the parade were 53,643 Volvos, most with throttles that might stick. Following closely were 47,945 products of British Leyland Motors, including 28,000 MGs whose headlights might fail to meet minimum height requirements, 5,394 Triumphs with possible ignition lock warning trouble and 4,378 Jaguars with the possibility of battery acid vapors spilling onto brake lines.

Tenth was the AM General Corp. with 32,614 postal delivery vehicles with either accelerator rod or engine mount troubles. Eleventh was Porshe-Audi Inc. with 30,394 recalls including 18,989 Porsches with possible seatbelt trouble and 9,920 Audis with incorrectly-stamped certification labels.

The 1972 callbacks brought to over 36,800,000 the total recalls since the Federal law went into effect in Sept. 1966.

Passenger Car Production, U.S. Plants

Source: Motor Vehicle Manufacturers Association of the U.S., Inc.

	1971	1972	1973 6 mos.		1971	1972	1973 6 mos.
American Motors Corp.				Lincoln	37,801	49,457	29,702
Gremlin	54,615	69,773	47,606	Mark III/IV	34,230	55,561	41,666
Hornet	67,875	83,213	59,556	**Total Lincoln**	**72,031**	**105,018**	**71,368**
Javelin/AMX	24,503	29,105	19,460	**Total Ford Motor Co.**	**2,176,335**	**2,400,871**	**1,417,861**
Matador	46,489	52,343	32,474				
Ambassador	42,187	44,698	29,766	**General Motors Corp...**			
Total American				Chevrolet	942,067	955,237	485,857
Motors Corp.	**235,669**	**279,132**	**188,862**	Corvette	26,844	27,376	17,051
Chrysler Corp.				Monte Carlo	136,515	186,171	131,899
Valiant	236,386	250,583	178,465	Chevelle	375,009	358,568	181,169
Barracuda	17,013	19,090	11,807	Camaro	148,379	35,943	64,761
Satellite	91,836	75,089	80,570	Nova	298,933	367,733	217,162
Fury	291,357	268,724	137,792	Vega	393,030	368,743	203,431
Total Plymouth	**636,592**	**613,486**	**408,634**	**Total Chevrolet**	**2,320,777**	**2,299,771**	**1,301,330**
Chrysler	188,360	204,881	128,235	Pontiac	300,587	304,545	195,133
Imperial	14,523	15,393	6,695	Grand Prix	89,512	98,587	93,141
Total Chrysler-				Le Mans/Tempest	195,721	198,411	125,968
Plymouth	**839,475**	**833,760**	**543,564**	Firebird	66,087	15,828	31,296
Challenger	28,901	27,770	17,397	Ventura	76,708	85,200	49,184
Dart	152,925	182,122	112,662	**Total Pontiac**	**728,615**	**702,571**	**494,722**
Coronet/Charger	159,951	178,261	104,252	Oldsmobile	390,173	389,089	223,557
Dodge	132,054	145,441	80,299	Tornado	46,352	51,267	31,721
Total Dodge	**473,831**	**533,594**	**314,610**	F-85/Cutlass	338,674	341,130	234,068
Total Chrysler Corp.	**1,313,306**	**1,367,354**	**858,174**	Omega		25,708	30,531
Ford Motor Co.				**Total Oldsmobile**	**775,199**	**807,194**	**519,877**
Ford	812,923	812,718	452,716	Buick	463,785	425,813	248,027
Torino	321,487	365,532	184,506	Riviera	45,464	36,210	15,508
Club Wagon	22,656	23,934	12,433	Century/Skylark	242,612	226,534	175,619
Maverick	127,414	165,934	111,372	Apollo			25,821
Pinto	299,867	322,338	196,680	**Total Buick**	**751,861**	**688,557**	**464,975**
Mustang	130,488	118,972	81,308	Cadillac	236,499	233,456	139,447
Thunderbird	46,277	58,582	52,119	Eldorado	40,064	43,795	29,038
Total Ford	**1,761,112**	**1,868,010**	**1,091,134**	**Total Cadillac**	**276,563**	**277,251**	**168,485**
Mercury	134,756	150,671	76,268	**Total General**			
Montego	76,786	140,477	89,586	**Motors Corp.**	**4,853,015**	**4,775,344**	**2,949,389**
Cougar	53,156	53,594	35,732	**Checkers Motors Corp.**	**5,328**	**5,504**	**3,401**
Comet	78,494	83,101	53,773				
Total Mercury	**343,192**	**427,843**	**255,359**	**Total Passenger Cars**	**8,583,653**	**8,828,205**	**5,417,687**

Total Road and Street Mileage in United States

Source: Federal Highway Administration, Dept. of Transportation 1971

State	Rural	Urban	Surfaced	Total	State	Rural	Urban	Surfaced	Total
Ala.	67,574	11,462	70,579	79,036	Neb.	92,084	6,681	76,969	98,765
Alaska	6,955	862	4,430	7,817	Nev.	47,783	1,919	16,130	49,702
Ariz.	40,919	6,166	21,967	47,085	N.H.	10,110	4,816	12,321	14,926
Ark.	69,449	9,231	61,136	78,680	N.J.	14,725	17,512	30,149	32,237
Calif.	119,993	45,997	121,470	165,990	N.M.	63,535	4,836	21,206	68,371
Colo.	74,289	7,581	51,762	81,870	N.Y.	65,872	40,618	102,346	106,490
Conn.	5,363	13,168	18,404	18,531	N.C.	72,593	13,885	79,234	86,478
Del.	4,338	766	5,080	5,104	N.D.	103,400	3,130	69,458	106,530
Fla.	71,035	22,275	65,426	93,310	Ohio	85,677	23,563	107,586	109,240
Ga.	85,186	15,028	69,671	100,214	Okla.	93,626	14,246	81,525	107,872
Hawaii	2,593	998	3,411	3,591	Ore.	91,105	6,348	61,265	97,453
Idaho	54,181	2,963	30,699	57,144	Pa.	91,487	24,171	96,854	115,658
Ill.	102,434	27,753	123,844	130,187	R.I.	1,017	4,444	5,243	5,461
Ind.	75,401	15,507	86,059	90,908	S.C.	52,791	6,838	40,891	59,629
Iowa	99,168	13,663	106,459	112,831	S.D.	81,105	2,973	60,182	84,078
Kan.	123,094	11,088	99,918	134,182	Tenn.	68,364	11,926	78,528	80,290
Ky.	63,271	5,852	61,470	69,123	Tex.	198,864	49,476	184,028	248,340
La.	42,347	10,993	49,477	53,340	Utah	36,569	4,412	23,304	40,981
Maine	18,975	2,449	19,861	21,424	Vt.	13,508	1,004	12,576	14,512
Md.	22,376	4,146	26,452	26,522	Va.	52,872	8,636	60,760	61,508
Mass.	7,497	21,858	28,993	29,355	Wash.	70,254	9,965	64,222	80,219
Mich.	94,949	20,115	97,108	115,064	W. Va.	32,329	3,612	26,815	35,941
Minn.	110,543	17,201	115,590	127,744	Wis.	89,130	14,222	97,755	103,352
Miss.	60,167	6,599	64,461	66,766	Wyo.	39,253	1,287	17,532	40,540
Mo.	100,158	15,386	108,283	115,544	D. of C.		1,087	1,087	1,087
Mon.	75,587	2,333	43,096	77,920	**Total**	**3,165,895**	**593,047**	**2,983,072**	**3,758,942**

Car, Truck and Bus Drivers in the U.S.A.

Source: Federal Highway Administration, estimated total licenses in force during 1972.

State	No. of drivers	State	No. of drivers	State	No. of drivers	State	No. of drivers
Alabama	1,805,801	Indiana	2,936,579	Nebraska	1,007,000	South Carolina	1,563,788
Alaska	153,631	Iowa	1,727,257	Nevada	369,595	South Dakota	423,880
Arizona	1,184,421	Kansas	1,564,697	New Hampshire	461,124	Tennessee	2,159,499
Arkansas	1,119,004	Kentucky	1,683,984	New Jersey	4,124,513	Texas	6,789,721
California	12,650,040	Louisiana	1,916,845	New Mexico	637,291	Utah	649,770
Colorado	1,535,918	Maine	556,881	New York	¹8,430,000	Vermont	280,408
Connecticut	1,797,821	Maryland	2,151,407	North Carolina	2,918,709	Virginia	2,670,493
Delaware	348,779	Massachusetts	¹3,141,000	North Dakota	347,310	Washington	2,007,862
Florida	4,360,625	Michigan	5,249,010	Ohio	6,140,623	West Virginia	1,016,060
Georgia	3,205,859	Minnesota	¹2,416,000	Oklahoma	1,630,647	Wisconsin	2,527,731
Hawaii	491,805	Mississippi	1,382,030	Oregon	1,512,657	Wyoming	217,251
Idaho	508,203	Missouri	2,775,589	Pennsylvania	6,367,388	Dist. of Col.	344,671
Illinois	6,003,602	Montana	444,376	Rhode Island	537,849	**Total**	**118,246,864**

¹Estimated

Auto Registrations, Taxes, Gasoline, Drivers' Ages
Source: Federal Highway Adm.

State	Drivers' Age Jan. 1, 1973 (1) Regular	1973 (2) Juvenile	Registered autos, buses & trucks est. (1972) Number	State Gas Tax per gal. (1972) Cents	Motor Fuel Gross Tax Collections $1,000 (1972)	Motor Fuel consumption (1972) Highway 1,000 Gallons	Non-highway 1,000 Gallons	Total 1,000 Gallons
Alabama	16		2,227,293	7	138,591	1,900,473	45,055	1,945,528
Alaska	16		148,756	8	10,133	109,500	69,121	178,621
Arizona	16		1,301,870	7	85,620	1,185,768	43,998	1,229,766
Arkansas	16		1,070,295	7.5	91,373	1,211,265	30,981	1,242,246
California	16/18	14	12,852,228	7	735,000	10,500,391	229,504	10,729,895
Colorado	21	16	1,679,702	7	91,009	1,323,303	61,048	1,384,351
Connecticut	16/18		1,860,385	10	140,426	1,383,077	24,669	1,407,746
Delaware	16/18		322,971	8	24,069	298,264	6,317	304,581
Florida	16/18		4,835,986	8	330,555	4,045,322	124,098	4,169,420
Georgia	16		2,959,454	7.5	222,566	2,929,489	49,600	2,979,089
Hawaii	15		447,409	5	13,622	267,386	11,420	278,806
Idaho	16	14	549,834	8.5	39,165	456,869	33,546	490,415
Illinois	18	16	5,643,853	7.5	390,970	5,075,195	225,804	5,300,999
Indiana	16/21		³2,908,543	8	243,541	2,961,899	105,670	3,067,569
Iowa	16/18	14	1,917,075	7	125,499	1,615,383	214,714	1,830,097
Kansas	16	14	1,691,501	7	96,993	1,328,874	136,639	1,465,513
Kentucky	16		1,967,620	9	140,707	1,730,819	30,647	1,761,466
Louisiana	17	15	1,942,263	8	144,203	1,760,676	51,609	1,812,285
Maine	15/17	15	564,782	9	49,957	545,081	11,899	556,980
Maryland	16/18		2,130,458	9	150,535	1,857,284	25,553	1,882,837
Massachusetts	18	16½	³2,821,596	7.5	³173,142	³2,370,480	³25,360	³2,395,840
Michigan	16/18	14	5,010,537	7	315,463	4,586,688	181,602	4,768,290
Minnesota	17/18	15	2,368,127	7	150,473	2,016,627	187,678	2,204,305
Mississippi	15		1,010,150	8	105,775	1,274,322	32,020	1,306,342
Missouri	16		2,618,164	7	153,252	2,727,251	137,503	2,864,754
Montana	15/16		584,116	7	35,354	463,627	42,185	505,812
Nebraska	16	14	1,080,885	8.5	81,189	911,350	64,381	975,731
Nevada	16	14	399,046	6	24,582	395,619	16,440	412,059
New Hampshire	16/18	16	436,158	9	36,289	398,128	6,329	404,457
New Jersey	17	16	3,858,631	8	253,913	3,377,996	61,343	3,439,339
New Mexico	15/16		710,765	7	51,021	728,144	16,346	744,490
New York	17/18	16	³7,118,566	8	500,310	6,054,788	257,640	6,312,428
North Carolina	16/18		3,219,776	9	262,619	2,872,824	79,730	2,952,554
North Dakota	16	14	463,622	7	30,133	338,404	113,008	451,412
Ohio	16/18	14	6,224,278	7	366,015	5,236,301	139,114	5,375,415
Oklahoma	16		1,887,210	6.5	107,676	1,644,961	49,614	1,694,575
Oregon	16	14	1,496,115	7	82,215	1,278,441	52,347	1,330,788
Pennsylvania	17/18	16	6,311,330	8	415,032	5,346,049	182,242	5,528,291
Rhode Island	16/18		536,284	8	31,477	384,938	11,973	396,911
South Carolina	16	15	1,497,389	8	111,812	1,503,127	34,235	1,537,362
South Dakota	16	14	462,613	7	35,224	421,660	79,742	501,402
Tennessee	16	14	2,293,635	7	163,442	2,257,277	43,275	2,300,552
Texas	16/18	15	7,315,711	5	378,841	7,290,467	160,346	7,450,813
Utah	16/17		740,507	7	44,702	640,514	25,382	665,896
Vermont	18	16	261,296	9	21,759	252,971	5,714	258,685
Virginia	16/18		2,602,773	9	196,942	2,552,093	52,129	2,604,222
Washington	16/18		2,242,060	9	159,203	1,700,364	56,756	1,757,120
West Virginia	16/18		873,606	8.5	71,145	808,827	9,690	818,517
Wisconsin	16/18	14	2,378,836	7	158,556	2,168,623	125,636	2,294,259
Wyoming	16		273,608	7	23,111	294,800	39,408	334,208
District of Columbia	18	16	259,492	8	18,282	253,681	4,461	258,142
Totals			**118,618,162**	**7.9**	**7,823,483**	**105,037,660**	**3,825,521**	**108,863,181**

(1) Unrestricted operation of private passenger car. When 2 ages are shown, license is issued at lower age upon completion of approved driver education course. (2) Juvenile license issued for use between home and school in Cal., Iowa, Kan., Me., Mich., Neb., Nev., N.H., N.D., Oreg. restricted to daylight or curfew hours in Idaho, Ill., La., Mass., Minn., N.Y., Pa., S.C., S.D., Tenn., Wisc.: hardship cases in Ohio and Texas: for agricultural pursuits in N.J. (3) Estimated.

Auto Registrations, Taxes, Gasoline, Driver's Ages in Canada
Source: Statistics Canada and Digest of Motor Laws, 1973

Province	Driver's Age Min. (1972)	Minor (1972)	Registered[1] autos, buses trucks & Motor cycles (1971)	Province Gas Tax per gal. (1971) cents	Motor Fuel Gross Tax Collections $1,000 (1971-72)	Motor Fuel Consumption (1971)[2] Public Roads & Highways 1,000 gallons	Non-highway 1,000 gallons	Total 1,000[3] gallons
Newfoundland	17	—	129,200	25	(a)	73,318	30,887	42,431
Prince Edward Island	16	*	42,691	21	6,120	27,408	4,050	31,458
Nova Scotia	16	*	310,383	21	42,189	185,114	10,981	196,095
New Brunswick	18	16-18	216,710	20	33,732	154,690	17,701	172,391
Quebec	17	16	2,279,722	19	319,445	1,417,193	27,210	1,444,403
Ontario	16	—	3,209,862	19	435,871	2,126,436	98,210	2,224,646
Manitoba	16	*	419,314	17	47,763	231,837	55,242	287,079
Saskatchewan	16	—	464,924	19	52,536	234,513	123,070	357,583
Alberta	16	14	813,395	15	83,700	474,884	122,085	596,969
British Columbia	19	16	1,115,028	15	108,830	577,612	98,194	675,806
Yukon & Northwest Territories	—	—	20,907	14	1,871 2,472	16,018	3,664	19,682
Total			**9,022,136**	**17.9**	**1,134,529**	**5,519,027**	**579,523**	**6,098,550**

(1) Registrations include: Passenger automobiles 6,967,247; Motor trucks and truck tractors 1,514,976; Buses 22,034; and Motorcycles 198,867. (2) Excludes aviation and aviation turbo fuels. (3) Total motor fuel consumed includes (in gallons) for private and commercial use. *No junior permit. (a) figures are not yet available.

U. S. Passport, Visa and Health Requirements

Source: Passport Office, U.S. Dept. of State and U.S. Public Health Service

Passports are issued by the United States Department of State to citizens and nationals of the United States for the purpose of documenting them for their foreign travel and to identify them as Americans. Some countries require a visa, or stamp of approval, to be affixed to the passport by the consulate of the country to be visited, while others waive this formality. Also some countries, which do not require visas, require tourist cards from visitors making a short stay.

Unless specifically endorsed, passports may not be used for travel into or through Cuba, North Korea or North Vietnam, or for travel into or through other countries or areas as determined to be in the national interest by the Secretary of State.

How to Obtain a Passport

An applicant for a passport who has never been previously issued a passport in his own name, must execute an application in person before (1) a Passport Agent; (2) a clerk of any Federal court; (3) a clerk of any State court of record or a judge or clerk of any probate court; (4) a postal clerk designated by the Postmaster General; or (5) a diplomatic or consular officer of the U.S. abroad. A wife/husband who is to be included in the application must appear with the applicant and execute the application. Passport Agencies are located at Boston (John F. Kennedy Bldg., Government Center), Chicago (Everett M. Dirksen Bldg., 219 S. Dearborn); Honolulu (Fed. Bldg.); Los Angeles (Hawthorne Fed. Bldg., 15000 Aviation Blvd., Rm. 2W16, Lawndale, Calif.); Miami (51 S.W. First Ave.); New Orleans (Medallion Tower Bldg., 344 Camp St.); New York (630 Fifth Ave.); Philadelphia (401 N. Broad St.); San Francisco (Fed. Bldg., 450 Golden Gate Ave.); Seattle (Logan Bldg., 500 Union St.): Washington D.C. (Passport Office, 1425 K St., N.W.).

A passport previously issued to, or one in which applicant was included, will be accepted as proof of citizenship in lieu of the following documents. A person born in the United States shall present his birth certificate. To be acceptable, the certificate must show the given name and surname, the date and place of birth and that the birth record was filed shortly after birth. The certificate must also be certified with the registrar's signature and the raised, impressed or multicolored seal of his office. Uncertified copies of birth certificates are not acceptable.

If such primary evidence is not obtainable, a notice from the registrar shall be submitted stating that no birth record exists. The notice shall be accompanied by the best obtainable secondary evidence such as a baptismal certificate, a certificate of circumcision, a hospital birth record, affidavits of persons having personal knowledge of the facts of the birth or other documentary evidence such as early census, school or family bible records, newspaper files and insurance papers. Secondary evidence should be created as close to the time of birth as possible.

A person in the U. S. who has been issued a passport in his own name within the last eight years may obtain a new passport by filling out, signing and mailing a passport by mail application together with his previous passport, two duplicate signed photographs taken within the last 6 months and the established fee to the nearest Passport Agency or to the Passport Office in Wash., D. C. If, however, an applicant is applying for a passport for the first time, if his prior passport was issued before his 18th birthday, if he wishes to include a person other than himself in the passport, or if he is applying for an official, diplomatic, or other no-fee passport, he must execute a passport application in person before a Passport Agent; a clerk of any Federal court, a clerk of any State court of record or a judge or clerk of any probate court; a postal clerk designated by the Postmaster General; or a diplomatic or consular officer of the U.S. abroad.

A naturalized citizen should present his naturalization certificate. A person born abroad claiming citizenship through either a native-born or naturalized citizen must submit a certificate of citizenship issued by the Immigration and Naturalization Service; or a Consular Report of Birth or Certification of Birth issued by the Dept. of State. If one of the above documents has not been obtained, he must submit evidence of citizenship of the parent(s) through whom citizenship is claimed and evidence which would establish the parent/child relationship. Additionally, if through birth to one American and one alien parent, an affidavit from parent(s) showing periods and places of residence in the United States and abroad, specifying periods spent abroad in the employment of the U.S. Government, including the Armed Forces, or with certain international organizations; if through naturalization of parents, evidence of admission to the United States for permanent residence.

A married woman must submit evidence of citizenship and, under certain conditions, marriage. Special regulations govern women married prior to Sept. 22, 1922; should be discussed with the person executing the application.

The applicant shall establish his identity to the satisfaction of the person executing the application. Proof of identity may be established through a personal knowledge of the applicant by the Clerk or Agent or by an item which contains the signature and either a physical description or photograph of the applicant. The following items of identification are acceptable; previous United States Passport; certificate of naturalization; driver's licence (not temporary or learner's license); a governmental (Federal, State, Municipal) identification card or pass.

If the applicant is not able to establish his identity by personal knowledge or by one of the above items, he shall have an identifying witness who has known him at least 2 years, and who is a U.S. citizen or a permanent resident alien of the U.S. The witness himself must have acceptable identification.

A person included in the passport of another may not use the passport for travel unless he is accompanied by the bearer.

Aliens—An alien leaving the U. S. must request passport facilities from his home government. He must have a permit from his local Collector of Internal Revenue, and if he wishes to return he should request a re-entry permit from the Immigration and Naturalization Service if it is required.

Contract Employees—Persons traveling because of a contract with the Government must submit with their applications letters from their employer stating position, destination and purpose of travel and Armed Forces contract number when pertinent.

Persons of military draft age may receive passports but should inform their draft boards of their travel plans.

Photographs and Fees

Photographs—Duplicate photographs taken within six months, both signed by the applicant and which are a good likeness, must accompany the passport application. A group photograph is preferred if more than one person is included in the passport. Photographs may be in color or in black and white. They must be full face, printed on a thin, nonglossy paper base on a light background and must be no smaller than 2½ x 2½ inches nor larger than 3 x 3 inches in size. They must also be capable of withstanding a mounting temperature of over 200°F.

Fees—The passport fee is $10. A fee of $2 shall be paid to the person executing the application. No execution fee is payable where a passport is applied for by mail. All applicants must pay the passport fee and, where applicable, the execution fee unless specifically exempted by law. If applying in person, service will be expedited by presenting exact fees. An emergency service fee of $10 is charged in addition to all other fees where work must be performed after hours. The only other fees are for special postage. "A passport is valid for five years. Upon expiration, passports may no longer be renewed. New passports must be obtained."

During the calendar year 1972 the Passport Office, Dept. of State, issued 2,728,021 passports to American citizens.

The loss of a valid passport is a serious matter and should be reported in writing immediately to the Passport Office, Dept. of State, Wash., D.C. 20524, or to the nearest consular office of the U.S. when abroad.

Foreign Regulations

A visa is an endorsement or a notation, usually rubber stamped in a passport by a representative of the country to be visited. It certifies that the bearer of the passport is to be permitted to enter that country for a certain purpose and length of time. With the exception of the Iron Curtain countries, no visas are required for brief tourist travel to Western European countries. Authoritative visa information can be obtained by writing directly to foreign consular officials. The locations of foreign consular offices in the U.S. may be obtained by consulting the Congressional Directory available in most libraries. (Check appropriate city telephone directories for complete address.)

Health Information

Smallpox – A Smallpox Vaccination Certificate is required for travel to most countries of the world except Europe. However, in the event of an outbreak of smallpox in any country in Europe, all countries remaining on the itinerary following a visit to the infected country will require a Certificate; the United States will also require a Certificate upon the traveler's return if, in the preceding 14 days, a traveler has visited a country reporting smallpox. The local health department can furnish current information on specific country requirements.

Regardless of the foreign country's requirements, the U.S. Public Health Service recommends that all travelers to Africa, Southeast Asia, and Brazil be vaccinated for their own protection.

A Vaccination Certificate is not required for travel from the U.S. **directly to and from** Europe, Canada, Mexico, Australia, and New Zealand. For travel to more than one island in the Caribbean, a Certificate will probably be required.

Yellow fever – A Yellow Fever Vaccination Certificate may be required for travel in yellow fever-infected countries.

Cholera – A Cholera Vaccination Certificate is required by most countries if a traveler has visited a cholera-infected country in the preceding 6 days. The U.S. has no cholera vaccination requirement.

Plague – Vaccination is not required by any country as a condition of entry. Selective immunization is advisable for travelers to Viet Nam, Cambodia, and Laos.

Yellow fever vaccine must be obtained at an officially designated Yellow Fever Vaccination Center, and the Certificate must be stamped by the Center. It remains valid for 10 years. Other vaccinations may be obtained from licensed physicians, and sometimes from local health departments. The Smallpox Certificate, valid for 3 years, and the Cholera Certificate, valid for 6 months, must be stamped by the State or local health department.

Vaccination must be recorded on approved version of PHS-731, International Certificates of Vaccination, which are available from State and local health departments, passport offices, travel agencies, and the Superintendent of Documents, U.S. Printing Office, Wash., D.C. 20402.

Recommended:

Antimalarial drug – chloroquine phosphate for travel to some countries in Africa, Southeast Asia, Central and South America.

Hepatitis prevention – Immune serum globulin for travel to most of Africa, Asia, Central and South America, and to any areas of poor sanitation.

Typhoid immunization – Travel to Africa, Asia, Central and South America.

Polio immunization – Travel to Africa, the Middle East (excluding Israel), Mexico, Central and South America.

Requirements and recommendations for international travel are subject to change. Current specific information is available from State and local health departments.

United States Immigration Law

The national origins quota system disappeared from United States immigration procedures July 1, 1968, as provided by the Act. of Oct. 3, 1965, which amended the Immigration and Nationality Act.

The Immigration and Nationality Act, as amended, provides for numerical limitations on immigration from the Eastern and Western Hemispheres. Not subject to any numerical limitations, however, are immigrants who are spouses or children of U.S. citizens, or parents of citizens who are 21 years of age or older; returning residents; certain former U.S. citizens; ministers of religion; and certain long-term U.S. Government employees.

The Act of Oct. 3, 1965, established new controls to protect the American labor market from an influx of skilled and unskilled foreign labor. The primary responsibility was placed on the would-be immigrant to obtain the Secretary of Labor's clearance, prior to the issuance of a visa, establishing that there are not sufficient workers in the U.S. at the alien's destination who are able, willing and qualified to perform the skilled or unskilled labor; and that the employment of the alien will not adversely affect wages and working conditions of workers in the U.S. similarly employed.

Eastern Hemisphere Immigrants

Persons born in countries of the Eastern Hemisphere and dependent areas thereof are subject to an annual limitation of 170,000. Within this numerical limitation there is an annual limitation of 20,000 for each country and 200 for each dependent area. Applicants are classified as either preference or nonpreference.

The preference visa categories are based on certain relationships to persons in the U.S.; i.e., unmarried sons and daughters of United States citizens, spouses and unmarried sons and daughters of resident aliens, married sons and daughters of U.S. citizens, and brothers and sisters of U.S. citizens (first, second, fourth, and fifth preference, respectively); certain professions and skills (third preference); and certain categories of workers which are in short supply in the U.S. (6th preference); refugees (7th preference). Spouses and children of preference applicants are entitled to the same preference if accompanying or following to join such persons.

Except for refugee status, preference status is based upon approved petitions, filed with the Immigration and Naturalization Service, by the appropriate relative or employer (or in the 3rd preference by the alien himself). Visa numbers for qualified preference applicants are made available in the order of the preference classes and, within such classes, in the order of the filing dates of the petitions.

Immigrants not entitled to classification within one of the above-mentioned preference groups are nonpreference applicants and receive only those visa numbers not needed by preference applicants.

A prerequisite for nonpreference classification is a labor certification under Section 212(a)(14) of the Immigration and Nationality Act, or satisfactory evidence that the provisions of that section do not apply to the alien's case. The availability of nonpreference visa numbers is contingent on the level of preference demand and cannot therefore be predicted with real accuracy. However, in some countries and dependent areas the higher preference categories may utilize the entire numerical limitation which will prevent any visa numbers from becoming available for persons from such countries or areas in the nonpreference category.

Western Hemisphere Immigrants

The Act establishes an annual ceiling of 120,000 on immigration by persons born in independent countries of the Western Hemisphere (Canada, Mexico, Central and South America and the Caribbean Area). Within this over-all ceiling there is no numerical limitation set for individual countries, and no preference classes have been established for such applicants. Visas within the 120,000 limitation will be made available to qualified applicants in the chronological order of their priority dates. An applicant's priority date is the date a labor certification for the applicant is accepted for processing by the Dept. of Labor or the date proof is received by a consular officer that a labor certification is not required.

Excludable Aliens

Aliens who are excludable on medical grounds are those who are mentally retarded, insane, psychopathic, mentally defective, sexual deviates, chronic alcoholics, narcotic addicts, and those who are afflicted with any dangerous contagious disease or who have a physical defect impairing the ability to earn a living. Also excludable are paupers, beggars, illiterates, stowaways, prostitutes, persons engaged in commercial vice, narcotics traffickers, persons convicted of crimes involving moral turpitude, persons who obtain or try to obtain a visa by fraud, or who left the U. S. to avoid military service. Those excludable on security grounds include persons who are anarchists, members or affiliates of certain proscribed organizations, and those who teach or advocate overthrow of the U. S. Government by force or violence.

For more detailed information consult the nearest office of the U. S. Immigration & Naturalization Service, or any U. S. Consul abroad.

Customs Exemptions and Advice to Travelers

United States residents returning after a stay abroad of at least 48 hours are, generally speaking, granted customs exemptions of $100 each. Each returning resident may bring home free of duty articles totaling $100 in fair retail value in the country of acquisition, subject to limitations on liquors and cigars. These articles must accompany the traveler at the time of his return, must be for his personal or household use, must have been acquired as an incident of his trip, and must be properly declared to Customs. Not more than one quart of alcoholic beverages may be included in the $100 exemption.

If a U.S. resident arrives directly or indirectly from American Samoa, Guam, or the Virgin Islands of the United States, his purchase may be valued up to $200 fair retail value, but not more than $100 of the exemption be applied to the value of articles acquired elsewhere than in such insular possessions, and one gallon of alcoholic beverages may be included in his exemption, but not more than 1 quart of such beverages may have been acquired elsewhere than in the designated islands.

The exemption for articles acquired in the Virgin Islands of the United States and in Mexico is not conditional upon the 48-hour absence requirement.

In either case, the exemption for alcoholic beverages is accorded only when the returning resident has attained 21 years of age at the time of his arrival. One hundred cigars may be included (except Cuban products) in either exemption.

The $100 or $200 exemption may be granted only if the exemption, or any part of it, has not been used within the preceding 30-day period.

Bona fide gifts costing no more than $10 fair retail value may be mailed to friends at home duty-free; addressee cannot receive in a single day gifts exceeding the $10 limit.

Air Travel

On a first-class trans-Atlantic flight a passenger may carry 66 lbs. of luggage free; a tourist class passenger, 44 lbs. free. A charge is made for extra weight.

Precautions for Travel

In some cases naturalized United States citizens desiring to visit the countries of their birth, and sometimes their American-born children traveling to those countries, may be subject to military service and other regulations there. The United States Department of State advises such travelers to get specific information from the consulates of the countries concerned before departure.

Service in Foreign Armed Forces

Voluntary service in the armed forces of a foreign state engaged in hostilities against the U.S. is highly persuasive evidence of an intention to relinquish citizenship and will normally result in loss of U.S. citizenship. Voluntary service in the armed forces of a foreign state not engaged in hostilities against the U.S. does not result in loss of U.S. citizenship unless there is persuasive evidence of an intent to transfer or abandon allegiance by reason of such military service.

Passports Issued and Renewed

Source: Passport Office, Dept. of State

Passports are actual count; other data based on sample. Projections are subject to error. While size of sample is constant from month to month total volume of passports by month may vary by a factor of four. In addition size of sample has not changed since 1955, but volume of passports has increased by 400%.

Item	1960	1965	1967	1968	1969[6]	1970	1971	1972
New and renewed passports	859,087	1,330,290	1,685,512	1,748,416	1,820,192	2,219,159	2,398,968	2,728,021
Object of Travel:[1]								
Government	115,910	119,140	161,122	210,116	167,562	146,169	98,938	136,901
Nongovernment	737,177	1,139,150	1,524,390	1,538,300	1,652,630	2,072,990	2,300,030	2,591,120
Personal reasons[2]	321,590	487,470	638,790	912,430	1,475,630	1,791,330	2,156,640	2,042,560
Pleasure[3]	350,897	535,150	670,880	442,770	130,670	216,700	109,210	441,010
Business[4]	24,540	76,201	140,700	103,560	25,180	39,940	15,570	68,700
Education	31,240	31,120	61,270	68,680	15,490	20,230	16,040	33,290
Religion	6,780	6,770	7,750	6,970	2,180	3,350	1,380	3,980
Health	1,460	500	2,280	1,530	220	640	130	800
Other	670	1,930	2,720	2,360	3,260	800	1,060	780
First area destination:								
Africa	8,440	19,580	19,580	21,450	19,760	18,790	14,820	29,750
Australia and Oceania	35,220	50,750	55,501	61,380	68,190	51,210	48,350	78,580
Europe	669,662	992,800	1,265,172	1,294,786	1,460,212	1,910,169	2,139,508	2,244,161
Far East	55,960	111,310	157,020	159,750	125,100	116,730	73,250	135,230
North, Central and South America	58,935	99,620	126,480	128,600	91,850	72,410	68,630	135,720
Middle-East	24,670	56,080	61,340	82,430	54,990	48,890	54,380	103,870
Not Stated[5]	200	150	....	....	....	....	30	710
Mode of Travel—departure:[7]								
Ship	226,245	39,340	37,793	15,498	2,766	....	....	....
Air	626,842	1,290,950	1,647,719	1,732,918	1,817,426	....	....	....
Sex of Passport Recipients:								
Male	419,615	700,080	870,383	902,840	945,520	1,123,620	1,266,770	1,358,530
Female	433,472	630,210	815,129	845,576	874,672	1,095,539	1,132,198	1,369,491
Citizenship of Passport Recipients:								
Native	710,172	1,236,791	1,535,313	1,603,074	1,702,320	2,072,560	2,270,610	2,553,750
Naturalized	142,915	93,493	150,199	145,342	117,872	146,599	128,358	174,271

(1.)Data not entirely comparable because of changes in classifications in 1961. (2.)Includes "Personal business," "Join husband," "Accompany husband," "Business and pleasure," "Visit family." (3.)Includes "Sightsee," "Vacation," "Visit," and "Tourist." (4.)Includes applicants formerly listed under "Employment" and "Commercial business." (5.)Beginning 1960, includes applicants who listed "World tour." (6.)Legislation effective Aug. 26, 1968 eliminated passport renewals. (7.)Data eliminated. Over 99% of passport recipients indicate departure by air.

Naturalization: How to Become an American Citizen
Source: The Federal Statutes

A person who desires to be naturalized as a citizen of the United States may obtain the necessary application form as well as detailed information from the nearest office of the Immigration and Naturalization Service or from the clerk of a court handling naturalization cases.

There are no racial bars to naturalization. Women have the same right as men to become naturalized.

An applicant must be at least 18 years old. He must have been a lawful resident of the United States continuously for 5 years. For husbands and wives of U.S. citizens the period is 3 years in most instances. Special provisions apply to certain veterans of the Armed Forces. An applicant must have been physically present in this country for at least half of the required 5 years' residence.

Every applicant for naturalization must:
(1) sign the petition in his own handwriting, if physically able to write:
(2) demonstrate an understanding of the English language, including an ability to read, write, and speak words in ordinary usage in the English language (persons physically unable to do so, and persons who were on December 24, 1952 over 50 years of age and had been residing in the United States for 20 years are excepted).
(3) have been a person of good moral character, attached to the principles of the Constitution, and well disposed to the good order and happiness of the United States for five years just before filing the petition or for whatever other period of residence is required in his case and continue to be such a person until admitted to citizenship; and
(4) demonstrate a knowledge and understanding of the fundamentals of the history, and the principles and form of government, of the U. S.

The petitioner also is obliged to have two credible citizen witnesses. These witnesses must have personal knowledge of the applicant.

A person not of good moral character includes a habitual drunkard, an adulterer, a polygamist, a violator of criminal law, a gambler, one who gave false testimony to obtain a benefit under the immigration law, one in prison for 180 days or more, one convicted of murder.

Naturalization is denied to any person who, within 10 years, has been subversive, including communists and others who favor totalitarian government, and who were members of a proscribed organization, unless the petitioner was under 16 or joined under duress.

A law approved Aug. 20, 1958, provides for the expeditious naturalization of alien spouses and adopted children of U.S. citizens who are missionaries or performing religious duties and are stationed abroad.

When the applicant files his petition he pays the court clerk $10. At the preliminary hearing he may be represented by a lawyer or social service agency. There is a 30-day wait. If action is favorable, there is a final hearing before a judge, who administers the following oath of allegiance:

Oath of Allegiance

I hereby declare, on oath, that I absolutely and entirely renounce and abjure all allegiance and fidelity to any foreign prince, potentate, state or sovereignty, of whom or which I have heretofore been a subject or citizen; that I will support and defend the Constitution and laws of the United States of America against all enemies, foreign and domestic; that I will bear true faith and allegiance to the same; that I will bear arms on behalf of the United States when required by the law; that I will perform noncombatant service in the armed forces of the United States when required by the law; that I will perform work of national importance under civilian direction when required by the law, and that I take this obligation freely without any mental reservation or purpose of evasion; so help me God.

Immigrants Admitted From All Countries
Source: Immigration and Naturalization Service, U. S. Dept. of Justice

Year	Number	Year	Number	Year	Number	Year	Number
1820	8,385	1881-1890	5,246,613	1951-1960	2,515,479	1967	361,972
1821-1830	143,439	1891-1900	3,687,564	1961	271,344	1968	454,448
1831-1840	599,125	1901-1910	8,795,386	1962	283,763	1969	358,579
1841-1850	1,713,251	1911-1920	5,735,811	1963	306,260	1970	373,326
1851-1860	2,598,214	1921-1930	4,107,209	1964	292,248	1971	370,478
1861-1870	2,314,824	1931-1940	528,431	1965	296,697	1972	384,685
1871-1880	2,812,191	1941-1950	1,035,039	1966	323,040	1820-1972	45,917,801

Status of American Woman Who Marries a Foreigner
Source: United Nations

She will automatically acquire the nationality of:

Afghanistan	Gabon*	Italy	Liechtenstein	Philippines	Spain
Austria	Greece*	Ivory Coast*	Monaco	Portugal*	Switzerland
Cambodia	Haiti	Jordan	Nepal	Rwanda (e)	Togo*
Ethiopia	Iran	Korea (Rep.)	Niger*	Saudi Arabia	Turkey
Finland	Iraq	Liberia	Peru	Somalia	

Automatically gains husband's nationality if she loses her own:

Belgium*	Cen. African	China	Costa Rica (b)	France*	Malagasy Rep. (b)	Somaliland
Cameroon*	Rep.*	Congo (a)	Dominican Rep.*	Laos*	Mauritania*	Tunisia

May acquire husband's nationality if she chooses:

Algeria (c)	Ecuador	Ireland	Libya	New Zealand	Senegal	Upper Volta
Andorra	Egypt	Jamaica	Luxembourg	Nicaragua	Sierra Leone	Venezuela
Barbados	Gambia	Kenya	Mali	Nigeria	Sudan	Vietnam, Rep.
Bolivia	Ghana	Kuwait	Mexico	Pakistan	Tanganyika	Zambia
Botswana	Guyana	Lebanon	Morocco	Poland	Thailand	
Chad (d)	Indonesia	Lesotho	Netherlands	San Marino	United Kingdom	

May acquire husband's nationality more easily than other aliens:

Australia	Colombia	Hungary	Malta	Syrian Arab	Rep. of S.
Brazil	Cuba	India	Norway	Rep.	Africa
Burma	Czechoslovakia	Israel	Panama	Trinidad-	Uruguay
Canada	Denmark	Japan	Singapore	Tobago	Western Samoa
Ceylon	El Salvador	Malawi	Swaziland	Uganda	Yugoslavia
Chile	Guatemala	Malaysia	Sweden (b)		

No effect on her nationality:

Albania, Argentina, Bulgaria, Germany (West), Honduras, Iceland, Paraguay, Romania, USSR.

*She may decline her husband's nationality. (A)She may acquire her husband's nationality if she resides in the country 5 years following the marriage and unless she declines before the expiration of this date. (B)She may acquire her husband's nationality by declaration. (C)She must formally declare before the marriage that she repudiates her nationality of origin. (D)Applies only to marriages celebrated in Chad. (E)Marriage must be registered in civil office of Rwanda Government, which reserves the right to oppose within one year the acquisition of nationality.

United States Population

Population Growth Rate Drops Sharply

By Vincent P. Barabba, Acting Director

Bureau of the Census, Social and Economic Statistics Administration, U.S. Dept. of Commerce

Population growth in the United States in 1972 dropped to its lowest level in 35 years. On Jan. 1, 1973 the population of the Nation was estimated at 209,717,000. This represented a gain of 1,628,000 — a growth rate of 7.8 persons per 1,000 of population, the lowest since the 1937 rate of 6.7 per 1,000.

During 1972 there were an estimated 3,256,000 births, more than one million under the 1957 peak of 4,332,000, and the lowest total of births since 1945.

Lowest Fertility

The number of births resulted in an estimated total fertility rate for the year of 2,025, lowest in American history. Total fertility rate is based on the total number of children each 1,000 women have in their lifetimes. Replacement level fertility is calculated at 2,100, meaning that, to achieve it, each 1,000 women would have 2,100 children in their lifetimes. This is the level required for the population to eventually reach zero growth if there were no immigration. The 1972 population increase included an estimated 338,000 due to net civilian immigration, the lowest since 1964, but a decline that may well be temporary.

A Bureau survey taken in June 1972 showed that 70% of wives in the 18-24 age group expect to have two children at the most. A year earlier the proportion expecting no more than two children was 64%, and in 1967 it was 44%. The proportion of young wives expecting 4 or more children dropped from 26% in 1967 to 9% in 1972, the survey also showed.

These declines in fertility and birth expectations are reflected in projecting the future population of the U.S. A new series of projections by Bureau demographers as 1972 came to a close, estimates that the population in the year 2000 will range from 251 to 300,000,000. This is down from a previous projected range of 271 to 322,000,000.

Growth Patterns Change

Another 1972 finding was that patterns of population growth which prevailed during the 1960 to 1970 decade seem to be changing. Provisional estimates of State populations for July 1, 1972 indicated that States which showed losses between 1960 and 1970 — West Virginia and North and South Dakota — gained at a rate not far below the national rate of growth since the 1970 census. No State lost population between 1970 and 1972, although the District of Columbia had a small decrease.

Rural northern States which showed very slow growth during the 1960's grew at or above the U.S. average during 1970-72.

During the same period, California's growth is estimated to have slowed to just above the national average. From 1900 to 1970, California grew at a rate at least twice the national average.

Incomes Up

Another 1972 survey finding was that for the first time in history, more than half of American families have annual incomes of $10,000 or more. The 1971 median family income was $10,290, up 4.2% from the 1970 figures of $9,870. For those families whose heads worked full time for the entire year, the median jumped to $12,440.

In 1971 there were 2,800,000 families with incomes of $25,000 and over and 10,400,000 with incomes of $15,000 to $24,999. About 19% of the total of 53,300,000 families had less than $5,000 in income.

Transportation is one of the major items of expense by Americans. A survey of automobile ownership showed 80% of all U.S. households own at least one car. About 30% own two or more cars, and 15% reported ownership of a truck. Of those with cars, 21% owned at least one 1971 or 1972 model, and 10% owned one or more imported cars.

Estimates of the Population of the United States

April 1, 1960 to April 1, 1973 (in thousands)

	Includes Armed Forces Overseas	Total Resident	Civilian Resident		Includes Armed Forces Overseas	Total Resident	Civilian Resident
April 1, 1973	210,036	209,470	207,685	April 1, 1971	206,511	205,614	203,629
March 1, 1973	209,915	209,330	207,555	April 1, 1970	204,766	203,185[1]	200,994
Feb. 1, 1973	209,826	209,256	207,434	April 1, 1969	202,084	200,810	198,575
Jan. 1, 1973	209,717	209,123	207,313	April 1, 1968	200,118	198,833	196,603
Dec. 1, 1972	209,583	208,971	207,152	April 1, 1967	198,608	197,430	195,159
Nov. 1, 1972	209,444	208,831	207,013	April 1, 1966	196,337	195,384	193,329
Oct. 1, 1972	209,293	208,702	206,878	April 1, 1965	194,032	193,310	191,346
Sept. 1, 1972	209,134	208,529	206,728	April 1, 1964	191,463	190,726	188,715
Aug. 1, 1972	208,981	208,369	206,586	April 1, 1963	188,741	187,998	186,000
July 1, 1972	208,842	208,230	206,457	April 1, 1962	185,979	185,208	183,092
June 1, 1972	208,706	208,095	206,321	April 1, 1961	183,043	182,350	180,496
May 1, 1972	208,562	207,934	206,146	April 1, 1960	180,007	179,323[1]	177,472
April 1, 1972	208,441	207,797	205,978	April 1, 1959	177,146	176,458	174,559

[1] Official census

Population of the United States, 1960-1970

Region, Division and State	1970 census	1960 census	Pct. + or −	1970 census Urban	1970 census Rural	Pct. Urban	Rank 1970	Rank 1960
United States	203,235,298	179,323,175	13.3	149,324,930	53,886,996	73.5		
Regions:								
Northeast	48,999,999	44,677,819	9.7	39,449,818	9,590,885	80.4	...	...
North Central	56,577,067	51,619,139	9.6	40,480,760	16,090,903	71.6	...	...
South	62,798,347	54,973,113	14.2	40,539,961	22,255,406	64.6	...	...
West	34,809,359	28,053,104	24.1	28,854,391	5,949,802	82.9	...	...
New England	**11,847,186**	**10,509,367**	**12.7**	**9,043,517**	**2,798,146**	**76.4**		
Maine	993,663	969,265	2.5	504,157	487,891	50.8	38	36
New Hampshire	737,681	606,921	21.5	416,040	321,641	56.4	42	45
Vermont	444,732	389,881	14.1	142,889	301,441	32.2	49	47
Massachusetts	5,689,170	5,148,578	10.5	4,810,449	878,721	84.6	10	9
Rhode Island	949,723	859,488	10.5	824,930	121,795	87.1	39	39
Connecticut	3,032,217	2,535,234	19.6	2,345,052	686,657	77.4	24	25
Middle Atlantic	**37,152,813**	**34,168,452**	**8.7**	**30,406,301**	**6,792,739**	**81.7**		
New York	18,241,266	16,782,304	8.4	15,602,486	2,634,481	85.6	2	1
New Jersey	7,168,164	6,066,782	18.2	6,373,405	794,759	88.9	8	8
Pennsylvania	11,793,909	11,319,366	4.2	8,430,410	3,363,499	71.5	3	3
East North Central	**40,252,678**	**36,225,024**	**11.1**	**30,091,847**	**10,160,629**	**74.8**		
Ohio	10,652,017	9,706,397	9.7	8,025,775	2,625,242	75.3	6	5
Indiana	5,193,669	4,662,498	11.4	3,372,060	1,821,609	64.9	11	11
Illinois	11,113,976	10,081,158	10.2	9,229,821	1,884,155	83.0	5	4
Michigan	8,875,083	7,823,194	13.4	6,553,773	2,321,310	73.8	7	7
Wisconsin	4,417,933	3,951,777	11.8	2,910,418	1,507,313	65.9	16	15
West North Central	**16,324,389**	**15,394,115**	**6.0**	**10,388,913**	**5,930,274**	**63.7**		
Minnesota	3,805,069	3,413,864	11.5	2,527,308	1,277,663	66.4	19	18
Iowa	2,825,041	2,757,537	2.4	1,616,405	1,207,971	57.2	25	24
Missouri	4,677,399	4,319,813	8.3	3,277,662	1,398,839	70.1	13	13
North Dakota	617,761	632,446	−2.3	273,442	344,319	44.3	46	44
South Dakota	666,257	680,514	−2.1	296,628	368,879	44.6	45	40
Nebraska	1,483,791	1,411,330	5.1	912,598	570,895	61.5	35	34
Kansas	2,249,071	2,178,611	3.2	1,484,870	761,708	66.1	28	28
South Atlantic	**30,671,337**	**25,971,732**	**18.1**	**19,523,920**	**11,147,417**	**63.7**	4?	46
Delaware	548,104	446,292	22.8	375,055	173,049	72.2	47	46
Maryland	3,922,399	3,100,689	26.5	3,003,935	918,464	76.6	18	21
District of Columbia	756,510	763,956	−1.0	756,510		100.0	41	...
Virginia	4,648,494	3,966,949	17.2	2,934,841	1,713,653	63.1	14	14
West Virginia	1,744,237	1,860,421	−6.2	679,491	1,064,746	39.0	34	30
North Carolina	5,082,059	4,556,155	11.5	2,285,168	2,796,891	45.0	12	12
South Carolina	2,590,516	2,382,594	8.7	1,232,195	1,358,321	47.6	26	26
Georgia	4,589,575	3,943,116	16.4	2,768,074	1,821,501	60.3	15	16
Florida	6,789,443	4,951,560	37.1	5,468,137	1,321,306	80.5	9	10
East South Central	**12,804,552**	**12,050,126**	**6.3**	**6,987,943**	**5,815,527**	**54.6**		
Kentucky	3,219,311	3,038,156	6.0	1,684,053	1,534,653	52.3	23	22
Tennessee	3,924,164	3,567,089	10.0	2,305,307	1,618,380	58.7	17	17
Alabama	3,444,165	3,266,740	5.4	2,011,941	1,432,224	58.4	21	19
Mississippi	2,216,912	2,178,141	1.8	986,642	1,230,270	44.5	29	29
West South Central	**19,322,458**	**16,951,255**	**14.0**	**14,028,098**	**5,292,462**	**72.6**		
Arkansas	1,923,295	1,786,272	7.7	960,865	962,430	50.0	32	31
Louisiana	3,643,180	3,257,022	11.9	2,406,150	1,235,156	66.1	20	20
Oklahoma	2,559,253	2,328,284	9.9	1,740,137	819,092	68.0	27	27
Texas	11,196,730	9,579,677	16.9	8,920,946	2,275,784	79.7	4	6
Mountain	**8,283,585**	**6,855,060**	**20.8**	**6,054,979**	**2,226,583**	**73.1**		
Montana	694,409	674,767	2.9	370,676	323,733	53.4	44	41
Idaho	713,008	667,191	6.9	385,434	327,133	54.1	43	42
Wyoming	332,416	330,066	0.7	201,111	131,305	60.5	50	48
Colorado	2,207,259	1,753,947	25.8	1,733,311	473,948	78.5	30	33
New Mexico	1,016,000	951,023	6.8	708,775	307,225	69.8	37	37
Arizona	1,772,482	1,302,161	36.1	1,408,864	362,036	79.6	33	35
Utah	1,059,273	890,627	18.9	851,472	207,801	80.4	36	38
Nevada	488,738	285,278	71.3	395,336	93,402	80.9	48	49
Pacific	**26,525,774**	**21,198,044**	**25.1**	**22,799,412**	**3,723,219**	**86.0**		
Washington	3,409,169	2,853,214	19.5	2,476,468	932,701	72.6	22	23
Oregon	2,091,385	1,768,687	18.2	1,402,704	688,681	67.1	31	32
California	19,953,134	15,717,204	27.0	18,136,045	1,817,089	90.9	1	2
Alaska	302,173	226,167	33.6	145,512	154,870	48.4	51	50
Hawaii	769,913	632,772	21.7	638,683	129,878	83.1	40	43

Urban and rural figures do not equal total 1970 population because of errors discovered by census bureau after tabulation.

Congressional Apportionment

State	1970 Census	1960 Census	State	1970 Census	1960 Census	State	1970 Census	1960 Census	State	1970 Census	1960 Census	State	1970 Census	1960 Census
Ala	7	8	Idaho	2	2	Minn.	8	8	N. D.	1	2	Vt.	1	1
Alaska	1	1	Ill.	24	24	Miss.	5	5	Ohio	23	24	Va.	10	10
Ariz.	4	3	Ind	11	11	Mo.	10	10	Okla.	6	6	Wash.	7	7
Ark.	4	4	Iowa	6	7	Mont.	2	2	Ore.	4	4	W. Va.	4	5
Calif.	43	38	Kan	5	5	Neb	3	3	Pa.	25	27	Wis.	9	10
Colo	5	4	Ky.	7	7	Nev.	1	1	R. I.	2	2	Wyo	1	1
Conn	6	6	La.	8	8	N. H.	2	2	S. C.	6	6			
Del	1	1	Me.	2	2	N. J.	15	15	S. D.	2	2	Totals	435	435
Fla	15	12	Md	8	8	N. M.	2	2	Tenn.	8	9			
Ga	10	10	Mass.	12	12	N. Y.	39	41	Texas	24	23			
Hawaii	2	2	Mich.	19	19	N. C.	11	11	Utah	2	2			

The chief reason why the Constitution provided for a census of the population every 10 years was to give a basis for apportionment of Representatives among the states. This apportionment has largely determined the number of electoral votes allotted to each state.

The number of Representatives of each state in Congress is determined by the state's population, except that each state is entitled to one Representative regardless of population. A Congressional apportionment has been made after each decennial census except that of 1920.

Under provisions of a law that became effective Nov. 15, 1941, apportionment of Representatives is made by the method of equal proportions. In the application of this method, the apportionment is made so that the average population per Representative has the least possible variation between one state and any other. The first House of Representatives, in 1790, had 65 members, or one Representative for each 30,000 of the estimated population, as provided by the Constitution. As the population grew, the number of Representatives was increased but the total membership has been fixed at 435 since 1912.

United States Population (Official Census), 1790-1880

Source: Bureau of the Census

State	1790	1800	1810	1820	1830[1]	1840[1]	1850	1860	1870	1880
Ala. . .	. . . . .	. . . . . .	9,046	127,901	309,527	590,756	771,623	964,201	996,992	1,262,505
Ariz. . .									9,658	40,440
Ark. . . .	. . . . .	. . . . . .	1,062	14,273	30,388	97,574	209,897	435,450	484,471	802,525
Calif. . .	. . . . .	. . . . . .					92,597	379,994	560,247	864,694
Colo. . . .								34,277	39,864	194,327
Conn. . .	237,946	251,002	261,942	275,248	297,675	309,978	370,792	460,147	537,454	622,700
Del. . . .	59,096	64,273	72,674	72,749	76,748	78,085	91,532	112,216	125,015	146,608
D.C. . . .		14,093	24,023	33,039	39,834	43,712	51,687	75,080	131,700	177,624
Fla. . . .					34,730	54,477	87,445	140,424	187,748	269,493
Ga	82,548	162,686	252,433	340,989	516,823	691,392	906,185	1,057,286	1,184,109	1,542,180
Ida									14,999	32,610
Ill.			12,282	55,211	157,445	476,183	851,470	1,711,951	2,539,891	3,077,871
Ind.		5,641	24,520	147,178	343,031	685,866	988,416	1,350,428	1,680,637	1,978,301
Iowa. . . .						43,112	192,214	674,913	1,194,202	1,624,615
Kans . .								107,206	364,399	996,096
Ky	73,677	220,995	405,511	564,317	687,917	779,828	982,405	1,155,684	1,321,011	1,648,690
La			76,556	153,407	215,739	352,411	517,762	708,002	726,915	939,946
Me	96,540	151,719	228,705	298,335	399,455	501,793	583,169	628,279	626,915	648,936
Md. . . .	319,728	341,548	380,546	407,350	447,040	470,019	583,034	687,049	780,894	934,943
Mass. . .	378,787	422,845	472,040	523,287	610,408	737,699	994,514	1,231,066	1,457,351	1,783,085
Mich. . .			4,762	8,896	31,639	212,267	397,654	749,113	1,184,059	1,636,937
Minn. . . .							6,077	172,023	439,706	780,773
Miss . . .		8,850	40,352	75,448	136,621	375,651	606,526	791,305	827,922	1,131,597
Mo			19,783	66,586	140,455	383,702	682,044	1,182,012	1,721,295	2,168,380
Mont. . . .									20,595	39,159
Neb. . . .								28,841	122,993	452,402
Nev. . . .								6,857	42,491	62,266
N. H. . . .	141,885	183,858	214,460	244,161	269,328	284,574	317,976	326,073	318,300	346,991
N. J. . . .	184,139	211,149	245,562	277,575	320,823	373,306	489,555	672,035	906,096	1,131,116
N. M. . . .							61,547	93,516	91,874	119,565
N. Y. . . .	340,120	589,051	959,049	1,372,812	1,918,608	2,428,921	3,097,394	3,880,735	4,382,759	5,082,871
N. C. . . .	393,751	478,103	555,500	638,829	737,987	753,419	869,039	992,622	1,071,361	1,399,750
N. D. . . .									*2,405	36,909
Ohio . . .		45,365	230,760	581,434	937,903	1,519,467	1,980,329	2,339,511	2,665,260	3,198,062
Okla										
Ore. . . .							13,294	52,465	90,923	174,768
Penn. . . .	434,373	602,365	810,091	1,049,458	1,348,233	1,724,033	2,311,786	2,906,215	3,521,951	4,282,891
R. I. . . .	68,825	69,122	76,931	83,059	97,199	108,830	147,545	174,620	217,353	276,531
S. C. . . .	249,073	345,591	415,115	502,741	581,185	594,398	668,507	703,708	705,606	995,577
S. D.								*4,837	*11,776	98,268
Tenn. . .	35,691	105,602	261,727	422,823	681,904	829,210	1,002,717	1,109,801	1,258,520	1,542,359
Tex.							212,592	604,215	818,579	1,591,749
Utah. . . .							11,380	40,273	86,786	143,963
Vt.	85,425	154,465	217,895	235,981	280,652	291,948	314,120	315,098	330,551	332,286
Va	747,610	880,200	974,600	1,065,366	1,211,405	1,239,797	1,421,661	1,596,318	1,225,163	1,512,565
Wash. . . .								11,594	23,955	75,116
W. Va. . . .									442,014	618,457
Wis. . . .						30,945	305,391	775,881	1,054,670	1,315,497
Wyo.									9,118	20,789
U.S.	3,929,214	5,308,483	7,239,881	9,638,453	12,866,020	17,069,453	23,191,876	31,443,321	38,558,371	50,155,783

[1] 1860 figure is for Dakota Territory; 1870 figures are for parts of Dakota Territory.
(1.) U.S. TOTAL INCLUDES PERSONS (5,318 in 1830 and 6,100 in 1840) on public ships in the service of the United States not credited to any region, division, or state.

U. S. Center of Population, From 1790

Center of population is that point which may be considered as center of population gravity of the U. S. or that point upon which the U. S. would balance if it were a rigid plane without weight and the population distributed thereon with each individual being assumed to have equal weight and to exert an influence on a central point proportional to his distance from that point.

Year	North latitude			West longitude			Approximate location
	°	′	″	°	′	″	
1790.	39	16	30	76	11	12	23 miles east of Baltimore, Md.
1800.	39	16	6	76	56	30	18 miles west of Baltimore, Md.
1810.	39	11	30	77	37	12	40 miles northwest by west of Washington, D. C. (in Va.)
1820.	39	5	42	78	33	0	16 miles east of Moorefield, W. Va.[1]
1830.	38	57	54	79	16	54	19 miles west-southwest of Moorefield W. Va.[1]
1840.	39	2	0	80	18	0	16 miles south of Clarksburg, W. Va.[1]
1850.	38	59	0	81	19	0	23 miles southeast of Parkersburg, W. Va.[1]
1860.	39	0	24	82	48	48	20 miles south by east of Chillicothe, Ohio.
1870.	39	12	0	83	35	42	48 miles east by north of Cincinnati, Ohio.
1880.	39	4	8	84	39	40	8 miles west by south of Cincinnati, Ohio (in Ky.)
1890.	39	11	56	85	32	53	20 miles east of Columbus, Ind.
1900.	39	9	36	85	48	54	6 miles southeast of Columbus, Ind.
1910.	39	10	12	86	32	20	In the city of Bloomington, Ind.
1920.	39	10	21	86	43	15	8 miles south-southeast of Spencer, Owen County, Ind.
1930.	39	3	45	87	8	6	3 miles northeast of Linton, Greene County, Ind.
1940.	38	56	54	87	22	35	2 miles southeast by east of Carlisie, Haddon township, Sullivan County, Ind.
1950 (Includes Alaska & Hawaii.)	38	48	15	88	22	8	3 miles northeast of Louisville, Clay County, Ill.
1960 (Includes Alaska & Hawaii.)	38	35	58	89	12	35	6½ miles northwest of Centralia, Ill.
1970 (Includes Alaska & Hawaii.)	38	27	47	89	42	22	5 miles east southeast of Mascoutah, St. Clair County, Ill.

(1) West Virginia was set off from Virginia Dec. 31, 1862, and admitted as a State June 20, 1863.

United States Population (Official Census), 1890-1970

Source: Bureau of the Census

State	1890	1900	1910	1920	1930	1940	1950	1960	1970
Alabama	1,513,401	1,828,697	2,138,093	2,348,174	2,646,248	2,832,961	3,061,743	3,266,740	3,444,165
Alaska								226,167	302,173
Arizona	88,243	122,931	204,354	334,162	435,573	499,261	749,587	1,302,161	1,772,482
Arkansas	1,128,211	1,311,564	1,574,449	1,752,204	1,854,482	1,949,387	1,909,511	1,786,272	1,923,295
California	1,213,398	1,485,053	2,377,549	3,426,861	5,677,251	6,907,387	10,586,223	15,717,204	19,953,134
Colorado	413,249	539,700	799,024	939,629	1,035,791	1,123,296	1,325,089	1,753,947	2,207,259
Connecticut	746,258	908,420	1,114,756	1,380,631	1,606,903	1,709,242	2,007,280	2,535,234	3,032,217
Delaware	168,493	184,735	202,322	223,003	238,380	266,505	318,085	446,292	548,104
Dist. of Col	230,392	278,718	331,069	437,571	486,869	663,091	802,178	763,956	756,510
Florida	391,422	528,542	752,619	968,470	1,468,211	1,897,414	2,771,305	4,951,560	6,789,443
Georgia	1,837,353	2,216,331	2,609,121	2,895,832	2,908,506	3,123,723	3,444,578	3,943,116	4,589,575
Hawaii								632,772	769,913
Idaho	88,548	161,772	325,594	431,866	445,032	524,873	588,637	667,191	713,008
Illinois	3,826,352	4,821,550	5,638,591	6,485,280	7,630,654	7,897,241	8,712,176	10,081,158	11,113,976
Indiana	2,192,404	2,516,462	2,700,876	2,930,390	3,238,503	3,427,796	3,934,224	4,662,498	5,193,669
Iowa	1,912,297	2,231,853	2,224,771	2,404,021	2,470,939	2,538,268	2,621,073	2,757,537	2,825,041
Kansas	1,428,108	1,470,495	1,690,949	1,769,257	1,880,999	1,801,028	1,905,299	2,178,611	2,249,071
Kentucky	1,858,635	2,147,174	2,289,905	2,416,630	2,614,589	2,845,627	2,944,806	3,038,156	3,219,311
Louisiana	1,118,588	1,381,625	1,656,388	1,798,509	2,101,593	2,363,880	2,683,516	3,257,022	3,643,180
Maine	661,086	694,466	742,371	768,014	797,423	847,226	913,774	969,265	993,663
Maryland	1,042,390	1,188,044	1,295,346	1,449,661	1,631,526	1,821,244	2,343,001	3,100,689	3,922,399
Massach'ts	2,238,947	2,805,346	3,366,416	3,852,356	4,249,614	4,316,721	4,690,514	5,148,578	5,689,170
Michigan	2,093,890	2,420,982	2,810,173	3,668,412	4,842,325	5,256,106	6,371,766	7,823,194	8,875,083
Minnesota	1,310,283	1,751,394	2,075,708	2,387,125	2,563,953	2,792,300	2,982,483	3,413,864	3,805,069
Mississippi	1,289,600	1,551,270	1,797,114	1,790,618	2,009,821	2,183,796	2,178,914	2,178,141	2,216,912
Missouri	2,679,185	3,106,665	3,293,335	3,404,055	3,629,367	3,784,664	3,954,653	4,319,813	4,677,399
Montana	142,924	243,329	376,053	548,889	537,606	559,456	591,024	674,767	694,409
Nebraska	1,062,656	1,066,300	1,192,214	1,296,372	1,377,963	1,315,834	1,325,510	1,411,330	1,483,791
Nevada	47,355	42,335	81,875	77,407	91,058	110,247	160,083	285,278	488,738
N. Hamp	376,530	411,588	430,572	443,083	465,293	491,524	533,242	606,921	737,681
New Jersey	1,444,933	1,883,669	2,537,167	3,155,900	4,041,334	4,160,165	4,835,329	6,066,782	7,168,164
New Mexico	160,282	195,310	327,301	360,350	423,317	531,818	681,187	951,023	1,016,000
New York	6,003,174	7,268,894	9,113,614	10,385,227	12,588,066	13,479,142	14,830,192	16,782,304	18,241,266
No. Carolina	1,617,949	1,893,810	2,206,287	2,559,123	3,170,276	3,571,623	4,061,929	4,556,155	5,082,059
No. Dakota	190,983	319,146	577,056	646,872	680,845	641,935	619,636	632,446	617,761
Ohio	3,672,329	4,157,545	4,767,121	5,759,394	6,646,697	6,907,612	7,946,627	9,706,397	10,652,017
Oklahoma	258,657	790,391	1,657,155	2,028,283	2,396,040	2,336,434	2,233,351	2,328,284	2,559,253
Oregon	317,704	413,536	672,765	783,389	953,786	1,089,684	1,521,341	1,768,687	2,091,385
Penn	5,258,113	6,302,115	7,665,111	8,720,017	9,631,350	9,900,180	10,498,012	11,319,366	11,793,909
Rhode Is	345,506	428,556	542,610	604,397	687,497	713,346	791,896	859,488	949,723
So. Carolina	1,151,149	1,340,316	1,515,400	1,683,724	1,738,765	1,899,804	2,117,027	2,382,594	2,590,516
So. Dakota	348,600	401,570	583,888	636,547	692,849	642,961	652,740	680,514	666,257
Tennessee	1,767,518	2,020,616	2,184,789	2,337,885	2,616,556	2,915,841	3,291,718	3,567,089	3,924,164
Texas	2,235,527	3,048,710	3,896,542	4,663,228	5,824,715	6,414,824	7,711,194	9,579,677	11,196,730
Utah	210,779	276,749	373,351	449,396	507,847	550,310	688,862	890,627	1,059,273
Vermont	332,422	343,641	355,956	352,428	359,611	359,231	377,747	389,881	444,732
Virginia	1,655,980	1,854,184	2,061,612	2,309,187	2,421,851	2,677,773	3,318,680	3,966,949	4,648,494
Washington	357,232	518,103	1,141,990	1,356,621	1,563,396	1,736,191	2,378,962	2,853,214	3,409,169
W. Virginia	762,794	958,800	1,221,119	1,463,701	1,729,205	1,901,974	2,005,553	1,860,421	1,744,237
Wisconsin	1,693,330	2,069,042	2,333,860	2,632,067	2,939,006	3,137,587	3,434,575	3,951,777	4,417,933
Wyoming	62,555	92,531	145,965	194,402	225,565	250,742	290,529	330,066	332,416
Tot. U.S.	62,947,714	75,994,575	91,972,266	105,710,620	122,775,046	131,669,275	150,697,361	179,323,175	203,235,298*

*Does not include members of the Armed Forces overseas or other U.S. nationals overseas.

American Indian Population Increases

Source: Bureau of the Census

The preliminary count of American Indians for the 1970 Census showed a greater than 50% growth since 1960. The count, of 792,730, was 269,139 over the 1960 figure. Fifty-three % of all Indians, in 1970, lived in 5 states, ranked as follows by their Indian population: Oklahoma, 98,468; Arizona, 95,812; California, 91,018; New Mexico, 72,788 and North Carolina, 44,406.

The following table gives the Indian population (preliminary) for 1970:

	1970	1960		1970	1960		1970	1960
United States	791,839	523,591	Iowa	2,992	1,708	North Carolina	44,406	38,129
			Kansas	8,672	5,069	North Dakota	14,369	11,736
Alabama	2,443	1,276	Kentucky	1,531	391	Ohio	6,654	1,910
Alaska	16,276	14,444	Louisiana	5,294	3,587	Oklahoma	98,468	64,689
Arizona	95,812	83,387	Maine	2,195	1,879	Oregon	13,510	8,026
Arkansas	2,014		Maryland	4,239	1,538	Pennsylvania	5,533	2,122
California	91,018	39,014	Massachusetts	4,475	2,118	Rhode Island	1,390	932
Colorado	8,836	4,288	Michigan	16,854	9,701	South Carolina	2,241	1,098
Connecticut	2,222	923	Minnesota	23,128	15,496	South Dakota	32,365	25,794
Delaware	656	597	Mississippi	4,113	3,119	Tennessee	2,276	638
District of			Missouri	5,405	1,723	Texas	17,957	5,750
Columbia	956	587	Montana	27,130	26,181	Utah	11,273	6,961
Florida	6,677	2,504	Nebraska	6,624	5,545	Vermont	229	57
Georgia	2,347	749	Nevada	7,933	6,681	Virginia	4,853	2,155
Hawaii	1,126	472	New Hampshire	361	135	Washington	33,386	21,076
Idaho	6,687	5,231	New Jersey	4,706	1,699	West Virginia	751	181
Illinois	11,413	4,704	New Mexico	72,788	56,255	Wisconsin	18,924	14,297
Indiana	3,887	948	New York	28,355	16,491	Wyoming	4,980	4,020

Full enumeration of the American Indian population was not made prior to 1890 because Indians living in Indian Territory or on reservations were not counted. The following is the count in each census since 1890.

1890	248,253	1920	244,437	1950	343,410			
1900	237,196	1930	332,397	1960	523,591			
1910	265,683	1940	333,929	1970	791,839			

How the Cities Grew

Source: Bureau of the Census

(Cities over 100,000 in the 1970 census)

Rank	Cities	1970	1960	1950	1900	1850	1790
1	New York, N.Y.	7,894,862	7,781,984	7,891,957	3,437,202	696,115	49,401
	Bronx boro.	1,471,701	1,424,815	1,451,277	200,507	8,032	1,781
	Brooklyn boro.	2,602,012	2,627,319	2,738,175	1,166,582	138,882	4,495
	Manhattan boro	1,539,233	1,698,281	1,960,101	1,850,093	515,547	33,131
	Queens boro.	1,987,174	1,809,578	1,550,849	152,999	18,593	6,159
	Richmond boro.	295,443	221,991	191,555	67,021	15,061	3,835
2	Chicago, Ill.	3,369,359	3,550,404	3,620,962	1,698,575	29,963	...
3	Los Angeles, Calif.	2,809,596	2,479,015	1,970,358	102,479	1,610	...
4	Phila., Pa.	1,950,098	2,002,512	2,071,605	1,293,697	121,376	28,522
5	Detroit, Mich.	1,513,601	1,670,144	1,849,568	285,704	21,019	...
6	Houston, Tex.	1,232,802	938,219	596,163	44,633	2,396	...
7	Baltimore, Md.	905,759	939,024	949,708	508,957	169,054	13,503
8	Dallas, Tex.	844,401	679,684	434,462	42,638	...	...
9	Washington, D.C.	756,510	763,956	802,178	278,718	40,001	...
10	Cleveland, Ohio	750,879	876,050	914,808	381,768	17,034	...
11	Indianapolis, Ind.	744,743	476,258	427,173	169,164	8,091	...
12	Milwaukee, Wis.	717,372	741,324	637,392	285,315	20,061	...
13	San Francisco, Calif.	715,674	740,316	775,357	342,782	[2]34,776	...
14	San Diego, Calif.	697,027	573,224	334,387	17,700	...	...
15	San Antonio, Tex.	654,153	587,718	408,442	53,321	3,488	...
16	Boston, Mass.	641,071	697,197	801,444	560,892	136,881	18,320
17	Memphis, Tenn.	623,530	497,524	396,000	102,320	8,841	...
18	St. Louis, Mo.	622,236	750,026	856,796	575,238	77,860	...
19	New Orleans, La.	593,471	627,525	570,445	287,104	116,375	...
20	Phoenix, Ariz.	581,562	439,170	106,818	5,544	...	...
21	Columbus, Ohio	540,025	471,316	375,901	125,560	17,882	...
22	Seattle, Wash.	530,831	557,087	467,591	80,671	...	...
23	Jacksonville, Fla.	528,865	201,030	204,517	28,429	1,045	...
24	Pittsburgh, Pa.	520,117	604,332	676,806	321,616	46,601	...
25	Denver, Colo.	514,678	493,887	415,786	133,859	...	...
26	Kansas City, Mo.	507,330	475,539	456,622	163,752	...	...
27	Atlanta, Ga.	497,421	487,455	331,314	89,872	2,572	...
28	Buffalo, N.Y.	462,768	532,759	580,132	352,387	42,261	...
29	Cincinnati, Ohio	452,524	502,550	503,998	325,902	115,435	...
30	Nashville, Tenn[3]	447,877	170,874	174,307	80,865	10,165	...
31	San Jose, Calif.	445,779	204,196	95,280	21,500	...	...
32	Minneapolis, Minn.	434,400	482,872	521,718	202,718	...	...
33	Fort Worth, Tex.	393,476	356,263	278,778	26,688	...	...
34	Toledo, Ohio	383,818	318,003	303,616	131,822	3,829	...
35	Newark, N.J.	382,288	405,220	438,776	246,070	38,894	...
36	Portland, Oreg.	380,555	372,676	373,628	90,426	...	...
37	Oklahoma City, Okla.	368,856	324,253	243,504	10,037	...	...
38	Louisville, Ky.	361,958	390,639	369,129	204,731	43,194	200
39	Oakland, Calif.	361,561	367,548	384,575	66,960	...	...
40	Long Beach, Calif.	358,633	344,168	250,767	2,252	...	...
41	Omaha, Nebr.	346,929	301,598	251,117	102,555	...	...
42	Miami, Fla.	334,859	291,688	249,276	1,681	...	...
43	Tulsa, Okla.	330,350	261,685	182,740	1,390	...	...
44	Honolulu, Hawaii	324,871	294,194	248,034	39,306	...	...
45	El Paso, Tex.	322,261	276,687	130,485	15,906	...	...
46	St. Paul, Minn.	309,828	313,411	311,349	163,065	1,112	...
47	Norfolk, Va.	307,951	304,869	213,513	46,624	14,326	2,959
48	Birmingham, Ala.	300,910	340,887	326,037	38,415	...	...
49	Rochester, N.Y.	296,233	318,611	332,488	162,608	36,403	...
50	Tampa, Fla.	277,767	274,970	124,681	15,839	...	...
51	Wichita, Kans.	276,554	254,698	168,279	24,671	...	...
52	Akron, Ohio	275,425	290,351	274,605	42,728	3,266	...
53	Tucson, Ariz.	262,933	212,892	45,454	7,531	...	...
54	Jersey City, N.J.	260,545	276,101	299,017	206,433	6,856	...
55	Sacramento, Calif.	257,105	191,667	137,572	29,282	6,820	...
56	Austin, Tex.	251,808	186,545	132,459	22,258	629	...
57	Richmond, Va.	249,430	219,958	230,310	85,050	27,570	3,761
58	Albuquerque, N. Mex.	243,751	201,189	96,815	6,238	...	...
59	Dayton, Ohio	243,601	262,332	243,872	85,333	10,977	...
60	Charlotte, N.C.	241,178	201,564	134,042	18,091	1,065	...
61	St. Petersburg, Fla.	216,232	181,298	96,738	1,575	...	...
62	Corpus Christi, Tex.	204,525	167,690	108,287	4,703	...	...
63	Yonkers, N.Y.	204,297	190,634	152,798	47,931	...	...
64	Des Moines, Iowa	201,404	208,982	177,965	62,139	...	...
65	Grand Rapids, Mich.	197,649	177,313	176,515	87,565	2,686	...
66	Syracuse, N.Y.	197,297	216,038	220,583	103,374	22,271	...
67	Flint, Mich.	193,317	196,940	163,143	13,103	...	...
68	Mobile, Ala.	190,026	194,856	129,009	38,469	20,515	...
69	Shreveport, La.	182,064	164,372	127,206	16,013	1,728	...
70	Warren, Mich.	179,260	89,246	727	350	...	...
71	Providence, R.I.	179,116	207,498	248,674	175,597	41,513	6,380
72	Fort Wayne, Ind.	178,021	161,776	133,607	45,115	4,282	...
73	Worcester, Mass.	176,572	186,587	203,486	118,421	17,049	2,095
74	Salt Lake City, Utah	175,885	189,454	182,121	53,531	...	...
75	Gary, Ind.	175,415	178,320	133,911	...	...	...
76	Knoxville, Tenn.	174,587	111,827	124,769	32,637	2,076	...
77	Virginia Beach, Va.	172,106	8,091	5,390	...	...	...
78	Madison, Wis.	172,007	126,706	96,056	19,164	1,525	...
79	Spokane, Wash.	170,516	181,608	161,721	36,848	...	...
80	Kansas City, Kans.	168,213	121,901	129,553	51,418	...	...
81	Anaheim, Calif.	166,408	104,184	14,556	1,456	...	...
82	Fresno, Calif.	165,972	133,929	91,669	12,470	...	...
83	Baton Rouge, La.	165,963	152,419	125,629	11,269	3,905	...
84	Springfield, Mass.	163,905	174,463	162,399	62,059	11,766	1,574
85	Hartford, Conn.	158,017	162,178	177,397	72,850	13,555	2,683
86	Santa Ana, Calif.	156,876	100,350	45,533	4,933	...	...

Rank	Cities	1970	1960	1950	1900	1850	1790
87	Bridgeport, Conn.	156,542	156,748	158,709	70,996	6,080	...
88	Tacoma, Wash.	154,581	147,979	143,673	37,714	...	...
89	Columbus, Ga.	155,028	116,779	79,611	17,614	5,942	...
90	Jackson, Miss.	153,968	144,422	98,271	7,816	1,881	...
91	Lincoln, Nebr.	149,518	128,521	98,884	40,159	...	...
92	Lubbock, Tex.	149,101	128,691	71,747	...	...	...
93	Rockford, Ill.	147,370	126,706	92,927	31,051	...	...
94	Paterson, N.J.	144,824	143,663	139,336	105,171	11,334	...
95	Greensboro, N.C.	144,076	119,574	74,389	10,035	...	...
96	Riverside, Calif.	140,089	84,332	46,764	7,973	...	...
97	Youngstown, Ohio	139,788	166,689	168,330	44,885	...	...
98	Fort Lauderdale, Fla.	139,590	83,648	36,328	...	...	...
99	Evansville, Ind.	138,764	141,543	128,636	59,007	3,235	...
100	Newport News, Va.	138,177	113,662	42,358	19,635	...	...
101	Huntsville, Ala.	137,802	72,365	16,437	8,068	2,863	...
102	New Haven, Conn.	137,707	152,048	164,443	108,027	20,345	4,487
103	Colorado Springs, Colo.	135,060	70,194	45,472	21,083	...	...
104	Winston-Salem, N.C.[4]	134,676	111,135	87,811	13,650	...	...
105	Torrance, Calif.	134,584	100,991	22,241	...	...	...
106	Montgomery, Ala.	133,386	134,393	106,525	30,346	8,728	...
107	Glendale, Calif.	132,752	119,442	95,702	...	...	...
108	Little Rock, Ark.	132,483	107,813	102,213	38,307	2,167	...
109	Lansing, Mich.	131,546	107,807	92,129	16,485	...	...
110	Erie, Pa.	129,231	138,440	130,803	52,733	5,858	...
111	Amarillo, Tex.	127,010	137,969	74,246	1,442	...	...
112	Peoria, Ill.	126,963	103,162	111,856	56,100	5,095	...
113	Las Vegas, Nev.	125,787	64,405	24,624	...	...	...
114	South Bend, Ind.	125,580	132,445	115,911	35,999	1,652	...
115	Topeka, Kans.	125,011	119,484	78,791	33,608	...	...
116	Raleigh, N.C.	123,793	93,931	65,679	13,643	4,518	...
117	Macon, Ga.	122,423	69,764	70,252	23,272	5,720	...
118	Garden Grove, Calif.	121,371	84,238	...	...	...	...
119	Hampton, Va.	120,779	89,258	5,966	2,764	...	...
120	Springfield, Mo.	120,096	95,865	66,731	23,267	415	...
121	Chattanooga, Tenn.	119,082	130,009	131,041	30,154	...	...
122	Savannah, Ga.	118,349	149,245	119,638	54,244	15,312	...
123	Beaumont, Tex.	117,548	119,175	94,014	9,427	...	...
124	Berkeley, Calif.	116,716	111,268	113,805	13,214	...	...
125	Huntington Bch, Calif.	115,960	11,492	5,237	...	...	...
126	Albany, N.Y.	115,781	129,726	134,995	94,151	50,763	3,498
127	Columbia, S.C.	113,542	97,433	86,914	21,103	6,060	...
128	Pasadena, Calif.	112,981	116,407	104,577	3,117	...	...
129	Elizabeth, N.J.	112,654	107,698	112,817	52,130	5,583	...
130	Independence, Mo.	111,630	62,328	36,963	6,974	...	...
131	Portsmouth, Va.	110,963	114,773	80,039	17,427	8,626	...
132	Alexandria, Va.	110,938	91,023	61,787	14,528	8,734	2,748
133	Cedar Rapids, Iowa	110,642	92,035	72,296	25,656	...	...
134	Livonia, Mich.	110,109	66,702	17,534	...	...	...
135	Canton, Ohio	110,053	113,631	118,912	30,667	2,603	...
136	Allentown, Pa.	109,527	108,347	106,756	35,416	3,779	...
137	Stamford, Conn.	108,798	92,713	74,293	15,997	...	...
138	Lexington, Ky.	108,137	62,810	55,534	26,369	8,159	834
139	Waterbury, Conn.	108,033	107,130	104,477	45,859	...	...
140	Hammond, Ind.	107,888	111,698	87,594	12,376	...	...
141	Hollywood, Fla.	106,873	35,237	14,351	...	...	...
142	San Bernardino, Calif.	104,783	91,922	63,058	6,150	...	...
143	Trenton, N.J.	104,638	114,167	128,009	73,307	6,461	...
144	Stockton, Calif.	104,463	86,321	70,853	17,506	...	...
145	Dearborn, Mich.	104,199	112,007	94,994	844	...	...
146	Scranton, Pa.	103,564	111,443	125,536	102,026	...	...
147	Camden, N.J.	102,551	117,159	124,555	75,935	9,479	...
148	Hialeah, Fla.	102,452	66,972	19,676	...	...	...
149	New Bedford, Mass.	101,777	102,477	109,189	62,442	16,443	3,313
150	Fremont, Calif.	100,869	43,790	...	...	...	...
151	Duluth, Minn.	100,578	106,884	104,511	52,969	...	...
152	Cambridge, Mass.	100,361	107,716	120,740	91,886	15,215	2,115
153	Parma, Ohio	100,216	82,845	28,897	...	...	...
	San Juan, P.R.	452,749	432,377	224,767	32,048	...	...
	Bayamon, P.R.	147,552	13,109	20,171	2,218	...	...
	Ponce, P.R.	128,233	114,286	99,492	27,952	...	...

(1) Population shown for years prior to 1900 is for New York and its boroughs as constituted under the act of consolidation in 1898. (2) Population shown is for 1862 as given in State census for that year. 1850 returns for San Francisco were destroyed by fire. (3) Figure for 1970 is for the Metropolitan Government of Nashville and Davidson County; figures for previous years are for Nashville city. (4) Winston city and Salem town consolidated as Winston-Salem city between 1910 and 1920. Figure for 1900 represents combined population of Winston and Salem.

The Good New Days

In 1947, one half of all American families made less than $5,480. In 1971, one half of American families made more than $10,290. Both dollar figures are in 1971 dollars to take inflation into account. That means that the purchasing power of U.S. families nearly doubled in 25 years.

According to the U.S. Census Bureau, the number of families making less than $4,000 (1971 dollars) declined from 11,900,000 to 6,900,000 between 1947 and 1971. At the same time, families with more than $10,000 annual income increased from 5,700,000 to 27,600,000, while the total number of families rose from 37,200,000 to 53,300,000.

Another Census Bureau report notes that between 1959 and 1971, the percentage of families with incomes below the federally defined low-income or poverty level fell from 18% to 10%. During this period the composition of the low-income population changed considerably. The proportion of poor people who were 65 years or older rose from 14% to 17%. During the same period the number of poor families headed by men decreased by about one-half, while the number headed by women rose by about one-tenth. As a result, 40% of low-income families were headed by women in 1971, as against 23% in 1959.

The rise in real income levels reflected a rise in wages and salaries. The Census Bureau also reported that, in 1969, 22,900,000 American families, or 45%, received only wages and salaries as their sole source of income. For these families, the average income was $10,206.

Foreign Born and 2nd Generation in U.S.; Countries of Origin

Source: Bureau of the Census

The table below shows, state by state, the country of origin of U.S. residents who were either foreign born or had at least one foreign-born parent.

In the table, Germany includes both East and West Germany, West Asia includes European Turkey, and China includes both the mainland and Taiwan.

	Ala.	Alaska	Ariz.	Ark.	Calif.	Colo.	Conn.	Del.	D. of C.	Fla.
Mixed parents	47,742	24,842	219,830	29,269	3,234,089	219,579	708,193	48,710	39,340	695,699
Foreign Born	15,988	7,763	76,570	8,287	1,757,990	60,311	261,614	15,648	33,562	540,284
U.K.	8,944	3,081	19,866	3,797	373,495	26,377	71,532	7,949	5,638	114,870
Ireland	1,912	804	5,670	1,056	109,888	7,804	60,366	4,244	3,553	36,389
Norway	643	2,501	4,745	408	69,278	4,787	5,513	510	504	12,288
Sweden	678	1,565	6,903	1,100	103,913	13,193	23,427	676	773	26,944
Denmark	555	632	3,180	559	61,757	5,508	5,471	231	426	9,944
Netherlands	526	215	2,947	537	63,772	3,609	3,586	485	408	10,800
Switzerland	408	201	1,629	989	44,483	2,419	4,291	309	533	6,909
France	1,799	630	2,972	1,010	63,449	3,695	8,388	686	1,881	14,833
Germany	12,074	3,526	25,653	9,806	360,656	43,172	60,290	5,991	5,642	123,429
Poland	2,097	765	7,930	1,331	115,833	7,882	103,820	7,263	2,787	50,591
Czecho.	989	536	3,483	1,170	44,964	5,074	19,871	865	804	16,222
Austria	1,556	603	5,370	1,027	77,382	9,242	24,595	1,819	1,612	35,896
Hungary	819	169	3,144	310	58,097	3,035	21,641	952	847	23,054
Yugo.	421	361	2,592	198	53,868	6,079	3,447	331	474	5,728
USSR	1,854	679	8,812	912	221,198	28,023	48,150	3,523	5,597	81,833
Lithuania	415	169	1,591	355	22,063	1,146	20,469	487	953	8,938
Greece	2,092	208	2,009	500	43,645	3,111	10,933	1,117	1,716	11,637
Italy	5,771	866	12,498	2,284	340,675	21,411	227,782	12,112	4,657	84,881
Other Europe	1,358	1,208	6,952	854	189,979	7,252	32,304	1,648	2,368	47,368
Western Asia	1,753	103	2,501	672	64,565	2,272	8,655	457	1,614	13,755
China	554	282	3,162	661	136,860	1,697	2,195	523	2,099	3,110
Japan	1,392	1,203	2,310	625	144,335	6,005	1,492	516	602	4,843
Other Asia	1,797	1,808	3,488	945	222,709	4,418	6,008	1,690	4,084	10,963
Canada	5,232	6,499	26,136	3,016	439,862	21,580	126,305	4,047	3,914	114,615
Mexico	975	766	113,816	862	1,112,008	24,759	1,220	246	611	11,047
Cuba	680	56	505	86	47,699	945	5,772	483	902	252,520
Other Amer.	2,146	576	3,586	572	176,586	3,519	18,844	1,239	11,514	44,411

	Ga.	Haw.	Ida.	Ill.	Ind.	Iowa	Kan.	Ky.	La.	Maine
Mixed parents	78,528	180,577	60,972	1,572,843	268,060	257,342	147,206	56,080	100,221	149,746
Foreign Born	32,988	75,595	12,572	628,898	83,198	40,217	27,842	16,553	39,542	43,014
U.K.	14,517	5,114	10,406	115,891	30,039	22,008	15,986	7,619	9,252	12,073
Ireland	3,461	1,056	1,653	101,856	9,931	9,441	4,853	3,156	3,240	6,528
Norway	933	664	3,534	34,922	2,934	20,418	1,920	457	1,331	1,234
Sweden	1,641	841	5,333	98,254	8,274	21,108	9,622	817	1,284	2,740
Denmark	759	532	3,627	22,021	2,269	20,024	3,200	473	729	1,050
Netherlands	971	355	1,568	27,189	6,760	19,213	1,692	555	1,005	448
Switzerland	517	275	1,736	11,827	3,710	3,476	3,256	1,650	608	222
France	2,684	811	865	19,266	5,372	2,911	2,775	1,848	5,420	1,052
Germany	20,951	5,112	9,894	312,070	64,883	101,974	43,252	21,438	14,237	4,488
Poland	4,574	775	684	299,316	34,590	3,323	4,046	2,147	2,771	2,532
Czecho.	1,456	385	1,118	88,259	13,681	10,995	4,978	857	977	741
Austria	2,646	746	1,091	65,026	10,441	3,347	5,581	1,627	1,751	826
Hungary	1,286	342	357	35,822	14,108	1,007	938	1,103	1,267	240
Yugo.	824	198	421	59,280	14,410	2,202	3,815	451	1,412	133
USSR	5,831	828	3,136	110,321	9,933	4,563	17,664	2,531	3,073	2,878
Lithuania	798	207	151	58,285	4,265	1,226	507	545	358	1,172
Greece	2,984	371	657	48,669	7,852	2,085	965	861	1,560	1,281
Italy	5,220	1,656	1,595	228,984	17,935	7,683	4,552	4,499	29,031	6,083
Other Europe	3,668	8,318	3,966	67,143	15,478	6,160	3,810	2,092	4,149	2,986
Western Asia	2,457	344	177	18,270	4,098	1,670	1,738	1,523	2,758	1,079
China	1,278	20,939	456	11,883	1,976	1,073	786	539	1,117	284
Japan	1,775	105,223	1,322	12,948	1,888	787	2,435	1,056	1,308	226
Other Asia	4,068	79,410	571	28,637	4,948	2,448	3,066	2,324	3,109	922
Canada	10,021	5,865	10,452	80,611	21,920	13,297	10,425	4,823	6,090	136,801
Mexico	1,562	1,159	5,669	117,268	18,325	4,546	13,728	692	4,865	277
Cuba	3,816	235	73	19,649	1,690	382	796	556	6,711	223
Other Amer.	3,880	1,371	371	31,276	4,208	1,538	2,011	1,998	18,235	808

	Md.	Mass.	Mich.	Minn.	Miss.	Mo.	Mont.	Neb.	Nev.	N.H.
Mixed parents	329,813	1,397,064	1,259,961	609,218	22,862	245,948	101,688	175,556	50,274	133,502
Foreign Born	124,345	494,660	424,309	98,056	8,125	65,744	19,634	28,796	18,179	37,048
U.K.	40,291	152,741	148,612	25,672	3,910	23,080	11,293	11,083	6,969	14,040
Ireland	18,267	218,798	28,667	11,900	816	15,470	5,274	4,846	1,991	8,436
Norway	3,385	8,969	12,899	114,221	347	2,257	14,595	3,183	1,163	1,219
Sweden	4,546	38,753	33,639	114,512	445	6,274	6,177	17,099	1,670	2,774
Denmark	2,461	5,163	11,951	22,762	294	2,879	4,302	13,202	1,485	593
Netherlands	3,312	5,656	72,763	13,166	237	2,425	2,731	1,754	796	616
Switzerland	2,437	3,845	5,442	4,282	160	5,204	1,225	2,054	1,103	422
France	6,519	12,342	12,149	3,766	733	5,297	1,160	1,296	1,959	1,265
Germany	59,680	54,846	184,192	137,442	4,960	77,748	15,593	62,726	7,023	6,308
Poland	39,334	117,992	214,085	26,931	730	15,469	1,781	8,333	1,578	6,886
Czecho.	11,111	6,434	32,176	17,905	377	7,504	2,171	19,551	796	428
Austria	13,516	16,898	40,730	17,266	576	11,755	3,464	3,612	1,483	1,297
Hungary	7,817	5,583	39,202	3,741	266	5,861	828	1,060	751	481
Yugo.	3,148	1,776	30,375	12,266	574	6,517	3,020	1,599	957	229
USSR	46,332	104,223	65,606	18,666	534	19,127	11,365	14,160	2,247	2,982
Lithuania	9,090	32,617	16,908	2,445	192	2,168	242	1,428	282	1,929
Greece	12,508	39,669	19,519	2,833	471	4,209	541	859	1,205	5,040
Italy	49,619	294,318	117,064	12,910	3,957	30,114	4,157	6,414	7,927	6,465
Other Europe	15,069	117,653	94,603	41,228	954	9,085		3,823	3,645	3,952
Western Asia	8,124	27,159	31,579	2,411	1,249	3,279	377	771	633	1,281
China	5,975	11,324	5,725	1,998	1,078	2,337	245	543	811	541
Japan	3,784	3,390	4,952	2,206	394	2,618	675	1,106	1,084	370
Other Asia	13,832	10,897	12,925	4,749	945	5,301	746	1,428	2,148	662
Canada	25,300	466,942	353,154	57,604	2,496	15,532	21,106	8,247	7,587	96,834
Mexico	2,714	2,136	31,067	4,575	783	8,353	1,485	5,552	5,760	209
Cuba	4,931	6,915	3,231	765	241	1,131	45	608	1,306	195
Other Amer.	19,309	27,299	13,339	3,390	1,427	3,857	426	1,017	1,147	728

Foreign Born and 2nd Generation in U.S.; Countries of Origin

	N.J.	N.M.	N.Y.	N.C.	N.D.	Ohio	Okla.	Ore.	Pa.	R.I.
Mixed parents	1,521,045	66,170	3,885,445	65,661	127,689	994,850	72,713	229,357	1,687,145	237,233
Foreign Born	634,818	22,510	2,109,776	28,620	18,437	316,496	20,160	66,149	445,895	74,374
U.K.	172,308	6,000	334,424	12,826	3,537	108,027	9,812	28,525	198,190	34,178
Ireland	122,600	1,718	386,403	2,506	1,248	37,941	2,386	7,175	118,174	21,041
Norway	17,474	872	47,605	773	38,722	4,382	901	18,085	5,251	1,093
Sweden	19,366	1,681	52,058	1,401	8,434	12,539	1,962	17,830	20,370	6,669
Denmark	11,000	721	20,911	728	3,442	4,492	1,396	8,792	4,935	574
Netherlands	28,440	655	32,043	1,444	1,120	6,539	1,101	4,776	5,691	749
Switzerland	13,219	557	23,773	678	426	12,337	1,200	6,816	8,039	522
France	22,152	1,219	56,861	1,820	402	13,640	1,669	3,263	18,484	3,261
Germany[1]	219,178	7,438	516,216	16,614	21,004	188,386	21,475	40,242	202,611	768
Poland	217,509	1,422	557,478	3,037	1,952	116,262	2,670	4,855	243,752	13,389
Czecho.	51,599	763	90,641	1,132	2,473	93,187	3,411	4,144	118,855	763
Austria	83,165	1,483	237,836	1,664	2,254	62,829	1,893	5,294	145,815	2,896
Hungary	70,424	687	115,474	1,190	1,590	82,944	793	2,298	62,014	589
Yugo.	16,202	899	41,756	449	194	73,843	400	3,220	54,424	278
USSR	143,234	1,725	569,813	2,928	33,177	54,520	5,463	15,709	157,348	11,198
Lithuania	22,658	371	42,863	545	117	13,979	559	778	43,183	1,459
Greece	25,703	747	90,886	3,883	168	22,210	667	3,480	23,198	2,242
Italy	515,889	3,916	1,330,057	4,658	485	166,629	3,531	9,644	444,841	73,255
Other Europe[2]	69,176	1,725	197,966	2,764	4,076	48,002	2,584	13,752	52,748	33,222
Western Asia[2]	23,415	865	87,036	2,536	770	18,246	2,488	2,348	20,191	4,211
China[3]	7,748	506	66,407	1,178	150	4,987	758	4,423	6,010	1,069
Japan	6,064	1,029	17,304	2,988	391	5,169	1,810	3,983	4,480	783
Other Asia	16,085	1,137	51,785	3,583	555	14,066	2,539	5,345	15,248	2,278
Canada	58,720	5,663	286,047	10,334	15,630	63,258	7,811	53,002	47,827	66,003
Mexico	3,301	37,822	12,249	1,770	276	13,349	6,071	7,739	4,707	407
Cuba	71,233	418	98,479	1,330	46	3,593	352	689	5,195	516
Other Amer.	54,867	1,484	415,906	3,012	378	11,679	2,114	2,887	20,183	2,788

	S.C.	S.D.	Tenn.	Tex.	Utah	Vt.	Va.	Wash.	W.Va.	Wis.
Mixed parents	25,436	90,147	40,889	889,010	184,800	84,660	170,810	401,880	97,550	617,479
Foreign Born	14,364	10,899	19,024	309,772	29,573	18,482	72,281	156,020	16,662	130,669
U.K.	7,779	4,562	8,682	49,185	28,531	7,008	32,737	60,522	8,259	28,446
Ireland	1,336	1,980	2,087	12,143	1,416	3,071	10,162	13,266	1,742	9,433
Norway	392	18,898	600	5,442	4,113	651	3,077	60,427	191	52,681
Sweden	686	7,790	1,081	10,873	7,477	1,142	4,144	45,251	601	27,352
Denmark	325	6,584	630	4,801	10,464	476	2,195	14,422	170	18,959
Netherlands	516	5,126	698	4,722	7,617	518	2,690	13,297	223	15,315
Switzerland	576	950	802	4,314	3,392	529	1,640	7,675	762	14,316
France	1,069	399	1,333	8,992	1,014	759	6,210	6,145	881	4,457
Germany[1]	9,193	26,792	11,675	104,726	14,179	4,195	32,596	71,353	6,960	234,767
Poland	1,701	1,052	2,789	16,328	904	2,797	9,423	9,821	6,360	71,534
Czecho.	704	3,507	776	29,536	668	393	4,675	6,137	2,996	26,465
Austria	935	1,305	1,354	13,397	1,436	614	6,827	10,332	2,572	27,343
Hungary	479	503	995	4,852	394	602	3,814	4,269	2,931	12,448
Yugo.	391	280	376	2,992	1,337	84	1,775	7,580	2,549	19,873
USSR	1,661	14,041	3,649	16,149	1,151	1,171	11,129	23,466	1,996	24,246
Lithuania	228	140	388	2,069	112	211	2,040	1,436	602	5,796
Greece	2,188	284	1,563	6,168	3,372	504	5,712	4,061	1,894	4,746
Italy	2,653	616	6,054	26,886	4,688	4,982	18,026	21,422	17,906	30,513
Other Europe[2]	1,658	2,659	1,678	15,713	2,396	1,707	8,005	24,907	2,564	22,142
Western Asia[2]	1,382	523	1,579	9,219	672	652	6,248	3,411	2,522	3,388
China[3]	408	270	1,032	7,606	983	165	2,936	8,107	135	2,141
Japan	892	273	1,352	8,388	2,834	66	4,691	15,777	433	1,871
Other Asia	2,106	403	2,726	12,465	1,533	449	14,060	18,701	1,704	4,928
Canada	4,805	6,617	6,213	35,900	11,194	46,176	24,048	136,546	2,492	36,888
Mexico	668	472	1,036	711,058	7,710	111	3,167	17,892	513	9,160
Cuba	860	58	894	7,749	116	7	4,479	570	110	787
Other Amer.	1,405	303	1,593	21,300	1,593	356	10,538	5,173	772	3,834

Wyoming

Mixed parents	31,014	Germany	5,721	Other Europe	1,194
Foreign born	6,989	Poland	1,033	Western Asia	177
U.K.	5,367	Czecho.	824	China	177
Ireland	1,066	Austria	1,300	Japan	341
Norway	1,257	Hungary	250	Other Asia	385
Sweden	2,156	Yugo.	1,263	Canada	3,069
Denmark	1,505	USSR	2,913	Mexico	2,638
Netherlands	332	Lithuania	82	Cuba	
Switzerland	563	Greece	728	Other Amer.	277
France	504	Italy	1,750		

New Housing Units Started in U.S.

Source: Bureau of the Census
Including Farm Housing

	1971	1972	Type of Structure:	1971	1972
Total private and public	2,084,500	2,378,500	1-family	1,151,000	1,309,200
Private	2,052,200	2,356,600	2-family	55,100	67,100
Public	32,300	21,900	3-4 family	65,200	74,200
Metropolitan	1,518,500	1,732,700	5 or more	780,900	906,200
Private	1,501,800	1,720,400	Regions:		
Public	16,700	12,200	Northeast	263,800	329,500
Nonmetropolitan	566,100	645,800	North Central	434,100	442,800
Private	550,400	636,200	South	868,700	1,057,000
Public	15,700	9,600	West	485,600	527,400

Origin of The Population By Age and Sex

Source: Bureau of the Census

About 102,000,000 of the 205,000,000 persons in the U.S. in a March 1972 survey by the Bureau of the Census reported that their origin or descent was one of 8 specific origin categories. The Spanish category includes persons who reported that they were of Mexican, Puerto Rican, Cuban, Central or South American or other Spanish origin.

Origin	Total population		Percent Distribution by age					Median age (years)
	Number	Percent	Under 14	14 to 24	25 to 44	45 to 64	65 and over	
Total	204,840,000	100.0	25.8	20.0	24.0	20.6	9.7	28.0
English, Scottish Welsh	29,548,000	14.4	23.6	16.2	23.1	23.7	13.3	33.1
French	5,420,000	2.6	28.5	16.1	25.0	20.6	9.8	28.2
German	25,543,000	12.5	28.1	16.3	24.3	20.3	11.1	28.9
Irish	16,408,000	8.0	26.3	16.2	23.7	22.7	11.0	30.9
Italian	8,764,000	4.3	24.2	16.9	23.6	26.3	9.0	32.0
Polish	5,105,000	2.5	23.7	15.5	23.5	27.8	9.5	32.9
Russian	2,188,000	1.1	20.8	13.2	21.3	29.5	15.2	39.7
Spanish	9,178,000	4.5	37.2	20.4	26.0	12.9	3.5	20.1
Other	85,130,000	41.6	26.3	23.7	23.4	18.4	8.2	25.0
Not reported	17,556,000	8.6	18.2	21.6	27.5	22.1	10.7	31.7
Male	**99,378,000**	**100.0**	**27.1**	**20.2**	**24.2**	**20.2**	**8.3**	**26.9**
English, Scottish, Welsh	14,302,000	14.4	25.0	16.4	23.6	23.8	11.1	31.2
French	2,572,000	2.6	28.5	16.4	26.0	20.7	8.4	27.9
German	12,812,000	12.9	28.1	16.2	24.7	21.2	9.7	29.2
Irish	7,762,000	7.8	28.6	16.3	23.1	22.5	9.2	28.9
Italian	4,432,000	4.5	24.3	16.9	24.9	25.2	8.7	31.8
Polish	2,424,000	2.4	24.3	16.0	23.7	27.8	8.2	31.8
Russian	1,052,000	1.1	21.2	13.4	22.8	27.3	15.2	38.2
Spanish	4,540,000	4.6	39.4	19.7	25.6	12.3	3.0	18.7
Other	40,850,000	41.1	28.0	24.4	23.1	17.6	6.9	23.7
Not reported	8,631,000	8.7	19.2	21.7	29.0	20.8	9.3	30.6
Female	**105,462,000**	**100.0**	**24.6**	**19.7**	**23.8**	**21.0**	**11.0**	**29.1**
English, Scottish Welsh	15,245,000	14.5	22.3	16.0	22.7	23.6	15.4	35.0
French	2,849,000	2.7	28.6	15.9	24.0	20.4	11.1	28.5
German	12,730,000	12.1	28.0	16.4	23.8	19.4	12.4	28.8
Irish	8,646,000	8.2	24.3	16.1	24.3	22.7	12.6	32.6
Italian	4,333,000	4.1	24.0	17.0	22.2	27.4	9.3	32.1
Polish	2,681,000	2.5	23.2	15.0	23.3	27.8	10.7	34.0
Russian	1,137,000	1.1	20.5	13.1	19.9	31.5	15.1	41.3
Spanish	4,638,000	4.4	35.0	21.1	26.3	13.6	4.0	21.4
Other	44,280,000	42.0	24.7	23.1	23.7	19.2	9.3	26.5
Not reported	8,925,000	8.5	17.3	21.5	26.0	23.3	12.0	33.0

Mother Tongue and Nativity, by Age (Nov., 1969)

	Number	Percent	Under 14	14 to 24	25 to 44	45 to 64	65 and over	Median age
Native	**187,333,000**	**100.0**	**28.8**	**19.1**	**23.4**	**20.4**	**8.3**	**26.8**
English	158,954,000	84.9	32.6	20.1	22.0	17.8	7.5	23.5
French	1,801,000	1.0	4.1	11.9	36.9	33.3	13.8	43.4
German	4,809,000	2.6	1.0	6.6	29.6	36.1	26.7	52.1
Italian	3,147,000	1.7	3.2	9.7	37.1	44.3	5.8	45.0
Polish	1,982,000	1.1	0.8	9.1	35.1	48.4	6.7	47.1
Spanish	4,878,000	2.6	29.5	25.5	29.2	13.5	2.2	22.7
Yiddish	1,142,000	0.6	0.4	7.0	29.4	50.6	12.7	50.2
Other	7,111,000	3.8	4.8	10.5	32.5	39.3	12.8	46.1
Not reported	3,506,000	1.9	5.1	20.5	22.0	35.0	17.4	46.3
Foreign born	**10,882,000**	**100.0**	**9.6**	**10.4**	**24.4**	**25.4**	**30.2**	**49.4**
English	2,833,000	26.0	25.1	12.0	19.9	22.8	20.3	38.1
French	378,000	3.5	7.5	11.9	33.0	28.7	19.1	43.6
German	1,025,000	9.4	0.4	6.3	30.0	29.0	34.4	54.2
Italian	1,218,000	11.2	2.0	6.9	17.8	25.0	48.2	63.6
Polish	399,000	3.7	1.7	3.8	9.3	25.7	59.5	65 +
Spanish	1,822,000	16.7	10.5	19.9	39.2	21.8	8.6	35.1
Yiddish	478,000	4.4	0.2	1.5	4.6	30.7	63.1	65 +
Other	2,655,000	24.4	1.4	7.9	24.7	27.9	37.2	55.8
Not reported	74,000	0.7	(B)	(B)	(B)	(B)	(B)	(B)

B Base less than 75,000

Country of Birth of the Foreign-Born Population, by Age and Sex (Nov., 1969)

(Numbers in thousands)

Age and sex	Total	Austria	Cuba	Germany	Ireland	Italy	Mexico	Poland	Russia	Sweden	United King.	Other
Total	10,882	236	504	1,004	277	1,353	938	550	412	166	1,006	4,434
Median age . . . . years	49.4	70.2	32.1	40.8	60.6	59.7	38.0	66.7	69.7	70.1	49.6	45.0
Male	**5,054**	**112**	**242**	**426**	**105**	**669**	**441**	**255**	**199**	**83**	**446**	**2,076**
Percent	100.0	100.0	100.0	100.0	100.0	100.0	100.0	100.0	100.0	100.0	100.0	100.0
Under 14 years	10.4	—	14.9	22.5	2.7	5.0	11.6	2.2	—	—	11.6	11.9
14 to 24 years	10.8	8.4	21.5	12.7	2.9	8.8	19.0	3.9	—	1.7	9.6	11.0
25 to 44 years	23.1	2.2	42.5	18.0	18.3	18.4	29.9	11.0	9.6	6.4	22.4	26.9
45 to 64 years	24.9	22.0	16.0	21.6	22.7	23.2	29.0	34.3	17.2	33.7	29.5	24.9
65 to 74 years	16.8	28.5	4.6	16.2	28.5	20.7	8.3	23.2	38.3	36.8	16.8	14.0
75 years and over	14.1	38.9	0.5	8.9	25.2	23.8	2.2	25.6	34.9	21.4	10.2	11.4
Median age . . . . years . . .	49.6	71.3	31.4	41.4	66.2	60.4	38.0	64.2	71.1	67.4	49.3	45.2
Female	**5,827**	**124**	**263**	**578**	**173**	**683**	**496**	**295**	**214**	**83**	**560**	**2,358**
Percent	100.0	100.0	100.0	100.0	100.0	100.0	100.0	100.0	100.0	100.0	100.0	100.0
Under 14 years	8.9	—	11.1	13.3	3.2	4.5	11.2	1.9	—	—	8.6	10.4
14 to 24 years	10.0	3.2	22.8	11.6	5.8	8.3	15.9	0.3	0.5	4.8	8.4	10.8
25 to 44 years	25.6	6.0	39.7	32.4	25.6	16.1	35.0	8.3	4.4	4.5	25.8	29.0
45 to 66 years	25.8	24.9	22.2	21.7	27.6	25.7	25.6	28.8	30.8	16.6	30.7	25.6
65 to 74 years	17.0	36.3	3.0	13.7	22.1	21.7	7.1	34.6	39.5	26.8	14.7	14.8
75 years and over	12.6	29.5	1.1	7.4	15.9	20.7	5.3	26.0	24.6	47.1	12.0	9.4
Median age . . . . years . . .	49.3	69.4	33.2	40.5	56.5	59.0	38.1	68.0	68.7	73.9	49.7	44.9

—Represents zero or rounds to zero.

Household and Family Characteristics by Race, for Regions

Source: Bureau of the Census

1970

WHITE POPULATION	Northeast Urban	Northeast Rural	North Central Urban	North Central Rural	South Urban	South Rural	West Urban	West Rural
All persons	34,883,058	9,427,446	35,772,964	15,868,219	32,212,232	18,207,876	25,904,386	5,472,194
In households	33,919,080	9,194,848	34,633,956	15,613,024	30,872,359	17,941,478	25,124,710	5,329,398
Head	11,339,522	2,751,979	11,413,201	4,749,933	10,427,974	5,619,044	8,574,651	1,653,070
14 to 24 years	628,661	134,336	926,403	251,702	917,782	361,226	774,936	95,240
25 to 34 years	1,813,323	503,239	2,083,148	807,526	1,991,622	987,740	1,714,363	290,835
35 to 44 years	1,998,345	560,192	2,024,370	864,230	1,929,128	1,025,004	1,601,758	318,790
45 to 64 years	4,503,811	1,042,062	4,122,728	1,750,327	3,654,347	2,072,639	2,979,055	629,661
65 years and over	2,395,382	512,150	2,256,552	1,076,148	1,935,095	1,171,435	1,504,539	318,544
Primary individual: Male	823,787	151,645	807,030	271,093	667,659	259,955	829,374	128,761
Female	1,596,600	232,131	1,596,602	426,444	1,369,490	468,847	1,208,160	131,619
Family head: Male	7,937,024	2,209,587	8,195,368	3,835,580	7,574,885	4,540,683	5,867,227	1,313,562
Female	982,111	158,616	814,201	216,816	815,940	349,559	669,890	79,128
Wife of head	7,652,346	2,146,061	7,985,311	3,727,274	7,389,352	4,410,024	5,702,582	1,278,242
Children Under 18 Years								
All families	8,919,135	2,368,203	9,009,569	4,052,396	8,390,825	4,890,242	6,537,117	1,392,690
With own children under 18 years	4,584,736	1,353,307	4,929,020	2,256,756	4,519,739	2,616,560	3,616,094	773,423
Number of own children under 18 years	10,274,201	3,258,604	11,370,142	5,624,725	9,645,885	5,796,905	8,093,135	1,884,319
Number of own children under 6 years	3,091,347	970,872	3,446,997	1,583,268	2,930,580	1,714,273	2,447,638	518,967
Husband-wife families	7,650,541	2,147,190	7,984,914	3,730,584	7,397,548	4,414,290	5,714,742	1,281,210
With own children under 18 years	4,103,377	1,259,810	4,469,719	2,125,638	4,038,238	2,422,233	3,137,802	711,254
Number of own children under 6 years	9,277,376	3,054,156	10,415,342	5,331,450	8,681,504	5,386,887	7,104,987	1,746,002
Families with female head	982,111	158,616	814,201	216,816	815,940	349,559	669,690	79,128
With own children under 18 years	422,250	75,841	401,874	104,394	424,036	156,464	423,452	49,388
Number of own children under 18 years	885,216	168,583	842,258	236,438	855,282	333,381	885,270	112,989
Number of own children under 6 years	211,287	34,890	189,300	46,409	183,691	64,603	214,217	24,559
Marital Status								
Male, 14 years old and over	12,444,611	3,313,507	12,556,025	5,643,203	11,578,384	6,593,397	9,309,611	2,020,714
Single	3,667,887	888,197	3,536,779	1,506,178	3,111,973	1,614,286	2,651,313	546,361
Married, except separated	7,934,969	2,226,080	8,204,714	3,824,546	7,730,080	4,591,228	5,936,659	1,336,333
14 to 19 years	30,276	10,475	55,828	22,606	75,925	44,876	45,153	9,197
20 to 34 years	1,898,608	589,533	2,355,174	973,070	2,369,546	1,265,235	1,793,987	340,711
35 to 64 years	4,889,678	1,344,570	4,752,271	2,236,440	4,316,711	2,605,898	4,390,869	798,569
Female, 14 years old and over	14,193,572	3,433,257	14,018,539	5,718,049	12,699,860	6,817,000	9,966,506	1,926,577
Single	3,544,700	722,927	3,264,869	1,122,496	2,547,782	1,185,662	2,112,525	360,334
Married, except separated	7,950,573	2,225,192	8,232,039	3,835,482	7,728,776	4,610,944	5,922,390	1,322,180
14 to 19 years	96,631	33,855	168,125	72,057	223,954	148,661	141,434	28,631
20 to 34 years	2,301,755	713,096	2,752,341	1,182,156	2,694,281	1,507,899	2,069,094	410,960
35 to 64 years	4,775,795	1,283,825	4,581,126	2,177,943	4,157,126	2,520,537	3,215,674	762,703

NEGRO POPULATION	Northeast Urban	Northeast Rural	North Central Urban	North Central Rural	South Urban	South Rural	West Urban	West Rural
All persons	4,214,819	129,334	4,446,946	124,604	8,063,781	3,906,180	1,641,772	52,853
In households	4,113,224	101,853	4,356,720	93,928	7,813,805	3,804,140	1,585,464	36,988
Head	1,252,116	27,332	1,257,211	26,662	2,211,638	898,624	495,961	10,716
14 to 24 years	102,634	1,232	113,019	1,199	171,929	43,647	50,323	697
25 to 34 years	301,696	4,640	277,381	3,274	429,513	128,908	124,988	1,860
35 to 44 years	289,793	6,129	280,349	4,329	436,296	153,667	110,814	2,174
45 to 64 years	415,546	10,520	424,432	10,231	789,399	351,415	159,703	4,055
65 years and over	142,447	4,811	162,030	7,629	384,501	220,987	50,133	1,930
Primary individual: Male	131,378	2,888	132,412	3,121	197,402	69,421	66,991	1,642
Female	173,301	2,394	149,733	2,859	289,059	77,648	63,335	963
Family head: Male	644,838	18,471	705,305	17,258	1,224,030	591,649	264,712	6,947
Female	302,599	3,579	269,761	3,424	501,147	159,906	100,923	1,164
Wife of head	596,969	16,896	656,384	16,217	1,142,114	550,493	240,529	6,268
Children Under 18 Years								
All families	947,437	22,050	975,066	20,682	1,725,177	751,555	365,635	8,111
With own children under 18 years	596,271	13,200	612,079	11,054	1,025,004	438,089	237,387	4,952
Number of own children under 18 years	1,497,438	37,370	1,669,460	34,413	2,801,365	1,429,001	606,081	14,548
Number of own children under 6 years	486,787	10,405	504,337	9,234	833,281	388,688	190,129	4,012
Husband-wife families	602,187	17,434	663,312	16,303	1,144,050	549,920	250,250	6,675
With own children under 18 years	365,431	10,522	397,377	8,599	676,726	334,434	153,588	3,956
Number of own children under 18 years	903,317	29,373	1,057,167	26,434	1,830,076	1,105,648	384,584	11,490
Number of own children under 6 years	305,037	8,353	333,361	7,264	582,554	315,117	126,918	3,324
Families with female head	302,599	3,579	269,761	3,424	501,147	159,906	100,923	1,164
With own children under 18 years	214,438	2,273	198,712	2,086	317,610	87,662	77,780	853
Number of own children under 18 years	558,423	6,920	571,991	6,950	897,508	278,616	207,650	2,688
Number of own children under 6 years	172,578	1,793	161,497	1,720	233,406	63,270	59,944	611
Marital Status								
Male, 14 years and over	1,277,559	53,049	1,372,041	54,551	2,480,076	1,225,388	531,947	26,474
Single	447,194	24,135	461,057	25,764	875,726	484,862	183,549	13,058
Married, except separated	656,462	22,715	712,719	21,376	1,263,589	612,567	270,736	9,809
14 to 19 years	5,552	190	7,587	191	15,919	6,745	2,801	177
20 to 34 years	221,380	6,821	227,474	5,549	403,805	157,508	99,430	3,627
35 to 64 years	373,635	13,137	407,395	11,566	694,912	344,160	149,122	5,041
Female, 18 years and over	1,586,269	40,213	1,593,961	38,286	2,971,088	1,310,701	567,758	13,190
Single	464,496	13,148	431,851	11,661	836,031	413,777	143,257	3,725
Married, except separated	654,616	18,837	705,092	17,953	1,265,790	610,506	257,396	6,875
14 to 19 years	16,998	384	23,842	450	48,514	22,246	8,577	206
20 to 34 years	260,754	5,720	265,367	4,384	466,842	184,828	106,480	2,247
35 to 64 years	343,257	11,262	374,945	10,632	663,376	340,465	130,638	3,843

Two types of household heads are distinguished, the head of a family and a primary individual. A family head is a household head living with one or more persons related to him by blood, marriage, or adoption. A primary individual is a household head living alone or with nonrelatives only.

Rankings of U.S. Standard Metropolitan Statistical Areas

Source: Bureau of the Census

The rankings of areas based on new SMSA definitions in order of population size according to the 1970 Census and a comparison with 1970 ranking. Includes all of the 267 Standard Metropolitan Statistical Areas (SMSA's) as currently defined by the Bureau of the Budget. There are 4 new SMSA's; 12 existing areas were combined into 6 new ones; boundary definitions were changed in 98 areas, and names were changed in 14 others.

The four new areas are Burlington, North Carolina; Fayetteville-Springdale, Arkansas; Kingsport-Bristol, Tennessee-Virginia; and St. Cloud, Minnesota. The 6 new areas resulting from mergers include Charlotte-Gastonia, North Carolina; Dallas-Fort Worth, Texas; Greenville-Spartanburg, South Carolina; Raleigh-Durham, North Carolina; Salt Lake City-Ogden, Utah; and Northeast Pennsylvania (a combination of the former Scranton and Wilkes-Barre-Hazleton SMSA's).

Nassau-Suffolk, N.Y., replaces Pittsburgh as the ninth largest metropolitan area in the new ranking. The Nassau-Suffolk SMSA was created out of the eastern Long Island counties formerly in the New York SMSA and has a population of 2.6 million.

The combined Dallas-Fort Worth SMSA now ranks 12th and has a population of 2.4 million persons. The former Dallas SMSA ranked 16th.

SMSA	1973 Rank	Pop.	1970 Rank	Pop.
New York, N.Y.-N.J.[3]	1	9,973,577	1	11,571,899
Los Angeles-Long Beach, Calif.	2	7,032,075	2	7,032,075
Chicago, Ill.	3	6,978,947	3	6,978,947
Philadelphia, Pa.-N.J.	4	4,817,914	4	4,817,914
Detroit, Mich.[1]	5	4,431,390	5	4,199,931
San Francisco-Oakland, Calif.	6	3,109,519	6	3,109,519
Washington, D.C.-Md.-Va.[1]	7	2,908,801	7	2,861,123
Boston, Mass.[1]	8	2,899,101	8	2,753,700
Nassau-Suffolk, N.Y.[4]	9	2,553,030		
St. Louis, Mo.-Ill.[1]	10	2,410,163	10	2,363,017
Pittsburgh, Pa.	11	2,401,245	9	2,401,245
Dallas-Fort Worth, Tex.[6]	12	2,377,979	16	1,555,950
Baltimore, Md.	13	2,070,670	11	2,070,670
Cleveland, Ohio	14	2,064,194	12	2,064,194
Newark, N.J.[1]	15	2,054,928	14	1,856,556
Houston, Tex.[1]	16	1,999,316	13	1,985,031
Minneapolis-St. Paul, Minn.-Wis[3]	17	1,965,159	15	1,813,647
Atlanta, Ga.[1]	18	1,597,816	20	1,390,164
Seattle-Everett, Wash.	19	1,421,869	17	1,421,869
Anaheim-Santa Ana-Garden Grove, Calif.	20	1,420,386	18	1,420,386
Milwaukee, Wis.	21	1,403,688	19	1,403,688
Cincinnati, Ohio-Ky.-Ind.	22	1,384,851	21	1,384,851
San Diego, Calif.	23	1,357,854	23	1,357,854
Buffalo, N.Y.	24	1,349,211	24	1,349,211
Kansas City, Mo.-Kans.[1]	25	1,271,515	26	1,253,916
Miami, Fla.	26	1,267,792	25	1,267,792
Denver-Boulder, Colo.[3]	27	1,228,801	27	1,227,529
Riverside-San Bernardino-Ontario, Calif.[2]	28	1,143,146	28	1,143,146
Indianapolis, Ind.	29	1,109,882	29	1,109,882
Tampa-St. Petersburg, Fla.[1]	30	1,088,549	32	1,012,594
San Jose, Calif.	31	1,064,714	30	1,064,714
New Orleans, La.	32	1,045,809	31	1,045,809
Columbus, Ohio[1]	33	1,017,847	35	916,228
Portland, Oreg.-Wash.	34	1,009,129	33	1,009,129
Phoenix, Ariz.	35	967,522	34	967,522
Rochester, N.Y.[1]	36	961,516	37	882,667
Providence-Warwick-Pawtucket, R.I.-Mass.[3]	37	905,558	36	910,781
San Antonio, Tex.[1]	38	888,179	38	864,014
Louisville, Ky.-Ind.[1]	39	867,330	40	826,553
Dayton, Ohio	40	850,266	39	850,266
Memphis, Tenn.-Ark.-Miss.	41	834,006	42	770,120
Sacramento, Calif.	42	800,592	41	800,592
Albany-Schenectady-Troy, N.Y.[1]	43	777,793	45	721,910
Birmingham, Ala.[1]	44	767,230	44	739,274
Toledo, Ohio-Mich.[1]	45	762,741	46	692,571
Greensboro—Winston-Salem—High Point, N.C.[1]	46	723,304	56	603,895
Hartford, Conn.[1]	47	720,581	49	663,891
Salt Lake City-Ogden, Utah[6]	48	705,458	57	557,635
Nashville-Davidson, Tenn.[3]	49	699,144	59	541,108
Oklahoma City, Okla.[1]	50	698,180	50	640,889
Norfolk-Virginia Beach-Portsmouth, Va.-N.C.[3]	51	687,576	47	680,600
Akron, Ohio	52	679,239	48	679,239
Syracuse, N.Y.	53	636,507	51	636,507
Gary-Hammond East Chicago, Ind.	54	633,367	52	633,367
Honolulu, Hawaii	55	629,176	53	629,176
Northeast Pennsylvania[6]	56	621,830	87	342,301
Jacksonville, Fla.[1]	57	621,519	64	528,865
Fort Lauderdale-Hollywood, Fla.	58	620,100	54	620,100
Jersey City, N.J.	59	609,266	55	609,266
Allentown-Bethlehem-Easton, Pa.-N.J.[1]	60	594,124	58	543,551
New Brunswick-Perth Amboy-Sayreville, N.J.[4]	61	583,813		
Charlotte-Gastonia, N.C.[6]	62	557,785	73	409,370
Tulsa, Okla.[1]	63	550,835	68	476,945
Richmond, Va.[1]	64	542,242	65	518,319
Springfield-Chicopee-Holyoke, Mass.-Conn.[1]	65	541,752	63	529,922
Omaha, Nebr.-Iowa	66	540,142	60	540,142
Grand Rapids, Mich.	67	539,225	61	539,225
Youngstown-Warren, Ohio	68	536,003	62	536,003
Flint, Mich.[1]	69	524,018	67	496,658
Wilmington, Del.-N.J.-Md.	70	499,493	66	499,493
Greenville-Spartanburg, S.C.[6]	71	473,226	101	299,502
Paterson-Clifton-Passaic, N.J.[1]	72	460,782	22	1,358,794
Long Branch-Asbury Park, N.J.[4]	73	459,379		
Orlando, Fla.[1]	74	453,270	69	428,003
Lansing-East Lansing, Mich[3]	75	424,271	77	378,423
Raleigh-Durham, N.C.[6]	76	418,841	135	228,453
New Haven-West Haven, Conn.[3]	77	413,722	83	355,538
Fresno, Calif.	78	413,053	70	413,053
Tacoma, Wash.	79	411,027	71	411,027
Harrisburg, Pa.	80	410,626	72	410,626
Knoxville, Tenn.[1]	81	409,409	74	400,337
Bridgeport, Conn.[1]	82	401,752	76	389,153
Canton, Ohio[1]	83	393,789	80	372,210
Wichita, Kans.	84	389,352	75	389,352
Mobile, Ala.	85	376,690	78	376,690
Oxnard-Simi Valley-Ventura, Calif.[2]	86	376,430	79	376,430
Baton Rouge, La.[1]	87	375,628	110	285,167
Worcester, Mass.[1]	88	372,144	86	344,320
Chattanooga, Tenn.-Ga.[1]	89	370,016	97	304,927
Davenport-Rock Island-Moline, Iowa-Ill.	90	362,638	81	362,638
Fort Wayne, Ind.[1]	91	361,984	112	280,455
El Paso, Tex.	92	359,291	82	359,291
Tucson, Ariz.	93	351,667	84	351,667
West Palm Beach-Boca Raton[2]	94	348,753	85	348,753
Beaumont-Port Arthur-Orange, Tex.[1]	95	345,939	95	315,943
Peoria, Ill.	96	341,979	88	341,979
Utica-Rome, N.Y.	97	340,670	89	340,670
Charleston, S.C.[1]	98	336,125	99	303,849
Shreveport, La.[1]	99	334,642	104	294,703
Albuquerque, N. Mex.[1]	100	333,266	96	315,774
Newport News-Hampton, Va.[1]	101	333,140	105	292,159
York, Pa.	102	329,540	90	329,540
Bakersfield, Calif.	103	329,162	91	329,162
Little Rock-North Little Rock..	104	323,296	92	323,296
Austin, Tex.[1]	105	323,158	103	295,516
Columbia, S.C.	106	322,880	93	322,880
Lancaster, Pa.	107	319,693	94	319,693
Des Moines, Iowa[1]	108	313,533	109	286,101
Trenton, N.J.	109	303,968	98	303,968
Binghamton, N.Y.-Pa.	110	302,672	100	302,672
Reading, Pa.	111	296,382	102	296,382
Madison, Wis.	112	290,272	106	290,272
Stockton, Calif.	113	290,208	107	290,208
Spokane, Wash.	114	287,487	108	287,487
Huntington-Ashland, W. Va.-Ky.-Ohio[1]	115	286,935	123	253,743
Evansville, Ind.-Ky.[1]	116	284,959	132	232,775
Corpus Christi, Tex.	117	284,832	111	284,832
Huntsville, Ala.[1]	118	282,450	136	228,239
South Bend, Ind.	119	280,031	113	280,031
Appleton-Oshkosh, Wis.	120	276,891	114	276,891
Augusta, Ga.-S.C.[1]	121	275,787	124	253,460
Las Vegas, Nev.	122	273,288	115	273,288
Rockford, Ill.	123	272,063	116	272,063
Lexington, Ky.[1]	124	266,701	160	174,323
Duluth-Superior, Minn.-Wis.	125	265,350	117	265,350
Santa Barbara-Santa Maria-Lompoc, Calif.[2]	126	264,324	118	264,324
Erie, Pa.	127	263,654	119	263,654

SMSA	1973 Rank	1973 Pop.	1970 Rank	1970 Pop.
Johnstown, Pa.	128	262,822	120	262,822
Jackson, Miss.	129	258,906	121	258,906
Lawrence-Haverhill, Mass.-N.H.[1]	130	258,564	133	232,415
Kalamazoo-Portage, Mich.[3]	131	257,723	147	201,550
Charleston, W. Va.[1]	132	257,140	134	229,515
Lorain-Elyria, Ohio	133	256,843	122	256,843
Salinas-Seaside-Monterey, Calif.[2]	134	250,071	125	250,071
Vallejo-Fairfield-Napa, Calif.[2]	135	249,081	126	249,081
Pensacola, Fla.	136	243,075	127	243,075
New London-Norwich, Conn.-R.I.[3]	137	241,556	143	208,412
Kingsport-Bristol, Tenn.-Va.[4]	138	241,123		
Colorado Springs, Colo.[1]	139	239,288	129	235,972
Columbus, Ga.-Ala.	140	238,584	128	238,584
Ann Arbor, Mich.	141	234,103	131	234,103
Melbourne-Titusville-Cocoa, Fla.[4]	142	230,006		
Lakeland-Winter Haven, Fla.[4]	143	227,222		
Macon, Ga.[1]	144	226,782	145	206,342
Hamilton-Middletown, Ohio	145	226,207	137	226,207
Montgomery, Ala.[1]	146	225,785	148	201,325
Poughkeepsie, N.Y.[4]	147	222,295		
Saginaw, Mich.[1]	148	219,743	138	219,743
Lowell, Mass.-N.H.[3]	149	218,268	140	212,860
Waterbury, Conn.[1]	150	216,808	142	208,956
Eugene-Springfield, Oreg.[2]	151	213,358	139	213,358
Fayetteville, N.C.	152	212,042	141	212,042
Lima, Ohio[1]	153	210,074	161	171,472
Savannah, Ga.[1]	154	207,938	152	187,767
Stamford, Conn.	155	206,419	144	206,419
Santa Rosa, Calif.	156	204,885	146	204,885
Roanoke, Va.[1]	157	203,153	156	181,436
Modesto, Calif.	158	194,506	149	194,506
Springfield, Ohio[1]	159	187,606	172	157,115
Salem, Oreg.	160	186,658	153	186,658
Wheeling, W. Va.-Ohio	161	182,712	154	182,712
McAllen-Pharr-Edinburg, Tex.	162	181,535	155	181,535
Topeka, Kans.[1]	163	180,619	173	155,322
Battle Creek, Mich.[3]	164	180,129		
Lubbock, Tex.	165	179,295	157	179,295
Muskegon-Muskegon Heights, Mich.	166	175,410	171	157,426
Terre Haute, Ind.[1]	167	175,143	158	175,143
Atlantic City, N.J.	168	175,043	159	175,043
Springfield, Ill.[1]	169	171,020	168	161,335
Racine, Wis.	170	170,838	162	170,838
Portland, Maine[1]	171	170,081	183	141,625
Galveston-Texas City, Tex.	172	169,812	163	169,812
Fall River, Mass.-R.I.[1]	173	169,549	176	149,976
Daytona Beach, Fla.[4]	174	169,487		
Springfield, Mo.[1]	175	168,053	174	152,929
Lincoln, Nebr.	176	167,972	164	167,972
Steubenville-Weirton, Ohio-W. Va.	177	165,627	165	165,627
Champaign-Urbana-Rantoul, Ill.[2]	178	163,281	166	163,281
Cedar Rapids, Iowa	179	163,213	167	163,213
New Bedford, Mass.[1]	180	161,288	175	152,642
Asheville, N.C.[1]	181	161,059	180	145,056
Fort Smith, Ark.-Okla.	182	160,421	169	160,421
Biloxi-Gulfport, Miss.[1]	183	160,070	188	134,582
Killeen-Temple, Tex.[4]	184	159,794		
Green Bay, Wis.	185	158,244	170	158,244
Brockton, Mass.[6]	186	150,416	151	189,820
Parkersburg-Marietta, W. Va.-Ohio[5]	187	148,132		
Waco, Tex.	188	147,553	177	147,553
Lake Charles, La.	189	145,415	178	145,415
New Britain, Conn.	190	145,269	179	145,269
Yakima, Wash.[4]	191	144,971		
Amarillo, Tex.	192	144,396	181	144,396
Jackson, Mich.	193	143,274	182	143,274
Brownsville-Harlingen-San Benito, Tex.	194	140,368	184	140,368
Anderson, Ind.	195	138,451	185	138,451
Provo-Orem, Utah	196	137,776	186	137,776
Altoona, Pa.	197	135,356	187	135,356
St. Cloud, Minn.[4]	198	134,585		
Lynchburg, Va.[1]	199	133,258	196	123,474
Waterloo-Cedar Falls, Iowa[2]	200	132,916	189	132,916
Manchester, N.H.[1]	201	132,512	211	108,461
Alexandria, La.[5]	202	131,749		
Mansfield, Ohio	203	129,997	190	129,997
Wichita Falls, Tex.[1]	204	129,941	193	127,621
Muncie, Ind.	205	129,219	191	129,219
Petersburg-Colonial Heights-Hopewell, Va.[2]	206	128,809	192	128,809
Fayetteville-Springdale, Ark.[4]	207	127,846		
Norwalk, Conn.[1]	208	127,516	200	120,099
Decatur, Ill.	209	125,010	195	125,010
Anchorage, Alaska[4]	210	124,542		
Santa Cruz, Calif.[4]	211	123,790		
Abilene, Tex.[1]	212	122,164	207	113,959
Vineland-Millville-Bridgeton, N.J.	213	121,374	197	121,374
Reno, Nev.	214	121,068	198	121,068
Sarasota, Fla.[4]	215	120,413		
Fargo-Moorhead, N. Dak.-Minn.	216	120,238	199	120,238
Pueblo, Colo.	217	118,238	201	118,238
Kenosha, Wis.[1]	218	117,917	202	117,917
Florence, Ala.[4]	219	117,743		
Bay City, Mich.	220	117,339	203	117,339
Sioux City, Iowa-Nebr.	221	116,189	204	116,189
Tuscaloosa, Ala.	222	116,029	205	116,029
Danbury, Conn.[1]	223	115,538	235	78,405
Monroe, La.	224	115,387	206	115,387
Williamsport, Pa[4]	225	113,296		
Texarkana, Tex.-Texarkana, Ark.[3]	226	112,392	217	101,198
[illegible]	227			
Lafayette, La.	228	109,716	209	109,716
Lafayette-West Lafayette, Ind.	229	109,378	210	109,378
Tallahassee, Fla.[3]	230	109,355	216	103,047
Lawton, Okla.	231	108,144	212	108,144
Wilmington, N.C.	232	107,219	213	107,219
Fort Myers, Fla.[4]	233	105,216		
Gainesville, Fla	234	104,764	214	104,764
Bloomington-Normal, Ill.	235	104,389	215	104,389
Elmira, N.Y.[4]	236	101,537		
St. Joseph, Mo.[1]	237	98,828	226	86,915
Fitchburg-Leominster, Mass.	238	97,164	218	97,164
Tyler, Tex.	239	97,096	219	97,096
Pittsfield, Mass.[1]	240	96,817	233	79,727
Albany, Ga.[1]	241	96,683	224	89,639
Burlington, N.C.[1]	242	96,362		
Sioux Falls, S. Dak.	243	95,209	220	95,209
Gadsden, Ala.	244	94,144	221	94,144
Richland-Kennewick, Wash.[4]	245	93,356		
Odessa, Tex.[1]	246	91,805	222	91,805
Dubuque, Iowa	247	90,609	223	90,609
Billings, Mont.	248	87,367	225	87,367
Nashua, N.H.[1]	249	86,280	239	66,458
Pine Bluff, Ark.	250	85,329	227	85,329
Rochester, Minn.	251	84,104	228	84,104
Sherman-Denison, Tex.	252	83,225	229	83,225
Great Falls, Mont.	253	81,804	230	81,804
Columbia, Mo.	254	80,911	231	80,911
La Crosse, Wis.	255	80,468	232	80,468
Owensboro, Ky.	256	79,486	234	79,486
Laredo, Tex.	257	72,859	236	72,859
Lewiston-Auburn, Maine	258	72,474	237	72,474
San Angelo, Tex.	259	71,047	238	71,047
Bristol, Conn.	260	69,878	240	65,808
Midland, Tex.	261	65,433	241	65,433
Bryan-College Station, Tex.	262	57,978	242	57,978
Meriden, Conn.	263	55,959	243	55,959

(1) Change in area definition since 1970 census, without change of title.
(2) Change in title since 1970 census.
(3) Change in area definition since 1970 census, with change of title.
(4) New SMSA established since 1970 census.
(5) New SMSA established in November 1971, and area definition changed in April 1973.
(6) Merger of two existing SMSAs since 1970 census; rank and population given for 1970 definition refer to the larger of the two merged SMSAs.

Value of New Construction Put in Place in U.S.

Source: Bureau of the Census

	Annual		First 3 mos.		Percent Change	
	1971	1972	1972	1973	1971 to 1972	1972 to 1973
Total new construction	$109,238,000,000	$123,836,000,000	$25,615,000,000	$28,620,000,000	+13	+12
Private construction	79,367,000,000	93,640,000,000	19,294,000,000	21,764,000,000	+18	+13
Private residential (incl. farm)	43,268,000,000	54,186,000,000	10,739,000,000	12,334,000,000	+25	+15
Public construction	29,871,000,000	30,196,000,000	6,321,000,000	6,856,000,000	+1	+8

Marital Status by Sex

Source: Bureau of the Census

Based on the results of the 1970 Census of the population.

State	Total 14 yrs. & over	Male Single	Married Tot.	Married Sep.	Widowed	Divorced	Total 14 yrs. & over	Female Single	Married Tot.	Married Sep.	Widowed	Divorced
Alabama	1,180,777	27.5	67.1	1.7	2.9	2.5	1,318,246	20.9	61.6	2.5	14.0	3.5
Alaska	113,657	33.8	60.7	1.1	1.4	4.0	89,907	20.6	71.4	1.2	4.1	3.9
Arizona	616,883	27.6	66.5	1.1	2.4	3.4	654,017	21.1	63.5	1.6	10.2	5.2
Arkansas	677,205	25.1	68.5	1.4	3.5	2.8	744,748	18.4	63.3	1.9	14.7	3.5
California	7,200,777	29.2	64.0	1.7	2.4	4.4	7,612,951	21.2	61.1	2.5	11.0	6.6
Colorado	784,269	29.3	65.0	1.1	2.3	3.3	824,381	22.5	62.3	1.5	10.2	4.9
Connecticut	1,066,148	28.7	66.3	1.3	2.9	2.0	1,171,577	24.1	61.1	2.1	11.6	3.1
Delaware	188,807	27.9	67.0	2.2	2.8	2.4	205,376	22.8	62.6	2.8	11.2	3.3
Dist. of Col.	263,148	38.0	54.2	6.4	3.7	4.1	317,659	33.9	46.8	8.1	13.5	5.8
Florida	2,448,895	24.4	68.9	1.9	3.3	3.4	2,718,123	18.0	63.1	2.5	13.9	5.0
Georgia	1,580,841	28.3	66.4	2.0	2.6	2.7	1,731,422	20.9	62.1	3.2	13.3	3.7
Hawaii	289,176	36.2	58.8	0.7	2.2	2.8	264,612	25.7	63.0	0.9	7.5	3.8
Idaho	253,439	27.4	66.9	0.7	2.4	3.3	258,988	20.0	66.0	1.0	10.3	3.7
Illinois	3,890,046	28.7	65.4	1.4	3.2	2.8	4,273,777	22.9	60.5	2.3	12.6	4.0
Indiana	1,850,978	26.4	67.7	0.9	2.8	3.1	1,964,067	20.9	63.0	1.3	11.8	4.4
Iowa	990,235	27.4	67.2	0.6	3.2	2.2	1,085,637	22.0	61.9	0.7	13.1	3.0
Kansas	811,073	27.5	66.9	0.7	2.8	2.8	865,667	20.5	63.0	1.0	12.8	3.7
Kentucky	1,141,799	27.9	66.3	1.1	3.0	2.7	1,221,486	20.5	62.5	1.5	13.1	3.8
Louisiana	1,225,885	30.3	64.7	2.2	2.9	2.1	1,340,100	23.2	60.6	3.5	12.9	3.2
Maine	346,929	28.0	65.5	0.9	3.5	3.0	379,054	22.2	60.5	1.1	13.2	4.1
Maryland	1,366,887	28.7	66.3	2.7	2.7	2.1	1,475,767	22.8	62.7	3.7	11.1	3.3
Massachusetts	1,974,450	31.5	63.0	1.3	3.4	2.1	2,255,547	27.5	56.2	2.0	13.1	3.2
Michigan	3,066,393	28.5	65.9	1.4	2.8	2.9	3,293,574	22.9	62.3	2.1	10.8	4.0
Minnesota	1,317,587	30.6	64.5	0.7	2.8	2.1	1,418,152	25.3	60.4	0.9	11.5	2.8
Mississippi	744,715	29.9	64.5	2.0	3.5	2.1	823,336	22.5	60.0	3.0	14.6	2.9
Missouri	1,645,308	26.5	67.3	1.3	3.2	3.0	1,833,614	20.8	61.2	1.8	13.8	4.3
Montana	249,067	30.0	63.7	0.7	2.9	3.4	252,855	21.4	63.2	0.9	11.7	3.7
Nebraska	525,680	28.7	66.0	0.7	3.1	2.2	567,722	22.5	61.7	0.9	12.9	3.0
Nevada	179,430	25.6	65.2	1.8	2.3	6.9	174,714	17.2	67.0	2.0	8.2	7.7
New Hampshire	258,217	28.4	65.9	1.1	3.2	2.5	279,376	22.7	61.6	1.3	12.2	3.4
New Jersey	2,521,425	28.1	67.0	2.0	3.2	1.6	2,792,336	22.9	61.8	3.2	12.7	2.6
New Mexico	341,352	30.0	64.7	0.9	2.4	2.9	359,801	23.4	62.6	1.5	9.4	4.6
New York	6,397,876	30.1	64.7	2.1	3.5	1.7	7,297,798	25.1	58.7	3.8	13.3	2.8
North Carolina	1,801,631	29.2	66.4	2.1	2.5	1.8	1,932,810	21.8	63.2	3.0	12.4	2.6
North Dakota	223,926	34.4	61.3	0.4	2.7	1.6	222,124	24.5	62.1	0.6	11.7	1.7
Ohio	3,690,880	27.2	66.8	1.1	3.0	3.0	4,074,270	22.5	61.4	1.6	11.8	4.3
Oklahoma	920,467	25.3	68.1	0.9	2.8	3.8	1,001,092	17.7	63.3	1.3	13.8	5.2
Oregon	754,947	26.1	67.2	1.1	2.6	4.1	809,409	20.3	63.5	1.4	11.3	4.9
Pennsylvania	4,163,587	28.5	65.7	1.8	3.7	2.0	4,683,918	24.1	59.6	2.6	13.5	2.8
Rhode Island	345,459	31.5	63.1	1.2	3.3	2.1	368,509	25.0	58.8	1.9	12.9	3.3
South Carolina	901,191	31.6	64.2	2.1	2.6	1.7	958,508	23.1	61.5	3.2	13.2	2.2
South Dakota	237,278	32.1	63.0	0.5	3.1	1.9	245,994	23.8	61.3	0.8	12.7	2.2
Tennessee	1,378,997	26.6	67.8	1.5	2.9	2.7	1,527,547	20.3	62.5	2.2	13.2	4.0
Texas	3,906,008	27.3	67.0	1.3	2.5	3.2	4,195,817	20.4	63.2	1.9	11.7	4.7
Utah	355,852	30.0	65.6	0.6	1.8	2.6	375,329	24.5	62.9	0.9	8.9	3.8
Vermont	154,288	30.8	63.8	1.1	3.1	2.3	167,774	24.8	59.4	1.4	12.7	3.1
Virginia	1,617,230	29.7	65.6	1.8	2.5	2.2	1,747,387	22.1	63.2	2.6	11.5	3.3
Washington	1,239,721	28.2	65.3	1.1	2.4	4.0	1,280,861	20.6	63.6	1.5	10.8	5.0
West Virginia	620,693	27.5	66.6	1.2	3.4	2.5	685,531	21.3	61.3	1.5	14.1	3.3
Wisconsin	1,541,822	30.4	64.3	0.7	3.2	2.2	1,650,691	24.9	60.6	1.0	11.7	2.9
Wyoming	120,033	27.6	65.8	1.1	2.5	3.6	120,911	19.6	66.1	0.9	10.3	3.9
United States	71,492,364	28.6	65.8	1.5	2.9	2.7	77,914,869	22.4	61.3	2.3	12.4	3.9

Density of Population by States

By Square Mile, Land Area Only

State	1920	1960	1970	State	1920	1960	1970	State	1920	1960	1970
Ala	45.8	64.2	67.9	Ky	60.1	76.2	81.2	N. D.	9.2	9.1	8.9
Alaska*	0.1	0.4	0.5	La	39.6	72.2	81.0	Ohio	141.4	236.6	260.0
Ariz	2.9	11.5	15.6	Maine	25.7	31.3	32.1	Okla	29.2	33.8	37.2
Ark	33.4	34.2	37.0	Md	148.5	313.5	396.6	Oregon	8.2	18.4	21.7
Calif	22.0	100.4	127.6	Mass	479.2	657.3	727.0	Pa	194.5	251.4	262.3
Colo	9.1	16.9	21.3	Mich	63.8	137.6	156.2	R. I.	566.4	819.3	905.5
Conn	286.4	520.6	623.7	Minn	29.5	43.0	48.0	S. C.	55.2	78.7	85.7
Del	113.5	225.2	276.5	Miss	38.6	46.0	46.9	S. D.	8.3	9.0	8.8
D. C.	7,292.9	12,523.9	12,401.8	Mo	49.5	62.6	67.8	Tenn	56.1	86.2	94.9
Fla	17.7	91.5	125.5	Mont	3.8	4.6	4.8	Texas	17.8	36.4	42.7
Ga	49.3	67.8	79.0	Neb	16.9	18.4	19.4	Utah	5.5	10.8	12.9
Hawaii*	39.9	98.5	119.8	Nev	.7	2.6	4.4	Vt	38.6	42.0	47.9
Idaho	5.2	8.1	8.6	N. H.	49.1	67.2	81.7	Va	57.4	99.5	116.9
Illinois	115.7	180.4	199.4	N. J.	420.0	805.5	953.1	Wash	20.3	42.8	51.2
Indiana	81.3	128.8	143.9	N. M.	2.9	7.8	8.4	W. Va.	60.9	77.2	72.5
Iowa	43.2	49.2	50.5	N. Y.	217.9	350.6	381.3	Wis	47.6	72.6	81.1
Kan	21.6	26.6	27.5	N. C.	52.5	93.2	104.1	Wyo	2.0	3.4	3.4
								U.S.	*29.9	*50.6	57.5

*For purposes of comparison, Alaska and Hawaii included in above tabulation for 1920 even though not states then.

Number of inhabitants per sq. mi. of Land Area in U. S. (1790) 4.5; (1800) 6.1; (1810) 4.3; (1820) 5.5; (1830) 7.4; (1840) 9.8; (1850) 7.9; (1860) 10.6; (1870) 13.0; (1880) 16.9; (1890) 21.2; (1900) 25.6; (1910) 31.0; (1920) 35.5; (1930) 41.2; (1940) 44.2; (1950) 50.7; (1960) 50.6; (1970) 57.5 (Alaska and Hawaii included in 1960 and 1970.)

Urban and Rural Population by Race and Sex*

Source: Bureau of the Census

Urban	Total**	Male—White	Negro	Total**	Female—White	Negro
United States	71,958,564	62,210,243	8,657,231	77,366,366	66,562,997	9,710,087
Regions						
Northeast.............	18,784,554	16,653,329	1,955,446	20,665,264	18,229,729	2,259,373
North Central...........	19,487,418	17,247,113	2,111,447	20,993,342	18,525,851	2,335,499
South..................	19,543,387	15,624,618	3,786,610	20,996,574	16,587,614	4,277,171
West..................	14,143,205	12,685,183	803,728	14,711,186	13,219,803	838,044
Northeast						
New England...........	4,316,939	4,114,117	175,407	4,726,578	4,502,322	197,237
Middle Atlantic..........	14,467,615	12,539,212	1,780,039	15,938,686	13,727,407	2,062,136
North Central						
East North Central.......	14,506,612	12,621,941	1,793,477	15,585,235	13,505,243	1,986,690
West North Central.......	4,980,806	4,625,172	317,970	5,408,107	5,020,608	348,809
South						
South Atlantic...........	9,415,616	7,359,956	1,999,619	10,108,304	7,809,142	2,244,906
East South Central.......	3,333,530	2,595,228	728,948	3,654,413	2,797,862	847,417
West South Central	6,794,241	5,669,434	1,058,043	7,233,857	5,980,610	1,184,848
West						
Mountain................	2,969,168	2,831,054	86,251	3,085,811	2,946,955	83,810
Pacific.................	11,174,037	9,854,129	717,477	11,625,375	10,272,848	754,234
Rural						
United States	26,953,628	24,510,744	2,091,085	26,933,368	24,464,991	2,121,888
Regions						
Northeast	4,778,491	4,690,208	71,498	4,812,434	4,731,240	97,838
North Central...........	8,075,281	7,956,592	70,774	8,015,622	7,911,627	53,830
South..................	11,044,454	9,059,936	1,915,492	11,210,952	9,147,940	1,990,688
West..................	3,055,442	2,804,010	33,321	2,894,360	2,668,184	19,532
Northeast						
New England...........	1,397,940	1,383,636	9,119	1,400,206	1,388,699	6,635
Middle Atlantic	3,380,511	3,306,570	62,379	3,412,228	3,348,541	15,201
North Central						
East North Central.......	5,095,788	5,024,915	54,096	5,064,841	5,008,036	38,642
West North Central.......	2,979,493	2,931,677	16,678	2,950,781	2,903,591	15,188
South						
South Atlantic...........	5,528,039	4,445,567	1,052,993	5,619,378	4,497,730	1,090,978
East South Central.......	2,879,338	2,390,214	484,092	2,936,189	2,419,506	510,834
West South Central	2,637,077	2,224,155	378,407	2,655,385	2,230,704	388,876
West						
Mountain................	1,132,632	1,029,436	6,454	1,093,951	990,642	3,867
Pacific.................	1,922,810	1,774,574	26,867	1,800,409	1,677,542	15,665

*Figures in this table have not been adjusted to reflect latest Census revisions. These revisions do not significantly affect the ratios indicated.
**The difference between the total and the total of white and negro represents other races.

Population 65 Years Old and Over, 1960 and 1970, and Increase

Source: Bureau of the Census (Population in 1,000s)

STATES	All races—Population 1970	1960	Increase Amt	Pct	Negro and other races Pop 1970	% Inc '60-'70	STATES	All races—Population 1970	1960	Increase Amt	Pct	Negro and other races Pop 1970	% Inc '60-'70
Ala...	326	261	65	24.8	86	15.6	Mont.	69	65	3	5.1	1	20.0
Alaska	7	5	2	27.9	2	43.0	Nebr.	184	164	19	11.8	3	33.1
Ariz..	161	90	71	79.0	9	41.1	Nev..	31	18	13	70.4	2	91.1
Ark...	238	194	44	22.3	44	12.0	N. H..	78	68	11	15.8	—	180.2
Calif..	1,801	1,376	425	30.9	118	108.2	N. J..	697	560	137	24.4	43	61.1
Colo..	188	158	30	18.8	5	47.8	N. M..	71	51	19	37.7	4	61.0
Conn.	289	243	46	19.1	8	85.2	N. Y..	1,961	1,688	273	16.2	127	81.5
Dela..	44	36	8	22.6	5	34.9	N. C..	414	312	102	32.7	82	29.7
D. of C.	71	69	2	2.4	30	49.1	N. D..	66	59	8	13.3	1	36.0
Fla....	989	553	436	78.9	70	51.0	Ohio .	998	897	101	11.2	68	51.5
Ga...	367	291	77	26.4	89	18.3	Okla..	300	249	51	20.5	27	38.5
Hawaii	44	29	15	51.3	32	46.4	Ore...	227	184	43	23.5	4	83.1
Idaho	68	58	10	16.3	1	6.8	Penn.	1,272	1,129	144	12.7	79	51.9
Ill. ...	1,094	975	119	12.2	84	53.0	R. I...	104	90	14	16.1	2	48.7
Ind...	494	446	48	10.8	24	46.2	S. C..	191	151	40	26.8	54	12.6
Iowa .	350	328	23	6.9	3	23.6	S. D..	80	72	9	12.5	2	24.4
Kan..	266	240	26	10.8	10	20.6	Tenn.	384	309	75	24.3	57	21.8
Ky...	337	292	45	15.4	24	10.4	Texas	992	745	247	33.1	116	32.1
La....	307	242	65	26.9	90	17.1	Utah .	78	60	18	29.4	1	55.4
Maine	115	107	8	7.6	—	46.4	Vt....	47	44	4	8.6	—	55.0
Md...	300	227	73	32.3	41	48.1	Va....	366	289	77	26.7	65	20.0
Mass.	636	572	65	11.3	12	50.3	Wash.	322	279	43	15.4	8	60.8
Mich.	753	638	115	18.0	59	83.0	W. Va.	194	173	22	12.7	10	11.9
Minn.	409	354	55	15.4	4	49.4	Wis....	473	403	70	17.4	6	101.1
Miss..	222	190	32	17.0	80	7.4	Wyo...	30	26	4	16.6	1	43.1
Mo. ...	561	503	57	11.4	41	31.3	**Tot. U.S.**	**20,066**	**16,560**	**3,506**	**21.2**	**1,735**	**38.2**

Zero Population Growth? Hardly!

Even if U.S. families limited themselves to an average of only 2.1 children per family for the next 70 years—thus achieving zero population growth—the U.S. population in 2043 would be about 320,000,000. That is 110,000,000 more people than in 1973.

The average of 2.1 births per family is considered the "replacement level," the level at which the population, once stabilized, will neither increase nor decline.

At present, however, there are nearly twice as many girls about to begin their child-bearing years as there are women about to leave those years behind. While there are only 1,100,000 women who were 39 in 1973, there are 2,100,000 girls who were age 13. Even if the 13-year-olds only replace themselves, they would produce nearly twice as many babies as the 39-year-olds.

Low 1972 Fertility Rates

In fact, however, in 1972, the fertility rate fell to its lowest level in history, well below the 2.1 "replacement level," to 2.03 children per family. In the last half of 1972, the rate was 1.98 per family compared with 2.08 during the first half of the year.

This sharp drop in the rates resulted in a decline in the number of actual births to 3,256,000, off 9% from 1971. This decline of 303,000 births occurred in spite of the fact that women of child-bearing years increased by 878,000. The decrease in births is even more striking when compared to the figures for 1946. In that year 33,290,000 women had 3,411,000 babies. In 1972, 33% more women—44,340,000 had 4% fewer babies—3,256,000.

The 1972 figures on population growth were remarkably low in several other respects. The general fertility rate—births per thousand women age 15 to 44—dropped from 82.3 in 1971 to 73.4 in 1972, a new low. The previous low was 75.8 in 1936, during the Depression.

The crude birth rate—births per thousand population—dropped to a new low of 15.6. The previous low was in 1971 when there were 17.3 births per thousand population.

The total population growth rate was lower in 1972 than in any year since 1945. The population in 1972 grew at a rate of 0.78 per cent. This was less than half the peak rate of 1.83 per cent in 1956. In 1945, the growth rate was 0.71 per cent.

ZPG is 70 Years Away

Does this mean that zero population growth is at hand? No, it does not. Fertility rates change very rapidly. With the disproportionate number of young women in the population, a slight upward change in rate would mean millions of additional people. That is why 70 years of low fertility rates are required to achieve population stability at about 320 million people.

There are some grounds for hope, however. Seventy per cent of U.S. wives in the 18- to 24-year age group surveyed in 1972 said they expected to have no more than two children. Only 5 years before, about 56% of wives in the same age group said they planned to have more than two children. The average number of births expected by this age group in 1972, however, was 2.3, considerably more than the 2.1 replacement level.

New Projections

The sharp drop in fertility rates and birth expectations led the Census Bureau to revise its projected population figures for the year 2,000. One series of projections, based on 3.1 fertility rate, was discontinued, and new projections were developed based on a very low fertility rate of 1.8. In all other series, the total population in the year 2,000 was scaled down.

Series	Assumed Fertility Rate	Projection New	Old
B	3.1	(discontinued)	322,277,000
C	2.8	300,406,000	305,111,000
D	2.5	285,969,000	288,293,000
E	2.1	264,430,000	271,082,000
F	1.8	250,686,000	...

All four active series show an increase of births into the early 1980's. This results from the increase in the number of women of prime child-bearing age. By the year 2000, however, a fertility rate of 1.8 would result in a population in which 50% of all people would be over 36 years old, and only 20% would be under 15. By contrast, a fertility rate of 2.8 would result in a population in which 50% of all people would be under 29 and 28% would be under 15. (All 4 series assume a continuing net immigration of 400,000 people per year)

Other factors are also working in favor of a low fertility rate continuing for a few years. Women are marrying later and getting divorced more. These patterns tend to hold down births. The increasing number of women who work in jobs outside the home also works against rising fertility rates.

Finally, improved information and availibility of contraceptives and their increasing use directly affects the fertility rate. Steady liberalization of abortion laws has the same result.

Annual Levels of Net Growth, Births, Deaths: 1930 to 1972.

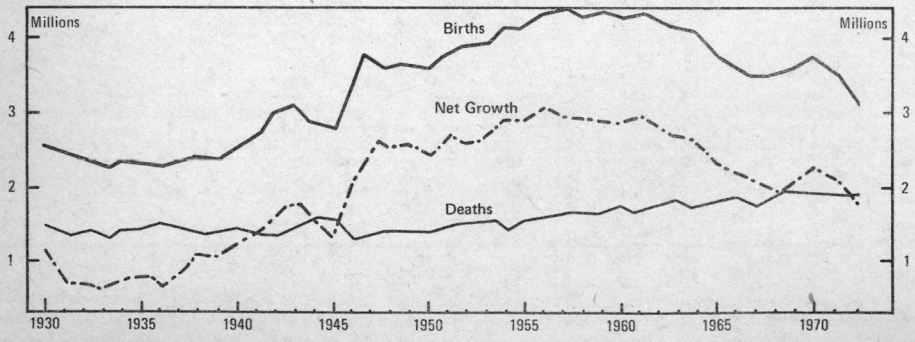

Special Censuses Made Between April 1, 1970 and Dec. 31, 1972

Source: Bureau of the Census

Place	Date	Census	Place	Date	Census
Arkansas			Lisle	Oct. 71	6,921
Bentonville	Dec. 72	6,391	Lombard	Aug. 71	37,052
Corning	June 72	3,136	Marion	Mar. 72	12,899
Fayetteville	Sept. 72	31,915	Mattoon	Nov. 72	19,270
Helena	Dec. 71	10,201	McHenry	Sept. 72	7,680
Jacksonville	Apr. 72	22,392	Milan	Sept. 72	5,053
Monticello	Nov. 72	7,034	Morris	Jan. 72	8,435
Sherwood	Nov. 72	3,576	Mundelein	Nov. 72	17,153
Springdale	July 72	18,848	Naperville	May 72	25,011
California			Niles	June 71	32,432
Firebaugh	Aug. 71	3,125	Normal	Nov. 72	31,343
Florida			Norridge	May 71	18,043
Sunrise (1)	Apr. 72	11,693	North Riverside	Oct. 71	7,849
Illinois			Oak Forest	Aug. 72	20,903
Addison	June 71	24,200	Oak Lawn	July 72	62,023
Arlington Hgts.	June 72	69,204	Orland Park	June 71	7,297
Auburn	Nov. 72	3,077	Palos Hills	Feb. 72	9,778
Barrington Hills	Aug. 71	2,920	*Park Forest So.	Apr. 72	3,232
Bartlett	Sept. 72	4,778	Richton Park	Mar. 72	4,786
Bellwood	Aug. 71	21,473	Romeoville	Oct. 71	15,336
Bethalto	Sept. 71	7,332	Round Lake Beach	Oct. 72	9,425
Bloomingdale	Oct. 71	4,434	Schaumburg	Feb. 72	25,155
Bolingbrook	Apr. 72	15,508	*Shorewood	June 72	2,809
Bradley	Oct. 72	10,631	Skokie	June 71	68,911
*Braidwood	May 72	2,503	South Holland	July 72	25,220
Bridgeview	Nov. 72	13,495	Villa Park	July 71	25,546
Broadview	Sept. 71	9,470	West Chicago	Oct. 71	11,624
Buffalo Grove	Apr. 72	15,653	Worth	Apr. 71	12,153
Calumet City	Sept. 72	35,808	**Minnesota**		
Carol Stream	Mar. 72	6,193	Brooklyn Park	July 72	29,945
*Channahon	Feb. 72	2,690	*Champlin	Sept. 72	6,298
Chatham	Apr. 72	3,252	Chanhassen	Nov. 71	5,054
Chicago Ridge	July 71	9,847	Chaska	Oct. 72	5,398
Crystal Lake	Nov. 72	16,049	**Nebraska**		
Deerfield	Aug. 72	18,867	La Vista	Sept. 71	6,388
Elgin	Aug. 72	56,937	**New York**		
Elk Grove Village	Nov. 72	22,860	Canadaigua	Apr. 71	10,753
Evergreen Park	July 71	25,981	New Windsor	Apr. 71	18,932
Galesburg	June 71	34,501	**North Dakota**		
Glenwood	Dec. 72	9,406	Grand Forks	Oct. 71	40,060
Greenville	Apr. 72	4,807	Jamestown	Nov. 71	15,078
Gurnee	Sept. 72	3,268	*Langdon	July 71	3,923
Hanover Park	July 72	19,609	Rugby	Oct. 72	3,150
Harwood Hgts.	July 71	8,837	West Fargo	Dec. 72	6,437
Hazel Crest	Jan. 72	11,657	**Pennsylvania**		
Hillside	June 71	9,466	Brackenridge	June 72	4,744
Hoffman Estates	Sept. 71	28,512	Rankin	May 71	3,550
Lake in the Hills	Mar. 72	4,081	**Wisconsin**		
Lake Zurich	Nov. 72	6,357	Fitchburg	Oct. 72	7,119
Lincolnshire	Aug. 72	3,238	Washington	May 72	6,452

*Prior to the special census these places were under 2,500 population. (1) Changed name June 4, 1971 from Sunrise Golf Village to Sunrise.

United States Area and Population: 1790 to 1970

Source: Bureau of the Census

Area figures represent area on indicated date including in some cases considerable areas not then organized or settled, and not covered by the census. Area figures have been adjusted to bring them into agreement with remeasurements made in 1940. *Changes in land and water area between 1960 and 1970 due to construction of dams and reservoirs. Also total area of Texas reduced approximately one square mile in the Chamizal agreement between U.S. and Mexico.

Census date	Area (square miles)			Population		Increase over preceding census	
	Gross	Land	Water	Number	Per sq. mile of land area	No.	%
1790 (Aug. 2)	888,811	864,746	24,065	3,929,214	4.5	(X)	(X)
1800 (Aug. 4)	888,811	864,746	24,065	5,308,483	6.1	1,379,269	35.1
1810 (Aug. 6)	1,716,003	1,681,828	34,175	7,239,881	4.3	1,931,398	36.4
1820 (Aug. 7)	1,788,006	1,749,462	38,544	9,638,453	5.5	2,398,572	33.1
1830 (June 1)	1,788,006	1,749,462	38,544	12,866,020	7.4	3,227,567	33.5
1840 (June 1)	1,788,006	1,749,462	38,544	17,069,453	9.8	4,203,433	32.7
1850 (June 1)	2,992,747	2,940,042	52,705	23,191,876	7.9	6,122,423	35.9
1860 (June 1)	3,022,387	2,969,640	52,747	[1]31,443,321	10.6	8,251,445	35.6
1870 (June 1)	3,022,387	2,969,640	52,747	[1]39,818,449	[1]13.4	8,375,128	26.6
1880 (June 1)	3,022,387	2,969,640	52,747	50,155,783	16.9	10,337,334	26.0
1890 (June 1)	3,022,387	2,969,640	52,747	62,947,714	21.2	12,791,931	25.5
1900 (June 1)	3,022,387	2,969,834	52,553	75,994,575	25.6	13,046,861	20.7
1910 (Apr. 15)	3,022,387	2,969,565	52,822	91,972,266	31.0	15,977,691	21.0
1920 (Jan. 1)	3,022,387	2,969,451	52,936	105,710,620	35.6	13,738,354	14.9
1930 (Apr. 1)	3,022,387	2,977,128	45,259	122,775,046	41.2	17,064,426	16.1
1940 (Apr. 1)	3,022,387	2,977,128	45,259	131,669,275	44.2	8,894,229	7.2
1950 (Apr. 1)[2]	3,615,211	3,552,206	63,005	151,325,798	42.6	19,161,229	14.5
1960 (Apr. 1)[2]	3,615,123	3,540,911	74,212	179,323,175	50.5	27,997,377	18.5
1970* (Apr. 1)[2]	3,615,122	3,536,855	78,267	203,211,926	57.5	23,888,751	13.3

X Not applicable. (1) Revised to include adjustments for underenumeration in Southern States; unrevised number is 38,558,371. (2) includes Alaska and Hawaii.

Incidence of Poverty for Families (in thousands)

Source: Bureau of the Census

Mar. 1971 Persons Below Low-Income Levels	Total	White	Black
U.S. Total	25,522	17,480	7,650
Metropolitan areas	13,378	9,017	4,129
Central cities	8.165	4,770	3,228
Outside central cities	5,213	4,247	901
Nonmetropolitan areas	12,142	8,464	3,520
North and West	14,039	11,377	2,357
Metropolitan areas	9,007	6,628	2,191
Central cities	5,414	3,363	1,901
Outside central cities	3,593	3,265	289
Nonmetropolitan areas	5,032	4,750	166
South	11,480	6,103	5,292
Metropolitan areas	4,371	2,390	1,938
Central cities	2,752	1,407	1,325
Outside central cities	1,619	982	612
Nonmetropolitan areas	7,109	3,714	3,354

Family Status	Below Low-Income Level Total	White	Black
In families	20,499	13,359	6,810
Male heads	3,280	2,604	625
Female heads	1,934	1,097	820
Members under 18 yrs.[1]	10,493	6,208	4,101
Other family members	4,792	3,450	1,264
Unrelated individuals	5,023	4,121	840
Nonfarm			
In families	18,690	12,007	6,385
Male heads	2,893	2,278	568
Female heads	1,887	1,066	805
Members under 18 yrs.[1]	9,654	5,634	3,857
Other family members	4,257	3,029	1,155
Unrelated Individuals	4,889	4,013	815
Farm			
In families	1,809	1,352	425
Male heads	388	326	57
Female heads	47	31	15
Members under 18 yrs.[1]	839	574	244
Other family members	535	421	109
Unrelated individuals	134	108	25

[1] Other than head or wife.

Family: A group of two or more persons related by blood, marriage, or adoption and residing together.

Head: One person in each family was designated as the head and usually regarded as head by members of the family. Women are not classified as heads if their husbands live with them.

Size of family: Number of persons living together who are related to each other by blood, marriage or adoption.

Unrelated individuals: Persons 14 years or older not living with relatives.

Low-Income Level by Family Size and Sex of Head

Number of Family members	Total	Total	Nonfarm Male	Female	Total	Farm Male	Female
1 member	$1,947	$1,954	$2,044	$1,898	$1,651	$1,697	$1,602
Under 65 yrs.	2,005	2,010	2,092	1,935	1,727	1,778	1,644
65 years and over	1,852	1,861	1,879	1,855	1,586	1,597	1,576
2 members	2,507	2,525	2,534	2,471	2,131	2,138	2,036
Head under 65 yrs.	2,569	2,604	2,619	2,522	2,218	2,225	2,104
Head 65 & over	2,328	2,348	2,349	2,336	1,994	1,996	1,972
3 members	3,080	3,099	3,113	3,003	2,628	2,635	2,511
4 members	3,944	3,968	3,970	3,948	3,385	3,387	3,345
5 members	4,654	4,680	4,684	4,639	4,000	4,002	3,963
6 members	5,212	5,260	5,263	5,220	4,490	4,491	4,441
7 or more members	6,407	6,468	6,486	6,317	5,518	5,521	5,472

Poverty by Age, Race and Sex (in thousands)

Age and Sex (Mar., 1971)	Total	White Number of Poor	% of Total	Total	Black Number of Poor	% of Total
Male[1]	86,276	7,359	8.5	10,750	3,318	30.9
Under 6 years	9,080	1,129	12.4	1,670	715	42.8
6 to 15 years[1]	17,723	1,853	10.5	2,823	1,187	42.0
16 to 21 years	8,901	756	8.5	1,250	405	32.4
22 to 44 years	25,111	1,316	5.2	2,752	442	16.1
45 to 54 years	10,103	439	4.3	949	161	17.0
55 to 59 years	4,313	253	5.9	389	75	19.3
60 to 64 years	3,575	340	9.5	304	80	26.3
65 years and over	7,470	1,273	17.0	613	253	41.3
Female[1]	91,076	10,123	11.1	11,967	4,321	36.1
Under 6 years	8,657	964	11.1	1,652	685	41.5
6 to 15 years[1]	17,031	1,802	10.6	2,809	1,152	41.0
16 to 21 years	9,464	916	9.7	1,404	470	33.5
22 to 44 years	26,023	2,023	7.8	3,296	922	28.0
45 to 54 years	10,818	691	6.4	1,153	340	29.5
55 to 59 years	4,747	452	9.5	477	173	36.3
60 to 64 years	4,122	565	13.7	368	150	40.8
65 years and over	10,214	2,710	26.5	808	429	53.1

[1] Excluding 14 and 15-year-old heads of household and spouses.

The tables above show several interesting facts about poverty in the U.S. In the North and West, poverty tends to be concentrated in the cities, while in the South most poverty is rural.

Among whites less than half the poor are children, while among blacks well over half are children. White persons living apart from relatives constitute a far larger proportion of the white poor than is the case with blacks. This is partly due to the longer life span of whites which tends to create a larger proportion of aged poor whites, as shown in the bottom table.

The middle table shows the upper limit of official poverty standards. A nonfarm family of four with only $3,968 annual income is classified as poor.

The bottom table suggests that women are less likely than men to begin their lives in poverty; but in old age, they are far more likely to be poor.

What Price Welfare?

Source: Department of Health Education and Welfare, Social and Rehabilitation Service

State	Per capita inc. 1971	Cost per inhabitant[1]	Federal funding %, FY72[10]	Recipients per 1,000 pop., 12-72	Avg. monthly payment per recipient, Dec., 1972 Old-age	Blind	Dis-abled	AFDC[2]	GA[3]
Ala.	$3,087	$39.77	78.3	83.7	$ 71.61	$102.36	$ 80.37	$21.28	$12.50
Alaska	4,875	43.24	25.4	51.1	125.46	167.16	170.30	71.51	38.72
Ariz.	3,913	25.06	69.1	50.3	79.97	88.13	88.94	34.60	69.62
Ark.	3,078	38.26	78.7	77.0	69.42	90.46	82.83	31.90	5.63
Cal.	4,640	88.59	46.9	99.4	111.94	166.41[9]	149.18	63.56	76.49
Colo.	4,153	45.18	54.4	63.8	76.10	77.46	81.32	54.06	86.11
Conn.	4,995	36.49	45.4	49.7	107.22	109.13	138.48	72.82	63.42
Del.	4,673	33.16	49.5	73.1	91.13	127.08	117.37	33.96	29.88
D.C.	5,870	77.38	47.6	161.8	86.91	120.72	110.62	58.37	120.32
Fla.	3,930	19.84	67.9	62.1	79.58	91.63	91.40	27.44	(5)
Ga.	3,599	38.25	73.3	99.2	57.83	74.00	68.16	30.01	24.87
Ha.	4,738	48.57	41.2	85.4	105.95	134.14	147.78	85.57	69.17
Idaho	3,409	22.84	69.5	37.1	70.78	92.84	95.52	53.21	(5)
Ill.	4,775	45.08	45.4	83.1	66.69	107.58	106.77	63.13	90.94
Ind.	4,027	13.02	55.3	36.9	54.81	82.29	61.30	40.54	(5)
Iowa	3,877	31.70	56.4	40.0	131.82	126.40	159.53	54.75	(5)
Kan.	4,192	30.67	51.9	42.9	66.19	79.92	79.44	58.69	70.03
Ky.	3,306	34.02	74.4	69.1	61.77	79.93	81.97	34.32	(5)
La.	3,252	50.89	73.8	107.1	73.98	85.77	64.12	23.81	51.36
Me.	3,375	40.46	66.3	95.5	83.76	110.72	110.02	39.39	21.76
Md.	4,522	30.27	44.5	64.9	66.12	100.33	91.56	45.35	90.67
Mass.	4,562	66.78	46.1	71.5	105.52	149.69	147.49	95.01[8]	83.80
Mich.	4,430	46.15	45.8	81.8	70.68	114.27	111.29	67.96	96.13
Minn.	4,032	32.90	52.5	42.6	64.98	104.15	93.91	74.34	51.13
Miss.	2,788	38.60	82.4	126.7	56.95	67.49	66.65	14.41	13.87
Mo.	3,940	38.75	62.7	76.3	82.99	104.95[9]	86.67	30.99	63.29
Mont.	4,000	21.10	60.5	40.0	81.01	97.50	98.50	40.10	20.99
Neb.	4,030	19.65	59.7	35.8	64.11	125.45	102.01	43.67	(5)
Nev.	4,822	17.45	52.0	34.0	75.88	97.87	(4)	36.90	(5)
N.H.	3,796	29.64	57.4	40.1	171.82	164.60	151.09	68.22	34.12
N.J.	4,811	50.16	47.0	62.7	78.46	97.98	111.65	71.68	(6)
N.M.	3,298	35.71	74.9	71.9	54.70	73.59	75.10	32.64	63.68
N.Y.	5,000	84.46	43.1	97.1	97.76	114.13	119.75	75.83	74.12
N.C.	3,424	22.52	72.1	45.2	77.73	90.78	84.07	32.71	11.98
N.D.	3,538	25.27	70.6	32.6	89.23	110.11	105.31	56.60	19.21
Ohio	4,175	28.05	46.5	60.0	62.21	83.46	86.09	44.94	47.24
Okla.	3,515	52.61	68.6	70.5	66.97	108.49	·101.51	39.69	7.74
Ore.	3,959	31.77	54.0	46.8	69.42	105.36	94.68	51.73	71.69
Pa.	4,147	54.16	44.4	69.9	122.85	144.51	108.19	65.29	108.60
P.R.	(5)	13.94	27.3	111.8	18.35	13.59	13.41	9.13	(5)
R.I.	4,126	49.00	46.8	76.2	70.19	103.53	108.19	62.84	43.46
S.C.	3,142	14.09	78.5	53.7	51.98	71.43	61.71	21.77	34.98
S.D.	3,441	25.00	65.0	40.8	61.31	91.09	76.76	50.37	12.53
Tenn.	3,300	29.01	75.2	67.7	55.48	76.84	72.58	30.76	11.82
Tex.	3,726	27.73	69.5	56.9	54.57	86.13	75.97	30.80	(5)
Utah	3,442	26.85	68.7	53.3	66.38	106.67	89.41	54.61	68.60
Vt.	3,638	39.17	63.4	54.5	72.53	107.38	114.18	66.86	(5)
Va.	3,899	19.92	60.2	43.9	74.87	97.34	94.90	47.73	60.98
Wash.	4,132	43.24	47.0	60.8	71.72	110.56	114.09	65.93	71.74
W. Va.	3,275	31.51	75.0	58.9	103.42	100.36	90.52	41.56	13.80
Wis.	3,912	26.82	51.5	40.8	154.28	102.03	142.89	81.24	53.85
Wyo.	3,929	15.92	56.7	27.6	65.89	(7)	80.98	47.78	27.12
U.S.	**4,156**	**45.33[11]**	**51.1[11]**	**71.8[11]**	**80.01[11]**	**112.83**	**106.05[11]**	**53.95[11]**	**72.72[12]**

(1) Amount expended per inhabitant in money payments to public assistance recipients in fiscal year 1971; does not include medical or miscellaneous payments. (2) Aid to Families with Dependent Children. (3) General Assistance: eligibility criteria vary greatly from state to state. (4) No program. (5) Data not available. (6) $145.33, including a variety of misc. payments not included in other states. (7) Fewer than 50 recipients. (8) Includes special payments for special needs in Mass. (9) Data includes payments made without federal participation. (10) Includes most medical payments. (11) Includes Guam and Virgin Islands. (12) Including Guam, the Virgin Islands, and an estimated portion of New Jersey payments.

Recipients and Payments, 1950-1971

Category	1955, Dec.	1960, Dec.	1965, Dec.	1967, Dec.	1969, Dec.	1970, Dec.	1971, Dec.
Old-age: Recipients	2,538,000	2,305,000	2,087,000	2,073,000	2,074,000	2,082,000	2,024,000
Total amt.	$127,003,000	$135,759,000	$131,674,000	$140,563,000	$153,278,000	$161,642,000	$156,585,000
Avg. amt.	$50.05	$58.90	$63.10	$70.15	$73.90	$77.65	$77.35
[1]Avg. real $	53.50	56.70	56.85	59.35	56.30	56.05	62.85
AFDC: Recipients[2]	2,192,000	3,073,000	4,396,000	5,309,000	7,313,000	9,660,000	10,651,000
Total amt.	$51,472,000	$87,051,000	$144,355,000	$184,577,000	$330,113,000	$486,232,000	$557,003,000
Avg. amt.	$23.50	$28.35	$32.85	$39.50	$45.15	$49.65	$51.65
[1]Avg. real $	25.10	27.25	29.60	33.40	34.40	35.85	41.95
Blind: Recipients	104,000	107,000	85,100	82,600	80,600	81,000	80,300
Total amt.	$5,803,000	$7,215,000	$6,922,000	$7,255,000	$7,956,000	$8,447,000	$8,548,000
Avg. amt.	$55.55	$67.45	$81.35	$90.45	$98.75	$104.35	$106.40
[1]Avg. real $	59.40	64.95	73.25	76.50	75.20	75.35	86.45
Disabled: Recipients	241,000	369,000	557,000	646,000	803,000	935,000	1,068,000
Total amt.	$11,750,000	$20,711,000	$37,035,000	$47,254,000	$72,412,000	$91,325,000	$108,947,000
Avg. amt.	$48.75	$56.15	$66.50	$80.60	$90.15	$97.65	$101.95
[1]Avg. real $	52.15	54.05	59.95	68.20	68.65	70.50	82.80

(1) Dollar amounts adjusted to represent actual purchasing power in terms of the average value of the dollar during the period 1957-1959 based on the consumers' price index for moderate-income families in large cities maintained by the Bureau of Labor statistics. (2) Includes as recipients the children and one or both parents or one caretaker relative other than a parent in families in which the requirements of such adults were considered in determining the amount of assistance.

Jewish Population by Countries and Cities

Source: Jewish Statistical Bureau, Dr. H. S. Linfield, Exec. Secy. Figures are 1971 estimates

North America	6,396,000	Australia and New Zealand	77,000
Central and South America	774,300	Africa	184,600
Europe	4,113,950		
Asia	3,233,050	**World Total (a)**	14,778,900

Europe

Albania	300
Austria	9,000
Belgium	41,000
Bulgaria	7,000
Czechoslovakia	15,000
Denmark	6,000
Finland	1,500
France	550,000
Germany	30,000
Gibraltar	650
Great Britain	450,000
Greece	6,500
Hungary	80,000
Irish Free State	5,500
Italy	35,000
Luxembourg	1,000
Malta	50
Netherlands	30,000
Norway	750
Poland	8,000
Portugal	700
Romania	100,000
Soviet Union	2,654,000
Spain	9,000
Sweden	15,000
Switzerland	20,000
Turkey	40,000
Yugoslavia	7,000

North America

Canada	300,000
United States	6,060,000
Mexico	36,000

Central and South America

Argentina	500,000
Barbados	100
Bolivia	2,000
Brazil	150,000
Chile	32,000
Colombia	10,000
Costa Rica	1,500
Cuba	1,700
Curacao	700
Dominican Rep.	350
Dutch Guiana	500
Ecuador	2,000
El Salvador	300
Guatemala	1,500
Haiti	200
Honduras	150
Jamaica	600
Nicaragua	200
Panama	2,000
Paraguay	1,200
Peru	5,000
Trinidad	300
Uruguay	50,000
Venezuela	12,000

Asia

Afghanistan	800
Burma	200
Cyprus	50
China	100
Hong Kong	200
India	15,000
Indonesia	100
Iran	80,000
Iraq	2,500
Israel	3,124,000
Japan	1,000
Lebanon	3,000
Pakistan	300
Philippines	500
Singapore	800
Syria	4,000
Yemen	500

Africa

Abyssinia	12,000
Algeria	1,500
Congo	500
Egypt	1,000
Kenya	700
Libya	100
Morocco	35,000
Rhodesia	5,000
Tunisia	8,000
Union of South Africa	120,000
Zambia	800

Australia and New Zealand

Australia	72,000
New Zealand	5,000

ESTIMATED JEWISH POPULATION IN FOREIGN CITIES

Amsterdam	12,000
Antwerp	13,000
Ascalon[1]	39,000
Ashdod[1]	40,000
Beersheba[1]	80,000
Berlin	6,000
Bet Shean[1]	12,500
Birmingham	6,300
B'nai B'rak	70,000
Bordeaux	6,500
Brussels	24,000
Bucharest	50,000
Budapest	65,000
Buenos Aires	350,000
Casablanca	22,000
Copenhagen	6,000
Czernowitz	70,000
Elat[1]	13,000
Glasgow	13,500
Haifa[1]	219,000
Istanbul	32,000
Jerusalem[1]	301,000
Johannesburg	57,500
Kharkov	80,000
Kiev	220,000
Leeds	18,000
Leningrad	165,000
Liverpool	7,500
Lod (Lydda)[1]	28,000
London (gr.)	280,000
Lyons	20,000
Marseilles	65,000
Manchester and Salford	31,500
Melbourne	35,000
Milan	9,500
Montreal	113,000
Moscow	285,000
Nazareth[1]	35,000
Nazareth Illet[1]	15,000
Nice	20,000
Ottawa	6,000
Paris	300,000
Petach Tikvah	80,000
Ramath Gan[1]	112,500
Rehovoth	35,000
Rio de Janeiro	50,000
Rome	15,000
Safed	13,000
Santiago	30,000
Sao Paulo	65,000
Stockholm	7,500
Strasbourg	12,000
Sydney	28,000
Teheran	50,000
Tel Aviv-Jaffa[1]	382,500
Tiberias[1]	23,500
Toronto	97,000
Toulouse	18,000
Vancouver	8,000
Vienna	8,000
Warsaw	5,000
Winnipeg	21,000
Zurich	6,200

(1.) Includes some Christians, Mohammedans and others.

ESTIMATED JEWISH POPULATION IN LARGE U. S. CITIES

Albany	13,500
Alexandria, Arlington & FairfaxCos.,Va.	13,000
Atlanta	16,000
Atlantic City*	10,000
Baltimore	100,000
Bergen County	100,000
Boston*	180,000
Bridgeport*	14,500
Buffalo	25,000
Camden	18,000
Chicago*	270,000
Cincinnati	28,000
Cleveland	80,000
Columbus	13,000
Dallas	22,000
Denver	25,000
Detroit	80,000
Elizabeth*	20,000
Hartford	24,000
Hollywood, Fla.	20,000
Houston	20,000
Jersey City	12,000
Kansas City	22,000
Long Beach, Cal.	15,000
Los Angeles*	535,000
Lynn	19,000
Miami*	188,000
Milwaukee	24,000
Minneapolis	22,000
Montg'y Co., Md	57,000
New Brunswick	13,500
New Haven	20,000
New Orleans	10,000
New York City	1,836,000
Manhattan	250,000
Bronx	395,000
Brooklyn	760,000
Queens	420,000
Richmond	11,000
N. Y. City environs:	
Nassau Co.	372,000
Suffolk Co	42,000
Westchester Co.	131,000
Newark:	
Essex Co	100,000
Oakland:	
Alameda and Contra Costa Co.*	19,000
Orange Co. Calif	30,000
Passaic	10,500
Paterson*	26,000
Philadelphia*	350,000
Phoenix*	13,500
Pittsburgh	45,000
Prince George County, Md	28,000
Providence*	23,000
Richmond, Va	10,000
Rochester	21,500
Rockland Co., N.Y.	25,000
St. Louis	60,000
St. Paul	10,000
San Diego	13,000
San Francisco*	73,000
Seattle	12,500
Springfield, Mass	11,000
Stamford	11,000
Syracuse	11,000
Trenton, N.J	10,000
Washington	112,000
Worcester	10,000

*Indicates greater area.

What to Do If You Cannot Get a Birth Certificate

Although a birth certificate is of great value in situations requiring documentation of date and place of birth, such as qualifying for Social Security or Medicare benefits, in obtaining a passport or in qualifying for certain jobs, many Americans do not possess such a certificate and may not be able to obtain one because the birth was not recorded or because records are not available.

In most instances a transcript from early census records is acceptable as a substitute for a birth certificate. The Bureau of the Census maintains a special office and a staff of trained researchers especially to provide this service, and charges a fee to cover the cost.

You may obtain an application form at your local Social Security Office or from the Personal Census Service Branch, Bureau of the Census, Pittsburg, Kan. 66762. Your application form should be accompanied by a check or money order in the amount of $5 for a regular search, or $6 for an expedited search, additional copies $1.00 each.

Transcripts from a regular search of census records usually are available within 4 to 6 weeks; from an expedited search in about 2 weeks.

Applications should be made by the person himself or by a legally authorized representative.

It is necessary to supply the information of the name of the street, city, county and State, and the name of the parent or head of the household with whom living at the time of a census, usually taken in the spring of years ending in zero, such as 1970. Rural residents should furnish rural route number and also the distance and direction of the residence from the nearest town. It is also necessary to tell why the record is needed, so the Census Bureau can determine which year would provide the most acceptable information.

Black Population by States

Source: Bureau of the Census

States (1970)

State	Number	State	Number	State	Number	State	Number
Ala.	903,467	Ill.	1,425,674	Mont.	1,995	R. I.	25,338
Alaska	8,911	Ind.	357,464	Neb.	39,911	S. C.	789,041
Ariz.	53,344	Iowa	32,596	Nev.	27,762	S. D.	1,627
Ark.	352,445	Kan.	106,977	N. H.	2,505	Tenn.	621,261
Calif.	1,400,143	Ken.	230,793	N. J.	770,292	Texas	1,399,005
Colo.	66,411	La.	1,086,832	N. M.	19,555	Utah	6,617
Conn.	181,177	Maine	2,800	N. Y.	2,168,949	Vt.	761
Del.	78,276	Md.	699,479	N. C.	1,126,478	Va.	861,368
D. of C.	537,712	Mass.	175,817	N. D.	2,494	Wash.	71,308
Fla.	1,401,651	Mich.	991,066	Ohio	970,477	W. Va.	67,342
Ga.	1,187,149	Minn.	34,868	Okla.	171,892	Wis.	128,224
Hawaii	7,573	Miss.	815,770	Ore.	26,308	Wyo.	2,568
Idaho	2,130	Mo.	480,172	Pa.	1,016,514	Total	22,580,289

50 Cities with the Largest Negro Population

Source: Bureau of the Census

City and State	Rank	1970 Number	%	1960 Number	City and State	Rank	1970 Number	%	1960 Number
New York City	1	1,666,636	21.2	1,087,931	San Francisco	27	96,078	13.4	74,383
Chicago, Ill.	2	1,102,620	32.7	812,637	Buffalo, N.Y.	28	94,329	20.4	70,904
Detroit, Mich.	3	660,428	43.7	482,223	Gary, Ind.	29	92,695	52.8	69,123
Philadelphia	4	653,791	33.6	529,240	Nashville-Davidson, Tenn.	30	87,851	19.6	76,437
Washington, D.C.	5	537,712	71.1	411,737	Norfolk, Va.	31	87,261	28.3	78,806
Los Angeles	6	503,606	17.9	334,916	Louisville, Ky.	32	86,040	23.8	70,075
Baltimore, Md.	7	420,210	46.4	325,589	Ft. Worth, Texas	33	78,324	19.9	56,440
Houston, Texas	8	316,551	25.7	215,037	Miami, Fla.	34	76,156	22.7	65,213
Cleveland, Ohio	9	287,841	38.3	250,818	Dayton, Ohio	35	74,284	30.5	57,288
New Orleans	10	267,308	45.0	233,514	Charlotte, N.C.	36	72,972	30.3	56,248
Atlanta, Ga.	11	255,051	51.3	186,464	Mobile, Ala.	37	67,356	35.4	65,619
St. Louis, Mo.	12	254,191	40.9	214,377	Shreveport, La.	38	62,152	34.1	56,607
Memphis, Tenn.	13	242,513	38.9	184,320	Jackson, Miss.	39	61,063	39.7	51,556
Dallas, Texas	14	210,238	24.9	129,242	Compton, Calif.	40	55,781	71.0	28,265
Newark, N.J.	15	207,458	54.2	138,035	Tampa, Fla.	41	54,720	19.7	46,244
Indianapolis	16	134,320	18.0	98,049	Jersey City, N.J.	42	54,595	21.0	36,692
Birmingham	17	126,388	42.0	135,113	Flint, Mich.	43	54,237	28.1	34,521
Cincinnati, Ohio	18	125,070	27.6	108,754	Savannah, Ga.	44	53,111	44.9	53,035
Oakland, Calif	19	124,710	34.5	83,618	San Diego, Calif.	45	52,961	7.6	34,435
Jacksonville, Fla.	20	118,158	22.3	105,655	Toledo, Ohio	46	52,915	13.8	40,015
Kansas City	21	112,005	22.1	83,146	Oklahoma City	47	50,103	13.7	37,529
Milwaukee	22	105,088	14.7	62,458	San Antonio	48	50,041	7.6	41,605
Pittsburgh	23	104,904	20.2	100,692	Rochester, N.Y.	49	49,647	16.8	23,586
Richmond, Va.	24	104,766	42.0	91,972	E. St. Louis, Ill.	50	48,368	69.1	36,338
Boston, Mass.	25	104,707	16.3	63,165					
Columbus, Ohio	26	99,627	18.5	77,140					

1970 Final Count of Japanese, Chinese and Filipino by State

Source: Bureau of the Census

State	Japanese	Chinese	Filipino	State	Japanese	Chinese	Filipino
Ala.	1,079	626	540	Mon.	574	289	236
Alaska	916	228	1,198	Neb.	1,314	661	324
Ariz.	2,394	3,878	1,253	Nev.	1,087	955	817
Ark.	587	743	289	N. H.	360	420	157
Calif.	213,280	170,131	138,859	N. J.	5,681	9,233	5,623
Colo.	7,831	1,489	1,068	N. M.	940	563	386
Conn.	1,621	2,209	2,177	N. Y.	20,351	81,378	14,279
Del.	359	559	392	N. C.	2,104	1,255	905
D. of C.	651	2,582	1,662	N. D.	239	165	204
Fla.	4,090	3,133	5,092	Ohio	5,555	5,305	3,490
Ga.	1,836	1,584	1,253	Okla.	1,408	999	612
Hawaii	217,307	52,039	93,915	Ore.	6,843	4,814	1,633
Idaho	2,255	498	206	Pa.	5,461	7,053	4,560
Ill.	17,299	14,474	12,654	R. I.	629	1,093	1,761
Ind.	2,279	2,115	1,365	S. C.	826	521	1,222
Iowa	1,009	993	614	S. D.	221	165	204
Kan.	1,584	1,233	758	Tenn.	1,160	1,610	846
Ken.	1,095	558	612	Texas	6,537	7,635	3,442
La.	1,123	1,340	1,249	Utah	4,713	1,281	392
Maine	348	206	453	Vt.	134	173	53
Md.	3,733	6,520	5,170	Va.	3,500	2,805	7,496
Mass.	4,393	14,012	2,361	Wash.	20,335	9,201	11,462
Mich.	5,221	6,407	3,657	W. Va.	368	373	722
Minn.	2,603	2,422	1,456	Wis.	2,648	2,700	1,209
Miss.	461	1,441	475	Wyo.	566	292	108
Mo.	2,382	2,815	2,010	Total	591,290	435,062	343,060

U.S. Places of 2,500 or More Population—with ZIP Codes

Source: U. S. Bureau of the Census; U.S. Post Office Department

The listings below show the official urban population of the United States. "Urban population" is defined as all persons living in (a) places of 2,500 inhabitants or more, incorporated as cities, villages, boroughs (except Alaska), and towns (except in New England, New York, New Jersey, Pennsylvania and Wisconsin), but excluding those persons living in the rural portions of extended cities; (b) unincorporated places of 2,500 inhabitants or more; and (c) other territory, incorporated or unincorporated, included in urbanized areas.

The non-urban portion of an extended city contains one or more areas, each at least 5 square miles in extent and with a population density of less than 100 persons per square mile. The area or areas constitute at least 25 percent of the legal city's land area or a total of 25 square miles or more."

In New England, New York, New Jersey, Pennsylvania, and Wisconsin, minor civil divisions called "towns" often include rural areas and one or more urban areas. Only the urban areas of these "towns" are included here, except in the case of New England where entire town populations, which may include some rural population, are shown in italics. Boroughs in Alaska may contain one or more urban areas which are included here.

The ZIP Code of each place appears before the name of that place, if it is obtainable.

CAUTION—Where an asterisk (*) appears before the ZIP Code, ask your local postmaster for the correct ZIP Code for a specific address within the place listed.

ZIP Code	Place	1970	1960
	Alabama		
36310	Abbeville	2,996	2,524
35007	Alabaster	2,642	1,623
35950	Albertville	9,963	8,250
35010	Alexander City	12,358	13,140
35442	Aliceville	2,851	3,194
36420	Andalusia	10,092	10,263
36201	Anniston	31,533	33,657
	Anniston Northwest	6,609	
35016	Arab	4,399	2,989
35611	Athens	14,360	9,330
36502	Atmore	8,293	8,173
35954	Attalla	7,510	8,257
36830	Auburn	22,767	16,261
36507	Bay Minette	6,727	5,197
36509	Bayou La Batre	2,664	2,572
35020	Bessemer	33,663	33,054
*35203	Birmingham	300,910	340,887
35226	Bluff Park	12,431	
35957	Boaz	5,635	4,654
36426	Brewton	6,747	6,309
35740	Bridgeport	2,908	2,906
36010	Brundidge	2,709	2,523
35215	Center Point	15,675	
35042	Centreville	2,235	1,981
36611	Chickasaw	8,447	10,002
35044	Childersburg	4,831	4,884
35045	Clanton	5,868	5,683
35550	Cordova	2,750	3,184
35055	Cullman	12,601	10,883
36853	Dadeville	2,847	2,940
36322	Daleville	5,182	693
35601	Decatur	38,044	29,217
36732	Demopolis	7,651	7,377
36301	Dothan	36,733	31,440
36323	Elba	4,634	4,321
36330	Enterprise	15,591	11,410
36027	Eufaula	9,102	8,357
35462	Eutaw	2,805	2,784
36401	Evergreen	3,924	3,703
36854	Fairfax	2,772	3,107
35064	Fairfield	14,369	15,816
36532	Fairhope	5,720	4,858
35555	Fayette	4,568	4,227
36442	Florala	2,701	3,011
35630	Florence	34,031	31,649
36535	Foley	3,368	2,889
35214	Forestdale	6,091	
36201	Fort McClellan	5,334	
35967	Fort Payne	8,435	7,029
36360	Fort Rucker	14,242	
35068	Fultondale	5,163	2,001
*35901	Gadsden	53,928	58,088
35071	Gardendale	6,537	4,712
36340	Geneva	4,398	3,840
35905	Glencoe	2,901	2,592
35073	Graysville	3,182	2,870
36744	Greensboro	3,371	3,081
36037	Greenville	8,033	6,894
35976	Guntersville	6,491	6,592
35565	Haleyville	4,190	3,740
35570	Hamilton	3,088	1,934
36344	Hartford	2,648	1,956
35640	Hartselle	7,355	5,000
36345	Headland	2,545	2,650
36264	Heflin	2,872	2,400
35209	Homewood	21,137	20,289
35020	Hueytown	8,673	5,997
35804	Huntsville	137,802	72,365
35210	Irondale	3,166	3,501
36545	Jackson	5,957	4,959
36265	Jacksonville	7,715	5,678
35501	Jasper	10,798	10,799
36862	Lafayette	3,530	2,605
36863	Lanett	6,908	7,674
35094	Leeds	6,991	6,162
36748	Linden	2,697	2,516
35020	Lipscomb	3,225	2,811
36863	Little Shawmut	2,682	
35758	Madison	3,086	1,435
36756	Marion	4,289	3,807
35228	Midfield	6,340	3,556
*36601	Mobile	190,026	194,856
36460	Monroeville	4,846	3,632
35115	Montevallo	3,719	2,755
*36104	Montgomery	133,386	134,393
35223	Mountain Brook	19,509	12,680
35660	Muscle Shoals	6,907	4,084
35476	Northport	9,435	5,245
35121	Oneonta	4,390	4,136
36801	Opelika	19,027	15,678
36467	Opp	6,493	5,535
36201	Oxford	4,361	3,603
36360	Ozark	13,555	9,534
35125	Pell City	5,602	4,165
36867	Phenix City	25,281	27,630
36272	Piedmont	5,063	4,794
35127	Pleasant Grove	5,090	3,097
36067	Prattville	13,116	6,616
36610	Prichard	41,578	47,371
35901	Rainbow City	3,107	1,625
36274	Roanoke	5,251	5,288
35020	Roosevelt City	3,663	
35653	Russellville	7,814	6,628
36571	Saraland	7,840	4,595
35768	Scottsboro	9,324	6,449
36701	Selma	27,379	28,385
35660	Sheffield	13,115	13,491
35150	Sylacauga	12,255	12,857
35160	Talladega	17,662	17,742
36078	Tallassee	4,809	4,934
35217	Tarrant City	6,835	7,810
36784	Thomasville	3,769	3,182
36081	Troy	11,482	10,234
35173	Trussville	2,985	2,510
35401	Tuscaloosa	65,773	63,370
35674	Tuscumbia	8,828	8,994
36083	Tuskegee	11,028	7,240
36089	Union Springs	4,324	3,704
35216	Vestavia Hills	8,311	4,029
35180	Warrior	2,621	2,448
36201	West End—Cobb	5,515	5,485
36092	Wetumpka	3,912	3,672
35594	Winfield	3,292	2,907
36925	York	3,044	2,932
	Alaska		
*99502	Anchorage	48,081	44,237
99701	College	3,434	1,755
99702	Eielson	6,149	
99506	Elmendorf	6,018	
99701	Fairbanks	14,771	13,311
99505	Fort Richardson	10,751	
99703	Fort Wainwright	9,097	
99801	Juneau	6,050	6,797
99611	Kenai	3,533	
99901	Ketchikan	6,994	6,483
99615	Kodiak	3,798	2,628
98790	Kodiak Station	3,052	
99502	Sand Lake	4,168	
99835	Sitka	3,370	3,237
99503	Spenard	18,089	9,074

ZIP Code	Place	1970	1960
	Arizona		
85321	Ajo	5,881	7,049
85323	Avondale	6,626	6,151
85602	Benson	2,839	2,494
85603	Bisbee	8,328	9,914
85326	Buckeye	2,599	2,286
85222	Casa Grande	10,536	8,311
85329	Cashion	2,705	....
85224	Chandler	13,763	9,531
85533	Clifton	5,087	4,191
85228	Coolidge	5,314	4,990
86326	Cottonwood	2,815	....
85607	Douglas	12,462	11,925
85335	El Mirage	3,258	1,723
85231	Eloy	5,381	4,899
86001	Flagstaff	26,117	18,214
85613	Fort Huachuca	6,659	....
85301	Glendale	36,228	15,893
85501	Globe	7,333	6,217
86025	Holbrook	4,759	3,438
85237	Kearny	2,829	902
86401	Kingman	7,312	4,525
85301	Luke	5,047	....
85201	Mesa	62,853	33,772
85539	Miami	3,394	3,350
85621	Nogales	8,946	7,286
85253	Paradise Valley	7,155	....
85345	Peoria	4,792	2,593
*85026	Phoenix	581,562	439,170
86301	Prescott	13,283	12,861
85546	Safford	5,333	4,648
85550	San Carlos	2,542	....
85631	San Manuel	4,332	10,028
85251	Scottsdale	67,823	10,026
85635	Sierra Vista	6,689	3,121
85713	South Tucson	6,220	7,004
85351	Sun City	13,670	....
85273	Superior	4,975	4,875
85282	Tempe	63,550	24,897
85353	Tolleson	3,881	3,886
*85702	Tucson	262,933	212,892
85364	West Yuma	5,552	2,781
85358	Wickenburg	2,698	2,445
85643	Willcox	2,568	2,441
85224	Williams	3,443	....
86047	Winslow	8,066	8,862
85364	Yuma	29,007	23,974
85364	Yuma Station	3,460	....
	Arkansas		
71923	Arkadelphia	9,841	8,069
71822	Ashdown	3,522	2,725
72006	Augusta	2,777	2,272
72501	Batesville	7,209	6,207
72012	Beebe	2,805	1,697
72015	Benton	16,499	10,399
72712	Bentonville	5,508	3,649
72315	Blytheville	24,752	20,797
72927	Booneville	3,239	2,690
72021	Brinkley	5,275	4,636
72023	Cabot	2,903	1,321
71701	Camden	15,147	15,823
72029	Clarendon	2,563	2,293
72830	Clarksville	4,616	3,919
72032	Conway	15,510	9,791
72422	Corning	2,705	2,192
71635	Crossett	6,191	5,370
72834	Dardanelle	3,297	2,098
71832	De Queen	3,863	2,859
71638	Dermott	4,250	3,665
72042	De Witt	3,728	3,019
71639	Dumas	4,600	3,540
72331	Earle	3,146	2,391
71730	El Dorado	25,283	25,292
72046	England	3,075	2,861
71640	Eudora	3,687	3,598
72701	Fayetteville	30,729	20,274
71742	Fordyce	4,837	3,890
72335	Forrest City	12,521	10,544
72901	Fort Smith	62,802	52,991
71646	Hamburg	3,102	2,904
72601	Harrison	7,239	6,580
72342	Helena	10,415	11,500
71801	Hope	8,810	8,399
71901	Hot Springs	35,631	28,337
72076	Jacksonville	19,832	14,488
72401	Jonesboro	27,050	21,418
71653	Lake Village	3,310	2,998
*72201	Little Rock	132,483	107,813
72086	Lonoke	3,140	2,359
71654	McGehee	4,683	4,448
71753	Magnolia	11,303	10,651
72104	Malvern	8,739	9,566
72360	Marianna	6,196	5,134
72365	Marked Tree	3,229	3,216
71953	Mena	4,530	4,388
71655	Monticello	5,085	4,412
72110	Morrilton	6,814	5,997
72653	Mountain Home	3,935	2,105
71852	Nashville	4,016	3,579
72112	Newport	7,725	7,007
71635	North Crossett	2,891	....
*72114	North Little Rock	60,040	58,032
72370	Osceola	7,204	6,189
72949	Ozark	2,592	1,965
72450	Paragould	10,639	9,947
72855	Paris	3,646	3,007
72254	Piggott	3,087	2,776
71601	Pine Bluff	57,389	44,037
72455	Pocahontas	4,544	3,665
71857	Prescott	3,921	3,533
72756	Rogers	11,050	5,700
72801	Russellville	11,750	8,921
72143	Searcy	9,040	7,272
72116	Sherwood	2,754	1,222
72761	Siloam Springs	6,009	3,953
72204	Southwest Little Rock	13,231	....
72764	Springdale	16,783	10,076
72160	Stuttgart	10,477	9,661
75501	Texarkana	21,682	19,783
72472	Trumann	6,023	4,511
72956	Van Buren	8,373	6,787
72476	Walnut Ridge	3,800	3,547
71671	Warren	6,433	6,752
72390	West Helena	11,007	8,385
72301	West Memphis	26,070	19,374
72396	Wynne	6,696	4,922
	California		
94501	Alameda	70,968	63,855
94507	Alamo-Danville	14,059	14,404
94706	Albany	14,674	14,804
91802	Alhambra	62,125	54,807
90249	Alondra Park	12,193	....
91001	Altadena	42,415	40,568
96101	Alturas	2,799	2,819
95116	Alum Rock	18,355	18,942
*92803	Anaheim	166,408	104,184
96007	Anderson	5,492	4,492
94508	Angwin	2,690	....
94509	Antioch	28,060	17,305
92307	Apple Valley	6,702	....
95003	Aptos	8,704	....
91006	Arcadia	43,237	41,005
95521	Arcata	8,985	5,235
95825	Arden-Arcade	82,492	73,352
93420	Arroyo Grande	7,454	3,291
90071	Artesia	14,757	9,993
93203	Arvin	5,199	....
94577	Ashland	14,810	....
93422	Atascadero	10,290	5,943
94025	Atherton	8,085	7,717
95301	Atwater	11,640	7,318
95603	Auburn	6,570	5,586
92505	August School Area	6,735	....
93204	Avenal	3,035	3,147
91746	Avocado Heights	9,810	....
91702	Azusa	25,217	20,497
*93302	Bakersfield	69,515	56,848
91706	Baldwin Park	47,285	33,951
92220	Banning	12,034	10,250
92311	Barstow	17,442	11,644
93401	Baywood-Los Osos	3,487	....
95903	Beale East	7,029	....
92223	Beaumont	5,484	4,288
90201	Bell	21,836	19,450
90706	Bellflower	51,454	45,909
90201	Bell Gardens	29,308	....
94002	Belmont	23,667	15,996
94920	Belvedere	2,599	2,140
94510	Benicia	7,349	6,070
95005	Ben Lomond	2,793	1,814
*94704	Berkeley	116,716	111,268
*90213	Beverly Hills	33,416	30,817
92314	Big Bear	5,268	1,562
93514	Bishop	3,498	2,875
92316	Bloomington	11,957	....
92225	Blythe	7,047	6,023
96001	Bonnyview	4,882	4,686
95416	Boyes Hot Springs	3,558	2,462
92227	Brawley	13,746	12,703
92621	Brea	18,447	8,487
94513	Brentwood	2,649	2,186
95005	Brisbane	3,003	....
95605	Broderick-Bryte	12,782	....
90620	Buena Park	63,646	46,401
*91505	Burbank	88,871	90,155
94010	Burlingame	27,320	24,036
92231	Calexico	10,625	7,992
93745	Calwa	5,191	....
93010	Camarillo	19,219	....
93010	Camarillo Heights	5,892	1,704
95154	Cambrian Park	5,316	....
95008	Campbell	24,770	11,863
92624	Capistrano Beach	4,149	2,026
95010	Capitola	5,080	2,021
92007	Cardiff By-The-Sea	5,724	3,149

ZIP Code	Place	1970	1960	ZIP Code	Place	1970	1960
92008	Carlsbad	14,944	9,253	95437	Fort Bragg	4,455	4,433
93921	Carmel-by-the-Sea	4,525	4,580	92311	Fort Irwin	2,991	.....
93924	Carmel Valley	3,026	1,143	95540	Fortuna	4,203	3,523
95608	Carmichael	37,625	20,455	94404	Foster City	9,522	.....
93013	Carpinteria	6,982	.....	92708	Fountain Valley	31,886	2,068
90744	Carson	71,150	.....	95019	Freedom	5,563	4,206
94546	Castro Valley	44,760	37,120	*94536	Fremont	100,869	43,790
95012	Castroville	3,235	2,838	*93721	Fresno	165,972	133,929
92234	Cathedral	3,640	1,855	*92631	Fullerton	85,987	56,180
95307	Ceres	6,029	4,406	95632	Galt	3,200	1,868
90701	Cerritos	15,856	3,508	*90247	Gardena	41,021	35,943
94541	Cherryland	9,969	.....	95205	Garden Acres	7,870	.....
92223	Cherry Valley	3,165	.....	*92640	Garden Grove	121,371	84,238
95926	Chico	19,580	14,757	92392	George	7,404	.....
95926	Chico North	6,656	.....	95020	Gilroy	12,665	7,348
95926	Chico West	4,787	.....	92509	Glen Avon	5,759	3,416
93555	China Lake	11,105	.....	*91209	Glendale	132,752	119,442
91710	Chino	20,411	10,305	91740	Glendora	31,349	20,752
93610	Chowchilla	4,349	4,525	93926	Gonzales	2,575	2,138
*92010	Chula Vista	67,901	42,034	92324	Grand Terrace	5,901	.....
95610	Citrus Heights	21,760	.....	95945	Grass Valley	5,149	4,876
91711	Claremont	23,464	12,633	93927	Greenfield	2,608	1,680
95422	Clearlake Highlands	2,836	.....	95948	Gridley	3,534	3,343
95425	Cloverdale	3,251	2,848	92041	Grossmont-Mt. Helix	8,723	.....
93612	Clovis	13,856	5,546	93433	Grover City	5,939	5,210
92236	Coachella	8,353	4,854	93434	Guadalupe	3,145	2,614
93210	Coalinga	6,161	5,965	95322	Gustine	2,793	2,300
92324	Colton	20,016	18,666	91745	Hacienda Heights	35,969	.....
95932	Colusa	3,842	3,518	94019	Half Moon Bay	4,023	1,957
90022	Commerce	10,536	9,555	93230	Hanford	15,179	10,133
*90220	Compton	78,611	71,812	90716	Hawaiian Gardens	9,019	.....
*94520	Concord	85,164	36,000	90250	Hawthorne	53,304	33,035
93212	Corcoran	5,249	4,976	*94544	Hayward	93,058	72,700
96021	Corning	3,573	3,006	95448	Healdsburg	5,438	4,816
91720	Corona	27,519	13,336	92343	Hemet	12,252	5,416
92118	Coronado	20,910	18,039	92343	Hemet East	8,598	1,936
94925	Corte Madera	8,464	5,962	90254	Hermosa Beach	17,412	16,115
92626	Costa Mesa	72,660	37,550	92345	Hesperia	4,592	.....
91722	Covina	30,380	20,124	92346	Highland	12,669	.....
95531	Crescent City	2,586	2,958	94010	Hillsborough	8,753	7,554
95531	Crescent North	3,053	3,086	95023	Hollister	7,663	6,071
92325	Crest Forest	3,509	.....	92250	Holtville	3,496	3,080
91730	Cucamonga	5,796	.....	91720	Home Gardens	5,116	1,541
90201	Cudahy	16,998	.....	92647	Huntington Beach	115,960	11,492
90230	Culver City	34,526	32,163	90255	Huntington Park	33,744	29,920
95014	Cupertino	18,216	3,664	92251	Imperial	3,094	2,658
93615	Cutler	2,503	2,191	92032	Imperial Beach	20,244	17,773
90630	Cypress	31,569	1,753	92201	Indio	14,459	9,745
*94017	Daly City	66,922	44,791	*90306	Inglewood	89,985	63,390
92629	Dana Point	4,745	1,186	93017	Isla Vista	13,441	.....
95616	Davis	23,488	8,910	94707	Kensington	5,823	.....
90250	Del Aire	11,930	.....	93630	Kerman	2,667	1,970
93215	Delano	14,559	11,913	93930	King City	3,717	2,937
92014	Del Mar	3,956	3,124	93631	Kingsburg	3,843	3,093
92240	Desert Hot Springs	2,738	.....	91011	La Canada-Flintridge	20,652	18,338
91766	Diamond Bar	12,234	.....	91214	La Crescenta-Montrose	19,594	.....
93618	Dinuba	7,917	6,103	90045	Ladera Heights	6,535	.....
95620	Dixon	4,432	2,970	94549	Lafayette	20,484	7,114
90810	Dominguez	5,980	.....	92651	Laguna Beach	14,550	9,288
*90241	Downey	88,445	82,505	92653	Laguna Hills	13,676	.....
91010	Duarte	14,981	13,962	92677	Laguna Niguel	4,644	.....
94566	Dublin	13,641	.....	90631	La Habra	41,350	25,136
93219	Earlimart	3,080	2,897	92352	Lake Arrowhead	2,682	.....
90220	East Compton	5,853	.....	95453	Lakeport	3,005	2,303
90638	East La Mirada	12,339	.....	92040	Lakeside	11,991	.....
90022	East Los Angeles	105,033	104,270	*90714	Lakewood	82,973	67,126
94303	East Palo Alto	17,897	.....	92041	La Mesa	39,178	30,441
93257	East Porterville	4,042	3,538	90638	La Mirada	30,808	22,444
93523	Edwards	10,331	.....	93241	Lamont	7,007	6,177
92020	El Cajon	52,273	37,618	93534	Lancaster	32,570	26,012
92243	El Centro	19,272	16,811	90620	La Palma	9,687	622
94530	El Cerrito	25,190	25,437	*91747	La Puente	31,092	24,723
93017	El Encanto Heights	6,225	.....	94939	Larkspur	10,487	5,710
95624	Elk Grove	3,721	2,205	91750	La Verne	12,965	6,516
*91731	El Monte	69,852	13,163	90260	Lawndale	24,825	21,740
93446	El Paso de Robles	7,168	6,677	92045	Lemon Grove	19,690	19,348
93030	El Rio	6,173	6,966	93245	Lemoore	4,219	2,561
90245	El Segundo	15,620	14,219	93245	Lemoore Station	9,210	.....
92330	Elsinore	3,530	2,432	90304	Lennox	16,121	31,224
92630	El Toro	8,654	.....	92311	Lenwood	3,834	2,407
92709	El Toro Station	6,970	.....	95648	Lincoln	3,176	3,197
94608	Emeryville	2,681	2,686	95207	Lincoln Village	6,112	.....
92024	Encinitas	5,375	2,786	95901	Linda	7,731	6,129
92025	Escondido	36,792	16,377	93247	Lindsay	5,206	5,397
95501	Eureka	24,337	28,137	95062	Live Oak (Santa Cruz)	6,443	3,518
93221	Exeter	4,475	4,264	95953	Live Oak (Sutter)	2,645	2,276
94930	Fairfax	7,661	5,813	94550	Livermore	37,703	16,058
94533	Fairfield	44,146	14,968	95334	Livingston	2,588	2,188
95628	Fair Oaks	11,256	.....	95240	Lodi	28,691	22,229
92028	Fallbrook	6,945	4,814	92354	Loma Linda	9,797	.....
93223	Farmersville	3,456	.....	90717	Lomita	19,784	.....
93015	Fillmore	6,285	4,808	93436	Lompoc	25,284	14,415
93622	Firebaugh	2,517	2,070	93436	Lompoc North	2,699	.....
90001	Florence-Graham	42,895	38,164	93436	Lompoc Northwest	4,874	.....
95828	Florin	9,646	.....	*90801	Long Beach	358,633	344,168
95630	Folsom	5,810	3,925	90720	Los Alamitos	11,346	4,312
92335	Fontana	20,673	14,659	94022	Los Altos	24,726	19,696
93268	Ford City	3,503	3,926	94022	Los Altos Hills	6,865	3,412
				*90052	Los Angeles	2,809,596	2,479,015

ZIP Code	Place	1970	1960
93635	Los Banos	9,188	5,272
95030	Los Gatos	23,735	9,036
90262	Lynwood	43,353	31,614
93250	McFarland	4,177	3,686
93637	Madera	16,044	14,430
90266	Manhattan Beach	35,352	33,934
95336	Manteca	13,845	8,242
93933	Marina	8,343	3,310
94553	Martinez	16,506	9,604
95901	Marysville	9,353	9,553
95655	Mather	7,027	
90270	Maywood	16,996	14,588
93023	Meiners Oaks-Mira Monte	7,025	
93640	Mendota	2,705	2,099
94025	Menlo Park	26,906	26,957
95340	Merced	22,670	20,068
94030	Millbrae	20,920	15,873
94941	Mill Valley	12,942	10,411
95035	Milpitas	27,149	6,572
91752	Mira Loma	8,482	3,982
92675	Mission Viejo	11,933	
*95350	Modesto	61,712	36,585
93501	Mojave	2,573	1,845
91016	Monrovia	30,015	27,079
91763	Montclair	22,546	13,546
90640	Montebello	42,807	32,097
93940	Monterey	26,302	22,618
91754	Monterey Park	49,166	37,821
95030	Monte Sereno	3,089	1,506
93021	Moorpark	3,380	2,902
95205	Morada	2,936	2,156
9___	Moraga	14,205	
9503?	Morgan Hill	6,485	3,151
93442	Morro Bay	7,109	
94040	Mountain View	54,206	30,889
92405	Muscoy	7,091	
94558	Napa	35,978	22,170
92050	National City	43,184	32,771
92363	Needles	4,051	4,590
94560	Newark	27,153	9,884
91321	Newhall	9,651	4,705
95360	Newman	2,505	2,148
*92660	Newport Beach	49,422	26,564
93444	Nipomo	3,642	
91760	Norco	14,511	
94025	North Fair Oaks	9,740	
95660	North Highlands	31,854	21,271
92135	North Island	6,002	
90650	Norwalk	91,827	88,739
94947	Novato	31,006	17,881
95361	Oakdale	6,594	4,980
*94615	Oakland	361,561	367,548
93022	Oak View	4,872	2,448
93445	Oceano	2,564	1,317
92054	Oceanside	40,494	24,971
93308	Oildale	20,879	
93023	Ojai	5,591	4,495
95961	Olivehurst	8,100	4,835
91761	Ontario	64,118	46,617
95060	Opal Cliffs	5,425	3,825
*92667	Orange	77,365	26,444
93646	Orange Cove	3,392	2,885
95662	Orangevale	16,493	
93454	Orcutt	8,500	1,414
94563	Orinda	6,790	5,568
95963	Orland	2,884	2,534
93647	Orosi	2,757	1,048
95965	Oroville	7,536	6,115
92010	Otay-Castle Park	15,445	
93030	Oxnard	71,225	40,265
94044	Pacifica	36,020	20,995
93950	Pacific Grove	13,505	12,121
93550	Palmdale	8,511	
93543	Palmdale East	3,560	
92260	Palm Desert	6,171	1,295
92262	Palm Springs	20,936	13,468
* 94302	Palo Alto	56,181	52,287
90274	Palos Verdes Estates	13,631	9,564
90274	Palos Verdes Peninsula	38,918	
95969	Paradise	14,539	8,268
90723	Paramount	34,734	27,249
95823	Parkway-Sacramento So.	28,574	
*91109	Pasadena	112,981	116,407
95363	Patterson	3,147	2,246
92055	Pendleton North	11,803	
92055	Pendleton South	13,692	
92370	Perris	4,228	2,950
94952	Petaluma	24,870	14,035
90660	Pico Rivera	54,170	49,150
94611	Piedmont	10,917	11,117
94564	Pinole	13,266	6,064
93449	Pismo Beach	4,043	1,762
94565	Pittsburg	20,651	19,062
92670	Placentia	21,948	5,861
95667	Placerville	5,416	4,439
94523	Pleasant Hill	24,610	23,844
94566	Pleasanton	18,328	4,203
93043	Point Mugu	3,351	
*91766	Pomona	87,384	67,157

ZIP Code	Place	1970	1960
93257	Porterville	12,602	7,991
93257	Porterville Northwest	2,517	
93257	Porterville West	6,200	
93041	Port Hueneme	14,295	11,067
94025	Portola Valley	4,943	
92064	Poway	9,422	1,921
93534	Quartz Hill	4,935	3,325
95971	Quincy	3,343	
92065	Ramona	3,554	2,449
95670	Rancho Cordova	30,451	7,429
95014	Rancho Rinconda	5,149	
91350	Rancho Santa Clarita	4,860	
96080	Red Bluff	7,676	7,202
96001	Redding	16,659	12,773
92373	Redlands	36,335	26,829
*90277	Redondo Beach	57,425	46,986
*94064	Redwood City	55,686	46,290
93654	Reedley	8,131	5,850
92376	Rialto	28,370	18,567
*94802	Richmond	79,043	71,854
93555	Ridgecrest	7,629	
95562	Rio Dell	2,817	
95673	Rio Linda	7,524	2,189
94571	Rio Vista	3,135	2,616
95366	Ripon	2,679	1,894
95367	Riverbank	3,949	2,786
*92502	Riverside	140,089	84,332
95677	Rocklin	3,039	1,495
94572	Rodeo	5,356	
94928	Rohnert Park	6,133	
95540	Rohnerville	2,781	2,268
90274	Rolling Hills Estates	6,735	3,941
91???	Rolling Hills	2,105	1,510
91770	Rosemead	40,972	15,476
95678	Roseville	18,221	13,421
94957	Ross	2,742	2,551
90720	Rossmoor	12,922	
91745	Rowland Heights	16,881	
92509	Rubidoux	13,969	
95501	Ryans Slough	3,922	3,634
*95813	Sacramento	257,105	191,667
94574	St. Helena	3,173	2,722
93901	Salinas	58,896	28,957
94960	San Anselmo	13,031	11,584
*92403	San Bernardino	104,783	91,922
94066	San Bruno	36,254	29,063
	San Buenaventura (See Ventura)		
94070	San Carlos	25,924	21,370
92672	San Clemente	17,063	8,527
*92101	San Diego	697,027	573,224
91773	San Dimas	15,692	
*91340	San Fernando	16,571	16,093
*94101	San Francisco	715,674	740,316
91776	San Gabriel	29,336	22,561
93657	Sanger	10,088	8,072
92383	San Jacinto	4,385	2,553
*95125	San Jose	445,779	204,196
92675	San Juan Capistrano	3,781	
*94577	San Leandro	68,698	65,962
94580	San Lorenzo	24,633	23,773
93401	San Luis Obispo	28,036	20,437
92069	San Marcos	3,896	
91108	San Marino	14,177	13,658
*94402	San Mateo	78,991	69,870
94806	San Pablo	21,461	19,687
*94901	San Rafael	38,977	20,460
94583	San Ramon	4,084	
*92711	Santa Ana	156,876	100,350
*93102	Santa Barbara	70,215	58,768
*95052	Santa Clara	87,717	58,880
95000	Santa Cruz	32,076	25,596
90670	Santa Fe Springs	14,750	16,342
93454	Santa Maria	32,749	20,027
93454	Santa Maria South	7,129	
*90406	Santa Monica	88,289	83,249
93060	Santa Paula	18,001	13,279
*95402	Santa Rosa	50,006	31,027
92071	Santee	21,107	
95070	Saratoga	27,110	14,861
94965	Sausalito	6,158	5,331
95060	Scotts Valley	3,621	
90740	Seal Beach	24,441	6,994
93562	Searles Valley	3,828	
93955	Seaside	35,935	19,353
95472	Sebastopol	3,993	2,694
93662	Selma	7,459	6,934
93263	Shafter	5,327	4,576
91024	Sierra Madre	12,140	9,732
90806	Signal Hill	5,582	4,627
93065	Simi Valley	59,832	
92075	Solana Beach	5,023	
93960	Soledad	4,222	2,837
95476	Sonoma	4,112	3,023
95370	Sonora	3,100	2,725
95073	Soquel	5,795	
91733	South El Monte	13,443	4,850
90280	South Gate	56,909	53,831
92677	South Laguna	2,566	2,000
95705	South Lake Tahoe	12,921	

ZIP Code	Place	1970	1960
95350	South Modesto.........	7,889	5,465
95965	South Oroville.........	4,111	3,704
91030	South Pasadena........	22,979	19,706
94080	South San Francisco....	46,646	39,418
91770	South San Gabriel......	5,051	......
91744	South San Jose Hill.....	12,386	......
90605	South Whittier.........	46,641	......
95991	South Yuba............	5,352	3,200
92077	Spring Valley..........	29,742	......
94305	Stanford..............	8,691	......
90680	Stanton...............	18,186	11,163
°95204	Stockton..............	109,963	86,321
94585	Suisun City...........	2,917	2,470
92381	Sun..................	5,519	......
92388	Sunnymead............	6,708	3,404
°94086	Sunnyvale.............	95,408	52,898
96130	Susanville............	6,608	5,598
93268	Taft..................	4,285	3,822
93561	Tehachapi............	4,211	3,161
91780	Temple City...........	31,040	......
95965	Thermalito............	4,217	......
°91360	Thousand Oaks........	35,873	......
94920	Tiburon..............	6,209	......
°90510	Torrance............_..	134,584	100,991
95376	Tracy................	14,724	11,289
93274	Tulare...............	16,235	13,824
95380	Turlock..............	13,992	9,116
92680	Tustin...............	21,178	2,006
92705	Tustin-Foothills........	26,598	......
92277	Twentynine Palms......	5,667	......
92278	Twentynine Palms Base.	5,647	......
95060	Twin Lakes...........	3,012	1,849
95482	Ukiah................	10,095	9,900
94587	Union City............	14,724	6,618
91786	Upland...............	32,551	15,918
95688	Vacaville.............	21,690	10,898
91355	Valencia..............	4,243	......
91744	Valinda..............	18,837	......
94590	Vallejo............ ..	71,710	60,877
93437	Vandenburg...........	13,193	......
93001	Ventura..............	57,964	29,114
92392	Victorville............	10,845	......
90043	View Park-Windsor Hills..	12,268	......
92667	Villa Park............	2,723	......
93277	Visalia...............	27,268	15,791
92083	Vista................	24,688	......
91789	Walnut...............	5,992	934
°94596	Walnut Creek..........	39,844	9,903
94596	Walnut Creek West.....	8,330	......
90255	Walnut Park..........	8,925	......
93280	Wasco...............	8,269	6,841
95076	Watsonville...........	14,569	13,293
96094	Weed................	2,983	......
90044	West Athens..........	13,286	......
90502	West Carson..........	15,501	......
90247	West Compton........	5,748	......
°91790	West Covina...........	68,034	50,645
90069	West Hollywood........	34,625	28,870
92683	Westminster..........	59,874	25,750
95351	West Modesto.........	6,135	1,897
90047	Westmont.............	29,310	......
94565	West Pittsburg.........	5,969	5,188
91746	West Puente Valley.....	20,733	......
95691	West Sacramento......	12,002	......
°90605	West Whittier-Los Nietos..	20,845	......
°90605	Whittier..............	72,863	33,663
95490	Willits...............	3,091	3,410
90222	WillowBrook..........	28,705	......
95988	Willows..............	4,085	4,139
95388	Winton...............	3,393	1,700
93286	Woodlake.............	3,371	2,623
95695	Woodland.............	20,677	13,524
94062	Woodside.............	4,734	3,592
92686	Yorba Linda...........	11,856	......
96097	Yreka City............	5,394	4,759
95991	Yuba City.............	13,986	11,507
92399	Yucaipa..............	19,284	......
92284	Yucca Valley..........	3,893	......

Colorado

ZIP Code	Place	1970	1960
81101	Alamosa.............	6,985	6,205
80401	Applewood...........	8,214	......
80002	Arvada..............	46,814	19,242
80010	Aurora..............	74,974	48,548
80302	Boulder..............	66,870	37,718
80601	Brighton.............	8,309	7,055
80020	Broomfield...........	7,261	......
80723	Brush...............	3,377	3,621
80807	Burlington............	2,828	2,090
81212	Canon City...........	9,206	8,973
80110	Cherry Hills Village.....	4,605	1,931
°80901	Colorado Springs......	135,060	70,194
80022	Commerce City........	17,407	8,970
81321	Cortez..............	6,032	6,764
81625	Craig...............	4,205	3,984
81416	Delta...............	3,694	3,832
°80202	Denver..............	514,678	493,887
80022	Derby...............	10,206	10,124

ZIP Code	Place	1970	1960
81301	Durango.............	10,333	10,530
80214	Edgewater...........	4,866	4,314
80110	Englewood...........	33,695	33,398
80620	Evans...............	2,570	1,453
81226	Florence.............	2,846	2,821
80913	Fort Carson..........	19,399	......
80521	Fort Collins..........	43,337	25,027
80701	Fort Morgan..........	7,594	7,379
80817	Fountain.............	3,515	1,602
81601	Glenwood Springs.....	4,106	3,637
80401	Golden..............	9,817	7,118
81501	Grand Junction........	20,170	18,694
80631	Greeley..............	38,902	26,314
80120	Greenwood Village.....	3,095	572
81230	Gunnison............	4,613	3,477
80026	Lafayette............	3,498	2,612
81050	La Junta.............	7,938	8,026
80215	Lakewood............	92,787	......
81052	Lamar...............	7,797	7,369
81054	Las Animas..........	3,148	3,402
80461	Leadville............	4,314	4,008
81212	Lincoln Park..........	2,984	2,085
80120	Littleton Southeast.....	22,899	......
80120	Littleton.............	26,466	13,670
80501	Longmont............	23,209	11,489
80537	Loveland.............	16,220	9,734
80829	Manitou Springs......	4,278	3,626
81144	Monte Vista..........	3,909	3,385
81401	Montrose............	6,496	5,044
80233	North Glenn..........	27,937	......
81501	Orchard Mesa.........	5,824	4,956
°81003	Pueblo..............	97,453	91,181
81067	Rocky Ford...........	4,859	4,929
81201	Salida..............	4,355	4,560
80911	Security-Widefield.....	15,297	9,017
80110	Sheridan.............	4,787	3,559
80221	Sherrelwood..........	18,868	......
80751	Sterling.............	10,636	10,751
80906	Stratton Meadows.....	6,223	......
80229	Thornton............	13,326	11,353
81082	Trinidad.............	9,901	10,691
81089	Walsenburg..........	4,329	5,071
80229	Welby...............	6,875	......
80030	Westminster..........	19,432	13,850
80221	Westminster East......	7,576	......
80033	Wheat Ridge..........	29,795	......

Connecticut

See Note on Page 166

ZIP Code	Place	1970	1960
06401	Ansonia.............	21,160	19,819
06001	Avon................	8,352	5,273
06403	Beacon Falls.........	3,546	2,886
06037	Berlin...............	14,149	11,250
06525	Bethany.............	3,857	2,384
06801	Bethel...............	10,945	8,200
06002	Bloomfield...........	18,301	13,613
06040	Bolton...............	3,691	2,933
06405	Branford.............	20,444	16,610
°06602	Bridgeport...........	156,542	156,748
06010	Bristol..............	55,487	45,499
06804	Brookfield............	9,688	3,405
06234	Brooklyn.............	4,965	3,312
06085	Burlington...........	4,070	2,790
06331	Canterbury...........	2,673	1,857
06019	Canton..............	6,868	4,783
06410	Cheshire.............	19,051	13,383
06412	Chester.............	2,982	2,520
06413	Clinton Center........	5,957	2,693
06413	Clinton..............	10,267	4,166
06415	Colchester Borough....	3,529	2,260
06415	Colchester...........	6,603	4,648
06022	Collinsville...........	2,897	1,682
06237	Columbia............	3,129	2,163
06340	Conning Towers-Nautilus Park.........	9,791	3,457
06238	Coventry.............	8,140	6,356
06416	Cromwell............	7,400	6,780
06810	Danbury.............	50,781	22,928
06239	Danielson Borough.....	4,580	4,642
06820	Darien..............	20,411	18,437
06417	Deep River...........	3,690	2,968
06418	Derby...............	12,599	12,132
06422	Durham.............	4,489	3,096
06026	East Granby..........	3,532	2,434
06423	East Haddam.........	4,676	3,637
06424	East Hampton........	7,078	5,403
06108	East Hartford.........	57,583	43,977
06512	East Haven...........	25,120	21,388
06333	East Lyme...........	11,399	6,782
06425	Easton..............	4,885	3,407
06016	East Windsor.........	8,513	7,500
06029	Ellington............	7,707	5,580
06082	Enfield..............	46,189	31,464
06426	Essex...............	4,911	4,057
06430	Fairfield.............	56,487	46,183
06032	Farmington...........	14,390	10,813
06033	Glastonbury..........	20,651	14,497
06035	Granby..............	6,150	4,968

ZIP Code	Place	1970	1960
06830	Greenwich	59,755	53,793
06351	Griswold	7,763	6,472
06340	Groton	38,244	29,937
06340	Groton Borough	8,933	10,111
06437	Guilford	12,033	7,913
06437	Guilford	3,632	2,420
06438	Haddam	4,934	3,466
06514	Hamden	49,357	41,056
*06101	Hartford	158,017	162,178
06790	Harwinton	4,318	3,344
06248	Hebron	3,815	1,819
06351	Jewett City	3,372	3,608
06239	Killingly	13,573	11,298
06249	Lebanon	3,804	2,434
06339	Ledyard	14,837	5,395
06351	Lisbon	2,808	2,019
06759	Litchfield	7,399	6,264
06443	Madison	9,768	4,567
06443	Madison	4,310	1,416
06040	Manchester	47,994	42,102
06250	Mansfield	19,994	14,638
06424	Marlborough	2,991	1,961
06450	Meriden	55,959	51,850
06762	Middlebury	5,542	4,785
06455	Middlefield	4,132	3,255
06457	Middletown	36,924	33,250
06460	Milford	50,858	41,662
06468	Monroe	12,047	6,402
06353	Montville	15,662	7,759
06354	Moosup	3,376	2,760
06385	Morningside Park	3,458	3,181
06355	Mystic	2,568	2,536
06111	‖‖‖‖‖‖	02,030	19,011
*06050	New Britain	83,441	82,201
06840	New Canaan	17,455	13,466
06810	New Fairfield	6,991	3,355
06057	New Hartford	3,970	3,033
*06510	New Haven	137,707	152,048
06111	Newington	26,037	17,664
06320	New London	31,630	34,182
06776	New Milford	14,601	8,318
06776	New Milford	4,606	3,023
06470	Newtown	16,942	11,373
06357	Niantic	3,422	2,788
06471	North Branford	10,778	6,771
06018	North Canaan	3,045	2,836
06473	North Haven	22,194	15,935
06359	North Stonington	3,748	1,982
06856	Norwalk	79,113	67,775
06360	Norwich	41,739	38,506
06371	Old Lyme	4,964	3,068
06475	Old Saybrook	8,468	5,274
06477	Orange	13,524	8,547
06483	Oxford	4,480	3,292
02891	Pawcatuck	5,255	4,389
06374	Plainfield	11,957	8,884
06374	Plainfield	2,923	2,044
06062	Plainville	16,733	13,149
06782	Plymouth	10,321	8,981
06258	Pomfret	2,529	2,136
06064	Poquonock Bridge	3,165	
06480	Portland	8,812	7,496
06360	Preston	3,593	4,992
06712	Prospect	6,543	4,367
06260	Putnam	6,918	6,952
	Putnam	8,598	8,412
06875	Redding	5,590	3,359
06877	Ridgefield	5,878	2,954
	Ridgefield	18,188	8,165
06067	Rocky Hill	11,103	7,404
06068	Salisbury	3,573	3,309
06483	Seymour	12,776	10,100
06484	Shelton	27,165	18,190
06070	Simsbury	4,994	2,745
	Simsbury	17,475	10,138
06071	Somers	6,893	3,702
06488	Southbury	7,852	5,186
06238	South Coventry	3,735	3,568
06489	Southington	30,946	22,797
06074	South Windsor	15,553	9,460
06330	Sprague	2,912	2,509
06075	Stafford	8,680	7,476
06076	Stafford Springs	3,339	3,322
*06904	Stamford	108,798	92,713
06378	Stonington	15,940	13,969
06268	Storrs	10,691	6,054
06497	Stratford	49,775	45,012
06078	Suffield	8,634	6,779
06787	Thomaston	6,233	5,850
06277	Thompson	7,580	6,217
06084	Tolland	7,857	2,950
06790	Torrington	31,952	30,045
06611	Trumbull	31,394	20,379
06066	Vernon	27,237	16,961
06492	Wallingford	35,714	29,920
06793	Washington	3,121	2,603
*06701	Waterbury	108,033	107,130
06385	Waterford	17,227	15,391
06795	Watertown	18,610	14,837
06498	Westbrook	3,820	2,399

ZIP Code	Place	1970	1960
06107	West Hartford	68,031	62,382
06516	West Haven	52,851	43,002
06388	West Mystic	3,415	3,268
06880	Weston	7,417	4,039
06880	Westport	27,414	20,955
06109	Wethersfield	26,662	20,561
06226	Willimantic	14,402	13,881
06279	Willington	3,755	2,005
06897	Wilton	13,572	8,026
06094	Winchester	11,106	10,496
06280	Windham	19,626	16,973
06095	Windsor	22,502	19,467
06096	Windsor Locks	15,080	11,411
06098	Winsted	8,954	8,136
06716	Wolcott	12,495	8,889
06525	Woodbridge	7,673	5,182
06798	Woodbury	5,869	3,910
06281	Woodstock	4,311	3,177

Delaware

ZIP Code	Place	1970	1960
19711	Brookside Park	7,856	.....
19703	Claymont	6,584	.....
19901	Dover	17,488	7,250
19901	Dover Base	8,106	.....
19805	Elsmere	8,415	7,319
19958	Lewes	2,563	3,025
19709	Middletown	2,644	2,191
19963	Milford	5,314	5,795
19711	Newark	21,078	11,404
19720	New Castle	4,814	4,469
19973	Seaford	5,537	4,430
19077	Smyrna	3,968	.....
*19899	Wilmington	80,386	95,827
19720	Wilmington Manor —Chelsea—Leedon	10,134	.....

District of Columbia

ZIP Code	Place	1970	1960
*20013	Washington	756,510	763,956
	Northeast	184,439	197,536
	Northwest	347,337	374,165
	Southeast	194,365	173,988
	Southwest	30,369	18,267

Florida

ZIP Code	Place	1970	1960
32701	Altamonte Springs	4,391	1,212
32320	Apalachicola	3,102	3,099
32703	Apopka	4,045	3,578
33821	Arcadia	5,658	5,889
33823	Auburndale	5,386	5,595
33825	Avon Park	6,712	6,073
32807	Azalea Park	7,367	.....
33830	Bartow	12,891	12,849
33154	Bay Harbor Islands	4,619	3,249
33507	Bayshore Gardens	9,255	2,297
33589	Beacon Squier	2,927	.....
33516	Belleair	2,962	2,456
33430	Belle Glade	15,949	11,273
32809	Belle Isle	2,705	2,344
33152	Biscayne Park	2,717	2,911
33040	Boca Chica	2,817	.....
33432	Boca Raton	28,506	6,961
33435	Boynton Beach	18,115	10,467
*33506	Bradenton	21,040	19,380
33511	Brandon	12,749	1,665
33314	Broadview Park-Rock Hill	6,049	.....
33512	Brooksville	4,060	3,301
33311	Browardale	17,444	.....
33142	Browns Village	23,442	.....
33137	Buena Vista	3,407	.....
33054	Bunche Park	5,773	.....
32401	Calloway	3,240	950
32533	Cantonment	3,241	2,499
32920	Cape Canaveral	4,258	.....
33904	Cape Coral	10,193	.....
33054	Carol City	27,361	21,749
33023	Carver Ranch Estates	5,515	.....
32707	Casselberry	9,438	2,463
33505	Cedar Hammock-Bradenton So.	10,820	3,089
32535	Century	2,679	2,046
32324	Chattahoochee	7,944	9,699
32428	Chipley	3,347	3,159
33516	Clearwater	52,074	34,653
32711	Clermont	3,661	3,313
33440	Clewiston	3,896	3,114
32922	Cocoa	16,110	12,294
32931	Cocoa Beach	9,952	3,475
32922	Cocoa West	5,779	3,975
33064	Collier Manor-Cresthaven	7,202	.....
33101	Combee Settlement	4,963	2,697
32809	Conway	8,642	.....
33314	Cooper City	2,535	550
33134	Coral Gables	42,494	34,793
32536	Crestview	7,952	7,467
33157	Cutler Ridge	17,441	7,005

ZIP Code	Place	1970	1960	ZIP Code	Place	1970	1960
33880	Cypress Gardens	3,757		33314	Melrose Park	6,111	
33525	Dade City	4,241	4,759	33561	Memphis	3,207	2,647
33004	Dania	9,013	7,065	32952	Merritt Island	29,233	3,554
33314	Davie	4,977		°33101	Miami	334,859	291,688
°32015	Daytona Beach	45,327	37,395	33139	Miami Beach	87,072	63,145
32713	DeBary	3,154	2,362	33153	Miami Shores	9,425	8,865
33441	Deerfield Beach	16,662	9,573	33166	Miami Springs	13,279	11,229
32433	De Funiak Springs	4,966	5,282	32570	Milton	5,360	4,108
32720	De Land	11,641	10,775	32754	Mims	8,309	1,307
33444	Delray Beach	19,366	12,230	33023	Miramar	23,973	5,485
32763	Deltona	4,868		32757	Mount Dora	4,543	3,756
33528	Dunedin	17,639	8,444	33860	Mulberry	2,701	2,922
33823	East Auburndale	2,621		32506	Myrtle Grove	16,186	
33610	East Lake-Orient Park	5,697		33940	Naples	12,042	4,655
33940	East Naples	6,152		33552	New Port Richey	6,098	3,520
32032	Edgewater	3,348	2,051	33552	New Port Richey East		
32542	Eglin	7,769			—Richey Lakes	2,758	
33614	Egypt Lake	7,556		32609	New Smyrna Beach	10,580	8,781
33533	Englewood	5,108	2,877	32578	Niceville	4,024	4,517
32726	Eustis	6,722	6,189	33555	Nokomis-Laurel	3,238	2,253
32034	Fernandina Beach	6,955	7,276	33308	North Andrews Terrace	7,082	
33030	Florida City	5,133	4,114	33141	North Bay Village	4,831	2,006
°33310	Fort Lauderdale	139,590	83,648	33903	North Fort Myers	8,798	
33841	Fort Meade	4,374	4,014	33161	North Miami	34,767	28,708
°33902	Fort Myers	27,351	22,523	33160	North Miami Beach	30,833	21,405
33931	Fort Myers Beach	4,305	2,463	33940	North Naples	3,201	
33901	Fort Myers Southeast	3,150		33403	North Palm Beach	9,035	2,684
33901	Fort Myers Southwest	5,086		33169	Norwood	14,973	
33901	Fort Myers Villas-Pine Manor	3,408		33307	Oakland Park	16,261	5,331
				32670	Ocala	22,583	13,598
33450	Fort Pierce	29,721	25,256	32548	Ocean	5,267	
33450	Fort Pierce Northwest	3,269		32761	Ocoee	3,937	2,628
32548	Fort Walton Beach	19,994	12,147	33472	Okeechobee	3,715	2,947
33843	Frostproof	2,814	2,664	33558	Oneco	3,246	1,530
32601	Gainesville	64,510	29,701	33054	Opa-Locka	11,902	9,810
32960	Gifford	5,772	3,509	32073	Orange Park	7,619	2,624
33170	Goulds	6,690	5,121	°32802	Orlando	99,006	88,135
32440	Graceville	2,560	2,307	32074	Ormond Beach	14,063	8,658
32043	Green Cove Springs	3,857	4,233	32074	Ormond By-The-Sea	6,002	3,476
32561	Gulf Breeze	4,190		33476	Pahokee	5,663	4,709
33581	Gulf Gate Estates	5,874		32077	Palatka	9,444	11,028
33737	Gulfport	9,730	9,730	32905	Palm Bay	7,199	2,808
33844	Haines City	8,956	9,135	33480	Palm Beach	9,086	6,055
33009	Hallandale	23,849	10,483	33403	Palm Beach Gardens	6,102	1
°33010	Hialeah	102,452	66,972	33561	Palmetto	7,422	5,556
32643	High Springs	2,787	2,329	33619	Palm River-Clair Mel	8,536	
32401	Hiland Park	3,691		33460	Palm Springs	4,340	2,503
32805	Holden Heights	6,206		32401	Panama City	32,096	33,275
32017	Holly Hill	8,191	4,182	32401	Parker	4,212	
°33022	Hollywood	106,873	35,237	33009	Pembroke Park	2,949	569
33509	Holmes Beach	2,699	1,143	33023	Pembroke Pines	15,520	1,429
33030	Homestead	13,674	9,152	°32502	Pensacola	59,507	56,752
33030	Homestead Base	8,257		33157	Perrine	10,257	6,424
33934	Immokalee	3,764	3,224	32347	Perry	7,701	8,030
32903	Indialantic	2,685	1,653	32808	Pine Hills	13,882	
32937	Indian Harbour Beach	5,371		33565	Pinellas Park	22,287	10,848
33535	Indian Rocks Beach	2,666	1,940	33566	Plant City	15,451	15,711
°32201	Jacksonville	528,865	201,030	33314	Plantation	23,523	4,772
33568	Jasmine Estates	2,967		°33060	Pompano Beach	38,544	15,992
32901	June Park	3,090	1,484	33064	Pompano Beach Highlands	5,014	
33458	Jupiter	3,136	1,058				
33156	Kendall	35,497		33950	Port Charlotte	10,769	3,197
33709	Kenneth City	3,862	2,114	32019	Port Orange	3,781	1,801
33577	Kensington Park	3,138	2,969	32456	Port St. Joe	4,401	4,217
33037	Key Largo	2,866		33950	Punta Gorda	3,879	3,157
33040	Key West	29,312	33,956	32351	Quincy	8,334	8,874
32741	Kissimmee	7,119	6,845	33156	Richmond Heights	6,663	4,311
33850	Lake Alfred	2,847	2,191	33581	Ridge Woods Heights	2,528	
	Lake Carroll	5,577		33312	Riverland-Lauderdale Isles	5,512	
32055	Lake City	10,575	9,465				
32208	Lake Forest	5,216		33404	Riviera Beach	21,401	13,046
°33803	Lake Holloway	6,227	3,172	32955	Rockledge	10,523	3,481
°33802	Lakeland	41,550	41,350	33572	Safety Harbor	3,103	1,787
33612	Lake Magdalene	9,266		32084	St. Augustine	12,352	14,734
33403	Lake Park	6,993	3,589	32769	St. Cloud	5,041	4,353
33853	Lake Wales	8,240	8,346	°33730	St. Petersburg	216,232	181,298
33460	Lake Worth	23,714	20,758	33706	St. Petersburg Beach	8,024	6,268
33460	Lantana	7,126	5,021	33505	Samoset	4,070	4,824
33540	Largo	22,031	5,302	32771	Sanford	17,393	19,175
33308	Lauderdale by the Sea	2,879	1,327	°33578	Sarasota	40,237	34,083
33313	Lauderdale Lakes	10,577		33579	Sarasota South	3,730	
33313	Lauderhill	8,465	132	33579	Sarasota Southeast	6,885	
32748	Leesburg	11,869	11,172	33577	Sarasota Springs	4,405	
33936	Lehigh Acres	4,394		32937	Satellite Beach	6,558	825
33614	Leto	8,458		33870	Sebring	7,223	6,939
33064	Lighthouse Point	9,071	2,453	33578	Siesta Key	4,460	
32060	Live Oak	6,830	6,544	33493	South Bay	2,958	1,631
32810	Lockhart	5,809		32021	South Daytona	4,979	1,954
33548	Longboat Key	2,850	1,000	33143	South Miami	11,780	9,846
32750	Longwood	3,203	1,689	33157	South Miami Heights	10,395	
32444	Lynn Haven	4,044	3,078	32937	South Patrick Shores	10,313	
32063	Macclenny	2,733	2,671	32016	South Peninsula	3,302	3,741
33738	Madeira Beach	4,342	3,943	32401	Springfield	5,949	4,628
32340	Madison	3,737	3,239	32091	Starke	4,848	4,806
32751	Maitland	7,157	3,570	33494	Stuart	4,820	4,791
33050	Marathon	4,397		33313	Sunrise Golf Village	7,403	
33063	Margate	8,867	2,646	33154	Surfside	3,614	3,157
32446	Marianna	6,741	7,152	33144	Sweetwater	3,357	645
32569	Mary Esther	3,192	780	33614	Sweetwater Creek	19,453	
°32901	Melbourne	40,236	11,982	°32302	Tallahassee	72,586	48,174

ZIP Code	Place	1970	1960	ZIP Code	Place	1970	1960
33513	Tamarac	5,078	.....	30905	Fort Gordon	15,589	.....
*33602	Tampa	277,767	274,970	30741	Fort Oglethorpe	3,869	2,251
33589	Tarpon Springs	7,118	6,768	31313	Fort Stewart	4,467	.....
32778	Tavares	3,261	2,724	31030	Fort Valley	9,251	8,310
33617	Temple Terrace	7,347	3,812	30501	Gainesville	15,459	16,523
33458	Tequesta	2,642	199	31408	Garden City	5,790	5,451
33905	Tice	7,254	4,377	30427	Glennville	2,965	2,791
32780	Titusville	30,515	6,410	31520	Glynco	2,558	.....
33740	Treasure Island	6,120	3,506	31031	Gordon	2,553	1,793
32401	Tyndall	4,248	.....	30642	Greensboro	2,583	2,773
32807	Union Park	3,166	.....	30223	Griffin	22,734	21,735
33620	University (Hillsborough)	10,039	.....	30813	Grovetown	3,169	1,396
32580	Valparaiso	6,504	5,975	30054	Hapeville	9,567	10,082
33595	Venice	6,648	3,444	30643	Hartwell	4,865	4,599
3959E	Venice South	4,680	.....	31036	Hawkinsville	4,077	3,967
32960	Vero Beach	11,908	8,849	31539	Hazlehurst	4,065	3,699
32960	Vero Beach South	7,330	.....	31313	Hinesville	4,115	3,174
33166	Virginia Gardens	2,524	2,159	30230	Hogansville	3,075	3,658
33880	Wahneta	2,733	1,796	31634	Homerville	3,025	2,634
32507	Warrington	15,848	16,752	30233	Jackson	3,778	2,545
32055	Watertown	3,624	2,109	31545	Jesup	9,091	7,304
33873	Wauchula	3,007	3,411	30236	Jonesboro	4,105	3,014
33505	West Bradenton	6,162	.....	30144	Kennesaw	3,548	1,507
32935	West Eau Gallie	2,705	.....	30728	La Fayette	6,044	5,588
32446	West End	5,289	3,124	30240	La Grange	23,301	23,632
32901	West Melbourne	3,050	2,266	31635	Lakeland	2,569	2,236
33144	West Miami	5,494	5,296	30245	Lawrenceville	5,115	3,804
*33401	West Palm Beach	57,375	56,208	30147	Lindale	2,768	.....
32505	West Pensacola	20,924	.....	30434	Louisville	2,691	2,413
33880	West Winter Haven	7,716	5,050	30436	Lyons	3,739	3,219
3316E	Westwood Lakes	12,811	22,517	30253	McDonough	2,675	2,224
32570	Whiting Field	3,439	.....	31055	McRae	3,151	2,738
33305	Wilton Manors	10,948	8,257	*31201	Macon	122,423	69,764
				30650	Madison	2,890	2,680
32787	Winter Garden	5,153	5,513	31816	Manchester	4,779	4,115
33880	Winter Haven	16,136	16,277	30060	Marietta	27,216	25,565
32789	Winter Park	21,895	17,162	30439	Metter	2,912	2,362
33599	Zephyrhills	3,369	2,887	31034	Midway-Hardwick	14,047	16,909
				31061	Milledgeville	11,601	11,117
	Georgia			30442	Millen	3,713	3,633
30101	Acworth	3,929	2,359	30655	Monroe	8,071	6,826
31620	Adel	4,972	4,321	31063	Montezuma	4,125	3,744
*31702	Albany	72,623	55,890	30260	Morrow	3,708	580
31510	Alma	3,756	3,515	31768	Moultrie	14,400	15,764
30161	Alto Park-Garden Lakes	2,963	2,526	31639	Nashville	4,323	4,070
31709	Americus	16,091	13,472	30263	Newnan	11,205	12,169
31714	Ashburn	4,209	3,291	30071	Norcross	2,755	1,605
30601	Athens	44,342	31,355	31774	Ocilla	3,185	3,217
*30304	Atlanta	497,421	487,455	31779	Pelham	4,539	4,609
*30901	Augusta	59,864	70,626	31069	Perry	7,771	6,032
30001	Austell	2,632	1,867	31407	Port Wentworth	3,905	3,705
31717	Bainbridge	10,887	12,714	30073	Powder Springs	2,559	746
30204	Barnesville	4,935	4,919	31643	Quitman	4,818	5,071
31513	Baxley	3,503	4,268	30274	Riverdale	2,521	1,045
31516	Blackshear	2,624	2,482	30153	Rockmart	3,857	3,938
31723	Blakely	5,267	3,580	30161	Rome	30,759	32,226
30110	Bremen	3,484	3,132	30741	Rossville	3,957	4,665
31520	Brunswick	19,585	21,703	30075	Roswell	5,430	2,983
30518	Buford	4,640	4,168	31558	St. Marys	3,408	3,272
31728	Cairo	8,061	7,427	31522	St. Simons	5,346	3,199
30701	Calhoun	4,748	3,587	31082	Sandersville	5,546	5,425
31730	Camilla	4,987	4,753	*31401	Savannah	118,349	149,245
30114	Canton	3,654	2,411	30080	Smyrna	19,157	10,157
30117	Carrollton	13,520	10,973	30457	Soperton	2,596	2,317
30120	Cartersville	9,929	8,668	30458	Statesboro	14,616	8,356
30125	Cedartown	9,253	9,340	30747	Summerville	5,043	4,706
30341	Chamblee	9,127	6,635	30401	Swainsboro	7,325	5,943
30705	Chatsworth	2,706	1,184	30467	Sylvania	3,199	3,469
30021	Clarkston	3,127	1,524	31791	Sylvester	4,226	3,610
30417	Claxton	2,669	2,672	30176	Tallapoosa	2,896	2,744
31014	Cochran	5,161	4,714	30286	Thomaston	10,024	9,336
30337	College Park	18,203	23,469	31792	Thomasville	18,155	18,246
*31902	Columbus	155,028	116,779	30824	Thomson	6,503	4,522
30529	Commerce	3,702	3,551	31404	Thunderbolt	2,750	1,925
30207	Conyers	4,890	2,881	31794	Tifton	12,179	9,903
31015	Cordele	10,733	10,609	30577	Toccoa	6,971	7,303
30531	Cornelia	3,014	2,936	30291	Union City	3,031	2,118
30209	Covington	10,267	8,167	31601	Valdosta	32,303	30,652
31740	Cuthbert	3,972	4,300	30474	Vidalia	9,507	7,569
30533	Dahlonega	2,658	2,604	30180	Villa Rica	3,922	3,450
30720	Dalton	18,872	17,868	31093	Warner Robins	33,491	18,633
31742	Dawson	5,383	5,062	30673	Washington	4,094	4,440
*30030	Decatur	21,943	22,026	31501	Waycross	18,996	20,944
31501	Deenwood	3,015	.....	30830	Waynesboro	5,530	5,359
31520	Dock Junction	6,009	5,417	31833	West Point	4,232	4,610
31745	Donalsonville	2,907	2,621	31404	Wilmington Island	3,284	.....
30340	Doraville	9,157	4,437	30680	Winder	6,605	5,555
31533	Douglas	10,195	8,736	31406	Windsor Forest	7,288	.....
30134	Douglasville	5,472	4,462				
31021	Dublin	15,143	13,814		**Hawaii**		
31023	Eastman	5,416	5,118	96701	Aiea	12,560	11,826
30344	East Point	39,315	35,633	96706	Barbers Pt. Housing	3,187	.....
31024	Eatonton	4,125	3,612	96706	Ewa	2,906	3,257
30635	Elberton	6,438	7,107	96706	Ewa Beach	7,765	4,627
30213	Fairburn	3,143	2,470	96818	Foster Village	3,755	.....
31750	Fitzgerald	8,187	8,781	96701	Halawa Heights	5,809	.....
30050	Forest Park	19,994	14,201	96712	Haleiwa	2,626	2,504
31029	Forsyth	3,736	3,697	96824	Hickam Housing	7,352	.....
31905	Fort Benning	27,495	.....	96720	Hilo	26,353	25,966

ZIP Code	Place	1970	1960
*96813	Honolulu	324,871	294,194
96706	Iroquois Point	4,572	......
96732	Kahului	8,280	4,223
96734	Kailua	33,783	......
96744	Kaneohe	29,903	14,414
96746	Kapaa	3,794	3,439
96761	Lahaina	3,718	3,423
96762	Laie	3,009	1,767
96766	Lihue	3,124	3,908
96792	Maili	4,397	......
96792	Makaha	4,644	......
96706	Makakilo City	3,499	......
96734	Maunawili	5,303	......
96734	Mokapu	7,860	......
96792	Nanakuli	6,506	2,745
96782	Pacific Palisades	7,846	......
96782	Pearl City	19,552	......
96786	Schofield Barracks	13,516	......
96786	Wahiawa	17,598	15,512
96791	Waialua	4,047	2,689
96792	Waianae	3,302	......
96793	Wailuku	7,979	6,969
96701	Waimalu	2,982	......
96795	Waimanalo Beach	3,045	......
96797	Waipahu	24,150	......

Idaho

ZIP Code	Place	1970	1960
83211	American Falls	2,769	2,123
83401	Ammon	2,545	1,882
83221	Blackfoot	8,716	7,378
*83707	Boise City	74,990	34,481
83316	Buhl	2,975	3,059
83318	Burley	8,279	7,508
83605	Caldwell	14,219	12,230
83201	Chubbuck	2,924	1,590
83814	Coeur D'Alene	16,228	14,291
83617	Emmett	3,945	3,769
83330	Gooding	2,599	2,750
83530	Grangeville	3,636	3,642
83401	Idaho Falls	35,776	33,161
83338	Jerome	4,183	4,761
83837	Kellogg	3,811	5,061
83501	Lewiston	26,068	12,691
83642	Meridian	2,616	2,081
83254	Montpelier	2,604	3,146
83843	Moscow	14,146	11,183
83647	Mountain Home	6,451	5,984
83648	Mountain Home Base	6,038	......
83651	Nampa	20,768	18,897
83544	Orofino	3,883	2,471
83661	Payette	4,521	4,451
83201	Pocatello	40,036	28,534
83263	Preston	3,310	3,640
83440	Rexburg	8,272	4,767
83350	Rupert	4,563	4,153
83445	St. Anthony	2,877	2,700
83861	St. Maries	2,571	2,435
83467	Salmon	2,732	2,944
83864	Sandpoint	4,144	4,355
83274	Shelley	2,614	2,612
83276	Soda Springs	2,977	2,424
83301	Twin Falls	21,914	20,126
83672	Weiser	4,108	4,208

Illinois

ZIP Code	Place	1970	1960
61401	Abingdon	3,936	3,469
60101	Addison	24,482	6,741
61231	Aledo	3,325	3,080
60102	Algonquin	3,515	2,014
62207	Alorton	3,573	3,282
60658	Alsip	11,141	3,770
62002	Alton	39,700	43,047
62906	Anna	4,766	4,280
60002	Antioch	3,189	2,268
*60004	Arlington Heights	64,884	27,878
62615	Auburn	2,594	2,209
*60507	Aurora	74,182	63,715
60010	Barrington	8,674	5,434
60010	Barrington Hills	2,712	1,726
60103	Bartlett	3,501	1,540
61607	Bartonville	7,221	7,253
60510	Batavia	8,994	7,496
62618	Beardstown	6,222	6,294
62220	Belleville	41,699	37,264
60104	Bellwood	22,096	20,729
61008	Belvidere	14,061	11,223
60106	Bensenville	12,956	9,141
62812	Benton	6,833	7,023
60162	Berkeley	6,152	5,792
60402	Berwyn	52,502	54,224
62010	Bethalto	7,074	3,235
60108	Bloomingdale	2,974	1,262
61701	Bloomington	39,992	36,271
60406	Blue Island	22,958	19,618
60439	Bolingbrook	7,643	......
60914	Bourbonnais	5,909	3,336

ZIP Code	Place	1970	1960
62230	Breese	2,885	2,461
60455	Bridge View	12,522	7,334
60153	Broadview	9,623	8,588
60513	Brookfield	20,284	20,429
60090	Buffalo Grove	11,799	1,492
60459	Burbank	29,900	......
60633	Burnham	3,634	2,478
61422	Bushnell	3,703	3,710
62206	Cahokia	20,649	15,829
62914	Cairo	6,277	9,348
60409	Calumet City	33,107	25,000
60643	Calumet Park	10,069	8,448
61520	Canton	14,217	13,588
62901	Carbondale	22,816	14,670
62626	Carlinville	5,675	5,440
62231	Carlyle	3,139	2,903
62821	Carmi	6,033	6,152
60187	Carol Stream	4,434	836
60110	Carpentersville	24,059	17,424
62016	Carrollton	2,866	2,558
62918	Carterville	3,061	2,643
62321	Carthage	3,350	3,325
60013	Cary	4,358	2,530
62420	Casey	2,994	2,890
62232	Caseyville	3,411	2,455
62801	Centralia	15,217	13,904
62206	Centreville	11,378	12,769
61820	Champaign	56,532	49,583
61920	Charleston	16,421	10,505
62629	Chatham	2,788	1,069
62233	Chester	5,310	4,460
*60607	Chicago	3,369,359	3,550,404
60411	Chicago Heights	40,900	34,331
60415	Chicago Ridge	9,187	5,748
61523	Chillicothe	6,052	3,054
62822	Christopher	2,910	2,854
60650	Cicero	67,058	69,130
60514	Clarendon Hills	6,750	5,885
61727	Clinton	7,570	7,355
60416	Coal City	3,040	2,852
61240	Coal Valley	3,088	435
62234	Collinsville	18,015	14,217
62236	Columbia	4,188	3,174
60477	Country Club Hills	6,920	3,421
60525	Countryside	2,864	......
60435	Crest Hill	7,460	5,887
60445	Crestwood	5,770	1,213
60417	Crete	4,656	3,463
61611	Creve Coeur	6,440	6,684
60014	Crystal Lake	14,541	8,314
61832	Danville	42,570	41,856
60559	Darien	7,789	......
*62521	Decatur	90,397	78,004
60015	Deerfield	18,876	11,786
60115	De Kalb	32,949	18,486
*60016	Des Plaines	57,239	34,886
60406	Dixmoor	4,735	3,076
61021	Dixon	18,147	19,565
60419	Dolton	25,937	18,746
60515	Downers Grove	32,751	21,154
62239	Dupo	2,842	2,937
62832	Du Quoin	6,691	6,558
60420	Dwight	3,841	3,086
62024	East Alton	7,309	7,630
60411	East Chicago Heights	5,000	3,270
60118	East Dundee	2,920	2,221
61244	East Moline	20,832	16,732
61611	East Peoria	18,455	12,310
*62201	East St. Louis	69,996	81,712
62025	Edwardsville	11,070	9,996
62401	Effingham	9,458	8,172
62930	Eldorado	3,876	3,573
60120	Elgin	55,691	49,447
60007	Elk Grove	21,907	6,608
60126	Elmhurst	48,887	36,991
60635	Elmwood Park	26,160	23,866
61530	Eureka	3,028	2,538
*60204	Evanston	79,808	79,283
60642	Evergreen Park	25,921	24,178
61739	Fairbury	3,359	2,937
62837	Fairfield	5,897	6,362
62207	Fairmont City	2,769	2,688
62232	Fairview Heights	8,625	......
61531	Farmington	2,959	2,831
62839	Flora	5,283	5,331
60422	Flossmoor	7,846	4,624
60130	Forest Park	15,472	14,452
60020	Fox Lake	4,511	3,700
60131	Franklin Park	20,348	18,322
61032	Freeport	27,736	26,628
61252	Fulton	3,630	3,387
60030	Gages Lake-Wildwood	5,337	......
61036	Galena	3,930	4,410
61401	Galesburg	36,290	37,243
61434	Galva	3,061	3,060
61254	Geneseo	5,840	5,169
60134	Geneva	9,115	7,646
60135	Genoa	3,003	2,330
61846	Georgetown	3,984	3,544
60936	Gibson City	3,454	3,453

ZIP Code	Place	1970	1960	ZIP Code	Place	1970	1960
62033	Gillespie	3,457	3,569	62864	Mount Vernon	16,382	15,566
60022	Glencoe	10,675	10,472	60060	Mundelein	16,128	10,526
60137	Glendale Heights	11,406	173	62966	Murphysboro	10,013	8,673
60137	Glen Ellyn	21,909	15,972	60540	Naperville	23,885	12,933
60025	Glenview	24,880	18,132	62263	Nashville	3,027	2,606
60425	Glenwood	7,416	882	60451	New Lenox	2,855	1,750
62040	Granite City	40,440	40,073	62448	Newton	3,024	2,901
60030	Grayslake	4,907	3,762	60648	Niles	31,432	20,393
61241	Green Rock	4,631	4,569	62075	Nokomis	2,532	2,476
62246	Greenville	4,631	4,569	61761	Normal	26,396	13,357
60031	Gurnee	2,738	1,831	60656	Norridge	17,020	14,087
62341	Hamilton	2,764	2,228	60542	North Aurora	4,833	2,088
60103	Hanover Park	11,916	451	60062	Northbrook	27,297	11,635
62946	Harrisburg	9,535	9,171	60064	North Chicago	47,275	22,938
60033	Harvard	5,177	4,248	60093	Northfield	5,010	4,005
60426	Harvey	34,636	29,071	60164	Northlake	14,212	12,318
60656	Harwood Heights	9,060	5,688	61111	North Park	15,679	
62644	Havana	4,376	4,363	60546	North Riverside	8,097	7,989
60429	Hazel Crest	10,329	6,205	60521	Oak Brook	4,164	324
61537	Henry	2,610	2,278	60452	Oak Forest	17,870	3,724
62948	Herrin	9,623	9,474	*60454	Oak Lawn	60,305	27,471
60457	Hickory Hills	13,176	2,707	*60301	Oak Park	62,511	61,093
62249	Highland	5,981	4,943	62024	Oakwood Heights	3,229	
60035	Highland Park	32,263	25,532	62269	O'Fallon	7,268	4,018
60040	Highwood	4,973	4,499	61348	Oglesby	4,175	4,215
62049	Hillsboro	4,267	4,232	62450	Olney	8,974	8,780
60162	Hillside	8,888	7,794	60461	Olympia Fields	3,478	1,503
60521	Hinsdale	15,918	12,859	61061	Oregon	3,539	3,732
60172	Hoffman Estates	22,238	8,296	60462	Orland Park	6,391	2,592
60456	Hometown	6,729	7,479	61350	Ottawa	18,716	19,408
60430	Homewood	18,871	13,371	60067	Palatine	25,904	11,504
60942	Hoopeston	6,461	6,606	60463	Palos Heights	9,915	3,775
60143	Itasca	4,638	3,564	60465	Palos Hills	6,629	3,766
60650	Jacksonville	20,553	21,690	60464	Palos Park	3,307	2,169
62052	Jerseyville	7,446	7,420	62557	Pana	6,326	6,432
62951	Johnston City	3,928	3,891	61944	Paris	9,971	9,823
*60431	Joliet	78,887	66,780	60085	Park City	2,855	1,408
60458	Justice	9,473	2,803	60466	Park Forest	30,638	29,993
60901	Kankakee	30,944	27,666	60068	Park Ridge	42,614	32,659
60043	Kenilworth	2,980	2,959	60957	Paxton	4,373	4,370
61109	Ken Rock	5,945		61554	Pekin	31,375	28,146
61443	Kewanee	15,762	16,324	*61601	Peoria	126,963	103,162
61448	Knoxville	2,930	2,560	61614	Peoria Heights	7,943	7,064
60525	La Grange	17,814	15,285	61354	Peru	11,772	10,460
60525	La Grange Park	15,459	13,793	62675	Petersburg	2,632	2,359
60525	La Grange Highlands	6,842		60426	Phoenix	3,596	4,203
60044	Lake Bluff	5,008	3,494	62274	Pinckneyville	3,377	3,085
60045	Lake Forest	15,642	10,687	62363	Pittsfield	4,244	4,089
60102	Lake in the Hills	3,240	2,046	60544	Plainfield	2,928	2,183
60047	Lake Zurich	4,082	3,458	60545	Plano	4,664	3,343
60438	Lansing	25,805	18,098	61064	Polo	2,542	2,551
61301	La Salle	10,736	11,897	61764	Pontiac	10,595	8,435
62439	Lawrenceville	5,863	5,492	60469	Posen	5,498	4,517
62254	Lebanon	3,564	2,863	61356	Princeton	6,959	6,250
60439	Lemont	5,080	3,397	60070	Prospect Heights	13,333	
61542	Lewistown	2,706	2,603	62301	Quincy	45,288	43,793
60048	Libertyville	11,684	8,560	61866	Rantoul	25,562	22,116
62656	Lincoln	17,582	16,890	62278	Red Bud	2,559	1,942
60015	Lincolnshire	2,531	555	60471	Richton Park	2,558	933
60645	Lincolnwood	12,929	11,744	60627	Riverdale	15,806	12,008
60046	Lindenhurst	3,141	1,259	60305	River Forest	13,402	12,695
60532	Lisle	5,329	4,219	60171	River Grove	11,465	8,464
62056	Litchfield	7,190	7,330	60546	Riverside	10,432	9,750
60441	Lockport	9,985	7,560	60472	Robbins	9,641	7,511
60148	Lombard	36,194	22,561	62454	Robinson	7,178	7,226
61111	Loves Park	12,390	9,086	61068	Rochelle	8,594	7,008
60534	Lyons	11,124	9,936	61071	Rock Falls	10,287	10,261
60050	McHenry	6,772	3,336	*61101	Rockford	147,370	126,706
62859	McLeansboro	2,630	2,951	61201	Rock Island	50,166	51,863
61455	Macomb	19,643	12,135	60008	Rolling Meadows	19,178	10,879
62060	Madison	7,042	6,861	60441	Romeoville	12,674	3,574
60950	Manteno	2,864	2,225	60172	Roselle	6,207	3,581
60152	Marengo	4,235	3,568	60018	Rosemont	4,000	978
62959	Marion	11,724	11,274	62024	Rosewood Heights	3,391	4,572
60426	Markham	15,987	11,704	60073	Round Lake Beach	5,717	5,011
61554	Marquette Heights	2,758	2,517	60073	Round Lake Park	3,148	2,565
61341	Marseilles	4,320	4,347	62681	Rushville	3,300	2,819
62441	Marshall	3,468	3,270	60174	St. Charles	12,928	9,269
62258	Mascoutah	5,045	3,625	62881	Salem	6,187	6,165
62664	Mason City	2,611	2,160	60548	Sandwich	5,056	3,842
60443	Matteson	4,741	3,225	60411	Sauk	7,479	4,687
61938	Mattoon	19,681	19,088	61074	Savanna	4,942	4,950
60153	Maywood	29,019	27,330	60172	Schaumburg	18,730	986
*60160	Melrose Park	22,716	22,291	60176	Schiller Park	12,712	5,687
61342	Mendota	6,902	6,154	62225	Scott	7,871	
62960	Metropolis	6,940	7,339	62565	Shelbyville	4,597	4,821
60445	Midlothian	15,939	6,605	61282	Silvis	5,907	3,973
61264	Milan	4,873	3,065	60076	Skokie	68,627	59,364
61265	Moline	46,237	42,705	61080	South Beloit	3,804	3,781
60954	Momence	2,836	2,949	60411	South Chicago Heights	4,923	4,043
61462	Monmouth	11,022	10,372	60177	South Elgin	4,289	2,624
60538	Montgomery	3,278	2,122	60473	South Holland	23,931	10,412
61856	Monticello	4,130	3,219	62650	South Jacksonville	2,950	2,340
60450	Morris	8,194	7,935	60459	South Stickney (see Burbank)		
61270	Morrison	4,387	4,159	62286	Sparta	4,307	3,452
61550	Morton	10,419	5,325	*62708	Springfield	91,753	83,271
60053	Morton Grove	26,369	20,533	61362	Spring Valley	5,605	5,371
62863	Mount Carmel	8,096	8,594	62088	Staunton	4,396	4,228
61054	Mount Morris	3,173	3,075	60475	Steger	8,104	6,432
60056	Mount Prospect	34,995	18,906	61081	Sterling	16,113	15,688

ZIP Code	Place	1970	1960
60402	Stickney	6,601	6,239
60165	Stone Park	4,429	3,038
60103	Streamwood	18,176	4,821
61364	Streator	15,600	16,868
61951	Sullivan	4,112	3,946
60501	Summit	11,569	10,374
62221	Swansea	5,432	3,018
60178	Sycamore	7,843	6,961
62568	Taylorville	10,927	8,801
60476	Thornton	3,714	2,895
61832	Tilton	2,544	2,598
60477	Tinley Park	12,382	6,392
61953	Tuscola	3,917	3,875
61801	Urbana	32,800	27,294
62471	Vandalia	5,160	5,537
60046	Venetian	2,554	2,084
62090	Venice	4,680	5,380
61956	Villa Grove	2,605	2,308
60181	Villa Park	25,891	20,391
62690	Virden	3,504	3,309
60555	Warrenville	3,268	
61571	Washington	6,790	5,919
62204	Washington Park	9,524	6,601
62298	Waterloo	4,546	3,739
60970	Watseka	5,294	5,219
60084	Wauconda	5,460	3,227
60085	Waukegan	65,269	55,719
60153	Westchester	20,033	18,092
60185	West Chicago	10,111	6,854
60118	West Dundee	3,295	2,530
61102	West End	7,554	
60558	Western Springs	12,147	10,838
62896	West Frankfort	8,854	9,027
60559	Westmont	8,920	5,997
61604	West Peoria	6,873	
61883	Westville	3,655	3,497
60187	Wheaton	31,138	24,312
60090	Wheeling	14,746	7,169
62092	White Hall	2,979	3,012
60480	Willow Springs	3,318	2,348
60091	Wilmette	32,134	28,268
60481	Wilmington	4,335	4,210
60190	Winfield	4,285	1,575
60093	Winnetka	13,998	13,368
60096	Winthrop Harbor	4,794	3,848
60097	Wonder Lake	4,806	3,543
60191	Wood Dale	8,831	3,071
60515	Woodridge	11,028	542
62095	Wood River	13,186	11,694
60098	Woodstock	10,226	8,897
60482	Worth	11,999	8,196
60099	Zion	17,268	11,941

Indiana

ZIP Code	Place	1970	1960
46001	Alexandria	5,600	5,582
*46011	Anderson	70,787	49,061
46703	Angola	5,117	4,746
47918	Attica	4,262	4,341
46706	Auburn	7,388	6,350
47001	Aurora	4,293	4,119
47102	Austin	4,902	
47006	Batesville	3,799	3,349
47421	Bedford	13,087	13,024
46107	Beech Grove	13,832	10,973
46711	Berne	2,988	2,644
47512	Bicknell	3,717	3,878
46408	Black Oak	9,624	
47424	Bloomfield	2,565	2,224
47401	Bloomington	43,262	31,357
46714	Bluffton	8,297	6,238
47601	Boonville	5,736	4,801
47834	Brazil	8,163	8,853
46506	Bremen	3,487	3,062
47012	Brookville	2,864	2,596
46112	Brownsburg	5,751	4,478
46032	Carmel	6,568	1,442
46303	Cedar Lake	7,589	
47111	Charlestown	5,933	5,726
46017	Chesterfield	3,001	2,588
46304	Chesterton	6,177	4,335
47130	Clarksville	13,806	8,088
47842	Clinton	5,340	5,843
46725	Columbia City	4,911	4,803
47201	Columbus	26,457	20,778
47331	Connersville	17,604	17,698
47112	Corydon	2,719	2,701
47932	Covington	2,641	2,759
47933	Crawfordsville	13,842	14,231
46407	Crown Point	10,931	8,443
46122	Danville	3,771	3,287
46733	Decatur	8,445	8,327
46923	Delphi	2,582	2,491
47366	Dunkirk	3,465	3,117
46311	Dyer	4,906	2,993
46312	East Chicago	46,982	57,669
46405	East Gary	9,858	9,309
46124	Edinburg	4,906	3,664
46514	Elkhart	43,152	40,274
46036	Elwood	11,196	11,793

ZIP Code	Place	1970	1960
*47708	Evansville	138,764	141,543
46928	Fairmount	3,427	3,080
47533	Fort Branch	2,535	1,983
*46802	Fort Wayne	178,021	161,776
47944	Fowler	2,643	2,491
46041	Frankfort	14,956	15,302
46131	Franklin	11,477	9,453
46738	Garrett	4,715	4,364
*46401	Gary	175,415	178,320
46933	Gas City	5,742	4,469
46526	Goshen	18,004	13,718
46135	Greencastle	8,852	8,506
47025	Greendale	3,783	2,861
46140	Greenfield	9,986	9,049
47240	Greensburg	8,620	7,492
46142	Greenwood	11,408	7,169
46319	Griffith	18,168	9,483
46970	Grissom	4,963	
46320	Hammond	107,888	111,698
47243	Hanover	3,018	1,170
47348	Hartford City	8,207	8,053
46322	Highland	24,947	16,284
46342	Hobart	21,485	18,680
47542	Huntingburg	4,794	4,146
46750	Huntington	16,217	16,185
*46206	Indianapolis	744,743	476,258
47546	Jasper	8,641	6,737
47130	Jeffersonville	20,008	19,522
46755	Kendallville	6,838	6,765
46534	Knox	3,519	3,458
46901	Kokomo	44,042	47,197
*47901	Lafayette	44,955	42,330
46350	La Porte	22,140	21,157
46226	Lawrence	16,646	10,103
47025	Lawrenceburg	4,636	5,004
46052	Lebanon	9,766	9,523
46767	Ligonier	3,034	2,595
47441	Linton	5,450	5,736
46947	Logansport	19,255	21,106
46360	Long Beach	2,740	2,007
47553	Loogootee	2,953	2,858
46356	Lowell	3,839	2,270
47250	Madison	13,081	10,488
46952	Marion	39,607	37,854
46151	Martinsville	9,723	7,525
46410	Merrillville		
	—Lottaville—Rexville	15,918	
46360	Michigan City	39,369	36,653
46544	Mishawaka	35,517	33,361
47446	Mitchell	4,092	3,552
47960	Monticello	4,869	4,035
46158	Mooresville	5,800	3,856
47620	Mount Vernon	6,770	5,970
*47302	Muncie	69,082	68,603
46321	Munster	16,514	10,313
46550	Nappanee	4,159	3,895
47150	New Albany	38,402	37,812
47362	New Castle	21,215	20,349
46774	New Haven	5,728	3,396
46184	New Whiteland	4,200	3,488
46060	Noblesville	7,548	7,664
46962	North Manchester	5,791	4,377
47265	North Vernon	4,582	4,307
47560	Oakland City	3,289	3,016
47454	Paoli	3,281	2,754
46970	Peru	14,139	14,453
47567	Petersburg	2,697	2,939
46168	Plainfield	8,211	5,460
46563	Plymouth	7,661	7,558
46368	Portage	19,127	11,822
46304	Porter	3,058	2,189
47371	Portland	7,115	6,999
47570	Princeton	7,431	7,906
47978	Rensselaer	4,688	4,740
47374	Richmond	43,999	44,149
46975	Rochester	4,631	4,883
47635	Rockport	2,565	2,474
47872	Rockville	2,820	2,756
46173	Rushville	6,686	7,264
47167	Salem	5,041	4,546
46375	Schererville	3,663	2,875
47170	Scottsburg	4,791	3,810
47172	Sellersburg	3,177	2,679
47274	Seymour	13,352	11,629
46176	Shelbyville	15,094	14,317
*46624	South Bend	125,580	132,445
46224	Speedway	16,052	9,624
47460	Spencer	2,553	2,557
47882	Sullivan	4,683	4,979
47586	Tell City	7,933	6,609
*47808	Terre Haute	70,335	72,500
46072	Tipton	5,313	5,604
46360	Trail Creek	2,697	1,552
47390	Union City	3,995	4,047
46989	Upland	3,202	1,999
46383	Valparaiso	20,020	15,227
47591	Vincennes	19,867	18,046
46992	Wabash	13,379	12,621
46580	Warsaw	7,506	7,234
47501	Washington	11,358	10,846

ZIP Code	Place	1970	1960	ZIP Code	Place	1970	1960
46408	West Glen Park	5,940		51201	Sheldon	4,535	4,251
47906	West Lafayette	19,157	12,680	51601	Shenandoah	5,968	6,567
47885	West Terre Haute	2,704	3,006	51249	Sibley	2,749	2,852
46391	Westville	2,614	789	51250	Sioux Center	3,450	2,275
46394	Whiting	7,247	8,137	*51101	Sioux City	85,925	89,159
47394	Winchester	5,493	5,742	51301	Spencer	10,278	8,864
46590	Winona Lake	2,811	1,928	51360	Spirit Lake	3,014	2,685
				50588	Storm Lake	8,591	7,728
	Iowa			52339	Tama	3,000	2,925
				52772	Tipton	2,877	2,862
52531	Albia	4,151	4,582	50322	Urbandale	14,434	5,821
50511	Algona	6,032	5,702	52349	Vinton	4,845	4,781
50009	Altoona	2,883	1,458	52353	Washington	6,317	6,037
50010	Ames	39,505	27,003	*50701	Waterloo	75,533	71,755
52205	Anamosa	4,389	4,616	52172	Waukon	3,883	3,639
50021	Ankeny	9,151	2,964	50677	Waverly	7,205	6,357
50022	Atlantic	7,306	6,890	50595	Webster City	8,488	8,520
50025	Audubon	2,907	2,928	52655	West Burlington	3,139	2,560
52208	Belle Plaine	2,810	2,923	50265	West Des Moines	16,441	11,949
52722	Bettendorf	22,126	11,534	52175	West Union	2,624	2,551
52537	Bloomfield	2,718	2,771	50311	Windsor Heights	6,303	4,715
50036	Boone	12,468	12,468	50273	Winterset	3,654	3,639
52601	Burlington	32,366	32,430				
52730	Camanche	3,470	2,225		**Kansas**		
51401	Carroll	8,716	7,682				
68100	Carter Lake	3,268	2,287	67410	Abilene	6,661	6,746
50613	Cedar Falls	29,597	21,195	67003	Anthony	2,653	2,744
*52401	Cedar Rapids	110,642	92,035	67005	Arkansas City	13,216	14,262
52544	Centerville	6,531	6,629	66002	Atchison	12,565	12,529
50049	Chariton	5,009	5,042	67010	Augusta	5,977	6,434
50616	Charles City	9,268	9,964	66006	Baldwin City	2,520	1,877
51012	Cherokee	7,704	7,701	66713	Baxter Springs	4,489	4,498
51632	Clarinda	5,420	5,901	66935	Belleville	3,063	2,910
50525	Clarion	2,972	3,232	67420	Beloit	4,121	3,837
50428	Clear Lake City	6,430	6,158	66012	Bonner Springs	3,662	3,171
52732	Clinton	34,719	33,589	66442	Camp Forsyth	3,290	
50053	Clive	3,005	752	66442	Camp Funston	4,147	
52240	Coralville	6,130	2,357	66720	Chanute	10,341	10,849
51501	Council Bluffs	60,348	55,641	67335	Cherryvale	2,609	2,783
52136	Cresco	3,927	3,809	67432	Clay Center	4,963	4,613
50801	Creston	8,234	7,667	67337	Coffeyville	15,116	17,382
*52802	Davenport	98,469	88,981	67701	Colby	4,658	4,210
52101	Decorah	7,458	6,435	66725	Columbus	3,356	3,395
51442	Denison	6,300	4,930	66901	Concordia	7,221	7,022
*50318	Des Moines	201,404	208,982	67037	Derby	7,947	6,458
52742	De Witt	3,647	3,224	67801	Dodge City	14,127	13,520
52001	Dubuque	62,309	56,606	67042	El Dorado	12,308	12,523
52040	Dyersville	3,437	2,818	66801	Emporia	23,327	18,190
50533	Eagle Grove	4,489	4,381	67045	Eureka	3,576	4,055
50627	Eldora	3,223	3,225	66205	Fairway	5,133	5,398
50536	Emmetsburg	4,150	3,887	66027	Fort Leavenworth	8,060	
51334	Estherville	8,108	7,927	66701	Fort Scott	8,967	9,410
50707	Evansdale	5,038	5,738	66736	Fredonia	3,080	3,233
52556	Fairfield	8,715	8,054	66739	Galena	3,712	3,827
50436	Forest City	3,841	2,930	67846	Garden City	14,790	11,811
50501	Fort Dodge	31,263	28,399	66032	Garnett	3,169	3,034
52627	Fort Madison	13,996	15,247	66743	Girard	2,591	2,350
51534	Glenwood	4,421	4,783	67735	Goodland	5,510	4,459
50112	Grinnell	8,402	7,367	67530	Great Bend	16,133	16,670
50638	Grundy Center	2,712	2,403	67601	Hays	15,396	11,947
50441	Hampton	4,376	4,501	67060	Haysville	6,483	5,836
51537	Harlan	5,049	4,350	67449	Herington	3,165	3,702
51023	Hawarden	2,789	2,544	66434	Hiawatha	3,365	3,391
50548	Humboldt	4,665	4,031	67063	Hillsboro	2,730	2,441
50644	Independence	5,910	5,498	67544	Hoisington	3,710	4,248
50125	Indianola	8,852	7,062	66436	Holton	3,063	3,028
52240	Iowa City	46,850	33,443	66951	Hugoton	2,739	2,912
50126	Iowa Falls	6,454	5,565	67501	Hutchinson	36,885	37,574
50129	Jefferson	4,735	4,570	67301	Independence	10,347	11,222
52632	Keokuk	14,631	16,316	66749	Iola	6,493	6,885
50138	Knoxville	7,755	7,817	66441	Junction City	19,018	18,700
50140	Lamoni	2,540	2,173	*66110	Kansas City	168,213	121,901
52753	Le Claire	2,520	1,546	67068	Kingman	3,622	3,582
51031	Le Mars	8,159	6,767	66043	Lansing	3,797	1,264
52057	Manchester	4,641	4,402	67550	Larned	4,567	5,001
52060	Maquoketa	5,677	5,909	66044	Lawrence	45,698	32,858
52302	Marion	18,028	10,882	66048	Leavenworth	25,147	22,052
50158	Marshalltown	26,219	22,521	66206	Leawood	10,349	7,446
50401	Mason City	30,379	30,642	66215	Lenexa	5,242	2,487
51555	Missouri Valley	3,519	3,567	67901	Liberal	13,789	13,813
52310	Monticello	3,509	3,190	67456	Lindsborg	2,764	2,609
52641	Mount Pleasant	7,007	7,339	67554	Lyons	4,355	4,592
52314	Mount Vernon	3,018	2,593	67460	McPherson	10,851	9,996
52761	Muscatine	22,405	20,997	66502	Manhattan	27,575	22,993
50201	Nevada	4,952	4,227	66508	Marysville	3,588	4,143
50659	New Hampton	3,621	3,456	67104	Medicine Lodge	2,545	3,072
50208	Newton	15,619	15,381	66221	Merriam	10,851	5,084
50662	Oelwein	7,735	8,282	66222	Mission	8,376	4,626
51040	Onawa	3,154	3,176	66205	Mission Hills	4,177	3,621
51041	Orange City	3,572	2,707	67110	Mulvane	3,185	2,981
50461	Osage	3,815	3,753	66757	Neodesha	3,295	3,594
50213	Osceola	3,124	3,350	67114	Newton	15,439	14,877
52577	Oskaloosa	11,224	11,053	66442	North Fort Riley	12,469	
52501	Ottumwa	29,610	33,871	67654	Norton	3,627	3,345
50219	Pella	6,668	5,198	66061	Olathe	17,917	10,987
50220	Perry	6,906	6,442	66523	Osage City	2,600	2,213
51566	Red Oak	6,210	6,421	66064	Osawatomie	4,294	4,622
51246	Rock Rapids	2,632	2,780	66067	Ottawa	11,036	10,673
50583	Sac City	3,268	3,354	66204	Overland Park	79,034	

ZIP Code	Place	1970	1960	ZIP Code	Place	1970	1960
66071	Paola	4,622	4,784	40361	Paris	7,823	7,791
67219	Park	2,529	2,687	41015	Park Hills	3,999	4,076
67357	Parsons	13,015	13,929	41501	Pikeville	4,899	4,754
67661	Phillipsburg	3,241	3,233	40977	Pineville	2,817	3,181
66762	Pittsburg	20,171	18,678	40258	Pleasure Ridge Park	28,566	10,612
67663	Plainville	2,627	3,104	41653	Prestonsburg	3,422	3,133
66208	Prairie Village	28,138	25,356	42445	Princeton	6,292	5,618
67124	Pratt	6,736	8,156	42450	Providence	4,270	3,771
66203	Roeland Park	9,974	8,949	40160	Radcliff	7,881	3,384
67665	Russell	5,371	6,113	40475	Richmond	16,861	12,168
67401	Salina	37,714	43,202	42276	Russellville	6,456	5,861
67871	Scott City	4,001	3,555	40207	St. Matthews	13,152	8,738
*66202	Shawnee	20,482	9,072	42164	Scottsville	3,584	3,324
*66601	Topeka	125,011	119,484	40065	Shelbyville	4,182	4,525
67880	Ulysses	3,779	3,157	40165	Shepherdsville	2,769	1,525
67147	Valley Center	2,551	2,570	40216	Shively	19,150	15,155
66547	Wamego	2,507	2,363	42501	Somerset	10,436	7,112
67152	Wellington	8,072	8,809	41071	Southgate	3,212	2,070
*67202	Wichita	276,554	254,698	40069	Springfield	2,961	2,382
67156	Winfield	11,405	11,117	41015	Taylor Mill	3,194	710
				40172	Valley Station	24,471	10,533
	Kentucky			40383	Versailles	5,679	4,060
				40175	Vine Grove	2,987	2,435
41001	Alexandria	3,844	1,318	40769	Williamsburg	3,687	3,478
41101	Ashland	29,245	31,283	40390	Wilmore	3,466	2,773
40906	Barbourville	3,549	3,211	40391	Winchester	13,402	10,187
40004	Bardstown	5,816	4,798				
42320	Beaver Dam	2,622	1,648		**Louisiana**		
42073	Bellevue	8,847	9,336				
42025	Benton	3,652	3,074	70510	Abbeville	10,996	10,414
40403	Berea	6,956	4,302	71301	Alexandria	41,557	40,279
42101	Bowling Green	36,253	28,338	71301	Alexandria Southwest	3,151	2,782
40218	Buechel	5,359	.....	70422	Amite City	3,593	3,316
42718	Campbellsville	7,598	6,966	71001	Arcadia	2,970	2,547
41008	Carrollton	3,884	3,218	70714	Baker	8,281	4,823
41129	Catlettsburg	3,420	3,874	71220	Bastrop	14,713	15,193
42330	Central City	5,450	3,694	*70821	Baton Rouge	165,963	152,419
42728	Columbia	3,234	2,255	70360	Bayou Cane	9,077	3,173
40701	Corbin	7,317	7,119	70380	Bayou Vista	5,121	.....
*41011	Covington	52,535	60,376	70342	Berwick	4,168	3,880
40823	Cumberland	3,624	4,271	70427	Bogalusa	18,412	21,423
41031	Cynthiana	6,356	5,641	71010	Bossier City	41,595	32,776
40422	Danville	11,542	9,010	70517	Breaux Bridge	4,942	3,303
42408	Dawson Springs	3,009	3,002	71322	Bunkie	5,395	5,188
41074	Dayton	8,751	9,050	70041	Buras Triumph	4,113	4,908
41017	Edgewood	4,139	1,100	70525	Church Point	3,865	3,606
42701	Elizabethtown	11,748	9,641	71101	Cooper Road	9,034	.....
41018	Elsmere	5,161	4,607	70433	Covington	7,170	6,754
41018	Erlanger	12,676	7,072	70526	Crowley	16,104	15,617
41040	Falmouth	2,593	2,568	71232	Delhi	2,887	2,514
41139	Flatwoods	7,380	3,741	70726	Denham Springs	6,752	5,991
41042	Florence	11,661	5,837	70633	De Quincy	3,448	3,928
42223	Fort Campbell North	13,616	.....	70634	De Ridder	8,030	7,188
41121	Fort Knox	37,608	.....	70346	Donaldsonville	7,367	6,082
41017	Fort Mitchell	6,982	525	71301	England	3,715	.....
41075	Fort Thomas	16,338	14,896	70535	Eunice	11,390	11,326
41011	Fort Wright-Lookout Hgts.	4,819	2,184	71241	Farmerville	3,416	2,727
40601	Frankfort	21,902	18,365	71334	Ferriday	5,239	4,563
42134	Franklin	6,553	5,319	70538	Franklin	9,325	8,673
42041	Fulton	3,250	3,265	70438	Franklinton	3,562	3,141
40324	Georgetown	8,629	6,986	70357	Golden Meadow	2,681	3,097
42141	Glasgow	11,301	10,069	70737	Gonzales	4,512	3,252
42345	Greenville	3,875	3,198	71245	Grambling	4,407	3,144
40831	Harlan	3,318	4,177	70052	Gramercy	2,567	2,094
40330	Harrodsburg	6,741	6,061	70053	Gretna	24,875	21,967
41701	Hazard	5,459	5,958	70401	Hammond	12,487	10,563
42420	Henderson	22,976	16,892	70123	Harahan	13,037	9,275
42050	Hickman	3,048	1,537	70058	Harvey	6,347	.....
41076	Highland Heights	4,400	3,496	71038	Haynesville	3,055	3,031
42748	Hodgenville	2,562	1,985	71040	Homer	4,483	4,665
42240	Hopkinsville	21,250	19,465	70360	Houma	30,922	22,561
40336	Irvine	2,918	2,955	70748	Jackson	4,697	1,824
40229	Jeffersontown	9,701	3,431	70544	Jeanerette	6,322	5,568
41537	Jenkins	2,552	3,202	70121	Jefferson Heights	16,489	19,353
41017	Lakeside Park	2,511	2,214	70546	Jennings	11,783	11,887
40444	Lancaster	3,230	3,021	71251	Jonesboro	5,072	3,848
40342	Lawrenceburg	3,579	2,523	71343	Jonesville	2,761	2,347
40033	Lebanon	5,528	4,813	70548	Kaplan	5,540	5,267
42754	Leitchfield	2,983	2,982	70062	Kenner	29,858	17,037
*40507	Lexington	108,137	62,810	70444	Kentwood	2,736	2,607
40741	London	4,337	4,035	70501	Lafayette	68,908	40,400
42001	Lone Oak	3,759	2,104	70501	Lafayette Southwest	5,498	6,682
*40201	Louisville	361,958	390,639	70549	Lake Arthur	3,551	3,541
41016	Ludlow	5,815	6,233	70601	Lake Charles	77,998	63,392
42431	Madisonville	15,332	13,110	71254	Lake Providence	6,183	5,781
42064	Marion	3,008	2,468	70068	Laplace	5,953	3,541
42066	Mayfield	10,724	10,762	70373	Larose	4,267	2,796
41056	Maysville	7,411	8,484	71446	Leesville	8,928	4,689
40965	Middlesborough	11,878	12,607	70123	Little Farms	15,713	.....
42633	Monticello	3,618	2,940	70070	Luling	3,255	2,122
40351	Morehead	7,191	4,170	70071	Lutcher	3,911	3,274
42437	Morganfield	3,563	3,741	70554	Mamou	3,275	2,928
40353	Mount Sterling	5,083	5,370	70448	Mandeville	2,571	.....
42071	Murray	13,537	9,303	71052	Mansfield	6,432	5,839
*41071	Newport	25,998	30,070	71449	Many	3,112	3,164
40356	Nicholasville	5,829	4,275	71351	Marksville	4,519	4,257
40219	Okolona	17,643	.....	70072	Marrero	29,015	.....
42301	Owensboro	50,329	42,471	*70004	Metairie	136,477	.....
42001	Paducah	31,627	34,479	71055	Minden	13,996	12,785
41240	Paintsville	3,868	4,025	71201	Monroe	56,374	52,219

ZIP Code	Place	1970	1960
70380	Morgan City	16,586	13,540
71457	Natchitoches	15,974	13,924
70560	New Iberia	30,147	29,062
*70113	New Orleans	593,471	627,525
70760	New Roads	3,945	3,965
70079	Norco	4,773	4,682
71459	North Fort Polk	7,955	
71463	Oakdale	7,301	6,618
70570	Opelousas	20,387	17,417
70392	Patterson	4,409	2,923
71360	Pineville	8,951	8,636
70764	Plaquemine	7,739	7,689
70454	Ponchatoula	4,545	4,727
70767	Port Allen	5,728	5,026
70083	Port Sulphur	3,022	2,868
70394	Raceland	4,880	3,666
70578	Rayne	9,510	8,634
71269	Rayville	3,962	4,052
70084	Reserve	6,381	5,297
71270	Ruston	17,365	13,991
70582	St. Martinville	7,153	6,468
71301	Samtown	4,210	4,008
70807	Scotlandville	22,557	
70764	Seymourville	2,506	1,788
*71102	Shreveport	182,064	164,372
70458	Slidell	16,101	6,356
71459	South Fort Polk	15,600	
71075	Springhill	6,496	6,437
70663	Sulphur	15,247	11,429
71282	Tallulah	9,643	9,413
71006	Thibodaux	13,382	
70361	Thibodaux		
71373	Vidalia	5,538	4,313
70586	Ville Platte	9,692	7,512
70668	Vinton	3,454	2,987
71082	Vivian	4,046	2,624
70591	Welsh	3,203	3,332
70669	Westlake	4,082	3,311
71291	West Monroe	14,868	15,215
70094	Westwego	11,402	9,815
71483	Winnfield	7,142	7,022
71295	Winnsboro	5,349	4,437
70791	Zachary	4,964	3,268

Maine

See Note on Page 166

ZIP Code	Place	1970	1960
04210	Auburn	24,151	24,449
04330	Augusta	21,945	21,680
04401	Bangor	33,168	38,912
04609	Bar Harbor	3,716	3,807
04530	Bath	9,679	10,717
04915	Belfast	5,957	6,140
03901	Berwick	3,136	2,738
04005	Biddeford	19,983	19,255
04412	Brewer	9,300	9,009
04009	Bridgton	2,967	2,707
04011	Brunswick	10,867	9,444
	Brunswick	16,195	15,797
04416	Bucksport	3,756	3,466
04093	Buxton	3,135	2,339
04619	Calais	4,044	4,223
04843	Camden	3,492	3,523
	Camden	4,115	3,988
04107	Cape Elizabeth	7,873	5,505
04736	Caribou	10,419	12,464
04021	Cumberland	4,096	2,765
04930	Dexter	2,732	2,720
	Dexter	3,725	3,951
04426	Dover-Foxcroft	4,178	4,173
04426	Dover-Foxcroft	3,102	2,481
04430	East Millinocket	2,564	2,295
	East Millinocket	2,567	2,392
03903	Eliot	3,497	3,133
04605	Ellsworth	4,603	4,444
04937	Fairfield	3,694	3,766
	Fairfield	5,684	5,829
04105	Falmouth	6,291	5,976
04938	Farmington	3,096	2,749
	Farmington	5,657	5,001
04742	Fort Fairfield	4,859	5,876
04743	Fort Kent	2,876	2,787
	Fort Kent	4,575	4,761
04032	Freeport	4,781	4,055
04345	Gardiner	6,685	6,897
04038	Gorham	3,337	2,322
	Gorham	7,839	5,767
04039	Gray	2,939	2,184
04347	Hallowell	2,814	3,169
04444	Hampden	4,693	4,583
04079	Harpswell	2,552	2,032
04730	Houlton	6,760	5,976
	Houlton	8,111	8,289
04239	Jay	3,954	3,247
04043	Kennebunk	2,764	2,804
	Kennebunk	5,646	4,551
03904	Kittery	7,363	8,051
	Kittery	11,028	10,689
04240	Lewiston	41,779	40,804

ZIP Code	Place	1970	1960
04750	Limestone	10,360	13,102
04457	Lincoln	3,482	3,616
	Lincoln	4,759	4,541
04250	Lisbon	6,544	5,042
04252	Lisbon Falls	3,257	2,640
04254	Livermore Falls	3,450	3,343
04750	Loring	7,881	
04756	Madawaska	4,452	4,035
	Madawaska	5,585	5,507
04950	Madison	2,920	2,761
	Madison	4,278	3,935
04257	Mexico	3,325	3,951
	Mexico	4,309	5,043
04462	Millinocket	7,558	7,318
	Millinocket	7,742	7,453
04463	Milo	2,572	2,756
04260	New Gloucester	2,811	3,047
04268	Norway	3,595	3,733
04963	Oakland	3,535	3,075
04064	Old Orchard Beach	5,273	4,431
	Old Orchard Beach	5,404	4,580
04468	Old Town	9,057	8,626
04473	Orono	9,146	3,234
	Orono	9,989	8,341
04474	Orrington	2,702	2,539
04271	Paris	3,739	3,601
04967	Pittsfield	3,398	3,232
	Pittsfield	4,274	4,010
*04101	Portland	65,116	72,566
04769	Presque Isle	11,452	12,886
04841	Rockland	8,505	8,769
	Rockland	9,100	7,022
	Rumford	9,363	10,005
04072	Saco	11,678	10,515
04073	Sanford	10,457	10,936
	Sanford	15,812	14,962
04074	Scarborough	7,845	6,418
04976	Skowhegan	6,571	6,667
	Skowhegan	7,601	7,661
03908	South Berwick	3,488	3,112
04106	South Portland	23,267	22,788
04083	Springvale	2,914	2,379
04084	Standish	3,122	2,095
04861	Thomaston	2,646	2,780
04086	Topsham	2,700	2,240
	Topsham	5,022	3,818
04785	Van Buren	3,429	3,589
	Van Buren	3,971	4,679
04989	Vassalborough	2,618	2,446
04572	Waldoboro	3,146	2,882
04901	Waterville	18,192	19,001
04090	Wells	4,448	3,528
04092	Westbrook	14,444	13,820
04294	Wilton	3,802	3,274
04082	Windham	6,593	4,498
04901	Winslow	5,389	3,640
	Winslow	7,299	5,891
04364	Winthrop	2,571	2,260
	Winthrop	4,335	3,537
04096	Yarmouth	4,854	3,517
03909	York	2,912	
03909	York	5,690	4,663

Maryland

ZIP Code	Place	1970	1960
21001	Aberdeen	12,375	9,679
21005	Aberdeen Proving Ground	7,403	
20331	Andrews	6,418	
*21401	Annapolis	30,095	23,385
21227	Arbutus	22,745	22,402
20853	Aspen Hill	16,799	
	Avenel-Hillandale	19,520	
21905	Bainbridge Center	5,257	
*21233	Baltimore	905,759	939,024
21014	Bel Air	6,307	4,300
21050	Bel Air North	2,771	
21014	Bel Air South	3,360	
20705	Beltsville	8,912	
20740	Berwyn Heights	3,934	2,376
20014	Bethesda	71,621	56,527
20021	Birchwood	9,558	
20715	Bladensburg	7,488	3,103
20715	Bowie	35,028	1,072
20722	Brentwood	3,426	3,693
21225	Brooklyn	13,896	
21716	Brunswick	3,566	3,555
20705	Calverton	6,543	
21613	Cambridge	11,595	12,239
20031	Camp Springs	22,776	
21401	Cape St. Clair	2,689	
20027	Capitol Heights	2,852	3,138
20027	Carmody Hills-Pepper Mill	6,245	
21228	Catonsville	54,812	37,372
20027	Chapel Oaks-Cedar Heights	6,049	
21620	Chestertown	3,476	3,602
20785	Cheverly	6,808	5,223
20015	Chevy Chase	16,424	2,405
20783	Chillum	35,656	
20904	Colesville	9,455	

ZIP Code	Place	1970	1960
20740	College Park	26,156	18,482
21043	Columbia	8,815	.....
20027	Coral Hills	7,105	.....
21817	Crisfield	3,078	3,540
21113	Crofton	4,478	.....
21502	Cumberland	29,724	33,415
20750	Damascus	2,638	.....
21222	Defense Heights	6,775	.....
20028	District Heights	8,424	7,524
21222	Dundalk	85,377	82,428
21601	Easton	6,809	6,337
21219	Edgemere	10,352	11,775
21040	Edgewood	8,551	1,670
21921	Elkton	5,362	5,989
21043	Ellicott	9,435	.....
21221	Essex	38,193	35,205
21061	Ferndale	9,929	.....
20028	Forest Heights	3,600	3,524
20028	Forestville	16,152	.....
20755	Fort Meade	16,699	.....
21701	Frederick	23,641	21,744
21532	Frostburg	7,327	6,722
20760	Gaithersburg	8,344	3,847
20801	Glenarden	4,447	1,336
21061	Glen Burnie	38,608	.....
20801	Good Luck	10,584	.....
20770	Greenbelt	18,199	7,479
21740	Hagerstown	35,862	36,660
21740	Halfway	6,106	4,256
20852	Halpine	5,912	.....
21078	Havre De Grace	9,791	8,510
20031	Hillcrest Heights	24,037	15,295
*20780	Hyattsville	14,998	15,168
21085	Joppatowne	9,092	.....
20904	Kemp Mill	10,037	.....
20785	Kentland	9,649	.....
20785	Landover	5,597	.....
20787	Langley Park	11,564	11,510
20801	Lanham-Seabrook	13,244	.....
21227	Lansdowne-Baltimore Highlands	17,770	13,134
20810	Laurel	10,525	8,503
21502	LaVale-Narrows Park	3,971	4,031
20653	Lexington Pk. Patuxent R	9,136	.....
21090	Linthicum	9,767	.....
21037	Londontowne	3,864	.....
21093	Lutherville-Timonium	24,055	12,265
20810	Maryland City	7,102	.....
21220	Middle River	19,935	10,825
20852	Montrose	6,140	.....
20822	Mount Rainier	8,180	9,855
20784	New Carrollton	14,870	3,385
20854	North Potomac	12,546	.....
20012	North Takoma Park	7,373	.....
21113	Odenton	5,989	1,914
21206	Overlea	13,086	10,795
21117	Owings Mills	7,360	3,810
20021	Oxon Hill	11,974	.....
20785	Palmer Park	8,172	.....
21234	Parkville	33,589	27,236
21128	Perry Hall	5,446	.....
21208	Pikesville	25,395	18,737
21851	Pocomoke City	3,573	3,329
20016	Potomac Valley	5,094	.....
21227	Pumphrey	6,433	.....
21133	Randallstown	33,683	.....
20853	Randolph	13,233	.....
21136	Reisterstown	14,037	4,216
20840	Riverdale	5,724	4,389
20840	Riverdale Hgts.-E. Pine	8,941	.....
21223	Riviera Beach	7,464	4,902
*20850	Rockville	41,564	26,090
21237	Rosedale	19,417	.....
21801	Salisbury	15,252	16,302
20027	Seat Pleasant	7,217	5,365
21146	Severna Park	16,358	3,728
*20907	Silver Spring	77,496	66,348
21061	South Gate	9,356	.....
20795	South Kensington	10,289	.....
20810	South Laurel	13,345	.....
20023	Suitland-Silver Hills	30,355	10,300
20012	Takoma Park	18,455	16,799
21204	Towson	77,799	19,090
20784	University Park	2,926	3,098
20601	Waldorf	7,368	1,048
20028	Walker Mill	6,322	.....
21562	Westernport	3,106	3,559
20810	West Laurel	4,478	.....
21157	Westminster	7,207	6,123
20902	Wheaton	66,247	54,635
20903	White Oak	19,769	.....
21207	Woodlawn-Woodmoor	28,821	.....

Massachusetts

See Note on Page 166

| 02351 | Abington | 12,334 | 10,607 |
| 01720 | Acton | 14,770 | 7,238 |

ZIP Code	Place	1970	1960
02743	Acushnet	7,767	5,755
01220	Adams	11,256	11,949
.....	Adams	11,772	12,391
01001	Agawam	21,717	15,718
01913	Amesbury	10,088	9,625
.....	Amesbury	11,388	10,787
01002	Amherst	17,926	10,306
.....	Amherst	26,331	13,718
01810	Andover	23,695	17,134
02174	Arlington	53,524	49,953
01430	Ashburnham	3,484	2,758
01721	Ashland	8,882	7,779
01331	Athol	9,723	10,161
.....	Athol	11,185	11,637
02703	Attleboro	32,907	27,118
01501	Auburn	15,347	14,047
02322	Avon	5,295	4,301
01432	Ayer	3,292	3,323
.....	Ayer	8,283	14,927
02630	Barnstable	19,842	13,465
01005	Barre	3,825	3,479
01730	Bedford	13,513	10,969
01007	Belchertown	2,636	.....
01007	Belchertown	5,936	5,186
02019	Bellingham	4,228	.....
02019	Bellingham	13,967	6,774
02178	Belmont	28,285	28,715
01915	Beverly	38,348	36,108
01821	Billerica	31,648	17,867
01504	Blackstone	6,566	5,130
*02109	Boston	641,071	697,197
02532	Bourne	12,636	14,011
01921	Boxford	4,032	2,010
01505	Boylston	2,774	2,367
02184	Braintree	35,050	31,069
02324	Bridgewater	4,032	4,296
.....	Bridgewater	11,829	10,276
*02403	Brockton	89,040	72,813
02147	Brookline	58,689	54,044
01803	Burlington	21,980	12,852
*02138	Cambridge	100,361	107,716
02021	Canton	17,100	12,771
01741	Carlisle	2,871	1,488
02632	Centerville	2,876	.....
01507	Charlton	4,654	3,685
02633	Chatham	4,554	3,273
01824	Chelmsford	31,432	15,130
02150	Chelsea	30,625	33,749
01225	Cheshire	3,006	2,472
01021	Chicopee	66,676	61,553
01510	Clinton	13,383	12,848
02025	Cohasset	6,954	5,840
01742	Concord	16,148	12,517
01226	Dalton	7,505	6,436
01923	Danvers	26,151	21,926
02714	Dartmouth	18,800	14,607
02026	Dedham	26,938	23,869
01342	Deerfield	3,850	3,338
02638	Dennis	6,454	3,727
02715	Dighton	4,667	3,769
01516	Douglas	2,947	2,559
02030	Dover	4,529	2,846
01826	Dracut	18,214	13,674
01570	Dudley	8,087	6,510
02332	Duxbury	7,636	4,727
02333	East Bridgewater	8,347	6,139
02536	East Falmouth	2,971	1,655
01027	Easthampton	13,012	12,326
01028	East Longmeadow	13,029	10,294
02334	Easton	12,157	9,078
01929	Essex	2,670	2,238
02149	Everett	42,485	43,544
02719	Fairhaven	16,332	14,339
*02722	Fall River	96,898	99,942
*02540	Falmouth	5,806	3,308
.....	Falmouth	15,942	13,037
01420	Fitchburg	43,243	43,021
01433	Fort Devens	12,951	.....
02035	Foxborough	4,090	3,169
.....	Foxborough	14,218	10,136
01701	Framingham	64,048	44,526
02038	Franklin Center	8,863	6,391
.....	Franklin	17,830	10,530
02702	Freetown	4,270	3,039
01440	Gardner	19,748	19,038
01830	Georgetown	5,290	3,755
01930	Gloucester	27,941	25,789
01519	Grafton	11,659	10,627
01033	Granby	5,473	4,221
01230	Great Barrington	3,203	2,943
.....	Great Barrington	7,537	6,624
01301	Greenfield	14,642	14,389
.....	Greenfield	18,116	17,690
01450	Groton	5,109	3,904
01830	Groveland	5,382	3,297
01035	Hadley	3,750	3,099
02338	Halifax	3,537	1,599
01982	Hamilton	6,373	5,488
01936	Hampden	4,572	2,345
02339	Hanover	10,107	5,923

ZIP Code	Place	1970	1960
02341	Hanson	7,148	4,370
01451	Harvard	12,536	2,563
02645	Harwich	3,842	
.....	Harwich	5,892	3,747
01038	Hatfield	2,825	2,350
01830	Haverhill	46,120	46,346
02043	Hingham	18,845	15,378
02343	Holbrook	11,775	10,104
01520	Holden	12,564	10,117
01746	Holliston	12,069	6,222
01040	Holyoke	50,112	52,689
01747	Hopedale	3,089	2,904
.....	Hopedale	4,292	3,987
01748	Hopkinton	5,981	4,932
01749	Hudson	14,283	7,987
.....	Hudson	16,084	9,666
02045	Hull	9,961	7,055
02601	Hyannis	6,847	5,139
01938	Ipswich	5,022	4,617
.....	Ipswich	10,750	8,544
02364	Kingston	3,772	1,301
02364	Kingston	5,999	4,302
02346	Lakeville	4,376	3,209
01523	Lancaster	6,095	3,958
01237	Lanesborough	2,972	2,933
*01842	Lawrence	66,915	70,933
01238	Lee	3,389	3,078
.....	Lee	6,426	5,271
01524	Leicester	3,173	1,750
.....	Leicester	9,140	8,177
01240	Lenox	5,804	4,253
01452	Leominster	32,939	27,929
02173	Lexington	31,886	27,691
01773	Lincoln	7,567	5,613
01460	Littleton	6,380	5,109
01460	Littleton Common	2,764	2,277
01106	Longmeadow	15,630	10,565
*01853	Lowell	94,239	92,107
01056	Ludlow	17,580	13,805
01462	Lunenburg	7,419	6,334
*01901	Lynn	90,294	94,478
01940	Lynnfield	10,826	8,398
02148	Malden	56,127	57,676
01944	Manchester	5,151	3,932
02048	Mansfield	4,778	4,764
.....	Mansfield	9,939	7,773
01945	Marblehead	21,295	18,521
02738	Marion	3,466	2,881
01752	Marlborough	27,936	18,819
02050	Marshfield Compact	2,562	
02050	Marshfield	15,223	6,748
02739	Mattapoisett	4,500	3,117
01754	Maynard	9,710	7,695
02052	Medfield	9,821	6,021
02155	Medford	64,397	64,971
02053	Medway	3,716	1,602
.....	Medway	7,938	5,168
02176	Melrose	33,180	29,619
01756	Mendon	2,524	2,068
01570	Merino Village	3,470	3,099
01860	Merrimac	4,245	3,261
01844	Methuen	35,456	28,114
02346	Middleborough	6,259	6,003
.....	Middleborough	13,607	11,065
01949	Middleton	4,044	3,718
01757	Milford	13,740	13,722
.....	Milford	19,352	15,749
01527	Millbury	11,987	9,623
02054	Millis	5,686	4,374
02054	Millis-Clicquot	3,217	2,588
02186	Milton	27,190	26,375
01057	Monson	7,355	6,712
01351	Montague	8,451	7,836
01908	Nahant	4,119	3,960
02554	Nantucket	3,774	3,559
01760	Natick	31,057	28,831
02192	Needham	29,748	25,793
*02741	New Bedford	101,777	102,477
01950	Newbury	3,804	2,519
01950	Newburyport	15,807	14,004
02158	Newton	91,263	92,384
02056	Norfolk	4,656	3,471
01247	North Adams	19,195	19,905
01059	North Amherst	2,854	1,009
01060	Northampton	29,664	30,058
01845	North Andover	16,284	10,908
*02760	North Attleborough	18,665	14,777
01532	Northborough	9,218	6,687
01534	Northbridge	3,321	2,128
.....	Northbridge	11,795	10,800
01535	North Brookfield	2,677	2,615
.....	North Brookfield	3,967	3,616
01360	Northfield	2,631	2,320
02358	North Pembroke	2,881	
02360	North Plymouth	3,434	3,467
01864	North Reading	11,264	8,331
02060	North Scituate	5,507	3,421
02766	Norton	9,487	6,818
02061	Norwell	7,796	5,207
02062	Norwood	30,815	24,898

ZIP Code	Place	1970	1960
01364	Orange	3,847	3,689
.....	Orange	6,104	6,154
02653	Orleans	3,055	2,342
01253	Otis	5,596	
01540	Oxford	6,109	6,985
.....	Oxford	10,345	9,282
01069	Palmer	3,649	3,888
.....	Palmer	11,680	10,358
01612	Paxton	3,731	2,399
01960	Peabody	48,080	32,202
02359	Pembroke	11,193	4,919
01463	Pepperell	5,887	4,336
01866	Pinehurst	5,681	1,991
01201	Pittsfield	57,020	57,879
02762	Plainville	4,953	3,810
02360	Plymouth	6,940	6,488
.....	Plymouth	18,606	14,445
02657	Provincetown Center	2,836	3,346
.....	Provincetown	2,911	3,389
02169	Quincy	87,966	87,409
02368	Randolph	27,035	18,900
02767	Raynham	2,526	
.....	Raynham	6,705	4,150
01867	Reading	22,539	19,259
02769	Rehoboth	6,512	4,953
02151	Revere	43,159	40,080
02370	Rockland	15,674	13,119
01966	Rockport	4,166	3,511
.....	Rockport	5,636	4,616
01969	Rowley	3,040	2,783
01543	Rutland	3,198	3,253
01970	Salem	40,556	39,211
01908	Salisbury	4,179	3,779
02563	Sandwich	5,239	2,082
01906	Saugus	25,110	20,666
02066	Scituate	3,738	3,229
.....	Scituate	16,973	11,214
02771	Seekonk	11,116	8,399
02067	Sharon	12,367	10,070
01770	Sherborn	3,309	1,806
01464	Shirley	4,909	5,202
02066	Shore Acres-Sand Hills	2,949	1,778
01545	Shrewsbury	19,196	16,622
02726	Somerset	18,088	12,196
02143	Somerville	88,779	94,697
01073	Southampton	3,069	2,192
01772	Southborough	5,798	3,996
01550	Southbridge	14,261	15,889
.....	Southbridge	17,057	16,523
01075	South Hadley	17,033	14,956
01561	South Lancaster	2,679	1,891
01077	Southwick	6,330	5,139
02664	South Yarmouth	5,380	2,029
01562	Spencer	5,895	5,593
.....	Spencer	8,779	7,838
*01101	Springfield	163,905	174,463
01564	Sterling	4,247	3,193
02180	Stoneham	20,725	17,821
02072	Stoughton	23,459	16,328
01775	Stow	3,984	2,573
01566	Sturbridge	4,878	3,604
01776	Sudbury	13,506	7,447
01527	Sutton	4,590	3,638
01907	Swampscott	13,578	13,294
02777	Swansea	12,640	9,916
02780	Taunton	43,756	41,132
01468	Templeton	5,863	5,371
01876	Tewksbury	22,755	15,902
01080	Three Rivers	3,366	3,082
01983	Topsfield	5,225	3,351
01469	Townsend	4,281	3,650
01376	Turner Falls	5,168	4,917
01879	Tyngsborough	4,204	3,302
01568	Upton	3,484	3,127
01569	Uxbridge	3,380	3,377
.....	Uxbridge	8,253	7,789
01880	Wakefield	25,402	24,295
02081	Walpole	18,149	14,068
02154	Waltham	61,582	55,413
01082	Ware	6,509	6,650
.....	Ware	8,187	7,517
02571	Wareham	11,492	9,461
01083	Warren	3,633	3,383
02172	Watertown	39,307	39,092
01778	Wayland	13,461	10,444
01570	Webster	12,432	12,072
.....	Webster	14,917	13,680
02181	Wellesley	28,051	26,071
01984	Wenham	3,849	2,798
01581	Westborough	4,474	4,011
.....	Westborough	12,594	9,599
01583	West Boylston	6,369	5,526
02379	West Bridgewater	7,152	5,061
01585	West Brookfield	2,653	2,053
01085	Westfield	31,433	26,302
01886	Westford	10,368	6,261
01473	Westminster	4,273	4,022
02193	Weston	10,870	8,261
02790	Westport	9,791	6,641
01089	West Springfield	28,461	24,924

ZIP Code	Place	1970	1960
02090	Westwood	12,750	10,354
02673	West Yarmouth	3,699	1,365
02188	Weymouth	54,610	48,177
01588	Whitinsville	5,210	5,102
02382	Whitman	13,059	10,485
01095	Wilbraham	3,540	.....
.....	Wilbraham	11,984	7,387
01267	Williamstown	4,285	5,428
.....	Williamstown	8,454	7,322
01887	Wilmington	17,102	12,475
01475	Winchendon	3,997	3,839
.....	Winchendon	6,635	6,237
01890	Winchester	22,269	19,376
02152	Winthrop	20,335	20,303
01801	Woburn	37,406	31,214
*01613	Worcester	176,572	186,587
02093	Wrentham	7,315	6,685
02675	Yarmouth	12,033	5,504

Michigan

ZIP Code	Place	1970	1960
49221	Adrian	20,382	20,347
49224	Albion	12,112	12,749
48001	Algonac	3,684	3,190
49010	Allegan	4,516	4,822
48101	Allen Park	40,747	37,494
48801	Alma	9,790	8,978
49707	Alpena	13,805	14,682
*48106	Ann Arbor	99,797	67,340
48413	Bad Axe	2,999	2,998
*49016	Battle Creek	38,931	44,169
48706	Bay City	49,449	53,604
49909	Beechwood	2,714	2,323
48809	Belding	5,121	4,887
49022	Benton Central	8,067	.....
49022	Benton Harbor	16,481	19,136
49022	Benton South	4,496	.....
48072	Berkley	21,879	23,275
49911	Bessemer	2,805	3,304
48009	Beverly Hills	13,598	8,633
49307	Big Rapids	11,995	8,686
*48012	Birmingham	26,170	25,525
49228	Blissfield	2,753	2,653
48013	Bloomfield Hills	3,672	2,378
49712	Boyne	2,969	2,797
49017	Brownlee Park	2,985	3,307
49107	Buchanan	4,645	5,341
49601	Cadillac	9,990	10,112
48723	Caro	3,701	3,534
48724	Carrollton	7,300	.....
48015	Center Line	10,379	10,164
49720	Charlevoix	3,519	2,751
48813	Charlotte	8,244	7,657
49721	Cheboygan	5,553	5,859
48118	Chelsea	3,858	3,355
48616	Chesaning	2,876	2,770
48617	Clare	2,639	2,442
48017	Clawson	17,617	14,795
49036	Coldwater	9,155	8,880
49041	Comstock	5,003	.....
49321	Comstock Park	5,766	.....
48817	Corunna	2,829	2,764
49508	Cutlerville	6,267	.....
48423	Davison	5,259	3,761
*48120	Dearborn	104,199	112,007
48127	Dearborn Heights	80,069	.....
*48233	Detroit	1,513,601	1,670,144
49047	Dowagiac	6,583	7,208
48020	Drayton Plains	16,462	.....
48429	Durand	3,678	3,312
48021	East Detroit	45,920	45,756
49506	East Grand Rapids	12,565	10,924
48823	East Lansing	47,540	30,198
49001	Eastwood	9,682	.....
48827	Eaton Rapids	4,494	4,052
48229	Ecorse	17,515	17,328
49829	Escanaba	15,368	15,391
48732	Essexville	4,990	4,590
49022	Fair Plain	3,680	3,744
48024	Farmington	10,329	6,881
48430	Fenton	8,284	6,142
48220	Ferndale	30,850	31,347
48134	Flat Rock	5,643	4,696
*48502	Flint	193,317	196,940
48433	Flushing	7,190	3,761
48734	Frankenmuth	2,834	1,728
48025	Franklin	3,344	2,262
48026	Fraser	11,868	7,027
49412	Fremont	3,465	3,384
48135	Garden City	41,864	38,017
49735	Gaylord	3,012	2,568
48173	Gibraltar	3,842	2,196
49837	Gladstone	5,237	5,267
48439	Grand Blanc	5,132	1,565
49417	Grand Haven	11,844	11,066
48837	Grand Ledge	6,032	5,165
*49501	Grand Rapids	197,649	177,313
49418	Grandville	10,764	7,975
48838	Greenville	7,493	7,440
48138	Grosse Ile	8,306	.....
48230	Grosse Point	6,637	6,631
48236	Grosse Pointe Farms	11,701	12,172
48236	Grosse Pointe Park	15,641	15,457
48236	Grosse Pointe Shores	3,042	2,301
48236	Grosse Pointe Woods	21,878	18,580
48212	Hamtramck	27,245	34,137
49930	Hancock	4,820	5,022
48236	Harper Woods	20,186	19,995
49057	Hartford	2,508	2,305
49058	Hastings	6,501	6,375
48030	Hazel Park	23,784	25,631
48203	Highland Park	35,444	38,063
49242	Hillsdale	7,728	7,629
49423	Holland	26,337	24,777
48442	Holly	4,355	3,269
48842	Holt	6,980	4,818
49931	Houghton	6,067	3,393
48843	Howell	5,224	4,861
49247	Hudson	2,618	2,546
49426	Hudsonville	3,523	2,649
48070	Huntington Woods	8,536	8,746
48141	Inkster	38,595	39,097
48846	Ionia	6,361	6,754
49801	Iron Mountain	8,702	9,299
49935	Iron River	2,684	3,754
49938	Ironwood	8,711	10,265
49849	Ishpeming	8,245	8,857
48847	Ithaca	2,749	2,611
*49201	Jackson	45,484	50,720
49428	Jenison	11,266	.....
*49001	Kalamazoo	85,555	82,089
48033	Keego Harbor	3,092	2,761
49508	Kentwood	20,310	.....
49788	Kincheloe	6,331	.....
49801	Kingsford	5,276	5,084
49843	K.I. Sawyer	8,224	.....
48035	Lake Orion Heights	2,552	1,918
48035	Lake Orion	2,921	2,698
48850	Lakeview	11,391	10,384
48144	Lambertville	5,721	1,168
49946	L'Anse	2,538	2,397
*48924	Lansing	131,546	107,807
48446	Lapeer	6,314	6,160
48503	Lapeer Heights	7,130	.....
48076	Lathrup Village	4,676	3,556
49913	Laurium	2,868	3,058
49017	Level Park-Oak Park	3,080	3,017
48146	Lincoln Park	52,984	53,933
*48150	Livonia	110,109	66,702
49331	Lowell	3,068	2,545
49431	Ludington	9,021	9,421
48071	Madison Heights	38,599	33,343
49660	Manistee	7,723	8,324
49854	Manistique	4,324	4,875
48039	Marine City	4,567	4,404
48855	Marquette	21,967	19,824
49068	Marshall	7,253	6,736
48040	Marysville	5,610	4,065
48854	Mason	5,468	4,522
48122	Melvindale	13,862	13,089
49858	Menominee	10,748	11,289
48640	Midland	35,176	27,779
48160	Milan	4,533	3,616
48042	Milford	4,699	4,323
48161	Monroe	23,894	22,968
48043	Mount Clemens	20,476	21,016
48458	Mount Morris	3,778	3,484
48858	Mount Pleasant	20,524	14,875
49862	Munising	3,677	4,228
*49440	Muskegon	44,631	46,485
49444	Muskegon Heights	17,304	19,552
49866	Negaunee	5,248	6,126
48047	New Baltimore	4,132	3,159
49117	New Buffalo	2,784	2,128
49120	Niles	12,988	13,842
49445	North Muskegon	4,243	3,855
48167	Northville	5,400	3,967
49441	Norton Shores	22,271	.....
49870	Norway	3,033	3,171
48050	Novi	9,668	6,390
48237	Oak Park	36,762	36,632
48864	Okemos	7,770	.....
48750	Oscoda-Au Sable	3,475	.....
49078	Otsego	3,957	4,142
48867	Owosso	17,179	17,006
48051	Oxford	2,536	2,357
49079	Paw Paw	3,160	2,970
49038	Paw Paw Lake	3,726	3,518
49770	Petoskey	6,342	6,138
48080	Plainwell	3,195	3,125
48069	Pleasant Ridge	3,989	3,807
48170	Plymouth	11,758	8,766
*48053	Pontiac	85,279	82,233
49081	Portage	33,590	.....
48060	Port Huron	35,794	36,084
48875	Portland	3,817	3,330
48024	Quakertown North	7,101	.....
48062	Richmond	3,234	2,667
48218	River Rouge	15,947	18,147
48192	Riverview	11,342	7,237

ZIP Code	Place	1970	1960
48063	Rochester	7,054	5,431
48173	Rockwood	3,225	2,026
49779	Rogers City	4,275	4,722
48065	Romeo	4,012	3,327
49444	Roosevelt Park	4,176	2,578
48066	Roseville	60,529	50,195
*48067	Royal Oak	86,238	80,612
*48605	Saginaw	91,849	98,265
48079	St. Clair	4,770	4,538
*48083	St. Clair Shores	88,093	76,657
49781	St. Ignace	2,892	3,334
48879	St. Johns	6,672	5,629
49085	St. Joseph	11,042	11,755
48880	St. Louis	4,101	3,808
48176	Saline	4,811	2,334
49783	Sault Ste. Marie	15,136	18,722
*48075	Southfield	69,285	31,501
48192	Southgate	33,909	29,404
49090	South Haven	6,471	6,149
48178	South Lyon	2,675	1,753
48161	South Monroe	3,012	2,919
49345	Sparta	3,094	2,749
49015	Springfield	3,994	4,605
49015	Springfield Place	4,831	5,136
49456	Spring Lake	3,034	2,063
*48077	Sterling Heights	61,365	
49091	Sturgis	9,295	8,915
48473	Swartz Creek	4,928	3,006
48180	Taylor	70,020	
49286	Tecumseh	7,120	7,045
49093	Three Rivers	7,355	7,092
13601	Tittabawassee Twp.	10,010	18,433
48183	Trenton	24,127	18,439
48084	Troy	39,419	19,402
48087	Utica	3,504	1,454
48768	Vassar	2,802	2,680
49968	Wakefield	2,757	3,231
49504	Walker	11,492	
48088	Walled Lake	3,759	3,550
*48089	Warren	179,260	89,246
48184	Wayne	21,054	16,034
48185	Westland	86,749	
49007	Westwood	9,143	
49461	Whitehall	3,017	2,590
48031	White Lake-Seven Harbors	4,504	2,748
48189	Whitmore Lake	2,763	
48895	Williamston	2,600	2,214
48088	Wolverine Lake	4,301	2,404
48183	Woodhaven	3,566	
48753	Wurtsmith	6,932	
48192	Wyandotte	41,061	43,519
49509	Wyoming	56,560	45,829
48197	Ypsilanti	29,538	20,957
49464	Zeeland	4,734	3,702

Minnesota

ZIP Code	Place	1970	1960
56007	Albert Lea	19,418	17,108
56308	Alexandria	6,973	6,713
55303	Anoka	13,489	10,562
55068	Apple Valley	8,502	
55112	Arden Hills	4,975	3,930
55705	Aurora	2,531	2,799
55912	Austin	25,074	27,908
55706	Babbitt	3,076	2,587
55003	Bayport	2,987	3,205
56601	Bemidji	11,490	9,958
56215	Benson	3,484	3,678
55433	Blaine	20,625	7,570
55420	Bloomington	81,970	50,498
56013	Blue Earth	3,965	4,200
56401	Brainerd	11,667	12,898
56520	Breckenridge	4,200	4,335
55429	Brooklyn Center	35,173	24,356
55429	Brooklyn Park	26,230	10,197
55313	Buffalo	3,275	2,322
55378	Burnsville	19,940	
55921	Caledonia	2,619	2,563
55008	Cambridge	2,720	2,728
55317	Chanhassen	4,879	244
55318	Chaska	4,352	2,501
55719	Chisholm	5,913	7,144
55014	Circle Pines	3,918	2,789
55720	Cloquet	8,699	9,013
55421	Columbia Heights	23,837	17,533
55433	Coon Rapids	30,505	14,931
55016	Cottage Grove	13,419	
56716	Crookston	8,312	8,546
55428	Crystal	30,925	24,283
55391	Deephaven	3,853	3,286
56501	Detroit Lakes	5,797	5,633
*55806	Duluth	100,578	106,884
55005	East Bethel	2,586	1,408
56721	East Grand Forks	7,607	6,998
55343	Eden Prairie	6,938	
55424	Edina	44,046	28,501
55731	Ely	4,904	5,438
55734	Eveleth	4,721	5,721
55331	Excelsior	2,563	2,020

ZIP Code	Place	1970	1960
56031	Fairmont	10,751	9,745
55113	Falcon Heights	5,641	5,927
55021	Faribault	16,595	16,926
55024	Farmington	3,104	2,300
56537	Fergus Falls	12,443	13,733
55025	Forest Lake	3,207	2,347
55421	Fridley	29,233	15,173
55336	Glencoe	4,217	3,216
56334	Glenwood	2,584	2,631
55427	Golden Valley	24,246	14,559
55744	Grand Rapids	7,247	7,265
56241	Granite Falls	3,225	2,728
55033	Hastings	12,195	8,965
55746	Hibbing	16,104	17,731
55343	Hopkins	13,428	11,370
55750	Hoyt Lakes	3,634	3,186
55350	Hutchinson	8,031	6,207
56649	International Falls	6,439	6,778
55075	Inver Grove Heights	12,148	
56143	Jackson	3,550	3,370
55947	La Crescent	3,296	2,624
55041	Lake City	3,594	3,494
55042	Lake Elmo	4,032	550
55044	Lakeville	7,556	924
55113	Lauderdale	2,571	
56058	Le Sueur	3,745	3,310
55014	Lino Lakes	3,692	2,329
55355	Litchfield	5,262	5,078
55110	Little Canada	3,481	3,512
56345	Little Falls	7,467	7,551
56156	Luverne	4,703	4,249
55115	Mahtomedi	2,640	2,127
55007	Mahtowa	3,011	
55369	Maple Grove	6,275	2,213
55109	Maplewood	25,222	18,519
56258	Marshall	9,886	6,681
55118	Mendota Heights	6,165	5,028
*55401	Minneapolis	434,400	482,872
55343	Minnetonka	35,737	25,037
55364	Minnetrista	2,878	
56265	Montevideo	5,661	5,693
56560	Moorhead	29,687	22,934
55051	Mora	2,582	2,329
56267	Morris	5,366	4,199
55364	Mound	7,572	5,440
55112	Mounds View	10,641	6,416
55112	New Brighton	19,507	6,448
55428	New Hope	23,180	3,552
55055	Newport	2,922	2,349
56071	New Prague	2,680	2,533
56073	New Ulm	13,051	11,114
55057	Northfield	10,235	8,707
56001	North Mankato	7,347	5,927
55109	North St. Paul	11,950	8,520
55119	Oakdale	7,304	
56277	Olivia	2,553	2,355
55391	Orono	6,787	5,643
56278	Ortonville	2,665	2,674
55369	Osseo	2,908	2,104
55060	Owatonna	15,341	13,409
56470	Park Rapids	2,772	3,047
56164	Pipestone	5,328	5,324
55427	Plymouth	18,077	9,576
55371	Princeton	2,531	2,353
55810	Proctor	3,123	2,963
55066	Red Wing	10,441	10,528
56283	Redwood Falls	4,774	4,285
55423	Richfield	47,231	42,523
55422	Robbinsdale	16,845	16,381
55901	Rochester	53,766	40,663
56751	Roseau	2,552	2,146
55113	Roseville	34,518	23,997
55414	St. Anthony	9,239	5,084
56301	St. Cloud	39,691	33,815
56081	St. James	4,027	4,174
55426	St. Louis Park	48,922	43,310
*55101	St. Paul	309,828	313,411
55071	St. Paul Park	5,587	3,267
56082	St. Peter	8,339	8,484
56378	Sauk Centre	3,750	3,573
56379	Sauk Rapids	5,051	4,038
55378	Savage	3,611	1,094
55379	Shakopee	6,876	5,201
55112	Shoreview	10,995	7,157
55331	Shorewood	4,223	3,197
55614	Silver Bay	3,504	3,723
56085	Sleepy Eye	3,461	3,492
55075	South St. Paul	25,016	22,032
56087	Springfield	2,530	2,701
55432	Spring Lake Park	6,417	3,260
55975	Spring Valley	2,572	2,628
56479	Staples	2,657	2,706
55976	Stewartville	2,802	1,670
55082	Stillwater	10,191	8,310
56701	Thief River Falls	8,618	7,151
56175	Tracy	2,516	2,862
55616	Two Harbors	4,437	4,695
55110	Vadnais Heights	3,391	2,459
55792	Virginia	12,450	14,034
56482	Wadena	4,640	4,381

ZIP Code	Place	1970	1960
56387	Waite Park	2,824	2,016
56093	Waseca	6,789	5,898
55391	Wayzata	3,700	3,219
56097	Wells	2,791	2,897
55118	West St. Paul	18,799	13,101
55110	White Bear Lake	23,313	12,849
56201	Willmar	12,869	10,417
56101	Windom	3,952	3,691
55987	Winona	26,438	24,895
55119	Woodbury	6,184	
56187	Worthington	9,916	9,015

Mississippi

ZIP Code	Place	1970	1960
39730	Aberdeen	6,507	6,450
38821	Amory	7,236	6,474
38606	Batesville	3,796	3,284
39520	Bay St. Louis	6,752	5,073
39038	Belzoni	3,394	4,142
*39530	Biloxi	48,486	44,053
38829	Booneville	5,895	3,480
39042	Brandon	2,685	2,139
39601	Brookhaven	10,700	9,885
39046	Canton	10,503	9,707
39051	Carthage	3,031	2,442
38921	Charleston	2,821	2,528
38614	Clarksdale	21,673	21,105
38732	Cleveland	13,327	10,172
39056	Clinton	7,289	3,438
39429	Columbia	7,587	7,117
39701	Columbus	25,795	24,771
39701	Columbus Base	4,074	
38834	Corinth	11,581	11,453
39059	Crystal Springs	4,195	4,496
39532	D'Iberville	7,288	3,005
38737	Drew	2,574	2,143
39063	Durant	2,752	2,617
39437	Ellisville	4,643	4,592
39074	Forest	4,085	3,917
38843	Fulton	2,899	1,706
38701	Greenville	39,648	41,502
38930	Greenwood	22,400	20,436
38901	Grenada	9,944	7,914
39501	Gulfport	40,791	30,204
39401	Hattiesburg	38,277	34,989
39083	Hazlehurst	4,577	3,400
38748	Hollandale	3,260	2,646
38635	Holly Springs	5,728	5,621
38851	Houston	2,720	2,577
38751	Indianola	8,947	6,714
*39205	Jackson	153,968	144,422
39090	Kosciusko	7,266	6,800
39440	Laurel	24,145	27,889
38756	Leland	6,000	6,295
39095	Lexington	2,756	2,839
39560	Long Beach	6,170	4,770
39339	Louisville	6,626	5,066
39648	McComb	11,969	12,020
39341	Macon	2,612	2,432
39111	Magee	2,973	2,039
38846	Marks	2,609	2,572
39301	Meridian	45,083	49,374
39117	Morton	2,672	2,260
39563	Moss Point	19,321	6,631
39120	Natchez	19,704	23,791
38652	New Albany	6,426	5,151
39345	Newton	3,556	3,178
39564	Ocean Springs	9,580	5,025
38860	Okolona	3,002	2,622
38655	Oxford City	13,846	5,283
39567	Pascagoula	27,264	17,155
39571	Pass Christian	2,979	3,881
39208	Pearl	9,623	5,081
39465	Petal	6,986	4,007
39350	Philadelphia	6,274	5,017
39466	Picayune	10,467	7,834
38863	Pontotoc	3,453	2,108
39150	Port Gibson	2,589	2,861
39355	Quitman	2,702	2,030
38663	Ripley	3,482	2,668
38769	Rosedale	2,599	2,339
38668	Senatobia	4,247	3,259
38773	Shaw	2,513	2,062
38774	Shelby	2,645	2,384
38671	Southaven	8,931	
39759	Starkville	11,369	9,041
39762	State College	4,595	
38801	Tupelo	20,471	17,221
39180	Vicksburg	25,478	29,143
38965	Water Valley	3,285	3,206
39576	Waveland	3,108	1,106
39367	Waynesboro	4,368	3,892
39501	West Gulfport	6,996	3,323
39773	West Point	8,714	8,550
39577	Wiggins	2,995	1,591
38967	Winona	5,521	4,282
39194	Yazoo City	10,796	11,236

Missouri

ZIP Code	Place	1970	1960
63123	Affton	24,898	
65605	Aurora	5,359	4,683
65608	Ava	2,504	1,581
63011	Ballwin	10,656	5,710
63137	Bellefontaine Neighbors	14,084	13,650
63133	Bel-Ridge	5,561	4,395
64012	Belton	12,179	4,897
63134	Berkeley	19,743	18,676
64424	Bethany	2,914	2,771
64015	Blue Springs	6,779	2,555
65613	Bolivar	4,769	3,512
63628	Bonne Terre	3,622	3,219
65233	Boonville	7,514	7,090
63334	Bowling Green	2,936	2,650
63114	Breckenridge Hills	7,011	6,299
63144	Brentwood	11,248	12,250
63044	Bridgeton	19,992	7,820
64628	Brookfield	5,491	5,694
64730	Butler	3,984	3,791
65018	California	3,105	2,788
64429	Cameron	3,960	3,674
63435	Canton	2,680	2,562
63701	Cape Girardeau	31,282	24,947
64633	Carrollton	4,847	4,554
64836	Carthage	11,035	11,264
63830	Caruthersville	7,350	8,643
65240	Centralia	3,618	3,200
63740	Chaffee	2,793	2,862
63834	Charleston	5,131	5,911
64601	Chillicothe	9,519	9,236
63105	Clayton	16,222	15,245
64735	Clinton	7,504	6,925
65201	Columbia	58,804	36,650
63128	Concord	21,217	
63126	Crestwood	15,123	11,106
63141	Creve Coeur	8,967	5,122
63019	Crystal City	3,898	3,678
63136	Dellwood	7,137	4,720
63601	Desloge	2,818	2,308
63020	De Soto	5,984	5,804
63131	Des Peres	5,333	4,362
63841	Dexter	6,024	5,519
63845	East Prairie	3,275	3,449
65026	Eldon	3,520	3,158
64744	Eldorado Springs	3,300	2,864
63011	Ellisville	4,681	2,732
64024	Excelsior Springs	9,411	6,473
63640	Farmington	6,590	5,618
65248	Fayette	3,520	3,294
63135	Ferguson	28,759	22,149
63028	Festus	7,530	7,021
63601	Flat River	4,550	4,515
63033	Florissant	65,908	38,166
65473	Fort Leonard Wood	33,799	
63645	Fredericktown	3,799	3,484
63131	Frontenac	3,920	3,089
65251	Fulton	12,248	11,131
64118	Gladstone	23,422	14,502
63122	Glendale	6,891	7,048
64030	Grandview	17,456	6,027
63133	Hanley Hills	2,726	3,308
63401	Hannibal	18,698	20,028
64701	Harrisonville	5,052	3,510
63851	Hayti	3,841	3,737
*63042	Hazelwood	14,082	6,045
65041	Hermann	2,658	2,536
64037	Higginsville	4,318	4,003
63133	Hillsdale	2,599	2,788
*64051	Independence	111,630	62,328
63755	Jackson	5,896	4,875
65101	Jefferson City	32,407	28,228
63136	Jennings	19,379	19,965
64801	Joplin	39,256	38,958
*64108	Kansas City	507,330	475,539
63857	Kennett	10,090	9,098
63140	Kinloch	5,629	6,501
63501	Kirksville	15,560	13,123
63122	Kirkwood	31,769	29,421
63124	Ladue	10,594	9,466
64759	Lamar	3,760	3,608
65536	Lebanon	8,616	8,220
64063	Lees Summit	16,230	8,267
63125	Lemay	40,516	
64067	Lexington	5,388	4,845
64068	Liberty	13,704	8,909
63353	Louisiana	4,533	4,286
63552	Macon	5,301	4,547
63863	Malden	5,374	5,007
63011	Manchester	5,031	2,021
63143	Maplewood	12,785	12,552
64658	Marceline	2,622	2,872
65340	Marshall	12,051	9,572
65706	Marshfield	2,961	2,221
63043	Maryland Heights	8,805	
64468	Maryville	9,970	7,807
65265	Mexico	11,807	12,889
65270	Moberly	12,988	13,170
63136	Moline Acres	3,722	3,132

ZIP Code	Place	1970	1960
65708	Monett	5,937	5,359
65711	Mountain Grove	3,377	3,176
65712	Mount Vernon	2,600	2,381
64850	Neosho	7,517	7,452
64772	Nevada	9,736	8,416
63869	New Madrid	2,719	2,867
63121	Normandy	6,183	4,452
64116	North Kansas City	5,183	5,657
63121	Northwoods	4,611	4,701
64076	Odessa	2,839	2,034
63366	O'Fallon	7,018	3,770
63132	Olivette	9,238	8,257
63114	Overland	24,949	22,763
63069	Pacific	3,247	2,795
63133	Pagedale	5,083	5,106
63461	Palmyra	3,188	2,933
63775	Perryville	5,149	5,117
63120	Pine Lawn	5,773	5,943
64080	Pleasant Hill	3,396	2,689
63901	Poplar Bluff	16,653	15,926
63873	Portageville	3,117	2,505
63664	Potosi	2,761	2,805
64133	Raytown	33,306	17,083
64085	Richmond	4,948	4,604
63117	Richmond Heights	13,802	15,622
63137	Riverview	3,741	3,706
63124	Rock Hill	6,815	6,523
65401	Rolla	13,245	11,132
63074	St. Ann	18,215	12,155
63301	St. Charles	31,834	21,189
63077	St. Clair	2,978	2,711
63670	Ste. Genevieve	4,468	4,443
65559	St. James	2,925	2,304
63114	St. John	8,960	7,342
*64501	St. Joseph	72,691	79,673
*63155	St. Louis	622,236	750,026
65560	Salem	4,363	3,870
63126	Sappington	10,603	.....
64485	Savannah	3,324	2,455
65301	Sedalia	22,847	23,874
63119	Shrewsbury	5,896	4,730
63801	Sikeston	14,699	13,765
65349	Slater	2,576	2,767
63138	Spanish Lake	15,647	.....
*65801	Springfield	120,096	95,865
64054	Sugar Creek	4,755	2,663
63080	Sullivan	5,111	4,098
63127	Sunset Hills	4,126	3,525
64491	Tarkio	2,517	2,160
63131	Town and Country	2,645	1,440
64683	Trenton	6,063	6,262
63379	Troy	2,538	1,779
63084	Union	5,183	3,937
63130	University City	46,309	51,249
63088	Valley Park	3,657	3,452
63382	Vandalia	3,160	3,055
63114	Vinita Park	3,657	2,204
64093	Warrensburg	13,125	9,689
63122	Warson Woods	2,544	1,746
63090	Washington	8,499	7,961
65583	Waynesville	3,375	2,377
64870	Webb City	6,923	6,740
63119	Webster Groves	27,455	28,990
63112	Wellston	7,050	7,979
63385	Wentzville	3,223	2,742
65775	West Plains	6,893	5,836
65301	Whiteman	5,040	.....
65360	Windsor	2,734	2,714
63134	Woodson Terrace	5,880	6,048

Montana

ZIP Code	Place	1970	1960
59711	Anaconda	9,771	12,054
59313	Baker	2,584	2,365
*59101	Billings	61,581	52,851
59715	Bozeman	18,670	13,361
59701	Butte	23,368	27,877
59912	Columbia Falls	2,652	2,132
59425	Conrad	2,770	2,665
59427	Cut Bank	4,004	4,539
59722	Deer Lodge	4,306	4,681
59725	Dillon	4,548	3,690
59701	Floral Park	5,113	4,079
59230	Glasgow	4,700	6,398
59330	Glendive	6,305	7,058
*59401	Great Falls	60,091	55,244
59034	Hardin	2,733	2,789
59501	Havre	10,558	10,740
59601	Helena	22,730	20,227
59901	Kalispell	10,526	10,151
59044	Laurel	4,454	4,601
59457	Lewistown	6,437	7,408
59923	Libby	3,286	2,828
59047	Livingston	6,883	8,229
59402	Malmstrom	8,374	.....
59301	Miles City	9,023	9,665
59801	Missoula	29,497	27,090
59801	Missoula South	4,886	.....
59801	Missoula West	9,148	.....

ZIP Code	Place	1970	1960
59474	Shelby	3,111	4,017
59270	Sidney	4,543	4,564
59701	Silver Bow Park	5,524	4,798
59937	Whitefish	3,349	2,965
59201	Wolf Point	3,095	3,585

Nebraska

ZIP Code	Place	1970	1960
69301	Alliance	6,862	7,845
68305	Auburn	3,650	3,229
68818	Aurora	3,180	2,576
68310	Beatrice	12,389	12,132
68005	Bellevue	21,953	8,831
68008	Blair	6,106	4,931
68822	Broken Bow	3,734	3,482
68826	Central City	2,803	2,406
69337	Chadron	5,921	5,079
68601	Columbus	15,471	12,476
69130	Cozad	4,225	3,184
68333	Crete	4,444	3,546
68352	Fairbury	5,265	5,572
68855	Falls City	5,444	5,598
68025	Fremont	22,962	19,698
69341	Gering	5,639	4,585
69138	Gothenburg	3,158	3,050
68801	Grand Island	31,269	25,742
68901	Hastings	23,580	21,412
68948	Holdrege	5,635	5,226
68847	Kearney	19,181	14,210
69145	Kimball	3,680	4,384
68128	La Vista	4,807	1,004
68850	Lexington	5,654	5,572
*68501	Lincoln	149,518	128,521
69001	McCook	8,285	8,301
68137	Millard	7,460	1,014
68959	Minden	2,669	2,383
68410	Nebraska City	7,441	7,252
68701	Norfolk	16,607	13,640
69101	North Platte	19,447	17,184
68113	Offutt East	5,195	.....
68113	Offutt West	8,445	.....
69153	Ogallala	4,976	4,250
*68108	Omaha	346,929	301,598
68763	O'Neill	3,753	3,181
68046	Papillion	5,606	2,235
68048	Plattsmouth	6,371	6,244
68027	Ralston	4,731	2,977
68661	Schuyler	3,597	3,096
69361	Scottsbluff	14,507	13,377
68434	Seward	5,294	4,208
69162	Sidney	6,403	8,004
68776	South Sioux City	7,920	7,200
68978	Superior	2,779	2,935
69201	Valentine	2,662	2,875
68066	Wahoo	3,835	3,610
68787	Wayne	5,379	4,217
68788	West Point	3,385	2,921
68467	York	6,778	6,173

Nevada

ZIP Code	Place	1970	1960
89005	Boulder City	5,223	4,059
89701	Carson City	15,468	5,163
89112	East Las Vegas	6,501	.....
89801	Elko	7,621	6,298
89301	Ely	4,176	4,018
89406	Fallon	2,959	2,734
89415	Hawthorne	3,539	2,838
89015	Henderson	16,395	12,525
*89114	Las Vegas	125,787	64,405
89110	Nellis	6,019	.....
89030	North Las Vegas	36,126	18,422
89109	Paradise	24,477	.....
*89501	Reno	72,863	51,470
89431	Sparks	24,187	16,618
89110	Sunrise Manor	10,886	.....
89109	Vegas Creek	8,970	.....
89101	Winchester	13,981	.....
89445	Winnemucca	3,587	3,453

New Hampshire

See Note on Page 166

ZIP Code	Place	1970	1960
03275	Allenstown	2,732	1,789
03031	Amherst	4,605	2,051
03102	Bedford	5,859	3,636
03570	Berlin	15,256	17,821
03301	Boscawen	3,162	2,181
03603	Charlestown	3,274	2,576
03743	Claremont	14,221	13,563
03301	Concord	30,022	28,991
03818	Conway	4,865	4,298
03038	Derry	6,090	.....
03038	Derry	11,712	6,987
03820	Dover	20,850	19,131
03824	Durham	7,221	4,688
	Durham	8,869	5,504
03833	Exeter	6,439	5,896

ZIP Code	Place	1970	1960
.....	Exeter	8,892	7,243
03835	Farmington	3,588	3,287
03835	Farmington	2,884	2,241
03235	Franklin	7,292	6,742
03246	Gilford	3,219	2,043
03045	Goffstown	9,284	7,230
03581	Gorham	2,998	3,039
03842	Hampton	5,407	3,281
.....	Hampton	8,011	5,379
03755	Hanover	6,147	5,649
.....	Hanover	8,494	7,329
03765	Haverhill	3,090	3,127
03244	Hillsborough	2,775	2,310
03451	Hinsdale	3,276	2,187
03049	Hollis	2,616	1,720
03106	Hooksett	5,564	3,713
03301	Hopkinton	3,007	2,225
03051	Hudson	10,638	5,876
03452	Jaffrey	3,353	3,154
03431	Keene	20,467	17,562
03848	Kingston	2,882	1,672
03246	Laconia	14,888	15,288
03584	Lancaster	3,166	3,138
03766	Lebanon	9,725	9,299
03561	Littleton	4,180	3,355
.....	Littleton	5,290	5,003
03053	Londonderry	5,346	2,457
*03101	Manchester	87,754	88,282
03253	Meriden	2,904	2,434
03054	Merrimack	8,595	2,989
03055	Milford	4,997	3,916
.....	Milford	6,622	4,863
03060	Nashua	55,820	39,096
03857	Newmarket	2,645	2,745
.....	Newmarket	3,361	3,153
03773	Newport	3,296	3,222
.....	Newport	5,899	5,458
03862	North Hampton	3,259	1,910
03076	Pelham	5,408	2,605
03275	Pembroke	4,261	3,514
03458	Peterborough	3,807	2,963
03263	Pittsfield	2,517	2,419
03865	Plaistow	4,712	2,915
03264	Plymouth	4,225	3,210
03264	Plymouth	4,225	3,210
03801	Portsmouth	25,717	26,900
03077	Raymond	3,003	1,867
03867	Rochester	17,938	15,927
03870	Rye	4,083	3,244
03079	Salem	20,142	9,210
03874	Seabrook	3,053	2,209
03878	Somersworth	9,026	8,529
03275	Suncook	4,280	2,318
03431	Swanzey	4,254	3,626
03276	Tilton	2,579	2,137
03608	Walpole	2,966	2,825
03470	Winchester	2,869	2,411
03087	Windham	3,008	1,317
03894	Wolfeboro	3,036	2,689

New Jersey

ZIP Code	Place	1970	1960
08201	Absecon	6,094	4,320
07401	Allendale	6,240	4,092
08865	Alpha	2,829	2,406
07712	Asbury Park	16,533	17,366
*08401	Atlantic City	47,859	59,544
07716	Atlantic Highlands	5,102	4,119
08106	Audubon	10,802	10,440
08007	Barrington	8,409	7,943
07002	Bayonne	72,743	74,215
08722	Beachwood	4,390	2,765
07109	Belleville	34,772	35,005
08030	Bellmawr	15,618	11,853
07719	Belmar	5,782	5,190
07823	Belvidere	2,722	2,636
07621	Bergenfield	29,000	27,203
07922	Berkeley Hts. Twp.	13,078	8,721
08009	Berlin	4,997	3,578
07924	Bernardsville	6,652	5,515
08010	Beverly	3,105	3,400
07003	Bloomfield	52,029	51,867
07403	Bloomingdale	7,797	5,293
07603	Bogota	8,960	7,965
07005	Boonton	9,261	7,981
08505	Bordentown	4,490	4,974
08805	Bound Brook	10,450	10,263
07720	Bradley Beach	4,163	4,204
08723	Brick Twp.	35,057	16,299
08302	Bridgeton	20,435	20,966
08730	Brielle	3,594	2,619
08203	Brigantine	6,741	4,201
08030	Brooklawn	2,870	2,504
08015	Browns Mills	7,144	....
07828	Budd Lake	3,168	1,520
08310	Buena	3,283	3,243
08016	Burlington	11,991	12,687
07405	Butler	7,051	5,414
07006	Caldwell	8,719	6,942
*08101	Camden	102,551	117,159

ZIP Code	Place	1970	1960
08701	Candlewood	5,629	....
08204	Cape May	4,392	4,477
07072	Carlstadt	6,724	6,042
07008	Carteret	23,137	20,502
07009	Cedar Grove Twp.	15,582	14,603
07928	Chatham	9,566	9,517
08034	Cherry Hill Twp.	64,395	31,522
08077	Cinnaminson Twp.	16,962	8,302
07066	Clark Twp.	18,829	12,195
08312	Clayton	5,193	4,711
08021	Clementon	4,492	3,766
07010	Cliffside Park	18,891	17,642
07721	Cliffwood-Cliffwood Beach	7,056	....
*07015	Clifton	82,437	82,084
07624	Closter	8,604	7,767
08108	Collingswood	17,422	17,370
07016	Cranford Twp.	27,391	26,424
07626	Cresskill	8,298	7,290
08075	Delran Twp.	10,065	5,327
07627	Demarest	5,133	4,231
07834	Denville Twp.	14,045	10,632
08096	Deptford Twp.	24,232	17,878
07801	Dover	15,039	13,034
07628	Dumont	20,155	18,882
08812	Dunellen	7,072	6,840
08816	East Brunswick Twp.	34,166	19,965
07019	East Orange	75,471	77,259
07407	East Paterson	20,511	19,344
07073	East Rutherford	8,536	7,769
08520	East Windsor Twp	11,736	2,298
07724	Eatontown	14,619	10,334
07020	Edgewater	4,987	4,113
08817	Edison Twp.	67,120	44,799
08215	Egg Harbor City	4,304	4,416
*07207	Elizabeth	112,654	107,698
07630	Emerson	8,428	6,849
07631	Englewood	24,985	26,057
07632	Englewood Cliffs	5,938	2,913
07021	Essex Fells	2,541	2,174
08053	Evesham Twp.	13,477	4,548
08618	Ewing Twp.	32,831	26,628
07706	Fairfield	6,731	....
07701	Fair Haven	6,142	5,678
07410	Fair Lawn	37,975	36,421
07022	Fairview	10,698	9,399
07023	Fanwood	8,920	7,963
08822	Flemington	3,917	3,232
08518	Florence-Roebling	7,551	....
07932	Florham Park	8,094	7,222
08640	Fort Dix	26,290	....
07024	Fort Lee	30,631	21,815
07416	Franklin	4,236	3,624
07417	Franklin Lakes	7,550	3,316
07728	Freehold	10,545	9,140
07026	Garfield	30,797	29,253
07027	Garwood	5,260	5,426
08026	Gibbsboro	2,634	2,141
08753	Gilford Park	4,007	1,560
08028	Glassboro	12,938	10,253
07028	Glen Ridge	8,518	8,322
07452	Glen Rock	13,011	12,896
08030	Gloucester City	14,707	15,511
07093	Guttenberg	5,754	5,118
*07602	Hackensack	36,008	30,521
07840	Hackettstown	9,472	5,276
08108	Haddon Twp.	18,192	17,099
08033	Haddonfield	13,118	13,201
08035	Haddon Heights	9,365	9,260
07508	Haledon	6,767	6,161
08037	Hammonton	11,464	9,854
07981	Hanover Twp.	10,700	9,329
07640	Harrington Park	4,841	3,581
07029	Harrison	11,811	11,743
07604	Hasbrouck Heights	13,651	13,046
07641	Haworth	3,760	3,215
07507	Hawthorne	19,173	17,735
07730	Hazlet Twp.	22,239	15,334
08829	High Bridge	2,606	2,148
08904	Highland Park	14,385	11,049
07732	Highlands	3,916	3,536
08520	Hightstown	5,431	4,317
07642	Hillsdale	11,768	8,734
07205	Hillside Twp.	21,636	22,304
07030	Hoboken	45,380	48,441
07423	Hohokus	4,348	3,988
07843	Hopatcong	9,052	3,391
08560	Hopewell Twp. (Mercer)	10,030	7,818
07111	Irvington	59,743	59,379
08527	Jackson Twp.	18,276	5,939
08831	Jamesburg	4,584	2,853
*07303	Jersey City	260,545	276,101
07734	Keansburg	9,720	6,854
07032	Kearny	37,585	37,472
08824	Kendall Park	7,412	....
07033	Kenilworth	9,165	8,379
07735	Keyport	7,205	6,440
07405	Kinnelon	7,600	4,431
07034	Lake Hiawatha	11,389	....
08733	Lakehurst	2,641	2,780
07871	Lake Mohawk	6,262	4,647

ZIP Code	Place	1970	1960	ZIP Code	Place	1970	1960
07054	Lake Parsippany	7,488		08865	Phillipsburg	17,849	18,502
08701	Lakewood	17,874	13,004	08021	Pine Hill	5,132	3,939
08530	Lambertville	4,359	4,269	08854	Piscataway Twp.	36,418	19,890
08021	Laurel Springs	2,566	2,028	08071	Pitman	10,257	8,644
08879	Laurence Harbor	6,715		*07061	Plainfield	46,862	45,330
08045	Lawnside	2,757	2,155	08232	Pleasantville	13,778	15,172
07605	Leonia	8,847	8,384	08742	Point Pleasant	15,968	10,182
07035	Lincoln Park	9,034	6,048	08742	Point Pleasant Beach	4,882	3,873
07036	Linden	41,409	39,931	07442	Pompton Lakes	11,397	9,445
08021	Lindenwold	12,199	7,335	08540	Princeton	12,311	11,890
08221	Linwood	6,159	3,847	08540	Princeton North	5,488	4,506
07424	Little Falls Twp.	11,727	9,730	07508	Prospect Park	5,176	5,201
07643	Little Ferry	9,042	6,175	*07065	Rahway	29,114	27,699
07739	Little Silver	6,010	5,202	08057	Ramblewood	5,556	
07039	Livingston Twp.	30,127	23,124	07446	Ramsey	12,571	9,527
07644	Lodi	25,213	23,502	07970	Randolph Twp.	13,296	7,295
07740	Long Branch	31,774	26,228	08869	Raritan	6,691	6,137
08865	Lopatcong	3,144	2,703	07701	Red Bank	12,847	12,482
07071	Lyndhurst Twp.	22,729	21,867	07657	Ridgefield	11,308	10,788
07940	Madison	16,710	15,122	07660	Ridgefield Park	13,990	12,701
08049	Magnolia	5,893	4,199	*07451	Ridgewood	27,547	25,391
07430	Mahwah Twp.	10,800	7,376	07456	Ringwood	10,393	4,182
08736	Manasquan	4,971	4,022	07457	Riverdale	2,729	2,596
08835	Manville	13,029	10,995	07661	River Edge	12,850	13,264
08052	Maple Shade Twp.	16,464	12,947	08075	Riverside Twp.	8,591	8,474
07040	Maplewood Twp.	24,932	23,977	08077	Riverton	3,412	3,324
08402	Margate City	10,576	9,474	07662	Rochell Park Twp.	6,380	6,119
07746	Marlboro Twp.	12,273	8,038	07866	Rockaway	6,383	5,413
08053	Marlton	10,180		07068	Roseland	4,453	2,804
07747	Matawan	9,136	5,097	07203	Roselle	22,585	21,032
07607	Maywood	11,087	11,460	07204	Roselle Park	14,277	12,546
08641	McGuire	10,933		07760	Rumson	7,421	6,405
08056	Medford Lakes	3,793	2,341	07786	Runnemede	10,475	9,461
07945	Mendham	3,729	2,371	07078	Rutherford	20,802	20,473
08619	Mercerville-Hamilton Sq.	24,465		07662	Saddle Brook Twp.	15,975	13,834
08109	Merchantville	4,425	4,075	08079	Salem	7,648	8,941
08840	Metuchen	16,031	14,041	08872	Sayreville	32,508	22,553
08846	Middlesex	15,038	10,520	07076	Scotch Plains Twp.	22,279	18,491
07748	Middletown Twp.	54,623	39,675	07094	Secaucus	13,228	12,154
07432	Midland Park	8,159	7,543	07850	Shore Hills	3,064	1,068
07041	Millburn Twp.	21,307	18,799	07701	Shrewsbury	3,315	3,222
08850	Milltown	6,470	5,435	08083	Somerdale	6,510	4,839
08332	Millville	21,366	19,096	08244	Somers Point	7,919	4,504
07434	Monroe Twp. (Gloucester)	14,071	9,396	08876	Somerville	13,652	12,458
*07042	Montclair	44,043	43,129	08879	South Amboy	9,338	8,422
07645	Montvale	7,327	3,699	08880	South Bound Brook	4,525	3,626
07045	Montville Twp.	11,846	6,772	07079	South Orange	16,971	16,175
07074	Moonachie	2,951	3,052	07080	South Plainfield	21,142	17,879
08057	Moorestown-Lenola	14,179		08882	South River	15,428	13,397
07950	Morris Plains	5,540	4,703	08753	South Toms River	3,981	1,603
07960	Morristown	17,662	17,712	07871	Sparta Twp.	10,819	6,717
07046	Mountain Lakes	4,739	4,037	08884	Spotswood	7,891	5,788
07092	Mountainside	7,520	6,325	07081	Springfield Twp.	15,740	14,467
07856	Mount Arlington	3,590	1,246	07762	Spring Lake	3,896	2,922
08059	Mount Ephraim	5,625	5,447	07762	Spring Lake Heights	4,602	3,309
08060	Mount Holly Twp.	12,713	13,271	07874	Stanhope	3,040	1,814
08063	National Park	3,730	3,380	08084	Stratford	9,801	4,308
07753	Neptune Twp.	27,863	21,487	07747	Strathmore	7,674	
07753	Neptune City	5,502	4,013	07901	Summit	23,620	23,677
07857	Netcong	2,858	2,765	07666	Teaneck Twp.	42,355	42,085
*07102	Newark	382,288	405,220	07670	Tenafly	14,827	14,264
08901	New Brunswick	41,885	40,139	08753	Toms River	7,303	6,062
08511	New Hanover	27,410	28,528	07511	Totowa	11,580	10,897
07646	New Milford	19,149	18,810	*08608	Trenton	104,638	114,167
07974	New Providence	13,796	10,243	07083	Union Twp.	53,077	51,499
07724	New Shrewsbury	8,395	7,313	07735	Union Beach	6,472	5,862
07860	Newton	7,297	6,563	07087	Union City	58,537	52,180
07032	North Arlington	18,096	17,477	07458	Upper Saddle River	7,949	3,570
07047	North Bergen Twp.	47,751	42,387	07044	Verona	15,067	13,782
08902	North Brunswick Twp.	16,691	10,099	08406	Ventnor City	10,385	8,688
07006	North Caldwell	6,425	4,163	08251	Villas	3,155	2,085
08204	North Cape May	3,019		08360	Vineland	47,399	37,685
08225	Northfield	8,875	5,849	07463	Waldwick	12,313	10,495
07508	North Haledon	7,614	6,026	07057	Wallington	10,284	9,261
07060	North Plainfield	21,796	16,993	07465	Wanaque	8,636	7,126
07647	Northvale	5,177	2,892	07882	Washington	5,943	5,723
08260	North Wildwood	3,914	3,598	07675	Washington Twp.		
07648	Norwood	4,398	2,852		(Bergen)	10,577	6,654
07110	Nutley	31,913	29,513	07060	Watchung	4,750	3,312
07755	Oakhurst	5,558	4,374	07470	Wayne Twp.	49,141	29,353
07436	Oakland	14,420	9,446	07087	Weehawken Twp.	13,383	13,504
08107	Oaklyn	4,626	4,778	07006	West Caldwell	11,887	8,314
08226	Ocean City	10,575	7,618	07091	Westfield	33,720	31,447
07757	Oceanport	7,503	4,937	07764	West Long Branch	6,845	5,337
08857	Old Bridge	25,176		07480	West Milford Twp.	17,304	8,157
07675	Old Tappan	3,917	2,330	07093	West New York	40,627	35,547
07649	Oradell	8,903	7,487	07052	West Orange	43,715	39,895
*07050	Orange	32,566	35,789	07424	West Paterson	11,692	7,602
07650	Palisades Park	13,351	11,943	08093	Westville	5,170	4,951
08065	Palmyra	6,969	7,036	07675	Westwood	11,105	9,046
07652	Paramus	28,381	23,238	07885	Wharton	5,535	5,006
07656	Park Ridge	8,709	6,389	08610	White Horse-Yardville	18,680	
07055	Passaic	55,124	53,963	07886	White Meadow Lake	8,499	
*07510	Paterson	144,824	143,663	08260	Wildwood	4,110	4,690
08066	Paulsboro	8,084	8,121	08260	Wildwood Crest	3,483	3,011
08110	Pennsauken Twp.	36,394	33,771	08094	Williamstown	4,075	2,722
08069	Penns Grove	5,727	6,176	08046	Willingboro Twp.	43,386	11,861
08070	Pennsville	11,014		08095	Winslow Twp.	11,202	9,142
07440	Pequannock Twp.	14,350	10,553	08270	Woodbine	2,625	2,823
08861	Perth Amboy	38,798	38,007	07095	Woodbridge Twp.	98,944	78,846

Zip Code	Place	1970	1960
08096	Woodbury	12,408	12,453
08097	Woodbury Heights	3,621	1,723
07675	Woodcliff Lake	5,506	2,742
08107	Wood-Lynne	3,101	3,128
07075	Wood-Ridge	8,311	7,964
08098	Woodstown	3,137	2,942
08562	Wrightstown	2,719	4,846
07481	Wyckoff Twp.	16,039	11,205

New Mexico

Zip Code	Place	1970	1960
88310	Alamogordo	23,035	21,723
*87101	Albuquerque	243,751	201,189
88210	Artesia	10,315	12,000
87410	Aztec	3,354	4,137
88023	Bayard	2,908	2,327
87002	Belen	4,823	5,031
88101	Cannon	5,461	
88220	Carlsbad	21,297	25,541
88415	Clayton	2,931	3,314
88101	Clovis	28,495	23,713
88030	Deming	8,343	6,764
87532	Espanola	4,136	1,976
88231	Eunice	2,641	3,531
87401	Farmington	21,979	23,786
87301	Gallup	13,779	14,089
87020	Grants	8,768	10,274
88240	Hobbs	26,025	26,275
88252	Jal	2,602	3,051
88001	Las Cruces	37,857	29,367
87701	Las Vegas (city)	7,528	7,790
87701	Las Vegas (town)	6,307	6,028
88045	Lordsburg	3,429	3,436
87544	Los Alamos	11,310	12,584
88260	Lovington	8,915	9,660
87107	North Valley	10,366	
88130	Portales	10,554	9,695
87740	Raton	6,962	8,146
88201	Roswell	33,908	39,593
87115	Sandia	6,867	
87501	Santa Fe	41,167	33,394
88061	Silver City	8,557	6,972
87801	Socorro	5,849	5,271
87105	South Valley	29,389	
87901	Truth or Consequences	4,656	4,269
88401	Tucumcari	7,189	8,143
88352	Tularosa	2,851	3,200
88001	University Park-Tortugas	4,165	
87544	White Rock	3,861	
88002	White Sands	4,167	
87327	Zuni Pueblo	3,958	3,585

New York

Zip Code	Place	1970	1960
14001	Akron	2,863	2,841
*12207	Albany	115,781	129,726
11507	Albertson	6,825	
14411	Albion	5,122	5,182
14004	Alden	2,651	2,042
14802	Alfred	3,804	2,807
11701	Amityville	9,794	8,318
12010	Amsterdam	25,524	28,772
14006	Angola	2,676	2,499
10502	Ardsley	4,470	3,991
12603	Arlington	11,203	8,317
14011	Attica	2,911	2,758
13021	Auburn	34,599	35,249
14414	Avon	3,260	2,772
11702	Babylon	12,897	11,062
11510	Baldwin	34,525	30,204
13027	Baldwinsville	6,298	5,985
12020	Ballston Spa	4,968	4,991
12550	Balmville	3,214	1,538
14020	Batavia	17,338	18,210
14810	Bath	6,053	6,166
11705	Bayport	8,232	
11706	Bay Shore	11,119	
11709	Bayville	6,147	3,962
12508	Beacon	13,255	13,922
11710	Bellmore	18,431	12,784
11713	Bellport	3,046	2,461
11714	Bethpage	18,555	20,515
14814	Big Flats	2,509	
*13902	Binghamton	64,123	75,941
14219	Blasdell	3,910	3,909
10913	Blauvelt	5,426	
11716	Bohemia	8,926	
11717	Brentwood	28,327	15,387
10510	Briarcliff Manor	6,521	5,105
11718	Brightwaters	3,808	3,193
14420	Brockport	7,878	5,256
10708	Bronxville	6,674	6,744
11545	Brookville	3,212	1,468
*14240	Buffalo	462,768	532,759
13316	Camden	2,936	2,694
13317	Canajoharie	2,686	2,681
14424	Canandaigua	10,488	9,370
13032	Canastota	5,033	4,896
14823	Canisteo	2,772	2,731
13617	Canton	6,398	5,046

ZIP Code	Place	1970	1960
11514	Carle Place	6,326	
10512	Carmel	3,395	
13619	Carthage	3,889	4,216
12414	Catskill	5,317	5,825
14850	Cayuga Heights	3,130	2,788
13035	Cazenovia	3,031	2,584
11516	Cedarhurst	6,941	6,954
11720	Centereach	9,427	8,524
11934	Center Moriches	3,802	2,521
11722	Central Islip	36,391	
13037	Chittenango	3,605	3,180
12065	Clifton Knolls	5,771	
14433	Clyde	2,828	2,693
12043	Cobleskill	4,368	3,471
12047	Cohoes	18,613	20,129
11724	Cold Spring Harbor	5,450	1,705
12205	Colonie	8,701	6,992
11725	Commack	24,138	9,613
10920	Congers	5,928	
11726	Copiague	19,578	14,081
12822	Corinth	3,267	3,193
14830	Corning	15,792	17,085
13045	Cortland	19,621	19,181
10520	Croton-on-Hudson	7,523	6,812
12929	Dannemora	3,735	4,835
14437	Dansville	5,436	5,460
11729	Deer Park	32,274	16,726
13753	Delhi	3,017	2,307
14043	Depew	22,158	13,580
13214	DeWitt	10,032	
11743	Dix Hills	9,840	
10522	Dobbs Ferry	10,353	9,260
13329	Dolgeville	2,872	3,058
14048	Dunkirk	16,855	18,205
14052	East Aurora	7,033	6,791
14850	East Cayuga Heights	2,611	
10709	Eastchester	21,330	
12302	East Glenville	5,898	
11746	East Half Hollow Hills	9,691	
11576	East Hills	8,624	7,184
11730	East Islip	6,819	
11758	East Massapequa	15,926	14,779
11554	East Meadow	46,252	46,036
10940	East Middletown	2,640	1,752
11743	East Neck	5,221	3,789
11731	East Northport	12,392	8,381
11772	East Patchogue	8,092	
14445	East Rochester	8,347	8,152
11518	East Rockaway	10,323	10,721
13057	East Syracuse	4,333	4,708
13902	East Vestal	10,472	
11596	East Williston	2,808	2,940
14057	Eden	2,962	2,366
12428	Ellenville	4,482	5,003
14059	Elma Center	2,784	
*14901	Elmira	39,945	46,517
14903	Elmira Heights	4,906	5,157
14903	Elmira Heights North	2,906	
11003	Elmont	29,363	30,138
10523	Elmsford	3,911	3,795
11731	Elwood	15,031	
13760	Endicott	16,556	18,775
13760	Endwell	15,999	
13219	Fairmount	15,317	
14450	Fairport	6,474	5,507
12601	Fairview	8,517	8,626
14733	Falconer	2,983	3,343
11735	Farmingdale	9,297	6,128
13066	Fayetteville	4,996	4,311
12801	Fernwood	3,659	2,108
12518	Firthcliffe	4,025	
*11001	Floral Park	18,422	17,499
11050	Flower Hill	4,236	4,594
12828	Fort Edward	3,733	3,737
13339	Fort Plain	2,809	2,809
13340	Frankfort	3,305	3,872
11010	Franklin Square	32,156	32,483
14063	Fredonia	10,326	8,477
11520	Freeport	40,374	34,419
13069	Fulton	14,003	14,261
11530	Garden City	25,373	23,948
11040	Garden City Park	7,488	
12550	Gardnertown	4,614	
14454	Geneseo	5,714	3,284
14456	Geneva	16,793	17,286
11542	Glen Cove	25,770	23,817
12801	Glens Falls	17,222	18,580
12078	Gloversville	19,677	21,741
10924	Goshen	4,342	3,906
13642	Gouverneur	4,574	4,946
14070	Gowanda	3,110	3,352
12832	Granville	2,784	2,715
11022	Great Neck	10,724	10,171
11021	Great Neck Estates	3,131	3,262
11020	Great Neck Plaza	5,921	4,948
12183	Green Island	3,297	3,533
11740	Greenlawn	8,493	5,422
11746	Half Hollow Hills	12,081	
14075	Hamburg	10,215	9,145

ZIP Code	Place	1970	1960
13346	Hamilton	3,636	3,348
10528	Harrison Town	21,509	19,201
10530	Hartsdale	12,226	.....
10706	Hastings-on-Hudson	9,479	8,979
11787	Hauppauge	13,957	.....
10927	Haverstraw	8,198	5,771
12538	Haviland	3,447	.....
°11551	Hempstead	39,411	34,641
13350	Herkimer	8,960	9,396
11040	Herricks	9,112	.....
11557	Hewlett	6,796	.....
°11802	Hicksville	49,820	50,405
10928	Highland Falls	4,638	4,469
10977	Hillcrest	5,357	.....
12603	Hillis	2,750	.....
11741	Holbrook-Holtsville	12,103	.....
13077	Homer	4,143	3,622
12090	Hoosick Falls	3,897	4,023
14843	Hornell	12,144	13,907
14845	Horseheads Village	7,989	7,207
12534	Hudson	8,940	11,075
12839	Hudson Falls	7,917	7,752
11743	Huntington	12,601	11,255
11743	Huntington Bay	3,258	1,267
11746	Huntington Station	28,817	23,438
12443	Hurley	4,081	.....
12538	Hyde Park	2,805	1,979
13357	Ilion	9,808	10,199
11696	Inwood	8,433	10,362
10533	Irvington	5,878	5,494
11558	Island Park	5,396	3,846
11751	Islip	7,692	.....
14850	Ithaca	26,226	28,799
14701	Jamestown	39,795	41,818
10535	Jefferson Valley-Yorktown	9,008	.....
11753	Jericho	14,010	10,795
13790	Johnson City	18,025	19,118
12095	Johnstown	10,045	10,390
14217	Kenmore	20,980	21,261
11754	Kings Park	5,555	4,949
11024	Kings Point	5,614	5,410
12401	Kingston	25,544	29,260
14218	Lackawanna	28,657	29,564
10512	Lake Carmel	4,796	2,735
14006	Lake Erie Beach	3,467	2,117
11755	Lake Grove	8,133	.....
12946	Lake Placid	2,731	2,998
11040	Lake Success	3,254	2,954
11552	Lakeview	5,471	.....
14750	Lakewood	3,864	3,933
14086	Lancaster	13,365	12,254
10538	Larchmont	7,203	6,789
12110	Latham	9,661	.....
11559	Lawrence	6,566	5,907
14482	Le Roy	5,118	4,662
11756	Levittown	65,440	65,276
14092	Lewiston	3,292	3,320
12754	Liberty	4,293	4,704
14223	Lincoln Park	2,851	2,707
11757	Lindenhurst	28,338	20,905
13365	Little Falls	7,629	8,935
13088	Liverpool	3,307	3,487
11743	Lloyd Harbor	3,371	2,521
14094	Lockport	25,399	26,443
11791	Locust Grove	11,626	11,558
11561	Long Beach	33,127	26,473
12211	Loudonville	9,299	.....
13367	Lowville	3,671	3,616
11563	Lynbrook	23,776	19,881
14489	Lyons	4,496	4,673
10541	Mahopac	5,265	1,337
12953	Malone	8,048	8,737
11565	Malverne	10,036	9,968
10543	Mamaroneck	18,909	17,673
11030	Manhasset	8,541	.....
13104	Manlius	4,295	1,997
11050	Manorhaven	5,488	3,566
11758	Massapequa	26,821	32,900
11762	Massapequa Park	22,112	19,904
13662	Massena	14,042	15,478
11951	Mastic Beach	4,870	3,035
13211	Mattydale	8,292	.....
12118	Mechanicville	6,247	6,831
14103	Medina	6,415	6,681
11746	Melville	6,641	.....
12204	Menands	3,449	2,314
11566	Merrick	25,904	18,789
10950	Merriewold Lake	2,564	.....
10940	Middletown	22,607	23,475
11501	Mineola	21,845	20,519
13407	Mohawk	3,301	3,533
10950	Monroe	4,439	3,323
10952	Monsey	8,797	.....
12701	Monticello	5,991	5,222
10549	Mt. Kisco	8,172	6,805
14510	Mount Morris	3,417	3,250
°10551	Mount Vernon	72,778	76,010
11030	Munsey Park	2,980	2,847
14866	Myers Corner	2,826	.....
10954	Nanuet	10,447	.....

ZIP Code	Place	1970	1960
11767	Nesconset	10,048	1,964
14513	Newark	11,644	12,868
12550	Newburgh	26,219	30,979
11590	New Cassel	8,721	.....
10956	New City	27,344	.....
14108	Newfane	2,588	1,423
11040	New Hyde Park	10,116	10,808
12561	New Paltz	6,058	3,041
°10802	New Rochelle	75,385	76,812
°12550	New Windsor	8,803	4,041
°10001	New York	7,895,563	7,781,984
°10451	Bronx	1,471,701	1,424,815
°11201	Brooklyn	2,602,012	2,627,319
°10001	Manhattan	1,539,233	1,698,281
°(Q)	Queens	1,987,174	1,809,578
	(Q)There are 4 Zip Codes for Queens: 11101 for L. I. City; 11691 Far Rockaway; 11351 Flushing and 11431 Jamaica.		
°10314	Richmond	295,443	221,991
13417	New York Mills	3,805	3,788
°14302	Niagara Falls	85,615	102,394
13901	Nimmonsburg-ChenangoBridge	5,059	.....
12309	Niskayuna	6,186	.....
11701	North Amityville	11,936	.....
11703	North Babylon	39,526	.....
11710	North Bellmore	22,893	19,639
11713	North Bellport	5,903	.....
14514	North Chili	3,163	.....
11752	North Great River	12,080	.....
11757	North Lindenhurst	11,117	.....
11758	North Massapequa	23,123	.....
11040	North Merrick	12,658	10,076
11040	North New Hyde Park	17,945	17,929
11772	North Patchogue	5,232	.....
10803	North Pelham	5,184	5,326
11768	Northport	7,494	5,972
13212	North Syracuse	8,687	7,412
10591	North Tarrytown	8,334	8,818
14120	North Tonawanda	36,012	34,757
11580	North Valley Stream	14,881	17,239
11793	North Wantagh	15,053	.....
13815	Norwich	8,843	9,175
10960	Nyack	6,659	6,062
11769	Oakdale	7,334	.....
11572	Oceanside	35,372	30,448
13669	Ogdensburg	14,554	16,122
11804	Old Bethpage	7,084	.....
11568	Old Westbury	2,667	2,064
14760	Olean	19,169	21,868
13421	Oneida	11,658	11,677
13820	Oneonta	16,030	13,412
12550	Orange Lake	4,348	.....
14127	Orchard Park	3,732	3,278
10562	Ossining	21,659	18,662
13126	Oswego	20,913	22,155
13827	Owego	5,152	5,417
11771	Oyster Bay	6,822	.....
14522	Palmyra	3,776	3,476
11772	Patchogue	11,582	8,838
10965	Pearl River	17,146	.....
10566	Peekskill	19,283	18,737
10803	Pelham Manor	6,673	6,114
14527	Penn Yan	5,293	5,770
14530	Perry	4,538	4,629
13135	Phoenix	2,617	2,408
11714	Plainedge	10,759	21,973
11803	Plainview	31,695	27,710
12901	Plattsburgh	18,715	20,172
12903	Plattsburgh Base	7,078	.....
10570	Pleasantville	7,110	5,877
10573	Port Chester	25,803	24,960
12466	Port Ewen	2,882	2,622
11777	Port Jefferson	5,515	.....
11776	Port Jefferson Station	7,403	1,041
12771	Port Jervis	8,852	9,268
11050	Port Washington	15,923	15,657
11050	Port Washington North	2,883	722
13676	Potsdam	9,985	7,765
°12601	Poughkeepsie	32,029	38,330
12143	Ravena	2,797	2,410
12603	Red Oaks Mill	3,919	.....
12144	Rensselaer	10,136	10,506
11901	Riverhead	7,585	5,830
°14603	Rochester	296,233	318,611
°11570	Rockville Centre	27,444	26,355
12205	Roessleville	5,476	.....
13440	Rome	50,148	51,646
11779	Ronkonkoma	7,284	4,220
11575	Roosevelt	15,008	12,883
11576	Roslyn	2,607	2,681
11577	Roslyn Heights	7,140	.....
12303	Rotterdam	25,214	16,871
10580	Rye	15,869	14,225
11780	St. James	10,500	3,524
14779	Salamanca	2,607	8,480
11050	Sands Point	2,916	2,161
11754	San Remo	8,302	3,160
12983	Saranac Lake	6,086	6,421
12866	Saratoga Springs	18,845	16,630

ZIP Code	Place	1970	1960
12477	Saugerties	4,190	4,286
12477	Saugerties South	3,159	
11782	Sayville	11,680	
10583	Scarsdale	19,229	17,968
°12305	Schenectady	77,958	81,682
12302	Scotia	8,224	7,625
11579	Sea Cliff	5,890	5,669
11783	Seaford	17,379	14,718
11784	Selden	11,613	1,604
13148	Seneca Falls	7,794	7,439
11733	Setauket-South Setauket	6,857	
13461	Sherrill	2,986	2,922
11967	Shirley	6,280	
13838	Sidney	4,789	5,157
14136	Silver Creek	3,182	3,310
13152	Skaneateles	3,055	2,921
14845	Slabtown	2,753	
14225	Sloan	5,216	5,803
10974	Sloatsburg	3,134	2,565
13209	Solvay	8,280	8,732
11968	Southampton	4,904	4,582
11735	South Farmingdale	20,464	16,318
12801	South Glens Falls	4,013	4,129
11741	South Holbrook	6,700	
11746	South Huntington	9,115	7,084
10960	South Nyack	3,435	3,113
14904	Southport	8,685	
11790	South Stony Brook	15,329	
11581	South Valley Stream	6,595	
11590	South Westbury	10,978	11,977
12603	Spackenkill	2,725	
14559	Spencerport	2,929	2,461
10977	Spring Valley	18,112	6,538
14141	Springville	4,350	3,852
11790	Stony Brook	6,391	3,548
10980	Stony Point	8,270	3,330
10901	Suffern	8,273	5,094
11791	Syosset	10,084	
°13201	Syracuse	197,297	216,038
10983	Tappan	7,424	
10591	Tarrytown	11,115	11,109
10594	Thornwood	6,874	
12883	Ticonderoga	3,268	3,568
14150	Tonawanda	21,898	21,561
°12180	Troy	62,918	67,492
10707	Tuckahoe	6,236	6,423
12936	Tupper Lake	4,854	5,200
11553	Uniondale	22,077	20,041
°13503	Utica	91,611	100,410
10989	Valley Cottage	6,007	
°11580	Valley Stream	40,413	38,629
12601	Van Keurens	3,292	
11731	Vernon Valley	7,925	5,998
13850	Vestal-Twin Orchards	8,303	
10901	Viola	5,136	
12186	Voorheesville	2,826	1,228
12586	Walden	5,277	4,851
13856	Walton	3,744	3,855
11793	Wantagh	21,873	34,172
12590	Wappingers Falls	5,607	4,447
12885	Warrensburg Center	2,743	2,240
14569	Warsaw	3,619	3,653
10990	Warwick	3,604	3,218
12188	Waterford	2,879	2,915
13165	Waterloo	5,418	5,098
13601	Watertown	30,787	33,306
12189	Watervliet	12,404	13,917
14891	Watkins Glen	2,716	2,813
14892	Waverly	5,261	5,950
14580	Webster	5,037	3,060
14895	Wellsville	5,815	5,967
11701	West Amityville	6,424	
11704	West Babylon	12,893	
11590	Westbury	15,362	14,757
14905	West Elmira	5,901	5,763
14787	Westfield	3,651	3,878
12801	West Glens Falls	3,363	2,725
10993	West Haverstraw	8,558	5,020
11552	West Hempstead	20,375	
11795	West Islip	17,374	
12203	Westmere	6,364	
10994	West Nyack	5,510	
11796	West Sayville	7,386	
13219	Westvale	7,253	
12887	Whitehall	3,764	4,016
°10602	White Plains	50,346	50,485
13492	Whitesboro	4,805	4,784
14221	Williamsville	6,835	6,316
11596	Williston Park	9,154	8,255
11598	Woodmere	19,831	14,011
11798	Wyandanch	15,716	10,952
11980	Yaphank	5,460	
°10701	Yonkers	204,297	190,634
10598	Yorktown Heights	6,805	2,478
13495	Yorkville	3,425	3,749

North Carolina

ZIP Code	Place	1970	1960
27910	Ahoskie	5,105	4,583
28001	Albemarle	11,126	12,261
27263	Archdale	4,844	1,520
27203	Asheboro	10,797	9,449
°28801	Asheville	57,681	60,192
28513	Ayden	3,450	3,108
28706	Balfour	4,836	3,805
28739	Barker Heights	2,933	2,184
28516	Beaufort	3,368	2,922
28012	Belmont	5,054	5,007
28016	Bessemer City	4,991	4,017
28711	Black Mountain	3,204	1,313
28607	Boone	8,754	3,686
28712	Brevard	5,243	4,857
27215	Burlington	35,930	33,199
27509	Butner	3,538	
28542	Camp Le Jeune Central	34,549	
28716	Canton	5,158	5,068
27510	Carrboro	5,058	1,997
27511	Cary	7,435	3,356
27514	Chapel Hill	25,537	12,573
°28202	Charlotte	241,178	201,564
28533	Cherry Point	12,029	
28021	Cherryville	5,258	3,607
27520	Clayton	3,103	2,656
28328	Clinton	7,157	7,461
28025	Concord	18,464	17,799
28613	Conover	3,355	2,281
28034	Dallas	4,059	3,270
28036	Davidson	2,931	2,573
28334	Dunn	8,302	7,566
°27701	Durham	95,438	78,302
28726	East Flat Rock	2,627	
28752	East Marion-Clinchfield	3,015	
28379	East Rockingham	2,858	3,211
27288	Eden	15,871	
27932	Edenton	4,956	4,458
27909	Elizabeth City	14,381	14,062
28621	Elkin	2,899	2,868
27823	Enfield	3,272	2,978
28339	Erwin	2,852	3,183
28340	Fairmont	2,827	2,286
27828	Farmville	4,424	3,997
°28302	Fayetteville	53,510	47,106
28043	Forest City	7,179	6,556
28307	Fort Bragg	46,995	
27526	Fuquay Varina	3,576	3,389
27529	Garner	4,923	3,451
28052	Gastonia	47,142	37,276
28052	Gastonia South	3,718	3,762
27215	Glen Raven	2,848	2,418
27530	Goldsboro	26,810	28,873
27253	Graham	8,172	7,723
°27420	Greensboro	144,076	119,574
27834	Greenville	29,063	22,860
28345	Hamlet	4,627	4,460
28532	Havelock	5,283	2,433
27536	Henderson	13,896	12,740
28739	Hendersonville	6,443	5,911
28601	Hickory	20,569	19,328
28601	Hickory East	4,181	3,274
°27260	High Point	63,259	62,063
28638	Hudson	2,820	1,536
28540	Jacksonville	16,289	13,491
28550	James	2,577	1,474
28081	Kannapolis	36,293	34,647
27284	Kernersville	4,815	2,942
28086	Kings Mountain	8,465	8,008
28501	Kinston	23,020	24,819
28551	LaGrange	2,679	2,133
28352	Laurinburg	8,859	8,242
28645	Lenoir	14,705	10,257
27292	Lexington	17,205	16,093
28092	Lincolnton	5,293	5,699
28601	Longview	3,360	2,997
27549	Louisburg	2,941	2,862
28098	Lowell	3,307	2,784
28358	Lumberton	16,961	15,305
28752	Marion	3,335	3,345
27027	Mayodan	2,875	2,366
28028	Mocksville	2,529	2,379
28110	Monroe	11,282	10,882
28115	Mooresville	8,808	6,918
28557	Morehead City	5,233	5,583
28655	Morganton	13,625	9,186
27215	Morgantown	3,547	
27030	Mount Airy	7,325	7,055
28120	Mount Holly	5,107	4,037
28365	Mount Olive	4,914	4,673
27855	Murfreesboro	3,508	2,643
28560	New Bern	14,660	15,717
28540	New River-Geiger	8,699	
28658	Newton	7,857	6,658
28012	North Belmont	10,678	8,328
28659	North Wilkesboro	3,357	4,197
27565	Oxford	7,178	6,978
27962	Plymouth	4,774	4,666
28376	Raeford	3,180	3,058
°27611	Raleigh	123,793	93,931
28377	Red Springs	3,383	2,767
27320	Reidsville	13,636	14,267
27870	Roanoke Rapids	13,508	13,320

ZIP Code	Place	1970	1960
28379	Rockingham	5,852	5,512
27801	Rocky Mount	34,284	32,147
27573	Roxboro	5,370	5,147
28139	Rutherfordton	3,245	3,392
28144	Salisbury	22,515	21,297
27330	Sanford	11,716	12,253
27874	Scotland Neck	2,869	2,974
27576	Selma	4,356	3,102
27530	Seymour-Johnson	8,172	......
28150	Shelby	16,328	17,698
27344	Siler City	4,689	4,455
27577	Smithfield	6,677	6,117
28387	Southern Pines	5,937	5,198
28159	Spencer	3,075	2,904
28160	Spindale	3,848	4,082
28390	Spring Lake	3,968	4,110
28677	Statesville	19,996	19,844
27886	Tarboro	9,425	8,411
27360	Thomasville	15,230	15,190
27049	Toast	2,635	2,023
28690	Valdese	3,182	2,941
28170	Wadesboro	3,977	3,744
27587	Wake Forest	3,148	2,664
28466	Wallace	2,905	2,285
28398	Warsaw	2,701	2,221
27889	Washington	8,961	9,939
28786	Waynesville	6,488	6,159
28025	West Concord	5,347	5,510
28752	West Marion	3,034	2,335
28472	Whiteville	4,195	4,683
27892	Williamston	6,570	6,924
28401	Wilmington	46,169	44,013
28174	Wingate	2,569	1,304
*27102	Winston-Salem	134,676	111,135

North Dakota

ZIP Code	Place	1970	1960
58501	Bismarck	34,703	27,670
58318	Bottineau	2,760	2,613
58301	Devils Lake	7,078	6,299
58601	Dickinson	12,405	9,971
58102	Fargo	53,365	46,662
58237	Grafton	5,946	5,885
58201	Grand Forks	39,008	34,451
58201	Grand Forks Base	10,474	......
58401	Jamestown	15,385	15,163
58554	Mandan	11,093	10,525
58257	Mayville	2,554	2,168
58701	Minot	32,290	30,604
58701	Minot Base	12,077	......
58368	Rugby	2,889	2,972
58072	Valley City	7,843	7,809
58075	Wahpeton	7,076	5,876
58078	West Fargo	5,161	3,328
58801	Williston	11,280	11,866

Ohio

ZIP Code	Place	1970	1960
45810	Ada	5,309	3,918
*44309	Akron	275,425	290,351
44601	Alliance	26,547	28,362
45213	Amberley	5,574	2,951
44001	Amherst	9,902	6,750
43502	Archbold	3,047	2,348
44805	Ashland	19,872	17,419
44004	Ashtabula	24,313	24,559
45701	Athens	24,168	16,470
44202	Aurora	6,540	4,049
44515	Austintown	29,393	......
44011	Avon	7,214	6,002
45404	Avondale	5,195	......
44012	Avon Lake	12,261	9,403
44203	Barberton	33,052	33,805
43713	Barnesville	4,292	4,425
44140	Bay Village	18,163	14,489
44122	Beachwood	9,631	6,089
44146	Bedford	17,552	15,223
44146	Bedford Heights	13,063	5,275
43906	Bellaire	9,655	11,502
43311	Bellefontaine	11,255	11,424
44811	Bellevue	8,604	8,286
45714	Belpre	7,189	5,418
44017	Berea	22,396	16,592
43209	Bexley	14,888	14,319
43004	Blacklick Estates	8,351	......
45107	Blanchester	3,080	2,944
45242	Blue Ash	8,324	8,341
45817	Bluffton	2,935	2,591
44512	Boardman	30,852	......
43402	Bowling Green	21,760	13,574
44141	Brecksville	9,137	5,435
43912	Bridgeport	3,001	3,824
45211	Bridgetown	13,352	......
44147	Broadview Heights	11,463	6,209
44144	Brooklyn	13,142	10,733
44142	Brook Park	30,774	12,856
45309	Brookville	4,403	3,184

ZIP Code	Place	1970	1960
44212	Brunswick	15,852	11,725
43506	Bryan	7,008	7,361
43008	Buckeye Lake	2,961	2,129
48820	Bucyrus	13,111	12,276
43907	Cadiz	3,060	3,259
43725	Cambridge	13,656	14,562
44405	Campbell	12,577	13,406
44406	Canfield	4,997	3,252
*44711	Canton	110,053	113,631
43316	Carey	3,523	3,722
45005	Carlisle	3,821	671
44615	Carrollton	2,817	2,786
45822	Celina	8,072	7,659
45459	Centerville	10,333	3,490
44022	Chagrin Falls	4,848	3,458
44024	Chardon	3,991	3,154
45211	Cheviot	11,135	10,701
45601	Chillicothe	24,842	24,957
44505	Churchill	7,457	......
*45202	Cincinnati	452,524	502,550
43113	Circleville	11,687	11,059
*44101	Cleveland	750,879	876,050
44118	Cleveland Heights	60,767	61,813
43410	Clyde	5,503	4,826
45638	Coal Grove	2,759	2,961
45828	Coldwater	3,533	2,766
44408	Columbiana	4,959	4,164
*43216	Columbus	540,025	471,316
44030	Conneaut	14,552	10,557
44410	Cortland	2,525	1,957
43812	Coshocton	13,747	13,106
45238	Covedale	6,639	......
44221	Cuyahoga Falls	49,678	47,922
44827	Crestline	5,947	5,521
43731	Crooksville	2,828	2,958
45341	Crystal Lakes	5,851	1,569
44222	Cuyahoga Falls	49,678	47,922
*45401	Dayton	243,601	262,332
45236	Deer Park	7,415	8,423
43512	Defiance	16,281	14,553
43015	Delaware	15,008	13,282
45833	Delphos	7,608	6,961
43515	Delta	2,544	2,376
44621	Dennison	3,506	4,158
44622	Dover	11,516	11,300
44112	East Cleveland	39,600	37,991
44094	Eastlake	19,690	12,467
43920	East Liverpool	20,020	22,306
43920	East Liverpool North	6,223	......
44413	East Palestine	5,604	5,232
45320	Eaton	6,020	5,034
44004	Edgewood	3,437	......
45216	Elmwood Place	3,525	3,813
44035	Elyria	53,427	43,782
45322	Englewood	7,885	1,515
44117	Euclid	71,552	62,998
45324	Fairborn	32,267	19,453
45227	Fairfax	2,705	2,430
45014	Fairfield	14,680	9,734
44313	Fairlawn	6,102	......
44077	Fairport	3,665	4,267
44126	Fairview Park	21,681	14,624
45840	Findlay	35,800	30,344
45405	Forest Park	15,139	......
45426	Fort McKinley	11,536	......
45806	Fort Shawnee	3,436	......
44830	Fostoria	16,037	15,732
45005	Franklin	10,075	7,917
43420	Fremont	18,490	18,767
43230	Gahanna	12,400	2,717
44833	Galion	13,123	12,650
45631	Gallipolis	7,490	8,775
44125	Garfield Heights	41,417	38,455
44041	Geneva	6,449	5,677
45121	Georgetown	3,087	2,674
45327	Germantown	4,088	3,399
43431	Gibsonburg	2,585	2,540
44420	Girard	14,119	12,997
45246	Glendale	2,690	2,823
45237	Golf Manor	5,170	4,648
43212	Grandview Heights	8,460	8,270
43023	Granville	3,963	2,868
45123	Greenfield	4,780	5,422
45218	Greenhills	6,092	5,407
45331	Greenville	12,380	10,585
43123	Grove City	13,911	8,107
*45012	Hamilton	67,865	72,354
45030	Harrison	4,408	3,878
43055	Heath	6,768	2,426
43526	Hicksville	3,461	3,116
44124	Highland Heights	5,926	2,929
43026	Hilliard	8,369	5,633
45133	Hillsboro	5,584	5,474
44425	Hubbard	8,583	7,137
45424	Huber Heights	18,943	......
44236	Hudson	3,933	2,438
44839	Huron	6,896	5,197
44131	Independence	7,034	6,868
45243	Indian Hill	5,651	4,526
45638	Ironton	15,030	15,745

ZIP Code	Place	1970	1960	ZIP Code	Place	1970	1960
45640	Jackson	6,843	6,980	43606	Ottawa Hills	4,270	3,870
44047	Jefferson	3,664	2,774	45431	Overlook-Pahe Manor	19,596	
43031	Johnstown	3,208	2,881	45056	Oxford	15,868	7,828
44240	Kent	28,183	17,836	44077	Painesville	16,536	16,116
43326	Kenton	8,315	8,747	44077	Painesville Southwest	5,461	
45236	Kenwood	15,789		44129	Parma	100,216	82,845
45429	Kettering	71,864	54,462	44130	Parma Heights	27,192	18,100
44094	Kirtland	5,530		45879	Paulding	2,983	2,936
45432	Knollwood	5,353		44124	Pepper Pike	5,933	3,217
44250	Lakemore	2,708	2,765	43551	Perrysburg	7,693	5,519
44107	Lakewood	70,173	66,154	45356	Piqua	20,741	19,219
43130	Lancaster	32,911	29,916	44514	Poland	3,097	2,766
45036	Lebanon	7,934	5,993	45769	Pomeroy	2,672	3,345
44904	Lexington	2,972	1,311	43452	Port Clinton	7,202	6,870
*45801	Lima	53,734	51,037	45662	Portsmouth	27,633	33,637
45215	Lincoln Heights	6,099	7,798	44266	Ravenna	11,780	10,918
43228	Lincoln	11,215		45215	Reading	14,303	12,832
44432	Lisbon	3,521	3,579	43068	Reynoldsburg	13,921	7,793
43217	Lockbourne Base	5,623		44286	Richfield	3,228	
45215	Lockland	5,288	5,292	44143	Richmond Heights	9,220	5,068
43138	Logan	6,269	6,417	45167	Ripley	2,745	2,174
43140	London	6,481	6,379	44270	Rittman	6,308	5,410
*44052	Lorain	78,185	68,932	44116	Rocky River	22,958	18,097
44842	Loudonville	2,865	2,611	43460	Rossford	5,302	4,406
44641	Louisville	6,298	5,116	45217	St. Bernard	6,080	6,778
45140	Loveland	7,144	5,008	43950	St. Clairsville	4,754	3,865
44124	Lyndhurst	19,749	16,805	45885	St. Marys	7,699	7,737
44056	Macedonia	6,375		44460	Salem	14,186	13,854
45243	Madeira	6,713	6,744	44870	Sandusky	32,674	31,989
44057	Madison North	6,882		44870	Sandusky South	8,501	4,724
*44901	Mansfield	55,047	47,325	44672	Sebring	4,954	4,439
44137	Maple Heights	34,093	31,667	44131	Seven Hills	12,700	5,708
45227	Mariemont	4,540	4,120	43947	Shadyside	5,070	5,028
45750	Marietta	16,861	16,847	44120	Shaker Heights	36,306	36,460
43302	Marion	38,646	37,079	45241	Sharonville	10,985	3,890
43935	Martins Ferry	10,757	11,919	44438	Sharon West	3,120	3,365
43040	Marysville	5,744	4,952	44054	Sheffield Lake	8,734	6,884
45040	Mason	5,677	4,727	44875	Shelby	9,847	9,106
44646	Massillon	32,539	31,236	44878	Shiloh	11,368	
43537	Maumee	15,937	12,063	45365	Sidney	16,332	14,663
44143	Mayfield	3,548	1,977	44221	Silver Lake	3,637	2,655
44124	Mayfield Heights	22,139	13,478	45236	Silverton	6,588	6,682
44437	McDonald	3,177	2,727	44139	Solon	11,519	6,333
44256	Medina	10,913	8,235	44001	South Amherst	2,913	1,657
44060	Mentor	36,912	4,354	44121	South Euclid	29,579	27,569
44060	Mentor-on-the-Lake	6,517	3,290	45065	South Lebanon	3,014	2,720
45342	Miamisburg	14,797	9,893	44022	South Russell	2,673	1,276
44017	Middleburg Heights	12,367	7,282	45066	Springboro	2,799	917
45760	Middleport	2,784	3,373	45246	Springdale	8,127	3,556
45042	Middletown	48,767	42,115	*45501	Springfield	81,941	82,723
45150	Milford	4,828	4,131	43952	Steubenville	30,771	32,495
44654	Millersburg	2,979	3,101	44224	Stow	19,847	12,194
44657	Minerva	4,359	3,833	44240	Streetsboro	7,966	
43938	Mingo Junction	5,278	4,987	44136	Strongsville	15,182	8,504
44260	Mogadore	4,825	3,851	44471	Struthers	15,343	15,631
45050	Monroe	3,492	1,475	43558	Swanton	2,927	2,306
45242	Montgomery	5,683	3,075	43560	Sylvania	12,031	5,187
43543	Montpelier	4,184	4,131	44278	Tallmadge	15,274	10,246
45439	Moraine	4,898	2,262	44883	Tiffin	21,596	21,478
44022	Moreland Hills	3,000	2,188	45371	Tipp City	5,090	4,267
43338	Mount Gilead	2,971	2,788	*43601	Toledo	383,818	318,003
45231	Mount Healthy	7,446	6,553	43964	Toronto	7,705	7,780
43050	Mount Vernon	13,373	13,284	45067	Trenton	5,278	3,064
44262	Munroe Falls	3,794	1,828	45426	Trotwood	6,997	4,992
43545	Napoleon	7,791	6,739	45373	Troy	17,186	13,685
45764	Nelsonville	4,812	4,834	44087	Twinsburg	6,432	4,098
43055	Newark	41,836	41,790	44683	Uhrichsville	5,731	6,201
45662	New Boston	3,325	3,984	45322	Union	3,654	1,072
44105	Newburgh Heights	3,396	3,512	44118	University Heights	17,055	16,641
45344	New Carlisle	6,112	4,107	43221	Upper Arlington	38,630	28,486
43832	Newcomerstown	4,155	4,273	43351	Upper Sandusky	5,645	4,941
45345	New Lebanon	4,248	1,459	43078	Urbana	11,237	10,461
43764	New Lexington	4,921	4,514	45377	Vandalia	10,796	6,342
45011	New Miami	3,273	2,360	45891	Van Wert	11,320	11,323
44663	New Philadelphia	15,184	14,241	44089	Vermilion	9,872	4,785
45157	New Richmond	2,650	2,834	44281	Wadsworth	13,142	10,635
44444	Newton Falls	5,378	5,038	43465	Walbridge	3,208	2,142
44446	Niles	21,581	19,545	44146	Walton Hills	2,508	1,776
45872	North Baltimore	3,143	3,011	45895	Wapakoneta	7,324	6,756
44720	North Canton	15,228	7,727	*44481	Warren	63,494	59,648
45239	North College Hill	12,363	12,035	44122	Warrensville Heights	18,925	10,609
44067	Northfield	4,283	1,055	43160	Washington	12,495	12,388
44070	North Olmsted	34,861	16,290	43566	Waterville	2,940	1,856
45414	Northridge	10,084		43567	Wauseon	4,932	4,311
44035	North Ridgeville	13,152	8,057	45690	Waverly	4,858	3,830
44133	North Royalton	12,807	9,290	44090	Wellington	4,137	3,599
43616	Northwood	4,222		45692	Wellston	5,410	5,728
43701	North Zanesville	3,399	2,201	43968	Wellsville	5,891	7,117
44203	Norton	12,308		45449	West Carrollton	10,748	4,749
44857	Norwalk	13,386	12,900	43081	Westerville	12,530	7,011
45212	Norwood	30,420	34,580	44145	Westlake	15,689	12,906
43449	Oak Harbor	2,807	2,903	45383	West Milton	3,696	2,972
45873	Oakwood City	10,095	10,493	45662	West Portsmouth	3,396	3,100
44014	Oakwood Village	3,127	3,283	44138	West View	2,523	1,303
44074	Oberlin	8,761	8,198	45694	Wheelersburg	3,709	2,682
44138	Olmsted Falls	2,504	2,144	43213	Whitehall	25,263	20,818
44862	Ontario	4,345	3,049	44092	Wickliffe	21,354	15,760
43616	Oregon	16,563	13,319	44890	Willard	5,510	5,457
44667	Orrville	7,408	6,511	44094	Willoughby	18,634	15,058
45875	Ottawa	3,622	3,245	44094	Willoughby Hills	5,247	4,241

ZIP Code	Place	1970	1960	ZIP Code	Place	1970	1960
44094	Willowick	21,237	18,749	74079	Stroud	2,502	2,456
45177	Wilmington	10,051	8,915	73086	Sulphur	5,158	4,737
44288	Windham	3,360	3,777	74464	Tahlequah	9,254	5,840
43952	Wintersville	4,921	3,597	74873	Techumseh	4,451	2,630
45215	Woodlawn	3,251	3,007	73120	The Village	13,695	12,118
43793	Woodsfield	3,239	2,956	73460	Tishomingo	2,663	2,381
44691	Wooster	18,703	17,046	74653	Tonkawa	3,337	3,415
43085	Worthington	15,326	9,239	*74101	Tulsa	330,350	261,685
45433	Wright-Patterson	10,151		74301	Vinita	5,847	6,027
45215	Wyoming	9,089	7,736	74467	Wagoner	4,959	4,469
45385	Xenia	25,373	20,445	73572	Walters	2,611	2,825
45387	Yellow Springs	4,624	4,167	73123	Warr Acres	9,887	7,135
*44501	Youngstown	140,909	166,689	73772	Watonga	3,696	3,252
43701	Zanesville	33,045	39,077	73096	Weatherford	7,959	4,499
				74884	Wewoka	5,284	5,954
	Oklahoma			74578	Wilburton	2,504	1,772
				73801	Woodward	9,412	7,747
74820	Ada	14,859	14,347	73099	Yukon	8,411	3,076
73521	Altus	23,302	21,225				
73717	Alva	7,440	6,258		**Oregon**		
73005	Anadarko	6,682	6,299				
74523	Antlers	2,685	2,085	97321	Albany	18,181	12,926
73401	Ardmore	20,881	20,184	97601	Altamont	15,746	10,811
74525	Atoka	3,346	2,877	97520	Ashland	12,342	9,119
74003	Bartlesville	29,683	27,893	97103	Astoria	10,244	11,239
73008	Bethany	21,785	12,342	97814	Baker	9,354	9,986
74008	Bixby	3,973	1,711	97005	Beaverton	18,577	5,937
74631	Blackwell	8,645	9,588	97701	Bend	13,710	11,936
74010	Bristow	4,653	4,795	97415	Brookings	2,720	2,637
74012	Broken Arrow	11,787	5,928	97720	Burns	3,293	3,523
74728	Broken Bow	2,980	2,087	97013	Canby	3,813	2,168
74834	Chandler	2,529	2,431	97223	Cedar Mill	1,991	0,000
74426	Checotah	3,074	2,614	97420	Coos Bay	13,466	7,084
73018	Chickasha	14,194	14,866	97423	Coquille	4,437	4,730
73020	Choctaw	4,750	623	97330	Corvallis	35,056	20,669
74017	Claremore	9,084	6,639	97424	Cottage Grove	6,004	3,895
74020	Cleveland	2,573	2,519	97338	Dallas	6,361	5,072
73601	Clinton	8,513	9,617	*97401	Eugene	78,389	50,977
74021	Collinsville	3,009	2,526	97116	Forest Grove	8,275	5,628
74339	Commerce	2,593	2,378	97301	Four Corners	5,823	4,743
74023	Cushing	7,529	8,619	97526	Fruitdale	2,655	2,158
73115	Del City	27,133	12,934	97027	Gladstone	6,254	3,854
74029	Dewey	3,958	3,994	97526	Grants Pass	12,455	10,118
74030	Drumright	2,931	4,190	97526	Grants Pass Southwest	3,431	
73533	Duncan	19,718	20,009	97030	Gresham	10,030	3,944
74701	Durant	11,118	10,467	97303	Hayesville	5,518	4,568
73034	Edmond	16,633	8,577	97838	Hermiston	4,893	4,402
73644	Elk City	7,323	8,196	97123	Hillsboro	14,675	8,232
73036	El Reno	14,510	11,015	97031	Hood River	3,991	3,657
73701	Enid	44,986	38,859	97351	Independence	2,594	1,930
73737	Fairview	2,894	2,213	97303	Keizer	11,405	5,288
73503	Fort Sill	21,217		97601	Klamath Falls	15,775	16,949
73542	Frederick	6,132	5,879	97850	La Grande	9,645	9,014
73044	Guthrie	9,575	9,502	97034	Lake Oswego	14,615	8,906
73942	Guymon	7,674	5,760	97630	Lakeview	2,705	3,260
74937	Heavener	2,566	1,891	97355	Lebanon	6,636	5,858
74437	Henryetta	6,430	6,551	97367	Lincoln City	4,198	
73651	Hobart	4,638	5,132	97128	McMinnville	10,125	7,656
74848	Holdenville	5,181	5,712	97501	Medford	28,425	24,425
73550	Hollis	3,150	3,006	97501	Medford West	3,919	
74743	Hugo	6,585	6,287	97862	Milton-Freewater	4,105	4,110
74745	Idabel	5,946	4,967	97222	Milwaukie	16,444	9,099
73750	Kingfisher	4,042	3,249	97361	Monmouth	5,237	2,229
73501	Lawton	74,470	61,697	97457	Myrtle Creek	2,733	2,231
73052	Lindsay	3,705	4,258	97458	Myrtle Point	2,511	2,886
73446	Madill	2,875	3,084	97132	Newberg	6,507	4,204
73554	Mangum	4,066	3,950	97365	Newport	5,188	5,344
73055	Marlow	3,995	4,027	97459	North Bend	8,553	7,512
74501	McAlester	18,802	17,419	97913	Nyssa	2,620	2,611
74354	Miami	13,880	12,869	97463	Oakridge	3,422	1,973
73110	Midwest City	48,212	36,058	97914	Ontario	6,523	5,101
73060	Moore	18,761	1,783	97045	Oregon City	9,176	7,996
74401	Muskogee	37,331	38,059	97801	Pendleton	13,197	14,434
73064	Mustang	2,637	198	*97208	Portland	380,555	372,676
73632	New Cordell	3,261	3,589	97754	Prineville	4,101	3,263
73116	Nichols Hills	4,478	4,897	97756	Redmond	3,721	3,340
73066	Nicoma Park	2,560	1,263	97467	Reedsport	4,039	2,998
73069	Norman	52,117	33,412	97470	Roseburg	14,461	11,467
74048	Nowata	3,679	4,163	97051	St. Helens	6,212	5,022
74859	Okemah	2,913	2,836	*97301	Salem	68,856	49,142
*73125	Oklahoma City	368,856	324,253	97138	Seaside	4,402	3,877
74447	Okmulgee	15,180	15,951	97381	Silverton	4,301	3,081
74055	Owasso	3,491	2,032	97501	South Medford	3,497	2,306
73075	Pauls Valley	5,769	6,856	97477	Springfield	27,220	19,616
74056	Pawhuska	4,238	5,414	97383	Stayton	3,170	2,108
73077	Perry	5,341	5,210	97479	Sutherlin	3,070	2,452
74601	Ponca City	25,940	24,411	97386	Sweet Home	3,799	3,353
74953	Poteau	5,500	4,428	97058	The Dalles	10,423	10,493
74361	Pryor	7,057	6,476	97223	Tigard	5,302	
73080	Purcell	4,076	3,729	97141	Tillamook	3,968	4,244
74955	Sallisaw	4,888	3,351	97391	Toledo	2,818	3,053
74063	Sand Springs	10,565	7,754	97068	West Linn	7,091	3,933
74066	Sapulpa	15,159	14,282	97071	Woodburn	7,495	3,120
73662	Sayre	2,712	2,913				
74868	Seminole	7,878	11,464		**Pennsylvania**		
74801	Shawnee	25,075	24,326				
74070	Skiatook	2,930	2,503	19001	Abington	8,594	
73084	Spencer	3,714	1,189	17501	Akron	3,149	2,167
74074	Stillwater	31,126	23,965				

ZIP Code	Place	1970	1960	ZIP Code	Place	1970	1960
19018	Aldan	5,001	4,324	15216	Dormont	12,856	13,098
15001	Aliquippa	22,277	26,369	19335	Downingtown	7,437	5,598
*18101	Allentown	109,527	108,347	18901	Doylestown	8,270	5,917
*16603	Altoona	63,115	69,407	15034	Dravosburg	2,916	3,458
19002	Ambler	7,800	6,765	15801	Du Bois	10,112	10,667
15003	Ambridge	11,324	13,865	18512	Dunmore	17,300	18,917
17003	Annville	4,704	4,264	18641	Dupont	3,431	3,669
18403	Archbald	6,118	5,642	15110	Duquesne	11,410	15,019
19003	Ardmore	5,801		18642	Duryea	5,264	5,626
15068	Arnold	8,174	9,437	15909	East Conemaugh	2,710	3,334
17921	Ashland	4,737	5,237	17701	East Faxon	4,175	3,641
18706	Ashley	4,095	4,258	19050	East Lansdowne	3,186	3,224
15215	Aspinwall	3,541	3,727	15035	East McKeesport	3,233	3,470
18810	Athens	4,173	4,515	18042	Easton	30,256	31,955
15202	Avalon	7,010	6,859	17520	East Petersburg	2,387	2,053
18641	Avoca	3,543	3,562	15112	East Pittsburgh	3,006	4,122
15005	Baden	5,536	6,109	18301	East Stroudsburg	7,894	7,674
19004	Bala-Cynwyd	6,483		15931	Ebensburg	4,318	4,111
15234	Baldwin	26,729	24,489	15005	Economy	7,176	5,925
18013	Bangor	5,425	5,766	19013	Eddystone	2,706	3,006
15714	Barnesboro	2,708	3,035	15218	Edgewood	5,138	5,124
15009	Beaver	6,100	6,160	17872	Edgewood (uninc.)	3,186	3,399
15010	Beaver Falls	14,375	16,240	16412	Edinboro	4,871	1,703
15522	Bedford	3,302	3,696	18704	Edwardsville	5,633	5,711
16823	Bellefonte	6,828	6,088	17022	Elizabethtown	8,072	6,780
15202	Bellevue	11,586	11,412	16117	Ellwood City	10,857	12,413
15202	Ben Avon	2,713	2,553	18049	Emmaus	11,511	10,262
15314	Bentleyville	2,714	3,160	15834	Emporium	3,074	3,397
18603	Berwick	12,274	13,353	15202	Emsworth	3,345	3,341
15102	Bethel Park	34,791	23,650	17522	Ephrata	9,662	7,688
*18016	Bethlehem	72,686	75,408	*16501	Erie	129,231	138,440
16157	Big Beaver	2,739	2,381	15223	Etna	5,319	5,519
19508	Birdsboro	3,196	3,025	18643	Exeter	4,670	4,747
15717	Blairsville	4,411	4,930	15538	Fairhope-Arnold City	3,239	2,803
18447	Blakely	6,391	6,374	17872	Fairview-Ferndale	3,723	4,067
17815	Bloomsburg	11,652	10,655	16121	Farrell	11,022	13,793
19512	Boyertown	4,428	4,067	16225	Fisher-Eldora	3,101	
15014	Brackenridge	4,796	5,697	19522	Fleetwood	3,064	2,647
15104	Braddock	8,795	12,337	19031	Flourtown	9,149	
16701	Bradford	12,672	15,061	19032	Folcroft	9,610	7,013
19406	Brandywine	11,411		16226	Ford City	4,749	5,440
15227	Brentwood	13,732	13,706	15221	Forest Hills	9,561	8,796
19405	Bridgeport	5,630	5,306	18704	Forty Fort	6,114	6,431
15017	Bridgeville	6,717	7,112	18015	Fountain Hill	5,384	5,428
19007	Bristol	12,085	12,364	15238	Fox Chapel	4,684	3,302
15824	Brockway	2,529	2,563	17931	Frackville	5,445	5,654
19015	Brookhaven	7,370	5,280	16323	Franklin	8,629	9,586
15825	Brookville	4,314	4,620	15143	Franklin Park	5,310	
15417	Brownsville	4,856	6,055	15042	Freedom	2,643	2,895
19010	Bryn Mawr	5,737		18224	Freeland	4,784	5,068
17009	Burnham	2,607	2,755	18052	Fullerton	7,908	
16001	Butler	18,691	20,975	17702	Garden View	2,662	2,418
15419	California	6,635	5,978	15904	Geistown	3,633	3,186
15621	Calumet-Norvelt	2,588			General Wayne	5,368	
17011	Camp Hill	9,931	8,559	17325	Gettysburg	7,275	7,960
15317	Canonsburg	11,439	11,877	16417	Girard	2,613	2,451
18407	Carbondale	12,800	13,595	15045	Glassport	7,450	8,418
17013	Carlisle	18,079	16,623	18617	Glen Lyon	3,408	4,173
17013	Carlisle Barracks	4,358		19036	Glenolden	8,697	7,249
15106	Carnegie	10,864	11,887	19038	Glenside	17,353	
15108	Carnot-Moon	13,093		17225	Greencastle	3,293	2,988
15234	Castle Shannon	11,899	11,836	15601	Greensburg	15,870	17,383
18032	Catasauqua	5,702	5,062	15220	Green Tree	6,441	5,226
19095	Cedarbrook-Melrose Park	9,980		16125	Greenville	8,704	8,765
19428	Cedar Heights	6,303		16127	Grove City	8,312	8,368
16404	Centerville	4,175	5,088	19526	Hamburg	3,909	3,747
17201	Chambersburg	17,315	17,670	17331	Hanover	15,623	15,538
15022	Charleroi	6,723	8,148	*17105	Harrisburg	68,061	79,697
19380	Chatwood	7,168	3,621	19044	Hatboro West	13,542	
*19013	Chester	56,331	63,658	19040	Hatboro	8,880	7,315
15024	Cheswick	2,580	2,734	18201	Hazleton	30,426	32,056
15221	Churchill	4,690	3,428	18055	Hellertown	6,613	6,716
15025	Clairton	15,051	18,389	17033	Hershey	7,407	6,851
16214	Clarion	6,095	4,958	16045	Highfield	2,994	2,471
18411	Clarks Summit	5,376	3,693	18042	Highland Park		
16830	Clearfield	8,176	9,270		(Northampton)	5,500	
19018	Clifton Heights	8,348	8,005	17034	Highspire	2,947	2,999
18218	Coaldale	3,023	3,949	15102	Hillcrest	3,897	3,541
19320	Coatesville	12,331	12,971	16648	Hollidaysburg	6,262	6,475
19426	Collegeville	3,191	2,254	16001	Homeacre Lyndora	8,415	
19023	Collingdale	10,605	10,268	15120	Homestead	6,309	7,502
17512	Columbia	11,237	12,075	18431	Honesdale	5,224	5,569
19023	Colwyn	3,169	3,074	17036	Hummelstown	4,723	4,474
15425	Connellsville	11,643	12,814	16652	Huntingdon	6,987	7,234
19428	Conshohocken	10,195	10,259	15701	Indiana	16,100	13,005
15027	Conway	2,822	1,926	15205	Ingram	4,902	4,730
18037	Coplay	3,642	3,701	15642	Irwin	4,059	4,270
15108	Coraopolis	8,435	9,643	15644	Jeannette	15,209	16,565
16407	Corry	7,435	7,744	15344	Jefferson	8,512	8,280
16915	Coudersport	2,831	2,889	19401	Jefferson-Trooper	13,022	
15205	Crafton	8,233	8,418	19046	Jenkintown	5,990	5,017
16833	Curwensville	3,189	3,231	17740	Jersey Shore	5,322	5,613
18612	Dallas	2,913	2,229	18434	Jessup	4,948	5,456
17313	Dallastown	3,560	3,615	18229	Jim Thorpe	5,456	5,945
17821	Danville	6,176	6,889	15845	Johnsonburg	4,304	4,966
19023	Darby	13,729	14,059	*15901	Johnstown	42,476	53,949
15627	Derry	3,338	3,426	16735	Kane	5,001	5,380
18519	Dickson City	7,698	7,738	19607	Kenhorst	3,482	2,815
15033	Donora	8,825	11,131	19348	Kennett Square	4,876	4,355

ZIP Code	Place	1970	1960
18704	Kingston	18,325	20,261
16201	Kittanning	6,231	6,793
17834	Kulpmont	4,026	4,288
19530	Kutztown	4,166	3,312
19444	Lafayette Hills-Plymouth Meeting	8,263	
*17604	Lancaster	57,690	61,055
19446	Lansdale	18,451	12,612
19050	Lansdowne	14,090	12,601
18232	Lansford	5,168	5,958
18704	Larksville	3,937	4,390
15650	Latrobe	11,749	11,932
19605	Laureldale	4,519	4,051
15650	Lawson Heights	3,844	
17042	Lebanon	28,572	30,045
17042	Lebanon South	3,457	
15656	Leechburg	2,999	3,545
18235	Lehighton	6,095	6,318
15401	Leith-Hatfield	2,668	1,622
16751	Lemont	2,547	1,153
17043	Lemoyne	4,625	4,662
17837	Lewisburg	6,376	5,523
17044	Lewistown	11,098	12,640
16930	Liberty	3,594	3,624
17543	Lititz	7,072	5,987
17340	Littlestown	3,026	2,756
17745	Lock Haven	11,427	11,748
15068	Lower Burrell	13,654	11,952
18709	Luzerne	4,504	5,118
17048	Lykens	2,506	2,527
19150	Lynnwood-Pricedale	3,191	2,230
18237	McAdoo	3,326	3,560
(illegible, smeared row)		4,703	3,138
15057	McDonald	2,879	3,141
15034	McKeesport	37,977	45,489
15136	McKees Rocks	11,901	13,185
17344	McSherrystown	2,773	2,839
17948	Mahanoy City	7,257	8,536
19355	Malvern	2,583	2,268
17545	Manheim	5,434	4,790
16933	Mansfield	4,114	2,678
19061	Marcus Hook	3,041	3,299
17547	Marietta	2,838	2,305
15461	Masontown	4,226	4,730
15347	Meadowlands-McGovern	3,609	1,967
16335	Meadville	16,573	16,671
17055	Mechanicsburg	9,385	8,123
*19063	Media	6,444	5,803
16137	Mercer	2,773	2,800
19066	Merion	5,686	
15552	Meyersdale	2,648	2,901
17057	Middletown	9,080	11,182
15059	Midland	5,271	6,425
17844	Mifflinburg	2,607	2,476
17061	Millersburg	3,074	2,984
17551	Millersville	6,396	3,883
15209	Millvale	5,815	6,624
17847	Milton	7,723	7,972
17954	Minersville	6,012	6,606
15061	Monaca	7,486	8,394
15062	Monessen	15,216	18,424
15063	Monongahela	7,113	8,388
15146	Monroeville	29,011	22,446
17754	Montoursville	5,985	5,211
18507	Moosic	4,273	4,243
19067	Morrisville	11,309	7,790
19070	Morton	2,602	2,207
17851	Mount Carmel	9,317	10,760
17552	Mount Joy	5,041	3,292
15210	Mount Oliver	5,487	5,980
19606	Mount Penn	3,465	3,574
15666	Mount Pleasant	5,895	6,107
17066	Mount Union	3,662	4,091
17756	Muncy	2,872	2,830
15120	Munhall	16,574	17,312
17067	Myerstown	3,645	3,268
18634	Nanticoke	14,632	15,601
15943	Nanty-Glo	4,298	4,608
19072	Narberth	5,151	5,109
18064	Nazareth	5,815	6,209
18240	Nesquehoning	3,338	
15066	New Brighton	7,637	8,397
*16101	New Castle	38,559	44,790
17070	New Cumberland	9,803	9,257
17557	New Holland	3,971	3,425
15068	New Kensington	20,312	23,485
16142	New Wilmington	2,721	2,203
*19401	Norristown	38,169	38,925
18067	Northampton	8,389	8,866
19003	North Ardmore	5,856	
15012	North Belle Vernon	2,916	3,148
15104	North Braddock	10,838	13,204
18032	North Catasauqua	2,941	2,805
16428	North East	3,846	4,217
19038	North Hills-Ardsley	13,173	
17857	Northumberland	4,102	4,156
19454	North Wales	3,911	3,673
19074	Norwood	7,229	6,729
19126	Oak Lane	6,192	
15139	Oakmont	7,550	7,504
16101	Oakwood	3,094	3,303
19117	Ogontz	5,463	2,254
15059	Ohioville	3,918	
16301	Oil City	15,033	17,692
18518	Old Forge	9,522	8,928
15472	Oliver	3,091	3,015
18447	Olyphant	5,422	5,864
19075	Oreland	9,114	
17961	Orwigsburg	2,661	2,131
19363	Oxford	3,658	3,376
18071	Palmerton	5,620	5,942
17078	Palmyra	7,615	6,999
19301	Paoli	5,835	
19365	Parkesburg	2,701	2,759
17331	Parkville	5,120	4,516
16668	Patton	2,762	2,880
18072	Pen Argyl	3,668	3,693
17103	Penbrook	3,379	3,671
19004	Pencoyd	6,650	
19401	Penn Sq.-Plymouth Valley	20,238	
19151	Penn Wynne	6,038	
18944	Perkasie	5,451	4,650
*19104	Philadelphia	1,950,098	2,002,512
16866	Philipsburg	3,700	3,872
19460	Phoenixville	14,823	13,797
15140	Pitcairn	4,741	5,383
*15219	Pittsburgh	520,117	604,332
*18640	Pittston	11,113	12,407
18705	Plains	6,606	
15236	Pleasant Hills	10,409	8,573
(illegible, smeared row) Plymouth		21,922	10,401
16342	Polk	3,673	3,574
15946	Portage	4,151	3,933
16743	Port Allegany	2,703	2,742
17965	Port Carbon	2,717	2,775
15133	Port Vue	5,862	6,635
19464	Pottstown	25,355	26,144
17901	Pottsville	19,715	21,659
19076	Prospect Park	7,250	6,596
15767	Punxsutawney	7,792	8,805
18951	Quakertown	7,276	6,305
15104	Rankin	3,704	5,164
*19603	Reading	87,643	98,177
17356	Red Lion	5,645	5,594
17764	Renovo	2,620	3,316
15851	Reynoldsville	2,771	3,158
15853	Ridgway	6,022	6,387
19078	Ridley Park	9,025	7,387
16673	Roaring Spring	2,811	2,937
15074	Rochester	4,819	5,952
19111	Rockledge	2,564	2,587
19001	Roslyn	18,317	
19468	Royersford	4,235	3,969
19046	Rydal	5,083	
17970	St. Clair	4,576	5,159
15857	St. Marys	7,470	8,065
18840	Sayre	7,473	7,917
17972	Schuylkill Haven	6,125	6,470
15683	Scottdale	5,818	6,244
*18503	Scranton	103,564	111,443
17870	Selinsgrove	5,116	3,948
18960	Sellersville	2,829	2,497
15143	Sewickley	5,660	6,157
17872	Shamokin	11,719	13,674
16146	Sharon	22,653	25,267
19079	Sharon Hill	7,464	7,123
15215	Sharpsburg	5,453	6,096
16150	Sharpsville	6,126	6,061
17976	Shenandoah	8,287	11,073
19607	Shillington	6,249	5,639
17257	Shippensburg	6,536	6,138
19608	Sinking Spring	2,862	2,244
18080	Slatington	4,687	4,316
16057	Slippery Rock	4,949	2,563
15501	Somerset	6,269	6,347
18964	Souderton	6,366	5,381
15601	South Greensburg	3,288	3,058
15905	Southmont	2,653	2,857
19464	South Pottstown	2,734	1,850
15401	South Uniontown	3,546	3,603
15601	Southwest Greensburg	3,186	3,264
17707	South Williamsport	7,153	6,972
15775	Spangler	3,109	2,658
19475	Spring City	3,578	3,162
15144	Springdale	5,202	5,602
16801	State College	33,778	22,409
17113	Steelton	8,556	11,266
19464	Stowe	3,596	2,765
18360	Stroudsburg	5,451	6,070
16623	Sugar Creek	5,944	
18250	Summit Hill	3,811	4,386
17801	Sunbury	13,025	13,687
19081	Swarthmore	6,156	5,753
15218	Swissvale	13,819	15,089
18704	Swoyersville	6,786	6,751
18252	Tamaqua	9,246	10,173
15084	Tarentum	7,379	8,232

ZIP Code	Place	1970	1960
18517	Taylor	6,977	6,148
18969	Telford	3,409	2,763
18512	Throop	4,307	4,732
16354	Titusville	7,331	8,356
18848	Towanda	4,224	4,293
15085	Trafford	4,383	4,330
15145	Turtle Creek	8,308	10,607
16686	Tyrone	7,072	7,792
16438	Union City	3,631	3,819
15401	Uniontown	16,282	17,942
19015	Upland	3,930	4,343
15690	Vandergrift	7,873	8,742
15147	Verona	3,737	4,032
15132	Versailles	2,754	2,297
16365	Warren	12,998	14,505
15301	Washington	19,827	23,545
15301	Washington North	2,855	2,077
15301	Washington West	3,297	3,951
17777	Watsontown	2,514	2,431
17268	Waynesboro	10,011	10,427
15370	Waynesburg	5,152	5,188
18255	Weatherly	2,554	2,591
16901	Wellsboro	4,003	4,369
16510	Wesleyville	3,920	3,534
19380	West Chester	19,301	15,705
18201	West Hazleton	6,059	6,278
15120	West Homestead	3,789	4,155
15122	West Mifflin	28,070	27,289
15905	Westmont	6,673	6,573
15089	West Newton	3,648	3,982
18643	West Pittston	7,074	6,998
19602	West Reading	4,578	4,938
15229	West View	8,312	8,079
18644	West Wyoming	3,659	3,166
17404	West York	5,314	5,526
18052	Whitehall	16,551	16,075
15131	White Oak	9,304	9,047
*18701	Wilkes-Barre	58,856	63,551
15221	Wilkinsburg	26,780	30,066
17701	Williamsport	37,918	41,967
19090	Willow Grove	16,494	....
15148	Wilmerding	3,218	4,349
15025	Wilson	8,482	8,465
15963	Windber	6,332	6,994
17043	Wormleysburg	3,192	1,794
17368	Wrightsville	2,668	2,345
18644	Wyoming	4,195	4,127
19610	Wyomissing	7,136	5,044
19067	Yardley	2,616	2,271
19050	Yeadon	12,136	11,610
*17405	York	50,335	54,504
15697	Youngwood	3,057	2,813
16063	Zelienople	3,602	3,284

Rhode Island

See Note on Page 166

ZIP Code	Place	1970	1960
02806	Barrington	17,554	13,826
02809	Bristol	17,860	14,570
02830	Burrillville	10,087	9,119
02863	Central Falls	18,716	19,858
02813	Charlestown	2,863	1,966
02816	Coventry	22,947	15,432
02910	Cranston	74,287	66,766
02864	Cumberland	26,605	18,792
02818	East Greenwich	9,577	6,100
02914	East Providence	48,207	41,955
02822	Exeter	3,245	2,298
02825	Foster	2,626	2,097
02814	Glocester	5,160	3,397
02833	Hopkinton	5,392	4,174
02835	Jamestown	2,911	2,267
02919	Johnston	22,037	17,160
02881	Kingston	5,601	2,616
02865	Lincoln	16,182	13,551
02840	Middletown	29,290	12,675
02882	Narragansett	7,138	3,444
02882	Narragansett Pier	2,686	1,741
02840	Newport	34,562	47,049
02843	Newport East	10,285	2,643
02852	North Kingstown	29,793	18,977
02908	North Providence	24,337	18,220
02876	North Smithfield	9,349	7,632
02859	Pascoag	3,132	2,983
*02860	Pawtucket	76,984	81,001
02871	Portsmouth	12,521	8,251
*02904	Providence	179,116	207,498
02812	Richmond	2,625	1,986
02857	Scituate	7,489	5,210
02917	Smithfield	13,468	9,442
02879	South Kingstown	16,913	11,942
02843	The Anchorage	3,441	....
02878	Tiverton	12,559	9,461
*02880	Wakefield-Peacedale	6,331	5,569
02885	Warren	10,523	8,750
02886	Warwick	83,694	68,504
02891	Westerly Center	13,654	9,698
02891	Westerly	17,248	14,267
02893	West Warwick	24,323	21,414
02895	Woonsocket	46,820	47,080

South Carolina

ZIP Code	Place	1970	1960
29620	Abbeville	5,515	5,436
29801	Aiken	13,436	11,243
29801	Aiken West	2,689	2,602
29810	Allendale	3,620	3,114
29621	Anderson	27,556	41,316
29510	Andrews	2,839	2,995
29407	Avondale-Moorland	5,236	....
29003	Bamberg	3,406	3,081
29812	Barnwell	4,439	4,568
29006	Batesburg	4,036	3,806
29902	Beaufort	9,434	6,298
29627	Belton	5,257	5,106
29512	Bennettsville	7,468	6,963
29611	Berea	7,186	....
29010	Bishopville	3,404	3,586
29020	Camden	8,532	6,842
29902	Capehart	4,490	....
29033	Cayce	9,967	8,517
*29401	Charleston	66,945	65,925
29404	Charleston Base	6,238	....
29408	Charleston Yard	13,565	....
29520	Cheraw	5,627	5,171
29706	Chester	7,045	6,906
29631	Clemson	5,578	1,587
29325	Clinton	8,138	7,937
29710	Clover	3,506	3,500
*29201	Columbia	113,542	97,433
29526	Conway	8,151	8,563
29532	Darlington	6,990	6,710
29042	Denmark	3,571	3,221
29536	Dillon	6,735	6,173
29640	Easley	11,175	8,283
29340	East Gaffney	3,750	4,779
29824	Edgefield	2,750	2,876
29501	Florence	25,997	24,722
29206	Forest Acres	6,808	3,842
29715	Fort Mill	4,505	3,315
29644	Fountain Inn	3,391	2,385
29340	Gaffney	13,253	10,435
29440	Georgetown	10,449	12,261
29445	Goose Creek	3,656	....
29055	Great Falls	2,727	3,030
*29602	Greenville	61,436	66,188
29646	Greenwood	21,069	16,644
29651	Greer	10,642	8,967
29924	Hampton	2,845	2,486
29410	Hanahan	8,376	....
29550	Hartsville	8,017	6,392
29654	Honea Path	3,707	3,453
29451	Isle of Palms	2,657	1,186
29832	Johnston	2,552	2,119
29556	Kingstree	3,381	3,847
29560	Lake City	6,247	6,059
29720	Lancaster	9,186	7,999
29720	Lancaster Mills	2,558	3,274
29360	Laurens	10,298	9,598
29657	Liberty	2,860	2,657
29102	Manning	4,025	3,917
29571	Marion	7,435	7,174
29662	Mauldin	3,797	1,462
29570	McColl	2,524	2,479
29464	Mount Pleasant	6,691	5,116
29574	Mullins	6,006	6,229
29577	Myrtle Beach	9,035	7,834
29577	Myrtle Beach Base	3,864	....
29108	Newberry	9,218	8,208
29809	New Ellenton	2,546	2,309
29841	North Augusta	12,883	10,348
29115	Orangeburg	13,252	13,852
29905	Parris Island	8,868	....
29670	Pendleton	2,615	2,358
29671	Pickens	2,954	2,198
29935	Port Royal	2,865	686
29730	Rock Hill	33,846	29,404
29407	St. Andrews	9,202	....
29301	Saxon	4,807	3,917
29678	Seneca	6,382	5,227
29150	Shannontown	7,491	7,064
29152	Shaw	5,819	....
29681	Simpsonville	3,308	2,282
29303	Southern Shops	2,864	....
*29301	Spartanburg	44,546	44,352
29720	Springdale (Lancaster)	3,193	2,981
29169	Springdale (Lexington)	2,638	1,002
29483	Summerville	3,704	3,633
29150	Sumter	24,555	23,062
29687	Taylors	6,831	1,071
29379	Union	10,775	10,191
29687	Wade-Hampton	17,152	....
29691	Walhalla	3,662	3,431
29488	Walterboro	6,257	5,417
29169	West Columbia	7,838	6,410
29693	Westminster	2,521	2,413
29303	Whitney	2,891	2,502
29697	Williamston	3,991	3,721
29853	Williston	2,594	2,722
29180	Winnsboro	3,411	3,479

ZIP Code	Place	1970	1960
29388	Woodruff	4,483	3,679
29745	York	5,081	4,758

South Dakota

ZIP Code	Place	1970	1960
57401	Aberdeen	26,476	23,073
57717	Belle Fourche	4,236	4,087
57006	Brookings	13,717	10,558
57013	Canton	2,665	2,511
57325	Chamberlain	2,626	2,598
57706	Ellsworth	6,207	
57747	Hot Springs	4,434	4,943
57350	Huron	14,299	14,180
57754	Lead	5,420	6,211
57042	Madison	6,315	5,420
57252	Milbank	3,727	3,500
57301	Mitchell	13,425	12,555
57601	Mobridge	4,545	4,391
57501	Pierre	9,699	10,088
57770	Pine Ridge	2,768	1,256
57701	Rapid City	43,836	42,399
57469	Redfield	2,943	2,952
*57101	Sioux Falls	72,488	65,466
57262	Sisseton	3,094	3,218
57783	Spearfish	4,661	3,682
57785	Sturgis	4,536	4,639
57069	Vermillion	9,128	6,102
57706	Villa Ranchaero	3,171	
57201	Watertown	13,388	14,077
57580	Winner	3,789	3,705
57078	Yankton	11,919	9,279

Tennessee

ZIP Code	Place	1970	1960
37701	Alcoa	7,739	6,395
37303	Athens	11,790	12,103
37650	Banner Hill	2,517	2,132
37660	Bloomingdale	3,120	
38008	Bolivar	6,674	3,338
37027	Brentwood	4,099	
37620	Bristol	20,064	17,582
38012	Brownsville	7,011	5,424
38320	Camden	3,052	2,774
37033	Centerville	2,592	1,678
*37401	Chattanooga	119,082	130,009
37642	Church Hill	2,822	769
37040	Clarksville	31,719	22,021
37311	Cleveland	20,651	16,196
37716	Clinton	4,794	4,943
37315	Collegedale	3,031	
38017	Collierville	3,651	2,020
37663	Colonial Heights	3,027	2,312
38401	Columbia	21,471	17,624
38501	Cookeville	14,270	7,805
38019	Covington	5,801	5,298
38555	Crossville	5,381	4,668
37321	Dayton	4,361	3,500
37055	Dickson	5,665	5,028
38330	Dyer	2,501	1,909
38024	Dyersburg	14,523	12,499
37801	Eagleton Village	5,345	5,068
37412	East Ridge	21,799	19,570
37643	Elizabethton	12,269	10,896
37650	Erwin	4,715	3,210
37331	Etowah	3,736	3,223
37334	Fayetteville	7,030	6,804
42223	Fort Campbell South	9,279	
37064	Franklin	9,497	6,977
37066	Gallatin	13,271	7,901
38138	Germantown	3,474	1,104
37075	Greater Hendersonville	11,996	
37743	Greeneville	13,722	11,759
37748	Harriman	8,734	5,931
38340	Henderson	3,581	2,691
37343	Hixson	6,188	
38462	Hohenwald	3,385	2,194
38343	Humboldt	10,066	8,482
38344	Huntingdon	3,661	2,119
38301	Jackson	39,996	34,376
37760	Jefferson City	5,124	4,550
37601	Johnson City	33,770	31,187
*37662	Kingsport	31,938	26,314
37665	Kingsport North	13,118	
37763	Kingston	4,142	2,010
*37901	Knoxville	174,587	111,827
37083	Lafayette	2,583	1,590
37766	La Follette	6,902	6,204
37416	Lake Hills-Murray Hills	7,806	
37086	La Vergne	2,825	
38464	Lawrenceburg	8,889	8,042
37087	Lebanon	12,492	10,512
37771	Lenoir City	5,324	4,979
37091	Lewisburg	7,207	6,338
38351	Lexington	5,024	3,943
38570	Livingston	3,050	2,817
37774	Loudon	3,728	3,812
38201	Mc Kenzie	4,873	3,780
37110	Mc Minnville	10,662	9,013
37354	Madisonville	2,614	1,812
37355	Manchester	6,208	3,930

ZIP Code	Place	1970	1960
38237	Martin	7,781	4,750
37801	Maryville	13,808	10,348
*38101	Memphis	623,530	497,524
38358	Milan	7,313	5,208
38053	Millington	21,177	6,059
37814	Morristown	20,318	21,267
37642	Mount Carmel	2,821	
38474	Mount Pleasant	3,530	2,921
37130	Murfreesboro	26,360	18,991
*37202	Nashville-Davidson	**447,877	170,874
37821	Newport	7,328	6,448
37830	Oak Ridge	28,319	27,169
37840	Oliver Springs	3,405	1,163
37841	Oneida	2,602	2,480
38242	Paris	9,892	9,325
37148	Portland	2,872	2,424
38478	Pulaski	6,989	6,616
37415	Red Bank	12,715	10,777
38063	Ripley	4,794	3,782
37854	Rockwood	5,259	5,345
37857	Rogersville	4,076	3,121
38372	Savannah	5,576	4,315
38375	Selmer	3,495	1,897
37862	Sevierville	2,661	2,890
37160	Shelbyville	12,262	10,466
37377	Signal Mountain	4,839	3,413
37166	Smithville	2,997	2,348
37167	Smyrna	5,698	3,612
37379	Soddy-Daisy	7,569	
37311	South Cleveland	5,070	1,512
42041	South Fulton	3,122	2,512
38483	Sparta	4,545	4,515
37172	Springfield	9,720	9,221
37874	Sweetwater	4,340	4,145
38382	Trenton	4,226	4,225
37388	Tullahoma	15,311	12,242
38261	Union City	11,925	8,837
37185	Waverly	3,794	2,891
37398	Winchester	5,256	4,760

**Comprises the Metropolitan Government of Nashville and Davidson County.

Texas

ZIP Code	Place	1970	1960
79311	Abernathy	2,625	2,491
*79604	Abilene	89,653	90,368
38516	Alamo	4,291	4,121
78209	Alamo Heights	6,933	7,552
78332	Alice	20,121	20,861
79830	Alpine	5,971	4,740
77511	Alvin	10,671	5,643
*79105	Amarillo	127,010	137,969
79714	Andrews	8,625	11,135
77515	Angleton	9,770	7,312
79501	Anson	2,615	2,890
78336	Aransas Pass	5,813	6,956
*76010	Arlington	89,723	44,775
75751	Athens	9,582	7,086
75551	Atlanta	5,007	4,076
*78710	Austin	251,808	186,545
76020	Azle	4,493	2,969
75149	Balch Springs	10,464	6,821
78201	Balcones Heights	2,504	950
76821	Ballinger	4,203	5,043
77532	Barrett	2,750	2,364
78602	Bastrop	3,112	3,001
77414	Bay City	11,733	11,656
77520	Baytown	43,980	28,159
*77704	Beaumont	117,548	119,175
76021	Bedford	10,049	2,706
78102	Beeville	13,506	13,811
77401	Bellaire	19,009	19,872
76505	Bellmead	7,698	5,127
76513	Belton	8,696	8,163
76126	Benbrook	8,169	3,254
79908	Biggs	4,226	
79720	Big Spring	28,735	31,230
78343	Bishop	3,466	3,722
75418	Bonham	7,698	7,357
79007	Borger	14,195	20,911
76230	Bowie	5,185	4,566
76825	Brady	5,557	5,338
76024	Breckenridge	5,944	6,273
77833	Brenham	8,922	7,740
77611	Bridge City	8,164	4,677
76026	Bridgeport	3,614	3,218
79316	Brownfield	9,647	10,286
78520	Brownsville	52,522	48,040
76801	Brownwood	17,368	16,974
77801	Bryan	33,719	27,542
77024	Bunker Hill	3,977	2,216
76354	Burkburnett	9,230	7,621
76028	Burleson	7,713	2,345
78611	Burnet	2,864	2,214
76520	Cameron	5,546	5,640
79015	Canyon	8,333	5,864
78834	Carrizo Springs	5,374	5,699
75006	Carrollton	13,855	4,242

ZIP Code	Place	1970	1960	ZIP Code	Place	1970	1960
75633	Carthage	5,392	5,262	79521	Haskell	3,655	4,016
78213	Castle Hills	5,311	2,622	77859	Hearne	4,982	5,027
75104	Cedar Hill	2,610	1,848	78361	Hebbronville	4,079	3,987
75935	Center	4,989	4,510	77024	Hedwig Village	3,255	1,182
79201	Childress	5,408	6,399	75652	Henderson	10,187	9,666
76437	Cisco	4,160	4,499	76365	Henrietta	2,897	3,062
75426	Clarksville	3,346	3,851	79045	Hereford	13,414	7,652
76031	Cleburne	16,015	15,381	75205	Highland Park	10,133	10,411
77327	Cleveland	5,627	5,838	77562	Highlands	3,462	4,336
76634	Clifton	2,578	2,335	76645	Hillsboro	7,224	7,402
77531	Clute City	6,023	4,501	77563	Hitchcock	5,565	5,216
75211	Cockrell Hill	3,515	3,104	78861	Hondo	5,487	4,992
76834	Coleman	5,608	6,371	75561	Hooks	2,545	2,048
77840	College Station	17,676	11,396	*77013	Houston	1,232,802	938,219
76034	Colleyville	3,368	1,491	77338	Humble	3,278	1,711
79512	Colorado City	5,227	6,457	77024	Hunters Creek	3,959	2,478
78934	Columbus	3,342	3,656	77340	Huntsville	17,610	11,999
76442	Comanche	3,933	3,415	76053	Hurst	27,215	10,165
75428	Commerce	9,534	5,789	78362	Ingleside	3,763	3,022
77301	Conroe	11,969	9,192	76367	Iowa Park	5,796	3,295
76522	Copperas Cove	10,818	4,567	*75060	Irving	97,260	45,985
*78408	Corpus Christi	204,525	167,690	77029	Jacinto City	9,563	9,547
75110	Corsicana	19,972	20,344	76056	Jacksboro	3,554	3,816
78014	Cotulla	3,415	3,960	75766	Jacksonville	9,734	9,590
79731	Crane	3,427	3,796	75951	Jasper	6,251	4,889
75835	Crockett	6,616	5,356	75657	Jefferson	2,866	3,082
76036	Crowley	2,662	583	76849	Junction	2,654	2,441
78839	Crystal City	8,104	9,101	78118	Karnes City	2,926	2,693
77954	Cuero	6,956	7,338	77450	Katy	2,923	1,569
75638	Daingerfield	2,630	3,133	75142	Kaufman	4,012	3,087
79022	Dalhart	5,705	5,160	78119	Kenedy	4,156	4,301
*75221	Dallas	844,401	679,684	76060	Kennedale	3,076	1,521
77535	Dayton	3,804	3,367	79745	Kermit	7,884	10,465
76234	Decatur	3,240	3,563	78028	Kerrville	12,672	8,901
77536	Deer Park	12,773	4,865	75662	Kilgore	9,495	10,092
78840	Del Rio	21,330	18,612	76541	Killeen	35,507	23,377
75020	Denison	24,923	22,748	78363	Kingsville	28,915	25,297
76201	Denton	39,874	26,844	78109	Kirby	2,558	680
79323	Denver City	4,133	4,302	75145	Kleberg	4,768	3,572
75115	De Soto	6,617	1,969	78236	Lackland	19,141	
78016	Devine	3,311	2,522	76705	Lacy-Lakeview	2,558	2,272
75941	Diboll	3,557		78559	La Feria	2,642	3,047
77539	Dickinson	10,776	4,715	78945	La Grange	3,092	3,623
79027	Dimmitt	4,327	2,935	77566	Lake Jackson	13,376	9,651
78537	Donna	7,365	7,522	79239	Lakeview	3,567	3,849
76446	Dublin	2,810	2,443	76135	Lake Worth Village	4,958	3,833
79029	Dumas	9,771	8,477	77568	La Marque	16,131	13,969
75116	Duncanville	14,105	3,774	79331	Lamesa	11,559	12,438
77434	Eagle Lake	3,587	3,565	76650	Lampasas	5,922	5,061
78852	Eagle Pass	15,364	12,094	75146	Lancaster	10,522	7,501
76448	Eastland	3,178	3,292	77571	La Porte	7,149	4,512
78538	Edcouch	2,656	2,814	78040	Laredo	69,024	60,678
78539	Edinburg	17,163	18,706	78840	Laughlin	3,458	
77957	Edna	5,332	5,038	77573	League City	10,818	
77437	El Campo	9,332	7,700	79336	Levelland	11,445	10,153
76360	Electra	3,895	4,759	75067	Lewisville	9,264	3,956
76621	Elgin	3,832	3,511	77575	Liberty	5,591	6,127
*79910	El Paso	322,261	276,687	79339	Littlefield	6,738	7,236
78543	Elsa	4,400	3,847	78233	Live Oak	2,779	
75119	Ennis	11,046	9,347	77351	Livingston	3,965	3,398
76039	Euless	19,316	4,263	78643	Llano	2,608	2,656
76140	Everman	4,570	1,076	78644	Lockhart	6,489	6,084
79838	Fabens	3,241	3,134	75601	Longview	45,547	40,050
78355	Falfurrias	6,355	6,515	*79408	Lubbock	149,101	128,691
75234	Farmers Branch	27,492	13,441	75901	Lufkin	23,049	17,641
78114	Floresville	3,707	2,126	78648	Luling	4,719	4,412
79235	Floydada	4,109	3,769	78501	McAllen	37,636	32,728
75701	Forest Hill	8,236	3,221	79752	McCamey	2,647	3,375
79906	Fort Bliss	13,288		76657	McGregor	4,365	4,642
76544	Fort Hood	32,597		75069	McKinney	15,193	13,763
78234	Fort Sam Houston	10,553		77864	Madisonville	2,881	2,324
79735	Fort Stockton	8,283	6,373	76063	Mansfield	3,658	1,375
76067	Fort Wolters	3,743		79843	Marfa	2,682	2,799
*76101	Fort Worth	393,476	356,268	76661	Marlin	6,351	6,918
78624	Fredericksburg	5,326	4,629	75670	Marshall	22,937	23,846
77541	Freeport	11,997	11,619	78368	Mathis	5,351	6,075
78357	Freer	2,804	2,724	79245	Memphis	3,227	3,332
77546	Friendswood	5,675		78570	Mercedes	9,355	10,943
79035	Friona	3,111	2,048	75149	Mesquite	55,131	27,526
76240	Gainesville	13,830	13,083	76667	Mexia	5,943	6,121
77547	Galena Park	10,479	10,852	79701	Midland	59,463	62,625
77550	Galveston	61,809	67,175	75773	Mineola	3,926	3,810
75040	Garland	81,437	38,501	76067	Mineral Wells	18,411	11,053
76528	Gatesville	4,683	4,626	78572	Mission	13,043	14,081
78626	Georgetown	6,395	5,218	77459	Missouri City	4,136	604
78942	Giddings	2,783	2,821	79756	Monahans	8,333	8,567
75644	Gilmer	4,196	4,312	79346	Morton	2,738	2,731
75647	Gladewater	5,574	5,742	75455	Mount Pleasant	9,459	8,027
78629	Gonzales	5,854	5,829	79347	Muleshoe	4,525	3,871
76046	Graham	7,477	8,505	75961	Nacogdoches	22,544	12,674
75050	Grand Prairie	50,904	30,386	77868	Navasota	5,111	4,937
76051	Grapevine	7,023	2,821	77627	Nederland	16,810	12,036
75401	Greenville	22,043	19,087	75570	New Boston	4,034	2,773
77619	Groves	18,067	17,304	78130	New Braunfels	17,859	15,631
77964	Hallettsville	2,712	2,808	76255	Nocona	2,871	3,127
76117	Haltom City	28,127	23,133	76118	North Richland Hills	16,514	8,662
76531	Hamilton	2,760	3,106	79760	Odessa	78,380	80,338
79520	Hamlin	3,325	3,791	76374	Olney	3,624	3,872
76541	Harker Heights	4,216		77630	Orange	24,457	25,605
78550	Harlingen	33,503	41,207	76943	Ozona	2,864	3,361

ZIP Code	Place	1970	1960
77465	Palacios	3,642	3,676
75801	Palestine	14,525	13,974
79065	Pampa	21,726	24,664
75460	Paris	23,441	20,977
*77501	Pasadena	89,277	58,737
77581	Pearland	6,444	1,497
77640	Pear Ridge	3,697	3,470
78061	Pearsall	5,545	4,957
79772	Pecos	12,682	12,728
79070	Perryton	7,810	7,903
78577	Pharr	15,829	14,106
79071	Phillips	2,515	3,605
77024	Piney Point	2,548	1,790
75686	Pittsburg	3,844	3,796
79072	Plainview	19,096	18,735
75074	Plano	17,872	3,695
78064	Pleasanton	5,407	3,467
77640	Port Arthur	57,371	66,676
78578	Port Isabel	3,067	3,575
78374	Portland	7,302	2,538
77979	Port Lavaca	10,491	8,864
77651	Port Neches	10,894	8,696
79356	Post	3,854	4,663
78065	Poteet	3,013	2,811
77445	Prairie View	3,589	2,326
78375	Premont	3,282	3,049
79252	Quanah	3,948	4,564
75475	Randolph	5,329	
76470	Ranger	3,094	3,313
78580	Raymondville	7,987	9,385
78377	Refugio	2,516	
75080	Richardson	48,582	16,810
76118	Richland Hills	8,865	7,804
77469	Richmond	5,777	3,668
78582	Rio Grande City	5,676	5,835
77019	River Oaks	8,193	8,444
76706	Robinson	3,807	2,111
78380	Robstown	11,217	10,266
76567	Rockdale	4,655	4,481
78382	Rockport	3,879	2,989
75087	Rockwall	3,121	2,166
77471	Rosenberg	12,098	9,698
78664	Round Rock	2,811	1,878
75088	Rowlett	2,579	
75785	Rusk	4,914	4,900
76901	San Angelo	63,884	58,815
*78205	San Antonio	654,153	587,718
75972	San Augustine	2,539	2,584
78586	San Benito	15,176	16,422
78384	San Diego	4,490	4,351
78589	San Juan	5,070	4,371
78666	San Marcos	18,860	12,713
76877	San Saba	2,555	2,728
76114	Sansom Park Village	4,771	4,175
78154	Schertz	4,061	
77586	Seabrook	3,811	
75159	Seagoville	4,390	3,745
77474	Sealy	2,685	2,328
78155	Seguin	15,934	14,299
79360	Seminole	5,007	5,737
76380	Seymour	3,469	3,789
79079	Shamrock	2,644	3,113
75090	Sherman	29,061	24,988
77656	Silsbee	7,271	6,277
78387	Sinton	5,563	6,008
79364	Slaton	6,583	6,568
78957	Smithville	2,959	2,933
79549	Snyder	11,171	13,850
77587	South Houston	11,527	7,523
78380	South San Pedro	3,065	
79081	Spearman	3,435	3,555
77024	Spring Valley	3,170	3,004
77477	Stafford	2,906	1,485
79553	Stamford	4,558	5,259
76401	Stephenville	9,277	7,359
77478	Sugar Land	3,318	2,802
75482	Sulphur Springs	10,642	9,160
77480	Sweeny	3,191	3,087
79556	Sweetwater	12,020	13,914
78390	Taft	3,274	3,463
79373	Tahoka	2,956	3,012
76574	Taylor	9,616	9,434
75860	Teague	2,867	2,728
76501	Temple	33,431	30,419
75160	Terrell	14,182	13,803
78209	Terrell Hills	5,225	5,572
75501	Texarkana	30,497	30,218
77590	Texas City	38,908	32,065
77375	Tomball	2,734	1,713
75862	Trinity	2,512	1,787
79088	Tulia	5,294	4,410
75701	Tyler	57,770	51,230
78148	Universal City	7,613	
76308	University Park	23,498	23,202
78801	Uvalde	10,764	10,293
79855	Van Horn	2,889	
76384	Vernon	11,454	12,141
77901	Victoria	41,349	33,047
77662	Vidor	9,738	

ZIP Code	Place	1970	1960
*76701	Waco	95,326	97,808
76248	Watauga	3,778	
75165	Waxahachie	13,452	12,749
76086	Weatherford	11,750	9,759
79095	Wellington	2,884	3,137
78596	Weslaco	15,313	15,649
77486	West Columbia	3,335	2,947
77630	West Orange	4,820	4,848
77005	West University Place	13,317	14,628
76114	Westworth	4,578	3,321
77488	Wharton	7,881	5,734
76273	Whitesboro	2,927	2,485
76108	White Settlement	13,449	11,513
*76307	Wichita Falls	96,265	101,724
75169	Wills Point	2,636	2,281
78239	Windcrest	3,371	441
75494	Winnsboro	3,064	2,675
79567	Winters	2,907	3,266
75979	Woodville	2,662	1,920
76710	Woodway	4,819	1,244
77098	Wylie	2,675	1,804
77995	Yoakum	5,755	5,761

Utah

ZIP Code	Place	1970	1960
84003	American Fork	7,713	6,373
84010	Bountiful	27,956	17,039
84302	Brigham City	14,007	11,728
84720	Cedar City	8,946	7,543
84014	Centerville	3,268	2,361
84015	Clearfield	13,316	8,833
84121	Cottonwood	8,404	
84025	Farmington		
84019	Granger-Hunter	9,029	
84106	Granite Park	9,573	
84029	Grantsville	2,931	2,166
84032	Heber	3,245	2,936
84117	Holladay	23,014	
84037	Kaysville	6,192	3,608
84118	Kearns	17,071	17,172
84041	Layton	13,603	9,027
84043	Lehi	4,659	4,377
84321	Logan	22,333	18,731
84044	Magna	5,509	6,442
84047	Midvale	7,840	5,802
84532	Moab	4,793	4,682
84117	Mount Olympus	5,909	
84107	Murray	21,206	16,806
84648	Nephi	2,699	2,566
84404	North Ogden	5,257	2,621
*84401	Ogden	69,478	70,197
84057	Orem	25,729	18,394
84651	Payson	4,501	4,237
84062	Pleasant Grove	5,327	4,772
84501	Price	6,218	6,802
84601	Provo	53,131	36,047
84701	Richfield	4,471	4,412
84401	Riverdale	3,704	1,848
84065	Riverton	2,820	1,993
84067	Roy	14,356	9,239
84770	St. George	7,097	5,130
*84101	Salt Lake City	175,885	189,454
84070	Sandy City	6,438	3,322
84335	Smithfield	3,342	2,512
84065	South Jordan	2,942	1,354
84403	South Ogden	9,991	7,405
84115	South Salt Lake	7,810	9,520
84660	Spanish Fork	7,284	6,472
84663	Springville	8,790	7,913
84015	Sunset	6,268	4,235
84074	Tooele	12,539	9,133
84337	Tremonton	2,794	2,115
84078	Vernal	3,908	3,655
84403	Washington Terrace	7,241	6,441
84084	West Jordan	4,221	3,009
84070	White City	6,402	
84087	Woods Cross	3,124	1,098

Vermont

See Note on Page 166

ZIP Code	Place	1970	1960
05641	Barre	10,209	10,387
	Barre	6,509	4,580
05822	Barton	2,874	3,066
05101	Bellows Falls	3,505	3,831
05201	Bennington (town)	14,586	13,002
	Bennington	7,950	8,023
05733	Brandon	3,697	3,329
05301	Brattleboro	9,055	9,315
	Brattleboro	12,239	11,734
05443	Bristol	2,744	2,159
05401	Burlington	38,633	35,531
05735	Castleton	2,837	1,902
05446	Colchester	8,776	4,718
05829	Derby	3,252	2,506
05451	Essex	10,951	7,090
05452	Essex Junction	6,511	5,340
05743	Fair Haven	2,777	2,378
05047	Hartford	6,477	6,355
05849	Lyndon	3,705	3,425
05254	Manchester	2,919	2,470

ZIP Code	*Place	1970	1960
05753	Middlebury.............	6,532	5,305
05468	Milton	4,495	2,022
05602	Montpelier............	8,609	8,782
05661	Morristown............	4,052	3,347
05855	Newport..............	4,664	5,019
05663	Northfield............	4,870	4,511
05764	Poultney.............	3,217	3,009
05060	Randolph.............	3,882	3,414
05101	Rockingham..........	5,501	5,704
05701	Rutland	19,293	18,325
05478	St. Albans...........	8,082	8,806
	St. Albans...........	3,270	2,303
05819	St. Johnsbury	8,409	8,869
05482	Shelburne............	3,728	1,805
05401	Shelburne Road Section..	2,591	2,037
05401	South Burlington	10,032	6,903
05156	Springfield...........	5,632	6,600
	Springfield...........	10,063	9,934
05488	Swanton.............	4,622	3,946
05488	Swanton.............	2,630	2,390
05676	Waterbury............	2,840	2,984
	Waterbury............	4,614	4,303
05495	Williston	3,187	1,484
05401	Williston Road Section...	5,375	3,259
05089	Windsor.............	4,158	4,468
05404	Winooski.............	7,309	7,420
05091	Woodstock...........	2,608	2,786

Virginia

ZIP Code	Place	1970	1960
24210	Abingdon.............	4,376	4,758
*22313	Alexandria............	110,938	91,023
24517	Altavista	2,708	3,299
22003	Annandale............	27,405	......
*22210	Arlington.............	174,284	163,401
23005	Ashland..............	2,934	2,773
22041	Bailey's Crossroads.....	7,295	......
24055	Bassett..............	3,058	3,148
24523	Bedford..............	6,011	5,921
22307	Belleview.............	8,299	......
24219	Big Stone Gap.........	4,153	4,688
24060	Blacksburg............	9,384	7,070
23824	Blackstone............	3,412	3,659
24605	Bluefield.............	5,286	4,235
23235	Bon Air..............	10,771	......
22812	Bridgewater...........	2,828	1,815
24201	Bristol...............	14,857	17,144
24416	Buena Vista...........	6,425	6,300
*22902	Charlottesville........	38,880	29,427
23924	Chase City	2,909	3,207
*23320	Chesapeake...........	89,580	......
23831	Chester..............	5,556	1,290
24073	Christiansburg.........	7,857	3,653
24422	Clifton Forge..........	5,501	5,268
24078	Collinsville...........	6,015	3,586
23834	Colonial Heights.......	15,097	9,587
24426	Covington............	10,060	11,062
22701	Culpeper.............	6,056	2,412
22191	Dale................	13,857	......
24541	Danville.............	46,391	46,577
23847	Emporia.............	5,300	5,535
22030	Fairfax..............	21,970	13,585
*22046	Falls Church..........	10,772	10,192
23901	Farmville	4,331	4,293
22060	Fort Belvoir	14,591	......
22308	Fort Hunt	10,415	......
23801	Fort Lee.............	12,435	......
23851	Franklin.............	6,880	7,264
22401	Fredericksburg.........	14,450	13,639
22630	Front Royal	8,211	7,949
24333	Galax...............	6,278	5,254
22306	Groveton.............	11,750	......
*23369	Hampton.............	120,779	89,258
22801	Harrisonburg..........	14,605	11,916
22070	Herndon.............	4,301	1,960
23075	Highland Springs.......	7,345	......
23860	Hopewell............	23,471	17,895
22303	Huntington...........	5,559	......
22042	Jefferson............	25,432	......
22041	Lake Barcroft.........	11,605	......
23228	Lakeside............	11,137	......
22075	Leesburg............	4,821	2,869
24450	Lexington............	7,597	7,537
22312	Lincolnia............	10,761	......
22030	Long Branch..........	21,634	......
22835	Luray...............	3,612	3,014
22134	Lyman Park-Thomason Park..............	3,765	......
*24505	Lynchburg............	54,083	54,790
22110	Manassas	9,164	3,555
22110	Manassas Park	6,844	5,342
22030	Mantua..............	6,911	......
24354	Marion..............	8,158	8,385
24112	Martinsville..........	19,653	18,798
22101	McLean..............	17,698	......
23111	Mechanicsville........	5,189	......
*23607	Newport News.........	138,177	113,662
*23501	Norfolk..............	307,951	304,869
22151	North Springfield......	8,631	......

ZIP Code	Place	1970	1960
24273	Norton..............	4,172	5,013
22960	Orange..............	2,768	2,955
23803	Petersburg...........	36,103	36,750
23362	Poquoson	5,441	4,278
*23705	Portsmouth...........	110,963	114,773
24301	Pulaski..............	10,279	10,469
22134	Quantico Station	6,213	......
24141	Radford	11,596	9,371
22070	Reston..............	5,723	......
24641	Richlands............	4,843	4,963
*23232	Richmond............	249,430	219,958
*24001	Roanoke	92,115	97,110
24151	Rocky Mount	4,002	1,412
24281	Rose Hill	14,492	......
24153	Salem	21,982	16,058
24370	Saltville	2,527	2,844
22044	Seven Corners	5,590	10,783
23430	Smithfield	2,713	917
24592	South Boston.........	6,889	5,974
23970	South Hill	3,858	2,569
*22150	Springfield...........	11,613	10,783
24401	Staunton............	24,504	22,232
22170	Sterling Park	8,321	......
23434	Suffolk..............	9,858	12,609
24651	Tazewell.............	4,168	3,000
22172	Triangle	3,021	2,948
22180	Vienna..............	17,146	11,440
24179	Vinton	6,347	3,432
*23458	Virginia Beach	172,106	8,091
22186	Warrenton	4,027	3,522
22980	Waynesboro...........	16,707	15,694
23181	West Point...........	2,600	1,678
22152	West Springfield.......	14,143	......
23185	Williamsburg	9,069	6,832
22601	Winchester...........	14,643	15,110
24293	Wise................	2,891	2,614
22191	Woodbridge-Marumsco...	25,412	......
24382	Wytheville	6,069	5,634
22110	Yorkshire............	4,649	......

Washington

ZIP Code	Place	1970	1960
98520	Aberdeen............	18,489	18,741
98221	Anacortes	7,701	8,414
98002	Auburn..............	21,817	11,933
98009	Bellevue.............	61,102	12,809
98225	Bellingham...........	39,375	34,688
98011	Bothell..............	4,883	2,237
98310	Bremerton...........	35,307	28,922
98036	Brier	3,093	......
98321	Buckley	3,446	3,538
98233	Burlington	3,138	2,968
98607	Camas	5,790	5,666
98531	Centralia	10,054	8,586
98520	Central Park	2,720	1,622
98532	Chehalis.............	5,727	5,199
98816	Chelan	2,684	2,402
99004	Cheney	6,358	3,173
99403	Clarkston............	6,312	6,209
98004	Clyde Hill	2,987	1,871
99111	Colfax..............	2,664	2,860
99324	College Place.........	4,510	4,031
99114	Colville.............	3,742	3,806
99328	Dayton..............	2,596	2,913
98188	Des Moines	4,099	1,987
99213	Dishman.............	9,079	......
98020	Edmonds	23,998	8,016
98926	Ellensburg	13,568	8,625
98312	Enetai	2,878	2,539
98022	Enumclaw	4,703	3,269
98823	Ephrata.............	5,255	6,548
*98201	Everett..............	53,622	40,304
99011	Fairchild.............	6,754	......
98466	Fircrest	5,651	3,565
98433	Fort Lewis	38,054	......
98902	Fruitvale............	3,275	3,345
98930	Grandview	3,605	3,366
98550	Hoquiam	10,466	10,762
98027	Issaquah	4,313	1,870
98626	Kelso	10,296	8,379
99336	Kennewick	15,212	14,244
98031	Kent	16,275	9,017
98033	Kirkland.............	15,249	6,025
98501	Lacey...............	9,696	......
98155	Lake Forest Park	2,530	......
98499	Lakes District	48,195	......
98632	Longview............	28,373	23,349
98264	Lynden	2,808	2,542
98036	Lynnwood	16,919	7,207
98270	Marysville...........	4,343	3,117
98438	McChord	6,515	......
99022	Medical Lake	3,529	4,765
98039	Medina	3,455	2,285
98040	Mercer Island.........	19,047	......
98354	Milton	2,607	2,218
98272	Monroe	2,687	1,901
98563	Montesano...........	2,847	2,486
98837	Moses Lake	10,310	11,299
98837	Moses Lake North	2,672	......
98043	Mountlake Terrace......	16,600	9,122

ZIP Code	Place	1970	1960	ZIP Code	Place	1970	1960
98273	Mount Vernon	8,804	7,921	24801	Welch	4,149	5,313
98310	Navy Yard	2,827	3,341	26070	Wellsburg	4,600	5,514
98166	Normandy Park	4,202	3,224	26452	Weston	7,323	8,754
98277	Oak Harbor	9,167	3,942	26505	Westover	5,086	4,749
*98507	Olympia	23,111	18,273	26003	Wheeling	48,188	53,400
98841	Omak	4,164	4,068	24986	White Sulphur Springs	2,869	2,676
99214	Opportunity	16,604	12,465	25661	Williamson	5,831	6,746
99344	Othello	4,122	2,669	26187	Williamstown	2,743	2,632
98444	Parkland	21,012					
99301	Pasco	13,920	14,522		**Wisconsin**		
99301	Pasco West	3,809	2,894				
98362	Port Angeles	16,367	12,653	54201	Algoma	4,023	3,855
98366	Port Orchard	3,904	2,778	54301	Allouez	13,753	
98368	Port Townsend	5,241	5,074	54720	Altoona	2,842	2,114
99350	Prosser	2,954	2,763	54409	Antigo	9,005	9,691
99163	Pullman	20,509	12,957	54911	Appleton	57,143	48,411
98371	Puyallup	14,742	12,063	54806	Ashland	9,615	10,132
98848	Quincy	3,237	3,269	54304	Ashwaubenon	9,323	
98577	Raymond	3,126	3,301	53913	Baraboo	7,931	7,660
98052	Redmond	11,031	1,426	53217	Bayside	4,461	3,181
98055	Renton	26,229	18,453	53916	Beaver Dam	14,265	13,118
99352	Richland	26,290	23,548	53511	Beloit	35,729	32,846
*98101	Seattle	530,831	557,087	54923	Berlin	5,338	4,838
98284	Sedro-Woolley	4,598	3,705	54615	Black River Falls	3,273	3,195
98942	Selah	3,070	2,824	54724	Bloomer	3,143	2,834
98584	Shelton	6,515	5,651	53805	Boscobel	2,510	2,608
98270	Shoultes	4,754	3,159	54110	Brillion	2,588	1,783
98290	Snohomish	5,174	3,894	53520	Brodhead	2,515	2,444
98903	South Broadway	3,298	3,661	53005	Brookfield	32,140	19,812
98387	Spanaway	5,768		53209	Brown Deer	12,582	11,280
*99210	Spokane	170,516	181,608	53105	Burlington	7,479	5,856
				53012	Cedarburg	7,697	5,191
	(illegible)		1,560		*(illegible)*		
98390	Sumner	4,325	3,156	54729	Chippewa Falls	12,351	11,708
98944	Sunnyside	6,751	6,208	54929	Clintonville	4,600	4,778
*98402	Tacoma	154,581	147,979	53925	Columbus	3,789	3,467
98501	Thompson Place-Tanglewilde	3,423		54113	Combined Locks	2,734	1,421
98948	Toppenish	5,744	5,667	53110	Cudahy	22,078	17,975
99268	Town and Country	6,484		53018	Delafield	3,182	2,334
98188	Tukwila	3,496	1,804	53115	Delavan	5,526	4,846
98502	Tumwater	5,373	3,885	54115	De Pere	13,309	10,045
98406	University Place	13,230		53533	Dodgeville	3,255	2,911
*98660	Vancouver	41,859	32,464	54701	Eau Claire	44,619	37,987
99362	Walla Walla	23,619	24,536	53534	Edgerton	4,118	4,000
99362	Walla Walla East	2,840	1,557	53121	Elkhorn	3,992	3,586
98951	Wapato	2,841	3,137	53122	Elm Grove	7,201	4,994
98671	Washougal	3,388	2,672	53536	Evansville	2,992	2,858
98801	Wenatchee	16,912	16,726	54935	Fond du Lac	35,515	32,719
99403	West Clarkston-Highland	3,797	2,851	53538	Fort Atkinson	9,164	7,908
*98901	Yakima	45,588	43,284	53217	Fox Point	7,939	7,315
				53132	Franklin	12,247	10,006
	West Virginia			53022	Germantown	6,974	622
				53209	Glendale	13,426	9,537
25801	Beckley	19,884	18,642	53024	Grafton	5,998	3,748
26031	Benwood	2,737	2,850	*54305	Green Bay	87,809	62,888
24701	Bluefield	15,921	19,256	53129	Greendale	15,089	6,843
26330	Bridgeport	4,777	4,198	53220	Greenfield	24,424	17,636
26201	Buckhannon	7,261	6,386	53130	Hales Corners	7,771	5,549
*25301	Charleston	71,505	85,796	53027	Hartford	6,499	5,627
25414	Charles Town	3,023	3,329	53029	Hartland	2,763	2,088
26034	Chester	3,614	3,787	53032	Horicon	3,356	2,996
26301	Clarksburg	24,864	28,112	54303	Howard	4,911	3,485
25064	Dunbar	9,151	11,006	54016	Hudson	5,049	4,325
26241	Elkins	8,287	8,307	53545	Janesville	46,426	35,164
26554	Fairmont	26,093	27,477	53549	Jefferson	5,429	4,548
26037	Follansbee	3,883	4,052	54130	Kaukauna	11,292	10,096
26354	Grafton	6,433	5,791	53140	Kenosha	78,805	67,899
25951	Hinton	4,503	5,197	54216	Kewaunee	2,901	2,772
*25701	Huntington	74,315	83,627	53042	Kiel	2,848	2,524
25526	Hurricane	3,491	1,970	54136	Kimberly	6,131	5,322
25530	Kenova	4,860	4,577	54601	La Crosse	51,153	47,575
26726	Keyser	6,586	6,192	54848	Ladysmith	3,674	3,584
26537	Kingwood	2,550	2,530	53147	Lake Geneva	4,890	4,929
25601	Logan	3,311	4,185	53551	Lake Mills	3,556	2,951
26040	McMechen	2,808	2,999	53813	Lancaster	3,756	3,703
26582	Mannington	2,747	2,996	54140	Little Chute	5,365	5,099
25401	Martinsburg	14,626	15,179	*53701	Madison	172,007	126,706
25136	Montgomery	2,525	3,000	54220	Manitowoc	33,430	32,275
26505	Morgantown	29,431	22,487	54143	Marinette	12,696	13,329
26041	Moundsville	13,560	15,163	54449	Marshfield	15,619	14,153
25637	Mount Gay	3,843	3,386	53948	Mauston	3,466	3,531
25882	Mullens	2,967	3,544	53050	Mayville	4,139	3,607
26155	New Martinsville	6,528	5,607	54451	Medford	3,454	3,260
25143	Nitro	8,019	6,894	54952	Menasha	14,905	14,647
25901	Oak Hill	4,738	4,711	53051	Menomonee Falls	31,697	18,276
26159	Paden City	3,674	3,137	54751	Menomonie	11,275	8,624
26101	Parkersburg	44,208	44,797	53092	Mequon	12,150	8,543
26416	Philippi	3,002	2,228	54452	Merrill	9,502	9,451
25550	Point Pleasant	6,122	5,785	53562	Middleton	8,286	4,410
24740	Princeton	7,253	8,393	53563	Milton	3,699	1,675
26164	Ravenswood	4,240	3,410	*53203	Milwaukee	717,372	741,324
26261	Richwood	3,717	4,110	53716	Monona	10,420	8,178
25271	Ripley	3,244	2,756	53566	Monroe	8,654	8,050
25177	St. Albans	14,356	15,103	53150	Muskego	11,573	
26426	Salem	2,597	2,366	54956	Neenah	22,892	18,057
26431	Shinnston	2,576	2,724	54556	Neillsville	2,750	2,728
25303	South Charleston	16,333	19,180	53151	New Berlin	26,910	15,788
26101	Vienna	11,549	9,381	53061	New Holstein	3,012	2,401
26062	Weirton	27,131	28,201	54961	New London	5,801	5,288
				54017	New Richmond	3,707	3,316

ZIP Code	Place	1970	1960	ZIP Code	Place	1970	1960
54935	North Fond Du Lac	3,286	2,549	54660	Tomah	5,647	5,321
53154	Oak Creek	13,928	9,372	54487	Tomahawk	3,419	3,348
53066	Oconomowoc	8,741	6,682	54241	Two Rivers	13,553	12,393
54153	Oconto	4,667	4,805	53182	Union Grove	2,703	1,970
54154	Oconto Falls	2,517	2,331	54665	Viroqua	3,739	3,926
53069	Okauchee Lake	3,134	1,879	53094	Watertown	15,683	13,943
54650	Onalaska	4,909	3,161	53186	Waukesha	40,274	30,004
53575	Oregon	2,553	1,701	54981	Waupaca	4,342	3,984
54901	Oshkosh	53,221	45,110	53963	Waupun	7,946	7,935
54552	Park Falls	2,953	2,919	54401	Wausau	32,806	31,943
53511	Perry Go Place	5,912	4,475	54401	Wausau West	6,399	4,105
54157	Peshtigo	2,836	2,504	53213	Wauwatosa	58,676	56,923
53072	Pewaukee	3,271	2,484	53214	West Allis	71,649	68,157
53072	Pewaukee West	3,401		53095	West Bend	16,555	9,969
53818	Platteville	9,599	6,957	53214	West Milwaukee	4,405	5,043
53073	Plymouth	5,810	5,128	54476	Weston	3,375	
53901	Portage	7,821	7,822	53217	Whitefish Bay	17,402	18,390
53074	Port Washington	8,752	5,984	53190	Whitewater	12,038	6,300
53821	Prairie Du Chien	5,540	5,649	54494	Wisconsin Rapids	18,587	15,042
*53401	Racine	95,162	89,144				
53959	Reedsburg	4,585	4,371				
54501	Rhinelander	8,218	8,790		**Wyoming**		
54868	Rice Lake	7,278	7,303				
53581	Richland Center	5,086	4,746	82834	Buffalo	3,394	2,907
54971	Ripon	7,053	6,163	82601	Casper	39,361	38,930
54022	River Falls	7,238	4,857	82001	Cheyenne	40,914	43,505
54474	Rothschild	3,141	2,550	82414	Cody	5,161	4,838
53207	St.Francis	10,489	10,065	82633	Douglas	2,677	2,822
54476	Schofield	2,577	3,038	82930	Evanston	4,462	4,901
54166	Shawano	6,488	6,103	82716	Gillette	7,194	3,580
53081	Sheboygan	48,484	45,747	82935	Green River	4,196	3,497
53085	Sheboygan Falls	4,771	4,061	82520	Lander	7,125	4,182
53211	Shorewood	15,576	15,990	82070	Laramie	23,143	17,520
53172	South Milwaukee	23,297	20,307	82701	Newcastle	3,432	4,345
54656	Sparta	6,258	6,080	82435	Powell	4,807	4,740
54481	Stevens Point	23,479	17,837	82301	Rawlins	7,855	8,968
53589	Stoughton	6,096	5,555	82501	Riverton	7,995	6,845
54235	Sturgeon Bay	6,776	7,353	82901	Rock Springs	11,657	10,371
53177	Sturtevant	3,376	1,488	82801	Sheridan	10,856	11,651
53590	Sun Prairie	9,935	4,008	82443	Thermopolis	3,063	3,955
54880	Superior	32,237	33,563	82240	Torrington	4,237	4,188
53089	Sussex	2,758	1,087	82001	Warren	4,527	
53092	Thiensville	3,182	2,507	82401	Worland	5,055	5,806

Nearly 10 Percent of Americans Are 65 or Over

A total of 20,000,000 persons 65 years and over (9.9% of the total population) was counted in the 1970 census by the Bureau of the Census. In the 1960 count there were 16,500,000 (9.2%). In the four census regions the Northeast had the highest proportion, 10.6% of the regional total. Other regions were: North Central States 10.1%; the South 9.6% and the West 8.9%.

The South in actual numbers led with 6,000,000 persons. In total numbers New York had the most with 2,000,000, three other states had over a million. California 1,800,000, Pennsylvania 1,300,000 and Illinois 1,100,000.

The following table gives the breakdown by regions, divisions and states.

Region, Division, and State	Persons 65 or Over 1970	Persons 65 or Over 1960	Region, Division, and State	Persons 65 or Over 1970	Persons 65 or Over 1960
United States, Total	20,049,592	16,559,580	Missouri	560,656	503,411
Regions			North Dakota	66,368	58,591
Northeastern States	5,193,059	4,498,283	South Dakota	80,484	71,513
North Central States	5,727,424	5,078,462	Nebraska	183,526	164,156
The South	6,033,048	4,582,014	Kansas	266,201	240,269
The West	3,096,061	2,400,821	**South Atlantic**		
Northeast			Delaware	43,833	35,745
New England	1,269,517	1,121,754	Maryland	299,697	226,539
Middle Atlantic	3,923,542	3,376,529	District of Columbia	70,803	69,143
North Central			Virginia	365,712	288,970
East North Central	3,810,977	3,358,486	West Virginia	194,120	172,516
West North Central	1,916,447	1,719,976	North Carolina	414,094	312,167
South			South Carolina	190,960	150,599
South Atlantic	2,932,280	2,099,469	Georgia	367,371	290,661
East South Central	1,267,652	1,052,360	Florida	985,690	553,129
West South Central	1,833,116	1,430,185	**East South Central**		
West			Kentucky	336,588	292,323
Mountain	695,221	527,371	Tennessee	383,017	308,861
Pacific	2,400,840	1,873,450	Alabama	325,727	261,147
New England			Mississippi	222,320	190,029
Maine	114,592	106,544	**West South Central**		
New Hampshire	78,412	67,705	Arkansas	237,201	194,372
Vermont	47,488	43,741	Louisiana	306,725	241,591
Massachusetts	636,185	571,609	Oklahoma	298,822	248,831
Rhode Island	103,932	89,540	Texas	990,368	745,391
Connecticut	288,908	242,615	**Mountain**		
Middle Atlantic			Montana	68,736	65,420
New York	1,954,427	1,687,590	Idaho	67,776	58,258
New Jersey	696,989	560,414	Wyoming	30,204	25,908
Pennsylvania	1,272,126	1,128,525	Colorado	187,891	158,160
East North Central			New Mexico	70,611	51,270
Ohio	997,694	897,124	Arizona	161,474	90,225
Indiana	493,809	445,519	Utah	77,561	59,957
Illinois	1,093,654	974,923	Nevada	30,968	18,173
Michigan	752,955	638,184	**Pacific**		
Wisconsin	472,865	402,736	Washington	322,061	279,045
West North Central			Oregon	226,799	183,653
Minnesota	408,919	354,351	California	1,800,977	1,376,204
Iowa	350,293	327,685	Alaska	6,887	5,386
			Hawaii	44,116	29,162

1970 Census & Areas of Counties and States

WITH NAMES OF COUNTY SEATS OR COURT HOUSES; LAND AREA IN SQUARE MILES
Source: Bureau of the Census

Alabama

(67 counties, 50,708-sq. mi. land; pop., 3,444,165)

County	Pop. April 1, 1970	County Seats or Court House	Land Area Sq. Mi.
Autauga	24,460	Prattville	599
Baldwin	59,382	Bay Minette	1,578
Barbour	22,543	Clayton	891
Bibb	13,812	Centreville	625
Blount	26,853	Oneonta	639
Bullock	11,824	UnionSprings	615
Butler	22,007	Greenville	773
Calhoun	103,092	Anniston	611
Chambers	36,356	Lafayette	597
Cherokee	15,606	Centre	556
Chilton	25,180	Clanton	699
Choctaw	16,589	Butler	911
Clarke	26,724	Grove Hill	1,232
Clay	12,636	Ashland	603
Cleburne	10,996	Heflin	574
Coffee	34,872	Elba	677
Colbert	49,632	Tuscumbia	596
Conecuh	15,645	Evergreen	850
Coosa	10,662	Rockford	650
Covington	34,079	Andalusia	984
Crenshaw	13,188	Luverne	611
Cullman	52,445	Cullman	730
Dale	52,938	Ozark	559
Dallas	55,296	Selma	976
De Kalb	41,981	Fort Payne	778
Elmore	33,661	Wetumpka	624
Escambia	34,912	Brewton	962
Etowah	94,144	Gadsden	555
Fayette	16,252	Fayette	627
Franklin	23,933	Russellville	644
Geneva	21,924	Geneva	577
Greene	10,650	Eutaw	627
Hale	15,888	Greensboro	662
Henry	13,254	Abbeville	554
Houston	56,574	Dothan	575
Jackson	39,202	Scottsboro	1,079
Jefferson	644,991	Birmingham	1,115
Lamar	14,335	Vernon	605
Lauderdale	68,111	Florence	662
Lawrence	27,281	Moulton	685
Lee	61,268	Opelika	612
Limestone	41,699	Athens	546
Lowndes	12,897	Hayneville	715
Macon	24,841	Tuskegee	616
Madison	186,540	Huntsville	803
Marengo	23,819	Linden	978
Marion	23,788	Hamilton	743
Marshall	54,211	Guntersville	571
Mobile	317,308	Mobile	1,240
Monroe	20,883	Monroeville	1,032
Montgomery	167,790	Montgomery	790
Morgan	77,306	Decatur	570
Perry	15,388	Marion	734
Pickens	20,326	Carrollton	887
Pike	25,038	Troy	673
Randolph	18,331	Wedowee	581
Russell	45,394	Phenix City	627
St. Clair	27,956	Ashville & Pell City	640
Shelby	38,037	Columbiana	798
Sumter	16,974	Livingston	915
Talladega	65,280	Talladega	750
Tallapoosa	33,840	Dadeville	704
Tuscaloosa	116,029	Tuscaloosa	1,333
Walker	56,246	Jasper	805
Washington	16,241	Chatom	1,066
Wilcox	16,303	Camden	899
Winston	16,654	Double Springs	615

Alaska

(29 divisions, 566,432 sq. mi. land; pop., 302,173)

Census Division	Pop. April 1, 1970	Land Area Sq. Mi.
Aleutian Islands	8,057	14,583
Anchorage	126,333	927
Angoon	503	2,825
Barrow	2,663	57,544
Bethel	7,767	19,642
Bristol Bay Borough	1,147	531
Bristol Bay	3,485	36,565
Cordova-McCarthy	1,857	15,481
Fairbanks	45,864	7,074
Haines	1,504	2,128
Juneau	13,556	1,286
Kenai-Cook Inlet	14,250	12,474
Ketchikan	10,041	1,345
Kobuk	4,434	42,978
Kodiak	9,409	5,375
Kuskokwim	2,306	56,562
Matanuska-Susitna	6,509	25,730
Nome	5,749	24,968
Outer Ketchikan	1,676	3,762
Prince of Wales	2,106	3,485
Seward	2,336	3,727
Sitka	6,109	2,296
Skagway-Yakutat	2,157	8,646
Southeast Fairbanks	4,179	17,713
Upper Yukon	1,684	84,142
Valdez-Chitina-Whittier	3,098	18,619
Wade Hampton	3,917	16,770
Wrangell-Petersburg	4,913	6,178
Yukon-Koyukuk	4,752	73,053

Arizona

(14 counties, 113,417 sq. mi. land; pop., 1,772,482)

County	Pop. April 1, 1970	County Seats or Court House	Land Area Sq. Mi.
Apache	32,304	Saint Johns	11,171
Cochise	61,910	Bisbee	6,255
Coconino	48,326	Flagstaff	18,540
Gila	29,255	Globe	4,748
Graham	16,578	Safford	4,618
Greenlee	10,330	Clifton	1,879
Maricopa	968,487	Phoenix	9,155
Mohave	25,857	Kingman	13,217
Navajo	47,559	Holbrook	9,910
Pima	351,667	Tucson	9,240
Pinal	68,579	Florence	5,364
Santa Cruz	13,966	Nogales	1,246
Yavapai	37,005	Prescott	8,091
Yuma	60,827	Yuma	9,983

Arkansas

(75 counties, 51,945 sq. mi. land; pop., 1,923,295)

County	Pop. April 1, 1970	County Seats or Court House	Land Area Sq. Mi.
Arkansas	23,347	DeWitt & Stuttgart	1,015
Ashley	24,976	Hamburg	928
Baxter	15,319	Mountain Home	537
Benton	50,476	Bentonville	851
Boone	19,073	Harrison	586
Bradley	12,778	Warren	651
Calhoun	5,573	Hampton	629
Carroll	12,301	Berryville and Eureka Sprg	626
Chicot	18,164	Lake Village	643
Clark	21,537	Arkadelphia	878
Clay	18,771	Corning Piggott	639
Cleburne	10,349	Heber Springs	554
Cleveland	6,605	Rison	601
Columbia	25,952	Magnolia	768
Conway	16,805	Morrilton	561
Craighead	52,068	Jonesboro and Lake City	716
Crawford	25,677	Van Buren	596
Crittenden	48,106	Marion	608
Cross	19,783	Wynne	625
Dallas	10,022	Fordyce	672
Desha	18,761	Arkansas City	736
Drew	15,157	Monticello	832
Faulkner	31,595	Conway	641
Franklin	11,301	Charleston and Ozark	613
Fulton	7,699	Salem	608
Garland	54,131	Hot Spgs. Nat'l Pk	658
Grant	9,711	Sheridan	631
Greene	24,765	Paragould	579
Hempstead	19,308	Hope	726
Hot Spring	21,963	Malvern	621
Howard	11,412	Nashville	569
Independence	22,723	Batesville	752
Izard	7,281	Melbourne	574
Jackson	20,452	Newport	629
Jefferson	85,329	Pine Bluff	873
Johnson	13,630	Clarksville	673
Lafayette	10,018	Lewisville	523
Lawrence	16,320	Walnut Ridge	590
Lee	18,884	Marianna	608
Lincoln	12,913	Star City	563
Little River	11,194	Ashdown	486
Logan	16,789	Boneville & Paris	718
Lonoke	26,249	Lonoke	796
Madison	9,453	Huntsville	832
Marion	7,000	Yellville	584
Miller	33,385	Texarkana	623
Mississippi	62,060	Blytheville and Osceola	904

County	Pop. April 1, 1970	County Seats or Court House	Land Area Sq. Mi.
Monroe	15,657	Clarendon	607
Montgomery	5,821	Mount Ida	775
Nevada	10,111	Prescott	616
Newton	5,844	Jasper	822
Ouachita	30,896	Camden	736
Perry	5,634	Perryville	551
Phillips	40,046	Helena	686
Pike	8,711	Murfreesboro	600
Poinsett	26,843	Harrisburg	760
Polk	13,297	Mena	859
Pope	28,607	Russellville	812
Prairie	10,249	Des Arc and De Valls Bluff	661
Pulaski	287,189	Little Rock	765
Randolph	12,645	Pocahontas	647
St. Francis	30,799	Forest City	635
Saline	36,107	Benton	724
Scott	8,207	Waldron	898
Searcy	7,731	Marshall	664
Sebastian	79,237	Fort Smith Greenwood	527
Sevier	11,272	De Queen	522
Sharp	8,233	Evening Shade & Hardy	581
Stone	6,838	Mountain View	608
Union	45,428	El Dorado	1,050
Van Buren	8,275	Clinton	699
Washington	77,370	Fayetteville	958
White	39,253	Searcy	1,041
Woodruff	11,566	Augusta	591
Yell	14,208	Danville and Dardanelle	929

California
(58 counties, 156,361 sq. mi. land; pop., 19,953,134)

County	Pop. April 1, 1970	County Seats or Court House	Land Area Sq. Mi.
Alameda	1,073,184	Oakland	733
Alpine	484	Markleeville	727
Amador	11,821	Jackson	583
Butte	101,969	Oroville	1,645
Calaveras	13,585	San Andreas	1,024
Colusa	12,430	Colusa	1,152
Contra Costa	555,805	Martinez	735
Del Norte	14,580	Crescent City	1,007
El Dorado	43,833	Placerville	1,715
Fresno	413,329	Fresno	5,966
Glenn	17,521	Willows	1,314
Humboldt	99,692	Eureka	3,586
Imperial	74,492	El Centro	4,241
Inyo	15,571	Independence	10,130
Kern	329,271	Bakersfield	8,152
Kings	66,717	Hanford	1,396
Lake	19,548	Lakeport	1,261
Lassen	16,796	Susanville	4,561
Los Angeles	7,036,887	Los Angeles	4,069
Madera	41,519	Madera	2,145
Marin	206,758	San Rafael	520
Mariposa	6,015	Mariposa	1,453
Mendocino	51,101	Ukiah	3,511
Merced	104,629	Merced	1,958
Modoc	7,469	Alturas	4,097
Mono	4,016	Bridgeport	3,027
Monterey	247,450	Salinas	3,324
Napa	79,140	Napa	787
Nevada	26,346	Nevada City	973
Orange	1,420,690	Santa Ana	782
Placer	77,632	Auburn	1,431
Plumas	11,707	Quincy	2,566
Riverside	459,074	Riverside	7,176
Sacramento	634,190	Sacramento	975
San Benito	18,226	Hollister	1,396
San Bernardino	681,535	San Bernardino	20,117
San Diego	1,357,854	San Diego	4,261
San Francisco	715,674	San Francisco	45
San Joaquin	289,564	Stockton	1,412
San Luis Obispo	105,690	San Luis Obispo	3,183
San Mateo	556,601	Redwood City	447
Santa Barbara	264,324	Santa Barbara	2,737
Santa Clara	1,066,421	San Jose	1,300
Santa Cruz	123,790	Santa Cruz	440
Shasta	77,640	Redding	3,788
Sierra	2,365	Downieville	958
Siskiyou	33,225	Yreka	6,262
Solano	171,815	Fairfield	823
Sonoma	204,885	Santa Rosa	1,604
Stanislaus	194,506	Modesto	1,511
Sutter	41,935	Yuba City	603
Tehama	29,517	Red Bluff	2,982
Trinity	7,615	Weaverville	3,173
Tulare	188,322	Visalia	4,812
Tuolumne	22,169	Sonora	2,252
Ventura	378,497	Ventura	1,863
Yolo	91,788	Woodland	1,028
Yuba	44,736	Marysville	639

Colorado
(63 counties, 103,766 sq. mi. land; pop., 2,207,259)

County	Pop. April 1, 1970	County Seats or Court House	Land Area Sq. Mi.
Adams	185,789	Brighton	1,237
Alamosa	11,422	Alamosa	719
Arapahoe	162,142	Littleton	797
Archuleta	2,733	Pagosa Springs	1,364
Baca	5,674	Springfield	2,563
Bent	6,493	Las Animas	1,519
Boulder	131,889	Boulder	748
Chaffee	10,162	Salida	1,038
Cheyenne	2,396	Cheyenne Wells	1,772
Clear Creek	4,819	Georgetown	394
Conejos	7,846	Conejos	1,268
Costilla	3,091	San Luis	1,213
Crowley	3,086	Ordway	802
Custer	1,120	Westcliffe	737
Delta	15,286	Delta	1,154
Denver	514,678	Denver	95
Dolores	1,641	Dove Creek	1,026
Douglas	8,407	Castle Rock	843
Eagle	7,498	Eagle	1,682
Elbert	3,903	Kiowa	1,864
El Paso	235,972	Colorado Springs	2,157
Fremont	21,942	Canon City	1,561
Garfield	14,821	Glenwood Springs	2,996
Gilpin	1,272	Central City	148
Grand	4,107	Hot Sulphur Spgs	1,854
Gunnison	7,578	Gunnison	3,220
Hinsdale	202	Lake City	1,054
Huerfano	6,590	Walsenburg	1,574
Jackson	1,811	Walden	1,622
Jefferson	233,031	Golden	783
Kiowa	2,029	Eads	1,767
Kit Carson	7,530	Burlington	2,171
Lake	8,282	Leadville	379
La Plata	19,199	Durango	1,683
Larimer	89,900	Fort Collins	2,611
Las Animas	15,744	Trinidad	4,794
Lincoln	4,836	Hugo	2,593
Logan	18,852	Sterling	1,822
Mesa	54,374	Grand Junction	3,301
Mineral	786	Creede	921
Moffat	6,525	Craig	4,743
Montezuma	12,952	Cortez	2,094
Montrose	18,366	Montrose	2,238
Morgan	20,105	Fort Morgan	1,278
Otero	23,523	LaJunta	1,254
Ouray	1,546	Ouray	540
Park	2,185	Fairplay	2,162
Phillips	4,131	Holyoke	680
Pitkin	6,185	Aspen	973
Prowers	13,258	Lamar	1,621
Pueblo	118,238	Pueblo	2,405
Rio Blanco	4,842	Meeker	3,263
Rio Grande	10,494	Del Norte	915
Routt	6,592	Steamboat Spgs	2,330
Saguache	3,827	Saguache	3,144
San Juan	831	Silverton	391
San Miguel	1,949	Telluride	1,283
Sedgwick	3,405	Julesburg	544
Summit	2,665	Breckenridge	604
Teller	3,316	Cripple Creek	553
Washington	5,550	Akron	2,526
Weld	89,297	Greeley	4,002
Yuma	8,544	Wray	2,379

Connecticut
(8 counties, 4,862 sq. mi. land; pop., 3,032,217)

County	Pop. April 1, 1970	County Seats or Court House	Land Area Sq. Mi.
Fairfield	792,814	Bridgeport	626
Hartford	816,737	Hartford	739
Litchfield	144,091	Litchfield	925
Middlesex	115,018	Middletown	372
New Haven	744,948	New Haven	604
New London	230,654	Norwich	667
Tolland	103,440	Rockville	416
Windham	84,515	Putnam	514

Delaware
(3 counties, 1,982 sq. mi. land; pop., 548,104)

County	Pop. April 1, 1970	County Seats or Court House	Land Area Sq. Mi.
Kent	81,892	Dover	594
New Castle	385,856	Wilmington	438
Sussex	80,356	Georgetown	950

District of Columbia
(61 sq. mi. land; pop., 756,510)

Florida
(67 counties, 54,090 sq. mi. land; pop., 6,789,443)

County	Pop. April 1, 1970	County Seats or Court House	Land Area Sq. Mi.
Alachua	104,764	Gainesville	916
Baker	9,242	Macclenny	585
Bay	75,283	Panama City	747
Bradford	14,625	Starke	294
Brevard	230,006	Titusville	1,011
Broward	620,100	Fort Lauderdale	1,219
Calhoun	7,624	Blountstown	561
Charlotte	27,559	Punta Gorda	703
Citrus	19,196	Inverness	560
Clay	32,059	Green Cove Spgs	593
Collier	38,040	Naples	2,006

County	Pop. April 1, 1970	County Seats or Court House	Land Area Sq. Mi.	County	Pop. April 1, 1970	County Seats or Court House	Land Area Sq. Mi.
Columbia	25,250	Lake City	784	Crisp	18,087	Cordele	292
Dade	1,267,792	Miami	2,042	Dade	9,910	Trenton	168
De Soto	13,060	Arcadia	648	Dawson	3,639	Dawsonville	211
Dixie	5,480	Cross City	692	Decatur	22,310	Bainbridge	575
Duval	528,865	Jacksonville	766	De Kalb	415,387	Decatur	269
Escambia	205,334	Pensacola	665	Dodge	15,658	Eastman	498
Flagler	4,454	Burnell	487	Dooly	10,404	Vienna	395
Franklin	7,065	Apalachicola	536	Dougherty	89,639	Albany	324
Gadsden	39,184	Quincy	512	Douglas	28,659	Douglasville	202
Gilchrist	3,551	Trenton	346	Early	12,682	Blakely	525
Glades	3,669	Moore Haven	753	Echols	1,924	Statenville	425
Gulf	10,096	Wewahitchka	565	Effingham	13,632	Springfield	480
Hamilton	7,787	Jasper	514	Elbert	17,262	Elberton	358
Hardee	14,889	Wauchula	629	Emanuel	18,357	Swainsboro	686
Hendry	11,859	La Belle	1,187	Evans	7,290	Claxton	186
Hernando	17,004	Brooksville	484	Fannin	13,357	Blue Ridge	394
Highlands	29,507	Sebring	997	Fayette	11,364	Fayetteville	199
Hillsborough	490,265	Tampa	1,038	Floyd	73,742	Rome	514
Holmes	10,720	Bonifay	482	Forsyth	16,928	Cumming	219
Indian River	35,992	Vero Beach	506	Franklin	12,784	Carnesville	263
Jackson	34,434	Marianna	935	Fulton	607,592	Atlanta	530
Jefferson	8,778	Monticello	605	Gilmer	8,956	Ellijay	439
Lafayette	2,892	Mayo	549	Glascock	2,280	Gibson	143
Lake	69,305	Tavares	961	Glynn	50,528	Brunswick	412
Lee	105,216	Fort Myers	785	Gordon	23,570	Calhoun	358
Leon	103,047	Tallahassee	670	Grady	17,826	Cairo	466
Levy	12,756	Bronson	1,083	Greene	10,212	Greensboro	403
Liberty	3,379	Bristol	839	Gwinnett	72,349	Lawrenceville	437
Madison	13,481	Madison	703	Habersham	20,691	Clarkesville	282
Manatee	97,115	Bradenton	739	Hall	59,405	Gainesville	378
Marion	69,030	Ocala	1,600	Hancock	9,019	Sparta	478
Martin	28,035	Stuart	550	Haralson	15,927	Buchanan	285
Monroe	52,586	Key West	1,034	Harris	11,520	Hamilton	465
Nassau	20,626	Fernandina Beach	650	Hart	15,814	Hartwell	231
Okaloosa	88,187	Crestview	944	Heard	5,354	Franklin	297
Okeechobee	11,233	Okeechobee	777	Henry	23,724	McDonough	331
Orange	344,311	Orlando	910	Houston	62,924	Perry	380
Osceola	25,267	Kissimmee	1,313	Irwin	8,036	Ocilla	372
Palm Beach	348,753	West Palm Beach	2,023	Jackson	21,093	Jefferson	346
Pasco	75,955	Dade City	742	Jasper	5,760	Monticello	373
Pinellas	522,329	Clearwater	265	Jeff Davis	9,425	Hazelhurst	331
Polk	227,697	Bartow	1,858	Jefferson	17,174	Louisville	530
Putnam	36,424	Palatka	779	Jenkins	8,332	Millen	351
St. Johns	31,035	Saint Augustine	605	Johnson	7,727	Wrightsville	313
St. Lucie	50,836	Fort Pierce	584	Jones	12,218	Gray	402
Santa Rosa	37,741	Milton	1,032	Lamar	10,688	Barnesville	181
Sarasota	120,413	Sarasota	587	Lanier	5,031	Lakeland	177
Seminole	83,692	Sanford	305	Laurens	32,738	Dublin	810
Sumter	14,839	Bushnell	555	Lee	7,044	Leesburg	355
Suwannee	15,559	Live Oak	686	Liberty	17,569	Hinesville	514
Taylor	13,641	Perry	1,051	Lincoln	5,895	Lincolnton	193
Union	8,112	Lake Butler	241	Long	3,746	Ludowici	402
Volusia	169,487	De Land	1,062	Lowndes	55,112	Valdosta	508
Wakulla	6,308	Crawfordville	601	Lumpkin	8,728	Dahlonega	292
Walton	16,087	De Funiak Spgs.	1,053	Mc Duffie	15,276	Thomson	253
Washington	11,453	Chipley	585	Mc Intosh	7,371	Darien	426

Georgia

(159 counties, 58,073 sq. mi. land; pop., 4,589,575)

County	Pop. April 1, 1970	County Seats or Court House	Land Area Sq. Mi.	County	Pop. April 1, 1970	County Seats or Court House	Land Area Sq. Mi.
				Macon	12,933	Oglethorpe	403
				Madison	13,517	Danielsville	281
Appling	12,726	Baxley	513	Marion	5,099	Buena Vista	365
Atkinson	5,879	Pearson	318	Meriwether	19,461	Greenville	499
Bacon	8,233	Alma	293	Miller	6,424	Colquitt	287
Baker	3,875	Newton	355	Mitchell	18,956	Camilla	510
Baldwin	34,240	Milledgeville	255	Monroe	10,991	Forsyth	398
Banks	6,833	Homer	231	Montgomery	6,099	Mount Vernon	237
Barrow	16,859	Winder	171	Morgan	9,904	Madison	356
Bartow	32,663	Cartersville	461	Murray	12,986	Chatsworth	342
Ben Hill	13,171	Fitzgerald	255	Muscogee	167,377	Columbus	220
Berrien	11,556	Nashville	468	Newton	26,282	Covington	271
Bibb	143,418	Macon	254	Oconee	7,915	Watkinsville	186
Bleckley	10,291	Cochran	219	Oglethorpe	7,598	Lexington	435
Brantley	5,940	Nahunta	447	Paulding	17,520	Dallas	318
Brooks	13,743	Quitman	491	Peach	15,990	Fort Valley	151
Bryan	6,539	Pembroke	443	Pickens	9,620	Jasper	225
Bulloch	31,585	Statesboro	685	Pierce	9,281	Blackshear	342
Burke	18,255	Waynesboro	831	Pike	7,316	Zebulon	230
Butts	10,560	Jackson	185	Polk	29,656	Cedartown	312
Calhoun	6,606	Morgan	289	Pulaski	8,066	Hawkinsville	253
Camden	11,334	Woodbine	653	Putnam	8,394	Eatonton	339
Candler	6,412	Metter	250	Quitman	2,180	Georgetown	156
Carroll	45,404	Carrollton	495	Rabun	8,327	Clayton	368
Catoosa	28,271	Ringgold	167	Randolph	8,734	Cuthbert	436
Charlton	5,680	Folkston	796	Richmond	162,437	Augusta	323
Chatham	187,816	Savannah	445	Rockdale	18,152	Conyers	128
Chattahoochee	25,813	Cusseta	253	Schley	3,097	Ellaville	162
Chattooga	20,541	Summerville	317	Screven	12,591	Sylvania	651
Cherokee	31,059	Canton	415	Seminole	7,059	Donalsonville	246
Clarke	65,177	Athens	116	Spalding	39,514	Griffin	201
Clay	3,636	Fort Gaines	200	Stephens	20,331	Toccoa	173
Clayton	98,043	Jonesboro	149	Stewart	6,511	Lumpkin	452
Clinch	6,405	Homerville	797	Sumter	26,931	Americus	488
Cobb	196,793	Marietta	343	Talbot	6,625	Talbotton	390
Coffee	22,828	Douglas	612	Taliaferro	2,423	Crawfordville	195
Colquitt	32,298	Moultrie	563	Tattnall	16,557	Reidsville	490
Columbia	22,327	Appling	290	Taylor	7,865	Butler	403
Cook	12,129	Adel	233	Telfair	11,394	MacRae	440
Coweta	32,310	Newnan	442	Terrell	11,416	Dawson	329
Crawford	5,748	Knoxville	315	Thomas	34,562	Thomasville	541
				Tift	27,288	Tifton	266
				Toombs	19,151	Lyons	368

County	Pop. April 1, 1970	County Seats or Court House	Land Area Sq. Mi.	County	Pop. April 1, 1970	County Seats or Court House	Land Area Sq. Mi.
Towns	4,565	Hiawassee	166	Cook	5,493,529	Chicago	954
Treutlen	5,647	Soperton	194	Crawford	19,824	Robinson	443
Troup	44,466	La Grange	415	Cumberland	9,772	Toledo	347
Turner	8,790	Ashburn	293	De Kalb	71,654	Sycamore	636
Twiggs	8,222	Jeffersonville	364	De Witt	16,975	Clinton	399
Union	6,811	Blairsville	309	Douglas	18,997	Tuscola	420
Upson	23,505	Thomaston	334	Du Page	492,181	Wheaton	331
Walker	50,691	La Fayette	445	Edgar	21,591	Paris	628
Walton	23,404	Monroe	330	Edwards	7,090	Albion	225
Ware	33,525	Waycross	912	Effingham	24,608	Effingham	481
Warren	6,669	Warrenton	284	Fayette	20,752	Vandalia	703
Washington	17,480	Sandersville	674	Ford	– 16,382	Paxton	488
Wayne	17,858	Jesup	645	Franklin	38,329	Benton	434
Webster	2,362	Preston	195	Fulton	41,900	Lewiston	877
Wheeler	4,596	Alamo	306	Gallatin	7,418	Shawneetown	328
White	7,742	Cleveland	243	Greene	17,014	Carrollton	543
Whitfield	55,108	Dalton	281	Grundy	26,535	Morris	432
Wilcox	6,998	Abbeville	383	Hamilton	8,665	McLeansboro	435
Wilkes	10,184	Washington	468	Hancock	23,664	Carthage	797
Wilkinson	9,393	Irwinton	458	Hardin	4,914	Elizabethtown	183
Worth	14,770	Sylvester	579	Henderson	8,451	Oquawka	376
				Henry	53,217	Cambridge	826

Hawaii

(4 counties, 6,425 sq. mi. land; pop., 769,913)

County	Pop. April 1, 1970	County Seats or Court House	Land Area Sq. Mi.
Hawaii	63,468	Hilo	4,037
Honolulu	630,528	Honolulu	596
Kauai	29,761	Lihue	619
Maui*	46,156	Wailuku	1,173

*Includes population of Kalawao County (279) shown separately in 1960 but included with Maui County in 1970.

Idaho

(44 counties, 82,677 sq. mi. land; pop., 713,008)

County	Pop. April 1, 1970	County Seats or Court House	Land Area Sq. Mi.
Ada	112,230	Boise	1,043
Adams	2,877	Council	1,371
Bannock	52,200	Pocatello	1,122
Bear Lake	5,801	Paris	984
Benewah	6,230	Saint Maries	788
Bingham	29,167	Blackfoot	2,084
Blaine	5,749	Hailey	2,647
Boise	1,763	Idaho City	1,910
Bonner	15,560	Sandpoint	1,733
Bonneville	52,457	Idaho Falls	1,836
Boundary	5,484	Bonners Ferry	1,275
Butte	2,925	Arco	2,239
Camas	728	Fairfield	1,054
Canyon	61,288	Caldwell	578
Caribou	6,534	Soda Springs	1,746
Cassia	17,017	Burley	2,544
Clark	741	Dubois	1,751
Clearwater	10,871	Orofino	2,521
Custer	2,967	Challis	4,929
Elmore	17,479	Mountain Home	3,048
Franklin	7,373	Preston	664
Fremont	8,710	Saint Anthony	1,806
Gem	9,387	Emmett	555
Gooding	8,645	Gooding	720
Idaho	12,891	Grangeville	8,516
Jefferson	11,740	Rigby	1,096
Jerome	10,253	Jerome	595
Kootenai	35,332	Coeur dAlene	1,249
Latah	24,898	Moscow	1,090
Lemhi	5,388	Salmon	4,580
Lewis	3,867	Nezperce	476
Lincoln	3,057	Shoshone	1,203
Madison	13,452	Rexberg	473
Minidoka	15,731	Rupert	750
Nez Perce	30,376	Lewiston	844
Oneida	2,864	Malad City	1,191
Owyhee	6,422	Murphy	7,641
Payette	12,401	Payette	402
Power	4,864	AmericanFalls	1,413
Shoshone	19,718	Wallace	2,609
Teton	2,351	Driggs	457
Twin Falls	41,807	Twin Falls	1,947
Valley	3,609	Cascade	3,676
Washington	7,633	Weiser	1,462

Illinois

(102 counties, 55,748 sq. mi. land; pop. 11,113,976)

County	Pop. April 1, 1970	County Seats or Court House	Land Area Sq. Mi.
Adams	70,861	Quincy	866
Alexander	12,015	Cairo	229
Bond	14,012	Greenville	378
Boone	25,440	Belvidere	283
Brown	5,586	Mount Sterling	306
Bureau	38,541	Princeton	866
Calhoun	5,675	Hardin	247
Carroll	19,276	Mount Carroll	456
Cass	14,219	Virginia	371
Champaign	163,281	Urbana	1,000
Christian	35,948	Taylorville	709
Clark	16,216	Marshall	505
Clay	14,735	Louisville	464
Clinton	28,315	Carlyle	434
Coles	47,815	Charleston	506

Illinois (continued)

County	Pop. April 1, 1970	County Seats or Court House	Land Area Sq. Mi.
Cook	5,493,529	Chicago	954
Crawford	19,824	Robinson	443
Cumberland	9,772	Toledo	347
De Kalb	71,654	Sycamore	636
De Witt	16,975	Clinton	399
Douglas	18,997	Tuscola	420
Du Page	492,181	Wheaton	331
Edgar	21,591	Paris	628
Edwards	7,090	Albion	225
Effingham	24,608	Effingham	481
Fayette	20,752	Vandalia	703
Ford	– 16,382	Paxton	488
Franklin	38,329	Benton	434
Fulton	41,900	Lewiston	877
Gallatin	7,418	Shawneetown	328
Greene	17,014	Carrollton	543
Grundy	26,535	Morris	432
Hamilton	8,665	McLeansboro	435
Hancock	23,664	Carthage	797
Hardin	4,914	Elizabethtown	183
Henderson	8,451	Oquawka	376
Henry	53,217	Cambridge	826
Iroquois	33,532	Watseka	1,122
Jackson	55,008	Murphysboro	605
Jasper	10,741	Newton	495
Jefferson	31,848	Mount Vernon	573
Jersey	18,492	Jerseyville	376
Jo Daviess	21,766	Galena	606
Johnson	7,550	Vienna	345
Kane	251,005	Geneva	520
Kankakee	97,250	Kankakee	678
Kendall	26,374	Yorkville	320
Knox	60,939	Galesburg	728
Lake	382,638	Waukegan	457
La Salle	111,409	Ottawa	1,150
Lawrence	17,522	Lawrenceville	374
Lee	37,947	Dixon	728
Livingston	40,690	Pontiac	1,043
Logan	33,538	Lincoln	622
Mc Donough	36,653	Macomb	582
Mc Henry	111,555	Woodstock	610
Mc Lean	104,389	Bloomington	1,173
Macon	135,010	Decatur	578
Macoupin	44,557	Carlinville	872
Madison	250,934	Edwardsville	733
Marion	38,986	Salem	579
Marshall	13,302	Lacon	391
Mason	16,180	Havana	541
Massac	13,889	Metropolis	245
Menard	9,685	Petersburg	312
Mercer	17,294	Aledo	556
Monroe	18,831	Waterloo	382
Montgomery	30,260	Hillsboro	705
Morgan	36,174	Jacksonville	561
Moultrie	13,263	Sullivan	326
Ogle	42,867	Oregon	758
Peoria	195,318	Peoria	623
Perry	19,757	Pinckneyville	439
Piatt	15,509	Monticello	437
Pike	19,185	Pittsfield	828
Pope	3,857	Golconda	381
Pulaski	8,741	Mound City	204
Putnam	5,007	Hennepin	160
Randolph	31,379	Chester	594
Richland	16,829	Olney	364
Rock Island	166,734	Rock Island	424
St. Clair	285,199	Belleville	673
Saline	25,721	Harrisburg	383
Sangamon	161,335	Springfield	879
Schuyler	8,135	Rushville	434
Scott	6,096	Winchester	251
Shelby	22,589	Shelbyville	752
Stark	7,510	Toulon	291
Stephenson	48,861	Freeport	568
Tazewell	118,649	Pekin	652
Union	16,071	Jonesboro	416
Vermilion	97,047	Danville	899
Wabash	12,841	Mt. Carmel	222
Warren	21,595	Monmouth	541
Washington	13,780	Nashville	564
Wayne	17,004	Fairfield	715
White	17,312	Carmi	502
Whiteside	62,877	Morrison	687
Will	247,825	Joliet	847
Williamson	49,021	Marion	429
Winnebago	246,623	Rockford	519
Woodford	28,012	Eureka	528

Indiana

(92 counties, 36,097 sq. mi. land; pop., 5,193,669)

County	Pop. April 1, 1970	County Seats or Court House	Land Area Sq. Mi.
Adams	26,871	Decatur	345
Allen	280,455	Fort Wayne	671
Bartholomew	57,022	Columbus	402
Benton	11,262	Fowler	409
Blackford	15,888	Hartford City	167
Boone	30,870	Lebanon	427
Brown	9,057	Nashville	319
Carroll	17,734	Delphi	374

County	Pop. April 1, 1970	County Seats or Court House	Land Area Sq. Mi.
Cass	40,456	Logansport	415
Clark	75,876	Jeffersonville	384
Clay	23,933	Brazil	364
Clinton	30,547	Frankfort	407
Crawford	8,033	English	312
Daviess	26,602	Washington	430
Dearborn	29,430	Lawrenceburg	306
Decatur	22,738	Greensburg	370
De Kalb	30,837	Auburn	366
Delaware	129,219	Muncie	396
Dubois	30,934	Jasper	433
Elkhart	126,529	Goshen	468
Fayette	26,216	Connersville	215
Floyd	55,622	New Albany	149
Fountain	18,257	Covington	397
Franklin	16,943	Brookville	394
Fulton	16,984	Rochester	368
Gibson	30,444	Princeton	498
Grant	83,955	Marion	421
Greene	26,894	Bloomfield	549
Hamilton	54,532	Noblesville	401
Hancock	35,096	Greenfield	305
Harrison	20,423	Corydon	479
Hendricks	53,974	Danville	417
Henry	52,603	New Castle	400
Howard	83,198	Kokomo	293
Huntington	34,970	Huntington	369
Jackson	33,187	Brownstown	520
Jasper	20,429	Rensselaer	562
Jay	23,575	Portland	386
Jefferson	17,000		266
Jennings	19,454	Vernon	377
Johnson	61,138	Franklin	315
Knox	41,546	Vincennes	516
Kosciusko	48,127	Warsaw	540
Lagrange	20,890	Lagrange	381
Lake	546,253	Crown Point	513
La Porte	105,342	La Porte	607
Lawrence	38,038	Bedford	459
Madison	138,451	Anderson	453
Marion	793,590	Indianapolis	392
Marshall	34,986	Plymouth	443
Martin	10,969	Shoals	345
Miami	39,246	Peru	377
Monroe	85,221	Bloomington	386
Montgomery	33,930	Crawfordsville	507
Morgan	44,176	Martinsville	406
Newton	11,606	Kentland	413
Noble	31,382	Albion	412
Ohio	4,289	Rising Sun	87
Orange	16,968	Paoli	405
Owen	12,163	Spencer	390
Parke	14,600	Rockville	445
Perry	19,075	Cannelton	384
Pike	12,281	Petersburg	335
Porter	87,114	Valparaiso	425
Posey	21,740	Mount Vernon	412
Pulaski	12,534	Winamac	433
Putnam	26,932	Greencastle	490
Randolph	28,915	Winchester	457
Ripley	21,138	Versailles	442
Rush	20,352	Rushville	409
St. Joseph	245,045	South Bend	466
Scott	17,144	Scottsburg	193
Shelby	37,797	Shelbyville	409
Spencer	17,134	Rockport	396
Starke	19,280	Knox	310
Steuben	20,159	Angola	309
Sullivan	19,889	Sullivan	457
Switzerland	6,306	Vevay	221
Tippecanoe	109,378	Lafayette	500
Tipton	16,650	Tipton	261
Union	6,582	Liberty	168
Vanderburgh	168,772	Evansville	241
Vermillion	16,793	Newport	263
Vigo	114,528	Terre Haute	415
Wabash	35,553	Wabash	398
Warren	8,705	Williamsport	368
Warrick	27,972	Boonville	391
Washington	19,278	Salem	516
Wayne	79,109	Richmond	405
Wells	23,821	Bluffton	368
White	20,995	Monticello	497
Whitley	23,395	Columbia City	337

Iowa

(99 counties; 55,941 sq. mi. land; pop., 2,825,041)

County	Pop. April 1, 1970	County Seats or Court House	Land Area Sq. Mi.
Adair	9,487	Greenfield	569
Adams	6,322	Corning	426
Allamakee	14,968	Waukon	636
Appanoose	15,007	Centerville	523
Audubon	9,595	Audubon	448
Benton	22,885	Vinton	718
Black Hawk	132,916	Waterloo	568
Boone	26,470	Boone	573
Bremer	22,737	Waverly	439
Buchanan	21,762	Independence	568
Buena Vista	20,693	Storm Lake	572
Butler	16,953	Allison	582
Calhoun	14,287	Rockwell City	571
Carroll	22,912	Carroll	574
Cass	17,007	Atlantic	559
Cedar	17,655	Tipton	585
Cerro Gordo	49,223	Mason City	575
Cherokee	17,269	Cherokee	573
Chickasaw	14,969	New Hampton	505
Clarke	7,581	Osceola	429
Clay	18,464	Spencer	570
Clayton	20,606	Elkader	779
Clinton	56,749	Clinton	693
Crawford	19,198	Denison	716
Dallas	26,085	Adel	597
Davis	8,207	Bloomfield	509
Decatur	9,737	Leon	530
Delaware	18,770	Manchester	572
Des Moines	46,982	Burlington	408
Dickinson	12,565	Spirit Lake	380
Dubuque	90,609	Dubuque	612
Emmet	14,009	Estherville	394
Fayette	26,898	West Union	728
Floyd	19,860	Charles City	503
Franklin	13,255	Hampton	586
Fremont	9,282	Sidney	524
Greene	12,716	Jefferson	596
Grundy	14,119	Grundy Center	501
Guthrie	12,243	Guthrie Center	569
Hamilton	18,383	Webster City	577
Hancock	13,492	Garner	570
Hardin	22,248	Eldora	574
Harrison	16,240	Logan	700
Henry	18,114	Mount Pleasant	440
Howard	11,442	Cresco	471
Humboldt	12,519	Dakota City	435
Ida	9,283	Ida Grove	431
Iowa	15,419	Marengo	584
Jackson	20,839	Maquoketa	644
Jasper	35,425	Newton	731
Jefferson	15,774	Fairfield	436
Johnson	72,127	Iowa City	619
Jones	19,868	Anamosa	585
Keokuk	13,943	Sigourney	579
Kossuth	22,937	Algona	979
Lee	42,996	Fort Madison and Keokuk	527
Linn	163,213	Cedar Rapids	717
Louisa	10,682	Wapello	403
Lucas	10,163	Chariton	434
Lyon	13,340	Rock Rapids	588
Madison	11,558	Winterset	564
Mahaska	22,177	Oskaloosa	572
Marion	26,352	Knoxville	498
Marshall	41,076	Marshalltown	574
Mills	11,832	Glenwood	447
Mitchell	13,108	Osage	467
Monona	12,069	Onawa	699
Monroe	9,357	Alba	435
Montgomery	12,781	Red Oak	422
Muscatine	37,181	Muscatine	443
O'Brien	17,522	Primghar	575
Osceola	8,555	Sibley	398
Page	18,537	Clarinda	535
Palo Alto	13,289	Emmetsburg	561
Plymouth	24,322	Le Mars	863
Pocahontas	12,757	Pocahontas	581
Polk	286,130	Des Moines	578
Pottawattamie	86,991	Council Bluffs	963
Poweshiek	18,803	Montezuma	589
Ringgold	6,373	Mount Ayr	538
Sac	15,573	Sac City	578
Scott	142,687	Davenport	454
Shelby	15,528	Harlan	587
Sioux	27,996	Orange City	766
Story	62,783	Nevada	568
Tama	20,147	Toledo	720
Taylor	8,790	Bedford	528
Union	13,557	Creston	425
Van Buren	8,643	Keosauqua	487
Wapello	42,149	Ottumwa	437
Warren	27,432	Indianola	558
Washington	18,967	Washington	568
Wayne	8,405	Corydon	532
Webster	48,391	Fort Dodge	718
Winnebago	12,990	Forest City	401
Winneshiek	21,758	Decorah	688
Woodbury	103,052	Sioux City	871
Worth	8,968	Northwood	400
Wright	17,294	Clarion	577

Kansas

(105 counties; 81,787 sq. mi. land; pop., 2,249,071)

County	Pop. April 1, 1970	County Seats or Court House	Land Area Sq. Mi.
Allen	15,043	Iola	505
Anderson	8,501	Garnett	577
Atchison	19,165	Atchison	427
Barber	7,016	Medicine Lodge	1,146
Barton	30,663	Great Bend	894
Bourbon	15,215	Fort Scott	639

County	Pop. April 1, 1970	County Seats or Court House	Land Area Sq. Mi.	County	Pop. April 1, 1970	County Seats or Court House	Land Area Sq. Mi.
Brown	11,685	Hiawatha	577	**Kentucky**			
Butler	38,658	El Dorado	1,442				
Chase	3,408	Cottonwood Falls	774	*(120 counties, 39,650 sq. mi. land; pop., 3,219,311)*			
Chautauqua	4,642	Sedan	647	Adair	13,037	Columbia	370
Cherokee	21,549	Columbus	586	Allen	12,598	Scottsville	351
Cheyenne	4,256	Saint Francis	1,027	Anderson	9,358	Lawrenceburg	206
Clark	2,896	Ashland	983	Ballard	8,276	Wickliffe	259
Clay	9,890	Clay Center	659	Barren	28,677	Glasgow	468
Cloud	13,466	Concordia	711	Bath	9,235	Owingsville	287
Coffey	7,397	Burlington	617	Bell	31,121	Pineville	370
Comanche	2,702	Coldwater	800	Boone	32,812	Burlington	249
Cowley	35,012	Winfield	1,136	Bourbon	18,476	Paris	300
Crawford	37,850	Girard	598	Boyd	52,376	Catlettsburg	159
Decatur	4,988	Oberlin	899	Boyle	21,090	Danville	183
Dickinson	19,993	Abilene	855	Bracken	7,227	Brooksville	204
Doniphan	9,107	Troy	388	Breathitt	14,221	Jackson	494
Douglas	57,932	Lawrence	471	Breckinridge	14,789	Hardinsburg	554
Edwards	4,581	Kinsley	617	Bullitt	26,090	Shepherdsville	300
Elk	3,858	Howard	647	Butler	9,723	Morgantown	443
Ellis	24,730	Hays	900	Caldwell	13,179	Princeton	357
Ellsworth	6,146	Ellsworth	717	Calloway	27,692	Murray	384
Finney	19,029	Garden City	1,301	Campbell	88,561	Alexandria	149
Ford	22,587	Dodge City	1,091	Carlisle	5,354	Bardwell	195
Franklin	20,007	Ottawa	577	Carroll	8,523	Carrollton	130
Geary	28,111	Junction City	374	Carter	19,850	Grayson	397
Gove	3,940	Gove	1,070	Casey	12,930	Liberty	435
Graham	4,751	Hill City	891	Christian	56,224	Hopkinsville	725
Grant	5,961	Ulysses	571	Clark	24,090	Winchester	259
Gray	4,516	Cimarron	872	Clay	18,481	Manchester	474
Greeley	1,819	Tribune	783	Clinton	8,174	Albany	190
Greenwood	9,141	Eureka	1,133	Crittenden	8,493	Marion	365
Hamilton	2,747	Syracuse	992	Cumberland	6,850	Burkesville	310
Harper	7,871	Anthony	801	Daviess	79,486	Owensboro	462
Harvey	27,236	Newton	540	Edmonson	8,751	Brownsville	298
Haskell	3,672	Sublette	580	Elliott	5,933	Sandy Hook	240
Hodgeman	2,662	Jetmore	860	Estill	12,752	Irvine	260
Jackson	10,342	Holton	656	Fayette	174,323	Lexington	280
Jefferson	11,945	Oskaloosa	510	Fleming	11,366	Flemingsburg	350
Jewell	6,099	Mankato	910	Floyd	35,009	Prestonsburg	399
Johnson	220,073	Olathe	476	Franklin	34,481	Frankfort	211
Kearny	3,047	Lakin	855	Fulton	10,183	Hickman	203
Kingman	8,886	Kingman	864	Gallatin	4,134	Warsaw	100
Kiowa	4,088	Greensburg	720	Garrard	9,457	Lancaster	236
Labette	25,775	Oswego	654	Grant	9,999	Williamstown	249
Lane	2,707	Dighton	720	Graves	30,939	Mayfield	560
Leavenworth	53,340	Leavenworth	466	Grayson	16,445	Leitchfield	496
Lincoln	4,582	Lincoln	725	Green	10,350	Greensburg	282
Linn	7,770	Mound City	606	Greenup	33,192	Greenup	351
Logan	3,814	Oakley	1,073	Hancock	7,080	Hawesville	187
Lyon	32,071	Emporia	841	Hardin	78,421	Elizabethtown	616
McPherson	24,778	McPherson	896	Harlan	37,370	Harlan	469
Marion	13,935	Marion	945	Harrison	14,158	Cynthiana	308
Marshall	13,139	Marysville	883	Hart	13,980	Munfordville	420
Meade	4,912	Meade	979	Henderson	36,031	Henderson	433
Miami	19,254	Paola	592	Henry	10,910	New Castle	289
Mitchell	8,010	Beloit	714	Hickman	6,264	Clinton	246
Montgomery	39,949	Independence	628	Hopkins	38,167	Madisonville	553
Morris	6,432	Council Grove	697	Jackson	10,005	McKee	337
Morton	3,576	Elkhart	728	Jefferson	695,055	Louisville	375
Nemaha	11,825	Seneca	708	Jessamine	17,430	Nicholasville	177
Neosho	18,812	Erie	587	Johnson	17,539	Paintsville	264
Ness	4,791	Ness City	1,081	Kenton	129,440	Independence	165
Norton	7,279	Norton	872	Knott	14,698	Hindman	356
Osage	13,352	Lyndon	707	Knox	23,689	Barbourville	373
Osborne	6,416	Osborne	896	Larue	10,672	Hodgenville	260
Ottawa	6,183	Minneapolis	723	Laurel	27,386	London	446
Pawnee	8,484	Larned	755	Lawrence	10,726	Louisa	425
Phillips	7,888	Phillipsburg	897	Lee	6,587	Beattyville	210
Pottawatomie	11,755	Westmoreland	820	Leslie	11,623	Hyden	409
Pratt	10,056	Pratt	729	Letcher	23,165	Whitesburg	339
Rawlins	4,393	Atwood	1,078	Lewis	12,355	Vanceburg	486
Reno	60,765	Hutchinson	1,260	Lincoln	16,663	Stanford	340
Republic	8,498	Belleville	718	Livingston	7,596	Smithland	311
Rice	12,320	Lyons	725	Logan	21,793	Russellville	563
Riley	56,788	Manhattan	597	Lyon	5,562	Eddyville	216
Rooks	7,628	Stockton	886	McCracken	58,281	Paducah	250
Rush	5,117	La Crosse	724	McCreary	12,548	Whitley City	418
Russell	9,428	Russell	867	McLean	9,062	Calhoun	257
Saline	46,592	Salina	720	Madison	42,730	Richmond	446
Scott	5,606	Scott City	724	Magoffin	10,443	Salyersville	303
Sedgwick	350,694	Wichita	1,007	Marion	16,714	Lebanon	343
Seward	15,744	Liberal	646	Marshall	20,381	Benton	303
Shawnee	155,322	Topeka	548	Martin	9,377	Inez	231
Sheridan	3,859	Hoxie	893	Mason	17,273	Maysville	238
Sherman	7,792	Goodland	1,055	Meade	18,796	Brandenburg	305
Smith	6,757	Smith Center	893	Menifee	4,050	Frenchburg	210
Stafford	5,943	Saint John	795	Mercer	15,960	Harrodsburg	256
Stanton	2,287	Johnson	676	Metcalfe	8,177	Edmonton	296
Stevens	4,198	Hugoton	731	Monroe	11,642	Thompkinsville	334
Sumner	23,553	Wellington	1,186	Montgomery	15,364	Mount Sterling	204
Thomas	7,501	Colby	1,070	Morgan	10,019	West Liberty	369
Trego	4,436	Wakeeney	901	Muhlenberg	27,537	Greenville	481
Wabaunsee	6,397	Alma	792	Nelson	23,477	Bardstown	437
Wallace	2,215	Sharon Springs	911	Nicholas	6,508	Carlisle	204
Washington	9,249	Washington	891	Ohio	18,790	Hartford	596
Wichita	3,274	Leoti	724	Oldham	14,687	La Grange	184
Wilson	11,317	Fredonia	574	Owen	7,470	Owenton	351
Woodson	4,789	Yates Center	497	Owsley	5,023	Booneville	197
Wyandotte	186,845	Kansas City	152	Pendleton	9,949	Falmouth	279

County	Pop. April 1, 1970	County Seats or Court House	Land Area Sq. Mi.
Perry	26,259	Hazard	341
Pike	61,059	Pikeville	782
Powell	7,704	Stanton	173
Pulaski	35,234	Somerset	653
Robertson	2,163	Mount Olivet	101
Rockcastle	12,305	Mount Vernon	311
Rowan	17,010	Morehead	290
Russell	10,542	Jamestown	238
Scott	17,948	Georgetown	284
Shelby	18,999	Shelbyville	383
Simpson	13,054	Franklin	239
Spencer	5,488	Taylorsville	193
Taylor	17,138	Campbellsville	277
Todd	10,823	Elkton	376
Trigg	8,620	Cadiz	408
Trimble	5,349	Bedford	146
Union	15,882	Morganfield	340
Warren	57,432	Bowling Green	546
Washington	10,728	Springfield	307
Wayne	14,268	Monticello	440
Webster	13,282	Dixon	339
Whitley	24,145	Williamsburg	459
Wolfe	5,669	Campton	227
Woodford	14,434	Versailles	193

Louisiana
(64 parishes, 44,930 sq. mi. land; pop. 3,643,180)

County	Pop. April 1, 1970	County Seats or Court House	Land Area Sq. Mi.
Acadia	52,109	Crowley	663
Allen	20,794	Oberlin	774
Ascension	37,086	Donaldsonville	301
Assumption	19,654	Napoleonville	356
Avoyelles	37,751	Marksville	832
Beauregard	22,888	De Ridder	1,181
Bienville	16,024	Arcadia	832
Bossier	63,703	Benton	849
Caddo	230,184	Shreveport	899
Calcasieu	145,415	Lake Charles	1,105
Caldwell	9,354	Columbia	551
Cameron	8,194	Cameron	1,441
Catahoula	11,769	Harrisonburg	742
Claiborne	17,024	Homer	763
Concordia	22,578	Vidalia	718
De Soto	22,764	Mansfield	894
East Baton Rouge	285,167	Baton Rouge	459
East Carroll	12,884	Lake Providence	436
East Feliciana	17,657	Clinton	454
Evangeline	31,932	Ville Platte	669
Franklin	23,946	Winnsboro	648
Grant	13,671	Colfax	670
Iberia	57,397	New Iberia	589
Iberville	30,746	Plaquemine	627
Jackson	15,963	Jonesboro	582
Jefferson	338,229	Gretna	369
Jefferson Davis	29,554	Jennings	658
Lafayette	111,745	Lafayette	283
Lafourche	68,941	Thibodaux	1,141
La Salle	13,295	Jena	643
Lincoln	33,800	Ruston	469
Livingston	36,511	Livingston	654
Madison	15,065	Tallulah	661
Morehouse	32,463	Bastrop	804
Natchitoches	35,219	Natchitoches	1,292
Orleans	593,471	New Orleans	197
Ouachita	115,387	Monroe	638
Plaquemines	25,225	Pointe a la Hache	1,030
Pointe Coupee	22,002	New Roads	563
Rapides	118,078	Alexandria	1,318
Red River	9,226	Coushatta	406
Richland	21,774	Rayville	576
Sabine	18,638	Many	873
St. Bernard	51,185	Chalmette	514
St. Charles	29,550	Hahnville	294
St. Helena	9,937	Greensburg	420
St. James	19,733	Convent	253
St. John The Baptist	23,813	Edgard	227
St. Landry	80,364	Opelousas	932
St. Martin	32,453	Saint Martinville	736
St. Mary	60,752	Franklin	624
St. Tammany	63,585	Covington	887
Tangipahoa	65,875	Amite	808
Tensas	9,732	Saint Joseph	626
Terrebonne	76,049	Houma	1,368
Union	18,447	Farmerville	885
Vermilion	43,071	Abbeville	1,205
Vernon	53,794	Leesville	1,351
Washington	41,987	Franklinton	665
Webster	39,939	Minden	615
West Baton Rouge	16,864	Port Allen	203
West Carroll	13,028	Oak Grove	356
West Feliciana	11,376	Saint Francisville	405
Winn	16,369	Winnfield	950

Maine
(16 counties, 30,920 sq. mi. land; pop., 993,663)

County	Pop. April 1, 1970	County Seats or Court House	Land Area Sq. Mi.
Androscoggin	91,279	Auburn	474
Aroostook	94,078	Houlton	6,821
Cumberland	192,528	Portland	879
Franklin	22,444	Farmington	1,709
Hancock	34,590	Ellsworth	1,536
Kennebec	95,306	Augusta	872
Knox	29,013	Rockland	369
Lincoln	20,537	Wiscasset	454
Oxford	43,457	South Paris	2,080
Penobscot	125,393	Bangor	3,390
Piscataquis	16,285	Dover-Foxcroft	3,892
Sagadahoc	23,452	Bath	257
Somerset	40,597	Skowhegan	3,894
Waldo	23,328	Belfast	737
Washington	29,859	Machias	2,554
York	111,576	Alfred	1,001

Maryland
(23 cos. 1 ind. city, 9,891 sq. mi. land; pop. 3,922,399)

County	Pop. April 1, 1970	County Seats or Court House	Land Area Sq. Mi.
Allegany	84,044	Cumberland	428
Anne Arundel	298,042	Annapolis	423
Baltimore	621,871	Towson	598
Calvert	20,682	Prince Frederick	217
Caroline	19,781	Denton	321
Carroll	69,006	Westminster	456
Cecil	53,291	Elkton	362
Charles	47,678	La Plata	459
Dorchester	29,405	Cambridge	594
Frederick	84,927	Frederick	665
Garrett	21,476	Oakland	659
Harford	115,378	Bel Air	453
Howard	62,394	Ellicott City	251
Kent	16,146	Chestertown	281
Montgomery	522,809	Rockville	495
Prince Georges	661,192	Upper Marlboro	485
Queen Annes	18,422	Centreville	375
St. Marys	47,388	Leonardtown	373
Somerset	18,924	Princess Anne	339
Talbot	23,682	Easton	261
Washington	103,829	Hagerstown	459
Wicomico	54,236	Salisbury	381
Worcester	24,442	Snow Hill	479
Baltimore Independent City	905,759		79

Massachusetts
(14 counties; 7,826 sq. mi. land; pop., 5,689,170)

County	Pop. April 1, 1970	County Seats or Court House	Land Area Sq. Mi.
Barnstable	96,656	Barnstable	393
Berkshire	149,402	Pittsfield	941
Bristol	444,301	Taunton	554
Dukes	6,117	Edgartown	104
Essex	637,887	Salem	494
Franklin	59,210	Greenfield	708
Hampden	459,050	Springfield	619
Hampshire	123,981	Northampton	529
Middlesex	1,398,355	Cambridge	825
Nantucket	3,774	Nantucket	46
Norfolk	604,854	Dedham	394
Plymouth	333,314	Plymouth	654
Suffolk	735,190	Boston	56
Worcester	637,079	Worcester	1,509

Michigan
(83 counties; 56,817 sq. mi. land; pop., 8,875,083)

County	Pop. April 1, 1970	County Seats or Court House	Land Area Sq. Mi.
Alcona	7,113	Harrisville	678
Alger	8,568	Munising	905
Allegan	66,575	Allegan	826
Alpena	30,708	Alpena	565
Antrim	12,612	Bellaire	478
Arenac	11,149	Standish	367
Baraga	7,789	L'Anse	901
Barry	38,166	Hastings	554
Bay	117,339	Bay City	447
Benzie	8,593	Beulah	316
Berrien	163,940	Saint Joseph	580
Branch	37,906	Coldwater	506
Calhoun	141,963	Marshall	709
Cass	43,312	Cassopolis	491
Charlevoix	16,541	Charlevoix	414
Cheboygan	16,573	Cheboygan	721
Chippewa	32,412	Sault Sainte Marie	1,590
Clare	16,695	Harrison	571
Clinton	48,492	Saint Johns	572
Crawford	6,482	Grayling	561
Delta	35,924	Escanaba	1,177
Dickinson	23,753	Iron Mountain	757
Eaton	68,892	Charlotte	571
Emmet	18,331	Petoskey	461
Genesee	445,589	Flint	642
Gladwin	13,471	Gladwin	503
Gogebic	20,676	Bessemer	1,107
Grand Traverse	39,175	Traverse City	462
Gratiot	39,246	Ithaca	566
Hillsdale	37,171	Hillsdale	600
Houghton	34,652	Houghton	1,017
Huron	34,083	Bad Axe	819
Ingham	261,039	Mason	559
Ionia	45,848	Ionia	575

County	Pop. April 1, 1970	County Seats or Court House	Land Area Sq. Mi.
Iosco	24,905	Tawas City	544
Iron	13,813	Crystal Falls	1,171
Isabella	44,594	Mount Pleasant	572
Jackson	143,274	Jackson	698
Kalamazoo	201,550	Kalamazoo	562
Kalkaska	5,272	Kalkaska	566
Kent	411,044	Grand Rapids	857
Keweenaw	2,264	Eagle River	538
Lake	5,661	Baldwin	571
Lapeer	52,361	Lapeer	658
Leelanau	10,872	Leland	345
Lenawee	81,951	Adrian	753
Livingston	58,967	Howell	572
Luce	6,789	Newberry	906
Mackinac	9,660	Saint Ignace	1,014
Macomb	625,309	Mount Clemens	480
Manistee	20,094	Manistee	553
Marquette	64,686	Marquette	1,828
Mason	22,612	Ludington	490
Mecosta	27,992	Big Rapids	560
Menominee	24,587	Menominee	1,038
Midland	63,769	Midland	520
Missaukee	7,126	Lake City	565
Monroe	118,479	Monroe	557
Montcalm	39,660	Stanton	712
Montmorency	5,247	Atlanta	555
Muskegon	157,426	Muskegon	501
Newaygo	27,992	White Cloud	849
Oakland	907,871	Pontiac	867
Oceana	17,984	Hart	536
Ogemaw	11,903	West Branch	571
Ontonagon	10,548	Ontonagon	1,316
Osceola	14,838	Reed City	581
Oscoda	4,726	Mio	563
Otsego	10,422	Gaylord	527
Ottawa	128,181	Grand Haven	563
Presque Isle	12,836	Rogers City	648
Roscommon	9,892	Roscommon	521
Saginaw	219,743	Saginaw	814
St. Clair	120,175	Port Huron	734
St. Joseph	47,392	Centreville	506
Sanilac	35,181	Sandusky	961
Schoolcraft	8,226	Manistique	1,181
Shiawassee	63,075	Corunna	540
Tuscola	48,603	Caro	815
Van Buren	56,173	Paw Paw	603
Washtenaw	234,103	Ann Arbor	711
Wayne	2,670,368	Detroit	605
Wexford	19,717	Cadillac	559

Minnesota

(87 counties; 79,289 sq. mi. land; pop., 3,805,069)

County	Pop. April 1, 1970	County Seats or Court House	Land Area Sq. Mi.
Aitkin	11,403	Aitkin	1,828
Anoka	154,595	Anoka	424
Becker	24,372	Detroit Lakes	1,297
Beltrami	26,373	Bemidji	2,507
Benton	20,841	Foley	402
Big Stone	7,941	Ortonville	490
Blue Earth	52,322	Mankato	737
Brown	28,887	New Ulm	610
Carlton	28,072	Carlton	862
Carver	28,331	Chaska	359
Cass	17,323	Walker	1,998
Chippewa	15,109	Montevideo	582
Chisago	17,492	Center City	419
Clay	46,608	Moorhead	1,045
Clearwater	8,013	Bagley	1,000
Cook	3,423	Grand Marais	1,346
Cottonwood	14,887	Windom	636
Crow Wing	34,826	Brainerd	995
Dakota	139,808	Hastings	576
Dodge	13,037	Mantorville	435
Douglas	22,910	Alexandria	647
Faribault	20,896	Blue Earth	711
Fillmore	21,916	Preston	859
Freeborn	38,064	Albert Lea	701
Goodhue	34,763	Red Wing	753
Grant	7,462	Elbow Lake	546
Hennepin	960,080	Minneapolis	567
Houston	17,556	Caledonia	565
Hubbard	10,583	Park Rapids	932
Isanti	16,560	Cambridge	438
Itasca	35,530	Grand Rapids	2,633
Jackson	14,352	Jackson	696
Kanabec	9,775	Mora	524
Kandiyohi	30,548	Willmar	783
Kittson	6,853	Hallock	1,123
Koochiching	17,131	International Falls	3,127
Lac Qui Parle	11,164	Madison	768
Lake	13,351	Two Harbors	2,062
Lake of the Woods	3,987	Baudette	1,311
Le Sueur	21,332	Le Center	440
Lincoln	8,143	Ivanhoe	531
Lyon	24,273	Marshall	709
McLeod	27,662	Glencoe	488
Mahnomen	5,638	Mahnomen	563
Marshall	13,060	Warren	1,789
Martin	24,316	Fairmont	703
Meeker	18,349	Litchfield	619
Mille Lacs	15,703	Milaca	571
Morrison	26,949	Little Falls	1,127
Mower	43,783	Austin	703
Murray	12,508	Slayton	703
Nicollet	24,518	Saint Peter	432
Nobles	23,208	Worthington	712
Norman	10,008	Ada	885
Olmstead	84,104	Rochester	656
Otter Tail	46,097	Fergus Falls	1,962
Pennington	13,266	Thief River Falls	622
Pine	16,821	Pine City	1,414
Pipestone	12,791	Pipestone	464
Polk	34,435	Crookston	2,013
Pope	11,107	Glenwood	669
Ramsey	476,350	Saint Paul	155
Red Lake	5,388	Red Lake Falls	432
Redwood	20,024	Redwood Falls	874
Renville	21,139	Olivia	979
Rice	41,582	Fairbault	496
Rock	11,346	Luverne	485
Roseau	11,569	Roseau	1,676
St. Louis	220,693	Duluth	6,092
Scott	32,423	Shakopee	353
Sherburne	18,344	Elk River	431
Sibley	15,845	Gaylord	583
Stearns	95,400	Saint Cloud	1,342
Steele	26,931	Owatonna	425
Stevens	11,218	Morris	558
Swift	13,177	Benson	739
Todd	22,114	Long Prairie	942
Traverse	6,254	Wheaton	568
Wabasha	17,224	Wabasha	522
Wadena	12,412	Wadena	536
Waseca	16,663	Waseca	415
Washington	82,948	Stillwater	386
Watonwan	13,298	Saint James	433
Wilkin	9,389	Breckenridge	762
Winona	44,409	Winona	620
Wright	38,933	Buffalo	674
Yellow Medicine	14,523	Granite Falls	753

Mississippi

(82 counties, 47,296 sq. mi. land; pop., 2,216,912)

County	Pop. April 1, 1970	County Seats or Court House	Land Area Sq. Mi.
Adams	37,293	Natchez	449
Alcorn	27,179	Corinth	405
Amite	13,763	Liberty	729
Attala	19,570	Kosciusko	724
Benton	7,505	Ashland	412
Bolivar	49,409	Cleveland and Rosedale	923
Calhoun	14,623	Pittsboro	575
Carroll	9,397	Carrollton & Vaiden	637
Chickasaw	16,805	Houston & Okolona	506
Choctaw	8,440	Ackerman	417
Claiborne	10,086	Port Gibson	489
Clarke	15,049	Quitman	697
Clay	18,840	West Point	414
Coahoma	40,447	Clarksdale	569
Copiah	24,764	Hazlehurst	780
Covington	14,002	Collins	416
De Soto	35,885	Hernando	476
Forrest	57,849	Hattiesburg	468
Franklin	8,011	Meadville	568
George	12,459	Lucedale	481
Greene	8,545	Leakesville	728
Grenada	19,854	Grenada	431
Hancock	17,387	Bay Saint Louis	482
Harrison	134,582	Gulfport	585
Hinds	214,973	Jackson & Raymond	876
Holmes	23,120	Lexington	769
Humphreys	14,601	Belzoni	421
Issaquena	2,737	Mayersville	414
Itawamba	16,847	Fulton	541
Jackson	87,975	Pascagoula	736
Jasper	15,994	Bay Springs and Paulding	683
Jefferson	9,295	Fayette	521
Jefferson Davis	12,936	Prentiss	414
Jones	56,357	Ellisville & Laurel	702
Kemper	10,233	De Kalb	757
Lafayette	24,181	Oxford	668
Lamar	15,209	Purvis	500
Lauderdale	67,087	Meridian	708
Lawrence	11,137	Monticello	433
Leake	17,085	Carthage	586
Lee	46,148	Tupelo	455
Leflore	42,111	Greenwood	592
Lincoln	26,198	Brookhaven	586
Lowndes	49,700	Columbus	508
Madison	29,737	Canton	727
Marion	22,871	Columbia	550
Marshall	24,027	Holly Springs	710
Monroe	34,043	Aberdeen	769
Montgomery	12,918	Winona	403

County	Pop. April 1, 1970	County Seats or Court House	Land Area Sq. Mi.	County	Pop. April 1, 1970	County Seats or Court House	Land Area Sq. Mi.
Neshoba	20,802	Philadelphia	568	Macon	15,432	Macon	798
Newton	18,983	Decatur	580	Madison	8,641	Fredericktown	496
Noxubee	14,288	Macon	695	Maries	6,851	Vienna	525
Oktibbeha	28,752	Starkville	454	Marion	28,121	Palmyra	438
Panola	26,829	Batesville & Sardis	693	Mercer	4,910	Princeton	455
Pearl River	27,802	Poplarville	828	Miller	15,026	Tuscumbia	600
Perry	9,065	New Augusta	653	Mississippi	16,647	Charleston	415
Pike	31,813	Magnolia	409	Moniteau	10,742	California	419
Pontotoc	17,363	Pontotoc	501	Monroe	9,542	Paris	669
Prentiss	20,133	Booneville	418	Montgomery	11,000	Montgomery City	534
Quitman	15,888	Marks	412	Morgan	10,068	Versailles	592
Rankin	43,933	Brandon	775	New Madrid	23,420	New Madrid	679
Scott	21,369	Forest	615	Newton	32,981	Neosho	629
Sharkey	8,937	Rolling Fork	436	Nodaway	22,467	Maryville	877
Simpson	19,947	Mendenhall	587	Oregon	9,180	Alton	784
Smith	13,561	Raleigh	642	Osage	10,994	Linn	608
Stone	8,101	Wiggins	448	Ozark	6,226	Gainesville	732
Sunflower	37,047	Indianola	694	Pemiscot	26,373	Caruthersville	493
Tallahatchie	19,338	Charleston and Sumner	644	Perry	14,393	Perryville	471
Tate	18,544	Senatobia	405	Pettis	34,137	Sedalia	679
Tippah	15,852	Ripley	464	Phelps	29,567	Rolla	677
Tishomingo	14,940	Iuka	443	Pike	16,928	Bowling Green	681
Tunica	11,854	Tunica	458	Platte	32,081	Platte City	427
Union	19,096	New Albany	422	Polk	15,415	Bolivar	637
Walthall	12,500	Tylertown	403	Pulaski	53,967	Waynesville	551
Warren	44,981	Vicksburg	581	Putnam	5,916	Unionville	518
Washington	70,581	Greenville	734	Ralls	7,764	New London	478
Wayne	16,650	Waynesboro	827	Randolph	22,434	Huntsville	473
Webster	10,047	Walthall	416	Ray	17,599	Richmond	573
Wilkinson	11,099	Woodville	677	Reynolds	6,106	Centerville	817
Winston	18,406	Louisville	606	Ripley	9,803	Doniphan	639
Yalobusha	11,915	Coffeeville and Water Valley	488	St. Charles	92,986	St. Charles	561
Yazoo	27,314	Yazoo City	938	St. Clair	7,667	Osceola	697

Missouri

(114 cos., 1 ind. city, 68,995 sq. mi. land; pop., 4,677,399)

County	Pop. April 1, 1970	County Seats or Court House	Land Area Sq. Mi.	County	Pop. April 1, 1970	County Seats or Court House	Land Area Sq. Mi.
				St. Francois	36,875	Farmington	457
				St. Louis	951,685	Clayton	499
				Ste. Genevieve	12,867	Ste. Genevieve	499
Adair	22,472	Kirksville	572	Saline	24,837	Marshall	757
Andrew	11,913	Savannah	436	Schuyler	4,665	Lancaster	306
Atchison	9,240	Rock Port	549	Scotland	5,499	Memphis	441
Audrain	25,362	Mexico	692	Scott	33,250	Benton	421
Barry	19,597	Cassville	783	Shannon	7,196	Eminence	999
Barton	10,431	Lamar	594	Shelby	7,906	Shelbyville	501
Bates	15,468	Butler	841	Stoddard	25,711	Bloomfield	823
Benton	9,695	Warsaw	735	Stone	9,921	Galena	449
Bollinger	8,820	Marble Hill	621	Sullivan	7,572	Milan	654
Boone	80,911	Columbia	685	Taney	13,023	Forsyth	615
Buchanan	86,915	Saint Joseph	404	Texas	18,320	Houston	1,183
Butler	33,529	Poplar Bluff	715	Vernon	19,065	Nevada	838
Caldwell	8,351	Kingston	430	Warren	9,699	Warrenton	426
Callaway	25,991	Fulton	835	Washington	15,086	Potosi	760
Camden	13,315	Camdenton	640	Wayne	8,546	Greenville	766
Cape Girardeau	49,350	Jackson	574	Webster	15,562	Marshfield	590
Carroll	12,565	Carrollton	697	Worth	3,359	Grant City	267
Carter	3,878	Van Buren	506	Wright	13,667	Hartville	684
Cass	39,448	Harrisonville	698	St. Louis Independent City	622,236		61
Cedar	9,424	Stockton	496				
Chariton	11,084	Keytesville	754				
Christian	15,124	Ozark	567		**Montana**		
Clark	8,260	Kahoka	506	*(56 counties, 145,587 sq. mi. land; pop., 694,409)*			
Clay	123,702	Liberty	412	Beaverhead	8,187	Dillon	5,560
Clinton	12,462	Plattsburg	420	Big Horn	10,057	Hardin	5,023
Cole	46,228	Jefferson City	384	Blaine	6,727	Chinook	4,275
Cooper	14,732	Boonville	566	Broadwater	2,526	Townsend	1,193
Crawford	14,828	Steelville	760	Carbon	7,080	Red Lodge	2,066
Dade	6,850	Greenfield	504	Carter	1,956	Ekalaka	3,313
Dallas	10,054	Buffalo	537	Cascade	81,804	Great Falls	2,661
Daviess	8,420	Gallatin	563	Chouteau	6,473	Fort Benton	3,927
De Kalb	7,305	Maysville	423	Custer	12,174	Miles City	3,756
Dent	11,457	Salem	756	Daniels	3,083	Scobey	1,443
Douglas	9,268	Ava	809	Dawson	11,269	Glendive	2,370
Dunklin	33,742	Kennett	543	Deer Lodge	15,652	Anaconda	740
Franklin	55,127	Union	934	Fallon	4,050	Baker	1,633
Gasconade	11,878	Hermann	519	Fergus	12,611	Lewistown	4,242
Gentry	8,060	Albany	488	Flathead	39,460	Kalispell	5,137
Greene	152,929	Springfield	677	Gallatin	32,505	Bozeman	2,517
Grundy	11,819	Trenton	435	Garfield	1,796	Jordan	4,455
Harrison	10,257	Bethany	720	Glacier	10,783	Cut Bank	2,964
Henry	18,451	Clinton	734	Golden Valley	931	Ryegate	1,176
Hickory	4,481	Hermitage	377	Granite	2,737	Philipsburg	1,733
Holt	6,654	Oregon	458	Hill	17,358	Havre	2,927
Howard	10,561	Fayette	472	Jefferson	5,238	Boulder	1,652
Howell	23,521	West Plains	920	Judith Basin	2,667	Stanford	1,880
Iron	9,529	Ironton	554	Lake	14,445	Polson	1,494
Jackson	654,178	Independence	603	Lewis & Clark	33,281	Helena	3,476
Jasper	79,852	Carthage	642	Liberty	2,359	Chester	1,439
Jefferson	105,647	Hillsboro	668	Lincoln	18,063	Libby	3,714
Johnson	34,172	Warrensburg	826	McCone	2,875	Circle	2,607
Knox	5,692	Edina	512	Madison	5,014	Virginia City	3,528
Laclede	19,944	Lebanon	770	Meagher	2,122	White Sulphur Springs	2,354
Lafayette	26,626	Lexington	632	Mineral	2,958	Superior	1,222
Lawrence	24,585	Mount Vernon	619	Missoula	58,263	Missoula	2,612
Lewis	10,993	Monticello	508	Musselshell	3,734	Roundup	1,887
Lincoln	18,041	Troy	625	Park	11,197	Livingston	2,626
Linn	15,125	Linneus	622	Petroleum	675	Winnett	1,655
Livingston	15,368	Chillicothe	530	Phillips	5,386	Malta	5,213
McDonald	12,357	Pineville	540	Pondera	6,611	Conrad	1,645
				Powder River	2,862	Broadus	3,288

County	Pop. April 1, 1970	County Seats or Court House	Land Area Sq. Mi.
Powell	6,660	Deer Lodge	2,336
Prairie	1,752	Terry	1,730
Ravalli	14,409	Hamilton	2,382
Richland	9,837	Sidney	2,079
Roosevelt	10,365	Wolf Point	2,385
Rosebud	6,032	Forsyth	5,037
Sanders	7,093	Thompson Falls	2,778
Sheridan	5,779	Plentywood	1,694
Silver Bow	41,981	Butte	715
Stillwater	4,632	Columbus	1,794
Sweet Grass	2,980	Big Timber	1,840
Teton	6,116	Choteau	2,294
Toole	5,839	Shelby	1,950
Treasure	1,069	Hysham	985
Valley	11,471	Glasgow	4,974
Wheatland	2,529	Harlowton	1,420
Wibaux	1,465	Wibaux	890
Yellowstone	87,367	Billings	2,642
Yellowstone Nat. Park	64		269

Nebraska
(93 counties, 76,483 sq. mi. land; pop., 1,483,791)

County	Pop.	County Seat	Land Area
Adams	30,553	Hastings	562
Antelope	9,047	Neligh	853
Arthur	606	Arthur	704
Banner	1,034	Harrisburg	738
Blaine	847	Brewster	710
Boone	8,190	Albion	683
Box Butte	10,094	Alliance	1,065
Boyd	3,752	Butte	538
Brown	4,021	Ainsworth	1,216
Buffalo	31,222	Kearney	949
Burt	9,247	Tekamah	483
Butler	9,461	David City	582
Cass	18,076	Plattsmouth	555
Cedar	12,192	Hartington	742
Chase	4,129	Imperial	800
Cherry	6,846	Valentine	5,966
Cheyenne	10,778	Sidney	1,186
Clay	8,266	Clay Center	570
Colfax	9,498	Schuyler	406
Cuming	12,034	West Point	571
Custer	14,092	Broken Bow	2,558
Dakota	13,137	Dakota City	255
Dawes	9,761	Chadron	1,386
Dawson	19,771	Lexington	975
Deuel	2,717	Chappell	436
Dixon	7,453	Ponca	475
Dodge	34,782	Fremont	528
Douglas	389,455	Omaha	335
Dundy	2,926	Benkelman	921
Fillmore	8,137	Geneva	577
Franklin	4,566	Franklin	578
Frontier	3,982	Stockville	962
Furnas	6,897	Beaver City	722
Gage	25,719	Beatrice	858
Garden	2,929	Oshkosh	1,678
Garfield	2,411	Burwell	569
Gosper	2,178	Elwood	464
Grant	1,019	Hyannis	764
Greeley	4,000	Greeley	570
Hall	42,851	Grand Island	537
Hamilton	8,867	Aurora	537
Harlan	4,357	Alma	556
Hayes	1,530	Hayes Center	711
Hitchcock	4,051	Trenton	712
Holt	12,933	O'Neil	2,405
Hooker	939	Mullen	722
Howard	6,807	Saint Paul	564
Jefferson	10,436	Fairbury	577
Johnson	5,743	Tecumseh	377
Kearney	6,707	Minden	512
Keith	8,487	Ogallala	1,032
Keya Paha	1,340	Springview	768
Kimball	6,009	Kimball	953
Knox	11,723	Center	1,107
Lancaster	167,972	Lincoln	845
Lincoln	29,538	North Platte	2,522
Logan	991	Stapleton	570
Loup	854	Taylor	574
McPherson	623	Tryon	856
Madison	27,402	Madison	572
Merrick	8,751	Central City	480
Morrill	5,813	Bridgeport	1,402
Nance	5,142	Fullerton	439
Nemaha	8,976	Auburn	400
Nuckolls	7,404	Nelson	579
Otoe	15,576	Nebraska City	619
Pawnee	4,473	Pawnee City	433
Perkins	3,423	Grant	885
Phelps	9,553	Holdrege	544
Pierce	8,493	Pierce	573
Platte	26,544	Columbus	667
Polk	6,468	Osceola	432
Red Willow	12,191	McCook	686
Richardson	12,277	Falls City	550
Rock	2,231	Bassett	1,009

County	Pop. April 1, 1970	County Seats or Court House	Land Area Sq. Mi.
Saline	12,809	Wilber	575
Sarpy	66,200	Papillion	239
Saunders	17,018	Wahoo	759
Scotts Bluff	36,432	Gering	726
Seward	14,460	Seward	571
Sheridan	7,285	Rushville	2,462
Sherman	4,725	Loup City	567
Sioux	2,034	Harrison	2,063
Stanton	5,758	Stanton	431
Thayer	7,779	Hebron	577
Thomas	954	Thedford	716
Thurston	6,942	Pender	388
Valley	5,783	Ord	569
Washington	13,310	Blair	386
Wayne	10,400	Wayne	443
Webster	5,396	Red Cloud	575
Wheeler	1,051	Bartlett	576
York	13,685	York	577

Nevada
(16 cos., 1 ind. city, 109,889 sq. mi. land; pop., 488,738)

County	Pop.	County Seat	Land Area
Churchill	10,513	Fallon	4,883
Clark	273,288	Las Vegas	7,874
Douglas	6,882	Minden	723
Elko	13,958	Elko	17,162
Esmeralda	629	Goldfield	3,570
Eureka	948	Eureka	4,182
Humboldt	6,375	Winnemucca	9,702
Lander	2,666	Austin	5,621
Lincoln	2,557	Pioche	10,649
Lyon	8,221	Yerington	2,010
Mineral	7,051	Hawthorne	3,765
Nye	5,599	Tonopah	18,064
Pershing	2,670	Lovelock	6,001
Storey	695	Virginia City	262
Washoe	121,068	Reno	6,375
White Pine	10,150	Ely	8,904
Carson City	15,468	Independent City Carson City	141

New Hampshire
(10 counties, 9,027 sq. mi. land, pop., 737,681)

County	Pop.	County Seat	Land Area
Belknap	32,367	Laconia	400
Carroll	18,548	Ossipee	938
Cheshire	52,364	Keene	715
Coos	34,291	Lancaster	1,820
Grafton	54,914	Woodsville	1,732
Hillsborough	223,941	Nashua	887
Merrimack	80,925	Concord	930
Rockingham	138,951	Exeter	691
Strafford	70,431	Dover	376
Sullivan	30,949	Newport	539

New Jersey
(21 counties, 7,521 sq. mi. land; pop., 7,168,164)

County	Pop.	County Seat	Land Area
Atlantic	175,043	Mays Landing	569
Bergen	897,148	Hackensack	234
Burlington	323,132	Mount Holly	819
Camden	456,291	Camden	221
Cape May	59,554	Cape May Court House	267
Cumberland	121,374	Bridgeton	500
Essex	932,299	Newark	130
Gloucester	172,681	Woodbury	329
Hudson	609,266	Jersey City	47
Hunterdon	69,718	Flemington	423
Mercer	303,968	Trenton	228
Middlesex	583,813	New Brunswick	312
Monmouth	461,849	Freehold	476
Morris	383,454	Morristown	468
Ocean	208,470	Toms River	642
Passaic	460,782	Paterson	192
Salem	60,346	Salem	365
Somerset	198,372	Somerville	307
Sussex	77,528	Newton	527
Union	543,116	Elizabeth	103
Warren	73,960	Belvidere	362

New Mexico
(32 counties, 121,412 sq. mi. land; pop., 1,016,000)

County	Pop.	County Seat	Land Area
Bernalillo	315,774	Albuquerque	1,169
Catron	2,198	Reserve	6,897
Chaves	43,335	Roswell	6,084
Colfax	12,170	Raton	3,764
Curry	39,517	Clovis	1,403
De Baca	2,547	Fort Sumner	2,356
Dona Ana	69,773	Las Cruces	3,804
Eddy	41,119	Carlsbad	4,167
Grant	22,030	Silver City	3,970
Guadalupe	4,969	Santa Rosa	2,998
Harding	1,348	Mosquero	2,134
Hidalgo	4,734	Lordsburg	3,447
Lea	49,554	Lovington	4,393
Lincoln	7,560	Carrizozo	4,858
Los Alamos	15,198	Los Alamos	108

County	Pop. April 1, 1970	County Seats or Court House	Land Area Sq. Mi.
Luna	11,706	Deming	2,957
McKinley	43,208	Gallup	5,454
Mora	4,673	Mora	1,940
Otero	41,097	Alamogordo	6,638
Quay	10,903	Tucumcari	2,875
Rio Arriba	25,170	Tierra Amarilla	5,843
Roosevelt	16,479	Portales	2,454
Sandoval	17,492	Bernalillo	3,714
San Juan	52,517	Aztec	5,500
San Miguel	21,951	Las Vegas	4,741
Santa Fe	53,756	Santa Fe	1,902
Sierra	7,189	Truth or Consequences	4,166
Socorro	9,763	Socorro	6,603
Taos	17,516	Taos	2,256
Torrance	5,290	Estancia	3,346
Union	4,925	Clayton	3,816
Valencia	40,539	Los Lunas	5,656

New York
(62 counties, 47,831 sq. mi. land; pop., 18,241,266)

County	Pop. April 1, 1970	County Seats or Court House	Land Area Sq. Mi.
Albany	286,742	Albany	526
Allegany	46,458	Belmont	1,047
Bronx	1,471,701	Bronx	41
Broome	221,815	Binghamton	714
Cattaraugus	81,666	Little Valley	1,318
Cayuga	77,439	Auburn	698
Chautauqua	147,305	Mayville	1,081
Chemung	101,537	Elmira	415
Chenango	46,368	Norwich	897
Clinton	72,934	Plattsburgh	1,059
Columbia	51,519	Hudson	645
Cortland	45,894	Cortland	502
Delaware	44,718	Delhi	1,443
Dutchess	222,295	Poughkeepsie	813
Erie	1,113,491	Buffalo	1,058
Essex	34,631	Elizabethtown	1,823
Franklin	43,931	Malone	1,674
Fulton	52,637	Johnstown	498
Genesee	58,722	Batavia	501
Greene	33,136	Catskill	653
Hamilton	4,714	Lake Pleasant	1,735
Herkimer	67,633	Herkimer	1,435
Jefferson	88,508	Watertown	1,294
Kings	2,602,012	Brooklyn	70
Lewis	23,644	Lowville	1,291
Livingston	54,041	Geneseo	638
Madison	62,864	Wampsville	661
Monroe	711,917	Rochester	675
Montgomery	55,883	Fonda	408
Nassau	1,428,838	Mineola	289
New York	1,539,233	Manhattan	23
Niagara	235,720	Lockport	532
Oneida	273,037	Utica	1,223
Onondaga	472,835	Syracuse	794
Ontario	78,849	Canandaigua	651
Orange	221,657	Goshen	833
Orleans	37,305	Albion	396
Oswego	100,897	Oswego	964
Otsego	56,181	Cooperstown	1,013
Putnam	56,696	Carmel	231
Queens	1,987,174	Jamaica	108
Rensselaer	152,510	Troy	665
Richmond	295,443	Saint George	58
Rockland	229,903	New City	176
St. Lawrence	111,991	Canton	2,768
Saratoga	121,764	Ballston Spa	818
Schenectady	161,078	Schenectady	207
Schoharie	24,750	Schoharie	624
Schuyler	16,737	Watkins Glen	330
Seneca	35,083	Ovid & Waterloo	330
Steuben	99,546	Bath	1,410
Suffolk	1,127,030	Riverhead	929
Sullivan	52,580	Monticello	980
Tioga	46,513	Owego	524
Tompkins	77,064	Ithaca	482
Ulster	141,241	Kingston	1,141
Warren	49,402	Lake George	887
Washington	52,725	Hudson Falls	836
Wayne	79,404	Lyons	606
Westchester	894,406	White Plains	443
Wyoming	37,688	Warsaw	598
Yates	19,831	Penn Yan	343

North Carolina
(100 counties, 48,798 sq. mi. land; pop., 5,082,059)

County	Pop. April 1, 1970	County Seats or Court House	Land Area Sq. Mi.
Alamance	96,362	Graham	428
Alexander	19,466	Taylorsville	259
Alleghany	8,134	Sparta	225
Anson	23,488	Wadesboro	533
Ashe	19,571	Jefferson	426
Avery	12,655	Newland	245
Beaufort	35,980	Washington	826
Bertie	20,528	Windsor	698
Bladen	26,477	Elizabethtown	883
Brunswick	24,223	Southport	856
Buncombe	145,056	Asheville	657
Burke	60,364	Morganton	511

County	Pop. April 1, 1970	County Seats or Court House	Land Area Sq. Mi.
Cabarrus	74,629	Concord	363
Caldwell	56,699	Lenoir	469
Camden	5,453	Camden	239
Carteret	31,603	Beaufort	536
Caswell	19,055	Yanceyville	428
Catawba	90,873	Newton	394
Chatham	29,554	Pittsboro	709
Cherokee	16,330	Murphy	452
Chowan	10,764	Edenton	173
Clay	5,180	Hayesville	209
Cleveland	72,556	Shelby	468
Columbus	46,937	Whiteville	945
Craven	62,554	New Bern	699
Cumberland	212,042	Fayetteville	654
Currituck	6,976	Currituck	246
Dare	6,995	Manteo	391
Davidson	95,627	Lexington	549
Davie	18,855	Mocksville	265
Duplin	38,015	Kenansville	815
Durham	132,681	Durham	295
Edgecombe	52,341	Tarboro	510
Forsyth	216,111	Winston-Salem	419
Franklin	26,820	Louisburg	491
Gaston	148,415	Gastonia	356
Gates	8,524	Gatesville	337
Graham	6,562	Robbinsville	292
Granville	32,762	Oxford	537
Greene	14,967	Snow Hill	267
Guilford	288,645	Greensboro	655
Halifax	53,884	Halifax	734
Harnett	49,667	Lillington	603
Haywood	41,710	Waynesville	553
Henderson	42,804	Hendersonville	378
Hertford	23,529	Winton	353
Hoke	16,436	Raeford	389
Hyde	5,571	Swanquarter	613
Iredell	72,197	Statesville	572
Jackson	21,593	Sylva	491
Johnston	61,737	Smithfield	797
Jones	9,779	Trenton	467
Lee	30,467	Sanford	256
Lenoir	55,204	Kinston	400
Lincoln	32,682	Lincolnton	297
McDowell	30,648	Marion	436
Macon	15,788	Franklin	513
Madison	16,003	Marshall	450
Martin	24,730	Williamston	455
Mecklenburg	354,656	Charlotte	530
Mitchell	13,447	Bakersville	215
Montgomery	19,267	Troy	488
Moore	39,048	Carthage	704
Nash	59,122	Nashville	544
New Hanover	82,996	Wilmington	185
Northampton	24,009	Jackson	536
Onslow	103,126	Jacksonville	765
Orange	57,707	Hillsboro	400
Pamlico	9,467	Bayboro	338
Pasquotank	26,824	Elizabeth City	228
Pender	18,149	Burgaw	871
Perquimans	8,351	Hertford	246
Person	25,914	Roxboro	401
Pitt	73,900	Greenville	655
Polk	11,735	Columbus	239
Randolph	76,358	Asheboro	798
Richmond	39,889	Rockingham	475
Robeson	84,842	Lumberton	949
Rockingham	72,402	Wentworth	569
Rowan	90,035	Salisbury	523
Rutherford	47,337	Rutherfordton	563
Sampson	44,954	Clinton	945
Scotland	26,929	Laurinburg	319
Stanly	42,822	Albemarle	398
Stokes	23,782	Danbury	457
Surry	51,415	Dobson	536
Swain	7,861	Bryson City	524
Transylvania	19,713	Brevard	382
Tyrrell	3,806	Columbia	390
Union	54,714	Monroe	639
Vance	32,691	Henderson	249
Wake	229,006	Raleigh	858
Warren	15,810	Warrenton	424
Washington	14,038	Plymouth	343
Watauga	23,404	Boone	317
Wayne	85,408	Goldsboro	557
Wilkes	49,524	Wilkesboro	757
Wilson	57,486	Wilson	375
Yadkin	24,599	Yadkinville	336
Yancey	12,629	Burnsville	312

North Dakota
(53 counties, 69,273 sq. mi. land; pop., 617,761)

County	Pop. April 1, 1970	County Seats or Court House	Land Area Sq. Mi.
Adams	3,832	Hettinger	989
Barnes	14,669	Valley City	1,479
Benson	8,245	Minnewaukan	1,403
Billings	1,198	Medora	1,139
Bottineau	9,496	Bottineau	1,677
Bowman	3,901	Bowman	1,170
Burke	4,739	Bowbells	1,119
Burleigh	40,714	Bismarck	1,625

County	Pop. April 1, 1970	County Seats or Court House	Land Area Sq. Mi.	County	Pop. April 1, 1970	County Seats or Court House	Land Area Sq. Mi.
Cass	73,653	Fargo	1,749	Marion	64,724	Marion	405
Cavalier	8,213	Langdon	1,512	Medina	82,717	Medina	425
Dickey	6,976	Ellendale	1,143	Meigs	19,799	Pomeroy	436
Divide	4,564	Crosby	1,300	Mercer	35,558	Celina	444
Dunn	4,895	Manning	1,992	Miami	84,342	Troy	407
Eddy	4,103	New Rockford	635	Monroe	15,739	Woodsfield	456
Emmons	7,200	Linton	1,503	Montgomery	608,413	Dayton	459
Foster	4,832	Carrington	645	Morgan	12,375	McConnelsville	420
Golden Valley	2,611	Beach	1,014	Morrow	21,348	Mount Gilead	403
Grand Forks	61,102	Grand Forks	1,438	Muskingum	77,826	Zanesville	651
Grant	5,009	Carson	1,666	Noble	10,428	Caldwell	398
Griggs	4,184	Cooperstown	710	Ottawa	37,099	Port Clinton	261
Hettinger	5,075	Mott	1,134	Paulding	19,329	Paulding	417
Kidder	4,362	Steele	1,358	Perry	27,434	New Lexington	410
La Moure	7,117	La Moure	1,136	Pickaway	40,071	Circleville	504
Logan	4,245	Napoleon	1,001	Pike	19,114	Waverly	443
McHenry	8,977	Towner	1,879	Portage	125,868	Ravenna	495
McIntosh	5,545	Ashley	992	Preble	34,719	Eaton	427
McKenzie	6,127	Watford City	2,735	Putnam	31,134	Ottawa	486
McLean	11,251	Washburn	2,065	Richland	129,997	Mansfield	496
Mercer	6,175	Stanton	1,042	Ross	61,211	Chillicothe	687
Morton	20,310	Mandan	1,920	Sandusky	60,983	Fremont	409
Mountrail	8,437	Stanley	1,819	Scioto	76,951	Portsmouth	608
Nelson	5,807	Lakota	995	Seneca	60,696	Tiffin	551
Oliver	2,322	Center	721	Shelby	37,748	Sidney	408
Pembina	10,728	Cavalier	1,124	Stark	372,210	Canton	576
Pierce	6,323	Rugby	1,038	Summit	553,371	Akron	408
Ramsey	12,915	Devils Lake	1,248	Trumbull	232,579	Warren	608
Ransom	7,102	Lisbon	861	Tuscarawas	77,211	New Philadelphia	569
Renville	3,828	Mohall	886	Union	23,786	Marysville	434
Richland	18,089	Wahpeton	1,449	Van Wert	29,194	Van Wert	409
Rolette	11,549	Rolla	913	Vinton	9,420	McArthur	411
Sargent	5,937	Forman	853	Warren	85,505	Lebanon	408
Sheridan	3,232	McClusky	989	Washington	57,160	Marietta	641
Sioux	3,632	Fort Yates	1,103	Wayne	87,123	Wooster	561
Slope	1,484	Amidon	1,225	Williams	33,669	Bryan	421
Stark	19,613	Dickinson	1,316	Wood	89,722	Bowling Green	619
Steele	3,749	Finley	710	Wyandot	21,826	Upper Sandusky	406
Stutsman	23,550	Jamestown	2,264				
Towner	4,645	Cando	1,042				
Traill	9,571	Hillsboro	861				
Walsh	16,251	Grafton	1,286				
Ward	58,560	Minot	2,044				
Wells	7,847	Fessenden	1,298				
Williams	19,301	Williston	2,064				

Ohio
(88 counties, 40,975 sq. mi. land; pop., 10,652,017)

Oklahoma
(77 counties, 68,782 sq. mi. land; pop., 2,559,253)

County	Pop. April 1, 1970	County Seats or Court House	Land Area Sq. Mi.	County	Pop. April 1, 1970	County Seats or Court House	Land Area Sq. Mi.
Adams	18,957	West Union	587	Adair	15,141	Stillwell	570
Allen	111,144	Lima	410	Alfalfa	7,224	Cherokee	868
Ashland	43,303	Ashland	424	Atoka	10,972	Atoka	991
Ashtabula	98,237	Jefferson	700	Beaver	6,282	Beaver	1,790
Athens	55,747	Athens	504	Beckham	15,754	Sayre	907
Auglaize	38,602	Wapakoneta	400	Blaine	11,794	Watonga	917
Belmont	80,917	Saint Clairsville	534	Bryan	25,552	Durant	889
Brown	26,635	Georgetown	490	Caddo	28,931	Anadarko	1,272
Butler	226,207	Hamilton	471	Canadian	32,245	El Reno	897
Carroll	21,579	Carrollton	390	Carter	37,349	Ardmore	830
Champaign	30,491	Urbana	432	Cherokee	23,174	Tahlequah	756
Clark	157,115	Springfield	402	Choctaw	15,141	Hugo	778
Clermont	95,887	Batavia	458	Cimarron	4,145	Boise City	1,843
Clinton	31,464	Wilmington	410	Cleveland	81,839	Norman	527
Columbiana	108,310	Lisbon	534	Coal	5,525	Colgate	526
Coshocton	33,486	Coshocton	562	Comanche	108,144	Lawton	1,084
Crawford	50,364	Bucyrus	404	Cotton	6,832	Walters	651
Cuyahoga	1,721,300	Cleveland	456	Craig	14,722	Vinita	764
Darke	49,141	Greenville	605	Creek	45,532	Sapulpa	936
Defiance	36,949	Defiance	412	Custer	22,665	Arapaho	980
Delaware	42,908	Delaware	450	Delaware	17,767	Jay	707
Erie	75,909	Sandusky	264	Dewey	5,656	Taloga	1,018
Fairfield	73,301	Lancaster	505	Ellis	5,129	Arnett	1,242
Fayette	25,461	Washington C. H.	404	Garfield	56,343	Enid	1,054
Franklin	833,249	Columbus	538	Garvin	24,874	Pauls Valley	814
Fulton	33,071	Wauseon	407	Grady	29,354	Chickasha	1,096
Gallia	25,239	Gallipolis	471	Grant	7,117	Medford	1,007
Geauga	62,977	Chardon	407	Greer	7,979	Mangum	633
Greene	125,057	Xenia	415	Harmon	5,136	Hollis	545
Guernsey	37,665	Cambridge	528	Harper	5,151	Buffalo	1,041
Hamilton	923,205	Cincinnati	414	Haskell	9,578	Stigler	602
Hancock	61,217	Findlay	532	Hughes	13,228	Holdenville	807
Hardin	30,813	Kenton	467	Jackson	30,902	Altus	810
Harrison	17,013	Cadiz	401	Jefferson	7,125	Waurika	780
Henry	27,058	Napoleon	416	Johnston	7,870	Tishomingo	638
Highland	28,996	Hillsboro	549	Kay	48,791	Newkirk	950
Hocking	20,322	Logan	421	Kingfisher	12,857	Kingfisher	904
Holmes	23,024	Millersburg	424	Kiowa	12,532	Hobart	1,027
Huron	49,587	Norwalk	497	Latimer	8,601	Wilburton	737
Jackson	27,174	Jackson	419	Le Flore	32,137	Poteau	1,560
Jefferson	96,193	Steubenville	411	Lincoln	19,482	Chandler	973
Knox	41,795	Mount Vernon	531	Logan	19,645	Guthrie	751
Lake	197,200	Painesville	231	Love	5,637	Marietta	513
Lawrence	56,868	Ironton	456	McClain	14,157	Purcell	573
Licking	107,799	Newark	686	McCurtain	28,642	Idabel	1,800
Logan	35,072	Bellefontaine	460	McIntosh	12,472	Eufaula	608
Lorain	256,843	Elyria	495	Major	7,529	Fairview	963
Lucas	484,370	Toledo	343	Marshall	7,682	Madill	366
Madison	28,318	London	463	Mayes	23,302	Pryor	648
Mahoning	304,545	Youngstown	415	Murray	10,669	Sulphur	423
				Muskogee	59,542	Muskogee	818
				Noble	10,043	Perry	743
				Nowata	9,773	Nowata	537
				Okfuskee	10,683	Okemah	637
				Oklahoma	527,717	Oklahoma City	700
				Okmulgee	35,358	Okmulgee	700
				Osage	29,750	Pawhuska	2,272

County	Pop. April 1, 1970	County Seats or Court House	Land Area Sq. Mi.
Ottawa	29,800	Miami	464
Pawnee	11,338	Pawnee	561
Payne	50,654	Stillwater	694
Pittsburg	37,521	McAlester	1,241
Pontotoc	27,867	Ada	714
Pottawatomie	43,134	Shawnee	794
Pushmataha	9,385	Antlers	1,420
Roger Mills	4,452	Cheyenne	1,140
Rogers	28,425	Claremore	685
Seminole	25,144	Wewoka	630
Sequoyah	23,370	Sallisaw	696
Stephens	35,902	Duncan	891
Texas	16,352	Guymon	2,062
Tillman	12,901	Frederick	901
Tulsa	399,982	Tulsa	573
Wagoner	22,163	Wagoner	563
Washington	42,302	Bartlesville	424
Washita	12,141	Cordell	1,009
Woods	11,920	Alva	1,298
Woodward	15,537	Woodward	1,251

Oregon

(36 counties, 96,184 sq. mi. land; pop., 2,091,385)

County	Pop. April 1, 1970	County Seats or Court House	Land Area Sq. Mi.
Baker	14,919	Baker	3,068
Benton	53,776	Corvallis	668
Clackamas	166,088	Oregon City	1,884
Clatsop	28,473	Astoria	805
Columbia	28,790	Saint Helens	639
Coos	56,515	Coquille	1,604
Crook	9,985	Prineville	2,975
Curry	13,006	Gold Beach	1,627
Deschutes	30,442	Bend	3,031
Douglas	71,743	Roseburg	5,063
Gilliam	2,342	Condon	1,208
Grant	6,996	Canyon City	4,530
Harney	7,215	Burns	10,166
Hood River	13,187	Hood River	523
Jackson	94,533	Medford	2,812
Jefferson	8,548	Madras	1,793
Josephine	35,746	Grants Pass	1,625
Klamath	50,021	Klamath Falls	5,970
Lake	6,343	Lakeview	8,231
Lane	215,401	Eugene	4,552
Lincoln	25,755	Newport	986
Linn	71,914	Albany	2,283
Malheur	23,169	Vale	9,859
Marion	151,309	Salem	1,166
Morrow	4,465	Heppner	2,060
Multnomah	554,668	Portland	423
Polk	35,349	Dallas	736
Sherman	2,139	Moro	830
Tillamook	18,034	Tillamook	1,115
Umatilla	44,923	Pendleton	3,227
Union	19,377	La Grande	2,032
Wallowa	6,247	Enterprise	3,178
Wasco	20,133	The Dalles	2,381
Washington	157,920	Hillsboro	716
Wheeler	1,849	Fossil	1,707
Yamhill	40,213	McMinnville	711

Pennsylvania

(67 counties, 44,966 sq. mi. land; pop., 11,793,909)

County	Pop. April 1, 1970	County Seats or Court House	Land Area Sq. Mi.
Adams	56,937	Gettysburg	526
Allegheny	1,605,133	Pittsburgh	728
Armstrong	75,590	Kittanning	652
Beaver	208,418	Beaver	440
Bedford	42,353	Bedford	1,018
Berks	296,382	Reading	862
Blair	135,356	Hollidaysburg	530
Bradford	57,962	Towanda	1,148
Bucks	415,056	Doylestown	614
Butler	127,941	Butler	794
Cambria	186,785	Ebensburg	692
Cameron	7,096	Emporium	401
Carbon	50,573	Jim Thorpe	404
Centre	99,267	Bellefonte	1,115
Chester	278,311	West Chester	761
Clarion	38,414	Clarion	597
Clearfield	74,619	Clearfield	1,139
Clinton	37,721	Lock Haven	899
Columbia	55,114	Bloomsburg	484
Crawford	81,342	Meadville	1,012
Cumberland	158,177	Carlisle	555
Dauphin	223,713	Harrisburg	518
Delaware	601,425	Media	184
Elk	37,770	Ridgeway	807
Erie	263,654	Erie	813
Fayette	154,667	Uniontown	802
Forest	4,926	Tionesta	419
Franklin	100,833	Chambersburg	754
Fulton	10,776	McConnellsburg	435
Greene	36,090	Waynesburg	578
Huntingdon	39,108	Huntingdon	895
Indiana	79,451	Indiana	825
Jefferson	43,695	Brookville	652
Juniata	16,712	Mifflintown	386
Lackawanna	234,107	Scranton	454
Lancaster	320,079	Lancaster	946
Lawrence	107,374	New Castle	367
Lebanon	99,665	Lebanon	363
Lehigh	255,304	Allentown	348
Luzerne	342,301	Wilkes-Barre	886
Lycoming	113,296	Williamsport	1,216
McKean	51,915	Smethport	992
Mercer	127,225	Mercer	670
Mifflin	45,268	Lewistown	431
Monroe	45,422	Stroudsburg	611
Montgomery	623,921	Norristown	496
Montour	16,508	Danville	130
Northampton	214,368	Easton	376
Northumberland	99,190	Sunbury	453
Perry	28,615	New Bloomfield	551
Philadelphia	1,950,098	Philadelphia	129
Pike	11,818	Milford	542
Potter	16,395	Coudersport	1,092
Schuylkill	160,089	Pottsville	784
Snyder	29,269	Middleburg	327
Somerset	76,037	Somerset	1,078
Sullivan	5,961	Laporte	478
Susquehanna	34,344	Montrose	833
Tioga	39,691	Wellsboro	1,146
Union	28,603	Lewisburg	318
Venango	62,353	Franklin	678
Warren	47,682	Warren	905
Washington	210,876	Washington	857
Wayne	29,581	Honesdale	741
Westmoreland	376,935	Greensburg	1,024
Wyoming	19,082	Tunkhannock	398
York	272,603	York	909

Rhode Island

(5 counties, 1,049 sq. mi. land; pop., 949,723)

County	Pop. April 1, 1970	County Seats or Court House	Land Area Sq. Mi.
Bristol	45,937	Bristol	25
Kent	142,382	East Greenwich	173
Newport	94,228	Newport	115
Providence	581,470	Providence	416
Washington	85,706	West Kingston	321

South Carolina

(46 counties, 30,225 sq. mi. land; pop., 2,590,516)

County	Pop. April 1, 1970	County Seats or Court House	Land Area Sq. Mi.
Abbeville	21,112	Abbeville	506
Aiken	91,023	Aiken	1,100
Allendale	9,783	Allendale	418
Anderson	105,474	Anderson	749
Bamberg	15,950	Bamberg	395
Barnwell	17,176	Barnwell	553
Beaufort	51,136	Beaufort	579
Berkeley	56,199	Moncks Corner	1,110
Calhoun	10,780	Saint Matthews	377
Charleston	247,650	Charleston	939
Cherokee	36,791	Gaffney	394
Chester	29,811	Chester	584
Chesterfield	33,667	Chesterfield	790
Clarendon	25,604	Manning	599
Colleton	27,622	Walterboro	1,049
Darlington	53,442	Darlington	543
Dillon	28,838	Dillon	407
Dorchester	32,421	Saint George	569
Edgefield	15,692	Edgefield	482
Fairfield	19,999	Winnsboro	696
Florence	89,636	Florence	805
Georgetown	33,500	Georgetown	812
Greenville	240,774	Greenville	792
Greenwood	49,686	Greenwood	446
Hampton	15,878	Hampton	562
Horry	69,992	Conway	1,154
Jasper	11,000	Ridgeland	652
Kershaw	34,727	Camden	781
Lancaster	43,328	Lancaster	502
Laurens	49,713	Laurens	711
Lee	18,323	Bishopville	409
Lexington	89,012	Lexington	717
McCormick	7,955	McCormick	360
Marion	30,270	Marion	487
Marlboro	27,151	Bennettsville	483
Newberry	29,273	Newberry	635
Oconee	40,728	Walhalla	654
Orangeburg	69,789	Orangeburg	1,106
Pickens	58,956	Pickens	492
Richland	233,868	Columbia	748
Saluda	14,528	Saluda	458
Spartanburg	173,631	Spartanburg	831
Sumter	78,885	Sumter	672
Union	29,133	Union	514
Williamsburg	34,203	Kingstree	935
York		York	684

South Dakota

(67 counties, 75,955 sq. mi. land; pop., 666,257)

County	Pop. April 1, 1970	County Seats or Court House	Land Area Sq. Mi.
Aurora	4,183	Plankinton	709
Beadle	20,877	Huron	1,259
Bennett	3,088	Martin	1,181
Bon Homme	8,577	Tyndall	560
Brookings	22,158	Brookings	800
Brown	36,920	Aberdeen	1,674
Brule	5,870	Chamberlain	818

County	Pop. April 1, 1970	County Seats or Court House	Land Area Sq. Mi.	County	Pop. April 1, 1970	County Seats or Court House	Land Area Sq. Mi.
Buffalo	1,739	Gannvalley	482	Hardeman	22,435	Bolivar	656
Butte	7,825	Belle Fourche	2,250	Hardin	18,212	Savannah	587
Campbell	2,866	Mound City	732	Hawkins	33,757	Rogersville	480
Charles Mix	9,994	Lake Andes	1,097	Haywood	19,596	Brownsville	519
Clark	5,515	Clark	964	Henderson	17,360	Lexington	515
Clay	12,923	Vermillion	405	Henry	23,749	Paris	567
Codington	19,140	Watertown	687	Hickman	12,096	Centerville	610
Corson	4,994	McIntosh	2,470	Houston	5,853	Erin	201
Custer	4,698	Custer	1,557	Humphreys	13,560	Waverly	530
Davison	17,319	Mitchell	432	Jackson	8,141	Gainesboro	323
Day	8,713	Webster	1,030	Jefferson	24,940	Dandridge	274
Deuel	5,686	Clear Lake	639	Johnson	11,569	Mountain City	293
Dewey	5,170	Timber Lake	2,351	Knox	276,293	Knoxville	508
Douglas	4,569	Armour	435	Lake	8,091	Tiptonville	167
Edmunds	5,548	Ipswich	1,154	Lauderdale	20,271	Ripley	477
Fall River	7,505	Hot Springs	1,743	Lawrence	29,097	Lawrenceburg	634
Faulk	3,893	Faulkton	996	Lewis	6,761	Hohenwald	285
Grant	9,005	Milbank	681	Lincoln	24,318	Fayetteville	580
Gregory	6,710	Burke	997	Loudon	24,266	Loudon	237
Haakon	2,802	Philip	1,816	McMinn	35,462	Athens	432
Hamlin	5,520	Hayti	511	McNairy	18,369	Selmer	569
Hand	5,883	Miller	1,432	Macon	12,315	Lafayette	304
Hanson	3,781	Alexandria	430	Madison	65,774	Jackson	560
Harding	1,855	Buffalo	2,682	Marion	20,577	Jasper	506
Hughes	11,632	Pierre	748	Marshall	17,319	Lewisburg	377
Hutchinson	10,379	Olivet	815	Maury	44,028	Columbia	614
Hyde	2,515	Highmore	863	Meigs	5,219	Decatur	191
Jackson	1,531	Kadoka	808	Monroe	23,475	Madisonville	660
Jerauld	3,310	Wessington Spgs.	527	Montgomery	62,721	Clarksville	539
Jones	1,882	Murdo	973	Moore	3,568	Lynchburg	124
Kingsbury	7,657	De Smet	818	Morgan	13,619	Wartburg	539
Lake	11,456	Madison	567	Obion	29,936	Union City	556
Lawrence	17,453	Deadwood	800	Overton	14,866	Livingston	441
Lincoln	11,761	Canton	576	Perry	5,238	Linden	411
Lyman	4,060	Kennebec	1,683	Pickett	3,774	Byrdstown	158
McCook	7,246	Salem	575	Polk	11,669	Benton	434
McPherson	5,022	Leola	1,147	Putnam	35,487	Cookeville	405
Marshall	5,965	Britton	848	Rhea	17,202	Dayton	312
Meade	17,020	Sturgis	3,465	Roane	38,881	Kingston	350
Mellette	2,420	White River	1,306	Robertson	29,102	Springfield	476
Miner	4,454	Howard	570	Rutherford	59,428	Murfreesboro	612
Minnehaha	95,209	Sioux Falls	813	Scott	14,762	Huntsville	544
Moody	7,622	Flandreau	523	Sequatchie	6,331	Dunlap	273
Pennington	59,349	Rapid City	2,779	Sevier	28,241	Sevierville	597
Perkins	4,769	Bison	2,860	Shelby	722,111	Memphis	755
Potter	4,449	Gettysburg	869	Smith	12,509	Carthage	323
Roberts	11,678	Sisseton	1,108	Stewart	7,319	Dover	470
Sanborn	3,697	Woonsocket	570	Sullivan	127,329	Blountville	413
Shannon	8,198	(Attached to Fall River)	2,100	Sumner	56,284	Gallatin	534
				Tipton	28,001	Covington	459
Spink	10,595	Redfield	1,505	Trousdale	5,155	Hartsville	114
Stanley	2,457	Fort Pierce	1,414	Unicoi	15,254	Erwin	185
Sully	2,362	Onida	1,004	Union	9,072	Maynardville	212
Todd	6,606	(Attached to Tripp)	1,388	Van Buren	3,758	Spencer	254
Tripp	8,171	Winner	1,620	Warren	26,972	McMinnville	439
Turner	9,872	Parker	612	Washington	73,924	Jonesboro	323
Union	9,643	Elk Point	452	Wayne	12,365	Waynesboro	739
Walworth	7,842	Selby	718	Weakley	28,827	Dresden	576
Washabaugh	1,389	(Attached to Jackson)	1,061	White	16,355	Sparta	382
				Williamson	34,423	Franklin	593
Yankton	19,039	Yankton	519	Wilson	36,999	Lebanon	567
Zeibach	2,221	Dupree	1,981				

Tennessee

(95 counties, 41,328 sq. mi. land; pop., 3,924,164)

Texas

(254 counties, 262,134 sq. mi. land; pop., 11,196,730)

County	Pop. April 1, 1970	County Seats or Court House	Land Area Sq. Mi.	County	Pop. April 1, 1970	County Seats or Court House	Land Area Sq. Mi.
Anderson	60,300	Clinton	335	Anderson	27,789	Palestine	1,072
Bedford	25,039	Shelbyville	482	Andrews	10,372	Andrews	1,504
Benton	12,126	Camden	392	Angelina	49,349	Lufkin	738
Bledsoe	7,643	Pikeville	404	Aransas	8,902	Rockport	275
Blount	63,744	Maryville	575	Archer	5,759	Archer City	913
Bradley	50,686	Cleveland	334	Armstrong	1,895	Claude	907
Campbell	26,045	Jacksboro	451	Atascosa	18,696	Jourdantown	1,206
Cannon	8,467	Woodbury	271	Austin	13,831	Bellville	663
Carroll	25,741	Huntingdon	596	Bailey	8,487	Muleshoe	835
Carter	43,259	Elizabethton	348	Bandera	4,747	Bandera	763
Cheatham	13,199	Ashland City	305	Bastrop	17,297	Bastrop	890
Chester	9,927	Henderson	285	Baylor	5,221	Seymour	845
Claiborne	19,420	Tazewell	444	Bee	22,737	Beeville	842
Clay	6,624	Celina	233	Bell	124,483	Belton	1,047
Cocke	25,283	Newport	424	Bexar	830,460	San Antonio	1,246
Coffee	32,572	Manchester	434	Blanco	3,567	Johnson City	719
Crockett	14,402	Alamo	269	Borden	888	Gail	907
Cumberland	20,733	Crossville	678	Bosque	10,966	Meridian	990
Davidson	447,877	Nashville	508	Bowie	67,813	Boston	891
Decatur	9,457	Decaturville	337	Brazoria	108,312	Angleton	1,423
De Kalb	11,151	Smithville	278	Brazos	57,978	Bryan	586
Dickson	21,977	Charlotte	485	Brewster	7,780	Alpine	6,204
Dyer	30,427	Dyersburg	529	Briscoe	2,794	Silverton	874
Fayette	22,692	Somerville	704	Brooks	8,005	Falfurrias	904
Fentress	12,593	Jamestown	498	Brown	25,877	Brownwood	938
Franklin	27,289	Winchester	553	Burleson	9,999	Caldwell	670
Gibson	47,871	Trenton	607	Burnet	11,420	Burnet	996
Giles	22,138	Pulaski	619	Caldwell	21,178	Lockhart	544
Grainger	13,948	Rutledge	282	Calhoun	17,831	Port Lavaca	527
Greene	47,630	Greeneville	613	Callahan	8,205	Baird	856
Grundy	10,631	Altamont	358	Cameron	140,368	Brownsville	896
Hamblen	38,696	Morristown	155	Camp	8,005	Pittsburg	192
Hamilton	254,236	Chattanooga	550	Carson	6,358	Panhandle	900
Hancock	6,719	Sneedville	230	Cass	24,133	Linden	941

County	Pop. April 1, 1970	County Seats or Court House	Land Area Sq. Mi.	County	Pop. April 1, 1970	County Seats or Court House	Land Area Sq. Mi.
Castro	10,394	Dimmitt	880	Kimble	3,904	Junction	1,274
Chambers	12,187	Anahuac	616	King	464	Guthrie	944
Cherokee	32,008	Rusk	1,049	Kinney	2,006	Brackettville	1,393
Childress	6,605	Childress	699	Kleberg	33,166	Kingsville	851
Clay	8,079	Henrietta	1,102	Knox	5,972	Benjamin	851
Cochran	5,326	Morton	783	Lamar	36,062	Paris	894
Coke	3,087	Robert Lee	911	Lamb	17,770	Littlefield	1,022
Coleman	10,288	Coleman	1,280	Lampasas	9,323	Lampasas	726
Collin	66,920	McKinney	836	La Salle	5,014	Cotulla	1,500
Collingsworth	4,755	Wellington	894	Lavaca	17,903	Halletsville	975
Colorado	17,638	Columbus	949	Lee	8,048	Giddings	637
Comal	24,165	New Braunfels	567	Leon	8,738	Centerville	1,102
Comanche	11,898	Comanche	944	Liberty	33,014	Liberty	1,180
Concho	2,937	Paint Rock	1,004	Limestone	18,100	Groesbeck	931
Cooke	23,471	Gainesville	905	Lipscomb	3,486	Lipscomb	934
Coryell	35,311	Gatesville	1,043	Live Oak	6,697	George West	1,055
Cottle	3,204	Paducah	900	Llano	6,979	Llano	941
Crane	4,172	Crane	795	Loving	164	Mentone	648
Crockett	3,885	Ozona	2,794	Lubbock	179,295	Lubbock	893
Crosby	9,085	Crosbyton	911	Lynn	9,107	Tahoka	915
Culberson	3,429	Van Horn	3,851	McCulloch	8,571	Brady	1,066
Dallam	6,012	Dalhart	1,494	McLennan	147,553	Waco	1,000
Dallas	1,327,321	Dallas	859	McMullen	1,095	Tilden	1,159
Dawson	16,604	Lamesa	902	Madison	7,693	Madisonville	480
Deaf Smith	18,999	Hereford	1,510	Marion	8,517	Jefferson	380
Delta	4,927	Cooper	276	Martin	4,774	Stanton	911
Denton	75,633	Denton	911	Mason	3,356	Mason	935
Dewitt	18,660	Cuero	910	Matagorda	27,913	Bay City	1,157
Dickens	3,737	Dickens	931	Maverick	18,093	Eagle Pass	1,289
Dimmit	9,039	Carrizo Springs	1,344	Medina	20,249	Hondo	1,352
Donley	3,641	Clarendon	930	Menard	2,646	Menard	914
Duval	11,722	San Diego	1,814	Midland	65,433	Midland	900
Eastland	18,092	Eastland	952	Milam	20,028	Cameron	1,028
Ector	91,805	Odessa	907	Mills	4,212	Goldthwaite	734
Edwards	2,107	Rocksprings	2,076	Mitchell	9,073	Colorado City	920
Ellis	46,638	Waxahachie	940	Montague	15,326	Montague	932
El Paso	359,291	El Paso	1,057	Montgomery	49,479	Conroe	1,090
Erath	18,141	Stephenville	1,085	Moore	14,060	Dumas	909
Falls	17,300	Marlin	764	Morris	12,310	Daingerfield	260
Fannin	22,705	Bonham	905	Motley	2,178	Matador	980
Fayette	17,650	La Grange	934	Nacogdoches	36,362	Nacogdoches	902
Fisher	6,344	Roby	904	Navarro	31,150	Corsicana	1,070
Floyd	11,044	Floydada	993	Newton	11,657	Newton	949
Foard	2,211	Crowell	676	Nolan	16,220	Sweetwater	922
Fort Bend	52,314	Richmond	869	Nueces	237,544	Corpus Christi	841
Franklin	5,291	Mount Vernon	293	Ochiltree	9,704	Perryton	907
Freestone	11,116	Fairfield	865	Oldham	2,258	Vega	1,478
Frio	11,159	Pearsall	1,116	Orange	71,170	Orange	359
Gaines	11,593	Seminole	1,489	Palo Pinto	28,962	Palo Pinto	948
Galveston	169,812	Galveston	399	Panola	15,894	Carthage	869
Garza	5,289	Post	914	Parker	33,888	Weatherford	903
Gillespie	10,553	Fredericksburg	1,055	Parmer	10,509	Farwell	859
Glasscock	1,155	Garden City	863	Pecos	13,748	Fort Stockton	4,740
Goliad	4,869	Goliad	871	Polk	14,457	Livingston	1,100
Gonzales	16,375	Gonzales	1,056	Potter	90,511	Amarillo	898
Gray	26,949	Pampa	934	Presidio	4,842	Marfa	3,892
Grayson	83,225	Sherman	940	Rains	3,752	Emory	210
Gregg	75,929	Longview	282	Randall	53,885	Canyon	914
Grimes	11,855	Anderson	801	Reagan	3,239	Big Lake	1,132
Guadalupe	33,554	Seguin	714	Real	2,013	Leakey	622
Hale	34,137	Plainview	979	Red River	14,298	Clarksville	1,033
Hall	6,015	Memphis	885	Reeves	16,526	Pecos	2,608
Hamilton	7,198	Hamilton	844	Refugio	9,494	Refugio	774
Hansford	6,351	Spearman	907	Roberts	967	Miami	899
Hardeman	6,795	Quanah	687	Robertson	14,389	Franklin	877
Hardin	29,996	Kountze	897	Rockwall	7,046	Rockwall	147
Harris	1,741,912	Houston	1,723	Runnels	12,108	Ballinger	1,058
Harrison	44,841	Marshall	894	Rusk	34,102	Henderson	939
Hartley	2,782	Channing	1,488	Sabine	7,187	Hemphill	456
Haskell	8,512	Haskell	877	San Augustine	7,858	San Augustine	473
Hays	27,642	San Marcos	650	San Jacinto	6,702	Coldspring	624
Hemphill	3,084	Canadian	904	San Patricio	47,288	Sinton	685
Henderson	26,466	Athens	943	San Saba	5,540	San Saba	1,120
Hidalgo	181,535	Edinburg	1,543	Schleicher	2,277	Eldorado	1,331
Hill	22,596	Hillsboro	1,010	Scurry	15,760	Snyder	904
Hockley	20,396	Levelland	908	Shackelford	3,323	Albany	887
Hood	6,368	Granbury	426	Shelby	19,672	Center	778
Hopkins	20,710	Sulphur Springs	793	Sherman	3,657	Stratford	916
Houston	17,855	Crockett	1,237	Smith	97,096	Tyler	934
Howard	37,796	Big Spring	911	Somervell	2,793	Glen Rose	197
Hudspeth	2,392	Sierra Blanca	4,554	Starr	17,707	Rio Grande City	1,211
Hunt	47,948	Greenville	826	Stephens	8,414	Breckenridge	899
Hutchinson	24,443	Stinnett	875	Sterling	1,056	Sterling City	914
Irion	1,070	Mertzon	1,073	Stonewall	2,397	Aspermont	926
Jack	6,711	Jacksboro	945	Sutton	3,175	Sonora	1,493
Jackson	12,975	Edna	850	Swisher	10,373	Tulia	896
Jasper	24,692	Jasper	907	Tarrant	716,317	Fort Worth	861
Jeff Davis	1,527	Fort Davis	2,259	Taylor	97,853	Abilene	912
Jefferson	246,402	Beaumont	951	Terrell	1,940	Sanderson	2,391
Jim Hogg	4,654	Hebbronville	1,143	Terry	14,118	Brownfield	899
Jim Wells	33,032	Alice	845	Throckmorton	2,205	Throckmorton	920
Johnson	45,769	Cleburne	740	Titus	16,702	Mount Pleasant	418
Jones	16,106	Anson	956	Tom Green	71,047	San Angelo	1,500
Karnes	13,462	Karnes City	758	Travis	295,516	Austin	1,012
Kaufman	32,392	Kaufman	815	Trinity	7,628	Groveton	707
Kendall	6,964	Boerne	670	Tyler	12,417	Woodville	919
Kenedy	678	Sarita	1,394	Upshur	20,976	Gilmer	584
Kent	1,434	Jayton	880	Upton	4,697	Rankin	1,312
Kerr	19,454	Kerrville	1,101	Uvalde	17,348	Uvalde	1,588

County	Pop. April 1, 1970	County Seats or Court House	Land Area Sq. Mi.
Val Verde	27,471	Del Rio	3,241
Van Zandt	22,155	Canton	845
Victoria	53,766	Victoria	892
Walker	27,680	Huntsville	790
Waller	14,285	Hempstead	509
Ward	13,019	Monahans	827
Washington	18,842	Brenham	594
Webb	72,859	Laredo	3,306
Wharton	36,729	Wharton	1,076
Wheeler	6,434	Wheeler	914
Wichita	120,563	Wichita Falls	611
Wilbarger	15,355	Vernon	952
Willacy	15,570	Raymondville	591
Williamson	37,305	Georgetown	1,104
Wilson	13,041	Floresville	802
Winkler	9,640	Kermit	887
Wise	19,687	Decatur	922
Wood	18,589	Quitman	721
Yoakum	7,344	Plains	830
Young	15,400	Graham	888
Zapata	4,352	Zapata	957
Zavala	11,370	Crystal City	1,291

Utah

(29 counties, 82,096 sq. mi. land; pop., 1,059,273)

County	Pop. April 1, 1970	County Seats or Court House	Land Area Sq. Mi.
Beaver	3,800	Beaver	2,584
Box Elder	28,129	Brigham City	5,603
Cache	42,331	Logan	1,174
Carbon	15,647	Price	1,476
Daggett	666	Manila	682
Davis	99,028	Farmington	297
Duchesne	7,299	Duchesne	3,255
Emery	5,137	Castle Dale	4,439
Garfield	3,157	Panguitch	5,158
Grand	6,688	Moab	3,682
Iron	12,177	Parowan	3,300
Juab	4,574	Nephi	3,412
Kane	2,421	Kanab	3,904
Millard	6,988	Fillmore	6,793
Morgan	3,983	Morgan	603
Piute	1,164	Junction	754
Rich	1,615	Randolph	1,023
Salt Lake	458,607	Salt Lake City	764
San Juan	9,606	Monticello	7,707
Sanpete	10,976	Manti	1,597
Sevier	10,103	Richfield	1,929
Summit	5,879	Coalville	1,849
Tooele	21,545	Tooele	6,923
Uintah	12,684	Vernal	4,487
Utah	137,776	Provo	2,014
Wasatch	5,863	Heber City	1,191
Washington	13,669	Saint George	2,427
Wayne	1,483	Loa	2,486
Weber	126,278	Ogden	581

Vermont

(14 counties, 9,267 sq. mi. land; pop., 444,732)

County	Pop. April 1, 1970	County Seats or Court House	Land Area Sq. Mi.
Addison	24,266	Middlebury	784
Bennington	29,282	Bennington	672
Caledonia	22,789	Saint Johnsbury	612
Chittenden	99,131	Burlington	533
Essex	5,416	Guildhall	663
Franklin	31,282	Saint Albans	660
Grand Isle	3,574	North Hero	83
Lamoille	13,309	Hyde Park	474
Orange	17,676	Chelsea	690
Orleans	20,153	Newport	715
Rutland	52,637	Rutland	927
Washington	47,659	Montpelier	707
Windham	33,476	Newfane	784
Windsor	44,082	Woodstock	962

Virginia

(96 cos. 34 ind. cities, 39,780 sq. mi.; pop., 4,648,494)

County	Pop. April 1, 1970	County Seats or Court House	Land Area Sq. Mi.
Accomack	29,004	Accomac	476
Albemarle	37,780	Charlottesville	740
Alleghany	12,461	Covington	444
Amelia	7,592	Amelia, C. H.	366
Amherst	26,072	Amherst	470
Appomattox	9,784	Appomatox	345
Arlington	174,284	Arlington	26
Augusta	44,220	Staunton	986
Bath	5,192	Warm Springs	540
Bedford	26,728	Bedford	727
Bland	5,423	Bland	369
Botetourt	18,193	Fincastle	548
Brunswick	16,172	Lawrenceville	579
Buchanan	32,071	Grundy	508
Buckingham	10,597	Buckingham	582
Campbell	43,319	Rustburg	529
Caroline	13,925	Bowling Green	545
Carroll	23,092	Hillsville	494
Charles City	6,158	Charles City	181
Charlotte	12,366	Charlotte Court- House	470
Chesterfield	77,046	Chesterfield	442
Clarke	8,102	Berryville	174

County	Pop. April 1, 1970	County Seats or Court House	Land Area Sq. Mi.
Craig	3,524	New Castle	336
Culpeper	18,218	Culpeper	389
Cumberland	6,179	Cumberland	291
Dickenson	16,077	Clintwood	332
Dinwiddie	25,046	Dinwiddie	507
Essex	7,099	Tappahannock	250
Fairfax	455,901	Fairfax	399
Fauquier	26,375	Warrenton	660
Floyd	9,775	Floyd	383
Fluvanna	7,621	Palmyra	288
Franklin	28,163	Rocky Mount	716
Frederick	28,893	Winchester	405
Giles	16,741	Pearisburg	363
Gloucester	14,059	Gloucester	228
Goochland	10,069	Goochland	289
Grayson	15,439	Independence	452
Greene	5,248	Stanardsville	153
Greensville	9,604	Emporia	299
Halifax	30,076	Halifax	796
Hanover	37,479	Hanover	465
Henrico	154,364	Richmond	229
Henry	50,901	Martinsville	381
Highland	2,529	Monterey	416
Isle of Wight	18,285	Isle of Wight	317
James City	17,853	Williamsburg	152
King and Queen	5,491	King and Queen	318
King George	8,039	King George	176
King William	7,497	King William	278
Lancaster	9,126	Lancaster	137
Lee	20,321	Jonesville	438
Loudoun	37,150	Leesburg	517
Louisa	14,004	Louisa	517
Lunenberg	11,687	Lunenburg	442
Madison	8,638	Madison	327
Mathews	7,168	Mathews	89
Mecklenburg	29,426	Boydton	612
Middlesex	6,295	Saluda	130
Montgomery	47,157	Christiansburg	394
Nansemond	35,166	Suffolk	408
Nelson	11,702	Lovingston	471
New Kent	5,300	New Kent	210
Northampton	14,442	Eastville	220
Northumberland	9,239	Heathsville	190
Nottoway	14,260	Nottoway	308
Orange	13,792	Orange	355
Page	16,581	Luray	316
Patrick	15,282	Stuart	464
Pittsylvania	58,789	Chatham	1,001
Powhatan	7,696	Powhatan	269
Prince Edward	14,379	Farmville	357
Prince George	29,092	Prince George	276
Prince William	111,102	Manassas	347
Pulaski	29,564	Pulaski	328
Rappahannock	5,199	Washington	267
Richmond	6,504	Warsaw	190
Roanoke	67,339	Salem	262
Rockbridge	16,637	Lexington	601
Rockingham	47,890	Harrisonburg	865
Russell	24,533	Lebanon	483
Scott	24,376	Gate City	539
Shenandoah	22,852	Woodstock	507
Smyth	31,349	Marion	435
Southampton	18,582	Courtland	602
Spotsylvania	16,424	Spotsylvania	409
Stafford	24,587	Stafford	270
Surry	5,882	Surry	277
Sussex	11,464	Sussex	494
Tazewell	39,816	Tazewell	522
Warren	15,301	Front Royal	219
Washington	40,835	Abingdon	574
Westmoreland	12,142	Montross	229
Wise	35,947	Wise	412
Wythe	22,139	Wytheville	460
York	33,203	Yorktown	129

Independent Cities

City	Pop. April 1, 1970	Land Area Sq. Mi.
Alexandria	110,938	15
Bedford	6,011	7
Bristol	14,857	4
Buena Vista	6,425	3
Charlottesville	38,880	10
Chesapeake	89,580	341
Clifton Forge	5,501	4
Colonial Heights	15,097	8
Covington	10,060	4
Danville	46,391	17
Emporia	5,300	2
Fairfax	21,970	6
Falls Church	10,772	2
Franklin	6,880	4
Fredericksburg	14,450	6
Galax	6,278	7
Hampton	120,779	55
Harrisonburg	14,605	6
Hopewell	23,471	9
Lexington	7,597	3
Lynchburg	54,083	25
Martinsville	19,653	11
Newport News	138,177	69
Norfolk	307,951	53

County	Pop. April 1, 1970	County Seats or Court House	Land Area Sq. Mi.
Norton.........	4,172		4
Petersburg.......	36,103		8
Portsmouth......	110,963		29
Radford........	11,596		5
Richmond.......	249,430		60
Roanoke........	92,115		27
Salem.........	21,982		14
South Boston	6,889		5
Staunton.......	24,504		9
Suffolk........	9,858		2
Virginia Beach....	172,106		259
Waynesboro.....	16,707		7
Williamsburg.....	9,069		5
Winchester	14,643		3

Washington
(39 counties 66,570 sq. mi. land; pop., 3,409,169)

County	Pop.	County Seats	Land Area
Adams.........	12,014	Ritzville	1,894
Asotin.........	13,799	Asotin	633
Benton........	67,540	Prosser	1,722
Chelan........	41,355	Wenatchee.....	2,926
Clallam........	34,770	Port Angeles ...	1,753
Clark.........	128,454	Vancouver	627
Columbia.......	4,439	Dayton	860
Cowlitz........	68,616	Kelso	1,144
Douglas........	16,787	Waterville	1,839
Ferry.........	3,655	Republic......	2,202
Franklin........	25,816	Pasco........	1,260
Garfield........	2,911	Pomeroy	713
Grant.........	41,881	Ephrata	2,681
Grays Harbor....	59,553	Montesano	1,910
Island.........	27,011	Coupeville	212
Jefferson.......	10,661	Port Townsend .	1,805
King..........	1,156,633	Seattle	2,131
Kitsap........	101,732	Port Orchard ..	393
Kittitas........	25,039	Ellensburg	2,320
Klickitat........	12,138	Goldendale.....	1,908
Lewis.........	45,467	Chehalis......	2,449
Lincoln........	9,572	Davenport	2,306
Mason........	20,918	Shelton	962
Okanogan......	25,867	Okanogan	5,301
Pacific........	15,796	South Bend ...	908
Pend Oreille.....	6,025	Newport	1,402
Pierce........	412,344	Tacoma......	1,676
San Juan.......	3,856	Friday Harbor...	179
Skagit........	52,381	Mount Vernon .	1,735
Skamania......	5,845	Stevenson	1,672
Snohomish.....	265,236	Everett.......	2,098
Spokane.......	287,487	Spokane......	1,758
Stevens.......	17,405	Colville......	2,481
Thurston.......	76,894	Olympia	714
Wahkiakum.....	3,592	Cathlamet	261
Walla Walla.....	42,176	Walla Walla	1,267
Whatcom.......	81,983	Bellingham	2,126
Whitman.......	37,900	Colfax	2,166
Yakima........	144,971	Yakima	4,271

West Virginia
(55 counties, 24,070 sq. mi. land; pop., 1,744,237)

County	Pop.	County Seats	Land Area
Barbour........	14,030	Philippi.......	341
Berkeley.......	36,356	Martinsburg....	316
Boone.........	25,118	Madison......	501
Braxton........	12,666	Sutton.......	511
Brooke........	29,685	Wellsburg......	88
Cabell.........	106,918	Huntington	279
Calhoun........	7,046	Grantsville	281
Clay.........	9,330	Clay........	343
Doddridge......	6,389	West Union ...	319
Fayette........	49,332	Fayetteville.....	663
Gilmer........	7,782	Glenville	339
Grant.........	8,607	Petersburg	478
Greenbrier......	32,090	Lewisburg.....	1,026
Hampshire......	11,710	Romney	639
Hancock.......	39,749	New Cumberland	83
Hardy.........	8,855	Moorefield	585
Harrison.......	73,028	Clarksburg	418
Jackson........	20,903	Ripley.......	461
Jefferson.......	21,280	Charles Town ...	211
Kanawha.......	229,515	Charleston	907
Lewis.........	17,847	Weston	392
Lincoln........	18,912	Hamlin	438
Logan.........	46,269	Logan	456
McDowell......	50,666	Welch	533
Marion........	61,356	Fairmont	311
Marshall.......	37,598	Moundsville ..	304
Mason........	24,306	Point Pleasant..	433
Mercer........	63,206	Princeton	417
Mineral........	23,109	Keyser......	330
Mingo.........	32,780	Williamson ...	423
Monongalia.....	63,714	Morgantown...	365
Monroe........	11,272	Union........	473
Morgan........	8,547	Berkeley Springs	233
Nicholas.......	22,552	Summersville ..	642
Ohio.........	64,197	Wheeling	106
Pendleton......	7,031	Franklin	695
Pleasants......	7,274	St. Marys	129
Pocahontas.....	8,870	Marlinton	943

County	Pop.	County Seats	Land Area
Preston	25,455	Kingwood.....	645
Putnam	27,625	Winfield	348
Raleigh	70,080	Beckley	605
Randolph........	24,596	Elkins........	1,036
Ritchie.........	10,145	Harrisville....	452
Roane.........	14,111	Spencer	486
Summers.......	13,213	Hinton	350
Taylor.........	13,878	Grafton	174
Tucker........	7,447	Parsons	421
Tyler.........	9,929	Middlebourne ...	256
Upshur........	19,092	Buckhannon ...	352
Wayne.........	37,581	Wayne	513
Webster........	9,809	Webster Springs .	551
Wetzel........	20,314	New Martinsville	363
Wirt.........	4,154	Elizabeth	235
Wood.........	86,818	Parkersburg	368
Wyoming	30,095	Pineville	504

Wisconsin
(72 counties, 54,464 sq. mi. land; pop., 4,417,933)

County	Pop.	County Seats	Land Area
Adams........	9,234	Friendship	646
Ashland........	16,743	Ashland	1,038
Barron.........	33,955	Barron	864
Bayfield........	11,683	Washburn	1,460
Brown.........	158,244	Green Bay	524
Buffalo........	13,743	Alma	711
Burnett........	9,276	Grantsburg....	840
Calumet........	27,604	Chilton	322
Chippewa......	47,717	Chippewa Falls..	1,018
Clark.........	30,361	Neillsville	1,221
Columbia.......	40,150	Portage	778
Crawford.......	15,252	Prairie du Chien.	568
Dane.........	290,272	Madison......	1,198
Dodge........	69,004	Juneau.......	889
Door.........	20,106	Sturgeon Bay ...	492
Douglas........	44,657	Superior	1,305
Dunn.........	29,154	Menomonie ...	853
Eau Claire......	67,219	Eau Claire	647
Florence........	3,298	Florence......	487
Fond Du Lac	84,567	Fond du Lac ...	725
Forest........	7,691	Crandon......	1,007
Grant.........	48,398	Lancaster	1,147
Green.........	26,714	Monroe	585
Green Lake	16,878	Green Lake ...	354
Iowa.........	19,306	Dodgeville ...	762
Iron..........	6,533	Hurley.......	747
Jackson........	15,325	Black River Falls	999
Jefferson.......	60,060	Jefferson	564
Juneau........	18,455	Mauston.....	774
Kenosha	117,917	Kenosha......	272
Kewaunee......	18,961	Kewaunee	330
La Crosse......	80,468	La Crosse.....	451
Lafayette.......	17,456	Darlington	643
Langlade.......	19,220	Antigo	856
Lincoln........	23,499	Merrill	892
Manitowoc.....	82,294	Manitowoc ...	590
Marathon......	97,457	Wausau	1,586
Marinette......	35,810	Marinette	1,378
Marquette......	8,865	Montello	455
Menominee.....	2,607	Keshena	360
Milwaukee.....	1,054,249	Milwaukee ...	237
Monroe........	31,610	Sparta	915
Oconto........	25,553	Oconto	1,101
Oneida........	24,427	Rhinelander ...	1,112
Outagamie.....	119,356	Appleton	634
Ozaukee.......	54,461	Port Washington	236
Pepin.........	7,319	Durand.......	235
Pierce.........	26,652	Ellsworth	590
Polk..........	26,666	Balsam Lake ...	931
Portage........	47,541	Stevens Point....	806
Price.........	14,520	Phillips	1,260
Racine........	170,838	Racine.......	337
Richland.......	17,079	Richland Center .	583
Rock.........	131,970	Janesville	721
Rusk.........	14,238	Ladysmith	906
St. Croix.......	34,354	Hudson	734
Sauk.........	39,057	Baraboo	841
Sawyer........	9,670	Hayward.....	1,259
Shawano	32,650	Shawano	919
Sheboygan.....	96,660	Sheboygan	505
Taylor.........	16,958	Medford	975
Trempealeau	23,344	Whitehall	735
Vernon........	24,557	Viroqua......	802
Vilas.........	10,958	Eagle River....	867
Walworth.......	63,444	Elkhorn	557
Washburn......	10,601	Shell Lake	817
Washington.....	63,839	West Bend	429
Waukesha......	231,338	Waukesha	554
Waupaca.......	37,780	Waupaca	751
Waushara......	14,795	Wautoma	627
Winnebago.....	129,934	Oshkosh......	448
Wood.........	65,362	Wisconsin Rapids	807

Wyoming
(23 counties, 97,203 sq. mi. land; pop., 332,416)

County	Pop.	County Seats	Land Area
Albany	26,431	Laramie	4,248
Big Horn........	10,202	Basin	3,157

County	Pop. April 1, 1970	County Seats or Court House	Land Area Sq. Mi.	County	Pop. April 1, 1970	County Seats or Court House	Land Area Sq. Mi.
Campbell	12,957	Gillette	4,756	Niobrara	2,924	Lusk	2,614
Carbon	13,354	Rawlins	7,905	Park	17,752	Cody	6,959
Converse	5,938	Douglas	4,281	Platte	6,486	Wheatland	2,086
Crook	4,535	Sundance	2,882	Sheridan	17,852	Sheridan	2,532
Fremont	28,352	Lander	9,196	Sublette	3,755	Pinedale	4,851
Goshen	10,885	Torrington	2,228	Sweetwater	18,391	Green River	10,429
Hot Springs	4,952	Thermopolis	2,022	Teton	4,823	Jackson	4,000
Johnson	5,587	Buffalo	4,175	Uinta	7,100	Evanston	2,086
Laramie	56,360	Cheyenne	2,703	Washakie	7,569	Worland	2,262
Lincoln	8,640	Kemmerer	4,085	Weston	6,307	Newcastle	2,407
Natrona	51,264	Casper	5,342				

1970 Population of Outlying Areas

Source: Bureau of the Census

Puerto Rico

Zip Code	Municipios	Pop. April 1	Land Area Sq. Mile	Zip Code	Municipios	Pop. April 1	Land Area Sq. Mile	Zip Code	Municipios	Pop. April 1	Land Area Sq. Mile
00601	Adjuntas	18,691	66	00653	Guanica	14,889	37	00720	Orocovis	20,201	63
00602	Aguada	25,658	30	00654	Guayama	36,249	65	00723	Patillas	17,828	48
00603	Aguadilla	51,355	36	00656	Guayanilla	18,144	42	00724	Penuelas	15,793	44
00607	Aguas Buenas			00657	Guaynabo	67,042	27	00731	Ponce	158,981	116
		18,600	30	00658	Gurabo	18,289	28	00742	Quebradillas	15,582	23
00609	Aibonito	20,044	31	00659	Hatillo	21,913	42	00743	Rincon	9,094	14
00610	Anasco	19,416	40	00660	Hormigueros			00745	Rio Grande	22,032	61
00612	Arecibo	73,468	127			10,827	11	00747	Sabana Grande		
00615	Arroyo	13,033	15	00661	Humacao	36,023	45			16,343	37
00617	Barceloneta	20,792	34	00662	Isabela	30,430	56	00751	Salinas	21,837	69
00618	Barranquitas	20,118	33	00664	Jayuya	13,588	39	00753	San German	27,990	54
00619	Bayamon	156,192	44	00665	Juana Diaz	36,270	61	*00936	San Juan	463,242	47
00623	Cabo Rojo	26,060	72	00666	Juncos	21,814	26	00754	San Lorenzo	27,755	53
00625	Caguas	95,661	58	00667	Lajas	16,545	60	00755	San Sebastian		
00627	Camuy	19,922	46	00669	Lares	25,263	62			30,157	71
00630	Carolina	107,643	48	00670	Las Marias	7,841	44	00757	Santa Isabel	16,056	34
00632	Catano	26,459	5	00671	Las Piedras	18,112	33	00758	Toa Alta	18,964	27
00633	Cayey	38,432	50	00672	Loiza	39,062	53	00759	Toa Baja	46,384	24
00635	Ceiba	10,312	27	00673	Luquillo	10,390	26	00760	Trujillo Alto	30,669	21
00638	Ciales	15,595	66	00701	Manati	30,559	46	00761	Utuado	35,494	115
00639	Cidra	23,892	36	00706	Maricao	5,991	37	00762	Vega Alta	22,810	28
00640	Coamo	26,468	77	00707	Maunabo	10,792	21	00763	Vega Baja	35,327	47
00642	Comerio	18,819	28	00708	Mayaguez	85,857	77	00765	Vieques	7,767	52
00643	Corozal	24,545	42	00716	Moca	22,361	51	00766	Villalba	18,733	37
00645	Culebra	732	10	00717	Morovis	19,059	39	00767	Yabucoa	30,165	55
00646	Dorado	17,388	23	00718	Naguabo	17,996	52	00768	Yauco	30,103	68
00648	Fajardo	23,032	31	00719	Naranjito	19,913	28	**Total**		**2,712,033**	**3,421**

Zip Code	Area	Pop. Apr. 1	Land Area Sq. Mile	Zip Code	Area	Pop. Apr. 1	Land Area Sq. Mile	Zip Code	Area	Pop. Apr. 1	Land Area Sq. Mile
	American Samoa				Inarajan	1,897	19	00801	Charlotte Amalie		
96920	American Samoa				Mangilao	3,228	10			12,220	
		27,159	76		Merizo	1,529	6	00820	Christiansted	3,020	
					Mongmong-Toto-			00840	Frederiksted	1,531	
	Canal Zone				Maiti	6,057	2				
	Canal Zone	44,198	362		Piti	1,284	7		**Trust Territory of**		
	Balboa	32,552	222		Santa Rita	8,109	17		**Pacific Islands**		
	Cristobal	11,646	140		Sinajana	3,506	1				
					Talofofo	1,935	17		Mariana district		
					Tamuning	10,218	6			9,640	184
	Guam				Umatac	813	6		Marshall district		
96910	Guam	84,996	209		Yigo	11,542	35			22,888	70
	Agana	2,119	1		Yona	2,599	20		Palau district		
	Agana Hgts.	3,156	1							11,210	192
	Agat	4,308	10		**Virgin Islands**				Ponape district		
	Asan	2,629	6							18,536	176
	Barrigada	6,356	9		Total	62,468	132		Truk district	21,041	49
	Chalan-Pago-				St. Croix	31,779	80		Yap district	7,625	46
	Ordot	2,931	6	00830	St. John	1,729	20		**Total**	**90,940**	**717**
	Dedeo	10,780	30	00801	St. Thomas	28,960	32				

Area and Population of the World

Source: Statistical Office of the United Nations, June, 1972

Continent	Area[1] (km²)*	Midyear 1971 Estimated	Continent	Area[1] (km²)*	Midyear 1971 Estimated
Africa	30,320,109	354,000,000	Europe[4]	4,936,247	466,000,000
America North[2]	24,246,904	327,000,000	Oceania	8,510,946	19,800,000
America, South	17,833,331	195,000,000	USSR	22,402,200	245,000,000
Asia[3]	27,532,130	2,104,000,000	World	135,781,867	$3,706,000,000

*One square kilometer (km²) equals 0.386 sq. mi. (1.)Including inland waters, but not some uninhabited polar regions and islands. (2.)Hawaii, Central America and Caribbean Islands included in N. A. (3.)Excluding USSR but including all of Turkey. (4.)Excluding USSR and European part of Turkey. (5.)Total is not the sum of the parts because an adjustment was made to the total figure to take into consideration the excess of projected immigration over projected emigration.

ASTRONOMY AND CALENDAR

Edited by Dr. Kenneth L. Franklin, Astronomer
Chairman, American Museum-Hayden Planetarium

Celestial Events Highlights, 1974
(All times are Greenwich Mean Time)

This year has several interesting and beautiful events in the sky for those in the right place or up at the right hour. Four eclipses occur, two of the moon and two of the sun. Each object experiences both a partial and a total eclipse. The partial solar eclipse in December will be seen over most of the United States and Canada. The moon occults no bright stars in 1974, but occults Saturn 6 times, Mars 3 times, Venus twice, Mercury once, and even manages to find Juno and occult it. A telescope will help in observing the close approach of Mercury to Jupiter in March, but brilliant Venus and Jupiter will be very obvious in the morning sky of April 15. They will still be near when the crescent moon passes by 3 mornings later. A telescope again will be necessary for another close approach by Venus, this time to Saturn at the end of July. Jupiter again dominates the entire night sky, when in September it passes opposition. Venus fades from view by summer, Mars becomes too faint to see even by Spring, and Saturn does not begin to be conspicuous until October, leaving the middle of the year for Jupiter. Thus to see most of the celestial scenery, one must arise early in the morning early in the year.

January

Mercury is busy and it's soon at superior conjunction on the 9th, and becomes an evening object. It is 6° south of the 26-hour moon on the 24th, and just 0°9 south of Jupiter on the 28th. All this month, the planet will probably be much too close to the sun to be seen.

Venus is at its eastern stationary point on the first day of this month, then rapidly closes to inferior conjunction on the 23rd to become a morning star.

Mars is fading rapidly, losing nearly a magnitude this month. It will be found 3° south of the moon on the 3rd and 2° south on the 31st.

Jupiter nearing conjunction may be found at magnitude −1.5 about 5° south of the thin crescent moon the evening of Jan. 24/25.

Saturn is still in retrograde motion this month. On the 7th at 9 hours Greenwich time, it will be less than 1° south of the moon. Observers in NE Asia, the Arctic and the northern and eastern parts of North America may be able to see an occultation of Saturn. This is the first of 6 occultations of Saturn this year and is a very interesting sight in even a modest telescope. Note that this one occurs quite early in the morning hours of the 7th.

Moon occults Saturn on the 7th; First Quarter, Jan. 1 at 12:06; Full Moon Jan. 8, 12:06; Third Quarter, Jan. 15, 7:04; New Moon, Jan. 23, 11:02. Perigee, Jan. 8; apogee, Jan. 21.

Jan. 3, 4— Quadrantid meteor shower best seen after moon set.

Jan. 4— Earth at perihelion, 91,400,000 miles from the sun

Jan. 7— Early morning occultation of Saturn.

Jan. 19— Sun enters Capricornus.

February

Mercury is 18° east of the Sun, its greatest elongation this time, on the 9th; stationary on the 15th; and in inferior conjunction on the 24th when it becomes a morning star.

Venus is stationary in the morning sky on the 12th, 4° north of the waning crescent moon in the dawn sky, and at greatest brilliancy, −4.3 magnitude on the 27th.

Mars, appearing as a first magnitude reddish star in Taurus, will be occulted by the first quarter moon the evening of Feb. 28-Mar. 1 if seen from the north Pacific, northern part of North America or the North Atlantic. Mars is 131,000,000 miles away from the earth during this event.

Jupiter is in conjunction on the 13th.

Saturn is occulted by the moon on the 3rd, seen from northern Europe, northern Asia and the Arctic. It is

stationary at the end of its retrograde motion on the 27th.

Moon occults Saturn on the 3rd and Mars, for western observers, on the 28th in the evening. Full Moon, Feb. 6; Third Quarter, 14; New Moon, 22; First Light, near apogee, 18th.

Feb. 3— Occultation of Saturn by the moon.

Feb. 16— Sun enters Aquarius.

Feb. 28-Mar. 1— Occultation of Mars by the moon.

March

Mercury is 4° south of Jupiter, but only 14° west of the Sun and looks like a 2nd magnitude star. It is stationary on the 9th ending its retrograde motion. On the 21st at 16 hours, it is seen by telescope 0°1 south of Jupiter as a +0.5 magnitude star. On the 23rd it reaches its greatest western elongation, 28° west of the sun, now resembling a star of +0.5 magnitude.

Venus, still very brilliant in the morning sky, will be joined by the waning crescent moon on the 19th. At 22 hours, Greenwich time on the 19th, the moon will occult Venus, if seen from eastern Asia, the north Pacific and Alaska.

Mars, a little fainter than first magnitude, is 7° north of Aldebaran as the 18th begins in Greenwich. The nearly First Quarter moon will occult Mars on the 29th as seen from the Indian Ocean.

Jupiter is probably too close to the sun to be seen in the dawn twilight, but it is 6° south of the waning crescent moon on the 21st. One hour earlier, at 16 hours Greenwich time, it is 0°1 north of Mercury. A telescope will be necessary to see this conjunction.

Saturn is occulted on the 2nd and the 30th. On the 2nd, the occultation can be seen from northern North America, Europe, the North Atlantic and northern Africa. On the 30th, the event may be seen from southeast Asia and the northern Pacific.

Moon occults Saturn, Mars, and Venus. First Quarter, Mar. 1; Full Moon, 8th; Third Quarter 15th; New Moon, 23rd; First Quarter, 31st. Perigee, 6th; Apogee, 18th.

Mar. 14— Sun enters Pisces.

Mar. 21— 00:07 at Greenwich, the sun passes the equator on its northern journey. Spring begins. At 16 hours, Mercury and Jupiter will be 0°1 apart.

April

Mercury spends all month as a morning star overtaking the sun.

Venus is at greatest western elongation 46° from the sun on the 4th. Still about 46° west of the sun, on the 15th, it is 1°1 from Jupiter. Venus is −3.9 magnitude. Venus

6° south of the crescent moon on the 18th.

Mars is 2° north of Saturn on the 20th and 3° north of the waxing crescent moon on the 26th.

Jupiter may now be easily seen in the morning sky as a bright star, −1.7 in magnitude. It will be 1°.1 south of Venus on the 15th.

Saturn is again occulted by the moon, in the 15th hour of the 26th day, seen from the northeast of South America, the mid Atlantic, central Africa, and the Malagasy Republic. It is 2° south of Mars on the 20th.

Moon is a waning crescent 6° north of the brilliant pair formed by Juniter and Venus in the morning twilight of the 18th. On the 26th it occults Saturn. Full Moon, 6th; Third Quarter, 14th; New Moon, 22nd; First Quarter, 29th. Perigee, 2nd and 27th; Apogee, 14th.

April 15—at 2 hours, Venus and Jupiter are in conjunction, 1°.1 apart.

April 18—Jupiter and Venus, now 3° apart will be passed by the crescent moon, 4 days before New, 6° north of the planets, a good picture opportunity. Sun enters Aries.

May

Mercury is in superior conjunction on the 4th and becomes an evening star. It is 7° north of Aldebaran on the 17th, and 2° north of the crescent moon on the 23rd.

Venus, still brilliant in the morning twilight, is 7° south of the moon on the 18th.

Mars now appears to be a 2nd magnitude star and is lost to all but the real searchers. It is 4° north of the moon on the 25th.

Jupiter has moved far to the west of Venus but is still a bright morning object.

Saturn is occulted by the moon on the 24th, an event seen from Australasia and the South Pacific.

Moon occults Saturn on the 24th. Full Moon, 6th; Third Quarter, 14th; New Moon, 21st; First Quarter, 28th. Apogee, 12; Perigee, 24.

May 12—Sun moves into Taurus.

May 24—Occultation of Saturn.

June

Mercury is 2° North of Saturn on the 2nd, stationary on the 17th, and in inferior conjunction on the 30th.

Venus is a −3.4 magnitude star, 5° south of the crescent moon on the morning of the 17th.

Mars is undistinguished as a second magnitude star 6° north of the moon on June 22-23.

Jupiter is 7° south of the moon on the 12th.

Saturn is in conjunction on the 30th.

Moon has a busy month. It is eclipsed on the 4th, and eclipses the Sun on the 20th. Full Moon, 4th; Third Quarter, 13th; New Moon, 20th; First Quarter, 26th. Apogee, 9; Perigee, 21.

June 4—Partial eclipse of the moon.

June 20—Sun moves into Gemini and is totally eclipsed.

June 21—At 18:38, the sun is above the Tropic of Cancer; Summer begins.

June 29—Delta Aquarid meteor shower. Check morning hours on either side of this date as well. A maximum of about 20 per hour may be expected.

July

Mercury is stationary at the end of its retrograde motion on the 12th. It is at greatest western elongation (20°) on the 22nd, a good opportunity to look for it with binoculars in the dawn twilight. It is a relatively faint object of +0.5 magnitude. On the 24th, it is 1°.2 south of Saturn, Mercury being brighter.

Venus is 4° north of Aldebaran on the 4th. It is occulted on the 17th, if seen from Central America, the eastern part of North America, southern Greenland, North Atlantic, Europe, the northern part of North Africa and southwest Asia. On the 31st, it is 0°.2 north of Saturn, a telescopic encounter, at 9 hours Greenwich time.

Mars is effectively lost from view, although still a second magnitude star in the evening sky, and 0°.7 north of Regulus on the 26th.

Jupiter is 7° south of the moon the morning of the 10th.

Saturn is slowly moving into the dawn twilight. An interesting telescopic view may be obtained at 9 hours on the 31st when it is 0°.2 south of Venus. It is +0.3 magnitude, 3.6 magnitudes fainter than Venus—a challenge to photographers.

Moon occults Venus on the 17th. Full Moon, 4th; Third Quarter, 12th; New Moon, 19th; First Quarter, 26th. Apogee, 6; Perigee, 19.

July 5—Earth at aphelion, 95,300,000 miles from the sun.

July 17—Occultation of Venus.

July 20—Sun enters Cancer.

August

Mercury is in superior conjunction on the 17th and becomes an evening star.

Venus may still be seen in the bright morning twilight but is gradually becoming fainter.

Mars is now lost in the evening twilight.

Jupiter dominates the morning sky, passing 7° south of the moon on the 6th.

Saturn is 1°.8 north of the crescent moon the 15th, but possibly will not be seen in the morning twilight.

Moon occults the asteroid Juno on the 6th at 7, Greenwich time. Juno is about 8th magnitude, so a good telescope is required to see this rare event. Full Moon, 3rd; Third Quarter, 11th; New Moon, 17th; First Quarter, 24th. Apogee 3rd and 30th; Perigee 17th.

Aug. 9—Sun enters Leo.

Aug. 10-14—Perseid meteor shower peaks during this period at about 50 per hour. Third Quarter moon may interfere with the fainter meteors.

September

Mercury is 0°.1 south of Mars on the 2nd, and 0°.3 north of Spica on the 22nd. A telescope with setting circles is a must to see these two events.

Venus is lost in the glare of the morning twilight.

Mars is lost in the glare of evening twilight.

Jupiter is at opposition of the 5th, at −2.5 magnitude, only 370,000,000 miles away; it becomes an evening star.

Saturn is 2° north of the moon on the 11th.

Moon. Full Moon, 1st; Third Quarter, 9th; New Moon, 16th; First Quarter, 23rd. Perigee, 14th; Apogee, 26th.

Sept. 15—Sun enters Virgo.

Sept. 23—Sun crosses the equator into southern hemisphere at 9:59 GMT. Autumn begins.

October

Mercury is at greatest eastern elongation (26°) on the 1st, stationary on the 13th, occulted by the moon on the 16th and at inferior conjunction on the 25th. The occultation may be seen from the North Pacific, the southwestern part of North America, Central America and the northern part of South America.

Venus is lost in the morning twilight.

Mars is in conjunction on the 14th.

Jupiter is still in retrograde motion in the evening sky.

Saturn is 3° north of the moon on the 9th, and stationary on the 31st, beginning its retrograde motion.

Moon occults Mercury on the 16th. Full Moon, 1st and 31st; Third Quarter, 8th; New Moon, 15th; First Quarter, 23rd. Perigee, 12th; Apogee, 24th.

Oct. 16—Mercury occulted.

Oct. 21—Orionid meteor shower peaks at 25 per hour. Moon sets before midnight, allowing a dark sky.

Oct. 29—Sun enters Libra.

November

Mercury is stationary on the 3rd, at greatest western elongation (19°) on the 10th, and 1°.1 north of faint Mars on the 24th.

Venus is in superior conjunction on the 6th.

Mars is lost in the glare of morning twilight, but might be found by telescope 1°.1 south of bright Mercury on the 24th.

Jupiter is stationary on the 3rd, ending its retrograde motion.

Saturn in retrograde is 3° north of the moon on the 5th.

Moon is in eclipse on the 29th. Last Quarter, 7th; New Moon, 14th; First Quarter, 21st; Full Moon, 29th. Perigee, 8th; apogee, 21st.

Nov. 22 — Sun enters Scorpius.

Nov. 29 — Sun enters Ophiuchus. Total eclipse of the moon.

December

Mercury is in superior conjunction on the 19th.

Venus is lost in the evening twilight.

Mars is lost in the morning twilight, but is occulted by the moon in an event observable from Antarctica.

Jupiter is prominent in the evening sky and passes 7° south of the moon on the 20th.

Saturn is 3° north of the moon on the 2nd and the 29th.

Moon partially eclipses the sun on the 13th after occulting Mars on the 12th. Last Quarter, 6th; New Moon, 13th; First Quarter, 21st; Full Moon, 29th. Perigee, 3rd & 31st; apogee, 19th.

Dec. 12 — Occultation of Mars.

Dec. 13 — Partial eclipse of Sun.

Dec. 14 — Geminid meteor shower peaks at 50 per hour. No moon to interfere with faint streaks among the fast occasionally bright meteors.

Dec. 18 — Sun enters Sagittarius.

Dec. 22 — At 05:57 GMT, the sun is over the Tropic of Capricorn. Winter begins.

Four Eclipses in 1974

Greenwich Mean Time

First Eclipse

A partial eclipse of the moon, June 4-5. The moon will pass through the southern part of the earth's shadow, the latter obscuring 83% of the moon's diameter at maximum eclipse. The beginning of the umbral phase, when the moon begins to enter the darkest part of the earth's shadow, will be visible in Australia, except the extreme eastern part; in Asia, except for the northern part; in the Indian Ocean, Africa, Europe, except the northern part; the eastern coast of South America, the South Atlantic Ocean, and Antarctica. The end of the umbral phase will be visible in Europe, except the northern part; the southwestern part of Asia, the Indian Ocean, Africa, the Atlantic Ocean, South America and Antarctica.

Circumstances of the Eclipse

Moon enters penumbra	June 4, 19:25
Moon enters umbra	20:40
Mid-eclipse (83%)	22:18
Moon leaves umbra	23:55
Moon leaves penumbra	June 5, 01:10

Second Eclipse

A total eclipse of the sun, June 20. Partial phases begin at dawn for the island of Madagascar, may be seen in Sumatra and most of the East Indies, all of Australia and Tasmania, and end at sunset at the extreme southeastern part of New Zealand. The path of totality is almost entirely in the Indian Ocean, only the extreme southeastern tip of Australia extending about one-third the way into the shadow toward the center line. This region will not experience the greatest duration of totality of approximately 5 minutes which will occur on the center line about 15 minutes earlier in the Indian Ocean.

Circumstances of the Eclipse

Eclipse begins	2:34
Central eclipse begins	3:50
Central eclipse at local apparent noon	4:56
Central eclipse ends	5:47
Eclipse ends	7:03

Third Eclipse

Total eclipse of the moon, Nov. 29. The center of the moon will pass somewhat north of the center of the earth's shadow, the northern edge of the shadow being about 30% of the moon's diameter farther north than the moon's northern limb. The beginning of the umbral phase is visible in the Arctic regions, the northwestern half of North America, the Pacific Ocean, except the southeastern part; Asia, except the extreme southwestern part; the northeastern part of Europe, the eastern part of the Indian Ocean, Australia and New Zealand. The end of the umbral phase will be visible in the Arctic, the extreme northwestern part of North America, the western part of the Pacific Ocean, Asia, Australia, Europe, except the extreme southwestern part; the northeastern part of Africa and the Indian Ocean.

Circumstances of the Eclipse

Moon enters penumbra	12:27
Moon enters umbra	13:30
Total eclipse begins	14:37
Mid-eclipse	15:15
Total eclipse ends	15:53
Moon leaves umbra	17:00
Moon leaves penumbra	18:03

Fourth Eclipse

Partial eclipse of the sun, Dec. 13. This eclipse will be seen in part over most of the United States, eastern Canada, the Central American and Caribbean area to the extreme northern part South America, and Portugal. The line connecting the center of the sun and the center of the moon misses the earth, passing above the Arctic. The greatest eclipse, 83% of the sun's diameter covered, will be seen with the sun due south on the horizon at west longitude 69°34' and north latitude 60°46'.

Circumstances of the Eclipse

Eclipse begins	14:04
Greatest eclipse	16:14
Eclipse ends	18:23

Morning and Evening Stars of 1974

MORNING

Mercury — Jan. 1-Jan. 9; Feb. 24-May 4; June 30-Aug. 17; Oct. 25-Dec. 19.

Venus — Jan. 23-Nov. 6.

Mars — Oct. 14-Dec. 31.

Jupiter — Feb. 13-Sept. 5.

Saturn — June 30-Dec. 31.

EVENING

Mercury — Jan. 9-Feb. 24; May 4-June 30; Aug. 17-Oct. 25; Dec. 19-Dec. 31.

Venus — Jan. 1-Jan. 23; Nov. 6-Dec. 31.

Mars — Jan. 1-Oct. 14.

Jupiter — Jan. 1-Feb. 13; Sept. 5-Dec. 31.

Saturn — Jan. 1-June 30.

Planets and the Sun

The planets of the solar system, in order of their distance from the sun are Mercury, Venus, Earth, Mars, Jupiter, Saturn, Uranus, Neptune and Pluto. Uranus, Neptune and Pluto are not included in the celestial list because they are too faint to be seen without optical aid. Both Uranus and Neptune are visible through good field glasses, but Pluto is so distant and so small that only large telescopes or long exposure photographs can make it visible.

Since Mercury and Venus are nearer to the sun than is the earth, their motions about the sun are seen from the earth as wide swings first to one side of the sun and then to the other, although they are both passing continuously around the sun in orbits that are almost circular. When their passage takes them either between the earth and the sun, or beyond the sun as seen from the earth, they are invisible to us. Because of the laws which govern the motions of planets about the sun, both Mercury and Venus require much less time to pass between the earth and the sun than around the far side of the sun, so their periods of invisibility are unequal.

The planets that lie farther from the sun than does the earth may be seen for longer periods of time and are invisible only when they are so located in our sky that they rise and set about the same time as the sun when, of course, they are overwhelmed by the sun's great brilliance. None of the planets has any light or exterior heat of of its own but each shines only by reflecting sunlight from its surface. Mercury and Venus, because they are between the earth and the sun, show phases very much as the moon does. The planets farther from the sun are always seen as full, although Mars does occasionally present a slightly gibbous phase—like the moon when not quite full.

The planets move rapidly among the stars because they are very much nearer to us than the stars are. The stars are also in motion, some of them at tremendous speeds, but they are so far away that their motion does not change their apparent positions in the heavens sufficiently for anyone to perceive that change in a single lifetime. The very nearest star is about 7,000 times as far away as the most distant planet.

Visible Planets of the Solar System

Mercury, Venus, Mars, Jupiter and Saturn

Mercury

Mercury, nearest planet to the sun, is also the smallest of the nine planets known to be orbiting the sun. Its diameter is 3,100 miles and its mean distance from the sun is 36,000,000 miles.

Mercury moves with great speed in its journey about the sun, averaging about 30 miles a second to complete its circuit of the sun in 88 of our days. Radar observations of Mercury by the 1,000-foot radio telescope at Arecibo, Puerto Rico, disclosed that Mercury rotates upon its axis over a period of nearly 59 days, thus exposing all of its surface periodically to the sun. For nearly 100 years, astronomy had accepted a rotational period for Mercury of 88 earth-days, synchronous with its period of revolution. A synchronous rotation-revolution period would have caused the same side of Mercury to face the sun continually and would have produced a temperature of between 750° and 1,000° on the sun-facing surface, while the perpetually dark side would have had a temperature of about –450° Fahrenheit.

Now, while it is believed that the surface passing before the sun may have a temperature of about 800° F., the temperature on the side turned temporarily away from the sun does not fall as low as might be expected. This night temperature has been described by Russian astronomers as "room temperature"–possibly about 70°. This would contradict the former belief that Mercury did not possess an atmosphere, for some sort of atmosphere would be needed to retain some of the fierce solar radiation that must strike Mercury at its small distance from the sun. A shallow but dense layer of carbon dioxide would produce the "greenhouse" effect in which heat accumulated during exposure to the sun, would not completely escape at night. The actual presence of a carbon dioxide atmosphere is in dispute.

This uncertainty about conditions upon Mercury and its motion arise from its short angular distance from the sun as seen from the earth, for Mercury is always too much in line with the sun to be observed against a dark sky, but is always seen during either morning or evening twilight.

Venus

Venus is slightly smaller than the earth. Its diameter is about 200 miles less than the earth's diameter. Venus moves about the sun at a mean distance of 67,000,000

miles in 225 of our days. Its synodical revolution–its return to the same relationship with the earth and the sun, which is a result of the combination of its own motion and that of the earth–is 584 days. Venus will, then, be nearer to the earth every 19 months than any of the other planets of the solar system. We have never been able to see the surface of Venus because the planet is covered with a dense, white cloudy atmosphere that conceals whatever is below it. This same cloud reflects sunlight efficiently so that when Venus is favorably situated, it is the third brightest object in the sky, exceeded only by the sun and the moon.

Ordinary telescopic observation has been unable to reveal much about the nature of the surface of Venus, nor even its period of axial rotation. Spectroscopic analysis of light reflected from the clouds indicates only carbon dioxide present above the cloud bank. Infrared spectroscopy from a balloon-borne telescope nearly 20 miles above the earth's surface gave indications of a small amount of water vapor present in the same region of the atmosphere of Venus. In 1956, however, a breakthrough in our knowledge came from radio astronomers at the Naval Research Laboratories in Wash., D. C. Their observations indicated a temperature for Venus of about 600 degrees Fahrenheit, in marked contrast to minus 125 degrees Fahrenheit, previously found at the cloud tops. Subsequent radio work confirmed a high temperature and produced evidence for this temperature to be associated with the solid body of Venus. With this peculiarity in mind, space scientists devised experiments for the U. S. space probe Mariner II to perform when it flew by in 1962. Mariner II confirmed the high temperature and the fact that it pertained to the ground rather than to some special activity of the atmosphere. In addition, Mariner II was unable to detect any radiation belts similar to the earth's so-called Van Allen belts. Nor was it able to detect the existence of a magnetic field even as weak as 1/100,000 of that of the earth, but it passed about 22,000 miles from the sunward surface.

An international scientific drama occurred in 1966 when a Russian space probe, Venus 4, and the American Mariner V arrived at Venus within a few hours of each other. Venus 4 was unique in that it was designed to allow an instrument package to land gently on the planet's surface via parachute. It ceased transmission of information after 75 minutes when the temperature it read went above 500 degrees Fahrenheit. After considerable controversy, it was agreed several years later that it still had 20 miles to go to reach the surface. In 1969, two more Russian probes dived into Venus' atmosphere, but ended reports after about ¾ hour. The Russians claimed these did make it to the surface and confirmed earlier findings of the Mariner probes. The U. S. probe, Mariner V, went around the dark side of Venus at a distance of about 6,000 miles. Again, it detected no significant magnetic field, but its radio signals passed to earth through Venus' atmosphere twice—once on the night side and once on the day side. The results are startling. Venus' atmosphere is nearly all carbon dioxide and must exert a pressure at the planet's surface of up to 100 times the earth's normal sea-level pressure of one atmosphere. Since the earth and Venus are about the same size, and were presumably formed at the same time by the same general process from the same mixture of chemical elements, one is faced with the question: which is the planet with the unusual history—earth or Venus?

But the apparent strangeness of Venus continues to enlarge. In the last several years, astronomers using radar techniques involving powerful transmitters as well as sensitive receivers and computers have suceeded in determining the rotation period of Venus. It turns out to be 243 days clockwise—in other words, contrary to the spin of most of the other planets and to its own motion around the sun. If it were exactly 243.16 days, Venus would always present the same face toward the earth at every inferior conjunction. This rate and sense of rotation allows a "day" on Venus of 117.4 earth days. Any part of Venus will receive sunlight on its clouds for over 58 days and will be in darkness for 58 days. The atmosphere here must be in sufficient motion to distribute much of the daytime heat to the night side, for little difference in temperature is detected between the two hemispheres. The mysteries of Venus have only been intensified by the knowledge we have recently gained about it.

Mars

Mars is the first planet beyond the earth, away from the sun. Mars's diameter is about 4,200 miles, although a determination of the radius and mass of Mars by the space-probe, Mariner IV, which flew by Mars on July 14, 1965 at a distance of less than 6,000 miles, indicated that these dimensions were slightly larger than had been previously estimated. While Mars's orbit is also nearly circular, it is not as nearly centered on the sun as are the orbits of many of the other planets, and Mars is more than 30 million miles farther from the sun in some parts of its year than it is at others. Mars takes 687 of our days to make one circuit of the sun, traveling at about 15 miles a second. Mars rotates upon its axis in almost the same period of time that the earth does—24 hours and 37 minutes. Mars's mean distance from the sun is 141 million miles, so that the temperature on Mars would be lower than that on the earth even if Mars's atmosphere were about the same as ours. The atmosphere is not, however, for Mariner IV reported that atmospheric pressure on Mars is between 1% and 2% of the earth's atmospheric pressure. This thin atmosphere appears to be largely carbon dioxide. No evidence of free water was found.

There appears to be no magnetic field about Mars. This would eliminate the previous conception of a dangerous radiation belt around Mars similar to the Van Allen Belt around the earth. The same lack of a magnetic field would expose the surface of Mars to an influx of cosmic radiation about 100 times as intense as that on earth.

Deductions from years of telescopic observation indicate that ⅗ths of the surface of Mars is a desert of reddish rock, sand and soil. The rest of Mars is covered by irregular patches that appear generally green in hues that change through the Martian year. These were formerly held to be some sort of primitive vegetation, but with the findings of Mariner IV of a complete lack of water and oxygen, such growth does not appear possible. The nature of the green areas is now unknown. They may be regions covered with volcanic salts whose color changes with changing temperatures and atmospheric conditions, or they may be gray, rather than green. Optical experiments show that when large gray areas are placed beside large

red areas, the gray areas will appear green to the eye.

Mars is inclined from a vertical to the plane of its orbit about the sun by about 25° and therefore has seasons as does the earth, except that the Martian seasons are longer because Mars's year is longer. White caps form about the winter pole of Mars, growing through the winter and shrinking in summer. These polar caps were thought to be frozen water which when it melted, nourished the green areas. In view of the negative findings of Mariner IV, however, the caps are thought to be carbon dioxide.

The canals of Mars have become more of a mystery than they were before the voyage of Mariner IV. Markings forming a network of fine lines crossing much of the surface of Mars have been seen there by men who have devoted much of their professional time to the study of the planet, but no canals have shown clearly enough upon previous photographs to be universally accepted. A few of the 21 photographs sent back to earth by Mariner IV covered areas crossed by canals. The pictures show faint, ill-defined, broad, dark markings, but no positive identification of the nature of the markings.

Mariners VI & VII in 1969 sent back many more photographs of higher quality than those of the pioneering Mariner IV. These pictures showed cratering similar to the earlier views, but in addition showed two other types of terrain. Some regions seemed featureless for many square miles, but others were chaotic, showing high relief without apparent organization into mountain chains or craters.

Mariner IX, the first artificial body to be placed in an orbit about Mars, has transmitted over 10,000 photographs covering 100% of the planet's surface. Preliminary study of these photos and other data shows that Mars resembles no other planet we know. Using terrestrial terms, however, scientists describe features that seem to be clearly of volcanic origin. One of these features is Nix Olympica, apparently a caldera over 300 miles in diameter. Some features may have been produced by cracking (faulting) of the surface and the sliding of one region over or past another. Many craters seem to have been produced by impacting bodies such as may have come from the nearby asteroid belt. Features near the south pole may have been produced by glaciers that are no longer present. Flowing water, non-existent on Mars at the present time, probably carved canyons, one 10 times longer and 3 times deeper than the Grand Canyon.

Mars's position in its orbit and its speed around that orbit in relation to the earth's position and speed bring Mars fairly close to the earth on occasions about two years apart and then move Mars and the earth too far apart for accurate observation and photography. Every 15-17 years, the close approaches are especially favorable for an all-out astronomical attack on Mars.

Mars has two satellites. They are small, estimated to be about 5 and 10 miles in diameter if their surfaces have properties similar to that of our moon. They were discovered in 1877 by Asaph Hall. The outer satellite is named Deimos and it revolves around Mars in about 31 hours. The inner satellite, Phobos, whips around Mars in a little more than 7 hours, making three trips around the planet each Martian day.

The Mariner flights of 1969 produced a photograph accidentally taken showing Phobos silhouetted against the planet. An analysis of the image gives dimensions of Phobos as about 14 miles by 8 miles, proportions resembling those of a potato. The ability of Phobos to reflect light appears to be even less than that of the earth's moon. Mariner IX has confirmed these results and added information that Phobos and Deimos are pitted with large craters and are of irregular shape, suggesting a history of fragmentation.

Jupiter

Jupiter is the largest of the planets. Its equatorial diameter is 88,000 miles, 11 times the diameter of the earth. Its polar diameter is about 6,000 miles shorter. This is caused by the almost fluid condition of its atmosphere and its extremely rapid rate of rotation. Jupiter's day is just under 10 hours long. For a planet of this size, this rotational speed is amazing, and it carries a point on Jupiter's equator along at a speed of 22,000 miles an hour, as compared with 1,000 miles an hour for a point on the earth's equator. Jupiter is at an average distance of 480 million miles from the sun and takes almost 12 of our years to make one complete circuit of the sun.

The only directly observable chemical constituents of Jupiter's atmosphere are methane (CH_4) and ammonia (NH_3), but it is reasonable to assume the same mixture of elements available to make Jupiter as to make the sun. This would mean a large fraction of hydrogen and helium must be present also, as well as water, H_2O. The temperature at the tops of the clouds may be about minus 260 degrees Fahrenheit. The clouds are probably ammonia ice crystals, becoming ammonia droplets lower down. There may be a space before water ice crystals show up as clouds; in turn, these become water droplets near the bottom of the entire cloud layer. The total atmosphere may be only a few hundred miles in depth, pulled down by the surface gravity (= 2.64 times earth's) to a relatively thin layer. Of course, the gases become denser with depth until they may turn into a slush or a slurry. Perhaps there is no solid surface–no real interface between solid and gas, but its temperature may approach 1,000 degrees Fahrenheit. Long before the center is reached hydrogen and helium–with the other elements regarded as impurities–become a fluid metal and perhaps a solid metal near the center. Jupiter's cloudy atmosphere is a fairly good reflector of sunlight and makes it far brighter than any of the stars among which it wanders. An extremely heavy radioactive belt has also been discovered surrounding Jupiter, similar to the earth's Van Allen Belt. This belt was discovered by radio astronomers following the identification of Jupiter as a source of radio emission by B.F. Burke and K.L. Franklin in 1955.

Jupiter has 12 satellites. Four of these are large and bright, rivaling our own moon and the planet Mercury in diameter, and may be seen through a field glass. They move rapidly around Jupiter and their change of position from night to night is extremely interesting to watch. The eight additional satellites are much smaller and, in all but one instance, much farther from Jupiter, and cannot be seen except through powerful telescopes. The 4 outermost satellites are revolving around Jupiter clockwise as seen from the north, contrary to the motions of the great majority of the satellites in the solar system and to the direction of revolution of the planets around the sun. The reason for this retrograde motion is not known, but one theory is that Jupiter's tremendous gravitational power may have captured 4 of the minor planets or asteroids, that move about the sun between Mars and Jupiter, and that these 4 may be running backwards. Jupiter's mass is more than twice the mass of all the other planets put together, and accounts for Jupiter's tremendous gravitational field and so, probably, for its numerous satellites and its dense atmosphere.

On March 2, 1972, the Pioneer 10 spacecraft was launched on a 21-month trip to Jupiter. Designed to take pictures of the planet and to measure its atmosphere, Pioneer 10 will make a 4-day swing around Jupiter and radio back the information collected before hurtling on into outer space. Some 50 years later, Pioneer 10 will become the first man-made object to leave our solar system. If the spacecraft is intercepted by intelligent beings in the far reaches of the universe millennia from now, they will find in it a 6 x 9 in. metal plaque etched with schematic drawings of a man and a woman and a code utilizing the radio properties of pulsars to indicate the location of Planet Earth. On April 5, Pioneer 11 was launched on a similar mission.

Saturn

Saturn, last of the planets visible to the unaided eye, is almost twice as far from the sun as Jupiter, almost 900 million miles. It is second in size to Jupiter but its mass is much smaller. Saturn's specific gravity is less than that of water. Its diameter is about 71,000 miles at the equator; its rotational speed spins it completely around in a little more than 10 hours, and its atmosphere is much like that of Jupiter, except that its temperature at the top of its cloud layer is at least 100° colder. At about 300° F. below zero, the ammonia would be frozen out of Saturn's clouds. The theoretical construction of Saturn resembles that of Jupiter; it is either all gas, or it has a small dense center surrounded by a layer of ice and a deep atmosphere.

Saturn has ten satellites, the 10th having been discovered by the French astronomer Audouin Dollfus in December, 1966. The newly found satellite is a few thousand miles outside of the edge of Saturn's ring system. Its discovery was made possible by an edge-on presentation of the rings. At such times, the rings virtually disappear to observers on earth. This aspect of the rings reduces their brilliance and permitted the hitherto unknown satellite to be seen.

Saturn's ring system begins about 7,000 miles above the visible disk of Saturn, lying above its equator and extending about 35,000 miles into space. The diameter of the ring system, including Saturn itself, is about 170,000 miles; the rings are estimated to be no thicker than 10 miles. In 1973, radar observation showed the ring particles to be large chunks of material averaging a meter on a side.

The rings cannot be seen except in a telescope of at least 3-inch aperture. Because of Saturn's inclination, as stated above, there are two periods during Saturn's journey around the sun when the rings are presented to us edge-on. At these times, the rings disappear. Nothing that is only 10 miles wide can be seen from a distance of nearly 900 million miles. The rings are approaching a favorable position to be seen. They were edge-on in 1966 and reached maximum visibility again in 1973.

Astronomical Signs and Symbols

☉ The Sun	⊕ The Earth.	♅ Uranus.	▫ Quadrature.
☾ The Moon.	♂ Mars	♆ Neptune.	☍ Opposition.
☿ Mercury.	♃ Jupiter.	♇ Pluto.	☊ Ascending Node.
♀ Venus.	♄ Saturn.	☌ Conjunction.	☋ Descending Node.

Two heavenly bodies are in "conjunction" (☌) when they are due north and south of each other, either in Right Ascension (with respect to the north celestial pole) or in Celestial Longitude (with respect to the north ecliptic pole). If the bodies are seen near each other, they will rise and set at nearly the same time. They are in "opposition" (☍) when their Right Ascensions differ by exactly 12 hours, or their Celestial Longitudes differ by 180°. One of the two objects in opposition will rise while the other is setting. "Quadrature" (▫) refers to the arrangement when the coordinates of two bodies differ by exactly 90°. These terms may refer to the relative positions of any two bodies as seen from the earth, but one of the bodies is so frequently the sun that mention of the sun is omitted; otherwise, both bodies are named. The geocentric angular separation between sun and object is termed "elongation". Elongation is limited only for Mercury and Venus; the "greatest elongation" for each of these bodies is noted in the appropriate tables and is approximately the time for longest observation. When a planet is in its "ascending" (☊) or "descending" (☋) node, it is passing northward or southward, respectively, through the plane of the earth's orbit, across the celestial circle called the ecliptic. The term "perihelion" means nearest to the sun, and "aphelion", farthest from the sun. An "occultation" of a planet or star is an eclipse of it by some other body, usually the moon.

Planetary Configurations, 1974

Greenwich Mean Time

(0 designates midnight; 12 designates noon)

Mo.	d.	h.	m.		
Jan.	1	16	–		♀ stationary
	3	13	–	☌ ♂ ☽	♂ 3° S
	4	10	–		⊕ at perihelion
	9	08	–	☌ ☿ ⊙	superior
	23	21	–	☌ ♀ ⊙	inferior
	24	13	–	☌ ☿ ☽	☿ 6° S
	25	00	–	☌ ♃ ☽	♃ 5° S
	28	01	–	☌ ☿ ♃	☿ 0°.9 S
	31	17	–	☌ ♂ ☽	♂ 2° S
Feb.	3	16	–	☌ ♄ ☽	♄ 0°.9 S
	9	08	–		☿ gr. elong. E (18°)
	12	23	–		♀ stationary
	13	16	–	☌ ♃ ⊙	
	15	05	–		☿ stationary
	19	03	–	☌ ♀ ☽	♀ 4° N
	24	21	–	☌ ☿ ⊙	inferior
	27	12	–		♀ gr. brilliancy
	27	22	–		♄ stationary
Mar.	1	01	–	☌ ♂ ☽	♂ 0°.5 S
	2	16	–	☌ ☿ ♃	☿ 4° N
	2	23	–	☌ ♄ ☽	♄ 0°.6 S
	9	03	–		☿ stationary
	19	22	–	☌ ♀ ☽	0°.9 S
	21	00	07		⊙ enters ♈ spring begins
	21	16	–	☌ ☿ ♃	☿ 0°.1 S
	21	17	–	☌ ♃ ☽	♃ 6° S
	21	17	–	☌ ☿ ☽	☿ 6° S
	23	20	–		☿ gr. elong. W (28°)
	29	10	–	☌ ♂ ☽	♂ 1°.1 N
	30	06	–	☌ ♄ ☽	♄ 0°.2 S
Apr.	4	04	–		♀ gr. elong. W (46°)
	15	02	–	☌ ♀ ♃	♀ 1°.1 N
	18	13	–	☌ ♃ ☽	♃ 6° S
	18	19	–	☌ ♀ ☽	♀ 6° S
	20	14	–	☌ ♂ ♄	♂ 2° N
	26	15	–	☌ ♄ ☽	♄ 0°.2 N
	26	21	–	☌ ♂ ☽	♂ 3° N
May	4	17	–	☌ ☿ ⊙	superior
	16	07	–	☌ ♃ ☽	♃ 7° S
	18	19	–	☌ ♀ ☽	♀ 7° S
	23	07	–	☌ ☿ ☽	☿ 2° N
	24	04	–	☌ ♄ ☽	♄ 0°.7 N
	25	10	–	☌ ♂ ☽	♂ 4° N
June	2	04	–	☌ ☿ ♄	☿ 2° N
	4	07	–		☿ gr. elong. E (24°)
	4	22	–		☽ partial eclipse
	12	22	–	☌ ♃ ☽	♃ 7° S
	17	14	–		☿ stationary
	17	15	–	☌ ♀ ☽	♀ 5° S
	20	05	–		⊙ total eclipse
	21	18	38		⊙ enters ♋ summer begins
	23	00	–	☌ ♂ ☽	♂ 6° N
	30	12	–	☌ ♄ ⊙	
	30	20	–	☌ ☿ ⊙	inferior
July	5	02	–		⊕ at aphelion
	8	08	–		♃ stationary
	10	07	–	☌ ♃ ☽	♃ 7° S
	12	01	–		☿ stationary
	17	11	–	☌ ♀ ☽	♀ 0°.4 S
	18	04	–	☌ ☿ ☽	☿ 2° S
	18	11	–	☌ ♄ ☽	♄ 1°.4 N
	21	15	–	☌ ♂ ☽	♂ 6° N
	22	09	–		☿ gr. elong. W (20°)
	24	16	–	☌ ☿ ♄	☿ 1°.2 S
	31	09	–	☌ ♀ ♄	♀ 0°.2 N
Aug.	6	10	–	☌ ♃ ☽	♃ 7° S
	15	03	–	☌ ♄ ☽	♄ 1°.8 N
	16	09	–	☌ ♀ ☽	♀ 4° N
	17	10	–	☌ ☿ ⊙	superior
	19	06	–	☌ ♂ ☽	♂ 7° N
Sept.	2	01	–	☌ ☿ ♂	☿ 0°.1 S
	2	09	–	☌ ♃ ☽	♃ 7° S
	5	20	–	☍ ♃ ⊙	
	11	16	–	☌ ♄ ☽	♄ 2° N
	17	21	–	☌ ☿ ☽	☿ 3° N
	23	09	59		⊙ enters ♎ autumn begins
	29	09	–	☌ ♃ ☽	♃ 7° S
Oct.	1	10	–		☿ gr. elong. E (26°)
	9	02	–	☌ ♄ ☽	♄ 3° N
	13	23	–		☿ stationary
	14	13	–	☌ ♂ ⊙	
	16	19	–	☌ ☿ ☽	☿ 0°.4 S
	25	13	–	☌ ☿ ⊙	inferior
	26	13	–	☌ ♃ ☽	♃ 7° S
	31	16	–		♄ stationary
Nov.	3	03	–		☿ stationary
	3	22	–		♃ stationary
	5	08	–	☌ ♄ ☽	♄ 3° N
	6	13	–	☌ ♀ ⊙	superior
	10	12	–		☿ gr. elong. W (19°)
	12	17	–	☌ ☿ ☽	☿ 6° N
	22	23	–	☌ ♃ ☽	♃ 7° S
	24	21	–	☌ ☿ ♂	☿ 1°.1 N
	29	15	–		☽ total eclipse
Dec.	2	13	–	☌ ♄ ☽	♄ 3° N
	12	02	–	☌ ♂ ☽	♂ 0°.9 N
	13	16	–		⊙ partial eclipse
	19	20	–	☌ ☿ ⊙	superior
	20	13	–	☌ ♃ ☽	♃ 7° S
	22	05	57		⊙ enters ♑ winter begins
	29	19	–	☌ ♄ ☽	♄ 3° N

Planetary Configurations, 1975

As a service to those who wish to consult the planetary configurations for early 1975 in the preceding fall, the WORLD ALMANAC publishes the configurations for January, February, March and April, 1975.

M.	d.	h.	m		
Jan.	2	–	–		⊕ at perihelion
	6	09	–	☍ ♄ ⊙	
	23	20	–		☿ gr. elong. E (19°)
	29	21	–		☿ stationary
Feb.	8	09	–	☌ ☿ ⊙	inferior
	17	19	–	☌ ♀ ♃	♀ 0°.2 S
	20	08	–		☿ stationary
Mar.	6	06	–		☿ gr. elong. W (27°)
	14	06	–		♄ stationary
	21	05	57		⊙ enters ♈ spring begins
	22	02	–	☌ ♃ ⊙	
Apr.	6	20	–	☌ ☿ ♃	☿ 1°.0 S
	18	21	–	☌ ☿ ⊙	superior

Moon's Perigee and Apogee, 1974

Greenwich Mean Time in 24 hour clock (0 is midnight; 12 is noon).

Perigee 1974								Apogee 1974							
		Hour				Hour				Hour				Hour	
Day		GMT	EST	Day		GMT	EST	Day		GMT	EST	Day		GMT	EST
Jan.	8	11	6 a.m.	July	19	22	5 p.m.	Dec.	25	22	5 p.m.**	July	6	21	4 p.m.
Feb.	6	00	7 p.m.*	Aug.	17	07	2 a.m.	Jan.	21	22	5 p.m.	Aug.	3	01	8 p.m.*
Mar.	6	06	1 a.m.	Sept.	14	16	11 a.m.	Feb.	18	08	3 a.m.	Aug.	30	05	12 Mid.
Apr.	2	16	11 a.m.	Oct.	12	16	11 a.m.	Mar.	18	02	9 p.m.*	Sept.	26	17	12 noon
Apr.	27	16	11 a.m.	Nov.	8	04	11 p.m.*	Apr.	14	22	5 p.m.	Oct.	24	11	6 a.m.
May	24	13	8 a.m.	Dec.	3	07	2 a.m.	May	12	17	12 noon	Nov.	21	08	3 a.m.
June	21	14	9 a.m.	Dec.	31	00	7 p.m.*	June	9	21	5 a.m.	Dec.	19	04	11 p.m.*

*Previous date
**1973

Largest Telescopes are in Northern Hemisphere

Most of the world's major astronomical installations are in the northern hemisphere, while many of astronomy's major problems are found in the southern sky. This imbalance has long been recognized and is being remedied at this time. For several years, large telescopes have been under construction in South America and Australia. Many of these will soon be in use.

In the northern hemisphere the very large reflectors include 3 in California: at Palomar Mtn., 200 inches; at Lick Observatory, Mt. Hamilton, 120 inches; and at Mt. Wilson Observatory, 100 inches. Also in the U.S. are a 158 inch reflector at Kitt Peak, Arizona, dedicated in June 1973, and a 107 inch telescope at the McDonald Observatory on Mt. Locke in Texas. A telescope at the Crimean Astrophysical observatory in the Soviet Union has a 104-inch mirror, and the USSR is building one with a mirror 236 inches in diameter which will be placed in operation soon.

At present the largest telescopes in the southern hemisphere are 74-inch reflectors in Pretoria, South Africa, and Mt. Stromlo, Australia. But the U. S. is erecting a 150-inch reflector at Cerro Tololo, in Chile. A 140-inch mirror at La Silla Mountain in Chile will be administered by the European Observatory Group. And Australia is building a telescope with a 150-inch aperture at Siding Spring.

Tremendous advances in the study of the central region of the Milky Way and of the Magellanic Clouds, as well as more detailed studies of many other regions hitherto unavailable to giant telescopes, will be made through the use of these new instruments.

Optical Telescopes

Optical astronomical telescopes are of two kinds, refracting and reflecting. In the first, light passes through a lens which brings the light rays to a focus, where the image may be examined after being magnified by a second lens, the eye-piece, or directly photographed.

The reflector consists of a concave parabolic mirror, generally of Pyrex or now of a relatively heat insensitive material, cervit, coated with silver or aluminum, which reflects the light rays back toward the upper end of the telescope, where they are either magnified and observed by the eye-piece or, as in the case of the refractors, photographed. In most reflecting telescopes, the light is reflected again by a secondary mirror and comes to a focus after passing through a hole in the side of the telescope, where the eye-piece or camera is located, or after passing through a hole in center of the primary mirror.

World's Largest Refractors

Location and diameter in inches.

Yerkes Obs., Williams Bay, Wisc	40
Lick Obs., Mt. Hamilton, Calif	36
Astrophys, Obs., Potsdam, E. Germany	32
Paris Observatory, Meuden, France	32
Allegheny Obs., Pittsburgh, Pa	30
Univ. of Paris, Nice, France	30
Royal Greenwich Obs., Herstmonceux, England	30
Union Obs., Johannesburg, South Africa	26.5
Universitats-Sternwarte, Vienna, Austria	26.5
University of Virginia	26
Obs., Academy of Sciences Pulkova, USSR	26
Astronomical Obs., Belgrade, Yugoslavia	26
Leander McCormick Obs., Charlottesville, Va	26
Obs. Mitaka, Tokyo-to, Japan	26

US Naval Obs., Washington, D. C	26
Mt. Stromlo Obs., Canberra, Australia	26

The Schmidt Telescopes are strictly cameras and cannot be used for visual observation. Light enters the upper end of the telescope tube, is refracted slightly by a correcting lens and is then reflected from a spherical mirror with a short focus. A camera, placed inside the telescope at the focus of the mirror can photograph large areas of the sky without distortion at the edges of the photograph. The diameters of Schmidt telescopes are given in two figures; first, the diameter of the correcting lens, followed by the diameter of the mirror.

The lists are partial lists including refractors from 26 inches and reflectors of 40-inches aperture or larger.

World's Largest Reflectors

Hale Obs., Palomar Mtn., Calif.	200
Kitt Peak National Obs., Tucson, Ariz.	158
Lick Obs., Mt. Hamilton, Calif.	120
McDonald Obs., Fort Davis, Texas	107
Crimean Astrophys. Obs., Nauchny, USSR	104
Hale Obs., Mount Wilson, Calif.	100
Royal Greenwich Obs., Herstmonceux, England	98
Mauna Kea Obs., Univ. of Hawaii, Hawaii	88
Kitt Peak National Obs., Tucson, Ariz	84
McDonald Obs., Fort Davis, Texas.	82
Saint Michel l'Observatoire, (Basses Alpes), Fr.	77
Tokyo Obs., Japan.	74
David Dunlap Obs., Ontario, Canada	74
Helwan Obs., Helwan, Egypt	74
Astrophys. Obs., Kamogata, Okayama-ken, Japan	74
Radcliffe Obs., Pretoria, South Africa	74
Dominion Astrophys. Obs., Victoria, B. C.	73
Perkins Obs., Flagstaff, Ariz.	72
Agassiz Station Harvard Obs., Cambridge, Mass	61
National Obs., Bosque Alegre Sta. Argentina	61
Arizona Univ. Obs., Tucson, Ariz	60
Boyden Obs., Bloemfontein, South Africa	60
Mt. Wilson Obs., Pasadena, Calif	60
Observatorium der Deutschen Tautenberg, Germany	(Schmidt)54-80
Mt. Stromlo Obs., Canberra, Australia	50
Observatorio Astronomica, Merate, Como, Italy	50
Sternberg Astronomical Inst., Crimea, USSR	50
Berlin-Babelsberg, Obs., Germany	49
Obs. Padua Univ., Asiago, Italy	48
Melbourne, Australia	48
Astrophy. Obs., Nauchny, Crimea, USSR	48
Dominion Astrophys. Obs., Victoria, B. C.	48
Saint Michel l'Observatoire, (Basses Alpes), Fr.	48
Nizamiah Obs., Osmania Univ., Hyderabad, India	48
Palomar Obs., Mt. Palomar, Calif.	(Schmidt)48-72
Paris Obs., St. Michel, France	47
Uccle Obs., Belgium	(Schmidt)33-46
Lowell Obs., Flagstaff, Ariz	42
Hamburg-Bergedorf Sterwarte, Germany	40
Kvistaberg Obs., Uppsala U., Sweden	(Schmidt)40-54
Observatoire Geneva, Switzerland	40
Observatorio Merate, Como, Italy	40
Royal Obs., Cape of Good Hope, S. Africa	40
Stockholm Obs., Saltsjobaden, Sweden	40
US Naval Obs., Flagstaff, Ariz	40
Pulkovo Obs., Russia	40
Mt. Stromlo, Canberra, Australia	40

Major Planetariums in the United States

A planetarium projector is perhaps the most complicated instructional device ever made. The first modern planetarium projector was designed and built in 1923 by Walter Bauersfeld of the Zeiss Optical Company. Other instruments had been attempted with only fair success before this time and modern projectors have developed from this beginning. There are now several manufacturers who make elaborate planetarium projectors frequently employing computers and industrial electronic circuitry.

A typical projector for a large auditorium can project the images of nearly 9,000 stars against the reflective surface of a hemispherical dome. In addition, the Milky

Way, star clusters, nebulae and other objects sufficiently bright to be seen under ideal conditions by the unaided eye are shown.

Planetarium projectors are usually in the form of two globes, one at either end of a latticed cylinder. The globes contain projectors for the stars, one for the northern hemisphere and the other for the south. In the latticed cylinder are projectors for the sun, the moon and the five planets visible to the eye. The motions of all of these objects are duplicated by the projector with amazing fidelity. First of all, the projector can be set in latitude so that it will produce the sky as it might be seen from any location on earth. The daily motion of the earth, which appears to move the sky throughout the day and night, is the most obvious effect produced. Then there is annual motion, the progress of the sun, moon and planets through the year, including the phasing of the moon. Finally, the precession of the equinoxes, the slow swing of the poles of the earth which is accomplished in 25,800 years and which slowly changes our view of the sky, is also built into the mechanism of these instruments.

The effects of the projector itself are usually supplemented by auxiliary projectors mounted around the edges of the auditorium to produce the color effects of sunrise and sunset, the aurora, clouds, rainbows, eclipses and many other phenomena. Most of the functions of the projector are controlled by the lecturer, who produces them from an array of switches and rheostats mounted in a control console usually situated near the north side of the auditorium.

There are literally hundreds of small planetarium projectors in schools and museums in the United States and several planetariums whose auditoriums will seat hundreds. Some of the major planetariums in the United States are listed below:

Academy Planetarium, U. S. Air Force Academy.
Adler Planetarium, Chicago, Ill.
American Museum-Hayden Planetarium, N. Y. C.
Buhl Planetarium, Pittsburgh, Pa.
Charles Hayden Planetarium, Boston, Mass.
Fels Planetarium, Philadelphia, Pa.
Fernback Science Center Planetarium, Atlanta, Ga.
Griffith Planetarium, Los Angeles, Calif.
La. Arts and Science Planetarium, Baton Rouge, La.
McDonnell Planetarium, St. Louis, Mo.
Morehead Planetarium, Chapel Hill, N. C.
Morrison Planetarium, San Francisco, Calif.
Robert T. Longway Planetarium, Flint, Mich.
Strasenburgh Planetarium, Rochester, N. Y.

Midnight To Dawn Best Time to See Meteors

In the earth's journey around the sun, the side from midnight to noon is the "front" of the earth. The hours from midnight to dawn are best for observing most meteors and meteor showers, for the earth is "running into" the meteoroids. It is common to see 5 to 10 meteors every morning hour. These sporadic meteors are unpredictable, appear in any part of the sky, and move in any direction. A meteor shower involves some organization. Many showers may exhibit 50 or more meteors each hour, but some events of weak showers may be hours apart. Shower meteors are distinguished by noting where the streak of light has come from. After three or more meteors have been traced back to a common point on the sky, one may suspect them of being part of a stream of meteoroids in space. The common point is called the radiant and is geometrically related to the vanishing point in perspective.

About a dozen meteor showers occur each year and the dates on which they take place may be found in the Calendar of Celestial Events. These showers are caused by the earth's passage through streams of meteoroids left in space by comets, of which they were a part. The meteoroids orbit the sun along the path originally followed by the comet and are encountered annually by the earth as it moves about the sun.

Canadian and American researchers have found evidence that the earth has been subjected to heavy bombardment from space on several occasions from 34,000,000 to 700,000 years ago.

The oldest of these catastrophes covered the eastern half of North America, the Atlantic Ocean and the northern half of Africa. Scars in the form of circular pits, sometimes a score of yards in diameter and often filled with water, have been located in northern Quebec, and fragments of metallic, stony and glassy objects define the area.

Central Europe received a fall of similar objects about 15,000,000 years ago and the most recent fall, about 700,000 years ago, struck the region including Australia and southeastern Asia.

The stony-metallic fragments are thought to originate in the asteroid belt, a region in space roughly between Mars and Jupiter in which travel thousands of minor planets ranging in size from 480 miles in diameter down to flying mountains a few miles across. Collisions among asteroids are believed to provide fragments, some of which may reach the earth. The glassy fragments, called tektites, were thought to be material resulting from collisions of large objects with the earth or the moon, scattered originally in liquid form and cooling in flight after initial impact into drop-shaped, glassy particles. Rocks recovered from the moon in the Apollo program show such a difference in chemical composition from tektites that most investigators feel that tektites did not come from the moon.

Meteorites

Meteoroids are celestial bodies, possibly associated with comets, that move through space with velocities up to 40 miles per second. Upon reaching the earth's atmosphere, they are vaporized by the heat of the friction of their passage into the atmosphere and are seen as meteors. An unusual number in a short period of time is called a meteor shower. Meteors are popularly known as falling stars or shooting stars. While most of them are consumed, a few fall to earth as fused metal or stone, and are called meteorites.

Many meteorites have been picked up in the United States, most of them small. A huge meteorite may lie embedded in the earth at Meteor Crater on U. S. 6 near Canyon Diablo in Arizona. The crater is 1 mi. in diameter at the surface and over 500 feet deep, and is surrounded by a wall of earth filled with pyrites presumably originating with the meteor. A lake in the Ungava region of northern Quebec fills the Chubb Crater, discovered 1943, which is 7½ mi. around. Vast destruction of timber was caused by a meteorite that hit in the vicinity of Lake Baikal, in Siberia, June 30, 1908. A large meteor that split into fragments of 80 to 820 pounds fell Feb. 17, 1930, 14 mi. sw of Paragould, Ark.

On display in the American Museum-Hayden Planetarium, New York, N. Y. are three meteorites: a 34 ton 85 pound iron-nickel meteorite and another 3-ton one brought from Cape York, Greenland, by Robert E. Peary in 1907 and a 14½ ton meteorite found in the Willamette region of Oregon in 1902.

Right Ascension of Mean Sun, 1974

0ʰ Greenwich Mean Time

Date	h m	Date	h m	Date	h m	Date	h m	Date	h m	Date	h m
Jan. 1	18:41.2	Mar. 2	22:37.7	May 1	2:34.3	July 10	7:10.0	Sept. 8	11:06.8	Nov. 7	15:03.2
11	19:20.4	12	23:17.2	11	3:13.7	20	7:49.5	18	11:46.3	17	15:42.6
21	19:59.8	22	23:56.6	21	3:53.0	30	8:29.0	28	12:25.7	27	16:21.9
31	20:39.2	Apr. 1	0:36.0	31	4:32.4	Aug. 9	9:08.5	Oct. 8	13:05.1	Dec. 7	17:01.3
Feb. 10	21:18.7	11	1:15.5	June 10	5:11.8	19	9:47.9	18	13:44.5	17	17:40.7
20	22:58.3	21	1:54.8	20	5:51.2	29	10:27.4	28	14:34.8	27	18:20.1
				30	6:30.7						

The Edge of the Universe?

For years people have been wondering if the universe had an edge, and if so, where it was. In 1973, observations of some of the most distant objects yet known, a few quasars, seemed to indicate that there was an edge and that the edge had been found. But this is a matter of interpretation, thus subject to considerable discussion and perhaps revision, before anyone is certain.

The term "edge" implies a brink—some discontinuity in the "here"—and a "beyond." Without observational evidence, a boundary such as an edge to the universe has had to be a theoretical concept. Most people would think that an edge would put a limit on the size of the universe, that the universe would be finite and bounded. This idea has been argued against, the argument going something like this: If the universe is finite, it must have a certain volume and thus a certain mass; but then, if we find the boundary, what can there be beyond the boundary if everything is on this side of it? Such an imponderable query is the direct result of experience with boundaries and "beyonds" and is implicit in the plane geometry of Euclid.

"Unbounded" Mind Boggling

So strong is the quandary about a "beyond" that some people have rejected "finite and bounded" in favor of "infinite and unbounded." This is another mind-boggler because it would permit no limit anywhere. Everything must become infinite: Volume, mass, time and energy, cycling and recycling.

A third possibility helps us out of the problems with these two dilemmas. Perhaps the universe is finite but unbounded. A little reflection here, however, shows a new problem. How can everything be limited if there are no limits anywhere? An answer is possible. We are used to living in a rectangular world, where Euclid's plane geometry applies very well. We are used to up-down, left-right, back-forth, and time. (We seldom think of time because we can't do anything with it, but it is a dimension of our world too.)

Unbounded but Finite

In our rectangular world, however, we can find something very familiar that is finite, yet has no boundary. This is the surface of the earth. The surface of the earth has a fixed, finite area, yet it has no boundary. The surface is strictly two dimensional, the curvature not counting because it's in the third dimension and is not part of the surface. In order for us to handle surveying problems, we must add complications to our plane geometry questions. These complications in the laws of surveying take account of this curvature of our surface.

In the universe we must conceive of a curvature

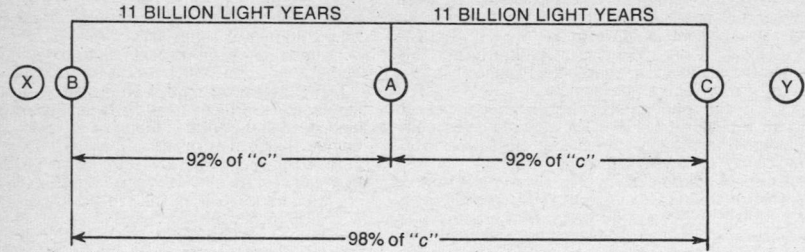

Two "edges" of the universe, as seen from galaxy A

One "edge" of the universe, as seen from galaxy C

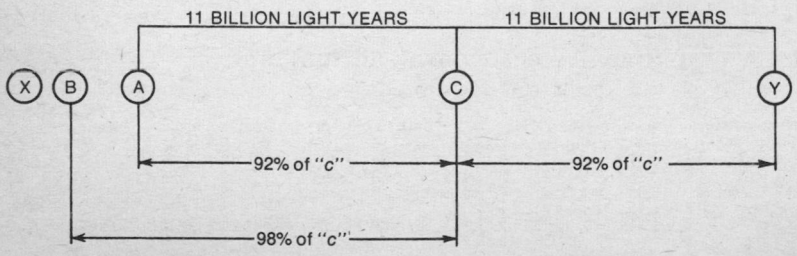

of our three dimensions—not just the two of our surface. This is very difficult to imagine, but the effects of this curvature will show up in the laws dealing with the geometry of space and affect our "surveying laws" of the universe. In this way we can conceive of a finite but unbounded universe. (A fourth possible concept—infinite but bounded—seems very difficult at this time.)

For over fifty years we have been aware that a certain class of astronomical object seemed to be moving away from us. Today, we know that these objects are galaxies and the farther away they are, the faster they seem to be moving away. This is usually described as the expanding universe, although it is possible to argue with the term. Actually, galaxies seem to be dispersing into the universe; the universe—a domain in which physical laws can operate—just seems to be waiting there for the galaxies to arrive.

The Red Shift

Their recessional velocity is observed by a technique known as spectroscopy. Light is emitted from atoms at certain well defined, narrow wave lengths or frequencies. These emissions have been measured in our laboratories. There is no reason to suppose that physical laws vary from place to place in the universe, and if we have determined them properly, we should be able to apply them everywhere. In the laboratory, we find that if a source of light or sound is moving toward the observer, the frequency is increased and the waves appear shorter. Moving away, the frequency is decreased and the waves appear longer. Higher frequency in sound is interpreted as higher pitch, while lower frequency is lower pitch. Long light waves are red and short ones are blue, so a shift toward longer light waves is called a red shift.

All galaxies show a red shift relative to our own galaxy, hence all galaxies must be moving away from us. If it is correct to interpret this red shift as an actual velocity (and there are some vague doubts), then the more distant galaxies, showing greater red shifts, are moving away faster than the nearer ones. Over forty years ago, Edwin Hubble found the relation between the distance and velocity of galaxies to be linear, that is: Twice the distance, twice the speed.

. Big Bang

This observation and this so-called law of the expanding universe has been turned around to answer the question: When was it all together? At the present time, the data seems to say it was all together about 12 billion years ago. The implication is that, at that time, some gigantic explosion propelled all matter outward from a central core. Our world today is the result of this "Big Bang," as the theory is named familiarly. In the original mass, all was in its very primitive state, an assemblage of nuclear particles. Very quickly, hydrogen and helium were formed. As the material cooled off and began to coalesce, stars were formed, then galaxies, and finally clusters of galaxies. The rest of the chemical elements were formed inside stars in processes that have become known in the last decade or two. Some stars have already lived out their lives and returned much of their material, now rich in heavy elements, to the clouds of interstellar dust from which new stars, like the sun, are formed.

Universal Speed Limit

In the early 1960's, radio astronomers called attention to small but bright sources of radio waves. Optical astronomers were first puzzled by their properties, but finally realized that the star-like images were much different from stars. They were called quasi-stellar radio sources, now shortened to quasars. The puzzle was solved when their strange spectra were interpreted as being affected by very great red shifts. As red shifts were observed to be greater and greater, implying greater and greater velocities, it became necessary to make corrections imposed by the theory of relativity. With this correction, it is possible for the red shift to increase without end, but the deduced velocity never quite reaches the velocity of light. This can be written algebraically as

$$\frac{v^2}{c^2} = \frac{(Z^2 - 1)}{(Z^2 + 1)}$$

where v is the velocity and Z is the red shift. Notice that Z can increase to any value, but the numerator is always smaller than the denominator, thus the fraction can never equal 1 and v can never equal c, the velocity of light. The fraction is often expressed as a percent of the velocity of light.

Quasars at the Edge

Recent observations of the red shift give a velocity of about 92% for 2 or 3 quasars. If the expansion law is still linear at this speed—and no one really knows—these quasars are about 11 billion light years away. They are faint, but not near the threshold of observation. Fainter ones could be seen if they exist and could be located. Fainter quasars might be farther away. If nothing is found beyond these recently detected objects, they might lie at the "edge" of our universe.

This interpretation must be interpreted even more, because there are problems in this view. Consider an observer on one of the distant quasars looking back at us. He will see us receding from him at 92% of c. If he looks beyond our galaxy to the "edge" we can see from here, will he not see objects going away from him at nearly twice the speed of light? No, because we must add the values of Z. That distant observer (C) looking beyond our galaxy (A) to another (B), which seems to us to be moving at 92% of c, will only see it moving at nearly 98% of c. This must be his interpretation, in spite of our belief that we are half way between A and B and each is 11 billion light years away from us. Thus galaxies at great distances would seem to be bunched up, and the appearance of an "edge" may only be a result of this curious visual compaction. (See diagrams.)

Beginning of Time

But perhaps we are not looking toward the distant edge, because in looking a distance of 11 billion light years, we are also looking backward in time, getting a view of the universe as it was 11 billion years ago when that light began its journey to our observatories. Perhaps, since we can see nothing beyond these particular quasars, we may be looking into the murk of the first billion years, into the time before anything as "primitive" as these brilliant bursts called quasars had time to form.

It makes one wonder.

The Sun

The sun, the controlling body of our solar system, is a star whose dimensions cause it to be classified among stars as average in size, temperature and brightness. Its proximity to the earth makes it appear to us as tremendously large and bright. A series of thermo-nuclear reactions involving the atoms of the elements of which it is composed produces the heat and light that make life possible on the earth.

The sun has a diameter of 864,000 miles and is distant, on the average, 92,900,000 miles from the earth. It is 1.41 times as dense as water. The light of the sun reaches the earth in 499.02 seconds or slightly more than 8 minutes. The average solar surface temperature has been measured by several indirect methods which agree closely on a value of 6,000° Kelvin or about 10,000° Fahrenheit. The interior temperature of the sun is about 35,000,000° Fahrenheit.

When sunlight is analyzed with a spectroscope, it is found to consist of a continuous spectrum composed of all the colors of the rainbow in order, crossed by many dark lines. The "absorption lines" are produced by gaseous materials in the atmosphere of the sun. More than 60 of the natural terrestrial elements have been identified in the sun, all in gaseous form because of the intense heat of the sun.

Spheres and Corona

The radiating surface of the sun is called the **photosphere**, and just above it is the **chromosphere**. The chromosphere is visible to the naked eye only at times of total solar eclipses, appearing then to be a pinkish-violet layer with occasional great prominences projecting above its general level. With proper instruments the chromosphere can be seen or photographed whenever the sun is visible without waiting for a total eclipse. Above the chromosphere is the **corona**, also visible to the naked eye only at times of total eclipse. Instruments also permit the brighter portions of the corona to be studied whenever conditions are favorable. The pearly light of the corona surges millions of miles from the sun. Iron, nickel and calcium are believed to be principal contributors to the composition of the corona, all in a state of extreme attenuation and high ionization that indicates temperatures on the order of a million degrees, Fahrenheit.

Sunspots

There is an intimate connection between sunspots and the corona. At times of low sunspot activity, the fine streamers of the corona will be much longer above the sun's equator than over the polar regions of the sun, while during high sunspot activity, the corona extends fairly evenly outward from all regions of the sun, but to a much greater distance in space. Sunspots are dark, irregularly-shaped regions whose diameters may reach tens of thousands of miles. The average life of a sunspot group is from two to three weeks, but there have been groups that have lasted for more than a year, being carried repeatedly around as the sun rotated upon its axis. The record for the duration of a sunspot is 18 months. Sunspots reach a low point every 11.3 years, with a peak of activity occurring irregularly between two successive minima.

The sun is 400,000 times as bright as the full moon and gives the earth 6 million times as much light as do all the other stars put together. Actually, most of the stars that can be easily seen on any clear night are brighter than the sun.

The Zodiac

The sun's apparent yearly path among the stars is known as the **ecliptic**. The zone 16° wide, 8° on each side of the ecliptic, is known as the **zodiac**. Inside of this zone are the apparent paths of the sun, moon, earth and major planets. Beginning at the point on the ecliptic which marks the position of the sun at the vernal equinox, and thence proceeding eastward, the zodiac is divided into twelve signs of 30° each, as shown herewith.

These signs are named from the twelve constellations of the zodiac with which the signs coincided in the time of the astronomer Hipparchus, about 2,000 years ago. Owing to the precession of the equinoxes, that is to say, to the retrograde motion of the equinoxes along the ecliptic, each sign in the zodiac has, in the course of 2,000 years, moved backward 30° into the constellation west of it; so that the sign Aries is now in the constellation Pisces, and so on. The vernal equinox will move from Pisces into Aquarius about the middle of the 26th Century. The signs of the zodiac with their Latin and English names are as follows:

Spring	1.♈Aries. The Ram.	Summer	5.♌Leo. The Lion.	Winter	10.♑Capricornus. The Goat.
Signs	2.♉Taurus. The Bull.	Signs.	6.♍Virgo. The Virgin.	Signs.	11.♒Aquarius. The Water Bearer.
	3.♊Gemini. The Twins.		7.♎Libra. The Balance.		12.♓Pisces. The Fishes.
	4.♋Cancer. The Crab.	Autumn	8.♏Scorpius. The Scorpion.		
		Signs.	9.♐Sagittarius. The Archer.		

The Moon

The moon completes a circuit around the earth in a period whose mean or average duration is 27 days 7 hours 43.2 minutes. This is the moon's sidereal period. Because of the motion of the moon in common with the earth around the sun, the mean duration of the lunar month—the period from one new moon to the next new moon—is 29 days 12 hours 44.05 minutes. This is the moon's synodical period.

The mean distance of the moon from the earth according to the American Ephemeris is 238,857 miles. Because the orbit of the moon about the earth is not circular but elliptical, however, the maximum distance from the earth that the moon may reach is 252,710 miles and the least distance is 221,463 miles. All distances are from the center of one object to the center of the other.

The moon's diameter is 2,160 miles. If we deduct the radius of the moon, 1,080 miles, and the radius of the earth, 3,963 miles from the minimum distance, or perigee, given above, we shall have for the nearest approach of the bodies' surfaces 216,420 miles.

The moon rotates on its axis in a period of time exactly equal to its sidereal revolution about the earth—27.321666 days. The moon's revolution about the earth is irregular because of its elliptical orbit. The moon's rotation, however, is regular and this produces together with the irregular revolution what is called "libration in longitude" which permits us to see first farther around the east side and then farther around the west side of the moon. The moon's variation north or south of the ecliptic permits us to see farther over first one pole and then the other of the moon and this is "libration in latitude." These two libration effects permit us to see a total of about 60% of the moon's surface over a period of time. The hidden side of the moon was photographed in 1959 by the Soviet space vehicle Lunik III. Since then many excellent pictures of nearly all of the moon's surface have been transmitted to earth by Lunar Orbiters launched by the U. S.

The tides are caused mainly by the moon, because of its proximity to the earth. The ratio of the tide-raising power of the moon to that of the sun is 11 to 5.

Astronomical Constants; Speed of Light

The following astronomical constants were adopted in 1968, in accordance with the resolutions and recommendations of the International Astronomical Union (Hamburg 1964): Velocity of light, 299,792.5 kilometers per second, or about 186,282 statute miles per second; solar parallax, 8".794; constant of nutation, 9".210; and constant of aberration, 20".496.

Comet Table 1974

Name	Year of Disc.	Due to Return	Period in Years	Perihelion Dist.	Aphelion Dist.	Inclination to Ecliptic Degree	Long.of Ascend. Node Degree	From.Asc. Node to Perihelion Degree
Encke...............	1786	Apr. 1974	3.30	0.34	4.10	12	334	186
Forbes...............	1929	May 1974	6.42	1.54	5.37	5	25	260
Reinmuth II	1947	May 1974	6.73	1.94	5.19	7	296	46
Finlay...............	1886	June 1974	6.90	1.08	6.17	4	42	322
Borrelly.............	1905	June 1974	6.99	1.45	5.87	31	76	351
Wirtanen............	1948	Aug. 1974	6.65	1.61	5.46	13	86	344
Schwassmann-Wachmann II	1929	Sept. 1974	6.52	2.15	4.83	4	126	358
Honda-Mrkos........	1948	Dec. 1974	5.22	0.56	5.46	13	233	184
Arend...............	1951	Mar. 1975	7.76	1.82	6.02	22	358	45
Perrine-Mrkos	1896	July 1975	6.72	1.27	5.85	18	240	166
Westphal............	1852	Oct. 1975	61.88	1.25	30.03	41	347	57
Gunn	1970*	Feb. 1976	6.80	2.44	4.74	10	68	197
Wolf................	1884	Feb. 1976	8.43	2.51	5.78	27	204	161
Churyumou-Gerasimenko	1969*	Mar. 1976	6.55	1.28	5.72	7	50	11
Harrington-Abell	1955	July 1976	7.19	1.77	5.68	17	146	338
Schaumasse.........	1911	Aug. 1976	8.18	1.20	6.92	12	86	52
Klemola.............	1965*	Aug. 1976	11.0	1.76	8.1	11	182	148
d'Arrest.............	1851	Aug. 1976	6.23	1.17	5.61	17	141	179
Pons-Winnecke	1819	Nov. 1976	6.34	1.25	5.61	22	93	172
Kojima..............	1970*	Dec. 1976	6.19	1.63	5.11	4	291	198
Johnson.............	1949	Jan. 1977	6.77	2.20	4.96	14	118	206
Dutoit-Neujmin	1941	Feb. 1977	6.31	1.68	5.15	3	188	116
Van Houten..........	1961	Feb. 1977	15.75	3.94	8.03	7	23	15
Kopff...............	1906	Mar. 1977	6.42	1.57	5.34	5	110	160
Faye	1843	Mar. 1977	7.39	1.62	5.98	9	199	204
Grigg-Skjellerup	1902	Apr. 1977	5.12	1.00	4.94	21	213	359
Encke...............	1786	Aug. 1977	3.30	0.39	4.10	12	334	186
Temple I	1867	Jan. 1978	5.50	1.50	4.73	10	68	179
Arend-Rigaux........	1951	Feb. 1978	6.84	1.44	5.76	18	122	329
Temple II	1873	Feb. 1978	5.26	1.36	4.68	12	119	191
Wolf-Harrington	1924	Mar. 1978	6.55	1.62	5.38	18	254	187
Whipple.............	1933	Mar. 1978	7.47	2.48	5.16	10	188	190
Tsuchinshan I	1965	May 1978	6.64	1.50	5.57	10	96	23
Comas-Sola	1926	May 1978	8.55	1.77	6.60	13	63	40
Daniel..............	1909	June 1978	7.09	1.66	5.72	20	68	11
Ashbrook-Jackson	1948	Aug. 1978	7.43	2.28	5.33	12	2	349
Tsuchinshan II.......	1965	Sept. 1978	6.80	1.78	5.40	7	288	203
Jackson-Neujmin	1936	Dec. 1978	8.39	1.43	6.83	14	163	196
VanBiesbroeck	1954	Dec. 1978	12.41	2.41	8.31	7	149	134
Halley..............	240BC	May 1986	76.1	0.59	35.3	162	58	112

*One appearance only.

Notes on the Comet Table

Most of the comets in the table will not be seen except by professional astronomers or by well-equipped amateurs. At any given time, these observers may be able to follow about a half dozen comets of which the public is unaware. An easily seen comet is rare, one or two every ten to fifteen years.

Comets are named for their discoverers, up to three independent observers being so honored. If a comet becomes unusual, it may be well-known by these names. Usually, however, a preliminary designation is used. This is the year followed by a letter of the alphabet assigned in the order of discovery during that year. About two years later, after any likely late discoveries, comets are given their permanent designation which states the year of their perihelion passage and a Roman numeral giving the order of passage during that year. Well-known periodic comets will receive these designations at each appearance, but the literature and the Comet Table will continue to identify them by their discoverers' names.

New Comet in 73-74 Winter Sky

The newly-discovered Kohoutek Comet may become visible to the naked eye during December 1973 and January 1974. The comet could be one-fifth as bright as the moon, depending on its reaction to its encounter with the sun. It can be seen in the southern sky until the last week of December and in the northern sky until it fades from view on its way into the outer solar system. It is not expected to return again.

Chronological Eras, 1974

The year 1974 of the Christian Era comprises the latter part of the 198th and the beginning of the 199th year of the independence of the United States of America.

Corresponding years of various chronological eras are shown in the tables below, together with the date in 1974 on which each year begins according to the Gregorian calendar.

Era	Year	Begins in 1974	Era	Year	Begins in 1974
Byzantine.................	7483	Sept. 14	Japanese (49th year of Showa) .	2634	Jan. 1
Jewish...................	5735	Sept. 16	Grecian (Seleucidae)............	2286	Sept. 14
Olympiads................	2750	July 1	(according to different sects) or		Oct. 14
(Second year of Olympiad 688)			Indian (Saka).................	1896	Mar. 22
Roman (Ab Urbe Condita)	2727	Jan. 14	Diocletian...................	1691	Sept. 11
Nabonassar (Babylonian)	2723	Apr. 30	Mohammedan (Hegira)	1394	Jan. 24

Chronological Cycles, 1974

Dominical Letter	F	Lunar Cycle or Golden Number	18	Roman Indiction	12
Epact	6	Solar Cycle	23	Julian Period	6687

The Earth; Size; Computation of Time; Seasons

SIZE AND DIMENSIONS

The earth is the fifth largest planet and the third from the sun. Its mass is 6 sextillion, 588 quintillion short tons. Using the parameters of an ellipsoid adopted by the International Astronomical Union in 1964 and recognized by the International Union of Geodesy and Geophysics in 1967, the length of the equator is 24,901.55 miles, the length of a meridian is 24,859.82 miles, the equatorial diameter is 7,926.41 miles, and the area of this reference ellipsoid is approximately 196,938,800 square miles.

The earth is considered a solid, rigid mass with a dense core of magnetic, probably metallic material. The outer part of the core is probably liquid. Around the core is a thick shell or mantle of heavy crystalline rock which in turn is covered by a thin crust forming the solid granite and basalt base of the continents and ocean basins. Over broad areas of the earth's surface the crust has a thin cover of sedimentary rock such as sandstone, shale, and limestone formed by weathering of the earth's surface and deposition of sands, clays, and plant and animal remains.

The temperature in the earth increases about 1°F. with every 100 to 200 feet in depth, in the upper 100 kilometers of the earth, and the temperature near the core is believed to be near the melting point of the core materials under the conditions at that depth. The heat of the earth is believed to be derived from radioactivity in the rocks, pressures developed within the earth, and original heat (if the earth in fact was formed at high temperature).

ATMOSPHERE OF THE EARTH

The earth's atmosphere is a blanket composed of gases and some water vapor. The principal gases are nitrogen, oxygen and argon, in amounts of about 78, 21 and 1% by volume. Also present in minute quantities are carbon dioxide, hydrogen, neon, helium, krypton and xenon.

Water vapor displaces other gases and varies from nearly zero to about 4% by volume. The height of the ozone layer varies from approximately 12 to 21 miles above the earth. Traces exist as low as 6 miles and as high as 35 miles. Traces of methane have been found.

The atmosphere rests on the earth's surface with the weight equivalent to a layer of water 34 ft. deep. For about 300,000 ft. upward the gases remain in the proportions stated. Gravity holds the gases to the earth. The weight of the air compresses it at the bottom, so that the greatest density is at the earth's surface. Pressure, as well as density, decreases as height increases because the weight pressing upon any layer is always less than that pressing upon the layers below.

The temperature of the air drops with increased height, until the tropopause is reached. This may vary from 25,000 to 60,000 ft. The atmosphere below the tropopause is the troposphere; the atmosphere for about twenty miles above the tropopause is the stratosphere, where the temperature generally increases with height except at high latitudes in winter. A temperature maximum near the 30-mile level is called the stratopause. Above this boundary is the mesosphere where the temperature decreases with height to a minimum, the mesopause, at a height of 50 miles. Extending above the mesosphere to the outer fringes of the atmosphere is the thermosphere, a region where temperature increases with height to a value measured in thousands of degrees Fahrenheit. The lower portion of this region, extending from 50 to about 400 miles in altitude, is characterized by a high ion density, and is thus called the ionosphere. The outer region is called exosphere; this is the region where gas molecules traveling at high speed may escape into outer space. Above 600 miles.

LATITUDE, LONGITUDE

Position on the globe is measured by means of meridians and parallels. Meridians, which are imaginary lines drawn around the earth through the poles, determine longitude. The meridian running through Greenwich, England, is the prime meridian of longitude, and all others are either east or west. Parallels, which are imaginary circles parallel with the equator, determine latitude. The length of a degree of longitude varies as the cosine of the latitude. At the equator a degree is 69.171 statute miles; this is gradually reduced toward the poles. Value of a longitude degree at the poles is zero.

Latitude is reckoned by the number of degrees north or south of the equator, an imaginary circle on the earth's surface everywhere equidistant between the two poles. According to the IAU Ellipsoid of 1964, the length of a degree of latitude is 68.708 statute miles at the equator and varies slightly north and south because of the oblate form of the globe; at the poles it is 69.403 statute miles.

COMPUTATION OF TIME

The earth rotates on its axis and follows an elliptical orbit around the sun. The rotation makes the sun appear to move across the sky from East to West. It determines day and night and the complete rotation, in relation to the sun, is called the apparent or true solar day. This varies but an average determines the mean solar day of 24 hours.

The mean solar day is in universal use for civil purposes. It may be obtained from apparent solar time by correcting observations of the sun for the equation of time, but when high precision is required, the mean solar time is calculated from its relation to sidereal time. These relations are extremely complicated, but for most practical uses, they may be considered as follows:

Sidereal time is the measure of time defined by the diurnal motion of the vernal equinox, and is determined from observation of the meridian transits of stars. One complete rotation of the earth relative to the equinox is called the sidereal day. The mean sidereal day is 23 hours, 56 minutes, 4.091 seconds of mean solar time.

The Calendar Year begins at 12 o'clock precisely local clock time, on the night of Dec. 31-Jan. 1. The day and the calendar month also begin at midnight by the clock. The interval required for the earth to make one absolute revolution around the sun is a sidereal year; it consists of 365 days, 6 hours, 9 minutes, and 9.5 seconds of mean solar time (approximately 24 hrs. per day) in 1900, and is increasing at the rate of 0.0001-second annually.

The Tropical Year, on which the return of the seasons depends, is the interval between two consecutive returns of the sun to the vernal equinox. The tropical year consisted of 365 days, 5 hours, 48 minutes, and 46 seconds. It is decreasing at the rate of 0.530 seconds per century. In 1956 the unit of time interval was defined to be identical with the second of Ephemeris Time, 1/31,556,925.9747 of the tropical year for 1900 January 0d 12th hour E. T. A physical definition of the second based on a quantum transition of cesium (atomic second) was adopted in 1964. The atomic second is equal to 9,192,631,770 cycles of the emitted radiation. In 1967 this atomic second was adopted as the unit of time interval for the Intern'l System of units.

THE ZONES AND SEASONS

The five zones of the earth's surface are the torrid, lying between the Tropics of Cancer and Capricorn; North Temperate, between Cancer and the Arctic Circle; South Temperate, between Capricorn and the Antarctic Circle; the Frigid Zones, between the polar Circles and the Poles.

The inclination or tilt of the earth's axis with respect to the sun determines the seasons. These are commonly marked in the North Temperate Zone, where spring begins at the vernal equinox, summer at the summer solstice, autumn at the autumnal equinox and winter at the winter solstice.

In the South Temperate Zone, the seasons are reversed. Spring begins at the autumnal equinox, summer at the winter solstice, etc.

If the earth's axis were perpendicular to the plane of the earth's orbit around the sun there would be no change of seasons. Day and night would be of nearly constant length and there would be equable conditions of temperature. But the axis is tilted 23° 27' away from a perpendicular to the orbit and only in March and September is the axis at right angles to the sun.

The points at which the sun crosses the equator are the equinoxes, when day and night are most nearly equal. The points at which the sun is at a maximum distance from the equator are the solstices. Days and nights are then most unequal.

In June the North Pole is tilted 23° 27' toward the sun and the days in the northern hemisphere are longer than the nights, while the days in the southern hemisphere are shorter than the nights. In December the North Pole is tilted 23° 27' away from the sun and the situation is reversed.

THE SEASONS IN 1974

In 1974 the 4 seasons will begin as follows according to EST; add one hour for Atlantic Time; subtract one hour for Central, two hours for Mountain, 3 hours for Pacific; 4 hours for Yukon; 5 hours for Alaska-Hawaii and 6 hours For Bering Time. Also shown in Greenwich Mean Time.

		Date	GMT	EST
Vernal Equinox	**Spring**	March 21	00:07	7:07 p.m.*
Summer Solstice	**Summer**	June 21	18:38	1:38 p.m.
Autumnal Equinox	**Autumn**	Sept. 23	09:59	4:59 a.m.
Winter Solstice	**Winter**	Dec. 22	05:57	0:57 a.m.

* March 20.

Poles and Rotation of the Earth

Poles of The Earth

Source: National Oceanic and Atmospheric Admn.

The geographic (rotation) poles, or points where the earth's axis of rotation cuts the surface, are not absolutely fixed in the body of the earth. The pole of rotation describes an irregular curve about its mean position.

Two periods have been detected in this motion: (1) an annual period due to seasonal changes in barometric pressure, load of ice and snow on the surface and to other phenomena of seasonal character; (2) a period of about 14 months due to the shape and constitution of the Earth.

In addition there are small but as yet unpredictable irregularities. The whole motion is so small that the actual pole at any time remains within a circle of 30 or 40 feet in radius centered at the mean position of the pole.

The pole of rotation for the time being is of course the pole having a latitude of 90° and an indeterminate longitude.

Magnetic Poles

The **north magnetic pole** of the earth is that region where the magnetic force is vertically downward and the **south magnetic pole** that region where the magnetic force is vertically upward. A compass placed at the magnetic poles experiences no directive force.

There are slow changes in the distribution of the earth's magnetic field. These changes were at one time attributed in part to a periodic movement of the magnetic poles around the geographical poles, but later evidence refutes this theory and points, rather, to a slow migration of "disturbance" foci over the earth.

There appear shifts in position of the magnetic poles due to the changes in the earth's magnetic field. The center of the area designated as the north magnetic pole was estimated to be in about latitude 70.5° N and longitude 96° W in 1905; from recent nearby measurements and studies of the secular changes, the position in 1970 is estimated as latitude 76.3° N and longitude 101° W. Improved data rather than actual motion account for at least part of the change.

The position of the south magnetic pole in 1912 was near 71° S and longitude 150° E; the position in 1970 is estimated at latitude 66° S and longitude 139.1° E.

The direction of the horizontal components of the magnetic field at any point is known as magnetic north at that point, and the angle by which it deviates east or west

of true north is known as the magnetic declination, or in the mariner's terminology the **variation of the compass.**

A compass without error points in the direction of magnetic north. (In general this is *not* the direction of the magnetic north pole.) If one follows the direction indicated by the north end of the compass, he will travel along a rather irregular curve which eventually reaches the north magnetic pole (though not usually by a great-circle route). However, the action of the compass should not be thought of as due to any influence of the distant pole, but simply as an indication of the distribution of the earth's magnetism at the place of observation.

Rotation of The Earth

Source: U.S. Naval Observatory

The speed of rotation of the earth about its axis has been found to be slightly variable. The variations may be classified as:

(A) **Secular.** Tidal friction acts as a brake on the rotation and causes a slow secular increase in the length of the day, about 1 millisecond per century.

(B) **Irregular.** The speed of rotation may increase for a number of years, about 5 to 10, and then start decreasing. The maximum difference from the mean in the length of the day during a century is about 5 milliseconds. The accumulated difference in time has amounted to approximately 44 seconds since 1900. The cause is probably motion in the interior of the earth.

(C) **Periodic.** Seasonal variations exist with periods of one year and six months. The cumulative effect is such that each year the earth is late about 30 milliseconds near June 1 and is ahead about 30 milliseconds near Oct. 1. The maximum seasonal variation in the length of the day is about 0.5 millisecond. It is believed that the principal cause of the annual variation is the seasonal change in the wind patterns of the Northern and Southern Hemispheres. The semi-annual variation is due chiefly to tidal action of the sun, which distorts the shape of the earth slightly.

The secular and irregular variations were discovered by comparing time based on the rotation of the earth with time based on the orbital motion of the moon about the earth and of the planets about the sun. The periodic variation was determined largely with the aid of quartz-crystal clocks. The introduction of the cesium-beam atomic clock in 1955 made it possible to determine in greater detail than before the nature of the irregular and periodic variations.

A Light Year Is a Lot of Miles

The distance that light travels in one year is called a **light year.** This is a unit of measure used to express the vast distances between stars and galaxies. Light travels at a speed of about 186,282 miles per second. In a 365-day year there are 31,536,000 seconds. Multiplying the speed of light per second by the number of seconds in a year produces 5,874,589,152,000 miles travelled by light in one

year, more easily expressed as one light year. Relatively few stars are less than 100 light years away from earth and the most distant galaxies are 1.6 billion light years away. By contrast, it takes only about 8.3 minutes for light to travel to the earth from the sun and 1.28 seconds from the moon.

Star Tables, 1974

These tables include stars of visual magnitude 2.5 and brighter. Co-ordinates are for the epoch Jan. 0.7, 1974. Where no parallax figures are given, the trigonometric parallax figure is smaller than the margin for error and the distance given is obtained by indirect methods. Stars of variable magnitude designated by V.

To find the time when star is on meridian, subtract R.A.M.S. of the sun table on page 229 from the star's right ascension, first adding 24h to the latter, if necessary. Mark this result P.M., if less than 12h; but if greater than 12h, subtract 12h and mark the remainder A.M.

Star	Magnitude	Parallax	Light Yrs.	Right Ascen. h. m.	Declination ° '	Star	Magnitude	Parallax	Light Yrs.	Right Ascen. h. m.	Declination ° '
α Andromedae (Alpheratz)	2.06	0.02	90	0 07.0	+28 57	α Ursae Majoris (Dubhe)	1.81	0.03	105	11 02.1	+61 54
β Cassiopeiae	2.26	0.07	45	0 07.8	+59 00	β Leunis (Denebola)	2.14	0.08	43	11 47.7	+14 43
α Phoenicis	2.39	0.04	93	0 25.0	42 28	γ Ursae Majoris (Phecda)	2.44	0.02	90	11 52.5	+53 50
α Cassiopeiae (Schedir)	2.16	0.01	150	0 39.0	+56 24	α Crucis	1.39	...	370	12 25.1	−62 57
β Ceti	2.02	0.06	57	0 42.3	−18 08	γ Crucis	1.69	...	220	12 29.7	−56 58
γ Cassiopeiae	2.13v	0.03	96	0 55.1	+60 35	γ Centauri	2.17	...	160	12 40.1	−48 49
β Andromedae	2.02	0.04	76	1 08.3	+35 29	β Crucis	1.28	...	490	12 46.2	−59 33
α Eridani (Achernar)	0.51	0.02	118	1 36.8	−57 22	ε Ursae Majoris (Alioth)	1.79	0.01	68	12 52.9	+56 06
γ Andromedae	2.14	...	260	2 02.3	+42 12	ζ Ursae Majoris (Mizar)	2.26	0.04	88	13 22.9	+55 04
α Arietis	2.00	0.04	76	2 05.7	+23 20	α Virginis (Spica)	0.91v	0.02	220	13 23.8	−11 02
α Ursae Min. (Pole Star)	1.99v	...	680	2 06.6	+89 09	ε Centauri	2.33	...	570	13 38.2	−53 20
ο Ceti	2.00v	0.01	103	2 18.0	−3 06	η Ursae Majoris (Alkaid)	1.87	...	210	13 46.5	+49 27
β Persei (Algol)	2.06v	0.03	105	3 06.5	+40 51	β Centauri	0.63	0.02	490	14 02.0	−60 15
α Persei	1.80	0.03	570	3 22.5	+49 46	θ Centauri	2.04	0.06	55	14 05.1	−36 15
α Tauri (Aldebaran)	0.86v	0.05	68	4 34.5	+16 28	α Bootis (Arcturus)	−0.06	0.09	36	14 14.5	+19 19
β Orionis (Rigel)	0.14v	...	900	5 13.3	−8 14	η Centauri	2.39v	...	390	14 33.9	−42 03
α Aurigae (Capella)	0.05	0.07	45	5 14.8	+45 58	α Centauri	0.01	0.75	4.4	14 37.8	−60 44
γ Orionis (Bellatrix)	1.64	0.03	470	5 23.7	+6 20	α Lupi	2.32	...	430	14 40.2	−47 17
β Tauri (El Nath)	1.65	0.02	300	5 24.7	+28 35	ε Bootis	2.37	0.01	103	14 43.9	+27 11
δ Orionis	2.20v	...	1500	5 30.7	−0 19	β Ursae Minoris	2.04	0.03	105	14 50.8	+74 16
ε Orionis	1.70	...	1600	5 34.9	−1 13	α Coronae Borealis	2.23v	0.04	76	15 33.6	+26 48
ζ Orionis	1.79	0.02	1600	5 39.5	−1 57	δ Scorpii	2.34	...	590	15 58.8	−22 33
κ Orionis	2.06	...	2100	5 46.6	−9 41	α Scorpii (Antares)	0.92v	0.02	520	16 27.8	−26 23
α Orionis (Betelgeuse)	0.41v	...	520	5 53.8	+7 24	α Trianguli Australis	1.93	0.02	82	16 45.9	−68 59
β Aurigae	1.86	0.04	88	5 57.6	+44 57	ε Scorpii	2.28	0.05	66	16 48.5	−34 15
β Canis Majoris	1.96	0.01	750	6 21.6	−17 57	η Ophiuchi	2.46	0.05	69	17 08.9	−15 42
αCarinae (Canopus)	−0.72	0.02	98	6 23.4	−52 41	λ Scorpii	1.60	...	310	17 31.8	−37 05
γ Geminorum	1.93	0.03	105	6 36.2	+16 25	α Ophiuchi	2.09	0.06	58	17 33.7	+12 35
α Canis Majoris (Sirius)	−1.42	0.38	8.7	6 44.0	−16 41	θ Scorpii	1.86	0.02	650	17 35.5	−42 59
ε Canis Majoris	1.48	...	680	6 57.6	−28 56	κ Scorpii	2.39	...	470	17 40.7	−39 01
δ Canis Majoris	1.85	...	2100	7 07.3	−26 21	γ Draconis	2.21	0.02	108	17 56.0	+51 29
η Canis Majoris	2.46	...	2700	7 23.1	−29 15	ε Sagittarii	1.81	0.02	124	18 22.5	−34 24
α Geminorum (Castor)	1.97	0.07	45	7 32.9	+31 57	α Lyrae (Vega)	0.04	0.12	26.5	18 36.0	+38 46
α Canis Minoris (Procyon)	0.37	0.29	11.3	7 37.9	+5 18	σ Sagittarii	2.12	...	300	18 53.7	−26 20
β Geminorum (Pollux)	1.16	0.09	35	7 43.7	+28 05	α Aquilae (Altair)	0.77	0.20	16.5	19 49.5	+8 48
ζ Puppis	2.23	...	2400	8 02.7	−39 56	γ Cygni	2.22	...	750	20 21.3	+40 10
γ Velorum	1.88	...	520	8 08.7	−47 15	α Pavonis	1.95	...	310	20 23.6	−56 49
ε Carinae	1.97	...	340	8 22.0	−59 26	α Cygni (Deneb)	1.26	...	1600	20 40.6	+45 11
δ Velorum	1.95	0.04	76	8 44.0	−54 37	ε Cygni	2.46	0.04	75	20 45.2	+33 52
λ Velorum	2.24	0.02	750	9 07.0	−43 20	α Cephei	2.44	0.06	52	21 18.0	+62 28
β Carinae	1.67	0.04	86	9 12.9	−69 37	ε Pegasi	2.31	...	780	21 42.9	+9 45
ι Carinae	2.25	...	750	9 16.4	−59 10	α Gruis	1.76	0.05	64	22 06.6	−47 05
κ Velorum	2.45	0.01	470	9 21.3	−54 54	β Gruis	2.17v	...	280	22 41.1	−47 01
α Hydrae	1.98	0.02	94	9 26.3	−8 33	α Piscis Austrinis (Fomalhaut)	1.19	0.14	22.6	22 56.2	−29 46
α Leonis (Regulus)	1.36	0.04	84	10 07.0	+12 06	β Pegasi	2.50v	0.02	210	23 02.5	+27 56
γ Leonis	1.99	0.02	90	10 18.5	+19 58	α Pegasi	2.50	0.03	109	23 03.5	+15 04
β Ursae Majoris (Merak)	2.37	0.04	78	11 00.3	+56 31						

Polar Star, 1974

Mean time of upper transit 0° Longitude, Greenwich Mean Time

Date	Upper Transit h. m. s.	Polar Dist. ° ' "	Date	Upper Transit h. m. s.	Polar Dist. ° ' "	Date	Upper Transit h. m. s.	Polar Dist. ° ' "
Jan. 1	19 23 15	0 50 53	May 1	11 29 44	0 51 11	Sept 1	3 28 42	0 51 18
Feb. 1	17 20 41	0 50 50	June 1	9 28 14	0 51 19	Oct. 1	1 31 16	0 51 08
Mar. 1	15 29 59	0 50 53	July 1	7 30 57	0 51 23	Nov. 1	23 25 43	0 50 58
Apr. 1	13 27 41	0 51 01	Aug. 1	5 29 51	0 51 22	Dec 1	21 27 38	0 50 46

Upper transit of Polaris occurs, on the average, 3m. 56s. earlier each day. The interval between lower and upper transit of Polaris is 11h.58m.2s. The greatest Eastern elongation of Polaris occurs 5h.56m. before upper transit and 6h.2m. after lower transit, while the greatest Western elongation occurs 5h.56m. after upper transit and 6h.2m. before lower transit.

Harvest Moon and Hunter's Moon

The Harvest Moon, the full moon nearest the Autumnal Equinox, ushers in a period of several successive days when the moon rises soon after sunset. This phenomenon gives farmers in temperate latitudes extra hours of light in which to harvest their crops before frost and winter come – hence the name. The 1974 Harvest Moon falls on Oct. 1. Harvest moon in the south temperate latitudes falls on Mar. 8.

The next full moon after Harvest Moon is called the Hunter's Moon, accompanied by a similar phenomenon but less marked.

New Calendar Tables: An Explanation

Attentive readers of this section of the World Almanac will notice several tables have been changed. Use of the World Almanac has spread to residents of all parts of North America, so, to serve them better, more astronomical data are presented than ever before.

To effect this change, it has been necessary to give times in the 24-hour system and to refer the information to the longitude of Greenwich (0°) rather than to the previous 75° of the Eastern Standard Time Zone.

The time of an event that occurs simultaneously for everyone on earth, such as the instant of an equinox, need be altered only by the zone time difference between Greenwich and the local standard time meridian (subtract 5 hours for EST; 6, CST; 7, MST; 8, PST; etc.), paying attention to any change of date arising from the arithmetic.

Times of purely local phenomena, such as the rising and setting of the moon, require different adjustment. The following step-by-step example shows you how to determine the rising and setting time of the sun or moon for any locality.

In this example, we wish to determine the time of moonrise over Washington, D.C. on Jan. 7.

A Find your latitude and longitude. See page 719, or consult your local newspaper, airport or weather station. For Washington, D.C.: the
 latitude is 38°53′ North
 the longitude is 77°01′ West

B Note that the calendar information is given for each 10° of latitude. In our example, you must determine what proportion Washington's latitude is between 30° and 40°. Washington's latitude is .89 of the 10° difference.

53′ = 53/60 of 1°
53/60 is near 54/60
54/60 = .9 of a degree
38°53′ = 38.9°
8° = .8 of 10°
8°53′ = .89 of 10°

C In 24 hours, the earth turns 360°. You must determine what proportion of a day is involved in turning from Greenwich, England, to Washington.

01′ = 1/60 of 1°
1/60 = 0.017
77°01′ = 77.017°
77.017 divided by 360
= 0.214 of a day

D Clock time is figured from the standard time meridians, not from exactly your longitude. For every degree east of a meridian, moonrise will occur 4 minutes earlier; for every degree west, it will occur 4 minutes later. The standard time meridians are: Atlantic 60°; Eastern 75°; Central 90°; Mountain 105°; Pacific 120°; Alaska-Hawaii 150°. Real time in Washington is 8.068 minutes later than clock time.

77.017° − 75°
= 2.017 times 4
= 8.068 minutes

The results of Steps B, C, and D will remain constant for a particular place. They need not be calculated again once you have calculated them for your location.

E From the calendar tables, read the time of moonrise on Jan. 7 for both 40° and 30° and find the difference between them.

30°−16 19 less
40°−15 51
=28 minutes

F The time of moonrise at 38.9° North latitude will lie between the times for 40° and 30° by the proportion determined in Step B.

28 times 0.89
= 25 minutes

G Add the result of Step F to the moonrise time for 30° on Jan. 7. This is the time the moon will rise at the Greenwich meridian (0°) at a latitude of 38.9° North. **Important Note:** If the moon rises earlier at the higher latitude (40° in this example), you must **subtract** the result of Step F from the lower latitude time. Always add or subtract from the lower latitude time.

16 19
less 25 minutes
=15 54

H Repeat Step E for Jan. 8.

17 31 less 17 07
=24 minutes

I Repeat Step F for Jan. 8.

24 times 0.89
= 21 minutes

K Repeat Step G for Jan. 8. The same **Important Note** for Step G applies here. This result gives the time when the moon will rise on Jan. 8 at Greenwich meridian at latitude 38°53′ North.

17 31 less
21 minutes
=17 10

L You must now determine the time of moonrise for Washington's meridian. Find the difference between Steps G and K.

17 10 less 15 54
=76 minutes

M Multiply L by C.

76 times 0.214
=16 minutes

N Add M to G. This is the real time that moonrise will occur at Washington, not clock time.

15 54 plus 16=16 10

O Add D to N. Remember, if you are east of your time zone meridian, **subtract** D from N. If you are on **daylight saving time**, add one hour.

16 10 plus
8.068 minutes
= 16 18 or 4:18 P.M. **Eastern Standard Time**

The calendar tables now show moonrise and set whenever they occur, not just during the night. These values appear just beneath the same information for the sun, so comparison of the times of these events is simplified. Since the moon moves rapidly against the background of stars, its rise time will occur any time of the day or night during a month. This action may initially confuse the reader. To resolve this, write the hours 0, 6, 12, 18, 24, evenly across a piece of paper. Note in this time scale when, for a particular day, the sun rises and sets. Then note the times when the moon rises and sets. You may even wish to include the same information for the planets, in order to have complete information for the day's events.

1st Month   January, 1974   31 Days

Greenwich Mean Time

NOTE: Light figures indicate Sun. **Dark** figures indicate **Moon.** *Degrees are North Latitude.*

CAUTION: Must be converted to local time. For instruction see page 237.

Day of month week year	Sun on meridian / Moon phase	20° Rise Sun/Moon	20° Set Sun/Moon	30° Rise Sun/Moon	30° Set Sun/Moon	40° Rise Sun/Moon	40° Set Sun/Moon	50° Rise Sun/Moon	50° Set Sun/Moon	60° Rise Sun/Moon	60° Set Sun/Moon
	h m s	h m	h m	h m	h m	h m	h m	h m	h m	h m	h m
1 Tu / 1	+3 30 18 06 D	6 35	17 31	6 56	17 10	7 22	16 44	7 59	16 08	9 03	15 03
		11 25		11 18		11 10		10 59		10 42	
2 We / 2	+3 58	6 35	17 32	6 56	17 11	7 22	16 45	7 59	16 09	9 03	15 05
		12 04	0 14	11 53	0 23	11 39	0 35	11 20	0 51	10 51	1 15
3 Th / 3	+4 26	6 35	17 33	6 56	17 12	7 22	16 47	7 58	16 10	9 02	15 07
		12 47	1 10	12 32	1 24	12 13	1 41	11 46	2 05	11 04	2 44
4 Fr / 4	+4 54	6 36	17 34	6 57	17 13	7 22	16 48	7 58	16 12	9 01	15 09
		13 36	2 10	13 17	2 28	12 53	2 50	12 19	3 22	11 23	4 16
5 Sa / 5	+5 21	6 36	17 35	6 57	17 14	7 22	16 49	7 58	16 13	9 00	15 11
		14 32	3 13	14 10	3 34	13 42	4 01	13 03	4 39	11 54	5 46
6 Su / 6	+5 47	6 36	17 35	6 57	17 14	7 22	16 50	7 57	16 14	8 59	15 13
		15 34	4 17	15 11	4 40	14 42	5 09	14 00	5 51	12 45	7 06
7 Mo / 7	+6 13	6 36	17 36	6 57	17 15	7 22	16 51	7 57	16 15	8 58	15 15
		16 41	5 21	16 19	5 44	15 51	6 12	15 12	6 53	14 02	8 04
8 Tu / 8	+6 39 12 36 O	6 37	17 37	6 57	17 16	7 22	16 52	7 56	16 17	8 57	15 17
		17 49	6 22	17 31	6 42	17 07	7 07	16 34	7 42	15 38	8 41
9 We / 9	+7 04	6 37	17 37	6 57	17 17	7 22	16 53	7 56	16 18	8 56	15 19
		18 57	7 17	18 43	7 33	18 25	7 53	18 01	8 20	17 21	9 04
10 Th / 10	+7 29	6 37	17 38	6 57	17 18	7 22	16 54	7 56	16 19	8 55	15 21
		20 01	8 07	19 52	8 18	19 42	8 32	19 26	8 50	19 03	9 19
11 Fr / 11	+7 53	6 37	17 38	6 57	17 19	7 21	16 55	7 55	16 20	8 54	15 23
		21 03	8 52	20 59	8 58	20 55	9 05	20 49	9 15	20 40	9 30
12 Sa / 12	+8 16	6 37	17 39	6 57	17 20	7 21	16 56	7 55	16 22	8 52	15 25
		22 01	9 34	22 03	9 35	22 05	9 35	22 08	9 37	22 13	9 38
13 Su / 13	+8 39	6 38	17 40	6 57	17 21	7 21	16 57	7 54	16 23	8 51	15 27
		22 58	10 14	23 04	10 09	23 13	10 04	23 25	9 57	23 43	9 47
14 Mo / 14	+9 01	6 38	17 40	6 57	17 22	7 21	16 58	7 54	16 25	8 50	15 29
		23 53	10 53		10 44		10 33		10 18		9 55
15 Tu / 15	+9 23 07 04 C	6 38	17 41	6 57	17 22	7 20	16 59	7 53	16 26	8 48	15 31
			11 33	0 04	11 20	0 19	11 03	0 38	10 41	1 10	10 05
16 We / 16	+9 44	6 38	17 42	6 57	17 23	7 20	17 00	7 53	16 27	8 47	15 33
		0 47	12 15	1 03	11 58	1 23	11 36	1 50	11 07	2 35	10 19
17 Th / 17	+10 04	6 38	17 42	6 57	17 24	7 20	17 01	7 52	16 29	8 45	15 36
		1 41	12 59	2 00	12 39	2 24	12 13	2 58	11 38	3 57	10 37
18 Fr / 18	+10 23	6 38	17 43	6 56	17 25	7 19	17 03	7 51	16 31	8 44	15 38
		2 34	13 45	2 56	13 23	3 23	12 55	4 02	12 15	5 12	11 05
19 Sa / 19	+10 42	6 38	17 44	6 56	17 25	7 19	17 04	7 50	16 32	8 42	15 41
		3 26	14 34	3 49	14 11	4 18	13 42	4 59	13 00	6 15	11 45
20 Su / 20	+11 00	6 38	17 45	6 56	17 27	7 18	17 05	7 49	16 34	8 40	15 43
		4 16	15 24	4 38	15 02	5 07	14 34	5 48	13 53	7 02	12 40
21 Mo / 21	+11 18	6 38	17 45	6 56	17 28	7 18	17 06	7 48	16 36	8 38	15 45
		5 03	16 15	5 24	15 55	5 51	15 29	6 29	14 52	7 35	13 47
22 Tu / 22	+11 34	6 38	17 46	6 55	17 29	7 17	17 07	7 46	16 37	8 36	15 48
		5 46	17 07	6 05	16 49	6 29	16 27	7 02	15 55	7 57	15 02
23 We / 23	+11 50 11 02 ●	6 37	17 47	6 55	17 29	7 16	17 09	7 45	16 39	8 34	15 50
		6 27	17 58	6 43	17 44	7 02	17 26	7 29	17 01	8 13	16 20
24 Th / 24	+12 05	6 37	17 47	6 55	17 30	7 16	17 10	7 44	16 41	8 32	15 53
		7 05	18 48	7 17	18 38	7 32	18 25	7 52	18 07	8 24	17 39
25 Fr / 25	+12 20	6 37	17 48	6 54	17 31	7 15	17 11	7 43	16 42	8 30	15 56
		7 41	19 38	7 49	19 32	7 59	19 24	8 12	19 14	8 32	18 58
26 Sa / 26	+12 33	6 37	17 49	6 54	17 31	7 15	17 12	7 42	16 44	8 29	15 59
		8 16	20 27	8 20	20 26	8 27	20 24	8 30	20 21	8 39	20 17
27 Su / 27	+12 46	6 37	17 49	6 53	17 32	7 14	17 13	7 40	16 46	8 26	16 01
		8 50	21 17	8 50	21 20	8 49	21 24	8 48	21 29	8 46	21 37
28 Mo / 28	+12 58	6 37	17 50	6 53	17 33	7 13	17 15	7 39	16 47	8 25	16 03
		9 26	22 09	9 21	22 16	9 14	22 26	9 06	22 39	8 53	22 59
29 Tu / 29	+13 09	6 36	17 50	6 53	17 34	7 12	17 16	7 38	16 49	8 22	16 06
		10 03	23 02	9 54	23 15	9 42	23 30	9 26	23 50	9 02	
30 We / 30	+13 19	6 36	17 51	6 52	17 35	7 11	17 17	7 37	16 51	8 19	16 09
		10 44	23 59	10 30		10 13		9 49		9 12	0 23
31 Th / 31	+13 28 07 39 D	6 36	17 51	6 52	17 36	7 10	17 18	7 36	16 52	8 16	16 12
		11 29		11 11	0 15	10 49	0 35	10 18	1 04	9 28	1 51

Moon Phases: 1st 18:06 1st Quarter D; 8th 12:36 Full O; 15th 7:42 Last Quarter C; 23rd 11:02 New ●; 31st 7:39 First Quarter D.

Morning Stars: Mercury (Jan. 1-9); Venus (Jan. 23-31). **Evening Stars:** Mercury (Jan. 9-31); Venus (Jan 1-23); Mars, Jupiter, Saturn.

2nd Month

February, 1974

28 Days

Greenwich Mean Time

NOTE: Light figures indicate Sun. **Dark** figures indicate **Moon.** *Degrees are North Latitude.*

CAUTION: Must be converted to local time. For instruction see page 237.

Day of month week year	Sun on meridian Moon phase	20° Rise Sun Moon	20° Set Sun Moon	30° Rise Sun Moon	30° Set Sun Moon	40° Rise Sun Moon	40° Set Sun Moon	50° Rise Sun Moon	50° Set Sun Moon	60° Rise Sun Moon	60° Set Sun Moon
	h m s	h m	h m	h m	h m	h m	h m	h m	h m	h m	h m
1 Fr 32	+13 37	6 36 / 12 19	17 52 / 0 58	6 51 / 11 58	17 37 / 1 18	7 09 / 11 32	17 19 / 1 43	7 34 / 10 55	16 53 / 2 18	8 14 / 9 52	16 14 / 3 19
2 Sa 33	+13 44	6 35 / 13 16	17 52 / 2 00	6 51 / 12 53	17 38 / 2 22	7 08 / 12 25	17 21 / 2 50	7 33 / 11 44	16 55 / 3 30	8 11 / 10 31	16 17 / 4 42
3 Su 34	+13 51	6 35 / 14 18	17 53 / 3 02	6 50 / 13 56	17 39 / 3 25	7 07 / 13 27	17 22 / 3 53	7 32 / 12 46	16 57 / 4 35	8 09 / 11 33	16 20 / 5 48
4 Mo 35	+13 57	6 35 / 15 24	17 54 / 4 02	6 49 / 15 04	17 40 / 4 24	7 06 / 14 38	17 23 / 4 51	7 30 / 14 01	16 59 / 5 29	8 07 / 12 57	16 22 / 6 35
5 Tu 36	+14 03	6 35 / 16 31	17 54 / 4 59	6 49 / 16 15	17 40 / 5 18	7 05 / 15 54	17 24 / 5 40	7 29 / 15 24	17 01 / 6 12	8 05 / 14 36	16 25 / 7 04
6 We 37	+14 07	6 34 / 17 38	17 55 / 5 51	6 48 / 17 26	17 41 / 6 05	7 04 / 17 11	17 26 / 6 23	7 27 / 16 51	17 03 / 6 46	8 02 / 16 18	16 27 / 7 23
7 Th 38	+14 11 ○ 23 24	6 34 / 18 42	17 55 / 6 39	6 48 / 18 35	17 42 / 6 48	7 04 / 18 27	17 27 / 6 59	7 25 / 18 16	17 05 / 7 14	7 59 / 17 59	16 30 / 7 36
8 Fr 39	+14 13	6 34 / 19 43	17 56 / 7 24	6 46 / 19 42	17 43 / 7 28	7 02 / 19 41	17 28 / 7 32	7 23 / 19 39	17 07 / 7 38	7 57 / 19 37	16 33 / 7 46
9 Sa 40	+14 15	6 33 / 20 42	17 56 / 8 06	6 45 / 20 47	17 44 / 8 04	7 01 / 20 52	17 29 / 8 02	7 22 / 21 00	17 08 / 8 00	7 55 / 21 11	16 35 / 7 55
10 Su 41	+14 16	6 33 / 21 40	17 56 / 8 47	6 45 / 21 50	17 44 / 8 41	7 00 / 22 01	17 30 / 8 32	7 20 / 22 17	17 10 / 8 21	7 53 / 22 43	16 38 / 8 04
11 Mo 42	14 17	6 32 / 22 37	17 57 / 9 29	6 44 / 22 51	17 45 / 9 17	6 58 / 23 08	17 31 / 9 03	7 19 / 23 32	17 12 / 8 44	7 51	16 41 / 8 14
12 Tu 43	+14 17	6 32 / 23 33	17 57 / 10 11	6 43 / 23 50	17 46 / 9 55	6 57	17 32 / 9 36	7 17	17 13 / 9 10	7 48 / 0 12	16 43 / 8 27
13 We 44	+14 16	6 31	17 58 / 10 55	6 42	17 47 / 10 36	6 56 / 0 13	17 33 / 10 12	7 15 / 0 44	17 15 / 9 39	7 45 / 1 37	16 45 / 8 44
14 Th 45	+14 14 ☾ 00 04	6 30 / 0 27	17 59 / 11 41	6 41 / 0 48	17 48 / 11 20	6 55 / 1 14	17 34 / 10 53	7 13 / 1 51	17 16 / 10 15	7 42 / 2 56	16 48 / 9 08
15 Fr 46	+14 11	6 30 / 1 20	17 59 / 12 29	6 41 / 1 43	17 48 / 12 07	6 54 / 2 11	17 35 / 11 38	7 10 / 2 51	17 18 / 10 57	7 39 / 4 04	16 51 / 9 44
16 Sa 47	+14 08	6 29 / 2 11	17 59 / 13 19	6 40 / 2 34	17 49 / 12 57	6 53 / 3 03	17 37 / 12 28	7 09 / 3 44	17 19 / 11 47	7 36 / 4 58	16 54 / 10 33
17 Su 48	+14 04	6 28 / 2 59	18 00 / 14 10	6 39 / 3 21	17 50 / 13 49	6 52 / 3 48	17 38 / 13 22	7 07 / 4 27	17 21 / 12 44	7 33 / 5 36	16 56 / 11 37
18 Mo 49	+14 00	6 28 / 3 44	18 00 / 15 02	6 38 / 4 04	17 51 / 14 43	6 50 / 4 28	17 39 / 14 19	5 03 / 5 03	17 23 / 13 46	6 02 / 5 36	16 59 / 12 49
19 Tu 50	+13 54	6 27 / 4 26	18 01 / 15 53	6 37 / 4 42	17 52 / 15 37	6 48 / 5 03	17 40 / 15 18	7 04 / 5 32	17 25 / 14 51	7 28 / 6 20	17 01 / 14 06
20 We 51	+13 49	6 27 / 5 05	18 01 / 16 43	6 36 / 5 18	17 52 / 16 32	6 47 / 5 34	17 41 / 16 17	7 02 / 5 57	17 27 / 15 57	7 25 / 6 32	17 03 / 15 25
21 Th 52	+13 42	6 26 / 5 42	18 02 / 17 34	6 35 / 5 51	17 53 / 17 26	6 45 / 6 02	17 43 / 17 17	6 18 / 6 18	17 04	6 42 / 7 23	16 44 / 17 06
22 Fr 53	+13 35 ● 05 34	6 25 / 6 17	18 02 / 18 24	6 34 / 6 22	17 53 / 18 20	6 43 / 6 29	17 44 / 18 17	6 58 / 6 37	17 30 / 18 11	7 20 / 6 50	17 08 / 18 03
23 Sa 54	+13 27	6 25 / 6 52	18 03 / 19 14	6 33 / 6 53	17 54 / 19 15	6 42 / 6 54	17 45 / 19 17	6 56 / 6 55	17 32 / 19 20	7 17 / 6 57	17 11 / 19 23
24 Su 55	+13 18	6 24 / 7 28	18 03 / 20 05	6 32 / 7 24	17 55 / 20 12	6 41 / 7 20	17 46 / 20 19	6 54 / 7 14	17 33 / 20 29	7 14 / 7 05	17 14 / 20 45
25 Mo 56	+13 09	6 24 / 8 05	18 03 / 20 59	6 31 / 7 57	17 55 / 21 09	6 39 / 7 47	17 47 / 21 22	6 52 / 7 33	17 35 / 21 40	7 11 / 7 13	17 16 / 22 09
26 Tu 57	+13 00	6 23 / 8 44	18 04 / 21 54	6 29 / 8 32	17 56 / 22 09	6 37 / 8 16	17 49 / 22 27	6 50 / 7 56	17 37 / 22 53	7 08 / 7 23	17 19 / 23 35
27 We 58	+12 50	6 22 / 9 27	18 04 / 22 52	6 28 / 9 11	17 57 / 23 10	6 36 / 8 51	17 50 / 23 33	6 48 / 8 23	17 38	7 05 / 7 37	17 21
28 Th 59	+12 39	6 21 / 10 15	18 04 / 23 51	6 27 / 9 55	17 58	6 35 / 9 31	17 51	6 46 / 8 56	17 40 / 0 06	7 02 / 7 58	17 24 / 1 02

Moon Phases: 6th 23:24 Full ○; 14th 00:04 Last Quarter ☾; 22nd 5:34 New ●.

Morning Stars: Mercury (Feb. 24-28); Venus; Jupiter (Feb. 13-28).
Evening Stars: Mercury (Feb. 1-24); Mars, Saturn; Jupiter (Feb. 1-13).

3rd Month   March, 1974   31 Days

Greenwich Mean Time

NOTE: Light figures indicate Sun. **Dark** figures indicate **Moon**. *Degrees are North Latitude.*

CAUTION: Must be converted to local time. For instruction see page 237.

Day of month / week / year	Sun on meridian / Moon phase	20° Rise Sun / Moon	20° Set Sun / Moon	30° Rise Sun / Moon	30° Set Sun / Moon	40° Rise Sun / Moon	40° Set Sun / Moon	50° Rise Sun / Moon	50° Set Sun / Moon	60° Rise Sun / Moon	60° Set Sun / Moon
		h m	h m	h m	h m	h m	h m	h m	h m	h m	h m
1 Fr	+12 27	6 20	18 05	6 26	17 59	6 34	17 52	6 44	17 42	6 59	17 27
60	18 03 D	11 08		10 46	0 12	10 19	0 39	9 40	1 17	8 31	2 25
2 Sa	+12 16	6 19	18 05	6 25	17 59	6 32	17 53	6 42	17 43	6 56	17 30
61		12 06	0 51	11 44	1 14	11 15	1 42	10 35	2 23	9 22	3 36
3 Su	+12 03	6 19	18 06	6 24	18 00	6 31	17 54	6 40	17 45	6 53	17 32
62		13 09	1 50	12 47	2 12	12 20	2 40	11 42	3 19	10 34	4 28
4 Mo	+11 50	6 18	18 06	6 23	18 00	6 29	17 55	6 38	17 47	6 50	17 35
63		14 13	2 46	13 55	3 06	13 31	3 31	12 59	4 05	12 03	5 03
5 Tu	+11 37	-6 17	18 06	6 22	18 01	6 27	17 56	6 36	17 49	6 47	17 37
64		15 17	3 39	15 03	3 55	14 46	4 15	14 21	4 42	13 41	5 26
6 We	+11 23	6 16	18 07	6 21	18 02	6 26	17 57	6 34	17 50	6 45	17 39
65		16 21	4 28	16 12	4 39	16 00	4 53	15 45	5 12	15 20	5 41
7 Th	+11 09	6 15	18 07	6 20	18 02	6 25	17 58	6 32	17 52	6 42	17 41
66		17 23	5 13	17 19	5 19	17 14	5 27	17 08	5 37	16 58	5 53
8 Fr	+10 54	6 14	18 07	6 19	18 03	6 23	17 59	6 29	17 53	6 39	17 44
67	10 03 O	18 23	5 56	18 25	5 57	18 27	5 59	18 29	6 00	18 33	6 03
9 Sa	+10 39	6 14	18 07	6 17	18 04	6 22	18 00	6 27	17 55	6 36	17 46
68		19 23	6 38	19 29	6 34	19 38	6 29	19 49	6 22	20 07	6 12
10 Su	+10 24	6 13	18 08	6 16	18 05	6 20	18 01	6 25	17 56	6 33	17 49
69		20 21	7 20	20 33	7 11	20 47	7 00	21 07	6 45	21 39	6 22
11 Mo	+10 08	6 12	18 08	6 15	18 06	6 19	18 02	6 23	17 58	6 30	17 52
70		21 19	8 03	21 35	7 49	21 54	7 33	22 22	7 10	23 08	6 34
12 Tu	+9 52	6 11	18 08	6 14	18 06	6 18	18 04	6 21	18 00	6 27	17 53
71		22 16	8 47	22 35	8 30	22 59	8 09	23 33	7 39		6 50
13 We	+9 36	6 10	18 09	6 12	18 07	6 16	18 05	6 19	18 01	6 24	17 55
72		23 11	9 34	23 32	9 14	23 59	8 48		8 13	0 32	7 12
14 Th	+9 20	6 10	18 09	6 11	18 07	6 14	18 06	6 17	18 03	6 21	17 58
73			10 22		10 00		9 33	0 38	8 53	1 47	7 43
15 Fr	+9 03	6 09	18 09	6 10	18 08	6 12	18 07	6 15	18 04	6 18	18 01
74	19 15 C	0 03	11 13	0 26	10 50	0 54	10 22	1 35	9 41	2 48	8 28
16 Sa	+8 46	6 08	18 10	6 09	18 09	6 11	18 08	6 12	18 06	6 15	18 04
75		0 53	12 04	1 15	11 42	1 43	11 15	2 22	10 36	3 32	9 26
17 Su	+8 29	6 07	18 10	6 08	18 09	6 09	18 09	6 10	18 07	6 11	18 06
76		1 39	12 55	2 00	12 35	2 25	12 11	3 01	11 36	4 03	10 36
18 Mo	+8 11	6 06	18 10	6 06	18 10	6 08	18 10	6 08	18 09	6 08	18 09
77		2 22	13 46	2 40	13 29	3 02	13 09	3 33	12 39	4 24	11 51
19 Tu	+7 54	6 06	18 10	6 05	18 11	6 06	18 11	6 05	18 10	6 05	18 12
78		3 02	14 37	3 17	14 24	3 35	14 07	3 59	13 45	4 39	13 08
20 We	+7 36	6 05	18 11	6 04	18 11	6 04	18 12	6 03	18 12	6 02	18 15
79		3 40	15 27	3 51	15 18	4 04	15 07	4 22	14 51	4 50	14 27
21 Th	+7 18	6 04	18 11	6 03	18 12	6 02	18 13	6 01	18 14	5 59	18 17
80		4 16	16 17	4 23	16 12	4 31	16 06	4 42	15 58	4 59	15 46
22 Fr	+7 01	' 6 03	18 11	6 01	18 12	6 01	18 14	5 59	18 16	5 56	18 19
81		4 51	17 08	4 54	17 07	4 57	17 07	5 01	17 07	5 07	17 06
23 Sa	+6 43	6 02	18 12	6 00	18 13	5 59	18 15	5 57	18 17	5 53	18 21
82	21 24 ●	5 27	17 59	5 25	18 04	5 23	18 09	5 19	18 16	5 15	18 28
24 Su	+6 25	6 01	18 12	5 59	18 13	5 57	18 16	5 54	18 19	5 50	18 24
83		6 04	18 53	5 58	19 02	5 50	19 13	5 39	19 28	5 23	19 52
25 Mo	+6 06	6 00	18 12	5 58	18 14	5 56	18 17	5 52	18 21	5 47	18 27
84		6 44	19 48	6 33	20 02	6 19	20 18	6 01	20 41	5 33	21 18
26 Tu	+5 48	5 59	18 13	5 57	18 15	5 54	18 18	5 50	18 22	5 44	18 29
85		7 26	20 46	7 11	21 03	6 53	21 25	6 27	21 55	5 47	22 46
27 We	+5 30	5 59	18 13	5 55	18 15	5 53	18 19	5 48	18 24	5 41	18 31
86		8 13	21 46	7 55	22 06	7 32	22 32	6 59	23 08	6 06	
28 Th	+5 12	5 58	18 13	5 54	18 16	5 51	18 20	5 46	18 25	5 38	18 34
87		9 05	22 46	8 44	23 08	8 18	23 36	7 40		6 35	0 11
29 Fr	+4 54	5 57	18 13	5 53	18 17	5 49	18 21	5 44	18 27	5 35	18 37
88		10 02	23 45	9 39		9 11		8 31	0 15	7 20	1 26
30 Sa	+4 36	5 56	18 14	5 52	18 18	5 48	18 22	5 42	18 29	5 32	18 39
89		11 02		10 40	0 07	10 13	0 34	9 34	1 14	8 25	2 24
31 Su	+4 18	5 55	18 14	5 51	18 18	5 46	18 23	5 40	18 30	5 29	18 41
90	01 44 D	12 04	0 41	11 45	1 01	11 21	1 27	10 46	2 02	9 48	3 03

Moon Phases: 1st 18:03 First Quarter D; 8th 10:03 Full O; 15th 19:15 Last Quarter C; 23rd 21:24 New ●; 31st 1:44 1st Quarter D.

Morning Stars: Mercury, Venus, Jupiter.
Evening Stars: Mars, Saturn.

4th Month   April, 1974   30 Days

Greenwich Mean Time

NOTE: Light figures indicate Sun. **Dark** figures indicate **Moon.** *Degrees are North Latitude.*

CAUTION: Must be converted to local time. For instruction see page 237.

Day of month/week/year	Sun on meridian / Moon phase	20° Rise Sun/Moon	20° Set Sun/Moon	30° Rise Sun/Moon	30° Set Sun/Moon	40° Rise Sun/Moon	40° Set Sun/Moon	50° Rise Sun/Moon	50° Set Sun/Moon	60° Rise Sun/Moon	60° Set Sun/Moon
		h m	h m	h m	h m	h m	h m	h m	h m	h m	h m
1 Mo 91	+4 00	5 54	18 14	5 50	18 19	5 44	18 24	5 38	18 31	5 26	18 44
		13 07	1 33	12 51	1 50	12 32	2 12	12 04	2 41	11 19	3 29
2 Tu 92	+3 42	5 53	18 14	5 49	18 19	5 43	18 25	5 36	18 33	5 23	18 47
		14 08	2 21	13 57	2 35	13 44	2 51	13 25	3 12	12 54	3 47
3 We 93	+3 24	5 52	18 15	5 47	18 20	5 41	18 26	5 34	18 34	5 20	18 49
		15 09	3 06	15 03	3 15	14 55	3 25	14 45	3 39	14 29	4 00
4 Th 94	+3 06	5 51	18 15	5 46	18 20	5 39	18 27	5 31	18 36	5 17	18 51
		16 08	3 49	16 07	3 52	16 06	3 57	16 05	4 02	16 03	4 10
5 Fr 95	+2 49	5 50	18 15	5 45	18 21	5 38	18 28	5 29	18 38	5 14	18 53
		17 07	4 31	17 11	4 29	17 16	4 27	17 24	4 24	17 35	4 20
6 Sa 96	21 00 ○ +2 32	5 50	18 16	5 44	18 21	5 36	18 29	5 27	18 40	5 11	18 55
		18 05	5 12	18 14	5 05	18 26	4 57	18 42	4 46	19 07	4 30
7 Su 97	+2 14	5 49	18 16	5 43	18 22	5 34	18 30	5 25	18 41	5 08	18 58
		19 03	5 54	19 17	5 43	19 34	5 29	19 30	0 10	20 27	4 41
8 Mo 98	+1 57	5 48	18 16	5 41	18 22	5 33	18 31	5 23	18 43	5 05	19 01
		20 01	6 38	20 18	6 23	20 40	6 04	21 12	5 37	22 04	4 55
9 Tu 99	+1 41	5 47	18 17	5 40	18 23	5 31	18 32	5 21	18 45	5 02	19 03
		20 57	7 24	21 18	7 06	21 44	6 42	22 20	6 09	23 24	5 14
10 We 100	+1 24	5 46	18 17	5 39	18 24	5 30	18 33	5 18	18 46	4 59	19 05
		21 52	8 13	22 14	7 52	22 42	7 25	23 21	6 48		5 42
11 Th 101	+1 08	5 46	18 17	5 38	18 24	5 28	18 34	5 16	18 48	4 56	19 08
		22 44	9 03	23 06	8 41	23 34	8 13		7 33	0 32	6 22
12 Fr 102	+0 52	5 45	18 17	5 37	18 25	5 27	18 35	5 14	18 49	4 53	19 11
		23 32	9 55	23 53	9 33		9 05	0 14	8 26	1 24	7 16
13 Sa 103	+0 37	5 44	18 17	5 36	18 25	5 25	18 36	5 12	18 50	4 50	19 13
			10 46		10 26	0 19	10 01	0 57	9 24	2 01	8 21
14 Su 104	14 57 ☾ +0 22	5 43	18 18	5 35	18 26	5 24	18 37	5 10	18 51	4 47	19 16
		0 17	11 38	0 35	11 20	0 59	10 58	1 31	10 27	2 26	9 34
15 Mo 105	+0 07	5 42	18 18	5 34	18 27	5 23	18 38	5 08	18 53	4 44	19 18
		0 58	12 29	1 14	12 14	1 33	11 56	2 00	11 31	2 43	10 51
16 Tu 106	−0 08	5 42	18 18	5 33	18 27	5 22	18 39	5 06	18 55	4 41	19 21
		1 36	13 19	1 48	13 08	2 03	12 55	2 24	12 37	2 56	12 08
17 We 107	−0 22	5 41	18 19	5 31	18 28	5 20	18 40	5 04	18 56	4 39	19 23
		2 13	14 08	2 21	14 02	2 31	13 54	2 45	13 43	3 06	13 26
18 Th 108	−0 35	5 40	18 19	5 30	18 28	5 18	18 41	5 02	18 58	4 36	19 26
		2 48	14 58	2 52	14 56	2 57	14 54	3 04	14 50	3 14	14 45
19 Fr 109	−0 49	5 39	18 19	5 29	18 29	5 17	18 42	5 00	19 00	4 33	19 28
		3 24	15 50	3 24	15 52	3 23	15 55	3 23	15 59	3 23	16 06
20 Sa 110	−1 02	5 38	18 20	5 28	18 30	5 15	18 43	4 58	19 01	4 30	19 30
		4 00	16 42	3 56	16 49	3 50	16 58	3 42	17 10	3 31	17 29
21 Su 111	−1 14	5 38	18 20	5 27	18 30	5 14	18 44	4 56	19 03	4 27	19 33
		4 39	17 38	4 30	17 49	4 19	18 04	4 04	18 23	3 41	18 55
22 Mo 112	10 17 ● −1 26	5 37	18 20	5 21	18 36	4 51	19 11	4 29	19 30	3 53	20 24
		5 21	18 36	5 08	18 51	4 51	19 11	4 29	19 30	3 53	20 24
23 Tu 113	−1 38	5 36	18 21	5 25	18 31	5 10	18 46	4 52	19 06	4 21	19 38
		6 08	19 36	5 50	19 55	5 29	20 19	4 59	20 54	4 11	21 52
24 We 114	−1 49	5 35	18 21	5 24	18 32	5 09	18 47	4 50	19 07	4 18	19 40
		6 59	20 37	6 39	20 59	6 13	21 26	5 38	22 05	4 37	23 13
25 Th 115	−1 59	5 35	18 21	5 23	18 33	5 08	18 48	4 48	19 09	4 15	19 42
		7 56	21 38	7 34	22 00	7 06	22 28	6 27	23 08	5 18	
26 Fr 116	−2 09	5 34	18 22	5 22	18 33	5 06	18 49	4 46	19 10	4 12	19 45
		8 56	22 36	8 34	22 57	8 07	23 23	7 27		6 18	0 17
27 Sa 117	−2 19	5 33	18 22	5 21	18 34	5 05	18 50	4 44	19 12	4 09	19 47
		9 58	23 30	9 38	23 48	9 13		8 38	0 00	7 36	1 03
28 Su 118	−2 28	5 33	18 22	5 20	18 35	5 04	18 51	4 43	19 14	4 07	19 50
		11 01		10 44		10 24	0 11	9 55	0 42	9 06	1 33
29 Mo 119	07 39 ☽ −2 37	5 32	18 23	5 19	18 36	5 03	18 52	4 41	19 15	4 04	19 53
		12 02	0 19	11 50	0 34	11 35	0 51	11 14	1 15	10 40	1 53
30 Tu 120	−2 45	5 32	18 23	5 18	18 37	5 02	18 53	4 39	19 17	4 01	19 55
		13 02	1 05	12 55	1 14	12 45	1 26	12 33	1 42	12 13	2 07

Moon Phases: 6th 21:00 Full ○, 14th 14:57 Last Quarter ☾; 22nd 10:17 New ●; 29th 7:39 1st Quarter ☽.

Morning Stars: Mercury, Venus, Jupiter.
Evening Stars: Mars, Saturn.

5th Month   May, 1974   31 Days

Greenwich Mean Time

NOTE: Light figures indicate Sun. **Dark** figures indicate **Moon.** *Degrees are North Latitude.*

CAUTION: Must be converted to local time. For instruction see page 237.

Day of month / week / year	Sun on meridian / Moon phase	20° Rise Sun/Moon	20° Set Sun/Moon	30° Rise Sun/Moon	30° Set Sun/Moon	40° Rise Sun/Moon	40° Set Sun/Moon	50° Rise Sun/Moon	50° Set Sun/Moon	60° Rise Sun/Moon	60° Set Sun/Moon
	h m s	h m	h m	h m	h m	h m	h m	h m	h m	h m	h m
1 We 121	−2 53	5 31	18 23	5 17	18 37	5 01	18 54	4 37	19 18	3 59	19 57
		14 00	1 47	13 58	1 52	13 55	1 58	13 50	2 06	13 44	2 18
2 Th 122	−3 00	5 31	18 24	5 16	18 38	4 59	18 55	4 35	19 19	3 56	20 00
		14 57	2 28	15 00	2 28	15 03	2 28	15 07	2 28	15 14	2 28
3 Fr 123	−3 07	5 30	18 24	5 15	18 38	4 58	18 56	4 34	19 21	3 53	20 02
		15 54	3 08	16 02	3 03	16 11	2 57	16 24	2 49	16 43	2 37
4 Sa 124	−3 13	5 30	18 25	5 15	18 39	4 57	18 57	4 32	19 23	3 50	20 05
		16 51	3 49	17 03	3 40	17 18	3 28	17 39	3 12	18 12	2 48
5 Su 125	−3 18	5 29	18 25	5 14	18 40	4 56	18 58	4 30	19 24	3 48	20 07
		17 48	4 32	18 04	4 18	18 24	4 01	18 53	3 38	19 39	3 01
6 Mo 126	−3 27 08 55 ○	5 29	18 25	5 13	18 40	4 55	18 59	4 28	19 26	3 45	20 10
		18 45	5 16	19 04	4 59	19 29	4 37	20 03	4 07	21 02	3 18
7 Tu 127	−3 28	5 28	18 26	5 12	18 41	4 53	19 00	4 27	19 28	3 43	20 12
		19 41	6 04	20 02	5 44	20 29	5 18	21 07	4 43	22 16	3 42
8 We 128	−3 32	5 27	18 26	5 12	18 41	4 52	19 01	4 25	19 29	3 40	20 15
		20 34	6 54	20 56	6 32	21 24	6 04	22 04	5 25	23 15	4 17
9 Th 129	−3 35	5 27	18 27	5 11	18 42	4 51	19 02	4 23	19 31	3 37	20 17
		21 24	7 45	21 46	7 23	22 12	6 55	22 51	6 16	23 58	5 05
10 Fr 130	−3 38	5 26	18 27	5 10	18 43	4 50	19 03	4 22	19 32	3 35	20 19
		22 10	8 37	22 30	8 16	22 55	7 50	23 29	7 13		6 07
11 Sa 131	−3 40	5 26	18 27	5 10	18 43	4 49	19 04	4 20	19 34	3 33	20 22
		22 53	9 29	23 10	9 11	23 31	8 47		8 14	0 27	7 18
12 Su 132	−3 41	5 25	18 28	5 09	18 44	4 48	19 05	4 19	19 35	3 31	20 24
		23 33	10 20	23 46	10 05		9 45	0 00	9 18	0 47	8 33
13 Mo 133	−3 42	5 25	18 28	5 08	18 45	4 47	19 06	4 17	19 37	3 28	20 27
			11 10		10 58	0 03	10 44	0 26	10 23	1 02	9 50
14 Tu 134	−3 43 09 29 ☾	5 24	18 28	5 08	18 45	4 46	19 07	4 16	19 38	3 26	20 29
		0 10	12 00	0 19	11 52	0 31	11 42	0 48	11 28	1 13	11 07
15 We 135	−3 43	5 24	18 29	5 07	18 46	4 45	19 08	4 15	19 39	3 23	20 31
		0 45	12 49	0 51	12 45	0 58	12 41	1 07	12 34	1 22	12 24
16 Th 136	−3 42	5 24	18 29	5 07	18 47	4 44	19 09	4 14	19 41	3 21	20 34
		1 20	13 39	1 22	13 40	1 23	13 40	1 26	13 41	1 30	13 43
17 Fr 137	−3 41	5 23	18 29	5 06	18 47	4 43	19 10	4 12	19 43	3 19	20 36
		1 56	14 30	1 53	14 35	1 49	14 42	1 45	14 50	1 38	15 04
18 Sa 138	−3 38	5 23	18 30	5 05	18 48	4 43	19 11	4 11	19 44	3 16	20 39
		2 33	15 24	2 26	15 34	2 17	15 45	2 05	16 02	1 47	16 28
19 Su 139	−3 36	5 23	18 30	5 05	18 48	4 42	19 12	4 10	19 45	3 14	20 41
		3 13	16 21	3 02	16 35	2 48	16 52	2 28	17 16	1 59	17 55
20 Mo 140	−3 33	5 22	18 31	5 04	18 49	4 41	19 13	4 08	19 46	3 12	20 43
		3 58	17 20	3 42	17 38	3 23	18 00	2 56	18 32	2 14	19 25
21 Tu 141	−3 29 20 34 ●	5 22	18 31	5 04	18 49	4 40	19 13	4 07	19 46	3 10	20 46
		4 48	18 22	4 28	18 43	4 05	19 09	3 32	19 46	2 36	20 51
22 We 142	−3 25	5 22	18 32	5 03	18 50	4 39	19 14	4 05	19 49	3 08	20 48
		5 43	19 25	5 22	19 47	4 55	20 15	4 17	20 54	3 11	22 04
23 Th 143	−3 20	5 22	18 32	5 03	18 51	4 39	19 15	4 04	19 50	3 06	20 50
		6 44	20 26	6 22	20 48	5 54	21 15	5 14	21 53	4 04	22 59
24 Fr 144	−3 15 ··	5 21	18 32	5 02	18 51	4 38	19 16	4 03	19 51	3 04	20 52
		7 47	21 23	7 27	21 43	7 01	22 06	6 23	22 39	5 19	23 35
25 Sa 145	−3 09	5 21	18 33	5 02	18 52	4 37	19 17	4 02	19 52	3 02	20 54
		8 52	22 16	8 34	22 31	8 12	22 50	7 41	23 16	6 48	23 58
26 Su 146	−3 03	5 21	18 33	5 02	18 52	4 37	19 17	4 01	19 53	3 00	20 56
		9 56	23 03	9 42	23 14	9 25	23 28	9 01	23 46	8 23	
27 Mo 147	−2 57	5 21	18 33	5 01	18 53	4 36	19 18	4 00	19 55	2 59	20 58
		10 57	23 47	10 48	23 53	10 37		10 22		9 58	0 14
28 Tu 148	−2 49 13 03 ☽	5 21	18 34	5 01	18 53	4 35	19 19	4 00	19 56	2 57	21 00
		11 56		11 52		11 47	0 01	11 40	0 11	11 30	0 27
29 We 149	−2 42	5 20	18 34	5 01	18 54	4 34	19 20	3 59	19 57	2 55	21 02
		12 53	0 28	12 54	0 30	12 55	0 31	12 57	0 33	13 00	0 37
30 Th 150	−2 34	5 20	18 35	5 00	18 55	4 34	19 21	3 58	19 58	2 53	21 04
		13 49	1 08	13 55	1 05	14 02	1 01	14 13	0 55	14 28	0 46
31 Fr 151	−2 26	5 20	18 35	5 00	18 55	4 33	19 21	3 57	19 59	2 52	21 06
		14 45	1 48	14 56	1 40	15 09	1 30	15 27	1 17	15 56	0 56

Moon Phases: 6th 8:55 Full ○; 14th 9:29 Last Quarter ☾; 21st 20:34 New ●; 28th 13:03 1st Quarter ☽.

Morning Stars: Mercury (May 1-4); Venus, Jupiter.
Evening Stars: Mercury (May 4-31); Mars, Saturn.

6th Month   June, 1974   30 Days

Greenwich Mean Time

NOTE: Light figures indicate Sun. **Dark** figures indicate **Moon.** *Degrees are North Latitude.*

CAUTION: Must be converted to local time. For instruction see page 237.

Day of month / week / year	Sun on meridian Moon phase	20° Rise Sun/Moon	20° Set Sun/Moon	30° Rise Sun/Moon	30° Set Sun/Moon	40° Rise Sun/Moon	40° Set Sun/Moon	50° Rise Sun/Moon	50° Set Sun/Moon	60° Rise Sun/Moon	60° Set Sun/Moon
		h m	h m	h m	h m	h m	h m	h m	h m	h m	h m
1 Sa 152	−2 17	5 20	18 35	5 00	18 56	4 33	19 22	3 56	20 00	2 50	21 07
		15 41	2 29	15 56	2 17	16 14	2 02	16 40	1 41	17 22	1 08
2 Su 153	−2 08	5 20	18 36	5 00	18 56	4 32	19 23	3 55	20 01	2 49	21 09
		16 37	3 13	16 55	2 56	17 18	2 36	17 50	2 08	18 45	1 23
3 Mo 154	−1 58	5 20	18 36	4 59	18 57	4 32	19 24	3 55	20 02	2 47	21 11
		17 32	3 58	17 53	3 39	18 19	3 15	18 56	2 41	20 02	1 44
4 Tu 155	22 10 ○ −1 48	5 20	18 37	4 59	18 58	4 32	19 25	3 54	20 03	2 45	21 12
		18 26	4 47	18 48	4 25	19 16	3 59	19 55	3 21	21 06	2 14
5 We 156	−1 38	5 20	18 37	4 59	18 58	4 32	19 26	3 53	20 03	2 44	21 14
		19 17	5 37	19 39	5 15	20 07	4 48	20 46	4 08	21 55	2 57
6 Th 157	−1 27	5 20	18 38	4 59	18 59	4 31	19 26	3 53	20 04	2 43	21 15
		20 05	6 29	20 26	6 08	20 51	5 41	21 27	5 02	22 29	3 54
7 Fr 158	−1 17	5 20	18 38	4 58	18 59	4 31	19 27	3 52	20 05	2 42	21 16
		20 49	7 21	21 07	7 02	21 30	6 37	22 01	6 02	22 52	5 02
8 Sa 159	−1 03	5 20	18 38	4 58	19 00	4 31	19 27	3 52	20 06	2 41	21 18
		21 30	8 13	21 45	7 56	22 03	7 35	22 28	7 06	23 09	6 16
9 Su 160	−0 54	5 20	18 39	4 58	19 00	4 31	19 28	3 51	20 07	2 40	21 19
		22 08	9 04	22 19	8 50	22 33	8 34	22 51	8 10	23 21	7 33
10 Mo 161	−0 42	5 20	18 39	4 58	19 00	4 31	19 29	3 51	20 07	2 39	21 20
		22 43	9 53	22 51	9 44	23 00	9 32	23 12	9 15	23 30	8 50
11 Tu 162	−0 30	5 20	18 39	4 58	19 01	4 30	19 29	3 51	20 08	2 39	21 21
		23 18	10 42	23 21	10 36	23 25	10 30	23 30	10 21	23 39	10 06
12 We 163	−0 18	5 20	18 40	4 58	19 01	4 30	19 29	3 50	20 09	2 38	21 22
		23 53	11 31	23 52	11 30	23 50	11 28	23 49	11 26	23 46	11 23
13 Th 164	−0 06 01 45 ☾	5 20	18 40	4 58	19 02	4 30	19 30	3 50	20 09	2 38	21 23
			12 20		12 24		12 27		12 33	23 55	12 41
14 Fr 165	+0 07	5 20	18 40	4 58	19 02	4 30	19 30	3 50	20 10	2 37	21 24
		0 28	13 12	0 23	13 19	0 17	13 29	0 08	13 42		14 02
15 Sa 166	+0 20	5 20	18 41	4 58	19 02	4 30	19 30	3 50	20 10	2 37	21 25
		1 06	14 06	0 57	14 18	0 45	14 33	0 29	14 53	0 05	15 26
16 Su 167	+0 33	5 20	18 41	4 58	19 03	4 30	19 31	3 50	20 11	2 36	21 26
		1 48	15 03	1 34	15 19	1 17	15 39	0 54	16 07	0 18	16 54
17 Mo 168	+0 46	5 21	18 41	4 59	19 03	4 30	19 31	3 50	20 11	2 36	21 26
		2 34	16 03	2 17	16 23	1 55	16 47	1 25	17 22	0 36	18 21
18 Tu 169	+0 59	5 21	18 42	4 59	19 03	4 31	19 31	3 50	20 12	2 35	21 27
		3 27	17 06	3 06	17 28	2 41	17 55	2 05	18 34	1 04	19 42
19 We 170	+1 12	5 21	18 42	4 59	19 04	4 31	19 32	3 50	20 12	2 35	21 27
		4 25	18 09	4 03	18 31	3 36	18 59	2 56	19 38	1 47	20 47
20 Th 171	+1 25 04 56 ●	5 21	18 42	4 59	19 04	4 31	19 32	3 50	20 12	2 35	21 27
		5 29	19 09	5 07	19 30	4 40	19 55	4 01	20 31	2 53	21 32
21 Fr 172	+1 38	5 21	18 42	4 59	19 04	4 31	19 32	3 50	20 12	2 35	21 28
		6 35	20 06	6 16	20 23	5 51	20 44	5 17	21 13	4 18	22 01
22 Sa 173	+1 51	5 22	18 43	4 59	19 04	4 31	19 33	3 51	20 13	2 35	21 28
		7 41	20 57	7 26	21 10	7 08	21 26	6 39	21 47	5 55	22 21
23 Su 174	+2 04	5 22	18 43	5 00	19 04	4 32	19 33	3 51	20 13	2 36	21 28
		8 46	21 44	8 35	21 52	8 22	22 01	8 03	22 15	7 34	22 35
24 Mo 175	+2 17	5 22	18 43	5 00	19 05	4 32	19 33	3 51	20 13	2 36	21 28
		9 48	22 27	9 42	22 30	9 35	22 34	9 25	22 38	9 10	22 46
25 Tu 176	+2 30	5 22	18 43	5 00	19 05	4 32	19 33	3 51	20 13	2 37	21 27
		10 47	23 08	10 46	23 06	10 46	23 04	10 45	23 01	10 43	22 56
26 We 177	+2 43 19 20 ☽	5 22	18 43	5 01	19 05	4 33	19 33	3 52	20 13	2 38	21 27
		11 44	23 49	11 49	23 42	11 54	23 34	12 02	23 23	12 14	23 06
27 Th 178	+2 56	5 22	18 43	5 01	19 05	4 34	19 33	3 52	20 13	2 38	21 27
		12 41		12 50		13 01		13 17	23 46	13 42	23 17
28 Fr 179	+3 08	5 23	18 43	5 01	19 05	4 34	19 33	3 52	20 13	2 39	21 27
		13 37	0 29	13 50	0 18	14 07	0 05	14 31		15 09	23 31
29 Sa 180	+3 20	5 23	18 43	5 02	19 05	4 34	19 33	3 53	20 13	2 40	21 26
		14 32	1 12	14 50	0 57	15 11	0 38	15 41	0 12	16 33	23 50
30 Su 181	+3 32	5 24	18 43	5 02	19 05	4 34	19 33	3 53	20 12	2 41	21 26
		15 27	1 56	15 47	1 38	16 13	1 15	16 48	0 43	17 51	

Moon Phases: 4th 22:10 Full ○; 13th 1:45 Last Quarter ☾; 20th 4:56 New ●; 26th 19:20 1st Quarter ☽.

Morning Stars: Mercury, Saturn (Jun. 30); Venus, Jupiter.
Evening Stars: Mercury, Mars, Saturn.

7th Month   July, 1974   31 Days

Greenwich Mean Time

NOTE: Light figures indicate Sun. **Dark** figures indicate **Moon.** *Degrees are North Latitude.*

CAUTION: Must be converted to local time. For instruction see page 237.

Day of month week year	Sun on meridian Moon phase	20° Rise Sun Moon	20° Set Sun Moon	30° Rise Sun Moon	30° Set Sun Moon	40° Rise Sun Moon	40° Set Sun Moon	50° Rise Sun Moon	50° Set Sun Moon	60° Rise Sun Moon	60° Set Sun Moon
	h m s	h m	h m	h m	h m	h m	h m	h m	h m	h m	h m
1 Mo 182	+3 44	5 24	18 44	5 02	19 05	4 35	19 33	3 54	20 12	2 42	21 25
		16 21	2 43	16 43	2 23	17 10	1 57	17 49	1 20	18 59	0 16
2 Tu 183	+3 55	5 24	18 44	5 02	19 05	4 35	19 32	3 55	20 12	2 43	21 25
		17.13	3 33	17 35	3 11	18 02	2 43	18 42	2 04	19 52	0 54
3 We 184	+4 06	5 25	18 44	5 03	19 05	4 35	19 32	3 56	20 12	2 44	21 24
		18 01	4 24	18 22	4 02	18 49	3 35	19 26	2 55	20 31	1 45
4 Th 185	+4 17 12 40 O	5 25	18 44	5 03	19 05	4 36	19 32	3 57	20 11	2 45	21 23
		18 47	5 16	19 06	4 55	19 29	4 30	20 02	3 53	20 58	2 50
5 Fr 186	+4 28	5 25	18 44	5 03	19 05	4 36	19 32	3 57	20 11	2 46	21 22
		19 28	6 07	19 44	5 50	20 04	5 27	20 32	4 56	21 16	4 02
6 Sa 187	+4 38	5 25	18 44	5 04	19 05	4 37	19 31	3 58	20 11	2 48	21 21
		20 07	6 58	20 20	6 44	20 35	6 25	20 56	6 00	21 30	5 18
7 Su 188	+4 48	5 26	18 43	5 04	19 05	4 37	19 31	3 59	20 10	2 49	21 20
		20 44	7 48	20 52	7 37	21 03	7 24	21 18	7 05	21 40	6 35
8 Mo 189	+4 57	5 26	18 43	5 05	19 04	4 38	19 31	4 00	20 10	2 50	21 19
		21 18	8 37	21 23	8 30	21 29	8 22	21 37	8 10	21 49	7 51
9 Tu 190	+5 06	5 27	18 43	5 06	19 04	4 39	19 31	4 01	20 09	2 52	21 17
		21 53	9 26	21 53	9 23	21 54	9 19	21 55	9 15	21 57	9 07
10 We 191	+5 15	5 27	18 43	5 06	19 04	4 39	19 30	4 02	20 09	2 53	21 15
		22 27	10 14	22 24	10 16	22 19	10 18	22 13	10 20	22 05	10 24
11 Th 192	+5 23	5 28	18 43	5 07	19 04	4 40	19 30	4 03	20 08	2 55	21 14
		23 03	11 04	22 56	11 10	22 46	11 17	22 33	11 27	22 14	11 42
12 Fr 193	+5 31 15 28 ☾	5 28	18 43	5 07	19 04	4 41	19 30	4 04	20 07	2 57	21 12
		23 42	11 56	23 30	12 06	23 16	12 18	22 56	12 36	22 25	13 03
13 Sa 194	+5 39	5 29	18 43	5 08	19 03	4 42	19 29	4 05	20 06	2 59	21 10
			12 50		13 04	23 50	13 22	23 23	13 47	22 40	14 27
14 Su 195	+5 46	5 29	18 43	5 08	19 03	4 43	19 29	4 06	20 05	3 01	21 09
		0 25	13 47	0 09	14 05		14 28	23 57	14 59	23 02	15 52
15 Mo 196	+5 52	5 29	18 43	5 09	19 03	4 43	19 28	4 07	20 04	3 03	21 07
		1 13	14 47	0 54	15 08	0 30	15 34		16 11	23 36	17 15
16 Tu 197	+5 58	5 29	18 42	5 09	19 02	4 44	19 27	4 09	20 03	3 05	21 05
		2 07	15 49	1 46	16 11	1 19	16 39	0 41	17 18		18 28
17 We 198	+6 04	5 30	18 42	5 10	19 02	4 45	19 27	4 10	20 02	3 07	21 04
		3 08	16.50	2 46	17 12	2 18	17 39	1 38	18 17	0 29	19 23
18 Th 199	+6 09	5 30	18 42	5 10	19 02	4 46	19 26	4 11	20 01	3 09	21 02
		4 12	17 49	3 52	18 08	3 26	18 32	2 49	19 05	1 44	20 00
19 Fr 200	+6 13 12 07 ●	5 30	18 42	5 11	19 01	4 47	19 25	4 12	20 00	3 11	21 00
		5 20	18 44	5 02	18 59	4 40	19 18	4 09	19 43	3 17	20 24
20 Sa 201	+6 17	5 31	18 41	5 11	19 01	4 48	19 25	4 13	19 59	3 14	20 58
		6 26	19 34	6 13	19 44	5 57	19 57	5 34	20 14	4 57	20 41
21 Su 202	+6 20	5 31	18 41	5 12	19 01	4 48	19 24	4 15	19 58	3 16	20 56
		7 31	20 20	7 23	20 26	7 13	20 32	6 59	20 41	6 38	20 54
22 Mo 203	+6 23	5 31	18 41	5 12	19 00	4 49	19 23	4 16	19 57	3 18	20 54
		8 34	21 04	8 31	21 04	8 28	21 04	8 23	21 04	8 16	21 05
23 Tu 204	+6 26	5 32	18 40	5 13	19 00	4 50	19 23	4 17	19 56	3 20	20 52
		9 34	21 46	9 37	21 41	9 40	21 35	9 44	21 27	9 50	21 15
24 We 205	+6 27	5 32	18 40	5 14	18 59	4 50	19 22	4 18	19 54	3 22	20 50
		10 33	22 28	10 40	22 18	10 50	22 07	11 02	21 51	11 22	21 26
25 Th 206	+6 28	5 32	18 40	5 14	18 59	4 52	19 21	4 19	19 53	3 25	20 48
		11 30	23 11	11 42	22 57	11 57	22 40	12 18	22 17	12 52	21 40
26 Fr 207	+6 29 03 51 ☽	5 33	18 40	5 15	18 58	4 52	19 20	4 21	19 52	3 27	20 45
		12 27	23 55	12 43	23 38	13 03	23 16	13 31	22 46	14 18	21 57
27 Sa 208	+6 28	5 33	18 39	5 16	18 58	4 53	19 19	4 22	19 50	3 29	20 43
		13 23		13 42		14 06	23 56	14 40	23 21	15 39	22 21
28 Su 209	+6 27	5 33	18 39	5 16	18 57	4 54	19 18	4 23	19 49	3 31	20 41
		14 17	0 41	14 38	0 21	15 05		15 43		16 50	22 54
29 Mo 210	+6 26	5 34	18 39	5 16	18 56	4 55	19 17	4 25	19 47	3 33	20 38
		15 09	1 30	15 31	1 08	15 59	0 41	16 38	0 03	17 49	23 41
30 Tu 211	+6 24	5 34	18 38	5 17	18 56	4 56	19 16	4 26	19 45	3 35	20 36
		15 59	2 20	16 20	1 58	16 47	1 31	17 25	0 51	18 32	
31 We 212	+6 21	5 34	18 38	5 18	18 55	4 57	19 15	4 27	19 43	3 37	20 34
		16 45	3 12	17 05	2 51	17 29	2 25	18 04	1 47	19 02	0 41

Moon Phases: 4th 12:40 Full O; 12th 15:28 Last Quarter ☾; 19th 12:07 New ●; 26th 3:51 1st Quarter ☽.

Morning Stars: Mercury, Venus, Jupiter, Saturn.
Evening Stars: Mars.

8th Month   August, 1974   31 Days

Greenwich Mean Time

NOTE: Light figures indicate Sun. **Dark** figures indicate **Moon.** *Degrees are North Latitude.*

CAUTION: Must be converted to local time. For instruction see page 237.

Rise/Set columns: top (light) figures = Sun, bottom (dark) figures = Moon. Units are h m.

Day (month / week / year)	Sun on meridian / Moon phase (h m s)	Body	20° Rise	20° Set	30° Rise	30° Set	40° Rise	40° Set	50° Rise	50° Set	60° Rise	60° Set
1 Th 213	+6 18	Sun	5 35	18 37	5 18	18 54	4 58	19 14	4 29	19 42	3 40	20 31
		Moon	17 28	4 03	17 45	3 45	18 06	3 21	18 35	2 48	19 23	1 51
2 Fr 214	+6 14	Sun	5 35	18 37	5 19	18 53	4 59	19 13	4 30	19 41	3 42	20 28
		Moon	18 07	4 54	18 21	4 39	18 38	4 19	19 01	3 51	19 38	3 05
3 Sa 215	+6 10 03 57 ○	Sun	5 36	18 36	5 20	18 52	5 00	19 12	4 32	19 40	3 45	20 26
		Moon	18 45	5 44	18 55	5 32	19 07	5 17	19 24	4 56	19 50	4 22
4 Su 216	+6 04	Sun	5 36	18 36	5 20	18 52	5 01	19 11	4 33	19 38	3 47	20 23
		Moon	19 20	6 34	19 26	6 25	19 34	6 15	19 44	6 01	19 59	5 39
5 Mo 217	+5 59	Sun	5 37	18 35	5 21	18 51	5 02	19 09	4 35	19 36	3 49	20 21
		Moon	19 54	7 22	19 56	7 18	19 59	7 13	20 02	7 06	20 08	6 55
6 Tu 218	+5 52	Sun	5 37	18 35	5 21	18 50	5 03	19 08	4 36	19 35	3 51	20 18
		Moon	20 29	8 11	20 27	8 11	20 24	8 11	20 21	8 11	20 16	8 11
7 We 219	+5 45	Sun	5 37	18 34	5 22	18 49	5 04	19 07	4 38	19 33	3 53	20 16
		Moon	21 04	9 00	20 58	9 04	20 50	9 10	20 40	9 17	20 24	9 20
8 Th 220	+5 38	Sun	5 38	18 33	5 23	18 48	5 05	19 06	4 39	19 31	3 56	20 13
		Moon	21 41	9 50	21 31	9 59	21 18	10 10	21 01	10 24	20 35	10 47
9 Fr 221	+5 30	Sun	5 38	18 33	5 23	18 47	5 05	19 05	4 40	19 29	3 58	20 10
		Moon	22 22	10 43	22 08	10 55	21 50	11 11	21 26	11 33	20 48	12 08
10 Sa 222	+5 21	Sun	5 38	18 32	5 24	18 46	5 06	19 03	4 42	19 27	4 01	20 08
		Moon	23 06	11 37	22 49	11 54	22 27	12 14	21 56	12 43	21 06	13 31
11 Su 223	+5 12 02 46 ☾	Sun	5 30	18 31	5 24	18 45	5 07	19 02	4 43	19 26	4 04	20 05
		Moon	23 56	12 35	23 36	12 54	23 11	13 19	22 35	13 53	21 34	14 53
12 Mo 224	+5 02	Sun	5 39	18 31	5 25	18 44	5 08	19 01	4 45	19 24	4 07	20 02
		Moon	—	13 34	—	13 55	—	14 22	23 24	15 00	22 16	16 08
13 Tu 225	+4 52	Sun	5 39	18 30	5 26	18 43	5 09	19 00	4 46	19 23	4 09	19 59
		Moon	0 52	14 34	0 30	14 55	0 03	15 23	—	16 01	23 18	17 10
14 We 226	+4 41	Sun	5 39	18 30	5 26	18 42	5 10	18 58	4 48	19 21	4 11	19 56
		Moon	1 53	15 32	1 31	15 52	1 04	16 18	0 26	16 53	—	17 54
15 Th 227	+4 30	Sun	5 40	18 29	5 27	18 41	5 11	18 57	4 50	19 19	4 14	19 53
		Moon	2 57	16 28	2 38	16 45	2 14	17 06	1 40	17 36	0 41	18 24
16 Fr 228	+4 18	Sun	5 40	18 29	5 27	18 41	5 12	18 55	4 51	19 17	4 16	19 51
		Moon	4 03	17 20	3 48	17 33	3 28	17 49	3 01	18 11	2 16	18 44
17 Sa 229	+4 06 19 02 ●	Sun	5 40	18 28	5 28	18 39	5 13	18 54	4 53	19 15	4 19	19 48
		Moon	5 09	18 08	4 59	18 17	4 45	18 26	4 26	18 40	3 57	19 00
18 Su 230	+3 53	Sun	5 41	18 27	5 29	18 38	5 14	18 53	4 54	19 13	4 21	19 45
		Moon	6 14	18 54	6 08	18 57	6 01	19 01	5 52	19 05	5 37	19 12
19 Mo 231	+3 40	Sun	5 41	18 27	5 29	18 37	5 15	18 51	4 56	19 11	4 23	19 42
		Moon	7 17	19 38	7 17	19 36	7 16	19 33	7 16	19 29	7 15	19 23
20 Tu 232	+3 26	Sun	5 41	18 26	5 30	18 36	5 16	18 49	4 57	19 09	4 26	19 39
		Moon	8 18	20 22	8 23	20 14	8 29	20 05	8 38	19 53	8 51	19 35
21 We 233	+3 11	Sun	5 41	18 25	5 30	18 35	5 16	18 48	4 59	19 07	4 28	19 37
		Moon	9 18	21 06	9 28	20 54	9 40	20 39	9 58	20 19	10 25	19 48
22 Th 234	+2 57	Sun	5 42	18 24	5 31	18 34	5 18	18 47	5 00	19 05	4 31	19 34
		Moon	10 17	21 51	10 31	21 35	10 49	21 15	11 14	20 48	11 55	20 04
23 Fr 235	+2 41	Sun	5 42	18 23	5 32	18 33	5 19	18 46	5 01	19 03	4 33	19 31
		Moon	11 15	22 37	11 33	22 18	11 55	21 55	12 27	21 22	13 20	20 26
24 Sat 236	+2 25 15 38 ☽	Sun	5 42	18 23	5 32	18 32	5 20	18 44	5 03	19 01	4 35	19 28
		Moon	12 11	23 26	12 31	23 05	12 57	22 39	13 33	22 01	14 37	20 57
25 Su 237	+2 09	Sun	5 42	18 22	5 33	18 30	5 21	18 43	5 04	18 59	4 38	19 25
		Moon	13 04	—	13 26	23 55	13 53	23 27	14 32	22 48	15 41	21 39
26 Mo 238	+1 53	Sun	5 43	18 21	5 33	18 29	5 22	18 42	5 06	18 57	4 40	19 22
		Moon	13 55	0 16	14 17	—	14 44	—	15 22	23 42	16 30	22 35
27 Tu 239	+1 36)	Sun	5 43	18 20	5 34	18 28	5 23	18 40	5 07	18 55	4 43	19 19
		Moon	14 42	1 08	15 03	0 47	15 28	0 20	16 04	—	17 05	23 41
28 We 240	+1 18	Sun	5 43	18 19	5 35	18 27	5 24	18 38	5 08	18 53	4 45	19 16
		Moon	15 26	1 59	15 44	1 40	16 06	1 15	16 37	0 41	17 29	—
29 Th 241	+1 00	Sun	5 43	18 19	5 35	18 26	5 24	18 37	5 10	18 50	4 48	19 13
		Moon	16 07	2 50	16 22	2 34	16 40	2 13	17 05	1 43	17 46	0 54
30 Fr 242	+0 42	Sun	5 44	18 18	5 36	18 25	5 25	18 35	5 11	18 48	4 51	19 10
		Moon	16 45	3 41	16 56	3 27	17 10	3 10	17 29	2 47	17 59	2 10
31 Sa 243	+0 24	Sun	5 44	18 17	5 36	18 24	5 26	18 34	5 13	18 46	4 53	19 07
		Moon	17 21	4 30	17 29	4 21	17 38	4 09	17 50	3 52	18 09	3 26

Moon Phases: 3rd 3:57 Full ○; 11th 2:46 Last Quarter ☾; 17th 19:02 New ●; 24th 15:38 1st Quarter ☽.

Morning Stars: Mercury (Aug. 1-17); Venus, Jupiter, Saturn.
Evening Stars: Mercury (Aug. 17-31); Mars.

9th Month   September, 1974   30 Days

Greenwich Mean Time

NOTE: Light figures indicate Sun. **Dark** figures indicate **Moon.** *Degrees are North Latitude.*

CAUTION: Must be converted to local time. For instruction see page 237.

In each day's pair of rows, the first (light) row gives the **Sun** rise/set and the second (dark) row gives the **Moon** rise/set.

Day of month / week / year	Sun on meridian / Moon phase (h m s)	20° Rise	20° Set	30° Rise	30° Set	40° Rise	40° Set	50° Rise	50° Set	60° Rise	60° Set
1 Su 244 (Sun)	+0 05	5 45	18 16	5 37	18 23	5 27	18 32	5 15	18 44	4 55	19 04
(Moon)	19 25 ○	17 56	5 19	18 00	5 14	18 04	5 07	18 09	4 57	18 18	4 42
2 Mo 245 (Sun)	−0 14	5 45	18 15	5 37	18 22	5 28	18 30	5 16	18 42	4 57	19 01
(Moon)		18 31	6 08	18 30	6 07	18 29	6 05	18 28	6 02	18 26	5 59
3 Tu 246 (Sun)	−0 34	5 45	18 14	5 38	18 20	5 29	18 28	5 18	18 40	4 59	18 58
(Moon)		19 06	6 57	19 01	7 00	18 55	7 04	18 47	7 08	18 35	7 16
4 We 247 (Sun)	−0 53	5 45	18 13	5 38	18 19	5 30	18 27	5 19	18 38	5 01	18 55
(Moon)		19 43	7 47	19 34	7 54	19 23	8 03	19 08	8 15	18 45	8 34
5 Th 248 (Sun)	−1 13	5 46	18 12	5 38	18 18	5 31	18 25	5 21	18 36	5 04	18 52
(Moon)		20 22	8 39	20 09	8 50	19 53	9 04	19 32	9 23	18 58	9 54
6 Fr 249 (Sun)	−1 33	5 46	18 11	5 39	18 17	5 32	18 23	5 22	18 34	5 06	18 49
(Moon)		21 05	9 33	20 49	9 48	20 28	10 07	20 00	10 33	19 15	11 16
7 Sa 250 (Sun)	−1 54	5 46	18 10	5 40	18 16	5 33	18 22	5 23	18 32	5 08	18 46
(Moon)		21 52	10 28	21 33	10 47	21 09	11 10	20 35	11 42	19 39	12 37
8 Su 251 (Sun)	−2 14	5 46	18 10	5 40	18 14	5 34	18 20	5 24	18 30	5 10	18 43
(Moon)		22 45	11 26	22 23	11 46	21 57	12 12	21 19	12 49	20 14	13 53
9 Mo 252 (Sun)	−2 35	5 46	18 09	5 41	18 13	5 35	18 18	5 26	18 27	5 13	18 40
(Moon)	12 01 ☾	23 41	12 24	23 20	12 45	22 53	13 12	22 15	13 51	21 07	14 58
10 Tu 253 (Sun)	−2 56	5 47	18 08	5 41	18 12	5 36	18 17	5 27	18 25	5 15	18 37
(Moon)			13 21		13 41	23 57	14 08	23 21	14 44	22 19	15 48
11 We 254 (Sun)	−3 17	5 47	18 07	5 42	18 11	5 37	18 15	5 29	18 23	5 18	18 34
(Moon)		0 42	14 16	0 22	14 34		14 57		15 29	23 46	16 22
12 Th 255 (Sun)	−3 38	5 47	18 06	5 43	18 10	5 38	18 14	5 31	18 21	5 20	18 31
(Moon)		1 46	15 08	1 28	15 23	1 07	15 41	0 36	16 06		16 46
13 Fr 256 (Sun)	−3 59	5 47	18 05	5 43	18 08	5 39	18 12	5 32	18 19	5 22	18 28
(Moon)		2 50	15 56	2 36	16 07	2 20	16 20	1 57	16 37	1 21	17 04
14 Sa 257 (Sun)	−4 20	5 47	18 04	5 44	18 07	5 40	18 11	5 34	18 17	5 25	18 25
(Moon)		3 53	16 43	3 45	16 48	3 35	16 55	3 21	17 04	2 59	17 18
15 Su 258 (Sun)	−4 41	5 48	18 03	5 44	18 06	5 41	18 09	5 35	18 14	5 27	18 22
(Moon)		4 56	17 27	4 53	17 28	4 50	17 28	4 44	17 29	4 37	17 30
16 Mo 259 (Sun)	−5 02	5 48	18 02	5 45	18 05	5 41	18 07	5 37	18 12	5 30	18 19
(Moon)	02 45 ●	5 58	18 12	6 01	18 07	6 04	18 01	6 07	17 53	6 14	17 41
17 Tu 260 (Sun)	−5 24	5 48	18 01	5 45	18 03	5 42	18 06	5 38	18 10	5 32	18 16
(Moon)		7 00	18 56	7 07	18 46	7 16	18 35	7 29	18 19	7 49	17 54
18 We 261 (Sun)	−5 45	5 48	18 01	5 46	18 02	5 43	18 04	5 40	18 08	5 35	18 13
(Moon)		8 01	19 42	8 13	19 28	8 28	19 11	8 49	18 47	9 23	18 10
19 Th 262 (Sun)	−6 06	5 48	18 00	5 46	18 00	5 44	18 03	5 41	18 06	5 37	18 10
(Moon)		9 00	20 29	9 17	20 12	9 37	19 50	10 05	19 20	10 53	18 30
20 Fr 263 (Sun)	−6 27	5 49	17 59	5 47	17 59	5 45	18 01	5 43	18 03	5 39	18 07
(Moon)		9 59	21 18	10 18	20 58	10 42	20 33	11 17	19 58	12 16	18 57
21 Sa 264 (Sun)	−6 49	5 49	17 58	5 48	17 58	5 46	17 59	5 44	18 01	5 41	18 04
(Moon)		10 55	22 09	11 16	21 48	11 43	21 21	12 20	20 43	13 27	19 36
22 Su 265 (Sun)	−7 10	5 49	17 57	5 48	17 57	5 47	17 58	5 46	17 59	5 43	18 01
(Moon)		11 48	23 01	12 09	22 40	12 36	22 13	13 15	21 35	14 22	20 28
23 Mo 266 (Sun)	−7 31	5 49	17 56	5 49	17 55	5 48	17 56	5 47	17 57	5 46	17 57
(Moon)	07 08 ☽	12 37	23 53	12 58	23 33	13 24	23 08	14 00	22 33	15 03	21 31
24 Tu 267 (Sun)	−7 52	5 49	17 55	5 49	17 54	5 49	17 54	5 49	17 54	5 48	17 54
(Moon)		13 23		13 41		14 05		14 37	23 34	15 31	22 42
25 We 268 (Sun)	−8 13	5 50	17 54	5 50	17 53	5 50	17 53	5 51	17 52	5 51	17 51
(Moon)		14 05	0 45	14 21	0 27	14 40	0 05	15 07		15 51	23 57
26 Th 269 (Sun)	−8 33	5 50	17 53	5 50	17 52	5 51	17 51	5 52	17 50	5 51	17 48
(Moon)		14 44	1 35	14 56	1 21	15 12	1 03	15 32	0 38	16 05	
27 Fr 270 (Sun)	−8 54	5 50	17 52	5 51	17 51	5 51	17 49	5 52	17 48	5 55	17 45
(Moon)		15 21	2 25	15 29	2 14	15 40	2 01	15 55	1 42	16 17	1 12
28 Sa 271 (Sun)	−9 14	5 50	17 51	5 51	17 50	5 53	17 47	5 54	17 46	5 58	17 42
(Moon)		15 56	3 14	16 01	3 07	16 07	2 59	16 15	2 47	16 27	2 28
29 Su 272 (Sun)	−9 34	5 50	17 50	5 52	17 48	5 54	17 45	5 56	17 43	6 00	17 39
(Moon)		16 31	4 03	16 32	4 00	16 33	3 57	16 34	3 52	16 36	3 44
30 Mo 273 (Sun)	−9 54	5 50	17 49	5 52	17 47	5 55	17 43	5 57	17 41	6 02	17 36
(Moon)		17 06	4 52	17 03	4 54	16 59	4 55	16 53	4 58	16 45	5 01

Moon Phases: 1st 19:25 Full ○; 9th 12:01 Last Quarter ☾; 16th 2:45 New ●; 23rd 7:08 1st Quarter ☽.

Morning Stars: Venus, Saturn; Jupiter (Sept. 1–5).
Evening Stars: Mercury, Mars; Jupiter (Sept. 5–30).

10th Month   October, 1974   31 Days

Greenwich Mean Time

NOTE: Light figures indicate Sun. **Dark** figures indicate **Moon.** *Degrees are North Latitude.*

CAUTION: Must be converted to local time. For instruction see page 237.

Day of month / week / year	Sun on meridian / Moon phase (h m s)	20° Rise	20° Set	30° Rise	30° Set	40° Rise	40° Set	50° Rise	50° Set	60° Rise	60° Set
1 Tu 274	−10 14 / 10 38 ○	5 51	17 48	5 53	17 46	5 56	17 42	6 00	17 39	6 05	17 33
(Moon)		17 43	5 43	17 36	5 48	17 26	5 55	17 14	6 05	16 55	6 20
2 We 275	−10 33	5 51	17 48	5 54	17 45	5 57	17 41	6 01	17 37	6 07	17 30
(Moon)		18 22	6 34	18 11	6 44	17 56	6 57	17 37	7 13	17 07	7 40
3 Th 276	−10 52	5 51	17 47	5 54	17 44	5 58	17 39	6 02	17 35	6 10	17 27
(Moon)		19 04	7 28	18 49	7 42	18 30	7 59	18 04	8 23	17 23	9 01
4 Fr 277	−11 10	5 51	17 46	5 55	17 42	5 59	17 38	6 04	17 32	6 12	17 24
(Moon)		19 51	8 24	19 32	8 41	19 10	9 03	18 38	9 33	17 45	10 23
5 Sa 278	−11 29	5 52	17 45	5 55	17 41	6 00	17 36	6 06	17 30	6 15	17 21
(Moon)		20 42	9 21	20 21	9 41	19 55	10 06	19 19	10 41	18 18	11 41
6 Su 279	−11 47	5 52	17 44	5 56	17 40	6 01	17 34	6 07	17 28	6 17	17 18
(Moon)		21 37	10 18	21 15	10 40	20 49	11 06	20 11	11 44	19 05	12 50
7 Mo 280	−12 04 / 10 01	5 50	17 43	5 57	17 39	6 02	17 33	6 09	17 26	6 19	17 15
(Moon)		22 35	11 15	22 15	11 36	21 49	12 02	21 13	12 39	20 03	10 41
8 Tu 281	−12 21 / 19 46 ☾	5 53	17 42	5 57	17 38	6 03	17 31	6 10	17 24	6 22	17 12
(Moon)		23 36	12 10	23 18	12 29	22 55	12 53	22 23	13 26	21 29	14 22
9 We 282	−12 38	5 53	17 41	5 58	17 36	6 04	17 30	6 12	17 22	6 24	17 10
(Moon)			13 01		13 17		13 37	23 40	14 05	22 59	14 49
10 Th 283	−12 54	5 53	17 40	5 58	17 35	6 05	17 28	6 13	17 20	6 27	17 07
(Moon)		0 38	13 49	0 23	14 01	0 05	14 16		14 37		15 08
11 Fr 284	−13 10	5 53	17 40	5 59	17 34	6 06	17 27	6 16	17 18	6 29	17 04
(Moon)		1 39	14 35	1 29	14 43	1 17	14 52	0 59	15 04	0 32	15 23
12 Sa 285	−13 25	5 54	17 39	6 00	17 33	6 07	17 26	6 17	17 16	6 31	17 01
(Moon)		2 41	15 19	2 35	15 22	2 29	15 25	2 20	15 29	2 06	15 35
13 Su 286	−13 40	5 54	17 38	6 00	17 32	6 08	17 24	6 19	17 14	6 33	16 58
(Moon)		3 41	16 02	3 41	16 00	3 41	15 57	3 41	15 53	3 40	15 47
14 Mo 287	−13 54	5 54	17 37	6 01	17 31	6 09	17 23	6 20	17 12	6 36	16 55
(Moon)		4 42	16 46	4 47	16 39	4 53	16 30	5 01	16 18	5 14	16 00
15 Tu 288	−14 08 / 12 25 ●	5 54	17 36	6 01	17 30	6 10	17 22	6 22	17 09	6 38	16 52
(Moon)		5 42	17 31	5 52	17 19	6 04	17 04	6 21	16 45	6 48	16 14
16 We 289	−14 21	5 55	17 36	6 02	17 29	6 11	17 20	6 23	17 07	6 41	16 49
(Moon)		6 43	18 18	6 57	18 02	7 15	17 42	7 39	17 16	8 20	16 32
17 Th 290	−14 33	5 55	17 35	6 03	17 28	6 12	17 18	6 25	17 05	6 44	16 46
(Moon)		7 43	19 07	8 00	18 48	8 23	18 25	8 54	17 52	9 47	16 57
18 Fr 291	−14 45	5 55	17 34	6 03	17 26	6 13	17 16	6 26	17 03	6 46	16 43
(Moon)		8 41	19 58	9 01	19 38	9 27	19 12	10 03	18 35	11 05	17 31
19 Sa 292	−14 56	5 56	17 34	6 04	17 25	6 15	17 15	6 28	17 01	6 49	16 41
(Moon)		9 37	20 51	9 58	20 30	10 25	20 03	11 03	19 25	12 09	18 18
20 Su 293	−15 07	5 56	17 33	6 04	17 24	6 16	17 13	6 29	16 59	6 51	16 38
(Moon)		10 29	21 44	10 49	21 24	11 16	20 58	11 53	20 22	12 57	19 18
21 Mo 294	−15 17	5 56	17 33	6 05	17 23	6 17	17 12	6 31	16 57	6 54	16 35
(Moon)		11 16	22 36	11 36	22 18	12 00	21 55	12 33	21 22	13 30	20 27
22 Tu 295	−15 27	5 57	17 32	6 06	17 22	6 18	17 11	6 33	16 56	6 56	16 32
(Moon)		12 00	23 28	12 17	23 12	12 38	22 53	13 07	22 26	13 54	21 41
23 We 296	−15 35 / 01 53 ☽	5 57	17 32	6 06	17 21	6 19	17 11	6 34	16 54	6 59	16 30
(Moon)		12 40		12 54		13 11	23 51	13 34	23 30	14 10	22 56
24 Th 297	−15 44	5 57	17 31	6 07	17 21	6 20	17 08	6 36	16 52	7 01	16 27
(Moon)		13 18	0 18	13 28	0 06	13 40		13 57		14 23	
25 Fr 298	−15 51	5 58	17 30	6 08	17 20	6 21	17 06	6 37	16 50	7 03	16 24
(Moon)		13 54	1 07	14 00	0 59	14 08	0 48	14 18	0 34	14 34	0 12
26 Sa 299	−15 58	5 58	17 30	6 09	17 19	6 22	17 05	6 39	16 48	7 06	16 21
(Moon)		14 29	1 56	14 31	1 52	14 34	1 46	14 38	1 39	14 43	1 27
27 Su 300	−16 04	5 59	17 29	6 09	17 18	6 23	17 04	6 41	16 46	7 09	16 18
(Moon)		15 04	2 45	15 02	2 45	15 00	2 44	14 57	2 44	14 53	2 43
28 Mo 301	−16 09	5 59	17 29	6 11	17 17	6 24	17 03	6 43	16 44	7 11	16 16
(Moon)		15 40	3 35	15 34	3 39	15 27	3 44	15 17	3 50	15 02	4 01
29 Tu 302	−16 13	5 59	17 28	6 11	17 16	6 26	17 02	6 44	16 43	7 14	16 13
(Moon)		16 19	4 26	16 09	4 34	15 56	4 44	15 40	4 58	15 14	5 20
30 We 303	−16 17	6 00	17 27	6 12	17 15	6 27	17 00	6 46	16 41	7 16	16 10
(Moon)		17 01	5 20	16 47	5 32	16 29	5 47	16 06	6 08	15 29	6 42
31 Th 304	−16 20 / 01 19 ○	6 00	17 27	6 13	17 14	6 28	16 59	6 47	16 39	7 19	16 08
(Moon)		17 46	6 15	17 29	6 31	17 08	6 53	16 38	7 19	15 49	8 05

Moon Phases: 1st 10:38 Full ○; 8th 19:46 Last Quarter ☾; 15th 12:25 New ●; 23rd 1:53 1st Quarter ☽; 31st 1:19 Full ○.

Morning Stars: Venus, Saturn; Mercury (Oct. 25-31); Mars (Oct. 14-31).
Evening Stars: Mercury (Oct. 1-25); Mars (Oct. 1-14); Jupiter.

11th Month   November, 1974   30 Days

Greenwich Mean Time

NOTE: Light figures indicate Sun. **Dark** figures indicate **Moon.** *Degrees are North Latitude.*

CAUTION: Must be converted to local time. For instruction see page 237.

Day of month week year	Sun on meridian Moon phase h m s	20° Rise Sun Moon	20° Set Sun Moon	30° Rise Sun Moon	30° Set Sun Moon	40° Rise Sun Moon	40° Set Sun Moon	50° Rise Sun Moon	50° Set Sun Moon	60° Rise Sun Moon	60° Set Sun Moon
1 Fr 305	−16 22	6 01	17 26	6 14	17 13	6 29	16 58	6 49	16 37	7 22	16 05
		18 37	7 13	18 17	7 32	17 52	7 56	17 17	8 29	16 19	9 27
2 Sa 306	−16 24	6 01	17 26	6 15	17 13	6 30	16 56	6 50	16 35	7 24	16 02
		19 32	8 12	19 10	8 33	18 44	8 59	18 07	9 36	17 02	10 40
3 Su 307	−16 25	6 02	17 25	6 16	17 12	6 32	16 55	6 52	16 33	7 27	16 00
		20 30	9 10	20 09	9 31	19 43	9 57	19 06	10 35	18 02	11 39
4 Mo 308	−16 24	6 02	17 24	6 16	17 12	16 33	16 54	6 55	16 32	7 29	15 57
		21 31	10 06	21 12	10 26	20 48	10 50	20 15	11 25	19 19	12 23
5 Tu 309	−16 23	6 03	17 24	6 17	17 11	6 34	16 53	6 56	16 30	7 32	15 55
		22 32	10 58	22 17	11 15	21 57	11 36	21 30	12 05	20 45	12 53
6 We 310	−16 21	6 04	17 23	6 18	17 10	6 35	16 52	6 58	16 29	7 35	15 52
		23 33	11 47	23 21	12 00	23 07	12 17	22 48	12 39	22 16	13 14
7 Th 311	−16 19 02 47 ☾	6 04	17 23	6 18	17 10	6 36	16 51	6 59	16 27	7 37	15 49
			12 33		12 42		12 52		13 07	23 48	13 30
8 Fr 312	−16 15	6 05	17 23	6 19	17 09	6 37	16 50	7 01	16 26	7 40	15 47
		0 33	13 16	0 26	13 20	0 17	13 25	0 06	13 32		13 43
9 Sa 313	−16 10	6 05	17 22	6 20	17 08	6 38	16 50	7 02	16 24	7 42	15 45
		1 32	13 58	1 30	13 57	1 27	13 57	1 24	13 56	1 19	13 54
10 Su 314	−16 05	6 06	17 22	6 21	17 07	6 39	16 49	7 04	16 23	7 45	15 42
		2 30	14 40	2 33	14 35	2 37	14 28	2 42	14 19	2 50	14 06
11 Mo 315	−15 59	6 06	17 22	6 22	17 06	6 40	16 48	7 06	16 22	7 47	15 40
		3 29	15 23	3 37	15 13	3 46	15 01	4 00	14 45	4 21	14 19
12 Tu 316	−15 52	6 07	17 21	6 22	17 06	6 41	16 47	7 07	16 20	7 49	15 38
		4 28	16 08	4 40	15 54	4 56	15 37	5 17	15 13	5 51	14 35
13 We 317	−15 44	6 07	17 21	6 23	17 05	6 42	16 46	7 09	16 18	7 52	15 35
		5 27	16 56	5 43	16 38	6 04	16 17	6 32	15 46	7 20	14 57
14 Th 318	−15 35 00 53 ●	6 08	17 21	6 23	17 05	6 43	16 45	7 10	16 17	7 54	15 33
		6 26	17 46	6 45	17 26	7 09	17 01	7 43	16 26	8 42	15 26
15 Fr 319	−15 25	6 08	17 21	6 24	17 05	6 45	16 44	7 12	16 16	7 57	15 31
		7 23	18 39	7 44	18 18	8 10	17 51	8 47	17 14	9 53	16 08
16 Sa 320	−15 15	6 09	17 20	6 26	17 04	6 46	16 43	7 14	16 15	8 00	15 29
		8 17	19 32	8 38	19 12	9 05	18 45	9 42	18 08	10 48	17 03
17 Su 321	−15 04	6 09	17 20	6 26	17 04	6 47	16 43	7 15	16 14	8 02	15 27
		9 08	20 26	9 28	20 07	9 53	19 42	10 28	19 08	11 28	18 09
18 Mo 322	−14 51	6 10	17 20	6 27	17 03	6 49	16 42	7 17	16 13	8 05	15 25
		9 54	21 18	10 11	21 02	10 34	20 41	11 04	20 11	11 56	19 22
19 Tu 323	−14 39	6 10	17 20	6 28	17 03	6 50	16 41	7 18	16 11	8 07	15 23
		10 36	22 09	10 51	21 56	11 09	20 39	11 34	21 16	12 15	20 38
20 We 324	−14 25	6 11	17 20	6 29	17 03	6 51	16 41	7 21	16 10	8 10	15 21
		11 15	22 59	11 26	22 49	11 40	22 37	11 59	22 20	12 29	21 53
21 Th 325	−14 10 22 39 ☽	6 12	17 19	6 30	17 02	6 52	16 40	7 22	16 09	8 12	15 19
		11 51	23 48	11 59	23 42	12 08	23 34	12 21	23 24	12 41	23 08
22 Fr 326	−13 55	6 12	17 19	6 30	17 02	6 53	16 40	7 23	16 08	8 15	15 17
		12 26		12 30		12 35		12 41		12 51	
23 Sa 327	−13 39	6 13	17 19	6 31	17 02	6 54	16 39	7 25	16 07	8 17	15 15
		13 01	0 36	13 00	0 34	13 00	0 32	13 00	0 29	13 00	0 23
24 Su 328	−13 22	6 13	17 19	6 32	17 01	6 55	16 38	7 26	16 07	8 20	15 14
		13 36	1 25	13 32	1 27	13 27	1 30	13 20	1 34	13 09	1 39
25 Mo 329	−13 04	6 14	17 19	6 33	17 01	6 56	16 38	7 28	16 06	8 22	15 12
		14 13	2 15	14 05	2 21	13 55	2 29	13 41	2 40	13 20	2 57
26 Tu 330	−12 46	6 15	17 19	6 34	17 00	6 57	16 37	7 29	16 05	8 24	15 10
		14 53	3 07	14 41	3 18	14 26	3 31	14 05	3 49	13 33	4 17
27 We 331	−12 27	6 15	17 19	6 34	17 00	6 58	16 37	7 31	16 04	8 26	15 09
		15 37	4 02	15 21	4 16	15 02	4 34	14 35	4 59	13 51	5 40
28 Th 332	−12 07	6 16	17 19	6 35	17 00	6 59	16 36	7 32	16 03	8 29	15 07
		16 26	4 59	16 07	5 17	15 44	5 39	15 11	6 11	14 16	7 03
29 Fr 333	−11 47 15 10 ○	6 17	17 19	6 36	17 00	7 00	16 36	7 34	16 03	8 31	15 06
		17 20	5 59	16 59	6 19	16 34	6 44	15 57	7 20	14 54	8 22
30 Sa 334	−11 25	6 18	17 19	6 37	17 00	7 01	16 36	7 35	16 02	8 33	15 04
		18 19	6 59	17 58	7 20	17 32	7 46	16 54	8 24	15 49	9 29

Moon Phases: 7th 2:47 Last Quarter ☾; 14th 0:53 New ●; 21st 22:39 1st Quarter ☽; 29th 15:10 Full ○.

Morning Stars: Mercury, Mars, Saturn; Venus (Nov. 1-6).
Evening Stars: Venus (Nov. 6-30); Jupiter.

12th Month   December, 1974   31 Days

Greenwich Mean Time

NOTE: Light figures indicate Sun. **Dark** figures indicate **Moon.** *Degrees are North Latitude.*

CAUTION: Must be converted to local time. For instruction see page 237.

Light figures = Sun, **dark figures = Moon**. For each day the first line is the Sun's Rise/Set, the second line (bold) is the Moon's Rise/Set.

Day of month / week / year	Sun on meridian / Moon phase	20° Rise	20° Set	30° Rise	30° Set	40° Rise	40° Set	50° Rise	50° Set	60° Rise	60° Set
1 Su 335	−11 03	6 19	17 19	6 38	17 00	7 02	16 35	7 37	16 01	8 35	15 03
		19 21	**7 57**	**19 01**	**8 18**	**18 37**	**8 43**	**18 02**	**9 19**	**17 02**	**10 20**
2 Mo 336	−10 41	6 19	17 20	6 38	17 00	7 03	16 35	7 38	16 01	8 37	15 02
		20 24	**8 53**	**20 07**	**9 11**	**19 46**	**9 33**	**19 17**	**10 04**	**18 28**	**10 55**
3 Tu 337	−10 18	6 20	17 20	6 39	17 00	7 04	16 35	7 40	16 00	8 39	15 01
		21 27	**9 44**	**21 14**	**9 59**	**20 58**	**10 16**	**20 36**	**10 41**	**20 00**	**11 20**
4 We 338	−9 54	6 20	17 20	6 40	17 00	7 05	16 35	7 41	16 00	8 41	15 00
		22 27	**10 31**	**22 19**	**10 42**	**22 09**	**10 54**	**21 55**	**11 11**	**21 33**	**11 37**
5 Th 339	−9 30	6 21	17 20	6 41	17 00	7 06	16 35	7 42	16 00	8 42	14 59
		23 27	**11 16**	**23 23**	**11 21**	**23 19**	**11 28**	**23 14**	**11 37**	**23 05**	**11 51**
6 Fr 340	−9 05 10 10 ☾	6 22	17 20	6 42	17 00	7 07	16 35	7 43	15 59	8 44	14 58
			11 58		**11 59**		**12 00**		**12 01**		**12 03**
7 Sa 341	0 00	0 00	17 01	6 42	17 00	7 08	16 35	7 44	15 59	8 45	14 57
		0 25	**12 39**	**0 26**	**12 35**	**0 20**	**12 37**	**0 31**	**12 21**		
8 Su 342	−8 13	6 23	17 21	6 43	17 00	7 09	16 35	7 45	15 59	8 47	14 56
		1 22	**13 21**	**1 29**	**13 13**	**1 37**	**13 02**	**1 47**	**12 48**	**2 04**	**12 27**
9 Mo 343	−7 46	6 24	17 21	6 44	17 01	7 10	16 35	7 46	15 58	8 49	14 55
		2 20	**14 04**	**2 31**	**13 52**	**2 44**	**13 36**	**3 03**	**13 15**	**3 33**	**12 41**
10 Tu 344	−7 19	6 25	17 21	6 45	17 01	7 11	16 35	7 47	15 58	8 50	14 55
		3 18	**14 50**	**3 33**	**14 34**	**3 51**	**14 13**	**4 17**	**13 45**	**5 00**	**13 00**
11 We 345	−6 52	6 25	17 22	6 46	17 01	7 12	16 35	7 48	15 58	8 52	14 54
		4 15	**15 38**	**4 34**	**15 19**	**4 56**	**14 55**	**5 29**	**14 22**	**6 23**	**13 25**
12 Th 346	−6 24	6 26	17 22	6 46	17 01	7 12	16 35	7 49	15 58	8 53	14 54
		5 12	**16 29**	**5 33**	**16 08**	**5 58**	**15 42**	**6 35**	**15 05**	**7 38**	**14 01**
13 Fr 347	−5 56 16 25 ●	6 26	17 22	6 47	17 01	7 13	16 35	7 50	15 58	8 54	14 54
		6 07	**17 22**	**6 28**	**17 01**	**6 55**	**16 34**	**7 33**	**15 56**	**8 39**	**14 50**
14 Sa 348	−5 27	6 27	17 23	6 48	17 01	7 14	16 35	7 51	15 58	8 56	14 54
		6 59	**18 15**	**7 20**	**17 55**	**7 45**	**17 30**	**8 22**	**16 54**	**9 25**	**15 52**
15 Su 349	−4 59	6 27	17 23	6 48	17 02	7 14	16 36	7 52	15 59	8 57	14 53
		7 47	**19 09**	**8 06**	**18 51**	**8 29**	**18 28**	**9 02**	**17 57**	**9 57**	**17 03**
16 Mo 350	−4 20	6 28	17 24	6 49	17 02	7 15	16 36	7 53	15 59	8 58	14 53
		8 31	**20 01**	**8 47**	**19 46**	**9 07**	**19 27**	**9 35**	**19 01**	**10 20**	**18 18**
17 Tu 351	−4 00	6 28	17 24	6 49	17 03	7 15	16 36	7 53	15 59	8 59	14 53
		9 11	**20 51**	**9 24**	**20 40**	**9 40**	**20 25**	**10 02**	**20 06**	**10 36**	**19 35**
18 We 352	−3 31	6 29	17 24	6 50	17 03	7 16	16 37	7 54	15 59	8 59	14 53
		9 49	**21 40**	**9 58**	**21 33**	**10 09**	**21 23**	**10 25**	**21 10**	**10 49**	**20 50**
19 Th 353	−3 01	6 29	17 25	6 50	17 04	7 17	16 37	7 55	15 59	9 00	14 54
		10 24	**22 28**	**10 30**	**22 25**	**10 36**	**22 20**	**10 45**	**22 14**	**10 59**	**22 05**
20 Fr 354	−2 31	6 30	17 25	6 51	17 04	7 17	16 37	7 55	16 00	9 01	14 54
		10 58	**23 16**	**11 00**	**23 17**	**11 02**	**23 17**	**11 04**	**23 18**	**11 08**	**23 19**
21 Sa 355	−2 02 19 43 ☽	6 30	17 26	6 52	17 05	7 18	16 38	7 56	16 00	9 02	14 54
		11 33		**11 30**		**11 27**		**11 24**		**11 18**	
22 Su 356	−1 32	6 31	17 26	6 53	17 05	7 18	16 38	7 57	16 01	9 02	14 55
		12 08	**0 05**	**12 02**	**0 10**	**11 54**	**0 15**	**11 44**	**0 23**	**11 27**	**0 35**
23 Mo 357	−1 02	6 31	17 27	6 53	17 06	7 19	16 39	7 57	16 01	9 03	14 55
		12 46	**0 55**	**12 36**	**1 04**	**12 23**	**1 15**	**12 06**	**1 29**	**11 39**	**1 52**
24 Tu 358	−0 32	6 32	17 27	6 53	17 06	7 19	16 39	7 57	16 02	9 03	14 56
		13 27	**1 48**	**13 13**	**2 00**	**12 56**	**2 16**	**12 32**	**2 37**	**11 54**	**3 12**
25 We 359	−0 02	6 32	17 28	6 54	17 07	7 20	16 40	7 58	16 02	9 04	14 57
		14 13	**2 43**	**13 56**	**2 59**	**13 34**	**3 19**	**13 04**	**3 47**	**12 15**	**4 34**
26 Th 360	+0 27	6 33	17 28	6 54	17 07	7 20	16 41	7 58	16 03	9 04	14 58
		15 04	**3 41**	**14 44**	**4 00**	**14 19**	**4 24**	**13 44**	**4 57**	**12 45**	**5 55**
27 Fr 361	+0 57	6 33	17 29	6 55	17 08	7 20	16 41	7 58	16 04	9 04	14 59
		16 01	**4 40**	**15 40**	**5 01**	**15 13**	**5 27**	**14 36**	**6 04**	**13 31**	**7 09**
28 Sa 362	+1 26	6 34	17 29	6 55	17 08	7 21	16 42	7 59	16 05	9 04	15 00
		17 02	**5 40**	**16 42**	**6 01**	**16 16**	**6 28**	**15 40**	**7 05**	**14 36**	**8 09**
29 Su 363	+1 56 03 51 ○	6 34	17 30	6 55	17 09	7 21	16 43	7 59	16 06	9 03	15 01
		18 07	**6 39**	**17 49**	**6 58**	**17 26**	**7 22**	**16 53**	**7 56**	**15 59**	**8 53**
30 Mo 364	+2 25	6 35	17 30	6 56	17 09	7 22	16 43	7 59	16 07	9 03	15 02
		19 12	**7 34**	**18 57**	**7 50**	**18 39**	**8 10**	**18 14**	**8 38**	**17 32**	**9 22**
31 Tu 365	+2 53	6 35	17 31	6 56	17 10	7 22	16 44	7 59	16 08	9 03	15 03
		20 16	**8 25**	**20 06**	**8 37**	**19 53**	**8 52**	**19 36**	**9 12**	**19 09**	**9 43**

Moon Phases: 6th 10:10 Last Quarter ☾; 13th 16:25 New ●; 21st 19:43 1st Quarter ☽; 29th 3:51 Full ○.

Morning Stars: Mercury (Dec. 1-19); Mars, Saturn.
Evening Stars: Mercury (Dec. 19-31); Venus, Jupiter.

PERPETUAL CALENDAR

(1800-2059)

Year-to-calendar key table:

1800...4	1826...1	1852...12	1878...3	1904...13	1930...4
1801...6	1827...4	1853...1	1879...4	1905...1	1931...6
1802...7	1828...6	1854...2	1880...12	1906...2	1932...8
1803...1	1829...7	1855...3	1881...7	1907...3	1933...4
1804...9	1830...1	1856...10	1882...1	1908...11	1934...6
1805...4	1831...3	1857...5	1883...2	1909...6	1935...7
1806...6	1832...8	1858...6	1884...10	1910...7	1936...8
1807...7	1833...3	1859...7	1885...5	1911...1	1937...3
1808...8	1834...4	1860...8	1886...6	1912...9	1938...5
1809...3	1835...6	1861...3	1887...7	1913...4	1939...6
1810...5	1836...13	1862...5	1888...8	1914...5	1940...7
1811...6	1837...1	1863...6	1889...3	1915...6	1941...4
1812...8	1838...2	1864...14	1890...4	1916...14	1942...9
1813...3	1839...3	1865...2	1891...6	1917...2	1943...5
1814...5	1840...11	1866...3	1892...9	1918...3	1944...13
1815...6	1841...6	1867...4	1893...1	1919...4	1945...1
1816...14	1842...7	1868...12	1894...2	1920...12	1946...2
1817...2	1843...1	1869...7	1895...3	1921...7	1947...3
1818...3	1844...9	1870...1	1896...11	1922...1	1948...11
1819...4	1845...5	1871...2	1897...6	1923...2	1949...6
1820...12	1846...6	1872...10	1898...7	1924...10	1950...7
1821...7	1847...7	1873...5	1899...1	1925...5	1951...1
1822...1	1848...8	1874...6	1900...2	1926...6	1952...9
1823...2	1849...3	1875...7	1901...3	1927...7	1953...4
1824...10	1850...5	1876...14	1902...4	1928...8	1954...6
1825...5	1851...6	1877...2	1903...5	1929...3	1955...7

1956...8	1982...6	2008...10	2034...1
1957...3	1983...7	2009...5	2035...5
1958...4	1984...8	2010...6	2036...10
1959...5	1985...3	2011...7	2037...7
1960...13	1986...5	2012...8	2038...1
1961...1	1987...6	2013...3	2039...2
1962...2	1988...14	2014...4	2040...10
1963...3	1989...2	2015...5	2041...5
1964...11	1990...3	2016...13	2042...6
1965...6	1991...4	2017...1	2043...7
1966...7	1992...12	2018...2	2044...8
1967...1	1993...7	2019...3	2045...3
1968...9	1994...1	2020...11	2046...5
1969...4	1995...2	2021...6	2047...6
1970...5	1996...10	2022...7	2048...14
1971...6	1997...5	2023...1	2049...2
1972...14	1998...6	2024...9	2050...3
1973...2	1999...7	2025...4	2051...4
1974...3	2000...8	2026...5	2052...12
1975...4	2001...3	2027...6	2053...7
1976...12	2002...4	2028...14	2054...1
1977...7	2003...5	2029...2	2055...2
1978...1	2004...13	2030...3	2056...10
1979...2	2005...1	2031...4	2057...5
1980...10	2006...2	2032...12	2058...6
1981...5	2007...3	2033...7	2059...7

Calendar tables (numbered 1–14 and sample years 1973, 1974, 1975), each showing the twelve months (JANUARY, FEBRUARY, MARCH, APRIL, MAY, JUNE, JULY, AUGUST, SEPTEMBER, OCTOBER, NOVEMBER, DECEMBER) with day columns S M T W T F S.

Sample calendars shown: **1973** (key 2), **1974** (key 3), **1975** (key 4).

DIRECTIONS: Pick desired year from box at top left. The number shown with each year indicates what calendar to use for that year.

Julian and Gregorian Calendars; Leap Year

Calendars based on the movements of sun and moon have been used since ancient times, but none has been perfect. The Julian calendar, under which western nations measured time until 1582 A. D., was authorized by Julius Caesar in 46 B.C., the year 709 of Rome. His expert was a Greek, Sosigenes. The Julian calendar, on the assumption that the true year was 365¼ days long, gave every fourth year 366 days. The Venerable Bede, an Anglo-Saxon monk, announced in 730 A.D. that the 365¼-day Julian year was 11 min. 14 sec. too long, making a cumulative error of about a day every 128 years, but nothing was done about it for over 800 years.

By 1582 the accumulated error was estimated to have amounted to 10 days. In that year Pope Gregory XIII decreed that the day following Oct. 4, 1582, should be called Oct. 15, thus dropping 10 days.

However, with common years 365 days and a 366-day leap year every fourth year, the error in the length of the year would have recurred at the rate of a little more than 3 days every 400 years. So 3 of every 4 centesimal years (ending in 00) were made common years, not leap years. Thus 1600 was a leap year, 1700, 1800 and 1900 were not, but 2000 will be one. Leap years are those divisible by 4 except centesimal years, which are common unless divisible by 400.

The Gregorian calendar was adopted at once by most predominantly Roman Catholic countries, but many Protestant countries did not accept it until the 18th Century.

The British Government imposed the Gregorian calendar on all its possessions, including the American colonies, in 1752. The British decreed that the day following Sept. 2, 1752, should be called Sept. 14, a loss of 11 days. All dates preceding were marked O.S., for Old Style: the British new year, which started Mar. 25, O.S., was changed to Jan. 1, 1752, New Style, as the switch was made to the Gregorian calendar. Therefore, George Washington's birth date, which was Feb. 11, 1731, O.S., became Feb. 22, 1732, N.S.

In 1793 the French Revolutionary Government adopted a calendar of 12 months of 30 days each with 5 extra days in September of each common year and a 6th extra day every 4th year. Napoleon reinstated the Gregorian calendar in 1806.

Japan adopted the Gregorian calendar in 1873, the Chinese Republic in 1912, Greece and Greek Orthodox communities in 1924, and Turkey (predominantly Moslem) in 1927.

To change from the Julian calendar to the Gregorian calendar, add 10 days to dates Oct. 5, 1582, through Feb. 28, 1700; after that date add 11 days through Feb. 28, 1800; after that date add 12 days through Feb. 28, 1900; and then 13 days through Feb. 28, 2100.

The Julian Period

How many days have you lived? To determine this, you must multiply your age by 365, add the number of days since your last birthday until today, and account for all the leap years. Chances are your answer would be wrong. Astronomers, however, find it very convenient to express dates and long time intervals in days rather than in years, months, and days. This is accomplished by use of the number of the day in the Julian Period.

In 1582, Joseph Scaliger introduced the Julian Period, an interval that is the least common multiple of 3 periods. The solar cycle is the interval of time between coincidences of Jan. 1 and Sunday. This is 28 Julian Years. The Lunar Cycle, 19 Julian years, is the cycle that brings full moon back to the same day of the year. The Roman Indiction is a 15-year cycle that was used on a rotating basis much as the oriental lunar calendar is used. The Julian Period so determined is 7980 Julian years. Scaliger computed the date when the 3 cycles were in step, i.e., when the full moon fell on Sunday, Jan. 1. This date is Jan. 1, 4713 B.C., long before any reliable astronomical records. Dec. 31, 1973 is Julian Day (JD) 2,442,047 since the beginning of the Julian Period. The JD of any day in 1974 may be found by adding the day of the year given in the calendar tables, pages 238 to 249, to this value. Tables available to astronomers make the conversion of dates to the JD system very simple.

Although this period was introduced in the year when the Gregorian Calendar replaced the Julian Calendar, the Julian Period was not named for Caesar, but for Julian Scaliger, Joseph's father.

Days Between Two Dates

Table covers period of two ordinary years. For leap year, one day must be added after Feb. 28.
Example—Days between Feb. 10, 1973 and Dec. 15, 1974; subtract 41 from 714; answer is 673 days.

Day Mo.	Jan.	Feb.	March	April	May	June	July	Aug.	Sept.	Oct.	Nov.	Dec.
1	1	32	60	91	121	152	182	213	244	274	305	335
2	2	33	61	92	122	153	183	214	245	275	306	336
3	3	34	62	93	123	154	184	215	246	276	307	337
4	4	35	63	94	124	155	185	216	247	277	308	338
5	5	36	64	95	125	156	186	217	248	278	309	339
6	6	37	65	96	126	157	187	218	249	279	310	340
7	7	38	66	97	127	158	188	219	250	280	311	341
8	8	39	67	98	128	159	189	220	251	281	312	342
9	9	40	68	99	129	160	190	221	252	282	313	343
10	10	41	69	100	130	161	191	222	253	283	314	344
11	11	42	70	101	131	162	192	223	254	284	315	345
12	12	43	71	102	132	163	193	224	255	285	316	346
13	13	44	72	103	133	164	194	225	256	286	317	347
14	14	45	73	104	134	165	195	226	257	287	318	348
15	15	46	74	105	135	166	196	227	258	288	319	349
16	16	47	75	106	136	167	197	228	259	289	320	350
17	17	48	76	107	137	168	198	229	260	290	321	351
18	18	49	77	108	138	169	199	230	261	291	322	352
19	19	50	78	109	139	170	200	231	262	292	323	353
20	20	51	79	110	140	171	201	232	263	293	324	354
21	21	52	80	111	141	172	202	233	264	294	325	355
22	22	53	81	112	142	173	203	234	265	295	326	356
23	23	54	82	113	143	174	204	235	266	296	327	357
24	24	55	83	114	144	175	205	236	267	297	328	358
25	25	56	84	115	145	176	206	237	268	298	329	359
26	26	57	85	116	146	177	207	238	269	299	330	360
27	27	58	86	117	147	178	208	239	270	300	331	361
28	28	59	87	118	148	179	209	240	271	301	332	362
29	29	...	88	119	149	180	210	241	272	302	333	363
30	30	...	89	120	150	181	211	242	273	303	334	364
31	31	...	90	...	151	...	212	243	...	304	...	365

Day Mo.	Jan.	Feb.	Mar.	April	May	June	July	Aug.	Sept.	Oct.	Nov.	Dec.
1	366	397	425	456	486	517	547	578	609	639	670	700
2	367	398	426	457	487	518	548	579	610	640	671	701
3	368	399	427	458	488	519	549	580	611	641	672	702
4	369	400	428	459	489	520	550	581	612	642	673	703
5	370	401	429	460	490	521	551	582	613	643	674	704
6	371	402	430	461	491	522	552	583	614	644	675	705
7	372	403	431	462	492	523	553	584	615	645	676	706
8	373	404	432	463	493	524	554	585	616	646	677	707
9	374	405	433	464	494	525	555	586	617	647	678	708
10	375	406	434	465	495	526	556	587	618	648	679	709
11	376	407	435	466	496	527	557	588	619	649	680	710
12	377	408	436	467	497	528	558	589	620	650	681	711
13	378	409	437	468	498	529	559	590	621	651	682	712
14	379	410	438	469	499	530	560	591	622	652	683	713
15	380	411	439	470	500	531	561	592	623	653	684	714
16	381	412	440	471	501	532	562	593	624	654	685	715
17	382	413	441	472	502	533	563	594	625	655	686	716
18	383	414	442	473	503	534	564	595	626	656	687	717
19	384	415	443	474	504	535	565	596	627	657	688	718
20	385	416	444	475	505	536	566	597	628	658	689	719
21	386	417	445	476	506	537	567	598	629	659	690	720
22	387	418	446	477	507	538	568	599	630	660	691	721
23	388	419	447	478	508	539	569	600	631	661	692	722
24	389	420	448	479	509	540	570	601	632	662	693	723
25	390	421	449	480	510	541	571	602	633	663	694	724
26	391	422	450	481	511	542	572	603	634	664	695	725
27	392	423	451	482	512	543	573	604	635	665	696	726
28	393	424	452	483	513	544	574	605	636	666	697	727
29	394	...	453	484	514	545	575	606	637	667	698	728
30	395	...	454	485	515	546	576	607	638	668	699	729
31	396	...	455	...	516	...	577	608	...	669	...	730

Twilight

Date 1974	20° Begin h m	20° End h m	30° Begin h m	30° End h m	40° Begin h m	40° End h m	50° Begin h m	50° End h m	60° Begin h m	60° End h m
Jan. 1	5 16	6 50	5 30	6 35	5 45	6 21	6 00	6 07	6 18	5 49
11	5 19	6 56	5 33	6 43	5 46	6 30	6 00	6 17	6 15	6 01
21	5 21	7 01	5 32	6 51	5 43	6 40	5 55	6 30	6 06	6 18
Feb. 1	5 21	7 07	5 29	6 58	5 38	6 51	5 45	6 44	5 51	6 38
11	5 18	7 11	5 24	7 05	5 29	7 01	5 32	6 59	5 32	7 01
21	5 13	7 15	5 17	7 12	5 17	7 12	5 16	7 14	5 09	7 23
Mar. 1	5 08	7 18	5 08	7 19	5 06	7 21	4 59	7 29	4 44	7 45
11	5 00	7 21	4 58	7 24	4 50	7 32	4 38	7 46	4 12	8 12
21	4 52	7 24	4 45	7 32	4 33	7 44	4 14	8 04	3 37	8 43
Apr. 1	4 42	7 28	4 31	7 39	4 14	7 57	3 47	8 25	2 53	9 21
11	4 32	7 32	4 18	7 47	3 56	8 09	3 20	8 47	2 03	10 10
21	4 23	7 36	4 04	7 54	3 37	8 23	2 52	9 11	0 37	11 44
May 1	4 14	7 41	3 52	8 04	3 19	8 37	2 22	9 39		
11	4 08	7 46	3 41	8 13	3 03	8 53	1 49	10 09		
21	4 02	7 52	3 32	8 22	2 48	9 07	1 13	10 46		
June 1	3 58	7 58	3 26	8 30	2 36	9 20	0 21	11 52		
11	3 56	8 03	3 22	8 36	2 29	9 30				
21	3 57	8 06	3 22	8 40	2 28	9 35				
July 1	3 59	8 07	3 25	8 41	2 30	9 35				
11	4 03	8 06	3 30	8 39	2 40	9 30				
21	4 08	8 03	3 39	8 33	2 52	9 18	1 12	11 23		
Aug. 1	4 15	7 56	3 48	8 18	3 06	9 01	1 49	10 20		
11	4 20	7 50	3 56	8 13	3 22	8 46	2 21	9 46		
21	4 24	7 41	4 05	8 01	3 34	8 27	2 47	9 15		
Sept. 1	4 29	7 31	4 14	7 46	3 51	8 08	3 13	8 43	1 40	10 02
11	4 32	7 20	4 20	7 33	4 02	7 50	3 33	8 16	2 36	9 12
21	4 35	7 11	4 26	7 19	4 14	7 31	3 52	7 52	3 11	8 31
Oct. 1	4 38	7 02	4 33	7 05	4 25	7 13	4 10	7 28	3 41	7 54
11	4 40	6 53	4 40	6 53	4 35	6 58	4 26	7 05	4 07	7 23
21	4 43	6 47	4 45	6 44	4 45	6 43	4 41	6 46	4 32	6 55
Nov. 1	4 46	6 41	4 52	6 34	4 56	6 30	4 58	6 27	4 56	6 27
11	4 50	6 38	4 59	6 28	5 06	6 21	5 13	6 14	5 17	6 08
21	4 55	6 36	5 06	6 25	5 16	6 15	5 26	6 04	5 37	5 52
Dec. 1	5 00	6 37	5 13	6 24	5 25	6 11	5 38	5 58	5 53	5 42
11	5 06	6 40	5 20	6 26	5 34	6 12	5 48	5 57	6 06	5 38
21	5 11	6 45	5 25	6 30	5 39	6 16	5 55	6 00	6 15	5 40
31	5 15	6 50	5 30	6 35	5 44	6 21	6 00	6 06	6 18	5 48

Rising and Setting of Sun and Moon; Twilight

The astronomical definition of the time of rising or setting of a body, such as the sun or moon, is the instant when the upper edge of the observable disk (upper limb) is exactly 90 degrees away from the observer's zenith, on the astronomical horizon. These are the times presented in the appropriate tables.

The calculations behind these tables must take into account several important effects. The basic calculations relate to the center of the sun's disk as seen from the center of the earth. Next a correction is applied for the apparent radius of the sun, which varies throughout the year as our distance from the sun changes. This locates the upper limb. The third step changes the viewpoint to the earth's surface where atmospheric refraction is encountered. This has the effect of elevating the upper limb an average of 34 minutes of arc.

The center of the sun's disk is usually about 50 minutes of arc below the astronomical horizon at the instant given for sunrise or sunset. This causes confusion in people's minds at the times of the equinoxes when it is expected that the durations of daylight and dark are equal. Ignoring refraction and the apparent size of the sun, one would find these periods to be equal at those times. Taking into account the proper definitions, the periods of daylight and dark are equal on some date prior to the vernal equinox and after the autumnal equinox, depending on the observer's latitude. At the times of the equinoxes, periods of light are equal all over the earth, and periods of dark are equal, but periods of light are not equal to periods of dark. At these times both poles see the sun continually, although this circumstance changes rapidly.

Users of the tables must remember that the instant sunlight will strike or leave a particular location will depend on that location, its height above sea level and the particular nature of the eastern or western horizon. It may be advisable to make personal observations of the event at the site a few days before the time required. It should be remembered that the direction of the sunrise or set also changes from day to day.

Similar calculations are made with respect to moonrise and set, but there are important differences. The atmospheric refraction is the same, but viewing the moon from the earth's surface involves a change of about 4,000 miles from the earth's center. This results in an apparent displacement (horizontal parallax) of the moon away from the zenith. This depression nearly cancels the refraction effect, but the parallax and the apparent radius of the moon vary significantly throughout the month, and must be accounted for.

Because the moon moves so rapidly through the sky, users of the tables must make an important adjustment to the given times.

The twilight tables give the times when the center of the sun's disk is 18° below the astronomical horizon, or 108° away from the observer's zenith. At this time, under ideal conditions, an observer should be able to see without optical aid a sixth magnitude star in the zenith. Navigators need to see bright stars and a horizon reference simultaneously. This condition no longer prevails when the sun is beyond 12° below the horizon, the limits of nautical twilight. The limits of civil twilight occur when the sun is greater than 6° below the horizon. The durations of twilight vary with season and latitude.

Rising and Setting of Planets, 1974

Greenwich Mean Time (0 designates midnight)

Venus, 1974

Date		20° N. Latitude		30° N. Latitude		40° N. Latitude		50° N. Latitude		60° N. Latitude	
		Rise	Set	Rise	Set	Rise	Set	Rise	Set	Rise	Set
Jan.	1	8:34	19:46	8:49	19:31	9:17	19:13	9:31	18:49	10:11	18:09
	15	7:19	18:39	7:31	18:27	7:46	18:12	8:05	17:53	8:37	17:21
Feb.	1	5:31	16:53	5:43	16:41	5:57	16:27	6:16	16:08	6:46	15:38
	15	4:27	15:45	4:39	15:33	4:54	15:18	5:14	14:58	5:47	14:25
Mar.	1	3:52	15:08	4:05	14:55	4:21	14:39	4:43	14:17	5:18	13:42
	15	3:36	14:54	3:49	14:41	4:04	14:26	4:26	14:04	5:00	13:30
Apr.	1	3:27	14:51	3:37	14:41	3:50	14:28	4:07	14:11	4:34	13:44
	15	3:21	14:59	3:29	14:51	3:38	14:42	3:50	14:30	4:08	14:12
May	1	3:16	15:08	3:18	15:06	3:21	15:03	3:25	14:59	3:31	14:53
	15	3:11	15:19	3:18	15:22	3:05	15:25	3:01	15:29	2:55	15:35
June	1	3:06	15:36	2:58	15:44	2:48	15:54	2:33	16:09	2:11	16:31
	15	3:08	15:52	2:54	16:06	2:38	16:22	2:15	16:45	1:39	17:21
July	1	3:13	16:13	2:56	16:30	2:33	16:53	2:02	17:24	1:10	18:16
	15	3:25	16:33	3:06	16:52	2:39	17:19	2:03	17:55	0:59	18:59
Aug.	1	3:45	16:55	3:25	17:15	2:59	17:41	2:21	18:19	1:13	19:27
	15	4:06	17:10	3:48	17:28	3:25	17:51	2:52	18:24	1:56	19:20
Sept.	1	4:33	17:19	4:19	17:33	4:02	17:50	3:39	18:13	3:01	18:51
	15	4:53	17:21	4:45	17:29	4:34	17:40	4:20	17:54	3:58	18:16
Oct.	1	5:15	17:21	5:13	17:23	5:11	17:25	5:08	17:28	5:03	17:33
	15	5:34	17:20	5:39	17:15	5:44	17:10	5:51	17:03	6:01	16:53
Nov.	1	5:59	17:21	6:11	17:09	6:25	16:55	6:43	16:37	7:13	16:07
	15	6:22	17:26	6:38	17:10	6:58	16:50	7:27	16:21	8:15	15:33
Dec.	1	6:50	17:40	7:10	17:20	7:37	16:53	8:15	16:15	9:21	15:09
	15	7:14	18:00	7:36	17:38	8:05	17:09	8:46	16:28	10:00	15:14

Mars, 1974

Date		20° N. Latitude		30° N. Latitude		40° N. Latitude		50° N. Latitude		60° N. Latitude	
		Rise	Set	Rise	Set	Rise	Set	Rise	Set	Rise	Set
Jan.	1	12:57	0:40	12:45	1:53	12:31	2:07	12:11	2:27	11:40	2:57
	15	12:21	1:09	12:06	1:24	11:49	1:40	11:26	2:04	10:48	2:40
Feb.	1	11:41	0:39	11:25	0:55	11:05	1:15	10:36	1:44	9:50	2:30
	15	11:11	0:17	10:54	0:34	10:31	0:56	9:58	1:30	9:05	2:22
Mar.	1	10:45	23:53	10:26	0:16	10:00	0:42	9:25	1:17	8:24	2:16
	15	10:21	23:33	10:00	23:54	9:32	0:24	8:53	1:03	7:44	2:12
Apr.	1	9:55	23:11	9:32	23:34	9:03	0:04	8:21	0:46	7:05	2:02
	15	9:35	22:53	9:12	23:16	8:42	23:46	7:59	0:30	6:39	1:50
May	1	9:14	22:32	8:51	22:55	8:22	23:24	7:39	0:08	6:21	1:26
	15	8:58	22:12	8:36	22:34	8:07	23:03	7:26	23:44	6:12	0:59
June	1	8:38	21:46	8:17	22:07	7:51	22:33	7:13	23:11	6:08	0:17
	15	8:21	21:25	8:04	21:42	7:40	22:06	7:06	22:40	6:10	23:36
July	1	8:03	20:57	7:47	21:13	7:27	21:33	6:59	22:01	6:13	22:47
	15	7:47	20:31	7:33	20:45	7:16	21:02	6:53	21:25	6:16	22:02
Aug.	1	7:26	20:00	7:16	20:10	7:03	20:23	6:47	20:39	6:20	21:06
	15	7:10	19:32	7:02	19:40	6:54	19:48	6:42	20:00	6:24	20:18
Sept.	1	6:48	19:00	6:45	19:03	6:42	19:06	6:36	19:12	6:27	19:21
	15	6:31	18:31	6:31	18:31	6:31	18:31	6:30	18:32	6:30	18:32
Oct.	1	6:12	18:00	6:15	17:57	6:19	17:53	6:26	17:46	6:35	17:37
	15	5:57	17:35	6:04	17:28	6:12	17:20	6:23	17:09	6:40	16:52
Nov.	1	5:40	17:04	5:50	16:54	6:03	16:41	6:21	16:23	6:48	15:56
	15	5:25	16:41	5:39	16:27	5:56	16:10	6:19	15:47	6:56	15:10
Dec.	1	5:13	16:15	5:28	16:00	5:49	15:39	6:17	15:11	7:05	14:23
	15	5:03	15:57	5:20	15:40	5:44	15:16	6:18	14:42	7:15	13:45

Jupiter, 1974

Date		20° N. Latitude		30° N. Latitude		40° N. Latitude		50° N. Latitude		60° N. Latitude	
		Rise	Set	Rise	Set	Rise	Set	Rise	Set	Rise	Set
Jan.	1	8:51	19:59	9:06	19:44	9:25	19:25	9:51	18:59	10:35	18:15
	15	8:08	19:18	8:22	19:04	8:40	18:40	9:05	18:21	9:45	17:41
Feb.	1	7:14	18:30	7:28	18:16	7:44	18:00	8:07	17:37	8:43	17:01
	15	6:31	17:49	6:43	17:37	6:58	17:22	7:19	17:01	7:52	16:28
Mar.	1	5:47	17:09	5:58	16:58	6:12	16:44	6:31	16:25	7:00	15:56
	15	5:02	16:28	5:13	16:17	5:25	16:05	5:43	15:47	6:09	15:21
Apr.	1	4:08	15:38	4:17	15:29	4:28	15:18	4:44	15:02	5:06	14:40
	15	3:23	14:55	3:31	14:47	3:41	14:37	3:54	14:24	4:15	14:03
May	1	2:28	14:06	2:36	13:58	2:45	13:49	2:57	13:37	3:15	13:19
	15	1:41	13:21	1:48	13:14	1:56	13:06	2:06	12:56	2:23	12:39
June	1	0:42	12:22	0:47	12:17	0:54	12:10	1:03	12:01	1:18	11:46
	15	23:51	11:33	23:56	11:28	0:02	11:22	0:11	11:13	0:25	10:59
July	1	22:51	10:33	22:56	10:28	23:02	10:22	23:10	10:14	23:23	10:01
	15	21:56	9:38	22:01	9:33	22:07	9:27	22:16	9:18	22:29	9:05
Aug.	1	20:46	8:28	20:52	8:22	20:59	8:15	21:08	8:06	21:22	7:52
	15	19:47	7:27	19:53	7:21	20:01	7:13	20:10	7:04	20:26	6:48
Sept.	1	18:33	6:11	18:40	6:04	18:48	5:56	19:00	5:44	19:17	5:27
	15	17:28	5:04	17:36	4:56	17:45	4:47	17:57	4:35	18:16	4:16
Oct.	1	16:19	3:53	16:27	3:45	16:38	3:34	16:50	3:22	17:11	3:01
	15	15:21	2:53	15:29	2:45	15:40	2:34	15:54	2:20	16:16	1:58
Nov.	1	14:13	1:43	14:21	1:35	14:31	1:25	14:46	1:10	15:08	1:48
	15	13:18	0:50	13:26	0:42	13:37	0:31	13:51	0:17	14:13	23:55
Dec.	1	12:19	23:51	12:27	23:43	12:37	23:33	12:50	23:20	13:11	22:59
	15	11:27	23:03	11:35	22:55	11:44	22:46	11:56	22:34	12:16	22:14

Date		20°N. Latitude		30°N. Latitude		40°N. Latitude		50°N. Latitude		60°N. Latitude	
		Rise	Set	Rise	Set	Rise	Set	Rise	Set	Rise	Set
Jan.	1	16:42	5:52	16:23	6:11	15:56	6:38	15:19	7:15	14:15	8:19
	15	15:43	4:53	15:24	5:12	14:57	5:39	14:20	6:16	13:16	7:20
Feb.	1	14:31	3:41	14:11	4:01	13:45	4:27	13:07	5:05	12:02	6:10
	15	13:34	2:44	13:14	3:04	12:48	3:30	12:10	4:08	11:05	5:13
Mar	1	12:39	1:49	12:19	2:09	11:53	2:35	11:15	3:13	10:09	4:19
	15	11:45	0:55	11:25	1:15	10:59	1:41	10:21	2:19	9:15	3:25
Apr.	1	10:41	23:51	10:21	0:11	9:54	0:38	9:16	1:16	8:10	2:22
	15	9:50	23:00	9:30	23:20	9:03	23:47	8:25	0:25	7:19	1:31
May	1	8:33	21:43	8:13	22:03	7:46	22:30	7:08	23:08	6:02	0:14
	15	8:04	21:16	7:45	21:35	7:19	22:01	6:39	22:41	5:33	23:47
June	1	7:06	20:16	6:46	20:36	6:20	21:02	5:41	21:41	4:35	22:47
	15	6:19	19:29	5:59	19:49	5:32	20:16	4:54	20:54	3:48	22:00
July	1	5:25	18:35	5:05	18:55	4:39	19:21	4:01	19:59	2:55	21:05
	15	4:38	17:48	4:18	18:08	3:52	18:34	3:14	19:12	2:09	20:17
Aug.	1	3:40	16:50	3:21	17:09	2:54	17:36	2:18	18:12	1:15	19:15
	15	2:53	16:01	2:33	16:21	2:07	16:47	1:31	17:23	0:27	18:27
Sept.	1	1:54	15:02	1:35	15:21	1:09	15:47	0:33	16:23	23:30	17:26
	15	1:04	14:12	0:45	14:31	0:19	14:57	23:44	15:32	22:41	16:35
Oct.	1	0:06	13:14	23:48	13:32	23:22	13:58	22:47	14:33	21:45	15:35
	15	23:13	12:21	22:55	12:39	22:29	13:05	21:54	13:40	20:52	14:42
Nov.	1	22:07	11:15	21:49	11:33	21:24	11:58	20:48	12:34	19:47	13:35
	15	21:11	10:19	20:53	10:37	20:27	11:03	19:52	11:38	18:50	12:20
Dec.	1	20:06	9:14	19:48	9:32	19:22	9:58	18:46	10:34	17:44	11:36
	15	19:07	8:15	18:48	8:34	18:22	9:00	17:47	9:35	16:44	10:38

(Left margin: Saturn, 1974)

The Planets and the Solar System

Name of Planet	Mean Daily Motion "	Orbital Velocity Miles Per Sec.	Sidereal Revolution Days	Synodical Revolution Days	Dist. from Sun in Millions of Miles Max.	Min.	Approx. miles from Earth in Millions Max.	Min.	Light at Peri-helion	Aphe-lion
Mercury..	14732.420	29.73	87.9686	116	43.355	28.566	136	50	10.58	4.59
Venus....	5767.668	21.75	224.7007	584	67.653	66.738	161	25	1.94	1.91
Earth	3548.329	18.50	365.2564	....	94.452	91.342	....	....	1.03	0.97
Mars	1886.519	14.98	686.9804	780	154.760	128.830	248	35	0.52	0.36
Jupiter...	299.128	8.11	4332.5870	399	506.710	459.940	600	367	0.41	0.034
Saturn ...	120.657	5.99	10759.2025	378	935.570	836.700	1028	744	0.012	0.010
Uranus ...	42.262	4.22	30685.93	370	1866.800	1698.800	1960	1606	0.001	0.0025
Neptune .	21.455	3.40	60187.64	367	2817.400	2769.600	2910	2677	0.001	0.001
Pluto.....	14.355	3.00	90737.	367	4600.000	2760.000	4700	2670	0.001	0.001

Jupiter has 4 large and 8 small satellites, (moons) revolving around it; Saturn has 10; Uranus 5; Neptune, 2; Mars, 2; Earth, 1.

Name of Planet	Mean Longitude of: * Ascending Node ° ' "	Perihelion ° ' "	Inclination * of Orbit to Ecliptic ° ' "	Mean Distance *	Eccentricity * of Orbit	Mean Longitude at the Epoch * ° ' "
Mercury....	48 01 17.5	77 02 56.0	7 00 15.3	0.387099	0.205629	72 33 26.9
Venus......	76 26 40.5	131 12 12.2	3 23 39.7	0.723332	0.006785	10 4 47.6
Earth	....	102 29 27.6	....	1.00000003	0.016720	52 57 17.3
Mars.......	49 20 21.5	335 34 40.9	1 50 59.4	1.523691	0.093381	33 26 59.4
Jupiter.....	100 10 47.3	13 53 32.3	1 18 20.5	5.202813	0.0480742	321 2 24.7
Saturn.....	113 26 52.8	91 43 34.4	2 29 21.6	9.528215	0.0538315	89 59 10.3
Uranus.....	73 51 53.8	171 22 28.6	0 46 23.4	19.17383	0.0460002	201 2 46.3
Neptune ...	131 31 49.7	26 46 30.0	1 46 16.2	30.12927	0.0078585	247 38 49.2
Pluto.......	110 01 51.6	224 17 39.1	17 08 53.0	39.36417	0.2480593	200 47 34.8

*Values are consistent at the epoch=1973 Nov. 14, 0 hours Greenwich Mean Time.

Sun and Planets	Semi-Diameter At Unit Dis-tance "	At Mean Least Dist. "	In Miles (Mean S.-D.)	Volume ⊕=1.	Mass. ⊕=1.	Den-sity ⊕=1.	Axial Rotation d. h. m. s.	Gravi-ty at Sur-face ⊕=1.	Re-flect-ing Power Pct.	Prob-able Tem-per-ature F.
Sun........	15 59.63	....	432000	1300000.	332000.	0.26	24 16 48	27.9	....	+10,000
Mercury....	3.34	5.45	1505	0.056	0.0543	0.68	59	0.38	0.07	+ 600
Venus.......	8.41	30.40	3805	0.910	0.8136	0.94	243 (R)	0.88	0.76	+ 100
Earth	....	....	3959	1.000	1.000	1.00	23 56 4.	1.00	0.39	+ 50
Moon	2.44	932.58	1080	0.020	0.0120	0.60	27 7 43 12	0.16	0.07	+ 215
Mars.......	4.68	8.94	2070	0.150	0.1069	0.71	24 37 23	0.39	0.15	0
Jupiter.....	1 35.19	22.60	43450	1312.	318.35	0.24	9 50	2.65	0.51	− 150
Saturn	1 18.95	9.24	35750	763.	95.3	0.12	10 14	1.17	0.50	− 250
Uranus.....	34.28	1.88	14750	53.	14.54	0.28	10 45 (R)	1.05	0.66	− 350
Neptune ...	36.56	1.26	15750	65.	17.2	0.26	15 48	1.23	0.62	− 400

The planet Pluto was located by C.W. Tombaugh of Lowell Observatory Mar. 13, 1930. Its mass is about 0.18 of the mass of the Earth. It rotates on its axis in 6 days 9 hours. Its average distance from the sun is 3,664,000,000 miles. On Mar. 23 at 21 hours, GMT, it is in opposition in Coma Berenices at right ascension 12 hrs. 37 mins. 12 secs. and declina-tion, north 14 degrees 33 minutes 26 seconds, Northeast of Messier 90. Pluto will have a magnitude of about 15. (R) Venus and Uranus are in retrograde motion, rotating in opposite direction from other planets.

Standard Time, Daylight Saving Time and Others

Source: Defense Mapping Agency Hydrographic Centre; Department of Transportation; National Bureau of Standards and U.S. Naval Observatory

STANDARD TIME

Standard time is reckoned from Greenwich, England, recognized as the Prime Meridian of Longitude. The world is divided into 24 zones, each 15° of arc, or one hour in time apart. The meridian of Greenwich (0°) extends through the center of the initial zone, and the zones to the eastward are numbered from 1 to 12 with the prefix "minus" indicating the number of hours to be subtracted to obtain Greenwich Time.

Zones westward are similarly numbered, but prefixed "plus" showing the number of hours that must be added to get Greenwich time. While these zones apply generally to sea areas, it should be noted that the Standard Time maintained in many countries does not coincide with zone time. A graphical representation of the zones is shown on the Standard Time Zone Chart of the World (N.O. 76) published by the Defense Mapping Agency Hydrographic Center, Washington, D.C. 20390.

The United States and possessions are divided into eight Standard Time zones, as set forth by the Uniform Time Act of 1966, which also provides for the use of Daylight Saving Time therein. Each zone is approximately 15° of longitude in width. All places in each zone use, instead of their own local time, the time counted from the transit of the "mean sun" across the Standard Time meridian which passes near the middle of that zone.

These time zones are designated as Atlantic, Eastern, Central, Mountain, Pacific, Yukon, Alaska-Hawaii, and Bering and the time in these zones is basically reckoned from the 60th, 75th, 90th, 105th, 120th, 135th, 150th, 165th meridians west of Greenwich. The line wanders to conform to local geographical regions. The time in the various zones is earlier than Greenwich Time by 4, 5, 6, 7, 8, 9, 10, and 11 hours respectively.

High Precision Time and Frequency are broadcast by U. S. Navy Stations which are maintained on frequency with the aid of Atomic Clocks (cesium beam and atomic hydrogen masers). The stations are as follows: NBA: NSS: NLK: NAA: NPM: NWC: NPN: NPG: NDT: Omega.

Loran-C Navigational Transmissions at 100 KHz of the East Coast, Central Pacific, Mediterranean, Northwest Pacific and the Norwegian sea chains may be used for time and frequency comparisons. These can be made to one microsecond.

STANDARD FREQUENCY STATIONS

The National Bureau of Standards (NBS) radio stations WWV at Fort Collins, Colorado, and WWVH on the island of Kauai, Hawaii, broadcast a number of technical services continuously night and day. These services are: 1. standard radio frequencies, 2.5, 5, 10, 15, 20 and 25 MHz (WWV) and 2.5, 5, 10, 15 and 20 MHz (WWVH); 2. standard time voice announcements (WWV — male, 7.5 seconds before the minute; WWVH — female, 15 seconds before the minute); 3. standard time intervals of one second and one minute; 4. corrections to adjust atomic time to astronomical time; 5. standard audio frequencies of 500 and 600 Hz on alternate minutes and a 440 Hz tone (the musical pitch A above middle C) once each hour; 6. a slow time code at 100 Hz giving the day, hour and minute in binary coded decimal form; 7. hourly radio propagation forecasts; 8. geophysical alerts on events in process and summaries of solar and geophysical events of the last 24 hours; and 9. storm warnings. The NBS also broadcasts time and frequency signals from its low frequency station (60kHz). WWVB, also located at Fort Collins, Colorado.

Each hour there are periods with no tone modulation during which the carrier, seconds ticks, minute time announcements, and 100 Hz time code continue. They occur during the 16th through the 20th minute on WWVH and the 46th through the 50th minute on WWV.

Storm warnings cover the waters of the Atlantic and Eastern Pacific from WWV and the Pacific from WWVH

and are given at the 8th, 10th and 12th minute of each hour from WWV and at the 49th and 51st minute of each hour from WWVH. Times of issue are 0500, 1100, 1600, and 2300 UT from WWV, and 0000, 0600, 1200, and 1800 UT from WWVH.

The time and frequency broadcasts are controlled by the NBS atomic frequency standards, which follow the internationally defined cesium resonance frequency with an accuracy of 2 parts in 10^{12}. (The cesium atom invariably resonates at a little over 9 billion oscillations per second.) The frequencies transmitted by WWV and WWVH are held stable to better than $+2$ parts in 10^{11} at all times. Deviations at WWV are normally less than 1 part in 10^{12} from day to day. Incremental frequency adjustments not exceeding one part in 10^{11} are made at WWV as necessary. Frequency adjustments made at WWVH do not exceed 2 parts in 10^{11}. Changes in the propagation medium (causing Doppler effect, diurnal shifts, etc.) result in fluctuations in the carrier frequencies as received which may be very much greater than the uncertainties described above.

The atomic time scale is uniform and does not reflect the variable rotational speed of the earth. The time signals are adjusted by introducing a leap second about once a year (at the end of June or December) so that the broadcast time never departs more than seven-tenths of a second from mean solar time which is determined by the rotational position of the earth.

Special Publication 236 describes in detail the standard frequency and time service of the National Bureau of Standards. Single copies may be obtained upon request from the National Bureau of Standards, Boulder, Colorado, 80302. Quantities may be obtained from the Superintendent of Documents, U.S. Gov. Printing Office, Wash., D.C. 20402, at 25¢ per copy.

DAYLIGHT SAVING TIME

Under the Uniform Time Act, which became effective in 1967, all states, the District of Columbia and U. S. possessions must observe Daylight Saving Time beginning at 2 a.m. on the last Sunday in April and ending at 2 a.m. on the last Sunday in October. Any state, by legislative action, can exempt itself from the law; Hawaii did so in 1967, Arizona in 1968, and Indiana in 1971. The 1972 amendment to the Uniform Time Act authorizes states split by time zones to take that into consideration in exempting themselves. As a result Indiana's exemption law applies only to the eastern portion of its state. The Dept. of Transportation, which oversees the act, has modified during the last 5 years some boundaries in Indiana, Michigan, Utah, North Dakota, Nebraska, Kansas, Oregon, Texas, and Alaska due to local problems. Daylight Saving Time is achieved by advancing the clock one hour.

24-HOUR TIME

24-hour time is widely used in scientific work throughout the world. In the United States it is used also in operations of the Armed Forces. In Europe it is used in preference to the 12-hour a.m. and p.m. system. With the 24-hour system the day begins at midnight and hours are numbered 0 through 23. Thus 8 a.m. is 0800, and 8:25 a.m. is 0825; 4 p.m. is 1600, and 7:52 p.m. is 1952, or 19 hours and 52 minutes past midnight.

INTERNATIONAL DATE LINE

The Date Line is a zig-zag line that approximately coincides with the 180th meridian, and it is where each calendar day begins. The date must be advanced one day when crossing in a westerly direction and set back one day when crossing in an easterly direction. The line is deflected between north latitude 48° and 75°, so that all Asia lies to the west of it and all North America, including the Aleutian Islands, to the east; between south latitude 5° and 51° the line is deflected so that Ellice and Chatham Island and the Tonga group lie to the west.

Standard Time Differences—North American Cities

Source: Dept. of Transportation

At 12 o'clock noon Eastern Standard Time, the standard time in N.A. cities is as follows:

City	Time		City	Time		City	Time	
Akron, Ohio	12.00	NOON	Fort Worth, Texas	11.00	A.M.	Philadelphia, Pa.	12.00	NOON
Albuquerque, N. Mex.	10.00	A.M.	Frankfort, Ky.	12.00	NOON	*Phoenix, Ariz.	10.00	A.M.
Atlanta, Ga.	12.00	NOON	Galveston, Tex.	11.00	A.M.	Pierre, S. Dak.	11.00	A.M.
Austin, Tex.	11.00	A.M.	Grand Rapids, Mich.	12.00	NOON	Pittsburgh, Pa.	12.00	NOON
Baltimore, Md.	12.00	NOON	Halifax, N.S.	1.00	P.M.	Portland, Me.	12.00	NOON
Birmingham, Ala.	11.00	A.M.	Hartford, Conn.	12.00	NOON	Portland, Oreg.	9.00	A.M.
Bismarck, N. Dak.	11.00	A.M.	Helena, Mont.	10.00	A.M.	Providence, R.I.	12.00	NOON
Boise, Idaho	10.00	A.M.	*Honolulu, Hawaii	7.00	A.M.	*Regina, Man.	11.00	A.M.
Boston, Mass.	12.00	NOON	Houston, Tex.	11.00	A.M.	Reno, Nev.	9.00	A.M.
Buffalo, N.Y.	12.00	NOON	*Indianapolis, Ind.	12.00	NOON	Richmond, Va.	12.00	NOON
Butte, Mont.	10.00	A.M.	Jacksonville, Fla.	12.00	NOON	Rochester, N.Y.	12.00	NOON
Calgary, Alta.	10.00	A.M.	Juneau, Alaska	9.00	A.M.	Sacramento, Calif.	9.00	A.M.
Charleston, S.C.	12.00	NOON	Kansas City, Mo.	11.00	A.M.	St. John's, Nfld.	1.30	P.M.
Charleston, W. Va.	12.00	NOON	Knoxville, Tenn.	12.00	NOON	St. Louis, Mo.	11.00	A.M.
Charlotte, N.C.	12.00	NOON	Lexington, Ky.	12.00	NOON	St. Paul, Minn.	11.00	A.M.
Charlottetown, P.E.I.	1.00	P.M.	Lincoln, Nebr.	11.00	A.M.	Salt Lake City, Utah	10.00	A.M.
Chattanooga, Tenn.	12.00	NOON	Little Rock, Ark.	11.00	A.M.	San Antonio, Tex.	11.00	A.M.
Cheyenne, Wyo.	10.00	A.M.	Los Angeles, Calif.	9.00	A.M.	San Diego, Calif.	9.00	A.M.
Chicago, Ill.	11.00	A.M.	Louisville, Ky.	12.00	NOON	San Francisco, Calif.	9.00	A.M.
Cincinnati, Ohio	12.00	NOON	*Mexico City	11.00	A.M.	Santa Fe, N.M.	10.00	A.M.
Cleveland, Ohio	12.00	NOON	Memphis, Tenn.	11.00	A.M.	Savannah, Ga.	12.00	NOON
Colorado Springs, Colo.	10.00	A.M.	Miami, Fla.	12.00	NOON	Seattle, Wash.	9.00	A.M.
Columbus, Ohio	12.00	NOON	Milwaukee, Wis.	11.00	A.M.	Shreveport, La.	11.00	A.M.
Dallas, Tex.	11.00	A.M.	Minneapolis, Minn.	11.00	A.M.	Sioux Falls, S. Dak.	11.00	A.M.
*Dawson, Yuk.	8.00	A.M.	Mobile, Ala.	11.00	A.M.	Spokane, Wash.	9.00	A.M.
Dayton, Ohio	12.00	NOON	Montreal, Que.	12.00	NOON	Tacoma, Wash.	9.00	A.M.
Denver, Colo.	10.00	A.M.	Nashville, Tenn.	11.00	A.M.	Tampa, Fla.	12.00	NOON
Des Moines, Iowa	11.00	A.M.	Newark, N.J.	12.00	NOON	Toledo, Ohio	12.00	NOON
Detroit, Mich.	12.00	NOON	New Haven, Conn.	12.00	NOON	Topeka, Kan.	11.00	A.M.
Duluth, Minn.	11.00	A.M.	New Orleans, La.	11.00	A.M.	*Tucson, Ariz.	10.00	A.M.
El Paso, Tex.	10.00	A.M.	New York, N.Y.	12.00	NOON	Tulsa, Okla.	11.00	A.M.
Erie, Pa.	12.00	NOON	Nome, Alaska	6.00	A.M.	Vancouver, B.C.	9.00	A.M.
Evansville, Ind.	11.00	A.M.	Norfolk, Va.	12.00	NOON	Washington, D.C.	12.00	NOON
Fairbanks, Alaska	7.00	A.M.	Okla. City, Okla.	11.00	A.M.	Wichita, Kan.	11.00	A.M.
Flint, Mich.	12.00	NOON	Omaha, Nebr.	11.00	A.M.	Wilmington, Del.	12.00	NOON
Fort Wayne, Ind.	12.00	NOON	Peoria, Ill.	11.00	A.M.	Winnipeg, Man.	11.00	A.M.

*Cities with an asterisk do not observe daylight savings time. During the summer it is necessary to add one hour to the cities observing daylight savings to get the proper time relation.

Standard Time Differences—World Cities

Source: Defense Mapping Agency Hydrographic Center

By government decree or proclamation Great Britain, Ireland, Spain, France, Netherlands, Portugal, and Belgium have advanced their time from the standard meridian by one hour throughout the year. The time indicated in table is fixed by law and is called the legal time, or, more generally, Standard Time. ˚Indicates morning of the following day.

At 12 o'clock noon Eastern Standard Time, the standard time in foreign cities is as follows:

City	Time		City	Time		City	Time		City	Time	
Alexandria	7:00	P.M.	Copenhagen	6:00	P.M.	Liverpool	5:00	P.M.	Seoul	2:00	A.M.˚
Amsterdam	6:00	P.M.	Dacca	11:00	P.M.	London	5:00	P.M.	Shanghai	1:00	A.M.˚
Athens	7:00	P.M.	Delhi	10:30	P.M.	Madrid	6:00	P.M.	Singapore	12:30	A.M.˚
Auckland	5:00	A.M.˚	Djakarta	12:00	MID.	Manila	1:00	A.M.˚	Stockholm	6:00	P.M.
Baghdad	8:00	P.M.	Dublin	5:00	P.M.	Melbourne	3:00	A.M.˚	Sydney		
Bangkok	12:00	MID.	Gdansk	6:00	P.M.	Montevideo	2:00	P.M.	(Australia)	3:00	A.M.˚
Belfast	5:00	P.M.	Geneva	6:00	P.M.	Moscow	8:00	P.M.	Tashkent	11:00	P.M.
Berlin	6:00	P.M.	Havana	12:00	NOON	Nagasaki	2:00	A.M.˚	Teheran	8:30	P.M.
Bogota	12:00	NOON	Helsinki	7:00	P.M.	Oslo	6:00	P.M.	Tel Aviv	7:00	P.M.
Bombay	10:30	P.M.	Hong Kong	1:00	A.M.˚	Paris	6:00	P.M.	Tokyo	2:00	A.M.˚
Bremen	6:00	P.M.	Istanbul	7:00	P.M.	Peking	1:00	A.M.˚	Valparaiso	1:00	P.M.
Brussels	6:00	P.M.	Jerusalem	7:00	P.M.	Prague	6:00	P.M.	Vladivostok	3:00	A.M.˚
Bucharest	7:00	P.M.	Johannesburg	7:00	P.M.	Rangoon	11:30	P.M.	Vienna	6:00	P.M.
Budapest	6:00	P.M.	Karachi	10:00	P.M.	Rio de Janeiro	2:00	P.M.	Warsaw	6:00	P.M.
Buenos Aires.	2:00	P.M.	Le Havre	6:00	P.M.	Rome	6:00	P.M.	Wellington		
Calcutta	10:30	P.M.	Leningrad	8:00	P.M.	Saigon	1:00	A.M.˚	(N. Z.)	5:00	A.M.˚
Cape Town	7:00	P.M.	Lima	12:00	NOON	Santiago			Yokohama	2:00	A.M.˚
Caracas	1:00	P.M.	Lisbon	6:00	P.M.	(Chile)	1:00	P.M.	Zurich	6:00	P.M.

Aurora Borealis and Aurora Australis

The Aurora Borealis, also called the Northern Lights, is a broad display of rather faint light in the northern skies at night. The Aurora Australis, a similar phenomenon, appears at the same time in southern skies. The aurora appears in a wide variety of forms. Sometimes it is seen as a quiet glow, almost foglike in character; sometimes as vertical streamers in which there may be considerable motion; sometimes as a series of luminous expanding arcs. There are many colors, with white, yellow and red predominating.

The auroras are most vivid and most frequently seen at about 20 degrees from the magnetic poles, along the northern coast of the North American continent and the eastern coast of the northern coast of Europe. They have been seen as far south as Key West and as far north as Australia and New Zealand, but such occasions are rare.

While the cause of the auroras is not known beyond question, there does seem to be a definite correlation between auroral displays and the sun-spot activity. It is thought that atomic particles expelled from the sun by the forces that cause solar flares speed through space at velocities of 400 to 600 miles per second. These particles are entrapped by the earth's magnetic field, forming what are termed the Van Allen belts. The encounter of these clouds of the solar wind with the earth's magnetic field weakens the field so that previously trapped particles are allowed to impact the upper atmosphere. The collisions between solar and terrestrial atoms result in the glow in the upper atmosphere called the aurora. The glow may be vivid where the lines of magnetic force converge near the magnetic poles.

The auroral displays appear at heights ranging from 50 to about 600 miles and have given us a means of estimating the extent of the earth's atmosphere.

The auroras are often accompanied by magnetic storms whose forces, also guided by the lines of force of the earth's magnetic field, disrupt electrical communication.

Tides and Their Causes

Source: National Ocean Survey (NOAA)

The tides are a natural phenomenon involving the alternating rise and fall in the large fluid bodies of the earth caused by the combined gravitational attraction of the sun and moon. The combination of these two variable force influences, as modified by certain factors such as depth of the water, configuration of the shoreline, and geographic location, produce the complex recurrent cycle of the tides. Tides may occur in both oceans and seas, to a limited extent in large lakes, the atmosphere, and, to a very minute degree, in the earth itself. The period between succeeding tides varies as the result of many factors and force influences.

The tide-generating force represents the difference between (1) the centrifugal force produced by the revolution of the earth around the common center-of-gravity of the earth-moon system and (2) the gravitational attraction of the moon acting upon the earth's overlying waters. Similar tide-producing forces exist in the earth-sun system. Since, on the average, the moon is only 238,857 miles from the earth compared with the sun's much greater distance of 93,000,000 miles, this closer distance outranks the much smaller mass of the moon compared with that of the sun, and the moon's tide-raising force is, accordingly, 2 1/5 times that of the sun.

The effect of the tide-generating forces of the moon and sun acting tangentially to the earth's surface (the so-called "tractive force"), tends to cause a maximum accumulation of the waters of the oceans at two diametrically opposite positions on the surface of the earth and to withdraw compensating amounts of water from all points 90°removed from the positions of these tidal bulges. The presence of the continents, as well as other factors, prevent the total free movement of water. However, as the earth rotates beneath the maxima and minima of these tide-generating forces, a sequence of two high tides, separated by two low tides, ideally is produced each day.

Twice in each lunar month, when the sun, moon, and earth are directly aligned, with the moon between the earth and the sun (at new moon) or on the opposite side of the earth from the sun (at full moon), the sun and the moon exert their gravitational force in a mutual or additive fashion. Higher high tides and lower low tides are produced. These are called *spring* tides. At two positions 90° in between, the gravitational forces of moon and sun –imposed at right angles–tend to counteract each other to the greatest extent, and the range between high and low tides is reduced. These are called *neap* tides. This semi-monthly variation between the spring and neap tides is called the *phase inequality*.

The inclination of the moon's orbit to the equator also produces a difference in the height of succeeding high tides and in the extent of depression of succeeding low tides which is known as the *diurnal inequality*. In extreme cases, this phenomenon can result in only one high tide and one low tide each day. The changing distance of the moon from the earth in each lunar month due to the elliptical orbit of the moon, produces a difference in the height of the tides known as the *lunar parallactic inequality*. The changing distance of the earth from the sun during the earth's annual revolution around the sun similarly introduces the *solar parallactic inequality*.

The actual amount of uplift of the waters in the deep ocean may amount to only one or two feet. However, as this tide approaches shoal waters and its effects are augmented, the tidal range may be greatly increased. In Nova Scotia, along the narrow channel of the Bay of Fundy, the range of tides, or difference between high and low waters, may reach 43½ feet or more (under spring tide conditions) due to resonant amplification.

At New Orleans, the periodic rise and fall of the tide varies with the state of the Mississippi, being about 10 inches at low stage and zero at high.The Canadian Tide Tables for 1972 gave a maximum range of nearly 50 feet at Leaf Basin, Ungava Bay.

In every case, actual high or low tide can vary considerably from the average due to weather conditions such as strong winds, abrupt barometric pressure changes, or prolonged periods of extreme high or low pressure.

The Average Rise and Fall of Tides

Source: National Ocean Survey (NOAA)

Places	Feet	In.	Places	Feet	In.	Places	Feet	In.
Baltimore, Md.	1	1	Mobile, Ala.	1	6	San Diego, Calif.	4	1
Boston, Mass.	9	6	New London, Conn.	2	7	Sandy Hook, N.J.	4	7
Charleston, S.C.	5	2	Newport, R.I.	3	6	San Francisco, Calif.	4	0
Colon, Panama	1	1	New York, N. Y.	4	6	Savannah, Ga.	7	5
Eastport, Me.	18	2	Old Pt. Comfort, Va.	2	6	Seattle, Wash.	7	7
Galveston, Tex.	1	5	Philadelphia, Pa.	5	11	Tampa, Fla.	2	10
Halifax, N.S.	4	5	Portland, Me.	9	0	Vancouver, B.C.	10	6
Key West, Fla.	1	4	St. John's, Nfld.	2	7	Washington, D.C.	2	11

Knots and Miles: Nautical Measures

Source: National Ocean Survey (NOAA)

A **Knot** is a measure of speed, one knot being a speed of one nautical mile an hour.

The **U.S. Statute Mile** is 5,280 feet. In Europe, the old miles, which varied in length from about 3,300 feet to over 36,000 feet, have been mostly replaced, officially at least, by the kilometer, which equals 0.6214 statute mile or 3,280.8 feet.

The **International Nautical Mile** is 1,852 meters or 6076.1033 feet; this distance is equivalent to 1.150777 statute miles.

To convert **statute miles into international nautical miles** multiply statute miles by 0.868978; to convert international nautical miles into statute miles multiply nautical miles by 1.150777 or 1 1/7.

A **Nautical, Geographic,** or **Sea Mile** at any place is considered, for purposes of navigation, to be equal to the length of one minute of the meridian at that place.

A **fathom**—6 feet, chiefly water depth.

A **cable**—100 fathoms or 600 feet or approximately 0.1 nautical mile (In U.S. Navy, 120 fathoms or 720 feet).

Using A Barometer

Your aching "tennis elbow" may have served your weather forecasting needs till now but your barometer and wind direction indicator can make you the weather seer of your neighborhood.

Weather systems in the northern hemisphere move from West to East. Since air moves from areas of high pressure to ones of low pressure, wind direction will show the location of highs and lows. For example, if the wind is from the East there is a high in the East and a low to the West. Because of the movement of systems West to East we can expect the low to move into our area bringing a period of bad weather. The barometer measures local air pressure. By a series of readings we can determine whether the pressure is rising or falling and how fast. A rising barometer signals the approach of a high, a falling one the approach of a low. The rate of change will indicate a gentle or abrupt change in the weather.

Make a chart of your observations of barometric pressure and wind direction. Morning and evening readings should be enough. Note the local weather at the same time. Soon you will be able to relate the wind direction and barometer movement to the next day's weather. Add cloud descriptions to your observations and you will soon be able to retire your weather forecasting "tennis elbow".

National Weather Service Watches and Warnings

National Weather Service forecasters issue a TOR-NADO WATCH for a specific area where it is reasonably possible that tornadoes may occur during the valid time of the watch. A WATCH is to alert people to watch for tornado activity and listen for a TORNADO WARNING. A TORNADO WARNING means that a tornado has been sighted or indicated by radar, and that safety precautions should be taken at once. The terms HURRICANE WATCH and HURRICANE WARNING are used similarly during hurricane season.

Definitions

Tornado—a violent rotating column of air pendant from a thundercloud, usually recognized as a funnel-shaped vortex accompanied by a loud roar. With rotating winds est. up to 300 mph., it is the most destructive storm. Tornado paths have varied in length from a few feet to nearly 300 miles (avg. 5 mi.); diameter from a few feet to over a mile (average 220 yards); average forward speed, 25-40 mph.

Cyclone—An atmospheric circulation of winds rotating counterclockwise in the northern hemisphere and clockwise in the southern hemisphere. Tornadoes, hurricanes and the LOWS shown on weather maps are all examples of cyclones having various sizes and intensities. Cyclones are usually accompanied by precipitation or stormy weather.

Hurricane—A severe cyclone originating over tropical ocean waters and having winds 74 miles an hour or higher. (In the western Pacific, such storms are known as typhoons.) The area of strong winds takes the form of a circle or an oval, sometimes as much as 500 miles in diameter. In the lower latitudes hurricanes usually move toward the west or northwest at 10 to 15 mph. When the center approaches 25° to 30° North Latitude, direction of motion often changes to northeast, with increased forward speed.

Blizzard—A severe weather condition characterized by low temperatures and by strong winds bearing a great amount of snow (mostly fine, dry snow picked up from the ground). The National Weather Service specifies, for blizzard, a wind of 35 miles an hour or higher, temperatures 20°F. or lower, and sufficient falling and/or blowing snow to reduce visibility to less than 1/4 of a mile. For "severe blizzard" wind speeds of 45 mph or more, temperature near or below 10°F., and visibility reduced by snow to near zero.

Monsoon—A name for seasonal winds (derived from Arabic "mausim," a season). It was first applied to the winds over the Arabian Sea, which blow for six months from northeast and six months from southwest, but it has been extended to similar winds in other parts of the world. The monsoons are strongest on the southern and eastern sides of Asia.

Flood—The condition that occurs when water over flows the natural or artificial confines of a stream or other body of water, or accumulates by drainage over low-lying areas.

National Weather Service Marine Warning and Advisories

Source: National Weather Service, NOAA, Dept. of Commerce

Small Craft Advisory: A Small Craft Advisory alerts mariners to sustained (exceeding two hours) weather and/or sea conditions either present or forecast, potentially hazardous to small boats. Hazardous conditions may include winds of 18 to 33 knots and/or dangerous wave or inlet conditions. It is the responsibility of the mariner, based on his experience and size or type of boat, to determine if the conditions are hazardous. When a mariner becomes aware of a Small Craft Advisory, he should immediately obtain the latest marine forecast to determine the reason for the Advisory. The visual signal is a RED pennant by day, a RED OVER WHITE light at night.

Gale Warning: Two RED pennants displayed by day and a WHITE light ABOVE a RED light at night to indicate that winds within the range 34 to 47 knots are forecast for the area.

Storm Warning: A single square RED flag with a BLACK center displayed during daytime and two RED lights at night to indicate that winds 48 knots and above, no matter how high the speed, are forecast for the area. However, if the winds are associated with a tropical cyclone (hurricane), the STORM WARNING display indicates that winds within the range 48 to 63 knots are forecast.

Hurricane Warning: Displayed only in connection with a hurricane or typhoon. Two square RED flags with BLACK centers displayed by day and a WHITE light between two RED lights at night to indicate that winds 64 knots and above are forecast for the area.

Primary sources of dissemination are by commercial radio, TV, U.S. Coast Guard Radio stations and NOAA VHF-FM broadcasts. These broadcasts on 162.40 and 162.55 MHz can usually be received 20-40 miles from the transmitting antenna site, depending on terrain and quality of the receiver used. Where transmitting antennas are on high ground, the range is somewhat greater, reaching 60 miles or more.

The frequencies 162.55 and 162.40 MHz require narrow band FM receivers of ± 5 kilohertz deviation. In selecting a suitable receiver, special attention should be paid to the manufacturer's rating of the receiver's sensitivity. Generally speaking, a receiver with a sensitivity of 1 microvolt or less should pick up a broadcast at a distance of about 40-50 miles depending upon antenna height and terrain.

Dissemination is also made by means of visual displays (flags, pennants and lights). These are indicated under each warning and advisory category.

Hurricane Names in 1974

The National Weather Service has used girls' names to identify hurricanes in the Atlantic, Caribbean and Gulf of Mexico since 1953. A semi-permanent list of 10 sets of names in aphabetical order was established in 1971. Hurricane season begins June 1 and ends Nov. 30.

Names assigned to potential hurricanes: **1974**—Alma, Becky, Carmen, Dolly, Elaine, Fifi, Gertrude, Hester, Ivy, Justine, Kathy, Linda, Marsha, Nelly, Olga, Pearl, Roxanne, Sabrina, Thelma, Viola, and Wilma.

Hurricanes and typhoons in the Eastern North Pacific are also identified by girls' names. **1974**—Aletta, Blanca, Connie, Dolores, Eileen, Francesca, Gretchen, Helga, Ione, Joyce, Kirsten, Lorraine, Maggie, Norma, Orlene, Patricia, Rosalie, Selma, Toni, Vivian and Winona.

1973—Year of the Tornado

Tornadoes struck the U.S. in record numbers in the first half of 1973. Preliminary figures showed that over 700 tornadoes occurred between Jan. 1 and May 29. The previous 5-month high was 504 in 1957. Tornadoes for April and May alone numbered 240 and 350.

The tornado activity is due to a stronger than normal jet stream flowing across the country from the southwest. The abnormal pressure of this high-altitude, high-speed air current keeps tornadoes at a Spring-like peak in the south. As it breaks, tornadoes move north.

Tornado safety depends on getting into small sturdy rooms or under sturdy furniture in the center of the building. In homes, a few windows should be left open, but always stay away from window areas. In a multi-story building, go to the basement or lowest floor. Get out of a mobile home. If no adequate shelter is available, lie down in a ditch or other depression and protect your head with your arms.

New Developments in U.S. Weather Satellite System

Source: National Oceanic and Atmospheric Administration

Since the successful launching of ESSA 1 and ESSA 2 (Environmental Survey Satellites) in Feb. 1966, the United States has had an operational weather satellite system providing both global and local cloud-cover pictures at least once every day.

The operational system is now based on the Improved TIROS Operational Satellite. The first of these, ITOS-1, was launched Jan. 23, 1970: the second, called NOAA-1 was launched Dec. 11, 1970; and the third, NOAA-2, was launched Oct. 15, 1972. The ITOS system is managed and operated by the National Environmental Satellite Service (NESS) of the National Oceanic and Atmospheric Administration (NOAA).

Although similar in appearance to previous ITOS satellites, NOAA-2 is the first in this series to fly with no cameras on-board and to rely entirely on scanning radiometers for imagery. NOAA-2 is also the first operational satellite to carry a sensor to obtain vertical temperature profile soundings of the atmosphere routinely on a near-global basis.

The 40 x 40 x 49-inch box, with a 3-panel solar cell array attached, contains instruments flown on earlier ITOS satellites—the 2-channel scanning radiometer and the solar proton monitor—and 2 new sensors flying for the first time on the operational satellites—the vertical temperature profile radiometer (VTPR) and the very high resolution radiometer (VHRR). Duplication of all sensors in the spacecraft ensures a more reliable service and longer lifetime.

The scanning radiometer system, similar to that on NOAA-1, obtains data in both visible and infrared channels. The visible channel observes only sunlit portions of the earth, while the infrared channel furnishes cloud pictures both night and day. The radiometer scans a 2000-nautical-mile-wide swath beneath the satellite's path. Picture resolution is 2 nautical miles in the visible channel and 4 nautical miles in the infrared.

The scanning radiometer replaces the 2 types of camera systems formerly carried on operational satellites, by providing both stored picture coverage of the earth's weather and direct transmission of cloud cover photographs from the satellite to more than 50 local receiving stations around the world. Its ability to photograph the dark side of the earth makes nighttime satellite observations available for use in preparing early morning forecasts and will ensure night as well as daytime coverage of hazardous weather, such as hurricanes and winter storms.

The very high resolution radiometer (VHRR) obtains observations similar to those taken by the scanning radiometer, but with a resolution of 1/2 mile in contrast to the 2-to-4-mile resolution of the scanning radiometer. In addition to providing images of cloud cover, the scanning radiometer and the VHRR obtain a measure of the sea surface temperature in cloud-free areas.

The vertical temperature profile radiometer, developed by NASA, is an instrument that measures infrared energy radiated at 6 levels of the atmosphere and at the earth's surface or cloud tops. These measurements are used to calculate the vertical temperature distribution of the atmosphere beneath the satellite. The radiometer also provides information on the total moisture content of the atmospheric column observed.

Nimbus III launched April 14, 1969, carried the first systems for gathering quantitative measurements through the column of atmosphere beneath the spacecraft. Called Satellite Infrared Spectrometer (SIRS) and Infrared Interferometer Spectrometer (IRIS), they provided vertical temperature measurements in the atmosphere, and additional information on atmospheric pressure can be derived from these soundings. NASA's Nimbus IV, launched April 8, 1970, and Nimbus V, launched December 11, 1972 (2:56 AM EST) carried other experiments designed to develop techniques for measuring, on a global basis, parameters needed for mathematical modeling.

The era of weather observation by satellite was inaugurated on April 1, 1960, with the successful launching and operation of the 270-lb. TIROS I.

The prototype satellite in NOAA's Geostationary Operational Environmental Satellite (GOES) system, NASA's Synchronous Meteorological Satellite A (SMS A), is scheduled for launch during the first half of 1974. A second satellite will follow within several months to complete the two-GOES system capable of viewing the 48 contiguous States and the adjacent waters from Puerto Rico to Hawaii.

NOAA's Ark

The National Oceanic and Atmospheric Administration, a part of the Dept. of Commerce, was created in 1970 to explore and chart the global oceans and their potential use to the nation; to monitor characteristics of the environment and predict changes in the earth, air, sun and sea; to warn against environmental hazards; and to ease the impact of destructive natural events.

Among its many activities, the NOAA reports the weather; prepares and issues aeronautical and nautical charts; conducts geodetic, oceanographic and marine geophysical surveys; predicts tides and currents; provides satellite observation of the environment; and collects and disseminates worldwide environmental data. One of its current projects is the establishment of a system of buoys to monitor the condition of U.S. coastal waters and the world's oceans.

NOAA consists of 6 major offices: National Marine Fisheries Service, National Ocean Survey, National Weather Service, Environmental Data Service, National Environmental Satellite Service, and Environmental Research Laboratories. It also includes the Office of Sea Grant, which administers a variety of grants.

Wind Chill Table

Source: National Oceanic and Atmospheric Administration

Degrees (Fahrenheit)	35	30	25	20	15	10	5	0	−5	−10	−15	−20	−25	−30	−35	−40	−45
MPH	Wind Chill Index: (Equivalent temperature) Equivalent in cooling power on exposed flesh under calm conditions.																
0	35	30	25	20	15	10	5	0	−5	−10	−15	−20	−25	−30	−35	−40	−45
5	33	27	21	16	12	7	1	−6	−11	−15	−20	−26	−31	−35	−41	−47	−54
10	21	16	9	2	−2	−9	−15	−22	−27	−31	−38	−45	−52	−58	−64	−70	−77
15	16	11	1	−6	−11	−18	−25	−33	−40	−45	−51	−60	−65	−70	−78	−85	−90
20	12	3	−4	−9	−17	−24	−32	−40	−46	−52	−60	−68	−76	−81	−88	−96	−103
25	7	0	−7	−15	−22	−29	−37	−45	−52	−58	−67	−75	−83	−89	−96	−104	−112
30	5	−2	−11	−18	−26	−33	−41	−49	−56	−63	−70	−78	−87	−94	−101	−109	−117
35	3	−4	−13	−20	−27	−35	−43	−52	−60	−67	−72	−83	−90	−98	−105	−113	−123
40	1	−4	−15	−22	−29	−36	−45	−54	−62	−69	−76	−87	−94	−101	−107	−116	−128
45	1	−6	−17	−24	−31	−38	−46	−54	−63	−70	−78	−87	−94	−101	−108	−118	−128
50	0	−7	−17	−24	−31	−38	−47	−56	−63	−70	−79	−88	−96	−103	−110	−120	−128

(Wind speeds greater than 40 mph have little additional chilling effect)

How Cold is Cold? Temperature and wind both affect the heat loss from the surface of the body. The effect of these two factors is expressed as an "equivalent temperature," which approximates the still-air temperature which would have the same cooling effect as the wind and temperature combination. For example, from the table above, with a temperature of 20°F. and a wind of 20 mph., the effect on exposed flesh is the same as −9°F. with no wind.

Monthly Normal Temperature and Precipitation

Source: National Climatic Center, NOAA, Dept. of Commerce

These normals are based on records for the thirty-year period 1931 to 1960 inclusive. See explanation on page 266. For stations that did not have continuous records from the same instrument site for the entire 30 years, the means have been adjusted to the record at the present site.

AP indicates airport station; those not so marked are city office stations.

T, Temperature in Fahrenheit; P, precipitation in inches; L, less than .05 inch.

Stations	Jan.		Feb.		Mar.		Apr.		May		June		July		Aug.		Sept.		Oct.		Nov.		Dec.	
	T.	P.	T.	P.	T.	P.	T.	P.	T.	P.	T.	P.	T.	P.	T.	P.	T.	P.	T.	P.	T.	P.	T.	P.
Albany, N. Y. (AP)	23	2.5	24	2.2	33	2.7	46	2.8	58	3.5	67	3.3	72	3.5	70	3.1	62	3.6	51	2.8	39	2.7	27	2.8
Albuquerque, N. M. (AP)	35	.4	40	.4	46	.5	56	.5	65	.8	75	.6	79	1.2	76	1.3	70	1.0	58	.8	44	.4	37	.6
Anchorage, Alaska (AP)	12	.8	19	.7	25	.5	37	.4	47	.5	56	1.0	58	1.9	56	2.6	48	2.5	36	1.9	22	1.0	14	.9
Asheville, N. C. (AP)	38	4.2	39	4.0	45	4.8	55	4.0	63	3.7	70	3.5	72	5.9	72	4.9	66	3.6	56	3.1	45	2.8	38	3.6
Atlanta, Ga. (AP)	45	4.4	46	4.5	51	5.4	60	4.5	69	3.2	77	3.8	79	4.7	78	3.6	73	3.3	62	2.4	51	3.0	45	4.4
Baltimore, Md. (AP)	35	3.4	36	2.9	43	3.8	54	3.6	64	4.0	73	3.3	77	4.2	75	5.2	68	3.3	57	3.2	46	3.1	36	3.0
Barrow, Alaska (AP)	-16	.2	-18	.2	-15	.1	0	.1	18	.1	33	.4	39	.8	38	.9	31	.6	17	.5	-1	.2	-11	.2
Birmingham, Ala. (AP)	47	5.0	49	5.3	55	6.0	63	4.5	72	3.4	79	4.0	82	5.2	81	4.9	76	3.3	66	3.0	53	3.5	47	5.0
Bismarck, N. D. (AP)	10	.4	14	.4	26	.8	44	1.2	56	2.0	65	3.4	72	2.2	69	1.7	59	1.2	47	.9	29	.6	18	.4
Boise, Idaho (AP)	29	1.3	34	1.3	41	1.3	50	1.2	58	1.3	65	.9	75	.2	72	.2	63	.4	53	.8	39	1.2	32	1.3
Boston, Mass. (AP)	30	3.9	30	3.3	38	4.2	48	3.8	59	3.3	68	3.5	74	2.9	72	3.7	65	3.5	55	3.1	45	3.9	33	3.6
Buffalo, N. Y. (AP)	25	2.8	24	2.7	32	3.2	44	3.0	55	3.0	65	2.5	70	2.6	68	3.1	61	3.1	51	3.0	39	3.6	28	3.0
Burlington, Vt. (AP)	16	2.0	17	1.8	27	2.1	41	2.6	54	3.0	64	3.5	69	3.9	67	3.4	58	3.3	48	3.0	35	2.6	22	2.1
Caribou, Maine (AP)	11	2.1	13	2.2	23	2.4	36	2.6	50	3.0	59	4.1	65	4.0	63	3.7	54	3.5	43	3.4	30	3.0	16	2.4
Charleston, S. C. (AP)	50	2.5	52	3.3	57	3.9	65	2.9	73	3.6	79	5.0	81	7.7	80	6.6	76	5.8	66	2.8	56	2.1	50	2.9
Chicago, Ill. (AP)	26	1.9	28	1.6	36	2.7	49	3.0	60	3.7	71	4.1	76	3.4	74	3.2	66	2.7	55	2.8	40	2.2	29	1.9
Cincinnati, Ohio	36	3.7	37	2.9	44	3.9	56	3.5	66	3.8	75	4.2	79	3.5	77	3.0	71	2.6	60	2.2	46	2.9	37	2.7
Cleveland, Ohio (AP)	28	2.7	29	2.3	35	3.1	47	3.4	58	3.5	68	3.4	72	3.3	70	3.3	64	2.9	53	2.4	41	2.6	31	2.3
Columbus, Ohio (AP)	32	3.2	33	2.3	41	3.2	52	3.5	63	4.0	73	4.2	76	3.9	75	2.9	68	2.7	57	2.1	43	2.5	34	2.3
Dallas, Texas (AP)	46	2.3	50	2.6	56	2.9	65	4.0	73	4.8	81	3.2	85	1.9	85	1.9	78	2.8	68	2.7	55	2.7	48	2.7
Denver, Colo. (AP)	29	.6	32	.7	36	1.2	46	2.1	56	2.7	67	1.4	73	1.5	72	1.3	63	1.1	51	1.0	38	.7	32	.5
Des Moines, Iowa (AP)	20	1.3	[illegible]	1.1	[illegible]	[illegible]	[illegible]	[illegible]	[illegible]	[illegible]	[illegible]	[illegible]	[illegible]	[illegible]	[illegible]	[illegible]	[illegible]	[illegible]	[illegible]	[illegible]	37	1.8	25	1.1
Detroit, Mich. (AP)	26	1.9	27	2.0	34	2.4	47	3.1	58	3.5	68	3.3	72	2.7	71	2.8	63	2.3	52	2.6	39	2.3	29	1.9
Dodge City, Kansas (AP)	31	.6	35	.7	42	1.2	54	1.8	64	3.2	74	3.0	80	2.3	79	2.4	70	1.5	58	1.4	43	.6	35	.5
Duluth, Minn. (AP)	9	1.2	11	1.0	21	1.6	37	2.4	49	3.3	59	4.3	66	3.5	64	3.8	54	2.9	45	2.2	27	1.8	14	1.2
Eureka, Calif	47	6.7	48	5.5	49	5.3	50	2.7	53	2.2	56	.7	56	.1	57	.1	56	.6	54	3.2	51	4.6	49	6.7
Fairbanks, Alaska (AP)	11	.9	-3	.5	9	.4	29	.3	47	.7	58	1.4	60	1.8	54	2.2	44	1.1	26	.9	4	.6	-8	.5
Ft. Worth, Tex. (AP)	46	2.0	49	2.2	56	2.5	65	3.6	73	4.6	82	3.0	85	1.8	85	1.7	78	2.5	68	2.6	55	2.5	48	2.4
Fresno, Calif. (AP)	46	2.0	51	2.2	55	2.0	61	1.1	68	.3	75	.1	81	L	79	L	74	.1	65	.4	54	1.0	47	2.0
Galveston, Texas	55	3.5	57	2.9	61	2.9	69	2.6	76	2.8	82	2.7	83	4.8	83	4.4	80	5.1	74	2.9	63	3.6	57	3.9
Grand Junct.,Colo.(AP)	26	.6	33	.7	42	.8	52	.8	62	.6	71	.4	78	.6	76	1.1	68	.9	55	.7	39	.6	29	.6
Gr. Rapids, Mich.(AP)	24	1.9	24	1.8	33	2.3	46	2.9	57	3.5	68	3.3	72	2.7	70	2.7	62	3.0	51	2.6	37	2.5	27	2.0
Helena, Mont. (AP)	19	.5	23	.4	31	.7	43	.8	53	1.6	60	2.2	68	1.0	66	.9	56	1.0	46	.7	32	.6	24	.5
Honolulu, Hawaii (AP)	73	3.8	72	3.3	73	2.9	74	1.3	76	1.0	78	.3	79	.4	79	.9	79	1.0	78	1.8	76	2.2	74	3.0
Houston, Tex. (AP)	54	3.8	56	3.4	61	2.7	69	3.2	76	4.3	82	3.7	83	4.3	83	4.3	79	4.3	71	3.8	61	3.9	56	4.4
Huron, S. D. (AP)	13	.5	17	.6	29	1.1	45	1.8	58	2.4	68	3.1	75	1.8	73	2.1	62	1.5	49	1.2	31	.7	19	.6
Indianapolis, Ind. (AP)	29	3.1	31	2.3	39	3.4	51	3.7	61	4.0	71	4.6	75	3.5	74	3.0	67	3.2	55	2.6	41	3.1	31	2.7
Jacksonville, Fla. (AP)	56	2.5	58	2.9	62	3.5	69	3.6	76	3.5	81	6.3	83	7.7	82	6.9	79	7.6	71	5.2	62	1.7	56	2.2
Juneau, Alaska (AP)	25	4.0	27	3.1	30	3.3	38	2.9	46	3.2	52	3.4	55	4.5	54	5.0	49	6.7	42	8.3	34	6.1	28	4.2
Kansas City, Mo. (AP)	29	1.3	34	1.3	42	2.6	54	3.5	64	4.3	74	5.6	80	4.4	78	3.8	69	4.2	58	3.2	42	1.5	33	1.5
Knoxville, Tenn. (AP)	41	4.9	43	4.8	50	4.7	59	3.7	68	3.5	76	3.3	78	4.8	77	3.5	72	2.5	61	2.6	49	3.2	42	4.2
Lander, Wyo. (AP)	19	.5	24	.7	32	1.2	43	2.5	53	2.7	62	1.4	71	.8	69	.5	59	1.0	47	1.2	31	.9	23	.4
Little Rock, Ark. (AP)	41	5.2	44	4.3	52	4.8	62	4.9	71	5.3	79	3.6	82	3.3	81	2.8	74	3.2	63	2.9	50	4.1	42	4.1
Los Angeles, Calif	56	3.1	57	3.3	59	2.3	62	1.2	65	.2	68	.1	73	L	73	L	72	.2	67	.4	63	1.1	58	2.9
Louisville, Ky. (AP)	35	4.1	36	3.3	43	4.6	55	3.8	64	3.9	73	4.0	78	3.4	76	3.0	70	2.6	58	2.3	45	3.2	36	3.2
Marquette, Mich	20	1.9	20	1.7	27	1.9	39	2.7	50	3.0	60	3.5	67	3.2	66	3.0	58	3.3	48	2.3	34	3.3	24	1.9
Memphis, Tenn. (AP)	42	6.1	44	4.7	51	5.1	61	4.6	70	4.2	79	3.7	81	3.5	81	3.0	74	2.8	63	2.7	50	4.4	43	4.9
Miami, Fla. (AP)	67	2.0	68	1.9	71	2.3	74	3.9	78	6.4	81	7.4	82	6.8	82	7.0	81	9.5	78	8.2	72	2.8	68	1.7
Milwaukee, Wisc. (AP)	21	1.8	22	1.4	31	2.3	44	2.5	53	3.2	63	3.6	69	3.0	68	3.1	60	2.7	50	2.1	36	2.2	25	1.6
Minneapolis, Minn. (AP)	12	.7	16	.8	27	1.5	44	1.9	57	3.2	67	4.0	72	3.3	70	3.2	60	2.4	49	1.6	31	1.4	18	.9
Mobile, Ala. (AP)	51	4.6	54	4.6	59	7.2	68	6.4	75	4.9	80	6.2	82	9.7	82	6.4	78	6.3	69	3.0	58	3.4	53	5.5
Moline, Ill. (AP)	23	1.6	26	1.4	35	2.4	50	3.2	61	3.8	71	4.4	76	3.3	74	3.5	65	3.3	55	2.5	39	2.0	27	1.7
Nashville, Tenn. (AP)	40	5.5	42	4.5	49	5.2	60	3.7	69	3.7	77	3.3	80	3.7	79	2.9	73	2.9	62	2.3	49	3.3	41	4.2
Newark, N. J. (AP)	32	3.3	33	2.8	41	4.1	51	3.5	62	3.7	71	3.4	76	3.7	74	4.4	67	3.8	57	3.1	45	3.4	35	3.2
New Haven, Conn. (AP)	30	4.0	30	3.2	37	4.6	47	3.9	57	3.7	66	3.5	72	3.4	71	4.2	64	3.9	54	3.5	43	4.1	32	4.0
New Orleans, La. (AP)	55	3.8	57	4.0	61	5.3	68	4.6	74	4.4	80	4.4	82	6.7	82	5.3	78	5.0	70	2.8	60	3.3	55	4.1
New York City, N. Y	33	3.3	33	2.8	41	4.0	51	3.4	62	3.7	71	3.3	77	3.7	75	4.4	69	3.9	58	3.1	47	3.4	36	3.3
Nome, Alaska (AP)	4	1.0	6	.9	8	.9	21	.8	35	.7	46	.9	50	2.3	49	3.8	42	2.7	30	1.7	17	1.2	6	1.0
Norfolk, Va. (AP)	41	3.3	42	3.2	48	3.5	58	3.2	68	3.4	76	3.6	79	5.9	78	6.0	73	4.2	62	2.9	51	3.1	43	2.7
Okla. City, Okla. (AP)	37	1.3	41	1.4	49	2.0	[illegible]	3.1	[illegible]	5.2	[illegible]	4.5	[illegible]	[illegible]	83	[illegible]	71	3.0	[illegible]	[illegible]	48	1.0	40	1.4
Omaha, Nebr. (AP)	21	.8	25	1.0	35	1.5	50	2.6	61	3.5	71	4.5	77	3.4	74	4.0	66	2.6	54	1.7	37	1.3	27	.8
Parkersburg, W. Va	35	3.3	36	2.8	43	3.5	54	3.3	64	3.7	73	4.3	76	4.1	74	3.8	68	2.7	57	2.1	45	2.4	36	2.8
Philadelphia, Pa. (AP)	32	3.3	33	2.8	41	3.8	52	3.4	63	3.7	71	4.1	76	4.2	74	4.6	67	3.5	56	2.8	44	3.4	34	2.9
Phoenix, Ariz. (AP)	50	.7	54	.9	59	.7	67	.3	75	.1	84	.1	90	.8	88	1.1	83	.7	71	.5	58	.5	52	.9
Pittsburgh, Pa. (AP)	29	3.0	29	2.2	37	3.3	49	3.1	60	3.9	68	3.8	72	3.9	71	3.3	64	2.5	53	2.5	41	2.2	31	2.4
Portland, Me. (AP)	22	4.4	23	3.8	31	4.3	43	3.7	53	3.4	62	3.2	68	2.9	67	2.4	59	3.5	49	3.2	38	4.2	26	3.9
Portland, Ore. (AP)	38	5.4	42	4.2	46	3.9	52	2.1	57	2.0	62	1.7	67	.4	67	.7	64	1.6	52	3.6	45	5.3	41	6.4
Providence, R. I. (AP)	29	3.8	30	3.1	37	4.1	47	3.8	58	3.4	66	2.8	72	2.9	71	4.0	63	3.5	53	3.1	43	4.1	32	3.6
Raleigh, N. C. (AP)	42	3.2	43	3.2	50	3.4	59	3.5	68	3.5	75	3.7	78	5.5	77	5.2	71	3.9	61	2.7	50	2.8	42	3.0
Rapid City, S. D. (AP)	22	.4	24	.5	31	1.0	45	1.7	56	2.7	65	3.1	74	1.8	72	1.2	62	1.0	50	.8	35	.4	27	.3
Reno, Nevada (AP)	30	1.2	36	1.0	42	.7	48	.5	54	.5	60	.4	68	.3	66	.2	59	.2	49	.5	38	.6	32	1.1
Richmond, Va (AP)	39	3.5	40	2.9	48	3.4	58	3.2	67	3.7	75	3.8	78	5.6	76	5.5	70	3.7	59	3.0	49	3.0	40	3.0
St. Louis, Mo. (AP)	32	2.0	35	2.0	43	3.1	55	3.7	64	3.7	74	4.3	78	3.3	77	3.0	70	2.8	58	2.9	44	2.6	35	2.0
Salt Lake City, Utah (AP)	27	1.4	33	1.2	40	1.6	50	1.8	59	1.4	67	1.0	77	.6	75	.9	64	.5	52	1.2	37	1.3	30	1.2
San Antonio, Tex. (AP)	52	1.7	55	1.7	61	1.7	68	2.8	75	3.5	82	3.0	84	2.1	84	2.4	79	3.5	71	2.5	60	1.4	54	1.8
San Diego, Calif. (AP)	55	2.0	56	2.2	59	1.6	62	.8	64	.2	66	L	70	L	72	.8	70	.2	66	.5	62	.9	57	2.1
San Francisco, Calif. (AP)	49	4.0	51	3.5	53	2.7	56	1.3	58	.5	61	.1	63	L	63	L	64	.2	61	.7	55	1.6	50	4.1
San Juan, P. R. (AP)	74	4.7	74	2.9	75	2.2	77	3.7	79	7.1	80	5.7	80	6.3	81	7.1	81	6.8	80	5.8	78	6.5	76	5.5
Sault Ste. Marie, Mich	16	2.1	16	1.5	24	1.8	38	2.2	50	2.8	59	3.3	65	2.5	64	2.9	56	3.8	46	2.8	33	3.3	21	2.3
Savannah, Ga. (AP)	52	2.8	53	3.7	58	4.0	66	3.7	73	3.8	80	5.1	81	6.6	81	6.6	77	5.3	67	2.6	57	2.1	51	2.8
Sea.-Tac., Wash. (AP)	38	5.7	41	4.2	44	3.8	49	2.4	56	1.7	60	1.6	65	.8	64	1.0	60	2.1	52	4.0	44	5.4	41	6.3
Spokane, Wash. (AP)	25	2.4	30	1.9	38	1.5	47	.9	56	1.2	62	1.5	71	.4	68	.4	61	.8	49	1.6	36	2.2	30	2.4
Springfield, Mo. (AP)	34	2.0	37	2.1	44	2.8	56	4.1	65	5.3	74	5.0	79	3.9	78	3.3	70	3.9	60	3.8	45	2.8	37	2.2
Syracuse, N. Y. (AP)	24	3.2	24	3.1	33	3.6	46	3.1	58	3.3	67	3.0	72	3.1	70	3.3	62	2.8	52	3.2	40	2.9	28	3.2
Tampa, Fla. (AP)	61	2.1	63	2.8	66	3.8	71	2.8	77	2.9	81	7.3	82	8.6	82	8.2	81	7.0	75	2.8	67	1.5	62	1.9
Trenton, N. J	33	3.1	33	2.6	41	3.8	52	3.2	62	3.6	71	3.6	76	4.2	74	4.8	67	3.5	57	2.8	46	3.2	35	2.9
Vicksburg, Miss	49	5.1	52	5.3	58	5.7	66	4.9	73	4.1	80	3.5	82	3.9	82	3.0	77	2.5	68	2.0	56	4.4	50	4.9
Washington, D. C. (AP)	37	3.0	38	2.5	45	3.2	56	3.2	66	4.1	74	3.2	78	4.2	77	4.9	70	3.8	59	3.1	48	2.8	38	2.8
Wilmington, Del. (AP)	33	3.4	34	3.0	41	4.0	52	3.3	63	3.5	71	4.1	76	4.3	74	5.6	68	4.0	57	2.9	45	3.5	35	3.0

Annual Climatological Data

Source: National Oceanic & Atmospheric Administration, National Climatic Center

1972

Station	Elev. ft	Temperature °F Highest	Date	Lowest	Date	Precipitation Total (in.)	Greatest in 24 hrs.	Date	Snow or Sleet Total (in.)	Greatest in 24 hrs.	Date	Wind Fastest MPH	Date	Clear*	Cloudy*	Prec. .01 in. or more	Snow, sleet 1 in. or more
Albany, N.Y.	275	91	7/19+	-16	2/23	47.18	2.66	10/6-7	102.3	17.1	11/14-15	42	2/20	53	221	158	23
Albuquerque, N.M.	5311	103	7/31	3	1/5	10.11	0.95	8/18	6.4	2.0	11/12	61	3/18	156	95	64	4
Anchorage, Alaska	114	80	7/6	-28	1/11	14.63	1.03	10/10-11	65.1	8.5	1/31-2/1	37	2/24+	86	224	99	18
Asheville, N.C.	2140	91	7/23+	0	1/16	48.02	3.54	6/19-20	15.4	5.0	3/25	60	2/19	92	159	133	6
Atlanta, Ga.	1010	94	7/23	5	1/16	50.61	3.22	12/14-15	T	T	3/25+	47	8/20	88	160	126	0
Baltimore, Md.	148	95	7/23+	5	1/16	52.33	5.23	6/21-22	13.0	4.0	2/23	38	12/16+	86	180	133	4
Barrow, Alaska	31	68	7/8	-42	2/15	4.92	0.50	8/9-10	41.0	5.3	10/11-12	40	11/1	65	168	80	13
Birmingham, Ala.	620	97	8/20	7	1/16	52.55	3.16	1/9-10	T	T	3/3+	36	4/16	89	159	124	0
Bismarck, N.D.	1647	100	8/15	-35	1/15	15.16	1.95	5/25-26	45.6	5.8	3/26-27	59	2/17	62	195	86	17
Boise, Idaho	2838	102	8/11	-23	12/10	11.31	0.76	3/1-2	23.3	4.2	12/6	44	5/20	121	157	90	10
Boston, Mass.	15	94	7/12	0	2/23	53.11	3.15	9/3	40.7	6.0	3/5	49	1/25	75	191	154	14
Buffalo, N.Y.	705	88	7/18+	-3	1/15	41.63	2.34	6/21-22	120.1	7.7	12/15-16	51	1/17	36	255	197	39
Burlington, Vt.	332	92	7/15+	-22	2/23	38.10	2.83	6/15-16	121.6	9.0	12/15-16	49	1/25	52	220	170	36
Charleston, S.C.	40	97	8/19+	17	1/17	42.86	3.83	11/29-30	0.0	0.0	...	56	2/3	99	140	100	0
Charleston, W. Va.	939	94	7/24+	-5	1/16	51.15	2.00	7/31	26.5	3.8	11/30-12/1+	43	5/2	36	238	183	9
Chicago, Ill.	607	96	7/22	-15	1/15	41.19	3.68	9/28-29	61.9	6.5	3/29	40	1/24	86	205	149	21
Cincinnati, Ohio	869	96	7/23	-13	1/16	45.30	2.24	10/31-1	21.4	5.5	2/6	32	8/19+	58	208	141	6
Cleveland, Ohio	777	91	7/23+	-14	1/16	48.34	4.00	6/22-23	66.9	6.4	12/15-16	47	7/18	65	236	184	25
Columbus, Ohio	812	92	7/23	-12	1/16	45.60	3.79	8/17-18	27.1	4.7	2/6	41	7/9	54	215	156	9
Concord, N.H.	342	92	7/15	-19	1/6	42.07	1.95	5/31-1	100.3	14.2	2/19-20	44	1/19	69	199	151	28
Dallas, Texas	481	104	7/25	15	1/15	24.36	2.71	4/27	0.9	0.5	1/4	47	6/21	132	133	70	0
Denver, Colo.	5283	100	7/30	-18	12/10	16.87	3.04	4/26	83.2	15.7	4/26	42	8/16+	91	156	99	21
Des Moines, Iowa	938	98	7/10	-18	2/9+	36.02	2.96	9/10-11	36.7	8.2	11/13-14	42	5/1	83	190	131	8
Detroit, Mich.	619	95	7/23+	-8	1/16	29.96	1.88	8/16-17	30.6	NA	NA	40	3/7	NA	NA	138	18
Dodge City, Kansas	2582	102	7/14	-8	1/15	31.00	3.52	7/15-16	13.4	4.4	11/17-18	51	3/1	106	162	93	5
Duluth, Minn.	1428	88	8/17+	-39	1/15	39.61	3.77	9/20	110.2	13.4	1/12	57	1/24	66	201	146	28
Fairbanks, Alaska	436	88	6/14	-49	1/17+	8.51	0.52	9/25-26	80.9	9.8	12/12-13	33	12/13	85	205	118	26
Fresno, Calif.	328	111	7/15	23	12/9	7.47	0.99	11/10-11	T	T	12/7+	32	6/9	181	104	36	0
Galveston, Texas	7	93	8/27+	29	1/5	39.95	2.95	5/12	0.0	0.0	...	38	9/29	NA	NA	103	0
Grand Rapids, Mich.	784	93	7/11	-16	1/16	37.38	3.28	6/14-15	92.9	6.0	12/12+	60	1/24	52	233	163	30
Helena, Montana	3828	93	8/9+	-35	12/8	8.22	0.62	8/22	40.0	5.9	12/2-3	50	1/11	64	197	97	15
Honolulu, Hawaii	7	90	8/15+	53	1/31	26.94	4.78	1/23-24	0.0	0.0	...	33	4/10	80	122	93	0
Houston, Texas	96	98	6/29	22	12/17+	50.80	7.47	3/20	T	T	1/4	37	11/13	83	167	106	0
Huron, S.D.	1281	96	8/17+	-29	1/15	26.46	2.00	11/1-2+	46.7	8.4	12/30-31	50	2/17	80	186	112	12
Indianapolis, Ind.	792	93	7/23+	-20	1/16	40.27	2.20	6/13	18.1	3.6	1/13	48	4/7	59	207	143	5
Jackson, Miss.	310	99	8/21	15	1/16	50.03	2.54	12/20-21	T	T	Feb.	41	3/27	100	140	118	0
Jacksonville, Fla.	26	97	7/28+	28	2/5	57.29	5.14	6/18-19	0.0	0.0	...	44	8/6	82	136	122	0
Juneau, Alaska	12	84	7/4	-22	1/12	53.67	2.27	10/5-6	150.2	10.2	12/13-14	41	10/2	57	266	202	39
Kansas City, Missouri	742	100	7/14	-9	1/15	27.75	2.00	6/14	15.9	2.5	3/31	49	12/30	101	172	105	6
Lander, Wyo.	5563	95	8/12	-26	12/11+	13.18	0.84	4/13-14	123.9	12.8	12/28-29	80	3/6	86	134	82	29
Little Rock, Ark.	257	103	8/21+	13	1/16+	45.01	3.90	11/6-7	1.1	0.4	12/10	40	6/25+	121	154	109	0
Los Angeles, Calif.	97	95	10/6	37	12/11+	7.12	1.77	10/18-19	0.0	0.0	...	45	12/4+	151	104	19	0
Louisville, Ky.	477	94	8/19+	-7	1/16	49.38	2.38	5/7-8	10.4	1.4	2/3	45	1/24	66	189	145	6
Marquette, Mich.	677	90	8/30	-19	1/15	33.70	1.86	11/2	140.9	10.7	1/24-25	38	9/6+	70	214	152	45
Memphis, Tenn.	258	96	9/19	6	1/16	58.95	3.64	11/6-7	0.4	0.3	1/4	40	5/16	110	155	123	0
Miami, Fla.	7	91	6/8	42	2/20	63.11	5.66	6/11-12	0.0	0.0	...	30	2/19	84	114	147	0
Milford, Utah	5028	101	7/29+	-32	12/10	10.65	1.05	8/27	54.7	9.6	12/28-29	...	...	146	128	53	15
Milwaukee, Wisc.	672	92	7/21	-22	1/15	36.68	2.31	9/17-18	50.2	6.7	3/13	46	9/18	77	203	141	17
Minneapolis, Minn.	834	97	8/20+	-29	1/15	23.77	1.57	7/22	54.6	6.0	1/24	39	1/12	74	205	122	16
Mobile, Alabama	211	99	8/7	21	1/16	49.76	4.47	5/7-8	0.0	0.0	...	40	6/25	84	158	117	0
Moline, Ill.	582	98	6/3	-19	2/9	46.65	4.33	8/5-6	63.2	11.0	3/28-29	49	7/14	82	191	128	19
Nashville, Tenn.	590	94	7/23+	-1	1/16	54.41	2.37	10/18-19	2.5	0.9	3/25	46	4/7	103	168	143	0
New Orleans, La.	4	96	8/5	24	1/16	63.98	4.70	5/12	0.0	0.0	...	30	3/16	101	132	116	0
New York, N.Y.	132	94	8/24+	5	1/16	67.03	5.60	11/8	22.9	5.7	2/19	50	11/8	...	...	145	8
Nome, Alaska	13	81	7/11	-32	3/22+	14.97	1.19	9/8-9	52.4	7.6	11/26-27	46	12/17	110	201	118	14
Norfolk, Va.	24	95	7/24	8	1/16	46.23	3.02	9/20-21	1.8	1.8	2/19	48	2/3	92	164	138	1
Okla. City, Okla.	1285	102	6/27+	1	1/15	27.63	3.70	10/21	14.6	5.5	11/18	46	3/20	130	140	72	4
Omaha, Nebraska	977	99	8/20	-15	1/15	35.56	3.16	9/10-11	27.1	7.9	11/13	47	1/24	89	181	121	7
Philadelphia, Pa.	5	96	8/26	6	1/16	49.63	3.22	6/21-22	12.1	3.7	2/19-20	43	8/26	82	192	138	5
Phoenix, Ariz.	1117	116	8/1	26	1/5	10.87	2.27	10/18-19	0.0	0.0	...	59	6/7	219	77	27	0
Pittsburgh, Pa.	1137	91	7/22	-10	1/16	40.07	2.18	9/13-14	51.5	7.5	2/13-14	46	4/16	52	237	174	15
Portland, Me.	43	87	7/16	-18	2/23	48.62	2.90	9/3	123.7	15.3	2/19-20	42	2.4+	77	188	148	25
Portland, Oregon	21	104	8/7	8	12/8	38.82	1.80	12/20-21	6.5	4.6	12/11-12	48	4/5	87	210	150	2
Providence, R.I.	51	91	7/12	0	2/23+	65.06	3.12	9/2-3	30.4	4.7	3/14-15	46	2/4	82	187	143	13
Raleigh, N.C.	434	94	7/23	4	1/16	51.74	2.77	9/29-30	4.0	2.6	3/25	54	5/3	92	165	128	1
Rapid City, S.D.	3162	98	8/13+	-23	12/8+	17.19	2.32	6/9-10	23.1	3.2	1/31-1	56	7/8	76	164	110	9
Reno, Nevada	4404	103	8/8+	-16	12/9	5.52	1.01	5/18-19	16.4	4.8	12/3-4	48	4/12	157	121	54	3
Richmond, Va.	164	95	7/23	3	1/16	59.34	3.91	6/18	14.3	5.3	2/1-2	40	4/15	84	178	135	3
Rochester, N.Y.	547	94	7/20	-3	2/23	38.28	2.19	6/21-22	119.9	9.9	2/19-20	50	1/25	41	227	179	38
St. Louis, Mo.	535	100	7/1	-7	1/15	33.74	2.87	11/1	12.5	5.2	11/19	40	2/18	79	188	119	4
Salt Lake City, Utah	4220	104	7/29	-15	12/15	15.74	1.82	12/28-29	76.8	18.1	12/28-29	55	9/5	109	155	89	20
San Antonio, Texas	788	98	7/30	17	1/5	31.49	6.53	5/6-7	T	T	12/11	35	11/12+	96	148	90	0
San Diego, Calif.	13	92	7/28	37	1/5	6.48	1.70	11/16-17	0.0	0.0	...	29	11/14	126	123	36	0
San Francisco, Calif.	8	98	7/14	24	12/9	16.97	2.11	10/10-11	T	T	12/12+	32	4/28	151	105	61	0
San Juan, P.R.	13	96	6/21	68	2/15	37.72	2.22	12/9-10	0.0	0.0	...	44	10/21	61	87	185	0
Sault Ste. Marie, Mich.	721	88	5/20	-23	1/16	35.45	1.24	7/31	190.5	14.2	1/24-25	39	1/19	62	224	171	57
Savannah, Ga.	46	98	8/8	19	1/17	48.57	4.41	8/28-29	0.0	0.0	...	41	6/10	81	154	110	0
Seattle, Wash.	400	95	8/7	12	1/27	48.36	2.86	3/4-5	22.2	9.7	1/24	38	4/5+	65	215	160	6
Sioux City, Iowa	1095	100	6/8	-18	2/15	33.72	5.50	7/17	28.1	5.8	12/11-12	52	6/27	91	182	125	6
Spokane, Wash.	2356	103	8/8	-12	2/2	13.53	0.99	5/8-9	31.3	8.2	1/24-25	59	1/9	97	179	106	12
Springfield, Mo.	1268	100	8/21+	-3	1/15	38.76	3.41	11/1	16.3	8.8	11/18-19	38	9/7	108	172	111	4
Syracuse, N.Y.	410	92	7/18+	-6	2/23	55.41	3.88	6/21-22	144.6	17.4	2/19-20	52	1/25	52	230	181	44
Tampa, Fla.	19	96	9/19+	34	12/17+	42.18	3.44	8/19	0.0	0.0	...	35	2/19	97	133	102	0
Trenton, N.J.	56	96	7/19	5	1/16	47.13	2.90	11/8-9	17.2	3.2	2/19	41	2/19	87	173	152	6
Washington, D.C.	10	95	7/21	3	1/16	51.97	7.19	6/21-22	15.3	5.5	2/19	43	6/21	90	187	134	4
Williston, N.D.	1899	100	8/12	-32	1/26	17.95	2.45	8/14	52.0	6.4	12/1-2	52	4/12	75	187	113	17
Wilmington, Delaware	74	95	7/23+	5	1/16	48.13	4.35	6/21-22	9.5	2.7	2/23+	42	12/16	81	185	123	5

* To get partly cloudy days deduct the total of clear and cloudy days from 365 (1 yr.). T-trace. (1) Date shown is the starting date of the storm (in some cases it lasted more than one day).

Normal Temperatures, Highs, Lows; Precipitation

Source: National Climatic Center, NOAA, Dept. of Commerce

These normals are based on records for the thirty-year period 1931-1960. (See explanation on page 266.) The extreme temperatures (thru 1971) are listed for the stations shown and may not agree with the state's records shown on page 264.

AP indicates airport station; those not so marked are city office stations. The minus (—) sign indicates temperatures below zero. Fahrenheit thermometer registration.

State	Station	January Max.	January Min.	July Max.	July Min.	Extreme temperature Highest	Extreme temperature Lowest	Normal annual precipitation (inches)
Alabama	Mobile (AP)	61	41	91	73	102	8	68.13
Alabama	Montgomery (AP)	59	38	92	72	102	5	50.69
Alaska	Juneau (A.P.)	30	20	63	48	86	—22	54.62
Arizona	Phoenix (AP)	64	35	105	75	116	19	7.20
Arkansas	Little Rock (AP)	51	31	93	71	108	—4	48.66
California	Los Angeles	65	47	83	63	110	30	14.68
California	San Francisco (AP)	55	42	72	54	106	29	18.69
Colorado	Denver (AP)	42	15	88	57	101	—25	14.81
Connecticut	°New Haven (AP)	37	22	81	63	100	—8	46.02
Delaware	Wilmington (AP)	41	26	86	66	102	—4	44.56
Dist. of Col	Washington (AP)	44	30	87	69	101	3	40.78
Florida	Jacksonville (AP)	67	45	92	73	105	12	53.36
Florida	Key West (AP)	74	65	87	79	95	46	39.99
Florida	Miami (AP)	76	58	89	75	96	34	59.76
Georgia	Atlanta (AP)	52	37	87	71	98	—3	47.14
Hawaii	Honolulu (AP)	79	66	85	73	91	54	21.89
Idaho	Boise (AP)	36	22	91	59	111	—17	11.43
Illinois	Chicago (AP)	33	19	84	67	101	—16	33.18
Indiana	Indianapolis (AP)	37	21	86	64	99	—18	39.25
Iowa	Des Moines (AP)	29	11	87	65	100	—24	30.37
Iowa	Dubuque (AP)	27	11	81	61	97	—29	35.71
Kansas	Wichita (AP)	42	22	92	69	113	—12	28.41
Kentucky	Louisville (AP)	44	27	89	67	101	—20	41.32
Louisiana	New Orleans (AP)	64	45	91	73	100	14	53.90
Maine	Portland (AP)	32	12	80	57	100	—39	42.85
Maryland	Baltimore (AP)	44	25	87	66	102	—7	43.05
Massachusetts	Boston (AP)	37	23	82	65	98	—4	42.77
Michigan	Detroit, City (AP)	33	21	84	65	105	—16	30.95
Michigan	Sault Ste. Marie	23	8	76	54	98	—28	31.22
Minnesota	Minn.-St. Paul (AP)	22	2	84	61	99	—34	24.78
Mississippi	**Vicksburg	57	11	90	73	101	2	49.50
Missouri	St. Louis (AP)	40	24	89	67	106	—11	35.31
Montana	Helena (AP)	29	8	84	52	105	—38	10.85
Nebraska	Omaha (AP)	32	13	90	67	107	—17	27.56
Nevada	Winnemucca (AP)	40	15	92	50	106	—24	8.63
New Hampshire	Concord (AP)	32	11	83	56	102	—29	38.80
New Jersey	Atlantic City (AP)	43	27	84	66	106	—8	42.36
New Mexico	Albuquerque (AP)	46	24	91	66	104	—17	8.13
New Mexico	Roswell (AP)	55	21	95	62	110	—8	11.62
New York	Albany (AP)	31	14	84	61	98	—28	35.08
New York	New York	40	27	85	68	106	—15	42.37
No. Carolina	Charlotte (AP)	51	34	89	70	100	2	43.38
No. Carolina	Raleigh (AP)	52	31	88	68	98	0	43.58
No. Dakota	Bismarck (AP)	20	0	86	58	108	—43	15.15
Ohio	Cincinnati	41	26	88	66	109	—17	39.51
Ohio	Cleveland (AP)	35	21	82	61	98	—19	35.35
Oklahoma	Oklahoma City (AP)	46	28	93	72	108	1	30.82
Oregon	Portland	44	33	79	56	107	—3	42.37
Pennsylvania	Harrisburg (AP)	39	24	87	65	107	—8	37.65
Pennsylvania	Philadelphia (AP)	40	24	86	65	104	—5	42.48
Rhode Island	Block Island (AP)	38	26	76	63	91	—4	40.45
So. Carolina	Charleston (AP)	61	38	89	72	103	8	49.16
So. Dakota	Huron (AP)	23	2	90	60	112	—39	17.33
So. Dakota	Rapid City (AP)	34	10	88	60	109	—27	14.71
Tennessee	Nashville (AP)	49	31	91	70	103	—6	45.14
Texas	Amarillo (AP)	50	24	94	67	104	—9	19.67
Texas	Galveston	61	49	87	80	101	8	41.81
Texas	Houston (AP)	64	44	92	74	106	17	45.95
Utah	Salt Lake City (AP)	37	18	91	60	107	—18	13.90
Vermont	Burlington (AP)	25	7	82	56	98	—27	33.21
Virginia	Norfolk (AP)	50	32	88	70	103	8	44.94
Washington	Seattle-Tacoma (AP)	44	33	76	54	99	6	38.94
Washington	Spokane (AP)	31	19	86	55	108	—25	17.19
West Virginia	Parkersburg	43	26	86	65	106	—27	38.77
Wisconsin	Madison (AP)	26	9	82	60	98	—30	30.16
Wisconsin	Milwaukee (AP)	28	13	79	58	98	—24	29.51
Wyoming	Cheyenne (AP)	37	14	85	55	96	—27	15.06
Puerto Rico	San Juan (AP)	81	67	87	74	95	60	64.21

° Closed June 14, 1969. °° Closed December 1966.

Mean Annual Snowfall (inches) based on record thru 1972; Boston, Mass. 42.8; Sault Ste. Marie, Mich., 108.2, Albany, N.Y., 67.3; Rochester, N.Y., 86.3, Burlington, Vt., 79, Cheyenne, Wyo., 51.7; Juneau, Alaska, 106.3.

Wettest Spot: Mount Waialeale, Hawaii, on the island of Kauai, is the rainiest place in the world, according to the National Geographic Society, with an average annual rainfall of 460 inches.

Highest Temperature: A temperature of 136° F. observed at Azizia, Tripolitania in Northern Africa on Sept. 13, 1922 is generally accepted as the world's highest temperature recorded under standard conditions.

The record high in the United States was 134° in Death Valley, Calif., July 10, 1913.

Lowest Temperature: A record low temperature of —126.9°F (—88.3°C.) was recorded at the Soviet Antarctic station Vostok on Aug. 24, 1960.

The record low in the United States was —80° at Prospect Creek, Alaska, Jan. 23, 1971.

The lowest official temperature on the North American continent was recorded at 81 degrees below zero in February, 1947, at a lonely airport in the Yukon called Snag.

These are the meteorological champions—the official temperature extremes—but there are plenty of other claimants to thermometer fame. However, sun readings are unofficial records, since meteorological data to qualify officially must be taken on instruments in sheltered and ventilated location.

Low and High Temp. Records of National Weather Service Thru 1971

State	Lowest °F	Highest	Latest Date	Location	Approximate Elevation
Alabama	−27		Jan. 30, 1966	New Market	725
		112	Sept. 5, 1925	Centerville	345
Alaska	−79.8		Jan. 23, 1971	Prospect Creek Camp	1,100
		100	June 27, 1915	Fort Yukon	*419
Arizona	−40		Jan. 7, 1971	Hawley Lake	8,180
		127	July 7, 1905	Parker	345
Arkansas	−29		Feb. 13, 1905	Pond	1,250
		120	Aug. 10, 1936	Ozark	396
California	−45		Jan. 20, 1937	Boca	5,532
		134	July 10, 1913	Greenland Ranch	−178
Colorado	−60		Feb. 1, 1951	Taylor Park	9,206
		118	July 11, 1888	Bennett	5,484
Connecticut	−32		Jan. 22, 1961	Coventry	480
		105	July 22, 1926	Waterbury	409
Delaware	−17		Jan. 17, 1893	Millsboro	535
		110	July 21, 1930	Millsboro	20
Dist. of Col	−15		Feb. 11, 1899	Washington	112
		106	July 20, 1930	Washington	112
Florida	−2		Feb. 13, 1899	Tallahassee	193
		109	June 29, 1931	Monticello	207
Georgia	−17		Jan. 27, 1940	CCC Camp F-16	1,000
		112	July 24, 1952	Louisville	337
Hawaii	18		Feb. 20, 1962	Mauna Loa Slope Obs	11,146
		100	Apr. 27, 1931	Pahala	850
Idaho	−60		Jan. 18, 1943	Island Park Dam	6,285
		118	July 28, 1934	Orofino	1,027
Illinois	−35		Jan. 22, 1930	Mount Carroll	817
		117	July 14, 1954	E. St. Louis	410
Indiana	−35		Feb. 2, 1951	Greensburg	954
		116	July 14, 1936	Collegeville	672
Iowa	−47		Jan. 12, 1912	Washta	1,157
		118	July 20, 1934	Keokuk	614
Kansas	−40		Feb. 13, 1905	Lebanon	1,812
		121	July 24, 1936	Alton (near)	1,651
Kentucky	−34		Jan. 24, 1963	Bonnieville (Closed Oct. 1966)	730
	−34		Jan. 28, 1963	Cynthiana	719
		114	July 28, 1930	Greensburg	581
Louisiana	−16		Feb. 13, 1899	Minden	194
		114	Aug. 10, 1936	Plain Dealing	268
Maine	−48		Jan. 19, 1925	Van Buren	510
		105	July 10, 1911	North Bridgton	450
Maryland	−40		Jan. 13, 1912	Oakland	2,461
		109	July 10, 1936	Cumberland and Frederick	623-325
Massachusetts	−34		Jan. 18, 1957	Birch Hill Dam	840
		106	July 4, 1911	Lawrence	51
Michigan	−51		Feb. 9, 1934	Vanderbilt	785
		112	July 13, 1936	Mio	963
Minnesota	−59		Feb. 16, 1903	Pokegama Dam	1,280
		114	July 6, 1936	Moorhead	940
Mississippi	−19		Jan. 30, 1966	Corinth	420
		115	July 29, 1930	Holly Springs	600
Missouri	−40		Feb. 13, 1905	Warsaw	700
		118	July 14, 1954	Warsaw	687
Montana	−70		Jan. 20, 1954	Rogers Pass	5,470
		117	July 5, 1937	Medicine Lake	1,950
Nebraska	−47		Feb. 12, 1899	Camp Clarke	3,700
		118	July 24, 1936	Minden	2,169
Nevada	−50		Jan. 8, 1937	San Jacinto	5,200
		122	June 23, 1954	Overton	1,240
New Hampshire	−46		Jan. 8, 1968	Mt. Washington	6,262
		106	July 4, 1911	Nashua	125
New Jersey	−34		Jan. 5, 1904	River Vale	70
		110	July 10, 1936	Runyon	18
New Mexico	−50		Feb. 1, 1951	Gavilan	7,350
		116	July 14, 1934	Orogrande	4,171
New York	−52		Feb. 9, 1934	Stillwater Reservoir	1,670
		108	July 22, 1926	Troy	35
North Carolina	−29		Jan. 30, 1966	Mt. Mitchell	6,525
		109	Sept. 7, 1954	Weldon	81
North Dakota	−60		Feb. 15, 1936	Parshall	1,929
		121	July 6, 1936	Steele	1,857
Ohio	−39		Feb. 10, 1899	Milligan	800
		113	July 21, 1934	Gallipolis (near)	673
Oklahoma	−27		Jan. 18, 1930	Watts	958
		120	July 26, 1943	Tishmoningo	670
Oregon	−54		Feb. 10, 1933	Seneca	4,700
		119	Aug. 10, 1898	Pendleton	1,074
Pennsylvania	−42		Jan. 5, 1904	Smethport	1,469
		111	July 10, 1936	Phoenixville	100
Rhode Island	−23		Jan. 11, 1942	Kingston	100
		102	July 30, 1949	Greenville	420
South Carolina	−13		Jan. 26, 1940	Longcreek (near)	1,631
		111	June 28, 1954	Camden	170
South Dakota	−58		Feb. 17, 1936	McIntosh	2,277
		120	July 5, 1936	Gannvalley	1,750
Tennessee	−32		Dec. 30, 1917	Mountain City	2,471
		113	Aug. 9, 1930	Perryville	377

State	Lowest °F	Highest	Latest Dates		Approximate Elevation	
Texas	−23		Feb.	8, 1933	Seminole.	3,275
		120	Aug.	12, 1936	Seymour	1,291
Utah	−50		Jan.	5, 1913	Strawberry Tunnel	7,650
		116	June	28, 1892	Saint George.	2,880
Vermont	−50		Dec.	30, 1933	Bloomfield	915
		105	July	4, 1911	Vernon	310
Virginia.	−29		Feb.	10, 1899	Monterey	3,008
		110	July	15, 1954	Balcony Falls	725
Washington	−48		Dec.	30, 1968	Mazama	2,120
	−48		Dec.	30, 1968	Winthrop.	1,755
		118	Aug.	5, 1961	Ice Harbor Dam.	475
West Virginia	−37		Dec.	30, 1917	Lewisburg.	2,200
		112	July	10, 1936	Martinsburg	435
Wisconsin	−54		Jan.	24, 1922	Danbury	908
		114	July	13, 1936	Wisconsin Dells.	900
Wyoming.	−63		Feb.	9, 1933	Moran.	6,770
		114	July	12, 1900	Basin	3,500

Low and High Temp. Records Thru 1967

Source: Atmospheric Environment Service, Dept. of Environment

Province	Lowest °F	Highest	Latest Dates		Station	Approximate Elevation
Alberta	−78		Jan.	11, 1911	Fort Vermilion	915
		108	July	12, 1886	Medicine Hat	2365
British Columbia	−74		Jan.	31, 1947	Smith River.	2208
		112	July	17, 1941	Chinook Cove	1324
		112	July	17, 1941	Lillooet	950
		112	July	17, 1941	Lytton	600
Manitoba	−63		Jan.	9, 1899	Norway House	720
		112	July	12, 1936	Emerson	792
		112	July	11, 1936	St. Albans	1180
Newfoundland	−56		Mar.	7, 1968	Twin Falls	1499
		107	Aug.	11, 1914	Northwest River	200
New Brunswick	−53		Feb.	1, 1955	Sisson Dam.	915
		103	Aug.	18, 1935	Nespisquit Falls	350
		103	Aug.	18, 1935	Woodstock	150
		103	Aug.	19, 1935	Rexton	20
Nova Scotia	−42		Jan.	31, 1920	Upper Stewiacke.	75
		101	Aug.	19, 1935	Collegeville	250
Ontario.	−73		Jan.	23, 1935	Iroquois Falls	830
		108	July	20, 1919	Biscotasing.	1300
		108	July	11, 1936	Atikokan	1289
		108	July	13, 1936	Fort Frances	1160
Prince Edward Island	−35		Jan.	26, 1884	Kilmahumaig	20
		98	Aug.	19, 1935	Charlottetown	74
Quebec	−66		Feb.	5, 1923	Doucet	1236
		104	July	6, 1921	Barrage Temiscaminigue	595
		104	Aug.	15, 1928	Bark Lake	1195
Saskatchewan	−70		Feb.	1, 1893	Prince Albert	1432
		113	July	5, 1937	Midale	1908
		113	July	5, 1937	Yellow Grass	1899
North West Territories	−71		Dec.	26, 1917	Fort Smith.	665
		103	July	18, 1941	Fort Smith.	680
Yukon Territory	−81		Feb.	3, 1947	Snag.	1925
		95	June	18, 1950	Mayo.	1625

Normal Temperatures, Highs, Lows, Precipitation

Source: Atmospheric Environment Service, Dept. of Environment

These normals are based on varying periods of record over the thirty-year period 1941 to 1970 inclusive.
Extreme temperatures are based on varying periods of record for each station thru 1970.
AP indicates airport station; those not so marked are city office stations. The minus (−) sign indicates temperatures below zero. Fahrenheit thermometer registration.

Province	Station	Normal January Max.	Normal January Min.	Normal July Max.	Normal July Min.	Extreme Highest	Extreme Lowest	Precipitation Normal Annual (inches)
Alberta	Calgary (AP)	23	3	74	49	97	−49	17.21
Alberta	Edmonton (Industrial AP)	14	3	74	53	94	−55	17.58
British Columbia	Prince George (AP)	19	2	72	46	94	−58	24.43
British Columbia	Victoria (AP)	43	32	71	52	97	4	33.72
British Columbia	Vancouver (AP)	41	31	72	55	92	0	42.05
Manitoba	Churchill (AP)	−11	−25	63	45	91	−49	15.61
Manitoba	Winnipeg (AP)	8	−10	79	56	105	−49	21.06
Newfoundland	Gander (AP)	28	14	71	52	96	−17	42.45
Newfoundland	St. John's (AP)	31	19	68	51	87	−10	59.50
New Brunswick	Fredericton (AP)	25	7	78	55	98	−35	41.74
New Brunswick	Moncton (AP)	26	9	76	55	99	−26	43.27
New Brunswick	Saint John (AP)	28	9	72	53	91	−34	55.13
Nova Scotia	Halifax (AP)	29	14	74	55	93	−14	54.94
Nova Scotia	Sidney (AP)	31	17	74	55	95	−13	52.78
Ontario.	Ottawa (AP)	21	4	80	59	100	−33	33.50
Ontario.	Sudbury (AP)	17	−1	77	55	97	−36	32.87
Ontario.	Toronto (AP)	28	13	81	58	101	−24	29.61
Ontario.	Windsor (AP)	31	18	82	62	101	−15	32.91
Prince Edward Island	Charlottetown (AP)	27	13	75	58	98	−23	41.69
Quebec	Montreal (AP)	22	6	79	61	96	−36	37.05
Quebec	Quebec City (AP)	19	3	77	56	96	−33	42.85
Quebec	Val-d'Or (AP).	12	−9	74	52	94	−47	35.52
Saskatchewan	Prince Albert (AP)	5	−17	77	51	100	−58	15.31
Saskatchewan	Regina (AP)	10	−9	79	53	110	−56	15.66
North West Territories	Alert	−19	−33	44	34	68	−57	6.15
North West Territories	Yellowknife (AP)	−12	−27	69	53	90	−60	9.84
Yukon Territory	Dawson	−13	−26	72	48	95	−73	12.81
Yukon Territory	Whitehorse	6	−9	68	47	94	−62	10.24

Canadian Monthly Normal Temperature and Precipitation

Source: Atmospheric Environment Service, Dept. of Environment

Normal refers to the mean daily temperature and total monthly precipitation based on varying periods of record over the thirty-year period 1941 to 1970 inclusive. In most cases no adjustment factor was used.

AP indicates airport station; those not so marked are city office stations

T, Temperature in Fahrenheit; P, Precipitation in inches; L, less than .05 inch.

Stations	Jan. T.	P.	Feb. T.	P.	Mar. T.	P.	Apr. T.	P.	May T.	P.	June T.	P.	July T.	P.	Aug. T.	P.	Sept. T.	P.	Oct. T.	P.	Nov. T.	P.	Dec. T.	P.
Calgary, Alta. (AP)	12	0.7	19	0.8	24	0.8	38	1.2	49	2.0	56	3.6	62	2.7	59	2.2	51	1.4	42	0.7	27	0.6	18	0.6
Charlottetown, P.E.I. (AP)	20	3.8	20	3.2	27	3.0	37	2.9	49	3.1	58	3.1	66	2.9	65	3.5	58	3.6	48	3.9	39	4.5	26	3.9
Churchill, Man. (AP)	-17	0.6	-16	0.5	-5	0.7	12	0.9	28	1.1	43	1.6	54	1.9	53	2.3	42	2.0	30	1.6	10	1.6	-7	0.8
Dawson, Yukon	-20	0.8	-9	0.6	7	0.5	29	0.4	46	0.9	57	1.5	60	2.1	55	2.0	44	1.1	26	1.1	2	1.0	-14	1.0
Edmonton, Alta. (Industrial AP)	6	1.0	13	0.8	22	0.7	39	0.9	52	1.4	58	2.9	63	3.2	61	2.8	52	1.4	42	0.7	24	0.7	.13	0.8
Fredericton, N.B. (AP)	16	3.7	17	3.6	28	2.7	39	2.9	51	3.2	61	3.1	67	3.4	64	3.4	56	3.2	46	3.4	35	4.3	21	4.4
Frobisher Bay, N.W.T. (AP)	-15	0.9	-13	1.1	-8	0.8	7	0.8	26	0.9	38	1.4	46	2.0	44	2.2	36	1.7	23	1.6	9	1.4	-5	1.0
Halifax, N.S. (AP)	21	5.3	20	5.0	28	4.0	37	4.2	48	3.8	58	3.1	64	3.1	64	4.2	57	3.7	48	4.6	39	6.4	27	7.0
Hamilton, Ont.	25	2.2	26	2.3	33	2.7	45	2.7	56	3.0	67	2.3	72	2.9	71	2.9	62	2.4	52	2.5	40	2.3	29	2.3
Kitchener, Ont.	20	2.3	21	2.1	30	2.8	44	2.7	54	3.2	65	3.2	69	3.5	68	3.0	60	2.8	49	2.8	37	3.0	25	2.9
London, Ont. (AP)	21	3.0	22	2.5	31	2.8	44	3.0	54	2.9	65	3.1	69	3.2	67	2.8	60	3.1	50	2.9	38	3.2	26	3.4
Moncton, N.B. (AP)	18	4.2	18	3.9	27	3.6	38	3.3	49	3.1	59	3.5	65	3.1	64	3.1	56	2.8	46	3.5	36	4.4	22	4.2
Montreal, Que. (AP)	14	2.9	16	2.7	28	2.7	43	2.9	55	2.6	65	3.2	70	3.3	68	3.4	59	3.1	49	2.9	36	3.4	20	3.4
Ottawa, Ont. (AP)	12	2.3	15	2.2	26	2.4	42	2.6	54	2.7	65	2.8	69	3.2	67	3.2	58	3.1	48	2.6	34	3.0	18	3.0
Quebec City, Que. (AP)	11	3.3	13	3.0	24	2.7	38	2.9	51	3.1	61	4.0	67	4.2	64	4.0	56	4.1	45	3.2	32	3.9	17	3.9
Regina, Sask. (AP)	1	0.7	6	0.6	17	0.5	36	1.1	51	1.6	59	3.2	66	2.2	64	1.9	53	1.4	41	0.7	23	0.7	9	0.6
Saint John, N.B. (AP)	19	5.7	18	5.1	27	4.1	37	4.4	48	4.0	56	3.7	62	3.5	61	3.8	54	4.0	46	4.3	37	6.0	24	6.1
St. John's, Nfld. (AP)	25	5.7	24	6.1	28	5.2	34	4.4	42	3.9	51	3.4	59	3.2	60	4.5	54	4.4	45	5.4	38	6.3	30	6.6
Saskatoon, Sask. (AP)	-2	0.7	5	0.7	16	0.6	38	0.8	51	1.3	60	2.2	66	2.0	63	1.7	52	1.3	41	0.7	22	0.7	7	0.7
Sault St. Marie, Ont. (AP)	13	3.2	11	2.1	23	2.2	38	2.2	48	3.3	58	3.4	64	2.8	62	2.6	56	3.7	47	3.1	34	4.1	20	3.7
Toronto, Ont. (AP)	21	2.1	22	1.9	30	2.3	43	2.5	54	2.8	65	2.4	69	2.9	68	2.8	60	2.9	52	2.3	38	2.4	26	2.2
Vancouver, B.C. (AP)	36	5.8	40	4.5	42	3.6	48	2.4	54	1.8	59	1.7	63	1.1	63	1.4	58	2.4	50	4.8	43	5.5	39	6.5
Victoria, B.C. (AP)	37	5.7	40	3.8	42	2.7	47	1.7	53	1.2	58	1.1	61	0.7	61	0.9	57	1.4	50	3.4	43	5.0	40	5.7
Whitehorse, Yukon (AP)	-2	0.7	8	0.5	18	0.5	32	0.4	45	0.5	54	1.1	57	1.3	54	1.4	40	1.1	33	0.7	16	0.8	-4	0.7
Windsor, Ont. (AP)	24	2.1	26	2.0	34	2.6	47	3.2	57	3.2	68	3.2	72	3.2	70	3.2	63	2.3	53	2.4	40	2.4	28	2.5
Winnipeg, Man. (AP)	-1	0.9	4	0.7	17	1.0	38	1.4	51	2.2	62	3.1	67	3.1	66	2.9	55	2.0	44	1.3	24	1.0	7	0.9
Yellowknife, N.W.T. (AP)	-19	0.5	-14	0.4	-1	0.4	18	0.4	39	0.5	54	0.6	61	1.3	57	1.4	44	1.1	30	1.2	6	0.9	-11	0.7

Annual Climatological Data

Source: Atmospheric Environment Service, Dept. of Environment

Station	Temperature					Precipitation			Snow or Sleet			Wind Fastest		No. of days	
	Elev. ft.	Highest	Date D./Mo.	Lowest	Date D./Mo.	Total (in.)	Greatest in 24 hrs.	Date D./Mo.	Total (in.)	Greatest in 24 hrs.	Date D./Mo.	MPH	Date D./Mo.	Prec. .01 in. or more	Snow, sleet 1 in. or more
1972															
Calgary, Alta.	3540	88	30/5	-36	26/1	18.95	1.39	9/6	83.3	7.5	1/12	55	16/2	127	77
Charlottetown, P.E.I.	186	86	16/7	-14	23/2	52.55	1.78	4/5	209.8	10.1	9/4	50	4/2	175	86
Churchill, Man.	115	87	25/8	-48	16/2	16.84	1.17	11/7	61.1	6.9	20/9	45	20/9	145	91
Dawson, Yukon	1062	89	13/6	-63	11/1	11.09	1.16	2/10	69.9	11.6	2/10	24	30/9	111	69
Edmonton, Alta.	2358	86	30/5	-42	26/1	20.33	1.19	24/6	64.5	5.1	23/3	35	17/1	141	72
Fredericton, N.B.	74	92	13/7	-21	1/1	53.71	2.27	3/3	184.6	14.6	16/12	38	26/1	180	78
Frobisher Bay, N.W.T.	68	70	24/7	-45	21/2	13.13	0.75	21/8	94.3	6.3	16/3	35	1/3	142	116
Halifax, N.S.	461	82	28/5	-8	23/2	67.81	2.81	23/3	124.1	8.9	26/2	39	19/2	175	77
Hamilton, Ont.	808	94	22/7	-4	15/1	36.8	3.57	7/8	75.2	6.2	14/12	31	25/1	161	69
Waterloo-Wellington (Kitchener) Ont.	1125	88	22/7	-8	5/1	35.38	1.52	21/6	82.6	4.5	20/1	38	13/12	170	74
London, Ont.	912	90	22/7	-10	15/1	41.31	2.35	7/8	99.5	6.1	4/2	42	18/7	175	81
Moncton, N.B.	248	89	13/7	-18	23/2	58.64	2.63	26/7	202.1	11.4	16/12	37	1/12	178	83
Montreal, Que.	98	90	15/7	-25	23/2	46.44	1.27	10/7	128.8	9.0	19/2	51	25/1	173	74
Ottawa, Ont.	413	88	12/7	-22	16/1	45.88	2.09	7/8	135.9	12.7	3/2	38	25/1	175	77
Quebec City, Que.	245	88	15/7	-27	23/2	53.90	1.51	30/9	201.7	10.7	22/3	40	4/2	186	95
Regina, Sask.	1884	100	29/8	-46	26/1	13.54	1.38	22/7	49.5	4.1	29/2	51	16/2	106	73
Saint John, N.B.	352	79	23/7	-18	23/2	63.85	2.85	7/10	154.2	7.9	26/2	50	2/12	183	87
St. John's, Nfld.	463	82	17/7	-8	24/2	56.77	2.76	11/11	157.3	14.1	23/11	50	27/2	207	97
Saskatoon, Sask.	1645	93	29/8	-51	25/1	12.03	0.90	9/7	40.7	4.3	8/1	50	11/6	117	62
Sault Ste. Marie, Ont.	620	88	20/5	-32	3/3	34.30	1.32	6/8	171.2	6.4	25/1	42	25/1	186	121
Thunder Bay, Ont.	644	91	30/8	-35	15/1	23.76	1.50	20/9	96.8	7.9	30/12	32	8/10	142	75
Toronto, Ont.	578	94	22/7	-5	16/1	37.02	1.64	12/12	76.8	7.2	15/12	42	25/1	144	52
Vancouver B.C.	16	81	8/8	12	27/1	48.96	3.52	25/12	23.1	6.0	10/1	43	2/1	165	21
Victoria, B.C.	67	86	4/7	17	25/1	29.99	2.67	5/3	17.8	2.6	18/1	50	27/2	148	18
Whitehorse, Yukon	2289	84	6/7	-49	11/1	11.38	0.72	6/7	73.5	5.0	1/6	25	16/1	130	88
Windsor, Ont.	637	95	21/7	-13	16/1	35.96	1.23	16/4	59.7	3.0	4/1	36	14/11	161	61
Winnipeg Man.	786	97	29/8	-38	25/1	16.68	1.41	15/8	44.9	4.6	27/10	36	15/1	126	62
Yellowknife, N.W.T.	682	83	25/6	-48	13/1	9.54	0.72	15/9	66.7	3.6	24/10	36	28/4	112	87

Explanation of Normal Temperatures

Normal temperatures listed in the tables on pages 261 and 263 are based on records of the National Weather Service for the 30-year period from 1931 to 1960 inclusive.

To obtain the average maximum temperature for any month, the daily maximum temperatures are added; the total is then divided by the number of days in that month. The average minimum temperature for the month is obtained by adding the daily minimum temperatures during that month and dividing by the number of days in that month.

The normal maximum temperature for January, for example, is obtained by adding the average maximums for January, 1931, January 1932, etc., through January, 1960. The total is then divided by 30. The normal minimum temperature is obtained in a similar manner by adding the average minimums for each January in the 30-year period and dividing by 30. The normal temperature for January is one-half of the sum of the normal maximum and minimum temperatures for that month.

The mean temperature for any one day is one-half the total of the maximum and minimum temperatures for that day.

Violence in the Air

As I was going up the stair,
I met a man who wasn't there.
He wasn't there again today;
I wish, I wish he'd go away.
(Hughes Mearns, 1875-1965)

The atmosphere of gases and water vapor is so insubstantial that we move through it with ease and say that nothing is there. Yet under certain conditions of temperature, pressure and electrical conductivity, this weakling air, which can't hold up a feather, can throw trains off their tracks, set buildings afire, and lift and carry the sea miles inland. Every year, violent weather kills several hundred Americans and is indirectly responsible for the deaths of many more.

The biggest killer year after year is heat. **Heat** takes the lives of about 175 Americans in an average year. In very hot summers the death toll can rise to well over 500 directly caused by heat.

Lightning, caused by an excessive positive charge on the ground and an excessive negative charge in a thunderstorm cloud, kills an average of 150 Americans every year, more than tornados and hurricanes combined. Property loss in damaged buildings and vehicles, livestock deaths, forest fires and disrupted communications is estimated at more than $100 million annually.

Tornados are another effect of **thunderstorms.** With winds estimated at up to 300 miles an hour inside its familiar funnel shape, the tornado is the most violent atmospheric phenomenon, and, over a small area, the most destructive. From 1953 to 1972, nearly 2,300 people were killed by tornados in the U.S. Oklahoma led the nation in the greatest number of tornados per 10,000 square miles in the same period. However, Mississippi, with only 2.8% of the total tornadoes, experienced the greatest percentage (13) of the total tornado-related deaths.

A third killer in a thunderstorm is the **flash flood.** Thunderstorms in June 1972 in the Black Hills caused a flood which took over 200 lives and damaged an estimated $120 million in property in Rapid City, South Dakota.

Storm surges are also the most violent effects of **hurricanes.** Not only can hurricane winds whip up waves over 50 feet high, but low atmospheric pressures at the storm center can literally lift the sea up several feet more and carry it over land.

But of all atmospheric phenomenon, the most persistently malevolent is the **winter storm** with its combinations of wind, snow, ice and freezing temperatures and its wake of auto accidents, heart attacks, exposure and freezing, fires, falls, etc. From 1936 through 1969, snowstorms caused more than 3,000 deaths. The worst year was 1960 with 354 winter storm deaths.

Speed of Winds in the United States

Miles per hour — average thru 1972. High thru 1972. Wind velocities in true values.
Source: National Climatic Center, NOAA, Dept. of Commerce

Stations	Avg.	High	Stations	Avg.	High	Stations	Avg.	High
Albany, N. Y.	8.8	71	Helena, Mont.	7.9	73	Pensacola, Fla	8.2 (b)	59
Albuquerque, N. M	8.9	90	Jacksonville, Fla.	8.8	82	Philadelphia, Pa.	9.6	73
Atlanta, Ga.	9.1	70	Key West, Fla	11.3	122	Pittsburgh, Pa.	9.4	58
Bismarck, N. D	10.7	72	Knoxville, Tenn	7.4	73	Portland, Ore	7.7	88
Boston, Mass.	12.9	65	Little Rock, Ark.	8.2	65	Rochester, N. Y	9.6	73
Buffalo, N. Y.	12.4	91	Louisville, Ky.	8.3	61	St. Louis, Mo	9.5 (b)	91
Cape Hatteras, N. C.	11.8 (b)	110	Memphis, Tenn	9.2	57	Salt Lake City, Utah.	8.7	71
Chattanooga, Tenn	6.3	82	Miami, Fla	9.0 (a)	74	San Diego, Calif	6.6	51
Chicago, Ill.	10.4	60	Minneapolis,Minn	10.6	92	San Francisco, Calif	10.5	58
Cincinnati, Ohio	7.1	49	Mobile, Ala.	9.4 (b)	63	Savannah, Ga.	8.3	66
Cleveland, Ohio	10.9	74	Montgomery,Ala	6.8	60	Spokane, Wash.	8.6	59
Denver, Colo	9.0	56	Nashville, Tenn	7.9	73	Toledo, Ohio	9.5	72
Detroit, Mich	10.1	77	New Orleans, La	8.4 (b)	98	Washington, D. C	9.3	78
Fort Smith, Ark	7.7	58	New York, N. Y.(c)	9.5	70	Mt. Wash'ton, N. H	35.2	231
Galveston, Texas	11.0 (d)	100	Omaha, Nebr	10.9	73			

(a) Highest velocity ever recorded in Miami area was 132 mph, at former station in Miami Beach in September, 1926. (b) Previous location. (c) Data for Central Park. Battery Place data through 1960, avg. 14.5, high 113. (d) Recorded before anemometer blew away. Estimated high 120.

WINDS, THEIR FORCE AND OFFICIAL DESIGNATIONS

Designation	MPH	Designation	MPH	Designation	MPH	Designation	MPH
Calm	Less than 1	Moderate breeze	13 to 18	Near gale	32 to 38	Storm	55 to 63
Light air	1 to 3	Fresh breeze	19 to 24	Gale	39 to 46	Violent storm	64 to 73
Light breeze	4 to 7	Strong breeze	25 to 31	Strong gale	47 to 54	Hurricane	74 and above
Gentle breeze	8 to 12						

Speed of Winds in Canada

Source: Atmospheric Environment Service, Dept. of Environment

Miles per hour-average in most cases is for the period of record 1955 to 1966. High is based on varying periods of record dependent on the origin of the station thru 1966.

Stations	Avg.	High	Stations	Avg.	High	Stations	Avg.	High
Calgary, Alta.	10.5	65	London, Ont.	10.5	63	Sault Ste. Marie, Ont.	10.0	55
Charlottetown, P.E.I.	12.0	64	Moncton, N.B.	12.5	62	Toronto, Ont.	9.9	67
Churchill, Man.	15.1	78	Montreal, Que.	10.1	50	Vancouver, B.C.	7.6	55
Dawson, Yukon	4.0	32	Ottawa, Ont.	9.4	54	Victoria, B.C.	7.5	48
Edmonton, Alta.	8.8	54	Quebec City, Que.	11.4	68	Whitehorse, Yukon	9.6	50
Fredericton, N.B.	8.8	43	Regina, Sask.	13.8	60	Windsor, Ont.	10.8	57
Frobisher Bay, N.W.T.	11.3	80	Saint John, N.B.	11.5	60	Winnipeg, Man.	12.4	56
Halifax, N.S.	11.1	53	St. John's, Nfld.	15.4	85	Yellowknife, N.W.T.	10.2	45
Hamilton, Ont.	7.9	41	Saskatoon, Sask.	11.3	65			

The Meaning of "One Inch of Rain"

An acre of ground contains 43,560 square feet. Consequently, a rainfall of 1 inch over 1 acre of ground would mean a total of 6,272,640 cubic inches of water. This is equivalent of 3,630 cubic feet.

As a cubic foot of pure water weighs about 62.4 pounds, the exact amount varying with the density, it follows that the weight of a uniform coating of 1 inch of rain over 1 acre of surface would be 226,512 pounds, or 113¼ short tons.

The weight of 1 U. S. gallon of pure water is about 8.345 pounds. Consequently a rainfall of 1 inch over 1 acre of ground would mean 27,154 gallons of water.

National Weather Service: National Oceanic and Atmospheric Admn.

The National Weather Service, formerly the Weather Bureau is a component of the National Oceanic and Atmospheric Administration (NOAA), a new agency created in the Dept. of Commerce on Oct. 3, 1970, under a Presidential reorganization plan.

The National Weather Service reports the weather of the U. S. and possessions, provides weather forecasts to the general public, issues warnings against tornadoes, hurricanes, floods, winter storms, and other atmospheric and hydrologic hazards, and provides a broad array of special services to aeronautical, maritime, astronautic, agricultural, and other weather-sensitive activities. These services are supported by a national network of observing and forecasting stations, communications links, aircraft, satellite systems, and computers. Some 300 NWS offices across the land ensure prompt and useful dissemination of weather information. **See also National Weather Service Watches and Warnings, Page 259.**

The River and Flood Forecasting Service is conducted through about 70 river district offices and 12 river forecasting centers and issues river stage and flood warnings for all the principal rivers and tributaries of the United States. The Water Supply Forecasting Service is conducted through 5 Water Supply Forecasting Centers for the Western and Northeastern United States on a water year or seasonal basis. Rainfall studies conducted in cooperation with the Army Corps of Engineers and the Department of Agriculture Soil Conservation Service assist in planning engineering works for flood control, water utilization, water-shed protection and local drainage design.

Weather service to aviation involves the responsibilities of providing current measurements and of forecasting conditions pertinent to conducting safe and efficient flight operations at airport terminals and along flight routes. Aviation weather forecasts and briefings are provided for transoceanic and domestic operations extending upward from the surface to include operational levels of civil jet aircraft.

The agricultural weather service program provides weather observations from representative agricultural areas, specialized forecasts of weather factors directly affecting agricultural production.

In addition, technical studies of the influence of weather on agriculture are coordinated jointly with agricultural experiment station personnel.

U. S. Department of Agriculture and the National Weather Service cooperate in issuing local weather-crop bulletins on an area basis.

The Fruit-frost Service provides detailed and localized forecasts and warnings to fruit growers on a cooperative basis in those states where winter and spring fruit and vegetable production is a major activity.

The marine weather service provides specialized weather forecasts, warnings, sea heights and data essential to the conduct of marine operations on the high seas and on coastal and inland waterways. In addition, it supplies forecasts for related phenomena, such as seiches and storm surges, for the protection of life and property.

The Weather Service also provides weather support for the U. S. manned space flight program and assists in the weather support to the Nation's other space programs.

The repository for all American and many international weather records and for large-scale tabulation, processing, and publication is the National Climatic Center, operated by NOAA's Environmental Data Service at Asheville, N. C. The Environmental Data Service also has an Agricultural Climatology Service Office which issues the Weekly Weather and Crop Bulletin jointly with the U.S. Dept. of Agriculture.

Temperature-Humidity Index

The purpose of the temperature-humidity index (THI) is to measure or estimate human discomfort in the summertime resulting from the combined effects of temperature and humidity. The THI is calculated by adding wet bulb and dry bulb temperature readings, multiplying the sum by 0.4 and adding 15.

At a THI value of 75, a majority of people will be uncomfortable; at an index of 80 or above, almost everyone will be very uncomfortable and many will be miserable. The following table, based on this calculation, lists those combinations of temperature and humidity which correspond to the **(A)** borderline of discomfort and **(B)** borderline of extreme discomfort. For example, a temperature of 85 degrees and a humidity of 33% or more will be uncomfortable for a majority of people: when the humidity at that temperature reaches or exceeds 71%, practically everyone will be acutely uncomfortable. The higher the temperature or humidity values, the greater will be the general discomfort.

Temp. Degrees F.	Relative Humidity in % A	B	Temp. Degrees F.	Relative Humidity in % A	B	Temp. Degrees F.	Relative Humidity in % A	B
75	100		86	29	65	96 Uncomfortable at any humidity		20
76	91		87	25	59			
77	82		88	20	54	97		16
78	75		89	17	49	98		13
79	68		90	14	43	99		11
80	61		91	10	38	100		8
81	55	100	92	7	34	101		6
82	49	93	93	5	30	102		3
83	43	86	94	3	26	103		1
84	38	78	95	1	23	104 Extremely uncomfortable at any humidity		
85	33	71						

How Degree Days are Measured

A degree day is a standard measure used by heating engineers to measure the heating season's coldness. The number of degree days in a calendar day is determined by subtracting the day's average from 65. If the high on a given day was 60 and the low was 40 the average temperature that day would be 50. Subtracted from 65, this would give 15 degree days for that calendar day.

Dew Point Explained

The dew point is the temperature to which air must be cooled to become saturated. When this temperature is below freezing, it is sometimes called the frost point.

The higher the air temperature, the more water vapor air can hold before saturation is reached and condensation occurs (fog, snow or rain). Thus, unsaturated air containing a given amount of water vapor will become saturated if its temperature decreases sufficiently.

The difference between the actual air temperature and the dew point temperature is an indication of how close the air is to saturation. Relative humidity increases as this difference decreases, reaching 100% when the spread is zero degrees.

United States — Associations and Societies

Source: World Almanac Questionnaire
Arranged according to key words in titles. Last figure indicates membership.

—A—

Aaron Burr Association (1946), Tremont, Inca Rd., Linden, VA 22642; 600.

Abortion, Assn. for the Study of (1965), 120 W. 57th St., N.Y., NY 10019; 25,000.

Accountants, Amer. Institute of Certified Public (1887), 666 5th Ave., N.Y., NY 90,000.

Accountants, Natl. Assn. of (1919), 919 Third Ave., N.Y., NY 10022; 64,000.

Accountants, Natl. Society of Public (1945), 1717 Pennsylvania Ave., N.W., Wash. DC 20006; 14,000.

Acoustical Society of America (1929), 335 E. 45 St., New York, NY 10017; 4,800.

Actors Equity Assn. (1913), 165 W. 46 St., New York, NY 10036; 16,844.

Actors' Fund of America (1882), 1619 Broadway, New York, NY 10019; 2,855.

Actuaries, Society of (1949), 208 S. La Salle St., Chicago, IL 60604; 4,300.

Adirondack Mountain Club (1922), RD #1, Ridge Rd., Glens Falls, NY 12801; 8,000.

Administrative Management Society (1919), Maryland Rd., Willow Grove, PA 19090; 13,780.

Adult Education Assn. of the U.S.A. (1951), Office of Education, 810 18th St., Wash., DC 20006; 7,000.

Adventurers' Club of New York (1912), 11 Seabert Lane, Kinnelon, NJ 07405; 203.

Advertisers, Assn. of National (1910), 155 East 44th St., New York, NY 10017; 421 companies.

Advertising Agencies, American Assn. of (1917), 200 Park Ave., N.Y., NY 10017; 385 agencies.

Advertising Club of New York (1906), 23 Park Ave., New York, NY 10016; 2,000.

Aeronautic Assn., Natl. (1905), 806 15th St., N.W., Washington DC 20005; 100,000.

Aeronautics and Astronautics, Amer. Institute of (1963), 1290 Ave., of the Americas, N.Y. NY 10019; 22,217.

Aerospace Industries Assn. of America (1919), 1725 DeSales St., N.W., Washington, DC 20036; 73.

Aerospace Medical Association (1929), Washington National Airport, Wash., DC 20001; 4,552.

Aesthetic Realism, Society for (1946), 39 Grove St., N.Y., NY 10014; 150.

African Violet Soc. of America (1946), 706 Hamilton Bank Bldg., Knoxville, TN 37901; 13,000.

Afro-American Life and History, Assn. for the Study of (formerly, **Assn. for the Study of Negro Life & History**) (1915), 1407 14th St., Wash., DC 20005; 35,000.

Aging Assn., Amer. (1970), Univ. of Neb. Medical Cntr., 42nd & Dewey Ave., Omaha, NE 68105; 500.

Agricultural Chemicals Assn., Natl. (1933), 1155 15th St., N.W., Wash. DC 20005; 105 companies.

Agricultural Economics Assn., American (1919), Univ. of Kentucky, Lexington, KY 40506; 5,000.

Agricultural Engineers, American Society of (1907), 2950 Niles Rd., St. Joseph, MI 49085; 6,500.

Agricultural History Society (1919), U.S. Dept. of Agriculture, Rm 144, 500 12th St. SW, Wash., DC 20250; 800.

Agronomy, American Society of (1907), 677 S. Segoe Rd., Madison, WI 53711; 7,700.

Ahepa, Order of (1922), 1422 K St., N.W., Washington, DC 20005; 28,500.

Air Force Aid Society (1942), 1117 N. 19th St., Arlington, VA 22209; 23,600.

Air Force Association (1946), 1750 Pennsylvania Ave., N.W., Washington, DC 20006; 110,000.

Air Force Sergeants Association (1961), Box 31050, Wash., DC 20031; 22,408.

Air Line Employees Assn. (1953), 5600 S. Central Ave., Chicago, IL 60638; 10,000.

Air Line Pilots Assn. (1931), 1625 Massachusetts Ave., Wash., DC, 20036; 31,000 pilots.

Air Pollution Control Assn. (1907), 4400 Fifth Ave., Pittsburgh, PA 15213; 6,500.

Air Transport Assn. of America (1936), 1000 Connecticut Ave., N.W., Wash., DC 20036; 29 airlines.

Air Transport Assn., Internatl. (1945), 1155 Mansfield St., Montreal 113, Canada; 108 airlines.

Aircraft Owners and Pilots Assn. (1939), 7315 Wisconsin Ave., Bethesda, MD 20014; 171,000.

Alcohol Problems, Amer. Council on (1895), 119 Constitution Ave., N.E., Wash. DC 20002.

Alcoholics Anonymous Box 459, N.Y., NY 10017; 650,000.

Alcoholism, Natl. Council on (1944), 2 Park Ave., New York, NY 10016; 175 groups.

Allergy, American Academy of (1943), 225 East Michigan St., Milwaukee, WI 53202; 2,300.

Allergy Foundation of America (1953), 801 Second Ave., New York, NY 10017; 55.

Allied Youth (1931), Rosslyn Building, 1901 Ft. Myer Drive, Arlington, VA 22209; 10,000.

Alpine Club, American (1902), 113 East 90th St., New York, NY 10028; 940.

Altrusa International (1917), 332 S. Michigan Ave., Chicago, IL 60604; 17,950.

Aluminum Assn. (1933), 750 Third Ave., New York, NY 10017; 69 companies.

Alumni Council, American (1913), One Dupont Circle, Washington, DC 20036; 1,600 schools.

American Citizens of German Descent, Federation of (1945), 460 Chapman St., Irvington, NJ 07111.

American Federation of Labor and Congress of Industrial Organizations (AFL-CIO) (Dec. 5, 1955, by merging **American Federation of Labor,** estab. 1881 and **Congress of Industrial Organizations** estab. 1935), 815-16th St., N.W., Wash., DC 20034; 13,500,000.

American Field Service (1947), 313 E. 43rd St., New York, NY 10017; 77,000.

American Indian Affairs, Assn. on (1923), 432 Park Ave. South, N.Y. NY 10016; 75,000.

American Legion, The (1919), 700 No. Pennsylvania St., Indianapolis, IN 46204; 2,700,000.

American Legion Auxiliary (1919), 777 No, Meridian St., Indianapolis, IN 46204; 942,000.

Amer. Society for Prevention of Cruelty to Animals (1866), 441 E. 92nd St., N. Y. NY 10028; 2,000.

American Veterans of World War II, Korea & Vietnam (AMVETS) (1947), 1710 Rhode Island Ave., N.W., Wash., DC 20036; 250,000. **AMVETS Natl. Auxiliary** (1946); Saco Rd., Old Orchard Beach, ME 04064; 26,000.

Amputation Foundation, National, (1919), 12-45 150th St., Whitestone, NY 11357; 2,000.

Animal Protection Institute (1968), 5894 S. Land Park Dr., Sacramento, CA 95822; 35,000.

Animal Welfare Institute (1951), P.O. Box 3650, Wash. DC 20007; 3,511.

Animals, Friends of (1957), 11 W. 60th St., N.Y., NY 10023; 45,000.

Animals, The Fund for (1967), 140 West 57th St, N.Y., NY 10019, 45,000.

Anthropological Assn., American (1902), 1703 New Hampshire Ave., N.W. Wash., DC 20009; 7,900.

Anti-Vivisection Society, American (1883), 1903 Chestnut St., Philadelphia, PA 19103; 11,500.

Antiquarian Society, American (1812), 185 Salisbury St., Worcester, MA 01609; 251.

Antique Automobile Club of America (1935), 501 West Governor Rd., Hershey, PA 17033; 30,000.

Appalachian Mountain Club (1876), 5 Joy St., Boston, MA 02108; 17,000.

Appalachian Trail Conference (1925), Box 236, Harpers Ferry, WV 25425; 76,000.

Appraisers, Society of (1952), Dulles Airport, P.O. Box 17265, Wash. DC 20041; 4,000.

Arbitration Association, American (1926), 140 W. 51st St., New York, NY 10020; 4,000.

Archaeological Institute of America (1879), 260 W. Broadway, N.Y., NY 10013; 6,500.

Archers Assn., Professional (1961), 1500 N. Chatsworth St., St. Paul, MN 55117; 350.

Archery Assn., Natl. (1879), 1951 Geraldson Dr., Lancaster, PA 17601; 5,168.

Architects, American Institute of (1857), 1735 New York Ave., N.W., Wash. DC 20006; 23,601.

Architectural Historians, Society of (1940), 1700 Walnut St., Philadelphia, PA 19103; 4,000.

Archivists, Society of American (1936), Rackham Bldg., U. of Michigan, Ann Arbor, MI 48104; 2,500.

Armed Forces Communications and Electronics Assn. (1946), Skyline Center, 5205 Leesburg Pike, Falls Church, VA 22124; 12,000.

Army and Navy Union of U.S.A. (1886), 1391 Main St., Lakemore, OH 44250; 28,000.

Art, Natl. Assn. of Schools of (1944), 1 Dupont Circle, NW, Suite 650, Wash. DC 20036; 65 schools.

Arthritis Foundation (1948), 1212 Ave. of the Americas, N.Y., NY 10036.

Artists of America, Allied (1914), 1083 Fifth Ave., New York NY 10028; 400.

Arts, American Federation of the (1909), 41 E. 65th St., New York NY 10021; 3,000.

Arts, Natl. Endowment for the (1965), 806 15th St., N.W., Washington, DC 20506.

Arts and Letters, American Academy of (1904), 633 West 155th St., New York, NY 10032; 48.

Arts and Letters, National Institute of (1898 as **Amer. Social Science Assn.**), 633 West 155th St., N.Y., NY 10032; 240.

Arts and Sciences, American Academy of (1780), 280 Newton St., Brookline, MA 02146; 2,689.

Arts, Associated Councils of the (1966), 1564 Broadway, N.Y., NY 10036; 600.

Assistance League, National (1935), 5627 Fernwood Ave., Hollywood, CA 90028; 11,000.

Associated Press, The (1848), 50 Rockefeller Plaza, New York, NY 10020.

Astrologers, Amer. Federation of (1938), #6 Library Ct., S.E., Wash., DC 20003; 3,000.

Astronautical Society, American (1954), 1629 K St. N.W., Washington, DC 20006; 600.

Astronomical Society, American (1899), Leander-Mc-Cormick Observatory, Box 3818 Univ. Sta., Charlottesville, VA 22903; 2,889.

Atheist Assn. (formerly, **Amer. Assn. for the Advancement of Atheism**) (1925), Box 2832, San Diego, CA 92112; 200.

Athletic Associations, Natl. Federation of State High School (1920), Box 98, Elgin, IL 60120; 50 States.

Athletic Conference, Eastern College (1938), Royal Manhattan Hotel, N.Y., NY 10036; 211 schools.

Athletic Union of the U.S., Amateur (1888), 3400 W. 86th St., Indianapolis, IN 46268; 300,000.

Attorneys General, National Assn. of (1907), Iron Works Pike, Lexington, KY 40505; 56.

Audit Bureau of Circulations (1914), 123 N. Wacker Dr., Chicago, IL 60606; 3,900 companies.

Audubon Society, National (1905), 950 3rd Ave., New York, NY 10022; 261,327.

Authors and Composers, American Guild of (1931), 50 W. 57th St., New York; NY 10019; 2,500. *

Authors League of America (1912), 234 W. 44th St., N.Y., NY 10036; 5,900.

Auto License Plate Collectors Assn. (1954), P.O. Box 1017, Chandler, AZ 85224; 1,462.

Automobile Association, American (1902), 8111 Gatehouse Rd., Falls Church VA 22042; 15,300,000.

Automobile Club, National (1924), 65 Battery St., San Francisco, CA 94111; 335,000.

Automobile Dealers Assn., National (1917), 2000 K St., N.W., Washington, DC 20006; 20,728.

Automobile Manufacturers Association (1913), 320 New Center Bldg., Detroit, MI 48202; 10 co's.

Automotive Booster Clubs Internatl. (1920), 1803 S. Busse Rd., Mt. Prospect, Il 60056; 3,076.

Automotive Engineers, Society of (1909), 2 Pennsylvania Plaza, New York, NY 10001; 25,984.

Automotive Organization Team (formerly **Automotive Old Timers**) (1939), Box 1742, Midland, MI 48640; 2,600.

Aviation Historical Society, Amer. (1956), P.O. Box 996; Ojai, CA 93023; 8,400.

Aztec Club of 1847 (1847), 5225 Westpath Way, Washington, DC 20016; 175.

— B —

Badminton Assn., American (1936), 1330 Alexandria Dr., San Diego, CA 92107; 4,000.

Ball Players of America, Assn. of Professional (1924), 530 E. Wardlow Rd., Long Beach, CA 90807; 5,500.

Bankers Assn., American (1875), 1120 Connecticut Ave., N.W., Wash., DC 20036; 18,059 banks, branch offices.

Bankers Assn. of America, Independent (1930), 1167 S. Main St., Sauk Centre, MN 56378; 7,026 banks.

Banker Assn., Internatl. (1968), 422 Washington Bldg., Washington, DC 20005; 1,700.

Bar Association, American (1878), 1155 East 60th St., Chicago, IL 60637; 163,748.

Bar Assn., Federal (1920), 1815 H Street, N.W., Wash., DC 20006; 14,000.

Barber Shop Quartet Singing in America, Society for the Preservation and Encouragement of (1938), 6315 Third Ave., Kenosha, WI 53141; 35,000.

Barbers and Beauticians of America, Associated Master (1924), 219 Greenwich Rd., Charlotte, NC 28211; 10,000.

Baseball Congress, American Amateur (1935), 212 Plaza Bldg., 2855 W. Market St., Akron, OH 44313.

Baseball Congress, National (1931), 338 S. Sycamore, Wichita, KS 67201; 5,000.

Baseball Leagues, Natl. Assn. of Professional (1901), 720 E. Broad St., Columbus, OH 43215; 18 leagues.

Basketball Assn., American (1967), 1700 Broadway, N.Y., NY 10019; 10 teams.

Basketball Assn., Natl. (1946), 2 Penn Plaza, N.Y., NY 10001; 17 teams.

Baton Twirling Assn., Internatl. (1967), Box 234, Waldwick, NJ 07463; 2000.

Battleship Assn., American (1964), P.O. Box 11247, San Diego, CA 92111; 1,500.

Beta Sigma Phi (1931), 1800 W. 91st Pl., Kansas City, MO 64114; 225,000.

Bible Society, American (1816), 1865 Broadway, N.Y., NY 10023; 200,000.

Biblical Literature, Society of (1880), Harvard Divinity School, 45 Francis Ave., Cambridge, MA 02138; 3,100.

Bibliographical Society of America (1904), P.O. Box 397, Grand Central Sta., N.Y., NY 10017; 1,625.

Bicycle Institute of America (1937), 122 East 42nd St., New York, NY 10017; 250.

Bide-A-Wee Home Assn. (1903), 410 East 38th St., N.Y., NY 10016; 21,500.

Big Brothers of America (1946), 341 Surburban Station Bldg., Phila. PA 19103; 208 agencies.

Billiard Congress of America (1948), 717 N. Michigan Ave., Chicago, IL 60611; 850.

Biological Chemists, American Society of (1906), 9650 Rockville Pike, Bethesda, MD 20014; 3,470.

Biological Sciences, Amer. Institute of (1947), 3900 Wisconsin Ave., N.W. Wash., DC 20016; 14,500.

Blind, American Foundation for the (1921), 15 W. 16th St., New York, NY 10011.

Blind, National Federation of the (1940), 218 Randolph Hotel, Des Moines, IA 50309; 50,000.

Blind and Visually Handicapped, Natl. Accreditation Council for Agencies Serving the (1967), 79 Madison Ave., N.Y., NY 10016; 47 agencies and schools.

Blinded Veterans Assn. (1945), 1735 DeSales St., NW, Wash., DC 20006; 1,600.

Blindness, Natl. Society for the Prevention of (1908), 79 Madison Ave., N.Y., NY 10016.

Blindness, Research to Prevent (1960), 598 Madison Ave., N.Y., NY 10022.

Blood Banks, American Assn. of (1947), 1818 L St., NW, Wash., DC 20036; 6,000.

Blueberry Council, North American (1966), P.O. Box 166, Marmora, NJ 08223; 2,350.

Blue Cross Assn. (1948), 840 N. Lake Shore Dr., Chicago, IL 60611.

Blue Shield Plans, Natl. Assn. of (1946), 211 E. Chicago Ave., Chicago, IL 60611; 72 plans.

B'nai B'rith (Oct. 13, 1843), 1640 Rhode Island Ave., N.W., Wash., DC 20036; 500,000. Component units include: **B'nai B'rith Hillel Foundations** (1923); **B'nai B'rith Youth Organization** (1924). Other units: **B'nai B'rith Women, Anti-Defamation League of B'nai B'rith, and B'rith Vocational Service.**

Board of Trade of the City of Chicago (1959), La Salle at Jackson Bvd., Chicago, IL 60604; 1,402.

Board of Trade, World (formerly, **New York Board of Trade**) (1973), 295 Fifth Ave., New York, NY 10016.

Boat Owners Assn. of the U.S. (1966), 1028 Connecticut Ave., Wash., DC 20036; 20,000.

Book Manufacturers' Institute (1920), Box 368, Ridgefield, CT 06877; 105 co's.

Booksellers Association, American (1900), 800 Second Ave., New York, NY 10017; 4,500.

Botanical Gardens and Arboreta, Amer. Assn. of (1941), Dept. of Horticulture, New Mexico State Univ., Las Cruces, NM 88001; 450.

Botanical Society of America (1906), Botany Dept., Rutgers Univ., New Brunswick, NJ 08903; 5,200.

Bottle Clubs, Federation of Historical (1969), c/o Babara Robertus, 5001 Queen Ave. N., Minneapolis, MN 55430; 125 clubs.

Bowling Congress, American (1896), 5301 S. 76th St., Greendale, WI 53129; 4,047,596.

Bowling Congress, Women's International (1916), 5301 S. 76th St., Greendale, WI 53129; 3,244,420.

Boy Scouts of America, National Council (Feb. 8, 1910), N. Brunswick, NJ 08902; 4,753,634.

Boys' Brigades of America, United (1893), P.O. Box 8406, Baltimore, MD 21234.

Boys' Clubs of America (1860), 771 First Ave., New York, NY 10017; 1,000,000.

Brand Names Foundation (1943), 477 Madison Ave., N.Y., NY 10022; 750.

Brewers Assn., U.S. (1862), 1750 K St. Washington, DC 20006.

Brick Institute of America (formerly, **Structural Clay Products Institute**) (1934), 1750 Old Meadow Rd., McLean, VA 22101; 110 co's.

Brith Sholom (1905), 121 S. Broad St., Philadelphia, PA 19107; 18,000.

Broadcasters, Natl. Assn. of (1922), 1771 N. St., N.W., Washington, DC 20036; 4,485.

Burroughs, Edgar Rice, Bibliophiles (1960), 454 Elaine Dr., Pittsburgh, PA 15236; 870.

Business Bureaus, Council on Better (1970), 845 Third Ave., New York, NY 10022; 137.

Business Clubs, Natl. Assn. of American (1922), P.O. Box 5127, High Point, NC 27262;5,100.

Business Communication Assn., American (1935), 317b David Kinley Hall, Urbana, IL 61801; 1000.

Business Education Assn., Natl. (1946), Dulles Airport, Box 17402, Wash., DC 20041; 23,000.

Business Law Association, American (1923), c/o Secretary, College of Business, 201 Johnson Hall, Colo. State Univ., Ft. Collins, CO 80521; 654.

Business Press Editors, Amer. Society of (1949), 9 S. Fairview Ave., Park Ridge, IL 60068; 100.

Button Society of America, Natl. (1938), 353 Stockton St., Hightstown, NJ 08520; 2,275.

Camp Fire Girls (1910), 1740 Broadway, New York, NY 10019; 600,000.

Campers & Hikers Assn., Natl. (1954) 7172 Transit Rd., Buffalo, NY 14221; 70,000 families.

Camping Assn., American (1910), Bradford Woods, Martinsville, IN 46151; 6,500.

Cancer Council, United (1963), 1803 N. Meridian St., Indianapolis, IN 46202; serves 27,500,000 people.

Cancer Society, American (1913), 219 E. 42nd St., New York, NY 10021; 228.

Candy Brokers Assn. of America, P.O. Box 34236, Washington, DC 20034; 402.

Canners Assn. National (1907), 1133 20th St., N.W., Washington, DC 20036; 540 companies.

Captive European Nations, Assembly of (1954), 29 West 57th St., New York, NY 10019; 150.

CARE (Cooperative For American Relief Everywhere) (1945), 660 1st Ave., N.Y., NY 10016; 26 agencies.

Carillonneurs in North America, Guild of (1936), 6231 Monero Dr., Palos Verdes, CA 90274; 250.

Carl Schurz Assn., Natl. (1930), 339 Walnut St.; Philadelphia, PA 19106, 2,766.

Cartoonists Society, Natl. (1946), 130 W. 44th St., New York, NY 10036; 450.

Casting Assn., American (1906), P.O. Box 51, Nashville, TN 37202; 3,000.

Catch Society (1968), Dept. of English, State Univ. College, Fredonia, NY 14063; 400.

Catholic Bishops, Natl. Conference (1966), 1312 Mass. Ave. N.W., Wash. DC 20005; 305.

Catholic Charities, Natl. Conference of (1910), 1346 Conn. Ave., N.W., Wash., DC 20036; 7,000.

Catholic Church Extension Society (1905), 1307 S. Wabash Ave., Chicago, IL 60605.

Catholic Conference, United States (1917), 1312 Massachusetts Ave., N.W., Wash., DC 20005.

Catholic Daughters of America (1903), 10 West 71st St., New York, NY 10023; 200,000.

Catholic Educational Assn., Natl. (1904), One Dupont Circle, Suite 350, N.W., Wash., DC 20036; 14,000.

Catholic Hospital Assn. (1915), 1438 So. Grand Blvd., St. Louis, MO 63104; 879.

Catholic Press Assn. (1911), 432 Park Ave., S. New York, NY 10016; 1,789.

Catholic Rural Life Conference, National (1923), 3801 Grand Ave., Des Moines, IA 50312; 3,500.

Catholic War Veterans of U.S.A. (1935), 2 Massachusetts Ave., N.W., Wash. DC 20001; 100,000.

Century Assn. (100th Infantry Div. Society) (1945), Chestnut Ridge Rd., Glens Falls, NY 12801; 3,300.

Ceramic Society, American (1899), 65 Ceramic Drive, Columbus, OH 43214; 10,500.

Cerebral Palsy Association, United (1949), 66 East 34th St., New York, NY 10016.

Chamber of Commerce of the U.S. (1912), 1615 H. St., N.W., Washington, DC 20006; 47,000 chapters.

Chartered Life Underwriters, Amer. Society of (1928), 270 Bryn Mawr Ave., Bryn Mawr, PA 19010; 17,100.

Chartered Property and Casualty Underwriters., Soc. of (1944), Penn State Bldg., Box 566, Media, PA 19063; 7,200.

Chautauqua Institution (1874), Chautauqua, NY 14722.

Chemical Engineers, American Institute of (1908), 345 East-47th St., New York, NY 10017; 38,800.

Chemical Society, American (1876), 1155 16th St., N.W., Washington, DC 20036; 110,000.

Chemists, Amer. Institute of (1923), 79 Madison Ave., New York, NY 10016; 8,500.

Chess Federation, U.S. (1938), 479 Broadway, Newburgh, NY 12550; 58,000.

Chief Warrant and Warrant Officers Assn., USCG (1928), Suite P-203, 955 L'Enfant Plaza N., S. W., Wash., DC 20024; 2,861.

Child Study Assn. of America (1888), 50 Madison Ave., N.Y., NY 10010; 7,000.

Child Welfare League of America (1920), 67 Irving Place, N.Y., NY 10003; 390 agencies.

Children of the American Revolution, Natl. Society (1895), 1776 D St., N.W., Wash. DC 20006; 15,000.

Children's Aid Society (1853), 105 East 22nd St., New York, NY 10010.

Children's Book Council (1945), 175 Fifth Ave., New York, NY 10010; 66.

Chinese Women's Association (1932), 54-32 152nd St., Flushing, NY 11355; 784.

Chiropractic Association, American (1963), 2200 Grand Ave., Des Moines, IA 50312; 8,000.

Chiropractors Association, International (1926), 741 Brady St., Davenport, IA 52808; 4,200.

Christian Anti-Defamation League (1956), P.O. Box 714, Mt. Vernon, NY 10551; 120,000.

Christian Laymans Counseling Board (1970), 8141 Plainfield Drive, Charlotte, NC 28202; 1,000,000.

Christians and Jews, Natl. Conference of (1928), 43 W. 57th St., N.Y., NY 10019; 200,000.

Cincinnati, Society of the (1783), 2118 Massachusetts Ave., N.W., Wash. DC 20008; 2,500.

Circus Fans Assn. of America (1926), P.O. Box 605, Aurora, IL 60507; 2,000.

Circus Historical Society (1939), 2515 Dorset Rd., Columbus, OH 43221; 1,400.

Cities, Natl. League of (1924), City Bldg., 1612 K St., N.W., Rm. 600, Wash. DC 20006; 14,883 municipalities.

City Management Assn., International (1914), 1140 Connecticut Ave., N.W., Wash., DC 20036; 4,000.

Citizens Against Legalized Murder (1966), P.O. Box 24, N.Y., NY 10024; 6,000.

Citizens for Clean Air (1965), 572 Madison Ave., N.Y., N.Y. 10022; 3,000.

Citizens for Conservation & Trustees of the Universe (1953), 1013 S. Washington Ave., Lansing, MI 48910.

Civil Engineers, American Society of (1852), 345 East 47th St., New York, NY 10017; 68,000.

Civil Liberties Union, Amer. (1920), 22 E. 40th St., N.Y., NY 10016; 180,000.

Civil Service League, Natl. (1881), 1825 K St., N.W. Wash., DC 20006; 1,428.

Civitan International (1920), 115 North 21st St., Birmingham, AL 35203; 53,500.

Classical League, Amer. (1919), Miami Univ., Oxford, OH 45056; 3,400.

Clinical Pathologists, American Society of (1922), 2100 W. Harrison, Chicago, IL 60612; 18,000.

Coal Association, National (1917), Coal Bldg., 1130 17th St., N.W., Wash. DC 20036; 150 co's.

Cocoa Exchange, New York (1925), 127 John St., New York, NY 10038; 183.

Coffee and Sugar Exchange, New York (1882), 79 Pine St., New York, NY 10005; 342.

Collectors Association, American (1939), 4040 W. 70th St., Minneapolis, MN 55435; 2,520 agencies.

College Entrance Examination Board (1900), 888 Seventh Ave., N.Y., NY 10019; 1,652 institutions.

College Physical Education Assn. for Men, Natl. (1897), 108 Cooke Hall, Univ. of Minn., Minneapolis, MN 55455; 1,250.

College Placement Council (1956), 65 E. Elizabeth Ave., Bethlehem, PA 18018; 1,400.

College Public Relations Assn., Amer. (1917), One Dupont Circle, N.W., Wash., DC 20036; 1,334.

College of Medical Technologists, American (1942), 5608 Lane, Raytown, MO 64133; 368.

College of Physicians, American (1915), 4200 Pine St., Philadelphia, PA 19104; 20,000.

College of Surgeons, American, (1913), 55 E. Erie St., Chicago, IL 60611; 34,000.

College of Surgeons, International, (1935), 1516 N. Lake Shore Dr., Chicago, IL 60610; 13,000.

Colleges, Assn. of American (1915), 1818 R St., N.W., Washington DC 20009; 795 colleges.

Collegiate Athletic Assn., National (1906), Box 1906, Shawnee Mission, KS 66222; 770.

Collegiate Schools of Business, Amer. Assembly of (1916), 101 N. Skinker Blvd., St. Louis MO 63130; 525 schools.

Colonial Dames of America (1890), 421 East 61 St., N.Y., NY 10021; 1,500.

Colonial Dames XVII Century, National Society (1915), 1300 New Hampshire Ave., N.W., Wash., DC 20036; 8,000.

Colonial Wars, General Soc. of (1893), c/o Lawson Whitesides, 840 Woodbine Ave., Glendale, OH 45246; 4,500.

Colored Women's Clubs, Natl. Assn. of (1896), 5808-16th St., N.W., Wash, DC 20011; 100,000.

Columbia Assns. in Civil Service, Grand Council of (1938), 299 Broadway, N.Y., NY 10007; 80,000.

Columbia University Club (1901), 4 West 43rd St., New York, NY 10036; 1,900.

Commerce and Industry Association of New York (1897), 99 Church St., N.Y., NY 10007; 3,500.

Commercial Law League of America (1895), 222 West Adams St., Chicago, IL 60606; 4,900.

Commercial Travelers of America, United (1888), 632 N. Park St., Columbus, OH 43215; 255,532.

Common Cause (1970), 2030 M St., Wash., DC 20036; 200,000.

Community Councils of the City of N.Y. (1917), 201 West 80th St., N.Y., NY 10024; 210 assns.

Community Service Society of N.Y. (1939 by merger of **Assn. for Improving Condition of the Poor**, 1843 and **Charity Organization Soc. of N.Y.**, 1882); 105 E. 22nd St., N.Y., NY 10010; 286.

Composers, Authors and Publishers, American Society of (ASCAP) (1914), One Lincoln Plaza, N.Y., NY 10023; 21,266 writers and publishers.

Composers and Conductors, Natl. Assn. for American (1933), 133 West 69th St., N.Y., NY 10023; 850.

Computing Machinery, Assn. for (1947), 1133 Ave. of Americas, N.Y., NY 10036; 26,406.

Concrete Institute, American 22400 W. Seven Mile Rd., Detroit, MI 48219; 15,432.

Conference Board (1916), 845 Third Ave., N.Y., NY 10022; 4,000.

Congress of Racial Equality (1942), 200 West 135th St., New York, NY 10035; 200,000.

Conscientious Objectors, Central Committee for (1948), 2016 Walnut St., Philadelphia, PA 19103.

Conservation Engineers, Assn. of (1961), Dept. of Natural Resources, Box 450, Madison, WI 53701; 150.

Conservation Foundation (1948), 1717 Massachusetts Ave., N.W., Washington, DC 20036.

Construction Industry Manufacturers Assn. (1921), 111 E. Wisconsin Ave., Milwaukee, WI 53202; 170.

Consulting Chemists and Chemical Engineers, Assn. of (1928), 50 E. 41st St., N.Y. NY 10017; 130.

Consulting Engineers, American Institute of (1910), 345 East 47th St., New York, NY 10017; 425.

Consulting Management Engineers, Assn. of (1933), 347 Madison Ave., N.Y., NY 10017; 41 firms.

Consumer Credit Assn., International (1912), 375 Jackson Ave., St. Louis, MO 63130; 52,000.

Consumer Federation of America (1967), 1012 14th St., Wash. DC 20005; 200 organizations.

Consumer Interests, American Council on (1953), 238 Stanley Hall, Univ. of Missouri, Columbia, MO 65201; 3,000.

Consumer Protection Council, Natl. Student (1970), Villanova Univ., Villanova, PA 19085; 250.

Consumers League, Natl. (1899), 1029 Vermont Ave., NW, Washington, DC 20005; 1,200.

Consumers Union of the U.S. (1936), 256 Washington St., Mount Vernon, NY 10550; 350,000.

Consumers Unions, Internatl. Organization of (1960), 9 Emmastraat, The Hague, Netherlands; 75 members in 35 nations.

Contract Bridge League, Amer. (1937), 2200 Democrat Rd., Memphis, TN 38131; 180,000.

Cooperative League of the U.S.A. (1916), 1828 L St., NW, Wash., DC 20036; 25,000,0J0.

Corporate Responsibility, Project Center on (1970), 1525 18th St., NW, Wash., DC 20036.

Correctional Administrators, Assn. of State (1955), Box 99, Huntsville, TX 77340; 56.

Correctional Assn., Amer. (1870), 4321 Hartwick Rd., College Park, MD 20740; 10,000.

Correctional Assn. of New York (1844), 135 East 15th St., New York, NY 10003; 500.

Cosmopolitan International (1933), P.O. Box 4588, Overland Park, KS 66204; 4,207.

Cotton Council of America, Natl. (1938), 1918 North Parkway, Memphis, TN 38112; 283.

Council of Churches of City of N.Y. (1815), 475 Riverside Drive, N.Y., NY 10027; 1,700 churches.

Country Music Assn. (1958), 700 16th Ave. South, Nashville, TN 37203; 3,000.

Credit Management, National Assn. of (1896), 475 Park Ave. South, N.Y., NY 10016; 36,000.

Credit Unions, World Council of (formerly **CUNA International**) (1970), 1617 Sherman Ave., Madison, WI 53701; 55,000 credit unions.

Crime and Delinquency, Natl. Council on (1907), 411 Hackensack Ave., Hackensack, NJ 07601; 60,000.

Criminology, American Assn. of (1953), Box 1115, North Marshfield, MA 02058; 2,500.

Crop Science Soc. of America (1953), 677 S. Segoe Rd., Madison, WI 53711; 3,000.

Cryptogram Assn., American (1932), 9504 Forest Rd., Bethesda, MD 20014; 800.

Customs Brokers & Forwarders Assn. of America, Natl. (1897), 1 World Trade Center, N.Y., NY 10048; 500.

Cyprus, Sovereign Order of (1192; in U.S. 1964), 835 Seventh Ave., N.Y., NY 10019; 416.

—D—

Dairy Council, Natl. (1915), 111 No. Canal St., Chicago, IL 60606; 700.

Dairy and Food Industries Supply Assn. (1919), 5530 Wisconsin Ave., Wash. DC 20015; 400 co's.

Dairy Goat Assn., Amer. (1904), P.O. Box 186, Spindale, NC 28160; 3,250.

Dairy Science Assn., Amer. (1906), 113 N. Neil St., Champaign, IL 61820; 3,000.

Dairylea Cooperative (formerly, **Dairymen's League Coop. Assn.**) (1907), One Blue Hill Plaza, Pearl River, NY 10965; 10,490.

Data Processing Management Assn. (1951), 505 Busse Highway, Park Ridge, IL 60068; 25,000.

Daughters of the American Revolution, Natl. Society (1890), 1776 D St., N.W., Wash., DC 20006; 196,000.

Daughters of the Confederacy, United (1894), 328 North Blvd., Richmond, VA 23220; 35,000.

Daughters of the Revolution Natl. Society (1891), 132 Nassau St., New York, NY 10038; 4,800.

Daughters of the Union Veterans of the Civil War 1861-1865 (1885), 503 S. Walnut St., Springfield, IL 62704; 10,000.

Deaf, Alexander Graham Bell Assn. for the (1890), 3417 Volta Place, Wash., DC 20007; 7,000.

Deaf, Conference of Executives of American Schools for the (1868), 5034 Wisconsin Ave., N.W. Wash., DC 20016; 250.

Deaf, Convention of Amer. Instructors of the (1850), 5034 Wisconsin Ave., N.W., Wash., DC 20016; 4,500.

Deaf, National Assn. of the (1880), 814 Thayer Ave., Silver Spring, MD 20910; 1,700.

Defenders of Bataan and Corregidor, American (1946), 34 Mt. View Ave., Hurley, NY 12443; 1,560.

Delta Kappa Gamma Society (1929), P.O. Box 1589, Austin, TX 78701; 122,000.

DeMolay, Order of (1919), 201 E. Armour Blvd., Kansas City, MO 64111; 3,000,000.

Dental Association, American (1859), 211 E. Chicago Ave., Chicago, IL 60611; 118,000.

Dental Assn., Natl. (1913), P.O. Box 197, Charlottesville, VA 22902; 800.

Descendants of the Colonial Clergy, Soc. of the (1933), 255 Madison St., Dedham, MA 02026; 725.

Descendants of the Signers of the Declaration of Independence (1907), 1300 Locust St., Philadelphia, PA 19107; 721.

Desert Protective Council (1954), Box 33, Banning, CA 92220; 700.

Diabetes Assn., American (1940), 18 E. 48th St., N.Y., NY 10017; 3,100.

Dialect Society, American (1889), 1611 N. Kent St., Arlington, VA 22209; 850.

Dietetic Assn. American (1917), 620 N. Michigan Ave., Chicago, IL 60611; 24,183.

Directors Guild of America (1936), 7950 Sunset Blvd., Los Angeles, CA 90046; 3,919.

Disabled American Veterans (1921), 3725 Alexandria Pike, Cold Spring, KY 41076; 400,000.

Disabled Officers Assn. (1919), 1612 K St., NW, Wash., DC 20006; 6,022.

Divorce Reform, United States (1961), P.O. Box 243, Kenwood, CA 95452; 6,000.

Dowsers, American Soc. of (1961), 957 Norwood Ave., Schenectady, NY 12303; 1,100.

Drug, Chemical and Allied Trades Assn. (1890), 350 Fifth Ave., Suite 3014, N.Y., NY 10001; 450 firms.

Duckpin Bowling Congress, Natl. (1927), 711 14th St., N.W., Washington, DC 20005; 250,000.

Ducks Unlimited (1937), P.O. Box 66300, Chicago, IL 60666; 80,000.

Duodecimal Society of America (1944), 4728 Cielo Dr., Huntington Beach, CA 92649; 150.

Dutch Settlers Soc. of Albany (1924), 1088 Cortland St., Albany, NY 12203; 269.

— E —

Eagles, Fraternal Order of (1898), 2401 W. Wisconsin Ave., Milwaukee, WI 53233; 850,000.

Earth, Friends of the (1969), 529 Commercial St., San Francisco, CA 94111; 19,500.

Easter Seal Society for Crippled Children and Adults, Natl. (1921), 2023 W. Ogden Ave., Chicago, IL 60612.

Eastern Star, Order of the (1876), 1618 New Hampshire Ave., Wash., DC 20009; 2,000,000.

Ecological Society of America (1915), c/o Frank Mc-Cormick, Univ. of N. Carolina, Chapel Hill, NC 27514; 4,500.

Economic Assn., American (1885), 1313 21st Ave. S., Nashville, TN 37212; 24,000.

Economic Development, Committee for (1942), 477 Madison Ave., N.Y., NY 10022; 200 trustees.

Edison Electric Institute (1933), 90 Park Ave., New York, NY 10016.

Education, American Council on (1918), One Dupont Circle, Wash., DC 20036; 1,380 schools.

Education, Council for Basic (1956), 725 15th St., N.W., Washington, DC 20005; 4,350.

Education Assn., Natl. (1857), 1201 16th St., N.W., Wash., DC 20036; 1,103,485.

Education, Society for the Advancement of (1939), 1800 Broadway, N.Y., NY 10023; 11,000.

Education, Natl. Society for the Study of (1902), 5835 Kimbark Ave., Chicago, IL 60637; 5,500.

Education of Young Children, Natl. Assn. for the (1926), 1834 Connecticut Ave., N.W., Wash., DC 20009; 18,000.

Education Society, Comparative and International (1958), c/o Edward Nemeth, Teachers College, Univ. of Neb., Lincoln, NE 68508; 1,000.

Educational Broadcasters, Natl. Assn. of (1925), 1346 Connecticut Ave., N.W., Wash., DC 20036; 4,500.

Educational Exchange, Council on Internatl. (1947), 777 UN Plaza, N.Y., NY 10017; 170 orgns.

Educational Research Assn., American (1915), 1126 16th St., N.W., Wash., DC 20036; 10,500.

Educators for World Peace, Internatl. Assn. of (1969), Huntsville, AL 35762; 6,800.

Electric Railroaders Assn. (1934), 145 Greenwich St., New York, NY 10006; 3,550.

Electrical and Electronics Engineers, Institute of (1884), 345 E. 47th St., N.Y., NY 10017; 160,000.

Electrical Manufacturers Assn., Natl. (1926), 155 East 44th St., N.Y., NY 10017; 525 companies.

Electrochemical Society (1902), P.O. Box 2071, Princeton, NJ 08540; 4,014.

Electronic Industries Assn. (1924), 2001 Eye St., N.W., Washington, DC 20006; 225 firms.

Electroplaters' Society, American (1909), 56 Melmore Gardens, E. Orange, NJ 07017; 7,500.

Elks, Benevolent and Protective Order of (1868), 2750 Lakeview Ave., Chicago, IL 60614; 1,531,912.

Elks, Improved Benevolent Protective Order of (1898), 1522 N. 16th St., Phila., Pa. 19121; 450,000.

Engine and Boat Manufacturers, Natl. Assn. of (1904), Box 503, Greenwich, CT 06830; 450 co's.

Engineering Education, Amer. Society for (1893), One Dupont Circle, Wash., DC 20036; 12,500.

Engineering, Natl. Academy of (1964), 2101 Constitution Ave., N.W., Wash., DC 20418; 429.

Engineering Society, German, VDI, North American Branch (1958), 2375 India St., San Diego, CA 92101; 60,000.

Engineering Trustees, United (1904), 345 East 47th St., New York, NY 10017.

Engineers Joint Council (1941), 345 East 47th St., New York, NY 10017; 38 societies.

Engineers, Natl. Society of Professional (1934), 2029 K St., N.W., Wash. DC 20006; 70,000.

English Association, College (1939), Oakland Univ., Rochester, MI 48063; 2,600.

English-Speaking Union of the U.S. (1920), 16 East 69th., New York, NY 10021; 37,000.

Entomological Society of America (1889), 4603 Calvert Rd., College Park, MD 20740; 6,400.

Environmental Defense Fund (1967), 162 Old Town Rd., E. Setauket, NY 11733; 38,000.

Epilepsy Foundation of America (1968 merger of Epilepsy Foundation and Epilepsy Assn. of America), 1828 L St., N.W., Wash., DC 20036.

Esperanto Assn. of No. Amer. (1905), 1837 N.E. 49th Ave., Portland, OR 97213; 508.

Esperanto League for No. America (1952), 410 Darrell Rd., Hillsborough Rd., CA 94010; 716.

Esperanto Society, American Catholic (1967), 7605 Winona Lane, Sebastopol, CA 95472; 50.

Evangelicals, Natl. Assn. of (1942), 350 S. Main Pl., Wheaton, IL 60187; 3,500,000.

Evangelism Crusades, International (1959), 7970 Woodman Ave., Van Nuys, CA 91402; 50,000.

Exchange Club, National (1917), 3050 Central Ave., Toledo, OH 43606; 50,000.

Executives' Secretaries (1938), 2188 Highland Dr., Salt Lake City, UT 84106; 3,500.

Experiment in International Living (1932), Brattleboro, VT 05301; 50,000.

Eye-Bank Assn. of America (1961), 3195 Maplewood Ave., Winston-Salem, NC 27103; 60.

Eye-Bank for Sight Restoration (1944), 210 E. 64th St., N.Y., NY 10021.

— F —

Fairs & Expositions, International Assn. (1920), 500 Ashland Ave., Chicago Heights, IL 60411; 325.

Family Physicians, Amer. Academy of (formerly American Academy of General Practice) (1947), 1740 W. 92nd St., Kansas City, MO 64114; 34,067.

Family Service Assn. of America (1911), 44 East 23rd St., New York, NY 10010; 330 agencies.

Farm Bureau Federation, Amer. (1919), 225 Touhy Ave., Park Ridge, IL 60068; 2,175,780.

Farmers Cooperatives, Natl. Council of (1929), 1129 20th St., N.W., Washington, DC 20036; 100.

Farmers' Educational and Co-Operative Union of America (National Farmers Union) (1902), 12025 E. 45th Ave., Denver, CO 80201; 250,000 families.

Federal Employees, Natl. Federation of (1917), 1737 H St., N.W., Wash., DC 200; 100,000.

Federal Employees Veterans Assn. (1957), 124 Union Ave., Bala, PA 19004; 540.

Feline Society, American (1938), 41 Union Square West, New York, NY 10003; 1,000.

Feminists for Life (1973), P.O. Box 5631, Columbus, OH 43221; 250.

Fencers League of America, Amateur (1891), 249 Elton Place, Westfield, NJ 07090; 6,500.

Film Library Assn., Educational (1943), 17 W. 60th St., N.Y., NY 10023; 1,800.

Financial Analysts Federation (1947), 219 E. 42nd St., New York, NY 10017; 14,000.

Financial Executives Institute (1931), 633 Third Ave., N.Y., NY 10017; 8,000.

Fire Chiefs, International Assn. of (1873), Suite 1108, 1725 K St., N.W. Wash., DC 20006; 7,500.

Fire Fighters, International Assn. of (1918), 905 16th St., N.W., Washington, DC 20006; 155,000.

Fire Marshals Assn. of No. America (1906), 470 Atlantic Ave., Boston, MA 02210; 800.

Fire Protection Assn., Natl. (1896), 470 Atlantic Ave., Boston, MA 02210; 28,000.

Fire Protection Engineers, Society of (1950), 60 Batterymarch St., Boston, MA 02110; 1,595.

First Cavalry Division Assn. (1944), P.O. Box 5129, Ft. Hood, TX 76544; 20,000.

First Division, Society of the (1919), 5 Montgomery Ave., Philadelphia, PA 19118; 17,500.

Fisheries Society, American (1870), 1319 18th St., N.W., Wash., DC 20036; 6,000.

Fishing Institute, Sport (1949), 608 13th St., N.W., Washington, DC 20005; 30,000.

Flag Day Assn., American (1888), P.O. Box 1121, Denver, CO 80201.

Flag Foundation, U.S. (1942), 115 East 86th St., New York, NY 10028; 500.

Florists, Society of American (1902), 901 N. Washington St., Alexandria, VA 22314; 4,300.

Fluid Power Society (1960), 432 E. Kilbourn Ave., Milwaukee, WI 53202; 3,000.

Folklore Society, Amer. (1888), Box 13, Logan Hall, U. of Pa., Phila., PA 19104; 1,300 institutions.

Food Processing Machinery and Supplies Assn. (1885), 7758 Wisconsin Ave., Wash., DC 20014; 325 firms.

Footwear Industries Assn., Amer. (1922), 1611 N. Kent St., Arlington, VA 22209; 400.

Foreign Policy Assn. (1918), 345 E. 46th St., New York, NY 10017.

Foreign Press Assn. (1918), 866 Second Ave., New York, NY 10017; 304.

Foreign Relations, Council on (1921), 58 E. 68th St., N.Y., NY 10021; 1,600.

Foreign Student Affairs, Natl. Assn. for (1948), 1860 19th St., N.W. Wash., DC 20009; 2,230.

Foreign Study, Amer. Institute for (1964), 102 Greenwich Ave., Greenwich, CT 06830; 55,000.

Foreign Trade Council, Natl. (1914), 10 Rockefeller Plaza, New York, NY 10020; 600 companies.

Forensic Sciences, American Academy (1948), 44 Medical Drive, Salt Lake City, UT 84113; 1,259.

Forensic League, Natl. (1925), Ripon College, Ripon, WI 54971; 270,000.

Forest Institute, American (1943), 1619 Massachusetts Ave., Wash., DC 20036; 35,000.

Forest Products Assn., Natl. (1902), 1619 Massachusetts Ave., N.W. Wash., DC 20036; 25 assns.

Forest Products Research Society (1947), 2801 Marshall Ct., Madison, WI 53705; 4,500.

Foresters, Society of American (1900), 1010 16th St., N.W., Washington, DC 20036; 18,000.

Forestry Assn., American (1875), 1319 18th St., NW, Washington, DC 20036; 72,000.

Forty and Eight, The (1920), 777 N. Meridian St., Indianapolis, IN 46204; 70,000.

Foster Parents Plan (1937), P.O. Box 400, Warwick, RI 02886; 50,000.

Founders and Patriots of America, Order of the (1896), Suite 833, 53 State St., Boston, MA 02109; 900.

Foundrymen's Society, American (1896), Golf & Wolf Roads, Des Plaines, IL 60016; 14,000.

4-H Clubs (betw. 1901-05), Federal Extension Service, Dept. of Agric., Wash., DC 20250; 5,000,000.

French Institute (1911), 22 East 60th St., New York, NY 10022; 6,000.

French Legion of Honor, American Society of the (1922), 22 East 60th St., N.Y., NY 10022; 442.

Friendly Sons of St. Patrick, Society of the (1784), 80 Wall St., N.Y., NY 10005; 1,300.

Friends Service Committee, American (1917), 160 North 15th St., Philadelphia, PA 19102; 517.

Future Farmers of America (1928), Natl. FFA Center, Box 15160, Alexandria, VA 22309; 432,288.

Future Homemakers of America (1945), 2010 Massachusetts Ave., Wash., DC 20036; 500,000.

— G —

Game Fish Assn., International (1939), 3000 E. Las Olas Blvd., Ft. Lauderdale, FL 33316; 700 clubs.

Garden Club of America (1913), 598 Madison Ave., New York, NY 10022; 13,000.

Garden Clubs of America, Men's (1932), 5560 Merle Hay Rd., Des Moines, IA 50323; 10,000.

Garden Clubs, Natl. Council of State (1929), 4401 Magnolia Ave., St. Louis, MO 63110; 373,656.

Gas Appliance Manufacturers Assn. (1935), 1901 N. Ft. Myer Drive, Arlington, VA 22209; 440 companies.

Gas Assn., American (1918), 1515 Wilson Blvd., Arlington, VA 22209; 6,000.

Genealogical and Biographical Society, N.Y. (1869), 122 E. 58th St., N.Y., NY 10022; 825.

Genealogical Society, National (1903), 1921 Sunderland Pl., N.W., Wash., DC 20036; 3,000.

General Contractors of America, Associated (1918), 1957 E. St., N.W., Wash., DC 20006; 9,415.

Genetic Assn., American (1903), 1028 Connecticut Ave., N.W., Wash., DC 20036; 1,600.

Geographers, Assn. of American (1904), 1710 16th St., N.W., Wash., DC 20009; 6,500.

Geographic Education, Natl. Council for (1914), 115 N. Marion St., Oak Park, IL 60301; 7,000.

Geographic Society, National (1888), 17th & M Sts., N.W., Washington, DC 20036; 8,500,000.

Geographical Society, American (1852), Broadway at 156th St., New York, NY 10032; 2,550.

Geological Institute, American (1948), 2201 M St., NW, Washington, DC 20037; 18 societies.

Geological Society of America (1888), 3300 Penrose Place, Boulder, CO 80301; 9,800.

Geophysical Union, American (1919), 1707 L St., N.W., Wash., DC 20036; 10,867.

Geriatrics Society, American (1942), 10 Columbus Circle, N.Y., NY 10019; 8,000.

Gideons International (1899), 2900 Lebanon Rd., Nashville, TN 37214; 39,381.

Gifted Children, American Assn. for (1946), 15 Gramercy Park, New York, NY 10003.

Gifted Children, Natl. Assn. for (1954), 8080 Springvalley Dr., Cincinnati, OH 45236; 2,000.

Girl Scout Council of Greater N.Y. (1941), 830 3rd Ave., N.Y., NY 10017; 63,000.

Girl Scouts of the U.S.A. (1912), 830 Third Ave., N.Y., NY 10022; 3,726,000 girls.

Girls Clubs of America (1945), 133 East 62nd St., New York, NY 10021; 151,000.

Gladiolus Council, North American (1943), 30 Highland, Peru, IN 46970; 2,000.

Gold Star Mothers, American (1928), 2128 Leroy Pl., N.W., Washington, DC 20008; 18,000.

Golf Association, U.S. (1894), Golf House, Far Hills, NJ 07931; 4,000 clubs.

Goose Island Bird & Girl Watching Soc. (1960), 301 Arthur Ave., Park Ridge, IL 60068; 857.

Gospel Music Assn. (1964), 817 18th Ave., So., Nashville, TN 37203; 1,600.

Government Effort Movement (1966), 565 Washington Ave., Rochester, NY 14617; 1,340.

Governmental Research Assn. (1914), P.O. Box 387, Ocean Gate, NJ 08740; 450.

Graduate Schools in the U.S., Council of (1961), One Dupont Circle, Wash., DC 20036; 307.

Grandmother Clubs of America, Natl. Federation of (1938), 203 N. Wabash Ave., Chicago, IL 60601; 20,000.

Grand Street Boys' Association (1920), 131-135 West 56th St., N.Y., NY 10019; 3,000.

Grange, The National (1867), 1616 H St., N.W., Washington, DC 20006; 600,000.

Graphic Artists, Society of American (1920), 1083 Fifth Ave., New York, NY 10028; 232.

Graphic Arts, American Institute of (1914), 1059 Third Ave., N.Y., NY 10021; 1,700.

Green Mountain Club (1910), 27-29 Center St., Rutland, VT 05773; 3,400.

Grocery Manufacturers of America (1908), 1425 K St., Washington, DC 20005; 200 firms.

Guide Dog Foundation for the Blind (1946), 109-19 72nd Ave., Forest Hills, NY 11375; 30,000.

Guild for Infant Survival, The Internatl. (1964), 6822 Brompton Rd., Baltimore, MD 21207; 600 families.

Gyro International (1912), 1096 Mentor Ave., Painesville, OH 44077; 5,700.

— H —

Hadassah (Women's Zionist Organization of America) (1912), 65 E. 52nd St., N.Y., NY 10022; 325,000.

Handball Assn., U.S. (1951), 4101 Dempster St., Skokie, IL 60076; 15,000.

Handicapped, Federation of the (1935), 211 West 14th St., New York, NY 10011; 1,000.

Handicapped, Natl. Assn. of the Physically (1958), 6473 Grandville, Detroit, MI 48228; 30 chapters.

Harvard Club of N.Y. City (1865), 27 West 44th St., New York, NY 10036; 7,095.

Hay Fever Relief Assn., Natl. (1923), 401 Broadway, New York, NY 10013; 1,500.

Health Assn., Amer. Social (1912), 1740 Broadway, N.Y., NY 10019; 1,900.

Health Council, Natl. (1920), 1740 Broadway, New York, NY 10019; 70 organizations.

Health Insurance Assn. of America (1956), 1701 K. St., N.W., Wash., DC 20006; 319 companies.

Health Insurance Institute (1956), 277 Park Ave., New York, NY 10017; 326 companies.

Health, Physical Education & Recreation, American Assn. for (1895), 1201 16th St., Wash., DC 20036; 45,000.

Hearing Aid Society, Natl. (1952), 24261 Grand River, Detroit, MI 48219; 3,500.

Hearing and Speech Agencies, Natl. Assn. of (formerly, **American Hearing Society**) (1919), 814 Thayer Ave., Silver Spring, MD 20910; 160 agencies.

Heart Association, American (1922), 44 E. 23rd St., New York, NY 10010; 104,397.

Heating Refrigerating and Air Conditioning Engineers, Amer. Soc. of (1894), 345 E. 47th St., N.Y., NY 10017; 28,268.

Helicopter Society, Amer. (1943), 30 East 42nd St., New York, NY 10017; 2,500.

Helicopter Assn. of America (1948), 1156 15th St., NW, Wash., DC 20005; 350 companies.

Hero Fund Commission, Carnegie (1904), 1932 Oliver Bldg., Pittsburgh, PA 15222.

Hias Service, United (1884), 200 Park Ave. South, N.Y., NY 10003; 15,000.

Historians, Organization of American (1907), (formerly, **Mississippi Valley Historical Assn.**) 112 N. Bryan St., Bloomington, IN 47401; 12,000.

Historians, The Society of Amer. (1939), 706 Hamilton Hall, Columbia Univ., N.Y., NY 10027; 200.

Historic Preservation, National Trust for (1949), 748 Jackson Place, N.W., Wash., DC 20006; 30,000.

Historical Assn., American (1889), 400 A St., S.E., Washington, DC 20003; 18,000.

Historical Assn., N.Y. State (1899), Fenimore House, Cooperstown, NY 13326; 8,000.

Historical Research Associates, Western (1971), Rt. 1, Box 192, Corvallis, MT 59828; 70.

Historical Society, Illinois State (1899), Old State Capitol, Springfield, IL 62706; 4,000.

Historical Society of Iowa, State (1857), 402 Iowa Ave., Iowa City, IA 52240; 9,000.

Historical Society of Missouri, State (1898), Hitt & Lowry Sts., Columbia, MO 65201; 14,185

Historical Society, New York (1804), 170 Central Park West, N.Y., NY 10024; 1,500.

Historical Society, Ohio (1885), Ohio Historical Center, Columbus, OH 43211; 7,000.

Historical Society, Oklahoma (1893), Historical Bldg., Lincoln Blvd. at NE 19th St., Okla. City, OK 73105; 2,500.

Historical Society of Pennsylvania (1824), 1300 Locust St., Philadelphia, PA 19107; 2,600.

Historical Society, Presbyterian (1852), 425 Lombard St., Philadelphia, PA 19147; 1,200.

Hockey Assn. of the U.S., Amateur (1937), 7901 Cedar Ave., Bloomington, MN 55420; 11,000 teams.

Hockey League, National, 922 Sun Life Bldg., Montreal, Quebec, Canada.

Holland Society of N.Y. (1885), 122 East 58th St., New York, NY 10022; 932.

Holy Cross of Jerusalem, Order of (1965), 853 Seventh Ave., N.Y., NY 10019; 1,025.

Home Builders, Natl. Assn. of (1940), 1625 L St., N.W., Washington, DC 20036; 68,140.

Home Economics Assn., Amer. (1909), 2010 Massachusetts Ave., Wash., DC 20036; 50,000.

Home Improvement Council, Natl. (1956), 11 E. 44th St., N.Y., NY 10017; 1,200.

Homoeopathy, American Foundation for (1924), 910 17th St., N.W. Wash., DC 20006; 800.

Homoeopathy, American Institute of (1844), 910 17th St., N.W., Wash., DC 20006; 105.

Horatio Alger Society (1961), 4907 Allison Dr., Lansing, MI 48190; 195.

Horse Show Assn., Natl. (1883), Empire Hotel, 44 West 63rd St., N.Y., NY 10023; 14.

Horse Shows Assn., American (1917), 527 Madison Ave., N.Y., NY 10022; 13,655, 73 assns.

Horticultural Society, American (1922), Mount Vernon, VA 22121; 20,000.

Horticultural Society of New York (1902), 128 W. 58th St., New York, NY 10019; 2,800.

Horticulture Society, Pennsylvania (1827), 325 Walnut St., Philadelphia, PA 19106; 5,000.

Hospital Association, American (1898), 840 N. Lake Shore Drive, Chicago, IL 60611; 19,380.

Hospital Fund of N.Y., United (1879), 3 East 54th St., N.Y., NY 10022; 55 hospitals.

Hospital Public Relations Directors, Amer. Society for (1965), 840 N. Lake Shore Dr., Chicago, IL 60611; 800.

Hotel & Motel Assn., Amer. (1925), 888 Seventh Ave., New York, NY 10019; 7,879 hotels & motels.

Humane Assn., American (1877), P.O. Box 1266, Denver, CO 80201, 2,000,000 in 1,050 societies.

Humane Legislation, Committee for (1967), 910 16th St., NW, Wash., DC 20006; 50,000.

Humane Society of the U.S. (1954), 1604 K St., N.W., Washington, DC 20006; 35,000.

Humane Studies, Institute for (1961), 1132 Crane St., Menlo Park, CA 94025.

Humanics Foundation, American (1948), 912 Baltimore Ave., Kansas City, MO 64105; 900.

Humanist Assn., American (1941), 125 El Camino del Mar, San Francisco, CA 94121; 5,000.

Humanities, Natl. Endowment for the (1965), 806 15th St., NW, Washington, DC 20506.

— I —

Iceland Veterans (1946), 2101 Walnut St., Philadelphia, PA 19103; 1,550.

Identification, International Assn. for (1915), P.O. Box 139, Utica, NY 13503; 2,000.

Illuminating Engineering Society (1906), 345 East 47th St., New York, NY 10017; 10,632.

Illustrators, Society of (1901), 128 East 63rd St., N.Y., NY 10021; 575.

Immigration and Nationality Lawyers, Assn. of (1946) 50 Court St., Brooklyn, NY 11201; 600.

Imperial Order of the Dragon (1900, in Temple of Agric., Peking, China; commemorating China Relief Expedition), 131 War Memorial Bldg., San Francisco, CA 94102; 2,000.

Indian Rights Assn. (1882), 1505 Race St., Philadelphia, PA 19102; 2,500.

Indoor Sports Club (1930), 3445 Trumbull St., San Diego, CA 92106; 2,500.

Industrial Advertisers, Assn. of (1922), 41 East 42nd St., N.Y., NY 10017; 3,000.

Industrial Democracy, League for (1905), 112 East 19th St., New York, NY 10003; 2,000.

Industrial Designers Society of America (1964), 60 W. 55th St., N.Y., NY 10019; 750.

Industrial Engineers, Amer. Institute of (1948), 25 Technology Park, Norcross, GA 30071, 18,520.

Industrial Health Foundation (1935), 5231 Centre Ave., Pittsburgh, PA 15232; 132 companies.

Industrial Management Society (1934), 570 N.W. Highway, Des Plaines, IL 60016; 700.

Information Industry Assn. (1969), 4720 Montgomery Lane, Bethesda, MD 20014; 70 corporations.

Instrument Society of America (1945), 400 Stanwix St., Pittsburgh, PA 15222; 19,000.

Insurance Assn., American (1866), 85 John St., N.Y., NY 10038; 125 companies.

Insurance Society of N.Y. (1901), 123 William St., New York, NY 10038; 800.

Insured Savings Associations, Natl. League of (1943), 1200 17th St., N.W., Suite 500, Wash., DC 20036; 500 assns.

Intercollegiate Athletics, Natl. Assn. (1940), 1205 Baltimore St., Kansas City, MO 64105; 565 schools.

Intercollegiate (Big Ten) Conference (1896) c/o Sheraton-Chicago Hotel, Chicago, IL 60611; 10 univ.

Intercollegiate Lacrosse Assn., U.S. (1883) Hall of Fame, Johns Hopkins Univ., Baltimore, MD 21218; 110 schools.

Interfraternity Conference, Natl. (1909), P.O. Box 40368, Indianapolis, IN 46040; 48 fraternities.

Interior Designers, Amer. Institute of (1931), 730 5th Ave., N.Y., NY 10019; 6,000.

Interior Designers, Natl. Society of (1957), 315 East 62nd St., N.Y., NY 10021; 5,100.

International Education, Institute of (1919), 809 United Nations Plaza, N.Y., NY 10017.

International Law, Amer. Society of (1906), 2223 Massachusetts Ave., Wash., DC 20008; 5,600.

Investment Clubs, Natl. Assn. of (1951), 1515 E. Eleven Mile Rd., Royal Oak, MI 48067; 176,500.

Iron Founders' Society, Gray and Ductile (1928), 20611 Center Rodge Rd., Rocky River, OH 44116; 200 co's.

Iron and Steel Engineers, Assn. of (1907), 3 Gateway Center, Pittsburgh, PA 15222; 12,000.

Iron and Steel Institute, American (1908), 150 East 42nd St., New York, NY 10017; 2,500.

Italian Historical Society of America (1949), 111 Columbia Heights, Brooklyn, NY 11201; 1,870.

Italy-America Chamber of Commerce, (1887), 350 Fifth Ave., N.Y., NY 10001; 1,100.

Izaak Walton League of America (1922), 1800 N. Kent St., Arlington, VA 22209; 56,000.

— J —

Jamestowne Society (1936), 3520 Hanover Ave., Richmond, VA 23221; 1,950.

Japanese American Citizens League (1930), 22 Peace Plaza, Suite 203, San Francisco, CA 94115; 27,000.

Jaycees, United States (1920), Box 7, 21st & Main, Tulsa, OK 74102; 300,000.

Jewish Appeal, United (1939), 1290 Ave. of the Americas, N.Y., NY 10019.

Jewish Center Workers, Assn. of (1918), 15 E. 26th St., N.Y., NY 10010; 1,000.

Jewish Committee, American (1906), 165 East 56th St., New York, NY 10022; 43,000.

Jewish Congress, Amer. (1918), 15 East 84th St., New York, NY 10028.

Jewish Federations and Welfare Funds, Council of (1932), 315 Park Ave. S., N.Y., NY 10010; 235 agencies.

Jewish Historical Society, Amer. (1892) 2 Thornton Rd., Waltham, MA 02154; 3,000.

Jewish Philanthropies of N.Y., Federation of (1917), 130 East 59th St., N.Y., NY 10022; 85,000.

Jewish War Veterans of the U.S.A. (1896), 1712 New Hampshire Ave., N.W., Wash., DC 20009; 100,000.

Jewish Welfare Board, National (1917), 15 East 26th St., New York, NY 10010; 1,000,000.

Jewish Women, National Council of (1893), 1 West 47th St., New York, NY 10036; 100,000.

Job's Daughters, Internatl. Order of (1921), 1820 Douglas, Masonic Temple, Omaha, NE 68102; 125,000.

Jockey Club (1894), 300 Park Ave., N.Y., NY 10022; 73.

John Birch Society, The (1958), 395 Concord Ave., Belmont, MA 02178; 60,000 to 100,000.

Judaism, American Council for (1943), 309 Fifth Ave., N.Y., NY 10016; 15,000.

Judicature Society, American (1913), 1155 East 60th St., Chicago, IL 60637; 47,000.

Junior Achievement (1919), 909 3rd Ave., N.Y., NY 10022; 160,000 children, 23,225 advisers.

Junior College Athletic Assn., Natl. Kansas Inn, Box 1586, Hutchinson, KS 67501; 533 colleges.

Junior Colleges, American Assn. of Community and (1920), 1 Dupont Circle, Wash., DC 20036; 905 colleges.

Junior Leagues, Assn. of (1921) 825 Third Ave., N.Y., NY 10022; 105,000.

—K—

Kennel Club, American (1884), 51 Madison Ave., New York, NY 10010; 380 clubs.

Key Club International (1925), 101 E. Erie St., Chicago, IL 60611; 80,000.

Kindergarten Assn., National (1909), 23 East 16th St., New York, NY 10003.

Kiwanis International (1915), 101 East Erie St., Chicago, IL 60611; 275,000.

Knights of Columbus (1882; merged with Supreme Council Catholic Benevolent Legion, 1968), 1 Columbus Plaza, New Haven, CT 06510; 1,157,847.

Knights of Pythias (1864), 47 N. Grant St., Rm. 201 Stockton, CA 95202; 170,065.

Knights Templar of the U.S.A. (1816), 14 East Jackson Blvd., Suite 1733, Chicago, IL 60604; 375,000.

—L—

La Leche League Internatl. (1956), 9616 Minneapolis Ave., Franklin Park, IL 60131; 50,000.

La Societe de Femme (1963), 777 N. Meridian St., Indianapolis, IN 46204; 2,100.

Lambs, The (1874), 128 West 44th St., New York, NY 10036; 1,153.

Landscape Architects, American Soc. of (1899), 1750 Old Meadow Rd., McLean, VA 22,101; 3,943.

Language Teachers Associations, Natl. Federation of Modern, (1916), 212 Crosby Hall, State Univ. of N.Y., Buffalo, NY 14214.

Latin, Assn. for Promotion of Study of (1929), P.O. Box 501, Elizabeth, NJ 07207; 5,100.

Law, Ralph Nader Center for Study of Responsive (1968), P.O. Box 19367, Wash., DC 20036.

Law Institute, American, (1923), 4025 Chestnut St., Philadelphia, PA 19104; 1,480.

Law and Social Policy, Center for (1969), 1751 N St., N.W., Wash., DC 20036.

Law Libraries, American Assn. of (1906), 52 W. Jackson Blvd., Chicago, IL 60604; 1,600.

Lawn Bowls Assn., Amer. (1915), 10337 Cheryl Dr., Sun City, AZ 85351; 6,100 men, 4,000 women.

Lawn Tennis Assn., U.S. (1881), 51 E. 42nd St., N.Y., NY 10017; 62,764.

League for Another Chance (1941), 1025 Vermont Ave., N.W., Wash., DC 20008.

Learned Societies, American Council of (1919), 345 East 46 St., N.Y., NY 10017; 39 societies.

Legal Aid and Defender Assn., National (1911), 1155 East 60th St., Chicago, IL 60637; 3,000.

Legal Secretaries, Natl. Assn. of (1929), 3005 E. Skelly Dr., Suite 120, Tulsa, OK 74105; 18,500.

Legion of Valor of the U.S.A. (1890), 621 S. Taylor St., Arlington, VA 22204; 950.

Leprosy, Leonard Wood Memorial for the Eradication of (American Leprosy Foundation) (1928), 2430 Pennsylvania Ave., NW, Wash., DC 20037; 35,000.

Leprosy Missions, American (1906), 297 Park Ave. So., New York, NY 10010; 50,000.

Letter Carriers, National Association of (1889), 100 Indiana Ave., N.W., Wash., DC 20001; 212,000.

Leukemia Society of America (1949), 211 E. 43 St., N.Y., NY 10017.

Liberty Lobby (1955), 300 Independence Ave., S.E., Wash., DC 20003; 20,000.

Libraries Association, Special (1909), 235 Park Ave. South, New York, NY 10003; 7,500.

Library Association, American (1876), 50 East Huron St., Chicago, IL 60611; 33,000.

Library Assn., Home and School (1938), 500 Wallace Ave., Covington, KY 41014.

Library Assn., Medical (1893), 919 N. Michigan Ave., Chicago, IL 60611; 3,010.

Life Insurance Agency Management Assn. (1916), 170 Sigourney St., Hartford, CT 06105; 545 co's.

Life Insurance Assn. of America 1730 Pennsylvania Ave., Wash., DC 20006; 350 co's.

Life Insurance, Institute of (1939), 277 Park Ave., New York, NY 10017; 189 companies.

Life Office Management Assn. (1924), 100 Park Ave., N.Y., NY 10017; 470 companies.

Lifespan (formerly, **People Taking Action Against Abortion**) (1972), Box 847, Wayne, MI 48184; 13,000.

Life Underwriters' Assn. of the City of N.Y. (1886), 500 Fifth Ave., N.Y., NY 10036; 3,000.

Life Underwriters, National Assn. of (1890), 1922 F St., N.W., Wash., DC 20006; 115,000.

Lions International (Intl. Assn. of Lions Clubs) (1917) York & Cermak Rds., Oak Brook, IL 60521; 996,599.

Little League Baseball (1939), P.O. Box 1127, Williamsport, PA 17701; 8,870.

Log Rolling Assn., International (1926), 5855 N. Sheridan Rd., Apt. 5-J, Chicago, IL 60660; 75.

Lone Indian Fellowship (1926), 1010 Huron Ave., Sheboygan, WI 53081; 800.

Long Island Assn. of Commerce and Industry (1926), 131 Jericho Turnpike, Jericho, NY 11753; 1,065 firms.

Lubrication Engineers, Amer. Society of (1945), 838 Busse Highway, Park Ridge, IL 60068; 3,000.

Lutheran Education Assn. (1942), 7400 Augusta St., River Forest, IL 60305; 2,900.

—M—

Macaroni Manufacturers Assn., Natl. (1948), 19 S. Bothwell, Box 336, Palatine, IL 60067; 65.

Magazine Publishers Assn. (1919), 575 Lexington Ave., N.Y., NY 10022; 130 companies.

Magazine Writers, Society of (1948), c/o Overseas Press Club, 123 W. 43rd., N.Y., NY 10036; 300.

Magicians Guild of America (1944), 20 W. 40th St., N.Y., NY 10018; 85.

Magicians, Society of American (1901), Aqueduct Rd. RD-2, Peekskill, NY 10566; 2,700.

Mail Advertising Assn., Direct (1917), 230 Park Ave., New York, NY 10017; 1,600 companies.

Mammalogists, Amer. Society of (1919), c/o Museum, Oklahoma State Univ., Stillwater, OK 74074; 3,533.

Management, American Institute of (1948), 125 East 38th St., New York, NY 10016; 5,000.

Management Assn., American (1923), 135 W. 50th St., N.Y., NY 10020; 50,000.

Management Assn., National (1925), 2210 Arbor Blvd., Dayton, OH 45439; 70,000.

Management Consultants, Institute of (1968), 347 Madison Ave., N.Y., NY 10017; 625.

Management Information Systems, Society for (1968), 221 N. La Salle St., Chicago, IL 60601; 1,000.

Management, Society for Advancement of (1912), 1472 Broadway, N.Y., NY 10036; 16,000.

Manufacturers' Agents National Assn. (1947), 3130 Wilshire Blvd., Los Angeles, CA 90010; 3,200.

Manufacturers, Natl. Assn. of (1895), 277 Park Ave., New York, NY 10017; 12,500.

Manufacturing Chemists' Assn. (1872), 1825 Connecticut Ave., N.W. Wash., DC 20009; 181 co's.

Manufacturing Engineers, Soc. of (formerly, **Amer. Soc. of Tool and Engineers**) (1932), 20501 Ford Rd., Dearborn, MI 48128; 40,000.

Manuscript Society (1948), 120 Prospect Ave., Princeton, NJ 08540; 1,150.

Marathon Swimming Federation, World Professional (1963), 10295 Windstream Dr., Columbia, MD 21044; 135.

March of Dimes, Natl. Foundation (1938), 1275 Mamaroneck Ave., White Plains, NY 10605; 1,000,000 volunteers.

Marine Corps Combat Correspondents Assn. (1943), 663 5th Ave., N.Y., NY 10022; 1,400.

Marine Corps League (1923), 933 N. Kenmore St., Arlington, VA 22201; 15,000.

Marine Historical Assn. (1929), Greenmanville Ave., Mystic, CT 06355; 11,500.

Marine Society of the City of N.Y. (1770), 80 Broad St., N.Y., NY 10004; 236.

Marine Surveyors, Natl. Assn. (1960), Box 55, Peck Slip Station, New York, NY 10038; 250.

Marine Technology Society (1963), 1730 M St., N.W., Washington, DC 20036; 5,000.

Marine Underwriters, Amer. Institute of (1898), 99 John St., NY 10038; 401.

Maritime Assn. Port of N.Y. (1873), 80 Broad St., N.Y., NY 10004; 650.

Marketing Assn., American (1915), 222 S. Riverside Plaza, Chicago, IL 60606; 18,000.

Masonic Service Assn. of the U.S. (1919), 8120 Fenton St., Silver Spring, MD 20910; 44 lodges.

Masons, Ancient Accepted Scottish Rite, Northern Masonic Jurisdiction, Supreme Council 33° (1813) 33 Marrett Rd., Lexington, MA 02173.

Masons, Ancient and Accepted Scottish Rite, Southern Jurisdiction, Supreme Council (1801), 1733 16th St., N.W., Wash., DC 20009; 600,000.

Masons of the State of N.Y., Grand Lodge of Free & Accepted (1781), 71 West 23rd St., N.Y., NY 10010; 225,000.

Masons, Royal Arch, General Grand Chapter (1797) Box 5320, Lexington, KY 40505; 525,000.

Mathematical Assn. of America (1915), 1225 Connecticut Ave., Wash., DC 20036; 19,000.

Mathematical Society, American (1888), P.O. Box 6248, Providence, RI 02904; 15,000.

Mathematics, Society for Industrial and Applied (1952), 33 S. 17th St., Phila., PA 19103; 3,800.

Mathematical Statistics, Institute of (1935), c/o Leo Katz, A-426 Wells Hall, M.S.U., E. Lansing, MI 48823; 3,000.

Mattachine Society (1951), 59 Christopher St., N.Y., NY 10014; 1,000.

Mayflower Descendants, General Soc. of (1897), 4 Winslow St., Plymouth, MA 02360; 15,196.

Mayors, U.S. Conference of (1933), 1620 Eye St., N.W., Washington, DC 20006.

Mechanical Engineers, American Society of (1880), 345 East 47th St., New York, NY 10017; 60,365.

Mechanics, Assn. of Chairmen of Departments of (1969), Technological Inst., Northwestern Univ., Evanston, IL 60201; 100 institutions.

Mechanics, Junior Order of United American (1853), Lodge Rd., Posquoson, VA 23662.

Mechanics and Tradesmen of the City of N.Y., Gen. Soc. of (1785) 20 W. 44th St., N.Y., NY 10036; 200.

Mediaeval Academy of America (1925), 1430 Massachusetts Ave., Cambridge, MA 02138; 3,300.

Medical Assn., American (1847), 535 N. Dearborn St., Chicago, IL 60610; 196,000.

Medical Association, National (1895), 2109 E St., N.W., Wash., D.C. 20037; 8,000.

Medical Colleges, Assn. of American (1876), 1 Dupont Circle, Washington, DC 20036; 2,900.

Medical Record Assn., American (1928), 875 N. Michigan Ave., Chicago, IL 60611; 11,442.

Medical Technologists, American (1939), 710 Higgins Rd., Park Ridge, IL 60068; 11,270.

Medical Vocabulary, Natl. Assn. on Standard (1960), 934 Monroe St., Charlestown, IN 47111; 4,200.

Medical Women's Association, American (1915), 1740 B'way, N.Y., NY 10019; 6,000.

Medicine, New York Academy of (1847), 2 E. 103 St., New York, NY 10029; 3,118.

Men Voters of the U.S., League of (1969), P.O. Box 225, Oroville, CA 95965.

Mensa (1946), 50 East 42nd St., N.Y., NY 10017; 12,500.

Mental Health, Natl. Assn. for (1909), 1800 N. Kent St., Arlington, VA 22209; 1,000,000.

Mental Health Program Directors, Natl. Assn. of State (1963), 15 E St., NW, Wash., DC 20001; 50.

Merchant Marine Library Assn., American (1921), 1 Bowling Green, N.Y., NY 10004; 4,560.

Metal Finishers, Natl. Assn. of (1955), 248 Lorraine Ave., Upper Montclair, NJ 07043; 859 co's.

Metals, American Society for (1913), Metals Park, OH 44073; 40,000.

Meteorological Society, American (1919), 45 Beacon St., Boston, MA 02108; 9,000.

Metric Assn. (1916), Sugarloaf Star Rte., Boulder, CO 80302; 2,500.

Microbiology, American Society for (1899), 1913 1 St., N.W., Washington, DC 20006; 17,000.

Microfilm Assn., Natl. (1945), 8728 Colesville, Rd., Silver Spring, MD 20910; 5,500.

Middle East, American Friends of (1952), 1717 Massachusetts Ave., N.W., Wash., DC 20036; 300.

Military Chaplains Assn. of the U.S.A. (1925), Suite 235; 2300 Connecticut Ave N.W., Wash., DC 20008; 3,000.

Military Engineers, Society of American (1920), 800 17th St., N.W., Wash., DC 20006; 21,948.

Military Institute, American (1933), Box 568, Benj. Franklin Sta., Wash., DC 20044; 975.

Military Order of the Carabao (1900, in Manila), 4829 Fairmont Ave., Bethesda, MD 20014; 1,250.

Military Order of the Loyal Legion of the U.S. (1865), 1805 Pine St., Phila., PA 19103; 850.

Military Order of the Purple Heart (1782, by Gen. George Washington; reactivated Feb. 22, 1932; by President Herbert Hoover and Chief of Staff Douglas MacArthur), 1444 Rhode Island Ave., N.W., Wash., DC 20005; 12,000.

Military Order of the World Wars (1920), 1100 17th St., N.W., Washington, DC 20006; 10,500.

Military Surgeons of the U.S., Assn. of (1891), 8502 Connecticut Ave., Chevy Chase, MD 20015; 8,086.

Mining, Metallurgical and Petroleum Engineers, Amer. Institute of (1871), 345 East 47th St., N.Y., NY 10017; 49,394.

Mining and Metallurgical Society of America (1908), 345 E. 47th St., N.Y., NY 10017; 365.

Ministerial Assn., American (1929), 446 Salem Ave., P.O. Box 1252, York, PA 17045; 6,288.

Minute Men of America (1918), P.O. Box 505, Stuart, FL 33494; 16,000.

Missouri Valley Conference (1907), 2815 E. Skelly Dr., S-821, Tulsa, OK 74105; 10 schools.

Model Railroad Assn., Natl. (1935), Box 1328 Station C, Canton, OH 44708; 23,000.

Modern Language Assn. of America (1883), 62 Fifth Ave., N.Y., NY 10011; 30,000.

Moose, Loyal Order of (1888), Mooseheart, IL 60539; 1,229,789.

Mothers Committee, Amer. (1935), Waldorf Astoria, N.Y., NY 10022; 3,000.

Motion Picture Arts and Sciences, Academy of (1927), 9038 Melrose Ave., Los Angeles, CA 90069; 3,800.

Motion Picture Assn. of America (1922), 522 Fifth Ave., New York, NY 10036.

Motion Picture and Television Engineers, Society of (1916), 862 Scarsdale Ave., Scarsdale, NY 10583; 10,000.

Motion Pictures, Natl. Board of Review of (1940), 210 E. 68th St., N.Y., NY 10021; 250.

Motor Bus Owners, Natl. Assn. of (1926) 1025 Connecticut Ave., Wash., DC 20036; 600.

Motor Vehicle Administrators, American Assn. of (1933), 1828 L St., N.W. Wash., DC 20036; 130.

Motorcycle Assn., American (1924), 33 Collegeview Ave., Westerville, OH 43081; 200,000.

Multiple Sclerosis Society, National (1946), 257 Park Ave. South, N.Y., NY 10010; 182,000.

Municipal Finance Officers Assn. of the U.S. & Canada (1906), 1313 E. 60th St., Chicago, IL 60637; 5,187.

Municipal League, National (1894), 47 East 68th St., New York, NY 10021; 6,000.

Mural Painters, Natl. Society of (1895), 41 E. 65th St., N.Y., NY 10021; 116.

Muscular Dystrophy Associations of America, (1950), 810 7th Ave., N.Y., NY 10019; 28,000.

Museums, American Assn. of (1906), 2233 Wisconsin Ave., N.W., Wash., DC 20007; 6,000.

Music Center, American (1940), 2109 Broadway, N.Y., NY 10023; 1,000.

Music Clubs, Natl. Federation of (1898), Suite 1215, 600 S. Michigan Ave., Chicago, IL 60605; 600,000.

Music Conference, Amer. (1947) 3505 E. Kilgore Rd., Kalamazoo, MI 49002.

Music Council, National (1940), 2109 Broadway, New York, NY 10023. 60 orgns.

Music Educators National Conference (1907), 1201 16th St., N.W., Washington, DC 20036; 61,425.

Music, Natl. Assn. of Schools of (1924), One Dupont Circle, N.W., Wash., DC 20036; 399 schools.

Music Players, Amateur Chamber (1947), Box 66A, Vienna, VA 22180; 7,000.

Music Publishers' Assn., Natl. (1917), 110 E. 59th St., New York, NY 10022; 68.

Music Teachers Natl. Assn. (1876), 1831 Carew Tower, Cincinnati, OH 45202; 14,000.

Musicians, American Fed. of (1896), 220 Mt. Pleasant Ave., Newark, NJ 07104; 300,000.

Musicological Society, Amer. (1934), 201 S. 34th St., Phila., PA 19104; 2,800.

Mutual Savings Banks, National Assn. of (1920), 200 Park Ave., N.Y., NY 10017; 485 banks.

—N—

NAAFA (Natl. Assn. to Aid Fat Americans) (1969), P.O. Box 745, Westbury, NY 11590; 1,000.

Name Society, American (1953) State University College, Potsdam, NY 13676; 950.

NAPAN (Natl. Assn. for the Prevention of Addiction to Narcotics) (1960), 175 5th Ave., N.Y., NY 10010; 125.

NASCAR (Natl. Assn. for Stock Car Auto Racing) (1948), Box K, Daytona Beach, FL 32015; 16,000.

NASTAR (National Standard Program) (1968), 126 Cresta Rd.,Colorado Springs, CO 80906; 30,000.

National Assn. for the Advancement of Colored People (NAACP) (1909), 1790 Broadway, N.Y., NY 10019; 420,000.

National Guard Assn. (1878), 1 Massachusetts Ave., Washington, DC 20001; 48,500.

Nationalities Service, American Council for (1918), 20 West 40th St., N.Y., NY 10018.

Natural Science for Youth Foundation (1961), 763 Silvermine Rd., New Canaan, CT 06840; 306.

Naturalists, Assn. of Interpretive (1961), 6700 Needwood Rd., Derwood, MD 20855; 800.

Nature Conservancy (1917), 1800 N. Kent St., Arlington, VA 22209; 25,000.

Nature and Natural Resources, Internatl. Union for Conservation of (1948), Box 19347, c/o Internatl. Commission on Natl. Parks, Wash., DC 20036; 293.

Nature Study Society, American (1908), Milewood Rd., Verbank, NY 12585; 800.

Naval Architects and Marine Engineers, Society of (1893), 74 Trinity Pl., N.Y., NY 10006; 10,000.

Naval Cadets of America, Junior (1958), 117 Bridge St., Groton, CT 06340; 2,500.

Naval Destroyermen, League of (1964), Drawer M, 146 Oakland Rd., S. Windsor, CT 06074; 6,050.

Naval Engineers, American Soc. of (1888), 1012 14th St., N.W., Wash., DC 20005; 3,750.

Naval Institute, U.S. (1873), U.S. Naval Academy, Annapolis, MD 21402; 63,000.

Naval Order of the U.S. (1890), Box 894, Oakland, CA 94604; 4,000.

Naval Reserve Assn. (1954), 1913 Eye St., M.W., Washington, DC 20006; 15,000.

Navigation, Institute of (1945), 815 15th St., N.W., Wash., DC 20005; 2,800.

Navy Club of the U.S.A. (1940), 1602 Wells St., Fort Wayne, IN 46801; 4,000. **Navy Club of the U.S.A. Auxiliary, Natl.** (1940), 418 W. Pontiac St., Fort Wayne, IN 46807; 10,000.

Navy League of the U.S. (1902), 818 18th St., N.W., Washington, DC 20006; 49,556.

Navy Mother's Clubs of America (1930), P.O. Drawer E, Fremont, NE 68025; 25,000.

Near East College Association (1927), 305 E. 45th St., New York, NY 10017; 5 colleges.

Needlework Guild of America (1885), 1736 Pine St., Philadelphia, PA 19107; 400,000.

Negro Business and Professional Women's Clubs, Natl. Assn. of (1935), 3411 Lynchester Rd., Baltimore, MC 21215; 10,000.

Negro College Fund, United (1944), 55 E. 52nd St., N.Y., NY 10022; 40 colleges.

New England Historic Genealogical Society (1845), 101 Newbury St., Boston, MA 02114; 4,000.

New York Chamber of Commerce and Industry (1768), 65 Liberty St., New York, NY 10005; 3,100.

New York Clearing House (1853), 100 Broad St., N.Y., NY 10004; 12 banks.

New York-New Jersey Trail Conference (1920), 15 E. 40th St., N.Y., NY 10017; 47 clubs.

New York Press Club (formerly, **Newspaper Reporters Assn. of N.Y.C.** (1948), Hotel Roosevelt, N.Y., NY 10017; 600.

Newspaper Editors, American Society of (1922), 1350 Sullivan Trail, Easton, PA 18042; 804.

Newspaper Guild, The (1933), Suite 835, 1125 15th St., N.W., Wash., D.C. 20036; 33,000.

Newspaper Promotion Assn., International (1938), 11600 Sunrise Valley Dr., Reston, VA 22090; 1,147.

Newspaper Publishers Assn., Amer. (1887), 11600 Sunrise Valley Dr., Reston, VA 22091; 1,080 co.s.

Newspaper Publishers Assn., Natl. (1940) 2400 S. Michigan Ave., Chicago, Il 60616; 80.

Newswomen's Club of N.Y. (1922), 4 West 43 St., New York, NY 10036; 200.

Ninety-Fifth Infantry Division Assn. (1950), P.O. Box 1274; Chicago, IL 60690; 2,000.

Ninety-Nines (1929), P.O. Box 59964, Will Rogers World Airport, Oklahoma City, OK 73159; 4,400.

Ninety-ninth Infantry Division Association, (1950), Chetwynd Apts., Rosemont, PA 19010; 2,500.

Ninety-Sixth Infantry Division Association (1958), 111 S. Hudson, Denver, CO 80222; 7,000.

Non-Commissioned Officers Assn. of U.S.A. (1960), Box 2268; San Antonio, TX 78298; 123,000.

Norway, Sons of (1895), 1455 West Lake St., Minneapolis, MN 55408; 84,000.

Notaries, American Society of (1965), 810 18th St., N.W., Washington, DC 20006; 4,064.

Nuclear Society, American (1955), 244 East Ogden Ave., Hinsdale, IL 60521; 10,000.

Numismatic Assn., American (1891), Box 2366, Colorado Springs, CO 80901; 28,000.

Numismatic Society, American (1858), Broadway between 155th & 156 Sts., N.Y., NY 10032; 1,664.

Nurse Education and Service, Natl. Assn. for Practical (1941), 122 E. 42nd St., N.Y., NY 10017; 37,000.

Nurses' Assn., American (1896), 2420 Pershing Rd., Kansas City, MO 64108; 200,000.

Nurses, Assn. of Operating Room (1949), 8085 E. Prentice Ave., Englewood, CO 80110; 17,127.

Nurses, Natl. Fed. of Licensed Practical (1949), 250 West 57th St., N.Y., NY 10019; 30,000.

Nursing, Natl. League for (1952), 10 Columbus Circle, New York, NY 10019; 15,000.

Nut Growers Assn., Northern (1910), 4518 Holston Hills Rd., Knoxville, TN 37914; 1,200.

Nutrition, Amer. Institute of (1928), 9650 Rockville Pike, Bethesda, MD 20014; 1,400.

—O—

Occupational Therapy, Assn., American (1914), 6000 Executive Blvd., Rockville, MD 20852; 13,725.

Odd Fellows, Independent Order of (1819), 16 W. Chase St. Baltimore, MD 21212; 1,200,000.

Old Crows, Assn. of (1965), 1225 Martha Custis Dr., Alexandria, VA 22302; 8,000.

Old Guard of City of New York (1868), 307 W. 91st St., New York, NY 10024; 65.

Olympic Committee, U.S. (1894), 57 Park Ave., N.Y., NY 10016.

Optical Society of America (1916), 2100 Pennsylvania Ave., N.W., Wash., DC 20037; 6,200.

Optimist International (1919), 4494 Lindell Blvd., St. Louis, MO 63108; 107,680.

Optometric Assn., American (1898), 7000 Chippewa St., St. Louis, MO 63119; 17,982.

Oral Surgeons, American Society of (1918), 211 E. Chicago Ave., Chicago, IL 60611; 2,589.

Order of the Rainbow for Girls, Supr. Assembly Internatl. (1922), 315 Carl Albert Parkway, McAlester, OK 74501; 165,000.

Ordnance Assn., American (1919), 819 Union Trust Bldg., Wash., DC 20005; 36,133.

Organists, American Guild of (1896), 630 Fifth Ave., New York, NY 10020; 16,000.

Organization of American States (1890), Pan American Union, 17th & Constitution Ave., N.W., Wash., DC 20006; 24 nations.

Oriental Society, American (1842), 329 Sterling Memorial Library, New Haven, CT 06520; 1,800.

ORT Federation, American (Organization for Rehabilitation through Training) (1922), 817 Broadway, N.Y., NY 10003; 120,000.

Ornithologists' Union, American (1883), c/o Museum of Natural History, Wash., DC 20560; 3,200.

Osteopathic Association, American, (1897), 212 E. Ohio St., Chicago, IL 60611; 10,834.

—P—

Paleontological Research Institution (1932), 1259 Trumansburg Rd., Ithaca, NY 14850; 435.

Paper Institute, American (1964),· 260 Madison Ave., New York, NY 10016; 200 companies.

Paper Stationery & Tablet Manufacturers Assn. (1934), 444 Madison Ave., N.Y., NY 10022; 40 co's.

Parasitologists, American Society of (1924), 1041 New Hampshire St., Box 368, Lawrence, KS 66044; 1,700.

Parents and Teachers, Natl. Congress of (1897), 700 N. Rush St., Chicago IL 60611; 8,236, 649.

Parents Without Partners (1958), 7910 Woodmont Ave., Wash., DC 20014; 85,000.

Parking Assn. Natl. (1951), 1101 17th St., N.W., Washington, DC 20036; 1,000.

Parkinson's Disease Foundation (1957), 640 W. 168th St., N.Y., NY 10032.

Parks & Conservation Assn., National (1919), 1701 18th St., N.W., Washington, DC 20009; 50,000.

Pathologists and Bacteriologists Amer. Assn. of (1900), c/o AAPB Central Office, 9650 Rockville Pike, Bethesda, MD 20014; 1,272.

Pay Toilets in America, Committee to End (1968), 1326 Amherst Pl., Dayton, OH 45406; 1,500.

P.E.N. American Center (1922), 156 Fifth Ave., N.Y., NY 10010; 1,200.

Pen Women, Natl. League of American (1897), 1300 17th St., N.W. Wash., DC 20036; 6,000.

Pennsylvania Society (1899), Suite 594, Waldorf-Astoria Hotel, 301 Park Ave., N.Y., NY 10022; 2,400.

P.E.O. Sisterhood (1869), 3700 Grand Ave., Des Moines, IA 50312; 180,000.

Performance Improvement, Amer. Society for (formerly, **Amer. Soc. for Zero Defects**) (1966), 790 Broad St., Newark, NJ 07102; 300.

Personnel Administration, Amer. Society for, 19 Church St., Berea, OH 44017; 10,500.

Personnel and Guidance Assn., Amer. (1952), 1607 New Hampshire Ave., Wash., DC 20009; 31,173.

Personnel Women, Internatl. Assn. (1950), 358 Fifth Ave. NY 10001; 1,000.

Petroleum Geologists, American Assn. of (1917), Box 979, Tulsa, OK 74101; 15,526.

Petroleum Institute, American (1919), 1801 K St., N.W., Washington, DC 20006; 7,500.

Petroleum Landmen, Amer. Assn. (1955), 2404 Continental Life Bldg., Fort Worth, TX 76101; 4,000.

Pharmaceutical Assn., American (1852), 2215 Constitution Ave., N.W., Wash., DC 20037; 53,341.

Philatelic Americans, Society of (1894), P.O. Box 42060, Cincinnati, OH 45242; 6,000.

Philatelic Society, American (1886) P.O. Box 800, State College, PA 16801; 28,375.

Philaticians, Society of (1972), Box 150, Clinton Corners, NY 12514; 160.

Philharmonic Symphony Society of New York (1928 by merger of **Philharmonic Soc. of N.Y.**, estab. 1842, and **Symphony Soc. of N.Y.** estab. 1887), Philharmonic Hall, Lincoln Center, N.Y., NY 10023; 1,400.

Philological Assn., American (1869), U. of Illinois, Foreign Languages Bldg., Urbana, IL 61801; 2,800.

Philological Association of the Pacific Coast, (1899), Dept. of For. Languages, San Fernando Valley State College, Northridge, CA 91324; 1,000.

Philosophical Assn., American (1900), Hamilton College, Clinton, NY 13323; 5,000.

Philosophical Society, American (1743), 104 S. 5th St., Philadelphia, PA 19106; 500.

Photographers of America, Professional (1880), 1090 Executive Way, Oak Leaf Commons, Des Plaines, IL 60018; 13,500.

Photographers in Communications, Society of (formerly, **Society of Magazine Photographers**) (1944), 60 East 42nd St., N.Y. NY 10017; 950.

Photographic Society of America (1934), 2005 Walnut St., Philadelphia, PA 19103; 15,000.

Physical Society, American (1899), 335 E. 45th St., N.Y., NY 10017; 28,000.

Physical Therapy Association, American (1921), 1156 15th St., N.W., Wash., DC 20005; 17,000.

Physics, American Institute of (1931), 335 East 45th St., New York, NY 10017; 58,000.

Physiological Society, American (1887), 9650 Rockville Pike, Bethesda, MD 20014; 4,000.

Pilgrim Society (1820), Pilgrim Hall, 75 Court St., Plymouth, MA 02360; 600.

Pilgrims of the United States (1903), 74 Trinity Pl., New York, NY 10006; 1,000.

Pilot Club International, (1921), Pilot Bldg., 244 College St., Macon, GA 31208; 17,500.

Pioneer Women (1926), 315 5th Ave., N.Y., NY 10016; 50,000.

Planned Parenthood Federation of America (1922 as **Amer. Birth Control League**; 1939, **Birth Control Fed. of Amer.**; renamed 1942) 810 7th Ave., N.Y., NY 10019; 190 Affiliates.

Planners, Amer. Institute of (1917), 917 15th St., N.W., Washington, DC 20005; 8,300.

Planning Assn., Natl. (1934), 1606 New Hampshire Ave., N.W., Washington, DC 20009; 3,500.

Planning Officials, American Society of (1934), 1313 E. 60th St., Chicago, IL 60637; 10,000.

Plastics Engineers, Society of (1942), 656 W. Putnam Ave., Greenwich, CT 06830; 16,500.

Plastics Industry, Society of (1937), 250 Park Ave., New York, NY 10017; 1,200.

Platform Assn., Internatl. (formerly **Amer. Lyceum Assn.**) (1831), 2564 Bershire Rd., Cleveland Heights, OH 44106; 12,000.

Plattsburg Society of (1935), c/o James MacLean, 14 Farmstead Lane, Brookville, NY 11545.

Podiatry Association, American (1912), 20 Chevy Chase Circle, N.W., Wash., DC 20015; 6,000.

Poetry Day Committee, Natl. (1965), 1110 N. Venetian Dr., Miami Beach, FL 33139; 10,000.

Poetry Society of America (1910), 15 Gramercy Park, N.Y., NY 10003; 700.

Poets, Academy of America (1934), 1070 Madison Ave., N.Y., NY 10028; 73.

Polar Society, American (1934); 98-20 62nd Dr., Apt. 7H, Rego Park, NY 11374; 2,500.

Police American Federation of (1966), 1100 NE 125th St., N. Miami, FL 33161; 33,000.

Police, International Assn. of Chiefs of (1893), Eleven Firstfield Rd., Gaithersburg, MD 20015; 9,500.

Police Officers Assn. of American, Natl. (1955), Police Hall of Fame Bldg., Venice, FL 33595; 35,000.

Policy Placers, Checkers and Raters of America, Natl. Assn. of (1968), 41-43 John St., N.Y., NY 10038; 5,031.

Polish Army Veterans Assn. of America (1921), 17 Irving Pl., N.Y., NY 10003; 9,500.

Polish Legion of American Veterans (1921), 3024 N. Laramie Ave., Chicago, IL 60641; 10,000.

Polish Natl. Alliance of Brooklyn (1903), 155 Noble St., Brooklyn, NY 11222; 16,388.

Political Items Collectors, Amer. (1945), 66 Golf St., Newington, CT 06111; 1,700.

Political Science, Academy of (1880), 49 Claremont Ave., N.Y., NY 10027; 10,200.

Political Science Assn., American (1903), 1527 New Hampshire Ave., N.W., Wash., DC 20036; 12,000.

Political and Social Science, Amer. Academy of (1889), 3937 Chestnut St., Philadelphia, PA 19104; 22,000.

Polo Association, U.S. (1890), Suite 706, 1301 W. 22nd St., Oak Brook, IL 60521; 1,750.

Population Assn. of America (1932), Box 14182, Benjamin Franklin Sta., Wash., DC 20044; 2,300.

Portuguese Continental Union of the U.S.A. (1929), 899 Boylston St., Boston, MA 02115; 9,276.

Postal Clerks, United Federation of (1906), 817 14th St., N.W., Washington, DC 20005; 285,000.

Postmasters of the U.S., Natl. Assn. of (1898), 425 13th St., N.W., Washington, DC 20004; 28,000.

Postmasters of the U.S., National League of (1904), 955 L'Enfant Plaza, S.W., Wash., DC 20024; 15,000.

Poultry Science Assn. (1908), c/o Dr. C. B. Ryan, Texas A & M Univ., College Sta., TX 77843; 1,700.

Power Boat Assn., American (1903), 22811 Greater Mack, St. Clair Shores, MI 48080; 7,275.

Power Conference, American (1938), Illinois Inst. of Technology, 10 W. 32nd St., Chicago, IL 60616.

Power Engineers, Natl. Assn. of (1882) 176 W. Adams St. Chicago, IL 60603; 12,296.

Power Squadron, U.S. (1914), 50 Craig Rd., Montvale, NJ 07645; 88,000.

Precancel Collectors, Natl. Assn. of (1950), 5121 Park Blvd., Wildwood, NJ 08260; 4,000.

Press Club of America, Overseas (1939), 1271 Ave. of the Americas, New York, NY 10020; 2,200.

Press Club, Natl. (1908), 529 14th St., N.W., Wash. DC 20004; 4,600.

Press Institute, International (1951), Münstergasse 9,8001 Zurich, Switzerland; 1,700.

Press Photographers Assn., N.Y. (1913), 150 Nassau St., N.Y., NY 10038; 300.

Press and Union League Club (1818); P. O. 7000 Montgomery, AL 36107; 696.

Press Women, National Fed. of (1937) 1105 Main St., Blue Springs, MO 64015; 3,700.

Princeton Club of N.Y. (1899), 15 West 43rd St., New York, NY 10036; 5,000.

Production and Inventory Control Society, Amer. (1957), Suite 504, 2600 Virginia Ave., N.W., Wash., DC 20037; 9,000.

Propeller Club of the U.S. (1927), 17 Battery Pl, New York, NY 10004; 12,500.

Psychiatric Association, American, (1844), 1700 18th St., N.W., Washington, DC 20009; 21,000.

Psychoanalytic Assn., American (1911), 1 East 57th St., N.Y., NY 10022; 1,333.

Psychological Assn., American, (1892), 1200 17th St., N.W., Wash., DC 20036; 34,000.

Psychological Assn. for Psychoanalysis, Natl. (1948), 150 W. 13th St., N.Y., NY 10011; 156.

Psychological Minorities, Soc. for the Aid of (1969), 42-25 Hampton St., Elmhurst, NY 11373; 150.

Psychotherapy Assn., American Group (1942), 1865 Broadway, N.Y., NY 10023; 2,700.

Public Health Assn., American (1872), 1015 18th St., NW, Wash., DC 20036; 26,610.

Public Relations Society of America (1948), 845 Third Ave., New York, NY 10022; 7,062.

Public Welfare Assn., American (1936), 1313 E. 60th St. Chicago, IL 60637; 7,900.

Publishers, Assn. of American (1970), One Park Ave., N.Y., NY 10016; 260 companies.

Pulp and Paper Industry, Technical Assn. of the (1915), 360 Lexington Ave., N.Y., NY 10017; 13,000.

—Q & R—

Quality Control, Amer. Society for (1946), 161 W. Wisconsin Ave., Milwaukee, WI 53203; 20,400.

Racing Commissioners, National Assn. of State (1935), P.O. Box 4216, Lexington, KY 40504; 285.

Racquetball Assn., Natl. (1973), 4101 Dempster St., Skokie, IL 60067; 3,500.

Radio Free Europe (1949), 2 Park Ave., N.Y., NY 10016; 1,543.

Radiological Society of North America (1915), 713 E. Genesee St., Syracuse, NY 13210; 6,500.

Radio Liberty (1951), 30 East 42nd St., N.Y., NY 10017.

Radio Relay League, American (1914), 225 Main St., Newington, CT 06111; 100,000.

Radio and Television Society, International, (1939), 420 Lexington Ave., N.Y., NY 10017; 1,200.

Radio Union, International Amateur (1925), 225 Main St., Newington, CT 06111; 84 societies.

Rail Passengers, Natl. Assn. of (1965), 417 New Jersey Ave., S.E., Wash., DC 20023; 56,000.

Railroads, Assn. of American (1934), 1920 L St., Rm. 211, Wash. DC 20036; 172 railroads.

Railway Engineering Assn., American (1899), 59 E. Van Buren St., Chicago, IL 60605; 3,400.

Railway Progress Institute (1908), 801 N. Fairfax St., Alexandria, VA 22314; 160 co's.

Rainbow Division Veterans, Natl. Assn. (1918), 1033 White Oak Ave., SW, Atlanta, GA 30310; 4,500.

Range Management, Society for (1948), 2120 S. Birch St., Denver, CO 80222; 4,500.

Real Estate Investment Funds, Natl. Assn. of (1960), 1101 17th St., N.W., Wash., DC 20036; 310.

Realtors, Natl. Assn. of (formerly, **Natl. Assn. of Real Estate Boards**) (1908), 155 E. Superior St., Chicago, IL 60611; 400,000.

Reconcilation, Fellowship of (1915), Box 271, Nyack, NY 10960; 23,467.

Recording Industry Assn. of America (1952), 1 East 57th St., New York, NY 10022; 51 firms.

Records Management Assn., Amer. (1956), Suite 823, 24 N. Wabash Ave., Chicago, IL 60602; 2,150.

Recreation and Park Assn., Natl. (1965), 1601 N. Kent St., Arlington, VA 22209; 14,829.

Red Cross, American National (1881), 17th & D Sts., N.W., Wash., DC 20006; 36,423,804.

Red Men, Improved Order of (1834), 1525 West Ave., Box 683, Waco, TX 77603; 67,000.

Regional Plan Assn. (1929), 235 East 45th St., N.Y., NY 10017; 4,000.

Rehabilitation Assn., Natl. (1925), 1522 K St., N.W., Washington, DC 20005; 30,000.

Religion, American Academy of (1909), Fla. State Univ., Tallahassee, FL 32306; 3,978.

Renaissance Society of America (1954), 1161 Amsterdam Ave., New York, NY 10027; 3,250.

Rescue Committee, Internatl. (1933), 386 Park Ave., SO., N.Y., NY 10016.

Reserve Officers Assn. of the U.S. (1922), 1 Constitution Ave., N.E., Wash., DC 20002; 73,000.

Restaurant Assn., Natl. 1919), 1530 N. Lake Shore Dr., Chicago, IL 60610; 11,251.

Retail Druggists, National Assn. of (1898), 1 East Wacker Dr., Chicago, IL 60601; 30,000.

Retail Grocers, National Association of (1893), 2000 Spring Rd., Oak Brook, IL 60521; 40,000.

Retail Merchants, Natl. Retail (1911), 100 West 31st St., N.Y., NY 10001; 26,000 stores.

Retarded Children, Natl. Assn. for (1955), 2709 Ave. E. East, Arlington, TX 76011; 210,000.

Retired Assn. for the Uniformed Services (1970), 4004 Hillsboro Rd., Nashville, TN 37215; 24,176.

Retired Officers Assn., (1929), 1625 Eye St., N.W., Washington, DC 20006; 165,000.

Retired Persons, Amer. Assn. of (1958), 1225 Connecticut Ave., N.W., Wash., DC 20036; 5,000,000.

Retired Teachers Assn., Natl., (1947), 1225 Connecticut Ave., N.W., Washington DC 20036; 362,555.

Retreads (World War I & World War II) (1947), 40-07 154th St., Flushing, NY 11354; 1,400.

Revolver Assn., U.S. (1900), 59 Alvin St., Springfield, MA 01104; 1,300.

Rhodes Scholars, Assn. of Amer. (1907), 1100 Phila. Natl. Bank Bldg., Phila., PA 19107; 1,493.

Rice Council for Market Development (1959), 3917 Richmond Ave., Houston, TX 77035; 19,000.

Rifle Assn. of America, Natl. (1871), 1600 Rhode Island Ave., N.W., Wash., DC 20036; 1,000,000.

Road Builders' Assn., American (1902), 525 School St., S.W. Washington, DC 20024; 6,000.

Rocketry, National Assn. of (1957), P.O. 178, McLean, VA 22101; 5,000.

Rodeo Cowboys Assn. (1936), 2929 W. 19th Ave., Denver, CO 80204; 3,144.

Roller Skating Assn., U.S. Amateur (1942), 152 W. 42nd St., New York, NY 10036; 11,000.

Roller Skating Rink Operators Assn. of America (1937), 7700 A St., Lincoln, NE 68510; 769 rinks.

Rose Society, American (1899), 4048 Roselea Pl., Columbus, OH 43214; 16,000.

Rosicrucian Fraternity (1614 in Germany, 1859 in U.S.), Beverly Hall, Quakertown, PA 18951.

Rosicrucian Order, AMORC (1915), Rosicrucian Park, San Jose, CA 95191; 120,000.

Rosicrucians, Society of (1909), 321 West 101st St., New York, NY 10025.

Rotary International (1905), 1600 Ridge Ave., Evanston, IL 60201; 732,000.

Round Table International (1922), 279 Bayview Ave., San Jòse, CA 95127; 1,000.

Rowing Assn., Intercollegiate (1895), Hotel Manhattan, 8th Ave. at 44th St., N.Y., NY 10036; 5.

Royal Arcanum, Supreme Council of the (June 23, 1877), 61 Batterymarch St., Boston, MA 02110; 30,918.

Rubber Manufacturers Assn., (1915), 444 Madison Ave., New York, NY 10022; 200 firms.

Ruritan National (1928), Box 487, Dublin, VA 24084; 37,000.

Russian Orthodox Clubs, Federated (1927), 84 East Market St., Wilkes-Barre, PA 18701; 4,500.

— S —

Safety Council, National (1913), 425 N. Michigan Ave., Chicago, IL 60611; 15,000.

Safety Engineers, American Society of (1911), 850 Busse Highway, Park Ridge, IL 60068; 11,000.

St. Andrew's Society of the State of N.Y. (1756), 281 Park Ave. South, N.Y., NY 10010; 1,107.

St. David's Society of the State of N.Y. (1835), 71 West 23rd St., N.Y., NY 10010; 250.

St. George's Society of N.Y. (1770), 15 East 26th St., New York, NY 10010; 832.

St. Paul, National Guilds of (1937), 601 Hill 'N Dale, Lexington, KY 40503; 13,750.

Sales Executives Club of N.Y. (1932), Hotel Roosevelt, N.Y., NY 10017; 3,500.

Salt Institute (1914), 206 N. Washington St., Alexandria, VA 22314; 25 companies.

Salvation Army (1880 in U.S.), 120 W. 14th St., N.Y., NY 10011; 335,684 in U.S.

Sane World, A Citizen's Organization for a (1957), 318 Massachusetts Ave., N.E., Wash., DC 20002; 25,000.

Save-the-Redwoods League (1920), 114 Sansome St., San Francisco, CA 94104; 55,000.

School Administrators, American Assn. of (1865), 1801 N. Moore St., Arlington, VA 22209; 20,000.

School Boards Assn., Natl. (1940), 800 State Natl. Bank Plaza, Evanston, IL 60201; 77,000.

School, College and University Staffing, Assn. for (1935), 14 E. Chcolate Ave., Box G, Hershey, PA 17033; 534 colleges, 395 schools.

School Counselor Assn., American (1952), 1607 New Hampshire Ave., N.W., Wash., DC 20009; 13,000.

School Principals, Natl. Assn. of Secondary (1916), 1904 Association Dr., Reston, VA 22091; 30,000.

Schools and Colleges, Amer. Council on (1929), 446 Salem Ave., Box 1252, York, PA 17405; 123 schools.

Schweitzer, Albert, Fellowship (1948), 866 United Nations Plaza, N.Y., NY 10017.

Schweitzer, Albert, Friendship House (1967), c/o Erica Anderson, Hurlburt Rd., Great Barrington, MA 01230; 50,000.

Science, Amer. Assn. for the Advancement of (1848), 1515 Massachusetts Ave., N.W., Wash., DC 20005; 127,402.

Science Service (1921), 1719 N St., N.W., Washington, DC 20036.

Science Teachers Assn., Natl. (1944), 1201 16th St., N.W., Wash., DC 20036; 20,000.

Science Writers, Natl. Assn. of (1934), Box H, Sea Cliff, NY 11579; 922.

Sciences, National Academy of — National Research Council (1863), 2101 Constitution Ave., N.W., Wash., DC 20418; 1,012.

Sciences, New York Academy of (1817), 2 East 63rd St., N.Y., NY 10021; 25,000.

Scientific Apparatus Makers Assn. (1918), 1140 Connecticut Ave., N.W., Wash., DC 20036; 200.

Scientists, Federation of American (1946), 203 C St., N.E., Washington, DC 20002; 5,500.

Scientists' Institute for Public Information (1963), 212 San Jose St., Salinas, CA 93901; 30.

Scottish Clans, Order of (1878), 111 Washington St., Brookline, MA 02146; 10,000.

Screen Actors Guild (1933), 7750 Sunset Blvd., Hollywood, CA 90046; 26,000.

Sculpture Society, Natl. (1893), 250 E. 51st. St., New York, NY 10022; 350.

Seamen's Service, United (1942), 17 Battery Place, N.Y., NY 10004.

Secretaries Assn., Natl. (1942), 616 E. 63 St., Kansas City, MO 64110; 29,000.

Secularists of America, United (1946), 377 Vernon St., Oakland, CA 94610; 950.

Securities Industry Assn. (1972 consolidation of **Investment Banker Assn.** and **Assn. of Stock Exchange Firms**), 20 Broad St., N.Y., NY 10005; 850 firms.

Security Industrial Assn., National (1944), 740 15th St., N.W., Wash., DC 20005; 275.

Seeing Eye, The (1929), Morristown, NJ 07960; 26,000.

Semantics, Institute of General (1938), White Hollow Rd., Lime Rock, CT 06039; 1,000.

Separation of Church and State, Americans United for (1947), 8120 Fenton St., Silver Spring, MD 20910; 130,000.

Separationists, Society of (1963), P.O. Box 2117, Austin, TX 78767; 35,000 families.

Sertoma International (1912) 1900 \E. Meyer Blvd., Kansas City, MO 64132; 29,000.

Settlements and Neighborhood Centers, Natl. Fed. of, (1911), 232 Madison Ave., N.Y., NY 10016; 1,350.

Sex Information & Education Council of the U.S. (SIECUS) (1964), 1855 Broadway, N.Y., NY 10023; 1,000.

Shade Tree Conference, Internatl. (1924), P.O. Box 71, Urbana, IL 61801; 2,500.

Sheriffs', Assn., Natl. (1940), Suite 209, 1250 Connecticut Ave., N.W., Wash., DC 20036; 31,000.

Shipbuilders Council of America (1921), Watergate 600, Wash., DC 20037; 40 co's.

Shoe Retailers Assn., Natl. (1912), 200 Madison Ave., New York, NY 10016; 3,200.

Shore & Beach Preservation Assn., Amer. (1926), 10 Rickenbacker Causeway, Miami, FL 33149; 600.

Showmen's League of America (1913), 300 W. Randolph St., Chicago, IL 60606; 1,350.

Shrine, Imperial Council of the A.A. Order of Nobles of the Mystic (1872), 323 N. Michigan Ave., Chicago, IL 60601; 896,750.

Sierra Club (1892), 1050 Mills Tower, 220 Bush St., San Francisco, CA 94107; 140,000.

Sigma Delta Chi, Professional Journalistic Soc. (1909), 35 E. Wacker Dr. Chicago, IL 60601; 55,000.

Silurians, Society of the (1924), 103 Park Ave., N.Y., NY 10017; 722.

Spelling Council, Phonemic (merged Simpler Spelling Assn.) (1971), Lake Placid Club, NY 12946; 100.

Skate Sailing Assn. of America (1922), 4 Manor Rd., Livingston, NJ 07039; 120.

Skating Union of the U.S., Amateur (1907), 4423 W. Deming Pl., Chicago, IL 60639; 4,000.

Skeet Shooting Assn., National (1946), Linwood Bldg., 2608 Inwood Rd., Dallas, TX 75235; 18,000.

Ski Assn., United States, (1904), 1726 Champa St., Denver, CO 80202; 130,000.

Small Business, Amer. Federation of (1963), 407 S. Dearborn, Chicago, IL 60605; 5,000.

Small Business Assn., Natl. (1937), 1225 19th St., N.W., Washington, DC 20036; 40,000.

Smoking & Health, Natl. Clearinghouse for (1965), 5401 Westbard Ave., Bethesda, MD 20016.

Soaring Society of America (1932), P.O. Box 66071, Los Angeles, CA 90066; 11,700.

Soccer Football Assn., U.S. (1913), 350 5th Ave., Suite 4010, N.Y., NY 10001; 42 state assns.

Social Biology, Society for the Study of (1926), N.Y. Psychiatric Institute, 722 W. 168th St., N.Y., NY 10032; 400.

Social Health Assn., American (1912), 1740 Broadway, New York, NY 10019; 1,200.

Social Science Research Council (1923), 230 Park Ave., New York, NY 10017; 30.

Social Sciences, Natl. Institute of (1899) 545 Madison Ave., NY., NY 10022; 721.

Social Welfare, Internatl. Council on (1928), 345 E. 46th St., N.Y., NY 10017; 68 natl. committees.

Social Welfare, Natl. Conference on (1874), 22 West Gay St., Columbus, OH 43215; 7,000.

Social Work Education, Council on (1952), 345 East 46th St., New York, NY 10017; 5,203.

Social Workers, National Assn., of (1955), 600 Southern Bldg., 15th & H Sts., NW, Wash., DC 20005; 60,000.

Sociological Assn., American (1905), 1722 N St., N.W., Wash., DC 20036; 14,140.

Softball Assn., Amateur (1933), 2801 N.E. 50th St., Oklahoma City, OK 73111; 1,500,000 players.

Soft Drink Assn., National (1919), 1101 16th St., N.W., Washington, DC 20036; 1,896.

Soil Conservation Society of America (1946), 7515 N.E. Ankeny Rd., Ankeny, IA 50021; 14,500.

Soil Science Soc. of America (1936), 677 S. Segoe Rd., Madison, WI 53711; 5,000.

Sojourners, National (1919), 4600 Duke St., Alexandria, VA 22304; 10,000.

Soldier's, Sailor's, and Airmen's Club (1919), 283 Lexington Ave., N.Y., NY 10016.

Sonic Boom, Citizens League Against the (1967), 19 Appleton St., Cambridge, MA 02138; 4,000.

Sons of the American Legion (1933), P.O. Box 1055, Indianapolis, IN 46206; 18,200.

Sons of the American Revolution, National Society (1889), 2412 Massachusetts Ave., N.W., Wash., DC 20008; 20,000.

Sons of Italy in America, Order (1905), 1226 S. Broad St., Philadelphia, PA 19146; 250,000.

Sons of Poland, Assn. of the (1903), 655 Newark Ave., Jersey City, NJ 07305; 20,000.

Sons of the Revolution (1876), Fraunces Tavern, 54 Pearl St., N.Y., NY 10004; 6,500.

Sons of Sherman's March to the Sea (1966), 1725 Farmers Ave., Tempe, AZ 85281; 144.

Sons of Shillelagh, The Order of the Friendly (1963), 1 Oak St., Old Bridge, NJ 08857; 400.

Sons of Union Veterans of the Civil War (1881), Box 24, Federal Bldg., Gettysburg, PA 17325; 3,000.

Soroptimist Federation of the Americas (1921), 1616 Walnut St., Philadelphia, PA 19103; 32,000.

Southern Christian Leadership Conference (1957), 334 Auburn Ave., N.E., Atlanta, GA 30303; 243 affiliate organizations.

Southern Regional Council (1944), 52 Fairlie St., N.W., Atlanta, GA 30303; 100.

Southern Society, N.Y. (1886), Plaza Hotel, Fifth Ave. at 59th St., N.Y., NY 10019; 900.

Spanish War Veterans, United (1899), P.O. Box 1915, Washington, DC 20013; 950.

Speech Communication Assn. (formerly, Speech Assn. of America) (1914), Statler Hilton Hotel, N.Y., NY 10001; 8,000.

Speech and Hearing Assn., Amer. (1925), 9030 Old Georgetown Rd., Wash., DC 20014; 15,500.

Speleological Society of America (1969), Dundridge, Rt. 1, Gunbarrel Lane, White Post, VA 22663; 3,800.

Speleological Society, Natl. (1939), Cave Ave., Huntsville, AL 35810; 4,500.

Sports Car Club of Amer. (1944), 2186 S. Holly, Denver, CO 80222; 23,000.

Sports Fans of America, Professional (1962), 324 Trade Sq. West, Troy, OH 45373; 109.

Stamp Dealers' Association, American (1914), 147 W. 42nd St., New York, NY 10036; 1,000.

Standards Institute, American National (1918), 1430 Broadway, New York, NY 10018.

State & Local History, American Assn. for (1940), 1315 8th Ave., So., Nashville, TN 37203; 4,000.

State Communities Aid Assn. (1872), 105 E. 22nd St., New York, NY 10010; 000.

State Governments, Council of (1933), Iron Works Pike, Lexington, KY 40505.

State High School Assns., Natl. Federation of (1920), 400 Leslie St., Elgin, IL 60014; 50 states.

State Legislative Leaders, Natl. Conference of (1959), 411 E. Mason St., Milwaukee, WI 53202; 47.

State Parks, Natl. Conference on (1921), 1601 N. Kent St., Arlington, VA 22209; 657.

State Universities and Land-Grant Colleges, Natl. Assn. of (1871), One Dupont Circle, N.W., Wash., DC 20036.

Statistical Assn., American (1839), 806 15th St., N.W., Washington, DC 20005; 10,500.

Steamship Historical Society of America (1935), 414 Pelton Ave., Staten Island, NY 10310; 1,735.

Steel Construction, American Institute of (1921), 101 Park Ave., N.Y., NY 10017; 349 companies.

Steel Founders' Society of America (1902), 20611 Center Ridge Rd., Rocky River, OH 44116; 126 foundries.

Steeplechase and Hunt Assn., Natl. (1895), Box 308, Elmont, NY 11003; 3,000.

Sterilization, Association for Voluntary (1943), 14 W. 40th St., N.Y., NY 10018; 7,500.

Steuben Society of America (1919), 369 Lexington Ave., New York, NY 10017.

Stock Exchange, American (1908), 86 Trinity Pl., New York, NY 10006; 852.

Stock Exchange, Midwest (1882), 120 S. LaSalle St., Chicago, IL 60603; 435.

Stock Exchange, N.Y. (1972), 11 Wall St., New York, NY 10005; 1,366.

Stock Exchange, Philadelphia-Baltimore-Washington (1790), 17th St. and Stock Exchange Pl., Phila., PA 19103; 450.

Student Assn., National (1947), 2115 S St., N.W., Washington, DC 20008; 500 colleges.

Student Councils, Natl. Assn. of (1931), 1904 Association Dr., Reston, VA 22091; 6,000 high schools.

Students of German, Natl. Federation of (1967), 339 Walnut St., Philadelphia, PA 19106; 15,000.

Sugar Association, (1949), 254 West 31st St., N.Y., NY 10001; 24.

Sugar Brokers Assn., National (1903), 76 Beaver St., N.Y., NY 10005; 301.

Sunbathing Assn., American (1929), 810 N. Mills Ave., Orlando, FL 32803; 20,000.

Sunday League (1933), 279 Highland Ave., Newark, NJ 07104; 35,000.

Sunday School Union, American (1817), 1816 Chestnut St. Phila., PA 19103; 1,586 schools.

Surveying and Mapping, American Congress on (1941), Suite 430, Woodward Bldg., 733 15th St., N.W., Washington, DC 20005; 6,000.

Symphony Orchestra League, American (1942), P.O. Box 66, Vienna, VA 22180; 2,000.

Systems Management, Assn. for (1947), 24587 Bagley Rd., Cleveland, OH 44138; 12,000.

—T—

Table Tennis Assn., U.S. (1933), Box 815, Orange, CT 06477; 5,500.

Tax Accountants, Natl. Assn. of Enrolled Federal (1960), 6108 N. Harding Ave., Chicago, IL 60659; 500.

Tax Administrators, Federation of (1937), 1313 East 60th St., Chicago, IL 60637.

Tax Assn., Natl.-Tax Institute of America (merged 1973), 21 E. State St., Columbus, OH 43215; 2,500.

Tax Foundation (1937), 50 Rockefeller Plaza, N.Y., NY 10020; 1,500.

Tea Assn. of the U.S.A. (1899), 230 Park Ave., N.Y., NY 10017; 250.

Tea Council of the U.S.A. (1953), 230 Park Ave., N.Y., NY 10017.

Teachers' Agencies, Natl. Assn. of (1915), 1825 K St., NW, Wash., DC 20006; 60.

Teachers, American Federation of (1916), 1012 14th St., N.W., Washington, DC 20005; 300,000.

Teachers of English, Natl. Council of (1911), 1111 Kenyon Rd., Urbana, IL 61801; 33,467.

Teachers of French, Amer. Assn. of (1927), 59 E. Armory Ave., Champaign, IL 61820; 11,200.

Teachers of German, Assn. of (1927), 339 Walnut St., Phila., PA 19106; 8,500.

Teachers of Spanish and Portuguese, Amer. Assn. of (1917), Wichita State Univ., Wichita, KS 67208; 14,000.

Technical Communication, Society for (formerly, **Society of Technical Writers and Publishers**) (1957), 1010 Vermont Ave., N.W., Wash., DC 20005; 3,000.

Television Arts and Sciences, Natl. Academy of (1946), 291 S. La Cienega, Beverly Hills, CA 90211; 7,000.

Television Bureau of Advertising (1955), 1 Rockefeller Plaza, N.Y., NY 10020; 350.

Television and Radio Arts, Amer. Federation of (1937), 1350 Ave. of Americas, N.Y., NY 10019; 29,000.

Telluride Assn. (1911), 217 West Ave., Ithaca, NY 14850; 75.

Tennis League, Youth (1968), 1701 Vandalia, Collinsville, IL 62234; 750.

Testing and Materials, American Society for (1898), 1916 Race St., Phila. PA 19103; 21,000.

Textile Association, Northern (1854), 211 Congress St., Boston, MA 02210; 200 companies.

Textile Manufacturers Institute, American (1949), 1501 Johnston Bldg., Charlotte, NC 28281.

Theatre Assn., Amer. (1936), 1317 F St., N.W., Washington, DC 20004; 4,500.

Theatre and Academy, American National (1935), 245 West 52nd St., New York, NY 10019; 1,650.

Theatre Organ Society, American (1955), Box 1002, Middleburg, VA 22117; 4,500.

Theatre Owners, Natl. Assn. of (1925), 1501 Broadway, N.Y., NY 10036; 8,000.

Theodore Roosevelt Assn. (1921), 28 East 20th St., New York, NY 10003.

Theological Library Assn., Amer. (1947), Lutheran Theological Seminary, 7301 Germantown Ave., Phila., PA 19119; 410.

Theological Schools, Amer. Assn. of (1936), P.O. Box 396, Vandalia, OH 45377; 196 schools.

Theosophical Society in America (1886), 1926 North Main St., Wheaton, IL 60187; 5,858.

37th Division Veterans Assn. (1919), 21 W. Broad St., Columbus, OH 43215; 3,500.

Thoreau Society (1941), State Univ. College, Geneseo, NY 14454; 1,000.

Thoroughbred Racing Assn. (1942), 5 Kadota Dr., Lake Success Quad, New Hyde Park, NY 11040; 54 race tracks.

Toastmasters International (1924), 2200 N. Grand, Santa Ana, CA 92701; 65,000.

Toastmistress Clubs, Internatl. (1938), 9068 E. Firestone Blvd., Downey, CA 90241; 21,000.

Topical Assn., American (1949), 3306 North 50th St., Milwaukee, WI 53216; 10,000.

Torch Clubs, Internatl. Assn. of (1924), Box 8670, University Sta., Knoxville, TN 37916; 5,200.

Toy Manufacturers of America (1916), 200 Fifth Ave., New York, NY 10010; 280.

Trade Relations Council (1885), 1001 Connecticut Ave., N.W., Washington, D.C. 20036; 75.

Traffic and Transportation, Amer. Society of (1946), 547 W. Jackson Blvd., Chicago, IL 60606; 2,646.

Traffic Engineers, Institute of (1930), 1815 N. Ft. Myer Dr., Arlington, VA 22209; 4,246.

Training Corps, American (1961), 107-12 Jamaica Ave., Richmond Hill, NY 11418; 700.

Training & Development, American Society for (1945), P.O. Box 5307, Madison, WI 53705; 9,000.

Transit Assn., Amer. (1882), 465 L'Enfant Plaza, S.W., Wash., DC 20024; 450 companies.

Transportation Assn. of America (1935), 1101 17th St., N.W., Washington, DC 20036; 850 co's.

Trapshooting Assn., Amateur (1924), 601 W. Natl. Rd., Vandalia, OH 45377; 70,000.

Travel Agents, American Society of (1931), 360 Lexington Ave., N.Y., NY 10017; 11,000.

Travel Organizations, Discover America (1969, merger of **Natl. Assn. of Travel Orgs. & Discover America**), 1100 Connecticut Ave., N.W., Wash., DC 20036; 1,000.

Travelers Aid-Internatl. Social Service of America (formerly, **Travelers Aid Assn. of America,** merged 1972), 345 E. 46th St., N.Y., NY 10017.

Travelers Aid Society of N.Y. (1905, 204 East 39th St., New York, NY 10016; 2,935.

Traveleers International (1943), P.O. Box 1017, Chandler, AZ 85224; 16,088.

Trotting Assn., U.S. (1932), 750 Michigan Ave., Columbus, OH 43215; 35,000.

Trucking Assns., American (1933), 1616 P St., N.W., Washington, DC 20036; 51 assns.

True Sisters, United Order (1846), 150 West 85th St., N.Y., NY 10024; 12,000.

Truly Absurd Corporation (1970), Box 613, Electric City, WA 99123; 215.

Turners, American (1848), 1550 Clinton Ave., N. Rochester, NY 14621; 14,000.

—U—

UNICEF, U.S. Committee for (1947), 331 East 38th St., N.Y., NY 10016; 3,000.

Unidentified Flying Objects, Natl. Investigations Committee on (1968), 7970 Woodman Ave., Van Nuys, CA 91402; 2,000.

Uniformed Services, Natl. Assn. for (1968), 956 N. Monroe St., Arlington, VA 22201; 33,000.

United Community Funds and Councils of America (1956), 345 46th St., N.Y., NY 10017; serves 36,000 agencies.

United Nations Assn. of the U.S.A. (1923 as **League of Nations Assn.;** renamed 1945), 833 UN Plaza, N.Y., NY 10017; 65,000.

United Nations, U.S. People for (1967), 777 United Nations Pl., N.Y., NY 10017.

United Press International (1907, formerly **United Press Assn.;** renamed 1958 after merger with **International News Service**), 220 East 42nd St., N.Y., NY 10017.

United Service Organizations (1941), 237 East 52nd St., New York, NY 10022; 130,000.

United States Army, Assn. of the (1892), 1529 18th St., N.W., Wash., DC 20036; 89,660.

United Way of America (1956), 801 N. Fairfax St., Alexandria, VA 22314.

Universities, Assn. of American (1900), One Dupont Circle, Wash., DC 20036; 48 universities.

Universities and Colleges, Assn. of Governing Boards of (1923), One Dupont Circle, N.W., Wash., DC 20036; 11,000.

University Extension Assn., Natl. (1915), One Dupont Circle, Suite 360, Wash., DC; 195 schools.

University Professors, American Assn. of (1915), One Dupont Circle, Wash., DC 20036; 87,000.

University Women, American Assn. of (1882), 2401 Virginia Ave., N.W., Wash., DC 20037; 173,000.

Up With People (1968), 3103 N. Campbell Ave., Tucson, AZ 85719.

Urban Coalition, The Natl. (1967), 2100 M St., N.W., Wash., DC 20037.

Urban League, National (1910), 55 East 52nd St., New York, NY 10022; 12,000.

Utility Commissioners, Natl. Assn. of Regulatory (1889), 1102 Interstate Commerce Comm. Bldg., Box 684, Wash., DC 20044; 57 agencies.

—V—

Variety Clubs International (1927), 7210 Red Rd., Suite 208, S. Miami, FL 33143; 10,327.

Vegetable Growers Assn. of America (1908), 1616 H. St., N.W., Wash., DC 20006; 1,200.

Veteran Motor Car Club of America (1938), 105 Elm St., Andover, MA 01810; 4,075.

Veterans Committee, American (1944), 1333 Connecticut Ave., Wash., DC 20036; 25,000.

Veterans of Foreign Wars of the U.S. (1899), 406 W. 34th St., Kansas City, MO 64111; 1,709,372.

Ladies Auxiliary to the VFW (1914), 406 W. 34th St., Kansas City, MO 64111; 483,000.

Veterans of World War I of the U.S.A. (1958), 916 Prince St., Alexandria, VA 22314; 160,000.

Veterinary Medical Assn., Amer. (1863), 600 S. Michigan Ave., Chicago, IL 60605; 22,800.

Victorian Society in America (1966), The Athenaeum, E. Washington Sq., Phila., PA 19106; 1,488.

Vocational Assn., American (1929), 1510 H St., N.W., Washington, DC 20005; 50,000.

Volleyball Assn., U.S. (1928), 13 State St., Schenectady, NY 12305; 6,000.

VOTES National Committee (formerly **Vindication of Twenty-Eighteen Suffrage**) (1961), Box 1991, Hartford, CT 06101; 240.

—W—

Walther League (1893), 119 W. Locust St., Chicago, IL 60610; 4,000.

War Dads Auxiliary, American (1945), 1123 Scarritt Arcade Bldg., Kansas City, MO 64106; 2,500.

War Mothers, American (1917), 2615 Woodley Pl. N.W., Washington, DC 20008; 14,000.

War of 1812, General Society of (1814), 3311 Columbia Pike, Lancaster, PA 17603; 1,169.

War of 1812, Military Society, (1826), Armory 643 Park Ave., N.Y., NY 10021; 100.

War of 1812, Veteran Corps of Artillery (1790), Armory, 643 Park Ave., N.Y., NY 10021; 178.

Watch and Clock Collectors, Natl. Assn. of (1943), NAWCC Bldg., 514 Popular St., Columbia, PA 17512; 35,000.

Water Pollution Control Administrators, Assn. of State & Interstate, c/o Alfred Peloquin, 607 Boyalston St., Boston, MA 02116.

Water Pollution Control Federation (1928), 3900 Wisconsin Ave. N.W., Wash., DC 20016; 20,000.

Water Ski Assn., Amer. (1939), 7th St. & Ave. G., S.W., Winter Haven, FL 33880; 10,765.

Water Resources Assn., Amer. (1964), 206 E. University, Urbana, IL 61801; 1,800.

Water Well Assn., Natl. (1948), 88 E. Broad St., Columbus, OH 43215; 3,200.

Water Works Assn., Amer. (1881), 2 Park Ave., New York, NY 10016; 22,000.

Welding Society, American (1919), 2501 N.W. 7th St., Miami, FL 33125; 22,908.

Wesleyan Service Guild (1921), 475 Riverside Dr., Rm. 1414; New York, NY 10027; 125,000.

Westbeth, The Artists Community (1970), 463 West St., New York, NY 10014; 1,200.

Western Forestry and Conservation Assn. (1909), 1326 American Bank Bldg., Portland, OR 97232; 600.

Wheelchair Athletic Assn. (1958), 40-42 62nd St., Woodside, NY 11377; 1,300.

Wilderness Society (1935), 729 15th St., N.W., Washington, DC 20005; 75,000.

Wildlife, Defenders of (1925), 2000 N. St., N.W., Washington, DC 20036; 40,000.

Wildlife Federation, Natl. (1936), 1412 16th St., N.W., Washington, DC 20036; 3,500,000.

Wildlife Foundation, N. American (1911), 709 Wire Bldg., Washington, DC 20005; 1,711.

Wildlife Fund, World (1961), 910 17th St., N.W., Washington, DC 20002; 48,000.

Wildlife Management Institute (1945), 709 Wire Bldg., Washington, DC 20005.

Wildlife Society, The (1937), S-176, 3900 Wisconsin Ave., N.W., Washington, DC 20016; 7,700.

William Penn Assn. (1886), 429 Forbes Ave., Pittsburgh, PA 15219, 67,311.

Wireless Pioneers, Society of (1967), P.O. Box 530, Santa Rosa, CA 95402; 1,487.

Women Geographers, Society of (1925), 1619 New Hampshire Ave., N.W., Wash., DC 20009; 450.

Woman's Assn., American, 19 West 44th St., New York, NY 10036.

Woman's Christian Temperance Union, Natl. (1874), 1730 Chicago Ave., Evanston, IL 60201; 250,000.

Women Artists, Natl. Assn. of (1889), 156 5th Ave., N.Y., NY 10010; 700.

Women Engineers, Society of (1952), 345 E. 47th St., New York, NY 10017; 1,500.

Women, Natl. Organization for (NOW) (1966), 1957 E. 73rd St., Chicago IL 60649; 30,000.

Women Strike for Peace (1961), 1 Union Square West, N.Y., NY 10003.

Women of the U.S., Natl. Council of (1888), 345 E. 46th St., N.Y., NY 10017; 1,500.

Women Voters of the U.S., League of (1920), 1730 M St., N.W., Wash., DC 20036; 160,000.

Women World War Veterans (1919), 237 Madison Ave., New York, NY 10016; 125,000.

Women's Army Corps Veterans Assn. (1946), 6049 Amboy Rd., Dearborn Heights, MI 48127; 1,500.

Women's Clubs, General Federation of (1891), 1734 N St., N.W., Wash., DC 20036; 10,000,000.

Women's Clubs, Natl. Federation of Business and Professional (1919), 2012 Massachusetts Ave., N.W., Wash., DC 20036; 170,000.

Women's Educational and Industrial Union (1877), 264 Boylston St., Boston, MA 02146; 2,260.

Women's Internatl. League for Peace and Freedom, (1915), 1213 Race St., Phila., PA 19107; 10,000.

Women's Natl. Republican Club (1921), 3 West 51st St., N.Y., NY 10019; 2,500.

Women's Overseas Service League (1921), 2456 20th St., N.W., Wash., DC 20009; 1,700.

Women's Veterinary Medical Assn. (1947), c/o Dr. Jane Robens, 2 Laurel Pl., Upper Montclair, NJ 07043; 250.

Woodmen of America, Modern (1883), 1710 1st Ave., Rock Island, IL 61201; 474,700.

Woodmen of the World (1890), 1450 Speer Blvd., Denver, CO 80204; 32,955.

Wool Growers Assn., Natl. (1865), 600 Crandall Bldg., Salt Lake City, UT 84101; 22 assns.

Workmen's Circle (1888), 175 East Broadway, New York, NY 10002; 52,000.

World Federalists, World Assn. of (1947), 63 Sparks St., Ottawa, Ontario, K1P 5A6, Canada; 40,000.

World Future Society (1966), 4916 St. Elmo Ave., Bethesda, MD 20014; 13,000.

World Health Organization, U.S. Committee for (1953), 777 United Nations Plaza, N.Y., NY 10017; 3,642.

World Ship Society (1946), c/o Dudley Thickens, 3319 Sweet Dr., Lafayette, CA 94549; 3,500.

Wrestling Foundation, U.S. Amateur (1959), 620 N. 48th St., Lincoln, NE 68504; 300.

Writers Assn. of America, Outdoor (1927), 4141 W. Bradley Rd., Milwaukee, WI 53209; 1,409.

Writers Guild of America, West (1954), 8955 Beverly Blvd., Los Angeles, CA 90048; 3,000.

—Y & Z—

Yale Club of N.Y. City (1897), 50 Vanderbilt Ave., New York, NY 10017; 6,300.

Yeomen F, National (1926), 10 Stuyvesant Oval, N.Y., NY 10009; 1,300.

Young Americans for Freedom (1960), 1221 Massachusetts Ave., Wash., DC 20005; 70,000.

YMHAs and Jewish Community Centers, World Federation of (1946), 15 East 26th St., N.Y., NY 10010; 17 nations.

YM-YWHAs of Greater New York, Associated (1957), 33 West 60th St., N.Y., NY 10023; 45,000.

Young Men's Christian Assns., Natl. Council of (1844 in London, 1851 in U.S.), 291 Broadway, N.Y., NY 10007; 7,000,000.

Young Women's Christian Assn. of the U.S.A. (1855 in England; 1858 in U.S.), 600 Lexington Ave., N.Y., NY 10022; 2,400,000 in the U.S.

Youth Hostels, Amer. (1934), Natl. Campus, Delaplane, VA 22025; 75,000.

Zero Population Growth (1968), 4080 Fabian Way, Palo Alto CA 94303; 25,000.

Zionist Organization of America (1897), 145 East 32nd St., New York, NY 10016; 110,000.

Zonta International (1919), 59 E. Van Buren St., Chicago, IL 60605; 22,000.

Zoological Parks & Aquariums, Amer. Assn. of (1924), Ogle Bay Park, Wheeling, WV 26003; 1,000.

Zoological Society, N.Y. (1895), c/o N.Y. Zoological Park, Bronx Park, NY 10460; 6,800.

Zoologists, American Society of (1913), Box 2730 Calif. Lutheran College, Thousand Oaks, CA 91360.

"The Americans of all ages, all conditions and all dispositions constantly form associations. They have not only commercial and manufacturing companies in which all take part but associations of a thousand other kinds, religious, moral, serious, futile, restricted, enormous or diminutive. The Americans make associations to give entertainments, to found establishments for education, to send missionaries to the antipodes. Wherever at the head of some new undertaking you see the government of France or man of rank in England, in the U.S. you will be sure to find an association."

Alexis de Tocqueville
1805-1859

Education
American Colleges and Universities

For Canadian Colleges and Universities see Page . . .

STUDENT AND FACULTY FIGURES FOR SPRING TERM, 1973
Source: World Almanac questionnaires and U.S. Office of Education

All coeducational unless followed by (M) for men only, or (W) for women only. Even though marked (M) or (W) some are coeducational at graduate level and in evening and summer divisions. Asterisk (*) denotes land-grant college.

Governing official is president unless otherwise designated. Year is that of founding. The word college is part of the name listed unless another designation is given.

Affiliation: C-County; D-religious denomination; Di-district; F-federal; Mu-municipal; P-private; S-state; T-territorial govt.; Y-YMCA.

Each institution listed has an enrollment of at least 100 students of college grade. Number of teachers is the total number of individuals on teaching staff. Enrollment and faculty in italics include all branches and campuses.

(A) Designates colleges that have not provided up-to-date information.
(See Index for typical tuition fees)

Senior Colleges

Name	Location	Year	Governing Official and Affiliation		Students	Teachers
Abilene Christian	Abilene, Tex.	1906	John C. Stevens	P	3,820	237
Adams State	Alamosa, Colo.	1921	John A. Marvel	S	2,500	160
Adelphi Univ.	Garden City, N.Y.	1896	Timothy Costello	P	8,000	501
Adrian	Adrian, Mich.	1859	John H. Dawson	P	1,097	109
Agnes Scott (W)	Decatur, Ga.	1889	Wallace M. Alston	P	625	84
Air Force Inst. of Tech.	Dayton, Ohio	1919	Gen. Frank Simokaitis	F	549	108
Akron, Univ. of	Akron, Ohio	1870	Dominic J. Guzzetta	S	18,139	1,362
Alabama A & M Univ.	Normal, Ala.	1875	Richard D. Morrison	S	3,313	187
Alabama State Univ.	Montgomery, Ala.	1874	Levi Watkins	S	3,272	127
Alabama, Univ. of	University, Ala.	1831	Forrest David Mathews	S	13,481	763
At Birmingham	Birmingham, Ala.	1966	J. F. Volker	S	8,097	750
At Huntsville	Huntsville, Ala.	1951	Benjamin B. Graves	S	2,687	147
Alaska Methodist Univ.	Anchorage, Alaska	1960	John O. Picton	D	968	64
Alaska, Univ. of*	Fairbanks, Alaska	1917	William R. Wood	S	9,978	517
Albany State	Albany, Ga.	1903	Charles L. Hayes	S	1,798	133
Albertus Magnus (W)	New Haven, Conn.	1925	Francis H. Horn	D	472	50
Albion	Albion, Mich.	1835	Bernard Tagg Lomas	P	1,751	132
Albright	Reading, Pa.	1856	Arthur Schultz	D	1,501	96
Albuquerque, Univ. of	Albuquerque, N.M.	1920	Frank Kleinhenz	P	3,200	150
Alcorn A. & M.	Lorman, Miss.	1871	Walter Washington	S	2,677	116
Alderson-Broaddus	Philippi, W. Va.	1871	Richard E. Shearer	P	931	69
Alfred Univ.	Alfred, N.Y.	1857	Leland Miles	P	2,354	180
Allegheny	Meadville, Pa.	1815	Lawrence L. Pelletier	P	1,692	120
Allen Univ.	Columbia, S.C.	1870	J. W. Hairston	D	381	43
Allentown	Center Valley, Pa.	1965	Rev. J. Stuart Dooling	P	600	60
Alliance	Cambridge Spgs., Pa.	1912	Walter Smietana (Act.)	P	585	50
Alma	Alma, Mich.	1886	Robert D. Swanson	P	1,168	80
Alvernia	Reading, Pa.	1958	Sis. M. Victorine	P	167	36
Alverno (W)	Milwaukee, Wis.	1936	Sister Joel Read	P	1,159	112
American Conservatory of Music	Chicago, Ill	1886	Leo Heim	P	431	24
American International	Springfield, Mass	1885	Harry J. Courniotes	P	2,546	129
American Univ.	Washington, D.C.	1893	George H. Williams	P	12,097	788
Amherst (M)	Amherst, Mass.	1821	John William Ward	P	1,276	146
Anderson	Anderson, Ind.	1917	Robert H. Reardon	P	1,565	121
Andrews Univ.	Berrien Spgs., Mich.	1874	Richard Hammill	D	2,051	170
Angelo State Univ.	San Angelo, Texas	1928	Lloyd Vincent	S	3,807	163
Anna Maria	Paxton, Mass.	1946	Sister Irene Socquet	D	612	54
Annhurst	Woodstock, Conn.	1941	Sister Cecile	P	385	85
Antioch	Yellow Spgs., Ohio	1852	James P. Dixon, Jr.	P	4058	587
Appalachian Bible Inst.	Bradley, W. Va.	1950	Lester E. Pipkin	D	204	16
Appalachian State Univ.	Boone, N.C.	1899	Herbert Wey	S	7,871	359
Aquinas	Grand Rapids, Mich	1923	Norbert J. Hruby	P	1,400	105
Arizona State Univ.	Temple, Ariz.	1885	John W. Schwada	S	27,322	1,034
Arizona, Univ. of*	Tucson, Arizona	1885	John Paul Schaefer	S	26,786	1,657
Arkansas Baptist	Little Rock, Ark.	1884	James C. Oliver	D	561	43
Arkansas College	Batesville, Ark.	1872	Dan C. West	D	403	34
Arkansas Polytechnic	Russellville, Ark.	1925	Kenneth Kersh	S	2,052	115
Arkansas State Univ.	State Univ., Ark.	1909	Carl R. Reng.	S	6,549	325
Arkansas, State Coll. of	Conway, Ark.	1907	Silas D. Snow	S	4,300	275
Arkansas, Univ. of*	Fayetteville, Ark.	1871	David W. Mullins	S	10,784	707
At Little Rock	Little Rock, Ark.	1927	Carey V. Stabler	S	4,171	148
at Pine Bluff	Pine Bluff, Ark.	1873	Lawrence David	S	2,540	167
Armstrong	Berkeley, Calif.	1918	John E. Armstrong	P	450	40
Armstrong State	Savannah, Ga.	1935	Henry L. Ashmore	S	2,800	120
Art Academy of Cincinnati	Cincinnati, Ohio	1887	P. R. Adams, Dean	P	170	18
Art Center Coll. of Design	Los Angeles, Calif.	1930	Donald R. Kubly	P	1,029	124
Art Institute of Chicago	Chicago, Ill.	1866	Donald Irving, Dir.	P	1,338	107
Asbury	Wilmore, Ky.	1890	Dennis F. Kinlaw	P	1,029	85
Ashland	Ashland, Ohio	1878	Glenn L. Clayton	Mu	2,441	169
Assumption	Worcester, Mass.	1904	Pasquale DiPasquale	D	1,632	102
Athenaeum of Ohio (M)	Norwood, Ohio	1829	Rev. J. Raymond Favret	D	237	47
Athens	Athens, Ala.	1822	Sidney Sandridge	D	784	57
Atlanta College of Art	Atlanta, Ga.	1927	William Voos	P	225	25
Atlantic Christian	Wilson, N.C.	1902	Arthur D. Wenger	D	1,689	117

Name	Location	Year	Governing Official and Affiliation		Stu-dents	Teach-ers
Atlantic Union	So. Lancaster, Mass.	1882	W. G. Nelson	D	690	75
Auburn Univ.*	Auburn, Ala.	1856	Harry Philpott	S	15,339	897
Augsburg	Minneapolis, Minn.	1869	Oscar A. Anderson	P	1,579	125
Augusta	Augusta, Ga.	1925	George A. Christenberry	S	2,604	125
Augustana	Rock Island, Ill.	1860	C. W. Sorensen	D	2,235	151
Augustana	Sioux Falls, S. Dak.	1860	Charles L. Balcer	P	1,991	156
Aurora	Aurora, Ill.	1893	James E. Crimi	P	921	57
Austin	Sherman, Tex.	1849	John D. Moseley	D	1,124	91
Austin Peay State Univ.	Clarksville, Tenn.	1927	Joe Morgan	S	3,470	174
Averett	Dansville, Va.	1859	Conwell A. Anderson	P	1,092	61
Avila	Kansas City, Mo.	1916	Sis. Olive Louis	P	948	88
Azusa Pacific	Azusa, Calif.	1899	Cornelius Haggard	P	1,022	62
Babson	Babson Park, Mass.	1919	Henry A. Kriebel	P	1,868	92
Baker Univ.	Baldwin, Kan.	1858	James E. Doty	P	756	68
Baldwin-Wallace	Berea, Ohio	1845	Alfred B. Bonds, Jr.	P	2,617	257
Ball State Univ.	Muncie, Ind.	1918	John J. Pruis	S	16,562	776
Baltimore Coll. of Commerce	Baltimore, Md.	1909	Deane Wyatt	P	675	37
Baltimore, Univ. of	Baltimore, Md.	1925	H. Mebane Turner	P	5,105	196
Baptist Coll. at Charleston	Charleston, S.C.	1965	John Hamrick	D	1,841	85
Barat (W)	Lake Forest, Ill.	1858	Sister Margaret Burke	P	625	55
Barber-Scotia	Concord, N.C.	1867	Jerome Lynwood Gresham	P	477	42
Bard	Annandale, N.Y.	1860	Reamer Kline	P	767	80
Barnard (W)	New York, N.Y.	1889	Martha E. Peterson	P	1,892	175
Barrington	Barrington, R.I.	1900	Charles Hummel	P	624	54
Barry (W)	Miami, Fla.	1940	Sister M. Dorothy Brown	D	1,353	126
Bartlesville Wesleyan	Bartlesville, Okla.	1909	Leo G. Cox	P	247	22
Bates	Lewiston, Me.	1864	Thomas H. Reynolds	P	1,204	86
Baylor Univ.	Waco, Tex.	1845	Abner V. McCall	P	7,451	413
Belhaven	Jackson, Miss.	1883	Howard J. Cleland	D	644	67
Belknap	Center Harbor, N.H.	1963	George Schlichte	P	408	40
Bellarmine	Louisville, Ky.	1950	Eugene Petrik	P	1,395	88
Bellevue	Bellevue, Nebr.	1966	Richard Winchell	P	1,019	37
Belmont	Nashville, Tenn.	1951	Herbert C. Gabhart	P	911	80
Belmont Abbey	Belmont, N.C.	1876	Rev. John Bradley	D	527	42
Beloit	Beloit, Wis.	1846	Miller Upton	P	1,754	123
Bemidji State	Bemidji, Minn.	1919	Robert Decker	S	4,500	196
Benedict	Columbia, S.C.	1870	Luns Richardson (Act.)	P	1,364	75
Benedictine	Atchison, Kans.	1971	Rev. Gerard Senecal	P	1,083	88
Benjamin Franklin Univ.	Washington, D.C.	1925	Clephane A. Kennedy	P	1,000	42
Bennett (W)	Greensboro, N.C.	1873	Isaac H. Miller	P	557	61
Bennington	Bennington, Vt.	1925	Gail Thain Parker	P	580	64
Bentley	Waltham, Mass.	1917	Gregory Adamian	P	3,700	105
Berea	Berea, Ky.	1855	W. D. Weatherford, Jr.	P	1,245	130
Berry	Mount Berry, Ga.	1902	John R. Bertrand	P	964	72
Bethany Bible	Santa Cruz, Calif.	1919	C. Morse Ward	D	450	28
Bethany	Lindsborg, Kan.	1881	Alvin Hahn	D	665	51
Bethany	Bethany, W. Va.	1840	Cecil Underwood	P	1,057	76
Bethany Nazarene	Bethany, Okla.	1899	Stephen Nease	D	1,355	75
Bethel	Mishawaka, Ind.	1947	Ray P. Pannabecker	P	383	31
Bethel	North Newton, Kan.	1887	Harold Schultz	P	452	56
Bethel	McKenzie, Tenn.	1842	James McKee	D	476	35
Bethel	St. Paul, Minn.	1947	Carl Lundquist	D	1,100	90
Bethune-Cookman	Daytona Beach, Fla.	1872	Richard V. Moore	D,P	1,127	61
Biola	La Mirada, Calif.	1908	J. Richard Chase	P	1,643	114
Birmingham-Southern	Birmingham, Ala.	1856	Ralph M. Tanner	P	880	69
Biscayne	Miami, Fla.	1962	Rev. John McDonnell	D	1,016	42
Bishop	Dallas, Tex.	1881	Milton K. Curry	D	2,085	99
Black Hills State	Spearfish, S. Dak.	1883	M. N. Freeman	S	1,746	115
Blackburn	Carlinville, Ill.	1837	Glenn L. McConagha	D	558	48
Bloomfield	Bloomfield, N.J.	1868	Merle F. Allshouse	P	1,600	103
Bloomsburg State	Bloomsburg, Pa.	1839	Charles Carson, act.	S	4,972	306
Blue Mountain (W)	Blue Mountain, Miss.	1873	E. Harold Fisher	P	342	31
Bluefield State	Bluefield, W. Va.	1895	Wendell G. Hardway	S	1,170	68
Bluffton	Bluffton, Ohio	1899	Robert S. Kreider	D	641	60
Bob Jones Univ.	Greenville, S.C.	1927	Bob Jones	P	4,150	249
Boise State	Boise, Idaho	1932	John Barnes	S	9,561	387
Boston	Chestnut Hill, Mass.	1865	Rev. J. Donald Monan	D	12,218	914
Boston State	Boston, Mass.	1852	Kermit C. Morrissey	S	8,800	540
Boston Conserv. of Music	Boston, Mass.	1867	George Brambilla	P	543	87
Boston Univ.	Boston, Mass.	1869	John Silber	P	21,925	2,700
Bowdoin	Brunswick, Me.	1794	Roger Howell, Jr.	P	1,152	103
Bowie State	Bowie, Md.	1965	Samuel L. Myers	S	3,115	166
Bowling Green State Univ.	Bowling Green, Ohio	1910	Hollis A. Moore	S	15,900	935
Bradley Univ.	Peoria, Ill.	1897	Martin G. Abegg	P	4,889	388
Brandeis Univ.	Waltham, Mass.	1948	Marver Bernstein	P	2,355	350
Brenau	Gainesville, Ga.	1878	James T. Rogers	P	453	51
Brescia	Owensboro, Ky.	1925	Sister J. Marie Lechner	P	903	81
Briar Cliff	Sioux City, Iowa	1930	Kasper Marking	P	807	60
Briarcliff (W)	Briarcliff Manor, N.Y.	1903	Thomas E. Baker	P	351	41
Bridgeport Eng. Inst.	Bridgeport, Conn.	1924	William J. Owens	P	310	50
Bridgeport, Univ. of	Bridgeport, Conn.	1927	Thurston E. Manning	P	7,861	549
Bridgewater	Bridgewater, Va.	1880	Wayne F. Geisert	P	794	70
Bridgewater State	Bridgewater, Mass.	1840	Adrian Rondileau	S	7,000	330
Brigham Young Univ.	Provo, Utah	1875	Dallin H. Oaks	D	25,175	1,060
Brooklyn Law School	Brooklyn, N.Y.	1901	Raymond Lisle, Dean	P	1,357	38
Brown Univ.	Providence, R.I.	1764	Donald F. Hornig	P	6,269	755
Bryan	Dayton, Tenn.	1930	Theodore Mercer	P	533	34
Bryant	Smithfield, R.I.	1863	Harry Evarts	P	2,308	93
Bryn Mawr (W)	Bryn Mawr, Pa.	1885	Harris L. Wofford, Jr.	P	1,421	234
Bucknell Univ.	Lewisburg, Pa.	1846	C. H. Watts	P	3,022	227
Buena Vista	Storm Lake, Iowa	1891	Wendell Q. Halverson	D	825	55
Butler Univ.	Indianapolis, Ind.	1855	Alexander E. Jones	P	4,250	235
Cabrini	Radnor, Pa.	1957	Sister Mary L. Sullivan	D	524	47
Caldwell	Caldwell, N.J.	1939	Sister Ann John	D	896	59
California Baptist	Riverside, Calif.	1950	James R. Staples	D	633	49
Calif. Coll. of Arts and Crafts	Oakland, Calif.	1907	Harry Xavier Ford	P	1,378	132

Name	Location	Year	Governing Official and Affiliation	Students	Teachers
Calif. College of Podiatric Medicine	San Francisco, Calif.	1914	H. D. Bailey	O	205	48
Calif. Inst. of the Arts	Valencia, Calif.	1961	William Lund	P	763	152
Calif. Inst. of Tech.	Pasadena, Calif.	1891	Harold Brown	P	1,387	478
Calif. Lutheran	Thousand Oaks, Calif.	1961	Mark Matthews	P	1,807	125
Calif. Maritime Academy	Vallejo, Calif.	1929	Adm. J. P. Rizza	S	200	23
Calif. State	Bakersfield, Calif.	1966	Paul Romberg	S	2,261	178
Calif. State	California, Pa.	1852	George Roadman	S	5,173	375
Calif. State	Dominguez Hills, Calif.	1960	Leo Cain	S	4,250	265
Calif. State	San Bernardino, Calif.	1965	John Pfau	S	2,581	167
Calif. State	Turlock, Calif.	1957	Carl Gatlin	S	2,588	159
Calif. State Polytechnic Univ.	San Luis Obispo, Calif.	1901	Robert Kennedy	S	11,468	686
Calif. State Polytechnic Univ.	Pomona, Calif.	1938	Robert C. Kramer	S	9,000	545
Calif. State Univ.	San Diego, Calif.	1897	Brage Golding	S	28,811	1,755
Calif. State Univ.	San Jose, Calif.	1857	John Bunzel	S	26,000	1,240
Calif. State Univ.	Northridge, Calif.	1958	James W. Cleary	S	24,130	1,750
Calif. State Univ.	Chico, Calif.	1887	Stanford Cazier	S	11,587	678
Calif. State Univ.	Fresno, Calif.	1911	Norman Baxter	S	15,100	1,000
Calif. State Univ.	Fullerton, Calif.	1958	L. Donald Shields	S	17,576	607
Calif. State Univ.	Hayward, Calif.	1957	Ellis McCune	S	12,038	766
Calif. State Univ.	Arcata, Calif.	1913	Cornelius H. Siemens	S	6,900	475
Calif. State Univ.	Long Beach, Calif.	1949	Stephen Horn	S	29,306	1,483
Calif. State Univ.	Los Angeles, Calif.	1947	J. A. Greenlee	S	23,036	1,483
Calif. State Univ.	Sacramento, Calif.	1947	Bernard Hyink	S	18,200	800
Calif. State Univ.	San Francisco, Calif.	1899	Vacant	S	21,337	1,233
Calif. Univ. of*	Berkeley, Calif.	1868	Charles J. Hitch	S	105,531	14,638
Berkeley Campus	Berkeley, Calif.	1873	Albert H. Bowker (Chan.)	S	27,700	2,000
Davis Campus	Davis, Calif.	1905	James Meyer (Chan.)	S	13,497	906
Irvine Campus	Irvine, Calif	1961	D. G. Aldrich (Chan.)	S	5,845	480
Los Angeles Campus	Los Angeles, Calif.	1919	Charles Young (Chan.)	S	27,460	1,945
Riverside Campus	Riverside, Calif.	1954	Ivan Hinderaker (Chan.)	S	5,125	600
San Diego Campus	La Jolla, Calif.	1912	William H. McElroy (Chan.)	S	6,630	550
San Francisco Campus	San Francisco, Calif.	1868	Philip R. Lee (Chan.)	S	2,184	1,100
Santa Barbara Campus	Santa Barbara, Calif.	1891	Vernon Cheadle (Chan.)	S	12,100	690
Santa Cruz Campus	Santa Cruz, Calif.	1965	D. E. McHenry (Chan.)	S	4,454	357
Calvary Bible	Kansas City, Mo.	1932	Wendell Grout, act.	P	345	24
Calvin	Grand Rapids, Mich.	1876	William Spoelhof	S	2,991	178
Cameron	Lawton, Okla.	1909	Don Owens	S	4,172	150
Campbell	Blues Creek, N.C.	1887	Norman A. Wiggins	P	2,056	147
Campbellsville	Campbellsville, Ky.	1906	William R. Davenport	P	656	48
Canisius	Buffalo, N.Y.	1870	V. Rev. James Demske	P	4,098	267
Capital Inst. of Tech.	Kensington, Md.	1932	Edward L. Fleckenstein	P	267	17
Capital Univ.	Columbus, Ohio	1850	Thomas H. Langevin	P	1,903	147
Cardinal Stritch	Milwaukee, Wis.	1937	Sister Mary Aquin Miller	P	740	75
Carleton	Northfield, Minn.	1866	Howard R. Swearer	P	1,643	154
Carlow	Pittsburgh, Pa.	1929	Sister Jane Scully	D	1,019	87
Carnegie-Mellon Univ.	Pittsburgh, Pa.	1900	Richard M. Cyert	P	2,998	500
Carroll	Helena, Mont.	1909	Rev. Joseph Harrington	P	986	72
Carroll	Waukesha, Wis.	1846	Robert V. Cramer	P	1,159	91
Carson-Newman	Jefferson City, Tenn.	1851	John A. Fincher	P	1,593	133
Carthage	Kenosha, Wis.	1847	Harold H. Lentz	D	1,637	95
Case Western Reserve Univ.	Cleveland, Ohio	1967	L. A. Toepfer	P	8,466	1,150
Castleton State	Castleton, Vt.	1787	Harold Abel	S	1,687	91
Catawba	Salisbury, N.C.	1851	M. L. Shotzberger	D	1,094	84
Cathedral	Douglaston, N.Y.	1967	Rev. Thomas Gradilone	D	274	58
Catholic Univ. of America	Washington, D.C.	1889	Clarence C. Walton	D	6,667	572
Catholic Univ. of Puerto Rico	Ponce, Puerto Rica	1948	F. J. Carreras	P	6,689	420
Cedar Crest (W)	Allentown, Pa.	1867	Pauline Tompkins	P	678	75
Cedarville	Cedarville, Ohio	1887	James Jeremiah	P	853	58
Centenary	Shreveport, La.	1825	John Horton Allen	P	715	90
Central Bible	Springfield, Mo.	1922	Rev. Philip Crouch	D	958	45
Central	Pella, Iowa	1853	Kenneth J. Weller	P	1,118	87
Central Connecticut State	New Britain, Conn.	1849	F. Don James	S	12,412	791
Central Methodist	Fayette. Mo.	1854	Harold Hamilton	D	722	60
Central Michigan Univ.	Mt. Pleasant, Mich.	1892	William Boyd	S	13,420	680
Central Missouri State Univ.	Warrensburg, Mo.	1871	Warren C. Lovinger	S	12,308	669
Central State Univ.	Edmond, Okla.	1890	Garland Godfrey	S	10,309	367
Central State Univ.	Wilberforce, Ohio	1887	Lionel H. Newsom	S	2,207	138
Central Tech. Inst.	Kansas City, Mo.	1931	C. L. Foster	P	396	19
Central Washington State	Ellensburg, Wash	1890	James E. Brooks	S	6,140	431
Central Wesleyan	Central, S.C.	1906	Claude Rickman	P	331	26
Centre Coll. of Kentucky	Danville, Ky.	1819	Thomas A. Spragens	P	730	65
Chadron State	Chadron, Nebr.	1911	Edwin Nelson	S	1,937	132
Chaminade Coll. of Honolulu	Honolulu, Hawaii	1955	Robert Maguire	P	1,711	104
Chapman (A)	Orange, Calif.	1861	John L. Davis	P	3,600	257
Charleston. Coll. of	Charleston, S.C.	1770	Theodore Stern	P	2,700	135
Chatham (W)	Pittsburgh, Pa.	1869	Edward D. Eddy	P	625	68
Chestnut Hill (W)	Philadelphia, Pa.	1924	Sister Mary Xavier Kirby	D	1,080	129
Cheyney State	Cheyney, Pa.	1837	Wade Wilson	S	2,275	224
Chicago College (Osteopathic)	Chicago, Ill	1913	Thaddeus Kawalek	P	330	150
Chicago Conservatory	Chicago, Ill.	1857	Francois D'Albert	P	200	60
Chicago-Kent Coll. of Law	Chicago, Ill.	1888	John Rettaliatta	P	701	35
Chicago State Univ.	Chicago, Ill.	1869	Milton B. Byrd	S	4,600	250
Chicago Technical (M)	Chicago, Ill.	1904	Leslie Morey	P	881	27
Chicago, Univ. of	Chicago, Ill.	1891	Edward H. Levi	P	9,083	1,125
Christian Brothers	Memphis, Tenn.	1871	Rev. Bernard Lococo	P	773	73
Cincinnati, Univ. of	Cincinnati, Ohio	1819	Warren G. Bennis	S,Mu	29,506	2,805
Citadel, The (Military) (M)	Charleston, S.C.	1842	James Duckett	S	2,606	158
Claflin	Orangeburg, S.C.	1869	Hubert V. Manning	P	731	55
Claremont Men's (M)	Claremont, Calif.	1946	Jack Lee Stark	P	784	97
Clarion State	Clarion, Pa.	1867	James Gemmell	S	4,325	309
Clark	Atlanta, Ga.	1869	Vivian Henderson	P	1,177	99
Clark Univ.	Worcester, Mass.	1887	Glenn W. Ferguson	P	2,995	264
Clarke (W)	Dubuque, Iowa	1843	Robert Giroux	P	652	68
Clarkson Coll. of Tech.	Potsdam, N.Y.	1896	John W. Graham, Jr.	D	2,324	183
Cleary	Ypsilanti, Mich.	1883	Walter Grieg	P	510	28
Clemson Univ.	Clemson, S.C.	1889	Robert C. Edwards	S	9,587	694
Cleveland Inst. of Art	Cleveland, Ohio	1882	Joseph McCullough	P	821	62
Cleveland Inst. of Music	Cleveland, Ohio	1920	Mrs. Frank Joseph	P	250	71
Cleveland State Univ.	Cleveland, Ohio	1964	Walter Waetjen	S	13,428	662

Name	Location	Year	Governing Official and Affiliation		Stu-dents	Teach-ers
Coe	Cedar Rapids, Iowa	1851	Leo Nussbaum	P	1,220	140
Coker	Hartsville, S.C.	1908	Gus Turbeville	P	497	40
Colby	Waterville, Me.	1813	Robert E. L. Strider	P	1,592	127
Colgate Univ.	Hamilton, N.Y.	1819	Thomas Bartlett	P	2,454	175
Colorado	Colo. Spgs., Colo.	1874	Lloyd E. Worner	P	1,869	125
Colorado Sch. of Mines	Golden, Colo.	1874	Guy McBride	S	1,425	125
Colorado State Univ. *	Fort Collins, Colo.	1870	A. R. Chamberlain	S	14,897	1,125
Colorado, Univ. of	Boulder, Colo	1876	Lawrence Silverman, (V.P.)	S	30,428	2,729
Denver Center	Denver, Colo.	1964	Joe Keen (V.P.)	S	6,621	615
Colorado Springs	Colorado Springs, Colo.	1965	Frederick P. Thieme	S	2,525	97
Colorado Women's (W)	Denver, Colo.	1888	Dumont F. Kenny	P	877	94
Columbia Bible	Columbia, S.C.	1923	J. Robertson McQuilkin	P	557	30
Columbia College	Columbia, S.C.	1854	R. Wright Spears	D	965	72
Columbia Union	Takoma Park, Md.	1904	George Akers	D	925	86
Columbia Univ.	New York, N.Y.	1754	William McGill	P	14,475	4,500
Teachers College	New York, N.Y.	1888	John H. Fischer	P	5,199	403
Columbus	Columbus, Ga.	1958	Thomas Y. Whitley	S	3,777	156
Columbus Business	Columbus, Ohio	1911	Richard Miller, Dir.	P	545	24
Columbus College of Art & Design	Columbus, Ohio	1879	Joseph Canzani (Dn.)	P	589	57
Concord	Athens, W. Va.	1872	Joseph F. Marsh, Jr.	S	1,673	105
Concordia	Bronxville, N.Y.	1881	Robert Schnabel	D	400	46
Concordia	Moorhead, Minn.	1891	Joseph Knutson	D	2,323	160
Concordia	St. Paul, Minn.	1893	Harvey Stegemoeller	D	614	55
Concordia Senior	Fort Wayne, Ind.	1957	Herbert Bredemeier	D	463	40
Concordia Teachers	River Forest, Ill.	1864	Martin L. Koehneke	D	1,500	93
Concordia Teachers	Seward, Nebr.	1894	W. T. Janzow	D	1,487	115
Connecticut	New London, Conn.	1911	Charles Shain	P	1,914	178
Connecticut, Univ. of *	Storrs, Conn.	1881	Edward Gant, act.	S	19,972	1,213
Converse (W)	Spartanburg, S.C.	1889	Robert T. Coleman, Jr.	P	900	70
Cooper	New York, N.Y.	1859	John White	P	1,011	177
Coppin State (A)	Baltimore, Md.	1900	Calvin W. Burnett	P	1,806	87
Cornell	Mt. Vernon, Iowa	1853	Samuel Stumpf	D	945	66
Cornell Univ.*	Ithaca, N.Y.	1865	Dale R. Corson	P	15,994	1,907
Corpus Christi, Univ. of*	Corpus Christi, Tex.	1947	K. A. Maroney	D	536	49
Covenant	Mt. Lookout, Tenn.	1955	Marion Barnes	D	472	30
Cranbrook Academy of Art	Bloomfield Hills, Mich.	1932	Wallace Mitchell	P	148	9
Creighton Univ.	Omaha, Nebr.	1878	Rev. Joseph Labaj	D	4,154	701
Culver-Stockton	Canton, Mo.	1853	Fred Helsabeck	P	580	48
Cumberland	Williamsburg, Ky.	1889	J. M. Boswell	D	1,688	100
Curry	Milton, Mass.	1879	John S. Hafer	P	1,000	78
Curtis Inst. of Music (A)	Philadelphia, Pa.	1924	William C. Bodine (Act.)	P	181	63
Dakota State	Madison, S.D.	1881	Gordon Foster	S	908	64
Dakota Wesleyan Univ.	Mitchell, S. Dak.	1885	Donald E. Messer	D	461	46
Dallas Baptist (A)	Dallas, Tex.	1898	Charles Pitts	D	1,375	89
Dallas, Univ. of	Irving, Tex.	1956	Donald A. Cowan	D	1,415	122
Dana	Blair, Nebr.	1884	Earl Mezoff	D	707	54
Daniel Payne	Birmingham, Ala.	1889	Daniel Grant	D	300	30
Dartmouth	Hanover, N.H.	1769	John George Kemeny	P	3,823	350
David Lipscomb	Nashville, Tenn.	1891	Athens C. Pullias	P	1,858	99
Davidson (M)	Davidson, N.C.	1837	Samuel R. Spencer, Jr.	P	1,092	92
Davis and Elkins	Elkins, W. Va.	1904	G. E. Hermanson	P	763	46
Dayton Art Institute	Dayton, Ohio	1919	Thomas Colt, Dir.	P	298	20
Dayton, Univ. of	Dayton, Ohio	1850	V. Rev. R. A. Roesch	D	7,755	450
Defiance	Defiance, Ohio	1850	W. Noel Johnston	P	840	70
Delaware State*	Dover, Del.	1891	Luna I. Mishoe	S	1,868	113
Delaware, Univ. of*	Newark, Del.	1833	E. A. Trabant	S	16,771	1,125
Del. Valley Coll. of S & A.	Doylestown, Pa.	1896	James Work	P	1,222	85
Delta State	Cleveland, Miss.	1924	Aubrey K. Lucas	S	3,251	175
Denison Univ.	Granville, Ohio	1831	Joel P. Smith	P	2,173	179
Denver, Univ. of	Denver, Colo.	1864	Maurice B. Mitchell	P	7,780	611
DePaul Univ.	Chicago, Ill.	1898	V. Rev. J. R. Cortelyou	P	9,311	520
DePauw Univ.	Greencastle, Ind.	1837	William E. Kerstetter	P	2,283	150
Detroit Bible	Detroit, Mich.	1945	Wendell Johnston	P	330	24
Detroit Coll. of Business	Dearborn, Mich.	1936	Robert W. Sneden	P	970	49
Detroit Coll. of Law	Detroit, Mich.	1891	G. Cameron Buchanan	P	955	37
Detroit Inst. of Technology	Detroit, Mich.	1891	Dewey F. Barich	P	1,200	94
Detroit, Univ. of	Detroit, Mich.	1877	V. Rev. M. Carron	P	8,672	597
DeVry Inst. of Tech.	Chicago, Ill.	1931	Edward I. Sobol	P	2,452	84
Dickinson	Carlisle, Pa.	1773	Howard L. Rubendall	P	1,665	120
Dickinson School of Law	Carlisle, Pa.	1834	Dale F. Shughart	P	422	22
Dickinson State	Dickinson, N. Dak.	1918	R. C. Gillund	S	1,146	73
Dillard Univ.	New Orleans, La.	1869	Broadus Butler	P	985	104
District of Columbia Teachers	Washington, D.C.	1851	Paul Cooke	Mu	2,323	127
Doane	Crete, Nebr.	1872	Philip C. Heckman	P	579	52
Dr. Martin Luther	New Ulm, Minn.	1884	Conrad Frey	D	645	70
Dominican	Racine, Wis.	1946	Thomas Stevens	D	774	62
Dominican	Houston, Texas	1945	Sis. A. Boykin	D	283	60
Dominican Coll. of Blauvelt	Blauvelt, N.Y.	1952	Sis. Natalie Casey	D	750	58
Dominican Coll of S. Rafael	San Rafael, Calif.	1889	Sis. M. Samuel Conlon	D	707	77
Dordt	Sioux Center, Iowa	1955	B. J. Haan	P	955	51
Drake Univ.	Des Moines, Iowa	1881	Wilbur C. Miller	P	6,944	304
Drew Univ.	Madison, N.J.	1866	Robert F. Oxnam	P	3,127	292
Drexel Univ.	Philadelphia, Pa.	1891	William W. Hagerty	P	9,045	298
Dropsie Univ.	Philadelphia, Pa.	1907	Abraham Katsh	P	105	16
Drury	Springfield, Mo.	1873	William Everheart	P	2,301	148
Dubuque, Univ. of	Dubuque, Iowa	1852	Walter F. Peterson	P	1,004	66
Duke Univ.	Durham, N.C.	1838	Terry Sanford	P	8,682	1,392
Duquesne Univ.	Pittsburgh, Pa.	1878	V. Rev. H. J. McAnulty	D	8,261	450
Dyke	Cleveland, Ohio	1848	John Corfias	P	853	55
D'Youville	Buffalo, N.Y.	1908	Sister Mary Charlotte	P.	1,236	75
Earlham	Richmond, Ind.	1847	Landrum Bolling	D	1,060	89
East Carolina Univ.	Greenville, N.C.	1907	Leo W. Jenkins	S	9,972	623
East Central State	Ada, Okla.	1909	Stanley Wagner	S	2,831	125
East Stroudsburg, State	E. Stroudsburg, Pa.	1891	Darrell Holmes	S	3,728	190
East Tennessee State Univ.	Johnson City, Tenn.	1911	Delos Culp	S	9,530	662
East Texas Baptist	Marshall, Texas	1912	Howard C. Bennett	D	649	42
East Texas State Univ.	Commerce, Texas	1889	F. H. McDowell	S	8,958	436

Name	Location	Year	Governing Official and Affiliation	Students	Teachers
Eastern	St. Davids, Pa.	1951	Henry Osgood, act.	D	562	55
Eastern Conn. State	Willimantic, Conn.	1889	Charles Richard Webb, Jr.	S	2,919	185
Eastern Illinois Univ.	Charleston, Ill.	1895	Gilbert C. Fite	S	7,804	654
Eastern Kentucky Univ.	Richmond, Ky.	1906	Robert R. Martin	S	10,110	525
Eastern Mennonite	Harrisonburg, Va.	1917	Myron S. Augsburger	P	883	88
Eastern Michigan Univ.	Ypsilanti, Mich.	1849	Harold E. Sponberg	S	17,690	795
Eastern Montana	Billings, Mont.	1927	Stanley Heywood	S	2,600	140
Eastern Nazarene	Quincy, Mass.	1918	Leslie Parrott	D	831	44
Eastern New Mexico Univ.	Portales, N. Mex.	1934	Charles Meister	S	5,502	180
Eastern Oregon State	La Grande, Ore.	1929	Vacant	S	1,400	108
Eastern Washington State	Cheney, Wash.	1890	Emerson C. Shuck	S	5,898	360
Eckerd	St. Petersburg, Fla.	1958	Billy O. Wireman	P	945	76
Edgecliff	Cincinnati, Ohio	1935	Sis. M. A. Molitor, act.	D	904	88
Edgewood	Madison, Wis.	1927	Sister Cecilia Carey	D	500	50
Edinboro State	Edinboro, Pa.	1857	Chester T. McNerney	S	7,153	489
Edward Waters	Jacksonville, Fla.	1866	Paul Driver, act.	D	635	39
Eisenhower	Seneca Falls, N.Y.	1966	John Rosenkrans	P	742	67
Elizabeth City State Univ.	Elizabeth City, N.C.	1891	Marion Dennis Thorpe	S	1,024	82
Elizabethtown	Elizabethtown, Pa.	1899	Morley J. Mays	P	1,431	109
Elmhurst	Elmhurst, Ill.	1871	Ivan Frick	P	2,427	166
Elmira	Elmira, N.Y.	1855	J. Ralph Murray	P	3,025	137
Elon	Elon College, N.C.	1889	J. E. Danieley	P	1,696	99
Embry-Riddle Aeronautical Univ.	Daytona Beach, Fla.	1926	Jack R. Hunt	P	1,650	150
Emerson	Boston, Mass.	1880	Richard Chapin	P	1,750	150
Emmanuel (W)	Boston, Mass.	1919	Sister Marie Barry	D	1,052	114
Emory & Henry	Emory, Va.	1836	Thomas F. Chilcote	D	847	70
Emory Univ.	Atlanta, Ga.	1915	S. S. Atwood	P	5,803	1,775
Emporia, Coll. of	Emporia, Kan.	1882	Robert Prins, act.	D	459	36
Erskine	Due West, S.C.	1839	Joseph Wightman	D	712	70
Eureka	Eureka, Ill.	1855	Ira W. Langston	P	541	37
Evangel	Springfield, Mo.	1955	J. Robert Ashcroft	P	1,120	62
Evansville, Univ. of	Evansville, Ind.	1854	Wallace B. Graves	P	5,369	265
Fairfield Univ.	Fairfield, Conn.	1943	Thomas Fitzgerald	P	3,993	245
Fairleigh Dickinson Univ.	Rutherford, N.J.	1942	J. O. Fuller	P	20,000	600
Fairmont State	Fairmont, W. Va.	1867	Eston K. Feaster	S	3,320	180
Faith Baptist Bible	Ankeny, Iowa	1952	David Nettleton	P	483	20
Fayetteville State Univ.	Fayetteville, N.C.	1877	Charles A. Lyons, Jr.	S	1,787	105
Federal City (A)	Washington, D.C.	1966	Harland Randolph	Mu	4,500	300
Ferris State	Big Rapids, Mich.	1884	Robert Ewigleben	S	7,497	422
Finch (W)	New York, N.Y.	1900	Rodney Felder	P	404	54
Findlay	Findlay, Ohio	1882	Glen R. Rasmussen	P	949	85
Fine Arts, School of	Ft. Wayne, Ind.	1922	Russell Oettel	P	251	14
Fisk Univ.	Nashville, Tenn.	1866	J. R. Lawson	P	1,473	120
Fitchburg State	Fitchburg, Mass.	1894	James Hammond	S	3,043	185
Flagler	St. Augustine, Fla.	1968	William L. Proctor	P	225	32
Florence State Univ.	Florence, Ala.	1872	Robert M. Guillot	S	3,226	164
Florida Atlantic Univ.	Boca Raton, Fla.	1962	C. L. Creech	S	5,089	340
Florida A. & M. Univ.*	Tallahassee, Fla.	1887	Benjamin Luther Perry, Jr.	S	4,011	295
Florida Inst. of Tech.	Melbourne, Fla.	1958	Jerome P. Keuper	P	2,041	175
Florida International Univ.	Miami, Fla.	1972	Charles E. Perry	S	4,500	300
Florida Memorial	Miami, Fla.	1892	Royal Puryear	D	687	50
Florida Southern	Lakeland, Fla.	1885	Charles T. Thrift, Jr.	D	1,280	100
Florida State Univ.	Tallahassee, Fla.	1857	Stanley Marshall	S	19,032	1,272
Florida, Univ. of*	Gainesville, Fla.	1853	Stephen O'Connell	S	20,240	2,260
Fontbonne (W)	St. Louis, Mo.	1917	Sister Jane Hassett	P	630	58
Fordham Univ.	Bronx, N.Y.	1840	Rev. James C. Finley	P	13,841	811
Ft. Hays Kansas State	Hays, Kan.	1902	John W. Gustad	S	4,566	272
Ft. Lauderdale Univ.	Ft. Lauderdale, Fla.	1969	Stanley Drake	P	350	26
Ft. Lewis	Durango, Colo.	1962	Rexer Berndt	S	2,400	143
Fort Valley State*	Fort Valley, Ga.	1939	W. W. E. Blanchet	S	1,992	136
Ft. Wayne Art Inst.	Fort Wayne, Ind.	1922	Russell Oettel	P	283	10
Fort Wayne Bible	Fort Wayne, Ind.	1904	Timothy Warner	D	599	37
Ft. Wright	Spokane, Wash.	1907	Sister Monica Schmidt	D	410	53
Framingham State	Framingham, Mass.	1839	D. Justin McCarthy	S	4,462	254
Francis Marion	Florence, S.C.	1970	Walter D. Smith	S	1,404	60
Franconia	Franconia, N.H.	1961	Leon Botstein	P	427	53
Franklin	Franklin, Ind.	1834	Wesley N. Haines	P	620	59
Franklin and Marshall	Lancaster, Pa.	1787	Keith Spalding	P	2,407	162
Franklin Pierce	Rindge, N.H.	1962	Frank S. DiPietro	P	814	74
Franklin Univ.	Columbus, Ohio	1902	Joseph Frasch	P	3,341	120
Free Will Baptist Bible	Nashville, Tenn.	1942	L. C. Johnson	D	480	25
Friends Univ.	Wichita, Kan.	1898	Harold C. Cope	P	922	63
Frostburg State	Frostburg, Md.	1898	Nelson Guild	S	2,837	170
Furman Univ.	Greenville, S.C.	1826	Gordon W. Blackwell	D	2,135	160
Gallaudet	Washington, D.C.	1864	Edward C. Merrill, Jr.	P	840	140
Gannon	Erie, Pa.	1944	Rev. W. J. Nash	P	3,395	202
Gardner-Webb	Boiling Springs, N.C.	1905	Ernest Eugene Poston	D	1,476	90
General Motors Institute	Flint, Mich.	1919	Harold P. Rodes	P	2,897	220
Geneva	Beaver Falls, Pa.	1847	Edwin C. Clarke	P	1,414	98
George Fox	Newberg, Ore.	1891	David La Shana	P	398	48
George Peabody Coll. for Teachers	Nashville, Tenn.	1785	John Claunch	P	1,980	235
Geo. Washington Univ.	Washington, D.C.	1821	Lloyd H. Elliott	P	14,242	1,175
George Williams	Downers Grove, Ill	1890	Richard E. Hamlin	P	1,141	95
Georgetown	Georgetown, Ky.	1829	Robert L. Mills	D	1,158	84
Georgetown Univ.	Washington, D.C.	1789	Rev. R. J. Henle	D	9,430	621
Georgia	Milledgeville, Ga.	1889	J. Whitney Bunting	S	2,435	108
Georgia Inst. of Technology	Atlanta, Ga.	1885	Joseph M. Pettit	S	7,199	556
Georgia, Medical Coll. of (A)	Augusta, Ga.	1828	Harry B. O'Rear	S	796	473
Georgia Southern	Statesboro, Ga.	1906	Pope A. Duncan	S	5,576	336
Georgia Southwestern	Americus, Ga.	1908	William B. King	S	2,100	139
Georgia State Univ.	Atlanta, Ga.	1913	Noah N. Langdale	S	16,380	796
Georgia Univ. of*	Athens, Ga.	1785	Fred. C. Davison	S	19,000	2,100
Georgian Court (W)	Lakewood, N.J.	1908	Sis. Mary Stephanie	P	716	70
Gettysburg	Gettysburg, Pa.	1832	Carl Arnold Hanson	P	1,824	160
Glassboro State	Glassboro, N.J.	1923	Mark Chamberlain	S	11,266	450
Glenville State	Glenville, W. Va.	1872	D. Banks Wilburn	S	1,444	82
Goddard	Plainfield, Vt.	1938	Gerald S. Witherspoon	P	1,600	68

Name	Location	Year	Governing Official and Affiliation		Stu-dents	Teach-ers
Golden Gate Univ.	San Francisco, Calif.	1901	Otto Butz	P	5,700	550
Gonzaga Univ.	Spokane, Wash.	1887	Rev. R. E. Twohy	P	2,800	210
Gordon	Wenham, Mass.	1889	Harold J. Ockenga	P	757	45
Goshen	Goshen, Ind.	1894	J. Lawrence Burkholder	D	1,220	105
Goucher (W)	Towson, Md.	1885	Marvin B. Perry, Jr.	P	945	106
Governors State Univ.	Park Forest South, Ill.	1969	William Engbretson	S	1,511	100
Grace	Winona Lake, Ind.	1948	Herman A. Hoyt	D	613	43
Grace Bible Institute	Omaha, Nebr.	1943	Robert Benton	D	482	28
Graceland	Lamoni, Iowa	1895	William Higdon	P	1,240	89
Grambling	Grambling, La.	1901	Ralph W. E. Jones	S	3,663	203
Grand Canyon	Phoenix, Ariz.	1949	William R. Hintze	D	750	34
Grand Valley State	Allendale, Mich.	1960	Arend Lubbers	S	5,218	265
Gratz	Philadelphia, Pa.	1895	Elazar Goelman	P	181	17
Great Falls, Coll. of	Great Falls, Mont.	1932	Msgr. A. M. Brown	P	964	78
Greensboro	Greensboro, N.C.	1838	David G. Mobberley	D	579	55
Greenville	Greenville, Ill.	1892	Orley R. Herron	P	852	61
Grinnell	Grinnell, Ia.	1846	Glenn H. Leggett	P	1,230	122
Grove City	Grove City, Pa.	1876	Charles S. MacKenzie	P	2,071	120
Guilford	Greensboro, N.C.	1837	Grimsley T. Hobbs	D	1,611	124
Gulf-Coast Bible	Houston, Tex.	1953	Max Gaulke	D	265	23
Gustavus Adolphus	St. Peter, Minn.	1862	Frank R. Barth	D	1,867	139
Gwynedd-Mercy (W)	Gwynedd Valley, Pa.	1948	Sister Isabelle Keiss	P	909	80
Hahnemann Medical	Philadelphia, Pa.	1848	Wharton R. Shober	P	957	1,234
Hamilton (M)	Clinton, N.Y.	1812	Vacant	P	950	97
Hamline Univ.	St. Paul, Minn.	1854	Richard Bailey	P	1,297	142
Hampden-Sydney (M)	Hampden-Sydney, Va.	1776	W. Taylor Reveley	D	695	55
Hampshire	Amherst, Mass.	1965	Charles Longsworth	P	1,000	90
Hampton Institute	Hampton, Va.	1868	Roy D. Hudson	P	2,401	181
Hanover	Hanover, Ind.	1827	John F. Horner	P	969	73
Hardin-Simmons Univ.	Abilene, Tex.	1891	Elwin L. Skiles	P	1,930	148
Harding	Searcy, Ark.	1924	Clinton L. Ganus, Jr.	P	2,005	125
Harris Teachers	St. Louis, Mo.	1857	Richard Stumpe	Mu	1,017	71
Hartford, Univ. of	W. Harford, Conn.	1877	A. M. Woodruff	P	7,959	539
Hartwick	Oneonta, N.Y.	1928	Adolph G. Anderson	P	1,594	110
Harvard, Univ. (B)	Cambridge, Mass.	1636	Derek Curtis Bok	P	22,000	5,700
Harvey Mudd	Claremont, Calif.	1957	Joseph B. Platt	P	373	65
Hastings	Hastings, Neb.	1882	Clyde B. Matters	P	681	58
Haverford (M)	Haverford, Pa.	1833	John R. Coleman	P	750	80
Hawaii, The Church Coll. of	Laie, Hawaii	1955	Stephen Brower	P	969	70
Hawaii, Univ. of*	Honolulu, Hawaii	1907	Wytze Gorter	S	27,016	1,612
Heald Engineering	San Francisco, Calif.	1863	James E. Deitz	P	800	70
Heidelberg	Tiffin, Ohio	1850	Leslie H. Fishel, Jr.	Mu	1,141	109
Henderson State	Arkadelphia, Ark.	1890	Martin Garrison	S	3,064	152
Hendrix	Conway, Ark.	1884	Roy Shilling	D	1,021	54
High Point	High Point, N.C.	1924	Wendell M. Patton	D	1,000	65
Hillsdale	Hillsdale, Mich.	1844	George C. Roche, 3rd	P	1,085	65
Hiram	Hiram, Ohio	1850	Elmer Jagow	P	1,222	115
Hobart & William Smith	Geneva, N.Y.	1822	Allan A. Kuusisto	P	1,535	130
Hofstra Univ.	Hempstead, N.Y.	1935	Robert J. Payton	P	12,144	704
Hollins (W)	Hollins Coll., Va.	1842	John A. Logan, Jr.	P	1,084	93
Holy Cross, Coll. of the	Worcester, Mass	1843	Rev. John Brooks	D	2,236	190
Holy Family	Philadelphia, Pa.	1954	Sister Mary Lillian	D	813	68
Holy Family	Manitowoc, Wis.	1939	Sister Ann Kennedy	D	542	51
Holy Names	Oakland, Calif.	1880	Sister M. Irene Woodward	P	755	104
Hood (W)	Frederick, Md.	1893	Ross Pritchard	P	601	74
Hope	Holland, Mich.	1866	Gordon Van Wylen	P	2,082	134
Houghton	Houghton, N.Y.	1883	Wilber T. Dayton	P	1,260	85
Houston Baptist	Houston, Tex.	1963	William Hinton	D	1,058	71
Houston, Univ. of	Houston, Tex.	1927	Philip G. Hoffman	S	25,727	1,543
Howard Payne	Brownwood, Tex.	1889	Roger L. Brooks	D	1,391	85
Howard Univ.	Washington, D.C.	1867	James E. Cheek	P	6,592	1,537
Huntingdon	Montgomery, Ala.	1854	Allen Jackson	D	604	49
Huntington	Huntington, Ind.	1897	E. DeWitt Baker	P	446	31
Huron	Huron, S. Dak.	1883	Richard H. Timmins	P	554	48
Husson	Bangor, Me.	1898	Barkey Kibarian	P	900	55
Huston-Tillotson	Austin, Tex.	1876	John T. King	D	648	56
Idaho, Coll. of	Caldwell, Idaho	1891	Warren B. Knox	P	850	65
Idaho State Univ.	Pocatello, Idaho	1901	William E. Davis	S	8,035	296
Idaho, Univ. of*	Moscow, Idaho	1889	Ernest W. Hartung	S	6,663	550
Illinois	Jacksonville, Ill.	1829	Donald Mundinger	P	758	53
Illinois Benedictine	Lisle, Ill.	1887	Rev. Daniel Kucera	D	1,022	75
Illinois Coll. of Optometry	Chicago, Ill.	1872	Alfred Rosenbloom	P	483	47
Illinois Inst. of Technology	Chicago, Ill.	1892	John T. Rettaliata	P	5,316	378
Illinois State Univ.	Normal, Ill.	1857	David K. Berlo	S	17,032	1,038
Illinois, Univ. of*	Urbana; Champaign, Ill	1867	John E. Corbally	S	54,684	5,075
Chicago Circle	Chicago, Ill.	1965	Warren Cheston, Chan.	S	18,735	1,034
Medical Center	Chicago, Ill.	1896	Joseph Begando, Chan.	S	3,556	694
Urbana–Champaign	Urbana, Ill.	1867	Jack W. Peltason, Chan.	S	32,393	3,347
Illinois Wesleyan Univ.	Bloomington, Ill.	1850	Robert C. Eckley	P	1,700	130
Immaculata (W)	Immaculata, Pa.	1920	Sister Mary Antione	D	1,000	130
Immaculate Heart	Los Angeles, Calif.	1916	Sister Helen Kelley	P	820	62
Incarnate Word (A)	San Antonio, Tex.	1881	Vacant	D	1,608	106
Indiana Central	Indianapolis, Ind.	1902	Gene Sease	P	2,118	119
Indiana Inst. of Tech.	Ft. Wayne, Ind.	1930	Charles W. Terrell	P	550	41
Indiana State Univ.	Terre Haute, Ind.	1865	Alan Rankin	S	14,472	775
Indiana Univ.	Bloomington, Ind.	1820	John W. Ryan	S	68,546	2,999
Indiana Univ. of Penn.	Indiana, Pa.	1875	William Hassler	S	10,500	600
Insurance, Coll. of	New York, N.Y.	1962	A. Leslie Leonard	P	1,549	141
Inter American Univ.	San German, P.R.	1912	Sol Luis Descartes	P	9,145	178
Iona (A)	New Rochelle, N.Y.	1940	Rev. Bro. McKenna	D	3,106	200
Iowa State Univ.*	Ames, Iowa	1858	W. Robert Parks	S	17,251	1,995
Iowa, Univ. of	Iowa City, Iowa	1847	Willard L. Boyd	S	19,055	2,655
Iowa Wesleyan	Mt. Pleasant, Iowa	1842	Louis Haselmayer	P	804	54
Ithaca	Ithaca, N.Y.	1892	Ellis L. Phillips	P	4,302	315

(B) Oldest college in the United States.

Name	Location	Year	Governing Official and Affiliation		Students	Teachers
Jackson State	Jackson, Miss.	1877	John A. Peoples	S	5,100	340
Jacksonville State Univ.	Jacksonville, Ala.	1883	Ernest Stone	S	5,056	253
Jacksonville Univ.	Jacksonville, Fla.	1934	Robert H. Spiro	P	2,239	115
Jamestown	Jamestown, N.D.	1883	Roy Joe Stuckey	P	507	60
Jarvis Christian	Hawkins, Tex.	1912	John Paul Jones	D	577	51
Jersey City State	Jersey City, N.J.	1928	James Mullen	S	8,300	450
John Brown Univ.	Siloam Springs, Ark.	1919	John E. Brown, Jr.	P	614	56
John Carroll Univ.	Cleveland, Ohio	1886	Rev. Henry Birkenhauer	P	3,700	180
John F. Kennedy Univ.	Martinez, Calif.	1965	Harry L. Morrison	P	225	75
John F. Kennedy	Wahoo, Nebr.	1965	Theodore Dillon	P	215	26
John Marshall Law School	Chicago, Ill.	1899	Noble W. Lee	P	1,657	50
John Wesley	Owosso, Mich.	1909	Kenneth Armstrong	P	250	15
Johns Hopkins Univ.	Baltimore, Md.	1876	Steven Muller	P	9,023	1,199
Johnson Bible	Knoxville, Tenn.	1893	David Lawson Eubanks	D	220	15
Johnson C. Smith Univ.	Charlotte, N.C.	1867	Wilbert Greenfield	D	993	87
Johnson State	Johnson, Vt.	1867	William Craig	S	1,103	96
Johnson & Wales	Providence, R.I.	1914	Morris J. Gaebe	P	2,000	50
Jones	Jacksonville, Fla.	1918	Jack H. Jones	P	1,618	70
Judson (W)	Marion, Ala.	1838	N. H. McCrummen	D	438	40
Juilliard School, The	New York, N.Y.	1905	Peter Mennin	P	1,165	183
Juniata	Huntingdon, Pa.	1876	John Stauffer	P	1,200	84
Kalamazoo	Kalamazoo, Mich.	1833	George N. Rainsford	D	1,050	70
Kans. City Art Inst.	Kansas City, Mo.	1885	John W. Lottes	P	825	62
Kan. City Coll. of Osteop. Med.	Kansas City, Mo.	1916	Rudolph Bremen	P	456	73
Kansas Newman	Wichita, Kansas	1933	Rev. Roman S. Galiardi	P	609	52
Kansas State	Pittsburg, Kan.	1903	George F. Budd	S	4,937	286
Kansas State Teachers	Emporia, Kan.	1863	John E. Visser	S	6,117	289
Kansas State Univ.*	Manhattan, Kan.	1863	James A. McCain	S	14,223	748
Kansas, Univ. of	Lawrence, Kan.	1864	Raymond Nichols	S	19,026	1,168
Kansas Wesleyan	Salina, Kan.	1886	Vacant	P	510	31
Kearney State	Kearney, Nebr.	1905	Brendon McDonald	S	5,297	255
Keene State	Keene, N.H.	1909	Leo Redfern	S	2,706	125
Kent State Univ.	Kent, Ohio	1910	Glenn A. Olds	S	17,816	940
Kentucky State Univ.*	Frankfort, Ky.	1886	Carl M. Hill	S	1,961	125
Kentucky, Univ. of*	Lexington, Ky.	1865	Otis A. Singletary	S	19,331	1,750
Kentucky Wesleyan	Owensboro, Ky.	1783	William James	P	933	71
Kenyon	Gambier, Ohio	1824	William Caples	P	1,383	113
Keuka (W)	Keuka Park, N.Y.	1890	G. Wayne Glick	P	650	59
King	Bristol, Tenn.	1867	Powell A. Fraser	D	300	38
King's	Briarcliff Manor, N.Y.	1938	Robert A. Cook	P	727	68
King's	Wilkes-Barre, Pa.	1946	Rev. L. D. Kilburn	P	2,428	135
Kirkland (W)	Clinton, N.Y.	1965	Samuel F. Babbitt	P	583	45
Kirksville Coll. of Osteopathic Med.	Kirksville, Mo.	1892	Morris Thompson	P	440	91
Knox	Galesburg, Ill.	1837	Sharvy G. Umbeck	P	1,349	104
Knoxville	Knoxville, Tenn.	1875	Robert Owens	D	1,100	100
Kutztown State	Kutztown, Pa.	1866	Lawrence M. Stratton	S	4,850	270
Ladycliff	Highland Falls, N.Y.	1933	Francis J. Breidenbach	P	427	51
Lafayette	Easton, Pa.	1832	K. R. Bergethon	P	2,004	198
LaGrange	LaGrange, Ga.	1831	Waights Henry, Jr.	D	590	42
Lake Erie	Painesville, Ohio	1856	Paul Weaver	P	784	77
Lake Forest	Lake Forest, Ill.	1857	Eugene Hotchkiss	P	1,055	91
Lakeland	Sheboygan, Wis.	1856	John B. Morland	P	475	42
Lake Superior State	Sault Ste. Marie, Mich.	1946	Kenneth Shouldice	S	1,630	101
Lamar Univ.	Beaumont, Tex.	1923	John E. Gray	S	10,069	511
Lambuth	Jackson, Tenn.	1843	James S. Wilder	D	748	67
Lander	Greenwood, S.C.	1872	Larry Jackson	S	867	51
Lane	Jackson, Tenn.	1882	Herman Stone	D	850	57
Langston Univ.*	Langston, Okla.	1897	William E. Sims	S	1,132	60
LaRoche	Pittsburgh, Pa.	1963	Sister De la Salle Mahler	D	400	47
La Salle	Philadelphia, Pa.	1863	Bro. Daniel Burke	D	7,948	450
La Verne	La Verne, Calif.	1891	Leland Newcomer	P	1,210	74
Lawrence Inst. of Tech.	Southfield, Mich.	1932	W. H. Buell	P	4,026	189
Lawrence Univ.	Appleton, Wis.	1847	Thomas S. Smith	P	1,275	122
Layton School of Art and Design	Milwaukee, Wis.	1920	Neil Lieberman	P	257	38
Lea	Albert Lea, Minn.	1966	Fred Glassburner	P	272	28
Lebanon Valley	Annville, Pa.	1866	Frederick Sample	P	1,093	93
Lee	Cleveland, Tenn.	1918	Charles Conn	Mu	1,024	61
Lehigh Univ.	Bethlehem, Pa.	1865	W. Deming Lewis	P	5,539	541
Le Moyne	Syracuse, N.Y.	1946	Rev. William L. Reilly	P	1,654	130
Le Moyne-Owen	Memphis, Tenn.	1862	Odell Horton	P	827	47
Lenoir Rhyne	Hickory, N.C.	1891	Raymond Bost	D	1,298	114
Lesley (W)	Cambridge, Mass.	1909	Don A. Orton	P	809	70
LeTourneau	Longview, Tex.	1946	Harry Hardwick	P	702	55
Lewis Univ.	Lockport, Ill.	1930	Lester Carr	D	2,450	139
Lewis & Clark	Portland, Ore.	1867	John R. Howard	D	2,352	120
Limestone	Gaffney, S.C.	1845	Melvin Stanyarne Bell	P	546	44
Lincoln Christian	Lincoln, Ill.	1944	L. H. Appel	D	939	36
Lincoln Memorial Univ.	Harrogate, Tenn.	1897	Charles West, act.	P	500	36
Lincoln Univ.	Jefferson City, Mo.	1866	Walter C. Daniel	S	2,345	147
Lincoln Univ.	Lincoln Univ., Pa.	1854	Herman Branson	S	996	100
Lincoln Univ.	San Francisco, Calif.	1919	T. Kong Lee	P	800	48
Lindenwood	St. Charles, Mo.	1827	John A. Brown	P	797	50
Linfield	McMinnville, Ore.	1849	Gordon Bjork	P	1,100	75
Livingston Univ.	Livingston, Ala.	1835	Asa Green	S	1,243	74
Livingstone	Salisbury, N.C.	1879	F. George Shipman	P	744	74
Lock Haven State	Lock Haven, Pa.	1870	Francis Hamblin	S	2,262	164
Loma Linda Univ.	Loma Linda, Calif.	1905	David J. Bieber	P	3,500	500
Lone Mountain	San Francisco, Calif.	1898	Sister Gertrude Patch	D	824	49
Long Island Univ.	Brooklyn, N.Y.	1926	Alexander Aldrich	P	6,985	400
C. W. Post	Greenvale, N.Y.	1954	Vacant	P	9,700	331
Longwood (W)	Farmville, Va.	1839	Henri I. Willett, Jr.	S	2,286	145
Loras	Dubuque, Iowa	1839	Msgr. Francis P. Friedl	D	1,452	96
Los Angeles Baptist	Newhall, Calif.	1927	John Dunkin	D	290	27
Loretto Heights	Denver, Colo.	1918	Ronald C. Hayes	P	746	63
Louisiana	Pineville, La.	1906	G. Earl Guinn	P	879	62
Louisiana Tech. Univ.	Ruston, La.	1894	F. J. Taylor	S	7,076	502

Name	Location	Year	Governing Official and Affiliation		Stu-dents	Teach-ers
Louisiana St. Univ.*	Baton Rouge, La.	1860	Martin Woodin	S	36,528	3,686
Baton Rouge Campus	Baton Rouge, La.	1860	C. G. Taylor (Chan.)	S	20,243	1,216
Medical Center	New Orleans, La.	1931	William H. Stewart (Chan.)	S	1,360	1,489
New Orleans Campus	New Orleans, La.	1956	Homer L. Hitt (Chan.)	S	11,305	496
Louisville, Univ. of	Louisville, Ky.	1798	Woodrow Strickler	S	10,781	1,402
Lowell State	Lowell, Mass.	1894	D. H. O'Leary	S	2,359	169
Lowell Technological Inst.	Lowell, Mass.	1895	Everett V. Olsen	S	7,000	440
Loyola	Baltimore, Md.	1852	V. Rev. J. A. Sellinger	D	3,588	185
Loyola Univ.	Chicago, Ill.	1870	Rev. R. C. Baumhart	D	13,787	630
Loyola Univ.	New Orleans, La.	1912	Rev. M. F. Kennelly	D	4,201	322
Loyola Marymount Univ.	Los Angeles, Calif.	1911	Rev. D. P. Merrifield	D	4,715	268
Lubbock Christian	Lubbock, Texas	1956	F. W. Mattox	D	946	76
Luther	Decorah, Iowa	1861	Elwin D. Farwell	P	1,960	162
Luther Rice	Alexandria, Va.	1967	Chester Bishop	P	175	28
Lycoming	Williamsport, Pa.	1812	Harold Hutson	P	1,592	85
Lynchburg	Lynchburg, Va.	1903	Carey Brewer	P	1,600	107
Lyndon State	Lyndonville, Vt.	1911	H. Franklin Irwin	S	642	58
Macalester	St. Paul, Minn.	1874	James A. Robinson	P	1,834	158
MacMurray	Jacksonville, Ill.	1846	John Wittich	P	980	62
Madison	Harrisonburg, Va.	1908	Ronald Carrier	S	5,315	350
Madison Business	Madison, Wisc.	1856	Otto J. Madland	P	293	19
Madonna	Livonia, Mich.	1947	Sister Mary Danatha	D	841	53
Maine Maritime Academy (M)	Castine, Me.	1941	E. A. Rodgers (Supt.)	S	552	54
Maine, Univ. of	Orono, Me.	1865	Winthrop C. Libby	S	8,782	545
at Farmington	Farmington, Maine	1864	Einar A. Olsen	S	1,803	89
at Ft. Kent	Ft. Kent, Maine	1878	Richard J. Spath	S	505	28
at Portland-Gorham	Portland, Maine	1970	W. P. Fridinger, act.	S	6,514	225
at Machias	Machias, Maine	1909	Arthur Buswell	S	536	48
at Presque Isle	Presque Isle, Maine	1903	Stanley Salwak	S	1,354	89
Malone	Canton, Ohio	1892	Lon D. Randall	D	800	50
Manchester	No. Manchester, Ind.	1889	Alfred B. Helman	P	1,270	99
Manhattan	Bronx, N.Y.	1853	Brother Gregory Nugent	P	4,127	314
Manhattan Sch. of Music	New York, N.Y.	1917	George Schick	P	968	193
Manhattanville	Purchase, N.Y.	1841	Elizabeth J. McCormack	P	2,091	142
Mankato State	Mankato, Minn.	1867	James F. Nickerson	S	11,300	662
Mannes College of Music	New York, N.Y.	1916	John Goldmark	P	186	90
Mansfield State	Mansfield, Pa.	1857	Lawrence Park	S	3,281	218
Marian	Indianapolis, Ind.	1851	Louis C. Gatto	P	835	81
Marian Coll. of Fond du Lac	Fond du Lac, Wis.	1936	James Hanlon	D	440	53
Marietta	Marietta, Ohio	1835	Frank E. Duddy	P	1,937	140
Marion	Marion, Ind.	1920	Woodrow Goodman	P	685	53
Marist	Poughkeepsie, N.Y.	1929	Linus Richard Foy	P	1,697	100
Marlboro	Marlboro, Vt.	1946	Thomas B. Ragle	P	207	34
Marquette Univ.	Milwaukee, Wis.	1880	V. Rev. J. P. Raynor	P	10,671	700
Mars Hill	Mars Hill, N.C.	1856	Fred Blake Bentley	P	1,407	106
Marshall Univ.	Huntington, W. Va.	1837	John G. Barker	S	7,794	399
Mary Baldwin (W)	Staunton, Va.	1842	William Watkins Kelly	D	740	55
Mary Hardin Baylor	Belton, Tex.	1845	Bobby E. Parker	D	1,063	64
Mary Manse	Toledo, Ohio	1922	Sister Rose Margaret	D	560	45
Mary Washington	Fredericksburg, Va.	1908	G. C. Simpson	S	2,040	167
Marycrest	Davenport, Iowa	1939	Sister Cathleen Real	D	1,065	75
Marygrove	Detroit, Mich.	1925	Raymond Fleck	D	1,128	97
Maryland Inst. of Art	Baltimore, Md.	1826	Eugene W. Leake	P	1,026	93
Maryland, Univ. of*	College Park, Md.	1807	Charles Bishop, Chan.	S	45,000	6,000
Eastern Shore	Princess Anne, Md.	1886	Archie Buffkins (Chan.)	S	600	55
Marylhurst	Marylhurst, Ore.	1893	Sister Marian D. Robinson	D	700	48
Marymount	Salina, Kan.	1922	Emerald Dechant	D	575	55
Marymount (W)	Tarrytown, N.Y.	1919	John Meng	P	1,007	101
Marymount Manhattan (W)	New York, N.Y.	1936	Sis. Colette Mahoney	D	1,283	83
Maryville	Maryville, Tenn.	1819	Joseph J. Copeland	D	669	63
Maryville	St. Louis, Mo.	1872	Sister Harriet Switzer	D	797	65
Marywood (W)	Scranton, Pa.	1915	Sister M. Coleman Nee	P	2,319	183
Massachusetts Coll. of Art	Boston, Mass.	1873	Jack Nolan	P	1,406	93
Mass. Coll. of Pharmacy	Boston, Mass.	1823	Raymond A. Gosselin	P	650	63
Mass. Institute of Tech.*	Cambridge, Mass.	1861	Jerome Wiesner	P	7,432	950
Mass. Maritime Academy (M)	Buzzards Bay, Mass.	1891	Adm. Lee Harrington	S	763	58
Massachusetts, Univ. of*	Amherst, Mass.	1863	Robert Wood	S	23,270	1,288
Boston Campus	Boston, Mass.	1964	F. L. Broderick (Chan.)	S	4,235	270
Mayville State	Mayville, N. Dak.	1889	T. S. Jenkins	S	600	40
McKendree	Lebanon, Ill.	1828	Eric N. Rackham	P	460	38
McMurry	Abilene, Tex.	1923	Tom K. Kim	D	1,380	92
McNeese State Univ.	Lake Charles, La.	1939	Thomas S. Leary	S	5,674	335
McPherson	McPherson, Kan.	1887	Galen Snell	D	436	37
Medaille	Buffalo, N.Y.	1937	Sister Alice Huber	P	453	34
Medical Coll. of Pa.	Philadelphia, Pa.	1850	Bernard Sigel	P	306	336
Meharry Medical	Nashville, Tenn.	1876	Lloyd C. Elam	P	622	239
Memphis Academy of Arts	Memphis, Tenn.	1936	Edwin C. Rust (Dir.)	P	204	27
Memphis State Univ.	Memphis, Tenn.	1909	John Richardson, act.	S	20,293	828
Menlo	Menlo Park, Calif.	1915	Richard O'Brien	P	555	50
Mercer Univ.	Macon, Ga.	1833	Rufus C. Harris	P	2,642	170
Mercy	Dobbs Ferry, N.Y.	1950	Donald Grunewald	P	1,716	107
Mercy Coll. of Detroit	Detroit, Mich.	1941	Sister Agnes Mary Mansour	D	1,914	120
Mercyhurst	Erie, Pa.	1926	Marion Shane	D	1,250	100
Meredith (W)	Raleigh, N.C.	1891	John Edgar Weems	D	1,350	82
Merrimack	No. Andover, Mass.	1947	Rev. John Aherne	P	2,606	194
Messiah	Grantham, Pa.	1909	D. Ray Hostetter	P	792	84
Methodist	Fayetteville, N.C.	1960	Stacy R. Weaver	P	704	52
Metropolitan State	Denver, Colo.	1965	James D. Palmer	S	7,509	320
Miami Univ.	Oxford, Ohio	1809	Phillip R. Shriver	S	15,807	770
Miami, Univ. of	Coral Gables, Fla.	1925	Henry K. Stanford	P	13,056	1,231
Michigan State Univ.*	East Lansing, Mich.	1855	Clifton R. Wharton, Jr.	S	41,349	3,201
Michigan Technological Univ.	Houghton, Mich.	1885	Raymond L. Smith	S	4,417	368
Michigan, Univ. of	Ann Arbor, Mich.	1817	Robben W. Fleming	S	41,178	4,904
at Dearborn	Dearborn, Mich.	1959	Leonard E. Goodall, Chan.	S	2,607	80
Mid-America Nazarene	Olathe, Kansas	1966	R. Curtis Smith	P	758	50
Middle Tennessee State Univ.	Murfreesboro, Tenn.	1911	M. G. Scarlett	S	8,719	535
Middlebury	Middlebury, Vt.	1800	James I. Armstrong	P	1,848	130
Midland Lutheran	Fremont, Nebr.	1883	L. Dale Lund	P	753	53
Midwestern Univ.	Wichita Falls, Tex.	1922	Travis A. White	S	4,008	179

Name	Location	Year	Governing Official and Affiliation		Stu-dents	Teach-ers
Miles	Birmingham, Ala.	1905	W. Clyde Williams	P	1,100	105
Millersville State	Millersville, Pa.	1855	William Duncan	S	5,900	334
Milligan	Milligan Coll., Tenn.	1881	Jess W. Johnson	P	685	52
Millikin Univ.	Decatur, Ill.	1903	J. Roger Miller	P	1,451	110
Mills (W)	Oakland, Calif.	1852	Robert J. Wert	P	1,005	106
Mills Coll. of Education (W)	New York, N.Y.	1909	Margaret Devine	P	425	63
Millsaps	Jackson, Miss.	1890	Edward Collins	D	888	59
Milton	Milton, Wis.	1867	Kenneth E. Smith	P	600	56
Milwaukee Sch. of Eng.	Milwaukee, Wis.	1903	Karl O. Werwath	P	1,880	98
Minneapolis Coll. of Art & Design	Minneapolis, Minn.	1886	Arnold Herstand	P	688	39
Minnesota, Univ. of*	Minneapolis, Minn.	1851	Malcolm C. Moos	S	44,756	6,659
Duluth Campus	Duluth, Minn.	1947	R. W. Darland (Prov.)	S	5,300	327
Morris Campus	Morris, Minn.	1960	John Imholte (Prov.)	S	1,745	102
Minot State	Minot, N. Dak.	1913	Gordon Olson	S	2,613	145
Misericordia (W)	Dallas, Pa.	1924	Sister Miriam Teresa	P	1,024	92
Mississippi	Clinton, Miss.	1826	Lewis Nobles	D	2,478	130
Mississippi Industrial	Holly Springs, Miss.	1905	E. E. Rankin	D	400	40
Miss. St. Coll. for Women (W)	Columbus, Miss.	1884	Charles P. Hogarth	S	2,583	160
Mississippi State Univ.*	State Coll., Miss.	1879	William L. Giles	S	9,111	767
Mississippi Univ. of	University, Miss.	1848	P. E. Fortune, Jr. (Chan.)	S	8,300	350
Mississippi Valley State	Itta Bena, Miss.	1950	E. A. Boykins	S	2,530	127
Missouri Southern State	Joplin, Mo.	1937	Leon Billingsly	S	2,794	132
Missouri Univ. of*	Columbia, Mo.	1839	C. Brice Ratchford	S	44,884	2,761
At Columbia	Columbia, Mo.	1839	H. W. Schooling (Chan.)	S	20,836	1,587
At Kansas City	Kansas City, Mo.	1929	James Olson (Chan.)	S	9,439	440
At Rolla	Rolla, Mo.	1870	Merl Baker (Chan.)	S	3,885	400
At St. Louis	St. Louis, Mo.	1963	Everett Walters, act.	S	10,724	330
Missouri Valley	Marshall, Mo.	1889	Willis Tompkins	P	597	50
Missouri Western	St. Joseph, Mo.	1915	Marvin Looney	S	3,056	177
Mobile	Mobile, Ala.	1961	William K. Weaver, Jr.	P	612	35
Molloy (A)	Rockville Ctre., N.Y.	1955	Vacant	D	1,127	106
Monmouth	Monmouth, Ill.	1853	Richard Stine	P	907	78
Monmouth	W. Long Branch, N.J.	1933	Richard J. Stonesifer	P	3,811	240
Montana Coll. of Mineral Science and Technology	Butte, Mont.	1893	Fred W. DeMoney	S	713	55
Montana State Univ.	Bozeman, Mont.	1893	Carl McIntosh	S	8,113	548
Montana, Univ. of	Missoula, Mont.	1895	Robert Pantzer	S	8,500	450
Montclair State	Upper Montclair, N.J.	1908	David W. D. Dickson	S	13,500	631
Monterey Inst. of Foreign Studies	Monterey, Calif.	1955	Fulton Freeman	P	355	55
Montevallo, Univ. of	Montevallo, Ala.	1896	Kermit Johnson	S	2,750	135
Moody Bible Institute	Chicago, Ill.	1886	George Sweeting	P	1,084	116
Moore Coll. of Art (W)	Philadelphia, Pa.	1844	Mayo Bryce	P	602	75
Moorhead State	Moorhead, Minn.	1885	Roland Dille	S	4,590	306
Moravian	Bethlehem, Pa.	1807	Herman E. Collier	D	1,440	92
Morehead State Univ.	Morehead, Ky.	1922	Adron Doran	S	6,220	300
Morehouse (M)	Atlanta, Ga.	1867	Hugh Gloster	P	1,029	94
Morgan State	Baltimore, Md.	1867	King V. Cheek	S	5,144	279
Morningside	Sioux City, Iowa	1894	Thomas S. Thompson	P	1,495	88
Morris Brown	Atlanta, Ga.	1881	John A. Middleton	P	1,417	102
Morris Harvey	Charleston, W. Va.	1888	Marshall Buckalew	P	2,417	145
Mt. Angel	Mt. Angel, Ore.	1887	Rev. Christian Mondor	P	267	40
Mt. Holyoke (W)	So. Hadley, Mass.	1837	David Truman	P	1,868	199
Mt. Marty	Yankton, S.D.	1936	Sister Evangeline Anderson	D	456	74
Mt. Mary (W)	Milwaukee, Wis.	1913	Sister Mary Nora Barber	P	825	98
Mt. Mercy	Cedar Rapids, Iowa	1928	Sister Mary Agnes	P	752	68
Mt. St. Joseph-on-the-Ohio (W)	Mt. St. Joseph, Ohio	1920	Robert Wolverton	P	843	67
Mt. St. Mary (W)	Hooksett, N. Hamp.	1934	Sister Amy Hoey	P	240	36
Mt. St. Mary	Newburgh, N.Y.	1954	William O'Hara	P	682	65
Mt. St. Mary's	Los Angeles, Calif.	1925	Sister Cecilia Louise	D	1,330	117
Mt. St. Mary's	Emmitsburg, Md.	1808	John J. Dillon	D	1,236	78
Mt. St. Vincent, Coll. of (W)	Riverdale, N.Y.	1847	Sister Mary David Barry	P	1,143	90
Mt. Senario	Ladysmith, Wis.	1962	Robert Lovett	P	243	27
Mt. Union	Alliance, Ohio	1846	Ronald Weber	P	1,278	107
Muhlenberg	Allentown, Pa.	1848	John H. Morey	P	1,815	126
Multnomah Sch. of the Bible	Portland, Ore.	1936	Willard M. Aldrich	P	675	34
Mundelein (W)	Chicago, Ill.	1930	Sister Ann Ida Gannon	P	1,138	94
Murray State Univ.	Murray, Ky.	1922	Harry Sparks	S	6,633	377
Muskingum	New Concord, Ohio	1837	William P. Miller	P	1,195	116
Nasson	Springvale, Me.	1912	John S. Bailey	P	829	60
Nathaniel Hawthorne	Antrim, N.H.	1962	Kenneth McLaughlin	P	800	55
National Coll. of Business	Rapid City, S.D.	1941	John Hauer	P	777	46
National Coll. of Chiropractic	Lombard, Ill.	1906	Joseph Janse	P	450	39
National Coll. of Education	Evanston, Ill.	1886	Calvin Gross	P	500	70
Nazareth	Kalamazoo, Mich.	1924	Sis. Mary L. Bader	P	1,917	111
Nazareth Coll. of Rochester (W)	Rochester, N.Y.	1924	Alice Foley	P	4,247	149
Nebraska, Univ. of*	Lincoln, Nebr.	1869	James H. Zumberge	S	21,581	1,103
At Omaha	Omaha, Nebr.	1908	Ronald Roskens, Chan.	S	12,224	720
Nebraska Wesleyan Univ.	Lincoln, Nebr.	1887	Vance D. Rogers	P	1,080	100
Nevada, Univ. of*	Reno, Nev.	1874	N. Edd Miller	S	6,908	409
At Las Vegas	Las Vegas, Nev.	1955	Roman J. Zorn	S	3,570	154
New	Sarasota, Fla.	1964	Arland Christ-Janer	P	564	55
New England	Henniker, N.H.	1946	Jere Chase	P	1,458	83
New England Cons. of Music	Boston, Mass.	1867	Gunther Schuller	P	602	128
New Hampshire	Manchester, N.H.	1932	Edward Shapiro	P	1,495	43
New Hampshire, Univ. of*	Durham, N.H.	1866	Thomas Bonner	S	10,529	734
New Haven, Univ. of*	New Haven, Conn.	1926	Marvin K. Petersen	P	5,100	250
New Mexico Highlands Univ.	Las Vegas, N. Mex.	1893	Frank Angel	S	2,400	120
N. Mex. Inst. of Min. & Tech.	Socorro, N. Mex.	1889	Stirling A. Colgate	S	816	72
New Mexico State Univ.*	Las Cruces, N. Mex.	1888	Gerald W. Thomas	S	10,727	490
New Mexico, Univ. of	Albuquerque, N. Mex.	1889	Ferrel Heady	S	18,853	1,560
New Rochelle, Coll. of (W)	New Rochelle, N.Y.	1904	Joseph McMurray	P	2,351	130
New Sch. for Social Research	New York, N.Y.	1919	John R. Everett	P	15,000	1,000
New York, City Univ. of	New York, N.Y.	1847	Robert J. Kibbee	Mu	155,414	11,727
Bernard M. Baruch	New York, N.Y.	1919	Clyde Wingfield	Mu	14,423	1,050
Brooklyn	Brooklyn, N.Y.	1930	John W. Kneller	Mu	34,348	2,694
City	New York, N.Y.	1847	Robert E. Marshak	Mu	20,654	1,938
Medgar Evers	Brooklyn, N.Y.	1968	Richard D. Trent	Mu	1,521	155
Hunter	New York, N.Y.	1870	Jacqueline G. Wexler	Mu	25,201	1,702
John Jay Coll. of Criminal Justice	New York, N.Y.	1964	D. H. Riddle	Mu	7,659	418

Name	Location	Year	Governing Official and Affiliation		Students	Teachers
Herbert H. Lehman	Bronx, N.Y.	1931	Leonard Lief	Mu	14,626	1,103
Queens	Flushing, N.Y.	1937	Joseph Murphy	Mu	30,027	2,213
Richmond	Staten Island, N.Y.	1965	Herbert Schueler	Mu	3,478	229
York	Jamaica, N.Y.	1966	Milton G. Bassin	Mu	3,477	225
N.Y. Inst. of Technology	Old Westbury, N.Y.	1955	Alexander Schure	P	4,520	200
New York Law School	New York, N.Y.	1891	Sylvester C. Smith, Jr.	P	800	10
New York Medical	New York, N.Y.	1860	Frederick L. Stone	P	613	1,200
New York, State Univ. of	Albany, N.Y.	1948	Ernest L. Boyer, (Chan.)	S	142,751	8,468
State Univ.	Albany, N.Y.	1844	Louis T. Benezet	S	13,571	762
" "	Buffalo, N.Y.	1846	Robert Ketter	S	20,963	949
" "	Binghamton, N.Y.	1946	C. Peter Magrath	S	7,930	418
" "	Stony Brook, N.Y.	1957	John Toll	S	12,058	601
State Univ. Colleges	Brockport, N.Y.	1867	Albert W. Brown	S	9,762	478
" " "	Buffalo, N.Y.	1867	Elbert K. Fretwell	S	10,660	526
" " "	Cortland, N.Y.	1866	Richard Jones	S	5,483	297
" " "	Fredonia, N.Y.	1867	Dallas Beal	S	5,334	287
" " "	Geneseo, N.Y.	1867	Robert Mac Vittie	S	5,699	291
" " "	New Paltz, N.Y.	1885	Stanley K. Coffman	S	8,225	383
" " "	Oneonta, N.Y.	1887	Clifford Craven	S	5,967	368
" " "	Oswego, N.Y.	1861	Sherwood Dunham, (Act.)	S	8,312	414
" " "	Old Westbury, N.Y.	1965	John Maguire	S	774	53
" " "	Plattsburgh, N.Y.	1889	George W. Angell	S	5,885	298
" " "	Potsdam, N.Y.	1867	Thomas Barrington	S	4,936	266
" " "	Purchase, N.Y.	1965	Abbott Kaplan	S	1,532	51
" " "	Utica, N.Y.	1966	William Kunsela	S	613	24
Empire State	Saratoga Springs, N.Y.	1971	James Hall	S	764	52
Agriculture & Life Sciences	Ithaca, N.Y.	1904	W. Keith Kennedy, Dean	S	3,665	393
Buffalo Health Sciences Center	Buffalo, N.Y.	1846	Clyde L. Randall, V.P.	S	2,189	429
College of Ceramics	Alfred, N.Y.	1900	W. G. Lawrence, Dean	S	556	42
Coll. of Sci. & Forestry	Ithaca, N.Y.	1911	Edward Palmer	S	1,867	94
College of Human Ecology	Ithaca, N.Y.	1925	David Knapp (Dean)	S	1,316	197
Downstate Medical Center	Brooklyn, N.Y.	1858	Calvin H. Plimpton	S	1,331	437
Health Sciences Center	Stony Brook, N.Y.	1957	Edmund Pellegrino	S	626	93
Maritime College (M)	Bronx, N.Y.	1874	Sheldon Kinney	S	803	59
School of Ind. & Labor Rel.	Ithaca, N.Y.	1944	Robert B. McKersie (Dean)	S	663	50
Upstate Medical Center	Syracuse, N.Y.	1834	Lewis H. Bluemle, Jr.	S	914	187
Veterinary Medicine	Ithaca, N.Y.	1894	G. C. Poppensiek (Dn.)	S	298	78
New York Univ.	New York, N.Y.	1831	James M. Hester	P	35,129	4,930
Newark Coll. of Engineering	Newark, N.J.	1881	William Hazell	S	4,267	315
Newark State	Union, N.J.	1855	Nathan Weiss	S	12,164	712
Newberry	Newberry, S.C.	1856	Fredric Brinker Irvin	D	753	61
Newton Coll. of Sacred Heart (W)	Newton, Mass.	1946	James Whalen	P	974	98
Niagara Univ.	Niagara Un., N.Y.	1856	Rev. K. F. Slattery	D	3,382	215
Nicholls State Univ.	Thibodaux, La.	1948	Vernon Galliano	S	5,407	231
Nichols	Dudley, Mass.	1815	Darcy C. Coyle	P	655	45
Norfolk State	Norfolk, Va.	1935	Lyman Brooks	S	5,621	300
North Adams State	North Adams, Mass.	1894	James Amsler	S	2,024	65
No. Carolina A. & T. State U.	Greensboro, N.C.	1891	Lewis Dowdy	S	4,456	265
North Carolina Central Univ.	Durham, N.C.	1910	Albert N. Whiting	S	3,470	269
North Carolina School of the Arts	Winston-Salem, N.C.	1963	Robert Ward	S	580	100
North Carolina, Univ. of						
at Asheville	Asheville, N.C.	1969	William Highsmith	S	1,091	71
at Chapel Hill	Chapel Hill, N.C.	1789	N. F. Taylor	S	19,500	1,800
at Charlotte	Charlotte, N.C.	1946	D. W. Colvard (Chan.)	S	5,200	268
at Greensboro	Greensboro, N.C.	1891	J. S. Ferguson (Chan.)	S	7,076	475
at Raleigh, State Univ.	Raleigh, N.C.	1887	J. T. Caldwell (Chan.)	S	12,829	913
at Wilmington	Wilmington, N.C.	1947	Wm H. Wagoner (Chan.)	S	2,206	132
North Carolina Wesleyan	Rocky Mount, N.C.	1956	Thomas A. Collins	D	581	43
North Central Bible	Minneapolis, Minn.	1930	Rev. E. M. Clark	D	420	25
North Central	Naperville, Ill.	1861	Arlo L. Schilling	D	779	63
North Dakota State Univ.	Fargo, N. Dak.	1890	L. D. Loftsgard	S	6,660	350
North Dakota, Univ. of	Grand Forks, N. Dak.	1883	Thomas Clifford	S	8,282	625
North Georgia	Dahlonega, Ga.	1873	John H. Owen	S	1,383	96
North Park	Chicago, Ill.	1891	Lloyd Ahlem	P	1,096	110
North Texas State Univ.	Denton, Tex.	1890	C. C. Nolen	S	14,582	1,004
Northeast Louisiana Univ.	Monroe, La.	1931	George T. Walker	S	8,362	483
Northeast Missouri St. Univ.	Kirksville, Mo.	1867	Charles T. McClain	S	5,894	278
Northeastern Illinois Univ.	Chicago, Ill.	1861	Jerome M. Sachs	S	8,200	471
Northeastern State	Tahlequah, Okla.	1846	Robert Collier	S	5,079	234
Northeastern Univ.	Boston, Mass.	1898	Asa S. Knowles	P	35,000	2,000
Northern Arizona Univ.	Flagstaff, Ariz.	1899	J. Lawrence Walkup	S	7,520	455
Northern Colorado, Univ. of	Greeley, Colo.	1890	Richard R. Bond	S	9,650	561
Northern Ill. Univ.	DeKalb, Ill.	1899	Richard Nelson	S	19,801	1,400
Northern Iowa, Univ. of	Cedar Falls, Iowa	1876	John Kamerick	S	9,011	502
Northern Michigan Univ.	Marquette, Mich.	1899	John X. Jamrich	S	8,053	284
Northern Montana	Harve, Mont.	1929	Joseph R. Crowley	S	1,005	84
Northern State	Aberdeen, S. Dak.	1901	Norbert Baumgart	S	2,392	163
Northland	Ashland, Wis.	1892	Malcolm McLean	P	610	50
Northrop Inst. of Tech.	Inglewood, Calif.	1942	B. J. Shell	P	1,335	72
Northwest	Kirkland, Wash.	1934	Rev. D. V. Hurst	D	452	28
Northwest Christian	Eugene, Ore.	1895	Barton A. Dowdy	D	435	21
Northwest Missouri State Univ.	Maryville, Mo.	1905	Robert P. Foster	S	5,039	304
Northwest Nazarene	Nampa, Idaho	1913	Vacant	D	921	67
Northwestern	Watertown, Wisc.	1865	Carleton Toppe	D	270	18
Northwestern	Orange City, Iowa	1882	Lars Granberg	P	643	54
Northwestern State Univ.	Natchitoches, La.	1884	Arnold R. Kilpatrick	S	6,327	335
Northwestern State	Alva, Okla	1897	R. W. Wygle	S	2,029	91
Northwestern Univ.	Evanston, Ill.	1851	James Miller, Chan.	P	14,418	2,400
Norwich Univ.	Northfield, Vt.	1819	Loring Hart	P	1,370	149
Northwood Institute	Midland, Mich.	1959	Arthur E. Turner	P	1,934	68
Notre Dame, Coll. of	Belmont, Calif.	1868	Sister Catharine Julie	D	1,141	136
Notre Dame (W)	St. Louis, Mo.	1954	Sister Barbara Brumleve	D	282	31
Notre Dame (W)	Manchester, N.H.	1950	Sister Jeannette Vezeau	D	413	47
Notre Dame (W)	Cleveland, Ohio	1922	Sister Mary Luke	P	526	79
Notre Dame of Maryland	Baltimore, Md.	1895	Sister Kathleen Feeley	D	631	78
Notre Dame, Univ. of (M)	Notre Dame, Ind.	1842	Rev. T. M. Hesburgh	D	8,344	625
Nova Univ. of Advanced Technology	Ft. Lauderdale, Fla.	1964	Abraham S. Fischler	D	377	39
Nyack	Nyack, N.Y.	1882	Harold W. Boon	D	596	50

Name	Location	Year	Governing Official and Affiliation		Stu-dents	Teach-ers
Oakland Univ.	Rochester, Mich.	1957	Donald D. O'Dowd	S	8,365	382
Oakland City	Oakland City, Ind.	1885	Bernard A. Loposer	D	670	38
Oakwood	Huntsville, Ala.	1896	C. B. Rock	D	775	65
Oberlin	Oberlin, Ohio	1833	Robert Fuller	P	2,696	262
Occidental	Los Angeles, Calif.	1887	Richard C. Gilman	P	1,741	145
Oglethorpe Univ.	Atlanta, Ga.	1835	Paul K. Vonk	P	981	40
Ohio Dominican	Columbus, Ohio	1911	Sister M. Suzanne Uhrhane	D	949	73
Ohio Coll. of Podiatric Medicine	Cleveland, Ohio	1916	Abe Rubin	P	399	75
Ohio Inst. of Technology	Columbus, Ohio	1952	Richard A. Czesniak	P	1,050	46
Ohio Northern Univ.	Ada, Ohio	1871	Samuel L. Meyer	D	2,336	157
Ohio State Univ.*	Columbus, Ohio	1870	Harold L. Enarson	S	45,074	5,348
Ohio Univ.	Athens, Ohio	1804	Claude R. Sowle	S	19,327	1,184
Ohio Wesleyan Univ.	Delaware, Ohio	1842	Thomas Wenzlau	P	2,411	150
Oklahoma Baptist Univ.	Shawnee, Okla.	1910	William G. Tanner	D	1,567	115
Oklahoma Christian	Oklahoma City, Okla	1950	James O. Baird	P	1,079	44
Oklahoma City Univ.	Oklahoma City, Okla.	1904	Dolphus Whitten, Jr.	P	2,300	140
Okla. Coll. of Liberal Arts	Chickasha, Okla.	1910	Bruce G. Carter	S	980	57
Oklahoma Panhandle State	Goodwell, Okla.	1909	Thomas L. Palmer	S	1,268	65
Oklahoma State Univ.*	Stillwater, Okla.	1890	Robert B. Kamm	S	16,888	904
Oklahoma, Univ. of	Norman, Okla.	1890	Paul F. Sharp	P	19,115	747
Old Dominion Univ.	Norfolk, Va.	1930	James Bugg	S	9,612	431
Olivet	Olivet, Mich.	1844	Ray. B. Loeschner	P	728	61
Olivet Nazarene	Kankakee, Ill.	1907	Harold W. Reed	P	1,670	88
Oral Roberts Univ.	Tulsa, Okla.	1965	Oral Roberts	P	1,900	120
Oregon College of Education	Monmouth, Ore.	1856	Leonard Rice	S	3,100	250
Oregon State Univ.*	Corvallis, Ore.	1868	Robert W. MacVicar	S	14,125	1,520
Oregon Technical Institute	Klamath Falls, Ore.	1947	W. D. Purvine	S	1,484	123
Oregon, Univ. of	Eugene, Ore.	1872	Robert Clark	S	14,418	1,390
Orlando, State Univ. at	Orlando, Fla.	1963	Charles N. Millican	S	6,335	404
Osteop., Med. & Surg., Coll. of	Des Moines, Iowa	1898	J. Leonard Azneer	P	434	126
Otis Art Institute of L.A. County	Los Angeles, Calif.	1918	A. S. Anderson (Dir.)	C	401	31
Ottawa Univ.	Ottawa, Kan.	1865	Peter H. Armacost	P	664	60
Otterbein	Westerville, Ohio	1847	Thomas Jefferson Kerr	D	1,296	88
Ouachita Baptist Univ.	Arkadelphia, Ark.	1885	Daniel R. Grant	P	1,461	88
Our Lady of Angels	Aston, Pa.	1965	Sister Madonna Marie	P	375	37
Our Lady of the Elms, Coll. of (W)	Chicopee, Mass.	1928	V. Rev. T. F. Devine	D	501	73
Our Lady of the Lake	San Antonio, Tex.	1911	Gerald Burns	D	2,293	158
Ozark Bible	Joplin, Mo.	1942	Don E. Boatman	P	717	52
Ozarks, Coll. of the	Clarksville, Ark.	1834	Don Davis	P	480	35
Ozarks, School of the	Pt. Lookout, Mo.	1906	M. Graham Clark	P	1,008	61
Pace	New York, N.Y.	1906	Edward J. Mortola	P	10,349	696
Pacific	Fresno, Calif.	1944	Arthur J. Wiebe	D	378	35
Pacific Christian	Long Beach, Calif.	1928	Medford Jones	P	277	19
Pacific Lutheran Univ.	Tacoma, Wash.	1890	Eugene Wiegman	P	3,164	190
Pacific Union	Angwin, Calif.	1882	J. W. Cassell	D	1,613	136
Pacific Univ.	Forest Grove, Ore.	1849	James Miller	P	1,103	110
Pacific, Univ. of the	Stockton, Calif.	1851	Stanley McCaffrey	P	5,409	637
Paine	Augusta, Ga.	1882	L. H. Pitts	D	717	63
Palmer Coll. of Chiropractic	Davenport, Iowa	1895	David Palmer	P	1,370	26
Pan American Univ.	Edinburg, Tex.	1927	Ralph Schilling	S	6,724	207
Panhandle State	Goodwell, Okla.	1909	Thomas L. Palmer	S	1,008	69
Park	Kansas City, Mo.	1875	Kenneth Beyer	P	497	43
Parsons School of Design	New York, N.Y.	1896	John R. Everett	P	700	150
Pasadena	Pasadena, Calif.	1902	W. S. Brown	D	1,276	63
Paul Quinn	Waco, Tex.	1872	S. E. Rutland	D	400	46
Peabody Cons. of Music	Baltimore, Md.	1857	Richard F. Goldman	P	421	85
Pembroke State Univ.	Pembroke, N.C.	1887	English E. Jones, Chan.	S	1,818	115
Penn. Coll. of Optometry	Philadelphia, Pa.	1919	Norman E. Willis	P	489	56
Penn. State Univ.*	University Park, Pa.	1855	John W. Oswald	S	52,360	2,939
Pennsylvania, Univ. of	Philadelphia, Pa.	1740	Martin Meyerson	P	17,339	1,726
Pepperdine Univ.	Los Angeles, Calif.	1937	William S. Banowsky	P	8,000	367
Peru State	Peru, Nebr.	1867	Max Smith, act.	S	820	54
Pfeiffer	Misenheimer, N.C.	1885	Douglas Reid Sasser	D	1,021	77
Phila. Coll. of Art	Philadelphia, Pa.	1876	George D. Culler	P	1,100	165
Phila. Coll. of Bible	Philadelphia, Pa.	1914	D. B. MacCorkle	P	1,050	53
Phila. Coll. of Osteopathic Med.	Philadelphia, Pa.	1898	Frederick H. Barth	P	575	180
Phila. Coll. of Pharm. & Science	Philadelphia, Pa.	1821	Arthur Osol	P	1,000	113
Phila. Coll. of Textiles & Science	Philadelphia, Pa.	1884	Lawson A. Pendleton	P	2,051	144
Philander Smith	Little Rock, Ark.	1877	Walter Hazzard	D	651	45
Phillips Univ.	Enid, Okla.	1905	Thomas Broce	D	1,432	83
Piedmont	Demorest, Ga.	1897	James E. Walter	P	378	19
Piedmont Bible	Winston-Salem, N.C.	1945	Donald Drake	P	390	24
Pikeville	Pikeville, Ky.	1889	Robert S. Cope	D	718	44
Pittsburgh, Univ. of	Pittsburgh, Pa.	1787	Wesley W. Posvar	S	25,562	1,901
Pitzer	Claremont, Calif.	1963	Robert Atwell	P	743	65
Plymouth State	Plymouth, N.H.	1871	Harold E. Hyde	S	2,440	122
Point Park	Pittsburgh, Pa.	1960	Arthur M. Blum	P	2,127	136
Polytechnic Inst. of Brooklyn	Brooklyn, N.Y.	1854	Norman P. Auburn	P	3,222	237
Pomona	Claremont, Calif.	1887	John David Alexander	P	1,293	133
Portland State Univ.	Portland, Ore.	1955	Gregory Baker Wolfe	S	12,050	642
Portland, Univ. of	Portland, Ore.	1901	Rev. P. E. Waldschmidt	P	1,985	135
Pratt Institute	Brooklyn, N.Y.	1887	Richardson Pratt, Jr.	P	4,139	445
Prescott	Prescott, Ariz.	1966	Frank Mertz, act.	P	390	37
Presbyterian	Clinton, S.C.	1880	Marc C. Weersing	D	777	60
Princeton Univ.	Princeton, N.J.	1746	William G. Bowen	P	5,501	1,052
Principia	Elsah, Ill.	1910	David K. Andrews	P	807	63
Providence	Providence, R.I.	1917	V. Rev. T. R. Peterson	P	3,635	210
Puerto Rico, Univ. of*	Rio Piedras, P.R.	1903	Jaime Benitez	S	42,516	2,785
Puget Sound, Univ. of	Tacoma, Wash.	1888	R. Franklin Thompson	P	2,974	245
Purdue Univ.*	Lafayette, Ind.	1869	Arthur G. Hansen	S	35,864	3,905
Queens (W)	Charlotte, N.C.	1857	John Smylie	P	642	69
Quincy	Quincy, Ill.	1859	Rev. Titus Ludes	D	1,845	110
Quinnipiac	New Haven, Conn.	1929	Leonard Kent	P	2,719	215
Racine, College of	Racine, Wisc.	1947	Thomas Stevens	P	720	64
Radcliffe (W)	Cambridge, Mass.	1879	Matina Souretia Horner	P	1,300	(c)

(c) Faculty at Harvard Univ. furnishes instruction.

Name	Location	Year	Governing Official and Affiliation		Students	Teachers
Radford	Radford, Va.	1910	Donald N. Dedmon	S	3,424	221
Ramapo College of New Jersey	Mahwah, N.J.	1968	George T. Potter	S	1,500	90
Randolph-Macon	Ashland, Va.	1830	Luther W. White	P	751	72
Randolph-Macon Woman's (W)	Lynchburg, Va.	1891	William F. Quillian, Jr.	P	758	82
Redlands, Univ. of	Redlands, Calif.	1909	Eugene Dawson	P	1,904	201
Reed	Portland, Ore.	1909	Paul Bragdon	P	1,208	113
Regis	Denver, Colo.	1877	Rev. David M. Clarke	D	1,249	98
Regis (W)	Weston, Mass.	1927	Sister M. Jeanne D'Arc	P	900	80
Rensselaer Poly. Inst.	Troy, N.Y.	1824	Richard Grosh	P	4,489	631
Rhode Island	Providence, R.I.	1854	Joseph Kauffman	S	7,058	341
R.I. School of Design	Providence, R.I.	1877	Talbot Rantoul	P	1,657	108
Rhode Island, Univ. of	Kingston, R.I.	1892	Werner Baum	S	10,049	840
Rice Univ.	Houston, Tex.	1912	Norman Hackerman	P	3,255	334
Richard Stockton State	Pomona, N.J.	1969	Richard Biork	S	2,007	100
Richmond, Univ. of	Richmond, Va.	1830	E. Bruce Heilman	P	5,290	302
Ricker	Houlton, Me.	1848	Robert Matson	P	450	40
Rider	Tenton, N.J.	1865	Frank N. Elliott	P	5,791	320
Rio Grande	Rio Grande, Ohio	1876	Alphus R. Christensen	P	667	43
Ripon	Ripon, Wis.	1851	Bernard S. Adams	P	983	87
Rivier (W)	Nashua, N.H.	1933	Sister Gloria Lemieux	P	1,010	54
Roanoke	Salem, Va.	1842	Perry F. Kendig	P	1,230	75
Robert Morris	Pittsburgh, Pa.	1921	Charles Sewall	P	3,773	96
Roberts Wesleyan	Rochester, N.Y.	1866	Lawrence Schoenhals	P	630	67
Rochester Inst. of Technology	Rochester, N.Y.	1829	Paul A. Miller	P	9,524	438
Rochester, Univ. of	Rochester, N.Y.	1850	Allan Wallis, Chan.	P	7,923	2,143
Rockefeller Univ.	New York, N.Y.	1901	Frederick Seitz	P	108	300
Rockford	Rockford, Ill.	1847	John A. Howard	P	1,139	85
Rockhurst	Kansas City, Mo.	1910	Rev. M. E. Van Ackeren	D	2,040	145
Rocky Mountain	Billings, Mont.	1878	Lawrence F. Small	P	510	45
Roger Williams	Bristol, R.I.	1948	Ralph Gauvey	P	2,800	198
Rollins	Winter Park, Fla.	1885	Jack B. Critchfield	P	2,500	200
Roosevelt Univ.	Chicago, Ill.	1945	Rolf A. Weil	P	6,532	700
Rosary	River Forest, Ill.	1901	Sister Candida Lund	P	1,256	105
Rosary Hill	Buffalo, N.Y.	1948	Sister Mary Angela	P	1,331	116
Rose-Hulman Inst. of Tech.	Terre Haute, Ind.	1874	John Logan	P	1,059	74
Rosemont	Rosemont, Pa.	1921	Sister Ann Marie	D	564	84
Russell Sage (W)	Troy, N.Y.	1916	Charles Walker	P	1,384	114
Rust	Holly Spgs., Miss	1866	W. A. McMillan	D	585	38
Rutgers, Univ.*	New Brunswick, N.J.	1766	Edward J. Bloustein	S	35,229	2,387
Douglass (W)	New Brunswick, N.J.	1918	Margery S. Foster, Dean	S	2,981	262
Sacred Heart, Coll. of the (W)	Santurce, P.R.	1935	Rafael Bottari	D	797	65
Sacred Heart Univ.	Bridgeport, Conn.	1963	Robert Kidera	P	2,129	122
Saginaw Valley	Univ. Center, Mich.	1963	Samuel Marble	S	2,073	65
St. Ambrose	Davenport, Iowa	1882	Rev. S. G. Menke	D	1,189	90
St. Andrews Presbyterian	Laurinburg, N.C.	1958	Donald J. Hart	D	813	69
St. Anselm's	Manchester, N.H.	1889	Joseph J. Gerry	D	1,765	132
St. Augustine's	Raleigh, N.C.	1867	Prezell R. Robinson	D	1,371	70
St. Benedict, Coll. of (W)	St. Joseph, Minn.	1913	Stanley Idzerda	D	1,050	75
St. Bernard	St. Bernard, Ala.	1892	Rev. Aloysius Plaisance	D	526	41
St. Bonaventure Univ.	St. Bonaventure, N.Y.	1856	V. Rev. D. McElrath	D	2,362	182
St. Catherine, Coll. of (W)	St. Paul, Minn.	1905	Sister Alberta Huber	P	1,422	134
St. Cloud State	St. Cloud, Minn.	1869	Charles J. Graham	S	9,811	422
St. Edward's Univ.	Austin, Tex.	1878	Bro. Stephen Walsh	D	1,282	91
St. Elizabeth, Coll. of (W)	Convent Station, N.J.	1899	Sister Fliz. Ann Maloney	D	677	91
St. Francis	Fort Wayne, Ind.	1890	Sister M. Jo Ellen Scheetz	D	1,641	97
St. Francis	Biddeford, Maine	1953	Robert L. Horn	P	485	42
St. Francis	Brooklyn, N.Y.	1859	Rev. Donald Sullivan	P	2,824	125
St. Francis	Loretto, Pa.	1847	Rev. Sean Sullivan	P	1,617	98
St. Francis (W)	Joliet, Ill.	1930	Francis Kerins	D	846	76
St. John Coll. of Cleveland	Cleveland, Ohio	1928	Rev. J. T. McManamon	D	733	73
St. John Fisher	Rochester, N.Y.	1948	V. Rev. C. J. Lavery	P	1,374	90
St. John's	Annapolis, Md.	1696	Richard D. Weigle	P	372	49
St. John's Univ. (M)	Collegeville, Minn.	1869	Rev. Michael P. Blecker	D	1,647	108
St. John's Univ.	Jamaica, N.Y.	1870	V. Rev. Joseph T. Cahill	P	13,113	632
St. Joseph (A) (W)	W. Hartford, Conn.	1932	Sister M. Theodore	D	986	87
St. Joseph's	Rensselaer, Ind.	1891	Rev. Charles Banet	P	1,068	81
Calumet Campus	E. Chicago, Ind.	1951	V. Rev. John Lefko	D	1,565	74
St. Joseph's	North Windham, Me.	1915	Bernard Currier	P	370	30
St. Joseph's	Philadelphia, Pa.	1851	Rev. Terrence Toland	D	6,387	265
St. Joseph's (A)	Brooklyn, N.Y.	1916	Sister George Aquin	P	560	76
St. Lawrence Univ.	Canton, N.Y.	1856	Frank Peter Piskor	P	2,169	144
St. Leo	St. Leo, Fla.	1965	Thomas Southard	P	1,100	72
St. Louis Coll. of Pharmacy	St. Louis, Mo.	1864	Charles C. Rabe	P	619	28
St. Louis Univ.	St. Louis, Mo.	1818	V. Rev. Paul Reinert	P	9,542	1,720
Parks Coll.	Cahokia, Ill.	1927	Leon Z. Seltzer (Dn.)	P	505	72
St. Martin's	Olympia, Wash.	1895	Rev. Matthew Naumes	D	766	80
St. Mary, Coll. of (W)	Omaha, Nebr.	1923	Sister Mary Angelica	D	543	71
St. Mary (W)	Leavenworth, Kan.	1923	Sister Mary Janet	D	525	54
St. Mary of the Plains	Dodge City, Kan.	1952	William V. Tucker	P	415	40
St. Mary-of-the-Woods (W)	St. Mary-of-the-Woods, Ind.	1840	Sister Jeanne Knoerle	D	361	63
St. Mary's	Notre Dame, Ind.	1884	Edward L. Henry	D	1,429	130
St. Mary's	Winona, Minn.	1925	Brother George Pahl	D	1,164	85
St. Mary's Coll. of Calif.	Moraga, Calif.	1863	Bro. Mel Anderson	P	1,019	101
St. Mary's Coll. of Maryland	St. Mary's City, Md.	1839	J. Renwick Jackson	S	949	71
St. Mary's Dominican (W)	New Orleans, La.	1910	Sister Mary Eugene	P	831	68
St. Mary's Univ.	San Antonio, Tex.	1852	Rev. James Young	P	3,700	209
St. Meinrad (M)	St. Meinrad, Ind.	1861	V. Rev. H. Ottensmeyer	D	218	36
St. Michael's	Winooski, Vt.	1904	Bernard Boutin	D	1,381	93
St. Norbert	De Pere, Wis.	1898	Robert Christin	D	1,422	90
St. Olaf	Northfield, Minn.	1874	Sidney A. Rand	D	2,661	232
St. Paul Bible	St. Paul, Minn.	1916	Francis W. Grubbs	D	374	30
St. Paul's	Lawrenceville, Va.	1888	James Alvin Russell, Jr.	P	541	43
St. Peter's	Jersey City, N.J.	1872	V. Rev. V. R. Yanitelli	D	4,369	301
St. Rose, Coll. of	Albany, N.Y.	1920	Thomas Manion	P	1,429	104
St. Scholastica, Coll. of	Duluth, Minn.	1912	Rev. F. X. Shea	D	1,000	100
St. Teresa, Coll. of	Winona, Minn.	1912	Sister Joyce Rowland	P	970	120
St. Thomas Aquinas	Sparkill, N.Y.	1952	Sister Mary Ann Biller	P	692	41

Name	Location	Year	Governing Official and Affiliation		Stu- dents	Teach- ers
St. Thomas, Coll. of (M)	St. Paul, Minn.	1885	Msgr. Terrence Murphy	D	1,813	138
St. Thomas, Univ. of	Houston, Tex.	1947	Rev. Patrick Braden	P	1,650	121
St. Vincent (M)	Latrobe, Pa.	1846	Rev. Cecil Diethrich	D	1,019	90
St. Xavier	Chicago, Ill.	1847	Sister M. Irenaeus	D	1,129	100
Salem (W)	Winston-Salem, N.C.	1772	John H. Chandler	P	609	65
Salem	Salem, W. Va.	1888	K. Duane Hurley	P	1,162	65
Salem State	Salem, Mass.	1854	Frank Keegan	S	6,916	414
Salisbury State	Salisbury, Md.	1925	Norman Crawford	S	2,305	92
Salve Regina (W)	Newport, R.I.	1947	Sister Lucille McKillon	P	1,112	98
Sam Houston State Univ.	Huntsville, Tex.	1879	E. T. Bowers	S	9,735	368
Samford Univ.	Birmingham, Ala.	1841	Leslie S. Wright	P	2,713	154
San Diego, Univ. of	San Diego, Calif.	1949	A. E. Hughes, Jr.	D	1,527	110
San Francisco Art Inst.	San Francisco, Calif.	1871	T. L. Eliot, Dir.	P	979	85
San Francisco, Univ. of	San Francisco, Calif.	1855	Rev. William McInnes	P	5,893	415
Sangamon State Univ.	Springfield, Ill.	1969	Robert Spencer	S	2,475	178
Santa Clara, Univ. of	Santa Clara, Calif.	1851	Rev. Thomas Terry	D	5,871	210
Santa Fe, Coll. of	Santa Fe, N.M.	1947	Bro. Cyprian Luke Roney	D	1,248	85
Sarah Lawrence	Bronxville, N.Y.	1928	Charles Dc Carlo	P	867	147
Savannah State (A)	Savannah, Ga.	1776	Howard Jordan, Jr.	S	2,120	105
Scarritt Coll. for Christian Workers	Nashville, Tenn.	1892	J. Richard Palmer	D	150	19
Scranton, Univ. of	Scranton, Pa.	1888	Rev. Dexter Hanley	D	3,724	156
Scripps (W)	Claremont, Calif.	1926	Mark H. Curtis	P	534	156
Seattle Pacific	Seattle, Wash.	1891	David L. McKenna	P	1,884	137
Seattle Univ.	Seattle, Wash.	1891	Rev. Louis Gaffney	P	2,900	160
Selma Univ.	Selma, Ala.	1878	Marshall C. Cleveland	D	435	30
Seton Hall Univ.	So. Orange, N.J.	1856	Rev. Thomas G. Fahy	D	9,200	500
Seton Hill (W)	Greensburg, Pa.	1883	Sister Mary Schmidt	P	750	74
Shaw Coll. at Detroit	Detroit, Mich.	1936	Romallus O. Murphy	P	932	65
Shaw Univ.	Raleigh, N.C.	1865	J. Archie Hargrave	D	1,047	84
Shenandoah Coll. & Cons. of Music	Winchester, Va.	1875	Robert Parker	D	518	85
Shepherd	Shepherdstown, W. Va.	1871	James Butcher	S	2,004	105
Shimer	Mt. Carroll, Ill.	1853	Robert S. Long	P	306	31
Shippensburg State	Shippensburg, Pa.	1871	Gilmore B. Seavers	S	5,336	313
Shorter	Rome, Ga.	1873	Randall H. Minor	P	498	47
Siena	Loudonville, N.Y.	1937	Matthew T. Conlin	P	1,916	116
Siena Heights	Adrian, Mich.	1919	Hugh L. Thompson	D	681	64
Simmons (W)	Boston, Mass.	1902	William J. Holmes, Jr.	P	2,513	329
Simpson	Indianola, Iowa	1860	Richard Lancaster	P	881	80
Simpson	San Francisco, Calif.	1921	Mark W. Lee	D	254	28
Sioux Falls	Sioux Falls, S. Dak.	1883	Ronald V. Wells	D	745	59
Skidmore	Saratoga Spgs., N.Y.	1911	Joseph C. Palamountain	P	1,820	159
Slippery Rock State	Slippery Rock, Pa.	1889	Albert A. Watrel	S	5,100	356
Smith (W)	Northampton, Mass.	1871	Thomas C. Mendenhall	P	2,755	240
South Alabama, Univ. of	Mobile, Ala.	1963	Frederick P. Whiddon	S	4,686	329
So. Carolina, Med. Coll. of	Charleston, S.C.	1824	William M. McCord	S	1,693	643
South Carolina St.*	Orangeburg, S.C.	1896	M. M. Nance	S	2,072	162
South Carolina, Univ. of	Columbia, S.C.	1801	Thomas F. Jones	S	23,080	1,596
S. Dak. Sch. of Mines & Tech.	Rapid City, S. Dak.	1885	Harvey R. Fraser	S	1,454	98
South Dakota State Univ.*	Brookings, S. Dak.	1889	H. M. Briggs	S	6,000	400
South Dakota, Univ. of	Vermillion, S. Dak.	1882	Richard L. Bowen	S	5,502	485
At Springfield	Springfield, S.D.	1897	Carrol Drause, Provost	S	1,134	90
South-Eastern Bible	Lakeland, Fla.	1930	Cyril Homer	D	655	20
South Florida, Univ. of	Tampa, Fla.	1956	Cecil Mackey	S	16,104	799
South, Univ. of the	Sewanee, Tenn.	1857	James J. Bennett, V. Chan.	D	967	82
Southeast Missouri State	Cape Girardeau, Mo.	1873	Mark Scully	S	7,050	356
Southeastern Louisiana Univ.	Hammond, La.	1925	Clea E. Parker	S	5,878	278
Southeastern Mass. Univ.	No. Dartmouth, Mass.	1895	Donald E. Walker	S	4,268	299
Southeastern State	Durant Okla.	1909	Leon Hibbs	S	3,610	195
Southeastern Univ.	Wash., D.C.	1879	Henry J. Duel	P	350	35
Southern California	Costa Mesa, Calif.	1912	Emil Balliet	D	631	45
Southern Calif., Univ. of	Los Angeles, Calif.	1880	John R. Hubbard	P	19,001	2,425
So. Calif. College of Optometry	Fullerton, Calif.	1904	Richard Hopping	P	260	65
Southern Coll. of Optometry	Memphis, Tenn.	1932	Spurgeon B. Eure	P	529	41
Southern Colorado State	Pueblo, Colo.	1964	Harry P. Bowes	S	4,950	356
Southern Conn. State	New Haven, Conn.	1893	Manson Van B. Jennings	S	11,844	684
Southern Illinois Univ.	Carbondale, Ill.	1869	David Derge	S	18,398	2,466
Southern Methodist Univ.	Dallas, Tex.	1915	Paul Hardin	P	10,021	726
Southern Missionary	Collegedale, Tenn.	1892	Frank Knittel	D	1,336	100
Southern Mississippi, Univ. of	Hattiesburg, Miss.	1912	William D. McCain	S	7,900	650
Southern Oregon	Ashland, Ore.	1926	James K. Sours	S	4,100	285
Southern State	Magnolia, Ark.	1909	Imon E. Bruce	S	1,808	115
Southern Univ.	Baton Rouge, La.	1880	G. Leon Netterville	S	8,107	534
Southern Utah State	Cedar City, Utah	1897	R. C. Braithwaite	S	1,640	104
Southwest, Coll. of the	Hobbs, N.M.	1957	Eugene E. Hughes	P	183	28
Southwest Baptist	Bolivar, Mo.	1878	James L. Sells	P	1,061	65
Southwest Minnesota State	Marshall, Minn.	1963	Jay Jones	S	2,368	150
Southwest Missouri State	Springfield, Mo.	1905	Duane Meyer	S	9,000	550
Southwest Texas State Univ.	San Marcos, Tex.	1899	Billy Mac Jones	S	11,352	469
Southwestern	Winfield, Kan.	1885	C. Orville Strohl	P	592	45
Southwestern La., Univ. of	Lafayette, La.	1898	Clyde Rougeou	S	10,753	616
Southwestern at Memphis	Memphis, Tenn.	1848	James Daughdrill	P	1,090	100
Southwestern State	Weatherford, Okla.	1901	Al Harris	S	4,860	230
Southwestern Union	Keene, Texas	1893	Leroy J. Leiske	D	535	48
Southwestern Univ.	Georgetown, Tex.	1840	Durwood Fleming	P	784	69
Spalding	Louisville, Ky.	1920	Sister Eileen Egan	P	1,081	100
Spelman (W)	Atlanta, Ga.	1881	Albert E. Manley	P	1,067	90
Spring Arbor	Spring Arbor, Mich.	1873	E. A. Voller	D	662	52
Spring Garden	Philadelphia, Pa.	1850	Robert H. Thompson	P	1,050	70
Spring Hill	Mobile, Ala.	1830	Rev. William Rimes	D	900	108
Springfield	Springfield, Mass.	1885	Wilbert Locklin	P	2,657	145
Stanford Univ.	Stanford, Calif.	1891	Richard W. Lyman	P	11,197	1,289
Stephen F. Austin State Univ.	Nacogdoches, Tex.	1923	Ralph W. Steen	S	9,585	415
Stephens (W)	Columbia, Mo.	1833	Seymour Smith	P	1,808	175
Sterling	Sterling, Kansas	1887	Robert Baptista	P	436	41
Stetson Univ.	De Land, Fla.	1883	John E. Johns	P	2,668	152
Steubenville, Coll. of	Steubenville, Ohio	1946	Rev. Kevin Keelan	P	1,118	70
Stevens Inst. of Tech.	Hoboken, N.J.	1870	Kenneth C. Rogers	P	1,995	168
Stillman	Tuscaloosa, Ala.	1876	Harold N. Stinson	D	610	46
Stonehill	No. Easton, Mass.	1948	Rev. Ernest Bartell	P	2,009	136

Name	Location	Year	Governing Official and Affiliation		Stu-dents	Teach-ers
Stratford (W)	Danville, Va.	1852	W. Hugh Moomaw	P	522	55
Strayer	Washington, D.C.	1904	Murray Donoho	P	1,000	120
Suffolk Univ.	Boston, Mass.	1906	Thomas Fulham	P	5,719	221
Sul Ross State Univ.	Alpine, Tex.	1917	Norman L. McNeil	S	2,510	140
Susquehanna Univ.	Selinsgrove, Pa.	1858	Gustave W. Weber	Mu	1,537	100
Swarthmore	Swarthmore, Pa.	1864	Edward Cratsley, act.	P	1,183	151
Sweet Briar (W)	Sweet Briar, Va.	1901	Harold B. Whiteman, Jr.	P	738	75
Syracuse Univ.	Syracuse, N.Y.	1870	M. A. Eggers (Chan.)	P	21,333	834
Tabor	Hillsboro, Kansas	1908	Roy Just	P	453	44
Talladega	Talladega, Ala.	1867	Herman H. Long	P	490	54
Tampa, Univ. of	Tampa, Fla.	1931	B. D. Owens	P	2,024	138
Tarkio	Tarkio, Mo.	1883	Eldon E. Breazier	P	580	42
Taylor Univ.	Upland, Ind.	1846	Milo Rediger	P	1,325	100
Temple Univ.	Philadelphia, Pa.	1884	Malvin Wachman	S	28,459	2,900
Tennessee State Univ.	Nashville, Tenn.	1912	A. P. Torrence	S	4,401	293
Tennessee Tech. Univ.	Cookeville, Tenn.	1915	William Everett Derryberry	S	6,002	432
Tennessee Temple	Chattanooga, Tenn.	1946	Lee Roberson	P	2,159	69
Tennessee, Univ. of*	Knoxville, Tenn.	1794	Edward Boling	S	41,742	2,755
At Chattanooga	Chattanooga, Tenn.	1886	William H. Masterson	S	4,847	280
At Knoxville	Knoxville, Tenn.	1794	Archie Dykes, Chan.	S	26,370	1,465
At Martin	Martin, Tenn.	1900	Larry T. McGhee, Chan.	S	4,365	243
At Memphis	Memphis, Tenn.	1851	Joseph E. Johnson, Chan.	S	1,562	501
Tennessee Wesleyan	Athens, Tenn.	1857	Charles Turner	D	550	38
Tex. A. & M.	College Station, Tex.	1876	Jack K. Williams	S	15,196	1,300
Prairie View A. & M.	Prairie View, Tex.	1878	Alvin Thomas	S	4,543	246
Tarleton State	Stephenville, Tex.	1899	William O. Trogden	S	2,741	157
Texas Christian Univ.	Fort Worth, Tex.	1873	J. M. Moudy (Chan.)	P	6,388	474
Texas	Tyler, Tex.	1894	Allen C. Hancock	P	614	39
Texas A & I Univ.	Kingsville, Tex.	1925	James C. Jernigan, Chan.	S	7,160	396
Texas Lutheran	Seguin, Tex.	1891	Joe M.	D	952	72
Texas Southern Univ.	Houston, Tex.	1947	Granville Sawyer	S	6,396	315
Texas, Univ. of	Austin, Tex.	1883	Charles A. LeMaistre, Chan.	S	68,534	6,379
At Arlington	Arlington, Tex.	1895	Wendell Nedderman, act.	S	14,028	787
At Austin	Austin, Tex.	1883	Stephen Spurr	S	39,900	3,337
El Paso	El Paso, Tex.	1913	Arleigh Templeton	S	10,550	453
Health Science Center	Houston, Tex.	1905	J. V. Olson	S	1,256	354
Medical Branch	Galveston, Tex.	1891	Truman G. Blocker, Jr.	S	1,056	326
Health Science Center	San Antonio, Tex.	1959	Frank Harrison	S	725	265
Health Science Center	Dallas, Tex.	1943	C. C. Sprague (Dean)	S	666	432
Texas Tech. Univ.	Lubbock, Tex.	1923	Grover Murray	S	19,787	1,329
Texas Wesleyan	Fort Worth, Tex.	1891	William Pearce	D	1,682	96
Texas Woman's Univ. (W)	Denton, Tex.	1901	John A. Guinn	S	5,602	300
Thiel	Greenville, Pa.	1866	Chauncey G. Bly	D	1,400	97
Thomas	Waterville, Maine	1894	John L. Thomas, Jr.	P	500	34
Thomas Jefferson Univ.	Philadelphia, Pa.	1824	Peter Herbut	D	1,399	1,150
Thomas More	Ft. Mitchell, Ky.	1921	Richard A. DeGraff	D	1,523	122
Thunderbird Graduate Sch. of Intl. Management	Glendale, Ariz.	1946	Charles W. Voris	P	632	55
Tiffin Univ.	Tiffin, Ohio	1918	Richard Pfeiffer	P	415	23
Tift (W)	Forsyth, Ga.	1847	Robert W. Jackson	P	607	36
Toccoa Falls Inst.	Toccoa Falls, Ga.	1911	Julian Bandy	P	335	21
Toledo, Univ. of	Toledo, Ohio	1872	William S. Carlson	S	14,903	670
Tougaloo	Tougaloo, Miss.	1869	George A. Owens	P	747	65
Towson State	Baltimore, Md.	1866	James L. Fisher	S	11,016	505
Transylvania Univ.	Lexington, Ky.	1780	Irvin E. Lunger	P	682	60
Trenton State	Trenton, N.J.	1855	C. B. Brower	S	10,600	500
Trevecca Nazarene	Nashville, Tenn.	1901	Mark Moore	P	730	46
Trinity	Hartford, Conn.	1823	Theodore Lockwood	P	2,029	131
Trinity	Burlington, Vt.	1925	Sister Elizabeth Candon	D	468	56
Trinity	Deerfield, Ill.	1897	Harry Evans	D	850	60
Trinity	Washington, D.C.	1897	Sister Margaret Claydon	P	550	80
Trinity Univ.	San Antonio, Tex.	1869	Duncan Wimpress	P	3,500	231
Tri-State	Angola, Ind.	1884	Richard Bateman	P	1,200	100
Troy State Univ. (A)	Troy, Ala.	1887	Ralph W. Adams	S	3,750	139
Tufts Univ.	Medford, Mass.	1852	Burton Hallowell	P	5,602	1,824
Tulane Univ.	New Orleans, La.	1834	H. E. Longenecker	P	8,212	830
Newcomb (W)	New Orleans, La.	1886	James F. Davidson (Dn.)	P	1,235	120
Tulsa, Univ. of	Tulsa, Okla.	1894	J. Paschal Twyman	P	5,541	320
Tusculum	Greenville, Tenn.	1794	Thomas Voss, Dean	P	356	35
Tuskegee Institute	Tuskegee Inst., Ala.	1881	Luther H. Foster	P	3,353	1,000
Union	Barbourville, Ky.	1879	Mahlon A. Miller	D	927	60
Union	Lincoln, Nebr.	1891	Robert H. Brown	D	819	85
Union	Schenectady, N.Y.	1795	Harold C. Martin	P	2,691	176
Union Univ.	Jackson, Tenn.	1825	Robert E. Craig	P	753	54
U.S. Air Force Academy (M)	Colo. Springs, Colo.	1954	Gen. Albert Clark, Supt.	F	3,836	570
U.S. Coast Guard Academy (M)	New London, Conn.	1876	Adm. J. S. Thompson	F	1,000	116
U.S. Dept. of Agric. Grad. Sch.	Washington, D.C.	1921	John B. Holden (Dir.)	F	4,570	600
U.S. International Univ.	San Diego, Calif.	1952	William Rust	P	5,000	260
U.S. Merchant Marine Acad. (M)	Kings Point, N.Y.	1938	Adm. Arthur Engel, Supt.	F	945	90
U.S. Military Academy (M)	West Point, N.Y.	1802	Gen. Wm. Knowlton,(Supt.)	F	3,894	525
U.S. Naval Academy (M)	Annapolis, Md.	1845	Adm. William P. Mack, Sup.	F	4,004	542
U.S. Naval Postgraduate Sch.	Monterey, Calif.	1909	Adm. M. B. Freeman	F	1,603	295
Unity	Unity, Maine	1966	Allan Karstetter	P	260	28
Upper Iowa	Fayette, Iowa	1857	Aldrich Paul	P	748	58
Upsala	E. Orange, N.J.	1893	Carl J. Fjellman	D	1,684	107
Urbana	Urbana, Ohio	1850	Paul Zehner	P	650	45
Ursinus	Collegeville, Pa.	1869	William Pettit	P	1,838	122
Ursuline (W)	Cleveland, Ohio	1871	Sister M. Kenan Dulzer	D	425	47
Utah State Univ.*	Logan, Utah	1888	Glen L. Taggart	S	7,900	528
Utah, Univ. of	Salt Lake City, Utah	1850	David P. Gardner	S	21,668	1,094
Valdosta State	Valdosta, Ga.	1906	S. Walter Martin	S	3,922	204
Valley City State	Valley City, N.D.	1890	Howard Rose	S	1,040	62
Valparaiso Univ.	Valparaiso, Ind.	1859	Albert Huegli	P	4,451	285
Vanderbilt Univ.	Nashville, Tenn.	1873	Alexander Heard (Ch.)	P	6,467	1,423
Vassar	Poughkeepsie, N.Y.	1861	Alan Simpson	P	2,232	240
Vermont, Univ. of*	Burlington, Vt.	1791	Edward C. Andrews	S	9,359	903

Name	Location	Year	Governing Official and Affiliation		Stu-dents	Teach-ers
Villa Maria (W)	Erie, Pa.	1925	Sister L. Antoun	P	721	50
Villanova Univ.	Villanova, Pa.	1842	Rev. Edward McCarthy	D	9,500	480
Virgin Islands, Coll. of the	St. Thomas, V.I.	1962	L. C. Wanlass	S	1,693	104
Virginia Commonwealth Univ.	Richmond, Va.	1838	Warren W. Brandt	S	15,068	2,000
Virginia Intermont	Bristol, Va.	1884	Floyd Turner	D	564	47
Virginia Military Institute (M)	Lexington, Va.	1839	Gen. Richard Irby (Supt.)	S	1,072	100
Virginia Poly. Inst. & Univ.* (A)	Blacksburg, Va.	1872	T. Marshall Hahn, Jr.	S	13,976	1,405
Virginia Union Univ. (A)	Richmond, Va.	1865	A. B. James	D	1,137	81
Virginia State*	Petersburg, Va.	1882	Wendell P. Russell	S	3,222	216
Virginia, Univ. of	Charlottesville, Va.	1819	Edgar F. Shannon, Jr.	S	12,300	1,200
Virginia Wesleyan	Norfolk, Va.	1961	Lambuth M. Clarke	P	626	51
Viterbo	La Crosse, Wis.	1931	Rev. J. Thomas Finucan	P	562	84
Voorhees	Denmark, S.C.	1897	Harry Graham	P	625	46
Wabash (M)	Crawfordsville, Ind.	1832	Thaddeus Seymour	P	719	74
Wagner	Staten Island, N.Y.	1883	Arthur O. Davidson	P	3,000	150
Wake Forest Univ.	Winston-Salem, N.C.	1834	James R. Scales	D	3,893	455
Walla Walla	College Place, Wash.	1892	Robert Reynolds	D	1,607	140
Walsh	Canton, Ohio	1960	Rev. Robert Francoeur	D	817	54
Walsh Coll. of Accounting	Troy, Mich.	1922	Jeffrey Barry	P	400	25
Warner Pacific	Portland, Ore.	1937	E. J. Gilliam	D	380	35
Warren Wilson	Swannanoa, N.C.	1894	Reuben H. Holden	P	358	50
Wartburg	Waverly, Iowa	1852	John W. Bachman	D	1,259	95
Washburn Univ.	Topeka, Kan.	1865	John W. Henderson	Mu	4,936	186
Washington	Chestertown, Md.	1782	Joseph McLain, act.	P	882	73
Washington and Jefferson	Washington, Pa.	1787	Howard J. Burnett	P	1,235	97
Washington and Lee Univ.	Lexington, Va.	1749	Robert Huntley	P	1,614	151
Washington State Univ.*	Pullman, Wash.	1890	W. Glenn Terrell, Jr.	S	13,770	878
Washington Univ.	St. Louis, Mo.	1853	W. H. Danforth (Chan.)	P	11,159	1,180
Washington, Univ. of	Seattle, Wash.	1861	Charles E. Odegaard	S	30,765	2,200
Wayland Baptist	Plainview, Tex.	1908	Roy C. McClung	D	941	54
Wayne State	Wayne, Nebr.	1910	Lyle Seymour, act.	S	1,970	133
Wayne State Univ.	Detroit, Mich.	1868	George Cullen	P	32,154	1,400
Waynesburg	Waynesburg, Pa.	1850	B. M. Rich	P	944	71
Weber State	Ogden, Utah	1889	Joseph Bishop	P	8,300	414
Webster	St. Louis, Mo.	1916	Leigh Gerdine	P	1,665	117
Wellesley (W)	Wellesley, Mass.	1875	Barbara W. Newell	P	1,796	217
Wells	Aurora, N.Y.	1868	John Wilson	P	620	74
Wentworth Coll. of Technology (M)	Boston, Mass.	1970	Edward Kirkpatrick	P	267	18
Wesleyan (W)	Macon, Ga.	1836	W. Earl Strickland	P	520	56
Wesleyan Univ.	Middletown, Conn.	1831	Colin G. Campbell	P	1,574	248
West Chester State	West Chester, Pa.	1812	Paul W. Rossey	S	7,000	512
West Coast Univ.	Los Angeles, Calif.	1909	Victor Elconin	S	1,450	125
West Florida, Univ. of	Pensacola, Fla.	1967	Harold Bryan Crosby	S	4,236	229
West Georgia	Carrollton, Ga.	1933	Ward Papport	S	5,213	283
West Liberty State	West Liberty, W. Va.	1837	James L. Chapman	S	2,697	170
West Texas State Univ.	Canyon, Tex.	1910	James Cornette	S	6,371	285
W. Va. Inst. of Technology	Montgomery, W. Va.	1895	Leonard C. Nelson	S	2,355	160
West Virginia State	Institute, W. Va.	1891	William J. L. Wallace	S	3,528	164
West Virginia Univ.*	Morgantown, W. Va.	1867	James G. Harlow	S	15,203	834
W. Virginia Wesleyan	Buckhannon, W. Va.	1890	John D. Rockefeller, IV	P	1,550	114
Western Baptist Bible	Salem, Ore.	1946	F. R. Brock	D	401	23
Western Carolina Univ. (A)	Cullowhee, N.C.	1889	Frank Brown, Jr. (Act.)	S	5,780	326
Western, (The)	Oxford, Ohio	1853	William Spencer	P	345	45
Western Conn. State	Danbury, Conn.	1904	Ruth A. Haas	S	4,336	231
Western Illinois Univ.	Macomb, Ill.	1889	John Bernhard	S	13,500	780
Western Kentucky Univ.	Bowling Green, Ky.	1906	Dero Dowling	S	11,300	780
Western Maryland	Westminster, Md.	1867	Ralph C. John	P	2,268	167
Western Mich. Univ.	Kalamazoo, Mich.	1903	James W. Miller	S	21,294	1,023
Western Montana	Dillon, Mont.	1897	James E. Short	S	950	50
Western New England	Springfield, Mass.	1919	Beaumont A. Herman	P	3,231	123
Western New Mexico Univ.	Silver City, N.M.	1893	John Snedeker	S	1,402	70
Western State	Gunnison, Colo.	1901	Harlan Bryant	S	2,665	136
Western Washington State	Bellingham, Wash.	1895	Charles Flora	S	7,653	495
Westfield State	Westfield, Mass.	1839	Leonard J. Savignano	S	2,609	144
Westmar	Le Mars, Iowa	1890	Laurence Smith	P	750	54
Westminster Choir	Princeton, N.J.	1926	Ray E. Robinson	P	449	61
Westminster	Fulton, Mo.	1851	Robert L. D. Davidson	P	692	59
Westminster	New Wilmington, Pa.	1852	Earland I. Carlson	P	1,484	107
Westminster	Salt Lake City, Utah	1875	Manford A. Shaw	P	741	47
Westmont	Santa Barbara, Calif.	1940	Lyle C. Hillegas	P	897	88
Wheaton	Wheaton, Ill.	1860	Hudson T. Armerding	P	2,029	162
Wheaton (W)	Norton, Mass.	1912	William H. C. Prentice	P	1,170	115
Wheeling	Wheeling, W. Va.	1954	Rev. Charles Currie	D	555	51
Wheelock	Boston, Mass.	1889	Gordon L. Marshall	P	791	63
White Plains, College of	White Plains, N.Y.	1923	Katherine Restaino	P	646	45
Whitman	Walla Walla, Wash.	1859	Donald Sheehan	P	1,140	94
Whittier	Whittier, Calif.	1901	Frederick M. Binder	P	1,821	97
Whitworth	Spokane, Wash.	1890	Edward B. Lindaman	P	1,570	105
Wichita State Univ.	Wichita, Kan.	1895	Clark Ahlberg	S	12,896	650
Wilberforce Univ.	Wilberforce, Ohio	1856	Rembert E. Stokes	D	1,217	46
Widener	Chester, Pa.	1821	Clarence R. Moll	P	2,762	214
Wiley	Marshall, Texas	1873	T. W. Cole, Sr.	P	468	41
Wilkes	Wilkes-Barre, Pa.	1933	Francis Michelini	P	2,760	198
Willamette Univ.	Salem, Ore.	1842	Roger J. Fritz	P	1,617	142
Willliam Carey	Hattiesburg, Miss.	1906	J. Ralph Noonkester	P	900	53
William Jewell	Liberty, Mo.	1849	Thomas Field	P	1,146	75
William and Mary, College of	Williamsburg, Va.	1693	Thomas A. Graves	S	5,381	458
William Mitchell Coll. of Law	St. Paul, Minn.	1900	Douglas Heidenreich (Dn.)	P	523	49
William Paterson Coll. of N.J.	Wayne, N.J.	1855	Frank Zanfino, act.	S	11,000	403
William Penn	Oskaloosa, Iowa	1873	Duane Moon	P	700	54
William Woods (W)	Fulton, Mo.	1870	Randall B. Cutlip	P	1,020	77
Williams	Williamstown, Mass.	1793	John W. Chandler	P	1,700	159
Wilmington	Wilmington, Ohio	1870	Robert E. Hinshaw	D	786	78
Wilmington	New Castle, Del.	1968	Donald E. Ross	P	525	29
Wilson (W)	Chambersburg, Pa.	1869	Charles C. Cole, Jr.	P	450	56
Windham	Putney, Vt.	1951	Eugene C. Winslow	P	792	63
Winona State	Winona, Minn.	1858	Robt. DuFresne	S	4,289	207
Winston-Salem State Univ.	Winston-Salem, N.C.	1892	Kenneth R. Williams	S	1,604	114

Name	Location	Year	Governing Official and Affiliation		Stu-dents	Teach-ers
Winthrop	Rock Hill, S.C.	1886	Charles S. Davis	S	3,761	212
Wisconsin, Univ. of*	Madison, Wis.	1848	John C. Weaver	S	34,000	3,000
Eau Claire	Eau Claire, Wisc.	1916	Leonard Haas, Chan.	S	8,073	567
La Crosse	La Crosse, Wisc.	1909	Kenneth Lindner, Chan.	S	6,785	424
Milwaukee	Milwaukee, Wis.	1956	Vacant	S	22,466	2,197
Oshkosh	Oshkosh, Wisc.	1871	Roger Guiles, Chan.	S	11,300	715
Platteville	Platteville, Wisc.	1866	Bjarne R. Ullsvik, Chan.	S	3,445	350
River Falls	River Falls, Wisc.	1874	George Field, Chan.	S	3,574	240
Stout	Menomonie, Wisc.	1893	Robert Swanson, Chan.	S	5,299	353
Superior	Superior, Wisc.	1893	Karl. W. Meyer, Chan.	S	2,658	220
Whitewater	Whitewater, Wisc.	1868	William L. Carter	S	7,712	490
Wittenberg Univ.	Springfield, Ohio	1845	G. Kenneth Andeen	P	2,771	279
Wofford	Spartanburg, S.C.	1854	J. M. Lesesne, Jr.	P	988	73
Woodbury	Los Angeles, Calif.	1884	Dora E. Kirby	P	1,900	75
Wooster, Coll. of	Wooster, Ohio	1866	J. G. Drushal	P	1,830	144
Worcester Polytechnic Inst.	Worcester, Mass.	1865	George W. Hazzard	P	2,474	183
Worcester State	Worcester, Mass.	1874	Robert Leestamper	P	3,820	181
Wright State Univ. (A)	Dayton, Ohio	1964	Vacant	S	9,950	440
Wyoming, Univ. of*	Laramie, Wyo.	1886	William Carlson	S	8,026	628
Xavier Univ. of Louisiana	New Orleans, La.	1925	Norman C. Francis	P	1,619	152
Xavier Univ.	Cincinnati, Ohio	1831	Rev. Robert Mulligan	P	6,236	286
Yale Univ.	New Haven, Conn.	1701	Kingman Brewster, Jr.	P	9,912	2,324
Yankton	Yankton, S. Dak.	1881	Alfred M. Gibbons	P	400	45
Yeshiva Univ.	New York, N.Y.	1886	Samuel Belkin	P	6,648	2,500
York College of Pa.	York, Pa.	1941	Ray A. Miller	P	2,593	127
Youngstown State Univ.	Youngstown, Ohio	1908	Albert L. Pugsley	S	13,353	760

Community and Junior Colleges

Enrollment and faculty figures in italics include all branches and campuses

Abraham Baldwin Agricultural	Tifton, Ga.	1908	J. Clyde Driggers	S	1,756	86
Adirondacks Community	Glens Falls, N.Y.	1960	Charles R. Eisenhart	S	1,380	57
Aeronautics, Academy of	Flushing, N.Y.	1932	Walter M. Hartung	P	860	57
Aims Community	Greeley, Colo.	1967	Ed Beaty	Di	4,090	213
Alabama Christian	Montgomery, Ala.	1942	E. R. Brannan	P	239	20
Alamance, Tech. Inst. of	Burlington, N.C.	1958	William Taylor	S	803	82
Albany Junior	Albany, Ga.	1963	B. R. Tilley	S	1,353	57
Albany, Junior Coll. of	Albany, N.Y.	1958	Charles Walker	P	545	32
Albemarle, Coll. of the	Elizabeth City, N.C.	1961	S. Bruce Petteway	S	811	65
Alexander City State Junior	Alexander City, Ala.	1965	W. Byron Causey	S	1,015	45
Alice Lloyd	Pippa Passes, Ky.	1923	Will Hayes	P	280	25
Allan Hancock Joint Comm.	Santa Maria, Calif.	1920	Walter E. Conrad	Di. C	7,263	349
Allegany Community	Cumberland, Md.	1961	W. Ardell Haines	S	1,077	73
Allegheny County, Comm. College of	Pittsburgh, Pa.	1966	John B. Hirt	C	16,000	350
Allen County Comm. Jr.	Iola, Kan.	1923	Bill Spencer	C	580	27
Alpena Community	Alpena, Mich.	1952	Herbert N. Stoutenburg	Di	1,264	65
Alphonsus	Woodcliff Lake, N.J.	1961	John Loftus	P	242	18
Altus Junior	Altus, Okla.	1926	E. T. Dunlap	S	642	35
Alvin Junior	Alvin, Tex.	1949	Thomas Jenkins	Di	1,593	93
Amarillo	Amarillo, Tex.	1929	Albert B. Martin	Mu	3,202	112
American Academy of Art	Chicago, Ill.	1923	Irving Shapiro, Dir.	P	700	18
American River	Sacramento, Calif.	1955	Kenneth Boettcher	Di	15,475	451
Anderson	Anderson, S.C.	1911	J. Cordell Maddox	D	983	46
Andrew	Cuthbert, Ga.	1854	J. C. Martinson, Jr.	P	300	21
Angelina	Lufkin, Tex.	1968	Jack W. Hudgins, Jr.	C	1,026	53
Anne Arundel Community	Arnold, Md.	1961	Robert P. Ludlum	S	4,061	190
Anson Tech. Inst.	Ansonville, N.C.	1962	H. B. Monroe	S	477	13
Anoka-Ramsey St. Jr.	Coon Rapids, Minn.	1965	Ronald Dennison	S	1,866	91
Antelope Valley	Lancaster, Calif.	1929	William Kepley, Jr.	S	3,933	147
Aquinas Junior	Milton, Mass.	1956	Sister Dorothy Wood	P	220	16
Aquinas Junior	Nashville, Tenn.	1961	Sister Henry Suso Fletcher	D	341	38
Arapahoe Community	Littleton, Colo.	1966	Allan P. Crawford	S	2,000	125
Arizona Western	Yuma, Ariz.	1963	Robert Garin	C	3,473	159
Asheville Buncombe Tech. Inst.	Asheville, N.C.	1959	Thomas Simpson	S	1,084	105
Atlantic Comm.	Mays Landing, N.J.	1966	L. R. Winchell	C	3,000	110
Auburn Community	Auburn, N.Y.	1953	Albert T. Skinner	C	2,749	85
Austin State Junior	Austin, Minn.	1940	Curtis C. Mac Donald	S	814	52
Bacone	Bacone, Okla.	1880	Garold D. Holstine	P	546	41
Bakersfield	Bakersfield, Calif.	1913	John J. Collins	C	12,905	334
Baltimore, Comm. College of	Baltimore, Md.	1947	Harry Bard	Mu	7,500	250
Barstow Community	Barstow, Calif.	1960	Mel Huden (Act.)	S	1,350	34
Barton County Comm. Jr.	Great Bend, Kansas	1969	Paul Hines	S	942	72
Bay de Noc Comm.	Escanaba, Mich.	1962	Edwin E. Wuehle	C	1,200	54
Bay Path Junior	Longmeadow, Mass.	1897	Randle Elliott	P	419	25
Beaufort County Tech. Inst.	Washington, N.C.	1968	James P. Blanton	S	1,762	136
Beaver County, Comm. Coll. of	Monaca, Pa.	1967	Richard Adams	C	1,400	75
Becker Junior	Worcester, Mass.	1887	Lloyd H. Van Buskirk	P	430	33
Beckley	Beckley, W. Va.	1933	John Saunders	P	984	38
Bee County	Beeville, Tex.	1965	Grady C. Hogue	S	1,181	51
Bell and Howell Schools	Chicago, Ill.	1969	George Doherty	P	7,200	350
Belleville Area	Belleville, Ill.	1946	H. J. Haberaecker	S	4,627	242
Bellevue Community	Bellevue, Wash.	1966	Merle Landerholm	S	3,662	212
Bennett (W)	Millbrook, N.Y.	1891	J. William Nystrom	P	324	46
Bergen Community	Paramus, N.J.	1965	Sidney Silverman	C	5,850	239
Berkeley-Charleston-DorchesterTEC	Charleston, S.C.	1964	Richard E. Waldroup	S, C	2,095	60
Berkshire Comm.	Pittsfield, Mass.	1960	T. E. O'Connell	S	2,073	88
Big Bend Community	Moses Lake, Wash.	1962	Robt. J. Wallenstien	S	900	54
Bismarck Junior	Bismarck, N. Dak.	1939	Ralph Werner	Mu	1,588	75
Black Hawk	Moline, Ill.	1946	Alban E. Reid	S	3,883	199
Bladen Tech. Inst.	Dublin, N.C.	1967	George Resseguie	S	275	23
Blinn	Brenham, Tex.	1883	James H. Atkinson	C	1,628	93
Bliss	Columbus, Ohio	1899	Gerald J. Wickham	P	300	20

Name	Location	Year	Governing Official and Affiliation		Stu-dents	Teach-ers
Bluefield	Bluefield, Va.	1922	Charles L. Tyer	D	340	26
Blue Mountain Community	Pendleton, Ore.	1962	Wallace C. McCrae	C	1,460	97
Blue Ridge Comm.	Weyers Cave, Va.	1965	James A. Armstrong	S	899	62
Bradford	Bradford, Mass.	1803	Robert Vogel	P	300	34
Brainerd State Junior	Brainerd, Minn.	1938	J. E. Chalberg	S	595	39
Brandywine	Wilmington, Del.	1965	Sidney Peters	P	1,200	50
Brazosport	Lake Jackson, Tex.	1968	J. R. Jackson	S	1,705	62
Brevard	Brevard, N.C.	1853	Robert A. Davis	P	423	48
Brevard Community	Cocoa, Fla.	1960	Maxwell King	S	6,650	336
Brewton Parker	Mt. Vernon, Ga.	1904	J. Theodore Phillips	D	442	24
Bristol Comm.	Fall River, Mass.	1965	Jack Hudnall	S	3,417	146
Bronx Community	Bronx, N.Y.	1957	James A. Colston	Mu	15,096	980
Broome Community	Binghamton, N.Y.	1946	Sigmund A. Smith	S	4,483	172
Broward Community	Ft. Lauderdale, Fla.	1960	Hugh Adams	S	9,635	529
Brunswick Junior	Brunswick, Ga.	1961	John W. Teel	S	887	56
Bryant & Stratton	Boston, Mass.	1865	L. P. White	P	645	46
Bucks County Comm.	Newtown, Pa.	1964	Charles Rollins	C	5,241	268
Burdett	Boston, Mass.	1879	F. G. Pfannenstiehl	P	200	20
Butler County Comm.	Butler, Pa.	1965	Thomas Ten Hoeve, Jr.	C	1,800	85
Butler County Comm. Jr.	El Dorado, Kansas	1927	Edwin J. Walbourn	C	1,800	75
Butte	Durham, Calif.	1966	Albert Schlueter	C	4,000	125
Cabrillo Comm.	Aptos, Calif.	1959	Robert E. Swenson	Di	6,947	228
Caldwell Comm. & TEC	Lenoir, N.C.	1964	H. Edwin Beam	S	750	75
Camden County	Blackwood, N.J.	1967	Otto R. Mauke	C	4,100	190
Canada	Redwood City, Calif.	1968	James W. Duke	C	3,037	196
Cape Cod Comm.	W. Barnstable, Mass.	1960	James F. Hall	S	2,547	130
Cape Fear Tech. Inst.	Wilmington, N.C.	1959	M. J. McLeod	S	546	52
Carl Albert Junior	Poteau, Okla.	1934	Norman McNabb	S	442	17
Carl Sandburg	Galesburg, Ill.	1967	Eltis Henson	Di	1,650	110
Carteret Tech. Inst.	Morehead City, N.C.	1963	E. D. Kearney, Act.	S	402	34
Casper	Casper, Wyo.	1945	Tilghman R. Aley	Di	2,476	152
Catawba Valley Tech. Inst.	Hickory, N.C.	1960	Robert E. Paap	S	1,200	100
Catonsville Community	Catonsville, Md.	1957	Robert Barringer	C	7,200	350
Cazenovia (W)	Cazenovia, N.Y.	1824	Vincent C. De Baun	P	468	42
Centenary Coll. for Women (W)	Hackettstown, N.J.	1967	Edward W. Seay	P	503	54
Centerville Community (A)	Centerville, Iowa	1930	Lyle Hellyer (Dn.)	S	700	45
Central	McPherson, Kan.	1884	Bruce L. Kline	D	169	21
Central Arizona	Coolidge, Ariz.	1969	Don Pence	C	4,161	76
Central Carolina Tech. Inst.	Sanford, N.C.	1958	James F. Hockaday	S	680	43
Central Florida Community	Ocala, Fla.	1957	Henry E. Goodlett	S	1,426	92
Central Oregon Community	Bend, Oregon	1949	Frederick Boyle	Di	892	62
Central Piedmont Comm.	Charlotte, N.C.	1963	Richard H. Hagemeyer	S	5,925	733
Central Texas	Killeen, Tex.	1967	L. M. Morton, Jr.	S	3,388	63
Central Virginia Comm.	Lynchburg, Va.	1966	M. Douglas Reed	S	1,602	87
Central Wyoming Comm.	Riverton, Wyo.	1967	Vacant	C	616	104
Central YMCA Comm.	Chicago, Ill.	1960	Donald A. Canar	P	4,700	225
Centralia	Centralia, Wash.	1925	Nels W. Hanson	S	3,200	160
Cerritos	Norwalk, Calif.	1955	Siegfried Ringwald	C	18,264	489
Chabot	Hayward, Calif.	1961	Reed L. Buffington	Di	11,957	478
Chaffey	Alta Loma, Calif.	1893	T. Stanley Warburton	S	8,400	500
Champlain	Burlington, Vt.	1878	C. Bader Brouilette	P	894	43
Charles Co. Community	La Plata, Md.	1958	J. N. Carsey	S	1,300	90
C. S. Mott Community	Flint, Mich.	1923	Charles Pappas	C	8,500	250
Chattanooga State Tech. Inst.	Chattanooga, Tenn.	1965	Edgar Sessions (Dir.)	S	975	90
Chemeketa Comm. (A)	Salem, Oregon	1955	Paul F. Wilmeth	Di	2,400	140
Chesapeake	Wye Mills, Md.	1965	George Silver	S	888	50
Chicago, City Colleges of	Chicago, Ill.	1911	Oscar Shabat	Mu	35,000	1,200
Loop College	Chicago, Ill.	1962	David Heller	Mu	10,628	246
Chipola Junior	Marianna, Fla.	1947	Raymond M. Deming	Di	1,267	90
Chowan	Murfreesboro, N.C.	1848	Bruce E. Whitaker	P	1,100	78
Cisco Junior	Cisco, Tex.	1941	Leland Willis	S	810	57
Citrus	Azusa, Calif.	1915	Robt. D. Haugh	S	8,367	141
Clackamas Comm.	Oregon City, Ore.	1966	John Hakanson	Di	4,300	191
Claremore Junior	Claremore, Okla.	1919	Richard Mosier	S	1,033	45
Clarendon Junior	Clarendon, Tex.	1898	Kenneth D. Vaughan	S	400	22
Clark	Vancouver, Wash.	1933	I. S. Hakanson	S	3,409	244
Clarke	Newton, Miss.	1908	W. L. Compere	P	280	22
Clatsop Community	Astoria, Ore.	1962	Philip Bainer	S	2,053	136
Clinton Community	Clinton, Iowa	1946	Gerald Clemmensen	Di	517	43
Clinton Comm.	Plattsburgh, N.Y.	1966	Albert Light	S	740	26
Cleveland State Comm.	Cleveland, Tenn.	1967	D. F. Adkisson	S	2,065	70
Cloud County Comm.	Concordia, Kansas	1965	Arley Bryant	C	581	32
Coahoma Junior	Clarksdale, Miss.	1949	James Earl Miller	S	1,072	60
Coastal Carolina Community	Jacksonville, N.C.	1964	James Henderson, Jr.	S	966	66
Cochise	Douglas, Ariz.	1962	John R. Edwards	C	2,269	139
Coffeyville Community Junior	Coffeyville, Kan.	1923	Russell Graham	S	623	44
Colby Comm.	Colby, Kansas	1964	James Tangeman	C	1,047	77
Colby (W)	New London, N.H.	1837	Louis Vaccaro	P	595	52
Colorado Mountain	Glenwood Spgs., Colo.	1967	Elbie L. Gann	Di	473	30
Columbia	Columbia, Mo.	1851	W. Merle Hill	P	800	50
Columbia Basin	Pasco, Wash.	1955	Fred L. Esvelt	S	4,500	175
Columbia-Greene Comm.	Athens, N.Y.	1966	Edward Owen	S	454	20
Columbia Junior	Columbia, Calif.	1968	Harvey Rhodes	S	1,683	71
Columbia State Comm.	Columbia, Tenn.	1966	Harold S. Pryor	S	1,200	80
Compton Comm.	Compton, Calif.	1927	Abel B. Sykes, Jr.	S	7,266	235
Concordia	Portland, Ore.	1905	Erhardt P. Weber	D	158	16
Concordia	Milwaukee, Wis.	1881	Walter W. Stuenkel	D	425	35
Concordia Lutheran	Austin, Tex.	1926	Ray F. Martens	D	260	25
Concordia Lutheran Jr.	Ann Arbor, Mich.	1962	P. A. Zimmerman	D	520	38
Connors State	Warner, Okla.	1908	Melvin Self	S	900	34
Contra Costa	San Pablo, Calif.	1948	Robert Wynne	S	7,600	175
Cooke County Jr. (A)	Gainesville, Tex.	1924	John H. Parker	C	1,279	65
Copiah-Lincoln Junior	Wesson, Miss.	1928	Billy Thames	C	1,148	95
Corning Community	Corning, N.Y.	1956	Robt. W. Frederick, Jr.	S	2,428	101
Cosumnes River	Sacramento, Calif.	1970	Douglas Burris	Di	1,953	77
Cottey	Nevada, Mo.	1884	Jon Hondrum	P	272	35
Cowley County Comm.	Arkansas City, Kans.	1921	Gwen Nelson	C	1,173	83

Name	Location	Year	Governing Official and Affiliation		Stu-dents	Teach-ers
Craven Tech. Inst.	New Bern, N.C.	1965	Thurman E. Brock	S	316	20
Crowder	Neosho, Mo.	1963	Dell Reed	Di	616	40
Cuesta	San Luis Obispo, Calif.	1964	Merlin Eisenbise	C	3,884	129
Cullman	Cullman, Ala.	1940	Sr. M. Lourdes Michel	D	196	29
Cumberland Coll. of Tenn.	Lebanon, Tenn.	1842	Ernest L. Stockton	P	341	23
Cumberland County	Vineland, N.J.	1966	William J. Sample	C	1,350	70
Cuyahoga Community	Cleveland, Ohio	1962	Charles E. Chapman	C, S	18,441	812
Dabney S. Lancaster Comm.	Clifton Forge, Va.	1967	John F. Backels	S	550	50
Dallas County Comm. Coll. System	Dallas, Texas	1965	Bill J. Priest	C	16,438	412
Dalton Jr.	Dalton, Ga.	1963	Derrell Roberts	S	1,016	56
Danville Junior	Danville, Ill.	1946	William Larigas	S	1,954	106
Davenport Coll. of Business	Grand Rapids, Mich.	1866	Robert W. Sneden	P	1,025	40
Davidson County Comm.	Lexington, N.C.	1958	Grady Love	S	1,444	91
Davis Junior	Toledo, Ohio	1858	Ruth L. Davis	P	325	13
Dawson	Glendive, Mont.	1940	James Hoffman	C, S	707	39
Daytona Beach Comm.	Daytona Beach, Fla.	1958	Roy F. Bergengren	S	2,569	68
Dean Junior	Franklin, Mass.	1865	Richard Crockford	P	910	68
De Anza	Cupertino, Calif.	1967	A. Robert DeHart	Di	11,111	475
DeKalb Community (A)	Clarkston, Ga.	1964	James Hinson, Jr.	C	2,917	118
Delaware Tech. & Comm.	Georgetown, Del.	1967	Paul K. Weatherly	S	2,600	125
Delgado Junior	New Orleans, La.	1921	Marvin E. Thames	S	5,768	208
Del Mar	Corpus Christi, Tex.	1935	Jean Richardson	S	5,649	258
Delaware County Community	Media, Pa.	1967	Douglas Libby, Jr.	C	2,606	129
Delta	University Ctr., Mich.	1957	Donald Carlyon	C	2,800	150
Des Moines Area Comm.	Ankeny, Iowa	1966	Paul Lowery, (Supt.)	S	2,700	100
Desert, Coll. of the	Palm Desert, Calif.	1958	Roy C. McCall	S	5,447	294
Diablo Valley	Pleasant Hill, Calif.	1948	William P. Niland	Di	14,020	280
Dixie Junior	St. George, Utah	1911	Ferron C. Losee	S	1,000	65
Dodge City Community	Dodge City, Kan.	1935	Chas. M. Barnes	C	780	35
Donnelly Coll. of	Kansas City, Kan.	1949	Rev. John Oldfield	D	525	35
Dundalk Comm.	Baltimore, Md.	1967	Rodney E. Berg	I	7,000	100
Durham Tech. Inst.	Durham, N.C.	1965	Harold Collins	S	992	75
Dutchess Community	Poughkeepsie, N.Y.	1957	James F. Hall	S	4,300	138
Dyersburg State Comm.	Dyersburg, Tenn.	1969	Edward Eller	S	810	44
East Central Junior	Decatur, Miss.	1928	Charles V. Wright	S	1,144	51
East Los Angeles	Los Angeles, Calif.	1945	J. M. Duling, act.	Di	14,300	567
East Mississippi Junior	Scooba, Miss.	1927	Earl A. Stennis	S	908	52
Eastern Arizona	Thatcher, Ariz.	1888	Dean Curtis	S, C	2,378	159
Eastern Iowa Comm.	Davenport, Iowa	1966	Gerald Clemmensen, (Supt.)	C	1,731	106
Eastern Oklahoma State	Wilburton, Okla.	1909	James Miller	S	1,565	60
Eastern Wyoming	Torrington, Wyo.	1948	Charles Rogers	C, S	359	28
Edison Community	Ft. Myers, Fla.	1962	David G. Robinson	S	1,813	86
Edmunds Community	Lynnwood, Wash.	1967	James Warren	S	1,500	150
El Camino	Torrance, Calif.	1947	Stuart E. Marsee	Di	22,647	583
El Paso Community	El Paso, Texas	1971	Alfredo de los Santos	Di	543	31
El Reno	El Reno, Okla.	1938	A. R. Harrison	S	472	23
Elgin Community	Elgin, Ill.	1949	Robert L. Appel, Jr.	Di	2,559	167
Elizabeth Seton	Yonkers, N.Y.	1960	Eileen Farley	D	410	38
Ellsworth Comm.	Iowa Falls, Iowa	1890	G. P. Warford (Dn.)	Di	832	53
Emmanuel	Franklin Spgs., Ga.	1919	C. Y. Melton	S	288	20
Endicott Junior (W)	Beverly, Mass.	1939	Eleanor Tupper	P	750	55
Erie Community	Amherst, N.Y.	1946	James Shenton	S	8,433	249
Essex Community	Baltimore, Md.	1967	Vernon Wanty	C	5,104	310
Essex County	Newark, N.J.	1968	J. Harry Smith	C	5,234	199
Everett Comm.	Everett, Wash.	1941	Jeanette Poore	S	5,000	250
Fayetteville Tech. Inst.	Fayetteville, N.C.	1961	Howard Boudreau	S	946	77
Fashion Inst. of Technology	New York, N.Y.	1944	Marvin J. Feldman	S, Mu	5,389	136
Fergus Falls State Jr.	Fergus Falls, Minn.	1960	W. A. Waage	S	577	43
Ferrum	Ferrum, Va.	1913	Joseph T. Hart	D	1,052	66
Finger Lakes, Comm. Coll. of	Canandaigua, N.Y.	1965	Charles Meder	S	1,288	45
Fisher Junior (W)	Boston, Mass.	1903	Scott Fisher	P	300	30
Flathead Valley Comm.	Kalispell, Mont.	1967	Larry Blake	S	1,298	65
Florence-Darlington TEC	Florence, S.C.	1963	Fred Fore	S	539	35
Florida	Temple Terrance, Fla.	1946	James R. Cope	P	396	26
Florida Jr. Coll. at Jacksonville	Jacksonville, Fla.	1966	Benjamin R. Wygal	S	9,148	283
Florida Keys Comm.	Key West, Fla.	1965	John S. Smith	S	1,030	42
Florissant Valley Community	St. Louis, Mo.	1962	Raymond J. Stith	Di	7,343	272
Floyd Junior	Rome, Ga.	1968	David McCorkle	S	904	44
Foothill	Los Altos Hills, Calif.	1958	Hubert H. Semans	Di	8,420	305
Forest Park Community	St. Louis, Mo.	1962	Ralph H. Lee	Di	6,905	326
Forsyth Tech. Inst.	Winston-Salem, N.C.	1963	Harley Affeldt	S	500	60
Fort Scott Comm.	Fort Scott, Kan.	1919	Leon Foster	C	589	27
Ft. Steilacoom Comm.	Tacoma, Wash.	1967	Marion O. Oppelt	S	4,775	200
Fox Valley Tech. Inst.	Appleton, Wisc.	1967	William Sirek, Dir.	Di	3,000	500
Frank Phillips	Borger, Tex.	1948	James W. Dillard	S	600	46
Franklin Inst. of Boston	Boston, Mass.	1908	L. J. Dunham Jr. (Dir.)	Mu	731	71
Freed-Hardeman	Henderson, Tenn.	1908	E. Claude Gardner	P	823	51
Fresno City	Fresno, Calif.	1918	Clyde McCully	S	13,795	320
Fullerton Junior	Fullerton, Calif.	1913	John Casey	S	16,000	470
Fulton-Montgomery Community	Johnstown, N.Y.	1963	Hadley S. DePuy	S	1,200	63
Gadsden State Junior	Gadsden, Ala.	1965	A. D. Naylor	S	2,627	150
Gainesville Junior	Gainesville, Ga.	1964	Hugh Mills, Jr.	S	1,050	48
Galveston	Galveston, Tex.	1967	Melvin M. Plexco	S	1,418	65
Garden City Community Junior	Garden City, Kan.	1919	Raymond Wamsley	C	906	55
Garland, Junior (W)	Boston, Mass.	1872	Alice J. Thurston	P	270	30
Gaston	Dallas, N.C.	1964	W. B. Sugg	S	1,813	97
Gateway Tech. Inst.	Kenosha, Wisc.	1912	Keith Stoehr	C	4,069	174
Gavilan	Gilroy, Calif.	1919	Ralph Schroder	Di	1,825	53
Genesee Community	Batavia, N.Y.	1966	Cornelius V. Robbins	C	1,873	91
George C. Wallace State Tech. Jr.	Dothan, Ala.	1965	Philip J. Hamm	S	945	52
Glen Oaks Comm.	Centreville, Mich.	1967	Justus Sunderman	C	653	56
Glendale	Glendale, Calif.	1927	John T. McCuen	Mu	5,871	110
Gloucester County	Sewell, N.J.	1968	William Apetz	C	1,839	103
Gogebic Community	Ironwood, Mich.	1932	James Perry	C	708	46
Golden West	Huntgtn. Bch., Calif.	1966	R. Dudley Boyce	Mu	13,471	300
Goldey Beacom	Wilmington, Del.	1886	Clarence A. Fulmer	P	477	33

Name	Location	Year	Governing Official and Affiliation		Students	Teachers
Gordon Junior	Barnesville, Ga.	1852	Jerry M. Williamson	S	554	40
Grahm Junior	Boston, Mass.	1950	Arthur Griffen	P	1,010	56
Grand Rapids Junior	Grand Rapids, Mich.	1917	Francis McCarthy (Dn.)	Mu	5,323	132
Grand View	Des Moines, Iowa	1896	K. F. Langrock	P	867	60
Grays Harbor	Aberdeen, Wash.	1930	Joseph Malik	S	2,000	67
Grayson County	Denison, Texas	1964	Truman Webster	S	3,145	150
Greater Hartford Comm.	Hartford Conn.	1967	Arthur C. Banks, Jr.	S	1,313	69
Greenfield Comm.	Greenfield, Mass.	1962	Lewis O. Turner	S	1,567	83
Green Mountain (W)	Poultney, Vt.	1834	Raymond A. Withey	P	614	46
Green River Comm.	Auburn, Wash.	1965	Melvin Lindbloom	S	5,200	250
Greenville TEC	Greenville, S.C.	1962	Thomas Barton, Jr. (Dir.)	S	1,667	100
Grossmont Community	El Cajon, Calif.	1961	Erv. F. Metzgar	S	13,100	374
Guilford Tech. Inst.	Jamestown, N.C.	1958	Luther R. Medlin	C	1,569	128
Gulf Coast Community	Panama City, Fla.	1957	Richard E. Morley	S	2,000	100
Hagerstown Junior	Hagerstown, Md.	1946	Atlee Kepler	C	1,352	93
Halifax County Tech. Inst.	Weldon, N.C.	1967	Phillip W. Taylor	S	380	45
Harcum Junior	Bryn Mawr, Pa.	1915	Michael A. Duzy	P	600	50
Harford Community	Bel Air, Md.	1957	Kenneth Oosting	S	5,618	279
Harrisburg Area Comm.	Harrisburg, Pa.	1964	Clyde Blocker	S	3,990	189
Hartford Coll. for Women (W)	Hartford, Conn.	1933	Laura A. Johnson	P	220	31
Hartford State Tech.	Hartford, Conn.	1946	Thomas Raimondi	S	471	56
Hartnell	Salinas, Calif.	1920	Gibb R. Madsen	Di	4,500	120
Hawkeye Inst. of Technology	Waterloo, Iowa	1966	Travis Martin, Supt.	Di	1,144	80
Haywood Tech. Inst.	Clyde, N.C.	1965	M. C. Nix	S	437	100
Henderson County Junior	Athens, Tex.	1946	T. M. Harvey	S	1,201	67
Henry Ford Community	Dearborn, Mich.	1938	Stuart M. Bundy	Mu	11,280	450
Herkimer County Comm.	Herkimer, N.Y.	1966	Robert McLaughlin	S	1,172	48
Hesston	Hesston, Kan.	1909	Laban Peachey	D	426	30
Hibbing State Junior	Hibbing, Minn.	1916	Curtis W. Johnson	S	750	49
Highland Comm.	Freeport, Ill.	1962	Kenneth E. Borland	Di	3,000	150
Highland Community Junior	Highland, Kan.	1858	T. E. Woodrum	S	320	22
Highland Park Comm.	Highland Park, Mich.	1918	Thomas Lloyd (Dean)	Mu	3,748	94
Highline Comm.	Midway, Wash.	1961	Orville Carnahan	S	5,999	383
Hilbert	Hamburg, N.Y.	1969	Sister Mary Edwina	P	585	45
Hill Junior	Hillsboro, Texas	1962	Oran Bailey	C	503	45
Hillsborough Comm.	Tampa, Fla.	1968	Morton S. Shanberg	C	4,600	175
Hinds Junior	Raymond, Miss.	1917	Robert Mayo	C	3,490	193
Hiwassee	Madisonville, Tenn.	1849	Horace N. Barker	D	488	32
Hocking Technical	Nelsonville, Ohio	1967	John J. Light	S	900	120
Holmes Junior	Goodman, Miss.	1925	Frank B. Branch	C, S	1,055	54
Holy Cross Junior	Notre Dame, Ind.	1966	Bro. John Driscoll	D	270	19
Holyoke Community	Holyoke, Mass.	1946	George E. Frost	S	2,965	208
Honolulu Business	Honolulu, Hawaii	1917	Francis Safford, Dir.	P	475	14
Honolulu Comm.	Honolulu, Hawaii	1926	James W. Thornton (Pro.)	S	2,215	117
Horry — Georgetown TEC	Conway, S.C.	1964	G. William Dudley (Dir.)	S	1,322	65
Hostos Community	Bronx, N.Y.	1968	Candito De Leon	S	1,140	130
Housatonic Comm.	Bridgeport, Conn.	1966	Edward J. Liston	S	1,634	110
Howard Community	Columbia, Md.	1970	Alfred J. Smith, Jr.	C	889	53
Howard County Junior	Big Spring, Tex.	1946	Thomas Salter	C	1,299	60
Hudson Valley Community	Troy, N.Y.	1953	James J. Fitzgibbons	S	6,089	248
Humphreys	Stockton, Calif.	1896	John R. Humphreys	P	282	21
Hutchinson Community Junior	Hutchinson, Kan.	1928	A. H. Elland	S	2,034	143
Illinois Central	E. Peoria, Ill.	1966	Kenneth L. Edwards	Di	7,968	367
Illinois Valley Comm.	Oglesby, Ill.	1924	R. Earl Trobaugh	Mu	2,448	100
Immaculata Coll. of Wash. (W)	Washington, D.C.	1905	Sister Marian Brady	D	160	23
Imperial Valley	Imperial, Calif.	1922	Terrel Spencer	S	3,225	132
Independence Comm. Jr.	Independence, Kan.	1925	Neil Edds	C	574	35
Indian Hills Community	Ottumwa, Iowa	1966	Mel Everingham	S	1,075	100
Indian River Community	Ft. Pierce, Fla.	1960	Herman Heise	S	1,559	289
Inver Hills State Junior	Inver Hills Hts., Minn.	1970	W. A. Gessner	S	1,300	75
Iowa Area Six Comm.	Marshalltown, Iowa	1966	Donald Skinner, Supt.	Di	2,012	120
Iowa Central Comm.	Ft. Dodge, Iowa	1966	Edwin Barbour	Di	2,001	142
Iowa Lakes Comm.	Esterville, Iowa	1967	Richard Blacker	S	1,050	70
Iowa Western Comm.	Clarinda, Iowa	1923	Robert Looft (Supt.)	S	375	28
Isothermal Comm.	Spindale, N.C.	1966	Fred J. Eason	S	516	30
Itasca State Junior	Grand Rapids, Minn.	1922	Harold E. Wilson	S	502	35
Itawamba Junior	Fulton, Miss.	1948	Winston O. Benjamin	S	1,620	164
Jackson Comm.	Jackson, Mich.	1928	Harold V. Sheffer	C	3,518	204
Jackson State Comm.	Jackson, Tenn.	1965	F. E. Wright	S	1,423	78
James H. Faulkner State Junior	Bay Minette, Ala.	1965	Lathem Sibert	S	1,197	45
Jamestown Community	Jamestown, N.Y.	1950	Roger Seager	S	2,532	88
Jefferson	Hillsboro, Mo.	1963	B. R. Henry	C	1,038	50
Jefferson Community	Watertown, N.Y.	1959	James F. McVean	S	1,452	51
Jefferson Davis State Jr.	Brewton, Ala.	1965	Woodfin Patterson	S	573	25
Jefferson State Jr.	Birmingham, Ala.	1965	George Layton	S	5,113	214
John A. Logan	Carterville, Ill.	1967	Nathan A. Ivey	S	1,150	50
John C. Calhoun St. Tech. Jr.	Decatur, Ala.	1965	Carlton Kelley	S	2,363	119
John Tyler Comm.	Chester, Va.	1967	James R. Walpole	S	1,738	132
Joliet Junior	Joliet, Ill.	1901	H. D. McAninch	S	4,431	269
Jones County Junior	Ellisville, Miss.	1927	T. Terrell Tisdale	S	1,800	107
Kalamazoo Valley Comm.	Kalamazoo, Mich.	1968	Dale B. Lake	C	3,364	153
Kankakee Comm.	Kankakee, Ill.	1966	John Samlin	S	1,494	87
Kan. City Kan. Comm. Junior	Kansas City, Kan.	1923	Jack M. Flint	C	2,156	90
Kansas Technical Inst.	Salina, Kansas	1965	James O. Thompson, Jr.	S	275	19
Kaskaskia	Centralia, Ill.	1965	Eugene McClintock	Di	1,500	75
Katherine Gibbs School	New York, N.Y.	1911	Fred Stapleford	P	1,750	78
Kauai Community	Lihue, Hawaii	1965	Edward White, Provost	S	1,021	43
Kellogg Community	Battle Creek, Mich.	1956	Richard F. Whitmore	S	3,135	140
Kendall	Evanston, Ill.	1934	Wesley M. Westerberg	P	747	73
Kennesaw Community	Marietta, Ga.	1966	Horace W. Sturgis	S	1,598	62
Kettering Coll. of Medical Arts	Kettering, Ohio	1967	Winton Beaven	D	300	44
Keystone Junior	La Plume, Pa.	1868	Harry K. Miller, Jr.	P	983	61
Kilgore Junior	Kilgore, Tex.	1935	Randolph C. Watson	Mu	2,575	124
King's	Charlotte, N.C.	1901	Richard H. Beasley	P	500	25
Kingsborough Community	Brooklyn, N.Y.	1963	Leon M. Goldstein	Mu	8,478	520

Name	Location	Year	Governing Official and Affiliation		Stu- dents	Teach- ers
Kirtland Comm.	Roscommon, Mich.	1966	Robert A. Stenger	Di	600	14
Kirkwood Comm.	Cedar Rapids, Iowa	1966	Selby Ballantyne (Supt.)	Di	3,094	210
Kishwaukee Comm.	Malta, Ill.	1967	W. Lamar Fly	Di	1,750	120
Kittrell	Kittrell, N.C.	1867	Nathaniel Gaylord, act.	P	392	31
Labette Community Jr.	Parsons, Kans.	1923	James J. Altendorf	C	519	33
Lackawanna Junior	Scranton, Pa.	1894	C. R. Walther Thomas	P	302	15
La Guardia Community	Long Island City, N.Y.	1970	Joseph Shenker	S	2,808	165
Lake City Comm.	Lake City, Fla.	1962	Herbert E. Phillips	S	1,815	110
Lake County, Coll. of	Grays Lake, Ill.	1969	Richard Erzen	C	4,789	220
Lake Land	Mattoon, Ill.	1966	Robert Webb	S	2,825	135
Lake Michigan	Benton Harbor, Mich.	1946	James Lehman	S	3,141	225
Lake Region Jr.	Devils Lake, N. Dak.	1941	Merril Berg	Di	750	50
Lake-Sumter Comm.	Leesburg, Fla.	1962	Paul P. Williams	Di	1,210	57
Lakewood State Junior	White Bear L., Minn.	1967	Carl Gerber	S	2,250	75
Lamar Community	Lamar, Colo.	1937	Don Keith	S	603	27
Lane Community	Eugene, Ore.	1964	Eldon G. Schafer	C	5,300	375
Laney	Oakland, Calif.	1954	Hebert Stein	C	12,200	450
Lansing Community	Lansing, Mich.	1957	Philip Gannon	S	7,500	400
Laramie County Community	Cheyenne, Wyo.	1969	H. D. Yarbrough	C	1,932	97
Laredo Junior	Laredo, Tex.	1947	Ray A. Laird	S	3,400	103
Lasell Junior (W)	Auburndale, Mass.	1851	Kenneth M. Greene	P	740	75
Lassen	Susanville, Calif.	1925	Robert Theiler	S	1,405	75
LDS Business College	Salt Lake City, Utah	1886	R. F. Kirkham	D	754	29
Lee	Baytown, Tex.	1934	Raymond C. Cleveland	Di	3,871	125
Lees Junior	Jackson, Ky.	1883	Troy R. Eslinger	Mu	321	34
Lees-McRae	Banner Elk, N.C.	1900	H. C. Evans, Jr.	D	675	60
Lehigh County Comm.	Schnecksville, Pa.	1966	John G. Berrier	C	2,023	113
Leicester Jr.	Leicester, Mass.	1784	Henry Borger	P	250	20
Lenoir Comm.	Kinston, N.C.	1960	Jesse L. McDaniel	S	1,455	102
Lewis and Clark Community	Godfrey, Ill.	1970		S	1,615	111
Lincoln Land Comm.	Springfield, Ill.	1967	Robert L. Poorman	S	4,147	225
Lincoln	Lincoln, Ill.	1865	J. Richard Stoltz	P	550	40
Lindsey Wilson	Columbia, Ky.	1903	L. R. McDonald	D	300	28
Lon Morris	Jacksonville, Tex.	1873	John E. Fellers	D	400	26
Long Beach City	Long Beach, Calif.	1927	Wiley Garner	Mu	*26,000*	*1,200*
Longview Community	Lee's Summit, Mo.	1969	William D. Hatley	Di	2,900	135
Lorain County Comm.	Elyria, Ohio	1963	Omar Olsen	S, C	3,802	162
Los Angeles City	Los Angeles, Calif.	1929	Louis Kaufman	Mu	17,517	700
Los Angeles Harbor	Wilmington, Calif.	1949	Eugene A. Pimenter	Di	8,980	415
Los Angeles Pierce	Woodland Hills, Calif.	1947	John Nicklin	Mu	16,278	483
Los Angeles Southwest	Los Angeles, Calif.	1967	Herbert Ravetch, act.	S	4,087	149
L.A. Trade - Techncal	Los Angeles, Calif.	1949	Fred Brinkman	C	15,391	255
Los Angeles Valley	Van Nuys, Calif.	1949	Robert Horton	Mu	19,000	320
Louisburg	Louisburg, N.C.	1787	C. W. Robbins	D	630	50
Lower Columbia	Longview, Wash.	1934	David Story	S	2,158	113
Luzerne County Comm.	Wilkes-Barre, Pa.	1967	Guy V. Ferrell	C, S	1,379	70
Macomb County Community	Warren, Mich.	1962	J. R. Dimitry	C, S	*16,736*	*508*
MacCormac Junior	Chicago, Ill.	1904	Gordon Borchardt	P	228	14
Macon Junior	Macon, Ga.	1968	Jack Carlton	S	1,231	45
Madison Area Technical	Madison, Wisc.	1912	Norman P. Mitby	Di	4,331	200
Madison Business	Madison, Wisc.	1856	Otto J. Madland	P	275	15
Manatee Junior	Bradenton, Fla.	1957	Samuel R. Neel	S	3,138	104
Manchester Comm.	Manchester, Conn.	1963	F. W. Lowe	S	3,150	143
Manhattan Comm.	New York, N.Y.	1963	Edgar Draper	S	10,615	462
Manor (W)	Jenkintown, Pa.	1947	Mother M. Olga	P	374	43
Maple Woods Community	Kansas City, Mo.	1969	John M. Gazda	S	1,650	60
Maria	Albany, N.Y.	1958	Sis. Mary B. Mahoney	P	500	60
Maria Regina (W)	Syracuse, N.Y.	1961	Sis. M. Rosalie Brady	P	319	36
Marin, Coll. of	Kentfield, Calif.	1926	John A. Grasham	S, C	*6,908*	*371*
Marion Institute (M)	Marion, Ala.	1889	Paul B. Robinson	P	374	75
Marshalltown Community	Marshalltown, Iowa	1927	James McKinstry	Di	850	51
Martin	Pulaski, Tenn.	1870	Tom E. Gray	D	375	29
Martin Tech. Inst.	Williamston, N.C.	1968	E. M. Hunt	S, C	300	23
Mary Holmes	West Point, Miss.	1892	Joseph Gore	D	414	42
Marymount	Boca Raton, Fla.	1963	Donald E. Ross	P	415	31
Marymount Coll. of Virginia (W)	Arlington, Va.	1950	Mother M. M. Berg	D	558	57
Massachusetts Bay Comm.	Watertown, Mass.	1961	J. F. McKenzie	S	*2,652*	*184*
Massasoit Comm.	Brockton, Mass.	1966	John Musselman	S	*2,868*	*175*
Mattatuck Community	Waterbury, Conn.	1967	Charles B. Kinney	S	2,146	100
Maui Community	Kahului, Hawaii	1966	Glen Fishbach	S	1,219	50
McCook	McCook, Nebr.	1926	M. L. Potter	Di	372	39
McDowell Tech. Inst.	Marion, N.C.	1964	John Price	S	197	17
McHenry County	Crystal Lake, Ill.	1967	James Davis	S	1,500	70
McLennan Comm.	Waco, Texas	1965	Wilbur Ball	S, C	4,000	170
Memphis, State Tech. Inst. at	Memphis, Tenn.	1967	Charles Whitehead (Dir.)	S	1,729	135
Meramec Community	St. Louis, Mo.	1962	Glynn E. Clark	Di	8,015	309
Merced	Merced, Calif.	1962	Lowell Barker	S	*5,987*	*212*
Mercer County Comm.	Trenton, N.J.	1966	Richard Greenfield	C	*5,458*	*209*
Meridian Jr.	Meridian, Miss.	1937	William F. Scaggs	Mu	1,500	90
Merritt	Oakland, Calif.	1953	John Carr, act.	S	9,706	269
Mesa	Gd. Junction, Colo.	1925	Theodore E. Albers	Di	2,726	189
Mesabi State Jr.	Virginia, Minn.	1921	Gilbert Staupe	S	667	41
Metropolitan State Jr.	Minneapolis, Minn.	1965	Howard Bergstrom	S	1,275	60
Miami-Dade Jr.	Miami, Fla.	1960	Peter Masiko, Jr.	S	28,025	*1,446*
Miami-Jacobs Jr. Coll. of Business	Dayton, Ohio	1860	Charles P. Harbottle	P	710	28
Michael J. Owens Tech.	Perrysburg, Ohio	1965	Jacob S. See	S	825	80
Michigan Christian	Rochester, Mich.	1959	Don Gardner	D	154	20
Mid Michigan Community	Harrison, Mich.	1965	Eugene W. Gillaspy	S	1,050	40
Middle Georgia	Cochran, Ga.	1884	Louis C. Alderman Jr.	S	1,556	92
Middlesex Comm.	Middletown, Conn.	1966	Philip Wheaton	S	1,340	92
Middlesex County	Edison, N.J.	1964	Frank M. Chambers	C	6,950	383
Midlands TEC	Columbia, S.C.	1963	Robert Grigsby	S	1,922	132
Midway (W)	Midway, Ky.	1944	Albert N. Cox	P	247	22
Miles Comm.	Miles City, Mont.	1939	Vernon R. Kailey	S	525	28
Milwaukee Area Technical	Milwaukee, Wis.	1951	William Ramsey (Dir.)	S	*8,978*	*507*
Mineral Area	Flat River, Mo.	1922	Richard Caster	Di	1,000	65
Mira Costa	Oceanside, Calif.	1934	John MacDonald	S	3,285	121

Name	Location	Year	Governing Official and Affiliation		Stu- dents	Teach- ers
Mississippi Delta Jr.	Moorhead, Miss.	1926	J. T. Hall	S	1,159	83
Mitchell	New London, Conn.	1939	Robert C. Weller	P	817	46
Mitchell	Statesville, N.C.	1852	Barton Herrscher	P	423	32
Moberly Area Junior	Moberly, Mo.	1927	Henry T. Morris	Di	928	35
Modesto Junior	Modesto, Calif.	1921	Kenneth Griffin	Di	11,265	400
Mohawk Valley Community	Utica, N.Y.	1946	W. Stewart Tosh	S	4,603	118
Monroe Community	Rochester, N.Y.	1961	LeRoy V. Good	S	8,943	288
Monroe County Comm.	Monroe, Mich.	1966	Ronald Campbell	C	1,465	70
Montcalm Comm.	Sidney, Mich.	1965	C. J. Bedore, Jr. (Act.)	Di	655	33
Monterey Peninsula Comm.	Monterey, Calif.	1947	George J. Faul	C	7,000	270
Montgomery Community	Rockville, Md.	1946	William Strasser	C	9,041	590
Montgomery County Comm.	Blue Bell, Pa.	1966	Leroy Brendlinger	C	3,335	175
Montgomery Tech. Inst.	Troy, N. C.	1968	Marvin G. Miles	S	300	30
Montreat-Anderson	Montreat, N. C.	1916	Silas M. Vaughn	D	303	24
Moorpark	Moorpark, Calif	1967	Robert A. Lombardi	C	8,500	350
Moraine Valley Comm.	Palos Hills, Ill.	1968	Robert E. Turner	S	3,806	198
Morris, County College of	Dover, N. J.	1968	Sherman H. Masten	C	5,000	120
Morristown	Morristown, Tenn.	1881	R. E. White	D	125	14
Morse School of Business	Hartford, Conn.	1860	Michael Taub	P	220	9
Morton	Cicero, Ill.	1924	Vincent A. Guarna	Mu	1,925	113
Motlow State Comm.	Tullahoma, Tenn.	1969	Sam H. Ingram	S	810	45
Mt. Aloysius Junior	Cresson, Pa.	1939	Sis. Mary Cecilia Meighan	P	476	59
Mt. Hood Comm.	Gresham, Ore.	1965	Earl L. Klapstein	S	8,000	375
Mt. Ida Junior	Newton Ctr., Mass.	1899	F. Roy Carlson	P	650	53
Mt. Olive	Mt. Olive, N. C.	1951	William B. Raper	D	311	34
Mt. St. Clare	Clinton, Iowa	1928	Sister Cecile Devereux	D	308	40
Mt. San Antonio	Walnut, Calif.	1945	Eldon Pearce	Di	15,292	566
Mt. San Jacinto	Gilman Hot Spgs., Cal.	1963	Milo P. Johnson	Di	1,585	65
Mt. Vernon (W)	Washington, D. C.	1875	Peter D. Pelham	P	270	22
Mt. Vernon Nazarene	Mt. Vernon, Ohio	1966	John A. Knight	D	455	40
Mt. Wachusett Comm.	Gardner, Mass.	1963	Arthur F. Haley	S	1,987	100
Murray State	Tishomingo, Okla.	1908	Clyde Kindell	S	738	40
Muscatine Community	Muscatine, Iowa	1929	Mark L. Hopkins	S	2,186	129
Muskegon Business	Muskegon, Mich.	1885	Robert Jewell	P	450	18
Muskegon Community	Muskegon, Mich.	1926	Charles Greene	C	3,890	129
Napa	Napa, Calif.	1946	George Clark	C	4,255	215
Nassau Community	Garden City, N. Y.	1959	George F. Chambers	S	18,012	358
Navarro Junior	Corsicana, Tex.	1946	Ben W. Jones	C	1,032	67
Nebraska Southern Community	Fairbury, Nebr.	1941	Ivan R. Simpson	Di	510	32
Nebraska Western	Scottsbluff, Nebr.	1928	William Ptacek	C	746	60
Neosho County Comm. Jr.	Chanute, Kans.	1936	J. C. Sanders	S	453	38
New England Aeronautical Inst.	Nashua, N. H.	1965	H. R. Thyng	P	366	22
New Hampshire Tech. Inst.	Concord, N. H.	1965	A. L. Fillion, act.	S	567	49
New Hampshire Voc. Tech.	Manchester, N. H.	1945	George C. Knox (Dir.)	S	485	41
New Hampshire Voc. Tech.	Portsmouth, N. H.	1945	E. A. McCourt (Dir.)	S	490	33
New Mexico Junior	Hobbs, N. M.	1965	Jodie C. Smith	C	964	60
New Mexico Military Inst. (M)	Roswell, N. M.	1891	Col. Robert Kemble	S	500	35
New River Community	Dublin, Va.	1966	W. Robert Sullins	S	870	50
N. Y. City Community Coll.	Brooklyn, N.Y.	1946	Herbert M. Sussman	Mu	17,531	1,385
New York, State Univ. of Agric. & Tech. Inst.	Alfred, N.Y.	1908	David H. Huntington	S	3,942	216
" " "	Canton, N.Y.	1906	Earl MacArthur	S	2,253	116
" " "	Cobleskill, N.Y.	1911	Walton A. Brown	S	2,454	127
" " "	Delhi, N.Y.	1913	William Kennaugh, act.	S	2,336	122
" " "	Farmingdale, N.Y.	1912	Charles W. Laffin	S	12,572	294
" " "	Morrisville, N.Y.	1908	Royson N. Whipple	S	2,766	132
Newton Junior	Newtonville, Mass.	1946	Charles W. Dudley	Mu	524	50
Niagara County Community	Niagara Falls, N.Y.	1962	Ernest Notar	S	3,087	115
Normandale State Jr.	Bloomington, Minn.	1968	Dale Lorenz	S	2,967	99
North Central Michigan	Petoskey, Mich.	1958	A. D. Shankland	S	973	43
North Central Tech. Inst.	Wausau, Wis.	1912	L. B. Hoyt (Dir.)	Di	9,216	280
North Country Comm.	Saranac Lake, N.Y.	1967	George Hodson	S	1,130	46
NDSU-Bottineau	Bottineau, N. Dak.	1907	Robert Johnson, Dean	S	538	25
N. Dak. St. Sch. of Science	Wahpeton, N. Dak.	1903	Clair T. Blikre	S	2,468	165
North Florida Junior	Madison, Fla.	1958	Stephen McMahon	S	1,300	65
North Greenville	Tigerville, S.C.	1892	Harold E. Lindsey	D	584	28
North Hennepin State Junior	Minneapolis, Minn.	1966	John F. Helling	S	2,141	100
North Idaho	Coeur d'Alene, Idaho	1939	Barry Schuler	C	1,127	81
North Iowa Area Comm.	Mason City, Iowa	1918	David Randall Pierce	S	1,593	108
North Platte Junior	North Platte, Nebr.	1965	William Hasewyeyer	Mu	407	27
North Shore Community	Beverly, Mass.	1965	Donald Beattie, act.	S	5,718	445
Northampton Junior	Northampton, Mass.	1896	Richard D. Pickett	S	433	27
Northampton County Area Comm.	Bethlehem, Pa.	1967	Richard Richardson, Jr.	Di	2,662	84
Northeast Alabama State Jr.	Rainsville, Ala.	1963	E. R. Knox	S	620	20
Northeast Iowa Vocational/Tech.	Calmar, Iowa	1966	Max Clark	Di	801	53
Northeast Miss. Junior	Booneville, Miss.	1948	Harold T. White	Di	1,442	68
Northeastern Christian Junior	Villanova, Pa.	1959	Elza Huffard	D	131	20
Northeastern Junior	Sterling, Colo.	1941	Ervin S. French	C	1,750	67
Northeastern Nebraska	Norfolk, Nebr.	1928	Robert P. Cox	Mu	600	40
Northeastern Okla. A. & M.	Miami, Okla.	1919	D. D. Creech	S	1,970	96
Northern Essex Comm.	Haverhill, Mass.	1960	Harold Bentley	S	4,245	281
Northern Okla.	Tonkawa, Okla.	1901	Edwin Vineyard	S	1,576	71
Northern Virginia Comm.	No. Springfield, Va.	1965	Richard Ernst	S	11,538	645
Northland State Junior	Thief R. Falls, Minn.	1965	Victor Charles	S	325	22
Northwest Community	Powell, Wyo.	1946	Sinclair Orendorff	C	737	59
Northwest Iowa Vocational	Sheldon, Iowa	1966	D. W. McPherson, Supt.	Di	500	32
Northwest Miss. Junior	Senatobia, Miss.	1927	R. D. McLendon	S	1,947	90
Northwestern Conn. Comm.	Winsted, Conn.	1965	Regina Duffy	S	1,354	68
Northwestern Michigan	Traverse City, Mich.	1951	Willard Smith, act	S	1,600	85
Norwalk Community	Norwalk, Conn.	1961	E. I. L. Baker	S	2,604	106
Norwalk State Tech.	Norwalk, Conn	1961	Frank Juszli	S	1,450	82
Oakland Community	Bloomfield Hills, Mich.	1964	Joseph Hill	C	9,000	333
Ocean City	Ocean City, Md.	1968	Walter Stencil	P	150	15
Ocean County	Toms River, N.J.	1966	Andrew S. Moreland	C,S	3,000	150
Ohlone	Fremont, Calif.	1967	Stephen E. Epler	S	4,181	172
Okaloosa-Walton Jr.	Niceville, Fla.	1963	J. E. McCracken	Di	2,169	96
Oklahoma Sch. of Business Accountancy, Law & Finance	Tulsa, Okla.	1919	H. Everett Pope	P	682	29

Name	Location	Year	Governing Official and Affiliation		Students	Teachers
Olney-Central	Olney, Ill.	1963	Gail L. Lathrop	S	2,400	120
Olympic	Bremerton, Wash.	1946	Henry Milander	S	4,000	110
Onondaga Community	Syracuse, N.Y.	1961	Marvin Rapp	S	4,373	150
Orange Coast	Costa Mesa, Calif.	1947	Robert Moore	S	21,872	614
Orange County Community	Middletown, N.Y.	1950	Robert T. Novak	S	3,519	116
Orangeburg Calhoun TEC	Orangeburg, S.C.	1966	Charles P. Weber	S	3,049	110
Oscar Rose	Midwest City, Okla.	1970	Jacob Johnson	S	2,200	64
Otero Junior	La Junta, Colo.	1941	William L. McDivitt	S	947	60
Ottumwa Heights	Ottumwa, Iowa	1925	Jerry Solloway	P	445	33
Owens Technical	Perrysburg, Ohio	1967	Jacob See	S	1,001	60
Paducah Comm.	Paducah, Ky.	1932	Donald J. Clemens	S	1,072	59
Palm Beach Junior	Lake Worth, Fla.	1933	Harold C. Manor	S	6,451	230
Palmer	Charleston, S.C.	1955	Charles E. Palmer	P	598	23
Palomar	San Marcos, Calif.	1946	Frederick R. Huber	Mu	7,366	178
Palo Verde	Blythe, Calif.	1947	George W. Pennell	S	715	48
Panola Junior	Carthage, Tex.	1947	Charles Hays	C	841	33
Paris Junior	Paris, Tex.	1924	Louis B. Williams	Di	1,303	75
Parkersburg Community	Parkersburg, W.Va.	1971	Robert Stauffer	S	2,512	127
Parkland	Champaign, Ill.	1967	William M. Staerkel	Di	4,463	300
Pasadena City	Pasadena, Calif.	1924	Armen Sarafian	S	16,631	762
Patrick Henry State Jr. (A)	Monroeville, Ala.	1965	B. E. Lee	S	500	26
Paul Smiths	Paul Smiths, N.Y.	1946	Chester L. Buxton	P	1,000	65
Peace (W)	Raleigh, N.C.	1857	S. David Frazier	D	470	31
Pearl River Junior	Poplarville, Miss.	1922	M. R. White	S, C	1,553	101
Peirce Junior	Philadelphia, Pa.	1865	Thomas M. Peirce	P	1,517	78
Peninsula	Port Angeles, Wash.	1961	E. John Maier	S	820	45
Penn Hall Junior (W)	Chambersburg, Pa.	1906	John J. Aulbach	P	140	22
Penn Valley Community	Kansas City, Mo.	1915	Thomas M. Law	Mu	4,867	103
Pensacola Jr.	Pensacola, Fla.	1948	T. Felton Harrison	S	7,995	441
Fermian Junior Bollege (Ijatam	Udeeea, Town	1940	Jay h. Dunoar, Dhon		3,549	270
Philadelphia, Comm. Coll. of	Philadelphia, Pa.	1965	Allen T. Bonnell	Mu	8,039	218
Phillips County Comm.	Helena, Ark.	1965	John Easley	S, C	1,427	50
Phoenix (A)	Phoenix, Ariz.	1920	William Berry, Dean	C	10,089	285
Piedmont TEC.	Greenwood, S.C.	1966	Lex Walters (Dir.)	S. C.	500	50
Pine Manor Junior (W)	Chestnut Hill, Mass.	1911	Frederick C. Ferry Jr.	P	493	55
Pitt Tech. Inst.	Greenville, N.C.	1961	W. E. Fulford, Jr.	S, C	635	50
Polk Comm.	Winter Haven, Fla.	1964	Frederick T. Lenfestey	S,C	3,100	149
Porterville	Porterville, Calif.	1927	O. H. Shires	Di	1,476	85
Portland Community	Portland, Ore.	1961	Amo De Bernardis	S	20,964	250
Post Junior	Waterbury, Conn.	1890	F. Burton Cook	P	600	42
Potomac St. Coll.	Keyser W. Va.	1901	Harold Doster (Dn.)	S	701	46
Prairie State	Chicago Hts., Ill.	1958	Ashley Johnson	Di	3,900	170
Pratt Community Jr.	Pratt, Kan.	1938	Donald Tolbert	S	546	36
Prentiss Institute	Prentiss, Miss.	1907	A. L. Johnson (Act.)	P	221	22
Presentation	Aberdeen, S.D.	1951	Sister Francis Mary Dunn	P	358	43
Prince George's Community	Largo, Md.	1958	Robert Bickford	C	7,736	377
Puerto Rico Junior	Rio Piedras, P.R.	1949	Ana G. Mendez	P	4,178	161
Queensborough Community	Bayside, N.Y.	1958	Kurt R. Schmeller	S	14,185	410
Quincy Junior (A)	Quincy, Mass.	1958	Kenneth P. White	Mu	1,800	135
Quinsigamond Comm.	Worcester, Mass.	1963	Paul Preus	S	3,667	200
R.C.A. Institutes	New York, N.Y.	1909	Robert F. Adams	P	3,100	103
Randolph Tech. Inst.	Asheboro, N.C.	1962	M. H. Branson	S	317	28
Ranger Junior	Ranger, Tex.	1926	Jack Elsom	S	525	28
Redwoods, Coll. of the	Eureka, Calif.	1964	Donald Weichert	S	5,000	220
Reedley	Reedley, Calif.	1926	Clifford M. Boyer	S	2,151	127
Reinhardt	Waleska, Ga.	1883	Allen Jernigan	P	252	20
Rend Lake	Ina, Ill.	1955	James Snyder	S	1,266	80
Rhode Island Jr.	Providence, R.I.	1964	William F. Flanagan	S	4,470	286
Richmond Tech. Inst.	Hamlet, N.C.	1965	Joseph Nanney	S	432	32
Ricks	Rexburg, Idaho	1888	Henry B. Eyring	S	4,500	275
Rio Hondo	Whittier, Calif.	1963	Walter Garcia	S	12,283	322
Riverside City	Riverside, Calif.	1917	Kenneth Harper	C	10,913	240
Robert Morris	Carthage, Ill.	1965	Charles W. Banta	P	187	18
Rochester State Junior	Rochester, Minn.	1915	Charles Hill	S	2,094	120
Rockland Community	Suffern, N.Y.	1957	Seymour Eskow	S	5,878	138
Rock Valley	Rockford, Ill.	1964	Karl Jacobs	Di	7,100	200
Rockingham Comm.	Wentworth, N.C.	1966	Gerald B. James	S, C	1,000	100
Sacramento City	Sacramento, Calif.	1916	Sam Kipp	Mu	11,920	370
St. Catharine	St. Catharine, Ky.	1931	Sister M. Marie Hofstetter	D	123	22
St. Clair County Comm.	Pt. Huron, Mich.	1923	Richard L. Norris	C	3,263	134
St. Gregory's	Shawnee, Okla.	1915	Rev. Michael Roethler	D	457	46
St. John's	Winfield, Kan.	1893	M. J. Stelmachowicz	D	309	30
St. John's River Junior	Palatka, Fla.	1958	Robert L. McLendon	S	962	75
St. Mary's Jr.	Minneapolis, Minn.	1964	Sis. Anne Joachim	D	755	71
St. Mary's (W)	Raleigh, N.C.	1842	Rev. Frank W. Pisani	P	490	51
St. Paul's	Concordia, Mo.	1883	Walter Rosin	P	125	23
St. Petersburg Junior	St. Petersburg, Fla.	1927	Michael Bennett	S	9,248	392
San Antonio	San Antonio, Tex.	1925	Jerome Weynand	S	15,664	755
San Bernardino Valley	San Bernardino, Calif.	1926	Arthur Jensen	S	14,020	474
San Diego City	San Diego, Calif.	1961	Allan Brooks, act.	Mu	4,394	163
San Diego Evening	San Diego, Calif.	1962	Robert S. Hamilton	Mu	13,781	712
San Diego, Mesa	San Diego, Calif.	1963	Ellis Bensen	Di	7,300	200
San Francisco, City Coll. of	San Francisco, Calif.	1935	Harry Buttimer	C	21,374	680
San Jacinto	Pasadena, Texas	1961	Thomas M. Spencer	S	6,423	212
San Joaquin Delta	Stockton, Calif.	1963	Joseph Blanchard	Di	13,510	411
San Jose City	San Jose, Calif.	1921	Otto Roemmich	S	14,500	650
San Mateo, Coll. of	San Mateo, Calif.	1922	David H. Mertes	Mu	13,779	513
Sandhills Comm.	Southern Pines, N.C.	1963	Raymond A. Stone	S	1,205	87
Santa Ana	Santa Ana, Calif.	1915	John E. Johnson	S	10,985	344
Santa Barbara City	Santa Barbara, Calif.	1908	Glenn Gooder	C, S	7,133	232
Santa Fe Community	Gainesville, Fla.	1966	Alan Robertson	C	4,054	187
Santa Monica	Santa Monica, Calif.	1929	Donald Click	Di	12,655	475
Santa Rosa Junior	Santa Rosa, Calif.	1918	Roy Mikalson	Di	11,000	310
Sauk Valley	Dixon, Ill.	1965	George C. Cole	S	1,990	112
Sayre Junior	Sayre, Okla.	1938	Harry Patterson	S	251	12

Name	Location	Year	Governing Official and Affiliation		Stu-dents	Teach-ers
Schenectady County Comm.	Schenectady, N.Y.	1967	Robert Larsson	S	2,173	46
Schoolcraft	Livonia, Mich.	1964	C. Nelson Grote	S	6,000	250
Schreiner	Kerrville, Tex.	1923	Sam Junkin	D	279	25
Seattle Central Community	Seattle, Wash.	1967	Nolen Ellison	S	6,839	251
Selma Univ.	Selma, Ala.	1878	Rev. M. Cleveland, Jr.	D	371	25
Seminole Junior	Sanford, Fla.	1966	E. S. Weldon	S	1,434	77
Sequoias, Coll. of the	Visalia, Calif.	1925	Ivan Crookshanks	Di	6,376	207
Shasta	Redding, Calif.	1950	Dale Miller	C	9,299	308
Shawnee	Ullin, Ill.	1968	Loren E. Klaus	S	1,000	66
Sheldon Jackson	Sitka, Alaska	1878	Robert Uddenberg	P	128	26
Sheridan	Sheridan, Wyo.	1948	Dana N. Peitersen	Di	413	29
Shoreline Community	Seattle, Wash.	1964	Richard S. White	S	6,197	376
Sierra	Rocklin, Calif.	1936	William M. Winstead	Di	4,500	140
Sinclair Community	Dayton, Ohio	1887	Marvin Knudson	S, C	4,200	188
Siskiyous, Coll. of the	Weed, Calif.	1959	Eugene Schumacher	Di	2,803	101
Skagit Valley	Mt. Vernon, Wash.	1926	Norwood Cole	S	3,700	150
Skyline	San Bruno, Calif.	1969	John C. Petersen	Di	5,164	198
Snead State Jr.	Boaz, Ala.	1935	Virgil McCain	S	1,017	92
Snow	Ephraim, Utah	1888	Floyd Holm	S	750	50
Solano Comm.	Suisun City, Calif.	1945	N. Dallas Evans	C	6,272	251
Somerset County	Somerville, N.J.	1966	Henry Evans	C	1,241	88
South Central Community	New Haven, Conn.	1968	W. De Homer Waller	S	1,279	52
South Florida Jr.	Avon Park, Fla.	1965	William A. Stallard	S	975	45
South Georgia	Douglas, Ga.	1906	Denton Coker	S	1,237	65
South Plains	Levelland, Tex.	1957	Marvin L. Baker	S	1,655	103
South Texas Junior	Houston, Tex.	1948	David Royce Reagan	P	2,827	91
Southeastern Community	Keokuk, Iowa	1953	C. W. Callison, Supt.	Di	361	27
Southeastern Community	Whiteville, N.C.	1965	Tom Cottingham	S	1,050	123
Southeastern Illinois (A)	Harrisburg, Ill.	1960	Joseph Deaton	Di	750	35
Southeastern Comm.	Burlington, Iowa	1966	C. W. Callison (Supt.)	S	2,500	100
Southern Baptist	Walnut Ridge, Ark.	1941	H. E. Williams	D	307	25
Southern Idaho, Coll. of	Twin Falls, Idaho	1965	James L. Taylor	C, S	2,897	120
Southern Union State Jr.	Wadley, Ala.	1922	L. Ray Jones	S	1,028	65
Southwest Mississippi Junior	Summit, Miss.	1918	Horace Holmes	S	815	45
Southwest Texas Junior	Uvalde, Tex.	1946	Wayne Matthews	S	1,316	65
Southwest Virginia Comm.	Richlands, Va.	1968	Charles King	S	1,350	80
Southwestern Comm.	Creston, Iowa	1966	John A. Smith, Supt.	S	580	35
Southwestern Oregon Comm.	Coos Bay, Ore.	1961	Jack E. Brookins	C	1,956	115
Southwestern Michigan	Dowagiac, Mich.	1966	Russell Owen	C	1,200	75
Southwestern Technical Institute	Sylva, N.C.	1964	Edward E. Bryson	S	260	26
Southwood	Salembury, N.C.	1926	Willard J. Blanchard	P	252	18
Spartanburg TEC	Spartanburg, S.C.	1961	Joe Gault (Dir.)	S	800	90
Spartanburg Junior	Spartanburg, S.C.	1911	James S. Barrett	D	963	52
Spokane Comm.	Spokane, Wash.	1963	Hobart Jenkins	S	3,905	250
Spokane Falls Community	Spokane, Wash.	1970	Max Snyder	S	3,142	106
Spoon River	Canton, Ill.	1959	Hearl C. Bishop	Di	918	66
Springfield Technical Comm.	Springfield, Mass.	1967	Edmund Garvey	S	4,500	271
Springfield Coll. in Illinois	Springfield, Ill.	1929	Sis. M. Patrick O'Brien	P	421	43
State Fair Comm.	Sedalia, Mo.	1968	Fred E. Davis	Di	1,303	72
Staten Island Community	Staten Island, N.Y.	1955	William M. Birenbaum	C	9,744	294
Stevens Henager (A)	Salt Lake City, Utah	1907	Jack Stevens	P	550	26
Sue Bennett	London, Ky.	1896	Earl F. Hays	D	213	18
Suffolk County Community	Selden, N.Y.	1959	Albert M. Ammerman	S	12,387	317
Sullins	Bristol, Va.	1870	Claude Pritchard, Jr.	P	273	24
Sullivan County Community	So. Fallsburg, N.Y.	1962	Richard F. Grego	S	1,484	59
Sumter Area TEC	Sumter, S.C.	1963	James Norris, Jr., Dir.	S	400	80
Suomi	Hancock, Mich.	1896	Ralph J. Jalkanen	P	309	21
Surry Community	Dobson, N.C.	1964	Swanson Richards	S	904	56
Sweetwater	Chula Vista, Calif.	1960	Chester De Vore	Di	4,356	165
Tacoma Comm.	Tacoma, Wash.	1965	Thornton Ford	S	4,500	243
Taft	Taft, Calif.	1922	Garlyn A. Basham	Di	935	46
Tallahassee Community	Tallahassee, Fla.	1965	Fred W. Turner	S	2,456	105
Tarrant County Junior	Ft. Worth, Tex.	1965	Joe B. Rushing	S	12,138	473
Temple Junior	Temple, Tex.	1926	H. M. Dawson	S	1,232	64
Texarkana	Texarkana, Tex.	1927	J. W. Cady	S	2,028	120
Texas Southmost	Brownsville, Tex.	1926	Arnulfo L. Oliveira	S	2,490	85
Thames Valley St. Tech.	Norwich, Conn.	1963	Donald Welter	S	866	40
Theodore Alfred Lawson St. Jr.	Birmingham, Ala.	1963	Leon Kennedy	S	1,388	54
Thomas Nelson Comm.	Hampton, Va.	1968	Gerald O. Cannon	S	2,200	153
Thornton Comm.	So. Holland, Ill.	1927	J. Philip Dalby	S	8,000	350
Three Rivers Community	Poplar Bluff, Mo.	1967	H. Tudor Westover	S	1,922	51
Tidewater Comm.	Portsmouth, Va.	1968	George Pass	S	4,000	175
Treasure Valley Comm.	Ontario, Ore.	1962	E. J. Skinner	S	920	57
Tomkins-Courtland Comm.	Groton, N.Y.	1967	Hushang Baher	S	1,501	34
Trinidad State Junior	Trinidad, Colo.	1925	Thomas Sullivan	S	1,222	80
Triton	River Grove, Ill.	1964	Herbert Zeitlin	Di	13,916	724
Truett McConnell	Cleveland, Ga.	1887	Ronald Weitman	D	228	25
Tulsa Junior	Tulsa, Okla.	1969	Alfred M. Phillips	S	3,066	75
Tunxis Community	Farmington, Conn.	1969	Benjamin G. Davis	S	2,040	111
Tyler Junior	Tyler, Tex.	1926	Harry E. Jenkins	S	3,843	193
Ulster County Community	Stone Ridge, N.Y.	1961	George B. Erbstein	S	2,160	84
Umpqua Comm.	Roseburg, Ore.	1964	Harry Jacoby	C	920	85
Union	Cranford, N.J.	1933	Kenneth Iverson	P	3,606	220
Utica Junior	Utica, Miss.	1903	A. H. Kinnard (Act.)	Di	899	58
Valencia Community	Orlando, Fla.	1967	James F. Gollattscheck	S	3,664	177
Ventura	Ventura, Calif.	1928	Ray C. Loehr	C	10,225	324
Vermilion State Junior	Ely, Minn.	1922	C. Donald Miller	S	307	20
Vermont	Montpelier, Vt.	1834	William L. Irvine	P	389	47
Vermont Technical	Randolph Center, Vt.	1957	Pierre Kieffer	S	480	47
Victor Valley	Victorville, Calif.	1961	B. W. Wadsworth	C, S	2,404	103
Victoria	Victoria, Tex.	1929	J. D. Moore	C	1,600	63
Villa Julie (W)	Stevenson, Md.	1952	Sister Mary Stephen	P	251	37
Vincennes Univ.	Vincennes, Ind.	1801	Isaac K. Beckes	S	3,125	186
Virginia Highlands Comm.	Abingdon, Va.	1969	Donald E. Puyear	S	700	70
Virginia Western Comm.	Roanoke, Va.	1966	Harold H. Hooper	S	2,650	124

Name	Location	Year	Governing Official and Affiliation		Students	Teachers
Wabash Valley	Mt. Carmel, Ill.	1969	John Cox	S	1,300	40
Waldorf	Forest City, Iowa	1903	Paul Mork	D	480	34
Walker	Jasper, Ala.	1938	David J. Rowland	P	733	45
Walla Walla Comm.	Walla Walla, Wash.	1967	Eldon Dietrich	S	1,500	90
Walters State Community	Morristown, Tenn.	1970	James W. Clark	S	895	61
Washtenaw Comm.	Ann Arbor, Mich.	1965	David Ponitz	C	3,758	110
Waterbury State Technical	Waterbury, Conn.	1964	Kenneth Fogg	S	1,250	42
Waubonsee Comm. (A).	Sugar Grove, Ill.	1966	James Nelson	S	2,291	145
Wayne Community	Goldsboro, N.C.	1957	Clyde Erwin, Jr.	S	1,507	99
Wayne County Comm.	Detroit, Mich.	1969	Reginald Wilson	S, C	11,500	854
Weatherford	Weatherford, Tex.	1869	E. W. Mince	C	966	40
Wenatchee Valley	Wenatchee, Wash.	1939	William Stewart	S	1,618	89
Wentworth Institute	Boston, Mass.	1904	Edward T. Kirkpatrick	P	1,474	99
Wentworth Military Acad. (M)	Lexington, Mo.	1923	Col. L. H. Ungles	P	120	30
Wesley	Dover, Del.	1873	Robert H. Parker	P	1,016	62
West Hills	Coalinga, Calif.	1932	Robert A. Annand	S	1,947	113
West Shore Comm.	Scottville, Mich.	1967	John Eaton	S, C	790	60
West Valley Comm.	Saratoga, Calif.	1964	James P. Hardy	C	13,749	525
Westbrook	Portland, Me.	1831	James F. Dickinson	P	485	40
Westchester Community	Valhalla, N.Y.	1946	Joseph N. Hankin	S	6,560	149
Western Iowa Technical	Sioux City, Iowa	1966	Robert Kiser, Supt.	Di	906	73
Western Piedmont Comm.	Morganton, N.C.	1966	Gordon Blank	S	998	56
Western Texas	Snyder, Texas	1971	Robert Clinton	C, S	778	40
Wharton County Junior	Wharton, Tex.	1946	Theodore Nicksick, Jr.	S	1,758	97
Wilkes Community	Wilkesboro, N.C.	1964	Howard Thompson	S	1,200	48
William Rainey Harper	Palatine, Ill.	1965	Robert E. Lahti	S	10,828	313
Williamsport Area Comm.	Williamsport, Pa.	1965	Kenneth Carl	S	3,300	216
Willmar State Jr.	Willmar, Minn.	1962	John Torgelson	S	714	42
Wilson County Tech. Inst.	Wilson, N.C.	1958	Ernest B. Parry	C	648	40
Wingate	Wingate, N.C.	1896	Budd E. Smith	D	1,483	78
Worcester Junior	Mathiston, Miss.	1886	Felix A. Sutphin	P	683	61
Worthington State Junior	Worthington, Minn.	1936	W. Donald Olsen	S	512	39
Yakima Valley	Yakima, Wash.	1929	Thomas E. Deem	S	3,600	150
Yavapai	Prescott, Ariz.	1966	Joseph Russo (Act.)	C	1,309	56
York	York, Nebr.	1890	Dale Larsen	P	308	24
York County TEC	Rock Hill, N.C.	1964	Baxter M. Hood	S	293	58
Young Harris	Young Harris, Ga.	1886	Ray Farley	P	380	30
Yuba Junior	Marysville, Calif.	1927	Daniel G. Walker	C	6,053	224

Students in Two-Year Colleges Likely To Be Older

Source: Bureau of the Census

There were 6,900,000 students 14 to 34 years old enrolled in the first four years of college in Oct. 1971. About 34% of these students reported they were enrolled in the first two years of 4-year colleges. Students enrolled in two-year colleges comprised 42% of the 4,300,000 students attending the first two years of all colleges. There were 631,000 Negroes enrolled in the first four years of college in Oct. 1971. About 25% of these Negroes were enrolled in two-year colleges.

Negro students comprised 9% of all undergraduates in two and four-year colleges in 1971.

Students at two-year colleges were nearly twice as likely to be 20 years old or over, twice as likely to be married, almost 3 times as likely to be attending classes on a part-time basis, and more likely to live in the West. About 17% were children of families in which the head had completed 4 years of college. For 65%, the family head had not completed a single year of college.

Type of College; Sex and Residence of Enrollees

(Numbers in thousands. Civilian non-institutional population)

Residence and sex	Total, enrollment	2-year colleges	Type of college 4-year colleges (year)		Not reported
			1st and 2nd	3rd and 4th	
Total, 14 to 34 years	6,895	1,830	2,359	2,407	299
Male	4,017	1,087	1,300	1,469	161
Female	2,878	743	1,059	938	138
Residence					
Metropolitan areas	4,822	1,349	1,567	1,684	222
Inside central cities	2,075	550	662	760	103
Outside central cities	2,746	799	905	923	119
Nonmetropolitan areas	2,073	481	792	723	77
Percent Distribution					
Total, 14 to 34 years	100.0	26.5	34.2	34.9	4.3
Male	100.0	27.1	32.4	36.6	4.0
Female	100.0	25.8	36.8	32.6	4.8
Residence					
Metropolitan areas	100.0	28.0	32.5	34.9	4.6
Inside central cities	100.0	26.5	31.9	36.6	5.0
Outside central cities	100.0	29.1	33.0	33.6	4.3
Nonmetropolitan	100.0	23.2	38.2	34.9	3.7

Youth Stays In School Longer

Young people are staying in school longer than in the past, according to the March 1972 Census Bureau national survey. As they replace the older, less well-educated population, the level of educational attainment in the U.S. is steadily rising.

Figures show that among American whites age 20-24, 85% have attained at least a high school education as compared to 60% for the age group 25 and over. Among blacks, 66% of the younger age group have a high school education while the figure for the group 25 and over is only 37%.

The 1972 survey also indicated considerable differences in length of schooling according to area of residence. Of the total metropolitan area population age 25 and over, 62% have high school diplomas. In nonmetropolitan areas, the proportion drops to 50%.

Degree Granting Canadian Colleges and Universities

All coeducational unless followed by (M) for men only, or (W) for women only. Even though marked (M) or (W) some are coeducational at graduate level and in evening and summer divisions.

Governing official is president unless otherwise designated. Year is that of founding. The word college is part of the name listed unless another designation is/given.

Each institution listed has an enrollment of at least 100 students of college grade. Number of teachers is the total number of individuals on teaching staff. Enrollment and faculty in italics include all branches and campuses.

Name	Location	Year	Governing Official	Stu-dents	Teach-ers
Acadia Univ.	Wolfville, Nova Scotia	1838	James M. R. Beveridge	2,400	160
Alberta, Univ. of	Edmonton, Calgary, Al.	1906	Max Wyman	22,188	2,149
Bishop's Univ.	Lennoxville, Que.	1843	D. M. Healy (Prin.)	622	81
Brandon Univ.	Brandon, Man.	1899	A. L. Dulmage	2,200	120
British Columbia, Univ. of	Vancouver, B.C.	1908	Walter Gage	20,583	1,621
Brock Univ.	St. Catharines, Ont.	1964	James A. Gibson	3,740	223
Calgary, Univ. of	Calgary, Alberta	1945	A. W. Carrothers	12,227	810
Carleton Univ.	Ottawa, Ont.	1942	Michael Oliver	13,659	530
College de Bathurst	Bathurst, N.B.	1889	Leopold Lanteigne, (Rect.)	950	50
Dalhousie Univ.	Halifax, Nova Scotia	1818	Henry D. Hicks	7,087	750
Guelph, Univ. of	Guelph, Ont.	1964	William C. Winegard	7,942	841
King's Coll., Univ. of	Halifax, Nova Scotia	1789	J. G. Morgan	263	16
Lakehead Univ.	Thunder Bay, Ont.	1965	Andrew D. Booth	3,158	250
Laurentian Univ.	Sudbury, Ont.	1961	Edward J. Monahan	5,078	200
Laval Universite	Quebec, Que.	1852	Larkin Kerwin	13,956	2,367
Lethbridge, Univ. of	Lethbridge, Alberta	1967	William Edwin Beckel	1,600	140
Manitoba, Univ. of	Winnipeg, Man.	1877	Ernest Sirluck	18,336	1,057
McGill Univ.	Montreal, Que.	1821	Robert Bell (Prin.)	17,176	3,125
McMaster Univ.	Hamilton, Ont.	1887	A. N. Bourns	14,601	882
Moncton, Univ. of	Moncton, N.B.	1963	Adélard Savoie	6,050	425
Montreal, Universite de	Montreal, Que.	1920	Roger Gaudry (Rector)	23,055	2,000
Mt. Allison Univ.	Sackville, N.B.	1840	Laurence H. Cragg	1,363	130
Mt. St. Vincent Univ.	Halifax, Nova Scotia	1925	Sister Catherine Wallace	1,400	100
New Brunswick, Univ. of	Fredericton, N.B.	1785	W. C. D. Pacey, Act.	7,031	387
Newfoundland, Mem. Univ. of	St. John's, Newfdld.	1925	Lord Taylor of Harlow	10,550	610
Notre Dame Univ. of Nelson	Nelson, B.C.	1963	Cecil L. Kaller	522	50
Nova Scotia Coll. of Arts & Design	Halifax, Nova Scotia	1887	G. N. Kennedy	400	70
Nova Scotia Technical	Halifax, Nova Scotia	1909	A. E. Steeves (Act.)	487	60
Ontario Inst. for Studies in Education	Toronto, Ont.	1965	R. W. B. Jackson (Dir)	377	144
Ottawa, Univ. of	Ottawa, Ont.	1848	V. Rev. R. Guindon (Rect.)	12,225	917
Quebec, Universite de	Montreal, Quebec	1968	Alphonse Riverin	10,500	410
Queens Univ.	Kingston, Ont.	1841	J. J. Deutsch	11,209	871
Prince Edward Island, Univ. of	Charlottetown, P.E.I.	1969	Ronald J. Baker	2,507	150
Royal Military Coll. of Canada (M)	Kingston, Ont.	1876	J. R. Dacey, Dir.	562	117
Ryerson Polytechnical	Toronto, Ont.	1948	D. L. Mordell	19,200	448
St. Anne	Church Pt. N.S.	1890	Raymond LeBlanc (Rector)	310	15
St. Francis Xavier Univ.	Antigonish, N.S.	1853	Rev. Malcolm MacDonell	2,899	209
St. Louis	Edmundston, N.B.	1946	Jean-Guy Lachonce (Dir.)	975	61
St. Mary's Univ.	Halifax, Nova Scotia	1841	D. Owen Carrigan	2,864	150
St. Michael's, Univ. of	Toronto, Ont.	1851	Rev. John Kelly	2,200	180
St. Paul Univ.	Ottawa, Ont.	1848	Rev. Marcel Patry	500	114
St. Thomas Univ.	Fredericton, N.B.	1934	Rev. Donald Duffie	1,040	66
Saskatchewan, Univ. of	Saskatoon, Sask.	1907	J. W. T. Spinks	11,888	798
Regina Campus	Regina, Sask.	1964	J. W. T. Spinks	5,400	350
Sherbrooke, Univ. of	Sherbrooke, Que.	1954	Msgr. Roger Maltais	8,109	660
Simon Fraser Univ.	Burnaby, B.C.	1965	Kenneth T. Strand	5,007	356
Sir George Williams Univ.	Montreal, Que.	1929	J. W. O'Brien	18,121	682
Toronto, Univ. of	Toronto, Ont.	1827	John Robert Evans	40,131	5,141
Trent Univ.	Peterborough, Ont.	1963	T. E. W. Nind	1,800	155
Trinity	Toronto, Ont.	1851	George Ignatieff, (Provost)	850	51
Victoria Univ.	Toronto, Ont.	1836	G. S. French	2,458	146
Victoria, Univ. of	Victoria, B.C.	1902	Hugh E. Farquhar	5,341	458
Waterloo Lutheran Univ.	Waterloo, Ont.	1923	Frank C. Peters	2,796	138
Waterloo, Univ. of	Waterloo, Ont.	1959	B. G. Matthews	14,826	796
Western Ontario, Univ. of	London, Ont.	1878	D. C. Williams	18,000	1,500
Windsor, Univ. of	Windsor, Ont.	1857	John F. Leddy	8,564	480
Winnipeg, Univ. of	Winnipeg, Man.	1871	Harry E. Duckworth	4,674	223
York Univ.	Downsview, Ont.	1959	D. W. Slater	23,316	888

Typical Tuition Fees at Selected Canadian Colleges and Universities

Source: Association of Universities and Colleges of Canada

Institution	Cost Range	Institution	Cost Range
Alberta, The University of	400-600	Ottawa, University of	636-806
British Columbia, The University of	457-693	Queen's University of Kingston	600-725
Calgary, The University of Alberta	400-800	Quebec, University du	250*
Carleton University, Ottawa	580-640	Ryerson Polytechnical Institute	212*
Dalhousie University	679-822	Saskatchewan, University of	460-685
Guelph, University of	585-645	Sir George Williams University	450-650
Laval, Universite	450-600	Toronto, University of	570-800
Manitoba, The University of	425-625	Victoria, University of	428-600
Montreal, Universite de	496-546	Waterloo, University of	625-780
Memorial University of Newfoundland	500-700	Western Ontario, The University of	588-773
McGill University	638-800	Windsor, University of	640-725
McMaster University	585-645	York University	660
New Brunswick, University of	612-642		

Universities with enrollment of 5,000 full day-time students or more. Fee is for 1972-73 academic year.
* Per semester

Typical Tuition Fee at Selected Colleges and Universities

Source: World Almanac Questionnare

The cost of a college education continues to mount. The United States Office of Education has estimated that the average cost in a private college in the fall of 1973, including tuition, board, and room, will be $3,281, a 7% increase over the previous year. The cost at a public college will average $1,492, a 6% increase.

Fees for tuition charged per year by colleges and universities for courses, use of libraries, laboratories and other facilities, are a major part of student expenses. Tuition varies considerably, depending on the type of institution, its control and location. The lowest tuition fees are those of state-controlled or other public-controlled institutions for residents of their state, city, etc. Students from other states or areas have to pay more. In the following list, such state or other public institutions are shown with two figures. The lower one is the tuition fee for residents, the higher one the tuition fee for students from other states or areas.

(Tuition does not include room, board or other expenses)

School	Tuition	School	Tuition	School	Tuition
Adrian	$1,894	Fairleigh Dickinson Univ.	2,050	Ohio State Univ.	630-1,680
Alabama, Univ. of	510-1,020	Fordham Univ.	2,200	Oklahoma State Univ.	484-1,308
Albuquerque, Univ. of	1,200	Furman Univ.	1,839	Oral Roberts Univ.	1,100
Amherst	4,205	Georgia, Univ. of	519-1,239	Oregon State Univ.	505-1,563
Anderson	1,770	Georgetown Univ.	2,500	Oregon, Univ. of	534-1,645
Antioch	3,335	Gonzaga Univ.	1,680	Penn. State Univ.	855-1,986
Arizona, Univ. of	411-1,301	Hampton Institute	1,630	Pittsburgh, Univ. of	970-1,960
Arizona State Univ.	320-1,210	Hartford, Univ. of	2,100	Portland State Univ.	516-1,575
Auburn Univ.	525-1,050	Hawaii, Univ. of	111-366	Portland, Univ. of	1,970
Avila	1,495	Holy Cross	2,730	Princeton Univ.	3,000
Baldwin-Wallace	2,568	Idaho State Univ.	1,445-2,195	Providence	2,145
Ball State Univ.	630-1,260	Illinois, Univ. of	686-1,676	Rice Univ.	2,200
Barrington	2,020	Iowa State Univ.	600-1,230	Richmond, Univ. of	1,925
Baylor Univ.	1,040	Iowa, Univ. of	620-1,250	Rochester, Univ. of	2,925
Bob Jones Univ.	765	Jacksonville Univ.	1,760	St. Bonaventure Univ.	2,150
Boston College	2,650	John Carroll Univ.	1,700	Santa Clara, Univ. of	2,175
Boston Univ.	2,600	Kansas State Univ.	526-1,316	Santa Fe	1,300
Bowdoin	2,700	Kansas, Univ. of	485-1,075	Seton Hall Univ.	2,500
Bowling Green State Univ.	780-1,923	Kent State Univ.	991-2,116	South Dakota State Univ.	548-1,288
Bradley Univ.	2,100	Kentucky, Univ. of	405-1,120	South, Dakota, Univ. of	553-1,249
Brandeis Univ.	2,900	Knoxville	2,300	Southern Calif., Univ. of	2,760
Brigham Young Univ. (A)	600	Louisville, Univ. of	950-1,950	Southern Illinois Univ.	600-1,500
Brown Univ.	3,250	Marquette Univ.	2,058	Southern Methodist Univ.	2,200
Bucknell Univ.	4,034	Maryland, Univ. of	698-1,698	Swarthmore	2,885
Butler Univ.	1,850	Massachusetts, Univ. of	469-1,695	Syracuse Univ.	2,880
Calif. Univ. of	638-938	Mass. Inst. of Tech.	3,100	Texas A & M Univ.	247-427
Carnegie-Mellon Univ.	2,500	Memphis State Univ.	348-1,068	Texas Christian Univ.	2,032
Case Western Reserve Univ.	2,720	Miami, Univ. of	2,633	Tufts Univ.	3,200
Cedar Crest	2,430	Michigan State Univ.	675-1,530	Utah State Univ.	438-948
Chicago, Univ. of	2,850	Michigan, Univ. of	740-2,400	Utah, Univ. of	480-1,155
Clemson Univ.	640-1,340	Minnesota, Univ. of	549-1,455	Valley City State	390-945
Coe	3,453	Mississippi, Univ. of	516-1,116	Vanderbilt Univ.	2,400
Colorado State Univ.	570-1,759	Montana, Univ. of	471-1,318	Vassar	2,900
Cooper Union	none	Morgan State	550-1,000	Vermont, Univ. of	1,085-2,685
Creighton Univ.	1,950	Nebraska, Univ. of	600-1,600	Villanova Univ.	2,350
Dana	1,770	Nevada, Univ. of	520-1,720	Wabash	2,470
Dartmouth	3,270	New Mexico Highlands Univ.	339-906	Wake Forest Univ.	2,000
Dayton, Univ. of	1,730	New Mexico State Univ.	466-1,296	Washburn Univ. of Topeka	575-845
Delaware, Univ. of	475-1,350	New Mexico, Univ. of	456-1,284	Washington State Univ.	730-907
Denver, Univ. of	2,700	New York Univ.	2,700	Weber State	405-810
Detroit, Univ. of	1,950	Niagara Univ.	2,200	Westmar	1,810
Dickinson	2,950	North Carolina State Univ.	236-2,033	Westmont	2,350
Doane	1,910	North Dakota, Univ. of	456-1,184	William and Mary	756-1,926
Drake Univ.	2,320	North Dakota State Univ.	435-1,164	Wisconsin, Univ. of	558-1,906
Duke Univ.	2,600	Notre Dame, Univ. of	2,600	Wyoming, Univ. of	390-1,356
Eastern Michigan Univ.	465-1,350	Oberlin	2,897	Youngstown State	570-1,050
Evansville, Univ. of	1,683				

(A) $300 additional for non-members of LDS church.

National Spelling Bee Champions

The National Spelling Bee, conducted by Scripps-Howard Newspapers and other newspapers since 1939, was instituted by the Louisville (Ky.) Courier-Journal in 1925. Children under 16 years of age sponsored by participating newspapers are eligible to compete for the cash prizes and prize trips. Recent winners are:

1971—1. Jonathan Knisely, 12, Mullica Hill, N.J. (Phila. Bulletin). 2. Susan O'Malley, 13, Phoenix, Ariz. (Arizona Republic). 3. Carolyn Cross, 13, Stow, Ohio (Akron Beacon Journal).

1972—1. Robin Kral, 14, Lamesa, Texas (Lubbock Avalanche-Journal). 2. Lauren Pringle, 13, Buffalo, N.Y.

(Buffalo Evening News). 3. Joseph J. Vissers, 13, Anchorage, Alaska (Anchorage Daily Times).

1973—1. Barrie Trinkle, 13, Fort Worth, Tex. (Fort Worth Press). 2. Stephen Hayes, 14, Oxon Hill, Md. (Washington, D.C., Star-News). 3. Camellia Jane Pratt, 12, Dickinson, Tex. (Houston Chronicle).

Scholarships, Fellowships, and Other Financial Aid

Scholarships are usually outright grants to undergraduates, while fellowships are awarded to graduate students. Scholarships, which may range from as little as $50 to as much as $3,000 annually, are usually given to students of proven talent and need.

To help assure that the available scholarships will go to those who deserve and need them, the College Scholarship Service was created 18 years ago as an agency of the College Entrance Examination Board. Most of the nation's colleges and universities are served by this agency. The College Scholarship Service, 888 Seventh Ave., New York, N.Y. 10019, requires parents to answer a confidential questionnaire on finances. Actual financial awards are made by the individual college or university.

Federal programs of financial assistance for students seeking post-secondary training at colleges, universities, and vocational training schools, take the form of grants, loans, and employment opportunities.

National Direct Student Loan Program permits total aggregate loans of up to $2,500 to be made to students in their first 2 years of college, $5,000 for students who have completed their first 2 years of undergraduate study and $10,000 for a graduate or professional student (including undergraduate loans). The financial aid officer on your campus is responsible for determining which students are eligible and the amount of the loan. Repayment begins 9 months after you cease at least half-time study and may extend over a 10-year period. Interest charges of 3% also begin at the start of the repayment period. No repayment is required and no interest is charged for any period up to 3 years during which you are serving in the Armed Forces, Peace Corps, or VISTA or if you are continuing your education in another institution. The program also provides for partial or total loan cancellation for students who enter certain eligible fields of elementary & secondary school teaching.

College Work-Study Program may assist you by providing a job opportunity for the college itself or for a public or private nonprofit agency or organization if the work is in the Public interest. Work averages 15 hours weekly while classes are in session and 40 hours per week may be worked during vacation periods. In general, the salary paid is at least equal to the current minimum wage, although, it is frequently higher. You are eligible if you are a full-time student with substantial financial need and could not otherwise attend college. The financial aid officer is responsible for determining the students to be employed, selecting suitable jobs for them, handling the payroll, and the general administration of the program.

Supplemental Educational Opportunity Grants Program is for undergraduate students of exceptional financial need in at least half-time attendance, who without this grant would be unable to continue their education. Grants of up to $1,500 a year are available for 4 years of undergraduate study. You do not need a superior academic record. This grant does not have to be repaid. The financial aid officer at your school selects those who will receive grants and determines the amount you will need.

Science Talent Search—administered annually by Science Service, Inc., identifies high school seniors in the United States talented in science, mathematics and engineering.

Greatest emphasis in the selection is placed on evaluation by scientists of an independent research project done by the student, and secondarily on answers to open-ended questions designed to elicit evidence of the students' interest and creativity in science.

Forty finalists are chosen from among 300 Honorable Mentions who in turn are selected from some 25,000 participants. The forty receive a five-day all-expense trip to Washington to compete for scholarships and awards totaling $67,500.

The Science Talent Search has been supported by the Westinghouse Educational Foundation since its inception. Information may be obtained from Science Service, 1719 N St., N.W., Washington, D.C. 20036.

National Merit Scholarship Program established in 1955 with grants from the Ford Foundation and the Carnegie Corp. of N.Y., awards about 3,000 scholarships annually to students who demonstrate extraordinary ability to benefit from a college education. Students may participate through their high schools. They become eligible by taking the qualifying test. Top scorers take a second examination, the Scholastic Aptitude Test of the College Entrance Examination Board and have to submit biographical information; family financial data optional. Financial need is not a factor in the selection of winners. About 1,000 nonrenewable National Merit $1,000 Scholarships are awarded annually. Approximately 2,000 four-year sponsored Merit Scholarships are offered each year. The stipends for the four-year sponsored awards range from $100 to $1,500 a year. Information may be obtained from Natl. Merit Scholarships Corp., 990 Grove St., Evanston, Ill., 60201.

Fulbright-Hays Scholarships— As part of an international educational exhange program, the U.S. Government, under the Fulbright-Hays Act provides scholarships for graduate study, research, lecturing and teaching abroad. There are full grants that cover transportation, tuition, books, living expenses and other costs, and there are grants which cover travel costs with tuition and other expenses fully or partly paid by foreign governments, universities, and other institutions.

Detailed information on these exchange grants may be obtained from the Fulbright Program Adviser at college and university campuses or one of the following agencies:

a) For graduate study and pre-doctoral research — Institute of International Education, 809 United Nations Plaza, New York, N.Y. 10017.

b) For teaching in elementary and secondary schools Teacher Exchange Section, Div. of International Exchange and Training, Institute of International Studies, Office of Education, Dept. of Health, Education & Welfare, Washington, D.C. 20202.

c) For university lecturing and post-doctoral research — Conference Board of Associated Research Councils' committee on Intl. Exchange of Persons, 2101 Constitution Ave., Washington D.C. 20418.

General Motors Scholarship Plan — Under this plan, about 135 4-year undergraduate scholarships are awarded annually to entering freshmen by 123 participating institutions throughout the nation. Scholarships range from $200 to $2,000 per year depending upon need. Applications are made through the directors of admission of participating colleges. General Motors Corp., Gen. Motors Bldg., Detroit, Mich. 48202.

Rhodes Scholarships — Thirty-two qualified American students, are chosen every year to receive Rhodes Scholarships for a minimum of two years of study at Oxford University. Rhodes Scholarships, estab. under the will of Cecil John Rhodes, carry a stipend of in excess of £1,600 a year. At Oxford work may be done in any field of study for which the university awards a degree. Applicants must be male, unmarried U.S. citizens, 18 to 24 years of age at the time of application, and with at least junior standing at a recognized degree-granting college or university at time of application. Information may be obtained from the Rhodes Scholarship Office, Wesleyan Univ, Middletown, Conn. 06457.

Canadian Scholarships, Fellowships, and Other Financial Aid

The Canada Council. The Canada Council offers various forms of assistance to students and scholars in the humanities and social sciences and to professionals in the arts. In the humanities and social sciences, it provides doctoral, leave, research and special M.A. fellowships through competitions held in the fall each year. Individuals may also apply for grants for advanced research and for travel to scholarly meetings and conferences. Senior arts grants and arts grants are awarded annually on a competitive basis to professional artists for six to twelve months' free work or advanced study, and short-term assistance in the arts is available in the form of short term grants, travel grants and project cost grants. Under cultural exchange agreements between Canada and various foreign countries, the Council administers several exchange programs, and in co-operation with the Foreign Area Fellowship Program (U.S.), it offers training fellowships in the social sciences for Canadian M.A. students who have a special interest in Latin America. Council assistance is available only to Canadian citizens and under certain conditions to landed immigrants in Canada. Further information may be obtained from The Canada Council, P.O. Box 1047, Ottawa, Ontario, K1P 5V8.

National Research Council of Canada. NRC offers a wide variety of awards, fellowships, and other forms of financial aid to students in science and engineering for further postgraduate and postdoctorate study. The main form of awards are the Postgraduate Scholarships and Postdoctorate Fellowships which are open to Canadian citizens or landed immigrants residing in Canada, and who have completed at least one year at a Canadian university. Award holders are decided through national competition. Some other significant awards are the Postgraduate Scholarships in Science Librarianship and Documentation, and the Industrial Postdoctorate Fellowships. For complete information as to the value, period and other award details write to The Scholarship Officer, Office of Grants and Scholarships, National Research Officer, Office Canada, Ottawa, Ontario, K1A 0R6.

Rhodes Scholarships. Eleven qualified Canadian students are chosen each year to receive Rhodes Scholarships. The number is based upon one student from each province, excluding Prince Edward Island, and 2 students from Ontario and Quebec. Students must be Canadian citizens, or must have been resident in a province for at least 5 years. The amount of the award is £1,500 a year. Information may be obtained from the Rhodes Scholarship Trust, P.O. Box 48, Toronto Dominion Centre, TORONTO, M5K 1E1.

Fall Enrollment and Teachers in Full-time Day Schools
Public Elementary and Secondary Day Schools—1971-72
Source: Statistics Canada

Province	Pupils Enrolled 5,640,515		Full-time Teachers o 262,517	
	Elementary (Kdgn to Gr 8)	Secondary (Grade 9 and up)	Elementary (Kdgn to Gr 8)	Secondary (Grade 9 and up)
Canada	3,988,501	1,652,014	162,894	98,623
Newfoundland	130,311	32,507	4,891	1,757
Prince Edward Island	22,416	8,154	1,123	516
Nova Scotia	160,446	54,334	6,501	3,368
New Brunswick	126,343	49,654	5,180	2,776
Quebec	1,084,340	484,331	46,500 e	31,500 e
Ontario	1,434,260	597,100	57,992 p	34,496 p
Manitoba	174,905	69,547	7,351	4,380
Saskatchewan	171,652	71,927	7,265	3,451
Alberta	299,868	128,100	12,995	7,526
British Columbia	370,516	153,789	13,412	8,700
Yukon	3,789	1,017	181	68
Northwest Territories	9,655	1,554	503	85

e = Estimate   p = Preliminary   o = Includes principals and supervisors

Cost Per Pupil by Province
Source: Statistics Canada

Expenditures of School Boards for Providing Elementary and Secondary Education in Canada (1972 and 1973)

Province	1972			1973		
	Total [1] Expenditures	Enrollment 1971-72	Cost per Pupil	Total [1] Expenditures	Enrollment 1972-73	Cost per Pupil
Canada	$4,863,591,000	5,640,515	$ 862	$5,182,162,000	5,613,611	$ 923
Newfoundland	80,516,000	162,818	495	87,783,000	161,712	543
Prince Edward Island	18,401,000	30,570	602	20,006,000	29,795	672
Nova Scotia	137,460,000	214,780	640	144,430,000	211,262	684
New Brunswick	91,070,000[2]	175,997	518	98,209,000[2]	173,851	565
Quebec	1,311,200,000	1,568,671 e	836	1,391,606,000	1,568,434 e	887
Ontario	1,968,560,000	2,031,360	969	2,083,790,000	2,028,114	1,028
Manitoba	199,397,000	244,452	816	214,050,000	238,861	896
Saskatchewan	176,721,000	243,579	726	189,970,000	234,152	811
Alberta	405,476,000	427,968	947	436,191,000	425,251	1,026
British Columbia	441,146,000	524,305	841	479,465,000	526,061	911
Yukon	6,742,000	4,806	1,403	7,482,000	4,749	1,576
Northwest Territories	26,902,000	11,209	2,400	29,180,000	11,369	2,567

(1) Provincial estimate
(2) Excludes capital expenditures, which used to be included in departmental expenditures in NB.
e Estimate

Income Discrimination: Male and Female, Black and White

Source: Bureau of the Census

Total Money Income (Includes full- and part-time workers, 25 and over, Mar. 1971)	Total	Years of Schooling					
		7 or less	8	9-11	12	13-15	16 or more
White Males with Income (1,000)	45,937	5,531	6,110	7,073	14,568	5,410	7,246
Percent	100.0	100.0	100.0	100.0	100.0	100.0	100.0
Loss to $2,999	14.0	40.7	24.9	13.6	6.7	6.9	5.1
$3,000 to $5,999	18.2	30.4	29.4	20.9	14.7	11.7	8.5
$6,000 to $7,999	16.1	14.1	17.0	19.9	19.0	13.9	8.7
$8,000 to $9,999	15.9	7.4	13.6	19.6	20.3	17.2	11.0
$10,000 to $14,999	23.3	5.8	11.9	20.6	29.8	31.9	29.3
$15,000 and over	12.6	1.4	3.3	5.4	9.6	18.4	37.4
Mean Income	$9,185	$4,651	$6,143	$7,902	$9,389	$11,081	$14,640
Black Males with Income (1,000)	4,382	1,490	419	972	1,025	264	211
Percent	100.0	100.0	100.0	100.0	100.0	100.0	100.0
Loss to $2,999	28.1	47.7	32.4	18.8	15.2	15.8	6.9
$3,000 to $5,999	31.9	32.0	38.4	36.6	31.0	19.6	16.1
$6,000 to $7,999	17.9	12.5	18.2	20.9	24.4	13.6	15.7
$8,000 to $9,999	11.7	5.4	6.4	14.1	16.3	24.6	17.6
$10,000 to $14,999	8.6	2.1	3.6	8.9	12.7	21.9	27.3
$15,000 and over	1.8	0.3	1.0	0.7	1.6	4.5	16.4
Mean Income	$5,429	$3,671	$4,633	$5,704	$6,523	$7,579	$10,155
Mean Income, Full-Time Males (65.9% of total)	**$10,697**	**$6,431**	**$7,947**	**$8,917**	**$10,080**	**$12,111**	**$15,946**
White Females with Income (1,000)	34,272	4,021	4,467	5,581	12,901	3,744	3,558
Percent	100.0	100.0	100.0	100.0	100.0	100.0	100.0
Loss to $2,999	53.5	79.5	70.7	58.0	45.7	44.7	32.1
$3,000 to $5,999	27.4	17.6	23.7	31.0	33.4	25.8	17.9
$6,000 to $7,999	10.1	1.9	3.8	7.5	13.0	15.8	14.7
$8,000 to $9,999	4.8	0.4	1.1	2.4	4.9	7.0	15.7
$10,000 to $14,999	3.3	0.4	0.5	0.8	2.5	4.7	15.2
$15,000 and over	0.9	0.2	0.2	0.3	0.5	2.0	4.2
Mean Income	$3,559	$1,947	$2,360	$2,938	$3,752	$4,334	$6,340
Black Females with Income (1,000)	4,492	1,276	469	1,117	1,110	294	226
Percent	100.0	100.0	100.0	100.0	100.0	100.0	100.0
Loss to $2,999	60.3	86.9	75.0	59.2	41.3	31.3	13.6
$3,000 to $5,999	27.2	11.7	21.9	34.0	40.4	34.6	18.3
$6,000 to $7,999	7.3	1.1	1.4	5.4	12.2	19.9	21.5
$8,000 to $9,999	3.1	0.1	1.8	0.7	4.0	8.2	22.9
$10,000 to $14,999	2.2	0.2	–	0.7	2.0	6.0	22.2
$15,000 and over	0.1	–	–	–	–	–	1.6
Mean Income	$2,945	$1,629	$2,088	$2,717	$3,706	$4,692	$7,284
Mean Income, Full-Time Females (33.1% of total)	**$6,046**	**$3,831**	**$4,277**	**$4,648**	**$5,820**	**$6,950**	**$8,940**

(Percentages may not add to 100.0 due to rounding; — represents zero or rounds to zero.)

Explanation: The tables above demonstrate that while income tends to rise with educational attainment, it rises far less for women and blacks than for white men. For every year of schooling, the black man tends to gain less than his white counterpart. (Black women appear to improve their incomes in comparison with white women, but this is probably because more black women tend to work full-time.)

Looking at the mean incomes for full-time workers, we can see that all women tend to make only a little more than half the earnings of men with the same educational attainments.

100 Years of Public Schools

Source: Office of Education. Dept. of Health, Education and Welfare

Pupils and teachers (in thousands)	1869-70	1899-1900	1909-10	1919-20	1929-30	1939-40	1949-50	1959-60	1967-68	1969-70
Total U.S. population	39,818	75,995	90,492	104,512	121,770	130,880	148,665	179,323	197,863	203,212
Population 5-17 years of age	12,055	21,573	24,009	27,556	31,417	30,150	30,168	43,881	51,584	52,490
Percent aged 5-17 years	30.3	28.4	26.5	26.4	25.8	23.0	20.3	24.5	26.1	25.8
Enrollment:										
Elementary and Secondary	6,872	15,503	17,814	21,578	25,678	25,434	25,111	36,087	43,891	45,619
Percent pop. 5-17 enrolled	17.3	20.4	19.7	20.6	21.1	19.4	16.9	20.1	22.2	22.4
Percent in high schools	1.2	3.3	5.1	10.2	17.1	26.0	22.7	23.5	27.9	28.5
High School graduates	....	62	111	231	592	1,143	1,063	1,627	2,395	2,589
Average school term (in days)	132.2	144.3	157.5	161.9	172.7	175.0	177.9	178.0	178.8	178.9
Total instructional staff	....	....	....	678	880	912	962	1,464	2,071	2,253
Teachers, librarians: Men	78	127	110	93	140	195	195	402	616	691
Women	123	296	413	565	703	681	719	985	1,341	1,440
Percent men	38.7	29.9	21.1	14.1	16.6	22.2	21.3	29.0	31.5	32.4
Receipts & Expenditures (in millions)										
Total receipts	....	$219	$433	$970	$2,088	$2,260	$5,437	$14,746	$31,903	$40,227
Total expenditures	$63	214	426	1,036	2,316	2,344	5,837	15,613[1]	32,977[1]	40,683
Current, elementary and secondary	....	179	356	861	1,843	1,941	4,687	12,329	26,877	34,218
Capital outlay	....	35	69	153	370	257	1,014	2,661	4,255	4,659
Interest on school debt	....	....	....	18	92	130	100	489	977	1,171
Other	....	....	....	3	9	13	35	132	866	636
Salaries and Pupil Cost	Data in unadjusted dollars					Data in adjusted dollars				
Average annual teacher salary[2]	$189	$325	$485	$1,554	$3,133	$3,894	$4,801	$6,651	$8,472	$8,840
Expenditure per capita total pop.	1.59	2.83	4.71	17.68	41.98	48.40	62.63	111.93	185.05	200.20
Current expenditure per pupil ADA[3]	....	16.67	27.85	95.15	191.27	238.05	333.06	482.24	730.87	815.98

(1.)Because of a modification of the scope "current expenditures for elementary and secondary schools" data for 1959-60 and later years are not entirely comparable with data for prior years. (2.)Includes supervisors, principals, teachers and other non-supervisory instructional staff. (3.)"ADA" means average daily attendance in elementary and secondary day schools.

Educational Attainment by Age, Race and Sex

Source: Bureau of the Census   (Number of Persons in thousands)

AGE RACE AND SEX March 1972	Total Pop.	ELEMENTARY 5 years	6&7 years	8 years	HIGH SCHOOL 1 year	2 years	3 years	4 years	COLLEGE 1 year	2 years	3 years	4 years	5 or more
White													
Total, 14 years and over	134,904	1,600	7,973	16,347	9,187	10,695	8,071	46,213	6,642	7,000	3,002	9,036	5,284
14 and 15 years	7,063	45	1,752	3,256	1,847	102	11	4	-	-	-	-	-
16 and 17 years	6,847	8	115	410	1,598	2,935	1,640	104	4	7	-	-	-
18 and 19 years	6,398	18	50	157	187	398	1,384	3,310	775	59	14	6	-
20 and 21 years	6,006	7	50	128	162	251	249	2,665	846	1,024	507	84	2
22 to 24 years	9,047	33	111	220	272	390	305	3,916	777	745	548	1,362	299
25 years and over	99,543	1,489	5,895	12,177	5,121	6,620	4,483	36,215	4,240	5,165	1,933	7,584	4,983
25 to 29 years	12,828	44	259	366	482	617	501	5,657	939	888	421	1,627	926
30 to 34 years	10,606	41	271	471	474	683	467	4,710	596	659	248	1,069	779
35 to 44 years	19,951	195	706	1,336	1,015	1,334	1,041	8,608	907	1,123	362	1,718	1,182
45 to 54 years	20,974	233	1,037	2,242	1,084	1,509	1,151	8,493	834	1,154	344	1,363	987
55 to 64 years	17,096	340	1,397	3,027	1,066	1,355	815	5,264	531	733	297	961	623
65 to 74 years	11,296	353	1,321	2,818	672	773	357	2,395	312	374	176	589	337
75 years and over	6,791	282	904	1,916	327	349	151	1,087	121	235	84	258	149
Male, 14 years and over	64,611	800	4,112	8,057	4,398	4,914	3,759	19,546	3,361	3,620	1,527	4,855	3,704
14 and 15 years	3,602	32	993	1,652	842	47	8	1	-	-	-	-	-
16 and 17 years	3,475	4	72	246	855	1,462	776	41	3	-	-	-	-
18 and 19 years	3,146	6	34	103	92	224	727	1,543	358	21	8	3	-
20 and 21 years	2,843	3	26	69	80	115	113	1,113	474	539	260	30	-
22 to 24 years	4,412	21	57	119	110	148	132	1,690	438	432	341	682	204
25 years and over	47,133	733	2,930	5,868	2,419	2,916	2,002	15,158	2,088	2,628	918	4,139	3,500
25 to 29 years	6,373	25	131	190	254	289	208	2,924	517	458	281	811	809
30 to 34 years	5,273	25	133	258	235	303	196	2,086	295	380	119	577	584
35 to 44 years	9,814	98	405	720	503	613	439	3,620	467	599	177	1,040	902
45 to 54 years	10,117	119	551	1,170	552	701	547	3,503	422	601	152	817	688
55 to 64 years	8,044	188	719	1,477	471	603	393	2,209	235	367	137	492	411
65 to 74 years	4,893	146	633	1,309	293	292	174	885	117	114	77	261	190
75 years and over	2,618	131	357	744	131	116	44	331	35	69	25	107	95
Female, 14 years and over	70,293	800	3,861	8,291	4,789	5,781	4,313	26,667	3,281	3,380	1,475	4,181	1,580
14 and 15 years	3,461	12	759	1,604	1,005	55	3	3	-	-	-	-	-
16 and 17 years	3,372	4	44	164	743	1,472	865	63	1	7	-	-	-
18 and 19 years	3,252	12	16	54	95	173	657	1,766	417	38	6	3	-
20 and 21 years	3,163	4	24	58	83	136	135	1,551	372	485	247	54	2
22 to 24 years	4,635	12	54	101	163	242	172	2,226	339	313	207	680	95
25 years and over	52,410	756	2,965	6,309	2,701	3,704	2,481	21,057	2,152	2,538	1,015	3,445	1,483
25 to 29 years	6,455	19	128	175	249	328	293	3,134	422	390	190	782	295
30 to 34 years	5,333	16	138	213	239	380	270	2,625	300	279	129	492	195
35 to 44 years	10,137	97	301	616	512	721	602	4,988	440	524	185	677	280
45 to 54 years	10,857	115	485	1,073	532	808	604	4,990	413	552	192	546	299
55 to 64 years	9,052	152	678	1,550	594	752	422	3,054	297	366	160	469	212
65 to 74 years	6,403	206	688	1,509	379	481	183	1,510	195	260	99	328	148
75 years and over	4,173	151	547	1,173	197	233	107	756	86	166	59	151	55
Negro & Other Races													
Total 14 years and over	17,129	561	1,847	1,864	1,627	1,755	1,410	4,312	560	535	220	528	357
14 and 15 years	1,193	23	392	483	252	20	3	3	-	-	-	-	-
16 and 17 years	1,146	7	56	139	306	405	209	17	-	-	-	-	-
18 and 19 years	1,014	3	21	50	60	150	238	403	70	4	1	-	-
20 and 21 years	923	3	25	35	67	70	90	368	102	96	44	6	-
22 to 24 years	1,263	7	27	58	65	112	112	565	86	68	65	68	16
25 years and over	11,590	517	1,326	1,099	876	998	758	2,956	301	368	110	455	341
75 years and over	580	71	95	78	13	24	2	33	2	3	1	4	1
Male, 14 years and over	7,857	265	903	879	690	774	603	1,848	245	257	98	240	214
14 and 15 years	595	18	226	234	98	5	-	3	-	-	-	-	-
16 and 17 years	569	3	37	82	166	182	90	7	-	-	-	-	-
18 and 19 years	483	3	14	32	28	85	114	163	33	4	1	-	-
20 and 21 years	416	3	14	17	30	33	40	158	52	42	19	-	-
22 to 24 years	576	3	15	24	28	49	44	251	41	35	36	30	9
25 years and over	5,218	234	598	491	341	420	315	1,267	119	177	42	210	205
25 to 29 years	744	4	38	39	40	66	59	298	40	44	12	48	42
30 to 34 years	640	6	36	41	65	62	40	242	13	36	6	44	38
35 to 44 years	1,174	42	114	97	102	121	86	314	37	33	13	57	61
45 to 54 years	1,095	66	157	134	67	107	79	227	20	37	8	39	27
55 to 64 years	804	58	134	102	48	37	40	120	4	11	3	15	27
65 to 74 years	517	38	78	52	15	18	12	55	5	17	-	4	9
75 years and over	244	20	41	27	4	9	-	11	-	-	-	3	1
Female, 14 years and over	9,272	296	944	985	936	980	808	2,464	314	278	122	288	143
14 and 15 years	598	5	166	249	155	15	3	-	-	-	-	-	-
16 and 17 years	577	4	19	57	140	223	119	10	-	-	-	-	-
18 and 19 years	531	-	7	18	33	65	124	241	37	-	-	-	-
20 and 21 years	507	-	11	19	37	37	50	210	50	53	25	6	-
22 to 24 years	687	4	12	34	37	62	67	314	45	34	29	38	7
25 years and over	6,372	283	728	608	535	578	443	1,689	182	191	68	244	137
25 to 29 years	906	7	36	39	59	77	68	393	49	48	23	74	28
30 to 34 years	793	7	37	50	70	87	64	334	36	26	7	31	30
35 to 44 years	1,477	29	129	115	154	171	153	463	49	56	16	65	26
45 to 54 years	1,285	56	161	154	126	143	77	294	31	35	15	36	28
55 to 64 years	932	66	178	123	91	60	57	127	11	19	6	21	14
65 to 74 years	643	68	134	75	26	24	22	56	4	4	-	17	11
75 years and over	336	51	54	51	8	16	2	22	2	3	1	1	-

The Principal Languages of the World

Source: Sidney S. Culbert, Assoc. Professor of Psychology, University of Washington

Total number of speakers of languages spoken by at least one million persons
Parenthesized numbers after names of languages refer to notes below table.

Language	Millions	Language	Millions	Language	Millions
Afrikaans (S. Africa)	5	Ijaw (W. Africa)	1	Pashto (see Pushtu)	
Albanian	3	Ilocano (Philippines)	4	Pedi (see Sotho, Northern)	
Amharic (Ethiopia)	9	Iloko (see Ilocano)		Persian	23
Annamese (see Vietnamese)		Indonesian (see Malay-Indonesian)		Polish	35
Arabic	117	Italian	60	Portuguese	116
Armenian	4	Japanese	108	Provencal (Southern France)	6
Assamese (1) (India)	12	Javanese	43	Punjabi (1) (India; Pakistan)	52
Azerbaijani (USSR; Iran)	8	Kamba (E. Africa)	1	Pushtu (mainly Afghanistan)	14
Bahasa (See Malay-Indonesian)		Kanarese (see Kannada)		Quechua (S. America)	5
Balinese	3	Kannada (1) (India)	27	Rajasthani (India)	20
Baluchi (Pakistan; Iran)	2	Kanuri (W. and Cent. Africa)	2	Romanian	21
Bashkir (USSR)	1	Kashmiri (1)	3	Rundi (S. Central Africa)	3
Batak (Indonesia)	2	Kazakh (USSR)	5	Russian (Great Russian only)	220
Bemba (S. Central Africa)	1	Khalkha (Mongolia)	1	Rwanda (S. Central Africa)	6
Bengali (1) (Bangladesh; India)	116	Kikongo (see Kongo)		Samar-Leyte (Philippines)	1
Berber (2) (N. Africa)		Kikuyu (or Gekoyo) (Kenya)	2	Sango (Central Africa)	1
Bhili (India)	4	Kimbundu (see Mbundu-Kim.)		Santali (India)	4
Bihari (India)	21	Kirghiz (USSR)	2	Sepedi (see Sotho, Northern)	
Bikol (Philippines)	2	Kituba (Congo River)	2	Serbo-Croatian (Yugoslavia)	18
Bisaya (see Cebuano, Panay-Hiligaynon, and Samar-Leyte)		Kongo (Congo River)	1	Shan (Burma)	1
		Konkani (India)	2	Shona (S.E. Africa)	4
Bugi (Indonesia)	2	Korean	50	Siamese (see Thai)	
Bulgarian	9	Kumauni (India)	1	Sindhi (India; Pakistan)	9
Burmese	22	Kurdish (S.W. of Caspian Sea)	6	Sinhalese (Sri Lanka)	10
Byelorussian (mainly USSR)	10	Kurukh (or Oraon) (India)	1	Slovak	4
Cambodian (Cambodia, Asia)	6	Lao (5) (Laos, Asia)	3	Slovene (Yugoslavia)	2
Canarese (see Kannada)		Latvian (or Lettish)	2	Somali (E. Africa)	4
Cantonese (China)	46	Lingala (see Ngala)		Sotho, Northern (S. Africa)	2
Catalan (Spain; France; Andorra)	5	Lithuanian	3	Sotho, Southern (S. Africa)	2
Cebuano (Philippines)	3	Luba-Lulua (Zaire)	3	Spanish	202
Chinese (3)		Luganda (see Ganda)		Sundanese (Indonesia)	14
Chuang (7) (China)		Luhya (or Luhia) (Kenya)	1	Swahili (E. Africa)	16
Chuvash (USSR)	2	Luo (Kenya)	1	Swedish	10
Czech	11	Macedonian (Yugoslavia)	1	Tagalog (Philippines)	20
Danish	5	Madurese (Indonesia)	7	Tajiki (USSR)	3
Dayak (Borneo)	1	Makua (S.E. Africa)	2	Tamil (1) (India; Sri Lanka)	50
Dutch (see Netherlandish)		Malagasy (Madagascar)	8	Tatar (or Kazan-Turkic) (USSR)	6
Edo (W. Africa)	1	Malay-Indonesian	90	Telugu (1) (India)	52
Efik	2	Malayalam (1) (India)	23	Thai (5)	29
English	345	Malinke-Bambara-Dyula (Africa)	5	Tibetan	7
Esperanto	1	Mandarin (China)	628	Tigrinya (Ethiopia)	4
Estonian	1	Marathi (1) (India)	48	Tiv (E. Central Nigeria)	1
Ewe (W. Africa)	2	Mbundu (Umbundu group) (S. Angola)	2	Tswana (S. Africa)	2
Finnish	5			Tulu (India)	1
Flemish (see Netherlandish)		Mbundu (Kimbundu group) (Angola)	1	Turkish	38
French	85	Mende (Sierra Leone)	1	Turkoman (USSR)	2
Fula (W. Africa)	7	Min (China)	38	Twi-Fante (or Akan) (W. Africa)	4
Galician (Spain)	2	Moldavian (inc. w/Rumanian)		Uighur-(Sinkiang, China)	4
Galla (Ethiopia)	7	Mongolian (see Khalkha)		Ukrainian (mainly USSR)	41
Ganda (or Luganda) (E. Africa)	3	Mordvin (USSR)	1	Umbundu (see Mbundu-Umbundu)	
Georgian (USSR)	3	Moré (see Mossi)		Urdu (1) (Pakistan; India)	56
German	120	Mossi (W. Africa)	3	Uzbek (USSR)	9
Gondi (India)	2	Ndongo (see Mbundu-Kimbundu)		Vietnamese	36
Greek	10	Nepali (Nepal; India)	10	Visayan (see Cebuano, Panay-Hiligaynon, and Samar-Leyte)	
Guarani (mainly Paraguay)	2	Netherlandish (Dutch and Flem.)		White Russian (see Byelorussion)	
Gujarati (1) (India)	29	Ngala (or Lingala) (Africa)	2	Wolot (W. Africa)	2
Hakka (China)	20	Norwegian	4	Wu (China)	41
Hausa (W. and Central Africa)	18	Nyamwezi-Sukuma (S.E. Africa)	1	Xhosa (S. Africa)	4
Hebrew	3	Nyanja (S.E. Africa)	2	Yi (China)	3
Hindi (1) (4)	200	Oraon (see Kurukh)		Yiddish (6)	
Hindustani (4)		Oriya (1) (India)	22	Yoruba (W. Africa)	11
Hungarian (or Magyar)	13	Panay-Hiligaynon (Philippines)	4	Zhuang (7) (China)	
Ibibio (see Efik)		Panjabi (see Punjabi)		Zulu (S. Africa)	4
Ibo (or Igbo) (W. Africa)	9				

(1.) One of the fourteen languages of the Constitution of India. (2.) Here considered a group of dialects. (3.) See Mandarin, Cantonese, Wu, Min, and Hakka. The "national language" (Guóyǔ) is a standardized form of Mandarin as spoken in the area of Peking. (4.) Hindi and Urdu are essentially the same language, Hindustani. As the official language of India it is written in the Devanagari script and called Hindi. As the official language of Pakistan it is written in a modified Arabic script and called Urdu. (5.) Thai includes Central, Southwestern, Northern and Northeastern Thai. The distinction between Northeastern Thai and Lao is political rather than linguistic. (6.) Yiddish is usually considered a variant of German, though it has its own standard grammar, dictionaries, a highly developed literature, and is written in Hebrew characters. Speakers number about 3,000,000. (7.) A group of Thai-like dialects with about 8 million speakers.

Roman and Arabic Numerals

I 1	VI 6	XI 11	XVI ...16	XXX 30	LXXX 80	CD 400	CM 900
II 2	VII 7	XII 12	XVII ...17	XL 40	XC 90	D 500	M 1000
III 3	VIII ...8	XIII 13	XVIII ..18	L 50	C 100	DC 600	MCM ..1900
IV 4	IX 9	XIV 14	XIX 19	LX 60	CC 200	DCC 700	MM ...2000
V 5	X 10	XV 15	XX 20	LXX 70	CCC 300	DCCC ..800	V 5000

Note — A dash line over a numeral multiples the value by 1,000; thus, $\overline{X}$ = 10,000; $\overline{L}$ = 50,000; $\overline{C}$ = 100,000; $\overline{D}$ = 500,000; $\overline{M}$ = 1,000,000; $\overline{CLIX}$ = 159,000; $\overline{DLIX}$ = 559,000.

Other general rules in Roman numerals are as follows: (1), repeating a letter repeats its value — XX = 20; CCC = 300; (2), a letter placed after one of greater value adds thereto — VI = 6; DC = 600; (3), a letter placed before one of greater value subtracts therefrom — IV = 4.

Cost Per Pupil by State

Source: Office of Education, Dept. HEW

Expenditures per pupil in average daily attendance in public elementary and secondary day schools, by State 1971-72.

State	Total[1]	Current	Capital outlay	Interest on school debt
United States ...	$1,091	$934	$119	$38
Alabama	629	543	72	14
Alaska	1,896	1,441	407	48
Arizona	1,003	911	71	21
Arkansas	688	601	66	21
California	1,049	932	86	31
Colorado	1,061	905	125	31
Connecticut	1,248	1,110	106	32
Delaware	1,511	1,097	358	56
Dist. of Col.	1,294	1,063	231	—
Florida	1,029	861	148	20
Georgia	887	788	70	29
Hawaii	1,197	1,020	169	8
Idaho	835	732	60	43
Illinois	1,181	986	146	49
Indiana	1,108	837	242	29
Iowa	1,157	970	161	26
Kansas	1,025	854	158	13
Kentucky	722	650	49	23
Louisiana	969	867	76	26
Maine	899	793	78	28
Maryland	1,252	962	244	40
Massachusetts	1,153	1,020	89	44
Michigan	1,410	1,175	146	89
Minnesota	1,271	1,134	83	54
Mississippi	706	634	61	11
Missouri	955	845	86	24
Montana	NA	NA	NA	NA
Nebraska	990	856	110	24
Nevada	1,113	917	140	56
New Hampshire	978	847	102	29
New Jersey	1,399	1,219	133	47
New Mexico	961	849	102	10
New York	1,669	1,466	145	58
North Carolina	773	695	66	12
North Dakota	824	740	60	24
Ohio	989	871	91	27
Oklahoma	757	686	62	9
Oregon	1,129	979	126	24
Pennsylvania	1,382	1,073	226	83
Rhode Island	1,151	1,023	91	37
South Carolina	806	700	90	16
South Dakota	891	796	83	12
Tennessee	744	659	56	29
Texas	775	650	95	30
Utah	828	707	107	14
Vermont	1,418	1,232	156	30
Virginia	1,052	875	144	33
Washington	1,009	866	107	36
West Virginia	794	713	70	11
Wisconsin	1,103	1,003	67	33
Wyoming	1,142	1,001	124	17
Outlying Areas				
American Samoa	818	738	48	32
Canal Zone	1,201	1,162	39	—
Guam	964	641	323	—
Puerto Rico	477	445	32	—

[1]Estimated.

Educational Attainment of Major Ethnic Origin Groups

Source: Bureau of the Census

A study of the educational attainment level of adults (25 yrs. old and over) in the U.S. by ethnic origin shows a wide range in the percent who had completed high school, some college, or 4 yrs. or more of college. These findings are based on the Nov. 1969 Current Population Survey of the Bureau of the Census. The educational data relate to the number of school years completed.

Since very few persons migrated to this country from Russia since 1930 when two-thirds of the Russian-born Americans reported they had spoken Yiddish in their childhood, it is likely that most persons of Russian origin had a Jewish cultural heritage.

	Total population	Number	Persons 25 years old and over		
			Years of school completed by percent		
			Less than 4 yrs. H.S	4 years of H.S. or more		
				Total	Some college	
					Total	4 or more
Total	198,214,000	106,284,000	44.8	55.2	21.3	11.0
English	19,060,000	11,999,000	39.8	60.2	26.6	14.4
German	19,961,000	12,825,000	42.4	57.6	20.4	10.5
Irish	13,282,000	8,630,000	44.7	55.3	20.0	10.2
Italian	7,239,000	4,683,000	54.3	45.7	13.7	7.0
Polish	4,021,000	2,769,000	49.1	50.9	15.8	8.8
Russian	2,152,000	1,584,000	30.9	69.1	35.4	22.9
Spanish:						
Central or South American	556,000	273,000	46.2	53.8	24.5	11.2
Cuban	565,000	320,000	47.8	52.2	24.7	12.7
Mexican	5,073,000	1,909,000	75.6	24.4	6.4	1.6
Puerto Rican	1,454,000	549,000	77.8	22.0	5.6	2.4
Other Spanish	1,582,000	766,000	47.7	52.2	19.8	8.7
All other	105,633,000	49,286,000	43.2	56.8	22.9	11.6
Not reported[1]	17,635,000	10,692,000	50.1	50.0	16.6	8.4

(1.)Includes persons who reported that they did not know their ethnic origin.

Learning and Earning

A man's income is generally directly related to his educational attainment. Of all employed men age 25 to 64 without high school diplomas, 33% had 1971 incomes of less than $6,000. Only 13% of this age group with diplomas had incomes below $6,000. Conversely, only 6% of the men without high school diplomas had incomes over $15,000, while 22% of men with diplomas and 43% of those with college degrees had incomes above $15,000.

Directly connected with these income figures is the type of work done by those who complete high school compared to those who do not. In 1972, only 9% of those without diplomas were working in professional, technical or managerial positions. But of those with a diploma, 21% held positions of this sort, while of those with a college degree an astonishing 80% were in these top white collar jobs.

Fall Enrollment and Teachers in Full Time Day Schools
PUBLIC ELEMENTARY AND SECONDARY DAY SCHOOLS 1972
Source: United States Office of Education

	Pupils Enrolled		Teachers[2]	1972 High School Graduates	
	Elementary	Secondary		Male	Female
United States[1]	27,326,000	18,428,000	2,097,000	1,347,000	1,361,000
Alabama	407,737	375,646	33,730	21,743	23,063
Alaska	52,278	33,054	4,142	1,929	1,831
Arizona	346,981	138,107	20,368	12,028	11,925
Arkansas	247,554	213,877	20,611	13,176	12,716
California	2,745,737	1,755,241	198,483	134,539	135,979
Colorado	311,530	262,718	24,879	16,553	16,901
Connecticut	425,768	238,993	34,077	18,248	19,556
Delaware	71,950	62,367	6,365	3,698	3,968
Dist. of Col	83,869	56,049	6,561	1,971	2,994
Florida	803,037	711,322	66,563	39,176	39,398
Georgia	690,947	399,333	44,536	28,186	30,172
Hawaii	100,316	81,663	8,310	5,579	5,606
Idaho	91,847	92,816	7,664	6,501	6,328
Illinois	1,652,200	697,000	110,516	67,210	69,200
Indiana	657,738	562,805	52,400	36,694	35,807
Iowa	357,597	288,811	32,749	22,623	21,803
Kansas	261,743	213,353	25,360	17,117	17,046
Kentucky	450,230	264,402	31,465	20,214	20,493
Louisiana	605,075	240,766	41,837	21,756	23,807
Maine	178,782	71,666	12,213	7,081	7,275
Maryland	507,973	412,923	41,681	24,052	26,318
Massachusetts	841,553	361,044	60,233	33,609	33,878
Michigan	1,138,365	1,059,372	89,969	62,829	63,580
Minnesota	469,833	439,820	43,354	31,812	31,323
Mississippi	302,248	224,118	23,329	12,764	13,765
Missouri	583,089	446,919	45,414	30,079	28,797
Montana		No report			
Nebraska	181,674	147,518	16,999	11,070	10,650
Nevada	72,456	59,204	5,411	3,127	3,079
New Hampshire	118,466	49,628	8,564	4,556	4,734
New Jersey		No report			
New Mexico	150,975	134,119	12,320	8,481	8,518
New York (est.)	1,892,250	1,631,925	179,334	99,470	101,480
North Carolina	812,207	349,119	49,571	34,618	35,624
North Dakota	83,866	57,669	7,454	5,304	5,211
Ohio	1,476,307	946,347	103,487	74,929	74,543
Oklahoma	333,145	273,939	27,401	19,781	18,628
Oregon	271,339	200,056	22,216	16,024	15,858
Pennsylvania	1,227,577	1,133,708	109,721	80,442	76,420
Rhode Island	116,937	72,756	9,484	5,203	5,706
South Carolina	380,190	243,588	26,957	17,923	19,148
South Dakota	83,021	79,377	8,253	6,072	5,873
Tennessee	541,221	350,554	36,200	25,087	26,535
Texas	1,955,050	783,081	127,237	76,747	76,906
Utah	163,724	142,192	12,090	9,567	9,404
Vermont	65,515	41,002	6,192	2,969	2,916
Virginia (est.)	659,219	410,126	49,743	29,727	32,645
Washington	412,792	377,710	32,733	25,773	25,790
West Virginia	229,426	180,563	17,958	11,279	10,880
Wisconsin	577,407	417,816	48,122	34,842	34,975
Wyoming	46,332	39,685	4,735	2,933	2,845
Outlying areas	481,748	297,919	27,290	12,312	14,831
American Samoa	5,981	2,184	NA	204	202
Canal Zone	7,088	5,428	532	404	401
Guam	16,907	10,015	1,183	509	522
Puerto Rico	439,337	271,901	24,552	11,195	13,706
Virgin Islands	12,435	8,391	1,023	NA	NA

[1]Estimates are included for nonreporting states. [2]Full and part-time classroom teachers.

Public School Attendance, Teachers, Expenditures
Source: U.S. Office of Education; Salaries cover supervisors, principals, and teachers

School Year	Pop. 5 to 17 yrs.	Pupils		Teachers[1]				Total Expend.
		Enrolled	Av. daily attend.	Male	Female	Total	Salary[2]	
1900	21,404,322	15,503,110	10,632,772	126,588	296,474	423,062	$325	$214,964,618
1910	24,239,948	17,813,852	12,827,307	110,481	412,729	523,210	485	426,250,434
1920	27,728,788	21,578,316	16,150,035	95,654	583,648	679,302	871	1,036,151,209
1930	31,571,322	25,678,015	21,264,886	141,771	712,492	854,263	1,420	2,316,790,384
1940	29,805,259	25,433,542	22,042,151	194,725	680,752	875,477	1,441	2,344,048,927
1950	30,788,000	25,111,427	22,283,845	194,968	718,703	913,671	3,010	5,837,643,000
1960	43,881,000	36,086,771	32,477,440	392,700	962,300	1,355,000	5,174	15,613,255,000
1968 (Fall)	52,288,000	44,961,662	41,157,000	617,805	1,324,980	1,942,785	8,200	35,511,170,000
1969 (Fall)	52,799,000	45,618,578	42,283,000	634,358	1,379,478	2,013,836	8,840	40,561,997,000
1970 (Fall	52,435,000	45,909,088	42,495,346	649,250	1,411,865	2,061,115	9,570	44,423,865,000
1971 (Fall)	52,133,000	46,081,000	42,544,000	668,000	1,395,000	2,063,000	10,100	48,513,986,000
1972 (Fall) (P)	51,637,000	45,754,000	42,408,000	679,000	1,418,000	2,097,000	10,608	51,905,025,000

(1.) Prior to 1954 includes other nonsupervisory instructional staff (librarians and guidance and psychological personnel)
(2.) Average annual salary per member of instruction staff. (P) Preliminary.

Number of Public School Systems Decline

The number of public school systems in the United States declined by more than 6,000 in the last 5 years while their pupil enrollment rose by 4,200,000. There were 17,237 public school systems in the 1971-72 school year, compared with 23,390 during the 1966-67 period.

The number of public school systems has consistently decreased over the past 30 years, primarily as the result of reorganization laws facilitating the consolidation and annexation of school districts.

Federal Funds for Education

Source: Office of Education, Dept. of Health, Education and Welfare.
(In thousands of dollars. Includes grants, loans, and directly administered services. Estimated.)

Type of support, level and program	1973	Type of support, level and program	1973
Total grants and loans	**$13,054,968**	General continuing education	115,219
Grants, total	**12,770,582**	Training State and local personnel	19,945
		Loans, total	**284,386**
Elementary-secondary education	**4,450,103**	Student loan program, Natl. Def. Ed. Act .	246,360
School asst. — federally affected areas .	478,347	College facilities loans	38,026
Economic Opportunity Programs	682,109	**Other Federal funds, total**	**5,157,199**
National Defense Education Act	36,760	Applied research and development	1,652,000
Supporting services	277,982	School lunch and milk programs	1,374,094
Asst. for eduationally deprived children	1,622,162	Training of Federal personnel	961,795
Teacher Corps	36,418	U.S. Academies	237,376
Vocational education	307,981	Professional training, military	700,703
Dependents' schools abroad	182,907	Civilian education and training in	
Public lands revenue for schools	92,008	non-Federal facilities	23,716
Assistance in special areas	179,520	**Library services**	**231,048**
Veterans' education	19,054	Grants to public libraries	47,169
Emergency school asst.	381,000	National library services	183,879
Revenue sharing	110,000	**International education**	**227,393**
Education Renewal	24,603	Educational exchange program	45,495
Other	19,252	AID projects	140,943
Higher education	**5,883,573**	Action (previously Peace Corps)	23,872
Basic Research	1,264,000	Other international education and train-	
Research facilities	166,000	ing	17,083
Training grants	1,044,768	**Other**	**710,869**
Fellowships and traineeships	256,580	Agricultural extension service	181,600
Facilities and equipment	321,730	Educational television facilities	5,152
Other institutional support	260,944	Education in Federal correctional insti-	
Other student assistance	2,558,501	tutions	9,305
Other higher education assistance	11,050	Other education and training	110,242
Vocational-tech. and continuing ed.	**2,436,906**	Value of surplus property transferred:	
Vocational-technical education	1,773,985	Acquisition cost of personal property	334,670
Veterans' education	527,757	Fair value of real property	17,900

New Federal Aid Grants to Students

More than $480,500,000 has been awarded for 1973-74 to higher education institutions in all 50 states, the District of Columbia, Puerto Rico and the Virgin Islands by the Office of Education of the Dept. of Health, Education and Welfare.

Approximately $210,300,000 will provide supplemental Educational Opportunity Grants to nearly 303,500 exceptionally needy students in 2,850 institutions. Ranging from $200 to $1500 a year for up to 4 years of full-time undergraduate work, the grants must be matched by the institution with other forms of assistance.

The remaining $270,200,000 will be used by College Work-Study programs at 2,950 institutions to create employment opportunities in 1973-74 for more than 560,000 students who must earn a portion of their expenses. Federal funds will provide 80% of student payrolls; matching funds from the institutions or other agencies will provide 20%.

Guaranteed Student Loan Program

The Office of Education sponsors a loan program which may enable you to borrow up to $2,500 per academic year from private lenders to help pay for the cost of education and training at universities, colleges, and vocational schools. Total loans outstanding may not exceed $7,500 for undergraduate or vocational students. This maximum may be extended to $10,000 for students who borrow for graduate study.

You may borrow under this program if you have been accepted for enrollment in an eligible school or are already in attendance and in good standing. Applications may be obtained from lenders, schools, State or private nonprofit guarantee agencies or regional offices of the Office of Education.

American Field Service (AFS) International Scholarship Program

The American Field Service (AFS) International Scholarships is a nonprofit, privately sponsored organization with no religious or political affiliations, which seeks, through its scholarship programs for students 16 to 18 years of age, to foster understanding of the differences which exist among peoples of the world.

It was founded in 1914 as a volunteer ambulance service with the French Armies. Between the two World Wars, AFS sponsored a "Fellowships for French Universities" program, and in 1939, reorganized its ambulance corps with the Allied Armies. In 1947 it established its present international scholarship programs on the teenage level when it brought 52 students from 11 countries to the United States.

During 1972-73, AFS brought more than 2,500 high school students to the USA from over 60 countries to participate in the life of an American community where they attend a secondary school and live in carefully selected homes as members of their host families. During the same period more than 2,000 American students were sent overseas to 56 countries for a similar experience. Since 1947, over 65,000 students in over 90 countries have participated in the AFS Scholarship Programs. Other programs include: interchange for teachers and school administrators to explore another country's educational system for 3 to 6 weeks, opportunities for students to meet new environments within their own countries for short periods of time.

Many organizations as well as individuals contribute to the AFS scholarship programs. Schools have waived nonresident tuition and other fees, and host families welcome students without pay. Local chapters contribute approximately 50% of the funds to administer the AFS. Approximately 35% of the budget comes from the natural families whose payments are adjusted according to their financial resources. The balance of AFS support is dependent upon general fund raising in the U.S. and abroad.

Stephen L. Rhinesmith is president of AFS, which has its international headquarters at 313 East 43rd Street, New York, N.Y. 10017.

Education Pays—Black or White

(— represents zero or rounds to zero. B means base less than 75,000.)

Race, Age, Income, Occupation (1971)	Total (1,000)	0-8	9-11	12	13-15	16	16+	Median Years
White employed,								
25-44 years old	**18,739**	**11.1**	**13.7**	**39.6**	**15.0**	**11.4**	**9.2**	**12.6**
Under $3,000	2,838	30.4	20.6	28.2	9.6	4.9	6.5	11.9
$3,000-$5,999	2,552	25.6	17.6	35.4	10.4	5.7	5.2	12.2
$6,000-$9,999	7,145	11.8	17.2	45.7	13.6	7.1	4.6	12.5
$10,000-$14,999	5,574	4.9	10.5	42.8	18.4	14.0	9.5	12.8
$15,000 & over	2,632	2.1	4.9	23.6	18.1	25.2	26.1	16.0
White-collar workers	**8,971**	**2.6**	**5.6**	**29.5**	**21.2**	**22.2**	**18.9**	**14.7**
Under $6,000	1,005	8.8	9.8	29.5	19.1	15.3	17.7	13.3
$6,000 & over	7,965	1.7	5.1	29.5	21.4	23.1	19.1	14.9
Blue-collar workers	**8,152**	**18.5**	**22.1**	**49.2**	**8.7**	**1.2**	**0.2**	**12.2**
Under $6,000	1,727	33.8	24.3	34.7	5.9	0.9	0.4	11.0
$6,000 & over	6,424	14.4	21.5	53.1	9.5	1.3	0.2	12.3
Service workers	**1,007**	**15.2**	**17.6**	**48.6**	**15.2**	**2.5**	**0.8**	**12.4**
Under $6,000	276	34.1	16.3	38.0	7.6	3.6	—	11.9
$6,000 & over	731	8.2	18.1	52.7	18.1	2.1	1.1	12.5
Farm workers	**608**	**30.4**	**13.3**	**43.6**	**9.1**	**3.0**	**0.7**	**12.1**
Under $6,000	380	37.4	15.3	36.8	7.6	2.4	0.5	11.5
$6,000 & over	229	18.8	9.6	59.6	11.4	4.4	0.9	12.4
Black employed,								
25-44 years	**1,885**	**23.2**	**29.0**	**33.0**	**8.1**	**4.4**	**2.4**	**11.8**
Under $3,000	269	40.9	28.0	22.6	5.6	1.6	1.2	10.0
$3,000-$5,999	659	28.4	35.7	29.6	4.1	1.3	0.9	10.8
$6,000-$9,999	715	17.7	26.4	40.6	9.3	5.1	0.9	12.1
$10,000-$14,999	197	4.5	21.7	33.6	19.6	12.9	7.6	12.7
$15,000 & over	44	B	B	B	B	B	B	B
White-collar workers	**370**	**3.2**	**15.2**	**33.2**	**18.1**	**18.7**	**11.6**	**13.0**
Under $6,000	93	6.5	28.0	32.3	14.0	10.8	8.6	12.5
$6,000 & over	277	1.8	10.8	33.6	19.5	21.7	12.6	13.6
Blue-collar workers	**1,236**	**27.5**	**32.7**	**33.8**	**5.0**	**0.7**	**0.1**	**11.1**
Under $6,000	645	34.1	33.2	28.7	3.6	0.2	0.2	10.4
$6,000 & over	590	20.5	32.4	39.5	6.4	1.4	—	11.7
Service workers	**223**	**20.1**	**32.5**	**35.1**	**10.5**	**1.8**	**—**	**11.8**
Under $6,000	134	23.2	42.5	29.9	3.7	1.5	—	10.8
$6,000 & over	88	14.7	18.2	44.3	20.5	2.3	—	12.4
Farm workers	**56**	**B**	**B**	**B**	**B**	**B**	**B**	**B**
Under $6,000	56	B	B	B	B	B	B	B
$6,000 & over	—	B	B	B	B	B	B	B
White employed,								
45-65 years old	**15,526**	**25.4**	**17.6**	**31.9**	**10.9**	**7.7**	**6.5**	**12.2**
Under $3,000	887	51.0	15.8	19.4	7.9	2.9	3.2	9.0
$3,000-$5,999	2,266	47.0	19.3	24.2	5.5	2.2	1.8	9.5
$6,000-$9,999	5,482	30.1	21.8	33.6	8.4	4.0	2.1	11.7
$10,000-$14,999	4,248	14.5	17.8	40.0	14.0	7.8	5.7	12.4
$15,000 & over	2,643	5.4	7.9	26.1	16.9	21.6	22.1	14.9
White-collar workers	**6,922**	**8.5**	**10.6**	**32.7**	**17.8**	**15.9**	**14.4**	**12.9**
Under $6,000	820	23.2	17.7	30.2	13.8	7.2	7.9	12.3
$6,000 & over	6,102	6.6	9.7	33.0	18.4	17.1	15.3	13.1
Blue-collar workers	**6,647**	**37.5**	**24.4**	**31.9**	**5.1**	**0.9**	**0.1**	**10.5**
Under $6,000	1,349	56.7	20.2	19.9	2.6	0.4	0.3	8.7
$6,000 & over	5,299	32.7	25.5	34.9	5.8	1.0	0.1	11.0
Service workers	**1,093**	**39.2**	**22.2**	**31.0**	**5.7**	**1.6**	**0.2**	**10.5**
Under $6,000	410	58.1	19.0	18.0	3.4	0.7	0.2	8.7
$6,000 & over	683	28.0	23.9	38.7	7.2	2.2	—	11.8
Farm workers	**865**	**49.1**	**15.3**	**26.7**	**6.5**	**2.2**	**0.3**	**9.2**
Under $6,000	574	56.6	14.1	22.6	5.4	1.2	—	8.8
$6,000 & over	290	34.5	17.2	34.8	8.6	4.5	0.7	11.7
Black employed,								
45-65 years old	**1,287**	**51.2**	**21.3**	**18.4**	**5.0**	**2.4**	**1.7**	**8.9**
Under $3,000	226	68.3	15.1	12.9	3.1	0.5	—	6.8
$3,000-$5,999	409	65.6	17.3	12.8	2.2	1.8	0.3	8.2
$6,000-$9,999	468	43.1	26.9	20.1	5.7	2.9	1.3	9.8
$10,000-$14,999	157	20.0	25.4	37.3	9.6	4.3	3.2	12.1
$15,000 & over	27	B	B	B	B	B	B	B
White-collar workers	**218**	**15.6**	**21.2**	**30.8**	**11.0**	**11.9**	**9.6**	**12.4**
Under $6,000	50	B	B	B	B	B	B	B
$6,000 & over	168	9.0	21.4	33.3	12.5	10.1	12.5	12.6
Blue-collar workers	**744**	**58.3**	**22.7**	**15.0**	**3.3**	**0.7**	**—**	**8.4**
Under $6,000	365	69.0	17.5	11.8	1.9	—	—	7.5
$6,000 & over	380	48.7	27.9	17.9	4.7	1.4	—	9.1
Service workers	**246**	**50.0**	**22.3**	**21.8**	**5.4**	**—**	**0.5**	**9.0**
Under $6,000	145	60.0	19.3	17.9	2.8	—	0.7	8.6
$6,000 & over	101	36.7	25.7	28.7	8.9	—	—	10.6
Farm workers	**78**	**86.8**	**4.5**	**5.4**	**3.3**	**—**	**—**	**4.2**
Under $6,000	75	88.0	5.3	4.0	2.7	—	—	2.3
$6,000 & over	2	B	B	B	B	B	B	B

Public Libraries in Selected North American Cities

Source: World Almanac Research

City	No. of Volumes	Circu- lation	Cost of Operation	City	No. of Volumes	Circu- lation	Cost of Operation
Akron, Ohio	759,545	1,920,995	$2,243,847	Nashville, Tenn.	409,320	1,291,540	1,327,573
Albany, N.Y.	242,117	550,570	593,697	New Haven, Conn.	468,684	476,677	821,882
*Albuquerque, N.M. (6)	258,000	1,068,000	560,000	New Orleans, La.	657,392	1,320,477	1,645,167
Augusta, Ga.	240,519	683,307	531,837	*New York	15,614,850	None	11,623,000
Baltimore, Md.	2,219,965	3,166,894	6,987,763	N.Y. branches (84)	5,272,381	11,082,692	18,939,075
*Baton Rouge, La. (8)	265,469	825,831	647,318	Brooklyn (55)	2,951,407	7,986,818	11,967,308
*Binghamton, N.Y. (5)	246,532	629,524	617,562	Queens (55)	2,533,218	7,592,572	10,233,529
Birmingham, Ala.	852,655	3,400,000	1,300,000	Norfolk, Va.	426,659	1,045,816	1,085,471
Boston, Mass.	3,092,424	49,584	6,470,628	Oklahoma City, Okla.	613,319	1,984,786	1,419,265
Bridgeport, Conn.	450,000	430,000	902,500	Omaha, Neb.	449,412	1,566,409	1,053,047
Buffalo, N.Y.	2,628,589	5,799,607	7,102,711	Orlando, Fla.	362,000	350,000	1,311,600
Calgary, Alberta	472,141	2,288,999	1,666,615	Ottawa, Ont.	500,000	1,706,801	1,500,000
Charleston, W. Va.	354,202	1,179,785	660,703	*Philadelphia, Pa. (44)	2,661,957	6,000,000	10,062,044
Charlotte, N.C.	533,006	1,365,411	1,290,483	Phoenix, Ariz.	704,940	2,371,232	1,928,142
Chattanooga, Tenn.	231,175	514,336	602,256	Pittsburgh, Pa.	2,266,112	4,495,283	5,779,537
Chicago, Ill.	4,184,500	9,742,570	14,014,727	Portland, Maine	220,043	259,443	393,542
Cincinnati, Ohio	3,007,575	5,132,744	5,412,701	Portland, Ore.	980,679	3,222,002	2,722,993
Cleveland, Ohio	3,273,948	4,212,844	7,286,899	Providence, R.I.	596,924	822,348	1,496,837
Columbus, Ohio	1,038,528	2,859,611	2,828,178	*Regina, Sask. (5)	230,827	1,063,827	945,038
Corpus Christi, Tex.	293,943	653,292	441,848	Richmond, Va.	449,225	1,119,021	888,996
*Dallas, Tex (16)	1,277,510	3,914,883	4,359,460	Roanoke, Va.	255,854	401,202	458,956
Dayton, Ohio	1,194,526	3,785,791	2,362,718	Rochester, N.Y.	829,696	1,752,592	2,714,314
Denver, Colo.	1,281,454	3,117,337	3,505,400	Sacramento, Calif.	750,319	3,276,075	3,236,271
Des Moines, Iowa	337,120	1,076,208	1,006,858	*St. Louis, Mo. (20)	1,426,175	2,772,464	3,234,655
*Detroit, Mich.	2,227,000	3,473,000	8,473,000	St. Paul, Minn.	780,000	2,000,000	1,600,000
*El Paso, Tex. (6)	381,318	962,930	727,133	St. Petersburg, Fla.	279,639	1,192,118	802,222
Erie, Pa.	240,000	404,000	410,000	Salt Lake City, Utah	430,045	863,160	912,828
Evansville, Ind.	444,629	1,325,575	818,214	*San Antonio, Tex. (8)	730,137	2,390,294	1,468,850
Halifax, Nova Scotia	298,691	1,227,548	801,107	San Diego, Calif.	1,519,960	6,103,493	4,761,684
Hamilton, Ont.	625,614	1,910,363	1,800,562	San Francisco, Calif.	1,355,966	3,233,782	4,730,390
*Hartford, Conn. (8)	453,697	589,409	1,054,000	San Jose, Calif.	1,358,453	5,036,422	3,892,911
Houston, Tex.	1,314,680	3,668,813	3,047,051	*Saskatoon, Sask. (3)	262,828	1,005,827	901,829
*Jacksonville, Fla. (10)	735,663	1,457,444	1,309,999	Seattle, Wash.	1,449,870	3,859,232	3,834,801
Kansas City, Kan.	243,279	358,920	522,901	Syracuse, N.Y.	1,081,537	2,135,943	1,801,678
Kansas City, Mo.	1,218,135	2,266,362	2,476,578	Tallahassee, Fla.	102,844	353,287	244,403
Kitchener-Waterloo, Ont.	332,812	1,351,276	975,626	Tampa, Fla.	343,596	1,534,317	1,563,317
Knoxville, Tenn.	445,623	1,293,511	899,411	Toledo, Ohio	1,270,607	2,762,514	2,687,870
Little Rock, Ark.	219,121	408,693	311,818	Tucson, Ariz.	392,948	1,750,535	1,696,143
London, Ont.	399,093	1,551,678	2,033,041	Tulsa, Okla.	577,642	1,647,270	1,496,577
Louisville, Ky.	917,000	1,693,827	2,602,215	Vancouver, B.C.	624,649	3,734,023	2,000,000
Memphis, Tenn.	980,008	2,334,287	2,763,546	*Washington, D.C. (20)	2,125,000	2,600,000	6,000,000
Miami, Fla.	741,832	2,413,400	3,494,099	Wichita, Kan.	314,985	1,157,401	1,068,172
Milwaukee, Wis.	2,145,825	3,996,258	5,326,369	Winnipeg, Manitoba	547,196	2,114,983	1,379,662
*Montreal, Quebec (17)	1,825,268	3,693,060	2,714,255	Winston-Salem, N.C.	292,500	900,000	860,000

*Figure in parentheses denotes number of branches.

Major American Academic Libraries

Source: Office of Education, Dept. of H.E.W. (1970-1)

Institution	Books Total	Books Added	Microform units	Staff Total	Staff Prof.	Expenditures
Harvard University	8,451,187	210,274	810,439	694	245	8,639,776
Yale University	5,829,035	200,793	816,523	501	171	6,980,819
University of Illinois (all campuses)	5,243,450	260,257	624,769	542	216	8,080,685
Columbia University (all campuses)	4,366,502	144,775	926,200	454	171	5,765,705
Cornell University (all campuses)	4,347,384	196,335	995,970	421	147	6,466,089
University of Michigan (all campuses)	4,312,093	176,963	781,479	461	163	6,467,345
University of California at Berkeley	4,009,595	165,405	647,290	425	160	6,668,760
University of Wisconsin (all campuses)	3,603,671	279,836	1,687,890	427	211	7,497,382
Stanford University	3,584,123	173,721	705,484	408	148	6,270,117
University of Minnesota (all campuses)	3,112,526	171,324	644,685	309	151	4,982,236
University of Chicago	3,090,127	129,338		104	76	3,711,429
University of California at Los Angeles	3,038,828	122,506	849,731	379	150	6,649,902
Indiana University (all campuses)	2,687,327	260,538	534,589	66	28	5,092,504
Ohio State University (all campuses)	2,539,716	158,255	756,493	179	98	4,530,421
University of Texas at Austin (all campuses)	2,444,112	162,823	583,515	156	115	6,240,765
University of Missouri (all campuses)	2,400,043	146,486	1,915,526	266	88	4,791,201
Northwestern University	2,364,720	75,012	397,533	202	83	3,082,653
University of Pennsylvania	2,329,401	93,674	812,617	269	87	3,633,008
Princeton University	2,314,323	121,356	411,764	276	80	3,363,494
Duke University	2,231,519	104,442	179,182	224	150	2,956,099
New York University	2,211,570	101,198	815,183	375	77	3,975,251
John Hopkins University	2,085,435	30,411	595,351	182	54	2,447,651
University of Virginia (all campuses)	2,019,680	119,312	954,413	252	79	3,556,424
Southern Illinois University (all campuses)	1,877,576	192,018	417,421	195	87	4,110,504
University of Washington	1,876,900	88,702	847,803	294	120	4,273,625
Louisiana State University (all campuses)	1,830,409	115,531	597,789	227	163	3,401,131
University of North Carolina at Chapel Hill	1,819,669	96,901	451,342	225	84	3,230,314
Michigan State University	1,759,942	132,422	440,294	190	75	2,835,304
Syracuse University (all campuses)	1,633,261	107,100	1,507,134	39	13	2,520,327
Rutgers University (all campuses)	1,611,649	103,855	755,206	233	88	3,753,833

Degrees Conferred by Higher Educational Institutions
UNITED STATES, 1970-71
Source: United States Office of Education
Major sub-classifications do not necessarily add to totals

Major field of study	Bachelor's degree		Master's degree		Doctor's (Ph.D., Ed.D., etc.)	
	Men	Women	Men	Women	Men	Women
Agriculture and natural resources	**12,136**	**536**	**2,313**	**144**	**1,055**	**31**
Agriculture, general	1,445	46	122	1	...	...
Agronomy	812	11	283	10	165	4
Animal science	2,222	223	318	26	140	5
Agricultural economics	1,165	10	403	14	209	3
Forestry	1,804	22	282	9	92	...
Architecture and environmental design	**4,906**	**664**	**1,469**	**236**	**33**	**3**
Architecture	3,284	175	578	47	6	...
City, community and regional planning	204	25	658	152	23	...
Area studies	**1,174**	**1,318**	**618**	**389**	**120**	**24**
Asian studies	122	118	150	63	15	2
Latin American studies	148	132	78	70	3	...
American studies	630	836	106	125	49	18
Biological sciences	**25,333**	**10,410**	**3,805**	**1,923**	**3,050**	**595**
Biology, general	18,253	8,041	1,746	919	405	131
Botany, general	349	197	212	99	195	28
Bacteriology	210	143	47	27	34	8
Zoology, general	4,314	1,066	451	240	346	72
Microbiology	596	526	224	158	264	59
Biochemistry	430	138	152	99	436	81
Business and management	**105,060**	**10,467**	**25,506**	**1,038**	**787**	**23**
General	27,208	2,979	8,316	377	188	2
Accounting	20,036	2,063	994	103	58	3
Banking and finance	5,757	165	1,741	40	23	...
Management and administration	26,096	1,932	9,253	318	296	10
Marketing and purchasing	14,696	1,289	1,325	58	25	...
Communications	**6,989**	**3,813**	**1,214**	**642**	**126**	**19**
Journalism	2,883	2,261	558	295	13	2
Computer and information sciences	**2,064**	**324**	**1,424**	**164**	**125**	**3**
Education	**45,089**	**131,482**	**38,899**	**49,817**	**5,043**	**1,355**
Elementary education, general	8,090	82,342	3,123	13,947	116	103
Secondary education, general	1,529	2,020	2,937	2,485	170	42
Special education, general	341	1,979	845	2,206	77	37
Pre-elementary education	47	3,358	34	499	2	7
Student personnel	3	4	6,589	6,746	440	116
Educational administration	4	1	6,127	1,575	875	82
Art education	1,598	4,063	334	664	37	16
Music education	3,064	4,200	837	727	95	14
Physical education	15,177	9,555	3,032	1,378	214	69
Business, commerce, and distributive education	2,627	5,923	777	1,147	56	26
Industrial arts, vocational and technical education	6,965	106	1,988	111	100	6
Home economics education	94	6,355	77	725	1	27
Engineering	**49,646**	**400**	**16,258**	**185**	**3,615**	**23**
Engineering, general	2,829	35	804	9	216	3
Aerospace, aeronautical, astronautical engineering	2,426	17	711	6	214	3
Chemical engineering	3,516	63	1,074	26	404	2
Civil, construction, and transportation engineering	6,474	52	2,397	28	443	3
Electrical, electronics, communications engineering	12,122	76	4,252	30	876	3
Mechanical engineering	8,817	41	2,232	5	438	...
Industrial and management engineering	3,152	19	1,898	23	136	3
Fine and applied arts	**12,256**	**18,138**	**3,510**	**3,165**	**483**	**138**
Foreign languages	**5,075**	**14,870**	**1,642**	**3,113**	**484**	**297**
French	1,140	6,166	331	1,106	103	89
German	962	1,639	296	394	95	49
Spanish	1,807	5,261	529	927	98	70
Health professions	**5,788**	**19,438**	**2,567**	**3,182**	**389**	**77**
Hospital and health care administration	56	4	436	60	14	...
Nursing	253	11,946	31	1,499	1	6
Dental specialties	5	...	428	22	14	...
Medical specialties	11	...	106	23	29	14
Pharmacy	3,636	913	154	40	93	1
Public health	91	36	772	472	66	19
Speech pathology and audiology	176	1,251	152	671	48	22
Medical laboratory technologies	386	2,711	13	32	3	1
Home economics	**301**	**10,866**	**88**	**1,364**	**48**	**75**
Law	**518**	**27**	**909**	**46**	**20**	....
Letters	**28,546**	**44,556**	**5,407**	**7,303**	**1,849**	**567**
English, general	17,002	34,560	2,852	4,658	708	300
Literature, English	1,599	2,942	365	520	190	84
Speech, debate and forensic science	2,983	3,987	700	1,015	180	55
Philosophy	4,620	1,165	449	149	358	36
Religious studies	1,506	855	445	283	152	8

Library science	81	932	1,311	5,690	28	11
Mathematics	15,369	9,432	3,673	1,518	1,106	93
Physical sciences	18,459	2,953	5,521	846	4,144	246
Physics, general	4,708	338	2,027	147	1,407	42
Chemistry, general	9,006	2,031	1,733	464	1,798	154
Astronomy	94	8	88	12	69	7
Atmospheric sciences and meteorology	245	4	149	4	61	...
Geology	2,097	262	544	62	279	10
Earth sciences, general	559	108	227	35	24	1
Psychology	21,029	16,851	2,783	1,648	1,355	427
Experimental psychology	44	...	44	16	57	15
Clinical psychology	16	8	119	72	104	29
Public affairs and services	4,723	4,497	4,274	3,986	135	43
Public administration	372	53	1,255	151	33	3
Parks and recreation management	1,058	563	153	65	1	1
Social work and helping services	1,139	3,469	2,415	3,604	87	39
Law enforcement and corrections	1,856	189	174	20	1	...
Social sciences	98,145	57,181	11,798	4,703	3,152	507
Social sciences, general	11,753	9,790	1,522	808	38	12
Economics	13,890	1,868	1,733	262	668	53
History	29,055	15,608	3,470	1,687	871	120
Political science and government	21,966	5,516	1,839	479	615	85
Sociology	13,610	19,653	1,131	677	455	119
Theology	2,727	1.017	2,049	661	305	6
Theological professions, general	1,644	247	1,204	138	246	3
Religious music	64	52	76	30	6	...
Religious education	722	643	551	386	31	3
Interdisciplinary studies	9,824	3,943	1,106	600	77	14
Total	475,594	364,136	138,146	92,362	27,520	1,533
Grand Total	839,730		230,509		32,107	

Air Force Library Service

The Air Force library program is designed to support all the missions of the Air Force. This includes not only support for education and training programs and scientific and technical research requirements but also providing opportunity for the constructive use of leisure time. Library service is worldwide. There are 180 main libraries and service centres. A total of 473 service units, including main libraries, branches and field collections are required to serve all Air Force personnel, whether on large Air Force bases or at small, remote or isolated sites. Over 5,574,961 volumes are in Air Force library collections. Annual book circulation is over 6,985,636. Reader services for 385,916 reference and bibliographic requests are provided each year. An annual library publicity contest is conducted.

Vocational Education

Source: United States Office of Education

All Federal funds expended for vocational education are matched by State and local funds. This does not include expenditures for buildings, except for construction of area vocational education school facilities allowable since 1965.

ENROLLMENT IN FEDERALLY AIDED VOCATIONAL CLASSES

Fiscal Year	Total Enrollment	Agriculture	Trades and Industry	Home Economics	Distributive Occupations	Health Occupations	Technical Education	Office Occupations	Other Programs
1935	1,178,896	325,685	503,865	349,346	......	......	......	......	......
1940	2,290,741	584,133	758,409	818,766	129,433	......	......	......	......
1945	2,012,931	446,953	522,733	890,464	152,781	......	......	......	......
1950	3,364,613	764,975	804,602	1,430,366	364,670	......	......	......	......
1955	3,314,255	776,138	870,954	1,431,808	235,355	......	......	......	......
1960	3,768,149	796,237	938,490	1,588,109	303,784	40,250	101,279	......	......
1965	5,430,611	887,529	1,087,807	2,098,520	333,342	66,772	225,737	730,904	......
1969	17,979,366	850,705	1,720,859	2,449,052	563,431	175,101	315,311	1,835,124	......
1970	18,793,960	852,983	1,906,133	2,570,410	529,365	198,044	271,730	2,111,160	354,135
1971	10,526,660	846,085	2,075,160	3,129,804	578,075	269,546	313,860	2,226,854	1,087,270
1972	11,602,144	896,460	2,397,968	3,445,698	640,423	336,652	337,069	2,351,878	1,304,619

(1.) Preliminary data.
(2.)Detail does not add to total, some students were enrolled in more than one program.

Fewer Young Men Going to College

There has been a drop in the proportion of young men attending college in 1973 in comparison to the peak reached in the late 1960s, according to a report made by the Bureau of Census based on a nation-wide survey.

College enrollment in the U.S. showed 38% of all 18- and 19-year old men going to college in the 1973 academic year compared to 44% in 1969; the rate of 20- and 21-year old men dropped from 45% to 36% in the same period.

Total school enrollment continued upward with 60,100,000 persons from 3 to 34 years old enrolled in schools during the same period. The number of elementary school students dropped 1,400,000 from the fall of 1971 to the fall of 1972, while pupils enrolled in nursery schools reached an all-time high of 1,300,000. College enrollment climbed from 8,100,000 to 8,300,000 between 1971 and 1972. During the decade between 1962 and 1972, enrollment rose from 1,400,000 to 2,000,000 in private colleges, while students at public colleges jumped from 2,800,000 to 6,300,000.

College-age women now make up a larger proportion of all college students. In 1962, 21% of women between 18 and 21 were enrolled; this rate increased to 30% in 1972. During the prior 4 years college enrollment rate for men 20 and 21 years old declined by 8%, but the rates for women increased by 5%.

Forms of Address for Persons of Rank and Public Office

In these examples John Smith is used as a representative American name. The salutation Dear Sir is always permissible when addressing a person not known to the writer.

President of the United States

Address: The President, The White House, Washington, D. C. Also, The President and Mrs. ____.
Salutation: Dear Sir or Mr. President or Dear Mr. President. More intimately: My dear Mr. President. Also: Dear Mr. President and Mrs.____
The Vice President takes the same forms as President.

Cabinet Officers

Address: Mr. John Smith, Secretary of State, Washington, D. C., or The Hon. John Smith. Similar addresses for other members of the Cabinet. Also: Secretary and Mrs. John Smith.
Salutation: Dear Sir, or Dear Mr. Secretary. Also:· Dear Mr. and Mrs. Smith.

The Bench

Address: The Hon. John Smith, Chief Justice of the United States. The Hon. John Smith, Associate Justice of the Supreme Court of the United States. The Hon. John Smith, Associate Judge, U. S. District Court.
Salutations: Dear Sir or Dear Mr. Chief Justice. Dear Mr. Justice. Dear Judge Smith.

Members of Congress

Address: The Hon. John Smith, United States Senate, Washington, D. C. Or Sen. John Smith, etc. Also The Hon. John Smith, House of Representatives, Washington, D. C. Or Rep. John Smith, etc.
Salutation: Dear Mr. Senator or Dear Mr. Smith; for Representative, Dear Mr. Smith.

Officers of Armed Forces

Address: Careful attention should be given to the precise rank, thus: General of the Army John Smith, Fleet Admiral John Smith. The rules for Air Force are same as Army.
Salutation: Dear Sir, or Dear General. All general officers, whatever rank, are entitled to be addressed as generals. Likewise a lieutenant colonel is addressed as colonel and first and second lieutenants are addressed as lieutenant.
Warrant officers and flight officers are addressed as Mister. Chaplains are addressed as Chaplain. A Catholic chaplain may be addressed as Father. Cadets of the United States Military Academy and Air Force Academy are addressed as Cadet. Noncommissioned officers are addressed by their titles. In the U. S. Navy all men from midshipman at Annapolis up to and including Lieut. Commander are addressed as Mister.

Ambassador, Governor, Mayor

Address: The Hon. John Smith, followed by his title. He can be addressed either at his embassy, or at the Department of State, Washington, D. C. A foreign ambassador is His Excellency.
Salutation: Dear Mr. Ambassador. A foreign ambassador is Your Excellency.
Governors and Mayors are often addressed as The Hon. John Smith, Governor of _____, or The Hon. John Smith, Mayor of _____; also Governor John Smith, State House, Albany, N. Y., or Mayor John Smith, City Hall, Erie, Pa.

The Clergy

Address: His Holiness, the Pope, or His Holiness Pope (name), State of Vatican City, Italy.
Salutation: Your Holiness or Most Holy Father.
Also: His Eminence, John, Cardinal Smith; salutation: Your Eminence. An archbishop or a bishop is addressed The Most Reverend, and the salutation is Your Excellency. A monsignor who is a papal chamberlain is The Very Reverend Monsignor and saluted as Very Reverend Monsignor; a monsignor who is a domestic prelate is The Right Reverend Monsignor and salutation is Right Reverend Monsignor. A priest is addressed Reverend John Smith, and saluted as Reverend Father, or Dear Reverend Father. A Brother of an order is addressed Brother _____, and saluted Dear Brother _____. A Sister takes the same form.
A bishop of the Protestant Episcopal Church is The Right Reverend John Smith; salutation is Right Reverend Sir, or Dear Bishop Smith. If a clergyman is a Doctor of Divinity, he is addressed: The Reverend John Smith, D. D., and the salutation is Reverend Sir, or Dear Dr. Smith. When a clergyman does not have the degree the salutation is Dear Mr. Smith.
A bishop of the Methodist Church is addressed Bishop John Smith with titles following.

Royalty and Nobility

An Emperor is to be addressed in a letter as Sir, or Your Imperial Majesty.
A King or Queen is addressed as His Majesty (Name), King of (Name), or Her Majesty (Name), Queen of (Name). Salutation: Sir, or Madam, or May it please Your Majesty.
Princes and Princesses and other persons of royal blood are addressed as His (or Her) Royal Highness, and saluted with May it please Your Royal Highness.
A Duke or Marquis is My Lord Duke (or Marquis), a Duke is His (or Your) Grace.

Famous Fairs and Expositions

1851 May 1	Great Exhibition opened, Crystal Palace, Hyde Park, London.
1853 July 14	New York World's Fair opened, Crystal Palace.
1867 Apr. 1	International Exhibition, Paris
1873 May 1	International Exhibition, Vienna
1876 May-Nov	Centennial Expos., Philadelphia
1889 May 6-Nov.6	Universal Exposition, Paris.
1893 May 1-Oct. 30	World's Columbian Exposition, Chicago.
1898 June 1-Oct. 31	Trans-Mississippi International Exposition, Omaha.
1900 Apr. 15	International Exposition, Paris
1901 May 1-Nov. 2	Pan-American Expo: Buffalo.
1904 Apr. 20-Dec. 1	Louisiana Purchase Exposition, St. Louis.
1905 June 1	Lewis and Clark Centennial Exposition opened, Portland, Ore.
1907 Apr. 26	Jamestown, Va., Tercentenary Exposition, opened.
1909 June 1-Oct. 16	Alaska-Yukon-Pacific Exposition, Seattle.
1909 Sept. 25-Oct. 2	Hudson-Fulton Celebration, N.Y.
1910 Apr. 23	International Exhibition, Brussels
1913 Apr. 26	International Exposition opened, Ghent, Belgium.
1915 Feb. 20-Dec. 4	Panama-Pacific International Exposition, San Francisco.
1915	Panama-California Exposition, San Diego.
1922-23	Brazilian Expos., Rio de Janeiro
1924-25	British Empire Expo. Wembley.
1926 May 31-Nov. 30	Sesquicentennial Exposition. Phila.
1931	International Colonial and Overseas Exposition, Paris.
1933 May 27-Nov. 12	Century of Progress, Chicago
1934 May 26-Oct. 31	Century of Progress, Chicago
1936	Texas Centennial Expos., Dallas
1936-1937	Great Lakes Expos., Cleveland
1939 Feb. 18-Oct. 29	Golden Gate International Exposition, San Francisco.
1939 Apr. 20-Oct. 31	New York World's Fair.
1940 May 11-Oct 21	New York World's Fair.
1957 Apr. 26-Oct. 30	Jamestown, Va., 350th Anniv.
1958 Apr. 17-Oct. 19	World's Fair, Brussels.
1962 Apr. 21-Oct. 21	Century 21 Exposition, Seattle
1964 Apr. 22-Oct. 18	New York World's Fair.
1965 Apr. 21-Oct. 17	New York World's Fair.
1967 Apr. 28-Oct. 27	Universal and International Exhibition (Expo. 67), Montreal
1968 Apr. 6-Oct. 6	HemisFair 1968, San Antonio
1970 Mar. 15 Sept. 13	Expo '70 (Japan World Exposition) Osaka, Japan.
1974 May-Oct	Expo 74, Spokane, Wash.

U.S. Bicentennial—1976

The 200th anniversary of the independence of the United States will be celebrated in 1976. Observances are planned in each of the 50 states and many cities, including reenactment of historic events and varied cultural and scientific projects.

Selected U.S. Daily Newspapers' Circulation

Source: Audit Bureau of Circulations' FAS-FAX Report of average paid circulation for 6 months ending Mar. 31, 1973. (†) Indicates 3 month circulation average.

As of Sept. 30, 1972 there were 1,728 English language daily newspapers in the U.S. (322 morning; 1,378 evening; 15 "all day") with a combined circulation of 62,353,381. Sunday newspapers numbered 585 with a total circulation of 50,391,861.

(m) Morning; (e) Evening; * Based on Monday to Friday average. Brackets indicate joint publication.

Newspaper	Daily	Sunday
Albany, N.Y., Times-Union (m)..	75,439	145,956
Albany, N.Y. Knickerbocker News-Union Star (e)........	70,517	.....
Akron Beacon Journal (e)...	175,302	214,375
Allentown Call-Chronicle (m&e)	*127,868	147,646
Atlanta Constitution (m)	216,624	.....
Atlanta Journal (e) & Sunday Journal Constitution	259,721	585,532
Baltimore News American	*207,775	294,565
Baltimore Sun (m & e)	*384,565	356,108
Birmingham News (e).........	181,051	223,626
Birmingham Post-Herald (m)...	77,059	
Boston Globe (m & e).......	*462,619	617,426
Boston Herald American (m) & Sunday Advertiser...........	371,365	503,045
Buffalo Courier-Express (m)....	127,767	292,280
Buffalo News (e).............	*281,162	.....
Charlotte News (e)...........	69,163	
Charlotte Observer (m).......	175,895	220,632
Chicago News (e)............	*448,314	
Chicago Sun-Times (m).......	*567,139	779,390
Chicago Today (e)...........	*441,775	
Chicago Tribune (m).........	735,734	1,106,947
Chi	100,010	
Cincinnati Enquirer (m)......	194,970	303,826
Cincinnati Post & Times-Star (e)	209,118	
Cleveland Plain Dealer (m).....	407,916	512,020
Cleveland Press (e).........	382,687	
Columbus Citizen-Journal (m)..	118,899	
Columbus Dispatch (e).......	225,450	346,133
Dallas News (m)............	267,164	312,364
Dallas Times Herald (e)......	*244,326	297,990
Dayton Journal Herald (m)....	113,117	
Dayton News (e)............	156,347	226,806
Denver Post (e).............	*256,439	368,912
Denver: Rocky Mt. News (m)...	214,490	236,903
Des Moines Register (m).....	245,060	484,909
Des Moines Tribune (e)......	107,325	
Detroit Free Press (m).......	605,216	706,312
Detroit News (e)............	683,452	852,801
Flint Journal (e)............	114,323	114,020
Ft. Worth Star-Telegram (m & e)	235,708	226,254
Fort Worth Press (e)........	48,257	52,456
Fresno Bee (e).............	115,589	140,716
Grand Rapids Press (e)......	130,636	134,500
Hackensack Record (e)......	*155,726	185,282
Harrisburg News (e).........	72,235	.....
Harrisburg Patriot (m) & Sun. News........	47,094	168,128
Hartford Courant (m)........	170,459	219,365
Hartford Times (e)..........	*123,376	122,857
Honolulu Advertiser (m)......	75,734	
Honolulu Star-Bulletin (e) & Sunday S-B & Advertiser	129,879	187,159
Houston Chronicle (e).......	*297,482	359,638
Houston Post (m)...........	*292,122	344,716
Indianapolis News (e)........	†176,715	
Indianapolis Star (m)........	†226,905	376,511
Jacksonville: Florida Journal (e)	62,697	
Jacksonville: Fla. Times Union (m)	151,216	184,570
Jersey City: Jersey Journal (e)..	*89,043	
Kansas City Star (e).........	315,560	404,519
Kansas City Times (m)........	335,361	
Knoxville Journal (m)........	63,756	
Knoxville News-Sentinel (e) ...	109,099	162,197
Little Rock: Ark. Democrat (m)	*69,342	92,613
Little Rock: Arkansas Gazette (m)	*115,576	141,125
Long Beach Independent (m) & Sunday Independent Press Telegram........	*56,426	146,268
Long Beach Press-Telegram (e)	*103,567	
Los Angeles Herald Examiner	*474,020	483,649
Los Angeles Times (m).......	*1,024,721	1,212,883
Louisville Courier-Journal (m) .	234,921	364,901
Louisville Times (e).........	174,666	
Memphis Commercial Appeal (m)	221,325	286,708
Memphis Press-Scimitar (e)...	125,865	
Miami Herald (m)...........	427,857	532,224
Miami News (e)............	*72,955	
Milwaukee Journal (e)........	357,077	551,017
Milwaukee Sentinel (m)......	180,140	
Minneapolis Star (e).........	258,169	
Minneapolis Tribune (m)......	237,033	646,158
Nashville Banner (e).........	99,895	
Nashville Tennessean (m).....	140,461	240,754
New Haven Register (e)......	*108,238	126,830
New Haven Journal-Courier (m)	*31,566	
New Orleans Times-Picayune (m)	*210,523	313,294
New Orleans States & Item (e)..	*127,353	
New York: Long Island Press (e)	†375,082	352,389
New York: Newsday (e)........	445,722	388,929
New York News (m)..........	*2,092,603	2,958,678
New York Post (e)...........	630,621	
New York Times (m).........	*877,962	1,486,902
Newark Star-Ledger (m)......	*355,065	576,902
Norfolk Ledger-Star (e)......	†105,296	
Norfolk Virginian-Pilot (m)...	†129,793	186,293
Oakland Tribune (e)...........	*191,149	221,844
Oklahoma City Oklahoman (m) .	(*190,325	292,488
Oklahoma City Times (e)......	*101,833	
Omaha World-Herald (m & e)..	*249,750	284,076
Orlando Sentinel-Star........	*199,869	209,291
Philadelphia Bulletin (e).....	*611,634	691,297
Philadelphia Inquirer (m).....	*450,293	833,302
Philadelphia News (e)........	*250,697	
Phoenix Republic (m)........	†211,962	318,539
Phoenix Gazette (e).........	†121,306	
Pittsburgh Post Gazette (m)...	*220,088	
Pittsburgh Press (e).........	*292,288	707,915
Portland, Me., Press-Herald (m)	52,957	
Portland, Me., Express (e) & Maine Sun-Telegram	29,854	407,076
Portland: Oregon Journal (e) ...	*128,032	
Providence Bulletin (e).......	*148,182	
Providence Journal (m).......	*67,975	206,826
Raleigh News & Observer (m)...	†135,065	157,811
Raleigh Times (e)...........	†32,698	
Richmond News Leader (e)	121,063	
Richmond Times-Dispatch (m) .	142,019	199,287
Rochester Democrat & Chronicle (m)	139,010	228,759
Rochester Times-Union (e).....	142,235	
Sacramento Bee (e).........	*181,960	217,629
Sacramento Union (m)........	*93,234	84,600
St. Louis Globe-Democrat (m)..	*291,074	295,040
St. Louis Post-Dispatch (e)....	*317,247	530,750
St. Paul Dispatch (e)........	127,533	
St. Paul Pioneer Press (m)....	108,675	235,890
St. Petersburg Independent (e)..	31,114	
St. Petersburg Times (m).....	199,443	239,671
Salt Lake City Tribune (m)....	110,635	185,847
Salt Lake City Deseret News (e)	79,965	
San Antonio Express-News & Sat.-Sun. Express-News	*84,329	133,052
San Antonio News (e).........	*63,048	
San Antonio Light (e)........	*123,560	170,121
San Diego Union (m)........	~175,298	289,911
San Diego Tribune (e)........	124,712	
San Francisco Examiner (e)...	*179,010	
San Francisco Chronicle (m) & Sunday Examiner Chronicle..	*461,164	661,016
San Jose Mercury (m) & Sunday Mercury-News...........	134,214	214,452
San Jose News (e)...........	77,519	
Santa Ana Register (m & e)....	*190,455	201,871
Seattle Post-Intelligencer (m) .	*200,451	250,841
Seattle Times (e)...........	*234,971	294,211
South Bend Tribune (e)......	117,075	126,714
Spokane Chronicle (e)........	68,133	
Spokane Spokesman Review (m)..	82,085	125,970
Springfield, Ill., Journal & State Register (m & e)......	81,182	73,692
Springfield, Mass., Union ...	81,519	
Springfield, Mass., News (e) & Sunday Republican.......	91,216	132,913
Syracuse Herald-Journal (e) & Sunday Herald-American....	125,416	241,404
Syracuse Post-Standard (m) ...	*92,305	
Tampa Tribune (m)..........	177,330	212,706
Tampa Times (e)...........	27,472	
Toledo Blade (e)...........	174,612	204,700
Toledo Times (m)..........	*29,565	
Tulsa Tribune (e)...........	†79,711	
Tulsa World (m)...........	†118,323	192,450
Wall St. Journal (m) (total)	1,313,146	
Washington (D.C.) Post (m) ...	*535,016	710,148
Washington Star & News (e)....	*418,126	344,011
Wichita Eagle (m) & Sunday Eagle-Beacon.............	†129,987	190,444
Wichita Beacon (e).........	59,604	
Winston-Salem Journal (m) & Sunday Journal Sentinel	80,406	100,734
Winston-Salem Sentinel (e) ...	47,212	
Worcester Gazette (e)........	†93,874	
Worcester Telegram (m)......	†58,936	111,038
Youngstown Vindicator (e)	†103,013	158,295

Canadian Daily Newspapers of Large Circulation

Source: Audit Bureau of Circulations' FAS-FAX Report of average paid circulation for 6 months ending Mar. 31, 1973. (†) Indicates 3 month circulation average.

As of Sept. 30, 1972, there were 102 English language and 15 French language daily newspapers in Canada (24 morning; 92 evening; 1 "all day") with a combined circulation of 4,780,385. Sunday newspapers numbered 11 with a total circulation of 784,899.

(m) Morning; (e) Evening; * Based on Monday to Friday average. Brackets indicate joint publication.

Newspaper	Daily	Sunday	Newspaper	Daily	Sunday
Calgary Albertan (m)	*34,216		St. Catharines Standard (e)	†38,142	
Calgary Herald (e)	111,755		St. John's Telegram (e)	*29,861	
Edmonton Journal (e)	168,692		Saint John Telegraph-Journal (m)	†30,544	
Halifax Chronicle-Herald (m)	67,862		Saint John Times Globe (e)	†27,264	
Halifax Mail-Star (e)	49,560		Saskatoon Star-Phoenix (e)	48,100	
Kitchener-Waterloo Record (e)	†59,871		Sherbrooke: La Tribune (e)	*43,272	
London Free Press (m & e)	126,797		Sudbury Star (e)	40,294	
Moncton Times (m)	†16,411		Toronto Globe and Mail (m)	*265,423	
Moncton Transcript (e)	†20,283		Toronto Star (e)	*518,874	
Montreal Gazette (m)	*134,654		Toronto Sun (m)	*82,870	
Montreal: La Presse (e)	*173,110		Trois Rivieres: Le Nouvelliste (m)	*49,853	
Montreal: Le Devoir (m)	*39,606		Vancouver Province (m)	115,448	
Montreal: Le Journal de Montreal (m)	*141,596	103,621	Vancouver Sun (e)	243,823	
Montreal-Matin (m)	*136,815	108,118	Victoria Colonist (m)[1]	41,616	47,522
Montreal Star (e)	*183,817		Victoria Times (e)	32,617	
Ottawa Citizen (e)	*90,046		Windsor Star (e)	85,249	
Ottawa Journal (e)	82,730		Winnipeg Free Press (e)	139,988	
Quebec: Le Soleil (e)	*169,493		Winnipeg Tribune (e)	*75,909	
Regina Leader Post (e)	66,063		(1) Excludes Monday.		

Circulation of Leading U.S. Magazines

Source: Audit Bureau of Circulations' FAS-FAX Report.

General and farm magazines, exclusive of groups and comics. Based on total average paid circulation during the 6 months prior to Dec. 31, 1972. * Indicates circulation for the 6 months prior to Dec. 31, 1971.

	Circulation		Circulation		Circulation
Reader's Digest	17,942,752	Popular Science	1,671,336	Flower & Garden Mag	724,066
TV Guide	17,698,537	Glamour	1,629,895	Lady's Circle	685,130
Women's Day	8,363,986	Elks Magazine	1,549,074	Family Handyman	645,133
Better Homes &		Mechanix Illustrated	1,540,848	Lion Magazine	640,936
Gardens	8,125,956	Seventeen	1,503,372	Forbes	628,122
Family Circle	8,032,110	Sports Afield	1,418,205	Car & Driver	618,825
National Geographic	7,729,571	Jr. Scholastic Unit	1,374,212	A.D.	618,327
McCall's	7,521,194	Sport	1,372,217	Weight Watchers	614,948
Ladies' Home		Scouting	1,368,368	Simplicity Fashion	614,111
Journal	7,007,827	Esquire	1,273,932	Motor Trend	610,564
Playboy	6,977,966	Ebony	1,237,352	Popular Photo'y	594,233
Good Housekeeping	5,687,864	Grit	1,211,312	Fortune	583,897
Mademoiselle	5,554,122	Today's Education	1,189,755	Golf Digest	582,388
Life	5,522,502	Argosy	1,151,428	Jet	559,836
Time	4,341,978	True	1,124,307	Presbyterian Life	550,539
Redbook	4,773,677	Photoplay	1,104,153	Gourmet	536,026
American Home	3,357,019	Sunset	1,088,454	Catholic Digest	524,591
Senior Scholastic		House & Garden	1,056,110	Lutheran, The	524,121
Unit	2,914,251	Holiday	1,016,479*	National Observer	497,676
Newsweek	2,716,508	Southern Living	931,262	National Lampoon	486,315
American Legion	2,685,866	Family Health	905,915	New Yorker	478,414
National Enquirer	2,636,599	Modern Screen	901,809	Golf Magazine	475,033
Boy's Life	2,305,688	Co-ed	893,395	Scientific American	474,496
Penthouse	2,217,207	Nation's Business	874,291	Hairdo & Beauty	465,585
Sports Illustrated	2,201,022	House Beautiful	867,238	Vogue Patterns	458,734
Parent's Magazine	2,010,727	Hot Rod	817,750	Vogue	458,555
U.S. News & World		TV Radio Mirror	801,775	Capper's Weekly	452,715
Report	1,940,947	American Girl	800,198	Skiing	450,713
True Story	1,824,619	Modern Romances	796,178	Rotarian	446,716
Outdoor Life	1,814,491	Signature	791,603	True Confessions	428,588
Workbasket	1,803,752	Ingenue	751,141	Motion Picture	427,263
Field & Stream	1,793,558	Saturday Review	750,391	Harper's Bazaar	426,034
Cosmopolitan	1,714,491	'Teen	750,021	Workbench	415,972
Popular Mechanics	1,701,742	Psychology Today	729,878	Intellectual Digest	401,135
V.F.W. Magazine	1,699,272	Business Week	726,433	Westways	391,065

Circulation of Leading Canadian Magazines

Source: Canadian Advertising Rates and Data (June 1973)

General and farm magazines, exclusive of groups and comics. Statistics based on figures for June 1973 unless where an (*) appears. For (*) statistics based on varying periods Dec. 1972 to May 1973).

The Canadian Magazine	2,101,060	Maclean's	769,194	County Guide	286,537
		The Canadian Star Weekly		Report on Farming	271,013
Weekend Magazine	1,631,509		739,439	*Travel Times	254,300
Homemaker's Magazine (English)	1,313,305	Star Week	705,015	Co-operative Consumer	250,059
		Quest	590,000	Canadian Churchman	243,293
The ABC's of Canadian Industry	1,250,000	Time Canada	493,047	This Week	210,000
		TV Times	450,506	Perspectives (French)	209,504
*Readers Digest	1,234,493	Legion Magazine	338,600	TV Hebdo (French)	205,591
Chatelaine (English)	1,005,679	Carguide	320,000	Miss Chatelaine	173,809
*Bottin Vert-Green Selector	990,000	*Travelplanner	298,505	*Famille d'Aujourd'hui	160,858
		Chatelaine (French)	290,444	*B. C. Motorist	147,704
TV Guide	889,768	United Church Observer	290,208	Canadian Motorist	112,938

Weights and Measures

Source: National Bureau of Standards, Department of Commerce

U.S. Moving, Inch by 25.4 mm, to Metric System

The U.S. is the only industrial country in the world which is not on the metric system and is not yet involved in an official changeover program. Sen. Claiborne Pell (D.-R.I.) has estimated that the U.S. loses $10 billion to $25 billion a year because U.S. measurements are not compatible with world standards.

On July 2, 1971, following the report of a metric conversion study committee, Commerce Secy. Maurice H. Stans recommended a gradual U.S. changeover during a 10-year period at the end of which the U.S. would be predominantly, but not exclusively, on the metric system. Proposals to that effect are now pending in Congress.

THE INTERNATIONAL SYSTEM (METRIC)

Two systems of weights and measures exist side by side in the United States today, with roughly equal but separate legislative sanction: the U. S. Customary System and the International (Metric) System. Throughout U. S. history, the Customary System (inherited from, but now different from, the British Imperial System) has been, as its name implies, customarily used; a plethora of Federal and State legislation has given it, through implication, standing as our primary weights and measures system. However, the Metric System (incorporated in the scientists new SI or Système International d'Unités is the only system that has ever received specific legislative sanction by Congress. The "Law of 1866" reads:

It shall be lawful throughout the United States of America to employ the weights and measures of the metric system; and no contract or dealing, or pleading in any court, shall be deemed invalid or liable to objection because the ~~weights or measures expressed or referred to therein are~~ weights or measures of the metric system.

Over the last 100 years, the Metric System has seen slow, steadily increasing use in the United States and, today, is of importance nearly equal to the Customary System.

On Feb. 10, 1964, the National Bureau of Standards issued the following bulletin:

Henceforth it shall be the policy of the National Bureau of Standards to use the units of the International System (SI), as adopted by the 11th General Conference on Weights and Measures (October 1960), except when the use of these units would obviously impair communication or reduce the usefulness of a report . . .

What had been the Metric System became the International System (SI), a more complete scientific system.

Seven units have been adopted to serve as the base for the International System as follows: **Length**—meter; **Mass**—kilogram; **Time**—second; **Electric Current**—ampere; **Temperature**—kelvin; **Amount of Substance**—mole; and **Light Intensity**—candela.

Prefixes

The following prefixes, in combination with the basic unit names, provide the multiples and submultiples in the International System. For example, the unit name "meter," with the prefix "kilo" added, produces "kilometer," meaning "1000 meters."

Prefix	Symbol	Multiples and Submultiples	Equivalent	Prefix	Symbol	Multiples and Submultiples	Equivalent
tera	T	10^{12}	trillionfold	centi	c	10^{-2}	hundredth part
giga	G	10^{9}	billionfold	milli	m	10^{-3}	thousandth part
mega	M	10^{6}	millionfold	micro	μ	10^{-6}	millionth part
kilo	k	10^{3}	thousandfold	nano	n	10^{-9}	billionth part
hecto	h	10^{2}	hundredfold	pico	p	10^{-12}	trillionth part
deka	da	10	tenfold	femto	f	10^{-15}	quadrillionth part
deci	d	10^{-1}	tenth part	atto	a	10^{-18}	quintillionth part

Tables of Metric Weights and Measures

Linear Measure

10 millimeters (mm)	= 1 centimeter (cm)
10 centimeters	= 1 decimeter (dm) = 100 millimeters
10 decimeters	= 1 meter (m) = 1,000 millimeters
10 meters	= 1 dekameter (dam)
10 dekameters	= 1 hectometer (hm) = 100 meters
10 hectometers	= 1 kilometer (km) = 1,000 meters

Area Measure

100 square milli- meters (mm²)	= 1 square centimeter (cm²)
10,000 square centi- meters	= 1 square meter (m²) = 1,000,- 000 square millimeters
100 square meters	= 1 are (a)
100 ares	= 1 hectare (ha) = 10,000 square meters
100 hectares	= 1 square kilometer (km²) = 1,000,000 square meters

Volume Measure

10 milliliters (ml)	= 1 centiliter (cl)
10 centiliters	= 1 deciliter (dl) = 100 milliliters

10 deciliters	= 1 liter (l) = 1,000 milliliters
10 liters	= 1 dekaliter (dal)
10 dekaliters	= 1 hectoliter (hl) = 100 liters
10 hectoliters	= 1 kiloliter (kl) = 1,000 liters

Cubic Measure

1,000 cubic milli- meters (mm³)	= 1 cubic centimeter (cm³)
1,000 cubic centi- meters	= 1 cubic decimeter (dm³) = 1,000,000 cubic millimeters
1,000 cubic deci- meters	= 1 cubic meter (m³) = 1 stere = 1,000,000 cubic centimeters = 1,000,000,000 cubic millimeters

Weight

10 milligrams (mg)	= 1 centigram (cg)
10 centigrams	= 1 decigram (dg) = 100 milligrams
10 decigrams	= 1 gram (g) = 1,000 milligrams
10 grams	= 1 dekagram (dag)
10 dekagrams	= 1 hectogram (hg) = 100 grams
10 hectograms	= 1 kilogram (kg) = 1,000 grams
1,000 kilograms	= 1 metric ton (t)

Tables of United States Customary Weights and Measures

LINEAR MEASURE

12 inches (in.)	= 1 foot (ft)
3 feet	= 1 yard (yd)
5½ yards	= 1 rod (rd), pole, or perch (16½ ft)
40 rods	= 1 furlong (fur.) = 220 yards = 660 feet
8 furlongs	= 1 statute mile (mi) = 1,760 yards = 5,280 feet
3 miles	= 1 league = 5,280 yards = 15,840 feet
6,076.11549 feet	= 1 International Nautical Mile

LIQUID MEASURE

When necessary to distinguish the liquid pint or quart from the dry pint or quart, the word "liquid" or the abbreviation "liq" should be used in combination with the name or abbreviation of the liquid unit.

4 gills	= 1 pint (pt) (=28.875 cubic inches)
2 pints	= 1 quart (qt) (=57.75 cubic inches)
4 quarts	= 1 gallon (gal) (=231 cubic inches) = 8 pints = 32 gills

AREA MEASURE

Squares and cubes of units are sometimes abbreviated by using "superior" figures. For example, ft² means square foot, and ft³ means cubic foot.

144 square inches	= 1 square foot (ft²)	
9 square feet	= 1 square yard (yd²) = 1,296 square inches	
30¼ square yards	= 1 square rod (rd²) = 272¼ square feet	
160 square rods	= 1 acre = 4,840 square yards = 43,560 square feet	
640 acres	= 1 square mile (mi²)	
1 mile square	= 1 section (of land)	
6 miles square	= 1 township = 36 sections = 36 square miles	

CUBIC MEASURE

1,728 cubic inches (in³)	= 1 cubic foot (ft³)
27 cubic feet	= 1 cubic yard (yd³)

GUNTER'S OR SURVEYORS' CHAIN MEASURE

7.92 inches (in.)	= 1 link
100 links	= 1 chain (ch) = 4 rods = 66 feet
80 chains	= 1 statute mile (mi) = 320 rods = 5,280 feet.

TROY WEIGHT

24 grains	= 1 pennyweight (dwt)
20 pennyweights	= 1 ounce troy (oz t) = 480 grains
12 ounces troy	= 1 pound troy (lb t) = 240 pennyweights = 5,760 grains

DRY MEASURE

When necessary to distinguish the dry pint or quart from the liquid pint or quart, the word "dry" should be used in combination with the name or abbreviation of the dry unit.

2 pints (pt)	= 1 quart (qt) (= 67.2006 cubic inches)
8 quarts	= 1 peck (pk) (= 537.605 cubic inches) = 16 pints
4 pecks	= 1 bushel (bu) (= 2,150.42 cubic inches) = 32 quarts

AVOIRDUPOIS WEIGHT

When necessary to distinguish the avoirdupois ounce or pound from the troy ounce or pound, the word "avoirdupois" or the abbreviation "avdp" should be used in combination with the name or abbreviation of the avoirdupois unit.

(The "grain" is the same in avoirdupois and troy weight.)

27 11/32 grains	= 1 dram (dr)
16 drams	= 1 ounce (oz) = 437½ grains
16 ounces	= 1 pound (lb) = 256 drams = 7,000 grains
100 pounds	= 1 hundredweight (cwt)°
20 hundredweights	= 1 ton = 2,000 pounds°

In "gross" or "long" measure, the following values are recognized:

112 pounds	= 1 gross or long hundredweight°
20 gross or long hundredweights	= 1 gross or long ton = 2,240 pounds°

°When the terms "hundredweight" and "ton" are used unmodified, they are commonly understood to mean the 100-pound hundredweight and the 2,000-pound ton, respectively; these units may be designated "net" or "short" when necessary to distinguish them from the corresponding units in gross or long measure.

Tables of Equivalents

When the name of a unit is enclosed in brackets thus, [1 hand], this indicates (1) that the unit is not in general current use in the United States, or (2) that the unit is believed to be based on "custom and usage" rather than on formal definition. *See above about superior figures in Area Measure.*

Equivalents involving decimals are, in most instances, rounded off to the third decimal place except where they are exact, in which cases these exact equivalents are so designated.

LENGTHS

1 Angstrom (A)	0.1 nanometer (exactly) / 0,000 1 micron (exactly) / 0.000 000 1 millimeter (exactly) / 0.000 000 004 inch
1 cable's length	120 fathoms / 720 feet / 219.456 meters (exactly)
1 centimeter (cm)	0.3937 inch
1 chain (ch) (Gunter's or surveyors)	66 feet / 20.1168 meters (exactly)
1 chain (engineers)	100 feet / 30.48 meters (exactly)
1 decimeter (dm)	3.937 inches
1 dekameter (dam)	32.808 feet
1 fathom	6 feet / 1.8288 meters (exactly)
1 foot (ft)	0.3048 meters (exactly)
1 furlong (fur.)	10 chains (surveyors) / 660 feet / 220 yards / ⅛ statute mile / 201.168 meters
[1 hand]	4 inches
1 inch (in.)	2.54 centimeters (exactly)
1 kilometer (km)	0.621 mile / 3,280.8 feet
1 league (land)	3 statute miles / 4,828 kilometers
1 link (Gunter's or surveyors)	7.92 inches / 0.201 meter
1 link (engineers)	1 foot / 0.305 meter
1 meter (m)	39.37 inches / 1.094 yards
1 micron (μ[the Greek letter mu])	0.001 millimeter (exactly) / 0.000 039 37 inch
1 mil	0.001 inch (exactly) / 0.025 4 millimeter (exactly)

1 mile (mi) (statute or land)	5,280 feet / 1.609 kilometers
1 International Nautical Mile (INM)	1.852 kilometers (exactly) / 1.150779 statute miles / 6,076.11549 feet
1 millimeter (mm)	0.039 37 inch
1 nanometer (nm)	0.001 micron (exactly) / 0.000 000 039 37 inch (exactly)
1 point (typography)	0.013 837 inch (exactly) / 0.351 millimeter
1 rod (rd), pole, or perch	16½ feet / 5½ yards / 5.029 meters
1 yard (yd)	0.9144 meter (exactly)

AREAS OR SURFACES

1 acre	43,560 square feet / 4,840 square yards / 0.405 hectare
1 are (a)	119.599 square yards / 0.025 acre
1 hectare (ha)	2.471 acres
[1 square (building)]	100 square feet
1 square centimeter (cm²)	0.155 square inch
1 square decimeter (dm²)	15.500 square inches
1 square foot (ft²)	929.030 square centimeters
1 square inch (in²)	6.452 square centimeters
1 square kilometer (km²)	247.105 acres / 0.386 square mile
1 square meter (m²)	1.196 square yards / 10.764 square feet
1 square mile (mi²)	258.999 hectares
1 square millimeter (mm²)	0.002 square inch
1 square rod (rd²), sq pole, or sq perch	25.293 square meters
1 square yard (yd²)	0.836 square meter

CAPACITIES OR VOLUMES

1 barrel (bbl), liquid .... 31 to 42 gallons°
°There are a variety of "barrels", established by law or usage. For example: Federal taxes on fermented liquors are based on a barrel of 31 gallons; many State laws fix the "barrel for liquids"

as 31½ gallons; one State fixes a 36-gallon barrel for cistern measurement; Federal law recognizes a 40-gallon barrel for "proof spirits"; by custom, 42 gallons comprise a barrel of crude oil or petroleum products for statistical purposes, and this equivalent is recognized "for liquids" by four States.

1 barrel (bbl), standard, for fruits, vegetables, and other dry commodities except cranberries............	7,056 cubic inches 105 dry quarts 3.281 bushels, struck measure
1 barrel (bbl), standard, cranberry..................	5,826 cubic inches 86 ⁴⁵/₆₄ dry quarts 2.709 bushels, struck measure
1 bushel (bu) (U.S.) (struck measure)............	2,150.42 cubic inches (exactly) 35.238 liters
[1 bushel, heaped (U.S.)].........	2,747.715 cubic inches 1.278 bushels, struck measure*

*Frequently recognized as 1¼ bushels, struck measure.

[1 bushel (bu) (British Imperial) (struck measure)]............	1.032 U.S. bushels, struck measure 2,219.36 cubic inches
1 cord (cd) (firewood)........................ 128 cubic feet	
1 cubic centimeter (cm³)................0.061 cubic inch	
1 cubic decimeter (dm³)...............61.024 cubic inches	
1 cubic foot (ft³)...............	7.481 gallons 28.317 cubic decimeters 0.554 fluid ounce
1 cubic inch (in.³)............	4.433 fluid drams 16.387 cubic centimeters
1 cubic yard (yd.³)...................	0.765 cubic meter
1 cup, measuring......	8 fluid ounces ½ liquid pint
[1 dram, fluid (fl dr) (British)]......	0.961 U.S. fluid dram 0.217 cubic inch 3.552 milliliters
1 dekaliter (dal).....................	2.642 gallons 1.135 pecks
1 gallon (gal) (U.S.)...........	231 cubic inches 3.785 liters 0.833 British gallon 128 U.S. fluid ounces
[1 gallon (gal) British Imperial]	277.42 cubic inches 1.201 U.S. gallons 4.546 liters 160 British fluid ounces
1 gill...........................	7.219 cubic inches 4 fluid ounces 0.118 liter
1 hectoliter (hl)................	26.417 gallons 2.838 bushels
1 liter......................	1.057 liquid quarts 0.908 dry quart 61.024 cubic inches
1 milliliter (ml)................	0.271 fluid dram 16.231 minims 0.061 cubic inch
1 ounce, liquid (U.S.).................	1.805 cubic inches 29.573 milliliters 1.041 British fluid ounces
[1 ounce, fluid (fl oz) (British)]..	0.961 U.S. fluid ounce 1.734 cubic inches 28.412 milliliters
1 peck (pk)........................ 8.810 liters	
1 pint (pt), dry..............	33.600 cubic inches 0.551 liter
1 pint (pt.) liquid..............	28.875 cubic inches (exactly) 0.473 liter

1 quart (qt.) dry (U.S.)........	67.201 cubic inches 1.101 liters 0.969 British quart
1 quart (qt). liquid.(U.S.)........	57.75 cubic inches (exactly 0.946 liter 0.833 British quart
[1 quart (qt) (British)]........	69.354 cubic inches 1.032 U.S. dry quarts 1.201 U.S. liquid quarts
1 tablespoon....................	3 teaspoons* 4 fluid drams ½ fluid ounce
1 teaspoon......................	⅓ tablespoon* 1¼ fluid drams*

*The equivalent "1 teaspoon = 1¼ fluid drams" has been found by the Bureau to correspond more closely with the actual capacities of "measuring" and silver teaspoons than the equivalent "1 teaspoon = 1 fluid dram" which is given by a number of dictionaries.

WEIGHTS OR MASSES

1 assay ton** (AT)........................29.167 grams

**Used in assaying. The assay ton bears the same relation to the milligram that a ton of 2000 pounds avoirdupois bears to the ounce troy; hence the weight in milligrams of precious metal obtained from one assay ton of ore gives directly the number of troy ounces to the net ton.

1 carat (c)...........................	200 milligrams 3.086 grains
1 dram avoirdupois (dr avdp)...	27 11/32 (=27.344) grains 1.772 grams
gamma, see microgram	
1 grain.............................64.799 milligrams	
1 gram (g)...........	15.432 grains 0.035 ounce, avoirdupois
1 hundredweight, gross or long*** (gross cwt)	112 pounds 50.802 kilograms
1 hundredweight, net or short (cwt. or net cwt.)...	100 pounds 45.359 kilograms
1 kilogram (kg).....................2.205 pounds	
1 microgram (γ [the Greek letter gamma]).........................0.000.001 gram (exactly)	
1 milligram (mg.)..................................0.015 grain	
1 ounce, avoirdupois (oz avdp)...........	437.5 grains (exactly) 0.911 troy ounce 28.350 grams
1 ounce, troy (oz t)...........	480 grains 1.097 avoirdupois ounces 31.103 grams
1 pennyweight (dwt).................1.555 grams	
1 pound, avoirdupois (lb avdp)...............	7,000 grains 1.215 troy pounds 453.592 37 grams (exactly)
1 pound, troy (lb t)...........	5,760 grains 0.823 avoirdupois pound 373.242 grams
1 ton, gross or long*** (gross tn).................	2,240 pounds 1.12 net tons (exactly) 1.016 metric tons

***The gross or long ton and hundredweight are used commercially in the United States to only a limited extent, usually in restricted industrial fields. These units are the same as the British "ton" and "hundredweight."

1 ton, metric (t)...............	2,204.623 pounds 0.984 gross ton 1.102 net tons
1 ton, net or short (sh ton)......	2,000 pounds 0.893 gross ton 0.907 metric ton

Density of Gases and Vapors
Source: National Bureau of Standards (Grams per liter)

Gas	Wt.	Gas	Wt.	Gas	Wt.
Acetylene................	1.171	Ethylene	1.260	Methyl fluoride.............	1.545
Air	1.293	Fluorine..................	1.696	Mono methylamine	1.38
Ammonia.................	.759	Helium...................	.178	Neon.....................	.900
Argon...................	1.784	Hydrogen.................	.090	Nitric oxide...............	1.341
Arsene	3.48	Hydrogen bromide	3.50	Nitrogen	1.250
Butane-iso	2.60	Hydrogen chloride........	1.639	Nitrosyl chloride..........	2.99
Butane-n	2.519	Hydrogen iodide..........	5.724	Nitrous oxide.............	1.997
Carbon dioxide...........	1.977	Hydrogen selenide	3.66	Oxygen...................	1.429
Carbon monoxide.........	1.250	Hydrogen sulfide.........	1.539	Phosphine................	1.48
Carbon oxysulfide.........	2.72	Krypton..................	3.745	Propane..................	2.020
Chlorine.................	3.214	Methane..................	.717	Silicon tetrafluoride........	4.67
Chlorine monoxide........	3.89	Methyl chloride...........	2.25	Sulfur dioxide.............	2.927
Ethane	1.356	Methyl ether.............	2.091	Xenon....................	5.897

Tables of Interrelation of Units of Measurement

Bold face type indicates exact values

UNITS OF LENGTH

Units		Links	Feet	Yards	Rods	Chains	Miles	Cm.	Meters
1 inch	=	1	0.126 263	0.083 333	0.027 778	0.005 051	0.001 263	0.000 016	2.54	0.025 4
1 link	=	7.92	1	0.66	0.22	0.04	0.01	0.000 125	20.117	0.201 168
1 foot	=	12	1.515 152	1	0.333 333	0.060 606	0.015 152	0.000 189	30.48	0.304 8
1 yard	=	36	4.545 45	3	1	0.181 818	0.045 455	0.000 568	91.44	0.914 4
1 rod	=	198	25	16.5	5.5	1	0.25	0.003 125	502.92	5.029 2
1 chain	=	792	100	66	22	4	1	0.012 5	2011.68	20.116 8
1 mile	=	63,360	8000	5280	1760	320	80	1	160 934.4	1609.344
1 cm	=	0.3937	0.049 710	0.032 808	0.010 936	0.001 988	0.000 497	0.000 006	1	0.01
1 meter	=	39.37	4.970 970	3.280 840	1.093 613	0.198 839	0.049 710	0.000 621	100	1

UNITS OF AREA

Units		Square inches	Square links	Square feet	Square yards	Square rods	Square chains
1 sq. inch	=	1	.015 942 3	0.006 944	0.000 771 605	0.000 025 5	0.000 001 594
1 sq. link	=	62.726 4	1	0.435 6	0.0484	0.0016	0.000 1
1 sq. foot	=	144	2.295 684	1	0.111 111 1	0.003 673 09	0.000 229 568
1 sq. yard	=	1296	20.661 16	9	1	0.033 057 85	0.002 066 12
1 sq. rod	=	39 204	625	272.25	30.25	1	0.062 5
1 sq. chain	=	627 264	10 000	4356	484	16	1
1 acre	=	6 272 640	100 000	43 560	4840	160	10
1 sq. mile	=	4 014 489 600	64 000 000	27 878 400	3 097 600	102 400	6400
1 sq. cm	=	0.155 000 3	0.002 471 05	0.001 076	0.000 119 599	0.000 003 954	0.000 000 247
1 sq. meter	=	1550.003	24.710 54	10.763 91	1.195 990	0.039 536 86	0.002 471 054
1 hectare	=	15 500 031	247,105	107 639.1	11 959.90	395.368 6	24.710 54

Units		Acres	Square miles	Square centimeters	Square meters	Hectares
1 sq. inch	=	0.000 000 159 423	0.000 000 000 249 10	6.451 6	0.000 645 16	0.000 000 065
1 sq. link	=	0.000 01	0.000 000 015 625	404.685 642 24	0.040 468 56	0.000 004 047
1 sq. foot	=	0.000 022 956 84	0.000 000 035 870 06	929.030 4	0.092 903 04	0.000 009 290
1 sq. yard	=	0.000 206 611 6	0.000 000 322 830 6	8 361.273 6	0.836 127 36	0.000 083 613
1 sq. rod	=	0.006 25	0.000 009 765 625	252 928.526 4	25.292 852 64	0.002 529 285
1 sq. chain	=	0.1	0.000 156 25	4 046 856	404.685 642 24	0.040 468 564
1 acre	=	1	0.001 562 5	40 468 564	4046.856 422 4	0.404 685 642
1 sq. mile	=	640	1	25 899 881 103	2 589 988.11	258.998 811 034
1 sq. centim'r	=	0.000 000 024 711	0.000 000 000 038 610	1	0.0001	0.000 000 01
1 sq. meter	=	0.000 247 105 4	0.000 000 386 102 2	10 000	1	0.0001
1 hectare	=	2.471 054	0.003 861 022	100 000 000	10 000	1

UNITS OF MASS NOT GREATER THAN POUNDS AND KILOGRAMS

Units		Grains	Pennyweights	Avdp. Drams	Avdp. Ounces
1 grain	=	1	0.041 666 67	0.036 571 43	0.002 285 71
1 pennyweight	=	24	1	0.877 714 3	0.054 857 14
1 dram avdp.	=	27.343 75	1.139 323	1	0.062 5
1 ounce avdp.	=	437.5	18.229 17	16	1
1 ounce troy	=	480	20	17.554 29	1.097 143
1 pound troy	=	5760	240	210.651 4	13.165 71
1 pound avdp.	=	7000	291.666 7	256	16
1 milligram	=	0.015 432	0.000 643 015	0.000 564 383	0.000 035 274
1 gram	=	15.432 36	0.643 014 9	0.564 383 4	0.035 273 96
1 kilogram	=	15 432.36	643.014 9	564.383 4	35.273 96

Units		Troy Ounces	Troy Pounds	Avoirdupois Pounds	Milligrams	Grams	Kilograms
1 grain	=	0.002 083 33	0.000 173 611	0.000 142 857	64.798 91	0.064 798 91	0.000 064 799
1 pennyw't	=	0.05	0.004 166 667	0.003 428 571	1555.173 84	1.555 173 84	0.001 555 174
1 dram avdp.	=	0.056 966 15	0.004 747 179	0.003 906 25	1771.845 195	1.771 845 195	0.001 771 845
1 oz. avdp.	=	0.911 458 3	0.075 954 86	0.062 5	28 349.523 125	28.349 523 125	0.028 349 52
1 oz. troy.	=	1	0.083 333 333	0.068 571 43	31 103.476 8	31.103 476 8	0.031 103 48
1 lb. troy	=	12	1	0.822 857 1	373 241.721 6	373.241 721 6	0.373 241 722
1 lb. avdp.	=	14.583 33	1.215 278	1	453 592.37	453.592 37	0.453 592 37
1 milligram	=	0.000 032 151	0.000 002 679	0.000 002 205	1	0.001	0.000 001
1 gram	=	0.032 150 75	0.002 679 229	0.002 204 623	1000	1	0.001
1 kilogram	=	32.150 75	2.679 229	2.204 623	1000 000	1000	1

UNITS OF MASS NOT LESS THAN AVOIRDUPOIS OUNCES

Units		Avdp. Ounces	Avdp. Pounds	Short Cwt.	Short Tons	Long Tons	Kilograms	Metric Tons
1 oz av.	=	1	0.0625	0.000 625	0.000 031 25	0.000 027 902	0.028 349 523	0.000 028 350
1 lb av.	=	16	1	0.01	0.0005	0.000 446 429	0.453 592 37	0.000 453 592
1 sh cwt.	=	1 600	100	1	0.05	0.044 642 86	45.359 237	0.045 359 237
1 sh ton	=	32 000	2000	20	1	0.892 857 1	907.184 74	0.907 184 74
1 long ton	=	35 840	2240	22.4	1.12	1	1016.046 908 8	1.016 046 909
1 kg	=	35.273 96	2.204 623	0.022 046 23	0.001 102 311	0.000 094 207	1	0.001
1 metric ton =		35 273.96	2204.623	22.046 23	1.102 311	0.984 206 5	1000	1

UNITS OF VOLUME

Units	Cubic inches	Cubic feet	Cubic yards	Cubic centimeters	Cubic decimeters	Cubic meters
1 cubic inch =	1	0.000 578 704	0.000 021 433	16.387 064	0.016 387	0.000 016 387
1 cubic foot =	1728	1	0.037 037 04	28 316.846 592	28.316 847	0.028 316 847
1 cubic yard =	46 656	27	1	764 554.857 984	764.554 858	0.764 554 858
1 cubic cm =	0.061 023 74	0.000 035 315	0.000 001 308	1	0.001	0.000 001
1 cubic dm =	61.023 74	0.035 314 67	0.001 307 951	1 000	1	0.001
1 cubic meter =	61 023.74	35.314 67	1.307 951	1 000 000	1000	1

UNITS OF CAPACITY (Liquid Measure)

Units	Minims	Fluid drams	Fluid ounces	Gills	Liquid pt.
1 minim =	1	0.016 666 7	0.002 083 33	0.000 520 833	0.000 130 208
1 liquid dram =	60	1	0.125	0.031 25	0.007 812 5
1 liquid ounce =	480	8	1	0.25	0.062 5
1 gill =	1920	32	4	1	0.25
1 liquid pint =	7680	128	16	4	1
1 liquid quart =	15 360	256	32	8	2
1 gallon =	61 440	1024	128	32	8
1 cubic inch =	265.974	4.432 900	0.554 112 6	0.138 528 1	0.034 632 03
1 cubic foot =	459 603.1	7660.052	957.506 5	239.376 6	59.844 16
1 milliliter =	16.230 73	0.270 512 18	0.033 814 02	0.008 453 506	.002 113 376
1 liter =	16 230.73	270.512 18	33.814 02	8.453 506	2.113 376

Units	Liquid quarts	Gallons	Cubic inches	Cubic feet	Liters
1 minim =	0.000 065 104 17	0.000 016 276 04	0.003 759 766	0.000 002 175 790	0.000 061 611 52
1 liq. dram =	0.003 906 25	0.000 976 562 5	0.225 585 9	0.000 130 547 4	0.003 696 691
1 liquid oz. =	0.031 25	0.007 812 5	1.804 687 5	0.001 044 379	0.029 573 53
1 gill =	0.125	0.031 25	7.218 75	0.004 177 517	0.118 294 118 25
1 liquid pt. =	0.5	0.125	28.875	0.016 710 07	0.473 176 473
1 liquid qt. =	1	0.25	57.75	0.033 420 14	0.946 352 946
1 gallon =	4	1	231	0.133 680 6	3.785 411 784
1 cubic in. =	0.017 316 02	0.004 329 004	1	0.000 578 703 7	0.016 387 064
1 cubic foot =	29.922 08	7.480 519	1728	1	28.316 846 592
1 liter =	1.056 688	0.264 172 05	61.023 74	0.035 314 67	1

UNITS OF CAPACITY (Dry Measure)

Units	Dry pints	Dry Quarts	Pecks	Bushels	Cubic inches	Liters
1 dry pint =	1	0.5	0.062 5	0.015 625	33.600 312 5	0.550 610 47
1 dry quart =	2	1	0.125	0.031 25	67.200 625	1.101 220 9
1 peck =	16	8	1	0.25	537.605	8.809 767 5
1 bushel =	64	32	4	1	2150.42	35.239 07
1 cubic inch =	0.029 761 6	0.014 880 8	0.001 860 10	0.000 465 025	1	0.016 387 064
1 liter =	1.816 166	0.908 083	0.113 510 37	0.028 377 59	61.023 74	1

Weight of Water

1	cubic inch	.0360	pound	1	imperial gallon	10.0 pounds
12	cubic inches	.433	pound	11.2	imperial gallons	112.0 pounds
1	cubic foot	62.4	pounds	224	imperial gallons	2240.0 pounds
1	cubic foot	7.48052	U. S. gals.	1	U. S. gallon	8.33 pounds
1.8	cubic feet	112.0	pounds	13.45	U. S. gallons	112.0 pounds
35.96	cubic feet	2240.0	pounds	269.0	U. S. gallons	2240.0 pounds

Temperature Conversion Table

The numbers in **bold face type** refer to the temperature either in degrees Celsius or Fahrenheit which are to be converted. If converting from degrees Fahrenheit to Celsius, the equivalent will be found in the column on the left, while if converting from degrees Celsius to Fahrenheit the answer will be found in the column on the right.

For temperatures not shown. To convert Fahrenheit to Celsius subtract 32 degrees and multiply by 5, divide by 9; to convert Celsius to Fahrenheit, multiply by 9, divide by 5 and add 32 degrees.

Celsius	Fahrenheit	Celsius	Fahrenheit	Celsius	Fahrenheit
—273.2	—459.7	....	— 17.8	0	32
—184	—300	....	— 12.2	10	50
—169	—273	—459.4	— 6.67	20	68
—157	—250	—418	— 1.11	30	86
—129	—200	—328	4.44	40	104
—101	—150	—238	10.0	50	122
— 73.3	—100	—148	15.6	60	140
— 45.6	— 50	— 58	21.1	70	158
— 40.0	— 40	— 40	23.9	75	167
— 34.4	— 30	— 22	26.7	80	176
— 28.9	— 20	— 4	29.4	85	185
— 23.3	— 10	14	32.2	90	194
			35.0	95	203
			36.7	98	208.4
			37.8	100	212
			43	110	230
			49	120	248
			54	130	266
			60	140	284
			66	150	302
			93	200	392
			121	250	482
			149	300	572

Water boils at 212° Fahrenheit at sea level. For every 550 feet above sea level, boiling point of water is lower by about 1° Fahrenheit. Methyl alcohol boils at 148° Fahrenheit. Average human oral temperature, 98.6° Fahrenheit. Water freezes at 32° Fahrenheit. Although "Centigrade" is still frequently used, the International Committee on Weights and Measures and the National Bureau of Standards have recommended since 1948 that this scale be called "Celsius."

Squares, Square Roots, Cubes and Cube Roots of Nos. 1 to 100

No.	Sq.	Cube	Sq. Root	Cube Root	No.	Sq.	Cube	Sq. Root	Cube Root	No.	Sq.	Cube	Sq. Root	Cube Root
1	1.000	1.000	1.000	1.000	35	1225	42875	5.916	3.271	68	4624	314432	8.246	4.081
2	4	8	1.414	1.259	36	1296	46656	6.000	3.301	69	4761	328509	8.306	4.101
3	9	27	1.732	1.442	37	1369	50653	6.082	3.332	70	4900	343000	8.366	4.121
4	16	64	2.000	1.587	38	1444	54872	6.164	3.362	71	5041	357911	8.426	4.140
5	25	125	2.236	1.710	39	1521	59319	6.245	3.391	72	5184	373248	8.485	4.160
6	36	216	2.449	1.817	40	1600	64000	6.324	3.420	73	5329	389017	8.544	4.179
7	49	343	2.645	1.913	41	1681	68921	6.403	3.448	74	5476	405224	8.602	4.198
8	64	512	2.828	2.000	42	1764	74088	6.480	3.476	75	5625	421875	8.660	4.217
9	81	729	3.000	2.080	43	1849	79507	6.557	3.503	76	5776	438976	8.717	4.235
10	100	1000	3.162	2.154	44	1936	85184	6.633	3.530	77	5929	456533	8.775	4.254
11	121	1331	3.316	2.224	45	2025	91125	6.708	3.556	78	6084	474552	8.831	4.272
12	144	1728	3.464	2.289	46	2116	97336	6.782	3.583	79	6241	493039	8.888	4.290
13	169	2197	3.605	2.351	47	2209	103823	6.855	3.608	80	6400	512000	8.944	4.308
14	196	2744	3.741	2.410	48	2304	110592	6.928	3.634	81	6561	531441	9.000	4.326
15	225	3375	3.873	2.466	49	2401	117649	7.000	3.659	82	6724	551368	9.055	4.344
16	256	4096	4.000	2.519	50	2500	125000	7.071	3.684	83	6889	571787	9.110	4.362
17	289	4913	4.123	2.571	51	2601	132651	7.141	3.708	84	7056	592704	9.165	4.379
18	324	5832	4.242	2.620	52	2704	140608	7.211	3.732	85	7225	614125	9.219	4.396
19	361	6859	4.358	2.668	53	2809	148877	7.280	3.756	86	7396	636056	9.273	4.414
20	400	8000	4.472	2.714	54	2916	157464	7.348	3.779	87	7569	658503	9.327	4.431
21	441	9261	4.582	2.758	55	3025	166375	7.416	3.803	88	7744	681472	9.380	4.448
22	484	10648	4.690	2.802	56	3136	175616	7.483	3.825	89	7921	704969	9.434	4.464
23	529	12167	4.795	2.843	57	3249	185193	7.549	3.848	90	8100	729000	9.486	4.481
24	576	13824	4.899	2.884	58	3364	195112	7.615	3.870	91	8281	753571	9.539	4.497
25	625	15625	5.000	2.924	59	3481	205379	7.681	3.893	92	8464	778688	9.591	4.514
26	676	17576	5.099	2.962	60	3600	216000	7.746	3.914	93	8649	804357	9.643	4.530
27	729	19683	5.196	3.000	61	3721	226981	7.810	3.936	94	8836	830584	9.695	4.546
28	784	21952	5.291	3.036	62	3844	238328	7.874	3.957	95	9025	857375	9.746	4.562
29	841	24389	5.385	3.072	63	3969	250047	7.937	3.979	96	9216	884736	9.798	4.578
30	900	27000	5.477	3.107	64	4096	262144	8.000	4.000	97	9409	912673	9.848	4.594
31	961	29791	5.567	3.141	65	4225	274625	8.062	4.020	98	9604	941192	9.899	4.610
32	1024	32768	5.656	3.174	66	4356	287496	8.124	4.041	99	9801	970299	9.949	4.626
33	1089	35937	5.744	3.207	67	4489	300763	8.185	4.061	100	10000	1000000	10.000	4.641
34	1156	39304	5.831	3.239										

Square Roots and Cube Roots, 1000 to 2000

No.	Square Root	Cube Root	No.	Square Root	Cube Root	No.	Square Root	Cube Root	No.	Square Root	Cube Root
1000	31.62	10.00	1255	35.43	10.79	1510	38.86	11.47	1765	42.01	12.09
1005	31.70	10.02	1260	35.50	10.80	1515	38.92	11.49	1770	42.07	12.10
1010	31.78	10.03	1265	35.57	10.82	1520	38.99	11.50	1775	42.13	12.11
1020	31.94	10.07	1275	35.71	10.84	1530	39.12	11.52	1785	42.25	12.13
1025	32.02	10.08	1280	35.78	10.86	1535	39.18	11.54	1790	42.31	12.14
1030	32.09	10.10	1285	35.85	10.87	1540	39.24	11.55	1795	42.37	12.15
1035	32.17	10.12	1290	35.92	10.89	1545	39.31	11.56	1800	42.43	12.16
1045	32.33	10.15	1300	36.06	10.91	1555	39.43	11.59	1810	42.54	12.19
1050	32.40	10.16	1305	36.12	10.93	1560	39.50	11.60	1815	42.60	12.20
1060	32.56	10.20	1315	36.26	10.96	1570	39.62	11.62	1825	42.72	12.22
1065	32.63	10.21	1320	36.33	10.97	1575	39.69	11.63	1830	42.78	12.23
1075	32.79	10.24	1330	36.47	11.00	1585	39.81	11.66	1840	42.90	12.25
1080	32.86	10.26	1335	36.54	11.01	1590	39.87	11.67	1845	42.95	12.26
1085	32.94	10.28	1340	36.61	11.02	1595	39.94	11.68	1850	43.01	12.28
1090	33.02	10.29	1345	36.67	11.04	1600	40.00	11.70	1855	43.07	12.29
1095	33.09	10.31	1350	36.74	11.05	1605	40.06	11.71	1860	43.13	12.30
1100	33.17	10.32	1355	36.81	11.07	1610	40.12	11.72	1865	43.19	12.31
1105	33.24	10.34	1360	36.88	11.08	1615	40.19	11.73	1870	43.24	12.32
1110	33.32	10.35	1365	36.95	11.09	1620	40.25	11.74	1875	43.30	12.33
1115	33.39	10.37	1370	37.01	11.11	1625	40.31	11.76	1880	43.36	12.34
1120	33.47	10.38	1375	37.08	11.12	1630	40.37	11.77	1885	43.42	12.35
1125	33.54	10.40	1380	37.15	11.13	1635	40.44	11.78	1890	43.47	12.36
1130	33.62	10.42	1385	37.22	11.15	1640	40.50	11.79	1895	43.53	12.37
1135	33.69	10.43	1390	37.28	11.16	1645	40.56	11.80	1900	43.59	12.39
1140	33.76	10.45	1395	37.35	11.17	1650	40.62	11.82	1905	43.65	12.40
1145	33.84	10.46	1400	37.42	11.19	1655	40.68	11.83	1910	43.70	12.41
1150	33.91	10.48	1405	37.48	11.20	1660	40.74	11.84	1915	43.76	12.42
1155	33.99	10.49	1410	37.55	11.21	1665	40.80	11.85	1920	43.82	12.43
1160	34.06	10.51	1415	37.62	11.23	1670	40.87	11.86	1925	43.87	12.44
1165	34.13	10.52	1420	37.68	11.24	1675	40.93	11.88	1930	43.93	12.45
1170	34.21	10.54	1425	37.75	11.25	1680	40.99	11.89	1935	43.99	12.46
1175	34.28	10.55	1430	37.82	11.27	1685	41.05	11.90	1940	44.05	12.47
1180	34.35	10.57	1435	37.88	11.28	1690	41.11	11.91	1945	44.10	12.48
1185	34.42	10.58	1440	37.95	11.29	1695	41.17	11.92	1950	44.16	12.49
1190	34.50	10.60	1445	38.01	11.31	1700	41.23	11.93	1955	44.22	12.50
1195	34.57	10.61	1450	38.08	11.32	1705	41.29	11.95	1960	44.27	12.51
1200	34.64	10.63	1455	38.14	11.33	1710	41.35	11.96	1965	44.33	12.53
1205	34.71	10.64	1460	38.21	11.34	1715	41.41	11.97	1970	44.38	12.54
1210	34.79	10.66	1465	38.28	11.36	1720	41.47	11.98	1975	44.44	12.55
1215	34.86	10.67	1470	38.34	11.37	1725	41.53	11.99	1980	44.50	12.56
1220	34.93	10.69	1475	38.41	11.38	1730	41.59	12.00	1985	44.55	12.57
1225	35.00	10.70	1480	38.47	11.40	1735	41.65	12.02	1990	44.61	12.58
1235	35.14	10.73	1490	38.60	11.42	1745	41.77	12.04	1995	44.67	12.59
1245	35.28	10.76	1500	38.73	11.45	1755	41.89	12.06	2000	44.72	12.60

Simple Interest Table

	Time	4%	5%	6%	7%	8%		Time	4%	5%	6%	7%	8%
$1.00	1 month	$.003	$.004	$.005	$.005	$.006	$100.00	4 days	$.045	$.053	$.066	$.077	$.089
"	2 months	.007	.008	.010	.011	.013	"	5 "	.056	.069	.082	.097	.111
"	3 "	.010	.013	.015	.017	.020	"	6 "	.067	.083	.100	.116	.133
"	6 "	.020	.025	.030	.035	.040	"	1 month	.334	.416	.500	.583	.667
"	12 "	.040	.050	.060	.070	.080	"	2 months	.667	.832	1.000	1.166	1.333
$100.00	1 day	.011	.013	.016	.019	.022	"	3 "	1.000	1.250	1.500	1.750	2.000
"	2 days	.022	.027	.032	.038	.044	"	6 "	2.000	2.500	3.000	3.500	4.000
"	3 "	.034	.041	.050	.058	.067	"	12 "	4.000	5.000	6.000	7.000	8.000

Mathematical Formulas

To find the CIRCUMFERENCE of a:
Circle–Multiply the diameter by 3.14159265 (usually 3.1416).

To find the AREA of a:
Circle–Multiply the square of the diameter by .785398 (usually .7854).
Rectangle–Multiply the length of the base by the height.
Sphere (surface)–Multiply the square of the radius by 3.1416 and multiply by 4.
Square–Square the length of one side.
Trapezoid–Add the two parallel sides, multiply by the height and divide by 2.
Triangle–Multiply the base by the height and divide by 2.

To find the VOLUME of a:
Cone–Multiply the square of the radius of the base by 3.1416, multiply by the height, and divide by 3.
Cube–Cube the length of one edge.
Cylinder–Multiply the square of the radius of the base by 3.1416 and multiply by the height.
Pyramid–Multiply the area of the base by the height and divide by 3.
Rectangular Prism–Multiply the length by the width by the height.
Sphere–Multiply the cube of the radius by 3.1416, multiply by 4 and divide by 3.

Common Fractions Reduced to Decimals

8ths	16ths	32ds	64ths		8ths	16ths	32ds	64ths		8ths	16ths	32ds	64ths	
			1	.015625				23	.359375				45	.703125
		1	2	.03125	3	6	12	24	.375			23	46	.71875
			3	.046875				25	.390625				47	.734375
	1	2	4	.0625			13	26	.40625	6	12	24	48	.75
			5	.078125				27	.421875				49	.765625
		3	6	.09375		7	14	28	.4375			25	50	.78125
			7	.109375				29	.453125				51	.796875
1	2	4	8	.125			15	30	.46875		13	26	52	.8125
			9	.140625				31	.484375				53	.828125
		5	10	.15625	4	8	16	32	.5			27	54	.84375
			11	.171875				33	.515625				55	.859375
	3	6	12	.1875			17	34	.53125	7	14	28	56	.875
			13	.203125				35	.546875				57	.890625
		7	14	.21875		9	18	36	.5625			29	58	.90625
			15	.234375				37	.578125				59	.921875
2	4	8	16	.25			19	38	.59375		15	30	60	.9375
			17	.265625				39	.609375				61	.953125
		9	18	.28125	5	10	20	40	.625			31	62	.96875
			19	.296875				41	.640625				63	.984375
	5	10	20	.3125			21	42	.65625	8	16	32	64	1.
			21	.328125				43	.671875					
		11	22	.34375		11	22	44	.6875					

Multiplication and Division Table

A number in the top line (19) multiplied by a number in the last column on the left (18) produces the number where the top line and the side line meet (342), and so on throughout the table.

A number in the table (342) divided by the number at the top of that column (19) results in the number (18) at the extreme left; also, a number in the table (342) divided by the number (18) at the extreme left gives the number (19) at the top of the column, and so on throughout the table.

1	2	3	4	5	6	7	8	9	10	11	12	13	14	15	16	17	18	19	20	21	22	23	24	25	1
2	4	6	8	10	12	14	16	18	20	22	24	26	28	30	32	34	36	38	40	42	44	46	48	50	2
3	6	9	12	15	18	21	24	27	30	33	36	39	42	45	48	51	54	57	60	63	66	69	72	75	3
4	8	12	16	20	24	28	32	36	40	44	48	52	56	60	64	68	72	76	80	84	88	92	96	100	4
5	10	15	20	25	30	35	40	45	50	55	60	65	70	75	80	85	90	95	100	105	110	115	120	125	5
6	12	18	24	30	36	42	48	54	60	66	72	78	84	90	96	102	108	114	120	126	132	138	144	150	6
7	14	21	28	35	42	49	56	63	70	77	84	91	98	105	112	119	126	133	140	147	154	161	168	175	7
8	16	24	32	40	48	56	64	72	80	88	96	104	112	120	128	136	144	152	160	168	176	184	192	200	8
9	18	27	36	45	54	63	72	81	90	99	108	117	126	135	144	153	162	171	180	189	198	207	216	225	9
10	20	30	40	50	60	70	80	90	100	110	120	130	140	150	160	170	180	190	200	210	220	230	240	250	10
11	22	33	44	55	66	77	88	99	110	121	132	143	154	165	176	187	198	209	220	231	242	253	264	275	11
12	24	36	48	60	72	84	96	108	120	132	144	156	168	180	192	204	216	228	240	252	264	276	288	300	12
13	26	39	52	65	78	91	104	117	130	143	156	169	182	195	208	221	234	247	260	273	286	299	312	325	13
14	28	42	56	70	84	98	112	126	140	154	168	182	196	210	224	238	252	266	280	294	308	322	336	350	14
15	30	45	60	75	90	105	120	135	150	165	180	195	210	225	240	255	270	285	300	315	330	345	360	375	15
16	32	48	64	80	96	112	128	144	160	176	192	208	224	240	256	272	288	304	320	336	352	368	384	400	16
17	34	51	68	85	102	119	136	153	170	187	204	221	238	255	272	289	306	323	340	357	374	391	408	425	17
18	36	54	72	90	108	126	144	162	180	198	216	234	252	270	288	306	324	342	360	378	396	414	432	450	18
19	38	57	76	95	114	133	152	171	190	209	228	247	266	285	304	323	342	361	380	399	418	437	456	475	19
20	40	60	80	100	120	140	160	180	200	220	240	260	280	300	320	340	360	380	400	420	440	460	480	500	20
21	42	63	84	105	126	147	168	189	210	231	252	273	294	315	336	357	378	399	420	441	462	483	504	525	21
22	44	66	88	110	132	154	176	198	220	242	264	286	308	330	352	374	396	418	440	462	484	506	528	550	22
23	46	69	92	115	138	161	184	207	230	253	276	299	322	345	368	391	414	437	460	483	506	529	552	575	23
24	48	72	96	120	144	168	192	216	240	264	288	312	336	360	384	408	432	456	480	504	528	552	576	600	24
25	50	75	100	125	150	175	200	225	250	275	300	325	350	375	400	425	450	475	500	525	550	575	600	625	25
2	3	4	5	6	7	8	9	10	11	12	13	14	15	16	17	18	19	20	21	22	23	24	25		

Electrical Units

The **watt** is the unit of power (electrical, mechanical, thermal, etc.). Electrical power is given by the product of the voltage and the current.

Energy is sold by the **joule**, but in common practice the billing of electrical energy is expressed in terms of the **kilowatt-hour**, which is 3,600,000 joules or 3.6 megajoules.

The **horsepower** is a non-metric unit sometimes used in mechanics. It is equal to 746 watts.

The **ohm** is the unit of electrical resistance and represents the physical property of a conductor which offers a resistance to the flow of electricity, permitting just 1 ampere to flow at 1 volt of pressure.

World Weights and Measures

Exclusive of the Metric System, which is used by many world countries, and for which see page 325

Source: National Bureau of Standards, Department of Commerce

Denominations	Where Used	Amer. Equiv.	Denominations	Where Used	Amer. Equiv.
Almude	Portugal	4.423 gal	Klafter	Austria	2.074 yd
Ardeb	Egypt	5.6189 bu	Klafter	Germany	1.90 yd
Arratel (Libra)	Portugal	1.012 lb	Koku	Japan	5.119 bu
Arroba	Argentina	25.32 lb	Kwan	Japan	8.2673 lb
"	Brazil	32.38 lb	Last	Belgium, Holland	85.134 bu
"	Cuba	25.36 lb	"	England	82.56 bu
"	Paraguay	25.32 lb	"	Germany	2 metric tons
"	Venezuela	25.40 lb	"	Prussia	112.29 bu
" (liquid)	Cuba, Spain and		League (land)	Paraguay	4.633 acres
	Venezuela	4.263 gal	Li	China	1890 ft
Arshine	USSR	28 in	"	China	0.01260 in
" (sq.)	"	5.44 sq ft			(1-1000 ch'ih
Artel	Morocco	1.12 lb	Libra (lb)	Argentina	1.0128 lb
Baril	Argentina and	20.077 gal	"	C. America, Chile	1.014 lb
	Mexico	20.0787 gal	"	Cuba	1.0143 lb
Barile (wine)	Malta	11.2 gal	"	Mexico	1.01467 lb
Berkovets	USSR	361.128 lb	"	Peru, Venezuela	1.0143 lb
Bongkal	Malaysia	832 grains	"	Uruguay	1.0127 lb
Bouw	Sumatra	7,096.5 sq meter	Load, timber	England	50 cu ft
Bu	Japan	0.12 inch	Manzana	Nicaragua	1.742 acres
Bushel	British	1.03205 U. S. bu	"	Costa Rica	1.727 acres
Caballeria	Cuba	33.162 acres	"	Salvador	1.727 acres
Caban (cavan)	Philippines	{2.13 bu	Marco	Bolivia	0.507 lb
		{19.8 gal	Maund	Bengal	82.¾ lb
Caffiso	Malta	5.40 gal	Mil	Denmark	4.68 miles
Candy	Bombay	560 lb	Milla	Nicaragua	1.1594 miles
"	India (Madras)	500 lb	"	Honduras	1.1493 miles
Cantaro	Malta	175 lb	Mina	Greece	0.95 lb
Carat (metric)	World	3.086 grains	Morgen	Germany	0.63 acre
Catty	China	1.333⅓ lb	Oka (Oke)	Greece	2.82 lb
" (see Kin)	Japan		Oke	Egypt	2.7514 lb
"	Java, Malacca	1.36 lb	"	Turkey	2.826 lb
"	Thailand	2⅔ lb	Pic	Egypt	22.83 inches
" (stand)	Thailand	1.32 lb	Picul	Borneo—Celebes	135.64 lb
"	Sumatra	2.12 lb	"	China	133⅓ lb
Centaro	Central America	4.2631 gal	"	Java	136.16 lb
Centner	Brunswick	117.5 lb	"	Philippines	139.44 lb
"	Bremen	127.5 lb	Pie	Argentina	0.9471 ft
"	Denmark, Norway	110.23 lb	"	Spain	0.91416 ft
"	Germany	113.44 lb	Pik	Turkey	27.9 inches
"	Sweden	93.7 lb	Pood	Russia	36.113 lb
Chetvert	USSR	5.957 bu	Pund (lb)	Denmark	1.102 lb
Ch'ih	China	12.60 in	Quart	British	1.20094 liq qt
" (metric)	China	39.37 in.=1 meter	"	"	1.03205 dry qt
Cho	Japan	2.451 acres	Quarter	"	8.256 bu
Coomb	England	4.1282 bu	Quintal	Argentina	101.3 lb
Coyan	Siam	2,645.5 lb	"	Brazil	129.54 lb
Cuadra	Argentina	4.2 acres	"	Castile, Peru, Chile	101.43 lb
"	Paraguay	94.71 yd	"	Mexico	101.47 lb
" (sq.)	Paraguay	1.85 acres	Rotl	Israel	6.35 lb
"	Uruguay	1.82 acres	Sagene	USSR	7 feet
Cwt. (hund. weight)	British	112 lb	Salm	Malta	8.26 bu
Dessiatine	USSR	2.6997 acres	Se	Japan	0.02451 acre
Drachma	Greece	49.38 grains	Seer	India	2 2-35 lb
Dunam	Israel	0.22239 acre	Shaku	Japan	11.9303 in
Fanega (dry)	Ecuador, Salvador	1.5745 bu	Sho	Japan	1.91 liq qt
"	Chile	2.75268 bu	Skalpund	Sweden	0.937 lb
" (dry)	Guatemala, Spain	1.57744 bu	Stone	British	14 lb
"	Mexico	2.57716 bu	Sun	Japan	1.193 inches
" (dry)	Spain	1.57501 bu	Tael (Kuping)	China	575.64 grs (troy)
" (liquid)	Spain	16 gal	Tan	Japan	0.25 acre
" (dry)	Trinidad & Tobago	110 lb	To	Japan	2.05 pecks
" (double)	Uruguay	7.776 bu	Tonde (cereal)	Denmark	3.9480 bu
" (single)	Uruguay	3.888 bu	Tonde (land)	Denmark	1.36 acres
"	Venezuela	3.334 bu	Tonne	France	2204.62 lb
Feddan	Egypt	1.04 acres	Tsubo	Japan	35.58 sq ft
Frail (raisins)	Spain	50 lb	Ts'un	China	1.26 inches
Frasco	Argentina	2.51 liq qt	Tunna (wheat)	Sweden	4.16 bu
Frasila	Zanzibar	35 lb	Tunnland	"	1.22 acres
Fuder	Luxembourg	264.18 gal	Vara	Argentina	34.0944 inches
Funt	USSR	0.9028 lb	"	Costa Rica, Salva.	32.913 inches
Gallon	British	1.20094 U. S. gal	"	Guatemala	32.909 inches
Garniec	Poland	1.0567 gal	"	Honduras	32.874 inches
Jerib	Iran	2.471 acres	"	Nicaragua	33.057 inches
Joch	Austria	1.422 acres	"	Chile and Peru	32.913 inches
"	Hungary	1.067 acres	"	Cuba	33.386 inches
Kantar	Egypt	99.05 lb	"	Mexico	32.992 inches
"	Morocco	112 lb	Vedro	USSR	3.249 gal
"	Turkey	124.45 lb	Verst	"	0.663 mile
Ken	Japan	5.97 feet	Vloka	Poland	41.50 acres
Kin	Japan	1.32 lb	Wey	Scotland, Ireland	40 bu

The metric carat of 200 milligrams is now very generally in use. The word carat also is used to denote the proportion of alloy in a metal. Thus, pure gold is 24 carats fine.

Chemical Elements, Discoverers, Atomic Weights

Atomic weights, based on the exact number 12 as the assigned atomic mass of the principal isotope of carbon, carbon 12, are provided through the courtesy of the International Union of Pure and Applied Chemistry and Butterworth Scientific Publications.

For the radioactive elements with the exception of uranium and thorium, the mass number of either the isotope of longest half-life (marked with a star) or the better known isotope (marked with two stars) is given.

Chemical element	Symbol	Atomic number	Atomic weight	Year discov.	Discoverer
Actinium	Ac	89	227*	1899	Debierne
Aluminum	Al	13	26.9815	1825	Oersted
Americium	Am	95	243*	1944	Seaborg, et al.
Antimony	Sb	51	121.75	1450	Valentine
Argon	Ar	18	39.948	1894	Rayleigh, Ramsay
Arsenic	As	33	74.9216	13th C.	Magnus
Astatine	At	85	210*	1940	Corson, et al.
Barium	Ba	56	137.34	1808	Davy
Berkelium	Bk	97	247*	1949	Thompson, Ghiorso, Seaborg
Beryllium	Be	4	9.0122	1798	Vauquelin
Bismuth	Bi	83	208.980	15th C.	Valentine
Boron	B	5	10.811a	1808	Davy
Bromine	Br	35	79.904b	1826	Balard
Cadmium	Cd	48	112.40	1817	Stromeyer
Calcium	Ca	20	40.08	1808	Davy
Californium	Cf	98	249**	1950	Thompson, et al.
Carbon	C	6	12.01115a	B.C.	
Cerium	Ce	58	140.12	1803	Klaproth
Cesium	Cs	55	132.905	1861	Bunsen, Kirchoff
Chlorine	Cl	17	35.453b	1774	Scheele
Chromium	Cr	24	51.996b	1797	Vauquelin
Cobalt	Co	27	58.9332	1735	Brandt
Copper	Cu	29	63.546b	B.C.	
Curium	Cm	96	247*	1944	Seaborg, et al.
Dysprosium	Dy	66	162.50	1886	Boisbaudran
Einsteinium	Es	99	254*	1952	Ghiorso, et al.
Erbium	Er	68	167.26	1843	Mosander
Europium	Eu	63	151.96	1901	Demarcay
Fermium	Fm	100	257*	1953	Ghiorso, et al.
Fluorine	F	9	18.9984	1771	Scheele
Francium	Fr	87	223*	1939	Perey
Gadolinium	Gd	64	157.25	1886	Marignac
Gallium	Ga	31	69.72	1875	Boisbaudran
Germanium	Ge	32	72.59	1886	Winkler
Gold	Au	79	196.967	B.C.	
Hafnium	Hf	72	178.49	1923	Coster, Hevesy
Hahnium	Ha	105	262*	1970	Ghiorso, et al.
Helium	He	2	4.0026	1895	Ramsay
Holmium	Ho	67	164.930	1879	Cleve
Hydrogen	H	1	1.00797a	1766	Cavendish
Indium	In	49	114.82	1863	Reich, Richter
Iodine	I	53	126.9044	1811	Courtois
Iridium	Ir	77	192.2	1804	Tennant
Iron	Fe	26	55.847b	B.C.	
Krypton	Kr	36	83.80	1898	Ramsay, Travers
Lanthanum	La	57	138.91	1839	Mosander
Lawrencium	Lr	103	260*	1961	Ghiorso, T. Sikkeland, A. E. Larsh, and R. M. Latimer
Lead	Pb	82	207.19	B.C.	
Lithium	Li	3	6.939	1817	Arfvedson
Lutetium	Lu	71	174.97	1907	Welsbach, Urbain
Magnesium	Mg	12	24.312	1830	Liebig, Bussy
Manganese	Mn	25	54.9380	1774	Gahn
Mendelevium	Md	101	258*	1955	Ghiorso, et al.
Mercury	Hg	80	200.59	B.C.	
Molybdenum	Mo	42	95.94	1782	Hjelm
Neodymium	Nd	60	144.24	1885	Welsbach
Neon	Ne	10	20.183	1898	Ramsay, Travers
Neptunium	Np	93	237*	1940	McMillan and Abelson
Nickel	Ni	28	58.71	1751	Cronstedt
Niobium (Form. Columbium)	Nb	41	92.906	1801	Hatchett
Nitrogen	N	7	14.0067	1772	Rutherford
Nobelium	No	102	259*	1958	Ghiorso, et al.
Osmium	Os	76	190.2	1804	Tennant
Oxygen	O	8	15.9994a	1774	Priestly, Scheele
Palladium	Pd	46	106.4	1803	Wollaston
Phosphorus	P	15	30.9738	1669	Brandt
Platinum	Pt	78	195.09	1735	Ulloa
Plutonium	Pu	94	242**	1940	Seaborg, et al.
Polonium	Po	84	210**	1898	P. and M. Curie
Potassium	K	19	39.102	1807	Davy
Praseodymium	Pr	59	140.907	1885	Welsbach
Promethium	Pm	61	147**	1945	Glendenin and Marinsky
Protactinium	Pa	91	231*	1917	Hahn and Meltner
Radium	Ra	88	226*	1898	P. & M. Curie, Bemont
Radon	Rn	86	222*	1900	Dorn
Rhenium	Re	75	186.2	1925	Noddack and Tacke
Rhodium	Rh	45	102.905	1803	Wollaston
Rubidium	Rb	37	85.47	1861	Bunsen, Kirchoff
Ruthenium	Ru	44	101.07	1845	Claus

Chemical element	Symbol	Number	Weight	Year	Discoverer
Rutherfordium	Rf	104	261*	1969	Ghiorso, et al.
Samarium	Sm	62	150.35	1879	Boisbaudran
Scandium	Sc	21	44.956	1879	Nilson
Selenium	Se	34	78.96	1817	Berzelius
Silicon	Si	14	28.086a	1823	Berzelius
Silver	Ag	47	107.868b	B. C.	
Sodium	Na	11	22.9898	1807	Davy
Strontium	Sr	38	87.62	1790	Crawford
Sulfur	S	16	32.064a	B. C.	
Tantalun	Ta	73	180.948	1802	Eckeberg
Technetium	Tc	43	99**	1937	Perrier and Segre
Tellurium	Te	52	127.60	1782	Von Reichenstein
Terbium	Tb	65	158.924	1843	Mosander
Thallium	Tl	81	204.37	1861	Crookes
Thorium	Th	90	232.038	1828	Berzelius
Thulium	Tm	69	168.934	1879	Cleve
Tin	Sn	50	118.69	B. C.	
Titanium	Ti	22	47.90	1789	Gregor
Tungsten (Alternate Wolfram)	W	74	183.85	1783	d'Elhujar
Uranium	U	92	238.03	1789	Klaproth
Vanadium	V	23	50.942	1830	Sefstrom
Xenon	Xe	54	131.30	1898	Ramsay, Travers
Ytterbium	Yb	70	173.04	1878	Marignac
Yttrium	Y	39	88.905	1794	Gadolin
Zinc	Zn	30	65.37	B. C.	
Zirconium	Zr	40	91.22	1789	Klaproth

a. Atomic weights so designated are known to be variable because of natural variations in isotopic composition. The observed ranges are: hydrogen ± 0.00001; boron ± 0.003; carbon ± 0.00005; oxygen ± 0.0001; silicon ± 0.001; sulfur ± 0.003.

b. Atomic weights so designated are believed to have the following experimental uncertainties: chlorine ± 0.001; chromium ± 0.001; iron ± 0.003; bromine ± 0.001; silver ± 0.001; copper ± 0.001.

Medical Signs and Abbreviations

Source: American Medical Association

℞ (Lat. Recipe) . . . . . take	gr . . . . grain	pulvis . . . . powder
ℨ . . . . drachm	a.c. . . . . before meals	q. 3 h . . every three hours
℥ . . . . fluid drachm	gtt . . . . drops	q.i.d. . . . . four times daily
℥ . . . . ounce	ad . . . . to, up to	q.s. . . . .
℥ . . . . fluid ounce	ad libitum . . . . at pleasure	h.s. . . . . at bedtime
℥ ss . . . . . . half an ounce	agit . . . . shake	inject . . . . injection	. as much as is sufficient
℥ i . . . . one ounce	aqua . . . . water	lb . . . . pound	sig . . . . sign, write
℥ iss . one ounce and a half	b.i.d. . . . . twice daily	m . . . . mix	solutio . . . . a solution
℥ ii . . . . two ounces	cap . . . . capsule	mg . . . . milligram	ss . . . . one-half
m . . . . . . minim, or drop	cum, or c . . . . with	ml . . . . milliliter	stat . . . . at once
O . . . . pint	e.m.p. . . . . . . as directed	non. rep. or n.r.	tab . . . . tablet
āā . . . . of each	fiant (ft) . . . . make		do not repeat	t.i.d. . . . three times daily
	gargarisma . . . . a gargle	p.c. . . . . after meals	ung . . . . ointment
	Gm . . . . gram	p.r.n. . . as circumstances	ut dict . . . . . . as directed
		may require	

Breaking the Sound Barrier; Speed of Sound

The prefix Mach is used to describe supersonic speed. It derives from Ernst Mach, a Czech-born German physicist, who contributed to the study of sound. When a plane moves at the speed of sound it is Mach 1. When twice the speed of sound it is Mach 2. When it is near but below the speed of sound its speed can be designated at less than Mach 1, for example, Mach .10. Mach is defined as "in jet propulsion, the ratio of the velocity of a rocket or a jet to the velocity of sound in the medium being considered."

When a plane passes the sound barrier–flying faster than sound travels–listeners in the area hear thunderclaps, but pilots do not hear them.

Sound is produced by vibrations of an object and is transmitted by alternate increase and decrease in pressures that radiate outward through a material media of molecules –somewhat like waves spreading out on a pond after a rock has been tossed.

The frequency of sound is determined by the number of times the vibrating waves undulate per second, and is measured in cycles per second. The slower the cycle of waves, the lower the sound. As frequencies increase, the sound is higher.

Sound is audible to human beings only if the frequency falls within a certain range. The human ear is usually not sensitive to frequencies of less than 20 vibrations per second, or more than about 20,000 vibrations per second–although this range varies among individuals. Anything at a pitch higher than the human ear can hear is termed ultrasonic.

Intensity or loudness is the strength of the pressure of these radiating waves, and is measured in decibels. The human ear responds to intensity in a range from zero to 120 decibels. Any sound with pressure over 120 decibels is painful.

The speed of sound is generally placed at 1088 ft. per second at sea level at 32°F. It varies in other temperatures and in different media. Sound travels faster in water than in air, and even faster in iron and steel. If in air it travels a mile in 5 seconds, it does a mile under water in 1 second, and through iron in ⅓ of a second. It travels through ice cold vapor at approximately 4,708 ft. per sec., ice-cold water, 4,938; granite, 12,960; hard wood, 12,620; brick, 11,960; glass, 16,410 to 19,690; silver, 8,658; gold, 5,717.

Bell Time on Shipboard

Source: Maritime Administration

Time, A.M.		Time, A.M.		Time, A.M.		Time, P.M.		Time, P.M.		Time, P.M.	
1 Bell	12:30	1 Bell	4:30	1 Bell	8:30	1 Bell	12:30	1 Bell	4:30	1 Bell	8:30
2 Bells	1:00	2 Bells	5:00	2 Bells	9:00	2 Bells	1:00	2 Bells	5:00	2 Bells	9:00
3 "	1:30	3 "	5:30	3 "	9:30	3 "	1:30	3 "	5:30	3 "	9:30
4 "	2:00	4 "	6:00	4 "	10:00	4 "	2:00	4 "	6:00	4 "	10:00
5 "	2:30	5 "	6:30	5 "	10:30	5 "	2:30	5 "	6:30	5 "	10:30
6 "	3:00	6 "	7:00	6 "	11:00	6 "	3:00	6 "	7:00	6 "	11:00
7 "	3:30	7 "	7:30	7 "	11:30	7 "	3:30	7 "	7:30	7 "	11:30
8 "	4:00	8 "	8:00	8 "	Noon	8 "	4:00	8 "	8:00	8 "	Midnight

Factors and Prime Numbers (*) The number 1 is usually excluded.

Factors are such numbers as multiplied together will produce a required number.
A Prime Number is one that cannot be resolved into two or more factors; or, it is a number exactly divisible only by itself and unity. A Composite Number is one that can be resolved into factors.

Table of Prime Numbers from 1 to 1000

(*)	59	139	233	337	439	557	653	769	883
2	61	149	239	347	443	563	659	773	887
3	67	151	241	349	449	569	661	787	907
5	71	157	251	353	457	571	673	797	911
7	73	163	257	359	461	577	677	809	919
11	79	167	263	367	463	587	683	811	929
13	83	173	269	373	467	593	691	821	937
17	89	179	271	379	479	599	701	823	941
19	97	181	277	383	487	601	709	827	947
23	101	191	281	389	491	607	719	829	953
29	103	193	283	397	499	613	727	839	967
31	107	197	293	401	503	617	733	853	971
37	109	199	307	409	509	619	739	857	977
41	113	211	311	419	521	631	743	859	983
43	127	223	313	421	523	641	751	863	991
47	131	227	317	431	541	643	757	877	997
53	137	229	331	433	547	647	761	881	

Playing Cards and Dice Chances

POKER HANDS (Four-Suit)

Hand	Number Possible	Odds Against
Royal Flush	4	649,739 to 1
Other Straight Flush	36	72,192 to 1
Four of a kind	624	4,164 to 1
Full House	3,744	693 to 1
Flush	5,108	508 to 1
Straight	10,200	254 to 1
Three of a kind	54,912	46 to 1
Two Pairs	123,552	20 to 1
One Pair	1,098,240	4 to 3(1.37 to 1)
Nothing	1,302,540	1 to 1
Total	**2,598,960**	

DICE
Totals Probabilities on Two Dice

Total	Odds Against (Single toss)		Odds Against (Single toss)
2	35 to 1	8	31 to 5
3	17 to 1	9	8 to 1
4	11 to 1	10	11 to 1
5	8 to 1	11	17 to 1
6	31 to 5	12	35 to 1
7	5 to 1		

DICE
Probabilities of Consecutive Winning Plays

No. Consecutive Wins	By 7, 11, or Point	No. Consecutive Wins	By 7, 11, or Point
1	244 in 495	6	1 in 72
2	24 in 100	7	1 in 141
3	3 in 25	8	1 in 287
4	1 in 17	9	1 in 582
5	1 in 34		

PINOCHLE AUCTION
Odds Against Finding in "Widow" of Three Cards

Open Places	Odds Against	Open Places	Odds Against
1	5 to 1	4	3 to 2 for
2	2 to 1	5	2 to 1 for
3	Even		

BRIDGE

The odds—Against suit distribution in a hand of 4-4-3-2 are about 4 to 1, against 5-4-2-2 about 8 to 1, against 6-4-2-1 about 20 to 1, against 7-4-1-1 about 254 to 1, against 8-4-1-0 about 2,211 to 1, and against 13-0-0-0 about 158,753, 389, 899 to 1.

Colors of the Spectrum

Color, an electromagnetic wave phenomenon, is a sensation produced through the excitation of the retina of the eye by rays of light. The colors of the spectrum may be produced by viewing a light beam refracted by passage through a prism, which breaks the light into its wave lengths.

Customarily, the primary colors of the spectrum are thought of as those six monochromatic colors which occupy relatively large areas of the spectrum: red, orange, yellow, green, blue and violet. However, Sir Isaac Newton named a seventh, indigo, situated between blue and violet on the spectrum. Aubert estimated (1865) the solar spectrum to contain approximately 1,000 distinguishable hues of which according to Rood (1881) 2,000,000 tints and shades can be distinguished; Luckiesh stated (1915) that 55 distinctly different hues have been seen in a single spectrum.

By many physicists only three primary colors are recognized: red, yellow and blue (Mayer, 1775); red, green and violet (Thomas Young, 1801); red, green and blue (Clerk Maxwell, 1860)

The color sensation of black is due to complete lack of stimulation of the retina, that of white to complete stimulation. The infra-red and ultra-violet rays, below the red (long) end of the spectrum and the violet end (short end) respectively, are invisible. Heat is the principal effect of the infra-red rays and chemical action that of the ultra-violet rays.

Braille Alphabet and Numerals

Braille is a system of raised dots for touch reading and writing by the blind, developed by Louis Braille (1809-1852), a French teacher of the blind who was himself blinded in an accident at the age of 3.

The Braille cell is three dots high and two dots wide. That means that 63 different characters can be formed.

The six dots of Braille are arranged and numbered thus:

```
1 •• 4     a  b  c  d  e  f  g  h  i  j  k  l  m  n  o  p  q  r  s  t  u  v  w  x  y  z
2 •• 5     1  2  3  4  5  6  7  8  9  0
3 •• 6
```

The first ten letters of the alphabet become numbers when preceded by the numeric indicator. Dots 2, 3, 5 and 6 are used for punctuation marks:

```
1 •• 4     ,  ;  :  .  !  (  )  "/?  "   Numeric Indicator   Dash  Apostrophe   Capital sign
2 •• 5                                                                (dot 3)    (dot 6)
3 •• 6
```

Discoveries and Innovations: Chemistry, Physics, Biology, Medicine

Product	Date	Discoverer	Nation
Acetylene gas	1892	Wilson	U. S.
ACTH	1949	Armour & Co.	U. S.
Adrenalin	1901	Takamine	Japan
Aluminum, electrolytic process	1886	Hall	U. S.
Aluminum, isolated	1825	Oersted	Danish
Analine dye	1856	Perkin	English
Anesthesia, ether	1842	Long	U. S.
Anesthesia, local	1885	Koller	Austria
Anesthesia, spinal	1898	Bier	German
Anti-rabies	1885	Pasteur	French
Antitoxin, diphtheria	1891	Von Behring	German
Antiseptic surgery	1867	Lister	English
Argyrol		Barnes	U. S.
Arsphenamine	1910	Ehrlich	German
Aspirin	1889	Dreser	German
Atomic numbers	1913	Moseley	English
Atomic theory	1803	Dalton	English
Atomic time clock	1947	Libby	U.S.
Atom-smashing theory	1919	Rutherford	English
Atabrine		Mietzsch, et al	German
Aureomycin	1948	Duggar	U. S.
Bacitracin	1945	Johnson et al	U. S.
Bacteria (described)	1676	Leeuwenhoek	Dutch
Barbital	1903	Fischer	German
Bleaching powder	1798	Tennant	English
Blood, circulation	1628	Harvey	English
Bordeaux mixture	1885	Millardet	French
Bromine from sea	1924	Edgar-Kramer	U. S.
Calcium carbide	1888	Wilson	U. S.
Calculus	1670	Newton	English
Carbon oxides	1925	Fisher	German
Carbomycin	1952	Tanner	U. S.
Camphor synthetic	1896	Haller	French
Canning (food)	1804	Appert	French
Chlorine	1810	Davy	English
Chloroform	1831	Guthrie,S.	U. S.
Chloromycetin	1947	Burkholder	U. S.
Classification of plants and animals	1735	Linnaeus	Swedish
Cocaine	1860	Niemann	German
Combustion, explained	1777	Lavoisier	French
Conditioned reflex	1914	Pavlov	Russian
Conteben	1950	Belmisch, Mietzsch, Domagh	German
Cortisone	1936	Kendall	U. S.
Cortisone, synthesis	1946	Sarett	U. S.
Cosmic rays	1910	Gockel	Swiss
Cyanide	1905	Caro, Frank.	German
Cyclotron	1930	Lawrence	U. S.
DDT	1874	Zeidler	German
(Not applied as insecticide until 1939)			
Deuterium (heavy hydrogen)	1932	Urey, Brick-Wedde, Murphy	U. S.
DNA (structure)	1951	Crick	English
		Watson	U. S.
		Wilkins	English
Electric resistance (law)	1827	Ohm	German
Electric waves	1888	Hertz	German
Electrolysis	1852	Faraday	English
Electromagnetism	1819	Oersted	Danish
Electron	1897	Thomson, J.	English
Electron diffraction	1936	Thomson, G	English
		Davisson	U. S.
Electroshock treatment	1938	Cerletti, Bini	Italy
Erythromycin	1952	McGuire	U. S.
Evolution, natural selection	1858	Darwin	English
Falling bodies, law	1590	Galileo	Italian
Gases, law of combining volumes	1808	Gay-Lussac	French
Geometry, analytic	1619	Descartes	French
Gold (cyanide process for extraction)	1887	MacArthur-Forest	British
Gravitation, law	1687	Newton	English
Holograph	1948	Gabor	British
Human heart transplant	1967	Barnard	S. Africa
Indigo, synthesis of	1880	Baeyer	German
Induction, electric	1830	Henry	U.S.
Insulin	1922	Banting, Best, MacLeod	Canada
Intelligence testing	1905	Binet and Simon	French
Isoniazid	1952	Hoffman-La-Roche	U. S.
		Domagh	German
Isotopes, theory	1912	Soddy	English

Product	Date	Discoverer	Nation
Laser (light amplification by stimulated emission of radiation)	1958	Townes, Schawlow	U.S.
Light, velocity	1675	Roemer	Danish
Light, wave theory	1690	Huygens	Dutch
Lithography	1796	Senfelder	Bohemia
Lobotomy	1935	Egas Moniz	Portugal
LSD-25	1943	Hoffman	Swiss
Mendelian laws	1866	Mendel	Austrian
Mercator's projection (map)	1568	Mercator (Kremer)	Flemish
Methanol	1925	Patard	French
Milk condensation	1853	Borden	U. S.
Molecular hypothesis	1811	Avogadro	Italian
Motion, laws of	1687	Newton	English
Neomycin	1949	Waksman & Lechevalier	U. S.
Neutron	1932	Chadwick	English
Nitric acid	1648	Glauber	German
Nitric oxide	1772	Priestley	English
Nitroglycerin	1846	Sobrero	Italian
Ohm's law	1827	Ohm, Georg	German
Oil cracking process	1891	Dewar	U. S.
Oxygen	1774	Priestley	English
Ozone	1840	Schonbein	German
Paper, from wood pulp, sulfate process	1884	Dahl	German
Paper, sulfite process	1867	Tilghman	U. S.
Penicillin	1929	Alex. Fleming	English
Practical use	1941	Florey-Chain	English
Periodic law and table of elements	1869	Mendelejeff	Russian
Planetary motion, laws	1609	Kepler	German
Plutonium fission	1940	Kennedy, J. W.	U. S.
		Wahl, A. C.	U. S.
		Seaborg, G. T.	U. S.
		Segre, Emilio.	U. S.
Polymixin	1947	Ainsworth	English
Positron	1932	Anderson	U.S.
Proton	1919	Rutherford	English
Psychoanalysis	1900	Freud	Austrian
Quantum theory	1900	Planck	German
Quasars	1963	Matthews & Sandage	U.S.
Quinine-synthetic	1918	Rabe	German
Radioactivity	1896	Becquerel	French
Radium	1898	Curie, Pierre	French
Radium	1898	Curie, Marie	Polish
Relativity theory	1905	Einstein	German
Reserpine	1949	Jal Vakil	India
Salvarsan (606)	1910	Ehrlich	German
Schick test, diphtheria	1913	Schick	U.S.
Silicon	1823	Berzelius	Swedish
Streptomycin	1945	Waksman	U. S.
Sulfanilamide theory	1908	Gelmo	German
Sulfanilamide	1934	Domagh	German
Sulfadiazine	1940	Roblin	U. S.
Sulfapyridine	1938	Ewins Phelps	English
Sulfathiazole		Fosbinder, Walter	U. S.
Sulfuric acid	1831	Phillips	English
Sulfuric acid, lead	1746	Roebuck	English
Terramycin	1950	Finlay, et al.	U. S.
Tuberculin	1890	Koch	German
Uranium fission (theory)	1939	Hahn, Strassmann	German
		Bohr	Danish
		Einstein	U. S.
		Fermi	Italian
		Pegram	U. S.
		Wheeler	U. S.
Uranium fission, atomic reactor	1942	Enrico Fermi	Italian
		Leo Szilard	U. S.
Vaccine, measles	1954	Enders, John	U. S.
		Peebies, T.	U. S.
Vaccine, polio	1955	Sabin, Alb. E.	U. S.
Vaccine, polio	1953	Salk, Jonas E.	U. S.
Vaccine, rabies	1885	Pasteur	French
Vaccine, smallpox	1796	Jenner, Edw.	English
Vaccine, typhus	1909	Nicolle, J.	French
Van Allen belts, radiation	1958	Van Allen	U.S.
Vitamin A	1913	McCollum, Davis	U. S.
Vitamin B	1916	McCollum	U. S.
Vitamin C	1912	Holst, Froelich	Norway
Vitamin D	1922	McCollum	U. S.
Wassermann test, syphilis	1906	Wassermann	German
Xerography	1938	Carlson	U. S.
X-ray	1895	Roentgen	German

Great Inventions and Scientific Discoveries

Invention	Date	Inventor	Nation
Adding machine	1642	Pascal	French
Adding machine	1885	Burroughs	U. S.
Addressograph	1892	Duncan	U. S.
Aerosol spray	1941	Goodhue	U. S.
Air brake	1868	Westinghouse	U. S.
Air conditioning	1911	Carrier	U. S.
Air pump	1650	Guericke	German
Airplane, automatic pilot	1929	Green	U.S.
Airplane, experim'tal	1896	Langley	U. S.
Airplane, jet engine	1937	Whittle	British
Airplane with motor	1903	Orville and Wilbur Wright	U. S.
Airplane, hydro	1911	Curtiss	U. S.
Airship	1852	Giffard	French
Airship, rigid dirigible	1900	Zeppelin	German
Arc tube	1923	Alexanderson	U. S.
Autogyro	1920	de la Cierva	Spanish
Automobile, differential gear	1885	Benz	German
Automobile, electric	1892	Morrison	U. S.
Automobile, experimental	1875	Marcus	Austrian
Automobile, gasoline	1887	Daimler	German
Automobile, gasoline	1892	Duryea, C. E.	U.S.
Automobile, magneto	1899	Daimler	German
Automobile, muffler		Maxim, H. P.	U. S.
Automobile, self-starter	1911	Kettering	U. S.
Automobile, steam	1889	Roper	U. S.
Babbitt metal	1839	Babbitt	U. S.
Bakelite	1907	Baekeland	Belg. U.S.
Balloon	1783	Montgolfier	French
Barometer	1643	Torricelli	Italian
Bicycle, modern	1884	Starley	English
Bifocal lens	1780	Franklin	U. S.
Block signals, railway	1867	Hall	U. S.
Bomb, depth	1916	Tait	U. S.
Bottle machine	1903	Owens	U. S.
Braille printing	1829	Braille	French
Burner, gas	1855	Bunsen	German
Calculating machine	1823	Babbage	English
Camera, Polaroid Land	1948	Land	U. S.
Car coupler	1873	Janney	U. S.
Carburetor, gasoline	1876	Daimler	German
Card time recorder	1894	Cooper	U. S.
Carding machine	1797	Whittemore	U. S.
Carpet sweeper	1876	Bissell	U. S.
Cash register	1879	Ritty	U. S.
Cathode ray tube	1878	Crookes	English
Cellophane	1911	Brandenberger	Swiss
Celluloid	1870	Hyatt	U. S.
Cement, Portland	1845	Aspdin	English
Chronometer	1735	Harrison	English
Circuit breaker	1925	Hilliard	U. S.
Clock, pendulum	1657	Huygens	Dutch
Coaxial cable system	1929	Affel & Espensched	U. S.
Coke oven	1893	Hoffman	Austrian
Compressed air rock drill	1871	Ingersoll	U.S.
Comptometer	1887	Felt	U. S.
Computer, automatic sequence	1939	Aiken et al	U. S.
Condenser microphone (telephone)	1920	Wente	U. S.
Cotton gin	1793	Whitney	U. S.
Cream separator	1880	DeLaval	Swedish
Cultivator, disc	1878	Mallon	U. S.
Cystoscope	1877	Nitze	German
Dental plate, rubber	1855	Goodyear	U. S.
Diesel engine	1895	Diesel	German
Dynamite	1866	Nobel	Swedish
Dynamo, continuous current	1860	Picinotti	Italian
Dynamo, hydrogen cooled	1915	Schuler	U. S.
Electric battery	1800	Volta	Italian
Electric fan	1882	Wheeler	U. S.
Electrocardiograph	1903	Einthoven	Dutch
Electroencephalograph	1929	Berger	German
Electromagnet	1824	Sturgeon	English
Electron spectrometer	1944	Deutsch, Elliott, Evans	U.S.
Electron tube multigrid	1913	Langmuir	U. S.
Electroplating	1805	Brugnatelli	Italian
Electrostatic generator	1929	Van de Graaff	U.S.
Elevator, brake	1852	Otis	U. S.
Elevator, push button	1922	Larson	U. S.
Engine, automobile	1879	Benz	German
Engine, gasoline	1872	Brayton, Geo.	U. S.

Invention	Date	Inventor	Nation
Engine, gas, compound	1926	Eickemeyer	U. S.
Engine, coal-gas 4 cycle	1877	Otto	German
Engine, compression ignition	1883	Daimler	German
Engine, electric ignition	1880	Benz	German
Engine, gasoline	1886	Daimler	German
Engine, steam, piston	1705	Newcomen	English
Engine, steam, piston	1769	Watt	Scottish
Engraving, half-tone	1893	Ives	U. S.
Filament, tungsten	1915	Langmuir	U. S.
Flanged rail	1831	Stevens	U.S.
Flatiron, electric	1882	Seeley	U. S.
Furnace, for steel	1861	Siemens	German
Galvanometer	1820	Sweigger	German
Gas discharge tube	1922	Hull	U. S.
Gas lighting	1792	Murdoch	Scottish
Gas mantle	1885	Welsbach	Austrian
Gasoline, (lead ethyl)	1922	Midgely	U. S.
Gasoline cracked	1913	Burton, W.M.	U. S.
Gasoline, high octane	1930	Ipatieff	Russian
Geiger counter	1913	Geiger	German
Glass, laminated	1909	Benedictus	French
Glider	1853	Cayley	English
Gun, breechloader	1811	Thornton	U.S.
Gun, Browning	1916	Browning	U. S.
Gun, magazine	1875	Hotchkiss	U. S.
Gun, ripower	1889	Maxim, H. P.	U. S.
Guncotton	1846	Schoenbein	German
Gyroscope	1852	Foucault	French
Gyrocompass	1911	Sperry	U. S.
Harvester	1836	Moore	U. S.
Harvester-Thresher	1888	Matteson	U. S.
Helicopter	1939	Sikorsky	U. S.
Hydrometer	1768	Baume	French
Ice-making machine	1851	Gorrie	U. S.
Iron Lung	1928	Drinker, Slaw	U.S.
Kaleidoscope	1817	Brewster	English
Kinetoscope	1887	Edison	U. S.
Kodak	1888	Eastman Walker	U. S.
Lacquer, nitrocellulose	1921	Flaherty	U. S.
Lamp, arc	1879	Brush	U. S.
Lamp, incandescent	1879	Edison	U. S.
Lamp, incand., frosted	1924	Pipkin	U. S.
Lamp, incand., gas	1916	Langmuir	U. S.
Lamp, Klieg	1911	Kliegl, A.&J.	U. S.
Lamp, mercury vapor	1912	Hewitt	U. S.
Lamp, miner's safety	1816	Davy	English
Lamp, Neon	1915	Claude	French
Lathe, turret	1845	Fitch	U. S.
Launderette	1934	Cantrell	U. S.
Lens, achromatic	1758	Dolland	English
Lens, fused bifocal	1908	Borsch	U. S.
Leydenjar (condenser)	1745	von Kleist	German
Lightning rod	1752	Franklin	U. S.
Linoleum	1860	Walton	English
Linotype	1885	Mergenthaler	U. S.
Lock, cylinder	1865	Yale	U. S.
Locomotive, electric	1851	Vail	U. S.
Locomotive, exper	1801	Trevithick	English
Locomotive, exper	1812	Fenton et al	English
Locomotive, exper	1813	Hedley	English
Locomotive, exper	1814	Stephenson	English
Locomotive practical	1829	Stephenson	English
Locomotive, 1st U. S.	1830	Cooper, P.	U.S.
Loom, power	1785	Cartwright	English
Loudspeaker, dynamic	1924	Rice-Kellogg	U. S.
Machine gun	1861	Gatling	U. S.
Machine gun, improved	1872	Hotchkiss	U. S.
Machine gun (Maxim)	1883	Maxim, H. S.	English
Magnet, electro	1828	Henry	U. S.
Mantle, gas	1885	Welsbach	Austrian
Mason Jar	1858	Mason, J.	U. S.
Match, friction	1827	John Walker	English
Mercerized textiles	1843	Mercer, J.	English
Meter, induction	1888	Shallenberger	U. S.
Meter, parking	1935	Magee	U. S.
Metronome	1816	Malzel	Austrian
Micrometer	1636	Gascoigne	English
Microphone	1877	Berliner	U. S.
Microscope, compound	1590	Janssen	Dutch
Microscope, electronic	1931	Knoll-Ruska	German
Monitor, warship	1861	Ericsson	U. S.
Monotype	1887	Lanston	U. S.

Invention	Date	Inventor	Nation
Motor, AC	1892	Tesla	U. S.
Motor, induction	1887	Tesla	U. S.
Motorcycle	1885	Daimler	German
Movie machine	1894	Jenkins	U. S.
Movie, panoramic	1952	Waller	U. S.
Movie, talking	1927	Warner Bros	U. S.
Mower, lawn	1868	Hills	U. S.
Mowing machine	1831	Manning	U. S.
Neoprene	1930	Carothers	U. S.
Nylon synthethic	1930	Carothers	U. S.
Nylon	1937	Du Pont lab	U. S.
Oil cracking furnace	1891	Gavrilov	Russian
Oil filled power cable	1921	Emanueli	Italian
Oleomargarine	1868	Mege-Mouries	French
Ophthalmoscope	1851	Helmholtz	German
Paper machine	1809	Dickinson	U. S.
Parachute	1785	Blanchard	French
Pen, ballpoint	1888	Loud	U. S.
Pen, fountain	1884	Waterman	U. S.
Pen, steel	1780	Harrison	English
Pendulum	1581	Galileo	Italian
Percussion cap	1814	Shaw	U.S.
Phonograph	1877	Edison	U. S.
Photo, color	1892	Ives	U. S.
Photo film, celluloid	1887	Goodwin	U. S.
Photo film transparent	1888	Eastman-Goodwin	U. S.
Photoelectric cell	1895	Elster	German
Photographic paper	1898	Baekeland	U. S.
Photography	1835	Fox-Talbot	English
Photography	1837	Daguerre	French
Photography	1839	Niepce, Jr	French
Photophone	1880	Bell	U. S.
Phototelegraphy	1925	Bell lab	U. S.
Piano	1709	Cristofori	Italian
Piano player	1863	Fourneaux	French
Pin, safety	1849	Hunt	U. S.
Pistol (revolver)	1835	Colt	U. S.
Plow, cast iron	1797	Newbold	U. S.
Plow, disc	1896	Hardy	U. S.
Pneumatic hammer	1890	King	U. S.
Powder, smokeless	1863	Schultze	German
Printing press, rotary	1846	Hoe	U. S.
Printing press, web	1865	Bullock	U. S.
Propeller, screw	1804	Stevens	U. S.
Propeller, screw	1837	Ericsson	Swedish
Punch card accounting	1884	Hollerith	U. S.
Radar	1922	Taylor and Young	U. S.
Radio amplifier	1907	De Forest	U. S.
Radio beacon	1928	Donovan	U. S.
Radio crystal oscillator	1918	Nicolson	U. S.
Radio receiver, cascade tuning	1913	Alexanderson	U. S.
Radio receiver, heterodyne	1913	Fessenden	U. S.
Radio transmitter, triode modulation	1914	Alexanderson	U. S.
Radio tube-diode	1905	Fleming	English
Radio tube oscillator	1915	De Forest	U. S.
Radio tube triode	1907	De Forest	U. S.
Radio, signals	1895	Marconi	Italian
Radio, magnetic detector	1902	Marconi	Italian
Radio FM 2-path	1929	Armstrong	U. S.
Rayon	1883	Swan	English
Razor, electric	1931	Schick	U. S.
Razor, safety	1895	Gillette	U. S.
Reaper	1834	McCormick	U. S.
Record, cylinder	1887	Bell-Tainter	U. S.
Record, disc	1887	Berliner	U. S.
Record, long playing	1948	Goldmark	U. S.
Record, wax cylinder	1888	Edison	U. S.
Refrigerants, low-boiling fluorine compound	1930	Midgely and co-workers	U. S.
Refrigerator car	1868	David	U. S.
Resin, synthetic	1931	Hill	English
Rifle, repeating	1860	Winchester	U.S.
Rocket engine	1929	R. H. Goddard	U. S.
Rubber, vulcanized	1839	Goodyear	U. S.
Saw, band	1808	Newberry	English
Saw, circular	1777	Miller	English
Searchlight, arc	1915	Sperry	U. S.
Sewing machine	1846	Howe	U. S.
Shoe-sewing machine	1860	McKay	U. S.
Shrapnel shell	1784	Shrapnel	English
Shuttle, flying	1733	Kay	English
Sleeping-car	1858	Pullman	U.S.
Slide rule	1620	Oughtred	English

Invention	Date	Inventor	Nation
Soap, hardwater	1928	Bertsch	German
Spectroscope	1859	Kirchoff-Bunsen	German
Spectroscope (mass)	1918	Dempster	U. S.
Spinning jenny	1767	Hargreaves	English
Spinning mule	1779	Crompton	English
Steamboat, exp'mtl	1783	Jouffroy	French
Steamboat, exp'mtl	1785	Fitch	U. S.
Steamboat, exp'mtl	1787	Rumsey	U. S.
Steamboat, exp'mtl	1788	Miller	Scot.
Steamboat, exp'mtl	1803	Fulton	U. S.
Steamboat, exp'mtl	1804	Stevens	U. S.
Steamboat, practical	1802	Symington	Scot.
Steamboat, practical	1807	Fulton	U. S.
Steam car	1770	Cugnot	French
Steam turbine	1884	Parsons	English
Steel	1856	Bessemer	English
Steel alloy	1891	Harvey	U. S.
Steel alloy, high speed	1901	Taylor-White	U. S.
Steel, electric	1900	Heroult	French
Steel, manganese	1884	Hadfield	English
Steel, stainless	1916	Brearley	English
Stereoscope	1838	Wheatstone	English
Stethoscope	1819	Laennec	French
Stethoscope, binaural	1840	Cammann	U. S.
Stock ticker	1870	Edison	U.S.
Storage battery, electric	1812	Ritter	German
Stove, electric	1896	Hadaway	U. S.
Submarine	1891	Holland	U. S.
Submarine, even keel	1894	Lake	U. S.
Submarine, torpedo	1776	Bushnell	U. S.
Tank, military	1914	Swinton	English
Tape recorder, magnetic	1899	Poulsen	Danish
Telegraph, magnetic	1837	Morse	U. S.
Telegraph, quadruplex	1874	Edison	U. S.
Telegraph, wireless, high frequency	1896	Marconi	Italian
Telephone	1876	Bell	U. S.
Telephone amplifier	1912	De Forest	U. S.
Telephone, automatic	1891	Strowger	U. S.
Telephone, radio	1902	Poulsen and Fessenden	U. S.
Telephone, radio	1906	De Forest	U. S.
Telephone, radio, l d.	1915	Am. T & T.	U. S.
Telephone, recording	1898	Poulson	Danish
Telephone, wireless	1899	Collins	U. S.
Telescope	1608	Lippershey	Neth.
Telescope	1609	Galileo	Italian
Telescope, astronomical	1611	Kepler	German
Teletype	1928	Morkrum-Kleinschmidt	U. S.
Television, iconoscope	1923	V. Zworykin	U S.
Television, electronic	1927	P. Farnsworth	U S.
Television, (mech. scanner)	1926	Baird	Scottish
Thermometer	1593	Galileo	Italian
Thermometer	1710	Reaumur	French
Thermometer, mercury	1714	Fahrenheit	German
Time recorder	1890	Bundy	U. S.
Time, self-regulator	1918	Bryce	U. S.
Tire, double-tube	1845	Thompson	English
Tire, pneumatic	1888	Dunlop	Irish
Toaster, automatic	1918	Strite	U. S.
Tool, pneumatic	1865	Law	English
Torpedo, marine	1804	Fulton	U. S.
Tractor, crawler	1900	Holt	U. S.
Transformer, A.C	1885	Stanley	U. S.
Transistor	1947	Shockley, Brattain, Bardeen	U. S.
Trolley car, electric	1884 -87	Van Depoel & Sprague	U. S.
Tungsten, ductile	1912	Coolidge	U. S.
Turbine, gas	1899	C. G. Curtis	U. S.
Turbine, hydraulic	1849	Francis	U. S.
Turbine, steam	1896	C. G. Curtis	U. S.
Type, movable	1450	Gutenberg	German
Typewriter	1868	Sholes and Glidden	U. S.
Vacuum cleaner, electric	1907	Spangler	U. S.
Washer, electric	1907	Hurley Co	U. S.
Welding, atomic hydrogen	1924	Langmuir-Palmer	U. S.
Welding, electric	1877	Thomson	U. S.
Wind tunnel	1923	Munk	U. S.
Wire, barbed	1874	Glidden	U. S.
Wire, barbed	1875	Haisn	U. S.
X-ray tube	1916	Coolidge	U. S.
Zipper	1891	Judson	U. S.

Copyright Law of the United States

Source: Copyright Office, Library of Congress

An author, or other owner who derives his rights from the author, may obtain protection for a literary, musical, or artistic work by complying with the provisions of the copyright law (Title 17 of the United States Code). The law gives the copyright owner the exclusive right to print, reprint, publish, copy and sell the copyrighted work; to revise or adapt it; and, with certain limitations, to perform and record it. Applications for registration of claims to copyright are filed with the Copyright Office, Library of Congress, Washington, D.C. 20540. Application forms and information circulars covering various subjects are furnished by the Copyright Office free upon request.

Categories of Works

The copyright law provides that the application for registration of any work shall specify to which of the following classes the work in which copyright is claimed belongs:

(A) Books, including composite and cyclopedic works, directories, gazetteers and other compilations; (B) periodicals, including newspapers; (C) lectures, sermons and addresses prepared for oral delivery; (D) dramatic or dramatico-musical compositions; (E) musical compositions; (F) maps; (G) works of art, models or designs for works of art; (H) reproductions of a work of art; (I) drawings or sculptural works of a scientific or technical character; (J) photographs; (K) prints and pictorial illustrations including prints or labels used for articles of merchandise; (L) motion-picture photoplays; (M) motion pictures other than photoplays; and (N) sound recordings.

How Copyright is Secured

Between the time a work is created and the time statutory copyright is secured, it is protected while unpublished, by the common law against unauthorized copying or other use, without any action being required by the Copyright Office.

Copyright in a published work is secured by publishing the work with the required notice of copyright, and it is important that all copies published bear the notice. The law provides that the notice shall consist of either the word "Copyright," or the abbreviation "Copr.," or the symbol ©, accompanied by the name of the copyright owner. If the work is a printed literary, musical or dramatic work, the notice shall include also the year in which the copyright was secured by publication. For example: © John Doe 1972. In the case, however, of copies of works specified in classes F through K above, the notice may consist of the symbol © accompanied by the initials, monogram, mark, or symbol of the owner, provided that his name appears on some accessible part of the copies.

Promptly after publication, there should be sent to the Copyright Office, Library of Congress, Washington, D.C. 20540, two copies of the best edition of the work, together with an application for registration and a $6 fee.

Manufacturing Requirements

For books and periodicals to be copyrightable if they are by American authors, or by foreign authors who are domiciled in the U.S. at the time of first publication, the typesetting, printing, and binding of the copies used for first publication must have been done in the U.S. The only general exception to this rule is that a book or periodical in the English language manufactured and first published abroad may secure a 5-year ad interim copyright, provided that registration is made within 6 months of the date of first publication abroad. If ad interim copyright is secured, the importation of 1,500 copies is permitted. Books by American authors manufactured abroad may generally not be imported while they are under U.S. copyright protection, unless an Import Statement issued by the Copyright Office at the time of the ad interim registration is presented to U.S. Customs at the port of entry. Further information may be obtained from the Copyright Office.

Copyright for Unpublished Works

Statutory copyright may be had for certain classes of unpublished works by depositing in the Copyright Office one copy of the work, together with an application for registration and the $6 fee. Works for which registration may be made in unpublished form include those in classes C,

D, E, G, I, J, L and M, above. There are special provisions concerning what should be deposited in the case of 3-dimensional works of art and motion pictures; information about them is obtainable from the Copyright Office. NOTE: Certain kinds of material are not registrable in unpublished form. These include "book material" such as fiction, nonfiction, poetry, directories and catalogs, as well as manuscripts of articles, stories and other works that are to be first published as contributions to periodicals. Such works are, as mentioned above, protected by the common law against unauthorized use while unpublished.

Duration of Copyright

The original term of copyright endures for 28 years, measured from the exact date of first publication of the work; or in the case of works registered in unpublished form, from the date of registration. During the last (the 28th) year of the first term, the copyright may be renewed by filing in the Copyright Office an application for renewal and a fee of $4. If they are not received by the Copyright Office before the original term has expired, the work falls into the public domain and the copyright cannot be restored.

Fees

All copyright fees are established by law. Remittances should be in the form of checks or money orders and be payable to the Register of Copyrights. The schedule of fees follows:

Registration of copyright claims (including a certificate bearing the Copyright Office seal) all classes of works, $6.

For registration of a claim to renewal, $4.

Each additional certificate, $2.

Other certifications, including certifications of photocopies of Copyright Office records, $3.

For recording each assignment, agreement or other document of 6 pages or fewer, listing no more than one title, $5. For each page over 6 and each title over one, 50c.

For recording a notice of use of copyrighted music on mechanical instruments such as phonograph records, where the notice contains 5 titles or fewer, $3. For each title over 5, in a single notice of intention to use, 50c.

Searches: for each hour spent by the Copyright Office staff in searching the official records, $5.

Sound Recordings

The law has been amended by a recent act of Congress to permit copyright protection for certain sound recordings, provided they are fixed and first published with the prescribed copyright notice on or after Feb. 15, 1972. The notice required to secure copyright for sound recordings is the symbol ℗, the year date of first publication of the sound recording, and the name of the copyright owner. For example: ℗ 1972 Doe Records, Inc. Registration should be made promptly after publication. SPECIAL NOTE: Copyright for a sound recording protects against unauthorized reproduction of the same series of sounds; it is not a substitute for registration of the musical or literary work recorded.

International Protection

The U.S. has copyright relations with some 60 countries, under which works of American authors are protected in those countries, and the works of their authors are protected in the U.S. The basic feature of this protection is "national treatment," under which the alien author is treated by a country in the same manner that it treats its own authors. Relations exist by virtue of bilateral agreements, or through the Buenos Aires Convention or the Universal Copyright Convention. Legislation implementing the latter convention, which became effective Sept. 16, 1955, gives the works of foreign authors the benefit of exemptions from the manufacturing requirements of the U.S. copyright law, provided the works are first published abroad with a copyright notice including the symbol ©, the name of the copyright owner and the year date of first publication, and that the work either is by an author who is a citizen of a foreign country which belongs to the Convention or is first published in a foreign member country. Conversely, works of U.S. authors are exempt from certain burdensome requirements in particular foreign member countries.

Trademarks: How to Obtain and Protect Them

U. S. Govt. Bureaus have adopted trademark as a single word compounded from the former trade mark.

A trademark, as defined by Act of Congress, "includes any word, name, symbol, or device, or any combination thereof, adopted and used by a manufacturer or merchant to identify his goods and distinguish them from those manufactured or sold by others." Rights in trademarks are acquired only by use, which must continue if those rights are to be preserved. In order to be eligible for registration a mark must be in use in commerce which may be lawfully regulated by Congress.

Trademarks are registered on the Principal Register and the Supplemental Register of the U.S. Patent Office. "Coined, arbitrary, fanciful or suggestive marks, usually called technical marks, if otherwise qualified," may be registered on the Principal Register. A trademark that is merely descriptive of goods, or their regional origin, or is primarily a surname, is placed on the Supplemental Register.

The Trademark Act of 1946 provides that "For the purposes of registration on the supplemental register, a mark may consist of any trademark, symbol, label package, configuration of goods, name, word, slogan, phrase, surname, geographical name, numeral, or device, or any combination of any of the foregoing, but such mark must be capable of distinguishing the applicant's goods or services."

A trademark cannot be registered if it comprises immoral, deceptive or scandalous matter, or matter that may disparage or falsely suggest a connection with persons living or dead, institutions, beliefs, or national symbols. It cannot use the flag or coat of arms or other insignia of the United States, any state, municipality or foreign nation. It cannot use a portrait, signature or name of a living individual without his consent, or those of a deceased President of the United States without consent of his widow.

An application for registration must be filed in the name of the owner of the mark, who may submit his case or be represented by an attorney at law, or other person authorized to practice in trademark matters. A complete application comprises a written application, a drawing of the mark, five specimens or facsimiles and the required filing fee.

The Patent Office publishes a pamphlet, General Information Concerning Trademarks, which describes the way applications and drawings are to be prepared and gives sample forms for applications. The Patent Office, upon request, will supply forms for the registration of a trademark in the name of (1) an individual, (2) a firm, and (3) a corporation. If facilities permit, the Office will make drawings from the applicant's direction and at his expense. If the application is allowed, the trademark will be published in the Official Gazette so that anyone who considers that he will be damaged by the new mark may file his opposition in 30 days.

The Trademark Act of 1946 also provides for the registration of service marks, certification marks and collective marks. A service mark is a title, symbol or name used in sale or advertising of services to identify them. A certification mark is used by others than the owner to certify origin or quality, such as work by a union. A collective mark is used by members of a cooperative, an association or other group and indicates membership in a union or other organization. A digest of registered trademarks may be inspected at the Patent Office.

A trademark is registered for 20 years and may be renewed for periods of 20 years if still in use in commerce regulated by Congress, or if nonuse is due to special circumstances which excuse nonuse and is not due to any intention to abandon the mark. The fee for the original application is $35, and for the renewal is $25, with lesser fees for corrections, amendments, abstracts of title and other services.

The pamphlet, General Information Concerning Trademarks, is a general guide. Pamphlet copies of the Trademark Laws and the Trademark Rules of Practice of the Patent Office also are published. The Official Gazette, issued weekly, contains information concerning trademarks published for opposition, registered, and renewed. The first pamphlet is available at the U.S. Patent Office, Washington, D.C. For the others inquiries may be addressed to the Supt. of Documents, Government Printing Office, Washington, D.C.

Patents and How to Apply for Them

A patent for an invention is granted by the United States Patent Office to the inventor of any new and useful process, machine, manufacture, or composition of matter, or any new and useful improvements in these categories. The grant to the patentee is of "the right to exclude others from making, using or selling the invention throughout the United States" for the term of 17 years. A patent is also granted for certain distinct and new varieties of plants, also for 17 years.

Patents for new, original and ornamental designs for articles of manufacture may be obtained for 3½, 7 and 14 years, as requested by the inventor. The filing fee on each design application is $20; the issue fee is $10 for a 3½-yr. term, $20 for 7 years and $30 for 14 years.

Except in special circumstances, an application must be made by the inventor; if two are associated in the invention both must apply; if the inventor is mentally ill or dead, application may be made by the guardian or administrator of the estate. The specification must include a written description of the invention and of the manner and process of making and using it, and is required to be in such full, clear, concise, and exact terms as to enable any person skilled in the art to which the invention pertains, or with which it is most nearly connected, to make and use the same. The claims are full descriptions of the subject matter of the invention. A drawing is required by the statute in all cases which admit of drawings. The filing fee is $65, with $2 additional for each claim in excess of 10, and $10 additional for each claim in independent form in excess of one.

The Patent Office examines the application to determine whether the invention is new and useful and whether the application otherwise complies with the law. If the application is allowed, a notice is sent the applicant and the final fee of $100, plus $10 for each page or portion thereof of specification as printed and $2 for each sheet of drawing, is due within 3 months. The terms "patent applied for" and "patent pending" have no legal significance but falsely using this marking is punishable by a fine.

If the Patent Office rejects an application, the applicant may ask for reconsideration, giving reason; if rejected again he may appeal to the Board of Appeals of the Patent Office, and if rejected there, may go to the Court of Customs and Patent Appeals or file a civil action in the U.S. District Court for the Dist. of Col.

Under certain conditions a license must be obtained before an application for a patent can be filed in a foreign country. The Commissioner of Patents may order an invention kept secret if publication would hurt the national safety or defense. Copies of the Patent Laws, the Rules of Practice of the U.S. Patent Office in Patent Cases, and General Information Concerning Patents, can be obtained from the Superintendent of Documents, Government Printing Office, Washington, D.C. 20402.

Delegates from over 40 nations took part in Washington May 25-June 19, 1970, in a diplomatic conference on a Patent Cooperation Treaty. It was unanimously approved and was signed by representatives of 20 governments, including the United States, Great Britain, Germany, Canada and Japan, with many others expected to sign later. The treaty will simplify the filing of patent applications on the same invention in different countries by means of centralized filing procedures and standardized formalities.

Religious Information

Census of Religious Bodies in the United States

Source: THE WORLD ALMANAC Questionnaire and Yearbook of American Churches

Membership figures in the following table are the latest available. Some denominations submitted carefully compiled data while others approached the task more casually. Some membership figures were obtained by WORLD ALMANAC Questionnaire, others from the Yearbook of American Churches for 1973. The number of churches is given in parentheses.

Denomination	Members	Denomination	Members
Adventist Bodies:	**480,457**	Chs. of Christ in Christn. Union (244)	8,741
Advent Christian Church (400)	30,969	**Churches of God:**	**635,108**
Church of God (Abrahamic Faith) (124)	6,700	Ch. of God (Anderson, Ind.) (2,271)	152,787
Primitive Advent Christian Ch. (10)	600	Ch. of God (Cleveland, Tenn.) (4,095)	287,099
Seventh-day Adventists (3,278)	448,888	Church of God of Prophecy (1,561)	51,527
Amana Church Society (7)	735	Ch. of God, Seventh Day (7)	2,000
American Rescue Workers (46)	5,410	Ch. of God, Seventh Day (Denver) (56)	5,500
Apostolic Faith (44)	4,835	Churches of God in N. Amer. (Gen.	
Armenian Church of America (55)	300,000	Eldership) (364)	37,024
Assemblies of God (8,871)	700,071	The Church of God (1,925)	74,171
		The (Original) Ch. of God (70)	20,000
		The Church of God by Faith (135)	5,000
Baptist Bodies:	**26,315,235**	**Churches of God, Holiness** (32)	**25,600**
American Baptist Assn. (3,321)	870,300	**Churches of the Living God:**	**47,570**
American Baptist Convention (6,090)	1,472,478	Church of the Living God (276)	45,320
Baptist General Conference (636)	100,297	House of God, which is the Church of the	
Baptist Missionary Assn. of Amer. (1,408)	187,246	Living God, the Pillar and Ground of	
Christian Unity Baptist Assn. (5)	345	Truth (107)	2,350
Conserv. Baptist Assn. of Amer. (1,127)	300,000	**Church of New Jerusalem, Gen.** (33)	**2,661**
Duck River (and Kindred) Assns. of		**Congregational Christian Churches,**	
Baptists (81)	8,492	Nat'l Assn. of (341)	80,000
Free Will Baptists (2,300)	205,000	**Congregational Holiness Ch.** (147)	**4,859**
Gen. Assn. of Regular Baptist Chs. (1,426)	204,357	**Conservative Cong. Christian Conf.** (120)	**19,416**
General Baptists (845)	65,000		
General Six-Principle Baptists (8)	308		
Natl. Baptist Conv. of Amer. (11,398)	2,668,799	**Eastern Orthodox Churches:**	**4,112,623**
Natl. Baptist Conv., U.S.A. (27,396)	6,487,003	Albanian Orthodox Archdio. in Am. (13)	62,000
Natl. Primitive Baptist Convention (2,198)	1,645,000	American Carpatho-Russian Orthodox	
No. Amer. Baptist Gen. Conf. (246)	41,516	Greek Catholic Church (70)	108,000
Progressive Natl. Baptist Conv. (655)	521,692	American Catholic Church	
Regular Bapt. Chs., Gen. Assn. of (1,443)	211,598	(Syro-Antiochian) (5)	1,090
Separate Baptists in Christ (84)	7,496	Antiochian Orthodox Archdiocese of	
Seventh Day Bapt. Gen. Conf. (66)	5,376	Toledo, O. (28)	45,000
Seventh Day Bapts. (German, 1728) (3)	150	Antiochian Orthodox Christian Archdio.	
Southern Baptist Convention (34,441)	11,826,463	(92)	32,500
Berean Fundamental Church (50)	2,419	Armenian Apostolic Ch. of America. (34)	125,000
Bethel Ministerial Association (25)	4,000	Bulgarian Eastern Orthodox Ch. (13)	86,000
Bible Protestant Church (42)	2,254	Church of East and of the	
Bible Way Chs. of Our Lord Jesus		Assyrians (12)	5,000
Christ World Wide (350)	30,000	Greek Archdio. of N. and S. America (490)	1,950,000
Brethren (German Baptists):	**235,157**	Holy Orthodox Church in America (Eastern	
Brethren Ch. (Ashland, Ohio) (119)	16,357	Cath. & Apostolic) (4)	260
Brethren Churches, Natl. Fellowship		Holy Ukrainian Autocephalic Orthodox Ch.	
of (226)	33,392	in Exile (15)	4,800
Church of the Brethren (1,036)	181,183	Orthodox Church in America (370)	1,000,000
Old German Baptist Brethren (54)	4,225	Romanian Orthod. Episc. of Amer. (47)	50,000
Brethren, Plymouth (740)	37,500	Russian Orthodox Catholic Ch. in the	
Brethren (River):	10,025	U.S.A., Patriarchal Parishes (67)	152,973
Brethren in Christ Church (151)	9,550	Russian Orthodox Church Outside Russia	
United Zion Church (17)	875	(110)	60,000
Buddhist Churches of America (60)	100,000	Serbian Eastern Orthodox Church (51)	250,000
		Syrian Orthodox Church of Antioch.	
		(Archdio. of the U.S.A. & Canada) (8)	35,000
Christadelphians (850)	15,800	Ukrainian Orthodox Ch. of the U.S.A. (100)	100,000
Christian Catholic Church (6)	3,000	**Ethical Union, American** (23)	5,000
Christian Church of North America, Gen. Council		**Evangelical Christian Churches** (118)	21,652
(110)	8,500	**Evangelical Congregational Ch.** (160)	29,682
Christian Church (Disciples of Christ)		**Evangelical Covenant Ch. of America** (526)	68,428
(4,569)	1,352,211	**Evangelical Free Ch. of America** (562)	70,490
Christian & Missionary Alliance (1,154)	77,991	**Evangelistic Associations:**	**64,470**
Christian Nation Church, U.S.A. (16)	2,000	Apostolic Christian Ch. of Amer. (77)	9,160
Christian Union (113)	6,006	Apostolic Christian Ch. (Nazarean) (43)	4,000
Ch. of Christ (Holiness) U.S.A. (159)	9,289	The Christian Congregation (263)	51,310
Church of Christ, Scientist (2,369)		Pillar of Fire (61)	5,100
(membership not recorded)			
The Church of God (2,025)	75,890		
Church of God in Christ (4,500)	425,000	**Free Christn. Zion Ch. of Christ** (742)	22,260
Church of Illumination (14)	9,000	**Friends:**	**124,581**
Church of the Nazarene (4,681)	404,732	Friends United Meeting (481)	65,892
Church of Revelation (5)	750	Northwest Yearly Meeting of Friends (63)	6,386
Churches of Christ (17,000)	2,290,000	Ohio Yearly Meeting of the Friends Ch. (83)	7,632

Denomination	Members
Pacific Yearly Meeting of Friends (40)	2,624
Religious Society of Friends (Conservative) (21)	1,696
Religious Society of Friends (General Conference) (342)	32,124
Religious Society of Friends (Kansas Yearly Meeting) (89)	8,227
Holiness Church of God (28)	927
Independent Fundamental Churches of America (596)	89,392
Internatl. Church of the Foursquare Gospel (736)	101,477
Jehovah's Witnesses (5,794)	431,179
Jewish Congregations:	5,450,000
Union of Amer. Hebrew Cong. (686)	1,000,000
Union of Orthod. Jewish Cong. of Amer. (3,000)	3,000,000
United Synagogue of Amer. (850)	1,450,000
Latter-Day Saints:	3,435,627
Church of Jesus Christ (Bickertonites) (42)	2,353
Church of Jesus Christ of Latter-Day Saints (Mormon) (5,394)	3,227,790
Reorganized Church of Jesus Christ of Latter-Day Saints	205,484
Lutheran Bodies:	8,833,232
Lutheran Church-Mo. Synod (5,886)	2,886,207
The American Lutheran Church (4,821)	2,491,590
The Lutheran Ch. in Amer. (5,758)	3,023,219
Other Lutheran Churches:	
Church of the Lutheran Brethren of America (90)	8,960
Evangelical Lutheran Synod (Norwegian Synod) (89)	16,210
Protestant Conference (Lutheran) (7)	2,600
Wisc. Evangelical Lutheran Synod (995)	388,244
Mennonite Bodies:	163,433
Beachy Amish Mennonite Chs. (62)	4,069
Ch. of God. in Christ (Mennonite) (38)	6,204
Evangelical Mennonite Brethren (33)	3,753
Evangelical Mennonite Church (20)	3,285
General Conf. Mennonite Ch. (192)	36,314
Hutterian Brethren (29)	3,405
Mennonite Church (1,032)	89,873
Old Order Amish Ch. (368)	14,720
Old Order (Wisler) Mennonite Ch. (38)	8,000
Reformed Mennonite Church (12)	500
Methodist Bodies:	12,930,573
African Meth. Episcopal Ch. (4,500)	940,000
African M.E. Zion Ch. (4,800)	1,035,421
African Union First Colored Methodist Protestant Church (41)	8,000
Christian Meth. Episcopal Ch. (2,598)	466,718
Evangelical Methodist Church (147)	9,602
Free Methodist Ch. of N.A. (1,091)	65,167
Fundamental Methodist Church (14)	722
The United Methodist Church (39,626)	10,334,521
Primitive Method. Ch. U.S.A. (86)	11,945
Reformed Meth. Union Episc. Ch. (20)	5,000
Reform. Zion Union Apostolic Ch. (50)	16,000
Southern Methodist Church (150)	9,917
Union Amer. Meth. Episcopal Ch. (256)	27,560

Denomination	Members
Moravian Bodies:	62,967
Moravian Ch. in Amer., North Prov. (99)	34,041
Moravian Ch. in Amer., South Prov. (49)	22,784
Unity of the Brethren (32)	6,142
New Apostolic Church of N. Amer. (262)	20,195
Old Catholic Churches:	63,524
American Catholic Church, Archdiocese of N.Y. (16)	3,435
No. Amer. Old R.C. Church (121)	60,098
Open Bible Standard Churches (250)	30,000
Pentecostal Assemblies:	572,950
Elim Fellowship (70)	5,000
Internatl. Pentecostal Assemblies (55)	10,000
Pent. Assemblies of the World (550)	45,000
Pentecostal Church of Christ (43)	1,209
Pentecostal Ch. of God of Amer. (1,250)	125,000
Pentecostal Fire-Baptized Holiness Church (41)	545
Pentecostal Free Will Baptist Ch. (150)	13,500
Pentecostal Holiness Church (1,341)	72,696
United Pentecostal Church (2,500)	300,000
Polish Natl. Catholic Ch. of Amer. (162)	282,411
Presbyterian Bodies:	4,134,806
Associate Reformed Presbyt. Church (General Synod) (147)	28,443
Cumberland Presbyterian Ch. (854)	90,368
Orthodox Presbyterian Ch. (116)	14,300
Presbyterian Ch. in the U.S. (4,284)	951,788
Reformed Presbyterian Ch. Evangelical Synod (133)	14,834
Reformed Presbyterian Church of N. Amer. (69)	5,704
United Presbyt. Ch. in the U.S.A. (8,813)	3,029,369
Protestant Episcopal Church (7,506)	3,385,436
Reformed Bodies:	680,115
Christian Reformed Church (519)	286,094
Hungarian Reformed Ch. in Am. (27)	11,250
Protestant Reformed Chs. of Amer. (19)	3,187
Reformed Church in America (939)	375,546
Reformed Church in the U.S. (25)	4,038
Reformed Episcopal Church (75)	7,085
Roman Catholic Church (23,796)	48,390,990
Salvation Army (1,174)	335,684
The Schwenkfelder Church (5)	2,250
Social Brethren (32)	1,685
Spiritualists:	9,392
Int. Gen. Assembly of Spiritualists (80)	1,200
Natl. Spiritual Alliance of the U.S.A. (34)	3,230
Natl. Spiritualist Assn. of Chs. (204)	4,962
Triumph the Church and Kingdom of God in Christ (495)	54,307
Unitarian Universalist Assn. (1,019)	210,648
United Brethren:	27,043
United Brethren in Christ (296)	26,643
United Christian Church (12)	400
United Church of Christ (6,635)	1,895,016
United Holy Ch. of America (470)	28,980
Vedanta Society of New York (13)	1,000
Volunteers of America (574)	30,730
Wesleyan Church, The (1,864)	86,854

Religious Population of the World

Source: The 1973 Encyclopedia Britannica Book of the Year.

Religion	N. America[1]	S. America	Europe[2]	Asia	Africa	Oceania[3]	Total
Total Christian	224,139,000	176,731,500	415,097,000	85,654,000	107,530,000	14,955,000	1,024,106,500
Roman Catholic	126,205,000	171,125,000	192,142,000	46,121,000	37,890,500	4,150,000	577,633,500
Eastern Orthodox	4,100,000	50,000	92,445,000	1,510,000	25,000,000	80,000	123,185,000
Protestant	93,834,000	5,556,500	130,510,000	38,023,000	44,639,500	10,725,000	323,288,000
Jewish	6,281,900	769,800	3,996,280	2,664,170	200,500	77,000	13,989,650
Muslim	200,000	85,000	25,065,000	376,269,500	126,735,000	525,000	528,879,500
Zoroastrian				180,000			180,000
Shinto	25,000	60,000		60,000,000			60,085,000
Taoist[5]	15,000	18,000		51,850,000			51,883,000
Confucian[5]	90,000	100,000	50,000	305,175,000		40,000	305,455,000
Buddhist	300,000	160,000	20,000	267,185,000			267,665,000
Hindu	60,000	710,000	200,000	475,541,500	772,000	375,000	477,658,500
Totals	231,110,900	178,634,300	444,428,280	1,624,519,170	235,237,500	15,972,000	2,729,902,150

(1) Includes Central America and the West Indies. (2) Includes the USSR where it is difficult to determine religious affiliation. (3) Includes Australia, New Zealand. (4) Protestant figures include "full members" rather than all baptized persons and are not comparable to those of ethnic religions or churches counting all adherents. (5) Statistics for Confucianism and Taoism are undeterminable in China since the Cultural Revolution.

Headquarters of U.S. Religious Bodies

(Year organized in parentheses)

Advent Christian Church (1854)—Pres., Rev. Joe Tom Tate. Exec. Sec. Rev. J. Howard Shaw, Box 23152, Charlotte, N.C. 28212.

Adventists, Seventh-day General Conference of (1863)—Pres. Robert H. Pierson, Secretary, C.O. Franz, 6840 Eastern Ave., N.W., Takoma Park, Wash., D.C. 20012.

African Methodist Episcopal Zion Church (1796)—Senior Bishop, Herbert Shaw. Sec., Board of Bishops, Bishop F. S. Anderson, 741 S. 44th St. Louisville, Ky. 40211.

Antiochian Orthodox Archdiocese of Toledo, Ohio (1936), Archbishop Metropolitan Michael G. Shaheen, 532 Bush St., Toledo, Ohio 43604.

Antiochian Orthodox Christian Archdiocese (formerly, Syrian Antiochian Orthodox Church) (1894)—Head of Archdiocese, Metropn. Archbishop Philip (Saliba), 358 Mountain Rd., Englewood, N.J. 07631.

Armenian Church of America, Diocese (1889)—Primate, Most Rev. Archbishop Torkom Manoogian. Sec., Very Rev. Zaven Arzoumanian, 630 Second Ave., New York, N.Y. 10016.

Assemblies of God (1914)—Gen. Supt., Thomas F. Zimmerman. Gen. Sec., Bartlett Peterson, 1445 Boonville Ave., Springfield, Mo. 65802.

Augustana Evangelical Lutheran Church. See *The Lutheran Church in America*.

Baha'i Faith—About 6,500 communities, groups and isolated centers in the U.S. Sec., Natl. Spiritual Assembly, Glenford E. Mitchell, 500 Ober dam Rd., Wilmette, Ill. 60091.

B_____ , Sec., Dr. A. L. Patterson, 214 E. Broad St., Texarkana, Tex. 75501.

Baptist Association of America, Conservative (1947)—Pres., Rev. John Berentschot, Corr. Sec., Rev. Charles W. Jewitt. P.O. Box 66, Wheaton, Ill. 60187.

Baptist Churches in the U.S.A., Amer. (1907)—Pres., Rev. Dr. Gene Bartlett. Gen. Sec., Rev. Dr. Robert Campbell, Valley Forge, Pa. 19481.

Baptist Convention, Southern (1845) Pres., Owen Cooper. Exec. Sec., Dr. Porter Routh, 460 James Robertson Parkway, Nashville, Tenn. 37219.

Baptists, General (1611)—Moderator, Rev. James Murray Clerk, Vern Whitten, 1629 Stinson Ave., Evansville, Ind. 47712.

Baptist General Conference (1879)—Gen. Sec., Warren Magnuson, 1233 Central St., Evanston, Ill. 60201.

Baptist General Conference, North American (1865)—Moderator, Rev. Aaron Buhler. Exec. Sec., Dr. G. K. Zimmerman, 7308 Madison St., Forest Park, Ill. 60130.

Baptists, Free Will (1727) Moderator, Dr. J. D. O'Donnell Exec. Sec., Rufus Coffey, P.O. Box 1088, Nashville, Tenn. 37202.

Baptist Missionary Assn. of America (formerly **North American Baptist Assn.**) (1950)—Pres., Rev. Lynn Stephens, Gen Sec., Craig Branham, 716 Main St., Little Rock, Ark. 72201.

Buddhist Churches of America (1914)—Bishop Takashi Tsuji, 1710 Octavia St., San Francisco, Calif. 94109.

Bulgarian Eastern Orthodox Church (1909)—Most Rev. Andrey, Metropolitan Archbishop, 312 West 101st St., N.Y., N.Y. 10025.

Calvary Grace Christian Churches of Faith (1898)—Internatl. Gen. Supt., Rev. Dr. Herman Keck, Jr., P.O. Box 1674, Ft. Lauderdale, Fla. 33302.

Calvary Grace Church of Faith (1874)—Rev. A. C. Spern, Internatl. Gen. Supt., P.O. Box 333, Rillton, Pa. 15678.

Christian Church (Disciples of Christ) (1809) General Min ister and Pres., Dr. A. Dale Fiers, Box 1986, Indianapolis, Ind. 46206.

Christian Endeavor, International Society of (1881)—Pres., Dr. LaVerne H. Roos. Gen. Sec., Rev. Charles W. Barner, 1221 East Broad St., P.O. Box 1110, Columbus, Ohio 43216.

Christian and Missionary Alliance (1887)—President, Dr. Nathan Bailey. Secretary, Dr. R. W. Battles, 260 West 44th St., New York, N.Y. 10036.

Christian Reformed Church (1857)—Stated Clerk, Rev. William P. Brink, 2850 Kalamazoo Ave., S.E., Grand Rapids, Mich. 49508.

Church of the Brethren (1719)—Gen. Sec., General Board, S. Loren Bowman, 1451 Dundee Ave., Elgin, Ill. 60120.

Church of Christ, Scientist, (1879)—Christian Science Mother Church. The First Church of Christ, Scientist, in Boston, Mass. Pres., Roy Garrett Watson. First Reader, William M. Correll. Clerk, Charles Henry Gabriel, Christian Science Center, Boston, Mass. 02115.

Church of God (Anderson, Ind.) (1880)—Exec. Secy., W. E. Reed. Box 2420, Anderson, Ind. 46011.

Church of God, The (1903) General Overseer, Bishop Voy M. Bullen, 2504 Arrow Wood Dr., S.E., Huntsville, Ala. 35803.

Church of Jesus Christ of Latter Day Saints (Mormon) (1830)—Pres., Harold B. Lee. President of the Council of Twelve Apostles, 47 East South Temple St., Salt Lake City, Utah 84111.

Church of Jesus Christ of Latter Day Saints, Reorganized (1830)—Pres., W. Wallace Smith. Comm. of Communications, Elroy Hanton, Saints Auditorium. Independence, Mo. 64051.

Church of the Nazarene (1908)—Gen. Sec., B. Edgar Johnson, 6401 The Paseo, Kansas City, Mo. 64131.

Churches of Christ—No central organization. B. C. Goodpasture, editor, the Gospel Advocate, 1006 Elm Hill Rd., Nashville, Tenn. 37210.

Churches of God in North America, General Eldership (1825)—Pres., Rev. Darrell Prichard. Sec., Rev. Harry G. Cadamore, 1210 Carlisle St., Natrona Heights, Pa. 15065.

Congregational Christian Churches, General Council. See *United Church of Christ*.

Congregational Christian Churches, Natl. Assn. of (1955)—Moderator, E. W. Adams. Sec., Rev. John H. Alexander, 176 W. Wisconsin Ave., Milwaukee, Wis. 53203.

Ethical Union, American (Ethical Culture Movement) Pres., Jack Tourin. Administrator, Jean Kotkin, 2 West 64th St., New York, N.Y. 10023. Member of Int. Humanist and Ethical Union.

Evangelical Christian Churches (1966)—Dir., Dr. Richard W. Hart, P.O. Box 5935, Los Angeles, Calif. 90055.

Evangelical Lutheran Synod (Norwegian Synod) (1918)—Pres., Rev. G. M. Orvick. Sec., Rev. Alf Merseth, 106 13th St., S., Northwood, Ia. 50459.

Evangelical Methodist Church (1946)—Gen. Supt. Dr. Ralph A. Fleetwood. Gen. Sec., Rev. R. D. Driggers, 3036 N. Meridian, Wichita, Kan. 67204.

Evangelical and Reformed Church. See *United Church of Christ*.

Finnish Evangelical Lutheran Church (Suomi Synod) See *The Lutheran Church in America*.

Foursquare Gospel, International Church of the (1927)—Pres., Dr. Rolf K. McPherson. Sec., Dr. Herman D. Mitzner, 1100 Glendale Blvd., Los Angeles, Calif. 90026.

Free Methodist Church of North America (1860)—Sec., Board of Bishops. Bishop W. Dale Cryderman, Winona Lake, Ind. 46590.

Friends, General Conference of the Religious Society of (1900)—Chmn., C. Lloyd Bailey. Gen. Sec., Howard W. Bartram, 1520 Race St., Philadelphia, Pa. 19102.

Friends United Meeting (formerly **Five Years Meeting of Friends**) (1902—Presiding Clerk, Thomas R. Bodine. Gen. Sec., Lorton Heusel, 101 Quaker Hill Dr., Richmond, Ind. 47374.

Greek Orthodox Church of North and South America (1864)—Primate, the Most Rev. Archbishop Iakovos. Chan., V. Rev. George J. Bacopulos, 10 East 79th St., New York, N.Y. 10021.

Harvest Fields Missionary and Evangelistic Assoc.—Pres., Rev. Joseph Morse. 3030 Mayhew Rd., Sacramento, Calif. 95826.

Hebrew Congregations, Union of American—Pres., Rabbi Alexander M. Schindler. 838 Fifth Ave., New York, 10021.

Independent Fundamental Churches of America (1930)—Pres., Rev. Robert L. Gray, Exec. Dir., Rev. Bryan J. Jones, Box 242, Westchester, Ill. 60153.

Jehovah's Witnesses (1884)—Pres., Nathan H. Knorr, 124 Columbia Heights. Brooklyn, N.Y. 11201.

Jewish Congregations of America, Union of Orthodox—Pres., Harold M. Jacobs. Natl. Dir., Rabbi Reuven Savitz, 116 E. 27th St.

Latter-day Saints. *See Church of Jesus Christ.*

Lutheran Church, The American (1961)—Pres., Dr. David W. Preus. Sec., A. R. Mickelson, 422 So. 5th St., Minneapolis, Minn. 55415.

Lutheran Church in America, The (estab. June 28, 1962 by consolidating Am. Evangelical Lutheran Ch., Augustana Evangelical Lutheran Ch., Finnish Evangelical Lutheran Ch., and The United Lutheran Ch. in Am.)—Pres., Rev. Robert J. Marshall. Sec., Rev. George F. Harkins, 231 Madison Ave., New York, N.Y. 10016.

Lutheran Church-Missouri Synod (1847)—Pres., Dr. J. A. O. Preus. Sec., Dr. Herbert A. Mueller, 500 N. Broadway, St. Louis, Mo. 63102.

Lutheran World Federation, U.S.A. National Committee of the (formed Jan. 1, 1967, former National Lutheran Council) Sec., Rev. Dr. Carl Mau, 315 Park Ave., N.Y.C. 10010.

Mennonite Church (1863)—Moderator, A. Don Augsburger, Sec., Paul N. Kraybill, 10600 West Higgins Rd., Rosemont, Ill. 60018.

Methodist Church, The United (1784)—Council of Bishops Pres., Bishop Charles F. Golden. Sec., Bishop Ralph T. Alton, 1100 W. 42nd St., Indianapolis, Ind. 46208.

Moravian Church in America (Unitas Fratrum) (1740)—Northern Province: Hq., 69 West Church St., Bethlehem, Pa. 18018; Pres., Provincial Elders' Conf., Dr. J. S. Groenfeldt. **Southern Province:** Hq., 459 So. Church St., Winston-Salem, N. C. 27101; Pres., Provincial Elders' Conf., Dr. Clayton H. Persons.

Open Bible Standard Churches (1919)–Gen. Supt., Raymond E. Smith, Sec.-Treas., O. Ralph Isbill, P. O. Box 1737, Des Moines, Ia. 50306.

Orthodox Church in America (formerly **Russian Orthodox Catholic Ch. of Amer.**) (1794)–Primate, Metropolitan-Archbishop Ireney. Sec., V. Rev. Daniel Hubiak, 59 East 2nd St., N.Y., N.Y. 10003.

New Jerusalem in the U. S. A., General Convention of the (1782)–Pres., Rev. Ernest O. Martin. Rec. Sec., Mrs. Wilfred G. Rice, 31 Poole St., Brockton, Mass. 02401.

Pentecostal Church of God of America (1919)–Gen. Supt., Dr. R. D. Heard, 316 Joplin Ave., Joplin, Mo. 64801.

Pentecostal Church, United (1945)–Gen. Supt., Stanley W. Chambers. Gen. Sec., Cleveland M. Becton, 8855 Dunn Rd., Hazelwood, Mo. 63118.

Presbyterian Church, Cumberland (1810)–Moderator, Claude D. Gilbert. Stated Clerk, H. Shaw Scates, Box 4149, Memphis, Tenn. 38104.

Presbyterian Church in the U. S. (1861)–Moderator, L. Nelson Bell. Stated Clerk, Dr. James A. Millard, Jr., 341 Ponce de Leon Ave., N.E., Atlanta, Ga. 30308.

Presbyterian Church in the U.S.A., United (formed 1958 through merger of the **Presbyterian Ch. in the U. S. A.** and the **United Presbyt. Ch. of No. America)**–Moderator, Clinton M. Marsh. Stated Clerk, Ruling Elder William P. Thompson, 475 Riverside Dr., N.Y., N.Y. 10027.

Protestant Episcopal Church, The (1789)–Presiding Bishop, Pres. of Exec. Council, Rt. Rev. John E. Hines; Sec., Gen. Convention, Rev. Canon Charles M. Guilbert, Sec., Exec. Council, Rev. John F. Stevens. 815 Second Ave., New York, N. Y. 10017.

Rabbinical Alliance of America–Pres., Rabbi Abraham Gross, 156 5th Ave., New York. N. Y. 10010.

Rabbinical Assembly, The–Pres., Rabbi Gershon Levy. Exec. V. P., Rabbi W. Kelman, 3080 Broadway, N.Y.C. 10027.

Rabbinical Council of America–Pres., Louis Bernstein. Exec. V. P., Rabbi Israel Klavan, 220 Park Ave., South, N.Y., N.Y. 10003.

Rabbis, Central Conference of American–Pres. Rabbi David Polish. Exec. Vice Pres., Rabbi Joseph B. Glaser. 790 Madison Ave., New York, N. Y. 10021.

Reformed Church in America (1628)–Pres., Harry De Bruyn. Gen Sec., Rev. Marion de Velder, D.D., 475 Riverside Dr., N. Y. 10027.

Reformed Episcopal Church (1873)–President and Presiding Bishop, Rev. Howard D. Higgins. Sec., Rev. D. Ellsworth Raudenbush, 560 Fountain St., Havre de Grace, Md. 21078.

Reformed Presbyterian Church, Evangelical Synod (April 6, 1965, union of the **Reformed Presbyterian Church, General Synod** and the **Evangelical Presbyterian Church**)–Moderator, Dr. William S. Barker. Stated Clerk, Rev. Paul R. Gilchrist, 107 Hardy Rd., Lookout Mountain, Tenn. 37350.

Regular Baptist Churches, General Assn. of (1932)–Natl. Rep., Dr. Joseph M. Stowell, 1800 Oakton Boulevard, Des Plaines, Ill. 60018.

Romanian Orthodox Episcopate of America (1929)–Bishop, His Grace Valerian D. Trifa. Sec., Rev. Eugene Lazar, 2522 Grey Tower Rd., Jackson, Mich. 49201.

Russian Orthodox Church Outside Russia (1920)–Pres., Council of Bishops, Most Rev. Metropolitan Philaret, 75 East 93rd St., New York, N.Y. 10028.

Salvation Army, The (1865 in Eng., 1880 in America)–Natl.

Cmdr., Commissioner, Paul J. Carlson. Natl. Chief Sec., Col. Ernest W. Holz. National Headquarters, 120-130 West 14th St., New York, N. Y. 10011.

Seamen's Church Institute of N. Y. (1834)–Director, Rev. John M. Mulligan. Sec., R. Thornton Wilson, Jr., 15 State St., New York, N. Y. 10004.

Serbian Eastern Orthodox Church–Diocese for U. S., Canada, and Europe. Bishops: Most Rev. Dionisije and Iriney. Sec., Very Rev. Aleksandar Ivanovich, St. Sava Monastery, Libertyville, Ill. 60048

Serbian Eastern Orthodox Church in U. S. and Canada–Bishops: Rt. Rev. Firmilian, Midwest Diocese, 8347 W. Summerdale Ave., Chicago, Ill. 60656; Rt. Rev. Gregory, Western Diocese, 2511 W. Garvey, Alhambra, Calif. 91803; Rt. Rev. Sava, Eastern U.S. and Canadian Diocese, 5095 Broadview Rd., Richfield, Ohio 44286.

Spiritualists, International General Assembly of (1936)–Pres., Fred Jordan. Sec., Charles Doyle, 1809 E. Bayview Blvd., Norfolk, Va. 23503.

Synagogue Council of America –Pres., Rabbi Irwin M. Blank. Exec. V. P. Rabbi Henry Siegman, 432 Park Ave., South, New York, N. Y. 10016.

Ukrainian Orthodox Church of the U.S.A. (1919)–Metropolitan Mstyslav S. Skrypnyk. Box 495, South Bound Brook, N. J. 08880.

Unitarian Universalist Assn. (formed May 11, 1961 by merger of the **American Unitarian Assn.** and the **Universalist Church of America**)–Pres., Rev. Robert Nelson West. Moderator, Dr. Joseph L. Fisher. Sec., Russel F. Benson, 25 Beacon St., Boston, Mass. 02108.

United Church of Christ (formed June 25, 1957 through union of the **General Council of the Congregational Christian Churches** with the **Evangelical and Reformed Church**)–President, Rev. Dr. Robert V. Moss, Jr. Sec., Rev. Dr. Joseph H. Evans, 297 Park Ave. South, New York, N.Y. 10010.

United Israel World Union–Pres. & Chmn. of the Board, David Horowitz. Natl. Sec., Peter Moyle, 507 Fifth Ave., N. Y. N. Y., 10017.

United Sons & Daughters of True Holiness Assn. (1912)–Gen. Sec., Elder B. W. Shoffner, 109 Daniel St., Greensboro, N. C. 27401.

United Synagogue of America–Pres., Jacob Stein, Exec. V.P., Dr. Bernard Segal, 3080 Broadway, New York, N. Y. 10027.

Volunteers of America (1896)–Commander-in-chief, Gen. John F. McMahon. Natl. Field Sec., Col. O. P. Strickland. Hq., 340 West 85th St., New York, N. Y. 10024.

Wesleyan Church, The (1968) (organized through the merger of the **Pilgrim Holiness Church** and the **Wesleyan Methodist Church of America**)–General Superintendents, Dr. B. H. Phaup, Dr. M. H. Snyder, Dr. J. D. Abbott, Dr. V. A. Mitchell. Secy., D. Wayne Brown, Box 2000, Marion, Indiana 46952.

Wesleyan Methodist Church of America, The (1894)–*See The Wesleyan Church.*

Wisconsin Evangelical Lutheran Synod (1850)–Pres., Rev. Oscar Naumann. Sec., Prof. Heinrich J. Vogel, 11757 N. Seminary Drive 65W, Mequon, Wisconsin 53092.

World Council of Churches, U. S. Conference for the–Chmn., Dr. John Coventry Smith. Exec. Sec., Dr. Eugene L. Smith, 475 Riverside Dr., New York, N. Y. 10027.

Volunteers of America 78 Years Old

The Volunteers of America, a religious and social welfare organization incorporated Nov. 6, 1896, in New York, is democratic in constitution and semi-military in administration. It has a staff of more than 5,200, and operates 728 mission chapels and program centers throughout the U.S. It was founded by Generals Ballington Booth and Maud Booth. Present head is General John F. McMahon.

The religious work includes meetings for adults for worship embracing the rituals of the Lord's Supper, baptism and marriage. The philanthropic work includes family counseling, health camps, day care centers, hospices for

working girls, maternity homes and adoption services, homes for transients, clubs and homes for the aged, sheltered workshops and rehabilitation departments, group homes for emotionally disturbed children, and halfway programs for released prisoners, for alcoholics and for drug addicts. During the past 4 years the VOA has developed a $80,000,000 housing program designed to accommodate 120,000 low or moderate income individuals and families.

Advisory boards associated with each post provide links with the communities served. The boards are composed of representative citizens.

Procedures for Adopting a Child

The United States Government has published factual reports on procedures for adopting a child. They are entitled **When You Adopt a Child; Legislative Guides for the Termination of Parental Rights** and **Responsibilities and the Adoption of Children.** The Supt. of Documents, Gov. Printing Office, Washington, D.C. 20402, supplies information on how to procure these issues.

Leading Protestant Bodies in the United States

Baptists

The Baptist church was formed in England in 1609 as part of the separatist movement from the Church of England.

The first Baptist Church in America was founded in 1638 in Providence, R.I., by Roger Williams. National Organization began in 1814, and a Missionary Convention was formed to permit followers to express themselves in terms of missionary activities. Baptist bodies throughout the United States have a membership of 26,315,235.

American Baptist Churches in the U. S. A. (formerly Northern Baptist Convention, renamed American Baptist Convention in 1950, and renamed American Baptist Churches in the U.S.A. in 1973) was organized in 1907. Renamed in 1950. Churches, 6,090, membership, 1,472,478. Headquarters at Valley Forge, Pa. 19481. Agencies operating under this convention of Baptists include the American Baptist Board of International Ministries, American Baptist Board of National Ministries, American Baptist Board of Educational Ministries, and the Ministers and Missionaries Benefit Board, all at Valley Forge, Pa. 19481.

National Baptist Convention of America, org. 1880. Churches, 11,398, membership, 2,668,799. The General Organization and JL others, Sec., Rev. Robert Wilson 1008 Hogan St., Jacksonville, Fla. 32202.

National Baptist Convention, U. S. A., Int., founded in 1880, in Montgomery, Alabama, is the oldest and parent convention of Negro Baptists. Churches, 27,396; membership, 6,487,003. Pres. Dr. J. H. Jackson; Sec., Rev. T. J. Jemison, 915 Spain St., Baton Rouge, La. 70802.

Southern Baptist Convention. In 1845 Southern Baptists withdrew from the General Missionary Convention over the question of slavery and other matters and formed the Southern Baptist Convention, largest of Baptist bodies. Churches in all 50 states are related to the Convention. 2,526 missionaries serve in 76 countries. Churches, 34,441, membership, 11,826,463. Executive Committee, 460 James Robertson Parkway, Nashville, Tenn. 37219. Pres., Owen Cooper. Sec., Dr. Porter Routh. Boards include Sunday School Board, Nashville, Tenn.; Foreign Mission Board, Richmond, Va.; Home Mission Board, Atlanta, Ga.; Annuity Board, Dallas, Tex.

Church of Christ, Scientist

First organized in 1879, under the direction of Mary Baker Eddy, The Christian Science Church took its present form in 1892 as the Mother Church, the First Church of Christ, Scientist, in Boston, Mass. Today there are 3,195 branches in 54 countries. There are 2,369 Christian Science churches in the United States. Membership figures are not recorded. Christian Science regards the Bible as its ultimate authority and includes spiritual healing as part of its teachings.

The denomination supports radio and television programs, charitable institutions, and a world-wide Board of Lectureship. It also maintains the Christian Science Publishing Society which publishes the Christian Science Monitor and various religious periodicals. The affairs of the denomination are administered by the Christian Science Board of Directors, Christian Science Center, Boston, Mass. 02115. Pres., Roy Garrett Watson.

Disciples of Christ

The Christian Church (Disciples of Christ) is an American communion arising out of a concern for Christian unity expressed by Barton W. Stone in 1804 and by Thomas Campbell and his son Alexander, in 1809. The first churches were Cane Ridge in Ky. and Brush Run near Washington, Pa. The "Christians" of Kentucky and the "Disciples" of Pennsylvania and Virginia united in 1832. The first General Convention was held in 1849. A missionary society was formed. The movement is congregational in government. Churches in the United States and Canada number 4,609, membership is 1,356,914. The communion is served by the General Office of the Christian Church (Disciples of Christ), 16 general units, 38 regional bodies and 31 educational institutions, General Minister and Pres., Dr. A. Dale Fiers, Box 1986, Indianapolis, Ind. 46206.

Evangelical Churches

The Evangelical and Reformed Church. See United Church of Christ.

The Evangelical United Brethren Church. See United Methodist Church.

Latter-Day Saints

The churches of the Latter-Day Saints do not consider themselves Protestants because they had no part in the 16th century Protestant Reformation and consider themselves to be the "restored" Church of Jesus Christ.

The Church of Jesus Christ of Latter-Day Saints, often called the "Mormon" church, regards the Bible, the Book of Mormon, the Doctrine and Covenants, and the Pearl of Great Price as the word of God. The church was organized Apr. 6, 1830, at Fayette, Seneca Co., N. Y., by Joseph Smith, first president. After settling in Kirkland, O., and Independence, Mo., the members located in Nauvoo, Ill., in 1839 to escape persecution. Attacks by a mob led to the fatal shooting of Joseph Smith and his brother Hyrum while they were in the Carthage, Ill., jail for protection from the mob, June 27, 1844. Beginning in 1847 most members under the leadership of Brigham Young, moved by covered wagons across the Plains to Utah.

The church is divided into stakes, wards, branches and missions. Highest authority is the First Presidency, consisting of the President and 2 counselors, assisted by 12 apostles. Harold B. Lee is the 11th and current president. Churches 5,394, membership, 3,227,790. Hq. at 47 East South Temple St., Salt Lake City, Utah, 84111.

Following the death of Joseph Smith Jr. in 1844, the scattered congregations that did not leave for the Far West formed the **Reorganized Church of Jesus Christ of Latter-Day Saints,** with the founder's son, Joseph Smith 3d, as president. Membership 205,484 (U. S., foreign missions). H/Q Saints Auditorium, Independence, Mo. 64051.

Lutherans

The church was started in Europe during the Protestant Reformation by the followers of Martin Luther.

Lutheranism was introduced into the United States by Dutch colonists on Manhattan, later by Swedes on the Delaware, by Palatines in Pennsylvania and New York and by Salzburgers in Georgia.

The American Lutheran Church was organized during a constituting convention at Minneapolis, Minn., in April 1960, merging the American Lutheran Church, The Evangelical Lutheran Church, and United Evangelical Lutheran Church. The merger brought together Lutherans of Danish, German and Norwegian heritage. A fourth body, The Lutheran Free Church, joined with The American Lutheran Church in February 1963. The American Lutheran Church has 2,492,355 members. Headquarters at 422 So. 5th St., Minneapolis. Dr. David W. Preus is president. The 4,825 congregations are divided territorially into districts in the U. S. The foreign mission program involves 473 missionaries (including wives) on 13 fields in South America, Africa and Asia. The church's Board of Publication operates the Augsburg Publishing House, 422 So. 5th St., Minneapolis 55415.

Augustana Evangelical Lutheran Church. See The Lutheran Church in America.

The Lutheran Church-Missouri Synod was organized in 1847. It is the leader in the conservative group among the Lutherans with 6,162 churches and a membership of 3,057,237. The Synod is divided into 40 districts (35 in the U.S.; 3 in Canada; 2 in South America). The Synod conducts a world-wide mission program and fosters a system of 16 ministerial and teacher training colleges to staff its congregations and its 1,258 parochial schools.

Affiliated are the Lutheran Laymen's League, Lutheran Women's Missionary League, and Walther League (a young people's organization). Valparaiso University, Valparaiso, Ind., is supported and controlled by the Lutheran University Assn. Headq. for the Synod; 500 N. Broadway, St. Louis, Mo. 63102.

The Lutheran Church in America was organized June 28, 1962 by the consolidation of the American Evangelical Lutheran Church, the Augustana Evangelical Lutheran Church, the Finnish Evangelical Lutheran Church and The United Lutheran Church in America. With 3,155,097 baptized members, the body is the largest of the Lutheran churches in the United States. The Lutheran Church in America has 6,120 congregations, organized in 33 synods in the U. S., Canada, Puerto Rico, and the Virgin Islands. The headquarters, of the denomination is at 231 Madison Ave., New York, N. Y. 10016, and principal agencies are at 2900 Queen Lane, Philadelphia, Pa., 327 South LaSalle St., Chicago Ill., and 608 Second Ave. S., 2nd floor, Minneapolis, Minn.

Wisconsin Evangelical Lutheran Synod, organized in 1850. It has 995 congregations, 388,244 members. Formerly the second largest body of the Synodical Conference. Wisconsin withdrew from the Conference in August 1963.

Methodists

The name Methodist was originally given to Charles and John Wesley and several other Oxford students, in 1729. It is thought that the term was selected due to the exact and "methodical" manner in which they performed various engagements which a sense of Christian duty induced them to undertake. The Methodist movement was carried to America in 1760 by emigrants from Ireland. Methodist bodies in the United States (19) have a membership of approximately 13,000,000.

The United Methodist Church has 39,626 churches and 10,334,521 members. The present organization of The United Methodist Church was formed Apr. 23, 1968, in Dallas, Tex., by the union of The Methodist Church and The Evangelical United Brethren Church. The two churches shared a common historical and spiritual heritage. The Methodist Church resulted in 1939 from the unification of three branches of Methodism–the Methodist Episcopal Church, the Methodist Episcopal Church, South, and the Methodist Protestant Church. The Methodist movement began in 18th Century England under the preaching of John Wesley, but the so-called Christmas Conference of 1784 in Baltimore is regarded as the date on which the organized Methodist Church was founded as an ecclesiastical organization. It was there that Francis Asbury was elected the first bishop in this country. The Evangelical United Brethren Church was formed in 1946 with the merger of the Evangelical Church and the Church of the United Brethren in Christ, both of which had their beginnings in Pennsylvania in the evangelistic movement of the 18th and early 19th centuries. Philip William Otterbein and Jacob Albright were early leaders of this movement among German-speaking settlers of the Middle Colonies.

The supreme policy-making body of The United Methodist Church is the quadrennial General Conference. Principal agencies are in the following cities: New York, N. Y., Evanston, Ill., Nashville, Tenn., Washington, D. C., Dayton, O., and Lake Junaluska, N. C.

African Methodist Episcopal Church, incorporated 1816 under Pennsylvania laws, is second largest of the Methodist bodies. Churches, 4,500; membership, 940,000.

President, Board of Bishops, Bishop Joseph D. Cauthen, 2843 Princess Ann Rd., Norfolk, Va. 23540.

Presbyterians

Presbyterianism is a system of representative church government by presbyters, or elders. John Calvin (1509-1564) has been regarded as the founder of Presbyterianism. Presbyterians were among the earliest colonists of America. Their first church was established about 1640 and the first presbytery in 1706. Nine Presbyterian bodies in the United States have a membership of more than 4,000,000.

The United Presbyterian Church in the U.S.A., largest of the Presbyterian bodies, was formed on May 28, 1958 by a merger of the Presbyterian Church in the U.S.A. and the United Presbyterian Church of North America. It has 8,813 churches and 3,029,369 members. Offices of the General Assembly, General Assembly's Mission Council, Support Agency, Program Agency, and Vocations Agency, 475 Riverside Dr., N.Y., N.Y. 10027.

Presbyterian Church in the United States, which established a separate existence in 1861, is sometimes miscalled the Southern Church. Churches, 4,284, membership 951,788. Office of the Gen. Assembly, 341 Ponce de Leon Ave., N.E. Atlanta, Ga. 30308. Moderator, Dr. Charles E. S. Kraemer. Stated Clerk, Rev. James E. Andrews.

Protestant Episcopal Church

An American religious denomination directly descended from the Church of England. Brought to America by the Jamestown colonists in 1607. Separated from English church and adopted present name in 1789. Alternate name, "The Episcopal Church" was adopted in 1967. Churches 7,069; membership, 3,285,826. Headquarters of the Exec. Council, 815 Second Ave., N. Y. N. Y. Presiding Bishop, Rt. Rev. John E. Hines; Exec. Officer of Gen. Convention, Rev. Canon Charles M. Guilbert.

United Church of Christ

Formed in 1957 by a union of the General Council of the Congregational Christian Church and the Evangelical and Reformed Church. It is the first union in the United States of churches with different forms of church government–congregational and modified presbyterian–and different historical backgrounds Congregationalism was brought to America by both the Pilgrims of the "Mayflower" and the Puritans of the Mass. Bay Colony. Eventually it became the dominant form of church organization in New England. The Evangelical and Reformed Church was started in 1934 with the union of the Evangelical Synod of North America and the Reformed Church in the U. S.

A constitution for the United Church of Christ was declared in force in July, 1961. The denomination has 1,895,016 members in 6,635 local congregations. The United Church Board for World Ministries has 300 missionaries and other personnel at work in 30 countries. In the United States, the United Church of Christ is active in Christian education, church extension, health and welfare, mass communication, race relations, and social action. Headquarters of United Church of Christ, 297 Park Ave. So., New York, N. Y. 10010; Office of Communication, 289 Park Ave. So., New York, N. Y. United Church Board for Homeland Ministries, 287 Park Ave. So. United Church Board for World Ministries, 475 Riverside Dr., New York, N. Y. 10027.

National Council of Churches

The National Council of the Churches of Christ in the U.S.A. is a cooperative federation of 32 Protestant and Orthodox churches which seeks to advance programs and policies of mutual interest to its members. The NCC was formed in 1950 by the merger of 12 interdenominational agencies. The Council's member churches now have an aggregate congregation totaling approximately 42,000,000. The NCC is not a governing body and has no control over the policies or operations

of any church belonging to it. The work of the Council is divided into 3 Divisions–Church and Society, Education and Ministry, Overseas Ministries, and 4 commissions on Faith and Order, Regional and Local Ecumenism, Broadcasting and Film, Stewardship. The chief administrative officer of the NCC is Dr. R. H. Edwin Espy. The main office is located at 475 Riverside Drive, N.Y., N.Y. 10027.

Leading Protestant Denominations in Canada

Source: Corpus Directory and Almanac of Canada 1972, and the Director of Christian Service, Ontario Bible College, Rev. Charles A. Tipp.

Anglicans

The Anglican Church of Canada was established in the early 1700s, and its first bishop Charles Inglis was appointed in 1789. The General Synod, created in 1893, acts to co-ordinate the various activities of the Church, and usually meets biennially. It is made up of the Church's Archbishops and Bishops together with the elected clerical and lay representatives from the 28 dioceses. The Anglican Church has 2,409,068 members.

Baptists

The two largest Baptist churches are the Federation of Canada and the Fellowship of Evangelical Baptist Churches. The Federation has about 410,000 members in 4 subdivisions: the Baptist Convention of Ontario and Quebec; the Baptist Union of Western Canada; the United Baptist Convention of the Atlantic Provinces; and the French Baptist Union. The Fellowship consists of about 110,000 members. Other large Baptist organizations are the Baptist General Conference, the North American Baptist Conference, and the Canadian Southern Baptist Conference. The Baptist faith in Canada has 593,553 adherents.

Lutherans

The first large settlement of Lutherans in Canada was in Halifax in 1749. There are 3 main Lutheran bodies: the Evangelical Lutheran Church of Canada, the Lutheran Church-Canada (Missouri Synod), and the Lutheran Church in America-Canada Section. These bodies co-operate through the Lutheran Council in Canada. The Lutheran churches of Canada have 662,744 members.

Presbyterians

The Presbyterian Church in Canada is connected historically to the Church of Scotland. It is organized into 8 synods and 44 presbyteries, and has 818,558 members.

United Church

The United Church of Canada is the largest Protestant denomination in Canada with 3,664,008 members. It was established in 1925 as a result of a merger among the Methodist Church, the Congregational Churches, and 70% of the Presbyterian Church. The Canada Conference of the Evangelical United Brethren Church joined this union in 1968. The highest policy making body of the United Church of Canada is the General Council which meets biennially.

Headquarters of Religious Bodies in Canada

Source: Corpus Directory and Ontario Bible College.

Anglican Church of Canada (creation of General Synod 1893)—Primate, Most Rev. E. W. Scott, Gen. Sec. of the General Synod, The Ven. E. S. Light, 600 Jarvis St., Toronto 285, Ontario.

Antiochian Orthodox Christian Church (Syrian)—Rev. Father E. Hanna, 555-575 Jean Talon E., Montreal 328.

Apostolic Church of Pentecost of Canada (Inc.), The—Moderator Rev. D. W. Breen; Clerk, Mr. F. Assman, 1612 Adelaide St. East, Saskatoon, Sask.

Associated Gospel Church of Canada (Christian Workers Church of Canada 1922)—Pres., Rev. L. K. Redinger, 280 Plains Rd. W., Burlington, Ont.

Baptist Federation of Canada—Gen. Sec.-Treasurer, Rev. R. Fred Bullen, 91 Queen St., Box 1298, Brantford, Ontario.

Brethren in Christ Church, Canada Conference—Box 65, Sherkston, Ontario.

British Israel World Federation—Office Manager and Secretary, Mrs. D. Cunningham, 313 Sherbourne St., Toronto 2, Ontario.

Buddhist Churches of Canada—Bishop, Rev. Neuton Ishiura, 918 Bathurst St., Toronto, Ontario.

Byelorussian Autocephalic Orthodox Church Abroad—Rt. Rev. Bishop Mikalay, 524 St. Clarens Ave., Toronto 172.

Canadian Council of Churches, The (1938)—Pres., Rev. Dr. A. B. B. Moore, 40 St. Clair Ave. E., Toronto 7.

Canadian Jewish Congress—Exec. Vice-Pres., Saul Hayes, Q.C., 1590 McGregor Ave., Montreal 109, Quebec.

Christian and Missionary Alliance in Canada, The (1889)—District Superintendent for Eastern and Central Canada, Rev. W. J. Newell, 125 Panin Road, Burlington, Ontario; District Superintendent for Canadian Midwest, Rev. A. H. Orthner, 2521 Parliament Avenue, Regina, Sask.; District Superintendent for Western Canada, Rev. Ray McIntyre, 2528 Chicoutimi Drive, N.W., Calgary, Alberta.

Christian Church (Disciples of Christ), (All Canada Committee formed 1922)—Chairman, Mr. R. K. Leland, 130 Merton St., Suite 301, Toronto 7, Ont.

Christian Reformed Churches, The Canadian Council of—Rev. John Van Hormelen, R.R. No. 8, London, Ontario.

Church of Jesus Christ of Latter Day Saints (Mormons), (1832)—Pres., Alberta Stake, Mr. F. N. Spackman, Cardston, Alberta; Pres., Ontario-Quebec Mission, Mr. R.R. Spackman, 338 Queen St., E., Suite 205, Brampton, Ontario.

Church of the Nazarene (1902)—Dist. Superintendent of Canada Central District, Rev. N. Hightower, 38 Riverhead Drive, Rexdale, Ont., Chairman of Exec. Board, Dr. Herman L. G. Smith, 2236 Capitol Hill Crescent, N.W., Calgary 44, Alta.

Evangelical Fellowship of Canada—Pres., Dr. R. N. Thompson M.P.; Sec., Rev. C. A. Tipp, 67 Harbord St., Toronto 4.

Fellowship of Evangelical Baptist Churches in Canada (merging of **Union of Regular Baptist Churches of Ontario and Quebec,** and **Fellowship of Independent Baptist Churches** 1953)—Gen. Sec., Dr. J. H. Watt, 74 Sheppard Ave. W., Willowdale, Ontario.

Free Methodist Church in Canada (1880)—11 Kingsview Blvd., Weston, Ont.

Greek Orthodox Church—Ninth Archdiocesan District, Canada, Titular Bishop of Ancona, His Grace Theodosios, 27 Teddington Park Ave., Toronto 12.

Independent Holiness Church: (Merger of former Holiness Movement of Canada with The Free Methodist Church in 1958)—Pres. Rev. Murdo Campbell, R.R. 3, Metcalfe, Ont.

Jehovah's Witnesses (Branch Office established in Winnipeg 1918)—Presiding Minister, Mr. Kenneth A. Little, 150 Bridgeland Ave., Toronto 390, Ontario.

Lutheran Church of Canada, The Evangelical—Pres., Dr. S. T. Jacobson, 212 Wiggins Ave., Saskatoon, Sask.

Lutheran Church-Canada—Pres., Rev. H. A. Merklinger, 7205 Sharon Ave., Niagara Falls, Ontario.

Lutheran Church in America—Canada Section—Pres., Dr. Otto A. Olson, Jr., 211-228 Portage Ave., Winnipeg 12, Man.

Lutheran Council in Canada—a joint body of the three main Churches, Gen. Sec., Dr. J. M. Zimmerman, 9901-107 St., Edmonton, Alta.

Mennonite Brethren Churches of North America, Canadian Conference—Moderator, Rev. J. H. Quiring, Clearbrook, B.C.

Mennonites in Canada, Conference of — Moderator, Rev. Jacob Tilitzky, 2201 Queen Rd., R.R. #1, Abbotsford, B.C.

Mennonite Church, The (Old) — First Mennonite Church, 117 King St. W., Kitchener, Ont. Mod. Elect., Newton W. Gingrick, Tavistock, Ont.

Missionary Church, The — (An Anabaptist body) — Dist. Supt. (Ontario) Rev. Grant Sloss, Ste. 203, Frederick St. Plaza, Kitchener, Ont.

National Spiritual Assembly of the Baha'is of Canada (incorporated 1949) — Gen. Sec. J.D. Martin, 7290 Leslie St., Thornhill, Ont.

Old German Baptist Brethren in Canada — c/o Elder Amos Baker, Gormley, Ont.

Northern Canada Evangelical Mission — 58 18th St., Prince Albert, Sask.

Overseas Missionary Fellowship (1887) — Gen. Dir., Mr. Michael C. Griffiths, 1058 Avenue Road, Toronto 12, Ontario.

Pentecostal Assemblies of Canada, The (Incorporated 1919) — General Superintendent, Rev. Robert W. Tartinger, 10 Overlea Blvd., Toronto 17, Ontario.

Pentecostal Holiness Church in Canada — Gen. Supt., Rev. G. H. Nunn, 4 Hobart Dr. S., Willowdale, Ont.

Presbyterian Church in Canada (1875) — Moderator, Rev. Max V. Putnam, Genl. Assembly Clerks, Rev. E. A. Thomson, Rev. L. H. Fowler, Rev. D. C. Mac-Donald, 50 Wynford Dr., Don Mills, Ont.

Religious Society of Friends (Quakers), (Canadian Yearly Meeting of the Religious Society of Friends formed 1955) — Sec. Treasurer, Mr. F. Baslam, 60 Lowther Ave., Toronto 180, Ontario.

Reorganized Church of Jesus Christ of Latter Day Saints, The — Regional Administrator, Mr. Lyle W. Woodstock, 189 Eramosa Road, Guelph, Ontario. Regional Administrator, Harry W. Black, 2035 31st St. Avenue, S.W., Calgary, Alta.

Roman Catholic Church in Canada — Apostolic Pro-Nuncio, His Grace Archbishop Guido Del Mestri, Apostolic Nunciature, 724 Manor Ave., Rockcliffe Park, Ottawa 2, Ontario.

Salvation Army, The (1882) — Territorial Commander, Commissioner Clarence D. Wiseman, 20 Albert St., Toronto 7.

Seventh-day Adventist Church in Canada — Pres., Pastor J. W. Bothe, 1148 King St. E., Oshawa, Ontario.

Ukrainian Greek Orthodox Church in Canada — Primate, The Most Rev. Archbishop Michael, 7 St. John's Avenue, Winnipeg, Man., R2W 1G8.

Unitarian Church, Canadian (1842) — Pres. Mr. C. Peterson, 175 St. Clair Ave. W., Toronto 7, Ont.

United Church of Canada, The (1925) — Sec. of General Council, Rev. G. Morrison, 85 St. Clair Ave. E., Toronto 7, Ontario.

Protestant Episcopal Calendar and Altar Colors

White — From the First Service (First Vespers) of Christmas Day to the Octave of Epiphany, inclusive (except on the Feasts of Martyrs); on Maundy Thursday (for the celebration); from the First Service of Easter Day to the Vigil of Pentecost (except on Feasts of Martyrs and Rogation Days); on Trinity Sunday, Conversion of St. Paul, Purification, Annunciation, St. John Baptist, St. Michael, All Saints, Saints not Martyrs, and Patron Saints (Transfiguration and Dedication of Church).

Red — From First Vespers of Pentecost to the First Vespers of Trinity Sunday (which includes Ember Days); Holy Innocents, and Feasts of all Martyrs, Apostles and Evangelists.

Violet — From Septuagesima to Maundy Thursday; Easter Even; Advent Sunday to Christmas Eve, Vigils, Ember Days (except in Whitsun Week); and Rogation Days.

An alternate Lenten color scheme: **Violet** — From Septuagesima to the Tuesday before Ash Wednesday; **Lenten White** — From Ash Wednesday to the Saturday after Fourth Lent; and **Crimson** — from Passion Sunday (Fifth Lent) to Easter Even (all inclusive).

Black — Good Friday and at funerals. **Green** — All other days.

Days, Etc.	1973	1974	1975	1976	1977	1978	1979
Golden Number	17	18	0	1	2	3	4
Sunday Letter	G	F	E	DC	B	A	G
Sundays after Epiphany	6	4	2	5	4	2	5
Septuagesima*	Feb. 18	Feb. 10	Jan. 26	Feb. 14	Feb. 6	Jan. 22	Feb. 11
Ash Wednesday	Mar. 7	Feb. 27	Feb. 12	Mar. 3	Feb. 23	Feb. 8	Feb. 28
First Sunday in Lent	Mar. 11	Mar. 3	Feb. 16	Mar. 7	Feb. 27	Feb. 12	Mar. 4
Passion Sunday*	Apr. 8	Mar. 31	Mar. 16	Apr. 4	Mar. 27	Mar. 12	Apr. 1
Palm Sunday	Apr. 15	Apr. 7	Mar. 23	Apr. 11	Apr. 3	Mar. 19	Apr. 8
Good Friday	Apr. 20	Apr. 12	Mar. 28	Apr. 16	Apr. 8	Mar. 24	Apr. 13
Easter Day	Apr. 22	Apr. 14	Mar. 30	Apr. 18	Apr. 10	Mar. 26	Apr. 15
Rogation Sunday*	May 27	May 19	May 4	May 23	May 15	Apr. 30	May 20
Ascension Day	May 31	May 23	May 8	May 27	May 19	May 4	May 24
Whitsunday	June 10	June 2	May 18	June 6	May 29	May 14	June 3
Trinity Sunday	June 17	June 9	May 25	June 13	June 5	May 21	June 10
Sundays after Trinity**	23	24	26	23	24	27	24
First Sunday in Advent	Dec. 2	Dec. 1	Nov. 30	Nov. 28	Nov. 27	Dec. 3	Dec. 2

In the Protestant Episcopal Church the days of fasting are Ash Wednesday and Good Friday. Other days of abstinence are the 40 days of Lent, the Ember Days, and all Fridays of the year except Christmas Day and the Epiphany and any Friday which may fall between them. Ember Days (12 annually at about the beginning of the four seasons) are days of abstinence and prayer for ordinands and the increase of the ministry. They fall on the Wednesday, Friday, and Saturday after the first Sunday in Lent, the Feast of Pentecost (Whitsunday), September 14, and December 13. Rogation Days are the three days from Rogation Sunday (the fifth after Easter) to Ascension Day, and are days of solemn supplication for God's blessing upon the fields and harvests of the world.

The Episcopal Church is studying, and trying out, a revised calendar of the Church Year. If adopted, the following changes in the foregoing list will obtain: * These Sundays will no longer be observed. ** This listing will carry the title "Sundays after Pentecost".

Roman Catholic Days of Obligation, Fast and Abstinence, 1974

Days of Obligation in the United States are Solemnity of the Holy Mother of God, Jan 1; Ascension Day, May 23; Assumption of the Blessed Virgin Mary, August 15; All Saints' Day, November 1; Immaculate Conception of the Blessed Virgin Mary, Dec. 8; Christmas Day, December 25. Also all Sundays.

Days of Fast. Ash Wednesday, Feb. 27, and Good Friday, Apr. 12. The law binds Catholics from the completion of their 21st year to the beginning of their 60th; i.e., from the ages of 21 to 59.

Days of Abstinence: Ash Wednesday, Good Friday and other Fridays in Lent. The law binds Catholics 14 years of age and older.

Ash Wednesday and Easter Sunday

Year	Ash Wed.	Easter Sunday	Year	Ash Wed.	Easter Sunday	Year	Ash Wed.	Easter Sunday	Year	Ash Wed.	Easter Sunday
1901	Feb. 20	April 7	1951	Feb. 7	Mar. 25	2001	Feb. 28	Apr. 15	2051	Feb. 15	Apr. 2
1902	Feb. 12	Mar. 30	1952	Feb. 27	April 13	2002	Feb. 13	Mar. 31	2052	Mar. 6	Apr. 21
1903	Feb. 25	April 12	1953	Feb. 18	April 5	2003	Mar. 5	Apr. 20	2053	Feb. 19	Apr. 6
1904	Feb. 17	April 3	1954	Mar. 3	April 18	2004	Feb. 25	Apr. 11	2054	Feb. 11	Mar. 29
1905	Mar. 8	April 23	1955	Feb. 23	April 10	2005	Feb. 9	Mar. 27	2055	Mar. 3	Apr. 18
1906	Feb. 28	April 15	1956	Feb. 15	April 1	2006	Mar. 1	Apr. 16	2056	Feb. 16	Apr. 2
1907	Feb. 13	Mar. 31	1957	Mar. 6	April 21	2007	Feb. 21	Apr. 8	2057	Mar. 7	Apr. 22
1908	Mar. 4	April 19	1958	Feb. 19	April 6	2008	Feb. 6	Mar. 23	2058	Feb. 27	Apr. 14
1909	Feb. 24	April 11	1959	Feb. 11	Mar. 29	2009	Feb. 25	Apr. 12	2059	Feb. 12	Mar. 30
1910	Feb. 9	Mar. 27	1960	Mar. 2	April 17	2010	Feb. 17	Apr. 4	2060	Mar. 3	Apr. 18
1911	Mar. 1	April 16	1961	Feb. 15	April 2	2011	Mar. 9	Apr. 24	2061	Feb. 23	Apr. 10
1912	Feb. 21	April 7	1962	Mar. 7	April 22	2012	Feb. 22	Apr. 8	2062	Feb. 8	Mar. 26
1913	Feb. 5	Mar. 23	1963	Feb. 27	April 14	2013	Feb. 13	Mar. 31	2063	Feb. 28	Apr. 15
1914	Feb. 25	April 12	1964	Feb. 12	Mar. 29	2014	Mar. 5	Apr. 20	2064	Feb. 20	Apr. 6
1915	Feb. 17	April 4	1965	Mar. 3	April 18	2015	Feb. 18	Apr. 5	2065	Feb. 11	Mar. 29
1916	Mar. 8	April 23	1966	Feb. 23	April 10	2016	Feb. 10	Mar. 27	2066	Feb. 24	Apr. 11
1917	Feb. 21	April 8	1967	Feb. 8	Mar. 26	2017	Mar. 1	Apr. 16	2067	Feb. 16	Apr. 3
1918	Feb. 13	Mar. 31	1968	Feb. 28	April 14	2018	Feb. 14	Apr. 1	2068	Mar. 7	Apr. 22
1919	Mar. 5	April 20	1969	Feb. 19	April 6	2019	Mar. 6	Apr. 21	2069	Feb. 27	Apr. 14
1920	Feb. 18	April 4	1970	Feb. 11	Mar. 29	2020	Feb. 26	Apr. 12	2070	Feb. 12	Mar. 30
1921	Feb. 9	Mar. 27	1971	Feb. 24	April 11	2021	Feb. 17	Apr. 4	2071	Mar. 4	Apr. 19
1922	Mar. 1	April 16	1972	Feb. 16	April 2	2022	Mar. 2	Apr. 17	2072	Feb. 24	Apr. 10
1923	Feb. 14	April 1	1973	Mar. 7	April 22	2023	Feb. 22	Apr. 9	2073	Feb. 8	Mar. 26
1924	Mar. 5	April 20	1974	Feb. 27	April 14	2024	Feb. 14	Mar. 31	2074	Feb. 28	Apr. 15
1925	Feb. 25	April 12	1975	Feb. 12	Mar. 30	2025	Mar. 5	Apr. 20	2075	Feb. 20	Apr. 7
1926	Feb. 17	April 4	1976	Mar. 3	April 18	2026	Feb. 18	Apr. 5	2076	Mar. 4	Apr. 19
1927	Mar. 2	April 17	1977	Feb. 23	April 10	2027	Feb. 10	Mar. 28	2077	Feb. 24	Apr. 11
1928	Feb. 22	April 8	1978	Feb. 8	Mar. 26	2028	Mar. 1	Apr. 16	2078	Feb. 16	Apr. 3
1929	Feb. 13	Mar. 31	1979	Feb. 28	April 15	2029	Feb. 14	Apr. 1	2079	Mar. 8	Apr. 23
1930	Mar. 5	April 20	1980	Feb. 20	April 6	2030	Mar. 6	Apr. 21	2080	Feb. 21	Apr. 7
1931	Feb. 18	April 5	1981	Mar. 4	April 19	2031	Feb. 26	Apr. 13	2081	Feb. 12	Mar. 30
1932	Feb. 10	Mar. 27	1982	Feb. 24	April 11	2032	Feb. 11	Mar. 28	2082	Mar. 4	Apr. 19
1933	Mar. 1	April 16	1983	Feb. 16	April 3	2033	Mar. 2	Apr. 17	2083	Feb. 17	Apr. 4
1934	Feb. 14	April 1	1984	Mar. 7	April 22	2034	Feb. 22	Apr. 9	2084	Feb. 9	Mar. 26
1935	Mar. 6	April 21	1985	Feb. 20	April 7	2035	Feb. 7	Mar. 25	2085	Feb. 28	Apr. 15
1936	Feb. 26	April 12	1986	Feb. 12	Mar. 30	2036	Feb. 27	Apr. 13	2086	Feb. 13	Mar. 31
1937	Feb. 10	Mar. 28	1987	Mar. 4	April 19	2037	Feb. 18	Apr. 5	2087	Mar. 5	Apr. 20
1938	Mar. 2	April 17	1988	Feb. 17	April 3	2038	Mar. 10	Apr. 25	2088	Feb. 25	Apr. 11
1939	Feb. 22	April 9	1989	Feb. 8	Mar. 26	2039	Feb. 23	Apr. 10	2089	Feb. 16	Apr. 3
1940	Feb. 7	Mar. 24	1990	Feb. 28	April 15	2040	Feb. 15	Apr. 1	2090	Mar. 1	Apr. 16
1941	Feb. 26	April 13	1991	Feb. 13	Mar. 31	2041	Mar. 6	Apr. 21	2091	Feb. 21	Apr. 8
1942	Feb. 18	April 5	1992	Mar. 4	April 19	2042	Feb. 19	Apr. 6	2092	Feb. 13	Mar. 30
1943	Mar. 10	April 25	1993	Feb. 24	April 11	2043	Feb. 11	Mar. 29	2093	Feb. 25	Apr. 12
1944	Feb. 23	April 9	1994	Feb. 16	April 3	2044	Mar. 2	Apr. 17	2094	Feb. 17	Apr. 4
1945	Feb. 14	April 1	1995	Mar. 1	April 16	2045	Feb. 22	Apr. 9	2095	Mar. 9	Apr. 24
1946	Mar. 6	April 21	1996	Feb. 21	April 7	2046	Feb. 7	Mar. 25	2096	Feb. 29	Apr. 15
1947	Feb. 19	April 6	1997	Feb. 12	Mar. 30	2047	Feb. 27	Apr. 14	2097	Feb. 13	Mar. 31
1948	Feb. 11	Mar. 28	1998	Feb. 25	April 12	2048	Feb. 19	Apr. 5	2098	Mar. 5	Apr. 20
1949	Mar. 2	April 17	1999	Feb. 17	April 4	2049	Mar. 3	Apr. 18	2099	Feb. 25	Apr. 7
1950	Feb. 22	April 9	2000	Mar. 8	April 23	2050	Feb. 23	Apr. 10	2100	Feb. 10	Mar. 28

A lengthy dispute over the date for the celebration of Easter was settled by the first Council of the Christian Churches at Nicaea, in Asia Minor, in 325 A.D. The council ruled that Easter would be observed on the first Sunday following the 14th day of the Paschal Moon, referred to as the Paschal Full Moon. The Paschal Moon is the first moon whose 14th day comes on or after March 21. Dates of the Paschal Full Moon, which are not necessarily the same as those of the real or astronomical full moon, are listed in the table below with an explanation of how to compute the date of Easter.

If the Paschal Full Moon falls on a Sunday, then Easter is the following Sunday. The earliest date on which Easter can fall is March 22; it fell on that date in 1761 and 1818 but will not do so in the 20th or 21st century. The latest possible date for Easter is April 25; it fell on that date in 1943 and will do so next in 2038.

Lent begins on Ash Wednesday, which comes 40 days previous to Easter Sunday, not counting Sundays. Originally it was a period of but 40 hours. Later it comprised 30 days of fasting, omitting all the Sundays and also all the Saturdays except one. Pope Gregory added Ash Wednesday to the fast, together with the remainder of that week.

The last seven days of Lent constitute Holy Week, beginning with Palm Sunday. Passion Week precedes Holy Week. The last Thursday—Maundy Thursday—commemorates the institution of the Eucharist.

The following day, Good Friday, commemorates the day of the crucifixion. Mohammedans celebrate Friday as the day of Adam's creation.

Easter is the chief festival of the Christian year, commemorating the resurrection of Christ. It occurs about the same time as the ancient heathen Roman celebration of the Vernal Equinox, the arrival of Spring. In the second century, A.D., Easter Day was among Christians in Asia Minor, the 14th of Nisan, the seventh month of the Jewish calendar. The Christians in Europe observed the nearest Sunday.

Date of Paschal Full Moon, 1900-2199

The Golden Number, used in the table, is greater by unity (one) than the remainder obtained upon dividing the given year by 19. For example, when dividing 1974 by 19, one obtains a remainder of 17. Adding 1 gives 18 as the Golden Number for the year 1974. From the table, then the date of the Paschal Full Moon is Apr. 7, 1974. This being a Sunday, the date of Easter is the following Sunday, Apr. 14.

Golden Number	Date	Golden Number	Date	Golden Number	Date	Golden Number	Date
1	April 14	6	April 18	11	Mar. 25	16	Mar. 30
2	April 3	7	April 8	12	April 13	17	April 17
3	Mar. 23	8	Mar. 28	13	April 2	18	April 7
4	April 11	9	April 16	14	Mar. 22	19	Mar. 27
5	Mar. 31	10	April 5	15	April 10		

Active Bishops of the Protestant Episcopal Church

Source: Rt. Rev. Scott Field Bailey, Sec., House of Bishops, 520 San Jacinto St., Houston, Tex. 77002
    PRESIDING BISHOP: Rt. Rev. John Elbridge Hines, 815 Second Ave., N.Y.C. 10017
Executive Council: Roger W. Blanchard, Ex. Vice-President of Executive Council; David E. Richards, Nat. Coordinator for House of Bishops Comm. on Pastoral Development; Clarence C. Hobgood, Suffragan Bishop to Armed Forces. Edmond L. Browning, Bishop of the Convocation of Episcopal Churches in Europe.

(M) Missionary Bishop; (C) Coadjutor; (S) Suffragan

Alabama: Furman C. Stough, Birmingham.
Alaska: William J. Gordon, Jr., Fairbanks.
Albany (N.Y.): Allen W. Brown, Charles B. Persell (S).
Arizona: Joseph M. Harte, Phoenix.
Arkansas: Christoph Keller, Little Rock.
Atlanta (Ga.): Bennet J. Sims, Milton L. Wood (S).
Bethlehem (Pa.): Lloyd E. Gressle.
California: C. K. Myers, G. R. Millard (S), San Fran.
    Northern California: Clarence R. Haden, Jr., Edward M. McNair (S), Sacramento.
Central Gulf Coast: George M. Murray.
Costa Rica: Jose Antonio Ramos (M), San Jose.
Chicago: J. W. Montgomery, Quinton E. Primo (S).
Colombia, South America: William A. Franklin (M), Bogota.
Colorado: William C. Frey, Denver.
Connecticut: Joseph Warren Hutchens, Morgan Porteus (S).
Dallas (Tex.): A. Donald Davies, Theodore H. McCrea (S).
Delaware: William H. Mead, Wilmington.
Dominican Republic: Telesford A. Issac (M), Santo Domingo.
East Carolina: Hunley A. Elebash, Wilmington, N.C.
Easton (Md): George A. Taylor.
Eau Claire (Wis.): Stanley Atkins.
Ecuador: Adrian D. Caceres (M).
Erie (Pa.): William Crittenden.
Florida: Hamilton West, Jacksonville.
    Central Florida: William H. Folwell, Winter Park.
    Southeast Florida: James L. Duncan, Miami.
    Southwest Florida: William L. Hargrave, St. Petersburg.
Fond du Lac (Wis.): William H. Brady.
Georgia: Geo. Paul Reeves, Savannah.
Guatemala: Anselmo Carral (M).
Haiti: Luc Anatole Jacques Garnier (M).
Hawaii: Edwin L. Hanchett.
Idaho: Hanford L. King Jr., Boise.
Indianapolis: John P. Craine.
    Northern Indiana: William C. R. Sheridan.
Iowa: Walter C. Righter, Des Moines.
Kansas: Edward C. Turner, Topeka.
    Western Kansas: William Davidson, Salina.
Kentucky: C. Gresham Marmion Jr., David B. Reed (C).
Lexington (Ky.): Addison Hosea.
Liberia: George D. Browne (M), Monrovia.
Long Island: Jonathan G. Sherman, Charles W. MacLean (S), R. B. Martin (S), Brooklyn, N.Y.
Los Angeles: Francis Bloy, Robert C. Rusack (C).
Louisiana: Iveson B. Noland, New Orleans.
Maine: Frederick B. Wolf, Portland.
Maryland: D. K. Leighton, Sr. Baltimore, William J. Cox (S).
Massachusetts: Boston, J. M. Burgess, Morris F. Arnold (S).
    Western Mass.: Alexander Stewart, Springfield.
Mexico: Jose G. Saucedo (M), Mexico City.
    Northern: Leonardo Romero (M), Monterey.
    Western: Melchor Saucedo (M), Guadalajara.
Michigan: H. Coleman McGehee Jr., Detroit.
    Northern Michigan: Samuel J. Wylie, Menominee.
    Western Michigan: Charles E. Bennison, Kalamazoo.
Milwaukee: Donald H. V. Hallock.
Minnesota: P. F. McNairy, Minn.
Mississippi: John Maury Allin.

Missouri: George L. Cadigan, St. Louis.
    West Missouri: Edward R. Welles, Edward A. Vogel (C).
Montana: Jackson E. Gilliam, Helena.
Nebraska: Robert P. Varley, Omaha.
Nevada: Wesley Frensdorff, Reno.
New Hampshire: Philip A. Smith, Concord.
New Jersey: A. L. Banyard, A. W. Van Duzer (S), Trenton.
New Mexico and S.W. Texas: Richard M. Trelease Jr., Albuquerque.
New York: Paul Moore, Jr., J. Stuart Wetmore (S), N.Y.C.
    Central New York: Ned Cole, Jr., Syracuse.
    Western New York: Harold B. Robinson, Buffalo.
Newark (N.J.): Leland Stark, George E. Rath (C).
Nicaragua: G. Edward Haynsworth (M).
North Carolina: Thomas A. Fraser, Jr., Raleigh, W. Moultrie Moore, Jr. (S).
    Western North Carolina: M. George Henry, Asheville, N.C.
North Dakota: George T. Masuda, Fargo.
Ohio: John H. Burt, Cleveland.
    Southern Ohio: John M. Krumm, Cincinnati.
Oklahoma: Chilton Powell, Frederick W. Putnam, Jr. (S), Oklahoma City.
Olympia, Wash.: Ivol I. Curtis, Seattle.
Oregon: James W. F. Carman, Hal R. Gross (S), Portland.
    Eastern Oregon: William B. Spofford, Bend.
Panama Canal Zone: Lemuel B. Shirley (M), Balboa.
Pennsylvania: Robert L. DeWitt, Philadephia.
    Central: Dean T. Stevenson, Harrisburg.
Philippines: Central—Benito C. Cabanban (M).
    Northern: Edward G. Longid (M).
    Southern: Constancio B. Manguramas (M).
Pittsburgh: Robert Appleyard.
Puerto Rico: Francisco Reus-Froylan, Santurce.
Quincy (Ill.): William Lickfield.
Rhode Island: Frederick H. Belden, Providence.
Rochester (N.Y.): Robt. R. Spears, Jr.
San Joaquin (Calif.): Victor M. Rivera, Fresno.
South Carolina: Gray Temple, Charleston.
    Upper South Carolina: George M. Alexander, Columbia.
South Dakota: Walter H. Jones, Harold S. Jones (S).
Spokane (Wash.): John R. Wyatt.
Springfield (Ill.): Albert W. Hillestad.
Taiwan: James T. Pong (M).
Tennessee: John Vander Horst, Nashville; William E. Sanders (C), Knoxville, William F. Gates Jr., (S), Memphis.
Texas: J. Milton Richardson, Houston; Scott F. Bailey (S), Houston.
    Northwest Texas: Willis R. Henton, Lubbock.
    West Texas: H. C. Gosnell, R. Earl Dicus (S), San Antonio.
Utah: Edgar O. Charles, Salt Lake City.
Vermont: Harvey D. Butterfield, Burlington.
Virgin Islands: Edward M. Turner, St. Thomas.
Virginia: Robert F. Gibson, Jr., Robert B. Hall (C), Philip A. Smith (S), Richmond.
    Southern Virginia: David S. Rose, Petersburg.
    Southwestern Virginia: William H. Marmion, Roanoke.
Washington (D.C.): W. F. Creighton, John T. Walker (S).
West Virginia: Wilburn C. Campbell, Charleston, Robt. P. Atkinson (C).
Wyoming: David R. Thornberry, Laramie.

The three Missionary Districts of Central, Southern and Southwestern Brazil became an independent branch of the Anglican Communion in 1965 fulfilling the action of the General Convention of 1964.

The World Council of Churches

The World Council of Churches is a fellowship of 263 Protestant, Anglican, Orthodox and Old Catholic churches from 90 countries and territories throughout the world. It was founded in Amsterdam in 1948 to promote Christian unity and to facilitate cooperation in mission work, doctrinal study and service projects such as aid to refugees. The Council has no judicial powers over its member churches. Denominations belonging to the Council have an estimated 400,000,000 members. The Roman Catholic Church is not a Council member, but increasingly cooperates in joint activities with the Council, particu-

larly in the areas of theological studies, relief work, development, justice and peace. World Council Assemblies were held in 1948 (Amsterdam), 1954 (Evanston, Ill.), 1961 (New Delhi), 1968 (Uppsala, Sweden). The Central Committee, policy making body of the WCC between assemblies met in the Netherlands Aug. 13-23, 1972. World headquarters of the Council are in Geneva, Switzerland where the offices of Gen. Sec., Dr. Philip A. Potter are located. The Council's New York office is located at 475 Riverside Drive, New York, N.Y. 10027.

Bishops of the United Methodist Church

Source: United Methodist Communications, 475 Riverside Drive, New York, N.Y. 10027

President: Bishop Charles F. Golden, Los Angeles, Calif.; President-designate, Bishop Dwight E. Loder, Detroit, Mich.; Secretary, Bishop Ralph T. Alton, 1100 W. 42nd Street, Indianapolis, Ind. 46208.

Allen, L. Scott, Knoxville, Tennessee
Alton, Ralph T., Indianapolis, Indiana
Armstrong, A. James, Aberdeen, South Dakota
Ault, James M., Philadelphia, Pennsylvania
Blackburn, Robert M., Raleigh, North Carolina
Borgen, Ole E., Stockholm, Sweden
Cannon, William R., Atlanta, Georgia
Carleton, Alsie H., Albuquerque, New Mexico
Carroll, Edward G., Boston, Massachusetts
Choy, Wilbur W., Seattle, Washington
Clymer, Wayne K., Minneapolis, Minnesota
Copeland, Kenneth W., Houston, Texas
Crutchfield, Finis A., New Orleans, Louisiana
de Carvalho, Emilio, Luanda, Angola
DeWitt, Jesse R., Sun Prairie, Wisconsin
Dixon, Ernest T., Topeka, Kansas
Ensley, F. Gerald, Columbus, Ohio
Finger, H. Ellis, Jr., Nashville, Tennessee
Frank, Eugene M., Little Rock, Arkansas
Golden, Charles F., Los Angeles, California
Goodrich, Robert E., Jr., St. Louis, Missouri
Goodson, W. Kenneth, Richmond, Virginia
Haertel, Armin, Dresden, Germany
Holter, Don W., Lincoln, Nebraska
Hunt, Earl G., Jr., Charlotte, North Carolina
Joshi, Ram Dutt, Bombay, India
Kulah, Francis E., Canton, Ohio
Lance, Joseph R., Lucknow, India
Loder, Dwight E., Detroit, Michigan
Mathews, James K., Washington, D.C.

McDavid, Joel D., Lakeland, Florida
Milhouse, Paul W., Oklahoma City, Oklahoma
Mitchell, Eric A., Delhi, India
Muzorewa, Abel T., Salisbury, Rhodesia
Nichols, Roy C., Pittsburgh, Pennsylvania
Onema, Fama S., Lodja Sakuru, Zaire
Pagura, Frederico, San Jose, Costa Rica
Peter, M. Elia, Hyderabad, India
Robertson, Frank L., Louisville, Kentucky
Sanders, Carl J., Birmingham, Alabama
Schaefer, Franz W., Zurich, Switzerland
*Short, Roy H., Nashville, Tennessee
Slater, O. Eugene, San Antonio, Texas
Sommer, C. Ernst, Frankfurt, Germany
Stokes, Mack B., Jackson, Mississippi
Stowe, W. McFerrin, Dallas, Texas
Stuart, R. Marvin, San Francisco, California
Taylor, Prince A., Jr., Princeton, New Jersey
Thomas, James S., Des Moines, Iowa
Tuell, Jack M., Portland, Oregon
Tullis, Edward L., Columbia, South Carolina
Ward, W. Ralph, New York, New York
Warman, John B., Harrisburg, Pennsylvania
Warner, Bennie D., Monrovia, Liberia
Washburn, Paul A., Chicago, Illinois
Webb, Lance, Springfield, Illinois
Wertz, D. Frederick, Charleston, West Virginia
Wheatley, Melvin E., Denver, Colorado
Yeakel, Joseph H., Syracuse, New York
Zunguze, Escrivao A., Lourenco Marques, Mozambique

* Interim administrator of the Baguio and Manila Areas in the Philippines.

The Ten Commandments

The Ten Commandments are an integral part of the Judaeo-Christian ethical system and represent the divine law, engraved on two stone tablets and given to Moses by God atop Mt. Sinai. Two varying versions of the Ten Commandments, or Decalogue, appear in the Bible. One is in Exodus 20, the other in Deuteronomy 5. The numbering of the Commandments differs in various religions. The following text is that of Exodus 20 as it appears in the Holy Bible, Revised Standard Version:

1—I am the Lord your God, who brought you out of the land of Egypt, out of the house of bondage. You shall have no other gods before me.

2—You shall not make for yourself a graven image, or any likeness of anything that is in heaven above, or that is in the earth beneath, or that is in the water under the earth; you shall not bow down to them or serve them; for I the Lord your God am a jealous God, visiting the iniquity of the fathers upon the children to the third and the fourth generation of those who hate me, but showing steadfast love to thousands of those who love me and keep my commandments.

3—You shall not take the name of the Lord your God in vain; for the Lord will not hold him guiltless who takes his name in vain.

4—Remember the sabbath day, to keep it holy. Six days you shall labor, and do all your work; but the seventh day is a sabbath to the Lord your God; in it you shall not do any work, you, or your son, or your daughter, your manservant, or your maidser-

vant, or your cattle, or the sojourner who is within your gates; for in six days the Lord made heaven and earth, the sea, and all that is in them, and rested the seventh day; therefore the Lord blessed the sabbath day and hallowed it.

5—Honor your father and your mother, that your days may be long in the land which the Lord your God gives you.

6—You shall not kill.

7—You shall not commit adultery.

8—You shall not steal.

9—You shall not bear false witness against your neighbor.

10—You shall not covet your neighbor's house; you shall not covet your neighbor's wife, or his manservant, or his maidservant, or his ox, or his ass, or anything that is your neighbor's.

World Bible Boom

The worldwide organization of United Bible Societies reported that 218,429,595 Bibles or parts of Bibles were distributed in 1972, a 27.6% increase over the 171,116,543 distributed in 1971. The 55 affiliated national publishing, translating

and distributing groups handed out 5,519,909 whole Bibles and 14,255,000 Testaments. Distributions of portions.—a complete book or more—reached 31,483,422. The bulk of distributions, 167,070,554, consisted of selections of short passages.

Chronological List of Popes

Source: Annuario Pontificio. Table lists year of consecration of each Pope.
The Roman Catholic Church names the Apostle Peter as founder of the Church in Rome. He arrived there C. 42, was martyred there C. 67, and raised to sainthood.

The Pope's temporal title is: Sovereign of the State of Vatican City.

The Pope's spiritual titles are: Bishop of Rome, Vicar of Jesus Christ, Successor of St. Peter, Prince of the Apostles, Supreme Pontiff of the Universal Church, Patriarch of the West, Primate of Italy, Archbishop and Metropolitan of the Roman Province and Sovereign of the State of Vatican City.

Anti-Popes are in *Italics*. Anti-Popes were illegitimate claimants of or pretenders to the papal throne.

Year	Name of Pope	Year	Name of Pope	Year	Name of Pope	Year	Name of Pope
See above	St. Peter	615	St. Deusdedit	974	Benedict VII	1305	Clement V
67	St. Linus		or Adeodatus I	983	John XIV	1316	John XXII
76	St. Anacletus or	619	Boniface V	985	John XV⁺	1328	*Nicholas V*
	Cletus	625	Honorius I	996	Gregory V	1334	Benedict XII
88	St. Clement I	640	Severinus	997	*John XVI*	1342	Clement VI
97	St. Evaristus	640	John IV	999	Sylvester II	1352	Innocent VI
105	St. Alexander I	642	Theodore I	1003	John XVII	1362	Urban V
115	St. Sixtus I	649	St. Martin I	1004	John XVIII	1370	Gregory XI
125	St. Telesphorus	654	St. Eugene I	1009	Sergius IV	1378	Urban VI
136	St. Hyginus	657	St. Vitalian	1012	Benedict VIII	1378	*Clement VII*
140	St. Pius I	672	Adeodatus II	1012	*Gregory*	1389	Boniface IX
155	St. Anicetus	676	Donus I	1024	John XIX	1394	*Benedict XIII*
166	St. Soterus	678	St. Agatho	1032	Benedict IX	1404	Innocent VII
175	St. Eleutherius	682	St. Leo II	1045	Sylvester III	1406	Gregory XII
189	St. Victor I	684	St. Benedict II	1045	Benedict IX	1409	*Alexander V*
199	St. Zephyrinus	685	John V	1045	Gregory VI	1410	*John XXIII*
217	St. Callistus I	686	Conon	1046	Clement II	1417	Martin V
217	*St. Hippolytus*	687	*Theodore*	1047	Benedict IX	1431	Eugene IV
222	St. Urban I	687	*Paschal*	1048	Damasus II	1440	*Felix V*
230	St. Pontian	687	St. Sergius I	1049	St. Leo IX	1447	Nicholas V
235	St. Anterus	701	John VI	1055	Victor II	1455	Callistus III
236	St. Fabian	705	John VII	1057	Stephen IX	1458	Pius II
251	St. Cornelius	708	Sisinnius	1058	*Benedict X*	1464	Paul II
251	*Novatian*	708	Constantine	1059	Nicholas II	1471	Sixtus IV
253	St. Lucius I	715	St. Gregory II	1061	Alexander II	1484	Innocent VIII
254	St. Stephen I	731	St. Gregory III	1061	*Honorius II*	1492	Alexander VI
257	St. Sixtus II	741	St. Zachary	1073	St. Gregory VII	1503	Pius III
259	St. Dionysius	752	Stephen II	1080	*Clement III*	1503	Julius II
269	St. Felix I	757	St. Paul I	1086	Victor III	1513	Leo X
275	St. Eutychian	767	*Constantine*	1088	Urban II	1522	Adrian VI
283	St. Caius	768	*Philip*	1099	Paschal II	1523	Clement VII
296	St. Marcellinus	768	Stephen III	1100	*Theodore*	1534	Paul III
308	St. Marcellus I	772	Adrian I	1102	*Albert*	1550	Julius III
309	St. Eusebius	795	St. Leo III	1105	*Sylvester IV*	1555	Marcellus II
311	St. Melchiades	816	Stephen IV	1118	Gelasius II	1555	Paul IV
314	St. Sylvester I	817	St. Paschal I	1118	*Gregory VIII*	1559	Pius IV
336	St. Mark	824	Eugene II	1119	Callistus II	1566	St. Pius V
337	St. Julius I	827	Valentine	1124	Honorius II	1572	Gregory XIII
352	Liberius	827	Gregory IV	1124	*Celestine II*	1585	Sixtus V
355	*Felix II*	843	*John*	1130	Innocent II	1590	Urban VII
366	St. Damasus I	844	Sergius II	1130	*Anacletus II*	1590	Gregory XIV
366	*Ursinus*	847	St. Leo IV	1138	*Victor IV*	1591	Innocent IX
384	St. Siricius	855	Benedict III	1143	Celestine II	1592	Clement VIII
399	St. Anastasius I	855	*Anastasius*	1144	Lucius II	1605	Leo XI
401	St. Innocent I	858	St. Nicholas I	1145	Eugene III	1605	Paul V
417	St. Zozimus	867	Adrian II	1153	Anastasius IV	1621	Gregory XV
418	St. Boniface I	872	John VIII	1154	Adrian IV	1623	Urban VIII
418	*Eulalius*	882	Marinus I	1159	Alexander III	1644	Innocent X
422	St. Celestine I	884	St. Adrian III	1159	*Victor IV*	1655	Alexander VII
432	St. Sixtus III	885	Stephen V	1164	*Paschal III*	1667	Clement IX
440	St. Leo I	891	Formosus	1168	*Callistus III*	1670	Clement X
461	St. Hilary	896	Boniface VI	1179	*Innocent III*	1676	Innocent XI
468	St. Simplicius	896	Stephen VI	1181	Lucius III	1689	Alexander VIII
483	St. Felix III or II	897	Romanus	1185	Urban III	1691	Innocent XII
492	St. Gelasius I	897	Theodore II	1187	Gregory VIII	1700	Clement XI
496	Anastasius II	898	John IX	1187	Clemente III	1721	Innocent XIII
498	St. Symmachus	900	Benedict IV	1191	Celestine III	1724	Benedict XIII
498	*Lawrence*	903	Leo V	1198	Innocent III	1730	Clement XII
	(501-505)	903	*Christopher*	1216	Honorius III	1740	Benedict XIV
514	St. Hormisdas	904	Sergius III	1227	Gregory IX	1758	Clement XIII
523	St. John I	911	Anastasius III	1241	Celestine IV	1769	Clement XIV
526	St. Felix IV or III	913	Landus	1243	Innocent IV	1775	Pius VI
530	Boniface II	914	John X	1254	Alexander IV	1800	Pius VII
530	*Dioscorus*	928	Leo VI	1261	Urban IV	1823	Leo XII
533	John II	928	Stephen VII	1265	Clement IV	1829	Pius VIII
535	St. Agapitus	931	John XI	1271	Gregory X	1831	Gregory XVI
536	St. Silverius	936	Leo VII	1276	Innocent V	1846	Pius IX
537	Vigilius	939	Stephen VIII	1276	Adrian V	1878	Leo XIII
556	Pelagius I	942	Marinus II	1276	John XXI	1903	St. Pius X
561	John III	946	Agapitus II	1277	Nicholas III	1914	Benedict XV
575	Benedict I	955	John XII	1281	Martin IV	1922	Pius XI
579	Pelagius II	963	Leo VIII	1285	Honorius IV	1939	Pius XII
590	St. Gregory I	964	Benedict V	1288	Nicholas IV	1958	John XXIII
604	Sabinianus	965	John XIII	1294	St. Celestine V	1963	Paul VI
607	Boniface III	973	Benedict VI	1294	Boniface VIII		
608	St. Boniface IV	974	*Boniface VII*	1303	Benedict XI		

Roman Catholic Hierarchy

Source: Apostolic Delegation, Washington, D. C.

SUPREME PONTIFF

At the head of the Roman Catholic Church is the Supreme Pontiff, Paul VI, Giovanni Battista Montini, born at Concesio, Italy, Sept. 26, 1897, ordained priest May 29, 1920, enthroned archbishop of Milan Jan. 6, 1955, proclaimed cardinal Dec. 15, 1958; elected Pope as successor of John XXIII, June 21, 1963; crowned June 30, 1963.

CARDINALS

Name	Office	Nationality	Born	Chosen
Alfrink: Bernard	Archbishop of Utrecht	Dutch	1900	1960
Antoniutti: Ildebrando	Prefect of the Sacred Congregation for Religious and Secular Institutes	Italian	1898	1962
Antonelli: Ferdinando		Italian	1896	1973
Aponte Martinez: Luis	Archbishop of San Juan in Puerto Rico	American	1922	1973
Arns: Paulo	Archbishop of Sao Paulo	Brazilian	1921	1973
Baggio: Sebastiano	Prefect of the Sacred Congregation for the Bishops	Italian	1913	1969
Beltrami: Giuseppe		Italian	1889	1967
Bengsch: Alfred	Archbishop-Bishop of Berlin	German	1921	1967
Bertoli: Paolo		Italian	1908	1969
Biayenda: Emile	Archbishop of Brazzaville	Congolese	1927	1973
Brandao Vilela: Avela	Archbishop of Sao Salvador da Bahia	Brazilian	1912	1973
Bueno y Monreal: Jose M	Archbishop of Seville	Spanish	1904	1958
Caggiano: Antonio	Archbishop of Buenos Aires	Argentinian	1889	1946
Carberry: John	Archbishop of St. Louis	American	1904	1969
Carpino: Francesco		Italian	1905	1967
Casariego: Mario	Archbishop of Guatemala	Guatemalan	1909	1969
Cento: Fernando	Titular Bishop of Vulturia	Italian	1883	1958
Cerejeira: Manuel Goncalves		Portuguese	1888	1929
Cicognani: Amleto	Titular Bishop of Frascati; Secretary of State Emeritus Dean of the Sacred College	Italian	1883	1958
Cody: John P	Archbishop of Chicago	American	1907	1967
Colombo: Giovanni	Archbishop of Milan	Italian	1902	1965
Concha: Luis		Colombian	1891	1961
Confalonieri: Carlo		Italian	1893	1958
Conway: William	Archbishop of Armagh	Irish	1913	1965
Cooke: Terence	Archbishop of New York	American	1921	1969
Cooray: Thomas B	Archbishop of Colombo in Ceylon	Ceylonese	1901	1965
Cordeiro: Joseph	Archbishop of Karachi	Pakistanian	1918	1973
da Costa Nunes: Jose		Portuguese	1880	1962
Danielou: Jean		French	1905	1969
Darmojuwono: Justin	Archbishop of Semarang	Indonesian	1914	1967
De Araujo Sales: Eugenio	Archbishop of St. Sebastian of Rio de Janeiro	Brazilian	1920	1969
Dearden: John	Archbishop of Detroit	American	1907	1969
de Furstenberg: Maximilian	Prefect of the Sacred Congregation for the Oriental Churches	Belgian	1904	1967
Di Jorio: Alberto		Italian	1884	1958
Dopfner: Julius	Archbishop of Munich	German	1913	1958
Duval: Leon-Etienne	Archbishop of Algiers	Algerian	1903	1965
Enrique y Tarancon: Vincenzo	Archbishop of Madrid	Spanish	1907	1969
Felici: Pericle	President of Pontifical Commission for the Revision of Code of Canon Law	Italian	1911	1967
Feltin: Maurice		French	1883	1953
Flahiff: George	Archbishop of Winnipeg	Canadian	1905	1969
Florit: Ermenegildo	Archbishop of Florence	Italian	1901	1965
Forni: Efrem		Italian	1889	1962
Freeman: James	Archbishop of Sydney	Australian	1907	1973
Frings: Joseph		German	1887	1946
Garrone: Gabriele M	Prefect of the Sacred Congregation for Catholic Education	French	1901	1967
Gilroy: Norman		Australian	1896	1946
Gonzalez Martin: Marcelo	Archbishop of Toledo	Spanish	1918	1973
Gouyon: Paul	Archbishop of Rennes	French	1910	1969
Gracias: Valerian	Archbishop of Bombay	Indian	1900	1953
Grano: Carlo		Italian	1887	1967
Gray: Gordon	Archbishop of St. Andrews and Edinburg	Scot.	1910	1969
Guerri: Sergio	Pro-President of the Pontifical Comm. for Vatican City State	Italian	1905	1969
Guyot: Louis	Archbishop of Toulouse	French	1905	1973
Heard: William		Scot.	1884	1962
Heenan: John	Archbishop of Westminster	English	1905	1965
Hoffner: Joseph	Archbishop of Cologne	German	1906	1969
Jaeger: Lorenz	Archbishop of Paderborn	German	1892	1965
Journet: Charles		Swiss	1891	1965
Jubany Arnau: Narciso	Archbishop of Barcelona	Spanish	1913	1973
Kim Sou Hwan: Stephan	Archbishop of Seoul	Korean	1922	1969
Knox: James	Archbishop of Melbourne	Australian	1914	1973
Koenig: Franz	Archbishop of Vienna	Austrian	1905	1958
Kominek: Boleslaw	Archbishop of Wroclaw	Polish	1903	1973
Krol: John	Archbishop of Philadelphia	American	1910	1967
Landazuri Ricketts: Juan	Archbishop of Lima	Peruvian	1913	1962
Leger: Paul		Canadian	1904	1953
Lercaro: Giacomo		Italian	1891	1953
Luciani: Albino	Patriarch of Venice	Italian	1912	1973
Malula: Joseph	Archbishop of Kinshasa	Congolese	1917	1969
Manning: Timothy	Archbishop of Los Angeles	American	1909	1973
Marella: Paolo		Italian	1895	1959
Martin: Joseph		French	1891	1965
Marty: Francis	Archbishop of Paris	French	1904	1969

Maurer: Jose	Archbishop of Sucre	Bolivian	1900	1967
McCann: Owen	Archbishop of Cape Town	So. African	1907	1965
McGuigan: James		Canadian	1894	1946
McIntyre: James		American	1886	1953
McKeefry: Peter	Archbishop of Wellington	New Zealand	1899	1969
Medeiros: Humberto	Archbishop of Boston	American	1915	1973
Meouchi: Paul	Maronite Patriarch of Antioch	Lebanese	1894	1965
Mindszenty: Jozsef	Archbishop of Esztergom	Hungarian	1892	1946
Miranda y Gomez: Miguel	Archbishop of Mexico	Mexican	1895	1969
Motta: Carlos Carmelo de Vasconcellos	Archbishop of Aparecida	Brazilian	1890	1946
Mozzini: Umberto		Italian	1904	1973
Munoz Vega: Paolo	Archbishop of Quito	Ecuadorian	1903	1969
Munoz Duque: Anibal	Archbishop of Bogota	Colombian	1908	1973
Nasalli Rocca: Mario		Italian	1903	1969
O'Boyle: Patrick		American	1896	1967
Oddi: Silvio		Italian	1910	1969
Ottaviani: Alfredo		Italian	1890	1953
Otunga: Maurice	Archbishop of Nairobi	Kenyan	1923	1973
Palazzini: Pietro		Italian	1912	1973
Pappalardo: Salvatore	Archbishop of Palermo	Italian	1918	1973
Parecattil: Joseph	Archbishop of Ernakulam	Indian	1912	1969
Parente: Pietro		Italian	1891	1967
Paupini: Giuseppe	Grand Penitentiary	Italian	1907	1969
Pellegrino: Michele	Archbishop of Turin	Italian	1903	1967
Philippe: Paul	Prefect of the Sacred Congregation for the Oriental Churches	French	1905	1973
Pignedoli: Sergio	President of the Secretariat for Non-Christians	Italian	1910	1973
Poletti: Ugo	Vicar General of His Holiness for the City of Rome	Italian	1914	1973
Poma: Antonio	Archbishop of Bologna	Italian	1910	1969
Primatesta: Francisco	Archbishop of Cordova	Argentinian	1919	1973
Quintero: Jose	Archbishop of Caracas	Venezuelean	1902	1961
Raimondi: Luigi	Prefect of the Sacred Congregation for Saints' Causes	Italian	1912	1973
Rakotomalala: Jerome	Archbishop of Tananarive	Madagascar	1913	1969
Renard: Alexandre	Archbishop of Lyon	French	1906	1967
Ribeiro: Antonio	Patriarch of Lisbon	Portuguese	1928	1973
Roberti: Francesco		Italian	1889	1958
Rosales: Julio	Archbishop of Cebu	Filipino	1906	1969
Rossi Agnelo	Prefect of the Sacred Congregation for the Evangelization of Peoples	Brazilian	1913	1965
Roy: Maurice	Archbishop of Quebec	Canadian	1905	1965
Rugambwa: Laurean	Archbishop of Dar es Salaam	Tanzania	1912	1960
Salazar: Lopez	Archbishop of Guadalajara	Mexican	1910	1973
Samore: Antonio	Prefect of Sacred Congregation of the Sacraments	Italian	1905	1967
Santos: Rufino	Archbishop of Manila	Filipino	1908	1960
Scherer: Alfredo	Archbishop of Porto Alegre	Brazilian	1903	1969
Seper: Franjo	Prefect of Sacred Congregation for the Doctrine of the Faith	Yugoslav	1905	1965
Shehan: Lawrence	Archbishop of Baltimore	American	1898	1965
Sidarouss: Stephanos	Coptic Patriarch of Alexandria	United Arab Republic	1904	1965
Silva Henriquez: Raul	Archbishop of Santiago	Chilean	1907	1962
Siri: Giuseppe	Archbishop of Genoa	Italian	1906	1953
Slipyj: Josyf	Ukrainian Archbishop of Lwow	Ukrainian	1892	1965
Staffa: Dinoa	Prefect of Supreme Tribunal of Apostolic Signatura	Italian	1906	1967
Suenens: Leo	Archbishop of Malines Brussels	Belgian	1904	1962
Tabera y Araoz: Arturo	Prefect of the Sacred Congregation of Divine Worship	Spanish	1903	1969
Taguchi: Paul	Archbishop of Osaka	Japanese	1902	1973
Taofinu'u	Bishop of Apia	Samoan	1923	1973
Traglia: Luigi	Chancellor of the Holy Roman Church	Italian	1895	1960
Trochta: Stepan	Bishop of Litomerice	Czechoslovak	1905	1973
Ursi: Corrado	Archbishop of Naples	Italian	1908	1967
Vagnozzi: Egidio	Pres. of the Prefecture of the Holy See's Economic Affairs	Italian	1906	1967
Villot: Jean	Secretary of State of His Holiness	French	1905	1965
Violardo: Giacomo		Italian	1898	1969
Willebrands: John	President of Secretariat for the Union of Christians	Dutch	1909	1969
Wojtyla: Karol	Archbishop of Krakow	Polish	1920	1967
Wright: John	Prefect of the Sacred Congregation for the Clergy	American	1909	1969
Wyszynski: Stefan	Archbishop of Gniezno-Warsaw	Polish	1901	1953
Yu Pin: Paul	Archbishop of Nanking	Chinese	1901	1969
Zerba: Cesare		Italian	1892	1965
Zoungrana: Paul	Archbishop of Ouagadougou	Upper Volta	1917	1965

Roman Catholic Hierarchy of the United States

Source: Apostolic Delegation, Washington, D. C.

Archdioceses

See	Archbishop	Cons.	See	Archbishops	Cons.
Anchorage	Joseph T. Ryan	1966	Chicago, Ill	John Cody (Card.)	1947
Atlanta, Ga	Thomas A. Donnellan	1964		Thomas J. Grady (Aux.)	1967
Baltimore, Md	Lawrence Shehan (Card.)	1945		William McManus (Aux.)	1967
	Thomas A. Murphy (Aux.)	1962		Michael R. Dempsey (Aux.)	1968
	F. Joseph Gossman (Aux.)	1968		Alfred Abramowicz (Aux.)	1968
Boston, Mass	Humberto S. Medeiros	1966		Nevin W. Hayes (Aux.)	1965
	Jeremiah F. Minihan (Aux.)	1954	Cincinnati, Ohio	Joseph Bernardin	1966
	Thomas J. Riley (Aux.)	1959		Nicholas Elko (Aux.)	1955
	Lawrence Riley (Aux.)	1972	Denver, Colo	James V. Casey	1957
	Joseph Maguire (Aux.)	1972		George R. Evans (Aux.)	1969

See	Archbishop	Cons.	See	Archbishop	Cons.
Detroit, Mich	John F. Dearden	1948		Edward Head (Aux.)	1970
	Walter J. Schoenherr (Aux.)	1968		James P. Mahoney (Aux.)	1972
	Thomas J. Gumbleton			Anthony F. Mestice (Aux.)	1973
	(Aux.)	1968	Oklahoma, Okla	John R. Quinn	1967
	Arthur H. Krawczak (Aux.)	1973	Omaha, Nebr	Daniel E. Sheehan	1964
	Joseph L. Imesch (Aux.)	1973	Philadelphia, Pa	John J. Krol (Card.)	1953
Dubuque, Iowa	James J. Byrne	1947		Gerald V. McDevitt (Aux.)	1962
	Francis Dunn (Aux.)	1969		John J. Graham (Aux.)	1964
Hartford, Conn	John F. Whealon	1961		Martin Lohmuller (Aux.)	1970
	John F. Hackett (Aux.)	1952		Thomas J. Welsh (Aux.)	1970
	Joseph Donnelly (Aux.)	1965	Portland, Ore	Robert J. Dwyer	1952
Indianapolis, Ind	George J. Biskup	1957	St. Louis, Mo	John J. Carberry (Card.)	1956
Kansas City, Kan	Ignatius J. Strecker	1962		George Gottwald (Aux.)	1961
Los Angeles, Calif.	Timothy Manning	1946		Joseph A. McNicholas	
	John J. Ward (Aux.)	1963		(Aux.)	1969
	William R. Johnson (Aux.)	1971		Charles R. Koester (Aux.)	1971
	Juan Arzurbe (Aux.)	1971		Edward O'Meara (Aux.)	1972
Louisville, Ky	Thomas J. McDonough	1947	St. Paul, Minn	Leo Binz	1942
	Charles G. Maloney (Aux.)	1955		Leo C. Byrne (Card.)	1954
Miami, Fla	Coleman F. Carroll	1953		Leonard Cowley (Aux.)	1958
	Rene Gracida	1972		John Roach (Aux.)	1971
Milwaukee, Wis	William E. Cousins	1952		Raymond Lucker (Aux.)	1971
	Leo Brust (Aux.)	1969	San Antonio, Tex	Francis Furey	1960
Newark, N. J.	Thomas A. Boland	1947		Patrick F. Flores (Aux.)	1970
	Martin W. Stanton (Aux.)	1957	San Francisco, Cal	Joseph T. McGucken	1941
	John J. Dougherty (Aux.)	1962		William McDonald (Aux.)	1964
	Joseph A. Costello (Aux.)	1962		Norman F. McFarland	
New Orleans, La	Philip M. Hannan	1956		(Aux.)	1970
	Louis A. Caillouet (Aux.)	1947	San Juan, P. R.	Luis Aponte Martinez	1960
	Harold R. Perry (Aux.)	1965		Juan de Dios Lopez de	
New York, N. Y.	Terence J. Cooke (Card.)	1965		Victoria (Aux.)	1963
	John J. Maguire (C..)	1959		James P. Davis	1943
	J. M. Pernicone (Aux.)	1954	Seattle, Wash	Thomas A. Connolly	1939
	Edward E. Swanstrom			Thomas E. Gill (Aux.)	1956
	(Aux.)	1960	Washington, D. C.	William W. Baum	1970
	Patrick Ahern (Aux.)	1970		Edward J. Hermann (Aux.)	1966

Canadian Archdioceses

See	Archbishop	Cons.	See	Archbishop	Cons.
Edmonton, Alta	Anthony Jordan	1964		Laurent Noel (Aux.)	1963
Grouard-McLennan, Alta	Henri Routhier	1967	Regina, Sask	Michael C. O'Neill	1948
Halifax, N.S.	James M. Hayes	1967	Rimouski, Que.	Louis Levesque	1967
Keewatin-Le Pas, Man.	Paul Dumouchel	1967	St. Boniface, Man.	Maurice Badoux	1955
Kingston, Ont.	Joseph L. Wilhelm	1966		Antoine Hacault (Aux.)	1964
Moncton, N.B.	Norbert Robichaud	1942	St. John's, Nfld.	Patrick J. Skinner	1951
Montreal, Que.	Paul Gregoire	1968	Sherbrooke, Que.	J. M. Fortier	1968
	Lawrence P. Whelan (Aux.)	1941	Toronto, Ont.	Philip F. Pocock	1971
	Leo Blais (Aux.)	1959		Francis V. Allen (Aux.)	1954
	Valerian Belanger (aux.)	1956		Thomas Fulton (Aux.)	1969
	Andre Cimichella (Aux.)	1964	Vancouver, B.C.	James F. Carney	1969
	Leonard Crowley (Aux.)	1971	Winnipeg, Man.	George B. Flahiff (Card.)	1961
Ottawa, Ont.	Joseph A. Plourde	1967			
Quebec, Que.	Maurice Roy (Card.)	1947	Ukrainian Byzantine Rite:		
	Lionel Audet (Aux.)	1968	Winnipeg, Man.	Maxim Hermaniuk	1956

1975 — A Holy Year

On Christmas Eve, 1974, with the ritual opening of the doors of the major basilicas in Rome, another Roman Catholic Holy Year will begin. Announced on May 9, 1973, by Pope Paul VI, the Year will last until Christmas Eve, 1975, when the basilica doors are closed.

During the Year, pilgrims to Rome who repent, confess, receive communion and fulfill other special obligations, such as visits to the major basilicas, are granted special indulgences — remission of punishment for sins. According to some estimates, the Holy Year may bring 25,000,000 visitors to Rome, compared to 2,100,000 in 1971.

To coordinate the Holy Year activities, Pope Paul appointed a commission headed by Maximilian Cardinal de Furstenberg. Vatican officials suggested that the Italian government and the city of Rome also set up special agencies to cope with the extraordinary problems of a 10-fold increase in pilgrims and tourists.

This Holy Year is thought to be the 21st or 22nd since the custom began. The first official Holy Year was in 1300, after Rome began to fill with pilgrims who had heard a rumor that anyone who visited St. Peters on Jan. 1, 1300, would receive full absolution. According to contemporary accounts, Vatican authorities found a 107-year-old peasant who vowed that his father had obtained such an absolution in 1200. Pope Boniface VIII thereupon issued a bull, **Antiquorem habet fidem,** dated Feb. 22, 1300, proclaiming a Holy Year. Thousands of pilgrims flocked to Rome for spiritual enrichment, and the church and city also profited.

In 1343, following a petition by the people of Rome, Pope Clement IV proclaimed that Holy Years would recur every 50 years. In 1389 Urban VI reduced the interval to 33 years, and in 1470 Pope Paul II set the interval at the present 25 years.

The scriptural basis for Holy Years is the Mosaic injunction that a sabbath year or Jubilee be proclaimed every 50 years (Leviticus XXV). During the Jubilee, according to Judaic law, all slaves were to be freed, debts remitted, and lands lost through debt or forced sale returned to their original owners.

Roman Catholic Statistics for the United States

Source: Official Catholic Directory, copyright 1973 by P. J. Kenedy & Sons

Archdioceses	Clergy	Parishes	Students	Cath. Pop.	Dioceses	Clergy	Parishes	Students	Cath. Pop.
Anchorage	24	17	3,534	30,000	Helena	153	58	17,334	70,550
Atlanta	157	38	20,041	63,250	Honolulu	161	66	32,975	195,046
Baltimore	788	143	99,596	418,460	Jefferson City	155	87	17,252	68,797
Boston	2,448	402	333,093	1,900,023	Joliet	367	110	77,246	323,626
Chicago	2,252	458	425,077	2,489,320	Juneau	12	7	1,032	4,022
Cincinnati	873	260	141,793	518,444	Kalamazoo	86	45	19,727	83,416
Denver	365	118	66,433	329,898	Kan. City-St. Joseph	364	94	37,053	130,365
Detroit	1,237	330	373,359	1,651,463	LaCrosse	347	178	51,849	197,142
Dubuque	497	201	66,281	230,407	Lafayette, Ind.	169	59	17,938	83,394
Hartford	721	218	151,263	837,491	Lafayette, La.	298	151	83,709	394,551
Indianapolis	425	164	38,950	204,757	Lansing	217	83	49,439	211,421
Kansas City, Kan.	279	96	36,541	137,775	Lincoln	146	94	15,151	59,997
Los Angeles	1,409	324	362,565	1,875,500	Little Rock	180	80	15,356	55,056
Louisville	409	124	51,861	189,671	Madison	237	137	46,191	197,861
Miami	434	116	78,514	569,543	Manchester	401	126	55,446	263,788
Milwaukee	1,185	265	158,370	696,269	Marquette	162	89	26,588	97,849
Newark	1,244	252	238,974	1,725,128	Memphis	74	28	12,551	40,026
New Orleans	599	161	124,863	587,105	Mobile	179	69	15,891	45,493
New York	2,119	406	302,504	1,800,000	Monterey	128	43	20,163	95,000
Oklahoma City	163	71	15,096	65,000	Nashville	99	56	14,614	54,465
Omaha	401	137	58,245	201,502	Natchez-Jackson	200	105	33,942	84,869
Philadelphia	1,663	311	299,705	1,372,441	New Ulm	126	84	21,594	69,039
Portland, Ore.	328	125	44,405	252,820	Norwich	213	70	45,492	186,950
St. Louis	1,080	248	126,691	535,180	Oakland	347	83	78,577	338,163
St. Paul & Minn.	558	217	141,818	537,471	Ogdensburg	252	122	41,622	174,347
San Antonio	393	156	88,282	535,164	Orlando	144	55	27,907	137,754
San Francisco	840	150	120,244	827,950	Owensboro	88	72	13,459	48,956
Santa Fe	246	92	61,017	284,558	Paterson	485	102	71,018	309,253
Seattle	412	126	63,603	339,721	Peoria	378	171	55,434	222,608
Washington, D.C.	1,140	126	113,257	389,482	Phoenix	211	60	40,348	216,156
Ukr. of Phila.	139	101	6,348	46,014	Pittsburgh	880	320	180,560	920,150
Byz. of Munhall	92	79	11,552	150,316	Portland, Me.	343	140	50,919	263,556
					Providence	606	155	111,760	603,919
Dioceses					Pueblo	159	60	19,000	105,601
					Raleigh	81	59	10,442	35,338
Albany	534	212	104,278	424,219	Rapid City	107	51	12,654	36,000
Alexandria, La.	175	85	20,070	73,500	Reno	95	38	12,778	50,683
Allentown	427	151	43,499	259,653	Richmond	357	125	72,195	253,616
Altoona-Johnstown	256	120	37,397	152,122	Rochester	486	160	97,738	318,430
Amarillo	90	57	16,477	65,170	Rockford	292	98	46,530	207,166
Austin	171	82	20,179	138,402	Rockville Centre	598	128	257,970	980,575
Baker, Ore.	53	31	5,984	23,488	Sacramento	266	89	37,269	222,153
Baton Rouge	154	65	37,491	152,923	Saginaw	182	105	43,022	172,152
Beaumont	86	36	15,426	74,775	St. Augustine	116	70	20,362	137,754
Belleville	220	130	26,000	113,862	St. Cloud	333	146	42,000	145,451
Belmont Abbey	27	1	568	436	St. Petersburg	234	70	29,753	155,621
Birmingham	140	58	13,530	41,355	Salina	135	99	15,429	59,183
Bismarck	133	84	25,409	72,685	Salt Lake City	88	38	11,236	50,683
Boise	105	67	12,400	62,432	San Angelo	71	46	13,927	58,654
Bridgeport	380	83	78,157	325,418	San Diego	531	165	76,201	543,907
Brooklyn	1,348	230	251,958	1,491,523	Santa Rosa	114	36	7,811	65,390
Brownsville	104	58	36,728	270,281	Savannah	113	42	11,420	35,275
Buffalo	1,069	288	172,947	926,531	Scranton	593	239	84,819	353,493
Burlington	244	102	34,063	136,241	Sioux City	218	141	33,875	106,591
Camden	453	123	76,898	322,543	Sioux Falls	197	126	30,916	100,936
Charleston	140	65	15,979	46,963	Spokane	200	58	17,651	69,397
Charlotte	73	53	11,344	35,585	Springfield, Ill.	295	143	43,069	184,163
Cheyenne	70	39	11,260	45,000	Springfield, Mass.	434	136	92,230	376,200
Cleveland	900	236	222,858	893,209	Springfield-Cape Gir.	112	59	10,453	40,492
Columbus	296	109	47,064	176,118	Steubenville	179	73	14,835	56,100
Corpus Christi	153	72	35,529	184,203	Stockton	84	31	15,567	88,035
Covington	213	82	26,201	103,500	Superior	138	86	22,064	84,055
Crookston	72	51	12,884	38,559	Syracuse	512	170	112,638	396,413
Dallas	211	52	32,059	111,835	Toledo	398	149	75,613	329,328
Davenport	230	119	29,430	105,333	Trenton	532	200	150,868	816,874
Des Moines	141	93	22,837	80,292	Tucson	160	55	31,138	175,157
Dodge City	71	49	8,739	33,452	Tulsa	90	50	9,188	51,000
Duluth	135	84	27,130	95,413	Wheeling	205	100	20,685	97,098
El Paso	185	72	59,374	226,453	Wichita	184	96	20,235	89,716
Erie	334	126	63,142	212,807	Wilmington	188	54	29,477	100,426
Evansville	148	75	21,445	86,228	Winona	210	130	36,097	117,285
Fairbanks	41	24	3,121	13,295	Worcester	515	131	82,622	342,173
Fall River	414	113	65,993	305,000	Yakima	72	38	9,034	50,384
Fargo	175	117	23,966	95,741	Youngstown	342	117	60,129	300,050
Fort Worth	96	47	16,842	68,230					
Ft. Wayne-So. Bend	543	81	42,748	150,723					
Fresno	165	84	40,314	274,761	**Eastern Rite:**				
Gallup	91	53	11,489	61,000	Passaic	102	83	9,360	98,750
Galveston-Houston	374	118	87,340	329,150	Stamford	80	57	3,584	87,820
Gary	246	86	46,145	186,206	Parma	58	45	6,749	28,700
Gaylord	79	58	18,614	71,676	St. Nicholas	48	36	2,228	29,810
Grand Island	86	56	13,537	51,680	Melkite	43	24	6	20,116
Grand Rapids	206	84	36,251	149,993	St. Maron	58	43	2,339	65,238
Great Falls	141	74	16,937	66,665					
Green Bay	503	193	91,351	319,482					
Greenburg	293	117	42,801	223,453	**Totals 1973**	**56,969**	**18,384**	**9,778,361**	**48,460,427**
Harrisburg	245	103	44,953	191,951	**Totals 1972**	**57,421**	**18,259**	**10,104,507**	**48,390,990**

There were 10 Cardinals (Balt., Boston, Chicago, Detroit, Los Angeles, N.Y., Phila., St. Louis, San Francisco, Wash. D.C.); 34 Archbishops; 261 Bishops; 58 Abbots; 56,969 Priests; 9,201 Brothers; 143,054 Sisters; 18,384 parishes with 17,775 resident pastors, and 609 parishes without resident clergy. Religious order seminars and novitiates 411 with 21,780 seminarians. Colleges and Universities 262, students 418,083; high schools 1,753, students 929,674; elementary schools 8,832, students 2,874,251; full-time teachers 183,258; protective institutions 118; 9,761 students. Orphanage and infant asylums 216 with 15,896 resident children; 702 general hospitals with 161,038 bed capacity; 111 special hospitals; 443 homes for the aged. Converts totaled 73,925; infant baptisms 975,071; 415,487 marriages and 426,340 deaths.

Islamic (Moslem) Calendar 1974-1975

The Islamic calendar, often referred to as Mohammedan, is a lunar reckoning from the year of the hegira, 622 A.D., when Mohammed fled from Mecca. It runs in cycles of 30 years, of which the second, 5th, 7th, 10th, 13th, 16th, 18th, 21st, 24th, 26th and 29th are leap years. Common years have 354 days, leap years 355, the extra day being added to the last month, Zu'lhijjah. Except for this case, the 12 months beginning with Muharram have alternately 30 and 29 days. The month begins at sunset on the day before that given in the tables.

Year	Name of the Month	Month Begins			Year	Name of the Month	Month Begins		
1394	Muharram (New Year)	Jan.	25,	1974	1395	Muharram (New Year)	Jan.	14,	1975
1394	Safar	Feb.	23,	1974	1395	Safar	Feb.	13,	1975
1394	Rabia I	Mar.	25,	1974	1395	Rabia I	Mar.	14,	1975
1394	Rabia II	Apr.	23,	1974	1395	Rabia II	Apr.	13,	1975
1394	Jumada I	May	23,	1974	1395	Jumada I	May	12,	1975
1394	Jumada II	June	21,	1974	1395	Jumada II	June	11,	1975
1394	Rajab	July	21,	1974	1395	Rajab	July	10,	1975
1394	Shaban	Aug.	19,	1974	1395	Shaban	Aug.	9,	1975
1394	Ramadan	Sept.	18,	1974	1395	Ramadan	Sept.	7,	1975
1394	Shawwai	Oct.	17,	1974	1395	Shawwai	Oct.	7,	1975
1394	Zu'lkadah	Nov.	16,	1974	1395	Zu'lkadah	Nov.	5,	1975
1394	Zu'lhijjah	Dec.	15,	1974	1395	Zu'lhijjah	Dec.	5,	1975

Greek Orthodox Church Calendar, 1974

Date		Holy Days	Date		Holy Days
Jan.	1	The Circumcision of Christ—The Feastday of St. Basil New Year's Day	June	2	Sunday of Pentecost
Jan.	6	The Epiphany, The Baptism of Jesus Christ The Sanctification of the Waters	June	29	Feast Day of Saints Peter and Paul
			June	30	Feast day of the Twelve Holy Apostles
Jan.	7	Feast day of St. John the Baptist	Aug.	6	The Transfiguration
Jan.	30	Feast day of Three Hierarchs: St. Basil, St. Gregory and St. John Chrysostom	Aug.	15	The Dormition of the Virgin Mary
			Aug.	29	Beheading of St. John The Baptist
Feb.	2	Presentation of Jesus in the Temple	Sept.	1	Beginning of the Church Year
Feb.	25	Easter Lent begins.	Sept.	8	Nativity of the Virgin Mary
Mar.	3	Sunday of Orthodoxy (1st Sun. of Lent)	Sept.	14	The Elevation of the Holy Cross
Mar.	25	The Annunciation of the Virgin Mary	Oct.	23	The Feast of St. James (Iakovos)
Apr.	7	Palm Sunday	Oct.	26	Feast Day of St. Demetrios the Martyr
Apr.	7-14	Holy Week	Nov.	15	The beginning of the Christmas Lent
Apr.	12	Good Friday—The Burial of Christ	Nov.	21	Presentation of Blessed Virgin Mary
Apr.	14	Easter Sunday	Nov.	30	The Feast of St. Andrew, Founder Ecumenical Patriarchate of Constantinople.
Apr.	23	Feast Day of St. George	Dec.	6	Feast Day of St. Nicholas, Bishop of Myra
May	23	The Ascension	Dec.	25	Christmas Day: The Birth of Jesus Christ.

The dates above are according to the Gregorian calendar, adopted by the Greek Church in 1923. First Greek Orthodox church in U. S. founded 1864, in New Orleans, La.

Lunar Calendar, Chinese New Years, Vietnamese Tet

The ancient Chinese lunar calendar is divided into 12 months of either 29 or 30 days (compensating for the fact that the mean duration of the lunar month is 29 days, 12 hrs., 44.05 mins.). Every 30 months the calendar is further adjusted by the addition of an extra month.

The Chinese calendar runs on a sexagenary cycle, i.e., 60 years. The cycles 1864-1923 and 1924-1983, with the years grouped under their 12 animal designations, are printed below. The year 1974 is found in the 3rd column, under Tiger, and is known as a "Year of the Tiger." Similarly, readers can find the animal name for the year of their birth, marriage, etc., in the same chart.

The lunar calendar is still used to set the dates for traditional festivals in the Republic of China (Taiwan), in Chinese communities around the world, and in Vietnam where the calendar was in use for many centuries.

The Chinese New Year, Hsin Nien, and the 3-day Vietnamese New Year festival, Tet, begin at the first new moon after the sun enters Aquarius. The day may fall, therefore, between Jan. 21 and Feb. 19 of the Gregorian calendar. The old-style Chinese year 4672 begins Jan. 23, 1974. The year 4673 (Hare) begins Feb. 11, 1975. (The date is fixed according to the date of the new moon in the Far East. Since this is west of the International Date Line the date may be one day later than that of the new moon in New York.)

Except for marking such traditional festivals, both Vietnam and the Republic of China use the western, Gregorian calendar.

Rat	Ox	Tiger	Hare (Rabbit)	Dragon	Snake	Horse	Sheep (Goat)	Monkey	Rooster	Dog	Pig
1864	1865	1866	1867	1868	1869	1870	1871	1872	1873	1874	1875
1876	1877	1878	1879	1880	1881	1882	1883	1884	1885	1886	1887
1888	1889	1890	1891	1892	1893	1894	1895	1896	1897	1898	1899
1900	1901	1902	1903	1904	1905	1906	1907	1908	1909	1910	1911
1912	1913	1914	1915	1916	1917	1918	1919	1920	1921	1922	1923
1924	1925	1926	1927	1928	1929	1930	1931	1932	1933	1934	1935
1936	1937	1938	1939	1940	1941	1942	1943	1944	1945	1946	1947
1948	1949	1950	1951	1952	1953	1954	1955	1956	1957	1958	1959
1960	1961	1962	1963	1964	1965	1966	1967	1968	1969	1970	1971
1972	1973	1974	1975	1976	1977	1978	1979	1980	1981	1982	1983

Jewish Holidays, Festivals and Fasts

Source: Synagogue Council of America
All Jewish holidays, etc., begin at sunset on the day previous. *Also observed the following day.

Festivals and Fasts	Hebrew Date		1973-1974 (5734)		1974-1975 (5735)		1975-1976 (5736)		1976-1977 (5737)	
Rosh Hashana (New Year)*	Tishri	1	Sept. 27	Th	Sept. 17	Tu	Sept. 6	Sa	Sept. 25	Sa
Fast of Gedalia	Tishri	3	....		Sept. 19	Th	Sept. 8	Mo	Sept. 27	Mo
Fast of Gedalia	Tishri	4	Sept. 30	Su	....		....		....	
Yom Kippur (Day of Atonement)	Tishri	10	Oct. 6	Sa	Sept. 26	Th	Sept. 15	Mo	Oct. 4	Mo
Sukkoth (Feast of Tabernacles), 1st Day*	Tishri	15	Oct. 11	Th	Oct. 1	Tu	Sept. 20	Sa	Oct. 9	Sa
Sukkoth, 8th Day	Tishri	22	Oct. 18	Th	Oct. 8	Tu	Sept. 27	Sa	Oct. 16	Sa
Simchat Torah (Rejoicing of the Law)	Tishri	23	Oct. 19	Fr	Oct. 9	We	Sept. 28	Su	Oct. 17	Su
Chanukah (Feast of Lights)	Kislev	25	Dec. 20	Th	Dec. 9	Mo	Nov. 29	Sa	Dec. 17	Fr
Fast of Tebet	Tebet	10	Jan. 4	Fr	Dec. 24	Tu	Dec. 14	Su	Dec. 31	Fr
Fast of Esther	Adar	13	Mar. 7	Th	Feb. 24	Mo	....		Mar. 3	Th
Fast of Esther	Adar II	13	....		....		Mar. 15	Mo	....	
Purim (Feast of Lots)	Adar	14	Mar. 8	Fr	Feb. 25	Tu	....		Mar. 4	Fr
Purim	Adar II	14	....		....		Mar. 16	Tu	....	
Pesach (Passover), 1st Day*	Nisan	15	Apr. 7	Su	Mar. 27	Th	Apr. 15	Th	Apr. 3	Su
Pesach, 7th Day	Nisan	21	Apr. 13	Sa	Apr. 2	We	Apr. 21	We	Apr. 9	Sa
Pesach, Last Day	Nisan	22	Apr. 14	Su	Apr. 3	Th	Apr. 22	Th	Apr. 10	Su
Lag B'Omer	Iyar	18	May 10	Fr	May 29	Tu	May 18	Tu	May 6	Fr
Shavuoth (Feast of Weeks)*	Sivan	6	May 27	Mo	May 16	Fr	June 4	Fr	May 23	Mo
Fast of Tammuz	Tammuz	17	July 7	Su	June 26	Th	July 15	Th	July 3	Su
Fast of Tammuz	Tammuz	18	....		....		....		....	
Tisha B'Av (Fast of Av)	Av	9	July 28	Su	July 17	Th	Aug. 5	Th	July 24	Su
Tisha B'Av	Av	10	....		....		....		....	

The months of the Jewish year are: 1 Tishri; 2 Chesvan (Also Marchesvan); 3 Kislev; 4 Tebet (Also Tebeth); 5 Sebat (Also Shebhat); 6 Adar; 6a, added month some years, Adar Sheni (II); 7 Nisan; 8 Iyar; 9 Sivan; 10 Tammuz; 11 Av (Also Abh); 12 Elul.

Canadian Holidays, 1974

New Year's Day, Jan. 1; Good Friday, April 12; Easter Monday, April 15; Queen's Birthday (Victoria Day), May 20; Dominion Day, July 1; Civic Holiday, August 5; Labor Day, Sept. 2; Thanksgiving Day, Oct. 14; Remembrance Day, November 11; Christmas Day, Dec. 25.

Calendar of Events and Anniversaries, 1974

For Revolutionary Calendar, 1774, see page 817; for approximate dates of other sports events, see under name of sport in Index.

Jan. 1	Rose Bowl
Jan. 13	Pro Superbowl
Jan. 21, 1924	Lenin died, near Moscow.
Jan. 21, 1954	1st atomic powered sub launched.
Jan. 25	Millrose Games
Feb. 8, 1924	1st coast-to-coast radio hookup.
Feb. 11-12 . .	Westminster Dog Show
Feb. 12, 1924	1st political speech by a president, Calvin Coolidge, on radio.
Feb. 22	AAU Indoor Track and Field games.
Feb. 26	Mardi Gras
Mar.	Emmy Awards
Mar. 10	Santa Anita Handicap
Mar. 18, 1949	North Atlantic Treaty signed.
Mar. 22, 1874	1st YMHA founded, in N.Y.C.
Mar., late	Sebring endurance race
Mar., late	Academy Awards (or early April)
Apr., early . . .	Stanley Cup playoffs (end mid-May)
Apr., early . . .	Masters Golf Tournament
Apr., early . . .	Baseball opening day
Apr. 17	Boston Marathon
Apr. 22, 1724	Immanuel Kant, philosopher, born.
May 4	Kentucky Derby
May 6	Pulitzer Prizes
May 6, 1924 .	Victor Herbert died, in N.Y.C.
May 18	Preakness
May, mid	Grand Prix of Monte Carlo
May 27	Indianapolis 500
June 8	Belmont Stakes
June 13-14 . .	AAU Outdoor Track and Field games.
June, mid . . .	U.S. Open Golf
June, late . . .	Wimbledon tennis (or early July)
June 30, 1924	1st major indictments in Teapot Dome scandal.
July, early . . .	British Open Golf
July 1, 1924 .	1st regular transcontinental airmail service begins.
July, late	Pocono 500
July, late	Miss Universe pageant

Aug., early . . .	PGA championship
Aug. 1, 1774 .	oxygen discovered by J. Priestley.
Aug. 3, 1924 .	Joseph Conrad, novelist, died.
Aug. 4, 1964 .	bombing of No. Vietnam began.
Aug., late	Tennis Amateur championships
Aug., late	Hambletonian
Sept., early . .	National Tennis Open
Sept. 7	Miss America pageant
Sept. 10, 1924	Leopold and Loeb sentenced to life for thrill murder of Robert Franks.
Sept. 23, 1949	1st Soviet atomic bomb test.
Sept. 28, 1924	2 U.S. planes completed 1st round-the-world flight, in Seattle.
Oct.	Nobel Prizes
Oct., early . . .	World Series, baseball
Oct. 9, 1874 . .	International Postal Congress, in Berne, established present international postal system.
Oct. 14, 1964	Khrushchev ousted by Brezhnev.
Oct. 16, 1964	1st Chinese Communist atomic bomb explosion.
Nov. 4, 1924 .	1st woman governor, Nellie T. Ross, elected in Wyoming.
Nov. 8, 1674 .	John Milton, poet, died.
Nov. 10, 1674	New Netherlands, surrendered to English, becomes New York.
Nov. 19, 1954	1st automatic toll collector, Garden State Parkway, N.J.
Nov., late	Grey Cup football game.
Nov. 24, 1874	Barbed wire patented.
Nov. 27, 1874	Chaim Weizmann, 1st Israel President, born.
Nov. 30, 1874	Winston Churchill born.
Dec., early . . .	Army-Navy football
Dec. 4, 1674 .	Father Marquette established mission at site of present Chicago.
Dec. 7, 1949 .	Nationalist Chinese government moved to Taiwan from mainland.
Dec. 13	Heisman Trophy

Legal or Public Holidays in the United States in 1974

Technically there are no national holidays in the United States; each state has jurisdiction over its holidays, which are designated by legislative enactment or executive proclamation. In practice, however, most states observe the Federal legal public holidays, even though the President and Congress can legally designate holidays only for the District of Columbia and for Federal employees.

Federal legal public holidays are New Year's, Washington's Birthday, Memorial or Decoration Day, Independence Day, Labor Day, Columbus Day, Veterans Day, Thanksgiving and Christmas.

1974

Chief Legal or Public Holidays

When a holiday falls on a Sunday it is usually observed on the following Monday.

Jan. 1 (Tuesday)— New Year's Day. All the states.

Feb. 12 (Tuesday)— Lincoln's Birthday. All the states except Ala., Ark., Fla., Ga., Idaho, Ky., La., Me., Mass., Miss., N.H., N.C., N.D., Okla., R.I., S.C., Tenn., Tex., Va. (In Del., Ill., Ore., the first Monday in Feb.).

Feb. 18 (Third Monday in Feb.)— Washington's Birthday. All the states. In Hawaii known as President's Day. In Ohio, S.D., Wisc., and Wyo. as Lincoln-Washington Day. Observed on Feb. 22 in Ariz., La., S.D., S.C. and W. Va.

April 12— Good Friday. Observed in all the states. A legal holiday in Conn., Del., Fla., Hawaii, Ind., La., N.J., N.D., Penn., Tenn. Partial holiday in Calif. and Wisc.

May 27 (Last Monday in May)— Memorial or Decoration Day. All the states except Ala., Miss., S.C. (Confederate Memorial Day in Virginia). Observed on May 30 in La.

July 4 (Thursday)— Independence Day. All the states.

Sept. 2— Labor Day. (First Monday in Sept.). All the states.

Oct. 14 (Second Monday in Oct.)— Columbus Day. All the states except Ark., Iowa, Maine, Miss., Nev., N.D., Okla., Ore., S.C., S.D. (Discover's Day in Hawaii; Discovery Day in Indiana and No. Dakota; Landing Day in Wisc.). (In La. and Wisc. on Oct. 12).

Oct. 28 (Fourth Monday in Oct.)— Veterans or Armistice Day. All the states except Kentucky. In Alaska, Conn., Ga., Maine, Miss., S.C., W. Va., and Wisc. on Nov. 11.

Nov. 5— General Election Day (First Tuesday after the first Monday in Nov.). All the states with the following exceptions—Ala., Alaska, Ark., Conn., Ga., Hawaii, Idaho, Iowa, Kan., Ky., Maine, Mass., Minn., Miss., Mo., Nebr., N.M., Ohio, Ore., R.I., S.D., Texas, Utah, Vt. (Observed usually only when presidential or general elections are held. Primary election days are observed in some states; see list of Days Usually Observed).

Nov. 28— Thanksgiving Day. (Always the fourth Thursday in Nov.). All the states. (Kentucky and Oklahoma observe day after Thanksgiving).

Dec. 25 (Wednesday)— Christmas Day. All the states. (Ky. and S.C. observe day after Christmas; Okla. observes Dec. 24).

Other Legal or Public Holidays

Jan. 8— Battle of New Orleans. In Louisiana.

Jan. 18— Arbor Day. In Florida (always third Friday in Jan.).

Jan. 19— Robert E. Lee's Birthday. Ark., Fla., Ga., La., N.C., S.C. In Ala. and Miss. the third Monday in Jan.

Jan. 19— Confederate Heroes Day. In Texas.

Jan. 20— Inauguration Day. The District of Columbia observed every fourth year.

Jan. 21— Lee-Jackson Day. In Virginia (third Monday in Jan.).

Feb. 14— Admission Day. In Arizona.

Feb. 26— Mardi Gras (Shrove Tuesday). Ala., Fla., La.

March 2— Texas Independence Day. In that state.

March 5— Town Meeting Day. In Vermont (first Tuesday in March).

March 17— Evacuation Day. In Boston and Suffolk County, Mass.

March 25— Seward's Day. In Alaska (always last Monday in March).

March 25— Maryland Day. In that state.

March 26— Kuhio Day. In Hawaii.

April 2— Pascua Florida Day. In that state.

April 12— Halifax Day. In North Carolina.

April 13— Thomas Jefferson's Birthday. In Missouri.

April 15— Patriot's Day. Maine and Mass. (always third Monday in April).

April 21— San Jacinto Day. In Texas.

April 22— Arbor Day. In Nebraska.

April 22— Fast Day. In New Hampshire (always fourth Monday in April).

April 26— Arbor Day. In Utah (always last Friday in April).

April 29— Confederate Memorial Day. Alabama & Miss. (always last Monday in April).

May ?— ?. ? Texas? independence Day. In that state.

May 10— Confederate Memorial Day. North Carolina & South Carolina.

May 20— Mecklenburg Day. In North Carolina.

June 3— Birthday of Jefferson Davis or* Confederate Memorial Day. In Ala., Fla., Ga., * La., Miss., and S.C. In Ala. and Miss. observed on the first Monday in June.

June 11— Kamehameha Day. In Hawaii.

June 14— Flag Day. In Penn.

June 20— West Virginia Day. In that state.

July 24— Pioneer Day. In Utah.

Aug. 5— Colorado Day. In that state (always first Monday in August).

Aug. 12— Victory Day. In Rhode Island (second Monday in August).

Aug. 16— Bennington Battle Day. In Vermont.

Aug. 16— Admission Day. In Hawaii (third Friday in August).

Aug. 27— Lyndon Johnson's Birthday. In Texas.

Aug. 30— Huey B. Long's Birthday. In Louisiana.

Sept. 9— Admission Day. In California.

Sept. 12— Defenders Day. In Maryland.

Oct. 14— Pioneer's Day— In So. Dakota (second Monday in Oct.).

Oct. 31— Nevada Day— In that state.

Nov. 1— All Saints' Day. In Louisiana.

Dec. 10— Wyoming Day. In that state.

Days Usually Observed

Not legal or public holidays:

American Indian Day (Sept. 27 in 1974). Always fourth Friday in September.

Arbor Day. Tree-planting day. First observed April 10, 1872, in Nebraska. Now observed in every state in the Union except Alaska (often on the last Friday in April). A legal holiday in Utah (always last Friday in April), in Florida (always third Friday in January) and in Nebraska (April 22).

Armed Forces Day (May 18 in 1974). Always third Saturday in that month, by Presidential proclamation. Replaced Army, Navy and Air Force Days.

Bill of Rights Day, Dec. 15. By Act of Congress. Bill of Rights took effect Dec. 15, 1791.

Bird Day. Often observed with Arbor Day.

Child Health Day (Oct. 7 in 1974). Always first Monday in October, by Presidential proclamation.

Citizenship Day, Sept. 17. President Truman, Feb. 29, 1952, signed bill designating Sept. 17 as annual Citizenship Day. It replaced I Am An American Day, formerly 3rd Sunday in May and Constitution Day, formerly Sept. 17.

Easter Sunday (April 14 in 1974).

Elizabeth Cady Stanton Day, Nov. 12. Birthday of pioneer leader for equal rights for women.

Father's Day (June 16 in 1974). Always third Sunday in that month.

Flag Day, June 14. By Presidential proclamation. It is a legal holiday in Pennsylvania.

Forefathers' Day, Dec. 21. Landing on Plymouth Rock, in 1620. Is celebrated with dinners by New England societies, especially "Down East."

Frances Willard Day, Sept. 28. Observed in Minnesota.

Nathan Bedford Forrest's Birthday, July 13. In Tennessee.

Four Chaplains Memorial Day, February 3.

Gen. Douglas MacArthur Day, Jan. 26. A memorial day in Arkansas.

Gen. Pulaski Memorial Day, Oct. 11. Native of Poland and Revolutionary War hero; died (Oct. 11, 1779) from wounds received at the siege of Savannah, Ga.

Gen. von Steuben Memorial Day, Sept. 17. By Presidential proclamation.

Georgia Day, Feb. 12—In that state.

Groundhog Day, Feb. 2. A popular belief is that if the groundhog sees his shadow this day he returns to his burrow and winter continues 6 weeks longer.

Halloween, Oct. 31. The evening before All Saints or All-Hallows Day. Informally observed in the United States with masquerading and pumpkin-decorations. Traditionally an occasion for children to play harmless pranks (trick or treat, ticktack).

Independence Sunday (June 30 in 1974). The Sunday preceding the Fourth of July. Observed in Iowa.

Andrew Jackson's Birthday, Mar. 15—in Tennessee.

Leif Ericsson Day, Oct. 9. Observed in Minnesota.

Loyalty Day, May 1. By act of Congress.

Martin Luther King's Birthday, Jan. 15—Observed by many schools and black groups.

May Day. Popularly given to May 1st.

Minnesota Day, May 11. In that state.

Mother's Day (May 12 in 1974). Always second Sunday in that month.

National Aviation Day, Aug. 19. By Presidential proclamation.

National Day of Prayer. By Presidential proclamation each year on a day other than a Sunday.

National Freedom Day, February 1. To commemorate the signing by President Lincoln, of the document to abolish slavery, Feb. 1, 1865. By Presidential proclamation.

National Maritime Day, May 22. First proclaimed 1935 in commemoration of the departure of the SS Savannah, from Savannah, Ga., on May 22, 1819, on the first successful transatlantic voyage under steam propulsion. By Presidential proclamation.

Pan American Day, April 14. In 1890 the First International Conference of American States, meeting in Washington, was held on that date. A resolution was adopted which resulted in the creation of the organization known today as the Pan American Union. By Presidential proclamation.

Poetry Day, Oct. 15.

Primary Election Day. A legal holiday in Ark., Cal., Ind., Me., Mont., N.D., Ore., Tenn., W. Va., and Wis. Observed usually only when presidential or general elections are held.

Reformation Day, Oct. 31. Observed by Protestant groups.

Sadie Hawkins Day, first Saturday after November 11.

St. Patrick's Day, March 17. Observed by Irish Societies and with parades.

St. Valentine's Day, Feb. 14. Festival of a martyr beheaded at Rome under Emperor Claudius. Association of this day with lovers has no connection with the saint and probably had its origin in an old belief that on this day birds begin to choose their mates.

Susan B. Anthony Day, Feb. 15. Birthday of a pioneer crusader for equal rights for women. Observed in Minn.

United Nations Day, Oct. 24. By Presidential proclamation, to commemorate founding of United Nations.

Verrazano Day, April 17. Observed by New York State, to commemorate the probable discovery of New York harbor by Giovanni da Verrazano in April, 1524.

Will Rogers Day, Nov. 4. In Oklahoma.

Wright Brothers Day, Dec. 17. By Presidential designation, to commemorate first successful flight by Orville and Wilbur Wright, Dec. 17, 1903.

Youth Honor Day, Oct 31. Iowa day of observance.

Weeks and Months

The following list contains special weeks and months designed to call to the attention of the public an event of importance. The dates usually change each year at the discretion of the sponsoring organization. Among the Weeks observed each year are American Art Week, American Education Week, American Heart Month, American Red Cross Fund Drive, Boys and Girls Week, Boy Scout Week, Brotherhood Week, Camp Fire Girls Birthday Week, Cancer Control Month, Christmas Seal Sale (sponsored by National Tuberculosis Association), Constitution Week, Earth Week, Fire Prevention Week, Girl Scout Week, Human Rights Week, Jewish Youth Week, March of Dimes (sponsored by National Foundation), Mutual Insurance Week, National Allergy Month, National Bible Week, National Boys' Club Week (sponsored by Boys Clubs of America), National Crime Prevention Week, National Drum Corps Week, National Employ the Physically Handicapped Week, National Heart Month, National Farm Safety Week, National 4-H Club Week, National Garden Week, National Highway Week, National Hospital Week, National Library Week, National Safe Boating Week, National Salvation Army Week, National School Lunch Week, National Stamp Collecting Week, National Transportation Week, National Wildlife Week (sponsored by National Wildlife Federation), National Youth Week, Poppy Week (sponsored by Veterans of Foreign Wars of the U.S.) Red Cross Month, Save Your Vision Week, United Nations Week, United States-Canada Good Will Week (sponsored by the Kiwanis International), World Trade Week, and Youth Week (sponsored by United Christian Youth Movement).

Old English Holidays

Jan. 6. Twelfth Day, or Twelfth-tide, sometimes called Old Christmas Day, the same as Epiphany (Feast of the Three Kings). It is celebrated in Spain as Christmas and in Italy as Epiphany (Befana Day). The previous evening is Twelfth Night. Since 1900 the Russian Orthodox Church has observed Jan. 7 as Christmas, inasmuch as 13 days instead of 12 now mark the difference between the old and the new or Gregorian calendar.

Feb. 2. Candlemas: Festival of the Purification of the Virgin. Consecration of the lighted candles to be used in the church during the year.

Feb. 14. Old Candlemas: St. Valentine's Day.

Mar. 25. Lady Day: Annunciation of the Virgin.

April 6 is Old Lady Day.

June 24, Midsummer Day: Feast of the Nativity of John the Baptist.

July 6 is Old Midsummer Day.

July 15. St. Swithin's Day. An old superstition: if rain fell it would continue forty days.

Aug. 1. Lammas Day. Originally in England the festival of the wheat harvest. In the church the festival of St. Peter's miraculous deliverance from prison. Old Lammas Day is August 13.

Sept. 29. Michaelmas—Feast of St. Michael the Archangel.

Nov. 1. Hallowmas. All-Hallows or All Saints Day. Previous evening is Hallowmas Eve.

Nov. 2. All Souls' Day. Day of prayer for the souls of the dead.

Nov. 11. Martinmas. Feast of St. Martin. Old Martinmas is Nov. 23.

Dec. 28. Childermas. Holy Innocents' Day.

Noted Personalities
American Statesmen of the Past

(Excluding Presidents, Vice Pres's., Sup. Ct. Justices, and most Signers of the Declaration of Independence; listed elsewhere.)

Born	Died	Name	Born	Died	Name	Born	Died	Name
1893	1971	Dean Acheson	1813	1861	Douglas, Stephen A.	1755	1835	Marshall, John
1807	1886	Adams, Charles Francis	1888	1959	Dulles, John Foster	1884	1968	Martin, Joseph W.
1841	1915	Aldrich, Nelson W.	1794	1865	Everett, Edward	1863	1941	McAdoo, William G.
1793	1836	Austin, Stephen	1808	1893	Fish, Hamilton	1874	1944	McNary, Charles L.
1877	1962	Austin, Warren R.	1892	1949	Forrestal, James V.	1891	1967	Morgenthau, Henry, Jr.
1871	1937	Baker, Newton D.	1706	1790	Franklin, Benjamin	1752	1816	Morris, Gouverneur
1874	1940	Bankhead, William B.	1813	1890	Fremont, John C.	1873	1931	Morrow, Dwight W.
1870	1965	Baruch, Bernard M.	1761	1849	Gallatin, Albert	1861	1944	Norris, George W.
1797	1869	Bell, John	1805	1879	Garrison, William Lloyd	1882	1965	Perkins, Frances
1782	1858	Benton, Thomas Hart	1858	1946	Glass, Carter	1757	1824	Pinckney, Charles
1862	1927	Beveridge, Albert J.	1757	1804	Hamilton, Alexander	1746	1825	Pinckney, Charles C.
1830	1893	Blaine, James G.	1737	1793	Hancock, John	1753	1813	Randolph, Edmund
1821	1875	Blair, Francis P.	1838	1905	Hay, John	1773	1833	Randolph, John
1835	1899	Bland, Richard P.	1879	1954	Hays, Will H.	1721	1775	Randolph, Peyton
1865	1940	Borah, William E.	1736	1799	Henry, Patrick	1882	1961	Rayburn, Sam
1760	1806	Breckinridge, John	1895	1967	Herter, Christian A.	1861	1944	Reed, James A.
1860	1925	Bryan, William Jennings	1890	1946	Hopkins, Harry L.	1872	1937	Robinson, Joseph T.
1891	1967	Bullitt, William C.	1895	1972	Hoover, J. Edgar	1884	1962	Roosevelt, Eleanor
1904	1971	Bunche Ralph	1858	1938	House, Edward M.	1845	1937	Root, Elihu
1887	1966	Byrd, Harry F.	1793	1863	Houston, Samuel	1829	1906	Schurz, Carl
1836	1926	Cannon, Joseph G.	1871	1955	Hull, Cordell	1733	1804	Schuyler, Philip J.
1808	1873	Chase, Salmon P.	1874	1952	Ickes, Harold L.	1801	1872	Seward, William H.
1799	1859	Choate, Rufus	1745	1829	Jay, John	1873	1944	Smith, Alfred E.
1850	1921	Clark, Champ	1866	1945	Johnson, Hiram W.	1814	1869	Stanton, Edwin M.
1777	1852	Clay, Henry	1874	1956	Jones, Jesse H.	1812	1883	Stephens, Alexander H.
1769	1828	Clinton, DeWitt	1903	1963	Kefauver, Estes	1900	1949	Stettinius, Edward R., Jr.
1829	1888	Conkling, Roscoe	1856	1937	Kellogg, Frank B.	1900	1965	Stevenson, Adlai E.
1877	1963	Connally, Tom	1925	1968	Kennedy, Robert F.	1867	1950	Stimson, Henry L.
1870	1957	Cox, James M.	1755	1827	King, Rufus	1889	1953	Taft, Robert A.
1787	1863	Crittenden, John J.	1071	1844	La Follette, Robert M.	1864	1956	Thomas, Norman M.
1862	1948	Daniels, Josephus	1855	1925	La Follette, Robert M.	1814	1886	Tilden, Samuel J.
1879	1945	Davis, Dwight F.	1882	1947	LaGuardia, Fiorello H.	1890	1961	Tydings, Millard E.
1808	1889	Davis, Jefferson	1807	1870	Lee, Robert E.	1884	1951	Vandenberg, Arthur H.
1873	1955	Davis, John W.	1878	1963	Lehman, Herbert H.	1877	1953	Wagner, Robert F.
1855	1926	Debs, Eugene V.	1850	1924	Lodge, Henry Cabot	1782	1852	Webster, Daniel
1902	1971	Dewey, Thomas E.	1786	1857	Marcy, William L.	1892	1961	Welles, Sumner
1896	1969	Dirksen, Everett M.	1880	1959	Marshall, George C.	1892	1944	Willkie, Wendell L.

AMERICAN BUSINESS LEADERS, PHILANTHROPISTS

Born	Died	Name	Born	Died	Name	Born	Died	Name
1884	1966	Arden, Elizabeth	1837	1904	Hanna, Marcus A.	1830	1891	Pratt, Charles
1832	1901	Armour, Phillip D.	1874	1940	Harkness, Edward S.	1808	1896	Pratt, Enoch
1764	1848	Astor, John Jacob	1848	1909	Harriman, Edward	1831	1897	Pullman, Geo. M.
1875	1967	Babson, Roger	1865	1957	Hartford, Geo. L. A.	1839	1937	Rockefeller, John D.
1894	1968	Bache, Harold L.	1839	1897	Havemeyer, Theo.	1874	1960	Rockefeller, J. D., Jr.
1870	1965	Baruch, Bernard M.	1838	1916	Hill, James J.	1862	1932	Rosenwald, Julius
1853	1924	Belmont, August	1795	1873	Hopkins, Johns	1740	1785	Salomon, Haym
1786	1844	Biddle, Nicholas	1821	1900	Huntington, C. P.	1891	1971	Sarnoff, David
1835	1919	Carnegie, Andrew	1882	1967	Jergens, Andrew	1847	1920	Schiff, Jacob H.
1821	1905	Cooke, Jay	1882	1967	Kaiser, Henry J.	1875	1966	Sloan, Alfred P.
1791	1883	Cooper, Peter	1876	1958	Kettering, Charles F.	1845	1912	Straus, Isidor
1834	1928	Depew, Chauncey M.	1879	1948	Knudsen, Wm. K.	1848	1931	Straus, Nathan
1806	1893	Drexel, Anthony J.	1867	1966	Kresge, S. S.	1839	1903	Swift, Gustavus
1856	1925	Duke, James B.	1863	1955	Kress, Samuel H.	1845	1920	Vail, Theo. N.
1739	1817	duPont, Pierre S.	1868	1948	Lamont, Robert P.	1794	1877	Vanderbilt, Cornelius
1890	1962	Fairless, Benjamin	1870	1948	Lamont, Thos. W.	1843	1899	Vanderbilt, Cornelius
1835	1906	Field, Marshall	1880	1952	Lasker, Albert D.	1849	1920	Vanderbilt, Wm. K.
1860	1937	Filene, Edward A.	1891	1969	Lehman, Robert	1835	1900	Villard, Henry
1894	1970	Folsom, Frank M.	1874	1938	Mackay, Clarence	1838	1922	Wanamaker, John
1863	1947	Ford, Henry	1831	1902	Mackay, John W.	1871	1937	Warburg, Felix M.
1879	1952	Fox, William	1855	1937	Mellon, Andrew W.	1896	1969	Warburg, James P.
1846	1927	Gary, Elbert H.	1899	1970	Mellon, Richard K.	1874	1956	Watson, Thomas J.
1870	1949	Giannini, Amadeo Peter	1884	1968	Mennen, William G.	1875	1957	Weir, Ernest T.
1885	1966	Gifford, Walter S.	1825	1910	Mills, Darius	1841	1904	Whitney, Wm. C.
1919	1964	Gilbert, A. C.	1837	1913	Morgan, J. Pierpont	1868	1951	Wiggin, Albert H.
1886	1966	Gimbel, Bernard F.	1868	1943	Morgan, J. P., Jr.	1886	1972	Wilson, Charles E.
1877	1965	Girdler, Tom M.	1875	1973	Mott, Charles Stewart	1890	1961	Wilson, Chas. Erwin
1836	1892	Gould, Jay	1875	1970	Neiman, Abraham	1879	1969	Wood, Robert E.
1834	1916	Green, Henrietta (Hetty)	1887	1963	Olds, Irving S.	1852	1919	Woolworth, Frank
1828	1905	Guggenheim, Meyer	1795	1869	Peabody, George			

AMERICAN EXPLORERS, NATURALISTS OF THE PAST

EXPLORERS

Born	Died	Name	Born	Died	Name	Born	Died	Name
1859	1930	Allen, Henry T.	1877	1948	Dickey, H. S.	1785	1843	Stuart, Robert
1884	1960	Andrews, Roy C.	1880	1951	Ellsworth, Lincoln	1799	1845	Sublette, William L.
1778	1838	Ashley, William Henry	1799	1854	Fitzpatrick, Thomas	1798	1876	Walker, Joseph R.
1875	1946	Bartlett, Robert A.	1813	1890	Fremont, John C.	1802	1847	Whitman, Marcus
1790	1847	Bent, Charles	1844	1935	Greely, Adolphus W.	1798	1877	Wilkes, Charles
1875	1956	Bingham, Hiram	1821	1871	Hall, Charles F.	1787	1849	Williams, W. S. (Old Bill)
1796	1878	Bonneville, Benj.	1884	1937	Johnson, Martin			
1734	1820	Boone, Daniel	1894	1953	Johnson, Osa			NATURALISTS
1796	1836	Bowie, James	1820	1857	Kane, Elisha K.			
1804	1881	Bridger, James	1774	1809	Lewis, Meriwether	1864	1926	Akeley, Carl Ethan
1888	1957	Byrd, Richard E.	1784	1864	Long, Stephen H.	1780	1851	Audubon, John J.
1809	1868	Carson, Kit	1874	1970	Macmillan, Donald	1850	1941	Beard, Daniel C.
1770	1838	Clark, William	1799	1877	Palmer, Nathaniel	1849	1926	Burbank, Luther
1775	1813	Colter, John	1856	1920	Peary, Robt. E.	1837	1921	Burroughs, John
1865	1940	Cook, Frederick A.	1779	1813	Pike, Zebulon M.	1838	1914	Muir, John
1844	1881	Cruzen, Richard H.	1834	1902	Powell, John W.	1887	1969	Osborn, Fairfield
1844	1881	De Long, G. W.	1793	1864	Schoolcraft, Hy. R.	1817	1862	Thoreau, Henry D.
			1849	1892	Schwatka, Frederick	1766	1813	Wilson, Alexander

American Military Leaders of the Past
All Army unless marked (N) Navy; (M) Marine; (AF) Air Force.
(Excluding Presidents)

Born	Died	Name	Born	Died	Name	Born	Died	Name
1737	1789	Allen, Ethan	1883	1959	Halsey, William F. (N)	1825	1875	Pickett, George E.
1741	1801	Arnold, Benedict	1818	1902	Hampton, Wade	1822	1892	Pope, John
1886	1950	Arnold, Henry F. (Hap) (AF)	1728	1777	Herkimer, Nicholas	1813	1891	Porter, David D. (N)
1816	1894	Banks, Nathaniel	1825	1865	Hill, Ambrose P.	1905	1970	Power, Thomas S. (AF)
1745	1803	Barry, John (N)	1892	1966	Hobbs, Leland	1809	1867	Price, Stirling
1818	1893	Beauregard, Pierre	1870	1937	Hobson, Richmond (N)	1819	1892	Rodgers, C. R. P. (N)
1853	1930	Bliss, Tasker H.	1887	1966	Hodges, Courtney	1773	1838	Rodgers, John (N)
1878	1967	Bloch, Claude C. (N)	1814	1879	Hooker, Joseph	1819	1898	Rosecrans, William S.
1817	1876	Bragg, Braxton	1831	1879	Hood, John B.	1736	1818	St. Clair, Arthur
1775	1828	Brown, Jacob J.	1773	1843	Hull Issac (N)	1840	1903	Sampson, William T. (N)
1888	1950	Buchanan, Pat (N)	1824	1863	Jackson, Thomas (Stonewall)	1831	1906	Schofield, John
1823	1914	Buckner, Simon B.	1803	1862	Johnston, Albert S.	1786	1866	Scott, Winfield
1886	1945	Buckner, Simon, Jr.	1807	1891	Johnston, Joseph	1835	1906	Shafter, William R.
1826	1863	Buford, John	1747	1792	Jones, John Paul (N)	1831	1888	Sheridan, Phillip
1861	1947	Bullard, Robert L.	1814	1862	Kearny, Philip	1896	1951	Sherman, Forrest P. (N)
1824	1881	Burnside, Ambrose	1794	1848	Kearny, Stephen	1820	1891	Sherman, William T.
1818	1893	Butler, Benjamin F.	1879	1956	King, Ernest J. (N)	1858	1936	Sims, William S. (N)
1817	1873	Canby, Edward	1781	1813	Lawrence, James (N)	1780	1867	Sloat, John D. (N)
1884	1970	Cates, Clifton B. (M)	1843	1899	Lawton, Henry	1882	1967	Smith, Holland M. (M)
1772	1840	Chauncey, Issac (N)	1875	1959	Leahy, William D. (N)	1895	1961	Smith, W. Bedell
1842	1914	Chaffee, Adna R.	1756	1818	Lee, Henry	1886	1969	Spruance, Raymond (N)
1890	1958	Chennault, Claire (AF)	1807	1870	Lee, Robert E.	1728	1822	Stark, John
1752	1818	Clark, George Rogers	1821	1904	Longstreet, James	1883	1946	Stilwell, Joseph W.
1786	1836	Crockett, David	1818	1861	Lyon, Nathaniel	1726	1783	Stirling (Alexander)
1819	1893	Crittenden, Thomas L.	1845	1912	MacArthur, Arthur	1890	1969	Stratemeyer, George (AF)
1828	1890	Crook, George	1880	1964	MacArthur, Douglas	1833	1864	Stuart, J. E. B.
1842	1874	Cushing, William B. (N)	1733	1795	Marion, Francis	1740	1795	Sullivan, John
1839	1876	Custer, George	1806	1873	Maury, Matthew F. (N)	1822	1880	Sykes, George
1779	1820	Decatur, Stephen (N)	1826	1885	McClellan, George B.	1827	1890	Terry, Alfred H.
1837	1917	Dewey, George (N)	1818	1885	McDowell, Irvin	1816	1876	Thomas, George H.
1857	1927	Dickman, Joseph T.	1828	1864	McPherson, James	1884	1955	Towers, John H. (N)
1879	1951	Drum, Hugh A.	1815	1872	Meade, George	1899	1954	Vanderberg, Hoyt (AF)
1816	1894	Early, Jubal A.	1839	1925	Miles, Nelson A.	1883	1953	Wainwright, Jonathan
1886	1961	Eichelberger, R.L.	1879	1936	Mitchell, Billy	1889	1950	Walker, Walton H.
1846	1912	Evans, Robley D. (N)	1887	1947	Mitscher, Marc A. (N)	1745	1796	Wayne, Anthony
1817	1872	Ewell, Richard	1736	1775	Montgomery, Richard	1836	1906	Wheeler, Joseph
1801	1870	Farragut, David G. (N)	1736	1802	Morgan, Daniel	1757	1825	Wilkinson, James
1806	1863	Foote, Andrew (N)	1730	1805	Moultrie, William	1837	1925	Wilson, James H.
1821	1877	Forrest, Nathan B.	1885	1966	Nimitz, Chester (N)	1860	1927	Wood, Leonard
1865	1917	Funston, Frederick	1896	1959	Parks, Floyd L.	1818	1897	Worden, John L. (N)
1728	1806	Gates, Horatio	1885	1945	Patton, George S.	1820	1899	Wright, Horatio G.
1805	1877	Goldsborough, L. M. (N)	1814	1881	Pemberton, J. C.	1876	1959	Yarnell, Hy. E. (N)
1742	1786	Greene, Nathaniel	1785	1819	Perry, Oliver H. (N)	1887	1964	York, Alvin C. (Sgt.)
1896	1970	Groves, Leslie R.	1860	1948	Pershing, John J.			
1815	1872	Halleck, Henry	1739	1817	Pickens, Andrew			

AMERICAN SCIENTISTS, PHYSICIANS, ENGINEERS OF THE PAST

Born	Died	Name	Born	Died	Name	Born	Died	Name
1838	1916	Abbe, Cleveland	1903	1973	Gibbon, John H.	1903	1966	Millikan, Clark
1876	1945	Albee, Fred H.	1839	1903	Gibbs, Josiah W.	1868	1953	Millikan, Robert
1807	1873	Agassiz, Louis	1858	1928	Goethals, Geo. W.	1866	1945	Morgan, Thos. H.
1832	1867	Baird, Spencer	1874	1929	Goldberger, Joseph	1819	1868	Morton, W. T. G.
1839	1883	Beard, George Miller	1854	1920	Gorgas, Wm. C.	1890	1967	Muller, Hermann J.
1785	1853	Beaumont, Wm.	1863	1914	Hall, Charles M.	1904	1967	Oppenheimer, J. Robert
1889	1967	Bigelow, Henry B.	1896	1965	Hench, Philip S.	1883	1962	Papanicolaou, Geo. N.
1899	1964	Blalock, Alfred	1883	1964	Hess, Victor F.	1903	1967	Pincus, Gregory
1773	1838	Bowditch, Nath.	1889	1953	Hubble, Edwin P.	1851	1902	Reed, Walter S.
1882	1961	Bridgman, Percy W.	1865	1958	Jackson, Chevalier	1846	1927	Remsen, Ira
1848	1908	Brooks, Wm. K.	1834	1913	Klebs, Edwin	1871	1910	Ricketts, Howard T.
1868	1939	Cabot, Richard C.	1834	1906	Langley, Samuel P.	1806	1869	Roebling, John A.
1873	1944	Carrel, Alexis	1881	1957	Langmuir, Irving	1837	1926	Roebling, Washington
1864	1943	Carver, Geo. W.	1884	1964	Lanza, Anthony J.	1879	1970	Rous, Peyton
1887	1968	Cobb, Stanley	1901	1958	Lawrence, Ernest O.	1745	1813	Rush, Benjamin
1892	1962	Compton, Arthur H.	1815	1878	Long, Crawford	1877	1967	Schick, Bela
1877	1954	Compton, Karl T.	1885	1916	Lowell, Percival	1885	1972	Shapley, Harlow
1869	1939	Cushing, Harvey W.	1806	1873	Maury, Matthew F.	1813	1883	Sims, James M.
1872	1946	Davis, John S.	1865	1939	Mayo, Charles H.	1865	1923	Steinmetz, Chas.
1927	1961	Dooley, Thomas	1898	1968	Mayo, Charles W.	1853	1943	Stevens, John Frank
1901	1965	Du Mont, Allen	1861	1939	Mayo, Wm. J.	1898	1964	Szilard, Leo
1820	1887	Eads, James P.	1845	1913	McBurney, Chas.	1899	1972	Theiler, Max
1879	1955	Einstein, Albert	1909	1968	McLean, John Milton	1894	1964	Wiener, Norbert
1706	1790	Franklin, Benjamin	1899	1966	Menninger, Wm. C.	1844	1930	Wiley, Harvey W.
1884	1967	Funk, Casimir	1852	1931	Michelson, Albert A.	1856	1931	Williams, Daniel Hale

AMERICAN SCULPTORS OF THE PAST

Born	Died	Name	Born	Died	Name	Born	Died	Name
1878	1949	Aitken, Robert I.	1805	1852	Greenouth, Horatio	1867	1917	Pratt, Bela
1887	1964	Archipenko, Alexander	1887	1967	Hoffman, Malvina	1868	1929	Quinn, Edmond T.
1881	1970	Baker, Bryant	1830	1908	Hosmer, Harriet	1816	1879	Rimmer, William
1819	1911	Ball, Thomas	1847	1914	Hoxie, Vinnie Ream	1825	1874	Rinehart, William H.
1863	1938	Barnard, George Grey	1825	1879	Jackson, John Adams	1829	1904	Rogers, John
1865	1925	Bartlett, Paul W.	1868	1925	Jaegers, Albert	1825	1892	Rogers, Randolph
1867	1915	Bitter, Karl T.	1892	1969	Jones, Thomas H.	1879	1922	Rumsey, Charles Cary
1913	1969	Boehm, Edward M.	1863	1947	Kitson, Henry Hudson	1756	1833	Rush, William
1871	1941	Borglum, Gutzon	1871	1932	Kitson, Theo Alice	1848	1907	St. Gaudens, Augustus
1868	1922	Borglum, Solon H.	1882	1935	Lachaise, Gaston	1871	1922	Shrady, Henry M.
1814	1886	Brown, Henry K.	1877	1954	Laessle, Albert	1839	1913	Simmons, Franklin
1898	1970	Bufano, Beniamino	1877	1963	Lawrie, Lee	1906	1965	Smith, David
1870	1945	Calder, Alexander S.	1871	1935	Lukeman, Henry A.	1819	1895	Story, William W.
1814	1857	Crawford, Thomas	1863	1937	MacMonnies, Fred W.	1860	1936	Taft, Lorado
1861	1944	Dallin, Cyrus	1885	1966	Manship, Paul	1830	1910	Ward, J. Q. A.
1884	1952	Davidson, Jo	1879	1947	MaCartan, Edward	1870	1952	Weinman, Adolph A.
1884	1953	Diederich, Hunt	1876	1916	Mears, Helen F.	1877	1942	Whitney, Gertrude
1895	1942	Flannagan, John	1883	1962	Mestrovic, Ivan	1877	1957	Young, Mahonri M.
1877	1953	Fraser, James E.	1875	1955	Milles, Carl	1863	1949	Zoinay, Geo. Julian
1790	1852	Frazee, John	1817	1904	Palmer, Erastus Dow	1887	1966	Zorach, William
1850	1931	French, Daniel C.	1805	1873	Powers, Hiram			

AMERICAN REFORMERS, SOCIAL-ECONOMIC LEADERS OF THE PAST

Born	Died	Name	Born	Died	Name	Born	Died	Name
1860	1935	Addams, Jane	1805	1879	Garrison, Wm. L.	1811	1886	Noyes, John H.
1909	1972	Alinsky, Saul O.	1887	1940	Garvey, Marcus	1801	1877	Owen, Robt. Dale
1847	1902	Altgeld, Peter	1839	1897	George, Henry	1810	1860	Parker, Theodore
1820	1906	Anthony, Susan B.	1837	1927	Gerry, Elbridge T.	1811	1884	Phillips, Wendell
1891	1969	Arnold, Thurman, W.	1850	1924	Gompers, Samuel	1849	1914	Riis, Jacob A.
1867	1961	Balch, Emily G.	1873	1952	Green, William	1816	1906	Sage, Russell
1821	1912	Barton, Clara H.	1887	1946	Hillman, Sidney	1828	1918	Sage, Margaret Olivia
1818	1895	Bloomer, Amelia J.	1801	1876	Howe, Samuel G.	1883	1967	Sanger, Margaret
1809	1890	Brisbane, Albert	1929	1968	King, Martin Luther	1747	1825	Shays, Daniel
1800	1859	Brown, John	1855	1925	LaFollette, Robt. M.	1797	1874	Smith, Gerrit
1859	1947	Catt, Carrie Chapman	1882	1947	La Guardia, Fiorello	1816	1902	Stanton, Eliz. Cady
1855	1926	Debs, Eugene	1880	1969	Lewis John L.	1818	1893	Stone, Lucy
1802	1887	Dix, Dorothea	1793	1880	Mott, Lucretia	1867	1960	Townsend, Francis E.
1817	1895	Douglass, Frederick	1886	1952	Murray, Philip	1893	1955	White, Walter
1868	1963	Du Bois, William E. B.	1846	1911	Nation, Carry	1839	1898	Willard, Frances E.

AMERICAN ETCHERS, ENGRAVERS, ILLUSTRATORS, CARTOONISTS

Born	Died	Name	Born	Died	Name	Born	Died	Name
1887	1953	Arms, John Taylor	1891	1969	Fitzpatrick, Daniel R.	1860	1919	Mielatz, C. F. Wm.
1904	1968	Arno, Peter	1878	1960	Flagg, Jas. Mont.	1869	1935	Mielziner, Leo
1856	1909	Bacher, Otto Henry	1883	1972	Fleischer, Max	1874	1948	Morgan, Wallace
1862	1951	Benson, Frank W.	1884	1964	Fox, Fontaine	1840	1902	Nast, Thomas
1909	1970	Breger, Dave	1851	1906	French, Edwin D.	1863	1928	Outcault, Richard F.
1875	1930	Briggs, Clare	1899	1969	Freyse, William	1870	1966	Parrish, Maxfield
1881	1966	Brown, Arthur Wm.	1851	1928	Frost, Arthur B.	1741	1827	Peale, Charles W.
1889	1968	Burger, Carl	1868	1945	Gibson, Chas. Dana	1857	1926	Pennell, Joseph
1877	1970	Cady, Harrison	1883	1970	Goldberg, Rube	1861	1933	Platt, Charles A.
1873	1952	Christy, H. Chandler	1861	1933	Kemble, E. W.	1877	1952	Robinson, Boardman
1852	1931	Cole, Timothy	1838	1895	Keppler, Joseph	1833	1909	Smillie, James D.
1822	1888	Darley, Felix O. C.	1876	1952	Kirby, Rollin	1887	1935	Smith, Sidney
1877	1968	Dirks, Rudolph	1872	1934	McCay, Winsor	1885	1952	Webster, H. T.
1796	1886	Durand, Asher Brown	1870	1949	McCutcheon, John T.	1887	1966	Westover, Russ
1901	1966	Edson, Gus	1858	1938	McDougall, Wait	1852	1916	Wolf, Henry
1885	1954	Fisher, H. C. (Bud)	1884	1954	McManus, George	1901	1973	Young, Chic

AMERICAN PAINTERS OF THE PAST

Born	Died	Name	Born	Died	Name	Born	Died	Name
1852	1911	Abbey, Edwin A.	1813	1894	Healy, George P. A.	1778	1860	Peale, Rembrandt
1779	1843	Allston, Washington	1865	1929	Henri, Robert	1851	1914	Pearce, Charles S.
1785	1851	Audubon, John James	1780	1849	Hicks, Edward	1884	1970	Peirce, Waldo
1893	1965	Avery, Milton C.	1823	1890	Hicks, Thomas	1912	1956	Pollock, Jackson
1912	1963	Baziotes, William	1880	1966	Hofmann, Hans	1823	1879	Powell, William H.
1855	1942	Beaux, Cecelia	1836	1910	Homer, Winslow	1861	1924	Prendergast, Maurice B.
1882	1925	Bellows, George W.	1882	1967	Hopper, Edward	1853	1911	Pyle, Howard
1828	1902	Bierstadt, Albert	1824	1879	Hunt, William M.	1801	1881	Quidor, John
1811	1879	Bingham, George Caleb	1816	1906	Huntington, Daniel	1913	1967	Reinhardt, Ad
1856	1943	Birch, Reginald B.	1801	1846	Inman, Henry	1861	1909	Remington, Frederic
1848	1936	Blashfield, Edwin H.	1825	1894	Inness, George	1871	1925	Reuterdahl, Henry
1847	1927	Bridgman, Frederic A.	1855	1914	Isham, Samuel	1838	1905	Richards, William T.
1855	1941	Brush, George de Forest	1843	1942	Jackson, William H.	1903	1970	Rothko, Mark
1893	1967	Burchfield, Charles E.	1781	1839	Jarvis, John Wesley	1864	1926	Russell, Charles M.
1845	1926	Cassatt, Mary	1824	1906	Johnson, Eastman	1847	1917	Ryder, Albert P.
1796	1872	Catlin, George	1874	1939	Johnson, Frank Tenney	1856	1925	Sargent, John Singer
1849	1916	Chase, William M.	1838	1911	Keith, William	1898	1969	Shahn, Ben
1826	1900	Church, Frederic	1818	1872	Kensett, John F.	1883	1965	Sheeler, Charles
1801	1848	Cole, Thomas	1877	1949	Kuhn, Walt	1876	1953	Shinn, Everett
1737	1815	Copley, John S.	1835	1910	La Farge, John	1871	1951	Sloan, John
1856	1919	Cox, Kenyon	1807	1889	Lambdin, James Reid	1883	1962	Speicher, Eugene E.
1823	1900	Cropsey, Jaspar F.	1873	1939	Lawson, Ernest	1880	1946	Stella, Joseph
1843	1909	Currier, J. Frank	1816	1868	Leutze, Emanuel	1755	1828	Stuart, Gilbert
1898	1946	Curry, John Steuart	1880	1940	Lie, Jonas	1783	1872	Sully, Thomas
1862	1928	Davies, Arthur B.	1853	1932	Low, Will Hicok	1861	1930	Symons, Gardner
1894	1964	Davis, Stuart	1867	1933	Luks, George B.	1849	1921	Thayer, Abbott H.
1883	1935	Demuth, Charles	1866	1912	MacCameron, Robert L.	1848	1933	Tiffany, Louis C.
1884	1958	Du Bois, Guy Pene	1860	1943	MacEwen, Walter	1756	1843	Trumbull, John
1796	1886	Durand, Asher Brown	1872	1953	Marin, John	1849	1925	Tryon, Dwight N.
1848	1919	Duveneck, Frank	1898	1954	Marsh, Reginald	1853	1902	Twachtman, John H.
1844	1916	Eakins, Thomas	1836	1897	Martin, Homer	1776	1852	Vanderlyn, John
1751	1801	Earle, Ralph	1813	1884	Matteson, Tompkins H.	1836	1923	Vedder, Elihu
1871	1956	Feininger, Lyonel	1868	1932	Maurer, Alfred H.	1858	1933	Vonnoh, Robert W.
1822	1884	Fuller, George	1860	1932	Melchers, Gari	1843	1929	Walker, Henry Oliver
1867	1934	Fuller, Henry Brown	1858	1925	Metcalf, Willard L.	1856	1928	Webb, J. Louis
1881	1952	Gallatin, Albert E.	1829	1901	Moran, Edward	1881	1961	Weber, Max
1870	1938	Glackens, William J.	1863	1935	Moran, Percy	1841	1903	Weir, John F.
1904	1948	Gorky, Arshile	1837	1926	Moran, Thomas	1852	1919	Weir, Julian Alden
1893	1959	Grosz, George	1860	1961	Moses, Grandma	1803	1889	Weir, Robert W.
1866	1946	Guerin, Jules	1807	1868	Mount, William S.	1738	1820	West, Benjamin
1865	1931	Hale, Philip L.	1907	1967	Murch, Walter T.	1834	1903	Whistler, James A. M.
1792	1866	Harding, Chester	1867	1940	Myers, Jerome	1820	1910	Whittredge, Worthington
1848	1892	Harnett, William M.	1847	1918	Nicoll, James Craig	1891	1942	Wood, Grant
1868	1933	Hart, George O.	1741	1827	Peale, Charles W.	1823	1903	Wood, Thomas W.
1877	1943	Hartley, Marsden	1749	1831	Peale, James	1836	1892	Wyant, Alexander H.
1860	1935	Hassam, Childe	1774	1825	Peale, Raphaelle	1882	1945	Wyeth, Newell
1872	1930	Hawthorne, Charles W.						

AMERICAN INVENTORS OF THE PAST

Born	Died	Name	Born	Died	Name	Born	Died	Name
1891	1954	Armstrong, Edwin	1882	1945	Goddard, Robert H.	1791	1872	Morse, S. F. B.
1847	1922	Bell, Alex. Graham	1800	1860	Goodyear, Chas.	1831	1897	Pullman, George M.
1890	1970	Bell, Herbert A.	1803	1855	Gorrie, John	1743	1792	Rumsey, Jas.
1906	1968	Carlson, Chester F.	1835	1901	Gray, Elisha	1889	1972	Sikorsky, Igor
1874	1961	De Forrest, Lee	1886	1964	Hazeltine, L. Alan	1894	1970	Spencer, Percy L.
1862	1938	Duryea, Charles E.	1797	1878	Henry, Jos.	1860	1930	Sperry, Elmer A.
1870	1967	Duryea, J. Frank	1812	1886	Hoe, Richard M.	1856	1943	Tesla, Nikola
1854	1932	Eastman, Geo.	1819	1867	Howe, Elias	1853	1937	Thomson, Elihu
1847	1931	Edison, Thos. A.	1866	1945	Lake, Simon	1846	1914	Westinghouse, Geo.
1803	1889	Ericsson, John	1881	1957	Langmuir, Irving	1765	1825	Whitney, Eli
1743	1798	Fitch, John	1826	1886	Loomis, Mahlon	1856	1910	Woods, Granville T.
1765	1815	Fulton, Robert	1809	1884	McCormick, Cyrus H.	1871	1948	Wright, Orville
1818	1903	Gatling, Rich. J.	1854	1899	Mergenthaler, Ottmar	1867	1912	Wright, Wilbur

AMERICAN EDUCATORS AND RELIGIOUS LEADERS

EDUCATORS

Born	Died	Name	Born	Died	Name	Born	Died	Name
1890	1970	Ackerman, Carl W.	1804	1894	Peabody, Eliz. P.	1748	1830	Hicks, Elias
1897	1967	Allport, Gordon	1870	1964	Pound, Roscoe	1879	1964	Holmes, John Haynes
1829	1916	Angell, James B.	1866	1916	Royce, Josiah	1886	1968	Holt, Ivan Lee
1870	1949	Angell, James R.	1774	1821	Seton, Elizabeth	1590	1643	Hutchinson, Anne
1811	1900	Barnard, Henry	1885	1963	Seymour, Charles	1883	1968	Jones, Bob
1827	1911	Bascom, John	1779	1864	Silliman, Benj.	1884	1973	Jones, E. Stanley
1862	1947	Butler, Nich. Murray	1917	1969	Smith, Courtney C.	1843	1926	Kohler, Kaufmann
1847	1909	Canfield, Jas. H.	1859	1934	Smith, Theobald	1866	1949	Manning, Wm. T.
1807	1874	Cornell, Ezra	1886	1967	Stace, Walter T.	1663	1728	Mather, Cotton
1862	1948	Cross, Wilbur	1840	1910	Sumner, Wm. Graham	1873	1970	McKay, David O.
1859	1952	Dewey, John	1893	1969	Tannenbaum, Frank	1890	1944	Aimee Semple McPherson
1868	1963	DuBois, Wm. E.	1858	1915	Washington, Booker T.	1837	1899	Moody, Dwight L.
1834	1926	Eliot, Chas. W.	1832	1918	White, Andrew D.	1711	1787	Muhlenberg, H. M.
1863	1940	Finley, John H.	1787	1870	Willard, Emma	1891	1963	Oxnam, G. Bromley
1903	1967	Gassner, John W.	1864	1935	Williams, Walter	1810	1860	Parker, Theodore
1831	1908	Gilman, Daniel C.				1842	1933	Parkhurst, C. H.
1906	1963	Griswold, A. Whitney			**RELIGIOUS LEADERS**	1913	1969	Pike, James A.
1844	1924	Hall, G. Stanley	1835	1922	Abbott, Lyman	1884	1968	Poling, Daniel A.
1856	1906	Harper, William R.	1745	1816	Asbury, Francis	1729	1796	Seabury, Samuel
1802	1887	Hopkins, Mark	1813	1887	Beecher, Henry Ward	1886	1969	Sheil, Bernard J.
1842	1910	James, William	1775	1863	Beecher, Lyman	1882	1968	Shipler, Guy E.
1880	1968	Keller, Helen	1835	1893	Brooks, Phillips	1881	1968	Silver, Eliezer
1797	1849	Lyon, Mary	1582	1658	Bulkeley, Peter	1805	1844	Smith, Joseph
1800	1873	McGuffey, Wm. H.	1802	1867	Bushnell, Horace	1876	1972	Smith, Joseph Fielding
1796	1859	Mann, Horace	1780	1842	Channing, Wm. Ellery	1889	1970	Sockman, Ralph W.
1738	1791	Manning, James	1584	1652	Cotton, John	1889	1967	Spellman, Francis
1872	1964	Meiklejohn, Alexander	1895	1970	Cushing, Richard	1863	1935	Sunday, Wm. (Billy)
1886	1964	Mott, Frank L.	1752	1817	Dwight, Timothy	1832	1902	Talmadge, T. Dewitt
1818	1901	Muhlenberg, Fred. A.	1821	1910	Eddy, Mary Baker	1886	1965	Tillich, Paul
1869	1946	Neilson, Wm. A.	1703	1758	Edwards, Jonathan	1862	1969	Welch, Herbert
1909	1969	Northrop, Eugene P.	1900	1968	Fry, Franklin C.	1599	1683	Williams, Roger
1827	1908	Norton, Chas. Eliot	1805	1879	Garrison, Wm. Lloyd	1874	1949	Wise, Stephen S.
1855	1902	Palmer, Alice Freeman	1834	1921	Gibbons, James	1801	1877	Young, Brigham
			1867	1938	Hayes, Patrick J.			

American Writers of the Past
Novelists, Poets, Historians, Journalists, Publishers, Biographers

A

Charles Francis Adams, biographer, diplomat, 1807-1886.

Charles Francis Adams, historian, lawyer, 1835-1915.

Franklin P. Adams, journalist, 1881-1960.

Henry Adams, historian, philosopher, 1838-1918.

James Truslow Adams, historian, 1878-1949.

Samuel Hopkins Adams, novelist, magazine writer, 1871-1958. It Happened One Night.

George Ade, humorist, dramatist, 1866-1944.

Louisa May Alcott, novelist, writer of children's books, 1832-1889. Little Women.

Thomas Bailey Aldrich, author, editor, 1836-1907.

Henry M. Alden, editor, 1836-1919. Harper's Magazine.

Horatio Alger, author of "rags-to-riches" boys' books, 1832-1899.

James Lane Allen, novelist, 1849-1925.

Charlotte Armstrong, mystery writer, 1905-1969.

Hamilton Fish Armstrong, journalist and editor of Foreign Affairs, 1893-1973. Black Oxen.

Gertrude Atherton, novelist, 1857-1948.

Mary Austin, novelist, playwright, 1868-1934.

B

Irving Bacheller, novelist, journalist, 1859-1950. Eben Holden.

Arthur (Bugs) Baer, humorous columnist, 1886-1969.

Dorothy Dodd Baker, novelist, 1907-1968. Young Man with a Horn.

Ray Stannard Baker, biographer, historian, 1870-1946.

George Bancroft, historian, diplomat, 1800-1891.

Margaret Ayer Barnes, novelist, 1886-1967. Years of Grace.

John Bartlett, publisher, 1820-1905. Familiar Quotations.

Bruce Barton, author, advertising executive, 1875-1967. The Man Nobody Knows.

Charles A. Beard, historian, 1874-1948.

Mary Ritter Beard, historian, 1876-1958.

Lucius M. Beebe, journalist, author, 1902-1966. N. Y. Herald Tribune.

Edward Bellamy, novelist, journalist, 1850-1898. Looking Backward: 2000-1887.

Robert C. Benchley, humorist, journalist, 1889-1945.

Stephen Vincent Benet, poet, novelist, 1898-1943.

William Rose Benet, poet, novelist, 1886-1950.

James Gordon Bennett, journalist, 1795-1872. Founded N. Y. Herald.

James Gordon Bennett, Jr., journalist, 1841-1918. N. Y. Herald. Evening Telegram.

Eric Berne, psychiatrist, author, 1910-1970. Games People Play.

John Berryman, poet, 1914-1972.

Albert J. Beveridge, historian, politician, 1862-1927.

Ambrose Bierce, short-story writer, journalist, 1842-1914.

Earl Derr Biggers, novelist, 1884-1933. Created Charlie Chan.

Josh Billings (H.W. Shaw), humorist, 1818-1885.

Louise Bogan, lyric poet, 1897-1970.

Samuel Bowles II, journalist, author, 1826-1878. Springfield Republican.

Gamaliel Bradford, biographer, 1863-1932.

Anne Bradstreet, poet, 1612-1672.

William Cowper Brann (Iconoclast), editor, reformer, 1855-1898.

Arthur Brisbane, journalist, 1864-1936. N. Y. Sun, Evening Sun, World and Hearst newspapers.

Louis Bromfield, novelist, essayist, 1896-1956.

Van Wyck Brooks, historian, critic, 1886-1963.

Heywood Broun, journalist, 1888-1939, N. Y. Morning Telegraph, Tribune, World.

John Mason Brown, drama, literary critic, 1900-1969.

Orestes Brownson, author, editor, clergyman, 1803-1876.

Katharine Brush, novelist, 1902-1952. Young Man of Manhattan.

William Cullen Bryant, poet, editor, 1794-1878.

Pearl Buck, author, won the Pulitzer and Nobel Prizes in literature, 1892-1973. The Good Earth.

Henry C. Bunner, poet, novelist, 1855-1896. Editor of Puck.

Ned Buntline, author of dime novels, 1823-1886. Gave "Buffalo Bill" Cody his nickname.

Edgar Rice Burroughs, novelist, 1875-1950. Tarzan of the Apes.

Struthers Burt, novelist, poet, 1882-1954.

C

George W. Cable, novelist, essayist, 1844-1925.

Henry Seidel Canby, editor, critic, 1878-1961. Saturday Review of Literature.

Will Carleton, poet, journalist, 1845-1912. Over the Hill to the Poorhouse.

David Lawrence, journalist, founder and editor of U.S. News & World Report, 1888-1973.

Victor F. Lawson, journalist, 1850-1925. Chicago Daily News.

Emma Lazarus, poet, essayist, 1849-1887. The New Colossus.

Charles Godfrey Leland, poet, journalist, 1824-1903.

William Ellery Leonard, poet, educator, 1876-1944.

Fulton Lewis, Jr., radio news commentator, 1903-1966.

Oscar Lewis, author, anthropologist, 1914-1970. La Vida.

Sinclair Lewis, novelist, playwright, 1885-1951. Babbitt, Arrowsmith, Dodsworth.

Ludwig Lewisohn, novelist, critic, 1883-1955.

Willy Ley, science writer, 1906-1969.

Vachel Lindsay, poet, 1879-1931.

Louis Lomax, author, 1922-1970. The Negro Revolt.

Jack London, novelist, journalist, 1876-1916. The Call of the Wild.

Henry Wadsworth Longfellow, poet, 1807-1882. The Wreck of the Hesperus, Evangeline, The Song of Hiawatha.

Benson John Lossing, historian, artist, 1813-1891. Pictorial Field Book of the Revolution.

Elijah P. Lovejoy, journalist, abolitionist, 1802-1837.

Amy Lowell, poet, critic, 1874-1925.

James Russell Lowell, poet, editor, 1819-1891.

Jim Lucas, journalist, 1914-1970. Scripps-Howard Newspapers.

Henry R. Luce, publisher, 1898-1967. Time, Life, Fortune magazines.

M

Elliot Beach Macrae, publisher, 1900-1968. E. P. Dutton & Co.

Edwin Markham, poet, 1852-1940. The Man with the Hoe.

John P. Marquand, novelist, 1893-1960. The Late George Apley.

Don Marquis, humorist, journalist, 1878-1937. The Old Soak.

Edgar Lee Masters, poet, biographer, 1869-1950. Spoon River Anthology.

James McClatchy, publisher, editor, 1824-1883. McClatchy Newspapers.

S. S. McClure, editor, publisher, 1857-1949.

Joseph Medill McCormick, journalist, politician, 1877-1925. Chicago Tribune.

Robert R. McCormick, editor, publisher, 1880-1955. Chicago Tribune.

Carson McCullers, novelist, 1917-1967. The Heart Is a Lonely Hunter.

Ralph E. McGill, editor, publisher, Atlanta Constitution, 1898-1969.

John B. McMaster, historian, 1852-1932.

Joseph Medill, journalist, 1823-1899. Chicago Tribune.

Herman Melville, novelist, poet, 1819-1891. Moby Dick.

Henry L. Mencken, editor, author, 1880-1956. Baltimore Sun, American Mercury.

Thomas Merton, poet, religious writer, 1915-1968. Seven Storey Mountain.

Edna St. Vincent Millay, poet, 1892-1950.

Joaquin Miller, poet, 1839-1913.

Max Miller, novelist, 1889-1967. I Cover the Waterfront.

Margaret Mitchell, novelist, journalist, 1900-1949. Gone With the Wind.

William Vaughn Moody, poet, dramatist, 1869-1910.

Clement C. Moore, poet, educator, 1779-1863. A Visit from Saint Nicholas.

Marianne Moore, poet, 1887-1972.

Christopher Morley, journalist, novelist, 1890-1957. Kitty Foyle.

John L. Motley, historian, diplomat, 1814-1877.

Willard Motley, novelist, 1912-1968. Knock at Any Door.

Edward R. Murrow, radio-TV commentator, 1908-1965.

N

Ogden Nash, poet, 1902-1971.

William Rockhill Nelson, journalist, 1841-1915. Kansas City Star.

John G. Nicolay, biographer, 1832-1901. Abraham Lincoln: A History.

Charles B. Nordhoff, novelist, 1887-1947. Co-author Mutiny on the Bounty.

Frank Norris, novelist, journalist, 1870-1902.

Frank Norris, novelist, 1907-1967. Tower in the West.

Kathleen Norris, novelist, 1880-1966.

Frank B. Noyes, newspaper executive, 1863-1948. Associated Press.

O

Edwin G. O'Connor, novelist, 1890-1968. Edge of Sadness, The Last Hurrah.

Adolph S. Ochs, journalist, 1858-1935. New York Times.

John O'Hara, novelist, 1905-1970. Butterfield 8, Ten North Frederick.

Fremont Older, journalist, 1856-1935. San Francisco Call-Bulletin.

James Oppenheim, poet, novelist, 1882-1932.

P

Thomas (Tom) Paine, author, political theorist, 1737-1809. Common Sense.

Dorothy Parker, poet, short-story writer, 1893-1967.

Francis Parkman, historian, 1823-1893.

James K. Paulding, poet, novelist, 1778-1860.

John Howard Payne, poet, dramatist, 1791-1852. Home, Sweet Home.

Frederick Palmer, war correspondent, 1873-1958.

Alicia Patterson, journalist, 1906-1963. Newsday.

Eleanor Medill Patterson, journalist, 1884-1948. Washington Times-Herald.

Joseph Medill Patterson, publisher, 1879-1946. Founded N. Y. Daily News.

Josephine P. Peabody, poet, dramatist, 1874-1922.

Drew Pearson, newspaper columnist, 1897-1969.

Westbrook Pegler, newspaper columnist, 1894-1969.

David G. Phillips, journalist, novelist, 1867-1911.

Edgar Allan Poe, poet, short-story writer, critic, 1809-1849.

Ernest Poole, journalist, novelist, 1880-1950.

Ezra Pound, poet, 1885-1972.

William H. Prescott, historian, 1796-1859.

Joseph Pulitzer, journalist, 1847-1911. St. Louis Post-Dispatch, N. Y. World.

Joseph Pulitzer, journalist, 1885-1955. St. Louis Post-Dispatch.

Ralph Pulitzer, journalist, 1879-1939, St. Louis Post-Dispatch, N. Y. World.

Ernie Pyle, journalist, war correspondent, 1900-1945.

R

James G. Randall, historian, 1881-1953.

Burton Rascoe, journalist, author, 1892-1957.

Marjorie Kinnan Rawlings, novelist, 1896-1953. The Yearling.

Thomas Buchanan Read, poet, painter, 1822-1872. Sheridan's Ride.

Lizette Woodworth Reese, poet, 1856-1935.

Ogden M. Reid, journalist, 1882-1947. N. Y. Herald Tribune.

Whitelaw Reid, journalist, diplomat, 1837-1912. N. Y. Tribune.

Erich Maria Remarque, novelist, 1898-1970. All Quiet on the Western Front.

Quentin Reynolds, journalist, author, 1902-1965.

James Ford Rhodes, historian, 1848-1927.

Alice Hegan Rice, novelist, 1870-1952. Mrs. Wiggs of the Cabbage Patch.

Cale Young Rice, poet, novelist, 1872-1943.

Grantland Rice, journalist, 1880-1954.

Conrad M. Richter, novelist, 1890-1968. The Town.

James Whitcomb Riley, poet, 1849-1916.

Mary Roberts Rinehart, novelist, dramatist, 1876-1958. The Circular Staircase (The Bat).

Elizabeth Madox Roberts, poet, novelist, 1886-1941.

Kenneth Roberts, novelist, 1885-1957. Northwest Passage.

Roy A. Roberts, journalist, 1887-1967. Kansas City Star.

Edwin Arlington Robinson, poet, 1869-1935.

Theodore Roethke, poet, 1908-1963.

Robert Ruark, journalist, author, 1915-1965.

Damon Runyon, short-story writer, journalist, 1884-1946. Guys and Dolls.

S

Carl Sandburg, poet, biographer, 1878-1967.

George Santayana, poet, essayist, philosopher, 1863-1952.

Lew Sarett, poet, 1888-1954.

Max L. Schuster, editor, publisher, 1897-1970. Simon & Schuster.

Edward W. Scripps, newspaper publisher, 1854-1926.

Robert P. Scripps, newspaper publisher, 1895-1938. Scripps-Howard Newspapers.

Alan Seeger, poet, 1888-1916. I Have a Rendezvous with Death.

Gilbert Seldes, author, critic, 1893-1970. The 7 Lively Arts, The Great Audience.

Ernest Thompson Seton, author, naturalist, 1860-1946. Wild Animals I Have Known.

Odell Shepard, author, politician, 1884-1967. Pedlar's Progress.

Frank Dempster Sherman, poet, educator, 1860-1916.

Lydia H. Sigourney, poet, 1791-1865.

Edward Rowland Sill, poet, educator, 1841-1887.

Upton Sinclair, novelist, 1878-1968. The Jungle, Dragon's Teeth.

Betty Smith, novelist, 1896-1972. A Tree Grows in Brooklyn.

Lillian Smith, novelist, 1897-1966. Strange Fruit.

Merriman Smith, newspaper correspondent, 1913-1970. United Press international.

Samuel Francis Smith, poet, clergyman, 1808-1895. America.

Jared Sparks, historian, educator, 1789-1866.

Keats Speed, newspaper editor, 1880-1952. New York Sun.

Burt L. Standish (Gilbert Patten), author, 1866-1945. Frank Merriwell series.

Frank L. Stanton, poet, journalist, 1857-1927. Mighty Lak' a Rose.

Lincoln Steffens, editor, author, 1866-1936. The Shame of the Cities.

Edmund C. Stedman, poet, critic, 1883-1908.

Gertrude Stein, author, 1874-1946. Three Lives.

John Steinbeck, novelist, 1902-1968. Of Mice and Men, The Grapes of Wrath.

George Sterling, poet, 1869-1926.

Wallace Stevens, poet, insurance executive, 1879-1955.

Frank R. Stockton, novelist, short-story writer, 1834-1902. The Lady or the Tiger?

Melville E. Stone, journalist, 1848-1929. Associated Press.

Harriet Beecher Stowe, novelist, 1811-1896. Uncle Tom's Cabin.

Edward Stratemeyer, author, 1862-1930. Creator of such series as the Rover Boys, Bobbsey Twins, Tom Swift.

Gene Stratton-Porter, novelist, 1863-1924. A Girl of the Limberlost.

Anna Louise Strong, journalist, 1885-1970.

Mark Sullivan, journalist, author, 1874-1952.

Arthur Hays Sulzberger, publisher, 1891-1968. The New York Times.

Herbert Bayard Swope, journalist, 1882-1958. N. Y. World.

T

John B. Tabb, poet, 1845-1909.

Genevieve Taggard, poet, 1894-1948.

Ida M. Tarbell, editor, author, 1857-1944. The History of the Standard Oil Company.

Booth Tarkington, novelist, 1869-1946. Seventeen.

Bayard Taylor, poet, novelist, 1825-1878. The Bedouin Love Song.

Edward Taylor, poet, c. 1642-1729.

Sara Teasdale, poet, 1884-1933.

Albert Payson Terhune, novelist, journalist, 1872-1942. Lad: A Dog.

Dorothy Thompson, journalist, author, 1894-1961.
James Thurber, humorist, artist, 1894-1961. The New Yorker.
Eunice Tietjens, poet, novelist, 1884-1944.
Ridgely Torrence, poet, dramatist, 1875-1950.
Charles Hanson Towne, poet, editor, 1877-1949.
George A. Townsend, journalist, war correspondent, 1841-1914.
Frederick J. Turner, historian, educator, 1861-1932.
Mark Twain (Samuel Clemens), novelist, humorist, 1835-1910. The Adventures of Huckleberry Finn.

V

Carl Van Doren, historian, critic, educator, 1885-1950.
Mark Van Doren, poet, author, critic, 1894-1972.
Henry Van Dyke, poet, educator, essayist, 1852-1933.
Hendrik Willem Van Loon, historian, journalist, 1882-1944.
Carl Van Vechten, novelist, music critic, 1880-1964.

Oswald G. Villard, editor, author, 1872-1949. The Nation.

W

Lew Wallace, novelist, diplomat, 1827-1905. Ben Hur.
Artemus Ward (Charles F. Browne), humorist, 1834-1867.
Henry Watterson, editor, author, 1840-1921. Louisville Courier-Journal.
Nathanael West, novelist, 1903-1940.
Edith Wharton, novelist, 1862-1937. The Age of Innocence.
Steward Edward White, novelist, 1873-1946.
William Allen White, editor, author, 1868-1944. Emporia (Kan.) Gazette.
Walt Whitman, poet, 1819-1892. Leaves of Grass.
John Greenleaf Whittier, poet, journalist, 1809-1892.
Kate Douglas Wiggin, children's author, educator, 1856-1923. Rebecca of Sunnybrook Farm.
Ella Wheeler Wilcox, poet, 1850-1919.
Ben Ames Williams, novelist, 1889-1953.
William Carlos Williams, poet, physician, 1883-1963.
Nathaniel P. Willis, journalist, author, 1806-1867.

Wilson, Edmund, literary and social critic, 1895-1972.
Lyle C. Wilson, journalist, 1899-1967. United Press International.
Walter Winchell, Broadway columnist, 1897-1972.
Thomas Wolfe, novelist, 1900-1938. Look Homeward, Angel.
Frederick E. Woltman, Pulitzer Prize winning journalist, 1907-1970. N. Y. World-Telegram & Sun.
Samuel Woodworth, poet, dramatist, 1784-1842. The Old Oaken Bucket.
Alexander Woollcott, journalist, critic, 1887-1943.
Harold Bell Wright, novelist, 1872-1944. The Shepherd of the Hills.
Richard Wright, novelist, 1908-1960. Native Son.
Elinor Wylie, poet, novelist, 1885-1928.
Philip Wylie, author, 1902-1971. Generation of Vipers.

Z

John Peter Zenger, journalist, printer, 1697-1746. N. Y. Weekly Journal.

Noted Canadians of the Past

Born	Died	Name	Born	Died	Name	Born	Died	Name
		STATESMEN	1895	1958	Dawson, R. MacGregor	1883	1922	Pickthall, Marj.
			1848	1917	Dionne, Narcisse	1883	1964	Pratt, Edwin J.
1821	1893	Abbott, John	....	1936	Doughty, Arthur G.	1749	1809	Quesnel, Joseph
1878	1943	Aberhart, William	1854	1907	Drummond, W. H.	1796	1852	Richardson, John
1804	1858	Baldwin, Robert	1862	1932	Duncan, Sara, J.	1860	1943	Roberts, Chas. G. D.
1912	1970	Beaudoin, Louis René	1864	1922	Edwards, Robert (Bob)	1885	1961	Roche, Mazo de la
1870	1957	Bennett, Richard B.	1799	1870	Faillon, Etienne	1839	1920	Routhier, Adolph
1833	1912	Blake, Edward	1805	1865	Ferland, Jean	1870	1943	Roy, Camille
1854	1937	Borden, Robert	1860	1936	Fraser, Alexander	1858	1913	Roy, Joseph E.
1823	1917	Bowell, Mackenzie	1839	1908	Frechette, Louis H.	1822	1893	Sangster, Charles
1884	1969	Bracken, John	1809	1866	Garneau, Francis X.	1862	1944	Scott, Duncan C.
1818	1880	Brown, George	1786	1871	Gaspe, Philippe de	1874	1958	Service, Robt. W.
1875	1940	Buchan, John	1824	1882	Gerin-Lajoie, Ant.	1859	1931	Short, Adam
1814	1873	Cartier, Georges	1871	1918	Gill, Charles	1878	1941	Skelton, O. D.
1890	1959	Duplessis, Maurice	1860	1937	Gordon, Chas. W.	1823	1910	Smith, Goldwin
1896	1969	Dupuy, Pierre			(Ralph Connor)	1841	1923	Sulte, Benjamin
1895	1973	Frost, Leslie	1878	1967	Groulx, Lionel A.	1888	1951	Trotter, R. G.
1817	1893	Galt, Alexander T.	1871	1948	Grove, Frederick	1856	1926	Weir, R. Stanley
1869	1953	Hepburn, Mitchell F.	1842	1910	Hannay, James	1860	1948	Wrong, George M.
1804	1873	Howe, Joseph	1796	1865	Haliburton, Thos. C.			
1874	1950	King, W. Mackenzie	1816	1876	Heavysege, Charles			**PAINTERS AND SCULPTORS**
1841	1919	Laurier, Wilfrid	1880	1913	Hemon, Louis	1863	1936	Ahrens, Carl
1887	1967	Massey, Vincent	1766	1844	Heriot, George	1876	1955	Allward, Walter S.
1795	1861	Mackenzie, Wm. Lyon	1894	1952	Innis, H. A.	1759	1830	Baillargé, François
1822	1905	McDougall, William	1881	1943	Kennedy, W. P. M.	1740	1794	Beaucort, Francois
1825	1868	McGee, Thomas D'Arcy	1859	1931	Kingsford, Wm.	1905	1960	Borduas, Paul-Emile
1874	1960	Meighen, Arthur	1817	1906	Kirby, William	1827	1916	Bourassa, Napoléon
1897	1972	Pearson, Lester B.	1862	1913	Johnson, Pauline	1855	1925	Brymner, William
1904	1968	Robertson, Norman A.	1871	1960	Laberge, Albert	1871	1945	Carr, Emily
1820	1914	Strathcona (Smith)	1861	1899	Lampman, Archibald	1866	1934	Cullen, Maurice
1844	1894	Thompson, John	1871	1936	Laut, Agnes	1769	1819	Field, Robert
1855	1927	Tupper, Charles H.	1869	1944	Leacock, Stephen	1810	1894	Fowler, Daniel
1888	1967	Vanier, George P.	1841	1907	Legendre, Napoleon	1881	1942	Gagnon, Clarence
1892	1969	Wilgress, Dana	1837	1918	Lemay, Pamphile	1817	1870	Hamel, Théophile
			1857	1954	Lighthall, William	1885	1970	Harris, Lawren Stewart
		AUTHORS	1909	1957	Lowry, Malcolm	1849	1919	Harris, Robert
1748	1784	Alline, Henry	1853	1931	Lucas, L. P.	1850	1917	Hebert, Louis P.
1850	1931	Beauchemin, Neree	1878	1924	Lozeau, Albert	1812	1901	Jacobi, Otto
1913	1966	Allen, Ralph	1874	1942	Macdonald, Lucy M.	1852	1908	Julien, Henri
....	1931	Beck, L. Adams	1876	1951	Mac Innes, Tom	1810	1871	Kane, Paul
1861	1924	Blake, W. H.	1862	1933	MacMechan, Archibald	1815	1872	Krieghoff, Cornelius
1827	1916	Bourassa, Napoleon	1840	1927	Mair, Charles	1873	1939	Lawson, Ernest
1840	1901	Buies, Arthur	1844	1945	Marmette, Joseph	1864	1955	Leduc, Ozias
1861	1918	Campbell, W. Wilfred	1864	1936	Marquis, Thomas	1795	1855	Legaré, Joseph
1861	1929	Carman, W. Bliss	1882	1958	Martin, Chester	1887	1968	Loring, Ernest
1831	1904	Casgrain, Henri-R.	1872	1918	McCrae, John	1847	1939	MacCarthy, Hamilton
1858	1946	Chapais, Thomas	1820	1907	McMullen, John	1873	1932	MacDonald, J. E. H.
1850	1917	Chapman, Wm.	1865	1944	Miner, John T. (Jack)	1882	1953	Milne, David
1820	1890	Chauveau, Pierre	1874	1942	Montgomery, Lucy	1865	1924	Morrice, James Wilson
1885	1953	Chopin, Rene	1803	1885	Moodie, Susanna	1832	1899	O'Brien, Lucius Richard
1850	1887	Crawford, Isabella	1889	1963	Morin, Paul	1860	1892	Peel, Paul
1827	1879	Cremazie, Octave	1879	1941	Nelligan, Emile	1802	1895	Plamondon, Antoine S.
1831	1904	Cosgrain, Abbe R.	1737	1818	Odell, Jonathan	1739	1819	Ranvoyzé, François
1866	1944	Dafoe, John Wesley	1895	1960	Panneton, Philippe	1816	1853	Ritter, Henry
1865	1945	Dantin, Louis	1862	1932	Parker, Gilbert	1869	1937	Suzor-Coté, Aurèle de Foy
			1887	1970	Phelps, Arthur L.	1877	1918	Thomson, Tom

Born	Died	Name
1798	1849	Valentine, William
1881	1969	Varley, F. H.
1858	1938	Walker, Horatio
1855	1936	Watson, Homer
1903	1966	Wood, Elizabeth Wynn
1881	1968	Wyle, Florence

SCIENCE, INDUSTRY

Born	Died	Name
1859	1942	Adams, Frank D.
1810	1882	Allan, Hugh
1891	1941	Banting, Fredk. G.
1877	1943	Beatty, Edward W.
1889	1966	Hilton, Hugh G.
1798	1875	Logan, Wm.
1849	1919	Osler, Wm.
1876	1935	Macleod, John J. R.
1863	1892	Stairs, Wm. Grant
1902	1967	Zimmerman, Adam

ANTHROPOLOGISTS, GEOLOGISTS AND NATURALISTS

Born	Died	Name
1876	1961	Anderson, Rudolph M.
1883	1969	Barbeau, Charles M.
1888	1938	Belaney, George Stansfeld (Grey Owl)
1841	1917	Bell, Robert
1820	1876	Billings, Elkanah
1874	1935	Brock, Reginald Walter
1878	1937	Collins, William Henry
1876	1957	Currelly, Charles Trick
1849	1901	Dawson, George Mercer
1846	1925	Dionne, Charles Eusibe
1817	1896	Hale, Horatio
1859	1944	Hill-Tout, Charles
1826	1892	Hunt, Thomas Sterry
1886	1969	Jenness, Diamond
1833	1881	LaRue, Francois A. H.
1875	1947	Laverner, Percy A.
1820	1892	Leon, Provancher

Born	Died	Name
1798	1875	Logan, Sir William E.
1861	1942	Low, Albert Peter
1858	1957	Lyrrell, Joseph Burr
1863	1945	Lyrrell, James Williams
1831	1920	Macoun, John
1862	1920	Macoun, James Melville
1869	1933	Macoun, William Lyrell
1885	1944	Marie-Victorin
1867	1947	Massicotte, Edouard Z.
1857	1942	McConnell, Richard G.
1905	1970	Rousseau, Jacques
1891	1957	Rowan, William
1870	1953	Roy, Pierre Georges
1836	1914	Saunders, William
1867	1937	Saunders, Sir Charles E.
1824	1902	Selwyn, Alfred R. C.
1860	1946	Seton, Ernest Thompson
1872	1940	Smith, Harlan I.
1872	1924	Waugh, Fredrick W.
1881	1964	Wilson, Alice Evelyn
1876	1941	Wintenberg, William J.

Composers of the Western World

Carl Philipp Emanuel Bach, 1714-1788. (G.) Prussian and Wurtembergian Sonatas.

Johann Christian Bach, 1735-1782. (G.) Concertos, sonatas.

Johann Sebastian Bach, 1685-1750. (G.) St. Matthew Passion; The Well-Tempered Clavichord.

Samuel Barber, b. 1910. (U.S.) Adagio for Strings; Vanessa.

Bela Bartok, 1881-1945. (H.) Concerto for Orchestra; The Miraculous Mandarin.

Ludwig Van Beethoven, 1770-1827. (G.) Concertos (Emperor); sonatas (Moonlight, Pastorale, Pathetique); symphonies (Eroica).

Vincenzo Bellini, 1801-1835, (It.) La Sonnambula; Norma; I Puritani.

Alban Berg, 1885-1935. (Aus.) Wozzeck; Lulu.

Hector Berlioz, 1803-1869, (F.) Damnation of Faust; Symphonie Fantastique; Requiem.

Leonard Bernstein, b. 1918. (U.S.) Jeremiah; West Side Story.

Georges Bizet, 1838-1875. (F.) Carmen; Pearl Fishers.

Ernest Bloch, 1880-1959 (Swiss) Schelomo; Voice in the Wilderness; Sacred Service.

Luigi Boccherini, 1743-1805 (It.) Cello Concerto in B Flat; Symphony in C.

Alexander Borodin, 1834-1887. (R.) Prince Igor; In the Steppes of Central Asia.

Johannes Brahms, 1833-1897. (G.) Liebeslieder Waltzes, Rhapsody in E Flat Major, Opus 119 for Piano, Academic Festival Overture; symphonies, quartets.

Benjamin Britten, b. 1913. (Br.) Peter Grimes, Turn of the Screw, Ceremony of Carols.

Anton Bruckner, 1824-1896. (Aus.) Symphonies (Romantic); Intermezzo for String Quintet.

Ferruccio Busoni, 1866-1924. (It.) Doctor Faust, Comedy Overture.

Dietrich Buxtehude, 1637-1707. (G.) Cantatas, Trio sonatas.

William Byrd, 1543-1623 (Br.) Masses, Sacred Songs.

Alexis Emmanuel Chabrier, 1841-1894. (Fr.) Le Roi Malgre Lui, Espana.

Gustave Charpentier, 1860-1956. (F.) Louise.

Frederic Chopin, 1810-1849. (P.) Concertos, Polonaise No. 6 in A Flat Major (Heroic), sonatas.

Aaron Copland, b. 1900. (U.S.) Appalachian Spring.

Claude Achille Debussy, 1862-1918. (F.) Pelleas et Mellisande, La Mer, Prelude to the Afternoon of a Faun.

C. P. Leo Delibes, 1836-1891, (F.) Lakme, Coppelia, Sylvia.

Norman Dello Joio, b. 1913. (U.S.), Triumph of St. Joan, Psalm of David.

Gaetano Donizetti, 1797-1848. (It.) Elixir of Love, Lucia de Lammermoor, Daughter of the Regiment.

Paul Dukas, 1865-1935. (Fr.) Sorcerer's Apprentice.

Antonin Dvorak, 1841-1904. (C.) Symphony in E Minor (From the New World)

Edward Elgar, 1857-1934. (Br.) Pomp and Circumstance.

Manuel de Falla, 1876-1946. (Sp.) La Vide Breve, El Amor Brujo.

Gabriel Faure, 1845-1924. (Fr.) Requiem, Ballade.

Friedrich vol Flotow, 1812-1883. (G.) Martha.

Cesar Franck, 1822-1890. (Belg.) D Minor Symphony.

George Gershwin, 1898-1937. (U.S.) Rhapsody in Blue, American in Paris, Porgy and Bess.

Umberto Giordano, 1867-1948 (It.) Andrea Chenier.

Alex K. Glazunoff, 1865-1936. (R.) Symphonies, Stenka Razin.

Mikhail Glinka, 1857-1904. (R.) Ruslan & Ludmilla.

Christoph W. Gluck, 1714-1787. (G.) Alceste, Iphigenie en Tauride.

Charles Gounod, 1818-1893. (F.) Faust, Romeo and Juliet.

Edvard Grieg, 1843-1907. (Nor.) Peer Gynt Suite; Concerto in A Minor.

George Frederick Handel, 1685-1759. (G.-Br.) Messiah, Xerxes, Berenice.

Howard Hanson, b. 1896. (U.S.) Symphonies No. 1 (Nordic) and 2 (Romantic).

Roy Harris, b. 1898. (U.S.) Symphonies, Amer. Portraits.

Joseph Haydn, 1732-1809. (Aus.) Symphonies (Clock); oratorios; chamber music.

Paul Hindemith, 1895-1963. (U.S.) Das Marienleben; Mathisder Mader.

Gustav Holst, 1874-1934. (Br.) The Planets, The Hymn of Jesus.

Arthur Honegger, 1892-1955. (Swiss) Judith, Le Roi David, Pacific 231.

Alan Hovhaness, b. 1911. (U.S.) Symphonies, Magnificat.

Engelbert Humperdinck, 1854-1921. (G.) Hansel and Gretel.

Charles Ives, 1874-1954. (U.S.) Third Symphony.

Aram Khachaturian, b. 1903. (R.) Gayane ballet, symphonies.

Zoltan Kodaly, 1882-1967. (Hung.) Hary Janos, Psalmus Hungaricus.

Fritz Kreisler, 1875-1962. (Aus.) Caprice Viennois, Tambourin Chinois.

Rodolphe Kreutzer, 1766-1831. (F.) 40 etudes for violin.

Edouard V. A. Lalo, 1823-1892. (F.) Fiesque, Symphonie Espagnole.

Ruggiero Leoncavallo, 1858-1919. (It.) I Pagliacci.

Franz Liszt, 1811-1886. (H.) 20 Hungarian Rhapsodies; symphonic poems.

Edward MacDowell, 1861-1908. (U.S.) To a Wild Rose.

Gustav Mahler, 1860-1911. (Aus.) Symphonies, Lied von der Erde.

Pietro Mascagni, 1863-1945. (It.) Cavalleria Rusticana.

Jules Massenet, 1842-1912. (F.) Manon, Le Cid, Thais, Don Quixote.

Mendelssohn-Bartholdy, 1809-1847. (G.) Midsummer Night's Dream, Songs Without Words.

Gian-Carlo Menotti, b. 1911. (It.-U.S.) The Medium, The Consul, Amahl and the Night Visitors.

Claudio Monteverdi, 1567-1643. (It.) Opera, masses, madrigals.

Wolfgang Amadeus Mozart, 1756-1791. (Aus.) Magic Flute, Marriage of Figaro, concertos, symphonies, etc.

Modest Moussorgsky, 1835-1881. (R.) Boris Godunov, Pictures at an Exhibition.
Jacques Offenbach, 1819-1880. (F.) Tales of Hoffman, operetta.
Karl Orff, b. 1895 (G.) Carmina Burana.
Ignace Paderewski, 1860-1941 (P.) Minuet in G.
Giovanni P. da Palestrina, 1524-1594. (It.) Masses, motets, madrigals.
Amilcare Ponchielli, 1834-1886. (It.) La Gioconda.
Francis, Poulenc, 1899-1963. (F.) La voix humaine, Les animaux modèles.
Serge Prokofiev, 1891-1953. (R.) Love for Three Oranges, It. Kije, Peter and the Wolf.
Giacomo Puccini, 1858-1924, (It.) La Boheme, Manon Lescaut, Tosca, Madame Butterfly.
Sergei Rachmaninov, 1873-1943. (R.) Prelude in C Sharp Minor.
Maurice Ravel, 1875-1937. (Fr.) Bolero, Daphne et Chloe, Rapsodie Espagnole.
Nickolai Rimsky-Korsakov, 1844-1908. (R.) Golden Cockerel, Cappriccio Espagnol, Scheherazade, Russian Easter overture.
Gioacchino Rossini, 1792-1868. (It.) Barber of Seville, Semiramide, William Tell.
Chas. Camille Saint-Saens, 1835-1921. (F.) Samson and Delilah, Danse Macabre.
Alessandro Scarlatti, 1659-1725. (It.) Cantatas; concer-
Arnold Schoenberg, 1874-1951. (Aus.) Pelleas and Melisande, Transfigured Night, De Profundis.

Franz Schubert, 1797-1828. (A.) Lieder; symphonies (Unfinished); overtures (Rosamunde).
William Schuman, b. 1910. (U.S.) Credendum, New England Triptych.
Robert Schumann, 1810-1856. (G.) Symphonies (Rhenish); Kinderszenen, songs.
Aleksandr Scriabin, 1872-1915. (R.) Prometheus.
Jean Sibelius, 1865-1957, (Finn.) Finlandia, Karelia.
Dimitri Shostakovich, b. 1906. (R.) Symphonies, Lady Macbeth of Minsk, The Nose.
Bedrich Smetana, 1824-1884. (C.) The Bartered Bride.
Karlheinz Stockhausen, b. 1928. (G.) Kontrapunkte, Kontakte.
Richard Strauss, 1864-1949. (G.) Salome, Elektra, Der Rosenkavalier, Thus Spake Zarathustra.
Igor F. Stravinsky, 1882-1971. (R.-U.S.) Oedipus Rex, Le Sacre du Printemps, Petrushka.
Peter I. Tchaikovsky, 1840-1893. (R.) Nutcracker Suite, Swan Lake, Eugen Onegin.
Ambroise Thomas, 1811-1896. (F.) Mignon.
Ralph Vaughan Williams, 1872-1958, (Br.) Job, London Symphony, Symphony No. 7 (Antarctica).
Giuseppe Verdi, 1813-1901. (It.) Aida, Rigoletto, Don Carlo, Il Trovatore, La Traviata, Falstaff, Macbeth.
Hector Villa Lobos, 1887-1959. (Brazil) Choros.
Antonio Vivaldi, 1669-1741. (It.) operas and cantatas.
Richard Wagner, 1813-1883. (G.) Rienzi, Tannhäuser, Lohengrin, Das Rheingold, Die Valkure, Siegfried, Göt-
terdämmerung, Tristan and Isolde, Parsifal.
Karl Maria von Weber, 1786-1826. (G.) Der Freischütz.

Composers of Operettas, Musicals and Popular Music.

Leroy Anderson, b. 1908. (U.S.) Syncopated Clock, Typewriter Serenade.
Harold Arlen, b. 1905. (U.S.) Stormy Weather, Over the Rainbow, Blues in the Night, That Old Black Magic.
Burt Bacharach, b. 1928. (U.S.) Raindrops Keep Fallin' on My Head, Blue on Blue, Walk on By, What the World Needs Now is Love.
Ernest Ball, 1887-1912. (U.S.) Mother Machree, When Irish Eyes are Smiling.
Irving Berlin, b. 1888. (U.S.) Ziegfield Follies; Face the Music; As Thousands Cheer; This is the Army; Annie Get Your Gun; Call Me Madam, God Bless America, White Christmas.
Sir Henry Rowley Bishop, 1786-1855. (Br.) Home Sweet Home.
Marc Blitzstein, 1905-1964 (U.S.) The Cradle Will Rock; No for an Answer; Regina; Reuben, Reuben.
Jerry Bock, b. 1928. (U.S.) Mr. Wonderful; Fiorello; Fiddler on the Roof; The Rothschilds.
Carrie Jacobs Bond, 1862-1946. (U.S.) I Love You Truly.
George M. Cohan, 1878-1942. (U.S.) Give My Regards to Broadway, You're A Grand Old Flag, Over There.
Sherman Edwards, b. 1919. (U.S.) See You in September; Wonderful! Wonderful!
Stephen Collins Foster, 1826-1864. (U.S.) My Old Kentucky Home, Old Folks At Home.
Rudolf Friml, 1879-1972. (naturalized U.S.) The Firefly; Rose Marie; Vagabond King; Bird of Paradise.
John Gay, 1685-1732. (Br.) The Beggar's Opera.
Edwin F. Goldman, 1878-1956. (U.S.) Marches.
Percy Grainger, 1882-1961. (Br.) Country Gardens.
Ferde Grofé, 1892-1972. (U.S.) Grand Canyon Suite.
W. C. Handy, 1873-1958. (U.S.) St. Louis Blues.
Victor Herbert, 1859-1924. (Ir.-U.S.) Mlle. Modiste; Babes in Toyland; The Red Mill; Naughty Marietta; Sweethearts, Princess Pat.
Jerry Herman, b. 1932. (U.S.) Milk and Honey, Hello Dolly!, Mame, Dear World.
Jerome Kern, 1885-1945. (U.S.) Sally; Sunny; Show Boat; Cat and the Fiddle; Music in the Air; Roberta.
Burton Lane, b. 1912. (U.S.) Three's a Crowd; Finnian's Rainbow; On A Clear Day You Can See Forever.
Franz Lehar, 1870-1948. (Hung.) Merry Widow, Count of Luxembourg.
Mitch Leigh, b. 1928. (U.S.) Man of La Mancha.
Frank Loesser, 1910-1969. (U.S.) Guys and Dolls; Where's Charley?; The Most Happy Fella.
Frederick Loewe, b. 1901. (Aust.-U.S.) The Day Before Spring; Brigadoon, Paint Your Wagon; My Fair Lady, Camelot.

Henry Mancini, b. 1924. (U.S.) Moon River, Days of Wine and Roses, Pink Panther theme.
Cole Porter, 1893-1964. (U.S.) Anything Goes; Jubilee; DuBarry Was a Lady; Panama Hattie; Mexican Hayride; Kiss Me Kate; Can Can; Silk Stockings.
Andre Previn, b. 1929. (U.S.) Coco.
Richard Rodgers, b. 1902. (U.S.) Garrick Gaieties; Connecticut Yankee; America's Sweetheart; On Your Toes; Babes in Arms; The Boys from Syracuse; Oklahoma!; Carousel; South Pacific; The King & I; Flower Drum Song; The Sound of Music; Two by Two.
Sigmund Romberg, 1887-1951. (Hung.) Maytime; The Student Prince; Desert Song; Blossom Time.
Harold Rome, b. 1908. (U.S.) Pins and Needles; Call Me Mister; Wish You Were Here; Fanny; Destry Rides Again; I Can Get It for You Wholesale.
Arthur Schwartz, b. 1900. (U.S.) The Band Wagon, Inside U.S.A., A Tree Grows in Brooklyn.
Stephen Sondheim, b. 1930, (U.S.) Follies; A Little Night Music.
John Phillip Sousa, 1854-1932. (U.S.) The Smuggler; Desiree; Queen of Hearts; El Capitan; The Bride-Elect.
Oley Speaks, 1875-1948. (U.S.) Sylvia, The Road to Mandalay.
Oskar Straus, 1870-1954. (Aus.) Waltz Dream, Chocolate Soldier.
Johann Strauss, 1825-1899. (Aus.) Gypsy Baron, Die Fledermaus. Waltzes. Blue Danube, Artist's Life.
Charles Strouse, b. 1928. (U.S.) Bye Bye, Birdie; All American; Golden Boy; Applause.
Jule Styne, b. 1905. (b. London-U.S.) High Button Shoes, Gentlemen Prefer Blondes; Bells Are Ringing; Say Darling; Gypsy; Funny Girl.
Arthur S. Sullivan, 1842-1900. (Br.) H.M.S. Pinafore, Pirates of Penzance, The Mikado, (with W. S. Gilbert, 1836-1911, librettist.)
Deems Taylor, 1885-1966. (U.S.) The King's Henchmen; Peter Ibbetson.
James Van Heusen, b. 1913. (U.S.) Moonlight Becomes You, Swinging on a Star.
Harry Warren, b. 1893. (U.S.) You're My Everything, We're in the Money, I Only Have Eyes for You, September in the Rain.
Kurt Weill, 1900-1950. (G.-U.S.) Three-Penny Opera; Down in the Valley; Lady in the Dark; Knickerbocker Holiday; One Touch of Venus; Lost in the Stars.
Meredith Willson, b. 1902, (U.S.) The Music Man.
Vincent Youmans, 1898-1946. (U.S.) Two Little Girls in Blue; Wildflower; No, No, Nanette; Hit the Deck; Rainbow; Smiles; Through the Years; Take A Chance.

Noted Black Americans—Past and Present

(Names of black athletes and entertainers are not included here as they are well known and are listed elsewhere in the World Almanac.)

Explorers and Settlers

Pedro Alonzo Nino, navigator of the Nina, one of Christopher Columbus' three ships on his first voyage of discovery to the New World, 1492.

Estevanico (also called Esteban) led the first Spanish explorations into the Arizona and New Mexico area, 1539.

Jean Baptiste Point du Sable, fur trader and first settler of Chicago, 1779.

James P. Beckwourth (1798-c.1867), western fur-trader, scout, after whom Beckwourth Pass in northern California is named.

Matthew A. Henson (1866-1955), with Robert E. Peary and 4 Eskimos, discovered the North Pole, 1909; Henson planted the U.S. flag at the Pole.

Soldiers, Patriots

Crispus Attucks, (c. 1723-1770), leader of a group fired on by British soldiers and one of the 5 slain in the "Boston Massacre," Mar. 5, 1770.

Peter Salem, one of the defenders at the Battle of Bunker Hill, June 17, 1775, shot and killed Maj. John Pitcairn, one of the British commanders.

(About 5,000 blacks served in the Continental Army, mostly in integrated units, some in all-black combat outfits.)

Harriet Tubman, after escaping from slavery made repeated trips to the South and led more than 300 slaves to freedom as an Underground Railroad conductor; served as nurse and spy for Union Army in the Civil War.

(Some 200,000 blacks served in the Union Army during the Civil War; 38,000 gave their lives: 22 won the Medal of Honor, the nation's highest award.)

Isaiah Dorman (19th Century), U.S. Army interpreter, killed with Col. George Custer at Battle of the Little Big Horn (1876).

Henry O. Flipper, first black to graduate from West Point (1877).

Pvt. Henry Johnson of Albany, N.Y., the first American decorated by France in World War I with the Croix de Guerre.

(Of 367,000 blacks in the Armed Forces in World War I, 100,000 served in France.)

Dorie Miller of Waco, Tex., a Navy mess attendant on the battleship Arizona during the Pearl Harbour attack, took over an anti-aircraft gun from a dying white sailor and shot down 4 Japanese bombers, Dec. 7, 1941; awarded the Navy Cross by President Franklin D. Roosevelt.

(More than 1,000,000 blacks served in the U.S. Armed Forces in World War II; all-black fighter and bomber AAF units and infantry divisions gave distinguished service. In 1954 the policy of all-black units was finally abolished.)

Brig. Gen. Benjamin O. Davis, Sr., born 1877, first black general (1940) in U.S. Army, rose through ranks to inspector general, retired 1948.

Lt. Gen. Benjamin O. Davis, Jr., b. 1912, West Point (1936), first Negro Air Force general (1954), had distinguished service as pilot and commander in World War II, retired 1970.

Admiral Samuel L. Gravely, Jr., first black admiral (1971), served in World War II, Korea and Vietnam.

Scientists, Inventors

Benjamin Banneker (1731-c. 1806), author of annual almanacs (1791-1802), served on commission which surveyed and helped lay out the future city of Washington, D.C.

Henry Blair (19th Century), obtained patent (believed the first issued to a black) for a corn-planter (1834) and for a cotton-planter (1836).

Norbert Rillieux (1806-1894), invented a vacuum pan evaporator which revolutionized the sugar-refining industry (1846).

Lewis H. Latimer (1848-1928), associate of Thomas Edison, wrote textbook on the Edison Co. lighting system in New York City; supervised installation of first electric street lighting in New York.

Jan Matzeliger (1852-1889), invented lasting machine which cut shoe industry costs in half and brought higher wages to shoe workers.

Dr. Daniel Hale Williams (1856-1931), performed one of first two open-heart operations (1893); founded Provident, Chicago's first Negro hospital; first black elected a fellow of the American College of Surgeons.

George Washington Carver (c. 1864-1943), agricultural scientist, philanthropist; brought about an agricultural revolution in the South, finding ways to enrich the soil, adding to its one-crop cotton economy not only emphasis on peanuts, sweet potatoes and soybeans, but discovering some 300 industrial uses for by-products he synthesized from them.

Dr. William A. Hinton (1883-1959), developed the Hinton and Davies-Hinton tests for detection of syphilis; first black professor at Harvard Medical School (1949).

Dr. Charles Richard Drew (1904-1950), pioneer in development of blood banks; director of American Red Cross blood donor project in World War II.

Writers, Educators

Jupiter Hammon (c. 1720-1800), a Long Island N.Y. poet, the first black American to have his works published.

Phillis Wheatley (c. 1753-1784), poet, second American woman and first black woman to have her works published; b. in Senegal, enslaved, taken to Boston, freed 1773.

John B. Russwurm (1799-1851) with **Samuel E. Cornish** (1793-1858), founded the nation's first black newspaper, Freedom' Journal (1827) in N.Y. City.

William Wells Brown (1815-1884), b. a slave, first American black to publish a novel (Clotel), as well as a drama, a travel book, 3 histories.

Frederick Douglass (1817-1895), author, editor, orator, diplomat; a runaway slave (b. Frederick Bailey), edited the abolitionist weekly, The North Star, in Rochester, N.Y., before the Civil War; became U.S. Minister and Consul General to Haiti.

Edward Bouchet (1852-1918), first black to earn a Ph.D. at a U.S. university (Yale, 1876); first to be elected to Phi Beta Kappa.

Booker T. Washington (1856-1915), founder and first president of Tuskegee Institute (1881); author of a dozen books including Up From Slavery; social reformer.

Charles Waddell Chestnutt (1858-1932), novelist; best-known for his short stories including The Conjure Woman.

William Edward Burghardt Du Bois (1868-1963), historian, sociologist, a found of the NAACP (1909) and founding editor of its magazine The Crisis; author of The Souls of Black Folk (1903) and other books.

James Weldon Johnson (1871-1938), poet, song-lyricist, novelist; first black admitted to Florida bar; a U.S. consul in Venezuela and Nicaragua.

Paul Laurence Dunbar (1872-1906), poet, novelist; won fame with Lyrics of Lowly Life (1896).

Dr. Carter G. Woodson (1875-1950), historian; founded Journal of Negro History and Assn. for Study of Negro Life and History (1915).

Langston Hughes (1902-1967), a major American poet; also author of stories and song lyrics.

Countee Cullen (1903-1946), poet, winner of numerous literary prizes.

Richard Wright (1908-1960), best-selling novels; Native Son (1940), Black Boy (1945), etc.

Willard Motley (1912-1965), novelist; wrote Knock on Any Door (1947).

Ralph Ellison, b. 1914, novelist, winner of 1952 National Book Award for Invisible Man.

Frank Yerby, b. 1916, most successful of American black novelists; some 19 novels with over 20,000,000 copies sold, including The Foxes of Harrow, Vixen.

Gwendolyn Brooks, b. 1917, poet, novelist; first black to win a Pulitzer Prize (1950), for Annie Allen.

Wilson C. Riles, b. 1917, elected California State Superintendent of Public Instruction (1970).

James Baldwin, b. 1924, best-seller author, playwright; Another Country (1962), The Fire Next Time (1963).

Charles Gordone, b. 1925, won 1970 Pulitzer Prize for Drama with play, No Place to Be Somebody.

Lorraine Hansberry (1930-1965), playwright; won N.Y. Drama Critics Circle Award with Raisin in the Sun (1959).

Imamu Amiri Baraka, b. LeRoi Jones, 1934; poet, playwright, community leader in Newark, N.J.

Public Officials

Hiram R. Revels (1822-1901), first black U.S. Senator, elected in Mississippi, served 1870-1871.

Joseph H. Rainey (1832-1887), first black elected to House of Representatives (1869-79 from South Carolina).

Dr. Mary McCleod Bethune (1875-1955), adviser to Presidents Franklin D. Roosevelt and Harry Truman; division administrator in National Youth Administration (1935); founder, president of Bethune-Cookman College.

William L. Dawson (1886-1970), Congressman from Illinois, first black chairman of a major House of Representatives committee.

William H. Hastie, b. 1904, first black Federal Judge (appointed 1937); Governor of Virgin Islands (1946-1949); Judge, U.S. Circuit Court of Appeals (1949).

Dr. Ralph Bunche (1904-1971), first black to win the Nobel Peace Prize (1950); became Undersecretary of the United Nations (1950).

Dr. Robert C. Weaver, b. 1907, first black member of the U.S. Cabinet; Secretary of the Department of Housing & Urban Development (1966).

Adam Clayton Powell (1908-1972), early civil rights leader (1930's), congressman (1945-1969); as head of House Committee on Education and Labor (1960-1967) was responsible for 48 major pieces of social legislation.

Thurgood Marshall, b. 1908, first black U.S. Solicitor General (1965); first black to be made a Justice of the U.S. Supreme

Court (1967); as a lawyer led the legal battery which won the historic decision from the Supreme Court declaring segregation of public schools unconstitutional (1954).

Edward W. Brooke, b. 1919; Attorney General of Massachusetts (1962); first black elected to U.S. Senate since 19th Century Reconstruction (1967).

Mrs. Constance Baker Motley, b. 1921; first black woman Borough President of Manhattan, N.Y. City (1965); Judge, U.S. District Court (1966).

Patricia Roberts Harris, first black woman U.S. Ambassador (1967), chairman Dem. party national convention credentials committee (1972).

Mrs. Shirley Chisholm, b. 1924, first black woman elected to House of Representatives (Brooklyn, N.Y. 1968).

Louis Stokes (Dem., Ohio), chairman of Black Caucus of the 13 black members of the House.

Carl T. Rowan, b. 1925, prize-winning journalist; public official; director of the U.S. Information Agency (1964), making him the first black to sit on the National Security Council; U.S. Ambassador to Finland (1963).

Benjamin Hooks, first black appointed to the Federal Communications Commission (1972).

Andrew F. Brimmer, b. 1926, first black member (1966) of the Federal Reserve Board, the U.S. central banking facility.

Robert C. Henry, elected Mayor of Springfield, Ohio (1965), first black Mayor of a moderate-sized city in the 20th Century.

Julian Bond, b. 1942, first black elected to Georgia legislature since Reconstruction.

Thomas Bradley, b. 1917, elected mayor of Los Angeles (1973). *(As of July 1, 1973, there were 82 black mayors, 928 city councilmen, 211 elected county officers, 42 state senators, 196 state representatives, 1 U.S. senator and 15 U.S. representatives. There are 2,621 blacks now holding elected office in the United States, an increase of 315 over the previous year and twice the number in office four years ago, according to a survey by the Joint Center for Political Studies, Washington, D.C.)*

Labor, Civil Rights Leaders

Sojourner Truth (1797-1883), born Isabella Baumfree; preacher, abolitionist; raised funds for Union in Civil War; worked for black educational opportunities.

Nat Turner (1800-1831), leader of the most significant of over 200 slave revolts in U.S. history, in Southhampton, Va.; he and 16 others were hanged.

Marcus Garvey (1887-1940), founded Universal Negro Improvement Assn. (1911) sought to promote a Back to Africa movement.

Willard Townsend (1895-1957), organized (1935) the United Transport Service Employees (redcaps, etc.); Vice President of AFL-CIO.

Elijah Muhammad, b. 1897, founded the Nation of Islam or Black Muslims (1931).

A. Philip Randolph, b. 1889, organized the Brotherhood of Sleeping Car Porters (1925); organizer of 1941 and 1963 March on Washington movements; Vice President of AFL-CIO.

Walter White (1893-1955), Executive Secretary, NAACP (1931-1955).

Roy Wilkins, b. 1901, became Executive Secretary, NAACP in 1955.

Bayard Rustin, b. 1910, an organizer of the 1963 March on Washington; Executive Director of the A. Philip Randolph Institute.

The Rev. Dr. Ralph David Abernathy, b. 1916, an organizer (1957) of the Southern Christian Leadership Conference; its President (1968).

James Farmer, b. 1920, a founder of the Congress of Racial Equality (1942); its National Director (1961-1965), Asst. Secretary of Health, Education and Welfare (1969).

Whitney M. Young, Jr., (1921-1971), Executive Director of the National Urban League (1961); author, lecturer, newspaper columnist.

Floyd McKissick, b. 1922, National Director of CORE (1966).

Malcolm X (1925-1965), founded the Organization of Afro-American Unity (1963), a leading spokesman for black pride.

The Rev. Dr. Martin Luther King, Jr. (1929-1968), led 382-day, Montgomery, Ala., boycott which brought 1956 U.S. Supreme Court decision holding segregation on buses unconstitutional; founder and President of the Southern Christian Leadership Conference (1957); leader of rights marches; won Nobel Peace Prize (1964).

Dr. George A. Wiley, b. 1931, Executive Director of National Welfare Rights Organization (founded 1966).

Roy Innis, b. 1934, National Director of CORE (1968).

Eldridge Cleaver, b. 1935, former Black Panther party leader, author of Soul on Ice

Bobby G. Seale, National Chairman, Black Panther party.

Jesse Jackson, National Director, Operation Bread Basket and major community leader in Chicago.

John Lewis, former chairman of Student Nonviolent Coordinating Committee, leader of Voter Education Project in the South.

Modern American Playwrights and Some of Their Plays

George Abbott, b. 1887. Co-author Three Men on a Horse, The Boys from Syracuse, Damn Yankees.

Edward F. Albee, b. 1928. Who's Afraid of Virginia Woolf?, Tiny Alice, A Delicate Balance.

William Alfred, b. 1922. Hogan's Goat.

Maxwell Anderson, 1888-1959. What Price Glory? Winterset, Saturday's Children, High Tor, Key Largo.

Philip Barry, 1886-1949. The Animal Kingdom, Holiday, The Philadelphia Story.

Abe Burrows, b. 1910. Co-author Guys and Dolls, How to Succeed in Business Without Really Trying.

Mary C. Chase, b. 1907. Harvey.

Paddy Chayefsky, b. 1923. Middle of the Night, The Tenth Man, Gideon, The Passions of Josef D.

Marc Connelly, b. 1890. The Green Pastures.

Russell Crouse, 1893-1966. Co-author State of the Union, Life With Father, Call Me Madam, The Sound of Music, Mr. President.

Edna Ferber, 1887-1968, Co-author Dinner at Eight, Stage Door.

Paul Foster, b. 1932. Tom Paine.

Jack Gelber, b. 1932, The Connection, The Cuban Thing.

William Gibson, b. 1914. Two for the Seesaw, The Miracle Worker.

Frank D. Gilroy, b. 1915. The Subject Was Roses, The Only Game in Town.

Charles Gordone, b. 1925. No Place to Be Somebody.

Paul Green, b. 1894. In Abraham's Bosom, Wilderness Road.

William Hanley, b. 1931. Slow Dance on the Killing Ground.

Lorraine Hansberry, 1930-1965. A Raisin in the Sun.

Moss Hart, 1904-1961. Co-author Once in a Lifetime, You Can't Take It With You.

Ben Hecht, 1884-1964. Co-author The Front Page.

Lillian Hellman, b. 1907. The Children's Hour, The Little Foxes, Watch on the Rhine.

Sidney Howard, 1881-1939. The Silver Cord, Yellow Jack, They Knew What They Wanted.

William Inge, b. 1913. Come Back, Little Sheba; Picnic, Bus Stop, The Dark at the Top of the Stairs, A Loss of Roses.

LeRoi Jones, b. 1934. Dutchman, The Slave.

George S. Kaufman, 1889-1961. Co-author Dinner at Eight, Stage Door, You Can't Take It With You, The Man Who Came to Dinner.

George Kelly, b. 1887. The Show-off, Craig's Wife.

Jean Kerr, b. 1923. Mary, Mary; Poor Richard; Finishing Touches.

Joseph Kesselring, 1902-1967. Arsenic and Old Lace.

Sidney Kingsley, b. 1906. Men in White, The Patriots, Dead End, Darkness at Noon.

Arthur Kopit, b. 1937. Oh Dad, Poor Dad, Mamma's Hung You in a Closet and I'm Feelin' So Sad.

Howard Lindsay, 1889-1968. Co-author State of the Union, Life With Father, Call Me Madam, The Sound of Music, Mr. President.

Charles MacArthur, 1895-1956. Co-author The Front Page.

Archibald MacLeish, b. 1892. J. B.

Terrence McNally, b. 1939. And Things That Go Bump in the Night, Sweet Eros.

Arthur Miller, b. 1915. All My Sons, Death of a Salesman, Crucible, View from the Bridge, After the Fall, Incident at Vichy, The Price.

Anne Nichols, 1891-1966. Abie's Irish Rose.

Clifford Odets, 1906-1963. Waiting for Lefty, Awake and Sing, Golden Boy, The Country Girl.

Eugene O'Neill, 1888-1953 The Long Voyage Home, The Emperor Jones, Anna Christie, Desire Under the Elms, Strange Interlude, Mourning Becomes Electra; Ah, Wilderness; The Iceman Cometh, Long Day's Journey Into Night.

John Patrick, b. 1905. The Hasty Heart, Teahouse of the August Moon.

Elmer Rice, 1892-1967. The Adding Machine, Street Scene, Counsellor-at-Law, Dream Girl.

Howard Sackler, b. 1930. The Great White Hope.

William Saroyan, b. 1908. My Heart's in the Highlands, The Time of Your Life.

Doré Schary, b. 1905. Sunrise at Campobello.

Murray Schisgal, b. 1926. The Typists and the Tiger, Luv.

Robert Sherwood, 1896-1955. Reunion in Vienna, the Petrified Forest, Idiot's Delight, There Shall Be No Night, Abe Lincoln in Illinois.

Neil Simon, b. 1927. Sweet Charity, Plaza Suite, The Odd Couple, Barefoot in the Park, Last of the Red Hot Lovers, The Gingerbread Lady; The Prisoner of Second Avenue; The Sunshine Boys.

Samuel A. Taylor, b. 1912. The Happy Time, The Pleasure of His Company, co-author Sabrina Fair and No Strings.

John Van Druten, 1901-1957. The Voice of the Turtle; I Remember Mama; Bell, Book and Candle; I Am a Camera.

Thornton Wilder, b. 1897. Our Town, The Skin of Our Teeth, The Matchmaker.

Tennessee Williams, b. 1914. The Glass Menagerie, A Streetcar Named Desire, Cat on a Hot Tin Roof, The Night of the Iguana, The Milk Train Doesn't Stop Here Anymore, Camino Real.

American Architects and Some of Their Achievements

Max Abramovitz, b. 1908. Philharmonic Hall at Lincoln Center, N. Y.

Henry Bacon, (1866-1924) Lincoln Memorial.

Pietro Belluschi, b. 1899. Juilliard School of Music, Lincoln Center, N. Y.

Marcel Breuer, b. Pecs, Hungary, 1902. Whitney Museum of American Art, N. Y. (with Hamilton Smith).

Charles Bulfinch, (1763-1844) State House, Boston; Capitol, Washington, (part).

Daniel H. Burnham, (1846-1912) Union Station, Washington; Flatiron, New York.

Ralph Adams Cram, (1863-1942) Cathedral of St. John the Divine, New York; U. S. Military Academy (part).

Alexander J. Davis, (1803-1892) Sub-treasury, N. Y.; capitols of Indiana, North Carolina, Illinois, Ohio.

R. Buckminster Fuller, b. 1895. U. S. Pavilion, Expo 67, Montreal (geodesic domes).

William F. Gibbs, (1886-1967) Designed liner United States.

Cass Gilbert, (1859-1934) Custom House, Woolworth Bldg., New York; Capitol, St. Paul.

Bertrand Goldberg, b. 1913. Marina City Towers, Chicago.

Bertram G. Goodhue, (1869-1924) Capitol, Lincoln, Nebr.; St. Thomas, St. Bartholomew, N. Y.

Walter Gropius, (1883-1969) Pan Am Building, N.Y. (with Pietro Belluschi).

Wallace K. Harrison, b. 1895. Metropolitan Opera House at Lincoln Center, N. Y.

Thomas Hastings, (1860-1929) Public Library, Frick Mansion, New York.

James Hoban, (1762-1831) The White House.

Raymond Hood, (1881-1934) Rockefeller Center (part); Daily News, N.Y.; Tribune, Chicago.

Richard M. Hunt, (1828-1896) Metropolitan Museum (part); The Breakers, Newport.

William Le Baron Jenney, (1832-1907) Home Insurance, Chicago (demolished).

Philip C. Johnson, b. 1906. N. Y. State Theater at Lincoln Center, N. Y.

Albert Kahn, (1869-1942) Athletic Club Bldg., General Motors Bldg., New York.

Louis Kahn, b. 1901. Salk Laboratory, Jolla, Calif.

Christopher Grant LaFarge, (1862-1938) Chapel, West Point; Cathedral, Seattle.

Benjamin H. Latrobe, (1764-1820) U. S. Capitol (part).

William Lescaze, (1896-1969) Philadelphia Savings Fund Society; Borg-Warner Bldg., Chicago.

Theodore C. Link, (1850-1923) Union Station, St. Louis.

Charles F. McKim, (1847-1909) Public Library, Boston; Columbia Univ. (part).

Charles M. McKim, b. 1920. KUHT-TV Transmitter Building, Houston; Lutheran Church of the Redeemer, Houston.

Medary, Milton B., (1874-1929) Bok Carillon Tower, Mountain Lake, Fla.

Ludwig Mies van der Rohe, (1886-1969). Seagram Building, N. Y. (with Philip C. Johnson); National Gallery, Berlin.

Robert Mills, (1781-1855) Washington Monument.

Richard J. Neutra, (1892-1970). Mathematics Park, Princeton; Orange Co. Courthouse, Santa Ana, Calif.

Frederick L. Olmsted, (1822-1903) Central Park, New York; Fairmount Park, Philadelphia.

Ieoh Ming Pei, b. Canton, China, 1917. Kips Bay Plaza, N. Y.; Earth Sciences Building (M.I.T.) Cambridge, Mass; National Center for Atmospheric Research, Boulder, Colo.

John Russell Pope, (1874-1937) National Gallery.

John Portman, B. 1924. Peachtree Center, Atlanta.

James Renwick, Jr., (1818-1895) Grace Church, St. Patrick's Cathedral, N. Y.; Smithsonian, Corcoran Galleries, Wash.

Henry H. Richardson, (1838-1886) Trinity, Boston.

Kevin Roche, b. 1922. Oakland, Calif., Museum; Fine Arts Center, U. of Mass.

James Gamble Rogers, (1867-1947) Columbia-Presbyterian Medical Center, New York; Northwestern Univ., Chicago.

John Weldon Root, b. 1887. Palmolive Building, Chicago; Hotel Statler, Washington; Hotel Tamanaco, Caracas.

Paul Rudolph, b. 1918. Jewitt Art Center, Wellesley College; Art & Architecture Bldg., Yale.

Eero Saarinen, (1910-1961) Gateway to the West arch, St. Louis; Trans World Flight Center, N. Y.

Louis Skidmore, (1897-1962) AEC town site, Oak Ridge, Tenn.; Terrace Plaza Hotel, Cincinnati.

Clarence S. Stein, b. 1882. Temple Emanu-El, New York.

Edward Durell Stone, b. 1902. U. S. Embassy, New Delhi, India; (H. Hartford) Gallery of Modern Art, N. Y.

Louis H. Sullivan, (1856-1924) Auditorium, Chicago.

Richard Upjohn, (1802-1878) Trinity Ch., N.Y.

Ralph T. Walker, (1889-1973). N.Y. Telephone hqrs., New York; IBM Research Lab., Poughkeepsie, N.Y.; General Foods Bldg., White Plains, N.Y.

Roland A. Wank, (1898-1970) Cincinnati Union Terminal; head architect TVA, 1933-44.

Stanford White, (1853-1906) Washington Arch. First Madison Square Garden, New York.

Frank Lloyd Wright, (1869-1959) Imperial Hotel, Tokyo; Guggenheim Museum, New York.

William Wurster, b. 1895. Ghirardelli Sq., San Francisco; Cowell College, U. Calif., Berkeley.

Minoru Yamasaki, b 1912. World Trade Center, New York City.

The Hall of Fame for Great Americans

The Hall of Fame for Great Americans was a gift to the American people by Mrs. Helen Gould Shepard. New York University acts as Trustee for the Shrine for the nation. Busts and tablets are donated. The Americans honored since 1900 are:

1900	Mary Lyon	James Buchanan Eads	Walter Reed
John Adams	James Madison	Patrick Henry	Booker T. Washington
John James Audubon	Maria Mitchell	William Thomas Green	
Henry Ward Beecher	William Tecumseh Sherman	Morton	**1950**
William Ellery Channing	John Greenleaf Whittier	Alice Freeman Palmer	
Henry Clay	Emma Willard	Augustus Saint-Gaudens	Susan B. Anthony
Peter Cooper		Roger Williams	Alexander Graham Bell
Jonathan Edwards	**1910**		Josiah Willard Gibbs
Ralph Waldo Emerson	George Bancroft	**1925**	William Crawford Gorgas
David Glasgow Farragut	Phillips Brooks		Theodore Roosevelt
Benjamin Franklin	William Cullen Bryant	Edwin Booth	Woodrow Wilson
Robert Fulton	James Fenimore Cooper	John Paul Jones	
Ulysses Simpson Grant	Oliver Wendell Holmes		**1955**
Asa Gray	Andrew Jackson	**1930**	
Nathaniel Hawthorne	John Lothrop Motley		Thomas Jonathan Jackson
Washington Irving	Edgar Allan Poe	Matthew Fontaine Maury	George Westinghouse
Thomas Jefferson	Harriet Beecher Stowe	James Monroe	Wilbur Wright
James Kent	Frances Elizabeth Willard	James Abbott McNeil	
Robert Edward Lee		Whistler	**1960**
Abraham Lincoln	**1915**	Walt Whitman	
Henry Wadsworth Longfellow			Thomas A. Edison
Horace Mann	Louis Agassiz	**1935**	Edward A. MacDowell
John Marshall	Daniel Boone		Henry D. Thoreau
Samuel Finley Breese Morse	Rufus Choate	Grover Cleveland	
George Peabody	Charlotte Saunders Cushman	Simon Newcomb	**1965**
Joseph Story	Alexander Hamilton	William Penn	
Gilbert Charles Stuart	Joseph Henry		Jane Addams
George Washington	Mark Hopkins	**1940**	Oliver Wendell Holmes, Jr.
Daniel Webster	Elias Howe		Sylvanus Thayer
Eli Whitney	Francis Parkman	Stephen Collins Foster	Orville Wright
1905	**1920**	**1945**	**1970**
John Quincy Adams	Samuel Langhorne Clemens	Sidney Lanier	Albert Abraham Michelson
James Russell Lowell	(Mark Twain)	Thomas Paine	Lillian D. Wald

British
POETS, DRAMATISTS, ESSAYISTS, HISTORIANS, NOVELISTS

Born	Died	Name	Born	Died	Name	Born	Died	Name
1672	1719	Addison, Joseph	1563	1631	Drayton, Michael	1882	1956	Milne, A. A.
1805	1882	Ainsworth, W. H.	1631	1700	Dryden, John	1608	1674	Milton, John
1721	1770	Akenside, Mark	1834	1896	Du Maurier, Geo. L.	1779	1852	Moore, Thomas
1832	1904	Arnold, Edwin	1819	1880	Eliot, George	1838	1923	Morley, John
1822	1888	Arnold, Matthew	1888	1965	Eliot, T. S.	1870	1916	Munro, H. H. (Saki)
1515	1568	Ascham, Roger	1620	1706	Evelyn, John	1880	1958	Noyes, Alfred
1775	1817	Austen, Jane	1707	1754	Fielding, Henry	1903	1950	Orwell, George
1561	1626	Bacon, Francis	1809	1883	Fitzgerald, Edward	1839	1894	Pater, Walter
1214	1294	Bacon, Roger	1908	1964	Fleming, Ian	1785	1866	Peacock, Thomas L.
1762	1851	Baillie, Joanna	1873	1939	Ford, Ford Madox	1632	1703	Pepys, Samuel
1860	1937	Barrie, James M.	1889	1966	Forester, C. S.	1688	1744	Pope, Alexander
1584	1616	Beaumont, Francis	1879	1970	Forster, E. M.	1900	1969	Potter, Stephen
673	735	Bede, the Venerable	1908	1967	Frankau, Pamela	1664	1721	Prior, Matthew
1872	1956	Beerbohm, Max	1867	1933	Galsworthy, John	1863	1944	Quiller-Couch, Arthur T.
1870	1953	Belloc, Hilaire	1685	1732	Gay, John	1552	1618	Raleigh, Sir Walter
1867	1931	Bennett, Arnold	1737	1794	Gibbon, Edward	1814	1884	Reade, Charles
1748	1832	Bentham, Jeremy	1857	1903	Gissing, George	1882	1957	Richardson, Dorothy
1662	1742	Bentley, Richard	1728	1774	Goldsmith, Oliver	1689	1761	Richardson, Samuel
1869	1951	Blackwood, Algernon	1716	1771	Gray, Thomas	1819	1900	Ruskin, John
1740	1795	Boswell, James	1840	1928	Hardy, Thomas	1872	1970	Russell, Bertrand
1844	1930	Bridges, Robert	1831	1923	Harrison, Frederic	1886	1967	Sassoon, Siegfried
1816	1855	Bronte, Charlotte	1778	1830	Hazlitt, William	1771	1832	Scott, Sir Walter
1818	1848	Bronte, Emily	1793	1835	Hemans, Felicia	1564	1616	Shakespeare, William
1806	1861	Browning, Elizabeth B.	1849	1903	Henley, Wm. Ernest	1856	1950	Shaw, G. Bernard
1812	1889	Browning, Robert	1591	1674	Herrick, Robert	1797	1851	Shelley, Mary W.
1838	1922	Bryce, James	1588	1679	Hobbes, Thomas	1792	1822	Shelley, Percy Bysshe
1628	1688	Bunyan, John	1770	1835	Hogg, James	1751	1816	Sheridan, Richard B.
1729	1797	Burke, Edmund	1799	1845	Hood, Thomas	1554	1586	Sidney, Sir Phillip
1759	1796	Burns, Robert	1859	1936	Housman, Alfred E.	1887	1964	Sitwell, Edith
1788	1824	Byron, (Geo. Gordon)	1722	1808	Home, John	1888	1969	Sitwell, Osbert
1777	1844	Campbell, Thomas	1894	1963	Huxley, Aldous	1771	1845	Smith, Sydney
1795	1881	Carlyle, Thomas	1825	1895	Huxley, Thos. H.	1721	1771	Smollett, Tobias
1832	1898	Carroll, Lewis	1889	1967	Irwin, Margaret	1774	1843	Southey, Robert
1888	1957	Cary, Joyce	1803	1857	Jerrold, Douglas W.	1552	1599	Spenser, Edmund
1340	1400	Chaucer, Geoffrey	1709	1784	Johnson, Samuel	1672	1729	Steele, Richard
1694	1773	Chesterfield, Earl of	1573	1637	Jonson, Ben	1713	1768	Sterne, Laurence
1874	1936	Chesterton, G. K.	1795	1821	Keats, John	1850	1894	Stevenson, Robert Louis
1911	1968	Churchill, Randolph	1896	1967	Kennedy, Margaret	1880	1932	Strachey, Lytton
1762	1835	Cobbett, William	1819	1875	Kingsley, Charles	1667	1745	Swift, Jonathan
1804	1865	Cobden, Richard	1865	1936	Kipling, Rudyard	1837	1909	Swinburne, Algernon C.
1772	1834	Coleridge, S. T.	1775	1834	Lamb, Charles	1809	1892	Tennyson, Alfred
1824	1889	Collins, Wilkie	1332	1400	Langland, William	1811	1863	Thackeray, W. M.
1670	1729	Congreve, William	1885	1930	Lawrence, David H.	1914	1953	Thomas, Dylan
1857	1924	Conrad, Joseph	1838	1903	Lecky, W. E. H.	1876	1962	Trevelyan, Geo. M.
1878	1957	Coppard, A. E.	1866	1947	LeGallienne, Richard	1815	1882	Trollope, Anthony
1864	1924	Corelli, Marie	1894	1957	Lewis, Wyndham	1884	1941	Walpole, Hugh
1731	1800	Cowper, William	1895	1970	Liddell Hart, Basil	1593	1683	Walton, Izaak
1890	1969	Crompton, Richmal	1632	1704	Locke, John	1851	1920	Ward, Mrs. Humphry
1809	1882	Darwin, Charles	1800	1859	Macaulay, Thomas B.	1674	1748	Watts, Isaac
1660	1731	Defoe, Daniel	1863	1947	Machen, Arthur	1903	1966	Waugh, Evelyn
1873	1956	De la Mare, Walter	1888	1923	Mansfield, Katherine	1866	1946	Wells, H. G.
1785	1859	De Quincey, Thomas	1564	1593	Marlowe, Christopher	1906	1964	White, T. H.
1812	1870	Dickens, Charles	1897	1969	Martin, Kingsley	1861	1947	Whitehead, Alfred N.
1804	1881	Disraeli, Benjamin	1878	1967	Masefield, John	1854	1900	Wilde, Oscar
1573	1631	Donne, John	1583	1640	Massinger, Phillip	1770	1850	Wordsworth, William
1868	1952	Douglas, Norman	1874	1965	Maugham, W. Somerset	1882	1941	Woolf, Virginia
1867	1900	Dowson, Ernest	1828	1909	Meredith, George	1640	1715	Wycherly, William
1859	1930	Doyle, Arthur Conan	1806	1873	Mill, John Stuart			

BRITISH PAINTERS AND SCULPTORS

Born	Died	Name	Born	Died	Name	Born	Died	Name
1836	1912	Alma-Tadema, Lawr.	1755	1826	Flaxman, John	1806	1870	Maclise, Daniel
1872	1898	Beardsley, Aubrey	1825	1899	Foster, Myles Birket	1829	1896	Millais, J. E.
1734	1808	Beauclerk, Lady Diana	1866	1934	Fry, Roger E.	1763	1804	Morland, George
1735	1839	Beechey, Wm.	1727	1788	Gainsborough, Thos.	1834	1896	Morris, William
1881	1967	Beresford, Frank E.	1648	1721	Gibbons, Grinling	1849	1933	Murray, David
1757	1827	Blake, William	1790	1866	Gibson, John	1835	1910	Orchardson, W. Q.
1802	1828	Bonington, R. P.	1817	1897	Gilbert, John	1878	1931	Orpen, William
1821	1893	Brown, Ford Madox	1775	1802	Girtin, Thomas	1839	1893	Pettie, John
1833	1898	Burne-Jones, Edw.	1786	1846	Haydon, Benj.	1836	1919	Poynter, E. J. Bt.
1799	1883	Calvert, Edward	1841	1917	Henry, C. N.	1756	1823	Raeburn, Henry
1781	1841	Chantrey, F. L.	1697	1764	Hogarth, William	1723	1792	Reynolds, Joshua
1896	1967	Charoux, Siegfried	1758	1810	Hoppner, John	1734	1802	Romney, George
1850	1934	Collier, John	1827	1910	Hunt, W. Holman	1828	1882	Rossetti, D. G.
1776	1837	Constable, John	1646	1723	Kneller, Godfrey	1891	1959	Spencer, Stanley
1803	1902	Cooper, Thos. Sidney	1802	1873	Lanseer, Edwin	1854	1935	Stokes, Adrian
1782	1842	Cotman, J. S.	1856	1941	Lavery, John	1775	1851	Turner, J. M. W.
1768	1821	Crome, John	1769	1830	Lawrence, Thomas	1817	1904	Watts, Geo. F.
1793	1865	Eastlake, Charles L.	1830	1896	Leighton, Fred'k, Lord	1775	1856	Westmacott, R.
1880	1959	Epstein, Jacob	1794	1859	Leslie, Charles R.	1785	1841	Wilkie, David
1787	1849	Etty, William	1864	1941	Llewellyn, William	1713	1782	Wilson, Richard

Poets Laureate of England

There is no authentic record of the origin of the office of Poet Laureate of England. According to Warton, there was a Versificator Regis, or King's Poet, in the reign of Henry III (1216-1272), and he was paid 100 shillings a year. Geoffrey Chaucer (1340-1400) assumed the title of Poet Laureate, and in 1389 got a royal grant of a yearly allowance of wine. In the reign of Edward IV (1461-1483), John Kay held the post. Under Henry VII (1485-1509), Andrew Bernard was the Poet Laureate, and was succeeded under Henry VIII (1509-1547) by John Skelton. Next came Edmund Spenser, who died in 1599; then Samuel Daniel, who died in 1619, and then Ben Jonson (appointed 1619). Sir William D'Avenant was appointed in 1638. He was a godson of William Shakespeare.

Others were John Dryden, 1670-1688; Thomas Shadwell, 1689; Nahum Tate, 1692; Nicholas Rowe, 1715; the Rev. Laurence Eusden, 1718; Colly Cibber, 1730; William Whitehead, 1758, on the refusal of Gray; Rev. Thomas Warton, 1785, on the refusal of Mason; Henry J. Pye, 1790; Robert Southey, 1813, on the refusal of Sir Walter Scott; William Wordsworth, 1843; Alfred Tennyson, 1850; Alfred Austin, 1896; Robert Bridges, 1913 (died 1930); John Masefield, 1930 (died 1967); Cecil Day Lewis (died May 22, 1972); Sir John Betjeman, 1972.

BRITISH ARMY (A), NAVY (N), AIR FORCE (F), EXPLORERS (E)

Born	Died	Name	Born	Died	Name	Born	Died	Name
1891	1969	Alexander, Harold R. (A)	1710	1759	Forbes, John (A)	1871	1951	Maurice, Frederick (A)
1861	1936	Allenby, Edmund (A)	1786	1847	Franklin, John (E)	1867	1948	Milne, Geo. (A)
1717	1797	Amherst, Jeffrey (A)	1852	1925	French, John (A)	1894	1967	Morgan, Frederick (A)
1584	1622	Baffin, William (E)	1535	1594	Frobisher, Martin (E)	1782	1853	Napier, Charles J. (A)
1871	1936	Beatty, David (N)	1721	1787	Gage, Thomas (A)	1810	1890	Napier, Robert C. (A)
1873	1967	Boyle, Wm. H. D. (N)	1833	1885	Gordon, Chas. G. (A)	1758	1805	Nelson, Horatio (N)
1695	1755	Braddock, Edward (A)	1541	1591	Grenville, Richard (N)	1696	1785	Oglethorpe, James (A)
1839	1908	Buller, Redvers (A)	1861	1928	Haig, Douglas (A)	1895	1968	Robb, James (F)
1723	1792	Burgoyne, John (A)	1853	1947	Hamilton, Ian (A)	1832	1914	Roberts, Frederick (A)
1663	1733	Byng, George (N)	1795	1857	Havelock, Henry (A)	1719	1792	Rodney, Geo. (N)
1675	1726	Cadogan, Wm. (A)	1745	1792	Hearne, Samuel (E)	1800	1862	Ross, James C. (E)
1593	1676	Cavendish, Wm. (A)	1536	1624	Howard, Charles (N)	1893	1969	Scobie, Ronald M. (A)
1873	1967	Chatfield, Alfred (N)	1726	1799	Howe, Richard (N)	1868	1912	Scott, Robert F. (E)
1738	1795	Clinton, Henry, (A)	1729	1814	Howe, William (A)	1874	1922	Shackleton, Ernest (E)
1892	1959	Cochrane, Edw. L. (N)	1575	1611	Hudson, Henry (E)	1891	1970	Slim, Wm. Joseph (A)
1770	1851	Codrington, Ed. (N)	1883	1966	Humphrey, Noel (E)	1841	1904	Stanley, Henry M. (E)
1727	1779	Cook, James (E)	1880	1959	Ironside, Wm. E. (A)	1869	1951	Swinton, Ernest (A)
1738	1805	Cornwallis, Chas. (A)	1859	1935	Jellicoe, John (N)	1890	1967	Tedder, Arthur W. (F)
1550	1605	Davis, John (E)	1715	1774	Johnson, Wm. (A)	1757	1798	Vancouver, George (E)
1896	1969	Dempsey, Miles (A)	1872	1945	Keyes, Roger (N)	1883	1950	Wavell, Archibald (A)
1883	1970	Dowding, Hugh C. (F)	1850	1916	Kitchener, H. H. (A)	1787	1834	Weddell, James (E)
1540	1596	Drake, Francis (N)	1888	1935	Lawrence, T. E. (A)	1769	1852	Wellington, Duke of (A)
1877	1967	Ellington, Edward (F)	1650	1722	Marlborough, Duke of (A)	1727	1759	Wolfe, James (A)
1841	1920	Fisher, John A. (N)						

BRITISH STATESMEN

Born	Died	Name	Born	Died	Name	Born	Died	Name
1852	1928	Asquith, Herbert H.	1725	1774	Clive, Robert	1858	1923	Law, A. Bonar
1879	1964	Astor, Viscountess	1889	1952	Cripps, Stafford	1863	1945	Lloyd George, David
1883	1967	Atlee, Clement	1599	1658	Cromwell, Oliver	1876	1947	Lytton, Victor
1867	1947	Baldwin, Stanley	1859	1925	Curzon of Kedleston	1866	1937	MacDonald, J. Ramsay
1848	1930	Balfour, Arthur J.	1804	1881	Disraeli, Benjamin	1854	1925	Milner, Alfred
1879	1964	Beaverbrook, Lord	1819	1886	Forster, Wm. E.	1732	1792	North, Frederick
1897	1960	Bevan, Aneurin	1749	1806	Fox, Chas. Jas.	1784	1865	Palmerston, Viscount
1881	1951	Bevin, Ernest	1906	1963	Gaitskell, Hugh	1788	1850	Peel, Robert
1838	1922	Bryce, James	1809	1898	Gladstone, Wm. E.	1867	1937	Peel, William
1884	1968	Cadogan, Alexander	1712	1770	Grenville, George	1759	1806	Pitt, William
1770	1827	Canning, George	1764	1845	Grey, Charles	1708	1778	Pitt, W. (Chatham)
1769	1822	Castlereagh, Robt.	1862	1933	Grey, Edward	1854	1932	Plunkett, Horace
1864	1958	Cecil, Edgar	1594	1643	Hampden, John	1853	1902	Rhodes, Cecil
1863	1937	Chamberlain, Austen	1732	1818	Hastings, Warren	1847	1929	Rosebery, Arch.
1836	1914	Chamberlain, Joseph	1863	1935	Henderson, Arthur	1792	1878	Russell, John
1869	1940	Chamberlain, Neville	1889	1969	Horsbrugh, Florence	1830	1903	Salisbury, Robt.
1874	1965	Churchill, Winston	1853	1917	Jameson, Leander S.	1676	1745	Walpole, Robert

BRITISH SCIENTISTS, ENGINEERS, PHYSICIANS

Born	Died	Name	Born	Died	Name	Born	Died	Name
1888	1967	Bamforth, Joseph	1898	1968	Florey, Howard W.	1903	1969	Powell, Cecil F.
1875	1968	Beatty, Chester	1892	1964	Haldane, J. B. S.	1733	1804	Priestley, Jos.
1813	1898	Bessemer, Henry	1578	1657	Harvey, Wm.	1857	1932	Ross, Ronald
1899	1966	Cameron, Roy	1792	1871	Herschel, John	1871	1937	Rutherford, Ernest
1881	1966	Campbell, Donald F.	1738	1822	Herschel, Wm.	1811	1870	Simpson, Jas. Y.
1731	1810	Cavendish, Henry	1897	1967	Hinshelwood, Cyril	1781	1848	Stephenson, Geo.
1905	1967	Cockcroft, John	1861	1947	Hopkins, Frederick	1624	1689	Sydenham, Thomas
1832	1919	Crooks, Wm.	1749	1823	Jenner, Edward	1820	1904	Thompson, Jos.
1875	1968	Dale, Henry H.	1815	1898	Jenner, William	1824	1907	Thomson, Wm. (Kelvin)
1766	1844	Dalton, John	1827	1912	Lister, Jos.	1820	1893	Tyndall, John
1809	1882	Darwin, Charles	1877	1969	Martin, William K.	1823	1913	Wallace, Alf. Russell
1791	1867	Faraday, Michael	1831	1879	Maxwell, Jas. Clerk	1736	1819	Watt, James E.
1881	1955	Fleming, Alexander	1663	1729	Newcomen, Thos.	1802	1875	Wheatstone, Chas.
1849	1945	Fleming, Ambrose	1642	1727	Newton, Isaac	1901	1966	Whinfield, John R.

BRITISH RELIGIOUS LEADERS

Born	Died	Name	Born	Died	Name	Born	Died	Name
1117	1170	Becket, Thomas a	1860	1954	Inge, William Ralph	1613	1667	Taylor, Jeremy
1685	1753	Berkeley, George	1874	1966	Johnson, Hewlett	1484	1536	Tyndale, William
1829	1912	Booth, William B.	1505	1572	Knox, John	1703	1791	Wesley, John
1566	1644	Brewster, William	1491	1555	Latimer, Hugh	1714	1770	Whitefield, Geo.
1489	1556	Cranmer, Thos.	1813	1873	Livingstone, David	1802	1865	Wiseman, Nicholas
1624	1691	Fox, George	1808	1892	Manning, Henry E.	1475	1530	Wolsey, Thomas
1554	1600	Hooker, Richard	1801	1890	Newman, John H.	1324	1384	Wycliffe, John

French

French Scientists, Physicians

Born	Died	Name	Born	Died	Name	Born	Died	Name
1775	1836	Ampere, Andre-Marie	1678	1761	Fauchard, Pierre	1864	1948	Lumière, Louis
1788	1878	Becquerel, A. C.	1842	1925	Flammarion, Camille	1852	1907	Moissan, Henri
1852	1908	Becquerel, H. A.	1778	1850	Gay-Lussac, Joseph	1745	1799	Montgolfier, Jacques
1827	1907	Berthelot, Marcelin	1900	1958	Joliot-Curie, Frederic	1740	1810	Montgolfier, Jos.
1812	1878	Bernard, Claude	1781	1826	Laennec, Rene	1807	1873	Nelaton, Auguste
1785	1870	Broglie, A. C. de	1736	1813	Lagrange, Jos. L.	1863	1933	Painleve, Paul
1872	1936	Bleriot, Louis	1744	1829	Lamarck, Jean B.	1647	1714	Papin, Denis
1825	1893	Charcot, Jean M.	1749	1827	Laplace, Pierre S.	1510	1590	Pare, Ambroise
1746	1823	Charles, Jacques	1743	1794	Lavoisier, Antoine	1822	1895	Pasteur, Louis
1786	1889	Chevreul, Michel	1822	1900	Lenoir, Etienne	1854	1912	Poincare, Henri
1859	1906	Curie, Pierre	1811	1877	LeVerrier, Urbain	1850	1936	Richet, Chas.
1890	1967	Danjon, Andre	1862	1954	Lumière, Auguste	1875	1965	Schweitzer, Albert

French Military Leaders and Explorers

Born	Died	Name	Born	Died	Name	Born	Died	Name
1769	1821	Bonaparte, Napoleon	1753	1800	Kleber, Jean-Bapt.	1611	1675	Turenne, Vicomte de
1753	1823	Carnot, Lazare	1757	1834	La Fayette, Marquis de			
1877	1969	Catroux, Georges	1902	1947	Leclerc, Jacques P.			**EXPLORERS**
1519	1572	Coligny, Gasp. de	1854	1934	Lyautey, Louis H.			
1621	1686	Conde, Prince de	1756	1817	Massena, Andre	1658	1730	Cadillac, Antoine
1881	1942	Darlan, Jean F.	1712	1759	Montcalm, Louis de	1491	1557	Cartier, Jacques
1722	1788	DeGrasse, Francois	1763	1813	Moreau, Jean V.	1567	1635	Champlain, Sam'l de
1773	1823	Dumouriez, Chas. F.	1769	1815	Ney, Michel	1867	1936	Charcot, Jean B.
1851	1929	Foch, Ferdinand	1856	1951	Petain, Henri Philippe	1868	1969	David-Neel, Alexandra
1489	1512	Foix, Gaston de	1725	1807	Rochambeau, Jean-Bapt.	1640	1701	Hennepin, Louis
1849	1916	Gallieni, Jos. S.	1579	1638	Rohan, Henri	1645	1700	Jolliet, Louis
1879	1949	Giraud, Henri H.	1696	1750	Saxe, Maurice de	1643	1687	LaSalle, Robt. de
1852	1931	Joffre, Jos.	1769	1851	Soult, Nicolas J.	1637	1675	Marquette, Jacques

French
FRENCH AUTHORS, DRAMATISTS, HISTORIANS, RELIGIONISTS

Born	Died	Name
1079	1142	Abélard, Pierre
1717	1783	Alembert, Jean d'
1885	1969	Allain, Marcel
1880	1918	Apollinaire, Guillaume
1820	1889	Augier, (Emile)
1902	1967	Ayme, Marcel
1799	1850	Balzac, Honoré de
1823	1891	Banville, Théodore de
1873	1935	Barbusse, Henri
1862	1923	Barrès, Maurice
1821	1867	Baudelaire, Charles
1732	1799	Beaumarchais, Pierre
1837	1899	Becque, Henry
1780	1857	Béranger, Pierre
1859	1941	Bergson, Henri
1888	1948	Bernanos, Georges
1866	1947	Bernard, Tristan
1876	1953	Bernstein, Henri
1876	1967	Birot, Pierre A.
1636	1711	Boileau, Nicolas
1627	1704	Bossuet, Jacques
1852	1935	Bourget, Paul
1867	1926	Boylesve, René
1858	1932	Brieux, Eugène
1707	1788	Buffon, Georges
1509	1564	Calvin, John
1913	1960	Camus, Albert
1541	1603	Charron, Pierre
[illegible]	[illegible]	[illegible]
1762	1794	Chénier, André
1895	1969	Chevallier, Gabriel
1889	1963	Cocteau, Jean
1873	1954	Colette, Sidonie
1445	1509	Comines, Philippe de
1798	1857	Comte, Auguste
1743	1794	Condorcet, Marquis de
1767	1830	Constant, Benjamin
1842	1908	Coppée, François
1845	1875	Corbière, Tristan
1606	1684	Corneille, Pierre
1854	1928	Curel, François de
1769	1832	Cuvier, Georges
1840	1897	Daudet, Alphonse
1596	1650	Descartes, René
1902	1969	De Vilmorin, Louise
1713	1784	Diderot, Denis
1881	1958	Du Gard, Roger M.
1803	1870	Dumas, Alexandre
1824	1895	Dumas, Alexandre fils
1926	1967	Fall, Bernard B.
1651	1715	Fénelon, François de
1821	1890	Feuillet, Octave
1821	1880	Flaubert, Gustave
1886	1914	Fournier, Alain
1844	1924	France, Anatole
1333	1400	Froissart, Jean
1811	1872	Gautier, Théophile
1869	1951	Gide, André
1882	1944	Giraudoux, Jean
1816	1882	Gobineau, Comte de
1822	1896	Goncourt, Edmond de
1830	1870	Goncourt, Jules de
1787	1874	Guizot, François
1570	1631	Hardy, Alexandre
1842	1905	Heredia, José-Maria de
1857	1915	Hervieu, Paul
1892	1955	Honegger, Arthur
1802	1885	Hugo, Victor
1848	1907	Huysmans, Joris-Karl
1876	1944	Jacob, Max
1868	1938	Jammes, Francis
1412	1431	Joan of Arc
1815	1888	Labiche, Eugene
1530	1568	La Boëtie, Etienne de
[illegible]	[illegible]	[illegible]
1621	1695	La Fontaine, Jean de
1860	1887	Laforgue, Jules
1744	1829	Lamarck, Jean-Baptiste
1790	1869	Lamartine, Alphonsede
1613	1680	La Rochefoucauld
1846	1870	Lautréamont, Comte de
1818	1894	Leconte de Lisle
1853	1914	Lemaitre, Jules
1668	1747	Lesage, Alain René
1850	1923	Loti, Pierre (J. Viaud)
1842	1898	Mallarmé, Stéphane
1688	1763	Marivaux, Pierre
1850	1893	Maupassant, Guy de
1885	1967	Maurois, Andre
1803	1870	Mèrimée, Prosper
1798	1874	Michelet, Jules
1622	1673	Moliére, Jean-Baptiste
1533	1592	Montaigne, Michel de
1689	1755	Montesquieu, Charles de
1810	1857	Musset, Alfred de
1808	1855	Nerval, Gerard de
1394	1465	Orleans, Charles d'
1623	1662	Pascal, Blaise
1873	1914	Péguy, Charles
1697	1763	Prévost (L'Abbé)
1871	1922	Proust, Marcel
1495	1553	Rabelais, François
1639	1699	Racine, Jean
1864	1936	Régnier, Henri de
1823	1892	Renan, Ernest
1849	1926	Richepin, Jean
1854	1891	Rimbaud, Arthur
1866	1944	Rolland, Romain
1524	1585	Ronsard, Pierre de
1868	1918	Rostand, Edmond
1760	1836	Rouget de Lisle, Claude
1712	1778	Rousseau, Jean-Jacques
1610	1703	Saint-Evremond, de
1900	1944	Saint-Exupéry, Ant. de
1675	1755	Saint-Simon, Duc de
1804	1869	Sainte-Beuve, Charles A.
1567	1622	Sales (Saint François de)
1804	1876	Sand, George (Lucile Dupin)
[illegible]	[illegible]	[illegible]
1791	1861	Scribe, Eugène
1626	1696	Sévigné, (Mme. de)
1875	1959	Siegfried, Andre
1766	1817	Staël, (Mme. de)
1783	1842	Stendhal, (Beyle)
1839	1907	Sully-Prudhomme, René
1828	1893	Taine, Hippolyte
1795	1856	Thierry, Augustin
1805	1859	Tocqueville, A. C. de
1871	1945	Valéry, Paul
1844	1896	Verlaine, Paul
1828	1905	Verne, Jules
1797	1863	Vigny, Alfred de
1838	1889	Villiers de l'Isle-Adam
1431	1484	Villon, François
1694	1778	Voltaire, (Arouet)
1840	1902	Zola, Emile

French Painters and Sculptors

Born	Died	Name
1834	1904	Bartholdi, F. A.
1848	1884	Bastien-Lepage, J.
1822	1899	Bonheur, Rosa
1867	1947	Bonnard, Pierre
1703	1770	Boucher, Francois
1825	1905	Bouguereau, W.
1876	1957	Brancusi, C.
1882	1963	Braque, Georges
1851	1933	Carrier-Belleuse, P.
1839	1906	Cézanne, Paul
1699	1779	Chardin, Jean-Bapt.
1600	1682	Claude Lorrain
1845	1902	Constant, Benj.
1796	1875	Corot, J. B. C.
1819	1877	Courbet, Gustave
1817	1878	Daubigny, C. F.
1808	1879	Daumier, Honore
1748	1825	David, Louis J.
1783	1856	David d'Angers, P. J
1834	1917	Degas, H. G. E.
1799	1863	Delacroix, Eugene
1797	1856	Delaroche, Paul
1880	1954	Derain, Andre
1807	1876	Diaz de la Pena, N. V.
1833	1883	Dore, Gustave
1877	1953	Dufy, Raoul
1811	1889	Dupre, Jules
1852	1931	Forain, Jean L.
1732	1806	Fragonard, Jean
1820	1876	Fromentin, Eugene
1848	1903	Gauguin, Paul
1770	1837	Gérard, F.
1791	1824	Gericault, J. L. A. T.
1824	1904	Gérôme, J. L.
1628	1715	Girardon, Fr.
1839	1883	Goupil, Jules A.
1725	1805	Greuze, J. B.
1741	1828	Houdon, J. A.
1780	1867	Ingres, J. A. D.
1755	1841	Lebrun, Marie
1887	1965	Le Corbusier
1798	1880	Lemaire, Ph. H.
1600	1682	Lorrain, Claude
1861	1944	Maillol, Aristide
1832	1883	Manet, Edouard
1869	1954	Matisse, Henri
1815	1891	Meissonier, J. L. E.
1815	1875	Millet, J. F.
1884	1920	Modigliani, Amadeo
1840	1926	Monet, Claude
1824	1898	Moreau, Gustave
1830	1903	Pissarro, Camille
1594	1665	Poussin, Nicolas
1758	1823	Prudhon, Pierre
1824	1898	Puvis de Chavanne
1840	1916	Redon, Odilon
1841	1919	Renoir, P. A.
1840	1917	Rodin, Auguste
1871	1958	Rouault, Georges
1812	1867	Rousseau, P. E. T.
1795	1858	Scheffer, Ary
1863	1927	Serusier, Paul
1859	1891	Seurat, Georges
1863	1935	Signac, Paul
1839	1899	Sisley, Alfred
1900	1955	Tanguy, Yves
1864	1901	Toulouse-Lautrec
1813	1865	Troyon, Constant
1883	1955	Utrillo, Maurice
1758	1835	Vernet, Carie
1714	1789	Vernet, Claude, J.
1789	1863	Vernet, Horace
1876	1958	Vlaminck, Maurice
1868	1940	Vuillard, Edouard
1684	1721	Watteau, Antoine

French Political Leaders

Born	Died	Name
1884	1966	Auriol, Vincent
1872	1950	Blum, Leon
1862	1932	Briand, Aristide
1841	1929	Clemenceau, Georges
1619	1683	Colbert, Jean-Bapt.
1884	1970	Daladier, Edouard
1759	1794	Danton, Georges
1890	1970	De Gaulle, Charles
1760	1794	Desmoulins, Camille
1763	1820	Fouche, Jos.
1620	1698	Frontenac, Louis de
1838	1882	Gambetta, Leon
1872	1957	Herriot, Edouard
1883	1945	Laval, Pierre
1871	1950	Lebrun, Albert
1744	1793	Marat, Jean-Paul
1602	1661	Mazarin, Jules
1749	1791	Mirabeau, Honore
1860	1934	Poincare, Raymond
1884	1970	Queuille, Henri
1878	1966	Reynaud, Paul
1585	1642	Richelieu, Cardinal de
1758	1794	Robespierre, Max.
1208	1265	Simon de Montfort
1754	1838	Talleyrand, Chas. de

GERMAN ARTISTS: PAINTERS, SCULPTORS, ARCHITECTS

Born	Died	Name
1480	1538	Altdorfer, Albrecht
1476	1545	Baldung, Hans
1870	1938	Barlach, Ernst
1884	1950	Beckmann, Max
1827	1901	Boecklin, Arnold
1726	1801	Chodowiecki, Dan'l
1858	1925	Corinth, Louis
1783	1867	Cornelius, Peter
1472	1553	Cranach, Lucas
1471	1528	Durer, Albrecht
1829	1880	Feuerbach, Anselm
1774	1840	Friedrich, Kaspar
1503	1529	Gruenewald, Matth.
1847	1921	Hildebrand, Adolf v.
1460	1524	Holbein, Hans (Sr.)
1497	1543	Holbein, Hans (Jr.)
1877	1947	Kolbe, Georg
1867	1945	Kollwitz, Kaethe
1847	1935	Liebermann, Max
1880	1916	Marc, Franz
1837	1887	Marees, Hans v.
1815	1905	Menzel, Adolf v.
1803	1884	Richter, Ludwig
1764	1850	Schadow, Johann
1781	1841	Schinkel, Karl
1868	1932	Slevogt, Max
1839	1924	Thoma, Hans
1848	1911	Uhde, Fritz v.
1455	1529	Vischer, Peter

Germans

GERMAN ENGINEERS, NATURALISTS, SCIENTISTS, INDUSTRIALISTS

Born	Died	Name	Born	Died	Name	Born	Died	Name
1840	1905	Abbe, Ernst	1400	1468	Gutenberg, Johannes	1848	1896	Lilienthal, Otto
1902	1958	Adler, Kurt	1834	1919	Haeckel, Ernst	1734	1815	Mesmer, Franz
1193	1280	Albertus Magnus	1844	1913	Hagenbeck, Carl	1855	1916	Neisser, Albert
1844	1929	Benz, Carl	1879	1968	Hahn, Otto	1899	1968	Nordhoff, Heinrich
1882	1970	Born, Max	1755	1843	Hahnemann, Samuel	1787	1854	Ohm, Geo. S.
1874	1940	Bosch, Karl	1821	1894	Helmholz, Hermann	1871	1948	Opel, Wilh. v.
1811	1899	Bunsen, Robert	1857	1894	Hertz, Heinrich	1853	1932	Ostwald, Wilhelm
1873	1941	Burger, Hans	1769	1859	Humboldt, Alex. v.	1858	1947	Planck, Max
1834	1900	Daimler, Gottlieb	1767	1835	Humboldt, Wilh. v.	1632	1694	Pufendorf, Samuel
1858	1913	Diesel, Rudolf	1859	1935	Junkers, Hugo	1845	1923	Roentgen, Wilh.
1895	1964	Domagk, Gerhard	1571	1630	Kepler, Johannes	1822	1890	Schliemann, Heinrich
1884	1969	Dornier, Claude	1843	1910	Koch, Robert	1816	1892	Siemens, Werner v.
1861	1935	Duisberg, Carl	1812	1887	Krupp, Alfred	1842	1926	Thyssen, Aug.
1868	1954	Eckener, Hugo	1907	1967	Krupp, Alfried	1821	1902	Virchow, Rudolf
1854	1915	Ehrlich, Paul	1900	1967	Kuhn, Richard	1866	1925	Wassermann, Aug. v.
1686	1736	Fahrenheit, Gabriel	1646	1716	Leibnitz, Gottfried v.	1853	1905	Wissmann, Hermann v.
1852	1919	Fischer, Emil	1742	1799	Lichtenberg, Georg	1838	1917	Zeppelin, Ferd. v.
1882	1964	Franck, James	1803	1873	Liebig, Justus v.	1883	1970	Warburg, Otto

GERMAN POLITICAL AND MILITARY LEADERS; ECONOMISTS

Born	Died	Name	Born	Died	Name	Born	Died	Name
1876	1967	Adenauer, Konrad	1863	1932	Hipper, Franz v.	1848	1916	Moltke, Helmuth von
1856	1921	Bethmann-Hollweg, T. v.	1889	1945	Hitler, Adolf	1879	1969	Papen, Franz V.
1815	1898	Bismarck, Otto v.	1882	1946	Keitel, Wilhelm	1876	1960	Raeder, Erich
1742	1819	Bluecher, Gebh. v.	1887	1960	Kesselring, Alb.	1867	1922	Rathenau, Walter
1885	1970	Bruning, Heinruch	1871	1919	Liebknecht, Karl	1891	1944	Rommel, Erwin
1849	1929	Buelow, Bernhar v.	1886	1966	Luckner, Felix V.	1876	1953	Rundstedt, Karl v.
1780	1831	Clausewitz, C. v.	1865	1937	Ludendorff, Erich	1877	1970	Schacht, Hjalmar
1875	1921	Erzberger, Matthias	1880	1919	Luxemburg, Rosa	1865	1939	Scheidemann, Philipp
1861	1922	Falkenhayn, E. v.	1849	1945	Mackensen, Aug. v.	1833	1913	Schlieffen, Alf. v.
1760	1831	Gneisenau, Aug.	1818	1883	Marx, Karl	1878	1929	Stresemann, Gustav
1847	1934	Hindenburg, Paul v.	1800	1891	Moltke, Helmuth von	1849	1930	Tirpitz, Alf. v.

GERMAN AUTHORS, DRAMATISTS, ESSAYISTS, RELIGIONISTS

Born	Died	Name	Born	Died	Name	Born	Died	Name
1769	1860	Arndt, Ernst Moritz	1802	1827	Hauff, Wilhelm	1804	1875	Moerike, Eduard
1886	1956	Benn, Gottfried	1862	1946	Hauptmann, Gerhart	1817	1903	Mommsen, Theodor
1898	1956	Brecht, Bertolt	1813	1863	Hebbel, Friedrich	1844	1900	Nietzsche, Friedrich
1778	1842	Brentano, Clemens	1760	1826	Hebel, Johann P.	1796	1835	Platten, Aug. v.
1491	1551	Bucer, Martin	1770	1831	Hegel, Georg W. F.	1795	1886	Ranke, Leopold, v.
1832	1908	Busch, Wilhelm	1797	1856	Heine, Heinrich	1810	1874	Reuter, Fritz
1740	1815	Claudius, Matthias	1744	1803	Herder, Johann v.	1763	1825	Richter, Jean Paul
1863	1920	Dehmel, Richard	1877	1962	Hesse, Hermann	1875	1926	Rilke, Rainer Maria
1837	1898	Elbers, Georg	1776	1822	Hoffman, E. T. A.	1899	1966	Ropke, Wilhelm
1788	1857	Eichendorff, Jos.	1770	1843	Hoelderlin, Friedrich	1788	1866	Rueckert, Friedrich
1820	1895	Engels, Friedrich	1878	1945	Kaiser, Georg	1494	1576	Sachs, Hans
1886	1933	Ernst, Paul	1724	1804	Kant, Immanuel	1775	1854	Schelling, Frederich v.
1170	1220	Eschenbach, Wolfram v.	1896	1966	Kasack, Hermann	1759	1805	Schiller, Friedrich
1884	1958	Feuchtwanger, Lion	1777	1811	Kleist, Heinrich v.	1767	1845	Schlegel, Aug. W.
1762	1814	Fichte, Johann G.	1724	1803	Klopstock, Friedr	1772	1829	Schlegel, Friedr.
1869	1966	Foerster, Friedrich	1791	1813	Koerner, Karl Th.	1768	1834	Schleiermacher, Fredrich
1819	1898	Fontane, Theodor	1875	1967	Kolb, Annette	1788	1860	Schopenhauer, Arthur
1816	1895	Freytag, Gustav	1646	1716	Leibnitz, Gottfried	1817	1888	Storm, Theodor
1868	1933	George, Stefan	1729	1781	Lessing, Gotthold	1857	1928	Sudermann, Hermann
1607	1676	Gerhardt, Paul	1844	1909	Liliencron, Detlev v.	1893	1939	Toller, Ernst
1749	1832	Goethe, Johann W. v.	1881	1948	Ludwig, Emil	1834	1896	Treitschke, Heinrich v.
1785	1863	Grimm, Jakob	1483	1546	Luther, Martin	1787	1862	Uhland, Ludwig
1786	1859	Grimm, Wilhelm	1871	1950	Mann, Heinrich	1873	1934	Wassermann, Jakob
1890	1941	Hasenclever, Walter	1875	1955	Mann, Thomas	1733	1813	Wieland, Chris. M.

Russians

AUTHORS—POETS

Born	Died	Name
1888	1966	Akhmatova, Anna A.
1871	1919	Andreyev, Leonid
1878	1927	Artsibashev, Mikhail
1880	1921	Blok, Alexander
1860	1904	Chekhov, Anton
1821	1881	Dostoievski, Feodor
1891	1967	Ehrenburg, Ilya G.
1809	1852	Gogol, Nicholas V.
1812	1891	Goncharov, Ivan A.
1868	1936	Gorky, Maxim
1812	1870	Herzen, Alexander
1809	1842	Koltsov, Alexei
1853	1921	Korolenko, Vladimir
1768	1844	Krylov, Ivan
1870	1938	Kuprin, Alexander
1814	1841	Lermontov, Michael
1831	1895	Leskov, Nicholas
1819	1883	Melnikov, Paul
1848	1936	Memirovich-Danchenko
1865	1942	Merezhkovsk, D. S.
1821	1877	Nekrasov, Nicholas
1824	1861	Nikitin, Vasili
1823	1886	Ostrovsky, Alexander
1890	1960	Pasternak, Boris
1857	1918	Piekhanov, Georgi
1799	1837	Pushkin, Alexander
1856	1919	Rozanov, Vasili
1820	1879	Soloviev, Sergei
1824	1919	Suvorin, Alexei
1883	1945	Tolstoy, Alexei

Born	Died	Name
1828	1910	Tolstoy, Leo
1818	1883	Turgenev, Ivan

ARTISTS

Born	Died	Name
1866	1924	Bakst, Leon S.
1866	1944	Kandinsky, Vasili
1783	1836	Kiprensky, Orest
1878	1927	Kostodiev, Boris
1861	1900	Levitan, Isaak
1844	1918	Repin, Ilya
1865	1911	Serov, Valentin
1842	1904	Vereshchagin, Vasili
1890	1967	Zadkine, Ossip

BALLET-STAGE

Born	Died	Name
1901	1968	Akimov, Nikolai
1872	1929	Diaghilev, Sergei
1898	1948	Eisenstein, Sergei
1890	1950	Nijinsky, Vaslav
1885	1931	Pavlova, Anna
1822	1910	Petipa, Marius
1863	1938	Stanislavsky, Konst.

POLITICAL LEADERS

Born	Died	Name
1746	1819	Baranov, Alexander
1875	1946	Kalinin, Mikhail
1881	1970	Kerensky, Alexander
1870	1924	Lenin, Vladimir
1877	1952	Litvinov, Maxim

Born	Died	Name
1845	1900	Muraviev, Michael
1744	1818	Novikov, Nicholas
1739	1791	Potemkin, G.
1772	1839	Speransky, Michael
1879	1953	Stalin, Josef
1863	1911	Stolypin, Peter
1895	1970	Timoshenko, Semyon
1879	1940	Trotzky, Leon (Bronstein)
1881	1969	Voroshilov, Klimenti Y.
1849	1915	Witte, Sergei

SCIENTISTS

Born	Died	Name
1877	1968	Arbuzov, Aleksandr
1898	1967	Balandin, Alcksei
1857	1927	Bekhterev, Vladimir
1779	1852	Bellingshausen, F.
1934	1968	Gagarin, Yuri
1862	1916	Golitzin, Boris
1842	1921	Kropotkin, Peter
1908	1968	Landau, Lev D.
1711	1765	Lomonosov, Michael
1909	1967	Maltsev, Anatoli
1834	1907	Mendeleyev, Dmitri
1845	1916	Metchnikov, Elie
1905	1970	Mikoyan, Artem I.
1849	1936	Pavlov, Ivan
1810	1881	Pirogov, Nicholas
1859	1905	Popov, Alexander
1907	1966	Sisakian, Norayr M.
1891	1969	Stechkin, Boris S.

Additional Foreign Personalities of the Past

Aus.-Austrian. Braz.-Brazilian. C.-Czech. Cong.-Congolese. D.-Danish. F.-French. G.-German. Gr.-Greek. H.-Hungarian. It.-Italian. Mex.-Mexican. N.-Norwegian. Port.-Portuguese. Sp.-Spanish. Sw.-Swedish. T.-Turkish.

S. Y. Agnon, Israeli novelist, 1888-1970.
Emilio Aguinaldo, Filipino revolutionary, 1869-1964.
Roald Amundsen, N. explorer, 1872-1928.
Hans Christian Andersen, D. writer, 1805-1875
Julius Andrassy, H. statesman, 1823-1890.
Pedro Aramburu, Argentine statesman, 1903-1970.
Sholem Asch, Polish-born Yiddish writer, 1880-1957.
Kemal Ataturk, T. statesman, 1881-1938.

Vasco Núñez de Balboa, Sp. explorer, 1475-1519.
Karl Barth, Swiss theologian, 1889-1966.
Brendan Behan, Irish playwright, 1923-1964.
Bjarni Benediktson, Icelandic statesman, 1908-1970.
Eduard Benes, C. statesman, 1884-1948.
Vitus J. Bering, D. explorer, 1681-1741.
Folke Bernadotte, Sw. statesman, 1895-1948.
Vicente Blasco-Ibáñez, Sp. novelist, 1867-1928.
Arnold Boecklin, Swiss painter, 1827-1901.
Niels Bohr, D. physicist, 1885-1962.
Simón Bolívar, South American revolutionary, 1783-1830.
José Bonifácio, Braz. statesman, 1763-1838.
Louis Botha, South African statesman, 1862-1919.
Constantin Brancusi, Romanian sculptor, 1876-1957.
Emil Brunner, Swiss theologian, 1889-1966.
Martin Buber, Aus.-born Jewish philosopher, 1878-1965.

Plutarco Calles, Mex. statesman, 1877-1945.
Constantine Canaris, Gr. statesman, 1790-1877.
Karel Čapek, C. writer, 1890-1938.
Lázaro Cárdenas, Mex. statesman, 1895-1970.
Venustiano Carranza, Mex. political leader, 1859-1920.
Roger Casement, Irish revolutionary, 1864-1916.
Humberto Castelo Branco, Braz. political leader, 1900-1967.
Miguel de Cervantes Saavedra, Sp. novelist, 1547-1616.
Henri Christophe, Haitian revolutionary, 1767-1820.
Nicholas Copernicus, Polish astronomer, 1473-1543.
Hernando Cortez, Sp. conqueror of Mexico, 1485-1547.
Marie Sklodowska Curie, Polish chemist, 1867-1934.

Hernando De Soto, Sp. explorer, 1500-1542.
Jean J. Dessalines, Haitian emperor, 1758-1806.
Porfirio Díaz, Mex. statesman, 1830-1915.
Ngo Dinh Diem, South Vietnamese president, 1901-1963.
Isak Dinesen, D. author, 1885-1962.
Engelbert Dollfuss, Aus. statesman, 1892-1934.
Christian Doppler, Aus. physicist, 1803-1853.

Robert Emmet, Irish patriot, 1778-1803.
Enver Pasha, T. political leader, 1881-1922.
Erasmus, Desiderius, Dutch author, 1466-1536.
Levi Eshkol, Israeli statesman, 1895-1969.

Manuel de Falla, Sp. composer, 1876-1946.
Ragnar Frisch, Norwegian economist, 1895-1973.

Vasco da Gama, Port. explorer, 1469-1524.
Mohandas K. Gandhi, Indian political leader, 1869-1948.
Alberto Giacometti, Swiss sculptor, 1901-1966.
Vincent van Gogh, Dutch painter, 1853-1890.
Francisco Goya y Lucientes, Sp. painter, 1746-1828.
El Greco, Greek painter in Spain, 1541-1614.
Lady Augusta Gregory, Irish dramatist, 1859-1932.
Edvard Grieg, N. composer, 1843-1907.

Franz Hals, Dutch painter, 1584-1666.
Dag Hammarskjold, Sw. statesman, 1905-1961.
Theodor Herzl, H. founder of modern Zionism, 1860-1904.
Ho Chi Minh, North Vietnamese president, 1890-1969.
Yukio Mishima, Japanese author, 1925-1970.
Andreas Hofer, Aus. patriot, 1767-1810.
Nicholas Horthy, H. statesman, 1868-1957.
Mikhailo Hrushevsky, Ukrainian statesman, 1866-1934.
Jan Huss, C. religionist, 1369-1415.

Henrik Ibsen, N. playwright, 1828-1906.

James Joyce, Irish author, 1882-1941.
Benito Juárez, Mex. statesman, 1806-1872.

Franz Kafka, C.-born Austrian author, 1883-1924.
Joseph Kasavubu, Cong. political leader, 1910-1969.
Abdul Karim Kassem, Iraqi politician, 1914-1963.
Yasunari Kawabata, Japanese novelist, 1899-1972.
Elizabeth (Sister) Kenny, Aus. nurse, 1886-1952.
Paul Klee, Swiss painter, 1879-1940.
Thaddeus Kosciusko, Polish general, 1746-1817.
Paul Kruger, South African statesman, 1825-1904.
Mikola Kulish, Ukrainian dramatist, 1892-1934.
Frank Kupka, C. painter, 1871-1957.

Selma Lagerlof, Sw. writer, 1858-1940.
Wanda Landowska, Polish harpsichordist, 1879-1959.
Francisco Largo Caballero, Sp. statesman, 1869-1946.
Louis Leakey, British archaeologist, 1903-1972.
Trygve Lie, N. statesman, 1896-1968.
Patrice E. Lumumba, Cong. political leader, 1925-1961.
Albert J. Luthuli, South African political leader, 1899-1967.

Francisco I. Madera, Mex. statesman, 1873-1913.
Maurice Maeterlinck, Belgian dramatist, 1862-1949.
Ferdinand Magellan, Port. explorer, 1480-1521.
Carl Gustav Mannerheim, Finnish statesman, 1867-1951.
José Marti, Cuban patriot, 1853-1895.
Jan Masaryk, C. statesman, 1886-1948.
Thomas G. Masaryk, C. statesman, 1850-1937.
Tom Mboya, Kenyan political leader, 1930-1969.
Lise Meitner, Aus. mathematician, 1878-1968.
Gregor J. Mendel, Aus. botanist, 1822-1884.
John Metaxas, Gr. statesman, 1871-1941.
Clemens W. N. L. Metternich, Aus. statesman, 1773-1859.
Draja Mikhailovich, Yugoslav soldier, 1893-1946.
Carl Milles, Sw. sculptor, 1875-1955.
Ferenc Molnar, H. dramatist, 1878-1952.
George Moore, Irish novelist, 1852-1933.
Thomas Moore, Irish poet, 1779-1852.
José M. Morelos y Pavón, Mex. revolutionary leader, 1765-1815.
Mohammed E. Mossadegh, Iranian statesman, 1880-1967.
Bartolomé E. Murillo, Sp. painter, 1618-1682.

Imre Nagy, H. statesman, 1895-1958.
Fridtjof Nansen, N. explorer, 1861-1930.
Juan Negrin, Sp. statesman, 1891-1956.
Jawaharlal Nehru, Indian statesman, 1889-1964.
Florence Nightingale, English nurse, 1820-1910.
Alfred Nobel, Sw. philanthropist, 1833-1898.

Alvaro Obregón, Mex. statesman, 1880-1928.
Sean O'Casey, Irish dramatist, 1884-1964.
Daniel O'Connell, Irish political leader, 1775-1847.
Frank O'Connor, Irish writer, 1903-1966.
Thomas P. O'Connor, Irish journalist, 1848-1929.
Bernardo O'Higgins, Chilean revolutionary, 1776-1842.

George Papandreou, Gr. statesman, 1888-1968.
Charles Stewart Parnell, Irish nationalist, 1846-1891.
Pablo Picasso, Spanish artist & sculptor, 1881-1973.
Joseph Pilsudski, Polish statesman, 1867-1935.
Miguel Primo de Rivera, Sp. dictator, 1870-1930.
Casimir Pulaski, Polish statesman, 1748-1779

Manuel L. Quezon, Philippine statesman, 1878-1944.

Adam Rapacki, Polish statesman, 1910-1970.
Fritz Reiner, Aus. orchestra conductor, 1888-1963.
Rembrandt van Rijn, Dutch painter, 1605-1669.
Syngman Rhee, South Korean president, 1875-1965.
José Rizal, Filipino patriot, 1861-1896.
Peter Paul Rubens, Flemish painter, 1577-1640.

Antonio de O. Salazar, Port. statesman, 1899-1970.
José de San Martin, South American revolutionary, 1778-1850.
Antonio L. de Santa Anna, Mex. general, 1794-1876.
Francisco de Paula Santander, Colombian politician, 1792-1840.
Arthur Schnitzler, Aus. dramatist, 1862-1931.
Dudley Senanayake, Ceylon statesman, 1911-1973.
Moshe Sharett, Israeli statesman, 1894-1965.
Richard B. Sheridan, Irish author, 1751-1816.
Taras Shevchenko, Ukrainian poet, 1814-1861.
Frans E. Sillanpaa, Finnish novelist, 1888-1964.
Jan C. Smuts, South African statesman, 1870-1950.
Paul Henri Spaak, Belgian statesman, 1899-1972.
Baruch Spinoza, Dutch philosopher, 1632-1677.
Antonio Stradivari, It. violin-maker, 1644-1737.
August Strindberg, Sw. writer, 1849-1912.
Sun Yat-Sen, Chinese statesman, 1866-1925.
Otto Sverdrup, N. explorer, 1854-1930.
Emanuel Swedenborg, Swedish scientist, scholar, 1688-1772.
John M. Synge, Irish author, 1871-1909.

Rabindranath Tagore, Indian poet, 1861-1941.
Vaino A. Tanner, Finnish statesman, 1881-1966.
Hideki Tojo, Japanese political & military leader, 1884-1948.
Rafael L. Trujillo Molina, Dominican dictator, 1891-1961.
Moise K. Tshombe, Cong. leader, 1919-1969.

Lesia Ukrainka, Ukrainian writer, 1871-1913.
Sigrid Undset, N. author, 1882-1949.

Anthony Van Dyck, Flemish painter, 1599-1641.
Getúlio D. Vargas, Braz. statesman, 1883-1954.
Diego Velazquez, Sp. painter, 1599-1660.
Eleutherios Venizelos, Gr. statesman, 1864-1936.
Jan Vermeer, Dutch painter, 1632-1675.
Hendrik F. Verwoerd, South African prime minister, 1901-1966.
Vladimir Vinnichenko, Ukrainian novelist, 1880-1951.
Franz Werfel, Aus. author, 1890-1945.
Chaim Weizmann, first Israeli president, 1874-1952.
William Butler Yeats, Irish poet, 1865-1939.
Emiliano Zapata, Mex. revolutionary, 1879-1919.
Stefan Zweig, Aus. author, 1881-1942.

Rulers of England and Great Britain

Name	ENGLAND	Began	Died	Age	Rgd

SAXONS AND DANES

Name	Description	Began	Died	Age	Rgd
Egbert	King of Wessex, won allegiance of all English	827	839	..	12
Ethelwulf	Son, King of Wessex,Sussex, Kent, Essex	839	858	..	19
Ethelbald	Son of Ethelwulf, displaced father in Wessex	858	860	..	2
Ethelbert	2nd son of Ethelwulf, united Kent and Wessex	858	866	..	8
Ethelred	3rd son, King of Wessex, defeated Danes	866	871	..	5
Alfred	The Great, 4th son, fought Danes, fortified London	871	901	52	30
Edward	The Elder, Alfred's son, united English, claimed Scotland	901	925	55	24
Athelstan	The Glorious, Edward's son, King of Mercia, Wessex	925	940	45	15
Edmund	3rd son of Edward, King of Wessex, Mercia	940	946	25	6
Edred	4th son of Edward	946	955	32	9
Edwy	The Fair, eldest son of Edmund, King of Wessex	955	959	18	3
Edgar	The Peaceful, son of Edmund, ruled all English	959	975	32	17
Edward	The Martyr, son of Edgar, murdered by stepmother	975	978	17	4
Ethelred II	The Unready, son of Edgar, married Emma of Normandy	978	1016	48	37
Edmund	Ironside, son of Ethelred II, King of London	1016	1016	27	0
Canute	The Dane, gave Wessex to Edmund, married Emma	1017	1035	40	18
Harold I	Harefoot, natural son of Canute	1035	1040	..	5
Hardicanute	Son of Canute by Emma: Danish King	1040	1042	24	2
Edward	The Confessor, son of Ethelred II (Canonized 1161)	1042	1066	62	24
Harold II	Edward's brother-in-law, last Saxon King	1066	1066	44	0

HOUSE OF NORMANDY

Name	Description	Began	Died	Age	Rgd
William I	The Conqueror, defeated Harold at Hastings	1066	1087	60	21
William II	Rufus, 3rd son of William I, killed by arrow	1087	1100	43	13
Henry I	Beauclerc, youngest son of William I	1100	1135	67	35

HOUSE OF BLOIS

Name	Description	Began	Died	Age	Rgd
Stephen	Son of Adela, 4th dau of William I. and Count of Blois	1135	1154	50	19

HOUSE OF PLANTAGENET

Name	Description	Began	Died	Age	Rgd
Henry II	Son of Goeffrey Plantagenet (Angevin) by Matilda, Dau. of Henry I.	1154	1189	56	35
Richard I	Coeur de Lion, son of Henry II, crusader.	1189	1199	42	10
John	Lackland, son of Henry II, signed Magna Carta, 1215	1199	1216	50	17
Henry III	Son of John, acceded at 9, under regency till 1227	1216	1272	65	56
Edward I	Longshanks, son of Henry III	1272	1307	68	35
Edward II	Son of Edward I, deposed by Parliament, 1327.	1307	1327	43	20
Edward III	Of Windsor, son of Edward II.	1327	1377	65	50
Richard II	Grandson of Edw. III, minor until 1389, deposed 1399.	1377	1400	34	22

HOUSE OF LANCASTER

Name	Description	Began	Died	Age	Rgd
Henry IV	Son of John of Gaunt, Duke of Lancaster, son of Edw. III	1399	1413	47	13
Henry V	Son of Henry IV, victor of Agincourt	1413	1422	34	9
Henry VI	Son of Henry V deposed 1461, died in Tower	1422	1471	49	39

HOUSE OF YORK

Name	Description	Began	Died	Age	Rgd
Edward IV	Great-grandson of Edward III, son of Duke of York	1461	1483	41	22
Edward V	Son of Edward IV, murdered in Tower of London	1483	1483	13	0
Richard III	Crookback, bro. of Edward IV, fell at Bosworth Field	1483	1485	35	2

HOUSE OF TUDOR

Name	Description	Began	Died	Age	Rgd
Henry VII.	Son of Edmund Tudor, Earl of Richmond, whose father had married the widow of Henry V; descended from Edward III through his mother, Margaret Beaufort via John of Gaunt. By marriage with dau. of Edward IV he united Lancaster and York	1485	1509	53	24
Henry VIII	Son of Henry VII See memorable dates	1509	1547	56	38
Edward VI	Son of Henry VIII, by Jane Seymour, his 3rd queen, Ruled under regents. Was forced to name Lady Jane Grey his successor. Council of State proclaimed her queen July 10, 1553. Mary Tudor won Council, was proclaimed queen July 19, 1553. Mary had Lady Jane Grey beheaded for treason, Feb., 1554.	1547	1553	16	6
Mary I	Daughter of Henry VIII, by Catharine of Aragon	1553	1558	43	5
Elizabeth	Daughter of Henry VIII, by Anne Boleyn, Designated Elizabeth I in 1952.	1558	1603	69	44

GREAT BRITAIN

HOUSE OF STUART

Name	Description	Began	Died	Age	Rgd
James I	James VI of Scotland, son of Mary, Queen of Scots. First to call himself King of Great Britain. This became official with the Act of Union, 1707	1603	1625	59	22
Charles I	Only surviving son of James I: beheaded Jan. 30, 1649	1625	1649	48	24

COMMONWEALTH, 1649-1660
Council of State, 1649: Protectorate, 1653

Name	Description	Began	Died	Age	Rgd
The Cromwells	Oliver Cromwell, Lord Protector	1653	1658	59	..
	Richard Cromwell, Lord Protector, resigned May 25, 1659	1658	1712	86	..

HOUSE OF STUART (RESTORED)

Name	Description	Began	Died	Age	Rgd
Charles II	Eldest son of Charles I, died without issue.	1660	1685	55	25
James II	Second son of Charles I. Deposed 1688. Interregnum Dec. 11, 1688, to Feb. 13, 1689	1685	1701	68	3
William III	Son of William, Prince of Orange, by Mary, dau. of Charles I	1702	51	13	
and Mary II	Eldest daughter of James II and wife of William III	1689	1694	33	6
Anne	Second daughter of James	1702	1714	49	12

HOUSE OF HANOVER

Name	Description	Began	Died	Age	Rgd
George I	Son of Elector of Hanover, by Sophia, grand-dau. of James I	1714	1727	67	13
George II	Only son of George I, married Caroline of Brandenburg	1727	1760	77	33
George III	Grandson of George II, married Charlotte of Mecklenburg	1760	1820	81	59
George IV	Eldest son of George III, Prince Regent, from Feb., 1811	1820	1830	67	10
William IV	Third son of George III, married Adelaide of Saxe-Meiningen.	1830	1837	71	7
Victoria	Dau. of Edward, 4th son of George III; married (1840) Prince Albert of Saxe-Coburg and Gotha, who became Prince Consort	1837	1901	81	63

HOUSE OF SAXE-COBURG AND GOTHA

Edward VII	Eldest son of Victoria, married Alexandra, Princess of Denmark.	1901	1910	68	9

HOUSE OF WINDSOR
Name Adopted July 17, 1917

George V	Second son of Edward VII, married Princess Mary of Teck . . .	1910	1936	70	25
Edward VIII	Eldest son of George V; acceded Jan. 20, 1936, abdicated Dec. 11.	1936	1972	77	1
George VI	Second son of George V; married Lady Elizabeth Bowes-Lyon .	1936	1952	56	15¾
Elizabeth II	Elder daughter of George VI, acceded Feb. 6, 1952	1952			

Rulers of France; Kings, Queens, Presidents

CAESAR TO CHARLEMAGNE

Julius Caesar subdued the Gauls, native tribes of Gaul (France) 57 to 52 B. C. The Romans ruled 500 years. The Franks, a Teutonic tribe, reached the Somme from the East C. 250 A. D. By the 5th Century the Merovingian Franks ousted the Romans. In 451 A. D., with the help of Visigoths, Burgundians and others, they defeated Attila and the Huns at Chalons-sur-Marne.

Childeric I became leader of the Merovingians 458 A. D. His son Clovis I (Chlodwig, Ludwig, Louis) crowned 481, founded the dynasty. After defeating the Alemanni (Germans) 496, he was baptized a Christian and made Paris his capital. His line ruled until Childeric III was deposed, 742.

The West Merovingians were called Neustrians, the eastern Austrasians. Pepin of Herstal (687-714) major domus, or head of the palace, of Austrasia, took over Neustria as dux (leader) of the Franks. Pepin's son, Charles, called Martel (the Hammer) defeated the Saracens at Tours-Poitiers, 732; was succeeded by his son Pepin the Short who deposed Childeric III and ruled as king until 768.

His son, Charlemagne, or Charles the Great, (742-814), became king of the Franks, 768, with his brother Carloman, who died 771. He ruled France, Germany, parts of Italy, Spain, Austria, enforced Christianity. Crowned Emperor of the Romans by Pope Leo III in St. Peter's, Rome, Dec. 25, 800 A.D. Succeeded by son, Louis, the Pious, 814. At death, 840, Louis left empire to sons, Lothair (Roman emperor); Pepin I (king of Aquitaine); Louis II (of Germany); Charles the Bald (France). They quarreled and by the peace of Verdun, 843, divided the empire.

A.D.   Name and year of accession.

THE CAROLINGIANS
840 Charles I, the Bald, Roman Emperor, 875
877 Louis II, the Stammerer, son
879 Louis III (died 882) and Carloman (bro.)
884 Charles II, the Fat; Roman Emperor, 881
888 Eudes (Odo) elected by nobles. Ceded land to
898 Charles III, the Simple, son of Louis II, defeated by
922 Robert, brother of Eudes, killed in war
923 Rodolph (Raoul) Duke of Burgundy
936 Louis IV, son of Charles III
954 Lothair, son, aged 13, defeated by Capet
986 Louis V, the Sluggard, left no heirs

THE CAPETS
987 Hugh Capet, son of Hugh the Great
996 Robert (the Wise), his son
1031 Henry I, his son, last Norman
1060 Phillip I (the Fair), son, king at 14
1108 Louis VI (the Fat), son
1137 Louis VII (the Younger), son
1180 Phillip II (Augustus), son, crowned at Reims
1223 Louis VIII (the Lion), son
1226 Louis IX, crusader; Louis IX (1214-1270) reigned 44 years, arbitrated disputes with English King Henry III; led crusades, 1248 (captured in Egypt 1250) and 1270, when he died of plague in Tunis. Canonized 1297 as St. Louis
1270 Philip III (the Hardy), son
1285 Phillip IV (the Fair), son, king at 17
1314 Louis X (the Headstrong), son. His posthumous son, John I, lived only 7 days
1316 Phillip V (the Tall), brother of Louis X
1322 Charles IV (the Fair), brother of Louis X

HOUSE OF VALOIS
1328 Phillip VI (of Valois), grandson of Phillip III
1350 John II (the Good), his son, retired to England
1364 Charles V (the Wise), son
1380 Charles VI (the Beloved), son
1422 Charles VII (the Victorious), son. In 1429 Joan of Arc (Jeanne d'Arc) promised Charles to oust the English, who occupied northern France. Joan won at Orleans and Patay and had Charles crowned at Reims July 17, 1429. Joan was captured May 24, 1430, and executed May 30, 1431, at Rouen for heresy. Charles ordered her rehabilitation, effected 1455. Agnes Sorel was Charles' mistress
1461 Louis XI (the Cruel), son, civil reformer

1483 Charles VIII (the Affable), son
1498 Louis XII, great grandson of Charles V
1515 Francis I, of Angouleme, nephew, son-in-law. Francis I (1494-1547) reigned 32 years, fought 4 big wars, was patron of the arts, aided Cellini, del Sarto, Leonardo da Vinci, Rabelais. Embellished Fontainebleau
1547 Henry II, son, killed at a joust in a tournament. He was the husband of Catherine de Medici (1519-1589)and the lover of Diane de Poitiers (1499-1566). Catherine was born in Florence, daughter of Lorenzo de Medici. By her marriage to Henry II she became the mother of Francis II, Charles IX, Henry III and Queen Margaret (Reine Margot) wife of Henry IV. She persuaded Charles IX to order the massacre of Huguenots on St. Bartholomew, Aug. 24, 1572, the day her daughter was married to Henry of Navarre
1559 Francis II, son of Henry II. In 1548, Mary, Queen of Scots married Francis, son of Catherine de Medici, Queen of France. They were married 1558. Francis died 1560, aged 16; Mary ruled Scotland, abdicated 1567.
1560 Charles IX, brother of Francis II
1574 Henry III, brother, assassinated

HOUSE OF BOURBON
1589 Henry IV, of Navarre, assassinated. Henry IV made enemies when he gave tolerance to Protestants by Edict of Nantes, 1598. He was grandson of Queen Margaret of Navarre, literary patron. He married Margaret of Valois, Catherine de Medici's daughter; was divorced; in 1600 married Marie de Medicis, Regent of France, 1610-17 for son, Louis XIII, and was exiled by Richelieu
1610 Louis XIII (the Just), son. Louis XIII (1601-1643) married Anne of Austria. His ministers were Cardinals Richelieu and Mazarin
1643 Louis XIV (The Grand Monarch), son. Louis XIV, was king 72 years. He exhausted a prosperous country in wars for thrones and territory. By revoking the Edict of Nantes (1685) he caused the emigration of the Huguenots. He said: "I am the state." His mistresses were Louise de la Valliere, Madame de Montespan and Madame de Maintenon
1715 Louis XV, great grandson. Louis XV (1710-1774) married a Polish princess. Lost Canada to the English. His favorites, Mme. Pompadour and Mme. DuBarry influenced policies. Noted for saying: Apres moi, le deluge. (After me, the deluge)
1774 Louis XVI, grandson; married Marie Antoinette, dau. of Empress Maria Therese of Austria. King and queen beheaded by Revolution, 1793. Their son, called Louis XVII, died in prison, never ruled

FIRST REPUBLIC
1792 National Convention of the French Revolution
1795 Directory, under Barras and others
1799 Consulate, Napoleon Bonaparte, First Consul. In 1802 elected Consul for life

FIRST EMPIRE
1804 Napoleon I, Emperor. Josephine (de Beauharnais) Empress, 1804-09; Marie Louise, Empress, 1810-1814. Her son, Francois (1811-1832) titular King of Rome, later Duke de Reichstadt and "Napoleon II," never ruled. Napoleon abdicated 1814, died 1821.

BOURBONS RESTORED
1814 Louis XVIII king; brother of Louis XVI
1824 Charles X, brother: reactionary, deposed by the July Revolution, 1830.

HOUSE OF ORLEANS
1830 Louis Philippe, the Citizen King

SECOND REPUBLIC
1848 Louis Napoleon. President, nephew of Napoleon I. He became:

SECOND EMPIRE
1852 Napoleon III, Emperor. Eugenie (de Montijo) Empress. Lost Franco-Prussian war, deposed 1870. Son, Prince Imperial (1856-79), died in Zulu War. Eugenie died 1920.

THIRD REPUBLIC-PRESIDENTS
1871 Thiers, Louis Adolphe (1797-1877), historian
1873 MacMahon Marshal Patrice M. (1808-1893)

1879 Grevy, Paul J. (1807-1891), resigned
1887 Sadi-Carnot, M. (1837-1894), assassinated
1894 Casimir-Perier, Jean P. P. (1847-1907), resigned
1895 Faure, Francois Felix (1841-1899)
1899 Loubet, Emile (1838-1929)
1906 Fallieres, Armand (1841-1931)
1913 Poincare, Raymond (1860-1934)
1920 Deschanel, Paul (1856-1922) resigned
1920 Millerand, Alexandre (1859-1943) resigned
1924 Doumergue, Gaston (1863-1937)
1931 Doumer, Paul (1857-1932) assassinated
1932 Lebrun, Albert (1871-1950) resigned 1940.

Vichy govt. under German armistice: Henry Philippe Petain (1856-1951) Chief of State, 1940-1944
Provisional govt. after liberation: Chas. de Gaulle (1890-1970) Oct., 1944-Jan. 21, 1946; Felix Gouin (1884-) Jan. 23, 1946; Georges Bidault (1899-) June 24, 1946.

FOURTH REPUBLIC—PRESIDENTS

1947 Auriol, Vincent (1884-1966)
1954 Coty, Rene (1882-1962)

FIFTH REPUBLIC—PRESIDENTS

1958 De Gaulle, Charles Andre M. J., (1890-1970)
1969 Pompidou, Georges J. R. (1911-)

Rulers of Middle Europe; Rise and Fall of Dynasties

CAROLINGIAN DYNASTY

Charles the Great, or Charlemagne, ruled France, Italy and Middle Europe; established Ostmark (later Austria); crowned Roman emperor by pope in Rome, 800 A.D. Died, 814.

Louis I (Ludwig) the Pious, son; crowned by Charlemagne 813, d. 840.

Louis the German, son, succeeded to East Francia (Germany) 843-876.

Charles the Fat, son, inherited East Francia and West Francia (France) 876, reunited empire, crowned emperor by pope, 881, deposed 887.

Arnulf, nephew, 887-899. Partition of empire.

Louis the Child, 900-911, last direct descendant of Charlemagne.

Conrad I, duke of Franconia, first elected German king, 911-918, founded House of Franconia.

SAXON DYNASTY; FIRST REICH

Henry I, the Fowler, duke of Saxony, 919-936.

Otto I, the Great, 936-973, son; crowned Holy Roman Emperor by pope, 962.

Otto II, 973-983, son; failed to oust Greeks and Arabs from Sicily.

Otto III, 983-1002, son. Crowned emperor at 16.

Henry II, duke of Bavaria, 1002-1024, great grandson of Henry the Fowler.

HOUSE OF FRANCONIA

Conrad II, 1024-1039, son-in-law of Otto I.

Henry III, 1039-1056, son; deposed 3 popes; annexed Burgundy.

Henry IV, 1056-1106, son; regency by his mother, Agnes of Poitou. Banned by Pope Gregory VII, he did penance at Canossa.

Henry V, 1106-1125, son; last of Salic House.

Lothair, duke of Saxony, 1125-1137. Crowned emperor in Rome, 1134

HOUSE OF HOHENSTAUFEN

Conrad III, duke of Suabia, 1138-1152. In 2nd Crusade.

Frederick I, Barbarossa, 1152-1190; son of Conrad's brother; in 3rd Crusade.

Henry VI, 1190-1196, took Lower Italy from Normans. Son became king of Sicily.

Philipp of Suabia, 1198-1208, son of Frederick I.

Otto IV, of House of Welf, 1198-1215; deposed.

Frederick II, 1215-1250, son of Henry VI; king of Sicily; crowned king of Jerusalem; in 5th Crusade.

Conrad IV, 1250-1254, son, lost Lower Italy to Charles of Anjou.

Conradin, son, king of Jerusalem and Sicily, was beheaded. Last Hohenstaufen.

Interregnum, 1250-1273. Rise of the Electors.

TRANSITION

Rudolph of Hapsburg, 1273-1291, defeated King Ottocar II of Bohemia. Bequeathed duchy of Austria to eldest son, Albert.

Adolphus, count of Nassau, 1291-1298, killed in war with Albert of Austria.

Albert I, German king, 1298-1308.

Henry VII, of Luxemburg, 1308-1313, crowned emperor in Rome. Seized Bohemia, 1310.

Louis IV of Bavaria (Wittelsbach), 1314-1347 Also elected was Frederick of Austria, 1314-1330 (Hapsburg). Abolition of papal sanction for election of Holy Roman Emperor.

Charles IV, of Luxemburg, 1347-1378, grandson of Henry VII, German emperor and king of Bohemia, Lombardy, Burgundy; took Mark of Brandenburg.

Wenceslaus, 1378-1400, deposed.

Rupert, Duke of Palatine, 1400-1410.

HUNGARY

Stephen I, house of Arpad, 907-1038. Crowned king by Pope Silvester II, 1001 A.D., converted Magyars. After several centuries of feuds Charles Robert of Anjou became Charles I, 1308-1342.

Louis I, the Great, son, 1342-1382, joint ruler of Poland with Casimir III, 1370. Defeated Turks.

Mary, daughter, 1385-1395, ruled with husband. Sigismund

of Luxemburg, 1387-1437, also king of Bohemia. As bro. of Wenceslaus he succeeded Rupert as Holy Roman Emperor, 1410.

Albert II, 1438-1439, son-in-law of Sigismund; also Roman emperor. *See under Hapsburg.*

Ulaszlo I of Poland, died in battle, 1444.

Ladislaus V, child. John Hunyadi (Hunyadi Janos) guardian, fought Turks, Czechs; died 1456.

Matthias I (Corvinus) son of Hunyadi, 1458-1490. Shared rule of Bohemia, captured Vienna, 1485, annexed Austria, Styria, Carinthia.

Ulaszlo II (King of Bohemia) 1490-1516.

Louis II, son, aged 10. 1516-1526. Wars with Soliman, Turk. In 1527 Hungary was split between Ferdinand I, Archduke of Austria, bro.-in-law of Louis II, and John Zapolya, of Transylvania. After Turkish invasion, 1547, Hungary was split between Ferdinand, Prince John Sigismund (Transylvania) and the Turks.

HOUSE OF HAPSBURG

Albert V of Austria, Hapsburg, crowned king of Hungary, Jan., 1438, Roman emperor, March, 1438, as Albert II; died 1439.

Frederick III, cousin, 1430-1493. Fought Turks.

Maximilian I, son, 1493-1519.. Assumed title of Holy Roman emperor (German), 1493.

Charles V, grandson, 1519-1556. King of Spain with mother co-regent; crowned Roman emperor at Aix 1520. Confronted Luther at Worms; attempted church reform and religious conciliation. Abdicated 1556.

Ferdinand I, king of Bohemia, 1526, of Hungary, 1527; disputed. German king, 1531. Crowned Roman emperor on abdication of Charles V, 1556.

Maximilian II, son, 1564-1576; Rudolph II, son, 1576-1612.

Matthias, brother, 1612-1619, king of Bohemia and Hungary.

Ferdinand II, of Styria, king of Bohemia, 1617, of Hungary, 1618, Roman emperor, 1619. Bohemian Protestants deposed him, elected Frederick V of Palatine, starting Thirty Years War.

Ferdinand III, son, king of Hungary, 1625, Bohemia, 1627, Roman emperor, 1637. Peace of Westphalia, 1648, ended war.

Leopold I, 1658-1705; Joseph I, 1705-1711; Charles VI, 1711-1740.

Maria Theresa, daughter, 1740-1780, Archduchess of Austria, queen of Hungary, ousted pretender, Charles VII, crowned 1742; in 1745 obtained election of her husband Francis I as Roman emperor and co-regent (d.1765). Fought Seven Years' war with Frederick II (the Great) of Prussia. Mother of Marie Antoinette, Queen of France.

Joseph II, son, 1765-1790, Roman emperor, reformer; powers restricted by Empress Maria Theresa until her death, 1780. First partition of Poland. Leopold II. 1790-1792.

Francis II, 1792-1835. Fought Napoleon. Proclaimed first hereditary emperor of Austria, 1806. Forced to abdicate as Roman emperor, 1806, last use of title. Ferdinand I, son, 1835-1848, abdicated during revolution.

AUSTRO-HUNGARIAN MONARCHY

Francis Joseph I, nephew, 1848-1916, emperor of Austria, king of Hungary. Dual monarchy of Austria-Hungary formed, 1867. After assassination of heir, Archduke Francis Ferdinand, June 28, 1914, Austrian diplomacy precipitated World War I.

Charles I, grandnephew, 1916-1918, last emperor of Austria and king of Hungary. Abdicated Nov. 11-13, 1918, died 1922.

RULERS OF PRUSSIA

Nucleus of Prussia was the Mark of Brandenburg. First margrave was Albert the Bear (Albrecht), 1134-1170. First Hohenzollern margrave was Frederick, burggrave of Nuremberg, 1415-1440.

Frederick William, 1640-1688, the Great Elector. Son, Frederick III, 1688-1713, was crowned Frederick I of Prussia, 1701.

Frederick II, the Great, 1740-1786, annexed Silesia, part of Austria.

Frederick William II, nephew, 1786-1797.

Frederick William III, 1797-1840. Napoleonic wars. Queen Louise.

Frederick William IV, 1840-1861. Uprising of 1848 and first parliament and constitution.

SECOND AND THIRD REICH

William I, 1861-1888, brother. Annexation of Schleswig and Hanover; Franco-Prussian war, 1870-71, proclamation of German Reich, Jan. 18, 1871, at Versailles; William, German emperor (Deutscher Kaiser), Bismarck, chancellor.

Frederick III, son, 1888.

William II, son, 1888-1918. Led Germany in World War I, abdicated as German emperor and king of Prussia, Nov. 9, 1918. Died in exile in Netherlands June 4, 1941. Minor rulers of Bavaria, Saxony, Wurttemberg also abdicated.

Germany proclaimed a republic at Weimar, July 1, 1919. Presidents: Frederick Ebert, 1919-1925, Paul von Hindenberg-Beneckendorff, 1925, reelected 1932, d. Aug. 2, 1934. Adolf Hitler, chancellor, chosen successor as Leader-Chancellor (Fuehrer & Reichskanzler) of Third Reich. Annexed Austria, March, 1938. Precipitated World War II, 1939-1945. Reported suicide May 1, 1945.

Rulers of Scotland

The Romans gave the name of Caledonia to present-day Scotland and called the people Caledonians. The Scots, a Celtic race that spoke Gaelic, came from Ireland, then called Scotia.

Kenneth I (S. C. MacAlpin) was the first Scot to rule both Scots and Picts, 843 A. D.

Duncan I was the first general ruler, 1034. Macbeth seized the kingdom 1040, was slain by Duncan's son, Malcolm Canmore (Malcolm III). 1058.

Malcolm married Margaret, English princess who had fled from the Normans. Queen Margaret introduced English language and English monastic customs. She was canonized. Her son Edgar, 1097, moved the court to Edinburgh. His brothers Alexander I and David I succeeded. Malcolm IV, grandson of David I, 1153, was followed by his brother, William the Lion, 1165, ... Alexander II, 1214. The latter's son, Alexander III, defeated the Norse and regained the Hebrides. When he died, 1286, his granddaughter, Margaret, child of Eric of Norway and grandniece of Edward I of England, known as the Maid of Norway, was chosen ruler, but died on the way, 1290.

John Baliol, 1292-1296. [Interregnum, 10 years].

Robert Bruce (The Bruce), 1306-1329, victor at Bannockburn, 1314.

David II only son of Robert Bruce ruled 1329-1371.

Robert II, 1371-1390, grandson of Robert Bruce, son of Walter, the Steward of Scotland, was called The Steward, first of the so-called Stuart line.

Robert III, son of Robert II, 1390-1406.

James I, son of Robert III, 1406-1437.

James II, son of James I, 1437-1460.

James III, 1460-1488, eldest son of James II.

James IV, 1488-1513, eldest son of James III.

James V, 1513-1542, eldest son of James IV.

Mary, daughter, born 1542, became queen when 1 week old; was crowned 1543. Married, 1558, Francis, son of Henry II of France, who became king 1559, died 1560. Mary ruled Scots 1561 until abdication. 1567. She also married (2) Henry Stewart, Lord Darnley, and (3) James, Earl of Bothwell. Imprisoned by Elizabeth I; beheaded 1587.

James VI, 1567-1625, son of Mary and Lord Darnley, became King of England on death of Elizabeth in 1603. Although the thrones were thus united, the legislative union of Scotland and England was not effected until the act of Union, May 1, 1707.

Rulers of Denmark, Sweden, Norway

Denmark

Earliest rulers invaded Britain; King Canute, who ruled in London 1017-1035, was most famous. The Valdemars furnished kings until the 15th century. In 1282 the Danes won the first national assembly, Danehof, from King Erik.

Most redoubtable medieval character was Margaret, daughter of Valdemar IV, born 1353, married at 10 to King Haakon VI of Norway. In 1375 she had her first infant son Olaf made king of Denmark. After his death, 1387, she was regent of Denmark and Norway. In 1388 Sweden accepted her as sovereign. In 1389 she made her grand-nephew, Duke Erik of Pomerania, titular king of Denmark, Sweden and Norway, with herself as regent. In 1397 she effected the Union of Kalmar of the three kingdoms and had Erik crowned. In 1439 the three kingdoms deposed him and elected Christopher of Bavaria king (Christopher III). On his death, 1448, the union broke up.

Succeeding rulers were unable to enforce their claims as rulers of Sweden until 1520, when Christian I conquered Sweden. He was thrown out 1522, and in 1523 Gustavus Vasa united Sweden. Denmark continued to dominate Norway until the Napoleonic wars, when Frederick VI joined the Napoleonic cause after Britain had destroyed the Danish fleet (1807). In 1814 he was forced to cede Norway to Sweden and Helgoland to Britain, receiving Lauenburg. Successors; 1839-Christian VIII; 1848-Frederick VII; 1863-Christian IX; 1906-Frederick VIII; 1912-Christian X; 1947-Frederick IX; 1972-Queen Margrethe.

Sweden

Early kings ruled at Uppsala, but did not dominate the country. Sverker (1134-1156) united the Swedes and Goths. In 1435 Sweden obtained the Riksdag, or parliament. After the Union of Kalmar, 1379, the Danes either ruled or harried the country until Christian II of Denmark conquered it anew, 1520. This led to a rising under Gustavus Vasa, who ruled Sweden 1523-1560, and established an independent kingdom. Charles IX (1594-1611, crowned 1607) conquered Moscow, Gustavus II Adolphus (1611-1633) was called the Great. Later rulers; 1633-Christina; 1654-Charles X; 1660-Charles XI; 1697-Charles XII(invader of Russia and Poland, defeated at Poltava, June 28, 1709); 1718-His sister, Unrika Eleanora, elected queen; 1720-Her husband, Frederick I (of Hesse); 1751-Aldolphus Frederick; 1771-Gustavus III; 1792-Gustavus IV; 1809-Charles XIII. (Union with Norway began, 1814). 1818-Charles XIV. He was Jean Bernadotte, Napoleon's Prince of Ponte Corvo, elected 1810 to succeed Charles XIII. He founded the present dynasty 1844-Oscar I; 1859-Charles XV; 1872-Oscar II; 1907-Gustavus V; 1950-Gustav VI Adolf.

Norway

Overcoming many rivals, Harald Haarfager (872-930) conquered Norway, Orkneys and Shetlands. Olaf, great-grandson (995-1000) brought Christianity into Norway, Iceland, Greenland. In 1035 Magnus the Good also became king of Denmark. Haakon V (1299-1319) had married his daughter to Erik of Sweden. Their son, Magnus, became ruler of Norway and Sweden at 6. His son, Haakon VI, married Margaret of Denmark; their son Olaf became king of Norway and Denmark, followed by Margaret's regency and the Union of Kalmar, 1397.

In 1450 Norway became subservient to Denmark. Christian IV (1588-1648) founded Christiania, now Oslo. After Napoleonic wars, when Denmark ceded Norway to Sweden, a strong nationalist movement forced recognition of Norway as an independent kingdom united with Sweden under the Swedish kings, 1814-1905. In 1905 the union was dissolved and Prince Carl of Denmark became Haakon VII. He died Sept, 21, 1957, aged 85; succeeded by son, Olav V, b. July 2, 1903.

Rulers of the Netherlands and Belgium

The Netherlands (Holland)

William Frederick, Prince of Orange, led a revolt against French rule, 1813, and was crowned King of the Netherlands, 1815. Belgium seceded Oct. 4, 1830, after a revolt, and formed a separate government. The change was ratified by the two kingdoms by treaty Apr. 19, 1839.

(1840) William II; (1849) William III; (1890) Wilhelmina (daughter of William III and his second wife Princess Emma of Waldeck); Wilhelmina abdicated Sept. 4, 1948, in favor of daughter Juliana, 39.

Belgium

A national congress elected Prince Leopold at Saxe-Coburg King; he took the throne July 21, 1831, as Leopold I. (1865) Leopold II; (1909) Albert I, nephew of Leopold II; (1934) Leopold III, son of Albert; (1944) Prince Charles, Regent, Leopold returned, 1950, yielded powers to son Baudouin, Prince Royal, Aug. 6, 1950, abdicated July 16, 1951. Baudouin I took throne July 17, 1951.

For political history prior to 1830 see articles on the Netherlands and Belgium.

Rulers of Modern Spain

From 8th to 11th centuries Spain was dominated by the Moors (Arabs and Berbers). The Christian reconquest established small competing kingdoms of the Asturias, Aragon, Castile, Catalonia, Leon, Navarre and Valencia. In 1474 Isabella (Isabel) B. 1451, became Queen of Castile & Leon. Her husband, Ferdinand, b. 1452, inherited Aragon 1474, with Catalonia, Valencia and the Balearic Islands, became Ferdinand V of Castile. By Isabella's request Pope Sixtus IV established the Inquisition, 1478. Last Moorish kingdom, Granada, fell 1492. Columbus opened New World of colonies, 1492. Isabella died 1504, succeeded by her daughter, Juana "the Mad," but Ferdinand ruled until his death 1516.

Charles I, b. 1500, son of Juana and grandson of Ferdinand & Isabella and of Maximilian I of Hapsburg; succeeded latter as Holy Roman Emperor, Charles V, 1520. Abdicated 1556. Philip II, son, 1556-1598, inherited only Spanish throne; conquered Portugal, fought Turks, persecuted non-Catholics, sent Armada vs. England. Was briefly married to Mary I of England, 1554-1558. Succession: Philip III, 1598-1621; Philip IV, 1621-1665; Charles II, 1665-1700, left Spain to Philip of Anjou, grandson of Louis XIV, who as Philip V, 1700-1746, founded Bourbon dynasty. Ferdinand IV, 1746-1759; Charles III, 1759-1788; Charles IV, 1788-1808, abdicated.

Napoleon now dominated politics and made his brother Joseph King of Spain but the Spanish ousted him finally in 1813. Ferdinand VII, 1814-1833, lost American colonies; succeeded by daughter, Isabella II, aged 3, with wife Maria Christina of Naples regent until 1843. Isabella deposed by revolution 1868.

Prince Amadeo of Savoy, 1870-1873. First republic, 1873-1874. Alphonso XII 1875-1885. His posthumous son was Alphonso XIII, with his mother, Queen Maria Christina regent; Spanish-American war, Spain lost Cuba, gave up Puerto Rico, Philippines, Sulu Isl., Marianas, Alphonso took throne 1902, aged 16, married British Princess Victoria Eugenia of Battenberg. The dictatorship of Primo de Rivera, 1923-30, precipitated the revolution of 1931. Alphonso agreed to leave without formal abdication. The monarchy was abolished and the second republic established, with strong socialist backing. Presidents were Niceto Alcala Zamora, to 1936, when Manuel Anzana was chosen.

In July, 1936, the army in Morocco revolted against the government and General Francisco Franco led the troops into Spain. The revolution succeeded by February, 1939, when Anzana resigned. Franco became chief of state, with provisions that if he is incapacitated the Regency Council by two-thirds vote may propose a king to the Cortes, which must have a two-thirds majority to elect him.

Alphonso XIII, died in Rome Feb. 28, 1941, aged 54. His property and citizenship had been restored.

A succession law theoretically restoring the monarchy was approved in a 1947 referendum. A new Constitution, approved by referendum Dec. 14, 1966, affirmed Spain's status as a monarchy under a king or a regent. Prince Juan Carlos was designated by Franco and the Cortes in 1969 as the future King and Chief of State. Juan Carlos is the son of the pretender to the throne, Don Juan of Bourbon.

Leaders in the South American Wars of Liberation

Simon Bolivar (1783-1830), Jose Francisco de San Martin (1783-1850) and Francisco Antonio Gabriel Miranda (1750-1816) are among the heroes of the early 19th century struggles of South American nations to free themselves from Spain. All three, and their contemporaries, operated in periods of intense factional strife, during which soldiers and civilians suffered.

Miranda, a Venezuelan, who had served with the French in the American Revolution and commanded parts of the French Revolutionary armies in the Netherlands, attempted to start a revolt in Venezuela in 1806 and failed. In 1810, with British and American backing, he returned and was briefly a dictator, until the British withdrew their support. In 1812 he was overcome by the royalists in Venezuela and taken prisoner, dying in a Spanish prison in 1816.

San Martin was born in Argentina and during 1789-1811 served in campaigns of the Spanish armies in Europe and Africa. He first joined the independence movement in Argentina in 1812 and then in 1817 invaded Chile with 4,000 men over the high mountain passes. Here he and General Bernardo O'Higgins (1778-1842) defeated the Spaniards at Chacabuco, 1817, and O'Higgins was named Liberator and became first dictator of Chile, 1817-1823. In 1821 San Martin occupied Lima and Callao, Peru, and became Protector of Peru.

Bolivar, the greatest leader of South American liberation from Spain, was born in Venezuela, the son of an aristocratic family. His organizing and administrative abilities were superior and he foresaw many of the political difficulties of the future. He first served under Miranda in 1812 and in 1813 captured Caracas, where he was named Liberator. Forced out next year by civil strife, he led a campaign that captured Bogota in 1814. In 1817 he was again in control of Venezuela and was named dictator. He organized Nueva Granada with the help of General Francisco de Paula Santander (1792-1840). By joining Nueva Granada, Venezuela and the present terrain of Panama and Ecuador, the republic of Colombia was formed with Bolivar president. After numerous setbacks he decisively defeated the Spaniards in the second battle of Carabobo, Venezuela, June 24, 1821.

In May, 1822, Gen. Antonio Jose de Sucre, Bolivar's trusted lieutenant, took Quito, Bolivar went to Guayaquil to confer with San Martin, who resigned as Protector of Peru and withdrew from politics. With a new army of Colombians and Peruvians Bolivar defeated the Spaniards in a saber battle at Juin in 1824 and cleared Peru.

De Sucre organized Charcas (Upper Peru) as Republica Bolivar (now Bolivia) and acted as president in place of Bolivar, who wrote its constitution. Sucre defeated the Spanish faction of Peru at Ayacucho, Dec. 19, 1824.

Continued civil strife finally caused the Colombian federation to break apart. Santander turned against Bolivar, but the latter defeated him and banished him. In 1828 Bolivar gave up the presidency he had held precariously for 14 years. He became ill from tuberculosis and died Dec. 17, 1830. He was honored as the great liberator and is buried in the national pantheon in Caracas.

Ancient Greeks and Latins

B. C. years are in black type; A. D. years in light. Herodotus believed Homer lived C. 850 B. C.

GREEKS

Born	Died	Name	Subj.	Born	Died	Name	Subj.	Born	Died	Name	Subj.
389	314	Aeschines	Orat.	450	....	Empedocles	Philos.	582	500	Pythagoras	Philos.
525	456	Aeschylus	Dram.	55	135	Epictetus	Philos.	600	....	Sappho	Poet
....	550	Aesop	Tales	342	270	Epicurus	Philos.	556	469	Simonides	Poet
563	478	Anacreon	Poet	480	406	Euripides	Dram.	469	399	Socrates	Philos.
500	428	Anaxagoras	Philos.	576	480	Heraclitus	Philos.	495	405	Sophocles	Dram.
287	212	Archimedes	Physi.	484	424	Herodotus	Hist.	63	24	Strabo	Geog.
448	380	Aristophanes	Dram.	....	735	Hesiod	Poet	600	540	Thales	Philos.
384	322	Aristotle	Philos.	460	377	Hippocrates	Medic.	530	460	Themistocles	Philos.
....	194	Athenaeus	Antiq.	....	....	Homer	Poet	....	255	Theocritus	Poet
460	370	Democritus	Philos.	342	292	Menander	Dram.	382	287	Theophrastus	Philos.
310	240	Callimachus	Poet	522	443	Pindar	Poet	471	401	Thucydides	Hist.
382	322	Demosthenes	Orat.	429	347	Plato	Philos.	280	....	Timon	Philos.
50	13	Diodorus	Hist.	49	120	Plutarch	Biog.	490	....	Zeno	Philos.
....	7	Dionysius	Hist.	207	122	Polybius	Hist.	430	357	Xenophon	Hist.

LATINS

Born	Died	Name	Subj.	Born	Died	Name	Subj.	Born	Died	Name	Subj.
330	390	Ammianus	Hist.	59	17	Livy	Hist.	35	95	Quintilian	Critic
125	200	Apuleius	Satir.	38	65	Lucan	Poet	86	34	Sallust	Hist.
130	175	Aulus Gellius	Satir.	180	103	Lucilius	Satir.	5	65	Seneca	Moral.
475	524	Boethius	Philos.	96	52	Lucretius	Philos.	25	100	Silius	Poet
100	44	Caesar, Julius	States.	43	104	Martial	Poet	61	96	Statius	Poet
234	149	Cato, (Elder)	Orat.	100	30	Nepos	Hist.	70	150	Suetonius	Biog.
87	54	Catullus	Poet	43	18	Ovid	Poet	55	117	Tacitus	Hist.
107	43	Cicero	Orat.	34	62	Persius	Satir.	185	159	Terence	Dram.
365	408	Claudian	Poet	254	184	Plautus	Dram.	54	18	Tibullus	Poet
65	8	Horace	Poet	23	79	Pliny	Natur.	70	19	Vergil	Poet
60	140	Juvenal	Satir.	62	113	Pliny (Younger)	Letters	70	16	Vitruvius	Arch.

Roman Rulers

From Romulus to the end of the Empire in the West. Rulers of the Roman Empire in the East sat in Constantinople and for a brief period in Nicaea, until the capture of Constantinople by the Turks in 1453, when it was succeeded by the Ottoman Empire.

B.C.	Name	A.D.	Name	A.D.	Name
	The Kingdom	81	Domitianus	324	Constantinus I (the Great)
753	Romulus (Quirinus)	96	Nerva	337	Constantinus II, Constans I, Constantius II
716	Numa Pompilius	98	Trajanus		
673	Tullus Hostillus	117	Hadrianus	340	Constantius II and Constans I
640	Ancus Marcius	138	Antoninus Pius	350	Constantius II
616	L. Tarquinius Priscus	161	Marcus Aurelius and Lucius Verus	360	Julianus II (the Apostate)
578	Servius Tullius	169	Marcus Aurelius (alone)	363	Jovianus
534	L. Tarquinius Superbus	180	Commodus		
		193	Pertinax; Julianus I		**West (Rome) and East**
	The Republic	193	Septimius Severus		**(Constantinople)**
509	Consulate established	211	Caracalla and Geta	364	Valentinianus I (West) and Valens
509	Quaestorship instituted	212	Caracalla (alone)		(East)
498	Dictatorship introduced	217	Macrinus	367	Valentinianus I with Gratianus
494	Plebeian Tribunate created	218	Elagabalus (Heliogabalus)		(West) and Valens (East)
494	Plebeian Aedileship created	222	Alexander Severus	375	Gratianus with Valentinianus II
444	Consular Tribunate organized	235	Maximinus (the Thracian)		(West) and Valens (East)
435	Censorship instituted	238	Gordianus I and Gordianus II; Pupienus and Balbinus	378	Gratianus with Valentinianus II (W.). Theodosius I (E.)
366	Praetorship established				
366	Curule Aedileship created	238	Gordianus III	383	Valentinianus II (West) and Theodosius I (East)
362	Military Tribunate elective	244	Philippus (the Arabian)		
326	Proconsulate introduced	249	Decius	394	Theodosius I (the Great)
311	Naval Duumvirate elective	251	Gallus and Volusianus	395	Honorius (West) and Arcadius (East)
217	Dictatorship of Fabius Maximus	253	Aemilianus		
133	Tribunate of Tiberius Gracchus	253	Valerianus and Gallienus	408	Honorius (West) and Theodosius II (East)
123	Tribunate of Gaius Gracchus	258	Gallienus (alone)		
82	Dictatorship of Sulla	268	Claudius II (the Goth)	423	Valentinianus III (West) and Theodosius II (East) and
60	First Triumvirate formed (Caesar, Pompeius, Crassus)	270	Quintillus		
		270	Aurelianus	450	Valentinianus III (West) and Marcianus (East)
46	Dictatorship of Caesar	275	Tacitus		
43	Second Triumvirate formed (Octavianus, Antonius, Lepidus)	276	Florianus	455	Maximus (West); Avitus (West); Marcianus (East)
		276	Probus		
		282	Carus	456	Avitus (W.) Marcianus (E.)
	The Empire	283	Carinus and Numerianus	457	Majorianus (W.), Leo I (E.)
27	Augustus (Gaius Julius Caesar Octavianus)	284	Diocletianus	461	Severus II (W.), Leo I (E.)
		286	Diocletianus and Maximianus	467	Anthemius (W.), Leo I (E.)
A.D.		305	Galerius and Constantius I	472	Olybrius (W.), Leo I (E.)
14	Tiberius I	306	Galerius, Maximinus II, Severus I	473	Glycerius (W.), Leo I (E.)
37	Gaius (Caligula)	307	Galerius, Maximinus II, Constantinus I, Licinius, Maxentius	474	Julius Nepos (W.) Leo II (E.)
41	Claudius I			475	Romulus Augustulus (West) and Zeno (East)
54	Nero				
68	Galba	311	Maximinus II, Constantinus I, Licinius, Maxentius	476	End of Empire in West; Odovacar, King, drops title of Emperor; murdered by King Theodoric of Ostrogoths 493 A. D.
69	Galba; Otho; Vitellius	312	Maximinus II, Constantinus I, Licinius		
69	Vespasianus	314	Constantinus I and Licinius		
79	Titus				

Rulers of Russia; Premiers of the USSR

First ruler to consolidate Slav tribes was Rurik, leader of the Russ, who established himself at Novgorod A.D. 862. He and his successors had Scandinavian affiliations. They moved to Kiev after 972 A.D. and ruled as **Dukes of Kiev.** In 988 Vladimir was converted and adopted the Byzantine Greek service, later modified by Slav influences. Important as organizer and lawgiver was Yaroslav, 1018-1054, whose daughters married kings of Norway, Hungary and France. His grandson, Vladimir II (Monomachos) 1113-1125, was progenitor of several rulers, but in 1160 Andrew Bogolubeki overthrew Kiev and began the line known as **Grand Dukes of Vladimir.**

Of the Grand Dukes of Vladimir Alexander Nevsky, 1245-1263, had a son, Daniel, first to be called **Duke of Muscovy** (Moscow) who ruled 1294-1303. His successors became **Grand Dukes of Muscovy.** After Demetrius III, Donskol, in 1380 defeated the Tartars, they also became Grand Dukes of all Russia. Independence of the Tartars and considerable territorial expansion was achieved under Ivan III, 1462-1505.

Czars of Muscovy—Ivan III was referred to in church ritual as Czar. He married Sofia, niece of the last Byzantine emperor. His successor, Basil, died in 1533 when Basil's son Ivan, was only 3. He became Ivan IV, "the Terrible," crowned 1547 as **Czar of all the Russias,** ruled till 1584. Under the weak rule of his son, Theodore, Boris Godunov had control. The dynasty died, and after years of tribal strife and intervention by Polish and Swedish armies, the Russians united under 17-year-old Michael Romanov, distantly related to the first wife of Ivan IV. He ruled 1613-1645 and established the Romanov line. Fourth ruler after Michael was Peter I.

Czars, or Emperors of Russia (Romanovs)—Peter I, 1682-1725, known as Peter the Great, took title of Emperor in 1721. His successors and dates of accession were: Catherine, his widow, 1725; Peter II, his grandson, 1727, d. 1730; Anne, Duchess of Courland, 1730, daughter of Peter the Great's brother. Czar Ivan; Ivan VI, 1740-1741, great grandson of Ivan V, child,

kept in prison and murdered 1764; Elizabeth, daughter of Peter I, 1741; Peter III, grandson of Peter I. 1761, deposed 1762 for his consort, Catherine II, former princess of Anhalt Zerbst (German) who is known as Catherine the Great, 1762-1796; Paul I, her son, 1796, killed 1801. Alexander I, son of Paul, 1801-1825, defeated Napoleon; Nicholas I, his brother, 1825; Alexander II, son of Nicholas, 1855, assassinated 1881 by terrorists; Alexander III, son, 1881-1894.

Nicholas II, son, 1894-1917, last Czar of Russia, was forced to abdicate by the Revolution that followed defeat by Germany. The Czar, the Czarina, the Czarevitch (Crown Prince) and the Czar's 4 daughters were murdered by the Bolshevists in Ekaterinburg, July 17, 1918.

Provisional Government—Prince Georgi Lvov and Alexander Kerensky, premiers, 1917.

Union of Soviet Socialist Republics

Bolshevist Revolution, Nov. 7, 1917, displaced Kerensky; Council of People's Commissars formed, Nicolai Lenin, premier. Lenin died Jan. 21, 1924. Alexei Rykov (executed 1938) and V. M. Molotov held the office, but actual ruler was Joseph Stalin (Joseph Vissarionovich Djugashvili), general secretary of the Central Committee of the Communist Party. Stalin became president of the Council of Ministers (premier) May 7, 1941, died Mar. 5, 1953. Succeeded by Georgi M. Malenkov, as head of the Council and premier and Nikita S. Khrushchev, first secretary of the Central Committee. Malenkov resigned Feb. 8, 1955, became deputy premier, was dropped July 3, 1957. Marshal Nikolai A. Bulganin became premier. Marshal Georgi K. Zhukov became minister of defense, was dropped Nov. 1, 1957. Bulganin was demoted and Khrushchev became premier Mar. 27, 1958. Krushchev was ousted Oct. 14-15, 1964, replaced by Leonid I. Brezhnev as first secretary of the party and by Aleksei N. Kosygin as premier.

Rulers of Modern Italy

After the fall of Napoleon in 1814 the Congress of Vienna, 1815, restored Italy as a political patchwork, comprising the Kingdom of Naples & Sicily, the Papal States, and smaller units. Piedmont and Genoa were awarded to Sardinia, ruled by King Victor Emmanuel I of Savoy.

United Italy emerged under the leadership of Camillo, Count of Cavour, (1810-1861)Sardinian prime minister. Agitation was led by Giuseppe Mazzini (1805-1872) and Giuseppe Garibaldi (1807-1882), soldier. Victor Emmanuel I abdicated 1821. After a brief regency for a brother, Charles Albert was King 1831-1849, abdicating when defeated by the Austrians at Novara. Succeeded by Victor Emmanuel II (1820-1878).

In 1859 France forced Austria to cede Lombardy to Sardinia, which gave rights to Savoy and Nice to France. In 1860 Garibaldi led 1,000 volunteers in a spectacular campaign, took Sicily and expelled the King of Naples. In 1860 the House of Savoy annexed Tuscany, Parma, Modena, Romagna, the Two Sicilies, the Marches and Umbria. Victor Emmanuel assumed the title of King of Italy at Turin Mar. 17, 1861. In 1866 he joined Prussia and Austria in the Triple Alliance and received Venetia from Austria. On Sept. 20, 1870, his troops under Gen. Raffaele Cardorna entered Rome and took over the Papal States, ending the temporal power of the Roman Catholic Church.

Succession. Humbert I, 1878, assassinated 1900; Victor Emmanuel III, 1900, abdicated 1946, died 1947; Humbert II, 1946, ruled a month. In 1921 Benito Mussolini (1883-1945) formed the Fascist party and became prime minister Oct. 31, 1922. He made the King Emperor of Ethiopia. 1937; entered World War II as ally of Hitler. He was deposed July 25, 1943.

At a plebiscite June 2, 1946, Italy voted for a republic. Premier Alcide de Gasperi became Chief of State June 13, 1946. On June 28, 1946, the Constituent Assembly elected Enrico de Nicola, Liberal, Provisional President of the Republic of Italy. Luigi Einaudi was elected President May 11, 1948. Giovanni Gronchi was elected Apr. 29, 1955, inaugurated May 11, 1955. Antonio Segni elected May 6, 1962, Giuseppe Saragat Dec. 28, 1964; Giovanni Leone Dec. 29, 1971.

Italians

AUTHORS, DRAMATISTS, POETS, PHILOSOPHERS, HISTORIANS

Born	Died	Name	Born	Died	Name	Born	Died	Name
1749	1803	Alfieri, Vittorio	1863	1938	D'Annunzio, Gabriele	1785	1873	Manzoni, Alessandro
1846	1908	Amicis, Edmond de	1265	1321	Dante Alighieri	1805	1872	Mazzini, Giuseppe
1227	1274	Aquinas, Thomas	1871	1936	Deledda, Grazia	1698	1782	Metastasio (P. Trapassi)
1492	1556	Aretino, Pietro	1817	1883	De Sanctis, Francesco	1672	1750	Muratori, Ludovico
1474	1533	Ariosto, Ludovico	1909	1967	Emanuelli, Enrico	1848	1923	Pareto, Vilfredo
1829	1907	Ascoli, Graziadio	1842	1911	Fogazzaro, Antonio	1855	1912	Pascoli, Giovanni
1791	1863	Belli, Giuseppe	1778	1827	Foscolo, Ugo	1788	1854	Pellico, Silvio
1313	1375	Boccaccio, Giovanni	1875	1944	Gentile, Giovanni	1304	1374	Petrarca, Francesco
1441	1494	Boiardo, Matteo Maria	1809	1850	Giusti, Giuseppe	1867	1936	Pirandello, Luigi
1548	1599	Bruno, Giordano	1707	1793	Goldoni, Carlo	1432	1484	Pulci, Luigi
1568	1639	Campanella, Tommaso	1713	1786	Gozzi, Gaspare	1901	1968	Quasimodo, Salvatore
1835	1907	Carducci, Giosué	1483	1540	Guicciardini, Francesco	1626	1698	Redi, Francesco
1725	1798	Casanova, Giacomo	1798	1837	Leopardi, Giacomo	1544	1595	Tasso, Torquato
1478	1529	Castiglione, Baldassarre	1836	1909	Lombroso, Cesare	1888	1970	Ungaretti, Giuseppe
1884	1966	Cecchi, Emilio	1469	1527	Machiavelli, Nicolo	1840	1922	Verga, Giovanni
1866	1952	Croce, Benedetto	1898	1957	Malaparte, Curzio	1668	1744	Vico, Giambattista
			1449	1515	Manuzio, Aldo (Aldus)			

ITALIAN EXPLORERS, SCIENTISTS, POLITICAL LEADERS

Born	Died	Name	Born	Died	Name	Born	Died	Name
1776	1856	Avogadro, Amado	1564	1642	Galileo (G. Galilei)	1859	1953	Nitti, Francesco
1738	1794	Beccaria, Cesare	1737	1798	Galvani, Luigi	1254	1324	Polo, Marco
1835	1900	Beltrami, Eugenio	1807	1882	Garibaldi, Giuseppe	1626	1698	Redi, Francesco
1476	1507	Borgia, Cesare	1882	1955	Graziani, Rodolfo	1878	1970	Ruini, Meuccio
16th	Cen	Cabot, John (Caboto)	1483	1540	Guicciardini, Francesco	1835	1910	Schiaparelli, Giovanni
1826	1910	Cannizzaro, Stanislao	1628	1694	Malpighi, Marcello	1818	1878	Secchi, Angelo
1810	1861	Cavour, Camillo Benso	1874	1937	Marconi, Guglielmo	1872	1952	Sforza, Carlo
1451	1506	Columbus, Christopher	1389	1464	Medici, Cosimo de' (1)	1729	1799	Spallanzani, Lazzaro
1830	1903	Cremona, Luigi	1519	1574	Medici, Cosimo de' (2)	1608	1647	Torricelli, Evangelista
1881	1954	De Gasperi, Alcide	1449	1492	Medici, Lorenzo de'	1485	1533	Verrazano, Giovanni
1901	1954	Fermi, Enrico	1846	1910	Mosso, Angelo	1454	1512	Vespucci, Amerigo
1847	1897	Ferraris, Galileo	1883	1945	Mussolini, Benito	1745	1827	Volta, Alessandro

ITALIAN PAINTERS, SCULPTORS AND ARCHITECTS

Born	Died	Name	Born	Died	Name	Born	Died	Name
1404	1472	Alberti, Leon Battista	1500	1571	Cellini, Benvenuto	1480	1528	Palma, Jacopo
1512	1572	Alessi, Galeazzo	1240	1302	Cimabue, Giovanni	1445	1523	Perugino, Pietro
1447	1522	Amadeo, Giovanni	1489	1534	Correggio, Antonio da	1720	1778	Piranesi, Giovanni
1387	1455	Angelico, Fra	1462	1521	Cosimo, Piero di	1454	1513	Pinturicchio
1591	1666	Barbieri, Giovanni	1486	1531	Del Sarto, Andrea	1483	1520	Raphael(Raffaelo)
1475	1517	Bartolomea, Fra	1386	1466	Donatello, Donato	1575	1642	Reni, Guido
1426	1507	Bellini, Gentile	1378	1455	Ghiberti, Lorenzo	1400	1482	Robbia, Luca della
1428	1516	Bellini, Giovanni	1449	1494	Ghirlandaio, Domenico	1615	1673	Rosa, Salvator
1400	1470	Bellini, Jacopo	1477	1510	Giorgione	1460	1529	Sansovino, Andrea
1467	1516	Beltraffio, Giovanni	1260	1336	Giotto di Bondone	1486	1570	Sansovino, Jacopo
1598	1680	Bernini, Gian Lor.	1420	1497	Gozzoli, Benozzo	1858	1899	Segantini, Giovanni
1598	1680	Bernini, Lorenzo	1406	1469	Lippi, Fra Fillippo	1883	1966	Severini, Gino
1445	1510	Botticelli, Sandro	1459	1504	Lippi, Filippino	1696	1770	Tiepolo, Giambattista
1444	1514	Bramante, Donato	1431	1506	Mantegna, Andrea	1518	1594	Tintoretto, Jacopo
1377	1446	Brunelleschi, Filippo	1401	1428	Masaccio, Tommaso	1477	1576	Titian (Tiziano)
1697	1768	Canaletto (Canale)	1827	1887	Mengoni, Giuseppe	1397	1475	Uccello, Paolo
1757	1822	Canova, Antonio	1475	1564	Michelangelo Buonarroti	1511	1574	Vasari, Giorgio
1570	1610	Caravaggio, Merisi	1826	1901	Morelli, Domenico	1528	1588	Veronese, Paolo
1450	1522	Carpaccio, Vittore	1518	1580	Palladio, Andrea	1435	1488	Verrocchio, Andrea
1881	1966	Carrá, Carlo				1452	1519	Vinci, Leonardo da

Concert Violinists of the Past

Born	Died	Name			Born	Died	Name	
1856	1943	Adamowski, T.		Pol.	1889	1934	Kichanski, Paul	Pol.
1845	1930	Auer, Leopold		Hung.	1875	1962	Kreisler, Fritz	Aus.
1795	1876	Boehm, Jos.		Czech.	1880	1940	Kubelik, Jan	Boh.
1810	1880	Bull, Ole		Nor.	1790	1861	Lipinski, Karl	Pol.
1653	1713	Corelli, Arcang		Ital.	1840	1927	Lotto, Isdor	
1891	1967	Elman, Mischa		U.S.	1722	1793	Nardini, Pietro	Ital.
1881	1955	Enesco, Georges		Rum.	1782	1840	Paganini, Nicolo	Ital.
1667	1762	Geminiani, F.		Ital.	1868	1920	Powell, Maud	U. S.
1716	1796	Giardini, F. di		Ital.	1830	1898	Remenyi, Edw.	Hung.
1858	1937	Hubay, Jeno		Hung.	1892	1936	Rigo, Jancsi	Hung.
1882	1947	Huberman, B.		Pol.	1774	1830	Rode, Jacques	Fr.
1831	1907	Joachim, Joseph		Hung.	1863	1946	Rosé, Arnold	Aus.

Born	Died	Name	
1844	1908	Sarasate, P. M	Span.
1815	1894	Sivori, Ern	Ital.
1888	1953	Spalding Albert	U.S.
1784	1859	Spohr, Ludwig	Ger.
1892	1973	Szigeti, Joseph	Hung.
1692	1770	Tartini, Gius.	Ital.
1880	1953	Thibaud, Jacq.	Fr.
1820	1881	Vieuxtemps, H	Belg.
1753	1824	Viotti, Giovanni	Ital.
1675	1741	Vivaldi, Antonio	Ital.
1835	1880	Wieniawski, H.	Pol.
1845	1908	Wilhelmj, Aug	Ger.
1858	1931	Ysaye, Eugene	Belg.

The Dynasties of China

(Until 221 B.C. and frequently thereafter, China was not a unified state. Where dynastic dates overlap, the rulers or events referred to appeared in different areas of China.)

Hsia	c.2000B.C.	-c.1500B.C.
Shang	c.1500B.C.	-c.1000B.C.
Western Chou	c.1000	- 771
Eastern Chou	770	- 256
Warring States	403	- 222
Ch'in (first unified empire)	221	- 206
Han	202B.C.-	220A.D.
Western Han (expanded Chinese state beyond the Yellow and Yangtze River valleys)	202B.C.-	9A.D.
Hsin (Wang Mang, usurper)	9A.D.-	23A.D.
Eastern Han (expanded Chinese state into Indo-China and Turkestan)	25A.D.-	220A.D.
Three Kingdoms (Wei, Shu, Wu)	220	- 264
Chin (western)	265	- 317
(eastern)	317	- 420
Northern Dynasties (followed several short-lived governments by Turks, Mongols, etc.)	386	- 581
Southern Dynasties (capital: Nanking)	420	- 589
Sui (reunified China)	581	- 618
T'ang (a golden age of Chinese culture; capital: Sian)	618	- 907
Five Dynasties (Yellow River basin)	907	- 959
Ten Kingdoms (southern China)	907	- 979
Liao (Khitan Mongols; capital: Peking)	947	- 1125
Sung	960	- 1279
Northern Sung (reunified central and southern China)	960	- 1127
Western Hsai (non-Chinese rulers in northwest)	990	- 1227
Chin (Tartars; drove Sung out of central China)	1114	- 1234
Southern Sung (capital: Hangchow)	1127	- 1279
Yuan (Mongols; Kublai Khan made Peking his capital in 1267)	1271	- 1368
Ming (China reunified under Chinese rule; capital: Nanking, then Peking in 1421)	1368	- 1644
Ch'ing (Manchus, descendents of Tartars)	1644	- 1912
Republic (disunity: provincial rulers, warlords)	1912	- 1949

Entertainment Personalities of the Past

Born	Died	Name
		A
1872	1953	Adams, Maude
1931	1968	Adams, Nick
1855	1926	Adler, Jacob P.
1858	1953	Adler, Sarah Levitzka
1898	1933	Adoree, Renee
1909	1964	Albertson, Frank
1885	1952	Alda, Frances
1894	1956	Allen, Fred
1906	1964	Allen, Gracie
1883	1950	Allgood, Sara
1882	1971	Anderson, Gilbert (Bronco Billy)
1886	1954	Anderson, John Murray
1859	1940	Anderson, Mary
1915	1967	Andrews, Laverne
1933	1971	Angeli, Pier
1876	1958	Anglin, Margaret
1887	1933	Arbuckle, Fatty (Roscoe)
1868	1946	Arliss, George
1900	1971	Armstrong, Louis
1890	1956	Arnold, Edward
1885	1946	Atwill, Lionel
1845	1930	Auer, Leopold
1905	1967	Auer, Mischa
1900	1972	Austin, Gene
1898	1940	Ayres, Agnes
		B
1864	1922	Bacon, Frank
1903	1951	Bailey, Mildred
1893	1968	Bainter, Fay
1895	1957	Baker, Belle
1898	1963	Baker, Phil
1882	1956	Bancroft, George
1903	1968	Bankhead, Tallulah
1890	1952	Banks, Leslie
1897	1950	Banks, Monty
1890	1955	Bara, Theda
1810	1891	Barnum, Phineas T.
1879	1959	Barrymore, Ethel
1882	1942	Barrymore, John
1878	1954	Barrymore, Lionel
1848	1905	Barrymore, Maurice
1897	1963	Barthelmess, Richard
1891	1962	Barton, James
1873	1951	Bauer, Harold
1893	1951	Baxter, Warner
1880	1928	Bayes, Nora
1904	1965	Beatty, Clyde
1901	1962	Reavers, Louise

Born	Died	Name
1887	1955	Beecher, Janet
1884	1946	Beery, Noah
1889	1949	Beery, Wallace
1901	1970	Begley, Ed.
1903	1931	Beiderbecke, Bix
1854	1931	Belasco, David
1906	1968	Benaderet, Bea
1906	1964	Bendix, William
1905	1965	Bennett, Constance
1924	1970	Benzell, Mimi
1873	1944	Bennett, Richard
1867	1944	Beresford, Harry
1899	1966	Berg, Gertrude
1863	1927	Bernard, Sam
1844	1923	Bernhardt, Sarah
1893	1943	Bernie, Ben
1889	1967	Bickford, Charles
1911	1960	Bjoerling, Jussi
1882	1951	Blaney, Charles E.
1900	1943	Bledsoe, Jules
1928	1972	Blocker, Dan
1888	1959	Blore, Eric
1899	1957	Bogart, Humphrey
1885	1965	Boland, Mary
1897	1969	Boles, John
1903	1960	Bond, Ward
1833	1893	Booth, Edwin
1796	1852	Booth, Junius Brutus
1894	1953	Bordoni, Irene
1888	1960	Bori, Lucrezia
1867	1943	Bosworth, Hobart
1905	1965	Bow, Clara
1874	1946	Bowes, Maj. Edward
1893	1939	Brady, Alice
1871	1936	Breese, Edmund
1898	1964	Brendel, El
1901	1948	Breneman, Tom
1875	1948	Brian, Donald
1891	1951	Brice, Fanny
1891	1959	Broderick, Helen
1898	1965	Brokenshire, Norman
1904	1951	Bromberg, J. Edward
1892	1973	Brown, Joe E.
1926	1966	Bruce, Lenny
1895	1953	Bruce, Nigel
1891	1957	Buchanan, Jack
1886	1957	Buck, Gene
1904	1965	Bunce, Alan
1863	1915	Bunny, John
1886	1970	Burke, Billie
1912	1967	Burnette, Smiley
1896	1956	Burns, Bob

Born	Died	Name
1902	1971	Burns, David
1882	1941	Burr, Henry
1883	1966	Bushman, Francis X.
1896	1946	Butterworth, Charles
1893	1971	Byington, Spring
		C
1905	1972	Cabot, Bruce
1895	1956	Calhern, Louis
1858	1942	Calve, Emma
1865	1940	Campbell, Mrs. Patrick
1892	1964	Cantor, Eddie
1878	1947	Carey, Harry
1866	1959	Carhart, Georgiana
1876	1941	Carle, Richard
1897	1954	Carney, "Uncle Don"
1878	1946	Carr, Alexander
1880	1961	Carrillo, Leo
1892	1972	Carroll, Leo G.
1905	1965	Carroll, Nancy
1910	1963	Carson, Jack
1862	1937	Carter, Mrs. Leslie
1873	1921	Caruso, Enrico
1894	1969	Castle, Irene
1887	1918	Castle, Vernon
1889	1960	Catlett, Walter
1874	1944	Cavalieri, Lina
1887	1950	Cavanaugh, Hobart
1868	1949	Cawthorn, Joseph
1873	1938	Chaliapin, Feodor
1919	1961	Chandler, Jeff
1883	1930	Chaney, Lon
1906	1973	Chaney, Jr., Lon
1893	1940	Chase, Charlie
1893	1961	Chatterton, Ruth
1888	1971	Chevalier, Maurice
1900	1951	Christians, Mady
1888	1960	Clark, Bobby
1914	1968	Clark, Fred
1887	1940	Clark, Marguerite
1885	1948	Clayton, Bessie
1874	1931	Clayton, Herbert
1887	1950	Clayton, Lou
1920	1966	Clift, Montgomery
1857	1934	Cline, Maggie
1900	1937	Clive, Colin
1932	1963	Cline, Patsy
1892	1967	Clyde, Andy
1877	1961	Coburn, Charles
1887	1934	Cody, Lew

Born	Died	Name
1838	1899	Coghlan, Charles
1851	1932	Coghlan, Rose
1878	1942	Cohan, George M.
1876	1916	Cohan, Josephine
1919	1965	Cole, Nat (King)
1878	1955	Collier, Constance
1866	1944	Collier, William, Sr.
1891	1958	Colman, Ronald
1908	1934	Columbo, Russ
1907	1944	Compton, Betty
1887	1940	Connolly, Walter
1855	1909	Conried, Henrich
1890	1964	Conroy, Frank
1904	1967	Conway, Tom
1901	1961	Cook, Donald
1890	1959	Cook, Joe
1893	1958	Cook, Phil
1901	1961	Cooper, Gary
1891	1971	Cooper, Gladys
1896	1973	Cooper, Melville
1914	1968	Corey, Wendell
1890	1972	Correll, Charles
1876	1951	Cossart, Ernest
1904	1957	Costello, Helene
1906	1959	Costello, Lou
1877	1950	Costello, Maurice
1899	1973	Coward, Noel
1890	1950	Cowl, Jane
1924	1973	Cox, Wally
1847	1924	Crabtree, Lotta
1875	1945	Craven, Frank
1916	1914	Cregar, Laird
1880	1942	Crews, Laura Hope
1910	1960	Cromwell, Richard
1865	1944	Crosman, Henrietta
1893	1966	Crouse, Russell
1878	1968	Currie, Finlay
1909	1953	Curtis, Alan

D

Born	Died	Name
1875	1927	Daly, Arnold
1838	1899	Daly, Augustin
1924	1965	Dandridge, Dorothy
1869	1941	Danforth, William
1894	1963	Daniel, Henry
1901	1971	Daniels, Bebe
1860	1935	Daniels, Frank
1921	1965	Darnell, Linda
1894	1967	Darwell, Jane
1858	1932	Davenport, Eva
1866	1949	Davenport, Harry
1900	1961	Davies, Marion
1908	1961	Davis, Joan
1931	1955	Dean, James
1881	1950	DeCordoba, Pedro
1905	1968	Dekker, Albert
1898	1965	Demarco, Tony
1881	1959	DeMille, Cecil B.
1891	1967	Denny, Reginald
1878	1949	Desmond, William
1878	1930	Destinn, Emmy
1942	1972	de Wilde, Brandon
1865	1950	de Wolfe, Elsie
1879	1947	Digges, Dudley
1890	1944	Dinehart, Alan
1901	1966	Disney, Walt
1895	1949	Dix, Richard
1856	1924	Dockstader, Lew
1892	1941	Dolly, Jennie
1892	1970	Dolly, Rosie
1905	1958	Donat, Robert
1903	1972	Donlevy, Brian
1904	1957	Dorsey, Jimmy
1905	1956	Dorsey, Tommy
1907	1959	Douglas, Paul
1889	1956	Draper, Ruth
1881	1965	Dresser, Louise
1869	1934	Dressler, Marie
1820	1897	Drew, Mrs. John
1853	1927	Drew, John (son)
1879	1920	Drew, Sydney
1909	1951	Duchin, Eddy
1940	1971	Duel, Peter
1900	1964	Dumke, Ralph
1890	1965	Dumont, Margaret
1873	1954	Duncan, Augustin
1877	1927	Duncan, Isadora
1905	1967	Dunn, James
1873	1947	Dupree, Minnie
1907	1968	Duryea, Dan
1859	1924	Duse, Eleanora

E

Born	Died	Name
1894	1929	Eagels, Jeanne
1896	1930	Eames, Clare
1865	1952	Eames, Emma
1902	1948	Eaton, Mary
1901	1967	Eddy, Nelson
1868	1931	Edeson, Robert
1893	1954	Edwards, Alan
1894	1971	Edwards, Cliff
1879	1945	Edwards, Gus
1874	1950	Elliott, Gertrude
1871	1940	Elliott, Maxine
1891	1967	Elman, Mischa
1883	1941	Eltinge, Julian
1881	1951	Errol, Leon
1903	1967	Erwin, Stuart
1913	1967	Evelyn, Judith

F

Born	Died	Name
1883	1939	Fairbanks, Douglas
1915	1970	Farmer, Frances
1870	1929	Farnum, Dustin
1876	1953	Farnum, William
1882	1967	Farrar, Geraldine
1904	1971	Farrell, Glenda
1868	1940	Faversham, William
1861	1939	Fawcett, George
1897	1960	Fay, Frank
1895	1962	Fazenda, Louise
1885	1961	Ferguson, Elsie
1903	1971	Fernandel
1905	1950	Field, Sidney
1867	1941	Fields, Lew
1884	1941	Fields, Stanley
1879	1946	Fields, W. C.
1869	1947	Fischer, Alice
1865	1932	Fiske, Minnie Maddern
1888	1961	Fitzgerald, Barry
1874	1941	Fitzgerald, Cissy
1895	1962	Flagstad, Kirsten
1900	1971	Flippen, Jay C.
1909	1959	Flynn, Errol
1880	1942	Fokine, Michel
1910	1968	Foley, Red
1905	1951	Forbes, Ralph
1853	1937	Forbes-Robertson
1887	1970	Ford, Ed (Senator)
1895	1973	Ford, John
1899	1965	Ford, Wallace
1859	1933	Forrest, Arthur
1806	1872	Forrest, Edwin
1904	1970	Foster, Preston
1854	1928	Foy, Eddie
1905	1968	Francis, Kay
1876	1941	Franklin, Irene
1893	1966	Frawley, William
1885	1938	Frederick, Pauline
1870	1955	Friganza, Trixie
1890	1958	Frisco, Joe
1860	1915	Frohman, Charles
1851	1940	Frohman, Daniel
1885	1947	Fyffe, Will

G

Born	Died	Name
1901	1960	Gable, Clark
1873	1929	Gallagher, Ed.
1900	1955	Gallagher, Richard
1889	1963	Galli-Curci, Amelita
1877	1967	Garden, Mary
1913	1952	Garfield, John
1922	1969	Garland, Judy
1893	1963	Gaxton, Wm.
1904	1954	George, Gladys
1879	1961	George, Grace
1892	1962	Gibson, Hoot
1890	1957	Gigli, Beniamino
1894	1971	Gilbert, Billy
1897	1936	Gilbert, John
1855	1937	Gillette, William
1867	1943	Gillmore, Frank

Born	Died	Name
1879	1939	Gilpin, Charles
1898	1968	Gish, Dorothy
1886	1959	Gleason, James
1888	1947	Gleason, Lucille
1864	1938	Gluck, Alma
1874	1955	Golden, John
1857	1919	Goodwin, Nat C.
1917	1969	Gorcey, Leo
1884	1940	Gordon, C. Henry
1887	1948	Gordon, Vera
1869	1944	Gottschalk, Ferdinand
1829	1869	Gottschalk, Louis
1916	1973	Grable, Betty
1901	1959	Gray, Gilda
1879	1954	Greenstreet, Sydney
1883	1944	Grey, Jane
1873	1950	Grey, Katherine
1874	1948	Griffith, David Wark
1858	1934	Griffith, Kate
1885	1957	Guitry, Sacha
1912	1967	Guthrie, Woody
1875	1959	Gwenn, Edmund

H

Born	Died	Name
1888	1942	Hackett, Charles
1869	1926	Hackett, James K.
1902	1958	Hackett, Raymond
1898	1939	Haig, Emma
1870	1943	Haines, Robert T.
1892	1950	Hale, Alan
1872	1933	Hale, Louise Closser
1847	1919	Hammerstein, Oscar
1895	1960	Hammerstein, Oscar, 2nd
1879	1955	Hampden, Walter
1873	1958	Handy, W. C.
1924	1964	Haney, Carol
1893	1964	Hardwicke, Sir Cedric
1892	1957	Hardy, Oliver
1883	1939	Hare, T. E. (Ernie)
1865	1940	Harlan, Otis
1911	1937	Harlow, Jean
1872	1946	Harned, Virginia
1844	1911	Harrigan, Edward
1905	1944	Harris, Mildred
1864	1935	Harrison, R. B.
1895	1943	Hart, Lorenz
1870	1946	Hart, William S.
1907	1955	Hartman, Grace
1902	1971	Hayward, Leland
1876	1945	Harwood, John
1910	1973	Hawkins, Jack
1855	1903	Haworth, Joseph
1885	1969	Hayes, Gabby
1896	1937	Healy, Ted
1910	1971	Heflin, Van
1879	1936	Heggie, O. P.
1873	1918	Held, Anna
1903	1947	Hellinger, Mark
1885	1955	Hempel, Frieda
1943	1970	Hendrix, Jimi
1913	1969	Henie, Sonja
1879	1942	Herbert, Henry
1887	1951	Herbert, Hugh
1868	1952	Herford, Beatrice
1883	1950	Herne, Crystal
1840	1901	Herne, James A.
1857	1943	Herne, Katherine
1886	1956	Hersholt, Jean
1895	1942	Hibbard, Edna
1857	1927	Hillard, Robert C.
1865	1929	Hitchcock, Raymond
1914	1955	Hodiak, John
1876	1957	Hofmann, Josef
1894	1973	Holden, Fay
1919	1959	Holliday, Billie
1923	1965	Holliday, Judy
1888	1951	Holt, Jack
1871	1947	Homer, Louise
1878	1950	Hopkins, Arthur
1858	1935	Hopper, DeWolf
1874	1959	Hopper, Edna Wallace
1890	1966	Hopper, Hedda
1916	1970	Hopper, William
1888	1970	Horton, Edward Everett
1874	1926	Houdini, Harry
1881	1965	Howard, Eugene
1867	1961	Howard, Joe
1893	1943	Howard, Leslie

Born	Died	Name
1886	1955	Howard, Tom
1886	1949	Howard, Willie
1914	1972	Hudson, Rochelle
1886	1957	Hull, Josephine
1907	1967	Hume, Benita
1895	1958	Humphrey, Doris
1895	1945	Hunter, Glenn
1925	1969	Hunter, Jeffrey
1901	1962	Husing, Ted
1884	1950	Huston, Walter

I

Born	Died	Name
1892	1950	Ingram, Rex
1895	1969	Ingram, Rex
1838	1905	Irving, Henry
1871	1944	Irving, Isabel
1872	1914	Irving, Laurence
1859	1930	Irwin, Flo
1862	1938	Irwin, May

J

Born	Died	Name
1875	1942	Jackson, Joe
1911	1972	Jackson, Mahalia
1889	1956	Janis, Elsie
1886	1950	Jannings, Emil
1800	1888	Jefferson, Joseph
1859	1923	Jefferson, Thomas
1862	1930	Jewett, Henry
1892	1962	Johnson, Chic
1878	1952	Johnson, Edward
1888	1950	Jolson, Al
1889	1940	Jones, Billy
1889	1942	Jones, Buck
1846	1931	Jones, Frank
1911	1965	Jones, Spike
1943	1970	Joplin, Janis
1897	1961	Jordan, Marian (Molly McGee)
1890	1955	Joyce, Alice

K

Born	Died	Name
1878	1965	Kaltenborn, Hans V.
1910	1966	Kane, Helen
1887	1969	Karloff, Boris
1893	1970	Karns, Roscoe
1811	1868	Kean, Charles
1806	1880	Kean, Mrs. Charles
1787	1833	Kean, Edmund
1885	1945	Keane, Doris
1895	1966	Keaton, Buster
1858	1929	Keenan, Frank
1830	1873	Keene, Laura
1841	1898	Keene, Thomas W.
1899	1960	Keith, Ian
1894	1973	Kellaway, Cecil
1899	1956	Kelly, Paul
1873	1939	Kelly, Walter C.
1909	1968	Kelton, Pert
1823	1895	Kemble, Agnes
1775	1854	Kemble, Charles
1809	1893	Kemble, Fannie
1848	1935	Kendal, Dame Madge
1843	1917	Kendal, Wm. H.
1926	1959	Kendall, Kay
1890	1948	Kennedy, Edgar
1885	1965	Kennedy, Tom
1886	1945	Kent, William
1880	1947	Kerrigan, J. Warren
1886	1956	Kibbee, Guy
1902	1966	Kiepura, Jan
1888	1964	Kilbride, Percy
1913	1965	Kilgallen, Dorothy
1863	1933	Kilgour, Joseph
1899	1965	King, Alexander
1894	1944	King, Charles
1897	1971	King, Dennis
1889	1938	Kohler, Fred
1897	1957	Korngold, Erich W.
1919	1962	Kovacs, Ernie

L

Born	Died	Name
1913	1964	Ladd, Alan
1895	1967	Lahr, Bert
1919	1973	Lake, Veronica
1904	1948	Landi, Elissa

Born	Died	Name
1919	1948	Landis, Carole
1904	1972	Landis, Jessie Royce
1884	1944	Langdon, Harry
1856	1929	Langtry, Lillian
1921	1959	Lanza, Mario
1881	1958	Lasky, Jesse L.
1870	1950	Lauder, Harry
1899	1962	Laughton, Chas.
1890	1965	Laurel, Stan
1892	1954	Laurie, Joe, Jr.
1872	1945	LaVerne, Lucille
1898	1952	Lawrence, Gertrude
1890	1929	Lawrence, Margaret
1907	1952	Lee, Canada
1914	1970	Lee, Gypsy Rose
1848	1929	Lehmann, Lilli
1896	1950	Lehr, Lew
1883	1949	Leiber, Fritz
1913	1967	Leigh, Vivien
1852	1908	Leighton, Margaret
1894	1931	Leitzel, Lillian
1831	1905	Lemoyne, W. J.
1870	1941	Leonard, Eddie
1911	1973	Leonard, Jack E.
1906	1972	Levant, Oscar
1881	1955	Levy, Ethel
1875	1925	Lewis, Ada
1847	1930	Lewis, Arthur
1903	1966	Lewis, Fulton, Jr.
1890	1971	Lewis, Joe E.
1891	1971	Lewis, Ted
1874	1944	Lhevinne, Josef
1889	1952	Lincoln, Elmo
1820	1887	Lind, Jenny
1889	1968	Lindsay, Howard
1869	1952	Lipman, Clara
1889	1971	Lloyd, Harold
1876	1922	Lloyd, Marie
1891	1957	Lockhart, Gene
1913	1969	Logan, Ella
1876	1943	Loftus, Cissie (Marie)
1909	1942	Lombard, Carole
1890	1950	Lord, Pauline
1888	1968	Lorne, Marion
1904	1964	Lorre, Peter
1917	1970	Louise, Anita
1914	1962	Lovejoy, Frank
1892	1971	Lowe, Edmund
1892	1947	Lubitsch, Ernst
1885	1956	Lugosi, Bela
1895	1971	Lukas, Paul
1902	1947	Lunceford, Jimmy
1853	1932	Lupino, George
1893	1942	Lupino, Stanley
1897	1957	Lyman, Abe
1926	1971	Lynn, Diana
1885	1954	Lytell, Bert
1867	1936	Lytton, Henry

M

Born	Died	Name
1907	1965	MacDonald, Jeanette
1902	1969	MacLane, Barton
1863	1931	Mack, Andrew
1878	1934	Mack, Willard
1909	1973	Macready, George
1861	1946	Macy, George Carleton
1896	1967	Mahoney, Will
1908	1973	Magnani, Anna
1865	1931	Mann, Louis
1933	1967	Mansfield, Jayne
1857	1907	Mansfield, Richard
1854	1927	Mantell, Robert B.
1920	1970	March, Hal
1897	1951	Margetson, Arthur
1865	1950	Marlowe, Julia
1890	1966	Marshall, Herbert
1864	1943	Marshall, Tully
1885	1969	Martinelli, Giovanni
1891	1961	Marx, Chico
1893	1964	Marx, Arthur (Harpo)
1862	1951	Maude, Cyril
1922	1972	Maxwell, Marilyn
1879	1948	May, Edna
1885	1957	Mayer, Louis B.
1895	1973	Maynard, Ken
1839	1896	Mayo, Frank
1884	1951	Mayo, Margaret
1884	1945	McCormack, John
1907	1962	McCormick, Myron
1888	1931	McCoy, Bessie

Born	Died	Name
1883	1936	McCullough, Paul
1895	1952	McDaniel, Hattie
1924	1965	McDonald, Marie
1879	1949	McIntyre, Frank J.
1857	1937	McIntyre, John
1879	1937	McKinley, Mabel
1886	1959	McLaglen, Victor
1907	1971	McMahon, Horace
1866	1932	McNaughton, Tom
1880	1946	Meek, Donald
1879	1936	Meighan, Thomas
1861	1931	Melba, Nellie
1890	1973	Melchior, Lauritz
1904	1961	Melton, James
1890	1963	Menjou, Adolphe
1902	1966	Menken, Helen
1882	1939	Mercer, Beryl
1890	1946	Merivale, Phillip
1904	1944	Miller, Glenn
1860	1926	Miller, Henry
1898	1936	Miller, Marilyn
1895	1927	Mills, Florence
1903	1955	Minnevitch, Borrah
1917	1955	Miranda, Carmen
1875	1957	Mitchell, Grant
1832	1918	Mitchell, Maggie
1892	1962	Mitchell, Thomas
1880	1940	Mix, Tom
1845	1909	Modjeska, Helena
1926	1962	Monroe, Marilyn
1910	1970	Montana, Vaughn
1875	1964	Monteux, Pierre
1824	1861	Montez, Lola
1919	1951	Montez, Maria
1886	1935	Moore, Florence
1903	1947	Moore, Grace
1861	1931	Moore, Mary
1885	1955	Moore, Tom
1876	1962	Moore, Victor
1882	1949	Moran, George
1884	1952	Moran, Polly
1890	1950	Morgan, Frank
1900	1941	Morgan, Helen
1888	1956	Morgan, Ralph
1866	1953	Morley, Victor
1901	1970	Morris, Chester
1849	1925	Morris, Clara
1914	1959	Morris, Wayne
1944	1971	Morrison, Jim
1885	1941	Morton, Jelly Roll
1897	1969	Mowbray, Alan
1897	1967	Muni, Paul
1894	1953	Munn, Frank
1906	1955	Munson, Ona
1924	1971	Murphy, Audie
1885	1965	Murray, Mae
1908	1965	Murrow, Edward R.

N

Born	Died	Name
1897	1970	Nagel, Conrad
1900	1973	Naish, J. Carrol
1902	1961	Naldi, Nita
1888	1950	Nash, Florence
1865	1945	Nash, George
1879	1945	Nazimova, Alla
1846	1905	Neilson, Ada
1848	1880	Neilson, Adelaide
1885	1967	Nesbit, Evelyn
1868	1957	Neilson-Terry, Julia
1870	1951	Nethersole, Olga
1874	1948	Niblo, Fred
1890	1950	Nijinsky, Vaslav
1898	1930	Normand, Mabel
1879	1959	Norworth, Jack
1905	1968	Novarro, Ramon
1893	1951	Novello, Ivor

O

Born	Died	Name
1898	1943	O'Connell, Hugh
1881	1959	O'Connor, Una
1872	1937	O'Dell, Maude
1878	1945	O'Hara, Fiske
1908	1968	O'Keefe, Dennis
1880	1938	Oland, Warner
1860	1932	Olcott, Chauncey
1885	1942	Oliver, Edna May
1892	1963	Olsen, Ole
1847	1920	O'Neill, James
1887	1949	Ouspenskaya, Maria
1887	1972	Owen, Reginald

Born	Died	Name
		P
1860	1941	Paderewski, Ignace
1889	1954	Pallette, Eugene
1881	1972	Parsons, Louella
1881	1940	Pasternack, Josef A.
1843	1919	Patti, Adelina
1840	1889	Patti, Carlotta
1885	1931	Pavlowa, Anna
1899	1973	Paxinou, Katina
1868	1934	Payton, Corse
1917	1986	Pearce, Alice
1885	1950	Pemberton, Brock
1899	1967	Pendleton, Nat
1904	1941	Penner, Joe
1888	1957	Percy, Esme
1892	1937	Perkins, Osgood
1883	1956	Peters, Brandon
1893	1931	Phillips, Norma
1915	1963	Piaf, Edith
1893	1957	Pinza, Ezio
1900	1963	Pitts, Zasu
1893	1964	Porter, Cole
1903	1969	Portman, Eric
1904	1963	Powell, Dick
1869	1931	Power, F. Tyrone
1914	1958	Power, Tyrone E.
1872	1935	Powers, Eugene
1900	1964	Price, George E.
1873	1943	Price, Kate
1856	1919	Primrose, George
1879	1956	Prouty, Jed
1871	1942	Pryor, Arthur
1908	1944	Purcell, Dick
1897	1958	Purviance, Edna
1925	1970	Pyne, Joe
		R
1873	1943	Rachmaninoff, Sergei
1906	1946	Ragland, John (Rags)
1890	1967	Rains, Claude
1893	1963	Raisa, Rosa
1889	1970	Rambeau, Marjorie
1900	1947	Rankin, Arthur
1892	1967	Rathbone, Basil
1897	1960	Ratoff, Gregory
1883	1953	Rawlinson, Herbert
1891	1943	Ray, Charles
1852	1901	Reed, Roland
1860	1916	Rehan, Ada
1893	1923	Reid, Wallace
1873	1943	Reinhardt, Max
1909	1971	Rennie, Michael
1870	1940	Richman, Charles
1895	1972	Richman, Harry
1872	1961	Ring, Blanche
1888	1958	Risdon, Elizabeth
1874	1930	Ritchie, Adele
1905	1969	Ritter, Thelma
1903	1966	Ritz, Al
1910	1938	Roberti, Lyda
1861	1928	Roberts, Theodore
1878	1949	Robinson, Bill
1893	1973	Robinson, Edward G.
1865	1942	Robson, May
1897	1933	Rodgers, Jimmy
1894	1958	Rodzinsky, Artur
1879	1935	Rogers, Will
1897	1937	Roland, Ruth
1887	1951	Romberg, Sigmund
1880	1962	Rooney, Pat
1899	1966	Rose, Billy
1882	1936	Rothafel, S. L. (Roxy)
1878	1953	Ruffo, Titta
1892	1970	Ruggles, Charles
1903	1972	Rushing, Jimmy
1864	1936	Russell, Annie
1861	1922	Russell, Lillian
1892	1972	Rutherford, Margaret
1902	1973	Ryan, Irene
1909	1973	Ryan, Robert
		S
1877	1968	St. Denis, Ruth
1884	1955	Sakall, S.K.
1885	1936	Sale (Chic), Charles
1906	1972	Sanders, George
1934	1973	Sands, Diana
1896	1960	Savo, Jimmy
1879	1954	Scheff, Fritzi
1892	1930	Schenck, Joe

Born	Died	Name
1895	1964	Schildkraut, Joseph
1865	1930	Schildkraut, Rudolph
1889	1965	Schipa, Tito
1882	1951	Schnabel, Artur
1910	1949	Schumann, Henrietta
1861	1936	Schumann-Heink, E.
1866	1945	Scott, Cyril
1914	1965	Scott, Zachary
1843	1896	Scott-Siddons, Mrs.
1873	1935	Sears, Zelda
1902	1965	Selznick, David O.
1858	1935	Sembrich, Marcella
1889	1928	Semon, Larry
1884	1960	Sennett, Mack
1856	1933	Seymour, William
1867	1954	Shannon, Effie
1907	1941	Shannon, Peggy
1881	1951	Shattuck, Arthur
1860	1829	Shaw, Mary
1868	1949	Shean, Al
1915	1967	Sheridan, Ann
1848	1908	Sheridan, John F.
1885	1934	Sherman, Lowell
1854	1935	Sherwin, Amy
1918	1970	Shriner, Herb
1883	1953	Shubert, Lee
1755	1831	Siddons, Mrs. Sarah
1882	1930	Sills, Milton
1914	1970	Silvera, Frank
1878	1946	Sis Hopkins (Melville)
1891	1934	Skelly, Hal
1858	1942	Skinner, Otis
1870	1952	Skipworth, Alison
1892	1970	Skulnik, Menasha
1894	1937	Smith, Bessie
1863	1948	Smith, C. Aubrey
1826	1881	Sothern, Edward A.
1859	1933	Sothern, Edward H.
1884	1957	Sothern, Harry
1854	1932	Sousa, John Philip
1884	1957	Sparks, Ned
1876	1948	Speaks, Oley
1890	1970	Spitalny, Phil
1888	1953	Spooner, Cecil
1875	1953	Spooner, Edna May
1855	1940	Spooner, Mary G.
1886	1958	Squire, Ronald
1873	1937	Standing, Guy
1898	1950	Starr, Muriel
1871	1956	Stephenson, Henry
1900	1941	Stephenson, James
1883	1939	Sterling, Ford
1882	1928	Stevens, Emily A.
1934	1970	Stevens, Inger
1896	1961	Stewart, Anita
1873	1959	Stone, Fred
1879	1953	Stone, Lewis
1871	1954	Straus, Oskar
1911	1960	Sullavan, Margaret
1903	1956	Sullivan, Francis L.
1862	1934	Summerville, Amelia
1904	1969	Swarthout, Gladys
		T
1897	1957	Talmadge, Norma
1917	1968	Talman, William
1878	1947	Tanguay, Eva
1899	1934	Tashman, Lilyan
1873	1940	Tate, Harry
1910	1956	Tatum, Art
1885	1966	Taylor, Deems
1899	1958	Taylor, Estelle
1887	1946	Taylor, Laurette
1911	1969	Taylor, Robert
1878	1938	Tearle, Conway
1884	1953	Tearle, Godfrey
1892	1937	Tell, Alma
1881	1934	Tellegen, Lou
1864	1942	Tempest, Marie
1910	1963	Templeton, Alec
1865	1939	Templeton, Fay
1848	1928	Terry, Ellen
1874	1940	Tetrazzini, Luisa
1899	1936	Thalberg, Irving
1857	1914	Thomas, Brandon
1892	1960	Thomas, John Charles
1835	1905	Thomas, Theodore
1861	1938	Thornton, James
1869	1936	Thurston, Howard
1896	1960	Tibbett, Lawrence

Born	Died	Name
1887	1940	Tinney, Frank
1909	1958	Todd, Michael
1906	1935	Todd, Thelma
1874	1947	Toler, Sidney
1905	1968	Tone, Franchot
1878	1933	Torrence, Ernest
1867	1957	Toscanini, Arturo
1898	1963	Tracy, Lee
1900	1967	Tracy, Spencer
1903	1972	Traubel, Helen
1853	1917	Tree, Herbert Beerbohm
1890	1973	Truex, Ernest
1883	1942	Tucker, Richard
1884	1966	Tucker, Sophie
1911	1970	Tufts, Sonny
1879	1945	Turner, Clara
1887	1946	Turner, Florence
1874	1940	Turpin, Ben
1908	1959	Twelvetrees, Helen
		U
1894	1970	Ulric, Lenore
		V
1895	1926	Valentino, Rudolph
1882	1927	Valli, Vallie
1870	1950	Van, Billy B.
1894	1943	Veidt, Conrad
1885	1944	Vivian, Robert
1886	1957	Von Stroheim, Erich
		W
1874	1946	Waldron, Charles D.
1904	1966	Walker, June
1919	1951	Walker, Robert
1904	1943	Waller, Thomas (Fats)
1873	1915	Walsh, Blanche
1876	1962	Walter, Bruno
1878	1936	Walthall, Henry B.
1872	1952	Ward, Fannie
1855	1935	Ward, Sallie
1877	1939	Ware, Helen
1866	1951	Warfield, David
1876	1958	Warner, H. B.
1911	1960	Warren, Leonard
1878	1964	Warwick, Robert
1924	1964	Washington, Dinah
1867	1945	Watson, Billy
1879	1962	Watson, Lucille
1890	1965	Watson, Minor
1896	1966	Webb, Clifton
1867	1942	Weber, Joe
1905	1973	Webster, Margaret
1900	1950	Weill, Kurt
1876	1926	Welch, Ben
1873	1918	Welch, Joe
1880	1952	Wenrich, Percy
1883	1953	Werrenrath, Reinald
1859	1934	West, Basil
1879	1942	Westley, Helen
1895	1968	Wheeler, Bert
1889	1938	White, Pearl
1890	1967	Whiteman, Paul
1869	1942	Whiteside, Walker
1882	1943	Whiting, George
1865	1948	Whitty, Dame May
1906	1966	Whorf, Richard
1895	1948	William, Warren
1877	1922	Williams, Bert
1867	1918	Williams, Evan
1923	1953	Williams, Hank
1872	1942	Williams, Hattie
1854	1935	Wilson, Francis
1917	1972	Wilson, Marie
1884	1969	Winninger, Charles
1904	1959	Withers, Grant
1881	1931	Wolheim, Louis
1907	1961	Wong, Anna May
1888	1963	Woolley, Monty
1889	1938	Woolsey, Robert
1881	1956	Wycherly, Margaret
1844	1919	Wyndham, Charles
1886	1966	Wynn, Ed
1906	1964	Wynyard, Diana
		Y
1869	1938	Yohe, May
1891	1960	Young, Clara Kimball
1887	1953	Young, Roland
1900	1956	Young, Victor
		Z
1869	1932	Ziegfeld, Florenz

Entertainment Personalities—Where and When Born
Actors, Actresses, Composers, Dancers, Musicians, Producers, Radio-TV Performers, Singers

Name	Birthplace	Born	Name	Birthplace	Born
A			**B**		
Abbott, Bud (Wm.)	Atlantic City, N.J.	1898	Bacall, Lauren	New York, N.Y.	1924
Abbott, George	Forestville, N.Y.	1887	Bacharach, Burt	Kansas City, Mo.	1928
Abel, Walter	St. Paul, Minn.	1898	Backus, Jim	Cleveland, Ohio	1913
Abner (Norris Goff)	Cove, Ark.	1906	Baclanova, Olga	Moscow, Russia	1899
Ackermann, Bettye	Cottageville, S.Car.	1928	Baer, Jr. Max	Oakland, Calif.	1937
Acuff, Roy	Maynardsville, Tenn.	1907	Baez, Joan	Staten Island, N.Y.	1941
Adams, Don	New York, N.Y.	1927	Bailey, Pearl	Newport News, Va.	1918
Adams, Edie	Kingston, Pa.	1929	Bailey, Raymond	San Francisco, Calif.	1905
Adams, Joey	New York, N.Y.	1911	Bain, Barbara	Chicago, Ill.	1934
Adams, Julie	Waterloo, Iowa	1926	Baird, William B.	Grand Island, Nebr.	1904
Addams, Dawn	Suffolk, England	1930	Baker, Carroll	Johnstown, Pa.	1935
Adderley, Cannonball	Tampa, Fla.	1928	Baker, Diane	Hollywood, Calif.	1938
Adler, Kurt H.	Vienna, Austria	1905	Baker, Josephine	St. Louis, Mo.	1906
Adler, Larry	Baltimore, Md.	1914	Baker, Kenny	Monrovia, Calif.	1912
Adler, Luther	New York, N.Y.	1903	Baker, Stanley	Glamorgan, Wales	1928
Agar, John	Chicago, Ill.	1921	Bakewell, William	Hollywood, Calif.	1908
Aherne, Brian	Worcestershire, Eng.	1902	Balanchine, George	St. Petersburg, Russia	1904
Aimee, Anouk	Paris, France	1932	Ball, Lucille	Jamestown, N.Y.	1911
Albanese, Licia	Bari, Italy	1913	Ballard, Kay	West Cleveland, Ohio	1926
Alberghetti, Anna	Pesaro, Italy	1936	Balsam, Martin	New York, N.Y.	1919
Albert, Eddie	Rock Island, Ill.	1908	Bampton, Rose	Cleveland, Ohio	1909
Albertson, Jack	Malden, Mass.	—	Bancroft, Anne	New York, N.Y.	1931
Albright, Lola	Akron, Ohio	1925	Bannon, Ian	Airdrie, Scotland	1928
Alda, Alan	New York, N.Y.	1936	Barber, Red	Columbus, Miss.	1908
Alda, Robert	New York, N.Y.	1914	Bardot, Brigitte	Paris, France	1934
Alexander, Jane	Boston, Mass.	1939	Bari, Lynn	Roanoke, Va.	1917
Alexander, Katherine	Arkansas	1901	Barnett, Vincent	Pittsburgh, Pa.	1902
Allan, Elizabeth	England	1910	Barrault, Jean-Louise	Le Vesinet, France	1919
Allbritton, Louise	Oklahoma City, Okla.	1920	Barrett, Sheila	Washington, D.C.	1909
Allen, Mel	Birmingham, Ala.	1913	Barrie, Mona	London, Eng.	1909
Allen, Steve	New York, N.Y.	1921	Barrie, Wendy	Hong Kong, China	1913
Allen, Woody	Brooklyn, N.Y.	1935	Barry, Gene	New York, N.Y.	1922
Allison, Fran	LaPorte City, Iowa	—	Barry, Jack	Lindenhurst, N.Y.	1918
Allyson, June	Lucerne, N.Y.	1923	Barrymore, John, Jr.	Beverly Hills, Calif.	1932
Alpert, Herb	Los Angeles, Calif.	1935	Bartholomew, Freddie	London, England	1924
Ameche, Don	Kenosha, Wis.	1908	Bartok, Eva	Budapest, Hungary	1929
Ames, Ed	Boston, Mass.	1929	Basehart, Richard	Zanesville, Ohio	1914
Ames, Leon	Portland, Ind.	1903	Basie, Count (Wm.)	Red Bank, N.J.	1904
Ames, Nancy	Washington, D.C.	1937	Bassey, Shirley	Cardiff, Wales	1937
Amos (F. F. Gosden)	Richmond, Va.	1904	Bates, Alan	Allestree, Eng.	1934
Amsterdam, Morey	Chicago, Ill.	1912	Baum, Kurt	Cologne, Germany	1908
Anderson, Judith	Adelaide, Australia	1898	Bavier, Frances	New York, N.Y.	1905
Anderson, Marian	Philadelphia, Pa.	1902	Baxter, Anne	Michigan City, Ind.	1923
Anderson, Mary	Birmingham, Ala.	1922	Beal, John	Joplin, Mo.	1909
Anderson, Michael, Jr.	London, England	1943	Bean, Orson	Cambridge, Mass.	1928
Anderson, Warner	Brooklyn, N.Y.	1911	Beatty, Robert	Hamilton, Ont.	1909
Andersson, Bibi	Stockholm, Sweden	1935	Beatty, Warren	Richmond, Va.	1938
Andress, Ursula	Switzerland	1938	Becker, Sandy	New York, N.Y.	1922
Andrews, Dana	Collins, Miss.	1909	Bedelia, Bonnie	New York, N.Y.	1948
Andrews, Edward	Griffin, Ga.	1915	Beery, Noah, Jr.	New York, N.Y.	1916
Andrews, Julie	Walton, England	1935	Belafonte, Harry	New York, N.Y.	1927
Andrews, Maxene	Minneapolis, Minn.	1918	Bel Geddes, Barbara	New York, N.Y.	1922
Andrews, Patty	Minneapolis, Minn.	1920	Bellamy, Ralph	Chicago, Ill.	1904
Angel, Heather	Oxford, England	1909	Belmondo, Jean-Paul	Neuilly-sur-Seine, Fr.	1933
Anka, Paul	Ottawa, Canada	1941	Benjamin, Dick	New York, N.Y.	1939
Ann-Margret	Stockholm, Sweden	1941	Bennett, Joan	Palisades, N.J.	1910
Annabella	Paris, France	1912	Bennett, Tony	Astoria, N.Y.	1926
Ansara, Michael	Lowell, Mass.	1922	Benny, Jack	Waukegan, Ill.	1894
Archer, John	Osceola, Nebr.	1915	Bentley, John	Warwickshire, Eng.	1916
Arden, Eve	Mill Valley, Calif.	1912	Bergen, Candice	Beverly Hills, Calif.	1946
Arkin, Alan	New York, N.Y.	1934	Bergen, Edgar	Chicago, Ill.	1903
Arlen, Harold	Buffalo, N.Y.	1905	Bergen, Polly	Knoxville, Tenn.	1930
Arlen, Richard	Charlottesville, Va.	1900	Berger, Senta	Vienna, Austria	1941
Arnaz, Desi	Santiago, Cuba	1917	Bergerac, Jacques	France	1927
Arnaz, Desi, Jr.	Los Angeles, Calif.	1953	Bergman, Ingmar	Uppsala, Sweden	1918
Arnaz, Lucie	Hollywood, Calif.	1951	Bergman, Ingrid	Stockholm, Sweden	1917
Arness, James	Minneapolis, Minn.	1923	Bergner, Elisabeth	Vienna, Austria	1900
Arnold, Eddy	Henderson, Tenn.	1918	Berkeley, Busby	Los Angeles, Calif.	1895
Arquette, Cliff	Toledo, Ohio	1905	Berle, Milton	New York, N.Y.	1908
Arrau, Claudio	Chillau, Chile	1903	Berlin, Irving	Temun, Russia	1888
Arroyo, Martina	New York, N.Y.	1937	Berlinger, Warren	Brooklyn, N.Y.	1937
Arthur, Beatrice	New York, N.Y.	—	Berman, Shelley	Chicago, Ill.	1926
Arthur, Jean	New York, N.Y.	1908	Bernardi, Hershel	New York, N.Y.	1923
Ashley, Elizabeth	Ocala, Fla.	1940	Bernstein, Elmer	New York, N.Y.	1922
Asner, Edward	Kansas City, Kansas	—	Bernstein, Leonard	Lawrence, Mass.	1918
Astaire, Fred	Omaha, Nebr.	1899	Berry, Ken	Moline, Ill.	—
Astin, John	Baltimore, Md.	1930	Bessell, Ted	Flushing, N.Y.	1936
Astor, Mary	Quincy, Ill.	1906	Best, Edna	Hove, England	1900
Attenborough, Richard	Cambridge, Eng.	1923	Bethune, Zina	New York, N.Y.	1945
Aumont, Jean-Pierre	Paris, France	1913	Bikel, Theodore	Vienna, Austria	1924
Autry, Gene	Tioga, Texas	1907	Bing, Rudolf	Vienna, Austria	1902
Avalon, Frankie	Philadelphia, Pa.	1940	Birney, David	Washington, D.C.	—
Ayres, Lew	Minneapolis, Minn.	1908	Bishop, Joey	Bronx, N.Y.	1918
Aznavour, Charles	Paris, France	1924	Bishop, Julie	Denver, Colo.	1917

Name	Birthplace	Born
Bisset, Jacqueline	Weybridge, Eng.	1944
Bixby, Bill	San Francisco, Calif.	—
Black, Karen	Park Ridge, Ill.	1942
Blackmer, Sidney	Salisbury, N.C.	1898
Blaine, Vivian	Newark, N.J.	1924
Blair, Janet	Altoona, Pa.	1921
Blair, June	San Francisco, Calif.	1937
Blake, Robert	Nutley, N.J.	1938
Blanc, Mel	San Francisco, Calif.	1908
Bloch, Ray	Alsace-Lorraine	1902
Blondell, Joan	New York, N.Y.	1909
Bloom, Claire	London, Eng.	1931
Blue, Ben	Montreal, Canada	1901
Blyden, Larry	Houston, Tex.	1925
Blyth, Ann	Mt. Kisco, N.Y.	1928
Boehm, Karl	Graz, Austria	1894
Bogarde, Dirk	London, Eng.	1921
Bolger, Ray	Boston, Mass.	1904
Bonaduce, Danny	Philadelphia, Pa.	1959
Bond, Sheila	New York, N.Y.	1928
Bondi, Beulah	Chicago, Ill.	1892
Bono, Cher	El Centro, Calif.	1946
Bono, Sonny	Detroit, Mich.	1940
Boone, Pat	Jacksonville, Fla.	1934
Boone, Richard	Los Angeles, Calif.	1917
Booth, Shirley	New York, N.Y.	1909
Borge, Victor	Copenhagen, Denmark	1909
Borgnine, Ernest	Hamden, Conn.	1917
Bosley, Tom	Chicago, Ill.	1927
Boswell, Connee	New Orleans, La.	—
Bowman, Lee	Cincinnati, Ohio	1914
Boyd, Stephen	Belfast, Ireland	1928
Boyer, Charles	Figeac, France	1899
Bracken, Eddie	Astoria, N.Y.	1920
Brand, Neville	Kewanee, Ill.	1921
Brando, Marlon	Omaha, Nebr.	1924
Brasselle, Keefe	Elyria, Ohio	1923
Brazzi, Rossano	Bologna, Italy	1916
Brennan, Eileen	Los Angeles, Calif.	1937
Brennan, Walter	Lynn, Mass.	1894
Brent, Evelyn	Tampa, Fla.	1899
Brent, George	Dublin, Ireland	1904
Brewer, Teresa	Toledo, Ohio	1931
Brian, David	New York, N.Y.	1914
Bridges, Beau	Hollywood, Calif.	—
Bridges, Lloyd	San Leandro, Calif.	1913
Britt, May	Sweden	1936
Britton, Barbara	Long Beach, Calif.	1923
Brolin, James	Los Angeles, Calif.	1942
Bronson, Charles	Scooptown, Pa.	1920
Brook, Clive	London, England.	1891
Brooks, Louise	Cherryvale, Kansas.	1906
Brooks, Mel	New York, N.Y.	1926
Brooks, Phyllis	Boise, Idaho	1914
Brooks, Stephen	Columbus, Ohio	1942
Brothers, Joyce	New York, N.Y.	1928
Brown, James	Augusta, Ga.	1934
Brown, Jimmy	St. Simons Island, Ga.	1936
Brown, Johnny Mack	Dothan, Ala.	1904
Brown, Les	Reinerton, Pa.	1912
Brown, Vanessa	Vienna, Austria	1928
Brubeck, Dave	Concord, Calif.	1920
Bruce, Carol	Great Neck, N.Y.	1919
Bruce, Virginia	Minneapolis, Minn.	1910
Bryant, Anita	Barnsdale, Okla.	1940
Brynner, Yul	Sakhalin, Japan	1920
Bubbles, John	Louisville, Ky.	1903
Buchanan, Edgar	Humansville, Mo.	1903
Bucholz, Horst	Berlin, Germany	1933
Bujold, Genevieve	Canada	1942
Burke, Paul	New Orleans, La.	1926
Burnett, Carol	San Antonio, Texas	1935
Burns, George	New York, N.Y.	1896
Burr, Raymond	New Westminster, B.C.	1917
Burrows, Abe	New York, N.Y.	1910
Burstyn, Ellen	Detroit, Mich.	1932
Burton, Richard	South Wales	1925
Bushell, Anthony	Kent, England.	1904
Buttons, Red	New York, N.Y.	1919
Buzzell, Eddie	Brooklyn, N.Y.	1897
Buzzi, Ruth	Westerly, R.I.	1936

C

Name	Birthplace	Born
Caan, James	New York, N.Y.	1939
Cabot, Sebastian	London, England.	1918
Caesar, Irving	New York, N.Y.	1895
Caesar, Sid	Yonkers, N.Y.	1922
Cagney, James	New York, N.Y.	1904
Cahn, Sammy	New York, N.Y.	1913

Name	Birthplace	Born
Caine, Michael	London, England.	1933
Caldwell, Zoe	Melbourne, Australia	1933
Calhoun, Rory	Los Angeles, Calif.	1922
Callahan, James	Grand Rapids, Mich.	1930
Callan, Michael	Philadelphia, Pa.	1940
Callas, Maria	New York, N.Y.	1923
Calloway, Cab	Rochester, N.Y.	1907
Calvert, Phyllis	London, England.	1917
Calvet, Corinne	Paris, France	1926
Cambridge, Godfrey	New York, N.Y.	1933
Cameron, Rod	Calgary, Canada	1912
Campbell, Glen	Billstown, Ark.	1936
Canary, David	Elwood, Ind.	1938
Cannon, Dyan	Tacoma, Wash.	1937
Canova, Judy	Jacksonville, Fla.	1916
Cantinflas	Mexico City, Mex.	1917
Capp, Al	New Haven, Conn.	1909
Capra, Frank	Palermo, Italy	1897
Cardinale, Claudia	Tunisia	1939
Carey, Macdonald	Sioux City, Iowa	1913
Carey, Phil	Hackensack, N.J.	1925
Carle, Frankie	Providence, R.I.	1903
Carlisle, Kitty	New Orleans, La.	1915
Carlson, Richard	Albert Lea, Minn.	1914
Carmichael, Hoagy	Bloomington, Ind.	1899
Carmichael, Ian	Hull, England	1920
Carne, Judy	Northampton, Eng.	1939
Carney, Art	Mt. Vernon, N.Y.	1918
Carnovsky, Morris	St. Louis, Mo.	1897
Caron, Leslie	Boulogne, France	1931
Carpenter, Karen	New Haven, Conn.	1950
Carpenter, Richard	New Haven, Conn.	1946
Carr, Vicki	El Paso, Texas.	1942
Carradine, David	Hollywood, Calif.	1945
Carradine, John	New York, N.Y.	1906
Carroll, Diahann	Bronx, N.Y.	1935
Carroll, Madeleine	W. Bromwich, Eng.	1906
Carroll, Pat	Shreveport, La.	1927
Carter, Jack	New York, N.Y.	1923
Carson, Jeannie	Yorkshire, Eng.	1929
Carson, Johnny	Corning, Iowa	1925
Carson, Mindy	New York, N.Y.	1927
Casadesus, Gaby	Marseilles, France	1902
Casals, Pablo	Vendrell, Spain	1876
Cash, Johnny	Kingsland, Ark.	1932
Cass, Peggy	Boston, Mass.	1926
Cassavetes, John	New York, N.Y.	1929
Cassidy, David	New York, N.Y.	1950
Cassidy, Jack	New York, N.Y.	1927
Cassidy, Ted	Pittsburgh, Pa.	1932
Caulfield, Joan	West Orange, N.J.	1922
Cavallaro, Carmen	New York, N.Y.	1913
Cavett, Dick	Kearny, Nebr.	1937
Chamberlain, Richard	Beverly Hills, Calif.	1935
Champion, Gower	Geneva, Ill.	1921
Champion, Marge	Los Angeles, Calif.	1926
Channing, Carol	Seattle, Wash.	1923
Chaplin, Charles	London, England.	1889
Chaplin, Geraldine	Santa Monica, Calif.	1944
Chaplin, Sydney	Beverly Hills, Calif.	1926
Charisse, Cyd	Amarillo, Texas.	1923
Charles, Ray	Albany, Ga.	1930
Chase, Ilka	New York, N.Y.	1905
Chayefsky, Paddy	New York, N.Y.	1923
Checker, Chubby	So. Phil., Pa.	1941
Christian, Linda	Tampico, Mexico	1924
Christie, Audrey	Chicago, Ill.	1912
Christie, Julie	Chukur, India	1940
Christopher, Jordon	Youngstown, Ohio.	1941
Christy, June	Springfield, Ill.	1925
Churchill, Sarah	London, England.	1916
Cilento, Diane	Queensland, Aust.	1933
Claire, Ina	Washington, D.C.	1892
Clark, Dane	New York, N.Y.	1913
Clark, Dick	Mt. Vernon, N.Y.	1929
Clark, Petula	Ewell, Surrey, Eng.	1934
Clayton, Jan	Tularosa, N.Mex.	1925
Cliburn, Van	Shreveport, La.	1934
Clooney, Rosemary	Maysville, Ky.	1928
Cobb, Lee J.	New York, N.Y.	1911
Coburn, James	Laurel, Nebr.	1928
Coca, Imogene	Philadelphia, Pa.	1920
Coco, James	New York, N.Y.	1929
Cohen, Myron	Grodno, Poland	1902
Colbert, Claudette	Paris, France	1907
Cole, Dennis	Detroit, Mich.	1943
Cole, Michael	Madison, Wis.	1945
Cole, Tina	Hollywood, Calif.	1943
Collins, Dorothy	Windsor, Ontario	1926

Name	Birthplace	Born	Name	Birthplace	Born
Collins, Joan	London, England	1933	Davis, Bette	Lowell, Mass.	1908
Collins, Judy	Seattle, Wash.	1939	Davis, Miles	Alton, Ill.	1927
Colonna, Jerry	Boston, Mass.	1903	Davis, Sammy, Jr.	New York, N.Y.	1925
Como, Perry	Canonsburg, Pa.	1912	Davis, Ossie	Cogdell, Ga.	1917
Conklin, Peggy	Dobbs Ferry, N.Y.	1912	Dawn, Hazel	Ogden, Utah	1898
Conley, Eugene	Lynn, Mass.	1908	Day, Dennis	New York, N.Y.	1917
Connelly, Marc	McKeesport, Pa.	1890	Day, Doris	Cincinnati, Ohio	1924
Conner, Nadine	Compton, Calif.	1913	Day, Laraine	Roosevelt, Utah	1920
Conniff, Ray	Attleboro, Mass.	1916	Dean, Jimmy	Plainview, Texas	1928
Connors, Michael	Fresno, Calif.	1925	De Camp, Rosemary	Prescott, Ariz.	1913
Connery, Sean	Edinburgh, Scotland	1930	De Carlo, Yvonne	Vancouver, B.C.	1924
Connors, Chuck	Brooklyn, N.Y.	1921	Dee, Frances	Los Angeles, Calif.	1907
Conrad, Robert	Chicago, Ill.	1935	Dee Joey	Passaic, N.J.	1940
Conrad, William	Louisville, Ky.	1919	Dee, Ruby	Cleveland, Ohio	1924
Conried, Hans	Baltimore, Md.	1917	Dee, Sandra	Bayonne, N.J.	1942
Considine, Tim	Los Angeles, Calif.	1940	DeFore, Don	Cedar Rapids, Iowa	1917
Conte, Richard	Jersey City, N.J.	1916	DeHaven, Gloria	Los Angeles, Calif.	1925
Converse, Frank	St. Louis, Mo.	1938	deHavilland, Olivia	Tokyo, Japan	1916
Conway, Gary	Boston, Mass.	1938	Dell, Gabriel	Brooklyn, N.Y.	1921
Conway, Shirl	Franklinville, N.Y.	1916	Della Chiesa, Vivienna	Chicago, Ill.	1920
Conway, Tim	Chagrin Falls, Ohio	1933	Delon, Alain	France	1935
Coogan, Jackie	Los Angeles, Calif.	1914	DeLuise, Dom	Brooklyn, N.Y.	1933
Cook, Barbara	Atlanta, Ga.	1927	Del Rio, Dolores	Durango, Mexico	1905
Cooke, Alistair	England	1908	Demarest, William	St. Paul, Minn.	1892
Cooper, Jackie	Los Angeles, Calif.	1922	De Mille, Agnes	New York, N.Y.	1905
Corey, Jeff	New York, N.Y.	1914	Deneuve, Catherine	Paris, France	1943
Cornell, Don	New York, N.Y.	1921	Denning, Richard	Poughkeepsie, N.Y.	1914
Cornell, Katharine	Berlin, Germany	1898	Dennis, Sandy	Hastings, Nebr.	1937
Cortez, Ricardo	Vienna, Austria	1899	Denver, Bob	New Rochelle, N.Y.	1935
Cosby, Bill	Philadelphia, Pa.	1937	Derek, John	Hollywood, Calif.	1926
Cosell, Howard	Winston-Salem, N.C.	1920	De Sica, Vittorio	Sora, Italy	1902
Costello, Dolores	Pittsburgh, Pa.	1905	Desmond, Johnny	Detroit, Mich.	1921
Cotsworth, Staats	Oak Park, Ill.	1908	Devine, Andy	Flagstaff, Ariz.	1905
Cotten, Joseph	Petersburg, Va.	1905	Dewhurst, Colleen	Montreal, Canada	1926
Courtenay, Tom	Hull, England	1937	de Wolfe, Billy	Wollaston, Mass.	—
Crabbe, Buster	Oakland, Calif.	1909	Diamond, Neil	Brooklyn, N.Y.	1941
Crain, Jeanne	Barstow, Calif.	1925	Dickinson, Angie	Kulm, N.Dak.	1936
Crane, Bob	Waterbury, Conn.	1928	Dietrich, Marlene	Berlin, Germany	1901
Crane, Les	New York, N.Y.	1934	Diller, Phyllis	Lima, Ohio	1917
Crawford, Broderick	Philadelphia, Pa.	1911	Dillman, Bradford	San Francisco, Calif.	1930
Crawford, Joan	San Antonio, Tex.	1908	Dixon, Ivan	New York, N.Y.	1931
Crawford, Michael	Salisbury, England	1942	Dixon, Jeane	Waterbury, Conn.	1905
Crenna, Richard	Los Angeles, Calif.	1927	Domino, Fats	New Orleans, La.	1928
Crisp, Donald	London, England	1880	Donahue, Troy	New York, N.Y.	1936
Cristal, Linda	Argentina	—	Donald, James	Aberdeen, Scotland	1917
Cronyn, Hume	London, Ont.	1911	Donald, Peter	Bristol, England	1918
Crosby, Bing (Harry)	Tacoma, Wash.	1904	Donnelly, Ruth	Trenton, N.J.	1896
Crosby, Bob	Spokane, Wash.	1913	Donovan	Glasgow, Scotland	1946
Cross, Milton	New York, N.Y.	1897	Dors, Diana	Swindon, England	1931
Crowley, Pat	Scranton, Pa.	1929	d'Orsay, Fifi	Montreal, Canada	1908
Cruz, Brandon	Bakersfield, Calif.	1962	Douglas, Donna	Baywood, La.	1939
Cugat, Xavier	Barcelona, Spain	1900	Douglas, Kirk	Amsterdam, N.Y.	1918
Cullen, Bill	Pittsburgh, Pa.	1920	Douglas, Melvyn	Macon, Ga.	1901
Culp, Robert	Berkeley, Calif.	1930	Douglas, Mike	Chicago, Ill.	1925
Cummings, Constance	Seattle, Wash.	1910	Downey, Morton	Wallingford, Conn.	1902
Cummings, Robert	Joplin, Mo.	1910	Downs, Hugh	Akron, Ohio	1921
Cummins, Peggy	Prestatyn, N. Wales	1925	Dragonette, Jessica	Calcutta, India	—
Curtin, Phyllis	Clarksburg, W.Va.	1930	Drake, Alfred	Bronx, N.Y.	1914
Curtis, Ken	Lamar, Colo.	1916	Drake, Betsy	Paris, France	1923
Curtis, Tony	New York, N.Y.	1925	Draper, Paul	Florence, Italy	1911
Cusack, Cyril	Durban, So. Africa	1910	Drew, Ellen	Kansas City, Mo.	1915
Cushing, Peter	Surrey, Eng.	1913	Dru, Joanne	Logan, W.Va.	1923
			Drury, James	New York, N.Y.	1934
D			Duchin, Peter	New York, N.Y.	1937
Dagmar (Egnor)	Huntington, W.Va.	1926	Duff, Howard	Bremerton, Wash.	1917
Dahl, Arlene	Minneapolis, Minn.	1927	Duke, Patty	New York, N.Y.	1946
Dailey, Dan	New York, N.Y.	1917	Dullea, Keir	Cleveland, Ohio	1936
Dalrymple, Jean	Morristown, N.J.	1910	Dunaway, Faye	Tallahassee, Fla.	1941
Dalton, Abby	Las Vegas, Nev.	1935	Duncan, Sandy	Henderson, Texas	1946
Daly, James	Wisconsin Rapids, Wis.	1918	Duncan, Todd	Danville, Ky.	1900
Daly, John	Johannesburg, S. Afr.	1914	Duncan, Vivian	Los Angeles, Calif.	1902
Damita, Lili	Paris, France	1907	Dunham, Katherine	Chicago, Ill.	1910
Damone, Vic	Brooklyn, N.Y.	1928	Dunn, Michael	Shattuck, Okla.	1935
Dana, Bill	Quincy, Mass.	1924	Dunne, Irene	Louisville, Ky.	1904
Dangerfield, Rodney	Babylon, L.I., N.Y.	1921	Dunninger, Joseph	New York, N.Y.	1898
Daniels, William	Brooklyn, N.Y.	1927	Dunnock, Mildred	Baltimore, Md.	1906
Danilova, Alexandra	Peterhof, Russia	1907	Durante, Jimmy	New York, N.Y.	1893
Danton, Ray	New York, N.Y.	1931	Durbin, Deanna	Winnipeg, Canada	1922
Darby, Kim	Hollywood, Calif.	1948	Duvall, Robert	San Diego, Calif.	1931
Darcel, Denise	Paris, France	1925	Dvorak, Ann	New York, N.Y.	1912
Darin, Bobby	Bronx, N.Y.	1936	Dylan, Bob	Duluth, Minn.	1941
Darren, James	Philadelphia, Pa.	1936			
Darrieux, Danielle	Bordeaux, France	1917	**E**		
Darrow, Henry	New York, N.Y.	1933	Eastwood, Clint	San Francisco, Calif.	1930
Da Silva, Howard	Cleveland, Ohio	1909	Eaton, Shirley	London, England	1937
Dassin, Jules	Middletown, Conn.	1911	Ebsen, Buddy	Belleville, Ill.	1908
Dauphin, Claude	Corbeil, France	1905	Eckstine, Billy	Pittsburgh, Pa.	1914
Davidson, John	Pittsburgh, Pa.	1941	Edelman, Herbert	Brooklyn, N.Y.	1933
Davis, Ann B.	Schenectady, N.Y.	1926	Eden, Barbara	Tucson, Ariz.	1934

Name	Birthplace	Born	Name	Birthplace	Born
Edwards, Douglas	Ada, Okla.	1917	Fosse, Bob	Chicago, Ill.	1927
Edwards, Joan	New York, N.Y.	1920	Foster, Norman	Richmond, Ind.	1900
Edwards, Ralph	Merino, Colo.	1913	Foster, Phil	Brooklyn, N.Y.	1914
Edwards, Vincent	Brooklyn, N.Y.	1928	Fountain, Pete	New Orleans, La.	1930
Egan, Richard	San Francisco, Calif.	1923	Fox, James	London, England	1939
Eggar, Samantha	London, England	1939	Foxx, Redd	St. Louis, Mo.	1922
Eggerth, Marta	Budapest, Hungary	1916	Foy, Eddie, Jr.	New Rochelle, N.Y.	1905
Ekberg, Anita	Malmo, Sweden	1931	Francescatti, Zino	Marseilles, France	1904
Ekland, Britt	Stockholm, Sweden	1942	Franciosa, Anthony	New York, N.Y.	1928
Eldridge, Florence	Brooklyn, N.Y.	1901	Francis, Arlene	Boston, Mass.	1908
Elgart, Larry	New London, Conn.	1922	Francis, Connie	Newark, N.J.	1938
Elgart, Les	New Haven, Conn.	1918	Franciscus, James	Clayton, Mo.	1934
Ellington, Duke	Washington, D.C.	1899	Frankenheimer, John	Malba, L.I., N.Y.	1930
Elliot, Mama Cass	Arlington, Va.	1943	Franklin, Aretha	Memphis, Tenn.	1942
Elliott, Bob	Boston, Mass.	1923	Franklin, Joe	New York, N.Y.	1926
Emerson, Faye	Elizabeth, L.A.	1917	Franz, Arthur	Perth Amboy, N.J.	1920
Erickson, Leif	Alameda, Calif.	1911	Freberg, Stan	Pasadena, Calif.	1926
Esmond, Jill	London, England	1908	Freed, Bert	New York, N.Y.	1919
Etting, Ruth	David City, Nebr.	1896	Freeman, Mona	Baltimore, Md.	1926
Evans, Dale	Uvalde, Texas	1912	Frizzell, Lefty	Corsicana, Texas	1938
Evans, Dame Edith	London, England	1888	Froman, Jane	St. Louis, Mo.	1911
Evans, Maurice	Dorchester, England	1901	Frost, David	Tenterden, England	1939
Everett, Chad	South Bend, Ind.	1937	Frye, David	Brooklyn, N.Y.	1934
Evers, Jason	New York, N.Y.	1927	Funicello, Annette	Utica, N.Y.	1942
Ewell, Tom	Owensboro, Ky.	1909	Funt, Allen	New York, N.Y.	1914
			Furness, Betty	New York, N.Y.	1916

Name	Birthplace	Born	Name	Birthplace	Born
F			**G**		
Fabares, Shelley	Santa Monica, Calif.	1944			
Fabian (Forte)	Philadelphia, Pa.	1943	Gabel, Martin	Philadelphia, Pa.	1912
Fabray, Nanette	San Diego, Calif.	1920	Gabin, Jean	Villette, Paris, France.	1904
Fadiman, Clifton	Brooklyn, N.Y.	1904	Gabor, Eva	Hungary	1924
Fairbanks, Doug., Jr.	New York, N.Y.	1909	Gabor, Zsa Zsa	Hungary	1923
Faith, Percy	Toronto, Ont.	1908	Gahagan, Helen	Boonton, N.J.	1900
Falk, Peter	New York, N.Y.	1927	Galloway, Don	Brooksville, Ky.	1937
Falkenburg, Jinx	Barcelona, Spain	1919	Gam, Rita	Pittsburgh, Pa.	1929
Farber, Barry	Baltimore, Md.	1930	Gambling, John A.	New York, N.Y.	1930
Farentino, James	Brooklyn, N.Y.	1938	Gambling, John B.	Norwich, England	1897
Farr, Felicia	Westchester, N.Y.	1932	Garagiola, Joe	St. Louis, Mo.	1926
Farrell, Charles	Onset Bay, Mass.	1901	Garbo, Greta	Stockholm, Sweden	1905
Farrell, Eileen	Willimantic, Conn.	1920	Gardiner, Reginald	Wimbledon, England	1903
Farrow, Mia	Los Angeles, Calif.	1946	Gardner, Ava	Smithfield, N.C.	1922
Faye, Alice	New York, N.Y.	1915	Gardner, Hy	New York, N.Y.	1908
Feeney, Joe	Grand Island, Nebr.	1931	Gargan, William	Brooklyn, N.Y.	1905
Feld, Fritz	Berlin, Germany	1900	Garfunkel, Art	New York, N.Y.	1941
Feldon, Barbara	Pittsburgh, Pa.	1941	Garland, Beverly	Santa Cruz, Calif.	1930
Feliciano, Jose	Puerto Rico	1945	Garner, Erroll	Pittsburgh, Pa.	1923
Fellini, Federico	Rimini, Italy	1920	Garner, James	Norman, Okla.	1928
Fellows, Edith	Boston, Mass.	1923	Garner, Peggy Ann	Canton, Ohio	1932
Fenton, Leslie	England	1903	Garroway, Dave	Schenectady, N.Y.	1913
Ferrer, Jose	Santurce, P.R.	1912	Garrett, Betty	St. Joseph, Mo.	1919
Ferrer, Mel	Elberon, N.J.	1917	Garson, Greer	Co. Down, No. Ireland	1908
Ferris, Barbara	London, England	1942	Garver, Kathy	Long Beach, Calif.	1948
Fetchit, Stepin	Key West, Fla.	1902	Gary, John	Watertown, N.Y.	1932
Fiedler, Arthur	Boston, Mass.	1894	Gavin, John	Los Angeles, Calif.	1932
Field, Sally	Pasadena, Calif.	1946	Gaynor, Janet	Philadelphia, Pa.	1906
Fields, Dorothy	Allenhurst, N.J.	1905	Gaynor, Mitzi	Chicago, Ill.	1931
Fields, Gracie	Rochdale, England	1898	Gazzara, Ben	New York, N.Y.	1930
Fields, Totie	Hartford, Conn.	1931	Gedda, Nicolai	Sweden	1925
Finch, Peter	London, England	1916	Geer, Will	Frankfort, Ind.	1902
Finney, Albert	Salford, England	1936	Geeson, Judy	Sussex, England	1948
Firkusny-Napajedla,			Genevieve (G. Auger)	Paris, France	1930
Rudolf	Czechoslovakia	1912	Genn, Leo	London, England	1905
Fisher, Eddie	Philadelphia, Pa.	1928	Gennaro, Peter	Metairie, La.	1924
Fisher, Gail	Orange, N.J.	—	Gentry, Bobby	Chickasaw Co., Miss.	1944
Fitzgerald, Ella	Newport News, Va.	1918	Gershwin, Ira	New York, N.Y.	1896
Fitzgerald, Geraldine	Dublin, Ireland	1914	Getz, Stan	Philadelphia, Pa.	1927
Fitzgerald, Pegeen	Norcatur, Kansas	1910	Ghostley, Alice	Eve, Mo.	1926
Fix, Paul	Dobbs Ferry, N.Y.	1902	Gibson, Henry	Germantown, Pa.	1935
Fleming, Rhonda	Hollywood, Calif.	1923	Gielgud, John	London, England	1904
Flynn, Joe	Youngstown, Ohio	1926	Gifford, Frank	Santa Monica, Calif.	1930
Foch, Nina	Leyden, Neth.	1924	Gillespie, Dizzy	Cheraw, N.C.	1917
Fonda, Henry	Grand Island, Nebr.	1905	Gillette, Anita	Baltimore, Md.	1936
Fonda, Jane	New York, N.Y.	1937	Gingold, Hermione	London, England	1897
Fonda, Peter	New York, N.Y.	1939	Gish, Lillian	Springfield, Ohio	1896
Fontaine, Frank	Cambridge, Mass.	1920	Givot, George	Omaha, Nebr.	1903
Fontaine, Joan	Tokyo, Japan	1917	Gleason, Jackie	Brooklyn, N.Y.	1916
Fontanne, Lynn	London, England	1887	Gobel, George	Chicago, Ill.	1919
Fonteyn, Margot	Reigate, England	1919	Godard, Jean Luc	Paris, France	1930
Foran, Dick	Flemington, N.J.	1910	Goddard, Mark	Lowell, Mass.	1936
Forbes, Bryan	London, England	1926	Goddard, Paulette	Great Neck, N.Y.	1911
Ford (Tenn.), Ernie	Bristol, Tenn.	1919	Godfrey, Arthur	New York, N.Y.	1903
Ford, Glenn	Quebec, Canada	1916	Goldwyn, Samuel	Warsaw, Poland	1882
Ford, Paul	Baltimore, Md.	1901	Goodman, Benny	Chicago, Ill.	1909
Ford, Ruth	Hazelhurst, Miss.	1915	Gordon, Gale	New York, N.Y.	1906
Forrest, Sally	San Diego, Calif.	1928	Gordon, Max	New York, N.Y.	1892
Forrest, Steve	Huntsville, Texas	1925	Gordon, Ruth	Wollaston, Mass.	1896
Forster, Robert	Rochester, N.Y.	1942	Gore, Lesley	Tenafly, N.J.	1946
Forsythe, John	Penns Grove, N.J.	1918	Gorin, Igor	Ukraine, Russia	1909

Name	Birthplace	Born	Name	Birthplace	Born
Gorme, Eydie	Bronx, N.Y.	1932	Hayden, Melissa	Toronto, Canada	1928
Gorshin, Frank	Pittsburgh, Pa.	1935	Hayden, Russell	Chico, Calif.	1912
Gould, Elliot	Brooklyn, N.Y.	1938	Hayden, Sterling	Montclair, N.J.	1916
Gould, Morton	Richmond Hill, N.Y.	1913	Haydon, Julie	Oak Park, Ill.	1910
Goulding, Ray	Lowell, Mass.	1922	Hayes, Helen	Washington, D.C.	1900
Goulet, Robert	Lawrence, Mass.	1933	Hayes, Peter Lind	San Francisco, Calif.	1915
Gowdy, Curt	Green River, Wyo.	1919	Hayes, Roland	Curryville, Ga.	1887
Grady, Don	San Diego, Calif.	1944	Haymes, Dick	Buenos Aires, Arg'tina	1918
Graham, Martha	Pittsburgh, Pa.	1902	Haynes, Lloyd	South Bend, Ind.	1934
Graham, Virginia	Chicago, Ill.	1913	Hayward, Louis	Johannesburg, S. Afr.	1909
Grahame, Gloria	Los Angeles, Calif.	1929	Hayward, Susan	Brooklyn, N.Y.	1919
Grahame, Margot	Canterbury, England	1911	Hayworth, Rita	New York, N.Y.	1918
Granger, Farley	San Jose, Calif.	1925	Healy, Mary	New Orleans, La.	1918
Granger, Stewart	London, England	1913	Heatherton, Joey	Rockville Centre, N.Y.	1944
Granville, Bonita	New York, N.Y.	1923	Heckart, Eileen	Columbus, Ohio	1919
Grant, Cary	Bristol, England	1904	Hefner, Hugh	Chicago, Ill.	1926
Grant, Kathryn	Houston, Texas	1933	Heifetz, Jascha	Vilna, Russia	1901
Grant, Lee	New York, N.Y.	1927	Hellman, Lillian	New Orleans, La.	1907
Grauer, Ben	New York, N.Y.	1908	Helmore, Tom	London, England	1912
Graves, Peter	Minneapolis, Minn.	1926	Helpmann, Robert	Mt. Gambier, Aust.	1909
Gray, Coleen	Staplehurst, Nebr.	1922	Henderson, Florence	Dale, Ind.	1934
Gray, Dolores	Chicago, Ill.	1924	Henderson, Marcia	Andover, Mass.	1932
Grayson, Kathryn	Winston-Salem, N.C.	1923	Henderson, Skitch	Halstad, Minn.	1918
Graziano, Rocky	New York, N.Y.	1922	Henning, David	Guildford, England	1941
Greco, Buddy	Philadelphia, Pa.	1926	Henning, Linda Kaye	Toluca Lake, Calif.	1944
Greco, Jose	Abruzzi, Italy	1918	Henreid, Paul	Trieste, Italy	1908
Greco, Juliette	Paris, France	—	Hepburn, Audrey	Brussels, Belgium	1929
Green, Eddie	Baltimore, Md.	1901	Hepburn, Katharine	Hartford, Conn.	1909
Green, Mitzi	London, England	1899	Herbert, Evelyn	Philadelphia, Pa.	1898
Greene, Lorne	Ottawa, Canada	1915	Herman, Woody	Milwaukee, Wis.	1913
Greenwood, Charlotte	Philadelphia, Pa.	1893	Hershfield, Harry	Cedar Rapids, Iowa	1885
Greenwood, Joan	London, England	1921	Heston, Charlton	Evanston, Ill.	1923
Greer, Jane	Washington, D.C.	1924	Heywood, Anne	Birmingham, England	1937
Gregory, Dick	St. Louis, Mo.	1933	Hildegarde	Adell, Wis.	1906
Grey, Joel	Cleveland, Ohio	1932	Hill, Arthur	Melfort, Sask., Canada	1922
Griffin, Merv	San Mateo, Calif.	1925	Hiller, Wendy	Stockport, England	1912
Griffith, Andy	Mount Airy, N.C.	1926	Hines, Earl (Fatha)	Duquesne, Pa.	1905
Griffith, Hugh	Wales	1912	Hines, Jerome	Hollywood, Calif.	1921
Grimes, Tammy	Lynn, Mass.	1936	Hines, Mimi	Vancouver, B.C.	1933
Grizzard, George	Roanoke Rapids, N.C.	1928	Hingle, Pat	Denver, Colo.	1924
Guardino, Harry	New York, N.Y.	1925	Hirt, Al	New Orleans, La.	1922
Guinness, Alec	London, England	1914	Hitchcock, Alfred	London, England	1899
Gunn, Moses	St. Louis, Mo.	1929	Ho, Don	Kakaako, Oahu, Hawaii	1930
Guthrie, Arlo	New York, N.Y.	1947	Hobart, Rose	New York, N.Y.	1906
			Hodges, Eddie	Hattiesburg, Miss.	1947
			Hoffman, Dustin	Los Angeles, Calif.	1937
H			Holbrook, Hal	Cleveland, Ohio	1925
			Holden, William	O'Fallon, Ill.	1918
Hackett, Buddy	Brooklyn, N.Y.	1924	Holder, Geoffrey	Trinidad	1930
Hackett, Joan	New York, N.Y.	1933	Holloway, Stanley	London, England	1890
Hackman, Gene	San Bernardino, Calif.	1931	Holloway, Sterling	Cedartown, Ga.	—
Hagen, Uta	Gottingen, Germany	1919	Holm, Celeste	New York, N.Y.	1919
Haggard, Merle	Bakersfield, Calif.	1937	Holtz, Lou	San Francisco, Calif.	1898
Hagman, Larry	Ft. Worth, Texas	1931	Homeier, Skip	Chicago, Ill.	1930
Hale, Barbara	DeKalb, Ill.	1922	Homolka, Oscar	Vienna, Austria	1903
Haley, Jack	Boston, Mass.	1899	Hooks, Robert	Washington, D.C.	1937
Hall, Huntz	New York, N.Y.	—	Hope, Bob	London, England	1903
Hall, Monty	Winnipeg, Canada	1923	Hopkin, Mary	Wales	1950
Hamilton, George	Memphis, Tenn.	1939	Hopper, Dennis	Dodge City, Kansas	1936
Hamilton, Margaret	Cleveland, Ohio	1902	Horne, Lena	Brooklyn, N.Y.	1917
Hamilton, Neil	Lynn, Mass.	1899	Horowitz, Vladimir	Kiev, Russia	1904
Hampshire, Susan	London, England	1941	Horton, Robert	Los Angeles, Calif.	1924
Hampton, Lionel	Birmingham, Ala.	1914	Howard, Clint	Burbank, Calif.	1959
Hampton, Ruth	Throop, Pa.	1932	Howard, Ronnie	Duncan, Okla.	1954
Hanley, Bridget	Minneapolis, Minn.	1943	Howard, Trevor	Kent, England	1916
Hanson, Howard	Wahoo, Nebr.	1896	Howes, Sally Ann	London, England	1934
Harding, Ann	Ft. Sam Houston, Tex.	1904	Hudson, Rock	Winnetka, Ill.	1925
Harper, Ron	Turtle Creek, Pa.	1935	Hull, Henry	Louisville, Ky.	1890
Harper, Valarie	Suffern, N.Y.	—	Hull, Warren	Gasport, N.Y.	1903
Harrington, Jr. Pat,	New York, N.Y.	1929	Humperdinck, Engelbert	Madras, India	1937
Harris, Barbara	Evanston, Ill.	1935	Hunnicutt, Arthur	Gravelly, Ark.	1911
Harris, Julie	Grosse Pte. Park, Mich.	1925	Hunt, Lois	York, Pa.	1925
Harris, Phil	Linton, Ind.	1906	Hunt, Marsha	Chicago, Ill.	1917
Harris, Richard	Co. Limerick, Ire.	1933	Hunter, Ian	Cape Town, S. Africa	1900
Harrison, George	Liverpool, England	1943	Hunter, Kim	Detroit, Mich.	1922
Harrison, Noel	London, England	1933	Hunter, Tab	New York, N.Y.	1931
Harrison, Rex	Huyton, England	1908	Hussey, Olivia	Buenos Aires, Arg.	1952
Harris, Rosemary	Ashby, England	1930	Hussey, Ruth	Providence, R.I.	1917
Hartman, David	Pawtucket, R.I.	1935	Huston, John	Nevada, Mo.	1906
Hartman, Elizabeth	Boardman, Ohio	1943	Hutchins, Will	Los Angeles, Calif.	1932
Hartman, Paul	San Francisco, Calif.	1904	Hutchinson, Josephine	Seattle, Wash.	1916
Harvey, Laurence	Yonishkis, Lithuania	1928	Hutton, Betty	Battle Creek, Mich.	1921
Hasso, Signe	Stockholm, Sweden	1915	Hutton, Ina Ray	Chicago, Ill.	1918
Haver, June	Rock Island, Ill.	1926	Hutton, Lauren	Charleston, S.C.	1944
Havoc, June	Vancouver, Canada	1916	Hyde-White, Wilfrid	England	1903
Hawn, Goldie	Washington, D.C.	1945	Hyer, Martha	Fort Worth, Texas	1929
Haworth, Jill	Sussex, England	1945	Hyland, Diana	Cleveland Hts., Ohio	1937
Hayakawa, Sessue	Japan	1890	Hyman, Earle	Rocky Mt. N.C.	1926

Name	Birthplace	Born	Name	Birthplace	Born
I			King, Alan	Brooklyn, N.Y.	1927
			King, B.B.	Itta Bena, Miss.	1925
Inescort, Frieda	Edinburgh, Scotland	1901	King, Henry	Christianburg, Va.	1896
Ingels, Marty	Brooklyn, N.Y.	1936	King, Peggy	Greensburg, Pa.	1931
Ireland, John	Vancouver, B.C.	1915	King, Walter Woolf	San Francisco, Calif.	1899
Iturbi, Jose	Valencia, Spain	1895	King, Wayne	Savannah, Ill.	1901
Ives, Burl	Hunt, Ill.	1909	King, Zalman	Trenton, N.J.	1942
			Kirby, Durward	Covington, Ky.	1912
J			Kirby, Michael	Canada	1925
Jackson, Anne	Allegheny, Pa.	1926	Kirk, Lisa	Brownsville, Pa.	1925
Jackson, Glenda	England	1938	Kirk, Phyllis	Syracuse, N.Y.	1930
Jacobi, Lou	Toronto, Ont., Canada	1912	Kirkland, Muriel	Yonkers, N.Y.	1903
Jaeckel, Richard	Long Beach, Calif.	1926	Kirsten, Dorothy	Montclair, N.J.	1919
Jaffe, Sam	New York, N.Y.	1891	Kitt, Eartha	North, S.C.	1928
Jagger, Dean	Columbus Grove, Ohio	1905	Klemperer, Werner	Cologne, Germany	1930
Jagger, Mick	Dartford, England	1944	Klugman, Jack	Philadelphia, Pa.	1922
James, Dennis	Jersey City, N.J.	1917	Knight, Ted	Terryville, Conn.	–
James, Harry	Albany, Ga.	1916	Knotts, Don	Morgantown, W.Va.	1924
Janney, Leon	Ogden, Utah	1917	Knowles, Patric	Horsforth, England	1911
Janney, William	New York, N.Y.	1908	Knox, Alexander	Strathroy, Canada	1907
Janssen, David	Naponee, Nebr.	1930	Korjus, Miliza	Warsaw, Poland	1912
Jason, Rick	New York, N.Y.	1926	Korman, Harvey	Chicago, Ill.	1927
Jeanmaire, Renee	Paris, France	1925	Kostelanetz, Andre	St. Petersburg, Russia	1910
Jeffreys, Anne	Goldsboro, N.C.	1923	Kramer, Stanley	New York, N.Y.	1913
Jeffries, Fran	San Jose, Calif.	1939	Kruger, Hardy	Berlin, Germany	1928
Jeffries, Lionel	England	1926	Kruger, Otto	Toledo, Ohio	1885
Jenkins, Allen	New York, N.Y.	1900	Krupa, Gene	Chicago, Ill.	1909
Jepson, Helen	Titusville, Pa.	1907	Kubelik, Rafael	Bychory, Czechoslovakia	1914
Jeritza, Maria	Brunn, Austria	1887	Kubrick, Stanley	Bronx, N.Y.	1927
Jessel, George	New York, N.Y.	1898	Kullman, Chas	New Haven, Conn.	1902
John, Elton	Middlesex, England	1947	Kulp, Nancy	Harrisburg, Pa.	1921
Johns, Glynis	Durban, So. Africa	1923	Kwan, Nancy	Hong Kong	1939
Johnson, Ben	Pawhuska, Okla.	–	Kyser, Kay	Rocky Mount, N.C.	1905
Johnson, Richard	Essex, England	1927	**L**		
Johnson, Van	Newport, R.I.	1916			
Johnston, Johnny	St. Louis, Mo.	1916	Laine, Frankie	Chicago, Ill.	1913
Jones, Allan	Scranton, Pa.	1907	Lamarr, Hedy	Vienna, Austria	1915
Jones, Anissa	W. Lafayette, Ind.	1958	Lamas, Fernando	Buenos Aires, Arg.	1915
Jones, Carolyn	Amarillo, Texas	1932	Lamb, Gil	Minneapolis, Minn.	1906
Jones, Chris	Jackson, Tenn.	1941	Lamour, Dorothy	New Orleans, La.	1914
Jones, Dean	Morgan Co., Ala.	1936	Lancaster, Burt	New York, N.Y.	1913
Jones, Grandpa	Henderson Co., Ky.	1913	Lanchester, Elsa	London, England	1902
Jones, Henry	Philadelphia, Pa.	1912	Landers, Harry	New York, N.Y.	1921
Jones, Jack	Hollywood, Calif.	1938	Landon, Michael	Forest Hills, N.Y.	1936
Jones, James Earl	Tate Co., Miss.	1931	Lane, Abbe	Brooklyn, N.Y.	1932
Jones, Jennifer	Tulsa, Okla.	1919	Lane, Lola	Macy, Ind.	–
Jones, Quincy	Chicago, Ill.	1933	Lane, Priscilla	Indianola, Iowa	–
Jones, Shirley	Smithtown, Pa.	1934	Lane, Rosemary	Indianola, Iowa	1916
Jones, Tom	Pontypridd, Wales	1940	Lane, Sara	New York, N.Y.	1949
Jory, Victor	Dawson, Yukon, Can.	1902	Lang, Harold	Daly City, Calif.	1924
Joslyn, Allyn	Milford, Pa.	1905	Lang, June	Minneapolis, Minn.	1915
Jourdan, Louis	Marseilles, France	1922	Lange, Hope	Redding Ridge, Conn.	1933
Judge, Arline	Bridgeport, Conn.	1912	Langella, Frank	Bayonne, N.J.	1940
Jurado, Katy	Guadalajara, Mexico	1927	Langford, Frances	Lakeland, Fla.	1913
			Lansbury, Angela	London, England	1925
K			Lansing, Robert	San Diego, Calif.	1929
Kamen, Milt	Harleyville, N.Y.	1924	Lanson, Snooky (Roy)	Memphis, Tenn.	1919
Kaminska, Ida	Odessa, Russia	1899	LaPlante, Laura	St. Louis, Mo.	1904
Kashi, Aliza	Tel-Aviv, Israel	1940	La Rosa, Julius	Brooklyn, N.Y.	1930
Kasznar, Kurt	Vienna, Austria	1913	La Rue, Jack	New York, N.Y.	–
Kaye, Danny	Brooklyn, N.Y.	1913	Laurie, Piper	Detroit, Mich.	1932
Kaye, Sammy	Lakewood, Ohio	1913	Law, John Philip	Hollywood, Calif.	1937
Kazan, Elia	Constantinople, Turkey	1909	Lawford, Peter	London, England	1923
Kazan, Lainie	New York, N.Y.	1940	Lawrence, Barbara	Carnegie, Okla.	1930
Keach, Stacy	Savannah, Ga.	1941	Lawrence, Carol	Melrose Park, Ill.	1934
Keaton, Diane	Santa Ana, Calif.	1946	Lawrence, Marjorie	Victoria, Australia	1909
Keel, Howard	Gillespie, Ill.	1917	Lawrence, Steve	Brooklyn, N.Y.	1935
Keeler, Ruby	Halifax, N.S., Canada	1910	Lawrence, Vicki	Inglewood, Calif.	1949
Keeshan, Bob	Lynbrook, N.Y.	1927	Leachman, Cloris	Des Moines, Iowa	–
Keith, Brian	Bayonne, N.J.	1921	Lean, David	Croydon, England	1908
Kellerman, Sally	Long Beach, Calif.	1938	Lederer, Francis	Prague, Czech.	1906
Kelley, DeForrest	Atlanta, Ga.	1920	Lee, Brenda	Atlanta, Ga.	1944
Kelly, Emmett	Sedan, Kansas	1898	Lee, Christopher	London, England	1922
Kelly, Gene	Pittsburgh, Pa.	1912	Lee, Lila	New York, N.Y.	1905
Kelly, Grace	Philadelphia, Pa.	1929	Lee, Michele	Los Angeles, Calif.	1942
Kelly, Jack	Astoria, N.Y.	1927	Lee, Peggy	Jamestown, N.D.	1920
Kelly, Nancy	Lowell, Mass.	1921	Lee, Pinky	St. Paul, Minn.	–
Kelly, Patsy	Brooklyn, N.Y.	1910	Le Gallienne, Eva	London, England	1899
Kennedy, Arthur	Worcester, Mass.	1914	Legrand, Michel	Paris, France	1932
Kennedy, George	New York, N.Y.	1926	Lehmann, Lotte	Perleberg, Germany	1888
Kennedy, Madge	Chicago, Ill.	–	Leigh, Janet	Merced, Calif.	1927
Kent, Allegra	Los Angeles, Calif.	1937	Leighton, Margaret	Worcestershire, Eng.	1922
Kenton, Stan	Wichita, Kansas	1912	Leinsdorf, Erich	Vienna, Austria	1912
Kenyon, Doris	Syracuse, N.Y.	1897	Lembeck, Harvey	New York, N.Y.	1923
Kerr, Deborah	Helensburgh, Scotland	1921	Lemmon, Jack	Boston, Mass.	1925
Kerr, John	New York, N.Y.	1931	Lennon, Dianne	Los Angeles, Calif.	1939
Kert, Larry	Los Angeles, Calif.	1930	Lennon, Janet	Culver City, Calif.	1946
Keyes, Evelyn	Port Arthur, Tex.	1925	Lennon, John	Liverpool, England	1940
Kiley, Richard	Chicago, Ill.	1922	Lennon, Kathy	Santa Monica, Calif.	1943
Kilian, Victor	Jersey City, N.J.	1898	Lennon, Peggy	Los Angeles, Calif.	1941

Name	Birthplace	Born
Leonard, Sheldon	New York, N.Y.	1907
Leontovich, Eugenie	Moscow, Russia	1894
LeRoy, Mervyn	San Francisco, Calif.	1900
Leslie, Joan	Detroit, Mich.	1925
Lester, Jerry	Chicago, Ill.	1911
Lester, Mark	Richmond, England	1958
Lester, Tom	Jackson, Miss.	1938
Levene, Sam	Russia	1905
Levenson, Sam	New York, N.Y.	1911
Lewis, Jerry	Newark, N.J.	1926
Lewis, Monica	Chicago, Ill.	1925
Lewis, Ramsey	Chicago, Ill.	1935
Lewis, Robert Q	New York, N.Y.	1924
Lewis, Shari	New York, N.Y.	1934
Liberace	West Allis, Wis.	1919
Lillie, Beatrice	Toronto, Canada	1898
Lincoln, Abbey	Chicago, Ill.	1930
Lindfors, Viveca	Uppsala, Sweden	1920
Lindsay, Margaret	Dubuque, Iowa	1910
Lindsey, Mort	Newark, N.J.	1923
Linkletter, Art	Saskatchewan, Can.	1912
Linn, Bambi	Brooklyn, N.Y.	1926
Lipton, Peggy	Lawrence, L.I., N.Y.	1948
Lisi, Virna	Italy	1937
List, Emanuel	Vienna, Austria	1891
Little, Cleavon	Chickasha, Okla.	1939
Little, Rich	Ottawa, Canada	1938
Livingston, Barry	Los Angeles, Calif.	1953
Livingston, Stanley	Los Angeles, Calif.	1950
Livingstone, Mary	Seattle, Wash.	1909
Lockhart, June	New York, N.Y.	1928
Lockwood, Margaret	Karachi, India	1916
Loden, Barbara	Marion, N.C.	1937
Loder, John	London, England	1898
Logan, Joshua	Texarkana, Texas	1908
Lollobrigida, Gina	Subiaco, Italy	1929
Lom, Herbert	Prague, Czech.	1917
Lombardo, Guy	London, Ont., Can.	1902
London, George	Montreal, Que., Can.	1920
London, Julie	Santa Rosa, Calif.	1926
Long, Richard	Chicago, Ill.	1927
Longet, Claudine	France	1942
Lopez, Perry	New York, N.Y.	1931
Lopez, Trini	Dallas, Texas	1937
Lopez, Vincent	Brooklyn, N.Y.	1895
Lord, Jack	New York, N.Y.	1930
Loren, Sophia	Rome, Italy	1934
Loring, Gloria	New York, N.Y.	1946
Loring, Lynn	New York, N.Y.	1944
Losch, Tilly	Vienna, Austria	1902
Loudon, Dorothy	Boston, Mass.	1932
Louise, Tina	New York, N.Y.	1934
Love, Bessie	Midland, Texas	1898
Loy, Myrna	Helena, Mont.	1905
Ludwig, Christa	Berlin, Germany	1934
Luke, Keye	Canton, China	1904
Lulu	Glasgow, Scotland	1948
Lum (Chester Lauck)	Allene, Ark.	1902
Lumet, Sidney	Philadelphia, Pa.	1924
Lund, John	Rochester, N.Y.	1913
Lundigan, William	Syracuse, N.Y.	1914
Lunt, Alfred	Milwaukee, Wis.	1892
Lupino, Ida	London, England	1918
Lynde, Paul	Mt. Vernon, Ohio	1926
Lynley, Carol	New York, N.Y.	1942
Lynn, Jeffrey	Auburn, Mass.	1909
Lynn, Loretta	Butcher Hollow, Ky.	—
Lyon, Ben	Atlanta, Ga.	1901
Lyon, Sue	Davenport, Iowa	1946

M

Name	Birthplace	Born
MacArthur, James	Los Angeles, Calif.	1937
MacGrath, Leueen	England	1914
MacGraw, Ali	Pound Ridge, N.Y.	1939
Mack, Ted	Greeley, Colo.	1904
MacKenzie, Gisele	Winnipeg, Man., Can.	1927
MacKay, Jim	Philadelphia, Pa.	1921
MacLaine, Shirley	Richmond, Va.	1934
MacMurray, Fred	Kankakee, Ill.	1908
MacRae, Gordon	East Orange, N.J.	1921
MacRae, Meredith	Houston, Texas	1945
MacRae, Sheila	London, England	1924
Macy, Bill	Revere, Mass.	1922
Madison, Guy	Bakersfield, Calif.	1922
Mahler, Fritz	Vienna, Austria	1901
Main, Marjorie	Acton, Ind.	1890
Malbin, Elaine	New York, N.Y.	1932
Malden, Karl	Gary, Ind.	1914
Malone, Dorothy	Chicago, Ill.	1925

Name	Birthplace	Born
Malone, Nancy	New York, N.Y.	1935
Mancini, Henry	Cleveland, Ohio	1924
Mann, Herbie	New York, N.Y.	1930
Mantovani, Annunzio	Venice, Italy	1905
Marceau, Marcel	France	1923
March, Fredric	Racine, Wis.	1897
Margo	Mexico City, Mexico	1918
Margolin, Janet	New York, N.Y.	1943
Markova, Alicia	London, England	1910
Marlowe, Hugh	Philadelphia, Pa.	1914
Marsh, Joan	Porterville, Calif.	1915
Marshall, Brenda	Philippines	1915
Marshall, E. G.	Awatonna, Minn.	1919
Marshall, Everett	Lawrence, Mass.	1901
Marshall, Sarah	London, England	1933
Marshall, William	Chicago, Ill.	1917
Martin, Dean	Steubenville, Ohio	1917
Martin, Dick	Detroit, Mich.	1928
Martin, Mary	Weatherford, Texas	1913
Martin, Ross	Poland	1920
Martin, Tony	San Francisco, Calif.	1913
Martini, Nino	Verona, Italy	1905
Marvin, Lee	New York, N.Y.	1924
Marx, Herbert (Zeppo)	New York, N.Y.	1901
Marx, Julius (Groucho)	New York, N.Y.	1891
Mason, Jackie	Sheboygan, Wisc.	1931
Mason, James	Huddersfield, England	1909
Mason, Pamela	Westgate, England	1918
Massey, Curt	Midland, Texas	—
Massey, Ilona	Hungary	1910
Massey, Raymond	Toronto, Canada	1896
Massine, Leonide	Moscow, Russia	1896
Mastroianni, Marcello	Italy	1924
Mathis, Johnny	San Francisco, Calif.	1935
Matthau, Walter	New York, N.Y.	1920
Matthews, Jessie	London, England	1907
Mature, Victor	Louisville, Ky.	1916
May, Billy	Pittsburgh, Pa.	1916
May, Elaine	Philadelphia, Pa.	1932
Mayehoff, Eddie	Baltimore, Md.	1914
Mayo, Virginia	St. Louis, Mo.	1920
Mazurki, Mike	Austria	1909
McBride, Mary Marg.	Paris, Mo.	1899
McCaffery, J. K. M.	Moscow, Idaho	1913
McCallum, David	Glasgow, Scotland	1933
McCambridge, Mercedes	Joliet, Ill.	1918
McCarthy, Kevin	Seattle, Wash.	1915
McCartney, Paul	Liverpool, England	1942
McClure, Doug	Glendale, Calif.	1935
McCord, Kent	Los Angeles, Calif.	1942
McCoy, Tim	Saginaw, Mich.	1891
McCrary, Tex (John)	Calvert, Texas	1910
McCrea, Joel	Los Angeles, Calif.	1905
McDowall, Roddy	London, England	1928
McDowell, Malcolm	Leeds, England	1943
McFarland, George	Dallas, Texas	1928
McGavin, Darren	San Joaquin, Calif.	1922
McGee, Fibber, Jordan	Peoria, Ill.	1896
McGiver, John	New York, N.Y.	1913
McGoohan, Patrick	Astoria, N.Y.	1928
McGuire, Sisters:		
Christine	Middletown, Ohio	1928
Dorothy	Middletown, Ohio	1930
Phyllis	Middletown, Ohio	1931
McGuire, Dorothy	Omaha, Nebr.	1919
McHugh, Frank	Homestead, Pa.	1899
McIntyre, John	Spokane, Wash.	1907
McKay, Scott	Pleasantville, Iowa	1915
McKenna, Siobhan	Belfast, Ireland	1923
McKuen, Rod	San Francisco, Calif.	1933
McLerie, Allyn	Grand Mere, Que., Can.	1926
McMahon, Ed	Detroit, Mich.	1923
McNair, Barbara	Chicago, Ill.	1939
McQueen, Butterfly	Tampa, Fla.	1911
McQueen, Steve	Indianapolis, Ind.	1930
Meadows, Audrey	Wu Chang, China	1929
Meadows, Jayne	Wu Chang, China	1926
Meara, Ann	New York, N.Y.	1929
Medford, Kay	New York, N.Y.	1920
Meeker, Ralph	Minneapolis, Minn.	1920
Melton, Sid	Brooklyn, N.Y.	1920
Menuhin, Yehudi	New York, N.Y.	1916
Mercer, Johnny	Savannah, Ga.	1909
Mercouri, Melina	Athens, Greece	1929
Meredith, Burgess	Cleveland, Ohio	1909
Merkel, Una	Covington, Ky	1903
Merman, Ethel	Astoria, N.Y.	1909
Merrick, David	Hong Kong	1911
Merrill, Dina	New York, N.Y.	1925
Merrill, Gary	Hartford, Conn.	1915

Name	Birthplace	Born
Merrill, Robert	Brooklyn, N.Y.	1919
Michell, Keith	Adelaide, Australia	1928
Middleton, Guy	Hove, England	1907
Middleton, Ray	Chicago, Ill.	1907
Midler, Bette	Hoboken, N.J.	—
Mielziner, Jo	Paris, France	1901
Milanov, Zinka	Zagreb, Yugoslavia	1908
Miles, Sarah	Ingatestone, England	1941
Miles, Vera	near Boise City, Okla	1930
Milland, Ray	Neath, Wales	1908
Miller, Ann	Houston, Tex.	1923
Miller, Cheryl	Sherman Oaks, Calif.	1943
Miller, Mitch.	Rochester, N.Y.	1911
Miller, Roger	Erick, Okla.	1936
Mills, Hayley	London, Eng.	1946
Mills, John	Suffolk, Eng.	1908
Mills, Juliet	London, Eng.	1941
Milner, Martin	Detroit, Mich.	1937
Milstein, Nathan	Odessa, Russia	1904
Mimieux, Yvette	Hollywood, Calif.	1942
Minnelli, Liza	Los Angeles, Calif.	1946
Mineo, Sal.	New York, N.Y.	1939
Mitchell, Cameron	Dallastown, Pa	1918
Mitchell, Guy	Detroit, Mich	1925
Mitchell, Joni	Alberta, Canada	1943
Mitchum, Robert	Bridgeport, Conn.	1917
Moffo, Ann	Wayne, Pa.	—
Montalban, Ricardo	Mexico City, Mex.	1920
Montand, Yves	Monsummano, Italy	1921
Montgomery, Eliz.	Hollywood, Calif	1933
Montgomery, George	Brady, Mont.	1916
Montgomery, Robt.	Beacon, N.Y.	1904
Moore, Colleen	Port Huron, Mich.	1902
Moore, Constance	Sioux City, Iowa	1922
Moore, Dickie	Los Angeles, Calif.	1925
Moore, Garry	Baltimore, Md.	1915
Moore, Mary Tyler	Brooklyn, N.Y.	1937
Moore, Melba	New York, N.Y.	1945
Moore, Roger	London, Eng.	1928
Moore, Terry	Los Angeles, Calif.	1932
Moorehead, Agnes	Clinton, Mass.	1906
Moran, Lois	Pittsburgh, Pa	1907
Moreau, Jeanne	Paris, France	1929
Moreno, Rita	Humacao, P.R.	1931
Morgan, Claudia	Brooklyn, N.Y.	1912
Morgan, Dennis	Prentice, Wis.	1910
Morgan, Harry	Detroit, Mich.	1915
Morgan, Henry	New York, N.Y.	1915
Morgan, Jane	Boston, Mass.	1920
Morgana, Nina	Buffalo, N.Y.	1895
Morini, Erika	Vienna, Austria	1910
Morison, Patricia	New York, N.Y.	1915
Morley, Robert	Wiltshire, England	1908
Morris, Greg	Cleveland, Ohio	1934
Morris, Howard	New York, N.Y.	1919
Morrow, Vic	Bronx, N.Y.	1932
Morse, Robert	Newton, Mass.	1931
Moss, Arnold	Brooklyn, N.Y.	1910
Mostel, Zero (Sam)	Brooklyn, N.Y.	1915
Muir, Gavin	Chicago, Ill.	1909
Muir, Jean	New York, N.Y.	1911
Mulhall, Jack	Wap'ing's Falls, N.Y.	1894
Mulhare, Edward	Ireland	1923
Mundy, Meg	London, England.	—
Munsel, Patrice	Spokane, Wash.	1925
Murray, Arthur	New York, N.Y.	1895
Murray, Don	Hollywood, Calif.	1929
Murray, Jan.	New York	1917
Murray, Kathryn	Jersey City, N.J.	1906
Murray, Ken	New York, N.Y.	1903
Myerson, Bess	Bronx, N.Y.	1924

N

Name	Birthplace	Born
Nabors, Jim	Sylacauga, Ala.	1933
Namath, Joe	Beaver Falls, Pa.	1943
Nardini, Tom.	Los Angeles, Calif.	1945
Natwick, Mildred	Baltimore, Md.	1908
Neal, Patricia	Packard, Ky	1926
Neff, Hildegarde	Ulm, Germany	1925
Negri, Pola	Lipno, Poland	1899
Nelson, Barry	Oakland, Calif.	1920
Nelson, David	New York, N.Y.	1936
Nelson, Ed.	New Orleans, La	1928
Nelson, Gene	Seattle, Wash.	1920
Nelson, Harriet	Des Moines.	—
Nelson, Lori	Santa Fe, N.M.	1933
Nelson, Ozzie	Jersey City, N.J.	1907
Nelson, Ricky	Teaneck, N.J.	1940
Nero, Peter	New York, N.Y.	1934

Name	Birthplace	Born
Nesbit, Cathleen	Cheshire, England	1889
Nevins, Natalie	Philadelphia, Pa.	1943
Newhart, Bob	Oak Park, Ill.	1929
Newley, Anthony	Hackney, England	1931
Newman, Paul	Cleveland, Ohio	1925
Newman, Phyllis	Jersey City, N.J.	1935
Newmar, Julie	California	1935
Newton, Wayne	Roanoke, Va.	1942
Nicholas, Denise	Detroit, Mich.	
Nichols, Mike	Berlin, Ger.	1931
Nicholson, Jack	Neptune, N.J.	1936
Nielson, Leslie	Regina, Canada	1926
Niesen, Gertrude	At sea	1913
Nillson, Anna Q.	Ystad, Sweden	1893
Nilsson, Birgit	W. Karop, Sweden	1918
Nimoy, Leonard	Boston, Mass.	1931
Niven, David	Kirriemuir, Scotland	1910
Noble, Ray	Sussex, England	1908
Nolan, Doris	New York, N.Y.	1916
Nolan, Jeannette	Los Angeles, Calif.	1911
Nolan, Kathy	St. Louis, Mo.	1934
Nolan, Lloyd	San Francisco, Calif.	1902
North, Jay	Hollywood, Calif.	1953
North, John Ringling	Baraboo, Wis.	1903
North, Sheree	Los Angeles, Calif.	1933
Norton, Judy	Santa Monica, Calif.	1958
Novak, Kim	Chicago, Ill.	1933
Nugent, Edward	New York, N.Y.	1904
Nugent, Elliott	Dover, Ohio	1899
Nureyev, Rudolf	Russia	1938
Nuyen, France	Marseilles, France	1939

O

Name	Birthplace	Born
Oakie, Jack	Sedalia, Mo.	1903
Oberon, Merle	Tasmania, Australia	1914
O'Brian, Hugh	Rochester, N.Y.	1930
O'Brien, Edmond	New York, N.Y.	1915
O'Brien, George	San Francisco, Calif.	1900
O'Brien, Margaret	San Diego, Calif.	1937
O'Brien, Pat	Milwaukee, Wis.	1899
Ochs, Phil	El Paso, Tex.	1940
O'Connell, Arthur	New York, N.Y.	1908
O'Connor, Carroll	New York, N.Y.	1925
O'Connor, Donald	Chicago, Ill.	1925
Odetta	Birmingham, Ala.	1930
O'Driscoll, Martha	Tulsa, Okla.	1922
O'Hara, Maureen	Dublin, Ireland	1920
O'Herlihy, Dan	Wexford, Ireland	1919
O'Keefe, Walter	Hartford, Conn.	1907
Olivier, Laurence	Dorking, England	1907
O'Malley, J. Pat	Burnley, Eng.	1901
O'Neal, Patrick	Ocala, Fla.	1927
O'Neal, Ryan	Los Angeles, Calif.	1941
O'Neill, Jennifer	Brazil	1948
Opatoshu, David	New York, N.Y.	1918
Orbach, Jerry	New York, N.Y.	1935
Ormandy, Eugene	Budapest, Hungary	1899
O'Shea, Kevin	Chicago, Ill.	1917
O'Sullivan, Maureen	Boyle, Ireland	1911
O'Toole, Peter	Connemara, Ireland	1934
Owens, Buck	Sherman, Texas	1929

P

Name	Birthplace	Born
Paar, Jack	Canton, Ohio	1918
Page, Geraldine	Kirksville, Mo.	1924
Page, Patti	Claremore, Okla	1927
Paige, Janis	Tacoma, Wash.	1923
Paige, Robert	Indianapolis, Ind.	1910
Palance, Jack	Lattimer, Pa.	1920
Palmer, Betsy	East Chicago, Ind.	1929
Palmer, Gregg	San Francisco, Calif.	1927
Palmer, Lilli	Posen, Germany	1914
Papas, Irene	Greece	1926
Parker, Eleanor	Cedarville, Ohio	1922
Parker, Fess	Ft. Worth, Tex.	1925
Parker, Frank	New York, N.Y.	1906
Parker, Jean	Deer Lodge, Mont	1916
Parker, Suzy	New York City	1934
Parkins, Barbara	Vancouver, Canada	1942
Parks, Bert	Atlanta, Ga.	1914
Parks, Larry	Olathe, Kans.	1914
Parsons, Estelle	Lynn, Mass.	1927
Pasternak, Joseph	Hungary	1901
Paterson, Pat.	Bradford, England	1911
Patterson, Melody	Los Angeles, Calif.	1947
Patterson, Neva	Nevada, Iowa	1922
Paulsen, Pat	South Bend, Wash.	—
Pavan, Marisa	Cagliari, Sardinia	1932
Payne, John	Roanoke, Va.	1912

Name	Birthplace	Born
Pearl, Jack	New York, N.Y.	1895
Pearl, Minnie	Centerville, Tenn.	1912
Peck, Gregory	La Jolla, Calif.	1916
Peerce, Jan	New York, N.Y.	1904
Pelletier, Wilfred	Montreal, Canada	1896
Penn, Arthur	Philadelphia, Pa.	1922
Peppard George	Detroit, Mich	1933
Perkins, Anthony	New York, N.Y.	1932
Perry, Margaret	Denver, Colo.	1913
Persoff, Nehemiah	Jerusalem	1920
Peters, Bernadette	Queens, N.Y.	1944
Peters, Brock	New York, N.Y.	1927
Peters, Jean	Canton, Ohio	1926
Peters, Roberta	New York, N.Y.	1930
Peterson, Dorothy	Hector, Minn.	1901
Petit, Pascale	France	1937
Pettet, Joanna	London, Eng.	1944
Phillips, Margaret	Wales	1923
Piatigorsky, Gregor	Russia	1903
Piazza, Ben	Little Rock, Ark.	1934
Piazza, Marguerite	New Orleans, La.	1926
Pickens, Jane	Macon, Ga.	—
Pickens, Slim	Kingsberg. Calif.	1919
Pickford, Mary	Toronto, Canada	1894
Picon, Molly	New York, N.Y.	1898
Pidgeon, Walter	E. St. John, N.B.	1898
Piston, Walter	Rockland, Me	1894
Platt, Edward	Staten Island, N.Y.	1916
Pleasence, Donald	Worksop, England	1919
Pleshette, Suzanne	New York City	1937
Plimpton, George	New York, N.Y.	1927
Plowright, Joan	Brigg, England	1929
Plummer, Christopher	Toronto, Canada	1929
Poitier, Sydney	Miami, Fla.	1927
Pollard, Michael	Passaic, N.J.	1939
Pons, Lily	Cannes, France	1904
Ponselle, Carmela	Schenectady, N.Y.	1892
Ponselle, Rosa	Meriden, Conn.	1897
Ponti, Carlo	Milan, Italy	1913
Poston, Tom	Columbus, Ohio	1927
Powell, Eleanor	Springfield, Mass.	1912
Powell, Jane	Portland, Ore.	1929
Powell, William	Pittsburgh, Pa.	1892
Powers, Mala	San Francisco, Calif.	1931
Powers, Stefanie	Hollywood, Calif.	1942
Preminger, Otto	Vienna, Austria	1906
Prentiss, Paula	San Antonio, Texas	1939
Presley, Elvis	Tupelo, Miss.	1935
Preston, Robert	Newton, Mass.	1918
Previn, Andre	Berlin, Germany	1929
Price, Leontyne	Laurel, Miss.	1927
Price, Ray	Perryville, Tex.	1926
Price, Roger	Charleston, W. Va.	1920
Price, Vincent	St. Louis, Mo.	1911
Pride, Charlie	Sledge, Miss.	1938
Prima, Louis	New Orleans, La	1912
Prince, William	Nichols, N.Y.	1913
Provine, Dorothy	Deadwood, S.D.	1937
Prowse, Juliet	Bombay, India	1937
Pryor, Roger	New York, N.Y.	1903
Puckett, Gary	Hibbing. Minn.	—
Pyle, Denver	Bethune, Colo.	1920

Q

Name	Birthplace	Born
Qualen, John	Vancouver, B.C.	1899
Quayle, Anthony	Lancashire, England	1913
Quillan, Eddie	Philadelphia, Pa.	1907
Quinn, Anthony	Chihuahua, Mexico	1916

R

Name	Birthplace	Born
Raft, George	New York, N.Y.	1895
Rainer, Luise	Vienna, Austria	1912
Raines, Ella	Snoqualmie Falls, Wash.	1921
Raitt, John	Santa Ana, Calif.	1917
Ralston, Esther	Bar Harbor, Maine	1902
Ralston, Vera	Prague, Czechoslovakia	1921
Rambo, Dack	Delano, Calif.	1941
Randall, Tony	Tulsa, Okla.	1920
Rawls, Lou	Chicago, Ill.	1935
Ray, Aldo	Pen Argyl, Pa	1926
Ray, Johnnie	Dallas, Ore.	1927
Rayburn, Gene	Christopher, Ill.	1917
Raye, Martha	Butte, Mont	1916
Raymond, Gene	New York, N.Y.	1908
Reddy, Helen	Melbourne, Aust.	1942
Redford, Robert	Santa Monica, Calif.	1937
Redgrave, Lynn	London, England	1943
Redgrave, Michael	Bristol, England	1908
Redgrave, Vanessa	London, England	1937
Redman, Joyce	Co. Mayo, Ireland	1918

Name	Birthplace	Born
Reed, Donna	Denison, Iowa	1921
Reed, Robert	Highland Park, Ill.	1932
Reese, Della	Detroit, Mich	1932
Regan, Phil	Brooklyn, N.Y.	1906
Reilly, Charles Nelson	New York, N.Y.	
Reiner, Bob	Bronx, N.Y.	1946
Reiner, Carl	Bronx, N.Y.	1922
Remick, Lee	Boston, Mass	1937
Renaldo, Duncan	Camden, N.J.	1904
Resnik, Regina	New York, N.Y.	1923
Reynolds, Burt	Georgia	1935
Reynolds, Debbie	El Paso, Texas	1932
Reynolds, Joyce	San Antonio, Texas	1924
Reynolds, Marjorie	Buhl, Idaho.	1921
Reynolds, William	Los Angeles, Calif.	1931
Rhodes, Hari	Cincinnati, Ohio	1932
Rich, Buddy	New York. N.Y.	1917
Rich, Irene	Buffalo, N.Y.	1897
Richardson, Ralph	Cheltenham, England	1902
Richardson, Tony	Shipley, England	1929
Rickles, Don	New York, N.Y.	1926
Riddle, Nelson	Hackensack, N.J.	1921
Rigg, Diana	England	1938
Ritchard, Cyril	Sydney, Australia	1898
Ritter, Tex.	Murvaul, Tex.	1907
Ritz, Harry	Newark, N.J.	1908
Ritz, Jimmy	Newark, N.J.	1905
Rivers, Joan	Brooklyn, N.Y.	1935
Robards, Jason, Jr.	Chicago, Ill.	1922
Robbins, Jerome	New York, N.Y.	1918
Robertson, Cliff	La Jolla, Calif.	1925
Robertson, Dale	Oklahoma City, Okla.	1923
Robeson, Paul	Princeton, N.J.	1898
Robinson, Jay	New York, N.Y.	1930
Robson, Flora	South Shields, England	1902
Rochester(E. Anders'n)	Oakland, Calif.	1905
Rockwell, Geo. (Doc.)	Providence, R.I.	1889
Rodgers, Richard	New York, N.Y.	1902
Rodgers, Jimmie	Camas, Wash.	1933
Rogers, Chas. (Buddy)	Olathe, Kans.	1904
Rogers, Ginger	Independence, Mo.	1911
Rogers, Roy	Cincinnati, Ohio	1912
Roland, Gilbert	Juarez, Mexico	1905
Roman, Ruth	Boston, Mass.	1924
Romero, Cesar	New York, N.Y.	1907
Rooney, Mickey	Brooklyn, N.Y.	1922
Rose Marie	New York, N.Y	
Rosenbloom, Maxie	New York, N.Y.	1906
Ross, David	St. Paul, Minn.	1924
Ross, Diana	Detroit, Mich.	1944
Ross, Katharine	Hollywood, Calif.	1943
Ross, Lanny	Seattle, Wash.	1906
Ross, Shirley	Omaha, Nebr.	
Roth, Lillian	Boston, Mass.	1910
Roundtree, Richard	New Rochelle, N.Y.	1942
Rowan, Dan	Beggs, Okla.	1922
Rowlands, Gena	Cambria, Wisc.	1936
Rubin, Benny	New York, N.Y.	1899
Rubinoff, David	Grodno, Russia	1897
Rubinstein, Artur	Lodz, Poland	1889
Rudolf, Max	Frankfurt, Germany	1902
Rule, Janice	Norwood, Ohio	1931
Rush, Barbara	Denver, Colo.	1930
Russell, Jane	Bemidji, Minn.	1921
Russell, Rosalind	Waterbury, Conn.	1911
Rutherford, Ann	Toronto, Canada	1924
Rydell, Bobby	Philadelphia, Pa.	1942

S

Name	Birthplace	Born
Sahl, Mort	Montreal, Que.	1927
Saint, Eva Marie	E. Orange, N.J.	1924
Sainte-Marie, Buffy	Craven, Sask.	1941
St. James, Susan	Los Angeles, Calif.	1946
St. John, Jill	Los Angeles, Calif.	1940
Sales, Soupy	Franklinton, No. Car.	1926
Sanders, Lugene	Oklahoma City, Okla.	1934
Sands, Tommy	Chicago, Ill.	1937
Sargent, Dick	Carmel, Calif.	1933
Sarnoff, Dorothy	New York, N.Y.	1919
Sarrazin, Michael	Quebec City, Quebec	1940
Saunders, Lori	Kansas City, Mo.	1941
Savalas, Telly	Garden City, N.Y.	1924
Saxon, John	Brooklyn, N.Y.	1935
Sayao, Bidu	Rio de Janeiro, Brazil	1908
Schallert, William	Los Angeles, Calif.	1925
Schary, Dore	Newark, N.J.	1905
Schell, Maria	Vienna, Austria	1926
Schell, Maximilian	Vienna, Austria	1930

Name	Birthplace	Born
Schenkel, Chris	Bippus, Ind.	1924
Scherman, Thomas	New York, N.Y.	1917
Schippers, Thomas	Kalamazoo, Mich.	1930
Schneider, Alexander	Vilna, Poland.	1908
Schneider, Romy	Austria	1938
Schuman, William	New York, N.Y.	1910
Schwartz, Arthur	Brooklyn, N.Y.	1900
Schwarzkopf, Elisabeth	Jarotschin, Poland	1915
Schofield, Paul	Hurst, Pierpont, England	1922
Scott, George C.	Wise, Va.	1927
Scott, Gordon	Portland, Ore.	1927
Scott, Hazel	Trinidad	1920
Scott, Lizabeth	Scranton, Pa.	1923
Scott, Martha	Jamesport, Mo.	1916
Scott, Randolph	Orange Co., Va.	1903
Scourby, Alexander	New York, N.Y.	1913
Seal, Elizabeth	England	1935
Sebastian, John	New York, N.Y.	1944
Seberg, Jean	Marshalltown, Iowa	1938
Seeger, Pete	New York, N.Y.	1919
Seeley, Blossom	San Pablo, Calif.	—
Segal, George	Great Neck, L.I., N.Y.	1934
Segal, Vivienne	Philadelphia, Pa.	1897
Seidel, Toscha	Odessa, Russia	1899
Sellers, Peter	Southsea, England	1925
Serkin, Rudolf	Eger, Austria	1903
Serling, Rod	Syracuse, N.Y.	1924
Severinsen, Doc.	Arlington, Ore.	1927
Shankar, Ravi	India	1920
Sharif, Omar.	Alexandria, Egypt	1932
Shatner, William	Montreal, Canada	1931
Shaw, Artie	New York, N.Y.	1910
Shaw, Rita	So. Paris, Maine	1912
Shaw, Robert	Red Bluff, Calif.	1916
Shaw, Robert	West Houghton, Eng.	1927
Shaw, Victoria	Sydney, N.S.W.	1935
Shaw, Winfred	San Francisco, Calif.	1899
Shearer, Moira	Scotland.	1926
Shearer, Norma	Montreal, Canada	1904
Shearing, George	London, Eng.	1920
Shepherd, Jean	Chicago, Ill.	1929
Sherman, Allan	Chicago, Ill.	1924
Sherman, Bobby	Santa Monica, Calif.	1945
Sherwood, Roberta	St. Louis, Mo.	1913
Shirley, Ann	New York, N.Y.	1918
Shore, Dinah	Winchester, Tenn	1920
Sidney, Sylvia	New York, N.Y.	1910
Siepi, Cesare	Milan, Italy.	1923
Signoret, Simone	Wiesbaden, Germany	1921
Sills, Beverly	Brooklyn, N.Y.	1929
Silvers, Phil	Brooklyn, N.Y.	1912
Sim, Alastair	Edinburgh, Scotland	1900
Simmons, Jean	London, England.	1929
Simone, Nina	Tyron, N.C.	1933
Simon, Paul	New York, N.Y.	1940
Simon, Simone	Marseilles, France	1914
Sinatra, Frank	Hoboken, N.J.	1917
Sinatra, Jr., Frank	Jersey City, N.J.	1944
Sinatra, Nancy	Jersey City, N.J.	1940
Singleton, Penny	Philadelphia, Pa.	1912
Skelton, Red (Richard)	Vincennes, Ind.	1913
Skinner, Cornelia Otis	Chicago, Ill.	1903
Slezak, Walter	Vienna, Austria	1902
Slick, Grace	Chicago, Ill.	1939
Smith, Alexis	Penticton, Canada	1921
Smith, Bob	Buffalo, N.Y.	1917
Smith, Connie	Elkhart, Ind.	1941
Smith, Ethel	Pittsburgh, Pa.	1921
Smith, Kate	Greenville, Va.	1909
Smith, Keely	Norfolk, Va.	1935
Smith, Lois	Topeka, Kan.	1931
Smith, Loring	Stratford, Conn.	1900
Smith, Maggie	Ilford, Eng.	1934
Smith, Muriel	New York, N.Y.	1933
Smith, Roger	South Gate, Calif.	1934
Smothers, Dick	New York, N.Y.	1939
Smothers, Tom	New York, N.Y.	1937
Snodgress, Carrie.	Park Ridge, Ill.	1945
Snow, Hank.	Nova Scotia	1914
Somes, Michael	nr. Stroud, England	1917
Sommer, Elke	Berlin, Ger.	1941
Sorvino, Paul	Brooklyn, N.Y.	1939
Sothern, Ann.	Valley City, N. Dak	1912
Specht, Bobby	Superior, Wis.	1921
Spewack, Bella	Hungary	1899
Spivak, Lawrence	Brooklyn, N.Y.	1900
Stack, Robert	Los Angeles, Calif.	1919
Stafford, Jo.	Coalinga, Calif.	1918
Stamp, Terence	London, England.	1940
Stang, Arnold	Chelsea, Mass.	1925
Stanley, Kim	Tularosa, N.M.	1925

Name	Birthplace	Born
Stanley, Pat	Cincinnati, Ohio	1931
Stanwyck, Barbara	Brooklyn, N.Y.	1907
Stapleton, Jean	New York, N.Y.	1923
Stapleton, Maureen	Troy, N.Y.	1925
Starr, Kay	Dougherty, Okla.	1924
Starr, Ringo	Liverpool, Eng.	1940
Steber, Eleanor	Wheeling, W. Va.	1916
Steele, Bob	Pendleton, Ore	1907
Steele, Karen	Hawaii	1934
Steele, Ted	Hartford, Conn.	1917
Steele, Tommy	London, England	1937
Steiger, Rod	W. Hampton, N.Y.	1925
Steinberg, David.	Winnipeg, Canada	1942
Stellman, Maxine	Brattleboro, Vt.	1906
Sterling, Jan	New York, N.Y.	1923
Sterling, Robert	New Castle, Pa.	1917
Stern, Isaac	Kreminisey, Russia	1920
Stevens, Cat	London, Eng.	1948
Stevens, Connie	Brooklyn, N.Y.	1938
Stevens, Kaye	Pittsburgh, Pa.	1935
Stevens, Mark	Cleveland, Ohio	1902
Stevens, Onslow	Los Angeles, Calif.	1902
Stevens, Rise	New York, N.Y.	1913
Stevens, Stella	Yazoo City, Miss.	1938
Stewart, Elaine	Montclair, N.J.	1929
Stewart, James	Indiana, Pa.	1908
Stewart, Rod	London, Eng.	1944
Stickney, Dorothy	Dickinson, N. Dak.	1903
Stockwell, Dean	Hollywood, Calif.	—
Stokowski, Leopold	London, England.	1887
Stone, Carol	New York, N.Y.	1916
Stone, Dorothy	Bensonhurst, N.Y.	1905
Stone, Ezra	New Bedford, Mass.	1917
Stone, Harvey	Detroit, Mich.	1911
Stone, Milburn	Burrton, Kans.	1904
Stone, Paula	New York, N.Y.	1916
Storch, Larry	New York, N.Y.	1925
Storm, Gale	Bloomington, Tex.	1922
Storrs, Suzanne	Salt Lake City, Utah	1934
Straight, Beatrice	Old Westbury, N.Y.	1918
Strasberg, Susan	New York, N.Y.	1938
Strauss, Robert	New York, N.Y.	1913
Streisand, Barbra	Brooklyn, N.Y.	1942
Stritch, Elaine	Detroit, Mich.	1925
Strode, Woody	Los Angeles, Calif.	1914
Struthers, Sally	Portland, Ore.	1948
Stuart, Gloria	Santa Monica, Calif.	1911
Sullivan, Barry	New York, N.Y.	1912
Sullivan, Ed.	New York, N.Y.	1902
Sumac, Yma	Ichocan, Peru	1928
Susskind, David	New York, N.Y.	1920
Sutherland, Donald	New Brunswick, Canada	1934
Sutherland, Joan	Sydney, Australia	1926
Sutton, Frank	Clarksville, Tenn.	1923
Suzuki, Pat	Cressey, Calif.	1931
Swanson, Gloria	Chicago, Ill.	1899
Swayze, John Cameron	Wichita, Kan.	1906
Sweet, Blanche	Chicago, Ill.	1896
Swenson, Inga	Omaha, Nebr.	1934

T

Name	Birthplace	Born
Talbot, Lyle.	Pittsburgh, Pa.	1902
Talbot, Nita	New York, N.Y.	1930
Tallchief, Maria	Fairfax, Okla.	1925
Talmadge, Constance.	Brooklyn, N.Y.	1900
Tamblyn, Russ	Los Angeles, Calif.	1935
Tandy, Jessica	London, England.	1909
Taylor, Billy	Greenville, N.C.	1921
Taylor, Elizabeth	London, England.	1932
Taylor, James	Boston, Mass.	1948
Taylor, Kent	Nashua, Iowa	1907
Taylor, Rod.	Sydney, Australia	1930
Tebaldi, Renata	Pesaro, Italy	1922
Temple, Shirley	Santa Monica, Calif.	1928
Terris, Norma	Columbus, Kans.	1904
Terry-Thomas	London, Eng.	1911
Teyte, Maggie	Wolverhampton, Eng.	1889
Thaxter, Phillis	Portland, Me.	1921
Thebom, Blanche	Monessen, Pa.	1919
Thibault, Conrad	Northbridge, Mass.	1898
Thinnes, Roy	Chicago, Ill.	1938
Thomas, B.J.	Houston, Tex.	1942
Thomas, Danny	Deerfield, Mich.	1914
Thomas, Lowell	Woodrington, Ohio	1892
Thomas, Marlo	Detroit, Mich.	1938
Thomas, Richard	New York, N.Y.	1951
Thompson, Marshall	Peoria, Ill.	1926
Thorndike, Sybil	Gainsborough, Eng.	1882
Thulin, Ingrid	Sweden.	1929
Tierney, Gene	Brooklyn, N.Y.	1920
Tierney, Lawrence	Brooklyn, N.Y.	1919

Name	Birthplace	Born
Tiffin, Pamela	Oklahoma City, Okla.	1942
Tillstrom, Burr	Chicago, Ill.	1917
Tiny Tim	New York, N.Y.	—
Tobias, George	New York, N.Y.	—
Todd, Richard	Dublin, Ireland	1919
Toomey, Regis	Pittsburgh, Pa.	1902
Tomkins, Angel	Albany, Calif.	1943
Tomlin, Lili	Detroit, Mich.	1940
Tomlinson, David	Scotland	1917
Torme, Mel	Chicago, Ill.	1925
Torn, Rip	Temple, Tex.	1931
Totter, Audrey	Joliet, Ill.	1923
Tracy, Arthur	Philadelphia, Pa.	1903
Travers, Mary	Louisville, Ky.	1936
Treacher, Arthur	Brighton, England	1894
Trevor, Claire	New York, N.Y.	1909
Truffaut, Francois	Paris, France	1932
Tryon, Tom	Hartford, Conn.	1926
Tucker, Forrest	Plainfield, Ind.	1919
Tucker, Orrin	St. Louis, Mo.	1911
Tucker, Richard	Brooklyn, N.Y.	1915
Tucker, Tommy	Souris, N.D.	1907
Turner, Lana	Wallace, Idaho	1921
Tushingham, Rita	Liverpool, Eng.	1942
Twiggy (Leslie Hornby)	London, Eng.	1949
Tyrrell, Susan	New Canaan, Conn.	1946

U

Name	Birthplace	Born
Uggams, Leslie	New York City	1943
Umeki, Miyoshi	Hokkaido, Japan	1929
Ure, Mary	Glasgow, Scotland	1933
Ustinov, Peter	London, England	1921

V

Name	Birthplace	Born
Vaccaro, Brenda	Brooklyn, N.Y.	1939
Vale, Jerry	New York, N.Y.	1931
Valentine, Karen	Santa Rosa, California	1947
Vallee, Rudy	Island Pond, Vt.	1901
Valli, Alida	Pola, Italy	1921
Vance, Vivian	Cherryvale, Kans.	1912
Van Cleef, Lee	Somerville, N.J.	1925
Van Doren, Mamie	Rowena, S.D.	1933
Van Dyke, Dick	West Plains, Mo.	1925
Van Dyke, Jerry	Danville, Ill.	1932
Van Fleet, Jo	Oakland, Calif.	1922
Vandervere, Trish	Tenafly, N.J.	1945
Varnay, Astrid	Stockholm, Sweden	1918
Varsi, Diane	San Francisco, Calif.	1938
Vaughn, Robert	New York, N.Y.	1932
Vaughn, Sarah	Newark, N.J.	1924
Venuta, Benay	San Francisco, Calif.	1911
Vera-Ellen	Cincinnati, Ohio	1926
Verdon, Gwen	Los Angeles, Calif.	1926
Vernon, Jackie	New York, N.Y.	1929
Vidor, King Louis	Galveston, Tex.	1895
Vinson, Helen	Beaumont, Tex.	1907
Vinton, Bobby	Canonsburg, Pa.	1935
Vogel, Mitch.	Alhambra, Calif.	1956
Voight, Jon	Yonkers, N.Y.	1938
Von Furstenberg, Betsy	Westphalia, Germany	1931
Von Sydow, Max	Lund, Sweden	1929
Von Zell, Harry R.	Indianapolis, Ind.	1906
Voorhees, Donald	Allentown, Pa.	1903

W

Name	Birthplace	Born
Waggoner, Lyle	Kansas City, Kansas	1935
Wagner, Robert	Detroit, Mich.	1930
Wain, Bea	Bronx, N.Y.	1917
Waite, Ralph	White Plains, N.Y.	1928
Walker, Clint	Hartford, Ill.	1927
Walker, Nancy	Philadelphia, Pa.	1922
Walker, Robert, Jr.	Long Island	1941
Wallace, Mike	Brookline, Mass.	1918
Wallach, Eli	Brooklyn, N.Y.	1915
Wallenstein, Alfred	Chicago, Ill.	1898
Wallis, Hal.	Chicago, Ill.	1899
Walston, Ray	New Orleans, La.	1918
Walters, Barbara	Boston, Mass.	1931
Ward, Burt	Los Angeles, Calif.	1946
Warden, Jack	Newark, N.J.	1920
Warfield, William	Helena, Ark.	1920
Warhol, Andy	Cleveland, Ohio	1931
Waring, Fred	Tyrone, Pa.	1900
Warner, David	Manchester, Eng.	1941
Warwicke, Dionne	E. Orange, N.J.	1941
Waters, Ethel	Chester, Pa.	1900
Watson, Debbie	Culver City, Calif.	1940
Watts, Andre	Germany	1946
Wayne, David	Traverse City, Mich.	1914
Wayne, John	Winterset, Iowa	1907
Weaver, Charley (Cliff Arquette)	Toledo, Ohio	1905

Name	Birthplace	Born
Weaver, Dennis	Joplin, Mo.	1924
Weaver, Fritz	Pittsburgh, Pa.	1926
Webb, Alan	York, England	1906
Webb, Jack	Santa Monica, Calif.	1920
Webb, Jimmy	Elk City, Okla	1946
Weissmuller, Johnny	Windber, Pa.	1904
Welch, Raquel	La Jolla, Calif.	1942
Weld, Tuesday	New York, N.Y.	1943
Welk, Lawrence	nr. Strasburg, N. Dak.	1903
Welles, Orson	Kenosha, Wis.	1915
Wells, Kitty	Nashville, Tenn.	1919
Werner, Oskar	Vienna, Austria	1922
West, Adam	Walla Walla, Wash.	1929
West, Mae	Brooklyn, N.Y.	1892
Westman, Nydia	New York City	1907
Whitaker, Johnny	Van Nuys, Calif.	1959
White, Jesse	Buffalo, N.Y.	1919
Whiting, Margaret	Detroit, Mich.	1924
Whitman, Stuart	San Francisco, Calif.	1926
Whitmore, James	White Plains, N.Y.	1921
Widmark, Richard	Sunrise, Minn.	1914
Wilcoxon, Henry	British West Indies	1905
Wilde, Cornel	New York, N.Y.	1918
Wilder, Billy	Vienna, Austria	1906
Wilder, Gene	Milwaukee, Wisc.	1934
Wilding, Michael	Essex, England	1912
Williams, Andy	Wall Lake, Iowa	1930
Williams, Barry	Santa Monica, Calif.	1954
Williams, Clarence	New York, N.Y.	1946
Williams, Emlyn	Mostyn, Wales	1905
Williams, Esther	Los Angeles, Calif.	1923
Williams, Joe	Cordele, Ga.	1918
Williams, Mason	Abilene, Tex.	1938
Williams, Roger	Omaha, Nebr.	1926
Williamson, Fred	Gary, Indiana	1937
Williamson, Nicol	Hamilton, Scotland	1936
Wills, Chill	Seagoville, Tex.	1903
Willson, Meredith	Mason City, Iowa	1902
Wilson, Demond	Valdosta, Ga.	
Wilson, Dolores	Philadelphia, Pa.	1929
Wilson, Don	Lincoln, Nebr.	1900
Wilson, Flip	Jersey City, N.J.	1933
Wilson, Julie	Omaha, Nebr.	1924
Wilson, Nancy	Chillicothe, Ohio	1937
Winchell, Paul	New York, N.Y.	1922
Windom, William	New York, N.Y.	1923
Winters, Jonathan	Dayton, Ohio	1925
Winters, Shelley	St. Louis, Mo.	1922
Winwood, Estelle	Lee, England	1884
Wiseman, Joseph	Montreal, Canada	1918
Withers, Jane	Atlanta, Ga.	1927
Wood, Helen	Clarksville, Tenn.	1937
Wood, Natalie	San Francisco, Calif.	1938
Wood, Peggy	Brooklyn, N.Y.	1892
Woodward, Joanne	Thomasville, Ga.	1930
Wonder, Stevie	Detroit, Mich.	1951
Worley, Jo Anne	Lowell, Ind.	1937
Wray, Fay	Alberta, Canada	1907
Wright, Martha	Seattle, Wash.	1926
Wright, Teresa	New York, N.Y.	1919
Wrightson, Earl	Baltimore, Md.	1916
Wyatt, Jane	Campgaw, N.J.	1912
Wyler, William	Mulhouse, France	1902
Wyman, Jane	St. Joseph, Mo.	1914
Wynette, Tammy	Tupelo, Miss.	1942
Wynn, Keenan	New York, N.Y.	1916
Wynter, Dana	London	1930

Y

Name	Birthplace	Born
Yarborough, Glenn	Milwaukee, Wisc.	1930
Yarrow, Peter	New York, N.Y.	1938
York, Dick	Ft. Wayne, Ind.	1928
York, Michael	Fulmer, England	1942
York, Susannah	London, England	1942
Young, Alan	Northumberl'd, Eng.	1919
Young, Gig	St. Cloud, Minn.	1917
Young, Loretta	Salt Lake City, Utah	1913
Young, Robert	Chicago, Ill.	1907
Young, Stephen	Toronto, Canada	1939
Youngman, Henny	Liverpool, England	1906
Yurka, Blanche	St. Paul, Minn.	1887

Z

Name	Birthplace	Born
Zanuck, Darryl F.	Wahoo, Nebr.	1902
Zimbalist, Efrem	Rostov, Russia	1889
Zimbalist, Efrem, Jr.	New York, N.Y.	1923
Zimmer, Norma	Larsen, Idaho	—
Zorina, Vera	Berlin, Germany	1917
Zukor, Adolph	Ricse, Hungary	1873

Widely Known Americans of the Present

Statesmen, Authors, Military Men and Other Prominent Persons Not Listed in Other Categories.

Name Birthplace	Birthdate	Name Birthplace	Birthdate
Abernathy, Ralph (Linden, Ala.)	3/11/26	Drury, Allan (Houston, Texas)	9/ 2/18
Abrams, Creighton (Springfield, Mass.)	9/15/14	Dubinsky, David (Brest-Litovsk, Poland)	2/22/92
Abzug, Bella (New York, N.Y.)	7/24/20	Durocher, Leo (West Springfield, Mass.)	7/27/06
Agnew, Spiro (Baltimore, Md.)	11/ 9/18		
Albee, Edward (Washington, D.C.)	3/12/28	Eagleton, Thomas (St. Louis, Mo.)	9/ 4/29
Albert, Carl (McAlester, Okla.)	5/10/08	Ehrlichman, John (Tacoma, Wash.)	3/20/25
Aldrin, Edwin E. (Buzz) (Glen Ridge, N.J.)	1/20/30	Eisenhower, Mamie (Boone, Iowa)	11/14/96
Ali, Muhammad (Louisville, Ky.)	1/18/42	Eisenhower, Milton, S. (Abilene, Kans.)	9/15/99
Alioto, Joseph (San Francisco, Calif.)	2/12/16	Ervin, Sam (Morganton, N.C.)	9/27/96
Alsop, Joseph W., Jr. (Avon, Conn.)	10/11/10	Evers, Charles (Decatur, Miss.)	9/11/22
Alsop, Stewart (Avon, Conn.)	5/17/14		
Alston, Walter (Butler Co., Ohio)	12/ 1/11		
Anderson, Jack (Long Beach, Calif.)	10/19/22	Farley, James A. (Grassy Point, N.Y.)	5/30/88
Arcaro, Eddie (Cincinnati, Ohio)	2/19/16	Farmer, James (Marshall, Texas)	1/12/20
Armstrong, Neil (Wapakoneta, Ohio)	8/ 5/30	Finch, Robert (Tempe, Ariz.)	10/ 9/25
Ashe, Arthur (Richmond, Va.)	7/10/43	Fischer, Bobby (Chicago, Ill.)	3/ 9/43
Askew, Reubin (Muskogee, Okla.)	9/11/28	Fong, Hiram (Honolulu, Hawaii)	10/ 1/07
		Ford, Gerald R. (Omaha, Nebr.)	7/14/13
		Friedman, Milton (Brooklyn, N.Y.)	7/31/12
Bailey, F. Lee (Waltham, Mass.)	1933	Fulbright, J. William (Sumner, Mo.)	4/ 9/05
Baker, Howard (Huntsville, Tenn.)	11/15/25		
Baker, Russell (Loudoun Co., Va.)	8/14/25		
Baldwin, Faith (New Rochelle, N.Y.)	10/ 1/93	Galbraith, John Kenneth (Ontario, Can.,)	10/15/08
Baldwin, James (New York, N.Y.)	8/ 2/24	Gardner, John (Los Angeles, Calif.)	10/ 8/12
Ball, George (Des Moines, Iowa)	12/21/09	Gavin, James (New York, N.Y.)	3/22/07
Barth, John (Cambridge, Md.)	5/27/30	Getty, J. Paul (Minneapolis, Minn.)	12/15/92
Bayh, Birch (Terre Haute, Ind.)	1/22/28	Glenn, John (Cambridge, Ohio)	7/18/21
Beame, Abraham (London, Eng.)	3/20/06	Goldberg, Arthur J. (Chicago, Ill.)	8/ 8/08
Belli, Melvin (Sonora, Calif.)	7/29/07	Goldwater, Barry M. (Phoenix, Ariz.)	1/ 1/09
Bellow, Saul (Quebec, Canada)	7/10/15	Graham, Billy (Charlotte, N.C.)	11/ 7/18
Benton, Thomas Hart (Neosho, Mo.)	4/15/89	Grange, Red (Forksville, Pa.)	6/13/04
Bishop, Jim (Jersey City, N.J.)	11/21/07	Gravel, Mike (Springfield, Mass.)	5/13/30
Blackmun, Harry (Nashville, Ill.)	11/12/08	Griffin, Robert P. (Traverse City, Mich.)	11/ 6/23
Bliss, Ray C. (Akron, Ohio)	12/16/07	Gurney, Edward (Portland, Maine)	1/12/14
Bok, Derek (Ardmore, Pa.)	3/22/30		
Bond, Julian (Nashville, Tenn.)	1/14/40	Haig, Alexander (Philadelphia, Pa.)	12/ 2/24
Borman, Frank (Gary, Ind.)	3/14/28	Harriman, W. Averell (New York, N.Y.)	11/15/91
Bowles, Chester (Springfield, Mass.)	4/ 5/01	Hart, Philip A. (Bryn Mawr, Pa.)	12/10/12
Bradley, Omar N. (Clark, Mo.)	2/12/93	Hatfield, Mark O. (Dallas, Ore.)	7/12/22
Bradley, Thomas (Calvert, Tex.)	12/29/17	Hayakawa, S. I. (Vancouver, B.C.)	7/18/06
Braun, Wernher von (Wirsitz, Germany)	3/23/12	Heller, Walter (Buffalo, N.Y.)	8/27/15
Brennan, William J. (Newark, N.J.)	4/25/06	Helms, Richard (St. Davids, Pa.)	3/30/13
Breslin, Jimmy (Jamaica, L.I., N.Y.)	10/17/30	Hickel, Walter (Ellinwood, Kansas)	8/18/19
Brewster, Kingman (Longmeadow, Mass.)	6/17/19	Hogan, Ben (Dublin, Tex.)	8/13/12
Brinkley, David (Wilmington, N.C.)	7/10/20	Hughes, Harold (Ida Grove, Iowa)	2/10/22
Brooke, Edward (Washington, D.C.)	10/26/19	Hughes, Howard (Houston, Tex.)	12/24/05
Buchanan, Patrick (Washington, D.C.)	11/ 2/38	Humphrey, Hubert (Wallace, S.D.)	5/27/11
Buchwald, Art (Mt. Vernon, N.Y.)	10/20/25		
Buckley, James (New York, N.Y.)	3/ 9/23	Inouye, Daniel (Honolulu, Hawaii)	9/ 7/24
Buckley, William F. (New York! N.Y.)	11/24/25		
Burns, Arthur F. (Stanislau, Aust.)	4/27/04	Jackson, Henry (Everett, Wash.)	5/31/12
Bundy, McGeorge (Boston, Mass.)	3/30/19	Javits, Jacob K. (New York, N.Y.)	5/18/04
Burger, Warren (St. Paul, Minn.)	9/17/07	Johnson, Luci Baines (Mrs. Patrick Nugent)	7/ 2/47
Bush, George (Milton, Mass.)	6/12/24	Johnson, Lynda Bird (Mrs. Charles Robb)	3/19/44
Butz, Earl (Albion, Ind.)	7/ 3/09	Johnson, Mrs. Lyndon B. (Karnack, Tex.)	12/22/12
Byrd, Robert (N. Wilkesboro, N.C.)	1/15/18	Jones, James (Robinson, Ill.)	11/ 6/21
Caldwell, Erskine (Coweta Co., Ga.)	12/17/03		
Capote, Truman (New Orleans, La.)	9/30/24	Kelley, Clarence M. (Kansas City, Mo.)	10/24/11
Case, Clifford (Franklin Park, N.J.)	4/16/04	Kennedy, Edward M. (Brookline, Mass.)	2/22/32
Casper, Billy (San Diego, Calif.)	6/24/31	Kennedy, Rose (Mrs. Joseph P.) (Boston)	1890
Celler, Emmanuel (Brooklyn, N.Y.)	5/ 6/88	Kerr, Walter (Evanston, Ill.)	7/ 8/13
Chamberlain, Wilt (Philadelphia, Pa.)	8/21/36	Kheel, Theodore (New York, N.Y.)	5/ 9/14
Chancellor, John (Chicago, Ill.)	7/14/27	Kissinger, Henry (Fuerth, Germany)	5/27/23
Chavez, Cesar (Yuma, Arizona)	3/31/27	Klein, Herbert (Los Angeles, Calif.)	4/ 1/28
Chisholm, Shirley (Brooklyn, N.Y.)	11/30/24	Kleindienst, Richard (Winslow, Ariz.)	8/ 5/23
Church, Frank (Boise, Idaho)	7/25/24	Koufax, Sandy (Brooklyn, N.Y.)	12/30/35
Clark, Ramsey (Dallas, Texas)	12/18/27	Kuhn, Bowie (Tacoma Park, Mo.)	10/28/26
Clay, Lucius D. (Marietta, Ga.)	4/23/97		
Conant, James B. (Dorchester, Mass.)	3/26/93	Laird, Melvin (Omaha, Nebr.)	9/ 1/22
Connally, John B. (Floresville, Tex.)	2/28/17	Landon, Alfred (West Middlesex, Pa.)	9/ 9/87
Considine, Bob (Washington, D.C.)	11/ 4/06	Lemnitzer, Lyman L. (Honesdale, Pa.)	8/29/99
Cooke, Terence (New York, N.Y.)	3/ 1/21	Lindbergh, Ann Morrow (Englewood, N.J.)	1906
Cooper, John Sherman (Somerset, Ky.)	8/23/01	Lindbergh, Charles A. (Detroit, Mich.)	2/ 4/02
Cousins, Norman (Union Hill, N.J.)	6/24/12	Lindsay, John V. (New York, N.Y.)	11/24/21
Cox, Archibald (Plainfield, N.J.)	5/17/12	Lippmann, Walter (New York, N.Y.)	9/23/89
Cranston, Alan (Palo Alto, Calif.)	6/19/14	Lodge, Henry Cabot (Nahant, Mass.)	7/ 5/02
Cronkite, Walter (St. Joseph, Mo.)	11/ 4/16	Long, Russell B. (Shreveport, La.)	11/ 3/18
		Louis, Joe (Lafayette, Ala.)	5/13/14
Daley, Richard (Chicago, Ill.)	5/15/02	Lowell, Robert (Boston, Mass.)	3/ 1/17
Davis, Angela (Birmingham, Ala.)	1/26/44	Lowenstein, Allard (Newark, N.J.)	1/16/29
Dempsey, Jack (Manassa, Colo.)	6/24/95	Luce, Clare Boothe (New York, N.Y.)	4/10/03
DiMaggio, Joe (Martinez, Calif.)	11/25/14		
Dole, Robert (Russell, Kans.)	7/22/23	MacGregor, Clark (Minneapolis, Minn.)	7/12/22
Doolittle, James H. (Alameda, Calif.)	12/14/96	MacLeish, Archibald (Glencoe, Ill.)	5/ 7/92
Douglas, William O. (Maine, Minn.)	10/16/98	Maddox, Lester (Atlanta, Ga.)	9/30/15

Name	Birthplace	Birthdate	Name	Birthplace	Birthdate
Mailer, Norman (Long Branch, N.J.)		1/31/23	Salinger, J. D. (New York, N.Y.)		1/ 1/19
Mansfield, Mike (New York, N.Y.)		3/16/03	Salinger, Pierre (San Francisco, Calif.)		6/14/25
Mantle, Mickey (Spavinaw, Okla.)		10/20/31	Salk, Jonas (New York, N.Y.)		10/28/14
Marchi, John (Staten Island, N.Y.)		5/20/21	Samuelson, Paul A. (Gary, Ind.)		5/15/15
Marshall, Thurgood (Baltimore, Md.)		7/ 2/08	Scali, John (Canton, Ohio)		4/27/18
Massell, Sam (Atlanta, Ga.)		8/26/27	Schlesinger, Arthur Jr. (Columbus, Ohio)		10/15/17
Mays, Willie (Fairfield, Ala.)		5/ 6/31	Schlesinger, James (New York, N.Y.)		2/15/29
McCarthy, Eugene (Watkins, Minn.)		3/29/16	Scott, Hugh (Fredericksburg, Va.)		11/11/00
McCormack, John W. (Boston, Mass.)		12/21/91	Scranton, William, W. (Madison, Conn.)		7/19/17
McGinley, Phyllis (Ontario, Ore.)		3/21/05	Seaborg, Glenn T. (Ishpeming, Mich.)		4/19/12
McClellan, John J. (Sheridan, Ark.)		2/25/96	Sevareid, Eric (Velva, N.D.)		11/26/12
McCloskey, Paul (San Bernardino, Calif.)		9/29/27	Sheen, Fulton J. (El Paso, Ill.)		5/ 8/95
McGovern, George (Avon, S.D.)		7/19/22	Shirer, William L. (Chicago, Ill.)		2/23/04
McNamara, Robert S. (San Francisco)		6/ 9/16	Shoemaker, Willie (Fabens, Texas)		8/19/31
Meany, George (New York, N.Y.)		8/16/94	Shor, Toots (Philadelphia, Pa.)		5/ 6/05
Menotti, Gian-Carlo (Cadegliano, Italy)		7/ 7/11	Shriver, Sargent (Westminster, Md.)		11/ 9/15
Michener, James A. (New York, N.Y.)		2/ 3/07	Shultz, George (New York, N.Y.)		12/13/20
Miller, Arthur (New York, N.Y.)		10/17/15	Smith, H. Allen (McLeansboro, Ill.)		12/19/06
Mills, Wilbur (Kensett, Ark.)		5/24/09	Smith, Howard K. (Ferriday, La.)		5/12/14
Mitchell, John (Detroit, Mich.)		9/15/13	Smith, Margaret Chase (Skowhegan, Me.)		12/14/97
Morse, Wayne (Madison, Wis.)		10/20/00	Sorenson, Theodore (Lincoln, Neb.)		5/ 8/28
Morton, Rogers (Lousville, Ky.)		9/19/14	Spillane, Mickey (Brooklyn, N.Y.)		3/ 9/18
Morton, Thruston (Louisville, Ky.)		8/19/07	Spock, Benjamin (New Haven, Conn.)		5/ 2/03
Moses, Robert (New Haven, Conn.)		12/18/88	Stassen, Harold (West St. Paul, Minn.)		4/13/07
Moynihan, Daniel P. (Tulsa, Okla.)		3/16/27	Steinem, Gloria (Toledo, Ohio)		3/25/36
Musial, Stan (Donora, Pa.)		11/21/20	Stengel, Casey (Kansas City, Mo.)		7/30/91
Muskie, Edmund (Rumford, Maine)		3/28/14	Stewart, Potter (Jackson, Mich.)		1/23/15
			Stokes, Carl (Cleveland, Ohio)		6/21/27
Nader, Ralph (Winsted, Conn.)		2/27/34	Stone, Irving (San Francisco, Calif.)		7/14/03
Nicklaus, Jack (Columbus, Ohio)		1/21/40	Symington, Stuart (Amherst, Mass.)		6/26/01
Nixon, Julie (Mrs. David Eisenhower)					
(Wilmington, D.C.)		7/ 5/48	Taft, Robert, Jr. (Cincinnati, Ohio)		2/26/17
Nixon, Mrs. Richard (Ely, Nevada)		3/16/12	Talmadge, Herman (Lovejoy, Ga.)		8/ 9/13
Nixon, Richard (Yorba Linda, Calif.)		1/ 9/13	Taylor, Maxwell D. (Keytesville, Mo.)		8/26/01
Nixon, Tricia (Mrs. Edward Cox) (Calif.)		2/21/46	Thomas, Lowell (Woodington, Ohio)		4/ 6/92
Nizer, Louis (London, England)		2/ 6/02	Thurmond, J. Strom (Edgefield, S.C.)		12/ 5/02
			Tower, John (Houston, Texas)		9/29/25
Oates, Joyce Carol (Lockport, N.Y.)		6/16/38	Truman, Mrs. Harry (Independence, Mo.)		2/13/85
O'Brien, Lawrence F. (Springfield, Mass.)		7/ 7/17	Truman, Margaret (Mrs. Clifton Daniel)		
Onassis, Jacqueline (Southampton, N.Y.)		7/28/29	(Independence, Mo.)		2/17/24
			Tuchman, Barbara (New York, N.Y.)		1/30/12
Paley, William S. (Chicago, Ill.)		9/28/01	Tunney, Gene (New York, N.Y.)		5/25/98
Palmer, Arnold (Youngstown, Pa.)		9/10/29	Tunney, John V. (New York, N.Y.)		6/26/34
Pauling, Linus (Portland, Ore.)		2/28/01			
Patterson, Floyd (Waco, N. Car.)		1/ 4/35	Unitas, John (Pittsburgh, Pa.)		5/ 7/33
Peale, Norman Vincent (Bowersville, Ohio)		5/31/98			
Percy, Charles H. (Pensacola, Fla.)		9/27/19	Vanderbilt, Alfred G. (London, England)		9/22/12
Perelman, S. J. (Brooklyn, N.Y.)		2/ 1/04	Van Buren, Abigail (Sioux City, Iowa)		7/ 4/18
Porter, Katherine Ann (Indian Creek, Tex.)		5/15/94	Veeck, Bill (Chicago, Ill.)		2/ 9/14
Powell, Lewis F. (Suffolk, Va.)		9/19/07	Vidal, Gore (West Point, N.Y.)		10/ 3/25
Proxmire, William (Lake Forest, Ill.)		1/11/15	Volpe, John (Wakefield, Mass.)		12/ 8/08
			Vonnegut, Kurt, Jr. (Indianapolis, Ind.)		11/11/22
Rand, Ayn (St. Petersburg, Russia)		1905			
Randolph, A. Philip (Crescent City, Fla.)		4/15/89	Wagner, Robert F. (New York, N.Y.)		4/20/10
Reagan, Ronald (Tampico, Ill.)		2/ 6/11	Walcott, Jersey Joe (Merchantville, N.J.)		1/31/14
Reasoner, Harry (Dakota City, Iowa)		4/17/23	Wallace, George (Clio, Ala.)		8/25/19
Rehnquist, William (Milwaukee, Wisc.)		10/ 1/24	Warren, Earl (Los Angeles, Calif.)		3/19/91
Reston, James (Clydebank, Scotland)		11/ 3/09	Warren, Robert Penn (Guthrie, Ky)		4/24/05
Ribicoff, Abe (New Britain, Conn.)		4/ 9/10	Weicker, Lowell (Paris, France)		5/16/31
Richardson, Elliot L. (Boston, Mass.)		7/20/21	Weinberger, Casper (San Francisco, Calif.)		8/18/17
Rickover, Hyman (Makowa, Poland)		1/27/00	Westmoreland, William (Spartanburg, S.C.)		3/26/14
Robertson, Oscar (Charlotte, Tenn.)		11/24/38	White, Byron R. (Ft. Collins, Colo.)		6/ 8/17
Rockefeller, David (New York, N.Y.)		6/12/15	White, Paul Dudley (Roxbury, Mass.)		6/ 6/86
Rockefeller, John D. 3rd (New York, N.Y.)		3/21/06	White, Theodore (Boston, Mass.)		5/ 6/15
Rockefeller, Laurance S. (New York, N.Y.)		5/26/10	Wicker, Tom (Hamlet, N.C.)		6/18/26
Rockefeller, Nelson A. (Bar Harbor, Me.)		7/ 8/08	Wilder, Thornton (Madison, Wisc.)		4/17/97
Rockwell, Norman (New York, N.Y.)		2/ 3/94	Wilkins, Roy (St. Louis, Mo.)		8/30/01
Rogers, William P. (Norfolk, N.Y.)		6/23/13	Williams, Ted (San Diego, Calif.)		8/30/18
Romney, George W. (Chihuahua, Mexico)		7/ 8/07	Williams, Tennessee (Columbus, Miss.)		3/26/14
Roosevelt, Elliot (New York, N.Y.)		9/23/10	Woodcock, Leonard (Providence, R.I.)		2/15/11
Roosevelt, Franklin D., Jr. (Canada)		8/17/14	Wouk, Herman (New York, N.Y.)		5/27/15
Roth, Philip (Newark, N.J.)		3/19/33			
Rozelle, Pete (South Gate, Calif.)		3/ 1/26	Yorty, Sam (Lincoln, Neb.)		10/ 1/09
Ruckelshaus, William (Indianapolis, Ind.)		7/24/32			
Rusk, Dean (Cherokee Co., Ga.)		2/ 9/09	Ziegler, Ronald (Covington, Ky.)		5/12/39
Ryun, Jim (Wichita, Kansas)		4/29/47			

Government Publications and How to Get Them

The United States Government, through the Government Printing Office issues a vast number of pamphlets, books and reports of studies and research conducted by departments and agencies. It has 391 periodicals or subscription services with more than 1,600,000 subscribers. It sells about 78,000,000 publications annually and distributes many more to libraries and offices. Receipts are more than $22,000,000 and more than $9,000,000 is turned over annually to the U.S. Treasury.

Catalogues and price lists are available to the public. Pamphlets dealing with every conceivable subject related to human living—the farm, the home, child care, education, business, fiscal matters—are published regularly. A list of selected publications, issued biweekly, can be had free on request. In addition to free price lists, the Monthly Catalogue of Publications is sold by subscription, $7, foreign $8.75. Address the Supt. of Documents, Government Printing Office, Washington, D.C. 20402.

Notable American Quotations

Wm. Penn—Truth often suffers more by the heat of its defenders, than from the arguments of its opposers. (Fruits of Solitude, 1693)

Benjamin Franklin— Remember that time is money. (1748)

They that can give up essential liberty to obtain a little temporary safety deserve neither liberty nor safety. (1759)

There never was a good war or a bad peace. (Sept. 11, 1773)

We must all hang together, or assuredly we shall all hang separately. (July 4, 1776)

Patrick Henry—Caesar had his Brutus; Charles the First his Cromwell; and George the Third ["Treason!" shouted a listener] may profit by their example. If this be treason make the most of it. (May 29, 1765)

I know not what course others may take, but as for me, give me liberty or give me death. (March 23, 1775)

John Parker— Stand your ground. Don't fire unless fired upon; but if they mean to have a war, let it begin here. (Lexington Green, Apr. 19, 1775)

Wm. Prescott— Don't fire until you see the whites of their eyes. (June 17, 1775)

Nathan Hale— I only regret that I have but one life to lose for my country. (At his execution, Sept. 22, 1776)

Thomas Paine—There are the times that try men's souls. The summer soldier and the sunshine patriot will, in this crisis shrink from the service of his country . . . (Dec. 23, 1776)

John Paul Jones— I have not yet begun to fight. (When asked to surrender, Sept. 23, 1779)

John Adams—A government of laws, not of men. (Original draft of Mass. Constitution, 1779)

Thomas Jefferson— Indeed, I tremble for my country when I reflect that God is just. (Notes on the State of Virginia, 1781-85)

Geo. Washington— It is our true policy to steer clear of permanent alliances with any portion of the foreign world. (Farewell Adress, Sept. 17, 1796)

Oliver Hazard Perry—We have met the enemy, and they are ours. (Sept. 10, 1813)

Daniel Webster—Liberty and Union, now and forever, one and inseparable. (Jan. 26, 1830)

Wm. Learned Marcy—They see nothing wrong in the rule that to the victor belong the spoils of the enemy. (Senate speech, January, 1832)

Col. Sidney Sherman— Remember the Alamo! (Apr. 21, 1836)

Ralph Waldo Emerson—A foolish consistency is the hobgoblin of little minds . . . (Essays, 1841)

Henry David Thoreau—Any man more right than his neighbors constitutes a majority of one. (Civil Disobedience, 1849)

If a man does not keep pace with this companions, perhaps it is because he hears a different drummer. (Walden, 1854)

The mass of men lead lives of quiet desperation. (Walden, 1854)

Henry Clay—Sir, I would rather be right than be President. (Senate speech, 1850)

John Babsone Lane Soule—Go west, young man! (1851)

Abraham Lincoln—As I would not be a slave, so I would not be a master. This expresses my idea of democracy. (Aug. 1, 1858?)

Accustomed to trample on the rights of others, you have lost the genius of your own independence and become the fit subjects of the first cunning tyrannt who rises among you. (Sept. 11, 1858)

It is true that you may fool all of the people some of the time; you can even fool some of the people all the time; but you can't fool all of the people all the time. (Date unknown)

David Glasgow Farragut—Damn the torpedoes! Captain Drayton, go ahead! Jouett, full speed! (Aug. 5, 1864)

Ulysses S. Grant— I propose to fight it out on this line if it takes all summer. (May 11, 1864)

Wm. Tecumseh Sherman— I am sick and tired of war. Its glory is all moonshine. It is only those who have neither fired a shot nor heard the shrieks and groans of the wounded who cry aloud for blood, more vengeance, more desolation. War is hell. (June 19, 1879)

Wm. H. Vanderbilt—The public be damned. (About 1883)

Adm. George Dewey—You may fire when you are ready, Gridley. (May 1, 1898)

Carl Schurz—Our country, right or wrong. When right to be kept right; when wrong, to be put right. (Oct. 17, 1899)

Henry Watterson—Things have come to a helluva pass when a man can't cudgel his own jackass. (On being rebuked for criticizing a government official; date unknown)

Justice Oliver Wendell Holmes, Jr.—Taxes are what we pay for civilization. (1904)

George Santayana—Fanaticism consists in redoubling your efforts when you have forgotten your aim. (The Life of Reason 1905-06)

Woodrow Wilson—The world must be made safe for democracy. (Apr. 2, 1917)

Mark Twain—Its name is Public Opinion. It is held in reverence. It settles everything. Some think it is the voice of God. (1925)

Calvin Coolidge—The business of America is business. (Jan. 17, 1925)

Will Rogers—All I know is what I read in the newspapers. (1930s)

Thomas A. Edison—Genius is one per cent inspiration and ninety-nine per cent hard work. (Life, 1932)

Franklin D. Roosevelt—The only thing we have to fear is fear itself. (March 4, 1933)

Ogden Nash—Candy / Is dandy / But liquor / Is quicker. (Date uncertain)

Wm. Thomas Cummings—There are no atheists in foxholes. (1942)

Gen. Douglas MacArthur— I shall return. (March 11, 1942)

Anthony Clement McAuliff—Nuts! (When called on to surrender, Dec. 23, 1944)

John F. Kennedy—Ask not what your country can do for you, ask what you can do for your country. (Jan. 20, 1961)

Awards — Medals — Prizes
The Alfred B. Nobel Prize Winners

Alfred B. Nobel, inventor of dynamite, bequeathed $9,000,000, the interest to be distributed yearly to those who had most benefited mankind in the fields of physics, chemistry, medicine - physiology, literature and peace. The first Nobel Prize in Economics was awarded in 1969. No awards given for years omitted.

PHYSICS

1972 John Bardeen, American
Leon N. Cooper, American
John R. Schrieffer, American
1971 Dennis Gabor, British
1970 Louis Neel, France
Hannes Alfven, Sweden
1969 Murray Gell-Mann, American
1968 Luis W. Alvarez, American
1967 Hans. A. Bethe, American
1966 Alfred Kastler, French
1965 Richard P. Feynman, American
Julian S. Schwinger, American
Shinichiro Tomanaga, Japan
1964 Nikolai G. Basov, Russian
Aleksander M. Prochorov, Russ.
Charles H. Townes, American
1963 Maria Goeppert-Mayer, Am.
J. Hans D. Jensen, German
Eugene P. Wigner, American
1962 Lev. D. Landau, Russian
1961 Robert Hofstadter, American
Rudolf L. Mössbauer, German
1960 Donald A. Glaser, American
1959 Owen Chamberlain, American
Emillo G. Segré, American
1958 Paval Cerenkov, Ilya Frank
Igor J. Tamm, All Russian
1957 Tsung-Dao Lee,
Chen Ning Yang, Both Am.
1956 John Bardeen, American
Walter H. Brattain, American
William Shockley, American
1955 Pólykarp Kusch, American

Willis E. Lamb, American
1954 Max Born, British
Walther Bothe, German
1953 Frits Zernike, Dutch
1952 Felix Bloch, American
Edward M. Purcell, American
1951 Sir John D. Cockroft, British
Ernest T. S. Walton, Irish
1950 Cecil F. Powell, British
1949 Hideki Yukawa, Japanese
1948 Patrick M. S. Blackett, British
1947 Sir Edward V. Appleton, British
1946 Percy Williams Bridgman, Am.
1945 Wolfgang Pauli, American
1944 Isidor Isaac Rabi, American
1943 Otto Stern, American
1939 Ernest O. Lawrence, American
1938 Enrico Fermi, American
1937 Clinton J. Davisson, American
George P. Thomson, British
1936 Carl D. Anderson, American
Victor F. Hess, Austrian
1935 James Chadwick, British
1933 Paul A. M. Dirac, British
Erwin Schrödinger, Austrian
1932 Werner Heisenberg, German
1930 Sir Chandrasekhara V. Raman, Indian
1929 Prince Louis-Victor de Broglie, French
1928 Owen W. Richardson, British
1927 Arthur H. Compton, American
Charles T. R. Wilson, British

1926 Jean B. Perrin, French
1925 James Franck,
Gustav Hertz, Both German
1924 Karl M. G. Siegbahn, Swedish
1923 Robert A. Millikan, American
1922 Niels Bohr, Danish
1921 Albert Einstein, American
1920 Charles E. Guillaume, French
1919 Johannes Stark, German
1918 Max K. E. L. Planck, German
1917 Charles G. Barkla, British
1915 Sir William H. Bragg, British
William L. Bragg, British
1914 Max von Laue, German
1913 Heike Kamerlingh-Onnes, Dutch
1912 Nils G. Dalén, Swedish
1911 Wilhelm Wein, German
1910 Johannes D. van der Waals, Dutch
1909 Carl F. Braun, German
Guglielmo Marconi, Italian
1908 Gabriel Lippmann, French
1907 Albert A. Michelson, American
1906 Sir Joseph J. Thomson, British
1905 Philipp E. A. von Lenard, Ger.
1904 Rayleigh, Lord (John W. Strutt), British
1903 Antoine Henri Becquerel, Fr.
Marie Curie, French
Pierre Curie, French
1902 Hendrik A. Lorentz,
Pieter Zeeman, Both Dutch
1901 Wilhelm C. Röntgen, German

CHEMISTRY

1972 Christian B. Anfinsen, Am.
Stanford Moore, American
William H. Stein, American
1971 Gerhard Herzberg, Canada
1970 Luis A. Leloir, Arg.
1969 Derek H. R. Barton, British
Odd Hassel, Norway
1968 Lars Onsager, American
1967 Manfred Eigen, German
Ronald G. W. Norrish, British
George Porter, British
1966 Robert S. Mulliken, American
1965 Robert B. Woodward, American
1964 Dorothy C. Hodgkin, British
1963 Giulio Natta, Italian
Karl Ziegler, German
1962 John C. Kendrew, British
Max F. Perutz, British
1961 Melvin Calvin, American
1960 Willard F. Libby, American
1959 Jaroslav Heyrovský, Czech
1958 Frederick Sanger, British
1957 Sir Alexander R. Todd, British
1955 Sir Cyril N. Hinchelwood, British
Nikolai N. Semenov, Russian
1955 Vincent du Vigneaud, American
1954 Linus C. Pauling, American

1953 Hermann Staudinger, German
1952 Archer J. P. Martin, British
Richard L. M. Synge, British
1951 Edwin M. McMillan, American
Glenn T. Seaborg, American
1950 Kurt Alder,
Otto P. H. Diels, Both German
1949 William F. Glauque, American
1948 Arne W. K. Tiselius, Swedish
1947 Sir Robert Robinson, British
1946 James B. Sumner, American
John H. Northrop,
Wendell M. Stanley, All Am.
1945 Artturi I. Virtanen, Finnish
1944 Otto Hahn, German
1943 Georg de Hevesy, Hungarian
1939 Adolf F. J. Butenandt, German
Leopold Ružicka, Swiss
1938 Richard Kuhn, German
1937 Walter N. Haworth, British
Paul Karrer, Swiss
1936 Peter J. W. Debye, Dutch
1935 Frédéric Joliot-Curie, French
Irène Joliot-Curie, French
1934 Harold C. Urey, American
1932 Irving Langmuir, American
1931 Friedrich Bergius, German
Carl Bosch, German

1930 Hans Fischer, German
1929 Arthur Harden, British
Hans von Euler-Chelpin, Swed.
1928 Adolf O. R. Windaus, German
1927 Heinrich O. Wieland, German
1926 Theodor Svedberg, Swedish
1925 Richard A. Zsigmondy, German
1923 Fritz Pregl, Austrian
1922 Francis W. Aston, British
1921 Frederick Soddy, British
1920 Walther H. Nernst, German
1918 Fritz Haber, German
1915 Richard M. Willstätter, German
1914 Theodore W. Richards, Am.
1913 Alfred Werner, Swiss
1912 Victor Grignard, French
Paul Sabatier, French
1911 Marie Curie, French
1910 Otto Wallach, German
1909 Wilhelm Ostwald, German
1908 Ernest Rutherford, British
1907 Eduard Buchner, German
1906 Henri Moissan, French
1905 Adolf von Baeyer, German
1904 Sir William Ramsay, British
1903 Svante A. Arrhenius, Swedish
1902 Emil Fischer, German
1901 Jacobus H. van't Hoff, Dutch

PHYSIOLOGY OR MEDICINE

1972 Gerald M. Edelman, Am.
Rodney R. Porter, British
1971 Earl W. Sutherland, Jr., American
1970 Julius Axelrod, American
Sir Bernard Katz, British
Ulf von Euler, Swedish
1969 Max Delbruck,
Alfred D. Hershey;
Salvador Luria; All Americans
1968 Robert W. Holley;
H. Gobind Khorana;
Marshall W. Nirenberg; All Am.
1967 Ragnar Granit, Swedish
Haldan Keffer Hartline, Am.
George Wald, American

1966 Charles B. Huggins,
Francis Peyton Rous, Both Am.
1965 Francois Jacob, French
André Lwoff, French
Jacques Monod, French
1964 Konrad E. Bloch, American
Feodor Lynen, German
1963 Sir John C. Eccles, Australian
Alan L. Hodgkin, British
Andrew F. Huxley, British
1962 Francis H. C. Crick, British
James D. Watson, American
Maurice H. F. Wilkins, British
1961 Georg von Bekesy, American
1960 Sir F. MacFarlane Burnet, Australian

Peter B. Medawar, British
1959 Arthur Kornberg, American
Severo Ochoa, American
1958 George W. Beadle, American
Edward L. Tatum, American
Joshua Lederberg, American
1957 Daniel Bovet, Italian
1956 André F. Cournand, American
Werner Forssmann, German
Dickinson W. Richards, Jr., Am.
1955 Alex H. T. Theorell, Swedish
1954 John F. Enders,
Frederick C. Robbins,
Thomas H. Weller, All American
1953 Hans A. Krebs, British
Fritz A. Lipmann, American

1952 Selman A. Waksman, American
1951 Max Theiler, American
1950 Philip S. Hench,
     Edward C. Kendall, Both Am.
     Tadeus Reichstein, Swiss
1949 Walter R. Hess, Swiss
     Antonio Moniz, Portuguese
1948 Paul H. Müller, Swiss
1947 Carl F. Cori,
     Gerty T. Cori, Both American
     Bernardo A. Houssay, Arg.
1946 Hermann J. Muller, American
1945 Ernst B. Chain, British
     Sir Alexander Fleming, British
     Sir Howard W. Florey, British
1944 Joseph Erlanger, American
     Herbert S. Gasser, American
1943 Henrik C. P. Dam, Danish
     Edward A. Doisy, American
1939 Gerhard Domagk, German

1938 Corneille J. F. Heymans, Belg.
1937 Albert Szent-Gyorgyi, American
1936 Sir Henry H. Dale, British
     Otto Loewi, American
1935 Hans Spemann, German
1934 George R. Minot, Wm. P. Mur-
     phy, G. H. Whipple, All Am.
1933 Thomas H. Morgan, American
1932 Edgar D. Adrian, British
     Sir Charles S. Sherrington, Bri.
1931 Otto H. Warburg, German
1930 Karl Landsteiner,American
1929 Christiaan Eijkman, Dutch
     Sir Frederick G. Hopkins, British
1928 Charles J. H. Nicolle, French
1927 Julius Wagner-Jauregg, Aus.
1926 Johannes A. G. Fibiger, Danish
1924 Willem Einthoven, Dutch
1923 Frederick G. Banting, Canada
     John J. R. Macleod, Canada

1922 Archibald V. Hill, British
     Otto F. Meyerhof, German
1920 Schack A. S. Krogh, Danish
1919 Jules Bordet, Belgian
1914 Robert Bárány, Hungarian
1913 Charles R. Richet,French
1912 Alexis Carrel, American
1911 Allvar Gullstrand, Swedish
1910 Albrecht Kossel, German
1909 Emil T. Kocher, Swiss
1908 Paul Ehrlich,German
     Elie Metchnikoff, French
1907 Charles L. A. Laveran, French
1906 Camillo Golgi, Italian
     Santiago Roman y Cajal, Sp.
1905 Robert Koch, German
1904 Ivan P. Pavlov, Russian
1903 Niels R. Finsen, Danish
1902 Sir Ronald Ross, British
1901 Emil A von Behring, German

LITERATURE

1972 Heinrich Böll, W. German
1971 Pablo Neruda, Chile
1970 Aleksandr I. Solzhenitsyn, Russ.
1969 Samuel Beckett, Irish
1968 Yasunari Kawabata, Japan
1967 Miguel Angel Asturias, Guate.
1966 Samuel Joseph Agnon, Israeli
     Nelly Sachs, Swedish
1965 Mikhail Sholokhov, Russian
1964 Jean Paul Sartre, French
     (Prize declined)
1963 Giorgos Seferis, Greek
1962 John Steinbeck, American
1961 Ivo Andric, Yugoslavian
1960 Saint-John Perse, French
1959 Salvatore Quasimodo, Italian
1958 Boris L. Pasternak, Russian
     (Prize declined)
1957 Albert Camus, French
1956 Juan Ramón Jiménez, Puerto
     Rican
1955 Halldór K. Laxness, Icelandic
1954 Ernest Hemingway, American
1953 Sir Winston Churchill, British
1952 Francois Mauriac, French

1951 Pär F. Lagerkvist, Swedish
1950 Bertrand Russell, British
1949 William Faulkner, American
1948 T. S. Eliot, British
1947 André Gide, French
1946 Hermann Hesse, Swiss
1945 Gabriela Mistral, Chilean
1944 Johannes V. Jensen, Danish
1939 Frans. E. Sillanpää, Finnish
1938 Pearl S. Buck, American
1937 Roger Martin du Gard, French
1936 Eugene O'Neill, American
1934 Luigi Pirandello, Italian
1933 Ivan A. Bunin, French
1932 John Galsworthy, British
1931 Erik A. Karlfeldt, Swedish
1930 Sinclair Lewis, American
1929 Thomas Mann, German
1928 Sigrid Undset, Norwegian
1927 Henri Bergson, French
1926 Grazia Deledda, Italian
1925 George Bernard Shaw, British
1924 Wladyslaw S. Reymont, Polish
1923 William Butler Yeats, Irish

1922 Jacinto Benavente, Spanish
1921 Anatole France, French
1920 Knut Hamsun, Norwegian
1919 Carl F. G. Spitteler, Swiss
1917 Karl A. Gjellerup, Danish
     Henrik Pontoppidan, Danish
1916 Verner von Heidenstam, Swed.
1915 Romain Rolland, French
1913 Rabindranath Tagore, Indian
1912 Gerhart Hauptmann, German
1911 Count Maurice Maeterlinck,
     Belgian
1910 Paul J. L. Heyse, German
1909 Selma Lagerlof, Swedish
1908 Rudolf C. Eucken, German
1907 Rudyard Kipling, British
1906 Giosue Carducci, Italian
1905 Henryk Sienkiewicz, Polish
1904 Frederic Mistral, French
     José Echegaray, Spanish
1903 Bjornsterne Bjornson, Norw.
1902 Theodor Mommsen, German
1901 René F. A. Sully Prudhomme,
     French

PEACE

1971 Willy Brandt, W. German
1970 Norman E. Borlaug, American
1969 Intl. Labor Organization
1968 Rene Cassin, French
1965 The United Nations Children's
     Fund (UNICEF)
1964 Martin Luther King, Jr., Am.
1963 International Red Cross
     League of Red Cross Societies
1962 Linus C. Pauling, American
1961 Dag Hammarskjöld, Swedish
1960 Albert J. Luthuli, South African
1959 Philip J. Noel-Baker, British
1958 Georges Pire, Belgian
1957 Lester B. Pearson, Canadian
1954 Office of the UN High Commis-
     sioner for Refugees
1953 George C. Marshall, American
1952 Albert Schweitzer, French
1951 Léon Jouhaux, French
1950 Ralph J. Bunche, American
1949 Lord John Boyd Orr of Brechin,
     British
1947 Friends Service Council, British
     American Friends Service Com-
     mittee, American

1946 Emily G. Balch,
     John R. Mott, Both American
1945 Cordell Hull, American
1944 International Red Cross
1938 Nansen International Office for
     Refugees
1937 Viscount Cecil of Chelwood
     (Lord Edgar A. R. G. Cecil), Brit.
1936 Carlos de Saavedra Lamas, Arg.
1935 Carl von Ossietzky, German
1934 Arthur Henderson, British
1933 Sir Norman Angell, British
1931 Jane Addams, American
     Nicholas Murray Butler, Amer.
1930 Nathan Söderblom, Swedish
1929 Frank B. Kellogg, American
1927 Ferdinand E. Buisson, French
     Ludwig Quidde, German
1926 Aristide Briand, French
     Gustav Stresemann, German
1925 Sir J. Austen Chamberlain, Brit.
     Charles G. Dawes, American
1922 Fridtjof Nansen, Norwegian
1921 Karl H. Branting, Swedish
     Christian L. Lange, Norwegian

1920 Léon V. A. Bourgeois, French
1919 Woodrow Wilson, American
1917 International Red Cross
1913 Henri La Fontaine, Belgian
1912 Elihu Root, American
1911 Tobias M. C. Asser, Dutch
     Alfred H. Fried, Austrian
1910 Permanent International Peace
     Bureau
1909 Auguste M. F. Beernaert, Belg.
     Paul H. B. B. d'Estournelles de
     Constant, French
1908 Klas P. Arnoldson, Swedish
     Fredrik Bajer, Danish
1907 Ernesto T. Moneta, Italian
     Louis Renault, French
1906 Theodore Roosevelt, American
1905 Baroness Bertha von Suttner,
     Austrian
1904 Institute of International Law
1903 Sir William R. Cremer, British
1902 Elie Ducommun,
     Charles A. Gobat, Both Swiss
1901 Jean H. Dunant, Swiss
     Frédéric Passy, French

ECONOMICS

1972 Kenneth J. Arrow, American
     John R. Hicks, British

1971 Simon Kuznets, American
1970 Paul A. Samuelson, American

1969 Ragnar Frisch, Norway; Jan
     Tinbergen, Netherlands

The Molson Prize

The Molson Prizes of the Canada Council for contributions to the arts, social sciences or humanities or to national unity. The value of the prize is $15,000 and 3 prizes are awarded each year.

1963 Donald Creighton; Alain Grandbois.
1965 Jean Gascon; Frank Scott.
1966 Rev. Georges-Henri Lévesque; H. McLennan.
1967 Arthur Erickson; Anne Hébert; Marshall
     McLuhan.
1968 Glenn Gould; Jean Le Moyne.

1970 Jean-Paul Audet; Morley Callaghan; Arnold
     Spohr.
1971 Maureen Forrester; Rina Lasnier; Norman
     McLaren.
1972 John Deutsch; Alfred Pellan; George Wood-
     cock.

Pulitzer Prizes in Journalism, Letters and Music

The Pulitzer Prizes were endowed by Joseph Pulitzer (1847-1911), publisher of The World, New York, N. Y., in a bequest to Columbia University, New York, N. Y., and are awarded annually by the trustees of the university on recommendation of the Advisory Board on Pulitzer Prizes for work done during the preceding year. Secretary of the Advisory Board is John Hohenberg of Columbia Univ. All prizes are $1,000 (originally $500) in each category, except Meritorious Public Service for which a gold medal is given. No awards given for years omitted.

Pulitzer Prizes in Journalism
Meritorious Public Service
For disinterested and meritorious public service by a United States newspaper.
1918—The New York Times. Also special award to Minna Lewinson and Henry Beetle Hough.
1919—Milwaukee Journal
1921—Boston Post
1922—The World, New York.
1923—Memphis (Tenn.) Commercial Appeal.
1924—The World, New York.
1926—Enquirer-Sun, Columbus, Ga.
1927—Canton (O.) Daily News.
1928—Indianapolis Times.
1929—Evening World, New York.
1931—Atlanta (Ga.) Constitution.
1932—Indianapolis (Ind.) News.
1933—New York World-Telegram.
1934—Medford (Ore.) Mail-Tribune.
1935—Sacramento (Calif.) Bee.
1936—Cedar Rapids (Iowa) Gazette.
1937—St. Louis Post-Dispatch.
1938—Bismarck (N. D.) Tribune.
1939—Miami (Fla.) Daily News.
1940—*illegible*
1941—St. Louis Post-Dispatch.
1942—Los Angeles Times.
1943—Omaha World Herald.
1944—The New York Times.
1945—Detroit Free Press.
1946—Scranton (Pa.) Times.
1947—Baltimore Sun.
1948—St. Louis Post-Dispatch.
1949—Nebraska State Journal.
1950—Chicago Daily News; St. Louis Post-Dispatch.
1951—Miami (Fla.) Herald and Brooklyn Eagle
1952—St. Louis Post-Dispatch.
1953—Whiteville (N. C.) News Reporter; Tabor City (N. C.) Tribune.
1954—Newsday, Garden City, N. Y.
1955—Columbus (Ga.) Ledger and Sunday Ledger-Enquirer.
1956—Watsonville (Calif.) Register-Pajaronian.
1957—Chicago Daily News.
1958—Arkansas Gazette, Little Rock.
1959—Utica (N. Y.) Observer-Dispatch and Utica Daily Press.
1960—Los Angeles Times.
1961—Amarillo (Tex.) Globe-Times.
1962—Panama City (Fla.) News-Herald.
1963—Chicago Daily News.
1964—St. Petersburg (Fla.) Times.
1965—The Hutchinson (Kans.) News.
1966—Boston Globe.
1967—The Louisville Courier-Journal and The Milwaukee Journal
1968—The Riverside (Calif.) Press-Enterprise.
1969—The Los Angeles Times.
1970—Newsday (Long Island, N.Y.)
1971—Winston Salem (N.C.) Journal & Sentinel
1972—The New York Times.
1973—The Washington Post.

Reporting
This category originally embraced all fields, local, national, and international. Later separate categories were created for the different fields of reporting.
1917—Herbert Bayard Swope, The World, N. Y.
1918—Harold A. Littledale, New York Evening Post.
1920—John J. Leary, Jr., The World, New York.
1921—Louis Seibold, The World, New York.
1922—Kirke L. Simpson, Associated Press.
1923—Alva Johnston, New York Times.
1924—Magner White, San Diego (Calif.) Sun.
1925—James W. Mulroy and Alvin H. Goldstein. Chi. Daily News.
1926—William Burke Miller, Louisville Courier-Journal.
1927—John T. Rogers, St. Louis Post-Dispatch.
1929—Paul V. Anderson, St. Louis Post-Dispatch.
1930—Russell D. Owens, New York Times. Also $500 to W. O. Dapping, Auburn (N. Y.) Citizen.
1931—A. B. MacDonald, Kansas City (Mo.) Star.
1932—W. C. Richards, D. D. Martin, J. S. Pooler, F. D. Webb, J. N. W. Sloan, Detroit Free Press.
1933—Francis A. Jamieson, Associated Press.
1934—Royce Brier, San Francisco, Chronicle.
1935—William H. Taylor, New York Herald Tribune
1936—Lauren D. Lyman, New York Times.
1937—John J. O'Neill, N. Y. Herald Tribune; William L. Laurence, N. Y. Times; Howard W. Blakeslee, A. P.; Gobind Behari Lal, University Service and David Dietz, Scripps-Howard Newspapers.

1938—Raymond Sprigle, Pittsburgh Post-Gazette.
1939—Thomas L. Stokes, Scripps-Howard Newspaper Alliance.
1940—S. Burton Heath, New York World-Telegram.
1941—Westbrook Pegler, New York World-Telegram.
1942—Stanton Delaplane, San Francisco Chronicle.
1943—George Weller, Chicago Daily News.
1944—Paul Schoenstein, N. Y. Journal-American.
1945—Jack S. McDowell, San Francisco Call-Bulletin.
1946—William L. Laurence, New York Times
1947—Frederick Woltman, N. Y. World-Telegram.
1948—George E. Goodwin, Atlanta (Ga.) Journal.
1949—Malcom Johnson, The Sun, New York.
1950—Meyer Berger, New York Times.
1951—Edward S. Montgomery, San Francisco Examiner.
1952—Geo. de Carvalho, San Francisco Chronicle.
Since 1953 two prizes are given for local reporting: (1) *to meet a deadline;* (2) *free of deadline.*
1953—(1) Providence (R. I.) Journal and Evening Bulletin; (2) Edward J. Mowery, N. Y. World-Telegram & Sun.
1954—(1) Vicksburg (Miss.) Sunday Post-Herald; (2) Alvin Scott McCoy, Kansas City (Mo.) Star.
1955—(1) Mrs. Caro Brown, Alice (Tex.) Daily Echo; (2) Roland K. Towery, Cuero (Tex.) Record.
1956—(1) Lee Hills, Detroit Free Press; (2) Arthur Daley, New York Times.
1957—(1) Salt Lake Tribune, Salt Lake City, Utah, (2) Wallace Turner and William Lambert, Portland Oregonian.
1958—(1) Fargo (N. D.) Forum; (2) George Beveridge, Evening Star, Washington, D. C.
1959—(1) Miss Mary Lou Werner, Evening Star, Washington, D.C.; (2) John Harold Brislin, Scranton (Pa.) Tribune, and The Scrantonian.
1960—(1) Jack Nelson, Atlanta (Ga.) Constitution; (2) Miriam Ottenberg, Evening Star, Washington, D. C.
1961—(1) Sanche de Gramont, N. Y. Herald Tribune; (2) Edgar May, Buffalo Evening News.
1962—(1) Robert D. Mullins, Desert News, Salt Lake City; (2) George Bliss, Chicago Tribune.
1963—(1) Shared by Sylvan Fox, William Longgood, and Anthony Shannon, N. Y. World-Telegram & Sun; (2) Oscar Griffin, Jr., Pecos (Tex.) Independent and Enterprise.
1964—(1) Norman C. Miller, Wall Street Journal; (2) Shared by James V. Magee, Albert V. Gaudiosi, and Frederick A. Meyer, Philadelphia Bulletin.
1965—(1) Melvin H. Ruder, Hungry Horse News (Columbia Falls, Mont.); (2) Gene Goltz, Houston, Post.
1966—(1) Los Angeles Times Staff; (2) John A. Frasca, Tampa (Fla.) Tribune.
1967—(1) Robert V. Cox, Chambersburg (Pa.) Public Opinion; (2) Gene Miller, Miami Herald.
1968—Detroit Free Press Staff; (2) J. Anthony Lukas, N. Y. Times.
1969—(1) John Fetterman, Louisville Courier-Journal and Times; (2) Albert L. Delugach, St. Louis Globe Democrat, and Denny Walsh, Life.
1970—(1) Thomas Fitzpatrick, Chicago Sun-Times; (2) Harold Eugene Martin, Montgomery Advertiser & Alabama Journal.
1971—(1) Akron Beacon Journal; (2) William Hugh Jones, Chicago Tribune.
1972—(1) Richard Cooper and John Machacek, Rochester (N.Y.) Times-Union; (2) Timothy Leland, Gerard M. O'Neill, Stephen A. Kurkjian and Anne De Santis, Boston Globe.
1973—(1) Chicago Tribune; (2) The Sun Newspapers of Omaha.

Criticism or Commentary
(1) *Criticism;* (2) *Commentary*
1970—(1) Ada Louise Huxtable, N. Y. Times; (2) Marquis W. Childs, St. Louis Post-Dispatch.
1971—(1) Harold C. Schonberg, N.Y. Times; (2) William A. Caldwell, The Record, Hackensack, N.J.
1972—(1) Mike Royko, Chicago Daily News; (2) Frank Peters Jr., St. Louis Post-Dispatch.
1973—(1) Ronald Powers, Chicago Sun-Times; (2) David S. Broder, Washington Post.

National Reporting
1942—Louis Stark, New York Times.
1944—Dewey L. Fleming, Baltimore Sun.
1945—James B. Reston, New York Times.
1946—Edward A. Harris, St. Louis Post-Dispatch.
1947—Edward T. Folliard, Washington Post.
1948—Bert Andrews, New York Herald Tribune; Nat S. Finney, Minneapolis Tribune.
1949—Charles P. Trussell, New York Times.
1950—Edwin O. Guthman, Seattle (Wash.) Times.
1952—Anthony Leviero, New York Times.
1953—Don Whitehead, Associated Press.

1954–Richard Wilson, Cowles Newspapers.
1955–Anthony Lewis, Washington Daily News.
1956–Charles L. Bartlett, Chattanooga Times.
1957–James Reston, New York Times.
1958–Relman Morin, A. P.; Clark Mollenhoff, Des Moines Register & Tribune.
1959–Howard Van Smith, Miami (Fla.) News.
1960–Vance Trimble, Scripps-Howard, Washington, D. C.
1961–Edward R. Cony, Wall Street Journal.
1962–Nathan G. Caldwell and Gene S. Graham, Nashville Tennessean.
1963–Anthony Lewis, New York Times.
1964–Merriman Smith, U.P.I.
1965–Louis M. Kohlmeier, Wall Street Journal.
1966–Haynes Johnson, Evening Star, Washington, D. C.
1967–Monroe W. Karmin and Stanley W. Penn, Wall Street Journal.
1968–Howard James, Christian Science Monitor; Nathan K. Kotz, Des Moines Register.
1969–Robert Cahn, Christian Science Monitor.
1970–William J. Eaton, Chicago Daily News.
1971–Lucinda Franks & Thomas Powers, UPI.
1972–Jack Anderson.
1973 – Robert Boyd and Clark Hoyt, Knight Newspapers.

International Reporting

1942–Laurence Edmund Allen, Associated Press.
1943–Ira Wolfert, No. Am. Newspaper Alliance.
1944–Daniel DeLuce, Associated Press.
1945–Mark S. Watson, Baltimore Sun.
1946–Homer W. Bigart, New York Herald Tribune.
1947–Eddy Gilmore, Associated Press.
1948–Paul W. Ward, Baltimore Sun.
1949–Price Day, Baltimore Sun.
1950–Edmund Stevens, Christian Science Monitor.
1951–Keyes Beech, Chicago Daily News; Homer Bigart and Marguerite Higgins, New York Herald Tribune; Relman Morin and Don Whitehead, A. P.; Fred Sparks, Chicago Daily News.
1952–John M. Hightower, Associated Press.
1953–Austin C. Wehrwein, Milwaukee Journal.
1954–Jim G. Lucas, Scripps-Howard Newspapers.
1955–Harrison Salisbury, New York Times.
1956–William Randolph Hearst, Jr., J. Kingsbury Smith, Frank Conniff, Hearst Newspapers.
1957–Russell Jones, United Press.
1958–The New York Times.
1959–Joseph Martin and Philip Santora, N. Y. Daily News.
1960–A. M. Rosenthal, New York Times.
1961–Lynn Heinzerling, Associated Press.
1962–Walter Lippmann, N. Y. Herald Tribune Synd.
1963–Hal Hendrix, Miami (Fla.) News.
1949–Malcolm W. Browne, A. P.; David Halberstam, N. Y. Times.
1965–J. A. Livingston, Philadelphia Bulletin.
1966–Peter Arnett, A. P.
1967–R. John Hughes, Crhistian Science Monitor.
1968–Alfred Friendly, Washington Post.
1969–William Tuohy, L. A. Times.
1970–Seymour M. Hersh, Dispatch News Service.
1971–Jimmie Lee Hoagland, Washington Post.
1972–Peter R. Kann, Wall Street Journal.
1973 – Max Frankel, N.Y. Times.

Correspondence

For Washington or foreign correspondence. Category was merged with those in national and international reporting in 1948.

1929–Paul Scott Mowrer, Chicago Daily News.
1930–Leland Stowe, New York Herald Tribune.
1931–H. R. Knickerbocker, Philadelphia Public Ledger and New York Evening Post.
1932–Walter Duranty, New York Times, and Charles G. Ross, St. Louis Post-Dispatch.
1933–Edgar Ansel Mowrer, Chicago Daily News.
1934–Frederick T. Birchall, New York Times.
1935–Arthur Krock, New York Times.
1936–Wilfred C. Barber, Chicago Tribune.
1937–Anne O'Hare McCormick, New York Times.
1938–Arthur Krock, New York Times.
1939–Louis P. Lochner, Associated Press.
1940–Otto D. Tolischus, New York Times.
1941–Bronze plaque to commemorate work of American correspondents on war fronts.
1942–Carlos P. Romulo, Philippines Herald.
1943–Hanson W. Baldwin, New York Times.
1944–Ernest Taylor Pyle, Scripps-Howard Newspaper Alliance.
1945–Harold V. (Hal) Boyle, Associated Press.
1946–Arnaldo Cortesi, New York Times.
1947–Brooks Atkinson, New York Times.

Editorial Writing

The test of excellence is clearness of style, moral purpose, sound reasoning and power to influence public opinion.

1917–New York Tribune.
1918–Louisville (Ky.) Courier-Journal.
1920–Harvey E. Newbranch, Omaha Evening World-Herald.
1922–Frank M. O'Brien, New York Herald.

1923–William Allen White, Emporia Gazette.
1924–Boston Herald, Frank Buxton. Special Prize. Frank I. Cobb, The World, New York.
1925–Charleston (S. C.) News and Courier.
1926–The New York Times, Edward M. Kingsbury.
1927–Boston Herald, F. Lauriston Bullard.
1928–Grover C. Hall, Montgomery Advertiser.
1929–Louis Isaac Jaffe, Norfolk Virginian-Pilot.
1931–Chas. Ryckman, Fremont (Nebr.) Tribune.
1933–Kansas City (Mo.) Star.
1934–E. P. Chase, Atlantic (Ia.) News Telegraph.
1936–Felix Morley, Washington Post. George B. Parker, Scripps-Howard Newspapers.
1937–John W. Owens, Baltimore (Md.) Sun.
1938–W. W. Waymack, Des Moines (Ia.) Register and Tribune.
1939–Ronald G. Callvert, Portland Oregonian.
1940–Bart Howard, St. Louis (Mo.) Post-Dispatch.
1941–Reuben Maury, Daily News, N. Y.
1942–Geoffrey Parsons, New York Herald Tribune.
1943–Forrest W. Seymour, Des Moines (Ia.) Register and Tribune.
1944–Kansas City (Mo.) Star, Henry J. Haskell.
1945–George W. Potter, Providence (R. I.) Journal-Bulletin.
1946–Hodding Carter, Greenville (Miss.) Delta Democrat-Times.
1947–William H. Brigmes, Wall Street Journal.
1948–Virginius Dabney, Richmond (Va.) Times-Dispatch.
1949–John H. Crider, Boston (Mass.) Herald, Herbert Elliston, Washington (D. C.) Post.
1950–Carl M. Saunders, Jackson Citizen-Patriot.
1951–William H. Fitzpatrick, New Orleans States.
1952–Louis LaCoss, St. Louis Globe Democrat.
1953–Vermont C. Royster, Wall Street Journal.
1954–Boston Herald, Don Murray.
1955–Detroit Free Press, Royce Howes.
1956–Lauren K. Soth, Des Moines (Ia.) Register and Tribune.
1957–Buford Boone, Tuscaloosa (Ala.) News.
1958–Harry S. Ashmore, Arkansas Gazette.
1959–Ralph McGill, Atlanta (Ga.) Constitution.
1960–Lenoir Chambers, Norfolk Virginian-Pilot.
1961–William J. Dorvillier, San Juan (Puerto Rico) Star.
1962–Thomas M. Storke, Santa Barbara (Calif.) News-Press.
1963–Ira B. Harkey, Jr., Pascagoula (Miss.) Chronicle.
1964–Hazel Brannon Smith, Lexington (Miss.) Advertiser.
1965–John R. Harrison, The Gainesville (Fla.) Sun.
1966–Robert Lasch, St. Louis Post-Dispatch.
1967–Eugene C. Patterson, Atlanta Constitution.
1968–John S. Knight, Knight Newspapers.
1969–Paul Greenberg, Pine Bluff (Ark.) Commercial.
1970–Philip L. Geyelin, Washington Post.
1971–Horance G. Davis, Jr., Gainesville (Fla.) Sun.
1972–John Strohmeyer, Bethlehem (Pa.) Globe-Times.
1973 – Roger B. Linscott, Berkshire Eagle, Pittsfield, Mass.

Cartoon

1922–Rollin Kirby, The World, New York.
1924–J. N. Darling, New York Herald Tribune.
1925–Rollin Kirby, The World, New York.
1926–D. R. Fitzpatrick, St. Louis Post-Dispatch.
1927–Nelson Harding, Brooklyn Eagle.
1928–Nelson Harding, Brooklyn Eagle.
1929–Rollin Kirby, The World, New York.
1930–Charles Macauley, Brooklyn Eagle.
1931–Edmund Duffy, Baltimore Sun.
1932–John T. McCutcheon, Chicago Tribune.
1933–H. M. Talburt, Washington Daily News.
1934–Edmund Duffy, Baltimore Sun.
1935–Ross A. Lewis, Milwaukee Journal.
1937–C. D. Batchelor, Daily News, New York.
1938–Vaughn Shoemaker, Chicago Daily News.
1939–Charles G. Werner, Daily Oklahoman.
1940–Edmund Duffy, Baltimore Sun.
1941–Jacob Burck, Chicago Times.
1942–Herbert L. Block, Newspaper Enterprise Assn.
1943–Jay N. Darling, New York Herald Tribune.
1944–Clifford K. Berryman, Washington Star.
1945–Bill Mauldin, United Feature Syndicate.
1946–Bruce Alexander Russell, Los Angeles Times.
1947–Vaughn Shoemaker, Chicago Daily News.
1948–Reuben L. (Rube) Goldberg, The Sun, N. Y.
1949–Lute Pease, Newark (N. J.) Evening News.
1950–James T. Berryman, Washington Star.
1951–Reginald W. Manning, Arizona Republic.
1952–Fred L. Packer, New York Mirror.
1953–Edward D. Kuekes, Cleveland Plain Dealer.
1954–Herbert L. Block, Washington Post & Times-Herald.
1955–Daniel R. Fitzpatrick, St. Louis Post-Dispatch.
1956–Robert York, Louisville (Ky.) Times.
1957–Tom Little, Nashville Tennessean.
1958–Bruce M. Shanks, Buffalo Evening News.
1959–Bill Mauldin, St. Louis Post-Dispatch.
1961–Carey Orr, Chicago Tribune.
1962–Edmund S. Valtman, Hartford Times.
1963–Frank Miller, Des Moines Register.
1964–Paul Conrad, Denver Post.
1966–Don Wright, Miami News.
1967–Patrick B. Oliphant, Denver Post.

1968—Eugene Gray Payne, Charlotte Observer.
1969—John Fischetti, Chicago Daily News.
1970—Thomas F. Darcy, Newsday
1971—Paul Conrad, L. A. Times.
1972—Jeffrey K. MacNelly, Richmond News-Leader.

Spot News Photography

1942—Milton Brooks, Detroit News.
1943—Frank Noel, Associated Press.
1944—Frank Filan, Associated Press; Earle L. Bunker, Omaha World-Herald.
1945—Joe Rosenthal, Associated Press, for photograph of planting American flag on Iwo Jima.
1947—Arnold Hardy, amateur, Atlanta, Ga.
1948—Frank Cushing, Boston Traveler.
1949—Nathaniel Fein, New York Herald Tribune.
1950—Bill Crouch, Oakland (Calif.) Tribune.
1951—Max Desfor, Associated Press.
1952—John Robinson and Don Ultang, Des Moines Register and Tribune.
1953—William M. Gallagher, Flint (Mich.) Journal.
1954—Mrs. Walter M. Schau, amateur (Calif.).
1955—John L. Gaunt, Jr., Los Angeles Times.
1956—New York Daily News.
1957—Harry A. Trask, Boston Traveler.
1958—William C. Beall, Washington Daily News.
1959—William Seaman, Minneapolis Star.
1960—Andrew Lopez, United Press Intl.
1961—Yasushi Nagao, Mainichi Newspapers, Tokyo.
1962—Paul Vathis, Associated Press.
1963—Hector Rondon, La Republica, Caracas. Venezuela.
1964—Robert H. Jackson, Dallas Times-Herald.
1965—Horst Faas, Associated Press.
1966—Kyoichi Sawada, U.P.I.
1967—Jack R. Thornell, Associated Press.
1968—Rocco Morabito, Jacksonville Journal.
1969—Edward Adams, A.P.
1970—Steve Starr, A.P.
1971—John Paul Filo, Valley Daily News & Daily Dispatch of Tarentum & New Kensington, Pa.
1972—Horst Faas and Michel Laurent, AP.
1973—Huynh Cong Ut, AP.

Feature Photography

1968—Toshio Sakai, UPI.
1969—Moneta Sleet, Jr., Ebony.
1970—Dallas Kinney, Palm Beach Post.
1971—Jack Dykinga, Chicago Sun-Times.
1972—Dave Kennerly, UPI.
1973—Brian Lanker, Topeka Capitol-Journal.

Special Citation

1938—Edmonton (Alberta) Journal, bronze plaque.
1941—New York Times.
1944—Byron Price and Mrs. William Allen White. Also to Richard Rodgers and Oscar Hammerstein, 2nd, for musical, Oklahoma!
1945—Press cartographers for war maps.
1947—(Pulitzer centennial year.) Columbia University and the Graduate School of Journalism, and the St. Louis Post-Dispatch.
1948—Dr. Frank Diehl Fackenthal.
1951—Cyrus L. Sulzberger, New York Times.
1952—Max Kase, New York Journal-American, and Kansas City (Mo.) Star.
1953—The New York Times, for Review of the Week section and Lester Markel, its founder.
1957—Kenneth Roberts, for his historical novels.
1958—Walter Lippmann, New York Herald Tribune.
1960—Garrett Mattingly, for The Armada.
1961—American Heritage Picture History of the Civil War
1964—The Gannett Newspapers.
1973—James T. Flexner, for "George Washington", a four-volume biography.

Pulitzer Prizes in Letters
Fiction

For fiction in book form by an American author, preferably dealing with American life.

1918—Ernest Poole, His Family.
1919—Booth Tarkington, The Magnificent Ambersons.
1921—Edith Wharton, The Age of Innocence.
1922—Booth Tarkington, Alice Adams.
1923—Willa Cather, One of Ours.
1924—Margaret Wilson, The Able McLaughlins.
1925—Edna Ferber, So Big.
1926—Sinclair Lewis, Arrowsmith. (Refused prize.)
1927—Louis Bromfield, Early Autumn.
1928—Thornton Wilder, Bridge of San Luis Rey.
1929—Julia M. Peterkin, Scarlet Sister Mary.
1930—Oliver LaFarge, Laughing Boy.
1931—Margaret Ayer Barnes, Years of Grace.
1932—Pearl S. Buck, The Good Earth.
1933—T. S. Stribling, The Store.
1934—Caroline Miller, Lamb in His bosom.
1935—Josephine W. Johnson, Now in November.
1936—Harold L. Davis, Honey in the Horn.
1937—Margaret Mitchell, Gone With the Wind.

1938—John P. Marquand, The Late George Apley.
1939—Marjorie Kinnan Rawlings, The Yearling.
1940—John Steinbeck, The Grapes of Wrath.
1942—Ellen Glasgow, In This Our Life.
1943—Upton Sinclair, Dragon's Teeth.
1944—Martin Flavin, Journey in the Dark.
1945—John Hersey, A Bell for Adano.
1947—Robert Penn Warren, All the King's Men.
1948—James A. Michener, Tales of the South Pacific.
1949—James Gould Cozzens, Guard of Honor.
1950—A. B. Guthrie, Jr., The Way West.
1951—Conrad Richter, The Town.
1952—Herman Wouk, The Caine Mutiny.
1953—Ernest Hemingway, The Old Man and the Sea.
1955—William Faulkner, A Fable.
1956—MacKinlay Kantor, Andersonville.
1958—James Agee, A Death in the Family.
1959—Robert Lewis Taylor, The Travels of Jaimie McPheeters.
1960—Allen Drury, Advise and Consent.
1961—Harper Lee, To Kill a Mockingbird.
1962—Edwin O'Connor, The Edge of Sadness.
1963—William Faulkner, The Reivers.
1965—Shirley Ann Grau, The Keepers of the House.
1966—Katherine Anne Porter, Collected Stories of Katherine Anne Porter.
1967—Bernard Malamud, The Fixer.
1968—William Styron, The Confessions of Nat Turner.
1969—N. Scott Momaday, House Made of Dawn.
1970—Jean Stafford, Collected Stories.
1972—Wallace Stegner, Angle of Repose.
1973—Eudora Welty, The Optimist's Daughter.

Drama

For an American play, preferably original and dealing with the life of the country.

1918—Jesse Lynch Williams, Why Marry?
1920—Eugene O'Neill, Beyond the Horizon.
1921—Zona Gale, Miss Lulu Bett.
1922—Eugene O'Neill, Anna Christie.
1923—Owen Davis, Icebound.
1924—Hatcher Hughes, Hell-Bent for Heaven.
1925—Sidney Howard, They Knew What They Wanted.
1926—George Kelly, Craig's Wife.
1927—Paul Green, In Abraham's Bosom.
1928—Eugene O'Neill Strange Interlude.
1929—Elmer Rice, Street Scene.
1930—Marc Connelly, The Green Pastures.
1931—Susan Glaspell, Alison's House.
1932—George S. Kaufman, Morrie Ryskind and Ira Gershwin, Of Thee I Sing.
1933—Maxwell Anderson, Both Your Houses.
1934—Sidney Kingsley, Men in White.
1935—Zoe Akins, The Old Maid.
1936—Robert E. Sherwood, Idiot's Delight.
1937—George S. Kaufman and Moss Hart, You Can't Take It With You.
1938—Thornton Wilder, Our Town.
1939—Robert E. Sherwood, Abe Lincoln in Illinois
1940—William Saroyan, The Time of Your Life.
1941—Robert E. Sherwood, There Shall Be No Night.
1943—Thornton Wilder, The Skin of Our Teeth.
1945—Mary Chase, Harvey.
1946—Russel Crouse and Howard Lindsay, State of the Union.
1948—Tennessee Williams, A Streetcar Named Desire.
1949—Arthur Miller, Death of a Salesman.
1950—Richard Rodgers, Oscar Hammerstein II, and Joshua Logan, South Pacific, based on James A. Michener's 1948 prizewinning book, Tales of the South Pacific.
1952—Joseph Kramm, The Shrike.
1953—William Inge, Picnic.
1954—John Patrick, Teahouse of the August Moon.
1955—Tennessee Williams, Cat on a Hot Tin Roof.
1956—Frances Goodrich and Albert Hackett, The Diary of Anne Frank.
1957—Eugene O'Neill, Long Day's Journey Into Night.
1958—Ketti Frings, Look Homeward, Angel.
1959—Archibald MacLeish, J. B.
1960—George Abbott, Jerome Weidman, Sheldon Harnick and Jerry Bock, Fiorello.
1961—Tad Mosel, All the Way Home.
1962—Frank Loesser and Abe Burrows, How To Succeed In Business Without Really Trying.
1965—Frank D. Gilroy, The Subject Was Roses.
1967—Edward Albee, A Delicate Balance.
1969—Howard Sackler, The Great White Hope.
1970—Charles Gordone, No Place to be Somebody.
1971—Paul Zindel, The Effect of Gamma Rays on Man-in-the-Moon Marigolds.
1973—Jason Miller, That Championship Season.

History

1917—J. J. Jusserand, With Americans of Past and Present Days.
1918—James Ford Rhodes, History of the Civil War.
1920—Justin H. Smith, The War with Mexico.
1921—William Sowden Sims, The Victory at Sea.
1922—James Truslow Adams, The Founding of New England.
1923—Charles Warren, The Supreme Court in United States History.

1924—Charles Howard McIlwain, The American Revolution: A Constitutional Interpretation.
1925—Frederick L. Paxton, A History of the American Frontier.
1926—Edward Channing, History of the U. S.
1927—Samuel Flagg Bemis, Pinckney's Treaty.
1928—Vernon Louis Parrington, Main Currents in American Thought.
1929—Fred A. Shannon, The Organization and Administration of the Union Army. 1961-65.
1930—Claude H. Van Tyne, The War of Independence.
1931—Bernadotte E. Schmitt, The Coming of the War, 1914.
1932—Gen. John J. Pershing, My Experiences in the World War.
1933—Frederick J. Turner, The Significance of Sections in American History.
1934—Herbert Agar, The People's Choice.
1935—Charles McLean Andrews, The Colonial Period of American History.
1936—Andrew C. McLaughlin, A Constitutional History of the United States.
1937—Van Wyck Brooks, The Flowering of New England.
1938—Carl Herman Buck, The Road to Reunion.
1939—Frank Luther Mott, A History of American Magazines.
1940—Carl Sandburg, Abraham Lincoln: The War Years.
1941—Marcus Lee Hansen, The Atlantic Migration.
1942—Margaret Leech, Reveille in Washington.
1943—Esther Forbes, Paul Revere and the World He Lived In.
1944—Merle Curti, The Growth of American Thought.
1945—Stephen Bonsal, Unfinished Business.
1946—Arthur M. Schlesinger, Jr., The Age of Jackson.
1947—Dr. James Phinney Baxter 3rd., Scientists Against Time.
1948—Bernard De Voto, Across the Wide Missouri.
1949—Roy F. Nichols, The Disruption of American Democracy.
1950—O. W. Larkin, Art and Life in America.
1951—R. Carlyle Buley, The Old Northwest, Pioneer Period 1815-1840.
1952—Oscar Handlin, The Uprooted.
1953—George Dangerfield, The Era of Good Feelings.
1954—Bruce Catton—A Stillness at Appomattox.
1955—Paul Horgan, Great River: The Rio Grande in North American History.
1956—Richard Hofstader, The Age of Reform.
1957—George F. Kennan, Russia Leaves the War.
1958—Bray Hammond, Banks and Politics in America—From the Revolution to the Civil War.
1959—Leonard D. White and Jean Schneider, The Republican Era; 1869-1901.
1960—Margaret Leech, In the Days of McKinley.
1961—Herbert Feis, The Triumphant Empire, Thunder-Clouds Gather in the West.
1963—Constance McLaughlin Green, Washington. Village and Capital. 1800-1878.
1964—Sumner Chilton Powell, Puritan Village: The Formation of A New England Town.
1965—Irwin Unger, The Greenback Era.
1966—Perry Miller, Life of the Mind in America.
1967—William H. Goetzmann, Exploration and Empire: the Explorer and Scientist in the Winning of the American West.
1968—Bernard Bailyn, The Ideological Origins of the American Revolution.
1969—Leonard W. Levy, Origin of the Fifth Amendment.
1970—Dean Acheson, Present at the Creation: My Years in the State Department.
1971—James McGregor Burns, Roosevelt: The Soldier of Freedom.
1972—Carl N. Degler, Neither Black Nor White.
1973—Michael Kammen, People of Paradox: An inquiry Concerning the Origins of American Civilization.

Biography or Autobiography

For a distinguished biography or autobiography by an American author, preferably on an American subject.
1917—Laura E. Richards and Maude Howe Elliott, assisted by Florence Howe Hall, Julia Ward Howe.
1918—William Cabell Bruce, Benjamin Franklin, Self-Revealed.
1919—Henry Adams, The Education of Henry Adams.
1920—Albert J. Beveridge, The Life of John Marshall.
1921—Edward Bok. The Americanization of Edward Bok.
1922—Hamlin Garland, A Daughter of the Middle Border.
1923—Burton J. Hendrick, The Life and Letters of Walter H. Page.
1924—Michael Pupin, From Immigrant to Inventor.
1925—M. A. DeWolfe Howe, Barrett Wendell and His Letters.
1926—Harvey Cushing, Life of Sir William Osler.
1927—Emory Holloway, Whitman, An Interpretation in Narrative.
1928—Charles Edward Russell, The American Orchestra and Theodore Thomas.
1929—Burton J. Hendrick, The Training of an American; The Earlier Life and Letters of Walter H. Page.
1930—Marquis James, The Raven. (Sam Houston).
1931—Henry James, Charles W. Eliot.
1932—Henry F. Pringle, Theodore Roosevelt.
1933—Allan Nevins, Grover Cleveland.
1934—Tyler Dennett, John Hay.
1935—Douglas Southall Freeman, R. E. Lee.
1936—Ralph Barton Perry, The Thought and Character of William James.
1937—Allan Nevins, Hamilton Fish, the Inner History of the Grant Administration.

1938—Divided between Odell Shepard, Pedlar's Progress; Marquis James, Andrew Jackson.
1939—Carl Van Doren, Benjamin Franklin.
1940—Ray Stannard Baker, Woodrow Wilson, Life and Letters.
1941—Ola Elizabeth Winslow, Jonathan Edwards.
1942—Forrest Wilson, Crusader in Crinoline.
1943—Samuel Eliot Morison, Admiral of the Ocean Sea (Columbus).
1944—Carleton Mabee, The American Leonardo: The Life of Samuel F. B. Morse.
1945—Russel Blaine Nye, George Bancroft: Brahmin Rebel.
1946—Linny Marsh Wolfe, Son of the Wilderness.
1947—William Allen White, The Autobiography of William Allen White.
1948—Margaret Clapp, Forgotten First Citizen. John Bigelow.
1949—Robert E. Sherwood, Roosevelt and Hopkins.
1950—Samuel Flag Bemis, John Quincy Adams and the Foundations of American Foreign Policy.
1951—Margaret Louise Colt, John C. Calhoun; American Portrait.
1952—Merlo J. Pusey, Charles Evans Hughes.
1953—David J. Mays, Edmund Pendleton 1721-1803.
1954—Charles A. Lindbergh, The Spirit of St. Louis.
1955—William S. White, The Taft Story.
1956—Talbot F. Hamlin, Benjamin Henry Latrobe.
1957—John F. Kennedy, Profiles in Courage.
1958—Douglas Southall Freeman (decd. 1953). George Washington, vols. I-VI; John Alexander Carroll and Mary Wells Ashworth, vol. VII.
1959—Arthur Walworth, Woodrow Wilson, American Prophet.
1960—Samuel Eliot Morison, John Paul Jones.
1961—David Donald. Charles Sumner and The Coming of the Civil War.
1963—Leon Edel, Henry James: Vol. II. The Conquest of London, 1870-1881; Vol. III, The Middle years, 1881-1895.
1964—Walter Jackson Bate, John Keats.
1965—Ernest Samuels, Henry Adams.
1966—Arthur M. Schlesinger, Jr., A. Thousand Days.
1967—Justin Kaplan, Mr. Clemens and Mark Twain.
1968—George F. Kennan, Memoirs (1925-1950).
1969—B. L. Reid, The Man from New York; John Quinn and his Friends.
1970—T. Harry Williams, Huey Long.
1971—Lawrance Thompson, Robert Frost: The Years of Triumph, 1915-1938
1972—Joseph P. Lash, Eleanor and Franklin.
1973—W. A. Swanberg, Luce and His Empire.

American Poetry

Before this prize was established in 1922, the following awards were made from gifts provided by the Poetry Society. 1918—Love Songs, by Sara Teasdale. 1919—Old Road to Paradise, by Margaret Widdemer; Corn Huskers, by Carl Sandburg.
1922—Edwin Arlington Robinson, Collected Poems.
1923—Edna St. Vincent Millay, The Ballad of the Harp-Weaver; A Few Figs from Thistles; Eight Sonnets in American Poetry, 1922; A Miscellany.
1924—Robert Frost, New Hampshire: A Poem with Notes and Grace Notes.
1925—Edwin Arlington Robinson, The Man Who Died Twice.
1926—Amy Lowell, What's O'Clock.
1927—Leonora Speyer, Fiddler's Farewell.
1928—Edwin Arlington Robinson, Tristram.
1929—Stephen Vincent Benet, John Brown's Body.
1930—Conrad Aiken, Selected Poems.
1931—Robert Frost, Collected Poems.
1932—George Dillon, The Flowering Stone.
1933—Archibald MacLeish, Conquistador.
1934—Robert Hillyer, Collected Verse.
1935—Audrey Wurdemann, Bright Ambush.
1936—Robert P. Tristram Coffin, Strange Holiness.
1937—Robert Frost, A Further Range.
1938—Marya Zaturenska, Cold Morning Sky.
1939—John Gould Fletcher, Selected Poems.
1940—Mark Van Doren, Collected Poems.
1941—Leonard Bacon, Sunderland Capture.
1942—William Rose Benet, The Dust Which Is God.
1943—Robert Frost, A Witness Tree.
1944—Stephen Vincent Benet, Western Star.
1945—Karl Shapiro, V-Letter and Other Poems.
1947—Robert Lowell, Lord Weary's Castle.
1948—W. H. Auden, The Age of Anxiety.
1949—Peter Viereck, Terror and Decorum.
1950—Gwendolyn Brooks, Annie Allen.
1951—Carl Sandburg, Complete Poems.
1952—Marianne Moore, Collected Poems.
1953—Archibald MacLeish, Collected Poems.
1954—Theodore Roethke, The Waking.
1955—Wallace Stevens, Collected Poems.
1956—Elizabeth Bishop, Poems, North and South.
1957—Richard Wilbur, Things of This World.
1958—Robert Penn Warren, Promises: Poems 1954-1956.
1959—Stanley Kunitz, Selected Poems 1928-1958.
1960—W. D. Snodgrass, Heart's Needle.
1961—Phyllis McGinley, Times Three: Selected Verse from Three Decades.
1962—Alan Dugan, Poems.

1963-William Carlos Williams, Pictures From Breughel.
1964-Louis Simpson, At the End of the Open Road.
1965-John Berryman, 77 Dream Songs.
1966-Richard Eberhart, Selected Poems.
1968-Anne Sexton, Live or Die.
1968-Anthony Hecht, The Hard Hours.
1969-George Oppen, Of Being Numerous.
1970-Richard Howard, Untitled Subjects.
1971-William S. Merwin, The Carrier of Ladders.
1972-James Wright, Collected Poems.
1973 — Maxine Winokur Kumin, Up Country.

General Non-Fiction

For best book by an American, not eligible in any other category.
1962-Theodore H. White, The Making of the President 1960.
1963-Barbara W. Tuchman, The Guns of August.
1964-Richard Hofstadter, Anti-Intellectualism in American Life.
1965-Howard Mumford Jones, O Strange New World.
1966-Edwin Way Teale, Wandering Through Winter.
1967-David Brion Davis, The Problem of Slavery in Western Culture.
1968-Will and Ariel Durant, the Story of Civilization (Vol. 10).
1969-Norman Mailer, The Armies of the Night; and Rene Jules Dubos, So Human an Animal;. How We Are Shaped by Surroundings and events.
1970-Eric H. Erikson, Gandhi's Truth.
1971-John Toland, The Rising Sun.
1972-Barbara W. Tuchman, Stilwell and the American Experience in China, 1911-1945.
1973 — Frances FitzGerald, Fire in the Lake: The Vietnamese and the Americans in Vietnam; and Robert Coles, Children of Crisis, Volumes 2 and 3.

Pulitzer Prize in Music

For composition in the larger forms of chamber, orchestral or choral music or for an operatic work including ballet, performed or published by a composer resident in the United States.

1943-William Schuman, Secular Cantata No. 2, A Free Song.
1944-Howard Hanson, Symphony No. 4, Op. 34.
1945-Aaron Copland, Appalachian Spring.
1946-Leo Sowerby, The Canticle of the Sun.
1947-Charles E. Ives, Symphony No. 3.
1948-Walter Piston, Symphony No. 3.
1949-Virgil Thomson, Louisana Story.
1950-Gian-Carlo Menotti, The Consul.
1951-Douglas Moore, Giants in the Earth.
1952-Gail Kubil, Symphony Concertante.
1954-Quincy Porter, Concerto for Two Pianos and Orchestra.
1955-Gian-Carlo Menotti, The Saint of Bleecker Street.
1956-Ernest Toch, Symphony No. 3.
1957-Norman Dello Joio, Meditations on Ecclesiastes.
1958-Samuel Barber, Vanessa.
1959-John La-Montaine, Concerto for Piano and Orchestra.
1960-Elliott Carter, Second String Quartet.
1961-Walter Piston, Symphony No. 7.
1962-Robert Ward, The Crucible.
1963-Samuel Barber, Piano Concerto No. 1.
1966-Leslie Bassett, Variations for Orchestra.
1967-Leon Kirchner, Quartet No. 3.
1968-George Crumb, Echoes of Time and the River.
1969-Karel Husa, String Quartet No. 3.
1970-Charles W. Wuorinen, Time's Encomium.
1971-Mario Davidovsky, Synchronisms No. 6.
1972-Jacob Druckman, Windows.

Special Awards

Awarded in 1973 unless otherwise designated
Books, Allied Arts

American Library Assn. Awards, for distinguished books for children. John Newbery Medal: Jean George for Julie of the Wolves. Randolph J. Caldecott Medal: Blair Lent for The Funny Little Woman.

Anisfield-Wolf Awards, for outstanding books on human relations, $1,500 each: Lee Rainwater for Behind Ghetto Walls; Betty Fladeland for Men and Brothers; and Pat Conroy for The Water is Wide.

Emily Clark Balch Poetry Prizes, by the Virginia Quarterly Review: Burke Davis 3rd for Points of Intersection; and Max Quertermous for The Artists of the Living Room. **Second Prize:** Richard Martin for Substitutes.

Bancroft Prizes, chosen by Columbia Univ. for best books in American History, diplomacy, and international relations, $4,000 each: Frances FitzGerald for Fire in the Lake: The Vietnamese and the Americans in Vietnam; John L. Gaddis for The U.S. and the Origins of the Cold War; and Louis R. Harlan for Booker T. Washington.

Berkshire Conference of Women Historians Award, for outstanding work by women historians: Patricia Bonomi for A Factious People: Politics and Society in Colonial New York; and Jessie Gregory for China and the Christian Colleges.

Bollingen Prize in Poetry, administered by Yale Univ., $5,000; James Merrill for Nights and Days.

The Governor General's Literary Awards, for excellence in Canadian writing, $2,500: Robertson Davies for The Manticore; Dennis Lee for Civil Elegies and Other Poems; John Newlove for Lies; Jean Hamelin and Yves Roby for Histoire economique du Quebec 1851-1896; Gilles Henault for Signaux pour les voyants; Antoine Maillet for Don l'orignal.

Delta Kappa Gamma Society's Educator's Award, $1,000: Rosalind Loring and Theodora Wells for Breakthrough: Women into Management.

Iowa School of Letters Award for Short Fiction, $1,000: H. E. Francis for The Itinerary of Beggars.

American Irish Foundation Award, $7,000: Seamus Heaney, Irish poet.

James Russell Lowell Prize, for outstanding literary or linguistic study, $1,000: Theodore J. Ziolkowski for Fictional Transfiguration of Jesus.

McKnight Awards, by the Univ. of Minnesota Press, for books published by the press, $1,000; Clarke A. Chambers for Paul U. Kellogg and 'Survey': Voices for Social Welfare and Social Justice; Second Prize, $750; Joseph L. Grabill for Protestant Diplomacy and the Near East: Missionary Influence on American Policy, 1810-1927.

Medical Journalism Award, by the American Medical Assn.: David Hendin for Death as a Fact of Life.

James Mooney Award, by the Southern Anthropological Society for studies of New World societies and cultures, $1,000: Dickson D. Bruce, Jr. for And They All Sang Hallelujah: Plain-Folk Camp-Meeting Religion, 1800-1845.

National Book Awards, for distinguished books by American authors, $1,000 for each award: Fiction: (tie) John Barth for Chimera, and John Williams for Augustus; Contemporary Affairs: Francis FitzGerald for Fire in the Lake; Biography: James Thomas Flexner for George Washington: Anguish and Farewell; Arts and Letters: Arthur M. Wilson for Diderot; Poetry: A. R. Ammons for Collected Poems: 1951-1971; Children's Books: Ursula Le Guin for The Farthest Shore; Philosophy and Religion: Sydney E. Ahlstrom for A Religious History of the American People; Science: George B. Schaller for The Serengeti Lion; Translation: Allen Mandelbaum for The Aeneid of Virgil.

National Institute of Arts and Letters, E. M. Forster Award, $5,000: Margaret Drabble. **Richard and Hinda Rosenthal Foundation Award,** $2,000: Thomas Rogers for The Confesion of a Child of the Century. **Marjorie Peabody Waite Award,** $1,500: A. Hyatt Mayor. **Zabel Award,** $2,500: Marjorie Hope Nicolson. **Gold Medal for Poetry:** John Crowe Ransom. **Awards in Literature,** $3,000 each: Marius Bewley, Maeve Brennen, Irving Feldman, Frances Fitzgerald, Dorothy Hughes, Philip Levine, Daniel P. Mannix, Cynthia Ozick, Jonathan Schell, Austin Warren.

National Jewish Book Awards, by the Jewish Book Council, $500 each: **Frank and Ethel S. Cohen Award:** Elie Wiesel for Souls on Fire; and Samuel Sandmel for Two Living Traditions: Essays on Religion and the Bible. **Bernard H. Marks Award,** for a book on Jewish history: Arthur J. Zuckerman for A Jewish Princedom in Feudal France, 768-900. **William and Janice Epstein Award,** for fiction: Robert Kotlowitz for Somewhere Else. **Charles and Bertie G. Schwartz Award:** Johanna Reiss for The Upstairs Room.

Phi Alpha Theta Award, for best book by a member of Phi Alpha Theta, $500: Horace Samuel Merrill and Marion Galbraith Merrill for *The Republican Command, 1897-1913.*

Phi Beta Kappa Awards, $2,500 each: Christian Gauss Award, literary scholarship and criticism, Hugh Kenner for *The Pound Era;* Ralph Waldo Emerson Award, for studies of the intellectual and cultural condition of man, John Rawls for *A Theory of Justice;* Phi Beta Kappa Award in Science, Barry Commoner for *The Closing Circle.*

Edgar Allan Poe Awards, by the Mystery Writers of America, best novel: Warren Kiefer for *The Lingala Case;* first novel, R. H. Shimer for *Squaw Point;* short story: Joyce Harrington for *The Purple Shroud;* fact crime: Stephen Fay, Lewis Chester and Magnus Linklater for *Hoax;* best paperback: Richard Wormser for *The Invader.*

San Francisco Foundation, Joseph Henry Jackson Award, $2,000: Russell Brandon for a collection of short stories. **James D. Phelan Award,** $2,000: Nels Hanson for *The Long Slow Death of Joe Dan Marten.*

Washington Monthly Awards: Francis FitzGerald for *Fire in the Lake;* and Daniel Ellsberg for *Papers on the War.*

Journalism Awards

Meyer Berger Award, by Columbia Univ. for distinguished local reporting in a New York daily, $750 each: John L. Hess, Times; Barry Cunningham, Post.

Heywood Broun Award, by The Newspaper Guild, $1,000: Carl Bernstein and Bob Woodward, Washington Post.

Canadian National Newspaper Awards: Spot News, John Zaritsky, Toronto Globe and Mail; Editorial Writing, Peter Worthington, Toronto Sun, Feature Writing, George Hutchinson, London Free Press; Spot News Photography, Frank Lennon, Toronto Star; Feature Photography, Jack Burnett, London Free Press; Cartooning, Duncan Macpherson, Toronto Star; Sports Writing, Tim Burke, Montreal Gazette; Critical Writing, David Billington, Montreal Gazette; Enterprise Reporting, David Crane, Toronto Star.

National Cartoonist Society, Reuben Award: Pat Oliphant, Denver Post. **Other Awards:** Syndicated Panel, Jim Berry, Newspaper Enterprise Assn.; Special Features, Jim Berry, Newspaper Enterprise Assn.; Editorial Cartoon, Dick Hodgins, Jr., N.Y. Daily News; Humor Strips, Dik Browne, KFS; Magazine Gag Cartoons, Don Orehek; Sports Cartoon, Bill Gallo, N.Y. Daily News; Story Strips, Stan Drake.

Roy W. Howard Public Service Awards, by The Scripps-Howard Foundation: (cash prizes as indicated) St. Louis Globe-Democrat ($2,500); WABC-TV, New York ($2,500); Sun Newspapers of Omaha ($1,000); WIND, Radio, Chicago ($1,000); WCKT-TV, Miami ($1,000); KING-AM-FM, Seattle ($1,000).

Elijah P. Lovejoy Award, by the Southern Illinois School of Journalism for courage in journalism: Bennie Scarton, Jr., Manassas (Va.) Journal-Messenger.

Edward J. Meeman Awards, by The Scripps-Howard Foundation for work in the field of conservation: First Prize, $2,500: Harry V. Martin, Napa (Calif.) Register. **Other Awards,** (cash prizes as indicated): Gordon Bishop, Newark Star-Ledger ($1,500); Harold Scarlett, Houston Post ($1,000); Robert C. Frederiksen, Providence Journal & Evening Bulletin ($1,000); Fred Jones, Pittsburgh Press ($750); Carson Brewer, Knoxville News-Sentinel ($500); Betty Klaric, Cleveland Press ($500); John Ed Pearce, Louisville Courier-Journal and Times Sunday Magazine ($500); Chet Hawes, Charleston Daily Mail ($250); Patrick T. Callahan, Seymour (Ind.) Daily Tribune ($250); John T. Opel, Palm Beach Post ($250); Arnold Friedman, Long Island Press ($250); Peter Tonge, Christian Science Monitor ($250); Bruce Ingersoll, Chicago Sun-Times ($250); Bob Poole, Winston-Salem Twin City Sentinel ($250).

New York Press Club, Schaefer Gold Typewriter Award, for public service: Richard Oliver, Daily News. **Byline Award:** Robert D. McGadden, N.Y. Times. **Other Awards:** Delos Smith, UPI; Selwyn Raab, WNET-TV.

Overseas Press Club of America Awards, for distinguished service in foreign journalism: Charlotte Saikowski, Christian Science Monitor; William L. Ryan, AP; Huynh Cong Ut, AP; Thomas J. Abercrombie, National Geographic; John Chancellor, NBC; Tom Streithorst, NBC; Joseph Kraft; James A. Michener; David Halberstam; Thomas F. Darcy, Newsday; Lewis H. Diuguid, Washington Post; Richard Dudman, St. Louis Post-Dispatch; Clive W. Limpkin, Sun (London).

Page One Awards, by the New York Newspaper Guild. National Reporting, Max Frankel, Times; Foreign Reporting, Bernard Weinraub, Times; Local Reporting, David K. Shipler, Times; Crusading Journalism, David K. Shipler, David Burnham and Nicholas Gage, Times; News Features, Phil Santora, News; Life-style Features, Judy Klemesrud, Times; News-magazine Writing, Frank J. Donner & Eugene Cerruti, The Nation; Feature Photography, Neal Boenzi, Times; Newsmagazine Photography, Wally McNamee, Newsweek; News Photography, Eddie Adams, AP; Sports Photography, Vic DeLucia, Post; Newspaper Cartoons, John Pierotti, Post; Sports Cartoons, Bruce Stark, News; Magazine Cartoons, Michael C. Witte, Time.

George Polk Memorial Awards, by Long Island Univ. for achievement in journalism: Foreign Reporting, Jean Thoraval and Jean LeClerc du Sablon, Agence France-Presse; National Reporting, Carl Bernstein and Robert Woodward, Washington Post; Metropolitan Reporting, Joseph Martin, Martin McLaughlin and James Ryan, New York Daily News; Local Reporting, Doris Ellen Olsen, Santa Monica (Calif.) Times; Community Service, Ronald Kessler, Washington Post; Investigative Reporting, Jean Heller, AP; Magazine Reporting, Frances Fitzgerald; Television Reporting, Jim McKay, ABC; News Photography, Huynh Cong Ut, AP; Special Award, Lesley Oelsner, New York Times.

Ernie Pyle Memorial Award, by The Scripps-Howard Foundation to the newspaperman most nearly exemplifying the style and craftsmanship of Ernie Pyle, $1,000: Bill Stokes, Milwaukee Journal.

Sigma Delta Chi Awards, for distinguished service in journalism: General Reporting, James M. Bolus and William F. Reed, Louisville Courier-Journal; Washington Correspondence Award, Carl Bernstein and Robert Woodward, Washington Post; Foreign Correspondence, Charlotte Saikowski, Christian Science Monitor; Public Service Award, Sun Newspapers, Omaha; News Photography, Huynh Cong Ut, AP; Editorial Cartoon, Bill Mauldin, Chicago Sun-Times; Research in Journalism, William J. Small; Editorial Writing, John R. Harrison, Lakeland (Fla.) Ledger; Magazine Reporting, Thomas Thompson, Life; Radio Reporting, Val Hymes, WTOP, Washington; Radio Public Service, WGAR, Cleveland; Radio Editorials, Frank Reynolds, ABC News; Television Reporting Laurens Pierce, CBS News; TV Public Service, WABC-TV, New York; TV Editorials, WCKT-TV, Miami:.

Silurian Awards, by the Silurians, a society of present and former New York newspapermen: Spot News, Patrick Doyle, News; Feature News, Marsha Kranes, Long Island Press; Public Service, Frank Lombardi, Hackensack Record; Spot News Photo, Ron Frehm, AP; Feature News Photo, Don Holway, Times; Editorial Cartoon, Warren King, News; Story by a newsman less than five years in the profession, Edmond Newton, Post and Penelope McMillan. **Television:** Documentary, WNET;. **Special Citation:** Delos Smith, UPI.

Thomas L. Stokes Journalism Award: Bob Poole, Winston-Salem Twin City Sentinel.

Paul Tobenkin Award, by Columbia Univ. for achievement in the field of newspaper writing in the fight against racial and religious hatred, intolerance, discrimination and bigotry: Howard Kohn, Detroit Free Press.

Television and Radio Awards

Emmy Awards, by the Academy of Television Arts and Sciences. **Actors Awards:** Continued performance in a dramatic series, Richard Thomas, The Waltons; Single performance in a drama, Laurence Olivier, A Long Day's Journey Into Night; Continued performance in a comedy series, Jack Klugman, The Odd Couple; Supporting Actor in a comedy Series, Ted Knight, The Mary Tyler Moore Show. **Actress Awards:** Continued performance in a comedy series, Mary Tyler Moore; Supporting Actress in a comedy series, Valarie Harper, The Mary Tyler Moore Show; Single performance in a drama, Cloris Leachman, A Brand New Life; Continued performance in a dramatic series, Miss Michael Learned, The Waltons; Supporting actress in a dramatic series, Ellen Corby, The Waltons. **Other Awards:** Best Variety Series, The Julie Andrews Show; Best Single Drama, A War of Children; Producing, Directing and Choreographing a Single Musical, Bob Fosse, Singer Presents Liza with a "Z"; Best Comedy Program, All in the Family; Comedy Writing, Michael Ross, Bernie West and Lee Kalcheim, All in the Family; Writing, single program in comedy, variety or music, Renee Taylor and Joseph Bologna, Acts of Love —and other Comedies; Writing, single drama, Eleanor Perry, The House Without a Christmas Tree; Sports Programming, ABC's Wide World of Sports, and 1972

Summer Olympic Games; Daytime Drama, The Edge of Night; Daytime Programming, Dinah's Place; Documentaries, Alistair Cooke's America and Jane Goodall and the World of Animal Behavior—The Wild Dogs of Africa.

George Foster Peabody Awards, for achievement in television and radio. **Television:** Alistair Cooke for his series America; Bill Monroe of "Today" for excellence in news reporting; The Waltons, CBS; NBC for programs devoted to American music; ABC Afternoon Specials; Captain Kangaroo, NBC; WNET, New York for The Restless Earth; WWL, New Orleans for China '72: A Hole in the Bamboo Curtain; NBC for The Pensions: The Broken Promise; WABC, New York for Willowbrook: The Last Great Disgrace; and ABC for coverage of the 1972 Summer Olympics. **Radio:** NBC for Monitor; KOAC, Corvallis, Ore. for Conversations with Will Shakespeare and Certain of His Friends; KGW, Portland, Ore. for Open Door; Westinghouse Broadcasting, New York for Breakdown.

TV Scout Awards, by Newspaper Enterprise Assn., Best Film: That Certain Summer; Best Actor: Hal Holbrook, That Certain Summer; Best Actress: (tie) Helen Hayes, The Snoop Sisters, and Cloris Leachman, A Brand New Life.

Theater Awards

Margo Jones Award, for significant contribution to the theater: Jules Irving, artistic director of the Repertory Theater of Lincoln Center.

Obie Awards, by The Village Voice, for the best theater piece of the Off Broadway season, $250 each: Lanford Wilson for The Hot l Baltimore and Joseph A. Walker for The River Niger.

New York Drama Critics Circle Award, for best productions during the season: Musical: A Little Night Music. Play: The Changing Room. American Play: The Hot l Baltimore.

Antoinette Perry Awards, (Tonys). By the League of New York Theaters, 1972-73 season. **Musical:** Actor,

Ben Veeren, Pippin; Actress, Glynis Johns, A Little Night Music; Supporting Actor, George S. Irving, Irene; Supporting Actress, Patricia Elliott, A Little Night Music; Best Musical, A Little Night Music; Costume Design, Florence Klotz, A Little Night Music; Director and Choreographer, Bob Fosse, Pippin; Score, Stephen Sondheim, A Little Night Music. **Drama:** Actor, Alan Bates, Butley; Actress, Julie Harris, The Last of Mrs. Lincoln; Supporting Actor, John Lithgow, The Changing Room; Supporting Actress, Leora Dana, The Last of Mrs. Lincoln; Best Play, That Championship Season; Director, A. J. Antoon, That Championship Season.

Miscellaneous Awards

The Order of Canada, to Canadian civilians for outstanding achievement, and acts of bravery or courage: The Hon. Fernand Choquette, The Hon. John Valentine, Dr. George F. Davidson, Dr. Robertson Davies, Air Chief Marshal Frank R. Miller, Mr. Marcel Vincent, Mr. John R. Bradfield, Hon. Thane A. Campbell, His Exce. Mr. Jules Leger, Dr. Moses Osborne Morgan, Dr. Norman McLaren and Dr. John Josiah Robinette.

Dance Magazine Awards: Rudolf Nureyev, William, Harold and Lew Christensen.

Frederick Douglass Awards, by the New York Urban League: Robert A. Bernhard and Jackie Robinson, posthumous.

Albert Einstein Commemorative Awards, by Yeshiva Univ. for contributions in a given field: Arthur Miller, playwright and author; Willem ·de Kooning, painter; Joseph Papp, producer; Dr. Paul Dudley White, cardiologist; Tom Wicker, columnist.

Freedoms Foundation Awards, given annually by the Freedoms Foundation at Valley Forge for contribution toward a better understanding and greater appreciation of the American way of life: **George Washington Award,** $5,000: Donald W. Hurrelbrink, Warren, Ohio. **Special Awards:** Sol Finestone, Washington Crossing, Pa.; Rev. Melvin Floyd, Philadelphia; James W.Walter, Tampa, Fla.; Armistead Maupin, Jr., San Francisco; George Mardikian, San Francisco. **Other Awards,** $500 each: Dr. Harry R. Butman, Los Angeles; Robert H. Rowland, Oklahoma City; Eugene Craig; George W. Kelly, Johnson City, Tenn.; Hon. Robert C. Byrd. **Defender of Freedom Awards,** $1,000 each: Lt. Col. Barbara J. Lee; Dan L. Johnston, Provo, Utah.

Sidney Hillman Awards, by the Sidney Hillman Foundation for achievement in mass communications,

$500 each: Carl Bernstein, Bob Woodward, Lucy Jarvis, Frances FitzGerald, Frank J. Donner and Eugene Cerruti.

Kittay International Award, for psychiatry, $25,000: Dr. Jean Piaget.

Laetare Medal, by the Univ. of Notre Dame to an outstanding Roman Catholic: Rev. John A. O'Brien.

McAlpin Research Achievement Award, by the National Assn. of Mental Health, $10,000: Robert Coles, psychiatrist.

Priestley Medal, by the American Chemical Society: Dr. Paul J. Flory.

American Institute of Public Service, for distinguished public service, $5,000 each; Henry A. Kissinger, John W. Gardner, Cesar Chavez, and Joseph A. Yablonski.

Sylvanus Thayer Award, by the United States Military Academy: General of the Army Omar N. Bradley.

Templeton Foundation Prize, for progress in religion, $85,000: Mother Teresa.

Vetlesen Prize, by Columbia Univ. for contributions toward understanding the origin and evolution of the earth and its place in the universe, $25,000: William A. Fowler, Calif. Inst. of Tech.

Westinghouse Science Talent Search (cash prizes as indicated): Arvind Narain Srivastava, Ft. Collins, Colo. ($10,000); Van Jay Wedeen, Brooklyn N.Y. ($8,000); Joshua L. Ribin, Long Island City, N.Y. ($8,000); June Anne Vayo, San Diego, Calif. ($6,000); Robert Jay Lipshutz, Freeport, N.Y. ($6,000); Laureen Pricilla Miller, Jacksonville, Fla. ($6,000); Esther Leila Zack, Los Angeles ($4,000); Glenn Greene, San Diego, Calif. ($4,000); Donald Schneider, Hartwell, Nebr. ($4,000); James Van Noto, Elmont, N.Y. ($4,000).

Academy Awards in Motion Pictures

For awards from 1927 to 1932-33 see 1972 edition of The World Almanac.

1934
Actor: Clark Gable, It Happened One Night.
Actress: Claudette Colbert, same.
Picture: It Happened One Night, Columbia.

1935
Actor: Victor McLaglen, The Informer.
Actress: Bette Davis, Dangerous.
Picture: Mutiny on the Bounty, MGM.

1936
Actor: Paul Muni, Story of Louis Pasteur.
Actress: Luise Rainer, The Great Ziegfeld.
Picture: The Great Ziegfeld, MGM.

1937
Actor: Spencer Tracy, Captains Courageous.
Actress: Luise Rainer, The Good Earth.
Picture: Life of Emile Zola, Warner.

1938
Actor: Spencer Tracy, Boys Town.
Actress: Bette Davis, Jezebel.
Picture: You Can't Take It With You, Columbia.

1939
Actor: Robert Donat, Goodbye Mr. Chips.
Actress: Vivien Leigh, Gone With the Wind.
Picture: Gone With the Wind, Selznick International.

1940
Actor: James Stewart, The Philadelphia Story.
Actress: Ginger Rogers, Kitty Foyle.
Picture: Rebecca, Selznick International.

1941
Actor: Gary Cooper, Sergeant York.
Actress: Joan Fontaine, Suspicion.
Picture: How Green Was My Valley, 20th Cent.-Fox.

1942
Actor: James Cagney, Yankee Doodle Dandy.
Actress: Greer Garson, Mrs. Miniver.
Picture: Mrs. Miniver, MGM.

1943
Actor: Paul Lukas, Watch on the Rhine.
Actress: Jennifer Jones, The Song of Bernadette.
Picture: Casablanca, Warner.

1944
Actor: Bing Crosby, Going My Way.
Actress: Ingrid Bergman, Gaslight.
Picture: Going My Way, Paramount.

1945
Actor: Ray Milland, The Lost Weekend.
Actress: Joan Crawford, Mildred Pierce.
Picture: The Lost Weekend, Paramount.

1946
Actor: Fredric March, Best Years of Our Lives.
Actress: Olivia de Havilland, To Each His Own.
Picture: The Best Years of Our Lives, Goldwyn, RKO.

1947
Actor: Ronald Colman, A Double Life.
Actress: Loretta Young, The Farmer's Daughter.
Picture: Gentleman's Agreement, 20th Cent.-Fox.

1948
Actor: Laurence Olivier, Hamlet.
Actress: Jane Wyman, Johnny Belinda.
Picture: Hamlet, Two Cities Film, Universal International.

1949
Actor: Broderick Crawford, All the King's Men.
Actress: Olivia de Havilland, The Heiress.
Picture: All the King's Men, Columbia.

1950
Actor: Jose Ferrer, Cyrano de Bergerac.
Actress: Judy Holliday, Born Yesterday.
Picture: All About Eve, 20th Century-Fox.

1951
Actor: Humphrey Bogart, The African Queen.
Actress: Vivien Leigh, A Streetcar Named Desire.
Picture: An American in Paris, MGM.

1952
Actor: Gary Cooper, High Noon.
Actress: Shirley Booth, Come Back, Little Sheba.
Picture: Greatest Show on Earth, Cecil B. DeMille, Paramount.

1953
Actor: William Holden, Stalag 17.
Actress: Audrey Hepburn, Roman Holiday.
Picture: From Here to Eternity, Columbia.

1954
Actor: Marlon Brando, On the Waterfront.
Actress: Grace Kelly, The Country Girl.
Picture: On the Waterfront, Horizon-American Corp., Columbia.

1955
Actor: Ernest Borgnine, Marty.
Actress: Anna Magnani, The Rose Tattoo.
Picture: Marty, Hecht and Lancaster's Steven Productions, U.A.

1956
Actor: Yul Brynner, The King and I.
Actress: Ingrid Bergman, Anastasia.
Picture: Around the World in 80 Days, Michael Todd Co., U.A.

1957
Actor: Alec Guinness, The Bridge on the River Kwai.
Actress: Joanne Woodward, The Three Faces of Eve.
Picture: The Bridge on the River Kwai, Columbia.

1958
Actor: David Niven, Separate Tables.
Actress: Susan Hayward, I Want to Live.
Picture: Gigi, Arthur Freed Production, MGM.

1959
Actor: Charlton Heston, Ben-Hur.
Actress: Simone Signoret, Room at the Top.
Picture: Ben-Hur, MGM.

1960
Actor: Burt Lancaster, Elmer Gantry.
Actress: Elizabeth Taylor, Butterfield 8.
Picture: The Apartment, Mirisch Co., U.A.

1961
Actor: Maximilian Schell, Judgment at Nuremberg.
Actress: Sophia Loren, Two Women.
Picture: West Side Story, United Artists.

1962
Actor: Gregory Peck, To Kill a Mockingbird.
Actress: Anne Bancroft, The Miracle Worker.
Picture: Lawrence of Arabia, Columbia.

1963
Actor: Sidney Poitier, Lilies of the Field.
Actress: Patricia Neal, Hud.
Picture: Tom Jones, Woodfall Prod., UA-Lopert Pictures.

1964
Actor: Rex Harrison, My Fair Lady.
Actress: Julie Andrews, Mary Poppins.
Picture: My Fair Lady, Warner Bros.

1965
Actor: Lee Marvin, Cat Ballou.
Actress: Julie Christie, Darling.
Picture: The Sound of Music, 20th Century-Fox.

1966
Actor: Paul Scofield, A Man for All Seasons.
Actress: Elizabeth Taylor, Who's Afraid of Virginia Woolf?
Picture: A Man for All Seasons, Columbia.

1967
Actor: Rod Steiger, In the Heat of the Night.
Actress: Katharine Hepburn, Guess Who's Coming to Dinner.
Picture: In the Heat of the Night.

1968
Actor: Cliff Robertson, Charly.
Actress: Katharine Hepburn, The Lion in Winter. Barbra Streisand, Funny Girl. (tie)
Picture: Oliver.

1969
Actor: John Wayne, True Grit.
Actress: Maggie Smith, The Prime of Miss Jean Brodie.
Picture: Midnight Cowboy.

1970
Actor: George C. Scott, Patton.
Actress: Glenda Jackson, Women in Love.
Picture: Patton.

1971
Actor: Gene Hackman, The French Connection.
Actress: Jane Fonda, Klute.
Picture: The French Connection.

1972
Actor: Marlon Brando, The Godfather.
Supporting Actor: Joel Grey, Cabaret.
Actress: Liza Minnelli, Cabaret.
Supporting Actress: Eileen Heckart, Butterflies Are Free.
Picture: The Godfather.
Foreign Language Film: The Discreet Charm of the Bourgeoisie.
Director: Bob Fosse, Cabaret.
Music: (score) Ralph Burns, Cabaret; (song) Al Kasha, Joel Hirschhorn, The Morning After, from The Poseidon Adventure.
Writing: (adapted) Mario Puzo and Francis Ford Coppola, The Godfather; (directly for screen) Jeremy Larner, The Candidate.
Cinematography: Geoffrey Unsworth, Cabaret.
Editing: David Bretherton, Cabaret.
Sound: Robert Knudson, David Hildyard, Cabaret.
Art Direction: Rolf Zehetbauer, Jurgen Kliebach, Herbert Strabl, Cabaret.
Documentary: (feature) Howard Smith, Sarah Kernochan, Marjoe; (Short) Charles & Martina Huguenot van der Linndenen, This Tiny World.
Costume Design: Anthony Powell, Travels with My Aunt.
Short Subject: (animated) Richard Williams, A Christmas Carol; (live action) Richard Barclay, Norman Rockwell's World ... An American Dream.
Jean Hersholt Humanitarian Award: Rosalind Russell.
Memorial Academy Award: Edward G. Robinson.
Special Effects: L. B. Abbot and A. B. Flowers, The Poseidon Adventure.

Canadian Film Awards

Source: Film Weekly Year Book

1969

Actor: Chris Wiggins, The Best Damn Fiddler from Calabogie to Kaladar
Acress: Jackie Burroughs, Dulcima
Picture: The Best Dam Fiddler from Calabogie to Kaladar

1970

Actor: Doug McGrath and Paul Bradley (tied), Goin' Down the Road
Actress: Genevieve Bujold, The Act of Heart
Picture: Psychocratie

1971

Actor: Jean Duceppe, Mon oncle Antoine
Actress: Ann Knox, The Only Thing You Know
Picture: Mon oncle Antoine

1972

Actor: Gordon Pinsent, The Rowdyman
Supporting Actor: Donald Pilon, Vrai nature de Bernadette
Actress: Micheline Lanctot, Vrai nature de Bernadette
Supporting Actress: Doris Petrie, Wedding in White
Picture: Wedding in White
Director: Gilles Carle, Vrai nature de Bernadette
Writer: (screen play) Gilles Carle, Vrai nature de Bernadette
Music: (score) Pierre Brault, Vrai nature de Bernadette
Grierson Award: Colin Low
Wendy Michener Award: Mireille Dansereau

National Teacher of the Year Award

Awarded by the Ladies' Home Journal magazine for distinguished service in elementary and secondary schools.

1952 — Geraldine Jomes, First grade, Hope Public School, Santa Barbara, Calif.
1953 — Dorothy Hamilton, Social studies, Milford H.S., Milford, Conn.
1954 — Willard Widerberg, Seventh grade, DeKalb Junior H.S., DeKalb, Ill.
1955 — Margaret Perry Teufel, Fourth grade, Monmouth Elementary, Monmouth, Ore.
1956 — Richard Nelson, Science, Flathead County H.S., Kalispell, Montana
1957 — (tie) Lugelle Guy Bizzell, speech, English & debate, A.N. McCallum H.S., Austin, Texas; and Mary Field Schwarz, Third grade, Bristol Elementary, Kansas City, Mo.
1958 — Jean Listebarger Humphrey, Second grade, Edwards Elementary, Ames, Iowa.
1959 — Edna Donley, mathematics and speech, Alva H.S., Alva, Okla.
1960 — Hazel Bragg Davenport, First grade, Central Elementary, Beckley, W. Va.
1961 — Helen Adams, Kindergarten, Cumberland Public School, Cumberland, Wisc.
1962 — Marjorie French, Mathematics, Topeka H.S., Topeka, Kansas.
1963 — Elmon Ousley, speech, American government & world problems, Bellevue Senior H.S., Bellevue, Wash.
1964   Lawana Trout, English, Charles Page H.S., Sand Springs, Okla.
1965 — Richard E. Klinck, Sixth grade, Reed Street Elementary, Wheat Ridge, Colo.
1966 — Mona Dayton, First grade, Walter Douglas Elementary, Tucson, Ariz.
1967 — Roger Tenney, music, Owatonna Junior-Senior H.S., Owatonna, Mich.
1968 — David E. Graf, vocational education & industrial arts, Sandwich Comm. H.S., Sandwich, Ill.
1969 — Barbara Goleman, language arts, Miami Jackson H.S., Miami, Fla.
1970 — Johnnie T. Dennis, physics, math analysis, Walla Walla H.S., Walla Walla, Wash.
1971 — Martha Marion Stringfellow, First grade, Lewisville Elementary, Chester Co., S.C.
1972 — James Marshall Rogers, American history & Black studies, Durham H.S., Raleigh, N.C.
1973 — John A. Ensworth, Sixth grade, Kenwood school, Bend, Ore.

Presidential Medal of Freedom

The Presidential Medal of Freedom is the nation's highest civilian award. It was instituted by President Kennedy and first awarded on July 4, 1963, to honor those "who contribute significantly to the quality of American life.

1969 Awards (By President Johnson)

Eugene R. Black (banker)
McGeorge Bundy (government official)
Clark M. Clifford (statesman)
Michael E. DeBakey (surgeon)
David Dubinsky (labor leader)
Henry Ford II (industrialist)
Ralph Ellison (author)
W. Averell Harriman (statesman)
Bob Hope (comedian)
Edgar Kaiser (industrialist)
Mary Lasker (philanthropist)
John W. Macy, Jr. (government official)
Gregory Peck (actor)
Laurance S. Rockefeller (conservationist)
Walt W. Rostow (government official)
Dean Rusk (statesman)
Merriman Smith (journalist)
Cyrus R. Vance (government official)
William S. White (journalist)
Roy Wilkins (social welfare executive)
Whitney M. Young (social welfare executive)

1969 Awards (By President Nixon)

Col. Edwin E. Aldrin, Jr. (astronaut)
Neil A. Armstrong (astronaut)
Lt. Col. Michael Collins (astronaut)
Duke Ellington (musician)

1970 Awards (By President Nixon)

Apollo 13 Mission Operations Team
Earl Charles Behrens (journalist)
Edward T. Folliard (journalist)
Fred Wallace Haise, Jr. (astronaut)
William M. Henry (journalist)*
Arthur Krock (journalist)
David Lawrence (journalist)
George Gould Lincoln (journalist)
James A. Lovell, Jr. (astronaut)
Raymond Moley (journalist)
Eugene Ormandy (conductor)
Adela Rogers St. Johns (journalist)
John Leonard Swigert, Jr. (astronaut)

1971 Awards (By President Nixon)

Sam Goldwyn (film producer)
Manlio Brosio (NATO secretary general)
William J. Hopkins (White House executive clerk)

1972 Awards (By President Nixon)

Lila and DeWitt Wallace (founders of Readers' Digest)
John Paul Vann (adviser in Vietnam war)

1973 Awards (By President Nixon)

John Ford (movie director)
*Awarded posthumously.

The Spingarn Medal

The Spingarn Medal has been awarded annually since 1914 by the National Association for the Advancement of Colored People for the highest achievement by an American Negro.

1945 — Thurgood Marshall	1955 — Jack Roosevelt Robinson	1963 — Roy Wilkins
1946 — Dr. Percy L. Julian	1956 — Martin Luther King, Jr.	1964 — Leontyne Price
1947 — Channing H. Tobias	1957 — Mrs. Daisy Bates and the Little	1965 — John H. Johnson
1948 — Ralph J. Bunche	Rock Nine	1966 — Edward W. Brooke
1949 — Charles Hamilton Houston	1958 — Edward Kennedy (Duke) Elling-	1967 — Sammy Davis, Jr.
1950 — Mabel Keaton Staupers	ton	1968 — Clarence M. Mitchell, Jr.
1951 — Harry T. Moore	1959 — Langston Hughes	1969 — Jacob Lawrence
1952 — Paul R. Williams	1960 — Kenneth B. Clark	1970 — Leon Howard Sullivan
1953 — Theodore K. Lawless	1961 — Robert C. Weaver	1971 — Gordon Parks
1954 — Carl Murphy	1962 — Medgar Wiley Evers	1972 — Wilson C. Riles

Engineering Wonders of North America

United States

Selected by American Society of Civil Engineers

In 1954 the American Society of Civil Engineers, after several years of research, selected the seven modern civil engineering wonders in the United States (shown listed in alphabetical order) and then selected one each year from 1960 on.

1973 — The Ludington Pumped Storage Project, Mich.	1963 — Ohio River Valley Clean Streams Program.
1972 — The California State Water Project.	1962 — Intercontinental Ballistic Missiles Program.
1971 — World Trade Center twin towers, N.Y.C.	1961 — John F. Kennedy (NY) Internatl. Airport.
1970 — Armco Steel Middletown Works in Ohio.	1960 — St. Lawrence Power and Seaway Project.
1969 — Oroville Dam on the Feather River and its accompanying Edward Hyatt Powerplant, California.	1954 — Chicago's sewage disposal system
1968 — San Mateo-Hayward Bridge over San Francisco Bay, Calif.	Colorado River Aqueduct
	Empire State Building
1967 — The Gateway Arch at St. Louis, Mo.	Grand Coulee Dam & Columbia Basin Project
1966 — NASA Complex 39, Apollo-Saturn V assembly.	Hoover Dam
1965 — Chesapeake Bay Bridge-Tunnel.	Panama Canal
1964 — Glen Canyon Dam on Colorado River.	San Francisco–Oakland Bridge

Canada

Selected with the aid of the Association of Professional Engineers

1972 — Churchill Falls Power Project. (Can.) Peace River Power Project.	1959 — St. Lawrence Seaway.
1971 — Pickering Nuclear Power Station.	1958 — Ripple Rock Blast. Trans-Canada Pipe Line.
1967 — Expo 67 Islands: Ile Sainte Helene and Ile Notre Dame. Gardiner Dam.	1954 — Kitimat Smelter.
	1951 — Cobalt Bomb.
	1950 — Avro C-102 Jetliner.
1965 — The 735 kv Transmission System of the Manicouagan Power Development.	1916 — C.P.R.'s Connaught Tunnel through the Rocky Mountains.
1962 — Alouette Satellite.	1909 — C.P.R.'s Spiral Tunnels through the Rocky Mountains.

Prize Bridges in U.S., 1972

Seven of the "most beautiful steel bridges" opened to traffic in the United States during 1972 were selected from 121 entries in the 45th annual competition sponsored by the American Institute of Steel Construction, the national association representing the structural steel fabricating industry.

The spans, chosen for designs showing concern "for human satisfaction, aesthetic needs, safety, social progress, and a sensitive concern for the environment" are:

Atchafalaya River Bridge, Simmesport, La.
LL Line over N. P. Ry. & LD 5 Line, Woodland, Wash.
Hatfield Bridge, Hatfield, Wisc.
Glen Lily Road No. 2 over B. O. P., Bowling Green, Ky.

Latah Creek Bridge, Spokane, Wash.
Harvey Canal Bridge, Jefferson Parish, La.
Pedestrian Overpass at Avenue Z, San Angelo, Texas.

Winners of 13th Annual Beautiful Steel Building Competition

Eight winners were named in the 13th Annual Competition for steel framed buildings sponsored by the American Institute of Steel Construction. The winners included a playground shelter, a substation, a bank, a school, an exhibition hall, a naval air station, a boiler plant and a vocational technical center. A list of the winners named in 1972 and located in 8 different states are listed below:

Naval Air Rework Facility P-108/P-110, Naval Air Station, North Island San Diego, Calif.
Boiler Plant Addition, Terre Haute, Indiana
McCormick Place On-The-Lake, Chicago, Ill.
Peoples Trust Company Mini Bank, Fort Wayne, Ind.

Cook Field, Yonkers, N.Y.
Calvert County Vocational-Technical Center, Prince Frederick, Md.
Monguagon School, Trenton, Mich.
Pardee Sub-Station, Valencia, Calif.

Miss America Pageant of Atlantic City, N.J.

The Miss America Pageant of Atlantic City, N.J., is a resort-promotion device developed since 1921, attracting thousands of visitors and getting national newspaper, radio and television coverage. Miss Ruth McCandliss is Executive Secretary. Local and state contestants are chosen by civic, educational and service organizations. A contestant must have a high school education and may come from any of the 50 states. The Scholarship Foundation, supported by industrial leaders, supplies $67,000 at the national finals, while nearly $1,000,000 is awarded at 3,500 local, state and national pageants. The 1973 finals were held at Atlantic City Sept. 3-9.

1973 Miss America Pageant Scholarship Winners

Miss America 1974—$15,000 Scholarship
*Rebecca Ann King, Sterling, Colorado
Miss Wisconsin—1st Runner-Up—$10,000
Scholarship   Judy Hieke, Menomonee Falls, Wisconsin
Miss New Jersey—2nd Runner-Up—$5,000
Scholarship   Suzanne Plummer, Wildwood, N.J.
Miss Louisiana—3rd Runner-Up—$3,000
Scholarship   Debbie Ward, Baton Rouge, La.
Miss Pennsylvania—4th Runner-Up—$2,000
Scholarship   Tina Thomas, Lancaster, Pa.
Miss California—Semi-Finalist—$1,500
Scholarship   Susan Kaye Shipley, Hillsborough, California

Miss Illinois—Semi-Finalist—$1,500
Scholarship   Colleen Ann Metternich, Carthage, Illinois
Miss Oklahoma—Semi-Finalist—$1,500
Scholarship   Andrea Jean Hanson, Tahlequah, Oklahoma
Miss Texas—Semi-Finalist—$1,500
Scholarship   Judy Mallett, Haltom City, Texas
Miss Washington—Semi-Finalist—$1,500
Scholarship   Leslie Ann Mays, Mercer Island, Washington
Miss Hawaii—"Miss Congeniality"—$1,000
Scholarship   Kanoe Lehua Kaumeheiwa, Hawaii Kai, Honolulu, Hawaii

Seven Non-finalist Scholarships for Most Talented Contestants

Miss Florida—$1,000 Scholarship   Ellen Rowena Moody, Bradenton, Florida
Miss Massachusetts—$1,000 Scholarship   Rena Diane Walmsley, North Attleboro, Massachusetts
Miss Montana—$1,000 Scholarship   Debbie Reber, Helena, Montana
Miss New Hampshire—$1,000 Scholarship   Michelle

Annette Cote, Manchester, New Hampshire
Miss Ohio—$1,000 Scholarship   Cheryl Ann Yourkvitch, Lorain, Ohio
Miss Utah—$1,000 Scholarship   Brenda Richardson, Provo, Utah
Miss Vermont—$1,000 Scholarship   Joylynn Frances McGraw, Barre, Vermont

All Other Contestants ($500 Scholarships)

Miss Alabama—Jane Rice, Huntsville
Miss Alaska—Jinny Adams, Anchorage
Miss Arizona—Susan May, Kingman
Miss Arkansas—Becky Jean Hume, Jonesboro
Miss Connecticut—Deborah Rhodes Blanchard, North Haven
Miss Delaware—Jackie LaGuardia, Milford
Miss Georgia—Gail Bullock, Thomasville
Miss Idaho—Sharon Lea Davis, Jerome
Miss Indiana—Karen Louise Rogers, Indianapolis
Miss Iowa—Lynette Marie Henninger, Bettendorf
Miss Kansas—Janie Schulte, Hays
Miss Kentucky—Lyda Lewis, Louisville
Miss Maine—Carlene Frances Quimby, Auburn
Miss Maryland—Kristi Maurine Reindl, LaVale
Miss Michigan—Sherry Lee Agnello, St. Clair Shores
Miss Minnesota—Joleen Marie Benoit, Farmington
Miss Mississippi—Kathy Coole, Gulfport

Miss Missouri—Terri Dodson, Fulton
Miss Nebraska—Sandy Cramer, Omaha
Miss Nevada—Echo Layne Rost, Sparks
(also won $250 Neat-as-a-Pin Award)
Miss New Mexico—Patti Nelms, Roswell
Miss New York—Jo Ann Miller, Cheektowaga
Miss North Carolina—Heather Lee Walker, Hendersonville
Miss North Dakota—Linda Joyce Cole, Lisbon
Miss Oregon—Nancy Jean Jackson, Nyssa
Miss Rhode Island—Pattie Garrahy, North Providence
Miss South Carolina—Fran Jean Riggins, Easley
Miss South Dakota—Gwen Resick, Clark
Miss Tennessee—Anne Randle Galloway, Knoxville
Miss Virginia—Gail Vandeventer, Pulaski
Miss West Virginia—Myra Elizabeth McVey, Huntingdon
Miss Wyoming—Pamela Jo Hill, Casper

Former Miss America Winners

For the winners of 1921 through 1958 see the 1972 issue of the World Almanac

		Height	Bust	Waist	Hips	Wgt.	Age	Hair	Eyes
1959	Mary Ann Mobley, Brandon, Miss	5-5	34½	22	35	114	21	Brown	Brown
1960	Lynda Lee Mead, Natchez, Miss	5-7	36	24	36	120	20	Brown	Green
1961	Nancy Fleming, Montague, Michigan	5-6	35	22	35	116	18	Brown	Green
1962	Maria Fletcher, Asheville, N.C.	5-5½	35	24	35	118	19	Brown	Hazel
1963	Jacquelyn Mayer, Sandusky, Ohio	5-5	36	22	36	115	20	Brown	Hazel
1964	Donna Axum, El Dorado, Arkansas	5-6½	35	23	35	124	21	Brown	Brown
1965	Vonda Kay Van Dyke, Phoenix, Ariz	5-6	36	24	36	124	21	Brown	Brown
1966	Deborah Irene Bryant, Overland Park, Kansas	5-7	36	23	36	115	19	Brown	Blue
1967	Jane Anne Jayroe, Laverne, Oklahoma	5-6	36	24	35	116	19	Brown	Green
1968	Debra Dene Barnes, Moran, Kansas	5-9	36½	24	36½	135	20	Brown	Blue
1969	Judith Anne Ford, Belvidere, Ill.	5-7	36	24½	36	125	18	Blonde	Blue
1970	Pamela Anne Eldred, Birmingham, Mich.	5-5½	34	21½	34	110	21	Blonde	Green
1971	Phyllis Ann George, Denton, Texas	5-8	36	23	36	121	21	Brown	Brown
1972	Laurie Lea Schaefer, Columbus, Ohio	5-7	36	24	34	118	22	Auburn	Green
1973	Terry Anne Meeuwsen, DePere, Wisconsin	5-8	36	25	36	120	23	Brown	Brown

Miss Black America

Arnice Russell, 22, of New York City became Miss Black America in Cherry Hill, N.J. Aug. 25, 1973. The winner received a personal appearance contract, a new wardrobe and other gifts.

Miss Universe 1973
Athens, Greece, July 21, 1973

Miss Universe—Margarita R. Moran, Philip. 2nd Runner-Up—Aina Walle, Norway. 4th Runner-Up—Limor Shreibman, Israel. 1st Runner-Up—Amanda Jones, U.S.A.   3rd Runner-Up—Rocio Martin, Spain. Miss Unity—Jeanette Robertson, Chile.

The Earth Sciences

Source: U.S. Geological Survey

Mineral Resource Problems: Most Americans are well aware how much the activity of their daily lives is dependent upon the use of raw or manufactured materials that have been made from, processed by, fertilized with, or in some other way affected by minerals or mineral products. The energy crisis is but a part of a larger mineral supply problem; without a steady supply of minerals our civilization as we have known it cannot survive. Indeed, the availability of mineral resources to meet expected demands will critically affect future events in a world where population is growing and national economies are expanding to provide more and more people with a greater abundance of goods.

Unlike most other natural resources, minerals are not renewable. Minerals are formed in the earth's crust by natural processes acting for thousands or millions of years. Once removed and used, mineral deposits cannot be formed again in our lifetime. The answer to the question of whether our supplies of minerals are running out should be of concern to every citizen.

A mineral resource may be defined as a concentration of elements in a particular location in or on the earth's crust (including the ocean floor) in such a form that a usable mineral commodity can be extracted from it. These usable commodities may be chemical elements, such as iron or aluminium; chemical compounds, such as salt or borax; minerals, such as emerald or asbestos; or rocks, such as marble, coal, or gypsum. But this definition has little practical value unless the particular commodity can be extracted at a profit, the basic standard for the success of any business enterprise.

A fundamental concept in the evaluation of mineral resources is the distinction between **resources** and **reserves**, and the principal distinction is based on current economic availability. **Reserves** are the known identified deposits of mineral-bearing rock from which the mineral or minerals can be extracted profitably with existing technology and under present economic conditions. **Resources,** however, include not only reserves but also other mineral deposits that may eventually become available—either known deposits that are not economically or technologically recoverable at present, or unknown deposits that may be inferred to exist but have not yet been discovered. A simple analogy from personal finance may help to clarify this important distinction. Reserves are represented by the funds in one's bank account and by other liquid assets. Resources include, in addition, all other assets and, more importantly, all income one may expect to receive, from whatever source, through the duration of one's lifetime. Reserves, therefore, are the only part of the total resource that is available now.

Reserves are of paramount concern to the mineral industry, and reserve estimates for most mineral commodities are generally available and are constantly revised as economic and technologic conditions change. For most minerals, however, current reserves are only a small part of the total resources.

More and more newspaper, magazine, and other news media accounts attempt to offer evaluations of the nation's mineral resources, and some even try to forecast economic or cultural trends that are dependent on mineral supplies. Most of these accounts discuss mineral resources from the perspective of economic availability under a given set of conditions, thereby overlooking the vital fact that reserves are but a part of resources.

Evaluations predicated only on knowledge (or estimates) of current reserves can easily lead to forecasts of the death of the industrial society in a short time. On the other hand, evaluations based on another kind of assumption suggest that a rise in prices will increase the reserves and bring much more material to market economically from lower and lower grade material in larger and larger deposits. This reasoning is also fallacious because elements are available in the earth's crust in very finite amounts. In both instances, the reasoning leads to serious misinterpretations because it does not give enough consideration to the single factor that finally determines all levels and degrees of mineral potential: geologic availability.

Geologic availability concerns the existence and concentration of elements or combinations of elements and is the most fundamental characteristic of a mineral commodity that governs its commercial use. Assessment of geologic availability of a commodity requires basic knowledge of the physical occurrence and chemistry of that material, the geologic environments in which it occurs, and the amount (concentration or grade, often expressed as a percentage of the material) in those environments. The technology of exploration, mining and beneficiation, recovery, and use is founded on this indispensable information.

Public concepts of the magnitude of mineral resources commonly are based on evaluations of economic rather than geologic availability, and even these are subject to numerous problems. Sound accurate estimates of reserves for large regions are very difficult to compile for many reasons. At some time, however, the pressures of economic and geologic factors will meet in crisis. Economic factors may be altered rapidly. Changes in demand and use alter established patterns of production and consumption, new deposits will be sought elsewhere, substitutes will be sought, and new technology will be developed as the ingenuity of man is focused on solving the problems. But there is no economic availability if there is no geologic availability.

A recent study by the U.S. Geological Survey concluded that, of more than 60 mineral and energy commodities in use, only evaporate salts, gypsum, sulfur, and molybdenum are available domestically in quantities needed to supply expected needs for hundreds of years. By no means is it too early to become concerned about future mineral supplies and to start planning. As larger lower grade ore deposits are mined, the impact on the environment will be considered and adjustments made to balance need against wishes. Greater consideration will be given to getting coproducts and byproducts to market rather than allowing them to be wasted (or become less available than they are now.)

Extraction and processing of all minerals require some form of energy, and it is a safe generalization to say that to produce a fixed amount of any given commodity, the lower the grade of the ore, the greater is the quantity of energy required.

416

As the mining industry turns to lower and lower grades of many ores, the cost and availability of the required energy are probably the most important factors that will ultimately determine whether or not a particular mineral deposit can be worked economically.

Reserves are created not by expanding the artificial boundaries of geologic knowledge and economic availability that separate reserves from resources, but by applied research. Development of new technologies will make economic extraction of some resources feasible. Innovative application of classic geologic theory and the creation of new concepts of ore formation can be expected to lead to the discovery of conventional mineral deposits in favorable regions. Research and exploration can be counted on to lead to the discovery of some new types of deposits in ore environments that we do not know about now. To these factors we must also add the factor of human ingenuity. Only by continuing efforts through vigorous exploration, research, and technologic development can we expect to convert geologically available materials into usable reserves.

Chemical Elements and Environmental Health: Our natural environment consists of chemical elements combined in various ways to form minerals, rocks, soils, water, air, and organic materials. Superimposed on this natural environment are the effects of chemical pollution which have altered it intensely at least in some regions. Some of the chemical elements are beneficial to human and animal health, some are neutral, and some are harmful whether present as natural constituents of the environment or as a result of pollution.

To evaluate changes in the chemistry of the environment that result from pollution, it is important to have geochemical data on the natural state, or what is called "baseline geochemical data." Such data have been obtained in parts of Georgia and Kentucky and are currently being collected in Missouri in collaboration with the Environmental Health Surveillance Center of the University of Missouri at Columbia.

Veterinarians of the University of Missouri found a small area in the central part of the state where beef cattle were suffering metabolic disorders apparently caused by an imbalance of minerals or other nutrients in the diets. A geochemical survey of the area showed that a number of chemical elements were being introduced into the local environment; the source of the elements was an abandoned clay-mining operation upstream from the pastures. The discovery was made by comparing the chemistry of local plants, soils, and water with the baseline data that had been accumulated for similar, but unpolluted, environments throughout the state. Accumulation of additional baseline data for other large regions of the nation is regarded as an important part of the Geological Survey's program in geochemistry.

Volcano Watch: In more than 4 years of almost continuous activity, Kilauea Volcano, Hawaii, has erupted huge volumes of lava in what scientists of the U.S. Geological Survey term the longest and most varied period of flank activity in the recorded history of the volcano. The activity at Kilauea, one of the world's most active volcanoes, is monitored by scientists of the Survey's Hawaiian Volcano Observatory, located at the summit of the volcano. Kilauea has erupted 3 times in 1967-68, and, since 1969, the volcano has been in almost a continuous state of activity. For much of the time, lava has welled quietly up to the surface, but for brief periods, it has jetted to great heights. During one episode in December 1969, lava fountains reached to heights of 1,600 feet, about three times the height of the Washington monument.

Since May 1969, Kilauea has produced a total of more than 440 million cubic yards of lava (an average of about 300,000 cubic yards per day), which has buried between 25 and 30 square miles of surrounding ranchland and forest. On 5 separate occasions during the period, parts of the erupted rivers of lava cascaded over steep terraced cliffs and poured into the Pacific Ocean, adding a total of about 210 acres of new land (part of which has already been removed by vigorous marine erosion) to the island of Hawaii. During the eruptions, a total of about 7,200 acres of forest have been burned by four major fires started by lava flows. The lava reaching the sea has quenched to black volcanic glass which forms a large delta-like mass. This process of eruption and entry of lava into the sea has taken place countless times in the recent geologic past, always adding more acreage to the island.

After Apollo—Geology of the Moon: The year 1973 saw the close of the Apollo program of manned exploration of the Moon. The U.S. Geological Survey was active in planning geological traverses and objectives on the 6 landing missions, in astronaut training and mission operations, and in analysis of the huge store of data collected on the Moon.

Rocks at the surface of the Moon proved to be markedly heterogeneous though probably not so much as comparable samples from the earth. Primitive material which might have dated back to the origin of the Moon and the solar system was not found at the sites visited. It is doubtful if such primitive material is present anywhere at the surface inasmuch as there has been considerable lateral redistribution of materials by meteoritic impact.

One distinct type of lunar material makes up the maria, or seas, the dark patches which are visible to the naked eye from Earth. These dark areas were sampled on the Apollo 11, 12, 15 and 17 missions and also by the Russian Luna 16 mission. The dark areas proved to be underlain by volcanic basalts rich in iron and titanium. The lavas of the maria were erupted over a period from about 3.1 to 3.8 billion years ago by partial melting in the Moon's interior. Orbital photographs taken under low sun illumination show a series of distinct lava flows making up the mare areas, indicating that eruption of each layer occurred after the preceding one had solidified.

The Apollo 15 mission visited the Hadley Rille, a huge meandering cleft in the maria. Several of the mare laval flows were exposed in the walls of the rille. Combined evidence from the lunar surface and orbit indicate that the rille is probably a collapsed lava tube through which lava drained toward the central part of the mare basin.

Rocks of the lunar highlands appear much brighter than the dark lavas of the maria. They make up about 80% of the moon's surface including virtually all of the far side. Apollos 14 and 16 and the Russian Luna 20 landed on the rolling hills and plains of the highlands; Apollos 15 and 17 landed near the base of steep highland mountains and collected fragments at the base of these hills. Some of the rocks sampled at the Apollo 17 site had obviously rolled down the mountain.

The highland rocks contain more feldspar and less iron and titanium than the mare rocks. Most of them are feldspathic breccias with a wide range of textures. Some are only slightly deformed and broken igneous rocks; others represent many cycles of reworking of rocks from several sources.

The so-called "genesis rock" collected at the Apollo 15 site is anorthosite (nearly pure feldspar) which has been shocked and broken but retains much of its original igneous texture. Like most of the highland rocks, its age lies close to 4 billion years so it does not apparently date back to the genesis of the moon at about 4.5 billion years. Whether these ages of highland rocks represent their time of crystallization or the time when they were involved in huge impacts which reset their radiometric clocks is an unsolved problem at this time.

One of the most distinctive materials returned from the moon was the "orange soil" from the Apollo 17 site. Rather than a young volcanic alteration product, as originally interpreted, it proved to be a deposit of orange glass the same age as the local mare basalts — 3.7 billion years. Its origin remains obscure. Another unusual material at the Apollo 17 site is a bright mantle of material extending from the South Massif 6 kilometers across the Taurus-Littrow Valley. It appears to be an avalanche deposit triggered by the formation of secondary impact craters high on the slopes of the South Massif.

Map of Mars: During the past year, the U.S. Geological Survey produced the first detailed map of the entire surface of the planet Mars. The map, based upon mosaics of thousands of photographs of the "red planet" returned by Mariner 9 spacecraft, was prepared in a shaded relief effect at a scale of 1:25,000,000 (1 inch to about 400 miles), and shows the major surface features of the entire planet — an area of about 55,700,000 square miles, or more than 18 times the area of the conterminous (48) United States.

The northern latitudes of Mars (north of about 20° N) are only sparsely cratered and include several large and relatively young volcanoes. Areas in the southern latitudes are more heavily cratered and include no large youthful volcanic features. Preliminary elevation data (not shown on the map) indicate that the northern portions of Mars are generally lower than the southern portions.

Among many unusual features depicted on the map is a volcanic mountain about 300 miles wide and rising to a height of about 10 miles with a 40-mile diameter summit crater or caldera. Another impressive feature shown on the map is a giant canyon that stretches for 2,600 miles, almost one-fourth of the entire circumference of Mars. Another feature — a huge basin — is about 1,400 miles in diameter, nearly twice as big as the largest basin on the Moon. Geologists speculate that internal heating and volcanism on Mars may just be beginning, and so far, has affected only the northern area. In contrast, volcanism on Earth has occurred throughout geologic time.

Meanwhile, two sites on Mars announced by NASA as landing areas for unmanned instrumented Viking spacecraft have been targets of intensive study by USGS geologists. Plans call for the first lander to touch down in the Chryse region (lat. 20° N, long. 33° W), an area located on a plain north of the lower end of a large channel, on or about July 4, 1976. About a month and a half later, a second lander will touch down in the Cydonia region (lat. 44° N, long. 10° W), not far from the southernmost extent of the north polar cap. The

search for life is an important factor in guiding the choice of landing sites, and geologists believe that the selected sites offer possibilities for evidences of either "fossil" water, or present water.

Geologic Aid to Foreign Nations: Scientific and technical cooperation between U.S. Geological Survey specialists and earth scientists in other countries has made an important contribution both to the Survey's domestic research program and to similar programs in counterpart agencies abroad. In addition to joint research and scientific exchange on subjects of mutual interest, the Survey has undertaken many cooperative assistance projects during the past 3 decades, mostly on behalf of the Agency for International Development of the Department of State.

The Survey's assistance has been oriented primarily toward helping the developing countries map and evaluate their resources and strengthen their resource institutions and programs. Such programs help the host countries achieve a more viable economy and keep abreast of the rapidly evolving earth-science technology. Some of the Survey programs have continued for long periods, with highly successful results, particularly in Brazil, Colombia, Chile, Pakistan, Turkey, Saudi Arabia, and Liberia.

Earthquake Research Staff Augmented: In May of 1973 the seismological and geomagnetic research groups from the Environmental Research Laboratories of the National Oceanic and Atmospheric Administration (NOAA), Department of Commerce joined forces with the U.S. Geological Survey, Department of the Interior. The more, part of an effort to consolidate Federal research in solid earth physics, involved about 75 scientists, engineers, and technicians.

The NOAA groups now part of the Geological Survey are:

The Earthquake Mechanism Laboratory, San Francisco, California, which conducts studies of strain, creep, and seismicity along the San Andreas and other active faults;

The Seismological Field Survey, San Francisco, California, which measures and analyses earthquake strong motion using an extensive network of specialized instruments;

The Special Projects Party, Las Vegas, Nevada, which conducts strong motion and seismicity studies, largely for the Atomic Energy Commission in connection with underground nuclear explosions;

The Seismological Research Group, Boulder, Colorado, which evaluates seismic risk and carries out other seismological research; and,

The Geomagnetic Research Group, Boulder, Colorado, which conducts research on rock magnetism analysis and monitors the earth's magnetic field.

The addition of these research specialists will bolster the Geological Survey's program activities directed toward important scientific goals, including: evaluation of seismic risk, prediction and control of earthquakes, and improvement of earthquake-resistant design for buildings.

The Geological Survey's earthquake program, conducted primarily from its National Center for Earthquake Research, Menlo Park, California, is keyed to the better understanding of fundamental seismological, geophysical, geological, tectonic, and soil mechanics principals. The Survey's program interfaces closely with that of the National Science Foundation, which has major responsibility for funding federal earthquake engineering research and also supports geophysical and geological research in the nation's colleges and universities.

Distribution of Elements in the Earth's Crust and Sea Water: The oceans and the earth's crust — the thin rocky "rind" of our planet — contain the raw elements that are the basic building blocks of our modern society. The following table provides an idea of the relative abundance of some of the more essential elements. Geologists of the U.S. Geological Survey emphasize that the estimates are necessarily crude and approximate, and that while some of the elements, such as aluminum, appear to be quite abundant, they can be mined and extracted only where they are concentrated favorably in accessible mineral deposits.

AVERAGE CONCENTRATIONS
(Tons per cubic mile)

Element	Crustal Rocks	Sea Water
Aluminum	910,000,000	39
Boron	110,000	18,000
Bromine	34,000	250,000
Chromium	2,200,000	0.2
Copper	780,000	12
Fluorine	3,300,000	5,500
Gold	50	0.01
Iron	560,000,000	39
Lead	150,000	0.4
Magnesium	230,000,000	5,000,000
Manganese	11,000,000	8
Nickel	830,000	8
Silver	900	1
Strontium	3,400,000	51,000
Tin	450,000	12
Zinc	1,500,000	39

Man's Water Supply: According to USGS hydrologists, man is presently able to utilize not more than one percent of the world's total supply of water. Most of the world's water — the estimate is more than 97 percent — is in the oceans. Most of the rest is locked up in the ice caps of Greenland and Antarctica — more than two percent. Therefore, man is left with only a small fraction of the total water supply to work with — except insofar as he has begun to tap the oceans for industrial cooling water and is beginning to desalinize a little ocean water for his use. Even so, there seems to be enough fresh, liquid water on the earth to supply present and projected needs far into the next century at least, providing we will bear the cost of making it clean, keeping it clean, storing and transporting it, and increasingly recycling it for more than one-time use.

It is rather convenient, and quite accurate, to look at the total supply of fresh water on the earth as recycled sea water — water that has evaporated from the surface of the oceans leaving the salt behind; water that is in the atmosphere and in lakes and rivers; or water that is in the soil or deeper in the aquifers (water-bearing strata) that underlie the land in many places and supply water to wells and springs. Wherever it is, and though it may take a while to get there, the fresh water is enroute back to the sea again.

Discharged Sediments: Rivers in the conterminous (48) United States discharge an average of about 1.3 million tons of sediment every day (491 million tons per year) into the oceans. Most of this soil and rock debris is deposited in the Gulf of Mexico. The Mississippi River alone discharges about 245 million tons of sediment every year into the Gulf — almost as much as all other U.S. rivers combined.

According to USGS measurements, the Eel River in northern California is the fastest eroding of the Nation's largest river basins, producing an average annual sediment yield of about 9,430 tons per square miles of basin. In contrast, the Colorado River, because of its highly developed reservoir system, has a sediment yield of only 0.04 tons per square mile, the lowest yield of any area draining into the oceans from the conterminous United States. The average sediment discharge to the oceans from the entire conterminous United States is 184.4 tons per square mile; in other words, an average of about 185 tons of sediment is eroded from each square mile of the United States.

Outer Continental Shelf: Among the responsibilities of the USGS are the classification of federal lands as to mineral character and water-power potential, the supervision of mining, drilling, and removal of minerals from leased federal and Indian lands, and the collection of royalties on behalf of the U.S. government from such operations. As reserves of oil and gas onshore of the U.S. continue to decline, reserves in the outer continental shelf are gaining greater attention. USGS scientists estimate that about half of the not-yet-discovered

World's Estimated Water Supply

Location	Surface area (square miles)	Water volume (cubic miles)[1]	Percentage of total water
Surface water:			
Fresh-water lakes	330,000	30,000	0.009
Saline lakes and inland seas	270,000	25,000	.008
Average in stream channels	—	300	.0001
Subsurface water:			
Water in unsaturated zone (includes soil moisture)	—	16,000	.005
Ground water within a depth of half mile	50,000,000	1,000,000	.31
Ground water — deep lying	—	1,000,000	.31
Other water locations:			
Icecaps and glaciers	6,900,000	7,000,000	2.15
Atmosphere (at sea level)			
	197,000,000	3,100	.001
World ocean	139,500,000	317,000,000	97.2
Totals (rounded)	—	326,000,000	100

[1] A cubic mile of water equals 1.1 trillion gallons.

covered crude oil reserves are offshore. The average oil discovery offshore contains 10 times the amount of oil and gas as the average onshore discovery. Less than 2% of the outer continental shelf has been leased. Total oil and gas production, and the royalty value from the outer continental shelf, principally off the coasts of the following states, through 1972, were as follows:

California	90,654,122	billion barrels of oil	$45,683,229
	43,579,743	million cubic feet of gas	$1,961,089
Louisiana	2,752,018,400	bbl oil	$1,591,139,647
	16,609,924,592	mcf gas	$502,568,780
Texas	15,370,364	bbl oil	$8,698,410
	786,839,669	mcf gas	$21,346,373

Since 1969, regulations governing outer continental shelf oil and gas operations have been revised and strengthened; the force for inspecting industry operations have been tripled, and their mobility and effectiveness increased by the use of helicopters and constant radio communication. These improvements, together with systemized inspection procedures, have resulted in a reduction of incidences of noncompliance of regulations, and of the numbers of low-level, chronic oil spills.

Mapping the Nation: One of the Geological Survey's major responsibilities is the preparation and updating of topographic maps which show the natural, as well as man-made features of the nation's land surface. These maps, produced by the agency's Topographic Division, provide a starting point for many high priority national activities including location and development of the nation's natural resources and land-use planning.

Modern map making requires teamwork; field survey engineers, who obtain the geographic data necessary to position the features on the map; photogrammetric specialists who obtain accurate map detail from aerial photographs through the use of the photogrammetric instruments; and cartographers, who scribe, edit and prepare the map manuscripts for publication.

The topographic mapping activity of the Geological Survey, conducted in part in cooperation with state and local government agencies produces the several series of standard quadrangle maps which constitute the National Topographic Program. These maps cover most of the area of the 50 States, Puerto Rico, American Samoa, the Virgin Islands, the Trust Territory of the Pacific Islands, and limited parts of Antarctica. Because maps become out of date, revision is necessary to show changes in terrain and additions to manmade features such as roads, buildings, and reservoirs. Through techniques such as photorevision procedures, the Survey carries out a continuous program to update its map series.

Most of the original topographic mapping now being done by USGS is published at a scale of 1/24000 (1 inch = 2,000 feet) in quadrangle units bounded by 7½ minutes of latitude and longitude. Mapping at this scale has been completed for about 57% of the country. In addition to the standard quadrangle maps, USGS provides special mapping products and services to meet national needs.

The Map Information Office collects, organizes, and distributes, without charge, information about the availability of map coverage, aerial photography, and geodetic control in the United States, and information about the activities of other federal mapping agencies and some state and private organizations.

The National Atlas of the United States, produced by the Geological Survey in cooperation with other federal agencies and private organizations, is a bound collection of color maps and charts showing the nation's physical features such as landforms, geology, soil, vegetation, and climate as well as economic, social and historical data.

In addition to the preparation and maintenance of the National Topographic Map Series, the Survey has developed new types of maps to meet special requirements. Some of these include orthophotomaps, a combination of photographic imagery and conventional map symbols, and clinometric maps showing slope zones generated from the contours of a standard map. A program is currently in progress for the publication of a series of topographic maps, each covering a complete county.

The Earth Resources Technology Satellite (ERTS-1) launched in July 1972, promises that satellite imagery will prove to be of value as a mapping aid. In addition to providing a means for the revision of small-scale maps, the imagery may provide an accurate and useful photo map. The U.S. Geological Survey is developing prototype ERTS image maps within the United States and parts of Antarctica.

Index maps of the National Topographic Map Series for each state, Puerto Rico and the Virgin Islands and Antarctica are available that show the areas covered by published maps. They also contain price information, ordering instructions and may be obtained without charge on request.

Eros Program: The Earth Resources Observation Systems program, administered by the U.S. Geological Survey, is coordinating departmental research activities using Earth Resources Technology Satellite (ERTS) and Skylab data. Attempts to identify geostructures of the continental crust in Alaska, particularly as they relate to mineral resources, has led to a greatly improved appreciation of the geologic structure of the area. Several experiments make use of ground data telemetered via ERTS and Goddard Space Flight Center to appropriate offices throughout the United States. Data on water temperature, acidity, oxygen concentration, ground water level and stream height in the Delaware River Basin are telemetered to the Basin Commission for use in their management of the river system. In south Florida, several data-collection platforms transmit information on water levels and cumulative rainfall used in devising a simplified "water budget" required for proper water management of the area, including the Everglades National Park. Assessment of the 1973 record-breaking Mississippi River flood using ERTS imagery, included measurement of areas flooded, movement of flood crests, limits of excessive soil moisture and its effect on the return of the flooded lands to agricultural use.

Pictures from Space: A cloud-free picture of your home town, taken from an altitude of 920 kb (570 miles), is probably now available from the Interior/Geological Survey EROS Data Center, Sioux Falls, South Dakota. Since its launch in July 1972, ERTS-1 (Earth Resources Technology Satellite) has acquired more than 15,000 scenes of the U.S., which provide cloud-free coverage (that is, 10 percent or less cloud cover) of at least 90 percent of the country, including Alaska and Hawaii. Each picture or image covers an area 185km (115 miles) on a side. Band 5, the red wavelength image from the multispectral scanner, is the best black and white picture for general purposes. A few scenes have been selected for special processing to make color pictures. Information on available pictures and prices can be obtained from the EROS Data Center, Sioux Falls, South Dakota 57198.

Land use Classification System: A new national land-use classification system has been proposed by geographers of the USGS for testing and review. The system has been developed to meet the needs of federal and state agencies for an up-to-date overview of land use throughout the nation on a basis that is uniform in date, scale, and categorization. The system is designed to accommodate the wealth of natural resource and environmental data being returned from earth-orbiting satellites and high-altitude aircraft. Rapid and complex changes in the use of land and water for a variety of purposes are placing a strain on the effectiveness of existing programs, which vary considerably in their identification of various land-use categories. The newly proposed system uses the best features of existing systems to the extent that they are amenable to use with remote sensing. The system is also "open-ended" so that regional, state, and local agencies may develop more detailed land-use classification systems to meet particular needs, and at the same time, remain compatible with each other and with the national system.

Oceanography—1973

Source: National Oceanic and Atmospheric Administration

Widespread contamination of the oceans received major attention in 1973. Oil globules and plastic debris in massive proportions infect nearly 700,000 square miles of blue water from Cape Cod to the Caribbean Sea, 3 ships of the National Oceanic and Atmospheric Administration (NOAA) discovered, and these materials are now part of the habitat of uncountable numbers of newborn blue marlin, tuna, bluefish, and other prized game and commercial species.

The cruises were made to assess distribution of fish eggs and larvae, but NOAA scientists often experienced difficulty with plankton-collecting nets from fouling by tar balls. One of the survey ships, **Albatross IV,** reported that 75 percent of the time its nets were befouled by oil clumps so thick they extruded through the mesh "like spaghetti". Laboratory analyses revealed that more than half the plankton (young fish and their food) collected from surface waters was oil-contaminated.

Following this announcement in February, a second report in March disclosed that thousands of pieces of plastic, ranging from tiny scraps to lengths of fishnet 100 feet long, litter Alaska's remote Amchitka Island beaches.

To learn how such pollutants affect plant and animal life in the world's oceans, the National Science Foundation in May announced a 6-year international program for which NSF initially granted more than $1,250,000. Total cost is projected at $6,000,000. Part of the International Decade of Ocean Exploration, the project is designed to learn specifically what effects chemical pollutants have on plankton. Scientists from Canada and the United Kindom will join in the project.

Increasingly, efforts to solve the riddles of the ocean became international. Antarctic icebergs that break off from the great southern continent and move north are tracked by a French satellite, EOLE-1, launched for the French by the National Aeronautics and Space Administration. American, Japanese, British, and New Zealand scientists are cooperating in the program, in which radio transmitters are placed on the icebergs for satellite tracking, giving the scientists information about ocean currents and circulation near the Antarctic continent.

An intensive 4-month study of a 40,000 square mile area of the Atlantic was carried on from March through June, involving 50 scientists from 15 oceanographic institutions in the United States, Britain, Sweden, and West Germany. Known as Mid-Ocean Dynamics Experiment (MODE), it was the most elaborate oceanographic field experiment ever attempted in the western world, and revealed much new information about the movements of medium-range ocean currents. For example, scientists have discovered that in many places the actual current, such as in the Gulf Stream, can flow in a direction opposite to the expected average for weeks at a time, and that large rotating masses of warm or cold water can drift around in the ocean for long periods of time.

U.S.-French Cooperation

The U.S.-French cooperative program in oceanography, led in France by the Centre Nationale pour l'Exploitation des Oceans and in the U.S. by NOAA, met in Miami in May to plan international projects on ocean pollution, aquaculture, and a joint program in the mid-Atlantic ridge. The latter program, called FAMOUS (French-American Mid-Ocean Undersea Study), began in September, with French submersibles diving off the Azores. Purpose of the program, which involves U.S. submersible **Alvin** operated by Woods Hole Oceanographic Institution for the Office of Naval Research, is to explore what many scientists believe to be the basic process responsible for shaping the earth's surface—the splitting-apart of the mid-ocean ridge and consequent seafloor spreading, a process that is slowly increasing the distance between New York and London.

Glomar Challenger, the drilling ship used in the National Science Foundation's famed Deep Sea Drilling Project, will conduct closely coordinated operations nearby during parts of Project FAMOUS.

The Deep Sea Drilling Program reported additional research findings during the year, and increased its international capability by for the first time bringing in a foreign oceanographic institution as part of its planning consortium— the P.P. Shirshov Institute of Oceanology of the USSR Academy of Sciences. At the end of Leg 31 of its cruise, **Glomar Challenger** reported in August from Hakodate, Japan, that the Philippine Sea and the Sea of Japan appear to be relatively young. The Philippine Sea appears no older than 60,000,000 years, while adjacent seafloor east of the Marianas Trench exceeds 100,000,000 years in age, according to evidence from recovered sediments and tiny entombed fossils.

Also in August, on the other side of the globe, 4 research ships—NOAA's **Researcher** from the United States, **Academician Korolov** and **Ernest Krenkel** from the Soviet Union, and **Cadete Virgilio Uribe** from Mexico—conducted a 10-day rehearsal of the complex GATE project planned for 1974. GATE—the GARP Atlantic Tropical Experiment—will be the first major international experiment in the Global Atmospheric Research Program (GARP), and will involve ships, aircraft, and satellites of 11 nations. The 4 ship rehearsal enabled scientists to correlate observations made by different sensors and with different observing techniques, and to adjust their procedures for common purposes.

A third international effort got under way in August when scientists from all over the world—including Dr. Edwin F. Danielson of the National Center for Atmospheric Research, Boulder, Colo. —met to seek solutions to some of the critical oceanic problems that threaten the survival of the city of Venice, Italy. The threat of high tides attacking Venice's ancient structures increases each year because the land is gradually subsiding, at the rate of about one inch every 5 years.

Manned undersea activities continued to provide information that cannot be obtained by indirect means, although the **Johnson Sea-Link** 4-man submersible suffered a tragedy in June. The small submersible, exploring off Key West, became entangled in a sunken destroyer's rigging. Before she could be brought up, two of the divers had expired.

Undersea Minerals

In another undersea operation, marine geologists headed by Dr. Robert Ginsburg of the University of Miami made 86 dives in 14 dive days, sampling areas of the Barrier Reef off British Honduras. They found the reef hardening into rock 600 feet underwater, and opened up new possibilities for oil prospecting on land. The expedition, jointly sponsored by NSF and NOAA, determined that even where coral reefs are nonporous, which oil prospectors earlier believed meant that they were devoid of oil, adjoining areas of the same reef may be porous and can contain oil. The team used the 2-man submersible **Nekton,** diving to depths as great as 1,050 feet.

During the year also, diving tables were successfully developed and tested by Union Carbide Corp, on contract to NOAA. These tables, provide scientist-divers with precise knowledge of how long they can work at various depths while saturated with a nitrogen-oxygen breathing mixture.

The new habitat **La Chalupa,** operated by the Puerto Rico Inter-National Undersea Laboratory (PRINUL), was successfully tested during the year, and regular scientific operations began in locations up to 100 feet in depth off Mayaguez, P.R. **La Chalupa** contains 4 scientists for up to 2 weeks while they perform underwater experiments.

Drs. Robert B. and Martha R. Scott, a husband-and-wife team of Texas A&M University scientists, collaborated with Dr. Peter A. Rona, research geophysicist of the Atlantic Oceanographic and Meteorological Laboratories, in analyses indicating that metal-concentrating processes in the ocean basins are many times more efficient than previously believed.

Other oceanographic research results during the year provided new clues both to the history of the earth and to the possibilities for increased use of the ocean's resources by man. Dr. Clement G. Chase of the University of Minnesota and Dr. Eugene C. Perry, Jr., of Northern Illinois University, after a close study of the chemistry of ancient oceanic rocks, have concluded that the world's oceans may be gradually shrinking. Ancient cherts—sedimentary rocks composed of pure silica that once was dissolved in ocean water—have a smaller ratio of heavy to light oxygen atoms than do modern day cherts. The changes in oxygen ratio is more rapid in a smaller volume, where the effect of the volcanic heavy oxygen is not as diluted, hence their conclusion.

Nine undersea mountains were discovered in the eastern Pacific off the Chilean coast, one of them towering more than two miles above the seabed. Ranging in height from 4,626 to 10,689 feet, the mountain chain in part surpasses in height the Pyrenees mountain range that separates France from Spain. The U.S. research ship **Discoverer** made the discoveries in the spring.

The cold water eddies that were a part of the MODE project may someday be used to speed shipping between the east coast of the United States and Bermuda, according to a Commerce Department oceanographer. Dr. Alan E. Strong said that surface currents near the edge of the eddies average about 2 miles per hour, and explained that if the speed and direction of these eddies was monitored and communicated to shipping lines, they could recommend slight course alterations to their vessels to permit them to take advantage of this extra "lift" provided by the ocean.

Drill of The Deep

Drill a hole in the New York City sidewalk with a wet noodle dangling from the top of the Empire State Building! Impossible? But that is a rough description of the task of *Glomar Challenger,* an ocean-going drilling rig.

In 1968, this ship began deep explorations of the ocean floor. By lowering into the open ocean over 20,000 feet of pipe and drilling into the floor, the *Glomar Challenger* can bring up cores, or samples, from the underlying sediment and rock. Less than 4 years on the job, the ship's crew has brought up cores which show astonishing facts about the oceans and their floors.

Cores taken from the Atlantic, for example, have proved that that ocean is expanding by about one inch a year as new earth material wells up from the Mid-Atlantic rift valley and pushes the Old and New Worlds apart. At the same time, the Mediterranean is growing smaller, according to the samples, because Africa is moving north. In time, the Mediterranean may return to the conditions of 6,000,000 years ago—a vast salt desert, two miles deep, separated from the Atlantic by a mountain chain across the Strait of Gibraltar. This view of the Mediterranean was also suggested by the evidence of the *Glomar Challenger's* samples.

Lately, the ship has been exploring the Pacific. It found that the oldest sediments in the Pacific are only 160,000,000 years old—about 1/25th as old as the planet. And the Pacific is shrinking as the Americas move north and west.

Research Minisub Trapped: 2 Oceanographers Die

Disaster struck a Smithsonian Institution project studying how subtropical fish had converted the wreck of a 2,425-ton destroyer into a 390-foot artificial reef. The project's research vessel, the Johnson-Sea-Link minisubmarine, became entrapped, **June 17,** in the scuttled destroyer, 360 feet below water level about 15 miles off Key West, Fla.

Rescue came 31 hours later when a grappling hook secured with the aid of remote control television cameras, **June 18,** yanked the sub to the surface. But, 2 members of the 4-man oceanographic crew were found dead of exposure when their bodies were removed from the aft section of the minisub where they had been trapped. Due to intricate decompression procedures, the bodies were taken from the sub 29 hours after it was hauled to the surface. Dead were Albert Stover, 51, considered a leading authority in the operation of such experimental vessels, and E. Clayton Link, 31, the son of the mini-sub's designer, Edwin A. Link.

The other 2 crew members, Archibald Menzies, the pilot-commander, and Robert Meek, a marine biologist, trapped in the forward section, a large, transparent acrylic bubble, were declared fit after 90 minutes in a decompression chamber. The acrylic bubble had served as insulation from the 40° temperature below water.

However, the aft section, made mostly of aluminum, conducted cold into the ship's air system and adversely affected the Baralyme, an ash-soda compound carried aboard to absorb carbon dioxide exhaled by the crew. The combination of cold and carbon dioxide build-up brought death to the entrapped crew members.

When commissioned 2 years ago, the Johnson-Sea-Link, equipped with over 100 safety innovations, was the most sophisticated diving craft of its kind—a small submersible vessel built to penetrate the shallow depth of the continental shelf. Boxy in shape, with stacks of glass cylinders and transparent bubble, it looks more like a helicopter than a submarine. The design, with its many appendages, may well have contributed to the accident.

Mountaineering 1972-1973

Japanese mountain climbers continued to make mountain-climbing history during the post-monsoon Himalayan climbing season in 1972. A 7-member Japanese team scaled 23,774-foot Putha Hiunchuli in late October. It was the first successful attempt on the mountain since a British team reached the summit in 1954.

On October 2, 1972, three members of a Japanese expedition became the first to surmount Annapurna South along the difficult east ridge. The 23,738-foot peak was first scaled in 1964 by another Japanese team using the northwest face. In 1970, a French team succeeded in climbing the south face.

Another French team, in late 1972, successfully scaled Cujra Himal peak. A woman was among the 4 team members in the final assault on the 23,600-foot summit.

A major British effort to conquer Mt. Everest along the unscaled southwest face was called off after persistent battering by wind and snow. The team, which aimed to put the first Briton on the peak, set up the highest camp ever placed on the mountain—at 27,000 feet—and that height was the greatest ever achieved in the post-monsoon season.

In the New World, 7 Americans from Los Angeles successfully climbed Aconcagua Peak (22,834 ft.) in early February, 1973. Their success followed tragedy for another U.S. expedition on the peak. Two climbers, Janet Johnson of Denver and John Cooper of East Houston, Texas, were killed in a snow storm on the Los Polacas glacier; 6 other members of the group were rescued.

Climbing Accidents Climb

In North America, climbing accidents seemed to be continuing the upward trend of the last 7 years. The increase is largely explained by greater numbers of inexperienced climbers who attempt climbs that would challenge the best mountaineers.

North American Climbing Accidents*

Year	Number	Deaths
1966	74	19
1967	84	38
1968	83	32
1969	105	33
1970	140	21
1971	127	42
1972	168	61

* Compiled by the American Alpine Club.

Of the 212 people involved in accidents in 1972, 93 were rated as having little or no experience. An additional 68 were reported to have only moderate experience. These figures were reflected in the youth of the climbers who had accidents: 81 were under 20 and an additional 55 were between the ages of 21 and 25.

Experts in mountaineering advise young people not to attempt long or difficult climbs beyond their experience. The experts also caution against climbing in unfamiliar areas where sharp weather changes or rapid nightfalls can find the unwary in dangerous situations. Above all, the experts say, young would-be mountain climbers should learn the sport from experienced mountaineers—not by trial and error.

Early Explorers of the Western Hemisphere

The first men to discover the New World or Western Hemisphere are believed to have walked across a "land bridge" from Siberia to Alaska, an isthmus since broken by Bering Strait. From Alaska, these ancestors of the Indians spread through North, Central and South America. Anthropologists have placed these crossings at between 18,000 and 14,000 B.C.; but evidence found in 1967 near Puebla, Mex., indicates mankind reached there as early as 35,000-40,000 years ago.

At first, these people were hunters using flint weapons and tools. In Mexico, about 7000-6000 B.C., they founded farming cultures, developing corn, squash, etc. Eventually, they created complex civilizations—Olmec, Toltec, Aztec and Maya and, in South America, Inca. Carbon-14 tests show men lived about 8000 B.C. near what are now Front Royal, Va.; Kanawha, W. Va., and Dutchess Quarry, N.Y. The Hopewell Culture, based on farming, flourished about 1000 B.C.; remains of it are seen today in large mounds in Ohio and other states.

Norsemen (Norwegian Vikings sailing out of Iceland and Greenland) are credited by most scholars with being the first Europeans to discover America, with at least five voyages around 1000 A.D. to areas they called Helluland, Markland and Vinland—possibly Labrador, Nova Scotia or Newfoundland, and New England.

The remains of a settlement at L'Anse-aux-Meadows, near the northern tip of Newfoundland, were uncovered by Dr. and Mrs. Helge Ingstad, Norwegian archeologists, 1960-63, with the aid of a grant from the National Geographic Society. They identified the settlement as Norse. Carbon-14 tests from hearths and the remains of a smithy indicated the site was occupied about 900 A.D. and during several hundred years before and after.

In 1965 Yale University announced the discovery of a map drawn about 1440 and apparently based on earlier maps, showing an area southwest of Greenland labeled Vinland. The map also bore an inscription crediting the discovery of Vinland to Leif Ericsson and Bjarni (Herjolfsson), who are among leaders named in early Norse sagas describing voyages to Vinland.

Christopher Columbus, most famous of the discoverers, was born at Genoa, Italy, but made his discoveries sailing for the Spanish rulers Ferdinand and Isabella. Dates of his voyages, places he discovered and other information follow:

1492 — First voyage. Left Palos, Spain, Aug. 3 with 88 men (est.) Discovered San Salvador (Guanahani or Watling Isl., Bahamas) Oct. 12. Also Cuba, Hispaniola (Haiti-Dominican Republic); built Fort La Navidad on latter.

1493 — Second voyage, first part, Sept. 25, with 17 ships, 1,500 men. Dominica (Lesser Antilles) Nov. 3; Guadaloupe, Montserrat, Antigua, San Martin, Santa Cruz, Puerto Rico, Virgin Islands. Settled Isabela on Hispaniola. Second part (Columbus having remained in Western Hemisphere), Jamaica, Isle of Pines, La Mona Isl.

1498 — Third voyage. Left Spain May 30, 1498, 6 ships. Discovered Trinidad. Saw South American continent Aug. 1, 1498, but called it Isla Sancta (Holy Island). Entered Gulf of Paria and landed, first time on continental soil. At mouth of Orinoco Aug. 14 he decided this was mainland.

1502 — Fourth voyage, 4 caravels, 150 men. St. Lucia, Guanaja off Honduras; Cape Gracias a Dios, Honduras; San Juan River, Costa Rica; Almirante, Portobelo and Laguna de Chiriqui, Panama.

A.D.	Explorer	Nationality and Employer	Discovery or Exploration
1497	John Cabot	Italian-English	Newfoundland or Nova Scotia
1498	John and Sebastian Cabot	Italian-English	Labrador to Hatteras
1499	Alonso de Ojeda	Spanish	South American coast, Venezuela
1500, Feb	Vicente y Pinzon	Spanish	South American coast, Amazon River
1500, Apr	Pedro Alvarez Cabral	Portuguese	Brazil (for Portugal)
1500-02	Gaspar Corte-Real	Portuguese	Labrador
1501	Rodrigo de Bastidas	Spanish	Central America

1513	Vasco Nunez de Balboa	Spanish	Pacific Ocean
1513	Juan Ponce de Leon	Spanish	Florida
1515	Juan de Solis	Spanish	Rio de la Plata
1519	Alonso de Pineda	Spanish	Mouth of Mississippi River
1519	Hernando Cortes	Spanish	Mexico
1520	Fernando Magellan	Portuguese-Spanish	Straits of Magellan, Tierra del Fuego
1524	Giovanni da Verrazano	Italian-French	Atlantic Coast-New York harbor
1526-27	Sebastian Cabot	Italian-Spanish	Rio de la Plata (river)
1527	Panfilo de Narvaez	Spanish	Florida
1531	Alfonso de Souza	Portuguese	Rio de Janeiro (river)
1532	Francisco Pizarro	Spanish	Peru
1534	Jacques Cartier	French	Canada, Gulf of St. Lawrence
1536	Pedro de Mendoza	Spanish	Buenos Aires (river)
1536	A. N. Cabeza de Vaca	Spanish	Texas coast and interior
1539	Francisco de Ulloa	Spanish	California coast
1539-41	Hernando de Soto	Spanish	Mississippi River near Memphis
1539	Marcos de Niza	Italian-Spanish	Southwest (now U. S.)
1540	Francisco V. de Coronado	Spanish	Southwest (now U. S.)
1540	Hernando Alarcon	Spanish	Colorado River
1540	Garcia de L. Cardenas	Spanish	Grand Canyon of the Colorado
1541	Francisco de Orellana	Spanish	Amazon River
1541-43	A. N. Cabeza de Vaca	Spanish	Brazil, Paraguay River
1542	Juan Rodriquez Cabrillo	Portuguese-Spanish	San Diego harbor
1565	Pedro Menendez	Spanish	St. Augustine
1573	Pedro Marquez	Spanish	Chesapeake Bay
1576	Martin Frobisher	English	Frobisher's Bay, Canada
1577-80	Francis Drake	English	California coast
1582	Antonio de Espejo	Spanish	Southwest (named New Mexico)
1584	Amadas & Barlow (for Raleigh)	English	Virginia
1585-87	Sir Walter Raleigh's men	English	Roanoke Isl., N. C.
1595	Sir Walter Raleigh	English	Orinoco River
1602	Bartholomew Gosnold	English	Martha's Vineyard and Massachusetts
1603-09	Samuel de Champlain	French	Canadian interior, Lake Champlain
1604	Samuel de Champlain	French	Mt. Desert Island
1607	Capt. John Smith	English	Atlantic coast
1609-10	Henry Hudson	English-Dutch	Hudson River, Hudson Bay
1634	Jean Nicolet	French	Lake Michigan; Wisconsin

Arctic Exploration

Early Explorers

1587—John Davis (England). Davis Strait to Sanderson's Hope, 72° 12′N.

1596—Willem Barents and Jacob van Heemskerck (Holland). Discovered Bear Island, touched northwest tip of Spitsbergen, 79° 49′N., rounded Novaya Zemlya, wintered at Ice Haven.

1607—Henry Hudson (England). North along Greenland's east coast to Cape Hold-with-Hope, 73° 30′, then north of Spitsbergen to 80° 23′. Returning he discovered Hudson's Touches (Jan Mayen).

1616—William Baffin and Robert Bylot (England). Baffin Bay to Smith Sound.

1728—Vitus Bering (Russia). Proved Asia and America were separate by sailing through strait.

1733-40—Great Northern Expedition (Russia). Surveyed Siberian Arctic coast.

1741—Vitus Bering (Russia). Sighted Alaska from sea, named Mount St. Elias. His lieutenant, Chirikof, discovered coast.

1771—Samuel Hearne (Hudson's Bay Co.). Overland from Prince of Wales Fort (Churchill) on Hudson Bay to mouth of Coppermine River.

1778—James Cook (Britain). Through Bering Strait to Icy Cape, Alaska, and North Cape, Siberia.

1789—Alexander Mackenzie (North West Co., Britain). Montreal to mouth of Mackenzie River.

1806—William Scoresby (Britain), North of Spitsbergen to 81° 30′.

1820-3—Ferdinand von Wrangel (Russia). Completed a survey of Siberian Arctic coast. His exploration joined that of James Cook at North Cape, confirming separation of the continents.

1845—Sir John Franklin (Britain) was one of many to seek the Northwest Passage–an ocean route connecting the Atlantic and Pacific via the Arctic. His two ships, (the Erebus and Terror), were last seen entering Lancaster Sound July 26.

1888—Fridtjof Nansen (Norway) crossed Greenland's icecap, 1893-96—Nansen in Fram drifted from New Siberian Isls. to Spitsbergen; tried Polar dash in 1895, reached Franz Josef Land.

1896—Salomon A. Andree (Sweden) and companion, in June, made first attempt to reach North Pole by balloon; failed and returned in August. On July 11, 1897, Andree and 2 others started in balloon from Danes Isl., Spitsbergen, to drift across Pole to America, and disappeared. Over 33 years later, Aug. 6, 1930, Dr. Gunnar Horn (Norway) found their frozen bodies on White Isl., 82° 56′N, 29° 52′E.

1903-06—Roald Amundsen (Norway) first sailed Northwest Passage.

Discovery of North Pole

Robert E. Peary began exploring in 1886 on Greenland, when he was 30. With his hq. at McCormick Bay he explored Greenland's coast 1891-92, tried for North Pole 1893, returned with large meteorites. In 1900 he reached northern limit of Greenland and 83° 50′N.; in 1902 he reached 84° 17′N; in 1906 he went from Ellesmere Isl. to 87° 06′N; He sailed in the Roosevelt, July, 1908, to winter off Cape Sheridan, Grant Land. The dash for the North Pole began Mar. 1 from Cape Columbia, Ellesmere Land. Peary reached the Pole, 90°N., April 6, 1909.

Peary had several supporting groups carrying supplies until the last group, under Capt. Robt. A. Bartlett, turned back at 87° 47′N. Peary, Matthew Henson and 4 Eskimos proceeded with dog teams and sleds. They crossed Pole several times, finally built an igloo at 90°, remained 36 hours. Started south Apr. 7 at 4 p.m. for Cape Columbia. Eskimos were Coqueeh, Ootah, Eginwah and Seegloo. Adm. Peary died Feb. 20, 1920. Henson, a Negro, born Aug. 8, 1866, died in New York, N. Y., Mar. 9, 1955, aged 88. Ootah, last survivor, died near Thule, Greenland, May, 1955, aged 80.

1914—Donald Macmillan (U.S.). Northwest, 200 miles, from Axel Heiberg Island to seek Peary's Crocker Land.

1915-17-Vihjalmur Stefansson (Canada) discovered Borden, Brock, Meighen and Lougheed Islands.

1918-20-Amundsen sailed Northeast Passage.

1926-Richard E. Byrd and Floyd Bennett (U.S.). reached 87° 44'N. in attempt to fly to North Pole from Spitsbergen.

1926-Richard E. Byrd and Floyd Bennett (U.S.) first over North Pole by air, May 9.

1926-Amundsen, Ellsworth, and Umberto Nobile (Italy) flew from Spitsbergen over North Pole May 12, to Teller, Alaska, in dirigible Norge.

1928-Nobile crossed North Pole in airship Italia May 24, crashed May 25. Amundsen lost while trying to effect rescue by plane.

1928-Sir Hubert Wilkins and Eielson. Flew from Point Barrow to Spitsbergen, 84°N.

Submarine Records

On Aug. 3, 1958, the Nautilus, under Comdr. William R. Anderson, became the first ship to cross the North Pole beneath the Arctic ice.

On Aug. 12, 1958, the nuclear submarine Skate, Comdr. James F. Calvert, became the second ship to make an underwater crossing of the North Pole.

In March, 1959, the Skate returned to the Arctic and, on its third attempt broke through at the North Pole, the first time any ship had been on the surface at 90° N.

The nuclear-powered U.S. submarine Seadragon, Comdr. George P. Steele II, made the first east-west underwater transit through the Northwest Passage during August, 1960. It sailed from Portsmouth, N.H., headed between Greenland and Labrador through Baffin Bay, then west through Lancaster Sound and McClure Strait to the Beaufort Sea. Traveling submerged for the most part, the submarine made 850 miles from Baffin Bay to the Beaufort Sea in six days. The vessel made a 300-foot dive to sail under an iceberg in Baffin Bay.

In February, 1960, the nuclear submarine Sargo traveled under the Arctic ice pack to and around the North Pole. The Sargo departed from and returned to Honolulu, and spent 31 days and 4 hours under the ice. The submarine successfully smashed its way through ice three feet thick.

Antarctic Exploration

Early History

Antarctica has been approached since 1773-75, when Capt. Jas. Cook (Britain) reached 71° 10' S. Many sea and landmarks bear names of early explorers, Bellingshausen (Russia), discovered Peter I and Alexander I Islands, 1819-21. Nathaniel Palmer (U.S.) discovered Palmer Peninsula, 60° W. 1820, without realizing that this was a continent. Jas. Weddell (Britain) found Weddell Sea, 74°15'S., 1823.

First to announce existence of the continent of Antarctic was Charles Wilkes (U.S.), who followed the coast for 1,500 mi., 1840. Adelie Coast, 140° E., was found by Dumont d'Urville (France). 1840. Ross Ice Shelf was found by Jas. Clark Ross (Britain), 1841-42.

1895-Leonard Kristensen, Norwegian whaling captain, landed a party on the coast of Victoria Land in Jan. 1895. They were the first ashore on the main continental mass. C. E. Borchgrevink, a member of that party, returned in 1899 with a British expedition, first to winter on Antarctica.

1902-04-Robert F. Scott (Britain), discovered Edward VII Peninsula. In 1902 he reached 82°17'S., 146°33'E. from McMurdo Sound.

1908-09-Ernest Shackleton in 1908 introduced the use of Manchurian ponies in Antarctic sledging. In 1909 he reached 88°23'S., discovering a route on to the plateau by way of the Beardmore Glacier and pioneering the way to the Pole.

Discovery of South Pole

1911-Roald Amundsen (Norway) with four men and dog teams reached the Pole Dec. 14, 1911.

1912-Capt. Scott reached the Pole from Ross Island Jan. 18, 1912, with four companions (Dr. E.A. Wilson, Lt. Bowers, Capt. Oates, and Petty Officer Edgar Evans), where they found Amundsen's tent. Of Scott's party, Oates and Evans died first; Scott, Wilson and Bowers died in a tent around March 29. They were found Nov. 12, 1912.

1928-First man to use an airplane over Antarctica was Hubert Wilkins (Britain).

1929-Richard E. Byrd (U.S.) established Little America on Bay of Whales. On 1600-mi. airplane flight begun Nov. 28 he crossed South Pole Nov. 29 with pilot Bernt Balchen, a radio operator and a photographer. Dropped U. S. flag over Pole, temp. 16° below zero.

1934-35-Richard E. Byrd (U.S.) led second expedition to Little America, which explored 450,000 sq. mi. Byrd wintered alone at an advance weather station in 80°08'S.

1934-37-John Rymill led British Graham Land expedition of 1934-37; discovered that Palmer Peninsula is part of Antarctic mainland.

1935-Lincoln Ellsworth (U.S.) flew south along Palmer Peninsula's east coast, then crossed continent to Little America, making four landings on unprepared terrain in bad weather, a new feat.

1939-41-U.S. Antarctic Service built West Base on Ross Ice Shelf under Paul Siple and East Base on Palmer Peninsula under Richard Black. U.S. Navy plane flights discovered about 150,000 sq. miles of new land.

1940-Richard E. Byrd (U.S.) charted most of coast between Ross Sea and Palmer Peninsula.

1946-47-U.S. Navy undertook Operation Highjump under Rear Admiral Byrd. Ships were commanded by Rear Admiral Richard H. Cruzen. Expedition included 13 ships and 4,000 men, 29 land-based flights from Little America and 35 by seaplanes from tenders, photo-mapped coastline and penetrated beyond Pole.

1946-48-Ronne Antarctic Research Expedition, Comdr. Finn Ronne, USNR, determined the Antarctic to be only one continent, with no strait between Weddell Sea and Ross Sea; discovered 250,000 sq. miles of land by flights to 79°S. Lat., and made 14,000 aerial photographs over 450,000 sq. miles of land. Mrs. Ronne and Mrs. H. Darlington, who accompanied their husbands, were the first women to winter on Antarctica.

1955-57-U. S. Navy's Operation Deep Freeze led by Adm. Richard E. Byrd. Supporting U. S. scientific efforts for the international Geophysical Year, the Operation was commanded by Rear Adm. George Dufek. It established five coastal stations fronting the Indian, Pacific, and Atlantic Oceans and also three interior stations; explored more than 1,000,000 sq. miles in Wilkes Land. Seven Navy men under Adm. Dufek landed by plane at the Pole Oct. 31, 1956, and landed radar reflectors.

1957-58-During the International Geophysical Year, July, 1957 through Dec., 1958, scientists from 12 countries conducted ambitious programs of Antarctic research. A network of some 60 stations on the continent and sub-Arctic islands studied oceanography, glaciology, meteorology, seismology, geomagnetism, the ionosphere, cosmic rays, aurora and airglow. A party from Ellsworth IGY station (US) south of Weddell Sea under the direction of Captain Finn Ronne explored beyond 1947 flight and delineated Berkner Island imbedded in the Filchner Ice Shelf. Pensacola Mountains, first sighted by Argentines in Oct., 1955 and seen by U.S. Navy in Jan, 1956, were accurately located. New mountain ranges about 11,609 ft. high were discovered in Edith Ronne Land.

Dr. V.E. Fuchs led a 12-man Trans-Antarctic Expedition on the first land crossing of Antarctica. Starting from the Weddell Sea, they reached Scott Station Mar. 2, 1958, after traveling 2,158 miles in 98 days.

1958-A group of 5 U.S. scientists led by Edward C. Thiel, seismologist, moving by tractor from Ellsworth Station on Weddell Sea, identified a huge mountain range, 5,000 ft. above the ice sheet and 9,000 ft. above sea level. The range, originally seen by a Navy plane, was named the Dufek Massif, for Rear Adm. George Dufek.

1959—Twelve nations—Argentina, Australia, Belgium, Chile, France, Japan, New Zealand, Norway, South Africa, the Soviet Union, the United Kingdom, and the U.S.—signed a treaty suspending any territorial claims for 30 years and reserving the continent for research.

1960-61—Scientists at Cape Adare found a wooden building erected in 1899 by the first men (led by C.E. Borchgrevink) to winter on the continent.

1961-62—Scientists discovered a trough, the Bentley Trench, running from Ross Ice Shelf, Pacific, into Marie Byrd Land, around the end of the Ellsworth Mtns., toward the Weddell Sea, which may be the long-suspected link between the Atlantic and Pacific Oceans.

1962—First nuclear power plant began operation at McMurdo Sound.

1963—On Feb. 22 a U.S. plane made the longest nonstop flight ever made in the S. Pole area, covering 3,600 miles in 10 hours. The flight was from McMurdo Station south past the geographical S. Pole to Shackleton Mtns., southeast to the "Area of Inaccessibility" and back to McMurdo Station.

1963—Three turbine-powered helicopters made the first copter landings on the S. Pole.

1964—A British survey team was landed by helicopter on Cook Island, the first recorded visit since its discovery in 1775.

1964—New Zealanders completed one of the last and most important surveys when they mapped the mountain area from Cape Adare west some 400 miles to Pennell Glacier.

1966-67—Fifteen Antarctic areas set aside as Specially Protected Areas for the conservation of flora and fauna.

Archeological Events of 1973

Kenya Skull Challenges Evolution Theory

What may be the oldest complete skull found by man, along with leg bones, was discovered in a desert region on the east side of Lake Rudolf in Kenya. The find may push back man's immediate ancestry by more than 1,000,000 years. Prior to the discovery, universally accepted evidence fixed the appearance of Homo erectus at about 1,000,000 years ago.

Current theory holds that Australopithecus, the apelike man who lived 2,500,000 to 3,000,000 years ago, and the beetle-browed Homo erectus represent the early stages of man's evolution. Now, according to Richard Leakey who headed the Kenya expedition, the newly discovered skull, which resembles modern man's more closely than the other two, displaces the other 2 creatures as representatives of the early stages of man's development. It was found in a layer of material deposited 2,600,000 years ago.

The leg bones, 2 intact thigh bones and parts of a lower leg, provide evidence that man had already evolved from the looping, stooped gait inherited from his arboreal relatives. This evolution was heretofore believed to have happened much later.

Leakey said his findings lead him to believe that "man walked from Africa out to all the other continents" and that if a Garden of Eden ever existed, it may well have been the African continent.

The skull, which was discovered crushed into hundreds of fragments, was pieced together by Dr. Maeve Leakey, Richard Leakey's wife. The skull structure indicates a brain size of 800 cubic centimeters—falling between the 500 cubic centimeters of the Australopithecus and modern man's 1,500-cubic-centimeter brain.

Leakey's expedition to Kenya, jointly led by Dr. Gynn Issac of the University of California at Berkeley, was supported by the National Geographic Society, the National Science Foundation and the National Museums of Kenya. The son of the late Louis S. B. Leakey and Dr. Mary Leakey, Richard Leakey is the administrative director of the National Museums of Kenya.

Leakey believes the skull, which is different from all other known forms of early man and does not fit any of the current theories of evolution, belongs to a creature of the genus Homo, but different from Homo sapiens. He said, "The whole shape of the brain case is remarkably suggestive of modern man, lacking the heavy and protruding eyebrow ridges and thick bone that is characteristic of Homo erectus known from younger deposits in both Africa and Asia."

"Fred": Earliest American Man?

Dr. David Davies, a Churchill scholar, isn't telling where in Ecuador he found "Fred," a skull that may belong to the earliest known man in America. He fears American archeologists may take over the site.

Reliable conjecture states that he and his wife actually discovered the skull in a small museum in Ecuador where it had remained unrecognized for many years.

They then located the site where the skull had originated and obtained permission to bring the skull back to Britain for tests.

To date, Cambridge tests on bone salt and aragonite deposits have placed the skull at 28,000± 750 years old and tests on the aragonite at Birmingham have placed the age at 25,000± 3,000 years old. Man was previously thought to have appeared in the Americas no earlier than 15,000 years ago.

Davies, who is in the Department of Zoology at University College, London, says "Fred" raises important questions about the origin of man in America: "Was an earlier, more primitive form of man present on the continent when the Indians as we know them, came? If so, was South America a cradle land for an early form of man, as Africa and Asia appear to have been? And if man was not indigenous to the continent, did he arrive there earlier than is now generally supposed?"

Early American Man Ages

In another investigation into the appearance of man in Early America, completion of carbon dating on 390 fossil vertebrae discovered at the Old Crow River site in the Yukon between 1966 and 1970 has also pushed the date back more than 10,000 years. W. N. Irving of the University of Toronto and C. R. Harington of the National Museums of Canada in Ottawa have completed the dating of the artifacts.

The specimens, of which 3 were dated at between 25,000 and 32,000 years old, include bone implements and a number of bone artifacts broken or otherwise modified by man. Dr. Louis S. B. Leakey and Ruth Dee Simpson have proposed an older and more controversial date—50,000 to 100,000 years—based on their excavations at the Calico Mountain site in California.

Man's arrival in North America was held to be coincidental with the existence of a land bridge across the Bering Strait about 15,000 years ago. However, the land bridge had opened and closed as the formation of glaciers lowered the sea level prior to 15,000 years ago. If Siberian hunter-nomads crossed during an earlier land opening, it could explain the findings of Irving and Harington and perhaps the dates suggested by Leaky and Simpson.

Stone Age Tools Found in New York

Joseph Timlin of Worcester, N.Y., went fishing near Cobleskill, N.Y., in 1970. Instead of fish, he came back with what appeared to be artifacts of an ancient culture.

Various studies of the silicified limestone, molded clay and quartzite tools have set their age at a minimum of 70,000 years. The tools bear much resemblance to 70,000-year-old flaked tools of old world origin. The patina of age and the profile of weathering also support the 70,000-year date. Further evidence lies in the fact that the soil in which the tools were found is believed to be 70,000 years old.

When concretely substantiated, the 70,000-year date would more than double the date previously set for human habitation in the Americas and perhaps confirm the date — 50,000 to 100,000 years — suggested by Louis Leakey and Ruth Dee Simpson. The Timlin tools are recognized to be of more obvious human origin than those found by Leakey and Simpson.

Domesticated Beans Found in Peruvian Caves

Vegetable remains found in a mountain cave in the Ancash Department of Peru offer evidence that Peruvian Indians practiced a well-developed system of farming some 10,000 years ago.

Drs. L. Kaplan of Massachusetts University, Thomas Lynch of Cornell University and C. E. Smith of Alabama University reported a find of full domesticated common beans, the Phaseolus vulgaris. Their study shows that by about 8,000 B.C. Peruvian Indians did more than gather and eat beans. The beans, larger and with thinner seed coats and pods than wild beans, and also lacking the heavy fibrous layer of wild beans, were definitely cultivated. The find points to the existence of selective cultivation on a sophisticated level. The best beans of this type were taken from an earth layer radiocarbon dated to 7,680 B.C. ± 280 years. Previously, the oldest date established for such sophisticated farming in the Americas was about 5,000 B.C.

Soviets Find 20,000-year-old House

Soviet archeologists believe Siberia was originally populated by people from the West as well as from the South. Their evidence reported by the Soviet press agency Tass, is a 20,000-year-old house discovered near Achinsk in Siberia. The dwelling was built by Paleolithic man from the bones of mammoths. The house was reported to have many characteristics common to other ancient dwellings discovered by other archeologists on the River Don in central Russia.

Clues Found to Prehistoric Sea Travel

The discovery of obsidian, a glassy volcanic stone, and large fish bones in a cave in southern Greece provides evidence of the world's earliest seafaring.

The proof, found at Franchthi, a cave near Koilada, by American archeologists puts the date for prehistoric seafaring at 7,500 to 7,000 B.C., 1,000 years before sea travel was thought to have been practiced.

The discovery of the obsidian, whose sources are limited, led to speculation about sea travel. Analysis concluded that the source of the rock was the Aegean Island of Melos, some 75 miles southeast of the cave. Since the island, an extinct volcano, was uninhabited during the period under consideration, it was concluded that the Franchthi cave dwellers had boats. Further corroboration came from the fish vertebrae which suggested that the inhabitants had done deep-sea fishing.

The Franchthi site, which was a home for humans almost without interruption from about 20,000 B.C. to 3,000 B.C., is considered by experts to be one of the most important prehistoric sites in Europe and the Middle East. Dr. Thomas W. Jacobsen of Indiana University, who has spent 6 years studying the area, said, "The cave produced evidence of continuous human activity from the upper Paleolithic through Mesolithic and Neolithic. In this sense it is unique. There is no such sequence anywhere else in the old world."

"Burnt City" Unearthed

Another dig in Iran, this time in a remote province in the southeast, has excavated some 15,000 square yards of the "Burnt City" of Sharh-Sokta, a Bronze Age city which may be 5,000 years old.

Iranian and Italian archeologists have discovered evidence that the city's early inhabitants practiced skills not directly related to food production. Artifacts indicate that cutters of local and imported precious stones, masons, coppersmiths, weavers, potters and dyers once practiced their trades in Sharh-Sokta.

Sharh-Sokta was locally known as the "Burnt City" because a thick layer of pottery shards in the area gave rise to the legend that the city had been destroyed by fire. Dr. Marizio Tosi, the archeologist in charge, described the city as being preserved like pickles in a pot due to the radical change in the Helmand River,

once the source of the city's prosperity.

Tosi believes the city was founded between 2,900-1,900 B.C., a period of extensive growth of urban communities. He holds that the evidence discovered, "a whole incredible collection of crafts that we had supposed were forever lost in Southwest Asia," will greatly enrich archeological research for the whole of southwestern Asia as well as provide new information on urban history.

Herodian Ruins Unearthed

Herod lived in magnificent style. Archeologists have unearthed a hilltop Herodian, built by the Biblical ruler 2,000 years ago, near Bethlehem. The ruins of the palace include a swimming pool, chariot race track and apartments for royal guests. Also discovered were pottery fragments with Hebrew inscriptions and columns with niches that once contained funerary ashes.

The preliminary results of a dig into another Herodian monument, the city of Caesaria Maritima, were announced by Dr. Robert Bull of Drew University. Located 41 miles from Tel Aviv, Caesaria Maritima was built by Herod to honor Caesar Augustus. Highlights of the excavation included a hippodrome seating 25,000, a ½-mile chariot race track, theaters, amphitheaters, temples, major aqueducts and a brilliantly-engineered "sea-flushed" sewer system with 10-foot wide tunnels. Bull considers the site an archeologist's dream. "I plan to devote the rest of my life to this project," he vowed.

Female Deity Figurines Found

A merchant ship carrying a routine cargo went down off the ancient Phoenician coast some 2,500 years ago. Today, that cargo, discovered north of the Israeli coast city of Haifa, bears great archeological interest.

Marine archeologists and divers from the University of Haifa have discovered artifacts, including earthen vases and votive figurines of the Phoenician goddess Tanit, which experts deem of "paramount importance to the study of cultural and economic relationships" between the Phoenician homeland and its principal colony at Carthage.

The votive figurines, according to Dr. Elisha Linder of the University of Haifa's Center for Maritime Studies, are the first of their kind. They should shed light on the extent of worship of Tanit, goddess of fertility and the only known female deity of the Phoenician world. The clay figurines range in height from 6 to 15 inches and appear to have been mass produced from molds. The pedestals bear the insignia of the goddess — a triangle topped by a disk and separated by a horizontal line. The symbol is common to many artifacts found at Carthage.

Frescoes Unveil Aegean History and Life

Digging on the Aegean Island of Thera has revealed a miniature frieze which dramatizes a punitive expedition by the Aegean fleet against a hostile Libyan city some 3,500 years ago.

Prof. Spyridon Marinatos, the inspector-general of Greek antiquities and leader of the dig, called the strip of miniature wall paintings the "most important historical document so far from the Bronze Age in Greece. The value, he said, lies in the illumination of the relations between the Aegean peoples and Libya in the second half of the 16th century B.C.

The site of the discovery is the city of wealthy homes at Akrotiri which was buried when the Thera volcano erupted in 1,500 B.C.

Frescoes previously discovered at the site had already provided a rare glimpse into daily life 3,500 years ago, long a matter of conjecture. The buildings, pottery, jewels and frescoes found, according to Prof. Marinatos, indicated an advanced civilization had existed on Crete and the other Aegean islands about 1,500 B.C. Among the frescoes was one showing the peaceful life of a fisherman. Marinatos called the paintings "an extraordinary discovery." "I would not exaggerate," he said, "if I said that we have learned more about life in that period from these paintings than in 100 years of excavations."

Volcanoes of the World

Source: National Geographic Society, Washington, D.C.

(E) Eruption year in parentheses (R) Rumbling (St.) Steaming (D) Dormant

Mt. Vesuvius, dominating the Bay of Naples, is the most famous of volcanoes. In August, 79 A.D., it buried Pompeii (c. 20,000 pop.) under hot ash and Herculaneum and Stabiae under mud flows. Three-fifths of Pompeii has been excavated; also part of Herculaneum, most of which lies under Resina. Stabiae lies under Castellammare. There was a big eruption in 1139, and a major one in December, 1631, when 5 towns were destroyed and 4,000 people killed. Minor eruptions have occurred in 1779, 1793, 1872, 1906 and 1944.

Krakatau on an island in the Sunda Strait between Sumatra and Java exploded Aug. 27, 1883, creating a depth of 1,000 ft. in the ocean. The explosion was heard 2,500 mi. away, and tidal waves killed 35,000. In 1927 Krakatau formed the island of Anak Krakatau, which exploded, 1929, depositing an island in the hole caused in 1883.

Mont Pelée, Martinique, destroyed St. Pierre and more than 30,000 people May 8, 1902. Eruptions slightly less powerful occurred May 20 and Aug. 30, 1902. A major eruption began Sept. 16, 1929, and lasted 3 years.

Mt. Agung, 10,308 ft., on the island of Bali, erupted in January, March and May, 1963; the last two eruptions claimed a total of more than 1,500 lives and a third of Bali's farm land, and left 85,000 homeless. Bali's **Mt Batur,** 5,636 ft., erupted in September, 1963, forcing 1,200 persons to leave their homes at its base; rumblings and explosions could be heard for 50 miles.

In Alaska's Valley of 10,000 Smokes, the lowest of **Mt. Trident's** 3 peaks erupted Apr. 1, 1963; the cloud of smoke and dust was visible 100 miles away.

Name	Location	Ht. Ft.
AFRICA		
Kilimanjaro (D)	Tanzania	19,340
Cameroon Mt. (E-1959)	Cameroon	13,350
Nyiragongo (E-1972)	Zaire	11,385
Nyamlagira (E-1971)	Zaire	10,028
Fogo (E-1951)	Cape Verde Is	9,281
Tristan da Cunha (E-1961)	Atlantic Ocean	6,760
San Juan (D)	Canary Is	2,612
Erta Ale (E-1972)	Ethiopia	1,660
ANTARCTICA		
Erebus (St.)		12,450
Melbourne (St.)		8,500
Deception Island (E-1970))		1,890
ASIA—OCEANIA		
Klyuchevskaya (E-1962)	U.S.S.R.	15,584
Kerintji (St)	Sumatra	12,467
Fuji (D)	Japan	12,388
Rindjani (E-1964)	Indonesia	12,224
Tolbachik (E-1941)	U.S.S.R.	12,080
Semeru (E-1963)	Java	12,060
Ichinskaya	U.S.S.R.	11,880
Kronotskaya (D)	U.S.S.R.	11,575
Koryakskaya (E-1957)	U.S.S.R.	11,339
Slamet (E-1953)	Java	11,247
Raung (St)	Java	10,932
Shiveluch (E-1964)	U.S.S.R.	10,771
Dempo (St)	Sumatra	10,364
Welirang (D)	Java	10,354
Agung (E-1964)	Bali	10,308
Sundoro (D)	Java	10,285
Tjareme (E-1938)	Java	10,098
Ontake (E-1970)	Japan	10,049
Gede (E-1949)	Java	9,705
Merapi (E-1969)	Java	9,551
Bezymyannaya (E-1961)	U.S.S.R.	9,514
Marapi (D)	Sumatra	9,485
Apo (D)	Philippines	9,369
Tambora (D)	Indonesia	9,353
Ruapehu (E-1971)	New Zealand	9,175
Peuetsagoe (D)	Sumatra	9,121
Bromo (St.)	Java	9,088
Avachinskaya (St.)	U.S.S.R.	9,026
Big Ben (E-1950)	Heard Island	9,007
Balbi (D)	Solomons	9,000
Papandajan (St)	Java	8,602
Guereudong (E-1924)	Sumatra	8,497
Asama (E-1973)	Japan	8,340
Sumbing (E-1926)	Sumatra	8,225
Tandikat (E-1924)	Sumatra	8,166
Mayon (E-1968)	Philippines	8,077
Yake Dake (E-1963)	Japan	8,064
Sinabung (St)	Sumatra	8,041
Idjen (D)	Java	7,828
Alaid (E-1972)	Kuril Is.	7,662
Ulawan (E-1970)	New Britain	7,532
Ngauruhoe (E-1956)	New Zealand	7,515
Guntur (D)	Java	7,379
Bamus (D)	New Britain	7,338
Galunggung (E-1920)	Java	7,113
Amburombu (E-1924)	Indonesia	7,051

Name	Location	Ht. Ft.
Sorikmarapi (E-1917)	Sumatra	7,037
Petarangan (E-1939)	Java	7,005
Sibajak (St)	Sumatra	6,870
Tokachi (E-1962)	Japan	6,813
Tangkubanperahu (R)	Java	6,637
Bagana (E-1966)	Solomons	6,560
Tongariro (E-1950)	New Zealand	6,458
Zheltovskaya (E-1972)	USSR	6,407
Sangeang (E-1953)	Indonesia	6,394
Kaba (E-1941)	Sumatra	6,358
Awu (E-1966)	Indonesia	6,102
Manam (E-1966)	Bismarck Arch.	6,000
Soputan (E-1947)	Celebes	5,994
Piton de la Fournaise (E-1973)	Reunion Is.	5,981
Siau (E-1949)	Indonesia	5,853
Kelud (E-1966)	Java	5,679
Batur (E-1963)	Bali	5,636
Belerang (St)	Sumatra	5,636
Ternate (E-1938)	Indonesia	5,627
Hibok Hibok (E-1960)	Philippines	5,619
Lewotobi Perampuan (E-1935)	Indonesia	5,591
Kirishima (St)	Japan	5,577
Karymskaya (E-1970)	U.S.S.R.	5,560
Mutu (D)	Indonesia	5,545
Lamongna (St)	Java	5,482
Boleng (E-1950)	Indonesia	5,443
Gamkonora (E-1949)	Indonesia	5,364
Aso (E-1970)	Japan	5,223
Lewotobi Lakilaki (E-1940)	Indonesia	5,217
Lokon (E-1970)	Celebes	5,184
Bulusan (E-1966)	Philippines	5,115
Sarycheva (E-1960)	Kuril Is.	4,960
Meakan (E-1959)	Japan	4,931
Ibu (D)	Indonesia	4,921
Lewotolo (D)	Indonesia	4,757
Lopevi (E-1960)	New Hebrides	4,755
Ambrim (E-1951)	New Hebrides	4,376
Mahawu (D)	Celebes	4,367
Long Island (E-1953)	Bismarck Arch	4,278
Tongkoko (D)	Celebes	3,770
Komaga Dake (E-1971)	Japan	3,740
Werung (E-1948)	Indonesia	3,678
Sakurajima (E-1970)	Japan	3,668
Langla (E-1965)	New Britain	3,586
Dukono (E-1950)	Indonesia	3,566
Lamington (E-1951)	New Guinea	3,500
Minami (E-1971)	Japan	3,478
Yasur (R)	New Hebrides	3,420
Lolobau (D)	Bismarck Arch	3,058
Asuncion (St)	Marianas	2,923
Paloë (E-1964)	Indonesia	2,871
Sirung (E-1947)	Indonesia	2,828
O Yama (E-1962)	Japan	2,674
Krakatua (E-1953)	Indonesia	2,667
Bam Island (D)	Bismarck Arch.	2,625
Nila (E-1932)	Indonesia	2,562
Batu Tara (St)	Indonesia	2,454
Alamagan (E-1945)	Marianas	2,441

Ruang (E-1949)	Indonesia......	2,379
Bango (D).............	New Britain	2,375
Tinakula (E-1971).......	Santa Cruz Is...	2,200
Ija (E-1969)	Indonesia......	2,162
Banda (D).............	Indonesia......	2,152
Teun (D)..............	Indonesia......	2,149
Serua (D)	Indonesia......	2,103
Mihara (E-1964)........	Japan.........	2,028
Pagan (D).............	Marianas	1,870
Tofua (D)	Tonga Islands ..	1,660
Unauna (E-1960)	Indonesia	1,640
Farallon de Pajaros (E-1952)	Marianas	1,096
White Island (E-1971)	NewZealand ...	1,075
Guguan (D)	Marianas	988
Taal (E-1971)	Philippines	984
Didicas (E-1952).......	Philippines.....	900
Niuafo'ou (E-1946)......	Tonga	853
Tavurvur (E-1941)	New Britain.....	741
Fonualei (E-1939).......	Tonga	600
Matthew Island (D)......	Loyalty Is......	580
Anak Krakatau (E-1960)..	Indonesia......	510

CENTRAL AMERICA—CARIBBEAN

Tajumulco (R).........	Guatemala	13,845
Tacaná (R)	Guatemala	13,428
Acatenango (R)	Guatemala	12,992
Fuego (E-1973)	Guatemala	12,582
Santa María (D)	Guatemala	12,362
Atitlan (R)............	Guatemala	11,565
Irazú (E-1964).........	Costa Rica	11,260
San Pedro (R).........	Guatemala	9,921
Poás (St).............	Costa Rica	8,930
Pacaya (E-1972)	Guatemala ...	8,346
San Miguel (E-1970)	El Salvador	6,988
Rincon de la Viej (E-1970)	Costa Rica	6,234
Izalco (E-1967)	El Salvador	6,184
El Viejo (E-1971)	Nicaragua	5,840
Ometepe (Concepción) (E-1957)	Nicaragua......	5,106
Arenal (E-1970)	Costa Rica	5,092
Pelée (D).............	Martinique	4,583
Momotombo (E-1952)...	Nicaragua.....	4,199
Conchagua (E-1947)....	El Salvador....	4,100
Soufriére (E-1972)	St. Vincent	4,048
Telica (E-1971).........	Nicaragua.....	3,409
Negro (E-1971)........	Nicaragua.....	3,204
Santiago (St)...........	Nicaragua.....	1,969

SOUTH AMERICA

Guallatiri (E-1959)	Chile.........	19,882
Lascar (E-1951)	Chile.........	19,652
Cotopaxi (St)..........	Ecuador	19,347
Misti (D).............	Peru.........	19,098
Cayambe (D)	Ecuador	18,996
Tupungatito (E-1959)....	Chile.........	18,504
Sangay (E-1946).......	Ecuador	17,159
Tungurahua (R)	Ecuador	16,512
Cotacachi (E-1955).....	Ecuador	16,204
Pichincha (D)	Ecuador	15,696
Purace (E-1950)........	Colombia	15,604
Lautaro (St)	Chile.........	11,090
Llaima (E-1955)	Chile.........	10,239
Villarrica (E-1972)......	Chile.........	9,318
Shoshuenco (E-1960)...	Chile.........	7,743
Ventisquero (E-1971)....	Chile.........	7,546
Puyehue (E-1972)......	Chile.........	7,349
Calbuco (E-1961)	Chile.........	6,611

Casablanca (E-1960)	Chile.........	6,529
Cauye (E-1960)........	Chile.........	4,692
Alcedo (E-1970)	Galapagos Is ..	3,599
Rininahue (E-1955)	Chile.........	1,004

MID-PACIFIC

Mauna Kea (D)........	Hawaii	13,796
Mauna Loa (E-1950)....	Hawaii ..	13,680
Kilauea (E-1972).......	Hawaii	4,077

EUROPE

Etna (E-1971).........	Sicily, Italy	10,902
Beeren Berg (E-1971) ...	Norway........	7,470
Askja (E-1961)	Iceland........	4,954
Hekla (E-1970)........	Iceland........	4,892
Vesuvius (St)	Italy	4,190
Katla (E-1918)........	Iceland........	3,182
Stromboli (E-1971).....	Italy	3,038
Thera (E-1956)........	Greece........	1,824
Vulcano (D)	Italy	1,637
Kirkjufell (E-1973).....	Iceland........	725
Surtsey (E-1965).......	Iceland........	568
Ilha Nova (E-1958)......	Azores	200

NORTH AMERICA

Citlaltepec (D).........	Mexico	18,700
Popocatépetl (St.)......	Mexico	17,887
Wrangell (St)..........	Alaska	14,163
Colima (St.)	Mexico	14,003
Torbert (E-1953).......	Alaska	11,413
Spurr (E-1953)........	Alaska	11,069
Lassen (D)	California	10,457
Redoubt (E-1966)......	Alaska	10,197
Iliamna (St)	Alaska	10,016
Shishaldin (St)	Aleutians	9,387
Pavlof (E-1950)........	Alaska	8,261
Veniaminof (D)........	Alaska	8,225
Griggs (St)	Alaska	7,600
Paricutin (D)..........	Mexico	7,451
Mageik (St)...........	Alaska	7,250
Douglas (St)..........	Alaska	7,064
Chiginagak (D)........	Alaska	6,900
Katmai (E-1962).......	Alaska	6,715
Kukak (St)...........	Alaska	6,700
Makushin (St)	Aleutians	6,680
Pogromni (E-1964).....	Aleutians	6,568
Martin (E-1960).......	Alaska	6,050
Trident (E-1963).......	Alaska	6,010
Tanaga (D)...........	Aleutians	5,925
Great Sitkin (St)	Aleutians	5,710
Cleveland (E-1944).....	Aleutians	5,675
Gareloi (D)...........	Aleutians	5,334
Korovin (D)...........	Aleutians	4,852
Kanaga (D)...........	Aleutians	4,416
Aniakchak (D).........	Alaska	4,400
Akutan (E-1952).......	Aleutians	4,275
Kiska (1962)..........	Aleutians	4,004
Augustine (E-1935).....	Alaska	3,927
Little Sitkin (St)	Aleutians	3,897
Okmok (E-1958).......	Aleutians	3,519
Seguam (D)	Aleutians	3,458
Yunaska (D)..........	Aleutians	3,133
Kagamil (D)	Aleutians	2,930
Novarupta (St)	Alaska	2,760
Cerberus (D)..........	Alaska	2,541
Boquerón (E-1955).....	Revillagigedo Is. (Mexico)	1,280

Indonesia's Paloe, 2871 ft., erupted in January, burning and destroying much of the surrounding vegetation.

Iceland's Kirkjufell (the new cone on Helgafell Mountain), 725 ft., erupted in late January. Helgafell had been inactive for 7,000 years. Volcanic activity continued until late April when the eruption began to slowly abate.

Japan's Asama, 8,340 ft., erupted in early February, after 11 year's silence, and continued sporadically through April.

Guatemala's Fuego, 12,582 ft., erupted in late February, preceded by a continuous gentle steam emission since the strong September 1971 eruption.

Chile's Mt. Hudson, 8,580 ft., erupted in April, in its first activity since 1971. The eruption was characterized by a gigantic fireball and thick columns of smoke.

Hawaii's Kilauea, 4,077 ft., erupted in early May amidst hundreds of volcanic tremors, 10 days after a 6.2 Richter magnitude earthquake shook the island.

The USSR's Tiatia, 6,013 ft., in the Kuril Islands, erupted in mid-July after 162 years of inactivity.

New Guinea's Mt. Langila, 3,924 ft., on the island of New Britain, erupted in mid-July.

Highest and Lowest Continental Altitudes

Source: National Geographic Society, Washington, D. C.

(In feet)

Continent	Highest Point	Elevation	Lowest Point	Below Sea Level
Asia	Mount Everest, Nepal-Tibet	29,028	Dead Sea, Israel-Jordan	1,299
South America	Mount Aconcagua, Argentina	22,834	Peninsula Valdés, Argentina	131
North America	Mount McKinley, Alaska	20,320	Death Valley, California	282
Africa	Kibo (Kilimanjaro) Tanzania	19,340	Lake Assal, Afars & Issas Terr.	512
Europe	Mount El'brus USSR Caucasus Mts	18,510	Caspian Sea, USSR	92
Antarctica	Vinson Massif	16,860	Sea level	
Australia	Mount Kosciusko, New South Wales	7,310	Lake Eyre, South Australia	52

Height of Mount Everest

Mt. Everest was considered to be 29,002 ft. tall when Edmund Hillary and Tenzing Norkay scaled it in 1953. This triangulation figure had been accepted since 1850. In 1954 the Surveyor General of the Republic of India set the height at 29,028 ft., plus or minus 10 ft. because of snow. The National Geographic Society accepts the new figure, but many mountaineering groups still use 29,002 ft.

High Peaks in United States, Canada, Mexico

Name	Place	Feet	Name	Place	Feet	Name	Place	Feet
McKinley	Alaska	20,320	Crestone	Colo	14,294	Columbia	Colo	14,073
Logan	Can.	19,850	Lincoln	Colo	14,286	Augusta	Alas. Can.	14,070
Citlaltepec (Orizaba)	Mexico	18,700	Grays	Colo	14,270	Culebra	Colo	14,069
St. Elias	Alas.-Can.	18,008	Antero	Colo	14,269	Missouri	Colo	14,067
Popocatépetl	Mexico	17,887	Torreys	Colo	14,267	Humboldt	Colo	14,064
Foraker	Alaska	17,400	Castle	Colo	14,265	Bierstad	Colo	14,060
Iztaccihuatl	Mexico	17,343	Evans	Colo	14,264	Sunlight	Colo	14,059
Lucania	Can.	17,147	Quandary	Colo	14,265	Split	Calif	14,058
King	Can.	16,971	Longs	Colo	14,255	Nauhcampatépetl		
Steele	Can.	16,644	McArthur	Can	14,253	(Cofre de Perote)	Mexico	14,049
Bona	Alaska	16,421	Mt. Wilson	Colo	14,246	Handies	Colo	14,048
Blackburn	Alaska	16,390	White	Calif	14,246	Culebra	Colo	14,047
Kennedy	Alaska	16,286	North Palisade	Calif	14,242	Lindsey	Colo	14,042
Sanford	Alaska	16,237	Shavano	Colo	14,229	Middle Palisade	Calif	14,040
South Buttress	Alaska	15,885	Belford	Colo	14,197	Little Bear	Colo	14,037
Wood	Can.	15,885	Princeton	Colo	14,197	Sherman	Colo	14,036
Vancouver	Alas.-Can.	15,700	Crestone	Colo	14,197	Redcloud	Colo	14,034
Churchill	Alaska	15,638	Yale	Colo	14,196	Langley	Calif	14,028
Fairweather	Alaska	15,300	Bross	Colo	14,172	Conundrum	Colo	14,022
Zinantecatl (Toluca)	Mexico	15,016	Kit Carson	Colo	14,165	Tyndall	Calif	14,018
Hubbard	Alas.-Can.	15,015	Wrangell	Alaska	14,163	Pyramid	Colo	14,018
Bear	Alaska	14,831	Shasta	Calif	14,162	Wilson Peak	Colo	14,017
Walsh	Can	14,780	Sill	Calif	14,162	Muir	Calif	14,015
East Buttress	Alaska	14,730	El Diente	Colo	14,159	Wetterhorn	Colo	14,015
Matlalcueyetl	Mexico	14,636	Maroon	Colo	14,156	North Maroon	Colo	14,014
Hunter	Alaska	14,573	Tabeguache	Colo	14,155	San Luis	Colo	14,014
Alverstone	Alas.-Can.	14,565	Oxford	Colo	14,153	Huron	Colo	14,005
Browne Tower	Alaska	14,530	Sneffels	Colo	14,150	Holy Cross	Colo	14,005
Whitney	Calif.	14,494	Point Success	Wash	14,150	Colima	Mexico	14,003
Elbert	Colo	14,433	Democrat	Colo	14,148	Sunshine	Colo	14,001
Massive	Colo	14,421	Liberty Cap	Wash	14,133	Grizzly	Colo	14,000
Harvard	Colo	14,420	Capitol	Colo	14,130	Barnard	Calif	13,990
Rainier	Wash	14,410	Lindsey	Colo	14,125	Stewart	Colo	13,980
Williamson	Calif	14,375	Pikes Peak	Colo	14,110	Keith	Calif	13,977
Blanca	Colo	14,345	Snowmass	Colo	14,092	Le Conte	Calif	13,960
La Plata	Colo	14,336	Windom	Colo	14,087	Meeker	Colo	13,911
Uncompahgre	Colo	14,309	Russell	Calif	14,086	Kennedy	Can	13,905
			Eolus	Colo	14,084			

South America

Peak	Country	Feet	Peak	Country	Feet	Peak	Country	Feet
Aconcagua, Argentina		22,834	Laudo, Argentina		20,997	Solo, Argentina		20,492
Bonete, Argentina		22,546	Ancohuma, Bolivia		20,958	Polleras, Argentina		20,456
Ojos del Salado, Arg.-Chile		22,539	Ausangate, Peru		20,945	Pular, Chile		20,423
Tupungato, Argentina-Chile		22,310	Toro, Argentina-Chile		20,932	Chañi, Argentina		20,341
Pissis, Argentina		22,241	Illampu, Bolivia		20,873	Aucanquilcha, Chile		20,295
Mercedario, Argentina		22,211	Tres Cruces, Argentina-Chile		20,853	Juncal, Argentina		20,276
Huascarán, Peru		22,205	Huandoy, Peru		20,852	Negro, Argentina		20,184
Llullaillaco, Argentina-Chile		22,057	Parinacota, Bolivia-Chile		20,768	Quela, Argentina		20,128
El Libertador, Argentina		22,047	Tórtolas, Argentina-Chile		20,745	Condoriri, Bolivia		20,095
Cachi, Argentina		22,047	Ampato, Peru		20,702	Palermo, Argentina		20,079
Yerupaja, Peru		21,765	Cóndor, Argentina		20,669	Solimana, Peru		20,068
Galán, Argentina		21,654	Salcantay, Peru		20,574	San Juan, Argentina-Chile		20,049
El Muerto, Argentina-Chile		21,457	Chimborazo, Ecuador		20,561	Sierra Nevada, Arg.-Chile		20,023
Sajama, Bolivia		21,391	Huancarhuas, Peru		20,531	Antofalla, Argentina		20,013
Nacimiento, Argentina		21,302	Gen. Manuel Belgrano, Arg		20,505	Marmolejo, Argentina-Chile		20,013
Illimani, Bolivia		21,201	Pumasillo, Peru		20,492	Licancabur, Argentina-Chile		19,425
Coropuna, Peru		21,079						

The highest point in the West Indies is in the Dominican Republic, Pico Duarte(10,417 ft.)

Africa, Australia and Oceania

Mountain and Country	Feet	Mountain and Country	Feet	Mountain and Country	Feet
Kibo (Kilimanjaro), Tanzania	19,340	Mandala, New Guinea	15,420	Toubkal, Morocco	13,665
Kenya, Kenya	17,058	Ras Dashan, Ethiopia	15,158	Kinabalu, Malaysia	13,455
Margherita Pk.,		Meru, Tanzania	14,979	Lesatima, Kenya	13,104
Uganda-Zaire	16,763	Wilhelm, New Guinea	14,793	Kerintji, Sumatra	12,467
Djaja, New Guinea	16,500	Karisimbi, Zaire-Rwanda	14,787	Cook, New Zealand	12,349
Pilimsit, New Guinea	15,748	Elgon, Kenya-Uganda	14,178	Teide, Canary Islands	12,198
Trikora, New Guinea	15,585	Batu, Ethiopia	14,131	Kosciusko, Australia	7,310
		Gughe, Ethiopia	13,780		

Europe

Peak	Feet	Peak	Feet	Peak	Feet	Peak	Feet
Alps		Hohberghorn	13,842	Fiescherhorn	13,283	**Pyrenees**	
Mont Blanc	15,771	Alphubel	13,799	Grünhorn	13,266	Aneto	11,168
Monte Rosa (high-		Rimpfischhorn	13,776	Lauteraarhorn	13,261	Posets	11,073
est peak of group)	15,203	Aletschhorn	13,763	Dürrenhorn	13,238	Perdido	11,007
Dom	14,911	Strahlhorn	13,747	Allalinhorn	13,213	Maladeta	10,866
Liskamm	14,852	Dent d'Hérens	13,686	Weissmies	13,199	Vignemale	10,820
Weisshorn	14,780	Breithorn	13,665	Lagginhorn	13,156	Long	10,479
Täschhorn	14,733	Bishorn	13,645	Fletschhorn	13,110	Estats	10,304
Matterhorn	14,690	Jungfrau	13,642	Zupó	13,109	Montcalm	10,105
Dent Blanche	14,293	Ecrins	13,461	Adlerhorn	13,081	**Caucasus (Europe-Asia)**	
Nadelhorn	14,196	Mönch	13,448	Gletscherhorn	13,068	El'brus	18,510
Grand Combin	14,154	Pollux	13,422	Schalihorn	13,040	Shkara	17,064
Lenzspitze	14,088	Schreckhorn	13,379	Scerscen	13,028	Dykh Tau	17,054
Finsteraarhorn	14,022	Ober Gabelhorn	13,330	Eiger	13,025	Kashtan Tau	16,877
Castor	13,865	Gran Paradiso	13,323	Jägerhorn	13,024	Kazbek	16,558
Zinalrothorn	13,849	Bernina	13,284	Rottalhorn	13,022	Dzhangi Tau	16,565

Asia

Peak	Country	Feet	Peak	Country	Feet
Everest	Nepal-Tibet	29,028	Jolmo Hari	Pakistan	24,240
K2 (Godwin Austen)	Kashmir	28,250	Tent Peak	Nepal-Sikkim	24,088
Kanchenjunga	Nepal-Sikkim	28,208	Chamlang	Nepal	24,012
Lhotse I (Everest)	Nepal-Tibet	27,923	Kabru	Nepal-Sikkim	24,002
Makalu I	Nepal-Tibet	27,824	Alung Gangri	Tibet	24,000
Lhotse II (Everest)	Nepal-Tibet	27,560	Chomo Lhari	Tibet-Bhutan	23,997
Dhaulagiri	Nepal	26,810	Baltoro Kangri	Kashmir	23,990
Manaslu I	Nepal	26,760	Mussu Shan	Sinkiang	23,890
Cho Oyu	Nepal-Tibet	26,750	Mana	India	23,860
Nanga Parbat	Kashmir	26,660	Baruntse	Nepal	23,688
Annapurna	Nepal	26,504	Amne Machin	China	23,490
Gasherbrum	Kashmir	26,470	Nepal Peak	Nepal-Sikkim	23,458
Broad	Kashmir	26,400	Pumori	Nepal-Tibet	23,442
Gosainthan	Tibet	26,287	Gauri Sankar	Nepal-Tibet	23,440
Annapurna II	Nepal	26,041	Badrinath	India	23,420
Gyachung Kang	Nepal-Tibet	25,910	Nunkun	Kashmir	23,410
Disteghil Sar	Kashmir	25,868	Lenina Peak	USSR	23,405
Himalchuli	Nepal	25,801	Api	Nepal	23,399
Nuptse (Everest)	Nepal-Tibet	25,726	Trisul	India	23,360
Masherbrum	Kashmir	25,660	Kangto	India-Tibet	23,260
Nanda Devi	India	25,645	Nyenchhen Thanglha	Tibet	23,255
Chomo Lonzo	Nepal-Tibet	25,640	Tirsuli	India	23,210
Rakaposhi	Kashmir	25,550	Dunagiri	India	23,184
Kamet	India-Tibet	25,447	Pauhunri	Sikkim-Tibet	23,180
Namcha Barwa	Tibet	25,445	Lombo Kangra	Tibet	23,165
Gurla Mandhata	Tibet	25,355	Saipal	Nepal	23,100
Ulugh Muz Tagh	Tibet-Sinkiang	25,340	Macha Pucchare	Nepal	22,958
Kungur	Sinkiang	25,325	Numbar	Nepal	22,817
Tirich Mir	Pakistan	25,230	Kanjiroba	Nepal	22,580
Makalu II	Nepal-Tibet	25,130	Ama Dablam	Nepal	22,494
Minya Konka	China	24,900	Pyramid	Nepal-Sikkim	22,430
Kula Gangri	Tibet-Bhutan	24,784	Cho Polu	Nepal	22,093
Changtse (Everest)	Nepal-Tibet	24,780	Lingtren	Nepal-Tibet	21,972
Muz Tagh Ata	Sinkiang	24,757	Khumbutse	Nepal-Tibet	21,785
Skyang Kangri	Kashmir	24,750	Hlako Gangri	Tibet	21,266
Communism Peak	USSR	24,590	Mt. Grosvenor	China	21,190
Jongsong Peak	Nepal-Sikkim	24,472	Thagchhab Gangri	Tibet	20,970
Pobedy Peak	Sinkiang-USSR	24,406	Damávand	Iran	18,934
Sia Kangri	Kashmir	24,350	Ararat	Turkey	16,946
Haramosh Peak	Pakistan	24,272			

Antarctica

Peak	Feet	Peak	Feet	Peak	Feet
Vinson Massif	16,860	Miller	13,650	Falla	12,549
Tyree	16,290	Long Gables	13,620	Rucker	12,520
Shinn	15,750	Dickerson	13,517	Goldthwait	12,510
Gardner	15,375	Giovinetto	13,412	Morris	12,500
Epperly	15,100	Wade	13,400	Erebus	12,450
Kirkpatrick	14,855	Fisher	13,386	Campbell	12,434
Elizabeth	14,698	Fridtjof Nansen	13,350	Don Pedro Christophersen	12,355
Markham	14,290	Wexler	13,202	Lysaght	12,326
Bell	14,117	Lister	13,200	Huggins	12,247
Mackellar	14,098	Shear	13,100	Sabine	12,200
Anderson	13,957	Odishaw	13,008	Astor	12,175
Bentley	13,934	Donaldson	12,894	Mohl	12,172
Kaplan	13,878	Ray	12,808	Frakes	12,064
Andrew Jackson	13,750	Sellery	12,779	Jones	12,040
Sidley	13,720	Waterman	12,730	Gjelsvik	12,008
Ostenso	13,710	Anne	12,703	Coman	12,000
Minto	13,658	Press	12,566		

Water Use in the United States
by C. Richard Murray
(Hydrologist, U.S. Geological Survey)

In 1970, an average of 370 bgd (billion gallons per day) was used for public supplies, commerce and industry, irrigation, rural domestic and livestock, or about 1,800 gallons per day for each individual in the country. According to the Geological Survey's 5-year assessments, the quantity of water withdrawn from water supplies for uses other than hydroelectric power generation has increased at a fairly uniform rate during the past 20 years: 200, 240, 270, 310, and 370 bgd for 1950, 1955, 1960, 1965, and 1970, respectively. At this rate of increase, daily water use in 1972 must be close to 400 bgd, or slightly more than the 395 bgd average daily flow of the Mississippi River.

Although water supplies in the humid eastern part of the United States generally are adequate for present and foreseeable future demands, the Columbia-North Pacific region is the only area west of the Mississippi that has an abundant supply in comparison to demand. Cumulative withdrawals exceeding dependably available supplies (based on the minimum monthly flow at major points of use under existing developmental conditions) are found in the Middle Atlantic, Texas-Gulf, Rio Grande, Lower Colorado, and California-South Pacific regions.

As the result of some uses, water is consumed, and thereby removed from the supply available for reuse. Water consumption in the United States in 1970 was estimated at 87 bgd, about 25 percent of withdrawals. Although consumption in the 31 Eastern States averaged only 14 percent of withdrawals, regional consumption in the West ranged from 30 to nearly 70 percent. In the Rio Grande and Lower Colorado regions, consumption exceeded the estimated dependable supply.

Nearly 19 percent of the water withdrawn, or 69 bgd, was derived from wells and springs; the remaining 300 bgd was from surface-water sources. About 53 bgd of the latter was saline (containing more than 1,000 milligrams per liter dissolved solids).

In the United States more water is withdrawn for industrial uses than for any other category. In 1970, the self-supplied industrial use was about 210 bgd, about 54 bgd of which was saline. The principal industrial use is thermoelectric power generation; in 1970, it constituted about 78 percent of industrial uses. About 3 percent of the fresh water withdrawn by industry was estimated to have been consumed, and 80 percent of the withdrawals took place in the Eastern United States.

Irrigation ranks second in the quantity of water withdrawn (130 bgd), but is by far the greatest consumer of water (73 bgd). Because of the large quantity of water consumed (nearly 60 percent of the water withdrawn for irrigation), increased use of water for this purpose can seriously deplete local water supplies. The nine Western regions used 95 percent of the irrigation water; about 36 percent of this water was withdrawn from ground water and 64 percent from surface-water sources.

Use of water for public supplies amounted to 27 bgd in 1970, an increase of 13 percent in the past 5 years and about 166 gpcd (gallons per capita per day) for people served in the United States and Puerto Rico. About 115 gpcd was for domestic and public uses; the remaining 51 gpcd was for commercial and industrial uses. Residents of the Western States used from 30 to 50 percent more water than those in the East. Lawn watering is an important factor in these high-use areas, but unusually large industrial use of public supplies also takes place, particularly in the Columbia-North Pacific region. About one-third of the public water supply was ground water and about one-fifth of the water withdrawn was consumed.

Of the various categories of water use, rural domestic and livestock use was the smallest, 4½ bgd, although showing a 13 percent increase from 1965 to 1970. Rural domestic use amounted to about 2.6 bgd for the 40,900,000 people supplying their own water, about 63½ gallons per capita per day, of which about 65 percent was consumed; about 96 percent of the rural domestic water was obtained from ground-water sources. Livestock water amounted to about 1.9 bgd, of which about 90 percent was consumed; ground water furnished about 58 percent of the stock water.

The average annual streamflow in the United States is about 1,200 bgd, which can be used as a simplified measure of the total potential water supply. Part of this supply, particularly during periods of flooding, reaches the oceans without having been used. The streamflow is about 3¼ times the cumulative water withdrawals, and nearly 14 times the estimated quantity of water consumed in 1970. Despite these favorable ratios, local water shortages occur as a result of varying amounts of precipitation, amount of reservoir storage, geographic requirements, and other supply and use factors.

World's Greatest Man-Made Lakes

UC—Under Construction 1. Formed by dam construction. 2. Represents increase in natural lake.

Name of dam	Capacity-acre-feet	Year	Name of dam	Capacity-acre-feet	Year
Owen Falls, Uganda (2)	166,000,000	1954	Bukhtarma, USSR	42,970,000	1960
Bratsk, USSR	137,214,000	1964	Tankiangkow, China	41,833,000	1962
Saad-El-Aali (High Aswan Dam)	133,000,000	1971	Irkutsk, USSR (2)	37,300,000	1956
Kariba, Rhodesia-Zambia	130,000,000	1959	Hoover, U.S.A. (Lake Mead)	29,755,000	1936
Akosombo, Ghana	120,000,000	1965	Volga-22nd Cong, USSR	27,200,000	1958
Daniel Johnson, Canada	115,000,000	1968	Glen Canyon, U.S.A. (Lake Powell)	27,000,000	1964
Krasnoyarsk, USSR	59,425,000	1972	Churchill Falls Storage, Canada	26,200,000	1971
W.A.C. Bennett, Canada	57,000,000	1968	Keban, Turkey	25,110,000	UC
Zeya, USSR	55,500,000	UC	Garrison, U.S.A.	24,300,000	1956
Sanmen Hsia, China	52,700,000	1962	Iroquois, U.S.A.-Canada (2)	24,288,000	1958
Cabora Bassa, Mozambique	51,900,000	UC	Oahe, U.S.A.	23,600,000	1963
Ust-Ilim, USSR	48,100,000	UC	Itaipu, Brazil-Paraguay	23,511,000	UC
Volga-V. I. Lenin, USSR	47,000,000	1955	Kossou, Ivory	23,308,000	UC

International Dams and Reservoirs

Source: International Boundary and Water Commission U.S. and Mexico

		Crest Hgt. Ft.	Vol. Lgth. Ft.	Cu. Yds.	Purpose	Year
Amistad Dam and Reservoir (C & E)	Tex.-Mex. Rio Grande	254	32,022	20,055	I-FC	1969
Falcon Dam and Reservoir (C & E)	Tex.-Mex. Rio Grande	150	26,294	13,242	I-FC-P	1954

How Deep Is the Ocean?

Principal Ocean Depths. **Source:** Defense Mapping Agency Hydrographic Center

Name of Area	Location	Depth Meters	Fathoms	Feet	Ship and/or Country	Year
PACIFIC OCEAN						
Mariana Trench	11°21′N, 142°12′E	11,034	6,033	36,198	Vityaz (USSR)	1957
	11°19′N, 142°15′E	10,863	5,939	35,631	HMS Challenger	1951
	11°20′N, 142°16′E	10,815	5,910	35,460	" " (UK)	1951
	11°21′N, 142°12′E	10,912	5,967	35,800	Bathyscaph Trieste	1960
Tonga Trench	23°15.3′S, 174°44.7′W	10,882	5,950	35,702	Vityaz (USSR)	1957
	24°00′S, 175°00′W	10,850	5,933	35,598	Nat'l Geographic	1965
	23°16′S, 174°46′W	10,633	5,814	34,884	US Horizon	1953
Kuril Trench	44°15.2′N, 150°34.2′E	10,542	5,764	34,587	Vityaz (USSR)	1954
	44°18′N, 150°30′E	10,382	5,677	34,062	Vityaz (USSR)	1953
Philippine Trench	10°24′N, 126°40′E	10,539	5,763	34,578	Galatheo (Danish)	1951
(Mindanao)	10°27′N, 126°39.5′E	10,497	5,740	34,440	USS Cape Johnson	1945
Izu Trench	30°32′N, 142°31′E	10,374	5,673	34,038	USS Ramapo	1932
	30°30′N, 142°30′E	9,985	5,459	32,751	Bathymetric Map (USSR)	1964
	31°54′N, 142°00′E	9,915	5,420	32,521	Bathymetric Map (USSR)	1964
	30°49′N, 142°18′E	9,441	5,159	30,954	Mansyu (Japan)	1924
Kermadec Trench	31°52.8′S, 177°20.6′W	10,047	5,494	32,964	Vityaz (USSR)	1957
	31°51′S, 177°02′W	9,994	5,465	32,790	Galathea (Danish)	1952
Bonin Trench	24°30′N, 143°24′E	9,156	5,005	30,032	Vityaz (USSR)	1964
	24°17′N, 143°23′E	9,150	5,002	30,012	USS Salt Lake City	1945
New Britain Trench	06°34′S, 153°55′E	9,140	4,998	29,988	Planet (German)	1910
	06°18′S, 153°48′E	9,103	4,976	29,858	Bathymetric Map (USSR)	1964
Yap Trench	08°33′N, 138°02′E	8,527	4,662	27,976	Vityaz (USSR)	1958
	08°08′N, 137°49′E	8,028	4,390	26,340	USCGC Kukui	1965
	07°55′N, 137°39′E	8,028	4,390	26,340	USS Greenfish	1965
Japan Trench	36°08′N, 142°43′E	8,412	4,597	27,591	Bathymetric Map (USSR)	1964
Palau Trench	07°40′N, 135°04′E	8,138	4,449	26,693	Stefan (Germany)	1905
	07°31′N, 134°56′E	7,324	4,005	24,030	USCGC Ironwood	1966
Aleutian Trench	50°53′N, 176°23′E	8,100	4,429	26,574	USCGC Bering Strait	1953
	51°13′N, 174°48′E	7,882	4,276	25,656	USCGC Chelan	1936
	50°51′N, 172°16′E	7,679	4,199	25,194	Coast & Geodetic	1036
	50°41′N, 177°11′E	7,666	4,192	25,152	Coast & Geodetic	1966
Peru Chile Trench	23°18′S, 71°41′W	8,064	4,409	26,454	US Spencer F. Baird	1957
(Atacama Trench)	23°27′S, 71°21′W	8,064	4,409	26,454	IGY	
	21°00′S, 71°15′W	7,920	4,330	25,980	US Atlantis	1955
New Hebrides Trench	20°36′S, 168°37′E	7,570	4,138	24,830	Planet (Germany)	1910
Ryukyu Trench	25°15′N, 128°32′E	7,507	4,105	24,629	Mansyu (Japan)	1925
	24°00′N, 126°48′E	7,181	3,926	23,554	Bathymetric Map (USSR)	1964
Mid. America Trench	14°02′N, 93°39′W	6,669	3,642	21,852	USS Epce	1965
ATLANTIC OCEAN						
Puerto Rico Trench	19°35′N, 68°17′W	8,648	4,729	28,374	US Archerfish	1961
	19°45′N, 67°49′W	8,528	4,663	27,978	US Rehoboth	1955
	19°44′N, 67°22′W	8,497	4,646	27,876	San Pablo, Rehoboth	1955
	19°53′N, 66°55′W	8,476	4,635	27,810	US San Pablo	1955
	19°41′N, 67°12′W	8,416	4,602	27,612	US San Pablo	1955
	19°45.5′N, 67°09.7′W	8,604	4,589	27,534	USNS Wyman	1972
	19°42′N, 67°05′W	8,381	4,583	27,498	US Vema	1954
Cayman Trench	19°12′N, 80°00′W	7,535	4,120	24,720	US Vema	1960
	18°59′N, 80°12′W	7,211	3,943	23,658	(British Admiralty)	1955
	18°59′N, 80°23′W	7,191	3,932	23,592	" "	1955
	19°03′N, 80°22′W	7,491	4,096	24,576	(Germany)	1937
So. Sandwich Trench	55°14′S, 26°29′W	8,252	4,512	27,072	USS Eltanin	1963
	55°08′S, 26°04′W	8,246	4,509	27,054	USS Eltanin	1963
	55°08′S, 26°05′W	8,210	4,494	26,964	USS Eltanin	1963
	55°07′S, 26°46′W	8,264	4,518	27,113	Meteor (Germany)	1926
Romanche Gap	00°16′S, 18°35′W	7,864	4,300	25,800	US Vema	1957
	00°13′S, 18°26′W	7,729	4,226	25,356	USS Albatross	1948
Brazil Basin	09°10′S, 23°02′W	5,119	3,346	20,076	US Vema	1956
INDIAN OCEAN						
Java Trench	10°15′S, 109°E (approx.)	7,725	4,224	25,344	Natl Geographic	1967
	10°20′S, 110°10′E	7,450	4,073	24,442	(British Admiralty)	1928
	10°19′S, 108°50′E	7,457	3,977	23,862	Australian Navy Hydrographer	1962
Ob Trench	(no position)	6,874	3,759	22,553	Nat'l Geographic	1967
Vema Trench	(no position)	6,402	3,501	21,004	Nat'l Geographic	1967
Agulhas Basin	(no position)	6,195	3,388	20,325	Nat'l Geographic	1967
Diamantina Trench	35°00′S, 105°35′E	6,062	3,315	19,890	Nat'l Geographic	1967
ARCTIC OCEAN						
Eurasia Basin	82°23′N, 19°31′E	5,450	2,980	17,880	Fidor Lithke (USSR)	1955
MEDITERRANEAN SEA						
Ionion Basin	36°32′N, 21°06′E	5,150	2,816	16,896	USS Taner	1955
	35°51′N, 22°18′E	5,005	2,737	16,420	Calypso (French)	1955

Ocean Area and Average Depth

Four major bodies of water are recognized by geographers and mapmakers. They are: the Pacific, Atlantic, Indian and Arctic Oceans. The Atlantic and Pacific Oceans are considered divided at the equator into the No. and So. Atlantic; the No. and So. Pacific. The Arctic Ocean is the name for waters north of the continental land masses in the region of the Arctic Circle.

	Sq. Miles	Avg. Depth		Sq. Miles	Avg. Depth
Pacific Ocean............	64,186,300	13,739	Hudson Bay..............	281,900	305
Atlantic Ocean...........	33,420,000	12,257	East China Sea	256,600	620
Indian Ocean............	28,350,500	12,704	Andaman Sea............	218,100	3,667
Arctic Ocean............	3,662,200	4,362	Black Sea...............	196,100	3,906
South China Sea.........	1,148,500	4,802	Red Sea.................	174,900	1,764
Caribbean Sea...........	971,400	8,448	North Sea...............	164,900	308
Mediterranean Sea.......	969,100	4,926	Baltic Sea...............	147,500	180
Bering Sea..............	873,000	4,893	Yellow Sea..............	113,500	121
Gulf of Mexico...........	582,100	5,297	Gulf of California........	59,100	2,375
Sea of Okhotsk...........	537,500	3,192	Persian Gulf.............	88,800	.328
Sea of Japan	391,100	5,468			

The Malayan Sea is not considered a geographical entity but a term used for convenience for waters between the South Pacific and the Indian Ocean.

Principal World Rivers

Source: National Geographic Society, Washington, D.C. (Length in miles)

River	Outflow	Lgth	River	Outflow	Lgth	River	Outflow	Lgth
Albany	James Bay ...	610	Japura	Amazon River .	1,750	Rio de la Plata	Atlantic Ocean	150
Amazon	Atlantic Ocean	4,000	Jordan	Dead Sea	200	Rio Grande ...	Gulf of Mexico	1,885
Amu	Aral Sea	1,578	Kootenay	Columbia Riv..	407	Rio Roosevelt .	Aripuana	400
Amur	Tatar Strait ..	2,705	Lena........	Laptev Sea ...	2,653	Saguenay	St. Lawrence R.	105
Angara	Yenisey River .	1,151	Loire........	Bay of Biscay .	634	St. John	Bay of Fundy..	418
Arkansas	Miss. River ...	1,450	Mackenzie ...	Arctic Ocean..	2,635	St. Lawrence..	Gulf of St. Law.	760
Back........	Arctic Ocean..	605	Madeira	Amazon River .	2,013	St. Maurice...	St. Lawrence R.	325
Brahmaputra .	Bay of Bengal .	1,800	Magdalena...	Caribbean Sea	956	Salween	Andaman Sea .	1,500
Bug (Southern)	Dnieper River .	532	Marne.......	Seine River...	326	São Francisco.	Atlantic Ocean	1,988
Bug (Western)	Wisla River...	481	Mekong	S. China Sea..	2,600	Saskatchewan	Lake Winnipeg	1,615
Canadian	Arkansas River	906	Meuse.......	North Sea	580	Seine	English Chan..	482
Churchill (Man.)	Hudson Bay ..	1,000	Mississippi ...	Gulf of Mexico	2,348	Shannon.....	Atlantic Ocean	230
Churchill (Que.)	Atlantic Ocean	408	Missouri.....	Miss. River ...	2,466	Snake.......	Columbia Riv..	1,038
Colorado.....	Gulf of Calif. .	1,450	Murray-Darling	Indian Ocean .	2,310	Sungari	Amur River ...	1,150
Columbia	Pacific Ocean.	1,214	Negro	Amazon	1,400	Syr	Aral Sea	1,370
Congo.......	Atlantic Ocean	2,716	Nelson	Hudson Bay ..	400	Tajo, Tagus...	Atlantic Ocean	626
Dahube......	Black Sea....	1,776	Niger	Gulf of Guinea	2,600	Tennessee ...	Ohio River....	652
Dnieper	Black Sea....	1,420	Nile	Mediterranean	4,187	Thames	North Sea	210
Dniester	Black Sea....	877	Ob-Irtysh	Gulf of Ob...	2,287	Tiber........	Tyrrhenian Sea	252
Don.........	Sea of Azov..	1,224	Oder	Baltic Sea....	567	Tigris	Euphrates....	1,180
Dráva	Danube River .	447	Ohio	Miss. River ...	975	Tisza	Danube River .	600
Dvina, North..	White Sea....	466	Orange	Atlantic Ocean	1,300	Tocantins	Pará River ...	1,677
Dvina, West...	Gulf of Riga ..	634	Orinoco......	Atlantic Ocean	1,281	Ural	Caspian Sea..	1,575
Ebro	Mediterranean	565	Ottawa	St. Lawrence R.	696	Uruguay	Rio de la Plata	1,000
Elbe	North Sea	724	Paraguay	Paraná River .	1,584	Usumacinta ..	Gulf of Mexico	270
Euphrates....	Persian Gulf .	2,235	Paraná	Rió de la Plata	1,827	Volga	Caspian Sea..	2,293
Fraser.......	St. of Georgia .	850	Peace	Slave River ...	1,195	Weser.......	North Sea	400
Gambia	Atlantic Ocean	700	Pilcomayo....	Paraguay River	1,000	Wisla	Bay of Danzig .	675
Ganges......	Bay of Bengal .	1,557	Po..........	Adriatic Sea..	405	Yangtze	E. China Sea..	3,434
Garonne	Bay of Biscay .	357	Purus	Amazon River .	2,100	Yellow (see Huang)		
Hsi	S. China Sea..	1,200	Red.........	Miss. River ...	1,018	Yenisey......	Kara Sea.....	2,566
Huang	Yellow Sea ...	3,000	Red River N...	Lake Winnipeg	355	Yukon	Bering Sea ...	1,979
Indus	Arabian Sea ..	1,800	Rhine	North Sea	820	Zambezi	Indian Ocean .	1,700
Irrawaddy....	Bay of Bengal.	1,300	Rhône.......	Gulf of Lions..	505			

Continental Statistics

Source: National Geographic Society, Washington, D.C.

Continents	Area (sq. mi.)	% of earth	Highest point (In feet)	Lowest point (In feet)	Population (est.)	% World total
Asia..................	16,988,000	29.5	1 Everest, 29,028	1 Dead Sea, −1,299	2,212,200,000	58.5
Africa................	11,506,000	20.0	2 Kilimanjaro, 19,340	2 Lake Assal, −512	364,000,000	9.6
North America.......	9,390,000	16.3	3 McKinley, 20,320	3 Death Valley, −282	330,000,000	8.7
South America.......	6,795,000	11.8	4 Aconcagua, 22,834	4 Valdés Penin., −131	201,000,000	5.3
Europe...............	3,745,000	6.5	5 El'brus, 18,510	5 Caspian Sea, −92	658,800,000	17.4
Australia.............	2,968,000	5.2	6 Kosciusko, 7,310	6 Lake Eyre, −52	13,000,000	.3
Antarctica...........	5,500,000	9.6	7 Vinson Massif, 16,860	Not Known		

Important Islands and Their Areas

Source: National Geographic Society, Washington, D.C.

Figure in parentheses shows rank among the world's ten largest islands. Some islands have not been surveyed accurately; in such cases estimated areas are shown. *See footnotes.

LOCATION-OWNERSHIP
Area in Square Miles

ARCTIC OCEAN
Canadian Islands
Axel Heiberg	15,779
Baffin (5)	183,810
Banks	23,230
Bathurst	7,609
Devon	20,861
Ellesmere (9)	82,119
Melville	16,369
Prince of Wales	12,830
Somerset	9,370
Southampton	15,700
Victoria (10)	81,930

USSR Islands
Franz Josef Land	6,400
Novaya Zemlya (two Is.)	31,900
Wrangel	2,800

Norwegian Islands
Bjørnøya	1,111
Nordaust Landet	5,792
Spitsbergen	15,251

ATLANTIC OCEAN
Anticosti, Canada	3,043
Ascension, UK	34
Azores, Portugal	888
Faial	66.2
São Miguel	299
Bahamas	5,380
Bermudas, UK	20.59
Block, Rhode Island	10.8
Canaries, Spain	2,808
Fuerteventura	670
Gran Canaria	634
Tenerife	919
Cape Breton, Canada	3,970
Cape Verde, Portugal	1,557
Faeroes, Denmark	540
Falklands, UK	4,618
Fernando de Noronha (Archipelago), Brazil	10
Fernando Póo, Equatorial Guinea	785

British Isles
Great Britain, mainland (8)	84,186
Channel Islands	75
Guernsey	30
Jersey	45
Sark	1.99
Hebrides	2,662
Ireland	32,598
Irish Republic	27,136
Northern Ireland	5,462
Man	227
Orkneys	375
Scilly	6.3
Shetlands	549
Skye	670
Wight	147
Greenland, Denmark (1)	840,000
Iceland	39,768
Long Island, N. Y.	1,723
Madeiras, Portugal	308
Marajo, Brazil	1,553
Martha's Vineyard, Mass	108.7

LOCATION-OWNERSHIP
Area in Square Miles

Mount Desert, Me	105.4
Nantucket, Mass	57
Newfoundland, Canada	43,359
Prince Edward, Canada	2,184
St. Helena, UK	47
South Georgia, UK	1,450
Tierra del Fuego, Chile and Argentina	18,800
Tristan da Cunha, UK	40

BALTIC SEA
Aland, Finland	572
Bornholm, Denmark	217
Gotland, Sweden	1,212

CARIBBEAN SEA
Antigua, UK	170
Aruba, Netherlands	74
Barbados	166
Cuba	44,217
Isle of Pines	1,180
Curacao, Netherlands	182
Dominica, UK	290
Guadeloupe, France	687
Hispaniola, (Haiti and Dominican Republic)	29,530
Jamaica	4,232
Martinique, France	425
Puerto Rico, U. S.	3,435
Tobago	116
Trinidad	1,864
Virgins, U. S.	133

INDIAN OCEAN
Andamans, India	2,500
Ceylon	25,332
Madagascar (Malagasy Republic) (4)	226,657
Mauritius	720
Pemba, Tanzania	380
Reunion, France	969
Seychelles, UK	145
Zanzibar, Tanzania	950

Persian Gulf
Bahrain	231

MEDITERRANEAN SEA
Balearics, Spain	1,936
Corfu, Greece	246
Corsica, France	3,367
Crete, Greece	3,207
Cyprus	3,572
Elba, Italy	87.4
Malta	122
Rhodes, Greece	545
Sardinia, Italy	9,194
Sicily, Italy	9,817
Euboea, Greece	1,508

PACIFIC OCEAN
Aleutians, U. S.	6,821
Adak	289
Amchitka	114
Attu	318
Kanaga	135
Kiska	110
Tanaga	185
Umnak	675
Unalaska	1,064
Unimak	1,600
Canton, U. S., UK*	
Carolines, U. S. trust terr.	463
Christmas, U.S., UK*	52

LOCATION-OWNERSHIP
Area in Square Miles

Diomede, Big, USSR	11.3
Diomede, Little, U. S	2.4
Easter, Chile	63.9
Formosa (Taiwan)	13,885
Funafuti, U. K., U. S.*	17
Galapagos, Ecuador	3,028
Guadalcanal, UK	1,130
Hainan, China	13,000
Hawaiian, U. S	6,450
Hawaii	4,037
Oahu	596
Hong Kong, UK	29
Japan	142,811
Hokkaido	30,077
Honshu (7)	89,008
Iwo Jima	7.8
Kyushu	13,768
Okinawa	454
Shikoku	6,857
Kodiak, U.S.	3,670
Marianas, U. S. trust terr., excluding Guam	184
Guam, U. S.	212
Marquesas, France	492
Marshalls, U. S. trust terr	69.8
Bikini*	
Nauru	8.2
New Caledonia, France	7,336
New Guinea (2)	305,577
New Hebrides, UK-Fr	5,700
New Zealand	103,739
Chatham	372
North	44,281
South	58,093
Stewart	670
Philippines	115,830
Leyte	3,090
Luzon	41,845
Mindanao	36,381
Mindoro	3,995
Negros	5,278
Palawan	5,751
Panay	4,749
Samar	5,184
Quemoy, Formosa	50
Sakhalin, USSR	29,498
Samoa Islands	1,173
American Samoa	76
Tutuila	53
Western Samoa	1,097
Savaii	662
Upolu	430
Santa Catalina, U.S.	74
Tahiti, France	402
Tasmania, Australia	26,383
Tongas	270
Vancouver, Canada	12,408
Vanua Levi (Fiji)	2,137
Viti Levu (Fiji)	4,010

East Indies
Bali, Indonesia	2,269
Borneo, Indonesia-Malaysia, UK (3)	280,107
Celebes, Indonesia	72,987
Java, Indonesia	48,763
Madura, Indonesia	2,113
Moluccas, Indonesia	28,767
New Britain, Aust	14,600
New Ireland, Aust	3,340
Sumatra, Indonesia (6)	182,860
Timor	13,071
Indonesian Timor	5,800
Portuguese Timor	5,763

Australia, often called an island, is a continent. Its mainland area is 2,968,000 sq. mi.

Islands in minor waters: Manhattan (31 sq. mi.), Staten (64 sq. mi.) and Governors (173 acres), all in New York Harbor, U.S.; Isle Royale (209.9 sq. mi.), Lake Superior, U.S.; Manitoulin (1,068 sq. mi.), Lake Huron, Canada; Penang (110 sq. mi.), Strait of Malacca, Malaysia; Singapore (224 sq. mi.), Singapore Strait, Singapore.

Atolls: Bikini (lagoon area, 280 sq. mi., land area 2.87 sq. mi.), U.S. Trust Territory of the Pacific Islands; Canton (lagoon 20 sq. mi. land 4.3 sq. mi.), U.S. and UK; Christmas (lagoon 89 sq. mi., land 52 sq. mi.), U.S. and UK; Funafuti (lagoon 84 sq. mi., land 17 sq. mi.), U.S. and UK.

Important Rivers of North America
Source: U.S. Geological Survey

River	Source or Upper Limit of Length	Outflow	Miles
Alabama	Junction of Coosa and Tallapoosa Rivers	Mobile River	735
Albany	Lake St. Joseph	James Bay	320
Allegheny	Potter County, Pa	Ohio River	325
Altamaha-Ocmulgee	Junction of Yellow and South Rivers, Newton County, Ga.	Atlantic Ocean	392
Androscoggin	Umbagog Lake, Maine	Atlantic Ocean	171
Apalachicola-Chattahoochee	Towns County, Ga.	Gulf of Mexico, Fla.	524
Assiniboine	Eastern Saskatchewan	Red River North	450
Arkansas	Lake County, Colo.	Mississippi River, Ark.	1,450
Atchafalaya	Red River, La.	Grand Lake, La.	170
Attawapiskat	Attawapiskat	James Bay	465
Back, N.W.T.	Contwoyto Lake	Chantrey Inlet	600
Big Black (Miss.)	Webster County, Miss.	Mississippi River	330
Big Horn	Junction of Wind and Popo Agie Rivers, Fremont County, Wyo.	Yellowstone Riv., Mont	336
Black (Mo.-Ark)	Jct. Middle & W. Forks, Reynolds Co., Mo.	White River	280
Bow	Rocky Mountains	South Saskatchewan River	315
Brazos	Junction of Salt and Double Mountain Forks, Stonewall County, Tex.	Gulf of Mexico	870
Canadian	Las Animas Co., Colo.	Arkansas Riv., Okla	906
Cape Fear	Junction of Haw and Deep Rivers, Chatham County, N.C.	Atlantic Ocean	202
Cedar (Iowa)	Dodge County, Minn.	Iowa River, Iowa	329
Cheyenne	Junction of Antelope Creek and Dry Fork, Converse Co., Wyo.	Missouri River	290
Churchill	Methy Lake	Hudson Bay	1,000
Cimarron	Colfax County, N. Mex.	Arkansas Riv., Okla	600
Clark Fork-Pend Oreille	Silver Bow County, Mont.	Columbia R., B.C., Can.	505
Colorado (Ariz.)	Rocky Mountain National Park, Colo. (90 miles in Mexico)	Gulf of Calif. Mexico	1,450
Colorado (Texas)	Borden County, Texas	Matagorda Bay	840
Columbia	Columbia Lake, British Columbia	Pac. Ocean, Bet. Ore. & W.	1,243
Columbia, Upper	Columbia Lake, British Columbia	To mouth of Snake River	890
Colville	Brooks Range	Beaufort Sea	350
Connecticut	Third Connecticut Lake, N.H.	L. I. Sound, Conn.	407
Coosa	Junction of Etowah and Oostanaula R., Floyd Co., Ga.	Alabama River	286
Coppermine, N.W.T.	Lac de Gras	Coronation Gulf (Arctic Ocean)	525
Cumberland	Junction of Poor and Clover Forks, Harlan County, Ky.	Ohio River	720
Delaware	Junction of E. & W. Branches, Hancock, N.Y.	Liston Point, Delaware Bay	390
Deschutes	Lava Lake, Deschutes County, Oreg.	Columbia River	250
Des Moines	Junction of E. and W. Forks, Humboldt Co., Iowa	Mississippi River	327
Dolores	Dolores County, Colo.	Colorado River	230
Flint	Hapeville City, Fulton Co., Ga.	Apalachicola River	265
Fraser	Near Mount Robson (On Continental Divide)	Strait of Georgia	850
French Broad	Junction of North and West Forks, Transylvania County, N.C.	Tennessee River	210
Gila	Catron County, N. Mex.	Colorado River, Ariz.	630
Grand (Mich.)	Jackson County, Mich.	Lake Michigan	260
Great Whale, Que.	Lake Bienville	Hudson Bay	230
Green (Ky.)	Lincoln County, Ky.	Ohio River, Ky.	360
Green (Utah-Wyo.)	Junction of Wells and Trail Creeks	Colorado River, Utah	730
Hamilton, Lab.	Lake Ashuanipi	Atlantic Ocean	600
Housatonic	Pittsfield, Mass.	Long Island Sound	111
Hudson	Henderson Lake, Essex County, N.Y.	Upper N.Y. Bay, NY-NJ	306
Humboldt	Wells, Nev.	Humboldt Lake	390
Illinois	Junction of Kankakee and Des Plaines Rivers, Grundy County, Ill.	Mississippi River	420
Iowa	Hancock Co., Ia.	Mississippi River	291
James (N. Dak.-S. Dak.)	Wells County, North Dakota	Missouri River, S.D.	710
James (Va.)	Junction of Jackson and Cowpasture Rivers, Botetourt County, Va.	Hampton Roads	340
Jefferson-Beaverhead-Red Rock	Source of Red Rock River in Beaverhead County, Mont.	Missouri River	217
John Day	Blue Mountains, Grant County, Oreg.	Columbia River	281
Kanawha-New	Junction of N. and S. Forks of New River, N.C.	Ohio River	352
Kentucky	Junction of N. and Middle Forks, Lee County	Ohio River	259
Klamath	Lake Ewauna, Klamath Falls, Oreg.	Pacific Ocean	250
Koyukuk	Brooks Range	Yukon River	470
Kuskokwim	Alaska Range	Kuskokwim Bay	680
Liard	Southern Yukon	Mackenzie River	570
Licking	Magoffin County, Kentucky	Ohio River	350
Little Colorado	Latitude 34°, Apache County, Ariz.	Colorado River	300
Little Missouri	Crook County, Wyo.	Missouri River	560
Mackenzie	Great Slave Lake	Arctic Ocean	900
Milk	Junction of N. and S. Forks, Alberta Province	Missouri River, Mont.	625
Minnesota	Big Stone Lake, Minn.	Mississippi R., St. Paul	332
Mississippi	Lake Itasca, Minn.	Mouth of S W Pass	2,348

River	Source or Upper Limit of Length	Outflow	Miles
Mississippi, Upper	Lake Itasca, Minn.	To mouth of Missouri R.	1,171
Mississippi-Missouri-Red Rk.	Source of Red Rock River, Mont.	Mouth of S W Pass	3,710
Missouri	Junction Jefferson, Madison and Gallatin Rivers, Madison County, Mont.	Mississippi River	2,315
Missouri-Red Rock	Source of Red Rock River, Mont.	Mississippi River	2,533
Mobile-Alabama-Coosa	Junction of Etowah and Oostanaula Rivers, Floyd County, Ga.	Mobile Bay	780
Neches	Van Zandt County, Tex.	Sabine Lake	280
Nelson, Man.	Lake Winnipeg	Hudson Bay	410
Neosho	Morris County, Kans.	Arkansas River, Okla.	460
Neuse	Junction of Eno, Little and Flat Rivers, Durham County, N.C.	Pamlico Sound	260
New	Junction of N. and S. Forks, Ashe Co., N.C.	Kanawha River	255
Niobrara	Niobrara County, Wyo.	Missouri River, Nebr.	431
Noatak	Brooks Range, Alaska	Kotzebue Sound	350
North Canadian	Union County, N. Mex	Canadian River, Okla.	760
North Platte	Junction of Grizzly and Little Grizzly Creeks, Jackson County, Colo.	Platte River, Nebr.	618
Nueces	Edwards County, Tex.	Nueces Bay	338
Ohio	Junction of Allegheny and Monongahela Rivers, Pittsburgh, Pa.	Mississippi R., Ill.-Ky.	981
Ohio-Allegheny	Potter County, Pa.	Mississippi River	1,306
Osage	Junction of Marais des Cygnes River and Little Osage River, Mo.	Missouri River, Mo.	250
Ottawa	Lake Capimitchigama	St. Lawrence	696
Ouachita	Polk County, Ark.	Red River, La.	605
Owyhee	Elko County, Nev.	Snake River	250
Pearl	Neshoba County, Miss.	Gulf of Mexico, Miss.-La.	241
Peace	Stikine Mountains	Slave River	1,054
Pecos	Mora County, N. Mex.	Rio Grande, Texas	735
Pee Dee	Junction of Yadkin and Uwharrie Rivers, Montgomery County, N.C.	Winyah Bay	233
Pee-Dee-Yadkin	Watauga County, N.C.	Winyah Bay, S.C.	435
Platte	Junction of N. and S. Platte Rivers, Nebr.	Missouri River, Nebr.	310
Porcupine	Yukon Territory (Canada)	Yukon River, Alaska	460
Potomac	Junction of North and South Branches, Hampshire County, W. Va.	Chesapeake Bay	287
Powder	Junction of S. and Middle Forks, Wyo.	Yellowstone River, Mont.	375
Red (Okla.-Tex.-La.)	Junction of Prairie Dog Town and N. Forks, Okla.	Mississippi River	1,270
Red River of the North	Junction of Otter Tail and Bois de Sioux Rivers, Wilkin County, Minn.	Lake Winnipeg, Man. Can.	545
Republican	Junction of N. Fork and Arikaree River, Nebr.	Kansas River, Kan.	445
Rio Grande	San Juan County, Colo.	Gulf of Mexico	1,885
Roanoke	Junction of N. and S. Forks, Montgomery Co., Va.	Albemarle Sound, N.C.	380
Rock (Ill.-Wis.)	Dodge County, Wis.	Mississippi River, Ill.	300
Sabine	Junction of South and Caddo Forks, Hunt County, Tex.	Sabine Lake, Tex.-La.	380
Sacramento	Siskiyou County, Calif.	Suisun Bay	377
St. Francis	Iron County, Mo.	Mississippi River, Ark.	425
St. Johns (Fla.)	Lake Washington, Brevard County, Fla.	Atlantic Ocean	276
St. Joseph	Hillsdale County, Mich.	Lake Michigan	210
St. Lawrence	Lake Ontario	Gulf of St. Lawrence (Atlantic Ocean)	800
Salmon (Idaho)	Custer County, Idaho	Snake River, Idaho	420
San Joaquin	Junction of South and Middle Forks, Madera County, Calif.	Suisun Bay	350
San Juan	Silver Lake, Archuleta County, Colo.	Colorado River, Utah	360
Santee-Wateree-Catawba	McDowell County, N.C.	Atlantic Ocean, S.C.	538
Saskatchewan, North	Rocky Mountains	Lake Winnipeg	1,100
Saskatchewan, South	Rocky Mountains	Lake Winnipeg	1,205
Savannah	Junction of Seneca and Tugaloo Rivers, Anderson County, S.C.	Atlantic Ocean, Ga.-S.C.	314
Severn, Ont.	Sandy Lake	Hudson Bay	610
Scioto	Auglaize County, Ohio	Ohio River	237
Skeena, B.C.	Skeena Mountains	Pacific Ocean	360
Smoky Hill	Cheyenne County, Colo.	Kansas River, Kan.	540
Snake	Ocean Plateau, Teton County, Wyo.	Columbia River, Wash	1,038
South Platte	Junction of South and Middle Forks, Park County, Colo.	Platte River, Nebr.	424
Stikine	Cassiar Mountains	Pacific Ocean	310
Susquehanna	Otsego Lake, Otsego County, N.Y.	Chesapeake Bay, Md.	444
Tallahatchie	Tippah County, Miss.	Yazoo River, Miss.	301
Tallapoosa	Near Embry in Paulding County, Ga.	Alabama River	268
Tanana	Wrangell Mts. (Yukon Territory, Can.)	Yukon River, Alaska	620
Tar-Pamlico	Person County, N.C.	Pamlico Bay	215
Tennessee	Junction of French Broad and Holston Rivers	Ohio River, Ky.	652
Tennessee-French Broad	Junction of N. and W. Forks of French Broad, N.C.	Ohio River	900
Tombigbee	Junction of E. and W. Forks, Itawamba Co., Miss.	Mobile River, Ala.	525
Tongue	Junction of N. and S. Forks, Sheridan Co., Wyo.	Yellowstone River	246
Trinity	Junction of E. and W. Forks, Dallas Co., Tex.	Galveston Bay, Texas	360
Wabash	Darke County, Ohio	Ohio River, Ill.-Ind.	529
Washita	Hemphill County, Tex.	Red River, Okla.	500
White (Ark.-Mo.)	Madison County, Ark.	Mississippi River	720
Wisconsin	Le Vieux Desert, Vilas County, Wis.	Mississippi River	430
Yellowstone	Park County, Wyo.	Missouri River, N.D.	671
Yukon	Junction of Lewes and Pelly Rivers, Yukon	Bering Sea, Alaska	1,770

Large Rivers in the United States

(Ranked according to average discharge in cubic feet per second (cfs) at mouth)
Source: U.S. Geological Survey (Average discharges for the period 1941-70.)

Rank	River	Average Discharge	Length [a] (miles)	Drainage Area	Most Distant Source	Maximum Discharge at Gaging Station Farthest Downstream	(date)
1	Mississippi	[b]640,000	[c]3,710	[d]1,247,300	Beaverhead Co., Montana	2,080,000	2-17-37
2	Columbia	262,000	1,243	258.000	Columbia Lake, B.C.	1,240,000	June 1894
3	Ohio	258,000	1,306	203,000	Potter Co., Pa.	1,850,000	2-01-37
4	St. Lawrence	[e]243,000	. . . .	[e]302,000	. . . . .	[f]314,000	May 1870
5	Yukon	[g]240,000	1,770	327,600	Coast Mountains, B.C.	1,030,000	6-22-64
6	[h]Atchafalaya	183,000	135	95,105	Curry Co., N.M.	. . . . .	. . . .
7	Missouri	76,300	2,533	529,400	Beaverhead Co., Montana	892,000	June 1844
8	Tennessee	64,100	900	40,910	SW Virginia	500,000	2-17-48
9	Red	[i]62,300	1,270	93,244	Curry Co., N.M.	233,000	4-17-45
10	Kuskokwim	62,000	680	49,000	Alaska Range, Alaska	392,000	6-05-64
11	Mobile	61,400	780	43,800	NW Georgia	. . . . .	. . . .
12	Snake	50,000	1,038	109,000	Teton Co., Wyoming	409,000	June 1894
13	Arkansas	45,100	1,450	160,600	Lake Co., Colorado	536,000	5-27-43
14	Copper	[j]43,000	280	24,000	Alaska Range, Alaska	[k]280,000	7-15-71
15	Tanana	[l]41,000	620	44,000	Wrangell Mtn., Alaska	186,000	8-18-67
16	Susitna	[m]40,000	300	20,000	Alaska Range, Alaska	90,700	6-07-64
17	Susquehanna	37,190	444	27,570	Otsego Co., N.Y.	787,000	3-19-36
18	Willamette	35,660	270	11,200	Douglas Co., Oregon	500,000	12-04-1861
19	Alabama	32,400	735	22,600	NW Georgia	267,000	3-07-61
20	White	32,100	720	28,000	Madison Co., Arkansas	343,000	4-17-45
21	Wabash	30,400	529	33,150	Darke Co., Ohio	428,000	3-30-13
22	Pend Oreille	29,900	490	25,820	near Butte, Montana	171,300	6-13-48
23	Tombigbee	27,300	525	20,100	Prentiss Co., Miss.	280,000	1874&1900
24	Cumberland	[n]26,900	720	18,080	Letcher Co., Kentucky	201,000	2-18-50
25	Stikine	[o]26,000	310	20,000	Stikine Range, B.C.	120,000	6-26-55
26	Appalachicola	24,700	524	19,600	Towns Co., Georgia	293,000	3-20-29
27	Sacremento	[p]22,500	377	27,100	Siskiyou Co., Calif.	[q]332,000	12-25-64
28	Illinois	22,800	420	27,900	St. Joseph Co., Ind.	123,000	May 1943
29	Koyukuk	[r]22,000	470	32,400	Endicott Mtns., Alaska	266,000	6-06-64
30	Porcupine	[s]20,000	460	45,000	Ogilvie Mtns., Alaska	217,000	3-03-68
31	Hudson	19,500	306	13,370	Essex Co., New York	215,000	3-19-36
32	Allegheny	19,290	325	11,700	Potter Co., Pa.	365,000	3-18-36
33	Delaware	[t]17,200	390	[t]11,440	Schoharie Co., N.Y.	329,000	8-20-55

(a)—Because river lengths and methods of measurement may change from time to time, the length figures given are subject to revision; (b)—About 25% of flow occurs in the Atchafalaya River; (c)—The length from mouth to source of the Mississippi River in Minnesota is 2,350 miles; (d)—at Baptiste Collette Bayou, Louisiana; (e)—At international boundary lat. 45°; (f)—Maximum monthly discharge; (g)—period 1956-66; (h)—Continuation of Red River; (i)—Flow of Ouachita River added; (j)—Period 1956-69; (k)—provisional; (l)—period 1962-69; (m)—Based on records of Chulitna, Talkeetna, and Yetna Rivers; (n)—period 1931-60; (o)—period 1948-68; (p)—American River and Yolo Bypass added; (q)—Discharge of American River not included; (r)—period 1960-69; (s)—period 1964-69; (t)—at Liston Point on Delaware Bay.

Large Rivers in Canada

Source: "Facts from Canadian Maps" Published by Canada Department of Energy Mines and Resources
(Ranked according to mean discharge in cubic feet per second (cfs))

Rank	River	Mean Discharge	Length (miles)	Drainage Area (sq. mi.)
1	St. Lawrence River	348,000	1,900	396,000[1]
2	Mackenzie (to head of Finlay)	343,000	2,635	697,000
3	Fraser.	125,000	850	84,800
4	Columbia (International Boundary to head of Columbia Lake) . . .	98,700	498	59,700[2]
5	Nelson (to head of Bow)	83,600	1,600	414,000[3]
6	Yukon (International Boundary to head of Nisutlin)	82,000	714	114,800[4]
7	Ottawa	69,000	790	56,500
8	Churchill (to head of Ashuanipi)	55,700	532	30,800
9	Churchill (to head of Churchill Lake)	42,400	1,000	108,600
10	Saskatchewan (to head of Bow) . . . .·. .	24,800	1,205	130,000

(1) Including 195,000 sq. mi. in U.S.A. (2) Including 20,000 sq. mi. in U.S.A. (3) Including 69,500 sq. mi. in U.S.A. (4) Including 9,000 sq. mi. in U.S.A.

The Largest Lake in Each Province of Canada

Source: Standard Encyclopedia of the World's Rivers and Lakes. 1965 & The Canada Yearbook. 1970-1971

Province	Largest within:	Largest partly in:	Shared with	Origin	Area sq. miles	Ft. above sea level
Alta.	Claire			Natural	545	699
		Athabasca	Sask.	Natural	940	699
B.C.	Kootenay			Natural	168	1,745
Man.	Winnipeg			Natural	9,465	713
Nfld.	Melville			Natural	1,133	S.L.
N.B.	Grand			Natural	65	Tidal
N.W.T. . . .	Great Bear			Natural	12,275	511
N.S.	Bras d'Or			Natural	360	Tidal
Ont.	Nipigon			Natural	1,870	855
		Huron	U.S.A. . . .	Natural	15,353	580
P.E.I.						
Que. . . .	Mistassini			Natural	840	1,220
Sask. . . .	Wollaston			Natural	796	1,300
		Athabasca	Alta. . . .	Natural	2,180	699

The Largest Lake in Each State of the United States

Source: National Geographic Society, Washington, D.C.

° indicates reservoir

State	Largest entirely within state	Largest partly in another state	Shared with	Origin	Total Area in square miles	Feet above sea level	Maximum depth feet	Shoreline length miles
Ala....	Wheeler			Man-made...	104.8	556	58	1,063
		Guntersville	Tenn	Man-made...	108	595	60	962
Alaska	Iliamna			Natural	1,010	44	980	297
Ariz...	Painted Rock*			Man-made...	83	661	181	....
		Powell	Utah	Man-made...	252	3,700	580	1,800
Ark ...	Ouachita			Man-made...	57	571	190	640
		Bull Shoals	Mo	Man-made...	71	654	203	740
Calif ..	Salton Sea			Natural	360	-235	48	....
		Tahoe	Nev	Natural	192	6,229	1,644	71
Colo ..	Blue Mesa*			Man-made...	14.3	7,519	333	96
		Navajo*	N. Mex	Man-made...	24.3	6,102	382	157
Conn..	Candlewood			Man-made...	8.5	429	85	65
Del ...	Lum's Pond			Man-made...	.31	50	10	6
Fla....	Okeechobee			Natural	700	14	20	117
Ga	Sidney Lanier			Man-made...	59.4	1,070	156	540
		Clark Hill	S.C.	Man-made...	109.4	330	150	1,200
Hawaii	Waita*			Man-made...	.66	233	23	3
Idaho .	Pend Oreille			Natural	146.9	2,064	1,400	120
Ill	Carlyle			Man-made...	40	445	40	83
		Michigan	Wis., Ind., Mich.	Natural	22,300	579	923	1,660
Ind ...	Monroe			Man-made...	16.8	538	45	142
		Michigan	Wis., Ill., Mich.	Natural	22,300	579	923	1,660
Iowa ..	Rathbun*			Man-made...	32.8	926	71	180
Kan...	Milford*			Man-made...	25.3	1,144	78	163
Ky....	Cumberland			Man-made...	78.5	723	183	1,085
		Kentucky	Tenn	Man-made...	247.3	359	60	2,025
La	Pontchartrain			Natural	621	Sea Lev.	15	117
Me....	Moosehead			Natural	117	1,058	246	....
Md...	Deep Creek			Natural	7.0	2,462	60	55
		Conowingo*	Penna	Man-made...	13.4	109	110	38
Mass..	Quabbin*			Man-made...	39.4	524	150	104
Mich .	Houghton			Natural	30.6	1,138	20	32
		Superior	Wis., Mich., Ont.	Natural	31,700	600	1,333	2,980
Minn..	Red			Natural	451.2	1,175	35	127
		Superior	Wis., Mich., Ont.	Natural	31,700	600	1,333	2,980
Miss ..	Ross Barnett*			Man-made...	51.5	297	50	150
Mo....	Lake of the Ozarks			Man-made...	91.5	660	120	1,150
Mont..	Fort Peck			Man-made...	385.9	2,234	220	1,520
Nebr..	McConaughy			Man-made...	54.7	3,270	142	105
Nev ...	Pyramid			Natural	168.7	3,789	330	66
		Mead	Ariz	Man-made...	247	1,221	432	550
N.H. ..	Winnipesaukee			Natural	69.6	504	169	240
N.J...	Hopatcong			Natural	4.2	915	60	22
N.M...	Elephant Butte*			Man-made...	58.9	4,450	193	250
N.Y...	Oneida			Natural	80	369	55	55
		Erie	Mich., Pa., Ont., Ohio.	Natural	9,910	570	210	856
N.C....	Norman			Man-made...	50.8	760	100	520
		John H. Kerr*	Va	Man-made...	76.4	320	120	800
N.D...	Sakakawea			Man-made...	609	1,850	180	1,605
		Oahe*	S.D.	Man-made...	579.7	1,620	200	2,250
Ohio ..	Grand			Man-made...	20	869	10	60
		Erie	Mich., Pa., N.Y., Ont.	Natural	9,910	570	210	856
Okla ..	Eufaula			Man-made...	160.1	585	87	600
Ore ...	Klamath			Natural	145.3	4,143	45	165
		Goose Lake	Calif	Natural	193.7	4,716	24	90
Pa	Wallenpaupack			Man-made...	9	1,182	50	45
		Erie	Mich., N.Y., Ohio, Ont.	Natural	9,910	570	210	856
R.I. ...	Scituate*			Man-made...	5.68	284	80	38
S.C....	Marion			Man-made...	157	75	35	299
S.D....	Francis Case			Man-made...	159.4	1,375	140	540
		Oahe	N.D.	Man-made...	579.7	1,620	200	2,250
Tenn ..	Watts Bar*			Man-made...	60.3	741	105	783
		Kentucky	Ky	Man-made...	250.5	359	88	2,380
Texas	Sam Rayburn			Man-made...	178.9	173	84	560
		Toledo Bend*	La	Man-made...	308.8	175	....	1,200
Utah ..	Great Salt Lake			Natural	1,650	4,200	30	....
Vt	Bomoseen			Natural	3.7	411	55	19
		Champlain	N.Y., Que	Natural	490	95	399	....
Va	Smith Mountain			Man-made...	32.2	795	217	500
		John H. Kerr*	N.C.	Man-made...	76.4	320	120	800
Wash.	F. D. Roosevelt			Man-made...	123.4	1,288	375	660
W.Va..	Tygart			Man-made...	5.44	1,010	....	106
Wis ...	Winnebago			Natural	215.26	747	21.6	91.96
		Superior	Minn., Mich., Ontario	Natural	31,700	600	1,333	2,980
Wyo ...	Yellowstone			Natural	139	7,733	309	110
		Flaming Gorge*	Utah	Man-made...	65.7	6,040	437	400

Large Lakes of Canada

Source: National Geographic Society, Washington, D.C.

Province/Lake	Total Area sq. miles	Elevation	Province/Lake	Total Area sq. miles	Elevation
Alberta			Nutarawit	350	—
Athabasca (part)	3,120	699	Gras, de	345	1,365
Claire	545	699	Aylmer	340	1,230
Lesser Slave	461	1,892	Pelly	331	501
British Columbia			**Nova Scotia**		
Atlin (part)	299	2,192	Bras d'Or	360	S.L.
Manitoba			**Ontario**		
Winnipeg	9,465	713	Huron (part)	23,100	580
Winnipegosis	2,103	833	Superior (part)	31,700	602
Manitoba	1,817	814	Erie (part)	9,910	572
Southern Indian	1,060	835	Ontario (part)	7,550	245
Island	550	744	Nipigon	1,870	855
Moose	525	838	Lake of the Woods		
Cedar	517	830	(part)	1,695	1,060
Reindeer (part)	2,467	1,150	Seul	539	1,172
Gods	319	585	Nipissing	350	640
Nuelton (part)	850	875	Abitibi (part)	369	868
Newfoundland			Rainy (part)	360	1,103
Melville	1,133	7	St. Clair (part)	402	575
Michikamau	566	1,510	**Quebec**		
Northwest Territory			Mistassini	840	1,220
Great Bear	12,275	511	Eau Claire	535	790
Great Slave	10,980	513	Minto	485	450
Nettilling	1,956	100	Saint-Jean	414	322
Dubawnt	1,600	774	Bienville	392	1,400
Baker	975	30	**Saskatchewan**		
Yathkyed	860	461	Athabasca (part)	3,120	699
La Martre	685	870	Reindeer (part)	2,467	1,150
Nueltin (part)	850	875	Wollaston	796	1,300
Aberdeen	475	261	Lac la Ronge.............	552	1,198
Hottah	377	640	Cree	446	1,570
Kaminuriak.............	360	320	Peter Pond	302	1,382

Lakes of the World

Source: National Geographic Society, Washington, D.C.

A lake is a body of water surrounded by land. Although some lakes are called seas, they are lakes by definition. The Caspian Sea is bounded by the Soviet Union and Iran and is fed by eight rivers.

Name	Continent	Area sq. mi.	Length mi.	Depth feet	Elev. feet
Caspian Sea	Asia-Europe	143,550	760	3,264	-92
Superior	North America	31,700	350	1,333	600
Victoria	Africa	26,828	250	265	3,720
Aral Sea................	Asia	25,300	280	223	174
Huron..................	North America	23,100	206	750	579
Michigan	North America	22,300	307	923	579
Tanganyika..............	Africa	12,700	420	4,650	2,534
Great Bear	North America	12,275	192	1,356	511
Baykal	Asia	11,780	395	5,315	1,493
Nyasa	Africa	11,430	360	2,226	1,550
Great Slave	North America	10,980	298	2,015	513
Erie	North America	9,910	241	210	570
Winnipeg...............	North America	9,465	266	60	713
Ontario.................	North America	7,550	193	802	245
Ladoga.................	Europe	6,835	120	738	13
Balkhash...............	Asia	6,720	373	85	1,115
Chad	Africa	6,300	175	24	787
Maracaibo..............	South America	5,127	96	108	Sea level
Onega..................	Europe	3,710	145	328	108
Volta	Africa	3,276	250	....	
Titicaca	South America	3,200	122	1,002	12,506
Athabasca	North America	3,120	208	407	699
Nicaragua	North America	3,100	102	230	102
Eyre	Australia	2,970	90	4	-52
Rudolf	Africa	2,473	154	240	1,230
Reindeer	North America	2,467	143	....	1,150
Issyk Kul	Asia	2,355	115	2,303	5,279
Torrens	Australia	2,230	130	....	106
Vänern.................	Europe	2,156	91	328	144
Winnipegosis	North America	2,103	141	38	833
Albert..................	Africa	2,075	100	54	2,030
Kariba	Africa	2,050	175	294	1,590
Nettilling	North America	1,956	67	Sea Level	100
Nipigon	North America	1,870	72	540	855
Gairdner	Australia	1,840	90	....	112
Manitoba...............	North America	1,817	140	12	814
Urmia..................	Asia	1,815	90	49	4,180
Mweru	Africa	1,770	76	84	3,010
Kyoga..................	Africa	1,710	50	25	3,400
Khanka	Asia	1,700	55	33	226
Lake of the Woods	North America	1,695	72	36	1,060
Koko (Tsing)	Asia	1,625	68	125	10,515
Dubawnt	North America	1,600	69	....	774
Great Salt	North America	1,600	75	48	4,200
Tungt'ing...............	Asia	1,430	75	....	36

Famous Waterfalls

Source: National Geographic Society, Washington, D. C.

Height=total drop in one or more leaps. †=falls of more than one leap; *=falls that diminish greatly seasonally; **=falls that reduce to a trickle or are dry for part of each year. If river names not shown, they are same as the falls. R.=river; L.=lake; (C)=cascade-type. See notes following list.

Name and Location	Ft.	Name and Location	Ft.	Name and Location	Ft.
AFRICA		**Norway—**		**Twin, Snake R	125
Angola		† Eastern Mardalsfoss	1,696	Kentucky	
Duque de Braganca,		Highest fall	974	Cumberland	68
Lucala R	344	Western Mardalsfoss	1,535	Maryland	
Ruacana, Cunene R	406	(Both on L. Eikesdal)		Great, Potomac R. (C)	90
Ethiopia		Skjeggedal	525	Minnesota	
Baratieri, Ganale		Skykkje, Skykkjua R	820	**Minnehaha	54
Dorya R	459	Vettis, Morkedöla R	1,214	Montana	
Dal Verme, Ganale		Highest fall	889	Missouri	75
Dorya R	98	Vöring, Bjoreia R	597	New Jersey	
Fincha	508	**Sweden**		**Passaic	70
*Tesissat, Blue Nile R	140	† Handöl, Handöl Cr	345	New York	
Lesotho		† *Stora Sjöfallet, Lule R	130	Taughannock	215
Maletsunyane	630	Tannforsen, Are R	120	Oregon	
Rhodesia-Zambia		**Switzerland**		† Multnomah	620
*Victoria, Zambezi R	355	† Giétroz (Glacier) (C)	1,640	Highest fall	542
South Africa		† Diesbach	394	Tennessee	
*Aughrabies, Orange R	400	† Giessbach	1,312	Fall Creek	256
Howick, Umgeni R	311	Handegg, Aare R	151	Rock House Creek	125
† Tugela (5 falls)	3,110	Iffigen	394	Washington	
Highest fall	1,350	Pissevache, La Salanfe R	213	Fairy Falls	700
Tanzania-Zambia		† Reichenbach	656	Mt. Rainier Nat. Pk.	
*Kalambo	726	Rhine	66	Narada, Paradise R	168
Uganda		† Simmen, Simme R	459	Sluiskin, Paradise R	300
Murchison, Victoria		Stäuber	590	Palouse	198
Nile R	140	Staubbach	984	Snoqualmie	270
Zambia		† Trümmelbach	1,312	Wisconsin	
Chirombo, Ieisa R	880	**NORTH AMERICA**		Manitou, Black R	165
ASIA		**Canada**		Wyoming	
India—Cauvery	330	British Columbia		Yellowstone Pk. Tower	132
† **Gersoppa (Jog),**		†Takakkaw (Daly Glacier)	1,650	Yellowstone (upper)	109
Sharavati R	830	Highest fall	1,200	Yellowstone (lower)	308
Japan		Della Falls	1,443	**Mexico**—El Salto	218
**Kegon, L. Chuzenji	330	Panther, Nigel Cr	600	**Juanacatlán, Rio	
Yudaki, L. Yuno	335	Labrador		Grande de Santiago	66
AUSTRALASIA		Churchill Falls, Churchill R	245	**SOUTH AMERICA**	
Australia		Mackenzie District		**Argentina—Brazil**	
New South Wales		Virginia, S. Nahanni R	315	† Iguazú	237
† Wentworth	518	Quebec		**Brazil**—Glass	1,325
Highest fall	360	Montmorency	274	Herval	400
Wollomombi	1,100	**Canada—United States**		Paulo Afonso, São Fran-	
Queensland		Niagara: American	193	cisco R	275
Coomera	210	Horseshoe	186	Patos-Maribondo, Rio	
Tully	450	**United States**		Grande	115
New Zealand		California		Urubupunga, Alto	
*Bowen (from Glaciers)	540	Feather, Fall R	640	Parana R	40
Helena	890	Yosemite National Park		**Brazil-Paraguay**	
Stirling	505	Bridalveil	620	Sete Quedas, or Guaira	
† Sutherland, Arthur R	1,904	Illilouette	370	Alto Paraná R	130
EUROPE		Nevada	594	**Colombia**—Tequendama,	
Austria—Upper Gastein	207	**Ribbon	1,612	Bogotá R	427
Lower Gastein	280	Silver Strand	1,170	Catarata de Candelas,	
(Both on Ache R.)		Vernal	317	Cusiana R	984
† Golling, Schwarzbach R	200	†Yosemite	2,425	**Ecuador**	
Krimml (Krimmler)	1,250	*Yosemite (upper)	1,430	Agoyan, Pastaza R	200
France—† Gavarnie (C)	1,385	*Yosemite (lower)	320	**Guyana**	
Great Britain—Wales		*Yosemite (middle)	675	Kaieteur, Potaro R	741
Pistyll Cain, Afon Gain R	150	Colorado		King George VI, Utshi R	1,600
Pistyll Rhaiadr	240	Seven	266	† Marina, Ipobe R	500
Scotland		Georgia		Highest fall	300
Glomach	370	† Tallulah	251	**Peru**	
Iceland—Detti, Jokul R	144	Hawaii		Sewerd, Cutibirene R	877
Gull, Hvita R	101	Akaka	442	**Venezuela**—† Angel	3,212
Italy—Toce (C)	470	Idaho		Highest fall	2,648
		Henry's Fork (upper)	96	Cuquenán	2,000
		Henry's Fork (lower)	70		
		**Shoshone, Snake R	195		

The earth has thousands of waterfalls, some of considerable magnitude. Their importance is determined not only by height but volume of flow, steadiness of flow, crest width, whether the water drops sheerly or over a sloping surface, and one leap or a succession of leaps. A series of low falls flowing over a considerable distance is known as a cascade.

Sete Quedas or Guaira is the world's greatest waterfall when its mean annual flow (estimated at 470,000 cusecs, cubic feet per second) is combined with height. A greater volume of water passes over Stanley Falls, though not one of its seven cataracts, spread over nearly 60 miles of the Congo River, exceeds 10 feet.

Estimated mean annual flow, in cusecs, of other major waterfalls are: Niagara, 212,200; Paulo Afonso, 100,000; Urubupunga, 97,000; Iguazú, 61,600; Patos-Maribondo, 53,000; Victoria, 38,400; Churchill, Labrador, 40,000; and Kaieteur, 23,400.

Notable Bridges in North America

Source: State Highway Engineers; Canadian Civil Engineering — ASCE

Asterisk (*) designates Railroad Bridge. Span of a bridge is distance (in feet) between its supports.

Suspension

Year	Bridge	Location	Longest Span
1964	Verrazano-Narrows	New York, N.Y.	4,260
1937	Golden Gate	San. Fran. Bay	4,200
1957	Mackinac	Sts. of Mackinac	3,800
1931	Geo. Washington	Hudson River	3,500
1952	Tacoma	Washington	2,800
1936	¹Transbay	San Fran. Bay	2,310
1939	Bronx-Whitestone	East R., N.Y.C.	2,300
1970	Quebec Road	Quebec	2,190
1951	Del. Memorial	Wilmington, Del.	2,150
1968	Del. Mem. (new)	Wilmington, Del.	2,150
1957	Walt Whitman	Phila., Pa.	2,000
1929	Ambassador	Detroit-Canada	1,850
1961	Throgs Neck	Long Is. Sound	1,800
1926	Benjamin Franklin	Philadelphia	1,750
1924	Bear Mt., N.Y.	Hudson River	1,632
1952	²Wm. Preston Lane Mem.	Sandy Point, Md.	1,600
1903	Williamsburg	East R., N.Y.C.	1,600
1969	Newport	Narragansett Bay, R.I.	1,600
1883	Brooklyn	East R., N.Y.C.	1,595
1930	Mid-Hudson, N.Y.	Poughkeepsie	1,500
1964	Vincent Thomas	Los Angeles Har	1,500
1909	Manhattan	East R., N.Y.C.	1,470
1936	Triborough	East R., N.Y.C.	1,380
1931	St. Johns	Portland, Ore	1,207
1929	Mount Hope	Rhode Island	1,200
1939	Deer Isle	Maine	1,080
1931	Maysville (Ky.)	Ohio River	1,060
1867	Cincinnati	Ohio River	1,057
1900	Miampimi	Mexico	1,030
1849	Wheeling, W. Va	Ohio River	1,010
1929	Royal Gorge	Colorado	880
1938	Thousand Islands	St. Lawrence R.	800
1933	Anthony Wayne	Ohio	782
1915	Belpre, O.-W. Va.	Ohio River	775
1904	E. Liv'p'l, O.-W. Va.	Ohio River	750
1933	South 10th St.	Pittsburgh, Pa	750
1932	Waldo-Hancock	Maine	750
1935	Memorial Twin (Ill.)	Mississippi R.	710
1921	Rondout	Kingston, N.Y.	705
1927	US-23	Ohio River, Ky	700

Cantilever

Year	Bridge	Location	Longest Span
1917	*Quebec (Railway)	Quebec	1,800
1970	Chester, Pa	Delaware River	1,644
1958	New Orleans, La.	Mississippi, R.	1,575
1936	Transbay	San. Fran. Bay	1,400
1968	Baton Rouge, La	Mississippi R.	1,235
1955	Nyack-Tarrytown	Hudson River	1,212
1930	Longview	Columbia River	1,200
1909	Queensboro	East R., N.Y.C.	1,182
1892	Muscatine, Iowa	Mississippi River	1,164
1932	Savanna-Sabvia, Ill.	Mississippi River	1,160
1927	Carquinez Strait	California	1,100
1958	Parallel Span		1,100
1968	Isaiah D. Hare	Jacksonville, Fla	1,088
1957	³Richmond	San Fran. Bay	1,070
1929	Grace Memorial	Charleston, S.C	1,050
1918	MacArthur, Ill.-Iowa	Mississippi River	1,000
1963	Newburgh-Beacon	Hudson R., N.Y.	1,000
UC(1975)	Caruthersville, Mo	Mississippi R	920
1969	Ohio River	Pt. Pleasant, W. Va.	900
1940	Natchez	Mississippi R.	875
1938	Blue Water	Pt. Huron, Mich	871
1972	Vicksburg	Mississippi River	870
1954	St. Petersburg, Fla.	Tampa Bay	864
1940	*Baton Rouge	Mississippi R	848
1899	*Cornwall	St. Lawrence R	843
1940	Greenville	Mississippi R	840
1961	Helena, Ark	Mississippi R	840
1963	Brent Spence	Covington, Ky.	831
1963	Cincinnati, O.	Ohio River	830
1956	Earl C. Clements	Ohio R., Ill-Ky	825⁶
1930	*Vicksburg	Mississippi R	825
1929	Louisville	Ohio River	820
1943	Jeff'rsonBarr'ks.,Mo.	Mississippi R.	804
1950	Maurice J. Tobin	Boston, Mass	800
1935	Rip Van Winkle	Catskill, N.Y	800
1938	Cairo, Ill	Ohio River	800
1940	Ludlow Ferry	Potomac R	800
1932	Washington Mem	Seattle, Wash	800
1930	Cairo, Ill	Mississippi R	800
1936	North Bend, Oreg	Coos Bay	793

Year	Bridge	Location	Longest Span
1936	McCullough	Coos Bay, Ore	793
1935	⁴Huey P. Long	New Orleans	790
1916	*Memphis(Harahan)	Mississippi R	790
1892	*Memphis	Mississippi R	790
1949	Memphis-Arkansas	Mississippi R	790
1904	*Mingo Jct., W. Va.	Ohio River	769
1910	*Beaver, Pa	Ohio River	767
1966	⁵S.N. Pearman	Charleston, S.C	760
1940	Owensboro	Ohio River	750
1911	Sewickley, Pa	Ohio River	750
1928	Outerbridge, N.Y.C	Arthur Kill	750
1964	Sunshine, Don'ville	Mississippi, La	750
1964	Ohio River	Henderson, Ky	720
1956	Talmadge Memorial	Savannah, Ga	710
1940	Bridge of the Gods	Oregon	705
1927	Bellaire, O	Ohio River	700
1955	Belpre, O.-W. Va	Ohio River	700
1927	Rim to Rim	Twin Falls, Ida	700
1928	Goethals, N.Y.C	Arthur Kill	672
1905	*Thebes, Ill	Mississippi R	671
1942	Chester, Ill	Mississippi R	670
1957	Rappahannock	White Stone, Va	648
1959	Corpus Christi	Nueces Co., Texas	620
1968	Reedy Point	Ches. & Del. Can	600
1960	Summit	Ches. & Del. Can	600
1959	Castleton	Hudson R., N.Y	600
1943	Gold Star	New London, Conn	540
1934	Gastineau Channel	Juneau, Alaska	516
1960	West River	Brattleboro, Vt.	440
1953	Luck Peak Reservoir	nr Boise, Idaho	432
1965	Jeremiah Morrow	Warren Co., Ohio	427
1952	Mormon Pioneer	Omaha	420
1930	Plattsmouth, Nebr.	Missouri River	403
1940	Main Avenue	Cleveland, Ohio	400
1959	Central Viaduct	Cleveland, Ohio	400

Simple Truss

Year	Bridge	Location	Longest Span
1917	*Metropolis	Ohio River	720
1929	Paducah, Ky	Ohio River	716
1922	*Tanana River	Nenana, Alaska	700
1911	MacArthur	St. Louis	668
1933	*Henderson	Ohio River	665
1967	IR 77, Ohio River	Marietta, Ohio	650
1919	Louisville	Ohio River	644
1933	Atchafalaya	Morgan City, La.	608
1924	*Castleton	Hudson River	598
1906	Elizabethtown	Great Miami R., O	586
1929	*Louisville	Ohio River	546
1889	*Cincinnati	Ohio River	542
1951	Allegheny River	Allegheny Co., Pa	533
1914	Pittsburgh	Allegheny R.	531
1930	*Martinez	California	528
1967	Tanana River	Alaska	500
1963	216 Nenana River	Rex, Alaska	406
1967	Tanana River	Big Delta, Alaska	399
1939	Rulo, Nebr.	Missouri River	379

Steel Truss

Year	Bridge	Location	Longest Span
1940	Gov. Nice Mem	Potomac River, Md	800
1937	US-60, Ky	Ohio River	800
1938	US-62, Ky	Green River	700
1952	US-62, Ky	Cumberland River	700
1940	Jamestown	Jamestown, R.I	640
1940	Greenville	Mississippi R., Ark	640
1949	Memphis	Mississippi R., Ark	621
1938	US-421	Ohio River, Ky	600
1960	Summit	Chespeak-Del. Canal	600
1938	US-22	Delaware River, N.J	540
1972	Mississippi River	Muscatine, Iowa	512
1896	Newport	Ohio River, Ky	511
1897	Missouri River	Sioux City, Neb-Ia	504
1931	US-60	Cumberland R., Ky	500
1958	Lake Oahe	Mobridge, S.D.	500
1958	Lake Oahe	Gettysburg S.D.	500
1910	McKinley, St. Louis	Mississippi River	500
1963	Millard E. Tydings	Susquehanna R., Md.	490
1930	Lake Champlain	Lake Champlain, N.Y	434
1952	Bellevue (GAR)	Missouri R., Nebr	420
1947	Mayo	Blountstown, Fla	420
1929	Clarendon	White River, Ark	400
1931	US-60	Tennessee R., Ky	400
1965	Moyie Springs	Moyie River, Idaho	378
1944	US-68	Tennessee R., Ky	368

Year	Name	Location	Length
1929	Augusta	White River, Ark.	360
1932	US-62	Kentucky River	360
1951	SR-80	Fishing Creek, Ky	360
1953	Lake Francis Case	Chamberlain, S.D	336
1876	High Bridge, Ky	Kentucky River	332
1963	US-68	Cumberland R., Ky	321
1939	US-431	Green & Rough R., Ky.	320
1940	Deep Creek Lake	Deep Creek Lake, Md	300
1953	Montague Twp	Delaware River, N.J	300
1958	Little Colorado	Cameron, Ariz	296
1950	Somerset	Cumberland R., Ky	280
1927	US-27	Kentucky River, Ky	275
1951	Comm. Isaac Hull	Housatonic R., Conn	254
1921	Yankton	Missouri R., S.D	250
1931	S. R. 627	Kentucky R., Ky	250

Continuous Truss

Year	Name	Location	Length
1959	Rocheport, Mo. (9)	Missouri River	2,500
1939	Lyons-Fulton	Mississippi R. Ill	1,340
1966	Astoria, Ore	Columbia R	1,232
1966	Marquam	Willamette R., Ore	1,044
UC(1975)	Mississippi R.	Dyersburg, Tenn.	900
1969	Irondequoit Bay	Rochester, N.Y.	891
1943	Dubuque, Ia	Mississippi R.	845
1953	John E. Mathews	Jacksonville, Fla	810
1957	Kingston-Rhinecliff	Hudson R., N.Y.	800
1961	Sherman Minton	New Albany, Ind	800
1918	*Sciotoville	Ohio River	775
1929	Madison-Milton	Ohio River	727
1973	I 275, Boone Co., Ky	Ohio River	720
1964	John F. Kennedy	Louisville, Ky	700
1966	Matthew E. Welsh	Mississippi R.	700
1929	Chain of Rocks	Mississippi R.	699
1966	Braga	Taunton R., Mass.	682
1938	Port Arthur-Orange	Texas	680
1929	*Cincinnati	Ohio River	675
1932	Mt. Carmel, Ill.	Wabash River	675
1928	CapeGirardeau, Mo.	Mississippi R.	672
1946	Chester, Ill.	Mississippi R.	670
1930	Quincy, Ill	Mississippi R.	628
1934	Bourne	Cape Cod Canal	616
1935	Sagamore	Cape Cod Canal	616
1965	Clarion River	Clarion Co., Pa.	612
1941	Rio Grande Gorge	Taos, N.M.	600
1962	Columbia River	Kettle Falls, Wash	600
1936	W. Br. Feather River	Oroville, Cal	576
1936	Meredosia	Illinois River	567
1937	Mark Twain Mem	Hannibal, Mo	562
1961	Homestead	Pittsburgh	553
1932	Ship Canal	Seattle, Wash.	552
1927	Pulaski Skyway	Passaic R., N.J	550
1936	Ross Island	Portland, Ore	535
1962	South Omaha	Mo. R., Neb-Iowa	525
1970	Columbia River	Beebe. Wash	520
1954	Snake River	Central Ferry, Wash.	520
1962	Columbia River	Pasco, Wash	520
1958	Columbia River	Vantage, Wash	520
1922	Stevenson, Ala	Tennessee R.	500
1962	Memorial	Missouri River, N.D.	475
1967	Martinez, Calif	Carquinex Str	475
1963	Mississippi River	Minneapolis, Minn	456
1956	I 75 Ky. (Twin)	Kentucky R.	448
1939	Decatur, Neb.	Missouri R.	420
1939	Florence, Ala	Tennessee R	420
1939	Brownville	Missouri R., Neb-Mo	420
1930	Nebraska City	Missouri R., Neb-Iowa	403

Continuous Box and Plate Girder

Year	Name	Location	Length
1953	Neches River	Orange County, Texas	850
1967	San Mateo-Hayward No. 2	San Fran. Bay, Cal.	750
1969	San Diego-Coronado	San Diego Bay, Calif.	660
1972	Ship Channel	Houston, Texas	630
1967	Poplar St.	St. Louis, Mo.	600
1971	Lake Koocanusa	Lincoln Co., Mont.	500
1967	La Crosse	Mississippi R., Wisc.	450
1967	Mississippi R.	LaCrescent, Minn.	450
1972	Sitka Harbor	Sitka, Alaska	450
1974	I-430	Arkansas R.	430
1972	Kansas City	Missouri R., Kan-Mo.	425
1967	Chattanooga	Tennessee R., Tenn.	420
1941	Susquehanna	Susquehanna R., Md.	400
1963	Lake Charles B'pass	Louisiana	399
1971	St. Croix River	Hudson, Minn.	390
1957	Conn. Turnpike	Quinnipiac R.	387
1960	Route 34	New Haven, Conn.	379
1971	S.H. No. 1	Pendleton, Ark.	377
1960	Tennessee River	Chattanooga, Tenn.	375
1966	LeClaire	LeClaire, Iowa	370
1971	Sacramento R.	Bryte, Cal.	370

Year	Name	Location	Length
1966	Benton-Humphrey	Tennessee R., Tenn	366
1967	San Mateo Creek	Hillsborough, Calif	360
	Gunnison River	Gunnison, Colo	360
1950	US-62	Tennessee R., Ky	350
1961	Whiskey Creek	Trinity Co., Calif	350
1972	Franklin Falls	Snoq'Imie Pass, Wash.	350
1971	Don Pedro Reserv.	Tuolumne Co., Calif	350
1970	Columbia River	Brewster, Wash	343
1968	Darmouth	Minneapolis	340
1967	Lexington Ave	St. Paul	340
1971	Cumberland River	Nashville, Tenn	330
1969	Buffalo Creek	Armstrong Co., Pa	325
1970	Arkansas R.	Dardanelle, Ark	325
1969	Arkansas R.	Morrilton, Ark.	322
1963	Western Ky. Pkwy	Green River, Ky	320
1965	Blue Grass Pkwy	Kentucky River, Ky	320
1964	Cumberland River	Nashville, Tenn	320
1967	Carroll County	Kentucky R., Ky	320
1936	Kentucky River	Frankfort, Ky	315
1966	Washington Ave.	Minneapolis	315
1959	William H. Putnam	Conn. River, Conn	311
1971	Copper River	Chitina, Alaska	310
1973	Main Street	Little Rock. Ark	303
1967	Rouge River	Detroit, Mich	300
1972	Mission Valley	San Diego, Cal	300
1953	Carrollton	Kentucky R., Ky	300
1950	Guthrie	Guthrie, Ariz	300
1942	Charter Oak	Hartford, Conn.	300
1970	Sacramento River	Elkhorn, Calif	285
1964	West Camas Slough	Camas, Wash	284
1950	US-231	Green River, Ky	276
1961	Rainier Ave. R.(Twins)	Seattle	275
1940	Lakefront	Cleveland, Ohio	271
1951	SR-61	Green River, Ky	260
1954	Wenatchee River	Wenatchee, Wash.	260
1971	Lake Bomoseen	Castleton, Vt.	260
1973	East 148 Street	Seattle, Wash	258
1966	Hansen	Hansen, Idaho	258
1965	Susitna River	Alaska	250
1940	Thomas A. Edison	Raritan River	250
1965	Barren River	165, Kentucky	250
1962	Snohomish River	Monroe, Wash	255
1954	Garden State Pkwy	Raritan River, N.J.	250
1958	P't. Wash'gt'n Narr.	Bremerton, Wash	250
1966	Lake Francis Case	Platte, S.D.	250
1973	Swinomish Slough	Mt. Vernon, Wash	246
1972	Arkansas River	Pine Bluff, Ark.	243
1948	Baldwin	Connecticut R.	240
1968	Sharon	Sharon, Vt.	239
1962	Lake Sharpe	Pierre, S.D.	235
1959	Mulholland Dr.	Los Angeles, Cal	235
1968	11th St. (Twins)	Anacostia R, Wash. DC	234
1967	White River	Hartford, Vt	233
1968	Royalton	Royalton, Vt	225
1964	Theodore Roosevelt	Potomac R., Wash. DC	222
1961	W'r'w. Wilson Mem	Potomac River	222
1969	Snohomish R	Monroe, Wash	222
1973	Chattahoochee R.	Ft. Gaines, Ga.	220
1940	Tallulah River	Tallulah Gorge, Ga	220
1970	Chulitna River	Alaska	220
1966	Green River	165-Kentucky	210
1938	Topeka Avenue	Topeka, Kan	217

Continuous Plate

Year	Name	Location	Length
1965	New Chain of Rocks	Mississippi R., Ill. (9)	2,755
1973	Great Congress Gty	Shenectady, N.Y.	1,870
1971	Congress St.	Troy, N.Y.	1,420
1965	Rock Island	Mississippi R., Ill	1,136
1955	Four Bears	Missouri R., N.D.	475
1966	I-480	Missouri R., Iowa-Neb.	425
1972	I-80	Missouri R, Iowa-Neb.	425
1970	Green River	Hendersonville, N.C.	350
1969	Fort Smith	Arkansas River	340
1957	Snake River	Alpine Jct., Wyo.	264
1973	Lewis & Clark	Williston, N.D.	235
1971	Washburn	Missouri R., N.D.	235
1965	Grant-Marsh	Missouri R., N.D.	235
1964	Galveston Bay	Galveston Co., Texas	215

I-Beam Girder

Year	Name	Location	Length
1941	US-31E	Rolling Fork R., Ky	340
1948	US-27	Licking River, Ky	316
1947	US-31E	Green River, Ky.	316
1941	US-62	Rolling Fork, Ky	240
1942	Licking River	Owingsville, Ky.	240
1954	Fuller Warren	Jacksonville, Fla	224
1957	Freeway	Arkansas River	210

Steel Arch

Year	Name	Location	Length
1931	Bayonne, N.J.	Kill Van Kull	1,652
1972	Fremont	Portland, Ore	1,255

1964	Port Mann	British Columbia	1,200
1959	Glen Canyon	Colorado River	1,028
1967	Trois-Rivieres	St. Lawrence R., P.Q.	1,100
1962	Lewiston-Queenston	Niagara River, Ont	1,000
1917	*Hell Gate	East R., N.Y.C.	977
1941	Rainbow	Niagara Falls	950
1970	Lake Quinsigamond	Worcester, Mass	849
1966	Charles Braga	Somerset, Mass	840
1967	Lincoln Trail	Ohio R., Ind.-Ky	825
1961	Sherman Minton	Louisville, Ky	800
1966	Lincoln Trail	Cannelton, Ind	806
1936	Henry Hudson	Harlem River	800
1936	French King	Conn. R. (Rt 2, Mass.)	782
1931	West End	Pittsburgh	778
1972	Piscataqua R	I-95, N.H.-Me.	756
1963	Cold Spring Canyon	Santa Barbara, Calif.	700
1964	John Kennedy	Ohio River, Ind.-Ky	700
1973	I-24, Paducah, Ky	Ohio River	700
1955	Pa.-N.J. Turnpike	Delaware River	682
1964	Burro Creek	(Wikieup) Ariz.	680
1954	Newark-Bayonne	Newark Bay, N.J.	670
1924	*Michigan Central	Niagara Falls	640
1955	Missouri River	Jefferson City, Mo	640
1929	Navajo	Colorado River, Ariz .	616
1961	Duluth Harbor	Lake Superior	600
1961	St. Louis Bay	Superior, Wis	600
1938	Middletown	Connecticut	600
1936	Yaquina Bay	Oregon	600
1954	Gt. So. Bay	West Islip, N.Y.	600
1963	Fire Isl. Inlet	Fire Isl., N.Y.	600
1916	Colorado River	Ariz.-Calif	592
1917	Cuyahoga River	Cleveland, Ohio	591
1929	Palmyra Boro	Delaware R., N.J.	550
1949	Chesapeake City	Ches. & Del. Can	540
1941	St. Georges	Ches. & Del. Can	540
1940	Centennial	Miss. R., Ill.-Iowa	539
1967	Gerald Desmond	Long Bea. H'b'r, Cal.	527
1874	Eads, St. Louis	Mississippi R.	520
1951	Hastings, Minn.	Mississippi R.	514
1888	Washington, N.Y.C.	Harlem River	509
1962	Alex'der Hamilton	Harlem R., N.Y.	505
1848	High Bridge, N.Y.C.	Harlem River	496
1956	Wabash Memorial	Wabash River, Ind	441
1959	Mississippi R.	Newport, Minn	420
1971	Hurricane Gulch	Alaska	407

Concrete Arch

1934	New River	Ripplemead, Va. (9)	1,321
1932	Clark Memorial	Wabash River (9)	1,033
1971	Selah Creek (twin)	Selah, Wash	549
1968	Cowlitz River	Mossyrock, Wash	520
1931	Westinghouse	Pittsburgh	425
1923	Cappelen	Minneapolis	400
1930	Jack's Run	Pittsburgh	400
1973	Elwha River	Port Angeles, Wash..	380
1931	Bixby Creek	Monterey Coast, Calif	330
1953	Arroyo Seco	Pasadena, Calif	320
1929	Chisholm Pk	Rumford, Me	210
1934	Waldport	Alsea Bay, Ore	210
1927	Mendota	Ft. Snelling, Minn	304
1915	Rocky River	Cleveland, Ohio	280
1929	10th Ave.	Minneapolis	266
1918	Third Ave.	Minneapolis	211
1925	Key	Potomac R., Wash.D.C.	208
1930	Cornwall, Conn	Housatonic R.	184
1928	Reynolds, Conn	Naugatuck R.	181
1932	Arlington Memorial	Potomac R.,Wash.D.C.	180

Twin Concrete Trestle

1963	Slidell, La	L. Pontchartrain	28,547[9]

Concrete Slab Dam

1927	Conowingo Dam	Maryland	4,611
1952	John H. Kerr Dam	Roanoke River, Va	2,785

1936	Hoover Dam	Boulder City, Nev	1,324

Drawbridges

Vertical Lift

1959	*Arthur Kill	N.Y.-N.J.	558
1935	*Cape Cod Canal	Massachusetts	544
1960	*Delair, N.J.	Delaware River	542
1937	Marine Parkway	New York City	540
1931	Burlington, N.J.	Delaware R.	534
1912	*A-S-B Fratt	Kansas City	428
1945	*Harry S. Truman	Kansas City	427
1932	*M-K-T R.R.	Missouri R.	414
1969	Wilm'gt'n Mem.	Wilmington, N.C.	408
1930	Duluth	Minnesota	386
1941	St. Johns River	Jack'ville, Fla	386
1941	Doremus	Passaic River, N.J.	366
1922	*Cincinnati	Ohio River	365
1967	Benj. Harrison Mem	James River, Va	363
1961	Corpus Christi, Tex	Port Aransas- R.R.-Highway Corpus Christi	344
1933	Troy-Menands	Hudson River	341
1962	Sand Island Aess	Oahu, Hawaii	340
1929	Carlton	Bath-Woolwich, Me..	328
1930	*Martinez	California	328
1960	West Bay	Panama City, Fla	327
1929	*Penn-Lehigh	Newark Bay	322
1920	*Chattanooga	Tennessee R.	310
1936	Triboro, N.Y.C.	East River	310
1936	Hardin	Illinois River	309
1960	Sacramento River	Rio Vista, Calif	306
1957	Claiborne Ave.	New Orleans	305
1927	Cochrane	Mobile, Ala	300
1928	James River	Newport News	300
1929	San Mateo	California	300
1926	*Missouri Pacific	Kragen, Ark.	300
1956	Sidney Lanier	Brunswick, Ga	295
1960	Interstate	Columbia River, Ore.-Wash.	279
1928	Jordan	Norfolk, Va	277
1959	Houghton-Hancock	Michigan	268
1955	Hackensack, N.J.	Hackensack River	222
1949	Newark, N.J.	Passaic River	222

Bascule

1926	*At,&SFRR(Iowa-III)	Mississippi R	525
1969	Pearl River	Slidell, La	482
1916	Keokuk Municipal	Mississippi R., Iowa	377
1940	Lorain, Ohio	Black River	295
1969	Elizabeth River	Chesapeake, Va	281
1957	Craig Memorial	IR-280, Toledo, Ohio	271
1952	Downtown	Norfolk, Va	230

Swing Bridges

1950	Douglass Memorial	Anac'tia R.,Wash.D.C.	386
1945	Lord Delaware	Mattaponi River, Va	252
1957	Eltham	Pamunkey River, Va	237
1939	Chickahominy River	Route 5, Va	222
1930	Nansemond River	Route 125, Va	200

Swing Span

1927	*Fort Madison	Mississippi R.	525
1908	*Willamette R	Portland, Ore	521
1903	*East Omaha	Missouri R.	519
1952	Yorktown	York River, Va.	500
1897	*Duluth, Minn	St. Louis Bay	486
1899	*C.M. & N.R.R.	Chicago	474
1895	Sioux City, Ia	Missouri R.	470
1914	*Coos Bay	Oregon	458

Floating Pontoon

1963	Evergreen Pt	Seattle, Wash	7,518
1940	Lacey V. Murrow	Seattle	6,561
1961	Hood Canal	Pt. Gamble, Wash	6,471

(1) The Transbay Bridge has 2 spans of 2,310 ft. each. (2) A second bridge in parallel will be completed in 1972. (3) The Richmond Bridge has twin spans 1,070 ft. each. (4) Railroad and vehicular bridge. (5) Two spans each 760 ft. (6) Two spans each 707 ft. (7) Two spans each 660 ft. (8) Two spans each 825 ft. (9) Total length of bridge. (10) Dumbarton has 7 spans each 225 ft. long.

Construction Details of Large and Unusual Bridges

Verrazano-Narrows Bridge, between Staten Island and Brooklyn, N. Y., has a suspension span of 4,260 ft., longest in the world and exceeding the Golden Gate Bridge, San Francisco, by 60 ft. One level in use November, 1964, second opened June 28, 1969. The name is a compromise; it spans the Narrows and commemorates a visit to New York harbor in April, 1524, deduced from certain general notes left by Giovanni da Verrazano, Italian navigator sailing for Francis I of France.

Allegheny River Bridge (Interstate 80) near Emlenton, Pa., 270 ft. above the water, tallest in eastern U. S., a continuous truss, 668 ft. long, 1968.

Angostura, suspension type, span 2,336 feet, 1967, at Ciudad Bolivar, Venezuela. Total length 5,507.

Charles Braga Bridge over Taunton River between Fall River and Somerset, Mass. It is 5,780 feet long.

Bendorf Bridge on the Rhine River, 5 mi. n. of Coblentz, completed 1965, is a 3-span cement girder bridge, 3,378 ft. overall length, 101 ft. wide, with the main span 682 ft.

Burro Creek Bridge with 4 spans over Burro Creek on highway 93 near Kingman, Arz. Main span steel truss 680 ft. Others plate girder, 110 and 2 of 85 ft. 1966.

Champlain Bridge at Montreal crossing the St. Lawrence River was opened 1962. It is 4 mi. long. Three other connect Montreal with the South Bank, the Jacques Cartier, Victoria and Mercier bridges.

Corpus Christi, Texas, has a high level port entrance bridge. It is a cantilever truss with anchor spans 310 ft. and main span 620 ft., total length approx. 5,862 ft.

Cross Bay Parkway Bridge (N. Y.) 3,000 feet long with 6 traffic lanes, 11 eight foot wide precast, prestressed concrete T girders to support spans 130 feet long each with main span 275 feet.

Delaware Memorial Bridge over Delaware River near Wilmington. A twin suspension bridge paralleling the original 250 ft. upstream has a 2,150-ft. main span suspended from 440-ft. towers.

Eads Bridge across the Mississippi R. between St. Louis and E. St. Louis, built in 1874 has 4 main spans 1,520 ft., 2,502 ft. and 1,118 ft. crossing Miss. R., a railroad and a road.

Evergreen Point Bridge in Wash., consists of 33 floating concrete pontoons weighing 4,700 tons each, held in place by 77 ton crete anchors. Pontoon structure is 6,561 ft. long, with approaches bridge is 12,596 ft. long.

Fremont Bridge part of Stadium Freeway, Portland, Ore., crossing Williamette R. 1,255 ft. steel arch span with two 452 ft. flanking steel arch spans. 1971.

Frontenac Bridge, Quebec, suspension, span 2,190 ft., open 1970.

Gladesville Bridge at Sydney, Australia, has the longest concrete arch in the world (1,000 ft. span).

George Washington Bridge, New York City, 4th longest suspension bridge in the world, spans the Hudson River between W. 178th St., Manhattan, and Ft. Lee, N. J.; 4,760 ft. between anchorages, two levels, 14 traffic lanes. **Triborough Bridge** connects Manhattan, the Bronx and Queens; project comprises a suspension bridge, a vertical lift bridge, and a fixed bridge, all connected by long viaducts. The famous **Brooklyn Bridge** over the East River, connecting Manhattan and Brooklyn, was completed in 1883, breaking all previous records by spanning 1,595 ft.

Golden Gate Bridge, crossing San Francisco Bay, has the second longest single span, 4,200 ft.

Hampton Roads Bridge-Tunnel, Va. A crossing completed in 1957 consisting of two man-made islands, two concrete trestle bridges, and one tunnel, under Hampton Roads with a length of 7,479 ft. A parallel facility is under construction with estimated completion date in 1974.

Hood Canal Floating Bridge, Wash., 23 floating concrete pontoons 4,980 tons ea. Roadway suspended on 5,000 T twin sections mounted on pontoons 30 feet above canal. Floating section is 6,471 ft. long, overall 7,866 ft.

International Bridge, a series of 8 arch and truss bridges crossing St. Mary's and the Soo Locks between Mich. and Ontario. 2-mile toll completed 1962.

Lacey V. Murrow Floating Bridge, Wash., 25 floating pontoons of 4,558 tons ea. Bridge with approaches is 8,583 ft.

Lake Pontchartrain Twin Causeway, Wash., a twin-span crete trestle bridge and 24-mile link within metropolitan New Orleans that connects the north and south shore. First span opened 1956, second 1969.

Lavaca Bay Causeway, Texas. 2.2 miles long, consisting of one 260 ft. continuous plate girder unit and 194 precast, prestressed concrete spans of 60 ft. length. 1961.

Newport Bridge between Newport and Jamestown, R. I. Total length 11,248 ft., a main suspension span of 1,600 feet, two side spans each 688 feet long. It has U.S.A.'s first prefabricated wire strands.

New York City bridges, *see Verrazano-Narrows Bridge and George Washington Bridge above.*

Ogdensburg-Prescott Internat'l Bridge across the St. Lawrence River from Ogdensburg, N. Y., to Johnston, Ont., opened 1960, is 13,510 ft. long with approaches and 7,260 ft. between abutments.

Oland Island Bridge under construction in Sweden will be completed in 1972. It will be 19,882 feet long when completed and will be Europe's longest.

Oosterscheldebrug, opened Dec. 15, 1965, is a 3.125-mile causeway for automobiles over a sea arm in Zeeland, the Netherlands. It completes a direct connection between Flushing and Rotterdam.

Poplar St. Bridge over the Mississippi at St. Louis, a 5-span continuous orthotropic deck plate girder bridge, longest span 600 ft. 8 lane 2,165 ft. long.

Quebec Road, suspension, span 2,190 feet, 1969, Quebec, Canada.

Robert Opie Norris Bridge, Rappahannock R. between Greys Pt. and White Stone, Va. 9,989 ft. long Main spans are two 144 foot cantilever truss spans with a 360 foot truss span suspended between them.

Rockville Bridge, world's longest 4-track stone arch bridge, 3,810 ft., with 48 arches. Part of the Penn-Central R.R. system west of Harrisburg, Pa. It contains 440,000,000 pds. of stone, 100,000 cubic yds. of masonry and crosses the Susquehanna River to Rockville, Pa.

Rio-Niteroi, Guanabara Bay, Brazil, under construction, will be world's longest continuous box and plate girder bridge, 8 miles, 3,363 feet long, with a center span of 984 feet and a span on each side of 656 feet.

Royal George Bridge, 1,053 ft. above the Arkansas River in Colorado, is the highest bridge above water. Opened Dec. 8, 1929, it is 1,260 ft. long with a main span of 880 ft., width 18 ft.

San Mateo-Hayward Bridge across San Francisco Bay is first major orthotropic bridge in U. S. It is 6.7 miles long, 4.9-mile low-level concrete trestle and 1.8 miles high-level steel bridge.

Sava I, Belgrade, Yugoslavia, 1956, a continuous box and plate girder bridge with a span of 856 feet.

Seven Mile Bridge is the longest of an expanse of bridges connecting the Florida Keys. It was built by the Florida East Coast Railway between 1904 and 1916, now a state highway.

Severn Bridge, with a main span of 3,240 ft., crosses the Severn River, linking England and Wales.

Shenandoah River Bridges, one spans the south fork, 1,924 ft. long, the other the north fork 1,090 ft. long, Warren County Va.

Straits of Mackinac Bridge, completed in 1957, is the longest suspension bridge betwen anchorages and with approaches extends nearly 5 mi. between Mackinaw City and St. Ignace, Mich.

Sunshine Skyway, a 15-mile-long bridge-causeway with twin roadbeds that crosses Tampa Bay at St. Petersburg, Fla., a system of twin bridges 864 feet long and 4 smaller bridges with 6 causeways.

Tagus River Bridge near Lisbon, Portugal, longest suspension bridge outside the United States, has a 3,323-ft. main span. Opened Aug. 6, 1966, it was named Salazar Bridge for the former premier.

Thatcher Ferry Bridge, opened 1962, spans Panama Canal 201 ft. above the water level near Balboa.

Thomas A. Edison Memorial Bridge (causeway) across Sandusky Bay between Martin Point and Danbury, Ohio, is 2.67 miles long. The main bridge is 2,044 feet long.

Thousand Island Bridge, St. Lawrence River. American span 800 ft.; Canadian 750 ft.

Union St. Bridge in Woodstock, Vt., a Timber Lattice Truss with a span of 122 feet built in 1969 using old time procedure of hand drilled holes and wooden pegs.

Vancouver Bridge, Canada's longest railway lift span connecting Vancouver and North Vancouver over Burrard Inlet. It is in 3 sections the longest 493 ft. Spans are part of a project that includes a 2-mile tunnel under Vancouver Hgts.

Woodrow Wilson Memorial Bridge across the Potomac R. at Alexandria, Va. is over a mile long.

Zoo Bridge across the Rhine at Cologne, with steel box girders, has a main span of 850 ft.

The **Interstate Highway 610** crossing of the Houston Ship Channel in Texas is 6,300 feet in length and consists of various lengths of prestressed concrete beam and slab approach spans and a 1,233 foot main unit of two 471' 6" plate girder units and one 290 ft. simple span.

Underwater Vehicular Tunnels in North America
Over 1,000 feet in length

Name	Location	Waterway	Lgth. Ft.
Bart Trans-Bay Tube (Rapid Transit)	San Francisco	S.F. Bay	3.6 miles
Brooklyn-Battery	New York, N.Y	East River	9,117
Holland Tunnel	New York, N.Y	Hudson River	8,557
Lincoln Tunnel	New York, N.Y	Hudson River	8,216
Baltimore Harbor Tunnel	Baltimore, Md.	Patapsco River	7,650
Hampton Roads	Norfolk, Va	Hampton Roads	7,479
Queens Midtown	New York, N.Y	East River	6,414
Thimble Shoal Channel	Cape Henry, Va	Chesapeake Bay	5,738
Sumner Tunnel	Boston, Mass	Boston Harbor	5,650
Louis-Hippolyte Lafontaine Tunnel	Montreal, Que.	St. Lawrence River	5,280
Detroit-Windsor	Detroit, Mich	Detroit River	5,135
Chesapeake Channel	Cape Charles, Va.	Chesapeake Bay	5,450
Callahan Tunnel	Boston, Mass	Boston Harbor	5,046
Midtown Tunnel	Norfolk, Va	Elizabeth River	4,194
Baytown Tunnel	Baytown, Tex.	Houston Ship Channel	4,111
Posey Tube	Oakland, Calif	Oakland Estuary	3,500
Downtown Tunnel	Norfolk, Va	Elizabeth River	3,350
Webster St	Alameda, Calif.	Oakland Estuary	3,350
Bankhead Tunnel	Mobile, Ala.	Mobile River	3,109
I-10 Twin Tunnel	Mobile, Ala.	Mobile River	3,000
Washburn Tunnel	Houston, Tex	Ship Channel	2,936

Land Vehicular Tunnels in United States (Over 1,000 feet long)

Name	Location	Lgth. Ft.	Name	Location	Lgth. Ft.
Eisenhower Memorial	Route 70, Colorado	8,941	Battery Park	New York City	2,300
Copperfield	Copperfield, Utah	6,989	Battery St.	Seattle, Wash	2,140
Allegheny (Twin)	Penna. Turnpike	6,070	Big Oak Flat	Yosemite Natl. Pk	2,083
Liberty Tubes	Pittsburgh, Pa	5,920	Prudential	Boston, Mass	1,980
Zion Natl. Park	Rte. 1, Utah	5,766	Internatl. Underpass	Los Angeles, Calif.	1,910
East River Mt. (Twin)	Interstate 77, W.Va.-Va	5,661	Street-Car	Providence, R.I.	1,793
Tuscarora (Twin)	Penna. Turnpike	5,326	Broadway	San Francisco, Calif	1,616
Kittatinny (Twin)	Penna. Turnpike	4,727	9th Street Expy	Washington, D.C.	1,610
Leigh	Penna. Turnpike	4,379	F.D. Roosevelt Dr.	42-48 Sts. NYC	1,600
Blue Mountain (Twin)	Penna. Turnpike	4,339	Lowry Hill	Minneapolis	1,496
Wawona	Yosemite Natl. Pk	4,233	Wheeling	Interstate 70, W. Va.	1,490
Squirrel Hill	Pittsburgh, Pa	4,225	Mt. Baker Ridge (3).	Seattle, Wash	1,466
Big Walker Mt	Route I-77, Va	4,200	Knowls Creek	Lane County, Ore	1,430
Fort Pitt	Pittsburgh, Pa	3,560	Mule Pass	Near Bisbee, Ariz	1,400
Mall Tunnel	Dist. of Columbia	3,400	Arch Cape	Oregon Coast Hwy. 9	1,228
Caldecott	Oakland, Calif	3,371	Queen Creek	Superior, Ariz.	1,200
Kalihi	Honolulu, Hawaii	2,780	West Rock	New Haven, Conn	1,200
Memorial	W. Va. Tpke. (I-77)	2,669	Green River	Route I-80, Wyo.	1,135
Cross-Town	178 St. N.Y.C.	2,414	Nouanu Pali	Koolau Mt. Oahu, Hawaii	1,080
F.D. Roosevelt Dr.	81-89 Sts. NYC	2,400	Elk Creek	Umpqua Hwy 45, Ore	1,080
Dewey Sq	Boston, Mass	2,400	Golden	Clear Cr'k Cany'n, Colo.	1,068

World's Longest Railway Tunnels
Source: 1969-1970 Railway Directory & Year Book. Tunnels over 4 miles in length.

Tunnel	Date	Miles	Yds	Operating Railway	Country
Simplon No. I and II	1922	12	559	Swiss Fed. & Italian St.	Switz.-Italy
Apennine	1934	11	892	Italian State	Italy
Gotthard	1882	9	562	Swiss Federal	Switzerland
Lötschberg	1913	9	140	Bern-Lötschberg-Simplon	Switzerland
Hokuriku	1962	8	1,089	Japanese National	Japan
Mont Cenis (Fréjus)	1871	8	855	Italian State	France-Italy
Cascade	1929	7	1,397	Great Northern	United States
Flathead Tunnel, Mont.	1970	6	1,758	Great Northern	United States
Arlberg	1884	6	650	Austrian Federal	Austria
Moffat	1928	6	373	Denver & Rio Grande	United States
Shimizu	1931	6	50	Japanese National	Japan
Kvineshei	1943	5	1,112	Norwegian State	Norway
Rimutaka	1955	5	821	New Zealand Gov.	New Zealand
Ricken	1910	5	608	Swiss Federal	Switzerland
Grenchenberg	1915	5	581	Swiss Federal	Switzerland
Otira	1923	5	564	New Zealand Gov.	New Zealand
Tauern	1909	5	551	Austrian Federal	Austria
Haegebostad	1943	5	467	Norwegian State	Norway
Ronco	1889	5	277	Italian State	Italy
Hauenstein (Lower)	1916	5	95	Swiss Federal	Switzerland
Connaught	1916	5	39	Canadian Pacific	Canada
Karawanken	1906	4	1,683	Austrian Federal	Austria-Yugo.
New Tanna	1964	4	1,663	Japanese National	Japan
Somport	1928	4	1,572	French National	France-Spain
Tanna	1934	4	1,493	Japanese National	Japan
Ulrikken	1964	4	1,338	Norwegian State	Norway
Hoosac	1875	4	1,230	Boston & Maine	United States
Monte Orso	1927	4	1,230	Italian State	Italy
Lupacino	1958	4	1,178	Italian State	Italy
Vivola	1927	4	1,004	Italian State	Italy
Monte Adone	1934	4	760	Italian State	Italy
Jungfrau	1912	4	750	Jungfrau	Switzerland
Borgallo	1884	4	700	Italian State	Italy
Severn	1886	4	628	Western Region	Great Britain
Lusse (Vosges)	1937	4	474	French National	France
Marianopoli	1885	4	42	Italian State	Italy
Turchino	1894	4	10	Italian State	Italy

Dams and Reservoirs; Water Conservation

Source: Bureau of Reclamation

The Bureau of Reclamation, an agency of the Department of the Interior, administers a multiple-purpose water resources program that develops projects for municipal, industrial and irrigation water supply, hydroelectric power generation, flood control, water quality improvement, fish and wildlife enhancement, outdoor recreation, and maintenance of a satisfactory natural environment. To these ends it builds dams, reservoirs, hydropower plants, canals, and tunnels in the 17 contiguous western states, and conducts a many-faceted water resources research program to develop new sources of water supply and also water and land conservation techniques.

Alaska Power Administration, located in Juneau, Alaska, is the agency of the Department of the Interior given charge of promoting development and use of the water, power and related resources of Alaska. The hydro power resources of Alaska are practically untouched. Of the 32 million kilowatts of hydroelectric power potential, the 30,000-kilowatt Eklutna Project is the only major operating project. When completed in 1972, the Snettisham Project will add 70,000 kilowatts of capacity to the APA system.

Colorado River Storage Project. Construction began in 1973 on the Crystal Dam and Powerplant on the Gunnison River in Colorado. A principal feature of the Curecanti Unit of the 5-state Colorado River Storage Project, authorized in 1956, the concrete, thin-arch Crystal Dam near Montrose, Colorado, will be 620 feet long at the crest and 340 feet high. It will be the thinnest dam of its type in the world. This dam and powerplant will be the third in a series of structures comprising the Curecanti Unit on the Gunnison River, the other two dams being Morrow Point and Blue Mesa. Morrow Point Dam, completed in 1968, was the first Bureau of Reclamation dam designed as a double-curvature, thin-arch structure and is also the first structure of the Bureau to locate the powerplant underground. Blue Mesa Dam and Powerplant have been in operation since 1966. Three other storage units of CRSP are fully in operation: **Glen Canyon Dam,** reservoir and power plant on the Colorado R. in Utah and Ariz. **Flaming Gorge Dam,** reservoir and power plant on the Green in Utah and Wyo.; and **Navajo Dam** and reservoir on the San Juan in N.M. and Colo.

High up on the eastern slope of the Rocky Mountains in N.M. construction has been completed on **Heron Dam,** a feature of the San Juan-Chama participating project. Water from the tributary streams of the Colorado R. west of the Rocky Mountains is brought under the Continental Divide by the Azotea Tunnel to be impounded by Heron Dam, then released to flow down the Rio Chama and Rio Grande for municipal and industrial use and for irrigation of farmlands.

Four other participating projects are under construction in the CRSP and 8 others are in operation.

Colorado River Basin Project. The first construction contract was awarded in 1973 on the $1.3 billion Central Arizona Project, which will mainly provide Colorado River water for municipal and industrial use in the vicinity of the urban areas of Phoenix and Tucson. Water will be pumped from the Colorado at Lake Havasu and transported some 300 miles, through a series of pumping plants, aqueducts, tunnels and canals for use in the Phoenix-Tucson areas. The Colorado River Basin Project, authorized by Congress in 1969, also provides for construction of **Hooker Dam** and Reservoir on the Gila R. in Western N. M. and construction of 7 participating projects of the Colorado R. Storage Project in Colo., N. M., and Utah.

Central Valley Project, California. Construction work is underway on the Bureau of Reclamation's $311,000,000 **Auburn Dam,** chief feature of the Auburn-Folsom South Unit of the Central Valley Project. On the North Fork of the American R., this structure will be Reclamation's longest and highest double curvature concrete dam, spanning 3,500 ft. at its crest 680 ft. above bedrock. Its reservoir, with 2,300,000 acre-feet storage capacity, will provide a full irrigation water supply for 29,340 acres and a supplemental supply for 300,000 acres, and will also supply municipal and industrial water for communities in the area, as well as to furnish recreational and fish and wildlife benefits. A power plant having an initial capacity of 300,000 kilowatts will be constructed at the toe of the dam. Construction has begun on another unit feature, the 69-mile-long Folsom South canal starting at the American River downstream from the dam which will deliver water to farmlands and communities.

Construction continues on the gigantic Westlands Irrigation Distribution system, a feature of the San Luis Unit of CVP. Ultimately this system will contain more than 1,000 miles of pipe. Wintertime runoff from northern Calif. streams is conveyed to the San Luis Unit, where it is stored in the reservoir behind **San Luis Dam,** the most massive earth-filled dam ever constructed by Reclamation. From there the water is channeled into the 102-mile long river-size San Luis Canal, which starts it on its way to beneficial use in the southern two-thirds of the state.

This unit, a unique joint Federal-State development, not only serves the Federal irrigation project, but stores and transports Calif. State Water Project water. **Orville Dam,** chief feature of the State project, is the highest earth-fill dam in the world. The 770-foot-high structure straddles the Feather R. about 60 miles north of Sacramento.

Third Powerplant at Grand Coulee Dam. A $57.8 million contract was awarded in 1973 for manufacture and installation of three giant turbines and generators at the Bureau's Third Powerplant at Grand Coulee Dam on the Columbia River. These 700,000 kilowatt generators and huge turbines, possibly the largest ever constructed, are the second group of three to be installed at the Third Powerplant. Work is progressing on manufacture of the first set of three 600,000 kilowatt generators and companion turbines for which contracts were let previously. When all six units are installed, the present 2,280,000 kilowatt capacity of the powerplant will be increased to 5,880,000 kilowatts. Work is also progressing on the Forebay Dam and on the powerplant which will house the big turbines and generators.

Fryingpan-Arkansas Project. Sugar Loaf and Ruedi Dams, major earth-fill impoundment structures were completed in 1969. The former, east of the Continental Divide, will result in the enlargement of Turquoise Lake from 17,000 to 130,000 acre-feet. **Ruedi Dam** on the western slope will create a 101,000 acre-foot impoundment on the Fryingpan R., compensating water users in western Colorado for the supply diverted at higher elevations through the Divide by the Charles H. Boustead Tunnel into Turquoise Lake for use in the Arkansas basin. The 5.4 mile-long tunnel under the Continental Divide is complete and construction work has commenced on **Pueblo Dam** and reservoir on the eastern slope. Pueblo Reservoir will impound 357,000 acre feet of water.

The multiple-purpose **Fryingpan-Arkansas Project** will provide water for supplemental irrigation of 280,000 acres and for domestic and industrial uses, initially will generate 111,000 kilowatts of hydroelectric power, and will provide flood control, fish and wildlife, and recreation benefits.

The **Palmetto Bend Project,** located in the central Gulf Coast area of Texas in Jackson County, was put under construction in 1972. **Palmetto Bend Dam and Reservoir No. 1** will store 182,000 acre-feet of water and provide 25 billion gallons of water annually for municipal and industrial use.

Construction was initiated in 1972 on the $25 million **Mountain Park Project,** located in southwestern Oklahoma. The project will provide 16,100 acre-feet of water annually for municipal and industrial use. Principal features of the project will be the **Mountain Park Dam and Reservoir** for storing 116,000 acre-feet of water, a 10.8 mile long diversion canal and 30 miles of pipeline for conveyance of stored water to the municipalities involved.

Pick-Sloan Missouri Basin Program. Construction is underway on the Snake Creek pumping plant, and the

McClusky canal, key features of the Garrison Diversion Unit, which will provide irrigation for 250,000 acres of land in N.D., will supply municipal and industrial water to 14 towns and cities, and will provide recreation and fish and wildlife enhancement benefits. The Snake Creek plant will pump water from the reservoir behind the Corps of Engineers **Garrison Dam** on the Missouri into an adjacent lake from where it will be conveyed to the farms and communities.

Yellowtail Dam on the Bighorn River in southern Mont. was dedicated in 1968. The 525-foot high dam, its 71-mile long reservoir, and its 250,000-kilowatt power plant comprise the Yellowtail unit of the P-SMBP.

Southern Nevada Water Project. A 4-mile tunnel has been bored through the River Mountains, which lie between the Las Vegas Valley and Lake Mead behind **Hoover Dam** on the Colorado R. Several pumping plants to lift water from Lake Mead to the tunnel, which will convey it to the valley to meet the municipal and industrial needs of the area have been completed and project put in operation. The first stage of the project delivers 132,000 acre-feet of Colorado R. water annually, and there is provision for enlarging the system as needs grow in the future. The project was turned over to the state of Nevada for operation in December, 1971.

Work got underway in 1972 on the **Teton Dam and Power and Pumping Plant,** located on the Teton River in southeastern Idaho. The first phase of this development, estimated to cost $65 million, will provide a supplemental water supply to 112,210 acres and a power supply of 20,000 kilowatts in 1976. The project will also provide recreation and downstream flood control benefits.

Southeastern Power Administration (Dept. of the Interior) with headquarters at Elberton, Ga., markets power produced at projects controlled by the Corps of Engineers in Va., W. Va., N. C., S. C., Ga., Fla., Ky., Ala., Miss., and Tenn. Power is sold to 188 customers from plants in operation at Allatoona, Ga.; Buford, Ga.; Clark Hill, Ga.-S. C.; Hartwell, Ga.-S. C.; Jim Woodruff, Ga.-Fla; Walter F. George, Ga.-Ala.; John H. Kerr, Va.-N. C.; Philpott, Va.; Wolf Creek, Ky.; Barkley, Ky.-Tenn.; Dale Hollow, Tenn.-Ky.; Center Hill, Tenn.; Old Hickory, Tenn.; Cheatham, Tenn.; Millers Ferry, Ala.; and J. Percy Priest, Tenn.; with a capacity of 1,910,000 kilowatts.

The following are under construction with capacity in kilowatts:

Carters, Georgia	500,000
Laurel, Kentucky	61,000
Cordell Hull, Tennessee	99,999
West Point, Georgia-Alabama	73,375

Jones Bluff, Alabama	68,000
Spewrell Bluff, Georgia	150,000

During the year ended June 30, 1973, Southeastern Power Administration sold 7.9 billion kilowatt-hours, gross revenue of $40,100,000.

Southwestern Power Administration, with hq. in Tulsa, Okla., is the agency of the Dept. of the Interior designated to market surplus hydroelectric power and energy generated at Federal multiple purpose reservoirs in a 6 state area of the southwest. Of 23 hydro-electric plants 19 are in commercial operation, and 4 are under construction.

SPA operates 1,633 miles of high-voltage transmission line and 32 substations and switching stations, including a 161,000 volt interconnection with the Bureau of Reclamation. This inter-tie, the first between federally owned systems, permits interchange of up to 60,000 kw between the two agencies by taking advantage of the daily and seasonal diversities between the two areas served.

Tennessee Valley Authority

TVA is a corporate agency of the Federal government, established by Congress in 1933 to develop the Tennessee River system and to aid in the development of other resources of the Tennessee Valley region. This includes resource development work in flood control, navigation, electric power, recreation, agriculture, forestry, and water quality.

TVA has built or acquired 27 major dams on the Tennessee and its tributary rivers, and by agreement with Alcoa controls water releases at 6 of its major dams. These structures make the main stream of the Tennessee navigable over its 650-mile length from Knoxville to the Ohio River, regulate flood waters, and generate hydroelectric power.

TVA is wholesale power supplier to 160 local electric systems serving 2 million customers in parts of 7 states, and sells power directly to several large atomic, military, and industrial installations. Fiscal year 1973 power sales were 103 billion kwh, about 70 times as much electricity as the region used in 1933. Since about 1950, when the region's hydroelectric potential was largely developed, most of the additional generating capacity built to meet this rapid growth in power demands has been in coalfired steam plants. In 1973 system capacity was 22,000,000 kw, with another 11,000,000 kw in nuclear, coal-fired and pumped storage plants scheduled for operation by the end of 1978.

The TVA Power System is financially self-supporting and self-liquidating.

California State Water Project
Source: California Resources Agency, Department of Water Resources.

California's State Water Project is the largest single water conservation and conveyance system ever built as a single unit, according to the California Department of Water Resources which conceived, designed, built and now is operating the system.

The Project is multi-purpose and provides for flood control, recreation and smog-free hydroelectric power generation as well as water conservation and distribution.

The Project stretches about 680 miles from the Upper Feather River in northern California to a terminal reservoir near Perris in the southern part of the State.

Oroville Dam, the highest in the United States and the key facility of the system, is located on the Feather River. Natural river channels convey the water to the San Joaquin-Sacramento rivers' Delta area. From that point State Water Project water travels uphill through the 444-mile-long California Aqueduct for distribution to homes, farms and factories in northern, central and

southern California.

The water at the Delta is 31 feet above sea level. At the highest point—the Pearblossom Pumping Plant in the Antelope Valley in southern California—the water has been lifted to 3,565 feet above sea level.

Water deliveries began in the San Francisco Bay area in 1962, in the south San Joaquin Valley in 1968 and to the Los Angeles area in southern California—through Castaic Lake—and the San Bernardino area—from the East Branch of the aqueduct—in 1972. Filling of the terminal reservoir started in 1973 permitting water distribution in Riverside County. Deliveries into San Diego County are scheduled for 1974.

At the Tehachapi Mountains, which the Aqueduct crosses enroute to southern California, the A. D. Edmonston Pumping Plant lifts more water higher than any other pumping plant in the world—120,000,000 gallons per hour one-third of a mile up.

Niagara Power Project

With a capability of 2,400,000 kw, the Niagara Power Project of the Power Authority of the State of New York is the largest in the Western World. That huge capacity is reached with the Robert Moses Niagara Power Plant, whose 13 generators have a nameplate rating of 1,950,000 kw., and the 12 generating units of the Lewiston Pump

Generating Plant, nominal rating 240,000 kw. The units have exceeded their nominal capacities to produce additional electricity. First power was delivered as scheduled on Feb. 10, 1961, and the final generating unit was placed on the line Nov. 11, 1962. The project was certified as completed Nov. 30, 1963.

Water for the operation is obtained from the Niagara River, 2½ miles above Niagara Falls. Two huge conduits convey water under the city of Niagara Falls to the plants 4 miles below the Falls. Under the 1950 treaty with Canada more water may be drawn at night and during winter than during daylight hours of the summer tourist season. Power is sold to municipalities, rural electric cooperatives, industries and private utilities.

Niagara Power Project was financed by $737,000,000 worth of bonds sold to private investors and no government credit or tax money is used.

The Power Authority also financed, built and is operating the United States half of the St. Lawrence Power Project, at Massena, N.Y., which has a total (United States and Canada) installed capacity of 1,824,000 kw. The Authority also constructed a 1,000,000 kw pumped storage plant 40 miles southwest of Albany and is completing a nuclear plant near Oswego that will generate more than 800,000 kw.

Major World Dams

Source: Bureau of Reclamation. Dept. of the Interior. Revised May 1973. * Replaces existing dam.

Volume in cubic yards. **Capacity** (Gross) in acre feet. **Year** of completion. **U.C.** under construction.
Type A—Arch. **B**—Buttress. **E**—Earthfill. **G**—Gravity. **R**—Rockfill. **MA**—Multi-arch.

Name of Dam	Type	Year	River and Basin	Country	Height Feet	Crest Length Feet	Volume (1,000 C.Y.)	Res. Cap. (1,000 A.F.)
Akosombo-Main	R	1965	Volta	Ghana	463	2,100	10,400	120,000
Almendra	A	UC	Tormes-Douro	Spain	649	13,438	3,267	2,025
Alpe Gera	G	1965	Comor-Adda-Po	Italy	584	1,710	2,265	53
Amir Kabir*	A	1962	Karadj-Caspian Sea	Iran	591	1,280	821	166
Auburn	MA	UC	N. F. American-Sacramento	U.S.A.	695	4,000	6,000	2,300
Balimela	E	UC	Sileru	India	230	15,200	29,600	3,100
Beas	E	UC	Beas-Indus	India	436	6,401	42,261	6,600
W.A.C. Bennett*	E	1967	Peace-Mackenzie	Canada	600	6,700	57,203	57,006
Bhakra	G	1963	Sutlent-Indus	India	742	1,700	5,400	8,000
Bhumiphol (Yanhee)	GA	1964	Ping-Chao Phraya	Thailand	505	1,594	1,307	9,891
Bratsk	GF	1964	Angara	USSR	410	17,105	1,530	137,314
Bukhtarma	A	1960	Irtish	USSR	295	1,247	1,530	42,970
Cabora Basa	A	UC	Zambezi	Portugal	550	994	589	129,389
Canelles	A	1960	Noguera Ribagorzana-Ebro	Spain	492	689	436	549
Castaic	E	1971	Castaic Cr.-Santa Clara	U.S.A.	340	5,200	44,000	350
Charvak	E	1970	Chirchik-Sir Darya	USSR	551	2,499	24,975	1,620
Chirkey	G	UC	Sulak-Caspian Sea	USSR	764	1,109	1,602	2,252
Cochiti	E	UC	Rio Grande	U.S.A.	251	28,200	41,100	602
Contra	A	1965	Verzasca-Ticino-Po	Switz.	754	1,246	863	70
Curnera	A	1967	Rein de Curnera-Rhine	Switz.	499	1,115	735	32.4
Dneprodzerzhinsk	GE	1964	Dneiper	USSR	115	119,038	35,857	1,985
Don Pedro*	ER	1970	Tuolume-San Joaquin	U.S.A.	585	1,900	16,760	2,030
Dworshak	G	UC	N. F. Clearwater Columbia	U.S.A.	717	3,287	6,500	3,453
Elephant Butte	G	1916	Rio Grande	U.S.A.	301	1,674	630	2,201
Emosson	A	UC	Barberine	Switz.	590	1,736	1,400	182
Esmeralda	E		Bota	Colombia	754	919	14,126	661
Flaming Gorge	GA	1964	Green-Colorado	U.S.A.	502	1,285	987	3,789
Fort Peck	E	1940	Missouri	U.S.A.	250	21,026	125,600	19,400
Fort Randall	E	1956	Missouri	U.S.A.	165	10,700	50,200	6,100
Gardiner*	E	1968	South Saskatchewan	Canada	223	16,700	85,739	8,000
Garrison	E	1956	Missouri	U.S.A.	210	11,300	66,500	24,500
Gatum	E	1912	Chagres	Panama	115	7,700	22,958	4,413
Gepatsch	A	1964	Faggenbach-Inn	Austria	500	2,070	9,250	114
Glen Canyon	A	1964	Colorado	U.S.A.	710	1,560	4,901	27,000
Gokcekaya	A	UC	Sakarya	Turkey	518	1,529	850	737
Gorky	EG	1955	Volga-Caspian S.	USSR	105	42,340	57,969	7,055
Goschernalp	E	1960	Goschenerreuss-Rhine	Switz.	508	1,771	12,230	61
Grand Coulee	G	1942	Columbia	U.S.A.	550	4,173	10,585	9,724
Grande Dixence	G	1962	Dixence-Rhone	Switz.	932	2,296	7,792	324
Gran Suarna	MA	UC	Navia	Spain	499	1,150	882	567
Guri	GER	1968	Caroni-Orinoco	Venezuela	348	2,264	4,917	14,349
High Aswan (Saad-El-Aali)	E	1971	Nile	U A R	364	12,565	55,747	133,000
Hirakud	GE	1956	Mahanadi	India	202	15,748	25,100	6,600
Hoover	A	1936	Colorado	U.S.A.	726	1,244	4,400	29,755
Hungry Horse	AG	1953	S.F. Flathead-Columbia	U.S.A.	564	2,115	3,086	3,468
Idikki	MA	UC	Periyar	India	561	1,201	609	1,182
Ihla Solteria	EG	UC	Parana Rio de la Plata	Brazil	291	20,300	35,741	17,172
Inguri	A	UC	Inguri	USSR	892	2,513	4,967	891
Irkutsk	GE	1956	Angara	USSR	144	8,080	10,220	37,200
Iroquois	G	1958	St. Lawrence	Canada	76	9,765		24,288
Ivankovo	E G	1937	Volga-Caspian S.	USSR	98	31,398	20,207	908
Jari	E	1967	Jari	Pakistan	234	5,700	42,400	400
Jaya Kwadi	E	UC	Godavari	India	120	32,493	15,409	2,110
Daniel Johnson*	MA	1968	Manicougan-St. Lawrence	Canada	703	4,311	2,950	115,000
Kakhovka	EG	1955	Dnieper	USSR	121	5,380	46,617	14,755
Kanev	E	UC	Dnieper	USSR	82	52,950	49,520	2,125
Kapchagay	E	1970	Ili	USSR	164	1,542	5,078	22,813
Kariba	G	1959	Zambesi	Rhodesia-Zambia	420	2,025	1,350	130,000
Keban	RG	UC	Firat (Euphrates)	Turkey	679	3,598	19,600	25,110
Kiev	E	1964	Dnieper	USSR	72	177,448	57,552	3,021
King Paul (Kremasta)	ER	1965	Acheloos	Greece	541	1,510	10,686	3,850
Krasnoyarsk	G	UC	Yenisei	USSR	407	3,493	5,685	59,425
Kremenchug	EG	1961	Dnieper	USSR	98	35,727	36,282	10,945
Kurobegawa No. 4	A	1964	Kurobe	Japan	610	1,603	1,782	162
Las Portas	A	UC	Camba	Spain	498	1,587	977	609
Luzzone	A	1963	Brenno di Luzzone-Ticino	Switz.	682	1,738	1,776	70
Mangla	E	1967	Jhelum	Pakistan	380	11,000	85,872	5,150
Marimbondo	E	UC	Grande	Brazil	295	11,970	24,328	5,184
Mauvoisin	A	1958	Drance de Bagnes-Rhone	Switz.	777	1,706	2,655	146
Mica	R	UC	Columbia	Canada	794	2,600	42,000	20,000
Mohamed Re Chah Pahlavi	A	1963	Dez-Karun	Iran	66	696	608	2,717
Mingechaur	E	1953	Kura	USSR	262	5,085	20,400	12,970
Monteynard	A	1962	Drac-Isere-Rhone	France	509	705	595	195
Montejaque	C	1924	Graduares	Spain	241	285	35,400	32.4
Mossyrock	MA	1968	Cowlitz-Columbia	U.S.A.	605	1,750	1,240	1,300
Mratinje	A	UC	Piva-Drina-Danube	Yugo	722	853	1,019	749

Name	Code	Year	River	Country	Ht	Lgth	Vol	
Nagwado	A	UC	Azua-Shinano	Japan ...	508	1,200	865	100
New Bullards Bar	A	1968	North Yuba-Sacramento	U.S.A. ...	635	2,200	2,700	930
New Melones	R	UC	Stanislaus-San Joaquin	U.S.A. ...	625	1,600	15,970	2,400
Nurek	E	1972	Vakhsh	USSR ...	1,040	2,390	75,864	8,424
Oahe	E	1963	Missouri	U.S.A. ...	245	9,300	92,000	23,600
Okutadami	G	1961	Tadami	Japan ...	515	1,575	2,145	487
Oroville	E	1968	Feather-Sacramento	U.S.A. ...	770	6,920	78,008	3,538
Owen Falls	G	1954	Lake Victoria - Nile	Uganda. ...	100	2,725		166,000
Place Moulin	AG	1965	Buthier-Dora Baltea	Italy ...	502	2,181	1,962	81
Reza Shah Kabir	A	UC	Karoun	Iran. ...	656	1,247	1,570	2,351
Roselend	AB	1961	Doronde Beaufort-Rhone	France ..	492	2,644	1,236	152
Ross	A	1949	Skagit	U.S.A. ...	540	1,300	909	1,405
Rybinsk	GE	1941	Volga-Caspian S.	USSR ...	98	2,060	3,329	20,590
Sakuma	G	1956	Tenryu	Japan ...	510	963	1,465	265
Sanmen Hsia	G	1962	Hwang Ho-Yellow	China ...	351	2,752		52,700
San Luis	E	1967	San Luis - San Joaquin	U.S.A. ...	382	18,600	77,670	2,110
Santa Giustina	A	1950	Noce-Adige	Italy ...	500	407	146	148
Saratov	E	UC	Volga-Caspian S.	USSR ...	131	4,130	34,531	10,458
Sayansk	A	UC	Yenisei	USSR ...	774	3,503	11,916	25,353
Shasta	G	1945	Sacramento	U.S.A. ...	602	3,460	8,711	4,500
Speccheri	A	1957	Leno Di Vallarsa - Adige	Italy ...	514	631	153	8
Swift	E	1958	Lewis-Columbia	U.S.A. ...	512	2,100	15,431	756
Tachien	A	UC	Tachia	Taiwan ...	656	853	940	235
Talbingo	R	1971	Tumut	Australia ..	530	2,300	18,500	747
Tankiangkow	G	1962	Tan & Han	China ...	427			41,833
Tarbela	ER	UC	Indus	Pakistan ..	470	9,000	186,000	11,100
Tignes	A	1952	Isere-Rhone	France ..	592	1,411	830	126
Toktogul	A	UC	Naryn-Syr Darya	USSR ...	705	1,352	3,438	15,800
Trinity	E	1962	Trinity-Klamath	U.S.A. ...	537	2,600	29,251	2,500
Tsimlyansk	EG	1952	Don	USSR ...	128	43,411	44,323	17,715
Tuttle Creek	ER	1962	Big Blue-Missouri	U.S.A. ...	157	7,500	21,000	2,367
Twin Buttes	E	1963	Concho-Colorado Texas	U.S.A. ...	134	42,460	21,442	641
Ust-Ilim	GE	UC	Angara	USSR ...	344	11,695	11,382	48,100
Vajont	MA	1961	Vaiont-Piave	Italy ...	858	624	460	137
Verkhne-Svirskaya	EG	1952	Svir	USSR ...	105	1,775	1,988	14,190
Vidraru	A	1965	Arges-Danube	Rumania ..	544	1,000	653	377
Volga-22nd Congress U.S.S.	ERG	1958	Volga-Caspian S.	USSR ...	144	13,038	33,020	27,160
Volga - V. I. Lenin	EG	1955	Volga-Caspian S.	USSR ...	148	12,405	44,298	47,020
Yellowtail	A	1966	Bighorn-Missouri	U.S.A. ...	525	1,480	1,456	1,375
Zervreila	A	1957	Valserrhein-Rhine	Switz. ...	495	1,653	819	81
Zeuzier	A	1957	Lienne-Rhone	Switz. ...	512	918	392	41
Zeya	G	UC	Zeya	USSR ...	371	2,312	10,456	55,080

Major Public and Private Dams and Reservoirs in U.S.

Source: Bureau of Reclamation, Dept. of the Interior; Corps of Engineers, U.S. Army and Tennessee Valley Authority

HEIGHT OVER 250 FEET, VOLUME OVER 1,000,000 CUBIC YARDS

Where reservoir name is different it is shown in italics

Height—Difference in elevation in feet, between lowest point in foundation and top of dam, exclusive of parapet or other projections.
Length—Overall length of barrier in feet; main dam and its integral features as located between natural abutments.
Volume—Total volume in cubic yards of all material in main dam and its appurtenant works.
Year—Date structure was originally completed for use. (1) Under construction subject to revision.
River—Mainstream.
Purpose: Irr or I—Irrigation; FC—Flood Control; P—Power Production; N—Navigation; WS—Water Supply; RR—River Regulation; DC—Debris Control.
Parentheses after name indicate type of dam as follows: (C)—Concrete; (E)—Earth; (G)—Gravity; (M)—Masonry; (R)—Rock Fill.
*Replacing existing dam.

Name of dam	State	River	Ht.	Lgth.	Vol. (1,000)	Purpose	Yr.
Oroville (E.)	Calif	Feather	770	6,920	80,300	Irr-WS-P-FC	1968
Hoover (C) *Mead*	Ariz.-Nev	Colorado	726	1,244	4,400	FC-I-P-RR-N-WS	1936
Dworshak (G)	Idaho	N. Fork Clearwater	717	3,287	6,500	FC-P-N	(1)
Glen Canyon (C) *Powell*	Ariz	Colorado	710	1,560	4,901	P-RR	1964
Auburn (C)	Calif	N. F. American	680	3,500	6,000	I-WS-FC-P	(1)
New Bullards Bar (C)	Calif	North Yuba	635	2,200	2,700	FC-WS-P	1968
Melones (R)	Calif	Stanislaus	625	1,600	15,970	I-P	(1)
Mossy Rock (C)	Wash	Cowlitz	605	1,750	1,240	P	1968
Shasta (C)	Calif	Sacramento	602	3,460	8,711	FC-I-P-RR-N	1945
Don Pedro (E.R.)	Calif	Tuolumne	585	1,900	16,760	I-FC-P-WS	1970
Hungry Horse (C)	Mont	South Fork Flathead	564	2,115	3,086	Irr-P-FC-N	1953
Grand Coulee (C) *F. D. Roosevelt*	Wash	Columbia	550	4,173	10,585	I-P-RR-FC-N	1942
Ross	Wash	Skagit	540	1,300	909	FC-P	1949
Trinity (E)	Calif	Trinity	537	2,600	29,251	I-P	1962
Yellowtail (C)	Mont	Bighorn	525	1,480	1,460	I-P-FC	1966
Swift (E)	Wash	Lewis	512	2,100	15,431	P	1958
Flaming Gorge	Utah	Green	502	1,285	987	....	1964
Fontana (C)	N.C	Little Tennessee	480	2,365	3,576	FC-P-RR	1944
New Exchequer (R)	Calif	Merced	490	1,240	5,300	I-P-FC	1966
Morrow Point	Colo	Gunnison	468	741	365	WS-D	1968
Anderson Ranch (E)	Idaho	South Fork, Boise	456	1,350	9,653	FC-Irr-P	1950
Detroit (C)	Oreg	North Santiam	454	1,528	1,357	FC-N-P-Irr-WS-RR	1953
Carters (R, E)	Georgia	Coosawattee	454	2,053	14,272	FC-P-RR	(1)
Cougar Reservoir (E)	Oreg	So. Fork McKenzie	445	1,730	12,572	FC-P-N-I-WS	1964
Libby (G)	Mont	Kootenia	445	2,955	3,800	FC-P	(1)
Pine Flat (C)	Calif	Kings	430	1,840	2,200	FC-Irr-RR-P	1954
Mud Mt. (Stevens) (E)	Wash	White	425	700	2,300	FC	1948
Union Valley (E)	Calif	Silver Creek	428	1,950	10,000	P	1963
Mammoth Pool (E, R)	Calif	San Joaquin	411	820	5,151	P	1960
Lower Hell Hole (R)	Calif	Rubicon	410	1,550	8,315	P-I-WS	1966
Navajo (E)	N. Mex	San Juan	402	3,648	26,841	I-FC	1963
Summersville (R)	W. Va	Gauley	398	2,280	11,494	FC	1966
Brownlee (R)	Idaho	Snake	395	1,700	6,700	P-FC	1959
Blue Mesa (E)	Colo	Gunnison	390	785	3,080	Irr-P-FC	1966

Name of Dam	State	River	Ht.	Lgth.	Vol.	Purpose	Yr.
Jocassee (ER)	S. Carolina	Kaowee	390	1,787	9,962	WS	(1)
San Luis (E)	Calif	San Luis Cr	382	18,600	77,670	I-P	1967
Folsom (C)	Calif	American	375	10,200	9,010	FC-Irr-P	1955
Green Peter (G)	Oreg	Mid. Santiam	365	1,380	942	I-P-FC-N	1967
Boundary (C)	Wash	Pend Oreille	360	740	150	P	1967
Grasshopper Hollow (E)	W. Va	Potomac (branch)	350	1,610	2,500	DC	(1)
Neversink (E)	N. Y	Neversink	275	2,820	10,500	WS-P-FC-RR	1952
Lucky Peak (E)	Idaho	Boise	316	1,700	6,300	FC-Irr	1955
Castaic (E)	Calif	Castaic Cr	340	5,200	44,000	WS-I-P	(1)
Hills Creek Dam (E, G, R)	Oreg	Mid. Fk. Willamette	338	2,170	11,789	FC-P-WS-N-Irr	1962
Casitas (E)	Calif	Coyote Creek	334	2,000	9,310	I-WS	1959
Hell's Canyon (G)	Ore	Snake	330	910	640	P	1968
Cherry Valley (E) *L. Lloyd*	Calif	Cherry Creek	330	2,600	7,000	I-WS-P-FC	1955
Salt Springs (R)	Calif	No. Fk., Mokelumne	328	1,300	3,000	P	1931
Abiquiu (E)	N. M.	Rio Chama	325	1,540	11,701	FC	1962
Yale (E)	Wash	Lewis	323	1,550	4,201	P	1953
Beardsley (E)	Calif	Stanislaus	320	960	3,250	IP	1957
Friant (C&G) *Millerton*	Calif	San Joaquin	319	3,488	2,135	Irr-FC	1942
Blue River (GER)	Oregon	Blue	319	1,420	5,180	FC-IN	(1)
Watauga (ER)	Tenn	Watauga	318	900	3,578	FC-P-RR	1948
San Gabriel #1 E (E, R)	Calif	San Gabriel	377	1,500	11,823	FC	1939
Courtright (R)	Calif	Helms Creek	310	850	1,450	P	1958
Sultan No. 1 (G)	Wash	Sultan	310				1952
Green Mountain (E)	Colo	Blue	309	1,150	4,360	Irr-P	1943
Kensico (G)	N. Y	Bronx	307	1,843	2,975	WS	1915
Hiwassee (C)	N. C	Hiwassee	307	1,376	801	FC-P-RR	1940
Lewis Smith (R)	Ala	Black Warrior	305	2,200	5,140	P	1961
Downsville (E)	N. Y	East branch, Delaware	254	2,450	9,900	FC-RR-WS-P	1955
Upper Baker (G)	Wash	Baker	308	1,200	628	P	1959
Elephant Butte	N.M.	Rio Grande	301	1,674	630	IH	1916
Gorge (C)	Wash	Skagit	300	656	280	P	1960
The Dalles (C & E)	Oreg-Wash	Columbia	300	8,875	5,061	N-P-I-R	1957
Granby (E)	Colo	Colorado	297	2,108	1,450	WS	1905
New Croton (G) *Croton*	N. Y	Croton	297	2,168	1,450	WS	1905
Winsor (E) *Quabbin*	Mass	Swift	295	2,640	4,000	PWS	1940
Blue River (E)	Oreg	Blue	319	1,420	5,180	I-FC-N	(1)
Wishon (R)	Calif	N. F., Kings	290	1,109	179	P	1958
Sly Creek (E)	Calif	Lost Creek	289	1,490	4,345	I-P	1961
South Holston (ER)	Tenn	South Fork, Holston	285	1,600	5,995	FC-P-RR	1950
Amistad (EC)	Texas-Mex	Rio Grande	285	32,022	16,955	WS-FC	1969
Ruedi (E, R)	Colo	Fryingpan	322	1,060	3,823		1968
Lemon (E)	Colo	Florida	284	1,360	3,042	I	1963
Alamo (E)	Ariz	Bill Williams	283	975	3,045	FC-WS	1968
Laurel River (R)	Ky	Laurel	282	1,420	3,200	P	(1)
Whiskeytown (E)	Calif	Clear Creek	282	4,070	4,535	I-P	1963
Cogswell (R)	Calif	West Fork, San Gabriel	280	585	1,045	FC-I	1934
Diablo (G)	Wash	Skagit	389	1,180	350	I-P-FC	1929
Cachuma (E)	Calif	Santa Ynez	279	3,350	6,695	Irr-FC-WS	1953
Marshall Ford (C & E) *Travis*	Texas	Colorado (Texas)	278	5,093	2,714	P-FC-RR-N-I	1942
Santa Felicia (E) *Piru*	Calif	Piru Creek	275	1,260	3,900	I-FC	1955
Dix River (RR)	Ky	Dix	275	1,032	1,747	P	1924
Palisades (E)	Idaho	South Fork, Snake	270	2,100	13,571	Irr-P-FC	1957
El Capitan (ER)	Calif	San Diego	270	1,200	2,680	WS	1934
Nacimiento (E)	Calif	Nacimiento	270	1,470	3,412	I-FC	1957
Briones (E)	Calif	Bear Creek	268	2,100	14,200	WS-I	1964
DeValle (E)	Calif	Arroyo Valle	268	880	4,200	WS-I	1968
Northfield (E)	Colo	W. Monument	267	4,600	3,883	WS	(1)
Ball Mountain Res. (E, R)	Vt	West	275	1,150	2,319	FC-WS	1961
Heron (E, R)	N. Mexico	Willow Cr	265	1,250	3,227	FC-WS-I	1969
Alcova (E)	Wyo	North Platte	265	763	1,635	Irr-P	1938
Norris (C)	Tenn	Clinch	265	1,860	1,184	FC-P-RR	1936
Mathews (E)	Calif	Cajalco Creek	264	2,584	3,600	WS	1938
Quabbin Dike (E)	Mass	Swift	264	2,140	2,500	WS	1937
Wyman (GE)	Me.	Upper Kennebec	263	2,650	2,610	P	1930
Table Rock (G)	Mo	White	261	6,423	4,550	FC-P	1959
Leroy Anderson(ER)	Calif	Coyote Ck.	260	1,385	3,320	FC	1950
Muddy Run (E)	Pa	Offstream	265	4,800	5,600	P	1967
Lookout Point (E, R, G)	Oregon	Middle Fork, Willamette	258	3,381	8,593	Irr-P-N-FC-WS-RR	1955
Bull Shoals (G)	Ark	White	258	2,256	2,036	FC-P	1951
Wolf Creek (E, G)	Ky	Cumberland	258	5,736	11,569	FC-P	1952
Gathright (R)	Va	Jackson	257	1,172	2,330	FC-RR-WS	(1)
John W. Flannagan (R)	Va	Pound	250	916	2,386	FC	1960
Ashokan (Olive Bridge) (G)	N. Y	Esopus Creek	252	4,650	2,472	WS-P	1912
Cochiti (E)	N. Mexico	Rio Grande	251	28,200	41,100	FC-WS	(1)
Fort Peck (E)	Mont	Missouri	250	21,026	125,600	FC-P-N-Irr	1940
Tygart River (G)	W. Va	Tygart	250	1,921	1,380	FC-RR-N	1938
Terminus (E)	Calif	Kaweah	255	2,375	6,450	FC-Irr	1962

World's Largest Dams

Source: Bureau of Reclamation, Dept. of the Interior

Based on total volume of structure. All dams listed are predominantly earthfill or rockfill and may contain concrete sections UC—Under Construction

Name of Dam	Cubic Yards	Completed	Name of Dam	Cubic Yards	Completed
Tarbela, Pakistan	186,000,000	U.C.	W. A. C. Bennett, Canada[2]	57,203,000	1968
Fort Peck, U.S.A.	125,612,000	1940	High Aswan (Saad-El-Aili), Egypt	55,747,000	1970
Oahe, U.S.A.	92,008,000	1963	Fort Randall, U.S.A.	50,205,000	1956
Mangla, Pakistan	85,872,000	1967	Kanev, U.S.S.R.	49,520,000	U.C.
Gardiner, Canada[1]	85,743,000	1968	Kakhovka, U.S.S.R.	46,617,000	1955
Oroville, U.S.A.	78,008,000	1968	Tsimlyanska, U.S.S.R.	44,323,000	1952
San Luis, U.S.A.	77,666,000	1967	Volga, V. I. Lenin, U.S.S.R.	44,298,000	1955
Nurek, U.S.S.R.	75,864,000	U.C.	Castaic, U.S.A.	44,000,000	1971
Nagarjuna Sagar, India	73,575,000	U.C.	Jari, Pakistan	42,400,000	1967
Garrison, U.S.A.	66,506,000	1956	Beas, India,	42,261,000	U.C.
Cochiti, U.S.A.	61,005,000	U.C.	Mica, Canada	42,001,000	U.C.
Gorky, U.S.S.R.	57,967,000	1955	Kremenchug, U.S.S.R.	41,192,000	1961
Kiev, U.S.S.R.	57,552,000	1964			

[1]Formerly South Saskatchewan [2]Formerly Portage Mt.

The Hispanic American Today

In April, 1973, the Bureau of the Census published a detailed statistical study describing the social and economic condition of persons of Spanish origin in the U.S. as of March, 1972. Among many other details, the following information is probably of most interest.

Age distribution: The average age of Hispanic Americans in 1972 was 20 years compared with 28 years for the U.S. population as a whole. Among persons of Mexican and Puerto Rican origin, children under 14 made up about 40% of their communities. Among Cubans and persons of Spanish origin other than Mexican or Puerto Rican, children under 14 were only about 30% of their communities. Only 25% of the total U.S. population is under 14 years of age.

Spanish speaking; About 65% of people of Spanish origin speak Spanish at home. Spanish use among Puerto Ricans is particularly high, with 72.5% speaking Spanish at home. Among those of Mexican descent, 65% use Spanish, while only 61% of other persons of Spanish origin use the language at home.

Use of Spanish at home has some relation to educational attainment. The following table shows that where Spanish is used at home, success in school declines, suggesting the necessity of bilingual education at the elementary and secondary levels.

Years of School Completed

(numbers in thousands)	Total, age 14 and over	5 to 8	High School 1 to 3	4	College 1 to 3	4	Median (approx.)
Total Spanish origin	5,765	1,724	1,372	1,260	386	210	9.8
Spanish in home	3,822	1,328	820	644	178	107	8.7
Mexican origin	3,171	930	774	647	177	53	9.3
Spanish in home	2,090	716	438	297	70	23	8.1
Puerto Rican origin	901	322	242	146	41	20	9.1
Spanish in home	671	261	183	92	18	5	8.7
Other Spanish origin	1,693	332	357	467	168	137	11.4
Spanish in home	1,061	351	199	256	90	79	10.5

Education: Young Hispanic Americans have more education than their elders. Of those between ages 25 and 30, 47.6% have completed high school, compared with only 23.2% of those between ages 45 and 65. In this respect, Hispanic Americans' education shows the same trend as U.S. education as a whole.

However, Americans of Mexican and Puerto Rican origins tend to have less education than the population as a whole. While 52.3% of the U.S. population over 25 has completed high school, only 25.8% of Mexican-Americans and only 23.7% of Puerto Ricans have done so. These education figures show significant differences between Hispanic Americans. Forty years ago Mexican-Americans were the least educated of all Hispanic groups; today, 42.9% of Mexican-Americans between ages 25 and 30 have completed high school as compared to 30.9% for Puerto Ricans.

This fact is particularly interesting because it runs contrary to a characteristic of the U.S. population as a whole. In general, persons living in urban areas are better educated than their rural cousins. But about 25% of Mexican Americans live in rural areas compared to only about 2.5% of Puerto Ricans.

Incomes and Occupations: Perhaps the most interesting figures are those which compare incomes and occupations of Hispanic Americans.

Income Levels by Sex and Spanish Origin, 1971

Income	Male U.S.	Mexican	P.R.	Other	Female U.S.	Mexican	P.R.	Other
Under $1,000	9.9%	10.1%	7.3%	8.9%	25.0%	32.0%	13.6%	21.1%
$1,000 to $1,999	7.6	10.4	4.7	6.4	19.2	22.2	20.4	18.7
2,000 to 2,999	7.2	10.0	9.4	5.8	12.3	15.4	20.4	11.0
3,000 to 3,999	6.7	9.7	5.9	7.2	10.3	13.1	19.2	16.5
4,000 to 4,999	6.4	9.2	14.4	9.3	4.9	6.5	15.6	10.4
5,000 to 6,999	12.8	16.2	27.3	17.3	12.6	7.6	7.6	13.9
7,000 to 7,999	7.3	8.4	12.9	11.9	3.9	1.7	1.6	2.4
8,000 to 9,999	12.5	11.0	6.2	14.4	4.4	1.0	1.2	3.9
10,000 to 14,999	19.0	13.2	8.5	13.9	3.0	0.5	–	2.0
15,000 to 24,999	8.1	1.6	2.9	4.3	0.6	–	–	–
25,000 and over	2.5	0.3	0.3	0.9	0.1	–	–	–
Median	$6,903	$5,073	$5,613	$6,492	$2,408	$1,810	$2,784	$2,931

— Represents zero or rounds to zero

Occupation Groups of Hispanic Americans, March 1972

(Numbers in thousands)

Employment status and occupation	Male Mexican origin	Puerto Rican origin	Other Spanish origin	Female Mexican origin	Puerto Rican origin	Other Spanish origin
Persons, 14 years old and over	1,567	432	752	1,604	469	941
Percent in labor force	76.1	67.4	76.3	34.4	23.7	45.1
Percent unemployed	7.9	8.8	5.4	9.4	17.8	8.9
Employed	1,097	265	543	500	91	386
Professional, technical, and kindred workers	4.7%	2.6%	12.9%	5.4%	7.7%	8.5%
Managers and administrators, except farm	5.6	6.8	8.3	3.6	–	3.6
Sales workers	2.7	2.3	4.1	4.6	3.3	4.9
Clerical and kindred workers	4.5	9.8	10.1	26.6	14.3	28.5
Craftsmen and kindred workers	20.9	15.1	19.3	0.6	1.1	1.3
Operatives, including transport	27.0	36.6	22.5	21.6	61.5	32.9
Laborers, excluding farm	14.7	7.2	7.7	1.2	2.2	1.0
Farmers and farm managers	0.5	–	0.6	–	–	–
Farm laborers and foremen	7.8	1.9	2.0	2.8	–	0.3
Service workers, except private household	11.8	18.5	12.5	25.4	8.8	15.0
Private household workers	–	–	–	8.0	1.1	3.9

— Represents zero or rounds to zero

American Indians, by Tribe, for the U.S. and Selected States

Source: U.S. Bureau of Census

Tribe	1970	Historic	Alas.	Ariz.	Calif.	Ill.	Mich.	Minn.	Mont.	New Mex.
Total, all Indians	763,594		16,080	94,310	88,263	10,304	16,012	22,322	26,385	71,582
Apache	22,993	6,000	4,245	10,515	2,089	155	42	6	41	2,963
Blackfeet	9,921	15,000	5	47	910	82	76	32	5,415	58
Cherokee	66,150	22,000	113	519	9,491	922	858	182	82	456
Cheyenne	6,872	3,500	–	41	473	16	–	15	2,383	56
Chickasaw	5,616	8,000	5	72	625	27	7	–	–	30
Chippewa	41,946	35,000	58	121	1,621	994	4,191	15,502	2,680	43
Choctaw and Houma	23,562	20,000	7	145	2,747	228	61	19	13	175
Comanche	4,250	7,000	–	40	506	28	–	15	–	40
Creek	17,004	22,500	5	184	1,630	188	71	–	35	19
Iroquois: Mohawk	6,105		8	8	301	60	505	29	38	29
Oneida	5,673	16,000	5	5	192	375	247	48	–	31
Seneca	4,644		7	15	218	16	11	–	5	6
Onondaga, etc.	5,051		–	15	306	27	209	39	6	20
Kaw, Omaha, Osage, etc.	6,849		–	83	581	14	13	54	5	66
Kiowa	4,337	2,000	–	168	224	19	–	–	–	120
Lumbee	27,520	16,000	11	–	78	22	92	–	4	–
Menominee	4,307	3,000	–	6	64	296	37	52	–	–
Navajo	96,743	8,000	70	44,306	4,770	318	58	23	23	37,450
Papago and Pima	16,600	10,000	–	14,964	1,357	18	–	–	–	52
Potawatomi	4,626	4,000	–	39	335	114	965	–	5	12
Hopi	7,236	3,000	–	5,823	582	31	–	–	–	294
Keresan	10,087	5,000	–	429	515	29	–	5	39	8,636
Tanoan	6,342	7,500	6	207	342	13	5	–	–	5,293
Zuni	7,306	2,500	3	179	899	36	51	–	5	5,425
Seminole	5,055	2,000	19	–	340	41	14	6	16	75
Shoshone, Piaute, Chemehuevi	14,248	14,500	9	555	4,085	23	37	11	40	52
Sioux (Dakota)	47,825	25,000	144	294	3,455	358	296	1,731	2,786	154
Ute	3,815	5,000	–	65	252	–	–	7	4	53
Yakima	3,856		10	32	106	–	–	–	7	16
Yuman	7,635		4	2,746	4,432	20	–	5	–	31
All other tribes	92,962		2,193	855	19,965	843	3,317	494	10,204	464
Tribe not reported	161,543		2,131	10,090	23,506	4,853	4,702	4,004	2,534	9,453

Tribe	N.Y.	N.C.	N.D.	Okla.	Ore.	S.D.	Tex.	Utah	Wash.	Wisc.
Total, all Indians	25,560	44,195	13,565	96,803	13,210	31,043	16,921	10,551	30,824	18,776
Apache	203	33	9	746	120	4	278	54	209	64
Blackfeet	506	37	7	89	306	50	151	13	994	65
Cherokee	1,613	6,075	50	27,197	848	50	2,663	81	868	266
Cheyenne	–	20	–	2,914	11	134	135	32	214	5
Chickasaw	21	–	5	3,772	26	11	595	–	52	8
Chippewa	267	186	6,721	65	598	498	133	26	1,372	4,940
Choctaw and Houma	53	30	–	12,859	144	12	1,868	51	100	48
Comanche	23	15	–	2,743	7	–	378	16	28	–
Creek	81	32	18	10,960	68	–	863	47	68	20
Iroquois: Mohawk	3,873	22	5	56	5	–	11	9	16	6
Oneida	557	42	35	10	15	–	10	5	18	3,587
Seneca	3,340	43	–	464	43	–	37	–	26	–
Onondaga, etc.	3,543	5	5	169	21	8	62	–	57	37
Kaw, Omaha, Osage, etc.	26	5	33	3,153	58	52	125	–	41	8
Kiowa	5	–	–	3,051	38	–	394	13	5	5
Lumbee	18	26,059	33	25	–	–	19	–	30	–
Menominee	17	5	–	4	24	59	18	–	10	3,592
Navajo	22	69	–	306	221	14	676	4,903	172	35
Papago and Pima	10	–	–	66	27	11	23	15	20	–
Potawatomi	4	–	–	1,006	47	44	147	–	102	518
Hopi	48	4	–	39	38	–	59	84	27	–
Keresan	61	–	7	17	–	–	85	9	–	4
Tanoan	4	6	–	20	4	14	164	26	10	–
Zuni	4	–	–	65	27	–	113	74	36	5
Seminole	208	18	–	2,821	9	–	160	–	17	11
Shoshone, Piaute, Chemehuevi	48	4	11	100	440	79	29	505	237	18
Sioux (Dakota)	282	144	3,655	348	471	26,090	420	148	1,071	208
Ute	–	3	5	40	30	–	11	1,972	–	6
Yakima	–	–	5	211	330	–	25	–	3,053	4
Yuman	35	34	–	20	16	–	11	17	70	–
All other tribes	1,556	599	1,602	9,617	5,970	455	1,187	265	14,090	2,401
Tribe not reported	8,812	10,694	1,359	13,835	3,115	3,458	5,510	2,157	6,167	2,863

(1) Population estimates are made from notes of explorers and other early whites in the area. The figures have been gathered from a variety of sources which vary considerably. In general, these are minimum estimates; other sources have estimated early Indian populations at 10% to 30% greater, with the larger increases going to the smaller tribes.

Agriculture

Total Net Income Per Farm by States, 1965-72[1]

Source: U.S. Department of Agriculture, Economic Research Service

State	1965	1966	1967	1968	1969	1970	1971	1972
Alabama	$ 2,893	$ 2,878	$ 2,681	$ 3,070	$ 3,700	$ 3,663	$ 3,716	$ 4,523
Alaska	1,346	1,803	382	2,609	1,397	2,222	2,635	2,594
Arizona	23,954	19,020	23,417	30,073	31,350	27,516	31,614	32,672
Arkansas	4,029	5,775	5,146	5,539	5,681	7,061	6,432	8,725
California	11,999	13,917	13,769	17,295	16,758	15,445	16,492	21,104
Colorado	5,723	5,377	4,190	5,709	6,326	7,793	8,177	8,998
Connecticut	6,952	8,605	6,543	8,455	9,194	9,962	8,723	7,438
Delaware	8,040	7,670	9,573	8,990	15,953	9,940	10,953	14,373
Florida	10,275	10,432	11,482	13,119	14,729	13,061	17,299	21,064
Georgia	4,499	5,186	5,214	4,810	6,331	5,981	6,450	7,020
Hawaii	16,348	18,399	17,953	19,321	17,356	17,232	19,084	19,348
Idaho	6,642	5,129	6,422	5,579	8,824	8,972	8,352	10,033
Illinois	6,404	6,822	6,875	5,431	6,451	5,403	6,971	10,344
Indiana	5,063	4,635	4,355	4,125	5,800	3,946	5,924	5,968
Iowa	7,537	8,102	6,682	7,029	8,717	8,781	7,216	11,626
Kansas	4,996	5,550	4,819	4,798	6,056	7,744	8,741	11,052
Kentucky	2,740	2,857	2,915	2,972	3,563	3,265	3,446	4,243
Louisiana	3,107	4,160	5,471	5,750	4,973	6,057	6,828	8,817
Maine	8,387	7,998	3,952	5,031	7,882	7,857	7,062	8,399
Maryland	4,516	4,202	5,130	5,032	7,455	6,694	4,835	6,620
Massachusetts	5,163	6,487	4,580	5,789	6,893	5,958	5,500	4,621
Michigan	2,674	3,509	2,937	2,873	3,294	3,331	2,636	4,202
Minnesota	4,277	4,962	4,598	4,615	5,225	6,923	5,811	6,886
Mississippi	3,375	3,691	4,267	4,448	4,589	4,903	5,142	8,402
Missouri	3,833	3,295	3,272	3,872	3,698	4,141	4,245	5,798
Montana	6,258	7,834	6,162	6,106	8,453	10,714	8,430	13,438
Nebraska	6,408	8,084	7,047	6,190	9,144	7,892	8,083	11,456
Nevada	2,896	5,843	3,772	4,117	11,474	12,173	13,421	18,099
New Hampshire	2,117	2,917	1,561	2,201	2,866	3,037	3,512	5,370
New Jersey	7,512	7,896	7,265	6,724	7,116	4,910	3,762	2,460
New Mexico	6,536	8,367	7,860	8,961	10,190	11,928	10,859	11,137
New York	4,398	5,688	5,242	5,320	6,284	5,667	5,238	3,916
North Carolina	2,967	3,762	3,840	3,516	4,480	4,518	4,332	5,387
North Dakota	6,492	6,017	5,362	4,610	7,102	5,039	8,272	8,450
Ohio	2,944	4,180	2,948	3,465	3,389	3,905	3,221	4,786
Oklahoma	3,210	3,171	3,145	2,515	3,359	4,207	3,378	4,466
Oregon	3,173	3,817	3,840	3,020	4,739	4,123	3,955	5,625
Pennsylvania	3,173	3,166	4,229	3,603	4,537	4,468	3,597	2,602
Rhode Island	3,190	4,062	1,246	2,349	4,753	4,864	3,669	2,030
South Carolina	2,682	3,117	3,392	2,735	3,365	3,403	3,621	4,556
South Dakota	5,879	7,297	6,612	7,363	7,879	7,138	7,996	11,044
Tennessee	1,967	2,062	1,861	1,803	2,091	2,139	2,129	2,580
Texas	4,573	5,206	4,246	5,117	5,308	6,513	5,165	6,645
Utah	2,388	2,571	3,443	3,375	4,099	4,570	4,643	5,748
Vermont	3,666	5,278	4,158	5,324	6,301	7,399	7,866	8,465
Virginia	2,406	2,036	2,592	2,203	2,614	2,465	2,162	2,945
Washington	4,719	6,813	6,828	6,466	8,238	5,842	6,048	9,898
West Virginia	749	544	928	599	841	515	395	709
Wisconsin	4,011	4,990	4,260	4,875	4,789	6,350	5,414	5,279
Wyoming	4,306	5,749	6,719	4,751	5,937	10,975	7,487	12,601
Total U.S.	4,465	4,990	4,707	4,828	5,620	5,725	5,817	7,089

(1.)Includes changes in inventories and represents income of farm operators.

Farm Income—Cash Receipts from Marketings (in $1,000)

1972 State	Crops	Live-stock	Gov't. Pay.	Total	1972 State	Crops	Live-stock	Gov't. Pay.	Total
Ala.	303,369	616,394	68,091	987,854	Neb.	765,031	1,915,112	233,324	2,913,467
Alaska	1,729	2,841	197	4,767	Nev.	16,207	94,313	2,619	113,139
Ariz.	342,253	479,986	49,013	871,252	N.H.	15,203	42,829	461	58,493
Ark.	730,139	673,596	81,624	1,485,359	N.J.	135,840	90,194	3,676	229,710
Calif.	3,268,272	2,205,784	122,443	5,596,499	N.M.	105,704	471,737	42,503	619,944
Colo.	303,291	1,396,479	70,906	1,770,676	N.Y.	270,757	830,801	19,939	1,121,497
Conn.	62,600	101,255	509	164,364	N.C.	1,016,828	642,372	57,529	1,716,729
Dela.	51,447	103,186	1,975	156,608	N.D.	534,455	365,261	208,122	1,107,838
Florida	1,198,524	464,033	18,183	1,680,740	Ohio	781,205	875,527	89,578	1,746,310
Georgia	634,392	786,774	81,064	1,502,230	Okla.	297,951	1,081,723	119,400	1,499,074
Hawaii	177,190	46,238	11,108	234,544	Ore.	355,433	288,767	24,558	668,758
Idaho	410,289	397,734	51,067	859,090	Pa.	249,047	840,966	22,892	1,112,905
Illinois	1,933,153	1,463,589	243,879	3,640,621	R.I.	8,204	8,946	57	17,207
Ind.	860,394	967,171	133,101	1,960,666	S.C.	345,150	214,337	49,285	608,772
Iowa	1,436,140	3,260,692	318,511	5,015,343	S.D.	238,269	969,470	111,519	1,319,258
Kansas	921,044	1,899,276	246,409	3,066,729	Tenn.	335,287	514,789	57,753	907,829
Ken.	492,067	593,327	36,837	1,122,231	Texas	1,368,752	2,564,846	528,567	4,462,165
La.	506,944	323,639	50,953	881,536	Utah	44,545	201,636	13,861	260,042
Maine	89,425	155,248	1,295	245,968	Ver.	18,349	160,981	828	180,158
Md.	134,834	278,085	9,572	422,491	Va.	273,833	385,752	19,563	679,148
Mass.	70,067	83,768	478	154,313	Wash.	692,160	332,331	56,411	1,080,902
Mich.	466,083	564,735	61,203	1,102,021	W.V.	26,928	90,209	3,324	120,461
Minn.	799,371	1,563,993	179,974	2,543,338	Wis.	251,644	1,598,147	57,106	1,906,897
Miss.	535,054	549,527	125,875	1,210,456	Wyo.	51,535	293,786	20,595	365,916
Mo.	701,799	1,237,845	150,203	2,089,847	Total U.S.	[1]25,075,158	35,595,544	3,961,109	[1]64,631,811
Mont.	266,536	495,517	103,169	865,222					

[1]Preliminary United States totals for crops and all cash receipts include an additional $180,427 not distributed to States.

Average Prices Received by U.S. Farmers
Source: Economic Research Service; Department of Agriculture

The figures represent dollars per 100 lbs. for hogs, beef cattle, veal calves, sheep, lamb and milk (wholesale); dollars per head for milk cows; cents per lb. for milk fat (in cream), chickens, broilers, turkeys and wool; cents for eggs per dozen. * Revised.

Year[1]	Hogs	Cattle (beef)	Calves (veal)	Sheep	Lambs	Cows (milk)	Milk (wholesale)	Milk fat (in cream)	Chickens (excl. broilers)	Broilers	Turkeys	Eggs	Wool
1930..	8.84	7.71	9.68	4.74	7.76	74.20	2.21	34.5	...	3	20.2	23.7	19.5
1940..	5.39	7.56	8.83	3.95	8.10	61.00	1.82	28.0	13.0	17.3	15.2	18.0	28.4
1950..	18.00	23.30	26.30	11.60	25.10	198.00	3.89	62.0	22.0	27.4	32.9	36.3	62.1
1960..	15.30	20.40	22.90	5.61	17.90	223.00	4.21	60.5	12.2	16.9	25.4	36.1	42.0
1965*	19.60	19.90	22.00	6.34	22.80	212.00	4.23	61.1	8.9	15.0	22.2	33.7	47.1
1967*	19.10	22.30	26.30	6.35	22.10	260.00	5.02	68.2	7.9	13.3	19.5	31.3	39.8
1968*	18.50	23.40	27.60	6.58	24.40	274.00	5.24	68.4	8.2	14.2	20.5	34.0	40.5
1969*	22.20	26.20	31.50	8.10	27.20	300.00	5.49	68.9	9.7	15.2	22.4	40.0	41.9
1970..	22.70	27.10	34.50	7.51	26.40	332.00	5.71	70.0	9.1	13.6	22.6	39.1	35.5
1971.	17.50	29.00	36.40	6.59	25.90	358.00	5.87	69.1	7.7	13.7	22.1	31.4	19.4
1972.	25.10	33.50	44.60	7.29	29.10	397.00	6.07	68.3	8.9	14.1	22.2	30.9	35.0

The figures represent cents per bushel for oats; cents per lb. for cotton, apples and peanuts; dollars per bushel for wheat, corn, barley and soybeans; dollars per 100 lbs. for rice, sorghum and potatoes; dollars per ton for cottonseed and baled hay.

Crop Year[2]	Wheat	Corn	Cotton	Oats	Barley	Rice	Soy-beans	Sor-ghum	Peanut	Cotton-seed	Hay	Potato§	Apples
1930.	.663	.550	9.46	31.1	.420	1.74	1.34	1.02	3.46	22.00	11.00	1.47	...
1940.	.674	.601	9.83	29.8	.393	1.80	.892	.873	3.33	21.70	9.78	.850	...
1950.	2.00	1.52	39.90	78.8	1.19	5.09	2.47	1.88	10.9	86.60	21.10	1.50	...
1960.	1.74	.997	30.08	59.8	.838	4.55	2.13	1.49	10.0	42.50	21.70	2.00	4.79
1965.	1.35	1.16	29.26	62.2	1.02	4.93	2.54	1.76	11.4	46.70	23.20	2.53	4.32
1967.	1.39	1.03	26.50	65.9	1.01	4.97	2.49	1.77	11.4	55.20	24.50	1.87	5.57
1968.	1.24	1.08	22.98	59.8	.921	5.00	2.43	1.69	11.9	50.50	23.60	2.23	6.11
1969*	1.25	1.16	21.86	58.4	.885	4.95	2.35	1.91	12.3	41.10	24.70	2.24	4.06
1970.	1.33	1.33	22.81	62.3	.973	5.17	2.85	2.03	12.8	56.50	26.10	2.21	4.54
1971.	1.34	1.08	28.07	60.5	.993	5.34	3.03	1.88	13.6	56.80	28.10	1.90	4.92
1972.	1.77	1.29	26.60	69.4	1.18	6.73	4.13	2.32	14.4	49.50	31.40	2.55	6.39

(1) Weighted calendar year prices for livestock and livestock products other than wool. 1943 through 1963, wool prices are weighted on marketing year basis. The marketing year has been changed (1964) from a calendar year to a Dec.-Nov. basis for hogs, chickens, broilers and eggs. (2) Weighted crop year prices. Crop years are as follows: apples, June-May; wheat, oats, barley, hay and potatoes, July-June; cotton, rice, peanuts and cottonseed, August-July; soybeans, September-August; and corn and sorghum grain, October-September. Beginning 1964, 480 lb. net weight bales.

Average Farm Wages

Cal. yr.	Per month Incl. board	Per month Excl. board	Per day Incl. board	Per day Excl. board	Cal. yr.	Per month Incl. board	Per month Excl. board	Per day Incl. board	Per day Excl. board	Cal. yr.	Per month Incl. board	Per month Excl. board	Per day Incl. board	Per day Excl. board
1910	$21.00	$28.00	$1.05	$1.35	1930.	$37.50	$48.00	$1.80	$2.15	1940.	$27.50	$37.50	$1.30	$1.60
1920...	51.00	65.00	2.80	3.30	1935...	22.00	30.50	1.10	1.35	1945...	79.00	101.00	3.85	4.35

New Series

Calendar year	Per month With house	Per month With board & room	Per week With board & room	Per week Without board or room	Per day With house	Per day With board & room	Per day Without board or room	Per hour With house	Per hour Without board or room
1950	$121.00	$99.00	$23.50	$31.00	$3.50	$4.45	$4.50	$.62	$.69
1955	154.00	123.00	29.75	38.00	4.20	5.40	5.30	.74	.82
1960	192.00	149.00	35.50	45.75	5.30	6.50	6.60	.88	.97
1965	223.00	171.00	40.25	51.50	6.20	7.40	7.60	1.03	1.14
1968	283.00	216.00	52.50	66.50	8.20	9.30	9.90	1.28	1.44
1969	307.00	234.00	56.75	73.00	9.00	10.10	10.90	1.42	1.58
1970	328.00	251.00	60.75	78.00	9.80	10.70	11.70	1.50	1.64
1971	340.00	263.00	64.50	81.00	10.30	11.20	12.20	1.56	1.73
1972	361.00	280.00	67.80	85.50	11.20	12.00	13.20	1.65	1.84

Index Numbers of Prices Received by Farmers
Source: Economic Research Service; Department of Agriculture index (1910-14 = 100 per cent)

Year	All Farm Products	All Crops	Livestock[1]	Food Grains	Feed Grains and Hay	Feed Grains	Cotton	Tobacco	Oil-bearing Crops	Fruit	Commercial Vegetables[2]	Potatoes Sweetpot[3]	Meat Animals	Dairy Products	Poultry and Eggs	Wool
1910	104	105	102	109	96	97	118	84	120	100	...	83	101	100	104	117
1920	211	235	190	249	202	209	262	233	208	188	...	294	171	202	222	214
1930	125	115	134	93	106	109	104	140	111	149	128	162	133	142	128	119
1940	100	90	109	84	85	86	83	134	103	81	122	89	108	120	98	160
1950	258	233	280	224	193	198	282	402	276	194	211	166	340	249	186	341
1960	239	222	253	203	152	151	254	500	214	244	230	203	296	259	160	235
1965	248	233	261	164	174	173	245	513	265	246	261	295	319	261	145	261
1970	280	227	326	163	177	176	183	604	266	233	294	222	405	345	151	194
1971	285	243	321	167	185	184	209	627	296	261	322	210	402	354	133	115
1972	320	261	371	192	183	176	243	685	320	280	327	233	494	366	137	202

(1.) Livestock and livestock products. (2.) For fresh market and processing beg. 1952. (3.) Including dry edible beans.

Government Payments by Programs, by States (in $1,000)

Source: Economic Research Service: Department of Agriculture

1972 State	Conservation[1]	Sugar Act	Wool Act	Feed Grain Program	Wheat Program	Cotton	Cropland Adjustment	Other[2]	Total
Alabama	5,054	.....	8	14,402	383	45,663	2,372	209	68,091
Alaska	90	.....	107	.....	.....	.....	.....	.....	197
Arizona	1,455	365	1,898	4,343	835	39,172	122	823	49,013
Arkansas	4,216	.....	22	2,252	1,128	73,540	255	211	81,624
California ...	4,653	15,270	7,912	11,802	4,862	76,765	128	1,051	122,443
Colorado	3,346	5,266	6,409	23,644	29,896	.....	887	1,458	70,906
Connecticut .	299	.....	23	114	1	.....	69	3	509
Delaware	217	.....	3	1,395	316	.....	44	.....	1,975
Florida	3,164	6,086	10	6,627	118	1,048	975	155	18,183
Georgia	6,110	.....	13	34,483	1,299	35,228	3,748	183	81,064
Hawaii	137	10,971	.....	.....	.....	.....	.....	.....	11,108
Idaho	2,023	7,415	5,714	4,798	30,757	.....	57	303	51,067
Illinois	6,125	.....	1,425	211,251	23,964	112	988	14	243,879
Indiana	4,361	.....	1,266	109,108	17,255	.....	1,101	10	133,101
Iowa	7,829	50	3,318	304,948	1,173	.....	1,166	27	318,511
Kansas	6,216	1,353	1,226	98,480	137,240	.....	1,096	798	246,409
Kentucky....	6,253	.....	363	26,213	2,213	385	1,408	2	36,837
Louisiana ...	3,756	8,624	46	2,138	262	35,832	101	194	50,953
Maine.......	1,071	.....	97	68	3	.....	44	12	1,295
Maryland ...	1,107	.....	99	6,524	1,749	.....	90	3	9,572
Massachusetts	353	.....	37	27	.....	.....	40	21	478
Michigan	3,760	3,106	1,130	34,496	16,009	.....	2,596	106	61,203
Minnesota...	5,104	3,984	2,401	147,890	17,762	.....	2,675	158	179,974
Mississippi ..	5,951	.....	21	9,207	593	108,985	571	547	125,875
Missouri.....	7,315	.....	1,172	98,121	20,800	2,532	.....	24	150,203
Montana	4,602	2,063	5,853	16,540	73,216	.....	215	680	103,169
Nebraska....	4,982	3,378	1,319	166,119	54,004	.....	2,256	1,266	233,324
Nevada.....	493	.....	1,383	71	424	245	.....	3	2,619
New Hampshire ..	405	.....	28	26	.....	.....	2	.....	461
New Jersey ..	631	.....	36	2,233	635	.....	136	5	3,676
New Mexico .	1,983	25	3,436	13,038	7,922	12,542	2,904	653	42,503
New York....	4,613	.....	524	8,998	4,911	.....	882	11	19,939
North Carolina	6,245	.....	67	30,520	4,802	14,637	1,236	22	57,929
North Dakota	5,763	2,761	2,048	53,587	141,244	.....	1,929	790	208,122
Ohio	4,711	1,476	3,384	58,597	19,731	.....	1,655	24	89,578
Oklahoma ...	6,032	.....	437	19,259	70,637	20,937	872	1,226	119,400
Oregon	2,828	995	3,271	3,399	13,880	.....	46	139	24,558
Pennsylvania	4,719	.....	753	11,691	4,721	.....	1,007	1	22,892
Rhode Island	48	.....	6	2	.....	.....	.....	1	57
South Carolina	3,043	.....	4	12,535	2,126	29,642	1,927	8	49,285
South Dakota	3,923	.....	6,638	57,714	40,720	.....	1,677	847	111,519
Tennessee ..	5,085	.....	149	18,366	1,542	31,246	1,353	12	57,753
Texas	18,943	882	25,948	153,621	54,157	265,553	6,400	3,063	528,567
Utah	1,379	1,099	6,073	1,198	3,965	.....	51	96	13,861
Vermont.....	668	.....	30	101	.....	.....	20	9	828
Virginia	4,588	.....	1,076	9,895	3,176	309	508	11	19,563
Washington .	3,050	3,950	886	5,823	41,542	.....	61	1,099	5,641
West Virginia	1,564	.....	889	662	169	.....	40	.....	3,324
Wisconsin ...	4,672	.....	689	47,704	575	.....	3,206	260	57,106
Wyoming	2,052	2,712	10,150	1,354	3,689	.....	61	577	20,595
Total U.S.....	**186,987**	**81,831**	**109,797**	**1,845,384**	**855,845**	**812,641**	**51,509**	**17,115**	**3,961,109**

(1) Includes amounts paid under other similar programs not listed separately.
(2) Includes Milk Indemnity, Great Plains Conservation.

Cooperative Farm Credit System

Loans outstanding to farmers and farmer's cooperatives from banks and associations supervised by the Farm Credit Admin.

Year ended Dec. 31	Farm mortgage loans Federal land banks	Farm production loans Production Credit ass'ns	Loans to co-operatives by banks for cooperatives	FICB loans and discounts other than interagency	Total
1950	946,469,000	455,472,000	344,979,000	70,020,000	1,816,940,000
1955	1,497,165,000	653,478,000	370,683,000	70,785,000	2,592,111,000
1960	2,563,772,000	1,490,138,000	648,859,000	91,951,000	4,794,720,000
1965	4,280,675,000	2,598,460,000	1,055,163,000	146,091,000	8,080,389,000
1969	6,714,172,000	4,533,393,000	1,731,972,000	224,425,000	13,203,962,000
1970	7,187,139,000	5,334,495,000	2,029,864,000	222,098,000	14,773,598,000
1971	7,918,185,000	6,115,524,000	2,013,491,000	238,931,000	16,286,131,000
1972	9,104,930,000	6,636,075,000	2,297,805,000	252,681,000	18,291,492,000

Farm Employment—Annual Averages

Source: Economic Research Service; Department of Agriculture

Yr.	Total Aver. No. (1,000)	Index %	Family Aver. No. (1,000)	Index %	Hired Aver. No. (1,000)	Index %	Yr.	Total Aver. No. (1,000)	Index %	Family Aver. No. (1,000)	Index %	Hired Aver. No. (1,000)	Index %
1920	13,432	99	10,041	99	3,391	100	1960	7,057	52	5,172	52	1,885	55
1930	12,497	92	9,307	92	3,190	94	1970	4,523	34	3,348	33	1,175	35
1940	10,979	81	8,300	82	2,679	79	1971	4,436	33	3,275	32	1,161	34
1950	9,926	73	7,597	75	2,329	69	1972	4,373	32	3,228	32	1,145	34

Index (1910-14 = 100 per cent)

Farm-Mortgage Debt Outstanding by Lender Groups

Source: National Economic Analysis Division, U.S. Department of Agriculture

Year (Jan. 1)	Total farm-Mortgage Debt[1]	Federal land Banks[2]	Farmers Home Administration[3]	Life Insurance Companies[4]	Commercial & Savings Banks[5]	Individuals and others[6]
	$1,000	$1,000	$1,000	$1,000	$1,000	$1,000
1961	12,812,210	2,538,425	481,610	2,974,609	1,686,139	5,131,427
1962	13,890,875	2,802,275	566,175	3,161,757	1,784,619	5,576,049
1963	15,159,843	3,023,149	585,263	3,391,183	2,053,369	6,106,879
1964	16,792,450	3,280,842	601,397	3,778,537	2,356,130	6,775,544
1965	18,880,151	3,685,501	615,463	4,284,921	2,662,479	7,631,787
1966	21,168,703	4,234,021	627,109	4,798,970	2,933,814	8,574,789
1967	23,283,052	4,908,094	581,589	5,210,915	3,164,223	9,418,231
1968	25,465,138	5,552,844	532,702	5,537,000	3,537,172	10,305,420
1969	27,117,924	6,070,619	490,264	5,761,200	3,851,297	10,944,544
1970	28,387,125	6,660,275	452,412	5,731,700	4,109,158	11,433,580
1971	29,506,876	7,128,323	343,967	5,608,300	4,440,766	11,985,520
1972	31,334,044	7,861,624	310,382	5,562,400	4,214,206	13,385,432
1973	34,500,181	9,017,183	270,864	5,686,429	4,783,681	14,742,024

(1.) Excludes Alaska, Hawaii, Territories and possessions.
(2.) Includes regular mortgages, purchase-money mortgages, and sales contracts.
(3.) Direct farm loans only. Includes farm-purchase, farm-enlargement, farm-development and loans primarily for refinancing purposes, project-liquidation, rural-housing (excludes nonfarm), and soil and water loans to individuals, and loans for these purposes from State Corporation trust funds. Farmers Home Administration also insures farm mortgage loans. They are held by miscellaneous lenders and are reported in the "Individuals and others" column, except for banks in years 1940-70.
(4.) Estimates based on direct reports from life insurance companies and official reports submitted to State insurance commissioners. Includes regular companies and sales contracts. Beginning 1965, excludes sales contracts.
(5.) All operating banks from 1961-71 includes bank holdings of soil and water loans and farm-ownership loans insured by the Farmers Home Administration. In 1971, a change in bank reporting procedures required banks to report F.H.A. insured loans they held as government securities rather than as farm loans as had been the case previously.
(6.) The amounts shown are residuals or differences between the amounts reported by institutional lenders and the estimates of total farm-mortgage debt. They may be taken as debt held by individuals and other nonreporting lenders.
(7.) Preliminary

Canadian Farm Cash Receipts[1]

Source: Statistics Canada

(in millions of dollars)

Crops

Year and quarter	Total cash receipts	Total crops	Wheat including C.W.B. payments[2]	Oats including C.W.B. payments[2]	Barley including C.W.B. payments[2]	C.W.B. net cash Advance payments	Other grains[3]	Sugar beets	Potatoes	Fruits	Vegetables	Tobacco	Other crops[4]
1971	4,529.76	1,713.13	721.18	33.70	208.88	−84.57	290.29	18.58	63.90	84.40	99.73	135.36	131.71
1972	5,307.43	2,081.89	948.20	31.85	221.41	−27.46	312.59	20.89	86.58	84.61	115.04	150.03	138.12
1972 2	1,216.84	392.53	186.99	11.03	77.46	−13.34	74.91	1.92	13.78	5.80	8.81	7.17	18.01
3	1,350.07	521.23	243.67	5.60	35.19	6.36	67.72	2.22	18.99	48.72	62.18	—	30.57
4	1,652.05	777.59	361.48	10.89	77.75	− 7.43	109.48	14.42	37.63	25.65	33.02	50.17	64.51
1973 1	1,331.45	510.56	179.10	6.99	33.63	− 4.31	124.35	3.07	40.38	5.00	11.55	84.75	26.04

Livestock and Products

Year & Quarter	Total	Cattle & Calves	Hogs	Sheep & Lambs	Dairy Products	Poultry	Eggs	Other	Total forest and maple products	Dairy supplementary payments	Deficiency payments[5]
1971	2,697.74	1,079.97	443.55	7.90	705.70	262.58	151.72	46.34	17.31	100.35	1.24
1972	3,076.66	1,106.84	676.71	9.06	778.82	295.85	163.77	57.31	24.48	101.41	23.10
1972 2	772.20	297.81	143.70	1.42	221.08	61.27	39.08	7.84	16.55	23.07	12.48
3	792.91	283.40	141.74	2.18	222.00	90.97	41.22	11.40	0.57	32.28	3.09
4	840.36	347.16	156.36	3.34	176.12	89.30	45.29	22.80	5.26	27.76	1.07
1973 1	800.55	312.12	184.58	2.50	161.78	70.56	51.74	17.29	2.38	17.91	0.6

[1]Cash receipts from farming operations excluding supplementary payments. Excludes Newfoundland. [2]Represents participation payments made by the Canadian Wheat Board direct to producers on crops delivered in previous years. [3]Includes rye, flaxseed, rapeseed, soybeans, and corn. [4]Includes clover and grass seed, hay, clover, greenhouse products, mustard seed, sunflower seed, hops, dry beans and dry peas and miscellaneous products. [5]Made under the authority of the Agricultural Stabilization Act.

Canada—Farm Cash Receipts from Farming Operations, 1968-72

Source: Statistics Canada

Province	1968	1969	1970	1971	1972
			(thousands of dollars)		
Prince Edward Island	34,476	37,870	44,198	38,868	43,897
Nova Scotia	55,026	63,380	66,507	63,604	68,319
New Brunswick	49,034	51,281	58,041	51,984	64,288
Quebec	636,814	672,495	651,976	682,548	766,441
Ontario	1,318,823	1,378,868	1,391,523	1,378,307	1,556,040
Manitoba	364,816	350,409	340,772	381,279	484,730
Saskatchewan	898,567	718,329	725,342	910,719	1,198,171
Alberta	802,090	729,598	713,925	801,594	913,836
British Columbia	204,823	197,589	210,324	225,208	245,503

Production of Chief United States Crops

Source: Economic Research Service: Department of Agriculture
1965-1969 Revised

Year	Corn, grain 1,000 bushels	Oats 1,000 bushels	Barley 1,000 bushels	Sorghums for grain 1,000 bushels	All Wheat 1,000 bushels	Rye 1,000 bushels	Flax-seed 1,000 bushels	Cotton Lint 1,000 bales	Cotton Seed 1,000 tons
1965..	4,102,867	929,554	393,055	672,698	1,315,603	33,307	35,402	14,938	6,237
1966..	4,167,608	803,324	392,108	714,992	1,304,889	27,791	23,390	9,557	3,960
1967..	4,860,372	793,800	373,745	755,344	1,507,598	23,949	20,036	7,443	3,210
1968..	4,449,542	950,689	426,151	731,277	1,556,635	22,971	26,983	10,926	4,640
1969..	4,687,057	965,863	427,055	729,919	1,442,679	30,204	34,929	9,990	4,068
1970..	4,151,938	917,159	416,139	683,571	1,351,558	36,840	29,548	10,192	4,068
1971..	5,641,112	881,227	463,601	875,752	1,617,789	49,288	18,198	10,477	4,244
1972..	5,473,727	694,967	423,461	826,604	1,544,775	29,536	13,909	13,567	5,557

Year	Tobacco 1,000 lbs.	All Hay 1,000 tons	Beans dry edible 1,000 cwt.	Peas dry field 1,000 cwt.	Peanuts 1,000 cwt.	Soy-beans 1,000 bushels	Pota-toes 1,000 cwt.	Sweet Pota-toes 1,000 cwt.	Five seed crops. 1,000 lbs.
1965..	1,854,568	125,610	16,457	3,031	2,389,596	845,608	291,109	15,469	302,592
1966..	1,884,627	120,930	19,964	2,532	2,415,731	928,481	307,242	13,669	281,254
1967..	1,967,911	125,134	15,215	2,563	2,477,255	976,439	305,766	13,486	234,511
1968..	1,710,348	124,244	17,435	2,727	2,546,591	1,106,958	295,401	13,378	219,015
1969..	1,803,272	126,026	18,913	3,736	2,535,394	1,133,120	312,418	14,370	229,455
1970..	1,906,453	126,971	17,399	3,315	2,979,465	1,127,100	325,752	13,409	254,429
1971..	1,707,612	129,119	15,917	3,930	3,005,118	1,175,989	319,354	11,718	222,554
1972..	1,748,759	128,389	18,015	2,103	3,289,045	1,276,290	294,490	12,440	169,256

Year	Sugar cane Sugar and Sugar seed* 1,000 tons	Syrup 1,000 gallons	Sugar beets 1,000 tons	Pecans 1,000 tons	Al-monds 1,000 tons	Wal-nuts 1,000 tons	Fil-berts 1,000 tons	Oranges and tan-gerines 1,000 boxes	Grape-fruit 1,000 boxes
1965......	23,663	2,923	20,918,100	125.6	72.9	80.3	7.7	139,650	46,695
1966......	24,515	2,121	20,342,200	80.8	85.1	96.0	12.2	187,810	55,676
1967......	26,651	2,346	19,197,000	116.0	76.6	76.4	7.5	128,080	44,058
1968......	24,825	2,661	25,363,300	96.2	74.5	95.6	7.6	188,090	54,170
1969......	22,615	Disc.	27,736,300	113.0	122.0	105.5	7.4	189,640	53,910
1970......	23,996	—	26,387,000	77.6	124.0	111.8	9.3	194,790	60,560
1971......	24,172	—	27,044,000	123.6	134.0	137.1	11.4	195,370	63,840
1972......	29,494	—	28,523,000	92.6	150.0	115.9	10.2	228,900	63,600

Agricultural Products, Production and Exports

Source: Foreign Agricultural Service, Dept. of Agriculture

Commodity[1]	Unit	Production U.S.	Production World	% U.S.	Exports U.S.	Exports World	% U.S.
Wheat, grain only	Mil. M.T.	44.0	322.6	13.6	15.7	50.0	31
Oats	Mil. M.T.	12.8	54.9	23.3	0.3	2.1	14
Corn	Mil. M.T.	143.3	291.0	49.3	16.7	30.1	55
Barley.....................	Mil. M.T.	10.1	130.4	7.7	1.1	15.5	7
Soybeans	Mil. M.T.	34.9	47.8	73.0	[2]11.5	[2 3]12.2	94
Rice	Mil. M.T.	3.9	299.4	1.3	[4 5]1.5	[4 5]7.5	20
Lard[5]	Mil. Lbs.	1,558.0	8,423.9	1.8	164.4	1,057.6	1.6
Tallow & Greases[5]	Mil. Lbs.	5,628.0	10,116.4	5.6	2,296.3	3,554.5	6.5
Tobacco, Unmftd	Mil. Lbs.	1,733.3	10,009.8	17.3	605.5	2,370.9	25.5
Edible Veg. Oils	Mil. M.T.	[6]6.5	[7]21.7	30.0	[8]3.1	[7 9]5.7	54
Cotton	1,000 Bales[10]	13,702.0	59,396.0	23.1	3,385.0	18,021.0	18.8

(1) Crop 1971-72 as follows: wheat, oats and barley year beginning July 1; corn, October 1; soybeans, September 1; rice and cotton, August 1; other commodities on calendar year 1972 and partially estimated. Excludes Alaska, Hawaii and Puerto Rico except for exports. (2) Calendar year. (3) Excludes estimates for Peoples Republic of China. (4) Milled rice. (5) Calendar year. (6) U.S. oil production figures include oil equivalent of exported oilseeds. (7) Excludes the palm oils. (8) Excludes re-exports and exports of oil produced from imported oilseeds. (9) Exports from producing countries. (10) Bales of 480 pounds net weight.

Canadian Harvested Acreage

Principal Crops,[1] (in thousands of acres.)
Source: Statistics Canada

Province	1970	1971	1972	Province	1970	1971	1972
Prince Edward Island ...	389	394	315	Manitoba..............	7,624	9,304	8,923
Nova Scotia	253	254	189	Saskatchewan	19,423	27,584	25,147
New Brunswick	378	373	282	Alberta................	15,729	18,406	17,302
Quebec	4,732	4,728	3,889	British Columbia	826	873	933
Ontario...............	7,538	7,618	7,798	Total[2]	56,891	69,532	85,803

[1] Crops included are winter wheat, spring wheat, oats, barley, fall rye, spring rye, flaxseed, mixed grains, corn for grain, buckwheat, peas, dry beans, soybeans, rapeseed, potatoes, mustard seed, sunflower seed, tame hay, fodder corn, field roots and sugar beets.
[2] Excluding Newfoundland.

Farms in United States by State—Number, Acreage and Value

Source: Bureau of the Census (Census of 1970)

State	Farms No.	Average Acreage	$ Value per Acre	2,000 Acres or more	10-49 Acres	Total Acreage
Alabama	72,491	188.3	$199.60	629	21,439	13,654,215
Alaska	322	4,831.9	12.73	35	32	1,604,211
Arizona	5,890	6,486.0	69.72	897	1,229	38,202,667
Arkansas	60,433	259.7	260.03	625	10,935	15,694,527
California	77,875	458.7	474.65	2,926	28,915	35,722,348
Colorado	27,950	1,312.9	94.58	4,166	3,048	36,697,132
Connecticut	4,490	120.5	921.19	6	1,245	541,372
Delaware	·3,710	182.0	499.00	14	872	673,895
Florida	35,586	394.3	354.58	1,062	12,413	14,031,998
Georgia	67,431	234.0	234.00	693	13,737	15,805,892
Hawaii	3,896	528.2	296.82	70	1,281	2,058,087
Idaho	25,475	565.9	176.55	1,218	4,382	14,416,521
Illinois	123,565	242.0	489.52	145	13,487	29,913,190
Indiana	101,479	173.0	406.00	65	19,522	17,572,865
Iowa	140,354	239.1	391.73	84	9,586	33,569,629
Kansas	86,057	573.9	158.78	3,341	5,231	49,390,369
Kentucky	125,069	127.6	253.05	114	26,761	15,968,243
Louisiana	42,269	231.5	321.33	536	13,610	9,788,662
Maine	7,971	220.7	160.79	25	948	1,759,700
Maryland	17,181	163.1	639.63	41	3,733	2,803,442
Massachusetts	5,703	122.8	564.63	7	1,622	700,578
Michigan	77,946	152.7	326.31	43	14,334	11,900,000
Minnesota	110,747	260.5	225.77	305	6,459	28,845,240
Mississippi	72,577	221.0	233.53	894	17,060	16,039,665
Missouri	137,067	236.5	224.22	396	16,823	32,420,284
Montana	24,953	2,521.0	59.57	7,596	1,485	65,800,000
Nebraska	72,257	634.3	154.38	3,509	3,113	45,833,953
Nevada	2,112	5,070.2	53.35	333	305	10,708,106
New Hampshire	2,901	211.1	288.78	0	443	612,790
New Jersey	8,493	122.0	1,092.00	13	2,471	1,036,000
New Mexico	11,641	4,019.6	41.87	2,660	1,704	46,792,302
New York	51,909	195.5	273.13	50	6,589	10,148,359
North Carolina	119,386	106.6	333.31	205	42,911	12,733,751
North Dakota	46,381	929.6	93.82	3,157	721	43,117,831
Ohio	111,332	153.6	398.51	53	19,729	17,111,459
Oklahoma	83,037	433.6	172.58	2,024	7,655	36,007,719
Oregon	29,063	619.9	150.22	1,739	9,000	18,017,850
Pennsylvania	62,824	141.6	372.88	38	10,428	8,900,767
Rhode Island	700	98.1	733.75	...	235	68,720
South Carolina	39,559	176.7	261.23	286	12,129	6,991,718
South Dakota	45,726	996.9	83.69	4,148	1,402	45,584,163
Tennessee	121,406	124.0	267.50	212	35,117	·15,056,907
Texas	213,550	668.0	148.49	9,941	27,315	142,566,826
Utah	13,045	867.2	91.90	849	3,159	11,313,000
Vermont	6,874	278.6	223.73	17	465	1,915,520
Virginia	64,572	164.9	286.13	206	15,169	10,649,862
Washington	34,033	515.9	223.83	1,693	10,817	17,559,187
West Virginia	23,142	187.5	135.69	67	3,808	4,340,554
Wisconsin	98,973	182.9	240.00	81	8,118	18,100,000
Wyoming	8,838	4,014.0	40.73	2,689	473	35,476,374
Total	**2,730,242**	**390.5**	**—**	**59,909**	**473,465**	**1,066,218,650**

Egg Production in Canada

Source: Statistics Canada

Province	1970 1,000 doz.	1971 1,000 doz.	1972 1,000 doz.	Province	1970 1,000 doz.	1971 1,000 doz.	1972 1,000 doz.
Newfoundland	9,147	8,736	7,536	Manitoba	58,239	55,540	52,068
Prince Edward Island	2,831	2,490	2,350	Saskatchewan	25,328	26,187	23,931
Nova Scotia	22,226	20,471	17,373	Alberta	43,547	42,143	41,315
New Brunswick	8,409	9,590	9,932	British Columbia	57,502	58,341	57,324
Quebec	75,945	73,547	64,490	**Total**	**490,705**	**489,663**	**467,410**
Ontario	187,471	192,618	191,091				

Gross income from farm eggs (1970) $185,701,000; (1971) $161,416,000; (1972) $173,419,000. Prices received by farmers per doz. taking the month of February (1970) 42.0¢; (1971) 29.4¢; (1972) 33.1¢; Gross income from farm chickens (1970) $177,876,000; (1971) $178,942,000; (1972) $211,851,000. Fowl produced (1970) 22,707,000, $10,768,000; (1971) 25,368,000, $10,539,000; (1972) 21,191,000, $8,631,000. Gross income from eggs and chickens (includes fowls) (1970) $371,393,000; (1971) $350,897,000; (1972) $393,901,000.

Canada—Production of Sawn Lumber [1]

(million feet, board measure)

Source: Canadian Statistical Review, June 1973

	Canada	N.S.	N.B.	Que.	Ont.	Sask.	Alta.	B.C.
1970	11,188.3	193.7	271.3	1,655.4	837.7	109.9	432.8	7,687.5
1971	12,723.0	157.9	298.8	1,808.6	960.7	111.0	470.0	8,916.0
1972 Jan.	1,093.0	13.2	24.1	163.9	79.4	11.7	83.0	717.7

[1] Excludes Newfoundland, P.E.I., Manitoba, the Yukon and the Northwest Territories which together account for less than 1% of the total.

Production of Principal Field Crops in Canada (1972)

Source: Statistics Canada

	Wheats 1,000 bushels	Oats 1,000 bushels	Barley 1,000 bushels	Ryes 1,000 bushels	Flaxseed 1,000 bushels
Canada[2]...................	533,288	300,208	518,413	13,524	19,017
Prince Edward Island....................	301	2,695	1,350	....	....
Nova Scotia.........................	159	884	363	....	....
New Brunswick......................	163	2,088	376	....	....
Quebec............................	758	23,392	1,289	44	....
Ontario............................	16,307	30,149	18,435	1,510	17
Manitoba..........................	69,000	55,000	85,000	1,830	6,500
Saskatchewan......................	326,000	79,000	177,000	5,030	9,800
Alberta............................	118,000	104,000	230,000	5,080	2,700
British Columbia....................	2,600	3,000	4,600	30	....

	Mixed Grains 1,000 bushels	Corn Grain 1,000 bushels	Soybeans 1,000 bushels	Rapeseed 1,000 bushels	Potatoes 1,000 c.w.t.
Canada[2].............................	104,285	104,597	11,745	57,300	41,437
Prince Edward Island................	3,819	....	....	....	8,268
Nova Scotia........................	402	....	....	....	597
New Brunswick.....................	344	....	....	....	11,220
Quebec............................	4,448	9,380	....	....	5,005
Ontario............................	51,442	94,517	11,745	....	6,772
Manitoba..........................	12,500	700	....	8,500	2,500
Saskatchewan......................	9,000	....	....	24,800	475
Alberta............................	22,000	....	....	24,000	4,100
British Columbia...................	330	....	....	....	2,500

	Mustard seed 1,000 pounds	Sunflower seed 1,000 pounds	Tame hay 1,000 tons	Fodder corn 1,000 tons	Sugar beets 1,000 tons
Canada[2]............................	151,500	170,000	23,929	10,369	1,070
Prince Edward Island...............	....	....	203	....	....
Nova Scotia.......................	....	....	285	....	....
New Brunswick....................	....	....	275	....	....
Quebec...........................	....	....	4,054	1,559	80
Ontario...........................	....	....	6,912	8,400	....
Manitoba..........................	12,500	152,000	2,000	160	330
Saskatchewan......................	115,000	15,000	2,500	....	....
Alberta............................	24,000	3,000	6,200	....	660
British Columbia...................	....	....	1,500	250	....

(2) Excluding Newfoundland.

Grain Receipts at Western Grain Centers (In bushels)

Crop Year 1971-72

Province	Wheat	Oats	Barley	Rye	Flaxseed	Rapeseed	Total
Manitoba.........	56,650,525	12,761,831	54,676,442	3,199,578	4,482,588	6,856,072	138,627,036
Saskatchewan....	350,789,295	11,227,216	151,574,559	8,975,652	12,589,014	29,750,518	564,906,254
Alberta..........	105,998,068	7,531,177	88,622,053	3,089,035	3,947,043	19,185,349	228,372,725
Total..........	513,437,888	31,520,224	294,873,054	15,264,265	21,018,645	55,791,939	931,906,015

Farmers' Marketing, Farm Supply, Related Service Cooperatives

Source: Farmer Cooperative Service, U.S. Dept. of Agriculture (Marketing Season 1969-70[1])

A marketing season includes the period during which the farm products of a specified year are moved into the channels of trade. Marketing seasons overlap.

State	Cooperatives	Memberships	Net business[2] $1,000	State	Cooperatives No.	Memberships	Net business[2] $1,000
Alabama.........	67	70,740	169,201	Montana.........	163	64,365	139,005
Alaska..........	2	420	2,820	Nebraska........	346	261,555	557,435
Arizona.........	17	84,085	157,579	Nevada.........	3	675	6,498
Arkansas........	106	99,455	318,259	New Hampshire...	6	2,885	32,119
California.......	321	86,970	2,113,428	New Jersey......	48	21,490	132,249
Colorado........	94	49,905	298,184	New Mexico......	25	7,835	40,624
Connecticut......	19	5,685	80,144	New York........	302	135,235	955,507
Delaware........	8	12,995	18,931	North Carolina....	38	155,680	314,919
Florida..........	96	50,720	433,694	North Dakota.....	495	229,645	418,466
Georgia.........	76	132,525	384,000	Ohio...........	214	246,255	717,700
Hawaii..........	21	1,750	17,251	Oklahoma........	158	139,030	282,259
Idaho...........	73	56,770	189,148	Oregon..........	78	66,620	329,706
Illinois.........	361	388,910	1,049,542	Pennsylvania.....	126	82,000	516,522
Indiana.........	117	419,800	624,338	Rhode Island.....	1	790	12,267
Iowa...........	478	418,775	1,259,908	South Carolina....	20	31,955	89,997
Kansas.........	283	209,000	555,587	South Dakota.....	282	172,700	274,700
Kentucky........	85	200,370	255,398	Tennessee.......	127	153,330	207,440
Louisiana.......	93	19,155	130,251	Texas...........	501	169,905	717,801
Maine..........	14	10,495	69,179	Utah...........	50	17,975	140,936
Maryland........	42	51,215	154,211	Vermont.........	15	8,630	128,176
Massachusetts...	18	8,990	96,874	Virginia.........	120	180,445	273,585
Michigan........	160	132,080	522,604	Washington......	164	114,205	480,114
Minnesota.......	984	562,815	1,270,271	West Virginia.....	66	48,680	60,006
Mississippi......	125	139,635	312,088	Wisconsin........	565	419,845	1,166,704
Missouri........	186	399,395	567,529	Wyoming.........	31	10,425	28,787

(1) Preliminary. (2) The volume of a Hawaiian sugar cooperative headquartered in Calif. is included in the dollar volume of Calif.

Grain, Hay, Potato, Cotton, Tobacco Production

Source: Economic Research Service; Department of Agriculture (preliminary)

1972 State	Barley 1,000 bushels	Corn; grain 1,000 bushels	Cotton[1] lint 1,000 bales	All Hay 1,000 tons	Oats 1,000 bushels	Potatoes 1,000 cwt.	Rye 1,000 bushels	Tobacco 1,000 pounds	All Wheat 1,000 bushels
Alabama		24,525	570	814	558	2,435		926	2,052
Alaska									
Arizona	7,739	525	610	1,372		2,400			11,390
Arkansas	35	1,120	1,465	1,159	7,800	91			10,952
California	50,930	21,500	1,750	8,159	6,783	21,991			23,340
Colorado	10,994	41,310		2,789	1,480	10,608	340		51,519
Connecticut				150		609		5,720	
Delaware	777	13,962		52	120	1,287	216		825
Florida		14,122	13	311	416	4,606		23,468	630
Georgia	464	77,480	360	912	2,470		1,500	114,386	2,800
Hawaii									
Idaho	39,744	2,175		3,715	3,024	78,795	84		44,226
Illinois	765	988,740	1	3,373	27,720	400	460		54,000
Indiana	645	479,612		1,946	11,859	1,458	300	15,000	39,648
Iowa	258	1,191,300		6,827	70,000	682	168		1,238
Kansas	4,620	130,000		5,549	7,348	95	500		314,900
Kentucky	2,800	83,248	4	2,772	410	150	87	437,581	7,020
Louisiana		4,816	715	632	616	218		120	690
Maine				362	1,984	33,280			
Maryland	3,936	35,440		568	1,225	350	230	26,000	3,850
Massachusetts				205		502		1,890	
Michigan	1,071	142,926		3,067	17,600	9,478	806		21,400
Minnesota	33,970	455,607		8,163	124,440	13,050	2,990		49,292
Mississippi		7,335	2,040	1,010	1,456	170			4,960
Missouri	630	220,000	425	5,533	6,900	66	322	5,980	36,075
Montana	64,013	468		4,362	11,808	1,650	69		98,831
Nebraska	1,292	537,680		7,203	19,698	1,393	1,800		94,572
Nevada	825		3	870	180				710
New Hampshire				163		141			
New Jersey	850	3,648		266	270	2,106	161		1,330
New Mexico	840	1,575	160	932		660			4,335
New York	396	18,900		4,503	12,600	10,830	377		5,180
North Carolina	2,562	108,000	130	509	3,375	1,930	294	679,230	6,975
North Dakota	104,680	10,653		5,030	107,407	17,400	4,615		216,818
Ohio	750	279,000		3,134	22,387	2,485	248	22,505	46,305
Oklahoma	8,775	6,319	320	2,899	5,813		1,260		89,700
Oregon	12,000	891		2,279	4,940	14,436	250		36,848
Pennsylvania	7,426	64,800		3,752	16,652	4,800	406	22,400	8,608
Rhode Island				17		907			
South Carolina	924	23,625	320	440	2,736		570	131,130	2,720
South Dakota	20,736	152,832		7,082	99,862	738	9,570		53,619
Tennessee	768	32,340	535	1,781	1,110	371	54	122,040	7,680
Texas	1,980	39,560	4,050	4,109	9,720	3,182	630		44,000
Utah	8,052	736		1,513	676	1,011			6,137
Vermont				851	108	209			
Virginia	4,515	41,666	2	1,817	1,806	4,145	408	114,260	8,066
Washington	14,190	5,406		2,467	2,030	30,495	432		122,083
West Virginia	470	3,975		981	630	259		2,880	490
Wisconsin	990	203,585		10,203	74,250	11,075	200	23,235	901
Wyoming	7,049	2,125		1,786	2,650	1,456	189		8,060
Total U.S.	423,461	5,473,727	13,473	128,389	694,967	294,790	29,536	1,748,759	1,544,775

(1) Equivalent 480 lbs. net weight.

Production and Consumption of Meat and Lard

Source: Economic Research Service: Department of Agriculture (in million lbs.)

Year	Beef Production	Beef Consumption	Veal Production	Veal Consumption	Lamb and Mutton Production	Lamb and Mutton Consumption	Pork (exclud. Lard) Production	Pork (exclud. Lard) Consumption	All Meats Production	All Meats Consumption	Lard Production	Lard Consumption
1940	7,175	7,257	981	981	876	873	10,044	9,701	19,076	18,812	2,288	1,901
1950	9,534	9,529	1,230	1,206	597	596	10,714	10,390	22,075	21,721	2,631	1,891
1960	14,753	15,147	1,109	1,093	768	852	11,607	11,566	28,237	28,658	2,562	1,358
1965	18,727	19,060	1,020	992	651	716	11,141	11,235	31,539	32,003	2,045	1,225
1969	21,158	22,065	673	654	550	687	12,953	12,938	35,334	36,344	1,904	1,011
1970	21,685	22,926	588	581	551	657	13,436	13,391	36,260	37,555	1,913	939
1971	21,904	23,086	546	546	554	644	14,795	14,907	37,799	39,183	1,960	880
1972	22,395	23,929	456	463	542	680	13,652	13,925	37,045	38,997	1,585	750

Harvested Acreage of Principal Crops

Source: Economic Research Service: Department of Agriculture. In thousands of acres

Harvested acreage of 20 crops (excluding duplications)

State	1970	1971	1972	State	1970	1971	1972
Alabama	2,692	2,920	2,852	Nebraska	15,408	16,271	15,766
Alaska	–	–	–	Nevada	547	505	471
Arizona	1,042	1,052	1,044	New Hampshire	112	112	111
Arkansas	7,322	7,253	7,163	New Jersey	374	280	360
California	5,751	5,779	5,626	New Mexico	1,029	1,063	1,020
Colorado	5,686	5,583	5,400	New York	3,925	3,866	3,733
Connecticut	144	149	142	North Carolina	4,022	4,371	4,147
Delaware	443	461	444	North Dakota	17,643	19,025	17,309
Florida	1,038	1,140	1,186	Ohio	8,792	9,548	7,828
Georgia	3,848	4,283	4,073	Oklahoma	8,166	8,111	8,003
Hawaii	120	122	116	Oregon	2,322	2,407	2,393
Idaho	3,904	3,890	3,872	Pennsylvania	4,242	4,396	5,726
Illinois	20,004	20,461	19,853	Rhode Island	18	18	18
Indiana	10,392	11,110	10,738	South Carolina	2,353	2,561	2,484
Iowa	20,687	21,820	20,784	South Dakota	14,185	15,110	13,603
Kansas	18,853	19,686	18,832	Tennessee	3,697	4,081	3,942
Kentucky	3,511	4,076	4,015	Texas	19,042	17,623	17,868
Louisiana	3,621	3,660	3,731	Utah	1,050	1,061	1,070
Maine	435	447	430	Vermont	577	584	574
Maryland	1,323	1,355	1,334	Virginia	2,612	2,724	2,661
Massachusetts	153	152	146	Washington	4,110	4,212	4,195
Michigan	5,297	5,757	5,564	West Virginia	723	751	735
Minnesota	16,958	18,580	17,187	Wisconsin	8,662	8,972	8,527
Mississippi	5,064	5,246	5,221	Wyoming	1,739	1,761	1,741
Missouri	11,273	12,085	11,531				
Montana	8,269	8,739	8,333	**Total U.S.**	**283,180**	**295,319**	**283,902**

(1) Includes barley, beans (dry edible), corn (all), cotton, flaxseed, hay (all), oats, peas (dry field), peanuts (harvested for nuts), potatoes (sweet), potatoes (white), rice, rye, sorghums (for grain), sorghums (for forage and silage), soybeans (for beans), sugar beets, sugarcane (all), tobacco, and wheat (spring and winter).

Livestock on Farms in the United States

Source: Economic Research Service; Dept. of Agriculture (in 1,000)

Year On Jan. I	All Cattle	Milk Cows	All Sheep	Hogs	Horses** and Mules	Year On Jan. i	All Cattle	Milk Cows	All Sheep	Hogs
1890	60,014	15,000	44,518	48,130	18,054	1962	100,369	18,963	30,969	56,619
1900	59,739	16,544	48,105	51,055	21,004	1963	104,488	18,379	29,176	57,993
1910	58,993	19,450	50,239	48,072	24,211	1964	107,903	17,647	27,116	56,757
1920	70,400	21,455	40,743	60,159	25,742	1965	109,000	215,380	25,127	50,792
1925	63,373	22,575	38,543	55,770	22,569	1966†	108,862	14,490	24,734	350,519
1930	61,003	23,032	51,565	55,705	19,124	1967†	108,783	13,725	23,953	357,125
1935	68,846	26,082	51,808	39,066	16,683	1968†	109,371	13,115	22,223	358,818
1940	68,309	24,940	52,107	61,165	14,478	1969†	110,015	12,550	21,350	360,829
1945	85,573	27,770	46,520	59,373	11,950	1970†	112,369	12,091	20,423	357,046
1950	77,963	23,853	29,826	58,937	7,781	1971†	114,578	11,909	19,686	367,433
1955	96,592	23,462	31,582	50,474	4,309	1972†	117,862	11,778	18,710	362,507
1960	96,236	19,527	33,170	59,026	3,089	³1973	121,990	11,651	17,726	361,502

** Discontinued in 1960. † Revised.

(1) Total estimated value on farms as of Jan. 1, 1973 was as follows (avg. val. per head in parenthesis): cattle and calves $30,691,129 ($252); Sheep and lambs $465,973 ($26.30); Hogs $2,575,029 ($41.90); Chickens $519,770,000 ($1.28); Turkeys not available.
(2) New series, milk cows and heifers that have calved beginning 1965.
(3) December 1, preceding year.

Egg Production in the U.S.

Source: Economic Research Service, Department of Agriculture (in millions of eggs)

State	1970	1971	1972	State	1970	1971	1972	State	1970	1971	1972	State	1970	1971	1972
Ala.	2,844	2,861	2,852	Ind.	2,705	2,993	3,036	Neb.	860	862	814	S.C.	1,301	1,341	1,381
Alas.	5	6	7	Iowa	2,473	2,406	2,256	Nev.	4	3	3	S.D.	914	901	814
Ariz.	226	195	164	Kansas	772	754	718	N.H.	300	312	313	Tenn.	1,064	1,012	1,113
Ark.	3,637	3,641	3,795	Ky.	572	566	537	N.J.	830	804	746	Texas	2,677	2,607	2,685
Calif.	8,657	9,012	8,652	La.	776	757	744	N.M.	220	219	234	Utah	271	287	295
Colo.	286	305	297	Me.	1,301	1,368	1,402	N.Y.	2,297	2,316	2,271	Vt.	85	96	114
Conn.	835	830	924	Md.	331	326	334	N.C.	3,440	3,377	3,433	Va.	849	858	825
Del.	126	131	130	Mass.	521	513	535	N.D.	179	168	153	Wash.	1,079	1,022	1,035
Fla.	2,545	2,802	2,840	Mich.	1,450	1,505	1,523	Ohio	2,160	2,338	2,324	W. Va.	268	271	261
Ga.	5,397	5,600	5,465	Minn.	2,249	2,493	2,584	Okla.	503	528	502	Wisc.	1,178	1,344	1,313
Hawaii	197	211	204	Miss.	2,474	2,317	2,299	Ore.	510	514	554	Wyo.	33	33	32
Idaho	190	186	167	Mo.	1,362	1,460	1,473	Pa.	3,218	3,541	3,599				
Ill.	1,820	1,799	1,778	Mont.	209	221	217	R.I.	82	70	57	**Total 68,282 70,082 69,804**			

Gross income from farm eggs (1970) $2,223,608,000; (1971) $1,833,187,000; (1972) 1,797,916,000. Prices received by farmers per dozen (1970) 39.1¢; (1971) 31.4¢ (1972) 30.9¢. Gross income from farm chickens (1970) $108,426,000; (1971) $95,956,000; (1972) $111,070,000. Commercial broilers produced (1970) 2,986,804,000, $1,474,728,000; (1971) 2,945,374,000, $1,487,091,000; (1972) 3,074,698,000, $1,622,000,000. Gross income from eggs and chickens (includes commercial broilers) (1970) $3,806,762,000; (1971) $3,416,234,000; (1972) $3,530,986,000.

Civilian Consumption of Major Food Commodities per Person

Source: Economic Research Service: Department of Agriculture

Commodity [1]	Avg. 1957-59 lbs.	1971 lbs.	1972 lbs.	Commodity [1]	Avg. 1957-59 lbs.	1971 lbs.	1972 lbs.
Meats (carcass wt.)	156.6	191.8	188.8	Apples (com.)	21.0	16.2	17.4
Beef	82.1	113.0	115.9	Other (exc. melons)	40.5	34.6	33.0
Veal	7.1	2.7	2.2	Processed:			
Lamb and mutton	4.4	3.1	3.3	Canned fruit	22.4	21.9	20.3
Pork (excl. lard)	63.0	73.0	67.4	Canned juice	13.5	15.4	15.6
Fish (edible wt.)	10.5	11.2	11.5	Frozen (inc. Juices)	8.6	10.2	10.4
Poultry products				Dried	3.3	2.6	1.8
Eggs (farm Basis)				Vegetables			
Number	356	322	315	Fresh [2]	104.1	98.6	98.2
Chicken (ready to				Canned, excl. potatoes			
cook)	27.5	41.4	42.9	and sweet pot.	43.3	51.2	51.6
Turkey (ready to				Frozen, excl. pot.	6.6	9.7	9.6
cook)	6.0	8.5	8.9	Potatoes, fresh equiv.	106.9	118.9	120.2
Dairy products				Sweet potatoes, fresh			
Cheese	7.9	12.2	13.1	equivalent	8.3	4.9	4.9
Condensed and				Grains			
evap. milk	14.8	6.8	6.2	Cornmeal and flour	7.4	7.4	7.4
Fluid milk and cream				Corn syrup	9.4	16.2	16.2
(milk equiv.)	337	259	258	Corn sugar	3.6	5.2	5.2
Ice Cream (prod. wt.)	18.4	17.6	17.9	Wheat flour [3]	120	110	110
Fats and Oils-Total,				Wheat cereals	2.8	2.9	2.9
fat content	45.3	52.1	53.1	Rice, milled	5.4	7.7	7.0
Butter (actual wt.)	8.2	5.1	5.0	Other			
Margarine (act. wt.)	8.9	11.1	11.3				
Lard	9.3	4.3	3.6	Coffee (green beans)	15.7	13.0	13.0
Shortening	11.4	16.8	16.9	Tea	.58	.77	.78
Other edible fats				Cocoa Beans	3.5	4.0	4.4
and oils	10.8	18.1	19.5	Peanuts (shelled)	4.6	5.9	6.1
Fruits				Dry edible beans	7.7	5.9	6.2
Fresh	95.5	80.0	77.7	Melons	25.1	22.7	22.0
Citrus	34.0	29.2	27.3	Sugar (refined)	96.1	102.4	102.4

[1]Quantity in pounds except for eggs. Data on calendar year basis except for dried fruits, which are on pack-year basis, fresh citrus fruits and peanuts on a crop-year basis, and rice on August 1 year. Fresh citrus year begins in previous October and rice year begins in previous August. [2]Commercial production for sale as fresh produce. [3]Includes white, whole wheat, and semolina flour.

Federal Food Program Costs, 1970-1973 (Calendar Years)

Source: U.S. Department of Agriculture, Food and Nutrition Service (millions of Dollars)

Year	Food Stamps Total Issued	Bonus Stamps [1]	Food Distribution [2] Needy Families	Supp. Food	Schools	Institutions	Child Nutrition School Lunch	School Bkfst.	Special Food	Special Milk	Total
1970	1,922	1,103	296	11	276	23	349	14	15	96	2,183
1971	3,105	1,699	318	13	296	26	647	22	34	92	3,147
1972 [3]	3,619	1,785	271	13	282	27	803	28	45	90	3,344
1st Qt.	847	460	76	3	120	6	252	9	4	29	959
2nd Qt.	870	472	72	3	44	8	195	7	8	22	831
1973											
1st Qt.	999	452	59	3	91	7	295	12	5	30	954

[1]Includes Food Certificate Program. [2]Cost of food delivered to state distribution centers. [3]Includes estimates for third and fourth quarters.

Recommended Daily Dietary Allowances

The Recommended Daily Dietary Allowances are amounts of nutrients recommended by the Food and Nutrition Board of the National Research council as adequate for maintenance of good nutrition in healthy persons in the U.S. The minimum daily requirements for the adult man are: Vitamin A, 4,000 I.U.; thiamin 1 milligram; riboflavin 1.2 mg.; niacin 10 mg.; ascorbic acid 30 mg., calcium 750 mg., iron 10 mg.

	Years From-up to	Wgt (lbs.)	Hgt (in.)	Calories	Protein (grams)	Calcium (grams)	Iron (mg.)	Vit. A (IU)	Thiamin (mg)	Riboflavin (mg)	Niacin (mg)	Ascorbic acid (mg)
Infants	0-1/6	9	22	lb. × 54.5	lb. × 1.0	0.4	6	1,500	0.2	0.4	5	35
	1/6-1/2	15	25	lb. × 50.0	lb. × .9	0.5	10	1,500	0.4	0.5	7	35
	1/2-1	20	28	lb. × 45.5	lb. × .8	0.6	15	1,500	0.5	0.6	8	35
Children	1-2	26	32	1,100	25	0.7	15	2,000	0.6	0.6	8	40
	2-3	31	36	1,250	25	0.8	15	2,000	0.6	0.7	8	40
	3-4	35	39	1,400	30	0.8	10	2,500	0.7	0.8	9	40
	4-6	42	43	1,600	30	0.8	10	2,500	0.8	0.9	11	40
	6-8	51	48	2,000	35	0.9	10	3,500	1.0	1.1	13	40
	8-10	62	52	2,200	40	1.0	10	3,500	1.1	1.2	15	40
Boys	10-12	77	55	2,500	45	1.2	10	4,500	1.3	1.3	17	40
	12-14	95	59	2,700	50	1.4	18	5,000	1.4	1.4	18	45
	14-18	130	67	3,000	60	1.4	18	5,000	1.5	1.5	20	55
Men	18-22	147	69	2,800	60	0.8	10	5,000	1.4	1.6	18	60
	22-35	154	69	2,800	65	0.8	10	5,000	1.4	1.7	18	60
	35-55	154	68	2,600	65	0.8	10	5,000	1.3	1.7	17	60
	55-75+	154	67	2,400	65	0.8	10	5,000	1.2	1.7	14	60
Girls	10-12	77	56	2,250	50	1.2	18	4,500	1.1	1.3	15	40
	12-14	97	61	2,300	50	1.3	18	5,000	1.2	1.4	15	45
	14-16	114	62	2,400	55	1.3	18	5,000	1.2	1.4	16	50
	16-18	119	63	2,300	55	1.3	18	5,000	1.2	1.5	15	50
Women	18-22	128	64	2,000	55	0.8	18	5,000	1.0	1.5	13	55
	22-35	128	64	2,000	55	0.8	18	5,000	1.0	1.5	13	55
	35-55	128	63	1,850	55	0.8	18	5,000	1.0	1.5	13	55
	55-75+	128	62	1,700	55	0.8	10	5,000	1.0	1.5	13	55
Pregnant				+200	65	+0.4	18	6,000	+0.1	1.8	15	60
Lactating				+1,000	75	+0.5	18	8,000	+0.5	2.0	20	60

Nutritive Value of Foods (Calories, Proteins, Etc.)

Source: Home and Garden Bulletin No. 72, U.S. Department of Agriculture

Available for 75ᶜ from Supt. of Documents, U.S. Government Printing Office, Washington, D.C. 20402

Food	Measure	Water%	Food Energy (Calories)	Protein (grams)	Fat (grams)	Carbohydrate (grams)	Calcium (mg)	Iron (mg)	Vit.A (I.U.)	Thiamin (mg)	Riboflavin (mg)	Niacin (mg)	Ascorbic acid (mg)
Milk, Cream, Cheese													
Milk, fluid, whole, 3.5% fat	1 cup	87	160	9	9	12	288	0.1	350	0.07	0.41	0.2	2
Milk, fluid nonfat (skim)	1 cup	90	90	9	T	12	296	.1	10	.09	.44	.2	2
Buttermilk, fluid, cultured, made from skim milk	1 cup	90	90	9	T	12	296	.1	10	.10	.44	.2	2
Cheese, Roquefort type	1 oz.	40	105	6	9	1	89	.1	350	.01	.17	.3	0
Cheese, Cottage, creamed	12 oz.	78	360	46	14	10	320	1.0	580	.10	.85	.3	0
Cream, half-and-half	1 cup	80	325	8	28	11	261	.1	1,160	.07	.39	.1	2
Cream, heavy	1 cup	57	840	5	90	7	179	.1	3,670	.05	.26	.1	2
Custard, baked	1 cup	77	305	14	15	29	297	1.1	930	.11	.50	.3	1
Yoghurt, whole milk	1 cup	88	150	7	8	12	272	.1	340	.07	.39	.2	2
Eggs (large)													
Raw	1 egg	74	80	6	6	T	27	1.1	590	.05	.15	T	0
Scrambled (milk and fat)	1 egg	72	110	7	8	1	51	1.1	690	.05	.18	T	0
Meat, Poultry													
Bacon	2 sli.	8	90	5	8	1	2	.5	0	.08	.05	.8	...
Beef, lean and fat	3 oz.	53	245	23	16	0	10	2.9	30	.04	.18	3.5	...
Hamburger, regular	3 oz.	54	245	21	17	0	9	2.7	30	.07	.18	4.6	...
Steak, broiled, lean and fat	3 oz.	44	330	20	27	0	9	2.5	50	.05	.16	4.0	...
Corned beef	3 oz.	59	185	22	10	0	17	3.7	20	.01	.20	2.9	...
Chicken, cooked:													
Flesh only, broiled	3 oz.	71	115	20	3	0	8	1.4	80	.05	.16	7.4	...
With bone, ½ breast, fried	3.3 oz.	58	155	25	5	1	9	1.3	70	.04	.17	11.2	...
Chicken, potpie, baked	8 oz.	57	535	23	31	42	68	3.0	3,020	.25	.26	4.1	5
Lamb chop, thick with bone	4.8 oz.	47	400	25	33	0	10	1.5	...	.14	.25	5.6	...
Lamb, lean and fat	3 oz.	54	235	22	16	0	9	1.4	...	.13	.23	4.7	...
Liver, beef, fried	2 oz.	57	130	15	6	3	6	5.0	30,280	.15	2.37	9.4	15
Ham, light cure, lean	3 oz.	54	245	18	19	0	8	2.2	0	.40	.16	3.1	...
Boiled ham, sliced	2 oz.	59	135	11	10	0	6	1.6	0	.25	.09	1.5	...
Pork roast, lean and fat	3 oz.	46	310	21	24	0	9	2.7	0	.78	.22	4.7	...
Frankfurter, heated	2 oz.	57	170	7	15	1	3	.8	...	.08	.11	1.4	...
Veal cutlet	3 oz.	60	185	23	9	...	9	2.7	...	.06	.21	4.6	...
Veal roast	3 oz.	55	230	23	14	0	10	2.9	...	.11	.26	6.6	...
Fish													
Bluefish, baked with fat	3 oz.	68	135	22	4	0	25	.6	40	.09	.08	1.6	...
Clams, raw, meat only	3 oz.	82	65	11	1	2	59	5.2	90	.08	.15	1.1	8
Crabmeat, canned	3 oz.	77	85	15	2	1	38	.7	...	.07	.07	1.6	...
Oysters, raw, meat	1 cup	85	160	20	4	8	226	13.2	740	.33	.43	6.0	...
Salmon, pink, canned	3 oz.	71	120	17	5	0	167	.7	60	.03	.16	6.8	...
Shrimp, canned, meat	3 oz.	70	100	21	1	1	98	2.6	50	.01	.03	1.5	...
Swordfish, broiled with butter	3 oz.	65	150	24	5	0	23	1.1	1,750	.03	.04	9.3	...
Tuna, canned in oil	3 oz.	61	170	24	7	0	7	1.6	70	.04	.10	10.1	...
Nuts													
Almonds, shelled, whole	1 cup	5	850	26	77	28	332	6.7	0	.34	1.31	5.0	T
Cashew nuts, roasted	1 cup	5	785	24	64	41	53	5.3	140	.60	.35	2.5	...
Peanuts, roasted	1 cup	2	840	37	72	27	107	3.0	...	.46	.19	24.7	0
Pecans, halves	1 cup	3	740	10	77	16	79	2.6	140	.93	.14	1.0	2
Walnuts, black or native, chopped	1 cup	3	790	26	75	19	T	7.6	380	.28	.14	.9	...
Vegetables & Products													
Asparagus, cooked, spears	4 sp.	94	10	1	T	2	13	.4	540	.10	.11	.8	16
Asparagus, canned	1 cup	94	45	5	1	7	44	4.1	1,240	.15	.22	2.0	37
Beans, lima, immature, cooked	1 cup	71	190	13	1	34	80	4.3	480	.31	.17	2.2	29
Beans, snap, green, cooked	1 cup	92	30	2	T	7	63	.8	680	.09	.11	.6	15
Beans, snap, canned, green	1 cup	94	45	2	T	10	81	2.9	690	.07	.10	.7	10
Beans, snap, yellow or wax	1 cup	93	30	2	T	6	63	0.8	290	.09	.11	.6	16
Beans, sprouted mung, cooked	1 cup	91	35	4	T	7	21	1.1	30	.11	.13	.9	8
Beets, cooked	2 beets	91	30	1	T	7	14	.5	20	.03	.04	.3	6
Broccoli, cooked	1 stalk	91	45	6	1	8	158	1.4	4,500	.16	.36	1.4	162
Brussels sprouts, cooked	1 cup	88	55	7	1	10	50	1.7	810	.12	.22	1.2	135
Cabbage, raw, shredded	1 cup	92	15	1	T	4	34	.3	90	.04	.04	.2	33
Cabbage, cooked	1 cup	94	30	2	T	6	64	.4	190	.06	.06	.4	48
Carrots, raw 5½ by 1 in.	One	88	20	1	T	5	18	.4	5,500	.03	.03	.3	4
Carrots, cooked, diced	1 cup	91	45	1	T	10	48	.9	15,220	.08	.07	.7	9
Cauliflower, cooked, flower buds	1 cup	93	25	3	T	5	25	.8	70	.11	.10	.7	66
Celery, raw, stalk, large	1 stalk	94	5	T	T	2	16	.1	100	.01	.01	.1	4
Corn, cooked, ear 5 by 1¾ in	1 ear	74	70	3	1	16	2	.5	310	.09	.08	1.0	7
Corn, canned	1 cup	81	170	5	2	40	10	1.0	690	.07	.12	2.3	13
Cucumbers, raw, pared	10 oz.	96	30	1	T	7	35	.6	T	.07	.09	.4	23
Lettuce, Boston type	1 head	95	30	3	T	6	77	4.4	2,130	.14	.13	.6	18
Mushrooms, canned	1 cup	93	40	5	T	6	15	1.2	T	.04	.60	4.8	4
Onions, mature, raw, 2½ in.	One	89	40	2	T	10	30	.6	40	.04	.04	.2	11
Peas, green, cooked	1 cup	82	115	9	1	19	37	2.9	860	.44	.17	3.7	33
Peas, green, canned	1 cup	83	165	9	1	31	50	4.2	1,120	.23	.13	2.2	22
Potatoes, medium, baked	One	75	90	3	T	21	9	.7	T	.10	.04	1.7	20
Potatoes, medium, boiled in skin	One	80	105	3	T	23	10	.8	T	.13	.05	2.0	22
Potatoes, mashed, milk added	1 cup	83	125	4	1	25	47	.8	50	.16	.10	2.0	19
Potato chips, medium	10 chips	2	115	1	8	10	8	.4	T	.04	.01	1.0	3
Sauerkraut, canned	1 cup	93	45	2	T	9	85	1.2	120	.07	.09	.4	33
Spinach, cooked	1 cup	92	40	5	1	6	167	4.0	14,580	.13	.25	1.0	50
Squash, summer, diced, cooked	1 cup	96	30	2	T	7	52	.8	820	.10	.16	1.6	21
Squash, winter, baked, mashed	1 cup	81	130	4	1	32	57	1.6	8,610	.10	.27	1.4	27
Sweet potatoes, baked	1	64	155	2	1	36	44	1.0	8,910	.10	.07	.7	24

Food	Measure	Water%	Food Energy (Calories)	Protein (grams)	Fat (grams)	Carbohydrate (grams)	Calcium (mg)	Iron (mg)	Vit.A (I.U.)	Thiamin (mg)	Riboflavin (mg)	Niacin (mg)	Ascorbic acid (mg)
Sweet potatoes, candied 3½ by 2¼ in ...	1	60	295	2	6	60	65	1.6	11,030	.10	.08	.8	17
Tomatoes, raw, medium.	1	94	40	2	T	9	24	.9	1,640	.11	.07	1.3	42
Tomato catsup, tablespoon	1 tbsp.	69	15	T	T	4	3	.1	210	.01	.01	.2	2
Tomato juice, canned.	1 cup	94	45	2	T	10	17	2.2	1,940	.12	.07	1.9	39

Fruits and Fruit Products

Food	Measure	Water%	Food Energy (Calories)	Protein (grams)	Fat (grams)	Carbohydrate (grams)	Calcium (mg)	Iron (mg)	Vit.A (I.U.)	Thiamin (mg)	Riboflavin (mg)	Niacin (mg)	Ascorbic acid (mg)
Apples, medium, raw	One	85	70	T	T	18	8	.4	50	.04	.02	.1	3
Apple juice, bottled or canned	1 cup	88	120	T	T	30	15	1.5	...	.02	.05	.2	2
Applesauce, canned, sweetened	1 cup	76	230	1	T	61	10	1.3	100	.05	.03	.1	3
Bananas, raw 6 by 1½ in	1	76	100	1	T	26	10	.8	230	.06	.07	.8	12
Blueberries, raw	1 cup	83	85	1	1	21	21	1.4	140	.04	.08	.6	20
Cantaloups, raw, medium	½ melon	91	60	1	T	14	27	.8	6,540	.08	.06	1.2	63
Cranberry sauce, sweetened, canned . . .	1 cup	62	405	T	1	104	17	.6	60	.03	.03	.1	6
Grapefruit, raw, medium, white	½	89	45	1	T	12	19	.5	10	.05	.02	.2	44
Grapefruit, canned, unsweetened . .	1 cup	89	100	1	T	24	20	1.0	20	.07	.04	.4	84
Grapes, raw, American type	1 cup	82	65	1	1	15	15	.4	100	.05	.03	.2	3
Grapejuice, canned.	1 cup	83	165	1	T	42	28	.8	...	.10	.05	.5	T
Lemons, raw, medium	One	90	20	1	T	6	19	.4	10	.03	.01	.1	39
Lemon juice, raw	1 cup	91	60	1	T	20	17	.5	50	.07	.02	.2	112
Lime juice, fresh	1 cup	90	65	1	T	22	22	.5	20	.05	.02	.2	79
Oranges, raw, 2⅝ in. diam	One	86	65	1	T	16	54	.5	260	.13	.05	.5	66
Orange juice, frozen, undiluted	1 can	55	360	5	T	87	75	.9	1,620	.68	.11	2.8	360
Peaches, raw, whole, medium	One	89	35	1	T	10	9	.5	1,320	.02	.05	1.0	7
Peaches, raw, halves or sliced	1 cup	79	200	1	T	52	10	.8	1,100	.02	.06	1.4	7
Pears, raw, 3 by 2½ in	One	83	100	1	T	25	13	.5	30	.04	.07	.2	7
Pineapple, canned, sliced	1 large slice	80	90	T	T	24	13	.4	50	.09	.03	.2	8
Plums, raw, 2 in. diam.	1 plum	87	25	T	T	7	7	.3	140	.02	.02	.3	3
Prune juice, canned	1 cup	80	200	1	T	49	36	10.5	...	.03	.03	1.0	5
Raisins, seedless, pkged. ½ oz	1 pkg.	18	40	T	T	11	9	.5	T	.02	.01	.1	T
Strawberries, raw, capped	1 cup	90	55	1	1	13	31	1.5	90	.04	.10	1.0	88
Watermelon, raw, wedge	1 wedge	93	115	2	1	27	30	2.1	2,510	.13	.13	.7	30

Grain Products

Food	Measure	Water%	Food Energy (Calories)	Protein (grams)	Fat (grams)	Carbohydrate (grams)	Calcium (mg)	Iron (mg)	Vit.A (I.U.)	Thiamin (mg)	Riboflavin (mg)	Niacin (mg)	Ascorbic acid (mg)
Bagel, 3 in. diam. egg	One	32	165	6	2	28	9	1.2	30	.14	.10	1.2	0
Biscuits, baking powder.	One	27	105	2	5	13	34	.4	T	.06	.06	.1	T
Bran flakes (40 % bran)	1 cup	3	105	4	1	28	25	12.3	0	.14	.06	2.2	0
Bread, cracked wheat	1 loaf	35	1,190	40	10	236	399	5.0	T	.53	.41	5.9	T
Bread, enriched, French:	1 loaf	31	1,315	41	14	251	195	10.0	T	1.27	1.00	11.3	T
Bread, enriched, Italian	1 loaf	32	1,250	41	4	256	77	10.0	0	1.32	.91	11.8	0
Bread, raisin, loaf	1 loaf	35	1,190	30	13	243	322	5.9	T	.23	.41	3.2	T
Bread, American, rye	1 loaf	36	1,100	41	5	236	340	7.3	0	.82	.32	6.4	0
Bread, white, enriched	1 loaf	36	1,225	39	15	229	381	11.3	T	1.13	.95	10.9	0
Cakes, Angelfood	1 cake	34	1,645	36	1	377	603	1.9	0	.03	.70	.6	0
Cupcakes, small, choc. icing	1 cake	22	130	2	5	21	47	.3	60	.01	.04	.1	T
Cakes, Boston cream pie	1 pce.	35	210	4	6	34	46	.3	140	.02	.08	.1	T
Cake pound	1 loaf	17	2,430	29	152	242	108	4.1	1,440	.15	.46	1.0	0
Saltines	4	4	50	1	1	8	2	.1	0	T	T	.1	0
Danish Pastry, round piece	1 pastry	22	275	5	15	30	33	.6	200	.05	.10	.5	T
Doughnuts, cake type	One	24	125	1	6	16	13	.4	30	.05	.05	.4	T
Macaroni, enriched, cooked	1 cup	64	190	6	1	39	14	1.4	0	.23	.14	1.8	0
Noodles, enriched	1 cup	70	200	7	2	37	16	1.4	110	.22	.13	1.9	0
Oatmeal, or rolled oats, cooked	1 cup	87	130	5	2	23	22	1.4	0	.19	.05	.2	0
Pie, apple ⅐ of 9 in. pie	1 sector	48	350	3	15	51	11	.4	40	.03	.03	.5	1
Pie, custard ⅐ of 9 in. pie	1 sector	58	285	8	14	30	125	.8	300	.07	.21	.4	0
Pie, lemon meringue ⅐ of 9 in. pie	1 sector	47	305	4	12	45	17	.6	200	.04	.10	.2	4
Pie, mince ⅐ of 9 in. pie	1 sector	43	365	3	16	56	38	1.4	T	.09	.05	.5	1
Pie, pumpkin ⅐ of 9 in. pie	1 sector	59	275	5	15	32	66	.7	3,210	.04	.13	.7	T
Pizza (cheese) ⅛ of 14 in. diam.	1 sector	45	185	7	6	27	107	.7	290	.04	.12	.7	4
Popcorn, plain	1 cup	4	25	1	T	5	1	.2	...	...	.01	.1	0
Rolls, home recipe	1 roll	26	120	3	3	20	16	.7	30	.09	.09	.8	T
Spaghetti, enriched, cooked	1 cup	72	155	5	1	32	11	1.3	0	.20	.11	1.5	0

Fats, Oils

Food	Measure	Water%	Food Energy (Calories)	Protein (grams)	Fat (grams)	Carbohydrate (grams)	Calcium (mg)	Iron (mg)	Vit.A (I.U.)	Thiamin (mg)	Riboflavin (mg)	Niacin (mg)	Ascorbic acid (mg)
Butter, regular	½ cup	16	810	1	92	1	23	0	3,750	...	...	...	0
Lard	1 cup	0	1,850	0	205	0	0	0	...	0	0	0	0
Vegetable fats	1 cup	0	1,770	0	200	0	0	0	...	0	0	0	0
Margarine	½ cup	16	815	1	92	1	23	0	3,750	...	...	...	0
Salad Dressing, French, regular	1 tbsp.	39	65	T	6	3	2	.1	...	...	...	...	...
Salad dressing, mayonnaise.	1 tbsp.	15	100	T	11	T	3	.1	40	T	.01	T	...
Salad dressing, 1,000 island	1 tbsp.	32	80	T	8	3	2	.1	50	T	T	T	T

Sugars, Sweets

Food	Measure	Water%	Food Energy (Calories)	Protein (grams)	Fat (grams)	Carbohydrate (grams)	Calcium (mg)	Iron (mg)	Vit.A (I.U.)	Thiamin (mg)	Riboflavin (mg)	Niacin (mg)	Ascorbic acid (mg)
Candy, milk chocolate, sweetened	1 oz.	1	145	2	9	16	65	.3	80	.02	.10	.1	T
Candy, plain fudge	1 oz.	8	115	1	4	21	22	.3	T	.01	.03	.1	T
Chocolate syrup, fudge type	1 oz.	25	125	2	5	20	48	.5	60	.02	.08	.2	T
Honey, strained or extracted	1 tbsp.	17	65	T	T	17	1	.1	0	T	.01	.1	T
Jellies	1 tbsp.	29	50	T	T	13	4	.3	T	T	.01	T	1
Sugars, brown	1 cup	2	820	0	0	212	187	7.5	0	.02	.07	.4	0
Sugars, granulated	1 cup	T	770	0	0	199	0	.2	0	0	0	0	0

Miscellaneous

Food	Measure	Water%	Food Energy (Calories)	Protein (grams)	Fat (grams)	Carbohydrate (grams)	Calcium (mg)	Iron (mg)	Vit.A (I.U.)	Thiamin (mg)	Riboflavin (mg)	Niacin (mg)	Ascorbic acid (mg)
Barbecue sauce	1 cup	81	230	4	17	20	53	2.0	900	.03	.03	.8	13
Beer	12 oz.	92	150	1	0	14	18	T	...	.01	.11	2.2	...
Alcoholic beverage, 86-proof	1½ fl. oz.	64	105	...	...	T	...	...	...	...	...	...	...
Cola type beverage.	12 fl. oz.	90	145	0	0	37	...	...	0	0	0	0	0
Ginger ale	12 fl. oz.	92	115	0	0	29	...	...	0	0	0	0	0
Soup, cream of chicken	1 cup	85	180	7	10	15	172	.5	610	.05	.27	.7	2
Soup, Tomato	1 cup	84	175	7	7	23	168	.8	1,200	.10	.25	1.3	15
Bean with pork	1 cup	84	170	8	6	22	63	2.3	650	.13	.08	1.0	3
Clam chowder	1 cup	92	80	2	3	12	34	1.0	880	.02	.02	1.0	...

T indicates a trace.

Giant Trees of the United States

Source: The American Forestry Association

There are 865 species of trees native to the continental U.S. including a few imports that have become naturalized to the extent of reproducing themselves in the wild state.

The oldest living trees in the world are reputed to be the bristlecone pines, the majority of which are found growing on the arid crags of California's White Mts. Some of them are estimated to be more than 4,600 years old. The largest known bristlecone pine is the "Patriarch," believed to be 1,500 years old.

The oldest known redwoods are about 3,500 years old.

Recognition as the National Champion of each species is determined by total mass of each tree, based on this formula: the circumference in inches as measured at a point 4½ feet above the ground plus the total height of the tree, plus ¼ of the average crown spread in feet. In case of a tie the Champion is determined on the basis of circumference. It is not possible, due to lack of space, to list all the 865 trees registered with the American Forestry Assn.

(Figure in parentheses is year tree was reported)

Species	Height (Ft.)	Location
Acacia, Koa (1969)	140	Kau, Hawaii
Ailanthus, Tree-of Heaven (1955)	80	Head of Harbor, L.I., N.Y.
Alder, European (1969)	87	Berks County, Pa.
Apple, Southern Crab (1968)	40	Columbia, S.C.
Ash, Blue (1970)	86	Danville, Ky.
Aspen, Bigtooth (1963)	93	Walker, N.Y.
Bald cypress, Common (1950)	122	nr. Sharon, Tenn.
Basswood, American (1971)	115	Grand Traverse Cty., Mich.
Bayberry, Pacific (1961)	38	Siuslaw Natl. Forest, Ore.
Beech, American (1970)	108	Ashtabula, Ohio
Birch, River (1968)	85	Germantown, Pa.
Blackbead, Catlaw (1972)	81	Ft. Myers, Fla.
Blackhaw, Rusty (1961)	25	Nr. Washington, Ark.
Bladdernut, American (1966)	36	nr. Utica, Mich.
Boxelder (1972)	95	Washtenaw Co., Mich.
Buckeye, Painted (1970)	144	Union County, Ga.
Buckthorn, Cascara (1945)	60	nr. Rockport, Wash.
Buckwheat tree (1967)	30	nr. Crooked Creek, Fla.
Buffaloberry, Silver (1970)	20.5	Inyo Natl. Forest Calif.
Bumelia, Gum (1964)	52	nr. Fairfield, Texas
Butternut (1968)	100	Portland, Ore.
Buttonbush, Common (1966)	29	nr. Clinton, Mich.
Button-Mangrove (1971)	49	Black Is. Lee City., Fla.
Cajeput (1968)	60	Miami, Fla.
Camphor-tree (1971)	65	nr. Zephyrhills, Fla.
Casuarina, Horsetail (1965)	81	No. Miami Beach, Fla.
Catalpa, Northern (1962)	94	Lansing, Mich.
Cedar, Port-Orford (1968)	219	Siskiyou Natl. Forest, Ore.
Cercocarpus, Birchleaf (1972)	34	Central Point, Ore.
Cherry, Black (1959)	114	Lawrence, Mich.
Chestnut, American (1964)	91	Oregon City, Ore.
Chinaberry (1970)	78	nr. Luverne, Alabama
Chinkapin, Golden (1954)	127	nr. Annapolis, Calif.
Coconut (1969)	63	Clewiston, Fla.
Coffeetree, Kentucky (1966)	101	Bryn Mawr, Pa.
(1973)	82	Lake County, Ohio
Chokecherry, Common (1967)	66	Ada, Mich.
Cottonwood, Black (1969)	147	Unionvalle, Ore.
Cypress, Monterey (1968)	63	Pt. Lobos St. Pk., Calif.
Dahoon (1971)	35	Berkeley Cty., S.C.
Desertwillow (1971)	40	Gila Nat'l. Forest, N.M.
Devil's-walkingstick (1949)	30	Great Smoky Nat'l. Pk., Tenn.
Devilwood (1967)	37	Mayo, Fla.
Dogwood, Pacific (1972)	60	Keizer, Ore.
Douglas Fir, Coast (1945)	221	Olympic Natl. Pk., Wash.
Doveplum (1965)	45	Miami, Fla.
Ebony, Mountain (1967)	46	Ellenton, Fla.
Elder, Blackbead (1954)	30	nr. Prescott, Ore.
Elm, American (1971)	130	Dundee, Kentucky
False-Mastic (1955)	56	nr. Miami, Fla.
Fig, Florida Strangler (1965)	51	Miami, Fla.
Fir, Noble (1964)	278	Gifford Pinchot Natl. Forest, Wash.
Franklinia (1968)	25	Wyndmoor, Pa.
Grapefruit (1967)	38	Ellenton, Fla.

Species	Height (Ft.)	Location
Gumbo-limbo (1972)	60	Ft. Myers, Fla.
Hackberry, Common (1972)	118	Wayland, Mich.
Hawthorn (1967)	50	Glenview, Ill.
Hemlock, Western (1954)	163	Olympic Natl. Pk., Wash.
Hercules-club (1961)	38	Little Rock, Ark.
Hickory, Pignut (1970)	125	nr. Brunswick, Ga.
Holly, Tawnyberry (1968)	55	Homestead, Fla.
Honeylocust, Thornless (1970)	128	Mt. Erie, Ill.
Hophornbeam, Eastern (1945)	78	nr. Winthrop, Me.
Hoptree, Common (1972)	31	Ada, Michigan
Hornbeam, American (1966)	42	Canton, Ohio
Joshua-tree (1967)	32	San Bernardino Natl. Forest, Calif.
Juniper, Western (1945)	87	Stanislaus Natl. Forest, Calif.
Larch, Western (1945)	177	nr. Kootenai Natl. Forest, Mont.
Laurelcherry, Carolina (1970)	44	Dellwood, Fla.
Lebbek (1970)	58	Princeton, Fla.
Loblolly-Bay (1963)	84	Hugh's Island, Fla.
Locust, Black (1972)	74	Albany, N.Y.
Lysiloma, Bahama (1955)	48	Key Largo, Fla.
Madrone, Pacific (1955)	80	Humboldt Cty., Calif.
Magnolia, Cucumber tree (1969)	97	Chester, Pa.
Mangrove, Red (1973)	60	North Miami, Fla.
Maple, Red (1964)	125	nr. Armada, Mich.
Mesquite, Velvet (1949)	55	Coronado Natl. Forest, Ariz.
Mountain-Ash, Showy (1968)	58	nr. Gould City, Mich.
Mountain-Laurel (1970)	20	Chattahoochee Natl. Forest, Ga.
Mulberry, White (1970)	77	St. Joseph Co., Mich.
(1973)	68	Logan Co., Ill.
Oak, California white (1967)	120	nr. Gridley, Calif.
Oleander, Common (1963)	22	Phoenix, Ariz.
Osage-Orange (1969)	51	Charlotte Cty., Va.
Palmetto, Cabbage (1965)	90	Highlands Hammock State Pk., Fla.
Paloverde, Blue (1967)	52	Ajo, Ariz.
Paulownia, Royal (1969)	105	Philadelphia Cty., Pa.
Pawpaw, Blue (1971)	41	nr. Smith Mills, Ky.
Pear (1966)	51	Clawson, Oakland Co., Mich.
(1972)	74	Leslie Co., Ky.
Pecan (1973)	128	Hopewell, Va.
Peppertree (1969)	47	San Juan Capistrano, Calif.
Pinckneya (1968)	21	nr. Mt. Pleasant, Fla.
Pine, ponderosa (1969)	161	nr. Lapine, Oregon
Planetree (1967)	77	nr. Chattahoochee, Fla.
Plum, American (1972)	35	Oakland Co., Mich.
Poison Sumac (1972)	20	Robin's Island, N.Y.
Pondcypress (1969)	135	nr. Newton, Ga.
Poplar, Balsam (1969)	98	So. Egremont, Mass.
Possumhaw (1970)	25	Richland Cty., S.C.
Redbay (1971)	58	Randolph Cty., Ga.
Redwood, Coast (1966)	362	Humboldt Redwoods State Pk., Calif.
Royalpalm, Florida (1972)	78	Collier Seminole Pk., Fla.
Sassafras (1954)	100	Owensboro, Ky.

Species	Height (Ft.)	Location	Species	Height (Ft.)	Location
Seagrape (1972)	57	Miami, Fla.	Tamarisk,		
Sequoia, Giant (1945)	272	Sequoia Natl. Pk., Calif.	Five-Stamen (1967)	37	Albuquerque, N.M.
Serviceberry,			Tanoak (1969)	100	Kneeland, Calif.
Downy (1966)	48	nr. Standish, Mich.	Tesota (1972)	31.6	nr. Quartzsite, Ariz.
Silk-oak (1972)	78	nr. La Belle, Fla.	Torreya, California (1945)	141	nr. Mendocino, Calif.
Silktree (1971)	41	Gilmer, Texas	Trifoliate-Orange (1968)	26	Harrisburg, Pa.
Silverbell, Two-wing (1971)	55	Tallahassee, Fla.	Tupelo, Black (1969)	117	Harrison Co., Texas
Smoketree, American (1963)	33	Dawes Arboretum, Ohio	(1971)	139	nr. Easterly, Texas
Soapberry, Western (1969)	67	Newton County, Tex.	Wahoo, Eastern (1971)	14	Carrollton, Mo.
Sourwood (1968)	118	nr. Robbinsville, N.C.	Walnut, California (1973)	116	Santa Rosa, Calif.
Sparkleberry tree (1970)	29	Keltys, Texas	Willow, Crack (1964)	112	nr. Utica, Mich.
Spruce, Sitka (1967)	248	"The Helen Clapp	Winterberry,		
		Spruce", Forks, Wash.	Common (1971)	40	Wildwood, Fla.
Sugarberry (1970)	148	Richland Cty., S.C.	Witch-Hazel,		
Sumac, Shining (1967)	47	nr. Chattahoochee, Fla.	Common (1967)	44	Franklin, Mich.
Sweetleaf,			Yaupon (1964)	45	nr. Devers, Texas
Common (1967)	55	Tallahassee, Fla.	Yellow-Poplar (1972)	124	Bedford, Va.
Sycamore, Calif. (1945)	116	nr. Santa Barbara, Calif.	Yellowwood (1964)	58	Morrisville, Pa.
Tallowtree (1967)	42	Polk County, Texas	Yew, Pacific (1959)	60	nr. Mineral, Wash.
Tamarack (1966)	95	Jay, Me.	Yucca, Aloe (1967)	15	Lakeland, Fla.

Grain Storage Capacity at Principal Grain Centers in U.S. and Canada

Source: Chicago Board of Trade

United States

Cities	Capacity Bushels	Cities	Capacity Bushels
Amarillo	27,883,534	Milwaukee	5,600,000
Buffalo	31,260,000	Minneapolis-St. Paul	120,341,100
California ports	16,473,000	New Orleans area	36,698,000
Chicago	60,658,000	Omaha-Council Bluffs	35,338,262
Des Moines	10,640,000	Peoria	6,820,000
Duluth-Superior	72,779,000	Portland-Columbia R.	31,499,535
Enid	66,102,000	Puget Sound	6,700,000
Fort Worth	57,565,398	Sioux City	13,406,000
Galveston-Houston	31,200,000	St. Joseph	20,584,000
Hutchinson	41,733,000	St. Louis	19,815,000
Kansas City	90,786,554	Toledo	32,200,000
Lincoln	42,812,584	Wichita	82,295,000
Lubbock	29,219,000		

Canada

Cities	Capacity	Cities	Capacity
Baie Comeau	13,853,000	Prescott, Ont.	5,500,000
Churchill, Man.	5,000,000	Prince Rupert, B.C.	2,250,000
Collingwood, Ont.	2,000,000	Quebec, Que.	8,000,000
Goderich, Ont.	4,600,000	Saint, John, N.B.	500,000
Halifax, N.S.	5,152,500	Sarnia, Ont.	5,400,000
Kingston, Ont.	2,350,000	Sorel, Que.	5,230,000
Midland, Ont.	11,550,000	Three Rivers, Que	6,000,000
Montreal, Que.	22,262,000	Thunder Bay	101,097,210
N. Vancouver, B.C.	6,972,000	Toronto, Ont.	4,000,000
Owen Sound, Ont.	4,000,000	Vancouver, B.C.	18,056,500
Port Cartier	10,462,000	Victoria, B.C.	1,040,000
Port Colborne, Ont.	5,250,000	West St. John, N.B.	2,576,800
Port McNicoll, Ont.	6,500,000		

Grain Receipts at Western Grain Centers

Source: Chicago Board of Trade (In thousands bushels)

1972	Wheat	Corn	Oats	Rye	Barley	Soybeans	Total
Chicago	17,024	92,285	2,221	9	860	32,257	144,656
Duluth	113,670	19,372	11,805	4,262	52,874	1,993	203,976
Enid	82,310	71	.....	.....	11	.....	82,392
Hutchinson	68,374	70	.....	.....	.....	.....	68,444
Kansas City	100,446	59,138	1,820	62	740	18,741	180,947
Milwaukee	143	26,700	111	.....	27,268	1,316	55,538
Minneapolis	136,826	26,906	64,448	8,123	82,382	5,058	323,743
Omaha	21,194	37,430	354	143	11	6,218	65,350
Peoria	72	28,238	298	206	.....	414	29,228
Sioux City	5,299	20,030	7,378	198	114	11,458	44,477
St. Joseph	1,538	5,748	1,674	.....	.....	2,582	11,542
St. Louis	25,585	15,337	12,646	.....	.....	6,643	60,211
Toledo	22,943	54,597	1,827	30	3	40,419	119,819
Wichita	17,375	900	12	.....	34	4,030	22,351
Total	**612,799**	**386,822**	**104,594**	**13,033**	**164,297**	**131,129**	**1,412,674**

The 1972 Wildfire Season

Source: Forest Service, U.S. Dept. of Agriculture

Federal, State and Private Protected Area

Drought again plagued southwestern United States in 1972. Precipitation was the lowest on record for January into May. During this critical period a careless person started the "Battle" fire on the Prescott National Forest, Arizona, an area which had been closed due to extreme fire danger. It spread out of control for seven days, threatening the town of Prescott and destroying 28,000 acres of watershed and timberland.

However, 96 percent of all fires were controlled at 10 acres or less in size on the 210 million acres of Forest Service protected lands. Less than one percent were large fires burning over 300 acres. These accounted for approximately 75 percent of burned acreage. Forest fires burned 0.6 acres for each 1,000 acres protected.

Late summer two fires in California severely endangered human lives and homes, besides damaging watershed and other valuable resources. Sadly, six firefighters lost their lives in a helicopter accident on one of these conflagrations, the "Bear" fire, Los Padres National Forest, California. All told, only three fires accounted for 42 percent of all acres burned in 1972.

Man-caused fires increased 15 percent over previous years. However 14,154 fires burned only 116,703 acres. Aggressive prevention measures followed by hard-hitting attack forces reduced the potential for major conflagrations on National Forests.

Success of this effort is borne out by the record. Only 4 percent of the fires escaped initial attack. An example of payoff from readiness and mobility occurred during a 5-day period in Southwest Idaho, when lighting ignited 250 fires in hazardous fuels. Only one of the fires reached large size. The rest were contained at less than ten acres.

On all Federal, State and private forest and non-forested watershed lands during 1972, a total of 124,554 fires were reported; an increase of 16,156

fires above the 108,398 reported during 1971. However, acreage burned on all lands totaled 2,641,166; a decrease of 1,637,306 acres below the 4,278,472 acres burned during 1971.

Through carelessness or incendiarism, man is blamed for the largest portion of wildfires. During 1972, some 84,516 fires, or 85 percent of the 98,947 reported as having burned on protected land were man-caused. Lightning-started fires amounted to 14,431 or 15 percent of the protected area fires. Causes of the 25,607 fires which occurred on unprotected lands are not known.

More than 631,162,000 acres of State and private forest and nonforested watershed lands are protected under the Federal-State cooperative Forest Fire Control Program. Since the area qualifying for protection under the program is 690,743,000 acres, the goal of the program is to bring protection to the more than 59,581,000 acres not now receiving protection. All States participate in the cooperative forest fire protection effort. The record on State and private protected lands for 1972 follows:

Group	Number of Fires	Acres Burned
Rocky Mountain	6,419	289,650
Pacific.	10,464	85,325
North Central	7,274	82,307
Southern.	50,212	567,157
Eastern	8,641	25,870
Total	**83,010**	**1,050,309**

The record on State and private unprotected lands is:

Rocky Mountain	544	7,465
North Central	1,070	46,500
Southern.	2,993	304,720
Eastern.	21,000	(no data)
Total	**25,607**	**358,685**

Total Fires and Acres Burned—National Forest Protection

Calendar Year	Lightning	Man Caused	Total	Acres Burned	Calendar Year	Lightning	Man Caused	Total	Acres Burned
1967..	6,790	4,981	11,771	204,106	1971..	5,876	6,363	12,239	171,867
1968..	4,808	4,923	9,731	212,420	Average				
1969..	4,726	5,308	10,034	92,126	1967-71	6,000	5,749	11,750	240,099
1970..	7,804	7,172	14,976	519,978	1972..	8,406	5,748	14,154	116,703

National Forest System

Administered by the Forest Service, U.S. Dept. of Agriculture, the National Forest System is made up of 155 National Forests, 19 National Grasslands, and other minor acreages which total 187,101,120 acres in 44 states, Puerto Rico, and the Virgin Islands. All lands within the National Forest System are managed under two guiding principles: multiple use–the management of lands to make each area yield the combination of uses best suited to public needs; and sustained yield–maintenance of a continuous supply of all forest resources through wise use, management, and protection.

National Forest lands which supply water for agriculture, industry, recreation, and domestic use, for example, also are managed to prevent erosion and help control floods, yet there also may be camping, skiing, and timber harvesting on the same land.

The scenic beauty and recreation opportunities available on National Forests yearly draw millions of Americans to these lands to hunt, fish, camp, picnic, boat, recreational play, swim, hike, ski, and to make pack trips into the wilderness. Use reached 183,958,300 visitor days during calendar year 1972.

National Forest Areas

Source: Forest Service, Dept. of Agriculture. (In Acres) Data as of June 30, 1973

States	Area	States	Area	States	Area	States	Area
Alabama	634,741	Iowa	360	N. Hampshire	683,203	Tennessee . .	613,780
Alaska	20,723,028	Kansas	107,914	N. Mexico . .	9,196,495	Texas	776,480
Arizona	11,422,784	Kentucky	616,757	New York . . .	13,779	Utah	8,042,711
Arkansas	2,457,685	Louisiana . . .	594,849	N. Carolina . .	1,135,448	Vermont	243,383
California	20,070,067	Maine	50,103	N. Dakota . .	1,105,234	Virgin Islands	147
Colorado	14,361,432	Michigan	2,687,578	Ohio	154,173	Virginia	1,538,438
Connecticut .	10	Minnesota . . .	2,796,564	Oklahoma . . .	290,672	Washington . .	9,067,260
Florida	1,081,459	Mississippi . .	1,136,313	Oregon	15,480,408	W. Virginia . .	950,055
Georgia	851,410	Missouri	1,441,016	Pennsylvania .	495,882	Wisconsin . .	1,489,590
Idaho	20,351,894	Montana	16,704,075	Puerto Rico .	27,998	Wyoming . . .	9,246,849
Illinois	247,572	Nebraska . . .	350,567	S. Carolina . .	598,276	**Total**	
Indiana	168,238	Nevada	5,108,731	S. Dakota . . .	1,985,702	**Acreage . . .**	**187,101,120**

Giant Trees of Canada
Source: Native Trees of Canada by R. C. Hosie
(Canadian Forestry Service. Dept. of Fisheries & Forestry)

There are nearly 140 species of trees native to Canada on which information is easily available. A "Native" tree is defined as a single-stemmed perennial woody plant growing to a height of more than ten feet, and which is indigenous to Canada. Most of the 'giant' trees in Canada are to be found in the Forest Regions. These regions reflect differences caused by terrain, soil, and climate. The nine Forest Regions are: The Grassland, Boreal, Great Lakes-St. Lawrence, Columbia, Deciduous, Coast, Subalpine, Acadian and Montane.

It is difficult to obtain precise records of single trees of outstanding heights. Given below are several common species of trees native to Canada showing the usual or normal height of the species. But many exceptions have been noted. For example the Douglas Fir whose average range in height is given at 150 to 200 ft. with diameters of up to 9 ft., occasionally may attain heights above 300 ft. and diameters of 15 ft. or more. The Sitka Spruce is also known to have reached heights of at least 280 ft., and the Western White Pine is recorded as having attained 200 ft.

Species	Height (Ft.)	Forest Region
Alpine Fir..........	65-100	Subalpine; N.W. Boreal
Amabilis Fir	80-125	Coast & coastal parts of Subalpine
Balsam Poplar	60-80	Boreal, Great Lakes-St. Lawrence & Acadian
Black Cottonwood..	80-125	Throughout B.C. and Western Alberta
Black Maple.......	80-90	Ontario to Montreal is.
Douglas-Fir........	150-200	Coast
Eastern Cottonwood	75-100	Gt. Lakes-St. Lawrence
Eastern White Pine.	100-175	Through east Canada
Engelmann Spruce.	100-120	Southern Subalpine
Grand Fir	100-125	S. Coast & Columbia
Mockernut Hickory.	75-90	Deciduous
Silver Maple	80-90	S.E. parts of G. Lakes-St. Lawrence

Species	Height (Ft.)	Forest Region
Sitka Spruce	125-175	Coast
Sugar Maple.......	80-90	Gt. Lakes-St. Lawrence
Sycamore	Up to 150	Deciduous
Western Hemlock ..	120-160	Coast & Columbia
Western Larch	100-180	Southern part of Columbia & Montane, B.C.
Western Red Cedar	150-200	Coast & Columbia
Western White Pine	50-110	S. Coast & Columbia
White Birch........	Med.- 80	Throughout Canada
White Elm	60- 80	G. Lakes-St. Lawrence & Acadian
White Oak	Med.-100	Southern Ontario
White Spruce	80-120	Boreal
Yellow Cypress.....	60- 80	Coast & in coastal parts of Subalpine

The 1971 Forest Fire Season in Canada

A rash of early spring fires wrought havoc throughout central Quebec as the province experienced one of its most disastrous forest fire season beginnings in history. By the end of June, fire had destroyed or damaged more than 500,000 acres of forest land. The hardest hit region, near Chibougamau, was subsequently declared a disaster area.

Ontario also reported severe burning conditions during the early part of June when a major portion of the total burned area in that province was hit by fire. One of the fires threatened the village of Moosonee and necessitated the evacuation of all residents of this northwestern Ontario community.

Extremely hot and dry conditions prevailed throughout most of British Columbia from about mid-July until the end of August. As a result of almost daily severe lightning storms, more than the normal number of large and difficult fires developed and suppression forces were taxed to the utmost.

A total of 9,173 forest fires were reported on all federal and provincial lands in 1971. This marks the second time in as many years when fire occurrence in Canada has surpassed the 9,000 level—an unprecedented 9,317 starts were recorded in 1970. The acreage burned on all lands totaled 4,188,320 in 1970, an increase of some 1,570,000 acres over the previous year.

The total area under some form of organized protection in 1971 rose 1,580,750 sq. mi. up 6,886 sq. mi. over 1970.

Forest Fires on Provincial and Federal Protected Lands, 1971

Provincial Lands	Number of Fires	Acres Burned	Provincial Lands	Number of Fires	Acres Burned
Newfoundland................	142	6,103	Alberta......................	854	155,819
Nova Scotia	425	1,157	British Columbia	2,896	868,036
Prince Edward Island.........	N.A.	N.A.	**Federal Lands**		
New Brunswick	344	3,372	Yukon......................	104	120,481
Quebec	1,331	647,648	Northwest Territories........	251	1,622,612
Ontario.....................	1,790	103,718	National Parks...............	165	424,597
Manitoba....................	490	21,030	Other Federal Lands	38	326
Saskatchewan...............	343	213,021	**Total all lands**	**9,173**	**4,188,320**

Total Fires and Acreage Burned by Causes

	MAN-CAUSED		LIGHTNING			MAN-CAUSED		LIGHTNING	
Year	Number of Fires	Acres Burned	Number of Fires	Acres Burned		Fires	Acres	Fires	Acres
1966*	5,782	494,566	1,686	649,873	1970..	6,018	400,609	3,299	2,217,690
1967*	6,429	586,583	2,221	1,625,371	Average 66-70 .	5,830	839,059	2,050	1,264,541
1968*	5,917	1,904,476	1,384	307,129	1971*	6,255	699,387	2,918	3,488,933
1969..	5,003	809,063	1,658	1,522,641	*Does not include Prince Edward Island.				

Theater — Opera — Films

Broadway's Principal Events of 1972-73

*still running July 1, 1973; (M) designates musicals; performers are original cast.

Play	Performers	Opened	Run
That Championship Season	Paul Sorvino, Charles Dunning, Michael McGuire, Richard Dysart	Sept. 12	499*
Dude (M)	Rae Allen, William Redfield, Allan Nicholls	Oct. 9	16
Hurry, Harry (M)	Samuel D. Ratcliffe, Mary Bracken Phillips	Oct. 12	1
6 Rms Riv Vu	Jerry Orbach, Jane Alexander, Ron Harper	Oct. 17	247
Mother Earth (M)	Kelly Garrett, Carol Kristy	Oct. 19	12
Pippin (M)	Irene Ryan, Ben Vereen, Leland Palmer	Oct. 23	289*
The Lincoln Mask	Fred Gwynne, Eva Marie Saint	Oct. 30	8
Butley	Alan Bates, Hayward Morse, Barbara Lester	Oct. 31	119
Lysistrata (M)	Melina Mercouri, Philip Bruns, Priscilla Lopez	Nov. 13	8
The Secret Affairs of Mildred Wild	Maureen Stapleton, Lee Wallace	Nov. 14	23
Ambassador (M)	Howard Keel, Danielle Darrieux, Carmen Mathews	Nov. 19	9
Via Galactica (M)	Irene Cara, Raul Julia	Nov. 28	1
The Creation of the World and other Business	Zoe Caldwell, Bob Dishy, George Grizzard, Stephen Elliott	Dec. 1	20
The Last of Mrs. Lincoln	Julie Harris	Dec. 12	63
The Sunshine Boys	Jack Albertson, Sam Levene, Lewis J. Stadlen	Dec. 19	221*
1973			
Tricks (M)	Rene Auberjonois, Christopher Murney	Jan. 8	8
Let Me Hear You Smile	Sandy Dennis, James Broderick, Paul B. Price	Jan. 16	1
The Jockey Club Stakes	Wilfrid Hyde-White, Robert Coote, Geoffrey Sumner	Jan. 24	69
Shelter (M)	Marcia Rodd, Terry Kiser, Susan Browning	Feb. 6	31
Finishing Touches	Barbara Bel Geddes, Robert Lansing	Feb. 8	164*
Warp	John Heard, Carolyn Gordon, Tom Towles	Feb. 14	7
Status Quo Vadis	Bruce Boxleitner	Feb. 18	1
No Sex Please, We're British	Tony Tanner, Maureen O'Sullivan	Feb. 20	16
A Little Night Music (M)	Glynis Johns, Hermione Gingold, Lou Cariou	Feb. 25	144*
Out Cry	Michael York, Cara Duff-McCormick	Mar. 1	12
The Changing Room	John Lithgow, Robert Murch, Tom Atkins	Mar. 6	135*
Irene (M)	Debbie Reynolds, George S. Irving, Patsy Kelly	Mar. 13	127*
Seesaw (M)	Michele Lee, Ken Howard, Tommy Tune	Mar. 19	121*
Emperor Henry IV	Rex Harrison	Mar. 28	37
The River Niger	Douglas Turner Ward, Les Roberts, Graham Brown	Mar. 28	111*
Cyrano (M)	Christopher Plummer	May 13	49
Nash at Nine (M)	E. G. Marshall, Virginia Vestoff	May 17	21

Record Long Run Broadway Plays   *Still running July 1, 1973

Fiddler on the Roof	3,242	Voice of the Turtle	1,558	Lightnin'	1,291
Life With Father	3,213	Barefoot in the Park	1,532	Promises, Promises	1,281
Tobacco Road	3,182	Mame	1,508	The King and I	1,246
Hello Dolly	2,844	Arsenic and Old Lace	1,444	Cactus Flower	1,234
My Fair Lady	2,717	The Sound of Music	1,442	"1776"	1,217
Man of La Mancha	2,328	How to Succeed in		Guys and Dolls	1,200
Abie's Irish Rose	2,327	Business Without Really		Cabaret	1,166
Oklahoma!	2,246	Trying	1,416	Mister Roberts	1,157
South Pacific	1,925	Hellzapoppin	1,404	Annie Get Your Gun	1,147
Harvey	1,775	The Music Man	1,376	Butterflies Are Free	1,128
Hair	1,750	Funny Girl	1,348	Pins and Needles	1,108
Born Yesterday	1,643	Oh! Calcutta!	1,314	*Sleuth	1,102
Mary, Mary	1,572	Angel Street	1,295	Plaza Suite	1,098

Record Long Runs Off-Broadway   *Still running July 1, 1973

*The Fantasticks	5,478	The Premise	1,490	*The Proposition	895
The Threepenny Opera	2,611	The Blacks	1,408	*Godspell	887
You're A Good Man Charlie Brown	1,597	Little Mary Sunshine	1,143	The Effect of Gamma Rays on Man-in-the Moon Marigolds	819
		The Boys in the Band	1,001	A View from the Bridge	780
Jacques Brel is Alive and Well and Living in Paris	1,847	*One Flew Over the Cuckoo's Nest	951	The Boy Friend	763
		Your Own Thing	933	The Pocket Watch	725
This Was Burlesque	1,509	Curley McDimple	931		
		Leave it to Jane	928		

New York Theater Productions

	Broadway			Off Broadway	
	1972/73	1971/72		1972/73	1971/72
Plays	42	35	Plays	54	64
Musicals	21	18	Musicals	22	30
Total	63	53	Revues	5	0
			Total	81	94

Plays in London * Still Running Aug. 15, 1973

* The Mousetrap 8,606	Blithe Spirit 1,997	Simple Spymen 1,404
Black and White Minstrels 4,354	Worms Eye View 1,745	Our Boys 1,362
Oliver 2,811	Me and My Girl 1,646	Knights of Madness 1,361
There's a Girl in my Soup 2,547	Reluctant Heroes 1,610	Maid of the Mountains 1,352
Sound of Music 2,385	Together Again 1,566	Arsenic and Old Lace 1,337
Salad Days 2,283	Seagulls Over Sorrento 1,551	The Farmer's Wife 1,329
My Fair Lady 2,281	Oklahoma 1,543	Annie Get Your Gun 1,304
Chu Chin Chow 2,238	Irma La Douce 1,512	The Little Hut 1,261
Charlie Girl 2,201	Dry Rot 1,475	A Little Bit of Fluff 1,241
The Boy Friend 2,084	Charley's Aunt 1,466	Sailor Beware 1,231
Canterbury Tales 2,082	The Secretary Bird 1,463	One for the Pot 1,221
Boeing Boeing 2,036	The Beggars Opera 1,463	* Oh Calcutta 1,187
Fiddler on the Roof 2,030	* Sleuth 1,454	Beyond the Fringe 1,184
* Hair 1,998	* The Man Most Likely To 1,429	

Symphony Orchestras of the United States and Canada

(As of Aug. 22, 1973)

Source: American Symphony Orchestra League, Inc.
Classifications are based on annual budgets of orchestras.

Major Symphony Orchestras

		Conductors
Atlanta Symphony	1280 Peachtree St., N.E., Atlanta, Ga. 30309	Robert Shaw
Baltimore Symphony	120 West Mount Royal Ave., Baltimore, Md. 21201	Sergiu Comissiona
Boston Symphony	Symphony Hall, Boston, Mass. 02115	Seiji Ozawa
Buffalo Philharmonic	26 Richmond Ave., Buffalo, N.Y. 14222	Michael Thomas
Chicago Symphony	220 S. Michigan Ave. Chicago, Ill. 60604	Georg Solti
Cincinnati Symphony	1313 Central Trust Tower, Cincinnati, Ohio 45202	Thomas Schippers
Cleveland Orchestra	11001 Euclid Ave., Cleveland, Ohio 44106	Lorin Maazel
Dallas Symphony	P.O. Box 8472, Dallas, Tex. 75205	Max Rudolf
Denver Symphony	1615 California St., Denver, Colo. 80202	Brian Priestman
Detroit Symphony	20 E. Jefferson Ave., Detroit, Mich. 48226	Aldo Ceccato
Houston Symphony	615 Louisiana, Houston, Tex. 77002	Lawrence Foster
Indianapolis Symphony	P.O. Box 88351, Indianapolis, Ind. 46208	Izler Solomon
Kansas City Philharmonic	210 W. 10th St. Kansas City, Mo. 64105	Jorge Mester
Los Angeles Philharmonic	135 North Grand, Los Angeles, Calif. 90012	Zubin Mehta
Milwaukee Symphony	929 N. Water St., Milwaukee, Wis. 53202	Ken Schermerhorn
Minnesota Orchestra	807 Hennepin Ave., Minneapolis, Minn. 55403	S. Skrowaczewski
Montreal Symphony	Place des Arts, Montreal 129, Que., Can.	Franz-Paul Decker
National Symphony	J.F.K. Center for the Performing Arts, Wash., DC 20566	Antal Dorati
New Orleans Philharmonic	333 St. Charles Ave., New Orleans, La. 70130	W. Torkanowsky
New York Philharmonic	Broadway at 65th St., New York, N.Y. 10023	Pierre Boulez
Philadelphia Orchestra	230 S. 15th St., Philadelphia, Pa. 19102	Eugene Ormandy
Pittsburgh Symphony	600 Penn Ave., Pittsburgh, Pa. 15222	William Steinberg
Rochester Philharmonic	60 Gibbs St., Rochester, N.Y. 14604	David Zinman
St. Louis Symphony	718 N. Grand Blvd., St. Louis, Mo. 63103	Walter Susskind
San Antonio Symphony	600 Hemisfair Plaza Way, San Antonio, Tex. 78205	Victor Alessandro
San Francisco Symphony	War Memorial Veterans' Bldg., San Fran., Calif. 94102	Seiji Ozawa
Seattle Symphony	305 Harrison St., Seattle, Wash., 98109	Milton Katims
Toronto Symphony	215 Victoria St., Toronto 2, Ontario, Can.	Victor Feldbrill
Utah Symphony	55 W. 1st So. St., Salt Lake City, Utah 84101	Maurice Abravanel

Metropolitan Orchestras

		Conductors
Akron Symphony	Thomas Hall, Hill & Center Sts., Akron, Ohio 44303	Louis Lane
Albany Symphony	19 Clinton Ave., Albany, N.Y. 12207	Julius Hegyi
Albuquerque Symphony	120 Madeira N.E., Albuquerque, N.M. 87108	Yoshimi Takeda
Austin Symphony	701 West 15th St., Austin, Tex. 78701	Walter Ducloux
Birmingham Symphony	710 N. 20th St., Birmingham, Ala. 35203	Amerigo Marino
Brooklyn Philharmonia	30 Lafayette Ave., Brooklyn, N.Y. 11217	Lukas Foss
Calgary Philharmonic	830 Ninth Ave., S.W., Calgary, Alberta, Can.	Maurice Handford
Cedar Rapids Symphony	P.O. Box 1903, Cedar Rapids, Iowa 52406	Richard D. Williams
Charlotte Symphony	827 F. Blvd., Charlotte, N.C. 28203	Jacques Brourman
Chattanooga Symphony	730 Cherry St., Chattanooga, Tenn. 37402	Richard Cormier
Clarion Music Soc.	415 Lexington Ave., New York, N.Y. 10017	Newell Jenkins
Colorado Springs Symphony	P.O. Box 1692, Colorado Springs, Colo. 80901	Charles Ansbacher
Columbus Symphony	200 East Town St., Columbus, Ohio 43215	Evan Whallon
Corpus Christi Symphony	P.O. Box 495, Corpus Christi, Tex. 78403	Maurice Peress
Dayton Philharmonic	Sheraton-Dayton Hotel, Dayton, Ohio 45402	Paul Katz
Duluth Symphony	401 Lonsdale Bldg., Duluth, Minn. 55802	Joseph Hawthorne
Eastern Music Festival	712 Summit Ave., Greensboro, N.C. 27405	Sheldon Morgenstern
Edmonton Symphony	P.O. Box 4232, Edmonton, Alberta, Can.	Pierre Hetu
Erie Philharmonic	720 G. Daniel Baldwin Bldg., Erie, Pa. 16501	Harold Bauer
Evansville Philharmonic	P.O. Box 84, Evansville, Ind. 47706	Minas Christian
Flint Symphony	1025 E. Kearsley St., Flint, Mich. 48502	William Byrd
Florida Gulf Coast Symphony	P.O. Box 569, St. Petersburg, Fla. 33731	Irwin Hoffman
Florida Symphony	P.O. Box 782, Orlando, Fla. 32802	Pavle Despalj
Florida West Coast Symphony	P.O. Box 1107, Sarasota, Fla. 33578	Paul C. Wolfe
Fort Lauderdale Symphony	450 E. Las Olas Blvd., Fort Lauderdale, Fla. 33301	Emerson Buckley

Fort Wayne Philharmonic	927 S. Harrison, Fort Wayne, Ind. 46802	Thomas Briccetti
Fort Worth Symphony	3505 W. Lancaster, Ft. Worth, Tex. 76107	John Giordano
Fresno Philharmonic	1362 N. Fresno St., Fresno, Calif. 93703	Guy Taylor
Glendale Symphony	121 W. Lexington Dr., Glendale, Calif. 91203	Carmen Dragon
Grand Rapids Symphony	Auditorium Center, Grand Rapids, Mich. 49502	Theo Alcantar
Hamilton Philharmonic	P.O. Box 514, Hamilton, Ont. Can.	Boris Brott
Hartford Symphony	15 Lewis St., Hartford, Conn. 06103	Arthur Winograd
Honolulu Symphony	1000 Bishop St., Honolulu, Hawaii 96813	Robt. LaMarchina
Hudson Valley Philharmonic	P.O. Box 191, Poughkeepsie, N.Y. 12602	Claude Monteux
Jackson Symphony	P.O. Box 4584, Jackson, Miss. 39216	Lewis Dalvit
Jacksonville Symphony	46 W. Duval St., Jacksonville, Fla. 32202	Willis Page
Kalamazoo Symphony	426 S. Park St., Kalamazoo, Mich. 49007	Pierre Hetu
Knoxville Symphony	618 Gay St., Knoxville, Tenn. 37902	Arpod Joo
Las Vegas Symphony	P.O. Box 15209, Las Vegas, Nev. 89114	Arthur Lief
Little Orchestra Soc.	1860 Broadway, New York, N.Y. 10023	Thomas Scherman
Louisville Orchestra	333 W. Broadway, Louisville, Ky. 40202	Jorge Mester
Madison Symphony	211 N. Carroll St., Madison, Wis. 53703	Roland Johnson
Memphis Symphony	1503 Monroe, Memphis, Tenn. 38104	Vincent DeFrank
Miami Beach Symphony	420 Lincoln Rd. Mall, Miami Beach, Fla. 33139	Barnet Breeskin
Miami Philharmonic	174 Flagler St., Miami, Fla. 33131	Alain Lombard
Midland Odessa Sym. & Chorale	P.O. Box 6266, Air Terminal Stn., Midland, Tex. 79701	Robert Krels
Nashville Symphony	1805 West End Ave., Nashville, Tenn. 37203	Thor Johnson
New Haven Symphony	254 College St., New Haven, Conn. 06510	Frank Brieff
New Jersey Symphony	1020 Broad St., Newark, N.J. 07102	Henry Lewis
New World, Symphony of the	250 W. 57th St., New York, N.Y. 10019	Everett Lee
Norfolk Symphony	P.O. Box 26, Norfolk, Va. 23501	Russell Stanger
North Carolina Symphony	P.O. Box 2508, UNC, Chapel Hill, N.C. 27514	John Gosling
Oakland Symphony	Latham Sq. Bldg., Oakland, Calif. 94612	Harold Farberman
Oklahoma City Symphony	Civic Center Music Hall, Oklahoma City, Okla. 73102	Ray E. Luke
Omaha Symphony	3929 Harney, Omaha, Neb. 68131	Yuri Krasnapolsky
Orchestra Da Camera	200 Emory Rd., Mineola, N.Y. 11501	
Oregon Symphony	320 S. W. Stark St., Portland, Ore. 97204	Lawrence Smith
Pasadena Symphony	301 E. Colorado Blvd., Pasadena, Cal. 91101	Daniel Lewis
Phoenix Symphony	6328 N. 7th St., Phoenix, Ariz. 85014	Eduardo Mata
Portland Symphony	30 Myrtle St., Portland, Me. 04111	Paul Vermel
Quebec Symphony	1115 Rue Claire Fontaine, Que., Can	Pierre Dervaux
Rhode Island Philharmonic	The Arcade, Providence, R.I. 02903.	Francis Madeira
Richmond Symphony	112 E. Franklin St., Richmond, Va. 23219	Jacques Houtmann
Sacramento Symphony	451 Parkfair Dr., Sacramento, Calif. 95825	Harry Newstone
San Diego Symphony	P.O. Box 3175, San Diego, Calif. 92103	Peter Eros
San Jose Symphony	St. Claire Hotel, San Jose, Calif. 95113	George Cleve
Santa Barbara Symphony	210 E. Figueroa, Santa Barbara, Calif. 93101	Ronald Ondrejka
Savannah Symphony	P.O. Box 9505, Savannah, Ga. 31402	Michael Charry
Shreveport Symphony	P.O. Box 4057, Shreveport, La. 71104	John Shenaut
Spokane Symphony	West 905 Riverside, Spokane, Wash. 99201	Donald Thulean
Springfield Symphony	49 Chestnut St., Springfield, Mass. 01103	Robert Gutter
Syracuse Symphony	113 E. Onondaga St., Syracuse, N.Y. 13202	Frederik Prausnitz
Toledo Orchestra	One Stranahan Sq., Toledo, Ohio 43604	Serge Fournier
Tri-City Symphony	P.O. Box 67, Davenport, Iowa 52801	James Dixon
Tucson Symphony	8 Paseo Redondo, Tucson, Ariz. 85705	Gregory Millar
Tulsa Philharmonic	2210 S. Main, Tulsa, Okla. 74114	Skitch Henderson
Vancouver Symphony	566 Hornby St., Vancouver 2, B.C., Can.	Kazuyoshi Akiyama
Vermont Symphony	P.O. Box 548, Middlebury, Vt. 05753	Alan Carter
Victoria Symphony	748 Johnson St., Victoria, B.C., Can.	Lazlo Gati
Wichita Symphony	225 W. Douglas, Wichita, Kan. 67202	Francois Huybrechts
Winnipeg Symphony	555 Main St., Winnipeg 2, Manitoba, Can.	Piero Gamba
Winston-Salem Symphony	610 Coliseum Dr., Winston-Salem, N.C. 27106	John Iuele
Youngstown Symphony	260 West Federal St., Youngstown, Ohio 44503	Franz Bibo

Chamber Orchestras

Los Angeles Chamber Orch.	1017 N. LaCienega Blvd., Los Angeles, Calif., 90069	Neville Marriner
St. Paul Chamber Orch.	109 W. 5th St., St. Paul, Minn. 55102	Leopold Sipe

1973 Opera Survey of the United States and Canada

Compiled from the Central Opera Service Directory of Opera Companies and Workshops in the U.S. and Canada. The directory is edited by Mrs. Maria F. Rich, Central Opera Service, Lincoln Center, New York, N.Y. 10023.

Atlanta Chamber Opera Society: F. Wolfe, Dir.

Augusta, Ga. Opera Co.: B. E. Evans, Gen. Mgr.

Baltimore Opera Co.: R. J. Collinge, Gen. Mgr.

Binghamton (N.Y.) Tri-Cities Opera Workshop, Inc.: G. E. Ravert, Bus. Mgr.

Birmingham Civic Opera Assn.: Mrs. J. V. Kidd, V-Pres.

Boston, Opera Company of: Miss Sarah Caldwell, Dir.

Boston Associate Artists Opera Co. of New England: E. Triplett, Gen. Dir.

Canadian Opera Company (Toronto): H. Geiger-Torel, Gen. Dir.

Central City, Colo., Opera Festival (summer): R. F. Lotitio, Exec. Mgr.

Charlotte Opera Assn.: C. Rosenkrans, Mus. Dir.

Chattanooga Opera Assn.: M. Allan, Mgr.

Chautauqua (N.Y.) Opera Assn.: L. Treash, Dir.

Chicago, Lyric Opera of: Miss Carol Fox, Gen. Mgr.

Cincinnati Summer Opera Assn.: J. deBlasis, Gen. Mgr.

Colorado Springs Opera Assn.: Baird & Jenkins, Co. Dirs.

Connecticut Opera Assn. (Hartford): F. Pandolfi, Exec. Dir.

Dallas Civic Opera Co.: Lawrence Kelly, Gen. Mgr.

Dayton Opera Assn.: L. Freedman, Gen. Dir.

Detroit Mich. Opera Theatre: D. DiChiera, Gen. Dir.

Detroit Piccolo Opera Company: M. Gordon, Dir.

Edmonton Opera Assn.: L. J. Moore, Gen. Mgr.

Florida Symphony, Opera Gala Guild, (Orlando): R. Landers, Music Dir.

Fort Worth Opera Assn.: Rudolf Kruger, Gen.

Mgr. & Music Dir.
Fresno Opera Assn.: N. Iacovetti, Music Dir.
Goldovsky Opera Theatre (New York) touring: E. Alley, Gen. Mgr.
Hawaii Opera Theatre of the Honolulu Symphony Soc.: R. La Marchina, Music Dir.
Houston Grand Opera Assn.: R. D. Gockley, Dir.
Jacksonville Opera Repertory Group: Miss A. Smith, Mng. Dir.
John F. Kennedy Center for the Performing Arts (Wash., D.C.): Julius Rudel, Music Dir.
Kansas City, Mo., Lyric Theater: R. Petterson, Dir.
Kentucky Opera Assn. (Louisville): M. Bomhard, Dir.
Lake George Opera Festival Assn. (Glen Falls): D. Lloyd, Gen. Dir.
Los Angeles Guild Opera Co.: J. Dahl, Mus. Dir.
Manhattan, Light Opera of, (New York).
Manitoba Opera Assn. (Winnipeg): I. Guttman, Art Dir.
Memphis Opera Theatre: G. Osborne, Dir.
Miami, Opera Guild of Greater: E. Buckley, Cond.
Milwaukee Florentine Opera Co.: J. Anello, Dir.
Minneapolis Minn. Opera Co.; J. Ludwig, Gen. Mgr.
Mississippi Opera Assn. (Jackson): Mrs. J. White, Prod. Dir.
Mobile Opera Guild: J. Yestadt, Gen. Mgr. & Mus. Dir.
Montreal Canadian Broadcasting Co., TV Opera Dept.: M. Charpentier
Music Center Opera Assn. (Los Angeles).
National Educational TV, NET Opera Theater (N.Y.): P. H. Adler, Music Dir.
Nevada Opera Co. (Reno): T. Puffer, Dir.
New Jersey, Opera Theatre of (Newark): A. Sillipigni, Dir.
New Orleans Opera House Assn.: A. Cosenza, Gen. Dir.
New York City Metropolitan Opera Assn.: S. Chapin, Gen. Mgr.
New York City Metropolitan Opera Studio (junior Co.): W. Mix, Dir.
New York City Opera Co.: Julius Rudel, Gen. Dir.
New York, Opera Orchestra of: Miss E. Queler, Dir.
Omaha Opera Company: L. Kopp, Music Dir.
Opera/South (Jackson, Miss.): D. Ardoyno, Mgr.
Ottawa National Arts Centre: M. Bernardi, Music Dir.
Palm Beaches, Civic Opera of the: P. Csonka, Music Dir.
Pennsylvania Opera Co. (Chester): K. Price, Mgr.
Philadelphia Grand Opera Co.: M. Leon, Pres.
Philadelphia Lyric Opera: I. Strasfogel, Art Dir.
Pittsburgh Opera: R. Karp, Gen. Dir.
Portland, Ore., Opera Assn.: S. Minde, Gen. Dir.
Providence, Artists Internationale: M. Ruffino, Art Dir.
L'Opèra du Quèbec, G. Beauline, Dir.
Opera Theatre of Rochester: Mrs. R. Rosenberg, Gen. Mgr. & Prod.
Raleigh, Natl. Opera Co. (touring): Y. Fletcher, Dir.
St. Paul Opera Assn. (summer): G. Schaefer, Gen. Mgr.
San Antonio Grand Opera Festival & Symphony: V. Alessandro, Music Dir.
San Carlo Opera of Florida (Tampa): Miss N. Russo, Dir.
San Diego Opera: Walter Herbert, Gen. Dir.
San Francisco Opera Assn.: Kurt Adler, Gen. Dir.
San Francisco Spring Opera Theater: Kurt Herbert, Gen. Dir.
San Francisco Western Opera Theater (junior touring): E. Corn, Mgr.
Santa Fe Opera Assn. of New Mexico (summer): J. Crosby, Gen. Dir.
Seattle Opera Assn.: Glynn Ross, Gen. Dir.
Toledo Opera Assn.: L. Freedman, Gen. Dir.
Toronto Canadian Broadcasting Co., TV Opera Dept.: J. Roberts, Supervisor.
Tulsa Opera: Mrs. J. Turner, Mgr.
Tucson Opera Co.: R. Miller, Art Dir.
Vancouver Opera Assn.: B. Hanson, Gen. Mgr.
Washington, Opera Society of: Ian Strasfogel, Gen. Dir.
West Virginia Opera Theatre (Charleston): D. Riggio, Music Dir.
Wolf Trap Company, Vienna, Va. (summer): F. Rizzo, Exec. Dir.

Summer Opera At Festivals in U.S. and Canada

Alaska—Alaska Festival of Music, Anchorage: June.
Ark.—Inspiration Point Fine Arts Colony, Eureka Springs: June-July.
Calif.—Cabrillo Music Festival, Aptos: Aug. Carmel Bach Festival, Carmel: July. Claremont Music Festival: June-Aug. Hollywood Bowl Assn., Los Angeles: July-Aug. Lyric Opera of Orange County, Laguna Beach: July. Music at the Vineyards, Saratoga: July-Aug. Ojai Festival. Redlands Bowl Summer Music Festival: July-Aug.
Colo.—Aspen Music Festival, Aspen: July-Aug. Central City Opera Festival, Central City: June-July. Colorado Opera Festival, Colorado Springs: June-July.
Fla.—Pensacola Jr. College Summer Opera: July-Aug.
Ill.—Grant Park Concerts, Chicago: June-Aug. Mississippi River Festival, Edwardsville: July-Aug. Ravinia Festival, Highland Park: July-Aug.
Ind.—Indiana University, Bloomington: July.
Ky.—Univ. of Ky. Opera Workshop, Lex. July-Aug.
Maine—Bar Harbor Festival, Bar Harbor: July-Aug. Quisiana, Center Lovell: June-Sept. Ram Island Arts Center, Portland: Aug.
Md.—Hartford Opera Theatre, Bel Air: June-Sept. Merriweather Post Pavilion of Music, Columbia: July-Aug.
Mass.—Berkshire Music Festival, Lenox: July-Aug.
Lenox Arts Center, Lenox. Tangelwood-Music Theatre Project, Lenox.
Mich.—Ann Arbor May Festival: May. Meadowbrook Music Festival, Rochester: July-Aug. National Music Camp, Interlochen: July-Aug. Univ. of Mich. School of Music Opera, Ann Arbor: July.
Minn.—St. Paul Opera Assn., St. Paul: June-July.
Nev.—Nevada Opera Co., Reno: July-Aug.
N.H.—Concerts at Dartmouth, Hanover: July-Aug. New Hampshire Music Festival, Center Harbor: July-Aug. White Mountain Festival, Franconia: July-Aug.
N.J.—Garden State Arts Center, Holmdel: June-Sept.
N.M.—Opera Assn. of N.M., Santa Fe; July-Aug.
N.Y.—Caramoor Festival, Katonah: June-July. Chautauqua Opera Assn., Chautauqua: July-Aug. Lake George Opera Festival, Glen Falls: July-Aug. Light Opera of Manhattan: June-Sept. Long Island Opera Showcase, Franklin Square: July. Metropolitan Opera Assn., "Concerts in the Park," New York: June-July. Mostly Mozart Festival, New York: July-Aug. Naumburg Concerts, New York: June-Aug. Opera Company of Nassau: July-Aug. Opera Under the Stars, Rochester: July. Saratoga Performing Arts Center, Saratoga Springs: June-Aug.
N.C.—Brevard Music Center Opera Co., Brevard: N.C. Summer Festival, Winston-Salem: July-Aug.

Ohio—Blossom Music Festival, Cuyahoga Falls: June-Aug. Briar Knoll Festival Opera Co., Loveland: June-July. Cincinnati Summer Opera, Cincinnati: July. Cincinnati Symphony-May Festival. Oberlin College Music Theatre, Oberlin: July-Aug.
Ore.—Portland Opera Assn., Portland: July.
Pa.—Ephrata Cloisters Assn., Ephrata: June-Aug. Robin Hood Dell, Philadelphia: June-July. Pennsylvania Opera Festival, Pittsburgh: Aug. Temple Music Festival and Institute, Ambler: July-Aug.
R.I.—Newport Music Festival, Newport: July-Aug.
Tex.—Houston Grand Opera Assn., "Opera in the Park," Houston: May. "Texas" Musical Drama, Canyon: June-Oct.
Va.—Department of Recreation and Parks, Rich-mond: Aug. Wolf Trap Foundation and Company, Vienna: June-Sept.
Wash.—Seattle Gilbert and Sullivan Society, Seattle: July.
W. Va.—Oglebay Institute, Wheeling: Aug.
Wis.—Music Under the Stars, Florentine Opera, Milwaukee: Aug. Peninsula Music Festival, Fish Creek: Aug. Skylight Comic Opera Co., Milwaukee: July-Sept.
Wyo.—Grand Teton Music Festival, Jackson Hole: July-Aug.
Canada—Banff Festival of the Arts, Alberta: Aug. Festival Canada, Nat'l Arts Centre, Ottawa: July. Guelph Spring Festival, Guelph, Ontario: May. Stratford Festival, Stratford: July-Aug.
Puerto Rico—Festival Casals, San Juan: June.

RECORDINGS

Disc and Tape Sales Zoom toward $2 Billion a Year

U.S. recording industry sales, including both phonograph records and pre-recorded tapes, headed for the $2 billion mark in 1973. Total sales in 1972 were $1.914 billion, up 10% from $1.744 in 1971, as reported by the Recording Industry Assn. of America.

Long-play albums went up 11% to $1.203 billion; singles rose 9% to $180,000,000; 8-track cartridges were up 10% to $425,000,000; pre-recorded cassettes rose 6% to $102,000,000; reel-to-reel tapes declined 33% to $8,000,000; sales of quadraphonic tapes, reported for the first time, were $6,000,000.

From Jan. 1, 1973, through Sept. 5, 1973, the RIAA issued 118 Gold Recording Awards. These awards are made in 2 categories: for single discs which RIAA certifies as having sold 1,000,000 copies, and for long-play albums and tape equivalents it certifies as having $1,000,000 in sales at the manufacturer's level. The awards for 12 months follow:

Artists and Recording Titles

(A) Album. (S) Single.

September 1972

The O'Jays: Back Stabbers. (S)
Roberta Flack & Donny Hathaway: Where Is the Love. (S)
Emerson, Lake & Palmer: Trilogy. (A)
Humble Pie: Smokin' (A)
Curtis Mayfield: Super Fly. (A)
Bill Withers: Still Bill. (A)
Ike & Tina Turner: What You Hear Is What You Get. (A)
The Hollies: Long Cool Woman in a Black Dress. (S)
Chuck Berry: My Ding-a-Ling. (S)
James Brown: Get on the Good Foot. (S)
Leon Russell: Carney. (A)
The Main Ingredient: Everybody Plays the Fool. (S)
Mac Davis: Baby Don't Get Hooked on Me. (S)
George Carlin: FM & AM. (A)

October 1972

Three Dog Night: Black and White. (S)
Grand Funk Railroad: Phoenix. (A)
Cat Stevens: Catch Bull At Four. (A)
Bill Withers: Use Me. (S)
Kris Kristofferson: The Silver Tongued Devil and I. (A)
Charley Pride: The Best of Carley Pride. (A)
Freddie Hart: Easy Loving. (A)
Chuck Berry: The London Chuck Berry Session. (A)
Elvis Presley: Burning Love. (S)
Uriah Heep: Demons and Wizards. (A)
The Spinners: I'll Be Around. (S)
Yes: Close to the Edge. (A)
Curtis Mayfield: Freddie's Dead (Theme from Super Fly). (S)

November 1972

Carole King: Rhymes & Reasons. (A)
Merle Haggard: The Best of Merle Haggard. (A)
The Band: Rock of Ages. (A)
Deep Purple: Machine Head. (A)
Raspberries: Go All the Way. (S)
Black Sabbath: Black Sabbath—Vol. IV. (A)
Alice Cooper: Love It to Death. (A)
Jethro Tull: Stand Up. (A)
Jethro Tull: Living in the Past. (A)
Santana: Caravanserai. (A)
Chicago: Saturday in the Park. (S)
Johnny Nash: I Can See Clearly Now. (S)
Bread: Guitar Man. (A)

Harold Melvin & the Blue Notes: If You Don't Know Me by Now. (S)
Moody Blues: Seventh Sojourn. (A)
Rick Nelson: Garden Party. (S)
It's a Beautiful Day: It's a Beautiful Day. (A)
Lobo: I'd Love You to Want Me. (S)
Al Green: I'm Still in Love with You. (A)

December 1972

Billy Paul: Me and Mrs. Jones. (S)
Soundtrack: Chilling, Thrilling Sounds of the Haunted House. (A)
Carly Simon: No Secrets. (S)
5th Dimension: The 5th Dimension Greatest Hits on Earth. (A)
Original Cast: Godspell. (A)
The Stylistics: I'm Stone in Love with You. (S)
Partridge Family: The Partridge Family at Home with Their Greatest Hits. (A)
London Symphony Orch. and Chamber Choir with Guest Soloists: Tommy. (A)
War: The World Is a Ghetto. (A)
Seals & Crofts: Summer Breeze. (A)
Grateful Dead: Europe '72. (A)
Al Green: You Ought to Be with Me. (S)
James Taylor: One Man Dog. (A)
America: Homecoming. (A)
Moody Blues: Nights in White Satin. (S)
Helen Reddy: I Am Woman. (S)
Peter Nero: Summer of '42. (A)
Duane Allman: An Anthology. (A)
Bread: Manna. (A)
Bread: On the Waters. (A)
Joni Mitchell: For the Roses. (A)
Neil Diamond: Hot August Night. (A)
Donny Osmond: Portrait of Donny. (A)
The Osmonds: The Osmonds 'Live'. (A)
Nilsson: Son of Schmilsson. (A)
John Denver: Rocky Mountain High. (A)

January 1973

Jefferson Airplane: Long John Silver. (A)
Donna Fargo: Funny Face. (S)
Carly Simon: You're So Vain. (S)
Albert Hammond: It Never Rains in Southern California. (S)
Rolling Stones: More Hot Rocks (Big Hits and Fazed Cookies). (A)
Curtis Mayfield: Super Fly. (S)
Uriah Heep: The Magician's Birthday. (A)
The Osmonds: Crazy Horses. (A)

Donny Osmond: Too Young. (A)
Creedence Clearwater Revival: Creedence Gold. (A)
John Rivers: Rockin' Pneumonia & the Boogie Woogie Flu. (S)
Donna Fargo: The Happiest Girl in the Whole U.S.A. (A)

February 1973

Loggins & Messina: Loggins & Messina. (A)
Elton John: Crocodile Rock. (S)
Brighter Side of Darkness: Love Jones. (S)
The O'Jays: Love Train. (S)
Billy Paul: 360 Degrees of Billy Paul. (A)
Elton John: Don't Shoot Me I'm Only the Piano Player. (A)
Elvis Presley: World Wide 50 Gold Award Hits, Vol. I. (A)
Elvis Presley: Elvis—Aloha from Hawaii Via Satellite. (A)
Barbra Streisand: Live Concert at the Forum. (A)
The Spinners: Could It Be I'm Falling in Love. (S)
Bobby Womack & Peace: Harry Hippie. (S)
The Stylistics: The Stylistics. (A)
Roberta Flack: Killing Me Softly With His Songs. (S)

March 1973

War: The World Is a Ghetto. (S)
War: Cisco Kid. (S)
Three Dog Night: Around the World with Three Dog Night. (A)
Helen Reddy: I Am Woman. (A)
Traffic: Shoot Out at the Fantasy Factory. (A)
Loggins & Messina: Your Mama Don't Dance. (S)
Eric Weissberg: Dueling Banjos. (S)
Soundtrack from "Deliverance" as performed by Eric Weissberg & Steve Mandel: Dueling Banjos. (A)
Mac Davis: Baby Don't Get Hooked on Me. (A)
Various Artists: Wattstax—The Living Word (A)
Edward Bear: Last Song. (S)
Gilbert O'Sullivan: Clair. (S)
Derek & the Dominos: In Concert. (A)
Alice Cooper: Billion Dollar Babies. (A)
Kenny Rogers & the First Edition: Kenny Rogers & The First Edition Greatest Hits. (A)

April 1973

Four Tops: Ain't No Woman. (S)
Vicki Lawrence: The Night the Lights Went Out in Georgia. (S)
Dawn: Tie a Yellow Ribbon Round the Old Oak Tree. (S)
Dr. Hook & The Medicine Show: The Cover of Rolling Stone. (S)
The Stylistics: Break Up to Make Up. (S)
Led Zeppelin: House of the Holy. (A)
Bread: The Best of Bread. (A)
Deep Purple: Who Do We Think We Are! (A)
The Beatles: The Beatles 1962-1966. (A)
The Beatles: The Beatles 1966-1970. (A)
Pink Floyd: The Dark Side of the Moon. (A)
Al Green: Call Me (Come Back Home). (S)
Bette Midler: The Divine Miss M. (A)
The Sweet: Little Willy. (S)
Edgar Winter: They Only Come Out at Night. (A)

May 1973

The O'Jays: Back Stabbers. (A)
Kenny Loggins with Jim Messina: Sittin' In. (A)
Ohio Players: Funky Worm. (S)
Yes: Yessongs. (A)
Yes: The Yes Album. (A)

The Carpenters: Sing. (S)
Sylvia: Pillow Talk. (S)
Independents: Leaving Me. (S)
The Nitty Gritty Dirt Band: William E. McEuen Presents Will the Circle Be Unbroken. (A)
Steely Dan: Can't Buy A Thrill. (A)
Deep Purple: Made in Japan. (A)

June 1973

George Harrison: Living in the Material World. (A)
Curtis Mayfield: Curtis. (A)
Curtis Mayfield: Back to the World. (A)
Barry White: I'm Gonna Love You Just a Little More Baby. (S)
The Carpenters: Now & Then. (A)
George Carlin: Class Clown. (A)
Charley Pride: The Sensational Charley Pride. (A)
Charley Pride: From Me To You. (A)
Charley Pride: The Country Way. (A)
The Stylistics: Round 2. (A)
Paul Simon: There Goes Rhymin' Simon. (A)
Edgar Winter Group: Frankenstein. (S)
Focus: Moving Waves. (A)
Seals & Crofts: Diamond Girl. (A)
Carole King: Fantasy. (A)
Billy Preston: Will It Go Round in Circles. (S)
Leon Russel: Leon 'Live'. (A)
Elvis Presley: Elvis—That's the Way It Is. (A)

July 1973

Isaac Hayes: Live at the Sahara Tahoe. (A)
Clint Holmes: Playground in My Mind. (S)
Doobie Brothers: The Captain and Me. (A)
Dobie Gray: Drift Away. (S)
Paul McCartney & Wings: My Love. (S)
Al Green: Call Me. (A)
Spinners: One of a Kind (Love Affair). (S)
Spinners: Spinners. (A)
Chicago: Chicago VI. (A)
Bloodstone: Natural High. (S)
Original Artists: Dick Clark/20 Years of Rock 'N Roll. (A)
Fred Wesley & The JB's: Doin' It to Death. (S)
Three Dog Night: Shambala. (S)
Jim Croce: Bad Bad Leroy Brown. (S)
Jethro Tull: A Passion Play. (A)
The Dells: Give Your Baby a Standing Ovation. (S)

August 1973

Cat Stevens: Foreigner. (A)
Carpenters: Yesterday Once More. (S)
Maureen McGovern: The Morning After. (S)
Original Soundtrack: Cabaret. (A)
Sly & The Family Stone: Fresh. (A)
Grand Funk Railroad: We're an American Band. (A)
Allman Bros. Band: Brothers and Sisters. (A)
Doobie Brothers: Toulouse Street. (A)
Stories: Brother Louie. (S)
Roberta Flack: Killing Me Softly. (A)
John Denver: Farewell Andromeda. (A)
Bobby Pickett: Monster Mash. (3)
Al Green: Here I Am (Come and Take Me). (S)
Deep Purple: Smoke on the Water. (S)
Helen Reddy: Delta Dawn. (S)
Paul McCartney & Wings: Live and Let Die. (S)

September 1973

Charlie Rich: Behind Closed Doors. (S)
Original Soundtrack: Jesus Christ Superstar. (A)
Carly Simon: Anticipation. (A)

Grammy Awards

On March 3, 1973, the Grammy Awards for what were judged the best efforts of the recording industry in 1972 were announced by the National Academy of Recording Arts and Sciences. The Grammys are golden statuettes of early gramophones. The categories and winners were:

Record of the Year and Song of the Year: The First Time Ever I Saw Your Face, Roberta Flack. Producer: Joel Dorn. Songwriter: Ewan MacColl.

Album of the Year: Concert for Bangladesh, George Harrison and Friends. Producers: George Harrison, Phil Spector.

Best New Artists of the Year: America.

Best Instrumental Arrangement: Theme from The French Connection. Arranger: Don Ellis.

Best Arrangement Accompanying Vocalist: What Are You Doing the Rest of Your Life, Sarah Vaughn. Arranger: Michel Legrand.

Best Engineered Recording (non-classical): Moods, Neil Diamond. Engineer: Armin Steiner.

Best Album Cover: The Siegel-Schwall Band, Siegel-Schwall Band. Art Director: Acy Lehman. Artist: Harvey Dinnerstein.

Best Album Notes: Tom T. Hall's Greatest Hits, Tom T. Hall. Annotator: Tom T. Hall.

Best Jazz Performance by a Soloist: Alone at Last, Gary Burton.

Best Jazz Performance by a Group: First Light, Freddie Hubbard.

Best Jazz Performance by a Big Band: Togo Brava Suite, Duke Ellington.

Best Pop Vocal Performance, Female: I Am Woman, Helen Reddy.

Best Pop Vocal Performance, Male: Without You, Nilsson.

Best Pop Vocal Performance by a Duo, Group or Chorus: Where Is the Love, Roberta Flack, Donny Hathaway.

Best Pop Instrumental Performance by an Instrumental Performer: Outa-Space, Billy Preston.

Best Pop Instrumental Performance by an Arranger, Composer, Orchestra and/or Choral Leader: Black Moses, Isaac Hayes.

Best Rhythm and Blues Vocal Performance, Female: Young, Gifted and Black, Aretha Franklin.

Best Rhythm and Blues Performance, Male: Me & Mrs. Jones, Billy Paul.

Best Rhythm and Blues Vocal Performance by a Duo, Group or Chorus; Best Rhythm and Blues Instrumental Performance; Best Rhythm and Blues Song: Papa Was a Rolling Stone, The Temptations. Songwriters: Barrett Strong, Norman Whitfield.

Best Soul Gospel Performance: Amazing Grace, Aretha Franklin.

Best Country Vocal Performance, Female: Happiest Girl in the Whole USA, Donna Fargo.

Best Country Performance, Male: Charley Pride Sings Heart Songs, Charley Pride.

Best Country Vocal Performance by a Duo or Group: Class of '57, The Statler Bros.

Best Country Instrumental Performance: Charlie McCoy/The Real McCoy, Charlie McCoy.

Best Country Song: Kiss an Angel Good Mornin'. Songwriter: Ben Peters.

Best Inspirational Performance (non-classical): He Touched Me, Elvis Presley.

Best Gospel Performance (other than soul): L-O-V-E, Blackwood Bros.

Best Ethnic or Traditional Recording: The London Muddy Waters Session, Muddy Waters.

Best Recording for Children: The Electric Company, Lee Chamberlin, Bill Cosby, Rita Moreno. Project Director: Christopher Cerf. Producer: Joe Raposo.

Best Comedy Recording: FM & AM, George Carlin.

Best Spoken Word Recording: Lenny. Producer: Bruce Botnick.

Best Instrumental Composition: Brian's Song. Composer: Michel Legrand.

Best Original Score for Motion Picture or TV Special: The Godfather. Composer: Nino Rota.

Best Score from an Original Cast Show Album: Don't Bother Me, I Can't Cope. Composer: Micki Grant. Producer: Jerry Ragavoy.

Album of the Year (classical), Best Choral Performance, Best Engineered Recording (classical), (Grammys to artists, producer, conductor, engineers): Mahler's Symphony No. 8 in E Flat Major, Georg Solti conducting Chicago Symphony Orchestra, Vienna Boys Choir, Vienna State Opera Chorus, Vienna Singverein Chorus and Soloists. Producer: David Harvey. Engineers: Gordon Parry, Kenneth Wilkinson.

Best Classical Performance—Orchestra (conductor's award): Mahler Symphony No. 7 in E Minor, Chicago Symphony Orchestra. Conductor: Georg Solti.

Best Opera Recording (conductor's and producer's awards): Berlioz's Benvenuto Cellini, BBC Symphony, Chorus of Covent Garden. Conductor: Colin Davis. Producer: Erik Smith.

Best Chamber Music Performance: Julian and John, Julian Bream and John Williams.

Best Classical Performance, Instrumental Soloist: Horowitz Plays Chopin, Vladimir Horowitz.

Best Classical Vocal Soloist Performance: Brahms' Die Schone Magelone, Dietrich Fischer-Dieskau.

Best Album Notes (classical): Vaughan Williams Symphony No. 2. Annotator: James Lyons.

Best Selling Books of 1972-1973

Listed according to frequency of citation in best-seller reports between Sept. 3, 1972 and Sept. 2, 1973

Fiction

1. *Jonathan Livingston Seagull, Richard Bach
2. *The Odessa File, Frederick Forsyth
3. *August 1914, Alexander Solzhenitsyn
4. Once is Not Enough, Jacqueline Susann
5. *Semi-Tough, Dan Jenkins
6. Breakfast of Champions, Kurt Vonnegut, Jr.
7. *The Winds of War, Herman Wouk
8. Green Darkness, Anya Seton
9. The Persian Boy, Mary Renault
10. The Camerons, Robert Crichton
11. *Captains and the Kings, Taylor Caldwell
12. The Taking of Pelham One Two Three, John Godey
13. The Matlock Paper, Robert Ludlum
14. Facing the Lions, Tom Wicker
15. On the Night of the Seventh Moon, Victoria Holt
16. Dark Horse, Fletcher Knebel
17. Evening in Byzantium, Irwin Shaw
18. The Hollow Hills, Mary Stewart
19. Harvest Home, Thomas Tryon
20. *My Name is Asher Lev, Chaim Potok
21. The Sunlight Dialogues, John Gardner
22. *The Word, Irving Wallace
23. To Serve Them All My Days, R. F. Delderfield
24. The Billion Dollar Sure Thing, Paul Erdman
25. Law and Order, Dorothy Uhnak

* One of the 10 best-sellers in calendar 1972 according to Publishers' Weekly.

General

1. *I'm O.K., Your're O.K., Thomas Harris
2. *Dr. Atkins' Diet Revolution, Robert C. Atkins
3. The Best and the Brightest, David Halberstam
4. The Joy of Sex, Alex Comfort
5. *The Peter Prescription, Laurence J. Peter
6. *Harry S. Truman, Margaret Truman
7. Supermoney, Adam Smith
8. Laughing All the Way, Barbara Howar
9. *Open Marriage, Nena and George O'Neill
10. Eleanor: The Years Alone, Joseph P. Lash
11. The Implosion Conspiracy, Louis Nizer
12. O Jerusalem!, Larry Collins and Dominique LaPierre
13. Sybil, Flora R. Schreiber
14. "Johnny We Hardly Knew Ye", Kenneth P. O'Donnell and David F. Powers
15. Hour of Gold, Hour of Lead, Anne Morrow Lindbergh
16. *Journey to Ixtlan, Carlos Castaneda
17. Weight Watchers Program Cookbook, Jean Nidetch
18. All Creatures Great and Small, James Herriot
19. The Superlawyers, Joseph C. Goulden
20. My Young Years, Arthur Rubinstein

Movies of the Year (Oct. 1, 1972, to Oct. 1, 1973)
Selected and Rated by the New York Daily News Film Critics

Listed below, alphabetically, are films rated by the New York Daily News star system, ★★★★ is for excellent, ★★★½ very good, ★★★ good, ★★½ mediocre, ★★ fair, ★½ poor, ★ very poor, 0★'s not worth rating.

Kathleen Carroll, N.Y. Daily News Movie Editor and Critic

Movie	Star Rating	Stars	Director
Across 110th Street	★★★	Anthony Quinn, Yaphet Kotto	Barry Shear
American Graffiti	★★★★	Richard Dreyfuss, Ronny Howard	George Lucas
Avanti!	★★½	Jack Lemon, Juliet Mills	Billy Wilder
Bad Company	★★★	Jeff Bridges, Barry Brown	Robert Benton
Badge 373	★★½	Robert Duvall, Verna Bloom	Howard W. Koch
Bang the Drum Slowly	★★★★	Robert De Niro, Michael Moriarty	John Hancock
Blume in Love	★★½	George Segal, Susan Anspach	Paul Mazursky
Charlotte's Web	★★★½	animated cartoon	Charles Nichols
Child's Play	★★★½	James Mason, Robert Preston	Sidney Lumet
Class of '44	★★★	Gary Grimes, Jerry Houser	Paul Bogart
Cries and Whispers	★★★★	Harriet Andersson, Ingrid Thulin	Ingmar Bergman
Cleopatra Jones	★★½	Tamara Dobson, Shelley Winters	Jack Starrett
Cops and Robbers	★★★	Cliff Gorman, Joe Bologna	Aram Avakian
Day of the Jackal	★★★½	Edward Fox, Terence Alexander	Fred Zinnemann
Discreet Charm of the Bourgeoisie, The	★★★½	Fernando Rey, Delphine Seyrig	Luis Bunuel
Doll's House, A	★★★½	Claire Bloom, Anthony Hopkins	Pat Garland
Effect of Gamma Rays on Man-in-the-Moon Marigolds, The	★★★½	Joanne Woodward, Neill Potts	Paul Newman
Emperor of the North Pole	★★½	Lee Marvin, Ernest Borgnine	Robert Aldrich
Fellini's Roma	★★★★	Peter Gonzales, Stefano Majore	Federico Fellini
40 Carats	★★★	Liv Ullmann, Edward Albert	Milton Katselas
Friends of Eddie Coyle, The	★★	Robert Mitchum, Peter Boyle	Peter Yates
Getaway, The	★★	Steve McQueen, Ali MacGraw	Sam Peckinpah
Godspell	★★★	Victor Garber, David Haskell	David Greene
Hail! To the Chief	★★★	Dan Resin, Richard B. Shull	Fred Levinson
Harrad Experiment, The	★★	James Whitmore, Tippi Hedren	Ted Post
Heartbreak Kid, The	★★★½	Charles Grodin, Cybill Shepherd	Elaine May
Heat	★★★	Joe Dallesandro, Sylvia Miles	Paul Morrissey
Hireling, The	★★★½	Robert Shaw, Sarah Miles	Alan Bridges
I Am a Dancer	★★½	Rudolf Nureyev, Margot Fonteyn	Pierre Jourdan
Images	★★★★	Susannah York, Rene Auberjonois	Robert Altman
Innocent Bystanders	★★½	Stanley Baker, Geraldine Chaplin	Peter Collinson
Jeremiah Johnson	★★★½	Robert Redford, Will Geer	Sydney Pollack
Jeremy	★★★½	Robby Benson, Glynnis O'Connor	Arthur Barron
Jesus Christ Superstar	★★★	Ted Neeley, Carl Anderson	Norman Jewison
Lady Caroline Lamb	★★★	Sarah Miles, Jon Finch	Robert Bolt
Lady Sings the Blues	★★★	Diana Ross, Billy Dee Williams	Sidney J. Furie
Last American Hero, The	★★★½	Jeff Bridges, Valerie Perrine	Lamont Johnson
Last of Sheila, The	★★★	James Coburn, Dyan Cannon	Herbert Ross
Last Tango in Paris	★★★★	Marlon Brando, Maria Schneider	Bernardo Bertolucci
Let the Good Times Roll	★★★½	Chuck Berry, Little Richard	Sid Levin & Bob Abel
Life and Times of Judge Roy Bean, The	★★★	Paul Newman, Victoria Principal	John Huston
Man of La Mancha	★★★	Peter O'Toole, Sophia Loren	Arthur Hiller
Mechanic, The	★★½	Charles Bronson, Jan-Michael Vincent	Michael Winner
Money, Money, Money	★★★	Lino Ventura, Jacques Brel	Claude Lelouch
Night Watch	★★★	Elizabeth Taylor, Laurence Harvey	Brian G. Hutton
Offence, The	★★★½	Sean Connery, Trevor Howard	Sidney Lumet
Oklahoma Crude	★★★	George C. Scott, Faye Dunaway	Stanley Kramer
O Lucky Man!	★★★½	Malcolm McDowell, Ralph Richardson	Lindsay Anderson
Paper Moon	★★★½	Ryan O'Neal, Tatum O'Neal	Peter Bogdanovich
Pat Garrett and Billy the Kid	★★★	James Coburn, Kris Kristofferson	Sam Peckinpah
Pete 'n' Tillie	★★★	Walter Matthau, Carol Burnett	Martin Ritt
Play It As It Lays	★★★½	Tuesday Weld, Anthony Perkins	Frank Perry
Poseidon Adventure, The	★★★	Gene Hackman, Ernest Borgnine	Ronald Neame
Pulp	★★★½	Michael Caine, Mickey Rooney	Michael Hodges
Rage	★★★	George C. Scott, Richard Basehart	George C. Scott
Savage Messiah	★★★	Dorothy Tutin, Scott Antony	Ken Russell
Save the Tiger	★★★	Jack Lemmon, Jack Gilford	John G. Avildsen
Scarecrow	★★★½	Gene Hackman, Al Pacino	Jerry Schatzberg
1776	★★★★	William Daniels, Howard Da Silva	Peter H. Hunt
Shamus	★★★★	Burt Reynolds, Dyan Cannon	Buzz Kulik
Sleuth	★★★★	Laurence Olivier, Michael Caine	Joseph L. Mankiewicz
Slither	★★½	James Caan, Peter Boyle	Howard Zieff
State of Siege	★★★★	Yves Montand, Renato Salvatori	Costa-Gavras
Tom Sawyer	★★★★	Johnny Whitaker, Celeste Holm	Don Taylor
Touch of Class, A	★★★½	George Segal, Glenda Jackson	Melvin Frank
Travels With My Aunt	★★★½	Maggie Smith, Alec McCowen	George Cukor
Ulzana's Raid	★★½	Burt Lancaster, Bruce Davison	Robert Aldrich
Under Milk Wood	★★★½	Richard Burton, Elizabeth Taylor	Andrew Sinclair
Up the Sandbox	★★½	Barbra Streisand, David Selby	Irvin Kershner
Valachi Papers, The	★★½	Charles Bronson, Jill Ireland	Terence Young
Visions of Eight	★★★	documentary	
Warm December, A	★★★½	Sidney Poitier, Esther Anderson	Sidney Poitier
Wattstax	★★★	Richard Pryor, Isaac Hayes	Mel Stuart
When the Legends Die	★★★½	Richard Widmark, Frederick Forrest	Stuart Millar
World's Greatest Athlete, The	★★★	Jan-Michael Vincent, Tim Conway	Robert Scheerer
Young Winston	★★★★	Robert Shaw, Anne Bancroft	Richard Attenborough

TV News and Commercials—A Community Report Card

In late 1972, just after the national presidential election, the Roper Organization polled 1,982 persons over 18 on their use of and attitudes toward television as a news source. When asked "Where do you usually get most of your news", 64% said television was their prime source of news. Television was the only source of news for 33%.

How much news can Americans get on television? Anywhere from 4½ hours to less than half an hour a day. Some cities have excellent TV news with all 3 network stations showing more than 17 hours of news and public affairs per week. While good TV news coverage is very expensive and must be paid for by showing commercials, there seems to be little relationship between the amount of news provided and the amount of time given to commercials during the week.

The raw data in the table which follows is derived from **Broadcasting in America: The Per-**formance of Network Affiliates in the Top 50 Markets. This study, prepared by Federal Communications Commissioner Nicholas Johnson, his staff and students, took its information directly from broadcast license renewal applications filed with the FCC since 1968. (Six stations were excluded from the study because of incomplete or out-of-date information.) The World Almanac has used only the data on news and public affairs programming and on the amount of commercials shown. Since some of the information given is over 3 years old, sharp changes for the better or worse may have occurred in the programming of some stations.

The entire report, which also gives advice on consumer action to improve television, is available for $1.75 from the Supt. of Documents, Government Printing Office, Washington, D.C. 20402. Ask for **Broadcasting in America**, FCC Reports, Vol. 42 (2nd series), No. 1.

	Station	Hrs N.-P.A.[1]	Hrs OC[2]		Station	Hrs N.-P.A.[1]	Hrs OC[2]		Station	Hrs N.-P.A.[1]	Hrs OC[2]
Excellent[3]				Tampa-St. Pete.	WTVT	21.99	47	Detroit	WWJ	19.55	49
Pittsburgh	KDKA	27.33	29		WFLA	19.08	50		WXYZ	14.12	50
	WIIC	22.33	42		WLYC	15.46	39		WJBK	13.33	46
	WTAE	21.45	20	Phoenix	KTAR	24.12	36	Cha'ston-Hunt'gton	WSAZ	19.75	37
Washington, D.C.	WTOP	27.04	47		KOOL	17.85	55		WHTN	13.70	25
	WRC	24.20	42		KTVK	14.33	33		WCHS[7]	10.85	27
	WMAL	18.10	32	Indianapolis	WISH	20.92	38	Gr'nville-Sptnbrg	WFBC	18.56	24
Philadelphia	KYW	30.48	26		WRTV[7]	20.09	31		WSPA	14.89	47
	WCAU	19.99	48		WLWI	15.00	49		WLOS	10.62	23
	WPV[7]	18.57	45	Seattle-Tacoma	KIRO	18.63	44	Charlotte	WBTV	18.43	40
Baltimore	WJZ	23.48	13		KOMO	18.18	35		WSOC	18.27	25
	WMAR	21.40	38		KING	17.98	18		WCCB	6.98	39
	WBAL	18.52	40	Providence	WJAR	20.75	37	Kalamazoo-Gr. Rap.	WOTV	21.10	43
Hartford-New Hav.	WTNH	21.79	35		WPRI	17.68	11		WKZO	11.88	40
	WHNB *	21.47	36		WTEV	16.28	32		WZZM	10.55	32
	WTIC	18.76	15	Birmingham	WAPI	20.53	25	Memphis	WMC	20.95	46
					WBRC	20.04	33		WREC	15.22	35
Good[4]					WBMG *	13.13	33		WHBQ	8.80	33
Chicago	WMAQ	29.08	50	St. Louis	KSD	23.52	37	Dayton	WLWD	19.75	51
	WBBM	19.85	56		KMOX	20.95	42		WHIO	10.83	50
	WLS	16.75	58		KTVI	8.70	27				
Houston	KHOU	23.35	44					**Poor[6]**			
	KPRC	23.12	38	**Fair[5]**				Milwaukee	WTMJ[7]	16.48	43
	KTRK	15.82	36	Buffalo	WBEN	23.35	35		WISN	13.03	48
Miami	WPLG	29.02	39		WGR	15.13	32		WITI	12.98	25
	WCKT	21.75	32		WKBW	14.57	25	Cleveland	WKYC	16.88	48
	WTVJ	17.12	30	Portland, Ore.	KGW	22.21	33		WJW	15.00	42
Los Angeles	KNBC	32.03	52		KOIN	17.10	35		WEWS	10.15	41
	KNXT	21.15	48		KATU	13.68	27	Gr'nsboro-Win. Sal.	WFMY	16.69	4
	KABC	14.58	40	San Antonio	WOAI	21.92	29		WXII	15.33	28
New York City	WNBC	26.21	40		KENS	15.92	39	Salt Lake City	KUTV	16.30	25
	WCBS	20.03	44		KSAT	14.75	28		KSL	14.34	40
	WABC	15.95	33	Denver	KOA	20.49	44		KCPX	10.75	36
Sacramento-St'kt'n	KCRA	27.82	37		KMGH[7]	15.90	47	Albany-Schen.	WRGB	14.47	31
	KXTV	21.29	48		KBTV[7]	13.17	58		WTEN	13.82	37
	KOVR	11.37	25	Oklahoma City	WKY	20.46	31		WAST	12.95	19
San Francisco	KPIX	27.34	2		KWTV	15.80	37	Louisville	WHAS	16.35	30
	KGO	21.20	41		KOCO[7]	11.58	39		WAVE	15.55	40
Boston	WBZ	26.31	33	Columbus, O.	WBNS	19.20	39		WLKY *	7.00	22
	WNAC	22.60	27		WLWC	19.00	48	Nashville	WSM	17.35	36
Dallas-Ft. Worth.	WBAP	23.14	31		WTVN	9.62	36		WLAC	13.16	46
	KDFW	19.87	48	Kansas City	WDAF	21.93	59		WSIX	8.00	29
	WFAA	15.87	37		KCMO	15.65	42	Cincinnati	WCPO	14.55	41
Atlanta	WAGA	22.69	48		KMBC	9.77	40		WLWT	14.42	49
	WSB	21.50	33	Minneap.-St. Paul	KSTP	19.72	35		WKRC	8.38	30
	WQXI	13.30	45		WCCO	17.38	53	Syracuse	WHEN	15.10	40
New Orleans	WWL	22.27	37		KMSP	10.23	24		WSYR	12.80	24
	WDSU	21.65	39	Norfolk-Newp. News.	WAVY	21.65	31		WNYS	8.48	19
	WVUE	13.40	32		WVEC	13.06	32	Toledo	WTOL	15.72	36
San Diego	KFMB	23.49	50						WSPD	12.18	32
	KGTV[7]	18.07	40						WDHO *	2.50	18

[1] Hrs. N.-P.A. = number of hours per composite broadcast week devoted to news and public affairs programs.
[2] Hrs. OC = number of hours per composite broadcast week in which 12 or more minutes of commercials were shown. [3] Half of the stations analyzed showed more than 17.53 hours of news per week. In cities ranked excellent all network affiliates ranked in the top half. [4] At least 2 network affiliates ranked among the top half. [5] Only one network affiliate ranked among the top half. [6] All affiliates ranked in the bottom half. [7] Data derived wholly from former licensee. * UHF station.

Television Stations Around the World

Source: World Almanac 1973 survey. * Privately-owned stations.

Note: Stations include central broadcast stations and local stations which contribute some local programing, but not automatic repeater stations.

Nation	Stations	Nation	Stations	Nation	Stations	Nation	Stations
Afghanistan	none	Greece	2	Malta*	1	Sweden	2
Andorra	none	Guatemala*	3	Mauritius	1	Tanzania	none
Austria	1	Guyana	none	Mexico	1	Thailand	9
Bahrain	1	Iceland	1	Mexico*	78	Tonga	none
Bangladesh	1	India	2	Morocco	3	Tunisia	1
Barbados	1	Indonesia	4	Nauru	none	Turkey	1
Belgium	2	Ireland	1	Nepal	none	USSR	127
Bhutan	none	Israel	1	Netherlands	2	United Kingdom	13
Bolivia	1	Italy	2	New Zealand	4	United Kingdom*	15
Botswana	none	Ivory Coast	1	Nigeria	5	United States (b).	1
Cameroon	none	Jamaica	1	Norway	1	United States*	931
Canada	35	Japan	2	Oman	none	Upper Volta	1
Canada*	60	Japan*	85	Pakistan	3	Venezuela	1
Cyprus	1	Jordan	1	Panama*	6	Venezuela*	6
Denmark	1	South Korea	1	Poland	19	South Vietnam	3
Ecuador*	10	South Korea*	2	Rhodesia	2	Western Samoa	none
Fiji	none	Kuwait	1	San Marino	none	Yemen Arab Rep.	none
Finland (a)	2	Liechtenstein	none	Saudi Arabia	5	Yugoslavia	8
France	3	Luxembourg*	1	South Africa	none		
West Germany	10	Madagascar	1	Swaziland	none		

(a) A private, commercial-supported company leases some time on both of Finland's stations. (b) WNYC-TV is owned by the City of New York.

Members of Global Communications System

Source: Department of State

The International Telecommunications Satellite Consortium (INTELSAT) has established a global operational system with satellites positioned above the Atlantic, Pacific and Indian Oceans. This system is transmitting live television, telephone, telegraph, data and facsimile communications linking six continents. As of July 1, 1973, there were 67 earth stations in 50 countries. It is expected there will be 73 earth stations in 55 countries at end 1973; 84 in 64 countries at end 1974 and 94 in 74 countries at end 1975. As of July 1, 1973, the 83 members were;

Afghanistan	Ecuador	Ivory Coast	Nicaragua	Syria
Algeria	Egypt	Jamaica	Nigeria	Tanzania
Argentina	Ethiopia	Japan	Norway	Thailand
Australia	Finland	Jordan	Pakistan	Trinidad & Tobago
Austria	France	Kenya	Peru	Tunisia
Barbados	Gabon	Korea, Rep. of	Philippines	Turkey
Belgium	Germany, Fed. Rep.	Kuwait	Portugal	Uganda
Brazil	Greece	Liechtenstein	Saudi Arabia	United Kingdom
Cameroon	Guatemala	Luxembourg	Senegal	United States
Canada	Iceland	Malagasy	Singapore	Vatican City
Central African Rep.	India	Malaysia	South Africa	Venezuela
Chile	Indonesia	Mauritania	Spain	Viet Nam, Rep. of
China, Republic of	Iran	Mexico	Sri Lanka	Yemen Arab Rep.
Colombia	Iraq	Monaco	Sudan	Yugoslavia
Costa Rica	Ireland	Morocco	Sweden	Zaire
Denmark	Israel	The Netherlands	Switzerland	Zambia
Dom. Republic	Italy	New Zealand		

Commercial Broadcast Stations on the Air

Source: Federal Communications Commission (January 1, 1972)

State	Total	AM	FM	TV	State	Total	AM	FM	TV
Total	7,289	4,324	2,258	707	Nebraska	79	48	17	14
United States	7,196	4,273	2,229	694	Nevada	38	21	10	7
Alabama	208	136	56	16	New Hampshire	43	27	13	3
Alaska	26	16	3	7	New Jersey	66	35	27	4
Arizona	88	59	18	11	New Mexico	83	57	19	7
Arkansas	133	84	41	8	New York	285	159	98	28
California	438	232	157	49	North Carolina	296	202	75	19
Colorado	106	65	30	11	North Dakota	49	27	10	12
Connecticut	64	38	21	5	Ohio	257	118	112	27
Delaware	15	10	5		Oklahoma	112	66	36	10
Dist. of Columbia	19	6	7	6	Oregon	111	78	20	13
Florida	316	194	97	25	Pennsylvania	312	171	118	23
Georgia	254	171	67	16	Rhode Island	24	15	7	2
Hawaii	38	24	4	10	South Carolina	155	102	42	11
Idaho	57	43	7	7	South Dakota	50	30	10	10
Illinois	252	121	107	24	Tennessee	232	148	68	16
Indiana	181	86	77	18	Texas	471	286	129	56
Iowa	128	72	43	13	Utah	45	32	10	3
Kansas	99	58	29	12	Vermont	26	18	6	2
Kentucky	182	106	64	12	Virginia	197	125	60	12
Louisiana	152	91	45	16	Washington	154	97	42	15
Maine	58	36	15	7	West Virginia	95	60	26	9
Maryland	94	53	34	7	Wisconsin	194	99	77	18
Massachusetts	114	63	40	11	Wyoming	33	29	1	3
Michigan	231	125	84	22					
Minnesota	144	87	45	12	Other areas	93	51	29	13
Mississippi	151	100	42	9	Puerto Rico	83	47	26	10
Missouri	180	106	50	24	Guam	3	1	1	1
Montana	61	41	8	12	Virgin Islands	7	3	2	2

Famous Paintings and Where You Can See Them

These paintings are listed because of their fame, not necessarily their artistic merit, and because they are in public collections. They are listed chronologically.

Giotto: Pieta, 1305, Arena Chapel, Padua.

Fra Filippo Lippi: Adoration of the Child, c. 1435, Staatliches Museum, Berlin.

Piero Della Francesca: Duke of Urbino, 1465, Uffizi Gallery, Florence.

Giovanni Bellini: Pieta, c. 1466, Brera, Milan.

Botticelli: The Birth of Venus, c. 1480, Uffizi Gallery, Florence.

Hieronymus Bosch: Christ Crowned with Thorns, c. 1500, National Gallery, London.

Leonardo da Vinci: Mona Lisa (La Gioconda), c. 1505, Louvre, Paris.

Michelangelo: Creation of Adam, 1508-12, Sistine Chapel, Vatican, Rome.

Giorgione: Sleeping Venus, c. 1508, Gemaldegalerie.

Raphael: The Sistine Madonna, 1515-19, Gemaldegalerie, Dresden.

Titian: The Tribute Money, 1516, Gemaldegalerie, Dresden.

Durer: The Four Apostles, 1523-26, Alte Pinakothek, Munich.

Holbein: Henry VIII, 1540, National Gallery, Rome.

Pieter Brueghel the Elder: Massacre of the Innocents, 1566, Kunsthistorisches Museum, Vienna.

El Greco: The Burial of Count Orgaz, 1586, Santo Tome, Toledo, Spain.

Rubens: Venus and Adonis, c. 1620, Met., N. Y.

Frans Hals: Laughing Cavalier, 1624, Wallace Collection, London.

Van Dyck: Charles I of England, c. 1635, Louvre, Paris.

Ribera: The Martyrdom of St. Bartholomew, 1630-39, Prado, Madrid.

Rembrandt: The Night Watch, 1642, Rijksmuseum, Amsterdam.

Velasquez: Maids of Honor, 1656, Prado, Madrid.

Vermeer: Young Woman with a Water Jug, c. 1658-64, Metropolitan, N. Y.

Ruisdael: View of Haarlem, c. 1670, Rijksmuseum, Amsterdam.

Murillo: Virgin and Child, c. 1672, Metropolitan, N. Y.

Watteau: The Embarkation for Cythera, c. 1712, Louvre.

Hogarth: The Orgy (Rake's Progress), 1734, Soane's Museum, London.

Fragonard: The Love Letter, c. 1769, Met., N. Y.

Gainsborough: The Blue Boy, c. 1770, Huntington Gallery, San Marino, Calif.

John Singleton Copley: Watson and the Shark, 1778, Museum of Fine Arts, Boston.

Joshua Reynolds: Mrs. Siddons as the Tragic Muse, 1784, Huntington Gallery, San Marino, Cal.

John Trumbull: The Declaration of Independence, 1786-94, Capitol, Washington, D. C.

Gilbert Stuart: George Washington, c. 1795, Museum of Fine Arts, Boston. (Others in Met., N. Y., etc.)

David: The Rape of the Sabines, 1799, Louvre, Paris.

Goya: The Naked Maja, 1799, Prado, Madrid.

Ingres: Odalisque, 1814, Louvre, Paris.

John Constable: The Hay Wain, 1821, National Gallery, London.

Thomas Lawrence: The Calmady Children, 1823, Metropolitan, N. Y.

John James Audubon: Birds of America (433 of the original 435 paintings), early 19th Century, New York Historical Society.

Joseph M. W. Turner: The Grand Canal, Venice, early 19th Century, Metropolitan, N. Y.

George Caleb Bingham: Fur Traders Descending the Missouri, 1845, Metropolitan, N. Y.

Emanuel Leutze: Washington Crossing the Delaware, 1851, Washington Crossing State Park, Pa.

Rosa Bonheur: The Horse Fair, 1855, Met., N. Y.

Jean-Baptiste Corot: Le Lac de Terni, 1861, Corcoran Gallery, Washington.

Honore Daumier: The Third-Class Carriage, c. 1862, Metropolitan, N. Y.

Jean-Francois Millet: Man with the Hoe, 1863, San Francisco Museum.

James McNeil Whistler: Arrangement in Grey and Black—The Artist's Mother, c. 1872, Louvre, Paris.

Thomas Eakins: The Gross Clinic, 1875, Jefferson Medical College, Philadelphia.

A.M. Willard: Spirit of '76, 1876 (3 versions): Cleveland City Hall: Western Reserve Historical Society, Cleveland; Abbot Hall, Marblehead, Mass.

Edgar Degas: La Danseuse au Bouquet, 1878, Rhode Island School of Design Museum, Providence.

Edouard Manet: In a Boat, 1879, Metropolitan, N. Y.

Pierre Auguste Renoir: Luncheon of the Boating Party, 1881, Phillips Collection, Washington.

Georges Seurat: Sunday Afternoon on the Grande Jatte, 1884-86, Art Institute of Chicago.

Paul Cezanne: Mont Sainte-Victoire, 1885-87, Met., N.Y.

Vincent Van Gogh: Wheat Field and Cypress Trees, 1889, National Gallery, London.

Albert Pinkham Ryder: Toilers of the Sea, c. 1890, Addison Gallery, Andover, Mass.

Paul Gauguin: Ia Orana Maria (Hail Mary),1891, Metropolitan, N. Y.

Henri de Toulouse-Lautrec: At the Moulin Rouge, 1892, Art Institute of Chicago.

Claude Monet: Rouen Cathedral, 1894, Met., N. Y.

Winslow Homer: Gulf Stream, 1899, Art Institute of Chi.

John Singer Sargent: The Wyndham Sisters, 1900, Metropolitan, N. Y.

Frederic Remington: Cavalry Charge on the Southern Plains, 1907, Metropolitan, N. Y.

Georges Braque: Head of a Woman, 1909, Musee d'Art Moderne, Paris.

Henri Rousseau: The Dream, 1910, Museum of Modern Art, N. Y.

Marc Chagall: I and the Village, 1911, Museum of Modern Art, N. Y.

Marcel Duchamp: Nude Descending a Staircase, 1912, Philadelphia Museum of Art.

Paul Chabas: September Morn, 1912, Met., N. Y.

Amadeo Modigliani: Portrait of Madame Zboroski, 1917-18, Rhode Island School of Design Museum, Providence.

Piet Mondrian: Composition, 1921, Kunstmuseum, Basel, Switzerland.

Paul Klee: Twittering Machine, 1922, Museum of Modern Art, N. Y.

George Bellows: The Dempsey-Firpo Fight, 1924, Whitney Museum of American Art, N. Y.

Vasily Kandinsky: Several Circles, 1926, Guggenheim Museum, N. Y.

Henri Matisse: Odalisque, 1928, Musee d'Art Moderne, Paris.

Grant Wood: American Gothic, 1930, Art Institute of Chi.

Joan Miro: Man, Woman and Child, 1931, Philadelphia Museum of Art.

Jose Clemente Orozco: Zapatistas, 1931, Museum of Modern Art, N. Y.

Maurice Utrillo: Sacred-Heart and Montmartre Square, 1932, Musee d'Art et d'Histoire, Geneva.

William Gropper: The Senate, 1935, Museum of Modern Art, N. Y.

Pablo Picasso: Guernica, 1937, Museum of Modern Art, N. Y.

Georges Rouault: The Old King, 1937, Carnegie Institute Museum, Pittsburgh.

Thomas Hart Benton: Threshing Wheat, 1939, Swope Gallery, Terre Haute, Ind.

John Steuart Curry: John Brown, 1939, Met., N. Y.

Anna (Grandma) Moses: The Thanksgiving Turkey, 1943, Metropolitan, N. Y.

Andrew Wyeth: Christina's World, 1948, Museum of Modern Art, N. Y.

Jackson Pollock: Autumn Rhythm, 1950, Met., N. Y.

Salvador Dali: Crucifixion, 1954, Metropolitan, N. Y.

Raphael Soyer: Portrait of Hugo Kastor, 1957, Met., N.Y.

Famous Sculptures and Where You Can See Them

The statues, monuments and other sculptures in the following list have been chosen because of the fame they have won, independent of the question of their individual artistic merit, and because they are on public view. They are listed chronologically, except for the group titled Non-Western. In a few cases, two works by the same artist have been listed. Some of the works are representative of a famed artist, many of whose works are equally well-known. The creators of some of the earliest works are unknown.

ANCIENT EGYPT

The Great Sphinx, c. 2900 B.C., limestone and masonry, Giza, United Arab Republic.
Queen Nofretete, c. 1365 B.C., painted limestone, State Museum, West Berlin.
Colossi of Ramses II, c. 1230 B.C., sandstone, Abu Simbel, United Arab Republic.

ANCIENT GREECE

Charioteer of Delphi, c. 470 B.C., bronze, Museum, Delphi, Greece.
Myron: Discobolus (Discus Thrower), marble Roman copy of Myron's bronze original of c. 450 B.C., Terme Museum, Rome.
Phidias: Parthenon Sculptures, c. 438 B.C., marble (by or under direction of Phidias), British Museum, London.
Polyclitus: Doryphorus (Spear Bearer), marble Roman copy of Polyclitus original of late 5th Century B.C., National Museum, Naples.
Praxiteles: Hermes with the Infant Dionysus, c. 350 B.C., Museum, Olympia; **Aphrodite of Cnidus,** marble Roman copy of Praxiteles' original of 330 B.C., Vatican, Rome.
Scopas: Head from the Temple at Tegea, c. 350 B.C., National Museum, Athens.
Lysippus: Apoxyomenos (athlete cleansing himself with a scraper), marble Roman copy of Lysippus' bronze original of 330 B.C., Vatican, Rome.
Nike of Samothrace (Winged Victory), c. 300 B.C., marble, Louvre, Paris.
Aphrodite of Melos (Venus de Milo), 2nd Century B.C., marble, Louvre, Paris.
Laocoon, 2nd Century B.C., marble, by Agesander, Athenodorus and Polydorus of Rhodes, Vatican, Rome.

ANCIENT ROME

Augustus, c. 20 B.C., marble, Vatican, Rome.
Caracalla, 211-217 A.D., marble, National Museum, Naples.

GOTHIC

Virgin of Paris, early 14th Century, stone, Notre Dame Cathedral, Paris.
Claus Sluter: Moses, c. 1400, stone, Champmol Monastery, near Dijon.
Tomb of Philippe Pot, c. 1480, painted stone, Louvre, Paris.

RENAISSANCE

Donatello: St. George, c. 1415, marble, National Museum, Florence; **Gattamelata,** 1445-50, bronze, Piazza del Santo, Padua.
Andrea del Verrocchio: Colleoni, c. 1485, bronze, Campo SS. Giovanni e Paolo, Venice.
Michelangelo Buonarroti: David, 1501-04, marble, Academy, Florence; **Pieta,** 1498-99, marble, St. Peter's, Rome.
Benvenuto Cellini: Perseus with the Head of Medusa, 16th Century, marble, Loggia dei Lanzi, Florence.
Gianlorenzo Bernini: Ecstasy of St. Theresa, 1645-52, marble, Church of Santa Maria della Vittoria, Rome.

NON-WESTERN

Buddha Vairocana, 8th Century A.D., bronze, Nara, Japan.
Thaloc (Toltec Rain God), 900 A.D. or earlier, stone, Anthropology Museum, Mexico City.

Amida Buddha, 1252, bronze, Kamakura, Japan.
Aztec Calendar Stone, 1427-29, painted volcanic rock, Anthropology Museum, Mexico City.
Stone Heads, 17th Century or earlier, Easter Island.
Mask with Horns, 19th Century, wood, from southeast Congo (Baluba), Royal Museum of Central Africa, Tervuren, Belgium.
Buddha, 1960, concrete, Changhua, Taiwan.

18th-19th CENTURIES

Jean Antoine Houdon: George Washington, 1788-92, marble, State Capitol, Richmond, Va.
Thomas Crawford: Statue of Freedom, bronze, 1863, atop the Capitol dome, Washington, D. C.
Frederic Auguste Bartholdi: Liberty Enlightening the World, 1886, copper on steel frame, Liberty Is., N. Y.
Auguste Rodin: The Thinker, 1879-89, bronze, Metropolitan Museum of Art, N. Y.
Augustus St. Gaudens: Abraham Lincoln, 1887, bronze, Lincoln Park, Chicago.
John Quincy Adams Ward: Henry Ward Beecher, bronze, 1891, Cadman Plaza, Brooklyn, N. Y.

20th CENTURY

Aristide Maillol: The Mediterranean, 1902-05, bronze, Museum of Modern Art, N. Y.
Mateo Alonso: Christ of the Andes, 1904, bronze, Uspallata Pass, Chile-Argentina border.
Ivan Mestrovic: My Mother, 1908, marble, State Museum, Belgrade.
Constantin Brancusi: The Kiss, 1908, stone Philadelphia Museum of Art; **Bird in Space,** 1927, bronze, Museum of Modern Art, N. Y.
Wilhelm Lehmbruck: Kneeling Woman, 1911, cast stone, Museum of Modern Art, N. Y.
Edvard Erichsen: The Little Mermaid, 1913, bronze, Copenhagen harbor.
Daniel Chester French: Abraham Lincoln, 1922, marble, Lincoln Memorial, Washington, D. C.
William Zorach: Child with Cat, 1926, marble, Museum of Modern Art, N. Y.
Gaston Lachaise: Standing Woman, 1912-27, bronze, Albright Art Gallery, Buffalo.
Ernst Barlach: Hovering Angel, 1927, bronze, Antoniter Church, Cologne.
Jacob Epstein: Madonna and Child, 1927, bronze, Riverside Church, N. Y.
Heitor da Silva Costa and Paul Landowski: Christ the Redeemer, 1931, reinforced concrete, Corcovado Mtn., Rio de Janeiro.
Vernon March: Canadian War Memorial, 1926-32 (dedicated 1939), bronze, Confederation Sq., Ottawa.
Paul Manship: Prometheus, 1934, bronze and goldleaf, Rockefeller Center, N. Y.
Alexander Calder: Lobster Trap and Fish Tail, 1939, steel wire, aluminum, Museum of Modern Art, N. Y.
Carl Milles: Meeting of the Waters Fountain, 1940, Aloe Plaza, St. Louis: **Millesgarden Sculptures,** Stockholm.
Gutzon Borglum: Mt. Rushmore Natl. Memorial, 1927-41, granite, near Keystone, S.D.
Gustav Vigeland: Sculpture Park, 1906-43, stone and bronze, Oslo.
Pablo Picasso: She-Goat, bronze, 1950, Museum of Modern Art, N. Y.
Felix de Weldon: Marine Corps War Memorial (Iwo Jima Flag-Raising), 1954, bronze, near Arlington Natl. Cemetery, Va.
Jose de Creeft: Alice in Wonderland, 1959, bronze, Conservatory Lake, Central Park, N. Y.
Henry Moore: Reclining Figure, 1963-65, bronze, Lincoln Center, N. Y.

U.S. Launches First Orbiting Space Station

Amidst a flurry of technical problems, the U.S., **May 14,** launched Skylab, its first orbiting space station. Deployment failure, 63 minutes after the unmanned launch, of the craft's solar-power wings delayed the launch of the Skylab 1 crew—Capt. Charles Conrad Jr., Cmdr. Joseph P. Kerwin and Cmdr. Paul J. Weitz, all Navy men—until **May 25.** However, despite the initial malfunctions, the Skylab 1 crew returned safely, **June 22,** having accomplished virtually all the flight's objectives and setting a duration record of 28 days and 40 minutes in space.

Crew Replaces Lost Sun Shield

Working closely with NASA ground personnel, the crew, **May 26,** attached a makeshift sunshield to compensate for the craft's thin aluminum micrometeoroid and thermal shield which had been lost in the launch malfunction. Loss of the shield had exposed Skylab to dangerous overheating from the sun's rays. A second major repair, on **June 7,** necessitated a "space walk" by Conrad and Kerwin; with difficulty, they removed an aluminum strap which had jammed a set of solarpower panels, robbing Skylab of nearly half its potential power.

Man Can Endure in Space

Beyond setting records—circling the earth 395 times in orbit, nearly 11.8 million miles traveled in space and first repair work done outside an orbiting craft—Skylab 1 presented evidence that man could live and work effectively in the weightless conditions of space for extended periods of time with no apparent damage to his health.

Other goals accomplished on the mission included a survey of the earth—aimed primarily at studying U.S. resources—with photographs and sensors. The crew also observed the sun from above the earth's obscuring atmosphere and, **May 31,** detected a "big hole" in the sun's corona. In a second "space walk," **June 19,** Conrad and Weitz retrieved 6 cannisters of exposed film and replaced them with fresh film for the Skylab 2 mission.

Skylab 2 Crew Goes Up

The success of Skylab 1 cleared the way for the almost flawless **July 28** launch of the Skylab 2 mission for a scheduled 58 days in space and a marathon journey of some 26 million miles. Again, the goal of the crew—Navy Capt. Alan L. Bean, Marine Maj. Jack R. Lousma and scientist Dr. Owen Garriott—was to study the physiology of man in space, the physics of the sun, and resources of the earth.

Technical Problems and Motion Sickness

However, like Skylab 1, the initial period of the Skylab 2 flight was riddled with problems. In the first maneuvers to catch up with Skylab, a leak was located in one of the 4 sets of small thruster rockets on the Apollo ferry craft. A malfunction, **Aug. 2,** in a second set raised concern over Apollo's ability to bring the astronauts back. Preparations to outfit a rescue ship were begun. Plans for the rescue were cancelled, **Aug. 21,** when it was determined that Apollo hardware was holding up well enough for the return flight. Another early problem was the failure of one of 9 gyroscopes on the space station. The Skylab 2 crew had brought along 6 back-up gyroscopes to be installed in event of such a failure. On **Aug. 6,** a leak was discovered in the air conditioning system; a check of the secondary system, however, found it to be in good shape.

Motion sickness curtailed the astronauts' activities during the first 3 days and forced delay of the first "space walk" to **Aug. 6.** On the walk, a record 6 hours, 31 minutes, Lousma and Garriott erected a new aluminum mylar sunshade to replace the makeshift shield installed by the Skylab 1 crew, put new film cassettes in the solar telescopes and inspected the leaking thrusters on the Apollo craft. On a second 4½-hour "space walk" on **Aug. 24,** Lousma and Garriott again replaced film and installed a new set of gyroscopes.

A spectacular performance by the sun, **Aug. 21,** highlighted the astronauts' survey of the sun. In what Houston scientists called "the most important, dynamic and interesting" event yet photographed from Skylab, the sun blew a bubble about three-fourths its own size. The bubble, in the sun's corona, was caused by an explosion on the other side of the sun. On **Sept. 7,** the astronauts photographed the "brightest and biggest" solar flare of the year; it was estimated to be 10 times the size of the earth.

Skylab Menagerie

The crew brought with them various experimental animals including 6 pocket mice, 2 common cross spiders named Arabella and Anita, 2 minnows, 50 minnow eggs, flies and more than 1,000 vinegar gnat pupae. Arabella quickly adjusted to zero-gravity living, spun her web, and, because she didn't like the insects aboard, ate raw meat. The minnows, after swimming around in circles for a few days, also adapted to the new environment.

Like the Skylab 1 crew, Skylab 2 astronauts made resource surveys of the earth and planned, in September, to survey Mali in Mauritania to collect data on possible water and food sources for that area of drought and famine.

The Skylab 2 mission was scheduled for Pacific Ocean splash down on **Sept. 25,** 59½ days after launch.

The Busiest Airports, 1971
(Total take-offs and landings)

United States Source: Dept. of Transportation		Canada Source: Dept. of Transport	
O'Hare (Chicago)	641,429(1)	St. Hubert (Montreal)	321,782
Long Beach, Calif.	587,845	Montreal	231,377(2)
Van Nuys, Calif.	562,030	Ottawa	219,938(5)
Santa Ana, Calif.	555,897	Toronto	213,876(1)
Los Angeles	493,234(3)	Calgary	180,009
Atlanta	438,704(2)	Edmonton	175,825
San Jose, Calif	408,252	Winnipeg	154,573(4)
Dallas	387,092	Quebec	148,292
JF Kennedy (New York)	380,000(4)	Vancouver	135,632(3)
San Francisco	366,766	London, Ontario	108,420
LaGuardia (New York)	(5)		

Numbers in parentheses indicate top 5 in air carrier operations only.

Aerial Piracy, 1948-72

Flight origin	1948-57	1958-67	1968	1969	1970	1971	1972	Total
North America	..	23	23	37	14	29	29	155
Latin America[1]	..	18	10	29	15	13	8	93
Western Europe[2]	..	..	1	4	4	4	10	23
Warsaw Pact	15	..	..	2	15	1	3	36
Middle East	..	..	1	3	14	5	5	28
Other	..	7	3	7	10	9	9	45
Diversion attempted to								
North America	..	..	..	..	..	5	14	19
Latin America[1]	..	41	32	63	28	26	19	209
(of which, Cuba)	..	(41)	(32)	(63)	(26)	(20)	(13)	(195)
Western Europe[2]	15	..	1	7	15	7	12	57
Warsaw Pact	..	..	..	..	..	..	3	3
Middle East[3]	..	..	..	4	16	4	6	30
Other[4]	..	7	5	8	13	19	10	62
Total attempts	15	48	38	82	72	61	64	380
Successful[5]	13	48	38	82	72	61	64	235
% Successful	86.7	64.6	86.8	85.4	63.9	39.3	28.1	61.8

Notes: [1]Including Caribbean countries.
[2]Including Austria, Turkey and Yugoslavia
[3]Including North Africa.
[4]Asia, Australasia, Sub-Saharan Africa and unknown.
[5]Success: hi-jackers reached desired destination or obtained ransom.

The downward trend in the number of aircraft hijacking attempts in 1970-71 was halted in 1972, although the number of successful attempts continued to fall. At the same time, there was a sharp increase in the number of attempts to exploit hijacking for personal enrichment by holding aircraft for ransom: from 3 cases in 1971 to some 20 in 1972. In only one of these cases, however, does a hijacker appear to have evaded subsequent capture and to have retained the ransom. Another notable trend was the increase in casualties, many of which were inflicted by exchanges of gunfire on the ground. During 1968-71, 12 passengers or crew members and 18 hijackers were killed during hijacking attempts, with an additional 71 people, including 13 hijackers, suffering injury. In 1972 alone, 13 passengers or crew members and 22 hijackers were killed and 29 others, including 5 hijackers, injured.

Pre-Flight Searches a Popular Success

In midsummer, 1973, a major national newspaper revealed that the Federal Aviation Administration was considering a plan to end the 100% screening and search procedures at airports across the U.S. in favor of a system of selective searches. Public reaction was so quick and intense, that the FAA dropped its plans.

The 100% screening began on Jan. 5, 1973, at the order of President Nixon, following 2 hijackings in which one person was killed, and one wounded, and $2,000,000 in ransom was collected by the hijackers. During the summer of 1972, U.S. planes were hijacked at a rate of more than 2 a month.

Since the institution of the 100% screen, no U.S. airliner has been hijacked. During the first 6 months of the screening, 1,337 potential airline passengers were arrested for a variety of crimes, including illegal possession of weapons. Over 890 guns were confiscated at airplane boarding gates. A few people refused to be searched and were denied permission to board their plane. About 1,500 people were turned away for this and other reasons

---

Consolidated Airline Traffic

Source: Civil Aeronautics Board Air Carrier Traffic Statistics, Dec. 1972.

	1970	1971	1972
Passenger Traffic			
Revenue passengers enplaned	169,922,000	173,667,000	195,305,000
Revenue passenger miles	131,710,018,000	135,651,780,000	164,015,261,000
Available seat miles	265,119,871,000	279,869,172,000	297,966,766,000
Cargo Traffic (ton miles)	4,984,197,000	5,108,616,000	6,388,595,000
Freight	3,407,552,000	3,712,257,000	5,110,974,000
Express	106,514,000	82,998,000	87,424,000
Priority U.S. Mail	606,492,000	595,666,000	581,704,000
Nonpriority U.S. Mail	863,639,000	717,695,000	608,493,000
Overall Traffic and Service			
Nonscheduled traffic-total	2,019,832,000	2,220,375,000	2,058,659,000
Total revenue ton miles	20,185,500,000	20,905,505,000	22,805,037,000
Total available ton miles	44,298,170,000	47,223,830,000	48,682,429,000
Scheduled revenue departures	5,119,556	4,999,252	5,046,438
Scheduled revenue miles	2,418,169,000	2,377,839,000	2,375,876,000
Scheduled revenue hours	5,846,195	5,703,310	5,728,496

Notable Ocean and Intercontinental Flights

Pilot, Plane	From	To	Mi.	Time	Date
		DIRIGIBLE BALLOONS			
British R-34 (1)....... {	East Fortune, Scot..	Mineola, N. Y.......	......	108 hrs.	July 2-6, 1919
	Mineola, N. Y......	Pulham, Eng........	......	75 hr.	July 9-13, 1919
Amundsen-Ellsworth-Nobile expedition ...	Spitsbergen.......	Teller, Alaska.......	......	80 hrs.	May 11-14, 1926
Graf Zeppelin........	Friedrichshafen	Lakehurst, N. J......	6,630	4d 15h 46m	Oct. 11-15, 1928
Hindenburg Zeppelin .. {	Germany	Lakehurst, N. J.......	......	51h 17m	June 30-July 2, 1936
	Lakehurst, N. J.....	Frankfort, Ger	......	42h 53m	Aug. 9-11, 1936
USN ZPG-2 Blimp..... {	S. Weymouth, Mass.	Africa..............	} 7,000	275h	Mar. 4-16, 1957
	Africa.............	Key West, Fla			
		AIRPLANES			
USN NC-4...........	Rockaway, L. I......	Lisbon, Port	......	....	May 8-27, 1919
John Alcock-A. W. Brown (2)	St. John's, Nfld......	Clifden, Ireland	1,960	16h 12m	June 14-15, 1919
Richard E. Byrd (3)...	Spitsbergen	North Pole	1,545	15h 30m	May 9, 1926
Chas. A. Lindbergh (4).	Mineola, N. Y.......	Paris...............	3,610	33h 29m 30s	May 20-21, 1927
Chas. A. Levine-Clarence D. Chamberlin (5).............	Roosevelt Field, Mineola, N. Y.....	Eisleben, Ger	3,911	42h 31m	June 4-6, 1927
Baron G. von Huenefeld, crew (6)	Dublin	Greenly Isl., Lab	......	37 hrs.	Apr. 12-13, 1928
Sir Hubert Wilkins (8) .	Point Barrow, Alaska .	Spitsbergen	......	....	April 16, 1928
Sir Chas. Kingsford-Smith, crew (7)......	Oakland, Calif	Brisbane, Aust	......	....	May 31-June8 1928
Amelia Earhart Putnam, W. Stultz, L. Gordon........	Trepassy, Nfld	Burry Port, Wales	......	20h 40m	June 17-18, 1928
Richard E. Byrd (9)....	Bay of Wales	South Pole	......	....	Nov. 28-29, 1929
Capt. D. Coste-M. Bellonte...........	Paris...............	Valley Stream, N. Y ..	4,100	37h 18m 30s	Sept. 1-2, 1930
Lt. L. Challe-Lt. T. L. Borres	Seville, Spain	Natal, Brazil	3,600	....	Dec. 15-17, 1930
Wiley Post-Harold Gatty.............	Harbor Grace, Nfld ...	England.............	2,200	16h 17m	June 23-24, 1931
Clyde Pangborn-Hugh Herndon, Jr. (10)	Tokyo.............	Wenatchee, Wash	4,458	41h 34m	Oct. 3-5, 1931
Amelia Earhart Putnam (11)	Harbor Grace, Nfld ...	Ireland.............	2,026½	14h 56m	May 20-21, 1932
James A. Mollison (12) .	Portmarnock, Ire	Pennfield, N. B	......	....	Aug. 18, 1932
Amelia Earhart Putnam (11)	Honolulu,...........	Oakland, Calif	2,408	18h 16m	Jan. 11-12, 1935
China Clipper (Pan Am. Airways) (13) ...	San Francisco......	Manila, P. I	......	....	Nov. 22-28, 1935
	Manila, P.I........	San Francisco.......	......	....	Dec. 1-6, 1935
Gromoff, Yumasheff, Danilin (USSR)......	Moscow, USSR......	San Jacinto, Calif....	6,262	62h 02m	July 12-14, 1937
Douglas C. Corrigan...	Floyd Bennett Field ..	Dublin, Ire	......	28h 13m	July 17-18, 1938
B-29 (Lt. Col. C. J. Miller).............	Honolulu,...........	Washington, D. C	4,640	17h 21m	Sept. 1, 1945
C-54 (Maj. G. E. Cain).	Tokyo.............	Washington, D. C	......	31h 25m	Sept. 3, 1945
William P. Odom	Honolulu,...........	Teterboro, N. J.......	5,300	36 hrs.	Mar. 8, 1949
USN Caroline Mars....	Honolulu,...........	San Diego, Calif	......	14h 17m	June 17-18, 1950
Col. David C. Schilling, USAF (14).........	England.............	Limestone, Me	3,300	10h 01m	Sept. 22, 1950
Chas. F. Blair, Jr	New York	London	3,500	7h 48m	Jan. 31, 1951
Canberra Bomber	Aldergrove, Belfast, N. I	Gander, Nfld	......	4h 40m	Feb. 21, 1951
Chas. F. Blair, Jr. (15)..	Bardufoss, Nor	Fairbanks, Alaska....	3,300	10h 29m	May 29, 1951
Chas. F. Blair, Jr	Fairbanks, Alaska....	New York	3,450	9h 31m	May 30, 1951
Canberra Bomber	England.............	Australia	......	20h 20m	Mar. 16, 1952
British Comet........	London	Johannesburg, S. Af...	......	23h 38m	May 2-3, 1952
Two U. S. S-55 Helicopters (16).........	Westover AFB, Mass..	Prestwick, Scot......	3,410	42h 30m	July 15-31, 1952
RB-45 Tornado (17)....	Anchorage, Alaska....	Yokoto AFB, Japan ...	3,460	9h 50m	July 29, 1952
Canberra Bomber (18).. {	Aldergrove, N. I	Gander, Nfld	2,073	4h 34m	Aug. 26, 1952
	Gander, Nfld	Aldergrove, N. I......	2,073	3h 25m	Aug. 26, 1952
B-47B..............	California	Hawaii.............	2,463	4h 52m	Sept. 20, 1952
British Comet........	London-Tokyo.......	Tokyo-London	20,400	74h 52m	April 3-7, 1953
U. S. B-47..........	Limestone AFB, Me ..	Fairford, Eng	2,925	4h 45m	July 28, 1953
U. S. B-47..........	Fairford, Eng	Tampa, Fla	4,450	9h 53m	Aug. 4, 1953
British Comet........	London	Rio de Janeiro	6,000	12h 30m	Sept. 13-14, 1953
Flt. Lieut. Roland Burton (Canberra PR-3 bomber in race)	England.............	New Zealand	12,270	23h 51m	Oct. 8-9, 1953
Comet II...........	London	Khartoum, Egypt.....	3,064	6h 22m	Jan. 22, 1954
Max Conrad (solo)....	New York	Paris, France	......	22h 23m	Nov. 7, 1954
10 U. S. F-84's.......	Stugate AFB, Eng ...	Bergstrom AFB, Austin, Texas	5,118	10h 48m	Aug. 17, 1955
Canberra Bomber	London (round trip) ..	New York	6,920	14h21m45.4s	Aug. 23, 1955
Capt. William F. Judd ..	New York	Paris...............	......	24h 11m	Jan. 29-30, 1956
Pan American DC-7 ...	New York	Shannon, Ire........	......	7h 45m	Dec. 10, 1956
Bristol Britannia......	New York	Rome	4,700	12h 20m	Mar. 8, 1957
Three USAF F-100 Cs .	London	Los Angeles, Calif....	6,710	14h 5m	May 13, 1957
Spirit of St. Louis II (USAF F-100F jet)...	McGuire AFB, N. J...	Le Bourget, Paris.....	......	6h 38m	May 21, 1957
Air France	Los Angeles	Paris...............	6,102	16h 21m	Aug. 25, 1957

Pilot, Plane	From	To	Mi.	Time	Date
Soviet TU-104	{ Vnukovo Airport, Moscow	McGuire AFB, N. J...	5,570	21h 54m	Sept. 3-4, 1957
	{ McGuire AFB, N. J.	Moscow	5,570	11h 13m	Sept. 7, 1957
Soviet TU-104	Moscow	McGuire AFB, N. J...	5,570	18h 30m	Sept. 13-14, 1957
Lockheed Super Starliner (19)	New York	Athens, Greece	5,000	14h 38m	Sept. 26, 1957
TWA Jetstream (20) ...	London	San Francisco	5,900	23h 19m	Oct. 1-2, 1957
6 USAF B-52 bombers .	U.S.-Argentina (no-stp)	Argentina-U. S	10,425	21h 42m	Nov. 16-17, 1957
4 USAF RF-101s (21) . .	Tokyo.	Honolulu	3,850	6h 35m	Dec. 2, 1957
El Al Britannia.	New York	London	......	7h 44m	Jan. 9, 1958
USAF KC-135.	Tokyo.	Lajes AFB, Azores....	10,230	18h 48m	Apr. 7-8, 1958
Max Conrad (solo)	New York	Palermo, Sicily.......	4,440	32h 55m	June 22-23, 1958
USAF KC-135.	New York	London	3,442	5h 27m 42.8s	June 27, 1958
USAF KC-135.	London	New York	3,460	5h 51m 24.8s	June 29, 1958
Capt. Mairon Boling ...	Manila, P. I	Pendleton, Oreg......	6,979	45h 42m	July 31-Aug. 1/58
Comet IV jet airliner ..	New York	London	3,496	6h 27m	Aug. 12, 1958
Boeing 707 Clipper....	New York	London	......	7h 28m	Sept. 8, 1958
USAF KC-135.	Yokota AB, Japan	Washington, D. C	7,100	12h 28m	Sept. 12, 1958
Comet IV jet airliner ..	New York	London	3,650	6h 12m	Oct. 4, 1958
Boeing 707 Clipper....	New York	Paris.	......	7h 1m	Nov. 4-5, 1958
Boeing 707	London	New York	3,700	7h 17m	Jan. 10, 1959
Max Conrad (solo).....	Chicago	Rome	5,000	34h 3m	Mar. 5-6, 1959
Boeing 707-320.	Seattle, Wash	Rome	5,800	11h 6m	May 29, 1959
Max Conrad (solo)	Casablanca, Africa....	Los Angeles	7,700	58h 36m	June 2-4, 1959
USSR TU-114 (22).....	Moscow	New York	5,092	11h 6m	June 28, 1959
Boeing 707 airliner	San Francisco	Sydney, Australia.....	7,630	16h 10m	July 2, 1959
Boeing 707-320.	New York	Moscow	c.5,090	8h 54m	July 23, 1959
Pan Amer. Clipper	Honolulu, Hawaii ...	San Francisco	2,410	4h 25m	Aug. 25, 1959
USAF F-100 (group) ...	Darwin, Australia	Itazuke, Japan	c.3,000	6h 35m	Nov. 4, 1959
Boeing 707	New York	Paris	5h 4m	5h 5m	Nov. 11, 1959
	New York	Shannon, Ireland	......	5h 5m	Nov. 11, 1959
Max Conrad (solo)	Casablanca, Mor	El Paso, Texas	6,911	56h 26m	Nov. 22-26, 1959
USAF B-58	New York	Paris.............	......	3h 10m 58s	May 26, 1961
Col. J. B. Swindal	Washington, D. C	Moscow	5,004	8h 39m 02.2s	May 19, 1963
Mrs. Jerrie Mock (23) ..	Columbus, Ohio......	Columbus, Ohio.......	23,206	29d 11h 59m	Mar. 19-Ap. 18/64
Joan Merriam (24)....	Oakland, Calif	Oakland, Calif	27,750	56d	Mar. 17-May 12/64
Sheila Scott (solo)	London	London	28,633	33d 03m	May 18-June 20/67
Elgen Long (solo)	San Francisco	San Francisco	38,896	28d 00h 43m	Nov. 5-Dec. 3/71

Notable first flights: 1, Atlantic aerial round trip. 2, Non-stop transatlantic flight. 3, Polar flight. 4, Solo transatlantic flight in the Ryan monoplane the "Spirit of St. Louis." 5, Transatlantic passenger flight. 6, East-West transatlantic crossing. 7, U.S. to Australia flight. 8, Trans-Arctic flight. 9, South Pole flight. 10, Non-stop Pacific flight. 11, Woman's transoceanic solo flight. 12, Westbound transatlantic solo flight. 13, Transatlantic airmail and U.S. to Philippines crossing. 14, Non-stop jet transatlantic flight. 15, Solo across North Pole. 16, Transatlantic helicopter flight. 17, Non-stop jet Pacific flight. 18, Transatlantic round trip on same day. 19, Non-stop between New York and Athens; carried 59 persons. 20, Non-stop London to San Francisco via polar route; carried 32 passengers. 21, Non-stop jet flight from Tokyo to Honolulu. 22, Non-stop between Moscow and New York. 23, First woman pilot to circle globe; first woman to fly both North Atlantic and Pacific, 24, Followed route Amelia Earhart partly completed in 1937. 25, Speed record around the world over both the earth's poles.

International Aeronautical Records

Source: The National Aeronautics Association, 806 15th St., N.W., Washington, D.C. 20005, representative in the United States of the Federation Aeronautique Internationale, certifying agency for world aviation and space records. The International Aeronautical Federation was formed in 1905 by representatives from Belgium, France, Germany, Great Britain, Spain, Italy, Switzerland and the United States, with headquarters in Paris. Regulations for the control of official records were signed Oct. 14, 1905. World records are defined as maximum performance, regardless of class or type of aircraft used. Records to Aug. 1, 1973.

WORLD AIR RECORDS—MAXIMUM PERFORMANCE IN ANY CLASS

Speed Over a Straight Course—3,331.507 km.p.m. (2,070.101 m.p.h.)—Col. R. L. Stephens, USAF, United States; Lockheed YF-12A; Edwards Air Force Base, Calif., May 1, 1965.

Speed Over a Closed Circuit—2,981.5 km.p.m. (1,850.61 m.p.h.)—Mikhail Komarov, USSR; E-266 Jet; Oct. 5, 1967.

Distance in a Straight Line—20,168.75 kms. (12,532.28 mi.)—Maj. Clyde P. Evely, USAF, United States; Boeing B52-H; Kadena, Okinawa, to Madrid, Spain, Jan. 11, 1962.

Distance Over a Closed Circuit—18,245.5 kms. (11,336.92 mi.)—Capt. William Stevenson, USAF, United States; Boeing B52-H; Seymour-Johnson, N. C.; Kindley, Bermuda; Sondrestrom, Greenland; Anchorage, Alaska; March AFB, Calif.; Key West, Fla.; Seymour-Johnson, N. C., June 6-7, 1962.

Altitude—95,935.99 meters (314,750 feet)—Maj. Robert M. White, USAF, United States; North American X-15-1; Edwards AFB, Calif., July 17, 1962.

Altitude in Horizontal Flight—24,462.596 meters (80,257.86 ft.)—Col. R. L. Stephens, USAF, United States; Lockheed YF-12A; Edwards Air Force Base, Calif., May 1, 1965.

MANNED SPACE CRAFT

Duration—28 days 49 min. 48 sec.-Charles Conrad, Jr., Joseph P. Kerwin, Paul J. Weitz, U.S.; Skylab 1; May 25-June 22, 1973.

Altitude—377,668.9 kms. (234,672.5 mi.)-Frank Borman, James A. Lovell, Jr., William Anders, United States; Spacecraft Apollo 8; Dec. 21-27, 1968.

Greatest Mass Lifted—127,980 kgs. (282,197 lbs.)-Frank Borman, James A. Lovell, Jr. William Anders, United States; Spacecraft Apollo 8; Dec. 21-27, 1968.

Distance—18,531,534 kms. (11,514,960 mi.)-Charles Conrad, Jr., Joseph P. Kerwin, Paul J. Weitz, U.S.; Skylab 1; May 25-June 22, 1973.

All other records, international in scope, are termed World "Class" records and are divided into classes: airships, free balloons, airplanes, seaplanes, amphibians, gliders, and rotorplanes. Airplanes (Class C) are sub-divided into four groups: Group I-Piston Engine Aircraft, Group II—Turbo-prop Aircraft, Group III—Jet Aircraft, Group IV—Rocket powered Aircraft. A partial listing of world records follows:

WORLD "CLASS" RECORDS

AIRPLANES (Class C, Group 1—Piston Engine)

Distance, Closed Circuit—14,441.26 kms. (8,974 mi.)—James R. Bede, United States; BD-2, 1 Continental IO 360-C engine, Columbus, Ohio to Kansas City Course, Nov. 7-9, 1969.

Distance, airline International—18,081.990 kms. (11,235.6 miles)-Comdr. Thomas D. Davies, USN; Comdr. Eugene P. Rankin, USN; Comdr. Walter S. Reid, USN, and Lt. Comdr. Ray A. Tabeling, USN: United States; Lockheed P2V-1; from Pearce Field, Perth, Australia, to Port Columbus, Columbus, Ohio, Sept. 29-Oct. 1, 1946 (United States)-same.

Maximum speed over 3-kilometer measured course (International)–776.449 km.p.h. (482.462 m.p.h.)–Darryl Greenamyer, United States, Grumman F8F, Edwards AFB, Calif., Aug. 16, 1969. **(United States)**–663.054 km.p.h. (412.002 m.p.h.)–Jacqueline Cochran, United States; North American F-51, Thermal, Calif., Dec. 17, 1947.

Speed for 100 Kilometers (62.137 miles) without payload (International)–755.668 km.p.h. (469.549 m.p.h.)–Jacqueline Cochran, United States; North American F-51, Coachella Valley, Calif., Dec. 10, 1947. **(United States)**–same.

Speed for 1,000 Kilometers (621.369 miles) without payload–693.78 km.p.h. (431.09 m.p.h.)–Jacqueline Cochran, United States; North American P-51; Santa Rosasummit, Calif.–Flagstaff, Arizona course, May 24, 1948.

Speed for 5,000 Kilometers (3,106.849) without payload–544.59 km.p.h. (338.39 m.p.h.)–Capt. James Bauer, USAF, United States; Boeing B-29; Dayton, Ohio, June 28, 1946.

Speed Around the World–318.28 km.p.h. (197.77 m.p.h.)–Trevor K. Brougham, Australia; Beechcraft Baron C-55, 2 Rolls-Royce Continental 10-470-L engines; Darwin, Australia; Aug. 5-10, 1971. Time: 5 days 5 hrs. 57 min.

AIRPLANES (Class C, Group II—Turbo-prop)

Distance in a Straightline–14,052.95 kms (8,732.09 miles)–Lt. Col. Edgar L. Allison, Jr., U.S. Lockheed HC-130 Hercules Aircraft; Feb. 20, 1972.

Speed Over a 15-25 Km. Course–Cdr. D. H. Lilienthal, USN, United States; Lockheed P3C Orion Aircraft; 806 km.p.h. (501 m.p.h.); Jan. 27, 1971.

Altitude–15,549 meters (51,014 ft.)–Donald R. Wilson, Greenville, Tex., LTV L450F Aircraft; Mar. 27, 1972.

Speed for 1,000 Kilometers (621.369 miles) without payload (International)–871.38 km.p.h. (541.449 m.p.h.)–Ivan Soukhomline, Boris Timochok and crew, USSR; TU-114 Swept Wing Monoplane, 4 turbo-prop TB-12 engines; Sternberg Course, Mar. 24, 1960.

Speed for 5,000 Kilometers (3,106.849 miles) without payload (International)–877.212 km.p.h. (545.072 m.p.h.)–Ivan Soukhomline, K. Sapielkine and crew, USSR; TU-114 Swept Wing Monoplane, 4 turbo-prop TB-12 engines; Sternberg-Svierdlovsk-Sebastopol-Sternberg, Apr. 9, 1960.

AIRPLANES (Class C, Group III—Jet-powered)

Distance in a Straight Line–20,168.78 kms. (12,532.28 mi.)–Maj. Clyde P. Evely, USAF, United States; Boeing B52-H, 8 Pratt & Whitney TF-33P-3 engines; Kadena, Okinawa, to Madrid, Spain. Jan. 10-11, 1962.

Distance in a Closed Circuit–18,245.05 kms. (11,336.92 miles)–Capt. William Stevenson, USAF, United States; Boeing B52-H, 8 Pratt & Whitney TF-33P-3 engines; terminal: Seymour-Johnson, N. C., June 6-7, 1962.

Altitude–34,714 meters (113,890.848 feet)–Gueorgui Mossolov, USSR; E-66A jet monoplane, triangular wing, T.R.D. and G.R.D. engines; Podmoskovnoe, USSR, Apr. 28, 1961.

Speed Over a 3-Kilometer Course–1,452.777 km.p.h. (902,769 m.p.h.)–Lt. Hunt Hardisty, USN, United States; McDonnell F4H Phantom, 2 GE J-79 jet engines; White Sands, N. M., Aug. 29, 1961.

Speed for 100 Kilometers–2,600 km.p.h. (1,615 m.p.h.)–Alexander Fedotov, USSR; E-266 Airplane, 2 RD jet engines; Apr. 8, 1973.

Speed for 500 Kilometers in a Closed Circuit–2,981.5 km.p.h. (1,852.61 m.p.h.)–Mikhail Komarov, USSR; E-266 Airplane, 2 RD jet engines; Oct. 5, 1967.

Speed for 1,000 Kilometers in a Closed Circuit–2,920.67 km.p.h. (1,814.81 m.p.h.)–Pyotr Ostapenko, USSR; E-266 Airplane, 2 RD jet engines; Oct. 27, 1967.

Speed for 2,000 Kilometers in Closed Circuit–1,708.817 km.p.h. (1,061.808 m.p.h.)–Maj. H. J. Deutchendorf, Jr., USAF, United States; Convair B-58 Hustler Bomber; Desert, Stoval, Boundary, Morris, Desert, Edwards AFB, Calif. Course; Jan. 12, 1961.

Sustained Altitude–24,462.596 meters (80,257.86 feet)–Col. R. L. Stephens, USAF; Lockheed YF-12A, 2 Pratt & Whitney J58 engines; Edwards AFB, California; May 1, 1965.

LIGHT AIRPLANES—Class C-1.d

Distance Airline (International)–12,341.26 kms. (7,668.48 miles)–Max Conrad, United States; Piper Comanche 250, Lycoming 0540-A1A5 250 hp.; Casablanca, Morocco to Los Angeles, June 2-4, 1959.

Speed for 100 Kilometers–(62.137 miles) in a Closed Circuit **(International)**–519.480km.p.h. (322.789 m.p.h.)– Miss. R.M. Sharpe, Great Britain; Vickers Supermarine Spitfire 5-B; Wolverhampton, June 17, 1950.

Gliders (Class D—Single-place)

Distance, Straight Line–1,460.8 kms. (907.7 miles)–Hans Werner Grosse, West Germany; ASK12 sailplane; Luebeck to Biarritz, Apr. 25, 1972.

Altitude above sea level–14,102 meters (46,267 feet)–Paul F. Bikle, United States; Sailplane Schweizer SGS 123E; Mojave, Lancaster, Calif. Feb. 25, 1961.

Helicopters (Class E-1)

Distance in a Straight Line–3,561.55 kms. (2,213.04 miles)–Robert G. Ferry, United States; Hughes YOH-6A Helicopter; Culver City, Calif., to Daytona, Fla., Apr. 6-7, 1966.

Speed over 3-Km. Course–348.971 km. p.h. (216.839 m.p.h.)–Byron Graham, United States; Sikorsky S-67 helicopter; Windsor Locks, Conn., December 14, 1970.

Free Balloons (Tenth category, 4001 cu. meters or more)

Altitude–34,668 meters (113,739.9 feet)–Cmdr. Malcolm D. Ross, USNR, United States; Lee Lewis Memorial Winzen Research Balloon; Gulf of Mexico, May 4, 1961.

F. A. I. COURSE RECORDS

Los Angeles to New York–1,954.79 km.p.h. (1,214.65 m.p.h.)–Capt. Robert G. Sowers, USAF, United States; Convair B-58 Hustler, 4 GE-J-79-5B engines, Elapsed time: 2 hrs. 58.71 secs., Mar. 5, 1962.

New York to Los Angeles–1,741 km.p.h. (1,081.80 m.p.h.)–Capt. Robert G. Sowers, USAF, United States; Convair B-58 Hustler. Elapsed time: 2 hrs. 15 min. 50.08 sec., Mar. 5, 1962.

Los Angeles-New York-Los Angeles–1,681.71 km.p.h. (1,044.46 m.p.h.)–Capt. Robert G. Sowers, USAF, United States; Convair B-58 Hustler; Elapsed time: 4 hrs. 41 min. 14.98 sec., Mar. 5, 1962.

New York to Paris–1,753.068 km.p.h. (1,089.36 m.p.h.)–Maj. W. R. Payne, United States; Convair B-58 Hustler; Elapsed time: 3 hrs. 10 min. 58 sec., May 26, 1961.

New York to London: (International)–1,164.865 km.p.h. (723.5 m.p.h.)–Lt. Cdr. Davies, U. K.; Phantom F-4K Airplane; May 11, 1969. Elapsed time: 4 hours; 46 mins. 57.6 secs.

London to New York (International)–945.423 km.p.h. (587.457 m.p.h.)–Maj. Burl B. Davenport, Lt. James J. Jones, and crew USAF, United States; Boeing KC-135 Stratotanker; London International Airport to Idlewild International Airport, Long Island, June 27, 1958. Elapsed time: 5 hours 29 minutes 14.64 seconds.

Baltimore to Moscow, USSR–906.64 km.p.h. (563.36 m.p.h.)–Col. James B. Swindal, USAF, United States; Boeing VC-137 (707), May 19, 1963. Elapsed time: 8 hours 33 minutes 45.4 seconds.

Moscow to Washington, D. C.–788.67 km.p.h. (490.06 m.p.h.)–Col. James B. Swindal, USAF, United States, Boeing VC-137 (707). Elapsed time: 9 hrs. 54 min. 48.5 sec. May 20-21, 1963.

Belfast to Gander, Newfoundland (International)–774.255 km.p.h. (481.099 m.p.h.)–Wing Commander R. P. Beamont and crew, Great Britain; Canberra bomber, two Rolls-Royce turbo-jet engines. Aug. 31, 1951. Elapsed time: 4 hours 18 minutes 24.4 seconds.

Fastest Trips Around the World

Fast circuits of the earth have been a subject of wide interest since Jules Verne, French novelist, described an imaginary trip by Phileas Fogg in Around the World in 80 Days, assertedly occuring Oct. 2, to Dec. 20, 1872. Notable actual such events follow:

Craft, pilot	Terminal	Miles	Time	Date
Nellie Bly	New York, N.Y.		72d 6h 11m	1889
George Francis Train	New York, N.Y.		67d 12h 03m	1890
Charles Fitzmorris	Chicago		60d 13h 29m	1901
J. W. Willis Sayre	Seattle		54d 09h 42m	1903

Craft, pilot	Terminal	Miles	Time	Date
Henry Frederick..			54d 07h 02m	1903
Col. Burnlay-Campbell...................................			40d 19h 30m	1907
Andre Jaeger-Schmidt...................................			39d 19h 42m 38s	1911
John Henry Mears.......................................			35d 21h 36m	1913
Two U.S. Army airplanes........	Seattle (57 hops, 21 countries)......	26,103	351h 11m	1924
Edward S. Evans and Linton				June 16-
Wells (New York World) (1).....	New York..................	18,400	28d 14h 36m 05s	July 14, 1926
John H. Mears and Capt.				June 29-
C. B. D. Collyer...............	New York...................		23d 15h 21m 03s	July 22, 1928
Graf Zeppelin	Friedrichshafen, Ger. via Tokyo,			Aug. 14-
	Los Angeles, Lakehurst, N.J.......	21,700	20d 04h	Sept. 4, 1929
Wiley Post and Harold Gatty	Roosevelt Field, via Arctic			June 23-
(Monoplane Winnie Mae).......	Circle	15,474	8d 15h 51m	July 1, 1931
Wiley Post (Monoplane Winnie	Floyd Bennett Field, via Arctic			
Mae) (2)..................	Circle	15,596	115h 36m 30s	July 15-22, 1933
H. R. Ekins (Scripps-Howard				
Newspapers in race) (Zeppelin				
Hindenburg to Germany, air-				Sept. 30-
planes from Frankfurt)........	Lakehurst, N. J., via Frankfurt, Ger.	25,654	18d 11h 14m 33s	Oct. 19, 1936
Howard Hughes and 4 assistants	New York, Paris, Moscow, Si-			
	beria, Fairbanks, Alaska.........	14,824	3d 19h 08m 10s	July 10-13, 1938
Mrs. Clara Adams (Pan Ameri-	Port Washington, N.Y., ret.			June 28-
can Clipper)..................	Newark, N.J.		16d 19h 04m	July 15, 1939
Globester, U.S. Air Transport				Sept. 28-
Command	Washington, D.C.............	23,279	149h 44m	Oct. 4, 1945
Capt. William P. Odom (A-26	New York, via Paris, Cairo,			
Reynolds Bombshell)...........	Tokyo, Alaska.............	20,000	78h 55m 12s	Apr. 12-16, 1947
America, Pan American 4-engine				
Lockheed Constellation (3).....	New York, eastward..........	22,219	101h 32m	June 17-30, 1947
Col. Edward P. F. Eagan.......	New York................	20,559	147h 15m	Dec. 13, 1948
USAF B-50 Lucky Lady II				Feb. 26-
(Capt. James Gallagher) (4)...	Fort Worth, Texas..............	23,452	94h 01m	Mar. 2, 1949
Thos. G. Lapphier, Jr..........	New York................	22,180	119h 47m	Dec. 2-7, 1949
Jean-Marie Audibert...........	Paris		4d 19h 38m	Dec. 11-15, 1952
Horace C. Boren..............	Idlewild Airport, New York		99h 16m	June 21-25, 1953
Pamela Martin	Midway Airport, Chicago		90h 59m	Dec. 5-8, 1953
Three USAF B-52 Stratofort-	Castle AFB, Merced, Calif., via			
resses (5)..................	Nfld., Morocco, Saudi Arabia,			
	India, Ceylon, P. I., Guam,			
	Riverside, Calif...............	24,325	45h 19m	Jan. 15-18, 1957
Joseph Cavoli	Cleveland, Ohio		80h 13m 37s	Jan. 31-Feb. 4, 1958
Miss K. Kanetake	Tokyo, via Bangkok, Karachi,			
	Rome, Anchorage........	18,580	73h 9m	July 28-31, 1958
Peter Gluckmann (solo).........	San Francisco	22,800	29d	Aug. 22-Sept. 20, 1959
Milton Reynolds	San Francisco		51h 45m 22s	Jan. 12-14 1960
Sue Snyder	Chicago	21,219	62h 59m	June 22-24, 1960
Max Conrad (solo)	Miami, Fla...............	25,946	8d 18h 35m 57s	Feb. 28-Mar. 8, 1961
Sam Miller & Louis Fodor	New York.................		46h 28m	Aug. 3-4, 1963
Jack Martin, Fred Austin, Harrison				
Finch, Robert Buck, James				
Gannett	Honolulu	26,230	62h 27m 35s	Nov. 15-17, 1965
Henry G. Beaird.............	Wichita, Kan.	22,992	65h 38m 49s	May 23-26, 1966
Robert & Joan Wallick (6)	Manila, Philippines	23,129	5d 6h 17m 10s	June 2-7, 1966
Arthur Godfrey, Richard Merrill				
Fred Austin, Karl Keller........	New York................	23,333	86h 9m 1s	June 4-7, 1966
Trevor K. Brougham	Darwin, Australia	24,800	5d 5h 57m	Aug. 5-Oct. 10, 1972

1. Mileage by train and auto, 4,100; by plane, 6,300; by steamship, 8,000. 2. First to fly solo around northern circumference of the world, also first to fly twice around the world. 3. Inception of regular commercial global air service. 4. First non-stop round-the-world flight, refueled 4 times in flight. 5. First non-stop global flight by jet planes; refueled in flight by KC-97 aerial tankers; average speed, approx. 525 m.p.h. 6. Official world record for light planes.

Aviation Hall of Fame

The Aviation Hall of Fame at Dayton, Ohio, is dedicated to honoring aviation's outstanding pioneers. It operates as a non-profit privately supported organization under a charter granted in 1964 by the Congress of the U. S.

1962
Orville Wright
Wilbur Wright

1963
Octave Chanute
Samuel Pierpont Langley
Frank Purdy Lahm
Benjamin Delahauf Foulois

1964
Thomas Scott Baldwin
Theodore Gordon Ellyson
Henry W. Walden
Glenn Hammond Curtiss
Calbraith Perry Rodgers
John Joseph Montgomery

1965
Alexander Graham Bell
Alfred Austell Cunningham
Albert Cushing Read
Eugene Burton Ely
A. Roy Knabenshue
Thomas Etholen Selfridge
Charles Edward Taylor
Edward Vernon Rickenbacker

1966
Lincoln Beachey
William Edward Boeing
Robert Hutchings Goddard
Glenn Luther Martin
William "Billy" Mitchell
John Henry Towers

1967
Henry Harley "Hap" Arnold
James Harold Doolittle
Charles Augustus Lindbergh
Carl Andrew Spaatz

1968
Richard Evelyn Byrd
Amelia Earhart Putnam
John Arthur MacReady
Igor Ivan Sikorsky

1969
Donald Wills Douglas
Grover Cleveland Loening
Wiley Hardeman Post
Juan Terry Trippe

1970
Alexander P. deSeversky
Ira Clarence Eaker
Robert Ellsworth Gross

1971
William McPherson Allen
Jacqueline Cochran (Odlum)
Harry Frank Guggenheim
George Churchill Kenney

1972
Claire Lee Chennault
Leroy Randle Grumman
J. H. "Dutch" Kindelberger
Curtis Emerson LeMay

1973
Colonel Bernt Balchen, USAF (Ret.): Authority on polar aviation; pilot on Admundsen-Ellsworth and Byrd Expeditions in 1920s and 1930s. Made first flight across the South Pole, first to pilot plane over both poles, created Arctic Rescue Squadron.
Howard Robard Hughes: Talented racing pilot, held world speed record, transcontinental speed records and round-the-world flight record. Aircraft manufacturer and promoter of airline development.
Dr. Elmer Ambrose Sperry, Sr.: Outstanding inventor and industrialist; developed gyroscopic aircraft controls and instruments including automatic stabilizer, turn and bank indicator, gyrocompass and automatic pilot.
Brigadier General Charles Elwood Yeager, USAF: Combat and test pilot credited with 13 victories in World War II. Experimental test pilot XI, first to exceed speed of sound (1947), first to exceed MACH II (1953).

Air Line Distances Between Selected Cities of the World

Source: Defense Mapping Agency Aerospace Center (Statute Miles)
Point-to-point measurements are usually from City Hall

	Bangkok	Berlin	Cairo	Capetown	Caracas	Chicago	Hong Kong	Honolulu	Lima	London
Bangkok	....	5,352	4,523	6,300	10,555	8,570	1,077	6,609	12,244	5,933
Berlin	5,352	....	1,797	5,961	5,238	4,414	5,443	7,320	6,896	583
Cairo	4,523	1,797	....	4,480	6,342	6,141	5,066	8,848	7,726	2,185
Capetown ...	6,300	5,961	4,480	....	6,366	8,491	7,376	11,535	6,072	5,989
Caracas.....	10,555	5,238	6,342	6,366	....	2,495	10,165	6,021	1,707	4,655
Chicago.....	8,570	4,414	6,141	8,491	2,495	....	7,797	4,256	3,775	3,958
Hong Kong ..	1,077	5,443	5,066	7,376	10,165	7,797	....	5,556	11,418	5,990
Honolulu ..	6,609	7,320	8,848	11,535	6,021	4,256	5,556	....	5,947	7,240
London	5,933	583	2,185	5,989	4,655	3,958	5,990	7,240	6,316	....
Madrid......	6,337	1,165	2,087	5,308	4,346	4,189	6,558	7,872	5,907	785
Melbourne ..	4,568	9,918	8,675	6,425	9,717	9,673	4,595	5,505	8,059	10,500
Mexico City ..	9,793	6,056	7,700	8,519	2,234	1,690	8,788	3,789	2,639	5,558
Montreal	8,338	3,740	5,427	7,922	2,438	745	7,736	4,918	3,970	3,254
Moscow.....	4,389	1,006	1,803	6,279	6,177	4,987	4,437	7,047	7,862	1,564
New Delhi ...	1,813	3,598	2,758	5,769	8,833	7,486	2,339	7,412	10,432	4,181
New York ...	8,669	3,979	5,619	7,803	2,120	714	8,060	4,969	3,639	3,469
Paris.......	5,877	548	1,998	5,786	4,732	4,143	5,990	7,449	6,370	214
Peking......	2,046	4,584	4,698	8,044	8,950	6,604	1,217	5,077	10,349	5,074
Rio de Janeiro	9,994	6,209	6,143	3,781	2,804	5,282	11,009	8,288	2,342	5,750
Rome.......	5,494	737	1,326	5,231	5,195	4,824	5,774	8,040	6,750	895
San Francisco	7,931	5,672	7,466	10,248	3,902	1,859	6,905	2,398	4,518	5,367
Singapore ...	883	6,164	5,137	6,008	11,402	9,372	1,605	6,726	11,689	6,747
Stockholm...	5,089	528	2,096	6,423	5,471	4,331	5,063	6,875	7,166	942
Tokyo	2,865	5,557	5,958	9,154	8,808	6,314	1,791	3,859	9,631	5,959
Warsaw	5,033	322	1,619	5,935	5,559	4,679	5,147	7,366	7,215	905
Washington..	8,807	4,181	5,822	7,895	2,047	596	8,155	4,838	3,509	3,674

	Madrid	Melbourne	Mexico City	Montreal	Moscow	Nairobi	New Delhi	New York	Paris	Peking
Bangkok	6,337	4,568	9,793	8,338	4,389	4,483	1,813	8,669	5,877	2,046
Berlin	1,165	9,918	6,056	3,740	1,006	3,949	3,598	3,979	548	4,584
Cairo	2,087	8,675	7,700	5,427	1,803	2,186	2,758	5,619	1,998	4,698
Capetown ...	5,308	6,425	8,519	7,922	6,279	2,542	5,769	7,803	5,786	8,044
Caracas.....	4,346	9,717	2,234	2,438	6,177	7,178	8,833	2,120	4,732	8,950
Chicago.....	4,189	9,673	1,690	745	4,987	8,011	7,486	714	4,143	6,604
Hong Kong ..	6,550	4,505	8,788	7,736	4,437	5,449	2,339	8,060	5,990	1,217
Honolulu ..	7,872	5,505	3,789	4,918	7,047	10,741	7,412	4,969	7,449	5,077
London	785	10,500	5,558	3,254	1,564	4,231	4,181	3,469	214	5,074
Madrid......	....	10,758	5,643	3,448	2,147	3,841	4,530	3,593	655	5,745
Melbourne ..	10,758	....	8,426	10,395	8,950	7,153	6,329	10,359	10,430	5,643
Mexico City ..	5,643	8,426	....	2,317	6,676	9,219	9,120	2,090	5,725	7,753
Montreal	3,448	10,395	2,317	....	4,401	7,267	7,012	331	3,432	6,519
Moscow.....	2,147	8,950	6,676	4,401	....	3,930	2,698	4,683	1,554	3,607
New Delhi ...	4,530	6,329	9,120	7,012	2,698	3,374	....	7,318	4,102	2,353
New York ...	3,593	10,359	2,090	331	4,683	7,364	7,318	....	3,636	6,844
Paris.......	655	10,430	5,725	3,432	1,554	4,022	4,102	3,636	....	5,120
Peking......	5,745	5,643	7,753	6,519	3,607	5,727	2,353	6,844	5,120	....
Rio de Janeiro	5,045	8,226	4,764	5,078	7,170	5,560	8,753	4,801	5,684	10,768
Rome.......	851	9,929	6,377	4,104	1,483	3,339	3,684	4,293	690	5,063
San Francisco	5,803	7,856	1,887	2,543	5,885	9,597	7,691	2,572	5,577	5,918
Singapore ...	7,080	3,759	10,327	9,203	5,228	4,638	2,571	9,534	6,673	2,771
Stockholm...	1,653	9,630	6,012	3,714	716	4,281	3,414	3,986	1,003	4,133
Tokyo	6,706	5,062	7,035	6,471	4,660	6,999	3,638	6,757	6,053	1,307
Warsaw	1,427	9,598	6,337	4,022	721	3,801	3,277	4,270	852	4,325
Washington..	3,792	10,180	1,885	489	4,876	7,551	7,500	205	3,840	6,942

	Rio de Janeiro	Rome	San Francisco	Singapore	Stockholm	Teheran	Tokyo	Vienna	Warsaw	Wash. D.C.
Bangkok	9,994	5,494	7,931	883	5,089	3,391	2,865	5,252	5,033	8,807
Berlin	6,209	737	5,672	6,164	528	2,185	5,557	326	322	4,181
Cairo	6,143	1,326	7,466	5,137	2,096	1,234	5,958	1,481	1,619	5,822
Capetown ...	3,781	5,231	10,248	6,008	6,423	5,241	9,154	5,656	5,935	7,895
Caracas.....	2,804	5,195	3,902	11,402	5,471	7,320	8,808	5,372	5,559	2,047
Chicago.....	5,282	4,824	1,859	9,372	4,331	6,502	6,314	4,698	4,679	596
Hong Kong ..	11,009	5,774	6,905	1,605	5,063	3,843	1,791	5,431	5,147	8,155
Honolulu ..	8,288	8,040	2,398	6,726	6,875	8,070	3,859	7,632	7,366	4,838
London	5,750	895	5,367	6,747	942	2,743	5,959	771	905	3,674
Madrid......	5,045	851	5,803	7,080	1,653	2,978	6,706	1,128	1,427	3,792
Melbourne ..	8,226	9,929	7,856	3,759	9,630	8,184	5,062	9,790	9,598	10,180
Mexico City ..	4,764	6,377	1,887	10,327	6,012	8,184	7,035	6,320	6,337	1,885
Montreal	5,078	4,104	2,543	9,203	3,714	5,880	6,471	4,009	4,022	489
Moscow.....	7,170	1,483	5,885	5,228	716	1,532	4,660	1,043	721	4,876
New Delhi ...	8,753	3,684	7,691	2,571	3,414	1,583	3,638	3,465	3,277	7,500
New York ...	4,801	4,293	2,572	9,534	3,986	6,141	6,757	4,234	4,270	205
Paris.......	5,684	690	5,577	6,673	1,003	2,625	6,053	645	852	3,840
Peking......	10,768	5,063	5,918	2,771	4,133	3,490	1,307	4,648	4,325	6,942
Rio de Janeiro	....	5,707	6,613	9,785	6,683	7,374	11,532	6,127	6,455	4,779
Rome.......	5,707	....	6,259	6,229	1,245	2,127	6,142	477	820	4,497
San Francisco	6,613	6,259	....	8,448	5,399	7,362	5,150	5,994	5,854	2,441
Singapore ...	9,785	6,229	8,448	....	5,936	4,103	3,300	6,035	5,843	9,662
Stockolm....	6,683	1,245	5,399	5,936	....	2,173	5,053	780	494	4,183
Tokyo	11,532	6,142	5,150	3,300	5,053	4,775	....	5,689	5,347	6,791
Warsaw	6,455	820	5,854	5,843	494	1,879	5,689	347	....	4,472
Washington..	4,779	4,497	2,441	9,662	4,183	6,341	6,791	4,438	4,472	....

Pollution Costs Billions

Source: President's Council on Environmental Quality, 4th Annual Report, September, 1973

The costs of pollution are divided into 4 types. Damage costs are those that result from the harm done by pollution—illness and property damage being the largest costs of air pollution, for example. These costs can be roughly estimated.

Estimated Air Pollution Damage Costs With No Controls
(in billions of dollars)

Damage to—	1968[1]	1977[2]
Health[3]	$ 6.1	$ 9.3
Residential property	5.2	8.0
Materials, vegetation[4]	4.9	7.6
Total	$16.2	$24.9

(1) In 1968 dollars. (2) In 1970 dollars. (3) Includes treatment and prevention of illnesses plus income lost by disability and early death. (4) Includes damage to approx. 50 materials most susceptible to air pollution damage, and direct visible damage affecting yield, quality and marketability of crops and forests.

Avoidance costs are those that people incur when they attempt to avoid or reduce damage costs. These costs are very difficult to determine. They include the costs of driving to a more distant beach, because the one nearby is polluted. Also included may be part of the cost of some clothes dryers; in some areas, the air is too dirty to hang clothes out to dry.

Transaction costs refer to expenditures for research and development, planning, monitoring the environment and specific polluters, the setting and enforcement of standards, etc. A large portion of federal anti-pollution funds are spent on transaction costs.

Monitoring is one of the major transaction costs. It is estimated that there are 70,000 to 100,000 major air pollution sources, each emitting over 25 tons of any one pollutant each year. A single measurement and analysis of emissions from one smoke stack can cost up to $5,000.

Abatement costs are those involved in attempting to reduce pollution at its source and decrease the damage it does to the environment. Abatement costs include the expense of buying, and paying interest on loans for, such items as "scrubbers" to clean smokestack emissions. They should also properly include such industrial costs as changes in production methods, lowered by-product revenues, etc. but these costs are hard to estimate.

The Environmental Protection Agency estimates that by 1981, the total annual cost of pollution abatement will more than triple to reach $39.5 billion dollars. (Their estimate is figured in 1972 dollars to take account of the effect of future inflation.)

Federal, state and local government expenditures will cover only about 35% of abatement costs between 1971 and 1981. The rest will be paid for out of private funds in the form of higher retail prices or lower stock dividends.

Given the costs of preventing further damage to the environment, is pollution control worth the price? If the costs of air pollution and prevention are any indication, the answer is a firm Yes.

While the table below shows an estimated savings of less than $2 billion, it should be noted that health damage costs from some auto emission pollutants are not included. Savings in direct health costs and indirectly through decreases in auto accident and insurance costs could be considerable.

Total Pollution Control Costs, 1971
(estimated, in billions of 1972 dollars)

	O&M[1]	Capital[2]	Total
Air pollution			
Public	0.2	—	0.2
Private			
Mobile[3]	1.1	—	1.2
Stationary	.4	.3	.7
Total	1.7	.4	2.1
Water pollution			
Public			
Federal	.2	na	na
State, local	1.2	3.8	5.0
Private			
Mfg.	.4	.3	.7
Utilities	.2	.1	.3
Total	2.0	4.2	6.0
Solid wastes			
Public	1.0	.2	1.2
Private	2.0	—	2.0
Total	3.0	.2	3.2
Grand Total	6.7	4.8	11.3[4]

(—) less than $50 million.
(1) Operating and maintaining pollution control devices. (2) Interest and depreciation. (3) Excluding heavy-duty vehicles. (4) Nothing was spent on control of water pollution from feedlots; no data are available on costs for noise and radiation control or for land reclamation after surface mining.

Air Pollution Damage and Control Costs, 1977
(estimated in billions of 1970 dollars)

Pollution source	Damages Without Controls	Damages With Controls	Control Costs
Mobile	2.2	1.2	8.4
Solid waste	.6	.2	.2
Stationary fuel use	12.8	3.4	2.5
Industry processes	7.0	3.7	1.2
Miscellaneous	2.3	2.3	0
Total	24.9	10.8	12.3

1972 Federal Transaction Costs
(in millions of dollars)

	Air	Water	Land	Other	Multi-media[1]	Total
Research and Development	136.5	70.2	26.3	82.3	32.8	348.1
Planning	2.2	19.8	.2	3.5	1.2	26.9
Monitoring	29.0	30.8	4.4	18.4	2.0	84.6
Administration, enforcement	82.2	72.8	0	16.6	27.4	199.0
Other	15.0	92.5	7.5	83.4	4.5	202.9
Total	264.9	286.1	38.4	204.2	67.9	861.5

[1] Two or more environmental factors: air and water, land and water, etc.

1973 EQ*

Twenty-six years ago the *Bulletin of Atomic Scientists* established a symbol on which to record their subjective collective judgment of our nearness to atomic war. Their symbol was a clock whose one hand indicated how many minutes remained before midnight. Recently, the hands on that clock moved backward several minutes: a reflection of East-West detente certainly, but perhaps also a reflection of the *Bulletin's* effort to arouse public attention to the danger of atomic war.

A few years ago, the National Wildlife Federation began to record a similar subjective collective judgment. Their symbols are 7 dials which measure year-to-year changes in 7 areas of environmental quality. Their measurements are rough. Their judgments regarding progress and decline are those of environmental protection advocates influenced by very high standards of environmental quality. But, the dials do provide some guidance for individual judgment. Over the coming years, they may engage our attention as they illustrate success or failure in achieving one set of goals.

TREND: We're still losing, but not as fast. Chance to turn corner in 1973.
GOOD NEWS:
- U.S. to spend new billions on water treatment.
- Public outcry spurs new clean water laws.
- Clean water can save your family $87 yearly.

BAD NEWS:
- More and more sewage dumped into streams.
- Many cities supply unsafe drinking water.
- Farm feedlot, new villain, is getting worse.

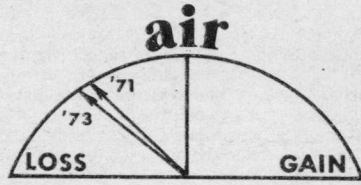

TREND: Rate of pollution has slowed. Now for long climb back to clean air.
GOOD NEWS:
- Emission control devices cut auto pollution.
- Air pollution cleanup could save average family $113 each year in cost of living.
- New laws, strict enforcement = cleaner air.

BAD NEWS:
- Health bill for dirty air: $6 billion annually.
- Auto emission controls use 15% more gasoline.
- Use of 'dirtier' fossil fuels increasing fast.

TREND: Static. Better management, but we're cutting too much timber.
GOOD NEWS:
- We're using 15% more of tree than in 1963.
- We're steadily raising timber yield per acre.

BAD NEWS:
- One-fourth of total tree is still wasted.
- 9.2 billion board feet of standing timber destroyed by insects and diseases in 1972.

TREND: Steady gain in food production, but we are losing valuable land.
GOOD NEWS:
- Soil resources, climate, good management, research make U.S. food production tops.

BAD NEWS:
- Concrete is covering more and more farmland.
- Uncertain dangers from buildup of fertilizer and herbicides in intensively farmed soil.

*Environmental Quality

TREND: Still going wrong way. Habitat destruction hurts wildlife.

GOOD NEWS:
- Public gradually realizing value of wildlife.
- Use of persistent pesticides greatly curtailed.
- 150,000 acres added to wildlife refuges in 1972.

BAD NEWS:
- Urban sprawl continues to gobble habitat.
- U.S. endangered species list stands at 101.
- No research, no management techniques can compensate for loss of wildlife living space.

TREND: Continued loss. U.S. is using energy and metals at alarming rate.

GOOD NEWS:
- High energy use gives us high living standard.
- Recycling of metals increasing slowly.

BAD NEWS:
- Use of non-renewable fuels is sky-rocketing.
- Strip mining despoils 4,000 acres weekly.
- Valuable fossil fuels not used efficiently.
- Research lags on alternate energy sources.

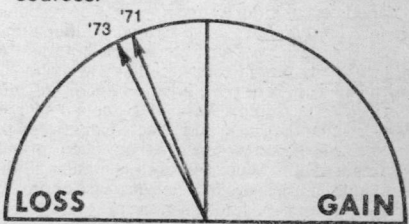

TREND: Down. Ecosystem damaged by too many people, wasteful life-style.

GOOD NEWS:
- U.S. population growth rate lowest ever.
- New areas set aside for recreation.
- Regional land use planning making headway.
- 'New cities' pioneer more pleasant living.

BAD NEWS:
- Even at 'replacement level,' U.S. population will continue to grow for at least 70 years.
- Dependence on autos strangling big cities.
- Wasteful life-style burdens entire ecosystem.

1973 EQ TREND

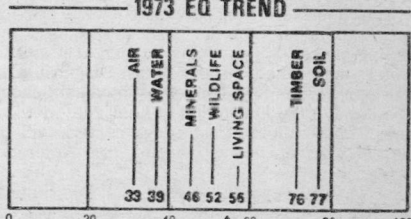

1973 EQ INDEX: 54.4

OVERALL

The National Wildlife Federation's 4th EQ Index stands at 54.4. (100 being the ideal environment). It is down from the 55.5 record by the 3rd Index in 1971. There have been losses in 6 of the 7 categories, though the rate of increase of air and water pollution has been slowed.

Medical News 1973

by David Hendin
Science Editor, Newspaper Enterprise Assn.

Some of the biggest medical stories of 1973 concerned the areas of biomedical ethics and the rights of patients to play a role in decision making where their own health is concerned.

However, the year was not without news of significant medical breakthroughs.

Twice in 1973, Dr. Irving S. Cooper of St. Barnabas Hospital, Bronx, N.Y., scored major victories over involuntary movement disorders through a type of brain surgery that has made him world-famous over the past 20 years. In an operation called "cryopulvinectomy", Cooper was able to reverse the spastic paralysis caused by strokes, cerebral palsy and similar brain damage in more than half of the patients on which it was performed. The operation destroys with deep cold an area of the brain called the pulvinar.

Later in the year, medical journals began to carry excited reports of another new Cooper procedure—a so-called brain pacemaker. The device is implanted in the brain and stimulated electrically at regular intervals by an external power source. So far the brain pacemaker has controlled intractable epilepsy and relieved spastic paralysis in several dozen patients.

Cancer Research

On the cancer front, Dr. Albert B. Sabin—known to the world as the developer of the oral polio vaccine—claimed proof that a common virus is a causative factor in 9 different kinds of human cancer. Sabin said that he didn't believe the virus—called herpes simplex and known to be responsible for common fever blisters among other things—was the exclusive cause of cancers, but said that other contributory factors weren't known yet.

A virus expert at the National Cancer Institute (NCI) praised Sabin's work, but stopped short of agreeing that the cause-and-effect link between the herpes viruses and cancers had been proved beyond a doubt. Major research continues in this field and scientists around the world are optimistic of more meaningful findings in the next few years.

In 1973, the first 3 of 20 planned breast cancer detection centers were announced. They will provide free examinations for the early detection of the leading cancer killer among women. The first 3 centers are at the Guttman Breast Diagnostic Institute, NYC; Emory University Medical School, Atlanta; and the University of Louisville Medical School in Kentucky. Cost of the centers will be shared between the NCI and the American Cancer Society.

In April, surgeons in Newark, N.J. and Bethesda, Md., implanted the first 16 American-developed nuclear-powered heart pacemakers. Similar devices developed by the French had been implanted earlier. The American devices have an expected lifetime of at least 10 years, alleviating the necessity of annual surgery to replace pacemaker batteries.

Acupuncture

Research into the still controversial and somewhat mysterious therapy called acupuncture picked up speed last year. Acupuncture was used in the United States to ease pain in Caesarean childbirth as well as abortions. A Hong Kong doctor reported success in using acupuncture to relieve drug addicts' withdrawal symptoms. Famed ear specialist Dr. Samuel Rosen of New York reported that he was carrying out a stringent study of whether acupuncture could help relieve nerve deafness.

In January, the 7,000-member American Hospital Assn. (AHA) approved a 12-point "Patient's Bill of Rights," which reaffirmed, among other important points, the patient's right to a full, clear explanation of his medical conditions, and an individual's right to choose death by rejecting medical treatment. The AHA document was seen as a giant step toward returning privacy and dignity to the care of patients.

Discussion continued this year on the controversial "Tuskegee Syphilis Study," which began in 1932 and allowed 430 Alabama blacks to suffer syphilis without treatment in order for doctors to study the long term effects of that venereal disease. Twenty-eight men apparently died as a direct result of the disease. As a result of study into the affair, a 9-man advisory panel studied the affair and reported to Congress, urging creation of a federal board to guide scientific research on human beings.

The bioethical debate of the year, however, concerned the reported involuntary sterilizations of 2 young black girls in Alabama. The girls' lawyer filed suit charging that a federally funded family planning clinic had sterilized the 12- and 14-years-olds without the knowledge or consent of their parents. After the disclosure of this case, there were at least a dozen other reports of similar cases of involuntary sterilizations of minors.

Psychosurgery Restricted

Another biomedical ethics issue that came to a head in 1973 concerned surgery on the brain which is aimed primarily at altering a person's behavior. In July, a 3-judge panel in Wayne County, Michigan ruled that experimental psychosurgery could not be performed on persons confined in state institutions, even if their consent was formally obtained. The courts left the door open for possible use of psychosurgery in these situations once the operations reach a point where benefits clearly outweigh risks. In the past, psychosurgery has been used to try to alter the behavior and emotional makeup of mentally ill patients who don't respond to conventional therapy.

In January, the U.S. Supreme Court overruled all of the various state laws that prohibited or restricted a women's right to have an abortion during her first 3 months of pregnancy. The high court issued a new set of national guidelines that have already considerably liberalized anti-abortion laws in 46 states where they existed. The court said that during the first 3 months of pregnancy the decision to have an abortion was strictly up to the woman and her doctor. During the next 6 months, the court said, the state "may regulate the abortion procedure in ways that are reasonably related to maternal health." For the last 10 weeks of pregnancy—the time during which the fetus is usually capable of surviving outside the womb—any state may prohibit abortions except when the mother's life or health are at risk.

To help disseminate objective information in all of these important areas of medical consumerism and biomedical ethics, a new organization, the National Center for Bioethics, Box 313, Ridgefield, NJ, has been formed.

Zoos Grow on Ecology Interest

by Edward Ricciuti

A spin-off of public interest in environmental matters during the past few years has been the increased popularity of zoos and aquariums, a trend that during the past year showed no signs of weakening. It was a year for opening of new institutions, development of new exhibits, and plans for more zoos to come.

Minnesota Governor Wendell Anderson signed a bill in May approving the $23,000,000 Minnesota State Zoo, to be built south of Minneapolis and St. Paul. A master plan calling for development of Bridgeport, Connecticut's Beardsley Park Zoo was unveiled during the summer. The plan provides for Beardsley Park to be redesigned as a zoo for New World animals, which visitors will view from open-roofed buses decorated in a circus motif—a reminder that Bridgeport is the city of P.T. Barnum. Beardsley Park Zoo, according to its master plan, opened outdoor exhibits for spider monkeys and ocelots, giving these tropical animals large open-air enclosure but allowing them access to heated quarters in the zoo's main building through specially-designed doors.

Mystic Marinelife

A brand new institution, the Mystic Marinelife Aquarium opened its doors this fall in the historic seaport and former whaling village of Mystic, Connecticut. Built at a cost of more than $5,000,000 and housing more than 2,000 sea creatures, the aquarium focuses on creatures from North American waters, housed in exhibits that provide information on ecology, behavior and how animals adapt to their environment. The Mystic Marinelife Aquarium is operated by Aquarium Systems, Inc., of East Lake, Ohio, which also operates the Niagara Falls (New York) Aquarium. The Mystic institution features 3 main exhibit sections, dealing with adaptation, aquatic communities and the open sea, as well as a 1,400-seat marine theater where sea mammals such as dolphins and whales will be used to demonstrate important facts of animal behavior.

The New England Aquarium, in Boston, opened a coral reef community in a 2,500-gallon tank that eventually will hold more than 400 colorful tropical fishes. The aquarium also announced that its marine mammal pavilion, a $2,000,000 project, will be open this June.

Several zoos completed major renovation projects, perhaps the largest being the expansion of Warner Bros. Jungle Habitat in West Milford, Milford, New Jersey. The $2,000,000 expansion was undertaken (at the end of Jungle Habitat's first season, which ended in January, 1973) to alleviate traffic congestion on local roads and to make the park more attractive to visitors. During the summer, Jungle Habitat added several new exhibits, including a section where visitors can drive their cars amidst tigers—12 Siberian and one Bengal.

Hippos and Dragons

Lion Country Safari near West Palm Beach, Florida, constructed a large lake for hippos, which had been exhibited in another section of the park. The 4 adult hippos, averaging 4,500 pounds each, were tranquilized, placed in slings, and lofted aboard a truck by a crane, for movement to the new lake.

The San Diego Zoo opened an exhibit of dragons —not the creatures of myth, but rare monitor lizards from the island of Komodo, the so-called Komodo dragons. The zoo's big reptiles, which can reach a length of 10 feet, now live in an exhibit that measures 60 by 30 feet, has quarters that are heated and a large pool.

Work moved apace in Columbia, South Carolina, where a new zoo will be opened this April. The zoo will feature a closed-circuit television system to give visitors a peek at bears and their cubs deep within their dens.

The San Diego Zoo also opened a new exhibit with a 350-foot-long river designed for aquatic African antelope and birds. Covering an acre, the exhibit holds red lechwe and sitatunga, both water-loving African antelope, and a number of ducks and geese. The river begins with a waterfall 25 feet high and contains a second fall 12 feet high.

Environmental Education

The Portland Zoo in Oregon completed construction of a new education building with an auditorium capable of seating 150 people. This project was one of several major educational efforts undertaken by zoos, which are emerging as environmental education institutions. The Storyland Zoo in Alberta, Canada, conducted 3 new summer programs for youngsters on the care and treatment of animals. Children were involved in feeding, medical care and observation of animals at the zoo. In addition, Storyland dispatched a traveling zoo on a truck to shopping centers, senior citizen's homes, and libraries.

The Philadelphia Zoo received grants totalling $16,000 for its educational programs, which focus on zoo visits by the city's school children. Cheyenne Mountain Zoo of Colorado Springs and Seattle's Woodland Park Zoo conducted training programs for volunteer teachers who aid these institutions in their educational efforts.

The Jacksonville Zoo in Florida conducted a series of 15-minute television programs on wildlife for school children. In Waco, Texas, the Cen-Tex Zoo began an animal story hour in public schools. Developed by the Baylor University Student Council for Exceptional Children, the program combines presentation of stories by a librarian and the exposure of children to animals in a petting zoo. The St. Paul Zoo has initiated a program of classes on Minnesota animals for youngsters in that city's schools.

Zoo Teaching Guides

Recently more zoos have been working with educators to improve the use of zoos as a teaching resource. Fresno Zoo in California and New Jersey's Jungle Habitat prepared packets of information to be used as teachers' guides for instructors visiting those zoos. Such guides assist teachers in preparing students for a zoo visit, and provide suggestions on what to look for and on projects to be conducted by students after the visit. This Spring, teachers in San Francisco were able to participate in a special training program conducted at that city's zoo.

Several zoos were active in education at a university level. The Oklahoma City Zoo and Oklahoma State University conducted a 2-week course dealing with the operation of a large zoo. The Fresno Zoo was the site of field trips by students from several California colleges. St. Louis

University conducted an entire animal behavior course at the St. Louis Zoo, where students observed behavior patterns of animals in the zoo's collection and discussed the experiences of zoo staff members in dealing with captive animals.

Shedd Aquarium of Chicago offered a combination of adventure and education by opening up its 75-foot collecting boat in the Florida Keys to students who wish to collect, observe and examine marine animals with the aquarium's instructors.

In Toronto, the Metropolitan Toronto Zoological Society moved ahead with its plans for a major new zoo. Queen Elizabeth II and Prince Phillip, during their 1973 Canadian visit, inspected a model of the planned Toronto zoo, which its backers claim will be the "world's finest." As part of the preparations, a large collection of live plants is being established. Greenhouses to hold the collection were donated to the zoo during the year and by mid-summer they were in operation.

Wildlife in The Human Environment

by Edward Ricciuti

When a research scientist at Harvard University imported a small, nondescript moth from Europe for a silk production experiment in 1869, he set off a chain of events that today creates havoc in the forests of the northeastern United States. The moth was the gypsy moth, whose caterpillars have stripped the leaves from countless square miles of northeastern forest. Each summer, with varying intensity in different regions, the gypsy moth plague denudes oaks, willows, birch, and even conifers such as pine, hemlock and spruce.

With few predators, the gypsy moth has flourished and fears are mounting that the creature will spread to other parts of the country. The

Some Endangered Species in North America
Source: U.S. Fish and Wildlife Service

Common Name	Scientific Name	Range
Mammals		
Wood Bison	Bison bison athabascae	Alberta, Canada
Black-Footed Ferret	Mustela nigripes	U.S., Canada
Northern Kit Fox	Vulpus velox hebes	Canada
West Indian (Florida) Manatee	Trichechus inunguis	Caribbean (once U.S.)
Sonoran Pronghorn	Antilocapra americana sonoriensis	U.S., Mexico
Eastern Timber Wolf	Canis lupus lycaon	(endangered in U.S. only)
Northern Rocky Mountain Wolf	Canis lupus irremotus	U.S., Canada
Red Wolf	Canis rufus	U.S.
Eastern Cougar	Felis concolor cougar	U.S., Canada
Birds		
Bald Eagle	Haliaetus leucocephalus	U.S., Canada
Masked Bobwhite	Colinus virginianus ridgwayi	U.S., Mexico
California Condor	Gymnogyps californianus	Southern California
Whooping Crane	Grus americana	Canada, U.S.
Eskimo Curlew	Numenius borealis	Canada to Argentina
American Peregrine Falcon	Falco peregrinus anatum	Canada to Mexico
Arctic Peregrine Falcon	Falco peregrinus tundrius	Canada to Mexico
Aleutian Canada Goose	Branta canadensis leucopareia	U.S. to Japan
Brown Pelican	Pelecanus occidentalis	Canada to Panama
Attwater's Greater Prairie Chicken	Tympanuchus cupido attwateri	U.S.
Bachman's Warbler	Vermivora bachmani	Southeast U.S., Cuba
Kirtland's Warbler	Dendroica kirtlandi	Michigan, Bahamas
Ivory-Billed Woodpecker	Campephilus principalis	Southeast U.S., Cuba

Some Other Endangered Species in the World
Source: U.S. Fish and Wildlife Service

Common Name	Scientific Name	Range
Mammals		
Asiatic Wild Ass	Equus hemionus	Iran to Mongolia
Dugong	Dugong dugon	East Africa to Okinawa
Slender-Horned Gazelle	Gazella leptoceros	North Africa, Arabia
Mountain Gorilla	Gorilla gorilla beringei	Central Africa
Orang Utan	Pongo pygmaeus	Indonesia, Malaysia
Great Indian Rhinoceros	Rhinoceros unicornus	India, Nepal
Javan Rhinoceros	Rhinoceros sondaicus	Indonesia
Sumatran Rhinoceros	Didermocerus sumatrensis	Bangladesh to Vietnam, Indonesia
Northern White Rhinoceros	Ceratotherium simum cottoni	Sudan, Zaire, Uganda
Blue Whale	Balaenoptera musculus musculus	Oceanic
Humpback Whale	Megaptera novaeangliae	Oceanic
Birds		
Great Indian Bustard (largest land bird)	Choriotis nigriceps	India, Pakistan
Japanese Crane	Grus japonicus	Japan (once all north Asia)
Chinese Egret	Egretta eulophotes	China (once all east Asia)
Japanese Crested Ibis	Nipponia nippon	Japan (once all north Asia)

damage caused by the gypsy moth has stimulated controversy over whether or not to combat the leaf-eating caterpillars with pesticides. Environmentalists have urged a ban on mass spraying, contending that natural controls—a viral disease and a handful of predators such as wasps and birds—will take hold. Indeed, in parts of Connecticut in the summer of 1973 gypsy moths seemed to give ground in face of disease and predatory wasps.

The U.S. Department of Agriculture is not counting on the help of predators and disease to dispose of the moth problem, however. In August, 1973, the USDA and the Massachusetts Department of Natural Resources began an effort to suppress the gypsy moth by using the insect's procreative urge to destroy it.

A Deadly Perfume

The key to the project is a tricky substance called "disparlure," an artificial reproduction of the sex attractant that the female gypsy moth uses to lure males. Developed by the USDA, disparlure will be used in the Massachusetts study to draw the males, possibly to traps, thereby removing large numbers of males from the breeding population. The fact that the female moths do not fly makes this approach especially attractive. In the Massachusetts study, the survival of gypsy moths in a 25-square-mile area treated with the artificial sex attractant will be compared with the survival rate in a similar but untreated tract. "Should the test be successful," says the USDA, "further spread of the gypsy moth may be prevented through the use of its sex attractant."

Another introduced animal is growing as a pest in the United States. Early in 1973 the Delaware Museum of Natural History called attention to the rapidly expanding populations of Chinese clams in waterways from coast to coast. The Chinese clam, a mite only three-quarters of an inch long, may have been introduced into California by Chinese immigrants from Canton during the 1880's. In Canton, the clam is eaten as part of the Chinese New Year meal. Vast accumulations of the clams' shells have been found in the Delta Mendota Canal in California's San Joaquin Valley. The clams also have been found in Georgia and South Carolina and now, according to the Delaware Museum, the clam is turning up in the Delaware River. Scientists worry that the clam shells may clog some waterways and necessitate costly removal programs.

Introduced animals generally end up as pests—witness the walking catfish and giant African land snail in Florida—but nevertheless people continue to release animals where they do not belong. For years there has been pressure from some sportsmen to introduce the peacock bass from South America into waters of the Southeastern United States.

Bass, Gambusia and Mosquito

It might not be such a good idea according to a report released this year by the National Science Foundation. The peacock bass was introduced in Panama from Brazil in the 1960's. Today the foot-long relative of the angel fish makes for good angling in Panamanian waters, but it also has been responsible for:

- exterminating a half-dozen other fish in Panama's Gatun Lake.
- reducing populations of herons, kingfishers and other birds that depend on the fish as food.
- interfering with the spring migration of Atlantic tarpon into Lake Gatun.

- increasing mosquito populations and possibly malaria cases.

The peacock bass has gobbled up all sorts of local fish, scientists say, including a species eaten by both tarpon and birds, and the little *Gambusia*, which eats mosquito larvae. The result: a totally lopsided environmental balance, and possible dire consequences, however good the fishing.

This same little *Gambusia*, however, which was introduced to southwestern waters to control mosquitoes, is responsible for endangering nearly a dozen other species of fish. In California, Arizona, New Mexico, Nevada, and Colorado, small fish which also eat mosquito larvae have found their food supplies stripped by the more aggressive *Gambusia*. One species, a relative of the *Gambusia*, was reduced to 3 individuals before its competitor was effectively kept out of a breeding pool in Nevada.

Whale Watch

For years scientists and laymen alike have wondered about what it is that makes some whales and dolphins suddenly strand themselves on the beach. One theory is that environmental conditions in the water interfere with the natural sonar system used by these creatures to navigate, and that they confuse directions. Whatever the cause, the Smithsonian Institution has organized a program to alert its scientists whenever a whale or dolphin is beached along the Atlantic Coast. The scientists will use these opportunities to study the whales, and possibly save them.

Early in the year—January 3, for that matter—the alert program enabled scientists to make observations on one of the rarest of whales, the Blainville's beaked whale, a 12-foot creature that has been little studied. One of these creatures was stranded on the shore at Beach Haven, New Jersey. Notified of the event, scientists rushed to the scene and were able to get the 1,000-pound creature into a swimming pool, then to the New York Aquarium. Critically ill, however, the whale died, but not before scientists learned something about the way in which it breathed. The whale directed its breath from its blowhole forward over its snout instead of straight up in the air, as in the case of larger whales.

Rebirth and New Birth

During June, the United States Department of the Interior recognized the return of the eastern cougar from alleged limbo by placing the creature, long thought to be extinct, on its endangered species list. Once common all through the Eastern half of the nation, the cougar was slaughtered by settlers, and its forest home eliminated. Apparently, however, a handful of cougars escaped. It is now certain that a few dozen cougars live in the Canadian maritime provinces and that a few more may roam the fastnesses of the Appalachian Mountains. Properly protected, the big cat may survive.

Protection is no guarantee of survival, however, for the eastern cougar's close cousin, the Florida cougar (or panther), has been protected for several years, yet according to the World Wildlife Fund it may become extinct. People still are killing the tawny cats in the Florida backwoods, the fund said in August, commenting on a study by scientists who said less than 50 cougars may survive in the Sunshine State. Increasingly, it appears, wild creatures and wild places are in short supply, despite growing public awareness of environmental problems.

The apparent return of the eastern cougar is complemented by the appearance of a dog-like wild animal in New England. Whether the animal is a hybrid coyote-dog or a distinct new species is a matter of controversy. Researchers at Hampshire College in Amherst, Mass., maintain it is a new species which they call the "new wolf." Other researchers in Connecticut, New York and elsewhere are certain it is basically a coyote with some strains of common dog. They call the animal a "coydog."

In any case, the animal is described as a little larger than a coyote and smaller than a wolf. It was first noted in the late 1950's and appears to have increased in population as much of upland New England reverted to forest after farmers abandoned the worked-out soil in the late 1900's. Classed as a predator, it also is an effective scavenger—which probably explains its capacity to survive and prosper on the fringes of the human environment.

Gestation, Longevity and Incubation

Note: The figures on gestation, incubation and longevity given below are averages based on estimates by leading authorities. The potential life span of mammals is rarely attained in nature. The longevity figures for wild animals listed below were based on experience with such animals in zoos.

Animal	Gestation (Days)	Longevity (Years)	Animal	Gestation (Days)	Longevity (Years)	Animal	Gestation (Days)	Longevity (Years)
Ass	365	24	Elephant	645	47	Puma	90	11
Baboon	187	27	Elk	250	22	Rabbit	37	5
Badger	60	15	Fox	52	8	Rhinoceros	450	27
Bat		6	Giraffe	425	10	Sea Lion	350	19
Bear			Goat (dom.)	151		Sheep	154	13
Black	219	19	Goat (mtn.)	184	9	Squirrel	44	8
Grizzly	225	31	Gorilla	257	25	Tiger	105	19
Polar	240	31	Guinea Pig	68	4	Whale	365	37
Beaver	122	13	Horse	330	27	Wolf	63	12
Buffalo	278	20	Kangaroo	42	19	Zebra	365	20
Camel	406	20	Leopard	98	17			
Cat (domestic)	63	15	Lion	100	15-29	**Incubation Time**		
Chimpanzee	231	30	Monkey	164	7	Chicken	21	
Chipmunk	31	7	Moose	240	8	Duck	30	
Cow	284	18	Mouse (meadow)	21	4	Goose	30	
Deer	201	17	Opossum	14-17	4	Pigeon	18	
Dog	61	16	Pig	112	14	Turkey	26	

A Collection of Animal Collectives

The English language boasts an abundance of nouns used to describe groups of things, particularly pairs or aggregations of animals. Some of these words have fallen into comparative disuse, but many of them are still in service, helping to enrich the vocabularies of those who like their language to be precise, who tire of hearing a group referred to as "a bunch of," or who enjoy the sound of words that aren't overworked.

Here is a lexicon of some of these "collectives":

band of gorillas
bed of clams, oysters
bevy of quail, swans
brace of ducks
brood of chicks
cast of hawks
cete of badgers
charm of goldfinches
chattering of choughs
cloud of gnats
clowder of cats
clutch of chicks
clutter of cats
colony of ants
congregation of plovers
covert of coots

covey of quail, partridge
cry of hounds
down of hares
draught of fish
drift of swine
drove of cattle, sheep
exaltation of larks
flight of birds
flock of sheep, geese
gaggle of geese
gam of whales
gang of elks
grist of bees
herd of curlews, elephants
hive of bees
horde of gnats

husk of hares
kindle or **kendle** of kittens
knot of toads
leap of leopards
leash of greyhounds, foxes
litter of pigs
murder of crows
muster of peacocks
mute of hounds
nest of vipers
nest, nide of pheasants
pack of hounds, wolves
pair of horses
pod of whales, seals
pride of lions
school of fish

sedge or **siege** of cranes
shoal of fish, pilchards
skein of geese
skulk of foxes
sleuth of bears
sounder of boars, swine
span of mules
spring of teals
swarm of bees
team of ducks, horses
tribe of goats
trip of goats
troop of kangaroos, monkeys
volery of birds
watch of nightingales
wing of plovers
yoke of oxen

Young of Animals have Special Names

The young of many animals, birds and fish have come to be called by special names. A young eel, for example, is an elver. Many young animals, of course, are often referred to simply as infants or babies. Some of the more distinctive names, and the animals, fish or birds of which these young are the offspring, follow.

bunny: rabbit.
calf: cattle, elephant, antelope, rhino, hippo, whale, etc.
cheeper: grouse, partridge, quail.
chick, chicken: fowl.
cockerel: rooster.
codling, sprag: codfish.
colt: horse (male).
cub: lion, bear, shark, fox, etc.
cygnet: swan.
duckling: duck.
eaglet: eagle.
elver: eel.
eyas: hawk, others.
fawn: deer.

filly: horse (female).
fingerling: fish generally.
flapper: wild fowl.
fledgling: birds generally.
foal: horse, zebra, others.
fry: fish generally.
gosling: goose.
heifer: cow.
joey: kangaroo, others.
kid: goat.
kit: fox, beaver, rabbit, cat.
kitten, kitty, catling: cats, other fur-bearers.
lamb, lambkin, cosset, hog: sheep.
leveret: hare.

nestling: birds generally.
owlet: owl.
parr, smolt, grilse: salmon.
piglet, shoat, farrow, suckling: pig.
polliwog, tadpole: frog.
poult: turkey.
pullet: hen.
pup: dog, seal, sea lion, fox.
puss, pussy: cat.
spike, blinker, tinker: mackerel.
squab: pigeon.
squeaker: pigeon, others.
whelp: dog, tiger, beasts of prey.
yearling: cattle, sheep, horse, etc.
younglet, youngling: animals generally.

National Defense
Data as of Aug., 1973

Chairman, Joint Chiefs of Staff
Adm. Thomas H. Moorer (Navy)

ARMY
Chief of Staff—General Creighton W. Abrams Jr.

General of the Army

	Date of Rank
Bradley, Omar N.	Sept. 20, 1950

Generals

Bennett, Donald V.	Sept.	1,	1972
Davison, Michael S.	May	26,	1971
DePuy, William E.	July	1,	1973
Goodpaster, Andrew J.	July	3,	1968
Kerwin, Walter T., Jr.	Feb.	1,	1973
Miley, Henry A., Jr.	Nov.	1,	1970
Palmer, Bruce, Jr.	Aug.	1,	1968
Rosson, William B.	May	15,	1969
Stilwell, Richard G.	July	31,	1973
Weyand, Frederick C.	Oct.	31,	1970
Zais, Melvin	Aug.	1,	1973

AIR FORCE
Chief of Staff—George S. Brown

Generals

Carlton, Paul K.	Oct.	9,	1972
Catton, Jack J.	Aug.	1,	1969
Clay, Lucius D., Jr.	Sept.	1,	1970
Dougherty, Russell E.	May	5,	1972
Eade, George J.	Apr.	18,	1973
Jones, David C.	Sept.	1,	1971
McKee, Seth J.	July	31,	1969
Meyer, John C.	July	31,	1969

Milton, Theodore R.	July	31,	1971
Momyer, William W.	Dec.	13,	1967
Vogt, John W., Jr.	Apr.	7,	1972
Wade, Horace M.	July	31,	1968

NAVY
Chief of Naval Operations
Admiral Elmo R. Zumwalt, Jr.

Admirals

Bringle, William F. (Aviation)	July	1,	1971
Clarey, Bernard A.	Jan.	17,	1968
Colbert, Richard G.	June	1,	1972
Cousins, Ralph W. (Aviation)	Oct.	30,	1970
Gayler, Noel A. M. (Aviation)	Sept.	1,	1972
Kidd, Isaac C., Jr.	Dec.	1,	1971
Weisner, Maurice F. (Aviation)	Sept.	1,	1972

MARINE
Corps Commandant, with rank of General

Cushman, Robert E., Jr.	Jan.	1,	1972

Asst. Commandant with rank of General

Anderson, Earl E.	Apr.	1,	1972

COAST GUARD
Commandant, with rank of Admiral

Bender, Chester R.	June	1,	1970

Vice Commandant, with rank of Vice Admiral

Sargent, Thomas R., 3rd	July	1,	1970

United States Unified and Specified Commands

Alaskan Command—Lt. Gen. James C. Sherrill, USAF.

Atlantic Command—Adm. Ralph Cousins, USN.

North American Air Defense Command & Continental Air Defense Command—Gen. Seth J. McKee, USAF.

European Command—Gen. Andrew J. Goodpaster, USA.

Pacific Command—Adm. Noel A. M. Gayler, USN.

Southern Command—Gen. William B. Rosson, USA.

Strat. Air Command—Gen. John C. Meyer, USAF.

U.S. Readiness Command—Gen. Bruce Palmer, Jr., USA.

North Atlantic Treaty Organization International Commands

Supr. Allied Commander, Europe (SACEUR)—Gen. Andrew J. Goodpaster, USA.

Deputy SACEUR—Gen. Sir Desmond Fitzpatrick (UK).

C-in-C, Allied Forces, Northern Europe—Gen. Sir Thomas Pearson (Britain).

C-in-C, Allied Force, Central Europe—Gen. Juergen Bennecke (Germany).

C-in-C. Allied Forces, Southern Europe—Adm. Richard G. Colbert, USN.

Comdr., Naval Forces, Southern Europe—Adm. G. Pighini (Italy).

Supr. Allied Comdr., Atlantic (SACLANT)—Adm. Ralph Cousins, USN.

Deputy SACLANT—V. Adm. E. G. N. Mansfield, (Britain).

Comdr. Striking Fleet Atlantic—V. Adm. Douglas C. Plate, USN.

Allied Comdr. in Chief, Channel—Adm. Sir Edward Ashmore (Britain).

Primary U.S. Military Training Centers
ARMY

Name, P.O. Address	Zip	Nearest City	Name, P.O. Address	Zip	Nearest City
Aberdeen Proving Ground, MD.	21005	Aberdeen	Fort Jackson, SC	29207	Columbia
Carlisle Barracks, PA	17013	Carlisle	Fort Knox, KY	40121	Louisville
Fort Belvoir, VA	22060	Alexandria	Fort Leavenworth, KS	66027	Leavenworth
Fort Benning, GA	31905	Columbus	Fort Lee, VA	23801	Petersburg
Fort Bliss, TX	79906	El Paso	Fort McClellan, AL	36201	Anniston
Fort Bragg, NC	28307	Fayetteville	Fort Monmouth, NJ	07703	Red Bank
Fort Devens, MA	01433	Ayer	Fort Ord, Cal.	93941	Seaside
Fort Dix, NJ	08640	Trenton	Fort Polk, LA	71459	Leesville
Fort Eustis, VA	23604	Newport News	Fort Rucker, AL	36362	Dothan
Fort Gordon, GA	30905	Augusta	Fort Sill, OK	73503	Lawton
Fort Hamilton, NY.	11252	Brooklyn	Fort Leonard Wood, MO	65473	Rolla
Fort Benjamin Harrison, IN.	46216	Indianapolis	Redstone Arsenal, AL	35809	Huntsville
Fort Sam Houston, TX.	78234	San Antonio	Rock Island Arsenal, IL	61202	Rock Island
Fort Huachuca, AZ	85613	Sierra Vista	The Judge Advocate General School, VA	22901	Charlottesville

NAVY

	Zip			Zip	
Great Lakes, Ill.	60088	Waukegan	Orlando, Fla.	32813	Orlando
San Diego, Calif.	92133	San Diego			

MARINE CORPS

Name, P.O. Address	Zip	Nearest City	Name, P.O. Address	Zip	Nearest City
Camp Lejeune, N.C.	28542	Jacksonville, N.C.	Marine Corps Development		
Marine Corps Air Station, NC	28533	Cherry Point, NC	and Education Command, Va.	22134	Quantico
Marine Corps Air Station, SC	29902	Beaufort	Parris Island, S.C.	29905	Beaufort
Marine Corps Air Station, CA	92630	El Torro	Camp Pendleton, Calif.	92055	Oceanside
Marine Corps Air Station, AZ	85364	Yuma	San Diego, Calif.	92140	San Diego

AIR FORCE

Name	Zip	Nearest City	Name	Zip	Nearest City
Chanute AFB, Ill.	61866	Rantoul	Maxwell AFB, Ala.	36112	Montgomery
Columbus AFB, Miss.	39701	Columbus	Moody AFB, Ga.	31601	Valdosta
Craig AFB, Ala.	36701	Selma	Nellis AFB, Nev.	89110	Las Vegas
Fairchild AFB, Wash.	99011	Spokane	Randolph AFB, Texas	78148	San Antonio
Keesler AFB, Miss.	39534	Biloxi	Reese AFB, Tex.	79489	Lubbock
Lackland AFB, Texas	78236	San Antonio	Sheppard AFB, Tex.	76311	Wichita Falls
Laughlin AFB, Tex.	78840	Del Rio	Vance AFB, Okla.	73701	Enid
Lowry AFB, Colo.	80230	Denver	Webb AFB, Texas	79720	Big Spring
Mather AFB, Calif.	95655	Sacramento	Williams AFB, Ariz.	85224	Chandler

Personal Salutes and Honors

The United States national salute, 21 guns, is also the salute to a national flag. The independence of the United States is commemorated by the salute to the Union—one gun for each state—fired at noon on July 4 at all military posts provided with suitable artillery.

A 21-gun salute on arrival and departure, with 4 ruffles and flourishes, is rendered to the President of the United States, to an ex-President and to a President-elect. The national anthem or *Hail to the Chief*, as appropriate, is played for the President, and the national anthem for the others. A 21-gun salute on arrival and departure, with 4 ruffles and flourishes, also is rendered to the sovereign or chief of state of a foreign country or a member of a reigning royal family; the national anthem of his or her country is played. The music is considered an inseparable part of the salute and will immediately follow the ruffles and flourishes without pause.

Rank	Salute—guns Arrive	Salute—guns Leave	Ruffles, flourishes	Music
Vice President of United States	19	..	4	Hail Columbia
Speaker of House	19	..	4	March
American or foreign ambassador	19	..	4	Nat. anthem of official
Premier or prime minister	19	..	4	Nat. anthem of official
Secretary of Defense, Army, Navy or Air Force	19	19	4	March
Other Cabinet members, Senate President pro tempore, Governor, or Chief Justice of U.S.	19	..	4	March
Chairman, Joint Chiefs of Staff	19	19	4	
Army Chief of Staff, Chief of Naval Operations, Air Force Chief of Staff, Marine Commandant	19	19	4	General's or Admiral's March
General of the Army; General of the Air Force; Fleet Admiral	19	19	4	
Generals, Admirals	17	17	4	
Assistant Secretaries of Defense, Army, Navy or Air Force	17	17	4	March
Chairman of a Committee of Congress	17	..	4	March

Other salutes (on arrival only) include 15 guns for American envoys or ministers and foreign envoys or ministers accredited to the United States; 15 guns for a lieutenant general or vice admiral; 13 guns for a major general or rear admiral (upper half); 13 guns for American ministers resident and ministers resident accredited to the U.S.; 11 guns for a brigadier general or rear admiral (lower half); 11 guns for American charges d'affaires and like officials accredited to U.S.: and 11 guns for consuls general accredited to U.S.

Military Units, U. S. Army and Air Force

Army units. Squad. In infantry usually ten men under a staff sergeant. **Platoon.** In infantry 4 squads under a lieutenant. **Company.** Headquarters section and 4 platoons under a captain. (Company in the artillery is a battery; in the cavalry, a troop.) **Battalion.** Hdqts. and 4 or more companies under a lieutenant colonel. (Battalion size unit in the cavalry is a squadron.) **Brigade.** Hdqts. and 3 or more battalions under a colonel. **Division.** Hdqts. and 3 brigades with artillery, combat support and combat service support units under a major general. **Army Corps.** Two or more divisions with corps troops under a lieutenant general. **Field Army.** Hdqts. and two or more corps with field Army troops under a general.

Air Force Units. Flight. Small components of a squadron organized for special purpose such as medical evacuation flights. **Squadron.** The basic organized unit of the Air Force, used by operational as well as support forces but not limited by numbers of personnel assigned; two to three tactical squadrons are assigned to a tactical wing. **Group.** Terminology used for special tactical forces and for many support elements. They do not necessarily have subordinate units assigned. **Wing.** Used for tactical and support forces. A tactical wing usually has two to three operational squadrons assigned. **Division.** An organizational component of operational numbered Air Forces consisting of two to three wings, also used to designate numerous support and research components. **Air Force.** An intermediate echelon of command directly under the headquarters of a large operational command, usually with four to seven subordinate divisions. **Major command.** A major subdivision of the Air Force that is assigned a major segment of the USAF mission, usually two or four subordinate Air Force elements.

Armed Services Senior Enlisted Adviser

The U.S. Army, Navy and Air Force in 1966-67 each created a new position of senior enlisted adviser whose primary job is to represent the point of view of his services' enlisted men and women on matters of welfare, morale and any problem concerning enlisted personnel. The senior adviser will have direct access to the military chief of his branch of service and policy-making bodies. The Marine Corps has had such a position for years.

The senior enlisted adviser for each Dept. is:
Army—Sgt. Major of the Army Silas L. Copeland.
Navy—Master Chief Petty Officer of the Navy John D. Whittet.
Air Force—Chief Master Sgt. of the Air Force Thomas N. Barnes.
Marines—Sgt. Major of the Marine Corps Clinton A. Puckett.

U.S. Army Insignia and Chevrons

Source: Department of the Army

Grade	Insignia

General of the Armies
(General John J. Pershing, the only person to have held this rank, was authorized to prescribe his own insignia, but never wore in excess of four stars. The rank originally was established by Congress for George Washington in 1799, but no record has been found to show that the appointment was made.)

General of the Army . . . . . . Five silver stars fastened together in a circle and the coat of arms of the United States in gold color metal with shield and crest enameled

General . . . . Four silver stars
Lieutenant General . . . . Three silver stars
Major General . . . . Two silver stars
Brigadier General . . . . One silver star
Colonel . . . . Silver eagle
Lieutenant Colonel . . . . Silver oak leaf
Major . . . . Gold oak leaf
Captain . . . . Two silver bars
First Lieutenant . . . . One silver bar
Second Lieutenant . . . . One gold bar

Warrant officers
Grade Four—Silver bar with 4 enamel black bands.
Grade Three—Silver bar with 3 enamel black bands.
Grade Two—Silver bar with 2 enamel black bands.
Grade One—Silver bar with 1 enamel black band.

Non-commissioned officers
Sergeant Major of the Army (E-9). Same as Command Sergeant Major (below). Also wears distinctive red and white shield on lapel.
Command Sergeant Major (E-9). Three chevrons above three arcs with a 5-pointed star with a wreath around the star between the chevrons and arcs.
Sergeant Major (E-9). Three chevrons above the three arcs with a five-pointed star between the chevrons and arcs.
First Sergeant (E-8). Three chevrons above three arcs with a lozenge between the chevrons and arcs.
Master Sergeant (E-8). Three chevrons above three arcs.
Platoon Sergeant or Sergeant First Class (E-7). Three chevrons above two arcs.
Staff Sergeant (E-6). Three chevrons above one arc.
Sergeant (E-5). Three chevrons.
Corporal (E-4). Two chevrons.

Specialists
Specialist Seven (E-7). Three arcs above the eagle device.
Specialist Six (E-6). Two arcs above the eagle device.
Specialist Five (E-5). One arc above the eagle device.
Specialist Four (E-4). Eagle device only.

Other Enlisted
Private First Class (E-3). One chevron above one arc.
Private (E-2). One chevron.
Private (E-1). None

United States Army

Source: Department of the Army

ARMY MILITARY PERSONNEL ON ACTIVE DUTY (a)

June 30 (b)	Total strength	Commissioned officers			Warrant officers		Enlisted personnel		
		Total	Male	Female (c)	Male (d)	Female	Total	Male	Female
1940	267,767	17,563	16,624	939	763	. . . . . .	249,441	249,441	. . . . . .
1942	3,074,184	203,137	190,662	12,475	3,285	. . . . . .	2,867,762	2,867,762	. . . . . .
1943	6,993,102	557,657	521,435	36,222	21,919	0	6,413,526	6,358,200	55,326
1944	7,992,868	740,077	692,351	47,726	36,893	10	7,215,888	7,144,601	71,287
1945	8,266,373	835,403	772,511	62,892	56,216	44	7,374,710	7,283,930	90,780
1946	1,889,690	257,300	240,643	16,657	9,826	18	1,622,546	1,605,847	16,699
1950	591,487	67,784	63,375	4,409	4,760	22	518,921	512,370	6,551
1955	1,107,606	111,347	106,173	5,174	10,552	48	985,659	977,943	7,716
1958	897,224	93,597	89,246	4,351	11,080	39	792,508	785,434	7,074
1959	860,148	91,048	86,756	4,292	10,603	39	758,458	750,621	7,837
1960	871,348	91,056	86,832	4,224	10,141	39	770,112	761,833	8,279
1961	856,853	90,066	85,853	4,213	9,817	38	756,932	748,372	8,560
1962	1,064,647	105,225	100,920	4,305	10,777	48	948,597	939,876	8,721
1963	974,070	98,622	94,810	3,812	9,640	40	865,768	857,476	8,292
1964	971,384	100,640	96,905	3,735	10,193	37	860,514	852,556	7,958
1965	967,049	101,812	98,029	3,783	10,285	23	854,924	846,409	8,520
1966	1,197,468	106,468	102,347	4,121	11,296	22	1,079,682	1,070,503	9,170
1967	1,440,120	127,400	122,700	4,700	16,090	34	1,296,600	1,256,900	9,709
1968	1,567,408	145,988	139,680	6,308	20,158	27	1,401,727	1,391,016	10,711
1969	1,534,200	147,338	141,899	5,439	23,930	20	1,359,562	1,347,162	12,400
1970	1,319,735	143,704	138,469	5,235	23,005	13	1,153,013	1,141,537	11,476
1971	1,120,822	130,261	125,240	5,021	18,670	19	971,872	960,047	11,825
1972	807,985	105,364	100,961	4,403	15,907	19	686,695	674,346	12,349

(a)Represents strength of the active Army, including Philippine Scouts, retired Regular Army personnel on extended active duty, and National Guard and Reserve personnel on extended active duty; excludes U. S. Military Academy cadets, contract surgeons, and National Guard and Reserve personnel not on extended active duty.
(b)Data for 1930 to 1947 include personnel in the Army Air Forces and its predecessors (Air Service and Air Corps).
(c)Includes: Women Doctors, Dentists and Medical Service Corps Officers for 1946 and subsequent years, Women in the Army Nurse Corps for all years, and the Women's Army Corps and Women's Medical Specialists Corps (dieticians, physical therapists and occupational specialists) for 1943 and subsequent years.
(d)Includes Army field clerks and field clerks, Quartermaster Corps as follows: 1925, 377. Act of Congress approved April 27, 1926, directed the appointment as warrant officers, of field clerks still in active service. Includes Flight Officers as follows: 1943, 5,700, 1944, 13,615, 1945, 31,117, 1946, 2,580.

ARMY EXPENDITURES FOR MILITARY FUNCTIONS (a)

(in millions of dollars)

Fiscal year	Amount	Fiscal year	Amount	Fiscal year	Amount	Fiscal year	Amount
1942	14,805	1952	15,708	1960	9,392	1967	21,010
1943	42,573	1953	16,337	1961	10,131	1968	25,223
1944	49,289	1954	12,910	1962	11,427	1969	25,035
1945	49,750	1955	8,899	1963	11,499	1970	24,749
1946	27,176	1957	9,063	1964	12,050	1971	23,077
1947	8,027	1958	9,051	1965	11,600	1972	22,596
1950	3,985	1959	9,468	1966	14,832	1973	20,576

(a)Excludes expenditures for all civil functions as defined in "The Budget of the United States Government." Data for fiscal years to 1947 include all Army Air Force expenditures.

U.S. Navy Insignia

NAVY
Stripes and corps device are of gold embroidery.

Stripes

Fleet Admiral . . . . 1 two inch with 4 one-half inch.
Admiral . . . . 1 two inch with 3 one-half inch.
Vice Admiral . . . . 1 two inch with 2 one-half inch.
Rear Admiral . . . . 1 two inch with 1 one-half inch.
Commodore
(war time only) . . . . . . 1 two inch.
Captain . . . . 4 one-half inch.
Commander . . . . 3 one-half inch.
Lieut. Commander . . . . . 2 one-half inch, with 1 one quarter inch between.
Lieutenant . . . . 2 one-half inch.
Lieutenant (j.g.) . . . . 1 one-half inch with 1 one quarter inch above.
Ensign . . . . 1 one-half inch.
Warrant Officers—One ½" (¼" for warrant officer W–1) broken with ½" intervals of blue as follows:
Chief Warrant Officer   W-4–1 break

Chief Warrant Officer   W-3–2 breaks, 2" apart
Chief Warrant Officer   W-2–3 breaks, 2" apart
Warrant Officer   W-1–3 breaks, 2" apart
(on ¼" gold)
The breaks are symmetrically centered on outer face of the sleeve. Enlisted personnel (non-commissioned petty officers) ... A rating badge worn on the upper left arm, consisting of a spread eagle, appropriate number of chevrons and centered specialty mark.

Marine Corps
Marine Corps and Army officer insignia are similar. Marine Corps and Army enlisted insignia, although basically similar, differ in color, design, and fewer Marine Corps subdivisions. The Marine Corps' distinctive cap and collar ornament is a combination of the American eagle, globe and anchor.

Coast Guard
Coast Guard insignia follow Navy custom, with certain minor changes such as the officer cap insignia. The Coast Guard shield is worn on both sleeves of officers and on the right sleeve of all enlisted men.

United States Naval Budget Outlays
Source: Department of the Navy

Fiscal year	Total amount expended	Shipbuilding conversion and modernizations	Aircraft and missile procurement	Military construction	All other expenditures
1940	$885,769,794	$328,819,394	$24,011,998	$72,503,151	$460,435,251
1945	29,380,421,832	7,228,192,871	3,541,009,589	1,576,096,922	17,035,122,450
1950	4,065,484,778	281,328,056	452,723,233	86,054,932	3,245,378,557
1955	9,637,637,835	903,303,717	1,834,511,038	238,631,005	6,661,192,075
1960	11,848,690,002	1,380,031,231	2,027,098,025	284,928,383	8,228,632,362
1967	19,291,496,288	1,398,414,838	3,006,902,022	522,638,470	14,363,540,958
1968	22,106,320,837	1,355,850,877	3,642,007,920	92,966,944	17,015,495,096
1969	22,507,495,249	1,948,577,741	3,315,166,323	424,837,766	16,818,733,419
1970	2,501,628,282	2,065,660,211	3,183,464,921	333,271,852	16,919,231,298
1971	22,046,000,000	2,592,000,000	3,273,000,000	327,000,000	15,854,000,000
1972	24,100,000,000	3,010,000,000	3,983,000,000	353,000,000	16,754,000,000
1973 (planned) . . .	25,600,000,000	2,971,000,000	3,685,000,000	539,000,000	18,405,000,000

United States Navy Personnel on Active Duty
Source: DOD Comptroller (* Excludes Nurses)

June 30	Officers*	Nurses	Enlisted	Off. Cand.	Total
1940	13,162	442	144,824	2,569	160,997
1945	320,293	11,086	2,988,207	61,231	3,380,817
1950	42,687	1,954	331,860	5,037	381,538
1955	72,423	2,104	579,864	6,304	660,695
1960	67,456	2,103	544,040	4,385	617,984
1965	75,996	1,870	587,183	6,399	671,448
1969	82,875	2,324	684,145	6,525	775,869
1970	78,488	2,273	605,899	6,000	692,660
1971	72,825	1,957	542,298	6,168	623,248
1972	71,041	2,114	510,669	4,219	588,043

Marine Corps Personnel On Active Duty
Source: DOD Comptroller

Yr.	Officers	Enl.	Total	Yr.	Officers	Enl.	Total	Yr.	Officers	Enl.	Total
1955	18,417	186,753	205,170	1965 . . .	17,258	172,955	190,213	1971 . .	21,765	190,604	212,369
1960	16,203	154,408	170,621	1970 . . .	24,941	234,796	259,737	1972 . .	19,843	178,395	198,238

The Federal Service Academies

U.S. Military Academy, West Point, N.Y. Founded 1802. Awards B.S. degree and Army commission for a 5-year service obligation. For admissions information, write Admissions Office, USMA, West Point, N.Y. 10996.

U.S. Naval Academy, Annapolis, Md. Founded 1845. Awards B.S. degree and Navy or Marine Corps commission for a 5-year service obligation. For admissions information, write Dean of Admissions, Naval Academy, Annapolis, Md. 21402.

U.S. Air Force Academy, Colorado Springs, Colo. Founded 1954. Awards B.S. degree and Air Force commission for a 5-year service obligation. For admissions information, write Registrar, U.S. Air Force Academy, Colo. 80840.

U.S. Coast Guard Academy, New London, Conn. Founded 1876. Awards B.S. degree and Coast Guard commission for a 5-year service obligation. For admissions information, write Admissions Office, Coast Guard Academy, New London, Conn. 06320.

U.S. Merchant Marine Academy, Kings Point, N.Y. Founded 1943. Awards B.S. degree, a license as a deck or engineer officer, and a U.S. Naval Reserve commission. Service obligations vary according to options taken by the graduating ensign. For admissions information, write Admission Office, U.S. Merchant Marine Academy, Kings Point, N.Y. 11024.

The Medal of Honor

The Medal of Honor is the highest military award for bravery that can be given to any individual in the United States. The first Army Medals were awarded on March 25, 1863, and the first Navy Medals went to sailors and Marines on April 3, 1863.

The Medal of Honor, established by Joint Resolution of Congress, 12 July 1862 (amended by Act of 9 July 1918 and Act of 25 July 1963) is awarded in the name of Congress to a person who, while a member of the Armed Forces, distinguishes himself conspicuously by gallantry and intrepidity at the risk of his life above and beyond the call of duty while engaged in an action against any enemy of the United States; while engaged in military operations involving conflict with an opposing foreign force; or while serving with friendly foreign forces engaged in an armed conflict against an opposing armed force in which the United States is not a belligerent party. The deed performed must have been one of personal bravery or self-sacrifice so conspicuous as to clearly distinguish the individual above his comrades and must have involved risk of life. Incontestable proof of the performance of service is exacted and each recommendation for award of this decoration is considered on the standard of extraordinary merit.

Prior to World War I, the 2,625 Army Medal of Honor awards up to that time were reviewed to determine which past awards met new stringent criteria. The Army removed 911 names from the list, most of them former members of a volunteer infantry group during the Civil War who had been induced to extend their enlistments when they were promised the Medal.

Since that review Medals of Honor have been awarded in the following numbers:
World War I 124   Korean War 131
World War II 431   Vietnam (to date) . 206
(For names of Vietnam winners of the Medal of Honor, see the 1972 and 1973 editions of the World Almanac.)

American Military Action, 1900-1973

1900—Occupation of Puerto Rico (ceded to U.S., 1899).
1900—500 Marines, 1,500 Army troops help relieve Peking in Boxer Rebellion.
1900-1902—Occupation of Cuba.
1900-1902—Guerrilla war in Philippines.
1903—Sailors and Marines from U. S. S. Nashville stop Colombian Army at Panama.
1904—Brief intervention in Dominican Republic.
1906-1909—Intervention in Cuba.
1909—Brief intervention in Honduras.
1910, 1912-1913—Intervention in Nicaragua.
1911—Intervention (to collect customs) in Honduras, Nicaragua, Dominican Republic.
1912-1917—Intervention in Cuba.
1914—Intervention in Dominican Republic.
1914—April 21 to Nov. 23. Marines in Vera Cruz; also Atlantic fleet and Brig. Gen. Fredk. Funston.
1914—Navy and Marines enter Haiti, stay until 1934.
1916—Gen. John J. Pershing and 10,000 into Northern Mexico to stop raids by Villa, Mar. 15-Nov. 24.
1916-1924—Marines in Dominican Republic.
1917—Apr. 6 to Nov. 11, 1918. War with Germany, Austria-Hungary.
1918-1920—Expeditions into North Russia, Siberia.
1918-1923—Occupation of Germany.
1922-24—Marines in Nicaragua.
1926-33—Marines in Nicaragua.
1927—1,000 U. S. Marines in China.

1941-1945—War with Japan, Germany, Italy and allies. Army units posted in Japan and West Germany.
1950-1953—U. S. and other U.N. countries aid the Republic of Korea to repel North Korean invaders; U. S. Navy protects Taiwan.
1956—U.S. Fleet evacuates U.S. nationals during Suez crisis.
1957—U. S. Fleet to Near East during Jordan crisis.
1958—Navy, Marines and Army units support Lebanon.
1960—Navy patrol in Caribbean to protect Guatemala and Nicaragua.
1961—Army units to Vietnam.
1962—Units of U. S. Navy on Cuban quarantine duty. Marines in Thailand.
1962-65—U. S. Military Assistance Command. Vietnam; units of U. S. Army, Navy, Air Force, Marine Corps, Coast Guard.
1965—Navy, Marines, U. S. Army units to Dominican Republic.
1965—American commanders in Vietnam authorized to send U. S. Armed Force into combat.
1969—President Nixon announces, June 8, first phase of withdrawal of U.S. troops from Vietnam.
1970—Army units participate in Cambodian sanctuary operations, Apr. 29-June 30.
1973—Last U.S. troops leave Vietnam, U.S. Military Assistance Command deactivated, March 29.
1973—End of all U.S. bombing operations over Indochina, Aug. 15.

Adjutant General's Figures of Civil War Deaths

Figures reported from the Adjutant General's Office previous to the above revision, and accepted for many years, are as follows:

Union Army, according to records in the office of the Adjutant General of the War Department in Washington—killed or died of wounds, 110,070 (6,365 officers, 103,705 men); died of disease, 224,586 (2,795 officers, 221,791 men); other deaths, 24,872 (424 officers, 24,448 men). Totals, 359,528 (9,584 officers, 349,944 men).

Confederate Army, estimated, no official records in the office of the Adjutant General of the War Department in Washington—killed in battle, 52,954 (2,086 officers, 50,868 men); died of wounds, 21,570 (1,246 officers, 20,324 men); died of disease, 59,297 (1,294 officers, 58,003 men). Total, 133,821 (4,626 officers, 129,195 men).

WORLD WAR II MERCHANT MARINE CASUALTIES
Source: U. S. Coast Guard

Died from direct causes while serving on American flag ships, 845; died in prisoner-of-war camps, 37; listed as missing, 4,780. There were 572 released prisoners of war, and one prisoner unaccounted for. Another 500 men died while serving on foreign flag ships under U. S. control.
The number of U. S. flag ships lost was 605 of 6,000,000 deadweight tons.

How the Military Hand Salute Originated

Hand-raising as a formal greeting originated with the cavemen, who wanted to prove to one another that they carried no weapons, according to the National Geographic Society. Later an armored knight raised his right arm to lift his helmet visor and to show friendship by keeping his sword hand away from the weapon. Before the 19th Century, British soldiers saluted by tipping their hats. In the modern U.S. military salute the right hand is raised smartly so the forefinger touches the forehead just above and to the right of the right eye, thumb and fingers extended, forearm and wrist at a 45-degree angle. This salute, with variations, is common among military forces around the world.

United States Air Force
Source: Department of the Air Force

The Army Air Forces were started Aug. 1, 1907, as the Aeronautical Division of the Signal Corps, U. S. Army. The division consisted of one officer and two enlisted men, and it was more than a year before it carried out its first mission in an airplane of its own. When the U. S. entered World War I (April 6, 1917), the Aviation Service, as it was called then, had 55 planes and 65 officers, only 35 of whom were fliers. On the day the Japanese struck at Pearl Harbor (Dec. 7, 1941), the Army Air Forces, as they had been renamed six months previously, had 10,329 planes, of which only 2,846 were suited for combat service. But when the Army's air arm reached its peak during World War II (in July, 1944), it had 79,908 of all types of aircraft and (in May, 1945) 43,248 combat aircraft and (in March, 1944) 2,411,294 officers and enlisted men. The Air Force was established under the Armed Services Unification Act of July 26, 1947.

USAF Personnel at Home and Overseas—Officers and Enlisted Men

June 30	Continental U. S.	Overseas	Total	June 30	Continental U. S.	Overseas	Total
1940	40,229	10,936	51,165	1966	641,957	245,396	887,353
1945	1,153,373	1,128,886	2,282,259	1967	617,632	279,862	897,494
1950	317,816	93,461	411,277	1968	616,163	285,035	901,198
1955	689,635	270,311	959,946	1969	566,475	291,936	858,411
1957*	651,674	268,161	919,835	1970	531,386	255,819	787,205
1960¹	607,383	207,369	814,752	1971	528,493	222,586	751,079
1965	635,430	189,232	824,662	1972	529,672	191,776	721,449

*Since 1957 continental U.S. includes Air Force Academy Cadets as follows: (1957) 504; (1960) 1,949; (1963) 2,660; (1964) 2,838; (1965) 2,907; (1966) 3,152; (1967) 3,361; (1968) 3,652; (1969) 3,941; (1970) 4,144; (1971) 2,997; (1972) 2,885.

(1.) Since 1960 Overseas includes Alaska and Hawaii. All figures include Mobilized Personnel. Officers 292, airmen 1,323.

USAF Military Personnel

June 30	Officers & Airmen	Male Commissioned Officers				Total Warrant Officers
		USAF (Reg.) & RA	USAFR & ORC	ANG & NG	AFUS & AUS	
1950	411,277	19,735	33,585	14	55	2,085
1955	959,946	23,463	105,587	984	2	3,961
1960	814,752	49,584	72,115	248	3	4,069
1965	824,662	62,076	62,537	280	54	2,532
1968	901,198	64,595	73,519	1,392	185	1,367
1969	858,411	65,265	68,778	233	132	1,067
1970	787,205	63,678	65,852	168	105	639
1971	624,980	63,903	61,817	154	45	398
1972	721,448	61,045	54,549	146	30	238

Female Commissioned Officers, and Enlisted Personnel

June 30	Female commissioned officers				Female WO	Enlisted personnel		
	Total	WAF	Nurses	WMSC		Total	Male	Female
1950	1,525	303	1,143	79	7	354,271	350,489	3,782
1960	3,858	679	3,020	159	5	685,063	679,412	5,651
1965	4,099	708	3,185	206	1	690,177	685,436	4,741
1968	4,991	893	3,863	235	....	761,507	755,384	6,123
1969	4,845	1,016	3,616	213	....	722,936	715,529	7,407
1970	4,667	1,072	3,407	188	....	657,402	648,415	8,987
1971	4,718	1,157	3,383	178	....	625,160	615,028	10,132
1972	4,766	1,214	3,391	161	....	599,774	588,049	11,725

Those Who Served in United States' Wars
Source: Veterans Administration

Revolution (1775-1784)
Participants 290,000
Deaths in Service 4,000
Last Veteran Died April 5, 1869 .... Age 109

War of 1812 (1812-1815)
Participants 287,000
Deaths in Service 2,000
Last Veteran Died May 13, 1905 .... Age 105

Mexican War (1846-1848)
Participants 79,000
Deaths in Service 13,000
Last Veteran Died September 3, 1929 ... Age 98

Civil War (1861-1865) (Union Forces Only)
Participants 2,213,000
Deaths in Service 364,000
Last Veteran Died August 2, 1956 ..... Age 109

Indian Wars (Approx. 1817-1898)
Participants 106,000
Deaths in Service 1,000
Living Veterans 1

Spanish-American War (1898-1902)
Participants 392,000
Deaths in Service 11,000
Living Veterans 2,202

World War I (1917-1918)
Participants 4,744,000
Deaths in Service 116,000
Living Veterans 1,233,000

World War II (1940-1947)
Participants .... 16,535,000[a]
Deaths in Service 406,000
Living Veterans 14,031,000

Korean Conflict (June 27, 1950-Jan. 31, 1955)
Participants .... 6,807,000[b]
Deaths in Service 55,000
Living Veterans 5,925,000

Service Between Korean Conflict and Vietnam Era (Jan. 31, 1955 – Aug. 5, 1964)
Participants 3,195,000
Deaths in Service 20,000
Living Veterans 3,109,000

Vietnam Era
(Active duty service after Aug. 4, 1964)
Participants .... 8,756,000[b]
On Active Duty 2,346,000

America's Wars
Total through December 31, 1972
Participants* 43,404,000
Deaths in Service 1,085,000
Living Veterans 28,927,000

*Persons who served in more than one war period are counted as participants in each.

[a] Includes 1,476,000 who served in both World War II and the Korean Conflict.

[b] Includes 1,260,000 who served in both the Vietnam Era and the Korean Conflict.

Veterans Administration Busy on Jobs, Education, Hospital Care

Source: Veterans Administration, Donald E. Johnson, Administrator, Washington, D.C. 20420

With the nation's veteran population climbing over the 29,100,000 mark, of which nearly 6,000,000 were veterans of the Vietnam era, the 1973 activity of the Veterans Administration dealt chiefly with problems of employment, education and hospital care.

Continuing its "Outreach" program, the V A sought returning veterans by mail, phone and personal visit and conducted a series of "job marts" in leading cities where employers and job hunters could meet in person.

As a part of the Nixon Administration's efforts to assist rural and disadvantaged veterans, the V A, with five other government agencies, started operation of National Assistance for Veterans mobile vans, manned with experts to give on-the-spot, one-stop aid and assistance to veterans seeking help in filling out forms, getting jobs, medical aid, etc. The mobile vans started in Texas and were expanded to 20 other states.

Legislation passed in 1966 had provided a permanent program of educational assistance and other benefits for those who served in the Armed Forces after Jan. 1, 1955. Another law in 1967 provided full wartime benefits to Vietnam veterans and increased benefits for older veterans.

V A research in medicine and surgery has 5,387 projects in most of its 169 hospitals. This V A research has resulted in advances in both techniques acclaimed by the medical profession. In 1972 the first nuclear-powered Pacemaker (heartbeat regulator) to be implanted in a patient in the United States was done at the Veterans Administration Hospital in Buffalo, N.Y. by the same team of surgeons who implanted the world's first Pacemaker in a human 12 years ago. That battery-powered device worked so successfully that the same patient was the one who received this nation's first nuclear-powered Pacemaker. Other advances included new treatment of hypertension, cancer, pulmonary ailments, and organ transplants.

Veterans of World War I, World War II, the Korean Conflict, and the Vietnam Era hold 8,467,833 V A-administered G.I. insurance policies with a total face value of $91.5 million.

The law also provided new programs of special assistance for educationally disadvantaged veterans to encourage those lacking high school diplomas to obtain them, to assist such veterans with tutorial aid and to encourage educational institutions to develop special tutorial or remedial programs for such veterans. The new law also permitted veterans' education at the elementary school level.

Another program encouraged and assisted those who had served at least 180 days to pursue a program of education or training while remaining in the service to prepare for future education, training or vocation.

Charged with the responsibility of seeking out eligible veterans (and eligible dependents) and providing them with information and assistance, the V A has increased its personnel in Vietnam and maintains contact representatives at all military discharge points in the United States as well as at all service hospitals.

Widows, wives and children of deceased or totally disabled veterans whose death or disabilities have been rated service connected are also eligible for this education program.

Monthly allowances for apprenticeships and on-the-job training have been provided. Monthly allowances for farm cooperative training cover institutional agricultural courses with a minimum of 12 clock hours per week in addition to related work on the farm.

Flight training leading to a commercial license was added to educational benefits by the 1967 legislation, which authorizes training at approved flying schools.

Under the current law, eligible veterans and servicemen may obtain GI loans made by private lenders and guaranteed by the V A for the purchase of homes, mobile homes or farms. In certain rural areas where ordinary lending facilities are not available, direct loans may be made by the V A for the purchase of homes and farmhouses. The effect of the Government's guarantee is intended to be to eliminate or reduce the amount of the down payment the lender normally requires.

The V A expends more than $6.5 billion annually in compensation and pension payments to 5.3 million disabled veterans and eligible dependents.

The overall number of loans guaranteed or insured by the V A since the program was launched in 1944 was 8,932,665 as of May 1972. Of these 1,383,746 had been made to veterans with service after the close of the Korean Conflict, Jan. 31, 1955.

Through its 169 hospitals the V A offers complete medical care to veterans of all wars with service connected disabilities and, if beds are available, to other veterans if they are unable to defray hospital costs. As of the end of Fiscal Year 1972, only about 15% of the V A patient population were veterans of Vietnam era service.

Veteran Population

		July 1973
1.	Veterans in civil life, end of month — Total	29,073,000
2.	War Veterans — Total	25,967,000
3.	Vietnam Era — Total[a]	6,557,000
4.	And service in Korean Conflict	406,000
5.	No service in Korean Conflict	6,151,000
6.	Korean Conflict — Total (includes line 4)	5,936,000
7.	And service in WW II	1,261,000
8.	No service in WW II	4,675,000
9.	World War II (includes line 7)	13,955,000
10.	World War I	1,184,000
11.	Spanish-American War	2,000
12.	Service between Korean Conflict (January 31, 1955) and Vietnam (August 5, 1964) Only[c]	3,106,000

(a) Service after Aug. 4, 1964; (b) includes 2,385,000 veterans who also served after the end of the Korean Conflict (Jan. 31, 1955); (c) excludes men who served on active duty for training only.

PENSION CASES AND COMPENSATION PAYMENTS

Fiscal year	Living veteran cases No.	Deceased veteran cases No.	Total cases No.	Total disbursement Dollars	Fiscal year	Living veteran cases No.	Deceased veteran cases No.	Total cases No.	Total disbursement Dollars
1890	415,654	122,290	537,944	106,093,850	1963	3,180,723	1,182,987	4,363,710	3,780,658,236
1900	752,510	241,019	993,529	138,462,130	1964	3,196,042	1,239,010	4,435,052	3,897,542,730
1910	602,622	318,461	921,083	159,974,056	1965	3,204,275	1,277,009	4,481,284	3,901,598,010
1920	419,627	349,916	769,543	316,418,029	1966	3,200,871	1,339,209	4,540,080	4,305,367,751
1930	542,610	298,223	840,833	418,432,808	1967	3,130,390	1,334,634	4,465,024	4,284,265,036
1940	610,122	239,176	849,298	429,138,465	1968	3,112,038	1,389,379	4,501,417	4,406,319,385
1950	2,368,238	658,123	3,026,361	2,009,462,298	1969	3,107,162	1,443,367	4,550,529	4,722,489,826
1955	2,668,786	808,303	3,477,089	2,634,292,537	1970	3,127,338	1,487,176	4,614,514	5,113,649,490
1960	3,008,935	950,802	3,959,737	3,314,761,383	1971	3,222,394	1,584,167	4,806,561	5,726,458,000
1962	3,130,856	1,096,708	4,227,564	3,649,870,466	1972	3,268,826	1,641,370	4,910,196	6,045,214,000

Modern Strategic Theory: A Layman's Guide to MAD

In the years ahead, one of the major public controversies will turn on arms control issues. Some knowledge of strategic theory will be required if citizens are to discuss the issues effectively. Strategic theory is a strange world of nightmare and paradox which calls for a complete change from traditional thinking about attack and defense. Herewith, The World Almanac presents a glossary of terms to help the concerned citizen understand this vital subject.

First strike capability means having enough missiles and bombers with enough nuclear warheads of enough destructive power to destroy or severely limit the enemy's ability to retaliate.

Second strike capability means having enough protected missiles and/or bombers to retaliate effectively after a first strike.

Assured destruction capability means having enough second strike capability to cause **unacceptable damage** to the opponent. The U.S. considers destruction of 25% of the Soviet population and 40% of Soviet industry to be unacceptable to Soviet leaders. Four hundred warheads of one megaton each (50 times more powerful than the Hiroshima bomb) reportedly would achieve this level of destruction if all warheads hit their targets.

Damage limitation capability means having the ability to knock out the enemy's nuclear strike forces (either before or after they are launched) and to provide adequate shelter for population and industry, so that the enemy would be unable to achieve assured destruction in either a first or second strike. Adequate damage limitation is thought by some theorists to be impossible at the present time.

Assured destruction and damage limitation are the central concepts of two competing strategic theories. Assured destruction proponents argue that pursuit of damage limitation capability, besides being technically impractical, could make nuclear war more likely. They argue that the other side could lose confidence in its own assured destruction capability and seek a first strike capability as an alternative. In any case, if one side goes for damage limitation capability, the other side will increase its nuclear arsenal and a new arms race would ensue. Damage limitation advocates argue that a lack of defense for population and industry, besides being unreasonable and immoral, puts cities and people in danger from accidental missile firings and from attack by an irrational enemy head of state.

Mutual assured destruction (MAD) refers to the ability of both sides to withstand a first strike and cause unacceptable damage to each other in a second strike. MAD is presently the aim of U.S. and Soviet arms control negotiations and agreements. Basically, MAD makes the population and industry of each side hostage to the other side.

Survivability refers to the ability of weapons systems to survive a first strike. Bombers have survivability because they can become airborne between the first warning and the arrival of enemy warheads. Submarines have survivability because they are hard to locate and destroy. (At present, no anti-submarine warfare, or ASW, techniques are reliable or effective.) Land-based missiles gain survivability by being protected in heavy concrete silos underground, by being defended by anti-ballistic missiles (ABMs), or by being made mobile on trucks or railroad cars.

Counter-force targets are the enemy's nuclear weapons, defense communications and command centers. Defense of these targets is called **hard-site or missile defense**.

Counter-value targets are the enemy's cities, population and industry. Defense of these targets is called **area defense**.

Stability is achieved when each side has sufficient information to be fairly sure that the other side is not seeking first-strike capability but has secure second-strike capability.

In the strategic theory that relies on assured destruction, certain offensive and defensive options are considered stabilizing and others are thought to be destabilizing. **Stabilizing options** are: nuclear submarines, because they can be counted easily by satellite while under construction and have great survivability; fixed land-based missiles, because they can be counted by satellite; hard-site defense, because it improves survivability of the second-strike force; and counter-value targeting, because it does not threaten second-strike capability. **Destabilizing options** are: mobile land-based missiles because they are hard to count; area defense and counter-force targeting, because they may prevent the other side from inflicting unacceptable damage in a second strike; and multiple independently-targetable re-entry vehicles (MIRV warheads), because they cannot be counted. Almost any weapons change, because it can cause confusion or doubt, is destabilizing.

The **3rd or n country problem** is exceptionally destabilizing. Two nuclear powers alone can be sure that their weapons are directed against each other and react appropriately. With the appearance of one or more additional nuclear powers with submarines or inter-continental missiles, the two major powers must build additional weapons to face both the major opponent and the 3rd country. But the major opponents cannot be certain that new missile strength really is targeted against the 3rd power and not against each other.

Crisis stability refers to the political value or reliability of strategic weapons in situations that mix tactical political issues and strategic threats. For example: Assume the U.S. and Soviet Union are engaged in a major political confrontation in Southeast Asia. Assume also that the U.S. is not sure that its land-based missiles could survive a first strike. If they were wiped out, would retaliation with U.S. submarine missiles be feasible? Or would that only provoke a Soviet second strike that would destroy a major part of U.S. population and industry? Fearing these alternatives, the U.S. might retreat in the political crisis and settle for a Soviet victory in Southeast Asia. At present, it is thought that U.S. land-based missiles might not be "crisis stable" when the Soviet Union develops accurate MIRV warheads.

Parity in nuclear arms suggests mutual assured destruction capability. Parity is most easily defined when the weapons of both sides have **symmetry**—that is, are roughly equal in range, destructive power, and intended use. The strategic weapons of the U.S. and the Soviet Union are **asymmetrical**: the Soviets have more land-based missiles with greater destructive power per warhead, while the U.S. has more warheads with greater accuracy; the Soviets will soon have more missile submarines than the U.S., but U.S. submarines can stay in attack position for a longer time and their missiles have a greater range. The U.S. and Soviet Union thus achieve parity not by symmetry or equality, but by **comparability**.

Strategic Nuclear Armaments: United States and Soviet Union

Source: International Institute for Strategic Services, London

United States				Soviet Union			
Type	Range[2] (statute miles)	Estimated warhead yield[3]	Deployed (July 1973)	Type	Range[2] (statute miles)	Estimated warhead yield[3]	Deployed (July 1973)
LAND-BASED MISSILES[1]				**LAND-BASED MISSILES[1]**			
ICBM Titan 2	7,250	5-10 MT	54	ICBM SS-7 Saddler	6,900	5 MT }	209
Minuteman 1	7,500	1 MT	140	SS-8 Sasin	6,900	5 MT }	
Minuteman 2	8,000	1-2 MT	510	SS-9 Scarp	7,500	20-25 MT[4]	288
Minuteman 3	8,000	3 × 200 KT	350	SS-11	6,500	1-2 MT[5]	970
				SS-13 Savage	5,000	1 MT	60
IRBM	–	–	–	IRBM SS-5 Skean	2,300	1 MT	100
MRBM	–	–	–	MRBM SS-4 Sandal	1,200	1 MT	500
SEA-BASED MISSILES				**SEA-BASED MISSILES**			
SLBM UGM-27B	–	–	–	SLBM SS-N-5 Serb	750	MT range	30
(nuclear Polaris A2	1,750	800 KT }		(nuclear SS-N-6	1,750	MT range	496
subs) UGM-27C		1 MT or }	336	subs) SS-N-8	4,000	MT range	36
Polaris A3[6]	2,880	3 × 200 KT }					
UGM-73A							
Poseidon	2,880	10 × 50 KT	320				
SLBM				SLBM			
(diesel subs)	–	–	–	(diesel SS-N-5 Serb subs)	750	MT range	30

United States				Soviet Union			
Type	Range[8] (statute miles)	Weapons load (lb)	Deployed (July 1973)	Type	Range (statute miles)	Weapons load (lb)	Deployed (July 1973)
AIRCRAFT[7]				**AIRCRAFT[7]**			
Long-range B-52 D-F	11,500	60,000 }	442[9]	Tu-95 Bear	7,800	40,000	100
B-52 G/H	12,500	75,000 }		Mya-4 Bison	6,050	20,000	40
Medium-range FB-111A	3,800	37,500	74	Tu-16 Badger	4,000	20,000	800
Strike aircraft: F-105D	2,100	16,500 }		Il-28 Beagle	2,500	4,850 }	
land-based F-4	2,300	16,000 }		Tu-22 Blinder	1,400	12,000 }	
F-11 A/E	3,800	25,000 }	1,300[10]	Yak-28 Brewer	1,750	4,400 }	1,300[10]
A-7D	3,400	15,000 }		Mig-21 Fishbed J	1,150	2,000 }	
				Mig-? Flogger	1,800	n.a. }	
Strike aircraft: A-4	2,055	10,000 }					
carrier- A-6A	3,225	18,000 }	1,300[10]				
based RA-5C	3,000	13,500 }					
A-7A/B/E	3,400	15,000 }					

(1) ICBM = intercontinental ballistic missile. IRBM = intermediate-range ballistic missile. MRBM = medium-range missile. SLBM = submarine-launched ballistic missile. (2) Operation range depends upon the payload carried; use of maximum payload may reduce missile range by up to 25%. (3) MT = megaton = 1,000,000 tons of TNT equivalent (MT range = 1 MT or over); KT = kiloton = 1,000 tons of TNT equivalent (KT range = less than 1 MT). (4) SS-9 missiles have also been tested with 3 warheads of 4-5 MT each. (5) SS-11 missiles have also been tested with 3 smaller warheads. (6) Most of all Polaris A3 missiles have been modified to carry 3 warheads. (7) All aircraft listed are dual-capable and many, especially in the categories of strike aircraft, would be more likely to carry conventional than nuclear weapons. (8) Theoretical maximum range, with internal fuel only, at optimum altitude and speed. Ranges for strike aircraft assume no weapons load. Especially in the case of strike aircraft, therefore, range falls sharply for flights at lower altitude, at higher speed or with full weapons load. (9) Including approximately 22 B-52 D-F and 43 G-H aircraft in active storage. (10) These aircraft are nuclear capable but may not have a nuclear role.

Women In The Armed Forces—An Increasing Role

Women are now eligible for 81% of all military job classifications and enlistments are coming in at a rate that strains the capacity of the armed forces to handle them. The services had planned on having 88,000 women in uniform by 1977. With enlistments coming in at 100% of the goals the services set themselves, there are plans to increase barracks space and other facilities to accomodate 110,000 by that date—double the present number.

Women's Army Corps—Brig. Gen. Mildred C. Bailey, WAC Director, Dept. of Army, Pentagon, Washington, D.C.; 1,109 officers, 16,455 enlisted women; wide variety of assignments, world-wide; subsidizes some college training.

Army Nurse Corps—Brig. Gen. Lillian Dunlap, Chief, Office of the Surgeon General, Dept. of Army, Washington, D.C. 20314; 2,818 officers; nursing and supervision assignments, world-wide; subsidizes some training; includes men.

Navy—Fully integrated, no commander; for information: Commander, Naval Recruiting, Dept. of Navy, Washington, D.C. 20370; 1,320 officers,

8,800 enlisted women; variety of assignments.

Navy Nurse Corps—Rear Adm. Alene B. Duerk, Director, Navy Nurse Corps, Bureau of Medicine and Surgery, Navy Dept. Washington, D.C.; 2,134 officers; nursing and supervision assignments at U.S. and foreign bases, and shipboard; subsidizes some training.

Air Force—Colonel Billie M. Bobbitt, Director, WAF, Hq. USAF, Pentagon, Washington, D.C. 20330; 1,400 officers, 16,500 enlisted women; variety of assignments, world-wide.

Air Force Nurse Corps—Brig. Gen. Ethel A. Hoefly, Chief, Office of the Surgeon General, USAF, Washington, D.C. 20333; 3,295 officers; nursing and supervision assignments, world-wide; subsidizes some training; includes men.

Women Marines—Col. Margaret A. Brewer, Director, Headquarters, Marine Corps, Washington, D.C. 20380; 300 officers, 2,000 enlisted women.

Coast Guard Spars—Capt. Eleanor L'Ecuyer, Commandant G-RA/82, U.S. Coast Guard, Washington, D.C. 20590; 9 officers, 385 enlisted women.

Monthly Pay Scale of the Army,

Commissioned Officers

Pay grade	Army or Air Force rank	Navy rank	Under 2	Over 2	Over 3	Over 4	Over 6	Over 8
0-10[1]	Chief of Staff........		$3,000.00	$3,000.00	$3,000.00	$3,000.00	$3,000.00	$3,000.00
0-10	General*............	Admiral................	2,415.00	2,500.20	2,500.20	2,500.20	2,500.20	2,595.90
0-9	Lieutenant General.	Vice Admiral........	2,140.50	2,196.90	2,243.70	2,243.70	2,243.70	2,300.40
0-8	Major General.......	Rear Admiral (upper half)	1,938.60	1,996.80	2,044.50	2,044.50	2,044.50	2,196.90
0-7	Brigadier General...	Rear Admiral (lower half).	1,610.70	1,720.80	1,720.80	1,720.80	1,797.30	1,797.30
0-6	Colonel..............	Captain..............	1,194.00	1,312.20	1,397.70	1,397.70	1,397.70	1,397.70
0-5	Lieutenant Colonel.	Commander.............	954.90	1,121.70	1,198.80	1,198.80	1,198.80	1,198.80
0-4	Major...............	Lieutenant Commander...	805.20	979.80	1,046.10	1,046.10	1,064.70	1,112.10
0-3	Captain.............	Lieutenant.............	748.20	836.40	893.70	989.40	1,036.50	1,073.70
0-2	First Lieutenant.....	Lieutenant (Junior Grade).	652.20	712.50	855.90	884.40	903.00	903.00
0-1	Second Lieutenant.	Ensign................	566.10	589.50	712.50	712.50	712.50	712.50

Commissioned officers with over 4 years service as enlisted members

0-3	Captain.............	Lieutenant.............	....	....	....	989.40	1,036.50	1,073.70
0-2	First Lieutenant.....	Lieutenant (Junior Grade).	....	....	....	884.40	903.00	931.50
0-1	Second Lieutenant.	Ensign................	....	....	....	712.50	760.80	789.30

Warrant Officers

W-4	Chief Warrant.......	Commissioned Warrant...	762.00	817.50	817.50	836.40	874.50	912.90
W-3	Chief Warrant.......	Commissioned Warrant...	693.00	751.50	751.50	760.80	770.10	826.50
W-2	Chief Warrant.......	Commissioned Warrant...	606.60	656.10	656.10	675.30	712.50	751.50
W-1	Warrant Officer.....	Warrant Officer...........	505.50	579.90	579.90	627.90	656.10	684.60

Enlisted Personnel[2]

E-9[3]	Sergeant Major**..	Master Chief Petty Officer	....	....	....	....	....	....
E-8[3]	Master Sergeant....	Senior Chief Petty Officer.	....	....	....	....	....	726.60
E-7	Sgt. 1st Class.......	Chief Petty Officer.........	507.30	547.20	567.60	587.40	607.80	627.00
E-6	Staff Sergeant......	Petty Officer 1st Class...	438.00	477.90	497.70	518.10	537.90	557.70
E-5	Sergeant............	Petty Officer 2nd Class...	384.60	418.80	438.90	458.10	488.10	507.90
E-4	Corporal............	Petty Officer 3rd Class....	369.90	390.60	413.10	445.50	463.20	463.20
E-3	Private 1st Class ...	Seaman................	355.80	375.30	390.30	405.60	405.60	405.60
E-2	Private.............	Seaman Apprentice.......	342.30	342.30	342.30	342.30	342.30	342.30
E-1	Private.............	Seaman Recruit...........	307.20	307.20	307.20	307.20	307.20	307.20

The pay scale also applies to: Coast Guard and Marine Corps, Coast and Geodetic Survey, Public Health Service, National Guard, and the Organized Reserves.

* Four star General or Admiral—personal money allowances of $2,200 per annum, or $4,000 if Chief of Staff or Chief of Naval Operations. Three star General or Admiral—personal money allowance of $500 per annum.

** A new title of Chief Master Sergeant created in 1965 rates E-9 classification.

(1) While serving as Chairman of Joint Chiefs of Staff, Chief of Staff of the Army, Chief of Naval Operations, Chief of Staff of the Air Forces, or Commandant of the Marine Corps, basic pay for this grade is $3,000 regardless of years of service.

(2) Air Force enlisted personnel pay grades, E-9, Chief Master Sergeant; E-8, Sr. Master Sergeant; E-7, Master Sergeant; E-6, Technical Sergeant; E-5, Staff Sergeant; E-4, Sergeant; E-3, Airman 1st Class; E-2, Airman; E-1, Basic Airman.

Marine Corps enlisted ranks are as follows: E-9, Sergeant Major and Master Gunnery Sergeant; E-8, First Sergeant and Master Sergeant; E-7, Gunnery Sergeant; E-6, Staff Sergeant; E-5, Sergeant; E-4, Corporal; E-3, Lance Corporal; E-2, Private First Class Marine; E-1, Private.

Marine Corps officer ranks are same as Army and AF.

(3) While serving as Sergeant Major of the Army, Master Chief Petty Officer of the Navy, Chief Master Sergeant of the Air Force, or Sergeant Major of the Marine Corps, basic pay for this grade is $1,355.40 regardless of years of service.

Hazardous Duty

Flying Duty (crew member) and Submarine Duty Additional Monthly Pay

	Under 2 yrs.	Over 2 yrs.	Maximum Over—Amt.
0-10	$165	$165	$165
0-9	165	165	165
0-8	155	155	165
0-7	150	150	160
0-6	200	200	18 yrs. —245
0-5	190	190	18 " —245
0-4	170	170	18 " —240
0-3	145	145	14 " —205
0-2	115	125	14 " —185
0-1	100	105	14 " —170
W-4	115	*	18 " —165
W-3	110	115	14 " —140
W-2	105	110	14 " —135
W-1	100	105	12 " —130
E-9	105	105	105
E-8	105	105	105
E-7	80	85	12 yrs. —105
E-6	70	75	14 " —100
E-5	60	70	12 " —95
E-4	55	65	8 " —80
E-3	55	60	2 " —60
E-2	50	60	2 " —60
E-1	50	55	2 " —55

Aviation Cadet under 2 years $50.

W-4 Under 6 years receives $115.

Incentive Pay

Officers and Warrant Officers	$110.00
Enlisted men	55.00

Types of duties for which these flat rates are payable are as follows—(1) Frequent and regular aerial flights not as a crew member. (2) Parachute jumping as an essential part of military duty. (3) Duty involving intimate contact with leprosy. (4) Duty involving demolition of explosives. (5, 6) Special pay is authorized for diving duty. Pay varies with rank and type of duty. (7) Human acceleration or deceleration duty. (8) High-or-low-pressure chamber duty. (9) Thermal stress duty. (10) Training for assignment to submarines of advanced design or for positions of increased responsibility aboard a submarine. Rates payable for this category are the same as those paid flying crew members listed under Hazardous Duty. (11) Flight Deck Duty.

Sea and Foreign Duty

Defense Secretary designates places where special duty pay may be awarded

(See Pay Guides listed above)

E-9	$22.50	E-4	13.00
E-8	22.50	E-3	9.00
E-7	22.50	E-2	8.00
E-6	20.00	E-1	8.00
E-5	16.00		

Navy and Air Force (1973)

Commissioned Officers

| Cumulative years of service | | | | | | | | Basic allowances for quarters | |
Over 10	Over 12	Over 14	Over 16	Over 18	Over 20	Over 22	Over 26	Without Dependents	With Dependents
$3,000.00	$3,000.00	$3,000.00	$3,000.00	$3,000.00	$3,000.00	3,000.00	$3,000.00	$	$
2,595.90	2,794.80	2,794.80	2,994.90	2,994.90	3,195.00*	3,195.00*	3,394.20	230.40	288.00
2,300.40	2,395.80	2,395.80	2,595.90	2,595.90	2,794.80	2,794.80	2,994.90	230.40	288.00
2,196.90	2,300.40	2,300.40	2,395.80	2,500.20	2,595.90	2,700.30	2,700.30	230.40	288.00
1,902.00	1,902.00	1,996.80	2,196.90	2,347.80	2,347.80	2,347.80	2,347.80	230.40	288.00
1,397.70	1,397.70	1,445.10	1,673.70	1,759.20	1,797.30	1,902.00	2,062.50	211.80	258.30
1,235.70	1,301.40	1,388.40	1,492.50	1,578.30	1,625.70	1,683.00	1,683.00	198.30	238.80
1,187.70	1,254.90	1,312.20	1,369.20	1,407.30	1,407.30	1,407.30	1,407.30	178.80	215.40
1,131.30	1,187.70	1,216.80	1,216.80	1,216.80	1,216.80	1,216.80	1,216.80	158.40	195.60
903.00	903.00	903.30	903.30	903.30	903.30	903.30	903.30	138.60	175.80
712.50	712.50	712.50	712.50	712.50	712.50	712.50	712.50	108.90	141.60
1,131.30	1,187.70	1,235.70	1,235.70	1,235.70	1,235.70	1,235.70	1,235.70	158.40	195.60
979.80	1,017.90	1,046.10	1,046.10	1,046.10	1,046.10	1,046.10	1,046.10	138.60	175.80
817.50	846.30	884.40	884.40	884.40	884.40	884.40	884.40	108.90	141.60

Warrant Officers

Over 10	Over 12	Over 14	Over 16	Over 18	Over 20	Over 22	Over 26	Without Dependents	With Dependents
950.70	1,017.90	1,064.70	1,102.50	1,131.30	1,169.10	1,207.80	1,301.40	172.50	207.90
874.50	903.00	931.50	959.70	989.40	1,027.20	1,064.70	1,102.50	155.40	191.70
780.00	808.20	836.40	865.50	893.70	922.20	959.70	959.70	137.10	173.70
712.50	741.60	770.10	798.60	826.50	855.90	855.90	855.90	123.90	160.80

Enlisted Personnel

Over 10	Over 12	Over 14	Over 16	Over 18	Over 20	Over 22	Over 26	Without Dependents	With Dependents
865.80	885.60	905.70	926.40	946.80	965.40	1,016.40	1,115.10	130.80	184.20
746.70	766.50	786.60	807.00	826.20	846.60	866.10	866.10	100.10	170.00
646.80	667.20	697.50	717.00	736.80	746.70	796.80	896.10	104.70	161.40
577.80	607.80	627.00	646.80	657.00	657.00	657.00	657.00	95.70	150.00
528.00	547.20	557.70	557.70	557.70	557.70	557.70	557.70	92.70	138.60
463.20	463.20	463.20	463.20	463.20	463.20	463.20	463.20	81.60	121.50
405.60	405.60	405.60	405.60	405.60	405.60	405.60	405.60	72.30	105.00
342.30	342.30	342.30	342.30	342.30	342.30	342.30	342.30	63.90	105.00
307.20	307.20	307.20	307.20	307.20	307.20	307.20	307.20	60.00	105.00

*Limited under existing law to $3,000

Basic Allowances for Subsistence

This allowance, the quarters allowance, and any other allowance are not subject to income tax.

Officers—Subsistence (food) is paid to all officers regardless of rank .... $47.88 per month

Enlisted members: When rations in kind are not available................................ $2.57 per day
When permission is granted to mess off the base .... $1.65 per day
When assigned to duty under emergency conditions where
no government messing facilities are available .... $3.42 per day (maximum rate)

Family Separation Allowance

Under certain conditions of family separation of more than 30 days, members in Pay Grades E-4 (with over 4 years' service) and above will be allowed $30 a month in addition to any other allowances to which he is entitled. When separated from family and required to maintain a home for his family and one for himself, the member is entitled to an additional monthly basic allowance for quarters at the "without dependents" rate for his grade.

Uniform Allowance

Enlisted personnel receive an initial uniform allowance valued at $164 to $285, with variations between Services. After 6 months and up to the 36th month maintenance allowance of $4.50 is paid. After 36 months the monthly allowance is $6.60. An officer is entitled to an initial allowance of not more than $300.00.

Enlistment Bonus

DOD currently authorizes a bonus of $2,500 for a four-year enlistment in certain combat arms skills.

Reenlistment Bonuses

Reenlistment Bonuses are paid to enlisted members who reenlist within a specified period of time following their discharge from active service. The Regular Reenlistment Bonus is paid to all reenlistees at each reenlistment point prior to completion of 20 years of service. It is paid in fractions of monthly basic pay multiplied by the number of years in the reenlistment contract. Maximum total amount for any one individual during a 20 year career is $2,000.

Members serving in critical military specialties may, as a special incentive, receive an additional bonus, the Variable Reenlistment Bonus. This retention incentive is paid at the first reenlistment point to individuals designated as having a critical military specialty. It is paid in multiples (not to exceed 4) of the Regular Reenlistment Bonus. Maximum allowable Variable Reenlistment Bonus is $8,000 which provides for a maximum combined total of $10,000 for both the Regular and Variable Reenlistment Bonuses.

Special Pay

Members of the uniformed services entitled to receive basic pay shall, in addition thereto, be entitled to receive incentive pay for the performance of hazardous duty required by competent orders. The President may, in time of war, suspend the payment of hazardous duty incentive pay. Officers receive no additional pay for overseas or sea duty.

Duty Subject to Hostile Fire

Except in time of war declared by the Congress, a special pay of $65 a month is authorized for any member of the Uniformed Services during any month in which he was subject to hostile fire.

Medical and Dental Corps

Commissioned officers in the Medical and Dental Corps of the Army, Navy and Air Force and commissioned medical, dental, and veterinary officers of the Regular Corps of the Public Health Service receive special pay based on cumulative years of service (0-2 years, $100; 2 to 6 years, $150; 6 to 10 years, $250; over 10 years, $350). In addition to basic pay and allowance. Optometrists and Veterinary Corps Officers receive $100 per month extra.

Casualties in Principal Wars of the United States

SEE INDEX FOR VIETNAM CASUALTIES

Data prior to World War I are based upon incomplete records in many cases. Casualty data are confined to dead and wounded personnel and therefore exclude personnel captured or missing in action who were subsequently returned to minitary control. Dash (−) indicates information is not available.

Wars	Branch of service	Number serving	Battle deaths	Casualties Other deaths	Wounds not mortal[8]	Total
Revolutionary War	Total	−	4,435	−	6,188	10,623
1775-1783	Army	184,000	4,044	−	6,004	10,048
	Navy	to	342	−	114	456
	Marines	250,000	49	−	70	119
War of 1812	Total	[9]286,730	2,260	−	4,505	6,765
1812-1815	Army	−	1,950	−	4,000	5,950
	Navy	−	265	−	439	704
	Marines	−	45	−	66	111
Mexican War	Total	[9]78,718	1,733	11,550	4,152	17,435
1846-1848	Army	−	1,721	11,550	4,102	17,373
	Navy	−	1	−	3	4
	Marines	−	11	−	47	58
Civil War	Total	[9]2,213,363	140,414	224,097	281,881	646,392
(Union forces only)	Army	2,128,948	138,154	221,374	280,040	639,568
1861-1865	Navy		2,112	2,411	1,710	6,233
	Marines	84,415	148	312	131	591
Confederate forces	Total	−	74,524	59,297	−	133,821
(estimate)[1]	Army	600,000	−	−	−	−
1863-1866	Navy	to	−	−	−	−
	Marines	1,500,000	−	−	−	−
Spanish-American	Total	306,760	385	2,061	1,662	4,108
War	Army[4]	280,564	369	2,061	1,594	4,024
1898	Navy	22,875	10	0	47	57
	Marines	3,321	6	0	21	27
World War I	Total	4,743,826	53,513	63,195	204,002	320,710
April 6, 1917-	Army[5]	4,057,101	50,510	55,868	193,663	300,041
Nov. 11, 1918	Navy	599,051	431	6,856	819	8,106
	Marines	78,839	2,461	390	9,520	12,371
	Coast Gd.	8,835	111	81	−	192
World War II	Total	16,353,659	292,131	115,185	670,846[1]	1,078,162
Dec. 7, 1941-	Army[6]	11,260,000	234,874	83,400	565,861	884,135
Dec. 31, 1946[2]	Navy[7]	4,183,466	36,950	25,664	37,778	100,392
	Marines	669,100	19,733	4,778	67,207	91,718
	Coast Gd.	241,093	574	1,343	−	1,917
Korean War	Total	5,764,143	33,629	20,617	103,284	157,530
June 25, 1950-	Army	2,834,000	27,704	9,429	77,596	114,729
July 27, 1953[3]	Navy	1,177,000	458	4,043	1,576	6,077
	Marines	424,000	4,267	1,261	23,744	29,272
	Air Force	1,285,000	1,200	5,884	368	7,452
	Coast Gd.	44,143	−	−	−	−

[1] Authoritative statistics for the Confederate Forces are not available. An estimated 26,000-31,000 Confederate personnel died in Union prisons.

[2] Data are for the period Dec. 1, 1941 through Dec. 31, 1946 when hostilities were officially terminated by Presidential Proclamation, but few battle deaths or wounds not mortal were incurred after the Japanese acceptance of Allied peace terms on Aug. 14, 1945. Numbers serving from Dec. 1, 1941-Aug. 31, 1945 were: Total—14,903,213; Army—10,420,000; Navy—3,883,520; and Marine Corps—599,693.

[3] Tentative final data based upon information available as of Sept. 30, 1954, at which time 24 persons were still carried as missing in action.

[4] Number serving covers the period April 21-Aug. 13, 1898, while dead and wounded data are for the period May 1-Aug. 31, 1898. Active hostilities ceased on Aug. 13, 1898, but ratifications of the treaty of peace were not exchanged between the United States and Spain until April 11, 1899.

[5] Includes Air Service. Battle deaths and wounds not mortal exclude casualties suffered by American forces in Northern Russia to Aug. 25, 1919 and in Siberia to April 1, 1920. Other deaths cover the period April 1, 1917-Dec. 31, 1918. [6] Includes Army Air Forces.

[7] Battle deaths and wounds not mortal include casualties incurred in Oct. 1941 due to hostile action.

[8] Marine Corps date for World War II, the Spanish-American War and prior wars represent the number of individuals wounded, whereas all other data in this column represent the total number (incidence) of wounds.

[9] As reported by the Commissioner of Pensions in his Annual Report for Fiscal Year 1903

American Military Cemeteries and Memorials on Foreign Soil

Administered by the American Battle Monuments Commission, Washington, D.C. 20315

(Numbers of graves, and numbers of commemorated missing in parentheses)

WORLD WAR I CEMETERIES

Aisne-Marne, near Belleau (Aisne) France (2288-1060)

Brookwood (Surrey) England (468-563)

Flanders Field, Waregem, Belgium (368-43)

Meuse-Argonne, Romagne (Meuse), France (14,246-954)

Oise-Aisne, Seringes (Aisne), near Fere-en-Tardenois (Aisne), France (6012-241)

St. Mihiel, Thiaucourt (M. et M.), France (4,153-284)

Somme, Bony (Aisne), France (1837-333)

Suresnes (Seine), France (1541-974). In this cemetery rest also 24 of our unknown Dead of World War II. The World War I chapel was, by the addition of two loggias, converted into a shrine to commemorate our Dead of both Wars. Senior representatives of the American and French governments assemble here on ceremonial occasions to pay homage to our military Dead of these wars.

WORLD WAR I MONUMENTS

Audenarde, Belgium.	Kemmel, near Ypres, Belgium.
Bellicourt (Aisne), France.	Montfaucon (Meuse), France.
Brest (Finistere), France.	Montsec (Meuse), France.
Cantigny (Somme), France.	Sommepy (Marne), France.
Château-Thierry (Aisne), Fr.	Tours (Indre et Loire), France.
Gii.....	

WORLD WAR II CEMETERY MEMORIALS

Ardennes, near Neuville-en-Condroz, Belgium (5,310-462)

Brittany, near St. James (Manche), France (4,410-498)

Cambridge, near Cambridge, England, (3,811-5,125)

Epinal, near Epinal (Vosges), France (5,255-424)

Florence, near Florence (Tuscany), Italy (4,402-1,409)

Henri-Chapelle, near Henri-Chapelle, Belgium (7,989-450)

Lorraine, St. Avold (Moselle), France (10,489-444)

Manila, near Manila, Rep. of the Philippines (17,206-36,279)

Netherlands, Margraten, Holland (8,301-1,722)

Normandy, near St. Laurent (Calvados), Fr. (9,386-1,557)

North Africa, Carthage, Tunisia (2,840-3,724)

Rhone, Draguignan (Var), France (861-293)

Sicily-Rome, Nettuno, Italy (7,862-3,094)

WORLD WAR II MEMORIALS

To commemorate those who met their deaths in the American coastal waters of the Atlantic and Pacific Oceans the Commission has erected a memorial in Battery Park, New York City, on which are inscribed 4,596 names, and at the Presidio of San Francisco, California, which carries 412 names. At the Honolulu Cemetery a memorial was erected which records the names of 18,093 Missing of World War II and 8,194 Missing resulting from the Korean operations.

The Commission also maintains a cemetery in Mexico City where the remains of 750 Americans who gave their lives in the Mexican War (1846-1848) are buried.

SERVICES

The Commission provides the following services: exact location and other information concerning place of interment or memorialization; best routes and modes of travel in-country to the cemeteries and memorials; escort service within the cemetery memorials for next-of-kin and members of the immediate families; letters authorizing "non-fee" passports for members of the immediate families; color lithographs of World War I and II cemeteries together with black-and-white photographs of the appropriate gravesite or section of the Tablets of the Missing; and arrangements for floral decorations of gravesites or the Tablets of the Missing.

National Cemeteries (with ZIP Code)

On June 18, 1973, Pres. Nixon signed the National Cemeteries Act. (Public Law 93-43) transferring 82 Dept. of the Army National Cemeteries to the Veterans Admin , effective Sept. 1, 1973. The two remaining with the Army are marked*.

ALABAMA
Mobile Natl. Cemetery
Mobile 36604

ALASKA
Sitka Natl. Cemetery
Sitka 99501

ARKANSAS
Fayetteville Natl. Cemetery
Fayetteville 72701
Fort Smith Natl. Cemetery
Fort Smith 72901
Little Rock Natl. Cemetery
Little Rock 72206

CALIFORNIA
Fort Rosecrans Natl. Cemetery
San Diego 92106
Golden Gate Natl. Cemetery
San Bruno 94067
San Francisco Natl. Cemetery
94129

COLORADO
Fort Logan Natl. Cemetery
Denver 80235

DIST. OF COLUMBIA
*Soldiers' Home Natl. Cemetery
Washington, D. C. 20011

FLORIDA
Barrancas Natl. Cemetery
Pensacola 32508
St. Augustine Natl. Cemetery
St. Augustine 32084

GEORGIA
Marietta Natl. Cemetery
Marietta 30060

HAWAII
Natl. Memorial Cemetery of the Pacific Honolulu 96813

ILLINOIS
Alton Natl. Cemetery
Alton 62004

Camp Butler Natl. Cemetery
Springfield 62707
Mound City Natl. Cemetery
Mound City 62963
Quincy Natl. Cemetery
Quincy 62301
Rock Island Natl. Cemetery
Rock Island 61201

INDIANA
Crown Hill Natl. Cemetery
Indianapolis 46208
New Albany Natl. Cemetery
New Albany 47150

IOWA
Keokuk Natl. Cemetery
Keokuk 52632

KANSAS
Fort Leavenworth Natl. Cem.
Fort Leavenworth 66027
Fort Scott Natl. Cemetery
Fort Scott 66701

KENTUCKY
Camp Nelson Natl. Cemetery
Nicholasville 40356
Cave Hill Natl. Cemetery
Louisville 40204
Danville Natl. Cemetery
Danville 40422
Lebanon Natl. Cemetery
Lebanon 40033
Lexington Natl. Cemetery
Lexington 40508
Mill Springs Natl. Cemetery
Nancy 42544
Perryville Natl. Cemetery
Perryville 40468
Zachary Taylor Natl. Cemetery
Louisville 40207

LOUISIANA
Alexandria Natl. Cemetery
Pineville 71360
Baton Rouge Natl. Cemetery
Baton Rouge 70806
Port Hudson Natl. Cemetery
Zachary 70791

MARYLAND
Annapolis Natl. Cemetery
Annapolis 21401
Baltimore Natl. Cemetery
Baltimore 21228
Loudon Park Natl. Cemetery
Baltimore 21229

MINNESOTA
Fort Snelling Natl. Cemetery
St. Paul 55111

MISSISSIPPI
Corinth Natl. Cemetery
Corinth 38834
Natchez Natl. Cemetery
Natchez 39120

MISSOURI
Jefferson Barracks Natl.
Cemetery
St. Louis 63125
Jefferson City Natl. Cemetery
Jefferson City 65101
Springfield Natl. Cemetery
Springfield 65804

NEBRASKA
Fort McPherson Natl.
Cemetery
Maxwell 69151

NEW JERSEY
Beverly Natl. Cemetery
Beverly 08010
Finn's Point Natl. Cemetery
Salem 08079

NEW MEXICO
Santa Fe Natl. Cemetery
Santa Fe 87501

NEW YORK
Cypress Hills Natl. Cemetery
Brooklyn 11208
Long Island Natl. Cemetery
Farmingdale 11735
Woodlawn Natl. Cemetery
Elmira 14901

NORTH CAROLINA
New Bern Natl. Cemetery
New Bern 28560

Raleigh Natl. Cemetery
Raleigh 27602
Salisbury Natl. Cemetery
Salisbury 28144
Wilmington Natl. Cemetery
Wilmington 28403

OKLAHOMA
Fort Gibson Natl. Cemetery
Fort Gibson 74434

OREGON
Willamette Natl. Cemetery
Portland 97266

PENNSYLVANIA
Philadelphia Natl. Cemetery
Philadelphia 19138

PUERTO RICO
Puerto Rico Natl. Cemetery
Bayamon 00620

SOUTH CAROLINA
Beaufort Natl. Cemetery
Beaufort 29904
Florence Natl. Cemetery
Florence 29501

SOUTH DAKOTA
Black Hills Natl. Cemetery
Sturgis 57785

TENNESSEE
Chattanooga Natl. Cemetery
Chattanooga 37401
Knoxville Natl. Cemetery
Knoxville 37917
Memphis Natl. Cemetery
Memphis 38122
Nashville Natl. Cemetery
Madison 37115

TEXAS
Fort Bliss Natl. Cemetery
Fort Bliss 79906
Fort Sam Houston Natl.
Cemetery
San Antonio 78209
San Antonio Natl. Cemetery
San Antonio 78202

VIRGINIA

Alexandria Natl. Cemetery
  Alexandria 22314
*Arlington Natl. Cemetery
  Arlington 22211
  Contains Tomb of the Un-
  known Soldier. *See Index.*
Balls Bluff Natl. Cemetery
  Leesburg 22075

City Point Natl. Cemetery
  Hopewell 23800
Cold Harbor Natl. Cemetery
  Mechanicsville 23111
Culpeper Natl. Cemetery
  Culpeper 22701
Danville Natl. Cemetery
  Danville 24541
Fort Harrison Natl. Cemetery
  Richmond 23231

Glendale Natl. Cemetery
  Richmond 23231
Hampton Natl. Cemetery
  Hampton 23369
Richmond Natl. Cemetery
  Richmond 23231
Seven Pines Natl. Cemetery
  Sandston 23150
Staunton Natl. Cemetery
  Staunton 24401

Winchester Natl. Cemetery
  Winchester 22601

WEST VIRGINIA

Grafton Natl. Cemetery
  Grafton 26354

Debt Owed U.S. Arising from World War I as of June 30, 1973

Source: Treasury Department

Country	Original Indebtedness	Interest thru June 30, 1972	Cumulative Payments — Principal	Interest	Unmatured Principal	Principal and Interest due and unpaid
Armenia	$11,959,917.49	$32,175,040.29	$32.49	$	$	$44,134,925.29
Austria[1]	26,843,148.66	44,058.93	862,668.00			26,024,539.50
Belgium	419,837,630.37	368,780,720.47	19,157,630.37	33,033,642.87	156,780,000.00	579,647,077.60
Cuba	10,000,000.00	2,286,751.58	10,000,000.00	2,286,751.58	. . . .	. . . .
Czechoslovakia	185,071,023.07	138,585,008.09	19,829,914.17	304,178.09	67,740,000.00	235,781,938.90
Estonia	16,466,012.87	25,304,960.01	10.66	1,248,432.07	6,600,000.00	33,922,530.15
Finland	8,999,999.97	12,337,320.96	5,550,099.97[2]	12,337,320.96[2]	3,449,000.00	. . . .
France	4,089,689,588.18	4,046,328,302.14	226,039,588.18	260,036,302.82	1,435,303,603.57	6,214,638,395.75
Great Britain .	4,802,181,641.56	7,891,531,958.11	434,181,641.56	1,590,672,656.18	1,789,000,000.00	8,879,859,301.93
Greece	34,319,843.67	5,045,224.32	1,398,868.34[3]	4,701,575.79	19,565,975.33[9]	13,698,648.53
Hungary[4]	1,982,555.50	3,173,639.66	73,995.50	482,924.26	822,590.00	3,776,685.40
Italy	2,042,364,319.28	444,456,220.22	37,464,319.28	63,365,560.88	945,900,000.00	1,440,090,659.34
Latvia	6,888,664.20	10,685,968.91	9,200.00	752,349.07	2,790,200.00	14,022,884.04
Liberia	26,000.00	10,471.56	26,000.00	10,471.56	. . . .	. . . .
Lithuania	6,432,465.00	9,905,518.12	234,783.00	1,003,173.58	2,777,467.00	12,322,559.54
Nicaragua[5] . .	141,950.36	26,625.48	141,950.36	26,625.48	. . . .	. . . .
Poland	207,344,297.37	322,437,184.38	1,287,297.37[6]	21,359,000.18	87,784,000.00	419,351,184.20
Romania	68,359,192.45	62,152,382.42	4,498,632.02[7]	292,375.20[7]	25,870,000.00	99,850,567.65
Russia	192,601,297.37	533,870,068.67	. . . .	8,750,311.88[8]	. . . .	717,721,054.16
Yugoslavia . . .	63,577,712.55	38,766,527.92	1,952,712.55	636,059.14	28,679,000.00	71,076,468.78
Totals	**12,195,087,259.92**	**13,947,903,952.24**	**762,710,244.32**	**2,001,299,711.59**	**4,573,061,835.90**	**18,805,919,420.85**

(1.) The Federal Republic of Germany has recognized liability for securities falling due between March 12, 1938 and May 8, 1945.
(2.) $8,480,090.26 has been made available for educational exchange programs with Finland pursuant to 22 U.S.C. 2455 (e).
(3.) Includes $13,155,921.00 refunded by the agreement of May 28, 1964. The agreement was ratified by Congress November 5, 1966.
(4.) Interest payments from December 15, 1932 to June 15, 1937 were paid in pengo equivalent.
(5.) The indebtedness of Nicaragua was canceled pursuant to the agreement of April 14, 1938.
(6.) Excludes claim allowance of $1,813,428.69 dated December 15, 1969.
(7.) Excludes payment of $100,000,00 on June 14, 1940 as a token of good faith.
(8.) Principally proceeds from liquidation of Russian assets in the United States.
(9.) Includes $12,813,601.32 on agreement of May 28, 1964.

Peak Strength of Armed Forces: Battle Deaths in World War II

Allies and Associated Powers

Country	Strength	Deaths	Country	Strength	Deaths
Australia	680,000	23,365	New Zealand	157,000	10,033
Belgium	650,000	7,760	Norway	45,000	1,000
Canada	780,000	37,476	Poland	1,000,000	320,000
China	5,000,000	[1]2,200,000	So. Africa, Union of	140,000	6,840
Denmark	25,000	3,006	United Kingdom	5,120,000	244,723
France	5,000,000	210,671	United States	12,300,000	291,557
Greece	414,000	[2]73,700	USSR	12,500,000	7,500,000
India	2,150,000	24,338	Yugoslavia	500,000	410,000
Netherlands	410,000	6,238			

(1.)1937-1945 against Japan. (2.)Includes 50,000 killed in guerrilla warfare.

Other Powers that Declared War on Axis

Country	Strength	Country	Strength	Country	Strength	Country	Strength
Albania	25,000	Czechoslovakia . . .	150,000	Honduras	3,500	Paraguay	10,000
Argentina	160,000	Dom. Republic . . .	5,000	Iran	120,000	Peru	40,000
Bolivia	10,000	Ecuador	9,000	Iraq	47,000	Philippines	200,000
Brazil	200,000	Egypt	54,000	Liberia	1,000	Turkey	850,000
Chile	60,000	El Salvador	3,500	Luxembourg	1,000	Uruguay	11,000
Colombia	19,000	Ethiopia	38,000	Mexico	70,000	Venezuela	15,000
Costa Rica	500	Guatemala	6,000	Nicaragua	3,500		
Cuba	20,000	Haiti	4,000	Forces engaged and losses,· if any, not available.			

Axis

Country	Strength	Deaths	Country	Strength	Deaths
Bulgaria	450,000	10,000	Italy	3,750,000	*77,494
Finland	250,000	82,000	Japan	6,095,000	1,219,000
Germany (inc. Austria) . . .	10,200,000	3,500,000	Romania	600,000	300,000
Hungary	350,000	140,000	*Includes 17,494 on Allied side.		

The Flag of the United States—The Stars and Stripes

The 50-star flag of the United States was raised for the first time officially at 12:01 a.m. on July 4, 1960, at Fort McHenry National Monument in Baltimore, Md. The 50th star had been added for Hawaii; a year earlier the 49th, for Alaska. Before that, no star had been added since 1912, when N. M. and Ariz. were admitted to the Union.

In the 50-star flag, the stars are arranged in alternate rows of 6 and 5, staggered; 5 rows of 6 and 4 rows of 5 stars.

HISTORY OF THE FLAG

The true history of the Stars and Stripes has become so cluttered by a volume of myth and tradition that the facts are difficult, and in some cases impossible, to establish. For example, it is not certain who designed the Stars and Stripes, who made the first such flag, or even whether it ever flew in any sea fight or land battle of the American Revolution. Historians disagree on many details of the history of the Stars and Stripes and the flags that preceded it.

One thing all agree on is that the Stars and Stripes originated as the result of a resolution offered by the Marine Committee of the Second Continental Congress at Philadelphia and adopted June 14, 1777. It read:

Resolved: that the flag of the United States be thirteen stripes, alternate red and white; that the union be thirteen stars, white in a blue field, representing a new constellation.

Congress gave no hint as to the design of the flag, no instructions as to the arrangement of the stars, and no information on its appropriate uses. Historians have been unable to find the basis of the resolution—the original flag law.

The resolution establishing the flag was not even published until Sept. 2, 1777, more than 11 weeks after its passage. Despite repeated requests by the American commander, Gen. George Washington, for the "Standard of the United States" for his army, he did not get the flags until 1783, after the Revolutionary War was over. And there is no certainty that they were the Stars and Stripes.

EARLY FLAGS

Although it was never officially adopted by the Continental Congress, many historians consider the first flag of the United States to have been the Grand Union (sometimes called Great Union) flag. This was a modification of the British Meteor flag, which had the red cross of St. George and the white cross of St. Andrew combined in the blue canton. For the Grand Union flag, 6 horizontal stripes were imposed on the red field, dividing it into 13 alternate red and white stripes. On Jan. 1, 1776, when the Continental Army came into formal existence, this flag was unfurled on Prospect Hill, Somerville, Mass. Washington wrote that "we hoisted the Union Flag in compliment to the United Colonies."

One of several flags about which controversy has raged for years is at Easton, Pa. Containing the devices of the national flag in reversed order, this has been in the public library at Easton for over 150 years. Supporters of the movement contend that this flag was actually the first Stars and Stripes, and that it was first displayed on July 8, 1776, on the occasion of the public reading of the Declaration of Independence at the court house in Easton. This flag has 13 red and white stripes in the canton, 13 white stars centered in a blue field.

A flag was hastily improvised from garments by the defenders of Fort Schuyler at Rome, N. Y., Aug. 3-22, 1777, and this has led to the assumption that it was the Stars and Stripes. Historians believe it was the Grand Union flag.

The Sons of Liberty had a flag of 9 red and white stripes, to signify 9 colonies, when they met in New York in 1765 to oppose the Stamp Tax. By 1775 the flag had grown to 13 red and white stripes, with a rattlesnake on it.

At Concord, Apr. 19, 1775, the minute men from Bedford, Mass., are said to have carried a flag having a silver arm with sword on a red field.

At Cambridge, Mass., the Sons of Liberty used a plain red flag with a green pine tree on it.

In June, 1775, Washington went from Philadelphia to Boston to take command of the army, escorted to New York by the Philadelphia Light Horse Troop. It carried a yellow flag which had an elaborate coat of arms—the shield charged with 13 knots, the motto "For These We Strive"—and canton of 13 blue and silver stripes.

In February, 1776, Col. Cristopher Gadsden, member of the Continental Congress, gave the South Carolina Provincial Congress a flag "such as is to be used by the commander-in-chief of the American Navy." It had a yellow field, with a rattlesnake about to strike and the words Don't Tread on Me. Benjamin Franklin's paper, the Pennsylvania Gazette, had suggested sending a cargo of rattlesnakes to London parks to retaliate for British injustice.

At the battle of Bennington, Aug. 16, 1777, patriots used a flag of 7 white and 6 red stripes with a blue canton extending down 9 stripes and showing an arch of 11 white stars over the figure 76 and a star in each of the upper corners. The stars are seven-pointed. This flag is preserved in the Historical-Museum at Bennington, Vt.

At the Battle of Cowpens, Jan. 17, 1781, the 3rd Maryland Regt. is said to have carried a flag of 13 red and white stripes, with a blue canton containing 12 stars in a circle around one star.

LEGENDS ABOUT THE FLAG

Who Designed the Flag? No one knows for a certainty. Francis Hopkinson, a signer of the Declaration of Independence and designer of seals for the State Department, the Treasury Board and of a naval flag, declared he also had designed the flag. He asked Congress to pay him for his services. Congress did not do so. Dumas Malone of Columbia Univ. wrote: "This talented man . . . designed the American flag."

Who Called the Flag Old Glory?—The flag is said to have been named Old Glory by William Driver, a sea captain of Salem, Mass. One legend has it that when he raised the flag on his brig, the Charles Doggett, in 1824, he said: "I name thee Old Glory." But his daughter, who presented the flag to the Smithsonian Institution, said he named it at his 21st birthday celebration Mar. 17, 1824, when his mother presented the homemade flag to him.

Washington Coat-of-Arms Legend—The idea that the flag was suggested by Washington's coat of arms was publicized by Martin F. Tupper, an English writer, in a play in the 1870s. It rests on a coincidence and has no validity.

Washington's Invocation Legend—Circulation has been given to this speech attributed to General Washington: "We take the stars from heaven, the red from our mother country, separating it by white stripes, thus showing that we have separated from her, and the white stripes shall go down to posterity representing liberty." There is no proof that Washington ever said this.

The Betsy Ross Legend—The widely publicized legend that Mrs. Betsy Ross made the first Stars and Stripes in June, 1776, at the request of a committee composed of George Washington, Robert Morris and George Ross, an uncle, was first made public in 1870 by a grandson of Mrs. Ross. Historians have been unable to find a historical record of such a meeting or committee. Dr. Milo Milton Quaife wrote: "No record has ever been found of the creation by Mrs. Ross of the first Stars and Stripes." The New Century Cyclopedia of Names (1954) says: "There is documentary evidence that she was paid in May, 1777, for 'making ships colours, etc.' but no direct documentary evidence has been found to link her with the flag adopted by the Continental Congress on June 14, 1777, as the national emblem, and most historians now doubt if she made it."

ADDING NEW STARS

The flag of 1777 was used until 1795. Then, on the admission of Vermont and Kentucky to the Union, Congress passed and President Washington signed an act that after May 1, 1795, the flag should have 15 stripes, alternate red and white, and 15 white stars on a blue field in the union.

When new states were admitted it became evident that the flag would become burdened with stripes. Congress thereupon ordered that after July 4, 1818, the flag should have 13 stripes, symbolizing the 13 original states; that the union have 20 stars, and that whenever a new state was admitted a new star should be added on the July 4 following admission. No law designates the permanent arrangement of the stars. However, since 1912 when a new state has been admitted, the new design has been announced by executive order. No star is specifically identified with any state.

Code of Etiquette for Display and Use of the U.S. Flag

Although the Stars and Stripes originated in 1777, it was not until 146 years later that there was a serious attempt to establish a uniform code of etiquette for the United States flag. The War Department issued Feb. 15, 1923, a circular on the rules of flag usage. These were adopted almost in their entirety June 14, 1923, by a conference of 68 patriotic organizations in Washington. Finally, on June 22, 1942, a joint resolution of Congress codified "existing rules and customs pertaining to the flag for civilians."

When to Display the Flag—The flag should be displayed on all days when the weather permits, especially on legal holidays and other special occasions, on official buildings when in use, in or near polling places on election days, and in or near schools when in session. A citizen may fly the flag at any time he wishes. It is customary to display the flag only from sunrise to sunset on buildings and on stationary flagstaffs in the open. However, it may be displayed at night on special occasions, preferably lighted. In Washington, the flag now flies over the White House both day and night. It flies over the Senate wing of the Capitol when the Senate is in session and over the House wing when that body is in session. It flies day and night over the east and west fronts of the Capitol, without floodlights at night but receiving light from the illuminated Capitol Dome. It flies 24 hours a day at several other places, including the Fort McHenry Nat'l Monument in Baltimore, where it inspired Francis Scott Key to write The Star Spangled Banner.

How to Fly the Flag—The flag should be hoisted briskly and lowered ceremoniously, and should never be allowed to touch the ground or the floor. When hung over a sidewalk from a rope extending from a building to a pole, the union should be away from the building. When hung over the center of a street it should have the union to the north in an east-west street and to the east in a north-south street. No other flag may be flown above or, if on the same level, to the right of the United States flag, except that at the United Nations Headquarters the UN flag may be placed above flags of all member nations and other national flags may be flown with equal prominence or honor with the flag of the United States. At services by Navy chaplains at sea, the church pennant may be flown above the flag.

When two flags are placed against a wall with crossed staffs, the U.S. flag should be at right—its own right, and its staff should be in front of the staff of the other flag; when a number of flags are grouped and displayed from staffs, it should be at the center and highest point of the group.

Church and Platform Use—In an auditorium, the flag may be displayed flat, above and behind the speaker. If on a staff in a church chancel or on a speaker's platform, it should be in the position of honor at the clergyman's or speaker's right as he faces the congregation or audience. Any other flag in the chancel or on the platform should be displayed at the clergyman's or speaker's left. If elsewhere than in chancel or on platform, the flag should be displayed at the right of the congregation or audience as they face the speaker.

When the flag is displayed horizontally or vertically against a wall, the stars should be at the observer's left.

When to Salute the Flag—All persons present should face the flag, stand at attention and salute on the following occasions: (1) When the flag is passing in a parade or in a review, (2) During the ceremony of hoisting or lowering,

(3) When the National Anthem is played and the flag is displayed, and (4) During the Pledge of Allegiance. Those present in uniform should render the military salute. When not in uniform, men should remove the hat with the right hand holding it at the left shoulder, the hand being over the heart. Men without hats should salute in the same manner. Aliens should stand at attention. Women should salute by placing the right hand over the heart.

On Memorial Day, May 30, the flag should fly at half-staff until noon, then be raised to the peak.

As provided by Presidential proclamation the flag should fly at half-staff for 30 days from the day of a death of a President or former President; for 10 days from the day of death of a Vice President, Chief Justice or retired Chief Justice of the U.S., or Speaker of the House of Representatives; from day of death until burial of an Associate Justice of the Supreme Court, Cabinet member, former Vice President, or Senate President pro tempore, Majority or Minority Senate Leader, or Majority or Minority House Leader; for a U.S. Senator, Representative, Territorial Delegate, or the Resident Commissioner of Puerto Rico, on day of death and the following day within the metropolitan area of the District of Columbia and from day of death until burial within the decedent's state, Congressional district, territory or commonwealth; and for the death of the governor of a state, territory or possession of the U.S., from day of death until burial within that state, territory or possession.

When used to cover a casket, the flag should be placed so that the union is at the head and over the left shoulder. It should not be lowered into the grave nor touch the ground.

Prohibited Uses of the Flag—The flag should not be dipped to any person or thing. It should never be displayed with the union down save as a distress signal. It should never be carried flat or horizontally, but always aloft and free.

It should not be displayed on a float, motor car or boat except from a staff.

It should never be used as a covering for a ceiling, nor have placed upon it any word, design, or drawing. It should never be used as a receptacle for carrying anything. It should not be used to cover a statue or a monument.

The flag should never be used for advertising purposes, nor be embroidered on such articles as cushions or handkerchiefs, printed or otherwise impressed on boxes or used as a costume or athletic uniform. Advertising signs should not be fastened to its staff or halyard.

The flag should never be used as drapery of any sort, never festooned, drawn back, nor up, in folds, but always allowed to fall free. Bunting of blue, white and red always arranged with the blue above and the white in the middle, should be used for covering a speaker's desk, draping the front of a platform, and for decoration in general.

An Act of Congress approved Feb. 8, 1917 provided certain penalties for the desecration, mutilation or improper use of the flag within the District of Columbia. A 1968 Federal law provided penalties of up to a year's imprisonment or a $1,000 fine or both, for publicly burning or otherwise desecrating any flag of the United States. In addition, many states have laws against flag desecration.

How to Dispose of Worn Flags—The flag, when it is in such condition that it is no longer a fitting emblem for display, should be destroyed in a dignified way, preferably by burning in private.

Pledge of Allegiance to the Flag

I pledge allegiance to the flag of the United States of America and to the republic for which it stands, one nation under God, indivisible, with liberty and justice for all.

This, the current official version of the Pledge of Allegiance, has developed from the original pledge, which was first published in the Sept. 8, 1892, issue of the Youth's Companion, a weekly magazine then published in Boston. The original pledge contained the phrase "my flag," which was changed more than 30 years later to "flag of the United States of America." An act of Congress in 1954 added the words "under God."

The authorship of the pledge has been in dispute for

many years. The Youths Companion stated in 1917 that the original draft was written by James B. Upham, an executive of the magazine who died in 1910. A leaflet circulated by the magazine later named Upham as the originator of the draft "afterwards condensed and perfected by him and his associates of the Companion force."

Francis Bellamy, a former member of the Youth's Companion editorial staff, publicly claimed authorship of the pledge in 1923. The United States Flag Assn., acting on the advice of a committee named to study the controversy, upheld in 1939 the claim of Bellamy, who had died 8 years earlier. The Library of Congress issued in 1957 a report attributing the authorship to Bellamy.

AFGHANISTAN	ALBANIA	ALGERIA	ANDORRA	ARGENTINA
AUSTRALIA	AUSTRIA	BAHAMAS	BAHRAIN	BANGLADESH
BARBADOS	BELGIUM	BHUTAN	BOLIVIA	BOTSWANA
BRAZIL	BULGARIA	BURMA	BURUNDI	CAMBODIA
CAMEROON	CANADA	CENTRAL AFRICAN REPUBLIC	CHAD	CHILE
CHINA (MAINLAND)	CHINA (TAIWAN)	COLOMBIA	CONGO	COSTA RICA
CUBA	CYPRUS	CZECHOSLOVAKIA	DAHOMEY	DENMARK
DOMINICAN REPUBLIC	ECUADOR	EGYPT	EL SALVADOR	EQUATORIAL GUINEA

Flags shown are *national* flags in common use and vary slightly from official
state flags, most particularly by omitting coats of arms in some cases.

ETHIOPIA	FIJI	FINLAND	FRANCE	GABON
GAMBIA	GERMANY, EAST	GERMANY, WEST	GHANA	GREECE
GUATEMALA	GUINEA	GUYANA	HAITI	HONDURAS
HUNGARY	ICELAND	INDIA	INDONESIA	IRAN
IRAQ	IRELAND	ISRAEL	ITALY	IVORY COAST
JAMAICA	JAPAN	JORDAN	KENYA	KOREA, NORTH
KOREA, SOUTH	KUWAIT	LAOS	LEBANON	
LESOTHO	LIBERIA	LIBYA	LIECHTENSTEIN	

LUXEMBOURG	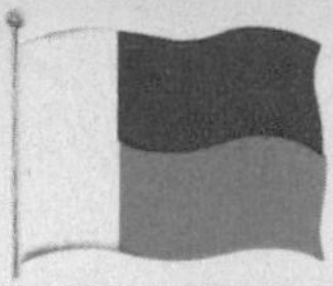 MALAGASY REPUBLIC	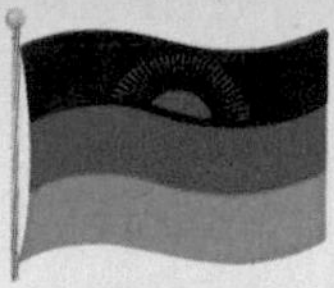 MALAWI	 MALAYSIA	 MALDIVES
 MALI	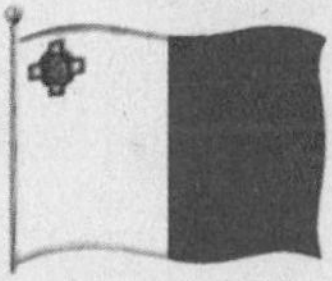 MALTA	 MAURITANIA	 MAURITIUS	 MEXICO
 MONACO	 MONGOLIA	 MOROCCO	 NAURU	 NEPAL
 NETHERLANDS	 NEW ZEALAND	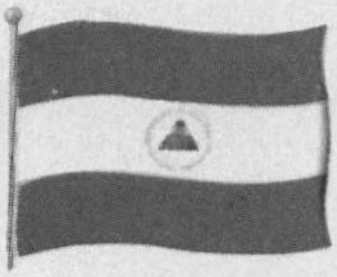 NICARAGUA	 NIGER	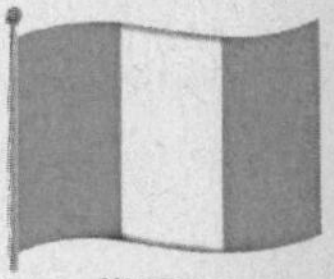 NIGERIA
 NORWAY	 OMAN	 PAKISTAN	 PANAMA	 PARAGUAY
 PERU	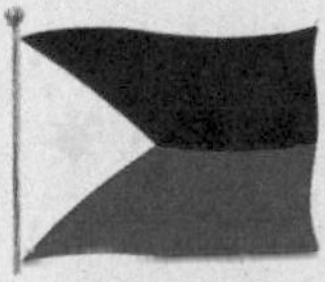 PHILIPPINES	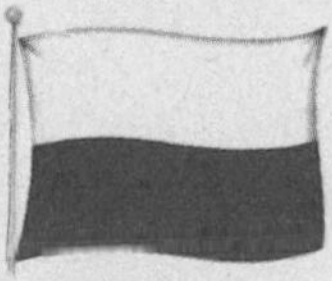 POLAND	 PORTUGAL	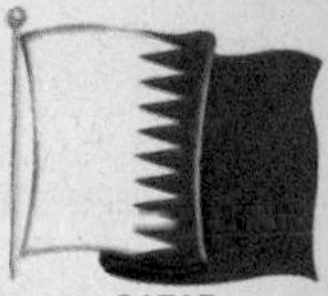 QATAR

RHODESIA

ROMANIA

RWANDA

SAN MARINO

SAUDI ARABIA

SENEGAL

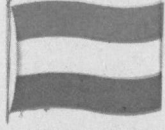

SIERRA LEONE

SINGAPORE

SOMALIA

SOUTH AFRICA

SPAIN

SRI LANKA

SUDAN

SWAZILAND

SWEDEN

SWITZERLAND

SYRIA

TANZANIA

THAILAND

TOGO

TONGA

TRINIDAD & TOBAGO

TUNISIA

TURKEY

UGANDA

U.S.S.R.

UNITED ARAB EMIRATES

UNITED KINGDOM

UNITED STATES

UPPER VOLTA

URUGUAY

VATICAN CITY

VENEZUELA

VIETNAM, NORTH

VIETNAM, SOUTH

WESTERN SAMOA

YEMEN

YEMEN, P.D.R. OF

YUGOSLAVIA

ZAIRE

ZAMBIA

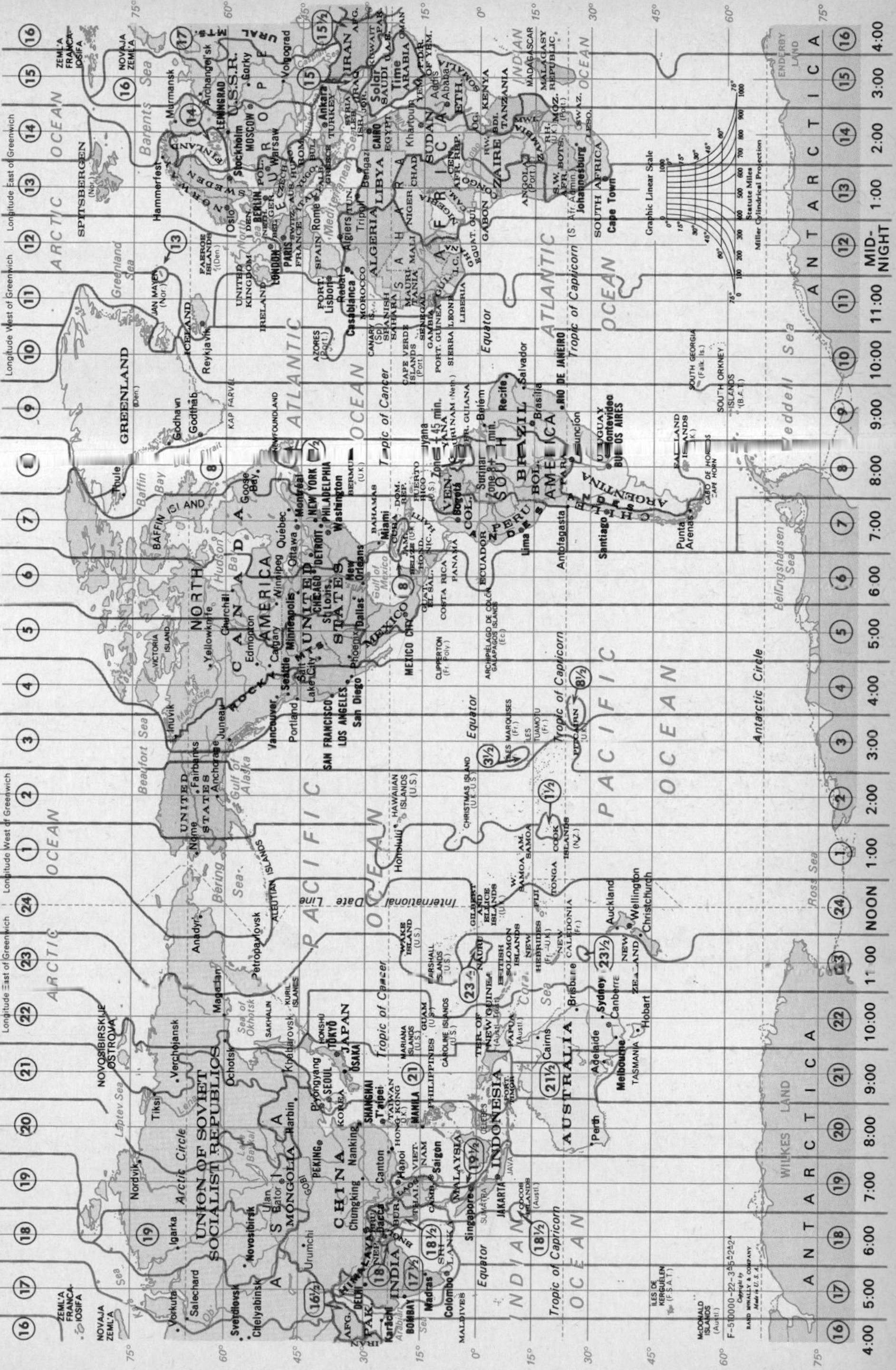

Longitude West of Greenwich
Longitude East of Greenwich
4:00
5:00
6:00
7:00
8:00
9:00
10:00
11:00
NOON
1:00
2:00
3:00
4:00
5:00
6:00
7:00
8:00
9:00
10:00
11:00
MID-NIGHT
1:00
2:00
3:00
4:00
ARCTIC OCEAN
PACIFIC OCEAN
ATLANTIC OCEAN
INDIAN OCEAN
ANTARCTICA
NORTH AMERICA
SOUTH AMERICA
AFRICA
EUROPE
ASIA
AUSTRALIA
UNION OF SOVIET SOCIALIST REPUBLICS
CHINA
INDIA
INDONESIA
UNITED STATES
CANADA
GREENLAND
BRAZIL
ARGENTINA
International Date Line
Tropic of Cancer
Equator
Tropic of Capricorn
Arctic Circle
Antarctic Circle
Graphic Linear Scale
Statute Miles
Miller Cylindrical Projection
F-510000-22-3-5-2-2-4
RAND McNALLY & COMPANY
Made in U.S.A.

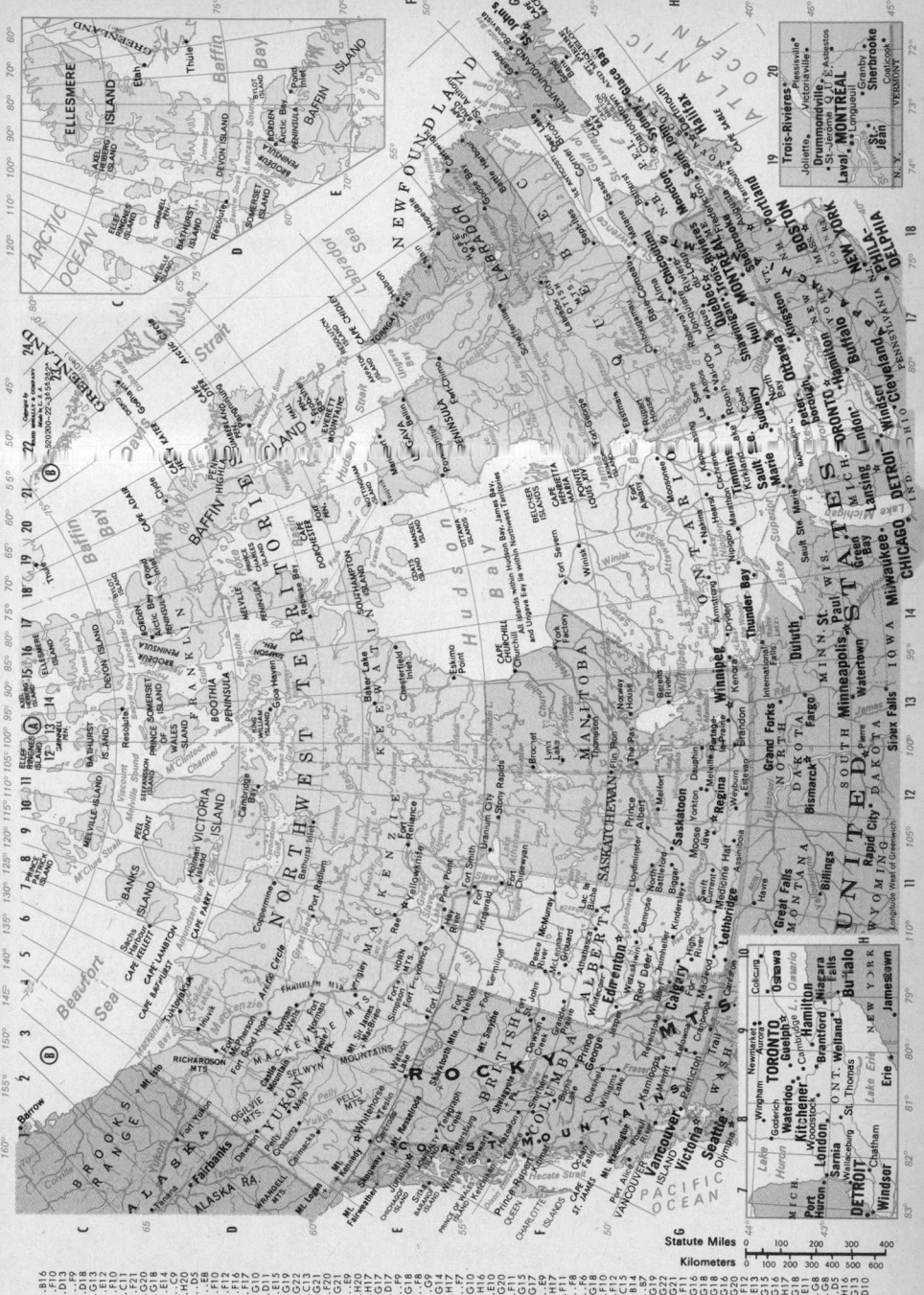

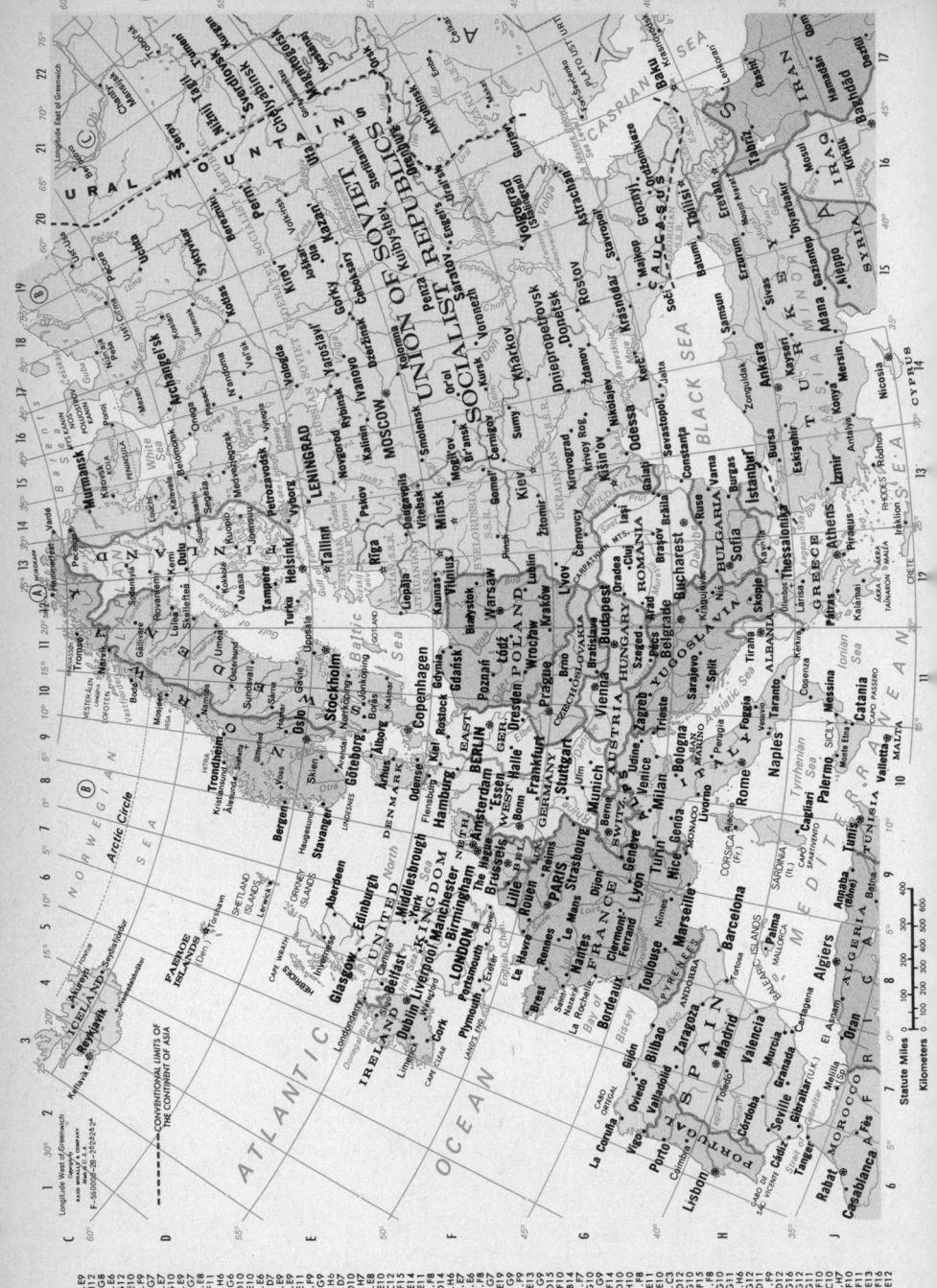

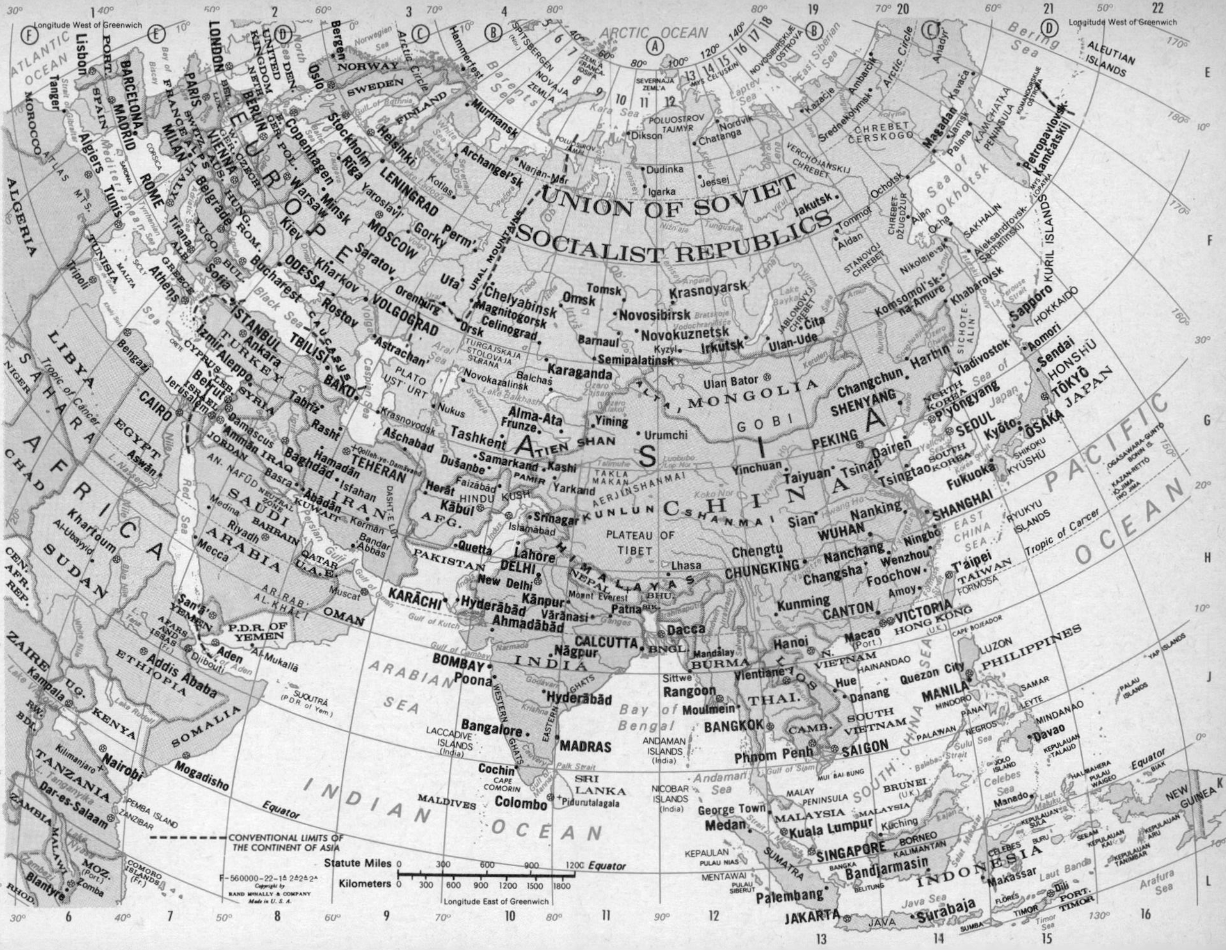

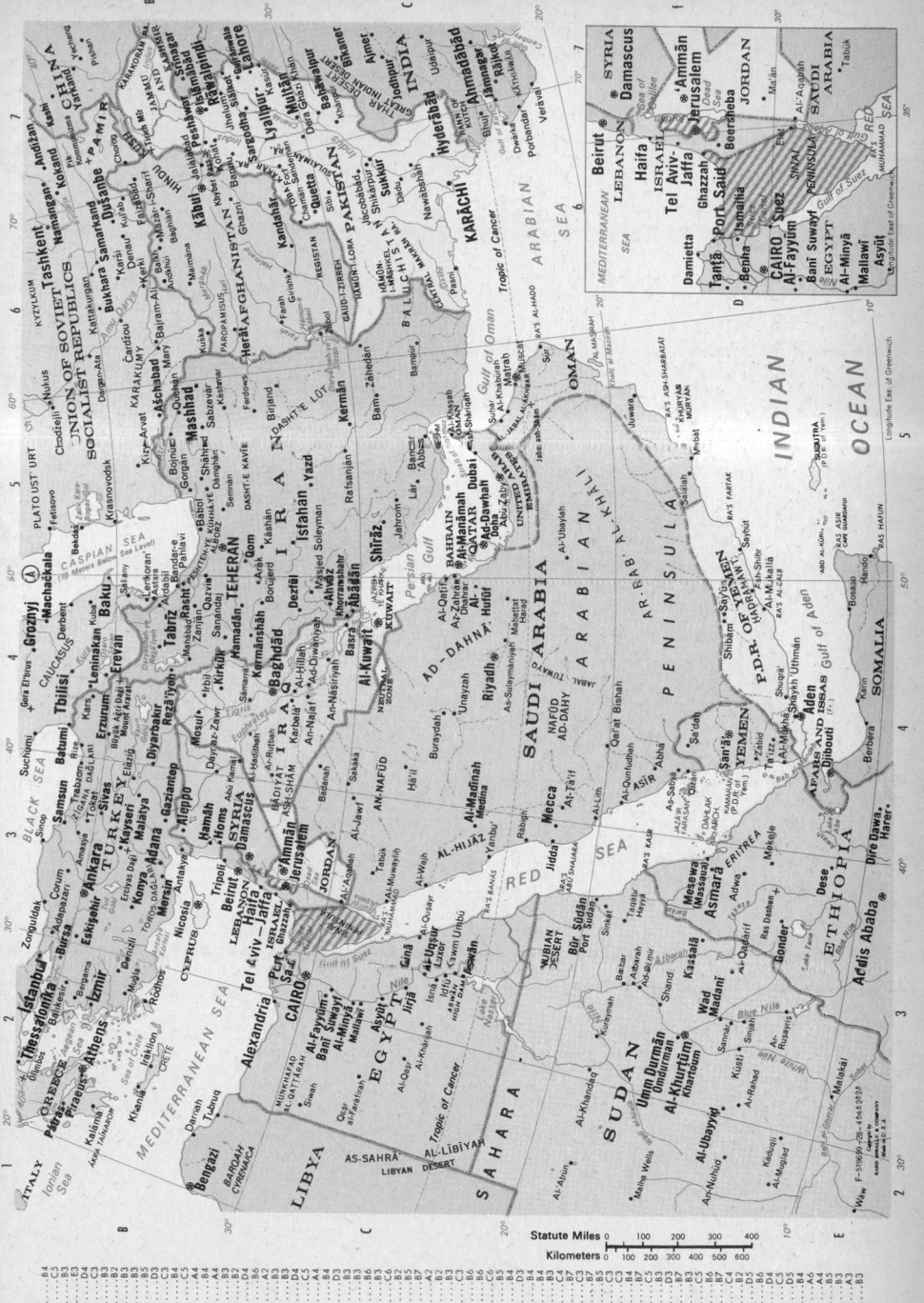

Statute Miles 0 100 200 300 400
Kilometers 0 100 200 300 400 500 600

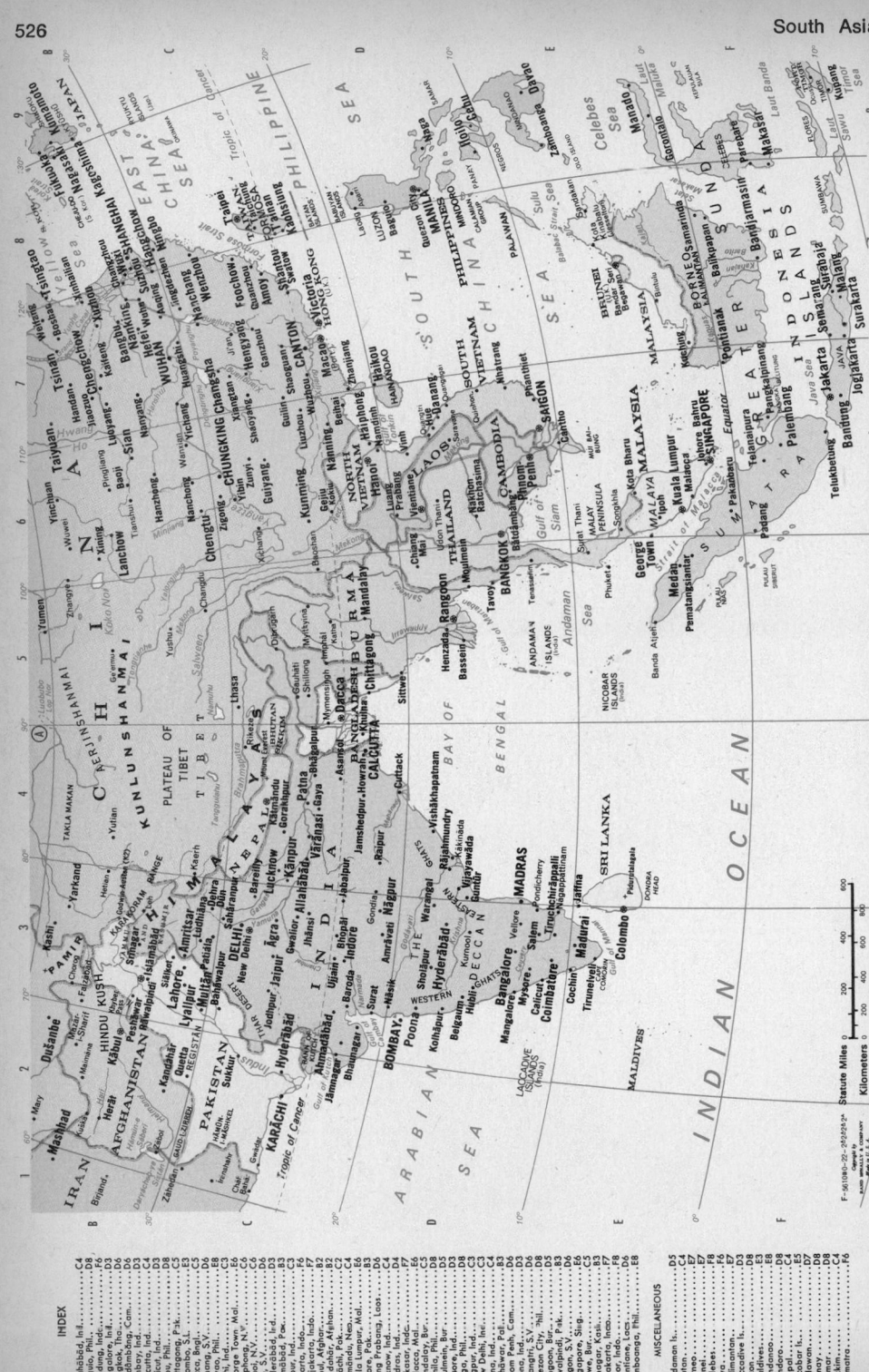

Canada: Minority Government

See Index for Calgary, Edmonton, Halifax, Hamilton, Kitchener-Waterloo, Lethbridge, London, Montreal, Ottawa, Quebec, Regina, Saskatoon, Toronto, Vancouver, Windsor, Winnipeg.

Capital: Ottawa. Area, 3,851,809 sq. mi. Population (Govt. est., April, 1973) 22,047,000. Monetary unit: Canadian dollar.

A cliffhanger to the end, Canada's 29th general election was the closest race in federal history. In several ridings, less than 100 votes separated the leading candidates for Parliament. When the final results were in, Prime Minister Trudeau's Liberals continued to hold power by a narrow margin of 109 seats to 107 seats won by the Progressive Conservatives led by Robert Stanfield.

A third party, the New Democrats headed by David Lewis, held the balance of power with 31 seats. Social Credit came fourth, but its 15 seats were not enough to allow it to be the king-maker. Two independents were also elected to the 264-seat House of Commons.

The Liberals' loss of 38 seats was thought to be due primarily to economic conditions—inflation and unemployment—and perhaps to an English-speaking backlash against Mr. Trudeau's efforts to upgrade the status of French. The Liberals held their 56 seats in Quebec, but lost 29 in Ontario, 8 in the prairie provinces, and 12 in British Columbia. The Liberals elected no members at all in Alberta. Since the Conservatives had only 2 candidates elected in Quebec, no party could form a secure nationally based government.

In Canada's 29th Parliament which opened on Jan. 4, 1973, the New Democrats consistently supported the Liberal minority government on all crucial votes, thereby keeping the government in power and avoiding the necessity of calling another election. The price of this support was the introduction of policies which the socialist-oriented N.D.P. could accept.

The government announced an increase in children's allowances from an average $7.21 a month to $20 a month, effective Jan. 1, 1974. For the first time, money paid in family allowances would be subject to income tax. The Liberals also announced a major overhaul in the national social security system which included long-term plans for higher old-age pensions and moves to encourage the working poor not to go on welfare. Less easy for the New Democrats to accept were the government's corporate tax cuts to spur industry.

On another front, the federal government offered the provincial governments a new procedure for the joint financing of costly higher education, hospital care, and medicare programs. The provinces were hesitant to commit themselves to the revised methods.

Despite indications that the public was opposed, a free vote in the House of Commons brought a narrow victory of 138-114 in favor of the government's proposal to extend for a further 5 years the ban on capital punishment for murder of all but policemen and prison guards.

The world-wide energy crisis had repercussions in Canada when the government in June imposed temporary controls on the export of Canadian gasoline and home heating oil. At the end of the month the government tabled a 639-page federal energy study which suggested that the solution to the energy crisis might be the creation of a state-run, publicly-owned national oil company, costing from $3 billion to $6 billion and taking 20 years to establish. Ottawa promised a white paper on the subject later, after public debate and consultations with the provinces and the energy industry.

The Economy

Canada's chief economic problem in 1973 was inflation. By mid-year the predicted increase in the cost of living for the year was more than 9%, which would be the largest annual increase since the Korean War in 1951. Soaring food prices were the major culprit. It was estimated that the 1973 increases in food costs would be about 15% or nearly double the 1972 jump of 7.9%.

Although Canadians had done well in 1972, securing an 11.5% average increase in their personal incomes, galloping inflation wiped out most of 1973's average wage gain of 8%.

In an effort to ease the pressure on low income groups, the government announced in August that it would amend the Canada Pension Plan to allow a 5.8% increase in payments starting in January, 1974. An increase in children's allowances was promised also.

At the same time Finance Minister John Turner adopted tougher controls on new government spending to prevent overheating the economy. The treasury tightened up on expenditures of $18.3 billion for 1973-74 which it had announced earlier. The budget had refrained from introducing new heavier taxes.

The government finished the fiscal year 1972-73 on March 31 with a $445-million surplus, the first in 3 years. By mid-1973 the economy was running well ahead of expectations. An anticipated budgetary deficit of $975 million for 1973-74 was reduced to $600 million. The merchandise trade surplus increased to $490 million in the second quarter while the seasonally adjusted unemployment rate dropped to 5.2% in July. Business capital investment was estimated to be 13% higher than in 1972. In the first quarter of 1973 profits of Canadian companies after taxes rose 30% above the comparable figure for 1972. Altogether, the finance minister's prediction of a real growth of 7% in the Gross National Product for the year seemed to be well founded.

Immigration to Canada increased by 12% in the first quarter of 1973. With immigration now amounting to about 100,000 annually, the United States continued to be the country supplying the largest number of new arrivals.

Foreign Relations

Canada's foreign relations have been altered significantly since the Trudeau government came to power first in 1968. The prime minister has put less stock in the traditional links with Western Europe and the U.S. and fostered closer relations with Far Eastern countries such as Japan and China. In mid-summer, 1973, the prime minister announced he would visit China in the autumn.

Mr. Trudeau has also reduced Canada's NATO commitments, trimmed the size of the armed forces, and insisted on establishing Canadian sovereignty in the Arctic. The government's reservations about peace-keeping were supported by the Canadian people when, after reluctantly providing troops for the international truce force in Viet-Nam, the Canadian government found its experience frustrating and pulled its troops out.

Initially cool towards the value of the Commonwealth, Mr. Trudeau has become a firm supporter. In August he hosted in Ottawa on behalf of Canada the 19th conference of Commonwealth heads, attended by Her Majesty Queen Elizabeth and representatives of 32 member-countries.

Since the U.S. is the country most involved in Canadian affairs, Canadian nationalism often smacks of anti-Americanism. There have been growing demands for limits on American ownership of Canadian industries and resources, for curbs on American investment, which now amounts to more than $24 billion, and for restraints on the importation of American culture.

The Land

Canada is the world's second largest country in land size, extending south from the North Pole to the U.S. border and including all the islands of the Arctic from near Greenland to near the Alaskan border. Its seacost, one of the longest in the world, includes 17,860 miles of mainland and 41,810 miles of islands. Canada's southernmost tip, Point Pelee in Lake Erie, is south of the Calif.-Ore. boundary.

A great sweep of the nation, stretching across the northern territories and prairies through northern Ontario and Quebec down to the Atlantic provinces, is known as the Canadian Shield, where past ice ages scraped most soil and vegetation off the land. This is the world's oldest surface rock, and it is here that most Canadian mineral discoveries have been made.

Canada's continental climate, while generally temperate, can run to freezing cold and blistering heat. The range is well beyond 100 degrees Fahrenheit.

History

French explorer Jacques Cartier is generally regarded as the founder of Canada. But his 1534 exploration of the Gulf of St. Lawrence followed by 37 years the sighting of Newfoundland in 1497 by English seaman John Cabot. Centuries prior to that, increasing evidence shows, Vikings had reached Newfoundland and Canada's Atlantic coast.

France pioneered Canadian settlement and the French have multiplied to become about 27% of the Canadian population today. Quebec was settled as early as 1608, Montreal in 1642; New France was declared a colony in 1663.

Britain and France clashed in Canada as a result of European rivalries and British expansion in America. Britain acquired Acadia (later Nova Scotia) in 1713, and captured Quebec in 1759, obtaining control of the rest of New France in 1763. The Quebec Act in 1774 gave the French rights to their own language, religion, and civil law. This was one reason why the French-Canadian settlers did not join American colonists in the War of Independence.

During the American Revolution, many former colonials moved north to settle in Canada, proudly calling themselves United Empire Loyalists.

The fur trade and exploration opened up the western plains and led Canadians across the continent to the Pacific. Alexander Mackenzie scrawled on a rock by the Pacific "From Canada, by land, 1793".

In Upper and Lower Canada (later called Ontario and Quebec) and in the Maritimes, legislative assemblies appeared in the 18th century and reformers called for responsible government. But the War of 1812 with the U.S. intervened. The war ended in a stalemate that was symbolic of the end to armed conflict between Canada and the U.S.

In 1837 political agitation for more democratic government culminated in rebellions in Upper and Lower Canada. The British sent Lord Durham to investigate and, in a famous report, he recommended union of the two parts into one colony called Canada. The union lasted until Confederation brought two additional colonies, Nova Scotia and New Brunswick, to join the new country in 1867. During the period 1840 to 1867, the Canadian colonies won the right to internal self-government.

The Dominion of Canada was launched on July 1, 1867, by the proclamation of the British North America Act, which became the country's written constitution, establishing a federal system of government on the model of a British parliament and cabinet structure under the crown. Canada was proclaimed a self-governing Dominion within the British Empire in 1931. Empire has now given way to Commonwealth, and Canada remains an independent member.

World War I had much to do with the development of Canadian nationhood. The pride it engendered and the industrial base it created in Canada led to the demand for full sovereignty.

But the achievement of nationhood was dulled by the blight of the Great Depression in the 1930s. It took World War II and Canada's accomplishments in it to revive the country's pride and sense of direction. It also fired the furnaces of industry, converting the country into an urban, industrial state.

Industrial Boom

On the Pacific coast a chain of rivers and lakes was reversed to flow backwards through the mountains to power electric generators for the huge aluminum smelters at Kitimat. The Columbia and Kootenay Rivers and Arrow Lakes were dammed to provide electricity. Oil wells and mineral strikes led to an El Dorado. Immense iron ore resources were discovered and developed in the wilds of Labrador. Uranium was unearthed in Northern Ontario and turned into nuclear power.

Canada joined with the U.S. to build the St. Lawrence River Seaway, and Ottawa shared costs with the provinces to complete the Trans-Canada Highway, the longest in the world. Two million immigrants arrived in Canada in the 2 decades after World War II and the country imported a billion dollars a year of foreign capital to finance a new industrial boom.

Economic System

The Canadian economy is a blend of private and public ownership. Despite a long historical tradition of state aid which has been necessary because of Canada's harsh climate and sparse population, private enterprise has flourished. But like Sweden, with which it vies for the second highest standard of living in the world, Canada accepts the idea of state capitalism and collectivism.

Most hydroelectric and many transportation and communication facilities are owned by either federal, provincial, or municipal governments. Air Canada, one of the largest airlines in the world, is a federal crown corporation, while the competing Canadian Pacific airline is privately owned. Canadian National Railways is another crown corporation. Its chief rival is the Canadian Pacific company. The Canadian Broadcasting Corp. is publicly owned, although independently managed.

There are also private radio chains and private television networks.

Welfare

Canada has a complex structure of social welfare. The federal government provides most of the cash, either through its own agencies or by assisting provincial governments and, through them, municipalities. The unemployment insurance program is contributory, as is the old age pension system, but there are additional private plans.

The two chief universal programs are the federally sponsored Family Allowances and Old Age Security plans. The former provides monthly allowances of from $6 to $8 (soon to be raised to a taxable average $20) per month per child, paid to mothers. The latter furnishes minimum pensions of $100 a month (to be raised to $105.30 January 1, 1974) to all persons 65 and over, regardless of need. There are supplementary benefits available to raise income to $179.16 per month for those without other resources. In addition, the federal government operates a compulsory contributory Canada Pension Plan whose payments are added to the basic old age security pension.

Canada has a publicly operated medical and hospital insurance scheme. Financed by federal assistance which runs to about $1.5 billion a year and covers about half the costs of operation, the 2 plans are managed by the provinces which put up the rest of the money.

Canadian Elections, Oct. 30, 1972

Final Election Results by Political Affiliation and by Province, of the Votes Cast

Source: Report of the Chief Electoral Officer, Dec., 1972.

Province	Lib.	P.C.	N.D.P.	S.C.	Ind.	None	Rejected Ballots	Totals
Ontario ...	1,366,593	1,399,161	768,328	12,859	7,893	23,007	69,809	3,647,650
Quebec ...	1,287,937	457,950	169,570	638,455	44,657	25,781	161,883	2,786,233
N.S.	130,322	204,399	47,066	1,310		499	7,477	391,073
N.B.	126,024	131,340	16,727	16,455	839	1,109	5,418	297,912
Nfld.......	78,502	85,962	8,165	266	616	1,635	7,164	182,310
P.E.I.	22,951	29,418	4,224	55			2,292	58,940
Man.......	137,085	184,366	116,440	3,225	517	1,674	10,330	453,637
B.C........	275,250	312,621	332,171	25,225	1,484	1,631	12,629	961,011
Sask.	109,493	159,586	155,156	7,717	201	420	9,625	442,198
Alta.	177,752	409,788	89,794	31,854	305	1,680	11,023	722,196
*Yukon	2,633	4,332	951		252		470	8,638
*N.W.T.....	4,112	4,354	5,616				268	14,350
TOTALS...	3,718,654	3,383,277	1,714,208	737,421	56,764	57,436	298,388	9,966,148
Total Vote ...... Valid	37.31%	33.95%	17.20%	7.40%	.57%	.58%	2.99%	100%
Votes ..... *Electoral District	38.46%	35.00%	17.73%	7.63%	.59%	.59%		100%

The Political Parties

Canadian parties, from whatever point in the political spectrum they begin, tend to move to the middle of the road where most of the votes lie. They all take much the same kind of moderate line.

Conservatives—The oldest party, they have adopted the prefix "Progressive" and moved to the left, advocating farm support programs and endorsing an extension of social welfare. Their support comes from older voters, Protestants, and English-speaking rural residents.

Liberals—Originally the Canadian equivalent of the American Jacksonian Democrats, favoring strict representation by population and the rural pioneer against the urban elite, they now get most of their electoral support from the middle and upper classes in cities, from ethnic voters, and among French-speaking Canadians. Liberals are cautious about extending the welfare state.

New Democratic Party—Successor to the Co-operative Commonwealth Federation, which combined the agrarian protest movement in western Canada with a democratic socialism of the British Labor party variety, the N.D.P. was founded in 1961. It now attempts to attract the vote of middle-class Canadians and fuse it with the party's labor support.

Social Credit—Adopting the unorthodox monetary theories of its English founder, Major C. H. Douglas, Social Credit has appealed to the have-nots, especially now in rural Quebec.

Supreme Court of Canada

The Supreme Court of Canada is the final court of appeal for civil and criminal appeals from lower courts. It sits in Ottawa and is comprised of a Chief Justice and 8 puisne judges, all appointed by the federal cabinet to hold office during good behavior until age 75. The court can render decisions on constitutional conflicts between the federal and provincial governments when they emerge in appeal cases or when asked to give an advisory opinion by either the federal or provincial governments. The Hon. Gerald Fauteux was appointed Chief Justice in 1970.

Other federal courts are the Federal Court, which replaced the former Exchequer Court in 1970 as a body to hear claims against the crown and income tax and shipping cases, the Court Martial Appeal Court, and the Territorial Courts in the Northwest Territories.

The Government of Canada

Canada is a constitutional monarchy with a parliamentary system of government. It is also a federal state. The head of state is Queen Elizabeth, so designated by the Canadian Parliament when she succeeded to the throne of the United Kingdom in 1952. The Queen is represented in Canada, a self-governing member of the Commonwealth of Nations, by a resident Governor-General, Rt. Hon. Roland Michener, appointed by Her Majesty in 1967 on the advice of the Canadian federal cabinet.

The cabinet is drawn from members of the party holding the largest number of seats in the House of Commons. Its members are appointed by the Governor-General on the advice of the prime minister, who is the leader of the party with the most Members of Parliament. The prime minister is the head of the executive branch of government which is composed of the cabinet and the Governor-General, the formal title of the body being "the governor-in-council", also known constitutionally as the Privy Council.

Canada has a bicameral Parliament. The House of Commons is the lower but more important chamber, being composed of 264 members elected federally at least every 5 years. The prime minister in reality chooses the date within this period.

The upper house is the Senate, comprised of 102 Senators who now are appointed to serve until 75. Prime ministers are free to choose appointees, the tradition being that they are party patronage nominations. The British North America Act requires that 30 members come from the Atlantic provinces, 24 from Quebec, 24 from Ontario, and 24 from the 4 western provinces.

Legislation becomes law by receiving three "readings" in the Commons, passing in the Senate and obtaining royal assent from the Governor-General. Financial bills can be introduced only in the Commons.

Each province has a modified version of the Ottawa pattern. The head of state in a province is the Lieutenant-Governor, representing the Queen but appointed by the federal cabinet. Each province has a unicameral legislature. The executive head in the province is referred to usually as the Premier.

Head of State

Queen Elizabeth— Succeeded to throne 1952.
Governor-General— Rt. Hon. Roland Michener, appointed 1967.

THE CABINET
(listed according to precedence) (Sept. 15, 1973)

Prime Minister— Pierre Elliott Trudeau
Leader of the Government in the Senate—
Paul Martin
Secretary of State for External Affairs—
Mitchell Sharp
President of the Privy Council—
Allan J. MacEachen
President of the Treasury Board—
Charles M. Drury
Transport (Minister)— Jean Marchand
Finance (Minister)— John N. Turner
Indian Affairs and Northern Development—
Jean Chrétien
Energy, Mines and Resources (Minister)—
Donald S. Macdonald
Labour (Minister)— John Munro
Communications (Minister)— Gérard Pelletier
Environment (Minister)— Jack Davis
Public Works (Minister)— Jean-Eudes Dubé
Minister of State for Urban Affairs—
Ronald Basford
Regional Economic Expansion (Minister)—
Donald C. Jamieson

Manpower and Immigration— Robert K. Andras
National Defence (Minister)—
James A. Richardson
Minister of Justice and Attorney General—
Otto Lang
Consumer and Corporate Affairs (Minister)—
Herb Gray
National Revenue (Minister)— Robert Stanbury
Supply and Services (Minister)—
Jean-Pierre Goyer
Industry, Trade and Commerce (Minister)—
Alastair W. Gillespie
Minister of State— Stanley Haidasz
Agriculture (Minister)— Eugene F. Whelan
Solicitor-General of Canada— Warren Allmand
Secretary of State— J. Hugh Faulkner
Postmaster General— André Ouellet
Veterans Affairs (Minister)— Daniel J. MacDonald
National Health and Welfare (Minister)—
Marc Lalonde
Minister of State for Science and Technology—
Jeanne Sauvé

Prime Ministers Since Confederation

Name	Party	Term	Name	Party	Term
Sir John A. Macdonald . .	Conservative	1867-1873	Arthur Meighen	Conservative	1920-1921
		1878-1891		Unionist	1926
Alexander Mackenzie . . .	Liberal	1873-1878	W.L.M. King	Liberal	1921-1926
Sir John J.C. Abbott	Conservative	1891-1892			1926-1930
Sir John S.D. Thompson	Conservative	1892-1894			1935-1948
Sir Mackenzie Bowell . . .	Conservative	1894-1896	R.B. Bennett	Conservative	1930-1935
Sir Charles Tupper	Conservative	1896	Louis St. Laurent	Liberal	1948-1957
Sir Wilfrid Laurier	Liberal	1896-1911	John G. Diefenbaker	Prog. Cons.	1957-1963
Sir Robert L. Borden	Conservative	1911-1920	Lester B. Pearson	Liberal	1963-1968
	Unionist		Pierre Elliott Trudeau . . .	Liberal	1968-

Governors-General

Since 1952, the Governors-General of Canada have been native born, replacing the former practice of appointing distinguished Britons. Canadian-born appointees have been:

Rt. Hon. Vincent Massey	1952-1959
Gen. Rt. Hon. Georges Vanier	1959-1967
Rt. Hon. Roland Michener . . . . : .	1967-

Provinces of Canada

Alberta

Alberta became a province in 1905, along with Saskatchewan. Nicknamed the "sunshine" province because of its good weather, it is one of the most beautiful in Canada. The south-eastern portion is flat or gently undulating prairie. The west of the province is notable for some of the finest cattle ranches in the world. The Rocky Mountains provide such famous tourist attractions as Banff and Jasper parks, Lake Louise and the Columbian ice fields.

Wheat and cattle gave Alberta its start but the economy was transformed by the discovery of huge petroleum and natural gas supplies at Leduc near Edmonton in 1947. Since then the province has become the 3rd wealthiest in Canada in terms of per capita income which was $3,756 in 1972. Its rate of population growth recently has been second only to British Columbia's, with estimated present population at about 1,700,000. The upsurge is concentrated in Alberta's 2 principal cities, Calgary and Edmonton, the capital.

Alberta was destined economically for another record year in 1973 with the provincial economy outperforming the national average. Real growth was expected to exceed the 6.5% to 7% predicted for Canada. The oil industry saw a 26.6% production increase over the first 6 months of 1972.

A Conservative government, headed by 45-year-old Premier Peter Lougheed, came to power in 1971 by defeating the Social Credit government that had been in power for 36 years. The annual provincial budget is now well in excess of $1 billion.

British Columbia

Canada's most westerly province is British Columbia. The 3rd largest in both area and population, 75% of its estimated 2,400,000 people are concentrated around the city of Vancouver, on Vancouver Island, and in the Kelowna valley—5% of B.C.'s total area. The interior is a series of rugged mountain ranges, including the Rockies. On the coast, the Pacific-warmed climate of Victoria, the capital, makes it a haven for tourists and retired people.

B.C. has the highest rate of population growth in Canada, increasing by 16.6% in 5 years, and the 2nd highest per capita income ($4,078). The budget now runs to $1.7 billion a year. Foreign capital has been pouring in, especially from Japan. Most of the private investment has been in primary extractive industries, such as coal, minerals, and lumber products. The port of Vancouver has been the busiest on the west coast, exporting more than 30 billion tons of cargo annually. The gross provincial product was estimated to be increasing by 12% to $13.3 billion in 1973.

For the first time in its history, B.C. elected a New Democratic party socialist government in 1972. Headed by Premier Dave Barrett, a 42-year-old former social worker, the government sought to maintain business confidence by maintaining the $575,000,000 reserve left behind by the outgoing Social Credit party which had been in power 20 years.

Manitoba

Manitoba, called the "keystone" province because it is the link between the eastern and western halves of the country, has a mixed economy. More than half of its population of about 1,000,000 lives in one large city, Greater Winnipeg. Another 30% lives in the arable section south of Lake Winnipeg and Lake Manitoba within 100 miles of the American border. The rest of the province is sparsely populated. The Canadian Shield covers most of it, making agriculture difficult but providing rich mineral deposits such as copper and zinc at Flin Flon and nickel at Thompson.

In recent years, Manitoba has suffered a relative decline from which it now seems to be emerging. To make up for recession in agriculture, the province has tried to develop its natural resources at a rapid rate. The most diversified industrially of the prairie provinces, its economy still depends heavily on agriculture. A 1973 provincial product estimated at $5 billion reflects the rapid expansion of the national economy.

Winnipeg, 5th largest city in Canada, is the provincial capital and the hub of business activity. The focal point of 2 east-west railways and a railway north to Churchill, a salt water port on Hudson Bay from which wheat is shipped to Europe, Winnipeg is also a strategic air center.

Manitoba's first socialist government was elected by a narrow margin in 1969. Premier Ed Schreyer, at 37 the youngest of Canada's premiers, has pursued a cautious policy. His attempt to win a larger majority in the Legislature in June 1973 gained only 2 seats.

New Brunswick

The rectangular Atlantic province has an extensive seacoast and the world's highest tides on the Bay of Fundy, but fishing takes second place to lumbering and pulp and paper mills. Heavily forested New Brunswick is home to an estimated 646,000 people.

New Brunswick has been traditionally one of the "have-not" provinces. With a per capita annual income of only $2,793, it ranks 3rd from the bottom. It also suffers from a chronically high rate of unemployment (9.8% in May, 1973). Although the number of jobs is increasing, young people looking for work outnumber openings. The federal government has launched several economic expansion projects. Most major industrial development takes place in the south around the principal cities of St. John and Moncton. Lorneville, near St. John, is the site of a new $184,000,000 electricity generating plant.

The present Conservative government, headed by Premier Richard Hatfield, was revamped in 1973, when its majority was reduced to 32 seats to the Liberals' 25.

Newfoundland

Newfoundland, the most recent addition to Canada, joined in 1949. The province consists of 2 parts: an Atlantic island of 43,359 sq. mi. and 112,826 sq. mi. of Labrador, east of Quebec. Both sections are rugged and generally barren. Newfoundland has more than 500,000 people but most of them reside in or near the capital, St. John's, or along the more verdant parts of the island's west coast.

For many years after joining Confederation, Newfoundland was the poorest province, but with a per capita income of $2,462 the province has now moved up to 9th in the prosperity list. However, 53.5% of the provincial governmental revenues still come from Ottawa. Unemployment hovers around 12%.

The province is heavily dependent upon massive industrial investment schemes; usually financed in part by the government. As a result, Newfoundland has the highest rate per capita debt in Canada; in 1973 it totalled $2,119. Among the development projects under way is a 300,000-barrels-a-day oil refinery costing $308,500,000 at Come-By-Chance, 90 miles west of St. John's.

The Conservative party led by 40-year-old Premier Frank Moores upset the charter Liberal administration of Joey Smallwood in 1972.

Nova Scotia

Nova Scotia includes a picturesque peninsula and Cape Breton Island. It has approximately 800,000 people, of whom about 40% live in the urban areas of Halifax-Dartmouth and Sydney-Glace Bay. The province has many excellent harbors, of which Halifax, the capital, is one of the most extensive and famous in the world.

Nova Scotia is the richest of the 4 Atlantic provinces, but its per capita income of $2,991 is only two-thirds that of Ontario. A natural gas strike on Sable Island in 1971 has raised hopes of sizable revenues in future, but a dispute still continues over ownership of offshore resources.

Traditionally a "have not" province, Nova Scotia has been striving to make itself financially independent of Ottawa, but in 1973 it was still dependent on the federal treasury for 25% of its provincial revenues. Premier Gerald Regan's Liberal government has attempted to attract industry by keeping corporate taxation at 10%, the lowest rate in Canada. But personal income tax rates and consumer taxes are among the highest. Unemployment, while dropping to 6.3% in May, 1973, was still higher than the national average.

Ontario

Ontario, the wealthiest province, had a per capita income of $4,324 in 1972. Ontario also has the largest population (about 8,000,000), more than one-third of Canada's people. The gross provincial product, now nearing $50 billion per year, accounts for about 40% of the GNP.

Ontario occupies the heartland of Canada, stretching from the Great Lakes to Hudson and James Bays in the north. The extensive Canadian Shield produces 40% of Canada's mineral output. Sudbury is the source of most of the world's nickel.

Ottawa, the national capital, is in Ontario. Toronto is the provincial capital and also the financial, commercial and manufacturing center of the province. As the center of a "Golden Horseshoe" of industrial activity, it is fast overtaking Montreal as the prime business city in Canada. Ontario accounts for 80% of all of Canada's manufactured exports.

The provincial economy continues to grow at an anticipated rate of about 6.8% for 1973. A 12.5% increase in retail sales is predicted for 1973. Unemployment remained at about 4%, one of the lowest rates in the country.

Satisfied that the economy was doing well, the provincial government's 1973 budget aimed at reducing the public debt. The retail sales tax was raised to 7%. The deficit was estimated at $5,000,000 on expenditures of $7.3 billion. The Conservative party, led by Premier Wm. Davis, continued in power for its 30th successive year.

Prince Edward Island

In 1973 the island celebrated its centenary as a Canadian province. P.E.I. hosted a meeting in Charlottetown, its capital, in 1864 which led to the Confederation of 4 provinces into Canada 3 years later, but P.E.I. did not join the new country until 1873. The smallest of the 10 provinces, the island has about 115,000 people. About 70% of the land is cultivated, the most popular crop being potatoes. Tourism is a major industry which is becoming more profitable each year.

The Liberal government, headed by 39-year-old Premier Alex Campbell, faces many problems. Per capita income, $2,442 in 1972 is the smallest in Canada. Per capita debt stood at $1,957 in 1972. The federal treasury provides 60% of total provincial revenues. It is also sharing with the province the cost of a current 15-year development program which will total $725,000,000.

Quebec

Quebec, one of the 4 charter provinces in Confederation, is the largest in size and the 2d largest in population (6,059,000 est. June 1972). Rocky and barren except for lakes and coniferous trees, the Canadian Shield spreads over the largest part of the province north of the St. Lawrence River. South of the river, the Appalachian Mountains run to the east and south to the U.S.A. A fertile agricultural band called the St. Lawrence Lowlands surrounds the western end of the river. Agriculture is declining rapidly in the province, which is now the 2d largest industrially.

Quebec City, the provincial capital, dates back 350 years to the founding of the colony by France. The walls and ancient buildings of the old town attract many tourists. Montreal, Canada's largest city, is the commercial and industrial hub of the province. Scene of Expo '67, Montreal has bid successfully for the Summer Olympics in 1976. About 87% of the population is of French maternal tongue.

During the "Quiet Revolution" of the 1960s, Quebec was transformed from a rural, agrarian, strongly traditional Roman Catholic society to a modern, urbanized, industrialized, secular society. The shock waves of this sudden change shook both Quebec and Canada. An upsurge of "nationalist" sentiment demanded separation and independence for Quebec. Inside the province the upheaval is apparent in the secularization of education (which was church-run until 1964), a rise in trade union militancy, and renewed insistence on the preservation of the French language.

A Liberal government headed by 40-year-old Robert Bourassa was elected in 1970. Taking economic development and prosperity as its theme to combat separatism, the government has pinned its hopes on stimulating the economy, providing 100,000 new jobs, and on making French the language of work. The government's most ambitious economic plan is a $5.8 billion hydro-electric development in the James Bay region. The 1973 budget calls for expenditures of more than $5 billion with a deficit of $278,000,000. Quebec's unemployment rate fell to 6.6 in May 1973, and the gross provincial product is predicted to rise 6.8% in real terms in 1973.

Saskatchewan

Saskatchewan, the granary of Canada, is the only province having trouble maintaining its present population of about 920,000. The southern portion of Saskatchewan is an arable plain devoted to wheat, but low rainfall and the need for large holdings with much capital equipment have squeezed out many small farmers. The majority of the province's land area lying to the north is not suited to agriculture and fewer mineral resources have been found here than in neighbouring provinces.

Regina, the "queen city", is the capital, and the center of the Royal Canadian Mounted Police, which in 1973 celebrated their centenary. Regina and Saskatoon are the largest urban centers.

Saskatchewan produces about 60% of the prairie grain crop. A sharp upturn in world demand for wheat brought a change in the province's fortunes in 1973. For the 3rd year in a row Canada is setting a record for the size of wheat exports. Estimates are that Canada will export about 860,000,000 bushels of wheat, and sell over 1 billion altogether. Bumper crops and sales of grain may bring as much as $1.4 billion to Saskatchewan farmers.

Saskatchewan had the first democratic socialist government in North America from 1944 to 1964. The New Democratic socialist party regained office from the Liberals in 1971 and Allan Blakeney, now 47, became Premier.

Floral Emblems of the Provinces of Canada

British Columbia (1948) . . . . Dogwood	New Brunswick (1936). . . . . Purple Violet
Alberta (1903). . . . . Wild Rose	Prince Edward Island (1947). . . . . Lady's slipper
Manitoba (1906). . . . . Prairie Crocus	Nova Scotia (1901). . . . . Trailing Arbutus
Saskatchewan (1941). . . . . Prairie Lily	or Mayflower
Ontario (1939). . . . . White Trillium	Newfoundland. . . . . Pitcher Plant
Quebec. White Garden Lily	Yukon . . . . Fireweed
or Fleur-de-lis	Northwest Territories . . . . Mountain Avens

Origins of Canadian Province Names

Canada—a term that was apparently derived from the Huron-Iroquois **Kanata,** meaning a village or community.

Alberta—named in honor of Princess Louise Caroline Alberta, daughter of Queen Victoria.

British Columbia—first named New Caledonia, the name was changed to avoid confusion with the French Pacific island.

Manitoba—probable derivation is from "Manitobau," the strait of the Manitu, the narrows of Lake Manitoba.

New Brunswick—named in honor of Britain's reigning House of Brunswick.

Newfoundland—derived from the charter given in 1496 by King Henry VII to explorer John Cabot, granting him the right to "sail to all parts . . . and to set up our banner on any new-found-land."

Nova Scotia—Latin for New Scotland, derived from the Latin charter by which New Scotland was granted to Sir William Alexander (afterwards Lord Stirling) in 1621.

Ontario—perhaps from "ontare," a Huron word for lake, and "io," meaning beautiful; or from "Entouhonorous," a name Champlain applied to the lake to designate it as the lake of the Seneca or Iroquois.

Prince Edward Island—named in honor of Prince Edward. Duke of Kent, father of Queen Victoria.

Quebec—(also Quebecq or Kèbec)—from an Algonquian word meaning "where the river narrows".

Saskatchewan—from the Cree Indian word for "swift-flowing," describing the Saskatchewan River of the prairies.

Superlative Canadian Statistics

Area for 10 provinces.	Total: Land 3,560,238 sq.mi.; Water 291,571 sq.mi.	3,851.809 sq.mi.
Largest province.	Quebec.	523,860 sq.mi.
Smallest province.	Prince Edward Island	2,184 sq.mi.
Largest city in area.	Whitehorse	162 sq.mi.
Smallest city in area (east). . . .	Thetford Mines, Que.	7 sq.mi.
Smallest city in area (west). . . .	Prince George, B.C.	17 sq.mi.
Northernmost point.	Cape Columbia, N.W.T.	83° 07′N.
Northernmost settlement.	Alert, Ellesmere Island	82° 31′N.
Northernmost town	Inuvik, N.W.T.	68° 21′N.
Southernmost point.	Middle Island (Lake Erie), Ont.	42° 41′N.
Southernmost settlement	Pelee Island South, Ont.	41° 45′N.
Southernmost town	Kingsville, Ont.	42° 02′N.
Westernmost point.	Mount St. Elias, Yukon.	141° W.
Westernmost settlement	Beaver Creek, Yukon.	140° 52′W.
Westernmost town	Dawson, Yukon.	139° 25′W.
Easternmost point	Cape Spear, Nfld.	52° 37′W.
Easternmost settlement.	Blackhead, Nfld.	52° 39′W.
Easternmost town.	St. John's, Nfld.	52° 43′W.
Highest city	Rossland, B.C. at R.R. Stn. (49°05′ 117°47′)	3,465 ft.
Highest settlement.	Mountain Park, P.O., Alta.	5,819 ft.
Highest town	Lake Louise, Alta.	5,051 ft.
Highest waterfall.	Takakkaw Falls, B.C. (51°30′ 116°29′)	1,248 ft.
Longest river	Mackenzie (from head of Finlay R.).	2,635 mi.
Highest mountain.	Mt. Logan.	19,850 ft.
Rainiest spot	Henderson Lake, Vancouver Is. yrly. avg. rainfall	262.0 inches
Highest lake.	Chilco Lake (51°20′ 124°05′) 75.1 sq.mi.	3,842 ft.
Largest man-made lake.	Manicouagan No. 5, Que.	115,000,000 acres
Biggest hydroelectric plant	Churchill Falls, Nfld.	5,225 megawatts

Canadian Armed Forces

In February, 1968, Canada carried out the unification of its traditionally separate services: the Royal Canadian Navy, the Canadian Army and the Royal Canadian Air Force. The first step towards a unified force was taken in 1964 when the 3 services were brought together under one control with common logistics and supply and training systems, but retaining their separate legal entities. The positions of Chairman of the Chiefs of Staff and Chiefs of the Navy, Army and Air Force were abolished and replaced by the Chief of the Defence Staff. On February 1, 1968, the 3 services ceased to exist. They were unified into the Canadian Armed Forces in which all officers, men and women are managed within a single body, with a common uniform.

Chief of the Defence Staff: General J. A. Dextraze

Air Defence Command—
    Maj. Gen. N. L. Magnusson
Air Transport Command—
    Maj. Gen. H. McLachlan
Communication Command—
    Col. L. H. Wylie

Canadian Forces Europe—
    Maj. Gen. W. C. Leonard
Maritime Command— Maj. Gen. R. W. Timbrell
(Pacific)—Maj. Gen. R. H. Leir
Mobile Command— Lt. Gen. W. A. Milroy
Training Command— Maj. Gen. R. S. Stephens

Regular Forces Strength

March 31	Navy	Army	Air Force	Total		Navy	Army	Air Force	Total
1940..	6,135	76,678	9,483	92,296	1968..	17,439	40,192	44,045	101,676
1945..	92,529	494,258	174,254	761,041	1969..	.....	.....	.....	98,340
1950..	9,259	20,652	17,274	47,185	1970..	.....	.....	.....	98,353
1955..	19,207	49,409	49,461	118,077	1971..	.....	.....	.....	89,563
1960..	20,675	47,185	51,737	119,597	1972..	.....	.....	.....	84,933
1965..	19,756	46,264	48,144	114,164	1973..	.....	.....	.....	82,402

Canadian Military Participation in Major Conflicts

Northwest Rebellion (1885)[1]
Participants—3,323
Killed—38
Last veteran died at the age of 104 in 1971.
South African War (1899-1902)
Participants—7,368[2]
Killed—89
Living Veterans—about 150
First World War (1914-1918)
Participants—626,636[3]

Killed—61,332[4]
Living Veterans—81,052
Second World War (1939-1945)
Participants—1,086,343 (inc. 45,423 women)
Killed—37,714 (inc. 8 women)
Living Veterans—769,175
Korean War (1950-1953)
Participants—25,583
Killed—314
Living Veterans—25,000

[1] First battle in history to be fought entirely by Canadian troops. [2] Includes Canadians in the South African constabulary and 8 nursing sisters. [3] Includes 2,854 nursing sisters. [4] Includes 21 nursing sisters and 1,563 airmen serving with the British air forces.

Department of National Defence Expenditures

(Thousands of Dollars)

	1964-65	1965-66	1966-67	1967-68	1968-69	1969-70	1970-71	1971-72	1972-73*
Defence Services	1,386,923	1,401,253	1,435,115	1,527,867	1,507,653	1,541,705	1,517,183	1,598,213	1,634,279
Defence Research	36,718	41,643	44,202	50,458	44,146	44,121	45,863	46,981	46,290
Administration .	3,925	4,647	5,696	6,277	6,317	7,529	6,960	9,054	10,367
Mutual Aid	27,541	14,663	18,720	17,976	15,250	14,112	14,384	13,833	14,324
Civil Emergency	–	–	–	–	6,346	4,991	5,017	4,929	5,388
Defence Construction ...	–	1,964	2,192	2,230	2,295	2,136	2,195	2,703	2,872
Pensions, etc...	80,528	84,277	134,453	148,674	178,789	174,914	226,274	219,462	267,750
Net Budgetary	**1,535,635**	**1,548,447**	**1,640,378**	**1,753,482**	**1,760,796**	**1,789,508**	**1,817,876**	**1,895,175**	**1,981,270**

*Estimated

Canadian Peacekeeping Operations

Canada has provided either policing or observer troops for every peacekeeping operation since World War II.

Nearly 900 Canadian soldiers served in the Gaza Strip following the Israeli-Egyptian crisis of 1956 until the force was disbanded in 1967.

In the Congo, a 300-man signals unit provided communications for the UN Force from 1960 to 1964.

In 1973, 20 officers served with the UN Truce Supervisory Organization, Palestine, observing the ceasefire and assisting parties in the observance of agreements between Egypt, Lebanon, Jordan, Syria and Israel.

There are 17 Canadian Forces personnel with

the UN Military Observer Group, India-Pakistan, to supervise the implementation of the ceasefire agreements between India and Pakistan in Kashmir.

The UN Force in Cyprus is Canada's largest UN military commitment. A Canadian contingent has served there since March, 1964, and in 1973 there were 580 officers and men on duty there.

One officer and a sergeant are in Korea with the UN Military Armistice Commission.

Canadian participation in the International Commission for Supervision and Control in Vietnam and Laos began in 1954 and at the high point of participation in 1973 there were 245 Canadian Forces personnel supervising the ceasefire.

Canadian Winners of the Victoria Cross

The Victoria Cross is Britain's highest military honor. It has been accorded to 94 Canadians since its inception in 1856. The cross was originally cast from metal of a Russian cannon captured during the Crimean War. Canadian winners in World War II:

Name	Unit	Theater of War & Date
Sgt. Mjr. J. R. Osborn	Winnipeg Grenadiers	Hong Kong, Dec. 19, 1941
Lt. Col. C. E. Merritt	S. Sask. Regiment	Dieppe, Aug. 19, 1942
Capt. J. W. Foote	Royal Hamilton Light Infantry	Dieppe, Aug. 19, 1942
Capt. F. T. Peters	Royal Navy	Oran, North Africa, Nov. 8, 1942
Capt. Paul Triquet	Royal 22nd Regiment	Casa Berardi, Dec. 14, 1943
Maj. C. F. Hoey	Lincolnshire Regiment	Burma, Feb. 16, 1944
Maj. John K. Mahoney	Westminster Regiment	Melfa River, May 24, 1944
P.O.A.C. Mynarksi	RCAF	Camria, France, June 12, 1944
Flt. Lieut. D. E. Hornell	RCAF	"Northern waters", June 25, 1944
Sqd. Ldr. Ian Bazalgette	RAF	Trossy St. Maximin, Aug. 4, 1944
Maj. D. V. Currie	South Alberta Regiment	Normandy, Aug. 20, 1944
Pvt. E. A. Smith	Seaforth Highlanders	Savio River, Italy, Oct. 22, 1944
Sgt. Aubrey Cosens	Queen's Own Rifles	Holland, Feb. 26, 1945
Maj. F. A. Tilston	Essex Scottish	Hochwald Forest, March 1, 1945
Cpl. F. G. Topham	1st Canadian Parachute Battalion	Germany, March 24, 1945
Lt. R. H. Gray	Royal Canadian Navy	Pacific, Aug. 9, 1945

Canadian Time Zones

There are seven time zones in Canada. In terms of the number of hours behind the Universal Time established on the zero meridian at Greenwich these are, from East to West:

Newfoundland Standard Time	3½ hours	Mountain Standard Time	7 hours
Atlantic Standard Time	4 hours	Pacific Standard Time	8 hours
Eastern Standard Time	5 hours	Yukon Standard Time	9 hours
Central Standard Time	6 hours		

The location of the time zone boundaries in Canada, together with other regulations governing time, is a matter of provincial jurisdiction. The adoption or rejection of Daylight Saving Time, therefore, is decided by provincial legislation except in those cases where the province leaves the decision to the the municipalities.

Canadian Road and Street Mileage

Source: Statistics Canada

1971	Paved	Gravel	Earth	Total	1972	Paved	Gravel	Earth	Total
Newfoundland	2,234	4,460	251	6,945	Saskatchewan	9,838	60,868	57,920	128,626
Prince Edward					Alberta	9,647	67,528	17,782	94,957
Island	1,769	1,012	611	3,392	British Columbia	14,248	17,408	6,548	38,204
Nova Scotia	6,194	10,667	78	16,939	Yukon Territory	41	2,371	−	2,412
New Brunswick	6,283	7,650	34	13,967	Northwest				
Quebec	26,503	25,952	13,660	66,115	Territories	18	969	4	991
Ontario	35,393	59,482	3,720	98,595					
Manitoba	6,456	27,907	12,812	47,175	Total	118,624	286,274	113,420	518,318

Canadian Shipping Traffic (thousand short tons)

Source: Canadian Statistical Review, June 1973

Cargo Handled

	Halifax	St. John	Quebec	Montreal	Toronto	Vancouver	All Ports	Coastwise
1970	11,072	6,401	8,552	22,376	5,163	26,923	290,708	126,318
1971	10,999	7,438	10,811	21,690	4,710	30,813	286,606	122,536
1972	11,355	10,263	14,901	20,431	4,534	29,894	298,076	122,403

Canadian Postal Code

The Canadian Postal Code consists of 6 alphanumeric characters with 2 components separated by a single space. The Area Code is a combination of letter-number-letter. The Local Code is a combination of number-letter-number.

The Postal Code precisely describes the location of the point of delivery for each item of mail. The Area Code makes it possible to sort mail into geographic areas, or forward sortation areas. The Local Code makes it possible to sort mail for Post Offices in rural areas, for letter carrier routes, large volume points of delivery, or forms of delivery service in urban areas.

As a matter of interest, only 18 letters are used in the first position, whereas 20 letters are used in 3rd and 5th position. There are a total of 7,200,000 possible codes, i.e., (18 x 10 x 20) (10 x 20 x 10) but only about 10% will be used initially.

Canadian Government Budgetary Expenditures by Principal Classes

(in millions of dollars)

Source: Canadian Statistical Review, June 1973

Fiscal Year and Month	National Defence	National Health and Welfare	Agriculture	Post Office	Public Works	Transport	Veterans Affairs	Fiscal, etc. Payments to provinces	Total Budgetary expenditures
1970-71	1,817.9	2,338.0	277.0	368.6	330.7	429.7	410.0	1,229.0	13,182.2
1971-72	1,895.2	2,706.1	286.1	413.3	336.8	512.4	423.3	1,425.5	14,840.9
1971-72									
Apr.	103.3	110.4	7.6	21.8	8.4	32.6	269.4	94.5	841.1
July	151.6	215.4	15.0	32.1	24.7	36.6	431.0	113.5	1,216.0
Dec.	176.2	230.0	23.1	36.7	30.3	40.1	370.5	146.4	1,253.4
Mar.	198.9	359.9	55.3	52.3	64.2	128.3	918.9	258.4	2,247.6
1972-73									
Apr.	88.1	145.3	7.7	19.1	9.4	37.5	31.5	95.0	941.7
July	171.0	227.1	14.9	33.6	25.1	60.7	41.5	135.3	1,340.4
Dec.	209.6	234.3	37.7	40.3	29.0	56.2	37.1	99.9	1,384.2

Canadian Government Budgetary Revenues

(million dollars)

Source: Canadian Statistical Review, June 1973.

Fiscal Year or Month	Personal Income Tax	Corporation Income Tax	Sales Tax	Other Excise Tax	Excise Duties	Customs Duties	Estate Taxes	Post Office	Total Budgetary Revenues
1970-71	3,778.5	2,218.5	1,707.5	403.2	561.0	814.5	120.2	337.6	12,803.1
1971-72	4,479.7	2,183.1	1,984.7	388.4	606.6	988.6	132.4	403.8	14,226.6
1971-72									
Apr.	168.4	368.5	115.4	21.5	39.1	65.6	9.1	27.8	1,140.2
Jul.	400.0	193.6	173.2	30.9	46.3	78.0	10.1	28.5	1,178.5
Dec.	440.2	155.3	177.4	31.3	57.2	81.0	14.4	46.2	1,280.5
Mar.	347.1	202.5	180.1	24.8	60.5	112.1	10.0	53.8	1,534.1
1972-73									
Apr.	243.4	492.1	124.2	22.1	42.2	76.2	7.3	27.4	1,306.7
Jul.	525.0	236.2	217.3	31.1	45.5	92.4	5.3	38.8	1,404.0
Dec.	552.3	189.4	200.7	16.7	49.3	91.8	3.0	54.5	1,436.2

Total Assets of Canada's Chartered Banks

Source: Supplement to the Canada Gazette (May 5, 1973)

Bank	Assets	Bank	Assets
Royal Bank of Canada (The)	$15,821,490,000	La Banque Provinciale du Canada	1,781,234,000
Canadian Imperial Bank of Commerce	14,050,082,000	The Mercantile Bank of Canada	482,357,000
Bank of Montreal	12,293,630,000	Bank of British Columbia	255,551,000
The Bank of Nova Scotia	9,340,199,000	Unity Bank of Canada	48,187,000
The Toronto-Dominion Bank	8,271,083,000	**Total**	**65,321,201,000**
Banque Canadienne Nationale	2,977,388,000		

Canadian Chartered Bank Deposits

(as of March 31, 1973)

Source: Department of Finance, Government of Canada

Rank	Bank	Deposits	Rank	Bank	Deposits
1	The Royal Bank of Canada	$14,426,912	6	Banque Canadienne Nationale	$2,713,157
2	Canadian Imperial Bank of Commerce	12,839,548	7	La Banque Provinciale du Canada	1,683,320
3	Bank of Montreal	11,263,511	8	The Mercantile Bank of Canada	429,287
4	The Bank of Nova Scotia	8,405,591	9	Bank of British Columbia	332,632
5	The Toronto-Dominion Bank	7,409,880			

Canadian Consumer Price Index (1961:100)

Source: Canadian Statistical Review, June 1973

	All Items	Food	Housing	Clothing	Health	Recreation	Commodities	Services
1969	125.5	127.1	124.7	124.5	133.6	126.8	120.3	132.3
1970	129.7	130.0	141.8	126.8	139.5	131.2	122.9	138.7
1971	133.4	131.4	149.7	128.7	142.4	135.6	125.1	144.1
1972	139.8	141.4	157.9	132.0	149.2	139.4	130.8	150.3
Jan.	136.7	136.4	154.1	130.2	146.3	136.5	127.8	147.7
Apr.	130.2	138.3	155.8	131.1	148.0	138.3	129.7	148.7
1973 Jan.	144.5	150.0	163.9	134.7	151.9	141.5	135.2	152.9
Apr.	147.3	156.2	166.6	136.4	154.1	143.0	138.8	154.7

Population and Area of Canada by Provinces

Source: Statistics Canada

Province, territory	Capital	Area in square miles Land	Fresh Water	Total	1966 Census	Population 1971 Census	Jan., 1973 Estmate
Newfoundland	St. John's ...	143,045	13,140	156,185	493,396	522,105	537,000
Prince Edward Island	Charlottetown	2,184	...	2,184	108,645	111,645	114,000
Nova Scotia	Halifax	20,402	1,023	21,425	756,039	788,960	802,000
New Brunswick ...	Fredericton..	27,835	519	28,354	616,788	634,555	648,000
Quebec	Quebec	523,860	71,000	594,860	5,780,845	6,027,765	6,068,000
Ontario..........	Toronto	344,092	68,490	412,582	6,960,870	7,703,110	7,893,000
Manitoba	Winnipeg....	211,775	39,225	251,000	963,066	988,245	993,000
Saskatchewan	Regina	220,182	31,518	251,700	955,344	926,245	910,000
Alberta..........	Edmonton ...	248,800	6,485	255,285	1,463,203	1,627,870	1,671,000
British Columbia ..	Victoria	359,279	6,976	366,255	1,873,674	2,184,620	2,291,000
Northwest Territories	Yellowknife..	1,253,438	51,465	1,304,903	28,738	34,805	37,000
Yukon Territory ...	Whitehorse ..	205,345	1,730	207,076	1,382	18,390	20,000
Total..........	....	3,560,238	291,571	3,851,809	20,014,880	21,568,315	21,984,000

Population by Mother Tongue, for Canada and Provinces, 1971

Source: Statistics Canada

Province	English	French	German	Indian, Eskimo	Italian	Dutch	Polish	Ukrainian	Other
Newfoundland	514,520	3,635	515	1,620	175	120	45	50	1,430
Prince Edward Island	103,105	7,360	140	145	35	280	40	30	510
Nova Scotia	733,560	39,330	2,000	2,710	1,495	1,850	555	435	7,020
New Brunswick	410,400	215,730	1,110	2,725	755	665	155	110	2,905
Quebec	789,185	4,867,250	31,025	21,050	135,455	4,660	15,480	11,385	152,265
Ontario............	5,971,570	482,045	184,880	28,590	344,285	77,475	73,985	80,230	460,050
Manitoba..........	662,720	60,550	82,720	31,665	7,265	10,385	15,900	72,925	44,130
Saskatchewan	685,920	31,605	75,885	26,020	2,045	4,695	7,675	53,385	39,025
Alberta............	1,263,935	46,500	92,800	29,920	15,570	20,670	13,730	70,895	73,855
British Columbia ...	1,807,250	38,035	89,020	18,550	31,030	23,955	7,100	20,055	149,620
Yukon.............	15,345	450	565	1,030	75	100	55	150	620
Northwest Territories	16,305	1,160	425	15,800	175	80	60	205	595
Total	12,973,810	5,793,650	561,085	179,825	538,360	144,920	134,780	309,855	932,020

Canadian Cities With Metropolitan Populations Over 100,000

Source: Statistics Canada

	Metro Area*	City		Metro Area*	City
Montreal, Que...........	2,743,208	1,214,352	Kitchener, Ont.	226,846	111,804
Toronto, Ont.	2,628,043	712,786	Halifax, N.S.	222,637	122,035
Vancouver, B.C.........	1,082,352	426,256	Victoria, B.C.	195,800	61,761
Ottawa, Ont.	602,510	302,341	Sudbury, Ont............	155,424	90,535
Winnipeg, Man.	540,262	246,246	Regina, Sask.	140,734	139,469
Hamilton, Ont.	498,523	309,173	Chicoutimi, Que.	133,703	33,893
Edmonton, Alta.	495,702	438,152	St. John's, Nfld.	131,814	88,102
Quebec, Que.	480,502	186,088	Saskatoon, Sask........	126,449	126,449
Calgary, Alta.	403,319	403,319	Oshawa, Ont.	120,318	91,587
St. Catharines, Ont.	303,429	109,722	Thunder Bay, Ont........	112,093	108,411
London, Ont.	286,011	223,222	Saint John, N.B.	106,744	89,039
Windsor, Ont.	258,643	203,300	*1971 Census Metropolitan Area		

Immigration to Canada, by province of (intended) destination

Source: Canadian Statistica Review (June, 1973)

Year and Quarter	Canada	Nfld.	P.E.I.	N.S.	N.B.	Que.	Ont.	Man.	Sask.	Alta.	B.C.	Yukon, N.W.T.
1971.....	121,900	819	172	1,817	1,038	19,222	64,357	5,301	1,426	8,653	18,907	183
1972.....	122,006	686	175	1,872	1,301	18,592	63,805	5,262	1,511	8,390	20,107	305

Immigration to Canada, by Country of last permanent residence

Source: Canadian Statistical Review, June 1973

Year and Quarter	Total	U.K. and Ireland	France	Germany	Netherlands	Greece	Italy
1971.....	121,900	16,281	2,966	2,275	1,301	4,769	5,790
1972.....	122,006	18,317	2,742	2,025	1,471	4,016	4,608

Year and Quarter	Portugal	Other Europe	Asia	Australasia	United States	West Indies	All Other
1971.....	9,157	9,294	22,369	2,906	24,366	10,843	9,583
1972.....	8,737	8,871	23,831	2,148	22,618	8,214	14,408

Births and Deaths in Canada by Province

Source: Statistics Canada

Province	Births 1970	1971	Deaths 1970	1971	Province	Births 1970	1971	Deaths 1970	1971
Nfld.	12,539	12,767	3,294	3,199	Sask.	16,443	16,054	7,472	7,413
P.E.I.	1,957	2,103	1,015	1,007	Alberta	31,967	30,545	10,112	10,525
Nova Scotia	14,159	14,250	6,723	6,682	B.C.	36,861	34,852	17,020	17,783
N.B.	11,545	12,187	4,945	4,943	Yukon	451	506	109	104
Quebec	91,757	89,210	40,392	40,738	N.W. Terr.	337	1,287	254	230
Ontario	134,724	130,395	56,769	56,623					
Manitoba	18,248	18,031	7,856	8,025	Total	371,988	362,187	155,961	157,272

Marriages and Divorces by Province, 1971

Province	Marriages	Divorces	Province	Marriages	Divorces
Newfoundland	4,685	150	Saskatchewan	7,813	813
Prince Edward Island	961	59	Alberta	15,614	3,652
Nova Scotia	6,883	721	British Columbia	20,389	4,942
New Brunswick	6,149	483	Northwest Territories	252	5
Quebec	49,695	5,195	Yukon	166	47
Ontario	69,590	12,189			
Manitoba	9,127	1,370	Total	191,324	29,626

Marriages, Divorces and Rates in Canada

(Rates per 1,000 population)

Year	Marriages No.	Rate	Divorces No.	Rate	Year	Marriages No.	Rate	Divorces No.	Rate
1936	82,941	7.4	1,570	0.14	1966	155,596	7.8	10,239	0.51
1940	125,797	10.8	2,416	0.21	1967	165,879	8.1	11,165	0.54
1945	111,376	9.0	5,101	0.42	1968	171,766	8.3	11,343	0.54
1950	125,083	9.1	5,386	0.39	1969	182,183	8.7	26,079	1.23
1955	128,029	8.2	6,053	0.38	1970	188,428	8.8	29,775	1.37
1960	130,338	7.3	6,980	0.39	1971	191,324	8.9	29,626	1.39
1965	145,519	7.4	8,974	0.45					

Immigration to Canada, by (intended) occupation group [1]

Source: Canadian Statistical Review (June, 1973)

Year and Quarter	Total Immigration	Managerial	Destined to the Labour Force Professional and Technical	Clerical	Commercial and Financial	Service and Recreation	Transport and communication	Agriculture
1971	121,900	3,464	16,307	9,909	2,486	6,387	740	2,160
1972	122,006	4,130	15,262	8,549	2,460	6,575	795	2,127
1971 4	27,895	874	3,746	1,774	504	1,409	172	479
1972 1	23,567	583	3,191	1,620	518	1,377	151	446
2	30,746	1,022	3,618	2,083	561	1,775	228	662
3	32,474	1,087	4,429	2,052	534	1,567	190	549
4	35,219	1,438	4,024	2,794	847	1,856	226	470

Year and Quarter	Destined to the Labour Force Mining and quarrying [2]	manufacturing [3]	Labourers	sub-Total [4]	Not Destined to the Labour Force Wives	Children	Students (18 years and over) [5]	sub-Total [6]
1971	324	16,166	1,324	62,606	21,333	29,684	3,153	60,618
1972	237	15,627	1,184	59,432	21,749	30,977	3,172	62,574
1971 4	69	3,087	291	12,905	5,218	7,441	577	14,990
1972 1	47	3,268	264	11,864	4,275	5,461	632	11,703
2	53	4,382	306	15,249	5,447	7,468	752	15,497
3	50	3,776	320	15,304	5,838	8,656	986	17,170
4	87	4,201	294	17,015	6,189	9,392	802	18,204

[1] The occupational status of the majority of the persons destined to the labour force is determined by immigration officials by an examination of documentary evidence provided by the immigrants. The classification of occupations is similar to that used in the 1961 Census; see Occupational Classification Manual, Census of Canada, 1961, Catalogue Number 12-506. [2] Includes logging, fishing, trapping and hunting. [3] Includes mechanical and construction. [4] Includes a small number in non-specified occupations. [5] Does not include students entering Canada on students' visas. [6] Includes also retired persons, elderly dependents, fiancés or fiancées and other unspecified persons not intending to enter the labour force. **Source: Quarterly Bulletin, Department of Manpower and Immigration.**

Canadian Foreign Trade ($1,000,000)

Source: Canadian Statistical Review, June 1973

Year and month	Exports including re-exports				Imports			
	All countries	U.S.	U.K.	All other countries	All countries	U.S.	U.K.	All other countries
1969.......	14,931	10,614	1,113	3,204	14,130	10,243	791	3,096
1970.......	16,820	10,917	1,485	4,404	13,951	9,917	738	3,296
1971.......	17,744	12,006	1,361	4,377	15,607	10,941	837	3,827
1972.......	19,977	13,922	1,328	4,727	18,654	12,870	949	4,836
1973 J.....	1,856.2	1,334.5	114.9	406.8	1,732.2	1,209.3	79.8	443.1
F.....	1,765.3	1,279.2	94.1	392.0	1,642.0	1,168.6	80.7	392.6
M	1,931.0	1,389.4	133.3	408.3	1,862.7	1,338.8	92.1	431.8

Canadian Sea Fish Catch and Exports

(in millions of pounds)

Source: Canadian Statistical Review—June, 1973.

Year and Month	Total Value ($1,000)	Total Quantity	Landings of Sea Fish						Exports by Country*			Exports by Type	
			Nfld	P E I	N S	N B	Que	B.C.	Total	United States	Other	Salmon	Lobster
1971...	192,993	2,466.1	871.6	97.5	658.1	370.1	240.2	228.7	607.6	438.3	169.3	58.5	22.5
1972...	210,779	2,084.8	559.2	56.9	634.6	325.8	176.3	331.8	642.0	443.6	169.3	77.6	19.8
1972 J	4,466	121.9	71.8	2.1	43.5	1.4	0.8	2.3	49.8	37.2	12.6	4.0	2.8
F	3,263	58.3	25.6	0.1	26.0	0.6	..	6.0	34.0	23.2	10.8	5.1	1.2
M	6,845	134.2	38.2	0.6	33.6	0.5	0.2	61.2	42.3	19.4	22.9	6.4	0.8
1973 J	4,701	68.5	28.3	0.3	34.1	2.2	0.1	3.6	44.1	37.2	6.9	4.6	2.3
F	5,103	60.4	26.1	0.2	21.5	0.9	0.2	11.5	39.5	23.9	15.6	8.0	0.7
M	13,720	164.4	33.2	0.2	22.7	3.7	0.4	104.2	70.2	33.8	36.4	6.1	1.4

*Exports include sea and freshwater fish and shellfish products but exclude bait, meal, oils, offal, livers, fish roe n.e.s. and fishery foods and fees n.e.s.

Value of Canadian Fishery Products and By-products[1]

Source: Statistics Canada ($1,000)

Province	1969	1970	1971
Total[2]	408,802	450,631	461,833
Newfoundland	72,302	85,104	94,943
Prince Edward Island	12,701	18,375	16,143
Nova Scotia	123,492	105,939	127,215
New Brunswick	64,820	67,404	68,629
Quebec	19,026	24,130	26,022
Ontario..........................	14,778	13,070	13,896
Manitoba.........................	6,700		
Saskatchewan	4,587	13,276	12,674
Alberta..........................	1,563		
Northwest Territories.............	946		
British Columbia	87,852	123,333	120,167
Yukon...........................	35		

(1) Final sales by fish processors, handlers and fishermen
(2) The sum of the provincial totals differ from the Canadian total as duplications (intershipments between provinces) have been removed from the Atlantic Coast totals.

Number of Canadian Households with Television Sets[1]

Source: Statistic Canada (May, 1972)

Province	Number Households	Black & White			Color		
		One Set	Two Sets or More	No Sets	One Set	Two Sets or More	No Sets
Newfoundland	114	87	11	16	12	*	102
Prince Edward Island	28	20	*	5	4	*	24
Nova Scotia	207	163	20	24	32	*	175
New Brunswick	157	120	18	20	26	*	131
Quebec........................	1,641	1,134	315	191	337	11	1,293
Ontario........................	2,280	1,595	311	375	589	13	1,678
Manitoba......................	287	209	33	46	60	*	227
Saskatchewan	261	184	23	54	62	*	198
Alberta........................	467	318	51	98	133	4	330
British Columbia	665	447	54	164	188	5	472
Total	6,108	4,278	838	992	1,443	35	4,629

(1) Estimates in thousands
*Less than 4,000

Nations of the World

The nations of the world are listed in alphabetical order, except for Canada and the United States (see Index for listings). .

Where figures on military strength are given "for 1972-1973," they are from The Military Balance 1972-73, published by the International Institute for Strategic Studies, London.

Some international groups of which various nations are members are referred to in the following articles, by initials (such as NATO). Articles on these groups may be found through the Index.

See special color section for maps and flags of all nations.

Afghanistan

DOULAT I GAMHOURIATE YE AFGHANISTAN

Capital: Kabul. Area: 253,861 sq. mi. Population (UN est. 1972): 17,880,000. Monetary unit: Afghani.

Afghanistan is a landlocked republic occupying a mountainous area much of which is 4,000 ft. and more above sea level. It is slightly smaller than Texas. Its neighbors are Iran, Pakistan, India and the USSR. The northeast tip of the country just touches China's Sinkiang Province.

The Hindu Kush mountains tower 16,000 ft. above the capital of Kabul and reach a height of more than 25,000 ft. some 200 miles to the east of the capital. Trade with India flows through the 35-mile long Khyber Pass from Kabul to Peshawar. The climate is dry, with extreme temperatures.

Ninety percent of the country's exports are agricultural products. Chief items are cotton, wool, karakul pelts, hides, casings, oilseeds and fresh and dried fruit. Hand-woven carpets, cotton, wool, fruits and nuts and sheepskin coats are exported. Some 4,000,000 head of broadtail karakul sheep are raised, as well as goats and camels. The sheep provide the principal meat item in the Afghan's diet and the tightly curled, glossy black coats of the newborn lambs are a valuable fur. Minerals include copper, lead, gas, coal, zinc, iron, silver, asbestos and oil. The country has received considerable economic aid from the U.S., USSR and mainland China. The USSR is Afghanistan's largest trading partner.

Textile mills, cement factories, highways and irrigation projects are among recent developments.

Famine, following a drought, brought death to thousands in 1972. The U.S. led other nations in gifts of relief wheat.

History and Government. Afghanistan was so named in about the middle of the 18th Century. In ancient times it was known as Aryana, in the Middle Ages as Khorasan. Pukhtuns (Pushtuns) comprise 53.5% of the population; Tajiks 36.7%; Uzbeks 6%; Hazaras 3%.

On Sept. 19, 1964 a Grand Assembly approved a new constitution providing for an elected Lower House, partly-elected Upper House, an independent judiciary, a prime minister chosen by the King. The last King was Mohammed Zahir Shah, who ascended the throne Nov. 8, 1933, on the assassination of his father, Mohammed Nadir Shah. In a July 17, 1973, coup, Gen. Mohammad Daud Khan, the King's brother-in-law, proclaimed Afghanistan a republic with himself as President and Premier.

Bordering on both Russia and China, Afghanistan has been traditionally neutral. Armed forces: over 80,000.

Education and Religion. Education is free and, where facilities are available, compulsory. The University of Kabul was established in 1932. Principal languages are Pushtu and Persian. English is taught. Islam is the predominant religion.

Albania

REPUBLIKA POPULLORE E SHQIPERISE

Capital: Tirana, Area: 11,100 sq. mi. Population (1972 est.): 2,230,000. Monetary unit: Lek.

Albania, a Balkan communist republic, is a narrow mountainous land, slightly larger than Maryland, extending for 225 mi. along the E coast of the Adriatic. Yugoslavia and Greece are its neighbors. Mt. Korab, 9,066 ft. is the tallest peak.

Resources and Industries. Still a preponderantly agricultural nation, Albania in the 1960s and 1970s pressed programs of industrialization and agricultural modernization with the aid of communist China. The government reported national income has grown a average of 7% annually since 1960.

New industrial installations included chemical fertilizer, textile, electric cable and electric power plants.

Principal exports include petroleum, bitumen, chrome, iron and copper; cotton textiles, wood products and tobacco. More than half of Albania's foreign trade is with communist China.

History and Government. Albania has been overrun by warring armies for over 2,000 years. It declared its independence from the Turks in 1912; this was backed by a conference of European powers which placed Prince William of Wied on the throne in 1914. He fled within months because of uprisings. During World War I armies of several nations occupied the land by turns. In 1920, a republic was set up. In 1925, Ahmed Zogu seized the presidency; in 1928 he proclaimed himself King, assuming the title Zog I.

King Zog fled in 1939 when Italy invaded and annexed Albania. When Italy surrendered to the Allies in 1943, German troops took over; they left in 1944 and communist partisans seized power. Gen. Enver Hoxha was named provisional president; a communist front won a 1945 election; in 1946 a new constitution, modeled on that of the USSR, was adopted under Hoxha's leadership.

The U. S. and Britain voted against Albanian admission to the UN in 1946; it finally won admission in 1955 with Britain voting "yes" and the U. S. abstaining. In 1955 it was admitted to the Warsaw Pact. Its policies have been strongly pro-Stalinist, anti-Khrushchev, procommunist China and hostile to Tito's Yugoslav regime. The USSR broke relations with Albania in Dec. 1961 and in 1962 barred it from Warsaw Pact meetings. Albania withdrew from the pact in 1968.

In 1970 communist China and Albania signed a new treaty providing for expanded trade and additional Chinese financial credits for Albania. In 1971, after years of mistrust, Albania resumed diplomatic relations with Yugoslavia and Greece.

Education and Religion. Historically, the largest segment of the population was Moslem, followed by Orthodox Christians and Roman Catholics. Primary education nominally is compulsory and free under the constitution. In 1969 there were 14,000 university and college students.

Racially the Albanians are mainly Ghegs in the north and Tosks in the south.

Defense. For 1972-73 military strength was Army, 28,000; Air Force, 4,000; Navy, 3,000.

Algeria

REPUBLIC OF ALGERIA

Capital: Algiers. Area: 919,591 sq. mi. Population (UN est. 1972): 15,270,000. Monetary unit: Dinar.

Algeria, an independent republic more than 3 times the size of Texas, is located in northern Africa extending for 640 mi. along the Mediterranean Sea between Tunisia and Morocco. The southern Saharan Departments extend into the Sahara Desert and border on Niger, Mali and Mauritania. The Tell, located on the coast, comprises fertile plains from 50 to 100 mi. wide. Several chains of the Atlas Mtns., running roughly E-W and reaching altitudes of 7,000 ft., separate the coast regions from inland plateaus and the Sahara. Algiers, the capital, is the largest city.

Resources and Industries. Agricultural products include wheat, barley, oats, corn, potatoes, artichokes, flax and tobacco. Wine and olive oil are produced. Dates, pomegranates and figs grow abundantly. Cattle raising is important. There are large deposits of oil, iron, zinc, lead, mercury, coal, copper and antimony.

Exports consist chiefly of wines, fruits, iron and zinc ores, phosphate rock, cork, tobacco products, vegetables, liquefied natural gas and petroleum. Algeria is the world's 10th largest oil-producing nation. Trade is mainly with France.

Exploitation of the Sahara's vast oil and gas deposits and its tourist potentiality is being pressed.

In 1967-68 foreign oil distribution companies were nationalized; in 1970-71 several foreign oil producing companies were nationalized.

In 1972, the government pressed its industrialization program with an oil refinery, natural gas liquefaction and iron and steel plants, and fertilizer and textile factories under construction or completed.

History and Government. The fertile Tell plains have attracted a succession of conquerors to Algeria from before the time of Christ. Once ruled over by Carthage, the country after 146 B.C. came under control of the Roman Empire. But it was the Arabs, who arrived in the 7th Century who were to have the most lasting influence on the country. In 1518 Algiers and the coastal area came under Turkish domination. France took control in 1830, annexed it in 1842 and began to develop the land.

From 1954-62 growing Arab nationalism led to outright warfare between the French and the Algerians. The political impasse was not broken until French President Charles de Gaulle negotiated with the Front de Liberatione Nationale (FLN). Algeria in a referendum July, 1962, voted overwhelmingly for independence; De Gaulle proclaimed it independent July 3.

Internal strife continued, however, between opposing Algerian factions, and Ahmed Ben Bella, with Army support, assumed control in Aug. 1962.

A constitution was approved Sept. 8, 1963, and Premier Ben Bella, sole candidate, was elected President for a 5-year term Sept. 15. Nationalization of lands and industries proceeded rapidly. Algeria received a $100,000,000 long-term industrial loan from the USSR in Sept. 1963, and continued to receive French aid.

President Ben Bella was arrested and deposed June 19, 1965, in a bloodless, army-backed coup d'etat led by Col. Houari Boumediene (born Mohammed Boukharouba), Defense Minister and Vice President. Col. Boumediene, on July 11, announced a new Cabinet with himself as President.

Algeria is a member of the UN, OAU and Arab League.

Education and Religion. The population before independence included approx. 1,000,000 Europeans, 80% of them Algerian-born, since reduced to about 80,000. Most Algerians are Arabs and Berbers, of Moslem faith. There are 3 universities and 21 technical institutes.

Defense. The armed forces are being expanded and modernized with aid from the USSR. Military strength for 1972-73 was 53,000 in the Army, 4,000 in the Air Force and 3,200 in the Navy.

Andorra

LES VALLS D'ANDORRA

Capital: Andorra la Vella. Area: 179 sq. mi. Population (1973 Census): 23,000. Monetary units: Franc, Peseta.

Andorra is a tiny principality of valleys and mountains set high in the Pyrenees on the border of France and Spain. It has two Co-Princes, the President of France and the Spanish Catholic Bishop of Urgel, whose representatives are charged with the administration of justice, but the country has enjoyed practical sovereignty since 1278. It pays an annual tribute of 960 francs to France and 460 pesetas to the Bishop of Urgel.

Actual government is in the hands of a Council-General of 24 members elected by universal suffrage, who enact laws and elect a Syndic General, the top administrator. Women won voting rights in 1970.

The main industry is tourism (189 hotels), followed by sheep-raising. Andorra has considerable iron, lead, alum, stone and timber. Skiing, trout fishing and chamois hunting are among tourist attractions.

The official language is Catalan; principal religion is Roman Catholicism.

Argentina

Capital: Buenos Aires. Area: 1,079,520 sq. mi. Population (UN est. 1972): 23,920,000. Monetary unit: Peso.

Argentina, 4 times the size of Texas, extends from Bolivia 2,300 miles to Tierra del Fuego and from the Andes to the South Atlantic, and is the 2nd largest and 2nd most populous country in South America, next to Brazil.

The mountains are grouped into 4 isolated systems: the Andean, Central, Misiones and Southern. Aconcagua is the highest peak in the Western Hemisphere, altitude 22,834 ft. (Official Arg. figure.) The southern Andes have lumpy, arear and hidden terrains.

East of the Andes are great plains, heavily wooded and called the Gran Chaco in the north, and the fertile, treeless Pampas, given over to wheat and cattle raising, in the central region. Patagonia, in the south, is bleak and arid; petroleum and sheep are its main products.

Rio de la Plata is the estuary of one of the world's great drainage systems. It is a wide gulf of mostly fresh water, 170 mi. long, 140 mi. wide at its mouth. On its banks are 3 important cities, Buenos Aires and La Plata in Argentina and Montevideo in Uruguay. Emptying into it are the Parana River, 2,500 mi. long, and the Uruguay, 1,000, both starting far to the north in Brazil. Further south, other large rivers flow from the Andes, in the west, to the Atlantic, including the Colorado and Negro.

Buenos Aires, the capital, is one of the largest cities in South America.

Resources and Industries. The mountains of Argentina contain deposits of coal, lead, zinc, iron, sulphur, silver, copper and gold. Argentina is the world's 15th largest petroleum producer.

Cotton, wheat, barley, rye, linseed, oats, alfalfa are important. Sugar, wine, cotton, fruit, corn, sorghum, tobacco and peanuts are cultivated. Sheep, cattle, horses, goats and pigs form the chief wealth of the ranches. In 1972 there were 55,000,000 cattle and 45,000,000 sheep, both high in world rankings. Meat processing is the chief industry. Flour milling is 2nd. Argentina is the world's 4th largest meat exporter.

Railroads and one domestic airline are state-owned.

Also important in the country's growing industrialization are chemicals, textiles, sugar-refining and machinery. In June 1973 price controls, moderate wage increases and a no-strike-for-two-years pledge by major unions were announced.

Foreign trade in thousands of U.S. dollars:

	Imports	Exports
1971	$1,869,000	$1,740,000
1972	$1,865,000	$1,885,000

History and Government. Discovered 1515-16 by Spanish explorers headed by Juan Diaz de Solis, Argentina remained under Spanish domination until the provinces, in a successful revolt May 25, 1810, established an independent republic. In 1853 a liberal constitution was adopted.

The present constitution, proclaimed May 1, 1956, is essentially that of 1853.

There are 22 provinces which elect their own governors and legislatures, and a Federal District, Buenos Aires (area 72 sq. mi.), whose Mayor is appointed by the President.

The President and Vice President must be Roman Catholic and Argentine by birth. They are elected for 4-year terms by direct popular vote. Congress consists of a Senate of 69 and a House of Deputies. Voting is compulsory for both men and women.

Beginning in 1944, and after the election of Juan D. Peron, an army officer, as President in 1946, Argentine democracy was replaced by a dictatorship. By concessions to labor Peron built a following; he then suppressed freedom of speech and of the press, religious schools and ran the country deeply into debt. Civilians, clericals and part of the armed forces unseated Peron Sept. 16, 1955, and he went into exile. A provisional government was replaced November, 1955, by a military junta, which chose Maj. Gen. Pedro Aramburu provisional President. He restored civil liberties, dissolved the Peronist party and returned expropriated property.

In the first free elections in 12 years, Feb. 22, 1958, Dr. Arturo Frondizi was elected President. Dissension among military leaders, democratic parties and the Peronist unions which had supported Dr. Frondizi resulted in a bloodless military coup Mar. 29, 1962. He was succeeded by Jose Maria Guido, head of the Senate. Elections were ordered and Dr. Arturo Illia was elected President, July 7, 1963, taking office Oct. 12, 1963.

On June 28, 1966, a 3-man military junta ousted Dr. Illia and named retired Lt. Gen. Juan Carlos Ongania President; the junta dissolved Congress and all political parties in a move against leftist activities. In 1969 workers battled police and troops in Cordoba and other cities.

In June 1970 the nation's military leaders deposed Pres. Ongania "to establish order" and named Gen. Roberto M. Levingston to succeed him. In March 1971 Lt. Gen. Alejandro A. Lanusse took over as President; he ordered a return to civilian government.

In March 1973 elections, Hector J. Campora, a follower of Peron, was elected President; he took office May 25. The 77-year-old Peron, after a visit in late 1972, returned to live again in Argentina on June 20, ending nearly 18 years of exile.

One of Campora's first acts was to resume diplomatic relations with Cuba. A rash of assassinations and kidnappings took place early in 1973.

Argentina is a member of the UN and OAS.

Education and Religion. The population is about 90% Roman Catholic, the constitutional religion since 1810. Primary education is free, secular, and compulsory. There are national universities in Cordoba (founded in 1613), Buenos Aires and 9 other cities, and numerous private universities. The language is Spanish. The people are of Spanish and Italian descent, with Basques, Swiss, Germans and British represented.

Defense. The 3 services total over 135,000 plus several hundred thousand reserves.

Australia

Capital: Canberra. Area: 2,967,741 sq. mi. Population (Govt. est. 1973): 13,026,300. Monetary unit: Australian dollar.

The continent of Australia, a huge island almost the size of the 48 conterminous U.S. states, is SE of Asia and below the islands of Indonesia. The Indian Ocean is W and S, the Pacific E and their waters meet N of Australia in the Timor and Arafura Seas. The Great Barrier Reef extends along the NE coast. About 150 mi. S of the state of Victoria lies the island state, Tasmania. Branches of the Pacific are the Coral Sea, NE, and the Tasman Sea, SE.

The Tropic of Capricorn bisects Australia. The Great Dividing Range along the E coast has Mt. Kosciusko, 7,316 ft., in New South Wales. The W plateau rises to 2,000 ft., with arid areas in the Great Sandy and Great Victoria Deserts. The NW part of Western Australia and Northern Territory are arid and torrid; Arnhem Land, in the latter, is a rugged wooded area reserved for aborigines. The NE has heavy rainfall and Cape York Peninsula has jungles. The Murray River rises in New South Wales, flows 1,600 mi. into the Indian Ocean and supplies hydro-electric plants.

States and territories of Australia with their areas in sq. mi. and 1972 est. populations were:

	Area	Population
New South Wales ..	309,433	4,680,700
Victoria	87,884	3,562,000
Queensland	667,000	1,883,900
South Australia	380,070	1,190,900
Western Australia .	975,920	1,059,000
Tasmania	26,215	393,000
Northern Territory .	520,280	94,800
Australian Capital Territory	939	162,000
Totals	2,967,741	13,026,300

The capitals are: New South Wales, Sydney; Victoria, Melbourne; Queensland, Brisbane; South Australia, Adelaide; Western Australia, Perth; Tasmania, Hobart; Northern Terr., Darwin; Capital Territory, Canberra.

Home of the kangaroo, Australia also is the habitat of other strange flora and fauna; the koala, or living teddy bear; the platypus, wombat, dingo, Tasmanian devil, a blind mole, and barking and frilled lizards.

By 1972, Australia had added more than 3,842,254 population from immigration since World War II. About one-half was British. Australia's aborigines in the tribal state are primitive and nomadic, but most now are detribalized. Programs are directed toward their ultimate assimilation.

The Melbourne Cup horse race is the biggest annual sports event; cricket, tennis and football are played extensively. Excellent beaches are numerous and surf riding is popular.

Resources and Industries. Almost from earliest days of settlement a primary producing country, Australia has become highly industrialized. More than 25% of the total labor force of approx. 5,550,000 work in factories; about 15% are engaged in rural occupations.

Wool and meat are important products. With an annual clip of more than 1.9 billion lbs., Australia produces 30% of the world's wool, 50% of its merino wool and is the largest exporter of both beef and lamb. It is also one of the largest wheat producers, with over 385,000,000 bu. annually. Over one-half is exported. Other important products are sugar, wine, fruit, vegetables, meat, grains, minerals, including uranium, gold, coal, copper, iron, silver, lead, bauxite, rutile and petroleum products.

Discovery of vast iron ore deposits in Western Australia brought a mining boom to desolate areas in the northwest in 1965. New oil and gas fields were discovered 1965-1968, nickel in 1969, uranium in 1972.

Principal manufactures include iron and steel, textiles, electrical and radio equipment, drugs, chemicals, paints, machinery, metal work, clothing, motor cars and engines, aircraft and ships. Unemployment in 1973 was est. at 1.5% of the work force. Gross national product in 1972 was est. at $46.4 billion, compared with $34.4 billion in 1971.

In recent years exports of mineral and industrial products have increased considerably.

Australia changed its currency from pounds-shillings-pence to dollars and cents Feb. 14, 1966, with its dollar worth half the old Australian pound. It will complete adoption of metric weights and measures by 1980.

Foreign trade, in thousands of U.S. dollars:

	Imports	Exports
1971	$4,633,000	$5,084,000
1972	$4,556,000	$6,329,000

Tourism is a rapidly expanding industry. In 1972 Australia had 426,400 overseas visitors, more than double the number 5 years earlier.

History and Government. Australia has been settled since 1788. The Commonwealth, proclaimed Jan. 1, 1901, is a self-governing federation of six states and two territories. Parliament consists of the Crown (represented by the Governor-General), the Senate and House of Representatives.

In Dec. 1972 elections, the Labor party won 67 seats in the House of Reps., ending 23 years of rule by the Liberal and Country parties coalition, which won 58 votes.

Gough Whitlam became Prime Minister. He ended

restrictions on non-white immigrants, ended the draft and military aid to South Vietnam, recognized China and North Vietnam.

Pension acts provide for payments of war, old age and invalid pensions; also cover the blind, the unemployed, victims of tuberculosis and, in some cases, dependents of former soldiers. The National Health Scheme provides free drugs and subsidizes hospital and medical expenses.

A maternity act provides for the payment of a maternity allowance for every child born in Australia. Social security for children includes child endowment payments for children under 16.

Education and Religion. Education is free and compulsory. There are 15 universities and 3 university colleges. The Church of England claims 37.7% of the population, the remainder being Roman Catholic, 23.3%; Presbyterian, 9.7%; Methodist, 10.8%, and others.

Defense. Australia adopted its first peacetime draft in 1966. Troops fighting alongside the U.S. in South Vietnam totaled 7,500 in 1971, but were withdrawn by the end of that year. The draft was ended in 1972. In June 1972 armed forces totaled 82,700 plus 32,500 in the Volunteer Citizen Forces.

AUSTRALIAN TERRITORIES

The jointly administered **Territory of Papua New Guinea,** originally two separate territories, is governed by a 1949 Act placing New Guinea under the UN Trusteeship system, but retaining the status of Papua as a Crown territory. Combined pop. of the two was est. in 1972 at 2,580,000.

New Guinea, once German New Guinea, later a League of Nations mandate and UN Trust Territory of Australia, occupies the NE quarter of the island of New Guinea, N of Australia, and includes nearby island groups: **New Britain, New Ireland** and the **Admiralty Islands** of the Bismarck Archipelago; **Bougainville,** 3,880 sq. mi.; **Buka,** 220 sq. mi., and smaller islands of the Solomons. Total area of the territory is about 93,000 sq. mi., with a population est. in 1972 at 1,840,000.

Papua is the southeastern part of the island. Area, 90,540 sq. mi.; population est. 1972, 740,000.

Papua New Guinea is governed by an Administrator, a cabinet and a legislative House of Assembly, with 96 of its 100 members elected by popular vote in 1972, an increase over the previous number. Australia was to grant it self-government except for defense, foreign affairs and internal security Dec. 1, 1973, with full independence a year or two later.

Principal products are timber, copra, cocoa, rubber and coffee. Gold and copper are mined.

Norfolk Island was taken over by Australia, 1914. It has an area of 13.5 sq. mi. and a population (est. 1973) of 1,380. The soil is very fertile and is suitable for the cultivation of citrus fruits, bananas and coffee. Many of the inhabitants are descendants of the Bounty mutineers; some descendants moved to Norfolk in 1856 from Pitcairn Is.; some stayed, some returned to Pitcairn.

Territory of Ashmore and Cartier Islands in the Indian Ocean came under the authority of Australia May, 1934 and are administered as part of Northern Territory. **Heard** and **McDonald Islands** are governed by Capital Territory.

Cocos-Keeling Islands, 27 small coral islands in the Indian Ocean 1,300 miles NW of Australia, are important for aviation use. Pop. (est. 1970): 611.

Christmas Island, 64 sq. mi., pop. 3,361 (est. 1970), 230 mi. S of Java, was taken over from Singapore in 1958. It has phosphate deposits.

Australian Antarctic Territory came under the authority of Australia in 1933. It claims 2,472,000 sq. mi. of territory S of 60th parallel S. Lat. and between 160th-45th meridians E. Long. except for French-claimed Adelie Land.

Austria
REPUBLIK OESTERREICH

Capital: Vienna. Area: 32,374 sq. mi. Population (UN est. 1972): 7,490,000. Monetary unit: Schilling.

Austria is a republic in the mountainous region of central Europe, 360 mi. long, 160 mi. wide—slightly smaller than Maine. It is bounded by Switzerland with the Rhaetian Alps, Liechtenstein, Italy's South Tyrol, Carnic Alps and Dolomite Mts., Yugoslavia and the Karawanken Mts., Czechoslovakia with the Little Carpathians, Bavaria (Federal Republic of Germany) and Hungary.

Near Switzerland are the Oetztal Alps, with Wildspitze, 12,309 ft. tall. The Hohe Tauern range has Grossglockner, 12,457 ft., and a 6-mile glacier. Mountain passes cross frontiers; the Brenner, below the Stubai Alps, has been a major route to Italy since ancient times. Austria has many forests, rich in conifers; the Wiener Wald is a forest belt near Vienna.

Principal river, the Danube, flows from Bavaria in NW to Czechoslovakia, E. Others are the Enns, Inn, Drau, Ill, Mur and Salzach, some furnishing hydroelectric power. There are numerous lakes and popular spas, such as Bad Gastein and Bad Ischl.

Resources and Industries. Austria produces iron ore, oil, timber, magnesite, aluminum, coal, lignite, cement and copper. It is an important source of high-grade graphite. Hydroelectric power, with high potential, is under extensive development. It manufactures steel, machinery, vehicles, electrical and optical instruments, glassware, sporting goods, paper, yarns, textiles, fertilizers, chemicals and atomic nuclear power.

Although farmland is limited, Austria produces about 85% of its foodstuffs. It grows wheat, rye, barley, oats, corn, potatoes, sugar beets. Vineyards flourish in Lower Austria and in Burgenland. Principal livestock: cattle, sheep, pigs.

Over 11,000,000 tourists visit annually. The Salzburg Festival, the Vienna State Opera, skiing and spas are among attractions.

Principal exports are iron, steel, paper, textiles, machinery, chemicals, metal products, vehicles, aluminum, electric power. Trade is heavy with West Germany, Italy and United States.

Foreign trade in thousands of U.S. dollars:

	Imports	Exports
1971	$4,189,000	$3,169,000
1972	$5,216,000	$3,883,000

History and Government. Austria, the East Mark (Ost Mark) of Charlemagne (788 A. D.) came under the Hapsburgs in 1278. Tyrol was added 1363, Bohemia (Czech) and Hungary, 1526. The Turks were twice turned back at Vienna, 1529 and 1683. Austrian dominance of German lands was challenged in the 18th Century and Empress Maria Theresa (ruled 1740-1780) lost Silesia to Frederick II (the Great) of Prussia. Austria took slices of Poland in the partitions of 1772, 1793 and 1795. Austria was the scene of major Napoleonic battles and helped defeat him. The Congress of Vienna, 1815, awarded it Istria, Illyria, and the Italian provinces of Lombardy and Venetia. Austria lost Lombardy to Italy 1859 and Venetia 1866, after Prussia defeated Austria in the Seven Weeks' War.

Under the Dual Monarchy of Austria-Hungary, estab. 1867, to recognize the aspirations of the Magyars, Francis Joseph was Emperor of Austria and King of Hungary. The country had an area of 261,259 sq. mi., population c. 51,000,000. It contained Austria, Hungary, Bohemia, Transylvania, Polish Galicia, Trentino, Slavonia, Croatia, Bosnia, Herzegovina, Banat. After Archduke Francis Ferdinand, heir to the Austrian throne, and his consort were assassinated in Sarajevo, Bosnia, June 28, 1914, Austria declared war on Serbia, which helped precipitate World War I. It was dismembered after that war; became a republic comprised of nine states in 1918.

Between the two world wars Austria had a turbulent political history. Socialists introduced some socio-economic changes. These were devised by Chancellor Engelbert Dollfuss, 1934. Dollfuss was murdered by Nazi conspirators July 25, 1934. Adolf Hitler, German Fuehrer, occupied Austria Mar. 13, 1938, and proclaimed its union with Germany. It was re-established as a republic in 1945, consisting of the states of Burgenland, Lower Austria, Upper Austria, Salzburg, Styria, Carinthia, Tyrol, Vorarlberg, and the city of Vienna.

Dr. Karl Renner was elected President of the provisional government after liberation by the Allies, 1945 (died 1950). After 17 years of occupation, delayed by tactics of the Soviet Union, a treaty of March 15, 1955 restored the frontiers existing Jan. 1, 1938, prohibited economic or political union with Germany, required support of democratic institutions. With final ratification July 27, 1955, Austria formally regained sovereignty. It declared its perpetual neutrality.

The President is elected by secret ballot for a 6-year term. He appoints the Chancellor and approves the ministers.

Parliamentary elections Oct. 10, 1971, gave the Socialist party a majority of seats.

Austria is a member of the UN and EFTA. In 1972 Austria and 5 other EFTA members joined with EEC (Common Market) members in agreements for mutual abolition of tariffs on industrial goods.

Education and Religion. The predominant religion is Roman Catholicism. Elementary education is free and compulsory between the ages of 6 and 15. There are universities in Vienna, Graz, Innsbruck and Salzburg. The language is almost entirely German.

Defense. Military strength for 1971-1972 was 48,300, of whom 44,000 were in the Army, 4,300 in Army air units.

The Bahamas

Capital: Nassau. Area: 4,404 sq. mi. Population (UN est. 1972): 190,000. Monetary unit: Bahamian dollar.

The Commonwealth of the Bahamas achieved full independence from Great Britain on July 10, 1973. The Bahamas comprise nearly 700 islands (30 inhabited) and over 2,000 islets in the western Atlantic. They extend 760 mi. NW to SE from a point 50 mi. off Florida to about 70 mi. from Haiti.

Christopher Columbus first set foot in the New World on the island of San Salvador (also called Watling Is.) on the eastern fringe of the Bahamas in 1492. British settlement started in 1647; the islands became a British colony in 1783. Internal self-government was granted by Britain in 1964. Elections to the Assembly in 1967 resulted in the selection if the islands' first black Prime Minister, Lynden O. Pindling.

The Prime Minister leads the majority part of the 38-member, elected Assembly. The 16-member Senate is appointed by the Governor-General (nominally representing the British Queen) on the advice of the Prime Minister and the opposition leader. The Bahamas joined the UN and Commonwealth.

Tourism is the main industry; second is international banking and investment management. Fruit and vegetables are grown mostly for local use. There are cement and pharmaceutical plants. Exports include salt, rock lobster, tomatoes, cucumbers and handicraft objects.

English is the language; Anglican is the predominant religion. Elementary schools are free and compulsory except on a few of the "Out Islands." About 84% of the population is of African descent.

Bahrain

Capital: Manama. Area: 231 sq. mi. Population: (Est. 1972): 220,000. Monetary unit: Dinar.

Bahrain, long a British Protected State, declared its complete independence Aug. 14, 1971. It includes the main island, Bahrain, and several smaller islands midway along the Persian (also called Arabian) Gulf, about 20 mi. off the Arabian Peninsula's NE coast.

Pearls, shrimp, fruit and vegetables were the mainstays of the economy until oil, discovered in 1932, gradually became most important. By the 1970s, oil reserves showed signs of depletion. Important contributions were made to the economy by a large refinery handling oil pumped by undersea pipeline from Saudi Arabia as well as the local product, by a large aluminum smelter using local natural gas, and by increased use of Bahrain as a trade transshipment center.

Long ruled by the Khalifa family, Bahrain signed a treaty in 1861 giving Great Britain responsibility for Bahrain's defense and foreign relations. When Britain an-

nounced it would remove its military forces from the Persian Gulf area by the end of 1971, Bahrain sought to form a federation with the 7 Trucial Sheikhdoms (now the United Arab Emirates) and Qatar, which were also British Protected States. The attempt failed and Bahrain declared itself an independent nation. It is ruled by an Emir, a Prime Minister and a Council of Ministers (cabinet). In 1973 a constitution to create "a basis for democracy" was under study. It is a member of the UN and Arab League.

Most of the Bahrainis are of northern Arabian descent, half of the Sunni branch of Islam, half of the Shi'ite branch. Arabic is the official language; Persian and English are also spoken. Education and health services are free.

The small U.S. Middle East Force uses naval facilities in part of the former British naval base.

Bangladesh

Capital: Dacca. Area: 55,126 sq. mi. Population: (Est. 1973): 75,000,000. Monetary unit: Taka.

East Pakistan, the smaller but more populous of the two sections of Pakistan, achieved independence as Bangladesh (Bengal Nation) during the Dec. 3-16, 1971, India-Pakistan war. Separated from West Pakistan by 1,000 mi. of India, it is mostly a low plain cut by the Ganges and Brahmaputra Rivers and is bounded by India, Burma and the Bay of Bengal. It is subject to heavy monsoon rains. A Nov. 13, 1970, cyclone killed at least 300,000 persons in coastal areas.

Resources and Industries. Bangladesh is primarily agricultural, with small, fertile farms. The area normally produces most of the world's jute, used in twine and sacks, and has large rice crops. Resources include rivers for irrigation and hydroelectric power, and natural gas. Small industries, many destroyed in 1971 fighting, were reestablished in 1972. Food shipments and other economic aid were provided by India, the U.S., USSR and others after the war. In Mar. 1972 Bangladesh announced nationalization of banks and some industries.

History and Government. British rule over the vast Indian sub-continent, dating from the 18th century, ended in Aug. 1947 when India and Pakistan became independent nations. Pakistan's government power was centered in West Pakistan, while East Pakistan, with about 56% of the population, demanded greater economic benefits and political reforms. There were riots in 1968-69.

In Dec. 1970 elections, the Awami League, which demanded greater autonomy for East Pakistan, won a majority of seats in the National Assembly, which was to draft a new Pakistan constitution. But Pakistan Pres. A.M. Yahya Khan postponed the Assembly sessions. A general strike and riots swept East Pakistan and on Mar. 25, 1971, West Pakistan troops launched attacks on rebellious Bengalis. Awami League leaders declared independence the next day. Months of fighting followed in which it was estimated 1,000,000 or more died as, it was charged, West Pakistan troops conducted repressive attacks on the populace and guerrilla forces. Some 10,000,000 Bengalis fled to India, which was supporting their cause.

Following border skirmishes, India and Pakistan each declared on Dec. 3, 1971, that the other had launched war. Pakistani troops surrendered Dec. 15 in the East; the Pakistan government accepted India's offer of a cease-fire on both East and West Pakistan fronts Dec. 16. India had recognized Bangladesh as independent Dec. 6. The U.S., which had earlier indicated sympathy with Pakistan, recognized Bangladesh Apr. 4, 1972.

Sheik Mujibur Rahman, Awami League leader arrested in Mar. 1971, was freed by Pakistan and became Bangladesh Prime Minister Jan. 12, 1972.

Bangladesh joined the Commonwealth but UN membership was vetoed by communist China, 1972.

A constitution providing for a parliamentary government took effect Dec. 16, 1972. In elections Mar. 7, 1973, Sheik Mujib's Awami League party won 305 of 313 seats.

In Aug. 1973 an India-Pakistan agreement on return of 1971 war prisoners paved the way for eventual recognition of Bangladesh by Pakistan and release of Bangladesh and Pakistani nationals stranded in each other's country.

Most of the Bangladesh people are Moslem Bengalis. The official language is Bengali.

Barbados

Capital: Bridgetown. Area: 166 sq. mi. Population (UN est. 1972): 240,000. Monetary unit: East Caribbean dollar.

Barbados achieved full independence from Great Britain Nov. 30, 1966. Furthest east of the West Indies, the island is about 2½ times the size of the District of Columbia; it lies alone in the Atlantic almost completely surrounded by coral reefs. Its highest point is Mt. Hillaby, 1,115 ft. The name Barbados (bearded) was believed given it by Portuguese or Spanish sailors, referring to bearded fig trees.

An English ship visited the island in 1605; English settlers arrived in 1627. Slaves were imported, but freed in 1834. Most of the islanders are Negroes, the language is English and the religion of most is Anglican.

A charter of 1652 provided for a Governor-General, council and assembly. Self-rule was achieved gradually; universal suffrage was granted in 1950, cabinet government in 1958, full internal self-government in 1961. It has a Parliament and Prime Minister and, as a member of the Commonwealth, a Governor-General.

Sugar, molasses, rum, cotton and building lime are the main products; there is a lively flying fish industry and, thanks mainly to the attractions of excellent beaches, the tourist business is booming. In 1973 it joined other West Indies states in the Caribbean Common Market.

With over 1,400 persons per sq. mi., the population density is one of the world's highest. Barbados also has one of the world's lowest illiteracy rates.

Belgium

ROYAUME DE BELGIQUE
KONINKRIJK BELGIË

Capital: Brussels. Area: 11,781 sq. mi. Population (Est. 1973): 9,691,000. Monetary unit: Franc.

Belgium's seacoast of 40 mi. borders on the North Sea at the Strait of Dover. Slightly larger than Maryland, the country shares borders with the Netherlands, Germany, Luxembourg and France. The Meuse (Maas) River crosses the country from France to the Netherlands. The Scheldt (Escaut Schelde) makes Antwerp an ocean port via the Netherlands.

Brussels, Bruges, Ghent and Antwerp are noted for art and architecture; Liege and Charleroi are important industrially. Antwerp is the world's 3rd largest port.

Resources and Industries. Coal is the nation's only important mineral. Although Belgium is essentially a manufacturing country, agriculture and forestry are profitable industries. The principal crops are oats, rye, wheat, potatoes, barley and sugar beets.

Important industries are mining, steel manufacture, glassware, diamond cutting, food and beverages, fishing, textiles and chemicals. Beurs voor Diamant in Antwerp is the world's largest diamond trading center.

Belgium lives by its foreign trade; about 40% of its entire production is sold abroad (75% of steel and glass). The Belgium-Luxembourg Economic Union is one of the world's foremost exporters of steel.

The gross national product rose from $30.5 billion in 1970 to $33 billion in 1972.

Foreign trade in thousands of U.S. dollars:

	Imports	Exports
1971	$15,726,575	$15,505,950
1972	$17,055,800	$17,603,375

History and Government. Belgium, land of the Belgae conquered by Julius Caesar, has a 2,000-year history during which it was ruled by the Romans, Merovingian Franks, Burgundy, Spain, Austria and France. After the fall of Napoleon, 1815, Belgium was made a part of the Netherlands. Its citizens demanded separation from the Dutch in 1830. Belgium became an independent constitutional monarchy in 1830 and chose Prince Leopold of Saxe-Coburg King, as Leopold I.

By the treaty of London, Apr. 19, 1839, Austria, France, Great Britain, Netherlands, Prussia and Russia guaranteed the inviolability of Belgium; this was the "scrap of paper" repudiated by Germany when its troops entered Belgium, Aug. 2, 1914. After World War I the Treaty of Versailles gave Belgium the cantons Eupen, Malmedy and Moresnet, 382 sq. mi., 64,250 population, added to the province of Liege in 1925.

Leopold II, son of Leopold I, was King 1865-1909, succeeded by his nephew, Albert I. Albert was killed while mountain climbing, Feb. 17, 1934; Leopold III, his son, succeeded.

During World War II, Leopold surrendered to Germany, May 28, 1940, to avoid further bloodshed. His cabinet maintained a government-in-exile in London. Nevertheless, Belgium suffered heavily. Ancient churches, houses and records were ruined at Nivelles, Mons, Tournai, Liege, Louvain; the University Library at Louvain, burned in 1914, restored with American aid, was again burned with 900,000 vols. About 50,000 Belgians died, some in Nazi prison camps.

In 1950 Belgians voted 57% in favor of recalling Leopold III (who had been in Switzerland since being freed from German internment), but Socialist opposition was so vehement that the King abdicated and his son became King Baudouin I July 17, 1951. Born Sept. 7, 1930, he was the son of Leopold's first wife, Princess Astrid of Sweden. Baudouin married (Dec. 15, 1960) Dona Fabiola de Mora y Aragon of Spain.

Universal suffrage is in force and those who fail to vote are fined. Women have voted since 1949.

Parliament consists of a Senate with members elected for four years, partly directly and partly indirectly; the number elected directly is equal to half the number of members of the House of Representatives. The Representatives are directly elected, for four years, by proportional representation (one for every 40,000 population).

The Flemings of northern Belgium speak Dutch while French is the language of the Walloons in the south. The language difference has been a perennial source of controversy, particularly as it affects education, with Flemish parents unwilling to have their children taught in French.

Disagreement between the two groups became embittered in Mar. 31, 1968, elections in which minority extremist parties increased their strength. In 1971 Belgium sought to solve the problem through creation of decentralized administrative and cultural communities.

Belgium is a member of the UN, NATO, EEC and the Benelux economic union.

Education and Religion. Roman Catholicism is the religion of the great majority. Part of the income of the ministers of the Catholic, Jewish, Church of England and Protestant Evangelical religions is paid by the government. There are universities in Ghent, Liege, Brussels, Mons, Antwerp and Louvain and agricultural, technical, art and music schools.

Defense: Military strength for 1972-73 was 66,000 in the Army; 20,000, Air Force; 4,000 Navy.

Bhutan

DRUK-YUL

Capital: Thimphu. Area: 18,147 sq. mi. Population (est. 1973): 1,150,000. Monetary unit: Indian rupee.

The tiny kingdom of Bhutan or Druk-Yul (Dragon-Country) is a constitutional monarchy in the eastern Himalayas, adjoining Tibet, Sikkim and the Indian provinces of West Bengal and Assam. It is 190 mi. long from east to west and 90 mi. across, with both mountains and jungles. Most of the people are Bhotias of Tibetan origin and are Buddhists; a minority are of Nepalese descent.

Agriculture is the chief industry. The principal products are rice, corn, yak butter, lac, wax, cloth, elephants, ponies and timber.

The ruler of the kingdom is the Dragon King, Jigme

Singye Wangchuk (born 1955), who ascended the throne July 24, 1972. The 150-member Tsongdu (Assembly) may remove the King by a two-thirds vote; he would be succeeded by his heir. Bhutan is guided by India in its foreign affairs. It joined the UN Sept. 21, 1971.

Modernization has begun, including the country's first road network usable by automobiles, linking central Bhutan and India. There is also airline service from India. Dzongs (castles), monasteries and a game sanctuary are among attractions.

Bolivia
REPUBLICA DE BOLIVIA
Capital: Sucre. Seat of gov't: La Paz. Area: 424,163 sq. mi. Population (UN est. 1972): 5,190,000. Monetary unit: Peso.

Bolivia is a landlocked nation, over 8 times the size of N. Y. State. It lies across the Andes, and its chief topographical feature is the great central plateau at an altitude of 12,000 ft., over 500 mi. long, lying between two great cordilleras having three of the highest peaks in South America. More than 65% of the population are Indians; 10% are white, and 25% are mixed (cholo).

Lake Titicaca, on the Peruvian-Bolivian border, is the highest lake in the world on which steamboats ply (12,506 ft.), and is the 2nd largest lake in South America (est. 3,200 sq. mi.).

The legal capital is Sucre, but La Paz, a city more accessible, is the actual seat of government. La Paz lies in the heart of a gigantic canyon about 3 mi. wide, 10 mi. long and 1,500 ft. deep, at an altitude of about 11,800 ft., and framed with high Andean peaks. Its huge cathedral seating 12,000, begun 1835, was dedicated 1933.

Resources and Industries. Agriculture claims 50% of the work force. Products include potatoes, sugar, coffee, barley, cocoa, highland rice, corn, bananas, citrus, rubber and cinchona bark.

The most important industry is mining. There are large deposits of tin, silver, copper, lead, zinc, petroleum, antimony, bismuth, wolfram, gold, iron, cadmium, borate of lime and natural gas. More than 12% of the world's output of tin is produced in Bolivia, running to 28,000 tons or more annually. The three largest tin producers were nationalized in 1952. The oilfields and plants of a U. S. company,were nationalized in Oct. 1969. A U.S. company's lead and zinc mine concession was canceled in April 1971.

Bolivian tin-miners' attempts to negotiate better working conditions with the Government-owned Bolivian Mining Corp. were led during 1967-68 by a group of Roman Catholic priests. An agreement was reached in March 1968 in which the corporation agreed to permit union activities and provide better working conditions and more housing and hospitals.

Bolivia receives economic aid from the U. S. and the Inter-American Development Bank, the World Bank and the International Monetary Fund. It is a member of the UN and OAS.

In May 1969 Bolivia joined Chile, Colombia, Ecuador and Peru in an Andean Common Market.

History and Government. Once part of the ancient Inca empire, Bolivia was under Spanish domination for centuries before it gained independence Aug. 6, 1825, naming itself after Simon Bolivar, famed liberator.

Bolivia's 16th constitution, adopted in 1967, provides for strong executive power, nationalization of mines, and agrarian reform. The Congress it provided for was dissolved in Sept. 1969.

Dr. Victor Paz Estenssoro, elected to a 3rd term as President May 31, 1964, was ousted Nov. 4 and the government was taken over by a military junta headed by Gen. Rene Barrientos Ortuno. On July 3, 1966, Gen. Barrientos was elected President in a constitutional election. He died in a helicopter crash Apr. 27, 1969.

On Sept. 26, 1969 a military junta seized power and Gen. Alfredo Ovando Candia was named President. He was ousted and succeeded by Gen. Juan Jose Torres, a leftist nationalist, Oct. 7, 1970. Military and civilian anti-Communist forces under Col. Hugo Banzer Suarez took over the Government in a brief conflict, Aug. 19-22, 1971.

In 1973 the government pressed school-building and oil-exploration programs.

Education and Religion. Primary education is free and compulsory. Adult illiteracy, estimated at 58%, is being lowered. There are 7 universities. Roman Catholicism is the predominant religion. Spanish is the official language.

Defense. Bolivia's armed forces total over 21,000.

Botswana
Capital: Gaborone. Area: 219,815 sq. mi. Population (UN est. 1972): 690,000. Monetary unit: South African rand.

The former British protectorate of Bechuanaland received full independence Sept. 30, 1966 and joined the UN Oct. 17, 1966.

In the center of southern Africa and populated predominantly by blacks, Botswana shares borders with the Republic of South Africa, South-West Africa (Namibia) and Rhodesia. It also claims to border on Zambia, its nearest black-ruled neighbor. It is slightly larger than Texas.

The Kalahari Desert, supporting only nomadic Bushmen and a few wild animals, spreads over the southwestern areas of Botswana; there are swamplands and farming areas in the north, and rolling plains in the east where livestock are grazed.

Cattle raising is the largest industry. Large copper and nickel deposits were discovered in 1967 and diamonds in 1969. Corn, sorghum, beans and peanuts are raised in the north. Tourism is flourishing; black-maned lions and swamp antelopes are hunted by safaris.

Many of the Botswana work as migrant labor in South Africa and much of the country's chief export, meat, goes to that country.

In 1885, Bechuanaland was made a British protectorate after local chiefs appealed to Great Britain for aid to halt encroachment on their territories by Boers of South Africa's Transvaal.

It is a republic with a President, a House of Chiefs (which handles questions of tradition) and a National Assembly.

Brazil
BRASIL
Capital: Brasilia. Area: 3,286,473 sq. mi. Population (Govt. est. 1973): 100,100,000. Monetary unit: Cruzeiro.

Brazil is the largest nation in South America in area and population. Larger in area than the 48 states in conterminous U.S., it is smaller than the 50 states. It has a coastline on the Atlantic Ocean of 4,603 mi., and extends approximately 2,689 from N to S and 2,684 from E to W. The northern part is the great, heavily-wooded basin of the Amazon (1,465,637 sq. mi. in Brazil) which rises in the Peruvian Andes and empties into the Atlantic.

The Amazon basin has a network of rivers which are navigable for 15,814 mi. The Amazon River by itself flows 2,093 mi. through Brazil, and is navigable for 2,300 mi., to the Peruvian riverport of Iquitos. The majestic falls of the Iguazu, 230 ft. high but extremely wide, are on the Brazil-Argentina border; Glass Falls, in Bahia west of Salvador, are 1,325 ft. high. Tallest mountain is Pico da Neblina, 10,046 ft., on the Venezuela border.

The south central region, favored by climate, resources and communications, has 45% of the population and produces 75% of agricultural goods and 80% of industrial output.

Brasilia, the capital city, was inaugurated Apr. 21, 1960, superseding Rio de Janeiro. Fast-growing Sao Paulo is the largest city in South America.

Resources and Industries: Brazil has vast mineral wealth and exploitation is being spurred. It leads the world in output of quartz crystal and beryl; is 2nd in sheet mica; 3rd in manganese, columbium and tantalum; 7th in iron ore. It has large deposits of iron (one-third of the world's reserves) and monazite, a source of thorium, alternate to uranium as a supplier of fissionable material. Gold output is about 142,000 troy oz. annually. Also important are oil, nickel, chrome, diamonds, coal, tungsten, tin, bauxite, various gem stones.

Cotton weaving is among important manufacturing industries, occupying 25% of workers. Brazil produces more than 5,000,000 tons of steel annually, about 40% in the Volta Redonda national mills. Automotive, aluminum, petrochemical, cement, pharmaceutical, plastics, food and beverage, electrical appliances, shipbuilding, ceramics, tires, paper, glass and heavy machinery industries are growing.

Brazil, world's greatest coffee grower, supplies about 30% of the coffee consumed in the U.S. Cotton, sugar, cocoa and iron ore are also important exports. There are large crops of bananas, manioc, oranges, pineapples, rice and corn. Also exported are castor oil and tobacco.

Brahman (zebu) cattle of India thrive in Brazil, which is 3rd among world leaders with 96,000,000 cattle and 66,000,000 hogs. It also has 25,000,000 sheep.

Brazil's economy boomed in the 1970s; the gross national product was up 10.4% in 1972. Exports showed strong gains in 1973. But inflation, though slowed, remained a problem. Brazil celebrated the 150th anniversary of its independence with Export 72, a world trade fair, in Sao Paulo. In 1973 Brazil pressed construction of its Trans-Amazon Highway, to run 3,400 mi. from the Atlantic to the Peruvian border, 1300 completed.

Foreign trade in thousands of U.S. dollars:

	Imports	Exports
1971	$3,370,000	$2,771,000
1972	$4,200,000	$3,990,000

History and Government. Pedro Alvares Cabral, a Portuguese navigator, is generally credited as the first European to reach Brazil, 1500.

Brazil was developed as a colony of Portugal until the royal house of Braganca, fleeing from Lisbon before Napoleon's army in 1807, transferred the seat of government to Rio de Janeiro, March, 1808. Brazil thereupon became a kingdom under Dom Joao VI. After his return to Portugal, his son Pedro I, proclaimed the independence of the country, Sept. 7, 1822, and was acclaimed emperor, Oct. 12, 1822. The second emperor, Dom Pedro II, was driven from the throne Nov. 15, 1889, by a revolution which established a republic, the United States of Brazil, which was the country's official name until Jan. 1967 when a new constitution shortened it to Brazil.

There are 22 states, with limited autonomy, a federal district and four territories: Roraima, Rondonia, Amapa and Fernando de Noronha Is.

Brazil took part in World Wars I and II on the Allied side. It is a member of both the UN and the OAS.

A military junta took control in 1930. Getulio Vargas became provisional President until 1933, when he was elected President under a new constitution. Out in 1945, he was reelected in 1950, but in 1954 the army forced him to retire.

In 1964, after a succession of Presidents, economic and social problems brought the ouster of Pres. Joao Goulart, in a part-military, part-civilian coup. Gen. Humberto Castelo Branco was named President. A new constitution, adopted in 1967, strengthened the powers of the Presidency, reducing those of Congress. Both Pres. Castelo Branco and his successor, Pres. Arthur da Costa e Silva, an army marshal elected by Congress in 1966, exercised at times rule by decree.

Pres. Costa e Silva suffered a stroke and died in 1969. Military leaders named Gen. Emilio G. Medici to succeed him and he was confirmed by Congress. In 1972 he said certain curbs on civil liberties would be continued.

In 1973 the military-backed government announced elections for a new President would be held Jan. 15, 1974, and said its choice was Gen. Ernesto Geisel. The election would be held by members of Congress and the state legislatures.

Education and Religion. Roman Catholicism is the predominant religion.

There are 53 universities in Brazil as well as other institutions of higher education. Primary, 5-year schools number more than 135,000 and there are more than 13,000 median level schools. Primary and secondary schools are free. The language is Portuguese.

Armed forces total almost 200,000.

Bulgaria

NARODNA REPUBLIKA BULGARIA

Capital: Sofia. Area: 42,729 sq. mi. population (UN est. 1972): 8,580,000. Monetary unit: Lev.

Bulgaria, fronting on the Black Sea, is about the size of Ohio. It is bounded by Romania, Turkey, Greece and Yugoslavia. The Balkan Mts. stretch across the center of the country with the Danubian Plain in the north and the Rhodope Mts. and Thracian Plain in the south.

Resources and Industries. Under Communism after World War II, farms were collectivized, resources nationalized and foreign trade made a government monopoly. The principal crops are wheat, fruit, rye, barley, oats, corn, potatoes and tobacco. Agriculture claimed a large percentage of the population, but the country is being industrialized under a nationalized planned economy which emphasizes electric power, chemicals, coal, machinery, metals, textiles, building materials, fur, leather goods and oil.

New economic reforms were launched Jan. 1, 1966, to decentralize planning and management, but were partly reversed in 1969-70. The index of industrial production (1963 = 100) reached 238 in 1971. Tourism is promoted and over 2,000,000 tourists visit Bulgaria annually.

About 80% of trade is with nations of the Communist bloc. Exports include maize, wheat, vegetables, chemicals, silver, textiles, hides, tobacco, rose attar, lead, zinc, cement, machinery, industrial vehicles (fork-lifts), wine.

Foreign trade in thousands of U.S. dollars:

	Imports	Exports
1971	$2,119,000	$2,182,000
1972	$2,548,000	$2,603,000

History and Government. The Bulgars, a Slavic people, settled Bulgaria in the 7th Century and became Christians in 865 A.D. The Turks conquered Bulgaria in 1396. It revolted in 1876 and in 1878 was made a principality. In 1908 it became an independent kingdom and Ferdinand of Saxe-Coburg-Gotha became Czar Ferdinand I of Bulgaria. It expanded after the first Balkan war but lost its Aegean coastline in World War I, when it sided with Germany.

Under the influence of King Boris III, Bulgaria joined the Axis in World War II, occupying considerable Balkan territory. King Boris died 1943 and a regency ruled for Simeon II, born 1937. In 1944 Bulgaria withdrew from the war, but the USSR refused to recognize its neutrality, declared war Sept. 5. Bulgaria asked for an armistice and declared war on Germany Sept. 7. In a plebiscite Sept. 8, 1946, the monarchy was abolished and a republic voted, which was established one week later. Georgi Dimitrov, Communist party leader, became the first premier.

A new constitution, adopted in May 1971, provides that the National Assembly, elected for 4 years, is the supreme organ of government. The Assembly chooses a Premier and a State Council whose President is the head of state.

Bulgaria was admitted to the UN in 1955 and is a member of the Warsaw Pact.

Education and Religion. Bulgarian is a Slavonic language. Elementary education is obligatory from 7 to 14 years of age. There are more than a score of universities and colleges, including the University of Sofia. The main religion is Eastern Orthodox. There are over 750,000 Moslems.

Defense. Military strength for 1972-73 was 117,000 in the Army; 22,000, Air Force; 7,000, Navy.

Burma

PYEE-DAUNG-SU MYANMA NAINGGAN-DAW

Capital: Rangoon. Area: 261,789 sq. mi. Population

(Est. 1972): 28,900,000. Monetary unit: Kyat.

The Union of Burma, slightly smaller than Texas, is a republic in the western part of the former Indochinese peninsula. It is bounded by China, Laos, Thailand, India, Bangladesh and the Bay of Bengal. Rivers flowing from the rugged mountains in the north provide habitable valleys down the peninsula. The largest is the Irrawaddy River which is navigable for 900 mi.

The **Burma Road,** extending from Lashio to Kunming in Yunnan province, China, was the principal military supply line from Burma into China 1938-1942. It winds for 700 mi. over an airline distance of 260 mi. It was completed by American help and protected by Gen. Claire Chennault's Flying Tigers. The **Ledo Road** was used when the Japanese closed the Burma Road.

Rangoon, on the Gulf of Martaban is the chief port; Mandalay is on the Irrawaddy River. Mingaladon airport, near Rangoon, handles international traffic.

Resources and Industries. Mineral wealth is great; included are petroleum, lead, silver, tin, tungsten, zinc, and gem stones, including rubies, sapphires and jade. The principal products are rice, cotton, maize, teakwood, tobacco, tin, silver and petroleum. In value of exports, rice accounts for 50%.

However, production in some industries declined in the 1960s. Exports, especially rice, fell off in 1970 but rose slightly in 1971 only to fall again in 1972.

History and Government. Burma was a Buddhist monarchy in the Middle Ages and came under the influence of the East India Co. (British) about 1612. Britain gained control of Lower Burma in 1824 and of Upper Burma in 1884 and administered them as part of India until 1937, when Burma became a self-governing unit of the British Commonwealth. It was overrun by the Japanese in World War II. Burma became an independent nation outside the Commonwealth by treaty effective Jan. 4, 1948 and a member of the UN in 1948.

Constituent units of the Union, resulting from amalgamations of a number of smaller states, are Shan State, Karen, Kachin, Kayah and Special Division of the Chins.

The constitution which went into effect in 1948 created a parliamentary democracy and provided for nationalization of certain industries. In a 1958 political crisis, Gen. Ne Win took over the government from Premier U Nu. Elections were held in 1960 and the Union party, headed by U Nu, won a large majority; he again became Premier in April, 1960.

Political and economic problems continued and the government was again taken over by Gen. Ne Win, Mar. 2, 1962; he set up a Revolutionary Council with himself as Chief of State, dissolving Parliament and setting aside the constitution. In 1972 he became Premier.

The Ne Win government pursued a socialist program and nationalized many industries. It continued a neutralist foreign policy, and isolated the nation from most foreign contacts.

Recurrent problems facing the government have been the need to stimulate production, rebellions staged by Chinese-backed Communist forces and pressures from extremist groups seeking greater autonomy for local ethnic groups.

Education and Religion. The Burmans are the main ethnic group; others are Karens, Shans, Kachins, Chins, etc. Burmese or one of its variants is spoken by nearly three-fourths of the population. Higher education is provided at the Universities of Rangoon, Mandalay and 5 smaller cities. A state-controlled system of schools was introduced after 1948.

The chief religion is Buddhism (about 90%).

Defense. Burma's armed forces for 1972-73 totaled 135,000 in the Army; 6,000, Navy; 7,000, Air Force.

Burundi

Capital: Bujumbura. Area: 10,747 sq. mi. Population (Est. 1972): 3,400,000. Monetary unit: Franc.

Burundi, a country the size of Maryland in east central Africa, became independent July 1, 1962. Formerly part of the Belgian UN Trusteeship of Ruanda-Urundi, it is bordered by Rwanda, Tanzania, Lake Tanganyika and Zaire. Much of the country is grasslands and mountains.

For 3 centuries in the present Burundi and Rwanda area, the Tutsi, a minority tribe, were overlords and political masters of the Hutu. (The Tutsi are an extremely tall race; the Hutu, the vast majority, are of average height; a 3rd tribe, the Twa, are pygmies.) Under German control in the late 19th Century, the area was taken over by Belgium in World War I; the League of Nations in 1923 gave the King of Belgium a mandate over the combined Ruanda-Urundi territory; Belgium received a UN Trusteeship in 1946.

Burundi became an independent constitutional monarchy in 1962 with Mwami Mwambutsa IV as King; there were a premier and cabinet, an Assembly elected by universal suffrage and a Senate. The government was mainly supported by the Uprena party, a coalition of moderate Tutsi and Hutu. Two premiers were slain by extremists and in Oct. 1965 a 3rd, Leopold Biha, was severely wounded. Hutu extremists opposed the power of the minority Tutsi in the government; Tutsi extremists, accused of receiving communist Chinese aid, opposed the government as too moderate.

In July 1966 the King's son, Prince Charles, 19, deposed him and ousted Premier Biha, appointing Michael Micombero Premier. Extremist Tutsi returned to power; on Sept. 1 Prince Charles was proclaimed King Mwami Ntare V. But in a coup d'etat Nov. 28, King Ntare was overthrown by Col. Micombero, who declared himself President. Burundi became a republic. Ntare was killed in April 1972, supposedly during an attempt to seize power.

A Hutu revolt, starting Apr. 29, 1972, was put down; it was estimated 10,000 Tutsi were slain by rebels and 100,000 Hutu by government troops. In May-June 1973, renewed fighting was reported and thousands of Hutus fled to Tanzania and Zaire.

The economy is agricultural, with 90% of the people farmers or livestock raisers. Coffee is the main crop and export. Much of the land is over-grazed and eroded. The nation receives aid from Belgium and the UN. It is a member of the UN and OAU.

Cotton production was becoming increasingly important in the late 1960s. With outside technical aid, tea plantations were set up.

Over half the population is Christian, mostly Roman Catholic. Many others believe in a supreme deity, Imana, called the Principle of Good. Kirundi, a Bantu tongue, and French are the official languages: Swahili is also widely used. (*See also Rwanda.*)

Cambodia

KHMER REPUBLIC

Capital: Phnom Penh. Area: 69,898 sq. mi. Population (Est. 1972): 7,250,000. Monetary unit: Riel.

Cambodia is in southeast Asia and, with Vietnam and Laos, comprised the former associated states of French Indochina. It is slightly larger than Utah. It is bordered by Laos, Thailand, the Gulf of Siam and South Vietnam. Three-fourths is forested; the central part is level, forming a basin for the Mekong River. The climate is tropical.

Resources and Industries. The country is largely undeveloped; 50% of the land is virgin forest. Main industries are forestry, fishing, and agriculture, rice occupying about 80% of the land usage. Other products are rubber, maize, pepper, kapok, palm-sugar, tobacco, cotton, silk, oil seeds, beans. Cattle flourish; the forests have valuable hardwoods. Some iron, copper, manganese and gold exist. Industry is developing, featuring textiles, paper, plywood. An oil refinery opened in 1968.

Continuing warfare created a rice shortage in Cambodia, a nation which until 1970 was an exporter of rice.

History and Government. Early kingdoms dating from that of Founan in the 1st Century A.D. culminated in the great Khmer civilization which flourished from the 9th Century to the 14th. The Khmer "God-Kings" built a series of monumental cities, distinguished for their temple tower architecture and striking wall sculptures. Most famous temple is that of Angkor Wat.

Cambodia came under French protection in 1863. A national constitution promulgated May 6, 1947, replaced the former absolutism. It became an associated state within the French Union by a treaty of Nov. 8, 1949, but declared its independence from France, Nov. 9, 1953. It is a UN member.

Prince Norodom Sihanouk was King, 1941-55; he abdicated in favor of his father, Norodom Suramarit, who died Apr. 3, 1960. On June 13, 1960, Sihanouk, refusing to become King again, was named Chief of State.

Sihanouk broke off diplomatic relations with the U.S. in 1965 after an attack by South Vietnamese planes on Vietcong forces fleeing into Cambodia. In 1968 Sihanouk said Vietnamese Communists were arming Cambodian insurgents. In July 1969 diplomatic relations between the U.S. and Cambodia were restored. In 1969-70 the U.S. bombed North Vietnamese forces in Cambodia but did not announce that action until 1973.

In Mar. 1970, while Sihanouk was in Europe, the Cambodian Government demanded, without result, that North Vietnam and the Vietcong withdraw their troops, estimated at 40,000, from Cambodia. On Mar. 18, 1970, Sihanouk's Premier, Lt. Gen. Lon Nol, seized control of the Government. Sihanouk later announced in Peking formation of a Government-in-exile.

The Lon Nol Government charged increasing attacks on its troops by the Communist forces and appealed for arms from other nations.

On Apr. 30, 1970, U.S. President Nixon announced that U.S. troops were moving into Cambodia to drive Communist forces from border area sanctuaries used for attacks on South Vietnam. South Vietnamese forces also moved into Cambodia. More than 30,000 U.S. troops and over 40,000 South Vietnamese took part in the operations.

On June 30 President Nixon announced the end of the U.S. incursion, reported huge enemy losses of military supplies as well as manpower and said the operation had insured the continued withdrawal of U.S. troops from Vietnam.

Despite the Jan. 1973 cease-fire in Vietnam, reaffirmed in June, fighting continued in Cambodia, with anti-Government forces pressing a siege of Phnom Penh. U.S. daily bombings ended Aug. 15. Cambodia described the rebel forces (the Khmer Rouge) as actually Vietnamese communists; the U.S. said some North Vietnamese were training and supplying the insurgents and manning heavy weapons.

On Oct. 9, 1970, by action of the legislature, the monarchy was abolished and Cambodia's name was officially changed to the Khmer Republic. In Apr. 1972 a new constitution, providing for a President and 2-house legislature, was approved by referendum. On June 4 Lon Nol was elected President.

Education and Religion. The national language is Cambodian, or Khmer; French is widely spoken and English is taught. In 1965 there were over 4,000 schools and 37 faculties of higher learning. Buddhism is the state religion.

Cameroon
REPUBLIQUE UNIE DU CAMEROUN

Capital: Yaounde. Area: 183,581 sq. mi. Population (Est. 1973): 6,000,000. Monetary unit: CFA Franc.

Cameroon, which became a republic in 1960, lies on the western coast of Africa, bounded N and NW by Nigeria, NE by Chad, E by Central African Republic, S by People's Republic of Congo, Gabon and Equatorial Guinea, W by Gulf of Guinea. It is larger than California.

Cameroon is comprised of two states: East Cameroon, formerly Republic of Cameroon, previously a French mandate and trusteeship; and West Cameroon, formerly British Southern Cameroons. Douala is the principal seaport and one of nine airports.

The population comprises some 200 tribes, including Bantus, Semitic and Sudanese peoples, Kirdis, Foulbes and Bamilekes. There are about 600,000 Christians and 600,000 Moslems; others are animists.

Resources and Industries. Mainly agricultural, Cameroon exports cocoa, coffee, palm products, leather, timber, rubber, peanut oil, tea, bananas, ginned cotton. Livestock includes cattle, horses, donkeys, pigs, sheep and goats.

Aluminum processing is the most important manufacturing industry. Trade is heavy with France and United Kingdom. Import and export totals are each over $200,000,000 annually.

New railroad and power dam construction and agricultural modernization were pressed in 1973.

History and Government. Cameroon embraces the larger part of the former German protectorate of Kamerun which was occupied by France and Britain in 1916, and placed under trusteeship, 1919. France passed a statute Dec. 31, 1958, conferring internal autonomy on the French trusteeship as a step toward complete independence which took effect Jan. 1, 1960.

Following a referendum by the UN in former British Cameroons, the southern section joined the Republic to form the Federal Republic of Cameroon, Oct. 1, 1961. The republic, composed of two federated states, is a member of the UN. (The northern section of British Cameroons voted to become part of Nigeria.)

The 120-member National Assembly is elected by direct universal suffrage.

Canada
See Index and special article preceding this section.

Central African Republic

Capital: Bangui. Area: 236,293 sq. mi. Population (Govt. est. 1973): 3,000,000. Monetary unit: CFA Franc.

The former French Overseas Territory of Ubangi-Shari in Equatorial Africa is 350 mi. NE of the Gulf of Guinea and is bounded by Chad, Sudan, Congo, Zaire and Cameroon. Slightly N of the Equator, it is mostly rolling plateau, average alt. about 2,000 ft. with rivers draining S to the Congo and N to Lake Chad. Landlocked, it is slightly smaller than Texas.

It achieved partial self-government in 1958. Complete independence was proclaimed Aug. 13, 1960, and the Republic became a UN member Sept. 20.

A few months after his election in 1960, Pres. David Dacko dissolved all political parties. He was re-elected Jan. 1965, running as the sole candidate. The country became a center for Chinese Communist activities.

On Jan. 1, 1966, the Army Chief of Staff, Col. Jean Bedel Bokassa, deposed Pres. Dacko; a few days later Pres. Bokassa broke off diplomatic relations with Peking. He was named President-for-life, Mar. 8, 1972.

French is the official language; Sangho is a lingua franca of the 4 ethnic groups: Banda, M'Baka, Zande, Mandjia-Baya.

Diamonds are the main export, accounting for about half the nation's total export earnings, which amount to about $30,000,000 annually. Uranium has been found; production was scheduled for 1972. Cotton, coffee and peanuts are the chief cash crops and production was increased in the late 1960s. There are large herds of cattle and sheep; lumber exports have increased. About 90% of the population makes its living from farming.

Small factories for textiles, food processing, soap and beer and for assembling motorbikes and radios have been given impetus.

CEYLON
See Sri Lanka

Republic of Chad

Capital: Fort-Lamy. Area: 495,753 sq. mi. Population (UN est. 1972): 3,790,000. Monetary unit: CFA Franc.

A former French Overseas Territory in Equatorial Africa, 500 mi. NE of the Gulf of Guinea, 550 mi. S of the Mediterranean, Chad is bounded N by Libya, E by Sudan, S by Central African Republic, W by Cameroon, Nigeria, Niger. It is four-fifths the size of Alaska.

Moslem groups predominate in the north, and black animists and others in the south. Chad has a southern wooded savannah, a steppe and a desert region, part of the Sahara, in the north. On the west is Lake Chad.

Chad proclaimed complete independence Aug. 11,

1960, and joined the UN Sept. 20. There is a President and a National Assembly elected by universal adult suffrage. Chad is a member of the OAU and UN. French is the official language. But in 1973 the nation began replacing French names with African ones.

Cotton is the main export; others are refrigerated meat, leather, dried fish and natron (sodium carbonate).

By mid-1973 a 5-year drought brought growing famine to the land. The U.S. and other nations donated grain.

In 1969-71, with the aid of French troops, government forces fought many skirmishes with rebellious Arab nomads in the northeast. French troops began leaving in 1972. Chad had accused Libya of aiding the rebels. In 1973 Chad broke off diplomatic relations with Israel, and Libya reportedly responded by halting aid to the rebels.

Chile

REPUBLICA DE CHILE

Capital: Santiago. Area: 292,257 sq. mi. Population (Est. 1973): 10,000,000. Monetary unit: Escudo.

The Republic of Chile lies along the southern half of the west coast of South America, a narrow strip of land 2,620 mi. long between the towering Andes and the South Pacific.

Most of Chile lies in the temperate zone, but the Atacama Desert in the north is one of the world's driest regions, with little or no rainfall. Chile itself is slightly larger than Texas; it also claims sovereignty over a large area of the Antarctic Continent, some 500,000 sq. mi.

The Christ of the Andes, a heroic-size statue in Uspallata Pass, symbolizes peace between Chile and Argentina.

Tierra del Fuego is the largest (18,800 sq. mi.) island in the archipelago of the same name at the southern tip of South America, an area of majestic mountains, tortuous channels and high winds. It was discovered 1520 by Magellan, who sailed through the strait (named after him) which separates the main island from the mainland; he named the island Land of Fire because of its many Indian bonfires. Part of the island is in Chile, part in Argentina. Punta Arenas, on a mainland peninsula in Chile, is a center of sheep-raising and the world's southernmost city (pop. over 64,000); Puerto Williams, pop. 949, at a Chilean naval base on Navarino Is., is the southernmost settlement. Beagle Channel, between Navarino and the main island, and Mt. Darwin were named after Chas. Darwin's visit to the area aboard the ship Beagle. The area's tallest mt. is Sarmiento, 7,546 ft. Cape Horn, about 1,400 ft., is a tiny island, named Hoorn by Dutch explorers after a town in the Netherlands.

Possessions in Pacific: Sala y Gomez and **Easter Is. (Rapa Nui),** with its huge stone statues, both over 2,000 mi. west; **San Ambrosio** and **San Felix,** 600 mi. west, and **Juan Fernandez Islands** (2 large, 1 small), center of lobster fishing and place where Alexander Selkirk, whose life reputedly was the inspiration for Defoe's Robinson Crusoe, lived 4 years.

Resources and Industries. The arid deserts of northern Chile contain incalculable mineral wealth. Mining industries account for more than 70% of Chile's exports. Nitrate production is about 100,000 metric tons a month. About 47% of the world's supply of iodine is a by-product of Chilean nitrate works. Chile produces about 12% of world copper output.

The provinces of Atacama and Coquimbo have enormous iron deposits estimated at a billion tons. Coal reserves are estimated at 2 billion tons. Oil wells, mostly in Tierra del Fuego, supply Chile's needs and offer an export potential. Other minerals are gold, silver, molybdenum, cobalt, zinc, manganese, borate, mica, mercury, iodine, salt, sulphur, marble, onyx. Chile has abundant waterpower. Patagonia, the sparsely-populated southern third of the nation, is undergoing extensive industrial development.

Agriculture is an important industry. There are many large dairy farms. Wheat, rice, barley, oats, beans, lentils, apples, melons, peaches, plums, nectarines, peas and potatoes are grown in abundance. Sugar beet, automotive, aviation and textile industries are being developed. Vineyards cover 250,000 acres and much wine is exported. Forests have large reserves of hard and soft woods. Coastal waters have shellfish, lobster, tuna, swordfish, sardines.

Manufacturing industries have developed greatly.

Besides minerals the exports are mainly fishmeal, barley, oats, wine, onions, garlic, leather, lentils, fruits, fish, sea-food, cellulose, newsprint, wood.

Chile has many airports and is served by 15 international airlines. The Pan American Highway runs 2,000 mi. from Arica in the N to Puerto Montt.

In the late 1960's the government pressed a wide program of social and economic reforms.

In 1970 Dr. Salvador Allende Gossens, a Marxist, was elected President and in July 1971 a Constitutional amendment provided for full nationalization of copper mines owned by 3 U.S. companies, with compensation to be negotiated. A policy of nationalizing large industries and banks and expropriating large farms was launched. In 1972 middle class groups staged street demonstrations protesting food shortages and socialist policies. Strikes and riots increased in 1973. Food shortages and inflation continued.

A U.S. Senate Foreign Relations subcommittee in 1973 accused the International Telephone & Telegraph Corp. and the U.S. Central Intelligence Agency of discussing, but not carrying out, plans to prevent Allende's election in 1970. The Allende government nationalized ITT phone systems in Chile, without compensation.

In an attack on the Presidential Palace, Sept. 11, 1973, a military junta seized power and said Allende killed himself. The junta named Gen. Augusto Pinochet Ugarte Pres., swore in a mostly-military cabinet and broke off diplomatic relations with Cuba, which Allende had resumed. Pinochet announced the junta would "exterminate Marxism."

History and Government. Diego de Almagro entered Chile for Pizarro 1536 and Valdivia completed Spanish conquest 1540. Sir Francis Drake raided the coast.

Independence was gained 1810-18, under Jose de San Martin and Bernardo O'Higgins; the latter as supreme director, 1817-1823, sought social and economic reforms until deposed. Chile defeated Peru-Bolivia in 1836-39 and 1879-84, taking Tacna and Arica provinces from Peru, returned Tacna, 1929. Arica (town) and Antofagasta are free ports for landlocked Bolivia.

Under the constitution the President is elected for 6 years, the 50 senators for 8 and 150 deputies for 4, all by direct popular vote. Voting age was lowered from 21 to 18 in 1970. Chile is a member of the UN and OAS.

About two-thirds of the Chileans are of mixed Spanish and Indian descent; about one-fourth of Spanish only; a small percentage are Indian only; there are some of German and other European descent.

Education and Religion. Education is free and compulsory between 7 and 15. There are 9 universities. The Roman Catholic religion is dominant. The language is Spanish.

China

The ancient land of China is split into two hostile parts, with the Republic of China limited to Taiwan (Formosa) and the mainland controlled by a communist regime called the People's Republic of China.

China, with about one-fourth of the world's population, occupies a territory in the eastern part of Asia about one-third larger than continental United States.

The mainland is of rolling topography, rising to high elevations in the N in the Khinghan Mtns., separating Manchuria and Mongolia; the Tarabagata Mtns. in Sinkiang; the Himalayan and Kunlun Mtns. in the SW in Tibet. Its length from N to S is 1,860 mi. and its breadth from E to W more than 2,000 mi.

The eastern half of China is one of the best-watered lands in the world. Three great river systems, the Yangtze, the Hwang (Yellow) and the Si (Si Kiang) provide water for vast farmlands.

Resources and Industry. Until communism prevailed,

China was chiefly agricultural. Wheat, barley, corn, koaliang, and millet and other cereals, peas and soy beans are produced in the north; rice, sugar and indigo in the south. Rice is the staple food of the Chinese. Fruit is grown in abundance. Fiber crops are important and include abutilon, hemp, jute, ramie and flax. Cotton is produced mostly in the Yangtze and Yellow River valleys. Tea is cultivated principally in the west and south. One of the most important industries of prewar China was silk culture which has flourished 4,000 years. Livestock is raised in large numbers. In years before World War II flour and rice milling had become extensive, together with tanning, cement and glass manufacture.

China is one of the foremost coal countries in the world. Other minerals are iron ore, tin, antimony, petroleum, tungsten, molybdenum, salt.

Education and Religion. Buddhism had the largest following. Confucianism, which reveres God but stresses ethical and philosophical principles rather than divine revelation, had wide acceptance. Taoism (after Lao-Tze, B. 604 B. C.) is more metaphysical and looks to immortality. Islam, at one time, had 50,000,000; there were 3,280,000 Roman Catholics and 700,000 Protestants. On the mainland foreign missionaries and church schools are no longer tolerated.

Republic of China

CHUNG-HUA MIN-KUO

Provisional Capital: Taipei, Taiwan. Area under control, 13,886 sq. mi. Population (Est. 1972): 15,000,000. Monetary unit: Taiwan dollar.

History and Government. One of the oldest of monarchies, with a history reaching back to 2205 B. C., China became a republic Jan. 1, 1912, following the Wuchang Uprising inspired by Dr. Sun Yat-sen, begun Oct. 10, 1911.

For a period of 50 years after the Sino-Japanese War, 1894-95, China was involved in conflicts with Japan. On Sept. 18, 1931, Japan seized the Northeastern Provinces (Manchuria) and set up a puppet state called Manchukuo. The border province of Jehol was cut off as a buffer state in 1933. Japan invaded China in the vicinity of Peiping (now Peking), July 7, 1937, precipitating war. After its defeat in World War II Japan returned all seized land.

After the war with Japan ended, Aug. 5, 1945, internal disturbances arose involving the Kuomintang, Communists and other factions. Manchuria was lost by the Nationalist regime in 1948, and China proper came under domination of Chinese Communist armies during 1949-1950. The Nationalist government moved to Taipei, Taiwan (Formosa), 90 mi. off the mainland Dec. 8, 1949.

China had concluded a treaty of friendship and alliance with the USSR, Aug. 14, 1945. After the Chinese Communists overran the mainland in 1949, the Soviet Union repudiated the treaty, withdrew its recognition of the Nationalist government, and signed a new treaty with the Communist regime, Feb. 15, 1950.

A new constitution became effective Dec. 25, 1947. The National Assembly is the supreme organ of the people. Members are elected on the basis of territorial and professional representation. They serve for a six-year term, subject to recall. The Assembly elects the President and Vice President, who likewise serve six-year terms; it also has the power to amend the constitution. A Yuan (Council), elected on the basis of regional and vocational representation, serves as the legislature. The cabinet, appointed by the President, is responsible to the Legislative Yuan.

Generalissimo Chiang Kai-shek, except for a period of semi-retirement, has been virtual ruler since 1927. He was elected President for a six-year term in April, 1948; reelected in 1954, 1960, 1966 and 1972. The Nationalist government was a founding member of the UN. On Oct. 25, 1971, the UN General Assembly expelled nationalist China from the UN and admitted communist China in its place. By 1973, only 37 nations, including the U.S., still recognized the nationalist regime.

Although agriculture remains a vital and growing part of the economy, industrial production has grown much more rapidly. Important industries include textiles, clothing, electrical and electronic equipment, TV sets, processed foods, chemicals, glass, metals and machinery.

Foreign trade, with imports and exports each above the $2 billion level, has also shown strong and steady growth. Gross national product was up 11% in 1972.

U.S. economic aid, begun in 1951 and totaling $1.5 billion, terminated June 30, 1965 (with exception of some funds previously committed through 1967). Military aid, which totaled $2.5 billion, continued, but at a reduced scale of about $90,000,000 a year. Textile products are the most important export. The republic has extended technical assistance to some 30 countries in Asia, Africa and Latin America.

Defense. Nationalist China has compulsory universal service. The armed forces have an estimated strength of about 550,000 on Taiwan and adjacent islands, including a Navy and an Air Force, largely equipped by the U. S.

The Nationalist government signed a mutual defense treaty with the U. S., in force Mar. 3, 1955. It provides for consultation on threats of attack and promises that if China is subject to unprovoked attack the U. S. will act according to its constitutional procedures.

TAIWAN (FORMOSA)

Taiwan is an island 110 mi. E of the mainland, but the term Taiwan is used by the nationalist government to include 14 other islands nearby and 64 others comprising the Penghu group.

Taiwan was ceded by China to Japan in 1895, after the Sino-Japanese War and was returned to China as a province, 1945, after the surrender of Japan. Japan renounced all claims to Taiwan and the Penghus in the Treaty of Peace, Sept. 8, 1951. China did not take part in the treaty, signing a separate treaty with Japan Apr. 27, 1952.

A range of mountains forms the backbone of the island. The eastern half is exceedingly steep and craggy but the western slope is flat, fertile and well cultivated, yielding two rice crops a year. The principal crops, besides rice, are tea, sugar, sweet potatoes, ramie, jute, turmeric and camphor. Minerals include gold, silver, copper and coal.

The Penghus (Pescadores), 50 sq. mi., pop. (1964) 108,800, lie between Taiwan and the coast of China, by which they were ceded to Japan in 1895. The islands remained under Japanese rule until restored to China, 1945.

The islands of **Quemoy** and **Matsu**, near the mainland, have been under communist artillery fire at intervals since 1958.

People's Republic of China

CHUNG-HUA JEN-MIN KUNG-HO KUO

Capital: Peking. Area under control; 3,746,453 sq. mi. Population (UN est 1972): 800,720,000. Monetary unit: Yuan.

The People's Republic of China was proclaimed in Peking (Peiping) Sept. 21, 1949, by the Chinese People's Political Consultative Conference under Mao Tse-tung, Communist leader. Chou En-lai was named premier and foreign minister Oct. 1, 1949. With defeat of the Nationalist armies, the Chinese mainland, the islands of Hainan and Chusan and the principal cities fell to the Communists.

Under the Communist regime, China comprises 22 provinces, including Taiwan, which it claims; 5 autonomous regions (Inner Mongolia, Sinkiang-Uighur, Kwangsi-Chuang, Ningsia-Hui, Tibet-Chamdo) and two municipalities—Peking and Shanghai. The government pressed birth control programs; without them experts said, China's population would reach 1 billion by 1980.

The Communist regime and the USSR signed a 30-year treaty of "friendship, alliance and mutual assistance," Feb. 15, 1950, repudiating the 1945 treaty between the Soviet Union and nationalist China authorized by the Yalta Agreement. Great Britain recognized the People's Republic in 1950 and France did so in 1964. By 1973, over 60 nations had recognized the regime.

United States Policies. The U. S. refused recognition, and after its consular officers met with abuse, withdrew them. On Nov. 26, 1950, when U. S. military forces and those of certain other UN members had the North Korean Communist rebels virtually defeated, the People's Republic sent armies of "volunteers" into Korea and, with the help of limitations on U.S. offensive action, forced a stalemate.

In April 1971, after the U.S. relaxed restrictions on visits by its citizens, a U.S. table tennis team was invited to the People's Republic.

On Oct. 25, 1971, the UN General Assembly ousted nationalist China from the UN and seated communist China in its place. The U.S. had announced support of the mainland's admission but opposed Taiwan's expulsion.

U.S. President Nixon visited China Feb. 21-28, 1972, on invitation from Premier Chou En-lai, ending years of antipathy between the two nations. They agreed to continue progress toward normalization of relations. In April, U.S. businessmen made purchases at the Canton export fair.

China and the U.S. moved close to formal diplomatic relations by opening liaison offices in each other's capitals, May-June 1973.

In 1973, because of food shortages, China ordered 6,000,000 tons of grain from the U.S., Australia and other countries.

Peking Foreign and Domestic Policies. On Feb. 27, 1957, Mao Tse-tung, then Chief of State, condemned the Stalinist terror but admitted an est. 800,000 anti-communist Chinese were executed 1949-54. Leniency for political criticism, proposed by Mao Tse-tung, led to a quick return to repressive measures. In 1958 the regime announced all "rightists" in govt. service had been removed. It endorsed the Soviet attack on Hungary, condemned Yugoslavia's independence. It pursued a more rigid communist ideology than the USSR and, with Albania, has maintained a continuous propaganda campaign against the USSR.

Early in 1966 a long, widespread purge of "anti-party intellectuals" was launched; it was viewed as a possible symptom of a struggle for power and the succession to the aging Mao. Premier Chou En-lai called the purge a "cultural revolution." Ousted from office and denounced were the Chief of the Army's General Staff, Minister of Culture, the party propaganda chief, 3 university presidents, newspaper editors and writers, opera producers, youth officials, economists, Peking's Mayor, etc.

In August, 1966 Defense Minister Lin Piao emerged as top deputy and heir apparent to Mao. But in 1972 China said Lin died in a 1971 plane crash trying to flee to the USSR after attempting a coup.

By late 1968-69 the long disruption had tapered off; much power was taken from the students and given to Revolutionary Committees and the military.

On Mar. 2, 1969, Chinese and Russian soldiers fought one of a series of border clashes on an island in the Ussuri River on the border between the two nations in the Far East, north of Vladivostok. The island, called Chenpao by Chinese and Damansky by Russians, was claimed by both nations. Both sides reported dead and wounded. There were later clashes on the island and reports of skirmishes far to the west on the Sinkiang-USSR border. In 1970, ambassadors were exchanged for the 1st time since 1966.

On Oct. 16, 1964, communist China exploded a low-yield atomic bomb in Sinkiang Province, becoming the 5th nation to possess such power. An explosion of a hydrogen bomb was announced June 17, 1967. The nation's first orbiting space satellite was launched Apr. 24, 1970.

Internationally, communist China has sought to promote revolutionary movements in Africa, Asia and South America. The program suffered serious setbacks, 1965-66. By the early 1970s, China was again reported sending military and economic aid to several nations.

Application of radical theories to industry and agriculture have resulted in erratic economic development. Serious food shortages existed beginning in 1959 after more than 148,000,000 acres of farm land were damaged by floods, drought and failure of the "Great Leap Forward" 5-year plan. The regime was forced to obtain grain from

Argentina, Mexico, Canada and Australia. Light industries dependent on agriculture for their raw materials also were affected—cotton textiles, knitted goods, vegetable oils, sugar and cigarets. The "people's commune" system of agriculture in effect since 1958 and which had disrupted family life, was drastically modified in 1960-61 to increase individual incentives to stimulate production, but the collectivization drive was renewed in 1963-1964. Many thousands fled to overcrowded Hong Kong.

In 1969-1972, after the "cultural revolution" eased off, both industry & agriculture showed production gains.

China leads all nations in number of hogs, is 3rd in sheep, 4th in cattle. Its fish catch is 2nd in value to Japan's.

Institutes of higher education include 15 universities, 48 engineering colleges and 31 agricultural colleges. English and Russian are required in high schools.

Defense. Missiles to carry nuclear warheads were under development. Military forces for 1972-73 totaled 2,880,000. The Army had 2,500,000; there were 150 divisions, including 5 armored, 3 cavalry and two airborne. Navy strength was 160,000; there were 33 submarines, 200 torpedo boats, 13 destroyers and escorts and numerous other ships. Air Force strength was 220,000; there were 3,600 combat aircraft and other planes of Soviet design.

Manchuria, 404,428 sq. mi., is administered as part of communist China. Seized by Japan in 1931, it was renamed Manchukuo, a puppet "independent" nation, Mar. 1, 1932. In 1945 it was returned to China.

Kwantung is the southern part of the Liaotung peninsula, the southernmost portion of Manchuria. Russia in 1898 forced China to lease it Kwantung and constructed the strongly fortified city of Port Arthur and the nearby commercial ice-free port of Dairen (Talien).

Japan seized Port Arthur in 1905, and at the close of the Russo-Japanese War took over the lease in the Treaty of Portsmouth. It was restored to the USSR by the Yalta Agreement, Feb. 11, 1945, which also internationalized Dairen. Following the 1950 Soviet-Chinese treaty the USSR returned the Changchun railroad, Port Arthur and Dairen to communist China.

Inner Mongolia was organized by the People's Republic as an Autonomous Region on May 12, 1947. Its boundaries have undergone frequent changes. In 1950 it comprised northern Chahar and parts of former Manchuria. Suiyan province was incorporated June 1954, and parts of Jehol in Aug. 1955. Population is about 6,200,000 of which less than 20% are Mongol. Capital: Huhehot (Kweisui).

Outer Mongolia: *For People's Republic of Mongolia, see Mongolia in Index.*

Sinkiang (New Dominion), in Central Asia, comprising Chinese Turkestan, Kulia and Kashgaria, is 633,802 sq. mi.; pop. (est. 1958), is 6,000,000, of whom 75% are Uighurs, a Turkic Moslem group, with a heavy Chinese increase in recent years. Tihwa (Urumchi), the capital, and Kuldja are the chief cities.

Sinkiang is considered China's richest region in strategic materials, including tungsten, wolfram, molybdenum, copper, zinc, coal, uranium and oil. The province was declared autonomous in 1953.

TIBET (PO)

Tibet, 470,000 sq. mi., is a thinly populated region of high plateaus and massive mountains, almost twice the size of Texas. The Himalayas ring it on the S, the Kunluns on the N. Lofty passes link it with India and Nepal to the S; roads lead into China proper. The capital is Lhasa. The average altitude is 15,000 ft. Jiachan, 15,870 ft., is believed to be the highest inhabited town on earth. Agricultural methods are primitive. Cereals are the main crops. The religion is Lamaism, a form of Buddhism. Pop. (1964 est.) 1,300,000.

With only token resistance, Tibet accepted suzerainty of the Chinese Communist regime under a pact signed May 23, 1951. A communist Tibetan Autonomous Government was announced Dec. 20, 1953, revising the quasi-religious administration of the Dalai and Panchen Lamas.

A revolt against the Communists occurred in 1959, when the latter attempted to arrest the Dalai Lama. The

Tibetan cabinet denounced the 1951 treaty. The Communists crushed the revolt and placed the Panchen Lama on the Tibetan throne. The Dalai Lama fled to India. The Panchen Lama was demoted Dec. 1964. A new ruler was sponsored by Peking Sept. 9,'1965, when it announced election of Ngapo Ngawang Jigme as chairman of the newly-established Tibet Autonomous Region. Revolts continued in 1965 and 1966.

A reform program, including land redistribution and abolition of serfdom (assertedly practiced in some monasteries) was announced July 3, 1959.

The International Commission of Jurists at Geneva in 1961 charged the Communist regime with genocide in Tibet. About 20,000 Tibetans have fled to India since the Chinese takeover.

Colombia
LA REBUBLICA DE COLOMBIA

Capital: Bogota. Area (UN est.): 455,335 sq. mi. Population (Govt. est. 1973): 23,000,000. Monetary unit: Peso.

The Republic of Colombia, situated in the extreme northwest of South America, extends up the Isthmus of Panama to the republic of Panama. It has a coast line of 913 mi. on the Pacific Ocean, and 1,094 mi. on the Caribbean Sea. It has no neighbors to the N and Brazil on the E, and Ecuador and Peru on the S. Its area is greater than the areas of Texas and California combined.

Three great ranges of the Andes, the Western, Central and Eastern Cordilleras, run through the country from N to S. The eastern range consists mostly of high table lands, cool and healthful, and densely populated. The Magdalena River, in the NE, rises in the high Andes and flows N into the Caribbean Sea near Barranquilla. It is navigable over 800 mi. The Magdalena Valley is a plain of rich alluvial land.

Snow-crested mountains standing almost directly over the Equator are one of many examples of scenic splendor in Colombia. Tourists are also attracted by the famous Tequendama Falls, a natural wonder near Bogota, 427 ft. high.

The Salt Cathedral of Zipaquira, 32 mi. N of Bogota, is an actual church carved with Gothic arches 1,300 ft. underground in a salt mine. It can accommodate 10,000 worshipers.

Bogota, the capital, founded in 1538, is in the Andes, 8,660 ft. above sea level.

Resources and Industries. Colombia is second to Brazil in exports of coffee, accounting for 50% of export trade. Rice, tobacco and cotton are cultivated, besides cocoa, sugar, tagua, wheat and bananas. Dyewoods, rubber, balsam and copaiba trees are important.

The country is rich in minerals. It has become a heavy producer of petroleum. Seventy-five miles from Bogota are the Muzo emerald mines which have been in operation for 4 centuries. Colombia produces 95% of the world's gem emeralds. Other minerals are gold, silver, copper, lead, mercury, cinnabar, manganese, platinum, coal, iron, nickel, salt. Colombia is accelerating expansion of its hydro-electric power which has est. potential of 85,000,000 kw. Food processing is the leading manufacturing industry; other products are textiles, rubber goods, steel, and chemicals. Textiles have become an important export.

Loans from international agencies have helped expand industry and modernize agriculture.

An Atlantic railroad, completed in 1961, running from Santa Marta on the Caribbean Sea to Salgar opened the Magdalena Valley to cultivation and improved travel between the coast and industrial cities of the interior. Aviation has done much to unify the country. An oil pipeline from the new Orito field in the SE, crosses the Andes to the Pacific port of Tumaco; it was finished in 1969.

The government has sought to reduce vast land holdings and increase the size of small farms. From 1961 to 1970 the Institute for Land Reform acquired or developed 9,800,000 acres; more than 95,000 families were given title to farm plots.

History and Government. The country, conquered and ruled by Spain for 300 years, won its freedom in the revolt of the Spanish-American colonies 1810-1824, the liberator, Simon Bolivar, establishing the Republic of Greater Colombia in 1819 from which Venezuela and Ecuador withdrew in 1829-1830. From the remainder of the confederation evolved New Granada, Confederation Granadina, and finally the Republic of Colombia under a constitution dated Aug. 5, 1886. Panama withdrew Nov. 3, 1903, becoming a separate republic.

The Congress consists of a Senate of 118 members, elected for a term of 4 years, and a House of Representatives with 210 members, elected directly by the people every 2 years. The President is elected by direct vote for 2 years and is ineligible for the following term.

Education and Religion. Most of the people are of mixed Indian and white descent; the next largest group is white; the smallest groups are Indians and Negroes. Education is free but not compulsory. The National Univ., founded 1572, is in Bogota. Roman Catholicism is the prevailing religion. Spanish is the language.

Defense. Armed forces total 50,000, Army; 7,200, Navy; 6,000 Air Force. Colombia is a member of the UN and OAS.

People's Republic of Congo

Capital: Brazzaville, Area: 132,046 sq. mi. Population (UN est. 1972): 980,000. Monetary unit: CFA Franc.

Formerly the French Middle Congo Overseas Territory, the People's Republic of the Congo straddles the Equator. It is bounded on the E and S by Zaire; on the W by Cabinda (Port.), the Atlantic and Gabon; on the N by Cameroon and Central African Republic. It is twice the size of Missouri.

Complete independence was proclaimed Aug. 15, 1960, and the Republic joined the UN Sept. 20. Fulbert Youlou was elected President Nov. 21, 1959, and resigned in Aug. 1963 in a coup sparked by trade unions. Under his successor, Pres. Alphonse Massamba-Debat, the country moved into the Red Chinese sphere of influence and announced a "scientific Socialist state" with one-party control.

In Aug. 1965 the U. S. withdrew its embassy staff, a step short of breaking off relations, charging harassment of American officials. Massamba-Debat was ousted in a military coup, Sept. 4, 1968. Maj. Marien Ngouabi became president Jan. 1, 1969.

In Jan. 1970, the earlier name, Republic of the Congo-Brazzaville, was changed to People's Republic of the Congo. The government advocates socialism.

The nation has received aid from both France and Communist China.

Forests are a prime resource, covering 54,000,000 acres, and wood products form a major export. Chief commercial agricultural products are palm oil and kernels, cocoa, bananas, and peanuts. Industrialization has progressed and its output now accounts for 11% of the total national product. Potash reserves are extensive.

DEMOCRATIC REPUBLIC OF CONGO
See Zaire

Costa Rica
REPUBLICA DE COSTA RICA

Capital: San Jose. Area: 19,575 sq. mi. Population (Est. 1972): 1,842,831. Monetary unit: Colon.

Costa Rica, in Central America, has Nicaragua for its neighbor on the N and Panama on the S. The lowlands by the Caribbean have a tropical climate. The interior plateau, with an altitude of about 4,000 ft., is temperate.

San Jose, the capital, situated inland–103 mi. by rail from Puerto Limon on the Atlantic; 93 by rail from Puntarenas on the Pacific–is the country's industrial and cultural center. Limon and Puntarenas are the principal ports. The crater atop Poas Volcano is the largest in the world. Puerto Limon occupies one of the sites where Columbus landed on his fourth and last visit to America.

Resources and industries. A 1962 law giving new industries a tax holiday of up to 10 years brought in a wide variety of factories. The Irazu volcano near San Jose erupted from March 1963 to Dec. 1964, dropping millions of tons of ash which severely damaged coffee, vegetable and dairy crops, but higher world coffee prices aided the economy. Coffee of a high quality is the chief crop and export, followed by bananas, sugar, cocoa, beef, cotton, fish and hemp.

Despite growing, small-scale industrialization, agriculture remains the mainstay of the economy, employing half the work force.

New industries include fiberglass products, aluminum processing, textiles, fertilizer, roofing and cement.

The forests are extensive, and the lumber industry is important. Gold and silver are mined on the Pacific slope. Other minerals are quartz, alabaster, granite, oil, alum, slate, onyx, mercury, sulphur, copper.

Chief imports are flour, industrial machinery, gasoline, leather, hardware and tools. Nearly half of the foreign trade is with the U. S. The balance of trade is adverse although increasing light industry and membership in the Central American Common Market have improved the situation.

The nation has a comparatively high standard of living and of social services.

History and Government. Although once a part of the Confederation of Central America, 1824-1829, Costa Rica has been independent since 1821.

An unusual Constitution was adopted Nov. 8, 1949. It abolishes the Army as a permanent institution. The legislative power is vested in a Chamber of Deputies, 57 in number, with 4-year terms, under universal suffrage. The President, elected for 4 years, appoints a Cabinet of 12. Deputies may not serve successive terms but may be reelected after an intervening 4 years. A President may not be reelected. There is a fine for not voting.

Religion and Education. Primary education is compulsory. Higher education is free. There are universities in Cartago, Heredia, San Jose and Turrialba. The language of the country is Spanish. English is taught in the public schools. Roman Catholicism is the predominant religion.

Defense. Order within the country is kept by a Civil Guard and police forces. Costa Rica is a member of the UN and OAS.

Cuba

Capital: Havana. Area: 44,218 sq. mi. Population (UN est. 1972): 8,750,000. Monetary unit: Peso.

Cuba, the Pearl of the Antilles, is both an island, the largest in the West Indies, and, including its offshore islands, a nation which is about the area of Pennsylvania. The Straits of Florida lie to the N, the Gulf of Mexico to the W, the Caribbean to the S.

Key West, Fla., is about 90 mi. N. The Windward Passage, 50 mi. wide, separates Cuba from Haiti to the E, and Jamaica lies 90 mi. to the S. Cuba's length is 730 mi.; its breadth averages 50 mi. The coastline, including the larger keys, is about 2,500 mi. It has numerous harbors, notably that of Havana, one of the finest in the world. **The Isle of Pines** (Isla de Pinos) is 1,180 sq. mi. in area.

Mountains rise in Pinar del Rio Province in the W, and in Oriente in the E where they reach about 3,000 ft., with Pico Turquino, 6,467 ft., the highest.

Havana (La Habana), pop. over 1,500,000, is the busiest port. Santiago de Cuba, on the SE coast, is the next largest port.

Resources and Industries. Chief barometer of the nation's economy is the sugar industry which represents about 80% of exports. U.S. sugar mills, seized by the revolutionary regime in 1960, represented an investment of approx. $275,000,000, producing about 40% of Cuba's output.

Tobacco raising and the manufacturing of cigars and cigarettes rank second. Other products are molasses, coffee, pineapples, bananas, citrus fruit and coconuts. Textiles, cabinet woods (mahogany and cedar), dyewoods, fibers, gums, resins and oils are important. Iron,

copper, manganese, nickel and salt are some of the minerals. Industries include rayon, cement, naphtha and gasoline, chemicals.

Poor sugar crops and food shortages resulted in collectivization of farms and stringent labor controls under the revolutionary government. Rationing of food, shoes, clothing, gasoline, was ordered. Some rationing continued in 1973.

Economic difficulties continued into the 1970s, despite massive aid from the USSR and assistance from other Communist countries.

History.—Cuba was discovered by Christopher Columbus, in Oct., 1492. Its name derives from the Indian Cubanacan. Except for British occupation of Havana, 1762-63, Cuba remained Spanish until 1898.

Under Spanish governors Cubans were denied citizenship, slavery was retained until 1886, and patriots who revolted were executed. On Oct. 10, 1868, Carlos Manuel de Cespedes led Cubans in a proclamation of independence. Their ten-years' war ended in 1878 with guarantees of rights by Spain, which Spain failed to carry out. A full-scale movement began Feb. 24, 1895, under Jose Marti, with the military under the command of Maximo Gomez, Antonio Maceo and Calixto Garcia. By 1897 over half the island was in Cuban hands. The Spanish governor, Valeriano Weyler, destroyed sugar plantations, banned export of tobacco and held patriots in "reconcentration camps." A U. S. offer to mediate was rejected by Spain.

The movement to help Cuba gain its independence was speeded up by the sinking of the U.S.S. Maine in Havana harbor. The U.S. declared war on Spain Apr. 25, 1898, and defeated it in the short Spanish-American War. In the Treaty of Paris, Dec. 10, 1898, Spain gave up all claims to Cuba. The U.S. formally withdrew May 20, 1902, when Tomas Estrada Palma was inaugurated first president of the republic.

Under 1903 and 1934 agreements, the U.S. leases a site for its naval base at Guantanamo Bay, on the SE coast.

In 1952 Fulgencio Batista seized control of the government and imposed a dictatorship.

Opposition to the corrupt Batista regime became vigorous in 1956 under leadership of Fidel Castro, born 1927, lawyer and former leader of student opposition. Known as the 26th of July Movement, the revolutionists in 1958 carried on intensified guerrilla warfare. Batista resigned Jan. 1, 1959. He died in Spain Aug. 6, 1973.

Castro proclaimed Dr. Manuel Urrutia Lleo Provisional President and Urrutia dissolved the Cuban Congress, Jan. 6, 1959. Castro became Premier Feb. 16. Pres. Urrutia resigned after accusing Communists of plotting treason.

The government, quickly dominated by left-wing extremists, began a program of sweeping economic and social changes, led by an agrarian reform law approved May 18, 1959. It executed hundreds of dissidents, and ousted moderates.

The National Institute of Agrarian Reform, principal agent for economic control, nationalized cattle and tobacco lands and instituted a system of cooperatives. All private enterprise was brought under control by a Central Planning Board created Feb. 20, 1960. By the end of 1960 all Cuban banks and industrial companies had been nationalized, including an est. $1 billion worth of U. S. owned properties.

Soviet, Communist Chinese and Czechoslovakian economic penetration was extended by trade and credit agreements, including sugar purchases and a USSR credit equiv. to $100,000,000 for construction of factories and other installations.

Citing the open hostility of the regime, the U. S. cut back Cuba's remaining 1960 sugar quota by 700,000 tons. The U. S., Oct. 19, imposed an extensive embargo on exports to Cuba and, Feb. 4, 1962, Pres. Kennedy ordered a total embargo.

The OAS nations voted July 26, 1964, 15-4, resolution for mandatory sanctions against Cuba and for strengthening defenses against Cuban subversion efforts. But by 1973 Latin American nations having diplomatic relations with Cuba included Mexico, Argentina, Peru, Trinidad-Tobago, Jamaica, Guyana, Barbados.

Bay of Pigs Raid. In April, 1961, Jose Miro Cardona, Pres., Cuban National Revolutionary Council, called on Cubans to unite to overthrow the Castro regime. On Apr. 17 about 1,400 Cuban patriots, who had trained in the U. S. and Guatemala, landed at the Bahia de Cochinos (Bay of Pigs) on Cuba's southern coast. They were overwhelmed by Castro forces and killed or imprisoned. The attempt created severe criticism in Congress of activities of the U. S. Central Intelligence Agency. Pres. Kennedy previously had declared there would be no intervention by the U. S. On Dec. 21, 1962, Castro agreed with James B. Donovan, representing welfare agencies, to release 1,113 prisoners in exchange for medical supplies worth a reputed $53,000,000. American drug concerns and religious groups raised the supply.

Kennedy vs. Soviet Missiles. In the fall, 1962, the U. S. ascertained that the Soviet Union was delivering nuclear missiles and other weapons to Cuba and building bases. On Oct. 22 Pres. Kennedy warned that any missile launched from Cuba would be regarded as an attack by the Soviet Union and would call for full retaliation. He asked Premier Khrushchev to halt this "clandestine, reckless and provocative threat to world peace." Khrushchev removed the missiles.

Cuba complained of numerous raids by infiltrators, 1964-70.

In Feb. 1973 Cuba and the U.S. signed an agreement providing for extradition or punishment of hijackers of planes or vessels, and for each nation to bar activity from its territory against the other.

More than 500,000 Cubans have gone into exile since the Castro takeover, most of them to the U.S., including 260,000 via an airlift paid for by the U.S. which started Dec. 1965 and ended April 1973.

Cuba is a member of the UN and Comecon.

Education and Religion. Education is compulsory between the ages of 6 and 14. Among the institutions of higher learning is the University of Havana, founded in 1721. The Roman Catholic religion is dominant. The language is Spanish with English widely understood.

Education was nationalized June 7, 1961, and many Catholic schools were seized. Many Catholic priests of Spanish origin were ordered deported.

Defense. Cuba's armed forces in 1973 totaled over 105,000, mostly Army. The Air Force had over 200 planes, the Navy had over 100 small ships.

Cyprus
KYPRIAKE DIMOKRATIA
KIBRIS CUMHURIYETI

Capital: Nicosia. Area: 3,572 sq. mi. Population (Govt. est. 1972): 651,000. Monetary unit: Pound.

Cyprus, former British Crown Colony, became a republic Aug. 16, 1960, and joined the Commonwealth, UN and Council of Europe. It is the third largest island in the Mediterranean Sea, 40 mi. S of Turkey, 60 mi. W of Syria, and 350 mi. E of Crete. Two mountain rangos run E W, separated by a wide, fertile plain. It is smaller than Connecticut.

Four-fifths of the inhabitants are Greek Orthodox Christians, nearly all the rest are Turkish Moslems. Greek and Turkish are official languages; English is widely spoken.

Resources and Industries. Cyprus is mainly agricultural, with cereals, grapes, wine, carobs, citrus fruits, potatoes and olives as principal crops. Agricultural products account for about 60% of the island's exports, but minerals are important—copper, iron pyrites, asbestos, gypsum, chrome and umber—making up 30% of total exports. Manufacturing is limited mainly to light industries. Cement and oil refining industries are under development.

The nation suffers an unfavorable balance of trade, offset by tourism, etc.

History and Government. Cyprus was inhabited as early as the New Stone Age in the 4th millennium B.C. Achaeans from Greece traded with the early Cypriots from 1600 B.C., set up colonies after the end of the Trojan War (c. 1184 B.C.). From the middle of the 8th Century B.C., Cyprus was dominated successively by Phoenicians, Assyrians, Egyptians, Persians, Alexander and the Ptolemies, Romans, Byzantines, Moslems, Crusaders, Venetians and Turks. Great Britain took over administration in 1878 under an agreement with Turkey, annexed the island in 1914, made it a Crown Colony in 1925.

Agitation for enosis (union) with Greece resulted in the British abolishing the legislative council in 1931. Demands for enosis were renewed after World War II; the Turkish minority, about 100,000, was opposed. Widespread violence in 1955-56, led by EOKA, an underground organization, brought harsh disciplinary measures, including the temporary exiling of Archbishop Makarios III, patriarch of the Orthodox Church in Cyprus and leader of the enosis movement.

In 1959, conflict was brought to a temporary halt by an agreement signed by British, Greek, Turkish and Cypriot leaders, under which Cyprus would become a republic, with a President elected from and by the ethnic Greek community, and a Vice President from and by the corresponding Turkish community. A 70-30% proportion of the Greek and Turkish communities was to be represented in the House of Representatives. Britain retained 2 military enclaves, Akrotiri and Dhekelia.

Separate Greek and Turkish Communal Chambers dealt with religious, educational and other communal affairs.

Archbishop Makarios was elected President for a 5-year term and Dr. Fazil Kutchuk Vice President, Dec. 14, 1959. The constitution was approved April 6, 1960; independence became final Aug. 16, 1960, and Pres. Makarios took office.

Communal strife again broke out in December, 1963, following proposals by Pres. Makarios to make changes in the constitution which the Turkish minority felt would reduce their rights.

The UN Security Council approved Mar. 4, 1964, a resolution providing for an international peace-keeping force and UN troops began action Mar. 27.

Tension worsened after Turkey charged that Turkish Cypriots had been massacred in a Greek push against the northwest coast and bombed and strafed Greek positions Aug. 7-10, 1964. Both sides accepted a cease-fire.

War between Greece and Turkey over Cyprus appeared imminent in Nov. 1967 but was averted mainly because of mediation work by Cyrus R. Vance, special envoy of U. S. President Johnson.

Archbishop Makarios, whose term as Pres. had been twice extended by Parliament, was re-elected Feb. 25, 1968, by an overwhelming popular vote, and again on Feb. 8, 1973.

In 1972, talks were planned to write a new constitution. Pres. Makarios resisted demands by Greece for more influence in Cypriote affairs.

Turkish Cypriots have not taken active part in the national government since the Dec. 1963 confrontation, but the Vice Pres. is a Turkish Cypriot.

Czechoslovakia

Capital: Prague (Praha). Area: 49,370 sq. mi. Population (UN est. 1972): 14,480,000. Monetary unit: Koruna.

Czechoslovakia is a central European socialist republic about 600 mi. long and 50 to 100 mi. wide—about the size of New York State. It is bounded by West Germany (Bavaria), East Germany (Saxony), Poland, the Soviet Union, Austria and Hungary.

The Vltava (Moldau) and Labe (Elbe) flow from Bohemia to Germany; the Danube separates Slovakia from Hungary. The Carpathian Mts. are in the E and NE; tallest are the Tatras, wtih Gerlachovka peak 8,737 ft.

Resources and Industries. Czechoslovakia has considerable natural resources, developed by farming, mining and industry. The nation is highly industrialized but agriculture remains important; chief crops are wheat, sugar beets, potatoes, rye, hops.

Coal is mined in the Ostrava-Karvina basin and at Plzen and Brno. Much iron is found in the Beroun basin and Slovakia. Oil, imported mainly from the USSR via the "Friendship Pipeline," is refined at Bratislava on the Danube. Jachymov (Joachimstal), has Europe's richest deposits of pitchblende (for radium) and uranium. Czechoslovakia is a major exporter of arms and machinery. Ostrava and Kosice are important steel centers.

There is a large glass and china industry; other products include chemicals, beer, aircraft, wood pulp, textiles, shoes.

Imports for 1972 were valued at $4.6 billion, exports at $5.12 billion.

History and Government. In February, 1948, Czechoslovakia became a unitary socialist republic composed of the Slav nations—the Czechs and the Slovaks—with a socialist constitution, nationalized industry and one-state elections. The Czechs make up 65% of the population and Slovaks about 30%. In addition, there are some 450,000 Hungarians, 200,000 Germans, 200,000 gypsies, 100,000 Ruthenian-Ukrainians and 100,000 Poles. Large numbers of Hungarians were moved out of Slovakia and many Slovaks were moved from Hungary to Slovakia in 1945-46. An estimated 3,000,000 Sudeten Germans were transferred to Germany under the Potsdam Agreement.

Bohemia, Moravia and Slovakia were part of the Great Moravian Empire when overrun by the Magyars 906 A.D. Bohemia and Moravia later became part of the Holy Roman Empire. Under the kings of Bohemia Prague in the 14th Century was the cultural center of Central Europe. The Hussite religious wars were fought here, 1420-36. In 1526 Ferdinand, brother of Emperor Charles V, became king of Bohemia and Hungary. Later the lands became part of Austria-Hungary.

In 1914-1918 Thomas G. Masaryk and Eduard Benes formed a provisional government with the support of Slovak leaders, of whom Milan Stefanik organized freedom fighters in foreign countries. When Austria fell, Oct. 28, 1918, they proclaimed the republic of Czechoslovakia Oct. 30. Masaryk became President, Benes Foreign Minister and Stefanik Minister of War. Benes succeeded Masaryk in 1935.

By 1938 Adolf Hitler of Nazi Germany had worked up disaffection among German-speaking citizens in Sudetenland and demanded its cession. To avoid war Prime Minister Neville Chamberlain of Great Britain, with the acquiescence of France, signed an agreement with Hitler at Munich, Sept. 30, 1938, agreeing to the cession, with a guaranty of peace by Hitler and Mussolini. Nazi Germany occupied Sudetenland Oct. 1-2. President Benes resigned Oct. 5.

Hitler on Mar. 15, 1939, dissolved Czechoslovakia, made protectorates of Bohemia and Moravia, and supported the autonomy of Slovakia, which was proclaimed independent Mar. 14, 1939, with Jozef Tiso as President.

Soviet troops with some Czechoslovak contingents entered eastern Czechoslovakia in 1944 and reached Prague in May 1945; Benes returned as President. In May 1946 elections, the Communists won 38% of the votes, largest for a single party, and Benes accepted Klement Gottwald, a Communist, as Prime Minister. Tiso was executed in 1947.

In Feb. 1948 a crisis resulted in the resignation of 12 anti-Communist ministers and Benes accepted a new Gottwald Cabinet Feb. 25. Jan Masaryk, son of Thomas Masaryk, had not resigned as Foreign Minister. He was found dead March 10, apparently a suicide but there was widespread speculation he was murdered.

In May 1948 a new constitution was approved by the constituent assembly; Benes refused to sign it. On May 30 the voters were offered a one-slate ballot and the Communists won full control. Benes resigned June 7, Gottwald became President and Benes died Sept. 3.

In Jan. 1968 a liberalization movement spread explosively through Czechoslovakia. Antonin Novotny, long the Communist boss of the nation, was deposed as party leader and succeeded by Alexander Dubcek, a Slovak, who declared he intended to make Communism democratic. On Mar. 22 Novotny resigned as President and was succeeded by Gen. Ludvik Svoboda. On Apr. 6, Premier Joseph Lenart resigned and was succeeded by Oldrich Cernik, whose new cabinet was pledged to carry out democratization and economic reforms.

In July 1968 the USSR and 4 hard-core Warsaw Pact nations demanded an end to liberalization. On Aug. 20, Russian, Polish, East German, Hungarian and Bulgarian military forces invaded Czechoslovakia.

Some Soviet troops remained and Soviet pressure in late 1968 and in 1969 brought agreements from officials that the liberal policies would be "normalized." Despite demonstrations and riots by students and workers, press censorship was imposed, many liberal leaders were ousted from office, promises of loyalty to Soviet policies were made by some old-line Communist party leaders.

On Apr. 17, 1969, Dubcek resigned as leader of the Communist party and was succeeded by Gustav Husak. In Jan. 1970, Premier Cernik was ousted. In 1972, more than 40 liberals were jailed on subversion charges. In 1973, amnesty was offered to some of the 40,000 who fled the country after the 1968 invasion.

On Jan. 2, 1969, Czechoslovakia became a federal state. In addition to a Federal President, Premier and Assembly for the Czechoslovak Socialist Republic, there were separate governments, a Czech Socialist Republic and a Slovak Socialist Republic, each with a National Council, a Premier and Cabinet. The central government retained control over foreign affairs, defense and finance. In the Federal Assembly, a House of People was chosen by electoral districts; a House of Nations had 75 Czech and 75 Slovak members.

West Germany and Czechoslovakia resumed diplomatic relations in 1973 and declared the 1938 Munich pact void.

Education and Religion. An estimated 75% of the population is Roman Catholic, the rest are Protestant (Hussite), Greek Orthodox, etc.

Institutions of higher learning are Charles University in Prague, founded in 1348; the Universities of Brno, Bratislava, Kosice, Hradec Kralove, Plzen; also technical universities. Czech and Slovak are official languages.

Defense. Military forces for 1972-73 numbered 145,000 in the Army and 40,000 in the Air Force plus 35,000 border troops and 120,000 in the militia.

Dahomey

Capitals: Porto-Novo, Cotonou. Area: 43,483 sq. mi. Population (UN est. 1972): 2,830,000. Monetary unit: CFA Franc.

The Republic of Dahomey, former Overseas Territory in French West Africa, is a narrow strip 415 mi. long and 77 mi. wide, bounded by the Republics of the Niger and Upper Volta, Nigeria, Gulf of Guinea and the Republic of Togo. It is about as large as Tennessee.

In accordance with the 1958 French constitution, Dahomey became fully independent Aug. 1, 1960, and became a member of the UN Sept. 20. It is a member of an economic alliance known as the Council of the Entente, formed May 29, 1959, the other members being Ivory Coast, Niger and Upper Volta. Dahomey signed agreements Apr. 24, 1961, providing for close ties with France.

Under the constitution the President and National Assembly are elected for five-year terms. Pres. Hubert Maga, elected Dec. 11, 1960, was deposed Oct. 28, 1963, and replaced by a provisional government headed by Gen. Christophe Soglo. The constitution of the second republic was adopted Dec. 19, 1963. Sourou Migan Apithy was elected Pres. Jan. 24, 1964: several more coups followed. In Oct. 1972 Maj. Mathieu Kerekou became President in a military coup.

Principal products: palm oil, kernels and nuts; peanuts, cotton, kapok, coffee, tobacco.

Small industries were constructed in the late 1960s, including a bicycle plant, cotton mill and peanut-oil plant. Oil was discovered offshore in 1969. France gives the nation an annual subsidy.

Denmark

KONGERIGET DANMARK

Capital: Copenhagen. Area: 16,619 sq. mi. Population including Faeroe Islands and Greenland (Govt. est. 1973): 5,100,000. Monetary unit: Krone.

Denmark occupies the peninsula of Jutland, thrusting out to the North from Germany, which is its only land neighbor, between the North Sea and the Baltic Sea, and adjacent islands. The Skagerrak separates it from Norway; the Kattegat and Oresund from Sweden. The country consists of low undulating plains. It is about the size of New Hampshire and Massachusetts combined.

The **Faeroe Islands** in the North Atlantic, about 300 mi. NE of the Shetlands, and 850 mi. from Denmark proper, 18 inhabited, have an area of 540 sq. mi. and pop. (est. 1971) of 40,000. They are part of the nation as is **Greenland,** described below.

Resources and Industries. About 10% of the population lives by agriculture on more than 70% of the usable land. Denmark exports much butter, cheese, poultry, eggs, bacon and beef. Fisheries are valuable. Tourist trade accounts for 10% of foreign exchange. Denmark exports machinery, ships, textiles, furniture, iron and steel goods. Most raw materials and fuels have to be imported, but manufactures have increased; industrial exports jumped 228%, 1956-66, surpassing agricultural exports.

Denmark is the world's largest exporter of pork and 3rd largest of meat in general.

The first cooperative consumers' society was established 1866; the system currently has about 1,650 affiliated societies and includes 863,000 households, about 51%.

More than 1,000,000 tourists visit Denmark annually. Many leave their children in Danish camps while visiting other countries.

Foreign trade in thousands of U.S. dollars:

	Imports	Exports
1971	$4,615,000	$3,685,000
1972	$5,054,000	$4,410,000

History and Government. The origin of Copenhagen dates back to ancient times, when the fishing and trading place named Havn (port) grew up on a cluster of islets in the Sound, but Bishop Absalon (1128-1201) is regarded as the actual founder of the city. On one of the islets he built a stronghold against the pirating Wends and the remnants of this still exist underground in front of Christiansborg. Elsinore (Helsingör) contains the reputed grave of Hamlet, the Danish prince immortalized by Shakespeare.

Denmark is a limited monarchy with a Queen, her ministers who form a Council of State, and a parliament. A new constitution, signed June 5, 1953, substituted a unicameral parliament, the Folketing, of 179 members for the former two-chamber Rigsdag.

The Queen of Denmark is Margrethe II (born Apr. 16, 1940) who succeeded to the throne Jan. 14, 1972, after the death of her father, King Frederik IX. She was married June 10, 1967, to Count Henri Marie Andre Laborde de Monpezat of France who became Prince Henrik of Denmark. They had two sons: Prince Frederik (born May 26, 1968) heir to the throne, and Prince Joachim (born June 7, 1969). Queen Margrethe had two sisters: Princess Benedikte (born Apr. 29, 1944), married to German Prince Richard Casimir of Sayn-Wittgenstein, and Princess Anne-Marie (born Aug. 30, 1946) who married King Constantine of Greece and became Queen of Greece.

Denmark has public assistance, health insurance, disability and old-age pensions, workmen's compensation and unemployment insurance. If a worker refuses to take an offered job, aid ceases. A pension is paid to men aged 67, widows and single women aged 62.

Denmark is a member of the UN and NATO, and joined the EEC Jan. 1, 1973.

Education and Religion. The Evangelical Lutheran is the established religion, but there is complete religious tolerance. Education is compulsory and includes vocational courses. Leading institutions are the Univ. of Copenhagen (1479), the Technical Univ. and the Univs. of Arhus, Odense and Roskilde.

Defense. Military forces for 1972-73 totaled 43,400 plus volunteer Home Guards of 52,000 and reserves.

GREENLAND

Greenland, a huge island between the North Atlantic and the Polar Sea, is separated from the North American continent by Davis Strait and Baffin Bay. Its total area is 840,000 sq. mi., 705,234 of which are ice-capped. Most of the island is a lofty plateau 9,000 to 10,000 ft. in altitude. The average thickness of the ice cap is 1,000 ft.

The population (est. 1972) is 50,000. The capital is Godthaab. Under the 1953 Danish constitution the colony became an integral part of the realm with representatives in the Folketing. Fish and fur are exported.

Denmark has built six Loran towers up to 1,345 ft. tall on Greenland and the Faeroe Islands to provide navigational aid to ships and planes.

Dominican Republic

REPUBLICA DOMINICANA

Capital: Santo Domingo. Area: 18,816 sq. mi. Population (UN est. 1972): 4,300,000. Monetary unit: Peso.

The Dominican Republic occupies the eastern two-thirds of the Island of Hispaniola (discovered by Columbus in 1492), second largest of the Greater Antilles, lying between Cuba on the W and Puerto Rico on the E. The boundary between it and the Republic of Haiti, which occupies the western part of the island, is 241 mi. long. It has a coastline of 979 mi. It is twice the size of New Hampshire. Climate is generally sub-tropical.

The city of Santo Domingo, founded 1496, is the oldest settlement by Europeans in the hemisphere and has the supposed ashes of Columbus in an elaborate tomb in its ancient cathedral.

Resources and Industries. The land is fertile. Chief products are sugar, cocoa, coffee, tobacco, corn, peanuts, bananas and livestock products.

The country has nickel, gold, copper, iron, salt, chalk, bauxite, marble, amber, kaolin.

Chief manufactures are sugar, molasses, rum, alcohol, cement, peanut oil, chocolate, tobacco products, cordage, textiles, apparel, lumber, furniture. The U. S. buys more than 50% of its exports, mostly sugar, cocoa and coffee, and supplies about 50% of imports.

Agricultural products, including sugar, showed strong gains in 1969-72. A large nickel refining plant opened in 1972.

History and Government. Spain ceded Santo Domingo to France, 1795. Toussaint L'Ouverture, Haitian leader, seized it, 1801. Spain returned intermittently 1803-1821, and several native republics came and went. From 1822 to 1844 Haiti governed it. The republic was formed 1844. Spain occupied it 1861-63.

The country was occupied by U.S. Marines from 1916 until 1924, when a constitutionally elected government was installed.

In 1930, Gen. Rafael Leonidas Trujillo Molina was elected President. Trujillo remained in power, ruling the nation with an iron hand (though turning the Presidency over to his brother, Hector, in 1952 and to Joaquin Balaguer in 1960) until his assassination May 30, 1961.

Pres. Balaguer resigned under pressure Jan. 17, 1962. Pending general elections, the country was governed by a 7-member Council of State headed by Rafael F. Bonnelly who was named President Jan. 18, 1962. He was succeeded by Juan Bosch, elected President Dec. 20, 1962, in first free elections in 38 years. Pres. Bosch was overthrown Sept. 25, 1963, and his regime replaced by an army-backed civilian triumvirate led by Donald Reid Cabral.

On April 24, 1965, a revolt was launched by followers of Bosch and others, including Communists, and led by Col. Francisco Caamano Deno. The Reid Cabral government was ousted, but the rebel regime was replaced Apr. 28 by a 3-man counter-revolutionary junta led by Gen. Elias Wessin y Wessin; on May 7 it was succeeded by a 5-man regime headed by Gen. Antonio Imbert Barreras, another anti-Bosch leader; fighting continued in Santo Domingo.

A force of 405 U. S. Marines landed by helicopter April 28, primarily, according to U. S. Pres. Johnson, to save American and other lives; U. S. forces were expanded to a high of 24,000 as the U. S. sought to restore order and prevent a Communist take-over.

At U. S. urging, the Organization of American States sent an Inter-American Peace Force to Santo Domingo starting May 23, under a Brazilian commander with the head of the U. S. forces as deputy commander. Some U. S. forces were withdrawn and the Inter-American Force consisted of 11,200 men, including 9,400 U. S. troops, 1,100 Brazilians, and units from Honduras, Nicaragua, Paraguay and Costa Rica.

On Sept. 3, Hector Garcia-Godoy became provisional President under sponsorship of the OAS with agreement by all major local groups.

An election was held June 1, 1966; former Pres. Balaguer defeated former Pres. Bosch, 754,409 votes to 517,783. The Balaguer Reformist party won control of both houses of Congress. The new President was inaugurated July 1. The Inter-American Peace Force began moving troops out and completed their departure Sept. 20. Pres. Balaguer was reelected, 1970.

Education and Religion. The population is mostly mixed white and Negro, plus about 15% whites and a slightly larger percentage of blacks. The people are mostly Roman Catholics. Education is free and compulsory. The language is Spanish, but English is widely spoken. The University of Santo Domingo was established 1538 by Dominican fathers.

Defense. The nation has an Army, Navy and Air Force totaling 15,000. It is a member of the UN and OAS.

Ecuador
REPUBLICA DEL ECUADOR
Capital: Quito. Area (govt est.): 116,270 sq. mi Population (Est. 1972): 6,598,300. Monetary unit: Sucre.

On the northwestern coast of South America, Ecuador (Sp. for Equator) straddles the world's midsection, extending 100 mi. into the Northern Hemisphere, 400 into the Southern. It is bounded by Colombia, Peru and the Pacific. Two ranges of the Andes run N and S, splitting the country into 3 zones—hot, humid lowlands on the coast; temperate highlands between the ranges, and rainy, tropical lowlands to the E. There are 22 peaks over 14,000 ft.; highest is Chimborazo, 20,561 ft.; many are snowcapped; some volcanoes have erupted in recent years. Ecuador is larger than Arizona.

The **Galapagos Islands**, 600 mi. to the W, are the home of huge tortoises and other unusual animals. Charles Darwin visited the islands aboard the Beagle in 1835; his studies of wildlife there provided most of the facts for his theory of evolution.

Ecuador has sought revision of its Amazon valley boundary with Peru. It claims jurisdiction over Pacific waters 200 mi. out from its coast. It has seized and fined U.S. fishing boats within that limit. In Jan. 1971 the U.S. in reply temporarily suspended military sales to Ecuador. But other U.S. aid continued.

Guayaquil, Ecuador's largest city, is the chief seaport and, together with Quito, is served by major airlines. Rail lines link Quito with Guayaquil and San Lorenzo on the coast. Quito is famed for its 17th Century churches.

Resources and Industries. The country is rich in undeveloped minerals. Large deposits of copper, iron, lead, coal and sulphur are known to exist. In Aug. 1972 Ecuador began exporting oil, brought by pipeline from eastern Ecuador to a Pacific coast terminal. Modern farm methods have speeded agricultural growth and made Ecuador the world's largest exporter of bananas. Other agricultural products are rice, cereals, potatoes, fruits, cocoa, coffee, kapok, rubber, mangrove bark.

Industry now contributes 20% to the national income, with large production increases in cement, edible oils, textiles, sugar, chemicals. Ecuador is the chief source of light but strong balsa wood. Ecuador was the original home of the Cinchona tree, source of quinine.

History and Government. Spain conquered the region, which was the northern Inca empire, in the 16th Century. Liberation forces defeated the Spanish May 24, 1822, near Quito. Ecuador became part of the Republic of Colombia but seceded, May 13, 1830, and became a republic. It has had a history of numerous coups.

In June 1968 elections, Dr. Jose Maria Velasco Ibarra, who had been elected Pres. 4 times but had been ousted 3 times by coups, was again chosen by the voters. In June 1970, he assumed dictatorial powers. On Feb. 15, 1972, he was ousted by a military junta which named Gen. Guillermo Rodriguez Lara president.

Education and Religion. Roman Catholicism is the chief religion. Primary education is compulsory. The language is Spanish. The population is over one-third Indian and one-third mixed; whites, mostly of Spanish descent, and Negroes are minority groups.

Defense. Armed forces total about 20,000.

Egypt
ARAB REPUBLIC OF EGYPT
Capital: Cairo. Area: 386,100 sq. mi. Population (Govt. est. 1972): 34,839,000. Monetary unit: Egyptian pound.

The United Arab Republic, a name adopted by Egypt and Syria during their brief union, Feb. 1, 1958, to Sept. 30, 1961, comprised only Egypt after Syria withdrew from the merger. In a pact approved Sept. 1, 1971, the UAR, Syria and Libya joined in a loose Federation of Arab Republics; the UAR changed its name to the Arab Republic of Egypt.

Egypt, itself a republic since 1953, occupies the NE corner of Africa on the Mediterranean. On the E lie Israel and 1,200 mi. of Red Sea separating Egypt from Saudi Arabia. Libya is to the W and Sudan to the S. Egypt's Sinai Peninsula extends into the Red Sea, with the Gulf of Aqaba on the E. The Gulf of Suez and the Suez Canal (connecting the Gulf with the Mediterranean) are in Egypt. Jurisdiction over a 28-mi. wide strip of Asia Minor west of Israel, including Gaza, was given Egypt by an armistice agreement, 1949, as a refuge for displaced Palestinian Arabs.

Alexandria, founded 332 B. C., is the chief port. Cairo, largest city, is rich in archeological treasures, cafes, bazaars. Tourist attractions include the pyramids, Sphinx, temple ruins at Karnak and Luxor, and other ancient monuments.

Resources and Industries. Productive acreage lies in the Valley of the Nile and in its delta, or Lower Egypt, north of Cairo. The Nile flows through 960 mi. in Egypt and covers 2,850 sq. mi. with waters and marshes. About 13,000 sq. mi. are cultivated for cereals, vegetables, cotton and sugar cane, and 1,900 sq. mi. have canals and fruit plantations. The Nile rises in June and reaches its peak by August, regulated by dams and networks of canals. Fruit is plentiful and includes grapes, dates, figs, pomegranates, peaches, apricots, oranges, lemons, bananas and olives. Egypt is one of the world's top producers of cotton.

The billion-dollar Aswan High Dam project, begun 1960, completed 1971, provided irrigation for more than 1,000,000 acres of additional land and 10 billion kwh of electricity per year. Artesian wells, drilled in the Western Desert, reclaimed 43,000 acres for cultivation, 1960-66.

A variety of minerals is found in Egypt; petroleum is most important. Oil production from new fields in the Red Sea and the Western Desert increased in 1970. Other minerals are phosphate rock, salt, iron, manganese, cement, gold, gypsum, kaolin, titanium. In 1972 new oil finds were made in the Western Desert.

A series of decrees in July, 1961, nationalized about 90% of industry and reduced land holdings to 52 acres per family.

Egypt has textile plants, chemical, steel, cement and fertilizer factories, and a film industry supplying the Middle East, Africa and Asia.

Principal exports are cotton, rice, petroleum, textiles, refrigerators, tires, cement, electrical instruments.

History and Government. Archeological records of ancient empires in Egypt go back to 4000 B.C. A high civilization of rulers and priests dominated the lowly serfs. Assyrians, Persians, Greeks (Alexander of Macedon), Romans, Saracens, Turks, French (Napoleon) and British invaded Egypt. Under Turkish sultans the khedive as hereditary viceroy had wide authority but repeated insolvency led to regulation by European powers. Britain, which supervised the administration after 1882, made Egypt a protectorate 1914-1922. Britain then recognized Egypt as a sovereign state but reserved defense, security of British communications, and the Sudan.

The sultan became King Fouad I in 1922 and a constitution was adopted in 1923. King Fouad I died in 1936 and was succeeded by his son, Farouk I. Farouk abdicated in 1952 and left the country. His son was named nominal ruler under a regency council, Aug. 5, 1952, but the crown was abolished when Egypt was declared a republic, June 18, 1953.

In 1936 an Anglo-Egyptian treaty of alliance revised the conditions of association. Britain agreed to a condominium over the Sudan, with British and Egyptian troops cooperating, and obtained the right to retain 10,000 soldiers and 400 airmen to defend the Suez Canal for 20 years until Egypt would take over, and also held naval bases in Alexandria and Port Said.

Egypt became a charter member of the UN and in 1944 led in organizing the Arab League. In 1947 Egypt brought before the UN Security Council a demand for unification of Egypt and Sudan and evacuation of all British troops from the Suez. In Oct. 1951 Egypt abrogated its 1936 treaty with Britain. The Sudan, with UN support, became independent in 1956.

Delays in reforms, corruption in public office and royal extravagance led to an uprising July 23, 1952, led by the Society of Free Officers which named Maj. Gen. Mohammed Naguib commander in chief and forced Farouk to abdicate. Naguib became Premier Sept. 7, 1952. When the republic was proclaimed June 18, 1953, Naguib became its first President and Premier. Lt. Col. Gamal Abdel Nasser, the principal influence behind the revolt, removed Naguib and succeeded him as Premier on Apr. 18, 1954.

On June 23, 1956, voters elected Col. Nasser President. A new constitution, guaranteeing individual rights, was approved by the voters Sept. 11, 1971.

In July, 1956, the United States, Great Britain and the International Bank withdrew support from loans to start the Aswan High Dam. President Nasser nationalized the Suez Canal and seized control of the assets of the Canal company. Later he obtained credits and technicians from the USSR to build the dam.

When the state of Israel was proclaimed in 1948, Egypt joined other Arab nations invading Israel and was defeated. No peace treaties were made and Egypt later denied Israeli shipping the use of the Suez Canal.

Border hostilities with Israel heightened and on Oct. 29, 1956, Israeli forces invaded Egypt's Sinai Peninsula. Egypt rejected a cease-fire demand by Britain and France; on Oct. 31 the two nations dropped bombs and on Nov. 5-6 landed forces. Egypt and Israel accepted a UN cease-fire, followed by Britain and France; fighting ended Nov. 7.

A UN Emergency Force guarded the 117-mile long border between Egypt and Israel until May 19, 1967, when it was withdrawn at Nasser's demand. Egyptian troops took over the Gaza Strip and the heights at Sharm el Sheikh and 3 days later closed the Strait of Tiran leading into the Gulf of Aqaba to all Israeli shipping. Full-scale war broke out June 5 and before it ended under a UN cease-fire 5 days later, Israel had captured Gaza and the Sinai Peninsula, controlled the east bank of the Suez Canal and reopened the gulf.

Sporadic fighting with Israel broke out late in 1968. In 1969-70 there were almost daily artillery duels across the Suez Canal, ground forays and air raids in which Israeli planes penetrated deep into Egypt. Military and economic aid was received from the USSR and it was est. in 1971 there were 19,000 or more Soviet military personnel in Egypt. Israel and Egypt agreed in 1970 to a cease-fire and peace negotiations proposed by the U.S. The cease-fire began Aug. 7; negotiations, pressed by the UN and U.S., failed to achieve results, but the cease-fire continued into 1973.

Pres. Nasser died Sept. 28, 1970. Anwar el-Sadat was elected President Oct. 14 by a 90% vote.

In July 1972 Sadat ordered most of the 20,000 Soviet military advisers and personnel to leave Egypt. They complied, leaving behind bases and equipment they had installed for the Egyptians. In Aug. 1972 Egypt and Libya agreed to prepare plans for unification of the two nations by Sept. 1, 1973. Instead, an Assembly of 50 Egyptians and 50 Libyans met that day to draft a constitution and nominate a President. In Mar. 1973 Sadat proclaimed himself Military Governor General and announced the start of "an era of total confrontation" with Israel.

Education and Religion. Three ethnic elements are represented: the Fellahin, basic Egyptian group; the Bedouin, nomadic Arabs; Nubians, a mixed group. Moslems form 92% of the population and Coptic Christians about 7%.

Education is compulsory for all children beginning at age 7 and free through high school. There is a famous seat of Moslem learning in the University of Al-Azhar in Cairo, founded about 968 A.D. Four modern universities are Cairo, Alexandria, Ein-Shams and Assiut. Arabic is the official language.

Defense. Military forces for 1972-73 totaled 325,000 plus 100,000 National Guard.

Cairo was the original site of the Arab League, formed in 1945 to foster the cause of the Arab nations.

THE SUEZ CANAL

The Suez Canal, 103 mi. long, links the Mediterranean and the Red Sea. It was begun April 25, 1859, by a French corporation under Ferdinand de Lesseps and opened Nov. 17, 1869. Benjamin Disraeli, British prime minister, obtained control for Britain Nov. 24, 1875, by buying 176,752 shares from the Khedive Ismail of Egypt for about $20,000,000. Prolonged agitation led to an agreement July 27, 1954, by which Britain agreed to withdraw all troops (est. 80,000) within 20 mos. after signing pact on Oct. 19, 1954. The 74-year British military occupation ended June 13, 1956. On July 26, Egypt proclaimed nationalization of the canal, seizing it from its French and British stockholders.

Egypt on Apr. 24, 1957, promised to abide by the Constantinople Convention of 1888, and to accept the jurisdiction of the International Court in differences arising from its interpretation. Citing Item 10 of the Convention, it continued to bar Israeli shipping and cargoes destined for Israel. Item 10 provides that freedom of passage "shall not interfere with measures Egypt might find necessary to take to secure the defense of Egypt."

A final agreement between Egypt and the Universal Suez Canal Co., signed July 13, 1958, called for payments to stockholders of $64,400,000. Final payments were made Jan. 1, 1963.

After nationalization, Egypt widened and deepened the canal. In the year before the seizure, the canal handled 14,666 ships, max. draft 35 ft., max. loaded capacity 30,000 tons, gross revenue $75,000,000. For the year ended June 30, 1966, the figures were 20,285 ships, 38 ft., 60,000 tons, $197,000,000.

The canal was closed to all shipping by Cairo at the height of the Israeli-Arab War in June 1967. In 1973 the canal was still closed. Subsidies to replace lost canal revenues were paid the UAR by Saudi Arabia, Kuwait and Libya.

El Salvador

REPUBLICA DE EL SALVADOR

Capital: San Salvador. Area: 8,260 sq. mi. Population (UN est 1972): 3,760,000. Monetary unit: Colon.

El Salvador, smallest of the 6 Central American or Middle American republics and the only one without an Atlantic seacoast, is bounded by Guatemala, Honduras and a Pacific coastline of about 160 mi. A country of mountains, including many volcanoes, and upland plains, it is entirely within the tropics, but tropic heat is modified by the elevation. It is about the size of Massachusetts.

The three racial types are white, 5%; mixed white and Indian descent, 85%; Indian, 10%.

Resources and Industries. Mountain slope plantations make El Salvador the world's 4th largest producer and a large exporter of coffee. Cotton production has made large strides; coffee represents 44% of the value of exports, cotton 8%. Primarily agricultural, the country is becoming industrialized; it produces cement, refined sugar and textiles.

Economic development has been helped by U.S. aid and membership in the Central American Common Market.

History and Government. El Salvador became independent of Spain in 1821; member of the Central American Federation until 1839. The constitution provides for a unicameral legislative system, the National Assembly of Deputies, elected by popular vote. Voting is compulsory for all over 18 years of age. Executive power is vested in the President who is elected for a 5-year term by direct, popular vote and is ineligible for immediate reelection.

In July 1969, a dispute over the presence of 300,000 Salvadorean workers and settlers in Honduras broke into open warfare between the two nations. After 5 days, the OAS arranged a truce. In 1970, after new clashes, a demilitarized zone was agreed on.

Education and Religion. Education is free but illiteracy rate is 50%. The language is Spanish. The dominant religion is Roman Catholicism.

Defense. Military forces number about 5,500. El Salvador is a member of the UN and OAS.

Equatorial Guinea

Capital: Santa Isabel. Area: 10,852 sq. mi. Population (Est. 1972): 300,000. Monetary unit: Peseta.

The Republic of Equatorial Guinea, which received its independence from Spain on Oct. 12, 1968, consists of the Province of Fernando Po, including Fernando Po Is. in the Gulf of Guinea off the west coast of Africa and Annobon Is., 370 mi. southwest, and the Province of Rio Muni, on the mainland facing the gulf. Santa Isabel, the capital, is on Fernando Po Is. which has an area of 780 sq. mi. and population (est. 1972) of 90,000.

Self-government and independence were achieved in steps, with local elections in 1960 and increased autonomy in 1964. The 1968 independence constitution provided for a President, a 35-member Assembly and two Provincial Councils, all elected by universal adult suffrage, and an advisory Council of the Republic chosen by the President. Francisco Macias Nguema was elected the first President. In 1971 he assumed complete control of the Government and in 1972 was named President for Life.

Important exports are cocoa and timber for plywood. Other exports are coffee, bananas and palm oil.

More than half the population is Roman Catholic. Spanish is the official language; numerous African languages are also spoken. Fernando Po natives were mostly Bubis; by the late 1960s Nigerian workers and settlers numbered almost half the island population. In Rio Muni, the Fangs were the largest group. Before a 1969 confrontation, there were about 7,000 Europeans, mostly Spanish, but many left during the dispute.

Equatorial Guinea is a member of the UN and OAU.

Ethiopia

YE ITIOPIA NEGUSE NEGUEST MENGUIST
(Abyssinia)

Capital: Addis Ababa. Area: 457,256 sq. mi. Population (Est. 1972): 25,930,000. Monetary unit: Ethiopian dollar.

Ethiopia is a ruggedly mountainous, independent empire in NE Africa. It faces on the Red Sea, but its main rivers are important tributaries of the Nile; the Abbai or Blue Nile, one of the two main branches of that mighty river, has its source in Ethiopia's Lake Tana. The country is as large as Texas, Oklahoma and New Mexico combined.

Resources and Industries. Economy is some 70% agricultural but industrial resources are potentially great, including vast hydroelectric power, surveys of which are under way with aid of the World Bank. Industries include food processing, cement, shoes, textiles.

Fertile soil and abundant rainfall produce two crops annually. Coffee, wheat, barley, millet, tobacco, and sugar are principal crops. Coffee of extremely high quality from Kaffa, in SW Ethiopia, reputed birthplace of the coffee plant, accounts for half of the country's foreign exchange. Over 100,000 tons are exported annually.

An unfavorable balance of trade continued in 1972. Value of exports rose to $168,000,000; imports totaled $189,000,000.

Cattle, sheep, mules and goats are raised. Hides and skins, oilseeds and vegetables also are exported. Mineral resources include platinum, gold, silver, manganese, tin, copper, asbestos, potash, sulphur, mica, cement and salt. There are known deposits of coal and iron; tests are in progress for petroleum.

Ethiopia has used large credits from the World Bank and other agencies for road building (it now has 4,000 mi. of all-weather roads). Aid and investment funds are received from the U. S. and other western nations and from Communist countries. Ethiopia is a member of the UN and Addis Ababa is hq. for the Organization of African Unity.

History and Government. Ethiopia is a constitutional monarchy derived from a number of earlier kingdoms, descendants of ancient Hamite and Semite tribes. Italy invaded the country in 1880 and acquired a sphere of influence and later organized its colony of Eritrea. In 1936 Italy invaded Ethiopia without declaring war. Emperor Haile Selassie fought until forced to withdraw. The League of Nations applied sanctions against Italy, which proved ineffective. Mussolini added Ethiopia to Italy. British forces freed Ethiopia in 1941.

The present Emperor, Haile Selassie I, 225th consecutive Solomonic ruler, was born July 23, 1892, crowned Nov. 2, 1930. He voluntarily established a parliament and judiciary system, 1931, and promulgated a new constitution 1955, incorporating a liberal bill of rights, and granting the franchise to all over 21. The Senate (Upper House) of 125 is appointed for 6-year terms; Chamber of Deputies, approx. 250, is elected for 4 years. In April 1966, the Emperor made further moves toward democracy, including empowering the Premier to appoint his own Cabinet.

At the 1973 meeting of the OAU a committee was set up to mediate a long-standing border dispute between Ethiopia and Somalia.

Education and Religion. Ethiopian culture has been influenced by Greece and Egypt. Christianity is the predominant religion, embraced in 330 A.D.; the Coptic, Monophysite branch is practiced. Until 1952 the Egyptian Coptic Patriarch was the head of the Church, but the Emperor now appoints the Ethiopian Archbishop. The population is largely composed of a mixture of Hamites, Semites and Negroes. The largest number are Coptic Christians; next are Moslems; others practice tribal religions.

There are two universities and a number of colleges. The official language is Amharic; English is widely taught.

Eritrea, which had been an Italian colony since 1890, was administered after World War II by Great Britain; the UN General Assembly voted to return it to Ethiopia and the action became effective Sept. 11, 1952. In 1970-72 secessionist guerrillas were active in Eritrea.

Fiji

Capital: Suva. Area: 7,055 sq. mi. Population (UN est. 1972): 540,000. Monetary unit: Fiji dollar.

The Fiji Islands lie in the South Pacific, E of Australia and N of New Zealand. There are about 840 islands (106 inhabited), many of them mountainous, with tropical forests and large fertile areas. The capital, Suva, is on Viti Levu, the largest island. (4,011 sq. mi.).

Descendants of the native Fijians (Melanesians and Polynesians) form about 43% of the population but have been protected by law in ownership of 83% of the land. Descendants of Indian contract laborers, brought to the islands in the late 19th Century, make up slightly over 51%. Most of the others are of Chinese or European descent. English is the official language. Most of the Fijians are Christians; the Indians are about 80% Hindu, 15% Moslem. Literacy is about 85%.

A British colony since 1874, Fiji received gradual measures of self-government in the 1960s. On Oct. 10, 1970, Fiji became a fully independent parliamentary democracy, with a Senate, a House of Representatives, a Prime Minister and, as a member of the Commonwealth, a Governor-General representing the British Queen. It is a member of the UN.

Sugar is a main export, along with coconut products, bananas and gold. Tourism is an important industry. A cement factory, shipyards and small manufacturing plants have been built.

Finland

SUOMEN TASAVALTA-REPUBLIKEN FINLAND

Capital: Helsinki. Area: 130,119 sq. mi. Population (UN est. 1972): 4,630,000. Monetary unit: Markka.

Finland is a republic in northern Europe, with Sweden, Norway and the USSR for neighbors. South and central Finland are mostly flat areas with low hills; there are mountainous areas, 3,000-4,000 ft., in the N. It is half the size of Texas.

About 70% of the land is forested. Lakes and canal waterways are navigable for 3,000 mi. Rail and air transport is well developed.

Aland Islands, constituting the autonomous department of Aland, is a group of small islands, 572 sq. mi., in the Gulf of Bothnia, 25 mi. from Sweden, 15 mi. from Finland. They are demilitarized. Mariehamn is the principal port.

Resources and Industries. Rapid industrialization has taken place, especially since World War II, but agriculture is still a vital factor. Principal crops are oats, barley, wheat, rye, potatoes, hay. Woodworking and paper and pulp products account for about 50% of total exports. Expansion is expected to increase pulp production to 5,430,000 metric tons annually. Other chief industries are shipbuilding, metals, machinery, food and beverages, textiles, leather, chemicals.

In 1972, 2,000,000 tourists visited Finland.

The cooperative system is carried on in Finland with marked success.

Foreign trade (in thousands of U.S. dollars):

	Imports	Exports
1971	$2,795,000	$2,357,000
1972	$3,198,000	$2,947,000

History and Government. The original Finns lived thousands of years ago, probably in the Ural area, and migrated in a northerly direction, first to the Baltic area and then, at about the beginning of the Christian era, to what is today Finland. Swedish settlers brought the country into the kingdom of Sweden, 1154 to 1809, when Finland became an autonomous grand duchy of the Russian Empire. Russian exactions created a strong national spirit; on Dec. 6, 1917, Finland declared its independence and on July 17, 1919, became a republic. On Nov. 30, 1939, the Soviet Union invaded Finland, and although the Finns took heavy toll, in March, 1940, were forced to cede 16,173 sq. mi., including the Karelian isthmus, Viipuri, and an area on Lake Ladoga. When Germany attacked the USSR June 22, 1941, Finland again was involved. An armistice was signed Sept. 19, 1944, and the USSR exacted the former cessions, plus Petsamo in the North and a lease for 50 years on Porkkala, near Helsinki, for a military base. The treaty of Feb. 10, 1947, also exacted $300,000,000 in goods in term payments. In April, 1948, Finland signed a treaty of mutual assistance and friendship with the USSR; in Jan. 1956 Russia returned Porkkala.

The President is chosen for a term of six years by an Electoral College of 300 named by direct vote: he appoints the Cabinet.

There is a single legislative chamber, the Eduskunta, numbering 200, elected to 4-year terms. The voting system is designed for proportional representation.

The Prime Minister and Cabinet normally represent a coalition of parties in the Eduskunta.

Education and Religion. The Evangelical Lutheran Church is the leading religion, and both Finnish and Swedish are official languages. The nation is considered completely free from illiteracy. There are 6 major universities (the oldest founded 1640) and six colleges of university level.

Defense. Military strength for 1972-73 was 39,500, including 34,000 in the Army, 3,000 in the Air Force and 2,500 in the Navy.

Finland is a member of the UN, Nordic Council and EFTA.

France

LA REPUBLIQUE FRANCAISE

Capital: Paris. Area: 212,918 sq. mi. Population (Govt. est. 1973): 51,915,000. Monetary unit: Franc.

France has coastlines on the Atlantic and Mediterranean and is about four-fifths the size of Texas. It shares borders with Belgium, Luxembourg, Germany, Switzerland, Italy, Andorra and Spain. It is separated from England by the English Channel and the Strait of Dover. The Rhine River is on the German boundary, the Jura Mts. form the Swiss boundary and the Pyrenees Mts. rise along the borders of Andorra and Spain.

Mont Blanc, on the Franco-Italian border, is the tallest mtn. W of the Caucasus, 15,771 ft. A highway tunnel, 7.25 mi. under Mont Blanc, was opened July 16, 1965, linking France and Italy.

The island of Corsica which lies in the Mediterranean W of Italy and N of Sardinia, forms an integral part of France. It has an area of 3,369 sq. mi. and a population of 269,831 (1968 Census). The capital is Ajaccio, birthplace of Napoleon.

There are four important rivers, the Seine, the Loire, the Garonne and the Rhone. There are some 5,005 mi. of navigable rivers and canals.

Resources and Industries. Agriculturally, France is a country of small diversified farms involving 45,800,000 acres and 15% of the employed, making France the biggest food producer in Western Europe. Agricultural exports are valued at more than $1.7 billion annually. Leading crops are wheat, barley, corn, oats, rice, and a wide variety of fruits and vegetables. Cattle, poultry, forestry and fishing are large-scale. France is the world's 8th ranking producer of beef. Approx. 1,500,000 farmers belong to cooperative unions, including farm machinery and marketing cooperatives.

The country is rich in minerals, and the basins of Pas de Calais and Lorraine are noted for their huge coal deposits, iron ore, bauxite, pyrites, mineral oils, auriferous ore, asphalt, rock salt and potash salts. The iron ore deposits in eastern France and the bauxite deposits in central France are among the richest in the world. Power stations produced about 149 billion kwh in 1972, up 10%.

Some of the basic principles of atomic energy were discovered by French scientists. France is the foremost uranium producer in Western Europe. Beginning in 1960, France exploded 5 atomic devices in the Sahara. On July 2, 1966, France exploded a small A-bomb over Mururoa, a tiny atoll 750 mi. SE of Tahiti; it was the 1st in a series of nuclear tests in succeeding years at Mururoa (France was not a signatory to the 1963 treaty banning such tests). In 1973, at the request of Australia and New Zealand, the International Court of Justice asked France to suspend the tests. France refused and exploded a nuclear device July 21 despite the presence of a New Zealand Navy protest frigate just outside the 12-mi. limit but within the test area.

Manufacturing includes chemicals, silk and cotton textiles, perfumes, automobiles, aircraft, ships, instruments, plastics, electronic equipment. Index of industrial production (1963=100) was 173 in 1972. Exports and industrial output showed large gains in 1972-73.

France leads the world in wine-making, producing almost 2 billion gallons a year. Names of French provinces and regions, such as Bordeaux, Champagne, Burgundy, identify wines highly esteemed.

Foreign trade in thousands of U.S. dollars

	Imports	Exports
1971	$21,137,000	$20,420,000
1972	$26,754,000	$26,052,000

History and Government. The monarchial system was

overthrown by the French Revolution (1789-1793) and succeeded by the First Republic; thereafter successively followed by the First Empire under Napoleon (1804-1814), a monarchy (1814-1848), the Second Republic (1848-1852), the Second Empire (1852-1870), the Third Republic (1871-1946), the Fourth Republic (1946-1958), Fifth Republic and French Community (1958).

France suffered severe losses in manpower and wealth in the first World War, 1914-1918, when it was invaded by the German Empire. With Britain and the U. S. as its principal allies it threw back the Germans and by the Treaty of Versailles exacted return of Alsace and Lorraine, French provinces seized by Germany in 1871. As Allied controls on Germany were reduced Adolf Hitler and the Nazi party gained power. Germany invaded France in May, 1940, occupied Paris June 14, 1940, and signed an armistice with a government that made its hq. in Vichy. Marshal Philippe Petain became chief of state, but underground forces (Resistance) operated as guerrillas while Gen. Charles de Gaulle formed an army in Africa. After France was liberated by the Allies Sept., 1944, Gen De Gaulle became Premier of the provisional government, serving from Nov. 1944 to Jan. 1946.

Gen. De Gaulle again became Premier June 1, 1958. His proposed constitution for the Fifth Republic and new French Community was approved by the voters by an overwhelming margin, Sept. 28, 1958.

Gen. De Gaulle was elected first President of the Fifth Republic Dec. 21, 1958; inaugurated Jan. 8, 1959.

Pres. De Gaulle ran for reelection Dec. 5, 1965; he failed to win a majority of the votes, getting about 44% compared to 32% for Francois Mitterand, left wing candidate. In a runoff election Dec. 19, Pres. De Gaulle won with about 55%.

The constitution provides for a strong executive branch headed by the President, a legislature composed of a National Assembly and a Senate.

A constitutional amendment adopted by referendum Oct. 28, 1962, provided that future Presidents be elected by popular vote rather than by an electoral college. The President, elected for 7 years, appoints the Premier (formerly invested by the Assembly), and may dissolve the Assembly and call for new elections; he may call for referendums on specific issues and may assume full powers in a national emergency.

Women, who had less than equal rights under provisions of the 1804 Code Napoleon, won the right to take jobs, open checking accounts and own their own businesses by a 1966 law.

In May 1968 rebellious students at the Sorbonne and elsewhere rioted, battled police and were joined by some 10,000,000 workers who launched nationwide strikes and took over many factories. The nation was almost completely paralyzed. The government awarded pay increases to the strikers May 26; on May 30 Pres. De Gaulle dissolved the Assembly. A threat of civil war was eased as Army tank units, loyal to the government, maneuvered in Paris outskirts. By early June, normalcy was returned.

In elections to the Assembly in late June 1968, Pres. De Gaulle's backers won a landslide victory.

In Nov. 1968 Pres. De Gaulle weathered an economic storm, refusing to devalue the franc. But on Apr. 28, 1969, he resigned from office after losing a nationwide referendum on his proposals for constitutional reform. He had asked approval as a personal vote of confidence but over 52% of the votes were against his proposals. Alain Poher, Senate President, became interim President.

A nationwide election for a successor, June 1, resulted in a runoff election June 15 in which the winner was Georges Pompidou, who had been Pres. De Gaulle's Premier from 1962 until July 1968. In the runoff, he took over 57% of the vote, defeating Poher. In 1973 elections the Gaullist coalition won 262 of the 473 seats in the National Assembly.

Education and Religion. Primary, secondary and higher edication are free and instruction is compulsory between the ages of 6 and 16.

The country is predominantly Roman Catholic, only about 800,000 being Protestants. The state recognizes no religion and tolerates all.

Both employers and employees contribute to the old-age pension fund. There is provision for family allowances and compulsory social insurance for illness, maternity, disability and death. A profit-sharing agreement was signed Jan. 7, 1959.

Defense. Compulsory military training has existed since 1798. Military strength for 1972-73 was 500,600. Of these, 328,000 were in the Army, 105,000 in the Air Force, 67,600 in the Navy. The Gendarmerie and security forces totaled 75,000.

France is a member of the U N, SEATO and EEC but announced in 1973 it would stop paying dues to SEATO after 1974.

Pres. De Gaulle announced Mar. 9, 1966, France would withdraw all its troops from the integrated military command of NATO and that NATO hq. and bases would have to be removed from France. But France maintained its membership in the political meetings of NATO.

AFARS & ISSAS TERRITORY
(Formerly French Somaliland)

The French Territory of the Afars and the Issas lies between Ethiopia and Somalia and is separated by the Straits of Bab-el-Mandeb from Yemen.

The area is 8,800 sq. mi. and population (est. 1973), 125,000; the capital is Djibouti. France took control of the area in gradual steps, beginning in 1862.

The Territory has few industries, except fishing and livestock. Salt is its most valuable product. Half of Ethiopia's foreign commerce passes along the rail line from Addis Ababa and through the port of Djibouti.

In a referendum Mar. 19, 1967, the Territory elected to remain French and by a decree signed by the High Commissioner French Somaliland changed its name to the French Territory of the Afars and the Issas. It sends a Deputy and a Senator to the French Parliament.

COMORO ISLANDS

Comoro Islands, an Overseas Territory, is an archipelago of small islands off SE Africa in Mozambique Channel NW of Madagascar. Chief islands are Grande Comore, Anjouan, Mayotte, Moheli. Total area, about 838 sq. mi.; population (est. 1970), 270,000. Capital: Moroni. Chief products are vanilla, coconuts and essential oils. It elects two Deputies, one Senator to the French Parliament.

REUNION

Reunion, Overseas Department is an island in the Indian Ocean, about 420 miles east of Madagascar, and has belonged to France since 1665. The area is 969 sq. mi.; the population (est. 1972) 470,000, is 30% of French extraction. Capital: Saint-Denis. The chief products are sugar, rum, corn, perfume essences, vanilla and spices. It elects 3 Deputies, two Senators to the French Parliament.

GUADELOUPE

Guadeloupe, Overseas Department in the West Indies' Leeward Islands, consists of two large islands, Basse-Terre and Grande-Terre, separated by the Salt River, plus Marie Galante and the Saintes group to the S and, to the N. Desirade, St. Barthelemy, and over half of St. Martin (the Netherlands portion is St. Maarten). A French possession since 1635, the department is represented in the French Parliament by two Senators and 3 Deputies; administration consists of a Prefect (Governor) and an elected General Council.

Area of the islands is 687 sq. mi.; population (est. 1972) 340,000, mainly descendants of slaves; capital is Basse-Terre on Basse-Terre Is. The land is fertile; sugar, rum and bananas are exported; tourism is an important industry.

MARTINIQUE

Martinique, one of the Windward Islands, in the West Indies, has been a possession since 1635, and a Department since March, 1946. It is represented in the French Parliament by two Senators and three Deputies. In Martinique is located the famous volcano, Mt. Pelee which erupted on May 8, 1902, destroyed the city of St. Pierre with more than 30,000 inhabitants. The island is the birthplace of the Empress Josephine.

Martinique has an area of 425 sq. mi. and population (est. 1972) 340,000 mostly descendants of slaves: The capital is Fort-de-France. It is a popular tourist stop.

The chief exports are sugar, rum, bananas, pineapples and cocoa. Trade is mainly with France and the United States.

ST. PIERRE AND MIQUELON

St. Pierre and Miquelon, an Overseas Territory, are two groups of rocky barren islands close to the south-western coast of Newfoundland, inhabited by fishermen. A Governor, assisted by a Council, rules the islands. The exports are chiefly cod, dried and fresh, and other fish products.

The St. Pierre group has an area of 10 sq. mi.; Miquelon, 83 sq. mi. Total population (est. 1967), 5,225. The capital is St. Pierre. A Deputy and a Senator are elected to the French Parliament.

FRENCH GUIANA

French Guiana, an Overseas Department, is on the NE coast of South America with Surinam (Netherlands Guiana) on the W and Brazil on the E and S. Its area is 37,740 sq. mi.; population (est. 1972), 60,000. Guiana sends one Senator and one Deputy to the French Parliament. Guiana has a Prefect and a Council-General of 15 elected members; capital is Cayenne.

In 1944 France closed the famous penal colony, Devil's Island, and repatriated 2,800 inmates.

Immense forests of rich timber cover 90% of the land. Very little of the land is cultivated. The principal crops are rice, corn, manioc, cacao, bananas, and sugar cane. Placer gold mining is the most important industry. Exports comprise cocoa, bananas, various woods, gold, fish glue, rum, rosewood essence, shrimp and hides.

FRENCH POLYNESIA

French Polynesia, Overseas Territory, comprises 130 islands widely scattered among 5 archipelagos in the South Pacific; administered by a Governor, Territorial Assembly and a Council with headquarters at Papeete, **Tahiti,** one of the **Society Islands.** A Deputy and a Senator are elected to the French Parliament.

Other groups are the **Marquesas Islands,** the **Tuamotu Archipelago,** the **Gambier Islands,** and the **Austral Islands.**

Total area of the islands administered from Tahiti is 1,544 sq. mi.; pop. (est. 1972), 130,000, more than half on Tahiti. Tahiti is picturesque and mountainous with a productive coastline bearing coconut, bananas and orange trees, sugar cane and vanilla.

Tahiti was visited by Capt. James Cook in 1769 and by Capt. Bligh in the Bounty, 1788-89. The beauty of its women and the landscape impressed Herman Melville, Paul Gauguin, Charles Darwin and Robert Louis Stevenson who called Tahitians "God's sweetest works."

NEW CALEDONIA

New Caledonia and its dependencies, an Overseas Territory, are a group of islands in the Pacific Ocean about 1,115 mi. E of Australia and approx. the same distance NW of New Zealand. Dependencies are the **Loyalty Islands,** the **Isle of Pines, Huon Islands,** and the **Chesterfield Islands.**

New Caledonia, the largest, has 6,530 sq. mi. Total area of the Territory is 7,374 sq. mi.; population (est. 1972) 110,000. The group was acquired by France in 1853.

The territory is administered by a Governor and government council. There is a popularly elected Territorial Assembly. A Deputy and a Senator are elected to the French Parliament. Capital: Noumea.

Mining is the chief industry. New Caledonia has large deposits of nickel. Other minerals found are chrome, cobalt, manganese, antimony, mercury, cinnebar, silver, gold, lead and copper. Agricultural products include coffee, copra, cotton, manioc (cassava), corn, tobacco, bananas and pineapples.

WALLIS AND FUTUNA ISLANDS

Wallis and Futuna Islands, two archipelagos raised to status of Overseas Territory July 29, 1961, are situated in the SW Pacific south of the Equator between Fiji and Samoa. The islands have a total area of 106 sq. mi. and

population (est. 1969) of 9,900. **Alofi,** attached to Futuna, is uninhabited. Capital: Mata-Utu. Chief products are copra, yams, taro roots, bananas. A Senator and a Deputy are elected to the French Parliament.

FRENCH ANTARCTICA

French Southern and Antarctic Lands, Overseas Territory, comprises **Adelie Land,** on Antarctica, and 4 island groups in the Indian Ocean. Adelie, discov. 1840, has 2 research bases, a coastline of 185 mi. and tapers 1,240 mi. inland to the South Pole. Heights rise to 8,200 ft. There are two huge glaciers, Ninnis, 22 mi. wide, 99 mi. long, and Mentz, 11 mi. wide, 140 mi. long. Climate varies from − 36° F. to 40° F.

Kerguelen Archipelago, discov. 1772, has 300 islands. The chief is 87 mi. long, 74 mi. wide, and has Mt. Ross, 6,429 ft. tall. Principal research station is Port-aux-Francais. Seals often weigh 2 tons; there are blue whales, coal, peat, semi-precious stones. **Crozet Archipelago** (discov. 1772), covers 195 sq. mi. Eastern Island rises to 6,560 ft. **Saint Paul,** in southern Indian Ocean, has warm springs and tropical climate, with earth at places heating to 120° to 390° F. **New Amsterdam,** nearby, has temperate climate, produces cod and rock lobster.

NEW HEBRIDES

New Hebrides, a condominium administered since 1906 by France and Great Britain, is a group of 11 main islands and about 69 islets 250 mi. northeast of New Caledonia and 500 mi. west of Fiji. It has an est. 5,790 sq. mi. and population (est. 1972) of 90,000, mostly Melanesian. It has two administrations—French and British. Chief products are copra, frozen fish, cocoa and coffee.

Gabon Republic

LA REPUBLIQUE GABONAISE

Capital: Libreville. Area: 102,089 sq. mi. Population (est. 1972): 500,000. Monetary unit: CFA franc.

A former French Overseas Territory, Gabon is on the west coast of Equatorial Africa, straddling the Equator and bounded by Cameroon, Equatorial Guinea, People's Republic of Congo and the Atlantic. Heavily forested, the country consists of coastal lowlands, plateaus in N, E and S, mountains in N, SE and center. It is about the size of Colorado.

Gabon's economy is thriving, with exports far exceeding imports in value. Valuable timber, plywood and veneers were the main export until the late 1960s when manganese, crude oil and uranium topped them in value. There are also large iron ore deposits.

Agriculture, roads, port facilities and hydroelectric power are being extensively developed. Main crops are cocoa, coffee, rice, peanuts, palm products, cassava, bananas. A new port, Owembo, and a railroad leading to iron mines in the NE were to be completed in 1974.

Gabon proclaimed independence Aug. 17, 1960; it became a UN member Sept. 20. It is a republic, with an elected President and unicameral National Assembly. The first President, Leon M'ba, died in 1967; he was succeeded Dec. 1 by Vice President Albert Bongo who declared a one-party state.

Dr. Albert Schweitzer, Nobel Peace Prize winner, physician, philosopher, musicologist and theologian, founded a hospital for lepers and others in 1913 at Lambarene. He died Sept. 4, 1965, at the age of 90 and was buried at the hospital.

The Gambia

Capital: Banjul. Area: 4,005 sq. mi. Population (Govt. est. 1972): 380,000. Monetary unit: Dalasi.

Gambia, Africa's smallest country in area, is a former British Colony and Protectorate in western Africa. It includes the island of Banjul at the mouth of the Gambia River and a 10-mile wide strip of territory on each side of the river. Except for its Atlantic coastline, Gambia is surrounded by Senegal.

Gambia attained internal self-government Oct. 4, 1963. Its legislature comprises a speaker and 32 elected members. Britain granted complete independence to the colony Feb. 18, 1965.

In April 1970, after a referendum, Gambia became a republic within the Commonwealth. Former Prime Minister Dawda K. Jawara became the first President.

Peanuts are the main export. Rice and other foods are also grown. Tourism has become important. Britain provides development aid.

English is the official language. Islam and animism are the main religions.

Germany

Area: 137,632 sq. mi. Population (UN est. 1972): 78,720,000. Now comprises two nations: Federal Republic of Germany (West Germany), German Democratic Republic (East Germany).

Germany is a central European nation composed of numerous states which had a common language and traditions but which did not become unified in one country until 1871; since World War II it has been split in two parts, West and East (see below).

The climate and terrain are varied. West Germany includes large parts of the Rhine basin, with hilly sections adjoining both banks of the Rhine river filling center of the country. North of Bonn are the plains of the lower Rhine and lowlands of Cologne. East Germany is composed largely of the region of the Elbe river and its tributaries and part of the Oder basin. Most of the territory is level, except for the hilly Erzgebirge and Riesengebirge. Its climate is cooler than that of West Germany with long, cold winters and short summers.

Resources and Industries. Some of more important crops are wheat, rye, barley, oats, potatoes, sugar beets and hay. Other commercial products are fruit, tobacco, hops, nuts.

Principal minerals are coal, lignite, iron, zinc, lead, copper, salt, potash and petroleum. Bulk of mining is in North Rhine-Westphalia, Central Germany, the Harz, and Westerwald. Oil comes chiefly from Emsland near Netherlands border, and Lower Saxony. Iron and steel production is greatest in the Ruhr and Saar.

History and Government. Germanic tribes were defeated by Julius Caesar, 55 and 53 B. C. but Roman expansion north of the Rhine was stopped with the wiping out of 3 legions under Varus in 9 A.D. Charlemagne, ruler of the Franks, consolidated Saxon, Bavarian, Rhenish, Frankish and other lands; after him the eastern part became the German Empire. The Thirty Years' War, 1618-1648, split Germany into small principalities and kingdoms. After Napoleon, Austria contended with Prussia for dominance, but lost the Seven Weeks' War to Prussia, 1866. Otto von Bismarck, Prussian chancellor, formed the North German Confederation, 1867.

In 1870 Bismarck maneuvered Napoleon III into declaring war. After the quick defeat of France Bismarck formed the **German Empire (Deutsches Reich)** and on Jan. 18, 1871, in Versailles, proclaimed King Wilhelm I of Prussia German Emperor (Deutscher Kaiser).

The German Empire reached its peak before World War I in 1914. At that time the homeland comprised 208,780 sq. mi., plus a colonial empire. After that war Germany ceded Alsace-Lorraine to France; Eupen and Malmedy to Belgium; parts of Silesia to Poland and Czechoslovakia; part of Schleswig to Denmark; lost all of its colonies as well as the ports of Memel and Danzig.

Republic of Germany, 1919-1933, adopted the Weimar constitution, met reparation payments and elected Friedrich Ebert and Gen. Paul von Hindenburg presidents.

Third Reich, 1933-1945. Adolf Hitler, born in Braunau, Austria, 1889, led the National Socialist German Workers' (Nazi) party after World War I. In 1923 with the help of Gen. Erich Ludendorff he attempted to unseat the Bavarian government in the "Beer Hall putsch," and was imprisoned. He wrote Mein Kampf while in prison. President von Hindenburg named Hitler chancellor Jan. 30,

1933; on Aug. 3, 1934, the day after Hindenburg's death, the cabinet joined the offices of President and Chancellor and made Hitler Fuehrer (Leader). Hitler abolished freedom of speech and assembly, and began a long series of persecutions climaxed by the mass extermination of Jews and opponents.

Hitler repudiated the Versailles treaty and reparations agreements. He remilitarized the Rhineland 1936 and annexed Austria (Anschluss, 1938). At Munich he made an agreement with Neville Chamberlain, British Prime Minister, enabling him to annex Czechoslovakia's Sudetenland. He signed a non-aggression treaty with the Soviet Union, 1939. He declared war on Poland Sept. 1, 1939, precipitating World War II.

With total defeat near, Hitler committed suicide in Berlin Apr. 30, 1945. The victorious Allies voided all acts and annexations of Hitler's Reich.

Postwar changes—The zones of occupation administered by the Allied Powers and later relinquished gave the Soviet Union Saxony, Saxony-Anhalt, Thuringia, and Mecklenburg, and the former Prussian provinces of Saxony and Brandenburg. The United States administered territory bounded on the East by the Russian zone and Czechoslovakia, on the North by the British zone, on the West by the French zone, and on the South by Austria, including Bavaria (except Lindau district), Wurttemberg (northern), Baden (northern), most of Hesse and Hesse-Nassau, and the city state of Bremen.

The territory east of the Oder-Neisse line within 1937 boundaries comprising the provinces of Silesia, Pomerania, West Prussia and the southern part of East Prussia, totaling about 41,220 square miles, population (1939) 9,600,000, is under Polish administration; northern East Prussia is under Soviet domination. The United States has not recognized these changes nor the East German regime.

The Western Allies ended the state of war with Germany in 1951. The USSR did so in 1955.

There was also created the area of Greater Berlin, within but not part of the Soviet zone, administered by the four occupying powers under the Allied Command. In 1948 the Soviet Union withdrew and established its single command in East Berlin. The Communists cut off supplies, whereupon the Allies utilized a gigantic airlift to bring food to West Berlin during 1948-1949. In Aug. 1961 the East Germans built a wall dividing Berlin.

West Germany

BUNDESREPUBLIK DEUTSCHLAND

Capital: Bonn. Area (including West Berlin): 95,633 sq. mi. Population (UN est. 1972): 61,670,000. Monetary unit: Deutsche Mark.

The Federal Republic of Germany was proclaimed May 23, 1949, in Bonn, after a constitution had been drawn up by a consultative assembly formed by representatives of the 11 Laender (states) in the French, British and American zones. Later reorganized into 9 units, the Laender number 10 with the addition of the Saar Jan. 1, 1957; Schleswig-Holstein, Hamburg, Lower Saxony, Bremen, North Rhine-Westphalia, Hesse, Rhineland-Palatinate, Baden-Wuerttemberg, Bavaria, Saarland. Berlin also was granted Land (state) status, but the 1945 occupation agreements placed restrictions on it.

The occupying powers, the United States, Britain and France, restored the civil status, Sept. 21, 1949. The U. S. resumed diplomatic relations July 2, 1951. The powers lifted controls and the republic became fully independent May 5, 1955.

Parliament has two chambers, serving 4-yr. terms. The Bundestag, lower house, is elected. It has 496 voting members from the republic and 22 nonvoting observers from West Berlin. The Bundesrat, upper house, represents the states; it has 41 delegates from the Laender and 4 non-voting members from West Berlin. The Bundesrat President serves one year and acts as deputy to the federal President.

The Federal President is elected for a 5-yr. term by the Federal Assembly, convened for this purpose only and made up of deputies of the Bundestag and an equal number of delegates from the Land parliaments. Re-election is possible only once. The President concludes treaties with foreign states, and signs laws, which must be countersigned by the Chancellor and the minister in charge. On proposal of the President the Chancellor is elected by majority vote of the Bundestag. Ministers are named by the President at the instance of the Chancellor.

Theodor Heuss, Free Democrat, was chosen first President Sept. 12, 1949, re-elected July 17, 1954. Succeeded by Heinrich Luebke, elected July 1, 1959, reelected July 1, 1964, and by Dr. Gustav Heinemann, elected Mar. 5, 1969.

Dr. Konrad Adenauer, Christian Democrat, was made Chancellor Sept. 15, 1949, reelected 1953, 1957, 1961. Dr. Ludwig Erhard, Christian Democrat, was elected 1963, 1965. Kurt Georg Kiesinger was elected Chancellor Dec. 1, 1966, heading a coalition government of Christian Democrats and Social Democrats.

Willy Brandt, heading a coalition of Social Democrats and Free Democrats, became Chancellor Oct. 21, 1969.

In 1970 Brandt signed friendship treaties with the USSR and Poland. In 1971, the U.S., Britain, France and the USSR signed an agreement on Western access to West Berlin. In 1972 the Bundestag approved the USSR and Polish treaties and East and West Germany signed their first formal treaty, implementing the agreement easing access to West Berlin. In 1973 a West Germany—Czechoslovakia pact nullified the 1938 "Munich Agreement".

West Germany is a member of NATO, EEC, European Coal and Steel Community and Council of Europe. Both West and East Germany gained full membership in the UN in Sept. 1973.

Resources and Industries. West Germany has experienced tremendous economic growth since 1950. It is one of the world's top industrial nations. The index of industrial production (1963=100) was 162 for 1972.

West Germany leads Western Europe as a steel producer. Shipyards annually produce more than 1,000,000 gross registered tons of shipping, more than half of it for export. The oil industry has a refining capacity of more than 133,000,000 tons annually.

Germany lost most of its merchant marine during World War II. However, the merchant fleet recovered rapidly and on Jan. 1, 1973, comprised 797 vessels over 1,000 gross tons each.

Frankfurt Rhine-Main airport, 3rd largest in Europe, handles annually about 5,000,000 passengers and is 2nd largest in freight shipments.

Foreign trade (in thousands of U.S. dollars):

	Imports	Exports
1971	$34,341,000	$39,034,000
1972	$39,776,000	$46,202,000

Education and Religion. The Federal Republic and West Berlin have 31 universities, 9 technical universities and over 100 musical, theological and other institutions of higher education. School attendance is compulsory, ages 6 to 15.

Complete religious freedom is guaranteed by the constitution. The country is 49% Protestant, 44.6% Roman Catholic. The Evangelical Church in Germany (EKD) was formed by the Lutheran, United and Reformed churches after World War II, supplanting an earlier group.

Defense. Strength of the German armed forces (Bundeswehr) for 1972-73 was 467,000, including 327,000 Army, 104,000 Air Force, 36,000 Navy. There are 650,000 reservists.

The Army included 13 armored, 12 armored infantry, 2 mountain and 3 airborne brigades; it had U.S. surface-to-surface missiles. The Air Force (Luftwaffe) had 459 combat aircraft including F-104G Starfighters, plus other planes. The Navy had 6 submarines, 11 destroyers, 40 patrol boats, about 200 other vessels and 100 combat aircraft.

Helgoland, an island of 130 acres in the North Sea, was taken from Denmark by a British Naval Force in 1807 and later ceded to Germany to become a part of Schleswig-Holstein province in return for rights in East Africa. The heavily fortified island was surrendered to Great Britain, May 23, 1945, demilitarized in 1947 and returned to West Germany, Mar. 1, 1952. It is a free port.

The Saar (Fr. Sarre), 10th Land (state) of the Federal Republic, is an industrial and mining area north of Lorraine, originally 738 sq. mi., now extended to about 991 and population (1970) of 2,567,520, mostly German. Capital: Saarbrucken. After World War II it had semi-autonomy and economic links to France. It became a German state again Jan. 1, 1957.

East Germany

DEUTSCHE DEMOKRATISCHE REPUBLIK

Capital: East Berlin. Area: 41,659 sq. mi. Population (UN est. 1972): 17,050,000. Monetary unit: DDR Mark.

The German Democratic Republic was proclaimed in the Soviet sector of Berlin Oct. 7, 1949. Wilhelm Pieck was named President, reelected Oct. 7, 1953, and Oct. 7, 1957 (died Sept. 7, 1960); Willi Stoph, Minister-President, or prime minister; Walter Ulbricht, Communist party secretary; deputy prime minister. The unicameral legislature is called the Volkskammer or People's Chamber. A ministry of state security, the SSD, and a militarized People's Police were organized.

The Soviet Union proclaimed East Germany a sovereign republic Mar. 25, 1954, but kept Soviet troops there on grounds of security and the four-power Potsdam agreement.

The Volkskammer approved a constitutional amendment Sept. 12, 1960, that abolished the Presidency, replacing it with a new Council of State designated as East Germany's highest governing body, with Walter Ulbricht as Chairman.

Ulbricht negotiated a treaty with Poland placing Poland's boundary at the line formed by the Oder and Neisse Rivers. The United States registered its disapproval, declaring that it violated the Potsdam agreement and that no boundaries could be settled "unilaterally or bilaterally" outside a peace treaty. The Republic also ratified an agreement with Czechoslovakia, accepting the expulsion of over 2,000,000 Germans from Sudetenland as "permanent and just." Its industry was integrated with that of the Soviet Union.

The Volkskammer abolished, 1952, the five traditional provinces of East Germany as administrative units in favor of 14 districts of 217 counties. Brandenburg, Mecklenburg, Saxony and Thuringia were divided into three districts each, Saxony-Anhalt into two.

Coincident with the entrance of West Germany into the European Defense Community, May 27, 1952, the East German government decreed a prohibited zone 3 miles deep along its 600-mile border with West Germany, separated Berlin's telephone system into 2 sections and cut many of its lines to the West. Berlin was further divided, 1953-1961, by reduction of crossing points and erection of a fortified wall, but the exodus of refugees from East Germany into Western sectors continued though on a much smaller scale.

The regime signed a 20-year treaty of friendship and co-operation with the USSR June 12, 1964.

East Germany suffered severe economic problems until the mid-1960s. A "new economic system" was introduced, easing the former central planning controls and allowing factories to make "profits" provided they were reinvested in operations or distributed to workers as bonuses. By the early 1970s, the economy was highly industrialized. In May 1972 the few remaining private firms were ordered sold to the government. The nation was credited with the highest standard of living among communist countries.

On Apr. 8, 1968, a new constitution, announced as approved by 94.49% of voters, went into effect. It reaffirmed Communist one-party rule and close ties with the USSR and declared German reunification could "take place only on the basis of Socialism."

In May 1971 Ulbricht resigned as leader of the Communist party and was replaced by Erich Honecker, but retained his post as Chairman of the Council of State. Ulbricht died Aug. 1, 1973.

Travel restrictions between the two Germanies were eased slightly in the first formal treaty signed by the two, in May 1972. East and West Germany gained admission to the UN in Sept. 1973.

Military service is compulsory. Military strength for 1972-73 was 131,000 plus 470,000 guards and armed workers groups. An estimated 20 Soviet divisions are stationed in East Germany.

Ghana

Capital: Accra. Area: 91,843 sq. mi. Population (UN est. 1972): 9,090,000. Monetary unit: Cedi.

The Republic of Ghana, a member of the UN and the Commonwealth, is composed of the former British Gold Coast colony with its territories of Ashanti and Northern Territories, and British Togoland, former UN trusteeship. Slightly smaller than Oregon, it faces on the Gulf of Guinea in Western Africa, bounded N by Upper Volta, E by Togo and W by the Ivory Coast.

Resources and Industries. Ghana is rich in mineral wealth. Ghana ranks among world leaders in production of diamonds (mostly industrial type), manganese, and bauxite.

Ghana is the world's leading cocoa producer; it exports over 350,000 tons annually, about 30% of world output. Timber is 2nd in value, including mahogany and rare woods.

The huge Akosombo hydroelectric project on the Volta River, partly financed by U. S., was completed in 1965 and began serving Ghana's 1st giant industry, an aluminum reduction plant near the port of Tema, built and owned by U.S. companies. In 1972-73 the government pressed a program of both small and large farms, "Operation Feed-Yourself," to cut costly food imports.

History and Government. Named after an earlier African state along the Niger River, 800-1076 A.D., Ghana has long been settled by the Adansi, Akwamu, Ga, and other tribes, and was ruled by Great Britain for 113 years. Its independence was gained by rapid steps after 1951 when Britain granted the colony a new constitution and its chief spokesman, Kwame Nkrumah, was elected Prime Minister. The UN General Assembly on Dec. 13, 1956, approved termination of the British Togoland trusteeship and merger of the territory with the new state following a 1956 plebiscite.

Full independence within the Commonwealth, with a British Governor-General, was effective Mar. 6, 1957. It became a republic July 1, 1960, but remained within the Commonwealth. Kwame Nkrumah became Pres.

In 1962 Parliament made Nkrumah Pres. for life. In 1964 a referendum gave him dictatorial powers and made Ghana a one-party Socialist state.

Pres. Nkrumah built hospitals and schools, raised the literacy rate, created a state-owned airline and ship line, but ran the country into debt, jailed hundreds of political dissenters and was accused of corruption.

On Feb. 24, 1966, a National Liberation Council of Army and police officers took over the government. The Council expelled Communist Chinese and East German teachers and technicians. It promised a "balanced neutrality" and slashed expenditures.

Elections were held in Aug. 1969 and Ghana returned to civilian rule, with an elected National Assembly, a Prime Minister and a President.

On Jan. 13, 1972, a National Redemption Council, headed by Army Col. Ignatius K. Acheampong, took over the government.

Greece

Capital: Athens. Area: 50,944 sq. mi. Population (est. 1972): 9,030,000. Monetary Unit: Drachma.

Greece occupies the southern part of the Balkan peninsula, reaching into the Mediterranean Sea with the Ionian Sea on the W and the Aegean Sea on the E. Its neighbors are Albania, Yugoslavia, Bulgaria and Turkey. The Pindus Mtns. run through the country N to S. Total length of the heavily indented coastline is 9,385 mi. Hundreds of islands account for 8,918 sq. mi. of the total land area, which is approx. that of Alabama; 166 islands are inhabited, among them Crete, Rhodes, Milos, Kerkira (Corfu), Chios, Lesbos, Samos. Principal seaport is Piraeus, near Athens.

Resources and Industries. Greece is still largely agricultural. Only one-fourth of the total area is arable: 13,350,000 of the total of 16,074,000 acres are covered by mountains, lakes and rivers. Four-fifths of the forests are state-owned. Chief agricultural products are wheat, rye, barley, oats, corn, rice, cotton, tobacco, olives, citrus fruits, raisins and figs. Sheep are the most important livestock.

Heavily damaged in World War II, Greece's industrial and agricultural output has far surpassed pre-war levels thanks to economic development programs helped in part by U. S. aid. Hydroelectric development is remedying the lack of coal. Principal industries are textiles, food-processing, wine, cement, chemicals, aluminum.

Greek-owned merchant marine tonnage is among world leaders, but most of it is registered under other flags.

Exports are mainly agricultural—tobacco, cotton, citrus fruits, raisins, vegetables. Ores, esp. bauxite, are also important. Aiding the economy is the tourist industry, which produces over $300,000,000 annually.

Foreign trade, in thousands of U.S. dollars:

	Imports	Exports
1971	$2,098,000	$662,000
1972	$2,145,000	$871,000

History and Government. The achievements of Ancient Greece in art, architecture, science, mathematics, philosophy, drama, literature and democracy became legacies for succeeding ages. Greece reached the height of its glory and power, particularly in the Athenian city-state, in the 5th Century B.C.

Greece fell under Roman domination in the 2nd and 1st Centuries B.C. In the 4th Century A.D. it became part of the Eastern Byzantine Empire and, after the fall of Constantinople to the Turks in 1453, part of the Ottoman Empire.

Greece won its war of independence from Turkey 1821-1829, and became a kingdom under guarantee of Britain, France and Russia, 1830. A republic was established 1925; the monarchy was restored, 1935, and George II, King of the Hellenes, resumed the throne. In Oct., 1940, Greece rejected an ultimatum from Italy and when attacked Greece drove the Italians back into Albania. Nazi support resulted in the defeat and occupation of Greece by Germans, Italians and Bulgarians. By the end of 1944 the invaders withdrew. Armed Communists attempted to seize the country but were thwarted by British liberation troops.

A plebiscite recalled King George II. He died Apr. 1, 1947, and was succeeded by his brother, Paul I. King Paul died Mar. 6, 1964, succeeded by his son, Crown Prince Constantine, born June 2, 1940. The King married Princess Ann-Marie of Denmark Sept. 18, 1964.

Communists waged guerrilla war 1947-49 against the government but were defeated with the aid of the U.S. (acting under the Truman Doctrine).

In Feb. 16, 1964, elections the coalition Center Union led by George Papandreou won 174 of 300 seats in the Chamber of Deputies. A prolonged government crisis was precipitated July 15, 1965, when Premier Papandreou resigned; at issue was a Papandreou plan to purge the Army of right-wing officers. King Constantine opposed the purge saying it would expose the armed forces to Communist influence. Leftists and backers of Papandreou staged riots in Athens as the King sought a new Premier who could win a Parliamentary majority over the opposition of the Papandreou bloc and the extreme leftists. He finally won with Stephanos Stephanopoulos, who was sworn in Sept. 17, 1965.

Continuing political crises ended in a pre-election coup d'etat Apr. 21, 1967, by rightist Army officers under Col. George Papadopoulos. They jailed hundreds of monarchists, Communists and political leaders. King Constantine on Dec. 13 sought to oust the junta but failed to rally military support and flew with his family to exile in Rome, Dec. 14. Papadopoulos was named Premier and a general was appointed "viceroy." In 1968 the Papadopoulos government freed some political prisoners but tightened its hold, replacing many officials including judges.

A new constitution, approved in a referendum, went into effect Nov. 10, 1968. It strengthened the powers of the Premier, weakened those of the King and Parliament. Certain provisions on civil rights were kept in abeyance.

In 1969 and in Apr. 1970, some of these rights were restored. In 1971, several colonels in the Cabinet were replaced with civilians.

Premier Papadopoulos abolished the monarchy and proclaimed Greece a republic with himself as President, June 1, 1973. He charged the exiled King Constantine had organized an unsuccessful mutiny by naval officers the previous week. A July 29 referendum, it was announced, approved the actions by a 78.4% vote. Papadopoulos promised parliamentary elections by the end of 1974 and freed hundreds.

Education and Religion. Greek Orthodox is the official church. Nine years of education is compulsory. There are 6 schools of university rank in Athens, and others in Thessaloniki, Patras and Ioannina.

Defense. Military strength for 1972-73 totalled 157,000. In 1972 Athens became a home port for U.S. Navy ships. Greece is a member of the UN and NATO and an associate member of EEC.

DODECANESE AND CRETE

The **Dodecanese** are a group of 13 islands in the southeastern Aegean Sea. They were occupied by Italy during the Balkan War of 1912 with Turkey and though claimed by Greece were retained by Italy. Rhodes is the capital.

After World War II the islands were ceded to Greece at the Paris Conference of Foreign Ministers, June 27, 1946, and annexed Mar. 7, 1948.

Crete, largest Greek island and 5th largest in Mediterranean, original site of Minoan civilization, lies south of the Peloponnesos peninsula and is 160 mi. long, 35 mi. wide, with area of 3,207 sq. mi. Principal towns: Heraklion (Candia) and Khania (Canea).

Guatemala

REPUBLICA DE GUATEMALA

Capital: Guatemala City. Area: 42,042 sq. mi. Population (UN est. 1972): 5,600,000. Monetary unit: Quetzal.

Guatemala is the most northerly country of Central America and about the size of Ohio. It faces on both the Caribbean and the Pacific. There are numerous volcanoes in the south, more than a half dozen over 11,000 ft. About 50% of the population is pure Indian and most of the remainder is of mixed Spanish and Indian descent.

There are famous Mayan ruins in Uaxatcun, Tikal and other sites in northern Guatemala. Other Mayan ruins of temples and monoliths are at Zaculeu in the west and at Quirigua, about 140 mi. from Guatemala City.

Santo Tomas and Puerto Barrios, main ports on the Atlantic, are connected by railroad and highway with Guatemala City in the highlands and ports on the Pacific.

Resources and Industries. Agriculture is the most important industry, the Guatemalan soil being exceedingly fertile. Coffee accounts for a third of the exports. Other important export crops are sugar, meat, bananas, cotton, chicle gum. Rare woods and cattle are important. Silver, gold, copper, iron, lead, zinc, and nickel are found. A search for oil is being pressed in the north, where natural gas has been found. Shoes and textiles are manufactured.

History and Government. The old Mayan Indian empire flourished in what is today Guatemala for over 1,000 years before the Spanish conquest.

Guatemala was a Spanish colony 1524-1821; briefly a part of Mexico and then of the U.S. of Central America; the republic was established in 1839.

Since 1945 when a labor government was elected to replace the long-term dictatorship of Jorge Ubico, the country has seen a swing toward Socialism, an allegedly U.S.-sponsored revolt, renewed attempts at social reform and a military coup. Communist-led guerrillas have terrorized parts of the nation and kidnaped officials.

Col. Enrique Peralta Azurdia, who became Pres. in the 1963 coup, sponsored free elections in March 1966. Prof. Julio Cesar Mendez Montenegro, a left-of-center reformist, won and was inaugurated Pres. July 1. He launched agrarian reforms. Col. Carlos Arana Osorio, who had led troops against guerrillas, was elected President and took office July 1, 1970.

Communist guerrillas killed U. S. Ambassador John Gordon Mein Aug. 18, 1968. West German Ambassador Count Karl Von Spreti was slain by leftist kidnapers Apr. 5, 1970.

Education and Religion. Roman Catholicism is the dominant religion. Education is compulsory. There are 4 universities in Guatemala City, with divisions in Quezaltenango. The language is Spanish.

Guatemala is a member of the UN and OAS.

Guinea

REPUBLIC OF GUINEA

Capital: Conakry. Area 94,925 sq. mi. Population (UN est. 1972): 4,110,000. Monetary unit: Sily.

Guinea, a former French Overseas Territory, is in western Africa with the Atlantic on the W; Portuguese Guinea, Senegal and Mali on the N, Ivory Coast on the E and Liberia and Sierra Leone on the S. Chief tribes are the Fullah, Malinké and Soussou. Guinea is about the size of Oregon.

Guinea has a variety of climates, from the humid coastal tropics (Conakry, the capital has an average annual rainfall of 169") to cooler plateaus and uplands. Wildlife is varied and abundant, including elephant, hippopotamus, buffalo, antelope, lion, leopard, chimpanzee.

Resources and Industries. Although Guinea is still primarily an agricultural country, the importance of minerals to its economy is growing. Bauxite, iron and diamonds (both gem and industrial) are the principal minerals. U.S. and European companies and the Guinean Government are engaged in a joint exploitation of one of the world's richest bauxite deposits, at Boke.

Economic progress has been aided by large grants from both Communist and non-Communist countries. Acceleration of agricultural output is a Government goal. Chief agricultural exports are bananas and pineapples. Production of rice, the staple food of the population, has been expanded. Other crops include corn, palm nuts, coffee and honey.

History and Government. Under provisions of the 1958 constitution of the Fifth Republic of France, Guinea voted Sept. 28, 1958, to secede from the French Community and proclaimed itself an independent republic Oct. 2. Premier Sekou Touré became first President. The nation's first constitution was adopted Nov. 12, 1958. It provided for rule by a President with a term of 7 years and a National Assembly elected by universal suffrage. The Political Bureau of the single legal party, the Parti Democratique de Guinee, exercises great power in making governmental decisions. Guinea is a member of the UN. French is the official language.

It has agreements with Czechoslovakia, East Germany, Poland, USSR and Communist China, and criticized U. S. "colonial" attitudes in Africa, but continues to avow a neutral course.

An unsuccessful invasion of Guinea, Nov. 22, 1970, was staged by forces from Portuguese Guinea, a UN mission charged, and the UN Security Council condemned Portugal for the action. Portugal denied the charge.

Guyana

Capital: Georgetown. Area: 83,000 sq. mi. Population (UN est. 1972): 750,000. Monetary unit: Guyana Dollar.

British Guiana, a British colony for 152 years, became the independent nation of Guyana on May 26, 1966. It was the first South American nation to become independent since Venezuela in 1830.

Fronting on the Atlantic in NE South America, Guyana borders on Venezuela, Brazil and Surinam. The nation is about the size of Kansas. The population is about 50% of East Indian (from India) descent, 31.5% of African descent, 12% of mixed descent, 4.6% American Indian descent, and small numbers of Chinese or European descent.

Dense tropical forests cover much of the land, although a flat coastal area about 50 mi. wide, where 90% of the population lives, provides space for agriculture.

Sugar and rice are the main cash crops and account for almost half of the total exports. Other products are: coconuts, coffee, cocoa, citrus fruits, timber and livestock.

The main industry is the mining of bauxite ore; Guyana is the 5th largest producer of the mineral, supplying over 7% of the world's needs. Also exported are gold and diamonds. Deposits of a wide range of other minerals have been found but not yet exploited.

Manufacturing has shown an average 5% annual growth; products include cigarettes, rum, clothing, furniture, drugs and insecticides.

Guyana was discovered in 1499 by Spanish sailors. The country became a British possession in 1814. African slaves and indentured servants from India were brought in to work on plantations. The Indians soon outnumbered the Negro population and still do today. Venezuela has claimed ownership of the western half of Guyana. In 1970 an agreement suspended the claim for 12 years.

A parliamentary democracy with a British Governor-General after becoming independent in 1966, Guyana became a republic, with a President, Prime Minister and National Assembly on Feb. 23, 1970. It is a UN and Commonwealth member. In 1973 it joined a new Caribbean Common Market.

Haiti

REPUBLIQUE D'HAITI

Capital: Port-Au-Prince. Area: 10,714 sq. mi. Population (UN est. 1972): 5,070,000. Monetary unit: Gourde.

Haiti, only French-speaking republic in the Americas, occupies the western third of the island known as Hispaniola, the second largest of the Greater Antilles, lying between Cuba on the W and Puerto Rico on the E. The boundary which separates Haiti from the Dominican Republic to the E is 241 mi. long. Haiti is a little larger in area than Maryland.

Blacks form over 90% of the population, the remainder being of mixed descent from former slaves and French settlers.

Resources and Industries. Major mineral exports are bauxite and copper. Other minerals are gold, silver and cement.

Coffee is the chief product, along with sisal, cotton, sugar, bananas, cocoa, tobacco and rice. Molasses and rum are produced; valuable woods are exported.

Haiti encourages tourism and is served by several major airlines, with an international jet airport at Port-au-Prince. However, tourist spending and private foreign investment in Haiti dwindled under the regime of Pres. Francois Duvalier. They revived in 1971 after his death. Economic improvement was reported in 1972.

History and Government. Haiti, discovered by Columbus, 1492, and a French colony from 1677, attained its independence, 1804, following the rebellion begun by Toussaint L'Ouverture and has been a republic since 1820. Following a period of political violence, 1910-1915, the United States occupied the country and restored order. The occupation terminated Aug. 14, 1934.

Five regimes failed between 1950-1957. In Sept. 1957, Dr. Duvalier was elected President for a 6-year term.

In June 1964 a new constitution made Dr. Duvalier President for life. There were unsuccessful outbreaks against his rule in 1963 and 1970. He died Apr. 21, 1971, and was succeeded by his son, Jean-Claude Duvalier, 19, as President for life.

In Jan. 1973 gunmen seized U.S. Ambassador Clinton Knox but freed him after Haiti paid a $70,000 ransom and freed 12 prisoners.

Haiti is a member of the UN and OAS.

Education and Religion. Roman Catholicism is the main religion. Education is compulsory, but illiteracy rate is est. at 90%. French is the official language of the country, but French Creole, a dialect, is spoken by the majority. The teaching of English and Spanish in the schools is obligatory.

Honduras

REPUBLICA DE HONDURAS

Capital: Tegucigalpa. Area (Govt. est.): 43,277 sq. mi. Population (est. 1972): 2,690,000. Monetary unit: Lempira.

Honduras is a republic in Central or Middle America, bounded on the N by the Caribbean; E and S by Nicaragua; S by Pacific Ocean and El Salvador; W by Guatemala. It is about the size of Pennsylvania.

The coast line on the Caribbean is 500 mi. long. On the Pacific side it has a coast line of 40 mi. on the Gulf of Fonseca. There are ports on both coasts. The country is mountainous, very fertile, with rich forests. The inhabitants are mostly of Spanish and Indian extraction.

At Copan, near the western border, are the imposing remains of a large Mayan city which flourished from the 4th Century A.D.; it had declined by the time Spaniards arrived in 1576.

Resources and Industries. Mineral resources are abundant but undeveloped and include gold, silver, copper, lead, zinc, iron, antimony and coal. The chief export is bananas, grown in the Caribbean coast. Coffee, timber, cotton, sugar, tobacco and cattle raising are important. The mountainous terrain has hindered development. There was a serious drought in 1973.

Manufacturing industries are small but growing; they include clothing, textiles, cement, chemicals, food products.

History and Government. Honduras became independent after freeing itself from Spain, Sept. 15, 1821, and from the Federation of Central America, 1838.

Pres. Roman Villeda Morales, elected Nov. 15, 1957, was overthrown in a military coup Oct. 3, 1963, and replaced by a regime headed by Col. Oswaldo Lopez Arellano.

The country returned to constitutional government and Lopez Arellano was inaugurated President June 6, 1965.

The 1965 constitution provided for a President, popularly elected for 6 years, and a unicameral Congress, also elected for 6 years.

In free elections, Mar. 28, 1971, Ramon Ernesto Cruz was chosen President. In Dec. 1972 Col. Lopez, now a general, seized the presidency again.

Honduras and El Salvador fought a 5-day war in July 1969 over the presence in Honduras of 300,000 Salvadorean workers and settlers. After new clashes in 1970, a demilitarized zone was agreed on.

Honduras is a member of the UN and OAS.

Education and Religion. Education is secular and free. The literacy rate is about 50%. The National University is in Tegucigalpa. Roman Catholicism is the prevailing religion. The language is Spanish.

Hungary

MAGYAR NEPKOZTARSASAG
HUNGARIAN PEOPLE'S REPUBLIC

Capital: Budapest. Area: 35,918 sq. mi. Population (UN est. 1972): 10,400,000. Monetary unit: Forint.

Hungary, a Communist republic in Central Europe, is bounded by Czechoslovakia, the USSR, Romania, Yugoslavia and Austria. It is about the size of Indiana.

The Danube forms the Czech border in the NW, then swings S to bisect the country. The eastern half of Hungary is mainly a great fertile plain, the Alfold; the west and north are hilly.

Resources and Industries. Before World War II, Hungary was primarily agricultural, but industry has surpassed it in value. The index of industrial production (1963 = 100) was 164 for 1972. Most means of production have been socialized.

Major economic reforms were launched early in 1968, switching from a central planning system to one where market forces and a profit principle control much of production. Productivity was boosted to a yearly average increase of 6%.

About 70% of foreign trade is with Eastern bloc countries. Value of imports rose from $2.99 billion in 1971 to $3.2 billion in 1972; exports rose from $2.5 billion to $3.3 billion.

In addition to a wide range of grains and vegetable crops, fruit production has been expanded. Near Tokay, in the northeast, the most famous Hungarian wines are vinted.

Industries include iron and steel, machines, machine tools, chemicals, vehicles, railways and communications equipment, milling and distilling. Hungary has become an important supplier of industrial products to Communist bloc countries.

Hungary produces large amounts of bauxite. Also important is natural gas.

History and Government. Earliest settlers, chiefly Slav and Germanic, were overrun by Huns and Magyars from the east. Stephen I (997-1038) was made King by Pope Silvester II in 1001 A.D. The country suffered repeated Turkish invasions in the 15th-17th Centuries. After the defeats of the Turks, 1686-1697, Austria dominated, but Hungary obtained concessions until it regained internal independence in 1867, with the Emperor of Austria as King of Hungary in a dual monarchy with a single diplomatic service. Defeated with the Central Powers in 1918, Hungary lost Transylvania to Romania, Croatia and Bacska to Yugoslavia, Slovakia and Carpatho-Ruthenia to Czechoslovakia. A republic under Michael Karoly and a bolshevist revolt under Bela Kun were followed by a vote for a monarchy in 1920 with Admiral Nicholas Horthy as regent.

Hungary joined Germany in World War II; Horthy was removed and Nazi supporters put in power, 1944. Russian troops captured most of the country, 1945. By terms of an armistice with the Allied powers Hungary agreed to give up territory acquired by the 1938 dismemberment of Czechoslovakia and to return to its borders of 1937.

Hungary declared for a republic Feb. 1, 1946, and elected Zoltan Tildy President. In 1947 the Communists forced Tildy out.

A Soviet-type constitution was adopted Aug. 18, 1949, which vests power in a President Council and a National Assembly of 349 members elected for 4-year terms. Hungary is a member of the UN and Warsaw Pact.

Premier Imre Nagy, in office since mid-1953, was ousted for his moderate policy of favoring agriculture and consumer production, April 18, 1955; succeeded by Andras Hegedus.

In 1956, popular demands for the ousting of Erno Gero, Hungarian Communist party secretary, and for formation of a new government by Imre Nagy, resulted in the latter's appointment Oct. 23, but demonstrations against Communist rule in Budapest developed into open revolt when the security police fired on the people. Gero called in Soviet armed forces to crush the rioting as Revolutionary Councils spread through the country. The insurrection appeared halted by Oct. 18 when Premier Nagy announced the Soviet Union had agreed to withdraw its troops from Hungary. However, by Nov. 1 Soviet forces again surrounded Budapest and launched a massive surprise attack against the city Nov. 4 with an estimated 200,000 troops, 2,500 tanks and armored cars.

The bid for free government was crushed. Estimates of casualties varied from 6,500 to 32,000 dead. Many rebels were reported executed and thousands deported. Between 170,000 and 196,000 persons fled the country. The U.S. received 38,248 under a refugee emergency program. In the spring of 1963 the regime freed many anti-

Communists and captives from the revolution in a sweeping amnesty.

Premier Nagy was removed in November, 1956, and Janos Kadar installed as the Soviet-sponsored Premier. Nagy was executed by the Russians. Kadar later became First Secretary of the Hungarian Workers (Communist) party.

In 1973 Hungary agreed to pay the U.S. $18,900,000 for nationalized U.S. properties in Hungary.

Education and Religion. There is no state religion, and all are tolerated. About two-thirds of the population are Roman Catholics; most of the remainder are Calvinists.

Public school education is compulsory and free for 8 years. Most church schools were nationalized in 1948. There are 91 institutes of higher learning. The language is Hungarian (Magyar).

Defense. Military strength for 1972-73 included an Army of 90,000 and an Air Force of 12,500. About 40,000 USSR troops are stationed in Hungary.

Iceland

LYDVELDID ISLAND

Capital: Reykjavik. Area: 39,768 sq. mi. Population (UN est. 1972): 210,000. Monetary unit: Krona.

The Republic of Iceland is an island of volcanic origin close to the Arctic Circle in the North Atlantic. There are geysers and hot springs and the climate is modified by the Gulf Stream. Iceland is about the size of Virginia.

Natural hot water from many of Iceland's volcanic springs is piped into towns and provides heat for office buildings, homes and hot houses. In Jan. 1973 a volcanic eruption on Heimaey forced evacuation of 5,500 residents of the small island off the SE coast of Iceland.

Resources and Industries. Agriculture engages about 13% of the population; industry and services 70%; fisheries 14%. About six-sevenths of the land is unproductive and only about 65,000 acres are under cultivation, producing potatoes, turnips and hay. The fishing industry is most important. It includes herring, cod and haddock. Fish products, in salted, smoked, canned or frozen form, account for 78% of exports.

Iceland's largest industrial plants include an ammonium nitrate factory, an aluminum smelter, a cement factory and a diatomite plant.

History and Government. Iceland was an independent republic, 930-1262; then it joined with Norway. The two came under Danish rule in 1380. When Norway separated from Denmark, 1814, Iceland remained under Denmark. Denmark acknowledged Iceland as a sovereign state, 1918, united with Denmark only in that the Danish King Christian X, was also King of Iceland. In 1941 the Althing (Parliament) voted to dissolve all ties with Denmark, and adopt the constitution of a republic. This was endorsed by popular vote, and the republic, with a President and Prime Minister, proclaimed June 17, 1944.

Iceland celebrated the 1,000th anniversary of the Althing, the oldest parliamentary assembly in the world, June 23-28, 1930. Under a constitutional amendment of 1959, the Althing increased from 52 to 60 members. The Prime Minister and his cabinet are responsible to the Althing. There is universal suffrage for men and women at age 20.

In 1972 Iceland barred foreign ships from fishing within 50 mi. of its coast. British trawlers defied the ban and in 1973 were fired on by Icelandic gunboats. British frigates were sent to the disputed waters; the confrontation won the name "cod war."

Iceland notified the U.S. in 1973 it would seek revision of the 1951 treaty under which 3,300 U.S. NATO Air Force and Navy personnel are stationed on the island.

Education and Religion. The Icelandic language has maintained its purity, as in Eddas and Sagas, for 1,000 years. Danish and English also are taught. Eight years of elementary education is compulsory. There is no illiteracy. There are 5 colleges and a university. The national church is Evangelical Lutheran, but there is complete religious freedom.

Defense: Iceland has no Army, Navy, Air Force or forts. It is a charter member of NATO. It is also a member of the UN, Council of Europe and Nordic Council.

India

BHARAT

Capital: New Delhi. Area: 1,261,597 sq. mi. Population (UN est. 1972): 563,490,000. Monetary unit: Rupee.

India, an independent republic since 1950 and a member of the Commonwealth, occupies the larger part of the subcontinent of India. It is a third the size of the U.S.

India's climate varies from tropical heat in the south to the nearly Arctic cold of the Himalayas. Approximately 22.3% of the area is forested.

The population is 80% rural, 20% urban. The annual increase rate, 2½%, poses food and housing shortages.

In 1967 the Government supplemented its birth control programs with monetary inducements to men to volunteer for sterilization. In 1973 the government reported 13,000,000 persons had undergone sterilization operations.

Sikkim, bordered by Tibet, Bhutan, Nepal and India, formerly British protected, became a protectorate of India in 1950. Area, 2,744 sq. mi.; population 1972, 208,000. The ruler is Chogyal (Maharaja) Palden Thondup Namgyal; in 1963, while Crown Prince, he married Hope Cooke, a New York debutante. He became ruler in 1964 but was not coronated until April 4, 1965, a date chosen as auspicious by court astrologers. In Apr. 1973 the Chogyal asked Indian troops to suppress demonstrations against his rule. In May he and India signed an agreement providing for a legislative assembly. Capital, Gangtok. Buddhism is the state religion.

Kashmir, a predominantly Moslem region in the northwest, has been in dispute between India and Pakistan since 1947 when British rule was ending and Indian and Pakistani troops entered the area. A cease-fire was negotiated by the UN, effective Jan. 1, 1949; it gave Pakistan control of one-third of the area, in the west and northwest, and India the remaining two-thirds, the Indian state of Jammu and Kashmir. In late Aug. 1965, clashes broke out along the line and soon involved the armed forces of the 2 nations in a spreading war.

On Sept. 20, 1965, the UN Security Council demanded a cease-fire and both sides agreed Sept. 22, to stop the fighting, but did not comply with a call for them to withdraw their forces across the old cease-fire line.

USSR Premier Aleksei N. Kosygin invited India Prime Minister Lal Bahadur Shastri and Pakistan Pres. Ayub Khan to a conference at Tashkent, USSR, and on Jan. 10, 1966, the two signed the "Tashkent Declaration," pledging to withdraw their armed forces in Kashmir to behind the cease-fire line by Feb. 28.

A new truce line, slightly altering the old cease-fire line, was agreed on in Dec. 1972, accommodating changes made during the Dec. 1971 war.

There were also clashes in April 1965 along the Assam-East Pakistan border and in the Rann (swamp) of Cutch area along the West Pakistan-Gujarat border near the Arabian Sea.

An international arbitration commission on Feb. 19, 1968, awarded 90% of the Rann to India, 10% to Pakistan.

France, 1952-54, peacefully yielded to India its 5 colonies on the Bay of Bengal, former **French India** comprising Pondicherry, Kirkal, Mahe, Yanaon and Chandernagor, totalling 196 sq. mi. and 346,000 pop.

Goa, 1,426 sq. mi., pop., 1962, 626,978, which had been administered by Portugal since 1505 A.D., first as a colony and later as a province, was taken by India by military action Dec. 18, 1961, together with two other Portuguese enclaves, Damao and Diu, located about 250 mi. S. of Bombay.

India is a union of 21 states and 9 centrally administered union territories.

Resources and Industries. Agriculture occupies 70% of the people and is being helped by government planning to reach eventual self-sufficiency.

Principal food products are rice, corn, millet, wheat, barley, coffee, sugar cane, spices, tea, cashew nuts. Other important products include cotton, copra, coir, jute, linseed, rubber, lumber.

A severe 2-year drought in Bihar and other northern areas threatened mass starvation and brought large shipments of grain from the U.S.; in July 1967, plentiful rains broke the drought; there were bumper crops, 1968-72; the drought and food shortages returned 1972-73.

Indian agriculture has made progress with high-yield seeds, with fertilizers, irrigation and limited mechanization.

For many years India has had large textile industries with a wide variety of cotton, woolen and silk products. In the 1960s, other industries, including steel, processed foods, cement, machinery, chemicals and fertilizers came into prominence, along with many finished products such as sewing machines, typewriters, bicycles, telephones and transportation equipment. The Tata Iron and Steel works in Jamshedpur is one of the largest in Asia.

India's 1st nuclear power plant, built with U. S. help, was dedicated in 1970 near Bombay.

The 1972 index of industrial production (1963 = 100) was 153.

Industrial production, distribution and prices are regulated by law. Railroads, airlines, banks, insurance and coal industries are state owned.

India is a leading producer of coal, mica and manganese; also important are salt, iron ore, bauxite and gypsum.

Exports include tea, sugar, raw and processed jute, cotton fabrics and other textiles, tanned hides and skins, manganese ore, pepper, tobacco. Largest trade is with the U. S.

Foreign trade, in thousands of U. S. dollars:

	Imports	Exports
1971	$2,433,000	$2,108,000
1972	$2,228,000	$2,439,000

History and Government. India has one of the oldest civilizations in the world. Excavations trace the Indus Valley civilization back for at least 5,000 years. Beautiful paintings in the mountain caves of Ajanta in South India, richly carved temples, the Taj Mahal in Agra and the Kutab Minar in Delhi are among relics of the glorious past.

Vasco da Gama established Portuguese trading posts 1498-99, 1502-03. The Dutch followed. The English East India Co. sent Capt. William Hawkins, 1609, to get concessions from the Mogul emperor for spices and textiles. The English founded Madras and Calcutta and acquired Bombay from Portugal. Operating as the East India Co. the British gained control of most of India. Warren Hastings, first Governor-General (1774-1785), set up civil government, later India Civil Service. The British Parliament assumed political direction. Under Lord Bentinck, 1828-35, misrule by rajahs was abolished, infanticide stopped, suttee—suicide of a widow on her husband's funeral pyre—made illegal.

Liberal policies were set back when the Sepoy troops mutinied, 1857-58. Thereafter the British supported the native rulers.

Indian nationalism grew rapidly after World War I. The National Congress and the Moslem League demanded constitutional reform. A leader emerged in Mohandas K. Gandhi (called Mahatma, or Great Soul), born Oct. 2, 1869, assassinated Jan. 30, 1948. A Hindu, trained in law in England, he began advocating self-rule, non-violence, pursuit of native handicrafts, removal of untouchability (which forced millions of poor to remain menials by heredity) in 1919. In 1930 he launched "civil disobedience," including boycott of British goods and rejection of taxes without representation.

In 1935 Britain gave India a constitution providing a bicameral federal congress, with a council of states and an assembly. Suffrage was granted about 30,000,000 in separate electorates. The Moslems objected that Hindu dominance injured their culture and freedom. Mohammed Ali Jinnah, head of the Moslem League, sought creation of a Moslem nation, Pakistan.

Following more than 40 years' active struggle for freedom by both Hindus and Moslems, the British government announced Feb. 20, 1947, its intention to partition India into two dominions and set June, 1948, for British withdrawal from India. Aug. 15, 1947, was designated

Indian Independence Day. India became a self-governing member of the Commonwealth and assumed charter membership British India had held in the UN. The dominion became a sovereign democratic republic under a constitution adopted Nov. 26, 1949, effective Jan. 26, 1950, but elected to remain a member of the Commonwealth. (*See Pakistan.*)

It has been estimated that more than 11,000,000 refugees (Hindus and Moslems) crossed the India-Pakistan borders in a mass transferral of some of the two peoples during 1947.

The constitution provides for a President, elected for a five-year term by an electoral college consisting of members of both houses of Parliament (Council of States and House of the People), and elected members of the lower houses of the federating states. A Council of Ministers (cabinet) is headed by a Prime Minister who is the practical head of the government. The federating states have governors, appointed by the President, at the head of state organizations similar to the federal system.

The Council of States is a permanent body, not subject to dissolution, but one-third of its members retire at the end of every second year. The House of the People may be dissolved by the President and new elections called.

Prime Minister Mrs. Indira Gandhi, named Jan. 19, 1966, succeeded Lal Bahadur Shastri, who on June 2, 1964, succeeded India's first Prime Minister, Jawaharlal Nehru. Mrs. Gandhi, Nehru's daughter, was no relation to Mahatma Gandhi. Nehru, Prime Minister from the beginning of India's independence in 1947, died May 24, 1964.

Long the dominant power in India's politics, the Congress party lost some of its near monopoly by 1967; its majority in the House of the People was smaller, and it lost control of several state legislatures. The Congress party split into New and Old Congress parties in 1969. Mrs. Ghandi's New Congress party won 350 of the 521 seats in the House of the People in March 1971 elections.

After Pakistan troops launched repression of Bengali separatists in East Pakistan, Mar. 25, 1971, some 10,000,000 refugees fled into India. Border skirmishes between India and Pakistan increased. On Aug. 9, India and the USSR signed a 20-year friendship pact while U.S.-India relations soured. India and Pakistan went to war Dec. 3, 1971, on both the East and West fronts. Pakistan troops in the East surrendered Dec. 16; Pakistan agreed to a cease-fire offer in the West Dec. 17. India recognized Bangladesh (East Pakistan) as a separate nation Dec. 6.

India and Pakistan signed a pact agreeing to withdraw troops from their borders and seek peaceful solutions to all problems, including Kashmir, July 3, 1972. In Aug. 1973 India agreed to release most of 93,000 Pakistanis held prisoner since 1971.

Education and Religion. The constitution provides for free, compulsory education through age 14. There are now 62 universities, 1,946 colleges, and 27 research institutes. There are 14 main languages, 12 originating from Sanskrit, with several hundred varied dialects. Hindi is spoken by nearly 50%, with Urdu, the principal Moslem language, spoken by 10%. Hindi became the official language in Jan. 1965 with English the associate official language. Much official government work and instruction at universities continues to be done in English.

The religion of 83% of the people is Hinduism. The constitution guarantees freedom of worship. Moslems are the largest minority, 61,417,934 in the 1971 Census; there were 14,223,382 Christians, 10,378,797 Sikhs, 3,812,325 Buddhists, 2,604,646 Jains. Hindus totaled 453,292,086.

Defense. Military strength for 1972-73 was 960,000, with 840,000 in the Army; 28,000, Navy; 92,000 Air Force.

Indonesia

REPUBLIK INDONESIA

Capital: Jakarta (Djakarta). Area: 735,865 sq. mi. Population (1972 est.): 120,400,000. Monetary unit: Rupiah.

Indonesia, world's largest archipelago, formerly the Netherlands East Indies, lies along the Equator SE of Asia, N and NW of Australia. Indonesia comprises about 13,000 islands, the largest being Java (one of the most densely populated areas in the world with 1,500 persons to the sq. mi.), Sumatra, Kalimantan (most of Borneo), Sulawesi (Celebes) and West Irian (Irian Jaya, the west half of New Guinea). Among others are Bangka, Billiton, Madura, Bali, Lombok, Sumbawa, part of Timor. The land area is 6 times that of New Mexico.

Many races are included, the principal ones being Achinese, Bataks, Menangkabaus, Javanese, Sundanese, Madurese, Balinese, Sasaks, Menadonese, Buginese, Dayaks and Papuans.

The capital, called Batavia by the Dutch, is Jakarta, on the island of Java.

Resources and Industries. Indonesia is one of the richest countries in natural resources. There are vast supplies of tin, oil and coal, and sizable deposits of bauxite, manganese, copper, nickel, gold and silver.

Agriculture occupies 80% of the population. Products include rice, maize, casava, ground nuts, soya beans, tobacco, coffee, rubber, cinchona, pepper, kapok, coconuts, palm oil, tea, sugar and indigo.

Inflation spiraled during the 1960's, but by 1969 comparative stability was achieved and a 5-year development plan was undertaken. Oil accounts for 35% of export income, followed by rubber and timber. Indonesia is the world's 11th largest oil producer. There are food processing, textile and other small factories.

History and Government. Until March, 1942, Indonesia was a Netherlands overseas territory. Following Japanese military occupation, 1942-1945, Nationalists, led by Dr. Sukarno and Dr. Hatta, proclaimed a republic Aug. 17, 1945. Four years of intermittent warfare between Netherlands and Indonesian forces ended with agreements signed Nov. 2, 1949, transferring sovereignty over all Indonesia, except Netherlands New Guinea (West Irian) to a new interim government effective Dec. 27, 1949. Dr. Sukarno was elected President, Dec. 16, 1949. On July 20, 1950, the member states agreed to form a strongly centralized government; a unitary state with an amended constitution was proclaimed Aug. 15 and its name formally changed to Republic of Indonesia. It joined the UN 1950.

After the Dutch in Nov. 1957 rejected proposals for new negotiations over West Irian, Indonesia's government stepped up the seizure of Dutch property. A U. S. mediator's plan was adopted in 1962, providing that West Irian be turned over temporarily to the UN, then to Indonesia. Under the agreement Indonesia pledged to hold a plebiscite allowing the people of West Irian the choice of staying with Indonesia or separating from it. The UN turned the area over to Indonesia May 1, 1963. In 1969, voting by tribal chiefs and other representatives favored staying with Indonesia.

Pres. Sukarno suspended the original elected 257-member Parliament Mar. 5, 1960, and announced a new 261-member appointed group, Mar. 27, and swept aside anti-Leftist criticism. He was named President for life May 18, 1963.

The USSR announced in 1964 plans to step up its contributions of modern arms to Indonesia to aid in attempting to "crush" the new nation, Malaysia, formation of which Indonesia opposed. In 1964 and 1965 Indonesia staged numerous guerrilla raids into Malaysia.

Indonesia withdrew from the UN in Jan. 1965. Many anti-American demonstrations were staged at U. S. consulates, including stonings, during the year.

Indonesia's large, pro-Peking Communist party tried to seize complete control Sept. 30, 1965, taking strategic points and murdering 6 high generals. The army smashed the coup and later intimated that Pres. Sukarno had played a role in it. Following the abortive putsch, anti-Communist rioters set fire to Communist hq. In Central and East Java, Reds seized control of several districts and fighting continued. It was later reported that many thousands of Communists were executed.

Gen. Suharto was named head of the Army; on Mar. 12, 1966, Pres. Sukarno turned over all government powers to him but continued as Pres., apparently in name only. Gen. Suharto was officially named President for a 5-year term by the Consultative Assembly Mar. 27, 1968. He was reelected in Mar. 1973.

On Aug. 11, 1966, Indonesia and Malaysia signed an

agreement ending the Sukarno policy of hostility to Malaysia. On Sept. 28 Indonesia resumed membership in the UN. The U. S. resumed economic aid.

In July 1971, in the first popular vote in 16 years, a coalition party backing the Suharto government won a strong majority in the House of Representatives.

Education and Religion. 90% of the inhabitants are Moslems, the remainder Christians, Hindus and Buddhists. There is compulsory primary education for children 6 to 12, plus optional secondary training and higher education. Major institutions of higher education are Univ. of Indonesia, Bandung Institute, Erlangga Univ., Gadjah Mada Univ., National Academy, Islam Univ., Pancasila Univ. Many languages are spoken; official language is Bahasa Indonesia, derived from Malay.

Iran

KESHVARE SHAHANSHAIYEIRAN
(Persia)

Capital: Tehran. Area: 636,293 sq. mi. Population (UN est. 1972): 30,550,000. Monetary unit: Rial.

A constitutional monarchy, Iran is a mountainous land, much of it a high plateau region, in southwestern Asia. Slightly larger than Alaska, it has coastlines on the Caspian Sea, Persian Gulf and Gulf of Oman. For neighbors it has the USSR, Afghanistan, Pakistan, Iraq and Turkey. Large salt deserts comprise 25% of the land but there are many beautiful oases.

Tehran, Isfahan, Shiraz and Abadan have jet airports. Shiraz is noted for ancient ruins of Persepolis.

Resources and Industries. Iran is the world's 4th largest oil producer; petroleum provides most of its foreign exchange and government income.

Other mineral wealth includes chromite, copper, iron, lead, manganese, zinc, barite, sulphur and coal. Also mined are emeralds and turquoise.

The first Iranian steel mill was under construction near Isfahan, built by the Soviet Union and paid for by natural gas piped to the USSR. Iran has contracted with the French for development of a petrochemical industry. There are cement, vehicle assembly and sugar refining plants.

Agriculture is a prime industry, wheat, barley, corn, rice, fruits, gums, wool, tobacco, raw silk, sugar beets and cotton being the chief products. Some wines are famous, as are Persian carpets. Sturgeon fishing in Caspian Sea is important, especially for caviar. Major dams built in the 1960s provide hydroelectric power and aid irrigation.

Under Shah Mohammed Reza Pahlavi's leadership, Iran has undergone an economic and social revolution to become a vigorous modern state. His improvements included major land reform, introduction of industry to towns, the spread of literacy and drastic gains in women's rights.

History and Government. Iran, derived from Aryan, is the correct name of the country long referred to as Persia. The Iranians, who came from the East during the 2nd millenium B. C., were Aryans, an Indo-European people related to the Aryans of India, and included Medes, Persians and other groups. Use of the name Iran became widespread in the 1920s and 1930s.

In 549 B.C. Cyrus the Great united the Medes and Persians in the Persian Empire, conquered Babylonia, 538 B.C.

Darius I began the invasion of Greece; crossed the Hellespont, fought Spartans at Thermopylae, was defeated at Salamis, 480 B.C. and Plataea, 479 B.C. Alexander of Macedon (the Great) invaded Persia, defeated Darius III at Issus, 333 B.C.

Subsequently Persia was ruled by the Seleucids; the Parthians beginning c. 250 B. C.; the Sassanians, c. 226 A.D.

Arabs brought Islam to Persia in the 7th Century and for many years the religious-political Caliphate ruled the land. Omar Khayyam (c. 1050- c. 1123) wrote his famous Rubaiyat and created a calendar renowned for its accuracy.

Mongols invaded the country in 1250 and again under Tamerlane c. 1370. After the downfall of the Mongols in

1502 Persia became a monarchy under a Shah.

In 1906 a constitution was enacted. It provided for an executive with power vested in a cabinet and government officials who act in the name of the Shah. The legislature has a national assembly (Majlis) elected for 4 years and a senate of 60, 30 elected and 30 nominated by the Shah. Women voted and were elected to the legislature for the first time in 1963.

The Shah is Mohammed Reza Pahlavi (born Oct. 26, 1919), ascended in 1941. He married Princess Fawzia, eldest sister of Farouk I of Egypt, March 15, 1939; divorced Nov. 19, 1948. The Shah married his 2nd wife, Soraya Esfandiary, Feb. 12, 1951, divorced Mar. 14, 1958. Both wives had failed to produce a male heir. The Shah married Farah Diba Dec. 21, 1959; Crown Prince Reza Pahlavi was born Oct. 31, 1960.

British and Russian forces entered Iran Aug. 25, 1941, withdrawing later. Britain and the USSR signed an agreement Jan. 29, 1942, to respect Iran integrity and give economic aid. In 1946 a Soviet attempt to take over the Azerbaijan region in northwest Iran was defeated when a puppet regime was ousted by force.

In 1951 the Majlis voted nationalization of the oil industry, the Anglo-Iranian Oil Co. closed its refinery and the industry was at a standstill until the Shah in 1954 signed an agreement with a consortium of British, U.S., Dutch and French companies. It gave the consortium the rights to Iran's oil, with much of the earnings going to Iran. In 1973 a new agreement gave the National Iranian Oil Co. greater control over all operations.

In 1969, Iran and Iraq were involved in a dispute over Iran's claimed right to use the Shatt al Arab, a border river estuary, for shipping. In 1972 there were renewed border clashes, reflecting rivalry for power in the Persian Gulf area. In late 1971, Iran occupied 3 islands at the mouth of the gulf, claimed by states of the United Arab Emirates. To protect oil shipments, Iran in the 1970s modernized its military forces, aided by sales of new equipment from the U.S.

Education and Religion. The Shiah branch of Islam predominates. Education is nominally compulsory. Higher education is available at the Universities of Tehran, Shiraz, Isfahan, Tabriz, Meshed, National Univ. and Ahwaz. A Literacy Corps is composed of high school and college graduates who teach in rural areas in lieu of military service. A Health Corps of graduate doctors and other graduates is patterned after the Literacy Corps. The language is Farsi (Persian), written in Arabic script.

Defense. Military strength for 1972-73 totaled 191,000. The Air Force had 160 combat aircraft.

Iran is a member of the UN and CENTO.

Iraq

Capital: Baghdad. Area: 173,259 sq. mi. Population (UN est. 1972): 10,070,000. Monetary unit: Dinar.

Iraq is the modern name for Mesopotamia, the area around the Euphrates and Tigris Rivers, about twice the size of Utah. It is bounded by Turkey, Iran, the Persian (also called Arabian) Gulf, Kuwait, Saudi Arabia, Jordan and Syria.

The country is mostly alluvial plain. The temperature varies widely: 120°F in the shade is common, contrasted with severe frosts in the winter.

Resources and Industries. Wheat, barley, rice, millet and cotton are the chief crops, with tobacco in the Kurdish hills. Dates are grown in the tidal stretches of the Shatt al Arab and beyond. Large flocks of sheep are raised in the north and wool and skins are exported.

Iraq is the world's 9th largest oil producer. About 70% of its national income is from oil. European and U.S. companies controlled the Iraq Petroleum Co. New fields were developed with USSR aid, 1970-72, and in June 1972 Iraq nationalized the Western-controlled company.

History and Government. The Tigris-Euphrates valley was the site of the ancient cities of Eridu, Ur, Nineveh and Babylon. The Sumerian culture of 3000 B. C. influenced Crete, Egypt and Greece.

Iraq, then known as Mesopotamia, was taken from

Turkey in World War I. The League of Nations gave a mandate to Britain, which ended 1932 when Iraq was recognized as a sovereign state.

Emir Faisal, then King of the Hejaz, was chosen ruler by a referendum in 1921. A constitutional monarchy was created in 1924. On his death, Sept. 1933, he was succeeded by his son, Ghazi Ibn Faisal. King Ghazi was killed in an automobile accident April 4, 1939; succeeded by his son, King Faisal II (born May 2, 1935).

King Faisal was assassinated July 14, 1958, when the Free Officers, led by Brig. Gen. Abdul Karim Kassem revolted and proclaimed Iraq "part of the Arab nation." Gen. Kassem became premier of a republic. Iraq received Soviet arms aid. It withdrew from the Baghdad pact and 3 U. S. arms agreements.

On June 7, 1967, Iraq broke diplomatic relations with the U.S. following Egyptian charges that America was aiding Israel in the 6-day, 1967 war.

After several coups, the government was taken over by a group headed by Gen. Ahmed Hassan al-Bakr, a member of the right wing of the international Baath Socialist party, July 17, 1968.

In 1969, in a series of trials, Iraq condemned and executed more than a score as spies for Israel, Iran and the U. S. It was involved with Iran in a dispute over navigation rights on the Shatt al Arab, a border river estuary. Iraq reportedly maintained 12,000 troops in Jordan as part of the general Arab confrontation with Israel. It withdrew them in 1971. In 1972 there were new border skirmishes with Iran. In April 1972 Iraq and the USSR signed a friendship pact. Soviet military aid was increased. In Mar. 1973 Kuwait charged Iraqi troops entered its territory in a border dispute.

Years of battling with the Kurds, a minority in the northeast area, ended in 1970 with recognition by the government of partial Kurdish autonomy and Kurdish representation in a legislature to be created in a new constitution. After a coup attempt failed in 1973, Gen. Bakr announced the legislature, an appointive body, would be created before the end of the year.

Education and Religion. Elementary and secondary education is free and compulsory. Arabic is the language of the majority. The people are preponderantly Moslems, divided between the Sunni and Shiah sects. Christians number 150,000.

Defense. Military strength for 1972-73 was 101,800.

Ireland
EIRE
POBLACHT NA H'EIREANN
Capital: Dublin. Area 27,136 sq. mi. Population (UN est. 1972): 3,010,000. Monetary unit: Irish pound.

Ireland, an island in the Atlantic near the European mainland, is a sovereign democratic republic about the size of W. Va. It is separated from Great Britain on the E by the Irish Sea and the North Channel and on the SE by St. George's Channel.

Ireland, the Emerald Isle, consists mainly of a central plateau surrounded by isolated groups of hills and mountains. Ireland's coastline is much indented by the sea, affording many inlets and coves. The mean annual temperature ranges from 48°F, in the N to 52°F, in the S. There are numerous lakes (called loughs); the best known are those of Killarney. The most important river is the Shannon, about 250 mi. long. Tallest mountains are in SW: Carrantuohill, 3,414 ft. in Kerry; Brandon Hill on the coast, 3,127 ft.

Tourist attractions include the scenery, historic houses, cultural and folk festivals and medieval banquets.

The famous Blarney stone is located in an old castle in the village of Blarney, 4 mi. NW of Cork. A legend says it confers oratorical powers on those who kiss it.

Emigration had been high and for years the population remained static. Since 1961, however, it has annually increased and emigration has recently decreased.

Resources and Industries. About 28% of the work force is employed in agriculture, forestry and fishing. The nearness of the Gulf Stream causes considerable rainfall; lush pastures support an extensive cattle and dairy

industry. Important crops are potatoes, wheat, oats, barley, sugar beets, fruits and vegetables. Food and animals comprised 43% of exports in 1972.

Industrialization increased, 1962-73, with over 750 new factories, many with foreign participation.

Major industries are tobacco, food processing, vehicle assembly, metals, textiles, chemicals and brewing. Marked gains have been recorded in electrical and non-electrical machinery, fertilizers and computers.

A mining boom, following discovery of zinc, lead and silver deposits, brought new strength to the economy in the mid-1960s. The index numbers of industrial production (1963=100) showed that the mining index jumped from 105 in 1965 to 267 in 1972. The index for general industrial production rose to 168 in 1972.

Tourism, growing annually, provides Ireland with earnings of over $250,000,000 annually.

Foreign trade, in thousands of U.S. dollars:

	Imports	Exports
1971	$1,835,000	$1,308,000
1972	$2,102,000	$1,611,000

A switch to decimal currency was made in 1971.

History and Government. Celtic tribes invaded the islands about the 4th Century B.C.; their Gaelic culture and literature flourished and spread to Scotland and elsewhere. In the 5th Century A.D., the country, in which St. Patrick converted the Irish to Christianity. Invasions by Norsemen began in the 8th Century, but were ended by defeat of the Danes by the Irish King Brian Boru in 1014. English invasions started in the 12th Century; for over 700 years the Anglo-Irish struggle continued with bitter rebellions and savage repressions.

The Easter Monday Rebellion (1916) failed but was followed by guerrilla warfare and harsh reprisals by British troops, the "Black and Tans." The Dail Eireann, or Irish parliament in Dublin, reaffirmed independence in Jan. 1919. The British offered dominion status to Ulster (6 counties) and southern Ireland (26 counties) Dec. 1921. The constitution of the Irish Free State, a British dominion, was adopted Dec. 11, 1922. By treaty with Great Britain Northern Ireland could vote itself out, which it did, Dec. 12, 1922.

A new constitution adopted by plebiscite came into operation Dec. 29, 1937. It declared the name of the state Eire in the Irish language and Ireland in the English and declared it a sovereign democratic state.

On Dec. 21, 1948, an Irish law declared the country a republic rather than a dominion and withdrew it from the Commonwealth. In 1949 the British Parliament recognized both actions, but re-asserted its claim to incorporate the six northeastern counties (Antrim, Armagh, Derry, Down, Fermanagh and Tyrone) in the United Kingdom. This claim has not been recognized by Ireland. *See United Kingdom—Northern Ireland.*

William T. Cosgrave was chosen President of the Executive Council, Dec. 1922. He was in office until Mar., 1932, when Eamon de Valera became President of the Executive Council and Minister for External Affairs, holding both offices until 1938. Leaders since 1938 have been:

Presidents: (7-year terms): Douglas Hyde, 1938-1945; Sean T. O'Kelly, 1945-1952, 1952-1959; Eamon de Valera, 1959-1966, 1966-1973; Erskine Childers, 1973-.

Prime Ministers: Eamon de Valera, 1937-1948; John A. Costello, 1948-1951; Eamon de Valera, 1951-1954; John A. Costello, 1954-1957; Eamon de Valera, 1957-1959; Sean Lemass, 1959-1966; John M. Lynch, 1966-1973; Liam Cosgrave, 1973-.

Following Feb. 28, 1973, elections the Fianna Fail party was ousted from power after 16 years, although it won 69 seats, by a coalition of Fine Gael, 54 seats, and Labor, 19. Independents won 2.

The parliament is composed of a house, Dail Eireann, of 144 elected members, and a senate, Seanad Eireann, of 60, 11 of them nominated by the prime minister, 6 by the universities and the rest elected from 5 panels of candidates representing public interests. The president, on nomination of the Dail, appoints the prime minister and on nomination of the latter with Dail approval names the other ministers.

Irish Governments have maintained that solution of Northern Ireland troubles can be reached only by peaceful unification of all Ireland.

Education and Religion. Roman Catholicism is the prevailing religion, claiming more than 90% of the population. In a 1972 referendum voters repealed a Constitutional provision giving the Roman Catholic Church a "special position."

Elementary education is free and compulsory, and the Irish language is a required study in all national schools. Institutions of higher learning include the National University, founded 1908, comprising the Constituent Colleges of Dublin, Cork, Galway and St. Patrick's, Maynooth; Trinity College, Dublin, founded 1591; the Dublin Institute for Advanced Studies; the Royal Irish Academy.

Defense. Recruitment is voluntary. Permanent force of the Army, Navy and Air Force is set at 13,000; first and second line reserves number 25,000. The Navy consists of small vessels.

Ireland is a member of the UN and Council of Europe.

It became a member of the EEC (Common Market) Jan. 1, 1973.

Israel

MEDINAT ISRAEL

Capital: Jerusalem. Area: 7,993 sq. mi. Population (Est. 1973): 3,200,000. Monetary unit: Israeli pound.

The nation of Israel was re-established, as a republic, in 1948. It occupies part of the ancient land first called Canaan, then Israel, then Palestine. About the size of New Jersey, it faces the Mediterranean to the W, Lebanon to the N, Syria and Jordan to the E, and Egypt to the SW.

The coastal plain on the W is 120 mi. long, 15 wide, fertile and well watered. In the center is the plateau of Judea. A triangular-shaped semi-desert region, the Negev, extends from south of Beersheba to an apex at the head of the Gulf of Aqaba. The eastern border drops sharply into the depressed valley of the River Jordan and the Dead Sea which is 46 mi. long, with an average width of 8 mi., 1,296 ft. below sea level, lowest point on the earth's surface.

Israel's area, as defined by armistices with the Arab nations, includes all the land assigned to it under the 1947 partition resolution of the UN General Assembly, as well as Western Galilee and a corridor to Jerusalem. By the terms of the armistice with Syria, July 20, 1949, last of the Arab states to end military action after the creation of modern Israel, demilitarized zones were set up on the eastern edge of Lake Huleh and the southeastern shore of the Sea of Galilee, site of Israel's Ein Gev settlement.

After the Israeli-Arab war of June 1967 in which Israel occupied the Sinai Peninsula, the west bank of the Jordan and a small area of Syria, Israel indicated it would not consider returning these areas unless the Arab states negotiated peace treaties directly with Israel and unless Egypt agreed Israel would have the same shipping rights as other nations in the Suez Canal.

Non-Jewish population: Moslem, 329,000; Christian, 76,000; Druse, 36,000.

The chief ports of Israel are Haifa, Elath and Ashdod.

Resources and Industries. Citrus fruit is the most valuable agricultural product. Other principal crops include wheat, barley, durra, olives, melons, grapes, figs, tomatoes, bananas, cotton. Since 1955 total cultivated area has been increased from 412,500 to more than 1,058,000 acres, of which 448,000 acres are under irrigation. Wine making is an extensive industry.

Israel has abundant deposits of some minerals including limestone, sandstone, gypsum, copper, iron, phosphates, magnesium, manganese, ceramic clays. The valley of Jordan and the Dead Sea yield rock salt, sulphur and potash.

Israel's over-all economy and industrialization have both grown rapidly. The economy has been aided by German reparations payments, U. S. aid, international loans and contributions. West Germany completed payment of $860,000,000 in reparations (cash and goods) in 1965. The

two countries also set up full diplomatic relations.

The index of industrial production (1963 = 100) reached 228 in 1971, 254 in 1972.

The Negev region in the South is Israel's primary development area, receiving nearly half of the immigrants. It has huge phosphate deposits, copper, oil, natural gas and diamonds.

A 150-mi. pipeline, major link in Israel's national water plan, was completed in June, 1964 and began carrying water from Lake Kinneret (Sea of Galilee) to the Negev. Several desalination plants have been built.

In 1970 Israel completed construction of a 160-mi., 42-inch, oil pipeline from Elath on the Gulf of Aqaba to Ashkelon on the Mediterranean.

Israel's first atomic reactor at Nahal Rubin began operations in July, 1960. The nation launched its first successful solid-fuel rocket 50 mi. into the atmosphere July 5, 1961, for meteorological study.

Israel's main exports are citrus fruits, polished diamonds, chemicals, textiles and fashion goods, machinery, plastics, tires and pharmaceutical products.

Tourism is second only to citrus products in earnings, over $150,000,000 annually.

Foreign trade in thousands of U. S. dollars:

	Imports	Exports
1971	$1,786,000	$ 915,000
1972	$1,922,200	$1,101,300

History and Government. The Jewish people lived in Israel from about 1200 B.C.; many were driven from the land by some of its various conquerors. The Judaic moral and ethical code and the Bible originated here. The modern Zionist movement for a homeland in Palestine, led by Dr. Chaim Weizmann (born in Motele, Russia, Nov. 27, 1874) caused the cabinet of Great Britain to give its support in the Balfour Declaration, Nov. 2, 1917. Under the Palestine Mandate, about four-fifths of historic Palestine was detached in 1922 to form Trans-Jordan, now the Kingdom of Jordan. When the Nazi persecutions began in Germany great numbers of Jews set out for Palestine. The UN General Assembly voted Nov. 29, 1947, to partition Palestine into two independent states by Oct. 1, 1948. A separate enclave of Jerusalem, area 289 sq. mi., was to be administered by a governor appointed by the UN. Great Britain gave up its mandate May 15, 1948.

A new Zionist state, the Republic of Israel, was proclaimed May 14, 1948. A few hours after Israel proclaimed its independence, the armies of Egypt, Jordan, Syria, Lebanon and Iraq, with Saudi Arabian contingents, crossed its frontiers at several points. They were defeated.

Separate armistices with the Arab nations were signed in 1949, but no general peace settlement was obtained. The Arab nations continued policies of economic boycott, blockade in the Suez Canal, political warfare and local incitement.

Saying an Arab attack was imminent, Israel invaded Egypt's Sinai, Oct. 29, 1956, aided briefly by British and French forces. A UN ceasefire was arranged Nov. 6.

An uneasy truce between Israel and the Arab countries, supervised by a United Nations Emergency Force, prevailed until May 19, 1967, when the UN force withdrew at the demand of Egypt's President Gamal Abdel Nasser. Egyptian forces rapidly reoccupied the Gaza Strip and closed the Gulf of Aqaba to Israeli shipping. In a full-scale 6-day war that started June 5, the Israelis took the Gaza strip, occupied the Sinai Peninsula to the Suez Canal, and captured Old Jerusalem, Syria's Golan Heights and Jordan's West Bank. The fighting was halted June 10 by UN-arranged cease-fire agreements.

By 1969-70 there were almost daily Egyptian-Israeli artillery duels across the Suez Canal as well as ground forays and air raids with Israeli planes penetrating deep into Egypt. Palestinian guerrilla raids and Israeli reprisals continued across the Jordanian, Syrian, and Lebanese frontiers; there were also encounters with Syrian and Jordanian forces.

It was est. in 1970 there were 10,000 or more Soviet military men in Egypt, and increasing supplies of Soviet planes and anti-aircraft missiles, some of which Israel charged were manned by Russians. In July 1972 the Russians, then est. at 20,000, were sent home by Egypt.

In June 1970 the U.S. proposed a 3-month, standstill cease-fire and peace negotiations. Israel, Egypt and Jordan agreed; the cease fire began Aug. 7; negotiations under UN auspices began Aug. 25. Palestinian guerrilla groups said they would continue attacks on Israel.

The cease-fire was formally ended by Egypt Mar. 7, 1971, but continued unofficially in effect as the U.S. and UN continued to seek peace agreements. Guerrilla terrorist attacks continued in 1972-73 and Israel made reprisal raids against guerrilla groups in Lebanon and Syria.

Israel is a parliamentary democracy. The first constituent assembly (Knesset), was formed Feb. 14, 1949, with 120 members, including 8 Arabs, The assembly elected Dr. Chaim Weizmann, who had been provisional President from the start, first President of Israel Feb. 17, 1949. He died Nov. 9, 1952. Israel's first Premier was David Ben-Gurion.

The Knesset (Parliament) members are elected by universal suffrage for 4-year terms by all citizens over 18, under proportional representation.

Israel maintains formal diplomatic relations with 100 nations. About 400 specialists in many fields share their knowledge with them in less developed nations in Africa and elsewhere. But several African nations broke off relations with Israel in 1972-73, reportedly at the urging of Libya.

Education. Israel has compulsory education from 5 years of age to 16. Total enrollment in 5,719 state schools in 1971 was 766,876. Of these, 116,733 were enrolled in Arab schools run by the state and 28,000 in non-state Arab schools. Total students in all educational institutions was close to 850,000 in 1971, compared to 130,000 in 1948.

Over 53,000 students attend 7 universities and other specialized institutes.

Defense. Military service is compulsory for men and, between ages 18-26, unmarried women. Military strength for 1972-73 was a regular force of 77,000 which could be raised rapidly to 300,000 by mobilization of reservists.

Israel became a member of the UN in 1949.

Italy

REPUBBLICA ITALIANA

Capital: Rome. Area: 116,303 sq. mi. Population (UN est. 1972): 54,350,000. Monetary unit: Lira.

The Republic of Italy occupies a long peninsula shaped like a boot, extending SE from the Alps into the Mediterranean, with the island of Sicily separated from the mainland by the 2-mi. Strait of Messina at the toe of the boot. The country is about 700 mi. long and not over 220 mi. wide. Its area is about the same as Arizona's. Lying directly W of mid-Italy is the major island of Sardinia, slightly smaller than Sicily.

Sicily, 9,927 sq. mi., pop. (1971) 2,985,678, is a triangular island 180 by 120 mi., seat of a Region that embraces the island of **Pantelleria,** 32 sq. mi., and the **Lipari** group, 44 sq. mi., pop. 14,000 including two with active volcanoes: **Vulcano,** 1,637 ft. and **Stromboli,** 3,038 ft. From prehistoric times Sicily has been settled by Mediterranean peoples; a strong Greek state had its capital at Syracuse. Rome took Sicily from Carthage 215 B.C. **Mt. Etna,** 10,705 ft. active volcano, is tallest peak. Sicily leads in citrus fruits, also produces wheat, grapes, wine, sulphur, salt, olives. Cattle and sheep are raised.

Sardinia, 9,283 sq. mi., pop. (1971), 1,406,345, lies in the Mediterranean, 115 mi. W of Italy and 7½ mi. S of Corsica. Like Sicily, it is under a regional administration. It is 160 mi. long, 68 mi. wide, mountainous, with mining of coal, zinc, lead, copper; it raises grapes, olives, tobacco, also cattle and sheep. In 1720 Sardinia was added to the possessions of the Dukes of Savoy in Piedmont and Savoy to form the Kingdom of Sardinia. Giuseppe Garibaldi is buried on the nearby isle of Caprera. Capital: Cagliari.

Elba, 87 sq. mi., pop. 30,000 6 mi. west of Tuscany. Industries include fishing, iron mining, wine making. Na-

poleon I lived here in exile, 1814-1815.

Capri, 4 sq. mi., pop. c. 9,000, 20 mi. SW of Naples, is famous for its beauty and equable climate.

The allure of historical monuments, great museums of painting and sculpture, imposing churches, as well as good living attracts about 28,600,000 tourists a year. Florence, with its galleries; Rome with its religious associations and ancient relics, Venice, and the resorts of the Riviera are the principal objectives.

The 3.4-mi. Great St. Bernard tunnel, between Italy and Switzerland, first auto tunnel in the Alps, was opened Mar. 19, 1964. The Mont Blanc tunnel, 7.25 mi. linking Italy and France, was opened July 16, 1965.

Resources and Industries. Italy has enjoyed an extraordinary industrial growth since World War II. Agriculture has also been improved through modernization. Grapes, olives, citrus fruits, vegetables, wheat, rice and cattle are the major agricultural products.

The wines of Italy have great variety. Chianti from Tuscany is popular, as are Asti Spumante, Orvieto, Capri.

White marble is quarried at Carrara, Volterra and Pisa; colored marble at Verona, Siena and Vicenza. Alabaster comes chiefly from Volterra.

Natural gas is found in the valley of the Po, the Marches, Abruzzi, Apulia, Basilicata and Sicily. In Sicily oil is carried by pipeline to the port of Augusta on the Gulf of Catania.

In 1972 electric plants produced 123.3 billion kwh. In 1971 there were 3 nuclear power plants and a 4th under construction. The electrical industry was nationalized in 1962.

Steel production was 19,784,000 metric tons in 1972. Italy is a heavy producer of industrial and electrical machinery, automobiles, steel products, typewriters, shoes, textiles, synthetic fabrics, machine tools. Its chemical industry has expanded rapidly.

The index of industrial production (1963 = 100) was 150 for 1972.

Italy's merchant marine ranks high. It has over 625 ships of more than 1,000 gross tons.

Tourism is important, bringing in $1.5 billion a year.

Foreign trade, in thousands of U.S. dollars:

	Imports	Exports
1971	$15,968,000	$15,111,000
1972	$19,282,000	$18,548,000

History and Government. Divided and dismembered for centuries, modern Italy began to develop after the war of 1859 when Lombardy came under the crown of King Victor Emmanuel II of Sardinia of the house of Savoy. By plebiscite in 1860, Parma, Modena, Romagna and Tuscany joined, followed by Sicily and Naples, and by the Marches and Umbria. The first Italian Parliament declared Victor Emmanuel King of Italy Mar. 17, 1861. Mantua and Venetia were added in 1866 as an outcome of the Austro-Prussian war. The Papal States were taken by Italian troops, Sept. 20, 1870, with the withdrawal of the French garrison. The states were annexed to the kingdom by plebiscite. The King entered Rome July 2, 1871. Italy recognized the State of Vatican City as independent Feb. 11, 1929.

Fascism appeared in Italy Mar. 23, 1919 when the original Fascisti organized an association against Communism and Socialism under the guidance of Benito Mussolini. They took over the government at the invitation of the King Oct. 28, 1922. Mussolini acquired dictatorial powers and was called Duce (Leader). He made war on Ethiopia and proclaimed Victor Emmanuel III emperor; defied the sanctions of the League of Nations; joined the Berlin-Tokyo axis; sent troops to fight for Franco against the Republic of Spain; joined Germany in World War II with defeat of France. After Fascism was overthrown in 1943, Italy declared war on Germany and Japan and contributed to the Allied victory. It surrendered conquered lands and lost colonies. Part of Venezia Giulia went to Yugoslavia and Trieste was made a free territory. Mussolini was put to death by a firing squad of Partisans near the village of Dongo on Lake Como, Apr. 28, 1945.

King, Victor Emmanuel III abdicated May 9, 1946; his

son Humbert II, was king until June 10, when Italy became a republic after a referendum, June 2-3.

The Constituent Assembly elected Enrico de Nicola provisional Head of State. He was succeeded by Luigi Einaudi, first President of the Republic, 1948-1955.

The Senate has 315 members, elected for 5-year terms, plus 5 whom the President may appoint for life. Ex-Presidents are eligible for life membership. The Chamber of Deputies has 630 members elected for 5 years. Titles of nobility are no longer recognized. Reorganization of the Fascist party is forbidden.

The Prime Minister and Cabinet normally represent a coalition of the Christian Democrats, largest of Italy's many parties, and one or two other parties.

Between 1948 and 1972, 15 regional governments were created, taking over some functions previously belonging to the central and local governments.

Trieste, part of which is now claimed as an Italian Department bounded E and S by Yugoslavia, was organized as a free territory by the Big Four in the peace treaty with Italy, Feb. 10, 1947, placed under jurisdiction of the UN Security Council, garrisoned by troops of the United States and Great Britain in the northern section (Zone A), and by Yugoslavia in the south (Zone B). It had about 320 sq. mi. Following prolonged negotiations an agreement was signed Oct. 5, 1954, by Italy and Yugoslavia which gave Italy provisional administration over the northern section and the seaport of Trieste, with 90 sq. mi. and about 300,000 pop., and Yugoslavia the Istrian peninsula it had occupied, 200 sq. mi. and 73,500 pop., and provision for emergency access to the port. The two areas are treated as parts of Italy and Yugoslavia.

Italy is a member of NATO, EEC and Council of Europe; admitted to the UN Dec. 14, 1955.

Education and Religion. Roman Catholicism is the state religion.

Italy has 26 state universities, including Bologna (founded 1088): Genoa (1471); Naples (1224); Padua (1222); Pisa (1338); Rome (1303), and Turin (1404). There are 22 other institutes of higher education. Education is compulsory between 6 and 14.

Defense. Military strength for 1972-73 was 427,000, plus security forces of about 80,000 and reserves of 660,000.

A large proportion of the forces are committed to NATO.

Ivory Coast

COTE D'IVOIRE

Capital: Abidjan. Area: 127,520 sq. mi. Population (UN est. 1972): 4,530,000. Monetary unit: CFA franc.

The Republic of the Ivory Coast, a former French Overseas Territory in West Africa, is on the northern coast of the Gulf of Guinea. Roughly square in shape and about the size of New Mexico, it is bounded by Liberia, Guinea, Mali, Upper Volta and Ghana. It has 340 mi. of coastline on the Atlantic. Abidjan, the capital, is the chief port. A new port, San Pedro, opened in 1971.

In accordance with provisions of the 1958 French constitution, Ivory Coast became fully independent Aug. 7, 1960; it became a member of the UN Sept. 20. Its present constitution was adopted Oct. 31, 1960. It signed a bilateral agreement Apr. 24, 1961, retaining close ties with France. Ivory Coast is a member of the West African economic community, formed June 1972, with Dahomey, Mali, Mauritania, Niger, Senegal and Upper Volta.

Agriculture, forestry, stock raising and fishing occupy 90% of the population. Chief export crops are coffee, cocoa, tropical woods and bananas; cotton, rice, oil palms also are raised. Electric power, lumbering and industrialization are being promoted.

The Ivory Coast has been the most prosperous of West African nations. It has a favorable balance of trade. Exports grew and continued to exceed imports in 1972. The number of small factories also increased.

About 18% of the people are Catholics or Protestants; 20% are Moslems and the rest animists. French is the official language.

Jamaica

Capital: Kingston. Area: 4,411 sq. mi. Population (UN est. 1972): 1,920,000. Monetary unit: Jamaican dollar.

Jamaica is a mountainous island in the Caribbean Sea, 90 mi. south of Cuba. Its area is 12% less than that of Connecticut.

Temperatures range from 80 to 86 on the coast and down to 40 in the Blue Mtns. Montego Bay and Ocho Rios are among popular resort areas; most of about 493,000 annual tourists are American.

Jamaica was discovered by Columbus, 1494, and ruled by Spanish (under whom native Arawak Indians died out) until captured by the English, 1655. The island figures largely in the history of the buccaneers of the West Indies before and during the time of Sir Henry Morgan, once its governor. Port Royal, old haunt of the pirate, at the entrance to Kingston harbor, was largely destroyed by earthquake, 1692.

Jamaica became independent within the Commonwealth Aug. 6, 1962, and joined the UN.

There is a Governor General representing the British crown, an elected House of Representatives and an appointed Senate; executive power lies with a Prime Minister and Cabinet.

Principal exports are bauxite (world's largest production) and alumina. Other products include sugar cane, coffee, bananas, rum, coconuts, ginger, cocoa, pimento, citrus fruits and cigars.

Value of imports exceeds that of exports but earnings from tourism help offset this. Manufacturing plants have grown in number, aided by government-sponsored incentives.

Japan

NIPPON—LAND OF THE RISING SUN

Capital: Tokyo. Area: 144,698 sq. mi. Population (Govt. est. 1972): 107,332,000. Monetary unit: Yen.

Japan consists of four main islands: Honshu ("mainland"), 88,952 sq. mi.; Hokkaido, 30,304; Kyushu, 16,191; and Shikoku, 7,240. Total area is about twice that of Missouri. The islands lie in the North Pacific separated from the Soviet Union and Korea by the Sea of Japan and from China by the East China Sea.

By the terms ending World War II, Japan was forced to surrender captured lands, including Manchuria (Manchukuo), the southern half of Sakhalin Is., the Kuriles, Korea, Taiwan, and the mandated islands in the Pacific, the Marshalls, the Carolines and the Marianas. (See Index for these.)

The Japanese coast is deeply indented, measuring 16,654 mi. The northern islands are a continuation of the Sakhalin mountain chain running through Hokkaido and the main island. The continuation of the Kunlun mountain range of China appears in the southern islands, the ranges meeting in the Japanese Alps. In the vast transverse fissure crossing the main island from the Sea of Japan to the Pacific rises a group of volcanoes, mostly extinct or dormant, with Fuji-San (Fujiyama), 60 mi. SW of Tokyo, lifting its white cone 12,388 ft.

Most important ports are Yokohama, Kobe, Nagoya, and Osaka. **Tokyo,** the capital, is one of the three largest cities of the world. It has a modern business section centering about the Ginza, a major avenue. The Imperial Palace, surrounded by a moat on a 250-acre site and the white-marble Diet building, erected in 1936, are also in Tokyo. Its International Airport is Asia's busiest.

Tokyo Tower is a 1,089-ft. steel structure built for radio-TV broadcasting and sightseeing.

At Kamakura, 30 mi. SW of Tokyo is the Great Buddha or Daibutsu, a bronze figure 42 ft. 6 in. tall with base, cast in 1252. The Hakone hot spring area is noted for the reflection in Lake Ashino of Fuji-San. Also famous is the Toshogu Shrine at Nikko, where a national park of 347,000 acres preserves the natural beauty of Japanese flora. Kyoto, for 1,000 years a capital city, with massive temples and colorful shrines, is a cultural center.

The 2.34-mi. Kanmon undersea highway tunnel connecting Honshu and Kyushu, is the world's first double-deck tunnel, with one level for vehicles and one for pedestrians.

Resources and Industries. More than half the arable land is used for growing rice, the chief food. Wheat, barley, sweet and white potatoes, tobacco, tea, beans, peaches, pears, apples, grapes, persimmons and mandarins are also produced. Minerals include gold, silver, copper, lead, zinc, chromite, white arsenic, coal, sulphur, salt and petroleum.

The principal industries are iron and steel products, transportation equipment, machinery, electronics, shipbuilding, precision instruments, chemicals, fertilizers, textiles (cotton, wool, silks, synthetics), ceramics, wood products, fisheries. The 1971 fish catch, valued at $2.7 billion, lead all nations.

Japan is 2nd to the U.S. in motor vehicle production; exports in 1972 totaled 1,965,490 autos, trucks and buses. It is also 2nd to the U.S. in number of telephones in use.

The index of industrial production (1963 = 100) zoomed to 270 for 1971, 290 for 1972.

Japan's shipyards lead the world, especially in construction of super tankers and bulk carriers of over 300,000 tons. Japan's own merchant fleet included over 2,210 ships of 1,000 or more gross tons, leading all nations.

Electric power production was about 384 billion kwh in 1972, about half from hydroelectric plants. An atomic power station at Tokai, near Tokyo, began commercial distribution of electricity in 1966.

Major exports are steel and related products, clothing, chemicals, motor vehicles, optical goods, ships, radio receivers, toys.

Tourism is an increasingly important source of foreign exchange; in 1972, 723,744 visitors spent over $210,000,000.

The U.S. is Japan's biggest customer, taking about one-third of all its exports. In 1972 Japan agreed to take steps to reduce the U.S. trade deficit with Japan.

Foreign trade in thousands of U.S. dollars:

	Imports	Exports
1971	$19,667,000	$24,090,000
1972	$23,481,000	$28,655,000

History and Government. According to Japanese legend, the empire was founded by Emperor Jimmu 660 B.C. Temporal power was exercised by successive families of Shoguns (military dictators), 1192-1867, until recovered by the Emperor Meiji in 1868. The Portuguese and Dutch had minor trade with Japan in the 16th and 17th Centuries. Commodore Matthew C. Perry, USN, opened it to U.S. trade in a treaty ratified 1854. Japan fought China, 1894-95, gaining Taiwan. In war with Russia, 1904-05, Russia's fleet was wiped out at Tsushima; Russia ceded S half of Sakhalin and gave concessions in China. Japan annexed Korea, 1910. In first World War Japan ousted Germany from Shantung, took over German Pacific islands as mandates from the League of Nations. Japan took Manchuria, 1931, started war with China 1932, taking Peking and Shanghai and bombing Nanking, Canton, Tientsin. Japan, frustrated in efforts to have a free hand in the East, started a war against the U.S. by attack on Pearl Harbor, Dec. 7, 1941. Japan surrendered Aug. 14, 1945, and Gen. Douglas MacArthur headed occupation of Japan as Supreme Commander for the Allied Powers.

In a new constitution adopted May 3, 1947, the Japanese people renounced the right to wage war; the Emperor was acknowledged as hereditary symbol of the nation, but gave up claims to divinity; the Diet became the sole law-making authority. The House of Councilors has 252 members elected for 6 yr. terms and the House of Representatives 491 members, elected for 4 yrs., both by popular vote. The constitution separates church and state. Japan has granted suffrage to women, lowered the voting age to 20.

The Emperor is Hirohito, the 124th of his line, born April 29, 1901, succeeded to the throne Dec. 25, 1926; married Jan. 26, 1924, to Princess Nagako Kuni. The Crown Prince is Akihito Tsugu No Miya, born Dec. 23, 1933;

married Apr. 10, 1959, Michiko Shoda. (First son: Prince Naruhito Hironomiya, born Feb. 23, 1960.)

Japan was elected 80th member of the UN Dec. 19, 1956. It is a member of UNESCO, World Court, International Monetary Fund and GATT.

The United States and 48 other non-Communist nations signed a peace treaty and the U. S. a bilateral defense agreement with Japan, in San Francisco, Sept. 8, 1951; ratified by the Senate, March 20; signed by President Truman, April 15, restoring Japan's sovereignty April 28, 1952. The Senate, in approving the treaty, Feb. 5, advised repudiation of the section of the Yalta agreement that gave to the USSR South Sakhalin, and the Kurile Islands. Under the treaty, Japan was reduced territorially to the four main islands, but it was to have an opportunity eventually to regain the Ryukyus and Bonin Islands. Japan signed separate treaties with Nationalist China, April 27, 1952; India, June 9, 1952; a declaration with USSR ending a technical state of war, Oct. 19, 1956; in Dec. 1965 Japan and South Korea agreed to resume diplomatic relations.

On June 26, 1968, the U. S. returned to Japanese control the Bonin Islands, the Volcano Islands (including Iwo Jima) and Marcus Island. On May 15, 1972, Okinawa and the other Ryukyu Islands and the Daito Islands were returned to Japan by the U.S., but it was agreed the U.S. would continue to maintain large military bases on Okinawa.

On Sept. 29, 1972, Japan and mainland China agreed to resume diplomatic relations; Japan and Taiwan severed relations.

Education and Religion. The principal forms of religion are Buddhism, with 12 sects, and Shintoism with 13. There are more than 100,000 Shinto shrines, 106,634 Buddhist temples and several thousand Christian churches.

Nine years of education is compulsory, consisting of 6 years of elementary and 3 years of lower secondary education. There were 382 colleges and universities, including 75 national universities, and 479 junior colleges in 1970. English is required study in lower secondary schools.

Defense. Legislation effective July 1, 1954, established new Self-Defense Forces. Military strength for 1972-73 totaled 260,000.

The Ground S-D Force had 180,000 uniformed personnel; it included one mechanized and 13 infantry divisions, 125 aircraft, 220 helicopters. The Maritime S-D Force had 39,000; it had 11 submarines, 40 destroyers, numerous other vessels, 200 planes, 60 helicopters. The Air S-D Force strength was 41,000; it had 406 combat planes plus other aircraft.

During 1969, the U. S. began turning over 50 military installation sites, a third of its facilities in Japan, to the Japanese. The U.S. reduced its forces in Japan in 1971.

Jordan
AL-MAMLAKAH
AL URDINIYAH AL HASHIMIYAH
Capital: Amman. Area: 37,500 sq. mi. Population (UN est. 1972): 2,470,000. Monetary unit: Dinar.

Jordan is a constitutional monarchy in southwest Asia, formerly under the Palestine Mandate. The country's former name, Transjordan, was dropped Apr. 26, 1949, after it occupied the West Bank lands, west of the Jordan River, in favor of the constitutional name, Hashemite Kingdom of Jordan. Hashemite is a family name and honors the loyalty of the original holder, disciple of Mohammed and "Guardian of Mecca."

About 12% of the land is fertile; the rest is arid. In the extreme south is its only port, Aqaba, on the Gulf of Aqaba. It shares the Dead Sea (1,296 ft. below sea level) with Israel. Jordan is slightly larger than Indiana.

Resources and Industries. The fertile western portions have a high agricultural potential. Principal crops are tomatoes, vegetables, wheat, barley, olives, grapes, citrus fruits and bananas.

Construction was started May 1966 on the Mokheiba Dam on the Yarmuk River, a tributary of the Jordan, to provide electric power and irrigation for 18,000 acres.

Industries include tobacco, flour milling, distilling, building materials, olive oil, soap, mother-of-pearl, textiles, plastics, cement, steel, batteries, leather. Airlines include Royal Jordan (ALYA).

Potash from the Dead Sea and phosphate rock are the main minerals. Phosphate is 30% of value of exports.

History and Government. Jordan was part of the Ottoman Empire from the 16th Century until World War I. It was set up within the Palestine Mandate Sept. 1, 1922, and gained its independence in 1946. Abdullah Ibn Al Hussein, born 1882, was proclaimed King, May 25, 1946; he was assassinated by an Arab extremist July 20, 1951. His eldest son was proclaimed King Talal I, Sept. 5, 1951.

Parliament removed King Talal on medical advice, installing his son King Hussein I (born Nov. 14, 1935), May 11, 1952. His first marriage to Sherifa Deena (a daughter, Princess Alya, was born 1956) was dissolved 1958. He married (May 25, 1961) Antoinette Avril Gardiner, of England, entitled Princess Muna. They had two sons, Prince Abdullah, b. 1962, Prince Feisal, b. 1964, and twin daughters, Zein and Aisha, born 1968, but in 1965 King Hussein designated one of his younger brothers, Hassan, to be Crown Prince and heir to the throne. In Dec. 1972 Hussein divorced Muna and married Alia Toukan, a Jordanian from the West Bank.

Legislature comprises a Senate of 30 nominated by the King and a lower house of 60 elected by manhood suffrage. Jordan is a member of the UN and Arab League.

After creation of the state of Israel, May 14, 1948, Jordan joined in the Arab attack on the new nation. An armistice was reached in 1949; Jordan took control of areas of central Palestine including the West Bank and the old city of Jerusalem. Several hundred thousand Palestinian refugees fled into Jordan.

In the 6-day Israeli-Arab war in June 1967 Israel took control of the old city of Jerusalem and the West Bank.

In 1968-70, Palestinian guerrillas based in Jordan continued raids on Israel, including artillery attacks. Israel staged reprisal raids against commando bases inside Jordan, including air attacks.

Fighting between Jordanian troops and Palestinian commandos in 1970 included a 10-day civil war in Sept. In renewed fighting in July 1971 Jordanian troops dispersed thousands of commandos from their bases. Syria, Algeria and Libya suspended relations with Jordan, and Iraq closed its border. Syria reopened its border in 1972.

Education and Religion. The population is chiefly Arab, of whom the majority are Arab Moslems, 250,000 Arab Christians, and 10,000 Moslem Circassians. The language is Arabic. Public school education is growing, with English and Arabic taught. The Jordanian Univ. was established in 1962 and offers 4-yr. courses in arts and sciences.

Defense. Military strength for 1972-73 was 69,000. The U.S. has provided military aid, including 2 squadrons of F-5E supersonic interceptors promised in 1973.

Kenya

Capital: Nairobi. Area: 224,960 sq. mi. Population (UN est. 1972): 12,070,000. Monetary unit: Kenya shilling.

Kenya, former British Colony and Protectorate which became independent in 1963, extends from its Indian Ocean coast NE to Somalia, N to Ethiopia, W to Uganda, and S to Tanzania. It has twice the area of New Mexico.

The northern three-fifths is arid. Most economic production is centered in the south, a low coastal area and a plateau varying from 3,000 to 10,000 ft. The main products are coffee, tea, cereals, cotton, sisal, dairy products, hides and skins, bark extract, timber and minerals. Kenya is the largest producer of tea in Africa.

In 1953 Kenya became the scene of terroristic activities of the Mau Mau, an oath-bound unit of some of the Kikuyu, Meru, Embu and other tribes which killed Africans and whites during an 8-year rebellion.

Kenya won independence within the Commonwealth Dec. 12, 1963, and joined the UN Dec. 16. Jomo Kenyatta, once imprisoned as a Mau Mau leader, became its first Prime Minister. It became a republic within the Commonwealth Dec. 12, 1964, and Kenyatta became its first President. The National Assembly is a unicameral legislature.

Since independence, Kenya's economy has continued to grow, including both agriculture and manufacturing. Tourism has boomed. Schools and health centers have increased. Drought caused setbacks in 1971 but eased off in 1972.

In Jan. 1968 Kenya and Somalia resumed diplomatic relations as efforts were made to end 4 years of skirmishes caused by "invasions" of nomadic Somali herders seeking grass and water.

From 1968 through 1973, thousands of Asians holding old British passports were ordered evicted from Kenya. In 1973 it was announced Swahili would become the national language, with English still used for international communications.

Republic of Korea

DAEHAN-MINKUK

Capital: Seoul. Area: 38,004 sq. mi. Population (UN est. 1972): 32,530,000. Monetary unit: Won.

Korea, Land of the Morning Calm, occupies a mountainous peninsula in northeast Asia separating the Yellow Sea from the Sea of Japan. South Korea is about the size of Indiana.

Resources and Industries. Once chiefly an agricultural country, South Korea has a cultivated area of about 5,095,655 acres. The main crops are rice, barley, wheat, tobacco and beans, but the mountainous terrain, poor soil and cold winters limit agricultural potential.

Division of Korea in 1945 left the South with only light industry and about 10% of the power generating capacity. Large infusions of foreign aid have since helped to build an industrial base especially in mining of tungsten (supplies 6% of world's needs), coal, iron ore, bismuth, fluorspar, graphite and cement. The fishing, timber, rubber, glass, shipbuilding, electronics and silk industries have expanded rapidly; chemical and fertilizer plants and oil refineries have been built. Industrial growth was at a record high in 1971-72.

U. S. support in South Korea has been military, financial, technical and educational. Since 1954 it has totaled more than $2.2 billion. Index of industrial production (1963 = 100) was 416 for 1972.

Foreign trade in thousands of U.S. dollars:

	Imports	Exports
1971	$2,394,000	$1,068,000
1972	$2,522,000	$1,633,000

History and Government. Korea, formerly the Hermit Kingdom, has a recorded history since the 1st Century B.C. and was united in a kingdom under the Silla Dynasty, 668 A.D. It was at times associated with the Chinese empire and the treaty that concluded the Sino-Japanese war of 1894-95 recognized Korea's complete independence. In 1910 Japan forcibly annexed Korea as Chosun.

At the Cairo conference, Nov. 1943, it was agreed that Korea should be "free and independent." At the Potsdam conference, July, 1945, the 38th parallel was designated as the line dividing the Soviet and the American occupation. Russian troops entered Korea Aug. 10, 1945, U. S. troops entered Sept. 8, 1945. The Soviet military organized Socialists and Communists and blocked efforts to let the Koreans unite their country. Although the Soviet Union, at a foreign ministers' conference in Moscow, Dec., 1945, agreed to a joint trusteeship for Korea, it thwarted efforts to put this into effect. A commission appointed by the UN to supervise elections in Korea in 1948 was denied admission to North Korea. (*See Index for Korean War.*)

The South Koreans formed the **Republic of Korea** in May, 1948, with Seoul as the capital. Dr. Syngman Rhee was chosen President July 20 and the republic was formally proclaimed Aug. 15, 1948. By June 29, 1949, the U. S. had withdrawn its troops, leaving behind a Korean constabulary. President Rhee was reelected to a 4th term, Mar. 15, 1960, when 85 years old. A national movement spearheaded by college students forced his resignation, Apr. 26, amid charges of corruption and election fraud.

A constitutional amendment passed June 15, 1960, replaced an autocratic presidential system with a cabinet system.

In an army coup, May 16, 1961, Gen. Park Chung Hee became chairman of the ruling junta. He was formally elected President Oct. 15, 1963 and reelected 1967 and 1971.

A referendum, Nov. 21, 1972, provided more Presidential powers and allowed him to be reelected for 6-year terms unlimited times. Pres. Park was reelected Dec. 23 by a National Conference and his party won control of the National Assembly in Feb. 1973.

North Korean raids across the border tapered off in 1971, but 2 South Korean soldiers were killed in Mar. 1973. In July 1972 South and North Korea agreed on a common goal of reunifying the two nations by peaceful means. Red Cross delegates from both nations met to find ways to aid divided families.

Education and Religion. Christianity, Confucianism, Buddhism and Chondogyo are the principal religions.

Primary education is compulsory. In 1970 there were 5,961 primary schools, 1,608 junior high schools, 889 high schools, 207 universities and colleges.

Defense. Military strength for 1972-73 was 634,000. By Mar. 1973, South Korea withdrew the last of 50,000 troops that had been aiding the Allies in South Vietnam.

During 1970-71 U.S. forces authorized in South Korea were reduced about a third to 40,000. South Korean troops replaced U.S. forces on the armistice border.

North Korea

CHOSON MINCHU-CHUI INMIN KONGHWA-GUK

Capital: Pyongyang. Area: 46,540 sq. mi. Population (UN est. 1972): 14,680,000. Monetary unit: Won.

The People's Democratic Republic of Korea was formed May 1, 1948. The U. S. did not recognize it.

North Korea has good mineral resources that are fairly well developed. The country ranks among the first 5 in the world in the output of tungsten, graphite and magnesite. Other products of significance include lead, zinc, pyrite, cement, iron ore, copper, gold, phosphate, salt and fluorspar. A well developed hydroelectric system and sizeable reserves of coal provide power needs for industry. Agriculture is collectivized and industry nationalized.

North Korea is slightly larger than N. Y. State.

The import and export trade is largely with Communist countries, particularly China and Russia.

The USSR signed a 10-year military aid treaty with North Korea July 6, 1961, pledging defense protection and financial help. A similar treaty was signed with Communist China. (*See Index for Korean War.*)

Soviet prestige declined in the early 1960s as North Korea sided with the Chinese in the Sino-Soviet dispute. In 1966 Pyongyang showed signs of trying to disengage from the dispute and maintain a more independent stand.

In March, 1967, North Korea and the Soviet Union signed a new defense agreement which was viewed as a further move to isolate the Chinese Communists.

North Korean patrol boats seized the U. S. Navy intelligence ship Pueblo on Jan. 23, 1968, charged it had entered North Korean territorial waters and held its crew captive. The 82 surviving crew members were freed Dec. 23 (Korean time).

North Korean planes shot down a U. S. Navy intelligence plane over the Sea of Japan Apr. 15, 1969 (Korean time). No survivors were found.

In July 1972 North and South Korea agreed they would seek reunification of the two nations by peaceful means.

North Korea's armed forces totaled over 400,000, including a large Air Force. (*See also predecing article, South Korea.*)

Kuwait

Capital: Kuwait City. Area: 6,178 sq. mi. Population (UN est. 1972): 910,000. Monetary unit: Kuwaiti dinar.

Kuwait, a small Arab state formerly under British protection, became fully independent June 19, 1961. It extends along the northwest coast of the Persian (also called Arabian) Gulf; bordered by Iraq and Saudi Arabia. Kuwait City is a principal Gulf port. In area, Kuwait is slightly larger than Connecticut.

Resources and Industries. Oil, discovered in 1938 and first exported in 1946, is Kuwait's economic mainstay and the nation has become the world's 6th largest producer. Reserves are estimated at 10 billion tons, about 15% of the world's total.

Crude oil production in 1972 was 151,200,000 tons. Annual payments to the Kuwait government in royalties and taxes exceed $1.3 billion, about 98% of the government's income. Per capita income was estimated at more than $3,000, among the world's highest.

Revenues from oil from a former Kuwaiti-Saudi neutral zone are split 50-50 with Saudi Arabia.

History and Government. Kuwait traditionally is governed by members of the Al-Sabah dynasty founded in 1756. Under a treaty of 1899 Great Britain administered its foreign relations and guaranteed its territorial integrity until it became fully independent June 19, 1961, by mutual agreement. It joined the Arab League 1961, the UN 1963. The nation's first constitution was proclaimed in January, 1963, and the first general elections for a 50-member National Assembly were held.

The Emir Sabah Al-Salim Al-Sabah became ruler Nov. 27, 1965, after the death of his older brother; the heir Abdulla Al-Salim Al-Sabah.

Iraqi troops crossed the Kuwait border in Mar. 1973 but soon withdrew; Iraq demanded possession of 2 islands claimed by Kuwait.

Education and Religion. The government has utilized its enormous national income from petroleum to create a welfare state that guarantees free medical care, education and social security for all. A $600,000,000 fund aids other Arab nations. There are no taxes except customs duties. Educational facilities are being rapidly expanded. There were, in 1973, 225 schools of all types, with 150,000 students and over 9,000 teachers. The University of Kuwait was opened in Oct. 1966. Islam is the official religion, about three-fourths Sunni, the remainder Shia.

Laos

Capital: Vientiane, Luang Prabang. Area: 91,429 sq. mi. Population (UN est. 1972): 3,110,000. Monetary unit: Kip.

Laos is a constitutional monarchy in southeast Asia, one of the three former French Indo-Chinese states. It is bounded by Communist China, North and South Vietnam, Cambodia, Thailand and Burma. It is landlocked, smaller than Oregon, largely jungle and mountains.

Laos became a French protectorate in 1893 and a member of the Indo-Chinese Union in 1899. As in Vietnam and Cambodia, nationalist aims grew in the 1940s and the King promulgated a constitution May 11, 1947, providing for a constitutional monarchy under the Luang Prabang dynasty, and a parliamentary government.

Laos became an independent sovereign state by a treaty with France, July 19, 1949.

The King is Sri Savang Vatthana, acceded Oct. 30, 1959, on the death of his father, King Sisavang Vong. The National Assembly is elected for 5 years.

Conflicts among neutralist, Communist and conservative factions created a chaotic political situation despite 1954 agreements. Although Laos was intended to be neutral, rivalry between the Communist Pathet Lao movement in the northern third of the country, led by Prince Souphanouvong, and rightwing and neutralist factions prevented integration of the Pathet Lao into the royalist army. Armed conflict increased after 1960 with the arrival of Soviet arms and North Vietnamese troops.

The 3 factions formed a coalition government in June 1962, with neutralist Prince Souvanna Phouma as Premier. A 14-nation conference in Geneva signed agreements July 23, 1962, guaranteeing neutrality and independence of Laos.

By 1964, the Pathet Lao had withdrawn from the coalition government and, with aid from North Vietnamese troops, renewed sporadic attacks on government positions. Both Laos and U. S. planes bombed the Ho Chi

Minh trail, supply line from North Vietnam to Communist forces in northern Laos and South Vietnam.

In 1970 Communist forces seized more territory in central and southeast Laos. On March 6, U.S. President Nixon urged the USSR and Britain to seek restoration of the 1962 accords; he confirmed that the U.S. had stepped up air support and military aid to Laos government forces. There were an est. 67,000 North Vietnamese troops in Laos, and some 15,000 Thai "irregulars" financed by the U.S.

On Feb. 8, 1971, South Vietnamese ground forces, with U.S. air and artillery support, launched a 44-day attack on the Ho Chi Minh trail in Laos. South Vietnam claimed heavy Communist losses and disruption of the North Vietnamese supply line. Laotian and North Vietnamese forces continued fighting in 1972.

Following a Feb. 21, 1973, ceasefire, the neutralists and Pathet Lao signed an agreement, Sept. 14, for a coalition government and withdrawal of foreign troops.

Chief products are tin, rice, maize, tobacco, cotton, opium, citrus fruits, benzoin, shellac, teakwood and coffee. The population comprises peoples of Thai, Indonesian and Chinese origin. Lao and French are the most important languages. Buddhism is the state religion.

Lebanon

AL-JUMHOURIYA AL-LUBNANIYA
Capital: Beirut. Area: 4,015 sq. mi. Population (UN est. 1972): 2,960,000. Monetary unit: Lebanese pound.

The Republic of Lebanon, in southwest Asia, occupies a strip along the Mediterranean coast about 120 mi. long and 30 to 35 mi. wide, extending from the Israeli frontier on the S to Syria on the E and N. It is smaller than Connecticut. There is a narrow coastal strip and two main mountain ranges running N and S with fertile land between. Beirut, with one-third of the country's population, is the chief seaport and has a jet airport.

Resources and Industries. Trade provides two-thirds of national income. Agriculture employs half the workers; chief crops are apples, citrus fruit, olives, tobacco, grapes, vegetables, cereals. Manufacturing is growing rapidly; important are food products, textiles, leather goods, cement, oil refining. Tripoli and Sidon are terminals of oil pipelines from Iraq and Saudi Arabia. Large hydroelectric and irrigation projects are being developed. Beirut is an Arab publishing center.

Lebanon has a free enterprise economy and banking secrecy laws. Fugitive capital from Arab Socialist states has poured into the country. Tourism is also important.

History and Government. Lebanon was formed from 5 former Turkish Empire districts and became, with Syria, an independent state Sept. 1, 1920, administered under French Mandate 1920-1941. In 1944 France yielded its powers to the Syrian and Lebanese governments. French troops were withdrawn in 1946.

Attempts by several factions to undermine the pro-western administration of Lebanon led to an open revolt in May, 1958. Lebanon became the center of international controversy when the U. S. sent Marines in reply to a government call for help. The revolt dwindled and American forces were withdrawn in Oct., 1958.

On Dec. 28, 1968, an Israeli helicopter raid on Beirut Airport destroyed 13 Lebanese airliners; Israel had accused Lebanon of aiding Arab terrorists who attacked an Israeli airliner at Athens, Dec. 26, killing an Israeli.

Lebanon's efforts to restrict Palestinian commandos caused armed clashes in 1969. Continued commando raids in 1970-71 brought Israeli reprisal raids. After more reprisal attacks by Israel in 1972 Lebanon announced that the commandos had agreed to restrict their activities.

Israeli commandos staged a reprisal raid Apr. 10, 1973, on Palestinian groups in Beirut, killing 3 guerrilla leaders. In May, the Lebanese Army and guerrilla forces battled for 2 weeks in and near Beirut; about 250 persons were killed. An agreement reportedly provided for Lebanese rule to supplant guerrilla control over the 90,000 Palestinian refugees in 15 refugee camps.

The republic's constitution instituted a democratic parliamentary regime. There is a unicameral legislature (Chamber of Deputies) of 99, elected every 4 years.

The President normally is elected for a 6-year term. Traditionally he is a Christian, the Premier a Moslem. Lebanon is a member of the UN and Arab League.

Education and Religion. Christians number about half the population, Moslems most of the remainder. There are 8 universities and institutions of higher learning in Beirut: American, French, Lebanese, and the private Academy of Arts. Arabic is the official language.

Lesotho

Capital: Maseru. Area: 11,716 sq. mi. Population (Govt. est. 1973): 1,200,000. Monetary unit: Rand.

The former British dependency, Basutoland, became independent as the Kingdom of Lesotho Oct. 4, 1966. An African state without white settlers or landowners, it is about the size of Maryland and completely surrounded by the Republic of South Africa.

The land is mountainous, altitudes ranging from 5,000 to 11,000 ft. There are air, rail and road links with South Africa. Agriculture has been advanced with U.S. and UN technical aid. Maize, sorghum, barley, beans and peas are grown. The main industry is livestock raising which produces wool and mohair, the chief exports. There are small industries including diamond polishing. About 40% of the men work in South Africa, many in the mines, earning about $2,800,000 a year. Tourism is being promoted.

In 1868, Lesotho became a British protectorate upon the request of Moshesh, the Paramount Chieftain, who sought protection against the Boers of South Africa. The British granted a constitution for the area in 1959 providing for a universally elected Legislative Council. The government consists of a King, an elected National Assembly of 60, a Senate, Cabinet and Prime Minister. In 1970, elections were suspended by Prime Minister Leabua Jonathan. A new constitution was planned in 1973.

Liberia

Capital: Monrovia. Area: 43,000 sq. mi. Population (est. 1973): 1,650,000. Monetary unit: U.S. dollar, also Liberian silver and copper coinage.

The independent Republic of Liberia lies on the southern side of the west African bulge adjacent to Sierra Leone, Guinea and the Ivory Coast and has an Atlantic coastline of about 350 mi. Much of the country is forest with valuable timber and mineral resources. It is slightly larger than Ohio.

Liberia has no natural harbors. The Free Port of Monrovia, built 1945-48 with U. S. funds, was turned over to the Liberian Government in 1964, with payments to be concluded by 1999. The country is served by several international airlines.

Resources and Industries. Iron ore and rubber are the main products.

Loans from the U. S. and other Western nations helped increase iron ore and rubber production in the 1960s. In 1970 a U. S. company began developing the nation's timber resources.

Diamonds and gold are also mined; other products are fibers, palm kernels, rice, cassava, coffee, cocoa and sugar. U. S. aid is promoting schools, hospitals, and food production.

History and Government. The population is entirely of African descent. Liberia was founded in 1822 when a settlement was made at Monrovia by black freedmen from the U. S. with the assistance of American colonization societies. It was declared a republic July 26, 1847. Its constitution is modeled on that of the U. S. Only persons of African descent may acquire citizenship and only citizens may own real estate.

There is a President elected for one 8-year term (thereafter for 4-year terms); a Senate of 18 elected for 6 years and a House of Representatives of 52, elected for 4 years. William V. S. Tubman, President since 1943, died July 23, 1971, and was succeeded by the Vice Pres., William R. Tolbert.

Education and Religion. Christianity predominates. There are nearly 4,000 schools, one university and two colleges. English is the official language.

Libya

Capital: Tripoli and Benghazi. Area: 679,358 sq. mi. Population (est. 1972): 2,080,000. Monetary unit: Libyan pound.

Libya, first country to receive independence fully under United Nations auspices, is an Arab republic comprising 10 provinces in the former states of Tripolitania, Cyrenaica and Fezzan. Larger than Alaska, it is on the north African coast, bounded by the Mediterranean, Egypt, Sudan, Chad, Niger, Algeria and Tunisia.

Resources and Industries. Discovery of major oil fields in the northern part of the country beginning in 1957 brought prosperity and an improved standard of living to the country.

By 1972, government revenues from taxes on oil companies were about $2 billion a year and the nation was the world's 7th largest petroleum producer. In 1973 it expropriated 51% of U.S. and other oil firms' assets.

In the 1960s-70s, several hundred schools were built, boosting enrollment from 40,000 to over 365,000. Homes, hospitals, roads and power stations were constructed. Per capita gross national product rose from $145 in 1959 to $2,036 in 1971. Education and health services are provided free.

Libya had been basically agricultural, producing dates, olives, lemons, almonds, figs, grapes and tobacco.

Carpets, leather goods and embroidered fabrics are also produced. Food processing and other factories have been built.

In 1973 "people's committees" took over many factories, firms, radio and TV stations, hospitals and farms, with government approval.

History and Government. Libya's strategic position has caused it to come under the domination successively of Carthage, Rome, the Vandals, the Ottoman Empire and Italy. After World War II Tripoli and Cyrenaica were placed under British administration, the Fezzan under French.

Emir Mohammed Idris El Senussi (born 1890), spiritual and temporal ruler of the Senussi tribesmen, was recognized by Great Britain as Emir of Cyrenaica, June, 1949. He promulgated a constitution and set up an interim government over internal affairs, Sept. 18, 1949. Libya, as a sovereign state, was approved by the UN, 1949, effective Jan. 2, 1952. A pre-independence constituent assembly chose the constitutional monarchy form of government and named the Emir as King of Libya, Dec. 3, 1950. A hereditary monarchy was proclaimed by King Idris I, Dec. 24, 1951.

On Sept. 1, 1969, a Revolutionary Command Council headed by Col. Muammar el-Qaddafi overthrew the government and announced formation of the Arab Republic of Libya.

On Sept. 1, 1971, Libya joined Egypt and Syria in a Federation of Arab Republics. Each nation retained its national sovereignty. In Aug. 1972 Libya and Egypt agreed to prepare unification of the 2 nations by Sept. 1, 1973. Instead, an Assembly of 50 Egyptians and 50 Libyans met that day to draft a constitution and nominate a President.

Education and Religion. Libya's population is mostly Arab Moslems and Islam is the state religion. Schools were taken over by the "people's committees" in 1973. There are two universities.

Defense. In 1970, Libya arranged to buy jet planes from France and received tanks and other arms from the USSR; the U.S. turned over its Wheelus Air Force Base to Libya. Armed forces total 25,000. In 1973 the U.S. charged Libya tried to shoot down a U.S. communications "eavesdropping" plane over the Mediterranean.

Liechtenstein

Capital: Vaduz. Area: 62 sq. mi. Population (Govt. est. 1972): 22,300. Monetary unit: Swiss franc.

Liechtenstein is a principality on the Upper Rhine between Austria and Switzerland. It is slightly smaller than the District of Columbia. It received independence in 1866 when the German Confederation dissolved and was in an economic union with Austria from 1852 to 1918. By treaty with Switzerland (1920-23) that country adminis-

ters its posts and telegraphs, customs and foreign interests. There is no army, only a police force of 33 with 31 auxiliaries.

Resources and Industries. The country is highly industrialized. Chief industries are machines and tools, cotton spinning and weaving, precision instruments, false teeth, ceramics and canned food. Finely engraved postage stamps are sold to philatelists around the world. Factories export about $133,000,000 in goods annually. Thousands of foreign workers are employed in Liechtenstein and constitute about 34% of the resident population.

History and Government. Liechtenstein is a hereditary monarchy. Under the constitution, granted in 1921, legislative powers rest in a Diet of 15 members, elected for four years by direct vote, on a basis of male suffrage and proportional representation. The reigning prince is Franz Joseph II. He succeeded his uncle, Prince Franz I, on the latter's abdication March 30, 1938. Taxes are very low and consequently many international corporations have made their headquarters there.

Education and Religion. The country is predominantly Catholic. German is the language.

Luxembourg

Capital: Luxembourg. Area: 999 sq. mi. Population (UN est. 1972): 350,000. Monetary unit: Luxembourg franc.

Luxembourg is a European Grand Duchy, bounded by Germany, Belgium and France. It measures only 55 mi. long by 34 mi. wide, smaller than Rhode Island.

Resources and Industries. About 9,500 farmers cultivate 336,000 acres. The principal crops are oats, wheat, rye, barley and potatoes.

Luxembourg's iron ore deposits, in the south, are the basis for an important steel industry. It employs nearly half the labor force, and accounts for 45% of total industrial production, and most of the value of exports. The country also produces chemicals, cement, beer, tires, tobacco and metal products, cement, roses and dairy products.

History and Government. Luxembourg, founded about 963, passed under the domination of Burgundy, Spain, Austria and France from 1443 to 1815; regained autonomy under the Treaty of Vienna, 1815. It left the Germanic Confederation in 1866, its integrity and neutrality guaranteed by the Treaty of London, May 11, 1867. Overrun by Germany in two World Wars, Luxembourg abolished its unarmed neutrality in 1948. Customs union with Netherlands and Belgium was adopted Jan. 1, 1948, expanded to the Benelux Economic Union, Feb. 3, 1958. Luxembourg is a member of the UN, NATO, OECD, Council of Europe, European Coal & Steel Community, Western European Union and the European Common Market.

As a Grand Duchy, Luxembourg is a constitutional monarchy, governed under the Constitution of 1868, with modifications. Legislative power rests with a Council of State of 21, chosen for life, and a Chamber of Deputies, 56 in number, elected by universal suffrage with executive power delegated to a Minister of State and a Cabinet. The country is headed by Grand Duke Jean (b. Jan. 5, 1921) who became Chief of State Nov. 12, 1964, when his mother, Grand Duchess Charlotte, abdicated in his favor after a 45-year reign. On April 9, 1953, he married Princess Josephine-Charlotte of Belgium. Their eldest son, Prince Henri (b. April 16, 1955) is hereditary Grand Duke.

The population is almost entirely Roman Catholic. Education is compulsory. Official languages are French and German; national language is Luxembourgeois.

Madagascar
MALAGASY REPUBLIC

Capital: Tananarive. Area: 228,000 sq. mi. Population (Govt. est. 1973): 7,655,134. Monetary unit: Ariary.

Formerly a French Overseas Territory, Madagascar is a large island off the SE coast of Africa, from which it is separated by the 240-mi. wide Mozambique Channel. It is about 980 mi. long and 360 mi. wide at its greatest breadth. It is a little smaller than Texas. There is a humid coastal strip on the E, fertile valleys in the mountainous center plateau region, and a wider coastal strip on the W.

The name of the nation and the island is Madagascar; the government is officially the Malagasy Republic.

The people, called the Malagasy, consist of many ethnic groups from succeeding waves of immigration, including those of SE Asian, Arab and African descent. They speak Malagasy, a language of Malayan origin. Over 3,000,000 are animists; 3,000,000 are Christians, about equally divided between Catholics and Protestants.

Madagascar came under a French protectorate, 1885, and was declared a French colony in 1896. It proclaimed itself an autonomous republic Oct. 14, 1958, and was granted full sovereignty effective June 26, 1960.

Discontent with inflation and French domination of the university led to student demonstrations, followed by a coup in May 1972. President Philibert Tsiranana was ousted. In Oct. a referendum approved a new government with Gen. Gabriel Ramanantsoa as Head of Government, a Superior Council and a National Popular Council.

Most of the population is engaged in agriculture. Chief crops are coffee, cloves, vanilla (producing 80% of the world's supply), rice, livestock, sugar, sisal, tobacco, peanuts etc. Small factories have been established.

Malawi

(FORMER NYASALAND)

Capital: Zomba. Area: 45,747 sq. mi. Population (UN est. 1972): 4,670,000. Monetary unit: Kwacha.

Malawi stretches more than 500 mi. north and south along the western and southern shores of Lake Nyasa (Lake Malawi) in southeast Africa. High mountains, dense forests and broad plains make it a scenic though landlocked country. It is about the size of N. Y. State.

Visited by Dr. David Livingstone in 1859, it became a British Protectorate in 1891. From 1953 to 1963 it was a member of the Federation of Rhodesia and Nyasaland. On Feb. 1, 1963, it became internally self-governing and, on July 6, 1964, achieved full independence from Britain. It became a republic within the Commonwealth July 6, 1966. It is a member of the UN.

Malawi is almost entirely an agricultural country with only a few light industries. Four crops—tea, tobacco, peanuts and cotton—account for 90% of the exports. Other important products are sugar, rubber, soybeans and coffee.

In 1967-68, factories were built for textiles, shoes, sugar, farm implements, and other products formerly imported.

Main trading partners are the United Kingdom, South Africa and the U.S. Malawi is dependent on Portuguese Mozambique for her rail trade routes to the sea. Construction continued in 1973 on a new capital at Lilongwe.

The Univ. of Malawi, which has 5 colleges, was built partly with U. S. aid; the first class graduated in July 1969.

Population is mostly African; there are about 12,000 Indians and 8,000 of European descent.

Malaysia

Capital: Kuala Lumpur. Area: 128,430 sq. mi. Population (UN est. 1972): 10,920,000. Monetary unit: Malaysian dollar.

Occupying the southern part of the Malay Peninsula in SE Asia and the northern part of the island of Borneo, Malaysia is the world's largest producer of rubber and tin. Total area is larger than Arizona.

Malaysia was created Sept. 16, 1963. It included the old Federation of Malaya (11 Malayan states which had become an independent constitutional monarchy and member of the Commonwealth Aug. 31, 1957), plus the formerly-British Singapore (an island and city off the southern tip of the Malay Peninsula), Sabah (former British North Borneo) and Sarawak (former British col-

ony in NW Borneo).

Indonesia harassed the new nation with guerrilla action 1963-65. After Indonesian Pres. Sukarno lost power, 1965-66, Malaysia and Indonesia agreed Aug. 11, 1966, to restore normal relations; full relations were restored Aug. 31, 1967.

On Aug. 9, 1965, the separation of Singapore from Malaysia was announced under an agreement by Malaysia and Singapore officials that this was the best way to end tensions between the ethnic Chinese, largest group in Singapore, and the Malays, who were in control of the Malaysia government. (*See Index for Singapore.*)

With Singapore's departure, the Malays numbered 44% of Malaysia's population and ethnic Chinese 36%.

The 11 Malay states, which form West Malaysia, and their capitals are: Johore (Johore Bahru), Kedah (Alor Star), Kelantan (Kota Bharu), Malacca (Malacca), Negri Sembilan (Seremban), Pahang (Kuantan), Penang (George Town), Perak (Ipoh), Perlis (Kangar), Selangor (Kuala Lumpur), Trengganu (Kuala Trengganu). Largest in area is Pahang, 13,820 sq. mi.

Forming East Malaysia are Sabah (former British North Borneo; capital, Kota Kinabalu) and Sarawak (capital, Kuching). They lie on the north coast of the island of Borneo and have a total pop. of 1,730,000 (1972) and area of 77,638 sq. mi.

A constitutional monarch, known as the Yang di-Pertuan Agong (Supreme Head of Malaysia) is elected by a council of hereditary rulers of the Malayan states every 5 years. There is a Senate, an elected House of Representatives, Prime Minister and Cabinet.

In May 1969 at least 180 persons died in riots between ethnic Chinese and Malays in Kuala Lumpur. Communist guerrillas renewed activities in 1971 and 1972.

Resources and Industries. Rubber, tin, timber, iron ore, palm oil and copra are the main products. Rubber, much of it produced by new high-yield trees, accounts for 41% of exports; tin, of which Malaysia produces 33% of the world output, amounts to 13% of her exports.

Other agricultural products are rice, coconuts, tapioca, sugar, pepper, camphor. Rubber trees were originally introduced from Brazil. Small-scale industry includes rubber goods, pottery, cement, pewterware, furniture, bricks, tiles, soap, fertilizers, processing plants.

Religion and Language. The Malays and some others are Moslems; other religions are Buddhist, Christian and Hindu. Malay is the national language and official in W. Malaysia; Malay and English are official in E. Malaysia.

Defense. In 1971 Malaysia increased its armed forces to 50,000 to compensate for reduction of British Southeast Asia forces. Britain, Australia and New Zealand maintain small forces in Malaysia to aid its defense.

Republic of Maldives

Capital: Malè. Area: 112 sq. mi. Population (Govt. est. 1973): 122,673. Monetary unit: Rupee.

The Maldive Islands are a group of 19 atolls containing 1,087 islands, 210 of which are inhabited. Totaling about twice the area of the District of Columbia, they are in the Indian Ocean 300 mi. SW of the southern tip of India. The country obtained full independence from Great Britain on July 26, 1965, in an agreement under which Britain retained its RAF base on Gan Is. in Addu Atoll in the southern Maldives. The Maldives became a member of the UN Sept.21, 1965.

The islands had been a British-protected state since 1887, with Britain responsible for their defense and foreign relations until the 1965 agreement. Long a Sultanate, the islands became briefly a republic in 1953 and a Sultanate again in 1954. After a referendum, the country became a republic once more, Nov. 11, 1968, with a popularly elected President and legislature (Majlis).

The people are Moslems and seafarers. Coconuts, fruit and millet are grown; the chief occupation is fishing. Production of processed fish, to be marketed in Ceylon, is the main industry. Also exported is coir, a coconut fiber, copra and cowries and other shells.

Mali

Capital: Bamako. Area: 464,000 sq. mi. Population (UN est. 1972): 5,260,000. Monetary unit: Franc.

The Republic of Mali, formerly the Sudanese Republic (1959-60) and a one-time French Overseas Territory in West Africa, is a landlocked nation which is larger than Texas but smaller than Alaska.

Mali is mostly a vast plain in the upper basins of the Senegal and Niger Rivers, extending N into the Sahara.

From the 11th to 15th Centuries the area was part of the great Mali Empire which stretched from the western Sudan to the Atlantic; Timbuktu was a renowned center of Islamic learning.

Under provisions of the 1958 French constitution French Sudan became the Sudanese Republic, an autonomous republic within the French Community and formed with neighboring Senegal Jan. 17, 1959, the Mali Federation. Complete independence was proclaimed June 20, 1960. Senegal withdrew from the federation Aug. 20, 1960, and Sudan took the name of Republic of Mali Sept. 22. It became a UN member Sept. 28, 1960. Mali signed economic and cultural agreements with France. On June 8, 1963, Mali and Senegal reached customs, trade and railway traffic agreements, with use of Senegalese harbors by Mali.

On Nov. 19, 1968, a coup ended the socialist regime of Pres. Modibo Keita; Lt. Moussa Traore became President Dec. 6, 1968.

The country is mainly agricultural and pastoral. Millet, rice and peanuts are the chief crops. Cotton, rubber and river fishing are also important. Livestock raising is a major prop of the economy. Famine, following a long drought, struck Mali and other sub-Saharan nations in 1973. Aid was sent by the U.S. and other nations.

The people are mostly Moslem, with a minority of Christians. French is the official language.

Malta

Capital: Valletta. Area: 122 sq. mi. Population (Govt. est. 1972): 322,070. Monetary unit: Pound.

Malta lies in the Mediterranean 58 mi. S of Sicily and 180 mi. from Africa. The island of Malta itself is 95 sq. mi.; the other two islands in the group are Gozo, 26 sq. mi., and Comino, one sq. mi.

For 35 centuries Malta was under successive rule by Phoenicians, Carthaginians, Romans, Arabs, Normans, the Knights of Malta, France and Britain (which annexed Malta in 1814). It achieved limited self-government in 1887; home rule on Oct. 24, 1961. On Sept. 21, 1964, it became independent, with the British monarch as head of state, represented by a governor general, and agreed to permit British forces to maintain a base for 10 years. It is a member of the Commonwealth, Council of Europe and UN. A House of Representatives with 55 members is elected by universal suffrage, the Prime Minister and Cabinet are chosen from the House.

Once a vital British stronghold, it withstood Axis air attacks for 3 years during World War II. Population density in 1968 was over 2,600 per sq. mi., there is continuous migration, much of it to Australia, the United Kingdom and Canada.

A Labor party victory in June 1971 elections brought a Maltese demand that NATO remove its naval hq. from Malta. NATO moved the hq. to Naples in Aug. In 1972 Malta agreed to Britain's use of its military bases for 7 more years in return for greatly increased payments; USSR forces would be barred.

Leading industries are ship repairing, food and beverages, textiles and tourism. Visiting tourists rose from 23,000 in 1962 to 178,704 in 1971. Historic sites, a casino and village fetes are among the attractions.

Mauritania

Capital: Nouakchott. Area: 419,231 sq. mi. Population (UN est. 1972): 1,230,000. Monetary unit: Ouguiya.

The Islamic Republic of Mauritania, former French Overseas Territory in West Africa, is bounded by the Atlantic Ocean, Spanish Sahara, Algeria, Mali and Senegal. Population is largely Moorish, Mauritania is about four-fifths the size of Alaska.

The economy has been agricultural and pastoral. Products include dates, grain, meat, fish. There are large herds of cattle, camels, sheep and goats and large deposits of iron and copper.

A large new iron mine was opened in 1968 to add to the nation's annual production of 8,000,000 tons of iron ore; fishing, which produced 270,000 tons of fish in 1970, was being expanded; a copper mine began production in 1971; a new cattle slaughterhouse and freezing plant was opened. It has received aid from France and Communist China. Drought and famine struck in 1973; aid was sent by the U.S. and others.

In accordance with the provisions of the 1958 French constitution, Mauritania became an autonomous state Nov. 28, 1958, and became fully independent Nov. 28, 1960. Prime Minister Mokhtar Ould Daddah, appointed June 26, 1959, became President by popular vote in August, 1962. Mauritania is a member of the UN.

Mauritius

Capital: Port Louis. Area: 720 sq. mi. Population (Gov't. est. 1972): 840,000. Monetary unit: Rupee.

Mauritius, an island in the Indian Ocean 550 mi. E of Malagasy (Madagascar), became an independent nation within the Commonwealth on Mar. 12, 1968, after 158 years of British rule. The country joined the UN Apr. 24, 1968. It has a parliamentary government.

Mauritius has one of the world's most complex racial, religious and political mixtures as well as one of the world's highest population densities. There are 4 main groups: over 408,000 Hindus; 224,000 of mixed European and African descent and whites; 130,000 Moslems and 25,000 Chinese. Although the official language is English, French is spoken by many persons, and Creole, a French patois, is the lingua franca. Chinese and several Indian languages are also spoken.

The country had a nearly one-crop economy, sugar. However, a flourishing tea industry has been developed and tourism is growing. Commonwealth subsidies support sugar prices and aid the economy. Unemployment was about 20% in 1971; the literacy rate is very high.

Mauritius was uninhabited until 1638 when the Dutch settled there and gave the island its present name in honor of Prince Maurice of Nassau. The French took over in 1721 and introduced sugar cane and African slaves. The British, who seized the island in 1810, brought Hindus and Moslems from India to work the sugar plantations.

Mauritius was the home of the famed dodo, a heavy, flightless bird which became extinct in the 17th Century.

Mexico

ESTADOS UNIDOS MEXICANOS

Capital: Mexico City. Area: 758,259 sq. mi. Population (UN est. 1972): 52,640,000. Monetary unit: Peso.

Second most populous nation in Latin America and third largest in area, Mexico compiled an enviable record for progress, social improvement and fiscal responsibility in the middle decades of the 20th Century.

With housing, health, farm and industrial programs, the nation has lifted itself and its people into the mainstream of the modern world; life expectancy, for example, was raised from 39 years in 1940 to 67 years in 1968.

Ever-growing streams of foreign visitors (958,000 in 1962; 2,234,682 in 1972) find spectacular scenery, striking art and architecture, cosmopolitan and colonial cities and luxurious resorts. The mountainous topography provides a variety of climates, from temperate to tropical.

The Sierra Madre Occidental Mtns. run NW-SE near the west coast. The Sierra Madre Oriental Mtns., a continuation of the Rockies, run near the Gulf of Mexico coast nearly as far S as Veracruz.

Between the two ranges lies the central plateau of Mexico, altitude from 5,000 to 8,000 ft. with a pleasant climate and with the vegetation and products of the temperate zone varying with the altitude. The lowlands along the coast are tropical, rising to subtropical in the foothills, with a heavy rainfall on the Gulf side. Along the Pacific slope and in the interior irrigation is needed. Mexico is nearly 3 times the size of Texas.

Tampico and Veracruz, on the Gulf, are the busiest of Mexico's 49 ocean ports.

Mexico's population is composed of descendants of the Toltecs, Aztecs, Mayas and the Spaniards who conquered and colonized the country. Archeological remains of the early Indian civilizations are important tourist attractions.

Resources and Industries. Mexico is rich in minerals and timber. It is one of the top two producers of silver; also important are gold, copper, lead, zinc, antimony, mercury, arsenic, amorphous graphite, molybdenum, sulphur, coal and opal. Mexico is the world's 13th largest petroleum producer. The industry is nationalized. Natural gas is supplied to the U.S. Electric power generated in 1972 rose to 33.6 billion kwh.

Farming, stock raising and fishing are important. The land is rich, but the rugged topography and lack of sufficient rainfall are major obstacles. Crops and farm prices are controlled, as are export and import. Large estates have been expropriated; since 1915 the government has distributed about 160,000,000 acres to small farmers through landholding communities (ejidos). Major irrigation projects in Sonora and Sinaloa have increased production of cotton and wheat.

Principal export crops are cotton, coffee, cane sugar, tomatoes, cattle, fruit, fresh and frozen meats.

Coffee is valued at more than $100,000,000 annually; other major crops are corn, rice, tobacco, garbanzos, cocoa, sisal, bananas. About 50% of the world supply of sisal comes from Yucatan, in southern Mexico.

Mexican industry is producing products formerly imported, especially in iron and steel, chemicals, electric goods. Other products are cotton, wool and synthetic textiles, flour, beverages, soap, cigarettes and cigars, rubber, paper, rubber products, cement, shoes, glass, furniture and tiles. Mexico is famous for industrial and native handicraft in silver, pottery, leather, wood, fibers and textiles. The U.S. buys a large portion of Mexico's exports.

Index of industrial production (1963=100) was 210 in 1972. The estimated gross national product (in U.S. dollars) was $26.7 billion for 1968, $38.3 billion for 1972.

Tourism is an important revenue source. Gross earnings in 1969 rose to $1.3 billion.

Foreign trade, in thousands of U.S. dollars:

	Imports	Exports
1971	$2,407,000	$1,471,000
1972	$2,936,000	$1,809,000

History and Government. Mexico was the site of advanced Indian civilizations before the Spanish conquest. The Mayas, an agricultural people, moved up from Yucatan and built immense stone pyramids and invented a calendar. The Toltecs were overcome by the Aztecs, who founded Tenochtitlan 1325 A.D., now Mexico City. Hernando Cortes, Spanish conquistador, destroyed the Aztec empire, 1519-1521.

After 3 centuries of misrule the people rose, under Fr. Miguel Hidalgo y Costilla (a priest), 1810, Fr. Morelos y Pavon (another priest), 1812, and Gen Agustin Iturbide, who made independence effectual Sept. 27, 1821, but made himself emperor as Agustin I. A republic was chosen in 1823; Iturbide was executed 1824.

Mexican authority extended into the present American Southwest and California until Texas revolted and established a republic in 1836; the Mexican legislature refused recognition but was unable to enforce its authority there. After numerous clashes, the U.S.-Mexican War, 1846-48, resulted in the loss by Mexico of the lands north of the Rio Grande, about half its total area.

French arms supported an Austrian archduke on the throne of Mexico as Maximilian I, 1864-67, but pressure from the U.S. forced France to withdraw troops, and led to his defeat by Mexican patriots under Benito Juarez, and subsequent execution. A dictatorial rule by Porfirio Diaz, president 1877-80, 1884-1911, led to fighting by rival forces until the new constitution of Feb. 5, 1917, provided social reform. Since then Mexico has developed large-scale programs of social security, labor protection and school improvement. A constitutional provision requiring

management to share profits with labor became effective Dec. 12, 1963.

Mexico is a federal democratic republic of 29 states, with President, legislature and judiciary elected by universal suffrage; two territories (Baja California Sur and Quintana Roo) with governors appointed by the President, and a federal district (Distrito Federal) containing Mexico City. The President is elected for 6 years and thereafter ineligible; 60 senators for 6 years and deputies for 3 years, ineligible for reelection until one term has intervened.

The Institutional Revolutionary party has been dominant in politics since 1929. In 1970 the legal voting age was lowered from 21 to 18.

Education and Religion. Education is secular, with primary education free and compulsory up to 15 years of age. Vocational instruction particularly in agriculture is promoted and there are many technical schools. The National University of Mexico continues an educational foundation of 1551 A.D. Spanish is the language.

Most of the people are Roman Catholics. All church real estate is vested in the nation, but care of church buildings is the responsibility of the clergy.

Defense. The armed forces total 73,000 regulars, 250,000 part-time.

Mexico is a member of the UN and OAS.

(See also Index for Mexico City.)

Monaco

Capital: Monaco. Area: 433 acres. Population (est. 1972): 24,300. Monetary unit: French franc.

Monaco is a small principality on the Mediterranean surrounded on all but the sea side by France. It is noted for an exceptionally mild climate and magnificent scenery.

There is a local police force of 200.

Resources and Industries. Monaco's fame as a tourist resort and international conference city is widespread. Its revenues derive from indirect taxation, a tobacco monopoly, postage and the gambling tables of the Monte Carlo Casino.

About a dozen subsidiaries of large drug manufacturers were established in Monaco and their drugs entered France free of duty. In October, 1962, when the customs union with France expired, France put up customs barriers pending imposition of taxes and ended domestic mail rates. By a 1963 agreement the customs barriers were eliminated in April and domestic mail rates restored. French citizens living in Monaco less than 5 years must pay income taxes to France.

Monaco endeavored to cover possible revenue losses by enacting a profits tax on Monaco companies that do 25% of their business outside Monaco. The company tax rate is now 35%.

History and Government. An independent principality for over 300 years, Monaco has belonged to the House of Grimaldi except during the French Revolution. It was placed under the protectorate of Sardinia in 1815 (Treaty of Vienna), and under that of France, 1861. The Prince of Monaco was an absolute ruler until a constitution was promulgated in 1911.

A new constitution, proclaimed Dec. 17, 1962, provided for female suffrage and abolition of capital punishment, and established a supreme tribunal to guarantee fundamental liberties. The legislature (National Council) consists of 18 members elected for 5 years.

The ruler of Monaco is Prince Rainier III who succeeded his grandfather, Prince Louis II, who died May 9, 1949. He married Grace Kelly, American motion picture actress, Apr. 18, 1956. A daughter, Princess Caroline Louise Marguerite, was born Jan. 23, 1957. The heir apparent, Prince Albert Alexander Louis Pierre, was born Mar. 14, 1958. Princess Stephanie Marie Elizabeth was born Feb. 1, 1965.

In 1967 the government purchased for $8,000,000 the holdings of Aristotle Onassis in the Societe des Bains de Mer, owner of the Casino and other interests. The Prince launched a program of reclaiming land from the sea and developing new tourist facilities.

Mongolia

Capital: Ulan Bator. Area: 604,000 sq. mi. Population (UN est. 1972): 1,320,000. Monetary unit: Tughrik.

The Mongolian People's Republic comprises Outer Mongolia in northeastern Asia. It is bounded on the N by the Siberian provinces of USSR, and on 3 other sides by Mainland China. It is larger than Alaska.

Much of Mongolia is a high plateau with vast grasslands; arid lands in the south are part of the Gobi Desert.

Resources and Industries. In the early 1970s Mongolia was changing from a nomadic culture to one of settled agriculture and growing industries with aid from the USSR and East European nations. Irrigation and scientific farming methods were pressed to increase grain crops and fodder for the large livestock herds which long were the mainstay of the economy. Food processing, textile, brick and cement factories were established in growing cities in the north. Electric power plants were built, running on coal; Mongolia has large coal deposits as well as tungsten, copper, gold, tin.

History and Government. One of the world's oldest countries, Mongolia reached the zenith of its power in the 13th Century when Genghis Khan and his successors conquered all of China and extended their influence as far W as Hungary and Poland. In later centuries, the empire dissolved and Mongolia came under the suzerainty of China.

With the advent of the 1911 Chinese revolution, Mongolia, with Russian backing, declared its independence. The Mongolian People's Republic was proclaimed July 11, 1921. China, however, continued to claim the country until 1945 when recognition of independence was given.

The Constitution vests power in the elected Great People's Khural from which is drawn a 7-member Presidium and a Council of Ministers. Actual power is in the hands of the Communist party and its 9-man Politburo.

Mongolia has sided with the Russians in the Sino-Soviet dispute. A Mongolian-Soviet mutual assistance pact was signed Jan. 15, 1966.

Mongolia is a UN member.

Education and Religion. There are primary, secondary and technical schools, and 7 higher educational institutes. Buddhist Lamaism is the leading religion. Khalka Mongol is the main language.

Morocco

Capital: Rabat. Area: 172,834 sq. mi. Population (UN est. 1972): 15,830,000. Monetary unit: Dirham.

The monarchy of Morocco lies on the NW tip of Africa separated from Europe by the 8-mile-wide Strait of Gibraltar. It is bounded by Algeria, Spanish Sahara, the Mediterranean and the Atlantic. Until 1956 it was a protectorate of France and Spain.

It consists of 5 natural regions: A series of mountain ranges (Riff, facing Gibraltar; Middle Atlas, extending NW of Marrakesh; Upper Atlas, and Anti-Atlas); a series of rich plains in the W; the alluvial plains of Haouz in the SW; the "mesata," a well-cultivated series of plateaus in the center; a pre-Saharan zone extending from S to E.

The inhabitants largely are a mixture of Arabs and the original Berbers.

Resources and Industries. Morocco is primarily agricultural and pastoral. Cereals rank 1st among agricultural products, including barley, wheat and corn. Fruit and vineyards are abundant and dates a staple crop. Carpets, leather goods, clothing and textiles are among the manufactures.

Morocco ranks 3rd in world production of phosphate rock and is 1st in phosphate exports. It produces 10% of the world's cobalt and 2% of manganese ore. Other minerals are antimony, zinc, lead ore, oil and anthracite.

In the late 1960s, a number of dams were under construction or planned to extend irrigation, including a large project built with U.S. aid. Foreign-owned agricultural lands were nationalized in 1973.

Tourism attracts 600,000 visitors annually to see Morocco's casbahs, Roman ruins, old fortresses and oases.

History and Government. Morocco is a remnant of an early empire founded by the Arabs at the close of the 7th Century which encompassed all NW Africa and most of the Iberian Peninsula.

It came under French influence because of its proximity to Algeria. A general uprising of tribes in 1910 culminated in the dispatch of a French expeditionary force that occupied Fez in 1911. Frequent uprisings continued for two decades until the exile of Abd-el-Krim in 1926 and the surrender of Sidi Ali Hociene in 1933.

Spain also held a protectorate over some areas.

Morocco became independent Mar. 2, 1956, after agreement by France to end its protectorate. Spain signed similar agreements.

Tangier, a seaport which had been internationalized during the protectorate, was turned over to Moroccan control in 1956. Ifni, a small Spanish enclave on the Atlantic coast, was turned over to Morocco June 30, 1969.

Mohammed V, Sultan since 1927 (with the title of King since 1957), died Feb. 26, 1961. His eldest son became King Hassan II.

Under a constitution approved by referendum Dec. 7, 1962, Morocco became a constitutional monarchy. The first Parliament was elected May 17, 1963.

The King suspended Parliament in June 1965. A new constitution was approved by voters in July 1970, providing for a unicameral, elected Chamber of Deputies. An attempted army revolt failed in July 1971. Air force pilots tried unsuccessfully to assassinate the King in Aug. 1972.

Morocco accepted U. S. and USSR military and economic aid on a basis of non-interference in its internal affairs. It has agreements with France on economic, technical and cultural cooperation. It is a member of the UN, OAU and Arab League.

Education and Religion. Trade schools and agricultural training centers have been developed, in addition to regular schools. The main university is in Rabat. Arabic is the official language. The population is Sunni Moslem.

Defense. Morocco's armed forces number more than 53,000.

Nauru

Area: 8 sq. mi. Population (est. 1973): 6,500. Monetary unit: Australian dollar.

Nauru, one of the world's smallest nations, became independent Jan. 31, 1968, after 80 years of foreign rule. In the southwest Pacific about 30 mi. S of the Equator and 1,300 mi. NE of Australia, Nauru is comfortably affluent because of its high-grade phosphate deposits.

Phosphate exports provide per capita revenue equal to over $6,000 a year for each of the 4,000 native Nauruans (about 1,300 foreigners work in the phosphate industry; there are about 1,200 other foreigners on the island). The deposits are expected to be depleted by 1990.

The island was discovered in 1798 by the British but was formally annexed to the German Empire in 1888. After World War I, Nauru became a League of Nations mandate administered by Australia. During World War II the Japanese occupied the island and shipped 1,200 Nauruans to the fortress island of Truk as slave laborers.

In 1947 Nauru was made a UN trust territory, administered by Australia on behalf of the three trust powers—Australia, Great Britain and New Zealand. Because of its small size Nauru has not sought UN membership.

There is an elected Parliament. Hammer De Roburt was elected first President.

Nepal

Capital: Katmandu. Area: 54,362 sq. mi. Population (est. 1972): 11,470,000. Monetary unit: Nepalese rupee.

Nepal is a monarchy in the Himalayas, bounded on the N by China (Tibet) and E, S and W by India. It is about the size of Arkansas.

There are many fertile valleys lying in the slopes of the lofty mountains, including Mt. Everest, on the Tibet border. The capital is in the fertile valley of Katmandu, 15 mi. long and 20 wide, which is noted for its many, lavishly decorated shrines.

Virtually closed to the outside world for centuries, Nepal is now linked to India and Pakistan by modern roads and air service and to Tibet by road.

Nepal has established a 500 sq. mi. game preserve for elephants, tigers, rhinoceroses, leopards, boars, crocodiles and over 500 species of birds.

Resources and Industries. Nepal has rich forests and quartz deposits. The country exports jute, rice, grain, cattle, hides, wheat and drugs. Trade is 90% with India. Tourism provides vital funds.

U.S. technical aid has made possible settlement of the fertile but once inaccessible Rapti Valley with a 53-mi. $500,000 highway. Nepal also receives financial aid from India, China and others. Its 4th 5-year plan stresses hydroelectric power and roads.

History and Government. Nepal was originally divided into petty principalities, the inhabitants of one of which, the Gurkhas, became dominant about 1769. Maharajadhiraja Tribhubana Bir Bikram (born June 30, 1906), member of the Shah family, returned from exile, ended the system of rule by hereditary premiers of the Ranas family, Hindu Rajputs, who kept the Kings virtual prisoners. He established a popular government Feb. 18, 1951.

King Tribhubana died Mar. 13, 1955, and was succeeded by his son, Mahendra Bir Bikram Shah Dev, who died Jan. 31, 1972, and was succeeded by his son, Birendra Bir Bikram Shah Dev.

King Mahendra promulgated a new constitution Dec. 16, 1962, providing for a three-tier system of indirectly elected councils topped by a National Assembly or National Panchayat.

Education and Religion. There are more than 2,400 English schools in addition to Sanskrit and Nepali schools and other institutions of learning. Buddha was born at Lumbini in South-Central Nepal. Hinduism and Buddhism are the main religions. Polygamy, child marriage and the caste system were abolished in 1963.

Nepal is a UN member.

The Netherlands

KONINKRIJK DER NEDERLANDEN

Capital: Amsterdam. Area (land): 14,125 sq. mi. Population (est. 1972): 13,371,000. Monetary unit: Guilder.

The Kingdom of the Netherlands, a constitutional monarchy in northwestern Europe, is bounded by Germany, Belgium, and the North Sea. Its surface is flat, with an average height above sea level of 37 ft., with much land below sea level, reclaimed and protected by dikes, of which there are 1,500 mi. The country is about the size of Vermont and Massachusetts combined.

Since the end of World War II the government has been draining the IJsselmeer, formerly Zuider Zee, and converting the reclaimed land into farms. The total will add over 550,000 acres. By 1972, 410,000 acres had been reclaimed.

The Hague is the seat of government, but Amsterdam is the sole capital of the kingdom and the inaugurations of sovereigns are held there.

Rotterdam, located along the principal mouth of the Rhine, handles the most cargo of any ocean port in the world.

Resources and Industries. About 46% of the land is given to pasture, farming takes 26%, heath, dunes and forest 7%, horticulture 5%. Of the arable land 80% is in holdings of fewer than 50 acres and about 25% of fewer than 10 acres. Cereals, potatoes, sugar beets and other crops are raised. Agriculture and fishing engage approx. 10% of the workers. Dairy products are an important industry. In pork exports the nation ranks 2d to Denmark. Tulips and other flowering bulbs and roots are grown.

The most important industries are shipbuilding, the manufacture of machinery, textiles (including rayon), and chemical products; also brewing and distilling and flour milling. Amsterdam is famous for diamond cutting; Delft for pottery. Eindhoven has electrical and radio factories. Coal, oil and salt are found. Natural gas reserves are large. Index of industrial production

(1963=100) was 203 for 1972.

Canals, of which there are 3,478 mi., are important in transportation. The Rhine, Meuse and Schelde reach the sea through the Netherlands and carry enormous traffic.

Foreign trade in thousands of U.S. dollars:

	Imports	Exports
1971	$15,510,000	$13,971,000
1972	$16,985,000	$16,826,000

History and Government. After the empire of Charlemagne (d. 814) fell apart, the Netherlands—Holland, Belgium, Flanders—split among counts, dukes and bishops, passed to Burgundy and thence to Charles V of Spain. His son, Philip II, sent the Duke of Alva as governor to check the Dutch drive toward political freedom and Protestantism (1568-1573). William the Silent, prince of Orange, led a confederation of the northern provinces, called Estates, in the Union of Utrecht, 1579. The Estates retained individual sovereignty, but were represented jointly in the States-General, a body that had control of foreign affairs and defense. In 1581 they repudiated allegiance to Spain. The rise of the Dutch republic to naval, economic and artistic eminence came in the 17th Century.

The United Dutch Republic ended 1795 when the French formed the Batavian Republic, ended 1798. Napoleon made his brother Louis King of Holland, 1806; Louis abdicated 1810 when Napoleon annexed Holland. In 1813 the French were expelled. In 1815 the Congress of Vienna formed a kingdom of the Netherlands, including Belgium, under William, I, with Brussels and The Hague as alternative capitals. In August, 1830, the Belgians revolted and formed a separate kingdom, which was recognized by the European powers in November, 1831.

The constitution, promulgated 1814, and subsequently revised, assures a hereditary constitutional monarchy. Executive power rests in the Crown (the Queen and ministers). Legislative powers are exercised jointly by the Crown and Parliament (States-General) of two chambers: First Chamber, 75 members, elected for 6 years (one half every third year) by the provincial legislatures, and the Second Chamber, 150 Deputies, elected for 4 years directly. Universal suffrage for citizens of both sexes over 18 years of age and proportional representation are in force. The sovereign exercises the executive authority through a Council of Ministers, the President thereof corresponding to a Prime Minister. There is a State Council named by the sovereign, of which she is president, to be consulted on all legislative and some executive matters.

The reigning sovereign is Queen Juliana Louise Emma Marie Wilhelmina, born April 30, 1909, only daughter of former Queen Wilhelmina. She succeeded to the throne, Sept. 6, 1948, on the abdication of her mother. Queen Juliana on Jan. 7, 1937, married Prince Bernhard of Lippe-Biesterfeld, born June 29, 1911, known as the Prince of the Netherlands since the accession of Juliana. They have 4 daughters, Princess Beatrix Wilhelmina Armgard, born Jan. 31, 1938, heir presumptive, married Claus von Amsberg, West German diplomat, Mar. 10, 1966; Princess Irene Emma Elisabeth, born Aug. 5, 1939, married Prince Carlos Hugo, Bourbon-Parma, Apr. 29, 1964; Princess Margriet Francisca, born Jan. 19, 1943, in Ottawa, Canada, married Pieter van Vollenhoven, Jan. 10, 1967, and Princess Maria-Christine, born Feb. 18, 1947.

On Apr. 27, 1967, Princess Beatrix gave birth to a son, Willem-Alexander, Prince of Orange, first male heir to the throne in three generations.

Education and Religion. There is complete liberty of worship. The royal family belongs to the Netherlands Reformed Church (Prot.). The population is 39.5% Roman Catholic; 30% Protestant; others 8%; non-church members 22.5%.

Education is obligatory from ages 6 to 15. Instruction is free or subject to a small fee, in both public and denominational schools and teachers are paid by the state. There are universities in Amsterdam (two), Utrecht, Leyden, Delft, Groningen, Wageningen, Rotterdam, Nijmegen, Enschede, Eindhoven and Tilburg.

Defense. Military forces in 1972 totaled 127,400. The Netherlands is a member of the UN, NATO, EEC, Council of Europe and Benelux.

SURINAM AND NETHERLANDS ANTILLES

A revision of the Netherlands charter, promulgated Dec. 15, 1954, raised Surinam and the Netherlands Antilles to equality with the Netherlands homeland in the Kingdom of the Netherlands, with complete internal autonomy and a voice in government of the kingdom. The kingdom is represented in each by the governor who also is head of government for the respective area. Local governments comprise the governor, council, ministers, and representative bodies (Staten), the latter elected by universal suffrage.

Surinam, also known as Dutch Guiana, is on the N coast of South America, between French Guiana on the E and Guyana on the W; forests and savannahs on the S stretch to the Tumuc Humac Mountains. The area is approximately 62,000 sq. mi. The population (Jan. 1, 1972) was 385,000. Capital: Paramaribo.

The country is rich in minerals and hydroelectric power is being developed on a large scale. Oil was discovered, 1966. Exports include bauxite, alumina, lumber, sugar, rice, citrus, coffee, bananas and shrimp.

The Dutch by the Treaty of Breda, 1667, ceded New Netherland (New York) to England in exchange for Surinam.

The **Netherlands Antilles** consist of two groups of islands in the West Indies **Curacao, Aruba** and **Bonaire** are near the South American coast; **St. Eustatius, Saba** and the southern part of **St. Maarten** are southeast of Puerto Rico. Northern two-thirds of St. Maarten belongs to French Guadeloupe; the French call the island St. Martin. Total area of the two groups is 395 sq. mi., including: Aruba 70, Bonaire 112, Curacao 180, St. Eustatius 12, Saba 5, St. Maarten (Dutch part) 16.

Tourism in recent years has been increasing, especially to the islands of Curacao and Aruba.

The Netherlands Antilles population (est. 1971) was 230,000. Willemstad is the capital. Chief products are corn, pulse, salt and phosphate; principal industry is the refining of oil. On Curacao and on Aruba there are large oil refineries, receiving crude oil from Venezuela.

New Zealand

Capital: Wellington. Area: 103,736 sq. mi. Population (est. 1973): 2,961,869. Monetary unit: New Zealand dollar.

The main islands of New Zealand lie in the South Pacific about 1,300 mi. E of Australia. The total area is about that of Colorado. Including remote islands to the N and the Ross Dependency to the S, the reach of New Zealand is from the tropics to Antarctica.

Snow-topped mountains, smoking volcanoes, deep fjords, boiling geysers, golden beaches and the glowworm caves of Waitomo are among attractions.

New Zealand comprises **North Island,** 44,281 sq. mi.; **South Island,** 58,093 sq. mi.; **Stewart Island,** 670 sq. mi.; **Chatham Islands,** 372 sq. mi. Both the North and South Islands slightly exceed 500 mi. in length. Cook Strait, separating the 2, is only 13 mi. wide at its narrowest.

In 1965, the **Cook Islands** (pop. 1972, 21,217; area 93 sq. mi.) became self-governing although New Zealand retains responsibility for defense and foreign affairs.

Wellington and Auckland, on North Is., are the chief ports. South Is. has the picturesque Southern Alps and Tasman, Fox and Franz Josef Glaciers. There are 15 named peaks over 10,000 ft., the highest being Mt. Cook, 12,349 ft. Christchurch and Dunedin are the main cities of South Is.

Resources and Industries. New Zealand is largely dependent on agricultural products for export income; wool, meat and dairy products account for 78% of the total value. Next to Australia, New Zealand is the world's largest exporter of meat (mostly lamb).

Imports totaled $1.5 billion (in U.S. dollars) in 1972; $1.3 billion 1971. Exports were $1.8 billion in 1972; $1.4 billion in 1971.

Agriculture engages 13% of the population, manufac-

turing industries 27%. Private enterprise is basic in the economy, but state ownership or regulation affects many industries. Railroads are largely state-owned.

Foor processing is the largest industry with value added amounting to about $180,000,000; forest products account for more than $126,000,000.

The pulp and paper industry on North Is. is partly powered by natural steam from volcanic areas. The first iron and steel plant commenced production in 1968. Natural gas was discovered at Kapuni, North Is., 1967, and was to be piped to several towns. A large hydroelectric plant at Lake Manapouri, South Is., began providing power for an aluminum smelter in 1971.

About 170,000 tourists visit New Zealand annually, over 40,000 of them from the U.S.

History and Government. New Zealand was discovered in 1642 by Abel Janszoon Tasman, a Dutch navigator, and its coasts were explored by Capt. James Cook, 1769-1770. British sovereignty was proclaimed in 1840, with organized settlement commencing in the same year. Representative institutions were granted in 1853. The Colony became a Dominion in 1907 and an independent member of the Commonwealth in 1947.

The native Maoris are Polynesians. Early in the 19th Century they numbered an est. 200,000; violence and European diseases cut them to 40,000 by the end of the century. Recently they have increased at 9% annually and totaled 236,066 in 1972.

Government consists of a governor-general, representing the British Crown; a House of Representatives whose members are elected by universal suffrage for a 3-year term; a Prime Minister and Cabinet who are members of the House and accountable to it. In Nov. 1972 elections the Labor party returned to power after 12 years of National (conservative) party rule.

In July 1973, to protest France's testing of nuclear devices above Mururoa Atoll, a New Zealand Navy frigate cruised just outside the French South Pacific island's 12-mi. limit but within the test area.

New Zealand is a member of the UN, Commonwealth, SEATO and ANZUS.

New Zealand's tax rates reach a maximum of 50 cents per dollar at the $12,000 income level. "Cradle-to-grave" social security includes maternity, school, medical, hospital, medicine, pension and other benefits.

Education and Religion. Education is free and compulsory between the ages of 7 and 15. There are universities in Dunedin, Christchurch, Wellington, Auckland, Hamilton, and Palmerston North. The Anglican and Presbyterian Churches have the largest followings.

Defense. Military forces in 1972 totaled 12,637. New Zealand had a force of 265 in Vietnam in 1971; they were withdrawn at the end of the year.

Ross Dependency, administered by New Zealand since 1923, comprises 160,000 sq. mi. of Antarctic territory.

Nicaragua
REPUBLICA DE NICARAGUA

Capital: Managua. Area: 53,938 sq. mi. Population (UN est. 1972): 1,990,000. Monetary unit: Cordoba.

Nicaragua, largest of the Central or Middle American States, lies between the Caribbean and the Pacific with more than 200 mi. of coastline on each. The country is bordered by Honduras on the N and Costa Rica on the S. The Cordillera range of mountains, including many volcanic peaks, runs NW-SE through the middle of the country. Between this range and a range of volcanic peaks to the W lie Lake Managua, 38 mi. by 15, and Lake Nicaragua, 100 mi. by 45, of great importance to the transport system. The government-owned Pacific railroad, Corinto to Leon and Managua to Granada, 171 mi., is the principal rail line.

Resources and Industries. The nation has valuable forests, some gold is mined. It is essentially an agricultural country, but industrialization, including oil refining, is growing. On the broad tropical plains of the east coast, bananas, cotton, fruit and yucca are cultivated. Products of the western half include coffee, sugar, corn, beans, cocoa, rice, tobacco and wheat.

Cotton, coffee and sugar acount for 70% of the value of exports.

A severe earthquake, Dec. 23, 1972, destroyed much of Managua; about 10,000 died and 200,000 were left homeless. The nation was also hit by severe drought, lasting into 1973.

History and Government. After gaining independence from Spain, 1821, Nicaragua was united for a short period with Mexico, then with the United Provinces of Central America, finally becoming an independent republic, 1838.

The constitution, revised in 1960, provided for a Congress of two chambers, a House of Deputies of 45 members and a Senate of 18 members, all elected by popular vote. Ex-Presidents also serve in the Senate and are appointed for life. The President is elected for 5 years and may not succeed himself.

Anastasio Somoza Debayle was elected president Feb. 5, 1967. He resigned May 2, 1972, and was succeeded by a 3-man National Junta, to rule until Dec. 1974 elections.

Education and Religion. Roman Catholicism is the prevailing religion. There are 3 universities. Spanish is the official language. Nicaragua is a UN and OAS member.

Niger

Capital: Niamey. Area: 489,189 sq. mi. Population (UN est. 1972) 4,210,000. Monetary unit: CFA franc.

The Republic of the Niger, a former French Overseas Territory in the heart of West Africa, is bounded by Libya, Algeria, Chad, Upper Volta, Dahomey, Nigeria and Mali. Chief access to the country, a vast plateau almost twice the size of Texas, is by air. The Niger River flows through the western corner.

Under provisions of the 1958 French constitution, Niger became fully independent Aug. 3, 1960, and joined the UN Sept. 20. It signed a bilateral agreement Apr. 24, 1961, retaining close ties with France. The republic has a President and National Assembly, elected for 5-year terms.

Niger is an agricultural and pastoral land. Peanuts are the principal cash crop; livestock (cattle, sheep, camels, donkeys, goats) are second in importance. Cotton is being promoted. Drought and famine struck in 1973; aid was sent by the U.S. and others.

Large, high-grade uranium deposits gave promise of economic improvement. Production started in 1971.

Nigeria

Capital: Lagos. Area: 356,669 sq. mi. Population (UN est. 1972) 58,020,000. Monetary unit: Naira.

The Federal Republic of Nigeria, Africa's most populous country, became independent of Britain in 1960. Larger than Texas and Oklahoma combined, it lies on the southern side of the West African bulge, between Dahomey and Cameroon, with Niger Republic to the N and Chad NE. It comprises nearly 250 tribal and linguistic groups, including the Hausas in the N, Ibos in the E, Yorubas in the W.

Nigeria's rich natural resources include oil, coal, iron, limestone and natural gas. It produces much of the world's columbium ore (for steel alloys).

By 1972, Nigeria became the world's 9th largest petroleum producer; oil accounted for 80% of export value with cocoa 2d. Other exports are tobacco, tin, palm oil, palm kernels, cotton lint, hides and skins, lumber, rubber and peanuts. Under an "indigenization" program, 55% of businesses were to be run by blacks only by 1974.

Nigeria became a sovereign country Oct. 1, 1960, and a republic within the British Commonwealth Oct. 1, 1963. It is a member of the UN. Its first constitution provided for 4 regions with local autonomy, and a federal Parliament and Prime Minister.

In 1966 there were two military coups and periods of interracial strife ending a long period of coalition governments of the majority Northern Region and other regions. On Jan. 15, junior Army officers seized control;

Gen. Johnson Aguyi-Ironsi, an easterner, made himself head of state, Prime Minister Abukabar Tafawa Balewa was assassinated. On Aug. 1, Col. Yakubu Gowon, a northerner, became head of state; Gen. Ironsi was assassinated.

On May 27, 1967, the military government created 12 new states, replacing the 4 regions. On May 30, the Eastern Region seceded, proclaiming itself the Republic of Biafra. The move plunged the country into civil war.

Casualties in the war were estimated at over 1,000,000, including many "Biafrans" (mostly Ibos) who died of starvation despite international efforts to provide relief. The secessionists, after steadily losing ground, capitulated Jan. 12, 1970; Gen Odumegwu Ojukwu, rebel leader, fled to the Ivory Coast. Gen. Gowon announced a general amnesty.

The northern parts of the nation are predominantly Moslem; there are many animists, Christians and Moslems in the south.

Norway
KONGERIKET NORGE

Capital: Oslo. Area: 125,181 sq. mi. Population (UN est. 1972) 3,930,000. Monetary unit: Krone.

Norway occupies the W part of the Scandinavian Peninsula in NW Europe. It shares borders with Sweden, Finland and the USSR. The rocky W coast is cut deep by fjords of scenic grandeur. Norway is about the size of New Mexico.

The country's greatest length is 1,100 mi.; its width varies from 270 to only 4 mi. at the narrowest point. The coastline, including the fjords and largest of the 150,000 islands, is 17,000 mi. long. The climate is mild and moist on the W coast, but fairly cold and dry in the E.

The midnight sun is a phenomenon of the northern area. The sun does not set from the middle of May until the end of July, nor does it rise above the horizon from approximately Nov. 20 to Jan. 24.

Resources and Industries. More than 72% of the land is unproductive and only 4,300 sq. mi. are cultivated; rivers and lakes occupy 5,000; forests 29,455.

Forests supply a sizable wood and paper industry. Large quantities of cod, herring, mackerel and salmon are caught. Norway has the world's 14th largest fish catch. Mining is a leading industry and the country yields copper, pyrites, nickel, iron, zinc, lead.

Lacking sufficient coal, Norway has harnessed its waterfalls to provide power. Manufacturing, mainly processing of mining, forest, fishing, and chemical products, consumes 65% of the hydroelectric output. Ferroalloys and aluminum are produced. North Sea oil production began in 1971.

Farm products include oats, rye, potatoes, dairy products and fruits.

Norway's merchant marine fleet is the world's 5th largest. It earnings help offset the unfavorable balance of trade.

Foreign trade in thousands of U.S. dollars:

	Imports	Exports
1971	$4,083,000	$2,563,000
1972	$4,369,000	$3,280,000

History and Government. The first supreme ruler of Norway was Harald the Fairhaired who came to power in 872 A.D. Between 800 and 1000, the Vikings raided and occupied parts of Europe. Christianity was introduced 1030.

The country was united with Denmark 1381-1814, and with Sweden 1814-1905. The Swedish union was dissolved in 1905 and a Danish prince was named King Haakon VII of Norway. Nazi Germany attacked Norway Apr. 9, 1940 and held it until liberation May 8, 1945.

Norway is a constitutional monarchy.

The King of Norway is Olav V (born July 2, 1903), son of Haakon VII. On the death of his father he became King Sept. 21, 1957. He married (Mar. 21, 1929) Princess Martha of Sweden (who died Apr. 5, 1954). The heir to the throne, Crown Prince Harald, was born Feb. 21, 1937.

Legislative power is vested in the Storting, whose 150 members are elected for four years. Executive power is held by a Premier; the King is titular chief of state.

Social security includes health and unemployment insurance and pensions.

Education and Religion. Evangelical Lutheran religion is endowed by the state and its clergy are nominated by the King. All religions enjoy complete freedom of worship.

Education is free and compulsory from ages 7 to 16. Universities are subsidized by the state.

Defense. The armed forces for 1972-73 totaled 36,000.

Norway is a member of UN, NATO, Nordic Council and Council of Europe.

Norway planned to join the European Economic Community but Norwegian voters rejected the plan in Sept. 1972. A trade agreement was reached with the EEC in 1973.

SPITSBERGEN
(Svalbard)

Spitsbergen is a group of mountainous islands in the Arctic Ocean, c. 23,957 sq. mi., pop. varying seasonally from 1,500 to 3,000, incorporated in Norway as Svalbard. The largest, West Spitsbergen, c. 15,000 sq. mi., seat of governor, is about 370 mi. N of Norway. Named Svalbard by Norse who discovered it in 1194, it was visited by Barents 1596 and became locale of whaling until 19th Century. By a treaty signed in 1920, four major European powers recognized the sovereignty of Norway, which incorporated it 1925. Sealing, fishing are followed; there are rich coal deposits. Mt. Newton (West Spitsbergen) is 5,633 ft. tall.

Oman

Capital: Muscat. Area: 82,000 sq. mi. Population (UN est. 1972): 700,000. Monetary unit: Riyal Omani.

The Sultanate of Oman (formerly Muscat and Oman) is an independent monarchy occupying the E corner of the Arabian Peninsula and including the tip of a nearby peninsula, Ruus-al-Jebal, to the N. The Sultanate has a coastline of 1,000 mi. along the Gulf of Oman to the NE and the Arabian Sea to the SE. Climate is generally hot and dry.

There is a narrow coastal plain up to 10 mi. wide, a range of barren mountains with Jebal Akhdar, the highest, reaching c. 9,900 ft., and a wide, stony, mostly waterless plateau averaging 1,000 ft. in altitude. The Sultanate is the size of Utah.

Exports are mainly oil, dates and some dried fish, limes and pomegranates. Cultivated areas also produce bananas, grapes, wheat, vegetables, coconuts and frankincense. Goats and sheep are raised.

Oil was discovered in 1964 and production began in 1967. By 1972 Oman was the world's 16th largest producer.

The people are predominantly Arab, but there are also Indians, Baluchi, Negroes and others. The language is Arabic, but Hindi, Urdu, Baluchi and others are also spoken. The religion is mainly Islam of the Ibadhi sect.

A long history of rule by other lands ended with ouster of the Persians in 1744. On July 23, 1970, Sultan Said bin Taimur was overthrown by his son, who became Sultan Qabus bin Said. The new Sultan changed the nation's name to Sultanate of Oman. He launched a domestic development program and battled leftist rebels in the southern Dhofar area. The Sultan received arms aid from Iran; the guerrillas reportedly got arms from Iraq and the Peoples Democratic Republic of Yemen.

Pakistan

Capital: Islamabad. Area: 310,403 sq. mi. Population (1972 Census prelim.): 64,892,000. Monetary unit: Rupee.

Pakistan became a sovereign nation Aug. 14, 1947, when what had been the British Empire of India achieved independence and was partitioned into two countries, Pakistan and India. At first a dominion, Pakistan declared itself a republic on Mar. 23, 1956.

Pakistan was divided into two sections, West Pakistan and East Pakistan. The two areas lie nearly 1,000 mi. apart on opposite sides of India.

East Pakistan became the separate, independent nation of Bangladesh as a result of its 1971 rebellion and the Dec. 3-17, 1971, Pakistan-India war.

Pakistan adjoins Iran, Afghanistan, India and the Arabian Sea. To the NE lies the disputed Kashmir region.

Pakistan is a land of rugged mountains and river valleys, where irrigation aids agriculture, the occupation of 80% of the people. The Indus flows for c.1,000 mi. from the base of the Himalayas to the Arabian Sea and with its tributaries supplies reservoirs, canals and hydroelectric plants. In the W are the Hindu Kush Mts., with Tirich Mir 25,230 ft. In the N is Mt. K2 (Godwin Austen), 28,250 ft., 2nd highest in the world. The climate is mostly dry with little rainfall and summer temperatures up to 120°F.

Resources and Industries. Rice, wheat, cotton, oilseeds, tobacco, sugar, flour, wool and fish are important products. Minerals include sulphur, gypsum, salt, chromite, cement, petroleum, gas, coal, asbestos, antimony, magnesite and silica.

Pakistan manufactures cotton textiles (its largest industry), wool, silk, rayon, cement, card and paper board, sugar, chemicals, dyes, synthetic fertilizers.

The Indus Basin irrigation project which Pakistan shares with India, a $2 billion development aided by Western nations, was nearing completion.

Foreign trade in thousands of U.S. dollars:

	Imports	Exports
1971	$925,000	$666,000
1972	$681,000	$697,000

History and Government. The land now called Pakistan shares the 5,000-year history of the India-Pakistan sub-continent. At the present day sites of Harappa and Mohenjo Daro, the Indus Valley Civilization, with large cities and elaborate irrigation systems, flourished c. 4000-2500 B.C.

A lasting influence on Pakistan was the arrival of Islam with the first Arab invasion of 711 A.D.

After World War I the Moslems of British India felt handicapped as a minority and began agitation for minority rights in elections.

Mohammad Ali Jinnah (1876-1948) was the principal architect of the Pakistan state. A lawyer who studied in England, he was a leader of the Moslem League from 1916, and worked for constitutional reform and dominion status for India. Convinced Moslem-Hindu relations in government were irreconcilable, he first advocated a separate Moslem state in 1940.

When the British withdrew Aug. 14, 1947, the Islamic majority areas of India acquired self-government with dominion status in the Commonwealth and Jinnah became the first Governor General (1947-1948). He died in 1948.

A republic was created in 1956. In Oct. 1958, Gen. Mohammad Ayub Khan took power in a coup and was declared President. He was elected to the post in 1960 and reelected in 1965. Pakistan had a National Assembly (legislature) with equal membership from East and West Pakistan, and two Provincial Assemblies.

Pres. Ayub resigned Mar. 25, 1969, after several months of violent rioting and unrest, most of it in East Pakistan, in which some 200 persons died. There were demands for a parliamentary form of government, for direct elections and economic reforms. In East Pakistan, which had about 56% of the population, there were demands for greater political power or autonomy.

The government was turned over to Gen. Agha Mohammad Yahya Khan and martial law was declared; Gen. Yahya assumed the Presidency.

The Awami League, which sought regional autonomy for East Pakistan, won a majority in Dec. 1970 elections to a National Assembly which was to write a new constitution. In March 1971 Yahya postponed the Assembly. Rioting and strikes broke out in the East.

On Mar. 25, 1971, government troops launched attacks in the East, allegedly to forestall an Awami League rebellion. The Easterners proclaimed the independent nation of Bangladesh. In months of widespread fighting estimates of those killed ran as high as 1,000,000. Some 10,000,000 Easterners fled into India. Pakistan charged India with aiding the rebels; India said Pakistan troops fired across the border.

Pakistan and India went to war Dec. 3, 1971, on both the East and West fronts. Pakistan troops in the East surrendered Dec. 16; Pakistan agreed to a cease-fire in the West Dec. 17. India recognized Bangladesh as a separate nation Dec. 6.

Yahya resigned as President Dec. 20 and Zulfikar Ali Bhutto, leader of the Pakistan People's party, which had won the most West Pakistan votes in the Dec. 1970 elections, became President. In 1972 he announced new land reforms and said the government would control management of major industries.

On July 3, 1972, Pakistan and India signed a pact agreeing to withdraw troops from their borders and seek peaceful solutions to all problems.

In Aug. 1973 India agreed to release 93,000 Pakistani prisoners, held since 1971; Pakistan agreed to release 175,000 Bengali nationals stranded in Pakistan, and agreed to accept Biharis (non-Bengalis) unwanted in Bangladesh.

A new constitution adopted Apr. 10, 1973, made Pakistan a federal Islamic republic, with a 2-chamber Parliament and a President, but with executive power given to the Prime Minister. Bhutto became Prime Minister Aug. 15; Fazal Elahi became President.

(*See article on India for disputes over Kashmir, Rann of Cutch, etc.*)

Education and Religion. Most of the population is Moslem. Free and compulsory education is a prime goal. Urdu is the national language.

Defense. Before the 1971 war, Pakistan armed forces totaled about 390,000.

Pakistan is a member of the UN and CENTO. Following border warfare between India and Communist China in 1962 and increase in U.S. aid to India, Pakistan made commercial and aid agreements with Communist China and Indonesia. The U.S. had provided Pakistan with nearly $4 billion in military and economic aid by 1965. U.S. aid to both Pakistan and India was suspended during the 1966 war over Kashmir but both economic aid and "nonlethal" military aid were resumed in 1966. Military aid was suspended again in 1971. The U.S. agreed in 1973 to sell "non-lethal" military equipment to both Pakistan and India.

Panama
REPUBLICA DE PANAMA
Capital: Panama. Area: 29,208 sq. mi. Population (UN est. 1972): 1,520,000. Monetary unit: Balboa.

The Republic of Panama occupies the isthmus of Panama, connecting Central and South America. It is smaller than South Carolina. It has a shoreline of 477 mi. on the Caribbean and a shoreline of 767 mi. on the Pacific. Its width varies from about 37 to 110 mi. It is bounded by Colombia and Costa Rica, and is bisected by the 10-mi. wide U.S. Canal Zone.

Resources and Industries. Panama has extensive forests, and exports mahogany. Only about half of the rich arable land is cultivated. Sufficient cement, clay and salt are produced for domestic needs. Bananas are the main export, rivaled by products of a large petroleum refinery (which imports crude oil). Also exported are pineapples, cocoa, coconuts, sugar, shrimp.

Due to easy Panama ship regulations and strictures in the U.S., merchant tonnage registered in Panama since World War II ranks high in size. Registered number of ships of more than 1,000 gross tons each is over 880.

History and Government. The coast of Panama was discovered by Rodrigo de Bastidas, sailing with Columbus for Spain in 1501, and was visited by Columbus in 1502. Vasco Nunez de Balboa crossed the isthmus and "discovered" the Pacific Ocean Sept. 13, 1513. Spanish colonies were ravaged by Francis Drake, 1572-95, and Henry Morgan, 1668-71. Morgan destroyed the old city of Panama which had been founded in 1519. Freed from Spain, Panama joined Colombia in 1821. Separatist forces in Panama sought to gain independence from Colombia several times.

Panama declared its independence from Colombia

Nov. 3, 1903, with U. S. recognition. U. S. Naval forces discouraged action by Colombia. On Nov. 18, 1903, Panama granted use, occupation and control of the Canal Zone to the U. S. by treaty, ratified Feb. 26, 1904. (*See also Canal Zone and Panama Canal.*)

Rioting began Jan. 9, 1964, in a dispute over the flying of the U. S. and Panamanian flags and terms of the 1903 treaty. A joint declaration by the two governments Apr. 3, 1964, called for action to pave the way for peaceful negotiations. At least 21 Panamanians and 3 U. S. soldiers died in the rioting.

In 1967 new treaties were proposed, but in 1970 Panama said the proposed treaties were unacceptable. New negotiations started in 1971. In 1973 the U.S. vetoed a Panama-backed resolution in the UN Security Council calling for a new treaty guaranteeing Panamanian sovereignty over all its territory. The U.S. said it wanted to negotiate with Panama "without outside pressure."

In a bitter election, May 12, 1968, Dr. Arnulfo Arias was elected President. Inaugurated Oct. 1, Dr. Arias was ousted Oct. 11 by a military junta.

Panama adopted its 4th constitution in 1972, providing for a President, Legislative Council and an elected Assembly. The Assembly gave Gen. Omar Torrijos powers as Head of Government.

Education and Religion. The Roman Catholic religion prevails but other faiths have representation. Education is compulsory for all children between 7 and 15. The National and Santa Maria de Antigua Universities are in Panama City. Spanish is the official language; English is widely spoken.

Paraguay
REPUBLICA DEL PARAGUAY
Capital: Asuncion. Area: 157,047 sq. mi. Population (UN est. 1972): 2,580,000. Monetary unit: Guarani.

Paraguay, one of the two landlocked countries of South America, is bounded by Bolivia, Brazil, and Argentina. The extensive plains are excellent for pasturage and agriculture, and the mountain slopes are covered with luxuriant forests. It is about the size of California and is one of the best watered countries in the world. The Paraguay River, the Republic's most important waterway, is 1,800 mi. long.

Resources and Industries. Timber resources are large. Most of the population is agricultural and pastoral, with cattle breeding the principal industry. Most important agricultural crops are corn, wheat, cotton, beans, peanuts, tobacco and citrus fruits.

Chief exports are beef and other food products: cotton, wood products, hides, tobacco, yerba mate (tea), vegetable oils.

The first stages of a large hydroelectric project were completed in 1968-70; a highway to Brazil to aid trade shipments for the landlocked nation was completed; earlier, new roads were built in the western Chaco cattle country. In 1973 Paraguay and Brazil agreed to build a $3 billion hydroelectric project on the Parana River. About 100,000 tourists spend $16,000,000 annually in Paraguay.

History and Government. Visited by Sebastian Cabot, 1527; settled as a Spanish possession in 1535, Paraguay gained its independence from Spain in 1811. After fighting Brazil, Argentina and Uruguay (War of the Triple Alliance 1865-1870) it adopted in 1870 a democratic constitution.

A new constitution, adopted in Aug. 1967, provided for a President, a Senate of 30 members and a House of Representatives of 60.

In elections held Feb. 11, 1973, Gen. Alfredo Stroessner, who had ruled Paraguay since 1954, was reelected President for a 5-year term.

Education and Religion. The Roman Catholic religion is established, but others are guaranteed freedom. Primary education is compulsory between the ages of 7 and 14. Spanish is the official language; both Spanish and Guarani, an Indian tongue, are designated national languages.

Peru
REPUBLICA DEL PERU

Capital: Lima. Area: 496,222 sq. mi. Population (UN est. 1972): 14,460,000. Monetary unit: Sol.

Peru, on the Pacific coast of South America, is bounded by Ecuador, Colombia, Brazil, Bolivia, Chile and the Pacific. It has a Pacific coastline of 1,410 mi. and an extreme width, from western coast to eastern jungle, of about 800 mi. It is about the size of Arizona, New Mexico and Texas combined.

Here the Andes reach 22,205 ft. (Mt. Huascaran); 7 peaks tower above 19,000 ft. The uplands of western slopes of the Andes are well watered as are the eastern slopes and lowlands reaching the Amazon basin, where the port of Iquitos loads ocean-going vessels for a 2,300-mi. trip down the Amazon through Peru and Brazil.

The coastal area on the west is almost rainless, but the soil is fertile and irrigation, using rivers pouring down from the Andes, has made the area highly productive.

Lima, the capital, is in the coastal region and is also the nation's commercial center. Callao, the chief seaport, is 7 mi. west of Lima.

Inca and earlier Chimu ruins make Peru a mecca for archeologists, notably at Cuzco, Chan Chan and the Andean city of Machu Picchu.

A severe earthquake hit northern Peru May 31, 1970, destroying many towns and killing an est. 50,000.

Resources and Industries. Agriculture and stock raising occupy half the population.

The leading agricultural product is cotton. Wool, hides, skins, sugar, coffee, rice, potatoes, beans, barley and tobacco also are produced. Corn, native to Peru, is a staple food.

Peru is normally the world's top fishing nation; it takes about a sixth of total world tonnage, mostly anchovies from the plankton-rich waters of the coastal Peru current. Most of the take is ground into fish meal for poultry and livestock feed. But in 1972 the industry was crippled by a disappearance of anchovies from offshore waters. In 1973 the government nationalized the crippled industry. Limited fishing was resumed in 1973.

The mountains are rich in minerals and many valuable mines, some dating back to the Incas, are being worked. The Toquepala copper mine in the southern Andes is one of the world's largest; another is at Cerro de Pasco. The steel industry is expanding. Petroleum production is important.

Fishmeal is the leading export with copper 2nd. Other exports are cotton, sugar, iron ore, lead.

In 1968-71, the military government converted large farmlands into cooperatives, expropriated a large U.S. oil company, forced foreign mining companies to expand investments and ordered local industries to turn over 50% of ownership to their workers.

History and Government. The powerful Inca empire had its seat at Cuzco in the Andes (alt. 11,000 ft.) when Francisco Pizarro, Spanish conquistador, began raiding Peru for its wealth, 1532. In 1533 he had the ruling Inca, Atahualpa, fill a room with gold, then executed him and enslaved the natives. In 1535 he established Lima and in 1537 its port, Callao.

Lima was the seat of Spanish viceroys until the Argentine liberator, Jose de San Martin, captured it in 1821; Spain was defeated by Simon Bolivar and Antonio J. de Sucre and recognized Peruvian independence, 1824. Chile defeated Peru and Bolivia, 1879-84, and took Tarapaca, Tacna and Arica; returned Tacna, 1929.

The constitution provided for a President and a bicameral legislature, all elected for 6-year terms. On Oct. 3, 1968, a military coup ousted Pres. Fernando Belaunde Terry and Gen. Juan Velasco Alvarado assumed the presidency.

Education and Religion. Religious liberty prevails but Roman Catholicism is the state religion.

About 47% of the population is Indian; most of the remainder are of Spanish descent, or mestizos (mixed), with small percentages of Negroes, Chinese and Japanese.

Education is free and compulsory between 7 and 14.

The University of San Marcos (founded 1551) is one of the oldest in the western hemisphere. There are 32 other universities.

Spanish is the official language, but many Indians speak Quechua or Aymara.

Peru is a member of the UN and OAS.

Philippines
REPUBLIKA NG PILIPINAS

Capital: Quezon City. Area: 115,707 sq. mi. Population (UN est. 1972): 39,040,000. Monetary unit: Piso.

The Republic of the Philippines occupies an archipelago in the western Pacific, 500 mi. from the SE coast of Asia, 7,000 mi. from San Francisco. About 7,100 islands extend 1,150 mi. N to S, 682 E to W.

Eleven of the islands comprise the bulk of the area. The country is about the size of Arizona.

The archipelago has a coastline of 10,850 mi. Manila Bay, with an area of 770 sq. mi., and a circumference of 120 mi., is the finest harbor in the Far East.

Resources and Industries. Agriculture, manufacturing, mining, lumbering and fishing are the main activities. Forests, which cover 42% of the area, provide a variety of products from lumber and resins to medicinal plants. In 1971 the nation had the world's 4th largest fish catch.

The islands are rich in mineral resources. Gold, silver, lead, zinc, nickel, copper, iron, coal, chromite, asbestos and manganese are mined.

The chief agricultural products are manila hemp, copra, sugar, rice, canned pineapple and tobacco.

In the late 1960s, self-sufficiency in rice production was achieved after introduction of "miracle" high-yield varieties. Manufacturing showed steady gains, mostly in processing or assembly of food, clothing, pharmaceuticals, paper products, appliances. Tourists number over 100,000 annually, providing further income.

In July 1972 floods destroyed crops in central Luzon and took hundreds of lives.

History and Government. The archipelago was visited by Magellan 1521. The Spanish founded Manila 1571 and began their conquest. The islands, named for King Philip II of Spain, were ceded to the U.S. by the Treaty of Paris (Dec. 10, 1898), following the Spanish-American War, the U.S. paying Spain $20,000,000 for the territory.

Japan attacked the Philippines Dec. 8, 1941 (Far Eastern time). Gen. Douglas MacArthur was put in command of the U.S.-Filipino forces (15,000 Americans, 40,000 in Filipino Army, 100,000 Filipino reservists). Japan conquered the islands in May, 1942, and was ousted by Sept. 1945.

On July 4, 1946, independence was proclaimed in accordance with an act passed by the U.S. Congress in 1934, providing for Philippine independence in 1946.

A republic, with a President, Senate and House, was established.

All natural resources of the Philippines belong to the state and their exploitation is limited to citizens of the Philippines or corporations and associations of which 60% of the capital is owned by citizens. In 1946 the right to develop natural resources and to own and operate public utilities until 1974 was extended to U.S. citizens.

President Ferdinand E. Marcos visited the U.S. Sept. 1966; concluded pact reducing U.S. base leases from 99 to 25 years. There were riots by radical youth groups and terrorism by leftist guerrillas and outlaws in 1970-71.

On Sept. 23, 1972, Pres. Marcos declared martial law to combat leftist terrorists. Ruling by decree, he ordered land reform, cut crime and stabilized prices.

On Jan. 17, 1973, he proclaimed a new constitution, establishing a parliamentary government with wide powers to himself as President and Premier and extending his term of office past Dec. 1973.

Government troops battled Moslem secessionists in 1973 in southern Mindanao.

Education and Religion. Primary and secondary education is free, instruction is in English. Institutions of higher education include the University of the Philippines, Far Eastern Univ., Univ. of Santo Tomas (founded 1611), and Silliman Univ.

The official national language is Pilipino, based on Tagalog. English and Spanish, also official, are commonly used in government and commerce.

About 83% of the inhabitants are Roman Catholics and about 10% belong to the Philippine Independent Church, organized by a Filipino priest, Fr. Gregorio Aglipay. Other Christians, Moslems, Buddhists are among minorities.

Defense. The Philippines and U.S. have treaties for U.S. military and naval bases and a 1951 Mutual Defense Treaty, pledging joint action against external attack. Military forces for 1971-72 numbered 34,600. The Republic is a member of the UN and SEATO. A battalion of 2,200 construction troops served with the U.S. in Vietnam, 1966-69.

Poland

POLSKA RZECZPOSPOLITA LUDOWA

Capital: Warsaw. Area: 120,664 sq. mi. Population (UN est. 1972): 33,070,000. Monetary unit: Zloty.

The Polish People's Republic, in Central Europe, is bounded by the Baltic Sea, USSR, Czechoslovakia and East Germany. It is about the size of New Mexico.

Its terrain consists largely of lowlands. Gdynia, Gdansk (once Danzig), Szczecin, Swinoujscie and Kolobrzeg are the principal ports.

Resources and Industries. About 22% of the population was still engaged in agriculture in the early 1970s. Chief crops are rye, wheat, barley, oats, potatoes, sugar beets, tobacco, flax. Coal mining, shipbuilding, textiles, chemicals, woodworking and metal industries are important. Products include automobiles, tractors, heavy machinery, aircraft. Key industries are nationalized and operate under a planned economy. About 85% of the farms and some businesses are privately operated. The index of industrial production (1963=100) was 212 for 1972.

Poland produces 6% of world coal output and much zinc. Other minerals are sulphur, cement, salt, cadmium, iron, copper. Imported raw materials supply aluminum plants and oil refineries.

History and Government. Poland, whose history dates from 966, was a great power from the 14th to the 17th Centuries. In 3 partitions (1772, 1793, 1795) it was apportioned among Prussia, Russia and Austria, and in 1939 between Germany and the USSR. Overrun by the Austro-German armies in World War I, its independence, self-declared on Nov. 11, 1918, was recognized by the Treaty of Versailles, June 28, 1919.

Nazi Germany and the Soviet Union invaded Poland Sept. 1-27, 1939, and divided the country. With Germany's defeat, a Polish government-in-exile in London was recognized by the U. S., but the Soviet Union pressed the claims of a Lublin group, the Polish Committee of National Liberation, to which a few members of the London committee were admitted. The U. S. and Britain opposed it but compromised with Stalin when he agreed to free elections in Poland. However, he rejected international supervision and the election of 1947 was completely dominated by the Communists.

Before World War II, Poland's population was 34,775,698 and its area 150,470 sq. mi. In compensation for 69,860 sq. mi. ceded to the USSR, 1945, Poland received aprox. 40,000 sq. mi. of German territory east of the Oder-Neisse line comprising Silesia, Pomerania, West Prussia and part of East Prussia.

The 1952 constitution describes Poland as a people's republic with a Sejm (Parliament) elected for 4-year terms by direct ballot. The Sejm elects a Council of State and a Council of Ministers (cabinet). Policy is decreed by the Communist party Politburo.

During 12 years of rule by Stalinist extremists large estates were abolished, industy was nationalized, schools secularized and some Roman Catholic prelates jailed. Farm production fell off. Harsh working conditions caused a riot by workmen in Poznan June 28-29, 1956.

A new Politburo, committed to development of a more independent Polish Communism, was elected Oct. 1956, with Wladyslaw Gomulka as First Secretary of the Communist party. Collectivization of farms was ended and many collectives were abolished.

In 1970, Poland and West Germany signed a treaty to normalize relations.

In Dec. 1970 workers in port cities rioted because of price rises and new incentive wage rules. On Dec. 20 Gomulka resigned as party leader; he was succeeded by Edward Gierek. In 1971 the incentive rules were dropped, price rises were revoked. In June 1971 a new 5-year plan was announced, placing more stress on housing and consumer goods production.

Parliamentary elections in March 1972 endorsed Gierek's policies. U.S. President Nixon visited Poland in May; later, a U.S. trade information office was opened in Warsaw and the U.S. said it would make loans available to Poland.

Education and Religion. Education is free and compulsory. There are 75 institutions of higher learning. Leading universities are at Warsaw, Lodz, Torun, Poznan, Krakow, Lublin and Wroclaw (Breslau).

Roman Catholicism is the religion of over 90%. A law promulgated Feb. 13, 1953, required government consent to high church appointments. In October, 1956, Gomulka released Stefan Cardinal Wyszynski from prison and agreed to permit religious liberty in public institutions and religious publications, provided the church kept out of politics. But in 1961 religious studies in public schools were halted.

The Government barred a Vatican visit by Cardinal Wyszynski in 1966 but permitted it in 1968. Government and church officials sought to normalize relations between church and state.

Defense. Military strength for 1972-73 was 274,000. Poland is a UN and Warsaw Pact member.

Portugal

REPUBLICA PORTUGUESA

Capital: Lisbon. Area: 35,510 sq. mi. Population (UN est. 1972): 8,830,000. Monetary unit: Escudo.

Portugal occupies the SW part of the Iberian Peninsula and is bordered by Spain and the Atlantic. It is about the size of Indiana. The Azores Islands, in the Atlantic, 740 mi. W of Portugal, have an area of 888 sq. mi. and population (1968) or 333,400. The Madeira Islands, 360 mi. off the NW coast of Africa, have an area of 308 sq. mi. and a population (1968) of 268,600. Other overseas areas in Africa, Asia and Oceania (see below) are provinces, similar to provinces of "metropolitan" Portugal.

Portugal is mountainous. About two-thirds of the land is cultivated.

Resources and Industries. Wheat, corn, oats, barley, rye and rice are important crops. Wines, olive oil, sardines, anchovies, resins and fruits are major industries. Forests of pine, oak and chestnut cover 19% of the country, and the nation leads the world in cork production. Portugal has lead, copper, tin, wolfram, kaolin, sulphur, iron, tungsten and cement. Textiles, pottery, canned seafood, olive oil, shipbuilding, petro-chemical products, paper and glassware are principal manufactures. Fishing and tourism are large industries. A trade agreement was signed with the EEC in 1973.

History and Government. Portugal, an independent state since the 12th Century, was a kingdom until a revolution in 1910 drove out King Manoel II and a republic was proclaimed.

A new constitution adopted by a plebiscite in 1933 and several times amended, provides some features of a corporative state. Two assemblies were created—the first, the National Assembly, 150 members, to exercise legislative powers, by direct election by heads of families regardless of sex for 4 years; the second, the Corporative Chamber, 205 members, chosen through a system of guild or syndical representation. The Corporative Chamber deals with economic and social matters, and advises the National Assembly.

The President is elected for 7 years, the method of

selection since 1959 being by an electoral college composed of members of the Assembly and Chamber and representatives from the various districts. He appoints the Premier.

Dr. Antonio de Oliveira Salazar, Premier and dominant figure in the government since 1932, suffered a stroke in Sept. 1968 and was replaced by Dr. Marcelo Caetano. Dr. Salazar died July 27, 1970.

Education and Religion. The dominant religion is Roman Catholicism; there is freedom of worship. Primary education is compulsory. There are 9 universities, 3 university schools, 4 colleges of music, 43 lyceums, a number of technical and art schools. Portugal went on year-long daylight saving time in 1966.

Defense. Military forces for 1972-73 totaled 218,000, with 179,000 in the Army; 18,000 Navy; 21,000 Air Force. A 1951 agreement gave the U.S. rights to use defense facilities in the Azores. Portugal is a member of NATO and the UN.

PORTUGUESE OVERSEAS PROVINCES

Intermittent guerrilla attacks were staged by rebel forces in Angola, Mozambique and Portuguese Guinea during the 1960s and early 1970s. Portugal had forces totaling 142,000 in these provinces in 1973, and sought to improve economic and social conditions. In May 1973 Portugal rejected a UN Security Council call for negotiations on independence for the African provinces, saying this was an internal affair.

Angola, Portuguese West Africa, has a 1,000 mi. coast line stretching S from the mouth of the Congo. It is governed by a Governor General and an elected Legislative Council. The Portuguese have owned it since 1575. Its area is 481,351 sq. mi., population est. (1972) 5,810,000, including about 340,000 Europeans. The capital is Luanda.

Large oil deposits discovered in Angola's northern coastal area, Cabinda, began production in 1969.

Chief products are coffee, fishmeal, corn, sisal, fish, sugar, cotton, coconuts, oilseeds, ivory, cattle, iron ore, diamonds. There are deposits of copper, manganese, sulphur, phosphates, gold. Manufacturing of alcohol, cotton goods, fish products, paper, footwear, soap, sugar, tobacco is growing. Metropolitan Portugal supplies nearly 50% of the imports.

Mozambique, Portuguese East Africa, faces the Indian Ocean and Mozambique Channel in SW Africa. Mozambique has 297,731 sq. mi., and a population est. at 8,510,000. The capital is Lourenco Marques. Chief products are cement, flour, sugar, coconuts, cotton, copra, sisal, and cashews. Minerals include tantalum, coal, copper, gold, asbestos.

The Cape Verde Islands in the North Atlantic 280 mi. W of Dakar, Africa, are 15 in number. The total area is 1,557 sq. mi. and the population 270,000. Chief products are coffee, medicinal products, hides fruits and grain.

Portuguese Guinea, on the W coast of Africa between Senegal and Guinea, has an area of 13,948 sq. mi. and a population est. at 480,000. Chief exports are peanuts, oils, ivory and hides. The capital is Bissau.

The Islands of Sao Tome and Principe are about 125 mi. off the W. coast of Africa on the Gulf of Guinea. The islands have an area of 372 sq. mi.; population about 70,000. Chief products are cocoa, coffee, coconut, copra, palm oil and cinchona.

Macao, with an area of 6 sq. mi., is an enclave, a peninsula and two small islands, at the mouth of the Canton River in China. Population is est. at 270,000.

Portuguese Timor occupies the E part of the island of Timor N of Australia in the Timor Sea. Indonesia owns the W part. The area is 7,330 sq. mi. and the population 630,000. Exports are coffee, sandlewood, sandal root, copra and wax. Capital, Dili.

Qatar

Capital: Doha (Al Dawhah). Area: 6,000 sq. mi. Population: (est. 1972): 115,000. Monetary unit: Qatar-Dubai Riyal.

Qatar, formerly a British Protected State, declared its complete independence Sept. 1, 1971. It occupies the Qatar Peninsula, extending into the Persian (also called Arabian) Gulf from the NE Arabian coast.

A mainly arid land, slightly larger than Connecticut, Qatar is the world's 15th largest petroleum producer. Production started in 1949 and provides an income of over $150,000,000 annually. Doha has become a modern city with seawater desalting plants. Commercial fishing, government-aided agriculture and herds of camels, sheep and goats are also important.

Qatar was under Turkish control from 1872 to 1915. In a treaty signed in 1916 Qatar gave Great Britain responsibility for its defense and foreign relations. After Britain announced it would remove its military forces from the Persian Gulf area by the end of 1971, Qatar sought a federation with other British Protected States in the area; this failed and Qatar declared itself independent. It is a monarchy, ruled by an Emir aided by a Prime Minister, Council of Ministers and Advisory Council. Its first ruler under independence, Emir Ahmed bin Ali al-Thani, was replaced by his cousin, Khalifa bin Hamad al-Thani, Feb. 22, 1972, in a bloodless coup. Qatar is a member of the UN and Arab League.

Most Qataris are Arabs of the Sunni branch of Islam. Arabic is the official language. Education is free and compulsory; ages 6-16.

Rhodesia

Capital: Salisbury. Area: 150,333 sq. mi. Population (UN est. 1972): 5,690,000. Monetary unit: Rhodesian dollar.

Rhodesia, which has declared itself independent of Great Britain, is mostly high plateau country, bordered by the Zambezi River and Zambia to the N, Mozambique to the E, the Republic of South Africa to the S and Botswana to the W. It is almost the size of California.

Victoria Falls on the Zambezi, partly in Zambia, are 355 ft. high, 5,580 ft. wide. They were discovered by Dr. David Livingstone in 1855.

The vast majority of the people are Africans (mostly Bantus); there are about 255,000 whites and small minorities of Asians and mixed descent. English is the official language but most Africans speak Bantu tongues.

Rich farmlands and mineral deposits are the mainstays of the economy. Tobacco is normally the leading export, followed by asbestos, meat, sugar, copper, clothing, iron, chemical products, cotton, coal and chrome.

Britain took over the area as Southern Rhodesia in 1923 from the British South Africa Co. and granted internal self-government. Under a 1961 constitution, there was a Governor representing the British Crown, a Prime Minister and Legislative Assembly with voting restricted to maintain whites in power. On Nov. 11, 1965, Prime Minister Ian D. Smith announced his country's unilateral declaration of independence. Britain termed the act illegal, demanding Rhodesia broaden voting rights to provide for eventual rule by the majority Africans.

The British government imposed sanctions, including embargoes on oil shipments to Rhodesia, which were backed by most nations including the U.S. Some oil and gasoline reached Rhodesia, however, from South Africa and Mozambique. Some African nations denounced Britain for refusing to use force against the Rhodesian government. In May 1968, the UN Security Council ordered a trade embargo against Rhodesia.

Rhodesia claimed the sanctions were ineffective. A new constitution came into effect Mar. 2, 1970, providing for a republic with a President and Prime Minister; a Senate of 23 members, and a House of Assembly elected by separate white and black voter rolls, eventually to have 50 representatives each (but effectively delaying full black representation through income tax requirements).

A proposed British-Rhodesian settlement was dropped in May 1972 when a British commission reported most Rhodesian blacks opposed it. In 1973 there were small clashes between black nationalist guerrillas and Rhodesian security forces.

Romania

REPUBLICA SOCIALISTA ROMANIA

Capital: Bucharest. Area: 91,699 sq. mi. Population (UN est. 1972): 20,770,000. Monetary unit: Leu.

Romania, a Balkan state in SE Europe is almost the size of Oregon. It is bounded by the USSR, the Black Sea, Bulgaria, Yugoslavia and Hungary. The Danube flows along the southern border and through eastern Romania into the Black Sea. The Carpathian Mts. enclose the north-central Transylvanian plateau. There are wide plains S and E of the mountains.

Resources and Industries. Romania has become heavily industrialized, industry accounting for more than half the total national product in the late 1960s. Industrial growth rate for 1972 was 11%. But 47% of labor was still agricultural.

Main industries are iron-steel, other metallurgy, machinery, oil and chemicals, building materials, timber, textiles, footwear, food processing.

There is considerable mineral wealth: oil, natural gas, coal, salt, bauxite, manganese, lead, zinc, gold, silver. Production in 1971 included 13,788,000 metric tons of crude oil, 6,804,000 of steel.

Farms and forests contributed 29% of the national product. State farms and cooperatives own 96.4% of arable land. Romania is the world's 6th largest corn producer; also important are wheat, sugar beets, grapes and fruits.

In 1973, Romania had over 14,000,000 sheep, 7,000,000 hogs, 5,000,000 cattle.

Imports in 1971 were valued at $2.103 billion, exports at $2.101 billion.

History and Government. Romania's earliest known people were merged with invading Proto-Thracians, preceding by centuries the Dacians. The Dacian kingdom was occupied by Rome 101 A.D.-271 A.D.; the people and language were Romanized. The principalities of Wallachia and Moldavia, dominated by Turkey, were united in 1859; became Romania in 1861. In 1866 the house of Hohenzollern-Sigmaringen placed a prince in control. In 1877 Romania proclaimed independence from Turkey, became an independent state by the Treaty of Berlin, 1870, and kingdom, 1881, under Carol I. In 1886 Romania became a constitutional monarchy with a bicameral legislature.

Romania's location on the border of warring states made it a frequent victim of strife. It helped Russia against Turkey, 1877-78. It was defeated by Germany and Austria-Hungary in World War I, 1914-15; later rejoined the Allies and won Bessarabia, Bukovina, Transylvania and Banat. In 1940 it ceded Bessarabia and Northern Bukovina to the USSR and part of Southern Dobrudja to Bulgaria.

King Carol II made himself dictator in 1938, abdicated 1940 (died 1953). Michael I (born Oct., 25, 1921) became king 1940.

Marshal Ion Antonescu, leader of militarist movement, came to power and forced Romania to join Germany against the USSR in World War II in 1941. In 1944 Antonescu was overthrown by King Michael with Soviet help and Romania joined the Allies.

With occupation by Soviet troops the National Democratic Front, headed by the Communist party, displaced the National Peasant party. A People's Republic was proclaimed, Dec. 30, 1947, and Michael was forced to abdicate. Land owners were dispossessed and practically all banks, factories and transportation units were nationalized. A new constitution on the Soviet model was voted Sept. 24, 1952. A modification, March 1961, replaced the Presidium with the State Council, elected by the Grand National Assembly from its own membership. A Council of Ministers is the administrative body. The Assembly has 465 Deputies, elected for 5-year terms.

On Aug. 22, 1965, a new Constitution proclaimed Romania a Socialist, rather than People's Republic. Since 1966, Romania has adopted an increasingly independent attitude toward the USSR, a stand pointed up by the visit of U. S. President Nixon in Aug. 1969. A friendship pact signed with the USSR in July 1970 did not alter this attitude. In 1972 economic relations with the USSR improved.

Education and Religion. Education is compulsory for 10 years, all education is free. There are universities in Bucharest, Jassy, Cluj, Craiova and Timisoara.

The language has a Latin base, with traces of French, Greek, Slav and Turkish influences.

Romanian Orthodox clergy are paid by the state, other clergy receive subsidies but church and state are called separated. Roman Catholic orders have been abolished and the Greek Catholic Church has been absorbed by the Romanian Orthodox.

Defense. Military forces for 1972-73 totaled 179,000. Romania is a member of the UN and Warsaw Pact.

Rwanda

REPUBLIQUE RWANDAISE

Capital: Kigali. Area: 10,166 sq. mi. Population (UN est. 1972): 3,900,000. Monetary unit: Rwanda Franc.

The Republic of Rwanda, which became independent July 1, 1962, had been part of the former Belgian UN Trusteeship of Ruanda-Urundi. Rwanda lies in East Central Africa, bounded N by Uganda, E by Tanzania, W by Zaire and S by Burundi.

The source of the Nile River, long sought by explorers and geographers, has been located in the headwaters of the Kagera River, SW of Kigali; from there it is 4,145 mi. to where the Nile empties into the Mediterranean.

About the size of Maryland, Rwanda is one of the most densely populated nations in Africa. The population includes the Hutu (90% of population), the Tutsi (Watusi, 8%) and the Twa (2%). For centuries the Tutsi (an extremely tall race) subjugated the Hutu (average height) and the Twa (pygmies). A civil war broke out in 1960 and Tutsi power was ended. *See Index for Burundi.*

The majority of Rwandans are Christians. French and Kinyarwanda are the official languages.

A Legislative Council, organized in Oct. 1960, declared Rwanda a republic Jan. 28, 1961, and a referendum, Sept. 25, abolished the monarchic system. The new government was dominated by the Hutu. A President and National Assembly are elected for 4-year terms. Rwanda is a member of the UN and OAU.

Coffee is the principal crop; cotton, tea, pyrethrum, tobacco, cattle and hides also are produced. Minerals include tin, gold, wolframite.

Kagera National Park, in the northeast, covers a tenth of the country; here the flora and fauna of East Central Africa are preserved intact. Lake Kivu, on the nation's western border with Zaire, is 4,788 ft. above sea level and considered one of Africa's most beautiful.

San Marino

REPUBBLICA DI SAN MARINO

Area: 23.5 sq. mi. Population (est 1972): 20,000. Monetary unit: Italian lira.

San Marino, one of the world's smallest nations, lies on the slopes of Mt. Titano in the Apennines near the Adriatic, in north central Italy. It is one-third the size of the District of Columbia.

Principal industries are printing postage stamps, tourism, woolen goods, paper, cement, industrial ceramics. There is no unemployment. Cradle-to-grave social security is provided. A ceremonial army of 180 men is maintained.

History and Government. The Republic claims to be the oldest state in Europe and to have been founded in the 4th Century. It has had a treaty of friendship with Italy since 1862. It is a member of the International Court of Justice.

San Marino is governed by a Grand Council of 60 members elected by popular vote, two of whom are chosen to exercise executive power for a term of 6 months. Women were allowed to vote for the first time Sept. 13, 1964.

Saudi Arabia

AL-MAMLAKA AL-'ARABIYA AS-SA'UDIYA

Capital: Riyadh. Area: 870,000 sq. mi. Population (Est. 1973): 8,000,000. Monetary Unit: Riyal.

Saudi Arabia occupies four-fifths of the Arabian Peninsula, with the Red Sea on most of its W coast and the Persian Gulf (also called Arabian Gulf) on the E. The highlands of the W, up to 9,000 ft., slope as an arid, barren desert to the Persian Gulf. Its neighbors are Jordan, Iraq, Kuwait, Bahrain, Qatar, United Arab Emirates, Oman, Yemen Arab Republic and PDR of Yemen. It is more than 3 times the size of Texas.

Saudi Arabia comprises four provinces: the former sultanate of Nejd, the old kingdom of Hejaz, Asir and El Hasa (now known as the Eastern Province).

The Hejaz contains the holy cities of Islam—Medina where the Mosque of the Prophet enshrines the tomb of Mohammed, who died in the city June 7, 632, and Mecca, his birthplace, containing a great mosque sheltering the sacred shrine, the Kaaba, which holds the black stone given by Gabriel to Abraham. More than 400,000 Moslems from 60 nations visit Mecca annually.

Two major airports, Dhahran and Jidda, handle the bulk of international traffic. Jidda, on the Red Sea, is the main seaport. A 357-mi. railroad runs from Dammam on the Persian Gulf to Riyadh.

Resources and Industries. Saudi Arabia possesses the world's largest oil reserves and is the 3d largest producer (after the U.S. and USSR). Production centers along the Persian Gulf. Refineries and piers for tankers are at Ras Tanura, and a pipeline runs from Abqaiq to Saida on the Lebanese coast. Operations are mostly in the hands of the Arabian American Oil Co. (Aramco), owned by several American companies. Most of the oil is shipped to Western Europe. Production is valued at over $4 billion a year and is about 11% of world output. In 1973, the Saudi government acquired 25% ownership of Aramco and will hike 51% by 1982.

Income from oil royalties defrays many expenses of the state, the cost of internal improvements and free medical care for its citizens.

An agricultural country except for oil, and recently discovered gold, silver and rich iron ore, Saudi Arabia's products are dates, wheat, barley, fruit, hides, wool. Camels, horses, donkeys and sheep are raised. Some hides, wool and gum are exported. It receives UN technical assistance. A steel mill and fertilizer plant have been built.

History and Government: Nejd, long an independent state and center of the Wahhabi sect, fell under Turkish rule in the 18th Century, but in 1913 Ibn Saud, founder of the Saudi dynasty, overthrew the Turks and captured the Turkish province of Hasa; took the Hejaz in 1925 and by 1926 most of Asir.

The form of government is a hereditary monarchy. King Saud ibn Abdul Aziz (born 1902) who succeeded his father Nov. 9, 1953, was stripped of his powers after a family council, Mar. 28, 1964, but was allowed to retain his title. Crown Prince Faisal, the King's half-brother, assumed title of Viceroy; on Nov. 2, was named King in place of Saud. There is no parliament or constitution.

Education and Religion. Elementary, secondary and higher education are free, but not compulsory. Development of education is extensive, taking more than 10% of the government budget. But illiteracy was still high in 1973. Population is almost entirely Moslem.

Defense. Military forces for 1972-73 numbered 41,000, mostly infantry with some tanks; there were coastal patrol boats and about 75 combat aircraft. Saudi Arabia is a member of the UN and Arab League. Arms purchases have been from Britain and the U.S.

Saudi Arabia and Egypt opposed each other during several years of warfare in Yemen, with Saudi Arabia supplying arms and other aid to the royalists and Pres. Gamal Abdel Nasser providing troops to fight for the republicans. By late 1967, Egyptian troops were withdrawn from Yemen. In 1969, Yemeni republican government claimed the civil war had ended.

Saudi Arabia has given financial aid to both Jordan and Palestinian guerrilla groups.

Senegal

Capital: Dakar. Area: 75,750 sq. mi. Population (UN est. 1972): 4,120,000. Monetary unit: CFA franc.

A former French Overseas Territory on the Atlantic coast of western Africa, Senegal has for neighbors Mauritania, Mali, Guinea and Portuguese Guinea and it almost surrounds tiny Gambia on 3 sides. It is about as large as South Dakota.

Senegal became an autonomous state in 1958 and with the Sudanese Republic formed the Mali Federation Jan. 17, 1959. The federation became completely independent June 20, 1960, but after political conflict arose Senegal withdrew from the federation Aug. 20, 1960. The Sudanese Republic assumed the name Mali. Senegal is a member of the UN. The President and National Assembly are elected by adult suffrage.

About 70% of the population is engaged in agriculture and stock raising; peanuts are the mainstay of the economy. Dakar is an important seaport, handling 4,000 ships annually. Phosphates are an important export, along with peanut oil. Developing industries include food processing, chemicals, cement. A long drought brought famine in 1973. Aid was sent by the U.S. and others. Also in 1973, a "nationalization" of jobs program was announced.

French is the official language, but the majority speak various tribal languages. About 80% of the population is Moslem.

Sierra Leone

Capital: Freetown. Area: 27,699 sq. mi. Population (UN est. 1972): 2,630,000. Monetary unit: Leone.

Sierra Leone, former British Colony and Protectorate which became an independent state within the Commonwealth Apr. 27, 1961, is in the SW corner of the West African bulge. The coast line on the Atlantic is about 210 mi.; the country extends inland about 180 mi., between Guinea and Liberia. It is a bit smaller than South Carolina. Its name, meaning Mountain of the Lion, was applied by an early Portuguese mariner because of thunderstorms around its coastal peaks.

Freetown, the capital, was founded in 1787 by the British government as a home for destitute freed slaves. Their descendants, known as Creoles, number more than 50,000. The city has one of the finest seaports in West Africa.

Principal exports are industrial diamonds, iron ore, bauxite, cocoa, coffee, palm kernels, kola nuts, ginger, piassava (palm fiber). More than 80% are employed in agriculture.

Successive steps toward independence followed introduction of the first constitution in 1951. The Sierra Leone People's party was dominant until a military coup d'etat Mar. 23, 1967.

The coup followed general elections in which the vote was almost equally divided between the People's party and the All People's Congress.

Col. A. T. Juxon-Smith who headed a ruling council, was himself ousted in another coup, Apr. 8, 1968, led by non-commissioned officers. The nation was returned to civilian rule with swearing-in of Siaka Stevens as Prime Minister, Apr. 26. Stevens, head of the All People's Congress party, had been Prime Minister for two hours at the time of the 1967 coup. Sierra Leone became a republic Apr. 19, 1971, and Stevens was named president.

Sierra Leone is a member of the UN and OAU.

English is the official language but the majority speaks Krio or tribal languages. Most of the people are animists; there are over 700,000 Moslems and over 100,000 Christians.

Singapore

Capital: Singapore. Area: 226 sq. mi. Population (UN est. 1972): 2,150,000. Monetary unit: Singapore dollar.

Singapore is an independent island republic 27 mi. long and 14 mi. wide at the southern tip of the Malay Peninsula in SE Asia. About 3 times the size of the District of Columbia, the main island is linked to the mainland by a three-quarter mile long causeway. The narrow Straits of Singapore separate it from its islets to the south.

Singapore, the capital, is the world's 4th largest port and the largest in SE Asia.

Founded in 1819 by Sir Thomas Stamford Raffles, Singapore was a British colony until 1959 when it became an internally autonomous state within the Commonwealth. On Sept. 16, 1963, it joined with Malaya, Sarawak and Sabah to form the Federation of Malaysia.

Tensions between Malayans, dominant in the federation, and ethnic Chinese, dominant in Singapore, led to an agreement under which Singapore became a separate nation, Aug. 9, 1965. It has a one-house Parliament, elected by compulsory suffrage; a President elected by Parliament, and a Prime Minister.

Singapore's population is 76% Chinese, 15% Malay and 9% Indians, Pakistanis, Ceylonese, Eurasians, etc. Industries include ship building, oil refining, textiles, and food, rubber, copra and lumber processing. Port activities are the basis of the economy but manufacturing has boomed.

Tourism is an important source of income; there were 783,000 visitors in 1972. Attractions include festivals, foods, Tiger Balm Gardens, some 500 Chinese temples, the harbor with its junks and sampans and Malay sea villages.

Primary education for 6 years is free but not compulsory. There are 2 universities, Singapore and Nanyang, and 2 technical colleges.

Singapore in 1971 increased its defense forces in preparation for reduction of British forces and joined Australia, Britain, Malaysia and New Zealand in a pact for consultation in case of an attack. Singapore is a member of the Commonwealth and UN.

Somalia
SOMALI DEMOCRATIC REPUBLIC

Capital: Mogadishu. Area: 246,201 sq. mi. Population (UN est. 1972): 2,940,000. Monetary unit: Somali shilling.

The Somali Democratic Republic is comprised of the former protectorate of British Somaliland and the former Italian UN trusteeship of Somalia in eastern Africa. It is bordered by the Gulf of Aden, Indian Ocean, Kenya, Ethiopia and the French Territory of Afars and Issas. It is about the size of Texas. The population is predominantly Moslem.

Resources and Industries. Somalia has a weak economy and long depended on outside aid, part of it from the U.S., Italy, Great Britain and the USSR. Principal occupations are livestock raising and agriculture. Products include incense, sugar, bananas, sorghum, corn, gum, hides, kapok.

Its mineral resources, largely undeveloped, include iron, tin, gypsum, sandstone, bauxite, meerschaum, titanium and others. In 1968 the Government announced discovery of large uranium deposits.

History and Government. Many of the Somali peoples are nomadic and include large numbers in Kenya and Ethiopia. The Italian Protectorate of Somalia, 194,000 sq. mi., extended along the Indian Ocean from the Gulf of Aden to the Juba River. It was proclaimed a protectorate by Italy, 1889. The UN General Assembly, Nov. 21, 1949, approved eventual creation of Somalia as a sovereign state and on April 1, 1950, Italy took over the trusteeship held by Great Britain since World War II.

British Somaliland, formed in the 19th Century in the northwest, had 68,000 sq. mi. Britain gave it independence June 26, 1960, and on July 1 it joined with the former Italian part to create the independent Somali Republic.

On Oct. 21, 1969, a Supreme Revolutionary Council seized power in an army and police coup, named a mainly civilian cabinet to aid it, and abolished the Assembly and offices of President and Prime Minister. In May 1970 several foreign companies were nationalized.

Republic of South Africa
REPUBLIEK VAN SUID-AFRIKA
Capitals: Pretoria and Cape Town. Area: 471,982 sq.

mi. **Population (UN est. 1972): 22,990,000. Monetary unit: Rand.**

The Republic of South Africa occupies the southern portion of the continent and includes the former colonies of the **Cape of Good Hope, Natal,** the **Transvaal** and the **Orange Free State,** which became provinces. It is about the size of Texas, Oklahoma and New Mexico.

Population growth of government-designated racial groups in terms of 1960 and 1970 censuses, was: Bantu, 10,907,789, 15,057,952; white, 3,088,492, 3,751,328; Colored (mixed) 1,509,258, 2,018,453; Asians, 477,125, 620,436.

Cape Town, seat of Parliament, is the legislative capital and Pretoria the administrative capital. Largest cities are Johannesburg, Cape Town and Durban.

Kruger National Park, an 8,000-sq. mi. wild game preserve; Cape Peninsula, and the Drakensberg Mtns., are among numerous tourist attractions.

Resources and Industries. Corn, wool, wheat, tobacco, sugar, fruit, peanuts, wine, karacul, butter and cheese are major agricultural products. Industry products include steel, tires, electric motors, textiles, furniture, plastics.

With vast mineral resources, South Africa leads the world in production of gold, gem diamonds and antimony; it is among top producers of platinum, chrome, uranium, vanadium, vermiculite, manganese and asbestos. Coal and iron resources are large. Annual production of more than 50 minerals is est. at over $2 billion.

South Africa has enjoyed an industrial boom. Index numbers of industrial production (1963 = 100) were 167 in 1972 for manufacturing and 127 for mining.

Air service is provided by 23 international lines. Railroads are state-controlled.

Foreign trade (in thousands of U.S. dollars) excluding gold:

	Imports	Exports
1971	$4,035,000	$2,176,000
1972	$3,647,000	$2,602,000

History and Government. The Union was formed by act of the British Parliament, effective May 31, 1910, 8 years after the British defeated the independent republics of the Transvaal and the Orange Free State in the Anglo-Boer War (1899-1902). The nation was settled by emigrants from Cape Colony, mostly of Dutch extraction in the Great Trek of 1831 and later. After gold was discovered in 1886 the Boers faced repeated difficulties from the Uitlanders (Outlanders) and the wildcat Jameson raid against the gold-bearing ridge, the Witwatersrand, at Johannesburg in 1896 increased the tension. The Anglo-Boer War made a national hero of Paul Kruger ("Oom Paul"), Pres. of the Transvaal, who died in exile, 1904.

With the election victory of Daniel Malan's National party in 1948, the policy of separate development of the races, or apartheid, already existing unofficially, became official. This called for separate development, separate residential areas and ultimate political independence for the whites, Bantus, Asians and Coloreds.

In 1959 the government passed acts providing the eventual creation of 9 Bantu nations or Bantustans. In 1963, the Transkei an area in the SE, became the first of these partially self-governing territories or "Homelands." By 1971 there were 7.

The nation became a Republic May 31, 1961. The government at first sought readmission to the Commonwealth in its new status (with a President instead of a Governor General representing the British Crown), but withdrew its application in the face of opposition by other Commonwealth governments to South Africa's apartheid policy. The nation is a member of the UN.

The white-operated government includes a President chosen for a 7-year term by the Senate and Assembly, and a Prime Minister who holds the actual executive power and who represents the party in power in the Assembly. Members of the partly appointed, partly indirectly-elected Senate, and of the elected Assembly, are chosen for 5-year terms; all members must be white. There is a separate, advisory Indian Council, partly elected, partly appointed, to represent those of Asian Indian descent. In 1969, a Colored People's Representative Council was created. There is an elected Provincial

Council in each of the 4 provinces.

Education and Religion. There are 16 universities, including 11 for white students, average enrollment exceeding 92,000 students. Primary education is free to all citizens and compulsory for white children over 7.

Dutch Protestant churches predominate, with Anglicans and Methodists next among whites. English and Afrikaans are official languages.

Defense. Military forces for 1972-73 totaled 109,300.

SOUTH-WEST AFRICA
NAMIBIA

South-West Africa, a sparsely populated land twice the size of California, became the object of international dispute in 1966. Made a German protectorate in 1884, it was surrendered to South Africa in 1915 and was administered by that country under an old League of Nations mandate. South Africa refused to accept UN authority under the trusteeship system.

Other African nations charged South Africa imposed apartheid, built military bases and exploited S-W Africa; 36 African states called on the UN to take over the mandate.

The UN General Assembly in May 1968 created an 11-nation council to take over administration of South-West Africa and lead it to independence. In April 1968 the council charged that South Africa had blocked its effort to unit South-West Africa.

In 1968 the UN General Assembly gave the area the name Namibia. In Jan. 1970 the UN Security Council condemned South Africa for "illegal" control of the area. In an advisory opinion in June 1971 the International Court of Justice declared South Africa was occupying the area illegally. In 1973, a South Africa-style "homeland," Ovamboland, in the northern area, was given limited self-government.

Most of S-W Africa is a plateau, 3,600 ft. high, with plains in the N, Kalahari Desert to the E, Orange River on the S, the Atlantic on the W. Area is 318,261 sq. mi.; population (UN est. 1972) 660,000 including over 96,000 whites; capital, Windhoek. There is a South African administrator; voters choose 18 members of a Legislative Assembly and send 6 members to the South African Assembly; 4 are appointed to the South Africa Senate. In 1972 South Africa began creation of "homelands", with partial self-government, in the area.

Products include cattle, sheep, diamonds, lead, zinc, vanadium, fish. People include Namas (Hottentots), Ovambos (Bantus), Bushmen and others.

Spain
ESTADO ESPANOL

Capital: Madrid. Area: 195,988 sq. mi. Population (UN est. 1972): 34,490,000. Monetary unit: Peseta.

Spain, a nominal monarchy, occupies the entire Iberian peninsula in Western Europe, except for Portugal. It is separated from France by the Pyrenees.

The interior is a high arid plateau traversed E and W by mountain ranges. Spain is twice the size of Wyoming.

The **Balearic Islands** in the western Mediterranean, 1,935 sq. mi., are a province of Spain; they include **Majorca**(Mallorca), with the capital, Palma; **Minorca, Cabrera, Ibiza** and **Formentera**. The **Canary Islands**, 2,807 sq. mi., in the Atlantic W of Morocco, form 2 provinces, including the islands of **Tenerife, Palma, Gomera, Hierro, Grand Canary, Fuerteventura** and **Lanzarote** with Las Palmas and Santa Cruz thriving ports. **Ceuta** and **Melilla**, small enclaves on Morocco's Mediterranean coast, are part of Metropolitan Spain.

Spanish Sahara is an overseas province on the W coast of Africa, S of Morocco; area 102,703 sq. mi., population (1970 est.) 60,000.

Spain has sought return of Gibraltar, in British control since 1704.

Resources and Industries. Only about 40% of the land is cultivable, the remainder is arid or mountainous. Farm mechanization and irrigation are increasing.

The principal agricultural products are wheat, barley, oats, rye, olives, grapes, lemons, oranges and other fruit, onions, almonds, esparto, flax, hemp, pulse and cork. Tobacco, cotton, and rice are also grown. Wine-making is a large and ancient industry. Spain possesses an abundance of minerals, including lead, iron, copper, zinc, coal, cobalt, mercury, silver, sulphur and phosphates.

Manufacturing includes cotton and woolen goods, shoes, paper, automobiles, cork and cement. Spain's commercial fish catch is the world's 6th largest. Coal production is more than 10,000,000 metric tons annually.

The index of general industrial production showed a large rise from 100 in 1963 to 250 for 1972. Electric power output rose from 37.7 billion kwh in 1966 to 68.1 billion in 1972; steel production from 3,800,000 metric tons to 9,528,000 tons. A trade pact with the USSR was signed in 1972. Spain recognized communist China in 1973.

More than 18,000,000 tourists spend $1.3 billion a year in Spain.

History and Government. Since Roman times Spain has had a major part in the political, religious and cultural fortunes of Europe. It was settled by Iberians, Basques and Celts, partly overrun by Carthaginian armies, conquered by Rome under Scipio Africanus c. 200 B.C. The Germanic Visigoths, in power by the 5th Century A.D., adopted Christianity but by 711 A.D. lost to the Islamic invasion from Africa. The Christian reconquest from the N led to a Spanish nationalist movement. Foremost Christian leader was the Cid Campeador (Lord Champion), d. 1099 A.D. In 1469 the kingdoms of Aragon and Castile were united by the marriage of Ferdinand II and Isabella I, and the last Moorish power broken by the fall of the kingdom of Granada, 1492. Spain became a bulwark of Roman Catholicism, and the Inquisition, under which non-believers were slain, converted or exiled, came into power.

Spain obtained a great colonial empire with the discovery of America by Columbus, 1492, the conquest of Mexico by Cortes and Peru by Pizarro. It also controlled the Netherlands and parts of Italy and Germany. Charles I (Charles V, Holy Roman emperor), 1519-1556, attempted to halt Luther's Reformation and reestablish religious unity. Philip II, 1556-1598, tried to uproot heresy. The Spanish Armada failed to subdue England, 1588. Napoleon seized control of Portugal and Spain, 1808, made his brother Joseph King of Spain and precipitated the Peninsular War. Spain lost Mexico, Peru and other American colonies in the 1820s. It lost Cuba, the Philippines and Puerto Rico during the Spanish-American War, 1898. It gained concessions in Morocco by 1912, but recognized Moroccan independence in 1956.

Primo de Rivera became dictator in 1923. King Alfonso XIII revoked the dictatorship, 1930, but was forced to leave the country Apr. 14, 1931. A republic was proclaimed which disestablished the church, curtailed its privileges and secularized education. A conservative reaction to these measures occurred 1933 but was followed by a Popular Front (1936-1939) composed of socialists, communists, republicans and anarchists.

Army officers headed a revolt against the government July 18, 1936, under Francisco Franco (b. Dec. 11, 1892). They established a provisional govt. at Burgos. In a destructive 3-yr. war, in which 1,000,000 are said to have died, Franco received help from Italy and Germany, while the Soviet Union, France and Mexico were active on behalf of the republic. About 600 Americans served in the Abraham Lincoln brigade for the republic. War ended when Madrid fell to Franco Mar. 28, 1939.

Franco was named caudillo, or leader of the nation, Chief of State, Commander in Chief, Prime Minister and head of the Falange party. The Cortes (Parliament) was reestablished July 1942, with elected, appointed and ex-officio members.

Spain was neutral in World War II but its relations with fascist countries and support for repressive measures caused its exclusion from the UN in 1946. It was admitted in 1955.

Dec. 14, 1966, a new constitution, called the "Organic Law," was approved by the people in a plebiscite. The new law implied a liberalization of government policy in the areas of religion, the press, trade unions and other social and political aspects of Spanish life.

In July 1969, Gen. Franco and the Cortes designated Prince Juan Carlos, then 31, as the future King and Chief of State, to assume office in the event of the death or incapacitation of Gen. Franco, who was then 76. Juan Carlos was the son of the pretender to the throne, Don Juan of Bourbon. In 1973, Franco, then 80, named Adm. Luis Carrero Blanco Premier but kept the title of Chief of State.

Education and Religion. Franco reestablished Catholicism as the state religion. The clergy are paid by the state. Primary education is compulsory and free. There are 13 universities. More than two-thirds speak Castilian; Basque is spoken in the N; Galician in the NW, and Catalan in the NE.

Defense. Military forces for 1972-73 totaled 301,000. Under an agreement with the U.S. signed in 1953, renewed in 1963 and 1970, Spain received military aid and the U.S. was granted use of military bases in Spain.

Sri Lanka

CEYLON

Capital: Colombo. Area: 25,332 sq. mi. Population (UN est. 1972): 13,030,000. Monetary unit: Rupee.

Ceylon, an independent nation within the Commonwealth, is an island in the Indian Ocean 20 mi. off the southern tip of India at its closest point. Its greatest length from N to S is 270 mi., and its greatest width, 140 mi. The coastal area of the island is flat, but the central part is mountainous with the highest peak, Pidurutalagala, 8,281 ft. The climate is hot, with high relative humidity. There are many mountain streams, which are navigable only by small river craft. Colombo is served by world airlines.

Resources and Industries. Minerals and metals include graphite, limestone, iron, precious and semi-precious stones, ilmenite, monazite, zircon, quartz. Manufactures include plywood, paper, glassware, ceramics, cement, chemicals, textiles, fertilizers and vegetable oil products.

Principal agricultural products are tea, rubber, coconuts, rice, cacao, cinnamon, citronella, tobacco. Accounting for 90% of exports are tea, rubber and coconuts.

A major source of precious stones, the island produces about 20 varieties including sapphires, star sapphires, rubies, alexandrites, topaz, tourmalines and cat's-eyes. Most are mined at pits in Ratnapura.

History and Government. Ceylon was known to the ancient Romans as Taprobane (copper-colored). It was first settled by colonists from the valley of the Ganges in India who immigrated about 543 B.C. and whose descendants, the Sinhalese, still form most of the population. Descendants of Tamil immigrants from Southern India account for one-fifth of the population. Parts of the maritime areas were occupied in turn by the Portuguese in 1505 and by the Dutch in 1658. The British annexed the island to the presidency of Madras, India, in 1796 and it became a Crown colony in 1802. Universal suffrage was granted in 1931 and a new constitution on the British model in 1946.

Ceylon became an independent member of the Commonwealth in 1948. It is a member of the UN.

Prime Minister W. R. D. Bandaranaike, appointed Apr. 12, 1956, was assassinated Sept. 25, 1959. After two short-lived regimes, new elections were held in which the Freedom party was victorious. Its leader, Mrs. Sirimavo Bandaranaike, widow of the former Prime Minister, was sworn in to the office.

The regime pledged itself to a neutralist policy and nationalized a number of industries. In April, 1962, the government expropriated service and terminal facilities of one British and two U.S. oil companies. In March 1965 elections the conservative, pro-Western United National party won the largest number of seats and its leader, Dudley Senanayake, became Prime Minister.

In Dec. 1965, the new government agreed to pay compensation for the seized oil companies. The U. S. in Feb. 1966, agreed to resume economic aid, which had been cut off when the oil companies were expropriated.

In May 1970 elections, a leftist coalition led by the Freedom party won control of the House of Representatives and Mrs. Bandaranaike became Prime Minister again. In 1971 the nation suffered economic problems and terrorist activities by ultra-leftists. Unemployment and food shortages plagued the nation in 1973.

On May 22, 1972, Ceylon became the Republic of Sri Lanka, a "socialist democracy" with a President, Prime Minister and a unicameral National Assembly.

Education and Religion. All education is free in government schools from kindergarten to university. The majority of the population, Sinhalese, belongs to the Buddhist faith. The Tamils, mostly Hindu, are est. at about 2,000,000. Sinhalese became the official language in 1961; Tamils have agitated for Tamil also to be made an official language.

Defense. Armed forces totaled 12,000 in 1973.

Sudan

Capital: Khartoum. Area: 967,500 sq. mi. Population (UN est. 1972): 16,490,000. Monetary unit: Sudanese pound.

Sudan, a former Anglo-Egyptian condominium in Africa, proclaimed itself a republic Jan. 1, 1956. It is bounded by Egypt, the Red Sea, Ethiopia, Uganda, Kenya, Zaire, the Central African Republic, Chad and Libya. It is about the size of Texas, Alaska and New Mexico combined.

The northern zone consists of the Libyan Desert, on the W, and the mountainous Nubian Desert, extending to the Red Sea on the E, separated by the narrow valley of the Nile; the central zone contains large fertile areas, including the rainlands of Kassala and Tokar, the Gezira Plain and the pastures and gum forests of Kordofan; in the southern equatorial belt the soil is richest and watered by tropical rains.

The White Nile flows N through the center of the country; the Blue Nile, rising in the mountains of Ethiopia, joins the White at Khartoum; the combined river flows N in a huge S curve to enter Egypt north of Wadi Halfa.

Resources and Industries. The Sudan is the world's principal source of gum arabic. Chief grain crop is durra (sorghum), the country's staple food. Cotton is the principal export; American and extra-long staple cottons are grown in the fertile Gezira, between the White and Blue Niles. Other important products are sesame, peanuts, rice, coffee, sugar cane, tobacco, dates, hides, mahogany, chrome. Live camels and sheep are exported to Egypt. There are textile and food processing factories.

History and Government. In the 1820s Egypt took over the Sudan, defeating the last of earlier empires, including the Fung. In the 1880s a revolution was led by Mohammed Ahmed who called himself the Mahdi (leader of the faithful) and his followers, the dervishes. British Gen. Charles Gordon (called Chinese Gordon for his exploits in China), who had earlier put down the slave trade in the Sudan, was sent by Egypt to evacuate its troops; he was besieged and finally slain at Khartoum, 1885.

In 1898 Horatio Kitchener (later titled Lord Kitchener of Khartoum) led an Anglo-Egyptian force which crushed the successors of the Mahdi at Omdurman.

In October, 1951, the Egyptian Parliament abrogated its 1899 and 1936 treaties with Great Britain, and amended the constitution, Oct. 16, to provide for a separate Sudanese constitution.

Sudan voted for complete independence effective Jan. 1, 1956. A five-member Supreme Commission (Council of State) and a Cabinet were sworn in.

A parliamentary government was set up but in 1958 Gen. Ibrahim Abboud took power; he resigned under pressure in 1964; a Constituent Assembly was elected in 1965 which approved a coalition government.

In May 1969, in a second military coup, a Revolutionary Council took power but a civilian Premier and Cabinet were appointed and the new government announced it would create a socialist state. It also announced plans to negotiate an end to guerrilla warfare which had beset the southern third of the nation for years. The northern 5 provinces are predominantly Arab-Moslem and have been dominant in the central government. The 3 southern provinces, in which there was a strong separatist movement, are Negro and predominantly pagan, with small Christian and Moslem minorities. A peace agreement, giving the South regional autonomy, was reached in 1972.

The government nationalized a number of businesses in May 1970. An attempted Communist coup in July 1971 failed but led to strained relations with the USSR. Diplomatic relations with the U.S., broken by Sudan during the 1967 Arab-Israeli war, were restored in 1972. On Mar. 2, 1973, the U.S. Ambassador and charge d'affaires and a Belgian diplomat were slain in Khartoum by Black September Palestinian terrorists.

Sudan is a member of the UN and Arab League.

Education and Religion. Sudanese inhabitants are Arabs, Negroes and Nubians of mixed Arab and Negro blood; the Arabs and Nubians are Mohammedans. Higher education is available at Khartoum Univ. (formerly Gordon College). Arabic is the national language.

Swaziland

Capital: Mbabane. Area: 6,704 sq. mi. Population (UN est. 1972): 430,000. Monetary unit: Rand.

The Kingdom of Swaziland is in SE Africa, almost completely surrounded by the Republic of South Africa except for part of the E border which adjoins Mozambique (Portuguese East Africa). The Swazis came under British protection in 1903.

The example of neighboring former British territories Bechuanaland and Basutoland, which became the independent nations of Botswana and Lesotho in 1966, encouraged the drive for Swazi independence; Swaziland was economically the most healthy of the 3. On Apr. 25, 1967, it achieved full internal self-government under a constitution and on Sept. 6, 1968, it became completely independent and a member of the Commonwealth.

The constitution provided for a partly elected, partly appointed Assembly and Senate, and a Prime Minister; the former Paramount Chief, Sobhuza II, became King Sobhuza, a constitutional head of state. The Royal house of Swaziland traces back 400 years, and remains one of Africa's last ruling dynasties. In April 1973 the King repealed the Constitution and assumed full powers.

Polygamy has been the common marital status. Women have the right to vote.

About 97% of the residents are Swazi, a Bantu group. South African whites constitute a small minority. English is the official language but Swazi is spoken by the vast majority.

The country is rich in mineral resources, including one of the world's largest asbestos mines, the Havelock Mine, and iron ore resources estimated at some 47,000,000 tons. In addition, there are gold, tin, coal, mica and other minerals.

In recent years Swaziland developed a multi-million-dollar timber and pulp industry, a railway link out of the landlocked country to ports in Mozambique, hydro-electric power and tarred roads. The major export items are asbestos, iron ore, beef, citrus fruits and sugar. The land is fertile and has abundant water, producing such other crops as corn, cotton, rice, pineapples and cattle.

About 8,000 Swazis hold jobs in South Africa and the currency is the South African rand.

Sweden
KONUNGARIKET SVERIGE

Capital: Stockholm. Area: 173,655 sq. mi. Population (Govt. est. 1973): 8,143,000. Monetary unit: Krona.

Sweden occupies the eastern and largest part of the Scandinavian peninsula in NW Europe. Its greatest N-S length is 977 mi.; greatest width 311 mi. The country is larger than Calif. but smaller than Texas. Sweden is separated from Norway on the W by the Kjolen Mtns., and from Finland on the E by the Baltic Sea except in the N where the 2 meet along the Tornea River.

Stockholm and Goteborg are the largest ports.

Resources and Industries. Although the topography is mountainous, Sweden contains much productive land, well watered, on which the Swedes have attained high efficiency in agriculture. Of Sweden's total land area, 9% is cultivated, 2.5% pasture, and 50% forests. About one-

third is unreclaimable. Chief agricultural products are milk, cheese, butter, beef, pork, wheat, rye, potatoes, sugar beets and vegetable oils.

Many industries flourish in Sweden, whose main natural resources are forests, iron ore and water power. Coal and oil have to be imported; oil constitutes 10% of all imports. Industry employs 37% of the work-population, agriculture 7%. Swedish steel is of especial value for tool making. Other metals produced are; lead, copper, zinc, gold and silver. In 1971, 66 billion kwh. were produced; the Stornorrforsen hydroelectric plant on the Ume River is the largest in Western Europe.

Although over 95% of the economy is in private hands, the government holds a large interest in water power production and the railroads are operated by a public agency.

Consumer cooperatives are in extensive operation, with 1,600,000 members served by about 2,650 stores. Cooperatives also are important in agriculture and housing.

Shipping is privately operated. The merchant marine totaled approx. 5,400,000 gross tons in 1972. The shipbuilding industry is 2d to Japan's. In 1971 49 ships were launched totaling 3,800,000 deadweight tons.

Sweden is one of the leading exporters of iron ore and cellulose. About one-fourth of the exports come from pulp, lumber, paper and other forestry products. Other important products are steel, automobiles, ships, airplanes, ball bearings, textiles, electrical goods, petrochemicals.

Foreign trade in thousands of U. S. dollars:

	Imports	Exports
1971	$7,080,000	$7,465,000
1972	$8,062,000	$8,749,000

History and Government. Sweden is a parliamentary democracy with a King as head of state and a prime minister as political chief executive. The Riksdag (Parliament) has, since 1970, a single chamber with 350 members elected for 3 years. All over 20 are entitled to vote.

The first peaceful consolidation of Sweden with other Scandinavian countries was the union of Kalmar, 1397. Sweden revolted 1434-1523.

King Gustaf VI Adolf died at the age of 90, Sept. 15, 1973, after a 23-year reign and was succeeded by his grandson, Carl XVI Gustaf, 27. Under a law proposed earlier but still awaiting final Parliamentary approval, the King's already minor role in government would be further curtailed to purely ceremonial functions as of Jan. 1, 1975.

In Parliamentary elections, Sept. 16, 1973, the Social Democrats, in power 41 years, and a non-Socialist coalition each won 175 of the 350 seats.

About 20% of the national income is redistributed through the social welfare system which includes compulsory health insurance. Unemployment during 1972 was about 2.7%.

The government has been critical of U.S. policy in Southeast Asia. About 450 U.S. deserters and draft resisters were given residency in Sweden. After the U.S.-Vietnam cease-fire, Sweden said no more would be admitted.

Sweden is a member of the Nordic Council, UN, EFTA, and GATT. In 1972 Sweden signed a trade agreement with the EEC for gradual elimination of tariffs on industrial goods.

Education and Religion. The population is homogeneous, being of the Scandinavian branch of the Germanic family, except for foreign workers. Approx. 95% of the people are Lutheran, which is the state religion. Education is compulsory and illiteracy is non-existent. There are state universities at Uppsala (founded 1477), Lund, Stockholm, Goteborg and Umea.

Defense. Military strength, if mobilized, was about 750,000 for 1972-73.

Switzerland
SCHWEIZ—SUISSE—SVIZZERA

Capital: Bern. Area: 151,941 sq. mi. Population (UN est. 1972): 6,420,000. Monetary unit: Franc.

Switzerland, a federal republic in Central Europe, is bounded by France, Germany, Austria, Liechtenstein and Italy. It is twice the size of New Jersey.

Switzerland is the most mountainous of all European countries. The Alps cover 61% of land area, the Jura 12%; running between them, NE to SW, are the midlands, about 27%. Highest peaks are Monte Rosa and Dufour, both 15,203 ft.; more than 70 are over 10,000 ft. Lakes famous for their beauty include Maggiore, Lucerne, Geneva, Neuchatel, Constance, Thun, Brienz. The Rhine, Rhone and feeders of the Danube and Po originate in Switzerland.

Resources and Industries. Switzerland's abundant water power is exploited by 431 major hydroelectric plants. Salt is the principal mineral. Watches (50% of the world's watch trade), machinery, and precision instruments are important manufactures; also textiles, iron, steel and electrical products; industrial chemicals, clothing, perfumes, and pharmaceuticals. Dairy products, especially cheese, lead agriculture, followed by cattle, pigs, fruit, poultry, tobacco, wheat, rye, oats, potatoes and wine. Machine making employs 26% of all factory workers and accounts for 34% of exports. Included are textile machinery, machine tools, dynamo-electric plants, transformers and diesels.

Switzerland is one of the world's greatest banking centers. Stability of its currency brings funds there from many quarters. Tourism is a vital part of the economy. Nearly 7,000,000 foreign tourists visit annually.

History and Government. Switzerland, the Helvetia of ancient times, is a federation of 22 cantons (19 full cantons and 6 half cantons), 3 of which once (1291) were members of a defensive league and later were joined by other districts. In 1648 the Swiss Confederation obtained its independence from the Holy Roman Empire. The cantons were joined under a Federal Constitution in 1848, with large powers of local control retained by each canton. Legislative authority vests in a parliament of 2 chambers, a Standerat or State Council to which each canton sends 2 members; and a lower house, Nationalrat or National Council, with 200 members.

Executive power is vested in the Bundesrat (Federal Council) of 7 members.

The President is selected from membership of the Federal Council, serves for one year and customarily is succeeded by the Vice President. Women won the right to vote in federal elections in 1971 and some were elected to parliament. —

Switzerland enters into no military alliance and is not a member of UN or NATO. It is however a member of various international agencies of the UN, such as the International Labor Org., World Health Org., UNESCO, FAO and others. In 1972 it signed an agreement with the EEC for gradual abolition of tariffs on industrial goods.

Geneva is the seat of a number of UN organizations, International Committee of the Red Cross, League of Red Cross Societies and Int'l Union for Telecommunications. The Universal Postal Union is in Bern.

Education and Religion. Primary education has been free and compulsory since 1874. There are 9 universities; the oldest is Basel, founded in 1460. Swiss German dialects are spoken by a majority of the people in 16 of the cantons; other languages are French, Italian, and Romansch.

There is complete freedom of worship. Of the population 52.7% are Reformed Protestants, 45.4% Roman Catholics.

Defense. Service in the national militia is compulsory. Its easily mobilized divisions comprise more than 600,000 men. The Air Force has about 300 combat craft.

Syria

SOURIYA

Capital: Damascus. Area: 72,234 sq. mi. Population (UN est. 1972): 6,680,000. Monetary unit: Syrian pound.

A land of Middle East contrasts, the Syrian Arab Republic has a short coastline on the Mediterranean, then stretches east and south with fertile valleys and plains alternating with mountainous and desert areas. The main rivers are the Euphrates and Orontes. Chief seaport is Latakia. The nation is about the size of South Dakota.

Resources and Industries. Syria is primarily an agricultural and stock-raising nation. Cotton, barley, wheat, fruits, vegetables, meat, textiles and wool are the main exports. Growing industries include flour milling, oil refining, textiles, cement, tobacco, glassware, sugar and brassware. In 1965 the Socialist regime nationalized most industries. Oil production, though small, has grown. Royalties are collected from Iraqi and Saudi Arabian pipelines crossing the nation to Mediterranean ports. In 1973 a $300,000,000 power and irrigation dam was completed on the upper Euphrates.

History and Government. One of the world's ancient inhabited lands, the state (later republic) of Syria was formed from former Turkish Empire Sanjaks (districts). Syria was made a separate entity by the Treaty of Sevres, Aug. 10, 1920, and divided into the states of Syria and Greater Lebanon Sept. 1, 1920. Both were administered under a French mandate 1920-1941.

Syria was proclaimed a republic by the occupying French authorities Sept. 16, 1941, and exercised full power effective Jan. 1, 1944. French troops left in 1946.

Syria joined with Egypt in Feb. 1958 in the United Arab Republic but seceded Sept. 30, 1961. The Socialist Baath party and military leaders seized power in March 1963. The Baath, an international Arab organization, became the only legal party. In Mar. 1973 voters approved, by 97%, a new constitution providing for a 186-member People's Council but giving most powers to the President.

In the Israeli-Arab war of June 1967, Israel seized and occupied the Golan Heights area inside Syria, from which Israeli settlements had for years been shelled by Syria.

Syria aided Palestinian guerrillas fighting Jordanian forces in Sept. 1970, and, after a renewal of that fighting in July 1971, broke off relations with Jordan.

Syria joined Egypt and Libya, Sept. 1, 1971, in a new Federation of Arab Republics.

There were continued border skirmishes with Israel in 1972-73 and Syria received large shipments of arms from the USSR.

Syria severed diplomatic relations with the U. S. after the 1967 war. It is a member of the UN. Military forces for 1971-72 were about 111,000.

Education and Religion. The population is composed mainly of Sunni Moslems but there are many Christians. Arabic is the official language. Syria has universities in Damascus and Aleppo.

Tanzania

(Formerly Tanganyika and Zanzibar)

Capital: Dar es Salaam. Area 363,708 sq. mi. Population (est. 1972): 14,000,000. Monetary unit: Tanzanian shilling.

The republic of Tanganyika in E. Africa and the republic of Zanzibar, a large island in the Indian Ocean off the coast of Tanganyika, joined in a single republic, Tanzania, Apr. 26, 1964. The new central government at Dar es Salaam (Haven of Peace), an important port and capital of Tanganyika, was given jurisdiction over defense, foreign affairs and public services.

Julius K. Nyerere, Tanganyika's President, became President of the new nation; Zanzibar's President became 1st Vice President.

In 1967 the government nationalized all banks, including some in which U. S. banks held a part interest, and many industries; some of the latter were taken over completely, in others the government took a part interest. The government also ordered that Swahili, not English, be used in all official business.

Tanzania is a member of the UN and Commonwealth. In 1972, a road to Zambia was being reconstructed with U.S. aid and a railroad to Zambia was being built with aid from the People's Republic of China.

In. Sept. 1972 Uganda accused Tanzania of aiding Ugandan rebels in an abortive invasion. Tanzania denied the charge. Burundi and Tanzania traded incursion charges in 1973.

TANGANYIKA

Tanganyika stretches from the Indian Ocean on the E to 3 of Africa's Great Lakes; Victoria, Tanganyika and Nyasa (now also called Malawi). Its area is 362,688 sq. mi., larger than Texas and Oklahoma combined; pop. (Govt. est. 1967): 13,000,000. Most of the people are Bantus and speak Swahili.

Snow-capped Mt. Kilimanjaro, tallest in Africa, rises 19,340 ft. in the N. Nearby are the famed Serengeti Plains, teeming with vast herds of wild animals, protected in one of Tanzania's several large national park game preserves. Safaris, sport fishing and mountain climbing are among attractions.

Principal products are sisal, cotton, coffee, tea, tobacco and hides. Both gem and industrial diamonds are mined as are gold, salt, tin and mica. Diamonds account for 77% of the mineral income, gold for 12%. Factories include food processing, clothing.

Arab colonization began in the 8th Century A.D.; Portuguese sailors explored the coast by about 1500. Other Europeans followed and it was under a mango tree at Ujiji on Lake Tanganyika that Henry M. Stanley found David Livingstone Nov. 10, 1871.

In 1885 Germany established German East Africa of ▓▓▓▓▓ Tanganyika Was formed also Dutta ▓▓▓▓ World War I it was taken and administered by Britain as a League of Nations mandate and after 1946 as a UN trust territory.

Constitutional changes gave it internal autonomy in Sept. 1960. It became fully independent Dec. 9, 1961, and was proclaimed a republic within the Commonwealth a year later.

ZANZIBAR

Zanzibar, the Isle of Cloves, lies 23 mi. off the coast of Tanganyika; its area is 640 sq. mi. The island of Pemba, 25 mi. to the NE, area 380 sq. mi., is included in the administration. The population is mainly Africans and Arabs. The total area of the two islands is about the size of Rhode Island; population (Govt. est. 1967): 354,360.

Attractions include public gardens and ancient palaces.

Chief industry is the production of cloves and clove oil of which Zanzibar and Pemba produce the bulk of the world's supply. Coconuts and copra also are exported. Pottery, coir fiber, rope, soap, oil, jewelry and mats are manufactured.

Portugal ruled Zanzibar for two centuries until ousted by Arabs around 1700. Zanzibar became an independent Sultanate in 1856 and a British Protectorate in 1890 by agreement with Germany and France.

Independence within the Commonwealth was attained Dec. 10, 1963. Rebel forces overthrew Sultan Seyyid Jamshid bin Abdullah bin Khalifa Jan. 12, 1964. The revolutionary government ousted American and British diplomats and newsmen and nationalized farms. Union with Tanganyika followed, 1964.

Thailand (Siam)

Capital: Bangkok. Area: 200,148 sq. mi. Population (UN est. 1972): 36,290,000. Monetary unit: Baht.

Thailand is a constitutional monarchy in SE Asia bordered by Burma, Laos, Cambodia, the Gulf of Thailand (or Siam) and Malaysia. It is about twice the size of Colorado with large areas under irrigation.

Bangkok, the capital, is a modern city. Its Don Muang airfield is one of the largest and most modern in Southeast Asia, served by 24 international airlines. It is also an important port. There is an extensive inland waterway system and network of roads.

Resources and Industries. There are many large forests, teakwood being an important article of export. Agriculture occupies 80% of the population.

Thailand is the world's 4th largest producer of tin ore; other minerals are iron, manganese, tungsten, antimony.

The chief crop is rice, the staple food of the people and heavily exported, accounting for about 17% of foreign exchange earnings. Other important exports are tin, rubber, corn, teak and tungsten. Coconuts, tobacco, pepper, tapioca flour, peanuts, beans and cotton are produced.

Foreign investment in industry is encouraged—auto assembly plants, pharmaceuticals, textiles, electrical goods. Tourism is important.

History and Government. Thailand, an ancient monarchy, noted for picturesque architecture and pageantry, is the only country in SE Asia never taken over by a colonial power, thanks to King Mongkut and his son King Chulalongkorn who ruled from 1851 to 1910, modernized the country and signed trade treaties with both Britain and France.

Thailand underwent a bloodless revolution in 1932. King Prajadhipok, a liberal, signed a new constitution, establishing a limited monarchy, but he refused to sign a measure abdicating the royal power of life and death and resigned. He was succeeded by his nephew, Prince Ananda, who was found dead of a bullet wound, June 9, 1946, and the legislature named his brother, Prince Phumiphol Aduldet (Bhumibol Adulyadej) (born 1927), to succeed him. The new King formally took the throne May 5, 1950, as Rama IX.

Since World War II there have been several military coups and changes in government. On June 21, 1968, a new constitution was promulgated, providing for an appointed Senate, and an elected House, with limited powers and a Premier.

In Nov. 1971 a military-civilian junta, headed by Premier Thanom Kittikachorn, took control of the government. In Dec. 1972 the King appointed a 299-member National Assembly and again named Thanom Premier.

There was sporadic Communist terrorism in the NE and far S. in 1965-73.

Education and Religion. Education is compulsory between 7 and 14. There are 9 universities, 31 training colleges and many vocational schools. The language is Thai, derived from Pali and Sanskrit. English is widely used. About 94% of the people are Buddhists; others are Moslems, Christians, etc.

Defense. Military strength for 1972-73 was 160,000. Thailand is a member of the UN and SEATO.

U.S. forces in Thailand, mostly airmen, totaled 45,000 in 1973; during the year, U.S. Southeast Asia military hq. was moved from Saigon to Nakhon Phanom in Thailand. The U.S. began withdrawing some forces from Thailand in Aug. About 15,000 Thai "irregular" forces, financed by the U.S., were still in Laos in 1973. The last of 11,000 Thai troops were withdrawn from South Vietnam in 1972.

Togo

Capital: Lomé. Area, 21,850 sq. mi. Population (UN est. 1972): 2,090,000. Monetary unit: CFA franc.

The republic of Togo, which became independent April 27, 1960, is comprised of part of the one-time German colony of Togoland, surrendered in 1914, and administered by France as a UN trusteeship, 1946-1960.

Togo is a thin sliver of land, about twice the size of Vermont, facing the Atlantic on the southern edge of the West African bulge. It is bounded by Upper Volta, Dahomey, the Atlantic and Ghana.

In 1958 France received UN approval to end its trusteeship and the republic was proclaimed Apr. 27, 1960. Official language is French. It is a member of the UN.

A draft constitution on the U. S. model was published Mar. 20, 1961. It provided for a President and a 46-member unicameral Parliament. First President, Sylvanus Olympio, elected Apr. 9, 1961, was assassinated by a military junta, Jan. 13, 1963. His successor was Nicolas Grunitzky, elected May 5, 1963. Grunitzky resigned Jan. 13, 1967, and was replaced by Etienne Eyadema, head of the armed forces.

Togo has received aid from France, the U.S. and West Germany. Tourism is a growing industry.

Principal products: phosphates, coffee, cocoa, palm kernels, copra, cotton, kapok and peanuts. There are textile and shoe factories.

Tonga

Capital: Nukualofa. Area: 269 sq. mi. Population (UN est. 1972): 90,000. Monetary unit: Pa'anga.

The Kingdom of Tonga, a constitutional monarchy, comprises 150 volcanic and coral islands (45 inhabited) in the South Pacific, NE of New Zealand and S of Samoa. The capital, Nukualofa, is on the main island, Tongatapu.

The islands were first visited by the Dutch in the early 17th Century. A series of civil wars ended in 1845 with establishment of the Tupou dynasty. In 1900 Tonga became a British protectorate. On June 4, 1970, Tonga became completely independent and a member of the Commonwealth.

Government consists of a King (Taufaahau Tupou IV at the time of independence), a Prime Minister and a partly elected Legislative Assembly.

Agriculture and fishing are the mainstays of the economy. Chief exports are coconut products and bananas. Tourism is being encouraged.

The Tongans are Polynesians; languages are Tongan and English. Education is free and compulsory, ages 6-14; medical care is free.

Trinidad and Tobago

Capital: Port of Spain. Area: 1,979 sq. mi. Population (UN est. 1972): 1,040,000. Monetary unit: Trinidad and Tobago Dollar.

Trinidad, area 1,864 sq. mi., is the most southerly of the West Indies, lying off the NE coast of South America approx. 7 mi. from Venezuela. It was discovered by Columbus in 1498. Tobago, 116 sq. mi. lies 20 mi. to the NE of Trinidad.

Second largest of the old British West Indies and a British possession since 1802, Trinidad and Tobago won independence Aug. 31, 1962. A Governor General represents the British crown. A Prime Minister is the actual executive. Parliament consists of a 24-member Senate appointed by the Gov. Gen. and a 36-member House of Representatives elected by universal suffrage. The country is a member of the UN, Commonwealth and OAS.

Import trade is heaviest with England, export trade with the U. S. Exports are mostly petroleum, sugar, asphalt, rum, cocoa, coffee, citrus, bananas, cement, bitters. In 1973 the country helped create a new Caribbean Common Market.

The nation is one of the most prosperous in the West Indies, but unemployment has been high, averaging 13%. In March-April 1970 there were riots in Port of Spain demanding Government action to solve economic problems, plus a brief mutiny by a group of soldiers.

Trinidad claims to have originated the steel band, calypso songs and the limbo dance. Tourism is an important source of revenue.

The population is mixed: Black 43%, East Indian (descended from immigrants from India) 36%; Lebanese, Syrians, Europeans and Chinese comprise the rest. Religions include Roman Catholic 36%, Protestant 34%, Hindu 23%, Moslem 6%.

Public primary and secondary education is free to age 18. Some units of the Univ. of West Indies are in Trinidad, some in Jamaica. There are two technical institutes.

Tunisia

AL-JOUMHOURIA ATTUNUSIA

Capital: Tunis. Area: 63,378 sq. mi. Population (UN est. 1972): 5,380,000. Monetary unit: Dinar.

Tunisia is a former French protectorate which became independent Mar. 20, 1956. It is on the Mediterranean coast of Africa wedged between Algeria and Libya. It is about the size of Florida. The people are mostly Arabs and Berbers.

Resources and Industries. The chief industry is agriculture and the fertile soil produces an abundance of grains, dates, olives, citrus fruits, almonds, figs, vegetables, alfa grass. Livestock is extensively raised. Phosphates, iron, oil, lead and zinc are leading minerals.

Industries include food processing, textiles, clothing, leather, oil refining, construction materials. Principal exports are olive oil, wine, iron ore, lead, phosphates, fruits, oil and grains. A 10-year economic development program was begun in 1962. A farm collectivization program was dropped in 1970.

Tourism is growing and attractions include numerous well-preserved Roman ruins, excellent beaches, and resorts on Djerba Is., reputed home of the Lotus Eaters of the Odyssey.

The tourist industry earns over $100,000,000 a year. Irrigation has aided agriculture. New industries include steel and auto-assembly plants, a paper mill and sugar refinery.

History and Government. A former Barbary state under the suzerainty of Turkey, Tunisia became a protectorate of France under a treaty signed May 12, 1881, after France sent a military force to combat the raiding Khroumer tribes. After receiving increasing measures of self-government since 1947, a constituent assembly, elected Mar. 25, 1956, chose a government headed by Habib Bourguiba of the dominant Neo-Destour party, named Premier Apr. 10. The basic law, adopted by the assembly, Apr. 13, vested sovereignty in the people, ignoring the titular ruler, Mohammed el Amim, Bey of Tunis. The assembly unanimously voted, July 25, 1957, to end the monarchy. It deposed the Bey and proclaimed a republic; Premier Bourguiba became President.

Under a U. S.-style constitution adopted June 1, 1959, the President is elected for 5 years, limited to 3 consecutive terms. The National Assembly also is elected for 5-year terms. A Prime Minister was added in 1969.

Although Tunisia is a member of the Arab League, Pres. Bourguiba in the 1960s urged negotiations to end Arab-Israeli disputes and was denounced by other members. In 1966 he broke relations with Egypt but resumed them after the 1967 Israeli-Arab war. He again urged negotiations with Israel in June 1973.

Education and Religion. The majority of the population is Moslem. Europeans number fewer than 100,000. Arabic is the national and official language. From 1956-1968 Tunisia raised the number of primary school students from 200,000 to 826,069, secondary from 15,500 to 124,607 and higher education from 1,350 to 11,224. The former Moslem University of Zitouna and the Institute of Advanced Studies are incorporated in the new University of Tunis.

Defense. The armed forces total over 24,000.

Turkey

TURKIYE CUMHURIYETI

Capital: Ankara. Area: 301,302 sq. mi. Population (Govt. est. 1973): 37,500,000. Monetary unit: Lira.

About 90% of Turkey's population lives in the Asian portion of the country on the Anatolian Peninsula—an area of 292,184 sq. mi. The remainder live in the European part which is bordered by Bulgaria and Greece. A republic since 1923, Turkey is a little larger than Texas and has extensive coastlines on the Black Sea, the Mediterranean and the Aegean. Its Asian neighbors are the USSR, Syria, Iraq and Iran.

Central Turkey has wide plateaus, with hot dry summers and cold winters with snow remaining until May. High mountains ring the interior on all but the W side. More than 20 peaks top 10,000 ft.

The world's 4th longest suspension bridge, linking Europe and Asia across the Bosporus, was to open in late 1973.

Resources and Industries. Approx. 67% of the labor force is engaged in agriculture, the products including tobacco (more than 350,000,000 lbs. annually), cereal, cotton, olive oil, wool, silk, figs, nuts, fruits, sugar, opium for medicinal purposes, and gums. About 45,000,000 acres are in forests.

In June 1971 Turkey agreed to stop all opium poppy production within a year to end smuggling.

There are large deposits of antimony, borate, copper and chrome (of which Turkey is one of the world's largest producers). Other minerals include manganese, lead, zinc, coal, iron, oil, silver, mercury, sulphur, molybdenum, magnesite and asbestos.

Turkey manufactures silk, cotton and woolen yarn and cloth, steel, foundry products, sugar, footwear, office furniture, cement, paper, glassware and appliances. About 18% of trade is with the U.S.

Foreign trade, in thousands of U.S. dollars:

	Imports	Exports
1971	$1,088,000	$677,000
1972	$1,508,000	$885,000

History and Government. Up to World War I, Turkey, or the Ottoman Empire, included European Turkey, Anatolia, Syria, Lebanon, Iraq, Jordan, Palestine, Arabia, Yemen and islands in the Aegean Sea.

Turkey joined Germany and Austria in World War I and its defeat resulted in loss of much territory and fall of the sultanate. A republic was declared Oct. 29, 1923, with Mustafa Kemal Ataturk first President. The Caliphate (spiritual leadership of Islam) was renounced 1924. Turkey was permitted (1936) to refortify the Dardanelles and Bosporus, to close them if threatened, but to permit free passage of merchant vessels in peace or war. The USSR has proposed joint control of the straits but Turkey has refused.

But in 1968 Turkey and the USSR agreed on a $200,000,000 loan from the Soviet to build factories in Turkey which would be paid for in Turkish products.

The present constitution, adopted July 9, 1961, provides for a bicameral legislature composed of a Senate of 150 and a National Assembly of 450 deputies. The President is elected by Parliament to a 7-year term and is ineligible for reelection. A Premier is chosen from the leading party.

Turkey is a member of the UN, CENTO, NATO, Council of Europe and an associate in EEC. Communism is outlawed, and many leftist terrorists have been jailed.

For years Turkey and Greece have been involved in a controversy over Cyprus (see Cyprus).

Education and Religion. About 98% of the population is Moslem. Public elementary education is free and compulsory; higher public education, through the university level, is free but optional. There are 9 universities in Istanbul, Ankara, Trabzon, Izmir and Erzurum.

Defense. Armed forces for 1972-73 totaled 449,000. Most of the forces were assigned to NATO.

Uganda

Capital: Kampala. Area: 91,134 sq. mi. Population (UN est. 1972): 10,460,000. Monetary unit: Uganda shilling.

Uganda, a former British protectorate, is in central Africa with Kenya to the E, Lake Victoria and Tanzania to the S, Lakes Albert and Edward (also called Lakes Sese Seko and Idi Amin) and Zaire to the W, Sudan to the N. It is about the size of Oregon. On the border with Zaire, the Ruwenzori Range, identified with the legendary "Mountains of the Moon," rises over 16,000 ft. In the SW there are several volcanoes over 11,000 ft. high; on their slopes is a gorilla sanctuary.

Uganda is the largest coffee producer in the Commonwealth. Cotton, tea, maize, peanuts, sisal, oil seeds, tobacco, sugar, are also produced. Copper and tin are important mineral exports. Textile, steel and chemical plants have been built.

Uganda became independent Oct. 9, 1962, a republic Oct. 9, 1963. Uganda is a member of the UN, OAU and the Commonwealth.

A long-standing political feud erupted Feb. 22, 1966, when Milton Obote, then Prime Minister, seized full power and on Mar. 2 ousted President Edward Mutesa (who earlier had been King).

A 1967 constitution provided for a President and National Assembly, both popularly elected.

Gen. Idi Amin seized government control Jan. 25, 1971, and was named President. In Sept. 1972 Uganda accused Tanzania of aiding Ugandan dissidents in an abortive invasion.

In 1972 Pres. Amin expelled all Asians holding British passports (Indians and Pakistanis). There were reportedly over 25,000, many of them business and professional men. Britain, the U.S. and some other nations accepted the deportees. In 1973 the U.S., Canada and Norway ended economic aid programs; Amin seized all British firms.

Nearly half the population is Christian (mostly Roman Catholics). English, Luganda, and Luo are the main languages.

Lake Victoria, 26,828 sq. mi., is Africa's largest lake. It is 3,720 ft. above sea level and over 200 mi. long. At Owen Falls on the Victoria Nile, outlet of Lake Victoria, a major dam and hydroelectric project has been constructed.

Union of
Soviet Socialist Republics

SOYUZ SOVYETSKIKH
SOTSIALISTICHESKIKH RESPUBLIK

Capital: Moscow. Area: 8,647,172 sq. mi. Population (Govt. est. 1973): 250,000,000. Monetary unit: Ruble.

The Union of Soviet Socialist Republics—in area the largest country in the world—stretches across two continents from the North Pacific to the Baltic Sea. It occupies the northern part of Asia and the eastern half of Europe. Its western borders brush against Norway, Finland, the Baltic, Poland, Czechoslovakia, Hungary and Romania. On the S it is bounded by Romania, the Black Sea, Turkey, Iran, Afghanistan, China, Mongolian Peoples Republic and North Korea. In the far NE, Bering Strait separates it from Alaska.

The vast territory of the USSR, one-sixth of the earth's land surface, contains every phase of climate, except the distinctly tropical, and a varied topography. The European portion is a vast low plain with the Ural Mtns. on its eastern edge, the Caucasus Mtns. and others on the S. The Urals, separating the European from the Asiatic portions of the country, stretch N and S for 2,500 mi. The Asiatic portion also consists largely of an immense plain, with mountain ranges on its E and S.

There are some 150,000 rivers and 250,000 lakes. The larger European rivers include the Dnieper, flowing into the Black Sea, the Volga and the Ural into the Caspian Sea, the Don into the Sea of Azov, the Western Dvina into the Baltic and the Northern Dvina into the White Sea. The Asiatic section is drained by the Ob, the Yenisei and the Lena, each over 2,000 mi. long, which flow into the Arctic Ocean, and the Amur, which flows into the Pacific.

The Caspian Sea, of which only the S end is in Iran, is the world's largest lake in surface area (143,550 sq. mi.). Other lakes are the Aral Sea (25,300 sq. mi.), Lake Baykal (11,780 sq. mi.), Lake Balkhash (6,720 sq. mi.), Lake Ladoga (6,835 sq. mi.).

In Moscow, the Kremlin, ancient citadel of the Czars, forms the nerve center of the federated republics. Leningrad (formerly St. Petersburg and Petrograd), in the delta of the Neva River, is the 2nd largest city. Kiev, the 1,000-year-old capital of the Ukrainian SSR, is the industrial center of the south. The Crimea and the eastern shore of the Black Sea, beneath the towering Caucasus Mtns., are a modern vacationland.

Beginning in 1939 the USSR by means of military action and negotiation overran contiguous territory and independent republics. Transfer of part of East Germany was approved at the Potsdam Conference. The Yalta Agreement conceded Soviet claims to Japanese territory in the Kurile islands and southern half of Sakhalin.

POLITICAL ORGANIZATION

The USSR is a federation consisting of 15 Union Republics, within certain of which are further subdivisions, such as Autonomous Soviet Socialist Republics, Autonomous Regions and National Districts. Four of the Union Republics contain 20 Autonomous Soviet Socialist Republics and 8 Autonomous Regions; the largest Union Republic, the Russian Soviet Federal Socialist Republic, has also 10 National Districts. The Union Republics are:

Republic	Area sq. miles	Pop. (Census prelim. 1970)
Russian SFSR	6,593,391	130,090,000
Ukrainian SSR	232,046	47,136,000
Kazakh SSR	1,064,092	12,850,000
Uzbek SSR	158,069	11,963,000
Byelorussian SSR	80,154	9,003,000
Azerbaijan SSR	33,436	5,111,000
Georgian SSR........	26,911	4,688,000
Moldavian SSR.......	13,012	3,572,000
Lithuanian SSR	26,173	3,129,000
Kirghiz SSR	76,642	2,933,000
Tadzhik SSR.........	54,019	2,900,000
Armenian SSR	11,306	2,493,000
Latvian SSR	24,695	2,365,000
Turkmen SSR........	188,417	2,158,000
Estonian SSR	17,413	1,357,000

The **Russian Soviet Federal Socialist Republic**, contains over 50% of the population of the Soviet Union and includes 76% of its territory. Its territories stretch from the Estonian, Latvian and Finnish borders and the Byelorussian and Ukrainian lines on the W, to the shores of the Pacific, and from the Arctic on the N to the Black and Caspian Seas and the borders of Kazakh SSR, Mongolia and Manchuria on the S. Siberia (Sibir), divided into a number of administrative units, encompasses a large part of the RSFSR area. Capital: Moscow.

In 1956 the USSR incorporated the **Karelo-Finnish Republic** as an autonomous republic within the RSFSR, reducing the federation by one to 15. It comprises territory ceded by Finland after World War II. The capital, Petrozavodsk, was founded in the 18th century by Peter the Great. Forests cover two-thirds of the area and the underground wealth includes non-ferrous metal and mineral deposits.

Eastern and Western Siberia of the RSFSR have been transformed by steel mills, huge dams, oil and gas industries, electric railroads and new highways.

Ukrainian SSR is the most densely populated of the constituent republics. It borders on the Black Sea, with Poland, Czechoslovakia, Hungary and Romania on the W and SW. The population is 80% Ukrainian. Capital: Kiev. Northern Bukovina was added to the Ukrainian SSR from Romania in 1940. The Crimea was transferred to the Ukraine, 1954.

The Ukraine contains the arable black soil belt, the chief wheat-producing section of the Soviet Union. Sugar beets and potatoes are important crops and livestock numbers are large.

The Donets Basin has a huge storage of coal, iron and other metals. Here are produced 34% of the coal mined in the country, 50% of the pig iron, 40% of the steel and 35% of the manganese. There are chemical and dye industries and salt mines.

Byelorussian SSR (White Russia), bordering on Poland, suffered greatly under the Czars from periodical pogroms and from inter-racial struggles. In the two World Wars it was a field for military operations. Minsk is the capital.

Chief industries include machinery, tools, appliances, tractors, clocks, cameras, steel, cement, textiles, paper, leather, glass. Main crops are grain, flax, potatoes.

Azerbaijan SSR boasts near Baku, the capital, important oil fields. Its natural wealth includes deposits of iron ore, cobalt, etc. Irrigation has boosted cotton production. A high-yield winter wheat also is grown. It produces iron, steel, cement, fertilizers, synthetic rubber, electrical and chemical equipment. It borders on Iran and Turkey.

Georgian SSR, which lies in the western part of Transcaucasia, contains the largest manganese mines in the world. There are rich timber resources and coal mines. Basic industries are food, textiles, iron, steel. Grain, tea, tobacco, fruits, grapes are grown. The capital is Tbilisi (Tiflis).

Armenian SSR is mountainous, sub-tropical, extensively irrigated with a wide range of crops. Copper, iron, marble are mined. Instrument making is important. Capital is Erevan.

Uzbek SSR, most important economically of the Central Asia republics, produces 68% of USSR cotton, 33% of

silk,34% of astrakhan, 85% of hemp. Industries include iron, steel, cars, tractors, TV and radio sets, textiles, food. Mineral wealth includes coal, sulphur, copper and oil. Capital: Tashkent, shaken by more than 600 earthquakes in 1966.

Turkmen SSR in Central Asia, produces cotton, grain, carpets, chemicals. Mineral wealth includes oil, coal, sulphur, barite, lime, gypsum. The Kara Kum desert occupies four-fifths of the territory. Capital: Ashkhabad.

Tadzhik SSR (Tadzhikistan), formed from the former regions of Bokhara and Turkestan, was admitted as a constituent republic on Dec. 5, 1929. Over half the population are Tadzhiks, mostly Sunnis, speaking an Iranian dialect. Chief occupations are farming and cattle breeding. Cotton, grain, rice and a variety of fruits are grown. Heavy industry, based on rich mineral deposits, coal and hydroelectric power, has replaced handicrafts. Dushanbe is the capital.

Kazakh SSR extends from the lower reaches of the Volga in Europe to the Altai Mtns. on the Chinese border. It has vast deposits of coal, oil, iron, tin, copper, etc. Fish for its canning industry are caught in Lake Balkhash and the Caspian and Aral Seas. Manufacturing, grains and cattle are important. The capital is Alma-Ata.

Kirghiz SSR is in the eastern part of Soviet Central Asia, on the frontier of Sinkiang (Western China). The people, once nomadic, breed cattle and horses and grow tobacco, cotton, rice, sugar beets. New industries include machine and instrument making, chemicals. Capital: Frunze.

Moldavian SSR in the SW part of the USSR, is a fertile black earth plain bordering Romania, and includes Bessarabia. It is an agricultural region that grows grains, fruits, vegetables and tobacco. Textiles, wine, food and electrical equipment industries have been developed. Capital: Kishinev.

Lithuanian SSR, on the Baltic, produces cattle, hogs, electric motors and appliances. The capital is Vilnius (Vilna). **The Latvian SSR** on the Baltic and the Gulf of Riga, has timber and peat resources estimated at 3,000,000,000 tons. In addition to agricultural products it produces rubber goods, dyes, fertilizers,glassware, telephone apparatus, TV and radio sets, railroad cars. The capital is Riga, on the Western Dvina River. **The Estonian SSR,** also on the Baltic, has textiles, shipbuilding, road-making and mining equipment industries and its shale refining industry is large. Tallinn is the capital. The 3 Baltic states were provinces of imperial Russia before World War I, were independent nations between World Wars I and II, and became SSRs, within the USSR, in 1940. They were occupied by Germany 1941-44. The U. S. has never formally recognized the incorporation of Lithuania, Latvia and Estonia into the USSR.

ECONOMICS AND PRODUCTION

The economic foundation of the USSR is the socialist ownership of the instruments and means of production. Socialist property exists in two forms: (1) State property; (2) Cooperative and collective farm property. State property includes the land, minerals, waters, forests, mills, factories, mines, rail, water and air transport, banks, communications, large agricultural enterprises and the bulk of dwellings.

The common enterprises of collective farms and cooperative organizations, their output and common buildings constitute their socialized property. Members may use small plots of land attached to their dwellings.

"Backyard" farms, from which farmers may sell produce and keep the profit, swelled in size and number in the 1960s.

Cultivated land and 1968 was est. at 515,249,900 acres. There were 36,800 collective farms and 12,783 state farms. In 1973 there were 104,000,000 cattle (2d to the U.S.), 66,500,000 hogs (2d to China) and 139,010,000 sheep (2d to Australia).

In 1963-5-6 the USSR was forced to make huge purchases of wheat in Canada and other countries, but a record surplus harvest was produced in 1966. It bought wheat from Canada again in 1971 and in 1972 reached agreement to make large purchases of U.S. grains, at least $175,000,000, over 3 years, but actually bought $1.1 billion worth in 1972 alone and ordered additional large amounts for 1973 and 1974. The nation's fish catch is the 3d largest, behind Japan and China.

The USSR is incalculably rich in natural resources. It claims to possess 57% of the world's coal deposits, 11.2% of its oil, 41% of iron ore, 88% of manganese, 54% of potassium salts, 30% of phosphates, and 25% of all timber land.

The USSR produces about 25% of world iron ore output, 19.5% of steel, 22% of coal, 13% of gold. Oil production in 1972 was 2d to the U.S., steel production led the world.

The index of industrial production (1963=100) was 201 for 1972.

In 1966 many major factories were put on an incentive profit-sharing system. In mid-1966 a system of bonuses to farms and farm workers (called "Socialist competition") was introduced to spur food production. In 1973 steps were taken to group factories into "production associations" partly resembling large U.S. corporations.

In 1971 a proposed new 5-year plan set goals of a 37-40% rise in national income, 42-46% in industrial output, 44-48% in consumer goods, 41-45% in capital goods, 20-22% in agricultural production. Premier Kosygin stressed growth in consumer goods.

But figures for 1972 showed fewer food and consumer production actually fell while heavy industry showed gains. National income growth rate for 1972 was 4%, lowest in 10 years.

FOREIGN TRADE

Exports include petroleum and its products, iron and steel, rolled non-ferrous metals, industrial plant equipment, lumber, cotton, asbestos, gold, manganese and others. Most of its trade is with Socialist nations, but trade with others is increasing. East Germany has been the Soviet Union's biggest customer.

Foreign trade, in thousands of U.S. dollars:

	Imports	Exports
1971	$12,479,000	$13,806,000
1972	$16,047,000	$15,361,000

The defense budget for 1972 was $19.9 billion, the same as for 1971, but it was lower percentagewise at 10.3% of the total budget (11.1% for 1971). Additional military spending was carried under other items in the budget.

Electric power output was est. at 800 billion kwh for 1972.

EARLY HISTORY

The first Russian state centered on Kiev in the 9th Century. In the 13th Century the Mongols overran the country. It recovered under the grand dukes and princes of Muscovy, or Moscow, and by 1480 freed itself from the Mongols. Ivan IV, the Terrible, was the first to be formally proclaimed Czar (1547). Peter the Great (1682-1725), extended the domain and in 1721 founded the Russian empire.

REVOLUTION OF 1917

The abortive Revolution of 1905 demonstrated the insecurity of the czarist regime and led to mild concessions. The 1917 Revolution began in March with a series of sporadic strikes for higher wages by factory workers. A provisional democratic government under Prince Georgi Lvov was established but was quickly followed in May by the second provisional government, led by Alexander Kerensky. The Kerensky government was overthrown in a Communist coup led by Vladimir Ilyich Lenin Nov. 7.

Lenin's death Jan. 21, 1924, resulted in an internal power struggle from which Joseph Stalin eventually emerged the absolute ruler of Russia. Stalin secured his position at first by exiling opponents such as Leon Trotsky. But in the 1930s he resorted to a series of "purge" trials in which virtually all opposition was directly eliminated.

KHRUSHCHEV, BREZHNEV

After Premier Stalin died, Mar. 5, 1953, Nikita Khrushchev was elected First Secretary of the Central Committee for 5 years; reelected 1956, 1959, 1961. In 1956 he condemned Stalin and his tyrannical methods before the Soviet Communist Party Congress in Moscow, said

Stalin cultivated a "cult of personality" and subverted Communist aims. Khrushchev lifted some restrictions, extended barter and trade policies. The names of Stalin, Molotov, Malenkov and other supporters of Stalin were eliminated from regions, cities and other sites in 1961-62 after Stalin's body was removed from the Lenin-Stalin tomb in Moscow.

Khrushchev was elected Premier by the Supreme Soviet, Mar. 27, 1958, succeeding Marshal Bulganin. He was reelected Apr. 24, 1962.

Under Khrushchev the open antagonism of Poland and Hungary against domination by Moscow was brutally suppressed in 1956. He advocated peaceful co-existence with the capitalist countries, but continued arming the USSR with nuclear weapons, promised aid to all "suppressed peoples" and so-called wars of liberation. He aided the Cuban revolution under Fidel Castro but withdrew Soviet missiles from Cuba during confrontation by U. S. President Kennedy, Sept.-Oct. 1962.

The USSR, the U. S. and Great Britain initialed a joint treaty July 25, 1963, which would ban all except underground nuclear tests.

The policy of co-existence alienated the leaders of Albania and Communist China. The latter continued to preach world revolution and denounced the Khrushchev methods as deviating from true Communism.

Khrushchev was suddenly deposed Oct. 14-15, 1964, and replaced as party First Secretary by Leonid I. Brezhnev, 57, and as Premier by Aleksei N. Kosygin, 60. (Brezhnev's title was changed in 1966 to General Secretary, and Khrushchev's de-Stalinization policy was relaxed.)

Communist China's Premier Chou En-lai visited the new USSR chiefs in Nov. 1964 but the visit failed to heal the growing rift between the two Communist powers.

In 1968, the U. S. and USSR joined 59 other nations in signing a treaty to bar spread of nuclear weapons.

In Aug. 1968 Russian, Polish, East German, Hungarian and Bulgarian military forces invaded Czechoslovakia to put a curb on liberalization policies of the Czech government. The USSR declared it had a duty to intervene in nations where socialism was "imperiled," the "Brezhnev Doctrine." Although the invasion succeeded in "normalizing" Czech policies, the action brought strong criticism from Communist parties in some nations.

In March 1969 troops of the USSR and Communist China fought the first of a series of clashes on a disputed island in the Ussuri River on the border between the two nations in the Far East, north of Vladivostok. In 1970 ambassadors were exchanged, after a lapse; but both nations increased their border forces. The USSR signed a treaty with West Germany in 1970 recognizing current European boundaries. In 1971 the USSR signed friendship pacts with Egypt, Canada and India, and joined in a Big 4 agreement on West Berlin.

The USSR in 1971 continued heavy arms shipments to Egypt. In July 1972 Egypt ordered most of the 20,000 Soviet military personnel in that country to leave. The USSR then increased arms shipments to Syria. A large Soviet fleet was maintained in the Mediterranean, about 55 ships in 1973, and smaller fleets in other seas.

During the May 1972 visit of U.S. Pres. Nixon, the U.S. and USSR reached agreements to freeze intercontinental missiles at their current levels, to limit defensive missiles to 200 each, to cooperate on health and environment problems, to stage a joint space flight and to set up commissions for trade and scientific cooperation.

In the June 1973 visit of Brezhnev to the U.S., agreements were signed to seek ways to promote trade, peace and cultural and scientific exchanges. Meanwhile, under Brezhnev, dissident intellectuals were repressed and purge-type trials resumed. Andrei Sakharov, creator of the USSR hydrogen bomb, warned Western nations that aid given Russia would be used against them.

GOVERNMENT

The first Soviet constitution was adopted in 1918 for the RSFSR. The USSR was formed in Dec., 1922, and the first Union constitution adopted in 1923. The current constitution, adopted in 1936, provides for universal direct suffrage with secret ballot. It was modified, 1944, to give each of the constituent republics the right to have separate commissions for defense and foreign affairs. Voting age is 18; candidates for election must have reached 23. Each Union republic is organized similarly to the central government.

The highest legislative authority is the Supreme Soviet consisting of two chambers, the Soviet of the Union and the Soviet of Nationalities. The first house is elected on the basis of one deputy for every 300,000 population; the second on the basis of 25 deputies from each Union republic, 11 from each autonomous republic, 5 from each autonomous region, and one from each national district. The Supreme Soviet normally meets twice a year, serves for a four-year term. It elects a 37-member Presidium which serves between sessions.

Titular chief of state, Chairman of the Presidium (President) of the Supreme Soviet, Nikolai V. Podgorny, was chosen Dec. 9, 1965.

Elections for the Supreme Soviet are by universal suffrage but from single slates of candidates approved by the party; voters are offered a choice only of striking out names.

The highest judicial organ is the Supreme Court, whose members are elected by the Supreme Soviet for five-year terms. Other courts are elected within the constituent republics. Since Feb. 1957, the Supreme Court has been restricted to appellate functions.

The highest executive and administrative organ of state power is the Council of Ministers (Premier and deputies) appointed by and theoretically responsible to the Supreme Soviet.

The Communist party of the USSR is the only legal party. Its highest organ is the Party Congress of about 1,500 elected representatives which normally meets once every 4 years. It elects a Central Committee, the party's directive body, and other committees. The Central Committee elects from its number a Politburo which makes party policy between Central Committee meetings; and a Secretariat, the party's chief executive body.

The Communist party Politburo normally consists of 15 full members and 6 candidate members.

Membership in the Communist party in 1971 was reported at about 14,500,000.

EDUCATION

Education is free. It is compulsory from ages 7 to 16. In 1968 there were 41,444,000 students in 8-year primary-polytechnical schools; 14,500,000 in secondary, evening and vocational schools and junior colleges; 4,300,000 in institutes of higher learning. Illiteracy was reduced to 1.5%.

SOCIAL BENEFITS

All workers are entitled to free public health services, paid vacations, sickness insurance, pensions for men at 60 and women at 55 (extended to collective farm members 1965). There are lower pension requirements for those in hazardous or difficult occupations. State payments are made to mothers on the birth of the 3rd and successive children. In 1968 there were 35,000,000 receiving pensions.

RELIGION

Separation of church and state was effected in 1918. Nine branches of Christianity are represented, led by the Orthodox Church, which in 1956 had 22,000 congregations. Islam has the second largest following. Jewish and Buddhist faiths are also present.

In 1970-72 many Jews sought to leave the USSR. In 1970 about 1,000 were permitted to leave; in 1971, 13,500; in 1972, 30,000; in 1973, another 30,000 was expected.

DEFENSE

Military forces for 1972-73 were est. to total 3,375,000. The Army had about 2,000,000 men, organized in 164 divisions. About 32 divisions were stationed in satellite nations (20 of them in East Germany). There were 60 divisions in European Russia; 28 in the Caucasus and central Asia; 44 in the Far East. The 164 divisions included 106 motorized rifle divisions, 51 tank divisions, 7 airborne. The Army was equipped with tactical missiles, including nuclear warheads.

Navy personnel totaled 475,000. The main power of the Soviet fleet was its 350 submarines, some 90 of which were nuclear-powered. Some were equipped with ballistic nuclear missiles. There were 22 cruisers, 210 destroyers, 2 helicopter carriers and hundreds of smaller craft.

Air Force personnel totaled 550,000; there was a total of about 9,000 combat aircraft. A long-range force had 140 intercontinental bombers and 700 medium-range bombers. Tactical forces included some 5,000 light bombers, interceptors and ground attack fighters, etc. The air defense command had about 3,300 fighter planes, the naval air force about 500 bombers and 500 other craft, the air transport force some 1,700 transport planes.

In 1972 the USSR was reportedly ahead of the U.S. in number of intercontinental ballistic missiles; the Soviet reportedly had 1,618 in place, the U.S. 1,054. The USSR reportedly had 710 submarine-borne missiles, the U.S. 656. But the U.S. had some missiles with multiple warheads (MIRVs). The USSR developed MIRVs in 1973.

The USSR is a member of the UN and Warsaw Pact.

United Arab Emirates

Capital: Abu Dhabi. Area: 32,278 sq. mi. Population (UN est. 1972): 200,000. Monetary unit: Dirham.

The United Arab Emirates, formerly known as the Trucial States or Trucial Sheikdoms, were British Protected States until they became an independent nation Dec. 2, 1971. It stretches 400 mi. along the Persian (also called Arabian) Gulf and the Gulf of Oman, from Qatar to Oman. Inland, it borders on Saudi Arabia.

The 7 sheikdoms signed treaties with Great Britain in the 19th Century giving Britain responsibility for defense and foreign relations. When Britain announced it would let the treaties lapse by the end of 1971, the 7 sought to form a federation with Bahrain and Qatar, also British Protected States. The attempt failed. The UAE was formed by 6 of the 7, Abu Dhabi, Dubai, Sharja, Ajman, Fujaira and Umm al Qaiwan. The 7th, Ras al Khaima, joined shortly. The city of Abu Dhabi became the capital and the Abu Dhabi ruler became President. There is a Prime Minister, a Supreme Council of Rulers and a National Council or legislature.

Abu Dhabi, Dubai and Sharja have large and increasing oil production, totaling the 14th largest in the world. Fujaira and Ras al Khaima have substantial food production. In 1971 Abu Dhabi launched an industrial development plan, including funds for projects in the other members of the UAE.

A 1968 census gave Dubai 59,000 inhabitants; Abu Dhabi, 49,000; Sharja, 31,500; Ras al Khaima, 24,500; Fujaira, 9,700; Ajman, 4,200; Umm al Qaiwan, 3,700. They are predominantly Arab, plus some Iranians, Indians and Baluchis.

The United Kingdom of Great Britain and Northern Ireland

Capital: London. Area: 94,209 sq. mi. Population (Govt. est. 1972): 55,788,000. Monetary Unit: Pound.

(See Index for Commonwealth)

The United Kingdom of Great Britain and Northern Ireland comprises England, Wales, Scotland and Northern Ireland.

The term British Isles is applied to these divisions and to the separately-governed island dependencies, Isle of Man and the Channel Islands.

The Isle of Man lies in the Irish Sea and the Channel Islands lie off the coast of France. The whole British Isles lie off the NW corner of Europe, with the North Atlantic on the N and W; separating England from the mainland are the North Sea on the E, the Strait of Dover on the SE and the English Channel on the S. The Thames, 210 mi. from its source to the North Sea, is England's longest river.

England has an area of 50,331 sq. mi. and Wales has 8,016 sq. mi., combined population (est. 1972), 49,029,000; Scotland, 30,411 sq. mi., 5,210,000; Northern Ireland,

5,451 sq. mi., 1,549,000.

The climate of the British Isles is equable, mild and somewhat warmer than that of the continent because of the Gulf Stream modifying the temperature, which has a mean of 48°. Rainfall averages 41 inches annually, and fogs are frequent.

On Apr. 1, 1965, new boundaries and a new government system for Greater London went into effect. The boundaries cut the size from 692 to 620 sq. mi. and the population from 8,176,810 (est. 1963) to 7,418,020 (est. 1972). A new Greater London Council administers most citywide services; local councils for 32 boroughs, formed from 100 former areas, conduct local services; the old City of London (675 acres), financial capital of the Commonwealth, retains independent status plus powers as a new borough.

QUEEN AND ROYAL FAMILY. The ruling sovereign is Elizabeth II of the House of Windsor, the former Princess Elizabeth Alexandra Mary, born April 21, 1926, eldest daughter of King George VI and Queen Elizabeth. She succeeded to the throne Feb. 6, 1952, and was crowned June 2, 1953. Her title in the United Kingdom and territories is: "Elizabeth II, by the Grace of God of the United Kingdom of Great Britain and Northern Ireland and of her other realms and territories, Queen, Head of the Commonwealth, Defender of the Faith." The title varies in other countries of the Commonwealth. The Queen is a great-great-granddaughter of Queen Victoria.

The Queen, as Princess Elizabeth, was married Nov. 20, 1947 to Lt. Philip Mountbatten, born June 10, 1921, former Prince of Greece. He was created Duke of Edinburgh Nov. 19, 1947, H.R.H. Prince Philip Nov. 20, 1947, and given the title Prince of the United Kingdom Feb. 22, 1957. He is a son of late Prince Andrew of Greece and Princess Alice, sister of Earl Mountbatten (former Governor-General of India); his grandfather, Prince Louis of Battenberg, became admiral in Royal Navy and changed the family name to Mountbatten; the Duke is great-grandson of Christian IX of Denmark and great-great-grandson of Queen Victoria.

They have four children: (1) Prince Charles Philip Arthur George, born Nov. 14, 1948, named Prince of Wales, July 26, 1958, (2) Princess Anne Elizabeth Alice Louise, born Aug. 15, 1950, (3) Prince Andrew Albert Christian Edward, born Feb. 19, 1960; (4) Prince Edward Antony Richard Louis, born Mar. 10, 1964, third in line for the throne. Prince Charles, the heir apparent, was invested Prince of Wales July 1, 1969.

The Queen has one sister, Princess Margaret Rose, born Aug. 21, 1930; married Antony Armstrong-Jones, a commoner, May 6, 1960. He received an Earldom as the Earl of Snowdon Oct. 3, 1961. Issue: David Albert Charles, Viscount Linley, born Nov. 3, 1961, sixth in line for the throne, and a daughter, Sarah Frances Elizabeth (Lady Sarah Armstrong-Jones), born May 1, 1964.

The late King George VI was born Dec. 14, 1895, son of King George V (died Jan. 20, 1936), and Queen Mary (died March 24, 1953). He succeeded to the throne on the abdication of his brother, Edward VIII, Dec. 11, 1936. As Prince Albert Duke of York, he married April 26, 1923, Lady Elizabeth Bowes-Lyon (born Aug. 4, 1900). He died Feb. 6, 1952.

His widow became Queen Elizabeth the Queen Mother. Two brothers and a sister also survived George VI.

They were H.R.H. Prince Edward Albert (born June 23, 1894) Prince of Wales; proclaimed King Edward VIII, acceded Jan. 20, 1936 but never crowned, abdicated Dec. 11, 1936; created Duke of Windsor (Dec. 12, 1936) married (June 3, 1937) Mrs. Wallis Warfield; appointed Governor of the Bahamas July 9, 1940; died, May 28, 1972; H.R.H. Prince Henry William (born March 31, 1900), created Duke of Gloucester (March 31, 1928), married (Nov. 6, 1935), Lady Alice Montagu-Douglas-Scott (born Dec. 25, 1901), daughter of the Duke and Duchess of Buccleuch and Queensbury—issue: William Henry Andrew Frederick (born Dec. 18, 1941, died Aug. 28, 1972), Richard Alexander Walter George (born Aug. 26, 1944); Princess (Victoria Alexandra Alice) Mary, Princess Royal (born April 25, 1897, died Mar. 28, 1965),

married (Feb. 28, 1922) Viscount Lascelles, later Earl of Harewood (died May 24, 1947)—issue; George Henry Hubert, Earl of Harewood (born Feb. 7, 1923), Gerald David (born Aug. 21, 1924).

A third brother, the Duke of Kent, was killed in an airplane accident in Scotland (Aug. 25, 1942). He was H.R.H. Prince George (born Dec. 20, 1902), married (Nov. 29, 1934) Princess Marina of Greece (born Nov. 30, 1906, died Aug. 27, 1968)—issue: Edward George Nicholas Patrick, Duke of Kent (born Oct. 9, 1935), married (June 8, 1961) Katharine Worsley; Alexandra Helen Elizabeth Olga Christabel (born Dec. 25, 1936) married Hon. Angus Ogilvy (April 1963); Michael George Charles Franklin (born July 4, 1942).

Queen Elizabeth announced Feb. 8, 1960, that her descendants, except princes and princesses of the royal family, would bear the surname Mountbatten-Windsor.

The Queen receives from Parliament an annuity of £980,000. The Civil List grants Prince Philip £65,000; Queen Mother Elizabeth £95,000; The Duke of Gloucester £45,000; Princess Margaret £35,000. Prince Charles receives an est. £110,000 from Duchy of Cornwall revenues.

PARLIAMENT is the legislative governing body for the United Kingdom, with certain powers over dependent units but none over the independent states. It consists of two Houses. The House of Lords is divided into (1) the Lords Temporal, consisting of hereditary peers and peeresses who have not disclaimed their titles, life peers created by the Crown, and Lords of Appeal; and (2) the Lords Spiritual who are the Archbishops of Canterbury and York and 24 diocesan bishops of the Church of England. Full membership of the House of Lords is over 1,000 but actual attendance is approximately 200.

Women became eligible to sit in the House of Lords for the first time, July 23, 1958. Previously, women had been eligible to sit only in Commons.

The House of Commons has 630 members, who are elected by direct ballot and divided as follows: England, 511; Wales and Monmouth, 36; Scotland 71; Northern Ireland, 12.

Clergymen of the Church of England, ministers of the Church in Scotland and Roman Catholic clergymen are disqualified from sitting as members, also certain government officers, and sheriffs. Women have had the right to vote since 1918.

Members of Parliament are paid £4,500. Most cabinet Ministers are paid £13,000. Ministers in the House of Commons draw an additional allowance of £1,250 from their pay as M.P.s.

The Conservative party ended nearly 6 years of Labor party rule by winning general parliamentary elections June 18, 1970. Conservative party leader Edward Heath became Prime Minister, succeeding Laborite Harold Wilson.

Popular vote and seats won in Commons were: Conservatives, 13,106,965 (46.4%), 330; Labor, 12,141,676 (43%), 287; Liberal, 2,109,218 (7.4%), 6; others, 900,473 (3.2%), 7.

RESOURCES AND INDUSTRIES. Great Britain's major occupations are manufacturing and trade. Metals and metal-using industries contribute more than 50% of the exports. Agriculture provides wheat, barley, oats, sugar beets, rye, livestock products and garden truck. Of about 60,000,000 acres of land in England, Wales and Scotland, 49,000,000 are farmed, of which 18,000,000 are arable, the rest pastures.

Large oil and gas fields have been found in the North Sea. There are large deposits of coal, the annual output is over 100,000,000 tons. Limestone, igneous rock and iron ore are valuable products. Other important minerals, in the order of their value, are gravel and sand, clay and shale, slate, sandstone, salt, China clay, fireclay, chalk, gypsum, oil shale, lead ore, tin ore and silica.

There are approximately 140 airports for civil use in Great Britain. British Airways is the state-owned airline.

The railroad lines, nationalized since 1948, have been reduced in total length, with a basic network of 11,000 mi. designated for modernization and development.

Telephone service is part of the postal system. There

are about 15,000,000 telephones.

Broadcast receiving licenses in 1972 totaled 14,167,000 for black-and-white TV, 2,815,000 for color.

The government, on July 28, 1967, took ownership of 14 steel companies which comprised 90% of the nation's steelmaking industry, paying shareholders in the companies more than $1.4 billion in government securities. The new British Steel Corp. became Britain's largest industrial enterprise.

The Labor government raised taxes several times, 1966-69; it devalued the pound from a value of $2.80 to $2.40 in 1967 and took various measures to improve exports and cut imports. The Conservative government put a freeze on prices, wages and rents in 1972 to combat inflation. In 1973 it substituted "restraints" for the freeze.

On Feb. 15, 1971, Britain completed a changeover to a system of decimal currency, continuing the same pound but dividing it into 100 new pence. By 1975 it plans to complete conversion to the metric system of measures.

Tourism ranks high in earnings. Visitors from abroad totaled more that 7,400,000 in 1972, of whom 1,612,000 were from the U.S.

Index of industrial production (1963=100) was 130 in 1972.

Industrial Production:

	1970	1971	1972
Coal (million tons)	142.3	151.2	119.9
Crude steel (million tons)	27.3	23.8	25.3
Automobiles (thousands)	1,640.1	1,741.5	1,921.3
Trucks, etc. (thousands)	457.5	456.2	408.1

The merchant marine totaled 27,114,000 gross registered tons in Jan. 1973, comprising over 10% of active world shipping. British shipyards have an estimated annual capacity of 1,259,000 tons.

The world's first power station using atomic energy to create electricity for civilian use began operation Oct. 17, 1956, at Calder Hall in Cumberland.

Britain's aid to less developed countries has more than doubled since 1956, totaling over $3 billion and amounting to $592,800,000 in 1971.

The United Kingdom is a member of the UN, Commonwealth, NATO, SEATO, CENTO, Council of Europe and, since Jan. 1, 1973, EEC.

Britain imports all of its cotton, rubber, sulphur, four-fifths of its wool, half of its food and iron ore, also certain amounts of paper, tobacco, chemicals. Manufactured goods made from these basic materials have been exported since the industrial age began.

Gross national product for 1972 was $151.6 billion.

Main exports are machinery, chemicals, woolen and synthetic textiles, autos and trucks, iron and steel, locomotives, jet aircraft, farm machinery, drugs, radio, TV, radar and navigation equipment, whisky.

Foreign trade in thousands of U.S. dollars:

	Imports	Exports
1971	$23,944,000	$22,353,000
1972	$27,860,000	$24,344,000

RELIGION AND CHURCHES. The Church of England is Protestant Episcopal. The Queen is supreme governor, with rights of appointment to archbishoprics, bishoprics and other offices. There are two provinces, Canterbury and York. The 100th Archbishop of **Canterbury** and Primate of All England is the Most Rev. Arthur Michael Ramsey (b. Nov. 14, 1904) whose seat is Lambeth Palace, London. Annual Salary £ 7,500. Dean is the Very Rev. Ian White-Thomson. The 114th Bishop of London is the Rt. Rev. Robert W. Stopford, £ 5,500. The Dean of Westminster is the Very Rev. Eric Symes Ab-

bott, £ 3,000.

The 93rd Archbishop of **York** and Primate of England is the Most Rev. Frederick Donald Coggan, Bishopthorpe, York; £6,000.

The Church of England has an est. 27,600,000 members. In 1970 there were some 14,300 parishes. Most famous church is Westminster Abbey (1050-1760), site of coronations; tombs of Elizabeth I, Mary of Scots, kings, poets and of the Unknown Warrior. St. Paul's Cathedral, London, 365 ft. to top of cross, has American War Memorial Chapel. Altogether, the Anglican Communion in the United Kingdom and overseas has over 47,000,000 members.

The **Roman Catholic Church**–Archbishop of Westminster, John Cardinal Heenan. Membership in the United Kingdom was approximately 5,300,000 in 1973.

The **Methodist Church**–This is headed by a conference governing body which has a President. There were about 14,000 churches and 651,000 members in 1971.

Others: There are an est. 410,000 Jews in Great Britain; 80% of them are Orthodox and more than half live in the London area. There are over 202,000 Baptists and about 167,000 Congregationalists. The Calvinistic Methodist (Presbyterian) Church of Wales has over 108,000 communicants. The Unitarians have 330 chapels. The Presbyterian Church of England has 318 congregations, 59,000 members. The Society of friends has over 440 meeting houses, nearly 21,000 members. The Church of Christ Scientist has 330 branches in Great Britain and Ireland. The Presbyterian Church in Ireland has a membership in Northern Ireland of about 143,000. The number of Moslems in Britain has been growing steadily.

The Church of Scotland is Presbyterian. It is presided over by a Moderator, chosen annually. Churches numbered 2,126, members 1,250,000 in 1973.

EDUCATION. Primary and secondary education is free and compulsory from 5 to 16.

The most celebrated of British universities are Oxford and Cambridge, each with colleges founded in the 13th Century. There are 40 other universities in England, Scotland, Wales and Northern Ireland.

SOCIAL WELFARE, TAXES. Under the Dept. of Health and Social Security, National Insurance provides for virtually universal compulsory insurance covering sickness, maternity, unemployment and industrial accidents, and death benefits and pensions for widows, orphans and the aged. The National Health Service provides free medical and nursing care, small dental fees and minimum charges for certain appliances and prescriptions. Under the Family Allowance Act the government pays 90 pence a week for each child of compulsory school age, after the first, and one pound each for the third or more.

Supplementary Benefits provide for those not fully protected by National Insurance. Contributions are made by purchase of National Insurance stamps, the amounts varying according to sex and classification (employed, self-employed, non-employed). In the case of employed, the employer pays slightly over one-half.

Under the 1973 unified (income) tax, the rate is 30% on the 1st £5,000, rising to a top of 75% on £20,000 and more.

DEFENSE: The government forecast that in Apr. 1974 total armed forces would number 353,100, comprising Army, 174,100; Navy, 77,900; RAF, 101,100.

The Territorial Army corresponds to the National Guard in the United States, is voluntary, and serves only at home in peacetime. The women's services are integrated into the three branches of the armed forces.

BUDGETS OF GREAT BRITAIN

Fiscal year ends March 31

Year	Revenues 1,000 £	Expendit's 1,000 £	Year	Revenues 1,000 £	Expendit's 1,000 £	Year	Revenues 1,000 £	Expendit's 1,000 £
1940	1,025,192	1,032,217	1963	6,794,000	6,441,000	1969	13,363,000	11,615,000
1950	3,924,031	3,356,569	1964	6,890,000	6,817,000	1970	15,521,000	12,518,000
1955	4,738,000	4,305,000	1965	8,157,000	7,712,900	1971	17,007,000	13,634,000
1960	5,630,529	5,222,996	1966	9,145,000	8,456,000	1972	19,374,000	15,325,000
1961	5,934,000	5,787,000	1967	10,279,000	9,541,000	1973	22,194,000	17,661,000
1962	6,645,000	6,235,000	1968	11,177,000	10,878,000	1974 (est.)	25,440,000	19,733,000

In 1973 the government reported 167 ships in the operational fleet, including 2 aircraft carriers, 2 commando ships, 8 guided-missile destroyers, 52 frigates, 27 subs, 42 minesweepers, 3 Polaris-firing submarines.

Britain exploded its 1st atomic bomb in 1952 and has a stockpile of these weapons. The Air Force is equipped with Blue Steel air-to-surface nuclear missiles.

Wales

The Principality of Wales and Monmouthshire in western Britain has an area of 8,016 sq. mi. and a population (est. 1971) of 2,723,596.

England and Wales are administered as a unit and Wales does not have a separate local government act, as has Scotland. More than one-fourth the population speak both English and Welsh and under 50,000 speak Welsh solely. Welsh nationalism is advocated by a small segment.

Early Anglo-Saxon invaders drove certain Celtic peoples into the mountains of Wales, terming them Waelise (Welsh, or foreign). There they developed a distinct nationality and culture. Members of the ruling house of Gwynedd in the 13th Century fought England for sovereignty but were crushed, 1282-1283. Edward of Caernarvon, son of Edward I of England, was created Prince of Wales Feb. 7, 1301.

Scotland

Scotland, a kingdom now united with England and Wales in Great Britain, occupies the northern 37% of the main British island, and the Hebrides, Orkney, Shetland and smaller islands. The Atlantic lies N and W; the North Sea, E. Length, 275 mi., breadth approx. 150 mi., area, 30,411 sq. mi., population (est. 1972) 5,210,000. Principal rivers are the Clyde, 106 mi.; the Tay, 117 mi., and the Tweed, 96 mi.

The Lowlands, a belt of land approximately 60 miles wide from the Firth of Clyde to the Firth of Forth, divide the farming region of the Southern Uplands from the granite Highlands of the north. Only one-tenth of the land area, the Lowlands contain three-quarters of the population and most of the industry. The Highlands, famous for hunting and fishing, have been opened to industry by many hydroelectric power stations.

Edinburgh, pop. (1971) 543,025, is the capital. It lies on the Firth of Forth in Midlothian County, 42 mi. from Glasgow, and has notable memorials of its royal and cultural history.

Glasgow, pop. (1971) 893,790, is the largest city, third largest in Britain, and Britain's greatest industrial center. It is a shipbuilding complex on the Clyde and an ocean port. Prestwick International Airport is a major transatlantic airport.

Aberdeen, pop. (1971) 181,785, 95 mi. N E of Edinburgh, is a major North Sea port, center of granite industry and fish processing.

Dundee, pop. (1971) 182,930, 40 mi. N E of Edinburgh, is an industrial and fish processing center on the Firth of Tay.

History. Scotland was called Caledonia by the Romans who battled early Picts and Celtic tribes and occupied southern areas from the 1st to the 4th Centuries. The Romans supposedly called one group Picti because they painted their bodies. The Scots were an Irish tribe from Scotia (an early name for Ireland). Missionaries from Britain introduced Christianity in the 4th Century; St. Columba, an Irish monk, converted most of Scotland to Christianity in the 6th Century.

The Kingdom of Scotland was established in the 11th Century. William Wallace, patriot leader, defeated an invading English army at Stirling Bridge, 1297, and Robert Bruce defeated another at Bannockburn, 1314.

In 1603 James VI of Scotland, son of Mary, Queen of Scots, succeeded Queen Elizabeth I on the throne of England as James I, and effected the Union of the Crowns. In 1707 Scotland received representation in the British Parliament, resulting from the union of former separate Parliaments. Its executive in the British cabinet is the Secretary of State for Scotland. John Knox led the Scottish church Reformation in the 16th Century. There is a small Scottish Nationalist party which urges independence for Scotland.

There are 8 universities, at Aberdeen, Edinburgh, Glasgow, St. Andrews, Dundee and Stirling. Education receives some support from trusts, founded by Andrew Carnegie. St. Andrews is the birthplace of golf.

Historic sites and literary associations, where memorials of Robert Burns, Sir Walter Scott, John Knox, Mary, Queen of Scots, are preserved, draw many tourists, as do the beauties of the Trossachs, Loch Katrine, Loch Lomond and abbey ruins that are now state property.

Industries. Engineering products are the most important industry, with growing emphasis on lighter products such as office machinery, autos, electronics and other consumer goods and less dependence on locomotives, boilers, pumps, valves and other industrial machinery. Scotland contributes about a third of all British shipbuilding.

Scotland produces fine woolens, worsteds, tweeds; silk textiles at Paisley and Glasgow; fine linens and jute. It is known for its Ayrshire, Aberdeen-Angus, Galloway, Belted Galloway, Highland and Scottish Shorthorn cattle. It raises Shetland, Highland and Cheviot sheep, Shetland ponies and Clydesdale draft horses. Fisheries have large hauls of herring, cod, whiting. Whisky remains the biggest export product.

Atomic projects to produce plutonium and electrical energy are at Dounreay, Chapelcross and Hunterston.

The Hebrides are a group of c. 500 islands, 100 inhabited, off the W coast. The Inner Hebrides include **Skye, Mull** and **Iona,** the last famous for the arrival of St. Columba, 563 A.D. The Outer Hebrides include **St. Kilda,** and **Harris.** Industries include sheep raising and weaving (Harris tweeds).

The Orkney Islands, c. 90, are separated from Scotland by the Pentland Firth. The capital is Kirkwall, on Pomona Is. Fish curing, sheep raising and weaving are occupations. Northeast of the Orkneys are the 200 **Shetland Islands,** 24 inhabited, home of the Shetland pony.

Northern Ireland

Six of the 9 counties of Ulster, the NE corner of Ireland, constitute Northern Ireland, with the parliamentary boroughs of Belfast and Londonderry; they are Antrim, Armagh, Down, Londonderry, Fermanagh and Tyrone. The country has an area of 5,451 sq. mi. and a population (1971 census prelim.) 1,528,000. Belfast is the capital and chief industrial center.

Industries. Shipbuilding, including large tankers, has long been an important industry, centered in Belfast, the largest port, which has 10 miles of wharves. Linen manufacture has also long been important, along with apparel and rope and twine. Growing diversification has added engineering products, synthetic fibers and electronics.

Agriculture is also important. There are large numbers of cattle, hogs and sheep; potatoes, poultry and dairy foods are also among the products. There is an agricultural surplus, most of which is shipped to England.

Government. An act of the British parliament, 1920, divided Northern from Southern Ireland, each with a parliament and government. When Ireland became a dominion, 1921, and later a republic, Northern Ireland chose to remain a part of the United Kingdom. It elects 12 members to the British House of Commons.

During 1968-69, large demonstrations were conducted by groups of Roman Catholics who charged they were discriminated against in voting rights, housing and employment. The Catholics, a minority comprising about a third of the population of Northern Ireland, demanded abolition of property qualifications for voting in local elections and demanded institution of "one man, one vote." Violence and terrorism intensified, involving branches of the Irish Republican Army (outlawed in the Irish Republic), Protestant groups, police and large British Army units. In 1972, over 18,000 British troops were on duty.

A succession of Northern Ireland prime ministers pressed reform programs but failed to satisfy extremists on both sides. By Sept. 1973 over 850 civilians and British soldiers (over 190 soldiers) had been killed in bombings and shootings. Britain suspended the Northern Ireland parliament Mar. 30, 1972, and imposed direct British rule under a Secretary of State.

In 1973 Britain's Parliament created a single-chamber Assembly to replace the old 2-chamber, Protestant-dominated Stormont Parliament in Northern Ireland. It was designed to insure Catholics a share of political power.

In June 28 elections moderate parties, pledged to make the system work, won nearly two-thirds of the 78 Assembly seats. But the first session, July 31, was disrupted by Protestant extremists.

Education and Religion. Northern Ireland is preponderantly Protestant. Elementary education is compulsory to age 15. Queens Univ. of Belfast (1908) had a 1968 enrollment of 5,527. The new Univ. of Ulster was opened in 1968.

Northern Ireland closely followed Britain in systems of social services, industrial accident and disability benefits, family allowances and pensions.

Dependencies
CHANNEL ISLANDS

The Channel Islands, area 75 sq. mi., est. pop. 1972 120,000, off the NW coast of France, the only parts of the one-time Dukedom of Normandy belonging to England, are **Jersey, Guernsey** and the dependencies of Guernsey—**Alderney, Brechou, Great Sark, Little Sark, Herm, Jethou and Lihou.** Jersey has a separate legal existence and a lieutenant governor named by the Crown. The islands were the only British soil occupied by German troops in World War II.

ISLE OF MAN

The Isle of Man, area 277 sq. mi., est. 1972 pop. 60,000, is in the Irish Sea, 20 mi. from Scotland, 30 mi. from Cumberland. It is rich in lead and iron. The island has its own laws and a lt. gov. who has wide constitutional powers, appointed by the Crown. The Tynwald (legislature) consists of the Legislative Council, partly elected, the House of Keys, elected. Capital: Douglas.

Farming, tourism and fishing are chief occupations. The mild climate is popular with tourists. Ronaldsway Airport handles 250,000 passengers a year. Herring (kippers) and scallops top fishing trade. Man is famous for the Manx tailless cat.

Mediterranean Dependency
GIBRALTAR

Gibraltar, a colony southeast of Spain, guards the entrance to the Mediterranean. The width of the strait dividing Europe from Africa varies from 7.75 mi. at the narrowest part to 23.75 at the widest. The Rock has been in British possession since 1704. There is a large harbor and as a naval base its position is of the greatest strategic importance. The Rock is 2.75 mi. long, ¾ of a mi. wide and 1,396 ft. in height; a narrow isthmus connects it with the mainland. Est. pop. 1972 was 30,000.

In 1966 Spain called on Britain to give "substantial sovereignty" of Gibraltar to Spain and imposed a partial blockade of the isthmus. On Sept. 10, 1967, in a referendum sponsored by Britain despite Spain's objection, the residents voted 12,138 for remaining under British rule against 44 for returning to Spain.

A new constitution, May 30, 1969, gave an elected House of Assembly more control in domestic affairs. A UN General Assembly resolution requested Britain to end Gibraltar's colonial status by Oct. 1, 1969. Britain did not do so.

British West Indies and Other American Dependencies
WEST INDIES

Swinging in a vast arc from the coast of Venezuela northeast, then north and northwest toward Puerto Rico are the Windward and Leeward Islands, forming a coral and volcanic barrier sheltering the Caribbean from the open Atlantic. Most of the islands are British possessions which have internal self-government. Universal suffrage was instituted 1951-4; ministerial systems of government were set up 1956-1960.

Moving northward from the southern end of the arc lie the **Windward Islands,** starting with **Grenada** (1972 pop. est.100,000, area 133 sq. mi., capital St. George's), **St. Vincent,** (1972 pop. 90,000, area 150 sq.mi., capital

Kingstown), **St. Lucia** (1972 pop. 120,000, area 238 sq. mi., capital Castries) and **Dominica** (1972 pop. 70,000, area 290 sq. mi., capital Roseau).

Further north, in the **Leeward Islands,** are **Montserrat** (1970 pop. 12,300, area 33 sq. mi., capital Plymouth), **Antigua** (1972 pop. 70,000, area 171 sq. mi., capital St. John's) and **St. Christopher-Nevis-Anguilla,** three islands also referred to as **St. Kitts** (1972 pop. 70,000, area 138 sq. mi., capital Basseterre on St. Christopher). Nearby are the small **British Virgin Islands.**

Britain granted self-government to 5 of these islands and island groups in 1967; each became an Associated State, with Britain retaining responsibility for the foreign affairs and defense of each. These 5 were Antigua, Dominica, Grenada, St. Lucia and the St. Christopher-Nevis-Anguilla Federation. Similar status was received by St. Vincent in 1969.

Britain agreed in 1973 to grant Grenada full independence Feb. 7, 1974.

Anguilla declared its independence June 16, 1967, but accepted appointment of a British administrator. Controversy continued and in March 1969 British paratroops were landed. They left in Sept. A commission was set up to administer the island. Anguilla's area is 35 sq. mi., its pop. 5,000. The main exports are lobsters and salt.

Sugar is the major crop of Antigua and St. Kitts; bananas are the main product of the Windwards; Dominica and Grenada produce cocoa; Antigua, Montserrat, St. Kitts and St. Vincent have Sea Island cotton; St. Vincent and Grenada have arrowroot; Grenada grows spices, and Dominica citrus fruits. Many of these products are exported; imports include other foods, clothing, machinery. Tourism is of mounting importance.

The three **Cayman Islands,** a colony, lie S of Cuba, NW of Jamaica. Population is 10,423 (1970), most of it on Grand Cayman, about 1,300 on Cayman Brac, about 16 on Little Cayman. It is a free port; in the 1970s Grand Cayman became a tax-free refuge for foreign funds and branches of many Western World banks were opened there in the 1970s to house such funds. Fishing, banking and tourism are the main industries. Total area: over 100 sq. mi. Capital: Georgetown.

The **Turks and Caicos Islands,** at the SE end of the Bahama Islands, are a separate British possession. There are about 30 islands, only 6 inhabited, 1967 pop. est. 6,000, area 166 sq. mi., capital Grand Turk. Salt, crayfish and conch shells are the main exports.

BERMUDA

Bermuda is a British possession governed by a royal governor and a representative legislature, the oldest legislative body among British dependencies. Capital is Hamilton.

It is a group of 360 small islands of coral formation, 20 inhabited, comprising 21 sq. mi. in the western Atlantic, 677 mi. SE of New York, 580 mi. E of North Carolina. Population, 1972, was 60,000 (about 63% are of African descent). Density is high, about 2,850 per sq. mi.

Bermuda's Parliament dates from 1620. In general elections May 22, 1968 the first on the basis of full universal adult suffrage without property qualifications, the predominantly white United Bermuda party won 30 of the 40 Assembly seats, the predominantly Black Progressive Labor party the other 10. Both sides ran white and black candidates; 16 of the 40 elected were blacks. A black member of the United Bermuda Party, Sir Edward Richards, became Prime Minister in 1971.

The British-appointed governor controls foreign and defense affairs and internal security. The Assembly, its members elected for 5-year terms, controls all local affairs. Bermuda adopted a dollar-decimal currency in 1970.

Gov. Richard Sharples and an aide-de-camp were slain by gunmen Mar. 10, 1973. The police commissioner was shot to death in 1972.

The U.S. maintains air and naval bases in the Bermudas, under long-term lease, and a NASA tracking station.

Bermuda boasts many modern resort hotels. Planes and cruise ships bring in upwards of 280,000 visitors a year, most of them from the U.S.

The government raises most of its revenue from import duties. There are also a real estate rental value tax, excise and other taxes, but none on income or inheritances.

Bermuda exports Easter lilies, drugs, essences, beauty preparations.

BELIZE (BRITISH HONDURAS)

Belize (formerly called British Honduras) is in Middle America facing the Caribbean to the E, with Mexico on the N and Guatemala on the W. Population (UN est. 1972) 130,000, area 8,867 sq. mi., capital Belmopan.

Internal self-government was granted by Britain in 1964.

The area has long been claimed by Guatemala, but also was promised independence by Britain. In Apr. 1968, a mediator proposed that British Honduras be made independent but have close association with Guatemala, consulting with it on foreign affairs of mutual concern. The proposal was rejected.

Main export is sugar, along with citrus fruits, mahogany and other hardwoods, chicle, lobsters and fish.

Atlantic Ocean Dependencies

Falkland Islands and Dependencies. British Colony, lies 300 mi. E of the Strait of Magellan at the southern end of South America.

The Falklands or Islas Malvinas include about 200 islands with an area of 4,618 sq. mi. and pop., est. 1970, of 2,045. Sheep-grazing is the main industry; wool is the principal export. The islands are also claimed by Argentina. **South Georgia,** area 1,450 sq. mi., and pop. 439, and the uninhabited **South Sandwich Islands** are dependencies of the Falklands.

Britain and Argentina discussed Argentine claims to the Falklands, but in Mar. 1968 officials of the islands declared their opposition to being ceded to Argentina.

British Antarctic Territory, south of 60° S lat., was made a separate Colony in 1962 and comprises mainly the **South Shetland Islands,** the **South Orkneys and Graham's Land.** A chain of meteorological stations is maintained.

St. Helena, an island 1,200 mi. off the W. coast of Africa and 1,800 E of South America, has 47 sq. mi. and est. pop., 1970 of 4,952. Flax, lace and rope making are the chief industries. After Napoleon Bonaparte was defeated at Waterloo the British exiled him to St. Helena, where he lived from Oct. 16, 1815, to his death, May 5, 1821. He was buried there until 1840, when his remains were transferred to Paris.

Tristan da Cunha is the principal of a group of islands of volcanic origin, total area 40 sq. mi., half way between the Cape of Good Hope and South America, which form one of the loneliest places on the globe. The other islands are Inaccessible, Gough (or Diego Alvarez) and the 3 Nightingale Islands. An ancient volcanic peak 6,760 ft. high erupted in Oct. 1961, and ruined the settlement. The 262 inhabitants were removed to England for resettlement, but most returned in 1963. The islands are administered as dependencies of St. Helena.

Ascension is an island of volcanic origin, 34 sq. mi. in area, 700 mi. NW of St. Helena, through which it is administered. It lies midway between Africa and South America and is an important communications relay center for Britain and has a U. S. satellite tracking center. Est. pop., 1971, was 1,232, about half of them communications workers. The island is noted for its sea turtles. ·

Asiatic States
BRUNEI

Brunei has been since 1888 a protected sultanate on the north side of the Island of Borneo, between the Malaysian states of Sarawak and Sabah. Its area is about 2,226 sq. mi., the size of Delaware, with population (1972 UN est), 140,000, two-thirds Malay and indigenous races, one-third of Chinese descent.

A 1959 constitution was amended, 1965, to provide for general elections to the Legislative Council, some members of which are appointed. There is a Sultan and a British High Commissioner. A Nov. 1971 agreement gave

Brunei full internal self-government.

Brunei's rich Seria oilfield provides tax revenues well in excess of government expenditures. Rubber is also exported. In recent years, some of the surplus has been spent on a growing program of school building and social services.

HONG KONG

Hong Kong is a Crown Colony at the mouth of the Canton River in China, 90 mi. south of Canton. Its nucleus is Hong Kong Island, 35½ sq. mi., acquired from China 1841, on which is located Victoria, the colonial capital. Opposite is Kowloon peninsula, 3 sq. mi. and Stonecutters Island, ¼ sq. mi., added to the colony by convention of Peking, 1860. An additional 355 sq. mi. known as the New Territories, comprised of an adjacent mainland area and numerous islands, were leased from China, 1898, for 99 years. Total area of the colony is 391 sq. mi., with a population, 1972 UN est., of 4,080,000, including many refugees from Communist China and fewer than 20,000 British. From 1949 to 1962 Hong Kong absorbed more than 1,000,000 refugees from the mainland. The flow of refugees continued, on a lesser scale, into the 1970s.

Hong Kong harbor, one of the finest in the East, was long an important British naval station and one of the world's greatest trans-shipment ports. It is served by many international airlines.

Principal industries are shipbuilding and textiles; also iron and steel, apparel, fishing, cement, and small manufactures. American tourists spend an est. $29,000,000 annually.

Since 1945 Hong Kong industry has zoomed from a few hundred factories to over 5,000. Its spinning mills, among the best in the world, and low wages compete with textiles elsewhere and have resulted in protective measures in some countries. It also has a booming electronics industry. The U. S. is the largest market for Hong Kong products.

During 1967 Communist China launched a campaign against British authority in Hong Kong, including demonstrations, strikes, riots, bombings, border incidents and slowdowns in supplying food from the mainland, accompanied by charges the British were mistreating Chinese residents.

Indian Ocean Dependencies

The Seychelles are a group of islands N of Madagascar, area 69 sq. mi., population 1972 UN est., 60,000. The capital is Victoria, on Mahe, a port with a coaling station. Coconuts are the chief product, followed by cinnamon, patchouli, mangrove bark, vanilla and tortoise shell. Copra is the chief export.

British Indian Ocean Territory was formed Nov. 1965, embracing islands formerly dependencies of Mauritius or Seychelles; the Chagos Archipelago (including Diego Garcia), Aldabra, Farquhar and Des Roches. Population, 558. In 1973 the U.S. Navy established a communications station on Diego Garcia.

British Pacific Islands
PITCAIRN ISLAND

Pitcairn Island is in the Pacific, halfway between South America and Australia. The island was discovered in 1767 by Carteret but was not inhabited until 23 years later when the mutineers of the Bounty landed there. The area is less than two sq. mi. and population, 1967, was about 90. It is a British Colony and is administered by a British Representative in New Zealand and a local Council. The uninhabited islands of **Henderson, Ducie** and **Oeno** are in the Pitcairn group.

Principal island groups administered by the British High Commissioner for the Western Pacific Islands, seated at Honiara, Guadalcanal, include the British Solomon Islands and the Gilbert and Ellice Islands:

BRITISH SOLOMON ISLANDS

The British Solomon Islands, a Protectorate, number 10 large islands and four groups of small islands with a total area of 11,500 sq. mi. and population, est. 1972, of 170,000, mostly Melanesians. The Solomons lie E of New

Guinea. The chief islands in the group are **Guadalcanal, Malaita, San Cristobal, New Georgia, Santa Ysabel, Choiseul, Shortland, Mono** or **Treasury, Vella Lavella, Ganongga, Gizo, Rendova, Russell, Florida** and **Rennel.** Among the groups of islands are the **Lord Howe, Santa Cruz, Tucopia, Mitre, Duff** or **Wilson,** and **Reef.** Some of the Solomons, including Bougainville, are an Australian UN Trusteeship.

Exports: copra, timber, nuts, and trochus shell.

GILBERT AND ELLICE ISLANDS

The **Gilbert and Ellice Islands** were proclaimed a protectorate in 1892 and, at the request of the native governments, were annexed as a colony. The Colony includes the **Gilbert Islands (16), Ellice Islands (9), Phoenix Islands, Ocean Island, Line Islands,** composed of **Fanning, Washington** and **Christmas Islands,** the last the largest atoll in the Pacific (also claimed by the United States). The total area is 375 sq. mi. and the population, 1970 est., 60,000. Exports: chiefly copra and phosphates.

NEW HEBRIDES

New Hebrides, a Condominium jointly administered since 1906 by Great Britain and France, is a group of 11 main islands and about 69 islets lying 500 mi. W of Fiji, with an aggregate area of approx. 5,700 sq. mi. Population, 1972 UN est. 90,000, mostly Melanesian. Chief products are copra, cotton, cocoa, fish and coffee.

British and French Resident Commissioners are joint heads of the administration.

Banks (309 sq. mi.) and **Torres** (40 sq. mi.) Islands, with pop. of 2,640, are attached to the New Hebrides for administration.

United States

(See Index for listings)

Upper Volta

Capital: Ouagadougou. Area: 105,869 sq. mi. Population (UN est. 1972): 5,610,000. Monetary unit: CFA franc.

The Republic of Upper Volta, one-time French Overseas Territory, is an inland plateau region in west Africa, bounded by Mali, Niger, the Ivory Coast, Ghana, Togo and Dahomey. It is the size of Colorado.

More than 90% of the people are subsistence farmers. Greatest wealth is in livestock, mostly cattle and sheep, accounting for 55% of exports. Principal market crops are cotton, rice, peanuts and karite. Climate is extremely dry but irrigation efforts, using water from the Black Volta, White Volta and pumped from underground, have been started with aid from the UN Special Fund. There are rich manganese deposits. A long drought brought famine in 1973; aid was sent by the U.S. and others.

In accordance with provisions of the 1958 French constitution, upper Volta became an autonomous state Dec. 11, 1958. It became fully independent Aug. 5, 1960 and a member of the UN Sept. 20. It signed a bilateral agreement Apr. 24, 1961, maintaining close ties with France.

A constitution, adopted Nov. 27, 1960, provides for a presidential form of government and a unicameral National Assembly. On Jan. 3, 1966, the army chief of staff, Lt. Col. Sangoule Lamizana, took control of the Presidency during demonstrations against austerity measures. A new constitution, providing for a prime minister, was adopted Dec. 20, 1970.

Uruguay

REPUBLICA ORIENTAL DEL URUGUAY

Capital: Montevideo. Area: 72,172 sq. mi. Population (UN est. 1972): 2,960,000. Monteray unit: Peso.

Uruguay is one of the smallest but most advanced republics in South America. Slightly larger than Missouri, it is a country of rich, rolling, grassy plains on the South Atlantic coast. Brazil and Argentina are its neighbors, with the Uruguay River forming the boundary line with Argentina.

Resources and Industries. Some 85% of Uruguay's area is devoted to stock raising; 9.6% to agriculture; 3.5% woods and forests; 1.8% is unproductive. The chief products are meat, wool, hides, corn, wheat, citrus fruits, rice, oats and linseed. Meat-packing, metalurgical, textile and wine-making industries are large.

More than one-third of the country's population lives in one city, Montevideo. More than one-third of the nation's workers are employed by the Government. The state owns the power, telephone, railroad, cement, oil-refining and other industries.

Uruguay's standard of living has been one of the highest in South America. Inflation, plus floods, drought and a cold wave in 1967 and a general strike in 1968 brought attempts by the Government to strengthen the economy through a series of devaluations of the peso and wage and price controls. But inflation continued. The cost of living rising 94% in 1972. In 1973 beef sales were banned for 3 months to promote meat exports.

History and Government. Uruguay, once a part of the Spanish Viceroyalty of Rio de la Plata and later a province of Brazil, declared its independence, Aug. 25, 1825, which was confirmed by a treaty with Brazil and Argentina, Aug. 27, 1828. The first constitution was adopted July 18, 1830. The constitution provides for a President, a Chamber of Deputies and a Senate elected for 5-year terms. Suffrage is universal.

Uruguay has one of the world's most extensive social welfare programs with old age pensions, child welfare.

Leftist guerrillas increased terrorist actions in 1970; a U.S. police adviser was slain in Aug. by the Tupamaros. In 1971 the guerillas kidnapped and, after 8 months, freed the British Ambassador. Violence continued and in Feb. 1973 Pres. Juan Maria Bordaberry agreed to permit military control of his administration. In June he abolished Congress and set up a Council of State in its place.

Education and Religion. Church and state are separate and there is complete religious tolerance. The preponderant religion is Roman Catholic. Education, including college is free; primary education is compulsory. Univ. of Montevideo was founded in 1849. The language is Spanish.

Defense. The armed forces total about 15,000, all paid volunteers. Uruguay is a member of the UN and OAS.

State of Vatican City

STATO DELLA CITTA DEL VATICANO

Area: 108.7 acres. Population: about 700.

The Popes for many centuries, with some slight interruptions, held temporal sovereignty over mid-Italy (the so-called Papal States), comprising an area of some 16,000 sq. mi., with a population in the 19th century of more than 3,000,000. This territory in the reign of Pius IX, was incorporated in the Kingdom of Italy, the sovereignty of the Pope being confined to the palaces of the Vatican and the Lateran in Rome and the villa of Castel Gandolfo, by an Italian law, May 13, 1871. This law also guaranteed to the Pope and his successors in the chair of St. Peter a yearly indemnity of 3,225,000 lire ($622,425 at par of exchange), which allowance, however, remained unclaimed.

Final settlement of the Roman question came when the Treaty of Conciliation, the Concordat and a financial convention were signed in the Lateran Palace, Feb. 11, 1929, by Cardinal Gasparri and Premier Mussolini. The Treaty and Concordat established the independent state of Vatican City, and gave the Catholic religion special status in Italy. The treaty (Lateran Agreement) became effective June 7.

The Lateran Agreement was made an integral part of the Constitution of Italy (Article 7) March 26, 1947.

Vatican City includes St. Peter's, the Vatican Palace and Museum covering more than 13 acres, the Vatican gardens, and neighboring buildings between Viale Vaticano and the Church. Thirteen buildings in Rome, although outside the boundaries, enjoy extra-territorial rights; these include buildings housing the congregations or officers necessary for the administration of the Holy See.

The legal system is based on the code of canon law, the apostolic constitutions and the laws especially promulgated for the Vatican City by the Sovereign Pontiff or those to whom he may delegate legislative power. In all cases not covered the Italian law of Rome applies. The Secretariat of State represents the Holy See in its diplomatic relations. By the Treaty of Conciliation the Pope is pledged to a perpetual neutrality unless his mediation is specifically requested by both parties in political disputes. This, however, does not prevent the defense of the Church whenever it is persecuted. A total of 70 nations maintain diplomatic representatives in Vatican City. The United States does not have an official ambassador, but in June 1970 President Nixon named Henry Cabot Lodge to be his personal envoy.

The present sovereign of the State of Vatican City is the Supreme Pontiff, Paul VI, Giovanni Battista Montini, born in Concesio, Italy, Sept. 26, 1897, elected Pope June 21, 1963, in succession to Angelo Giuseppe Roncalli, John XXIII, who died June 3, 1963.

Venezuela

REPUBLICA DE VENEZUELA

Capital: Caracas. Area: 352,148 sq. mi. Population (UN est. 1972): 10,970,000. Monetary unit: Bolívar.

Venezuela, a land of wide plains and lofty mountains, lies within the Torrid Zone in northern South America, with a 1,700 mile coastline on the Caribbean and the Atlantic. Its neighbors are Guyana, Brazil and Colombia. It includes 72 islands totaling 14,650 sq. mi., the largest being Margarita, 40 mi. by 20, which is one of Venezuela's 20 states and an important pearl center. Venezuela is more than twice the size of California.

The Orinoco River with its tributaries, drains about four-fifths of the country. About 1,700 mi. in length and 13.5 mi. across at its widest point, it is the 2nd largest river system in South America, and is navigable for about 700 mi.

Angel Falls, said to be the tallest in the world, 3,212 ft. in all, with one drop of 2,648 ft., was found on the Churun, a branch of the Caroni River by Jimmy Angel, American aviator, in 1937.

Caracas, the capital, is 12 mi. inland from its port, La Guaira. It has an international airport and airlines reach cities in the interior. It is noted for its modern architecture and luxury hotels. In its Pantheon are enshrined the ashes of Simon Bolivar, South American liberator (1783-1830).

Resources and Industries. Mining, agriculture, fishing and manufacturing are the chief industries. Venezuela in 1972 was the world's 5th largest oil exporter. Lake Maracaibo is the largest oil field in South America. Concessions are held by foreign interests, under state control, with 80% of the income going to the government. Other minerals are iron, gold, copper, coal, salt, nickel, manganese, asbestos, diamonds and mica. Iron ore production is more than 22,000,000 tons annually and is the 2nd most important export, next to oil.

Coffee is the major agricultural product. Exports also include cocoa, canned fish, fruit, sugar, steel products, rice. Industries include steel, petrochemicals, textiles, containers, tobacco products, paper, tires, shoes.

Tourists increased from 95,000 in 1965 to 175,000 in 1972. Attractions include resorts on Margarita Is.; Merida in the Andes with its cable car to snowcapped Mirror Peak, 15,000 ft.; beaches near Caracas.

Construction is booming, including skyscrapers in Caracas; a new $3.8 billion city, Ciudad Guyana, 300 mi. SE of Caracas, and a 4,175-ft. suspension bridge across the Orinoco which was opened in 1967 and is South America's largest.

Oil profits help finance the extensive industrial development. The gross national product rose from $8.9 billion in 1966 to $11.6 billion in 1972.

Oil exports have also provided Venezuela a favorable balance of trade. Oil production and proved reserves dwindled in the 1970s but there were large, undeveloped oil sand resources.

History and Government. Columbus first set foot on the South American continent on the peninsula of Paria, Aug. 1498; on the same voyage he found the mouth of the Orinoco. Alonso de Ojeda, 1499, found Lake Maracaibo, called the land Venezuela, or Little Venice, because na-

tives had houses on stilts. Venezuela was under Spanish domination until about 1821. The republic was formed after secession from the Colombian Federation in 1830.

The 1961 Constitution provided for a strong central government; a President, Senate and Chamber of Deputies elected for 5 years by direct universal vote, and a Supreme Court appointed by the Congress. Member: UN, OAS.

Education and Religion. The language is Spanish and Roman Catholic is the religion of the majority of the people, but religious freedom is guaranteed. All education, including college, is free. Primary education is compulsory.

Defense. Armed forces for 1972-73 totaled about 30,000.

Vietnam

Total area: 127,241 sq. mi. Total population (est. 1972): 41,339,000. Vietnam is split between two hostile governments, the Republic of Vietnam, which controls the southern half, and the Communist regime of North Vietnam.

Vietnam, one of 3 former French Indo-Chinese Associated States, is in SE Asia, bounded on the N by China, on the E and S by the South China Sea, and on the W by Cambodia and Laos. It consists of the former French protectorates of Tonkin and Annam, and former colony of Cochin China. Principal cities are Saigon, Hanoi, Haiphong, Hue and Danang.

Resources and Industries. Chief products are rice, principal food staple; rubber; and coal. Peacetime exports included rubber, rice, fish, coal, lumber, pepper, cattle and hides, corn, zinc and tin. Tea, coffee, and quinine are grown in the South. Rice and coal are chief products of the North; also coffee, tea, maize, sweet potatoes, tobacco, sugar cane and shellac.

History and Government. Vietnam's recorded history began in Tonkin before the Christian era; settled by the Viets who emigrated from central China. It was held by China, 111 B.C.-939 A.D., and was a vassal state during many subsequent periods. Vietnam defeated the armies of Kublai Khan at Bach Dang Giang, 1288. The French and Portuguese came in the late 16th Century. Piecemeal conquest by France began in 1858 and ended in 1884 with acceptance of a French protectorate.

In 1940 Vietnam was occupied by Japan and used as a base for the invasion of Malaya. During the occupation nationalist aims gathered force. A number of groups formed the Vietminh (Independence) League, headed by Ho Chi Minh, Communist guerrilla leader. In August, 1945, the Vietminh forced out Bao Dai, former Emperor of Annam, head of a short-lived regime sponsored by Japan. France, seeking to reestablish colonial control, battled Communist and nationalist forces, 1946-1954, incurring huge losses and was finally defeated at Dienbienphu, May 8, 1954. Meanwhile, on July 1, 1949, Bao Dai had formed a State of Vietnam, with its capital at Saigon and himself as Chief of State, with French approval. Communist China backed Ho Chi Minh.

A cease-fire accord signed in Geneva July 21, 1954, divided Vietnam along the Ben Hai River. It provided for a buffer zone, withdrawal of French troops from Northern Vietnam and elections to determine the country's future. Under the agreement the Communists gained control of the territory north of the 17th parallel, 22 provinces with an area of approx. 62,000 sq. mi. and 13,000,000 pop. (est.), with its capital at Hanoi, and Ho Chi Minh as President. South Vietnam was to comprise the 39 southern provinces with an area of 65,000 sq. mi. and pop. of 12,000,000 (est.). Approx. 800,000 North Vietnamese fled to South Vietnam. Neither South Vietnam nor the U. S. signed the agreement.

Republic of Vietnam

VIET NAM CONG HOA

Capital: Saigon. Area: 65,948 sq. mi. Population (est. 1972): 19,299,000. Monetary unit: Piastre.

On Oct. 26, 1955, Ngo Dinh Diem, Premier of the interim government of South Vietnam, proclaimed the

Southern Zone a republic and became its first President under a provisional constitution act, following a referendum Oct. 23 which ousted Bao Dai as Chief of State.

Fighting persisted from 1956, with the Communist Viet Cong, aided by North Vietnam, pressing a spreading war, and South Vietnam receiving increasing U. S. aid and, by June 1965, active U. S. combat participation.

A serious political conflict arose in 1963 when Buddhist groups charged the government with authoritarianism and brutality. This and government delays in reforms paved the way for a military coup Nov. 1-2, 1963, which overthrew the Diem regime and resulted in the deaths of Pres. Diem and two brothers.

A military triumvirate headed by Maj. Gen. Duong Van Minh formed the nucleus of a 23-member interim junta which was overthrown Jan. 30, 1964, in a bloodless coup led by Maj. Gen. Nguyen Khanh. Other governments followed; Air Force Commander Nguyen Cao Ky became Premier, on June 19, 1965, of the 9th regime since the fall of Pres. Ngo Dinh Diem.

On Sept. 11, 1966, South Vietnamese voters chose members of an assembly which was to draft a new constitution for a civilian government early in 1967.

In elections Sept. 3, 1967, Chief of State Nguyen Van Thieu was chosen Pres. and Premier Ky, Vice Pres. A 60-member Senate was also elected Sept. 3 and 137-member House on Oct. 22. Thieu was reelected Pres. in a one-candidate election, Oct. 3, 1971.

Following attacks on two U. S. destroyers by North Vietnamese PT boats in the Gulf of Tonkin Aug. 2-4, 1964, the U. S. retaliated with heavy air strikes against North Vietnam. Beginning in 1965, the raids were stepped up.

On Mar. 31, 1968, U. S. President Johnson announced the unilateral halting of bombing of North Vietnam, except for the southernmost area, and urged North Vietnam to join in peace talks. Hanoi agreed Apr. 3 to preliminary talks which began May 10 in Paris.

As of Nov. 1, 1968, President Johnson ended air, naval and artillery bombardment of North Vietnam. In Jan. 1969, the Paris peace talks were expanded to include South Vietnam and the National Liberation Front (Viet Cong). By April 1969, the number of U. S. battle deaths had passed the U.S. total in the Korean War (33,629).

U.S. troop strength in Vietnam, which reached a high of 543,400 in Apr. 1969, was ordered reduced by U.S. President Nixon in a series of withdrawals, beginning in June 1969.

On Mar. 30, 1972, North Vietnamese forces launched a massive offensive into South Vietnam across the demilitarized zone and from Laos and Cambodia. The U.S. resumed heavy bombing of North Vietnam military targets and on May 8 President Nixon announced he had ordered the mining of all North Vietnam ports to cut importing of arms. South Vietnamese troops halted the invasion forces after losing much of Quangtri Province.

A ceasefire agreement which President Nixon said would bring "peace with honor" was signed in Paris Jan. 27, 1973 (EST), by the U.S., North and South Vietnam and the Vietcong, to take effect the same day (Jan. 28 in Vietnam). It provided for withdrawal of U.S. troops (about 23,000 were still in Vietnam) and return of U.S. prisoners (590), both within 60 days, an International Commission to supervise the ceasefire, and for the U.S. and North Vietnam to respect the South Vietnamese people's right to self-determination.

Fighting between North and South Vietnamese forces continued, but on a reduced scale.

(See also Vietnam in Index.)

Most Vietnamese practice parts of several religions or mixtures of Confucianism, Taoism, Buddhism, ancestor worship and animism. About 20% practice Buddhism and about 12% Roman Catholicism. New indigenous religions include Cao Dai (1919) and Hoa Hao (1939). There are 7 universities.

Democratic Republic of Vietnam

VIET NAM DAN CHU CONG HOA

Capital: Hanoi. Area: 61,293 sq. mi. Population (UN est. 1971): 21,600,000. Monetary unit: Dong.

A Vietminh constitution, adopted Dec. 31, 1959, is based on Communist principles and calls for reunification of all Vietnam. It provides for a President elected by Parliament and a Prime Minister appointed by the President. President Ho Chi Minh, reelected July 15, 1960, by unanimous vote of the National Assembly, had held office since 1945. He died Sept. 3, 1969 and was succeeded as President by Ton Duc Thang.

North Vietnam sought to take over South Vietnam beginning in 1954. Aid to Viet Cong Guerrillas was intensified in 1959 and with large-scale troop infiltration in 1964. In that year U.S. response increased with bombing of military targets in North Vietnam; the bombings were ended in 1968 but renewed in 1972. North Vietnam had large forces in Laos and Cambodia and, at the time of the Vietnam ceasefire, Jan. 27, 1973 (EST), 145,000 troops in South Vietnam.

(See also Vietnam and Wars in Index.)

Western Samoa

Capital: Apia. Area: 1,110 sq. mi. Population (UN est. 1972): 150,000. Monetary unit: Tala.

Western Samoa, which became an independent nation Jan. 1, 1962, comprises 4 inhabited islands of a group in the South Pacific Ocean lying about 2,613 mi. SW of Hawaii. Largest of the islands are **Savaii** and **Upolu.** Eastern Samoa, the smaller portion of the group with its capital at Pago Pago, is a dependency of the U.S.

Western Samoa was a German colony, 1899 to 1914, when New Zealand landed troops and took over. It became a New Zealand mandate under the League of Nations and, in 1945, a New Zealand UN Trusteeship.

An elected local government took office in Oct. 1959 and the country became fully independent in 1962. New Zealand has continued economic aid and educational assistance. Western Samoa changed from pounds to decimal currency July 10, 1967.

The population is composed almost solely of Polynesians. The islands are fertile and life is leisurely. Chief products are tropical hardwoods, fish, cocoa, coconuts, bananas, taro, coffee, bark cloth (tapa), mats.

Robert Louis Stevenson's grave is on a hill near Apia.

People's Democratic Republic of Yemen

Capitals: Aden and Medina as-Shaab. Area: 112,000 sq. mi. Population (UN est. 1972): 1,510,000. Monetary unit: Dinar.

This nation became independent as the People's Republic of Southern Yemen Nov. 30, 1967, after 129 years of British rule. It changed it's name to People's Democratic Republic of Yemen on Nov. 30, 1970. It consists of the port city of Aden, 17 states of the former South Arabian Federation, 3 small sheikdoms, 3 larger sultanates, Quaiti, Kathiri and Mahri, which made up the Eastern Aden Protectorate, and Socotra, the largest island in the Arabian Sea.

One of the cities mentioned in the Bible, Aden has been a port for trade in incense, spices and silk between the East and West for 2,000 years. British rule began in 1839 when the British East India Co. seized control to put an end to the piracy threatening trade with India. Aden provided Britain with a controlling position at the southern entrance to the Red Sea.

With only 1% of the land fertile and few mineral deposits, the Port of Aden has been the area's most valuable natural resource. The port is 10 mi. across, well-sheltered and deep. In 1966 more than 6,000 ships put in at Aden for refueling, servicing and transshipment of goods, bringing over 227,000 visitors and $22,000,000.

But, with the closing of the Suez Canal because of the Israeli-Arab War in June 1967, the port lost much of its business. The nation is a UN member.

The struggle for independence began in earnest in

Dec. 1963, when two nationalist groups, the National Liberation Front (NLF) and the Egypt-supported Front for the Liberation of Occupied South Yemen, waged a guerrilla war against the British and local dynastic rulers. The two groups vied with each other for political control. The NLF succeeded in naming the first President, Qahtan al-Shaabi. In a June 1969 coup the left wing of the NLF seized power.

The new government broke off relations with the U. S. and nationalized some foreign firms. Aid has been furnished by the USSR and Communist China.

In 1972 there were border skirmishes with forces of the Yemen Arab Republic.

Yemen Arab Republic

Capital: Sana. Area: 75,289 sq. mi. Population (UN est. 1972): 6,060,000. Monetary unit: Yemeni rial.

Yemen is an ancient, mountainous country, near the southern tip of the Arabian Peninsula on the Red Sea. Its neighbors are the People's Democratic Republic of Yemen (formerly Southern Yemen) and Saudi Arabia. It is about the size of Nebraska.

Hodeida, Mocha and Loheiya are major ports. Marib and Sana are archeological sites.

Resources and Industries. On the plateau of El Jebel, the most fertile section of Arabia, coffee, barley and grain are grown. Mocha coffee, hides, dates, cotton, sesame, herbs, fruits and precious stones are exported.

Oil was discovered in 1972.

History and Government. Yemen's territory once was part of the ancient kingdom of Sheba, or Saba, a prosperous link in trade between Africa and India. A Biblical reference speaks of its gold, spices and precious stones as gifts borne by the Queen of Sheba to King Solomon.

Yemen was described as a democratic Islamic monarchy during the regime of the Imam Ahmed, who had ruled 1948-1962. The King was reported assassinated Sept. 26, 1962, and a revolutionary group headed by Brig. Gen. Abdullah al-Salal declared the country to be the Yemen Arab Republic. He became president.

The Imam Ahmed's heir, the Imam Mohamad al-Badr, fled to the mountains where tribesmen joined royalist forces; internal warfare between them and the republican forces continued. Egyptian Pres. Nasser sent 70,000 troops to aid the republicans; Saudi Arabia supported the royalists with military aid.

After Egypt's defeat in the June 1967 Israeli-Arab war, Egypt announced it would withdraw its troops from Yemen; the last of them left Nov. 29, 1967, and Saudi Arabia said it would stop aiding the royalists.

This was accompanied by a bloodless coup in which the government of Pres. al-Salal was overthrown, Nov. 5, 1967. Leadership was taken over by a Presidential Council headed by Abdul Rahman al-Iryani, who later became president.

Fighting continued between the Republican and royalist forces; troops from Southern Yemen aided those of the Republicans in 1968. Saudi Arabia announced in Feb. 1968 it was renewing its aid to the royalists, charging that both Soviet Russia and Syria, as well as Southern Yemen, were aiding the Republicans.

In April 1970 hostilities ended with an agreement between Yemen and Saudi Arabia and appointment of several royalists to the Yemen government.

There were border skirmishes with forces of the People's Democratic Republic of Yemen in 1972-73. The U.S. and Yemen in 1972 resumed diplomatic relations, broken by Yemen after the 1967 Arab-Israeli war.

Yemen is a member of the UN and Arab League.

Yugoslavia

Capital: Belgrade. Area: 98,766 sq. mi. Population (UN est. 1972): 20,770,000. Monetary unit: Dinar.

The Socialist Federal Republic of Yugoslavia is a rugged mountainous land, densely forested, which rises from the eastern shore of the Adriatic Sea. Its neighbors are Italy, Austria, Hungary, Romania, Bulgaria, Greece and Albania. It is about the size of Wyoming.

The federation comprises 6 republics: Serbia, Croatia, Slovenia, Montenegro, Bosnia-Herzegovina and Macedonia, and 2 autonomous provinces: Kosovo and Vojvodina.

Resources and Industries. Chief crops are cereals, maize, wheat, barley, rye, tobacco, oats, hops and fruits. The principal minerals are coal, iron, copper, chrome ore, antimony, manganese, lead, mercury, salt and bauxite.

Because of its intensive program of industrialization the country is gradually losing its predominantly agricultural character. Most industry is socialized and private enterprise is limited to small-scale production. Since 1952 workers are guaranteed a basic wage and a share in cooperative profits.

Management of industrial enterprises is handled by workers' councils. Farmland is 85% privately owned but farms are restricted to 25 acres.

Yugoslavia has conducted several large-scale programs to improve its economy. Beginning in the late 1950s, successful efforts were made to strengthen agriculture by improving fertilizers, grain varieties and livestock.

Tourism was promoted, particularly along the country's colorful Adriatic coast. Large numbers of visitors from nations of the West provided an important source of foreign income.

Beginning in 1965, reforms designed to decentralize the administration of economic development and to force industries to produce more efficiently in competition with foreign producers were introduced.

Yugoslavia has developed considerable trade with Western Europe as well as with the USSR and Eastern European countries and elsewhere. While its import-export balance has continued to show deficits, money earned by Yugoslavs working temporarily in Western Europe, and money brought in by tourists come close to making these up. In 1970 a trade treaty was signed with the European Common Market.

The index for industrial production (1963 = 100) was 200 for 1972.

Foreign trade in thousands of U.S. dollars:

	Imports	Exports
1971	$3,298,000	$1,837,000
1972	$3,233,000	$2,237,000

History and Government. Serbia, which had since the Battle of Kosovo (1389), been a vassal principality of Turkey, was established as an independent kingdom by the Treaty of Berlin, 1878. After the Balkan wars its boundaries were enlarged by the annexation of Old Serbia and Macedonia, 1913. When the Austrian Archduke Francis Ferdinand and wife were assassinated at Sarajevo June 28, 1914, the Austrian government forced war on Serbia, the onset of World War I, 1914-1918.

When the Austro-Hungarian empire collapsed, the Kingdom of the Serbs, Croats and Slovenes was formed from the former provinces of Croatia, Dalmatia, Bosnia, Herzegovina, Slovenia, Voyvodina and the independent state of Montenegro, with Peter I of Serbia as king. The name was later changed to Yugoslavia. Peter (d. 1921) was succeeded by his son Alexander I (assassinated at Marseille Oct. 9, 1934), after which Prince Paul became regent. He was overthrown in Mar. 1941 and Crown Prince Peter, born Sept. 6, 1923, was proclaimed king. Germany invaded April, 1941, and King Peter II fled to London.

But many Yugoslav troops continued to fight the Nazis from their mountainous strongholds. Among these guerrilla forces were the Chetniks led by Draja Mikhailovich, who became involved in open warfare with other partisan forces led by Josip Broz, known as Marshal Tito, for control of the resistance movement. Tito, backed by the USSR and Great Britain, won and by the time the Germans had been driven from Yugoslavia in 1944, was in control. Mikhailovich was captured and executed in Belgrade July 17, 1946, by the Tito regime.

The constituent assembly proclaimed Yugoslavia a republic Nov. 29, 1945. It became a federated republic Jan. 31, 1946, and Marshal Tito, a Communist, became head of the government. By terms of a treaty with Italy the greater part of Venezia-Giulia, Zara, Pelagosa and adjacent islands were ceded to Yugoslavia.

The Stalin policy of dictating the Communist line to all Communist nations was rejected by Marshal Tito. He accepted economic aid and military equipment from the U. S. and received aid in foreign trade also from France and Great Britain.

Yugoslavia is governed by the President, as chairman of a 22-man collective presidency (created in 1971), a Premier, and a parliament (Federal Assembly), from which cabinet members are drawn.

A new constitution was approved by Parliament, Apr. 7, 1963, replacing that in force since 1946. It made the country's official name the Socialist Federal Republic of Yugoslavia, limited political parties to the Communists and the Communist-dominated Socialist Alliance of Working People, and provided that future presidents be elected by parliament and restricted to two consecutive 4-year terms. The ballot is secret and freedom of worship is guaranteed. Tito was reelected President for 5 more years in July 1971.

Pres. Tito supported the liberalization government of Czechoslovakia in 1968 before its fall under Russian pressure. But Tito paid a friendship visit to Moscow in 1972.

A separatist movement among Croatians, 2nd to the Serbs in numbers, brought arrests and a change of government leaders in the Croatian Republic in Jan. 1972.

Education and Religion. All education is free; elementary training is compulsory to age 14. There are 7 universities. Principal languages are Slovene, Macedonian, Serbo-Croat. All religions are recognized and enjoy equal rights. Serbo-Orthodox comprises 42%, Roman Catholic 32%, Moslem 12%.

Complete free social security is in force, including unemployment, medical, maternity benefits.

Defense. Military forces in 1972-73 totalled 229,000.

Zaire
(DEMOCRATIC REPUBLIC OF CONGO)

Capital: Kinshasa (former Leopoldville). Area (estimated): 905,328 sq. mi. Population (UN est. 1972): 22,860,000. Monetary unit: Zaire.

The Democratic Republic of Congo changed its name to Republic of Zaire on Oct. 27, 1971; the Congo River was changed to Zaire and in 1972 Zairians with Christian names were ordered to change them to African names.

Until June 30, 1960, the Congo was a colony of Belgium in Equatorial Africa, entirely inland except for 25 mi. on the Atlantic Ocean, N of the mouth of the Congo (Zaire) River. It is larger than Texas and Alaska combined.

Along the eastern border lie several of Africa's Great Lakes. North of the Equator on the Uganda border, stand the Ruwenzori Mtns., believed to be the "Mountains of the Moon" of ancient legend. Mt. Margherita is 16,763 ft.

The Zaire River, one of the world's longest, rises near the Zambian border in the SE and flows 2,718 mi. N, then W and finally SW, emptying into the South Atlantic.

Wildlife is abundant and includes most of the species Africa is famous for: elephant, lion, gorilla, hippopotamus, crocodile, python, etc.

Resources and Industry. There are extensive mineral deposits in the Katanga, Ituri and Kivu highlands. Zaire normally produces 6% of the world's copper and over 45% of its cobalt and industrial diamonds. Also produced are cadmium, gold, silver, tin, germanium, zinc, iron, tungsten, manganese, uranium and radium.

Tropical rain forests cover much of the land; trees often are 150 to 200 ft. tall. They include mahogany, ebony, teak, copal, palms, cedars and gum and resin trees. Some livestock is raised in insect-free areas. Bananas, coffee, rubber, mangoes, plantain, coconuts are grown. Chief agricultural exports are fats and oils, timber, coffee, cotton, rubber, tea, cocoa, and bananas.

History and Government. Leopold II, King of the Bel-

gians, formed an international group to exploit the Congo in 1876. In 1877 Henry M. Stanley explored the Congo and in 1878 the King's group sent him back to organize the region and win over the native chiefs. Claims having been advanced by Portugal and others, the Conference of Berlin, 1884-85, organized the Congo Free State with Leopold as King and chief owner. Exploitation of native laborers on the rubber plantations caused international criticism and led to granting of a colonial charter, Oct. 18, 1908, whereby the state became a Belgian colony.

Belgian and Congolese leaders agreed Jan. 27, 1960, that the Congo would become independent June 30. In the first general elections, May 31, the National Congolese movement of Patrice Lumumba won 35 of 137 seats in the National Assembly, lower House of Parliament. He was appointed Premier June 21, and formed a coalition cabinet. Belgium's King Baudouin formally proclaimed the territory's independence at Leopoldville (now Kinshasa) June 30, 1960.

Widespread violence in which mutinous Congolese troops took part caused Europeans and others to flee the country. Pres. Moise Tshombe of Katanga seceded from the republic July 11, but ended the secession Jan. 15, 1963. Katanga was the seat of the copper-mining operations of the Union Miniere, which paid taxes formerly sufficient to defray one-half of the costs of the government. The UN Security Council Aug. 9, 1960, called on Belgium to withdraw its troops and sent a UN contingent to guard against civil war. Pres. Kasavubu removed Lumumba as premier and Lumumba fought for control with the backing of Ghana, Guinea and India. On Feb. 12, 1961, Lumumba was murdered by tribesmen in Katanga.

The last UN troops left the Congo June 30, 1964, and Cyrille Abdoula, Premier since Aug. 1, 1961, resigned, succeeded by Tshombe.

On Sept. 7, 1964, leftist rebels set up a "People's Republic" in Stanleyville with Christopher Gbenye as president. Premier Tshombe hired foreign mercenaries and sought to rebuild the Congolese Army. In Nov. and Dec. 1964 rebels slew scores of white hostages and thousands of Congolese: Belgian paratroops, dropped from U. S. transport planes, rescued hundreds. By July 1965 the rebels, though supplied with smuggled arms, had lost their effectiveness.

Growing rivalry between Pres. Kasavubu and Premier Tshombe ended when the former ousted the latter from office Oct. 13, 1965. Evariste Kimba became Premier but both he and Pres. Kasavubu were ousted Nov. 25 by Gen. Joseph D. Mobutu who was named President. He later changed his name to Mobutu Sese Seko.

In March 1966 Pres. Mobutu took over from Parliament all of its legislative powers. On July 1 he renamed Leopoldville Kinshasa; Stanleyville, Kisangani; and Elisabethville, Lubumbashi.

In 1967 a revolt, led by Belgian and French mercenaries, broke out in the eastern area. This revolt died and most of the mercenaries fled the country; the government was aided by 3 large U.S. transport planes sent to the area to help transport government troops and supplies.

In 1969-73, political stability under Pres. Mobutu was reflected in improved economic conditions. In 1970, he was elected to a 7-year term as President.

Education and Religion. The population is principally Bantu. More than 200 tribes are represented. Swahili, Lingala, Tshiluba and Kikongo are widely spoken; French is the official language. There are an estimated 9,000,000 African Christians, predominantly Roman Catholic. There are 3 universities.

Zambia

Capital: Lusaka. Area: 290,586 sq. mi. Population (UN est 1972): 4,420,000. Monetary unit: Kwacha.

The Republic of Zambia is the former British Protectorate of Northern Rhodesia. It is a land-locked country located in South Central Africa. Bordering it are Zaire, Tanzania, Malawi, Mozambique, Rhodesia, Botswana, South-West Africa (Namibia) and Angola. It is slightly larger than Texas.

The terrain is mostly high plateau covered with thin forest and suitable for both farming and grazing. The country is rich in minerals, including copper, zinc, cobalt, gold, vanadium, manganese, and coal. Zambia's wealth is mainly its copper; it is one of the world's largest copper producers.

Victoria Falls on the Zambezi River, the border with Rhodesia, is 3 times the width and more than twice the height of Niagara. Further down the river, the Kariba Dam, in 1961 created Lake Kariba, 175 mi. long.

As Northern Rhodesia, the country was under the administration of the South Africa Company, 1889 until 1924 when the office of governor was established, with an executive council and, subsequently, a legislature.

A new constitution, announced in 1963, granted internal self-government with a prime minister and cabinet, effective Jan. 22, 1964. The United National Independence party won the first elections Jan. 21 and its leader, Kenneth D. Kaunda, became the country's first Prime Minister. He was elected President and, on Oct. 24, 1964, Zambia became an independent republic within the Commonwealth. It has a National Assembly of 105

elected members and 5 nominated by the President. In 1973 a new constitution provided for a one-party system. Zambia is a member of the UN and the OAU.

After the white government of Rhodesia declared its independence from Britain Nov. 17, 1965, relations between Zambia and Rhodesia became strained and use of their jointly owned railroad was disputed.

Britain gave Zambia an extra $12,000,000 in 1966 after imposing an oil embargo on Rhodesia, and Zambia set up a temporary airlift to carry copper out from its mines and gasoline in. In Aug. 1968 a 1,958-mi. pipeline was completed, bringing oil from Tanzania. In 1973 a truck road to carry copper to Tanzania's port of Dar es Salaam was completed with U.S. aid; a railroad, being built with Chinese aid across Tanzania, reached the Zambian border.

As part of a program of government participation in major industries, a government corporation in 1970 took over 51% of the ownership of two foreign-owned copper mining companies, paying with bonds.

Gross National Product Estimates
(Non-Communist Nations)
For Calendar Year 1971 in Current Market Prices
Compiled by Agency for International Development

Nation	GNP Total $ Millions	GNP Per Capita $	Approx. Rate Per US $ 1971	Nation	GNP Total $ Millions	GNP Per Capita $	Approx. Rate Per US $ 1971
Afghanistan	1,575	90	45 afghanis	Ivory Coast	1,675	387	256 CFA francs
Algeria	5,300	370	4.55 dinars	Jamaica	1,386	729	.769 J $
Argentina	27,150	1,111	5 pesos	Japan	256,380	2,450	308 yen
Australia	43,300	3,370	.8224 A $	Jordan	575	286	.357 J pounds
Austria	17,840	2,411	23.3 schillings	Kenya	1,725	140	7 14 shillings
Bangladesh	4,300	60	.....	Korea, South	8,450	261	373 won
Barbados	177	745	1.84 EC $	Kuwait	3,460	4,170	.329 dinars
Belgium	31,660	3,274	44.82 francs	Laos	198	65	240 kips
Bolivia	1,072	225	12 pesos	Lebanon	1,770	580	3.16 L pounds
Botswana	67	105	.7134 rands	Lesotho	96	90	.7143 rands
Brazil	41,230	421	5.635 cruzeiros	Liberia	375	238	1 $
Burma	1,959	69	5.35 kyats	Libya	3,946	2,036	.329 dinars
Burundi	220	60	87.5 francs	Luxembourg	1,136	3,331	50 francs
Cambodia	655	90	55.54 riels	Malagasy Rep.	1,040	150	256 M francs
Cameroon	1,150	195	256 CFA francs	Malawi	406	89	.7675 kwacha
Canada	92,410	4,279	1 C $	Malaysia	4,298	384	2.82 M $
Cen. African Rep.	220	145	277.71 CFA francs	Mali	313	60	555.42 francs
Chad	290	76	277.71 CFA francs	Malta	280	862	.3744 pounds
Chile	7,540	795	15.8 escudos	Mauritania	215	180	.4167 pounds
China (Taiwan)	6,230	416	40 NT $	Mauritius	226	265	5.12 rupees
Colombia	6,860	315	21 pesos	Mexico	35,660	689	12.5 pesos
Congo (Brazza)	250	260	277.71 CFA francs	Morocco	4,011	245	4.66 dirhans
Costa Rica	1,024	570	6.65 colones	Nepal	903	80	10.125 rupees
Cyprus	673	1,053	.3838 pounds	Netherlands	39,440	2,990	3.245 guilders
Dahomey	250	97	277.71 CFA francs	New Zealand	7,610	2,670	.8224 NZ $
Denmark	18,240	3,612	6.98 kroner	Nicaragua	889	463	7 cordobas
Dominican Rep.	1,601	382	1 peso	Niger	400	100	277.71 CFA francs
Ecuador	1,684	261	25.25 sucres	Nigeria	6,730	120	.3571 pounds
Egypt	6,970	207	.435 E pounds	Norway	13,570	3,479	6.645 kroner
El Salvador	1,062	300	2.5 colones	Pakistan	4,740	79	11 rupees
Equatorial Guinea	80	277	.....	Panama	1,142	772	1 balboa
Ethiopia	2,031	79	2.3 E $	Paraguay	652	267	126 guaranies
Finland	11,500	2,457	4.1 markkaa	Peru	6,720	480	38.7 soles
France	176,770	3,449	5.116 francs	Philippines	7,660	194	6.43 pesos
Gabon	375	775	256 CFA francs	Portugal	7,430	756	27.25 escudos
Gambia	50	135	2.0833 dalasis	Rhodesia	1,573	273	.75 R $
Germany, West	235,460	3,791	3.223 marks	Rwanda	242	65	100 francs
Ghana	2,067	221	1.28 cedi	Saudi Arabia	3,910	708	4.145 riyals
Greece	10,770	1,222	30 drachmas	Senegal	800	205	277.71 CFA francs
Guatemala	1,955	355	1 quetzal	Sierra Leone	510	188	.7675 leones
Guinea	325	81	277.71 francs	Singapore	2,482	1,160	3.06 S $
Guyana	270	365	2 G $	Somali Rep.	250	88	7.143 shillings
Haiti	462	93	5 gourdes	South Africa	17,500	766	.75 rands
Honduras	733	262	2 lempiras	Spain	39,400	1,154	64.47 pesetas
Iceland	597	2,898	88 kronur	Sri Lanka (Ceylon)	2,130	167	5.95 rupees
India	57,830	100	7.28 rupees	Sudan	1,900	117	.348 pounds
Indonesia	8,430	69	415 rupees	Swaziland	91	210	.75 rands
Iran	12,750	428	75.75 rials	Sweden	38,040	4,690	4.813 kronor
Iraq	3,800	393	.329 dinars	Switzerland	26,280	4,158	3.84 francs
Ireland	4,967	1,672	.3838 pounds	Syria	1,978	307	3.82 pounds
Israel	5,554	1,823	4.2 I pounds	Tanzania	1,411	103	7.14 shillings
Italy	108,210	2,001	581.5 lire	Thailand	6,951	181	20.8 baht

Nation	GNP Total	GNP Cap.	Rate Per $	Nation	GNP Total	GNP Cap.	Rate Per $
Togo	300	149	256 CFA francs	Uruguay	2,039	697	370 pesos
Trinidad-Tobago	961	933	1.84 T&T $	Venezuela	11,170	1,004	4.4 bolivares
Tunisia	1,741	331	.484 dinars	Vietnam, South	2,350	125	275 piastres
Turkey	13,030	360	14 liras	Yemen (Aden)	165	110	......
Uganda	1,415	141	7.14 shillings	Yemen (Sana)	472	80	1.25 rials
United Kingdom	146,860	2,653	.3838 pounds	Zaire	2,072	114	.5 zaires
Upper Volta	353	64	256 CFA francs	Zambia	1,500	330	.714 kwacha

National Population Density, Growth Rate, Life Expectancy

Source: United Nations Demographic Yearbook 1971

Country	Density[1]	Growth Rate[2]	Life Expectancy[3]	Country	Density[1]	Growth Rate[2]	Life Expectancy[3]
Algeria	6	3.5	50.7 *†	Korea, South	324	2.2	62.04
Argentina	8	1.5	64.06 *	Kuwait	47	9.8	64.4 *†
Australia	2	1.9	68.46	Liberia	14		50.8 *
Austria	89	0.5	67.32	Mali	4	2.1	37.2 *
Belgium	319	0.6	68.39	Mexico	26	3.2	61.03 *
Bolivia	5	2.6	56.11	Mongolia	1	2.8	57.7 *†
Brazil	11	2.8	60.7 *†	Morocco	34		50.5 *†
Bulgaria	77	0.7	70.28	Netherlands	323	1.2	70.8
Canada	2	1.8	69.53	New Zealand	11	1.5	69.17
Ceylon	193	2.2	64.6	Nigeria	61	2.5	44.5
Chad	3	2.3	34.0	Norway	12	0.8	71.42
Chile	12	1.4	61.1	Panama	20	3.0	62.78
China	82	1.8	50.0 *†	Peru	11	3.1	52.59 *
Colombia	19	3.2	50.36	Philippines	127	3.0	54.74
Cuba	76	2.3	66.8 *†	Poland	105	0.8	68.98
Czechoslovakia	113	0.5	68.18	Portugal			68.63
Denmark	115	0.7	71.0	Puerto Rico	310	1.4	69.57
Egypt	34	2.5	56.2	Rhodesia	14	3.4	51.4 *†
Ethiopia	21	1.8	38.5 *†	Romania	86	1.1	69.02
Finland	14	0.4	65.8	Saudi Arabia	4	2.7	42.3 *†
France	94	0.9	67.9	Senegal	21	2.4	41.0 *†
Germany, East	148	−0.1	69.77	Singapore	3,632	2.2	68.2 *†
Germany, West	239	0.8	68.34	South Africa	18	3.1	49.0 *†
Ghana	37	3.0	47.95	Spain	68	1.1	69.15
Greece	68		70.47	Sudan	6	2.8	47.6 *†
Guatemala	49	3.1	52.49	Sweden	18	0.8	71.88
Guinea	16	2.2	33.0	Switzerland	154	1.2	69.43
Haiti	179	2.0	38.37 †	Syria	35	3.3	52.8 *†
Hong Kong	3,912	2.1	67.99	Tanzania	14	2.6	41.0 *†
Hungary	111	0.4	68.38	Thailand	69	2.7	53.6 *
Iceland	2	1.8	71.2	Turkey	46	2.5	53.7 *†
India	168	2.2	48.42	USSR	11	1.1	65.0 *
Indonesia	84	2.8	47.5 *	United Kingdom	228	0.4	69.1
Iran	18	3.0	50.0 *†	United States	22	1.1	71.2 *†
Ireland	42	0.5	69.33	Uruguay	16	1.2	67.99
Israel	146	3.0	70.34	Venezuela			68.75 †
Italy	180	0.8	69.59	Vietnam, North	136	2.4	50.0 *†
Jamaica	173	1.4	65.62	Vietnam, South			50.0 *†
Japan	283	1.1	69.26	Yugoslavia	80	1.0	67.59
Kenya	20	3.1	47.5 *†	Zaire	10	4.2	42.45
Korea, North	118	2.8	57.7 *†	Zambia	6	2.9	43.5 *†

(1) persons per sq. kilometer; (2) percent annual rate of increase, 1963-71; (3) for males at age one, except (*) at birth and (†) both sexes. Life expectancy figures are arrived at from statistics and estimates from a variety of years since 1950.

Population of World's Largest Urban Areas

City populations often cannot be used to compare urban areas because city limits may fall short of or exceed the built-up or urban area. The problem of comparison is compounded by the difficulty in obtaining reliable population data for a common year. The ranking of urban areas below represents one attempt at comparing the world's largest urban areas, taking into account, where necessary and within the limits of available data, urban development extending outward from the principal city named in the table. Thus, the Tokyo area included Tokyo plus neighboring smaller cities, towns and villages. (Some computations include Yokohama as part of Tokyo's urban population.) New York's urban area in 1970 included part or all the population of 10 New Jersey and 5 New York counties in addition to the 5 boroughs of New York city. However, the urban population figures reported for Bombay, Djakarta, Hamburg, Istanbul, Kiev, Madras, Peking, Seoul, Singapore, Shanghai and Tientsin did not run beyond the city limits.

*New York, N.Y. (census 1970)	16,206,841	Djakarta, Indonesia (census 1971)	4,576,009
Tokyo, Japan (census 1973)	11,324,417	Rio de Janeiro, Brazil (census 1970)	4,296,782
Shanghai, China (est. 1970)	10,820,000	Tientsin, China (est. 1970)	4,280,000
Paris, France (est. 1970)	9,250,647	Essen (Ruhr-Gebiet), W. Germany (est. 1966)	4,259,230
Mexico City, Mexico (census 1970)	8,541,070	Victoria-Hong Kong (est. 1970)	4,127,800
Buenos Aires, Argentina (census 1970)	8,408,930	Philadelphia, Pa.-N.J. (census 1970)	4,021,066
Los Angeles-Long Beach (census 1970)	8,351,266	Leningrad, USSR (est. 1971)	4,002,000
Osaka, Japan (census 1973)	7,838,722	Detroit, Mich. (census 1970)	3,970,584
Peking, China (est. 1970)	7,570,000	Delhi, India (census 1971)	3,629,842
London, England (est. 1971)	7,418,020	Karachi, Pakistan (est. 1971)	3,442,000
Moscow, USSR (est. 1971)	7,172,000	Berlin, E. & W. Germany (est. 1970)	3,218,028
Calcutta, India (census 1971)	7,005,362	Madrid, Spain (census 1970)	3,146,071
Chicago, Ill. (census 1970)	6,714,578	Bangkok, Thailand (census 1970)	3,051,000
Bombay, India (census 1971)	5,968,546	Manila, Philippines (census 1973)	3,000,000
Sao Paulo, Brazil (census 1970)	5,901,533	San Francisco-Oakland, Calif. (census 1970)	2,987,850
Seoul, Rep. of Korea (census 1970)	5,536,377	Bogota, Colombia (est. 1972)	2,800,000
Cairo, Egypt (est. 1970)	4,961,000	Rome, Italy (est. 1970)	2,755,135

Montreal, Canada (census 1971)	2,743,203	Singapore (census 1970)	2,074,507
Teheran, Iran (census 1966)	2,719,730	Nagoya, Japan (census 1970)	2,036,053
Sydney, Australia (census 1971)	2,717,069	Alexandria, Egypt (est. 1970)	2,032,000
Santiago, Chile (census 1970)	2,661,920	Lahore, Pakistan (est. 1971)	1,986,000
Boston, Mass. (census 1970)	2,652,575	Cleveland, Ohio (census 1970)	1,959,880
Toronto, Canada (census 1971)	2,628,043	Budapest, Hungary (census 1970)	1,940,200
Lima, Peru (est. 1970)	2,541,300	St. Louis, Mo.-Ill. (census 1970)	1,882,944
Athens, Greece (census 1971)	2,540,000	Pusan, Rep. of Korea (census 1970)	1,880,710
Washington, D.C.-Md.-Va. (census 1970)	2,481,489	Canton, China (est. 1958)	1,867,000
Madras, India (census 1971)	2,470,288	Vienna, Austria (census 1971)	1,858,700
Shengyang, (Mukden) China (est. 1958)	2,423,000	Pittsburgh, Pa. (census 1970)	1,846,042
Melbourne, Australia (census 1971)	2,388,941	Hamburg, W. Germany (est. 1970)	1,818,600
Manchester, England (census 1971)	2,386,774	Hyderabad, India (census 1971)	1,798,910
Birmingham, England (census 1971)	2,369,205	Barcelona, Spain (census 1970)	1,745,142
Istanbul, Turkey (census 1970)	2,247,630	Glasgow, Scotland (census 1971)	1,728,149
Yokohama, Japan (census 1970)	2,238,000	Leeds, England (census 1971)	1,726,097
Wuhan, China (est. 1958)	2,226,000	Rangoon, Burma (est. 1968)	1,717,649
Caracas, Venezuela (est. 1970)	2,175,400	Taipei, Taiwan (census 1970)	1,712,108
Chungking, China (est. 1958)	2,165,000	Milan, Italy (est. 1970)	1,707,576

* New York-Northeastern New Jersey urbanized area, including the 5 boroughs of New York City plus all or part of the counties of Nassau, Putnam, Rockland, Suffolk and Westchester in New State and all or part of the counties of Bergen, Essex, Hudson, Middlesex, Morris, Passaic, Somerset, Union, Mommouth and Ocean in New Jersey.

UNITED NATIONS
History, Membership, Organization and Purpose

The 28th regular session of the United Nations General Assembly opened Sept. 18, 1973. See Chronology for developments at UN sessions during 1973.

Foundations of the United Nations were laid at the Dumbarton Oaks Conference in Washington between the United States, the United Kingdom and the Soviet Union, Aug. 21-Sept. 28, 1944, and between the United States, the United Kingdom and the Republic of China (Nationalist) Sept. 29-Oct 7, 1944. Proposals to establish an organization of nations for maintenance of world peace led to the United Nations Conference on International Organization at San Francisco, Apr. 25-June 26, 1945, where the charter of the United Nations was drawn up. It was signed June 26 by 50 nations, and by Poland, one of the original 51, on Oct. 15, 1945. The charter came into effect Oct. 25, 1945, when the requisite ratification by the 5 permanent members of the Security Council, China, France, Soviet Union, United Kingdom and United States, and a majority of other signatories had been completed.

United Nations headquarters are located in New York, N. Y., between First Ave. and Roosevelt Drive and E. 42nd St. and E. 48th St. The General Assembly Bldg. (opened 1952), Secretariat, Conference and Library bldgs. are interconnected. The Dag Hammarskjold Library, built by a $6,200,000 grant from the Ford Foundation, was dedicated Nov. 16, 1961. It has room for 400,000 vols. To build the headquarters the U. S. Government advanced an interest-free loan of $65,000,000, payable in annual installments until 1982. John D. Rockefeller, Jr., contributed $8,000,000 for land and the City of New York contributed an est. $26,500,000 for adapting the site. United Nations has a post office originating its own stamps. See Postal Information.

Roster of the United Nations
(As of Sept. 18, 1973)
The 135 Members of the United Nations, with the dates on which they become Members.

Member	Date	Member	Date	Member	Date
Afghanistan	Nov. 19, 1946	Finland	Dec. 14, 1955	Mauritius	Apr. 24, 1968
Albania	Dec. 14, 1955	France	Oct. 24, 1945	Mexico	Nov. 7, 1945
Algeria	Oct. 8, 1962	Gabon	Sept. 20, 1960	Mongolia	Oct. 27, 1961
Argentina	Oct. 24, 1945	Gambia	Sept. 21, 1965	Morocco	Nov. 12, 1956
Australia	Nov. 1, 1945	Germany, East	Sept. 18, 1973	Nepal	Dec. 14, 1955
Austria	Dec. 14, 1955	Germany, West	Sept. 18, 1973	Netherlands	Dec. 10, 1945
Bahamas	Sept. 18, 1973	Ghana	Mar. 8, 1957	New Zealand	Oct. 24, 1945
Bahrain	Sept. 21, 1971	Greece	Oct. 25, 1945	Nicaragua	Oct. 24, 1945
Barbados	Dec. 9, 1966	Guatemala	Nov. 21, 1945	Niger	Sept. 20, 1960
Belgium	Dec. 27, 1945	Guinea	Dec. 12, 1958	Nigeria	Oct. 7, 1960
Bhutan	Sept. 21, 1971	Guyana	Sept. 20, 1966	Norway	Nov. 27, 1945
Bolivia	Nov. 14, 1945	Haiti	Oct. 24, 1945	Oman	Oct. 7, 1971
Botswana	Oct. 17, 1966	Honduras	Dec. 17, 1945	Pakistan	Sept. 30, 1947
Brazil	Oct. 24, 1945	Hungary	Dec. 14, 1955	Panama	Nov. 13, 1945
Bulgaria	Dec. 14, 1955	Iceland	Nov. 19, 1946	Paraguay	Oct. 24, 1945
Burma	Apr. 19, 1948	India	Oct. 30, 1945	Peru	Oct. 31, 1945
Burundi	Sept. 18, 1962	Indonesia	Sept. 28, 1950	Philippines	Oct. 24, 1945
Byelorussian Soviet Socialist Rep.	Oct. 24, 1945	Iran	Oct. 24, 1945	Poland	Oct. 24, 1945
Cambodia (Khmer Rep.)	Dec. 14, 1955	Iraq	Dec. 21, 1945	Portugal	Dec. 14, 1955
Cameroon	Sept. 20, 1960	Ireland	Dec. 14, 1955	Qatar	Sept. 21, 1971
Canada	Nov. 9, 1945	Israel	May 11, 1949	Romania	Dec. 14, 1955
Central African Rep.	Sept. 20, 1960	Italy	Dec. 14, 1955	Rwanda	Sept. 18, 1962
Chad	Sept. 20, 1960	Ivory Coast	Sept. 20, 1960	Saudi Arabia	Oct. 24, 1945
Chile	Oct. 24, 1945	Jamaica	Sept. 18, 1962	Senegal	Sept. 28, 1960
China[4]	Oct. 24, 1945	Japan	Dec. 18, 1956	Sierra Leone	Sept. 27, 1961
Colombia	Nov. 5, 1945	Jordan	Dec. 14, 1955	Singapore	Sept. 21, 1965
Congo, People's Rep.	Sept. 20, 1960	Kenya	Dec. 16, 1963	Somalia	Sept. 20, 1960
Costa Rica	Nov. 2, 1945	Kuwait	May 14, 1963	South Africa	Nov. 7, 1945
Cuba	Oct. 24, 1945	Laos	Dec. 14, 1955	Spain	Dec. 14, 1955
Cyprus	Sept. 20, 1960	Lebanon	Oct. 24, 1945	Sri Lanka (Ceylon)	Dec. 14, 1955
Czechoslovakia	Oct. 24, 1945	Lesotho	Oct. 17, 1966	Sudan	Nov. 12, 1956
Dahomey	Sept. 20, 1960	Liberia	Nov. 2, 1945	Swaziland	Sept. 24, 1968
Denmark	Oct. 24, 1945	Libya	Dec. 14, 1955	Sweden	Nov. 19, 1946
Dominican Rep.	Oct. 24, 1945	Luxembourg	Oct. 24, 1945	Syria[2]	Oct. 24, 1945
Ecuador	Dec. 21, 1945	Malagasy Rep.	Sept. 20, 1960	Thailand	Dec. 16, 1946
Egypt[2]	Oct. 24, 1945	Malawi	Dec. 1, 1964	Togo	Sept. 20, 1960
El Salvador	Oct. 24, 1945	Malaysia[1]	Sept. 17, 1957	Trinidad & Tobago	Sept. 18, 1962
Equatorial Guinea	Nov. 12, 1968	Maldives	Sept. 21, 1965	Tunisia	Nov. 12, 1956
Ethiopia	Nov. 13, 1945	Mali	Sept. 28, 1960	Turkey	Oct. 24, 1945
Fiji	Oct. 13, 1970	Malta	Dec. 1, 1964	Uganda	Oct. 25, 1962
		Mauritania	Oct. 27, 1961		

Ukrainian Soviet		United States	Oct. 24, 1945	Yemen Arab Rep	Sept. 30, 1947
Socialist Republic	Oct. 24, 1945	United Rep. of		Yemen, Peoples	
Union of Soviet		Tanzania[3]	Dec. 141961	Dem. Rep. of	Dec. 14, 1967
Socialist Repub's.	Oct. 24, 1945	Upper Volta	Sept. 20, 1960	Yugoslavia	Oct. 24, 1945
United Arab Emirates	Dec. 9, 1971	Uruguay	Dec. 18, 1945	Zaire	Sept. 20, 1960
United Kingdom	Oct. 24, 1945	Venezuela	Nov. 15, 1945	Zambia	Dec. 1, 1964

(1.) The Federation of Malaya joined the UN on Sept. 17, 1957. On Sept. 16, 1963, its name changed to Malaysia, following the admission to the new federation of Singapore, Sabah (North Borneo) and Sarawak. Singapore became an independent State Aug. 9, 1965 and a Member of the UN Sept. 21.

(2.) Egypt and Syria were original members of the United Nations from Oct. 24, 1945. Following a plebiscite held on Feb. 21, 1958, the United Arab Republic was established by a union of Egypt and Syria and continued as a single Member of the United Nations. On Oct. 13, 1961, Syria, having resumed its status as an independent State, resumed its separate membership in the Organization.

(3.) Tanganyika was a member of the United Nations from Dec. 14, 1961 and Zanzibar was a Member from Dec. 16, 1963, Following the ratification, on Apr. 26, 1964, of Articles of Union between Tanganyika and Zanzibar, the United Republic of Tanganyika and Zanzibar continued as a single Member of the United Nations, later changing its name to United Republic of Tanzania.

(4.) The General Assembly voted Oct. 25, 1971 to expel the Chinese National government of Taiwan and admit the Peking government in its place.

Operations of the United Nations Under Its Charter

The following article describes both the powers of the United Nations and its present organization. It is based on the provisions of the charter of the United Nations, and on an official report furnished by the Secretariat. The text of the Charter may be obtained from the Office of Public Information, United Nations, N. Y.

General Assembly

Pres. of 28th Session—Leopoldo Benites, Ecuador

The General Assembly is composed of representatives of all the member nations. Each nation may send not more than five representatives to each session. Each nation is entitled to one vote.

The General Assembly meets in regular annual sessions and in special session when necessary. Special sessions are convoked by the Secretary General at the request of the Security Council or of a majority of the members of the UN.

Any matter within the scope of the charter may be brought before the General Assembly, which may make recommendations on all except issues on the agenda of the Security Council. However, the General Assembly in November, 1950, decided that if the Security Council, because of lack of unanimity of the permanent members, fails to exercise its primary responsibility for the maintenance of international peace and security, in any case where there appears to be a threat to the peace, breach of the peace or act of aggression, the Assembly may consider it and recommend collective measures including, in the case of a breach of peace or act of aggression, the use of armed forces to maintain or restore peace. In such cases, the General Assembly may be convened within 24 hours in an emergency special session.

On important questions a two-thirds majority of members present and voting is required; on other questions a simple majority is sufficient. Questions that require a two-thirds majority include: recommendations on maintenance of international peace and security, election of non-permanent members of the Security Council, election of members of the Economic and Social Council, election of members of the UN that are to designate the members of the Trusteeship Council, admission of members to the UN, suspension and expulsion of members, trusteeship questions and budgetary matters.

The General Assembly must approve the budget and apportion expenses among members. A member in arrears will have no vote if the amount of arrears equals or exceeds the amount of the contributions due for the preceding two full years. The General Assembly may permit such a member to vote if it is satisfied that the failure is due to conditions beyond control.

A general or steering committee co-ordinates the proceedings of the Assembly and is composed of 26 members—the president of the Assembly, the 18 vice-presidents, and the chairmen of the seven main committees.

SECURITY COUNCIL

The Security Council consists of 15 members, 5 with permanent seats. The remaining 10 are elected for 2-year terms by the General Assembly; they are not eligible for immediate re-election.

Permanent members of the Council: China, France, USSR, United Kingdom, United States.

Non-permanent members are Australia, Austria, Guinea, India, Indonesia, Kenya, Panama, Peru, Sudan, Yugoslavia.

The Presidency of the Council is held monthly in turn by the member states in English alphabetical order.

The Security Council has the primary responsibility for maintaining international peace and security and members agree to carry out its decisions. The Council may investigate any dispute that threatens international peace and security. When the Security Council is handling a dispute or situation the General Assembly makes no recommendation unless the Council requests it.

The Security Council functions continuously, each member being represented at all times. It may change its place of meeting. Any member of UN at UN headquarters may participate in its discussions and a nation not a member of UN may appear if it is a party to a dispute.

Decisions on procedural questions are made by an affirmative vote of 9 members. On all other matters the affirmative vote of 9 members must include the concurring votes of all permanent members; it is this clause which gives rise to the so-called "veto." A party to a dispute must refrain from voting.

The Security Council may decide to enforce its decisions without the use of arms. Such measures include interruption of economic relations, break in transportation and communications, and severance of diplomatic relations. If such measures fail the Council may call on UN members to furnish armed forces, assistance and facilities, based on agreements made by the Council with the states and subject to ratification by the members of the UN "in accordance with their constitutional processes."

The right of individual or collective self-defense is not prohibited by membership in the UN, and if a member nation is attacked it may do what is necessary, reporting this to the Security Council, which may take independent action. However, the Council encourages regional arrangements or agencies by means of which local disputes can be settled without getting as far as the Council, after the Council has approved this method.

In the event of a conflict between the obligations of members to the UN and to other international bodies of which they may be members, then obligations to the UN are paramount.

ECONOMIC AND SOCIAL COUNCIL

The Economic and Social Council consists of 27 members elected by the General Assembly for 3-year terms of office. The council is responsible under the General Assembly for carrying out the functions of the United Nations with regard to international economic, social, cultural, educational, health and related matters. The council meets usually twice a year.

Membership of the Council

Until Dec. 31, 1973 — Haiti, Hungary, Lebanon, Madagascar, Malaysia, New Zealand, Niger, United States, Zaire.

Until Dec. 31, 1974 — Bolivia, Burundi, Chile, China, Finland, Japan, Poland, USSR, United Kingdom.

Until Dec. 31, 1975 — Algeria, Brazil, France, Mali, Mongolia, Netherlands, Spain, Trinidad & Tobago, Uganda.

The Economic and Social Council had the following commissions in 1971:

Functional Commissions

Statistical; Population; Social; Narcotic Drugs; Human Rights (and its Sub-Commission on the Prevention of discrimination and the protection of minorities); Status of Women.

Regional Economic Commissions

Economic Commission for Europe.
Economic Commission for Asia and the Far East.
Economic Commission for Latin America.
Economic Commission for Africa.

Also reporting to the Economic and Social Council are the Permanent Central Opium Board and the Drug Supervisory Body, the United Nations Children's Fund (UNICEF), the Council of the United Nations Development Program (UNDP) and the United Nations Special Fund, established to assist the economy of less-developed countries.

TRUSTEESHIP COUNCIL

The administration of Trust territories is subject to the supervision of the United Nations. Administering authorities are required to render an account of their stewardship to the Trusteeship Council. The Council may entertain petitions from private persons or organizations regarding conditions in the Trust territories and may dispatch missions to study conditions there.

The membership of the Council is made up of (1) countries which administer trust territories (Australia and the United States); (2) countries which are permanent members of the Security Council but which do not administer trust territories (China, France, the United Kingdom, USSR); and (3) as many other countries as may be necessary to ensure equal representation in the Council between administering and non-administering members. Those in the last named category are elected by the General Assembly for 3-year terms and are eligible for immediate reelection.

The Council usually meets once a year, in the spring.

The trust territories and the members administering them are: New Guinea (Australia), Pacific Islands (United States).

NON-SELF-GOVERNING TERRITORIES

Members of the United Nations responsible for the administration of non-self-governing territories not under trusteeships recognize the principle that the interests of the inhabitants are paramount and promote their welfare. They are bound by the charter to transmit to the Secretary-General technical information concerning economic, social and educational conditions in the territories. This information is summarized, analyzed and classified by the Secretariat. Since 1961 a committee has been studying the implementation of the 1960 General Assembly declaration on the granting of independence to colonial countries and peoples. This committee also receives the reports on non self-governing territories.

INTERNATIONAL COURT OF JUSTICE

The International Court of Justice is the principal judicial organ of the United Nations. All members are *ipso facto* parties to the statute of the Court. Other states may become parties to the Court's statute on conditions determined in each case by the General Assembly on the recommendation of the Security Council.

The jurisdiction of the Court comprises cases which the parties submit to it and matters especially provided for in the charter or in treaties. The Court gives advisory opinions and renders judgments. Its decisions, which are final, are only binding between the parties concerned and in respect to a particular dispute. If any party to a case fails to heed a judgment of the Court, the other party may have recourse to the Security Council, which may decide what is to be done.

The Court consists of 15 judges elected for 9-year terms by the General Assembly and the Security Council voting independently. No two of the judges may be nationals of the same state. Retiring judges are eligible for re-election. The Court remains permanently in session, except during the judicial vacations. A quorum of 9 judges suffices to constitute the Court. All questions are decided by majority. In the event of a tie, the President of the Court or the judge who acts in his place casts the deciding vote.

Judges

Nine year term in office ending Feb. 5, 1979:
Hardy C. Dillard, U.S.
Louis Ignacio-Pinto, Dahomey,
Federico de Castro, Spain
Platon D. Morozov, USSR
Eduardo Jimenez de Arechago, Uruguay

Nine-year term of office ending on Feb. 5, 1976:
Sture Petren, Sweden
Cesar Bengzon, Philippines
Fouad Ammoun, Lebanon
Manfred Lachs, Poland
Charles D. Onyeama, Nigeria

The president for 1973 is Manfred Lachs, Poland, and the vice president is Fouad Ammoun, Lebanon.

AGENCIES RELATED TO THE UNITED NATIONS

Working in partnership with the United Nations in various economic, social, scientific and technical fields is a group of intergovernmental organizations related to the United Nations by special agreements. Among these agencies (with their headquarters) are:

International Atomic Energy Agency (IAEA) aims to promote the peaceful uses of atomic energy. (Vienna)

International Labor Org. (ILO) aims to promote social justice; improve labor conditions and living standards; and promote economic stability. (Geneva)

Food & Agriculture Org. (FAO) aims to raise nutrition levels and living standards; secure improvements in production and distribution of food and agricultural products. (Rome)

United Nations Educational, Scientific & Cultural Org. (UNESCO) aims to promote collaboration among nations through education, science and culture in order to further human rights and freedoms without distinction of race, sex, language or religion. (Paris)

World Health Org. (WHO) aims to aid the attainment of the highest possible level of health. (Geneva)

International Bank for Reconstruction & Development (World Bank) aims to help in reconstruction and development of territories of members by facilitating investment of capital; promote foreign investment and supplement private investment by providing loans for productive purposes out of its capital funds raised by it and its other resources; and to promote growth of inter national trade and equilibrium in balance of payments. (Washington, D. C.)

International Development Assn. (IDA) aims to further economic development of members by financing on terms bearing less heavily on balance of payments than those of conventional loans. (Washington, D. C.)

International Finance Corp. (IFC) aims to further economic development by encouraging productive private enterprise, particularly in less developed areas. It is empowered to invest in private enterprises in association with private investors, and without government guarantee of repayment in cases where sufficient private capital is not available on reasonable terms; and to bring together private capital and management. (Washington, D. C.)

International Monetary Fund (Fund) aims to promote international monetary co-operation and expansion of international trade; to promote exchange stability and avoid competitive exchange depreciations; to assist in the establishment of a multilateral system of payments between members and in the elimination of foreign restrictions. (Washington, D. C.)

International Civil Aviation Org. (ICAO) promotes international standards and regulations. (Montreal)

Universal Postal Union (UPU) aims to perfect postal services and promote development of international collaboration. To this end, member countries are united in a single postal territory for reciprocal exchange of mail. (Berne)

International Telecommunication Union (ITU) sets up international regulations for radio, telegraph and telephone services and studies means to lower costs on international services. (Geneva)

World Meteorological Org. (WMO) aims to co-ordinate, standardize and improve world meteorological work. (Geneva)

Intergovernmental Maritime Consultative Org. (IMCO) aims to promote co-operation in technical problems of international shipping and to encourage the removal of discriminatory action by governments and restrictive practices by shippers. (London)

General Agreement on Tariffs and Trade (GATT) was drafted in 1946. Its functions are to ease trade barriers and establish rules of fair trade. In recent years, GATT has made special efforts to develop international trade and also has given particular emphasis to increasing the export trade of developing countries. (Geneva)

United Nation's Children's Fund (UNICEF) helps requesting countries meet the urgent needs of their children. Supported entirely by voluntary contributions from governments and individuals, UNICEF is currently helping 120 countries, mainly in the developing areas of the world. It is governed by a thirty-nation executive board. (New York)

SECRETARIAT

The Secretariat is composed of a Secretary-General appointed by the General Assembly upon the recommendation of the Security Council and such staff as the organization may require.

The Secretary General is the chief administrative officer of the UN. He may bring to the attention of the Security Council any matter that threatens international peace. He reports to the General Assembly.

Kurt Waldheim (Austria), Secretary General. He was chosen to succeed U Thant by the UN Security Council and General Assembly for a 5-year term beginning Jan. 1, 1972.

UNITED NATIONS BUDGET

The General Assembly voted a gross budget of $225,920,420 for 1973, $12,796,010 higher than the gross budget for 1972. It also approved estimates of income totalling $35,958,800 bringing the net budget for 1973 to $189,961,620.

SOURCES OF INFORMATION

Public Inquiries Unit, Office of Public Information, United Nations, N. Y. Provides pamphlets, study guides, speakers, films; arranges group visits. Telephones-Information on UN activities: PL 4-1234, Ext. 2526. Inquiries on tickets to meetings: Ext. 711.

UN Publications: UN Bookshop, United Nations, N.Y.

United Nations Assn. of the United States of America Inc., 345 E. 46th St., New York, N.Y. Tel. OX 7-3232. Publications Center, 78 Fifth Ave., New York, N.Y.

Cost of Living in Various Cities of the World

This comparison of the cost of living in various cities was drawn up in 1973 by the UN Statistical Office, based on prices for goods, services and housing for international officials stationed in these cities. Figures show relative costs, based on about 120 items. New York City was assigned the index figure 100. Thus, while expenditure for certain items might be $1,000 in New York, it would be $1,030 for them in Paris and $860 in Rio de Janeiro. Figures with an asterisk (*) omit cost of housing (rent, utilities and domestic service) in cities where they are furnished at nominal cost by governments.

Index	City	Index	City	Index	City
*113	Abidjan, Ivory Coast	78	Guatemala City, Guatemala	*113	Nouakchott, Mauritania
*82	Accra, Ghana	95	The Hague, Netherlands	99	Ouagadougou, Upper Volta
91	Addis Ababa, Ethiopa	81	Havana, Cuba	86	Panama City, Panama
83	Aden, Yemen (Dem.)	96	Jakarta, Indonesia	103	Paris, France
89	Algiers, Algeria	75	Kabul, Afghanistan	87	Port-au-Prince, Haiti
80	Amman, Jordan	*98	Kampala, Uganda	70	Port Louis, Mauritius
79	Ankara, Turkey	85	Karachi, Pakistan	74	Port-of-Spain, Trinidad
*90	Apia, Western Samoa	79	Katmandu, Nepal	75	Quito, Ecuador
78	Asuncion, Paraguay	87	Khartoum, Sudan	86	Rabat, Morocco
81	Athens, Greece	*105	Kigali, Rwanda	80	Rangoon, Burma
78	Baghdad, Iraq	86	Kingston, Jamaica	86	Rio de Janeiro, Brazil
*107	Bamako, Mali	*109	Kinshasa, Zaire	91	Riyadh, Saudi Arabia
79	Bangkok, Thailand	81	Kuala Lumpur, Malaysia	91	Rome, Italy
*117	Bangui, Cen. African Rep.	85	Kuwait, Kuwait	*90	Saigon, Vietnam
*87	Bathurst, Gambia	*107	Lagos, Nigeria	75	San Jose, Costa Rica
72	Beirut, Lebanon	76	La Paz, Bolivia	85	San Salvador, El Salvador
75	Belgrade, Yugoslavia	*108	Libreville, Gabon		
65	Bogota, Colombia	80	Lima, Peru	61	Santiago, Chile
99	Bonn, West Germany	91	Lome, Togo	92	Seoul, South Korea
*100	Brazzaville, Congo	85	London, United Kingdom	*77	Singapore, Singapore
80	Bridgetown, Barbados	*103	Lusaka, Zambia	75	Suva, Fiji
64	Buenos Aires, Argentina	88	Managua, Nicaragua	85	Sydney, Australia
96	Bujumbura, Burundi	72	Manila, Philippines	97	Tananarive, Malagasy
69	Cairo, Egypt	*74	Maseru, Lesotho	90	Tegucigalpa, Honduras
89	Caracas, Venezuela	70	Mbabane, Swaziland	85	Tehran, Iran
72	Colombo, Ceylon	85	Mexico City, Mexico	78	Tel Aviv, Israel
111	Conakry, Guinea	82	Mogadishu, Somalia	117	Tokyo, Japan
97	Copenhagen, Denmark	*94	Monrovia, Liberia	*111	Tripoli, Libya
91	Cotonou, Dahomey	52	Montevideo, Uruguay	91	Tunis, Tunisia
63	Damascus, Syria	84	Montreal, Canada	64	Valetta, Malta
80	Dar es Salaam, Tanzania	78	Nairobi, Kenya	87	Vienna, Austria
*110	Fort Lamy, Chad	77	New Delhi, India	86	Vientiane, Laos
*106	Freetown, Sierra Leone	100	New York, U.S.	90	Washington, D.C., U.S.
*77	Gaberone, Botswana	*109	Niamey, Niger	*96	Yaounde, Cameroon
91	Geneva, Switzerland	73	Nicosia, Cyprus	*70	Zomba, Malawi
66	Georgetown, Guyana				

U.S. Aid to Foreign Countries

Source: Bureau of Economic Analysis, U.S. Department of Commerce

Data shown by country do include the military supplies and services furnished under the Foreign Assistance Act and direct Defense Department appropriations. This aid is principally to the Southeast Asia countries. Data shown include credits which have been extended to private entities in the country specified.

Grants are largely outright gifts for which no payment is expected or which at most involve an obligation on the part of the receiver to extend aid to the United States or other countries to achieve a common objective.

Net grants and credits take into account all known returns to the U.S. Government, including reverse grants, returns of grants and payments of principal. A minus sign indicates that the total of these returns to the U.S. is greater than the total of grants or credits.

Other assistance represents the transfer of U.S. farm products in exchange for foreign currencies, less the Government's disbursements of the currencies as grants, credits, or for purchases. The net acquisitions of currencies represents net transfers of resources to foreign currencies, in addition to those classified as grants or credits.

Amounts do not include investments in international financial institutions in 1972 as follows: Asian Development Bank (ADB) $16,667,000; Inter-American Development Bank (IDB) $180,290,000; International Bank for Reconstruction and Development $1,335,000; International Development Association (IDA) $72,603,000.

(In millions of dollars or equivalent) (*Less than $500,000)

Calendar Year 1972	Total	Net grants	Net credits	Net other	Calendar Year 1972	Total	Net grants	Net credits	Net other
TOTAL	7,687	6,408	1,492	-213	Japan	-58	–	-56	-2
Military grants	4,235	4,235	–	–	Korea	221	41	200	-21
Other grants, credits, ass't.	3,452	2,173	1,492	-213	Laos	48	48	–	–
Western Europe	-158	-99	-56	-3	Malaysia	15	3	12	–
Austria	(*)	–	(*)	–	Philippines	70	30	41	(*)
Belgium-Luxembourg	-6	–	-6	–	Thailand	19	23	-5	–
Denmark	-1	–	-1	–	Trust Terr. Pacific	57	57	–	–
France	34	–	34	–	Vietnam	▓▓▓	▓▓▓	61	-13
Germany	0	–	-3	(0)	Other & unspecified	12	4	7	1
Ireland	-5	–	-5	–	Africa	259	136	125	-2
Italy	-15	–	-15	–	Cameroon	12	1	11	–
Malta	12	12	(*)	–	Ethiopia	14	7	7	–
Netherlands	38	–	38	–	Ghana	15	5	12	-2
Norway	42	–	42	–	Guinea	3	1	6	-4
Portugal	16	–	16	–	Ivory Coast	8	2	6	(*)
Spain	-16	–	-15	-1	Kenya	6	5	1	–
Sweden	5	–	5	–	Liberia	2	7	-5	–
United Kingdom	-208	–	-208	(*)	Morocco	21	17	3	1
Yugoslavia	55	–	56	-1	Nigeria	29	13	16	–
European Payments Union	-114	-114	–	–	Sudan	10	2	8	(*)
Other & unspecified	2	3	–	(*)	Tanzania	8	4	4	–
Eastern Europe	70	1	97	-28	Tunisia	36	8	25	3
Poland	-22	1	6	-28	Zaire	20	4	16	(*)
Romania	-10	–	-10	–	Other & unspecified	75	60	15	(*)
Soviet Union	102	–	102	–	Western Hemisphere	459	176	283	(*)
Near East & South Asia	1,115	643	612	-140	Bermuda	13	–	13	–
Afghanistan	22	21	1	(*)	Bolivia	38	7	31	(*)
Bangladesh	79	79	–	–	Brazil	53	25	28	(*)
Egypt	-6	3	-9	1	Canada	28	–	28	–
Greece	-9	(*)	-9	–	Chile	15	5	10	(*)
India	112	214	45	-146	Colombia	65	17	48	(*)
Iran	72	2	70	(*)	Costa Rica	11	6	5	–
Israel	249	61	188	-1	Dominican Republic	25	9	16	–
Jordan	107	74	33	(*)	Ecuador	8	7	1	(*)
Kuwait	-10	–	-10	–	El Salvador	9	4	5	–
Lebanon	5	2	3	–	Guatemala	18	9	9	–
Nepal	13	13	(*)	(*)	Guyana	6	2	4	–
Pakistan	154	15	130	9	Honduras	10	5	5	–
Sri Lanka (Ceylon)	20	2	18	(*)	Jamaica	8	4	4	–
Turkey	171	22	149	-1	Mexico	-11	1	-12	–
Other & unspecified	136	135	3	-2	Nicaragua	5	4	1	–
East Asia & Pacific	1,219	819	440	-40	Panama	18	6	12	–
Australia	39	–	39	–	Paraguay	7	5	2	(*)
Cambodia	72	62	9	1	Peru	48	11	37	(*)
China-Taiwan	26	10	21	-4	Uruguay	19	3	16	–
Indonesia	169	18	141	(*)	Other & unspecified	66	46	20	(*)
					International organizations & unspecified areas	488	497	-9	–

Major U.S. Foreign Aid, by Type

Grants and credits are generally goods delivered or shipped by, services rendered by, or funds disbursed by U. S. Government to or for account of a foreign government. Reverse grants and returns, and principal collections, are comprised of goods, services, and funds received by U. S. Government. Assistance through net accumulation of foreign currency claims represents transfer of U. S. farm products in exchange for foreign currencies, less U. S. disbursements of the currencies as grants, credits, or for purchases. **(In millions)**

Type—Post-war period (a)	1945-1972	Type—Post-war period (a)	1945-1972
Total, net	**148,750**	Gross grants	61,368
Investment in 5 international financial institutions (b)	2,446	Less: Reverse grants and returns	1,801
Under assistance programs, net	146,304	Net new credits (c)	28,362
Military grants (supplies and services), net	56,055	New credits	50,804
Gross grants	56,555	Less: Principal collections	22,442
Less: Reverse grants and returns	500	Other assistance (net accumulation of foreign currency claims), net	2,320
Other aid, net	90,249	Farm products sales (claims acquired) (d)	16,435
Net new grants (c)	59,567	Less: Currency disbursed	14,115

(a) July 1, 1945, through Dec. 31, 1972; all lend-lease from V-J Day (Sept. 2, 1945). (b) Asian Development Bank, Inter-American Development Bank, International Bank for Reconstruction & Development, International Development Assn., and International Finance Corp. (c) Net new grants have not been adjusted for post-war relief and other grants under agreements. Net new credits exclude prior grants converted into credits, totalling $3.7 billion. Repayments on these settlements are included in net new credits. (d) Includes foreign currencies acquired through second stage operations under farm sales legislation, such as principal and interest, amounting to $1,450,000,000.

Heads of States and Prime Ministers

Data to October 1, 1973

Country	Head of State, Title	Born	Acceded or Elected	Premier of Prime Minister
Afghanistan	Mohammed Daoud, Pres.		July 19, 1973	Mohammed Daoud
Albania	Maj.-Gen. Haxhi, Lleshi, Pres.	1913	July 1953	Maj. Gen. Mehmet Shehu
Algeria	Houari Boumediene, Pres.	1925	June 19, 1965	
Andorra	Pres. of France & Spanish Bishop of Urgel			
Argentina	Juan D. Peron, Pres.	Oct. 8, 1895	Sept. 23, 1973	
Australia (C)	Sir Paul Hasluck, Gov.-Gen(*)	Apr. 1, 1905	Apr. 30, 1969	Edward Gough Whitlam
Austria	Sir Franz Jonas, Pres.	Oct. 4, 1899	June 9, 1965	Dr. Bruno Kreisky
Bahamas (C)	Milo Butler, Gov. Gen. (*)	Aug. 11, 1906	Aug. 1, 1973	Lynden Pindling
Bahrain	Isa bin Sulman al-Khalifa	July 3, 1933	Dec. 16, 1961	Isa bin Sulman al-Khalifa
Bangladesh (C)	Abu Sayeed Choudhury	Jan. 31, 1921	Jan. 12, 1972	Sheik Mujibur Rahman
Barbados (C)	Sir A. W. Scott, Gov.-Gen. (*)	Mar. 17, 1900	May 18, 1967	E. W. Barrow
Belgium	Baudouin I, King	Sept. 7, 1930	July 17, 1951	Edmond Leburton
Bhutan	Jigme Singye Wangchuk, King	Nov. 11, 1955	July 24, 1972	
Bolivia	Col. Hugo Banzer Suarez	July 10, 1926	Aug. 22, 1971	
Botswana (C)	Sir Seretse Khama, Pres.	1921	Oct. 1, 1966	
Brazil	Gen. Emilio Garrastazu Medici	Dec. 4, 1905	Oct. 30, 1969	
Bulgaria	Todor Zhivkov, Pres.	1911	July 7, 1971	Stanko Todoro
Burma	Ne Win	1911	Mar. 2, 1962	
Burundi	Michel Micombero, Pres.	1939	Nov. 28, 1966	
Cambodia (Khmer Rep.)	Lon Nol, Pres.	1914	June 4, 1972	In Tam
Cameroon	Ahmadou Ahidjo, Pres.	Aug. 24, 1924	Jan. 1, 1960	
Canada (C)	Roland Michener, Gov.-Gen. (*)	Apr. 19, 1900	Apr. 5, 1967	Pierre E. Trudeau
Central African Rep.	Gen. Jean-Bedel Bokassa, Pres.	Feb. 22, 1920	Jan. 1, 1966	
Chad Rep.	N'Garta Tombalbaye, Pres.	1918	Aug. 11, 1960	
Chile	Gen. Augusto Pinochet Ugarte, Junta Pres.	Nov. 25, 1915	Sept. 11, 1973	
China, People's Republic				Chou En-lai
China (Taiwan)	Chiang Kai-shek, Pres.	1887	Apr. 1948	Chiang Ching-kuo
Colombia	Misael Pastrana Borrero	Nov. 14, 1923	July 15, 1970	
Congo, People's Rep.	Maj. Marien Ngouabi, Pres.	1937	Jan. 1, 1969	Maj. Alfred Raoul
Costa Rica	Jose Figueres Ferrer, Pres.	Sept. 25, 1906	May 8, 1970	
Cuba	Osvaldo Dorticos Torrado, Pres.	1919	July 17, 1959	Fidel Castro
Cyprus (C)	Archbishop Makarios, Pres.	Aug. 13, 1913	Dec. 14, 1959	
Czechoslovakia	Ludvik Svoboda, Pres.	Nov. 25, 1895	Mar. 30, 1968	Lubomir Strougal
Dahomey Rep.	Maj. Mathieu Kerekou, Pres.		Oct. 28, 1972	
Denmark	Margrethe II, Queen	Apr. 16, 1940	Jan. 14, 1972	Anker Jorgensen
Dominican Rep.	Dr. Joaquin Balaguer, Pres.	1908	July 1, 1966	
Ecuador	Guillermo Rodriguez Lara, Pres.		Feb. 15, 1972	
Egypt	Anwar el-Sadat, Pres.	Dec. 25, 1918	Oct. 15, 1970	Anwar el-Sadat
El Salvador	Arturo Armando Molina, Pres.	Aug. 6, 1927	July 1, 1972	
Equatorial Guinea	Francisco Macias Nguema, Pres.	Jan. 1, 1924	Oct. 12, 1968	
Ethiopia	Haile Selassie I, Emperor	July 23, 1892	Nov. 2, 1930	Aklilou Habte Wold
Fiji (C)	Ratu Sir George Cakobau, Gov.-Gen. (*)	Nov. 6, 1912	Jan. 13, 1973	Sir Kamisese Mara
Finland	Dr. Urho Kekkonen, Pres.	Sept. 3, 1900	Feb. 15, 1956	Kalevi Sorsa
France	Georges Pompidou, Pres.	July 5, 1911	June 20, 1969	Pierre Messmer
Gabon Rep.	Albert Bernard Bongo, Pres.	Dec. 30, 1935	Dec. 1, 1967	
Gambia (C)	Sir Dawda Kairaba Jawara, Pres.	May 16, 1924	Apr. 24, 1970	
Germany, Fed. Republic	Dr. Gustav Heinemann, Pres.	July 23, 1899	July 1, 1969	Willy Brandt
Germany, East	Friedrich, Ebert, acting Chmn.			Willi Stoph
Ghana (C)	Col. Ignatius K. Acheampong	Sept. 23, 1931	Jan. 13, 1972	Kofi A. Busia
Greece	George Papadopoulos, Pres.	May 5, 1917	June 1, 1973	Spyros Markezinis
Guatemala	Gen. Carlos Arana Osorio	July 17, 1918	July 1, 1970	
Guinea, Rep.	Sekou Toure, Pres.	Jan. 9, 1922	Oct. 2, 1958	Lansana Beavogui
Guyana (C)	Arthur Chung, Pres.	Jan. 10, 1918	Feb. 23, 1970	Forbes Burnham
Haiti	Jean-Claude Duvalier, Pres.	July 3, 1951	Apr. 21, 1971	
Honduras	Gen. Oswaldo Lopez Arellano, Pres.	1922	Dec. 4, 1972	
Hungary	Pal Losonczi, Pres.	1919	Apr. 14, 1967	Jeno Fock
Iceland	Kristjan Eldjarn, Pres.	Dec. 16, 1916	June 30, 1968	Olafur Johannesson
India (C)	V. V. Giri, Pres.	Aug. 10, 1894	Aug. 24, 1969	Indira Nehru Gandhi
Indonesia	Suharto, Pres.	Feb. 28, 1921	Mar. 11, 1967	
Iran	Mohammed Reza Pahlavi, Shah	Oct. 26, 1919	Sept. 18, 1941	Amir Abbas Hoveyda
Iraq	Ahmed Hassan al-Bakr, Pres.	1912	July 17, 1968	
Ireland	Erskine Childers, Pres.	Dec. 11, 1905	May 30, 1973	Liam Cosgrave
Israel	Ephraim Katzir, Pres.	May 16, 1916	Apr. 10, 1973	Mrs. Golda Meir
Italy	Giovanni Leone, Pres.	Nov. 3, 1908	Dec. 24, 1971	Mariano Rumor
Ivory Coast	Felix Houphouet-Boigny, Pres.	Oct. 18, 1905	Nov. 27, 1960	
Jamaica (C)	Florizel Glasspole, Gov.-Gen. (*)	Sept. 25, 1909	June 27, 1973	Michael Manley
Japan	Hirohito, Emperor	Apr. 29, 1901	Dec. 25, 1926	Kakuei Tanaka
Jordan	Hussein I, King	Nov. 14, 1935	May 2, 1952	Zaid al-Rifai
Kenya (C)	Jomo Kenyatta, Pres.	1890	Dec. 12, 1964	
Korea, Republic	Park Chung Hee, Pres.	Sept. 30, 1917	Nov. 26, 1963	Kim Jong Pil
Korea, People's Dem. Rep.	Choi Yung Kun, Presidium Chmn.	1903		Marshal Kim Il-Sung
Kuwait	Sabah al-Salim al-Sabah, Emir	1915	Nov. 27, 1965	Jaber al-Ahmed al-Jaber
Laos	Sri Savang Vatthana, King	Nov. 13, 1907	Oct. 30, 1959	Souvanna Phouma
Lebanon	Suleiman Franjieh, Pres.	1910	Aug. 17, 1970	Takieddin Solh
Lesotho (C)	Motlotlehi Moshoeshoe II, King	1898	Oct. 4, 1969	Chief Leabua Jonathan
Liberia	William R. Tolbert, Pres.	May 13, 1913	July 23, 1971	
Libya	Muammar el-Qaddafi	1944	Sept. 1, 1969	Abdel Salam Jalloud
Liechtenstein	Prince Franz Joseph II, Ruler	July 16, 1906	Mar. 30, 1938	Dr. Alfred Hilbe

Country	Head of State, Title	Born	Acceded or Elected	Premier or Prime Minister
Luxembourg	Grand Duke Jean	Jan. 5, 1921	Nov. 12, 1964	Pierre Werner
Madagascar	Gen. Bariel Ramanantsoa	1916	Oct. 9, 1972	
Malawi (C)	Dr. H. Kamuzu Banda, Pres.	1906	July 6, 1966	
Malaysia (C)	Abdul Halim Muazam, Paramount Ruler	1928	Sept. 21, 1970	Abdul Razak
Maldives, Rep. of	Ibrahim Nasir, Pres.	Sept. 2, 1926	Nov. 11, 1968	Ahmed Zaki
Mali	Moussa Traore, Pres.	Sept. 25, 1936	Nov. 19, 1968	
Malta (C)	Sir Anthony Mamo, Gov.-Gen. (*)	Jan. 9, 1909	July 3, 1971	Dom Mintoff
Mauritania	Moktar O. Daddah, Pres.	Apr. 25, 1925	Nov. 1958	Moktar Daddah
Mauritius (C)	Sir Abdool Raman Osman, Gov.-Gen. (*)	Aug. 1902	Dec. 27, 1972	Sir Seewoosagur Ramgoolam
Mexico	Luis Echeverria Alvarez	Jan. 17, 1922	July 5, 1970	
Monaco	Rainier III, Prince	May 31, 1923	May 9, 1949	
Mongolia	Sononym Luvsan, acting Pres.			Y. Tsedenbal
Morocco	Hassan II, King	July 11, 1929	Mar. 3, 1961	Ahmed Osman
Nauru (C)	Hammer De Roburt, Pres.	Sept. 25, 1922	Jan. 31, 1968	
Nepal	Birendra Bir Bikram, Shah	Dec. 28, 1945	Jan. 31, 1972	Nagendra Prashad Rijal
Netherlands	Juliana, Queen	Apr. 30, 1909	Sept. 4, 1948	Joop den Uyl
New Zealand (C)	Sir Denis Blundell, Gov.-Gen. (*)	May 29, 1907	Sept. 27, 1972	Norman E. Kirk
Nicaragua	3-man junta			
Niger	Hamani Diori, Pres.	June 16, 1916	Nov. 9, 1960	
Nigeria (C)	Gen. Yakubu Gowon, Head of Mil. Govt.	Oct. 19, 1934	Aug. 1, 1966	
Norway	Olav V, King	July 2, 1903	Sept. 21, 1957	
Oman	Sultan Qabus bin Said	Nov. 18, 1940	July 23, 1970	
Pakistan	Zulfikar Ali Bhutto	Jan. 5, 1928	Dec. 20, 1971	Zulfikar Ali Bhutto
Panama	Omar Torrijos Herrera, Govt. head	Feb. 13, 1929	Oct. 11, 1972	
Paraguay	Gen. Alfredo Stroessner, Pres.	Nov. 3, 1912	Aug. 15, 1954	
Peru	Gen. Juan Velasco Alvarado, Pres.	1910	Oct. 3, 1968	Gen. Edgardo Mercado
Philippines	Ferdinand Marcos, Pres.	Sept. 11, 1917	Dec. 30, 1965	Ferdinand Marcos
Poland	Henryk Jablonski, Chmn. Council of State	Apr. 23, 1911	Dec. 23, 1970	Piotr Jaroszewicz
Portugal	Americo R. Thomaz, Pres.	Nov. 19, 1894	July 22, 1958	Dr. Marcello Caetano
Qatar	Khalifa bin Hamad al-Thani	1936	Feb. 22, 1972	
Rhodesia	C. W. Dupont, Pres.	Dec. 6, 1905	Mar. 2, 1970	Ian Smith
Romania	Nicolae Ceausescu, State Council Pres.	Jan. 26, 1918	Dec. 7, 1967	Ion G. Maurer
Rwanda	Gregoire Kayibanda, Pres.	May 1, 1924	Oct. 26, 1961	
San Marino	Co-Regents			
Saudi Arabia	Faisal Abdel Aziz al Saud, King	1906	Nov. 2, 1964	
Senegal Rep.	Leopold S. Senghor, Pres.	1907	Sept. 1960	Abdou Diouf
Sierra Leone (C)	Siaka Stevens, Pres.	1906	Apr. 28, 1971	
Singapore (C)	Benjamin H. Sheares, Pres.	Aug. 12, 1907	Dec. 1970	Lee Kuan Yew
Somalia	Gen. Mohamed Siad Barre, Council Pres.		Oct. 15, 1969	
South Africa	Jacobus J. Fouche, Pres.	June 6, 1898	June 10, 1968	B. John Vorster
Spain	Gen. Francisco Franco Bahamonde, Chief of State	Dec. 4, 1892	Aug. 9, 1939	Luis Carrero Blanco
Sri Lanka (Ceylon) (C)	William Gopallawa, Pres.	Sept. 16, 1897	May 22, 1972	Mrs. Sirimavo Bandaranaike
Sudan	Gaafar al-Nimeiry, Pres.	1929	May 25, 1969	Ba Bakr Awadallah
Swaziland (C)	Sobhuza II, King	July 4, 1899	Apr. 25, 1967	Prince Makhosini
Sweden	Carl XVI Gustaf, King	Apr. 30, 1946	Sept. 15, 1973	Olof Palme
Switzerland (1)	Roger Bonvin, Pres.	Sept. 12, 1907	Jan. 1, 1973	Ernst Brugger, Vice Pres.
Syria	Hafez al-Assad, Chief of State	Mar. 1930	Mar. 14, 1971	Abd ar-Rahman Khulayfawi
Tanzania (C)	Julius K. Nyerere, Pres.	1922	Apr. 26, 1964	R. M. Kawawa
Thailand	Phumiphol Aduldet, King	Dec. 5, 1927	June 9, 1946	Thanom Kittikachorn
Togo	Gen. Etienne Eyadema, Pres.	1932	Jan. 13, 1967	
Tonga (C)	Taufaahau Tupou IV, King	July 4, 1918	July 5, 1967	Prince Tu'pelehake
Trinidad-Tobago (C)	Sir Ellis E. I. Clarke, Gov.-Gen. (*)	Dec. 28, 1917	Feb. 1973	Eric Williams
Tunisia	Habib Bourguiba, Pres.	Aug. 3, 1903	July 25, 1957	Hedi Nouira
Turkey	Fahri Koruturk, Pres.	1903	Apr. 6, 1973	Naim Talu
Uganda (C)	Maj. Gen. Idi Amin, Pres.	1925	Jan. 25, 1971	
USSR	Nikolai V. Podgorny, Pres. Presidium	Feb. 18, 1903	Dec. 9, 1965	Aleksei N. Kosygin
United Arab Emirates	Zayed bin Sultan	1923	Dec. 2, 1971	Marktum bin Rashid
United Kingdom (C)	Elizabeth II, Queen	Apr. 21, 1926	Feb. 6, 1952	Edward Heath
United States	Richard M. Nixon, Pres.	Jan. 9, 1913	Jan. 20, 1969	
Upper Volta	Gen. Sangoule Lamizana, Pres.	1921	Jan. 3, 1966	Gerard Kango Ouedraogo
Uruguay	Juan M. Bordaberry, Pres.	1928	Mar. 1, 1972	
Vatican City	Giovanni Battista Montini, Pope Paul VI	Sept. 26, 1897	June 21, 1963	
Venezuela	Dr. Rafael Caldera, Pres.	Jan. 1916	Mar. 11, 1969	
Vietnam, Dem. Republic of	Ton Duc Thang	1888	Sept. 23, 1969	Pham Van Dong
Vietnam, Rep. of	Nguyen Van Thieu, Pres.	Apr. 5, 1923	June 12, 1965	Tran Thien Khiem
Western Samoa	Malietoa Tanumafili II, Head of State	Jan. 4, 1913	Jan. 1, 1962	Fiame Mata'afa Faumuina Mulinuu II
Yemen, Peoples Dem. Rep. of	Salem Robaye Ali, Council Pres.	1934	June 23, 1969	Ali Nasser Hassani
Yemen Arab Rep.	Abdul Rahman al-Iryani, Pres.	July 18, 1917	Nov. 5, 1967	Abdullah al-Hajri
Yugoslavia	Marshall Tito (Josip Broz), Pres.	May 25, 1892	Jan. 31, 1946	Dzemal Bijedic
Zaire (Dem. Rep.)	Mobutu Sese Seko, Pres.	Oct. 30, 1939	Nov. 25, 1965	
Zambia (C)	Kenneth Kaunda, Pres.	1925	Oct. 24, 1964	

(1) President serves one-year term, the Vice President customarily succeeds him.
(C) Member of the Commonwealth of Nations.
(*) Gov.-Gen. acts as representative of the British monarch, who is recognized as head of state.

Population of Important World Cities

Source: Latest census reports and latest official estimates; * (asterisk) denotes capital;
Gr. denotes Greater, or metropolitan area
See index for U.S. and Canadian cities

Afghanistan
* Kabul 318,094
Kandahar 133,799
Albania
Tirana 169,300
Algeria
* Algiers 903,530
Constantine 243,558
Oran 327,493
Andorra
* Andorra La Vella . . . 8,062
Angola
Cabinda, Gr. 50,000
* Luanda, Gr. 224,540
Argentina
* Buenos Aires . . . 2,972,453
Cordoba, Gr. 798,663
La Plata, Gr. 506,287
Mendoza, Gr. 470,896
Rosario, Gr. 810,840
Santa Fe, Gr. 244,579
Tucuman, Gr. 365,757
Australia
Adelaide, Gr. 842,693
Brisbane, Gr. 867,784
* Canberra 141,795
Melbourne, Gr. . . 2,503,450
Newcastle, Gr. . . . 249,962
Perth, Gr. 703,199
Sydney, Gr. 2,807,828
Austria
Graz 249,211
Linz 204,627
Salzburg 127,455
* Vienna 1,603,408

Bahamas
* Nassau, Gr. 101,503
Bahrain
* Manama 88,785
Bangladesh
Chittagong 458,000
* Dacca 915,000
Khulna 403,000
Barbados
* Bridgetown 8,789

Belgium
Antwerp, Gr. 916,828
* Brussels, Gr. . . . 1,073,111
Charleroi, Gr. 217,349
Ghent, Gr. 220,100
Liege, Gr. 622,239

Belize (Br. Honduras)
* Belize 32,690

Bermuda
* Hamilton 3,000
Bolivia
* La Paz 700,000
Santa Cruz 200,000
* Sucre 53,000

Botswana
* Gaberone 15,000

Brazil
Belem 642,514
Belo Horizonte . . 1,232,708
* Brasilia 544,862
Curitiba 603,227
Fortaleza 842,231
Niteroi 324,367
Porto Alegre 885,567
Recife 1,078,819
Rio de Janeiro . . 4,296,782
Salvador 1,000,647
Santos 262,048
Sao Paulo 5,901,533

Bulgaria
Plovdiv 249,982
* Sofia 876,943

Burma
Mandalay 195,348
Moulmein 108,020
* Rangoon 1,717,649
Burundi
* Bujumbura, Gr. . . . 78,810

Cambodia (Khmer Rep.)
* Phnom-Penh 393,995
Cameroon
Douala, Gr. 250,000
* Yaounde 101,000
Central Africa Rep.
* Bangui, Gr. 187,000
Ceylon
* Colombo 583,000
Chad
* Fort-Lamy, Gr. . . . 99,000
Chile
Concepcion 191,746
* Santiago, Gr. . . . 2,661,920
Valparaiso 289,456
China
Amoy 224,300
Anshan 805,000
Canton 1,840,000
Changchun 975,000
Changsha 703,000
Chengchow 766,000
Chengtu 1,107,000
Chungking 2,121,000
Foochow 616,000
Fushun 985,000
Hangchow 784,000
Harbin 1,552,000
Lanchow 699,000
Nanking 1,419,000
* Peking 7,570,000
Port Arthur,
 Dairen 1,508,000
Shanghai 10,820,000
Shenyang 2,411,000
Sian 1,310,000
Taiyuan 1,020,000
Tientsin 4,280,000
Tsinan 862,000
Tsingtao 1,121,000
Tsitsihar 668,000
Wuhan 2,146,000
China (Taiwan)
Kaohsiung 784,502
Keelung 317,780
Taichung 428,426
Tainan 461,838
* Taipei 1,712,108
Colombia
Barranquilla 816,706
* Bogota, Gr. 2,800,000
Bucaramanga . . . 279,703
Cali 1,100,000
Cartagena 299,040
Medellin 967,825
Congo, People's Rep.
* Brazzaville, Gr. . . 136,200
Congo, Democratic Rep.
See Zaire
Costa Rica
* San Jose 203,148
Cuba
Camaguey 170,500
* Havana, Gr. . . . 1,565,700
Santa Clara 132,900
Santiago de Cuba . 249,600
Cyprus
* Nicosia, Gr. 115,000
Czechoslovakia
Bratislava 293,333
Brno 338,985
Ostrava 282,312
Plzen (Pilsen) . . . 147,650
* Prague 1,104,257

Dahomey
Cotonou 111,100
* Porto Novo 74,500
Denmark
Arhus 233,162
* Copenhagen, Gr. 1,383,073
Frederiksberg . . . 101,957
Odense 164,166
Dominican Republic
* Santo Domingo . . 671,402
Ecuador
Guayaquil 794,300
* Quito 528,100
Egypt
Alexandria 4,961,000
* Cairo 2,032,000
Giza 711,900
Port Said 313,000
Suez 315,000
El Salvador
* San Salvador . . . 337,171
Ethiopia
* Addis Ababa . . . 683,530
Asmara 192,330
Fiji
* Suva 54,157
Finland
* Helsinki 532,182
Tampere 153,990
Turku (bo) 153,347
France
Bordeaux 270,996
Le Havre 200,940
Lille 194,948
Lyon 535,000
Marseille 893,771
Nantes 265,009
Nice 325,400
* Paris 2,607,625
* Paris, Gr. 9,250,647
St. Etienne 216,020
Strasbourg 254,038
Toulouse 380,340

Gabon
* Libreville, Gr. . . . 57,000
Gambia
* Banjul 31,800
Germany
Aachen 177,600
Augsburg 214,400
Berlin (West) . . 2,134,300
Bielefeld 169,300
Bochum 346,900
* Bonn 299,400
Bremen 607,200
Brunswick 225,200
Cologne 866,300
Darmstadt 141,100
Dortmund 648,900
Duesseldorf . . . 680,000
Duisburg 457,900
Essen 704,800
Frankfurt 660,400
Gelsenkirchen . . 348,600
Hamburg 1,817,100
Hannover 517,800
Heidelberg 121,900
Karlsruhe 257,100
Kassel 213,500
Kiel 276,600
Krefeld 228,700
Luebeck 242,200
Ludwigshafen . . 174,700
Mannheim 330,900
Muelheim (Ruhr) . 191,100
Munich 1,326,300
Nuremberg . . . 477,100
Oberhausen . . . 249,000
Stuttgart 628,400
Wiesbaden . . . 260,600
Wuppertal 414,700

Germany (East)
* Berlin (East) . . . 1,083,728
Dresden 501,032
Halle 258,472
Karl Marx Stadt
 (Chemnitz) . . . 298,472
Leipzig 585,010
Magdeburg 270,027
Ghana
* Accra 615,800
Greece
* Athens (incl.
 Piraeus) . . . 2,800,000
Thessaloniki
 (Salonika) . . . 345,799
Guatemala
* Guatemala City . 730,991
Guinea
* Conakry, Gr. . . . 197,267
Guyana
* Georgetown 99,989
Haiti
* Port-au-Prince . . 386,250
Honduras
* Tegucigalpa . . . 232,276
Hungary
* Budapest 1,940,200
Debrecen 155,100
Miskolc 173,000
Iceland
* Reykjavik 81,603
India
Agra 594,858
Ahmedabad . . . 1,588,378
Allahabad 491,702
Amritsar 432,663
Bangalore 1,041,900
Bombay 5,968,546
Calcutta 3,141,180
Calcutta (Met.) . 7,005,362
* Delhi 3,279,955
Howrah 599,740
Hyderabad . . . 1,612,276
Kanpur 1,151,975
Lucknow 750,512
Madras 2,470,288
Madurai 548,298
Nagpur 866,144
Patna 474,349
Poona 853,226
Varanasi (Benares) 560,296
Indonesia
Bandung 1,201,730
* Jakarta 4,576,009
Jogjakarta 342,267
Makassar 434,766
Malang 422,428
Medan 635,562
Palembang 582,961
Semarang 646,590
Surabaja 1,556,255
Surakarta 414,285
Iran
Abadan 272,962
Isfahan 424,045
Mashhad 409,616
Shiraz 269,865
Tabriz 403,413
* Teheran 2,719,730
Iraq
* Baghdad 1,490,759
Basra 310,950
Mosul 264,146
Ireland
Cork 122,146
* Dublin 568,772
Israel
Ashkelon 22,700
Haifa 217,100
* Jerusalem 291,700
Ramat Gan . . . 115,500
Tel Aviv-Jaffa . . 384,000

Italy
Bari 354,338
Bologna 491,873
Catania 413,670
Florence 460,001
Genoa 841,978
Messina 273,526
Milan 1,707,576
Naples 1,277,438
Palermo 661,477
* Rome 2,755,135
Trieste 277,752
Turin 1,183,864
Venice 367,580

Ivory Coast
* Abidjan, Gr. 282,000

Jamaica
* Kingston 117,400

Japan
Amagasaki 553,696
Fukuoka 853,270
Hiroshima 541,998
Kawasaki 973,486
Kitakyushu 1,042,321
Kobe 1,288,937
Kyoto 1,419,165
Nagasaki 421,114
Nagoya 2,036,053
Osaka 2,980,487
Sapporo 1,010,123
Sendai 545,065
* Tokyo, Gr. 11,454,000
Yokohama 2,238,264

Jordan
* Amman 500,000

Kenya
Mombasa, Gr. 255,400
* Nairobi, Gr. 535,200

Korea, Dem. People's Rep. of
* Pyong Yang 653,100

Korea, Republic of
Inchon 646,013
Pusan 1,880,710
* Seoul 5,536,377
Taegu 1,082,750

Kuwait
* Kuwait 80,405

Laos
* Luang Prabang . . . 60,000
* Vientiane 132,253

Lebanon
* Beirut 700,000
Tripoli 127,611

Lesotho
* Maseru 16,312

Liberia
* Monrovia 96,226

Libya
* Bengazi 137,295
* Tripoli 213,506

Liechtenstein
* Vaduz 4,020

Luxembourg
* Luxembourg 78,000

Macau
* Macau 241,413

Malagasy Rep.
* Tananarive, Gr. . . 339,233

Malawi
Blantyre-Limbe, Gr. 109,461
* Zomba, Gr. 19,666

Malaysia
* Kuala Lumpur . . . 451,728
George Town 270,019

Maldives, Rep. of
* Male 11,760

Mali
* Bamako, Gr. 182,000

Malta
* Valletta 15,401

Mauritania
* Nouakchott 15,000

Mauritius
* Port Louis, Gr. . . . 139,700

Mexico
Chihuahua, Gr. . . . 363,850
Guadalajara, Gr. . . 1,196,218
Juarez, Gr. 436,054
Mexicali, Gr. 390,411
* Mexico 7,005,855
* Mexico, D.F. 8,541,070
Monterrey, Gr. . . . 1,177,361
Puebla, Gr. 521,885
Tijuana, Gr. 335,125
Torreon, Gr. 257,045
Veracruz, Gr. 242,351

Mongolian Rep.
* Ulan Bator 267,400

Morocco
Casablanca 1,506,373
Fez 325,327
Marrakech 332,741
Meknes 248,369
* Rabat—Sale 530,366
Tangier 187,994

Mozambique
* Lourenço Marques, Gr. 178,565

Namibia
* Windhoek 36,051

Nepal
* Katmandu 121,019

Netherlands
* Amsterdam 826,520
Eindhoven 189,230
Groningen 169,261
The Hague 545,076
Haarlem 172,268
Rotterdam 545,076
Utrecht 278,498

New Zealand
Auckland 151,900
Christchurch 166,800
* Wellington 136,400

Nicaragua
* Managua 398,514

Niger
* Niamey 78,991

Nigeria
Ibadan 758,332
Kano 357,098
* Lagos 900,969
Ogbomosho 386,650
Port Harcourt 217,043

Norway
Bergen 114,600
* Oslo 484,000
Trondheim 126,900

Oman
* Muscat 5,080

Pakistan
* Islamabad 50,000
Karachi, Gr. 3,442,000
Lahore, Gr. 1,986,000
Rawalpindi, Gr. . . 490,000

Panama
* Panama 418,013

Papua
* Port Moresby 41,848

Paraguay
* Asuncion, Gr. 411,500

Peru
Callao 335,400
Cuzco 108,900
* Lima, Gr. 2,541,300

Philippines
Cebu 359,200
Davao 406,100
Manila 1,377,000
* Quezon City 780,700

Poland
Gdansk (Danzig) . . 364,285
Krakow 583,444
Lodz 761,760
Poznan 469,085
* Warsaw 1,308,112
Wroclaw (Breslau) 523,318

Portugal
* Lisbon 786,500
Porto 306,800

Portuguese Guinea
* Bissau, Gr. 18,309

Qatar
* Doha 45,000

Rhodesia
* Salisbury, Gr. 280,090

Romania
* Bucharest 1,475,050
Ploesti 162,937
Timisoara 192,616

Saudi Arabia
Jidda 194,000
Mecca 185,000
* Riyadh 225,000

Senegal
* Dakar, Gr. 581,000

Sierra Leone
* Freetown 178,600

Somalia
* Mogadishu 172,677

South Africa
* Cape Town, Gr. . . 1,096,597
Durban Gr. 843,327
Johannesburg, Gr. 1,432,643
* Pretoria 543,950

Spain
Barcelona 1,745,142
Bilbao 410,490
Cordoba 235,632
* Madrid 3,146,071
Malaga 374,452
Murcia 243,759
Seville 548,072
Valencia 653,690
Zaragoza 479,843

Sudan
* Khartoum 261,840
Omdurman 258,532

Surinam
* Paramaribo 110,867

Sweden
Goteborg 451,806
Malmo 265,505
* Stockholm 740,486
* Stockholm, Gr. . . 1,344,748
Vasteras 116,849

Switzerland
Basel 212,857
* Berne 162,405
Geneva 173,618
Zurich 422,640

Syria
Aleppo 639,361
* Damascus 836,179

Tanzania
* Dar es Salaam . . . 343,911

Thailand
* Bangkok, Gr. 1,608,305
Thonburi, Gr. 459,555

Togo Rep.
* Lome 148,443

Trinidad and Tobago
* Port of Spain 73,900

Tunisia
* Tunis 468,997

Turkey
* Ankara 1,208,791
Istanbul 2,247,630
Izmir 520,686

Uganda
* Kampala 331,889

USSR
Alma-Ata 753,000
Baku 870,000
Barnaul 448,000
Chelyabinsk 891,000
Dniepropetrovsk . . 882,000
Donetsk 891,000
Erevan 791,000
Frunze 442,000
Gorky 1,189,000
Irkutsk 462,000
Ivanovo 426,000
Karaganda 530,000
Kazan 885,000
Khabarovsk 449,000
Kharkov 1,248,000
Kiev 1,693,000
Krasnodar 475,000
Krasnoyarsk 666,000
Krivoy Rog 581,000
Kuibyshev 1,069,000
Leningrad 3,563,000
Lyov 564,000
Makeyevka 394,000
Minsk 955,000
* Moscow 7,050,000
* Moscow, Gr. 7,172,000
Novoluznetsk 504,000
Novosibirsk 1,180,000
Odessa 913,000
Omsk 850,000
Perm 863,000
Riga 743,000
Rostov 808,000
Saratov 773,000
Sverdlovsk 1,048,000
Tashkent 1,424,000
Tbilisi 907,000
Ufa 796,000
Vladivostok 456,000
Volgograd 834,000
Voronezh 676,000
Yaroslavl' 527,000
Zaporozh'ye 690,000

United Kingdom
England
Birmingham 1,013,366
Bristol 425,203
Coventry 334,839
Leeds 494,971
Leicester 283,549
Liverpool 606,834
* London, Gr. 8,104,050
Manchester 541,468
Newcastle 222,153
Nottingham 299,758
Sheffield 519,703
Wales
Cardiff 278,221
Swansea 172,566
Scotland
Aberdeen 186,006
Dundee 182,084
Edinburgh 453,422
Glasgow 896,958
Northern Ireland
Belfast 360,150
Londonderry 53,744

Upper Volta
* Ouagadougou 77,500

Uruguay
* Montevideo 1,159,085

Venezuela
* Caracas, Gr. 2,175,000
Maracaibo 690,400
Valencia 224,800

Vietnam, Dem. Republic
Haiphong 182,490
* Hanoi 414,620

Vietnam, Republic of
Danang 334,229
Hue 156,537
* Saigon 1,681,893

Western Samoa
* Apia, Gr. 25,480

Peoples Dem. Rep. of Yemen
Aden 150,000

Yemen
* Sana 60,000

Yugoslavia
* Belgrade 772,000
Sarajevo 223,000
Skopje 290,000
Zagreb 565,000

Zambia
* Lusaka, Gr. 262,182

Zaire
Lubumbashi 318,000
* Kinshasa 1,288,122

North American Cities

Their History, Business and Industry, Educational Facilities, Cultural Advantages, Tourist Attractions and Transportation

Akron, Ohio

The World Almanac is sponsored in the Akron area by the Akron Beacon Journal, 44 E. Exchange St., Akron, Ohio 44328; phone (216) 375-8111; founded 1809 by Hiram Bowen; circulation 175,302 daily, 214,375 Sunday; John S. Knight president and editorial chairman, Ben Maidenburg publisher, Mark Ethridge vice president and editor, Robert Giles executive editor, William Ott vice president and general manager; winner of 1971 Pulitzer Prize for general reporting.

Population: 274,418 (city), 694,000 (metro area); 5th in state; total employed 271,000.

Area: 56 sq. mi. (city), 413 sq. mi. (metro) on Ohio Canal 30 mi. south of Lake Erie; founded 1825.

Industry: area produces more than $500,000,000 in products yearly; home offices and plants of Goodyear, General, Goodrich and Firestone employ 40,000, using 40% of entire world rubber supply; other products include auto bodies, wheel rims, salt, clay, matches, rubber toys, road building equipment, missile components, fishing tackle.

Transportation: major trucking center with 93 home-based carriers; bisected East-West, North-South by Interstate highways; served by 9 rail and trunk lines; 3 major carriers operate through Akron-Canton Airport; Akron Muni Airport for general aviation.

Sports: Derby Downs, home of All-American Soap Box Derby; 35,000-seat Univ. of Akron stadium; Firestone Country Club, home of World Series of Golf, twice scene of PGA championship.

New construction: $17,000,000 sports coliseum to house NBA Cleveland Cavaliers and WHA Crusaders; $5,000,000 post office; 6.7-acre Superblock urban renewal area with $17,000,000 Federal Office building and $80,000,000 Innerbelt Freeway system.

Medical facilities: Ohio State Fallsview Mental Health Center; 7 major hospitals including specialized children's treatment center.

Cultural attractions: Blossom Music Center, summer home of Cleveland Orchestra; Akron Art Institute; Akron Symphony Orchestra; Stan Hywet mansion; E. J. Thomas Performing Arts Center.

Other attractions: Goodyear Zeppelin Dock, Akron Airport; Goodyear Rubber Exhibit; Children's Zoo; 900 acres of city, 5,100 acres of state park.

Education: University of Akron; Kent State University; Firestone Conservatory of Music.

Further information: Akron Area Chamber of Commerce, Delaware Building, Akron, Ohio 44308; or Area Development Committee, First National Tower, Akron, Ohio 44308.

Albany, New York

The World Almanac is sponsored in the Albany-Schenectady-Troy area by The Times-Union and Knickerbocker News-Union Star, 645 Albany-Shaker Road, Albany, N.Y. 12201; telephone (518) 453-5454; Times-Union founded 1856; Knickerbocker News 1843; Union-Star 1855; circulation Times-Union (morn) 75,439, Sunday Times-Union 144,888, Knickerbocker News-Union Star (aft) 70,517; publisher Robert J. Danzig.

Population: 115,781 (city), 286,742 (county); total employed 99,047.

Area: 19.6 sq. mi. on west bank of Hudson River, 150 miles north of New York City.

Industry: chief products are felts, woolen goods, meat products, paper products, iron and brass castings, drugs and medicines; 295 manufacturing firms.

Commerce: 5 savings banks, 7 commercial banks.

Transportation: 2 major freight lines; 4 airlines at Albany County Airport; New York State Thruway, Adirondack Northway; Port of Albany.

Communications: 4 TV and 11 radio stations.

Medical facilities: 5 major hospital complexes including a Veteran's Administration installation.

Cultural facilities: Albany Symphony Orchestra, art museum, 90 church buildings, city libraries.

Educational facilities: Albany Law School, Albany College of Pharmacy, Albany Medical College, the State University of New York at Albany, Siena College, Saint Rose College, Albany Junior College and Maria College; 24 elementary schools, 2 senior high schools, 25 private and parochial schools.

New construction: Albany is in the midst of a major revamping of its downtown area. The $1-billion South Mall includes a 44-story state office tower, 4 large state agency buildings, as well as cultural buildings.

Recreational facilities: municipal golf course, private clubs, 2 large city parks with tennis, baseball, swimming facilities.

Other attractions: Dudley Observatory, Fort Crailo in Rensselaer; Joseph Henry Memorial Building, Ten Broeck Mansion, First Church in Albany (Reformed); Schuyler Mansion, the State Capitol and the new South Mall; 60 hotels and motels with over 5,000 rooms.

Sports: Bleecker Stadium (seating 7,000) is employed for professional and amateur baseball.

Government: 2nd only to Washington, Albany is the most important governmental city in the U.S.; home city of the governor, state officials and 30,000 state employes.

History: founded 1609 when Henry Hudson terminated his voyage in the Half Moon at the location where Albany was later settled by the Dutch.

Albuquerque, New Mexico

The World Almanac is sponsored in the Albuquerque area by The Albuquerque Tribune, 701 Silver Ave. SW, Albuquerque, N.M. 87103; telephone (505) 842-2300; founded June 22, 1922, by Carl Magee; a Scripps-Howard Newspaper since Sept. 24, 1923; circulation 37,259; editor Ralph Looney; sponsors Tribune Annual Spelling Bee, Charming Miss Charm Workshop.

Population: 285,000 (city), 346,000 (metro area), 1st in state, 58th in nation; total employed, 149,800.

Area: 81 sq. mi. on Rio Grande and U.S. 66.

Industry: electronics with Singer, GTE Lenkurt, Ampex, Gulton, Sparton; clothing with Levi Strauss, Pioneer Wear; movie production center.

Commerce: retail sales (1973) $1.219 billion; per capita income $3,532; bank resources $1.150 billion in 9 banks.

Transportation: Santa Fe Railway, Amtrak, Continental Trailways and Greyhound bus lines; Albuquerque International Airport, hub for 4 airlines, averages 583 air movements daily.

Communications: 4 TV and 15 radio stations.

Federal facilities: Kirtland AF Base, Bureau of Indian Affairs, Social Security, Forest Service.

Medical facilities: 7 major hospitals.

Cultural facilities: symphony orchestra, 26 art galleries, 4 museums, 7 library branches.

Educational facilities: University of New Mexico (18,852), University of Albuquerque (3,200), 117 public schools.

Recreational facilities: Sandia Peak Ski Area with longest tramway in North America; 80 city parks, 1 state park, Cibola National Forest; 8 golf courses, 83 tennis courts and 8 public swimming pools; Rio Grande Zoo.

Convention facilities: $9,200,000 convention center, 7,611 rooms in 104 motels and hotels.

Sports attractions: Dukes baseball, Thunderbirds football team, ice hockey.

History: Founded Feb. 7, 1706, and named for Duke of Albuquerque, Viceroy of New Spain.

Allentown, Pennsylvania

The World Almanac is sponsored in the Allentown-Bethlehem-Easton area by Call-Chronicle Newspapers, 101 N. 6th St., Allentown, Pa. 18105; phone (215) 433-4241; Call founded 1883; Chronicle 1870; Call circulation 104,500; Chronicle 24,500; Sunday 149,500; publisher Donald P. Miller, executive editor Edward D. Miller, sponsors Park & Shop, housing development, newspaper-in-the-classroom, newsprint recycling campaign.

Population: Allentown 109,871; Bethlehem 72,686; Easton 30,256; metro area 543,620; 3rd in state; total employed 229,934.

Area: 5,000 square miles (metro) in eastern Pa. at junction of Lehigh and Delaware Rivers.

Industry: Bethlehem Steel Corp., nation's 2d largest steel producer; area leads in textile and apparel production; home offices for Mack Truck Inc. and Air Products & Chemicals; New Jersey Zinc Co., Allen Products (ALPO), Lehigh-Portland Cement; transistor developed in Bell Labs here.

Commerce: retail center for central-eastern Pa.; retail sales (1971) $964,807,000; average family buying power $10,781.

Transportation: 3 major rail, 5 bus and 56 truck lines; 9 federal and state highways intersect area; jet airport averages 335 movements per day on 6 airlines.

Communications: 3 TV and 12 radio stations.

Medical facilities: 6 major hospitals.

Cultural facilities: Allentown Art Museum, Bethlehem Bach Choir, Allentown Symphony, 5 theater groups; Allentown Band is oldest continuing concert band in country; 10 colleges, including Lehigh University, Muhlenberg, Cedar Crest and Lafayette, serve 12,000 students.

Other attractions: center of "Pennsylvania Dutch" country; 1,400-acre park system; 1,170-acre game preserve, pre-Cambrian mountain range, access to Appalachian Trail, many historical preservations, folk fairs.

Sports: small game hunting, auto racing at Pocono Raceway, Olympic bicycle trials.

History: area settled in 1600's by Germans seeking religious freedom; Allentown founded 1762; hiding place for Liberty Bell during Revolutionary War; GAR founded Flag Day here in 1906.

Further Information: Chamber of Commerce, 462 Walnut St., Allentown, 18105; 420 Main St., Bethlehem, 18018; 63 N. 4th St., Easton, 18042.

Amarillo, Texas

The World Almanac is sponsored in the Amarillo area by the Amarillo Globe-News, 900 S. Harrison, Amarillo, Tex., 79166, telephone (806) 376-4488, a division of SouthWestern Newspapers Corp., and publisher of Daily News, Globe-Times and Sunday News-Globe; daily circulation 84,544, Sunday 75,755; James L. Whyte vice president and general manager.

Population: 127,010 (city), 144,396 (metro area), 13th in state, 181st in nation; total employed 66,500.

Area: 1,812 sq. mi. in Central Panhandle of Texas at junction of Interstates 40 and 27.

Industry: agribusiness—3-state hub of $8 billion market including wheat, beef, produce, value (1972) $17,300,000; refining—American Smelting &

Refining zinc plant and planned $100,000,000 copper refinery; Bell Helicopter, Levi Strauss, natural gas, petroleum, Iowa Beef Processors facility.

Commerce: wholesale-retail center for 3-state area; retail sales (1972) $337,302,000; bank resources $484,000,000 in 7 banks; 5 savings and loan associations.

Transportation: Air Terminal is base for 5 airlines with 168,000 passengers yearly; 5 key railroads; Continental, Greyhound bus lines; 25 truck lines; 6 state and federal highways intersect Amarillo.

Communications: 4 TV and 6 radio stations.

Medical: 5 hospitals including VA facility; paramedical training; mental health centers.

Culture, education, recreation: Amarillo Symphony; College Arts Complex; Civic Center Complex; summer musical "Texas"; area historical museum at West Texas State U. in Canyon; area lakes, 46 parks.

Sports: Giants baseball; college and school football, basketball.

History: settled 1887 as railroad crew camp, incorporated 1892. Named for yellow (Spanish: "amarillo") lake clay.

Anchorage, Alaska

The World Almanac is sponsored in the Anchorage area by the Anchorage Daily Times, 820 W. 4th Avenue, Anchorage, Alaska, 99510; telephone (907) 279-5622; founded 1915; circulation 43,000; editor-publisher Robert B. Atwood, general manager Bernard J. Kosinski; sponsors Spelling Bee, Airline Ski Races.

Population: 48,500 (1970), largest city in state; 138,500 (1973 est.) in census district, nearly half of Alaska's population.

Area: 927 sq. mi. (census district) at head of Cook Inlet on south central coast.

Industry & commerce: the business, transportation, communications, medical and cultural center for most of Alaska; aviation, oil companies, railroading, shipping, and national defense activities are largest elements in area's economy.

Transportation: Anchorage International Airport is a major refueling stop on transpolar Asia-Europe flights; thousands of small plane owners make Anchorage one of country's busiest air traffic centers; 5 airports and 25% of world's seaplanes in area; headquarters of Alaska Railroad; $10,000,000 port facility.

Communications: 3 TV and 7 radio stations; 2 daily newspapers.

Medical facilities: 5 hospitals.

Cultural facilities: Festival of Music with symphonic and opera music; community chorus, 2 symphony orchestras; 4 theatre groups; 2 foreign societies; community concert organization.

Educational facilities: 6 high schools, 4 junior high schools, 42 elementary schools enroll 34,500 pupils; Anchorage Community College (an extension of University of Alaska) and Alaska Methodist University.

Recreation: 3 major ski areas; annual Fur Rendezvous with dogsled races.

History: founded 1915 as construction camp for Alaska Railroad; twice winner of All America City award for coping with rapid growth and for swift recovery from catastrophic 1964 earthquake.

Atlanta, Georgia

Population: 500,800 (city), 1,700,900 (metro), 1st in state, 18th in nation; total employed 702,400 (metro).

Area: 136.0 sq. mi. in north central Georgia, on Piedmont plateau of Blue Ridge foothills, 1,050 ft. above sea level; 4,326 sq. mi. in 15-county metro area.

Industry: over 1,600 manufacturers produce more than 3,500 commodities; Over 4,250 of U.S.'s leading businesses operate in Atlanta; Ford assembly plant, 2 GM assembly plants, Lockheed-Ga Company; home base for Coca-Cola, Delta Air Lines, Retail Credit, Scripto, Genuine Parts.

Commerce; financial, retail and wholesale center of Southeast. Annual metro retail sales $4 billion. Massive Merchandise Mart. Headqtrs. 6th Federal Reserve District; 55 banks with resources of more than $5 billion; bank clearings of $67.382 billion (7th in U.S.); 20 savings and loan associations with 55 branches and with assets of over $2 billion.

Transportation: founded as railroad center, now served by 13 lines of 6 systems; Greyhound and Trailways maintain bus terminals used by 5 companies, 470 buses enter and leave daily carrying over 7,700 passengers; 9 combination airlines, 5 commuter with more than 900 scheduled mail, passenger, cargo flights daily, non-stop service to 93 citit+es from Hartsfield Internat'l Airport, 2nd busiest in U.S., handling 21,000,000 passengers in 1972. Approved rapid transit system to have 50 mi. of high speed rail, 14 mi. of busways co-ordinated with 1,500 mi. of surface street bus operations; 6 legs of 3 interstate highways intersect 100-acre downtown interchange; $7,000,000, 63-mile perimeter highway encircles city.

Communications: 5 commercial, 2 educational TV stations; 33 commercial, 1 educational radio stations; Protestant Radio and TV center; world's largest Bell system toll-free dialing area; one of nation's 5 TV and radio network control centers; 5 daily newspapers; 10th in nation in U.S. postal receipts.

New construction: boom in luxury hotels, office towers and parks, condominiums; total value 1972 city building permits $211,863,764, metro private construction $852,600,000.

Medical facilities: 41 hospitals, VA hospital, National Center For Disease Control.

Federal facilities: Washington of South with 26,000 federal employees; Ft. McPherson, hdqtrs. of 3rd Army, Dobbins A.F. Base, GSA Warehouse.

Cultural facilities: Memorial Arts Center with Museum, Symphony Orchestra, Ballet, School of Art; 24 degree-granting colleges and institutions of higher learning including Ga. Institute of Technology, Ga. State Univ., Emory Univ., Atlanta Univ.

Sports: NBA Braves, NFL Falcons, NHL Flames, ASL Chiefs. Stadium seats 52,000; Omni arena, 16,500.

Convention facilities: 504,000 delegates, 505 conventions (1972).

History: Named Atlanta 1845, chartered 1847; burned by General Wm. Sherman 1864.

Augusta, Georgia

The World Almanac is sponsored in the Augusta area by The Chronicle-Herald, 725 Broad St., 30901; (404) 724-8051; Chronicle established in 1785, circulation 50,000; Herald, 20,000; Sunday, 72,000. William S. Morris III publisher, Ed Skinner general manager, L. C. Harris editor, Robert W. Brown managing editor (Chronicle), David Playford (Herald).

Population: 58,483 (city), 282,300 (metro area); total employed 110,300 metro.

Area: 1,713 sq. mi. (metro: Richmond, Columbia counties, Ga.; Aiken County, S.C.) straddling the Savannah River.

Industry: diversified; Procter & Gamble, Continental Can, DuPont, Lily-Tulip, Monsanto, Olin, Dymo, American Cryogenics, river shipping.

Commerce: wholesale, retail center of 17 counties in 2 states; retail sales $546,492,000; per capita income $3,231; per family $11,015; effective buying income $912,053,000; 4 banks, 3 savings-loan associations; distribution center.

Transportation: 5 railroads; 26 truck lines; 3 airlines at modern airport and in-city field for small, executive planes; Interstate 20; several other federal highways; river shipping.

Communications: 2 TV and 10 radio stations.

Medical facilities: 5 major hospitals, including Eisenhower Memorial at Ft. Gordon; Medical College of Georgia, with Dental School.

Cultural facilities: Augusta College (state), Paine College (denominational); museum, art gallery, Arts Council with 25 affiliates.

Recreational facilities: 7 golf courses, hunting, fishing, boating, camping; home of The Masters Golf Tournament.

History: founded as fort 1717; named for wife of Prince of Wales 1735; temporary capital of Georgia, 1778.

Austin, Texas

The World Almanac is sponsored in the Austin area by The Austin American-Statesman, 308 Guadalupe St., Austin, Texas, 78701; telephone (512) 476-2661; Statesman founded 1871; American 1914; combined 1924; published by Newspapers, Inc.; circulation, American (morn.) 68,666, Statesman (aft.) 34,309, American-Statesman (Sunday) 104,122; Harlon M. Fentress chairman, Pat Taggart president, Richard F. Brown vice-president and publisher, Sam Wood editor, Bill Meroney, general manager.

Population: 283,700 (city), 334,000 (metro area), 6th in state, 56th in nation; total employed 158,500;

Area: 91 sq. mi. in mid-Texas on Colorado River.

Industry: electronics — Texas Instruments, IBM, Motorola, Tracor; Glastron (Conroy) boats, John Roberts jewelry, gas turbines by Westinghouse Electric; county has 360 manufacturing firms.

Commerce: wholesale, retail center for 10 counties (750,000 pop.) in triangle of Dallas-Fort Worth, San Antonio, Houston; retail sales (1972) $616,000,000; bank assets $1.3 billion in 13 banks; 7 savings associations with assets $442 million; 33 insurance home offices.

Transportation: 3 airlines; 3 railroads, Amtrak; 4 bus lines; 13 motor freight carriers; U.S. Interstate 35, State 71, 79, 183, 290.

Communications: 4 TV and cable, 12 radio stations.

Medical facilities: 7 hospitals, 1,032 beds; 389 physicians; 174 dentists.

Federal facilities: Bergstrom AF Base housing 6,000; Internal Revenue service center with 3,300 employees.

Cultural facilities: University of Texas System & UT at Austin with 40,000 students, 12,500 staff; Southwest conference football champions; Lyndon Baines Johnson Library dedicated 1971 with 1,700,000 visitors in 2 years; other libraries; Texas Memorial & Art Museums; theatres and auditoriums; 85,000-seat stadium; law and other graduate schools; campus in city center; 4 small colleges. O Henry Home, Laguna Gloria, Elizabet Ney & French Legation museums; 4 local theater companies, Austin Symphony, 2 ballet companies. City library, branches and mobile service. Austin public school district, 76 schools, 55,000 students, employes, 5,500.

State facilities: Capitol and office building complex for departments, agencies with 5 special schools for handicapped and psychiatric hospital 36,578 employes.

Convention facilities: $4,000,000 city center seats 5,000; transportation (city buses), hotels; near UT.

Recreational facilities: 2 lakes; 7,000 acres of parks, pools, 6 golf courses, tennis courts; 3 annual fiestas: Aqua (motor boat racing), Laguna Gloria, and Highland Lakes arts and crafts.

Baltimore, Maryland

The World Almanac is sponsored in the Baltimore area by the Baltimore News American, 301 E. Lombard St., Baltimore, Md. 21203; telephone (301) 752-1212; founded, 1773 as Maryland Journal and General Advertiser, Baltimore News founded 1872; adopted present name 1964; daily circulation 207,219, Sunday 296,044; publisher Mark F. Collins, executive editor Thomas J. White, general manager Roy W. Anderson; American Medical Association Award and Albert Lasker Award; sponsors I Am an American Day Parade.

Population: 905,759 (city), 2,070,670 (metro), 1st in state, 7th in U.S.; total employment 456,600 (city), 807,800 (metro).

Area: 91 sq. mi. (city) 2,225 sq. mi. (metro); on

Patapsco River, a tributary of Chesapeake Bay; 50 to 200 miles nearer mid-west than any other East Coast port.

Industry: highly diversified, none dominating; most important are steel fabricating, shipbuilding and repairing, manufacture of electrical equipment and food containers, processing foods, sugar, petroleum, chemicals, copper.

Commerce: metro area consists of city and 5 adjacent counties; estimated buying income $3,335 per capita; area has 208 shopping centers with 3,530 stores; auto ownership averages 1.3 per family; home ownership 58%.

Transportation: 3 railroads including Amtrak; Friendship International Airport used by 13 lines, 15 minutes from downtown; over 150 certified truck lines; tunnel carries motor traffic through city under Patapsco River; bus system operated by State Authority.

Port facilities: 84 steamship lines use port via 42-foot channel; 45 miles of waterfront; only port with 2 routes to Atlantic (Chesapeake Bay and Chesapeake and Delaware Canal); world's leading receiver of foreign autos; other leading imports are petroleum products, ores, grain, coal, bananas.

Communications: 3 daily newspapers in city, 2 more in metro area; 3 VHF TV stations and UHF public broadcast station; 25 radio stations.

Cultural facilities: Enoch Pratt Free Library, 24 branches, almost 2,000,000 volumes; metro county libraries have 25 branches, 600,000 volumes; Symphony Orchestra, Civic Opera Company, Art Museum, Walters Gallery, Peale Museum, Md. Academy of Sciences, Davis Planetarium, Morris A. Mechanic Theater and Center Theater.

Educational facilities: 30 colleges and 9 junior colleges, including John Hopkins University and medical institutions, University of Maryland Goucher College, Loyola College, Morgan State College, Peabody Institute of Music, Maryland

Institute College of Art, Ner Israel Rabbinical College, St. Mary's Seminary, Towson State College.

Medical facilities: 26 general hospitals, with 7,231 beds, in metro area, including world famous Johns Hopkins, University of Maryland and Greater Baltimore Medical Center.

Sports: Memorial Stadium, seating 62,000, is home of football Colts and baseball Orioles; horse racing, including annual Preakness at Pimlico track in city and International Race at Laurel; Bowie and Timonium tracks nearby. Chesapeake Bay's 1,700 sq. mi. of open water is noted for fishing, boating and wildfowl hunting; 18 ski resorts within 3 hours driving distance.

Convention facilities: Civic Center, 45 meeting rooms and 87,160 sq. ft. of exhibition space; 7 hotels in downtown area and 109 motels in or near city.

Other features: Fort McHenry Historic Shrine where Francis Scott Key wrote "The Star Spangled Banner"; historic U.S. frigate "Constellation"; Baltimore and Ohio railroad museum; Edgar Allan Poe grave; Babe Ruth home; annual "Preakness Festival Week". Most of central business district has been rebuilt in last 15 years; Inner Harbor project will provide World Trade Center, Science Building, marina, hotels. Naval Academy and new city of Columbia are in metro area.

History: founded 1729 by act of the Provincial Assembly of the Maryland Colony which was established by members of the Calvert family, Barons of Baltimore; early economy based on shipment of tobacco, grain and flour and on shipbuilding; privateering in War of 1812 caused British to try to capture the "nest of pirates" by land and sea. When Baltimore's economic growth was threatened by New York's completion of the Erie Canal, the city's business leaders countered by building the nation's first railroad, the Baltimore and Ohio.

Baton Rouge, Louisiana

The World Almanac is sponsored in the Baton Rouge area by The Morning Advocate and State-Times, 525 Lafayette, Baton Rouge, La. 70821; telephone (504) 348-0151; founded 1842; combined daily circulation, 104,934; Sunday 99,268; president Charles P. Manship, Jr. publisher Douglas L. Manship, associate editor-mechanical director Richard Palmer, business manager Charles Garvey, managing editors Edwin Price, Jr. (Morning Advocate) and Ernest Gueymard (State-Times).

Population: 165,963 (city), 392,400 (metro); 2nd in state, 86th in nation; total 1972 city-parish employment 132,375.

Area: city, 42.83 sq. mi.; parish, 407.01 sq. mi.; on east bank of Mississippi River, 80 mi. northeast of New Orleans.

Industry: northern anchor of 100-mile long petro-chemical complex along Mississippi River; largest refinery in the world; State capital; govt. employs 26,900; manufacturing employs 18,000.

Commerce: marketing center for major trade area of 400,000; bank resources $1.179 billion; 6 savings banks, 7 savings and loan associations.

Transportation: major transfer point on southern federal interstate system; 2 airports with 4 airlines; 2 bus lines; 4 railroad trunklines; Port of Baton Rouge is 7th largest deepwater port in nation, handling over 48,000,000 tons in 1971.

Communications: 3 TV and 9 radio stations.

Cultural facilities: 6 museums, art galleries, little theater, symphony, planetarium; La. Art Commission Galleries in historic Old State Capitol.

Educational facilities: Louisiana State University, founded 1860, center of 8-campus system; city enrollment 22,031, total system enrollment 39,542. Southern University, largest Negro land-grant college in U.S. and center of 3-college system; city enrollment 8,735, total system enrollment 9,091.

Sports attractions: LSU Tigers and Southern Jaguars home stadiums.

Other attractions: 34-story state capitol building; city-parish zoo and arboretum; 67 parks; major recreational lakes. Under construction, a new city-parish-federal civic complex.

History: first noted by French explorer Iberville in 1699, Baton Rouge (French for red stick) was then occupied by the Istrouma Indians; Louisiana's capitol since 1836. The government structure is a city-parish combination with a mayor-president and a city-parish council.

Billings, Montana

The World Almanac is sponsored in the Billings area by the Billings Gazette, 401 N. Broadway, Billings, Mont., 59101; telephone (406) 245-3071; founded 1885; member of Lee Enterprises, Inc., since 1960; circulation daily 56,598, Sunday, 58,129; publisher J. S. Hilleboe, editor D. W. Bowler.

Population: 65,331 (city), 79,406 (metro area), 1st in state; total employed 34,996.

Area: South central Montana on Yellowstone River.

Industry: 3 oil refineries, beet sugar refinery, 2 packing plants.

Commerce: wholesale and retail center for eastern Montana and northern Wyoming; retail sales (1971) $221,000,000; bank debits (1973) $274,003,000; 6 banks, 2 savings and loan associations; 200 wholesale firms, 800 retail firms; 2 national franchising operations (KOA and ABC Kiddie Shops) headquartered here; per capita income $3,545.

Transportation: 3 air lines; one railroad; 2 bus lines, 98 motor carriers, located on Interstates 90 and 94.

Communications: 2 TV and 5 radio stations; one weekly, one daily newspaper.

Medical facilities: 2 hospitals, 400 beds; 11 clinics; 116 doctors, 40 dentists.

Cultural facilities: 2 art galleries, symphony orchestra, 2 western museums, studio theater; 4-year liberal arts college, business college, private (church-related) college.

Other attractions: big game hunting, fishing, boating, skiing, within hour's drive; 21 city parks; 2,357 hotel motel rooms and facilities for conventions up to 5,000.

History: founded 1882 with arrival of railroad; named after Frederic Billings, then Northern Pacific president.

Binghamton, New York

The World Almanac is sponsored in the Binghamton area by The Evening and Sunday Press, Vestal Parkway East, Binghamton, N.Y. 13902; telephone (607) 798-1234; founded 1904; circulation daily 76,725, Sunday 81,113; president and publisher Robert R. Eckert, editor Laurence S. Hale, managing editor George R. Venizelos.

Population: 64,123 (city), 298,100 (metro area), 12th in state; total employed 115,500.

Area: 10.98 sq. mi. at junction of Chenango and Susquehanna Rivers.

Industry: GAF is 2d largest producer of film in country; computers, International Business Corp., electronics, simulators, Singer Co., shoes, Endicott Johnson Corp; a major railroad center.

Commerce: wholesale, retail center, center of area producing $400,000,000 a year; 5 banks; national headquarters of Security Mutual Life Insurance Co.

Transportation: 3 airlines, major being Allegheny, out of Broome County Airport; Intersection Inter state 81 and Route 17; Erie-Lackawanna and Delaware & Hudson freight rail carriers.

Communications: 3 TV and 4 radio stations.

Medical facilities: 2 major hospitals.

Cultural facilities: Roberson Center Arts & Sciences; State University at Binghamton; Tri-Cities Opera Co., symphony orchestra, Public Library; Civic Theater.

Other attractions: municipal parks zoo; major state park on outskirts; new War Memorial Arena.

Sports: semi-pro football, pro hockey.

History: Settled 1800, on main river route of General Washington's border fight against Indians in early 1700's; became rail center by 1848, with roads replacing old Chenango Canal that fed Erie Canal; named for Philadelphia patriot and multimillionaire William Bingham.

Birmingham, Alabama

The World Almanac is sponsored in the Birmingham area by The Birmingham Post-Herald, 2200 Fourth Ave., N, Birmingham, Ala. 35202; telephone (205) 325-2222; Post founded 1921 by Scripps-Howard Newspaper; Herald founded 1887; circulation, 75,630; editor Duard LeGrand, vice president W. H. Metz, managing editor George Cook; major public service projects include Goodfellow Christmas Fund, Alabama Favorite Teacher selection.

Population: 308,600 (city, 1972 est.), 744,300 (3-county metro area); employment, 312,700 (metro).

Area: 82 sq. mi. in north central Alabama.

Industry: heavy manufacturing in metals; U.S. Steel Corp. is area's largest employer; U.S. Pipe and Foundry and American Cast Iron Pipe Co. are in top 10 employers; South Central Bell's 5-state headquarters in city.

Commerce: wholesale and retail center for Alabama; retail sales (1972) $1.619 billion (county); bank deposits (1972) $1.810 billion; 11 banks, 8 savings and loan associations.

Transportation: 5 major rail freight lines; Amtrak; Greyhound and Continental Trailways bus lines; Eastern, United, Delta and Southern air lines serve modern Municipal Airport terminal completed in 1973; 70 truck line terminals. 3 interstate highways, I-59, I-65 and I-20.

Communications: 5 TV and 14 radio stations.

Medical facilities: University of Alabama in Birmingham Medical Center covers 60 sq. blocks; heart surgery team brings patients from all over the world. Veterans Administration hospital, in the same complex, is the base of an organ transplant program. Baprist Medical Centers, with 2 major hospitals, are expanding. There are 13 other hospitals.

Cultural facilities: Birmingham Symphony Orchestra, Oscar Wells Museum of Art with more than $4,000,000 in assets; Birmingham Civic Opera; 4 resident civic theaters; 2 resident ballet companies.

Education: Samford University, Birmingham-Southern College, Miles College, Daniel Payne College, Jefferson State and Lawson State Junior Colleges.

Convention facilities: new $50,000,000 civic center with exhibition hall, theater and music hall; coliseum to be added. New convention motel and other facilities under construction and planned.

Sports attractions: nicknamed "Football Capital of the South" from University of Alabama and Auburn University games played at municipal stadium, Legion Field; Birmingham A's, farm club of Oakland A's, play at Rickwood Field.

Other attractions: world's 2d largest cast iron statue, Vulcan, mythical god of the forge, overlooks Birmingham from Red Mountain as a symbol of steel industry; Arlington Shrine, antebellum home; Botanical Gardens complex with Japanese Garden; Jimmie Morgan Zoo; city park system.

History: chartered 1871, by 1900, Birmingham was known as the "Magic City" because of its rapid growth brought on by presence of the 3 ingredients in steelmaking — coal, iron ore and lime.

Bismarck, North Dakota

The World Almanac is sponsored in western North Dakota by The Bismarck Tribune, 222 Fourth St., Bismarck, N.D., 58501; telephone (701) 223-2500; founded 1873 as weekly, became daily 1881; circulation, 22,134; president Mrs. Stella I. Mann, publisher A. G. Sorlie, editor John O. Hjelle, advertising director J. Joe Miller.

Population: 37,000, 3rd in state; total employed 15,490.

Area: 11 sq. mi. on Missouri Riverbank.

Industry: agriculture, printing, trucking, farm machinery, state government, electric power, manufacturing, concrete products, railroad, insurance, livestock sales rings.

Commerce: retail trade area radius 100 miles, serving 150,000 people; retail sales (1972) $96,895,000; bank deposits (1972) $292,208,596; 4 banks, 4 building and loan associations.

Transportation: 2 railroad trunk lines, 1 transcontinental; 1,124-acre airport, hub for 3 airlines; 13 truck lines; 4 bus lines; U.S. Highways #10, #83 and I-94.

Communications: 2 daily newspapers, 3 AM, 2 FM radio stations, 2 TV stations.

Medical facilities: 2 hospitals, 500-bed capacity, served by 70 M.D.s.

New construction: 1972 building permits: $18,101,002.

Cultural facilities: Bismarck Junior College; 4-year Mary College; 6,500-seat Civic Center with 2,500 seats to be added; 67,000-volume public library; State Library.

Other attractions: State Capital; Dakota Zoo; 20 parks with over 1,250 acres.

History: founded 1872 as Edwinton, a railroad town; name changed to Bismarck to bring in German investment capital.

Bloomington, Illinois

The World Almanac is sponsored in Bloomington-Normal and Central Illinois by The Daily Pantagraph, 301 West Washington, Bloomington, Ill. 61701, telephone (309) 829-9411; founded 1837 by Jesse W. Fell; circulation 51,224; president and publisher Davis U. Merwin, editor Harold Liston; business manager William Diesel; managing editor Gene F. Smedley.

Population: 77,367 Bloomington-Normal, 106,400 (metro area) McLean County; mid-way between Chicago and St. Louis in central Illinois.

Industry: over 50 industries in county, ranks 9th in insurance cities in U.S., home offices of State Farm Insurance, Country Companies, Union Auto; uniform diversity of non-agricultural employment in all major work force areas. McLean County leads nation in corn production, 2d in soybeans.

Commerce: metro retail sales $248,412,000; per household income $12,850; per capita $3,853.

Transportation: new terminal at B-N Airport, 3 bus lines, 6 federal and state highways, 4 railroads, Amtrak, 35 interstate and 23 intrastate motor carriers.

Communications: 2 radio stations.

New construction: $35,500,000 in B-N in 1972.

Cultural facilities: Illinois Wesleyan University, 1,700 in Bloomington; Illinois State University, 18,000, in Normal; 49 churches; home of American Passion Play; B-N Symphony, Community Players, Amateur Musical.

Recreational facilities: 13 parks, city zoo, lakes, inter-collegiate and prep sports, American Legion Jr. Baseball, Y.M.C.A., Y.W.C.A.

History: incorporated 1850. Site of A. Lincoln's "Lost Speech" and David Davis mansion, state historical shrine; city's Stevenson family has produced 3 generations of leadership: vice president Adlai E.; governor, presidential candidate and U.N. Ambassador, Adlai E. II; and U.S. Senator Adlai E. III. Both Adlai E. and Adlai E. II buried in Bloomington.

Boise, Idaho

The World Almanac is sponsored in the Boise area by the Idaho Statesman, 1200 N. Curtis Road, Boise, Idaho 83707; telephone (208) 376-2121; founded 1864 as Tri-Weekly; daily circulation 60,539; Sunday 69,927; publisher Robert B. Miller, Jr., general manager C. Ralph Guilieri, managing editor Richard P. Hronek; a Gannett newspaper.

Population: 84,000 (city), 119,600 (metro area), 1st in state, 224th in nation; total employed 75,629.
Area: 1,054 sq. mi. on Boise River at foot of Salmon River Mountains.
Industry: mobile home and recreational trailers produced $100,000,000 in 1972; world headquarters Boise Cascade Corp., Morrison-Knudsen Co. and Albertson Food Stores.
Commerce: wholesale and retail center for southwest Idaho; retail sales (1971) $200,612,000; bank resources $500,000,000 in 16 banks with 16 branches; 4 savings and loan associations and 7 insurance company offices.
Transportation: 2 major airlines, 1 rail freight line,

4 bus lines and 17 common carrier truck lines.
Communications: 3 TV and 9 radio stations.
Medical facilities: 3 major hospital complexes including a Veteran's Administration facility.
Cultural facilities: Boise Philharmonic Orchestra, Art Gallery, State museum, Boise State College, Boise Little Theatre and a new $1,400,000 Public Library.
Other attractions: 33 parks, Southwestern Idaho Fairgrounds, 2 major recreational lakes, scenic mountain areas.
History: founded 1863; name derived from "les bois" (the trees), a description for area used by French furtrappers in 1811.

Boston, Massachusetts

The World Almanac is sponsored in the Boston area by The Boston Globe, 135 Morrissey Blvd., Boston, Mass. 02107; telephone (617) 288-8000; established 1872; combined daily circulation 462,619; Sunday 617,426. Chairman of the board and publisher William Davis Taylor, president John I. Taylor, general manager William O. Taylor, editor Thomas L. Winship. Two Pulitzer Prizes, Sigma Delta Chi public service, UPI and University of Missouri awards; sponsors Massachusetts Drama Festival, High School Art Competition, Science Fair, Newspaper in the Classroom and Boston Globe Book Festival.

Population: 641,071 (city); 2,899,401 (metro area of 92 cities and towns around Boston); 8th largest metro area in nation; total employed 266,505.
Area: 50 sq. mi. on central Atlantic coast of Massachusetts.
Commerce: major northeast center for finance and insurance; home for 50 insurance companies and regional headquarters for most U.S. and foreign companies based elsewhere. Banking center for New England with total deposits of $12.264 billion. Birthplace of the mutual fund, accounts for 35% of the nation's mutual fund holdings. Major industry in Boston area is electronics. Retail center for Northern New England; 1972 retail sales over 1.5 billion dollars; median family income $9,133 in city; $11,449 in metro area.
Transportation: terminating point for 2 railroads, Penn Central and Boston & Maine; Logan International Airport, terminal for 21 scheduled airlines, is 8th busiest airport in world with some 10,000,000 passengers a year; 5 interstate highways plus network of state highways.
Communications: 2 Boston newspapers; 7 TV and 31 radio stations (includes 11 FM).
New Construction: Now under construction: John Hancock Tower, National Shawmut Bank, Faneuil Hall Market Area, Boston Center for the Arts, University of Massachusetts Boston, Atlantic Ave. waterfront; proposed: Park Plaza, South Station Arena.
Medical facilities: in terms of dollars invested and spent, health is Boston's largest industry with Massachusetts General, Children's Medical Center, Boston City, Beth Israel, Peter Bent Brigham and Robert B. Brigham hospitals; Harvard, Boston University, and Tufts medical

schools; the Lahey Clinic.
Federal facilities: 50 federal agencies employ 45,700 persons (military facilities not included).
Cultural facilities: the "Athens of America", Boston's cultural scene is highlighted by the Boston Symphony Orchestra, the Boston Pops lead by Arthur Fiedler, numerous art museums including the Museum of Fine Arts, the Museum of Science, Hayden Planetarium, the Aquarium and the Boston Public Library with its newly completed auditorium.
Educational facilities: 16 degree-granting institutions of higher learning in the city plus 47 in the metropolitan area provide vast resources of intellectual, managerial, and technical talent.
Recreational facilities: 2,327 acres maintained by city for recreational purposes, includes historical Boston Common and Public Gardens. The Metropolitan District Commission also provides extensive recreational facilities.
Convention facilities: 49 hotels equipped to handle conventions; exhibition halls include Commonwealth Pier Exhibition Hall with 168,000 sq. ft. and John B. Hynes Auditorium at the Prudential Center with 154,000 sq. ft. plus auditorium seating for 5,200.
Sports attractions: Pro teams include Red Sox (baseball), Celtics (basketball), New England Patriots (football) and Bruins, Whalers, and Braves (hockey).
Other attractions: "The Freedom Trail" a 1½ mile walk through historical Boston; Boston Common and Public Gardens; Beacon Hill and Back Bay historical districts.
History: capital city of Commonwealth founded 1630; incorporated Feb. 23, 1822.

Bridgeport, Connecticut

The World Almanac is sponsored in the Bridgeport area by The Bridgeport Post (evening), The Bridgeport Telegram (morning) and The Bridgeport Sunday Post, published by The Post Publishing Co., 410 State Street, Bridgeport, Conn. 06602; telephone (203) 333-0161; circulation Post, 82,182, Telegram, 12,131; Sunday Post, 89,854; John E. Pfriem president and general manager, Leonard E. Gilbert managing editor.

Population: 156,542 (city), 311,130 (planning region); city 2nd in state, 87th in nation; labor force, 68,599 (1970 census).

Area: 17.5 sq. mi. on north shore of Long Island Sound at mouth of Pequonnock river.

Industry: "Industrial Capital of Connecticut;" products include metallic cartridges, tools, wiring devices, brass goods, valves, corsets, electrical apparatus and appliances; nearby are Sikorsky Aircraft and Avco Lycoming; General Electric company erecting corporate headquarters in Fairfield, 1 mile from city line.

Commerce: retail sales, $267,411,000 (1971), median family income, $9,840 (census); recently completed $50,000,000 downtown renewal boasts Gimbels and Sears stores, mall, 2,000-car parking garage, 2 office structures, Federal courthouse; new $20,000,000 business district complex, adjacent to state courthouse, slated for fall use.

Transportation: Connecticut Turnpike (Interstate 95) and historic U.S. 1 (Boston Post Road); 3 airlines at Bridgeport Municipal Airport; Penn Central Railroad; 2 national bus lines; summer ferry to Port Jefferson, L. I.

Medical facilities: 3 major hospitals, municipal hospital, state mental health center.

Cultural facilities: University of Bridgeport, Fairfield University, Sacred Heart University, Housatonic Community College; Museum of Art, Science and Industry; P. T. Barnum Museum; symphony orchestra; American Shakespeare Festival Theater in adjoining town of Stratford.

Recreational facilities: "The Park City" has 1,200 acres of parks, including Seaside with 2-mile shoreline; zoo; municipal indoor ice skating rink.

Other attractions: nationally-known annual Barnum Festival honoring former mayor and founder of famed circus, a 2-week celebration with largest July 4 street parade in U.S.

History: grew from Pequonnock Indian village, incorporated as town in 1821, as city in 1836.

Buffalo, New York

The World Almanac is sponsored in the Buffalo area by the Courier-Express, 785 Main St., Buffalo, N.Y. 14240; tel. (716) 847-5353; founded 1926, as merger of Courier and Express by William J. Conners, Sr.; circulation mornings 132,014, Sunday 301,902; publisher William J. Conners III, asst. to publisher Howard W. Clother, gen. mgr. R. C. Lyons, sponsors hole-in-one tournament, learn to swim program, ski school, Goodfellows.

Population: 1,349,211 (metro area), 462,768 (city) 2nd in state; metro area 24th in U.S.; employment over 540,000 (metro); hub of broad 8 county area with population of 1,758,000.

Area: 49.6 sq. mi. city, 1,567 sq. mi. metro; at western end of N.Y. State on Lake Erie, Niagara River, and U.S.-Can. boundary. Metro area includes cities of Buffalo, Niagara Falls, Lockport, Tonawanda, N. Tonawanda, Lackawanna.

Industry: 1,700 manufacturing establishments, Highly diversified; Leading categories are primary metals, transportation equipment, fabricated metals, machinery, chemicals, and food. Headquarters for National Gypsum, Carborundum, Buffalo Forge, Trico Products, Fisher-Price Toys. Large plants for Bethlehem Steel, Chevrolet, Ford, Westinghouse, Union Carbide.

Commerce: wholesale and financial center for western New York area; distribution center for northeastern U.S. and Canada; $5 billion in export-import trade between U.S. and Canada handled by area each year; 9 commercial banks, 3 savings banks, 17 savings and loans.

Transportation: Greater Buffalo Int. Airport served by 4 scheduled airlines with 1,212,021 passengers in, 1,204,515 out, 148,811 scheduled and nonscheduled flights in 1972; 6 major railroads, 10 freight terminals, 25,000 trains scheduled annually; about 150 motor carriers, Excellent highway system includes New York State Thruway. Direct highway and rail service to all parts of Canada; direct water service to entire Great Lakes-St. Lawrence Seaways system, overseas, and Atlantic seaboard.

Communications: morning and evening newspapers and one Sunday metropolitan newspaper; 3 additional dailies and one Sunday in surrounding cities; 4 TV and 25 AM and FM radio stations; 4 cable systems.

Cultural facilities: Buffalo Philharmonic has home in famous Kleinhans Music Hall; Albright-Knox Art Gallery; Studio Arena full time professional theater; Museum of Science; Historical Museum; Zoological Gardens (23 acres); Shaw Festival at Niagara-on-the-Lake, Ontario; Performing Arts Center in Lewiston.

Educational facilities: State University at Buffalo (now building $650,000,000 new campus), State College at Buffalo, Niagara University and Canisius College; 5 other colleges; At least 5 two-year institutions.

Sports attractions: Buffalo Bills football (AFL), Sabres hockey (NHL), Braves (NBA); new 80,000 seat stadium completed in 1973.

Recreation: unique to this area are abundant facilities for water and winter sports and activities; near to both U.S. and Canada vacationlands.

Special attractions: Niagara Falls and river areas from Buffalo to Lake Ontario; Robert Moses and Adam Beck hydro stations, St. Lawrence Seaways, Welland Canal Locks, Ceramics Center (Niag. Falls), Aquarium (Niag. Falls), Our Lady of Victory Basilica (Lackawanna); Old Fort Niagara; Letchworth and Allegany State Parks.

Further information: Chamber of Commerce, 238 Main, Buffalo 14202

Calgary, Alberta, Canada

The World Almanac is sponsored in the Calgary and southern Alberta area by the Calgary Albertan, 830 Tenth Ave., S.W., Calgary, Alberta, T2R 0B1; telephone (403) 263-7730; founded 1902; circulation 35,653; publisher Bruce L. Rudd; managing editor Tom Moore; business manager Al Vogt.

Population: 436,787.

Area: 157 sq. mi., one of Canada's highest cities (elevation 3,440 feet); in foothills of Rocky Mountains, 150 miles north of the Montana-Alberta border.

Industry: over 400 firms directly connected with the oil industry have headquarters in Calgary; also chemical, fertilizer and supply industries and older agricultural industries. Assistance in locating industrial information is provided by Ken Ford, Director, Industrial Development, City Hall, Calgary, Alberta.

Transportation: 2 railways, Greyhound Bus Lines, International Airport served by 6 airlines.

Communications: 2 TV and 6 radio stations; 2 cable TV channels.

Medical facilities: 6 major hospital complexes including a veteran's hospital.

New construction: building permits in 1972 totaled $233,624,315 with new convention center for 2,500 opening Sept. 1, 1974.

Cultural facilities: 2,700-seat auditorium, a gift of the province during Alberta's Jubilee year; Glenbow Museum; Allied Arts Centre; centennial planetarium; symphony orchestra and live theatre. University of Calgary enrolls over 12,800.

Other attractions: Calgary Exhibition and Stampede in July; Heritage Park reconstructs life in early days; Horseman's Hall of Fame recalls western historical events; Calgary Zoo and Natural History Park show life-size dinosaurs; 626-ft. rotating Calgary Tower gives panoramic view of city, seats 200 for dining and 300 in observation area.

Sports: every active sport; facilities for hockey, football and curling; Stampeders of Canadian Football League play in McMahon Stadium.

History: began as Mounted Police Outpost; as early as 1885, when the railway arrived, had a population of 1,000, discovery of oil in 1914 at Turner Valley contributed to Calgary's present prominence.

Charleston, West Virginia

The World Almanac is sponsored in the Charleston area by The Charleston Gazette, 1001 Virginia St., E., Charleston, W. Va. 25330; telephone (304) 348-5140; founded 1873 as the Kanawha Chronicle; became The Charleston Gazette 1898. W. E. Chilton III publisher; Harry G. Hoffmann editor; Dallas C. Higbee executive editor.

Population: 71,505 (city) 224,054 (Kanawha County), most populous county in state. City labor force 29,336.

Area: 29.3 sq. mi. at meeting place of Elk and Kanawha rivers.

Industry: diversified industrial complex, with coal and chemicals dominating; center for production of limestone, lumber, salt brines, vitreous clays and natural gas; also glass, petroleum products, alloys.

Commerce: wholesale, retail center for central and southern W. Virginia. Retail sales $407,487,000; median family income $9,321, mean family income $10,865.

Transportation: 2 rail freight lines, Amtrak, Greyhound lines, state's busiest airport with trunk and feeder lines, barge lines on Kanawha River; 3

interstate highways under construction will meet in city.

Communications: 3 TV and 7 radio stations.

Medical facilities: 6 hospitals, 2 of which are major complexes.

Cultural facilities: modern civic center and auditorium, Sunrise Cultural and Art Center, Symphony Orchestra, Community Music Assn., Light Opera Guild, Kanawha Players, State Museum, Morris Harvey College.

Other attractions: Coonskin Park, Kanawha State Forest, 6 golf courses.

Sports: Charleston Charlies, International League farm team of Pittsburgh Pirates.

History: First settlement Fort Lee, 1788; Virginia Assembly established Charles Town 1794; named Charleston 1818.

Charlotte, North Carolina

The World Almanac is sponsored in the Charlotte area by The Charlotte Observer, 600 S. Tryon St., Charlotte, N.C. 28201; telephone (704) 374-7070; founded 1886 as Charlotte Chronicle, changed to Charlotte Daily Observer 1892; sold to Knight Newspapers, Inc., 1955; circulation 175,895 daily, 220,632 Sunday; president and publisher James L. Knight, vice-president and general manager Beverly Carter, editor C. A. McKnight, executive editor James K. Batten.

Population: 241,178 (city) 354,656 (Mecklenburg County) 557,785 (metro); 2nd in state, 62nd in nation. Employment (metro) 287,650.

Area: 530 sq. mi. in Piedmont section of N.C., a rolling plateau extending from the foothills of the Appalachians to the flat Atlantic Coastal Plains.

Industry: electronic data processing, industrial chemicals, textiles, food products, machinery,

printing & publishing; 647 manufacturing companies.

Commerce: major distribution center; 1400 wholesale firms with annual business of $5 billion; retail sales (1972) $1.9 billion; effective buying income per household $12,579. A financial center; $9.1 billion banking resources in 16 banks, 11 mortgage

banks; 7 building and loan associations.
Transportation: 3 major railway lines; 4 buslines; 5 airlines with 190 air movements per day; 111 trucking firms operate from Charlotte.
Communications: 5 TV and 12 radio stations.
Medical facilities: Recognized as outstanding center in the Southeast; 5 general hospitals.
Cultural facilities: Opera Assoc.; Symphony Orchestra; Oratorio Society; Mint Museum (art); Coliseum-Auditorium; Civic Center; Johnson C. Smith University; University of North Carolina-Charlotte; Davidson College; Queens College; Central Piedmont Community College.

Sports attractions: Checkers (Eastern Hockey League); Motor Speedway (NASCAR) with World 600 and National 500 races; Kemper Open golf tournament.
Other attractions: 2 major recreational lakes, Lake Norman & Lake Wylie; nature museum.
History: Incorporated 1768; named for Queen Charlotte of England; played major part in American Revolution; gold mining capital of the country before the California Gold Rush of 1849; U.S. Mint built in Charlotte 1836.
Further information: Chamber of Commerce, 222 S. Church St., Charlotte, N.C. 28201.

Chattanooga, Tennessee

The World Almanac is sponsored in the Chattanooga area by the Chattanooga News-Free Press, 400 E. 11th St., Chattanooga, Tenn., 37401; telephone (615) 266-0171, circulation 63,000 daily and Sunday; publisher Roy McDonald, president Frank McDonald, senior vice president Everett Allen, vice president and editor Lee Anderson, managing editor Ralph Sanders.

Population: 119,923 (city), 370,857 (metro area); 4th in state, 89th in nation; 155,700 employed.
Area: 995 sq. mi. at juncture of Tennessee River and North Georgia boundary line.
Industry: over 590 manufacturers in vicinity employ 53,000. Value added by manufacture in 1969, $741,600,000. Agriculture grossed $19,181,268 in area.
Commerce: vital wholesale and retail center; wholesale sales (1967): $721,087,000; bank assets $1,044,957,563, in 12 banks, 2 mortgage banks, 8 building and loan associations, 3 major life insurance companies.
Transportation: 2 major freight lines; 2 bus lines; 35 truck lines; 10 federal and state highways intersect Chattanooga. Modern Municipal Airport

serves 5 airlines.
Communications: 5 TV and 16 radio stations.
Medical facilities: speech and hearing rehabilitation center; children and adults rehabilitation and education center; 7 major hospital complexes including psychiatric hospital.
Cultural facilities: University of Tenn. at Chattanooga; 3 liberal arts colleges, 1 state tech institute, 1 state area vocational-tech school; symphony orchestra, opera association, civic chorus, community concert, auditorium.
Other attractions: Recreational lakes, mountains, museums, tourist attractions abound.
History: Explored by DeSoto 1540, settled 1828 at Ross' landing, incorporated 1839.

Chicago, Illinois

The World Almanac is sponsored in the Chicago area by the Chicago Tribune, 435 N. Michigan Ave., Chicago, Ill., 60611; telephone (312) 222-3232; founded 1847 by Joseph Medill; circulation daily 702,736; Sunday 1,244,589; president, publisher and chief executive officer Stanton R. Cook; editor Clayton Kirkpatrick; major awards include 6 Pulitzer prizes won by staff members; sponsors college-pro All Star football game, academic honors dinner, high school press seminars, Silver Skates Derby and Chicago Tribune swimming meet.

Population: 3,369,359 (city), 2d largest in nation; 7,612,314 (8-county metro area in Illinois and Indiana); 1,137,854 households in city and 2,368,295 in metro area; total employed 3,534,000.
Area: 227 sq. mi. on southwest shore of Lake Michigan.
Industry: metro area is leading producer of steel, telephone equipment, radios, TV sets, confectionary products, household products, diesel engines, and frozen and canned foods. Largest industry is primary metals worth $7.1 billion; food and related products follow at $5.6 billion; then come electrical equipment, metal products, nonelectrical machinery, printing and publishing, transport equipment and paper products. Chicago accounts for 5.35% of the gross national product.
Commerce: 15,000 manufacturers have sales of $41 billion in metro area; 54,000 retailers do a $18.8-billion business; wholesale sales are estimated at $45.5 billion. Median family income $11,841. Midwest Stock Exchange markets 742 different stocks and bonds; 7th Federal Reserve District Bank; world's leading grain futures market; Chicago Board of Trade; Mercantile Exchange.
Transportation: 3 major airports with 30 commercial airlines handled 33,000,000 passengers in 1972;

O'Hare is world's largest and busiest commercial airport. Lake, ocean and river shipping makes city link between Mississippi River and St. Lawrence Seaway; Chicago handles one-third of Seaway cargo; 1972 overseas tonnage totaled 4,600,000 tons. Amtrak rail system headquarters. Over 12 major highways, expressways, tollways.
Convention facilities: 900 trade shows and conventions in 1972 attended by over 2,000,000 people.
Educational facilities: 93 institutions of higher learning, include University of Chicago, Illinois Institute of Technology, Northwestern University; 6 medical schools; 3 dental colleges and colleges of pharmacy and osteopathy.
Medical facilities: over 150 hospitals.
Cultural facilities: Art Institute; Museum of Science and Technology; Field Museum of Natural History; Shedd Aquarium is largest in world; Adler Planetarium; Lincoln Park and Brookfield Zoos; museums of Academy of Science and Historical Society.
Sports: National Football League Bears, American (baseball) League White Sox, National (baseball) League Cubs, National Hockey League Black Hawks, National Basketball Assoc. Bulls.
History: Indians named area Checagou after area's

strong-smelling wild onions; incorporated 1837 with population of 4,170.
Further information: Visitors Bureau and Infor-mation Center, Association of Commerce and Industry, 130 South Michigan Avenue, Chicago, IL 60603.

Cincinnati, Ohio

The World Almanac is sponsored in the Cincinnati area by The Post and Times-Star, a Scripps-Howard Newspaper, 800 Broadway, Cincinnati, Ohio 45202; telephone (513) 721-1111; founded 1881 by Alfred and Walter Wellman; evening circulation 209,118; editor Walter Friedenberg, business manager Joseph Williams.

Population: 452,524 (city), 1,412,063 (1972 estimate metro area), 3rd in state, 21st in nation; total employed 551,300.
Area: 2,150 sq. mi. (metro) in southwest corner of Ohio, southeast corner of Indiana and 3 north central counties in Kentucky.
Industry: no one industry dominates the city; home of Proctor & Gamble, world's largest soap maker; Federated Stores, world's largest department store chain; Kroger, 3rd largest food chain. Cincinnati Milacron is the biggest of several companies that make Cincinnati the world's largest producer of machine tools. A world leader in the production of jet engines, shoes, leather goods, playing cards, pianos, manufacturing, aluminum products, printing and publishing.
Commerce: retail sales (1972) $2.7 billion; bank resources $3 billion, 44 banks with 153 branches; 61 savings and loans with 72 branches and savings capital of $1.9 billion.
Transportation: hub linking the South, the Great Lakes and the trans-Appalachian East; served by 5 major rail lines and more than 100 truck lines; Amtrak; Greater Cincinnati Airport now in the midst of $40,000,000 expansion, 133 daily flights serve 5,000 passengers per day; Lunken Airport (municipal) had 177,953 operations in 1972, is the home base of 200 private planes; 4 Ohio River barge lines; metro freeway; 2 trans-continental bus lines and city-owned bus lines.
Communications: 5 TV, 12 AM, 22 FM radio stations.
New construction: "Town Center" on fringe of downtown to contain cultural, educational, commercial facilities, cost $40-$50,000,000 in private and public funds; Avondale $15,000,000 renewal, improvements to 7 urban neighborhoods, several multi-million dollar downtown and riverfront projects in the works.
Medical facilities: excellent; 28 hospitals with 9,569 beds; 120.7 physicians per 1,000 population; University of Cincinnati Medical Center where Sabin oral polio vaccine was discovered, Burn Institute VA Hospital.
Cultural facilities: Art Museum, Historical Society, Symphony Orchestra, Krohn Conservatory, Lloyd Library, May Festival, Taft Museum, Summer Opera, Museum of Natural History, Zoo.
Educational facilities: Universities: Cincinnati, Xavier, Northern Ky. State; Colleges: Edgecliff, Mt. St. Joseph, Hebrew Union, Thomas More.
Other attractions: Cincinnati Reds and football Bengals play in $44,000,000 Riverfront Stadium; Swords (1973 Calder Cup winner) play hockey in 14,000-seat Cincinnati Gardens; downtown focal points are Fountain Square Plaza and Convention-Exposition Center; Latonia and River Downs race tracks; Kings Island Amusement Park.

Cleveland, Ohio

The World Almanac is sponsored in the Cleveland area by The Cleveland Press, 901 Lakeside Ave., Cleveland, Ohio 44114; telephone (216) 623-1111; founded 1878 by E. W. Scripps; circulation 382,687; editor Thomas L. Boardman, managing editor Richard Campbell; business manager Robert H. Hartmann; major awards include Pulitzer Prize, Lasker Award.

Population: 750,879 (city), 2,064,194 (metro area), 1st in state, 10th in nation; total employed 838,000 (nonagricultural).
Area: 3,617 sq. mi., along southern shore of Lake Erie, east and west of Cuyahoga River.
Industry: city described by Newsweek as "an industrial powerhouse." City bills itself "The Best Location in the Nation." Within 500 miles are: more than 54% of populations of the U.S. and Canada, more than 60% of U.S. manufacturing plants, more than 55% of retail sales in U.S. and Canada and more than 66% of the nation's billion-dollar industrial markets. City has more corporate headquarters than any U.S. city of its size. No single industry dominates economy—steel and metal products are mainstays; manufacturing complex occupied essentially with primary metals, fabricated metal products, machinery, tools, automotive products. Important industries include making of electric motors, petroleum products, rubber, plastic, stone, clay and glass, chemicals, paints, wearing apparel, measuring instruments, electronic components, food products and publishing-printing. Value of Cleveland's products is $13 billion a year. Retail sales are almost $5 billion a year with average family spending about $6,000 on retail merchandise. City is a financial center, with 10 banks and 14 savings and loan associations in Cuyahoga County. Banks have nearly one-third of Ohio's total banking resources, deposits, loans and capital.
Transportation: Cleveland Hopkins Airport with more than 5,000,000 passengers each year; Burke Lakefront Airport, 5 minutes from Public Square and capable of handling intermediate jets; Cleveland Transit System. Port of Cleveland visited by more than 50 overseas steamship lines and Great Lakes Fleet; largest city on Lake Erie and third largest on Great Lakes.
Communications: Cleveland Press, evening daily, Cleveland Plain Dealer, morning daily plus Sunday, 6 television stations, 12 AM and 14 FM radio stations.
New construction: giant downtown rebuilding plan has seen completion of 29 facilities. Under construction now are two 23-story apartment towers, a $61,000,000 city-county justice center, a hotel and 5 other projects. Facilities to be built include a fire department headquarters, state office building, mall and education center. A proposed Lake Erie Gateway on the waterfront would consist of hotel, restaurant, shops, apartments and recreation area. Also proposed is Lake Erie International Jet-

port.

Cultural facilities: world-famous Cleveland Orchestra; Cleveland Play House, nation's oldest and largest resident professional theater; Cleveland Museum of Art with internationally-known collections; Karamu House, known for interracial artistic accomplishments; Western Reserve Historical Society; Cleveland Health Museum, Natural Science Museum, Cultural Gardens, Cleveland Zoo and Salvador Dali Museum, largest collection of his works in the world.

Educational facilities: Case Western Reserve University, Baldwin-Wallace College, Cleveland State University, Cuyahoga Community College, John Carroll University, Notre Dame College, St. John College and Ursuline College. More than 544,000 students attend 715 schools in Greater Cleveland.

Sports attractions: home of National Football League Browns, American League Indians (baseball), American Hockey League Barons, World Hockey League Crusaders, National Basketball Assn. Cavaliers. Also popular are tennis, horse and stock car racing, boating on lake.

Other attractions: downtown Convention Center is largest city-owned convention facility in country. Cleveland Public Library is 2d in size of book collection only to New York. Public Square, hub of city, marked by 52-story Terminal Tower. City, known as "Emerald Necklace" and "Forest City", is encircled by 18,000 acres of metropolitan parks.

History: Settlement established in summer, 1796 by Gen. Moses Cleaveland, was capital of the Western Reserve, became a city in 1836.

Columbus, Ohio

The World Almanac is sponsored in the Columbus area by the Columbus Citizen-Journal, 34 S. Third St., Columbus, Ohio, 43216; telephone (614) 461-5000; Citizen founded 1899, Ohio State Journal 1811; circulation 118,899 daily and Sat.; owned by E. W. Scripps Co.; editor Charles Egger, business manager Gregory A. Demski, managing editor Jack Keller.

Population: 539,677 (city), 1,017,847 (5-county metro area), 2nd in state, 33rd in nation; total employed 449,100.

Area: 155.8 sq. mi. in center of Ohio.

Industry: diversified; 987 manufacturers include General Motors, Rockwell International, Western Electric, Westinghouse, Borden (national headquarters); planes, missiles, refrigerators, mining machinery, telephones, auto parts; 1972 industrial payroll $765,526,112.

Commerce: wholesale, retail center for central, southern Ohio, parts of W. Va., Ky. Retail sales: $1,610,277,000; bank assets $3,900,000,000, 5 banks, 20 savings & loan associations; 44 insurance company home offices. Per capita income $4,076; average spendable family income $8,934.

Transportation: 71 truck lines, 6 intercity bus lines, 3 railroads; 8 airlines use Port Columbus International, with 750 air movements daily; 11 major highways intersect area.

Communications: 4 TV and 15 radio stations.

Government: state capital, Franklin County seat; federal installations include Lockbourne Air Force Base and Defense Construction Supply Center,

world's largest. Government is 21% of business total.

Medical facilities: 19 hospitals, medical centers. Children's Hospital led nation in children admitted. Ohio State University College of Medicine is nation's 5th largest.

Cultural facilities: Symphony Orchestra, Ohio Theatre, Columbus Public Library (20 branches), art museums, Center of Science and Industry, Ohio Historical Center.

Other attractions: Park of Roses (world's largest), zoo, Ohio Railway Museum, recreated 1840 village, 104 city parks, boating.

Educational facilities: Ohio State, Capital, and Franklin universities; Columbus College of Art and Design, Ohio Dominican College, Pontifical College Josephinum, Columbus Technical Institute.

Sports: 82,065 seats in Ohio Stadium; pro teams are Owls (hockey), Barons (football); Beulah Park (thoroughbreds) and Scioto Downs (harness).

History: founded 1812 as state capital; named for Christopher Columbus.

Corpus Christi, Texas

The World Almanac is sponsored in the Corpus Christi area by The Caller-Times, 820 Lower N. Broadway, Corpus Christi, TX., 78408; (512) 884-2011; Caller (a.m.) founded 1883; Times (p.m.) 1911; merged 1929. Caller circ. 67,973; Times 36,629; Sunday, 89,053; editor-publisher Edward Harte, gen. mgr. Allan Johnson, exec. ed. John Stallings, managing ed. John Anderson.

Population: 215,000 (city).

Area: 228 sq. mi., 250 miles south of Houston on Gulf of Mexico.

Commerce: Port of Corpus Christi handled 26,167,081 tons, 1972. Proposed $100-million Superport (1976) underway to handle foreign oil imports. City is economic hub of South Texas; farming, ranching, petroleum refining, King Ranch natural gas fields, and prosperous tourist business; 15 banks, have $496,556,539 total deposits.

Military: Corpus Christi Naval Air Station and Naval Air Training Command; Army Aeronautical Depot Maintenance Center, Army's only complete helicopter maintenance and overhaul facility. Combined annual payroll: $94,000,000.

Cultural facilities: museum, symphony, little theatre, Art Museum of South Texas on Corpus Christi Bay.

Sports and recreation: major tennis center, including Municipal Tennis Center with 15 lacold courts and center court stadium, 3 private clubs, numerous city facilities; site of world's largest tennis tourney, Texas Sectionals and Buccaneer Days Tournament, held each spring and summer. Sailing on Corpus Christi Bay, Municipal Marina with public launching ramps, yacht service; fishing off piers along waterfront; many facilities on Padre Island; swimming and surfing along miles of public beaches on bay and Padre Island Nat'l Seashore; 7 golf courses.

Dallas, Texas

The World Almanac is sponsored in Dallas by The Dallas Morning News, Communications Center, Dallas, Tex. 75222; telephone (214) 747-4611. Published by the oldest business in Texas, The News was founded in 1842 by Samuel Bangs; circulation, 312,364 Sunday, 267,164 daily. President Joe M. Dealey, executive editor Jack B. Krueger, managing editor Tom J. Simmons. Winner of numerous national awards, including Freedoms Foundation and National Headliner. Sponsors Dallas Beautification Award, Teen-age Citizenship Tribute, Fly-the-Flag campaign, Sports Show, etc.

Population: city, 882,400 (8th in nation); county, 1,421,000; Dallas-Fort Worth metro area, 2,544,900 (10th in nation); Total employed, 1,122,900 with 2.2% unemployment.

Area: 900 sq. mi. astride Trinity River in North Texas, about 75 miles south of Oklahoma border; elevation from 450 to 750 feet.

Industry: banking and insurance capital of the Southwest, Dallas ranks third among U.S. cities in the number of million-dollar-net-worth companies with 626 such firms. Manufacturing accounts for one-fourth of employment, about evenly divided between durable (including electronics, aviation, aerospace and machinery) and non-durable (including food products, apparel and printing-publishing).

Commerce: $2 billion wholesale market ($4 billion retail), Dallas ranks first nationally in giftware wholesaling, second in apparel and home furnishings; Metro retail sales totaled $5.5 billion in 1972, while estimated buying income reached $10.6 billion and bank deposits $11.2 billion.

Transportation: Dallas-Fort Worth Regional Airport, completed in 1973, is the world's largest. In 1972, Love Field was the nation's 4th busiest in itinerant operations; 5,816,250 passengers enplaned there. The city is served by 8 airlines, 9 railroads, 2 trans-continental bus lines and 37 motor freight lines; 7 interstate highway outlets.

Communications: 2 metropolitan daily newspapers, numerous suburban dailies, 4 commercial VHF TV stations, public television, 2 UHF stations, 16 AM and 21 FM radio stations.

Medical facilities: medical Mecca of the Southwest, Dallas has 40 accredited hospitals with 7,000 beds, 500 bassinets. Baylor University Medical Center recently chosen No. 4 among the country's top 13 "super hospitals."

Culture: Symphony Orchestra, Civic Opera, Summer Musicals, Civic Ballet, Sunday Concert Series — among others — offer varied programs. Drama at the Dallas Theater Center, Theater Three, National Children's Theater and 3 dinner theaters; 7

museums, SMU's Owens Fine Arts Center with a collection of paintings and sculpture, numerous art galleries.

Education: almost 100,000 students attend 32 colleges and universities within 50 miles of Dallas; Southern Methodist University, the University of Texas at Dallas, University of Dallas, North Texas State University, University of Texas at Arlington, Baylor University College of Dentistry, Southwestern Medical School and the Dallas County Junior College System with more than 30,000 students on 4 campuses and 3 more planned.

Convention facilities: 3 major convention centers, including new $37,300,000 expansion which offers more combined meeting-exhibit space (611,000 sq. ft.) than any other in U.S.; 21,000 air-conditioned hotel rooms. Dallas consistently ranks in top 5 convention cities. In 1972, 1,032,000 people attended 602 conventions in Dallas.

Sports attractions: Cotton Bowl is site of annual New Year's football game and SMU home games. Professional sports include football, baseball, tennis, golf, hockey, soccer.

Other attractions: Six Flags Over Texas, Marsalis Zoo, Seven Seas, Lion Country Safari. Fair Park is home of State Fair of Texas for 16 days each October; museums of fine arts, health and science, and natural history; Hall of State; Garden Center and Music Hall; excellent golf courses, lakes, parks, luxury hotels and fine restaurants.

History: First settler was Tennessee frontiers-man John Neely Bryan, who established a trading post and plotted the townsite in 1844; incorporated 1856; named for Vice President George Millifin Dallas. Since 1931, the city has had council-manager government. Spectacular population growth began after World War II, when aircraft manufacturing augmented an economy that had been built first on cotton, then on oil, banking and insurance. Diversified economic expansion fed the growth of the 1960s.

Further information: Dallas Chamber of Commerce, Fidelity Union Tower, Dallas, Tex. 75201.

Dayton, Ohio

The World Almanac is sponsored in the Dayton area by The Dayton Journal Herald, 37 South Ludlow Street, Dayton, Ohio 45401; telephone (513) 223-1111; founded 1808 as Dayton Repertory; circulation 113,615; editor and publisher Charles T. Alexander, managing editor Ralph Langer, editorial page editor Alvin P. Sanoff, sports editor Ritter Collett, Modern Living department editor Virginia Hunt.

Population: 245,000 (city), 881,900 (metro), 4th in state, 39th in nation; total employed 354,500.

Area: 41.72 sq. mi. at juncture of Miami, Mad and Stillwater rivers.

Industry: National Cash Register Co., McCall Printing Company, General Motors Corp. (Delco Moraine, Delco Products, Frigidaire and Inland Mfg.); over 800 other manufacturing facilities.

Commerce: retail sales (1971) $1.667 billion (4th in state, 41st in nation); average spendable household income $11,937.

Transportation: 5 airports, 6 airlines, 3 trunk rail systems, 6 bus lines and a city-owned trolley system.

Communications: 4 TV and 10 radio stations.

Medical facilities: 10 hospitals, including a Veteran's Administration facility.

Federal facilities: Wright-Patterson AFB (headquarters for Air Force Logistics Command and Aeronautical Systems Division); Defense Electronics Supply Center.

Convention facilities: downtown convention and

exhibition center completed and in operation.
New construction: downtown transportation center. Winters, First National Bank towers completed.
Educational facilities: University of Dayton, Wright State University; 2 junior colleges — Sinclair (new downtown campus) and Miami-Jacobs (a junior college of business); Dayton Art Institute School, United Theological Seminary.
Cultural facilities: Philharmonic Orchestra, Opera

Assoc., Civic Ballet, 4 amateur theatrical groups, 2 professional companies; Diehl Memorial Band Shell and Deed's Carillon.
Sports attractions: Dayton Gems (IHL); Amateur Trapshoot Assoc. Hdqtrs; college sports.
Other attractions: Air Force Museum; Carillon Park (Dayton historial exhibits), Paul Lawrence Dunbar homestead; Wright Brothers Memorial, Aviation Hall of Fame. A new center city Plaza planned at Old Courthouse Museum.

Denver, Colorado

The World Almanac is sponsored in the Denver area by the Rocky Mountain News, 400 W. Colfax Ave., Denver, Colo. 80201; telephone (303) 892-5000; founded 1859 by William N. Byers; circulation daily 214,490, Sunday 236,903; editor Vincent M. Dwyer, business manager William W. Fletcher; sponsors Colorado-Wyoming spelling bee, Golden Wedding party, Huck Finn Day, Ski School.

Population: 511,900 (city), 1,228,801 (metro area), 1st in state, 27th in nation; total employed 570,700.
Area: 100 sq. mi. on South Platte River at western edge of Great Plains, near foothills of Rocky Mountains.
Industry: Gates Rubber Co. is world's largest maker of V-belts and hose, 6th largest U.S. rubber company. Samsonite Corp. is world's largest luggage manufacturer, also makes folding furniture and toys. Adolph Coors Co. is nation's 4th largest brewer of beer. Center for "smokeless industries" with 1,550 manufacturing firms.
Commerce: largest distribution center in region embracing one-third of U.S. geographical area; retail sales (1972) $6.3 billion. Bank deposits $3.880 billion, 77 banks, 13 savings and loan associations and 43 insurance company home offices. Per capita income $4,675.
Transportation: 6 major rail freight lines, Amtrak; Continental and Greyhound bus lines; 3 Interstate highways intersect city. Stapleton International Airport is nation's 11th largest, with 600 daily commercial flights, hub for 6 trunk airlines; Frontier Airlines based here, as is United Air Lines Flight Training Center.
Communications: 5 TV and 22 radio stations.
Medical facilities: largest medical center between Kansas City and San Francisco; facilities include University of Colorado Medical Center, National Jewish Hospital, Childrens Asthma Research In-

stitute and Hospital (CARIH); 22 major hospitals.
Federal facilities: largest complex of federal offices outside Washington, D.C.; site of Atomic Energy Commission's Rocky Flats plant, U.S. Mint, Lowry Air Force Base, Air Force Accounting and Finance Center, Army's Rocky Mountain Arsenal, Fitzsimmons Army Medical Center.
Cultural facilities: Denver Symphony Orchestra, 3 nonprofessional orchestras, 2 choral groups, Denver Art Museum, 3 theater companies; 3-sq.-block convention center; 12,000-seat Red Rocks open-air theater.
Educational facilities: University of Denver, Colorado School of Mines, Colorado Womens College, Metropolitan State College, Loretto Heights College, Regis College, University of Colorado School of Medicine, Iliff School of Theology.
Recreational facilities: 150 named parks, 13,400 acres of mountain parks, 31 golf courses in metro area, City Park Zoo, 2 amusement parks; more than a dozen ski areas.
Sports: pro teams include Broncos (football), Bears (baseball), Rockets (basketball) and Spurs (Hockey).
Other attractions: Museum of Natural History, Botanic Gardens, State Historical Museum.
History: founded 1858 with discovery of gold, fast became supply center for mountain mining camps. Named for territorial governor.

Des Moines, Iowa

The World Almanac is sponsored in Iowa by the Des Moines Register and Tribune, 715 Locust St., Des Moines, Ia. 50304; telephone (515) 284-8000; founded 1849; circulation evening Tribune 111,562, morning Register 254,168, Sunday Register 507,603; president and publisher David Kruidenier, editor Kenneth MacDonald, managing editor A. Edward Heins, business manager Louis Norris, sales director J. R. Hudson; writers and photographers have won 11 Pulitzer Prizes.

Population: 201,404 (city), 286,101 (metro); 1st in state, 64th in nation; 145,400 employed.
Area: 66 sq. mi., at juncture of Racoon and Des Moines rivers, south central Iowa.
Industry: considered to be 2nd largest insurance center in nation (52 home companies) and 2nd largest tire center with Firestone, Armstrong plants. Publishing center — Meredith Co., Better Homes and Gardens, Wallace-Homestead and others. Farm implements — North American headquarters of Massey-Ferguson and John Deere. Lawn and garden equipment, sporting goods, cosmetics, food products, dental equipment, tools, automotive accessories, 700 wholesale and jobbing firms.
Commerce: retail sales $628,945,000 (1971), per

capita income $4,270 (1971); bank assets $700,000,000, 12 banks, 9 savings and loans.
Transportation: large, modern in-city airport, 3 major air lines; 38 regular truck lines, 27 special commodity truck lines; 4 bus lines; 5 railroads; junction Interstate Highways 35-80.
New construction: $114,055,000, 25-story financial center completed 1972; 36-story bank-office building under construction.
Medical facilities: 8 hospital complexes with over 2,500 beds, including VA hospital.
Cultural facilities: large art center, new Center of Science and Industry, Community Playhouse, Drama Workshop, Symphony Orchestra, Drake

University, Grand View Junior College, 2 Bible colleges, Community College, College of Osteopathic Medicine and Surgery, Technical High School, Iowa State University (at Ames).
Communications: 4 TV and 12 radio stations.
Recreational facilities: 1,400 acres of parks, 9 public golf courses, 11 public pools, tennis, new YWCA and YMCA buildings, huge Red Rock and Saylorville reservoirs.
Other attractions: AAA baseball, hockey, Drake Relays; Missouri Valley, Big 8 conferences; 15,000-seat auditorium, boys and girls state basketball tournaments, Iowa State Fair.
History: Founded 1843 as a fort to protect the rights of the Indians, incorporated 1853, became Iowa capital in 1857.

Detroit, Michigan

The World Almanac is sponsored in the Detroit area by The Detroit News, 615 W. Lafayette, Detroit, Mich. 48231; telephone (313) 222-2000; founded 1873 by James E. Scripps; circulation daily 683,452, Sunday 852,801; president and publisher Peter B. Clark, exec. v.p. Edwin K. Wheeler, gen. mgr. James T. Dorris, editor Martin S. Hayden; major awards won include Pulitzer Prize, Natl Headliners; 66 community projects include NCAA Indoor Track Championships, Policeman and Fire Fighter of the Month Awards, Science Fair, Scholastic Writing and Art Awards, Spelling Bee, Michigan Industrial Education Awards, Young Hunter Safety Clinic, Neighborhood Basketball Program, Free Golf School, Kid's Fishing Derby.

Population: 1,500,000 (city), 4,250,000 (metro area), (1972); first in state, 5th in U.S.
Area: 139.6 sq. mi. on the Detroit River, a Great Lakes connecting link and the world's busiest inland waterway; leads to the St. Lawrence Seaway.
Industry: "The Motor City" is the capital of the auto industry. Area plants produce 25% of the nation's cars and trucks, employing more than 210,000. Nonautomotive manufacturing and non-manufacturing firms employ more than 1,390,000. Other products are machine tools, gray iron products, metal stampings, hardware, industrial chemicals, drugs, paint, wire products, office machinery.
Commerce: total metro personel income was $18.173 billion, $14,111 per household (1971); area retail sales were $8.6 billion.
Transportation: Detroit is served by 6 railroads; over 200 intercity truck lines; 19 airlines offering both passenger and freight service and 31 scheduled steamship lines serving more than 40 countries. Air passengers totalled 7,073,171 (1971).
Communications: 7 TV and 18 radio stations.
New construction: a $500,000,000 riverfront development, "Renaissance Center," will be built on Detroit's eastside waterfront area, incorporating living units, business offices and hotels; other major urban rebuilding projects include 660 acres in the Lafayette and Elmwood downtown residential developments, valued at $284,000,000 when completed; and a 235-acre, $500,000,000 mid-town medical center.
Cultural facilities: Detroit Symphony Orchestra, International Institute, Meadow Brook music and drama programs, Institute of Arts, Detroit Concert Band, and the annual Freedom Festival, celebrating Canada's Dominion Day, July 1, and U.S. Independence Day, July 4.
Educational facilities: 11 colleges and universities are located in the metro area, including Wayne State Univ., Univ. of Detroit, and branches of the Univ. of Michigan and Michigan State University.
Convention facilities: hub of downtown business district is the 75-acre, $100,000,000 Civic Center, including Cobo Hall and Convention Arena with 400,000 sq. ft. of exhibit space; more than 24,000 rooms in 250 area hotels and motels.

Sports attractions: Tigers baseball (American League), Lions (National Football League), Red Wings (National Hockey League), and Pistons (National Basketball Assn.); 6 winter skiing areas are within short driving distance.
Other attractions: points of interest include Chrysler, Ford and General Motors auto plants, Henry Ford Museum and Greenfield Village historical displays, Cranbrook Institute (science museum and arts), Belle Isle (1,000-acre island park), Detroit Zoo (natural animal settings), Public Library, Historical Museum and Fort Wayne Military Museum. Neighboring Windsor, Canada, can be reached via Detroit-Windsor underwater tunnel or Ambassador Bridge.
History: founded 1701 by the Frenchman Cadillac as a strategic frontier fort and trading post, ceded to the British in 1763 and turned over to the U.S. in 1796 as a village of 2,500. Destroyed by fire in 1805 and rebuilt, it was reoccupied by the British for a year in the War of 1812. Completion of the Erie Canal in 1825 opened a cheap water transport route from New York to the Northwest and made Detroit an important commercial center. Rail service reached Chicago in 1852, New York in 1854. By 1880 Detroit was a major industrial city, with 116,000 people and 825 factories, with tobacco and metal products (stoves, railroad cars) leading industries. By 1900, thriving machine and foundry industries, carriage and wagon shops laid the foundation for Detroit's emergence as the nation's auto capitol. Several pioneer auto experimenters lived in Detroit: R.E. Olds, who built Detroit's first auto factory in 1899; and Henry Ford, who hand-built his first car in 1896, formed his first company in 1899, and the present Ford Motor Co. in 1903. Auto production, the World War I boom and the Roaring Twenties pushed Detroit's population from 285,000 in 1900 to 993,000 in 1920, and 1,568,000 in 1930. The area's industries made it the "Arsenal of Democracy" in World War II.
Further information: Greater Detroit Chamber of Commerce, 150 Michigan Ave., Detroit 48226; Cities Reporting and Information Dept., City-County Bldg., Detroit, 48226; Detroit Convention Bureau, 1400 Book Bldg., Detroit, 48226.

Edmonton, Alberta, Canada

Population: 441,530 (city), 507,000 (metro area), capitol of Alberta, largest Alberta city, 4th in Canada; total employed 228,864.
Area: 121 sq. mi., south central Alberta on North Saskatchewan River.
Industry: primary (agriculture, forestry, fisheries,

mining, quarries) 3.3%; manufacturing 13.3%; construction 9.5%; transportation, communications and other utilities 11.1%; trade 21.1%; finance, insurance and real estate 4.1%; service and public 35.2%; unclassified 2.4%.
Commerce: Distribution center for Western Canada and the Northern Territories; retail sales (1972) $940,000,000.
Transportation: Alaska and Mackenzie Highways are linked directly to Edmonton; Canadian Pacific, Canadian National, Pacific Northern, Great Slave and Alberta Resources railroad,; 4 airports, 113,279 itinerant movements making Edmonton 5th busiest in Canada.
Communications: 2 TV and 8 radio stations.
Medical facilities: 5 general and 5 auxiliary hospi-

tals, 2 rehabilitation centers, 9 nursing homes.
Cultural facilities: Edmonton Symphony Orchestra, Provincial Museum and Archives, University of Alberta, Northern Alberta Institute of Technology, Alberta and Edmonton ballet companies, Edmonton Opera, Northern Alberta Jubilee Auditorium, Queen Elizabeth Planetarium.
Other attractions: Klondike Days Annual Celebration; Edmonton Speedway; Storyland Valley Zoo;. Fort Edmonton, Mayfair and Elk Island parks; Alberta Game Farm; many lakes.
Sports: C.F.L. Edmonton Eskimos, W.H.L. Edmonton Oilers, Western Major Fastball League Monarchs; site of 1975 Commonwealth games.
History: Fort Edmonton erected 1795; named after town near London, England.

El Paso, Texas

The World Almanac is sponsored in the El Paso area by the El Paso Herald-Post, 401 Mills Ave., El Paso, Tex. 79999; telephone (915) 532-1661; Herald founded 1881, Post 1922, merged (under Scripps-Howard) 1931; circulation 47,370. Robert W. Lee, editor; Robert McBrinn, managing editor.

Population: 337,748 (city); with twin city, Juarez, Mexico, 837,000 (largest bilingual community on international border); 5th in state, 45th in nation; total employed 133,050.
Area: 130 sq. mi., at base of Franklin Mts., where Rio Grande cuts boundaries of Texas, New Mexico, Mexico; western tip of Texas.
Industry: clothing largest employer (17,000) including major manufacturers, Farah and Mann. Since 1967 60-plus assembly plants started in El Paso-Juarez twin-plant border industrialization, employ over 10,000, many in electronics. Home of El Paso Natural Gas; American Smelting & Refining (largest custom smelter in world); Phelps Dodge (copper) Standard and Texaco (oil-gasoline) refineries. Leather goods, dairies, processed Mexican foods, meat packing, nut processing, cattle, agriculture. 1972 manufacturing payroll $140 million.
Commerce: wholesale-retail center for West Texas, New Mexico, northern Mexico; retail sales (1971) $626,000,000; northbound border crossings (1972) 40.5 million. Bank deposits (1972)

$818,000,000; 13 banks, 5 savings-loan.
Transportation: 2 major rail lines, Amtrak, 8 buslines, 29 truck lines; 5 major highways, gateway to Mexico. International Airport, 4 airlines, 1972 operations 194,778.
Communications: 3 TV and 8 radio stations.
New construction: 1972 building permits $172,262,818 (up 40.9% over 1971).
Medical facilities: 6 major, 8 minor hospitals; University of Texas at El Paso Nursing School (formerly Hotel Dieu School).
Federal facilities: Ft. Bliss (U.S. Army Air Defense Center, Army Sgts. Major Academy) and William Beaumont Army Medical Center. Near White Sands Missile Range, N.M.
Cultural facilities: University of Texas at El Paso (10,000), El Paso Community College (4,000); El Paso Symphony, Museum of Art, university ballet, opera companies; theater groups; $20,000,000 Civic Center-convention facilities; 6 library branches.
Other attractions: Sun Carnival, Chamizal Park, Tigua Indians, historic missions, races.

Erie, Pennsylvania

The World Almanac is sponsored in the Erie area by the Erie Daily Times, 205 W. 12th Street, Erie, Pa., 16501; telephone (814) 456-8531; founded in 1888; circulation, 74,000 daily, 92,000 Sunday; publisher George J. Mead, executive editor Joseph Meagher, managing editor Len Kholos.

Population: 129,231 (city), 186,652 (metro area), 3rd in state; total employed 18,156.
Area: 19.53 sq. mi. at tip of northwestern Pa.
Commerce: tourism—more than 7 miles of beautiful beaches, good fishing, boating, winter sports bring thousands of tourists to the city annually; seaport—60 or more ocean-going vessels each year. Over 506 industrial plants, including General Electric and Hammermill Paper, producing machinery and parts, iron and steel forgings, hardware, meters, plastics, paper, furniture, and toys.
New construction: during the last 5 years, 5 bank buildings, 4 apartment complexes, 5 office buildings, and 2 enclosed-mall shopping centers, with a

downtown transitway mall to be completed in near future. Erie has been selected as one of 16 showcase planned variation cities across the country.
Special awards: recipient of the 1972 All America Cities Award (one of 11) for citizen participation in civic projects.
Transportation: 4 railroads, airport, 35 trucking companies, one taxi company, 4 bus lines.
Cultural facilities: Penn State University extension, Gannon, Mercyhurst, and Villa Maria colleges; Philharmonic Society, Council of the Arts, theatre groups.
History: Named after Eriez Indians; site of building of ship "Niagara," with which Oliver Hazard Perry defeated British in 1813.

Evansville, Indiana

The World Almanac is sponsored in Southwestern Indiana, Western Kentucky and Southeastern Illinois by The Evansville Press, 201 N.W. Second Street, Evansville, Ind. 47701; telephone (812) 424-7711; founded July 2, 1906 by E.W. Scripps and J. C. Harper; circulation, 46,498; editor Michael Grehl, managing editor William R. Burleigh.

Population: 138,764 (city), 288,300 (metro area), 4th in state, 120th in nation.
Area: 37 sq. mi., at a bend of the Ohio River.
Industry: Mead Johnson and Co., pharmaceutical firm, a division of Bristol-Myers Co.; 3 Whirlpool Corp. plants; Alcoa Warrick Operations just east of the city; several steel fabricating companies, furniture and fixture firms; 19 plastics firms; 303 manufacturing firms.
Commerce: retail sales (1972): $647,989,000 (114th in nation). Effective buying income per household after taxes (1972): $9,468; 5 banks, 7 savings and loan associations, home offices of CrediThrift of America, Inc.
Transportation: ranks 2nd in state in warehouse facilities because of strategic river location; world headquarters of Atlas Van Lines, moving and storage company; 5 commercial barge lines, 30 motor carriers, 4 interstate bus lines, 4 railroads, 3 airlines.
Communications: 2 daily newspapers, 3 TV and 6 radio stations.
Medical facilities: 5 general and mental hospitals and a 2-year branch of Indiana University Medical School.
Cultural facilities: Evansville Philharmonic Orchestra, Museum of Arts and Science, Mesker Zoo, University of Evansville, Indiana State University Evansville, and national headquarters of Phi Mu Alpha music fraternity. Abraham Lincoln boyhood home memorial nearby.
Sports: Evansville Triplets, Milwaukee Brewers' top farm team, site of NCAA college division basketball tournament for all 17 years.

Fort Wayne, Indiana

The World Almanac is sponsored in the Fort Wayne area by The Journal-Gazette, 600 W. Main St., Fort Wayne, Ind., 46802; (219) 423-3311. Established June 14, 1899 by consolidation of The Journal and The Daily Gazette. Circulation: 66,625 daily; Sundays 108,405; president-publisher Richard G. Inskeep, secretary-treasurer Miss Naomi Erb, editor Larry W Allen manpging editor James P Lovette

Population: 180,600 (city); 368,200 (metro area); total employed 132,800.
Area: 51.50 sq. mi. at confluence of St. Joseph, St. Mary's and Maumee rivers.
Industry: International Harvester and General Electric are largest employers; Magnavox and Essex International home offices as well as Central Soya, world's largest processor of soybeans. Several firms manufacture approximately 85% of world's diamond wire dies; magnet wire also a major product.
Commerce: wholesale and retail center for northeastern Indiana, southeastern Michigan and northwestern Ohio; retail sales (metro) $812,590,000. Bank deposits $1.156 billion, 5 banks, 4 savings-and-loan; 6 life insurance companies based here.
Transportation: 2 major rail freight lines; 56 motor freight lines including home-based North American Van, Elway Express, Scott and Transport Motor; I-69 connects city with Indianapolis and Indiana Toll Road; U.S. 30 now dual-laned to Chicago; modern municipal airport (United, Delta and Hub airlines) also headquarters 122nd Tactical Fighter Wing of Indiana Air National Guard.
Communications: 3 TV and 7 radio stations.
Medical facilities: 5 hospitals including Veteran's Admn., and TB hospital.
Cultural facilities: Fine Arts complex; Philharmonic orchestra; 9 universities and colleges; 4 museums.
Sports: Komet Hockey Team (IHL) plays at Allen Co. War Memorial Coliseum.
Other attractions: Children's Zoo; 61 parks and playgrounds; 11 golf courses; 33 shopping centers; 257 churches; Three Rivers Festival in late spring.
History: first white settlement in Indiana.

Fort Worth, Texas

The World Almanac is sponsored in the Fort Worth area by The Fort Worth Press, Fifth and Jones Sts., Fort Worth, Texas 76101; telephone (817) 332-5151; founded 1921 by Scripps-Howard Newspapers; editor Delbert Willis, business manager Leslie E. Yates, managing editor Jack Moseley.

Population: 401,800 (city, 1973 estimate); county 758,350 (1973); 4th largest Texas city. 310,500 employed of 320,100 work force.
Area: 233 sq. mi., on the Trinity River in North Central Texas.
Commerce: all types of manufacturing; metro wholesale and retail center for large area including West Texas; retail sales (estimated 1972) $1,641 billion; family buying income $8,411. Bank deposits $2,169 billion; 41 banks in the county, over 60 mortgage institutions, insurance companies and savings and loan associations.
Transportation: the first phase of the world's largest airport, The Dallas-Fort Worth Regional Airport, open in 1973, 17 miles from downtown. Meacham Field, general aviation airport; 9 railroads, Amtrak, 38 motor carriers, and 5 bus companies.
Communications: 2 TV stations and 18 area radio stations.
Medical facilities: over 20 hospitals.
Federal facilities: 14 federal agencies and Carswell Air Force Base; reserve training centers.
Cultural: Casa Manana, America's first permanent musical arena theater; symphony, opera, Van Cliburn Piano Competition. Museums: Kimball Art Museum, world acclaimed for its architecture and collection, Amon Carter Museum of Western Art, and others.
Educational facilities: 2 campuses of Tarrant County Junior College, Texas Christian University, University of Texas at Arlington, Texas Wesleyan College, Southwestern Baptist Seminary.
Recreation: 6 Flags over Texas in Arlington, Seven Seas, Forest Park and the Fort Worth Zoological Park; other parks.
Convention facilities: Tarrant County Convention Center, Will Rogers Memorial Center.
Sports attractions: Texas Rangers Baseball, Fort Worth Wings in hockey, and Colonial National Invitational Golf.
Other attractions: Fat Stock Show and Rodeo; Miss Texas Pageant.
History: founded 1849 as a frontier Army post on the Chisholm Trail; became major railhead.

Fresno, California

The World Almanac is sponsored in the Fresno area by The Fresno Bee, Van Ness and Calaveras, Fresno, Calif. 93721; telephone (209) 268-5221; founded 1922; circulation daily 115,589, Sunday 140,716; president Eleanor McClatchy, editor Walter Jones, managing editor George Gruner.

Population: 173,800 (city), 429,500 (county) total employed 176,000.
Area: one of largest counties in the state, 3,819,456 acres. Fresno is located in geographical center of the state midway between San Francisco and Los Angeles.
Agriculture: leading county in United States in annual value of agricultural production; State's leading county in production of grapes, barley, figs, turkeys, irrigated pasture, nectarines, cantaloupes, safflower, raisins and alfalfa. Peaches and oranges also major crops.
Industry: 478 diversified manufacturing establishments. Food processing is major industry. Canned, frozen, and dehydrated fruit and vegetable processing lead all other industrial sectors in employment; 2nd in importance is production of beverages, primarily wine, brandy and spirits.
Transportation: 2 airports, regularly scheduled daily service by 5 airlines. Freeways connect to all major metropolitan areas in California. Area served by 29 common truck carriers, 2 interstate bus lines and 2 mainline railroads with complete

freight handling facilities.
Communications: 6 TV and 16 radio stations.
Medical facilities: 4 general hospitals, including a Veteran's Administration installation.
Cultural facilities: $10,000,000 Community and Convention Center opened in 1967. Fresno has community philharmonic, opera, ballet and theater. Also California State University-Fresno, Pacific College and 3 community colleges.
Recreation: 3 National Parks: Yosemite, Sequoia and Kings Canyon with groves of giant Sequoia trees plus complete facilities for boating, sailing, hunting, fishing, skiing, hiking, pack trips and camping.
Other attractions: city zoo, nationally famous rodeo, county fair, underground gardens, Kearney museum and downtown Fresno malls with one of the best outdoor art displays in the west.
History: area explored by the Spaniards in the early 1800's and visited by fur trappers before 1840; settlement began when gold miners came in the 1850's; County created April 19, 1856, from parts of Mariposa, Merced and Tulare counties.

Halifax, Nova Scotia, Canada

The World Almanac is sponsored in Nova Scotia by The Chronicle-Herald and The Mail-Star, 1650 Argyle Street, Halifax; telephone (902) 426-2811; circulation Chronicle (morn.) 67,862, Mail-Star (aft.) 49,560; publisher and president Graham W. Dennis, chairman of the board Ira B. MacCallum, general-manager Fred G. Mounce, managing editor Alvin M. Savage, secretary-treasurer W. D. Coleman.

Population: 122,035 (city), 224,300 (metro), one of first 4 Canadian Provinces to enter Confederation.
Area: 15,620 acres of land, on the southeast coast of the province.
Industry: economy largely revolves around armed forces base industries, but offshore oil exploration programs are rapidly making industrial changes. Minimum expenditures on drilling and exploration are estimated to be $200,000,000 between 1972 and 1975. The Halifax Shipyards alone has contracts worth $86,000,000 for construction of 5 semi-submersible drilling rigs. Over $150,000,000 comes into the local area annually as a result of wages, services, warehousing, distribution and packaging originating at port.
Commerce: city is the leading commercial centre in Maritime provinces, handling over one-third of the retail trade and over two-thirds of the wholesale business in Nova Scotia. Retail sales (1971) in metro area over $380,000,000; average income in 1971 was $8,396. City has 51 bank branches, 6 trust

companies and 15 investment houses.
Transportation: 2 major rail freight lines, 6 container lines call regularly at port, and 65 steamship lines, coastal services, deep sea lines and passenger services make calls. The harbor easily handles ships with up to 250,000 dwt. International airport.
Communications: 2 TV and 3 radio stations.
Educational facilities: 6 degree-granting universities, 71 common schools, 3 private; 150 vocational schools and one technical institute.
Medical facilities: an $8,000,000 medical school and a $15,000,000 hospital for children offering finest facilities east of Montreal.
Cultural facilities: Atlantic Symphony Orchestra, 3 professional live theatres and one amateur; 2 public libraries.
Parks: 3 major parks (403 acres.)
Sports: home of Halifax Voyageurs of the American Hockey League.
History: founded in 1749; meeting place of the first legislative assembly in Canada, (1758).

Hamilton, Ontario, Canada

The World Almanac is sponsored in Hamilton and the Nigara Peninsula by The Spectator (a division of Southam Press Ltd.), 115 King Street East, Hamilton, Ontario; telephone (416) 522-8642; founded in 1846; circulation 135,000; publisher John D. Muir, business manager James S. Thomson, executive editor Gordon Bullock, managing editor, Paul Warnick.

Population: 307,473 (city), 495,864 (metro area), 3rd in province, 6th in Canada; total work force, 182,000 (1971).
Area: 54 sq. mi. at the westerly extremity of Lake Ontario.
Industry: 60% of all of Canada's steel is produced at 2 Hamilton plants, the Steel Company of Canada and Dominion Foundries and Steel Limited. City ranks 3rd in Canada in industrial production. About 750 plants in the metropolitan area, manu-

facturing wire, heavy machinery, various iron and steel goods, electrical apparatus, chemicals and textiles.
Commerce: retail sales (1972): $775,000,000; average wage per year: $7,040 (1972), 11th in Canada.
Transportation: served by both of Canada's transcontinental railways, Canadian National and Canada Pacific, as well as the Toronto, Hamilton and Buffalo line; provincial highways through

Toronto to Windsor and Buffalo pass metropolitan area; City has own airport 6 miles to south at Mount Hope, with commercial movements to Montreal, Ottawa and Pittsburgh.

Communications: one TV and 4 radio stations.

Medical facilities: new $73,000,000 medical center at McMaster University, with latest in teaching facilities; 4 other major hospitals in metropolitan area.

Educational facilities: McMaster University, one of Canada's largest post-secondary schools; Mohawk College of Applied Arts and Technology.

Cultural facilities: Hamilton Art Gallery; year-round Hamilton Philharmonic Orchestra, plus variety of theatrical groups; new theatre-auditorium.

Sports attractions: major sport is the Hamilton Tiger-Cats of the Canadian Football League.

Other attractions: Dundurn Castle, restored mansion of 1850 period; Royal Botanical Gardens display of flowers; Canadian Football League Hall of Fame.

History: Explorer Sieur de La Salle discovered Hamilton area on expedition in 1669.

Hartford, Connecticut

The World Almanac is sponsored in the Hartford area by The Hartford Times, 10 Prospect St., Hartford, Conn. 06101; telephone (203) 249-8211; founded 1817 by Frederick D. Bolles and John M. Niles; circulation 125,000 afternoons and Sunday; publisher Roger C. Coryell, executive editor Charles A. Betts, Pulitzer citation as Gannett Newspaper, Pulitzer Prize to staff member; community projects include series on tax reform, urban renewal and sponsorship of Times Farm Camp for less-privileged children.

Population: 158,017 (city), 738,800 (metro area); total employed in metro area 327,260.

Area: 17.2 sq. miles.

Industry: Known as "Insurance City", the Hartford area is headquarters for 33 insurance firms employing 45,000; East Hartford is the home office of United Aircraft Corp., one of the world's largest aircraft firms.

Commerce: total retail sales (metro area) in 1972 was $1.78 billion; per household consumer spendable income in 1972 was $14,314

Transportation: Hartford is at the intersection of highways 84 and 91. Rail passenger service is provided by Amtrak and freight service by Penn Central Railroad; Bradley International Airport services Hartford with 9 scheduled airlines, several providing cargo service.

New construction: to be completed by October, 1974—Hartford Civic Center complex, including $18,000,000 Aetna Life & Casualty shopping arcade, 20-story Sheraton Hotel, 10,000 seat coliseum, 70,000 sq. ft. exhibition hall and 17,000 sq. ft. assembly hall.

Communications: 6 radio and 4 TV stations.

Educational facilities: Trinity College, University of Hartford, Graduate Center of Rensselaer Polytechnic Institute, St. Joseph College, Hartford Seminary Foundation, University of Connecticut Law School.

Cultural facilities: Wadsworth Atheneum, the oldest public art museum in America; Mark Twain House; Hartford Symphony Orchestra; Connecticut Opera Association; Hartford Stage Company.

Sports: Hartford Knights (football); Hartford Capitols (basketball); Connecticut Wildcats (soccer).

History: City was founded in 1636 by Thomas Hooker and a company of settlers from Newtown (Cambridge), Mass. It became Connecticut's capital city in 1665.

Further information: Greater Hartford Chamber of Commerce, 250 Constitution Plaza, Hartford, Conn. 06103.

Honolulu, Hawaii

The World Almanac is sponsored in Hawaii by The Honolulu Advertiser, P.O. Box 3110, Honolulu, Hawaii, 96802; telephone (808) 537-2977; founded July 2, 1856, as the Pacific Commercial Advertiser by Henry M. Whitney; circulation 75,734 mornings, 187,159 Sunday; president and publisher Thurston Twigg-Smith, editor-in-chief George Chaplin, executive managing editor Buck Buchwach, major awards from American Political Science Assn., others.

Population: 345,000 (city), 660,100 (metro area), 1st in state, 44th in nation; total employed, 350,000.

Area: 595 sq. mi., encompassing the island of Oahu.

Commerce: major tourist destination for U.S. and Japan; tourists in 1972 numbered 2,244,377 and spent $755,000,000. National defense is slightly bigger in dollars than tourism. Pearl Harbor is headquarters for U.S. Pacific Fleet, with an estimated worth of more than $1.5 billion. Sugar and pineapple are the other big industries. Honolulu's retail sales (1972) $2.2 billion. There are 8 banks, 12 savings and loan associations; bank resources are more than $2.5 billion. City is business and financial center for the Pacific Basin.

Transportation: freight arrives by ship and air; passengers mostly by air; ocean liners call infrequently. Honolulu Airport served by 18 airlines: 8 domestic trunk carriers, 8 foreign, 2 inter-island; airport is 28th in nation in aircraft movements.

Communications: 5 TV and 22 radio stations.

Medical facilities: 18 hospitals, including U.S. Army's Tripler Hospital. University of Hawaii Medical School, and research laboratories specializing in tropical diseases.

Cultural facilities: University of Hawaii, a 9-campus system with more than 37,000 students, is especially noted for oceanography and tropical agriculture. East-West Center, co-sponsored by university and U.S. State Department, draws students from around the world. Other 4-year colleges: Chaminade College, operated by Catholic Church; Church College of Hawaii, run by the Mormon Church; Hawaii Loa College, founded by 4 Protestant denominations and publicly supported by community colleges. Bernice Pauahi Bishop Museum houses Pacific artifacts, is a center of archeological study of most Pacific cultures. Honolulu Symphony Orchestra.

Other attractions: Waikiki Beach and its famous view of the extinct volcano, Diamond Head. Honolulu best-known for its multi-racial population, Polynesian heritage.

History: Honolulu (Hawaiian for "sheltered bay") was small native village when first visited by 2 British ships in 1786, 8 years after Capt. James Cook discovered Hawaiian Islands.

Houston, Texas

The Houston Post, founded 1836, is the co-publisher of the Almanac in the Southwest. Located in ultra-modern facilities, the Post, 4747 Southwest Freeway, Houston, Texas, 77001, telephone (713) 621-7000, has a circulation of: daily, 291,622; Saturday, 323,544; Sunday, 344,216. Chairman of the board and editor Oveta Culp Hobby, president William P. Hobby, Jr. Awards include the Pulitzer Prize, Grand Prix and Editor & Publisher. Community service events include Science Fair, Spring Art Festival, travel fairs, as well as other civic and cultural activities.

Population: 1,341,000 (city), 6th in nation; 2,136,000 (metro), 13th in nation; total employed 933,600.

Area: 506.52 sq. mi. (city) on the upper center Gulf Coast prairies, 41 feet above sea level; county seat of Harris; connected to Gulf of Mexico by a 50-mile inland waterway.

Industry: nation's largest: manufacturer/distributer of petroleum equipment, pipeline transmissions, refineries; 2,683 manufacturing firms in metro area; 40% of all U.S. petrochemicals produced; 80% of all U.S. synthetic rubber.

Commerce: metro area retail sales $3.8 billion, 12th in nation; metro wholesale sales $6.6 billion, 9th in nation; 157 banks in metro area with resources of $10.4 billion and deposits of $8.5 billion.

Transportation: Port of Houston (nations 3rd largest seaport) moved 69,000,000 tons of cargo in 1972; 100 steamship lines; 20,000,000 short tons traveled on intracoastal waterways; 2 airports with 6 international carriers, 9 domestic carriers; 6 major rail systems moved 21,000,000 short tons of freight; 391 miles of freeways link metro area; 34 truck lines.

Communications: 5 commercial TV plus 1 educational station; 29 radio stations.

New construction: $806,100,000 in non-residential contracts; $611,300,000 value of residential units completed.

Medical facilities: Texas Medical Center with 28 institutions offering 3,507 beds serving 113,480 inpatients and over a million out-patients; 56 hospitals in metro area with 10,987 beds plus VA hospital with 1,332 beds.

Federal facilities: Lyndon B. Johnson Spacecraft Center, NASA, $202,000,000 complex on 1,640 acre site, 22 miles southeast; Center conceives, designs, develops, operates, controls manned spacecraft activities and trains astronauts, and is reason for nickname: "Space City, U.S.A."

Cultural facilities: nationally acclaimed 90-member Houston Symphony; Grand Opera Association; one of the 3 oldest resident theatres in U.S. — Alley Theatre — in its 27th season in a $3,000,000, two-theatre building; Miller Outdoor Theatre; 25 major art institutes; Natural Science Museum & planetarium; 27-branch library system, famous for collections on genealogy and Texana; Fine Arts Museum; Contemporary Arts Museum.

Educational facilities: 6th largest school district in nation, total enrollment of 432,539 in metro area; 25 colleges and universities in metro area, including University of Houston and Rice University.

Recreational facilities: Astroworld, 60-acre family amusement/entertainment park; botanical garden and arboretum; Herman Park and zoo; 245 municipal parks and playgrounds; 4 municipal golf courses; Gulf of Mexico with 70 miles of beaches.

Convention facilities: world's largest single level facility Astrohall (795,000 sq. ft.) next to famous Astrodome; downtown facilities include 300,000 sq. ft. Albert Thomas Center; 50,000 sq. ft. Coliseum and Music Hall, seating 14,536.

Sports attractions: pro-teams: Astros baseball, Oilers football, Aeros hockey, Rockets basketball. Rice Stadium site of 1974 Super Bowl; Astro-Bluebonnet college Bowl game.

Climate: Temperatures moderated by Gulf winds producing mild winters and relatively cool summer nights; rainfall abundant at 42″ annually; average yearly temperature 68° with highs in 90°s, lows in 40°s; average humidity 76%.

History: Founded 1836 by Allen brothers; named for General Sam Houston, first president of the Republic of Texas; an early capital of Republic; Battle of San Jacinto (1836) for Texas independence from Mexico fought nearby; oil discovered (1901) at Spindletop; Port opened in 1915.

Huntington, West Virginia

The World Almanac is sponsored in the Huntington area by The Herald-Dispatch (morn), and The Huntington Advertiser (aft), Huntington Publishing Company, 946 Fifth Avenue, Huntington, West Virginia 25720, member of the Gannett Group; circulation 69,038, Sunday 58,360. Publisher and president N. S. Hayden, business manager James D. Hoffman, executive editor John H. McMillan; managing editors, C. Donald Hatfield (Advertiser), and Donald G. Mayne (Herald-Dispatch).

Population: 74,315 (city), 286,935 (5-county metro area); largest city in the state.

Area: 15.86 sq. mi., on Ohio River near where West Virginia, Ohio and Kentucky meet.

Industry: home of Alloys Products division of the International Nickel Company, Inc.; center for handcrafted glass; coal transport center; headquarters for several railroad operations.

Commerce: largest port for inland vessels in U.S. handles nearly 23,000,000 tons of materials per year, moved by 7 freight companies; 1972 total retail sales in metro area $747,288,000.

Transportation: Tri-State Airport, now being expanded, is served by 2 airlines, 500 air movements

a month; 18 truck lines; urban bus transport system; 2 interstate bus lines.

Communications: 4 TV and 10 radio stations.

Cultural facilities: Marshall University with nearly 10,000 students; The Huntington Galleries of art.

Medical facilities: 5 general hospitals with 1,076 total beds; 3 specialty hospitals included a VA hospital.

New construction: $32,000,000 renewal program calls for large shopping mall, riverfront marina, civic auditorium and additional convention facilities.

Further information: Chamber of Commerce, 522 Ninth Street, Huntington, W. Va. 25701.

Indianapolis, Indiana

The World Almanac is sponsored in the Indianapolis area by The Indianapolis Star and The Indianapolis News, 307 North Pennsylvania Street, Indianapolis, Indiana 46206; (317) 633-1240; News founded 1869, Star 1903; circulation Star 226,187, News 176,866, Sunday 373,142; president-publisher Eugene C. Pulliam, asst. publisher Eugene S. Pulliam, Star editor Frank Crane, News editor M. Stanton Evans; Pulitzer Prize to News, National Headliners first prize to Star.

Population: 745,739 (1970) in Consolidated City, nation's 11th largest; 1,111,173 (1970) in area: labor force 479,100.

Area: 379.4 sq. mi., geographic center of state.

Industry: Over 1,400 diversified manufacturers including plane and auto engines and parts, electronics, pharmaceuticals, machinery; 1972 manufacturing payroll over $1.1 billion.

Commerce: commercial center for Indiana; state capital. Retail sales $2.3 billion; per capita personal income $4,861; 6 banks with resources over $4.3 billion; home offices of over 60 insurance companies.

Transportation: 9 airlines, 5 rail freight lines, Amtrak, 2 interstate buslines and over 100 truck lines; 7 interstate freeway routes.

Communications: 8 TV and 11 radio stations.

Medical facilities: 16 hospitals with 7,489 beds; location of the nation's largest private comprehensive rehabilitation center.

Cultural facilities: Museum of Art and Oldfields Museum of Decorative Arts; Indiana State Museum; Children's Museum, Children's Zoo;

Conner Prairie Pioneer Settlement and Museum of Indian Heritage; Clowes Hall for the performing arts, home of Indianapolis Symphony Orchestra. Civic Theatre, oldest U.S. amateur theatrical group; Indianapolis Repertory Theatre.

Education facilities: Butler University, Indiana Central College, Marian College, Christian Theological and St. Mauer's seminaries, and Indiana University-Purdue University at Indianapolis, with nation's largest medical school. Higher education enrollment about 23,000.

Recreational facilities: 9,000 park acres, 8 major swimming pools, 9 municipal golf courses; pro baseball and football in Sports Arena, home of ABA 1973 champion "Pacers."

Other attractions: Indianapolis 500, Yankee 300 and annual Drag Racing championships; new Convention-Exposition Center.

History: Sesquicentennial in 1971; important before Civil War, with nation's first union railway station (1853); home of James Whitcomb Riley, Booth Tarkington and President Benjamin Harrison.

Jacksonville, Florida

The World Almanac is sponsored in the Jacksonville area by The Florida Times-Union and the Jacksonville Journal, One Riverside Avenue, Jacksonville, Fla. 32202; telephone (904) 791-4111; Union founded 1864, Times 1881, merged 1883; Journal founded 1887 as Metropolis; circulation daily Times-Union 151,216, Journal 62,697, combined Sunday 184,570; president Robert R. Feagin, vice-president John A. Tucker, executive editor John S. Walters, managing editor Times-Union A. Bruce Manning, managing editor Journal Elvin Henson; Journal's Pulitzer Prize for news photography in 1967.

Population: 528,865 (1970); city includes entire metro area, largest in state.

Area: 827 sq. mi., largest incorporated developed area in Western Hemisphere.

Commerce: Florida's business capital, with emphasis on finance, insurance and distribution; home or regional headquarters for 34 insurance companies with total assets over $29 billion. Total retail sales in 1971 were $1.165 billion.

Transportation: served by 3 major railroads and 14 other lines, 16 truck lines; port handled 14,885,935 tons in 1972; 9 airlines into new airport with about 130 air movements per day; 2 interstate bus lines.

Communications: 4 TV and 14 radio stations.

Federal facilities: 2 air stations and a naval station add $250,000,000 a year to area economy.

Medical facilities: 10 general hospitals with a total of 2,456 beds, and one naval hospital.

Cultural facilities: Civic Auditorium, art museum, Cummer Art Gallery, Children's Museum, Jack-

sonville Symphony, Ballet Guild, Opera Repertory Group and 4 community theaters.

Educational facilities: Jacksonville University, Edward Waters College, Florida Junior College and University of North Florida.

New construction: since 1971, more than $140,000,000 of construction planned or begun, including 37-story Independent Life and Accident Insurance Co. building, 20-story addition to Florida Blue Cross-Blue Shield facilities, and a 21-story apartment building for the elderly.

Sports: Gator Bowl in 70,000-seat stadium; Greater Jacksonville Open, a $150,000 PGA tournament.

History: founded 1822 by Isiah Hart, city survived Seminole War of 1835, yellow fever epidemic in 1888 and a fire in 1901 that destroyed 2,368 buildings and left 10,000 people homeless; named for Andrew Jackson.

Further information: Chamber of Commerce, 604 Hogan St., Jacksonville, Fla. 32202.

Kalamazoo, Michigan

The World Almanac is sponsored in the Kalamazoo area by The Kalamazoo Gazette, 401 S. Burdick, Kalamazoo, Mich. 49003; telephone (616) 345-3511, founded 1833; circulation daily 57,581, Sunday 60,801; owned and operated by Booth Newspapers, Inc.; president Gordon H. Craig, editor Daniel M. Ryan, general manager Ralph H. Bastien, Jr.

Population: 85,555 (city), 201,000 (county); total employed in county, 82,800.

Area: located equidistant to the 3rd and 5th largest metro areas in nation—Chicago and Detroit, 140 miles away.

Industry: paper-making in area is the traditional industry, with 5 large plants here. Checker Motors Corp. manufacturers of cars; large Fisher Body Division body stamping plant; Upjohn Company, pharmaceuticals.

Commerce: shopping center for large part of Southwestern Michigan. In 1959, city became first in country to close downtown streets and create a pedestrian mall. Now known as "Mall City." Retail sales in (1972) $458 million. Four banks have combined assets in 1972 of $639,000,000, 4 savings and loan associations have assets of over $200,000,000.

Transportation: 2 railroads provide freight service, Amtrak passenger service; 33 general carriers provide trucking services; airport with freight and passenger service; 3 buslines.

Cultural facilities: 4 auditoriums offering music and theatrical performances, 6 live arts theaters, an art center, symphony orchestra, Kalamazoo Civic Players.

Educational facilities: 3 colleges and one university with combined student enrollment over 27,000.

Other attractions: Kalamazoo Nature Center, 83 lakes (county), National Junior Tennis Championships, 2 major hospitals.

Kansas City, Missouri

The World Almanac is sponsored in the Kansas City area by The Kansas City Star, 1729 Grand Ave., Kansas City, Mo. 64108; telephone (816) 421-1200; founded by William Rockhill Nelson; circulation morning 335,361, evening 315,560, Sunday 404,519; president Paul V. Miner, executive assistant to the president William T. Shields, general manager Frank S. McKinney, editor W. W. Baker, executive editor Cruise Palmer, advertising director W. W. Meyer.

Population: 511,600 (city); 1,323,800 (metro area), 27th in nation; total employed 592,200.

Area: 316.3 sq. mi., at confluence of Missouri and Kansas rivers.

Industry: 2d in nation in automotive assembly; 1st in production of vending machines, greeting cards, underground freezer space and winter wheat trading. Top employers: U.S. government, General Motors, TWA, Bendix, Western Electric, Ford. Presently Kansas City is a leading hard wheat center, stocker and feeder market, and is among the top 5 cities in flour production and grain elevator capacity.

Commerce: Total retail sales in 1972 $3.226 billion; the center of a 7-county metro area: Jackson, Clay, Platte, Cass and Ray counties in Missouri; Johnson and Wyandotte counties in Kansas.

Transportation: 8 airlines and 150 daily flights out of the new Kansas City International Airport; 169 truck lines and 4 barge companies. The city is one of the nation's major rail centers.

New construction: $200,000,000 Crown Center business and apartment complex covers 25 square blocks; new medical center of University of Missouri; American Royal Arena; Mercantile Bank Building; United Missouri Bank headquarters; 30-story office and retail building downtown. Worlds of Fun recreation center. More than 6 large hotels and several hospital additions.

Cultural facilities: Starlight Theater, nation's 2d largest outdoor theater; William Rockhill Nelson Gallery of Art, among the 10 top American museums with the 3rd largest Oriental collection outside China; Performing Arts Foundation formed in 1965 to present festival events; University of Missouri at Kansas City; Rockhurst College; Kansas City Art Institute; University of Kansas Medical Center. Within commuting distance are University of Kansas, Park College, William Jewell College and Central Missouri State College. Truman Library in Independence. Linda Hall Library of Science and Technology is one of the largest privately endowed technical reference libraries in the nation.

Recreational facilities: More than 100 parks cover 5,345 acres, including Swope Park, 2d largest in nation, with fine zoo.

Sports: The American Royal Livestock and Horse Show each fall attracts entries from throughout the country, Home of the Chiefs of the National Football League, Royals of American Baseball League, the Kings National Basketball Association team, and a National Hockey franchise that begins play in 1974.

History: Kansas City's beginnings can be traced to a trading post of French fur trappers about 1826. It became an important trade and transportation center as the overland routes of the Oregon and Santa Fe Trails spread westward. As agricultural production boomed, it became an important market and distribution center for crops from throughout the Middle West.

Kitchener-Waterloo, Ontario, Canada

The World Almanac is sponsored in the Kitchener-Waterloo area by the Kitchener-Waterloo Record, 225 Fairway Road South, Kitchener, Ont.; telephone (519) 579-2231; founded 1878; circulation 60,562; president and publisher John E. Motz, executive vice-president K. A. Baird, editor in chief Carl B. Schmidt.

Population: 119,483 (Kitchener) and 38,817 (Waterloo), 256,651 (metro area); total employed 92,500.

Area: 52.78 sq. mi. (Kitchener) and 25.28 sq. mi. (Waterloo), 65 miles west of Toronto.

Industry: Highly diversified industry (338 companies), tires, electronics, metal fabrication, brewing, distilling, automotive components. Budd Automotive Co., largest autoframe maker in Canada, capable of 1.4 million frames a year.

Commerce: Wholesale and retail centre for area; metro retail sales (1972): $335,100,000. Five banks, 54 branches, 6 trust companies, 16 branches; 28 life insurance offices, 19 other insurance offices; Waterloo, "The Hartford of Canada," head office for 6 insurance companies.

Transportation: 2 major rail lines, 34 truck lines, on Ontario's key highway 401; Waterloo-Wellington Airport; 45 mi. from Toronto International.

Communications: One TV and 4 radio stations.

Medical facilities: 2 major hospitals.

Cultural facilities: Kitchener-Waterloo Symphony Orchestra, Kitchener-Waterloo Art Gallery, Doon School of Fine Arts, Doon Pioneer Village; 28 mi. from famed Stratford Festival Theatre.

Educational facilities: University of Waterloo (13,100 students), Wilfrid Laurier University (2,800), Conestoga College (1,300).

Other attractions: Nationally-known farmers market; Canada's largest annual Oktoberfest celebration; Woodside national historic park, boyhood home of W. L. MacKenzie King, Canadian prime minister 22 years; nearby Amish Mennonite area.

History: Founded 1807 by Pennsylvania Dutch, followed by German settlers; retains strong Germanic flavor.

Knoxville, Tennessee

The World Almanac is sponsored in the Knoxville area by The Knoxville News-Sentinel, 204 West Church Avenue, Knoxville, Tenn. 37901; telephone (615) 523-3131; Sentinel founded in 1886 by John T. Hearn, News in 1921 by Scripps-Howard Newspapers, Sentinel purchased by Scripps-Howard in 1926 and combined with News; circulation 106,885 daily and 159,159 Sunday; editor Ralph L. Millett Jr., managing editor Harold E. Harlow.

Population: 174,587 (city), 409,000 (metro area); 3rd in state, 76th in nation.

Area: 77.6 sq. mi. located almost in the exact center of that portion of the United States lying east of the Mississippi River and south of the Great Lakes.

Industry: Major manufacturing industry is clothing with Standard Knitting Mills, the largest manufacturer of knitted clothing under one roof in the nation. Levi Strauss & Co. and Palm Beach Co. also have Knoxville plants. Nearly 1,000 industrial plants representing 51 diversified major industries, including Aluminum Company of America; Union Carbide Corp.'s Nuclear Division at Oak Ridge, are included in the Knoxville market.

Commerce: Trade center of a 42-county area in East Tennessee, Virginia, Kentucky and North Carolina; retail sales (1971) $556,999,000; average spendable family income $9,036.00.

Transportation: 2 rail lines, 5 airlines, 2 interstate bus lines, 23 motor freight carriers serve Knoxville. Interstate Highways I-40 and I-75 intersect in heart of city; I-40 and I-81 intersect several miles

east of city.

New construction: An $11-million development and expansion of McGhee-Tyson airport, serving Knoxville, scheduled for completion mid-1974.

Federal facilities: Administrative headquarters of the Tennessee Valley Authority, created by Congress in 1933, to develop navigation, flood control and power for Tennessee valley region.

Cultural facilities: University of Tennessee, Knoxville College, Knoxville Symphony Orchestra, 2 museums, art gallery, auditorium, coliseum, modern city library (480,829 book volume).

Sports: Neyland Stadium, seating 70,650, home of Tennessee Vols football team; Knoxville Sox, farm club of Chicago White Sox.

Other attractions: Great Smoky Mountains National Park, 39 miles from Knoxville, offers year-round scenic beauty, skiing in season. Within 30 miles of Knoxville, 6 TVA lakes have 2,320 miles of shoreline providing fishing, boating, etc.

History: Founded 1791. Homestead of John Sevier, first governor, is a state historical site.

Las Vegas, Nevada

The World Almanac is sponsored in the Las Vegas area by The Las Vegas Review-Journal, 1111 W. Bonanza, Las Vegas 89101; telephone (702) 385-4241; founded as a weekly 1909; purchased 1956 by Donald W. Reynolds, present publisher; member of Donrey Media Group; circulation morning, 16,000, evening 40,000, Sunday 69,000; general manager Wm. Wright, editor Don Digilio.

Population: 310,000 greater Las Vegas; approx. 12% over 55 years old; annual births 5,301, marriages 50,150, divorces 5,079; 133,500 employed 1972; unemployment rate 6.6%; annual payroll Las Vegas labor area $830,692,547.

Area: southeastern Nevada, approximately 30 mi. north of Boulder (Hoover) Dam.

Industry: 24-hour-a-day tourism, more than 17,400,000 visitors annually; 86% of possible sunshine; by 1975 city expects 40,000 hotel/motel rooms; total rooms 1973: 27,555; total annual tourist expenditure $602,026,950; gross gaming revenue $476,126,720.

Commerce: 4 savings and loan assocs., 5 banks.

Transportation: McCarran International Airport will handle 500,000 flights annually by 1980s; 7 major airlines; 3 bus lines; average daily traffic: I15 North 4,800, U.S. 95 north 1,150, U.S. 95 south 4,040, I15 south 10,140.

Communications: 10 radio and 5 TV stations.

New construction: greater Las Vegas building permits 1972: $323,517,119, up 41.9% over 1971.

Medical facilities: 9 hospitals greater Las Vegas with 1,497 beds.

Federal facilities: Nellis Air Force Base, nearly 9,000 assigned personnel, 1,000 civilians; U.S. Forest Service; Bureau of Land Management; Bureau of Reclamation; Natl. Park Service; EPA; FAA; AEC; Environmental Protection Agency.

Educational facilities: University of Nevada Las Vegas, more than 6,000 students, 265 fulltime professors; area public, private, parochial school enrollment 79,112; Clark County Community College (junior college).

Recreation: Lake Mead (fishing, boating, skiing, swimming, camping), Mt. Charleston, Valley of Fire, Kyle and Lee Canyons (skiing).

Convention facilities: $4,500,000 Convention Center served 100,000 in 1972; 45 acres, 515,000 sq. ft. under roof with 330,000 exhibit space.

Sports: 50 tournament-ready tennis courts; 11 golf courses; Las Vegas Stadium; university football, basketball, baseball; pro football team, Las Vegas Casinos.

Lethbridge, Alberta, Canada

The World Almanac is sponsored in the Lethbridge area by The Lethbridge Herald, 504 7th St. S., Lethbridge, Alta.; telephone (403) 328-4411; founded as weekly in 1905; became daily in 1907; circulation, weekdays 23,075, Saturdays 24,284; editor and publisher Cleo W. Mowers, general manager Thomas H. Adams, managing editor Don Pilling.

Population; 42,816, 3rd in province.
Area: 22 square miles; located 60 miles north of Montana border, 125 miles south of Calgary.
Industry: Heavily dependent on agriculture and allied industries. Lethbridge federally-inspected packing plants slaughtered about 30% per cent of the cattle slaughtered in Alberta in 1972—and the percentage increases every year. Serves large dryland grain growing and ranching area and extensive irrigation district. Brewery; new distillery will be completed by fall, 1973.
Commerce: 1972 retail sales of $120 million; 5 banks with 15 branches, 3 trust companies, 11 finance companies.
Transportation: Railway, 2 bus lines, depots for 48 trucking firms; regional airline flics out of Lethbridge Airport.

Communication: 2 radio and 2 TV stations.
Medical facilities: 2 general hospitals, one long-term care hospital, 4 nursing homes.
Cultural facilities: Canada Agriculture research station, University of Lethbridge, Lethbridge Community College, Alexander Galt Museum, Nikka Yuko Centennial Japanese Garden, symphony orchestra and chorus, theater groups.
Other attractions: 2 major parks plus neighborhood recreation areas, 2 artificial ice arenas, Stewart Game Farm.
Sports: Lethbridge will host 1975 Canada Winter Games, home of Lakers of the Montreal Expos farm system.
History: Early coal-mining center, named in 1885 after a coal executive.

Little Rock, Arkansas

The World Almanac is sponsored in Arkansas by the Arkansas Gazette, 112 West Third Street, Little Rock 72203, telephone 501-376-6161. Founded 1819 at Arkansas Post, A. T., by Wm. E. Woodruff, moved to Little Rock 1821; circulation 115,576 daily, 141,125 Sunday; Hugh B. Patterson Jr., publisher and president of company; J. O. Powell, editor; Robert R. Douglas, managing editor; J. R. Williamson, vice president-general manager.

Population: 166,100 (city), 333,287 (metro); 148,000 employed.
Area: 110 sq. mi. at point where Ozarks-Ouachita highlands meet central coastal plain at geographical center of state.
Industry: 376 manufacturing plants, employing 28,000 persons and including Allis-Chalmers, Armstrong Rubber Co., U.S. Time, AMF Cycle Division, Remington Arms, Jacuzzi Bros., Teletype and Westinghouse among others.
Commerce: Retail sales (1971 estimated), $662,975,000. Bank resources $1.076 billion. Building permits (1972), 6,471 with value of $113,769,446. Eleven banks, 6 building & loan associations, 4 oldline insurance companies. Postal receipts (1972), $16,705,705.
Transportation: 3 trunkline railroads, 5 federally

certified airlines, 8 bus lines, 14 common carrier barge lines.
Communications: 3 commercial TV stations, 1 ETV station, 11 radio stations.
Medical facilities: 9 hospitals including UA Medical Center, 2 VA hospitals and Ark. State Hospital for Nervous Diseases.
Cultural facilities: University of Arkansas at Little Rock, University of Arkansas Schools of Law, Medicine, Nursing and Pharmacy, UA School of Graduate Technology; Philander Smith, Shorter, and Arkansas Baptist colleges. Arkansas State Symphony, Arkansas Arts Center, 3 major public libraries, convention center-auditorium-hotel.
History: French explorer Bernard de la Harpe noted "le petit roche" on his map of the Arkansas River Valley in 1722.

London, Ontario, Canada

The World Almanac is sponsored in London and Southwestern Ontario by The London Free Press, 369 York St., London N6A 4G1, Ontario; (519) 679-1111. Founded 1849; combined morning-evening circulation, 124,000. Publisher Walter J. Blackburn, advertising director C. G. Fenn, editor W. C. Heine, production manager C. R. Turnbull, planning and development manager P. G. White.

Population: 230,100, 10th largest city in Canada; within an 80-mile radius population is 800,000.
Area: 43,929.6 acres, hub of prosperous industrial-agricultural area, 130 miles east of Detroit, 124 miles west of Toronto.
Industry: Diversified; 12 new industries settled in London in 1972 with total investment of $6,000,000; 35 existing industries expanded adding a capital investment for growth of $9,000,000. Recruitable labor force is estimated at 11,000. Surrounding city is prime farm land which supports a major beef and dairy industry, tobacco, fruit and vegetables. Nearby is the highly industrial area of Sarnia, St. Thomas, Woodstock and Chatham.
Commerce: Wholesale and retail center of the region, London is 10th largest in retail sales in Canada; 5th in automobile sales, and 6th in per capita income. Shoppers pour $415,000,000 annually into economy.
Transportation: 2 major railways, 3 major bus lines and 2 airlines serve London. There is direct

air and rail connection with the U.S. and all parts of Canada. St. Lawrence Seaway ports serve the region.
Communications: One TV and 4 radio stations.
Medical facilities: 4 major hospitals.
Federal facilities: London is headquarters for one of Canada's major military units— Royal Canadian Regiment. Historically the city has been a garrison town and today the military plays a major role in community life.
Cultural facilities: World-famous Stratford Shakespearian Festival, professional theatre, symphony orchestra, art museum and public library; University of Western Ontario with an enrollment of 14,000 students.
Recreational facilities: Extensive green belt, parks and recreational facilities; Fanshawe Park with 200 acres of parkland and 640 acres of water. Within a short distance, miles of sandy beaches and parkland are located on Lake Erie and Lake Huron.

Other attractions: Storybook Gardens, a major tourist attraction features storybook characters and items for family entertainment.

History: Incorporated as a city in 1855, London was once considered as the site for the capital of Upper Canada.

Los Angeles, California

Population: 2,894,911 (1972, City), 7,032,075 (county); 9.7 million (metro area); 1st in state, 3rd in nation; total employed, 3,214,700 (county).
Area: 463.7 sq. mi., on Pacific Coast 418 mi. south of San Francisco, 145 mi. north of Mexican border. Los Angeles is one of 77 cities in Los Angeles County.
Industry: Leading center aerospace industry; 17 of top 100 defense contractors in nation located in Southern California; County aerospace income (1972) $13.8 billion, workforce 917,000. Center entertainment industry, 617 firms in movie work, TV production. Important in women's clothing, leader sports wear, top electronics manufacturing locale, important center manufacture of rubber and tires, printing, furniture, paper, chemicals, autos and auto parts. Despite population, county is consistently among top 10 in nation in agriculture; farm income $106,000,000 (1969); slaughters more cattle than Kansas City and Chicago combined. Port of San Pedro, nation's top fishing port since 1948; fish catch 489,000,000 pounds (1969), worth $61,000,000.
Commerce: Total retail sales, $6,204,156 (city 1970), $15,953,701 (county 1970); average family income, $10,970; average per capita income $4,610 (county). More than 154,300 licensed retail stores; estimated 92 commercial banks with 1,167 branches; 79 savings and loans with 321 branches. Bank deposits $17,277,552,000; S & L $16,466,913,000.
Transportation: Santa Fe, Union Pacific and Southern Pacific railroads, Amtrak passenger rail, 76 trucking lines own world's largest concentration of trucks—57,813; 620 miles of freeway, more than 3,600,000 private autos; 36 domestic and international airlines serving Los Angeles International Airport, world's second busiest air travel center, handled 544,000 landings and takeoffs. 20,800,000 passengers (1970). More than 46 miles of commercial waterfront in Los Angeles and Long Beach harbors serves 141 steamship lines, 5,343 ships,

53,000,000 tons of cargo (1971).
Communications: 11 TV channels, more than 60 radio stations, more than 25 daily publications in English and foreign languages in the county and estimated 285 regular publications.
New construction: 46,465 private housing units authorized (1970).
Medical facilities: 168 hospitals, 26,757 beds.
Educational facilities: 435 elementary schools, 75 junior high schools, 56 high schools, 150 libraries, more than 150 private schools; University of California at Los Angeles (approx. 28,000 students), University of Southern California, California Institute of Technology, Loyola University, Pomona College, Whittier College, regional campuses of State University and Colleges.
Cultural facilities: 1,600 churches; Huntington Art Gallery and Library; Hollywood Bowl; Greek Theater, Griffith Park Planetarium, Mt. Wilson and Mt. Palomar Observatories; Los Angeles Museum; Music Center; County Art Museum; UCLA Botanical Gardens.
Recreational facilities: 206 parks and playgrounds; 6 public golf courses; 15 public beaches within 35 miles of downtown. Attractions within 2 hours driving time include mountains, lakes, winter ski resorts, desert regions, 4 national forests.
Convention facilities: More than 50,000 rooms; Convention Center.
Sports: Professional teams in baseball (Dodgers), football (Rams), basketball (Lakers), hockey (Kings and Sharks); Santa Anita and Hollywood Park thoroughbred racing; collegiate basketball and football, including Rose Bowl.
History: Discovered 1542 by Portugese navigator Juan Rodriguez Cabrillo. Mission San Gabriel founded September, 1771. City formally founded on Sept. 4, 1781 by Spanish colonial governor as El Pueblo de Nuestra Senora la Reina de los Angeles de Porciuncula.

Louisville, Kentucky

The World Almanac is sponsored in Kentucky and Southern Indiana by The Courier-Journal and The Louisville Times, 525 West Broadway, Louisville, Kentucky 40402; Courier-Journal founded 1868; Times 1884; Courier circulation 234,921; Times, 174,666; Sunday 364,901; chairman of the board Barry Bingham, Sr., editor and publisher Barry Bingham, Jr.; major awards include 5 Pulitzer Prizes, 11 National Headliner Awards, 34 national photo awards since 1963.

Population: 356,200 (city) 849,000 (metro area), 1st in state; total employed 357,400.
Area: Located southern bank of Ohio River. Incorporated City of Louisville 65.2 sq. mi., metro area 908 sq. mi.
Industry and commerce: One of top 20 industrial markets; famous for baseball bats, cigarettes, railroad repair shops, electrical appliances, farm machinery, motor vehicles, plumbing fixtures and whiskey; 900 manufacturing firms in area. Estimated retail sales, Jefferson County (1971), $1.622 billion. Business district and river-front in midst of $200,000,000 redevelopment.
Transportation: 7 trunk-line railroads, 2 terminal railroads, 85 inter-city trunk lines, 5 barge lines, 5 bus lines, 9 airlines, and 2 municipal airports.
Communications: 14 radio stations; 4 TV stations, one educational channel.
Medical facilities: 19 hospitals (2 under construction), 5,122 total beds.

Cultural and educational: 10 colleges and universities in area; Louisville Orchestra, Kentucky Opera Association, Art Center Association, J. B. Speed Art Museum, 20 private art galleries, Macauley Theatre, Actors Theatre, The Children's Theatre, Louisville Civic Ballet, Louisville and Jefferson County Youth Orchestra; 678 churches, 46 denominations.
Recreation: 147 public parks, covering 6,646 acres.
Convention facilities: The Kentucky Fair & Exposition Center, largest multi-purpose exposition building in U.S., with 22 acres under one roof, 20,000-plus seating, parking for 27,000 cars. Convention Center, downtown, handles up to 7,000.
Sports attractions: Kentucky Derby, held annually at Churchill Downs since 1875, attended annually by over 125,000. Kentucky Colonels, American Basketball Association franchise.
Other: Belle of Louisville excursion steamboat; Churchill Downs Museum; Louisville Zoo; Ameri-

can Printing House for the Blind.
History: Founded by explorer George Rogers

Clark, in 1778; named after King Louis XVI of France.

Lubbock, Texas

The World Almanac is sponsored in the Lubbock area by the Lubbock Avalanche-Journal, 8th St. and Ave. J, Lubbock, Texas, 79408; (806) 763-4343; founded 1900 as Leader, became Avalanche 1908, daily 1921; Plains Journal weekly founded 1923; consolidated 1926; circulation, (morn) 59,321, (eve) 22,024, Sat. 69,293, Sun. 76,102; member Southwestern Newspapers Corp.; general-manager Robert R. Norris; editor Jay Harris.

Population: 156,000 (city), 186,000 (metro area), 8th in state; total employed 79,400.
Area: 80 sq. mi. in the South Plains region of northwest Texas.
Industry: vegetable oils, cotton, cotton seed flour, grain sorghum, live stock; petroleum, sand and gravel; 228 manufacturing companies.
Commerce: wholesale and retail center for west Texas and eastern New Mexico; retail sales $324,315,000; bank resources: $679,000,000; 8 banks and 4 savings and loan associations.
Transportation: 12 regular motor freight carriers; 2 major railroads, and 3 bus lines; Lubbock Regional Airport served by 3 major airlines, averaging 68 air movements per day; 6 major federal and state highways intersect the city.
Communications: 4 TV and 9 radio stations.
Medical facilities: 8 hospitals, Lubbock State School for Mentally Retarded; medical school being constructed on Texas Tech campus.

Federal facilities: Reese Air Force Base, Federal Building, Federal Aviation Administration and a National Weather Service.
Cultural facilities: Lubbock Symphony Orchestra, Lubbock Theatre Centre; Museum of Texas Tech University, Moody Planetarium; Ranch Headquarters complex (authentic ranch houses dating to 1835); Lubbock Christian College; Memorial Convention Center under construction.
Recreational facilities: 39 city parks covering 1,750 acres; Mackenzie State Park, state's largest, with famed Prairie Dog Town, Buffalo Lakes; Municipal Auditorium, 3,200 seats; Municipal Coliseum, 10,000 capacity; annual Panhandle-South Plains Fair.
Sports: Texas Tech University and Lubbock Christian College, full sports schedules. Tech Jones Stadium, site of annual Coaches All-America football game.

Macon, Georgia

The World Almanac is sponsored in the Macon area by The Macon Telegraph and News, 120 Broadway, Macon, Ga., 31208; telephone (912) 743-2621; acquired by Knight Newspapers, Inc., 1969; circulation, Telegraph (morn) 53,165, News (eve) 24,375, Sunday 77,075; general manager Bert Struby, executive editor Don Carter, News editor Joseph Parham.

Population: 122,423 (city), 206,342 (metro area), 3rd in state; total employed 96,100.
Area: 52 sq. mi., 6 miles northeast of geographic center of Georgia.
Industry: textiles, Bibb Company, longtime industry leader, has headquarters and plants in area, and 2 textile-related industries began plant construction in 1973—YKK Zipper Co. of Japan and textile printing plant for Hawaiian Corp; forestry, Armstrong Cork Co. accoustical tile plant is area's largest and pulpwood also is used to manufacture cardboard, packaging. Kaolin (clay) deposits are mined in area and processed in numerous ways; Government Employes Insurance Co. is constructing regional office to employ 2,500.
Federal facilities: Warner Robins Air Materiel

Area and Robins Air Force Base, located 16 miles from Macon at Warner Robins, have been area's largest employers since World War II.
Educational facilities: Wesleyan College, nation's oldest college for women, and Mercer University, with leading law school and scholastic excellence, are among state's principal private institutions. State-supported Macon Jr. College opened in 1968. Other attractions: Ocmulgee National Monument displays archeological remains of 3 prehistoric Indian civilizations. A $4,500,000 coliseum seats 10,000. Tobesofkee Recreation Area around a 1,750-acre lake has water sports, campsites, etc.
History: Macon was first settled when government established Fort Hawkins in 1806. Chartered in 1823, city became home of many North Carolinians and was named for Nathaniel Macon of that state.

Madison, Wisconsin

The World Almanac is sponsored in Madison by Madison Newspapers, Inc., publisher of The Capital Times and Wisconsin State Journal, 115 S. Carroll St., Madison, Wis., 53701; (608) 256-5511; circulation, State Journal (morn) 73,574, Capital Times (eve) 45,029, Sunday Journal 112,843.

Population: 178,600 (city), 297,700 (metro), 2d in state; total metro work force 151,100.
Area: 50.4 sq.mi. (city), 1,197 sq.mi. (metro); in south-central Wisconsin.
Commerce: capital of Wisconsin. Home office of 29 insurance firms; 316 industrial firms; 17 banks, 5 savings and loans; retail sales, 1972: $419,458,000 (city), $630,616,000 (metro); average spendable family income, $11,820.
Transportation: municipal airport serves western and south-central Wisconsin with 3 airlines; 3

railroads, Amtrak; major north/south and east/west Interstate highway system; 3 bus lines; 10 truck lines.
Communications: 4 TV stations; 5 AM and 4 FM radio stations; 2 daily newspapers.
Medical facilities: 9 hospitals, including University hospital and V.A.; 22 clinics, about 500 physicians.
Federal facilities: Forest Products Laboratory; headquarters of U.S. Armed Forces Institute.
Cultural facilities: Dane County Coliseum (seats 10,134); 2 art centers, ballet company, 5 drama

groups, 7 music organizations including Madison and University symphonies. Churches: 14 Catholic, 120 Protestant, 2 synagogues, 1 Greek Orthodox.
Educational facilities: University of Wisconsin and

3 colleges; 34 elementary, 10 middle, 4 high schools, 17 parochial, 1 vocational-technical, 48 specialized; 6 city and 32 University libraries.
Convention facilities: Dane County Coliseum; 7 hotels with large convention facilities.

Memphis, Tennessee

The World Almanac is sponsored in the Memphis area by the Memphis Press-Scimitar, 495 Union Ave., Memphis, Tenn., 38101; telephone (901) 526-2141; Scimitar founded 1880 by G. P. M. Turner; Press 1906 by Scripps-McRae League, predecessor of Scripps-Howard newspapers; circulation 129,942; editor Charles H. Schneider, managing editor Ed. Ray.

Population: 623,530 (city), 830,304 (metro area), 1st in state, 17th in nation; total employed 361,100.
Area: 251.2 sq. mi., on east bank of the Mississippi River.
Industry: world's largest hardwood lumber center; manufacturing of furniture and flooring; world's largest inland spot cotton market; extensive cotton warehousing and processing of cotton seed into vegetable oil products; headquarters of Holiday Inns, Inc. Large industries include plants of Schering-Plough (drugs), Conwood Corp. (tobacco and food products), International Harvester (cotton pickers, hay balers), and Firestone (tires).
Commerce: wholesale-retail center for large parts of Tennessee, Arkansas and Mississippi. Retail sales (1971) $1,648 billion. Bank deposits $2,608 billion. There are 7 banks and 7 savings and loan associations. Average spendable income per family $10,288.
Transportation: 10 airlines with 150 arrivals a day; 7 trunk line railroads, 67 motor freight lines, 7 barge lines. One of the nation's largest inland river ports, handling 10,404,823 tons of freight in 1971.
Communications: 4 TV and 17 radio stations.
Medical facilities: University of Tennessee medi-

cal units and a Veterans Administration hospital in complex with public hospital. Also there are 3 private general hospitals and St. Jude Hospital, research center for children's illnesses, particularly leukemia.
Federal facilities: Naval Air Station, Naval Air Technical Training Center, Defense Depot Memphis and Air Force's 164th Air Transport Group.
Cultural facilities: Memphis Symphony Orchestra, Memphis Opera Theater, Memphis Little Theater, Brooks Art Gallery, Memphis Museum. Annual performances of Metropolitan Opera.
Educational facilities: Memphis State University, Southwestern College, Lemoyne-Owen College, Christian Brothers College, University of Tennessee Medical Units, Shelby State Community College, State Technical Institute, Southern College of Optometry and Mid South Bible College.
Recreational facilities: Meeman-Shelby Forest state park, 12,500 acres; 137 other parks.
Convention facilities: $27,000,000 Everett R. Cook Convention Center, with 1,300,000 sq. ft. and seating 16,500, completed in 1973.

Mexico City (Ciudad de Mexico), Mexico

Population: Federal District 8,541,070 (1970).
Area: About 53 sq. mi. within the 573 sq. mi. Distrito Federal; in central Mexico at an altitude of 7,349 ft.
Industry and commerce: Capital of Mexico; the political and economic hub of the nation. Manufactures include steel, automobiles, appliances, textiles, rubber goods, furniture and electrical equipment. Marketing center of Mexico.
Transportation: Center of modern highway and rail system. Served by most international air lines, Mexico City is 4 hrs. by jet from New York and 3 hrs. from Los Angeles.
Communications: Major media center for Mexico and parts of Latin America; city is a major film center.
Cultural facilities: Palace of Fine Arts and its Ballet Folklorico; National Palace (Diego Rivera murals); National University with over 90,000

students; National Museum of Anthropology. City itself is an architectural exhibit of Aztec ruins, Baroque cathedrals, and ultra-modern buildings.
Other attractions: Xochimilco with the "floating gardens" and gondolas; Chapultepec Castle, palace of the French-supported Emperor and Empress of Mexico, Maximilian and Carlotta; 22-ton Aztec Calendar Stone; 2 volcanoes, Popocatepetl and Iztaccihuatl.
History: Traditionally founded 1176 by Aztecs, city was called Tenochtitlan; captured by Spanish under Cortez in 1519 and again in 1521; occupied by the U.S. in 1847 and by the French from 1863 to 1867; Distrito Federal established 1824.
Further information: Mexican National Tourist Council, Mariano Escobedo 726, Mexico, D.F. or 677 5th Ave., New York 10022; or 9445 Wilshire Blvd., Beverly Hills 90212.

Miami, Florida

The World Almanac is sponsored in the Miami area by The Miami Herald, 1 Herald Plaza, Miami, Fla., 33101; telephone (305) 350-2111; founded Dec. 1, 1910 by Frank B. Shutts; circulation 407,000 daily, 508,000 Sunday; editorial chairman John S. Knight, editor Don Shoemaker, executive editor Larry Jinks, managing editor Ron Martin. Newspaper or staff writers have won or shared in 4 Pulitzer prizes, the latest in 1973, and numerous other honors.

Population: 334,859 (city), 1,267,792 (metro area); 1st in state, 24th in nation; total employed in metro area, 503,300.
Area: 53.8 sq. mi., land and water, on Biscayne Bay at mouth of Miami River.

Industry: tourism and aviation are mainstays of economy; 1,000 hotels and motels employ 50,000 and handle 12,000,000 visitors a year. Aviation accounts for 80,000 jobs. Eastern (largest industrial employer), National and Pan American operate bases; agricultural center.

Commerce: center of pan-American finance and commerce, with 80 banks, 16 savings and loan associations. Retail sales (1972) nearly $4 billion. Port of Miami busy in waterborne commerce as well as a cruise center, with 20 cruise sailings a week.

Transportation: Miami International, served by more than 100 air carriers, handled 12,000,000 travelers in 1972. Seaboard Coast Line (Amtrak) and all-freight Fla. East Coast Railroads operate in Miami, as do Greyhound and Trailways buses. Served by 40 truck lines.

Communications: 5 commercial and 5 educational or closed-circuit television stations, 36 radio stations.

New construction: major new office buildings downtown, topped by 40-story One Biscayne Tower, in a $500,000,000 building surge. Redevelopment underway at Miami International; boom in apartments, other rental structures.

Medical facilities: 37 hospitals provide 7,267 beds. More than 13,000 beds available at 54 nursing and convalescent homes in metro area. Jackson Memorial Hospital one of area's leading research facilities.

Cultural facilities: Greater Miami Philharmonic, Opera Guild of Greater Miami and other musical groups perform regularly; 18 auditoriums accommodate resident and touring theatrical productions; 4 major art museums. There are 7 playhouses, and 55 night clubs and theater restaurants.

Educational facilities: 8 colleges and universities, plus 3 campuses of Miami-Dade Junior College, count a total enrollment of 62,000. University of Miami is largest independent institution of higher learning in southeast. Florida International University opened in 1972. Public school system, with 300,000 students, is nation's 6th largest.

Recreational facilities: 14 miles of public beach on ocean and bay; 300 parks and playgrounds, 11 stadiums and grandstands. Resort-oriented, Miami offers 40 golf courses and 50 marinas for boaters, who have 36,000 pleasure craft. There are 72 movie houses.

Convention facilities: Miami Beach Convention Hall hosted both Republican and Democratic national conventions in 1972. Facilities also available in Miami and at major area hotels.

Sports attractions: pro football champion Miami Dolphins and U. of Miami play in Orange Bowl, which seats 75,000. Stadium also hosts Orange Bowl game, Orange Blossom Classic, North-South All-Star Shrine Game and other contests. Pari-mutuel wagering at 7 horse and greyhound tracks, jai alai fronton.

Other attractions: balmy subtropical climate, with mean annual temperature of 75.3°. There are 530 Protestant, 49 Catholic and 41 Jewish synagogues and churches. Marine Stadium features not only powerboat and regatta racing but twilight concerts, jazz and classical, as well. Everglades National Park, 40 miles south of Miami, features wildlife and trackless swamps.

History: America's newest big city, Miami had only 3 houses in 1895 in a community called Fort Dallas. Julia Tuttle persuaded Henry M. Flagler to extend his railroad from West Palm Beach south to Miami. The city was incorporated in 1896, the year the first trains arrived.

Further information: Miami, characterized as a Gateway to the Americas, is a bilingual city where Spanish is as commonly heard downtown as English. Some 400,000 residents are of Latin descent, many of them Cuban refugees who have become an integral part of the community. Jewish community also is one of the nation's largest.

Sports attractions: Liberty Bowl football game each December at Memphis Memorial Stadium, seating 50,000. Danny Thomas Memphis Classic golf tournament, on PGA tour. Mid-South Coliseum, seating 11,500, is home of Memphis State University basketball games. Memphis Blues baseball team, in Texas League.

Other attractions: Cotton Carnival each May. Beale St., home of the blues, where W. C. Handy, the composer, lived.

History: site of Memphis is where DeSoto stopped in 1541 when he discovered the Mississippi River. A U.S. military post, Ft. Adams, established there in 1797. Memphis incorporated in 1826. City was nearly depopulated by yellow fever epidemic in 1878 and temporarily surrendered its charter, but by 1890 had grown to population of 64,589.

Milwaukee, Wisconsin

The World Almanac is sponsored in the Milwaukee area by The Milwaukee Journal, Journal Square, Milwaukee, Wis. 53201; telephone (414) 224-2000; founded 1882 by Lucius W. Nieman; circulation 357,077 daily, 551,017 Sunday; chairman of the board Irwin Maier, publisher Donald B. Abert, president of The Journal Co. Donald D. Abert, editor Richard H. Leonard; major awards include 2 Pulitzer Prizes to the newspaper and 2 to staff members.

Population: 717,810 (city) 1,418,000 (metro area); city 12th and metro area 20th in U.S.; total employment 624,100 (metro area).

Area: 95.8 sq. mi. on shore of Lake Michigan.

Industry: largest U.S. producer of diesel and gasoline engines, outboard motors, motorcycles, tractors, padlocks, beer; 4th largest U.S. automaking center; graphic arts and food processing are largest non-durable goods employers; location for 10 "Fortune 500" industries.

Commerce: wholesale and retail trade center for Wisconsin, Upper Michigan: total retail sales $2.6 billion; wholesale trade $4 billion. Average household spendable income $12,901; 79 banks with $4.1 billion deposits; 53 savings and loan associations with $2.7 billion deposits.

Transportation: 4 major rail lines; Amtrak; 5 major airlines provide direct service to East and West Coasts, south, southeast and Florida for 2,000,000 users of Gen. Mitchell field; 30 U.S. and foreign-flag ship lines use Milwaukee's St. Lawrence seaway port, handling over 6,000,000 tons annually including 1,000,000 tons overseas cargo; port of Milwaukee gateway for 400 cities in 29 states and overseas ports, producing $240 million in exports 14th in total U.S. exports; 4 inter-city bus lines, 68 motor freight carriers; I-94, 5 federal and 14 state highways intersect Milwaukee.

Communications: morning, evening and sunday metropolitan newspaper; 4 commercial, 2 educational TV stations; 28 AM and FM radio stations.

Medical facilities: 21 major hospitals and medical centers, including new Veterans Administration hospital.

Cultural facilities: Milwaukee Symphony, Repertory Theater, 2 opera and one operetta companies;

Mid-America Ballet; nationally recognized Art Center; museum; University of Wisconsin — Milwaukee, Marquette University, Medical College of Wisconsin, 8 other colleges and vocational schools enroll 45,000 annually; new $13,000,000 Performing Arts Center; $15,900,000 addition to convention-arena-auditorium complex; Mitchell Park Conservatory and county zoo are parts of 13,000 acre County Park system.

Sports attractions: baseball, Milwaukee Brewers

(Amer. League); basketball, Marquette Univ. Warriors; Milwaukee Bucks (NBA); football, Green Bay Packers (NFL) play 3 of 11 home games in Milwaukee.

History: Founded by Solomon Juneau, one of many French trappers in area in early 1800s; incorporated as town 1837; as city 1846.

Further information: Metropolitan Milwaukee Association of Commerce, 828 N. Broadway, Milwaukee, Wisc. 53202.

Minneapolis, Minnesota

Population: 435,000 (city) 1,965,000 (metro area); 1st in state, 17th in nation; total employed: 853,000 (metro area).

Area: 200 sq. mi. (metro area) around St. Anthony Falls near junction of Mississippi and Minnesota Rivers.

Industry: marked by diversity; major electronics-computer manufacturing center, including Honeywell Inc., Control Data Corp., Medtronics Inc., Univac (Division of Sperry Rand). Headquarters for nation's 4 largest grain millers, including Pillsbury & General Mills.

Commerce: metro area 5th in nation in per household retail sales (1971) and 4th in median household income ($10,300). Total retail sales metro area (1972), $3.5 billion. City has 23 commercial banks, 7 savings & loan associations. Headquarters for Ninth Federal Reserve District. Metro area is world trade center, 12th among U.S. metro areas in exports.

Transportation: Amtrak regional terminal, 5 trunk railroads; 150 trucking firms; 5 major barge

lines headquartered in city. Mpls.-St. Paul International Airport, 650 flights daily.

Communications: 6 TV and 20 radio stations.

Medical facilities: 20 hospitals including one of nation's leading heart hospitals at University of Minnesota.

Cultural facilities: Minnesota Orchestra, 7 art galleries-museums, Tyrone Guthrie Theater, Walker Art Center, University of Minnesota.

Sports attractions: Minnesota Twins (American League) Minnesota Vikings (NFL) Minnesota North Stars (NHA).

New construction: General Hospital, beginning.

Other attractions: 153 parks, 22 lakes; 57-story IDS Tower; Mpls. Aquatennial celebration in July. Average yearly snowfall: 41 inches.

History: City site first visited in 1680s by Fr. Louis Hennepin who discovered and named St. Anthony Falls on the Mississippi River; Falls became the power source for lumbering & milling operations in 19th century. French fur traders used the region in the 18th century. The city incorporated in 1871.

Mobile, Alabama

The World Almanac is sponsored in the Mobile area by The Mobile Press Register, 304 Government St., 36630; telephone (205) 433-1551; published as a single paper, circulation 94,516, on Saturday and Sunday and as The Mobile Register (morning), 44,361, and The Mobile Press (evening), 59,319. The Press dates back to 1928 and the Register to 1813. William J. Hearin publisher and president, Fallon Trotter executive editor, John Fay associate executive editor.

Population: 190,026 (city), 376,690 (metro area), 2d city in state, 68th in nation; total employed (metro area), 123,300.

Area: 142 sq. mi. Located at the head of Mobile Bay, 31 miles from Gulf of Mexico.

Industry: home of Alabama State Docks, a $115,000,000 complex where 33 ocean-going ships can be docked at one time. Merchandise and raw products handled by the port include more than 10,000,000 tons of imported bauxite and iron ore annually. Over $500,000,000 is invested in diversified industry at Mobile, including paper and paper products, forest products, shipbuilding, chemicals, roofing, paints, alumina, oil, aircraft engines and metals.

Commerce: wholesale and retail center for large portion of southwest Alabama and southeast Mississippi; Mobile county retail sales (1972):

$543,855,000.

Transportation: served by 4 major railroads, one of the great river systems, 3 major airlines, about 100 steamship lines and 55 truck lines.

Communications: 2 TV and 12 radio stations.

Medical facilities: University of South Alabama Medical College and 3 modern hospitals.

Cultural facilities: $12,000,000 Municipal Auditorium-Theater complex that seats some 16,000 persons; art gallery; museum; amateur dramatic theater; public library and branches; University of South Alabama, Spring Hill College, Mobile College, and Bishop State Junior College.

Annual attractions: America's Junior Miss Pageant, Senior Bowl Football Game, and Mardi Gras.

History: Mobile was founded in 1702 by Jean Baptiste Le Moyne; 6 flags have flown over the city since then.

Montgomery, Alabama

The World Almanac is sponsored in the Montgomery area by The Advertiser-Journal, 200 Washington Street, Montgomery, Alabama 36102; telephone: (205) 262-1611; Advertiser founded 1828, Journal 1881, one ownership 1940; circulation Advertiser (morn) 58,551; Journal (eve) 27,073; combined Sunday 79,843; publisher Harold Martin, managing editor Ben R. Davis.

Population: 133,386 (city), 228,500 (metro area); 147th in nation; total employed 88,900.

Area: 45 sq. mi. (city), 442 sq. mi. (county).

Industry: machinery manufacture, glass products,

textiles, refrigeration equipment, axles, furniture, food products, paper, and fertilizers; over 230 industries.

Commerce: Wholesale and retail center for 13 counties in central Alabama; retail trade area sales (1971), $709,164,000; 6 banks, 3 savings & loans associations, and 6 insurance company home offices; state capital.

Transportation: 5 railroads, 3 airlines, 2 national bus lines; Interstate 65 and 85 intersect in the city; Alabama River is navigable to the Gulf of Mexico.

Medical facilities: 7 general hospitals and a VA hospital; over 2,000 beds.

Cultural facilities: Montgomery Art Guild, Montgomery Civic Ballet, Montgomery Little Theater, and a Community Concert Series; Montgomery Museum of Fine Arts; 5 major colleges and universities.

Sports: Rebels, farm team of Detroit, play at Patterson Field. Blue-Gray Football Classic, played in Montgomery's Cramton Bowl.

History: incorporated 1819; Jefferson Davis inaugurated President of the Confederate States of America, February 18, 1861, in Montgomery.

Montreal, Quebec, Canada

The World Almanac is sponsored in the Montreal area by The Gazette, a Southam newspaper, 1000 St. Antoine Street, Montreal 101, Quebec, Canada; telephone (514) 861-1111; founded 1778 by Fleury Mesplet; circulation 138,215 daily; publisher Mark Farrell; general manager J. Peter Kohl; editorial page editor Tim Creery; managing editor R. Lindsay Crysler. The Gazette sponsors an annual Christmas fund for needy families and participates in various community service projects.

Population: 1,214,300 (city), 2,743,200 (metro area); after Paris, the second largest French-speaking city in the world. The island city in the St. Lawrence River is Canada's largest urban center.

Area: an island of 60 sq. mi. located in the St. Lawrence River where the Ottawa and Richelieu Rivers flow into it at the head of the St. Lawrence Seaway.

Industry: Canada's industrial hub; oil refining, petrochemicals and chemicals, flour milling, meat packing, brewing, and construction products.

Commerce: Canada's financial, and commercial hub; two-thirds of its people are of French origin and 20% have an Anglo-Saxon heritage. $3.5 billion total retail sales; $13,000 average family income.

Transportation: The St. Lawrence Seaway, a $1-billion Canadian-American waterway and power project which runs 1,300 miles to the Great Lakes in the heart of North America. It has helped Montreal, 1,000 miles from the sea, become the world's 2d greatest island port, after Rotterdam. Montreal's harbor extends 42 miles. Air capital of the world, with the headquarters of both the International Civil Aviation Organization and the International Air Transport Association—the 2 global regulatory bodies—located in the city

and some 30 airlines serving its huge International airport. Canada's railroad hub, and a leading truck and bus center. **Subway:** The Metro, Montreal's $225,000,000, 16-mile subway system, the eighth largest in the world, opened in 1966. The system is being extended in all directions to be completed before the 1976 Summer Olympic Games.

Cultural facilities: a major cultural centre; Place des Arts, a 3,000-seat concert hall and 2 theatres, the home of the Montreal Symphony Orchestra, attracts the finest in drama, opera, ballet and music. The Montreal Museum of Fine Arts, the Musée de l'Art Contemporain. Some of the continent's most beautiful churches, including the Roman Catholic Mary Queen of the World Basilica, a half-size replica of St. Peter's in Rome. Home of 2 famous universities, McGill and l'Université de Montréal.

Sports: home of the National Hockey League Canadiens, the Canadian Football League Alouettes, and the Expos of baseball's National League.

History: Montreal was first visited by Jacques Cartier in 1535 and was founded under the name of Ville Marie in 1642. Old Montreal, some 1,000 acres in all, is the largest such area undergoing restoration in North America and retains the general atmosphere of the 18th century.

Nashville, Tennessee

The World Almanac is sponsored in the Nashville area by The Tennessean, 1100 Broadway, Nashville, Tenn., 37202; telephone (615) 255-1221; founded as the Tennessean, May 12, 1907, by Col. Luke Lea, but other incorporated publications date to 1812; circulation daily 142,511, Sunday 244,144; president Amon Carter Evans, publisher John L. Seigenthaler; major awards include 3 Pulitzer prizes, 8 Headliner awards and 2 Sigma Delta Chi awards to staff members.

Population: 465,400 (in unified Metro government), 2nd in state; labor force 236,700.

Area: 532 square miles, on the Cumberland river, in north central part of state.

Industry: recording, 52% of singles and 15% of U.S. albums are recorded in Nashville's 27 studio complexes, grossing $200 million annually; clothing, Nashville is headquarters of world's largest and most diversified clothing and footwear manufacturer; insurance, 2 of largest U.S. insurance companies located here; glass, world's largest auto glass plant; chemicals, printing and publishing (especially religious materials), aerostructures, heating equipment, tires.

Commerce: retail center for Middle Tennessee, South Kentucky; retail sales (1972) $1,079,000,000. Per capita income (1971) $3,993. Bank resources $2,658,797,983 in 8 banks, 79 branches.

Transportation: 9 U.S. highways and 6 branches of

the interstate system radiate from Nashville; municipal airport hosts 9 commercial airlines with 160 daily flights. Also 2 railroads, local and intercity bus lines, 71 motor freight lines.

Communications: 4 TV stations (one public) and 15 AM and FM radio stations.

Medical facilities: 15 hospitals, 2 with medical schools; speech-hearing center.

Cultural facilities: Nashville Symphony; replica of Parthenon with art gallery; public and state libraries; botanical gardens and art center at Cheekwood; Children's Museum; 2 theaters.

Educational facilities: 13 co-educational colleges and universities, 149 public schools, more than 40 commercial and vocational schools.

Convention facilities: 10,000-seat auditorium; Opryland convention center under construction.

Other attractions: Grand Ole Opry, Opryland ($28,000,000 theme park featuring music); Country

Music Hall of Fame; Hermitage (home of Andrew Jackson); Belle Meade antebellum mansion.
Recreation facilities: water sports, outdoor activity on Old Hickory and Percy Priest lakes.

History: Nashville was settled in 1780 as a fort in then western North Carolina. In 1784, incorporated with first written charter west of Alleghenies.

New Haven, Connecticut

The World Almanac is sponsored in the greater New Haven area by the New Haven Register (founded 1812) and the New Haven Journal-Courier (founded 1755); circulation Register evening 108,945, Sunday 126,158; Journal-Courier morning 32,898; Lionel S. Jackson president and publisher, Donald A. Spargo vice president and general manager, George S. Stearns, Jr. vice president and treasurer; Robert J. Leeney vice president and editor.

Population: 135,500 (city), 360,400 (metro area); 3rd in state.
Area: 18 sq. mi., southern coast of Conn. on north shore of Long Island Sound.
Industry: 1,000 firms in city and immediate area. Principle products—guns, hardware, rubber goods, paper products, machinery and tools.
Commerce: wholesale and retail center for southern Connecticut; retail city sales (1972) $370,312,-000; retail metropolitan sales (1972) $879,304,000. Serving 800,000 people within a radius of 25 miles. Harbor flourishes with trade ships and particularly with cargo ships dally moving oil.
Transportation: Penn Central, major freight lines, Amtrak Cosmopolitan turbotrain; 23 major truck lines; 14 federal and state highways. Tweed-New Haven Airport served by 3 airlines.
Communications: one TV and 6 radio stations.
Medical facilities: famed Yale Medical Center, Yale-New Haven Hospital and Hospital of St. Raphael.
Cultural facilities: Yale University Library, containing over 6,000,000 books, one of the world's largest collections; Yale's Peabody Museum with natural history exhibits and Yale's Art Gallery, oldest university museum in U.S.; Yale's Beinecke Rare Book Library; the New Haven Historical Society; under construction, the New Haven Cultural Center; 2 legitimate theatres, The Shubert Theatre and the Long Wharf Theatre; and The New Haven Symphony.
Educational facilities: Yale University and graduate schools, Albertus Magnus College, Southern Connecticut State College, South Central Community College, Quinnipiac College and University of New Haven.
Recreational facilities: Yale Bowl, Woolsey Hall, Ingalls Rink and the New Haven Coliseum; 15 parks, 50 playgrounds, West Rock Nature Center; one 18-hole golf course, 6 private golf courses; 00 tennis courts, 3 artificial outdoor skating rinks and 2 indoor rinks.
Convention facilities: New Haven Coliseum-convention center, the largest facility of its kind between Boston and New York, with a 19-story hotel nearby.
Sports attractions: New Haven Nighthawks of the American Hockey League.
History: New Haven founded in 1638 by Puritans led by John Davenport and Theophilus Eaton; named after Newhaven on the south coast of England. Incorporated 1638, New Haven became a part of Connecticut in 1662. First mayor was Roger Sherman, signer of the Declaration of Independence.

New Orleans, Louisiana

The World Almanac is sponsored in the New Orleans area by The States-Item, 3800 Howard Ave., New Orleans, La., 70140; telephone (504) 521-7011; founded Jan. 3, 1880, by Maj. Henry J. Hearsey; circulation 130,188 daily, 117,130 Saturday; editor Walter G. Cowan, associate editor Charles A. Ferguson, city editor William U. Madden; sponsors Women Against Crime Cursa Crusade and Football Fund for Underprivileged.

Population: 593,471 (city), 1,034,316 (metro area); first in state; total employed, 434,200.
Area: 363.5 sq. mi. of which 199.4 are land.
Industry: Port of New Orleans, second largest in nation, handled cargo with total value of $3.94 billion in 1972.
Commerce: trade center for lower Mississippi valley. Bank resources, $3.9 billion.
Transportation: rail hub for north, east and westbound commerce. Amtrak passenger service to Chicago, New York, Los Angeles. New Orleans International Airport serves major airlines; Lakefront Airport private aviation. Served by all major bus and truck lines.
New construction: hotel building booming in expectation of Dome opening and popularity of annual Mardi Gras festival; tallest building in South, 51-story One Shell Square opened at cost of $45,000,000.
Communications: 4 commercial TV stations and educational channel.
Medical facilities: City is major medical center with Charity Hospital, 2 schools of medicine and one of dentistry; Oschner Clinic, Touro Infirmary.
Cultural facilities: new Center for the Performing Arts seats 2,317 for operas, concerts. Museums include Louisiana State Museum, Isaac Delgado Museum of Art, the Middle American Research Institute of Tulane University and many small galleries.
Educational facilities: Tulane University, Louisiana State University in New Orleans, Loyola, Dillard, Southern University in New Orleans, Xavier, St. Mary's Dominican.
Other attractions: Louisiana Superdome scheduled for completion Jan. 1975 at a cost of more than $150,000,000, will seat 80,000 for major events. French Quarter remains major historic tourist attraction.
Sports: New Orleans Saints of the National Football League now play in Tulane Stadium, will move to dome by 1975. Sugar Bowl is major college attraction.
History: named after the Duke of Orleans, the city was founded on the edge of a swamp within crescent of the Mississippi River 100 miles upstream from the Gulf of Mexico by Jean Baptiste Le Moyne, Sieur de Bienville. Became capital of Louisiana Territory in 1722, when Adrien de Pauger laid out what is now the French Quarter. Became part of U.S. with signing of Louisiana Purchase in 1803.

New York, New York

The World Almanac is sponsored in the Greater New York City metropolitan area by the Daily News and Sunday News, 220 E. 42d St., New York, N.Y. 10017, telephone (212) MU 2-1234; New York News Inc., founded June 26, 1919 by Joseph Medill Patterson; circulation daily 2,092,603, Sunday 2,958,678; chairman of the board F. M. Flynn, president and publisher W. H. James, executive editor and senior vice president Floyd Barger, managing editor and vice president Michael J. O'Neill, treasurer and vice president R. J. Rohrbach, general manager and senior vice president Bruce G. McCauley, business manager, vice president and secretary V. E. Palmer; major awards include Pulitzer Prizes for news photography, international reporting, cartoon and editorial writing.

Population: 7,895,563 (city), 11,528,649 (metro area), 1st in state and nation; total employed 3,560,100; per capita personal income $5,292.
Area: 300 sq. mi., in southeast portion of the state at mouth of Hudson River leading into Atlantic Ocean. City embraces 5 boroughs — Manhattan, Bronx, Brooklyn, Queens and Richmond — and is host to United Nations.
Industry: Nation's leader in manufacturing and service industries. New York City produces 25.3% of America's apparel, 18.2% of printing and publishing, 10% of leather and leather products, 7% of jewelry, toys, notions and miscellaneous products; 4.6% of fabricated metal products and electrical machinery; 4.3% of textile mill products; 3.2% of food products. As of Jan. 1972, 38,129 manufacturing companies.
Commerce: Nation's richest port, handling annual 181,024,686 tons of maritime cargo. Wall Street is world's largest financial center, with New York and American stock exchanges. Wholesale and retail center for New York, New Jersey and southwestern Connecticut; retail sales $13.5 billion (1971). Thirty-five commercial banks, resources $110 billion; 43 savings banks, resources $39.5 billion. New $800,000,000 World Trade Center — two 110-story buildings that are world's largest.
Transportation: Kennedy International Airport handles 50% of nation's overseas air travel and 53% of export-import air tonnage, is served by 58 international air carriers. LaGuardia Airport served by 11 leading domestic airlines. City has 5 heliports. Penn Central Railroad, Amtrak; 2 major rail terminals, Pennsylvania and Grand Central stations. Served by 42 interstate bus lines. New York's subway network covers every borough except Richmond; ferry and the 4,260-ft. Verrazano-Narrows Bridge (world's longest suspension span) link Richmond to Manhattan and Brooklyn. More than 18 bridges connect Manhattan with other boroughs, and the George Washington Bridge over the Hudson River connects New Jersey. Brooklyn Bridge, opened to traffic in 1883, is the oldest. There are 5 tunnels under the Hudson and East rivers.
Communications: 12 TV stations (6 commercial, 2 educational, 1 municipal, 3 CATV); also 36 AM and FM radio stations. WPIX-TV and WPIX-FM are broadcast affiliates of The News.
Medical facilities: 124 hospitals (19 municipal, 32

private, 73 voluntary non-profit); 5 of the nation's major medical research centers specialize in cancer, heart diseases, sickle cell anemia and other research. Also Sloan-Kettering Institute for Cancer Research. City also has 3 VA hospitals.
Educational facilities: 7 universities, 31 colleges, 5 medical colleges and schools, 4 law schools, 3 colleges of pharmacy, 2 colleges of dentistry, 3 institutes of art and architecture; 926 schools in the public school system; more than 1,000 private schools. Public libraries total 189.
Cultural facilities: Lincoln Center for the Performing Arts (New York Philharmonic, New York Ballet Company, Metropolitan Opera and other theatrical arts), Carnegie Hall, Brooklyn Academy of Music. Broadway for varied theatrical productions; Off-Broadway plays are earning prestige. New York Shakespeare Festival at Delacorte Theater. Museum total of 34 includes the American Museum of Natural History, Metropolitan Museum of Art, Museum of the Performing Arts, Museum of Modern Art, Whitney Museum, and the National Art Museum of Sport.
Other attractions: Botanic gardens in the Bronx and Brooklyn; Central Park and Prospect Park are among scores of parks; 5 zoos including Central Park and Bronx zoos. City's recreational facilities include 15 municipal golf courses, over 200 tennis courts, 23 outdoor swimming pools.
Sports: NBA world champions New York Knicks, hockey teams N.Y. Rangers (NHL) and Golden Blades (WHA); NL baseball Mets, and football Jets play in Shea Stadium. AL New York Yankees and football Giants make Yankee Stadium their home. During 1973-74 stadium renovations, Giants play in Yale Bowl in New Haven, Conn.
History: Giovanni da Verrazano discovered New York in 1524. In 1626 Peter Minuit, 17 years after Henry Hudson first explored Manhattan Island, bought the island from the Manhattan Indians for about $24 in goods and trinkets. Settlement named New Amsterdam. In 1664, British troops occupied city without resistance and named it New York in honor of the Duke of York, brother of the King. Declaration of Independence read to the American troops July 9, 1776, in the presence of George Washington, near the present City Hall. On Jan. 1, 1898, Manhattan and large areas to the NE, E and S were consolidated into one City of New York.

Norfolk, Virginia

The World Almanac is sponsored in the Norfolk Metropolitan Area by The Virginian-Pilot and Ledger-Star, 150 W. Brambleton Ave., Norfolk, Va. 23501; tel: (703) 625-1431; Virginian founded 1865, Ledger, 1876; circulation: LS even. 105,604; VP morn. 130,013, VP Sun. 185,116; Frank Batten publisher, Charles Hauser vice president & general manager, Derek Dunn-Rankin vice president for operations, Perry Morgan executive editor, Robert H. Mason VP editor, George J. Hebert LS editor.

Population: 307,951 (city), 687,576 (SMSA — Norfolk, Virginia Beach, Portsmouth, Chesapeake). 1st in state; total civilian employment: 227,000.
Area: 915 sq. mi. in southeastern Virginia.

Industry: General Electric, Ford Motor Co., Norfolk Shipbuilding & Drydock Corp., Smith-Douglas.
Commerce: retail sales (1971): $1,077,727,000.

Median household income: $7,171.
Transportation: Port of Hampton Roads, world's finest natural harbor. Norfolk ranks first in export tonnage among Atlantic ports. Biggest coal port in world. Norfolk Regional Airport, housing 4 major airlines, is under $26,500,000 expansion program. Chesapeake Bay Bridge-Tunnel supplies direct northern highway route. Seven trunk line railroads, 50 major common carrier trucking companies, 2 bus companies.
Communications: 5 TV, 13 AM, 9 FM stations.
Medical facilities: 11 hospitals including oldest and 2d largest naval hospital in U.S.
Federal facilities: greatest concentration of naval installations in the world; 38 major commands in Norfolk include the Atlantic Fleet, the Second Fleet, NATO Supreme Allied Command Atlantic (SACLANT), Armed Forces Staff College and Commandant 5th Naval District.
Cultural facilities: Norfolk Symphony Orchestra, Feldman Chamber Quartet, repertory theater, dinner and little theaters, civic and university ballet. Chrysler Museum collections cover all cultures from Egyptian to pop art.
Educational facilities: Old Dominion University, Norfolk State College, Virginia Wesleyan College. Eastern Virginia Medical School to begin in 1973.
Recreational facilities: Norfolk Tour includes General Douglas MacArthur Memorial, Adam Thoroughgood House (1636), Gardens-by-the-sea, Naval Base. Dismal Swamp is located in Chesapeake and the famed resort city of Virginia Beach offers 38 miles of beach for swimming, fishing and surfing. Camping facilities at Seashore State Park.
Convention facilities: Scope—new $30,000,000 cultural and convention center.
Sports: Virginia Squires (ABA), Virginia Red Wings (AHL), Tidewater Tides (International League).

Oakland, California

Population: 362,100.
Area: 53.4 sq. mi. of land; county seat of Alameda County, located on the east side of San Francisco Bay and linked to San Francisco by the 8¼-mile Bay Bridge.
Industry: Food processing, fabricated metal products, transportation equipment, chemicals, paint and allied products rank high in industry. The Port of Oakland is the West Coast's leader in containerized cargo, 2d only to New York. Oakland is home base for Kaiser Industries and its aluminum, chemical, cement, gypsum and steel operations, as well as for Safeway Stores, Lucky Stores, Pacific Intermountain Express and Dymo Industries.
Commerce: There are 8,240 retail establishments in the City of Oakland with taxable sales of $1,025,425,000. The mean income for families is $11,279 per annum.
Transportation: The City is the western terminus for the Southern Pacific, Santa Fe and Western Pacific Railroads. More than 100 trucking companies have terminals in Oakland. The Port Authority operates Oakland International Airport, a major air-freight terminal. The airport is also the international center for supplemental air carriers. Headquarters for Bay Area Rapid Transit, an underground subway extending over a 75-mile network connecting 15 communities.
Medical facilities: 9 hospitals including Children's Hospital Medical Center, Kaiser Foundation and the Veteran's Administration.
New construction: Downtown Oakland is undergoing major redevelopment, with $100 million invested in construction.
Cultural facilities: Oakland/Alameda County Coliseum, site for many theatrical entertainments, exhibits, conventions and the circus. Oakland Museum, half garden, half gallery design, has divisions of Natural Science (ecology and environment), History (Indian culture to present), and Art. Also the Oakland Symphony, the Chinese Community Cultural Center and numerous theatrical, musical groups and drama workshops.
Educational facilities: Some of the colleges or universities serving the Oakland area are: University of California at Berkeley, Mills College, Peralta Community College, College of Holy Names, California College of Arts and Crafts, Cal State, Hayward and Chabot.
Sports attractions: Raiders (football), Athletics (baseball), Seals (hockey) and Golden State Warriors (basketball).
Other attractions: Lake Merritt, in the heart of Oakland, is surrounded by a botanical garden, a wildfowl refuge, a natural science center and Children's Fairyland. The 100-acre Zoo in Knowland State Park has a large collection of gibbon apes, the longest aerial tram in a California park and the African Veldt exhibit.
History: The Oakland Area was first explored in 1772, and was settled in 1850 when it attracted overflow from the Gold Rush. Oakland was incorporated as a town in 1852 and as a city in 1854.

Oklahoma City, Oklahoma

The World Almanac is sponsored in the Oklahoma City area by The Daily Oklahoman and The Oklahoma City Times, Oklahoma City, Oklahoma 73125; telephone (405) 232-3311; The Oklahoman founded in 1894; Times in 1888; Oklahoma Publishing Co. acquired The Oklahoman 1903 and The Times 1916. Circulation Oklahoman 185,750; Times 101,134; Sunday 286,880. Editor and publisher E. K. Gaylord, managing editor Charles L. Bennett.

Population: 368,856 (city), 699,092 (metro); largest city in state; labor force 346,000.
Area: city area, among nation's largest, is 647.5 sq. mi.; metro area, 3,491 sq. mi., located in state's center on N. Canadian River.
Industry: Oil, with about 1,800 producing wells in metro area. About 30,000 residents involved in oil industry. Tinker Air Force Base, one of world's largest air depots, employs 22,000 civilians and 2,500 military on $100,000,000 installation. FAA and Civil Aero-medical Institute. Some 37,000 other residents in aviation, with total annual payroll $300,000,000. Agricultural and ranching area. Manufactured goods include aircraft, telephone equipment, oil field machinery, oil and greases, building materials, feed, flour, meat and tires.
Commerce: Regional, national and international marketing center. Effective buying income $10,892 per household. Consumer sales near $1.7 billion.
Transportation: 5 passenger airlines; 4 primary federal and 3 major state highways, with I-35 and I-40 also intersecting the city, I-44 ends there. Fully planned urban expressway system; major bus, truck and rail lines.
Medical facilities: Oklahoma University Health

Sciences Center and 25 hospitals and clinics.

Cultural facilities: Oklahoma City Symphony and Junior Symphony; Oklahoma Art Center; Lyric Theater at Oklahoma City University; Warehouse Theater; Oklahoma Theater Center; Southwest Repertory Theater, University of Oklahoma.

Education: University of Oklahoma, Oklahoma City University, Central State University.

Convention facilities: New, $23,000,000 Myriad Convention Center, seating 15,000 in the center of a downtown redevelopment project costing nearly $300,000,000, hosts 350 conventions yearly with more than 150,000 delegates.

Other features: National Cowboy Hall of Fame, 130 municipal parks, major college sports. Pro sports; Oklahoma City 89ers, American Assn. baseball; Blazers, Central Hockey League; International Softball Headquarters.

History: Founded by land run, April 22, 1889.

Omaha, Nebraska

The World Almanac is sponsored in Nebraska by The Omaha World-Herald, World-Herald Square, Omaha, Nebraska 68102; telephone (402) 341-0300; Evening World, founded 1885 by G.M. Hitchcock, acquired Daily Herald, founded 1865; adopted present name 1889; circulation 251,792 daily, 290,064 Sunday. President Harold W. Andersen, vice-president-executive editor Louis G. Gerdes; awards include 3 Pulitzer Prizes; sponsors Midwest Spelling Bee, Newspapers in the Classroom, Publinks Golf Tournaments, Good Fellows Charities, college scholarships.

Population: 346,929 (city), 542,646 (metro area).
Area: 83 square miles of rolling hills.
Industry: Manufacturing accounts for $1.7 billion a year; 600 manufacturing plants employ 40,000 people. Western Electric, with 7,000 employees, is Nebraska's largest employer. Omaha ranks 2d in the nation in frozen food production and leads the world in salable receipts as the world's largest livestock market. Omaha received 75,000,000 bushels of grain in 1972.
Commerce: Center for 17 banks; 4th largest insurance center in nation; 36 insurance companies have home offices, including Mutual of Omaha, the largest provider of individual health insurance in the world, and Woodmen of the World Life Insurance Society, largest fraternal life company. Median family income $11,134. Retail sales over $1 billion.
Transportation: 4th largest in rail centers. Union Pacific and Burlington Northern main offices located here, transcontinental passenger trains daily, 75 freight trains daily. Over 750,000 tons carried on Missouri River annually. Six major airlines.
Medical facilities: 16 hospitals with 4,680 beds; 2 medical schools—University of Nebraska Medical School and Creighton School of Medicine; $2.5 million Eppley Institute for Research in Cancer is one of best in world. $100 million in medical construction planned or underway.
Federal facilities: Strategic Air Command's global headquarters at Offutt Air Base; Missouri River Division of the U.S. Army Corps of Engineers.
Cultural facilities: Omaha Symphony Orchestra, Omaha Opera Company, Omaha Ballet Society, 100 amateur and professional live theatre groups, 7 art galleries, 5 museums including $4,000,000 Joslyn Art Museum, 12 public libraries.
Educational facilities: 250 metro area schools, 6 colleges in the area teach 21,000 students, Voc-Tec program, College of Nursing.
Recreation: 120 public parks, 1,200 acre Fontenelle Forest Preserve and Nature Center, new $3,000,000 Henry Doorly Zoo, 3 dinner theatres, Civic Auditorium, professional basketball (NBA Kansas City-Omaha Kings), baseball, hockey, 55-day Ak-Sar-Ben pari-mutuel horseracing season. NCAA College World Series.
Further information: Omaha Chamber of Commerce, 1620 Dodge St., Omaha, Nebraska 68102.

Orange County, California

The World Almanac is sponsored in Orange County by The Register, 625 N. Grand, Santa Ana, CA, 92711; telephone (714) 835-1234; circulation combined daily 189,241, Sunday 201,871; purchased in 1935 by late R. C. Hoiles, president-founder Freedom Newspapers, Inc., now headed by son, Clarence H. Hoiles, also publisher of The Register. General manager David Threshie, executive editor Jim Dean, managing editor Mike Maloney.

Population: Estimated 1,596,000, up 4.2 percent in shift from fastest growing U.S. metropolitan area by rate to fastest numerically. Compares with 212,364 in '50; 2.5 million projected 1985.
Area: 500,000 acres stretching 25 mi. inland, 42 miles along Pacific Ocean from Long Beach past Huntington Beach surfing, Newport Beach yacht harbor, Laguna Beach art colony and Western White House to Camp Pendleton.
Industry and commerce: Bank deposits $2.55 billion; spendable income topped $7.1 billion as new business facilities opened at average of more than one per day. Housing construction reached 35,100 units or near 700 daily. Retail sales hit $3.66 billion as median family income was $13,760. Employment rose 6.2% to 554,000, with 134,100 in manufacturing, 116,300 in trade, 26,500 insurance, finance, real estate, 86,500 in services, 10,700 in $100-million agricultural output, and 79,900 in government. Biggest manufacturing employer Rockwell Intl's. Autonetics, Minuteman missiles and electronic calculators, sewing and reading machines firm. IR's Space Division built Apollo moon rocket second stage; McDonnell Douglas Astronautics, Apollo third stage and current Skylab. Other major employers include corporate or major unit headquarters for international firms such as Hughes, developer of NATO radar defense umbrella; Philco-Ford Aeronutronics, Beckman Instruments, AMF-Voit, Hunt-Wesson Foods, Santa Fe International, Westinghouse, ITT, Textron, Uniroyal, Cypress Mines, TRW and scores of others. County is center for such industries as sailboat construction, fiberglass products, glass con-

tainers, food processing, computers, construction both nationally and locally and even agriculture. One-fifth of U.S. strawberries produced here, cauliflower, oranges, and 90 percent of U.S. paprika. Tourism brought over 20,000,000 people to county in 1972, conventions several million more.

Transportation: 4 major freeways in county which is center of what apparently will be San Diego-to-Santa Barbara megalopolis. Nation's 4th busiest airport.

Communications: 7 major TV stations, half a dozen minor ones, and more than 40 radio stations.

Convention facilities: Anaheim Convention Center, Disneyland Hotel convention center and Newporter Inn building expanded facilities.

Other attractions: Disneyland, 10,000,000 in 1972 attendance; Knott's Berry Farm, 4,000,000; Movieland Wax Museum and Cars of Stars; Japanese Village; Lion Country Safari; air and car museums.

Cultural facilities: 2 major tax-supported universities, 4 private liberal arts colleges, multiple trade and special interest schools, 6 community colleges of more than 5,000 enrollment, and more than 50 high schools. Symphony orchestra, 2 master chorales, light opera, one pro and 5 amateur ballet companies, 32 community theater groups, 6 performing art support groups, 4 major art museums, art associations by score.

Sports attractions: American League Baseball Angels, pro teams in training, and heavy college, high school, amateur schedules.

Orlando, Florida

The World Almanac is sponsored in the Orlando area by the Sentinel Star, 633 N. Orange Ave., Orlando, Fla. 32802; telephone (305) 423-4411; Sentinel and Evening Star founded as dailies in 1913; merged in 1931, acquired by Tribune Company of Chicago in 1965; combined to create "all-day" newspaper in 1973; circulation, 199,870 daily, 199,994 Sunday; editor-publisher William G. Conomos.

Population: 114,500 (city), 595,015 (metro); 252,564 employed (metro).

Area: 30.1 sq. mi. in East Central Florida; 52 lakes inside city limit.

Industry: Center of citrus belt. Insurance headquarters for southeastern U.S.; 5 home and 8 regional insurance company offices. Martin Marietta Co., aerospace division, 2 General Electric plants, Westinghouse Electric Co. facility. Over 19,744 people employed by 466 manufacturers. 14 industrial parks. Third largest Naval Training Center in U.S.—7,800 personnel train over 40,000 recruits annually.

Commerce: 32 commercial banks in county; total deposits, $1,090,800,000. Tri-county metro area: 43 commercial banks; total deposits, $1,268,805,000. City has 4 building and loan associations. Three shopping malls each with more than 100 stores. Metro area retail sales, $1.4 billion.

Transportation: 6 airlines serve Orlando Jetport at McCoy with more than 205 scheduled flights daily; also Seaboard Coastline Railroad, 5 intercity bus lines, 22 common carrier truck lines and 9 freight forwarding services. Every major Florida market less than four hours away by highway.

Communications: 18 radio and 4 TV stations.

Medical facilities: 15 hospitals in metro area.

Cultural facilities: Loch Haven Art Center, John Young Museum and Planetarium; Florida Technological University, Seminole Junior College, Valencia Community College, Rollins College, Jones Business College.

Other attractions: Walt Disney World, 18 miles southwest of downtown Orlando; Sea World, $17,000,000 marine park on 125 acres; Bible World, $12,000,000 attraction to open Spring, 1974; Circus World opening 1975.

Convention facilities: 25,388 rooms as of Jan., 1974; 12,635 proposed. In 1972, 300 conventions with 65,000 attending.

Sports: Tinker Field, site of spring training for Minnesota Twins; Tangerine Bowl, post season football classic; 3 professional golf tournaments: $150,000 Florida Citrus Invitational in March, $150,000 Walt Disney World Tournament in Dec., $30,000 Lady Errol Classic in Nov. Ben White Raceways, training ground for trotters; Seminole Turf Club, harness racing.

Ottawa, Ontario, Canada

The World Almanac is sponsored in the Ottawa area by the Ottawa Journal, 365 Laurier Ave. West, Ottawa, Ontario; telephone (613) 563-3731; founded 1885 by A. S. Woodburn; circulation daily 84,288; Sat. 94,780; president and general manager Lucien A. Lalonde, managing editor George Paterson; affiliation, FP Publications; head office, Winnipeg.

Population: nearly 300,000 (city), 452,019 (region, including Carleton, Vanier and 14 other towns and villages); Canada's 5th largest city. Hull in neighboring Quebec adds another 130,000 to the metropolitan population.

Area: 30,481 acres (city), 1,100 sq. mi. (region) on Ontario-Quebec border at the Chaudiere Falls on the Ottawa River.

Industry: E. B. Eddy Co., producer of paper products, is largest private employer; Civil Service is the major employer.

Commerce: capital of Canada; large tourist business and developing convention capacity with 56 motels and hotels with 4,200 rooms.

Transportation: 45 miles of parkways in and around city; served by Canadian Pacific and Canadian National railways; International Airport, nation's 5th busiest, with 85 scheduled flights daily by 4 airlines and major operations by Canadian Armed Forces aircraft.

Cultural facilities: $45,000,000 National Arts Center with 2,300-seat opera house-concert hall, a theater and an experimental studio.

Other attractions: Gothic-style Parliament buildings, housing Canada's House of Commons and Senate; Peace Tower, memorial to Canada's war dead; Central Canada Exhibition, a 10-day summer fair at Lansdowne Park; Ottawa Winter Fair;

80 camping and trailer parks, and mountain and lake recreation facilities in the area.
Sports: Canadian Football League Ottawa Rough Riders and the Ottawa 67's, a junior hockey team, play in new $9,000,000 Civic Centre arena-stadium at Lansdowne Park.
History: founded 1827 as Bytown, incorporated as

Ottawa 1855; named after Outaouac (or Outaouais Indian tribe); became capital of Canada 1857. Governed by regional Chairman Denis Coolican and city Mayor Pierre Benoit.
Further information: Ottawa Tourist and Convention Bureau, 70 Besserer St., Ottawa, Ontario, Canada K1N 6A6.

Pensacola, Florida

The World Almanac is sponsored in the Pensacola area by the Pensacola News Journal, 101 E. Romana St., Pensacola, Fla. 32501; (904) 433-0041; predecessor The Floridian founded 1821, 1st daily News 1899, Journal 1898, merged 1924; combined circulation daily 59,884, Sunday 47,202; member Gannet Group; publisher Braden Ball, editor J. Earle Bowden.

Population: 61,900 (city), 213,500 (county) 425,200 (primary trade area).
Area: southern end of 759 sq. mi. Escambia County at west edge of Florida Panhandle.
Industry: U.S. Navy employs 15,200 military, 5,000 civilian personnel. Major manufacturers are Monsanto Corp., St. Regis Paper Co., Armstrong Cork, Tenneco Corp., Westinghouse; major industries are food and kindred products, lumber, printing and stone, clay, glass and concrete production.
Commerce: wholesale, retail center for 4 counties in west Florida, one in Alabama; effective buying income $1.132 billion; retail sales (1971) $666,241,000; 16 banks, 3 savings and loan banks, 26 mortgage firms; tourist industry $60,000,000, and farm and

forest income $5,400,000, annually.
Transportation: 2 railways, 2 airlines, 2 bus lines, 16 truck lines; 3 U.S. highways, Interstate 10.
Communications: one TV station, 8 radio stations.
Cultural facilities: Public Library, Historical Museum, Transportation Museum, symphony, Oratorio Society, Art Center, Little Theater.
Other attractions: historic forts, Pensacola Beach, Gulf Islands National Seashore.
Sports: Monsanto Open PGA tournament, Falstaff Classic Amateur Gold Classic, intercollegiate basketball.
History: colonized in 1559, failed; city founded in 1698, existing under 5 flags until ceded by Spain to U.S. in 1813.

Philadelphia, Pennsylvania

The World Almanac is sponsored in the Philadelphia area by The Philadelphia Inquirer, 400 N. Broad St., Philadelphia, Pa. 19101; telephone (215) 563-1600; lineage traced to Pennsylvania Packet, founded 1771; circulation 453,210 daily, 830,005 Sunday; published by Philadelphia Newspapers, Inc.; president Frederick Chait; vice president and general manager Sam S. McKeel; executive editor Eugene L. Roberts, Jr., editor Creed C. Black, managing editors, Gene Forman (news) and Will Jarrett (special projects); sponsors Delaware Valley Science Fair, Old Newsboys Day, Book & Author Luncheons.

Population: 1,933,700 (city); 4,854,200 (8-county metro area); 5,993,000 (14-county retail trading area); employment 2,052,600 (metro area).
Area: 129 sq. mi. (city); 3,575 sq. mi. (metro area); 5,900 sq. mi. (trading area); city located in southeastern Pa. on Delaware River, 90 mi. from New York City, 136 mi. from Washington, D.C.
Industry: diversified, with over 90% of all U.S. basic industries represented; major center for textiles and apparel, food processing, electrical machinery, petroleum (largest oil refining region on East Coast), instruments, transportation equipment, chemicals and pharmaceuticals; companies such as After Six, Campbell's Soup, Leeds & Northrup, RCA, Scott Paper, SmithKline, Sun Oil, Univac.
Commerce: retail sales in 1972 (metro area), $8.9 billion. Among commercial banks are 5 centenary institutions each with over $1 billion in deposits. Four of nation's largest savings banks. Large segment of American insurance industry (launched in Philadelphia).
Transportation: largest fresh-water port in world (50 mi. of waterfront); scheduled sailings to more than 200 ports in 100 countries; modern service for both bulk and packaged cargo. Penn Central, Reading and B&O rail lines provide extensive freight facilities (first 2 and Amtrak also provide passenger service). Over 250 motor truck lines,

vast network of highways and turnpikes. Completion of Cargo City, Philadelphia International Airport's $50,000,000 ultramodern freight facility, due by 1975; $400,000,000 passenger terminal expansion under way (7,400,000 passengers in 1972). Area transit (maintained by SEPTA) includes subway, elevated, bus and trolley lines.
Communications: 3 major daily newspapers, Inquirer, Bulletin and News (tabloid); 23 AM radio stations, 23 FM; 6 commercial TV stations.
New construction: Market Street East, $500,000,000 reconstruction of major retailing area); Franklin Town, privately financed $400,000,000 redevelopment of 50-acre midcity site, to provide 4,000 residential units, employment for 20,000; Centre Square, $86,000,000 dual-tower office building; Eighteen-Eighteen Market Street ($50,000,000 40-story office building).
Medical facilities: 117 hospitals, over 36,500 beds (metro area).
Federal facilities: Defense Industrial Supply Center: Defense Personnel Support Center; U.S. Naval Publications and Forms Center; Philadelphia Naval Base; U.S. Mint; Frankford Arsenal; U.S. Naval Home.
Cultural facilities: Philadelphia Orchestra, Pennsylvania Ballet, Lyric Opera Co., Grand Opera Co.; Academy of Music; Philadelphia Museum of Art; Franklin Institute; Pennsylvania Academy

of the Fine Arts; Rodin Museum; Academy of Natural Sciences; Barnes Foundation; Robin Hood Dell; Walnut Street Theater (oldest in America); Shubert, Forrest and New Locust theaters; many community and summer theaters.
Educational facilities: 54 colleges and universities within 25 mi. of City Hall; 6 medical schools in city (University of Pennsylvania's was nation's first); University City Science Center.
Recreational facilities: 4,100-acre Fairmount Park (largest municipal park in world); Zoological Gardens; swimming pools, parks, playgrounds; easy access to seashore and mountains.
Convention facilities: Philadelphia Civic Center (321,000 sq. ft. of air-conditioned exhibit space; 57 meeting rooms, including 12,500-seat Convention Hall, can accommodate 24,000 people); mod-

ern hotels and motels; fine restaurants.
Sports attractions: Phillies baseball team and Eagles football team play in Veterans Stadium; Flyers ice hockey club and 76ers basketball team play in Spectrum; local college teams; Army-Navy football game annually at John F. Kennedy Stadium.
Other attractions: City Hall (Philadelphia's tallest building, topped by huge statue of William Penn); restored Society Hill area; Elfreth's Alley; Longwood Gardens.
History: William Penn founded his "Greene Countrie Towne" as Quaker colony in 1682; gave it name that means "City of Brotherly Love"; national capital 1790-1800; historical shrines include Independence Hall, Liberty Bell, Carpenters' Hall, Betsy Ross House, Gloria Dei Church, Christ Church, USS Olympia, Fort Mifflin.

Phoenix, Arizona

The World Almanac is sponsored in the Phoenix area by The Phoenix Gazette, 120 East Van Buren Street, Phoenix, Arizona 85004; telephone (602) 271-8000; founded October 28, 1880 as Arizona Gazette by Charles H. McNeil; circulation 111,382; publisher Eugene C. Pulliam, managing editor Alan D. Moyer; sponsors Christmas Fund Drive, Music Memory Programs, Science Fair, Newspaper in the Classroom, Phoenix Suns Christmas Day Basketball Game, Family Symphony Concerts and other events.

Population: 701,000 (city), 1,140,000 (metro area), capital and largest city in state, 33rd in nation; total employed 451,500.
Area: 256.0 sq. mi. (city), 9,155 sq. mi. (metro area); in south central Arizona.
Industry: Electronic equipment manufacturers—Honeywell Information Systems and Motorola, Inc. each employ more than 2500; Aircraft and parts manufacturers—AiResearch, a division of The Garrett Corp., and Sperry Flight Systems each employ more than 2500; other major employers are E. L. Gruber (apparel), Goodyear Aerospace, General Electric, Western Electric Cable Mfg., Reynolds Metals, Marathon Steel Mfg., Arizona Public Service, Salt River Project, Mountain Bell, The Greyhound Corp. and Phoenix Newspapers.
Commerce: Wholesale and retail center for the state; retail sales (1972) $3.1 billion; effective buying income $11,384. Bank and S&L assets: $7.1 billion; there are 10 banks with 200 area offices and 4 S&L firms with 56 offices in the metro area.
Transportation: Phoenix is the transportation center of the southwest. Phoenix Sky Harbor International Airport is served by 10 airlines; in 1972, 3,364,933 passengers enplaned and deplaned there. Also served by 2 railroads; 2 transcontinental buslines; 10 transcontinental truck lines; 4 transcontinental heavy equipment haulers; 30 interstate and 39 intrastate truck lines.
Communications: 6 TV and 32 radio stations.
New construction: A record 36,427 new residential units permitted in 1972; total value, all types of

building permits: $820,973,656.
Medical facilities: Barrow Neurological Institute, one of nation's finest such facilities; 20 general-care hospitals; Veterans' Hospital; other special service facilities.
Cultural facilities: Art museum, public library, symphony orchestra, Indian museums, zoo, botanical gardens, community and professional theaters; Phoenix Civic Plaza, 6-sq. block convention center; Grady Gammage Auditorium.
Educational facilities: Arizona State University; Thunderbird Graduate School of International Management; 4 community colleges; Maricopa Technical College (vocational); 50 public and parochial high schools.
Sports attractions: 50 golf courses and $150,000 Phoenix Open; inland surfing beach; ice skating rinks; amusement park. Professional hockey, football, basketball, baseball teams; auto racing; greyhound and horse racing. Annual Fiesta Bowl (holiday football game).
Other attractions: Frank Lloyd Wright's Taliesin West; Paolo Soleri's Cosanti Foundation, Firebird Festival of the Arts; Dons' Club guided tours of Arizona; full calendar of events including state and county fairs, rodeos, horse shows, regattas, polo tournaments.
History: Founded in 1870, on site of ancient Indian settlement; the Hohokam tribe, which flourished ca. 500-1200 A.D., developed an intricate system of irrigation canals which form the base of the canal system in use today.

Pittsburgh, Pennsylvania

The World Almanac is sponsored in the Pittsburgh area by The Pittsburgh Press, 34 Boulevard of the Allies, Pittsburgh, Pa. 15222; telephone (412) 263-1100; founded June 23, 1884, as Evening Penny Press by Thomas J. Keehan; circulation 292,288 daily, 707,915 Sunday; editor John Troan, business manager and vice president Barney G. Cameron, executive editor Leo Koeberlein, managing editor Ralph Brem.

Population: 520,117 (city), 2,401,245 (4-county metro area), 2nd in state, 24th in nation; metro area labor

force, 997,300.
Area: 55.5 sq. mi., at juncture of the Allegheny and

Monongahela rivers which form the Ohio River; altitude, 702 feet.

Industry: One-fifth of nation's steelmaking capacity concentrated in metropolitan area; Western Pennsylvania mines produce 44,000,000 tons of bituminous coal annually; 6,000 different products made in area; home of world's first full-scale nuclear power plant, world's largest manufacturers of aluminum, steel rolls, rolling mill machinery, air brakes, plate and window glass and safety equipment; 3rd largest company headquarters city in country.

Commerce: Retail sales total over $4 billion a year; wholesale, about $4.6 billion a year; exports total over $372,000,000 yearly while river ports handle 66,800,000 tons annually, more than any other inland river area; average spendable family income, $10,789.

Transportation: 7 major airlines serve Greater Pittsburgh International Airport which is undergoing $250-million expansion; Amtrak and numerous major rail carriers; Continental Trailways and Greyhound Bus lines; over 400 common carriers; Port Authority Transit bus service; rapid and mass transit plan under development.

Communications: 2 daily newspapers, 5 TV (including country's first educational station) and 27 radio stations.

Medical facilities: 21 hospitals, including University of Pittsburgh Health and Medical complex where Dr. Jonas Salk developed polio vaccine; Veterans Administration installation.

Federal facilities: Federal Building on Liberty Avenue contains scores of U.S. government offices (Information Center 644-3456); U.S. Army Base at Oakdale; Air National Guard and Air Force Reserve bases at airport.

Cultural facilities: Civic Light Opera; 3 community and 2 commercial legitimate theaters; Pittsburgh Symphony and Pittsburgh Opera Company; Frick Art Museum; Carnegie Museum and Art Gallery, home of the triennial Carnegie International.

Educational facilities: University of Pittsburgh, Duquesne University, Point Park College, Chatham College, Carlow College, Robert Morris College, La Roche College, Carnegie-Mellon University, Community College of Allegheny County; 18 Carnegie public libraries, 3 bookmobiles, dozens of community libraries.

Sports: Baseball, National League Pirates; football, National Football League Steelers; hockey, National Hockey League Penguins.

Other attractions: Highland Park Zoo, Children's Zoo, Twilight Zoo, Aquarium, Aviary, Buhl Planetarium, Allegheny Observatory, Phipps Conservatory, 4 amusement parks, 2 operating passenger inclines, regional parks and dozens of parklets; Three Rivers Arts Festival every June; domed Civic Arena with retractable roof; 50,000-seat Three Rivers Stadium across the river from Golden Triangle.

History: First hunters and trappers came through here in 1714; city itself dates from Nov. 25, 1758 when English forces under Brig. Gen. John Forbes occupied the ruins of Fort Duquesne, which French soldiers had burned and abandoned, and built a new and bigger fortress called Fort Pitt. By the time it was incorporated in 1816, it already had reputation as a "Smoky City" from factories and coal-burning homes. Massive "Renaissance Plan" has cleared the skies and rebuilt heart of city during the last 25 years.

Further information: The Chamber of Commerce of Greater Pittsburgh, 411 Seventh Ave., Pittsburgh, Pa. 15222.

Portland, Maine

The World Almanac is sponsored in the Portland area by the Maine Sunday Telegram, 390 Congress, Portland, Me., 04104; phone (207) 775-5811; published by Guy Gannett Publishing Co., founded 1921; circulation 109,980; president Jean Gannett Hawley; editor Ernest Chard; also publishes morning Press Herald, circulation 53,743, and Evening Express, 29,538.

Population: 65,116 (city), 141,625 (metro area), 1st in state; total employed, 26,959.

Area: 21.6 sq. mi.; peninsula on Casco Bay.

Industry: Atlantic Coast's 2nd busiest oil shipping center, east terminus Montreal pipeline; fishing fleet base, seafood shipping center. Land-based products: printed materials, clothing, metal, processed food, wooden goods.

Commerce: Tourist center, regional retail and wholesale hub, large shopping complex, 1,000 retail, 350 wholesale, 600 service enterprises; retail sales (1971): 196,278,855. Median family income (1970): $8,456.

Transportation: Municipal jetport, Delta airline, 3 rail freight lines, integrated bus system, Greyhound and Continental bus terminals, 25 truck lines; Maine Turnpike, Interstate 95 and 295 highways connect to all New England; deep water anchorage, auto cruise ferries year round to Yarmouth, Nova Scotia.

Communications: 3 TV, 5 AM, 4 FM radio stations.

New construction: 2 banks, 2 hotels, housing.

Medical facilities: Medical center, 2 hospitals.

Cultural: Symphony Orch., Kotzschmar organ, one of world's largest; public, historical libraries; Victorian museums, Henry Longfellow home (1785); branch Univ. of Maine, Westbrook College, art, vocational and business schools; Portland Headlight, oldest lighthouse in the country.

Recreation: 18-hole municipal golf course, 9 others in area; scenic cruises; swimming, tennis, fishing within easy travel, scenic parks.

Convention facilities: 2 large assembly halls, meeting rooms in modern hotels and motels.

Portland, Oregon

The World Almanac is sponsored in the Portland area by The Oregon Journal, 1320 SW Broadway, Portland, Ore. 97201; telephone (503) 222-5511; founded March, 1902; circulation 129,913; editor Donald J. Sterling, Jr.; managing editor Edward F. O'Meara.

Population: 388,500 (city); 1,064,000 (metro area), in 1972; 1st in state; 33rd in nation; total employed, 443,400.

Area: 80 sq. mi., at juncture of Columbia and

Willamette Rivers.

Industry: Metal working, mostly aluminum, is big resource, plus some steel, clothing, paper, electronics. Ranks first in manufacture of equipment for logging-lumbering industry. Home of Georgia-Pacific, Louisiana-Pacific (forest products); Tektronix (electronic testing devices); Omark (saw cutting chain); Hyster (lifts, hoists, lumber handling); White Stag, Jantzen, Pendleton (clothing).

Commerce: Wholesale, retail center for large part of Oregon, SW Washington; retail sales metro area (1972), $2,436,639,000. There are 12 banks, 10 savings and loan associations.

Transportation: 3 major rail freight lines, Amtrak, Greyhound, Trailways buses. Tenth largest fresh-water port in U.S., with 27 miles frontage, 29 marine berths; 11,000,000 tons of cargo pass over docks annually. Portland, hub for 9 airlines with 261 daily scheduled flights, is major state terminal.

Communications: 4 TV and 17 radio stations.

Medical facilities: 9 major hospitals, University of Oregon Medical School, Veterans Administration Hospital.

Cultural facilities: Portland Art Museum, Oregon Symphony Orchestra, Portland Opera Association, Oregon Historical Society, Portland State University, University of Portland, Lewis & Clark College, Reed College, Marylhurst College and Concordia College.

Other attractions: Famed annual Rose Festival, Rose Show. Outstanding park system including Washington Park, Hoyt Arboretum, International Rose Test Garden, Portland Zoo, Oregon Museum of Science and Industry. Forest Park is largest forest area in a U.S. city's limits. Sports events and other attractions are presented in Memorial Coliseum.

History: Chartered in 1851 with population of 821; named after Portland, Me., rather than Boston, Mass., on flip of coin by 2 early citizens.

Providence, Rhode Island

The World Almanac is sponsored in the Providence area by The Providence Journal-Bulletin, 75 Fountain St., Providence, R.I. 02902; telephone (401) 277-7000; Journal founded 1829, Bulletin 1863, Sunday Journal 1883; circulation, Journal (m) 64,772, Bulletin (e) 146,219, Sunday Journal 201,492; president and publisher John C. A. Watkins, exec. VP Michael P. Metcalf, VP and asst. publ. Edwin P. Young, VP-admin. Charles P. O'Donnell, editor Michael J. Ogden.

Population: 179,116 (city), 942,000 (metro), 1st in state, 71st in nation; total employed in city, 111,776.

Area: 18.91 sq. mi., at the head of Narragansett Bay.

Industry: Jewelry, silverware, plated ware, costume jewelry are largest industries. Textron Inc., a multi-market company—one of largest in nation, is based in Providence. There are 1,314 manufacturing companies in the city.

Commerce: Wholesale and retail center for entire state; retail sales (1971, metro): $2,007,196,000. Consumer spendable income per household $10,897 (metro). Allendale Insurance, world's largest mutual insurer of industrial firms, is based outside of city in Johnston. Narragansett Capital Corp., largest small business investment company in nation, is based in city. One building-loan association, 3 mutual savings banks, 5 commercial banks.

Transportation: Penn Central Railroad, fast "Turbo-Liner" passenger service between Boston, Providence and N.Y.; 5 bus lines; 50 locally-based common carriers and contract truckers; 9 major highways link Providence to every corner of R.I.; 6 major airlines out of T.F. Green Airport in Warwick (15 min. from Prov.). Port is 3rd largest in New England; 27 wharves and docks, 10.5 miles of commercial waterfront on the bay.

Communications: 3 TV and 7 radio stations.

New construction: 27-story, $16,000,000 R.I. Hospital Trust National Bank office tower, just completed.

Medical facilities: 6 hospitals; one VA hospital.

Cultural facilities: R.I. Philharmonic, R.I. School of Design Musuem of Art; $13,000,000 Civic Center (seats 12,000).

Educational facilities: Brown University, founded 1764, is 7th oldest college in U.S. A 7-year M.D. program inaugurated 1973. Providence College, R.I. College and R.I. School of Design, one of nation's foremost art schools, all located within city.

Recreational facilities: One of America's most attractive recreational areas centers around Providence: 69 salt water beaches, 26 fresh water beaches, 49 golf and country clubs, 4 ski areas, 26 yacht clubs, 23 parks, all within 45 minutes of city.

Sports: America's Cup races held since 1930; Newport-Bermuda race, another major yachting event, starts at Newport every other year.

Other attractions: Largest collection of original early American homes of any city; located along Benefit St., they have been preserved by the Providence Preservation Society.

History: Founded 1636 by Roger Williams; incorporated 1832; official title of state is "Rhode Island and Providence Plantations."

Quebec City, Quebec, Canada

Population: 186,088 (city), 480,500 (metro area); the oldest city in Canada (1608) and the capital city of the Province of Quebec.

Area: A natural citadel on the north shore of the St. Lawrence River at confluence with St. Charles River; 400 miles from Gulf of St. Lawrence; 167 miles east of Montreal; covering an area of 30 sq. mi. The older part of the city is built on a cliff 360 ft. above the St. Lawrence.

Industry: Some 300 industrial firms, ranging from primary industry products to a variety of

consumer products, employ more than 16,000 people. Food and beverage, leather footwear and leather products, textiles, apparel, wood products, pulp and paper, printing and publishing, iron and steel products, non-ferrous metal products, chemical products.

Commerce: Quebec harbour, one of the busiest seaports of Canada, accommodates the largest ocean-going vessels with its year-round facilities, an important container terminal on the North Atlantic coast. The Provincial Government, with more than 15,000 employees, is the largest single

employer and consumer in the city.
Transportation: Railroads: Canadian Pacific and Canadian National. Airlines: Air Canada, Quebecair, Nordair. A major bus centre; Intercity Bus Lines; Quebec Autobus Ltée, Autobus Voyageur.
Medical facilities: 5 large general hospitals and many smaller ones serve the population of the metro area under the expert direction of world-renowned specialists in all fields.
Cultural facilities: Quebec's historic character, cultural appeal and natural beauty make tourism an important area of economic activity. Its annual "Carnaval" in February is internationally known, its annual summer Festival (July) changes the city into an open theatre for numerous artistic events. Expo-Quebec—an annual provincial exhibition (industrial, commercial and agricultural)—draws over 500,000 people a year.

Educational facilities: Laval University, the first in North America; Quebec University; 3 colleges for general and vocational training, numerous private schools.
History: Founded in 1608 by the French explorer Samuel de Champlain, Quebec City is recognized as the cradle of French civilization in America, and was once the key to the interior of the North American continent.
Other attractions: The only walled city in North America with fortifications standing today as they were 125 years ago. A main point of interest is the Citadel, built from 1823-1832. Within its walls are 25 buildings including the summer residence of the Governor General of Canada, the Parliament buildings (1886), the Quebec Museum, Battlefield Park, the Ursulines Museum, the Seminary (1663), the Talon cellars, Notre Dame des Victoires Church and Trésor Street.

Raleigh, North Carolina

The World Almanac is sponsored in eastern North Carolina by The News & Observer and the Raleigh Times, 215 S. McDowell St., Raleigh, NC 27601, (919) 832-4411; circulation News (morn) 133,415, Times (eve) 32,334; publisher Frank Daniels Jr., editorial director Claude Sitton, editor Times Herbert O'Keef, managing editor News Bob Brooks, Times Mike Yopp.

Population: 135,000 (city), 245,000 (county), 500,000 (metro area); 4th in state; 52,331 employed.
Area: 44 sq. mi. in geographical center of state where piedmont joins coastal plain; alt. 363 ft.
Industry: state capital, major industry is government, employing 24% of workforce; also electrical machinery, foods and textiles.
Commerce: financial, retail center of eastern N.C.; retail sales (1972) $817,000,000; 12 banks with $21.1 billion debits; income average per household $14,450, per capita $4,354.
Education: 6 colleges; N.C. State Univ. largest, with Univ. of N.C. (Chapel Hill) and Duke Univ. (Durham) within 30 mi. form Research Triangle; 5,000 acre Triangle Park employs 10,000 in drug, fiber, biomedical and engineering research.

Transportation: 5 rail and 4 bus lines; airport has 4 airlines and 50 daily flights.
Communications: 5 TV and 12 radio stations.
New construction: $90,000,000 (1972).
Medical facilities: 3 hospitals, 818 beds; major mental hospital, 2,765 beds, 350 doctors.
Convention facilities: 30 motels, 3,500 rooms.
Cultural facilities: 3 museums, state fairgrounds; Dorton Arena seats 9,111, Memorial Auditorium 3,000 and Reynolds Coliseum 12,000.
Recreational facilities: 4,200 acre Umstead Park; Carter Stadium seats 43,000; 98 city parks.
Sports: pro basketball Carolina Cougars; 3 pro golf tournaments; all college sports popular.
History: planned site founded 1792; named for Sir Walter Raleigh; Andrew Johnson birthplace.

Regina, Saskatchewan, Canada

The World Almanac is sponsored in southern Saskatchewan by The Leader-Post, 1964 Park St., Regina, Sask., telephone (306) 527-8511; founded 1885 by Nicholas Flood Davin; circulation 68,125; president, Michael Sifton, Toronto; executive vice-president, Max Macdonald; editor, W. Ivor Williams; managing editor, C. E. W. Bell; business manager, William Duffus; advertising manager, George Crawford; MacLaren Trophy for editorial page reproduction excellence.

Population: 140,734, first in province, 17th in nation; labor force, 58,000.
Area: 30.98 sq. mi., approximately 100 miles north of Canada-U.S. border, on a line with Calgary and Winnipeg; provincial capital.
Industry: Over 250 manufacturing industries; Gross production value (1971) $221,155,000, 36% of Saskatchewan total.
Commerce: Service centre for oil, potash, grain production area; retail sales (1972) $303,190,460, 22.92% of province; average disposable income per capita, $3,020.
Transportation: 2 railines, 2 airlines, 3 bus lines and 80 trucking companies; main east-west Trans-Canada highway bisects; city-run transit system, including Telebus, hybrid system with demand-response taxi service and multiple request of mass transit, provides to-and-from service to user's home.
Communications: 2 TV and 5 radio stations.

Medical facilities: 3 major hospitals, 1,483 beds.
Cultural facilities: Saskatchewan Centre of Arts, multi-purpose theatre-convention centre, main areas; Jubilee theatre (seats 450) stage, ballroom, reception hall and dining room; Centennial theatre (seats 2,029); Hanbidge Hall convention area, 12,200 square feet, 9 meeting rooms, seats 1,600 serves 1,200. Regina Symphony; Globe Repertory; Museum Natural History; Norman Mackenzie Art Gallery; RCMP Museum.
Educational facilities: Regina Campus, University of Saskatchewan; 13 collegiates; 76 elementary; Saskatchewan Institute of Applied Arts and Science.
Recreational facilities: Saskatchewan Roughriders (Canadian pro football team); 96 park areas and playgrounds; 9 golf courses; 5 swimming pools; 5 indoor ice rinks.
Other attractions: Wascana Centre, 2,000-acre development, man-made lake focal point with

public buildings, parks, recreation areas in heart of city.

History: Founded 1882, and since that time headquarters for RCMP training depot.

Reno, Nevada

The World Almanac is sponsored in the northern Nevada area by the Reno Evening Gazette and the Nevada State Journal, 401 West 2nd St., Reno, Nev. 89504; telephone (702) 323-3161; Journal founded 1870; Gazette 1876; combined daily circulation 44,894, Sunday 37,079. Publisher Richard J. Schuster, executive editor Warren L. Lerude.

Population: 1970 — 72,863 (city); 97,050 (metro area including Sparks). Estimated 10% annual increase to approximately (1972): 87,164 (city); 117,430 (metro area). Second largest in state. Average 1972 employment 72,000.

Area: 23.81 sq. mi.; Reno is the county seat of Washoe. Located in northwestern part of the state at eastern base of Sierra Nevada. Elevation 4,397 ft.

Industry: Gaming — 1972 gross revenue for county, $138 million. Tourism — Estimated 12,000,000 visitors in 1972, of which 103,413 were delegates to 275 conventions. Warehousing — 900,000 sq. feet; recent increase due to Nevada's liberal free port law. Marriages and divorces, 34,443 and 3,421 respectively.

Commerce: 4th fastest growing market in nation, Median household income $9,377. Total taxable sales for county $559,798,163. Bank resources, $1.25 billion.

Transportation: 2 major freight lines plus Amtrak and 3 commercial airlines. Airport is an International Port of Entry; 840,000 passengers passed through in 1972. Interstate 80 and U.S. 395 run through Reno.

Communications: 3 network TV stations, one cable TV; 10 radio stations.

Medical facilities: 3 hospitals including one Veteran's Administration.

Educational facilities: University of Nevada, Reno, enrollment about 9,000 in 1972 including a newly created 2-year medical school.

Sports: Reno Silver Sox, semi-pro baseball. Reno Aces, semi-pro ice hockey.

Cultural facilities: Fleischmann Atmospherium Planetarium and 180,000 volume library. Site of annual national Air Races. Harrah's Automobile Collection of 1,400 antique cars, Pioneer Theater Auditorium (1,428 seats) and Centennial Coliseum (8,000 seats).

Recreation: 19 ski resorts within 90 minutes, including Squaw Valley, site of 1960 Olympics. Fishing and water sports at Lake Tahoe and Pyramid.

History: Established 1868 with public auction of land by Central Pacific RR. Named after Civil War hero Gen. Jesse Lee Reno.

Richmond, Virginia

The World Almanac is sponsored in the Richmond area by the Richmond Times-Dispatch and News Leader, 333 E. Grace St., Richmond, Va. 23213; (804) 649-6000. Times-Dispatch founded 1850 by James A. Cowardin, circulation 140,693 daily, 195,235 Sunday; News Leader founded 1896 by Joseph Bryan, circulation 118,073; publisher D. Tennant Bryan, president Alan S. Donnahoe, executive editor John E. Leard, Times-Dispatch managing editor Alf Goodykoontz, News Leader managing editor J. A. Finch.

Population: 246,000 (city), 542,000 (metro area), total employed (non-agricultural) 250,100.

Area: 62.5 sq. mi. (city), located at fall line of James River, 90 miles from Atlantic Ocean.

Industry: Tobacco industry, with 17,200 workers, leads in employment; 9,300 in chemicals, second. Philip Morris cigarette plant being built will be world's largest. Printing, publishing, manufacturing of paper and allied products and food also major employers.

Commerce: Wholesale, retail center for central Virginia. Retail sales $1,435,000,000, per capita income $4,324, family $10,070, total income $2,308,000,000.

Transportation: 4 major railroads, 5 intercity bus lines, 3 commercial air lines, one commuter air line, 50 fixed motor truck lines. Three interstate routes, 6 U.S. highways, 9 state routes serve city. Deepwater terminal accessible to ocean-going vessels.

Communications: 4 TV and 16 radio stations.

Medical facilities: Medical College of Virginia known worldwide for heart, kidney transplants, medical research. Twenty other hospitals including McGuire VA Hospital.

Federal facilities: Defense General Supply Center at Bellwood, Ft. Lee (Quartermaster Corps headquarters) nearby Fifth Federal Reserve Bank, U.S. Fourth Circuit Court located here.

Cultural facilities: Va. Museum and Theatre with its company of professional artists make city a center for dramatic and other performing arts, along with a variety of other professional and amateur drama groups. Richmond Symphony Orchestra performs seasonally at city-owned Mosque auditorium.

Educational facilities: Virginia Commonwealth University has state's largest higher education enrollment. Private higher learning institutions are University of Richmond, Virginia Union University, Union Theological Seminary (Presbyterian), Randolph-Macon College.

Recreational Facilities: 12,000 seat Richmond Coliseum completed in 1971 can accommodate major athletic, entertainment events. Parker Field, City Stadium, numerous parks in city.

Convention facilities: Coliseum, Mosque, large downtown hotels attract numerous state convention groups.

Sports attractions: Richmond Braves (IL baseball), Richmond Robins (hockey), national ranked track and tennis events. Russian-American indoor track meets 1972, 1973.

Other attractions: St. John's Church, scene of Patrick Henry's "Liberty or Death" speech; Virginia Capitol designed by Thomas Jefferson; White House of Confederacy; Civil War battlefields.

History: Exploration here in 1607 by Capt. John Smith, others of Jamestown Colony; first settlement 1609; incorporated as town 1742, made Va. capital 1780, Confederate Capital 1861-65. Burned 1781 by Benedict Arnold, and 1865 when cotton, tobacco stockpiles fire set by fleeing Confederates spread to city. City suffered heavy damage from floods 1771, 1969, 1972.

Roanoke, Virginia

The World Almanac is sponsored in the Roanoke area by The Roanoke Times and The World-News, 201-203 Campbell Avenue, Roanoke, Va. 24010, telephone (703) 981-3000; Times founded 1886, World-News founded 1889; Lee C. Kitchin, president; Barton W. Morris, Jr., publisher; circulation combined daily, 115,699; Sunday 111,332.

Population: 92,115 (city), 185,000 (metro area), 4th largest metro area in Virginia; over 97,000 employed.
Area: Located at mouth of Shenandoah Valley.
Industry: Center of the furniture industry; distribution center for 2 major grocery chains; large industrial sites for General Electric, Eaton Corp., ITT, Johnson-Carper Division of Singer Co., and regional headquarters for All-State and Atlantic Cos life insurance.
Commerce: Retail shopping center for 20 counties and parts of West Virginia and North Carolina. Retail sales per household tops the state and U.S. southeastern Region.
Transportation: Roanoke is served by 2 airlines, Piedmont and Eastern; Trailways and Greyhound bus companies. Twelve major trucking firms have terminals in Roanoke. Connected to I-81 by spur I-

581. Hdqts., Norfolk & Western.
Communications: 3 TV and 12 radio stations.
Medical facilities: 5 major hospitals and large VA facility. New psychiatric hospital construction started in 1973.
Cultural facilities: Roanoke Symphony Orchestra, Children's Zoo and Transportation Museum; Roanoke Virginia Western and National Business and Hollins colleges. Barn Theatre and Theatre-in-the-Round; Civic Center and Auditorium.
Other attractions: Nearby Smith Mountain Lake and Claytor Lake State Park. Peaks of Otter; Blue Ridge Parkway.
Sports: Professional hockey and baseball.
History: First known as Big Lick, became Roanoke (Indian word for shell money) in 1882 with building of Shenandoah Valley Railroad to link with Norfolk & Western Railway.

Rochester, New York

The World Almanac is sponsored in the Rochester area by the Gannett Rochester Newspapers, 55 Exchange St., Rochester, N.Y. 14614; telephone (716) 232-7100; circulation, Democrat and Chronicle (morning), 138,940; The Times-Union (evening), 140,607; Democrat and Chronicle (Sunday), 223,389; publisher Eugene C. Dorsey; executive editor Stuart Dunham; director of advertising Cortland Peterson; 2 Times-Union reporters were awarded a 1972 Pulitzer Prize.

Population: 296,223 (1970); 5-county metropolitan area, 961,516; 395,959 employed.
Area: 178 sq. mi. (Monroe County) straddling Genesee River, on the shore of Lake Ontario.
Industry: World leader in production of photographic, optical and scientific instruments, with Eastman Kodak (45,000 employees), Xerox (15,000) and Bausch & Lomb (4,500), all founded in Rochester, the most prominent. Other fields: machinery, food products, apparel, printing and publishing. Annual industrial production growth rate: 12% since 1967.
Commerce: Retail sales (1972 estimate) over $1.7 billion, 16 commercial and savings banks, with assets of $5 billion; median household income (metropolitan area) $10,771, in 1972, 9th in the nation.
Transportation: Monroe County Airport with 3 major airlines and several freight companies; rail freight service by 4 lines and passenger service through Amtrak; port of Rochester; over 75 motor freight firms.
Communications: 4 TV and 11 radio stations.
Medical facilities: One of the nation's most ad-

vanced health care centers; 8 general hospitals, including Strong Memorial Hospital.
Cultural facilities: Eastman Theater, part of University of Rochester's Eastman School of Music, and home of Rochester Philharmonic Orchestra; Memorial Art Gallery; Rochester Museum and Science Center, including Strasenburgh Planetarium; George Eastman House of Photography.
Education facilities: 8 private and 2 public 4-year colleges, community colleges.
Recreation facilities: Finger Lakes area, with 13 parks, summer and winter sports, golf and bowling. 16-park Monroe County system, including Seneca Park Zoo and Highland Park "Lilac Festival" (May).
Sports: International League Red Wings, top Baltimore Orioles farm team; American Hockey League Amerks, North American Soccer League Lancers; thoroughbred racing at Finger Lakes Race Track.
Further information: Chamber of Commerce, 55 St. Paul St., Rochester, N.Y. 14604; or Convention and Publicity Bureau, 100 Exchange St., Rochester, N.Y. 14614.

Sacramento, California

The World Almanac is sponsored in the Sacramento area by The Sacramento Bee, 21st & Q, Sacramento, CA. 95816; telephone (916) 442-5011; founded 1857; circulation, daily 181,960, Sunday 217,629; president Eleanor McClatchy, editor Walter Jones, managing editor Martin Smith.

Population: 273,200 (City), 668,100 (county) total employed—318,400.
Area: 92 sq. miles (city), 997 sq. miles (county) located in Sacramento Valley 85 miles northeast of

San Francisco.
Industry: 475 manufacturing plants including Campbell Soup, Procter and Gamble, Libby Mc-Neil and Libby, California Almond Growers Exchange, Del Monte and Aerojet-General.
Commerce: State capital. Wholesale and retail center for large area of Sacramento Valley. Retail sales: (1972): $1,596,772,000.
Bank debits: $5,393,177,000 (city).
Transportation: New jet age Metropolitan Airport, $55-million Port of Sacramento gives access to the Pacific, major highways intersect in city.
Communications: 5 TV and 17 radio stations.
New construction: New Convention Center and Theater scheduled for opening in mid-1974. Downtown Sacramento Mall in final stages of redevelopment. Old Sacramento being restored as state and federal historical project.
Medical facilities: 11 major hospitals, University of California Medical School in nearby Davis.
Federal facilities: 2 large Air Force bases, Sacramento Army Depot, many regional federal offices.
Cultural facilities: Symphony orchestra, ballet; civic theater; Crocker Art Gallery; California State University, Sacramento; McGeorge College of Law, Lincoln University Law School and 3 community colleges.
Other attractions: City Zoo, many public parks and play grounds, 14 public and 4 private golf courses, Sutter's Fort, State Capitol, Stanford home, Pony Express Terminal and Governor's Mansion. Fishing, hunting, boating and skiing in nearby high Sierras. Site of Annual State Fair.
History: City founded by John Augustus Sutter in 1839. James Marshall discovered gold at Sutter's Mill in 1848 — 35 miles northeast of Sacramento. City became gateway to Mother Lode Country. Pony Express and the Central Pacific Railroad which crossed the Sierra Nevada were part of early Sacramento history.

St. Louis, Missouri

The World Almanac is sponsored in the St. Louis area by the Post-Dispatch, 900 N. 12th Blvd., 63101; telephone (314) 621 1111, founded Dec. 12, 1878 by Joseph Pulitzer; circulation, 317,247 daily, 530,750 Sunday; editor and publisher, Joseph Pulitzer Jr.; managing editor, Evarts A. Graham Jr.; general manager, Alex T. Primm; director of promotion and public affairs, William J. Isam; major awards include 5 Pulitzer prizes to newspaper, 11 to staff members; community projects include high school Scholar-Athlete program, Science Fair, Straight-A baseball tickets, Silver Skates, scholarships.

Population: 622,236 (city), 951,685 (county), 2,363,017 (metro area), 10th in nation, payroll employment 881,100.
Area: 4,935 sq. mi. metro area, just south of confluence of Missouri and Mississippi Rivers.
Industry: 2nd to Detroit in auto assembly with Ford, GM, and Chrysler plants; McDonnell Douglas Corp. headquarters, air and spacecraft manufacturer; other headquarters: nation's 2 largest shoemakers, Interco, Inc. and Brown Shoe Co.; Anheuser-Busch, world's largest brewer; Monsanto Co., General Dynamics, Ralston-Purina Co., Pet, Inc., Emerson Electric, Granite City Steel Co. and Peabody Coal. Grain market with 80 million bushel annual yield; 3300 manufacturing concerns employing 280,000 persons.
Commerce: $5.2 billion estimated retail sales for 1973 in metro area; $7,625 median family income; 142 banking institutions with resources of $7 billion.
Transportation: Served by 9 major airlines with 5,861,280 passenger movements in 1972; 2nd largest railroad center in nation served by 21 railroads; nation's largest inland Mississippi River port; 8 major highways; 40 motorbus lines; 300 freight lines.
Communications: 6 TV and 18 radio stations.
New construction: Industrial and commercial contracts totaled $240,431,000 (1972); residential totaled $292,029,000.
Medical facilities: 65 hospitals with 23,000 beds; Washington University and St. Louis University Medical Schools and affiliated hospitals provide specialized treatment in many areas.
Federal facilities: Military Personnel Records Center, Aeronautical Chart and Information Center, Granite City Army Installation, Scott Air Force Base.
Cultural facilities: City Art Museum; Museum of Science and Natural History; restored historic homes; St. Louis Symphony orchestra; Mississippi River Festival near Edwardsville in summer; Municipal Theatre Assoc. (Muny Opera) offers Broadway shows in one of nation's largest outdoor theatres in city's Forest Park.
Educational facilities: 4 major universities: Washington, St. Louis, University of Missouri at St. Louis and Edwardsville campus of Southern Illinois University; private colleges; 3-branch junior college system; numerous preparatory, vocational and theological schools.
Recreational facilities: Jefferson National Expansion Memorial with 630-foot Gateway Arch on the riverfront; 1,326-acre Forest Park with 3 golf courses, ball fields, floral displays, the McDonnell Planetarium and famous zoo; National Museum of Transportation; Six Flags Over Mid-America; Grant's Farm with President Grant's cabin and animal displays; Missouri Botanical Gardens with advanced research-display greenhouse, the Climatron.
Convention facilities: 12,000 hotel rooms; largest exhibit space: 45,000 sq. ft.; Kiel Auditorium seats 10,500; new convention center planned for city.
Sports attractions: 54,000 seat Busch Stadium is home of St. Louis Cardinals football and baseball teams and Soccer Stars; St. Louis Hockey Blues play in the Arena.
Other attractions: Climate has 4 distinct seasons; spring and autumn moderate, winters brisk, summers warm with 90-degree temperatures on 40 days; average annual temperature is 54.1 degrees; average precipitation 36.6 inches.
History: named for French King Louis IX by French fur trapper Pierre Laclede whose trading post became major fur market and gateway to the West; city became starting point for many expeditions including Lewis and Clark's exploration and Charles Lindbergh's Spirit of St. Louis flight.
Further information: Convention and Tourist Board of St. Louis, 911 Locust St., or Chamber of Commerce of Metropolitan St. Louis, 10 Broadway.

St. Paul, Minnesota

The World Almanac is sponsored in the St. Paul area by the St. Paul Pioneer Press and Dispatch, 55 E. 4th St., St. Paul, Minn. 55101; telephone, (612) 222-5011; founded 1868 as Minnesota Pioneer by James Goodhue; circulation, Pioneer Press (morning) 108,164, Dispatch (evening) 128, 804, Sunday Pioneer Press 237,101; Bernard H. Ridder, chairman of the board; Bernard H. Ridder Jr., president & publisher; John R. Finnegan, executive editor; William G. Sumner, editor.

Population: 309,828 (city), 1,874,380 (metro area), 2nd in state, 46th in nation, total employed, 186,000.
Area: 55 sq. mi. on banks of Mississippi River in eastern Minnesota; close to Minnesota and Wisconsin vacation lands.
Industry: 4th in printing and publishing, 5th in cosmetics, 4th in electronics. St. Paul Union Stock Yards is 2nd largest livestock center in nation with 3,326,439 head in 1972.
Commerce: Retail sales (1971): $3.574 billion. Average family income: $10,263. There are 25 banks and 7 savings and loan associations.
Transportation: 5 major and 2 regional rail lines, Amtrak, 21 intercity truck firms and 37 terminals, 3 interstate bus lines, 730-mile public transit system. Metropolitan Airport, hub of 8 commercial airlines, headquarters for Northwest and North Central Airlines, averages 824 air movements per day. Downtown Airport, off St. Paul's loop, serves area business firms. Sixty firms operate barges on the Mississippi River, using a 9-foot channel downtown.
Communications: 4 commercial TV and 2 educational stations, 29 radio stations.
Medical facilities: 12 private hospitals; a 611-bed community hospital and research center: St. Paul Ramsey Hospital.
Cultural facilities: Minnesota Symphony Orchestra, St. Paul Arts & Science Center; 8 higher education institutions: University of Minnesota Insti-

tute of Agriculture, Hamline University, Bethal College, College of St. Thomas, College of St. Catherine, Concordia College, Macalester College and William Mitchell College of Law. A $66,000,000 school system with 74 public schools and 61 private schools.
New construction: A $6,000,000 Federal Savings & Loan Building, $21,000,000 Civic Center Complex, $13,000,000 American National Bank Building. More than $250,000,000 in downtown construction since 1960.
Recreation facilities: More than 900 lakes in metro area, 438 tennis courts, 148 swimming beaches, 513 parks, 50 golf courses, 27 ski centers. There are 52 neighborhood recreation centers, 36 miles of parkways, 10 miles of hiking and biking trails.
Convention facilities: St. Paul Civic Center Complex with 101,000 sq. feet exhibit space, total seating for 35,000 in 4 main buildings, 15 meeting rooms. Fifty hotels and motels with 2,500 sleeping rooms.
Other attractions: St. Paul Winter Carnival, Minnesota State Fair, Como Park Zoo and Conservatory; onyx statue of Indian God of Peace in City Hall, State Capitol, Minnesota Historical Society Museums.
History: Pierre "Pig's Eye" Parrant, first settler, 1838; name changed from Pig's Eye when Father Lucien Galtier built chapel in name of St. Paul in 1841. Became a town, 1849, a city, 1854.

St. Petersburg, Florida

World Almanac sponsored in Florida Suncoast area by The St. Petersburg Times and Evening Independent, 490 1st Ave. S., St. Petersburg, Florida 33701; telephone (813) 894-1111; The Times founded 1884, Independent 1906. Circulation, The Times (mornings) 183,295; Independent 29,711; Sunday Times 219,841. Chairman of the Board, Nelson Poynter; editor and president. Eugene Patterson; Independent editor, Robert Stiff; The Times managing editor, Robert Haiman; publisher, John B. Lake.

Population: 255,437 (city); 1,319,661 (metro area); Employed (county) 160,100. Unemployment 1.8%.
Area: 59 sq. mi., midway on Florida's West Coast between Tampa Bay and Gulf of Mexico.
Industry and commerce: Tourism leads the way. Over 3,700,000 visitors spent $945,000,000 enjoying the good life in '72. Concentration of "smokeless" industry. GE, Minneapolis Honeywell, Electronics Communications, Inc., Jim Walter Research Corp., Milton Roy Co., 109-store shopping mall, Florida Regional office for Allstate Insurance Company.
Transportation: World's most modern air terminal 25 minutes from St. Petersburg downtown. Albert Whitted and Pinellas International airports also serve. Amtrak, Seaboard Coast Line Railroads, Greyhound and Trailways bus lines. Twin-span Sunshine Skyway, 15-mile bridge-causeway to south.
Communications: 6 TV and 46 radio stations.
Convention facilities: 52,000 units house 160,000 visitors at one time. Bayfront Center seats 9,400 in Arena, 2,200 in Auditorium. 361 days of sunshine a

year.
New construction: Highest ratio of building permits-to-population in nation's history in '71.
Medical facilities: Site of All-Children's Hospital for pediatrics. Affiliated with USF College of Medicine. Out-patient specialty clinics. 7 major hospitals. Bay Pines Veterans' Administration installation.
Cultural facilities: Fine Arts Museum, Gulf Coast Symphony, Historical Museum, amateur theaters, $5,000,000 Bayfront Center. Eckerd College Free Institutions Forums.
Educational facilities: Eckerd College, St. Petersburg Jr. College, University of South Florida Bay Campus, Florida Institute of Oceanography.
Recreational facilities: Downtown Bayfront city-owned. Yacht club, Nature Trail, Senior Citizens' Center, 54 parks and community centers.
Sports attractions: Cardinals and Mets spring training. Hockey, horse and greyhound racing, pro tennis, LPGA's Orange Blossom Open. Minor league baseball, watersports and drag racing.

Salt Lake City, Utah

The World Almanac is sponsored in the Salt Lake City area by the Salt Lake Tribune, 143 S. Main St., Salt Lake City, Utah 84110; telephone (801) 524-4545; founded Apr. 15, 1871; circulation 109,595 daily, 184,946 Sunday; publisher, John W. Gallivan; executive editor, Arthur C. Deck; major awards: 1957 Pulitzer Prize; civic projects: statewide civic beautification awards, Sub for Santa program, Community Christmas Tree, Intermountain Organ Bank, Organ Donor program.

Population: 1972 est. 175,700 (city); 589,000 (metro area), 1st in state, 66th in nation; 52% of the state's population lives within 30 miles of city.
Area: Nestled in a vast valley (ele. 4,327 ft.) surrounded by Wasatch and Oquirrh Mountains.
Industry: Labor force of 276,100. Effective buying income $1.8 billion in 1972, per family income $10,890. Major steps taken to unlock vast mineral wealth of Great Salt Lake, estimated to exceed 5.5 billion tons and to accumulate at the rate of 2,000,000 tons annually. Estimated the lake contains $50 billion in recoverable minerals. 55% of the state's construction in Salt Lake County. Residential housing growth in the Metro Area averaging higher than the U.S. Total construction value reached record high of $243 billion in 1972. Major employers are Hill Air Force Base, 30 miles to the north, local defense industries and Kennecott Copper Corp. Metro area becoming major center for electronics, apparel manufacturing. Mining, smelting, refining, distribution, warehousing center of West.
Commerce: Trade center of Mountain West with retail sales totaling $1,030,221,000 in 1972.
Transportation: 6 air lines, customs office. Passenger, cargo traffic at Salt Lake International Airport more than tripled in last 10 years. Crossroads of mountain travel, geographical center of 11 Western states. Hub of central transcontinental highway system. Served by 3 railroads, all major western truck, bus lines.
Communications: 2 daily newspapers, 3 commercial 2 public television stations, 18 radio stations.
Medical facilities: 10 hospitals, including University of Utah Medical Center, major researcher in transplant surgery.
Cultural facilities: Utah Symphony Orchestra, ranked among 12 best in U.S.; Mormon Tabernacle Choir, Ballet West, Repertory Dance Theatre.
Other Attractions: Temple Square, home of 3,500,000-member Church of Jesus Christ of Latter-Day Saints; 14,000-seat Salt Palace Civic Auditorium. 700 acres in parks, recreation areas; 22 parks, 25 playgrounds, 8 golf courses, 57 tennis courts. Near Great Salt Lake (7 times more salty than ocean), Pioneer Village, Hogle Zoological Gardens, Kennecott Copper Corp.'s Bingham Mine, world's largest open-pit copper mine and world's largest man-made excavation.
Sports: Near 9 major ski resorts, including famous Alta and Snowbird. Utah Stars (ABA), Salt Lake Golden Eagles (Western Hockey League), Salt Lake Angels (AAA Baseball), Bonneville Salt Flats west of city.
History: Founded July 24, 1847, by Brigham Young and contingent of pioneers.
Education: The University of Utah, Westminster College. State has highest percentage of high school graduates in the nation, is country's per capita leader in college enrollment, nearly 20% ahead of the second-ranking state.
Other: 4 well-defined seasons, mean annual temperature is 50.9°F.

San Antonio, Texas

The World Almanac is sponsored in the San Antonio area by San Antonio Express and San Antonio News, P.O. Box 2171, San Antonio, Tex. 78297; telephone (512) 225-7411; morning Express founded Sept. 27, 1865; evening News founded Sept. 4, 1918; circulation daily, Express 81,662, News 66,427, Sunday Express/News 128,784; president, James H. Smith; publisher and editor, Charles O. Kilpatrick; Express Publishing Co. is a division of Harte-Hanks Newspapers, Inc.

Population: 752,942 city; 928,490 metro area. Total employed, 324,100.
Area: Bexar County, 1,247 sq. mi., 2½ hours from Gulf Coast and Mexican border.
Industry: 5 military bases include Kelly AFB, city's largest employer; fast-growing medical industry; diverse manufacturing, tourism, construction, trade and service industries.
Commerce: Center for 50-county retail trade area, truck crops, livestock production; retail sales (1972), $2.1 billion.
Federal facilities: Kelly AFB, hq. AF Security Service; Randolph AFB, hq. AF Air Training Command & AF Personnel Center, Brooks AFB, hq. AF Aerospace Medical Division; Lackland AFB with Wilford Hall USAF Medical Center; Fort Sam Houston, hq. Fifth Army & Army Health Services Command, Brooke Army Medical Center.
Medical and research facilities: University of Texas Medical, Dental, Nursing Schools; new Audie Murphy VA Hospital; Southwest Research Institute; Southwest Foundation of Research and Education.
Transportation: International Airport, 9 major airlines; 3 rail freight, 2 Amtrak lines.
Education facilities: New University of Texas at San Antonio opens 1975; Trinity & St. Mary's Universities; Our Lady of the Lake and Incarnate Word Colleges; 2 jr. colleges, San Antonio College & St. Philip's College; permanent extension of National University of Mexico.
Convention facilities: Convention Center with large arena, theater, exhibit, meeting space.
Cultural facilities: Symphony orchestra; Institute of Texan Cultures, Mexican Cultural Institute, Witte Museums, McNay Art Institute.
Other attractions: Historic Alamo, old Spanish missions of San Jose, Concepcion, Capistrano, Espada; HemisFair Plaza with 622-foot observation tower-restaurant; downtown River Walk; zoo; annual events: Fiesta San Antonio, Livestock Show & Rodeo, Folklife Festival; professional sports: San Antonio Spurs of American Basketball Association plus minor league football (Toros) and baseball (Brewers).

San Bernardino, Calif.

The World Almanac is sponsored in the San Bernardino area by the Sun-Telegram, 399 North D St., San Bernardino, Cal. 92401, telephone (714) 889-9666, Telegram founded 1873, Sun founded 1894, daily circulation Sun 65,516, Telegram 15,800, Sunday Sun-Telegram 84,359, member Gannett chain; Marvin W. Reimer president, James Geehan editor-publisher, G. David Ackley vice president—civic affairs, O. Paul Balosso vice president—operations, Ted Warmbold managing editor.

Population: 114,684 (city), 1,143,146 (2-county metro area), 43rd in state, 145th in nation; total employed 34,299.
Area: 47.22 sq. mi. at base of Cajon Pass, 58 miles east of Los Angeles on major interstate routes.
Industry: 165 business and industrial firms including Culligan, Inc., Edginton Oil Co., Fleetwood Enterprises, Hanford Foundry, Knudsen Dairy, Mode O'Day, Pepsi-Cola and Seven-Up bottling plants, Santa Fe Railway, TRW Systems, Wander Homes, Inc.
Commerce: trading center for 20,189-sq. mi. San Bernardino County, largest county in the nation. Retail sales (1971) $426,647,000; 8 banks with 24 branches and 11 savings and loans associations; 2 major shopping center complexes each have parking for 5,000 or more cars.
Transportation: Santa Fe, Southern Pacific and Union Pacific railroad lines, Amtrak; Greyhound and Continental bus lines, major interstate highway routes leading from Mexico to Canada

and West Coast to East Coast; municipal airport and nearby Ontario International Airport (more than 1,000,000 passengers in 1972).
Communications: 15 radio stations and VHF educational television station, access to 5 major channels Los Angeles area.
Medical facilities: 3 major hospitals with 995 licensed beds; major research and training center for heart surgery and hip and knee replacement surgery.
Federal facilities: Norton Air Force Base, annual payroll $110,000,000 to 12,475 employees.
Cultural facilities: symphony orchestra, Civic Light Opera, nearby Redlands Bowl (summer concerts), National Orange Show with year-round activities and orange festival every spring, Convention Center-Exhibit Hall.
Educational facilities: California State College, junior college, 3 major universities nearby.
History: founded 1852 by Mormons who purchased land from Spanish grant holders.

San Diego, California

The World Almanac is sponsored in San Diego by The San Diego Union and Evening Tribune (Copley Newspapers), P.O. Box 191, San Diego 92112; (714) 299-3131; Union founded 1869 (pioneer daily of Southwest). Circulation, Union (morning) 175,298, Tribune (evening) 124,712, Sunday Union 289,911; publisher James S. Copley, general manager Al De Bakcsy, director of editorial and news policy Victor Krulak, Union editor Gene Gregston, Tribune editor Fred Kinne.

Population: 763,100 (1973, city); 1,492,600 (county); 11th largest U.S. city (official state estimate), total 1972 civilian employment 490,000.
Area: (county) 4,255 sq. mi., fronts Pacific for 70 miles from San Clemente to Mexican border.
Industry: Tourism, manufacturing, the military, and agriculture; manufactured products earn $1.7 billion.a year; non-military payroll $2.3 billion, military $593,900,000. Tourist spending $381,000,000. Corporations with bases or divisions include Bendix, Burroughs, Cohu, Control Data, Cubic, Fotomat, General Dynamics, Gulf, Honeywell, International Harvester's Solar division, National Cash Register, Pacific Southwest Airlines, Rohr, Sea World, Teledyne Ryan, TraveLodge, Wickes. Aerospace, rapid transit design and manufacture. Oceanography, marine biology, nuclear energy, medicine important. Also shipbuilding, tuna fishing, clothing, ocean shipping. Among top 20 counties in farm products (avocados, cut flowers, eggs). Marine Corps Recruit Depot, Naval Training Center, North Island and Miramar Naval Air Stations, Naval Electronics Lab and Undersea Center, Marine Corps base at Camp Pendleton.
Transportation: Freeway system state's second largest. Urban transit service, at 25-cent fare, Mexican border to 35 miles north. Amtrak, 9 airlines, bus lines. Primary airport Lindbergh Field.
Communications: Some 30 TV and radio stations.
Medical facilities: Salk Institute for Biological Studies, Scripps Clinic & Research Foundation;

Naval Hospital; many public, private hospitals.
Educational and cultural facilities: San Diego State University; U.S. International University; University of San Diego; University of California, San Diego (3 colleges and Scripps Institution of Oceanography); Point Loma College. San Diego Symphony Orchestra; Old Globe Theatre (functioning reproduction of Shakespeare's Globe Theatre); San Diego Opera; ballet; Fine Arts Gallery and Timken Gallery; La Jolla Museum of Contemporary Art.
Other attractions: World famous Zoo and Wild Animal Park; Balboa Park, central 1,400 acres containing museums, Zoo, new Fleet Space Theatre (computerized planetarium), many other attractions; Mission Bay Park includes Sea World; "Old San Diego" State Historical Park; "Star of India" ship-museum; visits to neighboring Mexico (Tijuana); 70 miles of beaches.
Sports: San Diego Chargers, NFL, play in 50,000-seat San Diego Stadium; San Diego Gulls, Western Hockey League; racing at Del Mar and Caliente.
History: Discovered 1542 by Cabrillo, founded in 1769 by Father Serra.
Other information: Climate sunny; summer and winter resort; average temp. 68 in summer, 57 in winter, rainfall mainly December to March. Famous "place names" include La Jolla (part of city of San Diego), Mount Helix and Rancho Santa Fe (unincorporated). 70 golf courses, including Torrey Pines, Tennis, yachting. Large convention facilities. Off-shore "whale watching."

San Francisco, California

The World Almanac is sponsored in the San Francisco-Oakland area by the San Francisco Examiner, P.O. Box 3100, Rincon Annex, San Francisco, CA. 94103; telephone (415) 781-2424; founded June 12, 1865, purchased in 1880 by Sen. George Hearst, who turned it over in 1887 to his son William Randolph Hearst; circulation daily Examiner 183,344, Sunday Examiner & Chronicle 655,649; publisher, Charles Gould; editor, Randolph A. Hearst; associate editor, Edmund J. Dooley; executive editor, Thomas Eastham; managing editor, Rene Cazenave; major awards include Pulitzer Prize, Freedoms Foundation Awards; Examiner sponsors the Examiner Games, Golden Gloves, Bay to Breakers Race and the Distinguished Ten Awards.

Population: 685,000, 2nd in state, 13th in nation; total employed: 693,300.

Area: 44.6 sq. mi. on the northern tip of a peninsula.

Industry: Food and kindred products, printing, publishing and allied arts, and fabricated metal products are leading industries. San Francisco is the West's financial capital and the administrative center for many of the nation's leading corporations. The City is also the West Coast operations' headquarters for a majority of the Federal agencies. Service industries, most notably finance, insurance and real estate, play an important role in the City's economy. S.F. is the chief port of the Pacific Coast.

Commerce: Wholesale and retail center for the Bay Area. Wholesale and retail trade employment for 1972: 273,400; services: 233,100; manufacturing: 186,800. There are 20,478 retail establishments in San Francisco with taxable sales of $2.41 billion (1972). Banks number 40 with 157 branches and there are 25 savings and loans with 39 branches. There is $10.7 billion on deposit in S.F. banks.

Transportation: 19 major airlines serve the San Francisco Bay Area. In 1972, San Francisco International Airport processed 16,611,000 passengers and moved 029,163,994 lbs. of cargo and 222,603,423 lbs. of mail. Other transportation serving San Francisco—rail: Southern Pacific, Western Pacific, Union Pacific, Santa Fe; truck: 396 carriers. Port of San Francisco services available: passenger ships, general cargo, containerization and barge service. Commute service: San Francisco Municipal Railway (intra city); Ac-Transit and Bay Area Rapid Transit System (BART) to the East Bay cities; Greyhound Bus and Southern Pacific Railroad to Peninsula area; Golden Gate Bridge District Bus and Ferry service to Marin County; Highways: U.S. 50, 101. Interstates 80, 280, 480, 580, 680.

Communications: 2 major newspapers, 18 local radio stations, 7 TV channels received direct, 1 TV cable system.

Medical facilities: San Francisco has 20 general hospitals with over 7,300 total bed capacity and 5 specialty hospitals with over 281 total bed capacity. The City also has 1,865 physicians-surgeons, 704 dentists, 120 optometrists and 75 chiropractors. Century old University of California Medical Center, one of the largest medical complexes in the world, consists of 42 buildings and is a general teaching and research institute. UC is the largest kidney transplant center in the United States, and its facilities include a neuro-psychiatric clinic, metabolic, immunization and pathology units, psychological testing and counseling and cancer, hormone and cardio-vascular research. The school has an enrollment of 600 medical students.

Cultural facilities: San Francisco Opera, Spring Opera, Western Opera Theater, symphony, ballet, Civic Light Opera, Japanese Cultural Center, Chinese Cultural Center, International Film Festival, 3 museums, 29 libraries, and 540 churches.

Educational facilities: 102 public elementary schools with a total enrollment of 39,916 students and 19 junior high and 12 high schools with a combined enrollment of 36,810 students. There are 5 colleges or universities: University of California, San Francisco; California State University, University of San Francisco, City College of San Francisco and Lone Mountain College.

Convention facilities: San Francisco has 103 hotels and motels with over 19,737 rooms. All are suitable for business visitors and conventions.

Sports attractions: Candlestick Park is the home of the San Francisco Giants, National Baseball League, and the San Francisco 49ers, National Football League. The Golden State Warriors of the National Basketball Assoc. is another professional team.

Other attractions: San Francisco is famous for its cable cars, Fisherman's Wharf and Chinatown, its sour dough frenchbread and exceptional restaurants. It is also known for such structures as the Ferry Building, Coit Tower, the Palace of Fine Arts and Grace Cathedral and for the historic Fairmont, Mark Hopkins and Sheraton-Palace Hotels. The San Francisco Zoo and the 1,013-acre Golden Gate Park containing the California Academy of Sciences, De Young Museum, the Japanese Tea Garden, lakes, deer and buffalo are also attractions. San Francisco's average maximum temperature ranges between 55 and 68 degrees. It rains on an average of 20 in. per year.

History: San Francisco Bay was discovered in 1769 by a Spanish scouting expedition headed by Sgt. Jose Ortega. The Presidio and Mission Dolores, both within present city limits, were founded in 1776 by Col. Juan Bautista de Anza. The pueblo of Yerba Buena was established on the site in 1834, and was renamed San Francisco on January 3, 1847. Its population was 800. San Francisco is located at the entrance to one of the world's finest natural harbors. It is built on 7 hills and has a breathtaking Bay view.

San Jose, California

The World Almanac is sponsored in the San Jose area by the Mercury and News, 750 Ridder Pk. Dr., San Jose, Calif. 95190; (408) 289-5000; Mercury founded June 20, 1851; News July 23, 1883; combined daily circulation, 214,871; Sunday Mercury-News, 216,000; publisher, Joseph B. Ridder; general manager, A. F. Peterson; business manager, P.A. Ridder; executive editor, Paul Conroy; editor emeritus, K. S. Conn; ad director L. E. Heindl; circ. director, D. J. Kelly.

Population: 495,000 (city), 1,140,000 (Santa Clara County), one of nation's 10 fastest growing metropolitan areas. Total employed: 450,000.

Area: A broad alluvial 832,256 acre valley at the south end of San Francisco Bay.

Industry: Broad based. Second in state for total manufacturing wages; third in manufacturing workers. Among over 250 firms are General Motors, Ford Motor Co., Lockheed Missile and Space; IBM; Hewlett-Packard; FMC Corp.; numerous electronic component firms; food processing, financial, agricultural and building trades companies. Manufacturing payroll: $1.3 billion. City accounts for 23% of all S.F. bay area new construction.

Commerce: Once called "fruit bowl of the world"; agriculture now dominated by floral industry; varied industry plus major urban renewal projects are transforming San Jose into a regional financial center. Fifteen local, national and international banks maintain 103 branches; 15 savings and loan companies with 52 branches. Retail sales: $2.5 billion in 1972.

Transportation: Municipal Airport served by 12 airlines. Interconnected with all interstate north/south, east/west highway systems; Southern Pacific and Western Pacific railroads; major truck and bus terminal.

Cultural facilities: San Jose Symphony, First State Capital Museum, Rosicrucian Planetarium & Science Museum, Lick Observatory, Egyptian Museum; Triton Museum of Art, Fujiyama Gardens, New Almaden Museum.

Sports: San Jose Bees, farm club for KC Royals;

Oakland A's and S.F. Giants, Warriors basketball; Seal's hockey nearby; 8 reservoirs with boat ramps, 2 with camping; outlet to S.F. Bay for ocean sports; Henry W. Coe State Park, camp sites in redwoods.

History: Santa Clara County is one of the original 27 California counties; named for mission dedicated to St. Clare of Assisi, first Franciscan nun. Mission and pueblo founded in 1777.

San Juan, Puerto Rico

The World Almanac is sponsored in Puerto Rico by The San Juan Star, G.P.O. Box 4187, San Juan, Puerto Rico 00936; telephone (809) 782-4200; founded Nov. 2, 1959; circulation 45,000 daily, 47,000 Sunday; president and general manager John A. Zerbe, Jr.; vice president and editor Andrew T. Viglucci; major awards include 1961 Pulitzer Prize for editorial writing; APME citations 1960, 1965; staff awards include 1970 IAPA Mergenthaler Award, 1972 Overseas Press Club Award; National Spelling Bee sponsor.

Population: 463,244 (city), 851,247 (metro area) 1st in commonwealth.

Area: 47 sq. mi. in Caribbean.

Industry: San Juan is the seat of Puerto Rico's tourism industry with more than 24 luxury hotels and several dozen high rise condominiums. City is also the commercial and shipping hub of the island, having pioneered in containerized shipping with 4 major lines operating and some 450 vessels docking in San Juan harbor monthly. Major industries are apparel and textiles, surpassed only by the growing petrochemical industry. Apparel account for 18% of exports to the U.S., with 516 plants and 43,000 workers. Footwear industry is currently in decline but still provides some 10,000 jobs in 70 plants. San Juan is center of the island's rum industry with the Bacardi distillery on San Juan Bay, the largest in the world. Electronics industry now ranks as 5th in terms of income, providing 12,500 jobs in 119 plants. Pharmaceuticals operate out of 84 plants with 4,000 workers.

Transportation: San Juan International Airport handles more than 450,000 passengers monthly with 6 major U.S. airlines and 11 foreign lines. Smaller airports handle light aircraft in San Juan, Ponce, Arecibo and Mayaguez, with Ramey Air Force Base in Aguadilla also being used commercially.

Education: seat of the Rio Piedras campus of the

University of Puerto Rico, a commonwealth institution, with 26,000 enrollment. Inter American University, World University, Sacred Heart University, UPR Medical Sciences Campus and Puerto Rico Junior College in San Juan with an additional 8-10,000 students.

Cultural facilities: Casals Festival, honoring Spanish cellist composer Pablo Casals, is held annually at the University of Puerto Rico Theater. San Juan is the seat of the Commonwealth government with the Governor's Mansion and the Capitol located here.

New construction: urban renewal of 2 distinct types—Old City historic restoration carried on by the Institute of Puerto Rican Culture, and the federally funded Model Cities program which has already spent $20,000,000 in improvements in 7 slum neighborhoods, with another $5,000,000 allotted for fiscal 1974, and a total $60,000,000 during 5 years.

Sports: Hiram Bithorn Stadium and the new Roberto Clemente Stadium are located in the city. A Clemente Sports City is now being planned to honor the late Pittsburgh Pirate star.

History: discovered by Christopher Columbus in 1493, colonized by Juan Ponce de Leon; since 1952, Puerto Rico has been a self-governing Commonwealth in association with the United States.

Santa Ana, California

See Orange County, California

Saskatoon, Saskatchewan, Canada

The World Almanac is sponsored in northern Saskatchewan by the Saskatoon Star-Phoenix, 204 Fifth Ave. North, Saskatoon, Sask., S7K 2P1; telephone (306) 652-9200; 2 papers, the Daily Star and the Phoenix, founded in 1906 and 1902 respectively, were merged in 1928 into the Star-Phoenix; circulation daily, 50,491; publisher Michael C. Sifton, executive vice president James K. Struthers.

Population: 129,000, 2d in prov.; labor force, 52,465.

Area: 38.586 sq. mi. land, 1,501 sq. mi. water, astride South Sask. River in transitional area between north forest and south wheat-plains.

Communications: 2 TV and 5 radio stations; one daily, one weekly; home of Western Producer, largest farm paper circulation in western Canada.

Transportation: 2 major rail lines; 2 airlines; 2 bus lines; on Yellowhead highway route, easiest access through Rockies to West Coast; because of terminus as transport and distribution center nicknamed the "Hub City".

Industry and Commerce: city retail sales (1971), $237,466,750; net effective buying income per capita, $2,909; per household, $9,018; 3 enclosed

malls, including one $20,000,000 mall; distribution center for 400,000 in 70,000-sq. mi. trading area. World's largest, richest potash reserves in Sask.; 6 of 10 Sask. mines within 60 miles of city. Meat packing and grain milling are major industries for agricultural-based trading area.

Cultural facilities: $7,000,000 auditorium with convention facilities; art gallery and civic conservatory; Western Development Museum, pioneer village, antique farm equipment, under 3-acre roof; $1,500,000 library, 4 branches.

Educational facilities: university (10,300 students) famed for agriculture, arctic space, physics, medicine; hospital associated; veterinary school for all western Canada. University is largest employer in city (3,600). Large technical school; school for deaf; animal farm.

Recreational facilities: 1,426 acres of parks; man-made ski mountain, 25 miles southwest; junior

football, Hilltops, several times Canada champs; junior Blades, hockey.

History: founded 1883 as Temperance colony; Inc. 1906. Battle sites of 1885 Riel Rebellion nearby.

Savannah, Georgia

The World Almanac is sponsored in the Savannah area by the Savannah News-Press, 111 W. Bay St., Savannah, Ga. 31401, telephone (912) 236-9511, publisher of the Savannah Morning News and Savannah Evening Press. Combined daily circulation 78,739; Sunday 70,633. Donald E. Harwood, general manager; Wallace M. Davis Jr., executive editor.

Population: 118,349 (city), 354,398 (metro area), 2nd in state.

Area: 37 sq. mi. on Savannah River 18 miles from Atlantic Ocean.

Industry: World's largest pulpwood-to-paper container plant is owned by Union Camp Corp. Savannah Sugar Refining Corp. is nation's 3rd largest seller. Jet aircraft manufacture (Grumman Aerospace Corp.), tea packaging (Tetley), fertilizer materials, ship repair, titanium dioxide production (American Cyanamid Co.).

Commerce: Hub of "Coastal Empire," economic center of 8 Georgia and 3 South Carolina counties; Southeast's leading foreign trade port; 75 steamship lines, 33 deep water terminals. Retail sales in 1972: $352,397,000. Five commercial banks, 3 savings banks, 2 savings and loan associations. Bank resources 1972: $5.368 billion.

Transportation: 3 rail freight lines; Amtrak; Greyhound, Trailways bus lines; 50 truck lines; Delta, National Air Lines.

Communications: 3 TV and 12 radio stations.

Medical facilities: 5 hospitals.

Cultural facilities: Telfair Academy of Arts and Sciences, Savannah Symphony Orchestra, Little Theatre, Dance Theatre of Savannah, the Savannah Ballet Guild, maritime museum, military museum, science museum, $10,400,000 Civic Center, Savannah State College, Armstrong State College.

Sports: Savannah Braves, Southern League baseball.

History: Founded 1733 by Gen. James Edward Oglethorpe, first planned city in the U.S. Much of old city is Registered National Historic Landmark, the largest area to be so designated.

Schenectady, New York

Population: 77,958; total employed, 38,000.

Area: 11.3 sq. mi., 13 miles northwest of Albany.

Industry: General Electric, employing about 27,000, is largest employer. Other firms manufacture industrial chemicals, pollution control and measuring devices, and military vehicles.

Commerce: There are 2,100 retail establishments with net sales of over $200,000,000; 8 banks, with to-

tal deposits over $450,000,000.

Cultural facilities: Union College, 66 homes and buildings built between 1700-1850; the Schenectady Museum and County Historical Society.

Other attractions: 5 hospitals, 87-acre Industrial Park; 65 schools; 175 churches; 25 parks, 5 golf courses, 30 tennis courts, 18 playgrounds; Schenectady Community College.

Seattle, Washington

The World Almanac is sponsored in the Seattle area by The Seattle Times, Fairview Ave. N. & John St., P.O. Box 70, Seattle, Wash. 98111; telephone (206) MA 2-0300; founded 1896 by Alden J. Blethen; circulation 234,971 daily, 294,211 Sunday; publisher, John A. Blethen; president, W. J. Pennington; vice president and general manager, Harold G. Fuhrman.

Population: 530,831 (city), 1,421,869 (metro area), 1st in state, 17th in nation, total employed (metro area) 570,000.

Area: 91.6 square miles (City of Seattle) between Lake Washington and Puget Sound.

Industry: Aerospace—The Boeing Co., with its headquarters in Seattle, employs about 50,000 persons, and is the largest single producer of commercial jet passenger planes in the world, having assembled more than half of the world's commercial jets. The Port of Seattle, a $126-million public agency, operates more than 9 mi. of port facilities. Seattle is also noted as a regional governmental and business headquarters center, particularly for retail trade and insurance. The wood products industry and ship building are important. Tourism is growing.

Commerce: Wholesale distribution and retail trading center for western Washington and Alaska, with important international connections. Department store sales (1972) $411,000,000; total retail sales (metro area), $2.8 billion. Area has 23 commercial banks, which have 207 branch offices (metro area). Deposits 1972: $2.17 billion (Seattle city).

Transportation: 3 transcontinental railroads; Am-

trak rail passenger service, Seattle-Chicago, Seattle-Vancouver, B.C., and Seattle-San Diego; Greyhound and Continental Trailways bus lines; 12 scheduled airlines serve Seattle-Tacoma International Airport; 8 commuter air lines; 4,780,000 passengers (1972). Interstate Highways 5 and 90 intersect in Seattle; 136 truck lines. Ferry system crosses Puget Sound.

Communications: 2 daily newspapers in Seattle, 3 in metro area; 6 television stations; 19 AM, 12 FM and 5 noncommercial FM radio stations.

Medical facilities: 34 hospitals including University of Washington Health Sciences Center; Northwest Kidney Center.

Cultural facilities: Seattle Symphony Orchestra; Seattle Opera Association; Seattle Art Museum; 10 other museums; 76 art galleries. University of Washington, Seattle University, Seattle Pacific College; 7 community colleges.

Other attractions: $50,000,000 Seattle Center, site of 1962 Seattle World's Fair, with 3,100-seat Opera House, 14,000-seat Coliseum, 5,200-seat Arena, Playhouse for Seattle Repertory Theater, Space Needle (605 feet), Pacific Science Center.

Sports: Seattle Super Sonics, National Basketball Association; Rainiers, Northwest League (baseball), Totems, Western Hockey League; $40,000,000 King County domed stadium seating 65,000 ready by September, 1974, in Seattle.
History: Seattle, settled in 1851, is named for an In-

dian chief who befriended the settlers. Downtown Seattle burned in 1889 but was rebuilt better than ever. The Gold Rush to Alaska and the Klondike in 1897-98 gave Seattle an economic impetus it never lost on the way to becoming the Pacific Northwest's principal city.

Shreveport, Louisiana

The World Almanac is sponsored in the Shreveport area by the Shreveport Journal (evening, except Sunday), 222 Lake St., Shreveport, La., 71120; telephone (318) 424-0373; founded 1895 as The Judge, given present name in 1897; circulation, 50,000; president Douglas F. Attaway, vice president D. Wesley Attaway, managing editor Jack F. Clark.

Population: 189,200; 2nd in state; total employed approximately 100,455.
Area: 80.286 sq.mi., on Red River in Caddo Parish, northwest Louisiana.
Industry: oil, gas, lumber, agriculture, manufacture of phone parts, steel products, glassware, chain saws, batterys. Barksdale Air Force Base, across river in Bossier Parish, contributes millions of dollars annually to area's economy.
Commerce: wholesale and retail center for Ark-La-Tex area. Retail sales (1972) more than $500,000,000; bank deposits of $909,920,551. City has 7 banks, 2 savings and loan companies, more than 100 insurance company offices.
Transportation: 6 railroads, 4 airlines, 1 busline, 14 motor-freight lines. City served by Interstate Hwy. 20; barge traffic on Red River expected by

the 1980's.
Communications: 3 TV and 8 radio stations.
Cultural facilities: State Exhibit Museum and Planetarium, Norton Art Gallery, Barnwell Art and Garden Center, symphony concerts, 295 churches, 5 colleges, 65 public and 35 private schools.

Other attractions: Shreve Town, Inc., multi-million-dollar restoration project on downtown riverfront; State Fair; Holiday-In-Dixie festival; 12 hospitals, including VA.

History: Founded 1836 as Shreve Town on bluff above Red River; named for riverboat Capt. Henry Miller Shreve, who cleared the Great Raft — driftwood clogging river for 214 miles; Louisiana capitol, 1863-1865.

Sioux Falls, South Dakota

The World Almanac is sponsored in the Sioux Falls area by the Sioux Falls Argus-Leader, 200 S. Minnesota Ave., 57102, tel. (605) 336-1130; a Speidel newspaper; founded 1885; circulation: 51,350 daily, 56,724 Sunday; publisher William H. Leopard, executive editor Anson Yeager.

Population: 72,444 (city), 95,209 (metro area) according to 1970 census; largest in state.
Area: 26 square miles in southeastern South Dakota at junction of interstates 29 and 90.
Federal facilities: The Earth Resources Observation Systems Data Center of the U.S. Department of Interior is located near Sioux Falls.
Industry and commerce: Located in the nation's breadbasket, Sioux Falls Stockyards is the 5th largest public market in the U.S. John Morrell & Co. is the largest of 170 manufacturers. There are 17 banks with clearings in excess of $1.3 billion and 3 savings and loan associations. Wholesale and retail center for South Dakota, parts of Minnesota and Iowa, Sioux Falls has yearly retail sales over $300,000,000, wholesale over $500,000,000.

Transportation: Served by 4 major rail lines, 4 bus lines, 5 major highways. Joe Foss Field with new modern terminal is within 2 miles of business district, has 3 major airlines offering 34 daily flights.
Medical facilities: 4 hospitals including Royal C. Johnson Veterans Hospital and a Crippled Children's Hospital and School.
Communications: 2 TV and 8 radio stations.
Culture & Education: New public library, Civic Fine Arts Center, Sioux Falls Symphony, Community Playhouse. Augustana College and Sioux Falls College, North American Baptist Seminary, the South Dakota School For the Deaf, a vocational school, business college, 2 nurses training schools and 3 high schools.

Springfield, Illinois

The World Almanac is sponsored in the Springfield area by the Illinois State Journal-Register, 313 S. 6th St., Springfield, Ill. 62701; (217) 544-5711; J. P. Clarke, publisher and Journal editor. Journal (morning), circ. 56,722, Dan. J. Cronin, managing editor; Register (evening), circ. 26,033, Edward H. Armstrong, editor, Patrick Coburn, managing editor.

Population: 91,753 (city), 161,335 (metro area), 4th in state; total employed 41,117.
Area: 38.5 sq. mi., located on Sangamon River in center of state.
Commerce: State capital with state and federal offices; 9 banks, 6 savings and loan associations; 14 insurance company home offices; 104 state and national organizations. Annual retail sales of $350,000,000.
Transportation: 5 railroads; 39 truck carriers; 1 airport; nearby barge facilities; interstate highways.

Communications: One TV and 6 radio stations.
Medical facilities: 2 hospitals, 1,281 beds, 509 doctors; 15 clinics; 11 nursing homes.
Cultural facilities: Municipal band, opera, symphony, chorus; Theatre Guild; State Capitol, Museum; Lincoln Historical Sites; New Salem Park.
Education: Sangamon State University; Lincoln Land College; Springfield College; Southern Ill. School of Medicine; Concordia Theological Seminary.
Recreation: 23 parks; swimming, boating, skiing

on Lake Springfield; public golf, tennis; 27 civic clubs; 36 social service organizations.
Special events: Illinois State Fair; Old Capitol Art Fair; NCAA College Division World Series; International Carillon Festival.

History: Settled 1818-1819. Became county seat 1823. Incorporated as a town 1832, chartered as a city in 1840. Selected as state capital 1837 through efforts of Abraham Lincoln and 8 other members of the Illinois Legislature.

Springfield, Massachusetts

The World Almanac is sponsored in the Springfield area by The Springfield Union, Springfield Sunday Republican, and Springfield Daily News, 1860 Main St., Springfield, Mass. 01101; tel: 413-787-2411; Union founded in 1864; Republican 1824; Daily News 1880; circulation, Union, 84,344; Republican, 133,669; Daily News, 92,506; publisher Sidney R. Cook; general manager Donald R. Newhouse; Union-Republican editor Joseph W. Mooney; Daily News, Richard Garvey.

Population: city-169,027; metro-529,922; 2nd in state (metro area), 4th in New England; total employed in city, 60,204.
Area: 33.1 sq. mi. in south central Massachusetts.
Industry and commerce: 236 manufacturing firms, a healthy retail and wholesale climate; Eastfield Mall, largest enclosed shopping plaza in western Mass., houses 75 retail outlets. Retail area population, 535,700; annual sales, $1.04 billion; 6 commercial banks, 5 savings institutions, 1 cooperative bank, 2 savings and loan associations, 2 major insurance companies; total bank resources $1.1 billion; Baystate West, a privately financed $50,000,000 combined shopping mall, office building and hotel; new $12,000,000 home of the sponsoring Springfield Newspapers; new federal building and a $9,300,000 civic center complete with convention facilities.
Transportation: All major bus lines, Amtrak, 2 rail lines—Penn central and Boston and Maine, Bradley International Airport (18 miles away), Mass. Turnpike and Interstate 91 give access to

New York, Boston and New England points.
Communications: 3 TV and 9 radio stations.
Medical facilities: 8 major hospital complexes.
Cultural facilities: American International College, Springfield College and Western New England College; Springfield Symphony Orchestra; Basketball Hall of Fame; many museums, 143 churches, and 7 synagogues. University of Massachusetts at Amherst, Smith College, Mt. Holyoke, Williams and Hampshire Colleges located within 25 miles. Famed Tanglewood festival in the Berkshires and winter ski slopes nearby.
Other attractions: 155 parks; 2,500 modern hotel rooms; Home of Springfield Kings hockey team.
History: Founded in 1636 by William Pynchon; known as the "City of Homes"; in 1795 the 1st U.S. musket was developed at the city's armory; in 1903, Springfield rifle was developed and produced here as was the Garand rifle. Springfield's armament contributions are commemorated in the Springfield Armory Museum.

Syracuse, New York

The World Almanac is sponsored in the Syracuse area by the Herald-Journal, Clinton Square, Syracuse, N.Y. 13201; telephone (315) 473-7700; founded Jan. 15, 1877 by Arthur Jenkins; circulation 125,416 daily, 241,404 Sunday Herald-American Post-Standard; publisher, Stephen Rogers; editor, William D. Cotter; sponsors college scholarship fund for police, sponsors teacher in Newspaper in Classroom course, awards medals to police and fire heroes.

Population: 197,297 (city), 636,507 (metro area), 5th in state, 66th in nation; total employed 263,000.
Area: 25.82 sq. mi. near center of state. Interstate Routes 90 and 81 intersect at Syracuse.
Industry: Major products of some 500 manufacturing plants are soda ash and by-products, air conditioning, candles, china and pottery, farm implements, electrical equipment, shoes, auto accessories, steel, pharmaceuticals. Major employers are General Electric, Carrier Corp., Crucible Steel Co., Crouse-Hinds Co. and Allied Chemical Corp.
Commerce: Retail center for Central New York; retail sales for 1972 estimated at $1.2 billion with average household spendable income for 1972 estimated at $8,600.
Transportation: Two major rail freight lines, Amtrak, Greyhound Bus Lines, 140 truck lines; Syracuse Hancock International Airport serves 3 major airlines, 1,401,107 passengers in 1972. Barge Canal system offers water transportation.
Communications: 4 TV, 14 radio stations.

New construction: Federal office building and combined county office-cultural center both were started in early 1973.
Medical facilities: 4 major hospital complexes including Upstate Medical Center of State University of New York and Veterans Administration installation.
Cultural facilities: Syracuse University, Le Moyne College, State University College of Environmental Science and Forestry, Maria Regina College, Onondaga Community College; Everson Museum of Art; Syracuse Symphony.
Sports: Syracuse University football at Archbold Stadium, Syracuse Chiefs of International League (baseball) at MacArthur Stadium.
Other Attractions: State Fairgrounds, War Memorial, 17th Century French fort, Salt Museum, Canal Museum, Burnet Park Zoo.
History: First explored 1615 by French. Salt deposits led to area development and even today Syracuse is known as "Salt City." A "cross-roads" since Indian days. Became city in 1847.

Tallahassee, Florida

The World Almanac is sponsored in the northern Florida-south Georgia panhandle area by the Tallahassee Democrat, 277 N. Magnolia Drive, Tallahassee, Florida 32302; telephone (904) 877-6181; founded 1905. Circulation: 39,666 evening and 41,883 Sunday; member Knight Newspapers, Inc. James L. Knight, president; Erwin R. Potts, vice-president and general manager; Malcolm B. Johnson, vice-president and editor; William M. Phillips, managing editor.

Population: 72,586 (city) 103,047 (metro-area). Total employment: 53,600.
Area: 26.14 sq. mi. located between the Gulf of Mexico and the Georgia state line.
Economic base: Tallahassee is Florida's capital and 44% of the economic base is state government. Small manufacturers, wholesalers, professional businesses and retailers comprise remaining economic base.
Commerce: Wholesale and retail center serving 17 counties. Two large regional shopping malls and 7 shopping centers containing 186 retail stores. Total retail sales (1972) of $244,682,000, 10th highest in state. The per household retail sales of $7,348 is highest in the state. Bank resources: $249,752,058. There are 8 commercial banks and 3 savings & loan.
Transportation: 3 major airlines, 2 commuter flight services, 1 railroad and 5 motor carriers.
Communications: 8 radio and 9 TV stations.
Medical facilities: One major hospital, a retardation hospital and 1 university hospital.
Recreational facilities: 5 recreation centers, 10 playgrounds, 45 ball fields, 21 tennis courts, salt water fishing in Gulf of Mexico, fresh water fishing in Lake Jackson, hunting for dove, quail, duck, geese, deer, bear, 4 golf courses and site of PGA Tallahassee Open Invitational.
Other attractions: College athletic events at Florida State University and Florida A&M. Tourists attractions include; 1845 historical capitol and many historical sites; Junior Museum, Wakulla Springs, Maclay Gardens State Park, Falling Waters State Park near Chipley and Ft. Gadsden near Telogia.
History: Established as state capital in 1823 and named Tallahassee, a Creek Indian term meaning 'old town'. Early settlers led by John McGiver established area which prospered through the years into large plantations and antebellum mansions, many of which still stand.
City government: Commission-City Manager with 5 elected city commissioners.
Additional information: Contact Tallahassee Area Chamber of Commerce, P.O. Box 1639, (904) 224-8116, Tallahassee, Florida 32302.

Tampa, Florida

The World Almanac is sponsored in the Tampa Bay area by The Tampa Tribune and The Tampa Times, 507 E. Kennedy Blvd., Tampa, Fla., 33602; telephone (813) 224-7711; Times founded 1893, Tribune 1895; combined circulation 189,543; Alan S. Donnahoe, president; J. C. Council, chairman of editorial board; R. F. Pittman, Jr., vice president and general manager; J. Stewart Bryan, III, exec. vice president; Tribune managing editor, Robert Hudson; Times managing editor, Doyle Harvill.

Population: 277,767 (city), 490,265 (county); 3rd in state, 50th in nation; total employed 103,742.
Area: 84.45 sq. mi., almost exactly halfway between the northern edge of Florida and its southern tip.
Industry: Tampa's port ranks 8th in the nation; principal export cargo, phosphate. The Ybor City section of Tampa is well-known for its cigar manufacturing, and has a total of 170 cigar factories.
Commerce: Retail sales (1972) $1.144 billion. Bank resources $1.482 billion. There are 15 banks and 12 savings and loan associations. First Financial Towers, the tallest building in Tampa, stands 458 feet and 36 stories high.
Transportation: 22 freight lines, Amtrak, 5 bus lines, city-owned bus system, and 48 truck lines; junction of Interstate 75 and Interstate 4. The new Tampa International Airport is served by 10 major airlines, with domestic and foreign service.
Communications: 5 TV and 15 radio stations.
New construction: First Financial Tower of Tampa; Busch Gardens expansion; General Telephone expansion; University Community Hospital expansion; University Square; Tampa Cultural Center; University of South Fla. Graduate Research Library and College of Medicine; Hillsborough Community College.
Medical facilities: 6 major hospital complexes; W. T. Edwards Tuberculosis Hospital.
Federal facilities: MacDill Air Force Base, U.S. Federal Building.
Cultural facilities: Fla. Gulf Coast Symphony Orchestra; 2 museums; University of South Fla., University of Tampa, Florida College, and Hillsborough Community College; Curtis Hixon Convention Center; a $2,400,000 library; Tampa Community Theatre.
Other attractions: Lowry Park Zoo; Busch Gardens zoo & gardens; Treasureland; sightseeing cruises aboard the Tom Sawyer; Ybor City — Tampa's Latin Quarter; 26 parks, 11 picnic areas; annual Gasparilla Pirate Invasion and Parade.
Sports: Tampa Tarpons, Cincinnati Reds farm team; Cincinnati Reds spring training at Al Lopez Field; Tampa Dog Track; Tampa Jai-Alai Fronton; 50,000 seat Tampa Stadium.
History: In 1824, Fort Brooke was established on the site of the present-day Tampa. Incorporated as a town in 1885.
Further information: Greater Tampa Chamber of Commerce, 801 E. Kennedy Blvd., Tampa, Florida, 33602.

Toledo, Ohio

The World Almanac is sponsored in the Toledo area by The Toledo Blade, 541 Superior St., Toledo, Ohio 43660; telephone (419) 259-6000; founded 1835; circulation, 174,612 daily, 204,177 Sunday; publishers Paul Block, Jr. and William Block; associate publisher, John D. Willey; general manager, Wayne G. Current; executive editor, Joseph O'Conor; managing editor, William Rosenberg. Winner of numerous awards including Silver Gavel, American Bar Assn.

Population: 387,568 (city), 774,000 (metro area), 5th in state, 45th in nation; total employed, 294,029.
Area: 85.3 sq. mi. at juncture of Maumee River and Lake Erie, in northwestern Ohio.
Industry: Glass — Glass capital of world, boasts headquarters for 3 largest glass companies: Owens-Illinois, Owens Corning & Libbey-Owens-Ford. Automotive parts — largest producer in nation. Home of American Motors Jeep, Toledo Scale and Haughton Elevator. Largest petroleum

refining center between Chicago and the East Coast, and is ranked first in Ohio in economic diversification.

Commerce: Growing port on Great Lakes ranking 2nd in international tonnage and 3rd in total tonnage. Toledo Port has only inland foreign trade zone in the nation and ranks 11th among all ports. Second largest on Lakes for the movement of grain, largest for movement of coal.. Annual overseas cargo normally runs to 500,000 tons.

Transportation: 9 railroads, 4 major airlines, 120 motor freight lines, 2 interstate bus lines. Thirteen major highways converge at Toledo, permitting the rapid flow of goods to almost 60% of the nation's consumers.

Communications: 3 television, 15 radio stations and 1 cablevision company.

Medical facilities: 12 major hospital complexes including the Medical College of Ohio Hospital.

Cultural facilities: Toledo Museum of Art, featuring the largest display of antique glass in the world. Museum also has a Peristyle used for the performing arts; the Toledo Symphony, the Toledo Opera Society.

Other attractions: Municipal Zoo ranks among top 10 in the nation; a modern 2,500 seat Masonic Auditorium with a Great Hall annex.

Sports: Toledo Mud Hens, farm club of the Detroit Tigers, headquarter at the Lucas County Recreation Center, a unique complex offering a wide variety of sports activities.

History: Founded in 1835; took its name from sister city, Toledo, Spain.

Toronto, Ontario, Canada

The World Almanac is sponsored in the Metropolitan Toronto area by The Toronto Star, One Yonge St., Toronto, Ontario, M5E 1E6. Tel: (416) 367-2000. Established 1892: Joseph E. Atkinson, publisher, 1899-1948. Circulation daily, 526,000; Saturday, 770,000. President and publisher, Beland H. Honderich; senior vice-president, Burnett M. Thall, editor-in-chief, Martin Goodman. Canada's largest newspaper in circulation, display and classified advertising linage; winner of 27 national newspaper awards and sponsors of the Santa Claus Fund and Fresh Air Fund.

Population: 712,786 (city), 2,609,638 (metro area); 2nd largest city in Canada, 10th in North America; total labor force: 800,000.

Area: 241 sq. mi., on northwest shore of Lake Ontario.

Industry: Canada's leading commercial and industrial centre; 5,800 industrial establishments. Value of 1971 factory shipments: $10.5 billion. Principal industries: slaughtering and meat packing, clothing, printing and publishing, machinery, electrical goods, furniture, food products, rubber goods, sheet metal products.

Commerce: Estimated retail sales for 1972: $4.8 billion. Headquarters for Eaton's and Simpson's, Canada's largest department store and mail order firms. Head offices of 10 trust companies and 4 of 10 federally chartered banks. Value of cheques cashed (1972): $446.4 billion. Toronto Stock Exchange, 4th largest in North America, traded shares worth $6.2 billion in 1972. Per capita disposable income: $3,910.

Transportation: 10 railway lines in and out of Toronto carry 250 freight and passenger trains daily and 6,500 trucks use 12 major highways to and from cities in every province. Toronto Transit Commission carries 346,000,000 passengers annually on 626 miles of routes, including 24 miles of subways. In 1972, 1,072 ships unloaded 3,800,000 tons of cargo at this major Great Lakes port. Thirteen internationally scheduled airlines handle close to 8,000,000 passengers annually at Toronto International Airport.

Communications: 5 TV stations including educational and French-language channels; 8 AM and 6 FM radio stations; 3 daily newspapers; 38 foreign-language papers.

New construction: Value of building permits issued in 1972: $1.2 billion. Work begun on Metro Centre, a $1-billion 190-acre commercial-residential project which will employ 50,000 office workers and provide 20,000 housing units.

Medical facilities: 27 active-treatment hospitals including world-famous Hospital for Sick Children. Special treatment centres: Clarke Institute for Psychiatry, Addiction Research Centre, Ontario Crippled Children's Centre.

Cultural facilities: Year-round entertainment centre; 20 local groups offer experimental, repertory and revue theatre. National Ballet of Canada and Canadian Opera Company perform in 3,200-seat O'Keefe Centre; Toronto Symphony Orchestra and Mendelssohn Choir at Massey Hall; original and touring productions at Royal Alexandra Theatre. 63 public libraries; Art Gallery of Ontario; Royal Ontario Museum.

Educational facilities: 2 universities: York and University of Toronto, Canada's largest (1972-73 enrollment on 3 campuses: 40,570). Ryerson Polytechnical Institute, 4 colleges of applied arts and technology, 2 teachers' colleges, Royal Conservatory of Music, Ontario College of Art, Osgoode Hall Law School.

Recreational facilities: Canadian National Exhibition, world's biggest annual fair; Ontario Place, 100 acres of offshore islands with restaurants, marina, exhibits and 1,000-seat Cinesphere for film showings. Toronto Islands park has 560 acres of swimming beaches, play and picnic grounds, wildlife areas and 3 yacht clubs.

Sports attractions: 8 public golf courses; thoroughbred and harness racing; track and field, hockey in 16,435-seat Maple Leaf Gardens, home of Toronto's National Hockey League team. Toronto Argonauts play Canadian Football League games at Exhibition Park Stadium.

Convention facilities; Canada's top convention centre; 244,625 visitors attended 350 conventions in 1972 and spent $38,000,000; 3 hotels opened in 1972 brought total rooms to 16,000.

Other attractions: Ontario Science Centre, a complex of exhibits designed for participation and involvement; Black Creek Pioneer Village, living displays of early life in Upper Canada; McMichael Conservation Collection of works by Canada's famed Group of Seven painters; Metropolitan Toronto Zoo, scheduled to open in 1974, will have 5,000 species roaming on 700 acres.

History: Town of York founded 1793 on site of French fort as capital of British colony of Upper Canada; incorporated as city 1834 and named Toronto from Indian word for meeting place.

Further information: Convention and Tourist Bureau, 85 Richmond St. West, Suite 300, Toronto, Ontario M5H 1H9

Troy, New York

Population: 62,918.
Area: 9.8 sq. mi., 8 miles northeast of Albany.
Industry: Known especially for its manufacture of collars and shirts; military equipment, precision machines, automobile parts, abrasive materials, metals.
Commerce: 7 banks.

Cultural facilities: Rensselaer Polytechnic Institute Fieldhouse (seating 7,500); Troy Music Hall, Junior Museum, Historical Society.
Other attractions: 21 playgrounds, 3 hospitals, Russell Sage College, Hudson Valley Community College, Emma Willard School for Girls, 31 public and parochial schools.

Tucson, Arizona

The World Almanac is sponsored in the Tucson area by The Arizona Daily Star, 4850 S. Park Ave., Tucson, Arizona, 85726: telephone 294-4433; founded 1877 as a weekly. Michael E. Pulitzer, editor and publisher; Frank E. Johnson, managing editor; Abe Chanin, editorial section director; Arnold A. Lewin, promotion director; sponsors the Sportsmen's Fund.

Population: 262,933 within city limits, 360,000 in Pima County (US Census, 1970).
Industry: Infilco (Westinghouse), Hughes Aircraft, Hamilton Aircraft. Tucson is the center of the Copper Circle: hundreds of millions of development dollars have been spent by Anaconda, Duval, American Smelting and Refining, Pima Mining, Kennecott and other companies.
Transportation: Tucson International Airport is a northern terminus of Aero Mexico and is served by most major airlines; 3 smaller airports serve Tucson; 2 bus lines and Southern Pacific Railroad; numerous motor freight lines.
Communications: 2 newspapers; 5 television and 17 radio stations.
Medical facilities: 10 hospitals including University Medical Center—a teaching hospital.

Climate: Mild, dry; rare freezing temperatures in winter; summer brings some rain, mostly after July 1, and temperatures to about 100°F.
Culture: Tucson Symphony Orchestra, several theatre groups, and programs by the University of Arizona.
Sports: Home of Tucson Toros of Pacific Coast League, farm club of the Oakland Athletics; spring training site for Cleveland Indians; home of Dean Martin Open Golf Tournament.
History: Original site was on the Santa Cruz river near the Mission of San Xavier del Bac. The Rev. Eusebio Francisco Kino, S. J., 17th century missionary to Northern Mexico and what is now called Southern Arizona, is generally credited with being the founder of the mission.

Tulsa, Oklahoma

The World Almanac is sponsored in the Tulsa area by The Tulsa Tribune, 315 South Boulder, Tulsa, Okla. 74102; telephone (918) 582-1101; founded in 1904 as The Tulsa Democrat, renamed The Tulsa Tribune in 1920; circulation, 88,500; editor, Jenkin Lloyd Jones; managing editor, Jenkin Lloyd Jones, Jr.; executive editor, Harmon Phillips.

Population: 330,350 (city), 476,945 (metro area), 2nd in state, 48th in nation; total employed, 224,800 (metro area).
Area: 175.71 sq. mi., on Arkansas River at 96th meridian.
Industry: Petroleum—about 30,000 persons are employed by 825 oil and oil-related firms with $180,000,000 total payroll annually; Sun Oil and Texaco refineries. Aviation—about 15,000 in aviation and aerospace industries; major plants include Rockwell International, McDonnell Douglas Aircraft and American Airlines Maintenance Center. Other—Tulsa is world's largest manufacturer of industrial heaters and winches; 1,200 diversified manufacturing plants.
Commerce: Retail sales (1972): $1.214 billion. Bank resources: $1.512 billion. There are 17 banks and 10 savings and loan associations.
Transportation: Tulsa Port of Catoosa, nation's most inland port, head of the Arkansas-Verdigris navigation channel, total 1972 barge tonnage, 329,589; 4 rail freight lines; 3 bus lines, 32 truck

lines, 6 airlines with 1,099,300 air passenger movements in 1972.
Communications: 2 daily newspapers, 3 TV and 15 radio stations.
Cultural facilities: University of Tulsa, Oral Roberts University, Tulsa Junior College, Tulsa Philharmonic, Opera, Civic Ballet, 2 art museums, including Thomas Gilcreas Institute of American History and Art.
Sports: Tulsa Oilers, top St. Louis Cardinals baseball farm team in American Association; professional ice hockey team in Central Hockey League; intercollegiate athletics, University of Tulsa and Oral Roberts University.
History: Founded 1848 as Creek Indian trading post; incorporated 1898; named for Creek word "Tulsey," or town; oil discovery at nearby Glenpool, Nov. 22, 1905, stimulated growth with subsequent hotel construction and civic effort to secure oil company headquarters assuring metropolitan status.

Vancouver, British Columbia, Canada

The World Almanac is published in the Vancouver area by The Vancouver Sun, 2250 Granville Street, Vancouver, B.C.; telephone (604) 732-2111; founded 1886; circulation 243,823; publisher, Stu Keate; editorial director, Bruce Hutchison; managing editor, Bill Galt; sponsors world's largest free Salmon Derby; free swim classes (annual enrollment 10,000); Sun Tournament of Soccer Champions and many other community services.

Population: 426,256 (city), 1,128,334 (metro area), 1st in province, third in Canada.

Area: 44 sq. miles on the Pacific coast at the mouth of the north arm of the Fraser River. Scenic

beauty of the city accented by the towering, snow-capped Rocky Mountains to the north and rich greenery of agricultural land to the east and south.
Industry: The city's 98 miles of waterfront, stretching up Burrard Inlet, makes it the largest cargo port on the Pacific and Canada's second busiest, with 36,700,000 tons handled in 1972. Major cargos: grain, lumber, coal, mineral ore, chemicals and manufactured goods. Tourism is also a major industry, with an estimated 6,000,000 visitors bringing in $290,000,000 in 1972.
Commerce: Retail sales: $2.85 billion in 1972. Value of shares traded on the Vancouver stock exchange: $784,103,000 in 1972.
Transportation: Vancouver is the western terminus of Canada's 2 national railways: Canadian National Railway and Canadian Pacific. It is also the headquarters of the provincially-operated British Columbia Railway (formerly the Pacific Great Eastern), and is linked to the U.S. by Amtrak along the Burlington Northern Railway right-of-way. The city is served by 2 major long-distance bus carriers: Provincial Stage Lines and Greyhound. Vancouver International Airport is served by 7 major airlines and handled more than 3.1 million passengers in 1972.
Communications: 12 radio stations and 2 local television stations. Also served by 4 major U.S.

network television outlets.
Medical facilities: Vancouver General and St. Paul's are the city's largest hospitals. Royal Columbian in New Westminster, Burnaby General, Lion's Gate in North Vancouver and Riverview Psychiatric Hospital are also major facilities.
Cultural facilities: Vancouver Symphony Orchestra, the opera association, several professional theatre groups, Centennial and Maritime Museums, and the Vancouver Art Gallery form the basis of a lively cultural scene. Queen Elizabeth Theatre is the major arts facility.
Other attractions: Pacific National Exhibition, Gastown, Chinatown, the H.R. MacMillan Planetarium, Bloedel Conservatory, Vancouver Public Aquarium, 1,000-acre Stanley Park, zoo, 18 golf courses, Grouse Mountain and Mount Seymour ski areas, University of British Columbia, Simon Fraser University, and 18 public beaches.
Sports: Home of the B.C. Lions (professional football); Vancouver Canucks (hockey); Exhibit-Racetrack (thoroughbreds); and several amateur teams and sports activities.
History: Discovered by the Spaniards; first mapped in 1791; taken possession of by Capt. George Vancouver for the British in 1792; Hudson's Bay Company post established early 1800s, city incorporated 1886.

Washington, District of Columbia

The World Almanac is sponsored in the Washington, D.C. area by the Evening Star and Washington Daily News, 225 Virginia Ave., S.E., Washington, D.C. 20003; telephone (202) 484-5000; founded Dec. 16, 1852 (The News came under Star ownership July 12, 1972); president John H. Kauffman, editor Newbold Noyes, managing editor Charles Seib; major awards received by the newspaper and staff members include 6 Pulitzer prizes.

Population: 745,000 (city), 3,200,000 (metro area) 1973 estimates; fastest growing metro area in nation includes D.C., 3 Maryland counties, 4 Virginia counties and 3 Virginia independent cities.
Area: 2,855 sq. mi. (metro area), 61 sq. mi. (D.C.), on Potomac River near Chesapeake Bay.
Industry: U.S. capital. Federal government employs 342,000, about one-fourth of labor force, with a payroll in excess of $5 billion a year. Government related activity—law, journalism, professional and trade associations (about 1,700), unions, lobbying groups and scientists—provide another large portion of the employment base. Tourism is a major industry, as is finance with Washington bank clearings surpassing $1 billion a year. Manufacturing is a minor part of the economy. Largest single private employer is Chesapeake and Potomac Telephone Company.
Commerce: Highest per capita and family income in nation; median household income in metro area is about $16,000, offset by high cost of living, particularly in housing, taxes, and professional services.
Transportation: Circumferential highway connects to all interstate highways north, west and south. A $3-billion, 98-mile rapid rail-transit system to be completed by 1980, with downtown subway to open in late 1974. Metroliner to New York, one of Amtrak's fastest growing passenger services. Over 1,000,000 passengers a month pass through National and Dulles International airports.
Communications: An information hub for the nation, the Washington area is headquarters for several national magazines, the Government Printing Office and news bureaus of major newspapers, wire services and radio and TV networks.

Area has 7 TV stations, 19 FM and 25 AM radio stations.
Education facilities: Major higher education institutions in the area include the University of Maryland in nearby College Park, Md., and American, Catholic, Georgetown, George Washington and Howard universities.
Medical facilities: about 40 hospitals, including Walter Reede Hospital (Army) and Bethesda Naval Medical Center; Children's Hospital specializes in children's ailments; 3 teaching hospitals.
Cultural facilities: Kennedy Center with 3 performance halls and Filene Center, an outdoor setting in nearby Vienna, Va., present major concerts, ballet, etc., Arena Stage and restored Ford's Theater are showcases for legitimate theater; National Symphony, Opera Society and National Ballet perform here; Smithsonian Institution provides one of largest and most varied museum facilities in the world, and includes major art collections; Corcoran Art Gallery displays many major works; Library of Congress, one of largest book collections in the world, and D.C. Public Library with 19 branches.
Sports: Professional sports now include football (Redskins), In 1974, a pro baseball team will move to Washington, to be followed by the pro basketball Bullets. A National Hockey League expansion team will take up quarters in Washington in 1975.
History: Washington, District of Columbia, was named for George Washington and Christopher Columbus. Laid out by Pierre L'Enfant, the city was founded by an Act of Congress in 1790 providing for the seat of the federal government. It is governed by 3 commissioners appointed by the President.

Wichita, Kansas

The World Almanac is sponsored in the Wichita area by The Wichita Eagle and Beacon Publishing Co., 825 East Douglas, Wichita, Kan. 67201; telephone (316) 268-6000; founded 1872 as weeklies; became dailies 1884, consolidated 1961; circulation, Eagle (morning) 126,969, Beacon (evening) 59,081; Sunday Eagle and Beacon 186,554; publisher Britt Brown, editor Don Boyett, Managing editors Keith Ashley and Lynn Holt.

Population: 264,801 (city), 372,791 (metro area), 1st in state, 75th in nation; employed 158,300.
Area: 90.74 square miles, at juncture of Big and Little Arkansas Rivers.
Industry: Aviation — 60% of all U.S. general aviation aircraft manufactured in Wichita by Beech Aircraft Corp., Cessna Aircraft Co., Gates Learjet Corp. and Boeing Co. Meat processing — Wichita is 12th largest processor of meat animals in the nation. Grain processing — Flour milling in 1972 7,264,268 cwt; Garvey elevator world's largest single-unit grain storage facility. Other — Petroleum, natural gas, chemicals; 600 manufacturing companies. Largest non-aero manufacturer is Coleman Co.
Commerce: Wholesale and retail center for large part of Kansas and northern Oklahoma; retail sales (1972): $948,094,000. Bank resources: $900,000,000. There are 15 banks, 2 mortgage banks, 10 building and loan associations and 5 insurance company offices.
Transportation: 4 major rail freight lines, Amtrak, Continental bus lines and 24 truck lines; 8 federal

and state highways intersect Wichita. Ultramodern Municipal Airport, hub for 5 airlines, averages 1,003 air movements per day. National Flying Farmers headquarters.
Communications: 4 TV and 10 radio stations.
Medical facilities: World's largest speech and hearing rehabilitation center (Institute of Logopedics); 5 major hospital complexes including a Veterans Administration installation.
Federal facility: McConnell Air Force Base.
Cultural facilities: Wichita Symphony Orchestra, 2 art museums, Wichita State University, Friends University, Kansas Newman (Sacred Heart) College; Century II auditorium and convention center with a $2,500,000 city library; 440 churches.
Other attractions: $3,000,000 city-county zoo, major recreational lakes, 52 parks, Cow Town (a restoration of 1872 Wichita), Wichita Historical Museum; averages 65% of possible sunshine.
Sports: Wichita Aeros, top Chicago Cubs farm team; National Baseball Congress tournament.
History: Founded 1870, became railhead on the Chisholm Trail; named after Wichita Indians.

Windsor, Ontario, Canada

The World Almanac is sponsored in Windsor and a large part of Southwestern Ontario including Essex, Kent and Lambton Counties, by The Windsor Star (circ, 85,000) 167 Ferry St., Windsor 12, Ontario; a division of Southam Press, Ltd.; published daily since 1890 (present name since 1957); publisher J. Patrick O'Callaghan, general manager A.H. Fast, editor R.M. Pearson.

Population: 203,000 (city), 258,643 (metro), 506,007 (tri-county); 10th in nation. Total employed 102,400.
Area: 50 sq.mi., one half mile across Detroit River from Detroit, Mich. Largest Canadian city on U.S.-Canada border.
Industry: Autos and auto parts, more than 25% national production (Chrysler, Ford, General Motors); scores of tool and die shops; alcoholic beverages (home office Hiram Walker and Sons); food processing (H.J. Heinz, Green Giant;) salt mining; zinc and plastic die-casting; pharmaceuticals; agriculture (rich producer early vegetables) — tomatoes, corn, soybeans, peaches, tobacco; tourism (largest port of entry in nation for visitors from U.S.).
Commerce: 10th in nation for retail sales ($484,504,000); effective buying income $1,060,131,000; average household effective buying income $11,662; per capita effective buying income

$3,591. Highest national average weekly earnings ($163.50). Six banks, 7 loan companies, 58 branches.
Transportation: 7 rail lines; 2 airlines; linked to Detroit by suspension bridge and underwater tunnel; western terminus Highway 401; major harbor terminal; private marinas, yacht club; municipal busline.
Communications: 5 radio and 1 TV stations; access to Detroit's 50 radio and 6 TV stations.
Medical facilities: 5 major hospital complexes including large hospital for chronically ill.
Cultural facilities: University of Windsor; St. Clair College of Applied Arts and Technology; Windsor Symphony Orchestra; Windsor Light Opera Association; Willistead Art Gallery; Hiram Walker Museum; new public library; Cleary Auditorium and convention center.
Other attractions: 60 parks and playgrounds; close access to Great Lakes resort areas.

Winnipeg, Manitoba, Canada

The World Almanac is sponsored in Winnipeg area by Winnipeg Free Press, 300 Carlton St., Winnipeg, Man., Canada; telephone (204) 943-9331; founded 1872; daily circulation 139,987; publisher and editor-in-chief R.S. Malone; executive editor Peter McLintock; managing editor A.E. Boothe; general manager R.H. Shelford; the newspaper and its staff have received numerous awards for outstanding journalism.

Population: 540,262, 1st in province, 5th in nation; capital of Manitoba.
Area: 161 sq. mi., junction of Red and Assiniboine rivers, near center of N. America.
Industry: manufacturing is single largest source of jobs. Winnipeg is 7th largest manufacturing center in Canada.
Commerce: trade is second largest source of jobs. Shipments in 1972 from 960 firms valued at $1.16 billion. Winnipeg Commodity Exchange is only gold futures market in Canada. Headquarters

Canadian Wheat Board, Canada Grain Council, Canadian Grain Institute, Canadian Grain Commission.
Transportation: Winnipeg International Airport Canada's 4th busiest. City served by 4 airlines; 2 national rail lines and freight link to U.S.; 5 national and regional bus lines; major trucking hub.
Communications: 3 TV and 5 radio stations.
New construction: Valued at $190,900,000 in 1972, up from $150,800,000 in 1971. A $23,700,000 convention center and $16,000,000 Royal Canadian Mint in

progress.

Medical facilities: One of Canada's largest medical teaching centres. Research: immunology; transplant-tissue rejection problems. Of Manitoba's 85 active treatment hospitals, 13 are in Winnipeg, including 2 major teaching centres.

Cultural facilities: Royal Winnipeg Ballet, Winnipeg Symphony Orchestra, Manitoba Theatre Centre, Winnipeg Art Gallery.

Educational facilities: 2 universities, 1 community college.

Sports attractions: Blue Bombers, member Canadian Football League, 25,000-seat stadium; first in Western Div., 1972. Winnipeg Jets, member

World Hockey Assoc., 10,000-seat arena; first, Western Div., 1972-73 under playing coach Bobby Hull.

Other attractions: major zoo; summer, winter festivals; planetarium; museums.

History: first colony, Lord Selkirk Settlers, 1812. Incorporated Nov. 8, 1873, as city. Jan. 1, 1972, amalgamated city government replaced 7 cities, 4 urban municipalities, 1 town and a metropolitan government; in central city is St. Boniface, largest French-Canadian center outside province of Quebec.

Additional information: Chamber of Commerce, 177 Lombard Ave., Winnipeg, Man., Canada.

Winston-Salem, North Carolina

The World Almanac is sponsored in the Piedmont Triad area by the Winston-Salem Journal and the Twin City Sentinel, 416-20 North Marshall Street, Winston-Salem, N.C. 27102. Telephone (919) 725-2311. The Sentinel was founded in 1856 and the Journal in 1897. They were brought under one ownership in 1927. They are now an affiliate of Media General, Inc. Wallace Carroll, editor and publisher; Charles W. Crowder, general manager.

Population: 137,100 (city), 222,800 (Forsyth County). Based on 1973 estimates.

Area: 57.5 square miles (city), 419 square miles (Forsyth County) in north central North Carolina.

Industry: R. J. Reynolds Industries, Inc., with diversified interests in tobacco, food, shipping, oil, packaging; Western Electric Co.,; Jos. Schlitz brewery; Westinghouse Corp.; Hanes Corp.; Hanes Dye and Finishing Co.; Du-plan Corp.; Brenner Industries; Bahnson Co.; Graveley Corp.; Dennis, Inc., the nation's biggest popcorn seller; Wachovia Corp., major financing institution.

Commerce: Products manufactured in Winston-Salem exceed $1.5 billion in value annually; city is part of the Piedmont Triad which, with Greensboro and High Point, comprise a rapidly-growing industrial and business area.

Transportation: Headquarters for Piedmont Airlines at Smith Reynolds Airport; city also served by regional airport with 4 airlines; Greyhound bus; McLean, Hennis and Pilot truck

lines have headquarters there; center for other trucking firms.

Communications: 3 television and 7 radio stations; television cable service.

Medical facilities: Bowman Gray School of Medicine of Wake Forest University; Baptist, Forsyth Memorial and Medical Park hospitals. Ardmore section contains one of the largest concentrations of medical facilities in the South

Cultural facilities: One of the nation's first arts councils formed in 1949; home of the N.C. School of the Arts. Salem Fine Arts Center one of the best in the nation. Home of Wake Forest University, Salem College and Winston-Salem State University. Old Salem, restoration of colonial town.

Sports: Wake Forest University teams play football at Grove Stadium, basketball at Memorial Coliseum; Winston-Salem Red Sox, professional baseball team, at Ernie Shore Field.

History: Salem founded in 1766; Winston founded in 1848; cities merged in 1913.

Youngstown, Ohio

The World Almanac is sponsored in the Youngstown area by The Vindicator, Vindicator Square, Youngstown, Ohio 44501; phone (216) 747-1471; founded in 1863 by J. H. Odell, passed as a weekly to William F. Maag, who began daily production Sept. 25, 1889; daily circulation 103,093, Sunday 161,713; president, publisher, general manager, William J. Brown; advertising manager, William Mittler; managing editor, Irving L. Mansell.

Population: 140,909 (city), 536,836 (metro area). Metro area 63rd largest in U.S., city Ohio's 7th largest; total employed in metro area, 225,800.

Area: 35 square miles in northeast Ohio at juncture of Ohio Turnpike and I-80.

Industry: Historically a strong iron and steel center, still important producer with Youngstown Sheet & Tube Co., Republic Steel Corp., and U.S. Steel Corp; local steel supplied to big nearby plants of General Motors Corp.—Packard Electric Div. in Warren and GMAD plant in Lordstown, where Chevrolet Vegas and trucks are made; GF Business Equipment sells office furnishings world wide; Commercial Shearing Inc. does world-wide tunnel frame and hydraulics business; other fabricators use local steel.

Commerce: Wholesale and retail center for large area of northeast Ohio and western Penn.; estimated retail sales for metro area $995,394,000 estimated value added by manufacture $1.589 billion.

Transportation: Rail and truck transport center with 7 railroads and 92 motor freight terminals;

airport served by 2 major airlines and is headquarters for Beckett Aviation, largest fleet of executive aircraft in U.S.

Communications: City has 3 TV, 5 radio stations.

New construction: New building permits for city in 1972 totaled $80,500,000.

Medical facilities: 6 large hospitals in city.

Federal facilities: Air Force Reserve base at municipal airport; Ravenna Arsenal nearby; Army, Navy reserve units in city, with bldgs.

Cultural facilities: Symphony orchestra with downtown bldg.; ballet guild; Youngstown Playhouse in own modern bldg.; Butler Institute of American Art with renowned collection.

Educational facilities: Youngstown State University with over 15,500 students and graduate program; 55 public and parochial schools; branches of Kent State Univ. in nearby Warren and Salem; Youngstown State U. has educational TV channel.

Recreational facilities: City park system has 10 parks, 44 playgrounds, golf courses, 6 swim pools; Mill Creek Park, 2,383 acres, 36-hole golf course.

Washington, Capital of the United States

THE CAPITOL

The Capitol (building) since 1961 has presented an entirely new East Central front, the central portion having been reconstructed and extended. It was moved forward 32½ ft. The former facade of Virginia sandstone was reproduced in Georgia marble, the original wall becoming an interior wall. The new section added 78 offices and other important facilities. The cost of the extension project was $11,400,000; improved illumination and other work brought the total to $24,000,000.

The original plan for the Capitol was drawn by Dr. William Thornton, of Tortola, West Indies, and accepted April 5, 1793. It had a central section, nearly square, a low dome and rectangular buildings north and south, 126 by 120 ft. The southeast cornerstone of the north section was laid by President Washington with Masonic ceremonies Sept. 18, 1793. Sandstone from Aquia Creek, Va., was used. The northern wing was completed first. The Congress occupied it in Nov. 1800. The Supreme Court met there in Feb. 1801, and other local courts also used the Capitol. In charge of early construction were architects Stephen H. Hallet, Geo. Hadfield, and James Hoban who was architect of the White House, Benjamin H. Latrobe was architect of the South or House wing which was occupied in 1807, but not completed until 1811. All the interiors were burned by the British in 1814. Latrobe had charge of the rebuilding until 1818 when Charles Bulfinch became the Architect for 11 years. Congress reoccupied the Capitol in 1819 and the central rotunda area was finished in 1829.

The present Senate and House wings were designed and constructed under the architect Thomas U. Walter in 1851-1863. The wing extensions are white marble from Lee, Mass., and the columns are from Maryland. Daniel Webster spoke at the laying of the cornerstone.

The House moved in Dec. 16, 1857; the Senate Jan. 4, 1859. In 1860 the Supreme Court moved into the former Senate Chamber, and in 1864 the old Hall of the House was designated Statuary Hall. The Court moved into its own building in 1935.

The original dome of the Capitol, wood covered with copper, was replaced, 1856, by the present dome of cast iron, completed 1865. Its greatest exterior diameter is 135 ft. 5 in. The rotunda is 96 ft. diameter, height from floor to base of lantern, 180 ft. 3 in. In the "eye" of the dome is a fresco by Constantino Brumidi, the "Apotheosis of Washington." Below the dome runs a 300-ft. frieze in fresco, portraying American history from Columbus, 1492, to Kitty Hawk, 1903. Brumidi painted part of it by 1880. Costaggini added panels by 1888. Allyn Cox completed the frieze in 1953 and it was dedicated in 1954.

The Statue of Freedom on the dome, 19½ ft. tall, is of bronze and weighs 14,985 pounds. At its base are the words "E Pluribus Unum" (Out of Many One). It was modeled in plaster by Thomas Crawford in Rome and cast in bronze. It cost $23,796, exclusive of erection.

Inaugurations of Presidents and Vice Presidents are usually held on a platform erected over the great steps on the East front. The oath of office of the President is usually given by the Chief Justice of the United States.

Prayer Room

A nondenominational room for meditation and prayer is located off the rotunda. Decorated in blue, it has a white oak altar with an open Bible, and candelabra, 10 seats and 2 kneeling benches.

National Statuary Hall

Statuary Hall was created in 1864 to occupy the former Hall of the House of Representatives. States were invited to contribute not more than two statues of distinguished persons judged worthy of national commemoration by the States. In 1933 the number of statues in Statuary Hall was limited to one statue from each state, others to be placed in other parts of the Capitol. To date 91 statues have been contributed by 50 states. The statues in Statuary Hall:

Alabama—Gen. Jos. Wheeler, USA, CSA.
Arizona—John C. Greenway, U. S. A.
Arkansas—Uriah M. Rose, jurist.
California—Junipero Serra, mission founder.
Colorado—Dr. Florence Rena Sabin, scientist.
Connecticut—Roger Sherman, statesman.
Delaware—Caesar Rodney, statesman.
Florida—Dr. John Gorrie, inventor.
Georgia—Alex. H. Stephens, statesman.
Hawaii—King Kamehameha I, (united islands)
Idaho—Geo. L. Shoup, first governor.
Illinois—Frances E. Willard, WCTU head.
Indiana—Lew Wallace, USA, author.
Iowa—Saml. J. Kirkwood, governor.
Kansas—John J. Ingalls, senator.
Kentucky—Henry Clay, statesman.
Louisiana—Huey P. Long, senator.
Maine—Hannibal Hamlin, vice president.
Maryland—Charles Carroll, signer, D. of I.
Massachusetts—Samuel Adams, statesman.
Michigan—Lewis Cass, statesman.
Minnesota—Henry M. Rice, senator.
Mississippi—Jefferson Davis, statesman.
Missouri—Thos. H. Benton, senator.
Montana—Charles Marion Russell, artist.
Nebraska—Wm. Jennings Bryan, statesman.
Nevada—Patrick A. McCarran, senator.
New Hampshire—Daniel Webster, statesman.
New Jersey—Richard Stockton, statesman.
New York—Robt. R. Livingston, statesman.
North Carolina—Zebulon B. Vance, governor.
North Dakota—John Burke, U. S. Treasurer.
Ohio—William Allen, senator, governor.
Oklahoma—Sequoyah, Cherokee leader.
Oregon—Rev. Jason Lee, pioneer.
Pennsylvania—Robert Fulton, inventor.
Rhode Island—Roger Williams, founder.
South Carolina—John C. Calhoun, statesman.
South Dakota—Gen. W.H.H. Beadle, educator.
Tennesse—John Sevier, first governor.
Texas—Sam Houston, pioneer leader.
Utah—Brigham Young, Mormon leader.
Vermont—Ethan Allen, Revolutionary leader.
Virginia—Robt. E. Lee, USA, CSA.
Washington—Dr. Marcus Whitman, pioneer.
West Virginia—Francis H. Pierpont, statesman.
Wisconsin—Robt. M. La Follette Sr., statesman.
Wyoming—Esther Hobart Morris, suffragette.

Located Elsewhere

Alaska—E. L. "Bob" Bartlett, senator.
New Mexico—Dennis Chavez, senator.

Under the dome in the Great Rotunda are statues and busts of Washington (Va.), Lincoln, Jefferson, Hamilton, Jackson (Tenn.), Lafayette, Grant, Garfield (Ohio) and Baker.

Adjoining it, the South Small Rotunda has statues of George Clinton (N.Y.), Stephen F. Austin (Tex.) and John Peter Muhlenberg (Pa.). The corridor leading from Statuary Hall to the House has statues of Jonathan Trumbull (Conn.), Wm. King (Me.), Father Jacques Marquette (Wis.), Wade Hampton (S. C.), Will Rogers (Okla.), E. L. "Bob" Bartlett (Alaska), and Dr. John McLoughlin (Ore.).

In the foyer of the former Senate and Supreme Court Chamber are statues of John Stark (N.H.), Dennis Chavez (N.M.), and Nathanael Greene (R.I.). In the corridor leading to the Senate wing are statues of Dr. Ephraim McDowell, (Ky.) and Dr. Crawford W. Long (Ga.), first to use ether as anaesthetic; John Hanson (Md.), 9th president of the Continental Congress, and John M. Clayton (Del.), Secy. of State; Wm. E. Borah (Idaho), Edward D. White (La.) and Maria L. Sanford (Minn.).

In the Hall of Columns on the first floor, House wing are statues of E. Kirby Smith (Fla.), Zachariah Chandler (Mich.), Jas. Harlan (Ia.), Francis P. Blair, Jr. (Mo.), Gen. Philip Kearny (N.J.), Gen. Jas. Shields

(Ill.), John Winthrop (Mass.), Oliver P. Morton (Ind.), J. Sterling Morton (Neb.), Rev. Thos. Starr King (Calif.), J. L. M. Curry (Ala.), J. P. Clarke (Ark.), Geo. W. Glick (Kan.), Jas. Z. George (Miss.), Chas. B. Aycock (N.C.), Jacob Collamer (Vt.), John E. Kenna (W. Va.), Joseph Ward (S. D.), Eusebio F. Kino, S. J. (Ariz.), and Father Damien (Hawaii).

Office Buildings for Members

Members of Congress meet constituents and transact other business in five office buildings on Capitol Hill, two for the Senate and three for the House.

The original Senate building, now named the Richard Brevard Russell Office Building, was completed in 1909, enlarged in 1933; the second Senate building, now named the Everett McKinley Dirksen Office Building, was constructed in 1958. A subway connects both with the Capitol.

The original House building (1908) was named for former Speaker Joseph G. Cannon (R.-Ill.), the second (1933) for former Speaker Nicholas Longworth (R.-Ohio), and the third (1964) for former Speaker Sam Rayburn (D.-Tex.). The Rayburn Building has underground transportation to the Capitol.

Also on Capitol Hill is the bell tower and statue memorial to Sen. Robert A. Taft of Ohio (1889-1953). It was erected by popular subscription and dedicated Apr. 14, 1959 by President Eisenhower.

Hours for Visiting

The Capitol is normally open from 9 a.m. to 4:30 p.m. daily. The Capitol is closed Christmas, New Year's Day and Thanksgiving Day. Should either the House or the Senate remain in session beyond closing time, the wing of the Capitol in use stays open until the session closes.

Tours, through the Capitol, including the House and Senate Galleries, are conducted from 9 a.m. to 4 p.m. without charge. It is not necessary to take a tour to see the Capitol. Visitors desiring to hear debate in either chamber for a longer period than the tour allows must obtain a visitor s card from their Senator or Representative.

The White House

The White House, the President's residence, stands on 18 acres on the south side of Pennsylvania Avenue, between the Treasury and the Executive Office Building. The main building, 170 by 85 ft, has 3 floors, with the East terrace, 135 by 35 ft., leading to the East Wing, a 3-story building, 139 by 82 ft., used for offices and as an entrance for official functions. The West Terrace, 174 by 35 ft., contains offices and new press facilities above the boarded over swimming pool, and leads to the Executive Office, 3 stories high, 148 by 98 ft., erected in 1902 and enlarged several times since.

The White House was designed by James Hoban, an Irish-born architect, in a competition that paid $500. The main facade resembles the Duke of Leinster's house in Dublin. President Washington chose the site, which was included on the plan of the Federal City prepared by the French engineer, Major Pierre L'Enfant. The cornerstone was laid Oct. 13, 1792. President Washington never lived in the house. President John Adams entered in November, 1800, and Mrs. Adams hung her washing in the uncompleted East Room.

The walls are of sandstone, quarried at Aquia Creek, Va. The exterior walls were painted during the course of construction, causing the building to be termed the "White House." For many years, however, it was generally referred to as the "President's House" or the "President's Palace." Thos. Jefferson developed the east and west terraces and built one-story offices, woodsheds and a wine cellar. On Aug. 24, 1814, during Madison's administration, the house was burned by the British. James Hoban completed rebuilding by Dec., 1817, and President Monroe moved in.

The south portico was added in 1824 and the north colonnade and porch in 1829 by Benjamin Latrobe, Surveyor of Public Buildings, based on sketches by Hoban, approved by Jefferson. In 1948 President Truman had a second-floor balcony built into the south portico. In 1948 he had Congress authorize complete rebuilding because the White House was unsafe. During its reconstruction he lived in Blair House, 1651 Pennsylvania Ave.

Reconstruction cost $5,761,000. The interior was completely removed, new underpinning 24 ft. deep was placed under the outside walls and a steel frame was built to support the interior. All original trim and metal work were preserved.

The Green Room, used for informal receptions, is in American Sheraton style, with green silk moire on the walls, a white marble fireplace and white enamel wainscoting and door trim. On the west wall hangs a portrait of Benjamin Franklin, painted in 1767. Most of the furniture now in the room was made in New York City about 1815-1825 by Duncan Phyfe or his contemporaries.

The Blue Room, an oval drawing room, is the main reception room. The parquet floor is exposed; the walls are covered with wallpaper reproduced from a French document of 1800. Portraits of Washington, Adams, Jefferson, Jackson, Monroe, Taylor and Tyler, as well as two sea-scapes by Fitz Hugh Lane of Boston harbor and Baltimore harbor decorate the walls. Gilton chairs and a French clock from Monroe's original 1817 furnishings remain in the room.

The Red Room, used as a parlor, is furnished in the Empire period, hung in red twill satin with gold scroll borders. There are a Savonnerie carpet of the period and a marble-topped gueridon labeled by Charles Honore Lannuier. There are portraits of Pierce, Polk, T. Roosevelt, Abigail Adams, Dolley Madison, Angelica Van Buren, Audubon, and Alexander Hamilton in the room. Also there is a marble bust of Martin Van Buren by Hiram Powers.

The State Dining Room has a large chief table. Other tables are brought in for large dinners but do not remain there. Centerpiece of the main table is a French bronze-doré plateau purchased by Monroe in 1817. China in use was ordered during the Lyndon B. Johnson Administration. Chairs are in Queen Anne style. The room is paneled in oak with Corinthian pilasters, painted white.

The Family Dining Room, used for breakfasts and luncheons, has the Healy portrait of John Quincy Adams.

The President's Dining Room is on the second floor. It has scenic wallpaper and is furnished with American Federal furniture, an 18th Century chandelier and blue silk window hangings. There is a mahogany sideboard once owned by Daniel Webster.

The Diplomatic Reception Room, an oval room on the ground floor, is used as the entrance to the mansion at state functions. It has scenic wallpaper based on 1820 engravings and a new Aubusson style rug with seals of the 50 states, installed in June, 1971.

The Library, on the ground floor, has the painted decor of an early American room. In August, 1963, 2,780 titles were selected to be placed in the library. All but a few are by American authors. They were chosen by a committee headed by the late James T. Babb, librarian emeritus of Yale University.

The Lincoln Bedroom, which contains an ornately carved bed and furniture of his period, is at the east end of the second floor. It served as Lincoln's cabinet room and in it he signed the Emancipation Proclamation of Jan. 1, 1863. A portrait of Jackson, admired by Lincoln, hangs there today. Seven pieces of furniture have Lincoln associations. The bed was used in the State Bedroom during the Lincoln administration. In the room is a copy of the Gettysburg Address, written out by Lincoln and donated to the White House by the will of Oscar B. Cintas, one-time Cuban ambassador, who died in 1957.

The Treaty Room, one door removed from Lincoln's cabinet room was used by Andrew Johnson as his cabinet room, and so used until 1902, when it became a sitting room. Here in 1899 was signed the peace protocol, a forerunner to the final treaty of peace with Spain. It is now a waiting or meeting room for the President and contains some of the original Victorian furniture. There are portraits of Presidents A. Johnson, Grant and Taylor and paintings of McKinley observing the signing of the treaty and of Lincoln and Grant in conference.

The Queen's Bedroom is assigned to distinguished women guests, and has sheltered five queens—Queen Mother Elizabeth, and Queen Elizabeth II of Britain, Wilhelmina and Juliana of the Netherlands, Queen Mother Frederika of Greece. The English overmantel mirror was presented by Princess Elizabeth in 1951.

The Yellow Oval Room, directly above the Blue Room is used as a private sitting room by the President and Mrs. Nixon.

The Map Room, on the ground floor, a top-secret war room during World War II, was redecorated in 1970 at the request of President and Mrs. Nixon. Furnished in American Chippendale style, it contains 4 American landscape paintings and a portrait of Benjamin Franklin which was taken from Franklin's Philadelphia home by a British officer quartered there during the American Revolution.

The President's Office, oval in form, is in the West Wing and looks out on the rose garden. The office was added in 1909 to the West Wing, which had been built 7 years earlier by Theodore Roosevelt. The West Wing also contains the Roosevelt Room and the Cabinet Room.

Visiting Hours

The White House is open from 10 a.m. to 12 noon, Tuesday through Friday, except on holidays. Also Saturdays, 10 a.m. to 2 p.m. June 1 through Labor Day, and 10 a.m. to noon Labor Day through May 31. Only the public rooms in the basement and the first floor rooms, may be visited. No permit is required.

President's Guest House

Blair House, the President's Guest House, fronts on Pennsylvania Ave., nw of the White House grounds. It is supervised by the Dept. of State and is the official residence of heads of state who visit Washington. Built 1824, it was the home of Francis Preston Blair (1791-1876), political leader and Lincoln advisor. President Truman lived there 1948-1952 during rebuilding of the White House, and two Puerto Rican fanatics tried to shoot their way in Nov. 1, 1950, killing one guard and wounding two others.

Restoration and refurnishing began in 1963 and the house was reopened Jan. 14, 1964, on the occasion of the visit of President Antonio Segni of the Italian Republic. The Blair House Fine Arts Committee is continuing providing for the house.

OTHER CENTERS OF INTEREST

Arlington National Cemetery

Arlington National Cemetery, on the former Custis Lee estate in Virginia, is the site of the **Tomb of the Unknown Soldier** and the final resting place of John Fitzgerald Kennedy, President of the United States, who was buried there Nov. 25, 1963. A torch burns day and night over his grave. The remains of his brother Sen. Robert F. Kennedy (N. Y.) were interred on June 8, 1968 in an area adjacent. Many other famous Americans also are buried at Arlington, as well as American soldiers from every major war.

Arlington National Cemetery, administered by the Department of the Army, was established June 15, 1864, on land originally the estate of George Washington Parke Custis. The land was a part of the District of Columbia. 1791 until 1847, when Arlington County was returned to Virigina.

The Unknown Soldier of World War I was entombed on the East front of the Arlington Memorial Amphitheater Nov. 11, 1921, in the presence of President Warren G. Harding. The tomb is inscribed: *Here rests in honored glory an American soldier known but to God.* The body had been chosen at Chalons-sur-Marne from unidentified dead in Europe. On Memorial Day, May 30, 1958, two unidentified servicemen, one of whom died in World War II and one in the Korean War, were placed in crypts beside the first, in ceremonies led by President Eisenhower and Vice President Nixon. The President placed the Medal of Honor on each of the two coffins.

As of Mar. 31, 1973, a total of 160,110 interments had been made in Arlington National Cemetery. Among the unknown dead are 2,111 who died on the battlefields of Virginia in the Civil War and 167 who lost their lives when the battleship Maine was blown up in Havana Harbor Feb. 15, 1898. The total of unknown dead interred in Arlington National Cemetery is 4,724.

Arlington House

On a hilltop above the cemetery, stands Arlington House, the Robert E. Lee Memorial, which from 1955 to 1972 was officially called the Custis-Lee Mansion. The house has a portico 60 ft. wide, with 6 Doric columns and faces the Potomac. With its two wings the house extends 140 ft. It was built by George Washington Parke Custis, grandson of Martha Washington and father of Mary Ann Randolph Custis, who married Lee in this house in 1831. Here Lee wrote his resignation from the U. S. Army, Apr. 20, 1861.The house became a military hq. and was confiscated by the Government. The U.S. Supreme Court restored it to the legal heir, George Washington Custis Lee, grandson of the builder, who

sold the entire estate (including the mansion) to the Government in 1883 for $150,000.

The mansion and grounds are administered by the National Park Service of the Dept. of the Interior.

U.S. Marine Corps War Memorial

North of the National Cemetery, approximately 350 yards, stands the bronze statue of the raising of the United States flag on Iwo Jima, executed by Felix de Weldon from the photograph by Joe Rosenthal, and presented to the nation by members and friends of the U.S. Marine Corps., at a cost of $850,000. It was dedicated Nov. 10, 1954, and is under the administration of the Dept. of the Interior, National Park Service.

Folger Shakespeare Library

The Folger Shakespeare Library on Capitol Hill, Washington, D. C., is a research institution devoted to the advancement of learning in the background of Anglo-American civilization in the 16th and 17th centuries and in most aspects of the continental Renaissance. It has the largest collection of Shakespeareana in the world with 79 copies of the First Folio. Its collection of English books printed before 1640 is the largest in the Western Hemisphere. It also has extensive source materials for the history of theatre and drama from the Middle Ages to the end of the 19th century, both English and American. The library owns approximately 250,000 books and manuscripts, about half of them rare.

The library was founded and endowed by Henry Clay Folger, a former president of the Standard Oil Co. of New York and his wife, Emily Jordan Folger. He left its administration to the trustees of his alma mater, Amherst College. The exhibition gallery and replica Elizabethan Theatre are open free every day except Federal holidays and Sundays from Labor Day to April 15.

Library of Congress

Established by and for Congress in 1800, the Library of Congress has extended its services over the years to other Government agencies and other libraries, to scholars, and to the general public, and it now serves as the national library. Two buildings, an ornate Italian Renaissance structure (1897) and a modern annex (1939), cover 6 acres of the 15²/₃-acre Library site and contain 35 acres of floor space. In addition the Library occupies 10 other buildings dispersed throughout the Metropolitan area. In October 1965, Congress passed a law authorizing construction of a third Library building, the James Madison Memorial Building; completion is expected in 1975.

L. Quincy Mumford, the 11th Librarian of Congress, took office September 1, 1954.

The Library had over 3,000 volumes when it was destroyed in the burning of the Capitol, August 24-25, 1814. In January 1815, Congress bought Thomas Jefferson's library of some 6,000 volumes. In 1851 fire destroyed about half the collections. In 1866 the science library of the Smithsonian Institution was transferred to the Library, and in 1870 the Library became the repository for materials deposited for copyright. Today the Library's collections contain over 80,000,000 items, including more than 16,000,000 volumes and pamphlets.

Many treasures of the Library are usually on exhibit, including the Gutenberg Bible, the first and second drafts of the Gettysburg Address, and Jefferson's so-called "rough draft" of the Declaration of Independence.

Important recent additions to the Library's collections include a collection of manuscripts relating to Spanish America donated by Hans P. Kraus; the papers of Helen Traubel, Agnes E. Meyer, Goodman Ace and Alma Gluck; letters of President Warren G. Harding (closed until the year 2014); the complete photographic files of Look magazine; holograph scores of compositions by Igor Stravinsky, Aaron Copland, Howard Hanson, Franz Liszt, and George Gershwin; and the original of President Calvin Coolidge's "I do not choose to run" message.

In addition to its world wide acquisitions programs, the Library acquires over 1,000,000 publications a year from 7 foreign countries for some 300 American libraries through U. S.-owned foreign currencies under Public Law 480 as amended. Under the Higher Education Act of 1965, the Library also launched the National Program for Acquisitions and Cataloging (NPAC) in 1966 to solve a national cataloging problem in research libraries by obtaining all foreign books of value to scholarship and cataloging them promptly for all libraries needing such catalog data.

By fiscal 1972 the Library had increased its total cataloging production from 109,000 titles in fiscal 1965 to 240,000 titles and was obtaining foreign cataloging information from 24 countries for use in publishing the Library's famous 3 X 5 printed catalog cards. As part of its automation program, the Library also is distributing machine-readable cataloging (MARC) on magnetic tapes to libraries subscribing to this service.

Tours in the Library of Congress begin at the office of the Captain of the Guard, Main Building, Monday through Friday.

Thomas Jefferson Memorial

The **Thomas Jefferson Memorial** stands on the south shore of the Tidal Basin in West Potomac park. It is a circular stone structure, with Vermont marble on the exterior and Georgia white marble inside and combines architectural elements of the dome of the Pantheon in Rome and the rotunda designed by Jefferson for the University of Virginia. The central circular chamber, 80.3 ft. in diameter, is dominated by a full-length figure of Thomas Jefferson 19 ft. tall, by the American sculptor Rudulph Evans. The architects were John Russell Pope and his associates Otto R. Eggers and Daniel P. Higgins. The Memorial was dedicated by President F. D. Roosevelt Apr. 13, 1943, the 200th anniversary of Jefferson's birth.

On the pediment over the portico is a sculptured group by Adolph A. Weinman showing Jefferson standing before the committee appointed by the Continental Congress to draft the Declaration of Independence. On the interior walls are four panels with inscriptions from Jefferson's writings. On the frieze of the main entablature are Jefferson's lines: "I have sworn upon the altar of God eternal hostility against every form of tyranny over the mind of man."

The Memorial is open daily from 8 a.m. to midnight, except Christmas Day.

John F. Kennedy Center

John F. Kennedy Center for the Performing Arts, on a 17-acre site on the Potomac River, is sole official memorial

to Pres. Kennedy in the capital and opened Sept. 8, 1971. Financed by both Government and private funds, the marble building designed by Edward Durell Stone houses a 2,200-seat Opera House, a 2,700 seat Concert Hall, a 1,100-seat Eisenhower Theater, an unfinished 500-seat studio playhouse, and other facilities.

Lincoln Memorial

The **Lincoln Memorial** in West Potomac Park, on the axis of the Capitol and the Washington Monument, consists of a large marble hall enclosing a heroic statue of Abraham Lincoln in meditation sitting on a large armchair. It was dedicated on Memorial Day, May 30, 1922. The Memorial was designed by Henry Bacon. The statue was made by Daniel Chester French. Murals and ornamentation on the bronze ceiling beams are by Jules Guerin.

The Memorial built on bedrock, is of white Colorado-Yule marble. There are two Doric columns at the entrance and 36 others in the colonnade. The frieze above the 36 columns bears the names of the 36 states existing at the time of Lincoln's death. On the attic parapet are recorded names of the 48 states existing in 1922.

Inside are three memorials to Lincoln. The seated figure of Lincoln is 19 ft. from head to foot and the classic armchair is 12½ ft. tall. Over the back of the chair a flag is draped in marble. The statue was fashioned out of 28 blocks of Georgia white marble. On the north wall is inscribed the Second Inaugural Address. On the south wall is the Gettysburg Address.

The walls of the interior are Indiana limestone. The panels between the overhead girders are of Alabama marble saturated with melted beeswax to produce translucency. The interior floor and the wall base are of pink Tennessee marble. The cost of the Memorial was $2,957,000 and of the statue $88,400.

The Memorial is open 24 hours daily, except Christmas Day.

Mount Vernon

Mount Vernon on the south bank of the Potomac, 16 miles below Washington, D. C., is part of a large tract of land in Northern Virginia which was originally included in a royal grant made to Lord Culpepper, who in 1674 granted 5,000 acres to Nicholas Spencer and John Washington. The division between Spencer and Washington put John Washington's son Lawrence in possession of the Washington half in 1690. Later it became the property of Lawrence Washington's son Augustine, the father of George Washington.

The present house is an enlargement of one apparently built on the site of an earlier one by Augustine Washington, who lived there 1735-1738. His son Lawrence came there in 1743, when he renamed the plantation Mount Vernon in honor of Admiral Vernon under whom he had served in the West Indies. Lawrence Washington died in 1752 and was succeeded as proprietor of Mount Vernon by his half-brother, George Washington.

To Mount Vernon in 1759 Washington brought his wife, Martha Dandridge Custis, having previously enlarged the house from 1½ to 2½ stories. Just before the Revolution he planned additions, and when he was called away to war his kinsman Lund Washington supervised the work, which was completed after Washington returned in 1783. During the Revolution Washington visited Mount Vernon only twice, on the way to and from Yorktown in 1781. In 1789 he left to become President and lived in New York and Philadelphia, with brief visits to the plantation. He came back in 1797 and died in Mount Vernon Dec. 14, 1799. He was buried in the old family vault. He had made plans for a new burial vault and this was built in 1831. Both his remains and those of Martha, who died in 1802, were transferred there.

Mount Vernon was left to Washington's nephew, U.S. Supreme Court Justice Bushrod Washington, and by him to his nephew, John Augustine Washington, whose son, John A. Washington, Jr., was the last private owner. In 1853 when the place was run down, Miss Ann Pamela Cunningham of South Carolina organized the Mount Vernon Ladies' Assn., which bought the mansion and 200 acres, since extended to just under 500 acres. The Association reassembled original Washington furniture and repaired the buildings. It restored the kitchen garden, flower garden and experimental botanical garden, reconstructed the greenhouse and built a museum. Several trees planted by Washington still exist, and the boxwood dates from 1798.

The Association preserves house and tomb with the visitor's fee. The Regent of the Mount Vernon Ladies' Association is Mrs. Thomas Turner Cooke. About 31 states are represented by vice regents. The Resident Director is Chas. C. Wall; the Assistant Director is Walter C. Densmore.

National Arboretum

The National Arboretum, established in 1927 for the study of trees and plants, has become one of Washington's great show places. Occupying 415 acres of rolling land along the Anacostia River in the northeastern section of the city, it is administered by the Secretary of Agriculture through the Plant Science Research Division of the Agricultural Research Service.

The Arboretum is open every day of the year except Christmas. The visiting hours are as follows: April through October–8 a.m. to 7 p.m. Monday through Friday; 10 a.m. to 7 p.m. Saturdays and Sundays, November through March–8 a.m. to 5 p.m. Monday through Friday; 10 a.m. to 5 p.m. Saturdays and Sundays.

National Archives

The Declaration of Independence, the Constitution of the United States and the Bill of Rights are now enshrined in the National Archives Exhibition Hall. They are sealed in glass-and-bronze cases filled with inert helium gas. They can be lowered at a moment's notice into a large shockproof and fireproof safe.

The National Archives holds all the permanently valuable Federal records of the United States Government, 1774 to the present. As a research institution, it is designed to preserve these records and make them available to scholars, students, writers, and the general public.

The National Archives and Records Service is a part of the General Services Administration. Through the Presidential Libraries Office it administers the Franklin D. Roosevelt Library at Hyde Park, N.Y., the Harry S. Truman Library at Independence, Mo., the Dwight D. Eisenhower Library at Abilene, Kan., the Herbert Hoover Library at West Branch, Iowa, the Lyndon Baines Johnson Library at Austin, Tex., and the John Fitzgerald Kennedy Library, temporarily at Waltham, Mass., later to be in Cambridge, Mass.

The National Archives and Records Service is headed by Dr. James B. Rhoads, Archivist of the United States, Pennsylvania Ave. and 8th St. N.W. For Research information, call 202-963-6411. For Visitor information, call 202-962-2000.

National Gallery of Art

The National Gallery of Art, situated in an area bounded by Constitution Avenue and the Mall, between Third and Seventh Streets, was established by Joint Resolution of Congress Mar. 24, 1937, and opened Mar. 17, 1941.

The collections comprise gifts of over 150 donors (none of the works were acquired with Government funds) and cover more than a dozen schools in the history of Western art from the 13th Century to the present.

The building was erected with funds given by Andrew W. Mellon, who also gave his collection, consisting of 126 paintings and 26 pieces of sculpture, the latter largely from the Dreyfus Collection. The paintings cover the various European schools from the 13th Century to the 19th, and include such masterpieces as Raphael's Alba Madonna, the Niccolini-Cowper

Madonna, and St. George and the Dragon; van Eyck's Annunciation; Botticelli's Adoration of the Magi; and 9 Rembrandts. Twenty-one paintings came from the Hermitage in Leningrad. Also in this collection are the Vaughan Portrait of George Washington, by Gilbert Stuart, and The Washington Family, by Edward Savage.

The Samuel H. Kress Collection includes the great tondo of the Adoration of the Magi by Fra Angelico and Fra Filippo Lippi, the Laocoön by El Greco, and fine examples by Giorgione, Titian, Grünewald, Durer, Memling, Bosch, Juan de Flandes, François Clouet, Poussin, Watteau, Chardin, Boucher, Fragonard, David and Ingres. Also included are a number of masterpieces of sculpture, especially of the Italian and French schools.

The Widener Collection of over 100 paintings includes 14 Rembrandts, 8 Van Dycks, two Vermeers and examples of Italian, Spanish, English and French painting; also Renaissance and French sculpture and examples of the decorative arts.

The Chester Dale Collection includes masterpieces by Manet, Cézanne, Renoir, Toulouse-Lautrec, Monet, Modigliani, Pissarro, Degas, van Gogh, Gauguin, Matisse, Picasso, Braque, and a group of American paintings.

Major works of art by some of the most important artists of the last hundred years, including Picasso, Cézanne, Gauguin, and the American painter, Walt Kuhn, have been given to the Gallery by the W. Averell Harriman Foundation in memory of Marie. N. Harriman.

Pictures to round out the collection have been bought with funds provided by the late Ailsa Mellon Bruce, daughter of Andrew W. Mellon. Preeminent among them is the portrait of Ginevra de' Benci, the only generally acknowledged painting by Leonardo da Vinci outside Europe, and Pablo Picasso's Femme Nue, the key work of the artist's analytical cubist period. Among others are: Rubens' Daniel in the Lions' Den; Claude Lorrain's Judgment of Paris; Saint George and the Dragon attributed to van der Weyden; and a number of American paintings, including Cole's second set of The Voyage of Life.

Cézanne's great early portrait of his father and 351 paintings by George Catlin, mostly of North and South American Indians, are among recent acquisitions given by Paul Mellon, president of the Gallery and son of Andrew Mellon. A fine collection of French Impressionist pictures are on loan to the Gallery from Mr. and Mrs. Mellon.

The National Gallery's rapidly expanding graphic arts holdings, in great part given by Lessing J. Rosenwald, numbers about 30,000 items and dates from the 12th century to the present. Mr. Rosenwald's gift, one of the world's great collections of prints and drawings, forms the nucleus of the Gallery's holdings in this field.

The Index of American Design contains over 17,000 watercolor renderings and 5,000 photographs of American crafts and folk arts.

The Gallery's Education Department gives daily talks on the collections in the galleries. The Extension Service lends audio-visual materials, films, slide lectures and exhibits to schools, colleges and civic groups in some 4,000 communities in the United States and Canada. Nearly all of the Gallery's services are available to the public free of charge.

Construction is in progress for the expansion of the National Gallery in the block immediately east of the present building. Funds for this project have come from the Mellon family. The architect is I. M. Pei. Expected to be finished in 1976, the East Building will provide space for temporary exhibitions, for the National Gallery's growing collection of 20th Century paintings and sculpture, for a Center for Advanced Study in the Visual Arts, and for a greatly expanded library and photographic archive.

Open daily except Christmas and New Year's. Hours 10 a.m. to 5 p.m. weekdays, noon to 9 p.m. Sundays. From April to Labor Day open weekdays 10 a.m. to 9 p.m., noon to 9 p.m. Sundays.

National Geographic Society

The National Geographic Society, founded in 1888 "for the increase and diffusion of geographic knowledge," is the world's largest nonprofit scientific and educational institution. The Society produces the illustrated monthly *National Geographic*, books, maps, globes, atlases, other educational materials, and television programs. Its activities are supported by the dues of nearly 8,500,000 members.

The Society's 10-story headquarters building in Washington, D. C., was dedicated by President Lyndon B. Johnson in 1964. It attracts many thousands of visitors, including members of the Society from all over the world. Explorers Hall offers exhibits, artifacts, and mementoes depicting the organization's research and exploration activities.

In 1968 the Society occupied its new Membership Center Building on a 100-acre tract near Gaithersburg, Md. The building accommodates 1,200 employees charged with handling membership files, correspondence, changes of address, and other clerical operations.

Executive officers are: Melville Bell Grosvenor, editor-in-chief and chairman of the Board of Trustees; Thomas W. McKnew, advisory chairman of the Board; Melvin M. Payne, president of the Society; Gilbert M. Grosvenor, vice president and editor; Robert E. Doyle, vice president and secretary; Leonard Carmichael, vice president for research and exploration; Thomas M. Beers, vice president and associate secretary; Hilleary F. Hoskinson, treasurer.

The Pentagon

The Pentagon, headquarters of the Department of Defense, is the world's largest office building, twice as large as the Merchandise Mart in Chicago and with 3 times the floor space of the Empire State Building in New York. Situated on the Virginia side of the Potomac River, it houses 30,000 employees in offices that occupy 3,707,745 square feet.

The Pentagon was completed Jan. 15, 1943, at a cost of about $83,000,000. It covers 34 acres and has 204 acres of lawns and terraces. It is 5 stories high and consists of 5 rings of buildings connected by 10 corridors, with a 5-acre pentagonal court in the center. Each of the outermost sides of the building is 921 ft. long and the perimeter is seven-eighths of a mile. Total length of corridors is 17½ miles. There is a partial mezzanine below the first floor and a partial basement below that.

Smithsonian Institution

The Smithsonian Institution is one of the world's great historical, scientific, educational and cultural establishments. It comprises numerous facilities, mostly in the metropolitan Wash. D.C. area. It was founded by an Act of Congress in 1846, pursuant to a bequest of James Smithson, a British scholar-scientist, to the United States to found at Washington "an establishment for the increase and diffusion of knowledge among men." The Smithsonian, ever since its founding, has been a center for basic scientific research; it engages in programs of education and it is also the largest museum-gallery complex in the world. More than 14,000,000 persons visit its halls annually. S. Dillon Ripley became the 8th secretary of the Smithsonian Feb. 1, 1964.

The Anacostia Neighborhood Museum opened in 1967 as a satellite museum located in a low-income urban setting. The first of its kind in the nation, it provides an environment for open, nondirected learning through actual contact with real things, for adults and children who rarely, if ever, use existing museums and other cultural resources. Its programs include exhibits drawn from Smithsonian collections in art, history, and science; workshops, clubs and classes related to the exhibits; and exhibits assembled or made by the residents of the neighborhood. A mobile unit brings small portable exhibitions to the schools and street corners of the Anacostia community.

The Freer Gallery of Art, the gift of Detroit industrialist Charles Lang Freer, is an outstanding museum of, and center for research in art of the Far and Near East. The gallery also houses the Whistler Peacock Room and his etchings and paintings.

The Joseph H. Hirshhorn Museum and Sculpture Garden scheduled to open in 1973, will house works in the Hirshhorn collection which were donated in 1966 to the people of the United States. Primary emphasis is on art of the 20th century although the sculpture section ranges from antiquity to works of the most significant European and American contemporaries.

The National Museum of History and Technology has exhibits illustrating American culture, civil and military history and the history of science and technology. The museum consists of 3 floors of exhibitions, and food facilities for its visitors. In the rotunda the visitor will find the original Star-Spangled Banner and a Foucault pendulum demonstrating the earth's rotation. The Growth of the United States exhibit portrays American civilization from its inception to modern times and includes such items as an early 18th-Century printing press used by Benjamin Franklin, Eli Whitney's model of the cotton gin, the locomotive John Bull and a uniform worn by Gen. George Washington. Other major exhibits feature gowns of the First Ladies, the Petroleum Hall, the history of two per annum. American political and military history, numismatics, philately, ceramics and glass, musical instruments, timekeeping, physical and medical sciences, graphic arts, electricity, photography and news reporting. National treasures on display include the desk on which Thomas Jefferson drafted the Declaration of Independence and Samuel Morse's first telegraph. A popular attraction is an authentic 19th century country store-post office where mail is hand-stamped with a "Smithsonian Station" postmark.

The National Museum of Natural History serves as a national and international center for the natural sciences. It maintains the largest reference collection in the nation and conducts a broad program of basic research on man, plants, animals, fossil organisms, rocks, minerals, and materials from outer space. Exhibits show aspects of life and cultures in Asia, Africa and the Pacific. Other exhibits include fossil plants and invertebrate animals, fishes, amphibians, dinosaurs, primitive reptiles and archaeology of the Americas, osteology, physical anthropology, geology, the World of Mammals, the Hall of Birds, the Fenykovi Elephant and the Hall of Gems and Minerals, including the 44½ carat blue Hope diamond and the largest gem emerald on public exhibit, the 858 carat Gachala emerald.

The National Air and Space Museum. Pending new construction, the Arts and Industries building and the temporary Air and Space building house the historic Wright Brothers' airplanes, Charles A. Lindbergh's "Spirit of St. Louis," spacecrafts of John Glenn and Alan Shepard, the Apollo 11 command module which carried Armstrong, Collins and Aldrin to the moon and back, and other significant air and space artifacts.

The National Collection of Fine Arts, opened its doors in 1968 in the renovated Old Patent Office Building, noted for its classical Greek architecture. In addition to its Two-Century Survey of American Art, there are special and loan exhibits of American sculpture, painting, and graphics. **The National Portrait Gallery,** also located in the Old Patent Office Bldg., exhibits the likenesses of persons who have made significant contributions to the history, development and culture of the people of the United States.

The Renwick Gallery, a division of the National Collection of Fine Arts, is a new national showcase for creativity in design, crafts and the decorative arts. Two permanent public rooms, restored and furnished in styles of the post-Civil War period, and special temporary exhibitions can be seen in the renovated building.

The National Zoological Park is noted for its outstanding collections including two giant pandas from China. Its research includes investigation in animal behavior, ecology, nutrition and reproduction physiology, pathology and clinical medicine. Conservation-oriented studies cover maintenance of wild population and long-term captive breeding and care of endangered species.

The **Smithsonian Associates** was founded to stimulate interest and active participation in Smithsonian's work. Its membership programs for adults and young people include seminars, lectures, workshops, demonstrations, concerts, theater, exhibition previews, dramas, films, tours, and field and camping trips. *Smithsonian*, a monthly magazine of the arts, sciences, and history is available to members of the Associates.

The **Smithsonian Institution Traveling Exhibition Service** (SITES) organizes and circulates exhibitions for art and science museums, colleges and other educational institutions around the United States and Canada. More than one hundred twenty-five exhibitions are on continuous tour, with fifty or sixty openings of these shows occurring monthly across the country.

Washington National Monument

The **Washington National Monument** is a tapering shaft or obelisk of white marble, 555 feet, 5⅛ inches in height and 55 feet, 1½ inches square at base. Eight small windows, two on each side, are located at the 500 foot level, where Washington points of interest are indicated.

The capstone weighs 3,300 lbs. and was placed Dec. 6, 1884. The monument was dedicated Feb. 21, 1885, and opened Oct. 9, 1888. It weighs 81,120 tons. It is dressed with white Maryland marble in 2-ft. courses. The first 150 ft. are backed by rubble masonry. From that point to 452 ft. Maine granite was used as backing, and above 452 ft. marble was used. The face of the monument is primarily marble from Maryland. Set into the interior wall are 190 memorial stones from states, foreign countries and organizations. An iron stairway has 50 landings and 898 steps. A modern elevator takes sightseers to the 500-foot level in one minute, compared with 12 "precarious minutes" in 1888.

The erection of the monument by the Washington National Monument society with funds obtained by popular subscription was authorized by Congress in 1848. The cornerstone was laid July 4 of the same year. Work progressed slowly until 1854 when $300,000 had been subscribed and 152 feet of the shaft erected. In that year the enterprise became controversial and contributions ceased. Work was resumed in 1880 at Government expense by the Corps of Engineers.

The Monument is open 7 days a week, 9 a.m. to 5 p.m. Extended summer hours are 8 a.m. to 12 midnight. It is closed Christmas Day.

Famous Churches

The **National Shrine of the Immaculate Conception,** at Fourth St. and Michigan Ave., NE, Washington, D. C. is the largest Catholic Church in the United States and one of the largest in the world. Built by all the Bishops and Catholics of the U. S. it honors the Blessed Virgin Mary as Patroness of the United States. The Shrine is impressive not only in size but also in beauty, its blue and gold dome and soaring bell-tower having become Washington landmarks. Open daily from 7 a.m. to 8 p.m., Sunday masses, 7, 8, 9, 10, 11 a.m. and noon, 1:15 and 4:30 p.m. Free guided tours 9 a.m. to 5 p.m. daily; Sunday tours 2 p.m. to 4 p.m. Carillon concerts on Sundays and preceding organ and choral concerts. Organ recitals every Sun. at 7:00 p.m. (June through August) and 4th Friday Organ Recitals (Sept. through May).

Washington Cathedral, Massachusetts and Wisconsin Aves., NW, is atop Mt. Saint Alban, the highest point in Washington, D.C. It is the seat of the Presiding Bishop of the Episcopal Church and of the Bishop of Washington. Started in 1907, it is only three-quarters complete, and when finished in 1985 is expected to be the 6th largest church in the world. Notables buried in the Cathedral include Woodrow Wilson, Adm. George Dewey, Cordell Hull and Frank B. Kellogg. The Cathedral is considered one of the finest examples of Gothic architecture in the country.

Several Protestant churches commemorate the association of Presidents with their congregations. **St. John's Episcopal Church,** across Lafayette Sq. from the White House, designed by Benj. Latrobe in 1815, was regularly attended by Madison and F. D. Roosevelt and at times by other Presidents. **New York Ave. Presbyterian Church,** 1313 New York Ave., NW, preserves the pew in which Lincoln sat, also an original manuscript of the first draft of his first proposal to abolish slavery. Church rebuilt on same site in 1950-51.

The **new National Presbyterian Church,** on a 13-acre tract, at Nebraska Ave. and Van Ness St., N. W., was dedicated on May 10, 1970. The Church traces its origin to a group of stonemasons who met in a carpenter's shop in the grounds of the White House in 1795, later becoming the First Presbyterian Church in the District of Columbia. The Church of the Covenant founded in 1883 united with the original Presbyterian body in 1930 to become the congregation of the National Presbyterian Church. President Eisenhower was baptized by the pastor, Dr. Edward L. R. Elson, and became a member of the Church on Feb. 1, 1953. He laid the cornerstone of the new Church on his 77th birthday, Oct. 14, 1967, and the Chapel of the Presidents is dedicated to him. The Chapel of the Presidents contains the Eisenhower pew, and pews representing 16 additional presidents who worshipped with the congregation. The oldest president's pew, occupied by Jackson, Polk, Pierce, Buchanan and Cleveland is on view together with much historic memorabilia.

The **Islamic Center,** 2551 Massachusetts Ave., N.W. A magnificent monument of Islamic culture and outstanding landmark for visitors, a Mosque for worship, and an institute for study of Islamic culture.

Cherry Blossom Time

Cherry blossom time in Washington is looked upon as the opening of spring. The famous cherry trees encircle the Tidal Basin in West Potomac Park and for 2 miles line the roadside in East Potomac Park. A gift by the Mayor of Tokyo to the city of Washington, the original 3,000 trees were propagated from the trees on the Arawaka River in a suburb of Tokyo. The first trees were planted by Mrs. William Howard Taft, wife of the President, and by Viscountess Chinda, wife of the Japanese Ambassador, Mar. 27, 1912. Today many of the 650 trees around the Tidal Basin have white blossoms, while some have pink; deep pink blossoms are in East Potomac Park. The trees usually are in full blossom the first week in April, but no precise date can be given earlier than 10 days prior to full blossom, which lasts about one week.

Other Points of Interest

Pan American Union, 17th St. and Constitution Ave., NW., houses the General Secretariat of the Organization of American States, the oldest major international organization in the world, representing 23 American republics. Of traditional Spanish architecture with a tropical garden courtyard, the building is one of the more gracious sights in Washington. It contains the Hall of the Americas assembly room, permanent and temporary exhibits of Latin American art, the Columbus Memorial Library and, behind the building, the Aztec Gardens.

National Society, Daughters of the American Revolution on a block bounded by 17th and 18th Sts., and C and D Sts., N.W.

American National Red Cross, 17th and D Sts., NW, occupies three white marble buildings of neoclassic design, embellished with a Corinthian portico, colonnades and bronze doors. The Red Cross Museum is in the East building.

Federal Reserve Building, Constitution Ave., between 20th and 21st Sts. NW, is a four story white marble building of Georgian design, with formal gardens and fountains and tasteful but relatively simple interiors, built 1937.

The **Corcoran Gallery of Art,** 17th St., between New York Ave., and E. St., NW, Washington, was donated by William Wilson Corcoran in 1859. Other donors, including Sen. W. A. Clark, have augmented its collection. The Gallery is open 11 a.m. to 5 p.m., Tuesday through Sunday; closed Mondays, and on Jan. 1, July 4, Thanksgiving, and Dec. 24, 25 and 31. Admission is $1.00; free on Tues. and Weds. and at all times to military personnel and senior citizens and children under 12 accompanied by an adult.

New York City Museums, Libraries, Centers of Interest

See Index for Statue of Liberty

THE NEW YORK AQUARIUM, in Coney Island, exhibits marine life from all climes, with over 3,000 live specimens including whales, sharks, seals, sea lions, fish, penguins, etc.

THE NEW YORK BOTANICAL GARDEN occupies 230 acres in the Bronx. An 11-greenhouse Main Conservatory features seasonal shows and permanent exhibits of palms, tropical and temperate plants, ferns, orchids. There are specialized gardens, a museum of plant evolution and uses and a botanical library.

THE NEW YORK CULTURAL CENTER, Columbus Circle, features exhibitions of painting, sculpture, photography and documentary work, changed periodically. The building was designed by Edward Durrell Stone.

THE FRICK COLLECTION, 1 E. 70th St., was founded by Henry Clay Frick (1849-1919). The principal part of the Collection consists of 14th-19th Century paintings as well as sculpture.

THE SOLOMON R. GUGGENHEIM MUSEUM, Fifth Ave. and 89th St.; permanent collection contains over 3,000 paintings, drawings, sculptures and graphic works by 19th and 20th Century artists. The museum's unique spiral building was designed by Frank Lloyd Wright.

THE HAYDEN PLANETARIUM, facing 81st St., near Central Park W., presents dramatic representations of the skies inside a large hemispheric dome with a Zeiss planetarium projector and other instruments; about 9,000 stars are shown. Also: astronomy, space, weather, time exhibits; Guggenheim Space Theater.

THE HISPANIC SOCIETY OF AMERICA is a free public museum and reference library devoted to the art and literature of Spain and Portugal. It is on Audubon Terrace, between 155th and 156th Sts., west of Broadway. Collections run from ancient to modern.

THE JEWISH MUSEUM, Fifth Ave. at 92nd St., offers exhibitions of Jewish art and ceremonial objects and exhibits of Jewish interest. The permanent collection of Judaica is considered the most comprehensive in the world. There are lectures and a book and print shop.

THE METROPOLITAN MUSEUM OF ART, Fifth Ave. at 82nd St. With over 1,000,000 works of art, the Museum's collection is the largest of its kind in the Western Hemisphere. Great masters of all the ages of art are included in the collections: Egyptian, Greek, Roman, Ancient Near Eastern, Islamic, Far Eastern, Medieval, Arms and Armor, European, Pre-Columbian, American, Contemporary Arts, Musical Instruments, Costume Institute and Junior Museum.

THE CLOISTERS, in Manhattan's Fort Tryon Park, is a branch of the Metropolitan devoted to Medieval art and architecture in 5 cloisters and other early European structures.

THE MUSEUM OF THE AMERICAN INDIAN, Heye Foundation, Broadway at 155th St., maintains the world's largest collection of American Indian materials, extensive archeological and ethnological displays from North, Central and South America, as well as study and photographic facilities.

THE MUSEUM OF MODERN ART, 11 W. 53rd St., est. 1929, presents 20th Century painting, sculpture, drawings, prints, architectural and industrial design, photography and film.

The library contains about 30,000 vols. and a reference collection of more than 100,000 photographs. The Film Dept. has more than 12,000,000 ft. of film. Bookstore, restaurant and gift shop.

THE AMERICAN MUSEUM OF NATURAL HISTORY occupies a group of buildings at Central Park West between 77th and 81st Sts. Here are large exhibits of man and beast from the most primitive times to the present, with extensive reconstruction of fossilized remains, dioramas of men and animals in their natural settings, dinosaurs, birds, Indians, Eskimos and glass models of protozoa, rotifers and coelenterates. The collections of gems and ocean life are famous. Visitors may handle artifacts in the People Center.

THE MUSEUM OF THE CITY OF NEW YORK on Fifth Ave. at 104th St., illustrates the history and life of the city. Its collections include dioramas, paintings, prints, maps, photographs, portraits, miniatures, vehicles, ship models, costumes, silver, furniture, theatrical and musical memorabilia, toys and rare books.

THE NEW-YORK HISTORICAL SOCIETY, founded 1804, is at 170 Central Park W. between 76th and 77th Sts. The society maintains a museum devoted to Americana; a large gallery of American portrait, landscape and genre paintings; a reference library of American and especially New York history; manuscripts from all periods of the nation's past; maps, prints, broadsides and photographs. Of special interest are the original water color drawings by John James Audubon for his *Birds of America.* Also, fire engine, carriage, toy collections.

THE AMERICAN NUMISMATIC SOCIETY, founded 1858, maintains a museum of coins and other currency, ancient and modern medals and decorations at Broadway and 156th St.

THE PIERPONT MORGAN LIBRARY, 29 E. 36th St., is a research-library museum based on collections formed by J. Pierpont Morgan (1837-1913). Its collections comprise medieval and renaissance illuminated and textual mss., incunabula, autograph mss., letters and documents, book-bindings, master drawings and Rembrandt etchings.

THE NEW YORK PUBLIC LIBRARY: In 1973, its resources were placed at more than 34,500,000 items of which over 9,000,000 were books, over 10,000,000 manuscripts, over 6,000,000 pictures, 3,500,000 posters, photographs and broadsides, 6,000,000 pamphlets, scrapbooks and clippings. Of this total, 4,000,000 books and the pictures are in the collections of the Branch Libraries which are maintained by the City of New York and which operate 83 branch libraries in Manhattan, the Bronx and Staten Island and 6 bookmobiles. The Research Libraries, based at Fifth Ave. and 42nd St., include the Performing Arts Research Center, in Lincoln Center, and the Schomburg Center for Research in Black Culture, 103 W. 135th St.

SEAMEN'S CHURCH INSTITUTE, facing Manhattan's Battery Park, has dining room, cafeteria, collections of ships' bells and marine paintings, gym, sauna, showers, all open to public.

SOUTH ST. SEAPORT MUSEUM, on the East River waterfront in Lower Manhattan, is a growing restoration of earlier eras of New York's port. At piers on South St. at Fulton, the museum has 9 ships, including an iron-hulled windjammer, a Hudson River sidewheeler and the original Ambrose Lightship. Ashore on Fulton St. are museum galleries and a bookshop. Special features include puppet and craft shows, songfests, plays for children and adults, and seminars on nautical subjects. Restorations will include 100 early buildings with art shops, retail stores, apartments, offices and restaurants.

THE STATEN ISLAND INSTITUTE OF ARTS AND SCIENCES, founded 1881, has a museum of art, natural science, conservation and Indian life at 75 Stuyvesant Pl., St. George, S. I., and a library at 51 Stuyvesant Pl. It offers lectures and classes for children and adults.

WHITNEY MUSEUM OF AMERICAN ART, Madison Ave. at 75th St., holds exhibitions of group and individual artists, historical and contemporary. Comprehensive permanent collection of American art.

ZOOS. One of the world's largest zoos is the N.Y. Zoological Park (the Bronx Zoo), Pelham Parkway and Southern Blvd., the Bronx. About 3,000 mammals, birds, reptiles are displayed in its 252 acres, including African Plains exhibit, World of Birds and Children's Zoo. The city's Parks Administration runs the Central Park Zoo and the adjoining Children's Zoo at Fifth Ave. and 64th St. in Manhattan, the Prospect Park Zoo and Children's Farmyard in Brooklyn, and the Queens Zoo and Children's Farm in Flushing Meadows-Corona Park, Queens. The Staten Island Zoological Society operates the Staten Island Zoo and Children's Zoo in Barrett Park, West New Brighton.

Brooklyn Centers

BROOKLYN ACADEMY OF MUSIC, 30 Lafayette Ave., is the Brooklyn Center for the Performing Arts. It presents music, dance, theater, lectures and special membership events.

BROOKLYN BOTANIC GARDEN, Eastern Parkway, Washington and Flatbush Aves., has 50 acres of gardens, including rose, herb, wild flower and Japanese, and a fragrance garden for the blind.

THE BROOKLYN MUSEUM, Eastern Parkway and Washington Ave., estab. 1897, has comprehensive exhibitions in all major fields of art. An Outdoor Sculpture Garden contains ornaments from razed N. Y. area buildings.

THE BROOKLYN PUBLIC LIBRARY occupies the Ingersoll Building, Grand Army Plaza, and 55 branches. It operates two bookmobiles. The Ingersoll Building has 5 major-subject divisions and Periodicals Division, Audio-Visual section, children's room and telephone reference service.

Churches

JOHN ST. UNITED METHODIST CHURCH, 44 John St., erected 1841, on site of Wesley Chapel of 1768, "first Methodist preaching-house in America," houses oldest Methodist Society, formed 1766. Has noontime services for office workers. It also has a museum.

LITTLE CHURCH AROUND THE CORNER is the name by which the Church of the Transfiguration (Episcopal), 1 East 29th St., has become famous. It was so called in 1870 by a rector of another church, who, unwilling to read the burial service for an actor, advised Joseph Jefferson to apply there. It became the actors' church.

MARBLE COLLEGIATE CHURCH (Collegiate Reformed Protestant Dutch), Fifth Ave. and W. 29th St., erected 1854, is notable for the preaching by Dr. Norman Vincent Peale.

PLYMOUTH CHURCH OF THE PILGRIMS (Congregational), Orange St., Brooklyn, is a National Historic Site, built 1847, present structure 1849. Has windows illustrating Puritan influence on America and pew where Lincoln sat to hear Henry Ward Beecher, the first minister. In 1860 Beecher raised funds at an auction here to purchase the freedom of a slave girl, Pinky.

RIVERSIDE CHURCH (Interdenominational—American Baptist and United Church of Christ), Riverside Drive and W. 122nd St. The chief donor was John D. Rockefeller, Jr. The Tower, reminiscent of Chartres, is 100 ft. square, rises 392 ft.

CATHEDRAL OF ST. JOHN THE DIVINE on Morningside Heights, Amsterdam Ave. and W. 112th St. (Protestant Episcopal), was begun 1892 as a Romanesque building; the design was changed to Gothic. The church is 601 ft. long, 146 wide at nave and will be 330 ft. wide at transept. Two front towers will rise to over 250 ft.

ST. BARTHOLOMEW'S (Protestant Episcopal), Park Ave. and E. 51st St., exemplifies Byzantine-Romanesque design, with a French Romanesque portico in colored marble and mosaic and the main structure in amber-colored brick and stone.

ST. MARK'S-IN-THE-BOWERY (Protestant Episcopal), 2nd Ave. and E. 10th St., originally a chapel built on the farm of Director General Peter Stuyvesant in 1660, rebuilt in 1799. A statue of Stuyvesant in the churchyard was presented by Queen Wilhelmina of the Netherlands in 1915. The church has a modern theater and poetry center.

ST. PATRICK'S CATHEDRAL (Roman Catholic) occupies a block facing Fifth Ave., between E. 50th and E. 51st Sts., opposite Rockefeller Center. It was begun in 1858 in granite and marble in a Gothic revival style designed by James Renwick. It was opened in part in 1877 and dedicated May 25,1879. It has two spires, 330 ft. tall, and a 26-ft. rose window. St. Patrick's is the cathedral church of the Archdiocese of N. Y.

ST. PAUL'S CHAPEL OF TRINITY PARISH (Protestant Episcopal), Broadway and Vesey St., is the oldest colonial church edifice in Manhattan. It was opened Oct. 30, 1766. Much of the interior decoration was by L'Enfant, who laid the plans for Washington, D.C. There is a unique collection of 14 Waterford Irish cut glass chandeliers.

ST. PETER'S CHURCH (Roman Catholic), Barclay and Church Sts., has the form of a Greek temple with large porch, wide steps, granite pillars, erected 1836-38 to replace the original church of 1785 of the first Catholic parish of New York.

ST. VARTAN ARMENIAN CATHEDRAL (Armenian Church of America), 2nd Ave. and 35th St. Steel arches support a gilded, conic dome.

TEMPLE EMANU-EL, Fifth Ave. and 65th St., was erected 1929 by Congregation Emanu-El (Reform), which dates from 1845. It was built of limestone in early Romanesque style, its auditorium 77 ft. wide by 150 ft. long and 103 ft. high, one of the largest temples in the world. Noteworthy are the high arch at the entrance, the rose window, mosaics and 3 bronze doors.

TRINITY CHURCH (Protestant Episcopal) faces Broadway at the head of Wall St. It was built 1841-46 of brown sandstone in perpendicular Gothic, designed by Richard Upjohn, is 78 ft. wide by 202 ft. long and has an octagonal brownstone spire 280 ft. high. The first church was opened in 1698. In the churchyard are buried Alexander Hamilton, Robert Fulton, Capt. James Lawrence and Revolutionary soldiers who died in British prisons.

Historic Sites

EDGAR ALLAN POE COTTAGE, Grand Concourse and Kingsbridge Road, Bronx, is a restored cottage, built 1812, in which Poe lived 1846-49, and in which his wife, Virginia Clem, died, 1847.

FEDERAL HALL NATIONAL MEMORIAL, Wall and Nassau Sts., is a Greek Revival structure of 1842, originally the Custom House, later the U. S. Sub-Treasury. On the site stood the Colonial City Hall and later Federal Hall, where the Stamp Act, Continental and U. S. Congresses met and George Washington took the oath of office as President.

FRAUNCES TAVERN, Broad and Pearl Sts., was erected 1719 as the DeLancey mansion, acquired 1762 by Samuel Fraunces and operated as the Queen's Head Tavern. The Long Room was the scene of Washington's farewell to his officers, Dec. 4, 1783. It was restored by the Sons of the Revolution in the State of New York and is their headquarters. It contains a Revolutionary War museum and art gallery, free to the public.

GOVERNORS ISLAND, in New York harbor south of the Battery, contains 173.35 acres. The picturesque old fort, Castle Williams, was built 1807-1811 by Col. Jonathan Williams, nephew of Benj. Franklin. It is 200 ft. in diameter, was used as a prison for Confederates during the Civil War. Fort Jay, built 1794-1806, marks the site of Revolutionary fortifications.

Long an Army installation, the island was turned over to the Coast Guard July 1, 1966; it became the Coast Guard's largest base. Group tours of historic points arranged on request.

GENERAL GRANT NATIONAL MEMORIAL (GRANT'S TOMB), Riverside Dr. and W. 122nd St., is a formal Roman-style mausoleum in which Gen. U. S. Grant, 18th President, and Mrs. Grant are buried. The tomb is 165 ft. tall.

THE JUMEL MANSION, W. 160th St. and Edgecombe Ave., is a 3-story colonial mansion with 4-pillared portico built in 1765 by Col. Roger Morris of the British Army. From Sept. 15-Oct. 19, 1776, it was the headquarters of Gen. George Washington.

In 1810 Stephen Jumel bought 63 acres of the property. In 1833, the widowed Mrs. Jumel married Aaron Burr. He lived there briefly.

WASHINGTON SQUARE, at the foot of Fifth Ave., is the best known landmark of **Greenwich Village**, a colorful community and tourist attraction. Facing the lower end of Fifth Ave. is the marble **Washington Arch**, designed by Stanford White to commemorate the centenary of the first inauguration and completed in 1895. To the east and south are buildings of **New York University**, which also owns many of the old redbrick houses of Federal design on the north side.

Important Buildings

THE CITY HALL, headquarters of the Mayor, the City Council and the Board of Estimate of the City of New York, is in City Hall Park (the original Common), bounded by Broadway, Park Row and Chambers St. Erected 1803-1812, it is an adaptation of French Renaissance with a clock cupola surmounted by a figure of Justice.

Other public buildings in the vicinity are **Hall of Records,** north of Chambers St., and **Municipal Bldg.,** 40 stories arched over Chambers St. North of these bldgs. is Foley Square, the site of Collect Pond of colonial days. It is boxed by public buildings: **United States Court House,** built 1936, designed by Cass Gilbert, 32 stories; the hexagonal **State Supreme Court Bldg.;** the **State Office Bldg.;** the **Health Services Bldg.** and the **Federal Bldg.,** 41 stories. North on Centre St. are the **Civil Court, Criminal Court** and **Men's House of Detention.**

THE COLISEUM, facing Columbus Circle between W. 58th and W. 60th Sts., is New York's principal center for national and international exhibitions. Opened Apr. 28, 1956, it cost about $35,000,000. The Coliseum has over 320,000 sq. ft. of exhibition space.

EMPIRE STATE BUILDING, Fifth Ave., between W. 33rd and 34th Sts., is one of the world's tallest buildings (see also World Trade Center, below), 1,250 ft. high plus a 222-ft. television and FM radio transmitting tower. The building was completed May 1, 1931. More than 1,500,000 persons annually visit the 86th and 102nd floor Observatories. On a clear day viewers can see a distance of 80 mi.

LINCOLN CENTER FOR THE PERFORMING ARTS was opened Sept. 23, 1962, with a concert in Philharmonic Hall. The Center is located between W. 62nd and 66th Sts., Amsterdam and Columbus Aves. It is a private, nonprofit tax-exempt corporation of 8 constituent organizations. The New York State Theater, facing Philharmonic Hall, opened in 1964. The Vivian Beaumont Theater, for repertory, and the Library-Museum of the Performing Arts opened in 1965. The Metropolitan Opera House opened in 1966. The Juilliard School of music, including Alice Tully Hall, opened in 1969.

MADISON SQUARE GARDEN CENTER, Pennsylvania Plaza (7th-8th Aves., 31st-33rd Sts.), opened in the 1967-68 season. The huge development, above the modernized underground Pennsylvania RR station, includes a 29-story office building and the Sports and Entertainment Center which has the Garden Arena seating over 20,000, the 5,000-seat Felt Forum, 48 bowling lanes, the National Art Museum of Sport, an Exposition Rotunda for trade and walk-around shows, and a 500-seat Cinema.

PAN AM BUILDING, north of Grand Central Station, is one of the world's largest commercial office buildings. It has 59 floors rising 808 ft., with provision for a rooftop heliport, and was erected over the tracks of Grand Central Terminal. It covers a ground area of 3½ acres. Estimated office population is 17,000.

ROCKEFELLER CENTER, the largest privately owned business and entertainment center in America was started Sept., 1931. Its area includes the three blocks from 48th to 51st Sts. between Fifth Ave. and the Ave. of the Americas, a large portion of the 51st-52nd St. block and 4 blockfronts on the west side of the Ave. of the Americas between 47th and 51st Sts. There are 20 buildings with one more under construction. It has 175,000 daily visitors; over 66,000 work there.

The surface area of Rockefeller Center covers 24 acres; almost one half are leased for a long period from Columbia University. Rockefeller Center pays Columbia an annual rental of nearly $4,000,000. The lease with options for renewal runs until 2069.

The part of Rockefeller Center comprising theaters and radio and television studios is often referred to as Radio City. Studios of the National Broadcasting Co. are located in the 70-story RCA building (850 ft. tall). There is an Observation Roof on the 70th floor.

RADIO CITY MUSIC HALL, Ave. of the Americas and W. 50th St., largest indoor theater in the world, seats 6,000 people. Its stage, 144 ft. wide by 67 ft. deep, has a proscenium arch 60 ft. high and 100 ft. wide. Has first-run films and stage spectacles featuring the Rockettes, Ballet Company, Symphony Orchestra and guest artists.

NEW YORK STOCK EXCHANGE, visitors' entrance 20 Broad St., has visitors' gallery, films, guided tours, Monday through Friday, 10 a.m. to market closing.

AMERICAN STOCK EXCHANGE, visitors' entrance 78 Trinity Pl., has visitors' gallery, guides, films and other exhibits. Mon. through Fri. during trading hours.

UNITED NATIONS HEADQUARTERS occupies over 16 acres between 1st Ave. and F.D.R. (East River) Drive, E. 42nd and E. 48th Sts. Most unusual is the **Secretariat Bldg.,** 505 ft. high at front entrance, 286 ft. long and only 72 ft. wide. The 2 sides have 5,400 windows; the end walls are of 2,000 tons of Vermont marble. **General Assembly Bldg.** has a hall 165 ft. long, 115 ft. wide. **Conference Bldg.** houses 3 Council chambers, etc. There are guided tours daily.

WORLD TRADE CENTER, dedicated Apr. 4, 1973, on Manhattan's lower West Side, has twin towers of 110 stories, 1,350 ft. each (2nd in height to Chicago's Sears Tower) and 4 other buildings. In 1973, over 7,000 of an eventual 50,000 persons worked in trade firms in the North and South Towers. Construction of this office complex for international trade, a Port of N.Y. Authority facility, is to be completed in 1975.

A Guide to Avenue Addresses in New York City

To find the location of a number on the following Avenues of Manhattan, cancel the last figure of the number, divide the remainder by 2 and add the given key number.
Thus: Where is 596 Seventh Avenue? Divide 59 by 2 = 30, plus 12 = 42nd Street.

Ave. A.	add	4	Up to 600	add	18	Above 1800	add	20
Ave. B.	add	3	Up to 775	add	20	8th Ave	add	9
Ave. C	add	3	From 775 to 1286			9th Ave	add	13
Ave. D	add	3	see exception below:			10th Ave	add	13
1st Ave	add	4	Up to 1500	add	45	11th Ave	add	15
2nd Ave	add	3	Up to 2000 Mt. Morris Pk.			Amsterdam Ave	add	59
3rd Ave	add	10	Above 2000	add	24	Audubon Ave	add	165
4th Ave	add	8	Ave. of Americas (6th)			Columbus Ave	add	60
5th Ave. to 200	add	13	subtract 12 or 13			Convent Ave	add	127
Up to 400	add	16	7th Ave	add	12	Edgecomb Ave	add	134

Ft. Wash. Ave	add	158
Lenox Ave	add	110
Lexington Ave	add	22
Madison Ave	add	27
Manhattan Ave	add	100
Park Ave	add	34
Pleasant Ave	add	101
St. Nicholas Ave	add	110
Wadsworth Ave	add	175
West End Ave	add	59

Exceptions

Broadway: Up to 754 below East 8th St.
Above 754, apply above rule but deduct following key numbers:
From 754 to 858 deduct 29.
From 857 to 958 deduct 25.
Above 1000 deduct 31.
Note: From Washington Square North most crosstown streets have 100 numbers to the block. Numbering of these streets starts east and west from Fifth Avenue.

Riverside Drive: Below 567, drop last figure, add 75; do not divide by two.
Above 577, drop last figure, add 78.
Central Park West: Drop last figure, add 60.
5th Avenue: From 775 to 1286, drop last figure and deduct 18 from remainder.

Notable Tall Buildings in North American Cities

Height from sidewalk to roof, including penthouse and tower if enclosed as integral part of structure: actual number of stories beginning at street level. Asterisks (*) denote buildings still under construction Jan. 1974.

City	Hgt. ft.	Stories
NEW YORK CITY, MANHATTAN		
World Trade Center (2 towers)	1,350	110
Empire State, 34th St., 5th Ave	1,250	102
TV tower, 222 ft., makes total	1,472	
Chrysler, Lexington Ave. & 42d St.	1,046	77
60 Wall Tower, 70 Pine St	950	67
40 Wall Tower	900	71
RCA, Rockefeller Center	850	70
Chase Manhattan Bldg	813	60
Pan Am Bldg., 200 Park Ave	808	59
Woolworth, 233 Broadway	792	60
1 Penn Plaza	764	57
U.S. Steel, 165 Broadway	743	50
20 Exchange Place	741	57
Esso, 1251 Ave., of the Americas	735	54
One Astor Plaza	730	54
9 W. 57th St.	725	50
Union Carbide Bldg., 270 Park Ave	707	52
General Motors Bldg	705	50
Metropolitan Life, 1 Madison Ave	700	50
500 Fifth Avenue	697	60
Chem. Bank N.Y. Trust Bldg	687	50
Marine Midland Bldg., 140 Bway	677	52
McGraw Hill, 1221 Ave. of the Am.	674	51
Chanin, Lexington Ave. and 42d St.	680	56
55 Water St.	680	53
Lincoln, 60 E. 42d Street	673	53
Gulf & Western Bldg., 15 Columbus Circle	679	44
1633 Broadway	670	50
American Tobacco, 245 Park Ave	648	47
Irving Trust, 1 Wall Street	640	50
345 Park Ave.	634	44
Monsanto Bldg., 1114 Ave. of the Am.	630	50
1 New York Plaza	630	50
Home Insurance Co. Bldg.	630	44
Waldorf-Astoria, 301 Park Ave	625	47
Burlington House, 1345 Ave. of the Americas	625	50
10 East 40th Street	620	48
General Electric, Lexington Ave	616	50
New York Life, 51 Madison Ave	615	40
Penney Bldg., 1301 6th Ave	609	46
Celanese Bldg., 1211 Ave. of the Am.	592	45
U. S. Court House, 505 Pearl St.	590	37
Federal Bldg., Foley Square	587	41
Time & Life, 1271 Ave. of the Am.	587	47
Cooper Bregstein Bldg., 1250 Bway	580	40
1185 Ave. of the Americas	580	42
Municipal, Park Row & Centre St.	580	34
Westvaco Bldg., 299 Park Ave	574	42
Socony Mobil Bldg., East 42nd St	572	45
Sperry Rand Bldg., 1290 Ave. of Am	570	43
600 3rd Ave.,	570	42
N. Y. General, 230 Park Ave	565	35
30 Broad Street	562	48
Sherry-Netherland, 5th Ave., 59th St	560	40
Continental Can, 633 Third Ave	557	39
Sperry & Hutchinson, 330 Madison	555	39
Interchem Bldg., 1133 Ave. of the Americas	552	44
919 3rd Ave.	550	47
Burroughs Bldg., 605 3rd Ave	550	44
Bankers Trust, 33 E. 48 St	547	41
Transportation,Bldg., 225 Bway	546	45
Equitable Life, 1285 Ave. of the Am	540	42
Ritz Tower, Park Ave. & 57th St	540	41
Bankers Trust, 6 Wall Street	540	39
Equitable, 120 Broadway	538	42
1700 Broadway	533	41
Downtown Athl. Club, 19 West St	530	45
Nelson Towers, 7th Ave. & 34th St	525	45
Hotel Pierre, Fifth Ave. & 61st St	525	44
House of Seagram, 375 Park Ave	525	38
Random House, 825 3rd Ave	522	40
Du Mont Bldg., 515 Madison Ave.	520	31
26 Broadway	520	31
Newsweek Bldg. 444 Madison Ave	518	43
Sterling Drug Bldg., 90 Park Ave	515	41
First Nat'l City Bank.	515	41
Bank of New York, 48 Wall Street	513	32
Navarre, 512 Seventh Avenue	513	43
Williamsburg Savings Bank, Bklyn	512	42

City	Hgt. ft.	Stories
ITT—American,437 Madison Ave	512	40
International, Rockefeller Center	512	41
1407 Broadway Realty Corp.	512	44
United Nations, 405 E. 42 St	505	39
2 New York Plaza	504	40
22 East 40th Street	503	43
60 Broad St	503	39
Americana Hotel	501	51
World Apparel Center, 1411 Bway.	501	42
AKRON, OHIO		
Cathedral Tower Restaurant	554	60
First National Tower Bldg	330	28
Cascade, 10 W. Bowery	316	24
ALBANY, N. Y.		
Office Tower, So. Mall	589	44
University Towers	480	40
State Office Building	388	34
Agency (four bldgs.), So. Mall	310	23
Capitol Hill Twin Towers	260	20
ATLANTA, GA.		
*Peachtree Center Plaza Hotel	721	71
First National Bank, 2 Peachtree St.	544	41
Equitable Building, 100 Peachtree St.	453	34
National Bank of Georgia, 34 Peachtree	439	32
*Atlanta Hilton Hotel, 255 Courtland St.	404	34
*Tower Place, 3361 Piedmont Road	401	29
Trust Company of Georgia, 26 Pryor St.	377	28
Coastal States Insurance, 260 Peachtree	377	27
Peachtree Center Cain Building, 229 Peachtree St.	376	30
Peachtree Center Building, 230 Peachtree	374	31
Life of Georgia Building, 600 West Peachtree St.	371	29
Peachtree Center South, 225 Peachtree	332	27
Gas Light Tower, 235 Peachtree Street.	331	27
Hyatt Regency Hotel, 265 Peachtree	330	23
100 Colony Square, 1175 Peachtree St.	328	25
Georgia Power Building, 270 Peachtree	318	22
*Fairmont Hotel, 180 Fourteenth St.	310	28
400 Colony Square, 1195 Peachtree St.	308	23
*260 Piedmont Building, 260 Piedmont Av.	301	23
Merchandise Mart, 240 Peachtree St.	300	22
AUSTIN, TEXAS		
*American Bank	313	21
State Capitol	309	
Univ. of Texas Admin. Bldg	307	29
J. Frank Dobie Univ. Center	299	29
Westgate Bldg	261	24
BALTIMORE, MD.		
U.S. Fidelity & Guaranty Company	529	40
Maryland National Bank Bldg.	509	34
Blaustein Bldg.	354	30
Arlington Federal Bldg.	338	28
2 Charles Center South	336	30
Tower Bldg.	330	16
222 Saint Paul	328	37
Emerson Tower	319	15
First National Bank	305	21
2 Charles Center North	301	27
British American Bldg.	300	21
Lord Baltimore Hotel	287	19
1 Charles Center	284	24
Baltimore Gas and Electric Company	283	22
First Presbyterian Church	273	
Mercy Hospital	267	20
Hilton Hotel (2 towers)	264	23, 29
Federal Building, 31 Hopkins Plaza	260	18
BATON ROUGE, LA.		
State Capitol	460	34
American Bank Bldg.	310	25
Hilton Hotel	290	28
La. Natl. Bank Bldg.	277	21
BIRMINGHAM, ALA.		
First Natl. Southern Natural Bldg.	390	30
South Central Bell Hdqts. Bldg.	390	30
City Federal Bldg.	325	27
Thomas Jefferson Hotel	287	21

City	Hgt. ft.	Stories
Daniel Bldg.	283	20
Bank for Savings Bldg.	264	19

BOSTON MASS.

City	Hgt. ft.	Stories
John Hancock Tower	790	60
Prudential Tower	750	52
Boston Co. Bldg., Court St.	601	41
First National Bank of Boston	591	37
Employers Commercial Union Co's	507	40
New England Merch. Bank Bldg	500	40
U. S. Custom House	496	32
John Hancock Bldg	495	26
State St. Bank Bldg	477	34
Keystone Custodian Funds	400	32
State Office Bldg	350	22
Federal Bldg. & Post Office	345	22
Suffolk County Courthouse	330	19
Sheraton-Boston Hotel	310	29
State Service Center	300	23

BUFFALO, N.Y.

City	Hgt. ft.	Stories
Marine Midland, Main St.	529	40
City Hall	378	32
Rand Bldg., not incl. 40-ft. beacon	351	29
Erie County Savings Bank, Main St.	350	26
Manuf. & Traders Trust Co.	317	21
Liberty Bank	305	23
Electric Tower	294	18
10 Lafayette Square	400	23

CALGARY, ALTA.

City	Hgt. ft.	Stories
Husky Tower (Calgary Tower)	626	...
*Sun Oil Bldg.	397	32
*Capitol Plaza	389	40
Western Centre	385	40
Two Bow Valley Square	378	39
Mobil Tower	362	32
One Palliser Square	350	28
Place Concorde	339	37
Mount Royal House	330	32
International Hotel	321	36
Standard Life Bldg.	316	27
Penthouse Towers	312	34
Two Calgary Place	300	28
Royal Bank Bldg.	299	24
O'Neil Towers	280	31
Dawson Bldg.	279	22
Pacific 66 Plaza	275	22

CHARLOTTE, N.C.

City	Hgt. ft.	Stories
*NCNB Plaza, 101 S. Tryon	508	38
Jefferson First Union Tower	433	32
*Wachovia Bldg., 400 S. Tryon	420	32
N. C. Natl. Bank Bldg., 200 S. Tyron	299	18
Baugh Building, 112 S. Tryon	280	20

CHICAGO, ILL.

City	Hgt. ft.	Stories
Sears Bldg.	1,454	110
Standard Oil (Indiana)	1,136	80
John Hancock Center	1,127	100
Water Tower Plaza	850	74
First Natl. Bank	850	60
IBM Bldg	695	52
Civic Center (City Hall)	662	31
Lake Point Tower	645	70
Board of Trade, incl. 81 ft. statue	605	44
Prudential Bldg., 130 E. Randolph Antenna tower, 311 ft., makes total	912	...
1000 Lake Shore Plaza Apts.	590	55
Marina City Apts., 2 buildings	588	61
Mid Continental Plaza	580	50
Pittsfield, 55 E. Washington St.	557	38
Kemper Insurance Bldg.	555	45
Newberry Plaza, State & Oak	553	56
LaSalle Bank, 135 S. LaSalle St.	535	44
One LaSalle Street	530	49
111 E. Chestnut St.	529	56
Pure Oil, 35 E. Wacker Drive	523	40
United Ins. Bldg., 1 E. Wacker Dr.	522	41
Lincoln Tower, 75 E. Wacker Dr.	519	42
Carbide & Carbon, 230 N. Mich.	503	37
Walton Colonnade	500	44
Edgewater Beach Apts., 5445 Sheridan.	499	39
LaSalle-Wacker, 221 N. LaSalle St.	491	41
Amer. Nat'l Bank, 33 N. LaSalle St	479	40
Bankers, 105 W. Adams St	476	41
Brunswick Bldg.	475	37

City	Hgt. ft.	Stories
Continental Companies	475	45
American Furniture Mart	474	24
Sheraton Hotel, 505 N. Mich. Ave.	471	42
Playboy Bldg., 919 N. Mich. Ave	468	37
188 Randolph Tower	465	45
Tribune Tower, 435 N. Mich. Ave.	462	36
Equitable Life, 401 N. Michigan	457	35
Roanoke, 11 S. LaSalle St.	452	37
Blue Cross, 233 N. Michigan	440	40
Willoughby Tower, 8 S. Mich. Ave.	438	38
111 E. Wacker Drive	432	30
LaSalle Plaza, Monroe & Dearborn	420	38
McClurg Court Center Apts.	418	45
1300 Lake Shore Apts.	404	40
777 N. Michigan Apts.	400	39
Illinois Bell Telephone Bldg.	400	30
Chicago Temple not incl. cross	400	21

CINCINNATI, OHIO

City	Hgt. ft.	Stories
Carew Tower	574	48
Central Trust Tower	495	34
Dubois Tower, 5th & Walnut	423	32
Kroger Bldg.	345	25
U. of Cinn., Sander Hall	297	27
Terrace Hilton Hotel	273	19
Cincinnati Gas & Electric Co.	268	18
Provident Tower	267	20

CLEVELAND, OHIO

City	Hgt. ft.	Stories
Terminal Tower	708	52
Erieview Plaza Tower	529	40
Federal Bldg.	419	32
Cleveland Trust Tower No. 1	383	29
Ohio-Bell Telephone	365	22
Central Natl. Bank Bldg.	305	23
CEI Bldg	300	22
Union Commerce Bldg.	289	21
Standard Bldg	282	21
Crystal Tower,	280	26
East Ohio Bldg.	275	21
Bond Court, 1300 E. 9th	270	20
B. F. Keith Bldg.	267	21
Cleveland State Univ.	265	21
Superior Bldg., 815 Superior Ave	265	21
Winton Place	264	30

COLUMBUS, OHIO

City	Hgt. ft.	Stories
Thirty East Broad Street	620	41
LeVeque-Lincoln Tower, 50 W. Broad	555	47
Borden Building, 180 E. Broad	438	34
Columbus Center, 100 E. Broad	357	26
Ohio Bell Building, 75 N. 4th St.	348	26
Motorists Building, 471 E. Broad	297	21
Midland Building, 250 E. Broad	278	21

CORPUS CHRISTI, TEX.

City	Hgt. ft.	Stories
Wilson Tower	263	21

DALLAS, TEXAS

City	Hgt. ft.	Stories
First International Bldg.	710	56
First National Bank	625	52
Republic Bank Tower	598	50
Southland Life Tower	550	42
2001 Bryan St.	512	40
Republic Bank Bldg., not incl. 150-ft. ornamental tower	452	36
One Main Place	445	34
Ling-Tempco-Vought Tower	434	31
Mercantile Natl. Bank Bldg., not incl. 115-ft. weather beacon	430	31
Mobil Bldg	430	31
Fidelity Union Tower	400	33
Southwestern Bell Toll Bldg.	372	22
Court House & Fed. Office Bldg.	362	16
Mercantile Dallas Bldg	360	22
Sheraton Hotel	352	38
Elm Place, 1005-09 Elm St.	341	22
Main Tower	336	26
Adolphus Tower	327	27
Bell Telephone Bldg	326	23
Davis Bldg.	323	21
Manor Bank, Bank of Service & Trust.	319	24
Preston Tower	316	29
Tower Petroleum Bldg	315	23
Adolphus Hotel.	312	25
Fairmont Hotel.	308	24
Baptist Annuity Center	303	17
Life Bldg	302	22
Santa Fe Bldg. (1st unit)	300	20

City	Hgt. ft.	Stories
DAYTON, OHIO		
Winters Bank Bldg.	404	30
Hulman Bldg.	295	23
Knott Bldg.	297	21
Grant-Deneau Bldg.	290	22
1 First National Plaza	265	21
DENVER COLO.		
Brooks Towers, 1020 15th St.	420	42
*First of Denver Plaza	415	32
Colorado Nat'l. Bank, 17th & Curtis	389	26
Security Life Bldg.	384	30
Lincoln Center	366	30
First National Bank	365	28
Western Fed. Savings Bldg.	354	24
Colorado State Bank	352	26
Tower Merchandise Mart	330	20
Prudential Tower Plaza	322	25
Hilton Hotel	299	21
Denver U.S. Natl. Bldg.	293	25
Denver Club Bldg	277	23
Brown Palace Hotel, West	269	22
State Social Services Bldg.	263	12
Federal Office Bldg	261	18
DES MOINES, IOWA		
Financial Center, 7th & Walnut	345	25
Equitable Bldg.	318	19
State Capitol.	275	4
DETROIT, MICH.		
Penobscot, 637 Griswold	557	47
Guardian, 500 Griswold	485	40
Book Tower, 1227 Wash Blvd	472	35
Cadillac Tower, 51 Cadillac Sq.	437	40
David Stott, 1150 Griswold	436	38
Mich. Cons. Gas Co. Bldg	430	32
Fisher, W. Grand Blvd. & 2d St	420	28
Detroit Bank & Trust Co. Bldg.	370	28
Walker Cisler	365	25
David Broderick Tower	358	34
Buhl, 535 Griswold	350	26
Michigan Bell Telephone	340	19
1st Federal Savings & Loan Assn.	338	23
Pontchartrain Motor Hotel	336	23
Michigan Bell Telephone	327	17
1300 Lafayette East	325	30
First National Bldg.	319	25
*The Executive Plaza, 1200 6th Ave.	313	21
Sheraton Cadillac Hotel	310	28
Mich. Blue Cross/Blue Shield	307	22
The Jeffersonian	305	29
EDMONTON, ALBERTA		
AGT Tower, 10020-100 St.	441	34
CN Tower, 10004-104 Ave.	365	26
Edmonton Centre, Tower One	325	25
Edmonton House, 9939 Bellamy Hill	315	34
Imperial Oil, 10025 Jasper Ave.	272	24
Centennial Bldg., 10015-103 Ave.	262	20
MacDonald Place, 9925 Jasper Ave.	261	26
FORT WAYNE, IND.		
Ft. Wayne Natl. Bank	339	26
Lincoln Natl. Bank.	312	23
FORT WORTH, TEXAS		
Ft. Worth Natl. Bank	454	37
Continental Natl. Bank Bldg.	380	30
Continental Life Ins. Bldg.	282	23
Ft. Worth Natl. Bank, 800 Main St.	275	20
Texas Electric, 7th & Lamar.	275	18
First Natl. Bank	272	22
W. T. Waggoner Bldg.	270	22
Service Life Center	270	19
HALIFAX, N.S.		
Fenwick Towers	300	31
HARRISBURG, PA.		
State Capitol.	272	6
Presbyterian Apts., 322 N. 2nd Ave.	260	23
HARTFORD, CONN.		
Travelers Ins. Co. Bldg.	527	34
Hartford Bldg.	420	22
Hartford Natl. Bank & Trust.	360	26
Bushnell Plaza	263	27

City	Hgt. ft.	Stories
HONOLULU, HAWAII		
Ala Moana Hotel	390	38
Pacific Trade Center	360	30
*Regency Tower, 2525 Date St.	350	42
Yacht Harbor Towers	350	40
Rainbow Plaza	348	37
Waipuna	343	38
*The Villa on Eaton Square	335	37
The Skyrise	333	38
Reed & Martin Apt. Bldg.	321	36
1350 Ala Moana	309	33
Ala Moana Bldg.	300	23
HOUSTON, TEXAS		
One Shell Plaza	714	50
*1100 Milam Bldg.	651	47
Exxon Bldg.	606	44
2 Houston Center	570	40
Dresser Tower.	550	40
United Gas Bldg.	518	35
Tenneco Bldg.	502	33
*Pennzoil, 700 Milam	495	34
Conoco Bldg	465	32
One Allen Center	452	34
Gulf Bldg.	428	37
First City Natl. Bank	410	32
Houston Lighting & Power	410	27
Neils Esperson Bldg.	409	31
Regency Hyatt Hotel	401	34
Houston Natural Gas Bldg	386	28
Bank of the Southwest.	369	24
Sheraton-Lincoln Hotel	352	28
Two Shell Plaza	341	26
American General Life	337	25
Transco	333	25
609 Fannin Bldg.	325	22
Holiday Inn	325	30
Capitol Natl. Bank	320	21
St. Luke's Hospital	316	26
500 Jefferson Bldg.	316	21
Marathon Manufacturing Co. Bldg.	313	21
Sterling Bldg.	312	22
Melrose Bldg.	308	21
Chamber of Commerce Bldg	306	22
Control Data Center	303	22
First National Life Bldg	302	22
Prudential Bldg.	300	21
Kellogg Bldg.	300	22
INDIANAPOLIS, IND.		
Indiana Natl. Bank Tower	504	37
City-County Bldg.	377	26
Indiana Bell Telephone	320	20
Riley Towers (2 bldgs).	294	30
Monument Circle.	284	—
JACKSONVILLE, FLA.		
Independent Life & Accident Ins. Co.	535	37
Gulf Life Ins. Co. Bldg.	432	28
Prudential Ins. Co. of America	295	22
Blue Cross-Blue Shield	287	20
Atlantic National Bank.	278	19
Universal Marion Bldg.	268	20
JERSEY CITY, N.J.		
Medical Center, Tuberculosis	320	24
Medical Center, 4 other bldgs	294	22
KANSAS CITY, MO.		
Kansas City Light and Power Bldg.	476	32
City Hall	443	29
Federal Office Bldg	413	35
Commerce Tower.	402	32
Southwest Bell Telephone Bldg.	394	27
Continental Bldg	365	30
A. T. & T. Long Line Bldg	331	20
Bryant Bldg.	319	26
Federal Reserve Bldg.	311	21
Holiday Inn	300	28
LAS VEGAS, NEV.		
International Hotel	346	30
Landmark Tower	308	27
Mint Hotel	268	26
LITTLE ROCK, ARK.		
*First National Bank	454	33
Worthern Trust	375	28
Bank Union National	331	24

City	Hgt. ft.	Stories
LOS ANGELES, CALIF.		
United Calif. Bank	858	62
Security Pacific Natl. Bank	738	55
Atlantic Richfield Plaza (2 bldgs.)	699	52
Crocker-Citizen Plaza	620	42
Theme Towers	571	44
Union Bank Square	516	41
City Hall	454	28
Equitable Life Bldg.	454	34
Occidental Life Bldg.	452	32
Mutual Benefit Life Ins. Bldg.	435	31
Broadway Plaza	414	33
1900 Ave. of Stars	398	27
1 Wilshire Bldg	395	28
Calif. Fed. Savings & Loan Bldg.	363	28
Century City Office Bldg.	363	24
Bunker Hill Towers	349	32
International Industries Plaza	347	24
City Natl. Bank Bldg.	344	24
Wilshire West Plaza	327	24
Luxury Towers	316	27
Getty Realty Bldg	312	22
Water & Power Bldg.	310	20
6312 Wilshire Office Bldg.	307	21
Los Angeles Fed. Savings Bldg	306	22
Barrington Plaza Bldg	300	25
LOUISVILLE, KY.		
First Natl. Bank	512	30
Citizen's Plaza	420	30
Liberty Natl. Bank & Trust Co. Tower	338	26
Galt House	325	25
Louisville Trust Bldg.	312	24
800 Apartments Bldg.	290	29
Lincoln Income Life Ins. Bldg.	289	16
Blanton House	260	20
MEMPHIS, TENN.		
100 N. Main Bldg.	430	37
Commerce Square	396	31
Sterick Bldg.	365	31
Clark, 5100 Poplar	365	32
First Natl. Bank Bldg	332	25
Lowenstein's Towers	296	25
Lincoln American Life Tower	290	22
White Station Tower	280	24
Exchange Bldg	264	22
MIAMI, FLA.		
One Biscayne Corp.	456	40
First Federal Savings & Loan	375	32
Dade County Court House	357	28
Ferre Bldg.	340	30
Palm Bay Club	279	24
MILWAUKEE, WIS.		
First Wisc. Center & Office Tower	601	40
City Hall	350	9
Wisconsin Telephone Co	313	19
Marine Plaza Bldg	288	22
Allen-Bradley Co.	280	17
Marshall & Ilsley Bank	277	21
Regency House Apts	274	27
Prospect Towers Apts.	268	23
Juneau Village Apts.	265	28
Schroeder Hotel	265	24
Carl Sandburg Dorm. (U. of Wisc.)	264	26
Locust Court Apts.	262	24
MINNEAPOLIS, MINN.		
IDS Center	772	57
Foshay Tower, not including 163-ft. antenna tower	447	32
Hennepin County Civic Center	403	24
First Natl. Bank Bldg	366	28
Municipal Building	355	14
North Western Bell Telephone	350	26
Batzli Cedar North Project	337	39
Rand Tower	311	26
Midwest Federal Savings & Loan	276	20
River Towers Apts	260	27
MONTREAL, P.Q.		
Place Victoria	624	47
Place Ville Marie	616	49
Canadian Imperial Bank of Commerce	580	45
Chateau Hotel	480	38
CIL House	429	32
La Tour Louriew	425	36
Banque Canadienne National	390	32
Place du Canada	372	33
Alex Nihon Plaza	331	33

City	Hgt. ft.	Stories
NASHVILLE, TENN.		
Natl. Life & Acc. Ins. Co	452	31
Nashville Life & Casualty Tower	409	30
Andrew Jackson State Office Bldg.	386	17
First American Tower	354	28
Third Natl. Bank Bldg.	292	20
Parkway Towers	261	21
NEWARK, N. J.		
National Newark & Essex Bank	465	36
Raymond-Commerce	448	36
Prudential Corporate Bldg.	369	27
Western Electric Bldg.	359	31
Gateway 1, tower	355	30
Prudential Insurance Company	353	21
American Insurance Company	326	21
N. J. Bell Telephone Co.	275	21
Gateway 2, Western Electric	272	20
Mutual Benefit Life Ins. Co	271	18
NEW HAVEN CONN.		
Knights of Columbus Hqs	320	24
NEW ORLEANS, LA.		
One Shell Square	697	50
Plaza Tower	531	45
Marriott Hotel	450	42
Bank of New Orleans	400	31
Intl. Trade Mart Bldg.	407	33
225 Baronne St.	362	28
Hibernia Bank Bldg.	355	23
American Bank Bldg.	330	23
Canal La Salle Bldg.	288	24
Charity Hospital of Louisiana	279	19
Lykes Center, 300 Poydras	276	22
OAKLAND, CALIF.		
Ordway Bldg. 2150 Valdez St.	404	28
Kaiser Bldg	390	28
City Hall	319	15
Tribune Tower	305	21
United Calif. Bank Bldg.	297	18
Blue Cross Bldg.	296	21
Telephone Bldg	289	15
565 Bellevue Apts	270	25
St. Paul Towers	267	22
OKLAHOMA CITY, OKLA.		
Liberty Tower	500	36
First National Bank	493	33
City National Bank Tower	440	32
Kerr-McGee Center	393	30
Fidelity Plaza	310	15
Southwestern Bell Telephone	303	15
Hotel Oklahoma	298	24
The Regency Tower	288	25
Southwestern Bell Telephone	265	16
Citizen's Tower Bldg.	265	20
United Founders Life Bldg.	264	20
OMAHA, NEBR.		
Woodmen Tower	453	30
Northwestern Bell Telephone Hdqrs.	334	16
Masonic Manor	320	22
First Natl. Bank	295	22
Mutual of Omaha	269	13
OTTAWA, ONT.		
Place de Ville, Tower C.	368	29
Place Bell Canada	318	26
D.B.S. Tower	308	26
Holiday Inn	308	28
Parliament Bldgs., Peace Tower	291	...
Skyline Hotel	286	25
Dept. of National Defense	261	22
PHILADELPHIA, PA.		
City Hall Tower incl. 37-ft. statue of Wm. Penn.	548	7
Fidelity Mutual Life Ins. Bldg.	490	38
Phila. Saving Fund Society	490	39
Central Penn Natl. Bank	490	36
Industrial Valley Bank Bldg	482	32
Philadelphia National Bank	475	25
Fidelity Bank Bldg.	410	30
Two Girard Plaza	404	30
2000 Market St.	399	29

City	Hgt. ft.	Stories
Lewis Tower, 15th & Locust	397	33
Fifteen Hundred Locust	390	44
Philadelphia Electric Co.	384	27
Penn Mutual Life	375	20
The Drake, 15th & Spruce	375	33
Medical Tower, 255 So. 17th	364	33
State Bldg., 1400 Spring Garden	351	18
Packard, 15th & Chestnut	340	25
Inquirer Building	340	18
Dorchester Aprt.	339	32
Transportation Centre	336	18
Land Title, Broad & Chestnut	331	22
Suburban Benefit Bldg.	330	...
Edison, 9th & Sansom	325	23
Penn Towers	320	31
1 East Penn Square	319	24
Architects, 17th & Sansom	316	24
1500 Walnut Street	313	23
Rittenhouse Towers	312	28
Society Hill Towers	309	32
1616 Walnut Street	309	25
Sheraton Hotel, inc. Tower	307	21
Kennedy House	306	29
Mutual Benefit Bldg.	304	20
Hopkinson House	301	35
1528 Walnut St.	300	21

PHOENIX, ARIZ.

Valley National Bank	483	40
First National Bank	372	27
First Federal Savings Bldg.	341	26
Mayer Central Plaza	315	25
Regency Apts.	297	21
Rosenzweig Center No. 2	280	22
Rosenzweig Center No. 1	271	17

PITTSBURGH, PA.

U.S. Steel Bldg.	841	64
Gulf, 7th Ave. and Grant St.	582	44
University of Pittsburgh	535	42
Mellon Bank Bldg.	520	41
1 Oliver Plaza	511	39
Grant, Grant St. at 3rd Ave.	485	40
Koppers, 7th Ave. and Grant	475	34
Pittsburgh National Bldg.	424	30
Alcoa Bldg., 425 Sixth Ave.	410	30
Westinghouse Bldg.	355	23
Oliver, 535 Smithfield St.	347	25
Gateway Bldg. No. 3	344	24
Smithfield Plaza	341	26
Federal Bldg., 1000 Liberty Ave.	340	23
Bell Telephone, 416 7th Ave.	339	21
Hilton Hotel	333	22
Frick, 437 Grant St.	330	20
301 Fifth Ave.	322	24
Washington Plaza Apts.	300	23
Commonwealth, 316 Fourth Ave.	300	21

PORTLAND, ORE.

First Natl. Bank of Oregon	538	41
Georgia Pacific Bldg.	367	27

PROVIDENCE, R.I.

Industrial National Bank	420	26
Rhode Island Hospital Trust Tower	408	30
First Hartford Realty Corp.	301	23

RICHMOND, VA.

City Hall	310	18
Central National Bank Bldg.	282	24
First National Bank Bldg.	262	19
Fidelity Bankers Life	261	23

ROCHESTER, N. Y.

Xerox Tower	443	30
Lincoln First Tower	390	26
Eastman Kodak Bldg	360	19
Marine Midland Bank Bldg	280	22
Lincoln Rochester Trust Bldg	261	15

ST. LOUIS, MO.

Gateway Arch	630	...
Laclede Gas Bldg., 8th & Olive	400	34
S. W. Bell Tele. Bldg	398	31
Civil Courts	387	13
*Mercantile Trust Bldg.	380	35
Queeny Tower	321	19

City	Hgt. ft.	Stories
Counsel House Plaza	320	27
Park Plaza Hotel	310	30
Riverfront Inn, 3rd St	301	30
Mansion House	285	28
500 Broadway	282	22
Continental Bldg.	277	23
Railroad Exchange Bldg.	277	21
Pierre Laclede Plaza Bldg.	276	23
77 Bonhomme Bldg.	275	25
*Boatman's Bank Tower	275	22
Equitable Bldg.	275	21
Lennox Hotel	275	25
500 Broadway Bldg.	270	22
Park Tower Apts.	264	24
Missouri Pacific Bldg.	264	23
Chromallay Bldg.	263	22
Gateway Towers, 1 Mem. Drive	261	20
City Towers Aprt.	260	22

ST. PAUL, MINN.

First Natl. Bank Bldg., not incl. 100-ft. sign	402	32
Osborn Bldg	368	20
Kellogg Square Apts.	366	32
Northwestern Bell Telephone Bldg.	340	15
*American National Bank Bldg.	335	25
St. Paul Cathedral	307	.....
U.S. Post Office Bldg.	274	12
St. Paul Hilton Hotel.	273	24
City Hall & Court House	261	18

SALT LAKE CITY, UTAH

L.D.S. Church Office Bldg.	420	30
*34 South State	351	27
City & County Bldg.	290	...
State Capitol	285	...
Univ. Club Bldg	277	24
Kennecott Bldg.	267	18
Walker Bank Bldg	262	18

SAN ANTONIO, TEXAS

Tower of the Americas	622	....
Tower Life	404	30
Nix Professional Bldg.	375	23
Natl. Bank of Commerce	310	24
Alamo National Bldg.	288	23
Milam Bldg.	280	20
Southwestern Bell Telephone Co	260	16

SAN DIEGO, CALIF.

So. Calif. First Natl. Bank Bldg.	388	25
U.S. Natl. Bank Bldg.	340	25
Financial Square, 6th & B Sts.	339	24
Union Bank	320	22
San Diego Gas & Electric Bldg.	293	21
Charter Oil Bldg.	281	23
Security Pacific Natl. Bank Bldg.	278	18
Home Tower	278	18

SAN FRANCISCO, CALIF.

Transamerica Pyramid	853	48
Bank of America	778	52
Security Pacific Bank	569	45
Wells Fargo Bldg.	561	43
Security Pacific Bank	569	45
*Standard Oil, 575 Market St.	551	39
Aetna Life	529	38
First & Market Bldg.	529	38
Metropolitan Life	524	38
Hilton Hotel	493	46
Pacific Gas & Electric	492	34
Union Bank	487	37
Pacific Insurance	476	34
Hartford Bldg.	465	33
Mutual Benefit Life	438	32
Russ Bldg.	435	31
Telephone Bldg.	435	26
*Levi Strauss	412	31
*Calif. State Automobile Assn.	399	29
Alcoa Bldg.	398	27
St. Francis Hotel	395	32
Shell Bldg.	386	29
Great Western Savings	359	26
Union Square Hyatt House Hotel	355	35
Equitable Life Bldg	355	25
Fox Plaza	354	29
International Bldg	350	22

City	Hgt. ft.	Stories	City	Hgt. ft.	Stories
450 Sutter Street	343	26	390 Bay Street	452	33
Cathedral Apartments	340	21	Commercial Union Tower, (T-D Centre)	440	32
Royal Towers	330	24	The Fairbanks	405	42
Fairmont Hotel	330	29	Royal York Hotel	400	23
Bechtel Bldg	327	23	Leaside Park Apts.	387	43
Standard Oil Bldg	327	22	Travellers Insurance Co.	369	27
Crown Zellerbach Bldg	320	20	Hyatt Regency Hotel	365	31
Standard Oil, 555 Market St	317	22	Summerhill Square	354	37
Sir Francis Drake Hotel	315	22	MacDonald Block	349	24
Eichler Summit	314	29	Richmond-Adelaide	340	26
Federal Office Bldg	312	20	*Royal Bank Plaza, No. Tower	336	25
Westbury Hotel	312	29	Toronto Star Bldg.	329	25
Bank of Calif.	311	21	City Hall, East Tower	327	27
100 McAllister Bldg.	310	28	Sutton Place	318	33
111 Sutter Bldg.	309	24	Prudential Bldg.	300	32
Mark Hopkins Hotel	306	19			
Mills Tower	302	22	**TULSA, OKLA.**		
City Hall	301	5			
1200 California Apts	300	27	1st National Tower	516	41
			4th Natl. Bank of Tulsa	412	32
SEATTLE, WASH.			National Bank of Tulsa	400	24
			Cities Service Bldg.	388	28
Seattle-1st Natl. Bank Bldg.	609	50	Univ. Club Tower	377	32
Space Needle	607	...	Philtower	343	23
Bank of Calif. 900 4th Ave.	548	42			
L.C. Smith Bldg.	522	42			
Federal Office Bldg.	487	37	**VANCOUVER, B.C.**		
Financial Center	414	30			
Washington Plaza Hotel	397	40	*Vancouver Square	538	32
*Safeco Ins. Co. Bldg.	630	23	*B.C. Tel Tower	517	40
Northern Life Tower	314	27	Royal Bank Centre	468	37
Norton Bldg	310	17	*Scotiabank Bldg.	462	36
Pacific Bldg.	298	22	T-D Bank Tower	410	31
Washington Bldg	289	21	Granville Square	403	30
IBM Bldg.	280	20	Sheraton-Landmark Hotel	394	41
Hilton Hotel	275	25	Bank of Montreal Tower	386	28
Exchange Bldg.	275	23	Regency-Hyatt House Hotel	357	36
Plaza 600	270	21	Hotel Vancouver	352	22
Park Place	270	20	Board of Trade Tower	342	26
Royal Crest Condominiums	267	26	MacMillan-Bloedel Bldg.	340	28
Tower 801	262	25	Guinness Tower	328	23
			Marine Bldg.	321	21
SYRACUSE, N.Y.			Martello Tower	300	31
			Denman Place	293	32
State Tower	315	22	BCFP Bldg.	292	21
Mony Office Bldg.	268	19	B.C. Hydro Bldg.	290	22
Carrier Tower	268	19	One Burnaby Centre	282	29
			Blue Horizon Hotel	282	30
TAMPA, FLA.			One Bentall Centre	281	22
			Sunset Plaza	280	28
First Financial Tower	458	36	The Imperial	273	28
Exchange Nat'l. Bldg.	280	22	Century Plaza Hotel	270	28
			Panorama Towers	261	28
TOLEDO, OHIO			*Plaza International Hotel	260	25
Owens-Corning Fiberglas Tower	400	30			
Owens Illinois Bldg	368	27	**WILMINGTON, DEL.**		
Toledo Trust Bldg	288	21			
			Hercules Tower	287	23
TORONTO, ONT.			American Life Ins. Co. Bldg	282	21
			Brandywine Bldg	259	19
*CN Tower, Metro Centre	1,805	...			
*Bank of Montreal Centre	930	73	**WINNIPEG, MAN.**		
Commerce Court	784	57			
Toronto-Dominion Bank Tower (T-D Centre)	740	56	Richardson Bldg., 1 Lombard Place	439	34
			55 Nassau St	354	39
Royal Trust Tower	588	46	North Star Inn	300	30
Manufacturers' Life Bldg.	535	52	1 Evergreen Place	294	32
*Royal Bank Plaza, So. Tower	480	37			
Bank of Commerce Bldg.	476	34	**WINSTON-SALEM, N.C.**		
Simpson Tower	470	33			
Four Seasons Sheraton Hotel	470	43	Wachovia Bldg.	410	30
Two Bloor Street West	463	34	Reynolds Bldg.	315	21

Tall Buildings In Other Cities

Figures denote number of stories. Height in feet is in parentheses.

Cape Canaveral, Fla., Vehicle Assembly Bldg., 40 (552); Albuquerque, N.M., National Bldg., 18 (272); Allentown, Pa., Power & Light Bldg., 23 (320); Amarillo, Texas, American Natl. Bank, 31 (374); Bethlehem, Pa., Martin Tower, 21 (332); Charleston, W. Va., Kanawha Valley Bldg., 20 (384); Frankfort, Ky., Capital Plaza Office Tower, 28 (338); Galveston, Tex., American National Ins., 20 (358); Greenville, S.C., Daniel Bldg., 22 (305); Knoxville, Tenn., Andrew Johnson Hotel, 18 (254); Lansing, Mich., Michigan Nat'l Tower, 25 (300, not including antenna tower); Lincoln, Neb., State Capital (432 incl. 32-ft. bronze statue); Long Beach, Calif. International Tower, 27 (277); Mobile, Ala., First Natl. Bank, 33 (420); Norfolk, Va., Va. Natl. Bank, 23 (304); Reading, Pa., Berks County Courthouse (280); Shreveport, La., Beck Bldg., 20 (266); So. Bend, Indiana, American National Bank Bldg., 25 (312); Springfield, Mass., Valley Bank Tower, (370); Tacoma, Wash., Washington Plaza, 23 (290); Waco, Tex., Amicable Life Bldg., 21 (282, incl. observation tower).

Latitude, Longitude and Altitude of North American Cities

Source: National Ocean Survey (NOAA) for geographic position.

Altitudes U.S. Geological Survey and various sources. *Approx. altitude at Downtown Business Area U.S.; in Canada at tower of major Airport.

Source for Canadian Cities: Geodetic Survey of Canada, Dept. of Energy, Mines and Resources.

City	Lat. (° ' ")	Long. (° ' ")	Alt.* (Feet)
Abilene, Texas	32 27 54	99 42 48	1710
Akron, Ohio	41 05 00	81 30 44	874
Albany, N.Y.	42 39 01	73 45 01	20
Albuquerque, N.M.	35 05 01	106 39 05	4,945
Allentown, Pa.	40 36 11	75 28 06	255
Alert, N.W.T.	82 29 50	62 21 15	95
Altoona, Pa.	40 30 55	78 24 03	1,180
Amarillo, Tex.	35 12 27	101 50 04	3,685
Anchorage, Alaska	61 10 00	149 59 00	118
Ann Arbor, Mich.	42 16 59	83 44 52	880
Asheville, N.C.	35 35 42	82 33 26	1,985
Ashland, Ky.	38 28 36	82 38 23	536
Atlanta, Ga.	33 45 10	84 23 37	1,050
Atlantic City, N.J.	39 21 32	74 25 53	10
Augusta, Ga.	33 28 20	81 58 00	143
Augusta, Me.	44 18 53	69 46 29	45
Austin, Tex.	30 16 09	97 44 37	.505
Bakersfield, Cal.	35 22 30	119 01 18	400
Baltimore, Md.	39 17 26	76 36 45	20
Bangor, Me.	44 48 13	68 46 18	20
Baton Rouge, La.	30 26 58	91 11 00	57
Battle Creek, Mich.	42 18 58	85 10 48	820
Bay City, Mich.	43 36 04	83 53 15	595
Beaumont, Tex.	30 05 20	94 06 09	20
Belleville, Ont.	44 09 30	77 22 30	280
Bellingham, Wash.	48 45 02	122 28 36	60
Berkeley, Cal.	37 52 10	122 16 17	40
Bethlehem, Pa.	40 37 16	75 22 34	235
Billings, Mont.	45 47 00	108 30 04	3,120
Biloxi, Miss.	30 23 48	88 53 00	20
Binghamton, N.Y.	42 06 03	75 54 47	865
Birmingham, Ala.	33 31 01	86 48 36	600
Bismarck, N.D.	46 48 23	100 47 17	1,674
Bloomington, Ill.	40 28 54	88 59 36	800
Boise, Idaho	43 37 07	116 11 58	2,704
Boston, Mass.	42 21 24	71 03 25	21
Bowling Green, Ky.	36 59 18	86 27 03	510
Brattleboro, Vt.	42 51 06	72 33 48	300
Brandon, Man.	49 51 00	99 57 00	1,265
Brantford, Ont.	43 07 30	80 15 30	705
Bridgeport, Conn.	41 10 49	73 11 22	10
Brockton, Mass.	42 05 02	71 01 25	130
Brownsville, Tex.	25 54 07	97 29 58	35
Buffalo, N.Y.	42 52 52	78 52 21	585
Burlington, Ont.	43 18 30	79 46 30	875
Burlington, Vt.	44 28 34	73 12 46	110
Butte, Mont.	46 01 06	112 32 11	5,765
Calgary, Alta.	51 02 46	114 03 24	3,557
Cambridge, Mass.	42 22 01	71 06 22	20
Camden, N.J.	39 56 41	75 07 14	30
Canton, Ohio	40 47 50	81 22 37	1,030
Carson City, Nev.	39 10 00	119 46 00	4,680
Cedar Rapids, Iowa	41 58 01	91 39 53	730
Central Islip, N.Y.	40 47 24	73 12 00	80
Champaign, Ill.	40 07 05	88 14 48	740
Charleston, S.C.	32 46 35	79 55 53	9
Charleston, W.Va.	38 21 01	81 37 52	601
Charlotte, N.C.	35 13 44	80 50 45	720
Charlottetown, P.E.I.	46 14 00	63 07 45	181
Chattanooga, Tenn.	35 02 41	85 18 32	675
Cheyenne, Wyo.	41 08 09	104 49 07	6,100
Chicago, Ill.	41 52 28	87 38 22	595
Churchill, Man.	58 45 15	94 10 00	94
Cincinnati, Ohio	39 06 07	84 30 35	550
Cleveland, Ohio	41 29 51	81 41 50	660
Colorado Springs	38 50 07	104 49 16	5,980
Columbia, Mo.	38 57 03	92 19 46	730
Columbia, S.C.	34 00 02	81 02 00	190
Columbus, Ga.	32 28 07	84 59 24	265
Columbus, Ohio	39 57 47	83 00 17	780
Concord, N.H.	43 12 22	71 32 25	290
Corpus Christi, Tex.	27 47 51	97 23 45	35
Dallas, Tex.	32 47 09	96 47 37	435
Dartmouth, N.S.	44 38 39	63 34 34	476
Davenport, Iowa	41 31 19	90 34 33	590
Dawson, Yukon	64 03 30	139 26 00	1,211
Dayton, Ohio	39 45 32	84 11 43	574
Daytona Beach, Fla.	29 12 44	81 01 10	7
Decatur, Ill.	39 50 42	88 56 47	682
Denver, Colo.	39 44 58	104 59 22	5,280
Des Moines, Iowa	41 35 14	93 37 00	805
Detroit, Mich.	42 19 48	83 02 57	585
Dodge City, Kans.	37 45 17	100 01 09	2,480
Dubuque, Iowa	42 30 10	90 40 30	620
Duluth, Minn.	46 46 56	92 06 24	610
Durham, N.C.	36 00 00	78 54 45	405
Eau Claire, Wis.	44 48 48	91 29 42	790
Edmonton, Alta.	53 32 45	113 29 15	2,373
El Paso, Tex.	31 45 36	106 29 11	3,695
Elizabeth, N.J.	40 39 43	74 12 59	21
Enid, Okla.	36 23 42	97 52 30	1,240
Erie, Pa.	42 07 15	80 04 57	685
Eugene, Ore.	44 03 16	123 05 30	422
Eureka, Cal.	40 46 54	124 09 24	45
Evansville, Ind.	37 58 20	87 34 21	385
Fairbanks, Alaska	64 48 00	147 51 00	448
Fall River, Mass.	41 42 06	71 09 18	40
Fargo, N.D.	46 52 30	96 47 18	900
Flagstaff, Ariz.	35 11 36	111 39 06	6,900
Flint, Mich.	43 01 18	83 41 00	750
Ft. Smith, Ariz.	35 23 06	94 25 06	440
Fort Wayne, Ind.	41 04 21	85 08 26	790
Fort Worth, Tex.	32 44 55	97 19 44	670
Fredericton, N.B.	45 57 40	66 38 30	67
Fresno, Cal.	36 44 12	119 47 11	285
Gadsden, Ala.	34 00 57	86 00 41	555
Gainesville, Fla.	29 39 36	82 19 48	175
Gallup, N.M.	35 31 30	108 44 30	6,540
Galveston, Tex.	29 18 10	94 47 43	5
Gary, Ind.	41 36 12	87 20 19	590
Grand Junction, Conn.	39 04 06	108 33 06	4,590
Grand Rapids Mich.	42 58 03	85 40 13	610
Great Falls, Mont.	47 30 06	111 17 06	3,340
Green Bay, Wis.	44 30 48	88 00 50	590
Greensboro, N.C.	36 04 17	79 47 25	839
Greenville, S.C.	34 50 50	82 24 01	966
Guelph, Ont.	43 32 30	80 15 30	1,075
Gulfport, Miss.	30 22 04	89 05 36	20
Halifax, N.S.	44 38 39	63 34 34	476
Hamilton, Ont.	43 15 17	79 52 28	776
Hamilton, Ohio	39 23 59	84 33 47	600
Harrisburg, Pa.	40 15 43	76 52 59	365
Hartford, Conn.	41 46 12	72 40 49	40
Helena, Mont.	46 35 33	112 02 24	4,155
Hilo, Hawaii	19 43 30	155 05 24	40
Holyoke, Mass.	42 12 29	72 36 36	115
Honolulu, Hawaii	21 18 22	157 51 35	21
Houston, Tex.	29 45 26	95 21 37	40
Hull, Que.	45 26 00	75 44 00	225
Huntington, W.Va	38 25 12	82 26 33	565
Huntsville, Ala.	34 43 54	86 35 12	640
Indianapolis, Ind.	39 46 07	86 09 46	710
Iowa City, Iowa	41 39 37	91 31 53	685
Jackson, Mich.	42 14 43	84 24 22	940
Jackson, Miss.	32 17 56	90 11 06	298
Jacksonville, Fla.	30 19 44	81 39 42	20
Jersey City, N.J.	40 43 50	74 03 56	20
Johnstown, Pa.	40 19 35	78 55 03	1,185
Joplin, Mo.	37 05 36	94 30 42	990
Juneau, Alaska	58 18 12	134 24 30	50
Kalamazoo, Mich.	42 17 29	85 35 14	755
Kansas City, Kan.	39 07 04	94 38 24	750
Kansas City, Mo.	39 04 56	94 35 20	750
Kenosha, Wis.	42 35 43	87 50 11	610
Key West, Fla.	24 33 30	81 48 12	5
Kingston, Ont.	44 13 30	76 30 00	310
Kitchener, Ont.	43 26 59	80 29 17	1,031
Knoxville, Tenn.	35 57 39	83 55 07	890
Lafayette, Ind.	40 25 11	86 53 39	550
Lancaster, Pa.	40 02 25	76 18 29	355
Lansing, Mich.	42 44 01	84 33 15	830
Laredo, Tex.	27 30 22	99 30 30	440
La Salle, Que.	45 25 30	73 38 30	100
Las Vegas, Nev.	36 10 20	115 08 37	2,030
Laval, Que.	45 35 30	73 45 30	100
Lawrence, Mass.	42 42 16	71 10 08	65
Lethbridge, Alta.	49 41 30	112 49 00	2,990
Lexington, Ky.	38 02 50	84 29 46	955
Lihue, Hawaii	21 58 48	159 22 30	210
Lima, Ohio	40 44 35	84 06 20	865
Lincoln, Nebr.	40 48 59	96 42 15	1,150
Little Rock, Ark.	34 44 42	92 16 37	286
London, Ont.	42 59 00	81 15 00	912
Long Beach, Cal.	33 46 14	118 11 18	35
Lorain, Ohio	41 28 05	82 10 49	610
Los Angeles, Cal.	34 03 15	118 14 28	340
Louisville, Ky.	38 14 47	85 45 49	450
Lowell, Mass.	42 38 25	71 19 14	100
Lubbock, Tex.	33 35 05	101 50 33	3,195
Macon Ga.	32 50 12	83 37 36	335
Madison, Wis.	43 04 23	89 22 55	860

City	Lat. ° ′ ″	Long. ° ′ ″	Alt. Feet
Manchester, N.H.	42 59 28	71 27 41	175
Marshall, Texas	32 33 00	94 23 00	410
Memphis, Tenn.	35 08 46	90 03 13	275
Meriden, Conn.	41 32 06	72 47 30	190
Mexico City, Mexico	19 25 45	99 7 00	7,347
Miami, Fla.	25 46 37	80 11 32	10
Milwaukee, Wis.	43 02 19	87 54 15	635
Minneapolis, Minn.	44 58 57	93 15 43	815
Minot, N.D.	48 14 18	101 17 48	1,550
Mississauga, Ont.	43 33 00	79 35 00	260
Mobile, Ala.	30 41 36	88 02 33	5
Moline, Ill.	41 30 31	90 30 49	585
Moncton, N.B.	46 05 30	64 47 30	75
Montgomery, Ala.	32 22 33	86 18 31	160
Montpelier, Vt.	44 15 36	72 34 41	485
Montreal, Que.	45 30 30	73 33 20	117
Moose Jaw, Sask.	50 23 30	105 32 30	1,810
Muncie, Ind.	40 11 28	85 23 16	950
Nashville, Tenn.	36 09 33	86 46 55	450
Natchez, Miss.	31 33 48	91 23 30	210
Newark, N.J.	40 44 14	74 10 19	55
New Bedford, Mass.	41 38 13	70 55 41	15
New Britain, Conn.	41 40 08	72 46 59	200
New Haven, Conn.	41 18 25	72 55 30	40
New Orleans, La.	29 56 53	90 04 10	5
New York, N.Y.	40 45 06	73 59 39	55
Niagara Falls, N.Y.	43 05 34	79 03 26	570
Niagara Falls, Ont.	43 05 30	79 03 30	585
Nome, Alaska	64 30 00	165 25 00	25
Norfolk, Va.	36 51 10	76 17 21	10
North Bay, Ont.	46 18 30	79 27 30	905
Oakland, Cal.	37 48 03	122 15 54	25
Ogden, Utah	41 13 31	111 58 21	4,295
Oklahoma City	35 28 26	97 31 04	1,195
Omaha, Nebr.	41 15 42	95 56 14	1,040
Orlando, Fla.	28 32 42	81 22 38	70
Oshawa, Ont.	43 54 00	78 52 00	350
Ottawa, Ont.	45 25 40	75 42 45	374
Paducah, Ky.	37 05 13	88 35 56	345
Pasadena, Cal.	34 08 44	118 08 41	830
Paterson, N.J.	40 55 01	74 10 21	100
Pensacola, Fla.	30 24 51	87 12 56	15
Peoria, Ill.	40 41 42	89 35 33	470
Peterborough, Ont.	44 18 00	78 19 30	685
Philadelphia, Pa.	39 56 58	75 09 21	100
Phoenix, Ariz.	33 27 12	112 04 28	1,090
Pierre, S.D.	44 22 18	100 20 54	1,480
Pittsburgh, Pa.	40 26 19	80 00 00	745
Pittsfield, Mass.	42 26 53	73 15 14	1,015
Pocatello, Idaho	42 52 24	112 27 00	4,460
Port Arthur, Texas	29 52 30	93 56 15	10
Portland, Me.	43 39 33	70 15 19	25
Portland, Ore.	45 31 06	122 40 35	77
Portsmouth, N.H.	43 04 30	70 45 24	20
Portsmouth, Va.	36 50 07	76 18 14	10
Prince Rupert, B.C.	54 19 00	130 19 00	125
Providence, R.I.	41 49 32	71 24 41	388
Provo, Utah	40 14 08	111 39 24	4,550
Pueblo, Col.	38 16 17	104 36 33	4,690
Quebec City, Que.	46 48 46	71 12 20	239
Racine, Wis.	42 43 49	87 47 12	630
Rapid City, S.D.	44 04 48	103 13 42	3,230
Raleigh, N.C.	35 46 38	78 38 21	365
Reading, Pa.	40 20 09	75 55 40	265
Regina, Sask.	50 27 02	104 36 30	1,894
Reno, Nev.	39 31 47	119 48 40	4,490
Richmond, Va.	37 32 15	77 26 09	160
Roanoke, Va.	37 16 13	79 56 44	905
Rochester, Minn.	44 01 21	92 28 03	990
Rochester, N.Y.	43 09 41	77 36 21	515
Rockford, Ill.	42 16 07	89 05 48	715
Sacramento, Cal.	38 34 57	121 29 41	30
Saginaw, Mich.	43 25 52	83 56 05	595
St. Catharines, Ont.	43 09 30	79 14 30	362
Saint John, N.B.	45 16 00	66 04 30	80
St. Cloud, Minn.	45 34 00	94 10 24	1,040
St. John's, Nfld.	47 34 00	52 43 30	200
St. Joseph, Mo.	39 45 57	94 51 02	850
St. Louis, Mo.	38 37 45	90 12 22	455
St. Paul, Minn.	44 57 19	93 06 07	780
St. Petersburg, Fla.	27 46 18	82 38 19	20
Salem, Ore.	44 56 24	123 02 00	155

City	Lat. ° ′ ″	Long. ° ′ ″	Alt. Feet
Salina, Kan.	38 50 06	97 36 30	1,229
Salt Lake City	40 45 23	111 53 26	4,390
San Angelo, Tex.	31 27 39	100 26 03	1,845
San Antonio, Tex.	29 25 37	98 29 06	650
San Bernardino, Cal.	34 06 30	117 17 28	1,080
San Diego, Cal.	32 42 53	117 09 21	20
San Francisco, Cal.	37 46 39	122 24 40	65
San Jose, Cal.	37 20 16	121 53 24	90
San Juan, P.R.	18 27 00	66 04 15	35
Santa Barbara, Cal.	34 25 18	119 41 55	100
Santa Cruz, Cal.	36 58 18	122 01 18	20
Santa Fe, N.M.	35 41 11	105 56 10	6,950
Sarasota, Fla.	27 20 12	82 31 54	20
Saskatoon, Sask.	52 07 50	106 39 41	1,653
Sault Ste. Marie, Ont.	46 31 30	84 20 00	650
Savannah, Ga.	32 04 42	81 05 37	20
Schenectady, N.Y.	42 48 42	73 55 42	245
Scranton, Pa.	41 24 32	75 39 46	725
Seattle, Wash.	47 36 32	122 20 12	10
Sheboygan, Wis.	43 45 36	87 44 54	630
Sherbrooke, Que.	45 24 00	71 53 30	625
Sheridan, Wyo.	44 47 48	106 57 42	3,740
Shreveport, La.	32 30 46	93 44 58	204
Sioux City, Iowa	42 29 46	96 24 30	1,110
Sioux Falls, S.D.	43 32 35	96 43 35	1,395
Somerville, Mass.	42 23 15	71 06 07	13
South Bend, Ind.	41 40 33	86 15 01	710
Spartanburg, S.C.	34 57 03	81 56 06	875
Spokane, Wash.	47 39 32	117 25 33	1,890
Springfield, Ill.	39 47 58	89 38 51	610
Springfield, Mass.	42 06 01	72 35 32	55
Springfield, Mo.	37 13 03	93 17 32	1,300
Springfield, Ohio	39 55 38	83 48 29	980
Stamford, Conn.	41 03 09	73 32 34	35
Steubenville, Ohio	40 21 42	80 36 53	660
Stockton, Cal.	37 57 30	121 17 16	20
Sudbury, Ont.	46 28 30	80 58 30	917
Superior, Wis.	46 43 14	92 06 07	630
Sydney, N.S.	46 08 30	60 11 00	50
Syracuse, N.Y.	43 03 04	76 09 14	400
Tacoma, Wash.	47 14 59	122 26 15	110
Tallahassee, Fla.	30 26 42	84 16 54	150
Tampa, Fla.	27 56 58	82 27 25	15
Terre Haute, Ind.	39 28 03	87 24 26	496
Texarkana, Texas	33 25 48	94 02 30	324
Thunder Bay, Ont.	48 25 00	89 14 00	650
Toledo, Ohio	41 39 14	83 32 39	585
Topeka, Kan.	39 03 16	95 40 23	930
Toronto, Ont.	43 39 12	79 23 00	532
Trenton, N.J.	40 13 14	74 46 13	35
Trois-Rivieres, Que.	46 21 00	72 33 00	115
Troy, N.Y.	42 43 45	73 40 58	35
Tucson, Ariz.	32 13 15	110 58 08	2,390
Tulsa, Okla.	36 09 12	95 59 34	804
Urbana, Ill.	40 06 42	88 12 06	725
Utica, N.Y.	43 06 12	75 13 33	415
Vancouver, B.C.	49 16 30	123 07 30	388
Victoria, B.C.	48 25 40	123 21 45	....
Waco, Tex.	31 33 12	97 08 00	405
Walla Walla, Wash.	46 04 08	118 20 24	936
Washington, D.C.	38 53 51	77 00 33	25
Waterbury, Conn.	41 33 13	73 02 31	260
Waterloo, Iowa	42 29 40	92 20 20	850
West Palm Beach, Fla.	26 43 00	80 03 12	15
Wheeling, W.Va.	40 04 03	80 43 20	670
Whitehorse, Yukon	60 43 15	135 03 15	2,305
White Plains, N.Y.	41 02 00	73 45 48	220
Wichita, Kan.	37 41 30	97 20 16	1,290
Wichita Falls, Tex.	33 54 34	98 29 28	945
Wilkes-Barre, Pa.	41 14 32	75 53 17	640
Wilmington, Del.	39 44 46	75 32 51	135
Wilmington, N.C.	34 14 12	77 55 24	35
Windsor, Ont.	42 19 50	83 03 00	590
Winnipeg, Man.	49 53 56	97 08 20	765
Winston-Salem, N.C.	36 05 52	80 14 42	860
Worcester, Mass.	42 15 37	71 48 17	475
Yakima, Wash.	46 35 42	120 30 48	1,060
Yellowknife, N.W.T.	62 28 15	114 22 00	674
Yonkers, N.Y.	40 55 55	73 53 54	10
York, Pa.	39 57 35	76 43 36	370
Youngstown, Ohio	41 05 57	80 39 02	840
Yuma, Ariz.	32 42 54	114 37 24	160
Zanesville, Ohio	39 56 18	82 00 30	720

World Cities

City	Lat. ° ′ ″	Long. ° ′ ″	Alt. Feet
London, U.K. (Greenwich)	51 30 00	0 0 0	245
Paris, France	48 50 14	2 20 14	300
Berlin, Germany	52 32 00	13 25 00	110
Rome, Italy	41 53 00	12 30 00	95
Warsaw, Poland	52 15 00	21 00 00	360
Moscow, U.S.S.R.	55 45 00	37 42 00	394
Athens, Greece	37 58 00	23 44 00	300
Jerusalem, Israel	31 47 00	35 13 00	2,500
Johannesburg, So. Afr.	26 10 00	28 02 00	5,740
New Delhi, India	28 38 00	77 12 00	770
Peking, China	39 54 00	116 28 00	600
Rio de Janeiro, Brazil	22 53 43	43 13 22	30
Tokyo, Japan	31 41 00	139 45 00	30
Sydney, Australia	33 52 00	151 12 00	25

States and Other Areas of the U.S.

Their Resources, Histories, Industries, Agriculture, Mineral Products, Tourist Attractions, Nicknames, State Symbols

Areas of the states are total land and water areas reported by the Geography Division, Bureau of the Census; gricultural figures are based on reports of the Dept. of Agriculture and state agencies; mineral statistics are those eported by the Bureau of Mines; manufacturing statistics are from the Bureau of the Census.

For maps and for descriptive articles on cities, see Index.

Alabama

Heart of Dixie, Cotton State

CAPITAL: Montgomery. AREA: 51,609 sq. mi., rank, 9th. POPULATION: (See Index for 1970 Census.) MOTTO: We Dare Defend Our Rights. FLOWER: Camllia. BIRD: Yellowhammer. FISH: Tarpon. TREE: outhern (Longleaf) Pine. SONG: Alabama. ADMIS-ION: 22nd.

Alabama lies in the cotton belt of the Old South but inroduction of new and diversified industries has given the tate a more balanced economy. Natural wealth inludes coal, which underlies about 7,000 sq. mi. in the lorthern Appalachian region, iron, bauxite and timber. Cheaha Mtn., 2,407 ft., is the state's highest point.

Abundant water for hydroelectric power and river hipping has contributed to the growth of Alabama's conomy. Three Tennessee Valley Authority dams and a arge nuclear power plant are in the northern part of the tate. Historic sites, fishing and hunting are among its atractions.

With two-thirds of the state's land area in timber, Alabama has important and expanding pulp, paper and paperboard production. It is a leader in production of outhern pine plywood and pulpwood.

Iron and steel production is the most important of Alaama's manufacturing industries; there is also a large egment of manufacturing devoted to primary metal roducts of wide diversity, particularly structural steel. Other important industry groupings include chemicals nd fertilizers, textile mill products and apparel, proessing of foods, stone-clay-glass products, transportaion equipment, electrical and other machinery. Value dded by manufacture is over $4.5 billion a year.

Industrial growth in 1972 saw over $838,290,000 invest-d in 682 new or expanded plants, providing 42,878 new obs.

Birmingham, center of the steel industry, has long een known as "the Pittsburgh of the South."

At Huntsville is the George C. Marshall Space Flight Center of NASA and a Space and Rocket museum.

Agriculture remains a vital part of the economy despite the increased importance of manufacturing. Cotton as long been king among Alabama's crops but is ivaled by corn, soybeans, pecans and peanuts. Among he states, Alabama ranked 3rd in production of pecans n 1972, 5th in peanuts. Also important are potatoes, vatermelons, tobacco and peaches.

Livestock, especially poultry, has grown in imporance. Alabama was 5th among the states in number of hickens in 1972. Farm receipts for livestock and livetock production in 1972 totaled $592,309,000; for crops, he total was $276,232,000. Forest product sales totaled 100,000,000 in 1972.

Alabama ranks 2nd behind Arkansas in production of auxite and is the 3rd largest producer of asphalt and nica. But bituminous coal accounts for over 50% of the alue of its total mineral production, which in 1972 eached a total estimated at $333,440,000. Also important are cement, stone and petroleum.

There are 56 institutions of higher education in Alaama. Among the largest are the Univ. of Alabama, Auurn Univ., Montevallo Univ., Jacksonville State Univ., Tuskegee Institute, the Univ. of South Alabama, Florence State and Samford Univs.

Alabama, first explored by De Narvaez, Spanish, 1528, s rich in historical markers and sites. Andrew Jackson lefeated the Creek Indians at Talledega and Horseshoe Bend. The Confederate States were organized at Montomery, Feb. 4, 1861, and Jefferson Davis took oath as resident at State Capital there Feb. 18. Davis' "first

White House" now is a state shrine; others include the house in Tuscumbia where Helen Keller was born June 27, 1880; Statue of Vulcan near Birmingham.

The state was organized as a Territory Mar. 3, 1817, and became a state Dec. 14, 1819.

Tourists spent an estimated $601,000,000 in Alabama in 1972.

At Russell Cave National Monument, near Bridgeport, may be seen a detailed record of occupancy by humans from about 7000 B.C. to 1650 A.D., including tools, weapons and pottery. The exhibit is free.

The George Washington Carver Museum at Tuskegee Institute, Tuskegee, contains records of the famous scientist's contributions to agronomy and dioramas of achievements by Negroes.

The University of Alabama Museum of Natural History, in Tuscaloosa, displays Alabama fossils, shells and aboriginal materials and collections of native and foreign beetles, birds, batrachians and reptiles. Mound State Monument, Moundville, an adjunct of the museum, shows aboriginal burials.

(See also Index for Birmingham, Mobile, Montgomery.)

Alaska

No official nickname

CAPITAL: Juneau. AREA: 586,412 sq. mi., rank 1st. POPULATION: (See Index for 1970 Census.) FLOWER: Forget-me-not. BIRD: Willow Ptarmigan. TREE: Sitka Spruce. SONG: Alaska's Flag. FISH: King Salmon. MOTTO: North to the Future. ADMISSION: 49th.

Alaska became the 49th state Jan. 3, 1959. Largest political division of the U.S., it is two and one-fifth times the size of Texas. Alaska occupies the NW part of North America, separated from the rest of the continental U.S. by Canada's British Columbia. Alaska's general coastline runs 6,640 mi.; including all its islands, 33,904 mi. It has mountain ranges, volcanoes, fjords and glaciers.

About one-fifth of the pop. are Eskimos and Indians.

Pt. Barrow in Arctic Alaska is the northernmost point of the state. The Yukon River flows E to W 1,200 mi. through Central Alaska, from the Canadian border to the Bering Sea. In South Central Alaska stands Mt. McKinley, 20,320 ft., highest point in North America.

In West Central Alaska, off the tip of the Seward Peninsula, lies Little Diomede Is., only 2.4 mi. from Big Diomede Is., owned by the USSR. The Alaska Peninsula and the Aleutian Islands into which it tapers, extended SW and W for 1,200 mi., with numerous volcanoes; at the base of the peninsula is Katmai National Monument, containing the Valley of 10,000 Smokes, scene of a 1912 eruption.

Alaska's Panhandle stretches SE; it is a narrow strip of mainland and islands, with fjords and Glacier Bay National Monument (containing the Muir Glacier, 2 mi. wide and 250 ft. high), facing the Pacific W of British Columbia.

History. Vitus Bering, a Dane employed by Russia, discovered Bering Strait, separating Asia and North America, in 1728, but may not have found Alaska until his second voyage, in 1741, when he explored Alaska's coast. Other early visits were made by Spanish explorers (1775, 1788); by the British Cook (1776), Vancouver (1791-94) and Mackenzie (1793); by the French LaPerouse (1786); and by the U.S. Capts. Robert Gray and John Kendrick (1788). Alexander Baranov, first Russian governor of Alaska, set up headquarters at New Archangel, near present Sitka, 1799.

William H. Seward, as Secy. of State under President Andrew Johnson, bought Alaska from Czarist Russia for

$7,200,000, a transaction some labeled at the time "Seward's Folly." The treaty was signed Mar. 30, 1867, the transfer of territory took place Oct. 18, 1867. Alaska was a District until Aug. 24, 1912, and an Organized Territory until becoming a state in 1959.

The "Gold Rush" began when gold was discovered near the Klondike River in Canada, Aug. 16, 1896. Out of 100,000 prospectors, 1897-1899, many died of exposure, others took up trading and farming. On the south coast of Seward Peninsula lies **Nome,** where gold-bearing sands were worked by placer mining.

Resources and Industries. The Good Friday, Mar. 27, 1964, earthquake, the most powerful ever recorded in North America, caused a temporary setback to the economic development of South Central Alaska, but reconstruction was speedily completed. Anchorage, Seward, Valdez and Kodiak benefited with new facilities.

Principal income is from fisheries, minerals (esp. oil), wood products, tourism and furs. Salmon, halibut, herring, cod and shellfish are frozen or canned; Alaska is a leading state in value of its commercial catch, about $80,733,000 in 1972.

Processing of fish and other foods is the largest manufacturing industry, followed by lumber and wood products.

Spruce, yellow cedar and hemlock are plentiful; there also are red cedar and birch. Commercial timberland of Alaska's vast forest totals 78,000,000 acres. The forest products industry in SE is expanding as pulp mills increase. Timber products value is over $118,000,000 yearly.

Furs produced are those of the seal, sable, ermine, wolverine, land otter, muskrat, beaver, mink, red fox, blue fox, lynx, marten. The black fox and white fox are less frequent. Wild life includes the gray wolf, moose, caribou, and 5 kinds of bear: black, grizzly, Polar, Kodiak and glacier. There are plenty of sea fowl, but whales, walrus, sea lion and sea otter have diminished.

The seal herd on the Pribilof islands is owned by the Government and seal harvesting is managed by the U.S. Commerce Dept. Reindeer herds are multiplying and their meat is marketed.

Oil production, mainly from offshore fields in Cook Inlet had an est. value of $237,340,000 in 1972. Total mineral production value was est. at $321,915,000.

Sale of leases for the vast North Slope oil discovery area at Prudhoe Bay brought the state $900,000,000 in 1969. A proposed 800-mi. pipeline to carry the oil to Valdez was held up by a controversy with ecologists.

The value of gold production in 1972 was $728,000. Alaska also has natural gas, tin, bituminous coal and mercury.

Principal ports are in the panhandle where Juneau, the capital, is on the mainland shore; N of it is Skagway, historic entry to Klondike gold fields via Chilkoot Pass and White Pass. Sitka, Wrangell and Ketchikan (center of salmon industry), are on islands of the Alexander group.

At the head of Cook inlet, in S. Central Alaska, is the state's largest city, Anchorage. Seward, S of Anchorage, is terminus for the govt-owned Alaska Railroad, which runs N to Fairbanks.

Nine domestic airlines serve Alaska. International lines flying via Arctic routes make stops.

Ships transport 90% of the goods and foods to and from Alaska, linking some 50 Alaskan ports with Seattle, etc.

More than 125,000 tourists visit Alaska annually, spending some $45,000,000.

There are now two motor routes to Alaska. The newer is by way of Marine Highway, a 450-mile ferry route from Prince Rupert, B.C., to Skagway, Alaska. Motorists leaving the ferry at Haines may drive to Fairbanks, Anchorage, etc., with part of the route passing through Canada. The older route is the Alaska Highway, from British Columbia. Fairbanks, largest city in Central Alaska, has the northernmost international airport on the continent. Nearby is Eielson AFB.

Higher education is provided by Univ. of Alaska, near Fairbanks, with 6 community colleges in other cities; Alaska Methodist Univ., Anchorage; Sheldon Jackson College, Sitka.

The Alaska State Museum in Juneau features Eskimo and Indian exhibits, mounted wildlife specimens, rocks and minerals and historical exhibits.

The University of Alaska Museum, in College, near Fairbanks, maintains cultural and natural history collections for research and for the public.

Arizona
Grand Canyon State

CAPITAL: Phoenix. AREA: 113,909 sq. mi., rank, 6th. POPULATION: (See Index for 1970 Census.) MOTTO: Ditat Deus, God Enriches. FLOWER: Giant Cactus or Saguaro. BIRD: Cactus Wren. TREE: Paloverde. SONG: Arizona. ADMISSION: 48th.

Arizona leads the nation in copper production with half of the total U. S. output, and ranks high among cotton-growing states, but its rapidly-growing manufacturing industries, such as machinery, aerospace and electronics, form the largest source of income. Mining, agriculture and tourism are also important.

Loads of sunshine and a wealth of scenic attractions give Arizona a steadily mounting tourist business est. at more than $600,000,000 a year.

The climate is dry in southern regions and the northern plateau, but high mountains and forests in central and northern areas have heavy snows in winter. Highest point is Humphreys Peak, 12,633 ft. Over 44% of the land is U. S. owned.

The only point in the U. S. at which 4 states meet is the juncture of Arizona, Utah, Colorado and New Mexico.

Arizona is noted for the Grand Canyon of the Colorado, an immense, vari-colored fissure 217 mi. long, 4 to 13 mi. wide at brim, 4,000 to 5,500 ft. deep. It also has one of man's greatest water barriers, Hoover Dam (formerly Boulder) in Black Canyon of the Colorado, 726 ft. high, 660 ft. wide at base, 1,244 ft. long at top, creating Lake Mead.

Nature has given Arizona the Painted Desert, extending for 30 mi. along U. S. 66; the Petrified Forest; Canyon Diablo, 225 ft. deep, 500 ft. wide, and Meteor Crater, 4,150 ft. across, 570 ft. deep, made by a prehistoric meteor, near U.S. 66. The state has 17 national monuments, 2 national parks. Rodeos and historic sites of Indian and Spanish eras are other attractions.

Copper is king among Arizona's many minerals and the state normally produces a half or more of the nation's copper output. The 1972 est. value of the state's copper production was $913,869,000. Arizona also ranks high among the states in pumice, silver, molybdenum and gold. Also important are helium, petroleum, mercury and vanadium. Total value of mineral production in 1972 was est. at $1.05 billion.

Cotton is a major crop; Arizona's harvest ranked 6th among the states in 1972. Cash receipts for all crops in 1972 were $318,589,000; receipts from livestock and livestock products, $503,729,000. The state ranks 12th in number of sheep. Fruit production is important; Arizona ranks high in lemons, oranges, grapefruit and grapes. Lettuce, melons and alfalfa are valuable crops.

Manufacturing has made large strides in recent years. Value added by manufacture is over $1.4 billion a year. Electrical machinery, including electronic components, accounts for over $281,000,000 of this total; other machinery is also highly important.

Federal spending on defense contracts, construction projects, air bases, etc., is an important factor in Arizona's economy.

Schools include the Univ. of Arizona at Tucson, Arizona State Univ. at Tempe and Northern Arizona Univ. at Flagstaff. The new observatory of the National Science Foundation is located on Kitt Peak near Tucson. Taliesin West is the Frank Lloyd Wright architectural school near Phoenix.

Originally part of the Territory of New Mexico, which was ceded in 1848 by Mexico with the Gadsden Purchase added in 1853, Arizona became a Territory itself in 1863 and a state Feb. 14, 1912.

Museums include Arizona State Museum, Tucson, which stresses the archeology and ethnology of the Southwest with exhibits on Hohakam pre-history, early elephant hunters, tree-ring dating of prehistoric cultures and Pima and Apache ethnology. The Museum of Northern Arizona, 3 mi. N of Flagstaff, has exhibits illustrating the geology and paleontology of the area, and the culture of prehistoric and modern Indians, with a Navajo rug display and a Hopi kiva.

The Southwestern Arboretum, on U. S. 60 and 70 near Superior, has over 6,000 plants and trees from arid regions of the world, from lowly cactus to lofty boojum tree. The Phoenix Zoo is one of the nation's largest.

The Arizona-Sonora Desert Museum, near Tucson, displays animals and plants of the desert.

(See also Phoenix and Tucson in Index.)

Arkansas
Land of Opportunity

CAPITAL: Little Rock. AREA: 53,104 sq. mi., rank, 27th. POPULATION: (See Index for 1970 Census.) MOTTO: Regnat Populus. Let the People Rule. FLOWER: Apple Blossom. BIRD: Mockingbird. TREE: Pine. SONG: Arkansas. ADMISSION: 25th.

Arkansas is an important agricultural state with growing industries, has large oil production, valuable thermal springs and is popular with sportsmen. Highest point is Magazine Mtn., 2,753 ft.

Arkansas became a state June 15, 1836; it seceded in 1861 and was readmitted to the Union in 1868.

Manufacturing is growing in importance with a 64% increase in employees from 1960 to 1970. Per capita income increased 103% from 1960 to 1970. Lumber, petroleum, bauxite and cotton are major products.

The $1.2 billion Arkansas River program, involving navigation, flood control and power developments and construction of 17 dams and locks in Arkansas and Oklahoma, was completed to Catoosa, near Tulsa, Okla., in 1971 and provided an important boost to the area's economy.

The state has 18,500,000 acres of oak, hickory, gum, cypress and pine, and forest industries have a $500,000,000 annual payroll. Cotton accounts for 48% of farm income and Arkansas ranked 4th in cotton production in the U.S. in 1972 with more than 1,465,000 bales. It was 2nd in rice. It was 3rd in number of chickens.

Arkansas accounts for by far the greatest amount of bauxite (aluminum ore) produced in the U.S. It also has the only diamond field in the U.S., ranks 1st in bromine and 2nd in vanadium.

But petroleum is the state's main mineral product; 1972 output was valued at $57,535,000; that of bauxite was $23,400,000. Natural gas and stone were also important. Total value of mineral production was est. at $258,121,000.

Arkansas has 24 institutions of higher learning, including colleges and universities, professional schools, teachers colleges and a number of junior colleges. It also has 16 vocational-technical schools.

Fresh-water fishing, duck-hunting in southeast lowlands, and recreation areas in 21 state parks and 3 national forests attract visitors. There are several reservoir-recreation areas, as at Norfork, Bull Shoals, Nimrod and Dardanelle, and others are being created. There are 47 hot springs in government-owned and operated Hot Springs National Park, which entirely surrounds the city of Hot Springs, about 50 mi. SW of Little Rock. Spring water ranges from 95° to 147° F. and is piped in insulated conduits for baths and drinking. The state has 93 airports.

Out-of-state visitors spend more than $533,000,000 annually in Arkansas.

Historic attractions in Little Rock include the Territorial Capital Restoration, a block of 13 original frame and brick buildings, furnished as in 1820-36, including the governor's home and an early print shop of the Arkansas Gazette, oldest newspaper west of the Mississippi. The Old State House in Little Rock was the state capitol 1836-1912; it houses many historical exhibits and the state archives.

The Little Rock Museum of Science and Natural History occupies the building where Gen. Douglas MacArthur was born; also in MacArthur Park is the Arkansas Museum of Fine Arts. (See also Index for Little Rock.)

California
Golden State

CAPITAL: Sacramento. AREA: 158,693 sq. mi., rank, 3rd. POPULATION: (See Index for 1970 Census.) MOTTO: Eureka, I Have Found It. FLOWER: California Poppy. BIRD: Valley Quail. TREE: Redwood. SONG: I Love You, California. ADMISSION: 31st.

California is the leading agricultural state and is 2nd only to New York in manufacturing.

Third largest in area, California also has, within only 85 mi. of each other, the highest and lowest points in the conterminous 48 states, Mt. Whitney, 14,494 ft., and Death Valley, 282 ft. below sea level.

The U. S. Bureau of the Census estimated California's population as of July 1, 1964, at 18,084,000 and New York's at 17,915,000, giving California 1st place; New York had been in 1st place from 1820 through the Census of 1960. In the 1970 Census, New York had 18,241,266; California, 19,953,134. California also has the most dogs and cats—an est. 50,000,000.

Among scenic regions are the Yosemite Valley, Lassen and Sequoia-Kings Canyon national parks, Lake Tahoe, the Mojave and Colorado deserts, San Francisco Bay and Monterey Peninsula. National forests cover one-fifth of the state.

Oldest living trees on earth are believed to be a stand of Bristlecone pine in the Inyo National Forest, est. to be 4,600 years old.

The world's tallest tree, the Howard Libbey redwood, 368 ft. with a girth of 44 ft., stands on Redwood Creek, Humboldt County.

California's huge fruit and vegetable production is fed by large irrigation systems. Receipts from crops in 1972 totaled $3.04 billion (tops in U.S.); from livestock, $2.04 billion (3rd in U.S.), total receipts were $5.09 billion (most in U.S.).

The state ranked 1st in numbers of chickens, 2nd in turkeys, 5th in sheep, 7th in cattle, as of Jan. 1, 1973.

California produces the most apricots, avocados, grapes and raisins, peaches, persimmons, pomegranates, plums, prunes, lemons, nectarines, olives, dates, almonds, walnuts and sugarbeets. Its total vegetable crop is the largest; it ranks 2nd to Florida in oranges and has large cotton, potato and rice crops.

It led all states in commercial fishing in 1972 with a catch valued at $91,898,000.

The state's giant aerospace industries employ a third of all its manufacturing employees. Value added by manufacture is over $27 billion annually; transportation equipment, especially aircraft and missiles, led; food products, particularly frozen and canned foods, were 2nd; electrical machinery, including electronic components, was 3rd, followed by ordnance, other machinery, metal products.

Gold, discovered at Sutter's sawmill Jan. 24, 1848, set off the historic Gold Rush and gave initial impetus to California's development, but petroleum is the leading mineral product today.

Oil output in 1972 was valued at an est. $945,472,000, over half the state's total mineral production value, $1.89 billion (3rd highest in the U. S. after Texas and Louisiana). Ranking 3rd in oil production, California is a leader in output of asbestos, cement, boron, gypsum and tungsten.

The Oroville Dam, main unit in the world's largest water project—the $2.8 billion Feather River Project—was dedicated May 4, 1968, N of Sacramento; electric power and water for irrigation were flowing even before completion.

Tourists spend about $3.5 billion a year in California.

There are some 200 institutions of higher learning in California, including 20 state colleges, a large number of junior colleges, and the University of California which has many divisions and an enrollment of over 120,000. Other well-known universities include Southern California, Stanford, Santa Clara and San Francisco.

Three of the world's largest observatories are located on Palomar Mtn., Mt. Hamilton and Mt. Wilson.

The Tournament of Roses and the Rose Bowl football game at Pasadena are held annually, Jan. 1. Winter sports are featured in many mountain areas.

Vandenberg AFB, 170 mi. NW of Los Angeles, is center of an interservice missile range extending from San Nicholas Island to Point Sur.

California, named by Spanish explorers, was Alta (Upper) California under Spain. Mexico took over, 1822, ceded it 1848. California Republic (Bear Flag) at Sonoma, June 14, 1846, was led by Gen. William B. Ide. Commander John D. Sloat raised U. S. flag at Monterey July 7, 1846. The state was admitted to the Union Sept. 9, 1850.

Among museums the Pasadena Art Museum has collections of modern German painting, American painting, Oriental art and prints. The Santa Barbara Museum of Art has exhibits of Greek and Roman sculpture, Oriental art, old master and modern paintings, primitive arts, American paintings and old and modern European drawings. The Santa Barbara Historical Society Museum displays and interprets objects of state and local history, owns several historic houses and operates the Gledhill Library for historical research. In Sacramento, the Crocker Art Gallery has collections of paintings, drawings, prints, sculpture and crafts representing all European schools from early Renaissance, American glass and a cross section of pottery from 5th Century B.C. to contemporary American.

The liner Queen Mary, retired from service, is a tourist attraction at Long Beach.

SPANISH MISSIONS. The 21 one churches built by Franciscans of the Roman Catholic Church, 1769-1823, have been restored, rebuilt or are in ruins. They are located on or near El Camino Real, the Royal Highway, U. S. 101. Father Junipero Serra led a missionary expedition from Mexico City and founded 9 churches between 1769 and his death, 1784. The missions converted Indians and raised livestock and grain. Mexico secularized and sold the missions in the 1830s. After the Mexican War the U. S. returned the missions to the church. The buildings suffered from fire, earthquake, military and secular use; some have been entirely rebuilt.

San Diego de Alcala, near San Diego. Restored.

San Luis Rey de Francia, near Oceanside. Seminary for priests.

San Juan Capistrano, 30 mi. from San Luis Rey. Famous for tradition that swallows arrive on St. Joseph's Day, Mar. 19, depart on St. John's Day, Oct. 23.

San Buenaventura, Ventura. Restored.

Santa Barbara, San Olivos St., Santa Barbara. Enlarged, restored since 1925 earthquake.

San Gabriel Arcangel, near Los Angeles.

San Fernando Rey de Espana, San Fernando. Oblate fathers. A museum.

Santa Ines, Solvang. Parish church.

La Purisima Concepcion, near Lompoc. State monument, rebuilt by CCC, 1935.

San Luis Obispo de Tolosa, San Luis Obispo.

San Miguel Arcangel, San Miguel.

San Antonio de Padua, 20 mi. SW of King City. Restored and rebuilt.

Nuestra Senora de la Soledad, Soledad. In course of restoration.

San Carlos de Borromeo de Carmelo, near Carmel, Tomb of Father Junipero Serra.

San Juan Bautista, 18 mi. N of Salinas.

Santa Cruz, Santa Cruz. New Church, 1858.

Santa Clara, Santa Clara. On campus of Univ.

San Jose, 15 mi. N of San Jose. Original destroyed; wooden church since 1891.

Mission Dolores (San Francisco de Asis) 16th and Dolores Sts., San Francisco. Restored chapel.

San Rafael Arcangel, A and Fifth Sts., San Rafael. New church, 1917.

San Francisco de Solano, Sonoma. Owned by state; chapel museum. Stands on plaza where Bear Flag was raised June 14, 1846.

Not one of the original 21 missions is **San Antonio de Pala,** originally a dependency of San Luis Rey de Francia, erected 1810, abandoned 1846, restored 1959.

(See also Index for Los Angeles, Oakland, Orange County, Sacramento, San Bernardino, San Diego, San Francisco, San Jose.)

Colorado
Centennial State

CAPITAL: Denver. AREA: 104,247 sq. mi., rank, 8th. POPULATION: (See Index for 1970 Census.). MOTTO: Nil Sine Numine. Nothing Without Deity. FLOWER: Columbine. BIRD: Lark Bunting. TREE: Colorado Blue Spruce. ANIMAL: Big Horn Sheep. SONG: Where the Columbines Grow. ADMISSION: 38th.

Once primarily a mining and grazing state, Colorado now draws the largest segment of its income from manufacturing, followed by agriculture, tourism and mining. Its snow-capped peaks, ski centers, ghost towns and health spas make it a popular vacation-recreation area.

Colorado was organized as a Territory Feb. 28, 1861, and was admitted to the Union Aug. 1, 1876, 100 years after the Declaration of Independence; hence its nickname, the Centennial State.

The total of value added by Colorado's varied manufacturing industries is over $2.08 billion yearly. Important industry groups are processing of meat, dairy and other food products, as well as machinery, metals and stone-clay-glass products. Research and aerospace industries are growing.

Farm receipts in 1972 totaled $1.48 billion, about 80% from livestock and livestock products. Colorado ranked 3rd among the states in the number of sheep in 1973, 11th in cattle. Its sugar beet crop is the 3rd largest in the U. S. Other important crops are wheat, corn, barley, alfalfa, potatoes, apples, peaches, pears. Large areas of the state have been made productive through irrigation.

Gold was discovered on the Platte in 1858 and at Leadville in 1860.

Climax, near Leadville, now produces most of the world's molybdenum. Colorado produces a rich variety of minerals and is a leader among the states in output of tin, vanadium, tungsten, carbon dioxide, uranium, lead, zinc and pyrites. Total 1972 mineral production was valued at $421,698,000; petroleum accounted for $109,836,000 of the total.

With Utah and Wyoming, Colorado shares the world's richest oil shale deposits, still to be developed.

Colorado is the highest state in the Union, with an average altitude of 6,800 ft. It has 52 of the nation's highest mountains and 1,500 peaks over 10,000 ft. Pikes Peak, 14,110 ft., was found by Lt. Zebulon M. Pike, 1806. Highest is Mt. Elbert, 14,433 ft. Frozen Lake, altitude 12,940 ft., is the highest lake in the 48 conterminous states.

The Continental Divide, which forms the crest of the continent and separates watersheds of the Pacific Ocean and the Gulf of Mexico, runs through the west-central part in a general N-S direction.

Six major rivers—the Colorado, Rio Grande, Arkansas, North Platte, South Platte and Republican—rise in Colorado, supply water to 19 states. The western rivers have cut great canyons; the Black Canyon of the Gunnison and the Royal Gorge of the Arkansas, 1,000 to 1,500 ft. deep. One of the world's highest bridges crosses the Arkansas 1,053 ft. above the river at Royal Gorge.

The Federal government owns 36.4% of the land, including two National Parks, 6 Monuments, two Recreation Areas, 12 forests, two Indian reservations, 7 major military reservations.

Colorado has 32 institutions of higher education, including 17 4-year schools and 13 2-year schools.

Colorado was the 1st of several states which in 1966 liberalized their abortion laws.

Tourist attractions include Rocky Mountain National Park, Garden of the Gods, Great Sand Dunes and Dinosaur National Monuments, Pikes Peak and Mt. Evans Highways, Mesa Verde National Park (pre-historic cliff dwellings). The Grand Mesa tableland comprises Grand Mesa Forest, 659,584 acres, with 200 lakes stocked with trout. Other attractions include the U. S. Air Force Academy near Colorado Springs, Denver Western Stock Show, Colorado State Fair, horse, dog and auto races, rodeos and pioneer celebrations. Thirty-one major ski areas operate from November to May.

The old mining towns of Aspen and Central City have become cultural centers.

Big game include deer, bear, elk, mountain lion, gray wolf, coyote. There are thousands of miles of trout streams and 2,000 fishing lakes.

Museums include the Colorado Springs Fine Arts Center which has paintings, prints and drawings by contemporary artists, exhibits of the cultural history of the SW and Latin America, and the John F. Huckel collection of 112 Navajo sand painting reproductions. The University of Colorado Museum, in Boulder, has more than a million objects in its exhibits of rocks, plants and early peoples as well as an art gallery.

(See also Index for Denver.)

Connecticut
Constitution State

CAPITAL: Hartford. AREA: 5,009 sq. mi., rank, 48th. POPULATION: (See Index for 1970 Census.) MOTTO: Qui Transtulit, Sustinet. He Who Transplanted, Sustains. FLOWER: Mountain Laurel. BIRD: American Robin. TREE: White Oak. Fifth of the Original 13 States to ratify Constitution.

Connecticut's heavily industrialized cities are in sharp contrast to its picturesque New England villages and scenic countryside. Despite its small size, the state has large and diverse manufacturing industries, mainly of high-value specialty products.

It is a leading maker of jet engines, helicopters, nuclear subs, pins and needles, silverware, hardware, clocks, typewriters, cutlery, and ball bearings. Ranking 48th in area, it is 14th in value added by manufacturing, a total of over $6.05 billion annually. Its factories employ over 34% of the working force. Hartford is headquarters for many of the nation's largest insurance companies.

Poultry and dairy products account for the largest part of farm receipts, which totaled $164,734,000 in 1972. Much of the soil is stony, but tobacco, potatoes, fruits and vegetables and nursery products are grown.

The vacation-recreation industry is important. Attractions include historic sites, charming villages, the American Shakespeare Festival in Stratford, Mystic Seaport and Marine Museum, trolley museums, skiing, boating on Long Island Sound. Greenhouse, nursery and forest products are valued at over $21,000,000 annually.

There are 85 state parks, recreation areas and historic sites, covering 25,519 acres.

Tourism brings Connecticut about $385,000,000 a year from out-of-state vacationers.

Mineral production is mostly of sand, stone and gravel for construction of roads and buildings. Total value for 1972 was $28,451,000.

Adriaen Block, Dutch, explored the Connecticut R., 1614. English from Massachusetts settled in 1630s. First practical constitution was the Fundamental Orders, adopted by Wethersfield, Windsor and Hartford, 1639; gave superior powers to legislature. The royal charter of 1662 was exceptionally liberal; when Gov. Edmund Andros tried to seize it, 1687, it was hidden in the Hartford Oak, commemorated in Charter Oak Place.

Free public schools were established in New Haven, 1642, Hartford, 1643. Compulsory education in elementary and Latin grammar schools was established in 1650.

Of 48 institutions of higher education, Yale Univ. (estab. 1701, named 1718) is the largest privately endowed. The public education system includes the University of Connecticut, with its main campus at Storrs. Trinity (Hartford), Wesleyan (Middletown) and the Univ. of Hartford are well known; Connecticut College and the U. S. Coast Guard Academy are at New London. Preparatory schools include Taft (Watertown), Choate (Wallingford), Hotchkiss (Lakeville), Kent (Kent) and Loomis (Windsor).

Museums include the P. T. Barnum Museum, Bridgeport; American Clock and Watch Museum, Bristol; Trolley Museums, East Haven and Warehouse Point; Hill-Stead Museum, a country house with paintings by famous Impressionists, Farmington; Museum of American Art, New Britain; Old Lighthouse, Stonington; Lyman Allyn Museum, New London; Bruce Museum, Greenwich; Wadsworth Atheneum, Hartford.

In New Haven museums include the Winchester Gun Museum, with 5,000 items from the 15th Century to present. The Yale University Art Gallery's collections illustrate the ancient civilizations of Greece, Rome, Egypt, Mesopotamia; far east and Italian Renaissance art; European and American painting and sculpture, African and pre-Columbian arts. The Peabody Museum at Yale has collections in paleontology, mineralogy, zoology, archeology and a leading collection of dinosaurs.

Mystic Seaport, Mystic, is a recreated 19th Century village, including smithy, chapel and schoolhouse. At the docks lie the wooden whaleship Charles W. Morgan, the squarerigger Joseph Conrad; the Gloucester fishing schooner L. A. Dunton.

(See also Index for Bridgeport, Hartford, New Haven)

Delaware
First State, Diamond State

CAPITAL: Dover. AREA: 2,057 sq. mi., rank, 49th. POPULATION: (See Index for 1970 Census.) MOTTO: Liberty and Independence. FLOWER: Peach Blossom. BIRD: Blue Hen Chicken. TREE: American Holly. SONG: Our Delaware. First of Original 13 States to ratify Constitution.

Delaware occupies part of the Delmarva Peninsula, so-called because Delaware and parts of Maryland and Virginia share the peninsula separating Delaware and Chesapeake Bays. Delaware is 96 mi. long and from 9 to 35 mi. wide. The land slopes from rolling hills (442 ft. highest elevation) in the N to a near sea-level plain.

Second smallest of the states in area, Delaware has a high level of income, with large chemical and other industries, the hqs. of many large corporations, prosperous farms and important shellfish production.

Important in Delaware's total of value added by manufacture are canned and frozen foods, leather and metal products, textiles and machinery. Total value added by manufacture is over $1.28 billion.

Broiler chickens are the largest item of farm income. Farm receipts for 1972 were $157,628,000. Truck farming produced $12,875,000, mainly fruit and vegetables.

Mineral production is mainly sand, gravel and stone used for construction. Total value in 1972 was est. at $2,388,000. There is also a sizable commercial fishing catch, valued at over $1,800,000.

Delaware's major tourist attractions include several famed beaches, racetracks and historic sites and museums. Annual value of tourism is $277,000,000.

Delaware Bay was reported in 1609 by Henry Hudson, under Dutch commission, and in 1610 by Samuel Argall, in Virginia service. The latter called the estuary after his Governor, Thomas West, Lord de la Warr, a name soon extended to the river and its lower western shore, and later adopted by the state.

An attempted Dutch settlement at Zwaanendael (Lewes) in 1631, failed. Swedish colonization began at Fort Christina (Wilmington) in 1638. New Sweden fell to Dutch forces in 1655. English conquered the area in 1664 under the Duke of York, who in 1682 transferred the Counties on Delaware to William Penn. Though in his proprietorship to 1776, they were separately governed from 1704 and fought during the Revolution as a state. On Dec. 7, 1787, Delaware became the first state to ratify the Federal Constitution.

Fort Christina Monument marks the site of founding of New Sweden in 1638. Holy Trinity (Old Swedes) Church erected 1698 is the oldest Protestant Church in the U. S. still in use. Center New Castle comprises a unique survival of a colonial capital nearly in its late 18th century form. The home of John Dickinson, "Penman of the Revolution," and drafter of the Articles of Confederation, has been restored near Dover.

Museums include the Delaware Art Center in Wilmington which has collections of Pre-Raphaelite English paintings. American paintings and manuscripts and drawings. The Henry Francis du Pont Winterthur Museum, at Winterthur near Wilmington, has 100 American period rooms from 17th to early 19th Centuries (reservations are required to visit some of them). The Hagley Museum at Wilmington includes many of the old du Pont powder mills and other exhibits illustrating the development of American industry. The Delaware Museum of Natural History is in Greenville.

The Delaware State Museum, Dover, has varied exhibits on Delaware history and life and the Eldridge Johnson Memorial collection on the development of the Victor Talking Machine and related sound recording.

Delaware has 7 institutions of higher education, including the University of Delaware in Newark.

WILMINGTON

Wilmington had a population of 80,386 (1970 Census). Laid out near Fort Christina, 1730-1736, by Thomas Willing and others, it was chartered in 1739 as Wilmington. Early a milling, shipping and manufacturing center, its business has remained varied. Notable current industries include vulcanized fibre, glazed kid and morocco leather, the largest braided hose plant, and the largest single cotton dyeing and finishing works. It is a world chemical center, with the home office and central laboratories of the I.C.I., du Pont and Hercules companies. The E. I. du Pont de Nemours Co., makers of over 1,400 products including many synthetics, maintains its executive department and a number of its research laboratories in Wilmington. In 1802, Eleuthere Irenee du Pont established a powder works on the Brandywine, the forerunner of the present corporation. Its original nylon plant is at Seaford, Del.

Florida

Sunshine State

CAPITAL: Tallahassee. AREA: 58,560 sq. mi., rank, 22nd. POPULATION: (See Index for 1970 Census.) MOTTO: In God We Trust. FLOWER: Orange Blossom. BIRD: Mockingbird. TREE: Sabal Palm. Song: Old Folks at Home. ADMISSION: 27th.

Florida's many miles of beaches and other resort areas offer fun in the sun to millions of vacationers, and its semi-tropical climate provides a pleasant retirement haven for thousands of oldsters. But the state also has a tremendous agricultural output, producing 80% of the nation's citrus fruits and ranking 2nd only to California in production of vegetables. And, its growing and diversified manufacturing industries provide even more income than its agriculture.

The Florida peninsula juts southward 500 mi. between the Atlantic and the Gulf of Mexico; Cuba is only 90 mi. from its southern tip. It has some 30,000 lakes; Okeechobee, covering 700 sq. mi., is the 4th largest natural lake inside the U. S. Highest elevation in the state is 345 ft., in the NW.

Florida was discovered by Ponce de Leon 1513; acquired from Spain 1819 by treaty ratified 1821. It was organized as a Territory Mar. 30, 1822, and admitted to the Union Mar. 3, 1845. It seceded 1861 and was readmitted 1868.

Tourism is a major industry; about 23,150,000 visitors spend some $3.6 billion annually in Florida. It offers a wide variety of tourist attractions in addition to climate, resorts and water sports.

Many of the tourists become permanent residents. Major tourist objectives are metropolitan Miami, with the nation's greatest concentration of luxury hotels at Miami Beach; Palm Beach; St. Augustine, founded 1565 and oldest city in U. S.; Daytona Beach, Fort Lauderdale, all on the E coast; Sarasota, Tampa, Key West, St. Petersburg on the W; Walt Disney World, an entertainment and vacation development near Orlando.

Everglades National Park, 1,400,533 acres of land and water, preserves the beauty of the vast Everglades swamp. Castillo de San Marcos (St. Augustine), Fort Matanzas, Fort Jefferson (Dry Tortugas), De Soto National Memorial (Bradenton), and Fort Caroline (Jacksonville) are national monuments.

The John F. Kennedy Space Center is another big tourist attraction. From it the nation's first earth satellite was launched Jan. 31, 1958, first U.S. manned space flight, May 5, 1961, and the first manned orbital flight, Feb. 20, 1962, by Col. John H. Glenn, as well as the first man-on-the-moon launch, July 16, 1969.

Key West became the 1st U. S. city to get its fresh water from the sea when a desalting plant, capable of producing 3,500,000 gallons a day, was opened in 1967.

Florida produces most of the nation's oranges and grapefruit; 1972 output was an est. 6,165,000 tons of oranges and 1,998,000 tons of grapefruit, both several times the amount produced by California. It ranks 2nd to California in fresh vegetables. It also produces avocados, watermelons, limes, tangerines, sugarcane, peanuts, cotton, tobacco, strawberries and honey. Florida also ranks high in number of chickens.

The cattle industry has grown in importance. Crop and livestock receipts for 1972 were $1.6 billion.

Manufacturing has made great gains and provides payrolls totaling $2.28 billion. Leading industries, in terms of value added by manufacturing, are food processing, chemicals, electrical equipment, transportation equipment, metal products, paper products.

Florida leads the U.S. in production of phosphate rock and is 2nd to New York in titanium. Total mineral production value in 1972 was est. at $396,538,000.

The commercial catch of fish and shellfish is worth over $55,000,000 a year, ranking high among the states.

Florida has 17 airports with scheduled service, 62 scheduled airlines and 5 major railroads. There are 14 deepwater ports which handle domestic and foreign trade valued at $1.8 billion a year.

Florida has 31 universities and 4-year colleges and 33 other institutions of higher education, including 2-year colleges. Among them are the Univ. of Florida (Gainesville), Florida State Univ. (Tallahassee), Univ. of Florida and Univ. of Tampa (Tampa), Univ. of Miami (Coral Gables), Jacksonville Univ. (Jacksonville), Rollins College (Winter Park), Stetson Univ. (Deland), Barry College (Miami).

Florida has no state income tax. Its excise taxes (beverage, tobacco, parimutuel), sales and other taxes account for 69% of total state revenue.

Museums include the Florida State Museum in Gainesville, which does field work in natural and social sciences in the southeast U.S. and Caribbean area, displays exhibits in archeology, ethnology, paleontology, ornithology, history and industry. Castillo de San Marcos in St. Augustine is a well-preserved Spanish fort built 1672-1696 which is now a national monument. Marineland of Florida, 18 mi. S of St. Augustine, has some 2,500 marine specimens ranging from sharks and porpoises to tiny tropical fish living in oceanarium tanks; visitors may view and photograph them through portholes; trained porpoises and pilot whales perform in shows. Miami's Seaquarium has similar shows.

At Pensacola is the Naval Aviation Museum with exhibits tracing flight development into the space age; also several forts, including Fort Pickens, built 1829, where Geronimo was imprisoned; the T. T. Wentworth Museum, with exhibits of local historical interest; the Pensacola Historical Museum and Spanish Village Museum.

In Sarasota, the John and Mable Ringling Museum of Art, willed to the state, contains works by Rembrandt, Rubens, Hals, Tiepolo, Velasquez, Murillo, Gainsborough, Reynolds and other masters. The Ringling Museum of the Circus includes elaborately decorated wagons, costumes and printed bills showing performers at fairs and circuses from the 16th to 20th centuries; the Asolo Theater presents plays and operas.

Also in Sarasota, the Circus Hall of Fame gives circus acts and puppet shows, displays mementos such as a coach given Tom Thumb by Queen Victoria, a sleigh P. T. Barnum gave Jenny Lind, costumes, rigging and circus equipment.

(See also Index for Jacksonville, Miami, Orlando, Pensacola, St. Petersburg, Tallahassee, Tampa.)

Georgia

Empire State of the South, Peach State

CAPITAL: Atlanta. AREA: 58,876 sq. mi., rank, 21st. POPULATION: (See Index for 1970 Census.) MOTTO: Wisdom, Justice, Moderation. FLOWER: Cherokee Rose. BIRD: Brown Thrasher. TREE: Live Oak. SONG: Georgia. Fourth of the Original 13 States to ratify Constitution.

Largest in area of the states east of the Mississippi, Georgia is rich in a number of natural resources and in its growing, diversified industries.

There are large deposits of marble in the mountainous N, along with fertile plains and industry centers in the NW. The Central Georgia Piedmont plateau boasts rich farmlands and a flourishing textile industry. The SE Coastal Plain produces pecans and peanuts and its forests yield a wealth of pulpwood and turpentine. Off its 100-mi. Atlantic coast lie its famed Golden Isles. The state also has large deposits of clay, limestone and talc.

Okefenokee in the SE is one of the largest swamps in the U. S., a wetland wilderness and peat bog covering 660 sq. mi. A large part of it is a National Wildlife Refuge, a home for wild birds, alligators, bear, deer, otter, etc.

Highest point in the state is Brasstown Bald in the NE, 4,784 ft.; Stone Mtn., near Atlanta, is 1,686 ft.

Manufacturing production has increased many times over since World War II, but the textile industry remains the largest, both in terms of number of workers and value added by manufacture. Also of great importance are paper products, transportation equipment, apparel, food products and chemicals.

Value added by manufacture totals over $6.5 billion a year.

Georgia ranks high among the states in forest products, particularly in its output of pulpwood and turpentine.

Georgia is by far the nation's largest producer of peanuts, harvesting 672,000 tons in 1972, more than twice that of any other state. It is among the leading growers of pecans, peaches and rye.

It ranked 2nd among the states in numbers of chickens, about 36,608,000 in 1972, and also had a large hog production. Farm receipts totaled over $1.3 billion in 1972, more than half from livestock and livestock products.

Georgia is also a leader in production of marble, zirconium, bauxite, barite and kyanite. Total value of mineral production in 1972 was an est. $268,236,000.

There are 62 institutions of higher education, including the Univ. of Georgia. Georgia Institute of Technology and Georgia State Univ.

Savannah and Brunswick are the main ports. The state is served by 6 major railroads and 10 airlines.

It is estimated that vacationers spend more than $930,000,000 a year in Georgia.

Notable among attractions are the Little White House in Warm Springs where President Franklin D. Roosevelt died Apr. 12, 1945, the 2,500-acre Callaway Gardens, Jekyll Island State Park, the restored 1850's farming community of Westville; Dahlonega, site of America's first gold rush; Helen, a mountain village with Alpine motif, Stone Mountain and Six Flags over Georgia.

Georgia has also become a sports center, with professional baseball, basketball, football and hockey teams.

Andersonville Prison Park and National Cemetery are on the site of the Confederate prison camp in which a total of 50,000 Union soldiers were confined, Feb. 1864 to Apr. 1865.

Georgia was visited by DeSoto, 1540. It was a part of land granted to the lords proprietors of Carolina, 1663 and 1685; became an independent colony by charter of 1732 with first permanent settlement under James Oglethorpe, 1733. Georgia ratified the Confederate constitution, Mar. 1861, was readmitted to the Union, July, 1870.

(See also Index for Atlanta, Augusta, Columbus, Macon, Savannah.)

Hawaii

Aloha State

CAPITAL: Honolulu. AREA: 6,450 sq. mi., rank, 47th. POPULATION: (See Index for 1970 Census.) MOTTO: The Life of the Land is Perpetuated in Righteousness. FLOWER: Hibiscus. BIRD: Nene (Hawaiian Goose). TREE: Kukui (Candlenut). OFFICIAL SONG: Hawaii Ponoi. ADMISSION: 50th.

Hawaii, prosperous paradise of the Pacific, became the 50th state Aug. 21, 1959, and the 50-star U. S. flag became official the following July 4.

The Hawaiian Islands lie in the North Pacific, 2,397 mi. from San Francisco (5 hrs. by commercial jet). They consist of 8 major islands (7 inhabited) and 124 minor islands.

The principal islands are Hawaii, the largest; Oahu, on which are Honolulu and Pearl Harbor; Lanai, Maui, Molokai, Kauai, Niihau and Kahoolawe (uninhabited).

The islands are volcanic. Highest point is Mauna Kea, on Hawaii, an extinct volcano 13,796 ft. above sea level. Its twin is Mauna Loa, about 100 ft. lower but an active volcano. Average annual rainfall is 22 inches at Honolulu Airport, 136.6 inches in Hilo, and 460 inches atop Waialeale, a mountain on Kauai. Honolulu is subtropical (all-time range, 57° to 88°) but Mauna Kea is often snow-capped.

Lake Waiau, at 13,020 ft. near the summit of Mauna Kea, is the highest lake in the U. S.

Ka Lae, or South Cape, on the island of Hawaii, is the southernmost point in the 50 states.

The islands were settled by Polynesians, probably about 700-750 A.D. These Polynesians are believed to have sailed to Hawaii from other islands, settled earlier, more than 2,000 mi. to the south, using large double canoes.

Hawaii was visited 1778 by British Capt. James Cook who called the group the Sandwich Islands. It was a kingdom until Jan. 17, 1893, when Queen Liliuokalani was deposed and annexation to the United States asked. President Cleveland blocked this on the ground of American collusion. Hawaii organized a republic, 1894, with Sanford B. Dole as president. Congress voted annexation July 7, 1898, under President McKinley. The Territory was established June 14, 1900.

Hawaii, among the states, has the most heterogeneous of populations, with Americans of Polynesian, Asian, European and African extraction.

Many of the Polynesians intermarried with the other racial groups, which arrived mainly in the 19th Century.

The 1970 Census gave as racial origins: Japanese, 28.3%; Caucasian, 39.2%; the remainder, Hawaiian, Chinese, Filipino, Korean, etc., with many of mixed racial descent.

Major sources of income are defense expenditures, tourism, sugar and pineapple production, in that order. Visitors totaled 2,245,000 in 1972, with an average 50,100 present daily.

Value added by manufacturing, led by food processing, was $435,000,000 in 1972. There were 4,300 farms, with a total of 2,340,000 acres; farm receipts for 1972 were $222,589,000.

Mineral production, mostly cement and stone for construction, was valued at $28,834,000 in 1972.

Science and technology have been promoted and more than 25,000 persons are employed in science-related work.

More than 1,700 ships put into Honolulu each year. Honolulu International Airport has an average of over 325,000 arrivals and departures annually.

A marine world exposition is scheduled for 1978, bicentennial of Capt. Cook's arrival in the islands.

(See also Index for Honolulu.)

Idaho

Gem State

CAPITAL: Boise. AREA: 83,557 sq. mi., rank, 13th. POPULATION: (See Index for 1970 Census.) MOTTO: Esto Perpetua. Let It Be Forever. FLOWER: Lewis Mock Orange (Syringa). BIRD: Mountain Bluebird. TREE: Western White Pine. SONG: Here We Have Idaho. GEM: Star Garnet. ADMISSION: 43rd.

A land of rugged grandeur, Idaho nevertheless ranks high in agricultural production.

Exploration of Idaho began with the visits of the Lewis and Clark Expedition, 1805-6. Fur traders and missionaries followed and the area became part of Oregon Territory, 1848; Idaho Territory, Mar. 3, 1863, and a state July 3, 1890.

Idaho was chiefly a farming, grazing, timber and mineral state for many years, but manufacturing has recently become second in importance to agriculture. There are rugged mountains, beautiful valleys, plateau regions, and extensive lava fields. Mt. Borah, in the Sawtooth Mts., is the highest peak, 12,662 ft.

The Snake River runs through Hells Canyon, which

averages 5,510 ft. in depth for 40 mi., at one point 7,900 ft., exceeding Grand Canyon, and is 10 mi. from rim to rim at widest point. The Snake has several noted waterfalls, among them Shoshone, Twin and American.

Idaho is the nation's leading potato producer, growing about 78,795,000 cwt. annually, worth more than $123,000,000. It ranks 2nd in sugar beets and 4th in barley and has large crops of wheat, hops and apples.

It ranks high in wool production and was 9th among the states in number of sheep in 1973 with 707,000. Farm marketing receipts in 1972 totaled $760,422,000, more than half from crops, the rest from livestock.

Manufacturing's gains were mainly in processing of potatoes and other foods, phosphates, paper, etc. Total value added by manufacturing was est. at over $669,000,000.

Discovery of silver in 1884 at Coeur d'Alene caused a stampede, and Idaho still leads the nation in production of that metal.

It also ranks high among the states in antimony, lead, cobalt, garnet, phosphate rock, vanadium, zinc and mercury. Total mineral production in 1972 was estimated at $112,629,000.

With 39% of its area in forests, Idaho produces much lumber, with the world's largest white pine lumber mill at Lewiston. Yellow pine, Douglas fir, white spruce, larch, hemlock abound; the DeVoto Grove has cedars 1,000 years old.

Total value of forest products is more than $151,000,000 a year.

Hells Canyon, Brownlee and Oxbow Dams, 3 recent hydro-electric projects on the Snake River, are in operation. The National Reactor Testing Station of the AEC on Upper Snake River Plains has more than a score of reactors in operation.

Tourism brings in an est. $215,000,000 or more annually, making it one of the state's important industries.

The state offers excellent hunting and fishing and Lake Pend Oreille, which has a 111-mile shoreline, is home of the world's largest trout, Kamloop rainbow. Craters of the Moon National Monument, 18 mi. W of Arco, is a jagged landscape. Lava covers the land and subterranean explosions have created many caves.

The Nez Perce National Historic Park, in northern Idaho, includes many sites visited by the Lewis and Clark Expedition.

The State Historical Museum in Boise has displays of early Idaho Indian life, the fur trade, mining, farm and household gear of the pioneers.

(See also Index for Boise.)

Illinois
The Inland Empire
CAPITAL: Springfield, AREA: 56,400 sq. mi., rank, 24th. POPULATION: (See Index for 1970 Census.) MOTTO: State Sovereignty, National Union. FLOWER: Native Violet. BIRD: Cardinal. TREE: White Oak. SONG: Illinois. SLOGAN: Land of Lincoln. ADMISSION: 21st.

Illinois ranks high among the states as both an agricultural and industrial empire. It is rich in coal and oil reserves and boasts highly developed rail, water and air transportation facilities.

The soil is rich and level, with the high point, Charles Mound near the Wisconsin line, only 1,235 ft.

Illinois ranks 4th highest among the states in terms of value added by manufacture with a total of close to $22.8 billion. Manufacturing payrolls total $11.7 billion.

Major manufacturing lines are machinery (particularly construction and farm), processing of food products (especially grain, beverages and bakery), electrical machinery (communications, electronic components and appliances), primary metals (mainly iron and steel), transportation equipment (for railroads, aircraft and cars) and chemicals. Rockford is one of the nation's largest machine-tool centers; Peoria is a distilling center.

In 1972 Illinois ranked 2nd to California in receipts from farm crops, $1.7 billion. It stood 8th in receipts for livestock and livestock products and was 4th among the states in total cash farm receipts, $3.1 billion.

Illinois and Iowa vie closely with each other for the largest corn crop. Illinois produces the most soybeans; in 1973 it ranked 2nd to Iowa in number of hogs and stood high in cattle and milk cows.

The state has large coal and oil reserves. It ranks high among the states in annual bituminous coal production, est. at $389,300,000 in 1972. Petroleum production, 2nd in value to coal, was est. to be worth $122,283,000. The state is a leader in output of fluorspar, tripoli, stone and peat. Total 1972 minerals were valued at $758,308,000.

A major research and development installation of the Atomic Energy Commission is the Argonne National Laboratory, Lemont, Ill., directed by the Univ. of Chicago, which also operates the Argonne Cancer Research Hospital in Chicago. Dresden Nuclear Power Station, using a boiling water type of reactor, has been built for Commonwealth Edison Co. and the seven other companies in Nuclear Power Group, Inc., near Joliet, Ill.

Illinois has 138 public and private institutions of higher education. The Univ. of Illinois has campuses in Chicago and Urbana and an enrollment of more than 54,000. Others with enrollments of more than 10,000 include the Univ. of Chicago and Loyola Univ. (Chicago), Illinois State Univ. (Normal), Northwestern Univ. (Evanston), Northern Illinois Univ. (DeKalb), Southern Illinois Univ. (Carbondale) and Western Illinois Univ. (Macomb).

The Illinois State Fair is held annually in August in Springfield. More than 37,000 entries compete for more than $270,000 in cash awards. Attendance is over 667,000.

State forests, parks and conservation areas cover 251,819 acres. Some are associated with the history of the Middle West, including Lincoln's home and tomb in Springfield; the restored Fort de Chartres, seat of French 18th Century authority; old settlements, such as Kaskaskia. Illinois, part of the territory taken from the British by George Rogers Clark, became a state in 1818.

The Illinois State Museum in Springfield has large collections of local art and archeology; art and architecture of the ancient Near East, and antique clocks, glass, china and furniture.

Located in Springfield is a state memorial including Abraham Lincoln's tomb and the Lincoln home which the family occupied for 17 years beginning in 1844. The Old State Capitol Building has been restored.

New Salem State Park, 20 mi. NW of Springfield, contains the restored pioneer village of New Salem where Lincoln lived as storekeeper, surveyor and postmaster, 1831-37. Annual performances are staged of Robert Sherwood's Abe Lincoln in Illinois.

(See also Index for Chicago, Springfield.)

Indiana
Hoosier State
CAPITAL: Indianapolis. AREA: 36,291 sq. mi., rank, 38th. POPULATION: (See Index for 1970 Census.) MOTTO: Cross-roads of America. FLOWER: Peony. BIRD: Cardinal. TREE: Tulip (Yellow Poplar). SONG: On the Banks of the Wabash. ADMISSION: 19th.

Indiana is heavily industrialized, yet is also important among the states for its agricultural output. It ranks among the top states in production of both steel and corn; it quarries much of the building limestone used in the U.S. and is a large producer of coal.

It was explored by LaSalle, 1679; French trading posts grew during the 18th Century. Vincennes, the 1st permanent settlement, was taken over by the British, 1763, and its capture by George Rogers Clark in 1779 led to the opening of the old N.W. Territories to the U.S. Indiana became a Territory July 4, 1800, and a state Dec. 11, 1816.

There are sand dunes and lakes in the N, a level plain through most of the central area, and hills in the S. Highest point is 1,257 ft. in Wayne Co., in the east central area.

The Calumet region in the state's NW corner, including Gary, Hammond, East Chicago and Whiting, has one of the world's greatest concentrations of heavy industry, especially steel, cement and oil refining plants. Gary was a sand dune in 1906 when U.S. Steel began constructing mills there; in 1970 it had a pop. of 175,415. Inland Steel and Youngstown have large plants in East Chicago.

Another vast steel complex has been developed further E along Lake Michigan, including a deepwater port at Burns Harbor in the famed Dunes area, a large plant of the Midwest Steel Div. of the National Steel Corp., and a large group of facilities of the Bethlehem Steel Corp.

While steel and other metal industries are responsible for $1.8 billion of the $12 billion in value added annually by manufacture, electrical machinery, including television sets and household appliances, is a close 2nd with $1.9 billion. Auto parts, aircraft and other transportation equipment is next, with $1.6 billion, followed by industrial farm and other machinery, 4th; chemicals, 5th; processing of food products, 6th.

Indiana is a leader in production of pre-fabricated wood products, mobile homes and band instruments. More than 40 cities are involved in the manufacture of furniture.

Corn is the principal crop and much of it goes to fatten the hogs. Among the states, Indiana ranks 3rd in hogs, 4th in corn, 4th in soybeans, 8th in chickens. Farm marketing receipts for 1972 totaled $1.8 billion, 10th highest among the states.

Coal accounts for over a third of the value of mineral production which in 1972 totaled $305,816,000. Portland cement, petroleum, limestone, clay and gypsum are also important.

Indiana limestone, from vast quarries in the southern part of the state, sheathes tens of thousands of buildings, including the Empire State, Rockefeller Center, the United Nations, the Pentagon, the National Cathedral, many Federal buildings and many state capitols.

Spending by out-of-state tourists is est. at $600,000,000 a year.

Indiana has 22 state parks and recreation areas, including Dunes State Park on Lake Michigan and prehistoric Indian mounds at Mounds State Park; over 1,000 lakes; French Lick and other mineral spas; Wyandotte Cave, 3rd largest in the U.S.; the Indianapolis 500-mile auto race, and the famous post-office, Santa Claus.

Lincoln's boyhood home in Spencer County and the grave of his mother, Nancy Hanks Lincoln, are part of the Lincoln Boyhood National Memorial. State memorials commemorate the capture of Vincennes by George Rogers Clark in the Revolution, the defeat of Tecumseh's Indians at Tippecanoe, and the Rappite and Robert Owen communities at New Harmony.

Spring Mill Village, 3 mi. E of Mitchell, is a restored pioneer settlement. The restored Whitewater Canal is in Brookville.

Among 44 institutions of higher education are Indiana Univ., Purdue Univ., Ball State Univ., Indiana State Univ., Univ. of Notre Dame, Indiana Central College, Valparaiso Univ., De Pauw Univ., Wabash College.

(See also Index for Bloomington, Evansville, Fort Wayne, Indianapolis.)

Iowa

Hawkeye State

CAPITAL: Des Moines. AREA: 56,290 sq. mi., rank, 25th. POPULATION: (See Index for 1970 Census.) MOTTO: Our Liberties We Prize and Our Rights We will Maintain. FLOWER: Wild Rose. BIRD: Eastern Goldfinch. TREE: Oak. SONG: Iowa. ADMISSION: 29th.

Iowa, the heart of the rich Midwest farm belt, is one of the nation's wealthiest agricultural states, but its industrial buildup has been so great that the value of its manufacturing output is far greater than that of its farms.

Many industries process farm products or produce farm implements. However, the fast-growing industrial economy includes a wide variety of manufacturing plants, with electronics items, home appliances, tires, railway equipment, furnaces, automobile accessories, chemicals and fertilizers, vending machines, office furniture, and gypsum wallboard among the diversified products. Value added by manufacture is over $3.9 billion a year.

Iowa's broad plains contain much of the finest soil in the world. Its huge harvests support the nation's richest livestock industry. Iowa had by far the most hogs, 14,556,000 on Dec. 1, 1972, more than twice as many as Illinois, the next largest raiser. In cattle, with 7,770,000 Iowa was 2nd only to Texas. It also had large numbers

of chickens, turkeys and sheep.

In field crops, Iowa ranked 1st in corn, 2nd in soybeans and 4th in alfalfa.

Receipts for livestock and livestock products totaled $3.19 billion in 1972, almost $1 billion more than Texas, the next ranking state. In receipts for crops, Iowa stood 4th. Its total farm receipts were $4.5 billion, 2nd only to California.

Iowa's forests produce hardwood lumber, particularly walnut.

Mineral production was valued at $136,012,000 in 1972. Products, in order of value, were cement, limestone, sand and gravel, gypsum and coal.

Visitors from other states add more than $344,000,000 to Iowa's economy annually.

Tourist attractions include the Herbert Hoover birthplace and library near West Branch, tulip festivals at Pella and Orange City in May, Iowa State Fair at Des Moines in August, several rodeos. The Little Brown Church in the Vale, near Nashua, inspired a well-known hymn and draws about 100,000 vistors annually. There are 91 state parks and other recreation areas. Effigy Mounds National Monument at Marquette is a prehistoric Indian burial site.

The Davenport Municipal Art Gallery has a collection of paintings and memorabilia of the Iowa painter Grant Wood, as well as other American, Mexican and European paintings, and a Haitian collection. Old masters include Breughel, Constable, Reynolds. The Davenport Public Museum displays the history of the area from prehistoric Indians to the steamboat and modern eras; archeology and ethnology of Egypt, Greece, Rome, Europe, South America and Asia; extensive collections of birds, mammals, insects, fossils, minerals and a herbarium of 20,000 plants.

In Decorah, the Norwegian-American Museum preserves homes, household utensils, etc., of pioneers who came from Norway.

Waterloo's Museum of History and Science has exhibits on Iowa history, pioneer life, Indian lore and earth sciences and a planetarium.

Iowa has 54 institutions of higher education. Among them are the Univ. of Iowa (Iowa City), Iowa State Univ. (Ames), Univ. of Northern Iowa (Cedar Falls), Coe College (Cedar Rapids), Drake Univ. (Des Moines), Grinnell College (Grinnell), St. Ambrose College (Davenport).

The first Europeans to visit the Iowa area were the French explorers, Father Jacques Marquette and Louis Jolliet, in 1673. It formed part of the Louisiana Purchase in 1803 and became a state Dec. 28, 1846.

(See also Index for Des Moines.)

Kansas

Sunflower State

CAPITAL: Topeka. AREA: 82,264 sq. mi., rank, 14th. POPULATION: (See Index for 1970 Census.) MOTTO: Ad Astra per Aspera. To the Stars Through Difficulties. FLOWER: Sunflower. BIRD: Western Meadow Lark. TREE: Cottonwood. ANIMAL: Buffalo. SONG: Home on the Range. ADMISSION: 34th.

Rolling fields of wheat, clusters of oil well derricks, great herds of cattle and towering grain storage elevators feature the landscape of Kansas, the geographical center of the 48 conterminous states. The land rises from broad plains in the E, 680 ft. above sea level, to slightly over 4,000 ft. in the W.

Manufacturing, farming and mining (especially petroleum and natural gas) are major factors in the Kansas economy. Large industry fields include transportation equipment, food processing, machinery and chemicals. Value added by manufacture is $2.5 billion a year.

Most of the land of Kansas is devoted to agriculture, and much of that to growing wheat. Kansas ranks 1st among the states in its wheat crop, which was est. at 314,900,000 bu. for 1972. It ranked 2nd in sorghum.

Kansas ranked 4th among the states in cattle with 6,850,000 on Jan. 1, 1973. Total farm receipts for 1972 were $2.6 billion, 5th highest in the U.S.

Forest products, particularly walnut lumber are valued at about $14,000,000 a year.

Wichita is one of the nation's largest aircraft manufacturing centers, and ranks 1st in production of private aircraft.

Kansas ranks high in petroleum production and has large reserves of natural gas and helium. Kansas ranks 1st among the states in helium production.

Petroleum production in 1972 was valued at an est. $262,592,000, almost half the total mineral production value, $587,678,000. Also important are natural gas and salt.

Coronado in 1541 headed a Spanish troop in a vain search for wealth in the area. France claimed all territory drained by the Mississippi through LaSalle's explorations, 1682. France ceded the vast area to Spain, 1763, and received it back in 1800. In 1803 the U.S. obtained the land through the Louisiana Purchase. The Kansas part of it became a Territory May 30, 1854; a state Jan. 29,1861.

During the fight over statehood Kansas was rent between free-state and pro-slavery forces. Kansas furnished one-fifth of her men for Union armies in the Civil War. Frontier posts were at Fort Leavenworth, now site of the U.S. Army Command and General Staff College; Fort Riley, Fort Scott, Fort Larned, Fort Hays, and other sites.

In Abilene, the boyhood home of the late President Dwight D. Eisenhower, is the Eisenhower Center, with the Eisenhower Home, Museum and Library. Near them, in a chapel named "Place of Meditation," the late President was buried April 2, 1969.

The Agricultural Hall of Fame and National Center, 14 mi. W of Kansas City, Kan., displays farm equipment of the past such as a wooden-wheeled corn planter, anvils, wheat drills, etc. In Dodge City are extensive reproductions of the original Front Street, saloons and Boot Hill cemetery.

The Wichita Art Museum has works by Bellows, Eakins, Copley, Sargent, Cassatt, Hopper, Ryder, Grosz, Marin, Andrew Wyeth, Stuart Davis, Lachaise, De Creeft, Zorach. The Kansas State Historical Society in Topeka has displays and period rooms of Midwest history and a library with newspaper and manuscript collections.

In Lawrence, the Univ. of Kansas has a Museum of Natural History which presents a panorama of North American mammals from the Arctic to the tropics; a Museum of Art, with European and American painting and sculpture and European and Oriental decorative arts; and the Snow Entomological Museum, with over 2,000,000 insects.

It is estimated that tourists spend over $527,000,000 a year in the state.

Kansas has 53 institutions of higher learning. Largest among them are the Univ. of Kansas (Lawrence), Wichita State Univ. (Wichita) and Kansas State Univ. of Agriculture and Applied Science (Manhattan).

Kansas has developed an extensive recreation system around its federal reservoirs, lakes and roadside parks. *(See also Index for Wichita.)*

Kentucky

Blue Grass State

CAPITAL: Frankfort. AREA: 40,395 sq. mi., rank, 37th. POPULATION: (See Index for 1970 Census.) MOTTO: United We Stand, Divided We Fall. FLOWER: Goldenrod. BIRD: Cardinal. SONG: My Old Kentucky Home. TREE: Tulip tree. ADMISSION: 15th.

Kentucky was the first area W of the Allegheny Mtns. settled by American pioneers, and one of the first of them to arrive was Daniel Boone, 1769. The first permanent settlement was that of James Harrod at Harrodsburg in 1774; the following year Boone blazed the Wilderness Trail and founded Boonesboro. Originally part of Fincastle Co., Va., the area became Kentucky Co., Va., in 1776, and an independent state in 1792.

Kentucky rises from an elevation of less than 260 ft., at the Mississippi, to over 4,000 ft. in the Cumberland and Pine mountains. Over 42% of the state is forested, and lumbering, particularly of hardwoods, is an important industry. Forest products were valued at $51,000,000 in 1972.

Manufacturing has shown important gains but agriculture and mining remain vital parts of Kentucky's economy.

Tobacco is the principal crop. With 436,581,000 lbs. in 1972, the Kentucky output was 2nd only to that of North Carolina.

Corn, soybeans, wheat, fruit, hogs and cattle, especially milk cows, are also important. Farm receipts in 1972 totaled $610,649,000 from livestock, $493,111,000 from crops.

In 1972 Kentucky produced more tons of coal than West Virginia but was 2nd in terms of its value. Kentucky also produces important amounts of petroleum, natural gas, fluorspar, clay and stone. But coal accounts for 90% of the total mineral value, est. at $1.05 billion for 1972.

Manufacturing has shown needed growth and diversity. Leading fields are food processing and beverages, tobacco products, machinery, chemicals, transportation equipment and apparel. Value added by manufacture is over $5.16 billion a year. Liquor distilling is important.

Tourists bring in an est. $635,000,000 a year. There are 48 state and national parks and shrines.

In 1966 Kentucky enacted a law requiring surface and strip miners of coal to restore and regrade earth removed by their operations.

Two of the largest man-made lakes in the world, Kentucky Lake and Lake Barkley, parallel each other in Western Kentucky, creating a 170,000-acre isthmus called the Land Between the Lakes National Recreation Area, developed by the Tennessee Valley Authority. Two major vacation resort parks, Kentucky Dam Village and Kenlake, are on the west shore of Kentucky Lake.

Lexington, heart of the Bluegrass country, is seat of Univ. of Kentucky and Transylvania, oldest college west of Alleghenies (1780), has a large tobacco market and holds annual trotting and running races and a horse show. Near Lexington are farms famous for blooded horses, including the Calumet, Castleton, Spendthrift, Walnut Hall, Greentree.

Fort Knox, repository of the nation's gold reserve, also contains the George S. Patton, Jr., Military Museum of World War II equipment.

Mammoth Cave, 40 mi. from Bowling Green, is in a national park. Discovered 1799, it has 150 mi. of passageways, rooms with 200-ft. ceilings, gypsum flowers, blind fish and an Echo River 360 ft. below ground.

Old Fort Harrod State Park, Harrodsburg, contains the reconstructed fort with stockade, blockhouses and cabins; the log cabin in which Thomas Lincoln and Nancy Hanks, Abraham Lincoln's parents, were married, and a museum with relics of Shakertown, Ky.

Abraham Lincoln Birthplace National Historic Site, 3 mi. from Hodgenville, contains the original Thomas Lincoln farm and the traditional Lincoln Birthplace cabin.

My Old Kentucky Home, 1 mi. E of Bardstown, was the home of John Rowan, senator and state chief justice. Stephen Foster, a relative, visited the Rowan family in 1852 and is said to have written My Old Kentucky Home on a desk preserved in the house.

(See also Index for Louisville.)

Louisiana

Pelican State

CAPITAL: Baton Rouge, AREA: 48,523 sq. mi., rank, 31st. POPULATION: (See Index for 1970 Census.) MOTTO: Union, Justice, Confidence. FLOWER: Southern Magnolia. BIRD: Eastern Brown Pelican. SONG: Give Me Louisiana. TREE: Bald Cypress. ADMISSION: 18th.

Louisiana blends a wealth of historic charm, rich natural resources and giant modern industries. Fertile soil, huge mineral deposits and over 7,000 mi. of navigable waterways linking the nation's heart with deepsea ports are factors basic to the state's wealth.

Mardi Gras and other festivals, the beat of Dixieland jazz in the land of its origin, and the nostalgic relics of the days of French and Spanish rule and the prosperous pre-Civil War era are among the attractions which bring Louisiana an est. $705,000,000 a year in tourist revenues.

In total value of its 1972 mineral output, $5.6 billion, Louisiana was 2nd only to Texas among the 50 states. It was 1st in value of its natural gas, sulphur and salt production, 2nd in petroleum. Much of the oil and sulphur comes from offshore deposits.

The lush Louisiana land produces one of the nation's largest crops of sweet potatoes. It is also a leader in rice and sugarcane. Also important are pecans, soybeans, cotton and corn.

Farm receipts in 1972 included $496,607,000 from crops, $305,276,000 from livestock.

Total value added by manufacture is over $3.5 billion annually.

Leading manufacturing industries include chemicals, food processing, petroleum and coal products (especially oil refining), paper (particularly paperboard), lumber and wood products, transportation equipment, stone-clay-glass products, apparel.

With 7,409 sq. mi. under water, Louisiana marshes supply most of the nation's muskrat fur; nutria has become the state's leading fur; there are also opossum, raccoon, mink, otter, and large numbers of game birds. The annual catch of fresh and salt water fish, shrimp and oyster is valued at about $72,000,000. Lake Pontchartrain covers 630 sq. mi., is the 5th largest natural lake wholly within the U.S.

Much of the land is a rich alluvial plain; there are also rolling hills, bluffs on the Mississippi and coastal marshes. The elevation ranges from 5 ft. below sea level, protected by vast levees, to 535 above.

Louisiana is rich in historical relics and traditions, with Spanish-French backgrounds, pirate lore, fashionable French society in the 18th Century, picturesque customs today. Early explorers were Pineda, 1519, de Vaca, 1528, De Soto, 1541, LaSalle, 1682. New Orleans was founded 1718. Louisiana became a French crown colony under Louis XV, 1731; was ceded to Spain, 1763, returned to France, 1801; sold by Napoleon to U.S. Dec. 20, 1803 (with large territory to N and NW). It became a U.S. Territory Mar. 26, 1804, effective Oct. 1. State was admitted to the union, Apr. 30, 1812; seceded Jan. 26, 1861, and joined Confederacy; readmitted June 25, 1868.

Louisiana has 25 institutions of higher education, among them Louisiana State Univ., with campuses in Baton Rouge, New Orleans and elsewhere, and Tulane Univ. in New Orleans.

Louisiana Creoles are descendants of early French and/or Spanish settlers. About 4,000 Acadians, French settlers in Nova Scotia, Canada, were forcibly transported by the British to Louisiana in 1755 (an event commemorated in Longfellow's Evangeline) and settled near Bayou Teche; their descendants became known as Cajuns. Another group, the Islenos, were descendants of Canary Islanders brought to Louisiana by a Spanish governor in 1770. Traces of Spanish and French survive in local dialects.

(See also Index for Baton Rouge, New Orleans, Shreveport.)

Maine
Pine Tree State

CAPITAL: Augusta. AREA: 33,215 sq. mi., rank, 39th. POPULATION: (See Index for 1970 Census.) MOTTO: Dirigo. I Direct. FLOWER: Pine Cone and Tassel. BIRD: Chickadee. TREE: Eastern White Pine. SONG: State of Maine Song. ADMISSION: 23rd.

Maine is noted for its scenic and vacation attractions, lobsters, potatoes, poultry and forest products, fishing and hunting.

Largest of the 6 New England states, it is the farthest NE and borders on only one other state, New Hampshire. Its rugged coast, because of deep indentations, measures 3,478 mi. Tides are often high; in Passamaquoddy Bay they average 20 ft.

Mt. Cadillac, on Mt. Desert Is., 1,532 ft., is the highest Atlantic seacoast point N of Brazil; West Quoddy Head, Long. 66° 57′ W, is the farthest east point on the U.S. Atlantic coast. Lubec is the most easterly town on the U. S. mainland.

John Cabot and his son, Sebastian, are believed to have visited the Maine coast in 1498. Long governed as a part of Massachusetts, Maine became a state in 1820.

Maine's coastal waters produce an annual 20,000,000 lbs. of lobsters, 75% of the nation's total, and 50% of its soft-shelled clams. The state packs over 150,000,000 cans of sardines a year. The fish and shellfish catch is worth $34,000,000 annually to the fisherman.

Maine grows about 12% of the nation's potatoes, 2nd to Idaho, and is the leading supplier of seed potatoes. It produces 90% of the nation's low bush blueberries. Also grown are apples, sweet corn, peas, beans. Farm income totaled $248,720,000 in 1972, with poultry and eggs the largest item.

With more than 80% of its area forested, Maine turns out wood products from boats to toothpicks, paper, lumber and Christmas trees. Over 98% of the forest land is privately owned. Forest products are valued at $714,617,000 a year. Spruce, white pine and birch are the most important woods. Also vital to Maine's economy are processed foods, shoes and textiles. It ranks high in shoe production.

Granite, cement and feldspar account for much of the 1972 value of mineral products, est. at $20,870,000.

Maine's scenic seacoast, beaches, lakes, mountains and resorts make it a popular vacationland; tourism is a $600,000,000-a-year industry. There are 20 state parks, including Baxter, where Mt. Katahdin, tallest of the state's 10 mountains over 4,000 ft., rises 5,268 ft. Maine has over 2,500 lakes, 1,300 wooded islands and 5,000 streams. Moosehead Lake is 40 mi. long and 2 to 10 mi. wide. Deer, grouse, black bear abound; game fish include salmon, tuna, trout, bass. There are over 45 public skiing facilities. Acadia National Park and the famed resort of Bar Harbor are on Mt. Desert Island.

Museums include the Bowdoin College Museum of Fine Arts, Brunswick, which has portraits by Gilbert Stuart, Smibert, Feke, Blackburn, Copley, Winslow Homer, Cassatt, etc.; also Assyrian, Greek and Roman sculpture.

The Colby College Art Museum, Waterville, has paintings by classic and contemporary Europeans and by Americans–Hassam, Homer, Denn, Inness, Moran, Poor, Sterne, Andrew Wyeth.

The Farnsworth Library and Museum, Rockland, has 19th and 20th Century American paintings, drawings, prints and sculpture.

The Portland Museum of Art comprises the Sweat Museum of American art and the Sweat Mansion, a Federal-style house built in 1800. Other historic homes in Portland are the Tate House, 1755, and the Victoria Mansion, 1859.

Colleges and universities include the Univ. of Maine, Bowdoin (1794), Colby and Bates.

(See also Index for Portland.)

Maryland
Old Line State, Free State

CAPITAL: Annapolis. AREA: 10,577 sq. mi., rank, 42nd. POPULATION: (See Index for 1970 Census.) MOTTO: Fatti Maschi. Parole Femine, Manly Deeds, Womanly Words. FLOWER: Black-eyed Susan. BIRD: Baltimore Oriole. TREE: White Oak. SONG: Maryland, My Maryland. Seventh of the Original 13 States to ratify Constitution.

Maryland stretches from the Atlantic Ocean to the Allegheny Mountains with 2 major interruptions, Chesapeake Bay and the District of Columbia. Both contribute importantly to the state's economy.

The bay cuts off the low coastal plain of the Eastern Shore from the rest of the state, provides both commercial and sports fishing and leads to the port of Baltimore, which handles some $3 billion in imports and exports a year. The 7.11-mi. Chesapeake Bay Highway Bridge spans the bay near Annapolis, S of Baltimore.

The national Capital area provides a market for much of Maryland's produce as well as adding to the crowds which enjoy the state's many recreational facilities.

Backbone Mtn. in the far W part of the state is its highest point, 3,360 ft.

Settlers, led by Leonard Calvert, brother of Cecilius Calvert, Lord Baltimore, arrived at St. Clements Island on March 25, 1634. They shortly moved to the mainland

and established the colony at St. Marys.

Maryland has a diversified economy. Leading industries in numbers of workers in 1972 were wholesale and retail trade, 326,400; government, 324,100; services, 254,100; manufacturing 250,400. Value added by manufacture totals over $4.28 billion annually. Important manufacturing industries are food products, primary metals, electrical equipment, printing and publishing, apparel, machinery.

Almost half of the land area is covered with forests. About 40% of timber cut is softwood. Stone and cement are leading mineral products; there is some coal mining. Mineral output was valued at $104,551,000 for 1972.

Seafood is an important industry. In a typical year, the fish and shellfish catch has a value of about $18,000,000. Striped bass is the principal contributor to the fin fish revenues, while oysters account for about 60% of the shellfish, followed by soft-shelled clams; Maryland is a leader in its catch of all three.

Much of Maryland's farmlands are fertile though not extensive. The state's largest cash crops are tobacco, corn, soybeans, apples and tomatoes. Commercial broilers and dairy products are important.

The 1st U. S. steam locomotive, Peter Cooper's Tom Thumb, was built in Baltimore and made its 1st run on the tracks of the Baltimore & Ohio R.R., 1830.

The Univ. of Maryland (1807) includes the Glenn L. Martin Institute of Technology. Other educational institutions: Johns Hopkins Univ. (estab. 1876), St. John's (1696), Goucher College (1885), U. S. Naval Academy (1845).

Famous racing events include the Preakness, at Pimlico track, Baltimore; the International at Laurel Race Course, and John B. Campbell Handicap at Bowie. Annapolis is a center for yacht races. Ocean City is a popular summer resort.

Famous historic sites include Fort McHenry, Baltimore, restored, where in 1814 waved the flag that inspired Francis Scott Key to write the Star-Spangled Banner; Antietam Battlefield near Hagerstown (1862); South Mountain (1862); Edgar Allan Poe house, Baltimore. The State House, Annapolis (1772), is the oldest in the U. S.

The U. S. Frigate Constellation, which was launched at Baltimore in 1797, has been made a National Historic Landmark and is a tourist attraction in Baltimore.

The Chesapeake Bay Maritime Museum in St. Michael's exhibits typical bay boats, including the last surviving oyster sloop, a cottage-type lighthouse and models of Baltimore clippers, log canoes, bugeyes and skipjacks.

The tourist industry is valued at over $300,000,000 a year. (See also Index for Baltimore, Washington, D. C.)

Massachusetts

Bay State, Old Colony

CAPITAL: Boston. AREA: 8,257 sq. mi., rank 45th. POPULATION: (See Index for 1970 Census.) MOTTO: Ense Petit Placidam Sub Libertate Quietem. By the Sword We Seek Peace, but Peace Only Under Liberty. FLOWER: Mayflower. BIRD: Chickadee. TREE: American Elm. SONG: All Hail to Massachusetts. Sixth of the Original 13 States to ratify Constitution.

Massachusetts has played important roles in the political, intellectual and economic development of the U. S. Here the Pilgrims, seeking religious freedom, founded Plymouth Colony in 1620.

As Massachusetts grew, it became a leader in resisting British oppression. Its citizens staged the Boston Tea Party in 1773 to protest unjust taxation. The Minutemen battled British troops at Lexington and Concord, Apr. 19, 1775, launching the American Revolution.

The state became the home of great universities such as Harvard and Massachusetts Institute of Technology. In the 19th Century its authors were giants among the nation's men of letters. It was also a hotbed of abolitionism.

In Massachusetts ports a great shipping industry, including the famed China trade, developed, along with vast whaling and fishing interests. Abundant waterpower helped create a variety of manufacturing industries.

While the Puritans demanded religious freedom for themselves, their leaders denied it to others; but some among them protested this, and the loudest protesters, Roger Williams, Anne Hutchinson and others were banished and settled Rhode Island in the 1630s as a haven for religious liberty. Meanwhile, in Massachusetts, Quakers and Baptists were persecuted and in Salem the infamous witchcraft trials and hangings were staged in 1692.

Eventually, religious freedom was achieved. In 1867, Mary Baker Eddy founded Christian Science in Lynn. Heavy immigration of Irish, Italians, Poles, Czechs and French Canadians brought many Catholics to the state.

In addition to Harvard (founded 1636) and Massachusetts Institute of Technology, other well known institutes of higher learning include Amherst, Andover Theological, Boston College, Boston Univ., Brandeis, Clark, Hebrew College, Holy Cross, Lowell Technological, Mt. Holyoke, Northeastern, Radcliffe, Simmons, Smith, Tufts, Univ. of Mass., Wellesley, Williams and Worcester Polytechnic.

The state had the first tax to support free schools and its first school at Dedham, 1649, and a uniform system in 1840.

Commercial fishing, in the rich waters off Massachusetts and the Grand Banks off Newfoundland, was one of the area's earliest industries. Whalers sailed the oceans around the world. Modern trawlers with huge nets help bring in a catch valued at about $48,000,000 a year, ranking high among the states.

Massachusetts was a pioneer in the manufacture of textiles and shoes and in creation of specialized machinery for them. The Bay State remains one of the top producers of shoes. A power loom, perfected by Francis Cabot Lowell in 1822, launched cotton manufacturing in Lowell.

Production of electrical machinery, including electronics and communications equipment, has become the leading manufacturing division, in terms of numbers of employees and value added by manufacture. It is closely followed by other types of machinery. Also important are processing of food products, leather, rubber and plastics, paper and paperboard, metal products.

Total value added by manufacture is over $9.4 billion a year, placing Massachusetts, despite its relatively small size, 10th among the states. A third of the state's workers are employed in manufacturing.

Massachusetts' cranberry crop is the nation's largest, 820,000 bbls. in 1972. Also important are dairy and poultry products, cigar wrapper tobacco, apples, peaches, maple syrup. Farm receipts totaled $162,934,000 in 1972. Mineral production for that year was valued at an est. $50,405,000, mostly of stone, sand nd gravel for construction industries.

Because of the state's numerous recreational areas and historic landmarks, tourism has become an important factor in the economy of the state. It is estimated that 2,500,000 out-of-state tourists visit Massachusetts annually, representing a value to the tourist industry of $1.25 billion.

Cape Cod has summer theaters, sports and an artists' colony at Provincetown. Tanglewood, in the Berkshires, has the summer concerts of the Boston Symphony Orch.

In New Bedford the Old Dartmouth Historical Society and Whaling Museum has a large and unique collection of whaling implements, scrimshaw and log-books as well as furniture, costumes, firearms, etc.

In Old Deerfield are Deerfield Memorial Hall (1799), Hall Tavern (1765), Parson Ashley House (1732) and other old buildings.

In Pittsfield, the Berkshire Athenaeum has memorabilia of Herman Melville, who lived there while writing Moby Dick, a scrimshaw and whaling collection and a large library. The Berkshire Museum, Pittsfield, has paintings by Rubens, Van Dyck, Reynolds, Murillo, the Hudson River artists, etc.; mineral and animal rooms; one of the sledges with which Robert E. Peary reached the North Pole.

In Plymouth, Pilgrim Hall contains relics of the Mayflower Pilgrims, including swords of Myles Standish, Bibles of Gov. William Bradford and John Alden, and the cradle of Peregrine White, first child born in the colony.

Old Sturbridge Village, in Sturbridge, is a recreated early New England village of 35 authentic homes and shops, shown functioning.

The Sterling and Francine Clark Art Institute, Williamstown, displays 14th-17th Century European paintings, a large collection of Impressionists, sculpture, silver and drawings.

The Worcester Art Museum presents a survey of art through 50 centuries, stressing early American painting, pre-Columbian and contemporary arts. Also in Worcester, the John W. Higgins Armory displays medieval armor, and the American Antiquarian Society has a collection of early printing, including newspapers and almanacs. (See also Index for Boston, Springfield.)

Michigan

Wolverine State

CAPITAL: Lansing. AREA: 58,216 sq. mi., rank, 23rd. POPULATION: (See Index for 1970 Census.) MOTTO: Si Quaeris Peninsulam Amoenam Circumspice. If You Seek a Pleasant Peninsula, Look About You. FLOWER: Apple Blossom. BIRD: Robin. TREE: White Pine. SONG: (unofficial) Michigan, My Michigan. ADMISSION: 26th.

Bordering on 4 of the 5 Great Lakes, Michigan is divided into an Upper and Lower Peninsula by the Straits of Mackinac, which link Lakes Michigan and Huron. The two parts of the state are connected by the Mackinac Bridge, which has the 3rd largest suspension span in the U. S. To the N, separating Michigan from Canada, is the Sault Ste. Marie (Soo) Ship Canal, one of the world's most heavily used waterways.

Michigan contains the world's greatest concentration of automobile manufacturers; its rich orchards near the shores of Lake Michigan grow large fruit crops; the Upper Peninsula produces important amounts of iron, copper and other minerals, and the state's lakes and forests make it a highly popular vacationland. The highest point is Mt. Curwood, 1,980 ft., in the Upper Peninsula.

While Michigan ranks 1st among the states in production of motor vehicles and parts, it is also a leader in many other manufacturing and processing lines including prepared cereals, machine tools, hardware, steel springs, public office furniture, padding and upholstering, industrial patterns, nonferrous castings, industrial leather belts, paperboard mills and gray iron foundries.

The state ranked 6th in the U.S. in the 1971 Survey of Manufactures in terms of value added by manufacture, $20.3 billion. Motor vehicles and equipment accounted for $7.4 billion of that and also provided the most jobs, about 286,000. Other major industry groups were primary metals and metal products, machinery, food and chemicals.

Tourist attractions are many and spending by tourists has been est. at over $1.5 billion a year. The state has 36,000 mi. of streams, over 11,000 lakes and the longest freshwater shoreline (facing 4 of the Great Lakes). Water sports, music festivals, skiing, winter carnivals, fishing and hunting are among attractions.

Isle Royale in Lake Superior is a national park with 539,339 acres. There are 5 national forests, 75 state parks and recreational areas and numerous canoe trails.

Farm receipts in 1972 totaled $1.09 billion, more than half from livestock products. The state ranked 8th in the U.S. in number of milk cows. It grew the most tart and sweet cherries and ranked high in apples, pears, grapes and sugar beets.

Iron ore is the largest source of Michigan's income from minerals. With continued depletion of high-grade iron ore deposits, production of high-grade pellets from low-grade taconite iron ore has increased, amounting to over 85% of the ore total.

Michigan was 2nd only to Minnesota among the states in value of iron ore output, $159,000,000 in 1972. It was also a leading producer of gypsum, peat, iodine, bromine, magnesium compounds, lime, gravel and cement. Other minerals include copper, petroleum and salt. Total output was est. at $670,457,000.

There are some 88 institutions of higher education, including the Univ. of Michigan, Michigan State Univ., Wayne State Univ., the Univ. of Detroit, Michigan Tech-

nological Univ., and Central Michigan, Eastern Michigan, Western Michigan and Northern Michigan Univs.

The Grand Rapids Art Museum, in addition to its permanent collections, holds special monthly and traveling exhibits and art classes conducted for adults by the Univ. of Michigan.

The state was originally explored by the French and many names (Detroit, Sault Ste. Marie) are of French origin. Etienne Brulé (1618), Jean Nicolet (1634), Pére Allouez (1666), Pére Marquette (1668) and Louis Jolliet (1669) were early visitors. France was ousted by Britain, 1763. Under the Ordinance of 1787 Michigan Territory embraced parts of other western states. It was organized as a separate territory 1805, admitted to the Union Jan. 26, 1837. (See Index for Detroit and Kalamazoo.)

Minnesota

North Star State, Gopher State

CAPITAL: St. Paul. AREA: 84,068 sq. mi., rank 12th. POPULATION: (See Index for 1970 Census.) MOTTO: L'Etoile du Nord, Star of the North. FLOWER: Showy Lady's-slipper. BIRD: Loon. TREE: Red (Norway) Pine. SONG: Hail! Minnesota. ADMISSION: 32nd.

Minnesota is a land rich in natural resources. Its fertile prairies support large crops and an important dairy industry, its mines yield most of the iron ore produced in the U.S., its forests produce mountains of pulpwood, its manufacturing is varied and vigorous, its thousands of lakes and other attractions lure millions of sportsmen and vacationers.

The headwaters of 3 great drainage systems lie within Minnesota; the Mississippi, leading to the Gulf of Mexico, with its source at Lake Itasca; the Red River of the North, which flows into Canada's Lake Winnipeg, draining into Hudson Bay; the St. Louis and other rivers draining into Lake Superior and thence through the Great Lakes and the St. Lawrence to the Atlantic.

Known as the "land of 10,000 lakes," Minnesota actually has 15,291 larger than 10 acres each. Two-thirds of the state is rolling prairie. Highest point is Eagle Mt. in the NE, 2,301 ft.

Fishing, hunting, water sports and winter sports are among attractions for more than 5,000,000 vacationers who spend some $886,000,000 annually.

Minnesota produces about 63% of the iron ore mined in the U.S., despite depletion of the high-grade ore in the famed Mesabi and other ranges in the NE part of the state. Lost production from the huge open pit and underground mines is being replaced by high-grade pellets refined from low-grade taconite iron ore. By 1972, shipments of taconite pellets comprised about 73% of the total iron ore value and were increasing.

Iron ore production in 1972 was valued at $564,000,000, the major part of the total mineral production value, $626,872,000.

Manufacturing has shown both growth and diversity. Largest industries are food processing and machinery. Also important are electrical machinery, chemicals, paper, stone-clay-glass products, apparel, lumber, fabricated metal products. Value added by manufacture is $4.8 billion.

Much of the land is richly fertile. With $2.4 billion in farm receipts for 1972, Minnesota ranked 7th among the states. Two-thirds of that income was from livestock products, the rest from crops. Ranking 2nd in number of milk cows in 1972, the state was a leader in dairy products. It ranked high in turkeys and hogs.

Minnesota's farms grew the most oats and it ranked among the top states in spring wheat, corn, rye, alfalfa and sugar beets.

Forest products have a yearly estimated value of over $400,000,000, most of it in pulpwood.

Nationally known is the Mayo Clinic at Rochester, founded by Drs. William J. and Charles H. Mayo.

Minnesota has 59 institutions of higher learning. Among them are the Univ. of Minnesota, 6 state colleges and 18 state junior colleges.

The Minnesota Orchestra, the Tyrone Guthrie Theater in Minneapolis and the St. Olaf College Choir in Northfield are well known.

Minnesota has a large system of state parks and recreation areas. Minnehaha Falls in Minneapolis became famous through Longfellow's "The Song of Hiawatha." Other attractions are the St. Paul Winter Carnival, the Minneapolis Aquatennial and the Minnesota State Fair. French traders and missionaries first penetrated Minnesota. Father Hennepin, 1680, named St. Anthony Falls, a 50-ft drop in the Mississippi in present-day Minneapolis. France ceded the land E of the Mississippi to Great Britain, 1763; Britain to U.S., 1783. It became part of Northwest Terr. The land W of the Mississippi was part of Louisiana Purchase, 1803. Henry R. Schoolcraft found source of Mississippi in Lake Itasca, July 13, 1832. Organized as a Territory in 1849, it became a state May 11, 1858. (See also Index for Minneapolis, St. Paul.)

Mississippi
Magnolia State

CAPITAL: Jackson. **AREA:** 47,716 sq. mi., rank, 32nd. **POPULATION:** (See Index for 1970 Census.) **MOTTO:** Virtute et Armis, By Valor and Arms. **FLOWER:** Magnolia. **TREE:** Magnolia. **BIRD:** Mockingbird. **SONG:** Go, Mississippi! **ADMISSION:** 20th.

Mississippi's economy, long based on one crop, "King Cotton," has become balanced and diversified, thanks to promotion of industry, varied crops, tourism and federal agency installations.

The land slopes from the NE hills, where the high point is Woodall Mt. (806 ft.), to the Delta, a cotton-producing alluvial plain in the W and NW lying between the Yazoo River and the Mississippi, which flows along the state's western border.

The land also slopes to the S where the sandy beaches on the Gulf of Mexico have created a popular vacationland.

Indian tribes, including the Chickasaw, Choctaw and Natchez, inhabited the Mississippi area when the 1st Europeans, under Spain's Hernando de Soto, passed through in 1540. The first permanent settlement by Europeans was by a French group under Pierre le Moyne, Sieur d'Iberville, in 1699, at Fort Maurepas near present-day Biloxi.

Great Britain took over the area in 1763 after the French and Indian War, ceding it to the U.S. in 1783 after the Revolution. Spain also claimed the land and did not relinquish it until 1798.

The population grew steadily and Mississippi became a state Dec. 10, 1817. It was the 2nd state to join the Confederacy, 1861, and was readmitted to the Union in 1870.

Soybeans have taken over as Mississippi's largest crop, although the state ranks 2nd only to Texas in cotton production. Other important farm products include large crops of pecans and sweet potatoes; other crops include rice and sugarcane syrup. Poultry and eggs are also important. Farm receipts totaled $1.1 billion in 1972.

Biloxi has a large seafood canning industry, operating deep-sea trawlers for shrimp and oysters. Value of the commercial catch is more than $11,000,000 a year.

With more than 60% of the land classified as forest, timber products yielded over $1 billion in 1972.

The state produces the most hardwood pulp wood, much hardwood lumber and slashpine products, including fiberboard, kraft paper, newsprint.

Petroleum production was valued at $192,938,000 for 1972; natural gas output was valued at $24,242,000; total value of mineral production was est. at $255,716,000.

Mississippi has achieved considerable industrial expansion. The main fields have been lumber, along with furniture and paper, food processing, apparel, chemicals, transportation equipment, machinery.

In 1972, $982,126,500 was invested in new and expanded plants, creating 21,749 new jobs; both record figures.

A $250,000,000 NASA space installation is used as a center for International Earth Sciences by NOAA and NASA.

Mississippi became the last state to abandon prohibition, adopting a local-option liquor law May 21, 1966.

Tourism is of growing economic importance. It is estimated that out-of-state tourists spend over $420,000,000 a year in the state.

Gulfport holds an annual yacht regatta and a fishing rodeo in July, Biloxi has a Mardi Gras, Pass Christian has a tarpon rodeo. Natchez holds a pilgrimage each spring which features visits to many of the city's ante bellum mansions. Also sponsoring such pilgrimages are Columbus, Holly Springs, Oxford, Carrollton, Jackson, Vicksburg, Woodville, Hatiesburg, Raymond, Meridian.

In Vicksburg National Military Park, visitors may see remains of forts, trenches and other works which featured the 1863 siege of the city.

The Old Court House Museum in Vicksburg, built in 1858 by slave labor, has a museum with relics of the siege of Vicksburg, including flags, documents, newspapers printed on the back of wallpaper, guns, swords, etc., and exhibits of the ante bellum South.

The Lauren Rogers Library and Museum of Art in Laurel contains works of 19th and early 20th Century Americans and Europeans, local artifacts and an unusual basket collection (about half of them Indian).

Missouri
Show Me State

CAPITAL: Jefferson City. **AREA:** 69,686 sq. mi., rank, 19th. **POPULATION:** (See Index for 1970 Census.) **MOTTO:** Salus Populi Suprema Lex Esto, The Welfare of the People Shall Be the Supreme Law. **FLOWER:** Hawthorn. **BIRD:** Eastern Bluebird. **TREE:** Dogwood. **SONG:** Missouri Waltz. **ADMISSION:** 24th.

The gateway through which the pioneers passed on their way West, Missouri today is a leading manufacturing state, with aerospace and a wide variety of other industries; it is the nation's largest producer of lead; it ranks high among the states in agricultural products; its areas of scenic and historic interest attract over 21,000,000 vacationers each year.

Gently rolling hills in the N and W produce large crops and support cattle, sheep and hogs. The Ozark highlands in the S are famed for fishing, hunting and rugged scenery, including numerous caves and springs. The "delta" area in the SE produces soybeans, cotton and melons.

The Mississippi forms the state's boundary on the E; the Missouri forms part of the boundary in the W, then flows across the state to join the Mississippi above St. Louis. Highest point in the state is Taum Sauk Mt., 1,772 ft., in the E central area.

Missouri has endeared itself to generations of Americans with its river lore, folk tales and especially the writings of Mark Twain (Samuel L. Clemens). Statues of two of his creations, Tom Sawyer and Huckleberry Finn, stand in Hannibal, his boyhood home. His birthplace near Florida, Mo., has been enshrined in Mark Twain State Park.

The farm birthplace of notorious bandit Jesse James (1847-1882) is near Excelsior Springs. A log cabin built by U.S. Grant is near St. Louis. The farm where George Washington Carver, agricultural scientist, was born near Diamond is now a National Monument. The Harry S. Truman Library, near Independence, contains Presidential papers and memorabilia. Mr. Truman, who died Dec. 26, 1972, is buried in the library courtyard.

Manufacturing, paced by the state's large aerospace industries, is the top income producer and employs more persons than any other segment of the economy. Value added by manufacture is over $7.5 billion yearly. Transportation equipment, including space capsules, rocket engines, aircraft and auto assemblies, ranks 1st, followed by food processing, esp. meat packing, grain milling, beer and other beverages. Also important are chemicals, printing, metal products, machinery, shoes. Corncob pipes and charcoal are well-known products.

Agriculture is also an important income producer. Farm receipts in 1972 totaled $1.9 billion, two-thirds from livestock products. Missouri ranked 4th among the states in hogs, 6th in cattle and 4th in turkeys. It has large soybean, corn and clover crops. Also important are winter wheat, tobacco, apples, peaches, alfalfa, popcorn, rye.

Tourism, described as the 3rd largest industry, produces $1 billion annually. Some 24,000,000 out-of-state tourists visit Missouri each year; more than 11,000,000 visit its many state park and recreation areas. There is a wide variety of vacation facilities; large resort areas include Lake of the Ozarks, Lake Taneycomo and Table Rock Lake.

Missouri is rich in minerals. Its output of lead, valued at $149,022,000 for 1972, was the largest in the U.S. Total mineral production value was worth $449,717,000. It was also a leader in barite and lime. Other products include cement, coal, iron ore, copper, zinc, asphalt.

There are 70 institutions of higher learning. The Univ. of Missouri has campuses at Columbia, Rolla, Kansas City and St. Louis. The Univ. of Missouri at Rolla was formerly the Missouri School of Mines & Metallurgy. The Univ. of Missouri at Columbia has the country's first School of Journalism, founded 1908 by Walter Williams.

De Soto visited the Missouri area in 1541. French fur traders founded Ste. Genevieve about 1735, St. Louis 1764. It was part of the Louisiana Territory purchased by the U.S. from France in 1803. Missouri was organized as a separate territory, 1812; admitted to the Union, Aug. 10, 1821.

The St. Joseph Museum in St. Joseph stresses the natural history and wildlife of the region and has exhibits on Indian tribes from Alaska to Florida. Also in St. Joseph is the Pony Express Museum.

(See also Index for Kansas City and St. Louis.)

Montana
Treasure State

CAPITAL: Helena. **AREA:** 147,138 sq. mi., rank, 4th. **POPULATION:** (See Index for 1970 Census.) **MOTTO:** Oro y Plata, Gold and Silver. **FLOWER:** Bitterroot. **TREE:** Ponderosa Pine. **BIRD:** Western Meadow Lark. **SONG:** Montana. **ADMISSION:** 41st.

The Rocky Mountains, with snow-capped peaks, forested slopes, broad valleys and many lakes, cover the western 40% of Montana; the rest is High Plains country devoted to grazing and farming. Montana is rich in minerals, hydroelectric power and impressive scenery. Highest mountain is Granite Peak, 12,799 ft.

Agriculture plays a vital role in Montana's economy, along with manufacturing, mining and tourism/recreation.

Oceans of grain cover much of Montana's plains; it ranks high among the states in wheat and barley output. Also grown are rye, oats, flaxseed, sugar beets and potatoes. Montana ranks 6th in sheep and 13th in cattle. Farm receipts totaled $715,249,000 in 1972, more than half from livestock.

Manufacturing industries have grown, with value added by manufacture over $330,400,000 a year. Processing of forest products and primary metal industries are most important and have the most employees, followed by food processing. Wood products include pulp, plywood and lumber; value is est. at $300,000,000 a year. The state ships more than 3,000,000 Christmas trees annually.

Total mineral production for 1972 was est. at $323,823,000, with petroleum accounting for $102,378,000 and copper $124,605,000. Other products include silver, gold, natural gas. Strip-mining for coal is increasing.

Out-of-state tourists spend an est. $210,000,000 annually.

Tourist attractions include hunting, fishing, skiing, dude ranching. Two large recreation-resort centers, Big Sky and Gregson Hot Springs, were being developed in 1973.

Hunters annually take about 100,000 deer, 11,000 antelope, 10,000 elk, 1,100 black bear, 500 moose, 350 mountain goats.

Glacier National Park, on the Continental Divide, is a scenic and recreational wonderland, with 60 glaciers, 200 lakes and many streams with good trout fishing.

Flathead Lake, in the NW, covers 189 sq. mi. and is the largest natural body of fresh water within a single state W of the Mississippi in conterminous U.S. Fort Peck Reservoir, in the NE, covers 382.8 sq. mi. and is one of the largest man-made lakes in the U.S.

Important historical site is Custer Battlefield National Cemetery, in Big Horn County (near Hardin), site of defeat of Custer by Sioux, June 25, 1876. First visited by the French Verendryes, father and sons, 1743; Lewis and Clark, 1805, Montana became a Territory, 1864, and a state Nov. 8, 1889.

There are 7 Indian reservations, covering over 5,000,000 acres; tribes are Blackfeet, Crow, Confederated Salish & Kootenai, Assiniboine, Gros Ventre, Sioux, Northern Cheyenne, Chippewa, Cree. Population of the reservations is approximately 25,500.

The Museum of the Plains Indian, on the Blackfeet Reservation near Browning, features exhibits of historic and contemporary arts and crafts of the Northern Plains Indians and an Indian craft shop; the museum is administered by the U.S. Interior Dept.

The Historical Society of Montana, in Helena, has paintings, dioramas and other exhibits of Montana's Indian and buffalo days, mining camps, frontier settlements, cattle roundups. Outstanding is the collection of nearly 100 Charles M. Russell paintings.

There are 12 colleges and universities, including the Univ. of Montana at Missoula and Montana State Univ. in Bozeman. *(See also Index for Billings.)*

Nebraska
Cornhusker State

CAPITAL: Lincoln. **Area:** 77,227 sq. mi., rank, 15th. **POPULATION:** (See Index for 1970 Census.) **MOTTO:** Equality Before The Law. **FLOWER:** Goldenrod. **TREE:** Cottonwood. **BIRD:** Western Meadow Lark. **SONG:** Beautiful Nebraska. **Admission:** 37th.

Fields of corn, wheat and sorghum cover the Nebraska plain, sloping gently toward the Missouri River, the eastern border of the state; vast herds of cattle roam the grassy sandhills which rise to the W, ending in the broken table lands which mark the foothills of the Rockies. Highest point, 5,426 ft., is in the far SW corner.

With more than 23,000,000 acres under cultivation, Nebraska is an agricultural stronghold, an important grain and livestock producer. Many of its manufacturing industries are agriculture-related.

But manufacturing has also become diversified, broadening the state's economic base. Firms making electronic components, auto accessories, pharmaceuticals and other sophisticated products have joined the older industries.

Processing of meat, grain and dairy products is by far the largest manufacturing field, accounting for more than a third of the total value added by manufacture, which is estimated at almost $1.5 billion, as well as for the largest number of workers.

Other important manufacturing fields are electrical machinery and other machinery, especially farm equipment; chemicals, metal products, transportation equipment, instruments and related products. Several score new plants and plant expansions are announced annually, continuing the industrial growth and adding new jobs.

Nebraska ranked 6th among the states in total farm receipts for 1972; $2.49 billion, with the larger part coming from livestock products. Its cattle herds ranked 3rd among the states; it had 6,915,000 cattle in 1973. It ranked 6th in hogs, with 3,455,000. Nebraska was also a leader in several crops, ranking high in sorghum, winter wheat, corn and rye. Also important are soybeans, sugar beets and oats.

Mineral production in Nebraska was valued at $74,124,000 for 1972. Oil continued to be the most important product, valued at $29,693,000. Other products included cement, lime, pumice, sand and gravel.

Nebraska has a unicameral or one-house legislature with 49 members elected on a nonpartisan ballot. All electric power facilities are state or municipally owned.

Nebraska has 27 institutions of higher education. Among them are the Univ. of Nebraska, with campuses in Lincoln and Omaha, Nebraska Wesleyan Univ. in Lincoln, and Creighton Univ. in Omaha.

Arbor Lodge State Park at Nebraska City is a memorial to J. Sterling Morton, founder of Arbor Day, which is observed as a legal holiday on his birthday, Apr. 22. Boys Town is 11 mi. W. of Omaha.

The Sheldon Memorial Art Gallery at the Univ. of Nebraska, Lincoln, housed in a building designed by Philip Johnson, has works by Bellows, Stuart Davis, Eakins, Gauguin, Homer, Hopper, Miro, O'Keeffe, Picasso, Ryder, Calder, Lachaise, Henry Moore, Rodin, Zorach, etc.

The Joslyn Art Museum, Omaha, has works by Titian, El Greco, Rembrandt, Goya, Renoir, etc.; exhibits of furniture, the early West, fur trade, Indian art, etc.

Pioneer Village, Minden, has some 30,000 items of Americana displayed in a rural schoolhouse, depot, general store, fort, fire house, sod house, Pony Express station, etc., plus old locomotives, tractors, a steam-powered merry-go-round.

The House of Yesterday, Hastings, has exhibits of pioneer days and natural science and the J. M. McDonald Planetarium.

French fur traders visited the Nebraska area about 1700. It was part of the Louisiana Purchase, 1803, and was visited by Lewis and Clark, 1804-06. The Union Pacific began its transcontinental railroad at Omaha in 1865 (completed 1869). The Territory of Nebraska was created by the Kansas-Nebraska Act. 1854; it became a state Mar. 1, 1867.

(See also Index for Omaha)

Nevada

Sagebrush State, Silver State

CAPITAL: Carson City. AREA: 110,540 sq. mi., rank, 7th. POPULATION: (See Index for 1970 Census.) MOTTO: All for Our Country. FLOWER: Sagebrush. BIRD: Mountain Bluebird. TREE: Single-leaf Pinon. SONG: Home Means Nevada. ADMISSION: 36th.

Nevada lies mostly in the Great Basin, a rugged plateau region broken by mountain chains running N-S. It is enclosed on the E by the Rockies and the Wasatch Range in Utah, and on the W by California's Sierra Nevada and Cascade Ranges which rob the clouds of moisture, making Nevada's climate extremely dry. Boundary Peak, near the SW border with California, is the state's highest point, 13,140 ft.

One of the smallest states in population, Nevada has attracted large numbers of outsiders, starting with the famed rush to the Comstock Lode (discovered 1859) and other fabulous gold and silver mines. Today, the attractions are legalized gambling, highly-developed entertainment and recreation facilities, and lenient divorce laws requiring only 6-weeks residence.

Spending by visitors is the biggest factor in Nevada's economy. More than 24,600,000 from out of state, about 49 times the state's population, visit Nevada annually.

Tourist-connected industries—hotels, casinos, amusement and recreation facilities—make up the largest employment category.

State collections from gaming were $54,880,112 in 1971-72, up $12,992,114 from the previous fiscal year. This income provides about 43% of the state's revenue. Gross gambling receipts for 1972 were $657,739,406.

There are big resort areas, with nearby skiing as well as sunbathing, near Lake Tahoe, Reno, Las Vegas and elsewhere. Ghost towns, rodeos, trout fishing, water skiing and deer hunting are other attractions.

Large recreation areas include those at Pyramid Lake, wholly within the state; Lake Tahoe, partly in California; Lake Mead, formed by Hoover Dam, and Lake Mohave, formed by Davis Dam, both in Lake Mead National Recreation Area, which is shared with Arizona.

Mineral production value for 1972 was est. at $184,800,000 with copper accounting for $108,201,000. Nevada is also a leader in gold, mercury, lithium, barite and silver.

Nevada is the largest manufacturer of gaming devices. Also important are electronic devices, chemicals, forest products, suntan lotion, stone-clay-glass products. About $161,800,000 is the est. value added annually by growing manufacturing industries.

Farm receipts totaled $100,139,000 for 1972, more than 80% from livestock products. The dry climate makes much of the state more suitable for grazing than for crops, although large-scale irrigation has expanded the growing areas.

The Nevada Test Site, NW of Las Vegas, is a proving ground for various atomic devices.

The Univ. of Nevada System administers the Univ. of Nevada, Reno, and the Univ. of Nevada, Las Vegas.

Trappers and traders entered the Nevada area in the 1820s, including Jedediah Smith and Peter Skene Ogden. It became U. S. territory at the end of the Mexican War. It became a state Oct. 31, 1864.

The Nevada State Museum, Carson City, occupies a former U. S. Mint, and exhibits coins, habitat groups of mammals and birds of the Great Basin area, Indian baskets, full-scale replicas of underground mining operations and thousands of arrowheads.

LAS VEGAS

Las Vegas (The Meadows), in southern Nevada, is the state's largest city and the seat of Clark County; 1970 Census pop. was 125,787, with a total of 273,288 in the county. About 17,399,000 tourists visited Las Vegas in 1972. Gross gaming revenues in 1972 totaled $476,126,720. The city has 22 major hotels, 293 motels, 35 other hotels, with a total of close to 28,000 rooms.

Las Vegas is served by 7 major airlines and passengers flying into McCarran Int. Airport in 1972 were 4,606,644. There is a Convention Center and hall seating 8,500. Nearby are Valley of Fire Park, Lakes Mead and Mohave, Mt. Charleston Recreation Area; Las Vegas Air Force Station, Nellis and Indian Springs Air Force Bases.

(See also Index for Reno.)

New Hampshire

Granite State

CAPITAL: Concord. AREA: 9,304 sq. mi., rank, 44th. POPULATION: (See Index for 1970 Census.) MOTTO: Live Free or Die. FLOWER: Purple Lilac. BIRD: Purple Finch. TREE: Paper (White) Birch. SONG: Old New Hampshire. Ninth of the Original 13 States to ratify Constitution.

One of the 6 New England states, New Hampshire is a land of impressive mountains, picturesque lakes, swift rivers and, in the north, thick forests. Mountain slopes provide excellent ski trails. Numerous lakes and streams afford fishing for trout, bass, pickerel, perch, whitefish.

Abundant water power early turned New Hampshire into an industrial state, with manufacturing the principal source of income. Soil and climate have curtailed agricultural growth, but scenic and recreation resources have been developed and the tourist-vacation business, about $400,000,000 a year, ranks 2nd in its contribution to the state's economy.

In 1964, to raise funds to support education, the state ran the 1st legal sweepstakes lottery in the U. S. since 1894 (in that year, a lottery in Louisiana was outlawed). Profits from the state lottery are turned over to local school districts.

Most important industrial products are shoes and boots, electrical and other machinery, wool and other textiles, and paper.

Most factories are concentrated along the Merrimack and Connecticut Rivers and in the seacoast area. Manufacturing employs about 100,000 workers. Value added by manufacture is over $1.09 billion a year.

Farm receipts for 1972 totaled $58,180,000, about four-fifths from dairy and poultry products. Crops include apples, peaches, maple sugar and syrup.

Mineral products, mainly sand, gravel and stone for construction, were valued at $10,555,000 for 1972.

Recreation and vacation attractions include Lake Winnipesaukee, largest of 1,300 lakes and ponds; the White Mountains, with skiing and scenic beauty; beaches on the Atlantic Coast and numerous historic sites.

One-third of the state is over 2,000 ft. above sea level. Highest land in Northeast U. S. is the Presidential range of the White Mountains, with Mt. Washington, 6,288 ft. (first cog railway in world opened 1869); Mt. Jefferson, 5,717 ft.; Mt. Adams, 5,789 ft. National forests cover 677,559 acres; 142 state forests and parks, 63,805 acres.

State-owned parks include areas in Crawford and Franconia Notches, the latter on Profile Mtn. where may be seen the Old Man of the Mountains, described by Nathaniel Hawthorne as the Great Stone Face.

Portsmouth is the state's only port. Manchester is the largest city.

New Hampshire was visited by Samuel Champlain in 1605. Under an English land grant, Capt. John Mason in 1623 sent two groups to establish a fishing colony at the mouth of the Piscataqua River. One group settled Little Harbor of Pannaway (now town of Rye); the other set up fishing stages at Northam, later named Dover. The colony was called after Hampshire, England, in 1629. It declared its independence Jan. 5, 1776, and contributed to the victories at Bennington and Saratoga, entering the Union June 21, 1788.

New Hampshire shared the educational pioneering of Massachusetts Bay from 1642; it established its first free public library at Dublin, 1822.

Its schools include the Univ. of N. H. and Dartmouth College. The MacDowell colony at Peterborough, established in 1908 in honor of Edward MacDowell, is a summer haven for writers, composers, artists.

The Currier Gallery of Art, Manchester, exhibits silver by Paul Revere and others, textiles, hooked rugs, pewter and glass and a rich collection of works by Tintoretto, Ruisdael, Monet, Corot, Constable, Picasso, Roualt, Copley, Stuart, Trumbull, Sargent, Homer, Wyeth, Marin, etc.

The New Hampshire Historical Society, Concord, has a museum displaying New Hampshire furniture, silver, pewter, glass, china, quilts, costumes, weapons, kitchen woodenware, etc.

New Jersey

Garden State

CAPITAL: Trenton. AREA: 7,836 sq. mi., rank, 46th. POPULATION: (See Index for 1970 Census.) MOTTO: Liberty and Prosperity. FLOWER: Purple Violet. BIRD: Eastern Goldfinch. TREE: Red Oak. Third of the Original 13 States to ratify Constitution.

Smallest of the Middle Atlantic states, New Jersey was settled by the Dutch early in the 17th Century and was the scene of much action during the American Revolution. Today it has the heaviest pop. per sq. mi. of the 50 states, ranks near the top in manufacturing, is rich in poultry and vegetable production, and has a flourishing resort industry.

There are vast shipping facilities and New Jersey divides authority over important airports, harbors, tunnels and bridges with the Port of New York Authority and the states of Delaware and Pennsylvania.

Much of the tonnage total of the Port of New York is loaded or unloaded at piers on the New Jersey side of the harbor.

About 63% of the state's land area is in farms and forests. Highest point is High Point, Sussex County, 1,803 ft.

Small in area, New Jersey has a heavy concentration of factories, highways, railroads and farms, and is a leader in many fields.

It also has the greatest population density among the 50 states, reaching that status in 1965, when it passed Rhode Island. In the 1970 Census, New Jersey had 953.1 persons per sq. mi., Rhode Island had 905.5.

Highly industrialized, New Jersey ranks 7th among the states in value added by manufacture, over $14 billion annually. It ranks 1st among the states in chemical products, having large pharmaceutical, basic chemical and paint industries.

It is also a leader in other manufacturing lines: apparel, food processing, electrical and other machinery, stone-clay-glass products, printing, rubber and plastics, petroleum products, leather products. It has a large concentration of research installations in many lines.

New Jersey also ranks high in the U.S. in gross income per farm acre. Chief crops are tomatoes, corn, asparagus, apples, cranberries, peaches, spinach. Poultry and dairy products are also important. The first dairy cattle artificial insemination project was launched in Hunterdon County; also the first common-carrier shipments of day-old chicks.

Total farm receipts in 1972 were $234,527,000, more than half from crops.

Mineral production showed gains in 1972. Of the total value, stone, sand and gravel, mainly for construction work, accounted for the largest part. Zinc, peat and clays were among other products.

Large refineries, which process oil from out of state, have a total crude capacity of more than 500,000 barrels a day.

The commercial fishing catch is valued at over $14,000,000 a year.

Among New Jersey's institutions of higher learning are Princeton and Rutgers (the state university); the Institute for Advanced Study; 3 other universities; 26 colleges, 23 junior and community colleges, 3 professional and technological colleges.

A state lottery, with proceeds to benefit education, was launched in 1971. It proved highly successful.

Atlantic City, Ocean City, Cape May, Asbury Park, Ocean Grove, Wildwood are among more than 100 resorts.

The resort industry generates over $2.6 billion in business annually. There are 40 state parks with 47,252 acres. The 10 state forests comprise 192,000 acres. There are several historic sites relating to the Revolutionary War period.

In Camden, the Walt Whitman House, home of the poet from 1884 until his death, Mar. 26, 1892, contains books, mementos and furnishings used by Whitman. The U. S. Army Signal Corps Museum, Fort Monmouth, contains communications equipment from the earliest visual methods to modern satellites.

The Montclair Art Museum exhibits art of many periods and lands, emphasizing the American. The Newark Museum is a museum of art, science and industry, including American paintings and sculpture; Chinese, Japanese and Tibetan art; collections of economic botany, birds, insects, minerals, shells, glass, ceramics and jewelry. The New Jersey Historical Society Museum, Newark, has old New Jersey rooms and collections of New Jersey furniture, paintings, china, silver, glass, costumes, etc.

The Garden State Arts Center, an amphitheater for concerts and stage shows, was opened at Telegraph Hill Park in 1968.

The Johnston Historical Museum, adjacent to the national hq. of the Boy Scouts of America, New Brunswick, depicts Scouting history, has a registered weather station, a ham radio station and a 22-acre Outdoor Museum of Nature and Conservation.

The Edison National Historic Site, West Orange, displays in buildings set up by Thomas Alva Edison his chemical laboratory, machine shop and library; a reproduction of the "Black Maria," Edison's 1st movie studio; originals or replicas of his phonograph, incandescent lamp and movie camera. In South Orange, the New Jersey Fire Museum displays 19th Century hand-pumpers, hose carts, helmets, etc.

In Trenton, the New Jersey State Museum displays the state's achievements in the arts, sciences, history, technology and industry, and has a planetarium.

Environmental protection activities have been aimed at eliminating pollution of shellfish areas, cutting air and water pollution and protecting beaches from erosion.

The New Jersey Meadowlands, lying close to the state's northeastern metropolitan centers, were the target of new development plans, including a New Jersey Sports Complex with a baseball-football stadium and race track. The N.Y. Giants plan to play their 1975 football season in the stadium.

The state's network of modern highways gives New Jersey more miles of roads per sq. mi. of area than any other state.

There are 16 airlines and 17 railroads. New Jersey has the most concentrated trackage per sq. mi. in the U.S.

New Mexico

Land of Enchantment

CAPITAL: Santa Fe. AREA: 121,666 sq. mi., rank, 5th. POPULATION: (See Index for 1970 Census.) MOTTO: Crescit Eundo, It Grows as It Goes. FLOWER: Yucca. BIRD: Road Runner. TREE: Pinon (Nut Pine). SONGS: O, Fair New Mexico, Asi Es Nuevo Mejico. ADMISSION: 47th.

New Mexico is a land of contrasts, presenting remnants of old Indian and Spanish cultures along with nuclear and space research centers; mountains over 13,000 ft. and a cavern 829 ft. below ground; ski slopes and desert resorts.

Vast areas are made fertile by irrigation via dams and reservoirs on the Rio Grande, San Juan, Pecos, Canadian, Cimarron, Gila, San Francisco Rivers. Wheeler Peak, 13,161 ft., is highest point.

The climate is dry and invigorating; annual rainfall is 7″ to 16″; mean temperature is 50°, reaching 100° on plains in summer.

National forests cover 13,281 sq. mi. Douglas fir, Ponderosa pine and spruce are cut for timber. Almost 34% of the land is Federally owned.

Minerals are New Mexico's richest natural resource and the state leads the U. S. in output of uranium and potassium salts.

Mineral production reached a total value of $1.06 billion in 1972. Petroleum accounted for the largest single part of this, $376,976,000, followed by natural gas, $194,080, and copper, $171,080. Also high in value were potassium salts, uranium. New Mexico ranks high among the states in perlite and carbon dioxide. Its rich variety of minerals also includes gold, silver, zinc, lead, molybdenum.

Farm receipts accounted for $541,079,000 for 1972, more than two-thirds from livestock products. New Mexico ranked 8th among the states in number of sheep. Cotton, pecans and sorghum are the most important field crops. Also grown are corn, peanuts, beans, onions and lettuce.

Manufacturing industries have grown and diversified. Principal lines are food products, chemicals, ordnance and transportation equipment, lumber, electrical machinery, stone-clay-glass products. Value added by manufacture is over $270,000,000 annually.

Federal government activities, especially nuclear and space research and testing, have played a large role in New Mexico's economic growth. Nuclear and space centers are at Los Alamos, White Sands, Holloman, Kirtland and Sandia.

New Mexico's most awe-inspiring natural wonder, Carlsbad Caverns, has more than a half-million visitors annually. A national park, the caverns are on 3 levels and have the largest natural cave "room" in the world, 1,500 by 300 ft., 300 ft. high.

There are 4 large Indian reservations and 19 inhabited pueblos, including Acoma, the "sky city," built atop a 357-ft. mesa. There are pueblo ruins from 1000 A.D. in Chaco Canyon.

Skiing, hunting, fishing, ghost towns and dude ranches help tourism show steady gains. Visitors spend more than $300,000,000 in the state annually.

Spaniards seeking gold explored New Mexico in the early 16th Century; the area was labeled New Mexico on a 1583 map. It was colonized 1598, with the 1st church at San Juan pueblo. The land remained under Spain until 1821, then under Mexico till U. S. troops occupied it in 1846.

It was formally ceded by Mexico to the U. S. in 1848, was made a Territory in 1850, was separated in 1863 from the part which was to become Arizona. New Mexico became a state in 1912.

New Mexico has 13 institutions of higher education. Among them are the Univ. of New Mexico, College of Santa Fe, New Mexico State Univ., Univ. of Albuquerque, Eastern and Western New Mexico Univs., New Mexico Highlands Univ.

Santa Fe (c. 1609) is the 2nd oldest city in the U. S. It and Taos have large artist colonies. Albuquerque (1706) is the state's largest city.

The Museum of Navaho Ceremonial Art, Santa Fe, housed in a modernized version of a ceremonial hogan, contains over 600 sandpaintings, recordings of some 2,000 Navaho chants, books, manuscripts, baskets, blankets, silver, etc.

The Museum of New Mexico, Sante Fe, maintains the oldest public building in the U. S., the Palace of the Governors (built 1610), a hall of modern Indian culture, collected works of artists of the SW, international folk art exhibits.

The Roswell Museum and Art Center, Roswell, has 19th and 20th Century art collections, archeology and geology exhibits, the Robert H. Goddard rocket collection.

(See also Index for Albuquerque.)

New York
Empire State

CAPITAL: Albany. AREA: 49,576 sq. mi., rank, 30th. POPULATION: (See Index for 1970 Census.) MOTTO: Excelsior. Ever Upward. FLOWER: Rose. BIRD: Bluebird. TREE: Sugar Maple. Eleventh of the Original 13 States to ratify Constitution.

New York is the nation's leading manufacturing state and within its borders are the financial capital of the nation, the largest city and port, the United Nations hq., the head offices of many of the greatest national corporations and insurance companies and a variety of industries.

New York's manufacturing industries outrank those of all other states in number, employees, payrolls and value added by manufacture ($28.46 billion annually).

Value added by manufacture in New York exceeded that of every other state in apparel ($3 billion), printing and publishing ($3.9 billion), instruments ($2.9 billion), paper and paper products ($844,200,000), and in the miscellaneous group, which includes jewelry, silverware, toys and sporting goods, pens and pencils, etc. ($1.01 billion).

The state produces more than 33% of the nation's instruments, 29% of apparel, 23% of printing and publishing and 90% of the miscellaneous category. It is the largest producer of both leather and paper products.

Average employment for 1972 was 7,805,000. Wages and salaries totaled over $60 billion.

The bi-state Port of New York (New York and New Jersey) handled 22% of the nation's foreign trade value in 1971 by U.S. Commerce Dept. figures. The 3 Customs Districts (New York, Buffalo and Ogdensburg) handled 30% of U.S. exports and imports by value in 1971.

Kennedy International Airport in N.Y. City handles about 50% of the nation's overseas air travel and is the nation's largest air cargo center, handling 53% of export-import air tonnage by value.

The state Barge Canal System is 800 mi. long. There are 33 railroads and 497 landing fields, including 26 seaplane bases and 62 heliports. The Verrazano-Narrows Bridge has the world's longest suspension span.

The Dewey Thruway runs from N.Y. City to the Pennsylvania border on Lake Erie, 559 mi., most of the state's 1,347-mi. portion of the Interstate Highway System was completed by 1972.

Tourism and business travel provide $3.7 billion a year to businesses in the state. Major vacation areas include the Adirondack and Catskill Mtns., Finger Lakes, Great Lakes, Thousand Islands, Long Island, N. Y. City and Niagara Falls.

Rich, rolling farmlands support a large agricultural output. New York usually ranks 1st among the states in production of clover and timothy, maple syrup and ice cream; it is 2nd to Washington in apples and 2nd to California in grapes (it has large wine and grape juice industries).

It is also a leader in milk production, with the 3rd largest number of milk cows in the U.S., and in vegetables and melons, sweet and tart cherries, pears and potatoes. Also important are corn, oats, wheat, peaches, peas, beans, beets, cabbages. Poultry and egg production is also high. Farm production supports large canning and freezing industries in the state.

Farm receipts for 1972 were est. at $1.13 billion, with more than two-thirds of the total from livestock and dairy products.

The state has a rich and varied mineral industry, normally ranking 1st in the U.S. in talc, titanium, emery, abrasive garnet and wollastonite; 2nd in zinc, and among the leaders in salt. Other products include lead, gypsum, petroleum, clay, stone, iron. Total value for 1972 was $299,554,000.

Highest point in the state is Mt. Marcy in the Adirondacks, 5,344 ft. The 128 state parks are visited annually by over 45,000,000 persons.

In 1967, a state lottery, with proceeds to be used for education, went into operation.

There are 219 institutions of higher education, with a total enrollment of more than 860,000 students. The State Univ. of N.Y. consisted of 72 colleges and university centers in 1972, with more planned. Included were 4 university centers, two medical centers, 13 colleges of arts and science, 3 specialized colleges, 6 two-year agricultural and technical colleges, 5 statutory colleges attached to other universities, one non-residential college and 38 locally-sponsored two-year community colleges.

New York was the nation's most populous state from 1820 through 1964. As of July 1, 1964, the U. S. Census Bureau estimated California's pop. reached 18,084,000, New York's 17,915,000 (including Armed Forces stationed in the 2 states; without them, New York still led 17,870,000 to 17,749,000). By July 1, 1965, the Bureau est. California led in both categories. In the 1970 census, California had 19,953,134; New York had 18,241,266.

Giovanni da Verrazano, Italian-born navigator sailing for France, probably saw what is now New York Bay in 1524. Henry Hudson, an Englishman sailing for the Dutch, reached the bay in 1609.

Sunnyside, the home of Washington Irving, "as full of angles and corners as an old cocked hat," is in Tarrytown. The Dutch Church of Sleepy Hollow (1697), North Tarrytown, overlooks a bridge commemorating Irving's story of the "headless horseman"; Irving is buried close by in Sleepy Hollow Cemetery. Also in Tarrytown is Lyndhurst, 19th Century mansion of Jay Gould, maintained by the National Trust for Historic Preservation.

The Franklin D. Roosevelt National Historic Site, in Hyde Park, includes the graves of President and Mrs. Roosevelt, the home occupied by the Roosevelt family from 1867, greenhouse, etc. The Roosevelt Library has historic papers, trophies and ship models.

Philipsburg Manor, in North Tarrytown, a trading center of the early 1700s, includes the restored Frederick Philipse home, a dam and grist mill. Van Cortlandt Manor, Croton-on-Hudson, has the restored Van Cortlandt home and ferry house.

In Kingston, the Senate House, seat of the 1st Senate of the state, exhibits early historical objects; its Museum has works by John Vanderlyn, local historical painter. In Newburgh, Washington's Hq., the Jonathan Hasbrouck House, has Revolutionary relics.

The Suffolk Museum and Carriage House, Stony Brook, L. I., has early American paintings and furniture, apothecary shop, tavern, Wells Fargo stage, Conestoga and gypsy wagons, etc.

In Cooperstown are the National Baseball Hall of Fame and Museum with a wide collection of mementos of the national game; nearby is Abner Doubleday Field, said to be where baseball originated in 1839. Near Cooperstown are Fenimore House, hq. of the State Historical Society, with collections including James Fenimore Cooper memorabilia and an art gallery; the Farmer's Museum, with craft demonstrations, and the Village Crossroads, with blacksmith shop, country store, etc.; the Carriage and Harness Museum preserves the stables and vehicles of the early 20th Century.

The restored Fort Ticonderoga, overlooking the waters connecting Lakes George and Champlain, has a museum of relics of the French and Indian War and the Revolution, in which the fort played important roles.

The New York State Museum in Albany has exhibits of natural resources, Indian life. Louis Agassiz Fuertes' paintings of birds, colonial houseware, etc.

The Corning Glass Center, Corning, has a museum and the Steuben factory, where visitors may see crystal glass formed and engraved. Also in the Finger Lakes area are the Curtiss Museum of aviation and the Wine Museum at Hammondsport and several wineries which offer tours to visitors. In Binghamton, the Roberson Center for the Arts and Sciences has art and historical collections.

In Utica, the Munson-Williams-Proctor Institute has a museum of 19th and 20th century art and Fountain Elms, a restored mid-19th Century home.

The Remington Art Memorial Museum, Ogdensburg, has paintings and bronzes by Frederic Remington (1861-1909), who was born in nearby Canton.

(See also Index for Albany, Binghamton, Buffalo, N.Y. City, Rochester, Schenectady, Syracuse, Troy.)

North Carolina

Tar Heel State, Old North State

CAPITAL: Raleigh. AREA: 52,586 sq. mi., rank, 28th. POPULATION: (See Index for 1970 Census.) MOTTO: Esse Quam Videri, To be, Rather Than To Seem. FLOWER: Dogwood. BIRD: Cardinal. TREE: Pine. SONG: The Old North State. Twelfth of the Original 13 States to ratify Constitution.

From a low coastal plain, with Capes Hatteras, Lookout and Fear jutting into the Atlantic, North Carolina rises to a central Piedmont plateau region and, in the W, to the scenic Blue Ridge and Great Smoky Mountains. Mt. Mitchell, 6,684 ft., is the highest peak E of the Mississippi.

Modernization of production methods has brought North Carolina increasing prosperity from its factories in recent years.

The state leads the U. S. in production of textiles, bricks and household furniture, and in both tobacco grown and cigarettes made.

In 1972, 157 new industrial plants opened and 326 expanded their facilities, creating an est. 26,222 new jobs through an investment of $645,694,000.

About 738,900 are employed in factories. The textile industry is the state's largest, with shipments valued at about $7.5 billion annually.

North Carolina ranks 1st among the states in tobacco production; in 1972 it totaled 339,615 tons. It was also 1st in sweet potatoes, 4th in peanuts. Other large crops are cotton, corn and soybeans. Also grown are wheat, oats, barley, peaches, apples. In crop receipts the state ranked 6th in 1972 with $997,526,000; livestock product receipts totaled $652,023,000.

There is a large poultry products business. The state ranked 3rd in turkeys, 4th in chickens in 1972.

Mineral production value was est. at $122,633,000 for 1972. North Carolina ranked 1st in mica, feldspar and lithium; it was also a leader in talc and asbestos.

Tourism is important; in 1972 travelers spent an est. $926,230,000 in the state. Sports include year-round golfing, skiing at mountain resorts, fishing in both fresh and salt water, hunting for both large and small game.

Among attractions are the Great Smoky Mtns. (half in Tennessee), the Blue Ridge Parkway (partly in Virginia) and the Cape Hatteras and Cape Lookout National Seashores.

Other attractions include the restored Fort Raleigh National Historic Site, Roanoke Is., where Virginia Dare, 1st child of English parents in the New World, was born Aug. 18, 1587; Wright Brothers National Memorial, near Kitty Hawk, has aviation exhibits and a reproduction of the plane in which Wilbur and Orville Wright made their 1st flights, 1903; Guilford Court House and Moore's Creek parks, sites of Revolutionary battles. The Battleship North Carolina, a war memorial, is berthed at Wilmington.

In Asheville is one of the world's largest rayon plants as well as Biltmore Industries, native craft plants set up by Mrs. George W. Vanderbilt in 1901 to continue handweaving traditions of the area. Just S of Asheville is the 19th Century Biltmore mansion of the Vanderbilts, which has a large collection of paintings, antiques and Ming china. Also in Asheville, the Thomas Wolfe Memorial was the home of the author.

Bennett Place, 6 mi. NW of Durham, is the site where Gen. Joseph E. Johnston surrendered the last Confederate army to Gen. William Tecumseh Sherman.

The Mint Museum of Art, Charlotte, has collections of paintings, sculpture, and ceramics. The North Carolina Museum of Art, Raleigh, exhibits American and European paintings, sculpture and decorative art. Tryon Palace, New Bern, is the reconstructed colonial capitol of 1770-1794, furnished with antiques.

Old Salem, in Winston-Salem, includes buildings erected by the Moravians from 1766 on. The R. J. Reynolds Tobacco Co. welcomes visitors at its plant and warehouses.

There are 98 institutions of higher education. Among the universities are Duke, Wake Forest, Western Carolina, East Carolina, the Univ. of North Carolina,

North Carolina Agricultural and Technical.

Verrazano, 1524, touched the coast. DeSoto went into the Great Smoky Mts. in 1540. Sir Walter Raleigh sent an expedition to Roanoke Is., 1584; colony was settled 1585, 1587; this, the Lost Colony, disappeared. Bath, oldest town in North Carolina, was settled in 1696. Revolutionary battles were fought in the state. North Carolina seceded from the Union May 20, 1861; revoked secession, 1865; was readmitted 1868.

(See also Index for Charlotte and Winston-Salem.)

North Dakota
Sioux State, Flickertail State

CAPITAL: Bismarck. AREA: 70,665 sq. mi., rank, 17th. POPULATION: (See Index for 1970 Census.) MOTTO: Liberty and Union, Now and Forever, One and Inseparable. FLOWER: Wild Prairie Rose. BIRD: Western Meadow Lark. TREE: American Elm. SONG: North Dakota Hymn. ADMISSION: 39th or 40th with South Dakota.

The eastern plains of North Dakota are rich in vast fields of grain and support large numbers of livestock, in sharp contrast to the rough, colorful Badlands in the W which have elements of scenic beauty and include Theodore Roosevelt National Memorial Park. Highest point is White Butte, 3,506 ft., in the SW.

North Dakota's economy is based on agriculture and mining, but manufacturing industries, especially processing of food, have grown in number and size. More than 90% of the usable land is in farms and ranches.

North Dakota led the other states in production of spring and durum wheat, barley and flaxseed in 1972. It was also a leader in rye, oats and potatoes. Farm receipts for 1972 totaled $920,724,000, more than half from its large grain crops. In 1973 there were 2,435,000 cattle in the state.

Mineral production in 1972 was valued at $99,546,000. The larger part of this was from petroleum. Other products include natural gas, natural gas liquids, coal (lignite), salt, peat.

North Dakota has 14 institutions of higher education. Among them are the Univ. of North Dakota, with its main campus in Grand Forks; North Dakota State Univ. in Fargo, Dickinson State College, Minot State College and Valley City State College.

Tourism brings in over $46,127,000 a year.

There are 65 state parks and historic sites. The International Peace Garden, on a 2,200-acre tract extending across the border into Manitoba, commemorates the friendly relations between the U. S. and Canada. The state is known for its waterfowl, grouse and deer hunting, and bass, trout and northern pike fishing. Lake Sakakawea, formed by the Garrison Dam across the Missouri River, is 609 sq. mi. in area.

A museum with exhibits of pioneer life, the Northern Plains Indians and natural history of the area, is maintained by the State Historical Society on the State Capitol grounds, Bismarck.

Explorations in what is now North Dakota were made as early as 1738-1740 by French-Canadians. The Lewis and Clark expedition (1804-1806) passed through the territory and established Fort Mandan. With South Dakota and parts of Montana and Wyoming it comprised Dakota Territory, organized Mar. 2, 1861. It became a separate state Nov. 2, 1889.

Fort Abraham Lincoln, now a state park near Mandan, was the base from which Col. George Custer set out in 1876 on the campaign which ended in the deaths of Custer and 5 companies of the 7th Cavalry at the hands of Sioux Indians at the Little Big Horn in Montana.

(See also Index for Bismarck.)

Ohio
Buckeye State

CAPITAL: Columbus. AREA: 41,222 sq. mi., rank, 35th. POPULATION: (See Index for 1970 Census.) MOTTO: With God, All Things Are Possible. FLOWER: Scarlet Carnation. BIRD: Cardinal. TREE: Ohio Buckeye. SONG: Beautiful Ohio. ADMISSION: 17th.

Ohio is the nation's 3rd greatest industrial state; it ranks among the wealthier states in livestock and crop receipts, and is a leader in output of lime, coal and coke.

Ohio leads the U.S. in a wide variety of products: tires, machine tools, playing cards, business machines, glassware, cutlery, dishwashers, clay and metal products. Industrial expansion has continued at a rapid pace; in 1972 new capital invested in manufacturing increased.

Total value added by manufacture was $23.1 billion in the 1971 Survey of Manufactures. Of this, autos, aircraft, boats and parts accounted for $2.9 billion; iron, steel and other metals, $2.9 billion; machinery, especially industrial, $3.4 billion; electrical machinery, especially household appliances, $2.4 billion. Also important are metal products, chemicals, rubber and plastic products, food processing.

Farm receipts for 1972 totaled over $1.5 billion, more than half of it from livestock products. Ohio has large numbers of milk cows, hogs and sheep; it ranks high in milk production. It is also a large producer of corn, grapes, clover, popcorn, oats, soybeans and other crops.

Mineral production was valued at a total $701,760,000 for 1972, with the largest item being bituminous coal. Ohio was the top state in lime production and one of the leaders in clays, salt, sand and gravel. Other important products include petroleum, cement, gypsum and natural gas.

It was estimated that the value of the mineral industry was more than $3.1 billion for 1972.

There are 56 state parks, over 300 roadside parks, and many historic memorials including Fallen Timbers Battlefield, prehistoric Indian mounds and the restored first settlement, Schoenbrunn (1772). The American Trapshooting Tournament is held annually at Vandalia.

The state is served by 18 railroads and 15 scheduled airlines. It has busy ports on Lake Erie and the Ohio River. Highest point is Campbell Hill, 1,550 ft., in the W. central area.

There are 97 institutions of higher education. Among the universities are Ohio, Ohio State, Ohio Wesleyan, Wittenberg, Case Western Reserve, Miami (Ohio), and the Universities of Akron, Cincinnati, Dayton and Toledo. Also large are Bowling Green State, Cleveland State, Kent State and Youngstown State.

George Rogers Clark defeated the Indians at Piqua, 1780; thereafter Ohio had British-Indian raids and battles; Gen. Anthony Wayne defeated Indians at Fallen Timbers Aug. 20, 1794, imposed Treaty of Greenville, 1795. Oliver Hazard Perry defeated British on Lake Erie near Put-in-Bay, Sept. 10, 1813. As governor of Northwest Territory, Gen. Arthur St. Clair sat at Marietta (1789) and Cincinnati (1791). Ohio became a state in 1803. Columbus became seat of government in 1816.

In Canton, the Pro Football Hall of Fame has a museum, library and daily movies; the Stark County Historical Society has science, industry and historical museums.

(See also Index for Akron, Cincinnati, Cleveland, Columbus, Dayton, Toledo, Youngstown.)

Oklahoma
Sooner State

CAPITAL: Oklahoma City. AREA: 69,919 sq. mi., rank, 18th. POPULATION: (See Index for 1970 Census.) MOTTO: Labor Omnia Vincit—Labor Conquers All Things. FLOWER: Mistletoe. BIRD: Scissortailed Flycatcher. TREE: Redbud. SONG: Oklahoma. ADMISSION: 46th.

Most of Oklahoma is a great, rolling plain sloping S and E with a mean altitude of 1,300 ft. There are 4 mountainous areas; the Ozark Plateau in the NE, the Ouachitas in the SE, the Arbuckles in the S central and the Wichitas in the SW. In the western Panhandle, the land rises toward the Rockies with Black Mesa, 4,973 ft., the highest point.

Oil, wheat and cattle are the basic ingredients of Oklahoma's economy, but manufacturing industries have gained increasing importance.

The $1.2 billion Arkansas River Navigation System, involving shipping, flood control and power dams, was completed to Catoosa, near Tulsa, in 1971. It made Catoosa a "seaport," with barge shipping to the Mississippi and beyond.

The state's output of petroleum was valued at $708,560,000 for 1972, accounting for much of the total value of mineral production, $1.22 billion. The state is one of the leaders in the U.S. in petroleum production, and in total mineral production.

Natural gas was 2nd most important among minerals; production was valued at $299,809,000. Other minerals include helium, in which the state is a leader, gypsum, zinc, cement, coal, copper, silver.

Oklahoma's rich plains produced the nation's 4th largest winter wheat crop in 1972 as well as large crops of sorghum, other grains and peanuts. Its cattle herd was the 5th largest in the U.S. Total farm receipts were $1.28 billion, more than half from livestock products.

While much of Oklahoma's manufacturing industry is based on processing of the state's own meat, wheat and oil, other lines have become important rivals. Value added by manufacture exceeds $1.7 billion annually. Important lines include food processing, machinery (especially construction and oil equipment), transportation equipment, metal products, petroleum and coal products.

There are 39 institutions of higher education. The largest include the Univ. of Oklahoma, Oklahoma State Univ. and Central State Univ.

Total tourist revenues are estimated at more than $494,000,000 annually. Attractions include 28 state parks, large lakes and reservoirs such as Eufaula (102,500 acres) and Lake Texoma (93,080 acres); Ouachita National Forest (176,000 acres), rodeos, Indian powwows, the National Cowboy Hall of Fame and Western Heritage Center in Oklahoma City, bass fishing and quail hunting.

The Will Rogers Memorial, Claremore, has collections of the great humorist's saddles and ropes, as well as trophies; his tomb is also here. In Anadarko, the Southern Plains Indian Museum and Crafts Center exhibits Indian arts and has a crafts sales shop. The Woolaroc Museum near Bartlesville has 55,000 exhibits in a panorama of New World history, and a collection of paintings of the West.

The restored Fort Gibson Stockade, with many of the original buildings, near Muskogee, was erected 1824 and was the army's largest outpost in the Indian lands.

Near Tahlequah is the Cherokee Cultural Center with a restored 1700 Cherokee village and a spring and summer pageant.

The 1st permanent white settlement in the area was made in 1796 by Maj. Jean Pierre Chouteau on the site of present-day Salina, Okla.

Part of the Louisiana Purchase, 1803, Oklahoma was known as Indian Territory (but was not given territorial government) after it became the home of the Five Civilized tribes—Cherokee, Choctaw, Chickasaw, Creek and Seminole—1828-1846. The land was also used by Comanche, Osage and other plains Indians. As white settlers pressed west, land was opened for homesteading by runs and lottery, a run being a race for a claim at a specific time. The first run took place Apr. 22, 1889; the most famous was the run to the Cherokee Outlet, 1893. The portion thus opened was organized as a Territory; this and Indian Territory were joined by Congress in the State of Oklahoma, admitted to the Union Nov. 16, 1907. Oklahoma's Indian population (1970 Census) was 97,731, largest in the U.S.

(See also Index for Oklahoma City and Tulsa.)

Oregon
Beaver State

CAPITAL: Salem. **AREA:** 96,981 sq. mi., rank, 10th. **POPULATION:** (See Index for 1970 Census.) **MOTTO:** The Union. **FLOWER:** Oregon Grape. **BIRD:** Western Meadow Lark. **COLORS:** Navy blue and gold. **FISH:** Chinook salmon. **ANIMAL:** Beaver. **TREE:** Douglas Fir. **SONG:** Oregon, My Oregon. **ADMISSION:** 33rd.

Oregon is rich in timber, fish and wildlife, water power and scenic beauty, with lofty mountain ranges, deep river gorges and broad, fertile valleys.

Half of Oregon, or about 30,000,000 acres, is thickly forested and the state leads the nation in value of forest products, over $1.8 billion a year. Production of lumber, furniture, paper and other forest products provides jobs for about 80,000 workers and is a major factor in the state's economy.

Also important are food processing, transportation equipment, machinery, fabricated metal products. Total value added by manufacture is over $2.8 billion a year.

Oregon's agriculture is rich and varied. While farmers grow fair-sized crops of wheat, oats, potatoes and other staples, the state is a leader in production of berries, pears, cherries, filberts, walnuts, vegetables. It also ranks high in number of turkeys and of sheep. Total farm receipts for 1972 were $630,885,000, more than half from crops, the rest from livestock.

Stone, nickel, cement, lime and pumice are important in mineral production, valued at $79,805,000 for 1972.

Hydroelectric power, from both privately-owned and publicly-owned utilities, is abundant. A Federal agency, the Bonneville Power Administration, markets electric power, much of it from a series of great dams across the Columbia River, to many of the utilities and to large industrial plants. Among users are plants for the refining and processing of metals from out of state, including aluminum.

The commercial fish catch, including salmon, tuna, halibut, sole, cod and shellfish, was worth over $24,000,000 in 1972.

Tourism is also an important industry, est. at over $438,000,000 annually. There are 221 state parks and both state and national forests. Crater Lake, a national park, is a body of sapphire blue water in a former volcano, 6 mi. in diameter and 1,932 ft. deep—deepest lake in the U.S. Oregon Dunes National Recreation Area was created in 1972.

Fort Clatsop National Memorial includes a replica of the fort in which the Lewis and Clark expedition spent the winter of 1805-06. Oregon Caves National Monument contains stone waterfalls. Skiing and the annual Pendleton Round-Up are other attractions.

A summer Shakespearean Festival is staged annually in Ashland.

Snow-capped Mt. Hood, which rises 11,235 ft., is the highest point in the state; nearby are scenic recreation areas.

The Columbia River brings ocean shipping to Portland, 100 miles inland but one of the Pacific Coast's principal ports, and to other river ports.

Oregon has 40 institutions of higher education, the largest of them being the Univ. of Oregon and Oregon State Univ.

The state is served by 5 major railroad systems and 10 airlines.

The Univ. of Oregon in Eugene has a Museum of Art with Oriental, Pacific Northwest and other art collections. It also has a Museum of Natural History.

Capt. Robert Gray, in the Columbia, discovered the river named after his ship May 11, 1792, and claimed the area for the U.S. President Jefferson sent the Lewis & Clark Expedition to the area, 1805-06. John Jacob Astor's fur depot, Astoria, was founded in 1811.

A provisional government was established in Champoeg, May 2, 1843, and U. S. title was established in 1846 in a settlement of U. S. and British claims to the area. Oregon became a state Feb. 14, 1859.

(See also Index for Portland.)

Pennsylvania
Keystone State

CAPITAL: Harrisburg. **AREA:** 45,333 sq. mi., rank, 33rd. **POPULATION:** (See Index for 1970 Census.) **MOTTO:** Virtue, Liberty and Independence. **FLOWER:** Mountain Laurel. **BIRD:** Ruffed Grouse. **TREE:** Eastern Hemlock. Second of Original 13 States to ratify Constitution.

Pennsylvania has extensive mineral resources and fertile farmlands, is a leader in manufacturing and boasts a wealth of historic landmarks and scenic attractions.

Roughly rectangular in shape, Pennsylvania has prosperous farmlands in the SE and the W; through the center, running NE-SW, are parallel mountain ridges with valleys between. Highest point is Mt. Davis in the SW, 3,213 ft.

Many of the nation's largest steel plants are in Pennsylvania, with the greatest concentration in the Pittsburgh area. Pennsylvania ranks 1st among the states in steel and iron production.

Mill and factory products are many and varied; value added by manufacture is over $21.9 billion. Primary metals are the most important, over $3.7 billion. Other large lines were machinery and electrical machinery, food processing, chemicals, metal products, transportation equipment, apparel and textiles.

The state ranks high in manufacturing of shoes and cigars.

Pennsylvania produces almost all of the nation's anthracite coal; it ranked 3rd in 1972 in output of bituminous coal. Also important are cement, stone, petroleum, natural gas, lime, clays, zinc, iron. Total mineral production value for 1972 was $1.2 billion.

Prosperous farms, such as those in the Pennsylvania Dutch country in the SE, brought in total livestock and crop receipts for the state of $1.09 billion in 1972, much of it from dairy and poultry products. The state ranked high in number of milk cows, chickens and turkeys.

The state ranks high in its output of grapes, peaches, apples and cherries. It claims 1st place in sausage products, scrapple, pretzels, and plantation-grown Christmas trees. It also ranks high in ice cream. Forest products are valued at over $1 billion annually.

The Commonwealth is rich in historic areas, including Valley Forge and the Gettysburg Battlefield, both national shrines. The Articles of Confederation, the Declaration of Independence and the Constitution were all adopted in Philadelphia.

Pennsylvania is among the leading states in hunting, fishing, golf and winter sports. Tourism, it was estimated, produces direct sales of $3.5 billion annually.

There are more than 150 state and federal parks, recreation areas and historic sites. Scenic attractions include the Delaware Water Gap in the east and the 1,000-ft. deep Pine Creek Gorge in the north. Dutch folk festivals, county fairs, and fall foliage in the Poconos draw many visitors.

Valley Forge State Park, 22 mi. NW of Philadelphia, preserves the site of Washington's encampment during the winter of 1777-78; of 11,098 soldiers, close to 3,000, ill-equipped, died during the bitter weather; there is a museum, restored buildings, etc. Washington Crossing State Park, where Continental troops crossed the Delaware to attack Hessian-British forces in Trenton, Christmas Night 1776, has restored buildings and picnic areas.

Longwood Gardens, near Kennett Square, include conservatories and rock, heather, flower and water gardens; arboretum, illuminated fountains, open-air theater; open every day of the year.

Lancaster County and nearby areas in the southeast are known as Pennsylvania Dutch Country. Descendants of early German (Deutsch) and Swiss settlers still maintain many of the early customs and "old world" culture which make their farms, festivals and market places attractive to tourists.

The William Penn Memorial Museum, Harrisburg, has collections of folk art, ironwork, glass, pewter, china, textiles, stage coaches, sleighs; replicas of artisans' shops, period rooms; fine arts exhibits and a planetarium.

There are 142 institutions of higher learning including Univ. of Pennsylvania (founded 1740), Univ. of Pittsburgh, Carnegie-Mellon Univ., Bryn Mawr, Swarthmore, Lehigh, Lafayette, Dickinson, Drexel Univ., Temple, Villanova, Bucknell, Penn State, Duquesne.

First permanent settlement was in 1643 on Tinicum Is., near Chester, as part of New Sweden. In 1655, the Dutch took over; in 1664, the English. In 1681, Charles II granted land to William Penn as payment for debts owed Penn's father. Penn made a treaty with the Indians, 1682, and called the land Pennsylvania (Penn's Woods) in honor of his father.

(See also Index for Allentown, Philadelphia, Pittsburgh.)

Rhode Island
Little Rhody

CAPITAL: Providence. AREA: 1,214 sq. mi., rank, 50th. POPULATION: (See Index for 1970 Census.) MOTTO: Hope. FLOWER: Violet. BIRD: Rhode Island Red. TREE: Red Maple. SONG: Rhode Island. Thirteenth of Original 13 States to ratify Constitution.

Rhode Island is the smallest of the 50 states but has the longest official name: State of Rhode Island and Providence Plantations. It is not an island, although its Narragansett Bay, extending from the Atlantic 28 mi. inland, contains many islands, the largest of which is named Rhode Is. Highest point, Jerimoth Hill in Providence County, is 812 ft.

Tiny Rhode Island is densely populated and highly industrialized. For many years, Rhode Island had the greatest density of population per square mile of all the states. By 1965, estimates showed it was 2nd to New Jersey in this respect. The 1970 Census showed New Jersey averaging 953.1 persons per sq. mi.; Rhode Island 905.5.

Industries show more than $1.4 billion in value added annually by manufacturing. Until 1940, textile mills, dating back to Samuel Slater's 1790 cotton mill, employed more workers than all other Rhode Island industries put together. Employment in the mills has fallen off sharply in recent years, but jobs in other fields have increased.

The state also pioneered in the manufacture of jewelry and silverware and remains tops in the U.S. Other leading industry groups are primary metal processing, metal products, machinery, rubber and plastics, food processing, chemicals, apparel.

The value of the tourist industry is est. at $90,000,000 annually

Only 1% of the labor force is engaged in farming, and farm receipts in 1972 totaled $18,911,000. Dairy and poultry (notably Rhode Island Reds) are the most important lines; potatoes and apples are principal crops. The fish and shellfish catch is valued at over $12,000,000 annually.

There are 14 institutions of higher education including the Univ. of Rhode Island, Brown Univ. (founded 1764), Rhode Island College and Providence College.

Rhode Island is distinguished historically for its battle for freedom of conscience and action, begun by Roger Williams, founder of Providence, who was exiled from Massachusetts Bay Colony in 1636. William Coddington, John Clark and other religious exiles founded Pocasset, now Portsmouth, in 1638 and Newport in 1639. The first Baptist church in the U.S. was founded in Providence in 1638. Rhode Island gave protection to Quakers in 1657 and to Jews from Holland in 1658.

The struggle for individual rights included defiance of British trade restrictions and taxation, and was climaxed in 1772 by the burning of the British revenue vessel Gaspee. Rhode Island declared its independence from Britain on May 4, 1776, before the Declaration of Independence. It ratified the U.S. Constitution May 29, 1790, last of the original 13 states. Rhode Island had prohibition of liquor in the 19th Century, but repealed it in 1889 and refused later to ratify the 18th Amendment.

Providence is a major manufacturing and educational center and a port handling over 9,000,000 tons of cargo per year.

The Rhode Island Historical Society in Providence occupies the historic John Brown House, with rooms containing furniture by 18th Century cabinet makers and other items of local origin. Also in Providence, the Rhode Island School of Design has a museum with collections of classic art, 18th Century American furniture, 19th Century paintings, etc.

Newport became famous as the summer capital of society in the mid-19th Century, when industrial magnates built showy mansions. Easton's Beach and Bailey's Beach are noted resorts and Ocean Drive and Bellevue Avenue are showplaces. Touro Synagogue (1763) is the oldest in the U. S. and is a national historic site. Music festivals and water sports are among attractions.

The Newport Historical Society has a marine museum; extensive exhibits of silver, furniture, china, etc.; a grist mill, several forts, a Seventh Day Baptist meeting house built 1729.

In Pawtucket, the Old Slater Mill Museum is a restored 1793 cotton mill, considered the 1st to spin yarn successfully in this country; it has demonstrations of hand spinning and weaving.

(See also Index for Providence.)

South Carolina
Palmetto State

CAPITAL: Columbia. AREA: 31,055 sq. mi., rank, 40th, POPULATION: (See Index for 1970 Census.) MOTTO: Dum Spiro, Spero—While I Breathe, I Hope, and Animis Opibusque Parati—Prepared in Spirit and Resources. FLOWER: Carolina (Yellow) Jessamine. BIRD: Carolina Wren. SONG: Carolina. TREE: Palmetto. Eighth of the Original 13 States to ratify Constitution.

In South Carolina the land slopes from the Blue Ridge Mountains in the NW, through thick pine forests and fertile farmlands with great fields of tobacco and cotton, to semi-tropic beaches and busy ports on the Atlantic. Deep-sea and inland fishing, hunting, the charm of ante bellum houses, public gardens and famed shore resorts are among the state's attractions. Highest point is Sassafras Mtn. in NW, 3,560 ft.

Efforts to diversify industry and expand foreign trade and tourism have been highly successful.

Manufacturing is by far the major source of income; value added by manufacture is over $4.2 billion annually. The textile industry is still the most important, comprising almost half of the value of all manufactured products and employing the most workers. South Carolina's mills rank high in cotton consumption and in out-put of yard goods. They are also a major producer of synthetic and woolen goods.

Other important manufacturing lines are chemicals, apparel, paper, lumber, food processing, machinery and stone-clay-glass products.

In 1972, new industrial investment was valued at $502,563,000; it was estimated this would provide 13,449 jobs. Major areas of expansion were in chemical, textile and metal-working fields.

Farms have become fewer but larger in recent years. South Carolina grows more peaches than any other state except California; it ranks 3rd in tobacco. Also grown are cotton, peanuts, sweet potatoes, pecans, etc. Poultry and eggs are important revenue producers; the state has large sales of chickens and turkeys.

Total farm receipts for 1972 were $526,651,000.

The state's mineral production value for 1972 was est. at $71,998,000. It is a leader in production of vermiculite, used in insulation, and of kyanite and kaolin used in ceramics. Also produced are mica, cement and stone, including Winnsboro blue granite.

Lumber for pulp and saw-timber is a major resource, especially the loblolly pine. Pulpwood production is over 3,500,000 cords annually.

Income from tourism has risen steadily, travelers spending an est. $443,000,000 in 1972.

Attractions include state parks, famed gardens, historic sites, coastal islands, shore resorts such as Myrtle Beach, fishing and quail hunting.

There are many historic churches and white-pillared houses in Charleston, Columbia and Beaufort. Gardens near Charleston include Middleton Place, Magnolia and Cypress; Brookgreen, south of Myrtle Beach, has 340 outdoor statues; other gardens are Edisto, at Orangeburg, Glencairn, at Rock Hill, Swan Lake, at Sumter.

Fort Sumter National Monument in Charleston harbor is the place where the Civil War began with bombardment of the fort by Confederate batteries, Apr. 12-13, 1861.

Charleston Museum, estab. 1773, has exhibits of interior paneling, furniture, arts, crafts and utensils from early South Carolina days.

The state has 45 institutions of higher learning, including the Univ. of South Carolina, Clemson, The Citadel and 13 technical education centers.

South Carolina played an important part in American

beginnings. First settled by Spaniards, 1526 and 1566, it was given by England's Charles I to Robert Heath as Carolina, 1629: the first permanent settlement by the English was Charles Town, now Charleston, 1670. Charles Pinckney helped frame the Constitution of the U. S., 1787. The state was 1st to secede, Dec. 20, 1860; readmitted in 1868.

South Dakota
Coyote State, Sunshine State

CAPITAL: Pierre. AREA: 77,047 sq. mi.; rank, 16th. POPULATION: (See Index for 1970 Census.) MOTTO: Under God, the People Rule. FLOWER: American Pasque. BIRD: Ringnecked Pheasant. SONG: Hail South Dakota. TREE: Black Hills Spruce. ADMISSION: 39th or 40th with North Dakota.

South Dakota is a rectangle split down the middle by the Missouri and a chain of huge lakes formed behind dams on the river. In the E are rich farmlands which produce large crops of rye, oats and other grains. In the W are rolling grasslands which support millions of cattle and sheep, as well as vast acreages of wheat. In the far W are the Black Hills with Harney Peak, 7,242 ft., the highest point in the nation E of the Rockies.

With more than 44,500 farms and ranches occupying most of the land area, agriculture is South Dakota's basic industry. Its livestock and livestock products account for the greater part of farm income. Mining and lumbering are also important natural resource industries.

The state normally ranks 1st in the U.S. in size of its rye crop and high in spring wheat, flaxseed, oats, barley. In 1973 South Dakota had 4,496,000 cattle and over a million sheep and 1,868,000 hogs. Total farm receipts for 1972 were $1.24 billion.

Large areas are reclaimed by irrigation and plans were under way for additional hundreds of thousands of acres to be fed from the Oahe Reservoir.

South Dakota leads the nation in gold production; the Homestake Mine in Lawrence County is the largest in the U.S. Gold accounted for $23,869,000 of the state's total mineral production value which was $69,894,000 for 1972. The state was also a leader in production of beryllium. Other products include silver, petroleum, uranium, cement.

Processing of foods produced by farms and ranches is the largest of South Dakota's manufacturing industries. Also important are lumber and wood products, and machinery, including farm equipment. Total value added by manufacture is over $226,200,000

South Dakota has 8,400 sq. mi. of Indian Reservations. The Indians, estimated to number about 32,365, are largely Sioux.

South Dakota has 16 institutions of higher education, including 7 state colleges and universities. There are 12 state parks, 35 recreation areas and 49 roadside parks totaling over 87,000 acres. Pheasant, duck and geese are abundant. There are large herds of white-tail and mule deer and elk and about 5,000 bison in state and private herds.

Mount Rushmore in the Black Hills has an altitude of 6,200 ft. Sculptured on its granite face are the heads of Washington, Jefferson, Lincoln and Theodore Roosevelt. These busts by Gutzon Borglum are proportionate to men 465 ft. tall. Rushmore is visited by about 2,000,000 persons annually.

Other tourist attractions include Custer State Park, with the world's largest herd of bison; the Black Hills Passion Play, staged from June to Sept. in an amphitheater at Spearfish,

The "Great Lakes of South Dakota" are 4 reservoirs created behind Oahe, Big Bend, Fort Randall and Gavins Point Dams on the Missouri River with total water surface area of 571,000 acres.

Out-of-state tourists, it is estimated, spend more than $250,000,000 a year in South Dakota.

Fort Sisseton State Park, 18 mi. SE of Britton, is a restored Army frontier post of 1864. The Sioux Indian Museum in Rapid City features historic and contemporary arts of the Sioux and an Indian craft sales shop.

Discovery of this area dates back to 1743 when the first

Europeans, the Verendrye brothers, Frenchmen, came in search of a route to the Pacific. South Dakota was admitted to the Union Nov. 2, 1889, together with its twin state, North Dakota, after 28 years as a part of Dakota Territory. South Dakota Historical Society asserts both states can be 39th or 40th state, since President Harrison intentionally shuffled the proclamations before signing.

(See also Sioux Falls.)

Tennessee
Volunteer State

CAPITAL: Nashville. AREA: 42,244 sq. mi., rank, 34th. POPULATION: (See Index for 1970 Census.) MOTTO: Agriculture, Commerce. FLOWER: Iris. BIRD: Mockingbird. TREE: Tulip Poplar. SONG: Tennessee Waltz. ADMISSION: 16th.

Eastern Tennessee is rugged country with the Great Valley separating the Great Smoky Mtns., on the state's E border, from the Cumberland Mtns.; the Central Basin is a rolling area containing the famed Bluegrass country; from there the state slopes W to the bottomlands on the Mississippi River. Clingman's Dome, in the Great Smokies, is the highest point, 6,643 ft.

Manufacturing has taken the top place in Tennessee's economy; products are many and varied. Among the most important are chemicals (especially plastic fibers), textiles, apparel, electrical machinery. Other important lines are food processing, furniture, lumber, paper, primary metals and metal products, leather goods.

Value added by manufacture is over $6.7 billion annually.

There are 24 research centers including Oak Ridge, TVA and Arnold Engineering Development Center for rocket research.

Tennessee ranks among the top states in tobacco production. Farm receipts for 1972 totaled $870,537,000, more than half of it from livestock, the rest from crops. It has large numbers of hogs and cattle.

Forest products are also important, providing full-time jobs to 40,000 persons and contributing over $500,000,000 annually to the state's economy. The state is known as the U.S. hardwood flooring center.

Tennessee produces a wide range of minerals and leads the other states in zinc. Other products include silver, cement, copper, coal and phosphate rock. Total mineral production was valued at $241,732,000 for 1972.

Tourism is of increasing importance; tourists spend about $750,000,000 annually in Tennessee. Folk music and the "Nashville sound" have made that city a leading recording center.

With 6 other states, Tennessee shares in Federal reservoir developments on the Tennessee and Cumberland River systems. About 41,000 sq. mi. are drawn on by the Tennessee Valley Authority, which built Norris Dam on the Clinch River and operates a number of other dams in the state. Their reservoirs cover 756,321 acres.

Tennessee has a number of natural wonders—Reelfoot Lake, the reservoir basin of the Mississippi River formed by an earthquake (1811); Lookout Mountain, a rock-faced promontory carved by the currents of the Tennessee River and overlooking Moccasin Bend, at Chattanooga; Fall Creek Falls, 256 ft. high; and the west half of Great Smoky Mountains National Park.

The American Museum of Atomic Energy in Oak Ridge has displays, models, lectures. The Hermitage, 13 mi. E of Nashville, home of Andrew Jackson, contains furniture and personal effects of the President. The Ancestral Home of James K. Polk, in Columbia, has portraits, furniture and various articles used by President Polk in the White House. The home, tailor shop and grave of President Andrew Johnson are a national monument at Greeneville. The Parthenon, in Centennial Park, Nashville, is a full-size replica of the Parthenon of Athens. There are 26 state parks.

There are 59 institutions of higher education; among universities are the Univ. of Tennessee, with its main campus in Knoxville; Vanderbilt and Fisk in Nashville; Memphis State in Memphis, and East Tennessee State in Johnson City.

Tennessee is believed to have been reached by De Soto in 1541. La Salle built a fort in 1682. It was part of the

Carolina grant of Charles II and home of Cherokee tribes. During 1784-1788 settlers formed the "state" of Franklin. North Carolina ceded it to the Federal government in 1790; it was part of the Territory South of the Ohio until it became a state in 1796. It seceded in 1861, was the site of more than 700 Civil War battles and skirmishes and was readmitted in 1866.

(See also Index for Chattanooga, Knoxville, Memphis, Nashville.)

Texas
Lone Star State

CAPITAL: Austin. AREA: 267,338 sq. mi., rank 2nd. POPULATION: (See Index for 1970 Census.) MOTTO: Friendship. (Carrying out meaning of Indian word, Tejas—friends, from which Texas derives name). FLOWER: Bluebonnet. TREE: Pecan. BIRD: Mockingbird. SONG: Texas, Our Texas. ADMISSION: 28th.

Texas leads all other states in many categories, among them oil, cattle, sheep, and cotton. While these are basic to the Texas economy, manufacturing, as measured in terms of value added, makes an even greater contribution than either mineral output or farm receipts.

It is 2nd only to Alaska in area.

Texas normally produces about 1/3 of the nation's total petroleum output. The state's 1972 petroleum production, 1.303 billion barrels, was valued at $4.54 billion. Texas is also the leading producer of asphalt, graphite, natural gas liquids and magnesium chloride; Louisiana and Texas are the leading producers of natural gas. Texas ranks 2nd among the states in output of sulphur, salt, helium and bromine, and 3rd in cement and clays. The total value of the state's annual mineral production is by far the greatest of any state, $7.3 billion in 1972.

Texas ranked 3rd among the 50 states in 1972 in cash receipts for crops, $1.4 billion; 2nd for livestock products, $2.4 billion; 3rd in total farm receipts, $3.8 billion.

It led all states in number of cattle, 15,350,000 (giving the state more cattle than people), and in sheep, 3,214,000; it ranked 6th in turkeys and 9th in chickens. It grew the largest crops of rice, pecans, sorghum and cotton, and ranked high in peanuts. It also grows large amounts of vegetables and melons; its varied output includes sweet potatoes, oranges, grapefruit, peaches and roses. Irrigation has reclaimed large arid areas in the west. Forest products are worth $115,000,000 yearly.

The largest of its many livestock expositions are held annually in Fort Worth, San Antonio, Houston and El Paso; the largest cattle auction in Amarillo.

Manufacturing industries have shown tremendous growth. Value added by manufacture was over $13.7 billion a year. About 20% of the total value is in chemicals, the largest manufacturing industry. Other important lines are petroleum refining, processing of foods, transportation equipment, machinery, primary metals and metal products.

Texas ranks high among the states in commercial fishing with the 1972 catch valued at over $85,011,000.

Tourists spend over $1.7 billion dollars annually in Texas. There are 70 state parks, recreation areas and historic sites, Big Bend and Guadalupe Mtns. National Parks, Padre Is. National Seashore and Fort Davis National Historic Site. Named for President Lyndon B. Johnson, who died Jan. 22, 1973, are a National Historic Site, a National Park and a State Park, marking his birthplace, boyhood home and ranch, all near Johnson City.

In 1973, Texas listed 310 museums with 40 more planned or being built; included were renowned art and historical collections and restored frontier buildings.

Texas has 132 institutions of higher education. Among the largest are the Univ. of Texas, Univ. of Houston, Texas Tech. Univ., Texas A & M. Univ., San Antonio College, North Texas State Univ., East Texas State Univ., Lamar Univ., Southern Methodist Univ. and Stephen F. Austin State Univ. Others include Texas Christian Univ., Rice Univ. and Baylor Univ.

Texas is the only state that was an independent republic, recognized by the U.S. before annexation. Over it have flown the flags of Spain, France, Mexico, the Lone

Star Flag of the Republic, the Confederate States and the United States.

The first Europeans to arrive in the area were Spaniards. Alonso de Pineda, in 1519, and Cabeza de Vaca, 1536, explored coastal areas; Francisco de Coronado crossed inland in 1541. Texas became a Spanish province in 1691 and a Mexican state in 1821.

American settlers revolted in 1835; after defeat at the Alamo, Mar. 6, 1836, they defeated the Mexicans at San Jacinto, Apr. 21, 1836. They formed the Republic of Texas and, in 1845, voted for annexation to the U.S. Texas was admitted as a state Dec. 29, 1845. It seceded and joined the Confederacy Feb. 1, 1861. It freed all slaves June 19, 1865, and was readmitted to the Union Mar. 30, 1870.

(See also Index for Austin, Amarillo, Corpus Christi, Dallas, El Paso, Fort Worth, Houston, Lubbock, San Antonio.)

Utah
Beehive State

CAPITAL: Salt Lake City. AREA: 84,916 sq. mi., rank, 11th. POPULATION: (See Index for 1970 Census.) MOTTO: Industry. FLOWER: Sego Lily. BIRD: California Gull. TREE: Blue Spruce. EMBLEM: Beehive. SONG: Utah We Love Thee. ADMISSION: 45th.

Wrested from the wilderness by Mormon settlers in the mid-19th Century, Utah is for the most part a mountainous area, broken by fertile irrigated valleys, several deserts and two large lakes, Great Salt Lake in the N and Lake Powell in the S.

Great Salt Lake is 4,200 ft. above sea level, but has no known outlet. Its salt density varies from 20 to 25%, 2nd only to that of the Dead Sea; it covers more than 1,500 sq. mi.; it is crossed by a 13-mi., rock-fill railroad causeway. Lake Powell, created by construction of the Glen Canyon Dam on the Colorado River just over the border in Arizona, is 186 mi. long, most of it in Utah. Highest point in Utah is Kings Peak in the NE, 13,528 ft.

Manufacturing has become the state's major industry, well ahead of mining, agriculture and tourism. Value added by manufacture in 1972 was over $864,200,000. Transportation equipment was the most important line, followed by food products, machinery, metal products, printing-publishing and electrical equipment.

Utah is an important center for research on and production of intercontinental missiles, rocket engines, solid fuel propellants, supersonic engines, aircraft navigational systems and military computer components. Many of the nation's largest aerospace firms have plants and divisions in Utah.

The state is a leading warehousing area and distribution center for much of the western U.S.

Utah is a rich storehouse of a wide variety of minerals. Among the states, it is a leading producer of copper, gold, silver, asphalt, molybdenum, lead, vanadium and potassium salts.

Copper has by far the greatest value among Utah's mineral products. In 1972, copper production was valued at $274,299,000 and total mineral production value was $536,795,000.

The nation's largest open-pit copper mine at Bingham Canyon, normally employs about 7,000 persons and produces about 20% of the newly-mined copper in the U.S. There are large smelters and refineries.

Petroleum has also been a large product; 1972 production was valued at $79,648,000. With Colorado and Wyoming, Utah shares what have been called the world's richest oil shale deposits. Studies of economical ways to recover this oil were under way.

Utah ranked 7th among the states in number of sheep in 1972 with nearly a million. It also raises large flocks of turkeys. It is a leader in apricots and cherries. Other crops include barley, sugar beets, alfalfa, winter wheat, potatoes. Farm receipts for 1972 included $201,241,000 from livestock, $40,792,000 from crops.

There are 13 institutions of higher education. The largest are Brigham Young Univ., the Univ. of Utah and Utah State Univ. and Weber State College.

Over 66% of the land is owned by the Federal government.

Tourists annually spend about $196,000,000 in the state. Utah is a great recreational area, with 11,000 mi. of fishing streams and 147,000 acres of lakes and reservoirs, numerous winter sports areas and camp grounds. Natural wonders may be seen at Zion, Canyonlands and Bryce Canyon National Parks and Arches, Capitol Reef, Dinosaur, Rainbow Bridge and Natural Bridges National Monuments. The Lake Powell Recreation Area and Flaming Gorge Dam are other attractions.

Works by Utah artists and archeological, botanical, mineral and fossil collections may be seen at the Brigham Young Univ. Collections in Provo.

The Latter-day Saints number about 72% of the population of the state. The Mormons reached Utah July 24, 1847.

Utah was organized as a Territory Sept. 9, 1850; admitted to the Union Jan. 4, 1896.

(See also Index for Salt Lake City.)

Vermont
Green Mountain State

CAPITAL: Montpelier. AREA: 9,609 sq. mi., rank, 43rd. POPULATION: (See Index for 1970 Census.) MOTTO: Freedom and Unity. FLOWER: Red Clover. TREE: Sugar Maple. BIRD: Hermit Thrush. ANIMAL: Morgan Horse. SONG: Hail, Vermont. ADMISSION: 14th.

Vermont, first state to join the Union after the original 13, was the home of the Green Mountain Boys who played heroic roles in several victories of the American Revolution. They took their name from the Green Mountains which form the N-S backbone of the state. There are rich marble quarries in the western part of the state and large granite beds in the E. The Connecticut River runs along the E boundary, Lake Champlain forms much of the W line; among the many lakes is Memphremagog which lies partly in Canada to the N. Seven peaks rise over 4,000 ft. with Mt. Mansfield, 4,393 ft., the highest.

Vermont has long been known for its stoneworking, forest and dairy industries. Manufacturing employs the most persons. Tourism is the 2nd industry, attracting 6,800,000 annually.

with aiding the industrial growth. Principal manufactured goods are machine tools, computer components, stone and clay products, lumber, furniture and paper. Value added by manufacture is over $562,000,000 a year.

Tourism is important; the accent is on recreation, which produces more than $250,000,000 a year. Skiing has accounted for a tremendous growth, with spending by skiers multiplying many times in recent years. There are more than 95 miles of ski lifts in the state and many ski areas, including Stowe, Killington, Mt. Snow, Stratton, Bromley, Jay Peak and Sugarbush.

Vermont has 72 state parks and forests covering over 130,000 acres. The Long Trail is popular for hiking and camping. There is fishing for trout, salmon, bass, muskellunge, and hunting for deer and game birds.

Vermont and New York are the largest producers of maple syrup. Large milk and butter production accounts for most of the total value of farm receipts which was $179,182,000 for 1972. For its small size, Vermont has a large number of milk cows.

The state ranks high in output of marble, granite and limestone; it is also a leader in production of asbestos and talc.

The Shelburne Museum, 7 mi. S of Burlington, preserves 35 early American buildings, including furnished homes, doctor's and dentist's offices, stagecoach inn; covered bridge, side-wheeler, old trains, folk art, etc.; Webb gallery of paintings by Rembrandt, Goya, Corot, Manet, Cassatt.

The Bennington Museum displays early American glass, furniture, pottery and what is said to be the oldest Stars and Stripes flag in existence.

The Vermont area was visited by Samuel de Champlain, 1609, and had its first permanent settlement at Fort Dummer near Brattleboro, 1724.

Jurisdiction over the area was disputed by New Hampshire and New York. During the Revolution, the Green Mountain Boys under Ethan Allen took Fort Ticonderoga and under Seth Warner captured Crown

Point; later they helped defeat the British in the Battle of Bennington and at Saratoga.

In 1777 the colonists declared their independence, adopted a constitution, the first giving universal manhood suffrage without property qualifications, elected a governor. They chose the name Vermont, suggested by Dr. Thomas Young, Philadelphia, from Vert Mont (Green Mountain). Vermont ratified the U.S. Constitution Jan. 1791, entered the Union Mar. 4, 1791. Vermonters were intense anti-slavery men and supported Lincoln over their native son Stephen Douglas.

Vermont has 23 institutions of higher education including the Univ. of Vermont at Burlington, Middlebury College in Middlebury and Norwich Univ. in Northfield.

Virginia

Old Dominion

CAPITAL: Richmond. AREA: 40,817 sq. mi., rank, 36th. POPULATION: (See Index for 1970 Census.) MOTTO: Sic Semper Tyrannis. Thus always to Tyrants. FLOWER: American Dogwood. BIRD: Cardinal. TREE: American Dogwood. SONG: Carry Me Back to Old Virginia. Tenth of the Original 13 States to ratify Constitution.

The Commonwealth of Virginia is famed for its colonial heritage, for the statesmen it produced, its historic homes and estates, and the great battlefields on which the fate of the nation was decided in both the 18th and 19th Centuries.

It was first settled, 1607, at Jamestown by English colonists and named for Elizabeth I, called the Virgin Queen. It had the New World's 1st representative legislature, the House of Burgesses, 1619; this assembly was elected by male suffrage. Virginia was active in resistance to the British Stamp Act and it provided much of the leadership that led to American independence and the writing of the Constitution.

Virginia's coastal plain, the Tidewater, consists mostly of 4 peninsulas formed by Chesapeake Bay and the Potomac, Rappahannock, York and James Rivers. The central Piedmont plateau rises, toward the W, to the Blue Ridge Mtns. Beyond the Blue Ridge and between it and the Alleghenies on the W border lies the Shenandoah Valley, a rich farming region. Highest point is Mt. Rogers in the SW, 5,729 ft.

Virginia's manufacturing industries have grown steadily and are diversified. They provide jobs for some 350,000, over 4 times the number employed in agriculture. Total value added by manufacture is more than $5.1 billion, with payrolls totaling $2.5 billion; value of shipments was estimated at $10.9 billion.

Largest lines were chemicals, textiles, food products and clothing. Other important lines were lumber, furniture, paper, electrical machinery, transportation equipment, cigarettes, metal products, stone-clay-glass products.

The Federal Government is a major employer with military installations at Hampton Roads and U.S. agencies near Washington, D.C.

Hampton Roads is the major port, a leader in bulk export tonnage.

Agriculture remains a vital factor in the economy. Virginia ranks among the leaders in the U.S. in its crops of tobacco, peanuts, apples and sweet potatoes. Other important crops are corn, vegetables, barley, peaches. It has large numbers of turkeys; its Smithfield hams are famous. Farm receipts for 1972 totaled $665,529,000, more than half from livestock, the rest from crops.

Coal is Virginia's leading mineral commodity, in terms of both tonnage and value, and usually accounts for more than half the value of total mineral production. Also important are lime, zinc, stone, cement. Total mineral production for 1972 was valued at $440,756,000.

The commercial fishing catch was worth $25,992,000 in 1972; tonnage was 2nd largest among the states.

With its wealth of historical attractions and recreational facilities such as Shenandoah National Park in the Blue Ridge Mts. and Virginia Beach, the state has a large tourist business, est. at about $1 billion a year. Tourism is 2nd to manufacturing and ahead of agriculture as a source of income.

Virginia was the birthplace of 8 Presidents: Washington, Jefferson, Monroe, Madison, Tyler, William H. Harrison, Taylor and Wilson—the last 3 elected from other states. It has many historic shrines, including Washington's birthplace, Wakefield; his home and grave at Mount Vernon; Jefferson's Monticello, near Charlottesville and the Univ. of Virginia he designed; Robert E. Lee's birthplace, Stratford Hall, and grave at Lexington.

Colonial Williamsburg is a restoration of the 18th century buildings and living conditions in what was the capital of Virginia when Washington, Jefferson, Patrick Henry and George Mason were young men. There are more than 800 buildings, many of them the originals.

At Jamestown, 1st permanent English settlement, are foundations and ruins of early buildings, relics, statues and monuments and a nearby exhibit of glassblowing.

At Yorktown, where the surrender of British Gen. Cornwallis to American and French forces, Oct. 19, 1781, virtually ended the American Revolution, may be seen Colonial buildings, the restored house in which terms of surrender were drawn up, earthworks and Revolutionary cannons.

In Fredericksburg, the James Monroe Law Office and Museum is the original building in which President Monroe practiced law in the 1780s; among other possessions is the desk at which he signed the Monroe Doctrine.

Appomattox Court House National Monument includes the rebuilt Wilmer McLean house in which Gen. Lee surrendered the Confederate Army of Northern Virginia to Lt. Gen Ulysses S. Grant, Apr. 9, 1865.

Fort Monroe Casemate Museum has relics of the imprisonment in the fort of Jefferson Davis and Chief Black Hawk and of the battle between the Monitor and Merrimac. The Quartermaster Museum, Fort Lee, exhibits clothing, saddles, etc., of American soldiers from the Revolution on. The War Memorial Museum of Virginia, in Newport News, displays World War I and II weapons and equipment of many nations.

In Lexington are Washington and Lee Univ. and Virginia Military Institute, both closely linked with leaders and action in the Civil War. Also in Lexington is the George C. Marshall Research Library and Museum with displays of the life of the famed World War II general and statesman.

At Staunton is the Woodrow Wilson Birthplace, with memorabilia of his family. The Gen. Douglas MacArthur Memorial in Norfolk contains the general's sarcophagus, flags of 30 units he commanded, documents and murals of important events in his life.

Virginia seceded from the Union Apr. 17, 1861, and Richmond became the capital of the Confederate States. Virginia was readmitted Jan. 26, 1870.

There are 70 institutions of higher education, including 39 universities and colleges and 31 junior and two-year colleges.

(See also Index for Norfolk, Richmond, Roanoke.)

Washington

Evergreen State

CAPITAL: Olympia. AREA: 68,192 sq. mi., rank 20th. POPULATION: (See Index for 1970 Census.) MOTTO: Al-Ki, By and By. FLOWER: Coast Rhododendron. TREE: Western Hemlock. BIRD: Willow Goldfinch. SONG: Washington, My Home. ADMISSION: 42nd.

The state of Washington in the Pacific Northwest is a leader in many ways—in lumber, in fruit and other crops, and in aircraft production; its ports on Puget Sound are gateways to Alaska and the Far East; the great dams on the Columbia River provide power for production of aluminum and irrigation for the rich Columbia Basin.

The lofty Cascade Range splits the state, running N-S. To the W, the Puget Sound lowlands support dairy, poultry and truck-farming; in the extreme W. the Olympic Peninsula is studded with the peaks of the Olympic Mtns. and the Coast Ranges. On the E slopes of the Cascades are the state's great fruit orchards; further E, plateau country provides sheep and cattle lands and a rich wheat belt. Highest peak is Mt. Rainier in the Cascades, 14,410 ft.

The Columbia River cuts a zig-zag course across Washington from the NE, then flows W along the Oregon border to the Pacific.

Puget Sound has many deep harbors beside which Seattle, Tacoma, Everett and other great cities have grown. Foreign trade, mainly with Japan and Canada, has increased greatly.

Manufacturing industries employ 220,700 workers with payrolls over $2 billion and value added by manufacture over $4.1 billion a year. Transportation equipment, mostly aircraft but including ships and trucks, accounts for $886,100,000.

Other important manufacturing lines are lumber, food processing, pulp and paper, metals and metal products, chemicals and machinery. The AEC plant at Hanford produces nuclear fuels and electricity.

Washington's large production of fruits, berries and other crops places it 1st among the states in apples, blueberries, hops and red raspberries; it is among the top producers of potatoes, winter wheat, pears, grapes, apricots, filberts, cranberries, cherries, asparagus, strawberries. Farm receipts for 1972 totaled $953,284,000; over half from crops, the rest from livestock products.

The commercial fishing catch is valued at over $38,000,000 a year. Salmon accounts for half the total, followed by halibut and bottomfish.

Mineral production in 1972 was valued at an est. $107,624,000. Sand and gravel, silver, cement, zinc and lead were the most important products.

Large aluminum reduction plants, using refined ore from out-of-state and low-cost electric power, have expanded. Aluminum output in 1970 was 1,000,000 tons, 25% of U. S. total.

A series of great dams on the Columbia, including the massive Grand Coulee in the NE and Bonneville on the Oregon border, provide power and irrigation.

More than half the state is in forests; one-sixth of the nation's standing sawtimber is in Washington. Towering Douglas firs and Ponderosa pines, western hemlocks and red cedars are among commercially important trees. Wood products are worth $1.2 billion a year.

There are 43 institutions of higher education, including 17 universities and 4-year colleges. Among the largest are the Univ. of Washington, Washington State Univ., Central Washington State College, Seattle Univ. and the Univ. of Puget Sound.

First visited by explorers in the late 18th Century, Washington was organized as a territory Mar. 2, 1853; admitted to the Union Nov. 11, 1889.

The state has 3 national parks, Mt. Rainier, North Cascades and Olympic National Park. Its state parks and national forests of nearly 10,000,000 acres have large hunting, fishing and recreation areas.

The Washington State Historical Society, Tacoma, has exhibits of the fur trade, Indian and Eskimo arts, and pioneer cabins, schoolhouse and covered wagon.

Tourists, it has been estimated, spend about $500,000,000 annually in the state.

(See also Index for Seattle.)

West Virginia
Mountain State

CAPITAL: Charleston. AREA: 24,181 sq. mi., rank, 41ST. POPULATION: (See Index for 1970 census.) MOTTO: Montani Semper Liberi. Mountaineers Always Free. FLOWER: Rhododendron Maximum. BIRD: Cardinal. TREE: Sugar Maple. ANIMAL: Black Bear. SONGS: The West Virginia Hills. This Is My West Virginia, and West Virginia, My Home, Sweet Home. ADMISSION: 35th.

West Virginia's fortunes have long been based on those of the bituminous coal industry; the state usually is 1st in coal production with about 25% of the U.S. total. Increased output of coal and natural gas, plus growth in the chemical, steel, glass and tourist industries, have aided the economy.

The terrain is mountainous with the Alleghenies running NE-SW in the eastern half of the state; the western half is a plateau sloping down to the Ohio River which forms most of the boundary on the W. Highest point is Spruce Knob in the NE, 4,863 ft.

West Virginia was part of Virginia until that state se-

ceded in 1861; delegates of 40 western counties adopted a state government at Wheeling. Nov. 27, 1861; West Virginia was admitted to the Union June 20, 1863.

Coal accounts for more than 88% of the total value of mineral production. In 1972 the total mineral production was valued at an est. $1.38 billion. Kentucky had a slight lead in tonnage but West Virginia led in its value.

West Virginia produces and markets more natural gas than any other state east of the Mississippi. Also important are petroleum, salt, stone, cement, lime and clays.

Production of a wide variety of chemicals, based in the state's resources of salt brine, gas, oil and coal, and including synthetic fibers and plastics, dominates the manufacturing field, accounting for about 35% of the $2.38 billion in value added annually by manufacture. Large plants are in the Ohio and Kanawha valleys, where electric power is abundant. The state is also a major producer of steel and iron, glass and pottery.

Farm receipts totaled $125,895,000 for 1972; the hilly terrain is not conducive to large-scale agriculture. Poultry, dairy products, cattle and sheep accounted for most of the receipts. Apples and peaches are profitable crops. About 65% of the state is in forests.

Tourism is being promoted and visitors spend over $700,000,000 annually. More than a million acres have been set aside for recreation in 34 state parks, 9 state forests, Monongahela and George Washington National Forests and large reservoir recreation areas.

Attractions include Harpers Ferry National Historical Park, mineral water resorts at White Sulphur and Berkeley Springs, trout fishing, turkey, deer and bear hunting.

Part of the town of Harpers Ferry has been restored to its condition in 1859, when John Brown seized the U. S. Armory. Still standing is the fire-engine house in which Brown and a score of followers were besieged and captured by a force of U. S. Marines under Robert E. Lee, then a U. S. colonel.

The State Museum in Charleston displays local relics and artifacts from prehistoric cultures (as early as 8,000 B.C.), Indians and pioneers, and the life of the area's people, past and present.

The Huntington Galleries, Huntington, has collections of 19th and 20th Century European and American paintings, furniture and decorative arts. The Oglebay Mansion-Museum displays Colonial furniture and 19th Century glassware.

There are 24 institutions of higher education. Among the larger ones are West Virginia Univ., West Virginia State College, West Liberty State College, Marshall Univ. and Fairmont State College.

(See also Index for Charleston, Huntington.)

Wisconsin
Badger State

CAPITAL: Madison. AREA: 56,154 sq. mi., rank 26th. POPULATION: (See Index for 1970 Census.) MOTTO: Forward. FLOWER: Butterfly Violet. BIRD: Robin. TREE: Sugar Maple. ANIMAL: Badger. FISH: Muskellunge. WILDLIFE ANIMAL: White-tailed deer. SONG: On, Wisconsin! ADMISSION: 30th.

Known as America's Dairyland, Wisconsin produces more milk and cheese than any other state and agriculture is a vital part of the state's economy. However, manufacturing, including processing of foods, has become the state's largest employer and biggest income producer.

Mining has declined with the near-cessation in 1965 of iron mining, but output of several other minerals has increased. Reforestation has kept the paper and wood product industries important. There are 14 ports on Lakes Michigan and Superior with access to the St. Lawrence Seaway.

The state has an abundance of recreation resources; water and winter sports, hunting and fishing are among its attractions. Vacationers, it is estimated, spend over $1,000,000 a year.

Highest point is Timms Hill in the N, 1,952 ft.

Wisconsin's rolling pasturelands and large crops support the nation's largest herd of milk cows, about 1,831,999; 80% of its farms are dairy farms.

The state produces the most milk, cheese, hay and alfalfa in the U.S. It is also a leading producer of butter, oats, corn, cranberries and maple syrup. In addition to cattle, it also has large numbers of hogs and turkeys.

Farm receipts for 1972 totaled $1.81 billion, 9th highest among the states, most of it from livestock products.

About 40% of income produced in Wisconsin comes from manufacturing and, with over 479,800 factory employees, the state ranks among the top 12. Value added by manufacturing is over $8.4 billion a year.

Most important products, in terms of value added, are: machinery, especially engines, turbines, industrial and construction; food products, including dairy, meat and beer; transportation equipment, especially motor vehicle parts and equipment and mobile homes; iron and steel, metal products, paper and lumber.

Mineral production for 1972 was valued at $82,660,000. Zinc, lime, cement and stone are important. Iron mining was resumed with production of pelletized low-grade taconite ore late in 1969.

Most of Wisconsin's timber production goes into pulp and paper, but the state is also a leading producer of hardwood plywood and veneer.

Wisconsin has over 8,500 lakes, of which Winnebago is the largest, and fronts on both Lakes Michigan and Superior. Water sports, ice-boating, and fishing for trout, bass and muskellunge are popular as are skiing and hunting for deer, bear and wildfowl. Public parks and forests take up one-seventh of the land area; there are 49 state parks, 9 state forests, two national forests.

Other attractions include small towns which preserve Swiss, Scandinavian, German and other European cultures, visits to breweries and cheese factories, Indian festivals and the Dells (scenic gorges) of the Wisconsin River.

The Circus World Museum in Baraboo has over 100 circus wagons and other displays, and presents circus shows daily, early May-early Sept.

There are 58 institutions of higher learning, among them the Univ. of Wisconsin, Wisconsin State Univ., Marquette and Lawrence Univs.; Beloit, Ripon, St. Norbert, Carthage and Carroll Colleges.

The 1st European to visit the Wisconsin area was Jean Nicolet in 1634; he was followed by French explorers and missionaries and the land became part of New France. The French surrendered it to the British in 1763; the British ceded it to the U. S. in 1783, but were not completely dislodged until 1815. Wisconsin became a state May 29, 1848.

(See also Index for Madison, Milwaukee.)

Wyoming
Equality State

CAPITAL: Cheyenne. AREA: 97,914 sq. mi., rank, 9th. POPULATION: (See Index for 1970 Census.) MOTTO: Equal Rights. FLOWER: Wyoming Paint Brush. BIRD: Western Meadow Lark. TREE: Plains Cottonwood (Balsam Poplar). SONG: Wyoming State Song. ADMISSION: 44th.

Wyoming's towering mountains and rolling plains provide spectacular scenery, grazing ranges for sheep and cattle, and a wealth of mineral resources.

Ranges of the Rockies cover the western two-thirds of the state; the eastern third is Great Plains country. Highest point is Gannett Peak in the W, 13,804 ft. The spectacular Teton Mtns. lie S of Yellowstone National Park, which is mostly carved out of Wyoming's NW corner.

The most important industry is mining, particularly of oil and natural gas. Agriculture, especially livestock, runs 2nd. Of growing importance are both tourism and manufacturing.

Wyoming has large reserves of coal, oil, gas, oil shale, iron ore and gypsum.

Production of petroleum in 1972 was valued at $440,820,000, about 60% of the total mineral production value for the year, $731,840,000. The state ranked 1st in the U.S. in sodium carbonate production, 2nd in uranium. Also important are coal, natural gas, clays and iron ore.

Wyoming is 2nd among the states in wool production and as of Jan. 1, 1973, its sheep numbered 1,565,000,

exceeded only by Texas; it also had 1,490,000 cattle. Principal crops include wheat, oats, sugarbeets, corn, potatoes, barley and alfalfa. Livestock receipts for 1972 totaled $254,278,000; receipts for crops were $43,892,000.

Much of Wyoming's manufacturing is based on its mining and agricultural products. Leading lines include petroleum and coal products, processed foods, timber and wood, construction materials, iron and steel, electronic components, equipment for farms and for food preparation. Value added by manufacture is about $119,400,000 annually.

Wyoming is a main source for 3 important river systems, the Missouri, Colorado and Columbia. Both power and irrigation are provided by a growing number of dams and reservoirs. Tourism produces an est. annual $175,000,000.

Wyoming was organized as a Territory July 25, 1868; admitted to the Union July 10, 1890. Women were given the right to vote, for the first time in the U. S., by the Territorial Legislature in 1869.

Grand Teton National Park, with mountains 13,000 ft. high, comprises 299,326 acres; the National Elk Refuge covers 25,000 acres. Devils Tower, a cluster of rock columns 865 ft. high, became the first National Monument in W. O. in 1906. Fort Laramie, partly preserved, partly restored, is a National Historic Site. The annual Cheyenne Frontier Days Celebration, last full week in July, is the state's largest rodeo. Hunting, fishing and skiing are other attractions.

The Buffalo Bill Historical Center in Cody has a museum with personal effects of William F. Cody (Buffalo Bill) and the Whitney Gallery of Modern Art with Indian art and paintings by Frederic Remington, Charles M. Russell, George Catlin, etc.

The Bradford Brinton Memorial Ranch, near Big Horn, has collections of western painting and sculpture, antiques, Indian arts, hunting trophies and firearms; open May 15-Sept. 15.

The University of Wyoming is in Laramie and there are seven community colleges.

(See Index for Yellowstone National Park).

District of Columbia

AREA: 67 sq. mi. POPULATION: (1970 Census) 756,510. MOTTO: Justitia Omnibus, Justice for All. FLOWER: American Beauty Rose. TREE: Scarlet Oak. BIRD: Wood Thrush. The City of Washington is coextensive with the District of Columbia.

The District of Columbia is the seat of the Federal Government of the United States. It lies on the west central edge of Maryland on the Potomac, opposite Virginia. Its area was originally 100 sq. mi. taken from the sovereignty of Maryland and Virginia. Virginia's portion south of the Potomac was given back to that state in 1846.

The 23rd Amendment, ratified in 1961, granted residents of the District the right to vote for President and Vice President for the first time and gave it three members in the Electoral College. Residents cast the first such votes in Nov. 1964.

Congress governed the District 1878-1967 through 3 Commissioners appointed by the President. The Reorganization Plan of 1967 substituted a single Commissioner (also called Mayor) and assistant and a 9-member City Council, all likewise appointed by the President; budgetary funds were still appropriated by Congress; residents had no vote in local government (except for recently granted right to elect school board members).

In Sept. 1970, Congress approved legislation giving the District one Delegate to the House of Representatives. The Delegate may vote in committee but not on the House floor. The first Delegate was elected Mar. 23, 1971.

Proposals for a "federal town" for the deliberations of the Continental Congress were made in 1783, four years before the adoption of the Constitution that gave the Confederation a national government. Rivalry between northern and southern delegates over the site appeared in the First Congress, meeting in New York in 1789. John Adams, presiding officer of the Senate, cast the deciding vote of that body for Germantown, Pa. In 1790 Congress compromised by making Philadelphia the temporary capital for ten years. The Virginia members of the House wanted a capital on the eastern bank of the Potomac; they were defeated by the Northerners, while the Southerners defeated the Northern attempt to have the nation assume the war debts of the 13 original states, the Assumption bill fathered by Alexander Hamilton. Hamilton and Jefferson arranged a compromise; the Virginia men voted for the Assumption Bill, and the Northerners conceded the capital to the Potomac. President Washington chose the site in October, 1790, and persuaded landowners to sell their holdings to the government at £ 25, then about $66, an acre. The capital was named Washington.

Washington appointed Pierre Charles L'Enfant, a French engineer who had come over with Lafayette, to plan the capital on an area not over 10 miles square. The L'Enfant plan was considered grandiose, for streets 100 to 110 feet wide and one avenue 400 feet wide and a mile long on the Potomac pastures seemed foolhardy. But

Washington endorsed his plans. When L'Enfant ordered a wealthy landowner to remove his new manor house because it obstructed his vista, and demolished it when the owner refused, Washington had to step in and dismiss L'Enfant. The official map was completed by Andrew Ellicott, surveyor, and Benjamin Banneker, black mathematician.

On Sept. 18, 1793, the cornerstone of the north wing of the Capitol was laid by President Washington. The occasion was expected to drum up sales of city lots, but there were few purchasers. Washington bought several lots. In the next few years Robert Morris and others invested. By 1799 the Senate wing of the Capitol had been roofed, the walls of the President's house were up and the Treasury building was ordered. On June 3, 1800, President John Adams moved to Washington and on June 10, Philadelphia ceased to be the temporary capital. The City of Washington was incorporated in 1802; the District of Columbia was created as a municipal corporation in 1871, embracing Washington, Georgetown and County of Washington. (*See also Washington, D. C.*)

OUTLYING U. S. AREAS

Commonwealth of Puerto Rico

Estado Libre Asociado de Puerto Rico
CAPITAL: San Juan. AREA: 3,435 sq. mi. POPULATION: (1970 Census) 2,712,033. FLAG: Three red, two white horiz. stripes; white star in blue triangle at staff. SONG: La Borinquena.

Puerto Rico is a hilly, tropical island lying between the Atlantic to the N and the Caribbean to the S; it is the easternmost of the West Indies group called the Greater Antilles, of which Cuba, Hispaniola and Jamaica are the larger units. It lies about 1,600 mi. SE of New York, 500 mi. N of Venezuela. It is roughly rectangular, 105 mi. long by 35 wide. Numerous small islands include Vieques, Culebra and Mona.

The soil of the coastal plain is fertile and there are many lush valleys, but there are dry areas in the S which need irrigation and an extensive system has been constructed by the government. The climate is mild, with a mean temperature of 76°; the mean maximum is 82° and the mean minimum 73°. Highest point is Cerro de Punta, 4,389 ft.,near the island's center.

President Truman, on Aug. 5, 1947, signed an act giving Puerto Rico the right to choose its chief executive by popular vote. An act of 1950, affirmed by special election, June 4, 1951, permitted Puerto Rico to draft its own constitution. One similar to that of the United States was approved in a convention Feb. 4, 1952, and ratified by a popular vote March 3, 1952. President Truman signed, July 3, 1952, a Congressional resolution approving the new constitution, elevating Puerto Rico to the status of a free commonwealth associated with the United States, effective July 25, 1952. In 1961 Pres. Kennedy appointed two Puerto Ricans to important posts in his administration.

In a July 23, 1967, referendum, Puerto Ricans strongly favored continuation of commonwealth status. The vote was: commonwealth, 425,081; statehood, 273,315; independence, 4,205.

The Legislative Assembly consists of a Senate and House of Representatives, elected by direct vote every 4 years. Eight senatorial districts elect two Senators each; 40 representative districts one member each; also 11 Senators and 11 Representatives at large. Its directly elected Resident Commissioner in the U.S. Congress has only committee voting privileges. Puerto Ricans were granted American citizenship under the Organic Act of 1917. They do not vote for President unless they move to the U.S., where they come under local laws.

Executive power is vested in a governor elected by direct vote. There are 12 executive departments each headed by a secretary: State, Justice, Education, Health, Treasury, Labor, Agriculture, Commerce, Social Services, Housing, Natural Resources and Transportation-Public Works. The judiciary is vested in a Supreme Court and lower courts.

The Commonwealth's "Operation Bootstrap" program for economic development has radically raised the standard of living; per capita income for 1972 was $1,713, up $948 from 1963.

Puerto Rico derives its largest income from manufacturing. $1.43 billion in 1972, up $186,000,000 from 1971. Products include textiles and apparel, electrical and electronic equipment, plastics and chemicals. The chemical products include pharmaceuticals, cosmetics, ammoniated superphosphate, ethylene glycol and potassium sulphate.

Gross capital investment in 1972 reached $1.93 billion; gross product was $5.82 billion.

Mineral production is mainly of construction materials, with cement accounting for a large part of the value; total value for 1972 was $96,831,000.

Agriculture, a large but declining source of income, rose by 7.1% in 1972 to $211,000,000. Income from dairy and livestock products has surpassed that from sugar. Also important are tobacco, coffee, pineapples, coconuts, fruits, garden truck, rum, molasses.

Off-island trade is chiefly with the United States.

	Imports	Exports
1971	$2,879,000,000	$1,797,000,000
1972	$3,108,000,000	$1,974,000,000

The flow of migrants to mainland U.S. after 1945 was reversed in 1963, reversed again in 1970, and in 1972 there was an excess of 41,098 arrivals over departures. These changes are caused mainly by employment conditions, mainland and Puerto Rican. Unemployment on the island is usually over 11%.

San Juan, with its international airport and resort hotels, is the center of the tourism industry. Visitors totaled 1,172,885 in 1972, up from 1,095,119 in 1971, and spending rose to $258,900,000 from $234,915,000.

Spanish is the official language but most persons also speak English. Public school education is free and compulsory at the elementary school level; English is taught as a language and is compulsory in all 8 grades. Chief religion is Roman Catholicism.

Puerto Rico (or Borinquen, after the original Indian name Boriquen) was discovered by Columbus, Nov. 19, 1493. Ponce de Leon conquered it for Spain, 1509, and established the first settlement at Caparra, across the bay from San Juan. Ruled by Spain until 1898, it was occupied by Maj. Gen. Nelson A. Miles in the Spanish-American war and ceded to the U. S. by the Treaty of Paris, Dec. 10, 1898. (*See also San Juan*)

Canal Zone and Panama Canal

For Panama Canal cargo traffic see Index.
The Canal Zone has been, in effect, a U. S. Government reservation. It is a strip of land extending 5 mi. on each side of the axis of the Panama Canal, under jurisdiction of the U.S. by treaty with the Rep. of Panama.

Efforts to change the Zone's status have been made by both nations for several years.

The canal connects the Caribbean with the Bay of Panama on the Pacific. Because of the geographic loop made by the Isthmus of Panama, the Caribbean end of the canal, which could be called the eastern end, is actually further west than the Pacific end.

The Zone has an area of 553 sq. mi. of which 362 are land. Population (1970 Census) was 44,198. About 11,000 U.S. Army, Air Force and Navy personnel are normally stationed in the Zone.

The Canal Zone Government and the Panama Canal Co. are the two operating agencies, both headed by an individual who acts as Governor of the Canal Zone and President of the Company. The governor is appointed by the President of the U. S. As governor he reports directly to the Secy. of the Army. As president of the company he reports to the board of directors, appointed by the Secy. of the Army. The Canal Zone Government maintains civil government. The Company operates the Canal, the Panama Railroad and a ship between New Orleans and the Canal Zone.

A French syndicate under Ferdinand de Lesseps failed to complete a canal, 1880-89, and a second French company failed in 1899. The U. S. bought their rights and offered Colombia compensation for a canal zone, but Colombia failed to ratify the treaty Oct. 1903. Panama declared itself independent of Colombia Nov. 3, 1903, and was recognized by President Theodore Roosevelt Nov. 6. American naval forces discouraged action by Colombia. On Nov. 18 Panama granted the Canal strip to the U. S. by treaty, ratified Feb. 26, 1904, compensation $10,000,000, with annual payments of $250,000 after 9 years, and a guarantee of Panama independence.

Under terms of the 1903 treaty, Panama granted the U. S. perpetual sovereignty over the Canal Zone "to the entire exclusion of the exercise by the Republic of Panama of any such sovereign rights, power or authority."

The canal was opened to traffic Aug. 15, 1914. In 1922 Colombia accepted $25,000,000 from the U. S. plus special land transportation privileges, and agreed to recognize Panama. The U. S. increased its annual payment to Panama to $430,000 and withdrew its guarantee of independence.

A further treaty regulating relations between the U. S. and Panama was signed Jan. 25, 1955, increasing the annuity paid Panama to $1,930,000. In addition, the U. S. gave Panama $28,000,000 worth of real estate and buildings no longer needed by the Canal Zone administration. U. S. citizen and non-citizen employees were guaranteed equality of pay and opportunity. In addition, the U. S. agreed to build the high level bridge over the Pacific entrance to the Canal, opened Oct. 12, 1962, as a link in the Inter-American Highway.

Negotiations for a new treaty began after Panamanian riots protesting the 1903 and 1955 treaties caused the death of 21 Panamanians and 3 U.S. soldiers, Jan. 9, 1964. Preliminary agreement was reached in 1967, but in 1970, after a change of government, Panama declared the proposed new treaty was unacceptable. Negotiations continued.

In March 1973, the U.S. vetoed a Panama-backed resolution in the UN Security Council which called on the U.S. and Panama to negotiate a new treaty to "guarantee full respect for Panama's effective sovereignty over all its territory." The U.S. said it wished to negotiate with Panama "without outside pressure."

Virgin Islands

CAPITAL: Charlotte Amalie, on St. Thomas Is. AREA: 133 sq. mi. POPULATION: (1970 Census) 62,468. FLOWER: Yellow Cedar.

The Virgin Islands of the United States, an unincorporated territory administered by the Interior Dept., lie to the E of Puerto Rico at the western end of the Lesser Antilles, 1,629 mi. SE of New York. There are about 100 islands in the Virgins, of which more than 50 islands and islets in the western area belong to the U. S.; the remainder are the British Virgin Islands.

The three largest and most populous of the U. S. islands are St. Croix, St. Thomas and St. John. Formerly the Danish West Indies, the islands were purchased by the U. S. from Denmark for $25,000,000 (effective Mar. 31, 1917) for defense purposes. The islands were discovered by Columbus in 1493. About 80% of the population is of Negro descent.

Mean winter temperature is 78°; summer, 82°. Virgin Islands National Park occupies about three-fourths of St. John, smallest of the three principal islands.

The inhabitants have been citizens of the U. S. since 1927. Legislation originates in a unicameral house of 15 senators, elected for 2 years.

The Governor, formerly appointed by the President of the U.S., was elected for a 4-year term in Nov. 1970 and took office Jan. 4, 1971. In 1972 a U.S. law gave the Virgin Islands one Delegate to the U.S. House of Representatives; the Delegate may vote in committee but not on the House floor.

Tourism is the largest industry and is growing. Principal exports are watch movements, jewelry, rum, wool textile products, thermometers, bay rum.

Minor Caribbean Islands

The tiny **Swan Islands**, 97 mi. N of Honduras and claimed by the U.S. since 1863, were turned over to Honduras by a treaty signed Nov. 22, 1971, and ratified by the U.S. Senate June 12, 1972. The 2 nations agreed to cooperate in maintaining a weather station and telecommunications facility on the islands, Great Swan and Little Swan, with a total area of under 3 sq. mi.

The **Corn Islands**, 30 mi. off the coast of Nicaragua and leased by the U.S. since 1914, were turned over to Nicaragua Apr. 25, 1971. The islands, Great Corn and Little Corn, have a population of over 1,800.

Quita Sueno Bank, Roncador Cay, Serrana Bank and **Seranilla Bank** lie in the Caribbean between Nicaragua and Jamaica. They are uninhabited. They were to be turned over to Colombia in 1973 under an agreement reached Sept. 8, 1972.

Navassa lies between Jamaica and Haiti, covers about 2 sq. mi., is reserved by the U.S. for a lighthouse.

American Samoa

CAPITAL: Pago Pago, Island of Tutuila. AREA: 76 sq. mi. POPULATION: (1970 Census) 27,159.

Blessed with spectacular scenery and delightful South Seas climate, American Samoa is the most southerly of all lands under U. S. ownership. It is an unincorporated territory consisting of 6 small islands of the Samoan group: Tutuila (where Pago Pago, the capital, lies by a crescent bay beneath tall mountains), Aunuu, the Manua Islands (Tau, Olosega and Ofu), and Rose. Also administered as part of American Samoa is **Swain's Is.,** 210 mi. to the NW, acquired by the U. S. in 1925. The islands are 2,300 mi. SW of Hawaii.

American Samoa became U. S. territory by a treaty with the United Kingdom and Germany in 1899, confirmed by local chiefs in 1900 and 1904. Pago Pago had been a U. S. Navy coaling station under an 1872 commercial treaty.

Western Samoa, comprising the larger islands of the Samoan group, was a New Zealand mandate and UN Trusteeship until it became an independent nation Jan. 1, 1962. (See Index.)

Tutuila has an area of 52 sq. mi. Tau has an area of 17 sq. mi., and the islets of Ofu and Olosega 5 sq. mi., with a population of a few thousand. Swain's Island has nearly 2 sq. mi. and about 100 population. Highest peak is Lata, on Tau Is., 3,056 ft.

About 70% of the land is forest. Chief products and exports are fish products, copra and handicrafts. Taro, bread-fruit, yams, coconuts, pineapples, oranges and bananas also are produced.

Formerly under jurisdiction of the Navy, since July 1, 1951, it has been administered by the Interior Dept., which appoints a Governor and a Secretary. It has a bicameral legislature.

The American Samoans are of Polynesian origin. They are nationals of the U. S.

Educational television was started in Sept., 1964, and serves an important role in Samoa's public schools.

Wake, Midway, Other Islands

Wake Island, and its sister islands, **Wilkes** and **Peale,** lie in the Pacific Ocean on the direct route from Hawaii to Hong Kong, about 2,000 mi. W of Hawaii and 1,290 mi. E. of Guam. The group is 4.5 mi. long, 1.5 mi. wide and totals about 3 sq. mi.

The United States flag was hoisted over Wake Island, July 4, 1898, by Gen. F. V. Greene, commanding Second Detachment, Philippine Expedition. Formal possession was taken Jan. 17, 1899; Wake is administered by the U.S. Air Force since 1972. Wake Island Air Base supports military flights.

The **Midway Islands,** acquired in 1867, are a group of two, **Sand** and **Eastern,** in the North Pacific, 1,150 mi. NW of Hawaii, with area of about 2 sq. mi., administered by the Navy Dept.

Johnston Atoll, SW of Hawaii, is under Air Force control, and **Kingman Reef,** S of Hawaii, is under Navy control.

Howland, Jarvis and **Baker Islands** south of the Hawaiian group, uninhabited since World War II, are under the Interior Dept.

Palmyra is an atoll SW of Hawaii, 4 sq. mi. Privately-owned, it has been under the Interior Dept. since 1961.

Certain islands taken from Japan in World War II were retained by the U.S. as possible military bases with the understanding they would eventually be returned.

On June 26, 1968, these islands were returned to Japanese control and administration. They included: the **Bonin Islands,** with an area of about 40 sq. mi., S of Japan: The **Volcano Islands,** S of the Bonins, including **Iwo Jima** (About 8 sq. mi.), scene of the famous World War II battle; **Marcus Island,** also called Minami Tori-Shima, about 1 sq. mi., E of the Volcanoes.

The 1968 agreement provided that the U. S. would continue the use of navigational stations on Iwo Jima and Marcus.

On May 15, 1972, the **Ryukyu Islands,** including **Okinawa** and the nearby **Daito Islands,** were returned by the U.S. to Japanese rule. The islands had been under U.S. administration beginning with the capture of Okinawa by the U.S. June 21, 1945, during World War II. Under the reversion agreement, the U.S. continued to maintain large military bases. Nuclear weapons stockpiled on Okinawa were withdrawn. The islands, stretching 400 mi. SW from Japan, have an area of 848 sq. mi. and pop. (1970 est.) of 945,465.

Guam

CAPITAL: Agana. AREA: 212 sq. mi. POPULATION: (1970 Census) 84,996.

Guam, the largest of the Mariana Islands, now an unincorporated territory, was ceded to the U. S. by Spain in the treaty of Paris, Dec. 10, 1898. It is 30 mi. long and 4 to 8½ mi. wide. Distance from Manila, 1,499 mi.; from San Francisco, 5,053 mi. Mean annual temp. is 81°, average annual rainfall, July to September, 70 in. The island is volcanic and mountains rise 700 to 1,329 ft. Highest peak is Mt. Lamlam.

Magellan discovered the group of islands, Mar. 6, 1521, and called them the Ladrones (thieves). They were colonized in 1668 by Spanish missionaries who renamed them the Mariana Islands in honor of Maria Anna, queen of Spain.

When Spain ceded Guam to the U. S., it sold the other Marianas to Germany. Japan obtained a League of Nations mandate over the German islands in 1919; in Dec. 1941 it seized Guam; the island was retaken by the U. S. in July 1944. Guam has Navy and Air Force Bases.

Guam is under the jurisdiction of the Dept. of the Interior. It is administered under the Organic Act of 1950, which provides for a governor, a 21-member unicameral legislature, elected biennially by the residents, who are American citizens but do not vote for President.

Beginning in Nov. 1970, Guamanians elected their own governor, previously appointed by the President of the U.S. He took office in Jan. 1971. In 1972 a U.S. law gave Guam one Delegate to the U.S. House of Representatives; the Delegate may vote in committee but not on the House floor.

School attendance is compulsory. The Univ. of Guam provides higher education. English is the official language. Chief religion is Roman Catholicism.

The Guamanians are of primarily Chamorro (Micronesian) stock, with some of mixed Spanish or Filipino descent.

Copra, fish and handicraft products are exported. Tourism has become a major aspect of Guam's economy. Over 90,000 tourists, most from Japan, visit annually.

Islands Under Trusteeship
CAROLINES, MARIANAS, MARSHALLS

The U.S. Trust Territory of the Pacific Islands, also called Micronesia, includes 3 major archipelagoes; the **Caroline Islands, Marshall Islands,** and **Mariana Islands (except Guam: See above).** There are 2,141 islands, 98 of them inhabited; land area total 717 sq. mi. but the islands are scattered over 3,000,000 sq. mi. of Micronesia in the western Pacific N of the Equator and E of the Philippines. Total pop. (1970 Census) was 94,940.

In 1885, many of the islands were claimed by Germany. Others, held by Spain, were sold to Germany at the time of the Spanish-American War, 1898. After the outbreak of World War I, Japan took over the islands and, after the war, League of Nations mandates over them were awarded to Japan.

After World War II, the United Nations assigned them (1947) as a Trust Territory to be administered by the U. S. They were placed under administration of the U. S. Interior Dept in 1951.

There is a High Commissioner, appointed by the U. S. President. Saipan is the headquarters of the administration. The Congress of Micronesia, an elected legislature with limited powers, held its first meeting in 1965. It has a Senate of 12 members and a House of Rep. of 21.

In 1969, a commission of the Congress of Micronesia recommended that Micronesia be given internal self-government in free association with the U. S.

A U.S. offer of commonwealth status, similar to Puerto Rico's, was rejected by Micronesian leaders in 1970.

In further talks in 1972, the U.S. proposed a plan for Micronesian self-government in free association with the U.S., leaving the U.S. responsible for foreign affairs and defense. The Marianas sought closer association with the U.S. than did the other groups.

Among the noted islands are: **Saipan** and **Tinian** in the Marianas, scene of a bitter engagement when they were taken by the U. S. from Japan in World War II; the former Japanese strongholds of **Palau, Peleliu, Truk** and **Yap** in the Carolines: **Bikini** and **Eniwetok,** where U. S. nuclear tests were staged, and **Kwajalein,** another World War II battle scene, all in the Marshalls.

Many of the islands are volcanic with luxuriant vegetation; others are of coral formation. Only a few are self-sustaining. Principal exports are copra, trochus shells, fish products, handicrafts and vegetables.

Disputed Pacific Islands

In the central Pacific, S and SW of Hawaii, lie 25 islands and atolls claimed by the U.S.; 18 of them are also claimed by the United Kingdom, and 7 by New Zealand. All are S of the Equator except Christmas Island.

Those claimed by the U. K. are:

The **Line Islands,** S of Hawaii, including Christmas, Flint, Malden, Starbuck and Vostok Islands and Caroline Atoll; only Christmas is inhabited. All are administered by the U. K.

Also, the **Phoenix Islands,** SW of Hawaii, including Canton and Enderbury Islands and Birnie, Gardner, Hull, McKean, Sydney and Phoenix Atolls. All are inhabited and administered by the U.K. except for Canton and Enderbury which are under joint U. S. and U. K. administration. A U. S. missile tracking station on Canton was discontinued in Dec. 1967.

Also, the **Ellice Islands,** further to the SW, including Funafuti, Nukufetau and Nukulailai Atolls and Nurakita; all inhabited and all administered by the U. K.

Those claimed by New Zealand are:

The **Tokelau (Union) Islands,** S of the Phoenix group, including Nukunono, Atafu and Fakaofu Atolls. All are inhabited and administered by New Zealand.

Also, the **Northern Cook Islands,** E of the Unions, including Danger, Manahiki, Rakahanga and Penrhyn (Tongareva) Atolls. All are inhabited and administered by New Zealand.

Confederate States and Secession, 1861-1865

The American Civil War, 1861-1865, grew out of sectional disputes over the employment of slavery in the South and the contention of southern legislators that the states retained many sovereign rights, including the right to secede from the Union.

The principal product of the South was cotton, harvested by slave labor. For 50 years Northern leaders had been trying to curtail slavery, but were checkmated in Congress by Southern legislators. Extreme partisans in the North, who demanded the immediate end of slavery for moral reasons, were called Abolitionists.

The Southern states argued that the U.S. Constitution was a contract between sovereign states, which could withdraw (secede) when state rights were violated. This has led Southern historians to call the Civil War the War Between the States. Actually the war was not fought by state against state but by one federal regime against another, the Confederate government in Richmond assuming control over the economic, political and military life of the South, under protest from Georgia and South Carolina.

The Census of 1860 gave the United States a population of 31,443,321. This included 487,690 free Negroes and 3,953,780 Negro slaves.

Earlier acts against slavery included the Missouri Compromise of 1820 which admitted Missouri as a slave state but prohibited slavery in the Louisiana Terr. N of Arkansas; the Compromise of 1850, which admitted California as a free state, omitted action on slavery in organizing Utah and New Mexico as territories, ended slave trade in Dist. of Columbia, amended Fugitive Slave Act to punish any who aided a fugitive and abolished trial by jury for fugitive; Kansas-Nebraska Act, 1854, which left choice of slavery in Kansas and Nebraska to residents there. (Squatter sovereignty)

Harriet Beecher Stowe's Uncle Tom's Cabin, 1851-52, intensified feeling against slavery.

Tension increased when the Supreme Court ruled Mar. 6, 1857, that Dred Scott, a Negro, did not become free when taken to a free state and did not have rights as a citizen; also that the Missouri compromise on slavery was unconstitutional.

John Brown's attempt to arm slaves at Harpers Ferry, Oct. 16-18, 1859, inflamed partisans.

Abraham Lincoln's stand for free soil (no slavery) in new states and territories, and his general condemnation of slavery, caused Southern fanatics to threaten secession if he were elected. When Sen. Stephen A. Douglas split the Democratic party by his stand against secession, Lincoln's election was assured. Even before inauguration Lincoln had Sen. Wm. H. Seward (N.Y.) offer a resolution that the Constitution never be altered to interfere with slavery where established, that the Fugitive Slave Law be amended to include trial by jury, that all states repeal laws contrary to the Constitution.

Secession of States

South Carolina voted an ordinance of secession from the Union, repealing its 1788 ratification of the U. S. Constitution, Dec. 20, 1860, proclaimed in effect Dec. 24. Other states seceding in 1861 and their votes in convention were:

Mississippi, Jan 9, 1861 by 84 to 15
Florida, Jan. 10, 1861, by 62 to 7.
Alabama, Jan. 11, 1861, by 61 to 39.

Georgia, Jan. 19, 1861, by 208 to 89.
Louisiana, Jan 26, 1861, by 113 to 17
Texas, Feb. 1, 1861, by 166 to 7, ratified by popular vote Feb. 23, 1861; for secession, 34,794; against 11,325.

Virginia had delayed action, but when President Lincoln called for troops after Sumter fell it voted for secession April 17, 1861, by 88 to 55, ratified by popular vote May 23, 1861; for secession, 128,884; against, 32,134.

Arkansas, May 6, 1861, by 69 to 1.

North Carolina, May 21, 1861, voted secession but refused by two-thirds vote to submit it to people for ratification.

Tennessee, May 7, 1861, entered a military league with the Confederacy; popular vote, June 8, for secession, 104,019; against 47,238.

Missouri Unionists stopped secession in the convention at Jefferson City Feb. 28 and at the second session in St. Louis Mar. 9. The legislature condemned secession Mar. 7. Under the protection of Confederate troops secessionist members of the legislature adopted a resolution of secession at Neosho, Oct. 31, 1861. The Confederate Congress seated representatives.

Kentucky did not secede and its government remained Unionist. In a part occupied by Confederate troops Kentuckians passed an act of secession and the Confederate Congress admitted representatives.

Maryland legislature voted against secession Apr. 27, 53 to 13. Delaware did not secede. Western Virginia held conventions at Wheeling, named a pro-Union governor June 11, 1861; admitted to Union as West Virginia June 30, 1863; its constitution provided for gradual abolition of slavery.

Confederate Government

Forty-two delegates from South Carolina, Georgia, Alabama, Mississippi, Louisiana and Florida met in convention at Montgomery, Ala., Feb. 4, 1861. Howell Cobb of Georgia was chosen to preside. On Feb. 6 delegates from North Carolina arrived to plead in vain for conciliation. The first delegate from Texas came Feb. 13. The congress adopted a provisional constitution of the Confederate States of America Feb. 8, 1861, and on the next day elected Jefferson Davis (Miss.), provisional president, and Alexander H. Stephens (Ga.), provisional vice president. Davis was inducted into office at Montgomery, Feb. 18, 1861.

A permanent constitution was adopted Mar. 11, 1861. It provided that the president should be elected for a single term of 6 years and abolished the African slave trade. The congress moved to Richmond, Va., July 20, 1861. Jefferson Davis was elected president, October, 1861, inaugurated Feb 22, 1862.

Jefferson Davis (1808-1889) was a West Point graduate, 1828; served in Black Hawk and Mexican wars; Senator from Mississippi, 1847-1851; Secretary of War, 1853-1857; Senator, 1857-1861.

The congress adopted a flag, consisting of a red field with a white stripe in the middle third, and a blue jack with a circle of white stars, going two-thirds of the way down the flag. This flag was unfurled in Montgomery Mar. 4, 1861. Later the more popular flag was the red field with blue diagonal cross bars that held 13 white stars, designed by Gen. P. G. T. Beauregard.

Dixie

The name Dixie is popularly associated with the southern states of the U.S. Several possible origins have been suggested.

One is said to be the French word Dix (10) which was printed on $10 bills used in early Louisiana and which were called "dixies" by Americans. Louisiana became known as "Dix's Land" or "land of the Dixie's."

Some sources suggest that the name originated from a kind-hearted Dutch farmer, Dixie (Dixye), who unsuccessfully tried to cultivate tobacco in Harlem, New York City in the late 1700s. When he sold his slaves to a farmer in Piedmont County, S.C. they are said to have longed to return to Dixie's farm and sang of its joys.

In the South many consider Dixie a derivation from the "Mason-Dixon Line" which divided the free and slave states.

The National Anthem–The Star-Spangled Banner

The Star-Spangled Banner was ordered played by the military and naval services by President Woodrow Wilson in 1916. It was designated the National Anthem by Act of Congress, March 3, 1931. It was written by Francis Scott Key, of Georgetown, D. C., during the bombardment of Fort McHenry, Baltimore, Md., Sept. 13-14, 1814. Key was a lawyer, a graduate of St. John's College, Annapolis, and a volunteer in a light artillery company. When a friend, Dr. Beanes, a physician of Upper Marlborough, Md., was taken aboard Admiral Cockburn's British squadron for interfering with ground troops, Key and J. S. Skinner, carrying a note from President Madison, went to the fleet under a flag of truce on a cartel ship to ask Beanes' release. Admiral Cockburn consented, but as the fleet was about to sail up the Patapsco to bombard Fort McHenry he detained them, first on H. M. S. Surprise, and then on a supply ship.

Key witnessed the bombardment from his own vessel. It began at 7 a.m., Sept. 13, 1814, and lasted, with intermissions, for 25 hours. The British fired over 1,500 shells, each weighing as much as 220 lbs. They were unable to approach closely because the Americans had sunk 22 vessels in the channel. Only four Americans were killed and 24 wounded. A British bomb-ship was disabled.

During the bombardment Key wrote a stanza on the back of an envelope. Next day at Indian Queen Inn, Baltimore, he wrote out the poem and gave it to his brother-in-law, Judge J. H. Nicholson. Nicholson suggested the tune, Anacreon in Heaven, and had the poem printed on broadsides, of which two survive. On Sept. 20 it appeared in the Baltimore American. Later Key made 3 copies; one is in the Library of Congress and one in the Pennsylvania Historical Society.

The copy that Key wrote in his hotel Sept. 14, 1814, remained in the Nicholson family for 93 years. In 1907 it was sold to Henry Walters of Baltimore. In 1934 it was bought at auction in New York from the Walters estate by the Walters Art Gallery, Baltimore, for $26,400. The Walters Gallery in 1953 sold the manuscript to the Maryland Historical Society for the same price.

The flag that Key saw during the bombardment is preserved in Smithsonian Institution, Washington. It is 30 by 42 ft., and has 15 alternate red and white stripes and 15 stars, for the original 13 states plus Kentucky and Vermont. It was made by Mary Young Pickersgill. The Baltimore Flag house, a museum, occupies her premises, which were restored in 1953.

THE STAR–SPANGLED BANNER

I

Oh, say can you see by the dawn's early light
What so proudly we hailed at the twilight's last gleaming?
Whose broad stripes and bright stars thru the perilous fight.
O'er the ramparts we watched were so gallantly streaming?
And the rocket's red glare, the bombs bursting in air.
Gave proof through the night that our flag was still there.
Oh, say does that star-spangled banner yet wave
O'er the land of the free and the home of the brave?

II

On the shore, dimly seen through the mists of the deep.
Where the foe's haughty host in dread silence reposes,
What is that which the breeze, o'er the towering steep,
As it fitfully blows, half conceals, half discloses?
Now it catches the gleam of the morning's first beam.
In full glory reflected now shines on the stream:
'Tis the star-spangled banner! O long may it wave
O'er the land of the free and the home of the brave!

III

And where is that band who so vauntingly swore
That the havoc of war and the battle's confusion,
A home and a country should leave us no more!
Their blood has washed out their foul footsteps' pollution
No refuge could save the hireling and slave
From the terror of flight, or the gloom of the grave:
And the star-spangled banner in triumph doth wave
O'er the land of the free and the home of the brave!

IV

Oh! thus be it ever, when freemen shall stand
Between their loved homes and the war's desolation!
Blest with victory and peace, may the heav'n rescued land
Praise the Power that hath made and preserved us a nation.
Then conquer we must, when our cause it is just,
And this be our motto: "In God is our trust."
And the star-spangled banner in triumph shall wave
O'er the land of the free and the home of the brave!

Yankee Doodle

The first known American printing of the popular song "Yankee Doodle" was as part of Benjamin Carr's *Federal Overture* in Baltimore in 1795. The origin of the song is unknown, but it is believed to have been composed in the 1750's and used to deride the colonials. It became instead a patriotic American air. Some of the verses are:

Father and I went down to camp	*Then I saw a swamping gun*	*Then they'd fife away like fun*
Along with Captain Gooding,	*As large as logs of maple*	*And play on cornstalk fiddles,*
And there we saw the men and boys	*Upon a very little cart,*	*And some had ribbons red as blood*
As thick as hasty pudding.	*A load for Father's cattle.*	*All bound around their middles.*
Yankee Doodle keep it up,	*Every time they shot it off*	*I can't tell you all I saw—*
Yankee Doodle Dandy,	*It took a horn of powder*	*They kept up such a smother.*
Mind the music and the step,	*And made a noise like father's gun*	*I took my hat off, made a bow,*
And with the girls be handy.	*Only a nation louder.*	*And scampered home to mother.*
There was Captain Washington	*There I saw a wooden keg*	
Upon a slapping stallion	*With heads made out of leather;*	
A-giving orders to his men—	*They knocked upon it with some sticks*	
There must have been a million.	*To call the folks together.*	

Origin of the Names of U. S. States

Source: State officials, and a study by John P. Harrington, Bureau of American Ethnology, Smithsonian Institute, Washington, D. C.

Alabama—Indian for tribal town, later tribe, of the Creek confederacy.

Alaska—Russian version of Aleutian (Eskimo) word for Alaska Peninsula.

Arizona—Spanish version of Pima Indian word for "little spring place," identified as in Arizona Creek.

Arkansas—French variant of Kansas, a Sioux Indian name for south wind people.

California—Bestowed by the Spanish Conquistadores, being the name of an imaginary island, near the earthly paradise, in "Las Serges de Esplandian," a romance of chivalry written by Montalvo, 1510. Baja California (Lower California, Mexico) was first penetrated 1533. The state later was Alta (Upper) California.

Colorado—Spanish, red, first applied to Colorado River.

Connecticut—From Mohican and other Algonquian words meaning "long river place."

Delaware—Lord De La Warre, first governor of Virginia Company, entered bay, 1610. Name first applied to river, then to Indian tribe and state.

District of Columbia—For Columbus, 1791.

Florida—Named by Ponce de Leon on Pascua Florida, feast of flowers, Easter Sunday, 1513.

Georgia—For King George II of England by James Ogle-thorpe, colonial administrator, 1733.

Hawaii—Possibly derived from native word for homeland.

Idaho—Shoshone derivation. State calls it "light on the mountains."

Illinois—French for Illini or land of Illini, Algonquian word meaning men or warriors.

Indiana—Named because Indians lived there.

Iowa—A Sioux word, meaning "one who puts to sleep."

Kansas—Sioux word for south wind people.

Kentucky—Wyandot word for plain, originally applied to Kentucky Plains, Clark County.

Louisiana—Part of territory called Louisiana by LaSalle for French King Louis XIV.

Maine—From Maine, ancient French province.

Maryland—For Queen Henrietta Maria, wife of Charles I of England.

Massachusetts—From Indian tribe named after "large hill place" identified by Capt. John Smith as near Milton, Mass.

Michigan—Alouet, 1672, makes it designate a clearing, but later writers mentioned Chippewa micigama, large water.

Minnesota—From Dakota Sioux word meaning "clouded or milky" water of Minnesota River.

Mississippi—Probably Chippewa; mici, large; zibi, river. Tonti wrote it Michi Sepe.

Missouri—Algonquian word, "canoe haver", applied to tribe on river which received their name.

Montana—Latin for mountainous.

Nebraska—From Omaha Indian name for Platte River, both meaning flat.

Nevada—Spanish, meaning snow-clad.

New Hampshire—Named 1629 by Capt. John Mason of Plymouth Council for county in England.

New Jersey—The Duke of York, 1664, gave a patent to John Berkeley and Sir Geo. Carteret to be called Nova Cae saria, or New Jersey.

New Mexico—Spaniards in Mexico applied term to land north and west of Rio Grande.

New York—For Duke of York and Albany who received patent to New Netherland from his brother Charles II and sent an expedition to capture it, 1664.

North Carolina—In 1619 Charles I gave a large patent to Sir Robt. Heath to be called Province of Carolana, from Carolus, Latin name for Charles. A new patent was granted by Charles II to Earl of Clarendon and others. Divided into North and South Carolina, 1710.

North Dakota—Dakota is Sioux for friend or ally.

Ohio—Indian, great, applied to river.

Oklahoma—Choctaw coined word meaning red man, proposed by Rev. Allen Wright, Choctaw-speaking Indian.

Oregon—In 1765 Maj. Robert Rogers proposed to George III to seek Northwest Passage by travel from Great Lakes to "a river called by the Indians Ouragon." In 1772 he spelled it Ourigan. In 1778 his associate, Jonathan Carver, wrote of "River Oregon or River of the West." In 1817 William Cullen Bryant wrote "where rolls the Oregon." In 1822 Rep. John Floyd (Va.) proposed creation of Oregon Terr. Wauregan is Algonquian for beautiful water. Presumably Rogers and Carver meant the Columbia.

Pennsylvania—William Penn, the Quaker, who was made full proprietor by King Charles II in 1681, suggested Sylvania, or woodland, for his tract. The king's government owed Penn's father, Admiral William Penn, £ 16,000, and the land being granted in part settlement, the king added the Penn to Sylvania, against the desires of the modest proprietor, in honor of the admiral.

Puerto Rico—Spanish for Rich Port.

Rhode Island—Red Island, first named by Adrian Block because of its red clay. Roger Williams suggested Island of Rhodes. His settlement, Providence Plantations, was also used.

South Carolina—See North Carolina.

South Dakota—See North Dakota.

Tennessee—From 1784 to 1788 this was the State of Franklin, or Frankland. Tanasi was the name of Cherokee villages on the Little Tennessee river.

Texas—Variant of word used by Caddo and other Indians meaning friends or allies, and applied to them by the Spanish in eastern Texas. Also written texias, tejas, teysas.

Utah—From a Navajo word meaning upper, or higher up, as applied to a Shoshone tribe called Utes. Spanish form is Yutta, English Uta or Utah. Proposed name Deseret, "land of honeybees," from Book of Mormon, was rejected by Congress.

Vermont—From French words Vert, green, and Mont, mountain. The Green Mountains were said to have been named by Samuel de Champlain. The Green Mountain Boys were Gen. Stark's men in the Revolution. When the state was formed, 1777, Dr. Thos. Young suggested combining vert and mont into Vermont.

Virginia—Named by Sir Walter Raleigh, who fitted out the expedition of 1584, in honor of Queen Elizabeth, the Virgin Queen of England.

Washington—Named after George Washington. When the bill creating the Territory of Columbia was introduced in the 32nd Congress, the name was changed to Washington because of the existence of the District of Columbia.

West Virginia—So named when western counties of Virginia rejected secession, 1863.

Wisconsin—An Indian name, spelled Outsconsin and Misconsing by early chroniclers. Means "grassy place" in Chippewa. Congress made it Wisconsin.

Wyoming—The word was taken from Wyoming Valley, Pa., which was the site of an Indian massacre and became widely known by Campbell's poem, Gertrude of Wyoming. In Algonquin it means "large prairie place."

Accession of Territory by The United States

Source: Statistical Abstract of the United States

Division	Yr.	Sq. mi.[1]	Division	Yr.	Sq. mi.[1]	Division	Yr.	Sq. mi[1]
Total (1960)		3,628,066	Texas	1845	390,143	American Samoa	1900	76
			Oregon	1846	285,580	Canal Zone[4]	1904	553
United States.		3,615,122	Mexican cession.	1848	529,017	Corn Islands[5]	1914	4
Territory of 1790[2]. . . .		888,685	Gadsden Purchase . . .	1853	29,640	Virgin Islands	1917	133
Louisiana Purchase . .	1803	827,192	Alaska	1867	586,412	Trust Territory of		
By treaty with			Hawaii	1898	6,450	the Pacific Isl.	1947	8,489
Spain			The Philippines[3].	1898	115,600	All other[6]		42
Florida	1819	58,560	Puerto Rico.	1899	3,435			
Other areas	1819	13,443	Guam	1899	212			

(1.)Gross area (land and water). (2.)Includes drainage basin of Red River on the North, south of 49th parallel, sometimes considered a part of the Louisiana Purchase. (3.)Area not included in totals; became Republic of the Philippines July 4, 1946. (4.)Under U.S. jurisdiction by treaty with Panama. (5.)Leased from Nicaragua for 99 years but returned April 25, 1971. (6.)See index for Outlying Areas; U.S.

Public Lands of the United States

Source: Bureau of Land Management, U. S. Dept. of the Interior

Acquisition of the Public Domain 1781-1867

Acquisition	Area*(In Acres)	Land	Water	Total	Cost[1]
State Cessions (1781-1802)		233,415,680	3,409,920	236,825,600	[2]$6,200,000
Louisiana Purchase (1803)[3]		523,446,400	6,465,280	529,911,680	23,213,568
Red River Basin[4]		29,066,880	535,040	29,601,920	
Cession from Spain (1819)		43,342,720	2,801,920	46,144,640	6,674,057
Oregon Compromise (1846)		180,644,480	2,741,760	183,386,240	
Mexican Cession (1848)		334,479,360	4,201,600	338,680,960	16,295,149
Purchase from Texas (1850)		78,842,880	83,840	78,926,720	15,496,448
Gadsden Purchase (1853)		18,961,920	26,880	18,988,800	10,000,000
Alaska Purchase (1867)		365,481,600	9,814,400	375,296,000	7,200,000
Total		**1,807,681,920**	**30,080,640**	**1,837,762,560**	**$85,079,222**

*All areas except Alaska were computed in 1912, and have not been adjusted for the recomputation of the area of the United States which was made for the 1950 Decennial Census.

(1.)Cost data for all except "State Cessions" obtained from U. S. Geological survey.
(2.)Paid by Federal Government for Georgia Cession, 1802 (56,689,920 acres).
(3.)Excludes areas eliminated by Treaty of 1819 with Spain.
(4.)Basin of the Red River of the North, south of the 49th parallel.

Disposition of Public Lands 1781 to 1970 (In acres)

Disposition by methods not elsewhere classified[1]		Granted to States for:	
Granted or sold to homesteaders	303,500,000	Support of common schools	77,600,000
Granted to railroad corporations	287,500,000	Reclamation of swampland	64,900,000
Granted to veterans as military bounties	94,300,000	Construction of railroads	37,100,000
Confirmed as private land claims[2]	61,000,000	Support of misc. institutions[6]	21,700,000
Sold under timber and stone law[3]	34,000,000	Purposes not elsewhere classified[7]	117,500,000
Granted or sold under timber culture law[4]	13,900,000	Canals and rivers	6,100,000
Sold under desert land law[5]	10,900,000	Construction of wagon roads	3,400,000
	10,700,000	**Total granted to States**	**328,300,000**
		Grand Total	**1,144,100,000**

(1.)Chiefly public, private, and preemption sales, but includes mineral entries, script locations, sales of townsites and townlots.
(2.)The Government has confirmed title to lands claimed under valid grants made by foreign governments prior to the acquisition of the public domain by the United States.
(3.)The law provided for the sale of lands valuable for timber or stone and unfit for cultivation.
(4.)The law provided for the granting of public lands to settlers on condition that they plant and cultivate trees on the lands granted.
(5.)The law provided for the sale of arid agricultural public lands to settlers who irrigate them and bring them under cultivation.
(6.)Universities, hospitals, asylums, etc.
(7.)For construction of various public improvements (individual items not specified in the granting act) reclamation of desert lands, construction of water reservoirs, etc.

Land Owned by the Federal Government (In acres)

Agency (June 30, 1971)	Public Domain	Acquired	Total
Bureau of Land Management	471,680,093.0	2,364,892.1	474,044,985.1
U.S. Forest Service	160,176,950.0	26,637,350.4	186,814,300.4
U.S. Fish and Wildlife Service	24,401,982.7	3,505,275.9	27,907,258.6
U.S. Park Service	19,587,492.2	4,883,982.8	24,471,475.0
U.S. Army	7,051,453.0	3,998,858.0	11,050,311.0
Bureau of Reclamation	5,829,133.1	1,749,102.4	7,578,235.5
U.S. Air Force	6,941,946.0	1,383,762.0	8,325,708.0
Corps of Engineers	787,232.7	6,599,510.2	7,386,742.9
Bureau of Indian Affairs	4,204,809.2	781,155.9	4,985,965.1
U.S. Navy	2,155,750.0	1,431,366.7	3,587,116.7
Atomic Energy Commission	1,446,299.6	678,684.5	2,124,984.1
Other Agencies	530,489.5	1,395,991.4	1,926,480.9
Totals	**704,793,631.0**	**55,409,932.3**	**760,203,563.3**

The Homestead Act; Sale of Public Land

The Homestead Act became effective Jan. 1, 1863, the same day that President Lincoln issued his Emancipation Proclamation. Its purpose was to open the vacant lands of America's vast public domain to agricultural settlement.

To qualify for a homestead a person had to be a citizen of the United States or express his intention of becoming one, be over 21 years of age or the head of a household, and own less than 160 acres of land.

To acquire title to 160 acres of public land the homesteader had to establish residence on the land and bring a portion under cultivation. After 6 months residence he could purchase the land for $1.25 per acre, or after 5 years residence he could acquire title for a $15 filing fee.

Originally passed by Congress on May 20, 1862, the Homestead Act was later amended to increase acreage limitations under certain conditions. Under the Homestead Act and its several amendments, more than a million families received title to over 248,000,000 acres of public land across the plains, prairies and mountains of western United States. But as subsequent waves of settlers moved onto vacant land the supply of arable land dwindled; by the late 1930s some homesteaders had settled on submarginal lands that would not support a farm family. In 1937 Congress passed the Bankhead-Jones Act authorizing the Government to repurchase bankrupt farms to relieve the plight of such families. Under this program about 2,000,000 acres of homestead land was returned to Federal ownership.

By the time of its 100th anniversary the Homestead Act had accomplished its purpose—the transformation of a wilderness into productive farmland. Now outdated, the Homestead Act will always be a part of the American heritage.

Public Land Sale

From time to time the Bureau of Land Management sells public land to private individuals. Public land is always sold for its fair market value as determined by public auction. The Federal Govt. offers no free land. Persons wishing to purchase public land should contact the Bureau of Land Management, Wash., D. C. 20240, or one of the Bureau's Land Offices in the public land states.

The Bureau stresses that it is the only authoritative source of information on the sale of land under its jurisdiction.

American Territorial Expansion

When the War of the Revolution ended the 13 original states—Massachusetts, Rhode Island, Connecticut, New Hampshire, New York, New Jersey, Pennsylvania, Delaware, Maryland, Virginia, North Carolina. South Carolina and Georgia had a land and water area of 892,135 sq. mi., comprising New England, all land from Canada to Florida and from the Atlantic to the Mississippi. At the request of Congress (acting under the Articles of Confederation) the states gave their unorganized land to the Congress, which passed the Northwest Ordinance of 1787, and formed Northwest Terr., north of the Ohio river and another territory south of it.

France originally occupied and fortified a large area from Canada to the Gulf via the Great Lakes and the Mississippi, which it lost to Britain by the Treaty of 1763 after the French and Indian War. Britain yielded this territory to the U. S. by the Treaty of Paris, 1783. After fighting Indians and British in border campaigns, the U. S. took possession July 11, 1796.

LOUISIANA PURCHASE

The first accession to the United States was the Louisiana Purchase, 827,192 sq. mi. west of the Mississippi. This was held by Spain until ceded to France in 1800, with the proviso that it go back to Spain if France gave it up. In order to free navigation on the Mississippi President Jefferson sent James Monroe and Robert R. Livingston to Paris to buy the isle of Orleans (New Orleans) and West Florida, for which Congress voted $2,000,000. Napoleon, defeated in San Domingo, offered the vast Louisiana area. The treaty was signed Apr. 30, 1803; Congress ratified it in October; the U. S. took possession at New Orleans Dec. 20, 1803. The U. S. paid $11,250,000 (60,000,000 francs), assumed claims of Americans against France, $3,750,000. Total cost $15,000,000.

Nobody knew the exact boundaries. After Mar. 10, 1804, the U. S. divided the Purchase into the Territory of Orleans, later the state of Louisiana, and the Territory of Louisiana. Included in the Purchase were the present state of Louisiana west to the Sabine River plus the port of New Orleans; the present areas of Arkansas, Missouri, Nebraska, Iowa and South Dakota; North Dakota except the northeast corner, held by Britain until the treaty of 1819; Minnesota west of the Mississippi; Kansas except a small part in the southwest; Oklahoma except the Panhandle no-man's-land; parts of Colorado and Montana. Sometimes Wyoming was claimed and the territory was thought to have run as far as the Pacific coast, but U. S., Britain, Spain and Russia had conflicting claims and settled them by treaty.

SPAIN GIVES UP FLORIDA

Spain, which still claimed East Florida and West Florida as far as Mobile, Ala., ceded all rights to the U. S. by treaty Feb. 22, 1819, ratified by Spain 1821. The U. S. gave up claims to an undetermined bound in Texas and on the Rio Grande and assumed $5,000,000 worth of Spanish obligations to Americans; total cost, $6,674,057.

Spain, Britain, France and the Americans had fought in this territory. Spain's title was recognized in 1783. In 1810 the U. S. took possession of large areas along the Gulf, except Mobile, and West Florida declared itself independent and asked annexation. In 1814 Gen. Andrew Jackson took Pensacola from the British.

OREGON TERRITORY ORGANIZED

Organization of the Territory of Oregon in 1848 was not called an accession because the U. S. claimed title by (1) discovery and occupation; (2) a free interpretation of the Louisiana Purchase; (3) treaties with Spain, 1819, Great Britain, 1818, Russia, 1824. The northern boundary was settled by treaty with Britain in 1846.

The Territory extended from the crest of the Rockies to the Pacific coast, north of 42° N. Lat. and included the present states of Oregon, Washington, Idaho and parts of Montana and Wyoming.

ADMISSION OF TEXAS AS STATE

The third accession came when the Republic of Texas was admitted to the Union as a state, Dec. 29, 1845. This was part of a Mexican state settled by many U. S. citizens. Texas declared its independence in 1836, was recognized by the U. S. and applied for admission into the Union. It was bounded by the Rio Grande on the Southwest, and the Sabine, Red and Arkansas Rivers on the North and Northeast, and roughly comprised parts of present New Mexico, Colorado, Wyoming and a bit of Kansas as well as Texas of

today, 390,144 sq. mi. Today the state has 267,339 sq. mi. Texas had declared for slavery and its admission was opposed by anti-slavery men. Since a two-thirds majority of the Senate could not be attained it was admitted, Mar. 1, 1845, by a joint resolution of Congress, requiring only a majority of both houses. Texas ratified the agreement July 4, 1845.

Texas formally became a state Dec. 29, 1845. Congress gave Texas the right to divide itself into as many as five states "of convenient size" and sufficient population, at its own discretion. The Lone Star flag of the republic has been retained as the state flag of Texas. It can be flown by the side of the Stars and Stripes, but not above it.

TERRITORY FROM MEXICO

At the end of the Mexican War the U. S. and Mexico signed the treaty of Guadalupe-Hidalgo, Feb. 2, 1848, which gave the fourth large accession of territory. This included the present states of Arizona, New Mexico, California, Nevada, Utah, and Colorado west of the Rockies. The Gila river was a boundary line. The U. S. paid $15,000,000 to Mexico and assumed claims of U. S. citizens against Mexico. The claim of Texas to part of New Mexico territory was settled in 1850 by paying Texas $10,000,000. Interest increased both totals.

Inexact boundaries and agitation by railroad men for the Gila river valley to build the Southern Pacific led President Franklin Pierce to send James Gadsden as ambassador to Mexico to negotiate concessions of land. Gadsden got the Mexican dictator, Santa Anna, to yield 29,640 sq. mi. for $10,000,000 in 1853. This made the Rio Grande the boundary line on the South and the Colorado river on the West.

ALASKA FROM RUSSIA

Russia, which operated Alaska as a fur and fishing station at a loss, first offered to sell it during President Pierce's administration, about 1856. President Buchanan wanted to pay $5,000,000 for it in 1860. Secy. Seward, an expansionist, signed a treaty with Baron Stoecki, Russian minister, Mar. 30, 1867, to buy it for $7,200,000. Senate ratified it Apr. 9, 1867, and it was transferred to U. S. at Sitka Oct. 18, 1867, before it had been paid for. The House, by 113 to 43, appropriated the money July 14, 1868. The legend that the U. S. bought Alaska to repay Russia for checkmating Britain during the Civil War is without foundation.

ACQUISITION OF HAWAII

A British naval officer seized the kingdom of Hawaii, 1843, but was disavowed. Britain and France recognized its independent status 1843. France seized it, 1849, but restored it at once. In 1851 the King offered it to the U. S.; Danl. Webster, Secy. of State, refused it. Annexation was urged, 1854, but rejected. A reciprocity treaty with U. S., 1875, increased trade; it was renewed 1884 to include lease of Pearl Harbor as naval base. Jas. G. Blaine, Secy. of State, in 1881 had practically extended Monroe Doctrine to Hawaii. After revolution, 1893 (with American connivance) the republic, 1894, asked annexation. U. S. voted this July 7, 1898, effective Aug. 12, 1898, and assumed a national debt of $4,000,000.

ISLANDS FROM SPAIN

After the 1898 war with Spain, Spain by treaty of Dec. 10, 1898, ceded Puerto Rico, Guam and the Philippine islands for $20,000,000. An additional $100,000 was paid later for islands of the Philippines not in the original treaty. Puerto Rico is a free commonwealth electing its own executives. Guam is administered by the Dept. of the Interior. The Philippine Islands received their independence July 4, 1946, as the Republic of the Philippines.

PACIFIC AND CARIBBEAN

American Samoa in the Pacific, Port of Pago Pago was ceded 1872. Tutuila and other islands ceded to U. S. by convention with Great Britain and Germany, Dec. 2, 1899. Swain's Isl. annexed 1925, Dept. of the Interior.

Wake annexed Jan. 17, 1899, from Spain.

Midway Islands (Sand Isl., Eastern Isl.) occupied Sept. 30, 1867. Under Navy Dept.

Baker Island, discovered 1832, U. S. since 1857. Also Jarvis and Howland. Under Interior Dept.

Virgin Islands in the Caribbean, the former Danish West Indies, comprising St. Croix, St. Thomas, St. John and islets, bought from Denmark Jan. 25, 1917, for $25,000,000.

Panama Canal Zone, acquired from the Republic of Panama.

States: Settled, Capitals, Entry into Union, Area, Rank

The Original Thirteen States—The 13 colonies that seceded from Great Britain and fought the War of Independence (American Revolution) became the 13 original states. They were Massachusetts, Rhode Island, Connecticut, New Hampshire, New York, New Jersey, Pennsylvania, Delaware, Maryland, Virginia, North Carolina, South Carolina and Georgia.

State	Set-tled*	Capital	Entered Union Date	Order**	Extent in Miles Long	Wide	Area in square miles Land	Inland water	Total	Rank In Area
Ala	1702	Montgomery	1819, Dec.	14	330	200	50,708	901	51,609	29
Alaska	1784	Juneau	1959, Jan.	3	(A) 900	800	566,432	19,980	586,412	1
Ariz.	1848	Phoenix	1912, Feb.	14	390	335	113,417	492	113,909	6
Ark.	1785	Little Rock	1836, June	15	275	240	51,945	1,159	53,104	27
Cal.	1769	Sacramento	1850, Sept.	9	770	375	156,361	2,332	158,693	3
Colo.	1858	Denver	1876, Aug.	1	390	270	103,766	481	104,247	8
Conn.	1635	Hartford	1788, Jan.	9	90	75	4,862	139	5,009	48
Del.	1638	Dover	1787, Dec.	7	110	35	1,982	75	2,057	49
Dist. Col.		Washington			...	...	61	6	67	51
Fla.	1565	Tallahassee	1845, Mar.	3	460	400	54,090	4,470	58,560	22
Ga.	1733	Atlanta	1788, Jan.	2	315	250	58,073	803	58,876	21
Hawaii		Honolulu	1959, Aug.	21	...	...	6,425	25	6,450	47
Idaho	1842	Boise	1890, July	3	490	305	82,677	880	83,557	13
Ill	1720	Springfield	1818, Dec.	3	380	205	55,748	652	56,400	24
Ind.	1733	Indianapolis	1816, Dec.	11	265	160	36,097	102	36,291	38
Iowa	1788	Des Moines	1846, Dec.	28	300	210	55,941	349	56,290	25
Kan.	1727	Topeka	1861, Jan.	29	400	200	81,787	477	82,264	14
Ky.	1774	Frankfort	1792, June	1	350	175	39,650	745	40,395	37
La.	1699	Baton Rouge	1812, Apr.	30	280	275	44.930	3,593	48,523	31
Me.	1624	Augusta	1820, Mar.	15	235	205	30,920	2,295	33,215	39
Md.	1634	Annapolis	1788, Apr.	28	200	120	9,891	686	10,577	42
Mass.	1620	Boston	1788, Feb.	6	190	110	7,826	431	8,257	45
Mich.	1668	Lansing	1837, Jan.	26	400	310	56,817	1,399	58,216	23
Minn.	1805	St. Paul	1858, May	11	400	350	79,289	4,779	84,068	12
Miss.	1699	Jackson	1817, Dec.	10	340	180	47,296	420	47,716	32
Mo.	1735	Jefferson City	1821, Aug.	10	300	280	68,995	691	69,686	19
Mont.	1809	Helena	1889, Nov.	8	580	315	145,587	1,551	147,138	4
Nebr.	1847	Lincoln	1867, Mar.	1	415	205	76,483	744	77,227	15
Nev.	1850	Carson City	1864, Oct.	31	485	315	109,889	651	110,540	7
N. H.	1623	Concord	1788, June	21	185	90	9,027	277	9,304	44
N. J.	1664	Trenton	1787, Dec.	18	160	70	7,521	315	7,836	46
N. M.	1605	Santa Fe	1912, Jan.	6	390	350	121,412	254	121,666	5
N. Y.	1614	Albany	1788, July	26	320	310	47,831	1,745	49,576	30
N. C.	1650	Raleigh	1789, Nov.	21	520	200	48,798	3,788	52,586	28
N. D.	1766	Bismarck	1889, Nov.	2	360	210	69,273	1,392	70,665	17
Ohio	1788	Columbus	1803, Mar.	1	230	205	40,975	247	41,222	35
Okla.	1889	Oklahoma City	1907, Nov.	16	585	210	68,782	1,137	69,919	18
Ore.	1811	Salem	1859, Feb.	14	375	290	96,184	797	96,981	10
Pa.	1682	Harrisburg	1787, Dec.	12	300	180	44,966	367	45,333	33
R. I.	1636	Providence	1790, May	29	50	35	1,049	165	1,214	50
S. C.	1670	Columbia	1788, May	23	285	215	30,225	830	31,055	40
S. D.	1856	Pierre	1889, Nov.	2	380	245	75,955	1,092	77,047	16
Tenn.	1757	Nashville	1796, June	1	430	120	41,328	916	42,244	34
Texas	1691	Austin	1845, Dec.	29	760	620	262,134	5,204	267,338(B)	2
Utah	1847	Salt Lake City	1896, Jan.	4	345	275	82,906	2,820	84,916	11
Vt.	1724	Montpelier	1791, Mar.	4	155	90	9,267	342	9,609	43
Va.	1607	Richmond	1788, June	26	425	205	39,780	1,037	40,817	36
Wash.	1811	Olympia	1889, Nov.	11	340	230	66,570	1,622	68,192	20
W. Va.	1727	Charleston	1863, June	20	225	200	24,070	111	24,181	41
Wis.	1766	Madison	1848, May	29	300	290	54,464	1,690	56,154	26
Wyo.	1834	Cheyenne	1890, July	10	365	275	97,203	711	97,914	9

*First permanent settlement. **The order for the original thirteen states is the order in which they ratified the constitution. (A.) Aleutian Islands and Alexander Archipelago are not considered in these lengths. (B.) Total area of Texas reduced 1 sq. mile by Chamizal boundary solution between U.S. and Mexico, 1963.

The Continental Divide

Source: U. S. Geological Survey, Department of the Interior

Continental Divide: watershed, created by mountain ranges or table-lands of the Rocky Mountains, from which the drainage is easterly or westerly; the easterly flowing waters reaching the Atlantic Ocean chiefly through the Gulf of Mexico, and the westerly flowing waters reaching the Pacific Ocean through the Columbia River, or through the Colorado River, which flows into the Gulf of California.

The location and route of the Continental Divide across the United States may briefly be described as follows:

Beginning at point of crossing the United States-Mexican boundary, near long. 108°45′ W., the Divide, in a northerly direction, crosses New Mexico along the western edge of the Rio Grande drainage basin, entering Colorado near long. 106°41′.

Thence by a very irregular route northerly across Colorado along the western summits of the Rio Grande and of the Arkansas, the South Platte, and the North Platte River basins, and across Rocky Mountain National Park, entering Wyoming near long. 106°52′.

Then in a northwesterly direction, forming the western rims of the North Platte, Big Horn, and Yellowstone River basins, crossing the southwestern portion of Yellowstone National Park.

Thence in a westerly and then a northerly direction forming the common boundary of Idaho and Montana, to a point on said boundary near long. 114°00′ W.

Thence northeasterly and northwesterly through Montana and the Glacier National Park, entering Canada near long. 114°04′ W.

Chronological List of Territories

Name of Territory	Date of Organic Act	Organic Act Effective	Admission as State	Yrs. Terr.
Northwest Territory (a)	July 13, 1787	No fixed date		
Territory south of Ohio River	May 26, 1790	No fixed date	June 1, 1796b	6
Mississippi	Apr. 7, 1798	When President acted	Dec. 10, 1817	19
Indiana	May 7, 1800	July 4, 1800	Dec. 11, 1816	16
Territory northwest of Ohio River	May 7, 1800	July 4, 1800	Mar. 1, 1803c	2
Orleans	Mar. 26, 1804	Oct. 1, 1804	Apr. 8, 1812d	7
Michigan	Jan. 11, 1805	June 30, 1805	Jan. 26, 1837	31
Louisiana-Missouri(E)	Mar. 3, 1805	July 4, 1805	Aug. 10, 1821	16
Illinois	Feb. 3, 1809	Mar. 1, 1809	Dec. 3, 1818	9
Alabama	Mar. 3, 1817	When Miss. became a State	Dec. 14, 1819	2
Arkansas	Mar. 2, 1819	July 4, 1819	June 15, 1836	17
Florida	Mar. 30, 1822	No fixed date	Mar. 3, 1845	23
Indian (organized 1834)*				
Wisconsin	Apr. 20, 1836	July 3, 1836	May 29, 1848	12
Iowa	June 12, 1838	July 3, 1838	Dec. 28, 1846	7
Oregon	Aug. 14, 1848	Date of act	Feb. 14, 1859	10
Minnesota	Mar. 3, 1849	Date of act	May 11, 1858	9
New Mexico	Sept. 9, 1850	On President's Proclamation	Jan. 6, 1912	61
Utah	Sept. 9, 1850	Date of act	Jan. 4, 1896	44
Washington	Mar. 2, 1853	Date of act	Nov. 11, 1889	36
Nebraska	May 30, 1854	Date of act	Feb. 9, 1867	12
Kansas	May 30, 1854	Date of act	Jan. 29, 1861	6
Colorado	Feb. 28, 1861	Date of act	Aug. 1, 1876	15
Nevada	Mar. 2, 1861	Date of act	Oct. 31, 1864	3
Dakota	Mar. 2, 1861	Date of act	Nov. 2, 1889	28
Arizona	Feb. 24, 1863	Date of act	Feb. 14, 1912	49
Idaho	Mar. 3, 1863	Date of act	July 3, 1890	27
Montana	May 26, 1864	Date of act	Nov. 8, 1889	25
Wyoming	July 25, 1868	When officers were qualified	July 10, 1890	22
Oklahoma	May 2, 1890	Date of act	Nov. 16, 1907	17
Hawaii	Apr. 30, 1900	June 14, 1900	Aug. 21, 1959	59
Alaska	Aug. 24, 1912	Nov. 5, 1912	Jan. 3, 1959	47

(A) Included present Ohio, Indiana, Illinois, Michigan, Wisconsin, Eastern Minnesota; (B) as the State of Tennessee; (C) as the State of Ohio; (D) as the State of Louisana; (E) organic act for Missouri Territory of June 4, 1812, became effective Dec. 7, 1812.

*Indian Territory was set aside in 1834 for the 5 civilized Indian tribes—Cherokee, Choctaw, Chickasaw, Creek and Seminole. In 1889 part of it was included in the Territory of Oklahoma. In 1906 Indian Territory and the Territory of Oklahoma were merged to form the state of Oklahoma.

Geographic Centers, United States and States

Source: U. S. Geological Survey, Department of the Interior

State	County	Locality

United States, including Alaska and Hawaii—South Dakota; Butte County, 17 miles west of Castle Rock, 14 miles east of junction of borders of South Dakota, Montana and Wyoming. Approx. Lat. 44°58'N, Long. 103°46'W.

Continental U. S. (49 States)—Near Castle Rock, Butte Co., South Dakota, Lat. 44°59'N, Long, 103°38'W.

Conterminous U. S. (48 States)—Near Lebanon, Smith Co., Kansas Lat. 39°50'N, Long. 98°35'W.

North American Continent—The geographic center is in Pierce County, North Dakota, 6 miles west of Balta, Latitude 48°10', Longitude 100°10'W.

STATES

Alabama—Chilton, 12 miles SW of Clanton
Alaska—Lat. 63°50'N, Long. 152°00'W. Approx. 60 mi. NW of Mt. McKinley.
Arizona—Yavapai, 55 miles ESE of Prescott.
Arkansas—Pulaski, 12 miles NW of Little Rock.
California—Madera, 38 miles E of Madera.
Colorado—Park, 30 miles northwest of Pikes Peak.
Connecticut—Hartford, at East Berlin.
Delaware—Kent, 11 miles south of Dover.
District of Columbia—near Fourth and "L" Streets. NW
Florida—Hernando, 12 miles NNW of Brooksville.
Georgia—Twiggs, 18 miles SE of Macon.
Hawaii—Hawaii, 20° 15' N; 156° 20' W, off Maui Island.
Idaho—Custer, at Custer, SW of Challis.
Illinois—Logan, 28 miles NE of Springfield.
Indiana—Boone, 14 miles NNW of Indianapolis.
Iowa—Story, 5 miles NE of Ames.
Kansas—Barton, 15 miles NE of Great Bend.
Kentucky—Marion, 3 miles NNW of Lebanon.
Louisiana—Avoyelles, 3 miles SE of Marksville.
Maine—Piscataquis, 18 miles north of Dover.

Maryland—Prince Georges, 4½ miles NW of Davidsonville.
Massachusetts—Worcester, north part of City.
Michigan—Wexford, 5 miles NNW of Cadillac.
Minnesota—Crow Wing, 10 miles SW of Brainerd.
Mississippi—Leake, 9 miles WNW of Carthage.
Missouri—Miller, 20 miles SW of Jefferson City.
Montana—Fergus, 12 miles west of Lewistown.
Nebraska—Custer, 10 miles NW of Broken Bow.
Nevada—Lander, 26 miles SE of Austin.
New Hampshire—Belknap, 3 miles east of Ashland.
New Jersey—Mercer, 5 miles SE of Trenton.
New Mexico—Torrance, 12 miles SSW of Willard.
New York—Madison, 12 miles south of Oneida and 26 miles SW of Utica.
North Carolina—Chatham, 10 miles NW of Sanford.
North Dakota—Sheridan, 5 miles SW of McClusky.
Ohio—Delaware, 25 miles NNE of Columbus.
Oklahoma—Oklahoma, 8 miles N of Oklahoma City.
Oregon—Crook, 25 miles SSE of Prineville.
Pennsylvania—Centre, 2½ miles SW of Bellefonte.
Rhode Island—Kent, 1 mile SSW of Crompton.
South Carolina—Richland, 13 miles SE of Columbia.
South Dakota—Hughes, 8 miles NE of Pierre.
Tennessee—Rutherford, ½ mi. NE of Murfreesboro.
Texas-McCulloch, 15 miles NE of Brady.
Utah—Sanpete, 3 miles north of Manti.
Vermont—Washington, 3 miles east of Roxbury.
Virginia—Buckingham, 5 miles SW of Buckingham.
Washington—Chelan, 10 mi. WSW of Wenatchee.
West Virginia—Braxton, 4 miles east of Sutton.
Wisconsin—Wood, 9 miles SE of Marshfield.
Wyoming—Fremont, 58 miles ENE of Lander.

There is no generally accepted definition of geographic center, and no satisfactory method for determining it. The geographic center of an area may be defined as the center of gravity of the surface, or that point on which the surface of the area would balance if it were a plane of uniform thickness.

No marked or monumented point has been established by any government agency as the geographic center of either the 50 states, the conterminous United States, or the North American continent. A monument was erected in Lebanon, Kan., by a group of citizens.

Highest and Lowest Altitudes in the United States

Source: U. S. Geological Survey. (Minus sign means below sea level; elevations are in feet.)

	Highest Point			Lowest Point		
State	Name	County	Elev.	Name	County	Elev.
Alabama	Cheaha Mountain	Cleburne	2,407	Gulf of Mexico		Sea level
Alaska	Mount McKinley		20,320	Pacific Ocean		Sea level
Arizona	Humphreys Peak	Coconino	12,633	Colorado R	Yuma	70
Arkansas	Magazine Mountain	Logan	2,753	Ouachita R	Ashley Union	55
California	Mount Whitney	Inyo-Tulare	14,494	Death Valley	Inyo	—282
Canal Zone	Cerro Galera	Balboa District	1,205	Atlantic Ocean		Sea level
Colorado	Mount Elbert	Lake	14,433	Arkansas R	Prowers	3,350
Connecticut	Mount Frissell	Litchfield	2,380	L. I. Sound		Sea level
Delaware	On Ebright Road	New Castle	442	Atlantic Ocean		Sea level
Dist. of Col	Tenleytown	N. W. part	410	Potomac R		1
Florida	West boundary	Walton	345	Atlantic Ocean		Sea level
Georgia	Brasstown Bald	Towns-Union	4,784	Atlantic Ocean		Sea level
Guam	Mount Lamlam	Agat District	1,329	Pacific Ocean		Sea level
Hawaii	Mauna Kea	Hawaii	13,796	Pacific Ocean		Sea level
Idaho	Borah Peak	Custer	12,662	Snake R	Nez Perce	710
Illinois	Charles Mound	Jo Daviess	1,235	Mississippi R	Alexander	279
Indiana	Franklin Township	Wayne	1,257	Ohio R	Posey	320
Iowa	NE of Sibley	Osceola	1,670	Mississippi R	Lee	480
Kansas	Mount Sunflower	Wallace	4,039	Verdigris R	Montgomery	680
Kentucky	Black Mountain	Harlan	4,145	Mississippi R	Fulton	257
Louisiana	Driskill Mountain	Bienville	535	New Orleans	Orleans	—5
Maine	Mount Katahdin	Piscataquis	5,268	Atlantic Ocean		Sea level
Maryland	Backbone Mountain	Garrett	3,360	Atlantic Ocean		Sea level
Massachusetts	Mount Greylock	Berkshire	3,491	Atlantic Ocean		Sea level
Michigan	Mount Curwood	Baraga	1,980	Lake Erie		572
Minnesota	Eagle Mountain	Cook	2,301	Lake Superior		602
Mississippi	Woodall Mountain	Tishomingo	806	Gulf of Mexico		Sea level
Missouri	Taum Sauk Mt	Iron	1,772	St. Francis R	Dunklin	230
Montana	Granite Peak	Park	12,799	Kootenai R	Lincoln	1,800
Nebraska	Johnson Township	Kimball	5,426	S.E. cor. State	Richardson	840
Nevada	Boundary Peak	Esmeralda	13,140	Colorado R	Clark	470
New Hampshire	Mt. Washington	Coos	6,288	Atlantic Ocean		Sea level
New Jersey	High Point	Sussex	1,803	Atlantic Ocean		Sea level
New Mexico	Wheeler Peak	Taos	13,161	Red Bluff Res	Eddy	2,817
New York	Mount Marcy	Essex	5,344	Atlantic Ocean		Sea level
North Carolina	Mount Mitchell	Yancey	6,684	Atlantic Ocean		Sea level
North Dakota	White Butte	Slope	3,506	Red River	Pembina	750
Ohio	Campbell Hill	Logan	1,550	Ohio R	Hamilton	433
Oklahoma	Black Mesa	Cimarron	4,973	Little River	McCurtain	287
Oregon	Mount Hood	Clackamas-Hood, R.	11,235	Pacific Ocean		Sea level
Pennsylvania	Mt. Davis	Somerset	3,213	Delaware R	Delaware	Sea level
Puerto Rico	Cerro de Punta	Ponce	4,389	Atlantic Ocean		Sea level
Rhode Island	Jerimoth Hill	Providence	812	Atlantic Ocean		Sea level
Samoa	Lata Mtn	Tau Island	3,160	Pacific Ocean		Sea level
South Carolina	Sassafras Mountain	Pickens	3,560	Atlantic Ocean		Sea level
South Dakota	Harney Peak	Pennington	7,242	Big Stone Lake	Roberts	962
Tennessee	Clingmans Dome	Sevier	6,643	Mississippi R	Shelby	182
Texas	Guadalupe Peak	Culberson	8,751	Gulf of Mexico		Sea level
Utah	Kings Peak	Duchesne	13,528	Beaverdam Cr	Washington	2,000
Vermont	Mount Mansfield	Lamoille	4,393	Lake Champl'n	Franklin	95
Virginia	Mount Rogers	Grayson-Smyth	5,729	Atlantic Ocean		Sea level
Virgin Islands	Crown Mt	Is. St. Thomas	1,556	Atlantic Ocean		Sea level
Washington	Mount Rainier	Pierce	14,410	Pacific Ocean		Sea level
West Virginia	Spruce Knob	Pendleton	4,863	Potomac R	Jefferson	240
Wisconsin	Timms Hill	Price	1,952	Lake Michigan		581
Wyoming	Gannett Peak	Fremont	13,804	B. Fourche R	Crook	3,100

U. S. Coastline by States*

Source: NOAA, Department of Commerce

State	Coastline[1]	Shoreline[2]	State	Coastline[1]	Shoreline[2]
Atlantic Coast	2,069	28,673	Gulf coast	1,631	17,141
Connecticut	(—)	618	Alabama	53	607
Delaware	28	381	Florida	770	5,095
Florida	580	3,331	Louisiana	397	7,721
Georgia	100	2,344	Mississippi	44	359
Maine	228	3,478	Texas	367	3,359
Maryland	31	3,190	Pacific coast	7,623	40,298
Massachusetts	192	1,519	Alaska	5,580	31,383
New Hampshire	13	131	California	840	3,427
New Jersey	130	1,792	Hawaii	750	1,052
New York	127	1,850	Oregon	296	1,410
North Carolina	301	3,375	Washington	157	3,026
Pennsylvania	(—)	89	Arctic coast, Alaska	1,060	2,521
Rhode Island	40	384			
South Carolina	187	2,876	United States	12,383	88,633
Virginia	112	3,315			

*In statute miles (April 1, 1961). (—). Represents zero.

(1.)Figures are lengths of general outline of seacoast. Measurements were made with a unit measure of 30 minutes of latitude on charts as near the scale of 1:1,200,000 as possible. Coastline of sounds and bays is included to a point where they narrow to width of unit measure, and includes the distance across at such point.

(2.)Figures obtained in 1939-40 with a recording instrument on the largest-scale charts and maps then available. Shoreline of outer coast, offshore islands, sounds, bays, rivers, and creeks is included to the head of tidewater or to a point where tidal waters narrow to a width of 100 feet.

International Boundary Lines of the United States

The length of the northern boundary of the conterminous United States the U.S.-Canadian border, excluding Alaska—is 3,987 miles according to the U. S. Geological Survey, Dept. of the Interior. The length of the Alaskan-Canadian border is 1,538 miles. The length of the U.S.-Mexican border, from the Gulf of Mexico to the Pacific Ocean, is approximately 1,933 miles (1963 boundary agreement).

Superlative United States Statistics

Source: National Geographic Society, Washington, D.C.

Area for fifty states	Total	3,615,122 sq. mi.
	Land 3,536,855 sq. mi..... Water 78,267 sq. mi.	
Largest state	Alaska	586,412 sq. mi.
Smallest state	Rhode Island	1,214 sq. mi.
Largest county	San Bernardino County, California	20,119 sq. mi.
Smallest county	New York, N.Y.	23 sq. mi.
Largest city in area	Jacksonville, Florida	827 sq. mi.
Smallest cities in area	Belvedere, Calif.; Bonne Terre, Mo.;	
	Montgomery, W. Va.	each .4 sq. mi.
Smallest independent cities	Clifton Forge, Emporia, Falls Church	
(all in Virginia)	South Boston, Suffolk	Each 2 sq. mi.
Northernmost city	Barrow, Alaska	71° 17′N.
Northernmost point	Point Barrow, Alaska	71° 23′N.
Southernmost city	Hilo, Island of Hawaii	19° 43′N.
Southernmost town	Naalehu, Island of Hawaii	19° 03′ N.
Southernmost point	Ka Lae (South Cape), Island of Hawaii	18° 56′ N. (155° 41′ W.)
Easternmost city	Eastport, Maine	66° 59.5′ W.
Easternmost town	Lubec, Maine	66° 59′ W.
Easternmost point	West Quoddy Head, Maine	66° 57′ W.
Westernmost city	Lihue, Island of Kauai, Hawaii	159° 22′ W.
Westernmost town	Adak, Aleutians, Alaska	176° 45′ W.
Westernmost point	Cape Wrangell, Attu Island, Aleutians, Alaska	172° 27′ E.
Highest city	Leadville, Colo.	10,200 ft.
Lowest town	Calipatria, Calif.	−183 ft.
Highest point on Atlantic coast	Cadillac Mountain, Mount Desert Isl., Maine	1,530 ft.
Largest and oldest national park	Yellowstone National Park (1872), Wyoming	3,472 sq. mi.
	Montana, Idaho	
Largest national monument	Glacier Bay, Alaska	
Highest waterfall	Yosemite Falls, Cal., in three sections	2,425 ft.
	Upper Yosemite Fall	1,430 ft.
	Cascades in middle section	675 ft.
	Lower Yosemite Fall	320 ft.
Longest river	Mississippi-Missouri	3,710 mi.
Highest mountain	Mount McKinley, Alaska	20,320 ft.
Lowest point	Death Valley, California	−282 ft.
Deepest lake	Crater Lake, Oregon	1,932 ft.
Highest lake	Lake Waiau, Hawaii	13,020 ft.
Rainiest spot	Mt. Waialeale, Hawaii; Annual Aver. rainfall 460 inches	
Largest gorge	Grand Canyon, Colorado River, Arizona; 217 miles	
	long, 4 to 13 miles wide, 1 mile deep	
Deepest gorge	Hells Canyon, Snake River, Idaho;	7,900 ft.
Strongest surface wind	Mount Washington, New Hampshire recorded 1934	231 mph.
Biggest dam	Ft. Peck, Missouri River, Mont.; 125,628,000 cu. yds. material used	
Tallest building	Sears Tower, Chicago, Ill.	1,454 ft.
Largest building	Boeing 747 Manufacturing Plant, Everett, Wash. 205,600,000	
	cu. ft.; covers 47 acres.	
Tallest structure	TV tower, Blanchard, N. Dakota	2,063 ft.
Longest bridge span	Verrazano-Narrows, New York;	4,260 ft.
Highest bridge	Royal Gorge, Colorado;	1,053 ft. above water
Deepest well	Oil well, Beckham County, Oklahoma	30,050 ft.

THE FORTY-NINE STATES, INCLUDING ALASKA

Area for forty-nine states	Total	3,608,672 sq. mi.
	Land 3,530,430 sq. mi..... Water 78,242 sq. mi.	

THE FORTY-EIGHT STATES

Area for forty-eight states	Total	3,022,260 sq. mi.
	Land 2,963,998 sq. mi.... Water 58,262 sq. mi.	
Largest state	Texas	267,338 sq. mi.
Northernmost cities	Portal, North Dakota	48° 59′ N.
	Sumas, Washington	48° 59′ N.
Northernmost town	Angle Inlet, Minnesota	49° 22′ N.
Northernmost point	Northwest Angle, Minnesota	49° 23′ N.
Southernmost city	Key West, Florida	24° 33′ N.
Southernmost mainland town	Florida City, Florida	25° 27′ N.
Southernmost point	Key West, Florida	24° 33′ N.
Westernmost city	Gold Beach, Oregon	124° 25′ W.
Westernmost town	La Push, Washington	124° 38′ W.
Westernmost point	Cape Alava, Washington	124° 44′ W.
Highest mountain	Mount Whitney, California	14,494 ft.

Note to users: The distinction between cities and towns varies from state to state. In this table the U.S. Bureau of the Census usage was followed.

Statistical Information About the United States

In the *Statistical Abstract of the United States* the Bureau of the Census of the Social and Economic Statistics Administration, U.S. Dept. of Commerce annually publishes a summary of social, political and economic information. A book of more than 1,000 pages, it presents in 33 sections comprehensive data on population, housing, health, education, employment, income, prices, business, banking, science, defense, trade, government finance, foreign country comparison, and other subjects. Special features include comprehensive data for metropolitan areas and a summary of recent trends. The book is prepared under the direction of William Lerner, Data User Services Office, Bureau of the Census. Supplements to the *Statistical Abstract* are *Pocket Data Book, USA, 1973. County and City Data Book, 1972; Congressional District Data Book, 93rd Congress; Historical Statistics of the United States, Colonial Times to 1970.* Information concerning these and other publications may be obtained from the Supt. of Documents, Government Printing Office, Wash., D.C. 20402, or from the U.S. Bureau of the Census, Data User Services Office, Wash., D.C. 20233.

Geodetic Datum Point of North America

The geodetic datum point of the United States is the National Ocean Survey's triangulation station Meades Ranch in Osborne County, Kansas, at latitude 39° 13′26″. 686 N and longitude 98° 32′30″. 506 W. (Frequently this is referred to as the geodetic center of the U.S., which has no meaning.) This geodetic datum point is a fundamental point from which all latitude and longitude computations originate for North America and Central America.

National Wild and Scenic Rivers System

Eight national wild and scenic rivers and one State wild river area are included in the National Wild and Scenic Rivers System, established by 1968 Federal legislation (P.L. 90-542). Unspoiled sections of the Clearwater (middle fork), Idaho; Eleven Point, Mo.; Feather, Calif.; Rio Grande, N. Mex.; Rogue, Ore.; Saint Croix, Minn., and Wis.; Salmon (middle fork), Idaho; and Wolf, Wis., were immediately included as national wild, scenic or recreation rivers. The Allagash Wilderness Waterway in Maine was designated in 1970 as a State wild river area in the national system. The lower Saint Croix, Minn. and Wis., was added to the system in October 1972 by act of Congress.

Studies of 27 additional rivers by the Depts. of the Interior and Agriculture for possible later inclusion in the national system were authorized in the Act. Interior's study of the Upper Iowa, Iowa, was submitted to the President and the Congress in 1972. Reports on 11 other completed studies are in various phases of review prior to being submitted — Interior's reports on the Suwannee, Ga., and Fla.; segments of the Allegheny and the Clarion, Pa.; lower St. Croix, Minn. and Wis.; Missouri, Mont.; Little Miami, Ohio; Delaware, Pa. and NY; Obed, Tenn.; and the Dept. of Agriculture studies of the Pere Marquette, Mich.; Flathead, Mont.; Chattooga, N.C., S.C. and Ga.

National Trails System

The Appalachian Trail, running about 2,000 miles from Maine to Georgia, and the Pacific Crest Trail, extending 2,350 miles from Mexico to British Columbia, were established as National Scenic Trails by 1968 legislation (P.L. 90-543). Thirty-six recreation trails in 20 States and the District of Columbia were added to the national system by the end of April 1973; under provisions of the law, these are administered by Federal, State or local governments or private organizations.

Fourteen trails were authorized by the Trails Act for study as potential national scenic trails. Studies of the Potomac Heritage and Continental Divide Trails were completed in 1971 and the Oregon and North Country Trails studies are under way. Reconnaissance studies have been completed on the Mormon, Mormon Battalion, and the El Camino Real Trails.

Legacy of Parks

President Nixon's "Legacy of Parks" program, announced in February 1971, is being implemented in part through the Land and Water Conservation Fund program and through conveyance at up to 100% discounts of surplus Federal properties to State and local governments for public parklands.

Land and Water Conservation Fund — Since inception of the Land and Water Conservation Fund program in fiscal year 1965 through fiscal year 1973, almost $700,000,000 has been used to acquire approximately 1,100,000 acres for national parks, forests, wildlife refuges and other national recreation areas. During this period, over $900,000,000 in L&WCF monies was apportioned to State and local governments for recreation planning, acquisition and development projects. Total Federal investments in national, State and local park and recreation resources through the Fund rose to $1.6 billion by the end of fiscal 1973.

Federal Surplus Property for Parks — By the end of fiscal year 1973, 300 surplus Federal properties had been added to the Nation's recreation estate to serve State and local park and recreation needs. The total fair market value approached $40,000,000 and acreage approximated 50,000 acres. The properties are in all 50 States, the District of Columbia and the Commonwealth of Puerto Rico. The Secretary of the Interior is authorized to convey properties under Public Law 91-485, enacted October 22, 1970, amending the Federal Property and Administrative Service Act of 1949.

Golden Eagle and Golden Age Passport Program

The Passport program, recently restored under Public Law 92-347, provides for the sale of Golden Eagle Passports and the distribution of free Golden Age Passports to persons 62 years of age or older. The Golden Eagle Passport costs $10 and admits the bearer and all those accompanying him in a single noncommercial vehicle to designated Federal recreation areas.

The Golden Age Passport entitles the bearer the same entry privileges as well as a fifty percent reduction in Federal special recreation use fees in designated areas. Neither Passport covers fees charged by private concessionaires.

Both Passports are good for one calendar year. They may be obtained at first and second class Post Offices throughout the country and at Federal recreation areas where entrance fees are charged. Receipts from Passport sales and special recreation use fees go into Federal outdoor recreation programs.

Smokey the Bear's Successor Ready

The Smokey Bear symbol was created by an Advertising Task Force in 1944 for use in the National Cooperative Forest Fire Prevention Program. He first appeared as a "poster bear" in 1945. Smokey Bear came on the scene in 1950, when a young cub was rescued from a fire in the Lincoln National Forest in New Mexico. He was brought to the National Zoo in Wash., D.C., shortly after his rescue and now, at the age of 22, is in reasonably good health. Goldie, a female black bear from New Mexico, was brought to Washington in 1962 with the vain hope that she would provide progeny for Smokey. Little Smokey is a young male bear abandoned by his mother last year in the same forest in which Smokey was found. He was turned over to Forest Service officials who brought him to the National Zoo in November 1971, where he joined Smokey and Goldie. Little Smokey will serve as an understudy of Smokey Bear until the older bear dies or becomes permanently incapacitated. At that time, Little Smokey will assume the role of the living symbol of forest fire prevention.

National Parks, Other Areas Administered by Nat'l Park Service

National Parks

Acadia, Me. (1916) 41,651. Includes Mount Desert Island, half of Isle au Haut, Schoodic Point on mainland. Highest elevation on Eastern seaboard.

Arches, Utah (1929) 73,389. Contains giant red sandstone arches and other products of erosion.

Big Bend, Texas (1935) 708,118. On Rio Grande River.

Bryce Canyon, Utah (1923) 36,034. Spectacularly colorful and unusual display of erosion effects in Southwestern Utah.

Canyonlands, Utah (1964) 344,482. At junction of Colorado and Green Rivers, extensive evidence of prehistoric Indians.

Capitol Reef, Utah (1937) 241,866. A 70-mile uplift of sandstone cliffs dissected by high-walled gorges.

Carlsbad Caverns, N.M. (1923) 46,756. Largest known underground caverns, not yet fully explored.

Crater Lake, Ore. (1902) 160,290. Extraordinary blue lake in crater of extinct volcano encircled by lava walls 500 to 2,000 feet high.

Everglades, Fla. (1934) 1,400,533. Largest remaining subtropical wilderness in Continental U.S., abundant wildlife includes rare birds.

Glacier, Mont. (1910) 1,013,277. Superb Rocky Mountain scenery, numerous glaciers and glacial lakes. Part of Waterton-Glacier International Peace Park established by U.S. and Canada in 1932.

Grand Canyon, Ariz. (1908) 673,561. Most spectacular part of Colorado River. ⟨illegible⟩

Grand Teton, Wyo. (1929) 310,463. Most impressive part of the Teton Mountains, winter feeding ground of largest American elk herd.

Great Smoky Mountains, N.C.-Tenn. (1926) 516,860. Largest eastern mountain range, magnificent forests.

Guadalupe Mountains, Texas (1966) 79,972. Extensive and significant Permian limestone fossil reef; tremendous earth fault. INFORMATION OFFICE OPEN: **NO OTHER FACILITIES.**

Haleakala, Hawaii (1960) 27,283. 10,023 foot dormant volcano on Maui.

Hawaii Volcanoes, Hawaii (1916) 229,174. Contains Kilauea and Mauna Loa, active volcanoes on the island of Hawaii.

Hot Springs, Ark. (1832) 5,729. Government supervised bath houses use waters of 45 of the 47 natural hot springs.

Isle Royale, Mich. (1931) 539,498. Largest island in Lake Superior, noted for its wilderness area and wildlife.

Kings Canyon, Calif. (1890) 460,134. Mountain wilderness, dominated by Kings River canyons and High Sierra, contains giant sequoias.

Lassen Volcanic, Calif. (1907) 106,446. Contains Lassen Peak, most recently active volcano in continental U.S., and other volcanic phenomena.

Mammoth Cave, Ky. (1926) 51,311. 144 miles of surveyed underground passages, beautiful natural formations, river 360 feet below surface.

Mesa Verde, Colo. (1906) 52,036. Most notable and best preserved prehistoric cliff dwellings in the United States.

Mount McKinley, Alaska (1917) 1,939,493. Highest mountain in North America, large glaciers, and unusual wildlife.

Mount Rainier, Wash. (1899) 235,404. Greatest single-peak glacial system in the U.S. radiates from this dormant volcano.

North Cascades, Wash. (1968) 505,000. Spectacular mountainous region with many glaciers, lakes, and rugged peaks.

Olympic, Wash. (1900) 897,960. Mountain wilderness containing finest remnant of Pacific Northwest rain forest, active glaciers, Pacific shoreline, rare elk.

Petrified Forest, Ariz. (1906) 94,189. Extensive petrified wood and Indian artifacts. Contains part of Painted Desert.

Platt, Okla. (1906) 912. Numerous natural springs.

Redwood, Calif. (1968) 56,238. Forty miles of Pacific coastline, virgin groves of ancient redwoods.

Rocky Mountain, Colo. (1915) 261,973. Beautiful scenery on the continental divide includes 107 named peaks over 11,000 feet.

Sequoia, Calif. (1890) 386,822. Groves of giant sequoias, largest mountain in conterminous United States — Mount Whitney (14,494 feet).

Shenandoah, Va. (1926) 194,248. Portion of the Blue Ridge Mountains; this park overlooks much of the famous Shenandoah Valley.

Virgin Islands, Virgin Islands (1956) 14,470. Covers ¾ of St. John Island. Lush growth, lovely beaches, Indian relics, evidence of colonial Danes.

Voyageurs, Minn. (1971) 219,128. Abundant lakes, forests, wildlife, unusual recreation. **LIMITED FACILITIES.**

Wind Cave, S.D. (1903) 28,060. Limestone caverns in Black Hills. Extensive wildlife includes a herd of bison.

Yellowstone, Ida., Mont., Wyo., (1872) 2,219,823. Oldest and largest National Park. World's greatest geyser area has about 3,000 geysers and hot springs; the spectacular falls and impressive canyons of the Yellowstone River are major attractions.

Yosemite, Calif. (1890) 761,155. Yosemite Valley, the nation's highest waterfall, 3 groves of giant sequoias, and mountainous terrain.

Zion, Utah (1909) 146,845. Unusual shapes and landscapes have resulted from the effects of erosion and faulting activity. Zion Canyon, with sheer walls ranging up to 2,500 feet, is readily accessible.

National Historical Parks

Appomattox Court House, Va. (1930) 995. Where Lee surrendered to Grant.

Chalmette, La. (1907) 142. Scene of part of the Battle of New Orleans.

Chesapeake and Ohio Canal, Md.-W. Va-D of C. (1961) 20,239. 185 mile historic canal; D.C. to Cumberland, Md.

City of Refuge, Hawaii (1955) 181. Until 1819, a sanctuary for Hawaiians vanquished in battle, and those guilty of crimes or breaking taboos.

Colonial, Va. (1930) 9,146. Includes most of Jamestown Island, site of first successful English colony; Yorktown, site of Cornwallis' surrender to George Washington; Cape Henry Memorial, approximate site of the first landing of the Jamestown colonists; and Colonial Parkway.

Cumberland Gap, Ky. — Tenn. — Va. (1940) 20,267. Mountain pass of the Wilderness Road which carried the first great migration of pioneers into America's interior.

George Rogers Clark, Ind. (1966) 26. Commemorates American defeat of British in West during Revolution.

Harpers Ferry, Md., W. Va. (1944) 1,530. At the confluence of the Shenandoah and Potomac Rivers, the site of John Brown's 1859 raid on the Army arsenal. Scene of several Civil War Battles.

Independence, Pa., (1948) 18. Contains several properties in Philadelphia associated with the Revolutionary War and the founding of the U.S.

Minute Man, Mass. (1959) 746. Where the colonial Minute Men battled the British, April 19, 1775. Also contains Nathaniel Hawthorne's home.

Morristown, N.J. (1933) 1,377. Sites of important military encampments during the Revolutionary War; Washington's headquarters 1777, 1779-80.

Nez Perce, Ida. (1965) 2,213. Illustrates the history and culture of the Nez Perce Indian country. 22 separate sites.

San Juan Island, Wash. (1966) 1,752. Commemorates the peaceful relations of the U.S., Canada and Great Britain since the 1872 boundary disputes at this site.

Saratoga, N.Y. (1938) 3,337. Scene of a major battle which became a turning point in the War for Independence.

Sitka, Alaska. (1910) 108. Scene of last major resistance of the Tlingit Indians to the Russians, 1804.

International Park

Roosevelt-Campobello, New Brunswick, Canada (1964) 2,722. Administered by U.S. — Canadian joint commission. FDR's vacation home.

National Memorial Park

Theodore Roosevelt, N.D. (1947) 70,403. Part of T.R.'s Elkhorn Ranch along the Little Missouri River. Has bison and some original prairie.

National Battlefields

Big Hole, Mont. (1910) 1,383. Site of major battle with Nez Perce Indians.

Cowpens, S.C. (1929) 846. Revolutionary War battlefield.

Fort Necessity, Pa. (1931) 500. First battle of French and Indian War.

Petersburg, Va. (1926) 2,310. Scene of 10-month Union campaign 1864-65.

Stones River, Tenn. (1927) 331. Civil War battle leading to Sherman's "March to the Sea."

Tupelo, Miss. (1929) 1.5. Crucial battle over Sherman's supply line.

Wilson's Creek, Mo. (1960) 1,728. Civil War battle for control of state of Missouri.

National Battlefield Parks

Kennesaw Mountain, Ga. (1917) 3,683. Two major battles of Atlanta campaign.

Manassas, Va. (1940) 3,283. Two early Civil War battles.

Richmond, Va. (1936) 742. Site of battles defending Confederate capital.

National Battlefield Sites

Antietam, Md. (1890) 1,829. End of first Confederate invasion of North.

Brices Cross Roads, Miss. (1929) 1. Civil War Battlefield.

National Military Parks

Chickamauga and Chattanooga, Ga. — Tenn. (1890) 7,976. Four Civil War Battlefields.

Fort Donelson, Tenn. (1928) 538. Site of first major Union victory.

Fredericksburg and Spotsylvania County, Va. (1927) 4,660. Sites of several major Civil War battles and campaigns.

Gettysburg, Pa. (1895) 3,788. Major Confederate defeat in North.

Guilford Courthouse, N.C. (1917) 220. Revolutionary War battle.

Horseshoe Bend, Ala. (1956) 2,040. On Tallaposa River, place where Gen. Andrew Jackson broke the power of the Creek Indian Confederacy.

Kings Mountain, S.C. (1931) 3,950. Revolutionary War battle.

Moores Creek, N.C. (1926) 50. Pre-Revolutionary War Battle.

Pea Ridge, Ark. (1956) 4,279. Civil War battle.

Shiloh, Tenn. (1894) 3,702. Major Civil War battle; site includes some well-preserved Indian burial mounds.

Vicksburg, Miss. (1899) 1,741. Union victory gave North control of the Mississippi and split the Confederacy in two.

Historic Areas

Fort Scott, Kan. (1965) 7. Commemorates historic events in Kansas.

National Memorials

Arkansas Post, Ark. (1960) 305. First permanent French settlement in the lower Mississippi River Valley.

Benjamin Franklin, Philadelphia, Pa. (1972) 0.12. Colossal seated statue of inventor-statesman.

Chamizal, El Paso Texas (1966) 55. Commemorates 1963 settlement of 99-year border dispute with Mexico.

Coronado, Ariz. (1952) 2,834. Commemorates first European exploration of the Southwest under Francisco Vasquez Coronado.

Arlington House, The Robert E. Lee Memorial (Custis-Lee Mansion), Va. (1925) 3. 19th century mansion.

De Soto, Fla. (1948) 30. Commemorates 16th-century Spanish explorations.

Federal Hall, N.Y. (1939) 0.45. First seat of U.S. government.

Fort Caroline, Fla. (1950) 141. On St. Johns River, overlooks site of second attempt by French Huguenots to colonize. N.A.

Fort Clatsop, Ore. (1958) 125. Lewis and Clark encampment 1805-06.

Frederick Douglass Home, D. of C. (1962) 8. 19th-century black leader, ex-slave and Ambassador to Haiti.

General Grant, N.Y. (1958). 76. Tombs of Gen. and wife.

Hamilton Grange, N.Y. (1962) .71. Home of Alexander Hamilton.

Johnstown Flood, Pa. (1964) 108. Commemorates tragic flood.

Lincoln Boyhood, Ind. (1962) 200. Farm Lincoln grew up on.

Lincoln Memorial, D. of C. (1911) 164.

Mount Rushmore, S.D. (1925) 1,278. World famous sculpture of 4 presidents.

Perry's Victory and International Peace Memorial, Ohio (1936) 26. American naval victory, War of 1812.

Roger Williams, Providence, R.I. (1965) 5. Memorial to founder of R. I., early proponent of religious freedom. **NOT OPEN TO PUBLIC.**

Thaddeus Kosciuszko, Phila. Pa. (1972) 0.01. Polish hero of American Revolution. **NOT YET OPEN TO PUBLIC.**

Thomas Jefferson Memorial, D. of C. (1934) 18.

Washington Monument, D. of C. (1848) 106.

Wright Brothers, N.C. (1927) 431. First powered flight.

National Historic Sites

Abraham Lincoln Birthplace, Hodgenville, Ky. (1916) 117.

Adams, Quincy, Mass. (1946) 8. Home of Presidents John Adams, John Quincy Adams, and celebrated descendants.

Allegheny Portage Railroad, Pa. (1964) 767. Part of the Pennsylvania Canal system.

Andersonville, Andersonville, Ga. (1970) 494. Noted Civil War prison. **LIMITED FEDERAL FACILITIES.**

Andrew Johnson, Greeneville, Tenn. (1935) 17. Home of the President.

Ansley Wilcox House, Buffalo, N.Y. (1966) 1. Where President Theodore Roosevelt took the oath of office.

Bent's Old Fort, Colo. (1960) 178. Old West fur-trading post.

Carl Sandburg Home, Flat Rock, N.C. (1968) 247. Home of the poet. **NOT YET OPEN TO THE PUBLIC.**

Chicago Portage, Chi., Ill. (1952) 91. Part of original trader's link between the Great Lakes and the Mississippi River.

Chimney Rock, Nebr. (1956) 83. Landmark and campsite on Oregon Trail.

Christiansted, St. Croix; Virgin Islands (1952) 27. Commemorates Danish colony.

Dorchester Heights, Boston, Mass. (1951) 5. Memorial tower to colonial batteries, 1776.

Edison, West Orange, N.J. (1955) 20. Home and laboratory.

Eisenhower, Gettysburg, Pa. (1967) 493. Home of former President and World War II Allied Supreme Commander. **NOT OPEN TO PUBLIC.**

Ford's Theatre, Washington, D.C. (1866) 0.25. Includes theater, now restored, where Lincoln was assassinated, house where he died, and Lincoln Museum.

Fort Bowie, Ariz. (1964) 970. Focal point of operations against Geronimo and the Apaches. **LIMITED FACILITIES.**

Fort Davis, Texas (1961) 460. Frontier outpost battled Comanches and Apaches.

Fort Laramie, Wyo. (1938) 563. Military post on Oregon Trail.

Fort Larned, Kan. (1964) 681. Military post on Santa Fe Trail.

Fort Point, San Francisco, Calif. (1970) 96. Largest West Coast fortification.

Fort Raleigh, N.C. (1941) 160. First English settlement.

Fort Smith, Ark. (1961) 19. Active post from 1817 to 1890.

Fort Union Trading Post, Mont. — N.D. (1966) 446. Principal fur-trading post on upper Missouri, 1828-1867. **LIMITED FACILITIES.**

Fort Vancouver, Wash. (1948) 170. Hdqts. for Hudson's Bay Company in 1825. Early military and political seat of Pacific N.W.

Gloria Dei Church, Philadelphia, Pa. (1942) 3. Second oldest Swedish church in U.S., founded 1677, built approx. 1700.

Golden Spike, Utah (1957) 2,172. Commemorates completion of first transcontinental railroad in 1869.

Grant-Kohrs Ranch, Mass. (1972) 1,564. Archeological remains of pre-Columbian Hohokam culture. **NOT YET OPEN TO PUBLIC.**

Hampton, Md. (1948) 45. 18th-century Georgian mansion.

Herbert Hoover, West Branch, Iowa (1965) 148. Home of the President.

Home of Franklin D. Roosevelt, Hyde Park, N.Y. (1944) 188. Birthplace, home and "Summer White House".

Hopewell Village, Pa. (1938) 848. 19th-century iron making.

Hubbell Trading Post, Ariz. (1965) 160. Indian trading post.

Jamestown, Va. (1940) 21. First permanent English settlement.

Jefferson National Expansion Memorial, St. Louis, Mo. (1935) 94. Commemorates westward expansion with park and memorial arch.

John Fitzgerald Kennedy, Brookline, Mass. (1967) .09. Birthplace and childhood home of the President.

John Muir, Martinez, Calif. (1964) 9. Early conservationist and writer.

Lincoln Home, Springfield. Ill. (1971) 12. Residence when he was elected President, 1860. **NO FEDERAL FACILITIES.**

Longfellow, Cambridge, Mass. (1972) 2. Longfellow's home, 1837-82, and Washington's hq during Boston Siege, 1775-76. **NO FEDERAL FACILITIES.**

Lyndon B. Johnson, Johnson City, Texas (1969) 8. Birthplace and boyhood home of the 36th President.

Mar-A-Lago, Palm Beach, Fla. (1969) 17. 1920's mansion. **NOT OPEN TO PUBLIC.**

McLoughlin House, Oregon City, Ore. (1941) .63. Home of Dr. John McLoughlin, "The father of Oregon."

Pennsylvania Avenue, Wash. D.C. (1965) Area between the White House and the Capitol.

Puukohola Heiau, Island of Hawaii, Hawaii (1972) 77. Temple built by King Kamehameha, 1791. **NOT YET OPEN TO PUBLIC.**

Sagamore Hill, Oyster Bay, N.Y. (1962) 85. Home of President Theodore Roosevelt until his death in 1919.

Saint-Gaudens, Cornish, N.H. (1964) 86. Home, studio and gardens of American sculptor Augustus Saint-Gaudens.

Saint Paul's Church, Mount Vernon, N.Y. (1943) 6. Architectural landmark, had important role in Revolutionary War and the establishment of the freedom of the press.

St. Thomas, Charlotte Amalie, V.I. (1960) 2. Contains Fort Christian, oldest (1680) structure in the Virgin Islands, part of Danish settlement. **NO VISITOR FACILITIES.**

Salem Maritime, Mass. (1938) 11. Only port never seized from the Patriots by the British. Major fishing and whaling port.

San Jose Mission, San Antonio, Texas (1941) 4. Spanish mission established in 1720.

San Juan, Puerto Rico (1949) 48. 16th-century Spanish fortifications.

Saugus Iron Works, Mass. (1968) 9. Reconstructed 17th-century colonial ironworks.

Theodore Roosevelt Birthplace, N.Y., N.Y. (1962). 11.

Theodore Roosevelt Inaugural, Buffalo, N.Y. (1966) 1. Wilcox House where he took oath of office, 1901. **NO FEDERAL FACILITIES.**

Touro Synagogue, Newport, R.I. (1946) .23. Colonial Syn.

Vanderbilt Mansion, Hyde Park, N.Y. (1940) 212. Mansion of 19th-century financier.

Whitman Mission, Wash. (1936) 98. Site where Dr. and Mrs. Marcus Whitman ministered to the Indians until slain, 1847.

William Howard Taft, Cincinnati, Ohio (1969) 0.78. Birthplace and early home of the 27th President, 1909-13; Chief Justice, 1921-30. **LIMITED FACILITIES.**

National Capital Parks

District of Columbia — Maryland — Virginia (1790) 7,052. Includes 704 reservations.

White House

Washington, D.C. (1961) 18. Presidential residence since November 1800.

National Monuments

Name	State	Year	Acreage	Name	State	Year	Acreage
Agate Fossil Beds	Nebr.	1965	3,050	Gila Cliff Dwellings	N.M.	1907	533
Alibates Flint Quarries and				Glacier Bay	Alaska	1925	2,805,269
Texas Panhandle				Grand Canyon	Ariz.	1932	198,260
Pueblo Culture*	Tex.	1965	93	Grand Portage	Minn.	1951	710
Aztec Ruins	N.M.	1923	27	Gran Quivira	N.M.	1909	611
Badlands	S.D.	1929	243,508	Great Sand Dunes	Colo.	1932	36,696
Bandelier	N.M.	1916	29,661	Hohokam Pima*	Ariz.	1972	1,555
Biscayne**	Fla.	1968	95,127	Homestead National Monument			
Black Canyon of the Gunnison	Colo.	1933	13,671	of America	Nebr.	1936	195
Booker T. Washington	Va.	1956	218	Hovenweep	Colo.-Utah	1923	505
Buck Island Reef	Virgin Isls.	1961	850	Jewel Cave	S.D.	1908	1,275
Cabrillo	Calif.	1913	123	Joshua Tree	Calif.	1936	558,234
Canyon de Chelly	Ariz.	1931	83,840	Katmai	Alaska	1918	2,792,137
Capulin Mountain	N.M.	1916	775	Lava Beds	Calif.	1925	46,239
Casa Grande Ruins	Ariz.	1892	473	Lehman Caves	Nev.	1922	640
Castillo de San Marcos	Fla.	1924	20	Marble Canyon	Ariz.	1969	26.080
Castle Clinton	N.Y.	1946	1	Montezuma Castle	Ariz.	1906	842
Cedar Breaks	Utah	1933	6,155	Mound City Group	Ohio	1923	68
Chaco Canyon	N.M.	1907	21,510	Muir Woods	Calif.	1908	554
Channel Islands	Calif.	1938	18,167	Natural Bridges	Utah	1908	8,011
Chiricahua	Ariz.	1924	10,648	Navajo	Ariz.	1909	360
Colorado	Colo.	1911	17,669	Ocmulgee	Ga.	1934	683
Craters of the Moon	Idaho	1924	53,545	Oregon Caves	Ore.	1909	480
Custer Battlefield	Mont.	1879	765	Organ Pipe Cactus	Ariz.	1937	330,690
Death Valley	Calif.-Nev.	1933	1,913,985	Pecos	N.M.	1965	341
Devils Postpile	Calif.	1911	700	Petrified Forest	Calif.	1908	14,498
Devils Tower	Wyo.	1906	1,347	Pipe Spring	Ariz.	1923	40
Dinosaur	Colo.-Utah	1915	207,398	Pipestone	Minn.	1937	282
Effigy Mounds	Iowa	1949	1,467	Rainbow Bridge	Utah	1910	160
El Morro	N.M.	1906	1,279	Russell Cave	Ala.	1961	310
Florissant Fossil Beds**	Colo.	1969	5,992	Saguaro	Ariz.	1933	78,986
Fort Frederica	Ga.	1936	215	Saint Croix Island**	Me.	1949	35
Fort Jefferson	Fla.	1935	47,125	Scotts Bluff	Nebr.	1919	3,060
Fort McHenry National Monu-				Statue of Liberty	N.J.-N.Y.	1924	58
ment and Historic Shrine	Md.	1925	43	Sunset Crater	Ariz.	1930	3,040
Fort Matanzas	Fla.	1924	299	Timpanogos Cave	Utah	1922	250
Fort Pulaski	Ga.	1924	5,517	Tonto	Ariz.	1907	1,120
Fort Stanwix*	N.Y.	1935	18	Tumacacori	Ariz.	1908	10
Fort Sumter	S.C.	1948	34	Tuzigoot	Ariz.	1939	52
Fort Union	N.M.	1954	721	Walnut Canyon	Ariz.	1915	1,879
Fossil Butte*	Wyo.	1972	8,178	White Sands	N.M.	1933	144,855
G. Washington Birthplace	Va.	1930	456	Wupatki	Ariz.	1924	35,253
George Washington Carver	Mo.	1943	210	Yucca House*	Colo.	1919	10

National Cemeteries

Antietam	Md.	1870	11
Battleground	D. of C.	1867	1
Fort Donelson	Tenn.	1867	15
Fredericksburg	Va.	1865	12
Gettysburg	Penn.	1870	21
Poplar Grove	Va.	1866	9
Shiloh	Tenn.	1866	10
Stones River	Tenn.	1865	20
Vicksburg	Miss.	1865	118
Yorktown	Va.	1866	3

National Seashores

Assateague Island	Md.-Va.	1965	39,631
Cape Cod	Mass.	1961	44,600
Cape Hatteras	N.C.	1937	28,500
Cape Lookout**	N.C.	1966	24,500
Cumberland Island*	Ga.	1972	39,494
Fire Island	N.Y.	1964	19,311

Gulf Islands, Fla.-Miss. (1971) 124,690. White sand beaches, primitive off-shore islands, historic forts**.

Padre Island	Texas	1962	133,918
Point Reyes	Calif.	1962	64,546

National Lakeshores

Apostle Islands, Wis. (1970) 42,826. Picturesque islands and coastal portion of Bayfield Peninsula on south shore of Lake Superior**.

Indiana Dunes**	Ind.	1966	8,330
Pictured Rocks**	Mich.	1966	67,000

Sleeping Bear Dunes, Mich. (1970) 71,105. Notable for its beaches, massive sand dunes, forests, lakes. **Benzie and D. H. Day State Parks open to public.**

National River

Buffalo	Ark.	1972	95,840

National Scenic Riverways

Lower Saint Croix**	Minn.-Wis.	1972	7,845
Ozark	Mo.	1964	82,321
Saint Croix**	Minn.-Wis.	1968	67,747
Wolf**	Wis.	1968	5,516

National Recreation Areas

Amistad	Texas	1965	65,000
Arbuckle	Okla.	1965	5,631
Bighorn Canyon	Mont.-Wy.	1964	140,459
Coulee Dam	Wash.	1946	100,059
Curecanti	Colo.	1965	41,572
Delaware Water Gap**	N.J.-Pa.	1965	58,985
Gateway**	N.Y.-N.J.	1972	26,172
Glen Canyon	Ariz.-Utah	1958	1,236,880
Golden Gate**	Calif.	1972	34,202
Lake Chelan	Wash.	1968	62,000
Lake Mead	Ariz.-Nev.	1936	1,936,978
Ross Lake	Wash.	1968	107,000
Lake Meredith	Texas	1965	41,097
Shadow Mountain	Colo.	1952	18,240
Whiskeytown-Shasta-Trinity	Calif.	1962	42,445

National Scenic Trail

Appalachian	Me. to Ga.	1968	50,000

National Scientific Reserve

Ice Age	Wis.	1964	32,500

National Parkways

Baltimore—Washington	Md.	1950	2,431
Blue Ridge	N.C.-Va.-Ga.	1933	90,083
Geo. Washington Memorial	Md.-Va.	1930	7,142
John D. Rockefeller, Jr.	Wyo.	1972	23,700
Natchez Trace	Ala.-Miss.-Tenn.	1934	46,805
Suitland	D. of C.-Md.	1949	731

Other Areas

Catoctin Mountain Park	Md.	1936	5,769
John F. Kennedy Center for the Performing Arts	D.C.	1972	17
Piscataway Park	Md.	1961	4,014
Prince William Forest Park	Va.	1936	18,572
Theodore Roosevelt Island	D. of C.	1932	88
Wolf Trap Farm Park for the Performing Arts	Va.	1966	130

*Not Open to the Public. **Limited or No Federal Facilities.

Statue of Liberty National Monument

Since 1886 the Statue of Liberty Enlightening the World has stood on Liberty Island in New York harbor as a symbol of freedom. It also commemorates Franco-American friendship for it was given by the people of France and designed by Frederic Auguste Bartholdi (1834-1904). A $2,500,000 building housing the American Museum of Immigration was opened by Pres. Nixon Sept. 26, 1972, at the base of the statue. Exhibit halls, a library and study rooms as well as a Hall of Records will be grouped within the star-shaped Fort Wood which encompasses the statue. The statue is a National Monument, administered by the National Park Service.

Edouard de Laboulaye, French historian and admirer of American political institutions, suggested that the French present a monument to the United States, the latter to provide pedestal and site. In June, 1871, Bartholdi came to the United States to investigate the project. He visualized the idea of a colossal statue at the entrance of New York harbor, welcoming the peoples of the world with the torch of liberty. Bartholdi was then 37 years old.

The French approved the idea and formed the Franco-American Union to raise funds, which eventually reached $250,000. Bartholdi began work about 1874 in Paris. He made several models and one, 36 ft. tall, enabled him to compute the statue in sections. Wooden battens were made and sheets of copper 3/32 of an inch thick were hammered into shape on them by hand. A framework of four steel supports was designed by Gustave Eiffel, creator of the Eiffel tower.

On Washington's birthday, Feb. 22, 1877, Congress approved the use of a site on Bedloe's island suggested by Bartholdi. This island of 12 acres had been owned in the 17th century by a Walloon named Isaac Bedloe, who came to New Amsterdam in 1639. He died in 1673 and his wife sold the island for £80. In later years it was owned by the City of New York and the U.S. Government. It was called Bedloe's until Aug. 3, 1956, when President Eisenhower approved a resolution of Congress changing the name to Liberty Island.

The hand of the statue holding aloft the torch was exhibited at the Centennial exposition in Philadelphia in 1876 and later in Madison Square.

The head was shown at the Paris exposition of 1878. When framework and base were put in place in Paris the American minister, Levi P. Morton, drove the first rivet on Oct. 24, 1881, in honor of the centennial of the battle of Yorktown, in which French and Americans were allies.

The statue was finished May 21, 1884, and formally presented to U.S. Minister Morton July 4, 1884, by Ferdinand de Lesseps, head of the Franco-American Union and promoter of the Panama Canal.

On Aug. 5, 1884, the Americans laid the cornerstone for the pedestal. This was to be built on the foundations of Fort Wood, which had been erected by the Government in 1811. The American committee had raised $125,000, but when the pedestal was 15 ft. high, this was found to be inadequate. Joseph Pulitzer, owner of the World of New York City, on Mar. 15, 1885, called for general subscriptions. By Aug. 11, 1885, he had raised $100,000. The pedestal was made of concrete with granite facing, and steel girders were built into it to connect with the framework of the statue.

The statue arrived dismantled, in 214 packing cases, in the steamship Isere, which reached New York from Rouen, France, in June, 1885. The first rivet of the statue was driven July 12, 1886, and the last on Oct. 28, 1886, when President Grover Cleveland dedicated the statue in the presence of the sculptor. The total cost of statue and pedestal was estimated at $500,000.

The torch was originally maintained by the Lighthouse Service. Funds for permanently lighting the statue were raised by subscription by the World of New York in 1916 and President Wilson turned on the lights Dec. 2, 1916.

At the celebration of the statue's 50th anniversary, in 1936, President Franklin D. Roosevelt said: "The realization that we are all bound together by hope of a common future rather than by reverence for a common past has helped us to build upon this continent a unity unapproached in any similar area or similar-size population in the whole world. For all our millions of people, there is a unity in language and speech, in law and economics, in education and in general purpose which nowhere finds its match.

"It was the hope of those who gave us this statue and the hope of the American people in receiving it that the Goddess of Liberty and the Goddess of Peace were the same."

The statue weighs 450,000 lbs. or 225 tons. The copper sheeting weighs 200,000 lbs. There are 167 steps from the land level to the top of the pedestal, 168 steps inside the statue to the head, and 54 rungs on the ladder leading to the arm that holds the torch. Visitors may enter the head, which holds from 30 to 40 persons, but not the torch. The statue is open daily.

DIMENSIONS OF THE STATUE	Ft.	In.
Height from base to torch	151	1
Foundation of pedestal to torch	305	1
Heel to top of head	111	1
Length of hand	16	5
Index finger	8	0
Circumference at second joint	3	6
Size of finger nail .... 13x10 in.		
Head from chin to cranium	17	3
Head, thickness from ear to ear	10	0
Distance across the eye	2	6
Length of nose	4	6
Right arm, length	42	0
Right arm, greatest thickness	12	0
Thickness of waist	35	0
Width of mouth	3	0
Tablet, length	23	7
Tablet, width	13	7
Tablet, thickness	2	0

EMMA LAZARUS' FAMOUS POEM

A poem by Emma Lazarus is graven on a tablet within the pedestal on which the Goddess stands:

THE NEW COLOSSUS

Not like the brazen giant of Greek fame,
With conquering limbs astride from land to land;
Here at our sea-washed, sunset gates shall stand
A mighty woman with a torch, whose flame
Is the imprisoned lightning, and her name
Mother of Exiles. From her beacon-hand
Glows world-wide welcome; her mild eyes command
The air-bridged harbor that twin cities frame.
"Keep ancient lands, your storied pomp!" cries she
With silent lips. "Give me your tired, your poor,
Your huddled masses yearning to breathe free,
The wretched refuse of your teeming shore.
Send these, the homeless, tempest-tost to me,
I lift my lamp beside the golden door!"

Nearby Ellis Island, abandoned as an immigration center in 1954 after serving as the gateway to America for 16,000,000, was proclaimed by President Johnson in 1965 part of the Statue of Liberty National Monument. The National Park Service plans to develop the island as a visitor site.

LAWS AND DOCUMENTS
DECLARATION OF INDEPENDENCE

The Declaration of Independence was adopted by the Continental Congress in Philadelphia, on July 4, 1776. John Hancock was president of the Congress and Charles Thomson was secretary. A copy of the Declaraton, engrossed on parchment, was signed by Members of Congress on and after August 2, 1776. On January 18,1777, Congress ordered that "authenticated copies, with the names of the Members of Congress subscribed the same, be sent to each of the United States, and that they be desired to have same put upon record." Authenticated copies were printed in broadside form in Baltimore, where the Continental Congress was then in session. The following text is that of the original printed by John Dunlap at Philadelphia for the Continental Congress.

IN CONGRESS, July 4, 1776.
A DECLARATION
By the REPRESENTATIVES of the
UNITED STATES OF AMERICA,
In GENERAL CONGRESS assembled

When in the Course of human Events, it becomes necessary for one People to dissolve the Political Bands which have connected them with another, and to assume among the Powers of the Earth, the separate and equal Station to which the Laws of Nature and of Nature's God entitle them, a decent Respect to the Opinions of Mankind requires that they should declare the causes which impel them to the Separation.

We hold these Truths to be self-evident, that all Men are created equal, that they are endowed by their Creator with certain unalienable Rights, that among these are Life, Liberty, and the Pursuit of Happiness–That to secure these Rights, Governments are instituted among Men, deriving their just Powers from the Consent of the Governed, that whenever any Form of Government becomes destructive of these Ends, it is the Right of the People to alter or to abolish it, and to institute new Government, laying its Foundation on such Principles, and organizing its Powers in such Form, as to them shall seem most likely to effect their Safety and Happiness. Prudence, indeed, will dictate that Governments long established should not be changed for light and transient Causes; and accordingly all Experience hath shewn, that Mankind are more disposed to suffer, while Evils are sufferable, than to right themselves by abolishing the Forms to which they are accustomed. But when a long Train of Abuses and Usurpations, pursuing invariably the same Object, evinces a Design to reduce them under absolute Despotism, it is their Right, it is their Duty, to throw off such Government, and to provide new Guards for their future Security. Such has been the patient Sufferance of these Colonies; and such is now the Necessity which constrains them to alter their former Systems of Government. The History of the present King of Great-Britain is a History of repeated Injuries and Usurpations, all having in direct Object the Establishment of an absolute Tyranny over these States. To prove this, let Facts be submitted to a candid World.

He has refused his Assent to Laws, the most wholesome and necessary for the public Good.

He has forbidden his Governors to pass Laws of immediate and pressing Importance, unless suspended in their Operation till his Assent should be obtained; and when so suspended, he has utterly neglected to attend to them.

He has refused to pass other Laws for the Accommodation of large Districts of People, unless those People would relinquish the Right of Representation in the Legislature, a Right inestimable to them, and formidable to Tyrants only.

He has called together Legislative Bodies at Places unusual, uncomfortable, and distant from the Depository of their public Records, for the sole Purpose of fatiguing them into Compliance with his Measures.

He has dissolved Representative Houses repeatedly, for opposing with manly Firmness his Invasions on the Rights of the People.

He has refused for a long Time, after such Dissolutions, to cause others to be elected; whereby the Legislative Powers, incapable of Annihilation, have returned to the People at large for their exercise; the State remaining in the mean time exposed to all the Dangers of Invasion from without, and Convulsions within.

He has endeavoured to prevent the Population of these States; for that Purpose obstructing the Laws for Naturalization of Foreigners; refusing to pass others to encourage their Migrations hither, and raising the Conditions of new Appropriations of Lands.

He has obstructed the Administration of Justice, by refusing his Assent to Laws for establishing Judiciary Powers.

He has made Judges dependent on his Will alone, for the Tenure of their Offices, and the Amount and Payment of their Salaries.

He has erected a Multitude of new Offices, and sent hither Swarms of Officers to harrass our People, and eat out their Substance.

He has kept among us, in Times of Peace, Standing Armies, without the consent of our Legislatures.

He has affected to render the Military independent of and superior to the Civil Power.

He has combined with others to subject us to a Jurisdiction foreign to our Constitution, and unacknowledged by our Laws; giving his Assent to their Acts of pretended Legislation:

For quartering large Bodies of Armed Troops among us:

For protecting them, by a mock Trial, from Punishment for any Murders which they should commit on the Inhabitants of these States:

For cutting off our Trade with all Parts of the World:

For imposing Taxes on us without our Consent:

For depriving us, in many Cases, of the Benefits of Trial by Jury:

For transporting us beyond Seas to be tried for pretended Offences:

For abolishing the free System of English Laws in a neighbouring Province, establishing therein an arbitrary Government, and enlarging its Boundaries, so as to render it at once an Example and fit Instrument for introducing the same absolute Rule into these Colonies:

For taking away our Charters, abolishing our most valuable Laws, and altering fundamentally the Forms of our Governments:

For suspending our own Legislatures, and declaring themselves invested with Power to legislate for us in all Cases whatsoever.

He has abdicated Government here, by declaring us out of his Protection and waging War against us.

He has plundered our Seas, ravaged our Coasts, burnt our Towns, and destroyed the Lives of our People.

He is, at this Time, transporting large Armies of foreign Mercenaries to compleat the Works of Death, Desolation, and Tyranny, already begun with circumstances of Cruelty and Perfidy, scarcely paralleled in the most barbarous Ages, and totally unworthy the Head of a civilized Nation.

He has constrained our fellow Citizens taken Captive on the high Seas to bear Arms against their Country, to become the Executioners of their Friends and Brethren, or to fall themselves by their Hands.

He has excited domestic Insurrections amongst us, and has endeavoured to bring on the Inhabitants of our Frontiers, the merciless Indian Savages, whose known Rule of Warfare, is an undistinguished Destruction, of all Ages, Sexes and Conditions.

In every stage of these Oppressions we have Petitioned for Redress in the most humble Terms: Our re-

751

peated Petitions have been answered only by repeated Injury. A Prince, whose Character is thus marked by every act which may define a Tyrant, is unfit to be the Ruler of a free People.

Nor have we been wanting in Attentions to our British Brethren. We have warned them from Time to Time of Attempts by their Legislature to exter. I an unwarrantable Jurisdiction over us. We have reminded them of the Circumstances of our Emigration and Settlement here. We have appealed to their native Justice and Magnanimity, and we have conjured them by the Ties of our common Kindred to disavow these Usurpations, which, would inevitably interrupt our Connections and Correspondence. They too have been deaf to the Voice of Justice and of Consanguinity. We must, therefore, acquiesce in the Necessity, which denounces our Separation, and hold them, as we hold the rest of Mankind, Enemies in War, in Peace, Friends.

We, therefore, the Representatives of the UNITED STATES OF AMERICA, in GENERAL CONGRESS, Assembled, appealing to the Supreme Judge of the World in the Rectitude of our Intentions, do, in the Name, and by Authority of the good People of these Colonies, solemnly Publish and Declare, That these United Colonies are, and of Right ought to be, FREE AND INDEPENDENT STATES; that they are absolved from all Allegiance to the British Crown, and that all political Connection between them and the State of Great-Britain, is and ought to be totally dissolved; and that as FREE AND INDEPENDENT STATES, they have full Power to levy War, conclude Peace, contract Alliances, establish Commerce, and to do all other Acts and Things which INDEPENDENT STATES may of right do. And for the support of this declaration, with a firm Reliance on the Protection of divine Providence, we mutually pledge to each other our lives, our Fortunes, and our sacred Honor.

JOHN HANCOCK, President.

ATTEST.

CHARLES THOMSON, Secretary.

Signers of the Declaration of Independence

Delegate and State	Vocation	Birthplace	Born	Died
Adams, John (Mass.)	Lawyer	Braintree (Quincy), Mass	1735, Oct. 30	1826, July 4
Adams, Samuel (Mass.)	Politician	Boston, Mass.	1722, Sept. 27	1803, Oct. 2
Bartlett, Josiah (N. H.)	Phys., Law	Amesbury, Mass	1729, Nov. 21	1795, May 19
Braxton, Carter (Va.)	Farmer	King & Queen C. H., Va	1736, Sept. 10	1797, Oct. 10
Carroll, Chas. of Carrollton (Md.)	Lawyer	Annapolis, Md	1737, Sept. 19	1832, Nov. 14
Chase, Samuel (Md.)	Jurist	Princess Anne, Md	1741, April 17	1811, June 19
Clark, Abram (N. J.)	Law., Fin	Elizabeth, N. J.	1726, Feb. 15	1794, Sept. 15
Clymer, George (Pa.)	Merchant	Philadelphia, Pa.	1739, March 16	1813, Jan. 23
Ellery, William (R. I.)	Jurist	Newport, R. I.	1727, Dec. 22	1820, Feb. 15
Floyd, William (N. Y.)	Soldier	Brookhaven, N. Y.	1734, Dec. 17	1821, Aug. 4
Franklin, Benjamin (Pa.)	Print., Pub	Boston, Mass.	1706, Jan. 17	1790, April 17
Gerry, Elbridge (Mass.)	Merchant	Marblehead, Mass	1744, July 17	1814, Nov. 23
Gwinnett, Button (Ga.)	Merchant	Down Hatherly, Eng.	1732	1777, May 19
Hall, Lyman (Ga.)	Phys., Jurist.	Wallingford, Conn.	1724, April 12	1790, Oct. 19
Hancock, John (Mass.)	Merchant	Braintree (Quincy), Mass	1737, Jan. 12	1793, Oct. 8
Harrison, Benjamin (Va.)	Farmer	Berkeley, Va	1726, April 5	1791, April 24
Hart, John (N. J.)	Farmer	Stonington, Conn	(1707-1711?)	1779, May 11
Hewes, Joseph (N. C.)	Merchant	Kingston, N. J.	1730, Jan. 23	1779, Nov. 10
Heyward, Thos. Jr. (S. C.)	Law., Farm	St. Luke's Parish, S. C	1746, July 28	1809, March 6
Hooper, William (N. C.)	Lawyer	Boston, Mass.	1742, June 28	1790, Oct. 14
Hopkins, Stephen (R. I.)	Mer., Judge	Providence, R. I.	1707, March 7	1785, July 13
Hopkinson, Francis (N. J.)	Jur., Music	Philadelphia, Pa.	1737, Sept. 21	1791, May 9
Huntington, Samuel (Conn.)	Jurist	Windham County, Conn	1731, July 3	1796, Jan. 5
Jefferson, Thomas (Va.)	Lawyer	Old Shadwell, Va.	1743, April 13	1826, July 4
Lee, Richard Henry (Va.)	Farmer	Stratford, Va.	1732, Jan. 20	1794, June 19
Lee, Francis Lightfoot (Va.)	Farmer	Stratford, Va.	1734, Oct. 14	1797, Jan. 11
Lewis, Francis (N. Y.)	Merchant	Landaff, Wales.	1713, March	1803, Dec. 30
Livingston, Philip (N. Y.)	Merchant	Albany, N. Y.	1716, Jan. 15	1778, June 12
Lynch, Thomas, Jr. (S. C.)	Farmer	Winyah, S. C	1749, Aug. 5	1779, (at sea)
McKean, Thomas (Del.)	Lawyer	New London, Pa	1734, March 19	1817, June 24
Middleton, Arthur (S. C.)	Farmer	Charleston, S. C.	1742, June 26	1787, Jan. 1
Morris, Lewis (N. Y.)	Farmer	Morrisania, N.Y. (N.Y.C.)	1726, April 8	1798, Jan. 22
Morris, Robert (Pa.)	Merchant	Liverpool, Eng.	1734, Jan. 20	1806, May 8
Morton, John (Pa.)	Jurist	Ridley, Pa.	1724	1777, April
Nelson, Thos. Jr. (Va.)	Soldier	Yorktown, Va	1738, Dec. 26	1789, Jan. 4
Paca, William (Md.)	Jurist	Abingdon, Md	1740, Oct. 31	1799, Oct. 23
Paine, Robert Treat (Mass.)	Rev., Jurist	Boston, Mass.	1731, March 11	1814, May 12
Penn, John (N. C.)	Lawyer	Near Port Royal, Va	1741, May 17	1788, Sept. 14
Read, George (Del.)	Jurist	Near North East, Md	1733, Sept. 18	1798, Sept. 21
Rodney, Caesar (Del.)	Jurist	Dover, Del.	1728, Oct. 7	1784, June 29
Ross, George (Pa.)	Jurist	New Castle, Del	1730, May 10	1779, July 14
Rush, Benjamin (Pa.)	Physician	Byberry, Pa. (Philadelphia)	1745, Dec. 24	1813, April 19
Rutledge, Edward (S. C.)	Lawyer	Charleston, S. C.	1749, Nov. 23	1800, Jan. 23
Sherman, Roger (Conn.)	Lawyer	Newton, Mass.	1721, April 19	1793, July 23
Smith, James (Pa.)	Lawyer	Dublin, Ireland	1713	1806, July 11
Stockton, Richard (N. J.)	Lawyer	Near Princeton, N. J.	1730, Oct. 1	1781, Feb. 28
Stone, Thomas (Md.)	Lawyer	Charles County, Md	1743	1787, Oct. 5
Taylor, George (Pa.)	Ironmonger	Ireland	1716	1781, Feb. 23
Thornton, Matthew (N. H.)	Phys., Jurist	Ireland	1714	1803, June 24
Walton, George (Ga.)	Jurist	Prince Edward County, Va	1741	1804, Feb. 2
Whipple, William (N. H.)	Mer., Jurist	Kittery, Maine	1730, Jan. 14	1785, Nov. 28
Williams, William (Conn.)	Mer., Jurist	Lebanon, Conn	1731, April 23	1811, Aug. 2
Wilson, James (Pa.)	Jurist	Carskerdo, Scotland.	1742, Sept. 14	1798, Aug. 28
Witherspoon, John (N. J.)	Educator	Gifford, Scotland.	1723, Feb. 5	1794, Nov. 15
Wolcott, Oliver (Conn.)	Jurist	Windsor, Conn.	1726, Dec. 1	1797, Dec. 1
Wythe, George (Va.)	Lawyer	Elizabeth City, Va.	1726	1806, June 8

The American's Creed

Written by William Tyler Page, clerk of the U.S. House of Representatives, in 1917.

I believe in the United States of America as a government of the people, by the people, for the people; whose just powers are derived from the consent of the governed; a democracy in a republic; a sovereign nation of many sovereign states, a perfect union, one and inseparable; established upon those principles of freedom, equality, justice and humanity for which American patriots sacrificed their lives and fortunes. I therefore believe it is my duty to my country to love it; to support its Constitution; to obey its laws; to respect its flag, and to defend it against all enemies.

How the Declaration of Independence Was Adopted

On June 7, 1776, **Richard Henry Lee,** who had issued the first call for a congress of the colonies, introduced in the Continental Congress at Philadelphia a resolution declaring "that these United Colonies are, and of right ought to be, free and independent states, that they are absolved from all allegiance to the British Crown, and that all political connection between them and the state of Great Britain is, and ought to be, totally dissolved."

The resolution, seconded by John Adams on behalf of the Massachusetts delegation, came up again June 10 when a committee of five, headed by Thomas Jefferson, was appointed to express the purpose of the resolution in a declaration of independence. The others on the committee were John Adams, Benjamin Franklin, Robert R. Livingston, and Roger Sherman.

Drafting the Declaration was assigned to Jefferson, who worked on a portable desk of his own construction in a room at Market and 7th Sts. The committee reported the result June 28, 1776. The members of the Congress suggested a number of changes, which Jefferson called "deplorable." They didn't approve Jefferson's arraignment of the British people and King George III for en-'couraging and fostering the slave trade, which Jefferson called "an execrable commerce." They made 8° ⬛⬛⬛⬛ ul⬛⬛⬛⬛⬛ ⬛⬛⬛ ⬛⬛⬛⬛⬛ and leaving 1,00⬛ in the final form capitalization was erratic. Jefferson had written that men were endowed with "inalienable" rights; in the final copy it came out as "unalienable" and has been thus ever since.

The Lee-Adams resolution of independence was adopted by 12 yeas July 2–the actual date of the act of independence. The Declaration, which explains the act, was adopted the evening of July 4.

After the Declaration was adopted, July 4, 1776, it was turned over to John Dunlap, printer, to be printed on broadsides. The original copy was lost and one of his broadsides was attached to a page in the journal of the Congress. It was read aloud July 8 in Philadelphia, Easton, Pa. and Trenton, N. J. On July 9 at 6 p.m. it was read by order of Gen. George Washington to the troops assembled on the Common in N. Y. C. (City Hall Park).

The Continental Congress on July 19, 1776, adopted the following resolution:

"Resolved, That the Declaration passed on the 4th, be fairly engrossed on parchment with the title and stile of 'The unanimous Declaration of the thirteen united States of America' and that the same, when engrossed, be signed by every member of Congress."

Not all delegates who signed the engrossed Declaration were present on July 4. Robert Morris (Pa.), William Williams (Conn.) and Samuel Chase (Md.) signed on Aug. 2. Oliver Wolcott (Conn.), George Wythe (Va.), Richard Henry Lee (Va.) and Elbridge Gerry (Mass.) signed in August and September. Matthew Thornton (N.H.) joined the Congress Nov. 4 and signed later. Thomas McKean (Del.) rejoined Washington's Army before signing and said later that he signed in 1781.

Charles Carroll of Carrollton was appointed a delegate by Maryland on July 4, 1776, presented his credential Jul) 18, ⬛⬛⬛ signed the engrossed ⬛⬛⬛ declaration Aug. 2. Born Sept. 19, 1737, he was 95 years old and the last surviving signer when he died Nov. 14, 1832.

Two Pennsylvania delegates who did not support the Declaration on July 4 were replaced.

The four New York delegates did not have authority from their state to vote on July 4. On July 9 the New York state convention authorized its delegates to approve the Declaration and the Congress was so notified on July 15, 1776. The four signed the Declaration on Aug. 2.

The original engrossed Declaration is preserved in the National Archives Building in Washington.

The Liberty Bell; Its History and Significance

The Liberty Bell, in Independence Hall, Philadelphia, is an object of great reverence to Americans because of its association with the historic events of the War of Independence.

The original Province bell, ordered to commemorate the 50th anniversary of the Commonwealth of Pennsylvania, was cast by Thomas Lister, Whitechapel, London, and reached Philadelphia in August, 1752. It bore an inscription from Leviticus XXV, 10: "Proclaim liberty throughout all the land unto all the inhabitants thereof."

The bell was cracked by a stroke of its clapper in September, 1752, while it hung on a truss in the State House yard for testing. Pass & Stow, Philadelphia founders, recast the bell, adding 1½ ounces of copper to a pound of the original metal to reduce brittleness. It was found that the bell contained too much copper, injuring its tone, so Pass & Stow recast it again, this time successfully.

In June, 1753, the bell was hung in the wooden steeple of the State House, erected on top of the brick tower. In use while the Continental Congress was in session in the State House, it rang out in defiance of British tax and trade restrictions, and proclaimed the Boston Tea Party and the first public reading of the Declaration of Independence.

On Sept. 18, 1777, when the British Army was about to occupy Philadelphia, the bell was moved in a baggage train of the American Army to Allentown, Pa., where it was hidden in Zion Reformed Church until June 27, 1778. It was moved back to Philadelphia after the British left.

In July, 1781, the wooden steeple became insecure and had to be taken down. The bell was lowered into the brick section of the tower. Here it was hanging in July, 1835, when it cracked while tolling for the funeral of John Marshall, Chief Justice of the United States. Because of its association with the War of Independence it was not recast but remained mute in this location until 1846, the year of the Mexican War, when it was placed on exhibition in the Declaration Chamber of Independence Hall.

In 1876, when many thousands of Americans visited Philadelphia for the Centennial Exposition, it was placed in its old walnut frame in the tower hallway. In 1877 it was hung from the ceiling of the tower by a chain of 13 links. It was returned again to the Declaration Chamber and in 1896 taken back to the tower hall, where it occupied a glass case. In 1915 the case was removed so that the public might touch it. It remains there today.

The measurements of the bell follow: Circumference around the lip, 12 ft.; circumference around the crown, 7 ft. 6 in.; lip to the crown, 3 ft.; height over the crown, 2 ft. 3 in.; thickness at lip, 3 in.; thickness at crown, 1¼ in.; weight, 2080 lbs.; length of clapper, 3 ft. 2 in.; cost. £ 60 14s 5d.

Origin of the United States National Motto

In God We Trust, designated as the U. S. National Motto by Congress in 1956, originated during the Civil War as an inscription for U. S. coins, although it was used by Francis Scott Key in a slightly different form when he wrote The Star-Spangled Banner in 1814. On Nov. 13, 1861, when Union morale had been shaken by battlefield defeats, the Rev. M. R. Watkinson, of Ridleyville, Pa., wrote to Secy. of the Treasury Salmon P. Chase, "From my heart I have felt our national shame in disowning God as not the least of our present national disasters," the minister wrote, suggesting "recognition of the Almighty God in some form on our coins." Secy. Chase ordered designs prepared with the inscription *In God We Trust* and backed coinage legislation which authorized use of this slogan. It first appeared on some U. S. coins in 1864, disappeared and reappeared on various coins until 1955, when Congress ordered it placed on all paper money and all coins.

CONSTITUTION OF THE UNITED STATES

The Original Seven Articles

PREAMBLE

We, the people of the United States, in order to form a more perfect Union, establish justice, insure domestic tranquility, provide for the common defense, promote the general welfare, and secure the blessings of liberty to ourselves and our posterity, do ordain and establish this Constitution for the United States of America.

ARTICLE 1.

Section 1—Legislative powers; in whom vested:
All legislative powers herein granted shall be vested in a Congress of the United States, which shall consist of a Senate and House of Representatives.

Section 2—House of Representatives, how and by whom chosen. Qualifications of a Representative. Representatives and direct taxes, how apportioned. Enumeration. Vacancies to be filled. Power of choosing officers, and of impeachment.

1. The House of Representatives shall be composed of members chosen every second year by the people of the several States, and the electors in each State shall have the qualifications requisite for electors of the most numerous branch of the State Legislature.

2. No person shall be a Representative who shall not have attained to the age of twenty-five years, and been seven years a citizen of the United States, and who shall not, when elected, be an inhabitant of that State in which he shall be chosen.

3. Representatives and direct taxes shall be apportioned among the several States which may be included within this Union, according to their respective numbers, which shall be determined by adding to the whole number of free persons, including those bound to service for a term of years, and excluding Indians not taxed, three-fifths of all other persons. The actual enumeration shall be made within three years after the first meeting of the Congress of the United States, and within every subsequent term of ten years, in such manner as they shall by law direct. The number of Representatives shall not exceed one for every thirty thousand, but each State shall have at least one Representative; and until such enumeration shall be made, the State of New Hampshire shall be entitled to choose three, Massachusetts eight, Rhode Island and Providence Plantations one, Connecticut five, New York six, New Jersey four, Pennsylvania eight, Delaware one, Maryland six, Virginia ten, North Carolina five, South Carolina five, and Georgia three.

4. When vacancies happen in the representation from any State, the Executive Authority thereof shall issue writs of election to fill such vacancies.

5. The House of Representatives shall choose their Speaker and other officers; and shall have the sole power of impeachment.

Section 3—Senators, how and by whom chosen. How classified. State Executive, when to make temporary appointments, in case, etc. Qualifications of a

---

Origin of the Constitution

The War of Independence was conducted by delegates from the original 13 states, called the Congress of the United States of America and generally known as the Continental Congress. In 1777 the Congress submitted to the legislatures of the states the Articles of Confederation and Perpetual Union, which were ratified by New Hampshire, Massachusetts, Rhode Island, Connecticut, New York, New Jersey, Pennsylvania, Delaware, Virginia, North Carolina, South Carolina and Georgia, and finally, in 1781, by Maryland.

The first article of the instrument read: "The stile of this confederacy shall be the United States of America." This did not signify a sovereign nation, because the states delegated only those powers they could not handle individually, such as power to wage war, establish a uniform currency, make treaties with foreign nations and contract debts for general expenses, such as paying the army. Taxes for the payment of such debts were levied by the individual states. The president under the Articles signed himself "President of the United States in Congress assembled," but here the United States were considered in the plural, a cooperating group. Canada was invited to join the union on equal terms but did not act.

When the war was won it became evident that a stronger federal union was needed to protect the mutual interests of the states. The Congress left the initiative to the legislatures. Virginia in January, 1786, appointed commissioners to meet with representatives of other states, with the result that delegates from Virginia, Delaware, New York, New Jersey and Pennsylvania met at Annapolis. Alexander Hamilton prepared their call asking delegates from all states to meet in Philadelphia in May, 1787, "to render the Constitution of the Federal government adequate to the exigencies of the union." Congress endorsed the plan Feb. 21, 1787. Delegates were appointed by all states except Rhode Island.

The convention met May 14, 1787. George Washington was chosen president (presiding officer). The states certified 65 delegates, but 10 did not attend. The work was done by 55, not all of whom were present at all sessions. Of the 55 attending delegates, 16 failed to sign, and 39 actually signed Sept. 17, 1787, some with reservations. Some historians have said 74 delegates were named and 19 failed to attend. These 9 additional persons refused the appointment, were never delegates and never counted as absentees. Washington sent the Constitution to Congress with a covering letter and that body, Sept. 28, 1787, ordered it sent to the legislatures, "in order to be submitted to a convention of delegates chosen in each state by the people thereof."

The Constitution was ratified by votes of state conventions as follows: Delaware, Dec. 7, 1787, unanimous; Pennsylvania, Dec. 12, 1787, 43 to 23; New Jersey, Dec. 18, 1787, unanimous; Georgia, Jan. 2, 1788, unanimous; Connecticut, Jan. 9, 1788, 128 to 40; Massachusetts, Feb. 6, 1788, 187 to 168; Maryland, April 28, 1788, 63 to 11; South Carolina, May 23, 1788, 149 to 73; New Hampshire, June 21, 1788, 57 to 46; Virginia, June 25, 1788, 89 to 79; New York, July 26, 1788, 30 to 27. Nine states were needed to establish the operation of the Constitution "between the states so ratifying the same" and New Hampshire was the ninth state. The government did not declare the Constitution in effect until the first Wednesday in March, 1789, which was March 4. After that North Carolina ratified it Nov. 21, 1789, 197 to 77; and Rhode Island May 29, 1790, 34 to 32. Vermont in convention ratified it Jan. 10, 1791, and by act of Congress approved Feb. 19, 1791, was admitted into the Union as the 14th state, Mar. 4, 1791.

Senator. President of the Senate, his right to vote. President pro tem., and other officers of the Senate, how chosen. Power to try impeachments. When President is tried, Chief Justice to preside. Sentence.

1. The Senate of the United States shall be composed of two Senators from each State, chosen by the Legislature thereof, for six years; and each Senator shall have one vote.

2. Immediately after they shall be assembled in consequence of the first election, they shall be divided as equally as may be into three classes. The seats of the Senators of the first class shall be vacated at the expiration of the second year, of the second class at the expiration of the fourth year, and of the third class at the expiration of the sixth year, so that one-third may be chosen every second year; and if vacancies happen by resignation, or otherwise, during the recess of the Legislature of any State, the Executive thereof may make temporary appointments until the next meeting of the Legislature, which shall then fill such vacancies.

3. No person shall be a Senator who shall not have attained to the age of thirty years, and been nine years a citizen of the United States, and who shall not, when elected, be an inhabitant of that State for which he shall be chosen.

4. The Vice-President of the United States shall be President of the Senate, but shall have no vote, unless they be equally divided.

5. The Senate shall choose their other officers, and also a President pro tempore, in the absence of the Vice-President, or when he shall exercise the office of President of the United States.

6. The Senate shall have the sole power to try all impeachments. When sitting for that purpose, they shall be on oath or affirmation. When the President of the United States is tried, the Chief Justice shall preside: and no person shall be convicted without the concurrence of two-thirds of the members present.

7. Judgment in cases of impeachment shall not extend further than to removal from office, and disqualification to hold and enjoy any office of honor, trust or profit under the United States: but the party convicted shall nevertheless be liable and subject to indictment, trial, judgment and punishment, according to law.

Section 4—Times, etc., of holding elections, how prescribed. One session in each year.

1. The times, places and manner of holding elections for Senators and Representatives, shall be prescribed in each State by the Legislature thereof; but the Congress may at any time by law make or alter such regulations, except as to the places of choosing Senators.

2. The Congress shall assemble at least once in every year, and such meeting shall be on the first Monday in December, unless they shall by law appoint a different day.

Section 5—Membership, Quorum, Adjournments, Rules. Power to punish or expel. Journal. Time of adjournments, how limited, etc.

1. Each House shall be the judge of the elections, returns and qualifications of its own members, and a majority of each shall constitute a quorum to do business; but a smaller number may adjourn from day to day, and may be authorized to compel the attendance of absent members, in such manner, and under such penalties as each House may provide.

2. Each House may determine the rules of its proceedings, punish its members for disorderly behavior, and, with the concurrence of two-thirds, expel a member.

3. Each House shall keep a journal of its proceedings, and from time to time publish the same, excepting such parts as may in their judgment require secrecy; and the yeas and nays of the members of either House on any question shall, at the desire of one-fifth of those present, be entered on the journal.

4. Neither House, during the session of Congress, shall, without the consent of the other, adjourn for more than three days, nor to any other place than that in which the two Houses shall be sitting.

Section 6—Compensation, Privileges, Disqualifications in certain cases.

1. The Senators and Representatives shall receive a compensation for their services, to be ascertained by law, and paid out of the Treasury of the United States. They shall in all cases, except treason, felony and breach of the peace, be privileged from arrest during their attendance at the session of their respective Houses, and in going to and returning from the same; and for any speech or debate in either House, they shall not be questioned in any other place.

2. No Senator or Representative shall, during the time for which he was elected, be appointed to any civil office under the authority of the United States, which shall have been created, or the emoluments whereof shall have been increased during such time; and no person holding any office under the United States, shall be a member of either House during his continuance in office.

Section 7—House to originate all revenue bills. Veto. Bill may be passed by two-thirds of each House, notwithstanding, etc. Bill, not returned in ten days, to become a law. Provisions as to orders, concurrent resolutions, etc.

1. All bills for raising revenue shall originate in the House of Representatives; but the Senate may propose or concur with amendments as on other bills.

2. Every bill which shall have passed the House of Representatives and the Senate, shall, before it become a law, be presented to the President of the United States; if he approve he shall sign it, but if not he shall return it, with his objections to that House in which it shall have originated, who shall enter the objections at large on their journal, and proceed to reconsider it. If after such reconsideration two-thirds of that House shall agree to pass the bill, it shall be sent, together with the objections, to the other House, by which it shall likewise be reconsidered, and if approved by two-thirds of that House, it shall become a law. But in all such cases the votes of both Houses shall be determined by yeas and nays, and the names of the persons voting for and against the bill shall be entered on the journal of each House respectively. If any bill shall not be returned by the President within ten days (Sundays excepted) after it shall have been presented to him, the same shall be a law, in like manner as if he had signed it, unless the Congress by their adjournment prevent its return, in which case it shall not be a law.

3. Every order, resolution, or vote to which the concurrence of the Senate and House of Representatives may be necessary (except on a question of adjournment) shall be presented to the President of the United States; and before the same shall take effect, shall be approved by him, or being disapproved by him, shall be repassed by two-thirds of the Senate and House of Representatives, according to the rules and limitations prescribed in the case of a bill.

Section 8—Powers of Congress.

1. The Congress shall have power

To lay and collect taxes, duties, imposts and excises, to pay the debts and provide for the common defense and general welfare of the United States; but all duties, imposts and excises shall be uniform throughout the United States;

2. To borrow money on the credit of the United States;

3. To regulate commerce with foreign nations, and among the several States, and with the Indian tribes;

4. To establish a uniform rule of naturalization, and uniform laws on the subject of bankruptcies throughout the United States;

5. To coin money, regulate the value thereof, and of foreign coin, and fix the standard of weights and measures;

6. To provide for the punishment of counterfeiting the securities and current coin of the United States;

7. To establish post-offices and post-roads;

8. To promote the progress of science and useful arts, by securing for limited times to authors and inventors the exclusive right to their respective writings and discoveries;

9. To constitute tribunals inferior to the Supreme Court;

10. To define and punish piracies and felonies committed on the high seas, and offenses against the law of nations;

11. To declare war, grant letters of marque and reprisal, and make rules concerning captures on land and water;

12. To raise and support armies, but no appropriation of money to that use shall be for a longer term than two years;

13. To provide and maintain a navy;

14. To make rules for the government and regulation of the land and naval forces;

15. To provide for calling forth the militia to execute the laws of the Union, suppress insurrections and repel invasions;

16. To provide for organizing, arming, and disciplining the militia, and for governing such part of them as may be employed in the service of the United States, reserving to the States respectively, the appointment of the officers, and the authority of training the militia according to the discipline prescribed by Congress;

17. To exercise exclusive legislation in all cases what-

soever, over such district (not exceeding ten miles square) as may, by cession of particular States, and the acceptance of Congress, become the seat of the Government of the United States, and to exercise like authority over all places purchased by the consent of the Legislature of the State in which the same shall be, for the erection of forts, magazines, arsenals, dockyards, and other needful buildings; —And

18. To make all laws which shall be necessary and proper for carrying into execution the foregoing powers, and all other powers vested by this Constitution in the Government of the United States, or in any department or officer thereof.

Section 9—Provision as to migration or importation of certain persons. Habeas Corpus, Bills of attainder, etc. Taxes, how apportioned. No export duty. No commercial preference. Money, how drawn from Treasury, etc. No titular nobility. Officers not to receive presents, etc.

1. The migration or importation of such persons as any of the States now existing shall think proper to admit, shall not be prohibited by the Congress prior to the year one thousand eight hundred and eight, but a tax or duty may be imposed on such importation, not exceeding ten dollars for each person.

2. The privilege of the writ of habeas corpus shall not be suspended, unless when in cases of rebellion or invasion the public safety may require it.

3. No bill of attainder or ex post facto law shall be passed.

4. No capitation, or other direct, tax shall be laid, unless in proportion to the census or enumeration herein before directed to be taken.

5. No tax or duty shall be laid on articles exported from any State.

6. No preference shall be given by any regulation of commerce or revenue to the ports of one State over those of another; nor shall vessels bound to, or from, one State, be obliged to enter, clear, or pay duties in another.

7. No money shall be drawn from the Treasury, but in consequence of appropriations made by law; and a regular statement and account of the receipts and expenditures of all public money shall be published from time to time.

8. No title of nobility shall be granted by the United States; and no person holding any office of profit or trust under them, shall, without the consent of the Congress, accept of any present, emolument, office, or title, of any kind whatever, from any king, prince, or foreign state.

Section 10—States prohibited from the exercise of certain powers.

1. No State shall enter into any treaty, alliance, or confederation; grant letters of marque and reprisal; coin money; emit bills of credit; make anything but gold and silver coin a tender in payment of debts; pass any bill of attainder, ex post facto law, or law impairing the obligation of contracts, or grant any title of nobility.

2. No State shall, without the consent of the Congress, lay any imposts or duties on imports or exports, except what may be absolutely necessary for executing its inspection laws: and the net produce of all duties and imposts, laid by any State on imports or exports, shall be for the use of the Treasury of the United States; and all such laws shall be subject to the revision and control of the Congress.

3. No State shall, without the consent of Congress, lay any duty of tonnage, keep troops, or ships of war in time of peace, enter into any agreement or compact with another State, or with a foreign power, or engage in war, unless actually invaded, or in such imminent danger as will not admit of delay.

ARTICLE II.

Section 1—President: his term of office. Electors of President; number and how appointed. Electors to vote on same day. Qualification of President. On whom his duties devolve in case of his removal, death, etc. President's compensation. His oath of office.

1. The Executive power shall be vested in a President of the United States of America. He shall hold his office during the term of four years, and together with the Vice President, chosen for the same term, be elected as follows

2. Each State shall appoint, in such manner as the Legislature thereof may direct, a number of electors, equal to the whole number of Senators and Representatives to which the State may be entitled in the Congress: but no Senator or

Representative, or person holding an office of trust or profit under the United States, shall be appointed an elector.

(The electors shall meet in their respective States, and vote by ballot for two persons, of whom one at least shall not be an inhabitant of the same State with themselves. And they shall make a list of all the persons voted for, and of the number of votes for each; which list they shall sign and certify, and transmit sealed to the seat of the Government of the United States, directed to the President of the Senate. The President of the Senate shall, in the presence of the Senate and House of Representatives, open all the certificates, and the votes shall then be counted. The person having the greatest number of votes shall be the President, if such number be a majority of the whole number of electors appointed; and if there be more than one who have such majority, and have an equal number of votes, then the House of Representatives shall immediately choose by ballot one of them for President; and if no person have a majority, then from the five highest on the list the said House shall in like manner choose the President. But in choosing the President, the votes shall be taken by States, the representation from each State having one vote; a quorum for this purpose shall consist of a member or members from two-thirds of the States, and a majority of all the States shall be necessary to a choice. In every case, after the choice of the President, the person having the greatest number of votes of the electors shall be the Vice President. But if there should remain two or more who have equal votes, the Senate shall choose from them by ballot the Vice President.)

(This clause has been superseded by the 12th amendment.)

3. The Congress may determine the time of choosing the electors, and the day on which they shall give their votes; which day shall be the same throughout the United States.

4. No person except a natural born citizen, or a citizen of the United States, at the time of the adoption of this Constitution, shall be eligible to the office of President; neither shall any person be eligible to that office who shall not have attained to the age of thirty-five years, and been fourteen years a resident within the United States.

(For qualification of the Vice President, see Article XII of the amendments.)

5. In case of the removal of the President from office, or of his death, resignation, or inability to discharge the powers and duties of the said office, the same shall devolve on the Vice President, and the Congress may by law provide for the case of removal, death, resignation or inability, both of the President and Vice-President, declaring what officer shall then act as President, and such officer shall act accordingly, until the disability be removed, or a President shall be elected.

(This clause has been amended by Article XX, sections 3 and 4, of the amendments.)

6. The President shall, at stated times, receive for his services, a compensation, which shall neither be increased nor diminished during the period for which he shall have been elected, and he shall not receive within that period any other emolument from the United States, or any of them.

7. Before he enter on the execution of his office, he shall take the following oath or affirmation:

"I do solemnly swear (or affirm) that I will faithfully execute the office of President of the United States, and will to the best of my ability, preserve, protect, and defend the Constitution of the United States."

Section 2—President to be Commander-in-Chief. He may require opinions of Cabinet Officers, etc., may pardon. Treaty-making power. Nomination of certain officers. When President may fill vacancies.

1. The President shall be Commander-in-Chief of the Army and Navy of the United States, and of the militia of the several States, when called into the actual service of the United States; he may require the opinion, in writing, of the principal officer in each of the executive departments, upon any subject relating to the duties of their respective offices, and he shall have power to grant reprieves and pardons for offenses against the United States, except in cases of impeachment.

2. He shall have power, by and with the advice and consent of the Senate, to make treaties, provided two-thirds of the Senators present concur; and he shall nominate, and by and with the advice and consent of the Senate, shall appoint ambassadors, other public ministers and consuls,

judges of the Supreme Court, and all other officers of the United States, whose appointments are not herein otherwise provided for, and which shall be established by law: but the Congress may by law vest the appointment of such inferior officers, as they think proper, in the President alone, in the courts of law, or in the heads of departments.

3. The President shall have power to fill up all vacancies that may happen during the recess of the Senate, by granting commissions, which shall expire at the end of their next session.

Section 3—President shall communicate to Congress. He may convene and adjourn Congress, in case of disagreement, etc. Shall receive Ambassadors, execute laws, and commission officers.

He shall from time to time give to the Congress information of the state of the Union, and recommend to their consideration such measures as he shall judge necessary and expedient; he may, on extraordinary occasions, convene both Houses, or either of them, and in case of disagreement between them, with respect to the time of adjournment, he may adjourn them to such time as he shall think proper; he shall receive ambassadors and other public ministers; he shall take care that the laws be faithfully executed, and shall commission all the officers of the United States.

Section 4—All civil offices forfeited for certain crimes.

The President, Vice President, and all civil officers of the United States, shall be removed from office on impeachment for and conviction of treason, bribery, or other high crimes and misdemeanors.

ARTICLE III

Section 1—Judicial powers. Tenure. Compensation.

The judicial power of the United States, shall be vested in one Supreme Court, and in such inferior courts as the Congress may from time to time ordain and establish. The judges, both of the Supreme and inferior courts, shall hold their offices during good behavior, and shall at stated times, receive for their services, a compensation, which shall not be diminished during their continuance in office.

Section 2—Judicial power; to what cases it extends. Original jurisdiction of Supreme Court Appellate. Trial by jury, etc. Trial, where.

1. The judicial power shall extend to all cases, in law and equity, arising under this Constitution, the laws of the United States, and treaties made, or which shall be made, under their authority; to all cases affecting ambassadors, other public ministers and consuls; to all cases of admiralty and maritime jurisdiction; to controversies to which the United States shall be a party; to controversies between two or more States; between a State and citizens of another State; between citizens of different States, between citizens of the same State claiming lands under grants of different States, and between a State, or the citizens thereof, and foreign states, citizens, or subjects.

(This section is abridged by Article XI of the amendments.)

2. In all cases affecting ambassadors, other public ministers and consuls, and those in which a State shall be party, the Supreme Court shall have original jurisdiction. In all the other cases before mentioned, the Supreme Court shall have appellate jurisdiction, both as to law and fact, with such exceptions, and under such regulations as the Congress shall make.

3. The trial of all crimes, except in cases of impeachment, shall be by jury; and such trial shall be held in the State where the said crimes shall have been committed; but when not committed within any State, the trial shall be at such place or places as the Congress may by law have directed.

Section 3—Treason defined. Proof of. Punishment of.

1. Treason against the United States, shall consist only in levying war against them, or in adhering to their enemies, giving them aid and comfort. No person shall be convicted of treason unless on the testimony of two witnesses to the same overt act, or on confession in open court.

2. The Congress shall have power to declare the punishment of treason, but no attainder of treason shall work corruption of blood, or forfeiture except during the life of the person attainted.

ARTICLE IV.

Section 1—Each State to give credit to the public acts, etc., of every other State.

Full faith and credit shall be given in each State to the public acts, records, and judicial proceedings of every other State. And the Congress may by general laws prescribe the manner in which such acts, records and proceedings shall be proved, and the effect thereof.

Section 2—Privileges of citizens of each State. Fugitives from Justice to be delivered up. Persons held to service having escaped, to be delivered up.

1. The citizens of each State shall be entitled to all privileges and immunities of citizens in the several States.

2. A person charged in any State with treason, felony, or other crime, who shall flee from justice, and be found in another State, shall on demand of the Executive authority of the State from which he fled, be delivered up, to be removed to the State having jurisdiction of the crime.

3. No person held to service or labor in one State, under the laws thereof, escaping into another, shall in consequence of any law or regulation therein, be discharged from such service or labor, but shall be delivered up on claim of the party to whom such service or labor may be due.

(See 13th amendment.)

Section 3—Admission of new States. Power of Congress over territory and other property.

1. New States may be admitted by the Congress into this Union; but no new State shall be formed or erected within the jurisdiction of any other state; nor any State be formed by the junction of two or more States, or parts of States, without the consent of the Legislatures of the States concerned as well as of the Congress.

2. The Congress shall have power to dispose of and make all needful rules and regulations respecting the territory or other property belonging to the United States; and nothing in this Constitution shall be so construed as to prejudice any claims of the United States, or of any particular State.

Section 4—Republican form of government guaranteed. Each State to be protected.

The United States shall guarantee to every State in this Union a Republican form of government, and shall protect each of them against invasion; and on application of the Legislature, or of the Executive (when the Legislature cannot be convened) against domestic violence.

ARTICLE V.

Constitution: how amended, Proviso.

The Congress, whenever two-thirds of both Houses shall deem it necessary, shall propose amendments to this constitution, or, on the application of the Legislatures of two-thirds of the several States, shall call a convention for proposing amendments, which, in either case, shall be valid to all intents and purposes, as part of this Constitution, when ratified by the Legislatures of three-fourths of the several states, or by conventions in three-fourths thereof, as the one or the other mode of ratification may be proposed by the Congress; provided that no amendment which may be made prior to the year one thousand eight hundred and eight shall in any manner affect the first and fourth clauses in the Ninth Section of the First Article; and that no State, without its consent, shall be deprived of its equal suffrage in the Senate.

ARTICLE VI.

Certain debts, etc., declared valid, Supremacy of Constitution, treaties, and laws of the United States. Oath to support Constitution, by whom taken. No religious test.

1. All debts contracted and engagements entered into, before the adoption of this Constitution, shall be as valid against the United States under this Constitution, as under the Confederation.

2. This Constitution, and the laws of the United States which shall be made in pursuance thereof; and all treaties made, or which shall be made, under the authority of the United States, shall be the supreme law of the land; and the judges in every State shall be bound thereby, any thing in the Constitution or laws of any State to the contrary notwithstanding.

3. The Senators and Representatives before mentioned, and the ..embers of the several State Legislatures, and all executive and judicial officers, both of the United States and of the several States, shall be bound by oath or affirmation, to support this Constitution; but no religious test shall ever be required as a qualification to any office or public trust under the United States.

ARTICLE VII.
What ratification shall establish Constitution.

The ratification of the Conventions of nine States shall, be sufficient for the establishment of this Constitution between the States so ratifying the same.

Done in convention by the unanimous consent of the States present the Seventeenth day of September in the year of our Lord one thousand seven hundred and eighty seven, and of the independence of the United States of America the Twelfth. In witness whereof we have hereunto subscribed our names.

George Washington. President and deputy from Virginia.

New Hampshire—John Langdon, Nicholas Gilman.
Massachusetts—Nathaniel Gorham, Rufus King.
Connecticut—Wm. Saml. Johnson, Roger Sherman.
New York—Alexander Hamilton.
New Jersey—Wil: Livingston, David Brearley, Wm. Paterson, Jona: Dayton.
Pennsylvania—B. Franklin, Thomas Mifflin, Robt. Morris, Geo. Clymer, Thos. FitzSimons, Jared Ingersoll, James Wilson, Gouv. Morris.
Delaware—Geo: Read, Gunning Bedford, Jun., John Dickinson, Richard Bassett: Jaco: Broom.
Maryland—James McHenry, Daniel of Saint Thomas Jenifer, Danl. Carroll.
Virginia—John Blair, James Madison, Jr.
North Carolina—Wm. Blount, Rich'd. Dobbs, Spaight, Hugh Williamson.
South Carolina—J. Rutledge, Charles Cotesworth Pinckney, Charles Pinckney, Pierce Butler.
Georgia—William Few. Abr. Baldwin.
Attest: William Jackson, Secretary.

Ten Original Amendments—The Bill of Rights

In force December 15, 1791

The First Congress, at its first session in the City of New York, Sept. 25, 1789, submitted to the states 12 amendments to clarify certain individual and state rights not named in the Constitution. They are generally called the Bill of Rights.

Influential in framing these amendments was the Declaration of Rights of Virginia, written by George Mason (1725-1792) in 1776. Mason, a Virginia delegate to the Constitutional Convention, did not sign the Constitution and opposed its ratification on the ground that it did not sufficiently oppose slavery or safeguard individual rights.

In the preamble to the resolution offering the proposed amendments, Congress said: "The conventions of a number of the States having at the time of their adopting the Constitution, expressed a desire, in order to prevent misconstruction or abuse of its powers, that further declaratory and restrictive clauses should be added, and as extending the ground of public confidence in the government will best insure the beneficent ends of its institution, be it resolved," etc.

Ten of these amendments now commonly known as one to 10 inclusive, but in reality three to 12 inclusive were ratified by the states as follows: New Jersey, Nov. 20, 1789; Maryland, December 19, 1789; North Carolina, Dec. 22, 1789; South Carolina, Jan. 19, 1790; New Hampshire, Jan. 25. 1790; Delaware. Jan. 28, 1790; New York, Feb. 24, 1790; Pennsylvania, March 10, 1790; Rhode Island, June 7, 1790; Vermont, Nov. 3, 1791; Virginia, Dec. 15, 1791; Massachusetts, March 2, 1939; Georgia, March 18. 1939; Connecticut, April 19, 1939. These original 10 ratified amendments follow as Article I to X inclusive.

The two of the original proposed amendments which were not ratified by the necessary number of States related, the first, to apportionment of Representatives; the second, to compensation of members.

ARTICLE I.
Religious Establishment Prohibited. Freedom of Speech, of the Press, and Right to Petition.

Congress shall make no law respecting an establishment of religion, or prohibiting the free exercise thereof; or abridging the freedom of speech, or of the press; or the right of the people peaceably to assemble, and to petition the Government for a redress of grievances.

Article II.
Right to Keep and Bear Arms.

A well-regulated militia, being necessary to the security of a free State, the right of the people to keep and bear arms, shall not be infringed.

ARTICLE III.
Conditions for Quarters for Soldiers.

No soldier shall, in time of peace be quartered in any house, without the consent of the owner, nor in time of war, but in a manner to be prescribed by law.

ARTICLE IV.
Right of Search and Seizure Regulated.

The right of the people to be secure in their persons, houses, papers, and effects, against unreasonable searches and seizures, shall not be violated, and no warrants shall issue, but upon probable cause, supported by oath or affirmation, and particularly describing the place to be searched, and the persons or things to be seized.

ARTICLE V.
Provisions concerning prosecution. Trial and Punishment—Private Property not to Be Taken for Public Use Without Compensation.

No person shall be held to answer for a capital, or otherwise infamous crime, unless on a presentment or indictment of a Grand Jury, except in cases arising in the land or naval forces, or in the militia, when in actual service in time of war or public danger; nor shall any person be subject for the same offense to be twice put in jeopardy of life or limb;

nor shall be compelled in any criminal case to be a witness against himself, nor be deprived of life, liberty, or property, without due process of law; nor shall private property be taken for public use without just compensation.

ARTICLE VI.
Right to Speedy Trial, Witnesses, etc.

In all criminal prosecutions, the accused shall enjoy the right to a speedy and public trial, by an impartial jury of the State and district wherein the crime shall have been committed, which district shall have been previously ascertained by law, and to be informed of the nature and cause of the accusation; to be confronted with the witnesses against him; to have compulsory process for obtaining witnesses in his favor, and to have the assistance of counsel for his defense.

ARTICLE VII.
Right of Trial by Jury.

In suits at common law, where the value in controversy shall exceed twenty dollars, the right of trial by jury shall be preserved, and no fact tried by a jury shall be otherwise re-examined in any court of the United States, than according to the rules of the common law.

ARTICLE VIII.
Excessive Bail or Fines and Cruel Punishment Prohibited.

Excessive bail shall not be required, nor excessive fines imposed, nor cruel and unusual punishments inflicted.

ARTICLE IX.
Rule of Construction of Constitution.

The enumeration in the Constitution, of certain rights, shall not be construed to deny or disparage others retained by the people.

ARTICLE X.
Rights of States Under Constitution.

The powers not delegated to the United States by the Constitution, nor prohibited by it to the States, are reserved to the States respectively, or to the people.

Amendments Since the Bill of Rights

ARTICLE XI.
Judicial Powers Construed.

The following amendment was proposed to the Legislature of the several States by the Third Congress on the 4th of March 1794, and was declared to have been ratified in a message from the President to Congress, dated Jan. 8, 1798.

The judicial power of the United States shall not be construed to extend to any suit in law or equity, commenced or prosecuted against one of the United States by citizens of another State, or by citizens or subjects of any foreign state.

(It was on Jan. 5, 1798, that Secretary of State Pickering received from 12 of the States authenticated ratifications, and informed President John Adams of that fact.)

As a result of later research in the Department of State, it is now established that the Eleventh Amendment became part of the Constitution on Feb. 7, 1795, for on that date it had been ratified by twelve States as follows:

(1) New York, (March 27, 1794); (2) Rhode Island, (March 31, 1794); (3) Connecticut, (May 8, 1794); (4) New Hampshire, (June 16, 1794); (5) Massachusetts, (June 26, 1794); (6) Vermont, (between Oct. 9, 1794 and Nov. 9, 1794); (7) Virginia, (Nov. 18, 1794); (8) Georgia, (Nov. 29, 1794); (9) Kentucky, (Dec. 7 1794); (10) Maryland, (Dec. 26, 1794); (11) Delaware (Jan. 23, 1795); (12) North Carolina, (Feb. 7, 1795).

On June 1, 1796, more than a year after the Eleventh Amendment had become a part of the Constitution (but before anyone was officially aware of this), Tennessee had been admitted as a State; but not until Oct. 16, 1797, was a certified copy of the resolution of Congress proposing the amendment sent to the Governor of Tennessee (John Sevier) by Secretary of State Pickering, whose office was then at Trenton, New Jersey, because of the epidemic of yellow fever at Philadelphia; it seems, however, that the Legislature of Tennessee took no action on the Eleventh Amendment, owing doubtless to the fact that public announcement of its adoption was made soon thereafter.

Besides the necessary twelve States, one other, South Carolina, ratified the Eleventh Amendment, but this action was not taken until Dec. 4, 1797; the two remaining States, New Jersey and Pennsylvania, failed to ratify.

ARTICLE XII.
Manner of Choosing President and Vice-President.

Proposed by Congress Dec. 9, 1803; ratification completed June 15, 1804.

The Electors shall meet in their respective States and vote by ballot for President and Vice-President, one of whom, at least, shall not be an inhabitant of the same State with themselves; they shall name in their ballots the person voted for as President, and in distinct ballots the person voted for as Vice-President, and they shall make distinct lists of all persons voted for as President, and of all persons voted for as Vice-President, and of the number of votes for each, which lists they shall sign and certify, and transmit sealed to the seat of the Government of the United States, directed to the President of the Senate; the President of the Senate shall, in the presence of the Senate and House of Representatives, open all the certificates and the votes shall then be counted;—The person having the greatest number of votes for President, shall be the President, if such number be a majority of the whole number of Electors appointed; and if no person have such majority, then from the persons having the highest numbers not exceeding three on the list of those voted for as President, the House of Representatives shall choose immediately, by ballot, the President. But in choosing the President, the votes shall be taken by States, the representation from each State having one vote; a quorum for this purpose shall consist of a member or members from two-thirds of the States, and a majority of all the States shall be necessary to a choice. And if the House of Representatives shall not choose a President whenever the right of choice shall devolve upon them, before the fourth day of March next following, then the Vice-President shall act as President, as in case of the death or other constitutional disability of the President. The person having the

greatest number of votes as Vice-President, shall be the Vice-President, if such number be a majority of the whole number of Electors appointed, and if no person have a majority, then from the two highest numbers on the list, the Senate shall choose the Vice-President; a quorum for the purpose shall consist of two-thirds of the whole number of Senators, and a majority of the whole number shall be necessary to a choice. But no person constitutionally ineligible to the office of President shall be eligible to that of Vice-President of the United States.

TITLES OF NOBILITY—*Not Ratified*

Congress, May 1, 1810, proposed to the States the following Amendment to the Constitution:

"If any citizen of the United States shall accept, claim, receive, or retain any title of nobility or honor, or shall, without the consent of Congress, accept and retain any present, pension, office, or emolument of any kind whatever, from any emperor, king, prince or foreign power, such person shall cease to be a citizen of the United States and shall be incapable of holding any office of trust or profit under them or either of them."

It was ratified by Maryland, (Dec. 25, 1810); Kentucky, (Jan. 31, 1811); Ohio, (Jan. 31, 1811); Delaware, (Feb. 2, 1811); Pennsylvania, (Feb. 6, 1811); New Jersey, (Feb. 13, 1811); Vermont, (Oct. 24, 1811); Tennessee, (Nov. 21, 1811); Georgia, (Dec. 13, 1811); North Carolina, (Dec. 23, 1811); Massachusetts, (Feb. 27, 1812); New Hampshire, (Dec. 10, 1812).

Rejected by New York (Senate), (March 12, 1811); Connecticut, (May session, 1813); South Carolina approved by Senate Nov. 28, 1811, reported unfavorably in House and not further considered Dec. 7, 1813; Rhode Island (Sept. 15, 1814). The amendment failed, not having sufficient ratifications.

THE CORWIN AMENDMENT—*Not Ratified*

Congress March 2, 1861, in a joint resolution signed by President James Buchanan, proposed to the States the following Amendments to the Constitution:

"No amendment shall be made to the Constitution which will authorize or give to Congress the power to abolish or interfere, within any State, with the domestic institutions thereof, including that of persons held to labor or service by the laws of said State."

Ratified by Ohio, (March 13, 1861); Maryland, (Jan. 10, 1862); Illinois (convention), (Feb. 14, 1862). The amendment failed, for lack of a sufficient number of ratifications.

THE RECONSTRUCTION AMENDMENTS

The 13th, 14th, and 15th Amendments to the Constitution are commonly known as the Reconstruction Amendments, inasmuch as they followed the Civil War, and were drafted by Republicans who were bent on imposing their own policy of reconstruction on the South. Post-bellum legislatures there—Mississippi, South Carolina, Georgia, for example—had set up laws which, it was charged, were contrived to perpetuate Negro slavery under other names.

ARTICLE XIII.
Slavery Abolished.

Proposed by Congress Jan. 31, 1865; ratification completed Dec. 6, 1865.

The Amendment when first proposed by a resolution in Congress, was passed by the Senate, 38 to 6, on April 8, 1864, but was defeated in the House, 95 to 66 on June 15, 1864. On reconsideration by the House, on Jan. 31, 1865, the resolution passed, 119 to 56. It was approved by President Lincoln on Feb. 1, 1865, although the Supreme Court had decided, in 1798, that the President has nothing to do with the proposing of amendments to the Constitution, or their adoption.

1. Neither slavery nor involuntary servitude, except as a punishment for crime whereof the party shall have been duly convicted, shall exist within the United States, or any place subject to their jurisdiction.

2. Congress shall have power to enforce this article by appropriate legislation.

ARTICLE XIV
Citizenship Rights Not to Be Abridged.

The following amendment was proposed to the Legislatures of the several States by the Thirty-ninth Congress (June 13, 1866), and was declared to have been ratified in a proclamation by the Secretary of State (July 28,1868).
The 14th amendment was adopted only by virtue of ratification subsequent to earlier rejections. Newly constituted legislatures in both North Carolina and South Carolina, respectively (July 4 and 9, 1868), ratified the proposed amendment, although earlier legislatures had rejected the proposal. The Secretary of State issued a proclamation, which, though doubtful as to the effect of attempted withdrawals by Ohio and New Jersey, entertained no doubt as to the validity of the ratification by North and South Carolina. The following day (July 21, 1868), Congress passed a resolution which declared the 14th Amendment to be a part of the Constitution and directed the Secretary of State so to promulgate it. The Secretary waited, however, until the newly constituted legislature of Georgia had ratified the amendment, subsequent to an earlier rejection, before the promulgation of the ratification of the new amendment.

1. All persons born or naturalized in the United States, and subject to the jurisdiction thereof, are citizens of the United States and of the State wherein they reside. No State shall make or enforce any law which shall abridge the privileges or immunities of citizens of the United States; nor shall any State deprive any person of life, liberty, or property, without due process of law; nor deny to any person within its jurisdiction the equal protection of the laws.

2. Representatives shall be apportioned among the several States according to their respective numbers, counting the whole number of persons in each State, excluding Indians not taxed. But when the right to vote at any election for the choice of Electors for President and Vice-President of the United States, Representatives in Congress, the executive and judicial officers of a State, or the members of the Legislature thereof, is denied to any of the male inhabitants of such State, being twenty-one years of age, and citizens of the United States, or in any way abridged, except for participation in rebellion, or other crime, the basis of representation therein shall be reduced in the proportion which the number of such male citizens shall bear to the whole number of male citizens twenty-one years of age in such State.

3. No person shall be a Senator or Representative in Congress, or Elector of President and Vice-President, or hold any office, civil or military, under the United States, or under any State, who, having previously taken an oath, as a member of Congress, or as an officer of the United States, or as a member of any State Legislature, or as an executive or judicial officer of any State, to support the Constitution of the United States, shall have engaged in insurrection or rebellion against the same, or given aid or comfort to the enemies thereof. But Congress may by a vote of two-thirds of each House, remove such disability.

4. The validity of the public debt of the United States, authorized by law, including debts incurred for payment of pensions and bounties for services in suppressing insurrection or rebellion, shall not be questioned. But neither the United States nor any State shall assume or pay any debt or obligation incurred in aid of insurrection or rebellion against the United States, or any claim for the loss or emancipation of any slave; but all such debts, obligations and claims shall be held illegal and void.

5. The Congress shall have power to enforce, by appropriate legislation, the provisions of this article.

ARTICLE XV.
Equal Rights for White and Colored Citizens.

The following amendment was proposed to the Legislatures of the several States by the Fortieth Congress (Feb. 26, 1869), and was declared to have been ratified in a proclamation by the Secretary of State (March 30, 1870).
1. The right of citizens of the United States to vote shall not be denied or abridged by the United States or by any

State on account of race, color, or previous condition of servitude.

2. The Congress shall have power to enforce this article by appropriate legislation.

ARTICLE XVI.
Income Taxes Authorized.

Proposed by Congress July 12, 1909; ratification completed Feb. 3, 1913.
The Congress shall have power to lay and collect taxes on incomes, from whatever sources derived, without apportionment among the several States, and without regard to any census or enumeration.

ARTICLE XVII.
United States Senators to Be Elected by Direct Popular Vote.

Proposed by Congress May 13, 1912; ratification completed Apr. 8, 1913.
1. The Senate of the United States shall be composed of two Senators from each State, elected by the people thereof, for six years; and each Senator shall have one vote. The electors in each State shall have the qualifications requisite for electors of the most numerous branch of the State Legislatures.

2. When vacancies happen in the representation of any State in the Senate, the executive authority of such State shall issue writs of election to fill such vacancies: Provided, That the Legislature of any State may empower the Executive thereof to make temporary appointments until the people fill the vacancies by election as the Legislature may direct.

3. This amendment shall not be so construed as to affect the election or term of any Senator chosen before it becomes valid as part of the Constitution.

ARTICLE XVIII.
Liquor Prohibition Amendment.

Proposed by Congress Dec. 18, 1917; ratification completed Jan. 16, 1919.
1. After one year from the ratification of this article the manufacture, sale, or transportation of intoxicating liquors within, the importation thereof into, or the exportation thereof from the United States and all territory subject to the jurisdiction thereof for beverage purposes is hereby prohibited.

2. The Congress and the several States shall have concurrent power to enforce this article by appropriate legislation.

3. This article shall be inoperative unless it shall have been ratified as an amendment to the Constitution by the Legislatures of the several States, as provided in the Constitution, within seven years from the date of the submission hereof to the States by the Congress.

The total vote in the Senates of the various States was 1,310 for, 237 against—84.6% dry. In the lower houses of the States the vote was 3,782 for, 1,035 against-78.5% dry.

The amendment untimately was adopted by all the States except Connecticut and Rhode Island.

Repealed by Article XXI effective Dec. 5, 1933.

ARTICLE XIX.
Giving Nation-Wide Suffrage to Women.

Proposed by Congress June 4, 1919; ratification certified by Secretary of State Aug. 26, 1920.
1. The right of citizens of the United States to vote shall not be denied or abridged by the United States or by any State on account of sex.

2. Congress shall have power to enforce this Article by appropriate legislation.

CHILD LABOR—*Not Ratified*

Congress, in a joint resolution passed by the House of Representatives Apr. 26, 1924, and by the Senate June 2, 1924, submitted to the states the following proposed amendment:
1. The Congress shall have power to limit, regulate and

prohibit the labor of persons under 18 years of age.

2. The power of the several States is unimpaired by this article except that the operation of State laws shall be suspended to the extent necessary to give effect to legislation enacted by the Congress.

It was ratified by Arizona (1925), Arkansas (1924), California (1925), Colorado (1931), Idaho (1935), Illinois (1933), Indiana (1935), Iowa (1933), Kansas (1937), Kentucky (1937), Maine (1933), Michigan (1933), Minnesota (1933), Montana (1927), Nevada (1937), New Hampshire (1933), New Jersey (1933), New Mexico (1937), North Dakota (1933), Ohio (1933), Oklahoma (1933), Oregon (1933), Pennsylvania (1933), Utah (1935), Washington (1933), West Virginia (1933), Wisconsin (1925), Wyoming (1925). With ratification by 36 states necessary, only these 28 had ratified it by 1938, when Congress passed the Fair Labor Standards Act, prohibiting labor of children under 16 in industries whose products entered interstate commerce. When the constitutionality of this act was upheld the proposed child labor amendment became virtually a dead issue.

ARTICLE XX.

Terms of President and Vice-President to Begin on Jan. 20; Those of Senators and Representatives

Proposed by Congress Mar. 2, 1932; ratification completed Jan. 23, 1933.

1. The terms of the President and Vice-President shall end at noon on the 20th day of January, and the terms of Senators and Representatives at noon on the 3rd day of January, of the years in which such terms would have ended if this article had not been ratified; and the terms of their successors shall then begin.

2. The Congress shall assemble at least once in every year, and such meeting shall begin at noon on the 3rd day of January, unless they shall by law appoint a different day.

3. If, at the time fixed for the beginning of the term of the President, the President elect shall have died, the Vice-President elect shall become President. If a President shall not have been chosen before the time fixed for the beginning of his term, or if the President elect shall have failed to qualify, then the Vice-President elect shall act as President until a President shall have qualified; and the Congress may by law provide for the case wherein neither a President elect nor a Vice-President shall have qualified, declaring who shall then act as President, or the manner in which one who is to act shall be selected, and such person shall act accordingly until a President or Vice-President shall have qualified.

4. The Congress may by law provide for the case of the death of any of the persons from whom the House of Representatives may choose a President whenever the right of choice shall have devolved upon them, and for the case of the death of any of the persons from whom the Senate may choose a Vice-President whenever the right of choice shall have devolved upon them.

5. Sections 1 and 2 shall take effect on the 15th day of October following the ratification of this article (Oct., 1933).

6. This article shall be inoperative unless it shall have been ratified as an amendment to the Constitution by the Legislatures of three-fourths of the several States within seven years from the date of its submission.

ARTICLE XXI.

Repeal of the Eighteenth (Prohibition) Amendment by Conventions in the States.

Proposed by Congress Feb. 20, 1933; ratification completed Dec. 5, 1933.

1. The eighteenth article of amendment to the Constitution of the United States is hereby repealed.

2. The transportation or importation into any State, Territory, or Possession of the United States for delivery or use therein of intoxicating liquors, in violation of the laws thereof, is hereby prohibited.

3. This article shall be inoperative unless it shall have been ratified as an amendment to the Constitution by conventions in the several States, as provided in the Constitution, within seven years from the date of the submission hereof to the States by the Congress.

ARTICLE XXII.

Limiting Presidential Terms of Office.

Proposed by Congress Mar. 21, 1947; ratification completed Feb. 27, 1951.

1. No person shall be elected to the office of the President more than twice, and no person who has held the office of President, or acted as President, for more than two years of a term to which some other person was elected President shall be elected to the office of the President more than once. But this Article shall not apply to any person holding the office of President when this Article was proposed by the Congress, and shall not prevent any person who may be holding the office of President, or acting as President, during the term within which this Article becomes operative from holding the office of President or acting as President during the remainder of such term.

2. This article shall be inoperative unless it shall have been ratified as an amendment to the Constitution by the Legislatures of three-fourths of the several States within seven years from the date of its submission to the States by the Congress.

ARTICLE XXIII.

Presidential Vote for District of Columbia

Proposed by Congress June 17, 1960; ratification completed Mar. 29, 1961.

1. The District constituting the seat of Government of the United States shall appoint in such manner as the Congress may direct:

A number of electors of President and Vice President equal to the whole number of Senators and Representatives in Congress to which the District would be entitled if it were a State, but in no event more than the least populous State; they shall be in addition to those appointed by the States, but they shall be considered, for the purposes of the election of President and Vice President, to be electors appointed by a State; and they shall meet in the District and perform such duties as provided by the twelfth article of amendment.

2. The Congress shall have power to enforce this article by appropriate legislation.

ARTICLE XXIV

Barring Poll Tax in Federal Elections

Proposed by Congress Aug. 27, 1962; ratification completed Jan. 23, 1964.

1. The right of citizens of the United States to vote in any primary or other election for President or Vice President, for electors for President or Vice President, or for Senator or Representative in Congress, shall not be denied or abridged by the United States or any State by reason of failure to pay any poll tax or other tax.

2. The Congress shall have power to enforce this article by appropriate legislation.

ARTICLE XXV

Presidential Disability and Succession

Proposed by Congress July 6, 1965; ratification completed Feb. 10, 1967.

1. In case of the removal of the President from office or of his death or resignation, the Vice President shall become President.

2. Whenever there is a vacancy in the office of the Vice President, the President shall nominate a Vice President who shall take office upon confirmation by a majority vote of both houses of Congress.

3. Whenever the President transmits to the President pro tempore of the Senate and the Speaker of the House of Representatives his written declaration that he is unable to discharge the powers and duties of his office, and until he transmits to them a written declaration to the contrary, such powers and duties shall be discharged by the Vice President as Acting President.

4. Whenever the Vice President and a majority of either the principal officers of the executive departments or of

such other body as Congress may by law provide, transmit to the President pro tempore of the Senate and the Speaker of the House of Representatives their written declaration that the President is unable to discharge the powers and duties of his office, the Vice President shall immediately assume the powers and duties of the office as Acting President.

Thereafter, when the President transmits to the President pro tempore of the Senate and the Speaker of the House of Representatives his written declaration that no inability exists, he shall resume the powers and duties of his office unless the Vice President and a majority of either the principal officers of the executive department or of such other body as Congress may by law provide, transmit within four days to the President pro tempore of the Senate and the Speaker of the House of Representatives their written declaration that the President is unable to discharge the powers and duties of his office. Thereupon Congress shall decide the issue, assembling within forty-eight hours for that purpose if not in session. If the Congress, within twenty-one days after receipt of the latter written declaration, or, if Congress is not in session, within twenty-one days after Congress is required to assemble, determines by two-thirds vote of both houses that the President is unable to discharge the powers and duties of his office, the Vice President shall continue to discharge the same as Acting President; otherwise, the President shall resume the powers and duties of his office.

Article XXVI
Lowering Voting Age to 18 yrs.
Proposed by Congress Mar. 23, 1971; ratification completed June 30, 1971.

1. The right of citizens of the United States, who are 18 years of age or older, to vote shall not be denied or abridged by the United States or any state on account of age.
2. The Congress shall have the power to enforce this article by appropriate legislation.

Article XXVII
Equal Rights
Proposed by Congress Mar. 22, 1972; ratification completed, as of June 1, 1973, by 30 states, rejected by 12; needs total of 38 for adoption.

1. Equality of rights under the law shall not be denied or abridged by the United States or by any State on account of sex.
2. The Congress shall have the power to enforce, by appropriate legislation, the provisions of this article.
3. This amendment shall take effect two years after the date of ratification.

Independence Hall, American Patriotic Shrine

Independence Hall is the central and main building of a group located in Philadelphia, located in Independence Square and facing Chestnut St. It is connected by arcades with two 2-story buildings, the East and West Wings, and two separate corner buildings. Of the latter Congress Hall is at Sixth St., and Old City Hall at Fifth St.

Independence Hall originally was the State House. It was begun in 1732, and completed in 1759. The East and West Wings were intended to house offices. Tower and spire were completed by June 1753.

The Pennsylvania Assembly occupied Assembly Hall in 1735, before the whole structure was completed. In 1775 it gave the use of the room to the Second Continental Congress. Here, on June 16, 1775, George Washington accepted command of the Continental Army. Here the Declaration of Independence was adopted on July 4, 1776; the Articles of Confederation and Perpetual Union were signed beginning on July 9, 1778, and the Constitution of the United States was framed by the Constitutional Convention in 1787.

Congress Hall, at the west end of the group, was erected in 1787 and was the seat of the United States Congress from 1790 to 1800, when the Congress moved to Washington, D.C. The Court House, or Old City Hall, at the east end, was built in 1790 for the municipal courts, and was the first seat of the United States Supreme Court.

Independence Hall and the other buildings in Independence Square form the nucleus around which has been developed the Independence National Historical Park, established in 1956. Much restoration work has been done.

The Monroe Doctrine; Its Origin and Meaning

President James Monroe, in his annual message to Congress on Dec. 2, 1823, made the statement of policy since known as the Monroe Doctrine. Its major assertion is that the United States would consider as dangerous to its peace and safety any attempt of the European powers to extend their political system to any portion of the western hemisphere.

Balancing this statement in the same message is Monroe's declaration that in regard to Europe it is the policy of the United States "not to interfere in the internal concerns of any of its powers, to consider the government de facto as the legitimate (one) for us . . ."

Statesmen besides Monroe associated in the development of the Doctrine were John Quincy Adams, Secretary of State; Richard Rush, American Minister in London, and George Canning, British Secretary for Foreign Affairs. Consulted were Thomas Jefferson, John C. Calhoun, Secretary of War, and William Wirt, Attorney General.

History of Its Origin. The message grew out of two complications. The first was the decree of Russia reserving exclusively to Russian subjects the whole of the northwest coast of North America, from the Bering Straits to 51° N. Lat. and from the Aleutians to Siberia, for commerce, whaling, fishery and other industries, and prohibiting any foreign ship from approaching within 100 miles, on penalty of seizure. Secretary Adams rejected this, and after negotiations Russia reversed itself. In the message President Monroe said the American continents, "by the free and independent condition which they have assumed and maintain, are henceforth not to be considered as subjects for colonization by any European power."

The other part originated in the threat of foreign encroachment on Latin-American states, the independence of which had been recognized by the United States. George Canning, British Foreign Secretary, on Aug. 20, 1823, suggested to Rush, the American Minister, that the British and American governments declare "in the face of the world" their attitude toward the Spanish-American countries. He believed the two governments entertained similar views, and cited that the British conceived the recovery of the colonies by Spain to be hopeless; thought recognition of them as independent states to be a matter "of time and circumstances"; would not interfere with amicable negotiation between them and their mother country (Spain); did not wish to possess any portion of them or see it go to any other power with indifference.

Canning thought such a declaration might forestall any military attempts to coerce Latin America. When the United States did not act by October he addressed a similar statement to the French ambassador in London, Prince de Polignac, and received the assurance that France did not intend to take any of the Spanish colonies in America.

Secretary Adams, writing to Minister Rush Nov. 29, 1823, endorsed Canning's views but urged as indispensable the recognition of the independence of the new governments by Britain. He thought a unilateral statement better, and the joint declaration was never issued.

Lincoln's Address at Gettysburg, 1863

Fourscore and seven years ago our fathers brought forth on this continent a new nation, conceived in liberty and dedicated to the proposition that all men are created equal.

Now we are engaged in a great civil war, testing whether that nation or any nation so conceived and so dedicated can long endure. We are met on a great battle field of that war. We have come to dedicate a portion of that field, as a final resting-place for those who here gave their lives that that nation might live. It is altogether fitting and proper that we should do this.

But, in a larger sense, we can not dedicate—we can not consecrate—we can not hallow—this ground. The brave men, living and dead, who struggled here, have consecrated it, far above our poor power to add or detract. The world will little note, nor long remember, what we say here, but it can never forget what they did here. It is for us the living, rather, to be dedicated here to the unfinished work which they who fought here have thus far so nobly advanced. It is rather for us to be here dedicated to the great task remaining before us —that from these honored dead we take increased devotion to that cause for which they gave the last full measure of devotion—that we here highly resolve that these dead shall not have died in vain—that this nation, under God, shall have a new birth of freedom—and that government of the people, by the people, for the people, shall not perish from the earth.

President Lincoln delivered his address at the dedication of the military cemetery at Gettysburg, Pa., Nov. 19, 1863. The battle had been fought July 1-3, 1863. He was preceded by Edward Everett, former president of Harvard, pro[...] of Greek and Latin from Massachusetts, then 69 and one of the nation's great orators. Everett gave a full resume of the battle, Lincoln's speech was so short that the photographer did not get his camera adjusted in time. The report that newspapers ignored Lincoln's address is not entirely accurate; Everett's address swamped their columns, but the greatness of Lincoln's speech was immediately recognized. Everett wrote him: "I should be glad if I could flatter myself that I came as near the central idea of the occasion in two hours as you did in two minutes."

Five copies of the Gettysburg address in Lincoln's hand are extant. The first and second draft, prepared in Washington and Gettysburg just before delivery, are in the Library of Congress. The third draft, written at the request of Everett to be sold at a fair in New York for the benefit of soldiers, was given the Illinois State Historical Library by popular subscription.

The fourth copy was written out by Lincoln for George Bancroft, the historian, and remained in custody of the Bancroft family until 1929, when it was acquired by Mrs. Nicholas H. Noyes, of Indianapolis, Ind. In 1949 Mrs.

Noyes presented this copy to the Cornell University Library, Ithaca, N.Y. The fifth copy, usually described as the clearest and best, was also made by Lincoln for George Bancroft, for facsimile reproduction in a volume to be sold for the benefit of soldiers and sailors in Baltimore, where Bancroft lived. It is the second Bancroft copy. It passed to Bancroft's stepchildren, named Bliss, and was sold for $54,000 by the estate of Dr. William J. A. Bliss in New York April 27, 1949, to Oscar B. Cintas, former Cuban ambassador to the United States. He died in May, 1957, and willed it to the Lincoln room of the White House, where 'it was placed in March, 1959. Lincoln's spelling of battle field and can not as separated words in that version is reproduced above.

Sen. John Sherman Cooper (R.-Ky.) president of the Lincoln Sesquicentennial Commission, on June 17, 1959 presented a Latin translation of Lincoln's Gettysburg Address to the Apostolic Delegation of the Roman Catholic Church, in Washington, D. C. It was engrossed on vellum and was to be sent to Pope John XXIII for deposit in the Vatican Library. The presentation took place in the presence of Government officials and members of the Diplomatic Corps. The translation was made by the Rt. Rev. Edwin Ryan of White Plains, N. Y. The Latin Version was ordered printed in the Congressional Record.

Washington's Letter on Bigotry and Persecution

During a tour of various New England states in 1790, then President George Washington was greeted by various leaders in Newport, R.I. Among the clergy was Moses Seixas, the Warden of the Hebrew Congregation, who greeted Washington and praised the new government for its opposition to bigotry. Washington acknowledged the greeting in a letter to the congregation:

Gentlemen:

While I received with much satisfaction, your address replete with expressions of affection and esteem; I rejoice in the opportunity of assuring you, that I shall always retain a grateful remembrance of the cordial welcome I experienced in my visit to Newport, from all classes of Citizens.

The reflection on the days of difficulty and danger which are past is rendered the more sweet, from a consciousness that they are succeeded by days of uncommon prosperity and security. If we have wisdom to make the best use of the advantages with which we are now favored, we cannot fail, under the just administration of a good Government, to become a great and happy people.

The Citizens of the United States of America have a right to applaud themselves for having given to mankind examples of an enlarged and liberal policy; a policy worthy of imitation. All possess alike liberty of conscience and immunities of citizenship. It is now no more that toleration is spoken of, as if it was

by the indulgence of one class of people, that another enjoyed the exercise of their inherent natural rights. For happily the Government of the United States, which gives to bigotry no sanction, to persecution no assistance, requires only that they who live under its protection, should demean themselves as good citizens, in giving it on all occasions their effectual support.

It would be inconsistent with the frankness of my character not to avow that I am pleased with your favorable opinion of my administration, and fervent wishes for my felicity. May the Children of the Stock of Abraham, who dwell in this land, continue to merit and enjoy the good will of the other Inhabitants; while everyone shall sit in safety under his own vine and fig tree, and there shall be none to make him afraid. May the father of all mercies scatter light and not darkness in our paths, and make us all in our several vocations useful here, and in his own due time and way everlastingly happy.

Go. Washington

Election Statistics

Popular and Electoral Vote for President 1972

Compiled by The World Almanac from official returns of the States.
Blank and void ballots are excluded from all totals.

States	Electoral Vote Nixon	McGovern	Republican Nixon	Democrat McGovern	American Schmitz	Soc. Labor Fisher	Soc. Worker Jenness or Reed	Communist Hall	Others**	Total
Ala. . . .	9		728,701	256,923	11,918				8,551	1,006,093
Alaska	3		55,349	32,967	6,903					95,219
Ariz. . .	6		402,812	198,540	21,208		30,945†			653,505
Ark. . . .	6		445,751	198,899	3,016					647,666
Calif. . .	45		4,602,096	3,475,847	232,554	197	574	373	56,218	8,367,859
Colo. . .	7		597,189	329,980	17,269	4,361	666	432	3,981	953,878
Conn. .	8		810,763	555,498	17,239				777	1,384,277
Del. . . .	3		140,357	92,298	2,638				238	235,516
D. of C.	. . .	3	35,226	127,627			316	252		163,421
Fla. . . .	17		1,857,759	718,117					7,407	2,583,283
Ga. . . .	12		881,496	289,529	2,288	3			1,456	1,174,722
Hawaii	4		168,865	101,409						270,274
Idaho .	4		199,384	80,826	28,869		397		903	310,379
Ill.	26		2,788,179	1,913,472	2,471	12,344		4,541	2,229	4,723,236
Ind. . . .	13		1,405,154	708,568		1,688	5,575		4,544	2,125,529
Iowa . .	8		706,207	496,206	22,056	195	488	272	520	1,225,944
Kansas	7		619,812	270,287	21,808				4,188	916,095
Ky.	9		676,446	371,159	17,627		685	464	1,118	1,067,499
La.	10		686,852	298,142	52,099		14,398			1,051,491
Me. . . .	4		256,458	160,584					229	417,271
Md. . . .	10		829,305	505,781	18,726					1,353,812
Mass. .	. . .	14	1,112,078	1,332,540	22,877	129	10,600	46	486	2,458,756
Mich. .	21		1,961,721	1,459,435	63,381	2,437	1,603	1,210		3,489,727
Minn. .	10		898,269	802,346	31,407	4,261	940	662	3,767	1,741,652
Miss. . .	7		505,125	126,782	11,598		2,458			645,963
Mo. . . .	12		1,154,058	698,531						1,852,589
Mont. .	4		183,976	120,197	13,430					317,603
Nebr. .	5		406,298	169,991					817	577,225
Nev. . .	3		115,750	66,016						181,766
N.H. . .	4		213,724	116,435	3,386		368		142	334,055
N.J. . . .	17		1,845,502	1,102,211	34,378	4,544	2,233	1,263	7,098	2,997,229
N.M. . .	4		235,606	141,084	8,767		474			385,931
N.Y. . . .	41		4,192,778	2,951,084		4,530	7,797	5,641		7,161,830
N.C. . . .	13		1,054,889	438,705	25,018					1,518,612
N.D. . .	3		174,109	100,384	5,646		288	87		280,514
Ohio . .	25		2,441,827	1,558,889	80,067	7,107		6,437	460	4,094,787
Okla. . .	8		759,025	247,147	23,728					1,029,900
Ore. . . .	6		486,686	392,760	46,211				2,289	927,946
Pa. . . .	27		2,714,521	1,796,951	70,593		4,639	2,686	2,715	4,592,105
R.I. . . .	4		218,290	191,981			729			411,000
S.C. . . .	8		477,044	186,824	10,075				17	673,960
S.D. . . .	4		166,476	139,945			994			307,415
Tenn. .	10		813,147	357,293	30,373				369	1,201,182
Texas .	26		2,298,896	1,154,289	6,039		8,664		3,393	3,471,281
Utah . .	4		323,643	126,284	28,549					478,476
Vt. . . .	3		117,149	68,174			296		1,328	186,947
Va.* . .	11		988,493	438,887	19,721	9,918				1,457,019
Wash. .	9		837,135	568,334	58,906	1,102	623	566	4,181	1,470,847
W. Va. .	6		484,964	277,435						762,399
Wisc. .	11		989,430	810,174	47,525	998	506	663	3,594	1,852,890
Wyo. . .	3		100,464	44,358	748					145,570
Total U.S.	521	17	47,165,234	29,168,110	1,101,052	53,814	97,256	25,595	123,015	77,734,195

* One elector in Virginia voted for John Hospers and Theodora Nathan.
** **Dr. Benjamin Spock, People's Party:** Calif. 55,167, Col. 2,403, Idaho 903, Ind. 4,544, Ky. 1,118, Mass. 101, Minn. 2,805, N.J. 5,355, Wash. 2,644, Wis. 2,701. Total 77,741. In Vermont, under label of Liberty Party, 1,010. **John Mahalchik, America First:** New Jersey 1,743. **Earle H. Munn, Prohibition:** Alabama 8,551, Calif. 50, Colo. 467, Dela. 238, Kansas 4,188. Total 13,494. **John Hospers, Libertarian:** Calif. 980, Colo. 1,111, Mass. 43, Wash. 1,537. Total 3,671. **Gabriel Green, Universal Party:** Calif. 21, Iowa 199. Total 220. **Scattered:** Conn. 777, Fla. 7,407, Ga. 1,456, Ill. 2,229, Iowa 321, Maine 229, Minn. 962, Nebr. 817, N.H. 142, Ohio 460, Ore. 2,289, Pa. 2,715, S.C. 17, Tenn. 369, Texas 3,393, Vt. 318, Wis. 893. Total 25,136.
† Due to a confused ballot, thousands of Arizonians mistakenly voted for two candidates. See County-by-county returns.

Major Parties' Popular and Electoral Vote for President

(F) Federalist; (D) Democrat; (R) Republican; (DR) Democrat Republican; (NR) National Republican; (W) Whig; (P) People's; (PR) Progressive; (SR) States' Rights; Asterisk (*)—See notes below

Year	President Elected	Popular	Elec.	Losing Candidate	Popular	Elec.
1789	George Washington (F)	Unknown	69	No opposition		
1792	George Washington (F)	Unknown	132	No opposition		
1796	John Adams (F)	Unknown	71	Thomas Jefferson (DR)	Unknown	68
1800	Thomas Jefferson (DR)	Unknown	73	Aaron Burr (DR)	Unknown	73
	Elected by House of Representatives (due to tie vote)					
1804	Thomas Jefferson (DR)	Unknown	162	Charles Pinckney (F)	Unknown	14
1808	James Madison (DR)	Unknown	122	Charles Pinckney (F)	Unknown	47
1812	James Madison (DR)	Unknown	128	DeWitt Clinton (F)	Unknown	89
1816	James Monroe (DR)	Unknown	183	Rufus King (F)	Unknown	34
1820	James Monroe (DR)	Unknown	231	John Quincy Adams (DR)	Unknown	1
1824	John Quincy Adams (NR)	105,321	84	Andrew Jackson (D)	155,872	99
	Elected by House of Representatives (no			Henry Clay (DR)	46,587	37
	candidate having polled a majority)			William H. Crawford (DR)	44,282	41
1828	Andrew Jackson (D)	647,231	178	John Quincy Adams (NR)	509,097	83
1832	Andrew Jackson (D)	687,502	219	Henry Clay (DR)	530,189	49
	First national Presidential convention					
1836	Martin Van Buren (D)	762,678	170	William H. Harrison (W)	548,007	73
1840*	William H. Harrison (W)	1,275,017	234	Martin Van Buren (D)	1,128,702	60
1844	James K. Polk (D)	1,337,243	170	Henry Clay (W)	1,299,068	105
1848*	Zachary Taylor (W)	1,360,101	163	Lewis Cass (D)	1,220,544	127
1852	Franklin Pierce (D)	1,601,474	174	Winfield Scott (W)	1,386,578	42
1860	Abraham Lincoln (R)	1,866,352	180	Stephen A. Douglas (D)	1,375,157	12
				John C. Breckinridge (D)	845,763	72
				John Bell (Const. Union)	589,581	39
1864*	Abraham Lincoln (R)	2,216,067	212	George McClellan (D)	1,808,725	21
1868	Ulysses S. Grant (R)	3,015,071	214	Horatio Seymour (D)	2,709,615	80
1872	Ulysses S. Grant (R)	3,597,070	286	Horace Greeley (D-L)	2,834,079	....
1876*	Rutherford B. Hayes (R)	4,033,950	185	Samuel J. Tilden (D)	4,284,757	184
1880*	James A. Garfield (R)	4,449,053	214	Winfield S. Hancock (D)	4,442,030	155
1881	Grover Cleveland (D)	4,911,017	219	James G. Blaine (R)	4,848,334	182
1888*	Benjamin Harrison (R)	5,444,337	233	Grover Cleveland (D)	5,540,050	168
1892	Grover Cleveland (D)	5,554,414	277	Benjamin Harrison (R)	5,190,802	145
				James Weaver (P)	1,027,329	22
1896	William McKinley (R)	7,035,638	271	William J. Bryan (D-P)	6,467,946	176
1900*	William McKinley (R)	7,219,530	292	William J. Bryan (D)	6,358,071	155
1904	Theodore Roosevelt (R)	7,628,834	336	Alton B. Parker (D)	5,084,491	140
1908	William H. Taft (R)	7,679,006	321	William J. Bryan (D)	6,409,106	162
1912	Woodrow Wilson (D)	6,286,214	435	Theodore Roosevelt (Pr)	4,216,020	88
				William H. Taft (R)	3,483,922	8
1916	Woodrow Wilson (D)	9,129,606	277	Charles E. Hughes (R)	8,538,221	254
1920*	Warren G. Harding (R)	16,152,200	404	James M. Cox (D)	9,147,353	127
1924	Calvin Coolidge (R)	15,725,016	382	John W. Davis (D)	8,385,586	136
				Robert M. LaFollette(Pr)	4,822,856	13
1928	Herbert Hoover (R)	21,392,190	444	Alfred E. Smith (D)	15,016,443	87
1932	Franklin D. Roosevelt (D)	22,821,857	472	Herbert Hoover (R)	15,761,841	59
				Norman Thomas(Socialist)	884,781	....
1936	Franklin D. Roosevelt (D)	27,751,597	523	Alfred Landon (R)	16,679,583	8
1940	Franklin D. Roosevelt (D)	27,243,466	449	Wendell Willkie (R)	22,304,755	82
1944*	Franklin D. Roosevelt (D)	25,602,505	432	Thomas E. Dewey (R)	22,006,278	99
1948	Harry S. Truman (D)	24,105,812	303	Thomas E. Dewey (R)	21,970,065	189
				J. Strom Thurmond(SR)	1,169,021	39
				Henry A. Wallace (PR)	1,157,172	....
1952	Dwight D. Eisenhower (R)	33,936,252	442	Adlai E. Stevenson (D)	27,314,992	89
1956*	Dwight D. Eisenhower (R)	35,585,316	457	Adlai E. Stevenson (D)	26,031,322	73
1960*	John F. Kennedy (D)	34,227,096	303	Richard M. Nixon (R)	34,108,546	219
1964	Lyndon B. Johnson (D)	43,126,506	486	Barry M. Goldwater (R)	27,176,799	52
1968	Richard M. Nixon (R)	31,785,480	301	Hubert H. Humphrey (D)	31,275,166	191
				George C. Wallace (3rd party)	9,906,473	46
1972	Richard M. Nixon (R)	45,767,218	520	George S. McGovern (D)	28,357,668	17

1840—President Harrison died on April 4, 1841, and Vice President Tyler became President.

1848—President Taylor died in office on July 9, 1850, was succeeded by Vice President Fillmore.

1864—President Lincoln was shot April 14, 1865 at Ford's Theatre, Washington, by actor J. Wilkes Booth, and died April 15, whereupon Vice President Andrew Johnson became President.

1872—Greeley died Nov. 29, 1872. His electoral votes were split among 4 individuals.

1876—Fla., La., Ore., and S.C. election returns were disputed. Congress in joint session (Mar. 2, 1877) declared Hayes and Wheeler elected President and Vice-President.

1880—President Garfield was shot July 2, 1881, at Washington, D. C., by Charles J. Guiteau of New York and died Sept. 19, whereupon Vice President Chester A. Arthur became President.

1888—On the result of the popular vote Cleveland had more votes than Harrison but the 233 electoral votes cast for Harrison against the 168 for Cleveland elected Harrison president.

1900—President McKinley was shot, Sept. 6, 1901, at the Pan American Exposition, Buffalo, N. Y. He died on Sept. 14, and Vice President Theodore Roosevelt became President. The assassin, Leon Czolgosz, was executed Oct. 29, 1901.

1920—President Harding died at San Francisco, Calif., Aug. 2, 1923, succeeded by Vice President Coolidge.

1944—President Roosevelt died at Warm Springs, Ga., on April 12, 1945, succeeded by Vice President Truman.

1956—Democrats elected 74 electors but one from Alabama refused to vote for Stevenson, voted for Walter B. Jones.

1960—Sen. Harry F. Byrd (D-Va.) received 15 electoral votes. President Kennedy was shot and fatally wounded by an assassin Nov. 22, 1963, in Dallas, Tex.; he was succeeded by Lyndon B. Johnson.

1972—John Hospers of Calif. and Theodora Nathan of Ore., received one vote from an elector of Virginia.

PRESIDENTIAL ELECTION RETURNS BY STATES
Compiled by the World Almanac from official state returns.
Some County figures may not add to total shown.

Alabama

County	1968 Hum- phrey (D)	Nixon (R)	Wal- lace (I)	1972 McGov- ern (D)	Nixon (R)
Autauga	1,553	606	5,523	1,593	5,367
Baldwin	1,821	2,154	14,167	2,923	15,104
Barbour	1,898	386	5,491	1,846	4,985
Bibb	652	263	3,746	837	3,332
Blount	331	2,013	6,536	1,582	6,486
Bullock	1,964	190	2,161	2,321	2,178
Butler	1,240	500	5,601	1,401	4,685
Calhoun	4,146	3,061	19,211	5,832	20,364
Chambers	1,358	1,082	7,885	2,076	8,716
Cherokee	462	343	4,773	1,182	3,179
Chilton	566	1,602	6,611	1,356	7,349
Choctaw	1,641	176	4,250	1,934	3,055
Clarke	1,717	488	6,168	2,031	5,256
Clay	256	706	4,048	507	3,948
Cleburne	160	485	3,314	581	3,420
Coffee	1,071	682	8,885	2,160	9,076
Colbert	2,291	1,727	11,341	4,811	11,215
Conecuh	1,151	186	3,828	1,042	3,214
Coosa	623	330	2,830	773	2,672
Covington	791	831	11,419	1,547	9,278
Crenshaw	726	209	4,513	1,085	3,129
Cullman	1,115	4,964	11,063	3,571	14,390
Dale	862	607	8,109	1,594	8,346
Dallas	6,516	1,246	8,798	5,427	8,644
DeKalb	1,274	5,314	8,144	3,759	9,434
Elmore	1,745	801	9,038	1,891	8,461
Escambia	1,491	680	8,474	1,598	8,883
Etowah	4,613	4,351	21,416	7,372	20,851
Fayette	676	827	4,683	836	4,240
Franklin	588	2,524	5,909	1,840	5,877
Geneva	380	284	7,871	1,049	5,851
Greene	2,229	180	1,555	3,235	1,404
Hale	2,003	266	2,934	1,779	2,859
Henry	955	84	4,233	853	3,414
Houston	1,488	974	13,872	2,358	12,622
Jackson	1,022	1,191	8,504	2,985	6,202
Jefferson	55,845	39,752	106,233	57,288	135,095
Lamar	302	364	5,229	766	3,283
Lauderdale	2,166	2,952	13,467	5,112	14,410
Lawrence	650	580	6,253	1,416	4,433
Lee	2,803	2,366	7,721	3,622	11,571
Limestone	889	870	8,430	2,079	6,188
Lowndes	1,127	234	1,822	2,559	1,990
Macon	4,450	257	1,619	3,636	1,931
Madison	8,004	13,213	29,823	13,108	38,899
Marengo	3,479	457	5,185	2,645	5,156
Marion	365	1,492	6,415	986	5,927
Marshall	955	2,725	12,742	3,894	12,090
Mobile	18,615	10,509	61,673	20,694	62,639
Monroe	1,673	375	5,217	1,636	5,155
Montgomery	12,088	6,746	27,202	12,723	35,353
Morgan	1,878	3,043	16,841	5,004	18,100
Perry	2,457	308	2,768	2,718	2,800
Pickens	1,434	321	4,549	1,933	4,071
Pike	1,565	658	6,038	1,624	5,690
Randolph	666	839	5,103	1,330	4,427
Russell	2,707	704	7,584	2,644	6,034
St. Clair	869	1,635	7,050	1,859	6,952
Shelby	1,105	1,706	7,736	1,538	9,390
Sumter	2,336	303	2,158	2,737	2,686
Talladega	3,099	1,935	13,505	4,567	12,763
Tallapoosa	1,331	1,205	9,043	2,113	8,535
Tuscaloosa	5,556	3,822	18,611	8,272	21,172
Walker	1,971	2,628	14,416	3,724	14,581
Washington	902	200	4,545	1,096	3,282
Wilcox	1,658	237	2,511	3,254	2,641
Winston	258	2,174	3,032	779	4,971
Totals	**196,579**	**146,923**	**691,425**	**256,923**	**728,701**

ALABAMA VOTE SINCE 1924
1924 (Pres.), Davis, Dem., 112,966; Coolidge, Rep., 45,005; LaFollette, Prog., 8,084; Faris, Proh., 538.
1928 (Pres.), Smith, Dem., 127,797; Hoover, Rep., 120,725; Thomas, Soc., 460.
1932 (Pres.), Roosevelt, Dem., 207,910; Hoover, Rep., 34,675; Foster, Com., 406; Thomas, Soc., 2,030; Upshaw, Proh., 13.
1936 (Pres.), Roosevelt, Dem., 238,195; Landon, Rep., 35,358; Colvin, Proh., 719; Browder, Com., 679; Lemke, Union, 549; Thomas, Soc., 242.
1940 (Pres.), Roosevelt, Dem., 250,726; Willkie, Rep., 42,174; Babson, Proh., 698; Browder, Com., 509; Thomas, Soc., 100.
1944 (Pres.), Roosevelt, Dem., 198,918; Dewey, Rep., 44,540; Watson, Proh., 1,095; Thomas, Soc., 190.
1948 (Pres.), Thurmond, States' Rights, 171,443; Dewey,

Rep., 40,930; Wallace, Prog., 1,522; Watson, Proh., 1,085.
1952 (Pres.), Eisenhower, Rep., 149,231; Stevenson, Dem., 275,075; Hamblen, Proh., 1,814.
1956 (Pres.), Stevenson, Dem., 290,844; Eisenhower, Rep., 195,694; Independent electors, 20,323.
1960 (Pres.), Kennedy, Dem., 324,050; Nixon, Rep., 237,981; Faubus, States' Rights, 4,367; Decker, Proh., 2,106; King, Afro-Americans, 1,485; Scattering, 236.
1964 (Pres.), Dem., 209,848 (electors unpledged); Goldwater, Rep., 479,085; Scattering, 105.
1968 (Pres.), Nixon, Rep. 146,923; Humphrey, Dem., 196,579; Wallace, 3rd party, 691,425; Munn, Proh. 4,022.
1972 (Pres.), Nixon, Rep., 728,701; McGovern, Dem. 219,108 plus 37,815 Natl. Demo. Party of Alabama; Schmitz, Conservative 11,918; Munn, Proh. 8,551.

Alaska

Election District	1968 Hum- phrey (D)	Nixon (R)	Wal- lace (I)	1972 McGov- ern (D)	Nixon (R)
No. 1	1,871	2,151	517	1,526	2,529
No. 2	828	940	112	967	1,386
No. 3	1,236	1,110	151	1,393	1,549
No. 4	2,767	2,532	365	2,968	4,277
No. 5	646	590	136	903	1,689
No. 6	635	878	282	849	2,384
No. 7	893	1,075	350	2,854	4,527
No. 8	13,005	13,833	3,831	2,454	5,275
No. 9	449	371	88	2,501	6,759
No. 10	1,717	1,671	892	2,854	6,882
No. 11	862	986	247	1,337	2,686
No. 12	363	419	69	727	1,117
No. 13	553	591	100	178	293
No. 14	1,147	835	137	843	1,042
No. 15	848	964	305	1,235	919
No. 16	4,569	5,743	1,863	1,004	902
No. 17	962	785	98	5,535	7,672
No. 18	943	849	104	640	1,202
No. 19	559	274	64	1,515	1,114
*	558	1,003	313	† 1,044	† 1,145
Totals	**35,411**	**37,600**	**10,024**	**32,967**	**55,349**

*Ballot cast for president only by voters ineligible to vote in local elections. †20th Election district.

ALASKA VOTE SINCE 1960
1960 (Pres.), Kennedy, Dem., 29,809; Nixon, Rep., 30,953.
1964 (Pres.), Johnson, Dem., 44,329; Goldwater, Rep., 22,930.
1968 (Pres.), Nixon, Rep., 37,600; Humphrey, Dem., 35,411; Wallace, 3rd party, 10,024.
1972 (Pres.), Nixon, Rep., 55,349; McGovern, Dem., 32,967; Schmitz, American, 6,903.

Arizona

County	1968 Hum- phrey (D)	Nixon (R)	Wal- lace (I)	1972 McGov- ern (D)	Nixon (R)
Apache	1,668	2,092	402	3,145	3,394
Cochise	6,597	7,619	2,393	6,023	11,706
Coconino	3,504	6,765	1,049	6,250	10,611
Gila	4,831	3,610	1,222	4,295	5,673
Graham	1,726	2,327	859	1,863	3,575
Greenlee	2,434	1,026	276	2,013	1,758
Maricopa	86,204	162,262	24,941	95,135	244,593
Mohave	2,109	3,208	883	2,588	6,755
Navajo	2,930	4,596	1,438	4,003	6,999
Pima	39,786	49,479	7,221	56,223	73,154
Pinal	7,409	6,883	1,869	6,404	10,584
Santa Cruz	1,557	1,702	242	1,866	2,137
Yavapai	3,989	8,296	1,837	3,977	12,277
Yuma	5,770	6,856	1,941	4,755	9,596
Totals	**170,514**	**266,721**	**46,573**	**198,540**	**402,812**

ARIZONA VOTE SINCE 1924
1924 (Pres.) Coolidge, Rep., 30,516; Davis, Dem., 26,235; LaFollette, Prog., 17,210.
1928 (Pres.), Hoover, Rep., 52,533; Smith, Dem., 38,537; Foster, Com., 184.
1932 (Pres.), Roosevelt, Dem., 79,264; Hoover, Rep., 36,104; Thomas, Soc., 2,030; Foster, Com., 406.
1936 (Pres.), Roosevelt, Dem., 86,722; Landon, Rep., 33,433; Lemke, Union, 3,307; Colvin, Proh., 384; Thomas, Soc., 317.
1940 (Pres.), Roosevelt, Dem., 95,267; Willkie, Rep., 54,030; Babson, Proh., 742.
1944 (Pres.), Roosevelt, Dem., 80,926; Dewey, Rep., 56,287; Watson, Proh. 421.

1948 (Pres.), Truman, Dem., 95,251; Dewey, Rep., 77,597; Wallace, Prog., 3,310; Watson, Proh., 786; Teichert, Soc. Lab., 121.
1952 (Pres.), Eisenhower, Rep., 152,042; Stevenson, Dem., 108,528.
1956 (Pres.), Eisenhower, Rep., 176,990; Stevenson, Dem., 112,880; Andrews, Ind. 303.
1960 (Pres.), Kennedy, Dem., 176,781; Nixon, Rep., 221,241; Hass, Soc. Lab., 469.
1964 (Pres.), Johnson, Dem., 237,753; Goldwater, Rep., 242,535; Hass, Soc. Labor, 482.
1968 (Pres.), Nixon, Rep., 266,721; Humphrey, Dem., 170,514; Wallace, 3rd party, 46,573; McCarthy, New Party, 2,751; Halstead, Soc. Worker, 85; Cleaver, Peace and Freedom, 217; Blomen, Soc. Labor, 75.
1972 (Pres.), Nixon, Rep., 402,812; McGovern, Dem., 198,540; Schmitz, American, 21,208; Soc. Worker, 30,945. (Due to ballot peculiarities in 3 counties (particularly Pima), thousands of voters cast ballots for the Socialist Workers Party *and* one of the major candidates. Court ordered both votes counted as official.

Arkansas

County	1968 Humphrey (D)	1968 Nixon (R)	1968 Wallace (I)	1972 McGovern (D)	1972 Nixon (R)
Arkansas	2,019	1,806	1,775	1,018	4,440
Ashley	1,952	3,461	1,513	2,677	6,754
Baxter					
Benton	4,088	8,104	4,036	4,083	14,621
Boone	1,907	3,349	2,169	1,862	5,484
Bradley	1,457	802	2,546	1,368	3,218
Calhoun	688	287	1,215	707	1,298
Carroll	1,298	2,596	1,174	1,401	3,565
Chicot	2,595	865	2,187	1,469	2,858
Clark	2,733	1,642	2,776	2,741	4,173
Clay	1,663	2,410	2,285	1,933	4,381
Cleburne	1,202	1,301	1,657	1,400	2,870
Cleveland	407	312	1,751	734	1,837
Columbia	2,487	1,916	3,843	2,193	5,801
Conway	2,560	1,973	1,958	3,009	4,187
Craighead	3,738	5,047	6,742	5,843	11,312
Crawford	1,578	2,723	2,917	1,520	6,974
Crittenden	3,475	2,454	4,657	3,246	7,971
Cross	1,555	1,093	3,056	1,221	3,743
Dallas	1,253	672	1,722	1,402	2,152
Desha	2,270	972	2,474	1,665	3,385
Drew	1,324	1,040	2,307	1,168	3,334
Faulkner	3,756	2,791	4,375	4,604	6,746
Franklin	1,149	1,333	2,111	1,252	3,678
Fulton	1,019	1,198	1,080	960	2,030
Garland	5,655	7,674	6,955	5,207	15,602
Grant	852	627	2,194	1,147	2,414
Greene	2,197	2,859	3,021	2,263	6,128
Hempstead	2,322	1,783	3,136	2,047	4,963
Hot Spring	2,137	1,780	4,139	2,872	5,378
Howard	1,061	1,286	1,660	1,069	2,682
Independence	2,289	2,782	2,770	2,630	5,076
Izard	948	931	1,109	1,108	2,001
Jackson	2,051	1,356	3,525	2,092	4,196
Jefferson*	5,798	3,163	4,698	10,346	16,888
Johnson	1,747	1,667	1,693	2,045	4,107
Lafayette	1,208	672	1,704	952	2,460
Lawrence	1,613	1,788	2,813	1,751	3,981
Lee	2,135	834	1,907	1,907	3,540
Lincoln	1,209	408	2,084	1,115	2,318
Little River	1,095	745	1,473	1,091	2,550
Logan	1,998	2,341	2,160	1,956	4,964
Lonoke	2,014	1,677	4,002	2,504	5,298
Madison	1,574	2,320	1,028	1,889	3,372
Marion	990	1,385	877	1,108	2,331
Miller	2,929	2,662	5,062	2,855	8,355
Mississippi	4,993	4,369	6,147	3,544	10,931
Monroe	1,783	804	2,406	1,578	2,897
Montgomery	649	885	992	688	1,555
Nevada	1,308	840	1,773	1,179	2,513
Newton	852	1,467	567	831	1,924
Ouachita	4,603	2,209	5,031	3,931	6,620
Perry	634	740	916	810	1,445
Phillips	5,039	2,154	4,279	4,283	6,235
Pike	656	1,104	1,535	798	2,316
Poinsett	1,672	2,140	4,074	1,908	7,010
Polk	1,290	2,094	1,812	1,120	3,609
Pope	2,578	3,319	2,769	3,302	6,917
Prairie	875	693	2,014	873	2,186
Pulaski	27,597	26,709	25,844	33,611	57,576
Randolph	1,367	1,237	1,610	1,525	2,578
St. Francis	3,284	1,608	4,254	2,674	5,692
Saline	3,111	2,614	5,569	4,503	7,972
Scott	1,000	1,162	1,238	771	2,424
Searcy	724	1,909	726	853	3,163
Sebastian	6,320	12,073	8,649	5,770	25,219
Sevier	1,129	1,217	1,501	1,048	2,526
Sharp	1,025	1,136	1,299	1,154	2,677
Stone	698	987	979	958	1,989
Union	4,426	4,919	7,853	3,531	11,925
Van Buren	1,149	1,325	1,224	1,594	2,622
Washington	6,131	10,640	5,092	7,108	17,523
White	3,198	3,887	5,054	4,161	8,701
Woodruff	1,270	625	1,734	1,183	1,989
Yell	1,513	1,819	1,949	1,669	3,310
Totals	184,901	189,062	235,627	198,899	445,751

*Official vote only. Actual vote was higher.

ARKANSAS VOTE SINCE 1924

1924 (Pres.), Davis, Dem., 84,795; Coolidge, Rep., 40,564; LaFollette, Prog., 13,173.
1928 (Pres.), Smith, Dem., 119,196; Hoover, Rep., 77,751; Thomas, Soc., 429; Foster, Com., 317.
1932 (Pres.), Roosevelt, Dem., 189,602; Hoover, Rep., 28,467; Thomas, Soc., 1,269; Harvey, Ind., 1,049; Foster, Com., 175.
1936 (Pres.), Roosevelt, Dem., 146,765; Landon, Rep., 32,039; Thomas, Soc., 446; Browder, Com., 164; Lemke, Union, 4.
1940 (Pres.), Roosevelt, Dem., 158,622; Willkie, Rep., 42,121; Babson, Proh., 793; Thomas, Soc., 305.
1944 (Pres.), Roosevelt, Dem., 148,965; Dewey, Rep., 63,551; Thomas, Soc. 438.
1948 (Pres.), Truman, Dem., 149,659; Dewey, Rep., 50,959; Thurmond, States' Rights, 40,068; Thomas, Soc., 1,037; Wallace, Prog., 751; Watson, Proh., 1.
1952 (Pres.), Eisenhower, Rep., 177,155; Stevenson, Dem., 226,300; Hamblen, Proh., 886; MacArthur, Christian Nationalist, 458; Hass, Soc., ...
1956 (Pres.), Stevenson, Dem., 213,277; Eisenhower, Rep., 186,287; Andrews, Ind., 7,008.
1960 (Pres.), Kennedy, Dem., 215,049; Nixon, Rep., 184,508; National States' Rights, 28,952.
1964 (Pres.), Johnson, Dem., 314,197; Goldwater, Rep., 243,264; Kasper, Nat'l. States Rights, 2,965.
1968 (Pres.), Nixon, Rep., 189,062; Humphrey, Dem., 184,901; Wallace, 3rd party, 235,627.
1972 (Pres.), Nixon, Rep. 445,751; McGovern, Dem., 198,899; Schmitz, Amer. Party, 3,016.

California

County	1968 Humphrey (D)	1968 Nixon (R)	1968 Wallace (I)	1972 McGovern (D)	1972 Nixon (R)
Alameda	219,545	153,285	28,426	259,254	201,862
Alpine	83	150	20	195	366
Amador	2,440	2,269	660	2,705	3,533
Butte	12,887	22,225	3,891	18,401	28,819
Calaveras	2,134	3,042	643	2,268	4,119
Colusa	1,858	2,361	344	1,810	2,715
Contra Costa	101,668	97,486	18,330	111,718	139,044
Del Norte	2,236	2,387	495	2,156	2,927
El Dorado	6,054	7,468	1,676	8,654	11,330
Fresno	65,153	59,901	11,292	72,682	79,051
Glenn	2,466	3,848	808	2,681	4,569
Humboldt	16,476	16,719	2,759	21,132	22,345
Imperial	7,481	10,818	2,100	7,982	14,178
Inyo	2,314	3,641	714	2,006	4,873
Kern	49,284	53,990	12,309	41,937	71,686
Kings	8,643	7,796	1,640	7,274	10,509
Lake	3,777	4,464	838	4,715	6,477
Lassen	2,930	2,553	712	3,134	3,618
Los Angeles	1,223,251	1,266,480	151,050	1,189,977	1,549,717
Madera	6,932	6,229	1,720	6,580	7,835
Marin	38,278	41,422	3,801	47,414	54,123
Mariposa	1,187	1,496	302	1,487	2,122
Mendocino	7,935	8,305	1,554	9,435	11,128
Merced	14,453	11,595	2,248	13,914	17,737
Modoc	1,264	1,713	284	1,271	2,085
Mono	465	1,130	156	828	1,872
Monterey	28,261	33,670	4,800	32,545	47,004
Napa	14,762	14,270	3,476	14,529	23,403
Nevada	4,607	6,061	1,078	5,693	8,004
Orange	148,869	314,905	33,034	176,847	448,291
Placer	14,050	12,427	2,574	16,911	18,597
Plumas	2,961	2,097	529	3,057	2,952
Riverside	61,146	83,414	12,432	71,591	108,120
Sacramento	118,769	97,177	16,269	137,287	141,218
San Benito	2,809	2,961	447	2,582	3,961
San Bernardino	89,418	111,974	21,187	85,986	144,689
San Diego	167,669	261,540	33,340	206,455	371,627
San Francisco	177,509	100,970	17,332	170,882	127,461
San Joaquin	42,073	47,293	8,923	44,062	61,646
San Luis Obispo	15,828	19,420	2,416	20,779	28,566
San Mateo	106,519	98,654	14,720	109,745	135,377
Santa Barbara	37,565	50,068	5,083	50,609	67,071
Santa Clara	173,511	163,446	18,754	208,506	237,334
Santa Cruz	20,492	25,365	3,465	32,336	34,799
Shasta	14,510	11,821	2,815	17,214	16,618
Sierra	559	548	85	658	629
Siskiyou	6,260	6,334	1,088	6,434	7,563
Solano	27,271	17,683	5,810	24,766	31,314
Sonoma	33,587	38,088	5,875	43,746	57,697
Stanislaus	31,316	29,573	3,973	35,005	39,521
Sutter	4,624	8,665	1,228	5,409	10,224

Tehama	4,565	5,198	1,216	5,175	6,054
Trinity	1,433	1,426	432	1,621	1,868
Tulare	22,180	29,314	4,580	21,775	36,048
Tuolumne	3,913	4,330	865	4,596	5,894
Ventura	47,794	59,705	8,234	49,307	95,310
Yolo	15,833	11,123	1,742	23,694	17,969
Yuba	4,461	5,371	1,296	4,435	6,623
Totals	**3,244,318**	**3,467,664**	**487,270**	**3,475,847**	**4,602,096**

CALIFORNIA VOTE SINCE 1924

1924 (Pres.), Coolidge, Rep., 733,250; Davis, Dem., 105,514; LaFollette, Prog., 424,649; Faris, Proh. 18,365.

1928 (Pres.), Hoover, Rep., Proh., 1,162,323; Smith, Dem., 614,365; Thomas, Soc., 19,595; Varney, Proh. 14,394 (incl. in Hoover vote); Foster, Com., 216.

1932 (Pres.), Roosevelt, Dem., 1,324,157; Hoover, Rep., 847,902; Thomas, Soc., 63,299; Upshaw, Proh., 20,637; Harvey, Liberty, 9,827; Foster, Com., 1,023.

1936 (Pres.), Roosevelt, Dem., 1,766,836; Landon, Rep., 836,431; Colvin, Proh., 12,917; Thomas, Soc., 11,325; Browder, Com., 10,877.

1940 (Pres.), Roosevelt, Dem., 1,877,618; Willkie, Rep., 1,351,419; Thomas, Prog., 16,506; Browder, Com., 13,586; Babson, Proh., 9,400.

1944 (Pres.), Roosevelt, Dem., 1,988,564; Dewey, Rep., 1,512,965; Watson, Proh., 14,770; Thomas, Soc., 3,923; Teichert, Soc. Lab., 327.

1948 (Pres.), Truman, Dem., 1,913,134; Dewey, Rep., 1,895,269; Wallace, Prog., 190,381; Watson, Proh., 16,926; Thomas, Soc., 3,459; Thurmond, States' Rights, 1,228; Teichert, Soc. Lab., 195; Dobbs, Soc. Wkr. 133.

1952 (Pres.), Eisenhower, Rep., 2,897,310; Stevenson, Dem., 2,197,548; Hallinan, Prog., 24,106; Hamblen, Proh., 15,653; MacArthur, (Tenny Ticket), 3,326; (Kellems Ticket) 178; Hass, Soc. Lab., 273; Hoopes, Soc., 206; Scattered, 3,249.

1956 (Pres.), Eisenhower, Rep., 3,027,668; Stevenson, Dem., 2,420,136; Holtwick, Proh., 11,119; Andrews, Constitution, 6,087; Hass, Soc. Lab., 300; Hoopes, Soc., 123; Dobbs, Soc. Workers, 96; Smith, Christian Nat'l., 8.

1960 (Pres.), Kennedy, Dem., 3,224,099; Nixon, Rep., 3,259,722; Decker, Proh., 21,706; Hass, Soc. Lab., 1,051.

1964 (Pres.), Johnson, Dem., 4,171,877; Goldwater, Rep., 2,879,108; Hass, Soc. Labor, 489; DeBerry, Soc. Worker, 378; Munn, Proh., 305; Hensley, Universal, 19.

1968 (Pres.), Nixon, Rep., 3,467,664; Humphrey, Dem., 3,244,318; Wallace, 3rd party, 487,270; Peace and Freedom party, 27,707; McCarthy, Alternative, 20,721; Gregory, write-in, 3,230; Mitchell, Communist, 260; Munn, Prohibition, 59; Blomen, Socialist, 341; Soeters, Defense, 17.

1972 (Pres.), Nixon, Rep., 4,602,096; McGovern, Dem., 3,475,847; Schmitz, Amer., 232,554; Spock, Peace and Freedom, 55,167; Hall, Communist, 373; Hospers, Libertarian, 980; Munn, Prohibition, 53; Fisher, Soc. Labor, 197; Jenness, Soc. Workers, 574; Green, Universal, 21.

Colorado

County	1968			1972	
	Humphrey (D)	Nixon (R)	Wallace (I)	McGovern (D)	Nixon (R)
Adams	25,111	24,343	5,702	24,170	40,372
Alamosa	1,574	2,277	287	1,540	2,916
Arapahoe	18,569	33,712	3,953	18,631	52,283
Archuleta	409	486	83	300	606
Baca	719	1,441	340	527	1,645
Bent	1,126	1,228	231	787	1,525
Boulder	17,422	27,671	2,497	29,484	40,766
Chaffee	1,667	2,121	358	1,354	2,859
Cheyenne	392	664	136	400	815
Clear Creek	719	1,011	183	815	1,557
Conejos	1,492	1,361	117	1,140	1,658
Costilla	933	477	32	744	602
Crowley	565	775	196	414	1,094
Custer	204	433	77	154	495
Delta	2,327	3,692	618	1,903	4,890
Denver	106,081	92,003	11,408	98,062	121,995
Dolores	217	392	131	166	498
Douglas	857	1,910	327	1,048	3,625
Eagle	927	1,049	160	1,306	1,920
Elbert	484	1,043	185	451	1,416
El Paso	21,232	32,066	6,199	21,234	53,892
Fremont	3,292	4,908	967	2,813	6,701
Garfield	2,273	3,157	607	2,088	4,452
Gilpin	218	358	99	362	516
Grand	433	1,167	127	685	1,721
Gunnison	866	1,411	139	1,187	2,231
Hinsdale	43	127	22	44	172
Huerfano	1,934	1,133	150	1,341	1,620
Jackson	177	474	51	178	623
Jefferson	31,392	50,847	6,767	31,555	80,082

County	1968			1972	
	Humphrey (D)	Nixon (R)	Wallace (I)	McGovern (D)	Nixon (R)
Kiowa	423	689	112	372	849
Kit Carson	1,026	1,977	232	824	2,316
Lake	1,550	1,025	287	1,263	1,556
La Plata	2,523	4,269	673	2,830	5,691
Larimer	9,152	18,438	1,819	13,731	27,462
Las Animas	4,602	2,499	388	3,222	3,659
Lincoln	809	1,407	247	685	1,678
Logan	2,521	4,323	736	2,426	5,352
Mesa	8,775	10,745	2,076	6,358	15,527
Mineral	126	116	22	96	247
Moffat	765	1,785	322	591	1,928
Montezuma	1,349	2,461	545	1,223	3,391
Montrose	2,394	3,547	753	1,870	4,571
Morgan	2,310	4,598	593	2,081	5,365
Otero	3,891	4,690	723	2,929	6,016
Ouray	250	401	120	186	669
Park	286	601	134	386	1,001
Phillips	723	1,237	211	687	1,480
Pitkin	728	1,135	136	2,531	2,064
Prowers	2,329	2,741	503	1,860	3,272
Pueblo	27,215	16,646	3,823	19,620	25,607
Rio Blanco	502	1,294	204	414	1,586
Rio Grande	1,562	2,442	182	1,029	2,787
Routt	1,076	1,602	292	1,613	2,629
Saguache	648	824	97	578	1,062
San Juan	134	165	59	140	238
San Miguel	311	422	60	426	583
Sedgwick	546	1,007	100	485	1,129
Summit	301	536	95	707	1,082
Teller	403	722	249	535	1,440
Washington	694	1,634	352	643	1,837
Weld	10,420	17,101	2,189	11,690	24,695
Yuma	1,175	2,529	330	1,066	2,873
Total	**335,174**	**409,345**	**60,813**	**329,980**	**597,189**

COLORADO VOTE SINCE 1924

1924 (Pres.), Coolidge, Rep., 195,171; Davis, Dem., 75,238; LaFollette, Prog., 57,368; Faris, Proh., 966; Foster, Workers, 562; Johns, Soc. Lab., 378.

1928 (Pres.), Hoover, Rep., 253,872; Smith, Dem., 133,131; Thomas, Soc., 3,472; Foster, Com., 675; Farm.-Lab., 1,092.

1932 (Pres.), Roosevelt, Dem., 250,877; Hoover, Rep., 189,617; Thomas, Soc., 14,018; Upshaw, Proh., 1,928.

1936 (Pres.), Roosevelt, Dem., 295,081; Landon, Rep., 181,267; Lemke, Union, 9,962; Thomas, Soc., 1,593; Browder, Com., 497; Aiken, Soc. Labor, 336.

1940 (Pres.), Roosevelt, Dem., 265,554; Willkie, Rep., 279,576; Thomas, Soc., 1,899; Babson, Proh., 1,597; Browder, Com., 378.

1944 (Pres.), Roosevelt, Dem., 234,331; Dewey, Rep., 268,731; Thomas, Soc., 1,977.

1948 (Pres.), Truman, Dem., 267,288; Dewey, Rep., 239,714; Wallace, Prog., 6,115; Thomas, Soc., 1,678; Dobbs, Soc. Workers, 228; Teichert, Soc. Lab., 214.

1952 (Pres.), Eisenhower, Rep., 379,782; Stevenson, Dem., 245,504; MacArthur, Constitution, 2,181; Hallinan, Prog., 1,919; Hoopes, Soc., 365; Hass, Soc. Lab., 352.

1956 (Pres.), Eisenhower, Rep., 394,479; Stevenson, Dem., 263,997; Hass, Soc. Lab., 3,308; Andrews, Ind., 759; Hoopes, Soc., 531.

1960 (Pres.), Kennedy, Dem., 330,629; Nixon, Rep., 402,242; Hass, Soc. Lab., 2,803; Dobbs, Soc. Workers, 572.

1964 (Pres.), Johnson, Dem., 476,024; Goldwater, Rep., 296,767; Hass, Soc. Labor, 302; DeBerry, Soc. Worker, 2,537; Munn, Proh., 1,356.

1968 (Pres.), Nixon, Rep., 409,345; Humphrey, Dem., 335,174; Wallace, 3rd party, 60,813; Blomen, Soc., 3,016; Gregory, New-party, 1,393; Munn, Proh., 275; Halstead, Soc. Wrk., 235.

1972 (Pres.), Nixon, Rep., 597,189; McGovern, Dem., 329,980; Fisher, Soc. Labor, 4,361; Hospers, Libertarian, 1,111; Hall, Com., 432; Jenness, Soc. Wrks, 666; Munn, Proh., 467; Schmitz, American, 17,269; Spock, Peoples, 2,403.

Connecticut

County	1968			1972	
	Humphrey (D)	Nixon (R)	Wallace (I)	McGovern (D)	Nixon (R)
Fairfield	139,364	173,108	21,477	125,128	233,188
Hartford	190,865	131,740	16,779	174,837	194,095
Litchfield	29,340	31,429	3,526	27,929	43,478
Middlesex	23,727	21,999	2,706	23,573	33,249
New Haven	159,653	130,501	23,985	135,132	200,818
New London	41,507	37,116	4,879	32,935	58,516
Tolland	18,007	16,666	1,918	19,505	25,798
Windham	19,098	14,162	1,380	16,459	21,621
Totals	**621,561**	**556,721**	**76,650**	**555,498**	**810,763**

CONNECTICUT VOTE SINCE 1924

1924 (Pres.), Coolidge, Rep., 246,322; Davis, Dem., 110,184; LaFollette, Prog., 42,416; Johns, Soc. Lab., 1,373.
1928 (Pres.), Hoover, Rep., 296,614; Smith, Dem., 252,040; Thomas, Soc., 3,019; Foster, Com., 730; Reynolds, Soc. Lab., 622.
1932 (Pres.), Roosevelt, Dem., 281,632; Hoover, Rep., 288,420; Thomas, Soc., 22,767.
1936 (Pres.), Roosevelt, Dem., 382,129; Landon, Rep., 278,685; Lemke, Union, 21,805; Thomas, Soc., 5,683; Browder, Com., 1,193.
1940 (Pres.), Roosevelt, Dem., 417,621; Willkie, Rep., 361,021; Browder, Com., 1,091; Aiken, Soc. Lab., 971; Willkie, Union, 798.
1944 (Pres.), Roosevelt, Dem., 435,146; Dewey, Rep., 390,527; Thomas, Soc., 5,097; Teichert, Soc. Lab., 1,220.
1948 (Pres.), Truman, Dem., 423,297; Dewey, Rep., 437,754; Wallace, Prog., 13,713; Thomas, Soc., 6,964; Teichert, Soc. Lab., 1,184; Dobbs, Soc. Workers, 606.
1952 (Pres.), Eisenhower, Rep., 611,012; Stevenson, Dem., 481,649; Hoopes, Soc., 2,244; Hallinan, Peoples, 1,466; Hass, Soc. Lab., 535; Write-in, 5.
1956 (Pres.), Eisenhower, Rep., 711,837; Stevenson, Dem., 405,079; Scattered, 205.
1960 (Pres.), Kennedy, Dem., 657,055; Nixon, Rep., 565,813.
1964 (Pres.), Johnson, Dem., 826,269; Goldwater, Rep., 390,996; Scattered, 1,313.
1968 (Pres.), Nixon, Rep., 556,721; Humphrey, Dem., 621,561; Wallace, 3rd party, 76,650; ~~~~~~ 1,000.
~~~~~~~~~~~~~~~~~~~~ ~~~~~~~ ~~~~~~~~~~~~ ~~~~, 888,499;
Schmltz, Amer. Party, 17,239; Scattered 777.

Delaware

County	1968			1972	
	Humphrey (D)	Nixon (R)	Wallace (I)	McGovern (D)	Nixon (R)
New Castle	68,468	70,014	17,931	70,190	100,681
Kent	9,055	11,082	4,751	10,463	17,712
Sussex	11,671	15,618	5,777	11,630	21,964
Totals	89,194	96,714	28,459	92,283	140,357

DELAWARE VOTE SINCE 1924

1924 (Pres.), Coolidge, Rep., 52,441; Davis, Dem., 33,445; LaFollette, Prog. & Soc., 4,979.
1928 (Pres.), Hoover, Rep., 68,860; Smith, Dem., 36,643.
1932 (Pres.), Hoover, Rep., 57,074; Roosevelt, Dem., 54,319; Thomas, Soc., 1,376; Foster, Com., 133.
1936 (Pres.), Roosevelt, Dem., 69,702; Landon, Rep., 54,014; Lemke, Union, 442; Thomas, Soc., 179; Browder, Com., 52.
1940 (Pres.), Roosevelt, Dem., 74,599; Willkie, Rep., 61,440; Babson, Proh., 220; Thomas, Soc., 115.
1944 (Pres.), Roosevelt, Dem., 68,166; Dewey, Rep., 56,747; Watson, Proh., 294; Thomas, Soc., 154.
1948 (Pres.), Truman, Dem., 67,813; Dewey, Rep., 69,688; Wallace, Prog., 1,050; Watson, Proh., 343; Thomas, Soc., 250; Teichert, Soc. Lab., 29.
1952 (Pres.), Eisenhower, Rep., 90,059; Stevenson, Dem., 83,315; Hass, Soc. Lab., 242; Hamblen, Proh., 234; Hallinan, Prog., 155; Hoopes, Soc., 20.
1956 (Pres.), Eisenhower, Rep., 98,057; Stevenson, Dem., 79,421; Holtwick, Proh., 400; Hass, Soc. Lab., 110.
1960 (Pres.), Kennedy, Dem., 99,590; Nixon, Rep., 96,373; Faubus, States' Rights, 354; Decker, Proh., 284; Hass, Soc. Lab., 82.
1964 (Pres.), Johnson, Dem., 122,704; Goldwater, Rep., 78,078; Hass, Soc. Lab., 113; Munn, Proh., 425.
1968 (Pres.), Nixon, Rep., 96,714; Humphrey, Dem., 89,194; Wallace, 3rd party, 28,459.
1972 (Pres.), Nixon, Rep., 140,357; McGovern, Dem., 92,283; Schmitz, Amer. Party, 2,638; Munn, Proh., 238.

District of Columbia

County	1968			1972	
	Humphrey (D)	Nixon (R)	Wallace (I)	McGovern (D)	Nixon (R)
Dist. of C	139,566	31,012		127,627	35,226
Totals	139,566	31,012	......	127,627	35,226

DISTRICT OF COLUMBIA

1964 (Pres.), Johnson, Dem., 169,796; Goldwater, Rep., 28,801.
1968 (Pres.), Nixon, Rep., 31,012; Humphrey, Dem., 139,566.
1972 (Pres.), Nixon, Rep., 35,226; McGovern, Dem., 127,627; Reed, Soc. Worker, 316; Hall, Communist, 252.

Florida

County	1968			1972	
	Humphrey (D)	Nixon (R)	Wallace (I)	McGovern (D)	Nixon (R)
Alachua	10,060	9,670	8,696	17,245	22,536
Baker..........	487	294	1,962	379	1,943
Bay	4,020	5,121	15,161	3,914	20,245
Bradford	1,173	718	2,840	1,217	3,652
Brevard	18,281	37,124	21,909	16,854	62,773
Broward.......	56,613	106,122	31,992	74,127	196,528
Calhoun	398	356	2,375	461	2,069
Charlotte	3,647	6,056	2,270	3,874	12,888
Citrus..........	1,775	2,767	2,606	2,607	8,848
Clay...........	1,954	3,251	4,046	1,748	10,467
Collier	2,230	5,362	2,952	3,201	13,501
Columbia.......	1,750	1,553	4,046	1,664	6,723
Dade	176,689	135,222	53,391	177,693	256,529
De Soto........	937	1,103	2,054	852	2,958
Dixie	325	217	1,546	367	1,628
Duval	54,834	51,585	60,559	46,530	122,154
Escambia.......	16,281	15,089	37,000	14,078	56,071
Flagler.........	601	360	817	493	1,409
Franklin........	699	529	1,909	490	2,277
Gadsden.......	3,274	1,337	4,446	3,829	5,995
Gilchrist	208	183	1,119	247	1,306
Glades	230	261	600	253	1,019
Gulf	711	364	2,725	713	2,628
Hamilton	820	337	1,574	626	1,741
Hardee	~~~~	~~~~	~~~~	~~~	~~~~
Hendry........	~~~~	~~~	~~~~	~~~	~~~~
Hernando......	1,524	2,053	2,387	2,110	6,296
Highlands	2,582	4,560	3,475	2,458	9,645
Hillsborough ...	45,848	49,441	46,913	45,305	106,956
Holmes	312	377	4,700	309	3,819
Indian River...	3,179	6,518	3,022	3,316	11,741
Jackson	2,472	1,236	8,622	2,220	8,904
Jefferson	1,066	459	1,567	1,049	2,108
Lafayette	215	137	1,125	173	1,060
Lake	4,599	11,763	8,442	4,803	23,079
Lee	7,978	14,376	8,741	9,404	36,738
Leon	10,440	9,288	12,878	15,555	27,479
Levy..........	767	745	2,449	862	3,273
Liberty........	242	154	1,322	222	1,199
Madison.......	1,378	654	2,703	1,187	3,236
Manatee	8,286	18,247	8,214	8,058	32,664
Marion........	5,798	7,468	9,600	5,397	19,505
Martin	2,580	5,179	2,471	2,946	11,296
Monroe	5,534	5,094	4,271	4,469	11,688
Nassau........	1,598	1,301	3,634	1,293	5,078
Okaloosa	3,059	5,525	12,237	2,843	23,303
Okeechobee.....	542	862	1,604	621	2,581
Orange........	22,548	50,874	27,247	23,840	94,516
Osceola	1,870	4,172	3,462	1,875	9,320
Palm Beach.....	32,837	62,191	21,894	40,825	108,670
Pasco.........	6,292	9,743	6,966	11,330	29,249
Pinellas	68,209	109,235	33,814	77,197	179,541
Polk..........	15,898	27,839	31,540	16,419	60,748
Putnam	2,920	2,955	5,150	2,901	8,741
St. Johns......	2,748	3,880	4,682	2,549	8,919
St. Lucie	5,232	7,281	4,410	4,593	14,258
Santa Rosa	1,600	2,567	8,549	1,491	12,669
Sarasota	10,127	30,160	7,041	12,235	48,939
Seminole	6,120	10,821	7,275	6,503	27,658
Sumter........	1,277	910	2,879	1,107	3,695
Suwannee	1,182	845	3,955	1,027	4,435
Taylor	941	794	3,318	754	4,109
Union.........	290	179	1,192	253	1,314
Volusia........	24,987	28,024	17,209	21,637	52,656
Wakulla	440	247	1,668	539	2,466
Walton........	1,064	963	5,135	988	6,217
Washington.....	722	528	3,682	606	3,777
Totals	676,794	886,804	624,207	718,117	1,857,759

FLORIDA VOTE SINCE 1924

1924 (Pres.), Davis, Dem., 62,083; Coolidge, Rep., 30,633; LaFollette, Prog., 8,625; Faris, Proh., 5,498; Nations, Amer. 2,315.
1928 (Pres.), Hoover, Rep., 144,168; Smith, Dem., 101,764; Thomas, Soc., 4,036; Foster, Com., 3,704.
1932 (Pres.), Roosevelt, Dem., 206,307; Hoover, Rep., 69,170; Thomas, Soc., 775.
1936 (Pres.), Roosevelt, Dem., 249,117; Landon, Rep., 78,248; Thomas, Soc., 775.
1940 (Pres.), Roosevelt, Dem., 359,334; Willkie, Rep., 126,158.
1944 (Pres.), Roosevelt, Dem., 339,377; Dewey, Rep., 143,215.
1948 (Pres.), Truman, Dem., 281,988; Dewey, Rep., 194,280; Thurmond, States' Rights, 89,755; Wallace, Prog., 11,620.
1952 (Pres.), Eisenhower, Rep., 544,036; Stevenson, Dem., 444,950; Scattered, 351.
1956 (Pres.), Eisenhower, Rep., 643,849; Stevenson, Dem., 480,371.
1960 (Pres.), Kennedy, Dem., 748,700; Nixon, Rep., 795,476.

1964 (Pres.), Johnson, Dem., 948,540; Goldwater, Rep., 905,941.
1968 (Pres.), Nixon, Rep., 886,804; Humphrey, Dem., 676,794; Wallace, 3rd party, 624,207.
1972 (Pres.), Nixon, Rep., 1,857,759; McGovern, Dem., 718,117; scattered 7,407.

Georgia

County	1968			1972	
	Humphrey (D)	Nixon (R)	Wallace (I)	McGovern (D)	Nixon (R)
Appling	760	795	2,678	512	2,755
Atkinson	686	288	1,554	309	924
Bacon	279	586	1,935	192	1,771
Baker	548	99	1,067	345	965
Baldwin	2,109	2,318	2,678	1,435	4,826
Banks	296	398	1,434	356	1,336
Barrow	1,070	1,377	2,731	867	3,423
Bartow	2,149	2,045	4,052	1,590	4,836
Ben Hill	876	661	1,833	703	2,104
Berrien	451	566	2,810	371	2,285
Bibb	10,579	13,490	17,328	10,201	27,402
Bleckley	396	756	2,458	377	2,308
Brantley	317	237	1,709	338	1,587
Brooks	787	589	2,404	643	2,430
Bryan	560	381	1,428	263	1,409
Bulloch	1,788	2,113	3,953	1,524	5,683
Burke	1,676	1,416	1,802	1,058	2,846
Butts	959	584	1,490	727	1,968
Calhoun	697	234	979	495	892
Camden	1,146	751	1,988	753	2,380
Candler	587	552	1,624	238	1,427
Carroll	2,326	3,135	6,509	2,158	8,296
Catoosa	901	2,043	6,449	894	6,008
Charlton	455	332	1,157	310	1,244
Chatham	18,201	18,106	17,238	15,566	38,079
Chattahoochee	148	70	303	121	345
Chattooga	1,255	1,087	3,024	923	3,188
Cherokee	1,434	2,675	3,351	1,159	5,509
Clarke	5,543	5,800	3,452	6,090	11,465
Clay	516	133	608	283	632
Clayton	3,510	8,256	11,665	3,740	23,681
Clinch	334	304	1,142	239	1,127
Cobb	8,755	18,649	17,805	7,688	43,977
Coffee	1,331	1,241	3,785	607	3,934
Colquitt	1,119	1,882	6,325	930	6,900
Columbia	905	1,636	2,207	946	4,839
Cook	603	521	2,438	525	2,135
Coweta	1,204	2,442	3,791	1,560	5,751
Crawford	489	246	886	512	1,167
Crisp	1,017	935	3,271	682	3,623
Dade	282	613	2,460	148	2,110
Dawson	246	509	845	230	828
Decatur	1,729	749	4,576	1,196	4,292
DeKalb	27,796	52,485	23,954	30,671	104,750
Dodge	1,230	1,055	3,406	884	4,346
Dooly	879	454	1,803	590	1,904
Dougherty	3,831	5,611	9,317	3,625	12,878
Douglas	1,242	1,848	4,159	982	6,610
Early	785	327	2,797	513	2,396
Echols	56	53	533	68	404
Effingham	635	769	2,561	497	3,175
Elbert	1,216	914	3,252	884	2,875
Emanuel	1,508	1,297	3,307	916	3,684
Evans	492	543	1,475	375	1,666
Fannin	1,229	3,475	1,188	949	3,783
Fayette	551	867	1,888	450	3,401
Floyd	4,036	7,470	10,001	3,372	15,485
Forsyth	647	1,389	2,397	549	2,968
Franklin	766	716	2,691	435	2,022
Fulton	77,847	64,153	36,995	74,329	96,256
Gilmer	690	2,074	1,259	768	2,729
Glascock	47	185	733	41	578
Glynn	3,247	3,725	5,341	3,002	9,443
Gordon	1,161	1,815	3,077	870	4,344
Grady	1,425	561	3,817	874	3,732
Greene	1,635	652	1,223	919	1,679
Gwinnett	3,226	5,350	8,909	2,896	18,181
Habersham	1,070	1,611	3,008	172	971
Hall	3,174	4,923	5,546	2,440	10,686
Hancock	2,165	381	1,104	1,502	1,595
Haralson	771	1,451	3,251	767	3,460
Harris	1,072	1,021	1,851	701	2,617
Hart	979	586	3,208	784	2,308
Heard	356	303	1,153	276	1,239
Henry	2,317	2,017	3,604	1,460	5,155
Houston	2,831	4,285	7,339	2,556	13,576
Irwin	474	430	1,955	335	1,851
Jackson	1,537	1,139	3,473	1,055	4,124
Jasper	835	456	926	463	1,289
Jeff Davis	376	577	1,958	302	1,857
Jefferson	1,899	1,227	2,090	1,184	2,777
Jenkins	704	574	1,249	484	1,769
Johnson	446	381	2,041	417	2,201
Jones	1,105	693	1,770	861	2,483
Lamar	790	575	1,440	666	1,844
Lanier	277	241	1,024	193	850
Laurens	3,451	2,738	6,649	2,130	7,350
Lee	673	389	1,201	390	1,441

County	1968			1972	
	Humphrey (D)	Nixon (R)	Wallace (I)	McGovern (D)	Nixon (R)
Liberty	1,572	592	1,365	1,217	2,337
Lincoln	491	408	1,290	340	1,246
Long	574	156	1,037	236	764
Lowndes	2,402	3,073	5,679	2,015	7,812
Lumpkin	396	687	1,048	385	1,477
Macon	954	598	1,559	837	2,005
Madison	621	600	2,529	572	2,606
Marion	247	186	849	164	850
McDuffie	991	1,324	1,709	996	2,990
McIntosh	943	315	841	833	1,367
Meriwether	1,760	1,120	2,571	1,213	3,420
Miller	171	249	1,862	118	1,269
Mitchell	1,255	731	3,647	1,120	2,400
Monroe	1,028	770	1,422	789	2,181
Montgomery	503	352	1,433	337	1,370
Morgan	973	616	1,391	668	2,007
Murray	818	1,278	1,750	644	2,643
Muscogee	7,591	11,193	15,804	8,234	28,449
Newton	1,996	1,660	3,017	1,380	4,647
Oconee	414	713	1,405	464	2,029
Oglethorpe	483	383	1,737	326	1,712
Paulding	1,023	977	3,054	1,004	2,814
Peach	1,362	904	1,638	2,413	3,747
Pickens	677	1,659	1,392	520	2,101
Pierce	507	579	2,144	269	1,982
Pike	632	345	1,442	423	1,432
Polk	2,007	1,729	4,240	1,317	4,929
Pulaski	514	595	1,569	444	1,966
Putnam	972	594	1,177	604	1,963
Quitman	198	90	459	140	502
Rabun	590	680	1,407	366	1,477
Randolph	1,028	502	1,438	798	1,603
Richmond	11,770	14,993	9,532	9,219	24,362
Rockdale	1,213	1,195	2,215	791	3,560
Schley	309	164	619	162	694
Screven	1,411	916	1,830	575	2,402
Seminole	369	201	1,922	376	1,851
Spalding	2,949	3,077	4,953	1,702	7,183
Stephens	1,035	1,295	2,802	871	3,773
Stewart	489	233	932	353	1,020
Sumter	1,701	1,383	3,489	1,268	4,533
Talbot	510	317	688	508	990
Taliaferro	678	232	508	372	585
Tattnall	957	852	3,405	492	2,892
Taylor	691	393	1,626	514	1,580
Telfair	1,038	720	2,502	687	2,245
Terrell	1,275	545	1,798	686	2,057
Thomas	2,583	2,261	5,039	2,171	6,668
Tift	1,187	1,692	3,942	816	4,591
Toombs	896	1,397	3,405	675	4,080
Towns	770	1,492	589	404	1,573
Treutlen	341	474	1,081	210	1,346
Troup	2,896	3,239	6,232	2,056	8,350
Turner	412	419	1,845	437	2,120
Twiggs	812	336	1,167	1,113	1,363
Union	974	1,221	906	742	2,317
Upson	1,480	1,494	3,599	896	4,892
Walker	1,930	3,664	8,725	1,574	8,728
Walton	1,552	1,399	4,047	1,140	3,994
Ware	2,255	2,047	5,895	1,724	6,578
Warren	582	406	767	475	1,175
Washington	1,443	1,247	2,029	1,246	3,901
Wayne	980	1,313	3,422	733	3,677
Webster	147	72	494	108	483
Wheeler	488	251	934	294	1,093
White	435	762	1,157	343	1,537
Whitfield	2,723	4,828	3,954	1,955	8,591
Wilcox	465	381	1,822	315	1,863
Wilkes	953	873	1,709	646	2,195
Wilkinson	829	685	1,870	751	2,196
Worth	719	603	3,049	542	2,942
Totals	**334,440**	**380,111**	**535,550**	**289,529**	**881,496**

GEORGIA VOTE SINCE 1924

1924 (Pres.), Davis, Dem., 123,200; Coolidge, Rep., 30,300; LaFollette, Prog., 12,691; Faris, Proh., 231; Nations, Amer., 155.
1928 (Pres.), Smith, Dem., 129,602; Hoover, Rep., 63,498; Hoover (anti-Smith, Dems.), 35,871; Hoover total, 99,369; Thomas, Soc., 124; Foster, Com., 64.
1932 (Pres.), Roosevelt, Dem., 234,118; Hoover, Rep., 19,863; Upshaw, Proh., 1,125; Thomas, Soc., 461; Foster, Com., 23.
1936 (Pres.), Roosevelt, Dem., 255,364; Landon, Rep., 36,942; Colvin, Proh., 660; Lemke, Union, 141; Thomas, Soc., 68.
1940 (Pres.), Roosevelt, Dem., 265,194; Willkie, Rep., 23,934; Ind. Dem., 22,428; total, 46,362; Babson, Proh., 983.
1944 (Pres.), Roosevelt, Dem., 268,187; Dewey, Rep., 56,506; Watson, Proh., 36.
1948 (Pres.), Truman, Dem., 254,646; Dewey, Rep., 76,691; Thurmond, States' Rights, 85,055; Wallace, Prog., 1,636; Watson, Proh., 732.

1952 (Pres.), Eisenhower, Rep., 198,979; Stevenson, Dem., 456,823; Liberty Party, 1.
1956 (Pres.), Stevenson, Dem., 444,388; Eisenhower, Rep., 222,778; Andrews, Ind., write-in, 1,754.
1960 (Pres.), Kennedy, Dem., 458,638; Nixon, Rep., 274,472; write-in 239.
1964 (Pres.), Johnson, Dem., 522,557; Goldwater, Rep., 616,600.
1968 (Pres.), Nixon, Rep., 380,111; Humphrey, Dem., 334,440; Wallace, 3rd party, 535,550; write-in votes 162.
1972 (Pres.), Nixon, Rep., 881,496; McGovern, Dem., 289,529; Schmitz, Amer. Party, 2,288; scattered 1,459.

1944 (Pres.), Roosevelt, Dem., 107,399; Dewey, Rep., 100,137; Watson, Proh., 503; Thomas, Soc., 282.
1948 (Pres.), Truman, Dem., 107,370; Dewey, Rep., 101,514; Wallace, Prog., 4,972; Watson, Proh., 628; Thomas, Soc., 332.
1952 (Pres.), Eisenhower, Rep., 180,707; Stevenson, Dem., 95,081; Hallinan, Prog., 443; Write-in, 23.
1956 (Pres.), Eisenhower, Rep., 166,979; Stevenson, Dem., 105,868; Andrews, Ind., 126; Write-in, 16.
1960 (Pres.), Kennedy, Dem., 138,853; Nixon, Rep., 161,597.
1964 (Pres.), Johnson, Dem., 148,920; Goldwater, Rep., 143,557.
1968 (Pres.), Nixon, Rep., 165,369; Humphrey, Dem., 89,273; Wallace, 3rd party, 36,541.
1972 (Pres.), Nixon, Rep., 199,384; McGovern, Dem., 80,826; Schmitz, American, 28,869; Spock, Peoples, 903; Jenness, Soc. Worker, 397.

Hawaii

County	1968 Humphrey (D)	Nixon (R)	Wallace (I)	1972 McGovern (D)	Nixon (R)
Hawaii	15,819	9,625	283	11,652	16,832
Honolulu	108,141	71,259	2,794	7,399	11,618
Kauai	7,051	4,140	155	76,957	132,844
Maui	10,313	6,401	237	5,401	7,571
Totals	141,324	91,425	3,469	101,409	168,865

HAWAII VOTE SINCE 1960
1960 (Pres.), Kennedy, Dem., 92,410; Nixon, Rep., 92,295.
1964 (Pres.), Johnson, Dem., 163,249; Goldwater, Rep., 44,022.
1968 (Pres.), Nixon, Rep., 91,425; Humphrey, Dem., 141,324; Wallace, 3rd party, 3,469.
1972 (Pres.), Nixon, Rep., 168,865; McGovern, Dem., 101,409.

Idaho

County	1968 Humphrey (D)	Nixon (R)	Wallace (I)	1972 McGovern (D)	Nixon (R)
Ada	11,529	30,185	6,167	36,665	12,687
Adams	360	844	227	963	293
Bannock	9,084	10,234	2,016	12,856	7,840
Bear Lake	1,058	1,866	177	2,213	716
Benewah	1,160	1,125	248	1,494	1,062
Bingham	2,988	6,484	1,293	6,886	2,476
Blaine	815	1,337	332	2,113	1,240
Boise	205	450	154	676	256
Bonner	3,063	3,240	779	4,405	2,599
Bonneville	5,178	13,582	2,290	13,134	4,199
Boundary	883	1,084	330	1,587	860
Butte	521	681	144	788	387
Camas	118	271	93	344	95
Canyon	5,717	14,995	3,186	18,383	5,630
Caribou	727	1,731	327	2,069	614
Cassia	1,350	4,187	988	4,576	1,080
Clark	87	271	49	339	64
Clearwater	1,838	1,287	343	1,590	1,412
Custer	385	711	327	989	274
Elmore	1,230	1,980	631	3,078	1,153
Franklin	831	2,509	455	2,787	611
Freemont	961	2,297	667	2,621	819
Gem	1,183	2,314	500	2,717	1,069
Gooding	1,018	2,349	861	3,124	1,030
Idaho	1,883	2,317	714	3,235	1,622
Jefferson	955	2,927	879	2,983	715
Jerome	976	2,785	841	3,661	888
Kootenai	6,207	7,092	1,472	9,958	5,162
Latah	3,782	4,708	636	6,043	4,548
Lemhi	547	1,476	539	1,812	526
Lewis	927	697	177	961	635
Lincoln	350	972	223	1,120	313
Madison	904	2,971	513	3,606	710
Minidoka	1,332	3,182	1,140	4,097	1,423
Nez Perce	6,502	5,019	1,058	6,232	5,081
Oneida	465	1,114	105	1,204	402
Owyhee	562	1,385	376	1,630	463
Payette	1,216	3,032	708	3,577	1,113
Power	582	1,222	224	1,405	625
Shoshone	3,850	3,080	657	3,868	3,020
Teton	376	694	128	932	298
Twin Falls	4,001	11,564	2,808	13,075	3,344
Valley	534	1,160	308	1,324	537
Washington	1,033	2,020	451	2,264	935
Totals	89,273	165,369	36,541	199,384	80,826

IDAHO VOTE SINCE 1924
1924 (Pres.), Coolidge, Rep., 69,879; LaFollete, Prog., 54,160; Davis, Dem., 24,256.
1928 (Pres.), Hoover, Rep., 99,848; Smith, Dem., 53,074; Thomas, Soc., 1,308.
1932 (Pres.), Roosevelt, Dem., 109,479; Hoover, Rep., 71,312; Harvey, Lib., 4,712; Thomas, Soc., 526; Foster, Com., 491.
1936 (Pres.), Roosevelt, Dem., 125,683; Landon, Rep., 66,256; Lemke, Union, 7,684.
1940 (Pres.), Roosevelt, Dem., 127,842; Willkie, Rep., 106,553; Thomas, Soc., 497; Browder, Com., 276.

Illinois

County	1968 Humphrey (D)	Nixon (R)	Wallace (I)	1972 McGovern (D)	Nixon (R)
Adams	11,521	17,444	3,115	9,055	20,731
Alexander	2,929	2,540	1,443	2,482	3,669
Bond	2,516	3,674	758	2,704	4,010
Boone	1,265	1,629	247	1,203	1,780
Bureau	6,304	11,216	1,171	6,133	12,786
Calhoun	1,329	1,542	266	1,299	1,705
Carroll	2,558	5,275	440	2,571	6,041
Cass	3,302	3,411	424	2,803	4,414
Champaign	18,425	26,027	3,857	24,743	33,700
Christian	8,465	7,486	1,730	7,556	10,072
Clark	2,813	4,809	949	2,965	5,706
Clay	2,878	4,429	672	2,844	5,283
Clinton	4,453	6,561	1,180	4,756	7,931
Coles	7,337	10,449	1,973	7,988	13,936
Cook	1,181,316	960,493	186,921	1,063,268	1,234,307
Crawford	3,383	5,870	840	3,477	6,568
Cumberland	1,828	2,671	512	2,083	3,257
DeKalb	6,974	14,535	1,238	12,375	18,910
DeWitt	2,823	4,247	759	2,672	5,025
Douglas	2,824	5,058	651	2,656	5,840
DuPage	48,492	124,893	13,814	57,043	172,341
Edgar	3,565	6,281	1,292	3,889	7,195
Edwards	1,095	2,633	403	1,055	3,017
Effingham	4,496	6,698	777	4,431	8,752
Fayette	4,011	5,449	939	4,192	6,574
Ford	2,216	5,233	550	1,934	5,656
Franklin	10,095	9,036	1,930	8,545	10,121
Fulton	9,622	9,582	1,234	7,529	12,328
Gallatin	1,980	1,802	404	1,844	2,148
Greene	3,094	3,944	660	2,824	4,673
Grundy	3,407	6,607	1,085	3,584	8,725
Hamilton	1,951	2,912	643	2,006	3,282
Hancock	3,720	6,866	806	3,592	7,519
Hardin	1,199	1,492	187	1,140	1,915
Henderson	1,635	2,224	288	1,744	2,689
Henry	8,455	12,524	1,725	8,368	14,796
Iroquois	3,897	10,885	1,225	3,723	11,995
Jackson	8,856	9,134	1,645	13,146	12,393
Jasper	2,012	2,944	728	2,114	3,461
Jefferson	6,476	7,367	1,612	6,396	9,448
Jersey	3,350	3,806	971	3,317	5,104
JoDaviess	3,228	5,563	607	3,318	5,763
Johnson	1,143	2,406	421	1,293	2,826
Kane	26,609	54,144	6,340	27,525	64,546
Kankakee	14,460	20,025	3,735	13,434	26,866
Kendall	2,228	7,184	780	2,525	9,373
Knox	9,707	14,216	2,394	9,323	17,315
Lake	43,409	68,999	8,738	47,416	92,052
LaSalle	22,940	26,054	2,590	21,405	31,190
Lawrence	3,075	4,883	972	2,818	5,347
Lee	4,727	9,598	925	4,788	10,636
Livingston	5,234	11,963	950	5,110	13,217
Logan	4,552	8,638	1,083	4,395	10,277
Macon	23,369	21,027	5,163	20,296	29,596
Macoupin	10,750	10,262	2,325	9,662	13,583
Madison	46,384	39,622	14,987	43,289	55,385
Marion	7,737	8,134	1,680	6,968	10,755
Marshall	2,455	3,897	313	2,141	4,452
Mason	3,365	3,899	572	2,901	4,897
Massac	1,934	3,578	926	1,831	4,313
McDonough	3,885	8,496	628	5,143	10,573
McHenry	10,896	27,245	2,701	12,090	36,114
McLean	12,779	22,284	2,351	14,824	31,060
Menard	1,640	2,980	372	1,587	3,657
Mercer	3,143	4,844	607	3,477	5,452
Monroe	2,822	5,086	1,253	2,958	6,479
Montgomery	7,318	7,547	1,468	6,858	9,025
Morgan	6,281	8,902	1,137	5,674	11,103
Moultrie	2,447	3,094	571	2,350	3,143
Ogle	4,399	12,168	1,060	4,743	13,512
Peoria	30,937	37,021	5,648	27,264	50,324
Perry	4,449	5,384	1,144	4,084	6,968
Piatt	2,447	3,973	636	2,394	5,057

County	1968 Humphrey (D)	Nixon (R)	Wallace (I)	1972 McGovern (D)	Nixon (R)
Pike	4,191	5,035	697	3,883	5,940
Pope	732	1,307	226	773	1,440
Pulaski	2,076	1,741	815	1,683	2,485
Putnam	988	1,351	162	1,112	1,665
Randolph	5,953	7,681	1,607	6,440	9,761
Richland	2,495	4,781	853	2,553	5,558
Rock Island	34,506	30,404	5,054	32,529	37,548
St. Clair	50,726	34,442	15,260	46,636	50,519
Saline	5,985	6,913	939	5,226	7,660
Sangamon	29,542	36,510	6,586	25,720	50,458
Schuyler	1,475	2,760	346	1,534	2,994
Scott	1,252	1,971	325	1,145	2,228
Shelby	4,528	5,487	1,115	4,389	7,217
Stark	1,128	2,292	239	993	2,529
Stephenson	7,040	11,821	1,050	6,404	13,584
Tazewell	20,712	22,971	4,711	15,576	31,937
Union	3,603	3,889	871	3,428	5,034
Vermilion	16,238	21,391	5,726	14,413	24,863
Wabash	2,244	3,529	614	1,985	4,310
Warren	3,085	5,877	824	2,969	7,021
Washington	2,093	4,793	671	2,327	5,179
Wayne	2,993	5,532	745	2,763	6,400
White	3,837	5,351	761	3,678	6,052
Whiteside	8,132	15,177	1,179	7,909	17,305
Will	31,576	43,630	12,595	33,633	65,155
Williamson	9,660	11,886	2,031	9,202	14,101
Winnebago	36,702	47,646	6,176	35,937	57,682
Woodford	4,005	7,876	856	3,558	9,622
Totals	**2,039,814**	**2,174,774**	**390,958**	**1,913,472**	**2,788,179**

ILLINOIS VOTE SINCE 1924

1924 (Pres.), Coolidge, Rep., 1,453,321; Davis, Dem., 576,975; LaFollette, Prog., 432,027; Johns, Soc. Lab., 2,334; Foster, Workers, 2,622; Faris, Proh., 2,367; Wallace, Comm. Land., 421.

1928 (Pres.), Hoover, Rep., 1,768,141; Smith, Dem., 1,313,817; Thomas, Soc., 19,138; Reynolds, Soc. Lab., 1,812; Foster, Com., 381.

1932 (Pres.), Roosevelt, Dem., 1,882,304; Hoover, Rep., 1,432,756; Thomas, Soc., 67,258; Foster, Com., 15,582; Upshaw, Proh., 6,388; Reynolds, Soc. Lab., 3,638.

1936 (Pres.), Roosevelt, Dem., 2,282,999; Landon, Rep., 1,570,393; Lemke, Union, 89,439; Thomas, Soc., 7,530; Colvin, Proh., 3,439; Aiken, Soc. Lab. 1,921.

1940 (Pres.), Roosevelt, Dem., 2,149,934; Willkie, Rep., 2,047,240; Thomas, Soc., 10,914; Babson, Proh., 9,190.

1944 (Pres.), Roosevelt, Dem., 2,079,479; Dewey, Rep., 1,939,314; Teichert, Soc. Lab., 9,677; Watson, Proh., 7,411; Thomas, Soc., 180.

1948 (Pres.), Truman, Dem., 1,994,715; Dewey, Rep., 1,961,103; Watson, Proh., 11,959; Thomas, Soc., 11,522; Teichert, Soc. Lab., 3,118.

1952 (Pres.), Eisenhower, Rep., 2,457,327; Stevenson, Dem., 2,013,920; Hass, Soc. Lab., 9,363; Write-in, 448.

1956 (Pres.), Eisenhower, Rep., 2,623,327; Stevenson, Dem., 1,775,682; Hass, Soc. Lab., 8,342; Write-in, 56.

1960 (Pres.), Kennedy, Dem., 2,377,846; Nixon, Rep., 2,368,988; Hass, Soc. Lab., 10,560; Write-in, 15.

1964 (Pres.), Johnson, Dem., 2,796,833; Goldwater, Rep., 1,905,946; Write-in, 62.

1968 (Pres.), Nixon, Rep., 2,174,774; Humphrey, Dem., 2,039,814; Wallace, 3rd party, 390,958; Blomen, Soc. Labor, 13,878, write-ins 325.

1972 (Pres.), Nixon, Rep., 2,788,179; McGovern, Dem., 1,913,472; Fisher, Soc. Labor, 12,344; Schmitz, Amer., 2,471; Hall, Communist, 4,541; Others 2,229.

Indiana

County	1968 Humphrey (D)	Nixon (R)	Wallace (I)	1972 McGovern (D)	Nixon (R)
Adams	4,667	5,774	762	3,971	7,549
Allen	40,411	59,211	9,121	38,621	76,924
Bartholomew	8,268	13,628	2,438	6,974	17,365
Benton	1,854	3,326	400	1,566	3,703
Blackford	2,898	3,052	534	2,311	3,876
Boone	4,118	7,905	1,346	3,235	9,874
Brown	1,327	1,881	587	1,443	2,737
Carroll	2,816	4,796	918	2,214	5,885
Cass	7,142	9,441	1,678	5,317	12,681
Clark	11,493	10,305	4,982	10,838	16,111
Clay	3,956	5,743	1,569	3,742	7,146
Clinton	5,714	7,929	1,033	4,283	9,849
Crawford	1,536	2,132	589	1,801	2,623
Daviess	4,071	7,036	1,274	3,538	8,490
Dearborn	4,842	6,208	1,704	4,137	7,689
Decatur	3,602	5,474	731	2,994	6,761
Dekalb	4,790	7,650	931	4,354	8,834
Delaware	19,532	23,554	6,349	17,936	32,468

County	1968 Humphrey (D)	Nixon (R)	Wallace (I)	1972 McGovern (D)	Nixon (R)
Dubois	6,725	5,865	958	6,365	6,637
Elkhart	14,222	24,484	3,440	12,659	31,009
Fayette	4,549	5,286	1,413	3,519	7,273
Floyd	10,671	9,714	3,266	9,243	13,198
Fountain	3,237	5,110	1,280	2,977	5,979
Franklin	2,386	3,468	775	2,131	4,324
Fulton	2,561	5,145	757	2,150	6,170
Gibson	6,777	7,645	1,497	5,633	9,115
Grant	10,938	16,170	3,602	7,912	20,969
Greene	5,493	6,525	1,419	4,450	8,453
Hamilton	4,586	14,250	2,202	4,151	20,247
Hancock	3,902	7,516	1,896	3,069	11,019
Harrison	3,725	4,410	1,557	3,927	5,910
Hendricks	5,155	12,597	3,231	4,384	17,699
Henry	8,045	11,626	2,366	5,610	14,538
Howard	11,026	15,905	4,507	8,083	23,089
Huntington	6,238	9,002	1,250	4,908	10,858
Jackson	5,140	7,710	1,891	4,984	9,546
Jasper	2,201	4,996	1,003	1,920	6,369
Jay	4,290	5,460	918	3,349	6,090
Jefferson	4,635	5,731	1,196	4,267	6,722
Jennings	2,996	4,416	1,214	2,903	5,156
Johnson	5,946	12,089	3,021	5,067	17,537
Knox	7,297	8,369	2,053	6,089	11,940
Kosciusko	5,342	12,633	1,700	4,233	16,216
LaGrange	1,691	3,328	380	1,658	4,152
Lake	99,897	77,911	35,099	88,510	115,480
LaPorte	15,780	20,295	4,587	13,222	26,243
Lawrence	5,349	8,830	1,995	4,278	10,936
Madison	23,886	28,726	6,613	20,921	39,036
Marion	115,715	162,503	32,043	102,166	206,065
Marshall	5,385	9,290	1,685	4,349	11,908
Martin	2,315	2,512	604	2,021	3,470
Miami	5,019	7,295	1,294	3,889	9,477
Monroe	10,789	13,752	2,361	15,241	19,953
Montgomery	4,752	9,085	1,309	3,431	10,997
Morgan	4,042	8,944	3,122	3,390	11,980
Newton	1,453	3,145	483	1,252	3,771
Noble	5,075	6,699	1,253	4,250	7,916
Ohio	991	1,053	243	922	1,368
Orange	2,918	4,666	915	2,932	5,715
Owen	1,932	2,898	776	1,708	3,896
Parke	2,472	3,738	907	2,207	5,014
Perry	4,343	4,211	547	4,277	5,204
Pike	2,953	3,087	745	2,648	4,252
Porter	8,914	17,328	6,126	8,943	26,877
Posey	3,889	5,045	1,204	3,586	6,771
Pulaski	2,071	3,361	681	1,863	4,243
Putnam	3,692	5,873	1,826	3,339	7,879
Randolph	3,962	7,238	1,431	3,409	8,754
Ripley	3,787	5,389	1,215	3,601	6,594
Rush	2,636	5,004	761	1,764	5,965
St. Joseph	47,414	47,114	11,948	41,629	64,808
Scott	2,796	2,671	784	2,785	3,564
Shelby	5,417	8,574	2,205	4,028	10,794
Spencer	3,767	4,603	612	3,867	5,518
Starke	3,208	4,011	1,097	2,994	5,520
Steuben	2,268	4,762	577	2,401	5,636
Sullivan	4,453	4,266	1,135	3,624	5,338
Switzerland	1,466	1,515	452	1,612	1,872
Tippecanoe	14,528	24,352	2,000	14,598	31,565
Tipton	2,646	4,270	861	2,095	5,674
Union	920	1,691	404	765	2,043
Vanderburgh	31,326	38,231	7,737	22,163	48,806
Vermillion	3,845	3,607	1,175	3,515	4,764
Vigo	20,328	20,814	5,386	18,898	29,730
Wabash	4,598	8,611	836	4,601	10,011
Warren	1,375	2,475	483	1,164	2,746
Warrick	4,784	5,742	1,503	4,296	8,520
Washington	2,936	3,891	1,143	3,086	4,758
Wayne	10,686	17,335	4,240	7,655	21,610
Wells	3,827	5,361	882	3,244	6,425
White	3,395	5,932	965	2,675	7,419
Whitley	3,848	5,684	1,120	3,838	7,489
Totals	**806,659**	**1,067,885**	**243,108**	**708,568**	**1,405,154**

INDIANA VOTE SINCE 1924

1924 (Pres.), Coolidge, Rep., 703,042; Davis, Dem., 492,245; LaFollette, Prog., 71,700; Faris, Proh., 4,416; Foster, Workers, 987.

1928 (Pres.), Hoover, Rep., 848,290; Smith, Dem., 562,691; Varney, Proh., 5,496; Thomas, Soc., 3,871; Reynolds, Soc. Lab., 645.

1932 (Pres.), Roosevelt, Dem., 862,054; Hoover, Rep., 677,184; Thomas, Soc., 21,388; Upshaw, Proh., 10,399; Foster, Com., 2,187; Reynolds, Soc. Lab., 2,070.

1936 (Pres.), Roosevelt, Dem., 943,974; Landon, Rep., 691,570; Lemke, Union, 19,407; Thomas, Soc., 3,856; Browder, Com., 1,090.

1940 (Pres.), Roosevelt, Dem., 874,063; Willkie, Rep., 899,466; Babson, Proh., 6,437; Thomas, Soc., 2,075; Aiken, Soc. Lab., 706.

1944 (Pres.), Roosevelt, Dem., 781,403; Dewey, Rep., 875,891; Watson, Proh., 12,574; Thomas, Soc., 2,223.

1948 (Pres.), Truman, Dem., 807,833; Dewey, Rep.,
821,079; Watson, Proh., 14,711; Wallace, Prog., 9,649;
Thomas, Soc., 2,179; Teichert, Soc. Lab., 763.
1952 (Pres.), Eisenhower, Rep., 1,136,259; Stevenson,
Dem., 801,530; Hamblen, Proh., 15,335; Hallinan,
Prog., 1,222; Hass, Soc. Lab., 979?
1956 (Pres.), Eisenhower, Rep., 1,182,811; Stevenson,
Dem., 783,908; Holtwick, Proh., 6,554; Hass, 1,334.
1960 (Pres.), Kennedy, Dem., 952,358; Nixon, Rep.,
1,175,120; Decker, Proh., 6,746; Hass, Soc. Lab., 1,136.
1964 (Pres.), Johnson, Dem., 1,170,848; Goldwater, Rep.,
911,118; Munn., Proh., 8,266; Hass, Soc. Lab. 1,374.
1968 (Pres.), Nixon, Rep., 1,067,885; Humphrey, Dem.,
806,659; Wallace, 3rd party, 243,108; Munn, Prohibition, 4,616; Halstead, Soc. Worker, 1,293; Gregory, 36.
1972 (Pres.), Nixon, Rep., 1,405,154; McGovern, Dem.,
708,568; Reed, Soc. Worker, 5,575; Fisher, Soc.
Labor, 1,688; Spock, Peace & Freedom, 4,544.

Iowa

| County | 1968 | | | 1972 | |
	Hum-phrey (D)	Nixon (R)	Wal-lace (I)	McGov-ern (D)	Nixon (R)
Adair	1,559	2,789	234	1,642	3,041
Adams	993	1,868	260	1,161	1,814
Allamakee	2,245	4,449	407	2,271	4,150
Appanoose	3,005	3,497	540	2,283	4,321
Audubon	1,710	2,592	198	1,533	2,515
Benton	3,944	5,016	602	4,282	5,273
Black Hawk	21,097	25,594	2,621	21,721	30,920
Boone	5,219	5,260	602	5,105	6,211
Bremer	2,481	5,604	423	3,122	6,333
Buchanan	3,670	4,541	454	3,609	5,277
Buena Vista	3,051	5,599	386	3,460	5,685
Butler	1,673	4,651	252	1,682	4,615
Calhoun	2,361	3,715	335	2,446	3,821
Carroll	4,809	3,927	412	4,608	4,415
Cass	2,136	5,223	369	1,923	5,234
Cedar	2,675	4,494	438	2,465	4,452
Cerro Gordo	8,554	10,661	1,036	9,460	11,856
Cherokee	2,705	4,436	340	2,780	4,726
Chickasaw	2,966	3,510	286	3,134	3,836
Clarke	1,655	2,059	286	1,590	2,214
Clay	2,840	4,325	369	2,887	4,564
Clayton	3,168	5,132	541	3,366	5,447
Clinton	9,515	11,513	1,059	9,895	12,768
Crawford	2,851	4,287	539	3,018	4,493
Dallas	5,062	5,549	640	5,085	6,143
Davis	1,904	2,016	355	1,806	2,287
Decatur	2,057	2,261	262	1,880	2,638
Delaware	2,760	4,650	412	2,944	4,848
Des Moines	10,164	8,452	1,318	8,869	10,216
Dickinson	2,286	3,472	281	2,373	3,739
Dubuque	18,664	14,197	1,701	18,417	17,272
Emmet	2,163	3,444	230	1,970	3,436
Fayette	4,098	6,935	636	4,413	7,263
Floyd	2,971	4,792	390	3,338	4,726
Franklin	1,777	3,604	240	1,986	3,643
Fremont	1,484	2,385	396	1,210	2,642
Greene	2,208	3,208	269	2,152	3,371
Grundy	1,675	4,866	290	1,844	4,706
Guthrie	2,063	3,346	335	2,258	3,655
Hamilton	3,058	4,607	301	2,913	4,803
Hancock	2,131	3,544	249	2,349	3,706
Hardin	3,227	5,308	407	3,516	5,869
Harrison	2,410	3,867	540	2,369	4,721
Henry	2,532	4,613	503	2,721	5,066
Howard	2,420	3,141	253	2,439	2,980
Humboldt	1,940	3,229	217	2,062	3,622
Ida	1,463	2,753	208	1,490	2,819
Iowa	2,586	4,133	367	2,578	4,202
Jackson	3,413	4,535	489	3,704	4,975
Jasper	6,556	7,901	742	7,007	9,133
Jefferson	2,411	4,130	377	2,362	4,628
Johnson	13,541	11,384	736	20,922	14,823
Jones	3,415	4,513	475	3,468	4,962
Keokuk	2,807	3,588	332	2,619	3,831
Kossuth	4,392	5,350	310	4,393	5,841
Lee	8,076	8,883	1,052	7,510	9,748
Linn	29,898	30,918	3,182	31,370	36,503
Louisa	1,632	2,529	323	1,707	2,806
Lucas	1,942	2,543	290	1,759	2,851
Lyon	1,403	4,195	151	1,407	3,788
Madison	2,192	3,151	327	2,234	3,480
Mahaska	3,721	5,670	420	3,382	6,374
Marion	4,618	5,791	597	4,643	6,583
Marshall	6,362	9,402	819	6,618	10,798
Mills	1,216	2,916	532	1,060	3,531
Mitchell	2,103	3,533	192	2,449	3,395
Monona	2,184	2,980	437	2,189	3,277
Monroe	2,240	2,143	312	1,736	2,357
Montgomery	1,892	4,155	425	1,559	4,391
Muscatine	4,726	7,361	643	4,917	8,436
O'Brien	2,146	5,594	322	2,224	5,159
Osceola	1,420	2,516	164	1,317	2,262
Page	2,128	5,907	634	1,790	6,200
Palo Alto	2,874	3,114	234	2,845	3,141
Plymouth	3,234	6,236	557	4,033	6,339

| County | 1968 | | | 1972 | |
	Hum-phrey (D)	Nixon (R)	Wal-lace (I)	McGov-ern (D)	Nixon (R)
Pocahontas	2,364	2,940	254	2,241	3,138
Polk	52,731	51,814	9,524	59,169	70,245
Pottawattamie	9,495	16,038	2,758	8,074	19,722
Poweshiek	3,250	4,470	367	3,718	4,785
Ringgold	1,237	1,986	256	1,003	2,264
Sac	2,207	4,182	280	2,452	4,017
Scott	24,596	25,783	4,133	23,810	34,135
Shelby	2,365	3,886	330	2,259	4,052
Sioux	2,181	10,010	315	2,867	10,721
Story	9,456	13,327	772	13,972	16,517
Tama	3,767	4,955	494	3,693	5,058
Taylor	1,501	2,765	368	1,247	3,042
Union	2,137	3,365	374	2,112	3,734
Van Buren	1,331	2,294	237	1,268	2,272
Wapello	9,375	7,825	1,355	8,348	9,301
Warren	4,613	5,619	919	5,143	7,332
Washington	2,679	4,899	349	2,784	5,187
Wayne	1,723	2,553	283	1,574	2,681
Webster	8,572	9,349	1,026	8,358	11,133
Winnebago	2,163	3,543	246	2,324	4,300
Winneshiek	3,364	5,600	344	4,401	5,877
Woodbury	18,281	21,159	2,153	16,974	23,757
Worth	1,815	2,383	214	2,034	2,564
Wright	2,969	4,299	248	2,780	4,778
Total	**476,699**	**619,106**	**66,422**	**496,206**	**706,207**

IOWA VOTE SINCE 1924

1924 (Pres.), Coolidge, Rep., 537,635; LaFollette, Pro-
272,243; Davis, Dem., 160,000; Foster, Workers, 4,037.
1928 (Pres.), Hoover, Rep., 623,818; Smith, Dem.,
378,936; Thomas, Soc., 2,960; Webb, Farm-Lab., 3,088;
Foster, Com., 328; Reynolds, Soc. Lab., 230.
1932 (Pres.), Roosevelt, Dem., 598,019; Hoover, Rep.,
414,433; Thomas, Soc., 20,467; Upshaw, Proh., 2,111;
Coxey, Farm-Lab., 1,094; Foster, Com., 559.
1936 (Pres.), Roosevelt, Dem., 621,756; Landon, Rep.,
487,977; Lemke, Union, 29,687; Thomas, Soc., 1,373;
Colvin, Proh., 1,182; Browder, C., 506; Aiken, S., 252.
1940 (Pres.), Roosevelt, Dem., 578,800; Willkie, Rep.,
632,370; Babson, Proh., 2,284; Browder, Com., 1,524;
Aiken, Soc. Lab., 452.
1944 (Pres.), Roosevelt, Dem., 499,876; Dewey, Rep.,
547,267; Watson, Proh., 3,752; Thomas, Soc., 1,511;
Teichert, Soc. Lab., 193.
1948 (Pres.), Truman, Dem., 522,380; Dewey, Rep.,
494,018; Wallace, Prog., 12,125; Teichert, Soc. Lab.,
4,274; Watson, Proh., 3,382; Thomas, Soc., 1,829;
Dobbs, Soc. Workers, 256.
1952 (Pres.), Eisenhower, Rep., 808,906; Stevenson, Dem.,
451,513; Hallinan, Prog., 5,085; Hamblen, Proh., 2,882;
Hoopes, Soc., 219; Hass, Soc. Lab., 139; Scattering, 29.
1956 (Pres.), Eisenhower, Rep., 729,187; Stevenson, Dem.,
501,858; Andrews (A.C.P. of Iowa), 3,202; Hoopes, Soc.,
192; Hass, Soc. Lab., 125.
1960 (Pres.), Kennedy, Dem., 550,565; Nixon, Rep.,
722,381; Hass, Soc. Lab., 230; Write-in, 634.
1964 (Pres.), Johnson, Dem., 733,030; Goldwater, Rep.,
449,148; Hass, S. L., 182; DeBerry, S. W. 159; Munn,
P., 1,902.
1968 (Pres.), Nixon, Rep., 619,106; Humphrey, Dem.,
476,699; Wallace, 3rd party, 66,422; Munn, Pro. 362;
Halstead, Soc. Worker, 3,377; Cleaver, Peace and
Freedom, 1,332; Blomen, S.L., 241.
1972 (Pres.), Nixon, Rep., 706,207; McGovern, Dem.,
496,206; Schmitz, American, 22,056; Jenness, Soc.
Worker, 488; Fisher, Soc. Labor, 195; Hall, Communist, 272; Green, Universal, 199; scattered 321.

Kansas

| County | 1968 | | | 1972 | |
	Hum-phrey (D)	Nixon (R)	Wal-lace (I)	McGov-ern (D)	Nixon (R)
Allen	1,875	3,520	492	1,610	3,938
Anderson	1,242	2,168	397	1,035	2,718
Atchison	3,379	3,644	888	2,404	5,471
Barber	1,027	2,023	283	727	2,308
Barton	4,464	6,700	1,017	3,481	8,479
Bourbon	2,241	3,983	769	1,912	4,776
Brown	1,199	3,748	463	1,038	4,314
Butler	5,952	7,893	1,671	4,669	11,045
Chase	462	1,038	154	315	1,184
Chautauqua	478	1,537	329	378	1,546
Cherokee	3,597	4,211	1,054	2,806	6,019
Cheyenne	412	1,423	174	399	1,440
Clark	446	920	210	311	1,142
Clay	926	3,335	357	887	3,562
Cloud	2,132	3,282	412	1,806	3,832
Coffey	933	2,223	367	782	2,667
Comanche	451	906	85	281	1,052
Cowley	5,014	8,070	1,751	3,592	10,332

County	1968 Humphrey (D)	Nixon (R)	Wallace (I)	1972 McGovern (D)	Nixon (R)
Decatur	652	1,654	206	616	1,707
Dickinson	2,399	5,574	675	1,957	6,515
Doniphan	958	2,402	425	690	2,856
Douglas	6,936	10,533	2,080	11,646	15,316
Edwards	832	1,243	182	757	1,534
Elk	503	1,327	216	428	1,522
Ellis	3,809	3,944	671	4,113	5,463
Ellsworth	1,060	1,776	246	1,028	2,087
Finney	2,521	2,295	496	2,062	4,335
Ford	3,191	4,645	935	2,804	6,232
Franklin	2,524	4,875	825	2,056	6,011
Geary	2,228	2,954	625	1,708	4,299
Gove	538	1,018	164	466	1,226
Graham	597	1,308	243	488	1,440
Grant	618	1,121	217	476	1,469
Gray	61?	952	151	511	1,235
Greeley	227	465	82	212	639
Greenwood	1,122	2,937	381	951	3,157
Hamilton	410	751	170	394	941
Harper	1,015	2,351	297	729	2,628
Harvey	3,351	6,682	780	3,555	8,287
Haskell	476	762	167	383	1,036
Hodgeman	387	756	130	331	853
Jackson	1,225	2,678	501	1,191	3,363
Jefferson	1,355	2,781	774	1,237	3,679
Jewell	842	2,172	252	716	2,242
Johnson	26,034	55,060	6,635	24,324	76,161
Kearny	423	721	95	325	876
Kingman	1,201	2,318	319	1,107	2,756
Kiowa	481	1,484	123	406	1,559
Labette	3,974	5,503	1,251	3,210	6,399
Lane	385	781	118	294	943
Leavenworth	5,546	7,081	2,000	4,727	10,762
Lincoln	583	1,721	217	476	1,649
Linn	893	2,250	419	876	2,593
Logan	411	1,120	221	428	1,164
Lyon	4,020	6,558	847	3,720	9,157
Marion	1,494	4,287	304	1,478	4,373
Marshall	1,949	3,835	731	1,823	4,127
McPherson	2,893	6,420	543	2,858	7,457
Meade	572	1,511	196	526	1,712
Miami	2,739	3,614	1,023	2,140	5,234
Mitchell	1,144	2,428	283	1,030	2,830
Montgomery	5,210	9,697	2,456	3,685	11,717
Morris	976	1,938	313	704	2,471
Morton	475	770	262	363	1,165
Nemaha	1,925	3,003	628	1,777	3,422
Neosho	2,725	3,950	784	2,559	5,034
Ness	767	1,352	192	652	1,539
Norton	841	2,543	193	776	2,688
Osage	1,664	3,157	792	1,522	4,073
Osborne	793	2,073	301	724	2,182
Ottawa	777	1,740	253	705	2,065
Pawnee	1,416	2,037	300	1,110	2,370
Phillips	844	2,567	340	827	2,919
Pottawatomie	1,368	3,267	490	1,298	3,947
Pratt	1,490	2,670	435	1,214	3,253
Rawlins	553	1,438	153	560	1,553
Reno	9,872	11,804	1,710	8,183	15,714
Republic	1,187	2,841	240	1,059	2,421
Rice	2,049	3,141	386	1,825	3,843
Riley	4,258	8,296	772	5,333	11,120
Rooks	1,012	2,252	307	904	2,457
Rush	864	1,471	217	806	1,639
Russell	1,261	3,177	290	1,011	3,168
Saline	6,286	9,324	1,169	5,406	12,592
Scott	500	1,374	193	449	1,547
Sedgwick	44,041	60,853	12,255	39,220	83,949
Seward	1,291	3,065	550	989	3,866
Shawnee	21,735	31,140	6,817	20,383	43,727
Sheridan	563	1,002	144	552	1,134
Sherman	954	1,803	368	785	2,225
Smith	939	2,558	279	818	2,600
Stafford	1,205	1,851	253	844	2,200
Stanton	288	541	78	259	754
Stevens	528	1,157	296	408	1,392
Summer	3,562	5,622	1,116	2,685	6,941
Thomas	1,074	1,971	241	943	2,300
Trego	623	1,211	226	621	1,369
Wabaunsee	695	1,979	402	662	2,461
Wallace	235	608	144	214	782
Washington	1,131	3,177	332	996	3,301
Wichita	364	757	130	288	794
Wilson	1,276	3,340	640	1,043	3,568
Woodson	639	1,450	222	550	1,592
Wyandotte	34,189	23,091	11,510	28,206	34,157
Totals	**302,996**	**478,674**	**88,921**	**270,287**	**619,812**

KANSAS VOTE SINCE 1924

1924 (Pres.), Coolidge, Rep., 407,671; Davis, Dem., 156,319; LaFollette, Prog., 98,461.

1928 (Pres.), Hoover, Rep., 513,672; Smith, Dem., 193,003; Thomas, Soc., 6,206; Foster, Com., 320.

1932 (Pres.), Roosevelt, Dem., 424,204; Hoover, Rep., 349,498; Thomas, Soc., 18,276.

1936 (Pres.), Roosevelt, Dem., 464,520; Landon, Rep., 397,727; Thomas, Soc., 2,766; Lemke, Union, 494.

1940 (Pres.), Roosevelt, Dem., 364,725; Willkie, Rep., 489,169; Babson, Proh., 4,056; Thomas, Soc., 2,347.

1944 (Pres.), Roosevelt, Dem., 287,458; Dewey, Rep., 442,096; Watson, Proh., 2,609; Thomas, Soc., 1,613.

1948 (Pres.), Truman, Dem., 351,902; Dewey, Rep., 423,039; Watson, Proh., 6,468; Wallace, Prog., 4,603; Thomas, Soc., 2,807.

1952 (Pres.), Eisenhower, Rep., 616,302; Stevenson, Dem., 273,296; Hamblen, Proh., 6,038; Hoopes, Soc., 530.

1956 (Pres.), Eisenhower, Rep., 566,878; Stevenson, Dem., 296,317; Holtwick, Proh., 3,048.

1960 (Pres.), Kennedy, Dem., 363,213; Nixon, Rep., 561,474; Decker, Proh., 4,138.

1964 (Pres.), Johnson, Dem., 464,028; Goldwater, Rep., 386,579; Munn, Proh., 5,393; Hass, Soc. Labor, 1,901.

1968 (Pres.), Nixon, Rep., 478,674; Humphrey, Dem., 302,996; Wallace, 3rd, 88,921; Munn, Proh., 2,192.

1972 (Pres.), Nixon, Rep., 619,812; McGovern, Dem., 270,287; Schmitz, Cons. 21,808; Munn, Proh. 4,188.

Kentucky

County	1968 Humphrey (D)	Nixon (R)	Wallace (I)	1972 McGovern (D)	Nixon (R)
Adair	1,362	3,239	844	1,610	3,859
Allen	927	2,952	905	1,259	3,025
Anderson	1,334	1,594	657	1,302	2,298
Ballard	1,632	564	1,197	1,411	1,542
Barren	3,464	4,209	2,140	3,384	6,070
Bath	1,394	1,277	658	1,347	1,919
Bell	4,138	4,905	1,204	3,219	6,518
Boone	2,725	4,081	2,240	2,595	7,355
Bourbon	2,566	1,848	1,023	1,860	3,180
Boyd	7,914	8,632	2,443	6,434	12,812
Boyle	2,663	2,715	1,356	2,395	4,317
Bracken	1,067	1,115	548	873	1,628
Breathitt	2,954	1,361	361	2,677	1,346
Breckinridge	2,024	2,779	1,067	1,921	3,574
Bullitt	2,135	1,965	2,180	2,827	4,517
Butler	691	2,637	634	835	2,941
Caldwell	1,439	2,139	1,426	1,345	2,952
Calloway	3,854	2,672	2,150	3,468	5,167
Campbell	9,747	13,681	4,750	8,585	20,025
Carlisle	1,144	479	807	872	1,169
Carroll	1,765	868	514	1,308	1,228
Carter	2,344	3,234	926	2,591	4,082
Casey	879	3,698	649	913	3,727
Christian	4,281	3,788	4,527	4,063	7,414
Clark	2,385	2,698	1,722	2,020	4,506
Clay	1,213	4,663	327	1,709	4,046
Clinton	568	2,572	280	659	2,632
Crittenden	838	1,942	748	859	2,248
Cumberland	646	2,116	355	686	2,294
Daviess	9,947	10,111	5,015	8,168	17,234
Edmonson	679	2,280	516	722	2,327
Elliott	1,387	515	280	1,499	782
Estill	1,261	2,236	675	1,322	3,054
Fayette	16,902	24,948	8,354	19,828	42,362
Fleming	1,406	2,220	535	1,455	2,484
Floyd	8,333	3,550	1,150	7,544	6,099
Franklin	6,396	4,057	2,655	5,601	7,781
Fulton	1,204	1,079	1,526	1,024	1,807
Gallatin	685	413	304	612	719
Garrard	1,000	2,205	675	1,441	3,143
Grant	1,169	1,386	941	1,054	2,086
Graves	5,103	3,239	3,829	3,701	6,098
Grayson	1,595	3,598	657	1,839	4,155
Green	1,003	2,448	712	1,209	2,755
Greenup	4,689	4,698	1,365	4,491	6,828
Hancock	867	1,049	419	791	1,583
Hardin	4,470	5,329	2,845	4,060	8,740
Harlan	6,389	4,572	2,099	4,349	6,527
Harrison	2,373	1,637	839	1,780	2,732
Hart	1,657	2,817	1,002	2,307	3,582
Henderson	5,062	3,512	2,132	3,889	6,231
Henry	1,978	1,271	711	1,688	1,919
Hickman	880	623	1,154	976	1,430
Hopkins	4,391	3,791	3,668	3,129	7,133
Jackson	304	3,098	149	436	5,303
Jefferson	90,242	95,942	35,561	88,143	142,436
Jessamine	1,334	2,338	1,440	1,269	3,819
Johnson	2,142	4,046	344	1,840	4,907
Kenton	14,656	17,263	7,612	12,872	28,076
Knott	3,335	1,098	428	2,774	1,479
Knox	2,244	4,388	944	1,805	5,017
Larue	1,251	1,862	776	1,483	2,449
Laurel	1,756	6,251	1,236	2,274	7,276
Lawrence	1,825	1,946	476	1,529	2,392
Lee	674	1,339	285	744	1,629
Leslie	828	2,615	236	913	3,299
Letcher	3,499	3,243	920	2,908	4,213
Lewis	1,017	2,760	472	1,200	3,524
Lincoln	1,736	2,591	1,129	1,882	3,623

County	1968 Humphrey (D)	Nixon (R)	Wallace (I)	1972 McGovern (D)	Nixon (R)
Livingston	1,272	1,079	953	1,065	1,673
Logan	3,339	3,402	1,881	2,459	3,573
Lyon	719	579	619	687	1,030
McCracken	9,741	5,887	5,810	7,567	11,260
McCreary	759	2,670	479	684	3,203
McLean	1,373	1,372	1,084	1,191	2,298
Madison	3,884	5,325	2,558	4,328	8,659
Magoffin	1,927	1,967	229	2,024	2,243
Marion	2,436	1,620	849	2,351	2,370
Marshall	3,301	2,432	2,183	2,806	4,290
Martin	759	1,943	136	661	2,495
Mason	2,772	2,661	1,131	2,459	3,529
Meade	1,926	1,385	886	1,541	2,492
Menifee	554	509	247	732	596
Mercer	1,950	2,432	1,227	1,707	3,575
Metcalfe	1,001	1,566	469	1,308	1,896
Monroe	693	4,086	590	768	3,770
Montgomery	1,408	2,113	980	1,657	2,868
Morgan	2,222	1,341	398	1,815	1,535
Muhlenberg	3,688	3,853	2,198	3,246	5,596
Nelson	3,420	2,373	1,104	2,828	3,495
Nicholas	911	725	413	804	1,076
Ohio	1,695	3,504	1,263	906	2,392
Oldham	1,399	1,655	937	1,311	3,041
Owen	1,608	827	697	1,161	1,456
Owsley	303	1,417	157	251	1,328
Pendleton	1,156	1,614	760	909	1,966
Perry	4,562	3,993	983	3,601	5,373
Pike	11,663	8,911	1,933	9,513	12,535
Powell	934	1,167	000	1,230	1,766
Pulaski	2,823	8,290	1,780	3,080	10,602
Robertson	406	416	186	421	456
Rockcastle	868	3,072	644	968	3,437
Rowan	1,898	2,017	541	2,169	3,245
Russell	961	3,035	718	1,169	3,992
Scott	1,961	1,748	1,242	1,642	3,255
Shelby	2,579	2,287	1,185	2,074	3,893
Simpson	1,505	1,435	1,390	1,325	2,285
Spencer	564	733	448	481	1,120
Taylor	1,367	3,032	1,554	1,859	4,035
Todd	1,082	1,433	1,932	1,222	1,964
Trigg	1,330	1,100	1,180	1,514	1,767
Trimble	1,045	511	406	757	935
Union	2,616	1,371	1,804	1,855	2,701
Warren	5,200	8,084	4,365	5,934	12,481
Washington	1,675	1,863	472	1,552	2,378
Wayne	1,467	3,055	475	1,853	3,514
Webster	2,114	1,446	1,337	1,712	2,396
Whitley	2,134	5,639	1,650	2,199	6,788
Wolfe	1,162	758	282	957	936
Woodford	1,646	1,901	894	1,268	3,363
Totals	**397,541**	**462,411**	**193,098**	**371,159**	**676,446**

KENTUCKY VOTE SINCE 1924

1924 (Pres.), Coolidge, Rep., 398,966; Davis, Dem., 374,855; LaFollette, Prog., 38,465; Johns, Soc. Lab., 1,499; Nations, Amer., 1,299; Wallace, Comm., 248.

1928 (Pres.), Hoover, Rep., 558,064; Smith, Dem., 381,070; Thomas, Soc., 837; Reynolds, Soc. Lab., 340; Foster, Com., 293.

1932 (Pres.), Roosevelt, Dem., 580,574; Hoover, Rep., 394,716; Upshaw, Proh., 2,252; Thomas, Soc., 3,853; Reynolds, Soc. Lab., 1,396; Foster, Com., 272.

1936 (Pres.), Roosevelt, Dem., 541,944; Landon, Rep., 360,702; Lemke, Union, 12,501; Colvin, Proh., 929; Thomas, S., 627; Aiken, S. L., 294; Browder, Com., 204.

1940 (Pres.), Roosevelt, Dem., 557,222; Willkie, Rep., 410,384; Babson, Proh., 1,443; Thomas, Soc., 1,014.

1944 (Pres.), Roosevelt, Dem., 472,589; Dewey, Rep., 392,448; Watson, Proh., 2,023; Thomas, Soc., 535; Teichert, Soc. Lab., 326.

1948 (Pres.), Truman, Dem., 466,756; Dewey, Rep., 341,210; Thurmond, States' Rights, 10,411; Wallace, Prog., 1,567; Thomas, Soc., 1,284; Watson, Proh., 1,245; Teichert, Soc. Lab., 185.

1952 (Pres.), Eisenhower, Rep., 495,029; Stevenson, Dem., 495,729; Hemblen, Proh., 1,161; Haas, Soc. Lab., 893; Hallinan, Proh., 336.

1956 (Pres.), Eisenhower, Rep., 572,192; Stevenson, Dem., 476,453; Byrd, States' Rights, 2,657; Holtwick, Proh., 2,145; Hass, Soc. Lab., 358.

1960 (Pres.), Kennedy, Dem., 521,855; Nixon, Rep., 602,607.

1964 (Pres.), Johnson, Dem., 669,659; Goldwater, Rep., 372,977; John Kasper, Nat'l States Rights, 3,469.

1968 (Pres.), Nixon, Rep., 462,411; Humphrey, Dem., 397,547; Wallace, 3rd p., 193,098; Halstead, S.W., 2,843.

1972 (Pres.), Nixon, Rep., 676,446; McGovern, Dem., 371,159; Schmitz, Amer., 17,627; Jenness, Soc. Worker, 685; Hall, Comm., 464; Spock, Peoples, 1,118.

Louisiana

Parish	1968 Humphrey (D)	Nixon (R)	Wallace (I)	1972 McGovern (D)	Nixon (R)
Acadia	4,098	3,178	9,715	4,406	9,698
Allen	2,026	1,004	4,229	2,029	3,581
Ascension	3,203	1,338	6,004	3,324	5,187
Assumption	2,085	1,222	2,898	2,065	3,751
Avoyelles	2,973	2,459	6,760	3,395	6,225
Beauregard	1,569	1,615	4,048	1,728	4,955
Bienville	1,768	941	3,466	1,890	3,384
Bossier	2,782	3,745	9,249	2,914	12,856
Caddo	17,675	21,224	28,463	15,649	47,215
Calcasieu	14,593	9,520	20,250	15,330	24,778
Caldwell	973	490	2,252	508	2,306
Cameron	533	405	1,655	739	1,391
Catahoula	769	755	2,677	823	2,683
Claiborne	1,545	1,117	3,311	1,551	3,432
Concordia	1,983	974	4,542	2,142	4,521
DeSoto	3,400	974	4,190	2,596	4,017
E. Baton Rouge	21,770	21,661	35,250	23,617	52,648
East Carroll	1,926	586	1,706	1,661	1,736
East Feliciana	1,409	457	2,225	1,603	1,992
Evangeline	2,647	1,549	7,362	2,910	5,500
Franklin	991	1,032	5,394	1,272	4,967
Grant	532	1,113	3,470	859	3,626
Iberia	5,510	5,448	8,071	5,143	11,812
Iberville	4,084	1,413	4,290	3,650	3,972
Jackson	1,525	1,104	3,941	1,477	4,152
Jefferson	20,193	29,478	41,902	20,981	75,348
Jefferson Davis	2,641	2,213	4,897	2,551	5,903
Lafayette	7,983	10,669	11,723	8,740	22,939
Lafourche	5,516	4,797	10,910	5,713	13,936
LaSalle	710	1,258	3,878	651	3,858
Lincoln	2,009	2,643	4,225	2,589	6,736
Livingston	1,400	947	9,907	1,898	7,481
Madison	2,659	649	2,380	2,249	2,420
Morehouse	1,793	1,772	5,377	2,355	5,770
Natchitoches	3,945	2,352	5,505	3,180	6,994
Orleans	72,451	47,728	58,489	60,790	88,075
Ouachita	6,470	10,089	15,145	6,920	24,860
Plaquemines	1,144	968	6,430	990	6,595
Pointe Coupee	3,139	850	3,508	3,133	3,192
Rapides	8,793	10,199	16,239	8,422	22,306
Red River	914	380	2,477	957	2,245
Richland	1,017	1,031	4,415	1,335	4,304
Sabine	1,159	1,125	4,526	1,332	4,935
St. Bernard	2,485	3,486	13,056	3,189	15,198
St. Charles	3,070	1,675	4,383	2,788	5,469
St. Helena	1,351	219	1,800	943	1,446
St. James	2,987	778	2,765	2,633	3,112
St. John	3,245	940	3,246	2,815	3,525
St. Landry	9,075	3,508	12,659	7,421	12,510
St. Martin	3,321	1,625	4,759	3,202	6,337
St. Mary	5,312	4,586	6,761	4,435	11,117
St. Tammany	4,445	4,846	11,470	3,949	15,438
Tangipahoa	4,983	2,907	13,088	5,227	11,607
Tensas	845	503	1,290	1,568	1,729
Terrebonne	4,627	5,214	8,836	4,415	13,753
Union	1,336	1,113	4,297	1,465	4,322
Vermillion	3,806	3,278	8,124	3,876	8,909
Vernon	1,496	1,574	5,536	1,345	6,225
Washington	3,021	1,606	11,002	2,947	8,162
Webster	2,871	2,496	8,646	2,859	8,829
W Baton Rouge	2,016	669	2,569	1,849	2,626
West Carroll	395	289	3,574	571	2,997
West Feliciana	1,303	296	1,073	1,079	1,001
Winn	1,230	1,050	4,015	1,490	4,235
Totals	**309,615**	**257,535**	**530,300**	**298,142**	**686,852**

LOUISIANA VOTE SINCE 1924

1924 (Pres.), Davis, Dem., 93,218; Coolidge, Rep., 24,670; LaFollette, Prog., 4,063.

1928 (Pres.), Smith, Dem., 164,655; Hoover, Rep., 51,160.

1932 (Pres.), Roosevelt, D., 249,418; Hoover, R., 18,863.

1936 (Pres.), Roosevelt, D., 292,894; Landon, R., 36,791.

1940 (Pres.), Roosevelt, D., 319,751; Willkie, R., 52,446.

1944 (Pres.), Roosevelt, D., 281,564; Dewey, R., 67,750.

1948 (Pres.), Thurmond, States' Rights, 204,290; Truman, D., 136,344; Dewey, R., 72,657; Wallace, Prog., 3,035.

1952 (Pres.), Eisenhower, R., 306,925; Stevenson, D., 345,027.

1956 (Pres.), Eisenhower, Rep., 329,047; Stevenson, Dem., 243,977; Andrews, States Rights, 44,520.

1960 (Pres.), Kennedy, Dem., 407,339; Nixon, Rep., 230,980; States' Rights (unpledged) 169,572.

1964 (Pres.), Johnson, D., 387,068; Goldwater, R., 509,225.

1968 (Pres.), Nixon, Rep., 257,535; Humphrey, Dem.,

309,615; Wallace, 3rd party, 530,300.
1972 (Pres.), Nixon, Rep., 686,852; McGovern, Dem., 298,142; Schmitz, American, 52,099; Jenness, Soc. Worker, 14,398.

Maine

County	1968 Humphrey (D)	Nixon (R)	Wallace (I)	1972 McGovern (D)	Nixon (R)
Androscoggin.....	26,820	10,390	542	19,509	19,406
Aroostook	15,044	13,919	273	11,474	19,051
Cumberland......	44,697	32,275	1,076	33,326	51,268
Franklin.........	4,307	4,127	162	2,988	5,958
Hancock	4,979	8,929	277	4,191	11,889
Kennebec	21,752	16,009	531	16,379	24,617
Knox	5,119	6,585	214	3,601	8,478
Lincoln	3,380	5,659	222	2,903	7,580
Oxford..........	10,870	8,030	375	6,661	12,114
Penobscot	24,327	20,011	661	18,552	30,186
Piscataquis	3,561	3,199	158	2,518	4,617
Sagadahoc......	5,553	4,126	209	3,414	6,463
Somerset........	8,312	6,720	324	5,921	10,079
Waldo	3,525	4,821	234	2,941	6,480
Washington	6,249	5,523	208	3,742	7,820
York	28,817	18,931	904	22,464	30,452
Totals........	217,312	169,254	6,370	160,584	256,458

MAINE VOTE SINCE 1924

1924 (Pres.), Coolidge, Rep., 138,440; Davis, Dem., 41,964; LaFollette, Prog., 11,382; Johns, Soc. Lab., 406.
1928 (Pres.), Hoover, Rep., 179,923; Smith, Dem., 81,179; Thomas, Soc., 1,068.
1932 (Pres.), Roosevelt, Dem., 128,907; Hoover, Rep., 166,631; Thomas, Soc., 2,439; Reynolds, Soc. Lab., 255; Foster, Com., 162.
1936 (Pres.), Landon, Rep., 168,823; Roosevelt, Dem., 126,333; Lemke, Union, 7,581; Thomas, Soc., 783; Colvin, Proh., 334; Browder, Com., 257; Aiken, Soc. Lab., 129.
1940 (Pres.), Roosevelt, Dem., 156,478; Willkie, Rep., 165,951; Browder, Com., 411.
1944 (Pres.), Roosevelt, Dem., 140,631; Dewey, Rep., 155,434; Teichert, Soc. Lab., 335.
1948 (Pres.), Truman, Dem., 111,916; Dewey, Rep., 150,234; Wallace, Prog., 1,884; Thomas, Soc., 547; Teichert, Soc. Lab., 206.
1952 (Pres.), Eisenhower, Rep., 232,353; Stevenson, Dem., 118,806; Hallinan, Prog., 332; Hass, Soc. Lab., 156; Hoopes, Soc., 138; Scattered, 1.
1956 (Pres.), Eisenhower, Rep., 249,238; Stevenson, Dem., 102,468.
1960 (Pres.), Kennedy, Dem., 181,159; Nixon, Rep., 240,608.
1964 (Pres.), Johnson, Dem., 262,264; Goldwater, Rep., 118,701.
1968 (Pres.), Nixon, Rep., 169,254; Humphrey, Dem., 217,312; Wallace, 3rd party, 6,370.
1972 (Pres.), Nixon, Rep., 256,458; McGovern, Dem., 160,584; scattered 229.

Maryland

County	1968 Humphrey (D)	Nixon (R)	Wallace (I)	1972 McGovern (D)	Nixon (R)
Allegany	13,227	13,561	5,122	10,808	20,687
Anne Arundel	25,381	36,557	15,687	26,082	71,707
Baltimore	80,798	108,930	29,283	70,309	175,897
Calvert	2,032	1,946	1,471	2,232	4,024
Caroline	1,697	3,120	1,414	1,567	4,325
Carroll..........	4,658	11,888	3,085	4,408	16,847
Cecil	4,517	6,462	3,235	4,113	10,759
Charles	4,247	4,645	3,173	4,502	9,665
Dorchester	2,714	4,183	3,217	2,136	6,859
Frederick........	8,316	13,649	4,348	8,235	19,907
Garrett	1,933	4,021	818	1,510	5,480
Harford	9,914	15,799	4,978	8,737	25,141
Howard	5,752	9,957	2,796	10,668	19,265
Kent	2,243	2,946	1,146	2,168	4,036
Montgomery	92,026	84,651	14,726	100,228	133,090
Prince George's ..	71,524	73,269	32,867	79,914	116,166
Queen Anne's ...	1,969	2,888	1,298	1,712	4,380
St. Mary's.......	3,280	3,348	2,547	3,571	7,689
Somerset........	2,319	2,829	1,899	2,036	4,342
Talbot	2,609	4,902	1,372	2,181	6,620
Washington	11,266	16,050	6,737	10,039	24,234
Wicomico........	5,392	8,707	4,356	5,510	13,115

County	1968 Humphrey (D)	Nixon (R)	Wallace (I)	1972 McGovern (D)	Nixon (R)
Worcester	2,046	3,541	1,871	1,792	5,584
BALTIMORE CITY	178,450	80,146	31,288	141,323	119,486
Totals........	538,310	517,995	178,734	505,781	829,305

MARYLAND VOTE SINCE 1924

1924 (Pres.), Coolidge, Rep., 162,414; Davis, Dem., 148,072; LaFollette, Prog., 47,157; Johns, Soc. Lab., 987.
1928 (Pres.), Hoover, Rep., 301,479; Smith, Dem., 223,626; Thomas, Soc., 1,701; Reynolds, Soc., Lab., 906; Foster, Com., 636.
1932 (Pres.), Roosevelt, Dem., 314,314; Hoover, Rep., 184,184; Thomas, Soc., 10,489; Reynolds, Soc. Lab., 1,036; Foster, Com., 1,031.
1936 (Pres.), Roosevelt, Dem., 389,612; Landon, Rep., 231,435; Thomas, Soc., 1,629; Aiken, Soc. Lab., 1,305; Browder, Com., 915.
1940 (Pres.), Roosevelt, Dem., 384,546; Willkie, Rep., 269,534; Thomas, Soc., 4,093; Browder, Com., 1,274; Aiken, Lab., 657.
1944 (Pres.), Roosevelt, Dem., 315,490; Dewey, Rep., 292,949.
1948 (Pres.), Truman, Dem., 286,521; Dewey, Rep., 294,814; Wallace, Prog., 9,983; Thomas, Soc., 2,941; Thurmond, States' Rights, 2,476; Wright, Write-in 2,294.
1952 (Pres.), Eisenhower, Rep., 499,424; Stevenson, Dem., 395,337; Hallinan, Prog., 7,313.
1956 (Pres.), Eisenhower, Rep., 559,738; Stevenson, Dem., 372,613.
1960 (Pres.), Kennedy, Dem., 565,808; Nixon, Rep., 489,538.
1964 (Pres.), Johnson, Dem., 730,912; Goldwater, Rep., 385,495; Write-in, 50.
1968 (Pres.), Nixon, Rep., 517,995; Humphrey, Dem., 538,310; Wallace, 3rd party, 178,734.
1972 (Pres.), Nixon, Rep., 829,305; McGovern, Dem., 505,781; Schmitz, American Party, 18,726.

Massachusetts

County	1968 Humphrey (D)	Nixon (R)	Wallace (I)	1972 McGovern (D)	Nixon (R)
Barnstable.......	16,546	24,296	1,242	22,636	36,340
Berkshire	38,497	23,078	2,593	35,391	30,380
Bristol	119,439	56,672	6,999	103,163	84,390
Dukes...........	1,540	1,576	75	2,001	2,312
Essex...........	171,901	99,721	9,236	157,324	138,040
Franklin.........	12,072	12,345	893	11,968	16,088
Hampden	111,376	55,783	9,846	94,945	86,164
Hampshire.......	26,666	16,270	2,314	28,572	24,529
Middlesex.......	370,310	188,304	16,561	345,343	269,064
Nantucket.......	744	991	52	952	1,418
Norfolk.........	160,513	95,858	9,080	150,232	134,459
Plymouth........	67,771	54,644	5,342	69,124	76,062
Suffolk.........	203,406	48,952	15,121	166,250	85,272
Worcester	168,437	88,354	7,734	144,139	127,560
Totals........	1,469,218	766,844	87,088	1,332,540	1,112,078

MASSACHUSETTS VOTE SINCE 1924

1924 (Pres.), Coolidge, Rep., 703,489; Davis, Dem., 280,884; LaFollette, Prog., 141,225; Foster, Workers, 2,637; Johns, Soc. Lab., 1,668.
1928 (Pres.), Smith, Dem., 792,758; Hoover, Rep., 775,566; Thomas, Soc., 6,262; Foster, Com., 2,464; Reynolds, Soc. Lab., 773.
1932 (Pres.), Roosevelt, Dem., 800,148; Hoover, Rep., 736,959; Thomas, Soc. 34,305; Foster, Com., 4,821; Reynolds, Soc. Lab., 2,668; Upshaw, Proh., 1,142.
1936 (Pres.), Roosevelt, Dem., 942,716; Landon, Rep., 768,613; Lemke, Union, 118,639; Thomas, Soc., 5,111; Browder, Com., 2,930; Aiken, Soc. Lab., 1,305; Colvin, Proh. 1,032.
1940 (Pres.), Roosevelt, Dem., 1,076,522; Willkie, Rep., 939,700; Thomas, Soc., 4,091; Browder, Com., 3,806; Aiken, Soc. Lab., 1,492; Babson, Proh., 1,370.
1944 (Pres.), Roosevelt, Dem., 1,035,296; Dewey, Rep., 921,350; Teichert, Soc. Lab., 2,780; Watson, Proh., 973.
1948 (Pres.), Truman, Dem., 1,151,788; Dewey, Rep., 909,370; Wallace, Prog., 38,157; Teichert, Soc. Lab., 5,535; Watson, Proh., 1,663.
1952 (Pres.), Eisenhower, Rep., 1,292,325; Stevenson, Dem., 1,083,525; Hallinan, Prog., 4,636; Hass, Soc. Lab., 1,957; Hamblen, Proh., 886; Scattered, 69; Blanks, 41,150.
1956 (Pres.), Eisenhower, Rep., 1,393,197; Stevenson,

Dem., 948,190; Hass, Soc. Lab., 5,573; Holtwick, Proh., 1,205; Others, 341.
1960 (Pres.), Kennedy, Dem., 1,487,174; Nixon, Rep., 976,750; Hass, Soc. Lab., 3,892; Decker, Proh., 1,633; Others, 31; Blank and void 26,024.
1964 (Pres.), Johnson, Dem., 1,786,422; Goldwater, Rep., 549,727; Hass, Soc. Lab., 4,755; Munn, Proh., 3,735; scattered 159; Blank 48,104.
1968 (Pres.), Nixon, Rep., 766,844; Humphrey, Dem., 1,469,218; Wallace, 3rd party, 87,088; Blomen, Soc. Labor, 6,180; Munn, Prohibition, 2,369; scattered 53; blanks 25,394.
1972 (Pres.), Nixon, Rep., 1,112,078; McGovern, Dem., 1,332,540; Jenness, Soc. Worker, 10,600; Fisher, Soc. Labor, 129; Schmitz, American, 2,877; Spock, Peoples, 101; Hall, Communist, 46; Hospers, Libertarian, 43; scattered 342.

Michigan

County	1968			1972	
	Hum-phrey (D)	Nixon (R)	Wal-lace (I)	McGov-ern (D)	Nixon (R)
Alcona	958	1,852	338	1,195	2,434
Alger	1,927	1,406	173	1,803	2,035
Allegan	7,276	14,769	2,389	7,883	18,407
Alpena	4,788	5,717	747	5,104	6,513
Antrim	1,690	3,002	374	2,000	4,068
Arenac	1,573	2,089	324	1,829	2,588
Baraga	1,680	1,508	116	1,517	1,905
Barry	5,200	9,118	1,074	5,484	10,393
Bay	21,410	18,779	2,291	21,712	23,094
Benzie	1,147	2,138	219	1,310	2,686
Berrien	21,266	32,136	9,333	18,597	43,047
Branch	4,518	7,071	1,037	4,887	8,388
Calhoun	22,633	26,181	5,944	22,154	32,531
Cass	5,616	6,996	2,257	4,982	10,398
Charlevoix	2,446	3,696	556	2,831	4,522
Cheboygan	2,840	3,422	634	2,985	4,529
Chippewa	4,132	5,359	793	4,744	7,028
Clare	1,909	3,315	602	2,434	4,402
Clinton	5,548	9,416	1,591	5,770	13,438
Crawford	845	1,266	187	1,143	1,953
Delta	7,821	5,829	700	8,003	7,647
Dickinson	5,726	4,920	533	5,339	5,989
Eaton	8,347	14,184	2,252	8,986	20,413
Emmet	2,624	4,405	446	3,081	4,288
Genesee	75,174	63,948	24,539	73,896	85,747
Gladwin	1,668	2,840	511	2,016	3,484
Gogebic	5,839	4,140	434	4,984	5,631
Grand Traverse	4,741	8,960	843	5,810	11,421
Gratiot	4,040	8,404	949	4,370	9,904
Hillsdale	3,803	8,506	1,107	3,942	9,261
Houghton	6,988	6,639	473	6,402	9,053
Huron	3,607	8,743	1,178	4,456	9,832
Ingham	37,362	46,805	6,432	53,458	63,376
Ionia	6,055	8,625	1,261	6,240	10,898
Iosco	2,533	4,068	736	3,065	5,750
Iron	4,130	3,292	340	3,512	3,630
Isabella	4,450	7,111	808	7,446	9,682
Jackson	18,205	27,828	5,689	19,350	34,220
Kalamazoo	26,437	39,796	7,398	33,324	50,405
Kalkaska	753	1,190	288	924	1,855
Kent	61,891	85,810	11,584	67,587	104,041
Keweenaw	602	525	65	456	715
Lake	1,482	1,094	220	1,548	1,532
Lapeer	5,199	8,866	2,081	5,531	11,615
Leelanau	1,562	2,798	297	1,855	3,809
Lenawee	10,552	16,280	2,197	11,018	19,125
Livingston	7,052	10,034	2,543	7,634	16,856
Luce	855	1,351	109	862	1,579
Mackinac	1,751	2,507	317	1,937	3,096
Macomb	114,552	63,139	29,239	82,346	147,777
Manistee	3,671	4,007	614	3,625	5,070
Marquette	11,199	8,960	802	11,555	13,249
Mason	3,660	5,311	854	3,697	6,811
Mecosta	2,738	5,053	625	3,799	7,158
Menominee	4,877	4,599	620	4,657	6,060
Midland	7,428	14,329	1,849	9,504	16,473
Missaukee	736	2,161	292	924	2,647
Monroe	18,921	15,685	4,873	17,726	23,263
Montcalm	5,303	8,329	1,244	5,402	9,591
Montmorency	810	1,279	260	914	1,798
Muskegon	24,492	28,233	5,808	22,804	36,428
Newaygo	3,369	6,626	1,042	3,978	8,245
Oakland	154,630	156,538	33,024	129,400	241,613
Oceana	2,152	3,911	876	2,525	4,992
Ogemaw	1,647	2,526	454	2,056	3,367
Ontonagon	2,462	2,290	252	2,140	3,040
Osceola	1,509	3,705	583	1,706	4,441
Oscoda	563	1,124	157	678	1,561
Otsego	1,661	1,871	259	1,912	2,854
Ottawa	12,431	33,356	3,460	15,119	42,169
Presque Isle	2,300	2,565	385	2,440	3,372
Roscommon	1,639	2,635	431	2,187	4,136
Saginaw	32,266	38,070	6,906	29,424	47,920
St. Clair	16,251	21,084	5,261	15,712	23,471
St. Joseph	5,413	10,445	1,759	5,119	18,438

County	1968			1972	
	Hum-phrey (D)	Nixon (R)	Wal-lace (I)	McGov-ern (D)	Nixon (R)
Sanilac	3,193	9,273	1,692	3,780	11,031
Schoolcraft	1,869	1,745	227	1,759	2,310
Shiawassee	8,619	11,465	2,377	3,932	15,489
Tuscola	4,698	10,205	1,682	5,449	12,198
Van Buren	7,304	10,676	2,560	7,159	13,903
Washtenaw	33,073	36,432	7,456	55,350	50,535
Wayne	654,157	270,566	105,606	514,913	435,877
Wexford	2,832	4,364	535	3,048	5,221
Totals	**1,593,082**	**1,370,665**	**331,968**	**1,459,435**	**1,961,721**

MICHIGAN VOTE SINCE 1924

1924 (Pres.), Coolidge, Rep., 874,631; Davis, Dem., 152,238; LaFollette, Prog., 122,014; Faris, Proh., 6,085; Johns, Soc. Lab., 5,330.
1928 (Pres.), Hoover, Rep., 965,396; Smith, Dem., 396,762; Thomas, Soc., 3,516; Foster, Com., 2,881; Proh, 2,728; Soc. Lab., 799.
1932 (Pres.), Roosevelt, Dem., 871,700; Hoover, Rep., 739,894; Thomas, Soc., 39,205; Foster, Com., 9,318; Upshaw, Proh., 2,893; Reynolds, Soc. Lab., 1,041; Harvey, Lib., 217.
1936 (Pres.), Roosevelt, Dem., 1,016,794; Landon, Rep., 699,733; Lemke, Union, 75,795; Thomas, Soc., 8,208; Browder, Com., 3,384; Aiken, Soc. Lab., 600; Colvin, Proh., 579.
1940 (Pres.), Roosevelt, Dem., 1,032,991; Willkie, Rep., 1,039,917; Thomas, Soc., 7,593; Browder, Com., 2,834; Babson, Proh., 1,795; Aiken, Soc. Lab., 795
1944 (Pres.), Roosevelt, Dem., 1,106,899; Dewey, Rep., 1,084,423; Watson, Proh., 6,503; Thomas, Soc., 4,598; Smith, America First, 1,530; Teichert, Soc. Lab., 1,264.
1948 (Pres.), Truman, Dem., 1,003,448; Dewey, Rep., 1,038,595; Wallace, Prog., 46,515; Watson, Proh., 13,052; Thomas, Soc., 6,063; Teichert, Soc. Lab., 1,263; Dobbs, Soc. Workers, 672.
1952 (Pres.), Eisenhower, Rep., 1,551,529; Stevenson, Dem., 1,230,657; Hamblen, Proh., 10,331; Hallinan, Prog., 3,922; Hass, Soc. Lab., 1,495; Dobbs, Soc. Workers, 655; Scattered, 3.
1956 (Pres.), Eisenhower, Rep., 1,713,647; Stevenson, Dem., 1,359,898; Holtwick, Proh., 6,923.
1960 (Pres.), Kennedy, Dem., 1,687,269, Nixon, Rep., 1,620,428; Dobbs, Soc. Workers, 4,347; Decker, Proh., 2,029; Daly, Tax Cut, 1,767; Hass, Soc. Lab., 1,718, Ind. American 539.
1964 (Pres.), Johnson, Dem., 2,136,615; Goldwater, Rep., 1,060,152; DeBerry, Soc. Worker, 3,817; Hass, Soc. Lab., 1,704; Proh. (no candidate listed), 669; Scattering, 145.
1968 (Pres.), Nixon, Rep., 1,370,665; Humphrey, Dem., 1,593,082; Wallace, 3rd party, 331,968; Halstead, Soc. Worker, 4,099; Blomen, Soc. Labor, 1,762; Cleaver, New Politics, 4,585; Munn, Prohib., 60; Scattering 29.
1972 (Pres.), Nixon, Rep., 1,961,721; McGovern, Dem., 1,459,435; Schmitz, Amer., 63,321; Fisher, Soc. Labor, 2,437; Jenness, Soc. Worker, 1,603; Hall, Communist, 1,210.

Minnesota

County	1968			1972	
	Hum-phrey (D)	Nixon (R)	Wal-lace (I)	McGov-ern (D)	Nixon (R)
Aitkin	3,094	2,254	286	2,687	3,241
Anoka	30,656	16,358	3,073	28,031	29,546
Becker	4,875	4,728	568	4,695	6,033
Beltrami	5,034	3,912	599	5,194	5,947
Benton	4,022	3,470	514	4,282	4,652
Big Stone	2,119	1,645	176	2,185	1,748
Blue Earth	9,254	9,571	686	10,638	12,702
Brown	4,585	7,039	703	4,347	7,791
Carlton	8,538	3,016	444	7,116	5,445
Carver	4,590	6,649	528	4,852	8,546
Cass	3,569	3,888	486	3,347	4,906
Chippewa	3,701	3,195	243	3,630	3,787
Chisago	4,102	3,053	492	4,174	4,718
Clay	7,987	7,910	640	9,076	11,089
Clearwater	2,046	1,284	217	1,751	1,819
Cook	777	853	96	742	1,047
Cottonwood	3,046	4,050	293	2,802	4,396
Crow Wing	7,411	6,687	672	7,328	8,774
Dakota	28,416	19,290	2,142	28,479	34,967
Dodge	2,437	3,064	201	1,921	3,863
Douglas	4,826	5,464	536	5,501	6,678
Faribault	4,335	5,662	379	3,519	6,503
Fillmore	3,918	6,257	426	3,155	7,101
Freeborn	8,671	7,315	558	6,147	9,747
Goodhue	7,220	8,283	451	6,147	11,107
Grant	1,982	1,929	179	2,085	1,899
Hennepin	220,078	170,002	15,659	205,943	228,951
Houston	2,703	4,450	521	2,467	5,186

County	1968 Humphrey (D)	Nixon (R)	Wallace (I)	1972 McGovern (D)	Nixon (R)
Hubbard	1,920	2,720	304	2,136	3,294
Isanti	3,439	2,429	451	3,660	3,715
Itasca	10,512	4,898	780	8,683	7,558
Jackson	3,515	2,886	359	3,304	3,599
Kanabec	2,154	1,847	240	1,969	2,395
Kandiyohi	7,639	5,086	658	7,241	6,624
Kittson	1,894	1,436	179	1,584	1,832
Koochiching	4,697	2,104	299	3,396	3,681
LacQuiParle	2,937	2,672	212	2,845	2,773
Lake	4,266	1,351	263	3,640	2,575
Lake O' Woods	875	607	69	672	877
Le Sueur	5,094	4,189	292	4,725	5,388
Lincoln	2,109	1,732	187	2,148	1,881
Lyon	5,317	4,331	306	5,614	5,820
McLeod	4,861	6,619	576	4,538	7,820
Mahnomen	1,508	893	201	1,397	1,246
Marshall	3,161	2,367	418	2,790	3,264
Martin	4,271	7,115	580	3,816	7,569
Meeker	4,213	4,044	438	3,601	5,097
Mille Lacs	3,494	2,990	399	3,221	4,291
Morrison	6,111	4,511	612	5,993	5,714
Mower	11,022	7,736	692	10,286	9,929
Murray	2,662	2,906	316	2,893	2,959
Nicollet	4,244	4,671	312	4,680	6,230
Nobles	5,171	4,451	477	5,464	4,951
Norman	2,828	1,981	200	2,444	2,536
Olmsted	13,417	17,292	1,103	9,817	23,806
Otter Tail	7,400	12,483	802	7,881	13,519
Pennington	2,998	2,247	212	2,892	3,548
Pine	4,044	2,591	463	3,794	3,881
Pipestone	2,234	3,241	260	2,758	3,543
Polk	8,380	6,074	700	7,366	8,139
Pope	2,592	2,504	265	2,910	2,610
Ramsey	122,568	64,068	8,543	108,392	95,716
Red Lake	1,467	718	130	1,409	1,052
Redwood	3,680	5,134	462	3,177	5,776
Renville	4,535	4,821	543	4,499	5,329
Rice	7,785	7,037	477	8,065	9,195
Rock	2,084	3,056	232	2,089	3,470
Roseau	2,649	2,048	326	2,396	2,844
St. Louis	72,267	25,981	3,255	61,103	41,435
Scott	6,656	4,632	540	6,745	7,310
Sherburne	3,481	2,737	369	4,070	4,332
Sibley	2,540	4,250	361	2,433	4,543
Stearns	15,990	15,422	2,081	19,315	18,951
Steele	4,631	6,193	358	4,010	7,678
Stevens	2,247	2,560	246	2,870	2,830
Swift	3,716	2,476	247	3,823	2,673
Todd	3,992	4,883	572	4,270	5,387
Traverse	1,669	1,277	137	1,744	1,276
Wabasha	3,452	4,081	346	3,017	5,158
Wadena	2,198	2,912	269	2,430	3,408
Waseca	3,057	4,292	244	2,767	5,064
Washington	16,449	10,921	1,527	16,102	19,142
Watonwan	2,701	3,446	278	2,229	3,960
Wilkin	1,946	2,037	181	1,739	2,292
Winona	8,627	7,998	781	8,080	10,910
Wright	8,793	6,321	627	8,695	9,996
Yellow Med	3,587	3,060	406	3,462	3,683
Totals	**857,738**	**658,643**	**68,931**	**802,346**	**898,269**

MINNESOTA VOTE SINCE 1924

1924 (Pres.), Coolidge, Rep., 420,759; LaFollette, Prog., 339,192; Davis, Dem., 55,913; Foster, Workers, 4,427; Johns, Soc. Lab., 1,855.

1928 (Pres.), Hoover, Rep., 560,977; Smith, Dem., 396,451; Thomas, Soc., 6,774; Foster, Com., 4,853; Industrial, 1,921.

1932 (Pres.), Roosevelt, Dem., 600,806; Hoover, Rep., 363,959; Thomas, Soc., 25,476; Foster, Com., 6,101; Coxey, Farm.-Lab., 5,731; Reynolds, Ind., 770.

1936 (Pres.), Roosevelt, Dem., 698,811; Landon, Rep., 350,461; Lemke, Union, 74,296; Thomas, Soc., 2,872; Browder, Com., 2,574; Aiken, Soc., 961.

1940 (Pres.), Roosevelt, Dem., 644,196; Willkie, Rep., 596,274; Thomas, Soc., 5,454; Browder, Com., 2,711; Aiken, Ind., 2,553.

1944 (Pres.), Roosevelt, Dem., 589,864; Dewey, Rep., 527,416; Thomas, Soc., 5,073; Teichert, Ind., Gov't., 3,176.

1948 (Pres.), Truman, Dem., 692,966; Dewey, Rep., 483,617; Wallace, Prog., 27,866; Thomas, Soc., 4,646; Teichert, Soc. Lab., 2,525; Dobbs, Soc. Workers, 606.

1952 (Pres.), Eisenhower, Rep., 763,211; Stevenson, Dem., 608,458; Hallinan, Prog., 2,666; Hass, Soc. Lab., 2,383; Hamblen, Proh., 2,147; Dobbs, Soc. Workers, 618.

1956 (Pres.), Eisenhower, Rep., 719,302; Stevenson, Dem., 617,525; Hass, Soc. Lab. (Ind. Gov.), 2,080; Dobbs, Soc. Workers, 1,098.

1960 (Pres.), Kennedy, Dem., 779,933; Nixon, Rep., 757,915; Dobbs, Soc. Workers, 3,077; Industrial Gov., 962.

1964 (Pres.), Johnson, Dem., 991,117; Goldwater, Rep., 559,624; DeBerry, Soc. Workers, 1,177; Hass, Industrial Gov., 2,544.

1968 (Pres.), Nixon, Rep., 658,643; Humphrey, Dem., 857,738; Wallace, 3rd party, 68,931; scattered 2,443; Halstead, Soc. Worker, 808; Blomen, Ind. Govt., 285; Mitchell, Communist, 415; Cleaver, Peace, 935; McCarthy, write-in 585; scattered 170.

1972 (Pres.), Nixon, Rep. 898,269; McGovern, Dem., 802,346; Schmitz, American, 31,407; Spock, Peoples, 2,805; Fisher, Soc. Labor, 4,261; Jenness, Soc. Worker, 940; Hall, Communist, 662; scattered 962.

Mississippi

County	1968 Humphrey (D)	Nixon (R)	Wallace (I)	1972 McGovern (D)	Nixon (R)
Adams	5,214	1,475	6,812	3,697	8,500
Alcorn	1,122	1,760	6,304	982	5,732
Amite	1,533	393	3,206	1,185	2,846
Attala	1,588	599	4,776	1,103	4,738
Benton	850	185	1,630	701	1,483
Bolivar	4,696	1,790	5,018	3,616	7,397
Calhoun	276	394	4,823	245	3,023
Carroll	925	138	2,131	580	1,777
Chickasaw	720	381	4,062	579	3,753
Choctaw	417	211	2,543	326	2,301
Claiborne	2,129	230	1,143	2,076	1,521
Clarke	878	298	4,214	954	4,561
Clay	1,510	494	3,505	1,410	4,035
Coahoma	5,352	1,875	3,671	3,708	6,602
Copiah	2,724	704	4,951	1,803	5,498
Covington	691	445	3,668	642	3,842
DeSoto	1,898	1,092	5,346	1,557	7,917
Forrest	2,957	3,294	9,975	2,933	14,418
Franklin	782	231	2,429	561	2,361
George	214	171	3,992	270	3,979
Greene	449	132	2,744	513	2,884
Grenada	2,050	718	4,335	1,471	4,800
Hancock	904	1,065	4,072	745	5,133
Harrison	4,549	6,542	18,157	4,761	28,962
Hinds	14,880	13,488	32,366	12,679	49,877
Holmes	3,881	520	3,008	3,459	3,158
Humphreys	1,219	258	2,151	892	2,334
Issaquena	527	44	534	395	701
Itawamba	417	569	5,204	509	4,419
Jackson	2,236	2,942	15,261	2,534	22,204
Jasper	987	373	3,100	935	3,597
Jefferson	2,121	147	1,112	1,457	1,131
Jefferson Davis	1,465	297	2,614	1,005	2,830
Jones	2,476	3,242	12,276	2,790	16,489
Kemper	655	167	2,530	837	2,748
Lafayette	1,578	1,235	3,329	1,545	5,391
Lamar	351	546	4,422	493	5,022
Lauderdale	3,195	2,328	14,842	3,453	18,337
Lawrence	740	329	2,825	709	3,394
Leake	1,295	453	4,568	1,053	4,217
Lee	1,912	2,522	9,232	1,632	10,730
Leflore	4,386	1,514	5,732	2,038	6,779
Lincoln	1,585	1,057	7,276	1,070	7,593
Lowndes	2,229	1,968	6,829	2,398	10,098
Madison	4,515	876	4,071	3,464	5,047
Marion	1,722	763	5,848	1,693	6,805
Marshall	2,907	577	2,794	1,875	3,326
Monroe	1,506	1,167	7,856	1,279	7,273
Montgomery	896	475	2,988	925	3,210
Neshoba	867	531	6,417	812	6,815
Newton	799	542	5,561	597	5,585
Noxubee	1,387	232	2,040	1,052	2,239
Oktibbeha	1,826	1,276	4,127	1,880	6,160
Panola	2,743	1,098	4,133	2,091	5,284
Pearl River	926	1,298	6,050	901	7,487
Perry	439	227	2,541	446	2,689
Pike	2,848	1,460	5,846	2,332	6,542
Pontotoc	599	733	4,798	488	4,476
Prentiss	440	723	5,055	398	4,607
Quitman	1,502	434	2,443	790	2,524
Rankin	1,975	1,124	9,224	1,913	12,187
Scott	1,067	604	5,093	1,213	5,244
Sharkey	972	249	1,188	655	1,426
Simpson	1,079	875	5,064	871	5,669
Smith	352	437	4,367	329	4,419
Stone	314	258	2,140	293	2,467
Sunflower	2,602	1,036	3,932	1,874	5,389
Tallahatchie	1,477	577	3,076	835	3,442
Tate	1,162	605	2,810	1,151	3,966
Tippah	663	589	4,627	569	3,937
Tishomingo	358	617	4,569	443	4,177
Tunica	1,133	413	783	858	1,446
Union	624	948	5,198	658	5,477
Walthall	1,233	387	3,186	747	3,110
Warren	4,503	2,392	7,217	3,480	10,420
Washington	5,520	3,500	6,300	4,623	9,634
Wayne	739	247	4,089	975	4,648
Webster	295	330	3,398	403	3,624
Wilkinson	2,144	272	1,503	1,409	1,608
Winston	911	508	4,635	1,354	5,155

County	1968 Humphrey (D)	Nixon (R)	Wallace (I)	1972 McGovern (D)	Nixon (R)
Yalobusha	873	562	2,725	797	2,944
Yazoo	2,163	958	4,939	2,008	5,555
Totals	150,644	88,516	415,349	126,782	505,125

MISSISSIPPI VOTE SINCE 1924

1924 (Pres.), Davis, Dem., 100,475; Coolidge, Rep., 8,546; LaFollette, Prog., 3,494.

1928 (Pres.), Smith, Dem., 124,539; Hoover, Rep., 27,153.

1932 (Pres.), Roosevelt, Dem., 140,168; Hoover, Rep., 5,180; Thomas, Soc., 686.

1936 (Pres.), Roosevelt, Dem., 157,318; Landon, Rep., Howard faction, 2,760; Rowlands faction, 1,675; total, 4,435; Thomas, Soc., 329.

1940 (Pres.), Roosevelt, Dem., 168,252; Willkie, Ind. Rep., 4,550; Rep., 2,814; total, 7,364; Thomas, Soc., 103.

1944 (Pres.), Roosevelt, Dem., 158,515; Dewey, Rep., 3,742; Reg. Dem., 9,964; Ind. Rep., 7,859.

1948 (Pres.), Thurmond, States' Rights, 167,538; Truman, Dem., 19,384; Dewey, Rep., 5,043; Wallace, Prog., 225.

1952 (Pres.), Eisenhower, Ind. vote pledged to Rep. candidate, 112,966; Stevenson, Dem., 172,566.

1956 (Pres.), Stevenson, Dem., 144,498; Eisenhower, Rep., 56,372; Black and Tan Grand Old Party, 4,313; total, 60,685; Byrd, Independent, 42,966.

1960 (Pres.), Democratic unpledged electors, 116,248; Kennedy, Dem., 108,362; Nixon, Rep., 73,561. Mississippi's victorious slate of 8 unpledged Democratic electors cast their votes for Sen. Harry F. Byrd (D.-Va.).

1964 (Pres.), Johnson, Dem., 52,618; Coldwater, Rep., 356,528.

1968 (Pres.), Nixon, Rep., 88,516; Humphrey, Dem., 150,644; Wallace, 3rd party, 415,349.

1972 (Pres.), Nixon, Rep., 505,125; McGovern, Dem., 126,782; Schmitz, American, 11,598; Jenness, Soc. Worker, 2,458.

Missouri

County	1968 Humphrey (D)	Nixon (R)	Wallace (I)	1972 McGovern (D)	Nixon (R)
Adair	2,645	4,624	592	2,286	6,157
Andrew	2,005	3,398	359	1,686	4,180
Atchison	1,752	2,206	337	1,509	2,927
Audrain	4,806	5,005	1,012	3,706	7,197
Barry	3,398	5,537	758	3,167	7,295
Barton	1,832	2,928	499	1,140	4,026
Bates	3,370	4,087	801	3,020	5,314
Benton	1,345	2,899	498	1,423	3,537
Bollinger	1,693	2,283	583	1,818	3,069
Boone	11,771	11,917	2,015	13,666	17,488
Buchanan	15,860	16,101	2,752	11,395	21,850
Butler	4,379	6,326	2,759	3,466	9,198
Caldwell	1,490	2,631	430	1,231	3,167
Callaway	3,738	4,277	1,276	3,036	6,313
Camden	1,605	3,500	633	1,761	4,996
Cape Girardeau	6,656	10,298	2,351	6,280	15,693
Carroll	2,473	3,680	645	1,927	4,100
Carter	738	861	289	565	1,257
Cass	4,468	5,271	1,938	3,731	9,242
Cedar	1,218	2,940	430	1,152	3,520
Chariton	2,371	2,404	509	1,999	2,812
Christian	1,586	4,019	633	1,945	6,305
Clark	1,489	2,111	342	1,403	2,499
Clay	17,547	19,643	6,972	14,538	33,017
Clinton	2,525	2,659	619	1,944	3,924
Cole	5,916	11,575	1,625	4,754	16,685
Cooper	2,798	4,115	530	2,332	5,172
Crawford	2,123	3,525	671	2,248	4,595
Dade	917	2,250	330	747	2,624
Dallas	1,237	2,835	465	1,085	3,120
Daviess	1,676	2,288	334	1,430	2,840
DeKalb	1,452	2,112	285	1,339	2,766
Dent	1,810	2,369	469	1,710	3,024
Douglas	978	2,836	412	1,209	3,773
Dunklin	5,063	4,366	2,903	2,776	5,926
Franklin	7,566	9,823	1,960	7,464	13,785
Gasconade	1,131	4,400	364	1,226	4,944
Gentry	2,189	2,286	216	1,642	2,984
Greene	19,659	32,638	6,751	20,155	48,348
Grundy	1,976	3,213	419	1,428	3,969
Harrison	1,688	3,092	412	1,383	3,574
Henry	3,514	3,824	682	3,125	5,802
Hickory	537	1,484	209	622	1,851
Holt	1,211	2,031	379	1,011	2,578
Howard	2,333	1,825	507	2,041	2,613
Howell	2,763	5,631	1,444	2,795	7,253
Iron	1,755	1,600	491	1,346	2,203
Jackson	112,154	91,086	28,980	92,830	129,989
Jasper	10,987	16,794	3,181	7,652	22,482
Jefferson	13,230	11,708	6,115	13,787	21,947
Johnson	3,484	4,834	1,018	3,044	7,228
Knox	1,257	1,562	350	1,031	1,896
Laclede	2,958	4,860	852	2,186	6,152
Lafayette	4,859	6,840	1,105	4,063	9,187
Lawrence	3,710	6,834	898	3,130	8,445
Lewis	2,067	2,038	537	1,695	2,738
Lincoln	3,142	3,185	1,297	2,784	5,127
Linn	3,933	3,795	513	3,073	4,595
Livingston	3,467	3,827	518	2,662	5,253
McDonald	2,188	3,025	681	1,787	4,339
Macon	3,462	3,804	821	2,844	4,538
Madison	1,521	2,164	615	1,451	2,837
Maries	1,185	1,438	403	1,219	2,082
Marion	5,416	4,732	1,221	4,171	7,197
Mercer	783	1,406	125	607	1,592
Miller	1,727	4,425	668	1,598	5,682
Mississippi	2,303	1,421	1,575	1,470	2,727
Moniteau	1,687	3,210	586	1,395	3,963
Monroe	2,776	1,349	516	2,299	2,141
Montgomery	1,891	2,903	623	1,691	3,707
Morgan	1,649	2,906	504	1,685	4,021
New Madrid	4,195	2,317	2,984	3,500	4,735
Newton	5,064	7,343	1,481	4,291	10,701
Nodaway	4,494	4,736	615	3,322	5,942
Oregon	1,726	1,213	625	1,352	2,118
Osage	1,540	3,107	394	1,485	4,266
Ozark	606	1,967	304	625	2,119
Pemiscot	2,681	2,191	3,060	0,111	4,031
Perry	1,558	3,858	462	1,953	4,736
Pettis	6,334	6,738	1,549	5,016	10,065
Phelps	4,211	5,577	1,995	3,567	7,598
Pike	3,192	3,072	803	2,659	4,452
Platte	4,665	4,836	1,815	4,183	8,764
Polk	2,170	4,145	614	2,245	5,409
Pulaski	2,303	2,555	718	1,903	4,243
Putnam	952	1,971	169	571	2,112
Ralls	1,900	1,175	478	1,371	1,827
Randolph	4,810	3,582	893	3,814	5,195
Ray	3,541	2,587	1,078	2,844	4,205
Reynolds	1,245	898	438	1,031	1,541
Ripley	1,440	1,973	677	1,361	2,810
St. Charles	10,374	13,533	5,752	11,034	25,677
St. Clair	1,496	2,271	411	1,410	2,847
St. Francois	6,379	7,492	1,867	4,658	8,812
Ste. Genevieve	2,225	1,937	440	2,247	2,900
St. Louis	165,786	180,355	39,234	160,801	264,147
Saline	4,646	4,698	704	3,460	6,641
Schuyler	969	1,291	168	991	1,495
Scotland	1,340	1,554	210	1,269	1,918
Scott	4,313	3,856	2,474	3,646	7,316
Shannon	1,216	1,048	446	1,134	1,623
Shelby	2,045	1,693	358	1,569	2,057
Stoddard	3,150	3,919	1,751	2,636	6,282
Stone	1,004	3,006	455	1,094	4,180
Sullivan	1,907	2,332	225	1,588	2,611
Taney	1,219	3,289	414	1,435	4,982
Texas	3,117	4,022	981	2,737	5,104
Vernon	3,557	3,590	783	3,057	4,892
Warren	1,033	2,669	565	1,225	3,530
Washington	2,292	2,641	776	2,229	3,818
Wayne	1,714	2,156	641	1,746	3,091
Webster	2,547	4,118	572	2,343	5,095
Worth	853	924	126	727	1,170
Wright	1,337	3,576	487	1,368	4,350
ST. LOUIS CITY	143,010	58,252	19,652	119,817	77,402
Write-in Vote				1,484	206
Totals	791,444	811,932	206,126	698,531	1,154,058

MISSOURI VOTE SINCE 1924

1924 (Pres.), Coolidge, Rep., 648,486; Davis, Dem., 572,753; LaFollette, Prog., 84,160; Faris, Proh., 1,418; Johns, Soc. Lab., 909; Wallace, Comm. Land, 259.

1928 (Pres.), Hoover, Rep., 834,080; Smith, Dem., 662,562; Thomas, Soc., 3,739; Reynolds, Soc. Lab., 340.

1932 (Pres.), Roosevelt, Dem., 1,025,406; Hoover, Rep., 564,713; Thomas, Soc., 16,374; Upshaw, Proh., 2,429; Foster, Com., 568; Reynolds, Soc. Lab., 404.

1936 (Pres.), Roosevelt, Dem., 1,111,403; Landon, Rep., 697,891; Lemke, Union, 14,630; Thomas, Soc., 3,454; Colvin, Proh., 908; Browder, Com., 417; Aiken, Soc. Lab., 292.

1940 (Pres.), Roosevelt, Dem., 958,476; Willkie, Rep., 871,009; Thomas, Soc., 2,226; Babson, Proh., 1,809; Aiken, Soc. Lab., 209.

1944 (Pres.), Roosevelt, Dem., 807,357; Dewey, Rep., 761,175; Thomas, Soc., 1,750; Watson, Proh., 1,175; Teichert, Soc. Lab., 221.

1948 (Pres.), Truman, Dem., 917,315; Dewey, Rep., 655,039; Wallace, Prog., 3,998; Thomas, Soc., 2,222.

1952 (Pres.), Eisenhower, Rep., 959,429; Stevenson, Dem., 929,830; Hallinan, Prog., 987; Hamblen, Proh., 885; MacArthur, Christian Nationalist, 302; America First, 233; Hoopes, Soc., 227; Hass, Soc. Lab., 169.

1956 (Pres.), Stevenson; Dem., 918,273; Eisenhower, Rep., 914,299.
1960 (Pres.), Kennedy, Dem., 972,201; Nixon, Rep., 962,221.
1964 (Pres.), Johnson, Dem., 1,164,344; Goldwater, Rep., 653,535.
1968 (Pres.), Nixon, Rep. 811,932; Humphrey, Dem., 791,444; Wallace, 3rd party, 206,126.
1972 (Pres.), Nixon, Rep., 1,154,058; McGovern, Dem., 698,531.

Montana

County	1968			1972	
	Humphrey (D)	Nixon (R)	Wallace (I)	McGovern (D)	Nixon (R)
Beaverhead	853	1,896	357	775	2,460
Big Horn	1,319	1,789	209	1,552	2,148
Blaine	1,198	1,291	165	1,151	1,513
Broadwater	439	671	125	411	916
Carbon	1,353	1,972	258	1,292	2,378
Carter	269	624	110	218	726
Cascade	13,507	11,588	1,539	12,899	16,159
Chouteau	1,216	1,695	247	1,149	2,027
Custer	1,760	2,831	275	1,875	3,486
Daniels	688	826	69	570	973
Dawson	1,695	2,650	220	1,685	3,207
Deer Lodge	4,208	1,554	308	3,979	2,373
Fallon	477	990	97	531	1,034
Fergus	2,070	3,367	616	1,652	4,082
Flathead	5,253	7,215	1,524	5,412	10,417
Gallatin	3,818	7,433	706	5,096	10,663
Garfield	190	542	112	173	695
Glacier	1,723	1,643	295	1,469	2,143
Golden Valley	194	332	26	170	359
Granite	502	626	135	422	804
Hill	3,386	2,970	305	3,061	3,759
Jefferson	820	798	152	904	1,281
Judith Basin	606	804	106	557	961
Lake	1,956	3,358	679	2,260	4,172
Lewis & Clark	5,379	7,979	723	6,081	10,719
Liberty	390	670	83	365	808
Lincoln	2,677	2,355	765	2,402	3,276
Madison	734	1,289	261	669	1,780
McCone	589	733	82	562	854
Meagher	218	543	102	230	674
Mineral	576	483	108	659	706
Missoula	8,398	9,745	1,638	13,784	15,557
Musselshell	795	953	111	689	1,202
Park	1,815	3,063	460	1,923	3,771
Petroleum	98	211	26	87	232
Phillips	1,100	1,353	177	828	1,659
Pondera	1,149	1,530	205	1,215	1,890
Powder River	258	699	118	267	844
Powell	1,206	1,301	231	1,050	1,720
Prairie	270	635	30	303	685
Ravalli	2,080	3,183	709	2,480	4,611
Richland	1,399	2,381	228	1,438	2,645
Roosevelt	1,771	1,947	162	1,464	2,304
Rosebud	711	1,190	204	777	1,486
Sanders	1,242	1,459	292	1,197	1,779
Sheridan	1,275	1,180	115	1,197	1,500
Silver Bow	12,626	5,488	1,120	11,704	7,967
Stillwater	676	1,347	177	716	1,698
Sweet Grass	336	1,043	110	350	1,260
Teton	1,228	1,697	179	1,121	1,991
Toole	1,048	1,407	249	897	1,679
Treasure	188	298	41	176	377
Valley	1,926	2,290	393	1,973	3,210
Wheatland	525	673	101	445	761
Wibaux	252	347	56	283	390
Yellowstone	11,682	19,898	2,124	13,602	25,205
Totals	114,117	138,835	20,015	120,197	183,976

MONTANA VOTE SINCE 1924

1924 (Pres.), Coolidge, Rep., 74,138; LaFollette, Prog., 61,105; Davis, Dem., 33,805; Foster, Workers, 357; Johns Soc. Lab., 247.
1928 (Pres.), Hoover, Rep., 113,300; Smith, Dem., 78,578; Thomas, Soc., 1,667; Foster, Com., 563.
1932 (Pres.), Roosevelt, Dem., 127,286; Hoover, Rep., 78,078; Thomas, Soc., 7,891; Foster, Com., 1,775; Harvey, Lib., 1,449.
1936 (Pres.), Roosevelt, Dem., 159,690; Landon, Rep., 63,598; Lemke, Union, 5,549; Thomas, Soc., 1,066; Browder, Com., 385; Colvin, Proh. 224.
1940 (Pres.), Roosevelt, Dem., 145,698; Willkie, Rep., 99,579; Thomas, Soc., 1,443; Babson, Proh., 664; Browder, Com., 489.
1944 (Pres.), Roosevelt, Dem., 112,556; Dewey, Rep., 93,163; Thomas, Soc., 1,296; Watson, Proh., 340.
1948 (Pres.), Truman, Dem., 119,071; Dewey, Rep., 96,770; Wallace, Prog., 7,313; Thomas, Soc., 695; Watson, Proh., 429.
1952 (Pres.), Eisenhower, Rep., 157,394; Stevenson, Dem.,

106,213; Hallinan, Prog., 723; Hamblen, Proh., 548; Hoopes, Soc. 159.
1956 (Pres.), Eisenhower, Rep., 154,933; Stevenson, Dem., 116,238.
1960 (Pres.), Kennedy, Dem., ·134,891; N ixon, Rep., 141,841; Decker, Proh., 456; Dobbs, Soc. W orkers, 391.
1964 (Pres.), Johnson, Dem., 164,246; Goldwater, Rep., 113,032; Kasper, Nat'l States Rights, 519; Munn, Proh., 499; DeBerry, Soc. Worker, 332.
1968 (Pres.), Nixon, Rep. 138,835; Humphrey, Dem., 114,117; Wallace, 3rd party, 20,015; Halstead, Soc. Worker, 457; Munn, Prohibition, 510; Caton, New Reform, 470.
1972 (Pres.), Nixon, Rep., 183,976; McGovern, Dem., 120,197; Schmitz, American, 13,430.

Nebraska

County	1968			1972	
	Humphrey (D)	Nixon (R)	Wallace (I)	McGovern (D)	Nixon (R)
Adams	3,524	7,191	647	3,359	8,841
Antelope	952	2,805	360	851	3,228
Arthur	47	218	15	45	236
Banner	72	350	69	96	404
Blaine	64	344	25	56	343
Boone	934	2,179	291	883	2,406
Box Butte	1,052	2,728	263	960	3,431
Boyd	437	1,250	247	506	1,419
Brown	369	1,340	162	330	1,462
Buffalo	2,875	6,786	733	2,988	8,587
Burt	937	2,615	263	900	2,937
Butler	1,544	1,646	324	1,812	2,301
Cass	1,739	3,185	605	1,805	4,503
Cedar	1,444	2,853	340	1,807	2,995
Chase	363	1,171	193	307	1,318
Cherry	582	2,199	222	463	2,610
Cheyenne	993	2,725	414	950	3,120
Clay	935	2,273	206	861	2,542
Colfax	932	2,264	315	1,107	2,799
Cuming	935	3,254	296	1,019	3,810
Custer	1,407	4,325	401	1,147	4,836
Dakota	1,541	2,383	286	1,748	2,879
Dawes	741	2,600	273	711	2,987
Dawson	1,614	5,221	419	1,424	6,211
Deuel	250	997	78	224	1,001
Dixon	890	2,051	183	941	2,299
Dodge	3,755	8,059	822	3,826	9,837
Douglas	51,617	69,808	15,739	48,201	101,579
Dundy	281	1,001	128	221	1,003
Fillmore	1,297	2,213	203	1,270	2,511
Franklin	626	1,447	152	599	1,510
Frontier	345	1,183	157	324	1,315
Furnas	701	2,137	223	676	2,282
Gage	3,704	5,465	637	3,588	6,298
Garden	206	1,120	99	204	1,161
Garfield	183	797	63	209	903
Gosper	229	701	57	242	829
Grant	84	311	20	69	376
Greeley	739	882	142	760	1,005
Hall	4,571	8,457	833	4,218	10,987
Hamilton	918	2,592	144	907	2,960
Harlan	579	1,392	203	539	1,549
Hayes	127	496	73	123	486
Hitchcock	387	1,173	193	364	1,339
Holt	1,278	3,319	430	1,053	4,147
Hooker	36	350	12	52	394
Howard	1,003	1,256	186	945	1,691
Jefferson	1,572	2,793	272	1,476	3,008
Johnson	759	1,508	215	917	1,637
Kearney	825	1,806	191	759	2,203
Keith	694	2,126	178	665	2,513
Keya Paha	109	531	50	146	563
Kimball	414	1,423	237	437	1,650
Knox	1,131	3,129	328	1,289	3,318
Lancaster	23,539	33,051	2,940	25,924	42,573
Lincoln	3,491	5,996	782	3,220	7,502
Logan	130	363	54	73	320
Loup	64	331	38	58	345
McPherson	40	236	34	42	247
Madison	2,364	7,066	614	2,224	8,580
Merrick	840	2,031	212	887	2,418
Morrill	480	1,516	285	520	1,740
Nance	677	1,316	172	641	1,413
Nemaha	1,023	2,290	295	909	2,600
Nuckolls	1,127	1,894	172	999	2,089
Otoe	1,508	3,840	474	1,718	4,815
Pawnee	583	1,209	213	524	1,299
Perkins	360	1,165	127	354	1,165
Phelps	825	2,976	254	735	3,356
Pierce	674	2,408	197	653	2,451
Platte	2,999	5,817	768	2,855	7,871
Polk	690	1,795	201	827	2,050
Red Willow	1,145	3,066	364	931	3,701
Richardson	1,591	3,133	527	1,508	3,662
Rock	146	791	94	138	937
Saline	2,543	2,341	350	2,654	2,828
Sarpy	3,506	6,019	1,945	3,904	11,514
Saunders	1,990	3,429	556	2,501	4,302
Scotts Bluff	2,649	7,356	946	2,764	8,649

County	1968			1972	
	Hum-phrey (D)	Nixon (R)	Wal-lace (I)	McGov-ern (D)	Nixon (R)
Seward	1.658	2.939	254	2,087	3,707
Sheridan	454	2.236	241	481	2,386
Sherman	851	955	180	811	1,099
Sioux	157	565	69	129	639
Stanton	411	1.408	154	478	1,662
Thayer	1.061	2.331	177	978	2,274
Thomas	76	354	31	73	397
Thurston	802	1.341	210	840	1,565
Valley	793	1.759	179	771	2,011
Washington	1.279	3.063	492	1,401	4,290
Wayne	786	2.582	192	902	2,659
Webster	781	1.521	186	696	1,631
Wheeler	131	323	49	84	361
York	1.237	3.923	259	1,318	4,651
Totals	**170,784**	**321,163**	**44,904**	**169,991**	**406,298**

NEBRASKA VOTE SINCE 1924

1924 (Pres.), Coolidge, Rep., 218,585; Davis, Dem., 137,289; LaFollette, Prog., 106,701; Faris, Proh., 1,594.

1928 (Pres.), Hoover, Rep., 349,745; Smith, Dem., 197,959; Thomas, Soc., 3,434.

1932 (Pres.), Roosevelt, Dem., 359,082; Hoover, Rep., 201,177; Thomas, Soc., 9,876.

1936 (Pres.), Roosevelt, Dem., 347,454; Landon, Rep., 248,731; Lemke, Union, 12,847.

1940 (Pres.), Roosevelt, Dem., 263,677; Willkie, Rep., 352,201.

1944 (Pres.), Roosevelt, Dem., 233,246; Dewey, Rep., 329,880.

1948 (Pres.), Truman, Dem., 224,165; Dewey, Rep., 264,774.

1952 (Pres.), Eisenhower, Rep., 421,603; Stevenson, Dem., 188,057.

1956 (Pres.), Eisenhower, R., 378,108; Stevenson, D., 199,029.

1960 (Pres.), Kennedy, D., 232,542; Nixon, R., 380,553.

1964 (Pres.), Johnson, D., 307,307; Goldwater, R., 276,847.

1968 (Pres.), Nixon, Rep., 321,163; Humphrey Dem. 170,784; Wallace, 3rd party, 44,904.

1972 (Pres.), Nixon, Rep., 406,298; McGovern, Dem., 169,991; scattered 817.

Nevada

County	1968			1972	
	Hum-phrey (D)	Nixon (R)	Wal-lace (I)	McGov-ern (D)	Nixon (R)
*Churchill	1.211	1.954	575	1,038	2,970
*Clark	33.225	31.522	10.318	36,807	53,101
Douglas	670	1.801	327	983	2,898
Elko	1.686	2.687	559	1,467	3,886
Esmeralda	118	138	97	127	273
Eureka	149	277	64	139	371
Humboldt	885	1.287	353	713	1,659
Lander	301	461	147	468	798
Lincoln	414	555	144	382	841
Lyon	939	1.616	444	959	2,813
Mineral	1.242	927	700	768	2,111
Nye	728	843	500	802	1,287
Ormsby	1.770	3.169	662	(a)	(a)
Pershing	466	567	180	365	853
Storey	172	222	50	226	508
Washoe	14.560	23.492	4.936	17,100	33,539
White Pine	2.062	1.670	376	1,546	2,446
CARSON CITY	(a)	(a)	(a)	2,120	5,396
Totals	**60,598**	**73,188**	**20,432**	**66,016**	**115,750**

(a) Ormsby county merged with Carson City, July 1, 1969.

NEVADA VOTE SINCE 1924

1924 (Pres.), Coolidge, Rep., 11,243; LaFollette, Prog., 9,769; Davis, Dem., 5,909.

1928 (Pres.), Hoover, Rep., 18,327; Smith, Dem., 14,090.

1932 (Pres.), Roosevelt, Dem., 28,756; Hoover, Rep., 12,674.

1936 (Pres.), Roosevelt, Dem., 31,925; Landon, Rep., 11,923.

1940 (Pres.), Roosevelt, Dem., 31,945; Willkie, Rep., 21,229.

1944 (Pres.), Roosevelt, Dem., 29,623; Dewey, Rep., 24,611.

1948 (Pres.), Truman, Dem., 31,291; Dewey, Rep., 29,357; Wallace, Prog., 1,469.

1952 (Pres.), Eisenhower, Rep., 50,502; Stevenson, Dem., 31,688.

1956 (Pres.), Eisenhower, Rep., 56,049; Stevenson, Dem., 40,640.

1960 (Pres.), Kennedy, Dem., 54,880; Nixon, Rep., 52,387.

1964 (Pres.), Johnson, Dem., 79,339; Goldwater, Rep., 56,094.

1968 (Pres.), Nixon, Rep., 73,188; Humphrey, Dem., 60,598; Wallace, 3rd party, 20,432.

1972 (Pres.), Nixon, Rep., 115,750; McGovern, Dem., 66,016.

New Hampshire

County	1968			1972	
	Hum-phrey (D)	Nixon (R)	Wal-lace (I)	McGov-ern (D)	Nixon (R)
Belknap	4.942	8.642	454	4,610	11,536
Carroll	2.163	6.795	348	2,395	8,525
Cheshire	9.135	10.702	441	9,157	13,390
Coos	8.261	6.822	399	5,829	9,468
Grafton	7.813	12.881	727	8,388	16,605
Hillsborough	45.423	42.409	4.231	34,739	65,274
Merrimack	12.711	19.289	1.201	11,737	25,354
Rockingham	21.195	28.842	2.333	21,998	38,825
Strafford	13.129	12.427	650	12,028	16,846
Sullivan	5.817	6.094	389	5,554	7,901
Totals	**130,589**	**154,903**	**11,173**	**116,435**	**213,724**

NEW HAMPSHIRE VOTE SINCE 1924

1924 (Pres.), Coolidge, Rep., 98,575; Davis, Dem., 57,201; LaFollette, Prog., 8,993.

1928 (Pres.), Hoover, Rep., 115,404; Smith, Dem., 80,715; Thomas, Soc., 455; Foster, Com., 173.

1932 (Pres.), Roosevelt, Dem., 100,680; Hoover, Rep., 103,629; Thomas, Soc., 947; Foster, Com., 264.

1936 (Pres.), Roosevelt, Dem., 108,460; Landon, Rep., 104,642; Lemke, Union, 4,819; Browder, Com., 193.

1940 (Pres.), Roosevelt, Dem., 125,292; Willkie, Rep., 110,127.

1944 (Pres.), Roosevelt, Dem., 119,663; Dewey, Rep., 109,916; Thomas, Soc., 46.

1948 (Pres.), Truman, Dem., 107,995; Dewey, Rep., 121,299; Wallace, Prog., 1,970; Thomas, Soc., 86; Teichert, Soc. Lab., 83; Thurmond, States' Rights, 7.

1952 (Pres.), Eisenhower, R., 166,287; Stevenson, D., 106,663.

1956 (Pres.), Eisenhower, R., 176,519; Stevenson, D., 90,364; Andrews, Const., 111.

1960 (Pres.), Kennedy, D., 137,772; Nixon, R., 157,989.

1964 (Pres.), Johnson, D., 182,065; Goldwater, R., 104,029.

1968 (Pres.), Nixon, Rep., 154,903; Humphrey, Dem., 130,589; Wallace, 3rd party, 11,173; New Party, 421; Halstead, Soc. Worker, 104.

1972 (Pres.), Nixon, Rep., 213,724; McGovern, Dem., 116,435; Schmitz, American, 3,386; Jenness, Soc. Worker, 368; Scattered 142.

New Jersey

County	1968			1972	
	Hum-phrey (D)	Nixon (R)	Wal-lace (I)	McGov-ern (D)	Nixon (R)
Atlantic	35.581	32.807	7.528	28,203	45,667
Bergen	162.182	224.911	23.663	147,155	285,458
Burlington	41.651	46.177	11.635	41,520	70,805
Camden	87.347	77.642	23.111	75,202	111,935
Cape May	9.664	14.970	3.498	8,729	22,621
Cumberland	21.661	18.388	5.356	18,692	26,409
Essex	185.440	140.084	26.823	161,270	170,036
Gloucester	27.438	30.596	10.626	25,509	44,806
Hudson	124.939	91.324	23.138	87,977	136,895
Hunterdon	8.755	15.851	2.749	9,031	21,282
Mercer	63.218	45.354	16.104	62,180	69,303
Middlesex	103.339	96.515	24.138	88,397	149,033
Monmouth	69.669	87.311	13.047	63,176	124,830
Morris	52.398	85.512	9.659	50,937	113,469
Ocean	26.909	41.995	8.520	27,710	77,979
Passaic	74.442	79.862	16.617	62,302	108,511
Salem	11.172	11.407	3.647	8,609	16,371
Somerset	27.580	42.459	7.331	26,537	56,524
Sussex	8.325	18.043	2.843	8,585	25,977
Union	109.674	110.309	19.963	90,482	148,290
Warren	12.822	13.950	2.191	10,008	19,301
Totals	**1,264,206**	**1,325,467**	**262,187**	**1,102,211**	**1,845,502**

NEW JERSEY VOTE SINCE 1924

1924 (Pres.), Coolidge, Rep., 676,277; Davis, Dem., 298,043; LaFollette, Prog., 109,028; Faris, Proh., 1,660; Foster, Workers, 1,560; Johns, Soc. Lab., 358.

1928 (Pres.), Smith, Dem., 616,517; Hoover, Rep., 926,050; Foster, Com., 1,257; Reynolds, Soc. Lab., 500.

1932 (Pres.), Roosevelt, Dem., 806,630; Hoover, Rep., 775,684; Thomas, Soc., 42,998; Foster, Com., 2,915; Reynolds, Soc. Lab., 1,062; Upshaw, Proh., 774.

1936 (Pres.), Roosevelt, Dem., 1,083,549; Landon, Rep., 719,421; Lemke, Union, 9,405; Thomas, Soc., 3,895; Browder, Com., 1,590; Colvin, Proh., 916; Aiken, Soc. Lab., 346.

1940 (Pres.), Roosevelt, Dem., 1,016,404; Willkie, Rep., 944,876; Browder, Com., 8,814; Thomas, Soc., 2,823; Babson, Proh., 851; Aiken, Soc. Lab., 446.
1944 (Pres.), Roosevelt, Dem., 987,874; Dewey, Rep., 961,335; Teichert, Soc. Lab., 6,939; Watson, Nat'l Proh., 4,255; Thomas, Soc., 3,385.
1948 (Pres.), Truman, Dem., 895,455; Dewey, Rep., 981,124; Wallace, Prog., 42,683; Watson, Proh., 10,593; Thomas, Soc., 10,521; Dobbs, Soc. Workers, 5,825; Teichert, Soc. Lab., 3,354.
1952 (Pres.), Eisenhower, Rep., 1,373,613; Stevenson, Dem., 1,015,902; Hoopes, Soc., 8,593; Hass, Soc. Lab., 5,815; Hallinan, Prog., 5,589; Krajewski, Poor Man's, 4,203; Dobbs, Soc. Workers, 3,850; Hamblen, Proh., 989.
1956 (Pres.), Eisenhower, Rep., 1,606,942; Stevenson, Dem., 850,337; Holtwick, Proh., 9,147; Hass, Soc. Lab., 6,736; Andrews, Conservative, 5,317; Dobbs, Soc. Workers, 4,004; Krajewski, American Third Party, 1,829.
1960 (Pres.), Kennedy, Dem., 1,385,415; Nixon, Rep., 1,363,324; Dobbs, Soc. Workers, 11,402; Lee, Conservative, 48,708; Hass, Soc. Lab., 4,262.
1964 (Pres.), Johnson, Dem., 1,867,671; Goldwater, Rep., 963,843; DeBerry, Soc. Workers, 8,181; Hass, Soc. Labor, 7,075.
1968 (Pres.), Nixon, Rep., 1,325,467; Humphrey, Dem., 1,264,206; Wallace, 3rd party, 262,187; Halstead, Soc. Worker, 8,667; Gregory, Peace Freedom, 8,084; Blomen, Soc. Labor, 6,784.
1972 (Pres.), Nixon, Rep., 1,845,502; McGovern, Dem., 1,102,211; Schmitz, American, 34,378; Spock, Peoples, 5,355; Fisher, Soc. Labor, 4,544; Jenness, Soc. Worker, 2,233; Mahalchik, Amer. First, 1,743; Hall, Communist, 1,263.

New Mexico

County	1968 Humphrey (D)	Nixon (R)	Wallace (I)	1972 McGovern (D)	Nixon (R)
Bernalillo	40,835	56,234	4,920	48,753	79,993
Catron	278	674	128	271	829
Chaves	3,612	8,866	1,425	4,296	11,493
Colfax	2,477	2,212	263	1,855	2,663
Curry	2,915	5,562	1,754	2,416	8,392
De Baca	345	658	130	270	752
Dona Ana	7,658	10,824	1,453	9,416	14,562
Eddy	6,093	7,193	1,671	5,040	9,921
Grant	3,817	2,908	793	4,081	4,431
Guadalupe	1,027	1,176	77	1,202	1,297
Harding	284	450	44	220	522
Hidalgo	678	606	257	562	1,051
Lea	4,751	7,415	3,025	3,429	12,478
Lincoln	802	2,004	287	696	2,528
Los Alamos	2,552	3,447	268	2,435	5,039
Luna	1,438	1,952	490	1,560	2,958
McKinley	4,491	4,376	547	5,124	5,366
Mora	1,069	1,155	35	1,135	1,165
Otero	3,978	4,475	1,688	2,981	7,033
Quay	1,399	2,123	567	1,161	3,224
Rio Arriba	4,799	3,935	269	5,642	4,351
Roosevelt	1,547	3,256	773	1,612	4,727
Sandoval	2,609	1,959	129	3,293	3,507
San Juan	4,036	7,664	2,304	4,296	10,788
San Miguel	4,088	4,027	195	4,663	4,434
Santa Fe	9,544	9,359	492	10,761	12,211
Sierra	930	1,624	282	934	2,074
Socorro	1,871	2,230	173	1,994	2,658
Taos	2,993	3,119	124	3,472	3,617
Torrance	974	1,316	188	908	1,758
Union	678	1,217	279	496	1,545
Valencia	5,513	5,676	707	6,110	8,239
Totals	**130,081**	**169,692**	**25,737**	**141,084**	**235,606**

NEW MEXICO VOTE SINCE 1924

1924 (Pres.), Coolidge, Rep., 54,745; Davis, Dem., 48,542; LaFollette, Prog., 9,543.
1928 (Pres.), Hoover, Rep., 69,645; Smith, Dem., 48,211; Foster, Com., 158.
1932 (Pres.), Roosevelt, Dem., 95,089; Hoover, Rep., 54,217; Thomas, Soc., 1,776; Harvey, Lib., 389; Foster, Com., 135.
1936 (Pres.), Roosevelt, Dem., 105,838; Landon, Rep., 61,710; Lemke, Union, 942; Thomas, Soc., 343; Browder, Com., 43.
1940 (Pres.), Roosevelt, D., 103,699; Willkie, R., 79,315.
1944 (Pres.), Roosevelt, Dem., 81,389; Dewey, Rep., 70,688; Watson, Proh., 148.
1948 (Pres.), Truman, Dem., 105,464; Dewey, Rep., 80,303; Wallace, Prog., 1,037; Watson, Proh., 127; Thomas, Soc., 83; Teichert, Soc. Lab., 49.
1952 (Pres.), Eisenhower, Rep., 132,170; Stevenson, Dem., 105,661; Hamblen, Proh, 297; Hallinan, Ind. Prog., 225; MacArthur, Christian National, 220; Hass, Soc. Lab., 35.

1956 (Pres.), Eisenhower, Rep., 146,788; Stevenson, Dem., 106,098; Holtwick, Proh., 607; Andrews, Ind., 364; Hass, Soc. Lab., 69.
1960 (Pres.), Kennedy, Dem., 156,027; Nixon, Rep., 153,733; Decker, Proh., 777; Hass, Soc. Lab., 570.
1964 (Pres.), Johnson, Dem., 194,017; Goldwater, Rep., 131,838; Hass, Soc. Labor, 1,217; Munn, Proh., 543.
1968 (Pres.), Nixon, Rep., 169,692; Humphrey, Dem., 130,081; Wallace, 3rd party, 25,737; Chavez, 1,519; Halstead, Soc. Worker, 252.
1972 (Pres.), Nixon, Rep., 235,606; McGovern, Dem., 141,084; Schmitz, Amer., 8,767; Jenness, S. W., 474.

New York

County	1968 Humphrey (D-L*)	Nixon (R)	Wallace (I)	1972 McGovern (D-L*)	Nixon (R-C**)
Albany	80,724	52,498	5,025	67,297	81,848
Allegany	4,986	11,222	851	4,812	13,426
Broome	37,451	46,872	4,618	37,154	55,736
Cattaraugus	12,733	16,594	1,674	10,909	21,906
Cayuga	14,604	16,167	1,826	11,907	22,774
Chautauqua	26,431	28,561	3,273	26,253	37,158
Chemung	15,820	20,693	2,807	12,650	26,200
Chenango	5,706	11,785	887	5,695	13,770
Clinton	10,153	11,951	931	9,703	17,048
Columbia	7,762	13,857	1,372	7,558	17,995
Cortland	5,791	10,209	720	5,234	12,885
Delaware	5,360	12,366	1,121	5,243	15,136
Dutchess	31,025	45,032	5,662	27,872	64,864
Erie	250,054	167,853	33,402	218,105	256,462
Essex	5,218	9,377	701	4,955	11,763
Franklin	6,678	8,314	544	5,266	10,959
Fulton	8,871	11,895	989	7,303	15,200
Genesee	9,533	12,418	1,141	8,631	17,107
Greene	5,499	10,954	1,421	5,260	14,313
Hamilton	762	2,123	163	731	2,597
Herkimer	10,940	15,192	1,455	9,487	20,194
Jefferson	13,438	18,552	1,016	11,629	23,123
Lewis	3,205	5,524	430	2,987	6,591
Livingston	6,989	11,659	775	7,031	15,886
Madison	7,056	13,819	1,053	6,241	18,392
Monroe	141,437	143,233	10,875	120,031	196,579
Montgomery	11,449	12,566	1,147	9,460	16,640
Niagara	41,999	38,796	6,617	38,991	54,777
Oneida	44,685	52,875	5,666	33,642	78,549
Onondaga	83,576	95,806	9,459	61,895	140,039
Ontario	11,719	17,114	1,180	11,012	23,828
Orange	28,122	44,955	6,473	25,778	63,556
Orleans	4,786	8,509	696	4,371	10,938
Oswego	14,636	20,041	1,962	11,317	29,109
Otsego	7,981	13,543	1,091	7,898	17,364
Putnam	8,472	13,293	2,388	7,747	21,673
Rensselaer	30,232	34,674	3,461	24,019	48,864
Rockland	36,948	40,880	5,028	35,771	64,753
St. Lawrence	15,662	20,982	1,178	15,286	26,145
Saratoga	17,766	25,658	2,220	17,899	40,582
Schenectady	34,786	33,687	3,246	29,619	47,529
Schoharie	3,883	6,166	689	3,730	8,644
Schuyler	2,034	4,105	522	1,937	4,945
Seneca	5,222	7,083	635	4,441	9,368
Steuben	12,229	24,189	2,194	9,462	28,708
Sullivan	10,860	11,657	1,487	9,847	17,035
Tioga	5,336	10,441	1,127	5,470	13,396
Tompkins	10,343	13,446	1,236	12,344	17,605
Ulster	20,886	34,798	4,183	21,371	46,883
Warren	6,460	12,963	807	5,760	16,649
Washington	6,806	12,694	930	5,677	16,136
Wayne	8,907	17,470	1,211	8,203	23,379
Wyoming	4,477	8,459	799	4,365	11,184
Yates	2,158	5,482	440	1,958	6,639
Outside N.Y Metro	**1,220,646**	**1,371,502**	**142,804**	**1,068,404**	**1,914,829**
Nassau	278,599	329,792	30,860	252,831	438,723
Suffolk	122,590	218,027	31,304	132,441	316,452
Westchester	173,954	201,652	22,115	154,412	262,901
N.Y. Suburban	**575,143**	**749,471**	**84,279**	**539,684**	**1,018,076**
Bronx	277,385	142,314	21,950	243,345	196,754
Kings	489,174	247,936	33,563	387,768	373,903
New York	370,806	135,458	12,958	354,326	178,515
Queens	410,546	306,620	44,198	328,316	426,015
Richmond	34,770	54,631	9,112	29,241	84,686
Greater N.Y Metro	**1,582,681**	**886,959**	**121,781**	**1,342,996**	**1,259,873**
D/R Total	3,066,8q8			2,767,956	3,824,642
2d Party (Lib/Con)	311,622			183,128	368,136
Totals	**3,378,470**	**3,007,932**	**358,864**	**2,951,084**	**4,192,778**

*Democratic and Liberal   **Republican and Conservative

NEW YORK VOTE SINCE 1924

1924 (Pres.), Davis, Dem., 950,796; Coolidge, Rep., 1,820,058; LaFollette, Prog., 268,510; LaFollette, Soc., 198,783; Johns, Soc. Lab., 9,928; Foster, Workers, 8,228.

1928 (Pres.), Hoover, Rep., 2,193,344; Smith, Dem., 2,089,863; Thomas, Soc., 107,332; Reynolds, Soc. Lab., 4,206; Foster, Com., 10,884.
1932 (Pres.), Roosevelt, Dem., 2,534,959; Hoover, Rep., 1,937,963; Thomas, Soc., 177,397; Foster, Com., 27,956; Reynolds, Soc. Lab., 10,339.
1936 (Pres.), Roosevelt, Dem., 3,018,298; American Lab., 274,924; total, 3,293,222; Landon, Rep., 2,180,670; Thomas, Soc., 86,879; Browder, Com., 35,609.
1940 (Pres.), Roosevelt, Dem., 2,834,500; American Lab., 417,418; total 3,251,918; Willkie, Rep., 3,027,478; Thomas, Soc., 18,950; Babson, Proh., 3,250.
1944 (Pres.), Roosevelt, Dem., 2,478,598; American Lab., 496,405; Liberal, 329,325; total, 3,304,238; Dewey, Rep., 2,987,647; Teichert, Ind. Gov't, 14,352; Thomas, Soc., 10,553.
1948 (Pres.), Truman, Dem., 2,557,642; Liberal, 222,562; total, 2,780,204; Dewey, Rep., 2,841,163; Wallace, Amer. Lab., 509,559; Thomas, Soc., 40,879; Teichert, Ind. Gov't. 2,729; Dobbs, Soc. Workers, 2,675.
1952 (Pres.), Eisenhower, Rep., 3,952,815; Stevenson, Dem., 2,687,890, Liberal, 416,711; total, 3,104,601; Hallinan, American Lab., 64,211; Hoopes, Soc., 2,664; Dobbs, Soc. Workers, 2,212; Hass, Ind. Gov't. 1,560; Scattering, 178; Blank and void, 87,813.
1956 (Pres.), Eisenhower, Rep., 4,340,340; Stevenson, Dem., 2,458,212; Liberal, 292,557; total, 2,750,769. Write-in votes for Andrews, 1,027; Werdel, 492; Hass, 150; Hoopes, 82; Others, 476.
1960 (Pres.), Kennedy, Dem., 3,423,909; Liberal 406,176; total, 3,830,085; Nixon, Rep., 3,446,419; Dobbs, Soc. Workers, 14,319; Scattering, 256; Blank and void, 88,896.
1964 (Pres.), Johnson, Dem., 4,913,156; Goldwater, Rep., 2,243,559; Hass, Soc. Labor, 6,085; DeBerry, Soc. Worker, 3,215; Scattering, 188; Blank and void, 151,383.
1968 (Pres.), Nixon, Rep., 3,007,932; Humphrey, Dem., 3,378,470; Wallace, 3rd party, 358,864; Blomen, Soc. Labor, 8,432; Halstead, Soc. Worker, 11,851; Gregory, Freedom and Peace, 24,517; blank, void and scattering, 171,624.
1972 (Pres.), Nixon, Rep. 3,824,642 Conservative 368,136; McGovern, Dem. 2,767,956 Liberal 183,128; Reed, Soc. Worker, 7,797; Fisher, Soc. Labor, 4,530; Hall, Communist, 5,641; blank, void or scattered 161,641.

North Carolina

County	1968 Humphrey (D)	1968 Nixon (R)	1968 Wallace (I)	1972 McGovern (D)	1972 Nixon (R)
Alamance	8,241	12,310	13,139	6,833	22,046
Alexander	1,834	4,379	2,203	2,468	5,865
Alleghany	1,102	1,695	904	1,304	2,158
Anson	2,969	1,474	3,571	2,188	3,551
Ashe	3,426	4,894	888	3,313	5,784
Avery	631	3,197	690	627	3,510
Beaufort	3,232	2,669	5,686	2,901	6,915
Bertie	3,207	811	3,108	1,819	2,874
Bladen	2,754	1,746	3,897	2,201	4,205
Brunswick	2,972	2,404	3,358	2,500	6,153
Buncombe	14,624	21,031	11,889	12,626	32,001
Burke	5,704	11,068	5,892	6,197	14,447
Cabarrus	5,501	13,226	6,538	5,336	18,384
Caldwell	4,746	10,433	5,095	4,886	12,976
Camden	707	180	1,100	556	909
Carteret	3,762	4,593	3,061	2,805	8,463
Caswell	2,137	1,036	2,851	1,922	2,983
Catawba	6,974	18,393	7,285	7,744	24,106
Chatham	3,532	3,845	3,239	3,624	6,175
Cherokee	2,402	3,768	915	2,411	4,113
Chowan	1,201	798	1,696	936	1,906
Clay	847	1,390	293	797	1,545
Cleveland	5,661	7,298	9,649	4,994	13,726
Columbus	4,243	3,881	6,693	3,305	8,468
Craven	4,240	2,991	6,509	2,384	9,372
Cumberland	9,938	9,143	9,539	9,853	24,376
Currituck	738	363	1,471	718	1,578
Dare	700	1,035	844	634	1,986
Davidson	7,594	16,678	11,544	7,691	24,875
Davie	1,502	3,866	2,515	1,578	5,613
Duplin	3,451	2,724	6,082	2,857	7,153
Durham	16,563	12,705	13,542	15,566	25,576
Edgecombe	5,243	3,198	5,861	4,635	8,244
Forsyth	20,281	31,623	15,681	20,928	46,415
Franklin	2,855	1,375	5,525	2,341	5,431
Gaston	10,100	18,741	13,973	8,462	27,956
Gates	1,151	406	1,227	1,177	1,264
Graham	1,061	1,570	363	1,057	1,699
Granville	2,638	1,837	4,071	2,918	6,037
Greene	1,560	650	2,906	847	2,788
Guilford	25,604	38,996	19,751	25,800	61,381
Halifax	4,927	3,148	7,116	4,241	8,908
Harnett	4,007	5,184	6,531	3,347	10,259
Haywood	5,703	6,205	3,898	4,515	8,903
Henderson	3,053	9,334	3,861	2,701	12,134
Hertford	3,275	1,125	2,203	1,928	2,794
Hoke	2,185	812	1,545	1,466	1,927
Hyde	769	401	833	403	1,112
Iredell	4,878	10,557	9,021	5,088	16,736
Jackson	2,956	3,747	1,080	3,169	4,709
Johnston	4,492	6,764	9,212	3,488	14,272
Jones	1,225	361	1,780	1,093	1,650
Lee	2,524	2,586	3,711	2,024	5,836
Lenoir	3,853	3,844	8,036	3,672	11,065
Lincoln	4,044	6,188	3,161	5,100	8,597
Macon	2,070	3,295	1,162	1,749	4,134
Madison	2,201	3,130	1,034	2,039	3,273
Martin	3,118	1,221	3,818	1,840	4,188
McDowell	2,543	4,740	3,018	2,348	6,570
Mecklenburg	31,102	56,325	20,070	33,730	77,546
Mitchell	819	3,778	603	800	4,240
Montgomery	2,410	3,070	2,259	2,175	4,417
Moore	3,583	5,322	3,263	3,627	9,406
Nash	5,283	4,602	9,230	4,503	12,679
New Hanover	7,750	10,020	9,291	5,894	19,060
Northampton	4,072	860	2,986	3,233	2,997
Onslow	3,281	3,444	5,542	2,424	10,343
Orange	8,366	6,097	7,816	12,004	11,652
Pamlico	1,280	745	1,447	919	1,847
Pasquotank	2,564	1,430	3,597	2,115	3,906
Pender	1,942	1,007	2,720	1,415	3,327
Perquimans	1,023	468	1,554	723	1,299
Person	2,644	2,138	4,065	2,246	5,941
Pitt	7,696	5,745	9,167	5,858	14,406
Polk	1,523	2,550	1,484	1,416	3,121
Randolph	5,351	13,450	6,892	5,346	18,724
Richmond	4,257	2,865	5,457	3,508	5,692
Robeson	8,248	4,526	6,441	7,391	11,362
Rockingham	6,774	8,095	9,324	5,530	14,519
Rowan	8,074	15,207	9,220	6,834	20,735
Rutherford	4,622	7,785	4,476	4,140	9,506
Sampson	4,797	6,597	4,527	4,888	9,684
Scotland	2,252	1,717	2,016	1,938	3,485
Stanly	4,199	9,428	4,706	5,218	12,459
Stokes	2,374	4,781	3,410	3,254	7,118
Surry	5,088	9,638	4,103	4,706	10,497
Swain	1,227	1,494	537	1,101	2,052
Transylvania	2,210	4,033	2,365	2,321	5,860
Tyrrell	581	291	415	459	676
Union	3,630	5,290	4,761	3,886	10,264
Vance	3,852	2,252	5,244	3,117	6,491
Wake	20,979	28,928	17,250	22,807	56,808
Warren	2,293	796	2,294	1,698	2,603
Washington	1,898	1,016	1,866	1,546	2,559
Watauga	2,952	5,081	1,060	3,451	6,017
Wayne	5,338	5,678	8,709	5,234	14,352
Wilkes	4,497	11,195	2,876	4,634	13,105
Wilson	4,173	4,053	7,903	4,166	12,060
Yadkin	1,443	5,885	2,397	1,592	6,824
Yancey	2,215	2,448	752	2,278	3,106
Totals	464,113	627,192	496,188	438,705	1,054,889

NORTH CAROLINA VOTE SINCE 1924

1924 (Pres.), Davis, Dem., 284,270; Coolidge, Rep., 191,753; LaFollette, Prog., 6,651; Faris, Proh., 13.
1928 (Pres.), Hoover, Rep., 348,923; Smith, Dem., 286,227.
1932 (Pres.), Roosevelt, Dem., 497,566; Hoover, Rep., 208,344; Thomas, Soc., 5,591.
1936 (Pres.), Roosevelt, Dem., 616,141; Landon, Rep., 223,283; Thomas, Soc., 21; Browder, Com., 11; Lemke, Union, 2.
1940 (Pres.), Roosevelt, Dem., 609,015; Willkie, Rep., 213,633.
1944 (Pres.), Roosevelt, Dem., 527,399; Dewey, Rep., 263,155.
1948 (Pres.), Truman, Dem., 459,070; Dewey, Rep., 258,572; Thurmond, States' Rights, 69,652; Wallace, Prog., 3,915.
1952 (Pres.), Eisenhower, Rep., 558,107; Stevenson, Dem., 652,803.
1956 (Pres.), Eisenhower, Rep., 575,062; Stevenson, Dem., 590,530.
1960 (Pres.), Kennedy, Dem., 713,136; Nixon, Rep., 655,420.
1964 (Pres.), Johnson, Dem., 800,139; Goldwater, Rep., 624,844.
1968 (Pres.), Nixon, Rep., 627,192; Humphrey, Dem., 464,113; Wallace, 3rd party, 496,188.
1972 (Pres.), Nixon, Rep., 1,054,889; McGovern, Dem., 438,705; Schmitz, American, 25,018.

North Dakota

County	1968 Humphrey (D)	Nixon (R)	Wallace (I)	1972 McGovern (D)	Nixon (R)
Adams	641	1,020	116	665	1,177
Barnes	2,623	3,831	348	2,804	4,518
Benson	1,772	1,707	164	1,635	2,050
Billings	174	395	69	192	509
Bottineau	1,520	2,633	230	1,369	3,263
Bowman	559	927	156	643	1,111
Burke	808	1,239	132	651	1,446
Burleigh	5,139	10,661	818	5,841	13,909
Cass	10,819	15,240	1,167	14,073	21,770
Cavalier	1,631	1,953	257	1,867	2,898
Dickey	1,098	2,087	161	1,266	2,277
Divide	914	1,032	102	774	1,230
Dunn	772	1,207	169	644	1,438
Eddy	893	1,018	76	911	1,022
Emmons	756	1,991	311	1,115	2,194
Foster	897	1,119	123	861	1,352
Golden Val	348	735	115	362	774
Grand Forks	7,695	9,802	1,332	9,416	13,361
Grant	488	1,648	157	596	1,569
Griggs	1,008	1,110	109	901	1,312
Hettinger	638	1,424	163	726	1,511
Kidder	548	1,204	192	557	1,315
La Moure	1,269	2,008	189	1,399	2,110
Logan	459	1,416	135	554	1,408
McHenry	1,595	2,226	281	1,554	2,765
McIntosh	342	2,258	129	521	2,440
McKenzie	935	1,625	164	937	1,913
McLean	2,050	2,764	216	1,703	3,575
Mercer	730	2,039	169	784	2,567
Morton	3,156	4,465	489	3,312	5,494
Mountrail	1,662	1,494	212	1,391	2,038
Nelson	1,477	1,526	157	1,358	1,625
Oliver	269	616	85	293	669
Pembina	1,686	2,574	335	1,801	3,317
Pierce	1,048	1,700	229	973	1,970
Ramsey	2,384	3,189	269	2,384	3,954
Ransom	1,286	1,943	153	1,355	2,056
Renville	880	851	84	702	1,121
Richland	3,098	4,224	443	3,367	5,194
Rolette	1,870	1,211	172	1,803	1,713
Sargent	1,308	1,386	154	1,331	1,616
Sheridan	350	1,295	79	334	1,460
Sioux	525	482	58	557	561
Slope	238	379	64	249	413
Stark	2,577	4,365	500	2,636	5,115
Steele	991	952	88	892	1,063
Stutsman	3,532	5,162	477	3,589	6,269
Towner	990	1,109	124	944	1,349
Traill	1,740	2,692	243	1,892	3,118
Walsh	2,948	3,410	453	2,908	3,991
Ward	7,105	9,079	896	6,706	13,900
Wells	1,265	2,266	247	1,297	2,519
Williams	3,263	3,980	483	2,989	4,800
Totals	**94,769**	**138,669**	**14,244**	**100,384**	**174,109**

NORTH DAKOTA VOTE SINCE 1924

1924 (Pres.), Coolidge, Rep., 94,931; LaFollette, Prog., 89,922; Davis, Dem., 13,858; Foster, Workers, 370.

1928 (Pres.), Hoover, Rep., 131,441; Smith, Dem., 106,648; Thomas, Soc., 842; Foster, Com., 936.

1932 (Pres.), Roosevelt, Dem., 178,350; Hoover, Rep., 71,772; Harvey, Lib., 1,817; Thomas, Soc., 3,521; Foster, Com., 830.

1936 (Pres.), Roosevelt, Dem., 163,148; Landon, Rep., 72,751; Lemke, Union, 36,708; Thomas, Soc., 552; Browder, Com., 360; Colvin, Proh., 197.

1940 (Pres.), Roosevelt, Dem., 124,036; Willkie, Rep., 154,590; Thomas, Soc., 1,279; Knuttson, Com., 545; Babson, Proh., 325.

1944 (Pres.), Roosevelt, Dem., 100,144; Dewey, Rep., 118,535; Thomas, Soc., 943; Watson, Proh., 549.

1948 (Pres.), Truman, Dem., 95,812; Dewey, Rep., 115,139; Wallace, Prog., 8,391; Thomas, Soc., 1,000; Thurmond, States' Rights, 374.

1952 (Pres.), Eisenhower, Rep., 191,712; Stevenson, Dem., 76,694; MacArthur, Christian Nationalist, 1,075; Hallinan, Prog., 344; Hamblen, Proh., 302.

1956 (Pres.), Eisenhower, Rep., 156,766; Stevenson, Dem., 96,742; Andrews, American, 483.

1960 (Pres.), Kennedy, Dem., 123,963; Nixon, Rep., 154,310; Dobbs, Soc. Workers, 158.

1964 (Pres.), Johnson, Dem., 149,784; Goldwater, Rep., 108,207; DeBerry, Soc. Worker, 224; Munn, Proh., 174.

1968 (Pres.), Nixon, Rep., 138,669; Humphrey, Dem., 94,769; Wallace, 3rd party, 14,244; Halstead, Soc. Worker, 128; Munn, Prohibition, 38; Troxell, Ind., 34.

1972 (Pres.), Nixon, Rep., 174,109; McGovern, Dem., 100,384; Jenness, Soc. Worker, 288; Hall, Communist, 87; Schmitz, American, 5,646.

Ohio

County	1968 Humphrey (D)	Nixon (R)	Wallace (I)	1972 McGovern (D)	Nixon (R)
Adams	2,685	3,973	1,049	2,709	4,980
Allen	10,994	23,124	4,231	10,184	26,966
Ashland	4,526	9,745	1,323	4,302	12,470
Ashtabula	16,738	17,058	2,753	15,052	22,762
Athens	7,351	7,837	1,207	9,977	9,735
Auglaize	5,550	9,368	1,528	4,617	11,900
Belmont	22,056	11,512	2,478	14,800	17,628
Brown	3,610	4,700	2,307	3,770	6,772
Butler	23,649	35,962	14,188	21,194	50,380
Carroll	3,119	4,634	1,092	2,755	5,984
Champaign	4,264	6,863	1,621	3,626	8,756
Clark	24,029	23,748	6,710	19,725	34,447
Clermont	8,859	15,299	7,690	8,276	22,936
Clinton	2,982	6,265	1,830	2,709	8,140
Columbiana	19,382	19,947	3,832	15,683	27,308
Coshocton	5,013	7,256	1,270	3,790	8,082
Crawford	6,737	11,898	2,373	5,518	14,632
Cuyahoga	363,540	238,791	71,360	317,670	329,493
Darke	7,371	10,926	2,015	6,534	13,862
Defiance	5,686	7,348	925	4,377	8,914
Delaware	4,056	9,029	2,557	4,452	12,950
Erie	11,388	13,023	2,437	10,889	16,714
Fairfield	9,533	14,810	4,124	7,746	21,909
Fayette	2,966	5,339	1,962	2,344	6,970
Franklin	101,240	148,933	37,390	117,562	219,771
Fulton	3,338	7,817	1,033	3,615	8,387
Gallia	2,660	5,134	1,039	2,341	6,506
Geauga	7,825	11,857	3,226	7,329	15,624
Greene	15,178	17,589	5,999	12,736	25,349
Guernsey	5,815	7,336	1,685	4,757	9,648
Hamilton	135,057	183,611	46,742	119,054	239,212
Hancock	6,918	15,032	2,659	6,084	18,111
Hardin	4,180	6,963	1,794	3,535	8,713
Harrison	3,594	3,532	574	2,388	4,554
Henry	3,256	6,970	799	3,145	8,099
Highland	3,828	6,489	2,208	3,464	8,524
Hocking	3,701	3,998	1,003	2,874	5,407
Holmes	1,898	3,350	479	1,507	3,752
Huron	6,515	9,456	1,741	5,491	10,942
Jackson	4,021	5,870	1,077	3,410	7,351
Jefferson	21,917	12,949	3,740	16,198	21,531
Knox	5,725	9,072	1,695	5,370	10,705
Lake	27,932	28,450	9,160	27,523	42,488
Lawrence	8,671	9,782	2,470	7,112	15,125
Licking	15,021	19,542	5,405	12,460	28,070
Logan	4,889	8,362	1,647	3,786	10,938
Lorain	42,642	34,252	8,825	36,634	51,102
Lucas	91,346	69,403	17,260	90,142	88,401
Madison	2,780	5,882	1,631	2,484	8,372
Mahoning	68,433	42,948	12,189	62,428	64,144
Marion	8,611	12,887	2,772	7,970	17,197
Medina	9,194	14,089	3,632	10,643	21,010
Meigs	2,921	4,759	774	2,335	5,961
Mercer	6,801	6,313	1,095	5,798	8,587
Miami	13,228	16,997	3,348	9,121	21,226
Monroe	3,105	2,686	562	2,483	3,721
Montgomery	96,082	84,766	26,232	82,231	120,998
Morgan	1,789	3,030	450	1,554	3,679
Morrow	2,405	4,898	1,509	2,527	6,886
Muskingum	13,089	15,260	3,356	10,313	19,897
Noble	1,726	2,615	587	1,449	3,274
Ottawa	6,319	7,149	1,647	6,465	9,772
Paulding	2,703	4,074	908	2,283	4,553
Perry	4,811	4,815	1,084	3,728	6,716
Pickaway	3,536	6,690	2,335	2,978	9,661
Pike	3,445	3,247	1,423	3,531	5,037
Portage	16,348	15,064	5,093	20,769	23,294
Preble	3,817	6,544	2,073	3,472	8,993
Putnam	3,530	7,188	1,387	3,729	8,185
Richland	14,988	23,484	5,311	13,468	31,117
Ross	6,873	11,284	4,087	5,879	15,573
Sandusky	8,581	11,696	1,745	8,308	15,489
Scioto	13,836	15,310	3,171	11,008	19,998
Seneca	8,970	12,040	2,010	8,180	13,939
Shelby	6,479	7,248	1,499	4,721	9,089
Stark	57,675	68,414	16,775	51,565	92,110
Summit	100,068	82,649	26,157	108,534	112,419
Trumbull	40,365	33,076	9,314	35,278	47,680
Tuscarawas	15,617	14,102	2,741	12,255	18,413
Union	2,431	6,415	1,392	2,447	8,389
Van Wert	4,360	7,835	1,332	3,644	9,545
Vinton	1,608	2,219	414	1,537	2,725
Warren	6,756	12,663	6,595	6,941	20,210
Washington	6,922	11,888	1,597	5,814	14,023
Wayne	8,891	15,151	1,924	9,260	20,368
Williams	4,456	8,059	970	4,278	9,083
Wood	10,867	16,111	2,952	13,494	21,080
Wyandot	2,919	5,265	910	2,771	6,414
Totals	**1,700,586**	**1,791,014**	**467,495**	**1,558,889**	**2,441,827**

OHIO VOTE SINCE 1924

1924 (Pres.), Coolidge, Rep., 1,176,130; Davis, Dem., 477,888; LaFollette, Prog., 357,948; Johns, Soc. Lab., 3,025; Wallace, Comm. Land., 1,246.

1928 (Pres.), Hoover, Rep., 1,627,546; Smith, Dem., 864,210; Thomas, Soc., 8,683; Foster, Com., 2,836; Reynolds, Soc. Lab., 1,515; Varney, Proh., 3,556.

1932 (Pres.), Roosevelt, Dem., 1,301,695; Hoover, Rep., 1,227,679; Thomas, Soc., 64,094; Upshaw, Proh., 7,421; Foster, Com., 7,221; Reynolds, Soc. Lab., 1,968.

1936 (Pres.), Roosevelt, Dem., 1,747,122; Landon, Rep., 1,127,709; Lemke, Union, 132,212; Browder, Com., 5,251; Thomas, Soc., 117; Aiken, Soc. Lab., 14.

1940 (Pres.), Roosevelt, Dem., 1,733,139; Willkie, Rep., 1,586,773.

1944 (Pres.), Roosevelt, Dem., 1,570,763; Dewey, Rep., 1,582,293.

1948 (Pres.), Truman, Dem., 1,452,791; Dewey, Rep., 1,445,684; Wallace, Prog., 37,596.

1952 (Pres.), Eisenhower, Rep., 2,100,391; Stevenson, Dem., 1,600,367.

1956 (Pres.), Eisenhower, Rep., 2,262,610; Stevenson, Dem., 1,439,655.

1960 (Pres.), Kennedy, Dem., 1,944,248; Nixon, Rep., 2,217,611.

1964 (Pres.), Johnson, Dem., 2,498,331; Goldwater, Rep., 1,470,865.

1968 (Pres.),· Nixon, Rep., 1,791,014; Humphrey, Dem., 1,700,586; Wallace, 3rd party, 467,495; Gregory, 372; Munn, Prohibition, 19; Blomen, Soc. Labor, 120; Halstead, Soc. Worker, 69; Mitchell, Communist, 23.

1972 (Pres.), Nixon, Rep., 2,441,827; McGovern, Dem., 1,000,000; Fisher, Soc. Labor, 1,101; Hall, Communist, 6,437; Schmitz, American, 80,067; Wallace, Ind., 460.

Oklahoma

County	1968			1972	
	Hum-phrey (D)	Nixon (R)	Wal-lace (I)	McGov-ern (D)	Nixon (R)
Adair	1,549	2,877	1,000	1,601	4,720
Alfalfa	865	2,672	310	641	3,208
Atoka	1,400	1,131	1,613	993	2,905
Beaver	624	2,114	339	522	2,562
Beckham	2,354	2,935	1,550	1,608	4,472
Blaine	1,285	3,036	732	963	3,958
Bryan	3,214	2,727	2,264	3,144	5,397
Caddo	4,212	4,712	1,858	2,921	7,683
Canadian	3,577	5,891	2,525	2,751	11,400
Carter	5,807	5,127	3,414	4,577	9,368
Cherokee	2,554	3,971	1,866	2,899	7,080
Choctaw	2,268	1,414	1,751	1,798	3,399
Cimarron	436	1,122	527	323	1,350
Cleveland	8,617	12,446	4,711	11,126	25,777
Coal	963	669	625	680	1,461
Comanche	8,061	9,225	5,879	4,559	19,759
Cotton	1,192	1,016	905	798	2,050
Craig	2,098	2,686	1,229	1,642	4,163
Creek	5,151	6,934	3,913	3,705	12,396
Custer	2,717	4,709	936	2,298	7,267
Delaware	2,129	3,168	1,402	2,135	5,476
Dewey	773	1,508	540	626	2,106
Ellis	533	1,601	426	473	2,059
Garfield	5,802	14,370	3,011	4,557	19,348
Garvin	3,845	3,786	2,670	2,685	7,245
Grady	4,760	4,242	2,117	3,440	7,762
Grant	1,047	2,403	437	805	2,829
Greer	1,419	1,225	830	1,004	2,154
Harmon	1,097	644	403	568	1,319
Harper	518	1,483	353	385	1,976
Haskell	1,563	1,516	1,013	1,408	2,815
Hughes	2,578	1,897	1,170	1,787	3,497
Jackson	3,371	2,248	1,786	2,054	5,519
Jefferson	1,628	780	701	969	1,709
Johnston	1,216	1,048	974	983	2,205
Kay	6,031	12,751	2,809	4,246	17,244
Kingfisher	1,226	3,558	720	912	4,861
Kiowa	2,219	2,418	957	1,495	3,711
Latimer	1,350	1,091	892	1,239	2,520
Le Flore	4,020	3,600	3,345	3,433	7,932
Lincoln	2,304	3,855	1,969	1,919	6,512
Logan	2,508	3,960	1,689	2,760	6,543
Love	931	677	766	671	1,407
McClain	1,842	2,047	1,647	1,350	4,241
McCurtain	2,944	2,795	2,880	2,568	6,441
McIntosh	1,759	1,532	1,254	1,686	3,216
Major	594	2,550	357	512	3,203
Marshall	1,191	1,209	986	1,113	2,273
Mayes	2,855	4,260	2,431	2,656	7,535
Murray	1,773	1,454	1,027	1,294	2,983
Muskogee	9,377	8,707	4,596	7,380	15,161
Noble	1,412	2,911	618	999	4,085
Nowata	1,314	2,116	1,080	1,096	3,293
Okfuskee	1,777	1,686	981	1,328	2,862
Oklahoma	60,395	93,212	33,834	46,986	156,437
Okmulgee	6,089	4,709	2,728	4,494	8,706
Osage	3,919	5,499	2,407	2,968	9,288
Ottawa	4,820	5,000	1,421	3,657	8,348
Pawnee	1,343	2,437	990	1,135	4,280

County	1968			1972	
	Hum-phrey (D)	Nixon (R)	Wal-lace (I)	McGov-ern (D)	Nixon (R)
Payne	5,772	9,577	2,475	5,644	17,019
Pittsburg	6,112	3,978	3,726	4,748	9,989
Pontotoc	4,291	4,161	2,425	3,160	8,762
Pottawatomie	6,721	6,899	3,873	4,822	13,308
Pushmataha	1,232	1,225	1,287	1,016	2,456
Roger Mills	720	1,102	610	420	1,696
Rogers	2,665	4,631	3,141	2,607	9,697
Seminole	3,889	3,711	2,142	2,746	6,879
Sequoyah	2,618	2,797	2,158	2,519	6,842
Stephens	5,249	5,508	3,566	3,623	10,309
Texas	1,176	3,729	954	924	5,726
Tillman	1,771	1,748	1,376	1,256	3,331
Tulsa	32,748	81,476	28,443	32,779	125,278
Wagoner	2,183	3,187	2,262	2,257	6,569
Washington	4,641	12,812	3,091	3,658	16,347
Washita	1,771	2,592	858	1,305	3,578
Woods	1,439	3,449	517	1,234	4,413
Woodward	1,444	3,748	663	1,014	5,350
Totals	**301,658**	**449,697**	**191,731**	**247,147**	**759,025**

OKLAHOMA VOTE SINCE 1924

1924 (Pres.), Davis, Dem., 259,798; Coolidge, Rep., 226,242; LaFollette, Prog., 41,141; Johns, Soc. Lab., 5,234.

1928 (Pres.), Hoover, Rep., 394,046; Smith, Dem., 219,174; Thomas, Soc., 3,924; Farm-Lab., 1,283.

1932 (Pres.), Roosevelt, Dem., 516,468; Hoover, Rep., 188,165.

1936 (Pres.), Roosevelt, Dem., 501,069; Landon, Rep., 245,122; Thomas, Soc., 2,221; Colvin, Proh., 1,328.

1940 (Pres.), Roosevelt, Dem., 474,313; Willkie, Rep., 348,872; Babson, Proh., 3,027.

1944 (Pres.), Roosevelt, Dem., 401,549; Dewey, Rep., 319,424; Watson, Proh., 1,663.

1948 (Pres.), Truman, Dem., 452,782; Dewey, Rep., 268,817.

1952 (Pres.), Eisenhower, Rep., 518,045; Stevenson, Dem., 430,939.

1956 (Pres.), Eisenhower, Rep., 473,769; Stevenson, Dem., 385,581.

1960 (Pres.), Kennedy, Dem., 370,111; Nixon, Rep., 533,039.

1964 (Pres.), Johnson, Dem., 519,834; Goldwater, Rep., 412,665.

1968 (Pres.), Nixon, Rep., 449,697; Humphrey, Dem., 301,658; Wallace, 3rd party, 191,731.

1972 (Pres.), Nixon, Rep., 759,025; McGovern, Dem., 247,147; Schmitz, American, 23,728.

Oregon

County	1968			1972	
	Hum-phrey (D)	Nixon (R)	Wal-lace (I)	McGov-ern (D)	Nixon (R)
Baker	2,464	3,311	480	2,047	3,441
Benton	6,538	11,654	749	10,842	14,906
Clackamas	27,939	32,363	3,659	32,540	41,767
Clatsop	6,243	5,810	651	6,017	5,998
Columbia	6,064	4,208	728	5,997	5,348
Coos	10,984	8,230	1,767	11,778	10,370
Crook	1,611	1,727	256	1,743	2,167
Curry	1,934	2,323	436	2,108	2,832
Deschutes	4,859	5,599	738	6,319	7,747
Douglas	9,186	13,410	3,433	9,009	15,881
Gilliam	436	619	65	355	665
Grant	934	1,632	239	932	1,781
Harney	1,036	1,617	197	1,004	1,693
Hood River	2,385	2,597	323	2,330	3,152
Jackson	12,714	19,577	2,446	14,529	24,003
Jefferson	1,160	1,669	180	1,229	1,816
Josephine	4,351	8,456	1,800	5,090	9,911
Klamath	5,629	9,604	1,735	5,719	11,169
Lake	730	1,538	229	777	1,619
Lane	34,521	39,563	5,830	46,177	47,739
Lincoln	5,009	5,031	659	5,117	6,112
Linn	10,032	12,604	1,648	11,178	15,079
Malheur	2,021	5,447	892	1,870	5,908
Marion	22,327	30,417	2,756	23,908	36,441
Morrow	797	1,068	102	718	1,059
Multnomah	124,651	106,831	11,054	125,470	118,219
Polk	4,961	6,997	581	5,908	8,985
Sherman	384	646	59	330	677
Tillamook	3,609	3,261	394	3,544	4,120
Umatilla	6,402	8,975	956	6,090	10,470
Union	3,409	3,796	521	3,272	5,073
Wallowa	1,006	1,527	194	899	1,909
Wasco	3,918	3,842	514	3,749	4,537
Washington	22,943	34,105	2,566	27,890	43,958
Wheeler	292	443	27	267	474
Yamhill	5,487	7,936	819	6,008	9,660
Totals	**358,866**	**408,433**	**49,683**	**392,760**	**486,686**

OREGON VOTE SINCE 1924

1924 (Pres.), Coolidge, Rep., 142,579; LaFollette, Prog. 68,403; Davis, Dem., 67,589; Johns, Soc. Lab., 917.

1928 (Pres.), Hoover, Rep., 205,341; Smith, Dem., 109,223; Thomas, Soc., 2,720; Reynolds, Soc. Labor, 1,564; Foster, Com., 1,094.

1932 (Pres.), Roosevelt, Dem., 213,871; Hoover, Rep., 136,019; Thomas, Soc., 15,450; Reynolds, Soc. Lab., 1,730; Foster, Com., 1,681.

1936 (Pres.), Roosevelt, Dem., 266,733; Landon, Rep., 122,706; Lemke, Union, 21,831; Thomas, Soc., 2,143; Aiken, Soc. Lab., 500; Browder, Com., 104; Colvin, Proh., 4.

1940 (Pres.), Roosevelt, Dem., 258,415; Willkie, Rep., 219,555; Aiken, Soc. Lab., 2,487; Thomas, Soc., 398; Browder, Com., 191; Babson, Proh., 154.

1944 (Pres.), Roosevelt, Dem., 248,635; Dewey, Rep., 225,365; Thomas, Soc., 3,785; Watson, Proh., 2,362.

1948 (Pres.), Truman, Dem., 243,147; Dewey, Rep., 260,904; Wallace, Prog., 14,978; Thomas, Soc., 5,051.

1952 (Pres.), Eisenhower, Rep., 420,815; Stevenson, Dem., 270,579; Hallinan, Ind., 3,665.

1956 (Pres.), Eisenhower, Rep., 406,393; Stevenson, Dem., 329,204.

1960 (Pres.), Kennedy, Dem., 367,402; Nixon, Rep., 408,060.

1964 (Pres.), Johnson, Dem., 501,017; Goldwater, Rep., 282,779; Write-in, 2,509.

1968 (Pres.), Nixon, Rep., 408,433; Humphrey, Dem., 358,866; Wallace, 3rd party, 49,683; Write-ins, McCarthy, 1,496; N. Rockefeller, 69; others 1,075.

1972 (Pres.), Nixon, Rep., 486,686; McGovern, Dem., 392,760; Schmitz, American, 46,211; Write-in 2,289.

Pennsylvania

County	1968 Humphrey (D)	Nixon (R)	Wallace (I)	1972 McGovern (D)	Nixon (R)
Adams	5,993	11,303	1,579	5,529	13,593
Allegheny	364,906	264,790	79,776	282,496	371,737
Armstrong	13,921	14,132	2,256	10,490	17,557
Beaver	45,396	28,264	7,974	31,570	43,637
Bedford	4,725	10,482	1,301	3,836	11,243
Berks	49,877	50,623	8,093	36,563	66,172
Blair	15,803	28,780	3,644	10,023	33,126
Bradford	6,373	13,308	1,347	5,204	15,050
Bucks	57,634	69,646	15,211	56,784	99,684
Butler	19,415	21,618	4,139	14,695	29,665
Cambria	41,225	33,280	4,485	27,950	43,825
Cameron	1,104	1,822	159	828	1,935
Carbon	10,634	9,954	952	7,774	11,639
Centre	11,163	15,865	1,389	13,194	20,683
Chester	32,606	56,073	9,142	31,118	72,726
Clarion	5,341	8,077	981	4,509	10,073
Clearfield	12,369	14,471	2,252	9,246	16,780
Clinton	6,301	6,563	625	4,772	8,205
Columbia	8,187	12,202	1,797	7,222	14,187
Crawford	11,345	14,991	1,832	9,371	18,393
Cumberland	15,467	32,908	4,893	14,562	42,099
Dauphin	25,480	48,394	7,534	22,587	54,307
Delaware	106,695	133,777	25,051	94,144	175,414
Elk	6,886	6,193	945	4,710	7,900
Erie	51,604	43,134	4,868	42,022	61,542
Fayette	34,340	18,921	5,984	22,475	27,288
Forest	669	1,172	129	509	1,374
Franklin	11,451	19,146	4,557	9,456	24,093
Fulton	1,174	2,200	592	1,192	2,515
Greene	8,198	5,099	1,094	5,562	7,790
Huntingdon	4,128	8,276	962	3,394	9,606
Indiana	12,175	14,899	2,078	10,833	18,122
Jefferson	6,839	10,214	1,278	5,024	11,631
Juniata	2,321	4,039	507	2,156	4,412
Lackawanna	66,297	44,388	3,538	45,465	58,838
Lancaster	29,870	69,953	8,194	24,223	81,036
Lawrence	21,027	18,360	3,635	17,595	23,712
Lebanon	9,529	21,832	2,584	6,683	25,008
Lehigh	44,033	47,255	3,900	33,325	58,023
Luzerne	79,040	57,044	6,857	51,128	81,358
Lycoming	16,888	23,830	2,761	11,999	28,913
McKean	6,326	10,506	745	4,513	11,958
Mercer	22,814	23,131	3,033	18,087	27,961
Mifflin	5,681	8,133	859	3,667	9,989
Monroe	6,946	9,465	1,267	5,619	12,701
Montgomery	102,464	141,621	15,599	91,959	173,662
Montour	2,239	3,289	438	1,755	4,386
Northampton	42,554	32,033	3,276	32,335	41,822
Northumberland	17,013	22,366	2,456	13,885	25,912
Perry	2,944	6,655	1,222	2,731	8,082
Philadelphia	525,768	254,153	63,506	431,736	344,096
Pike	1,617	3,719	441	1,385	4,568
Potter	1,860	4,019	451	1,710	4,422
Schuylkill	34,982	37,194	4,381	26,077	44,071
Snyder	1,993	6,784	676	1,834	7,308
Somerset	11,515	17,511	1 845	8,743	19,739
Sullivan	1,035	1,629	200	885	1,886
Susquehanna	4,364	8,705	929	4,154	9,476
Tioga	3,488	9,298	1,065	3,733	10,028
Union	2,178	6,422	581	2,278	6,905
Venango	8,319	12,323	1,262	6,302	13,991
Warren	6,368	8,889	676	4,877	10,018
Washington	47,805	28,023	9,016	34,781	42,587
Wayne	3,176	7,827	754	2,733	8,948
Westmoreland	81,833	52,206	14,436	59,322	75,085
Wyoming	2,366	5,207	539	2,112	6,423
York	33,328	51,631	8,054	27,520	63,606
Totals	2,259,405	2,090,017	378,582	1,796,951	2,714,521

PENNSYLVANIA VOTE SINCE 1924

1924 (Pres.), Coolidge, Rep., 1,401,481; Davis, Dem., 409,192; LaFollette, Soc., 93,441; Labor, 214,126; Nations, Amer., 13,035; Faris, Proh., 9,779; Foster, Workers, 2,735.

1928 (Pres.), Hoover, Rep., 2,055,382; Smith, Dem., 1,067,586; Thomas, Soc., 18,647; Foster, Labor, (Workers, 2,687; Com., 2,039), 4,726.

1932 (Pres.), Roosevelt, Dem., 1,295,948; Hoover, Rep., 1,453,540; Thomas, Soc., 91,119; Upshaw, Proh., 11,319; Foster, Com., 5,658; Cox, Jobless, 725; Reynolds, Indust., 659.

1936 (Pres.), Roosevelt, Dem., 2,353,788; Landon, Rep., 1,690,300; Lemke, Royal Oak, 67,467; Thomas, Soc., 14,375; Colvin, Proh., 6,691; Browder, Com., 4,060; Aiken, Ind. Lab., 1,424.

1940 (Pres.), Roosevelt, Dem., 2,171,035; Willkie, Rep., 1,889,848; Thomas, Soc., 10,967; Browder, Com., 4,519; Aiken, Ind. Gov., 1,518.

1944 (Pres.), Roosevelt, Dem., 1,940,479; Dewey, Rep., 1,835,054; Thomas, Soc., 11,721; Watson, Proh., 5,750; Teichert, Ind. Gov., 1,789.

1948 (Pres.), Truman, Dem., 1,752,426; Dewey, Rep., 1,902,197; Wallace, Prog., 55,161; Thomas, Soc., 11,325; Watson, Proh., 10,338; Dobbs, Militant Workers, 2,133; Teichert, Ind. Gov., 1,461.

1952 (Pres.), Eisenhower, Rep., 2,415,789; Stevenson, Dem., 2,146,269; Hamblen, Proh., 8,771; Hallinan, Prog., 4,200; Hoopes, Soc., 2,684; Dobbs, Militant Workers, 1,502; Hass, Ind. Gov., 1,347; Scattered, 155.

1956 (Pres.), Eisenhower, Rep., 2,585,252; Stevenson, Dem., 1,981,769; Hass, Soc. Lab., 7,447; Dobbs, Militant Workers, 2,035.

1960 (Pres.), Kennedy, Dem., 2,556,282; Nixon, Rep., 2,439,956; Hass, Soc. Lab., 7,185; Dobbs, Soc. Workers, 2,678; Scattering 440.

1964 (Pres.), Johnson, Dem., 3,130,954; Goldwater, Rep., 1,673,657; De Berry, Soc. Worker, 10,456; Hass, Soc. Labor, 5,092; Scattering, 2,531.

1968 (Pres.), Nixon, Rep., 2,090,017; Humphrey, Dem., 2,259,405; Wallace, 3rd party, 378,582; Blomen, Soc. Labor, 4,977; Halstead, Soc. Worker, 4,862; Gregory, 7,821; others 2,264.

1972 (Pres.), Nixon, Rep., 2,714,521; McGovern, Dem., 1,796,951; Schmitz, American, 70,593; Jenness, Soc. Worker, 4,639; Hall, Communist, 2,686; Others 2,715.

Rhode Island

County	1968 Humphrey (D)	Nixon (R)	Wallace (I)	1972 McGovern (D)	Nixon (R)
Bristol	11,561	7,403	483	9,928	12,009
Kent	35,609	22,493	2,519	29,004	40,534
Newport	16,251	10,504	1,043	12,844	19,142
Providence	169,246	70,320	10,347	129,232	129,418
Washington	13,851	11,639	1,286	13,637	19,280
Totals	246,518	122,359	15,678	194,645	220,383

RHODE ISLAND VOTE SINCE 1924

1924 (Pres.), Coolidge, Rep., 125,286; Davis, Dem., 76,606; LaFollette, Prog., 7,628; Foster, Workers, 280; Johns, Soc. Lab., 268.

1928 (Pres.), Smith, Dem., 118,973; Hoover, Rep., 117,522; Reynolds, Soc. Lab., 416; Foster, Com., 283.

1932 (Pres.), Roosevelt, Dem., 146,604; Hoover, Rep., 115,266; Thomas, Soc., 3,138; Foster, Com., 546; Reynolds, Soc. Lab., 433; Upshaw, Proh., 183.

1936 (Pres.), Roosevelt, Dem., 165,238; Landon, Rep., 125,031; Lemke, Union, 19,569; Aiken, Soc. Lab., 929; Browder, Com., 411.

1940 (Pres.), Roosevelt, Dem., 182,182; Willkie, Rep., 138,653; Browder, Com., 239; Babson, Proh., 74.

1944 (Pres.), Roosevelt, Dem., 175,356; Dewey, Rep., 123,487; Watson, Proh., 433.

1948 (Pres.), Truman, Dem., 188,736; Dewey, Rep.,

135,787; Wallace, Prog., 2,619; Thomas, Soc., 429; Teichert, Soc. Lab., 131.
1952 (Pres.), Eisenhower, Rep., 210,935; Stevenson, Dem., 203,293; Hallinan, Prog., 187; Hass, Soc. Lab., 83.
1956 (Pres.), Eisenhower, Rep., 225,819; Stevenson, Dem., 161,790.
1960 (Pres.), Kennedy, D., 258,032; Nixon, R. 147,502.
1964 (Pres.), Johnson, D., 315,463; Goldwater, R. 74,615.
1968 (Pres.), Nixon, Rep., 122,359; Humphrey, Dem., 246,518; Wallace, 3rd party, 15,678; Halstead, Soc. Worker, 383.
1972 (Pres.), Nixon, Rep., 220,383; McGovern, Dem., 194,645; Jenness, Soc. Worker, 729.

South Carolina

County	1968 Humphrey (D)	Nixon (R)	Wallace (I)	1972 McGovern (D)	Nixon (R)
Abbeville	1,425	1,213	3,201	1,347	3,265
Aiken	6,319	12,264	8,815	5,745	21,117
Allendale	1,538	997	820	1,383	1,740
Anderson	5,218	5,661	12,384	5,241	17,514
Bamberg	1,845	1,327	1,618	1,680	2,537
Barnwell	1,716	1,849	2,351	1,560	3,955
Beaufort	3,740	2,983	1,498	3,237	5,929
Berkeley	5,089	4,021	4,808	4,497	9,345
Calhoun	1,216	885	978	1,148	1,887
Charleston	18,343	24,282	13,255	16,856	39,832
Cherokee	1,998	2,853	5,642	2,107	7,570
Chester	2,865	2,862	2,762	2,352	4,724
Chesterfield	3,180	2,564	4,324	2,938	5,230
Clarendon	3,606	2,201	2,097	3,276	3,958
Colleton	2,651	2,824	2,670	2,376	5,738
Darlington	3,803	4,947	5,231	4,414	11,756
Dillon	2,178	2,396	2,132	1,604	4,364
Dorchester	3,855	3,354	3,539	3,606	8,095
Edgefield	1,225	1,688	1,006	1,326	2,812
Fairfield	3,011	1,619	1,336	2,491	2,608
Florence	8,079	8,917	7,642	7,451	18,107
Georgetown	4,110	3,269	2,642	4,446	6,114
Greenville	12,928	31,652	15,241	10,163	46,360
Greenwood	3,741	4,891	6,024	3,400	9,370
Hampton	2,107	1,671	1,452	2,086	2,891
Horry	3,924	3,924	6,701	4,437	15,324
Jasper	1,402	633	1,081	1,203	1,650
Kershaw	2,539	4,079	3,960	2,531	8,035
Lancaster	3,151	4,874	4,886	2,461	9,016
Laurens	3,016	4,813	4,279	2,650	8,141
Lee	2,151	1,219	2,113	1,996	3,076
Lexington	4,058	12,204	8,907	4,069	25,327
Marion	2,821	2,512	1,484	844	1,302
Marlboro	2,294	2,024	2,140	2,535	4,719
McCormick	988	466	757	2,999	3,838
Newberry	2,444	4,538	3,734	2,035	7,325
Oconee	2,009	2,618	4,742	1,739	6,825
Orangeburg	8,971	5,144	7,144	7,652	11,711
Pickens	2,016	6,873	4,424	2,255	11,776
Richland	18,198	26,215	7,030	20,875	38,500
Saluda	1,200	1,466	2,136	1,022	3,095
Spartanburg	11,467	18,183	17,346	9,723	31,187
Sumter	6,103	5,451	4,754	5,795	10,892
Union	2,271	3,011	4,590	2,676	8,337
Williamsburg	5,106	3,029	2,652	5,213	5,729
York	5,571	7,596	7,102	6,374	14,441
Totals	**197,486**	**254,062**	**215,430**	**186,824**	**477,044**

SOUTH CAROLINA VOTE SINCE 1924

1924 (Pres.), Davis, Dem., 49,008; Coolidge, Rep., 1,123; LaFollette, Prog., 620.
1928 (Pres.), Smith, Dem., 62,700; Anti-Smith, 2,670; Hoover, Rep., 3,188; Thomas, Soc., 44.
1932 (Pres.), Roosevelt, Dem., 102,347; Hoover, Rep., 1,978; Thomas, Soc., 82.
1936 (Pres.), Roosevelt, Dem., 113,791; Landon, Rep., Tolbert faction (953), Hambright faction (693), total, 1,646.
1940 (Pres.), Roosevelt, Dem., 95,470; Willkie, Rep., 1,727.
1944 (Pres.), Roosevelt, Dem., 90,601; Dewey, Rep., 4,547; Southern Democrats, 7,799; Watson, Proh., 365; Rep. (Tolbert faction), 63.
1948 (Pres.), Thurmond, States' Rights, 102,607; Truman, Dem., 34,423; Dewey, Rep., 5,386; Wallace, Prog., 154; Thomas, Soc., 1.
1952 (Pres.), Eisenhower ran on two tickets. Under State law vote cast for two Eisenhower slates of electors could not be combined. Eisenhower, Ind., 158,189; Rep., 9,793; total 168,082; Stevenson, Dem., 173,004; Hamblen, Proh., 1.
1956 (Pres.), Stevenson, Dem., 136,372; Byrd, Inc., 88,509; Eisenhower Rep., 75,700; Andrews, Ind., 2.
1960 (Pres.), Kennedy, Dem., 198,129; Nixon, Rep., 188,558; Write-in, 1.

1964 (Pres.), Johnson, Dem., 215,700; Goldwater, Rep., 309,048; Write-ins: Nixon, 1; Wallace, 5; Powell, 1; Thurmond, 1.
1968 (Pres.), Nixon, Rep., 254,062; Humphrey, Dem., 197,486; Wallace, 3rd party, 215,430.
1972 (Pres.), Nixon, Rep., 477,044; McGovern, Dem., 184,559 United Citizens 2,265; Schmitz, American, 10,075; Write-in 17.

South Dakota

County	1968 Humphrey (D)	Nixon (R)	Wallace (I)	1972 McGovern (D)	Nixon (R)
Aurora	1,060	1,043	130	1,257	1,075
Beadle	5,357	4,214	307	4,297	5,922
Bennett	457	665	111	476	808
Bon Homme	1,773	2,411	199	2,368	2,116
Brookings	3,202	4,674	205	4,701	5,182
Brown	7,302	6,685	560	8,216	8,134
Brule	1,425	1,237	153	1,665	1,421
Buffalo	265	261	28	275	221
Butte	1,017	2,090	196	1,085	2,452
Campbell	245	1,216	73	361	1,169
Chas. Mix	2,369	2,093	213	2,691	2,020
Clark	1,325	1,596	119	1,336	1,617
Clay	2,006	2,249	131	2,821	2,518
Codington	4,235	3,929	288	4,601	4,936
Corson	821	1,108	80	689	975
Custer	727	1,143	100	798	1,476
Davison	3,585	3,869	265	4,710	3,796
Day	2,463	2,062	182	2,719	1,971
Deuel	1,076	1,398	151	1,370	1,357
Dewey	721	941	123	699	1,008
Douglas	592	1,613	77	887	1,434
Edmunds	1,225	1,534	181	1,646	1,567
Fall River	965	1,843	286	1,107	2,374
Faulk	819	997	199	986	1,004
Grant	1,890	2,259	211	2,231	2,247
Gregory	1,266	1,810	251	1,555	1,670
Haakon	377	759	109	366	1,021
Hamlin	1,149	1,649	128	1,276	1,693
Hand	1,136	1,650	226	1,307	1,806
Hanson	826	901	72	1,022	876
Harding	266	564	65	253	637
Hughes	1,666	3,204	343	2,037	4,231
Hutchinson	1,412	3,544	175	2,248	3,092
Hyde	499	713	113	533	789
Jackson	267	480	98	261	581
Jerauld	745	1,002	56	829	988
Jones	358	562	88	346	642
Kingsbury	1,491	2,300	146	1,632	2,320
Lake	2,294	2,876	188	2,886	2,919
Lawrence	2,425	4,185	338	2,533	4,795
Lincoln	1,961	3,259	222	2,617	3,201
Lyman	643	1,063	131	774	1,166
Marshall	1,518	1,471	140	1,646	1,500
McCook	1,653	1,959	188	1,993	1,963
McPherson	389	2,105	126	579	1,950
Meade	1,522	2,392	343	1,633	3,146
Mellette	407	611	79	433	637
Miner	1,255	1,045	92	1,337	1,059
Minnehaha	16,462	20,141	1,177	22,386	22,447
Moody	1,614	1,689	153	1,895	1,648
Pennington	7,303	9,671	1,174	8,592	13,654
Perkins	869	1,498	114	900	1,691
Potter	780	1,273	149	858	1,389
Roberts	2,651	2,225	337	2,976	2,187
Sanborn	956	1,024	80	1,074	1,064
Shannon	1,202	533	61	1,246	356
Spink	2,669	2,068	178	2,321	2,547
Stanley	439	572	98	492	779
Sully	356	676	93	414	773
Todd	987	683	91	907	806
Tripp	1,362	2,242	245	1,538	2,592
Turner	1,350	3,246	205	1,993	3,007
Union	2,014	2,212	225	2,554	2,271
Walworth	1,276	2,204	182	1,287	2,416
Washabaugh	203	224	22	211	245
Yankton	2,733	3,977	382	3,835	4,366
Ziebach	350	449	55	378	486
Totals	**118,023**	**149,841**	**13,400**	**139,945**	**166,476**

SOUTH DAKOTA VOTE SINCE 1924

1924 (Pres.), Coolidge, Rep., 101,299; LaFollette, Prog., 75,355; Davis, Dem., 27,214.
1928 (Pres.), Hoover, Rep., 157,660; Smith, Dem., 102,660; Thomas, Soc., 443; Foster, Com., 232; Farm-Lab., 927.
1932 (Pres.), Roosevelt, Dem., 183,515; Hoover, Rep., 99,212; Harvey, Lib., 3,333; Thomas, Soc., 1,551; Upshaw, Proh., 463; Foster, Com., 364.
1936 (Pres.), Roosevelt, Dem., 160,137; Landon, Rep., 125,977; Lemke, Union, 10,338.
1940 (Pres.), Roosevelt, D., 131,362; Willkie, R., 177,065.
1944 (Pres.), Roosevelt, D., 96,711; Dewey, R., 135,365.
1948 (Pres.), Truman, Dem., 117,653; Dewey, Rep., 129,651; Wallace, Prog., 2,801.

1952 (Pres.), Eisenhower, Rep., 203,857; Stevenson, Dem.,
90,426.
1956 (Pres.), Eisenhower, Rep., 171,569; Stevenson, Dem.,
122,288.
1960 (Pres.), Kennedy, Dem., 128,070; Nixon, Rep.,
178,417.
1964 (Pres.), Johnson, Dem., 163,010; Goldwater, Rep.,
130,108.
1968 (Pres.), Nixon, Rep., 149,841; Humphrey, Dem.,
118,023; Wallace, 3rd party, 13,400.
1972 (Pres.), Nixon, Rep., 166,476; McGovern, Dem.,
139,945; Jenness, Soc. Worker, 994.

Tennessee

County	1968 Hum-phrey (D)	1968 Nixon (R)	1968 Wal-lace (I)	1972 McGov-ern (D)	1972 Nixon (R)
Anderson	7,198	10,233	4,323	6,713	13,865
Bedford	2,416	1,870	4,099	2,565	4,262
Benton	1,059	1,468	2,255	1,479	2,614
Bledsoe	957	1,477	732	899	1,952
Blount	5,176	12,753	4,407	5,303	16,078
Bradley	2,762	6,924	4,159	2,804	10,440
Campbell	2,268	4,024	1,367	1,629	4,909
Cannon	809	780	1,464	911	1,615
Carroll	1,932	3,757	3,298	2,290	5,784
Carter	2,160	9,467	3,009	2,191	11,102
Cheatham	778	669	2,497	1,321	2,235
Chester	849	1,408	2,037	961	2,787
Claiborne	1,314	3,101	775	1,230	3,632
Clay	667	814	451	648	982
Cocke	950	5,645	1,159	805	5,268
Coffee	3,040	3,337	4,794	2,973	6,416
Crockett	703	932	2,865	735	2,642
Cumberland	1,428	3,115	1,469	1,482	4,593
Davidson	44,543	44,175	47,889	48,869	82,636
Decatur	877	1,409	1,544	1,187	2,368
De Kalb	847	1,532	1,516	1,243	2,014
Dickson	2,034	1,291	3,475	2,619	3,645
Dyer	2,033	2,826	5,842	1,600	6,066
Fayette	2,236	740	2,570	2,067	3,264
Fentress	671	2,026	808	665	2,154
Franklin	2,489	1,700	4,939	2,896	4,136
Gibson	3,962	4,093	7,233	3,625	9,900
Giles	2,203	1,264	3,966	1,875	2,914
Grainger	761	2,788	596	828	2,842
Greene	2,947	7,957	2,753	2,764	9,772
Grundy	1,307	618	1,642	1,005	1,364
Hamblen	2,390	6,382	2,259	2,563	8,879
Hamilton	23,441	29,302	32,080	20,657	58,469
Hancock	318	1,489	236	393	1,813
Hardeman	1,709	1,171	2,924	1,550	3,494
Hardin	1,153	2,910	2,325	1,202	4,401
Hawkins	2,213	6,217	1,798	2,608	7,791
Haywood	1,709	1,152	2,757	1,966	3,123
Henderson	1,230	3,591	2,086	1,313	5,122
Henry	3,149	2,068	3,439	2,694	4,613
Hickman	1,152	760	2,473	1,393	1,943
Houston	636	232	941	870	800
Humphreys	1,391	866	2,095	1,973	2,263
Jackson	1,122	673	908	1,085	956
Jefferson	1,494	5,494	1,199	1,357	5,925
Johnson	450	3,107	375	450	3,362
Knox	24,528	47,202	18,277	24,076	64,747
Lake	737	409	1,262	536	1,147
Lauderdale	2,108	1,080	3,566	1,771	3,597
Lawrence	2,191	4,343	3,993	2,824	6,438
Lewis	1,088	455	997	1,138	1,056
Lincoln	1,848	1,167	4,214	1,867	3,266
Loudon	1,581	4,299	1,996	1,604	5,357
McMinn	2,889	6,098	2,535	2,838	7,423
McNairy	1,377	2,979	2,872	1,610	4,774
Macon	530	2,173	1,041	653	2,295
Madison	5,517	6,143	9,420	5,203	15,481
Marion	1,661	1,959	2,784	1,929	3,711
Marshall	1,527	1,202	3,379	1,526	2,593
Maury	3,401	3,048	8,148	3,262	7,371
Meigs	493	729	442	539	1,052
Monroe	2,926	4,749	1,222	2,870	5,657
Montgomery	5,538	3,248	5,638	5,691	7,839
Moore	346	224	856	356	608
Morgan	968	1,803	1,028	1,084	2,531
Obion	2,235	2,420	4,680	2,243	5,800
Overton	1,592	1,258	1,176	1,573	1,947
Perry	726	519	784	937	900
Pickett	405	884	199	357	957
Polk	1,454	1,808	754	1,431	2,285
Putnam	3,541	3,693	3,073	3,738	6,038
Rhea	1,301	2,428	2,237	1,312	3,842
Roane	3,258	6,033	3,898	3,433	8,742
Robertson	2,315	1,802	3,904	2,985	4,175
Rutherford	4,921	4,168	7,773	5,811	11,256
Scott	991	2,406	734	679	2,775
Sequatchie	549	663	1,011	629	1,298
Sevier	1,112	7,629	1,476	1,128	8,273
Shelby	81,486	73,416	76,996	81,089	161,922
Smith	1,443	1,089	1,831	1,260	1,812
Stewart	1,041	443	1,057	1,098	790

County	1968 Hum-phrey (D)	1968 Nixon (R)	1968 Wal-lace (I)	1972 McGov-ern (D)	1972 Nixon (R)
Sullivan	9,783	20,251	9,991	10,007	27,593
Sumner	4,376	4,519	7,592	4,596	10,020
Tipton	2,071	1,422	4,943	1,853	5,542
Trousdale	694	252	649	539	663
Unicoi	910	3,327	843	822	3,877
Union	527	1,956	449	570	1,927
Van Buren	282	327	507	364	629
Warren	2,046	1,858	3,814	2,118	3,565
Washington	4,930	12,882	4,925	5,284	17,343
Wayne	506	2,417	1,208	673	2,898
Weakley	1,988	2,858	4,525	2,027	5,836
White	1,584	1,423	1,750	1,392	2,252
Williamson	2,063	2,788	4,867	2,616	7,556
Wilson	2,916	2,736	5,648	3,096	6,486
Totals	351,233	472,592	424,792	357,293	813,147

TENNESSEE VOTE SINCE 1924

1924 (Pres.), Davis, Dem., 158,404; Coolidge, Rep.,
130,882; LaFollette, Prog., 10,656; Farris, Proh., 115.
1928 (Pres.), Hoover, Rep., 195,388; Smith, Dem., 167,343;
Thomas, Soc., 631; Foster, Com., 111.
1932 (Pres.), Roosevelt, Dem., 259,817; Hoover, Rep.,
126,806; Upshaw, Proh., 1,995; Thomas, Soc., 1,786;
Foster, Com., 234.
1936 (Pres.), Roosevelt, Dem., 327,083; Landon, Rep.,
146,516; Thomas, Soc., 685; Colvin, Proh., 632; Browder, Com., 319; Lemke, Union, 296.
1940 (Pres.), Roosevelt, Dem., 351,601; Willkie, Rep.,
169,153; Babson, Proh., 1,606; Thomas, Soc., 463.
1944 (Pres.), Roosevelt, Dem., 308,707; Dewey, Rep.,
200,311; Watson, Proh., 882; Thomas, Soc., 892.
1948 (Pres.), Truman, Dem., 270,402; Dewey, Rep.,
202,914; Thurmond, States' Rights, 73,815; Wallace,
Prog., 1,864; Thomas, Soc., 1,288.
1952 (Pres.), Eisenhower, Rep., 446,147; Stevenson, Dem.,
443,710; Hamblen, Proh., 1,432; Hallinan, Prog., 885;
MacArthur, Christian Nationalist, 379.
1956 (Pres.), Eisenhower, Rep., 462,288; Stevenson, Dem.,
456,507; Andrews, Ind., 19,820; Holtwick, Proh., 789.
1960 (Pres.), Kennedy, Dem., 481,453; Nixon, Rep.,
556,577; Faubus, States' Rights, 11,304; Decker, Proh.,
2,458.
1964 (Pres.), Johnson, Dem., 635,047; Goldwater, Rep.,
508,965; Write-in, 34.
1968 (Pres.), Nixon, Rep., 472,592; Humphrey, Dem.,
351,233; Wallace, 3rd party, 424,792.
1972 (Pres.), Nixon, Rep., 813,147; McGovern, Dem.,
357,293; Schmitz, American, 30,373; Write-in 369.

Texas

County	1968 Hum-phrey (D)	1968 Nixon (R)	1968 Wal-lace (I)	1972 McGov-ern (D)	1972 Nixon (R)
Anderson	3,447	2,828	3,196	2,233	5,826
Andrews	922	1,400	1,312	677	2,615
Angelina	5,174	4,645	6,111	4,970	11,453
Aransas	1,222	1,076	417	844	2,037
Archer	1,308	636	413	632	1,494
Armstrong	301	434	206	177	768
Atascosa	2,522	1,805	771	1,804	3,400
Austin	1,299	1,971	1,084	1,043	3,084
Bailey	820	1,174	563	465	1,837
Bandera	535	842	423	434	1,796
Bastrop	2,687	1,455	975	1,906	3,097
Baylor	1,064	657	443	598	1,190
Bee	2,957	1,995	589	2,067	3,779
Bell	11,893	5,705	3,547	6,848	17,525
Bexar	95,325	72,951	16,598	91,662	137,572
Blanco	620	614	223	460	1,215
Borden	157	117	112	96	330
Bosque	1,817	1,377	727	1,014	2,947
Bowie	6,468	5,966	7,165	5,227	14,722
Brazoria	11,439	10,631	8,026	11,350	21,045
Brazos	6,299	6,839	2,437	5,692	14,243
Brewster	958	790	342	904	1,524
Briscoe	528	411	219	349	642
Brooks	1,904	534	166	1,657	1,117
Brown	3,999	2,997	1,606	2,171	5,990
Burleson	1,678	891	694	1,361	1,762
Burnet	1,876	1,459	643	1,227	3,438
Caldwell	2,889	1,402	837	1,974	3,171
Calhoun	2,612	1,672	1,065	1,936	3,614
Callahan	1,437	921	737	665	2,223
Cameron	15,726	11,759	2,042	13,340	20,816
Camp	1,272	555	1,074	1,041	1,599
Carson	904	1,211	570	561	1,868
Cass	2,536	1,930	2,883	1,981	5,303
Castro	1,181	1,033	623	751	1,685
Chambers	1,217	1,061	1,329	1,206	2,390
Cherokee	3,242	2,575	3,791	2,467	5,743

County	1968 Humphrey (D)	Nixon (R)	Wallace (I)	1972 McGovern (D)	Nixon (R)
Childress	1,093	1,045	621	729	1,716
Clay	1,573	936	665	1,023	1,893
Cochran	633	548	449	415	1,106
Coke	563	387	208	358	761
Coleman	1,449	1,507	1,153	721	2,386
Collin	5,918	6,494	3,850	4,783	17,667
Collingsworth	746	712	475	501	1,250
Colorado	1,976	2,296	1,163	1,502	3,495
Comal	2,338	3,646	724	1,823	6,761
Comanche	1,980	1,436	708	1,176	2,608
Concho	502	411	197	350	709
Cooke	2,711	3,799	1,412	1,702	6,317
Coryell	2,987	1,698	1,172	1,235	5,077
Cottle	742	268	266	571	564
Crane	498	493	712	349	1,123
Crockett	571	509	279	329	851
Crosby	1,574	865	401	1,021	1,503
Culberson	330	298	145	238	555
Dallam	588	990	430	327	1,271
Dallas	123,809	184,193	55,552	129,662	305,112
Dawson	1,522	2,091	900	846	3,247
Deaf Smith	1,545	2,474	691	1,240	3,690
Delta	1,037	370	475	581	957
Denton	7,463	8,222	3,178	9,720	19,138
DeWitt	1,871	2,589	784	1,357	3,755
Dickens	811	428	295	534	708
Dimmit	896	584	177	1,078	1,172
Donley	547	816	208	250	1,220
Duval	3,978	384	121	3,729	623
Eastland	2,884	2,453	1,013	1,630	4,106
Ector	5,312	10,557	8,671	5,449	21,386
Edwards	148	409	82	109	520
Ellis	5,431	3,794	2,838	3,839	8,779
El Paso	32,658	30,347	5,111	32,435	49,981
Erath	2,915	2,209	935	1,648	4,777
Falls	2,990	1,345	1,364	1,825	3,017
Fannin	3,931	1,585	1,661	2,295	3,826
Fayette	1,833	2,380	1,562	1,400	3,882
Fisher	1,560	555	268	933	1,207
Floyd	1,305	1,465	847	841	2,181
Foard	594	216	168	312	369
Fort Bend	4,493	4,573	2,447	4,541	10,475
Franklin	1,001	481	507	546	1,059
Freestone	2,066	958	1,069	1,283	2,459
Frio	1,330	795	307	1,588	1,904
Gaines	1,087	1,401	1,037	669	1,923
Galveston	26,041	16,229	10,322	22,565	30,936
Garza	662	615	383	446	1,153
Gillespie	725	2,945	432	526	3,490
Glasscock	106	169	172	75	288
Goliad	690	707	156	464	1,018
Gonzales	1,930	1,476	983	1,164	2,707
Gray	2,374	5,994	2,427	1,367	7,968
Grayson	10,379	8,007	4,615	6,952	16,769
Gregg	5,733	9,278	8,109	5,325	19,927
Grimes	1,473	1,076	976	1,116	2,243
Guadalupe	3,529	4,332	1,241	3,404	8,287
Hale	3,293	4,696	2,309	2,135	7,051
Hall	1,038	753	434	607	1,303
Hamilton	1,116	1,266	452	685	1,931
Hansford	392	1,359	437	202	1,947
Hardeman	1,145	873	531	614	1,357
Hardin	2,894	1,986	3,979	2,952	5,190
Harris	182,546	202,079	86,412	215,916	365,672
Harrison	4,959	3,668	5,324	4,333	9,600
Hartley	299	597	264	206	967
Haskell	1,888	713	610	950	1,744
Hays	3,546	1,993	643	4,068	5,406
Hemphill	400	699	201	214	942
Henderson	3,119	2,315	2,497	2,741	6,263
Hidalgo	20,087	14,455	2,569	18,366	22,920
Hill	3,415	1,809	1,751	1,882	4,481
Hockley	2,426	2,265	1,456	1,625	4,084
Hood	1,155	593	411	949	1,743
Hopkins	2,700	1,860	1,932	1,710	3,903
Houston	2,782	1,391	2,062	1,844	3,317
Howard	3,897	3,812	2,789	2,714	7,343
Hudspeth	289	285	132	250	467
Hunt	4,785	4,651	3,469	3,655	9,535
Hutchinson	2,416	4,813	2,919	1,405	7,411
Irion	187	211	92	111	363
Jack	1,133	966	512	775	1,719
Jackson	1,698	1,438	1,145	1,163	2,743
Jasper	2,438	1,839	2,906	2,746	4,575
Jeff Davis	239	191	66	202	382
Jefferson	30,032	26,007	21,824	29,909	45,819
Jim Hogg	1,276	223	53	848	765
Jim Wells	6,304	2,827	913	4,404	5,283
Johnson	5,330	4,372	2,709	3,968	10,042
Jones	2,372	1,676	931	1,050	3,202
Karnes	2,271	1,342	686	1,780	2,639
Kaufman	3,311	2,431	2,350	2,795	5,100
Kendall	538	1,569	364	484	2,681
Kenedy	100	76	7	88	124
Kent	303	143	188	223	465
Kerr	1,878	3,692	1,073	1,511	6,039
Kimble	463	640	264	266	971
King	109	44	71	75	143
Kinney	333	198	68	234	425
Kleberg	4,633	2,713	670	4,481	5,312
Knox	1,222	580	325	638	1,148
Lamar	4,635	3,395	2,903	2,865	7,736
Lamb	2,267	2,595	1,460	1,350	3,981
Lampasas	1,423	935	460	688	2,251
LaSalle	645	324	112	567	1,073
Lavaca	2,165	1,698	1,451	1,429	3,288
Lee	1,283	1,075	631	920	1,877
Leon	1,536	659	880	863	1,699
Liberty	3,469	2,746	3,393	3,311	6,111
Limestone	2,796	1,485	1,402	1,452	2,949
Lipscomb	279	1,079	187	156	1,226
Live Oak	922	938	484	610	1,745
Llano	1,282	1,079	464	766	2,164
Loving	18	23	40	7	55
Lubbock	15,430	25,646	9,078	15,353	43,564
Lynn	1,333	1,005	544	697	1,766
Madison	994	608	765	561	1,540
Marion	1,260	637	957	1,106	1,680
Martin	373	343	539	287	935
Mason	560	789	169	369	1,096
Matagorda	3,595	3,094	1,777	2,473	5,003
Maverick	1,570	771	165	1,710	1,477
McCulloch	1,353	947	359	753	1,769
McLennan	22,388	15,958	8,268	15,947	33,377
McMullen	160	168	88	88	304
Medina	2,471	2,058	722	1,507	4,059
Menard	362	491	118	273	644
Midland	4,756	12,789	5,675	4,388	18,905
Milam	3,269	1,614	1,525	2,159	3,554
Mills	722	645	296	388	1,089
Mitchell	1,589	893	499	699	1,790
Montague	2,555	1,736	914	1,286	3,463
Montgomery	4,021	4,353	4,879	4,358	15,067
Moore	1,359	2,378	1,258	863	3,620
Morris	1,701	1,064	1,323	1,162	2,699
Motley	397	415	295	230	657
Nacogdoches	3,449	3,235	3,196	3,656	8,757
Navarro	5,296	2,845	2,245	3,246	6,039
Newton	1,476	555	1,509	1,636	1,946
Nolan	2,784	1,969	1,185	1,338	3,654
Nueces	39,025	21,307	7,159	33,277	41,682
Ochiltree	432	2,208	492	298	2,861
Oldham	237	320	230	173	666
Orange	6,485	5,886	8,845	7,172	13,234
Palo Pinto	3,552	2,627	1,257	2,181	5,058
Panola	1,711	1,586	2,650	1,511	4,324
Parker	4,301	3,068	1,934	3,184	7,152
Parmer	833	1,539	730	495	2,304
Pecos	1,592	1,524	900	847	2,419
Polk	1,841	1,013	1,712	1,760	3,048
Potter	8,238	13,338	5,486	6,264	18,891
Presidio	969	481	132	674	785
Rains	558	340	306	532	865
Randall	4,060	11,400	3,128	3,470	18,557
Reagan	370	454	288	244	703
Real	277	290	136	150	483
Red River	2,245	1,305	1,554	1,361	3,112
Reeves	1,456	1,310	743	1,510	2,427
Refugio	1,699	1,114	486	1,060	1,937
Roberts	90	311	113	71	467
Robertson	2,833	965	944	1,976	1,977
Rockwall	778	614	582	610	1,890
Runnels	1,448	1,707	668	739	2,752
Rusk	4,078	3,739	4,729	2,867	8,179
Sabine	1,078	455	935	936	1,333
San Augustine	817	506	1,137	753	1,508
San Jacinto	1,235	381	693	1,020	1,296
San Patricio	6,818	3,717	1,876	5,097	7,179
San Saba	1,140	535	465	567	1,106
Schleicher	378	396	178	250	630
Scurry	2,031	1,745	1,084	1,223	3,777
Shackelford	673	557	277	331	909
Shelby	2,511	1,127	3,285	1,792	4,292
Sherman	297	723	376	169	996
Smith	8,897	12,079	9,595	8,041	23,671
Somervell	384	313	204	284	703
Starr	3,922	1,374	71	3,320	2,389
Stephens	1,239	1,287	525	678	2,259
Sterling	151	170	54	94	286
Stonewall	635	213	262	394	662
Sutton	351	412	147	245	705
Swisher	1,760	1,177	623	1,300	1,790
Tarrant	79,705	81,786	29,256	69,187	151,596
Taylor	9,107	12,218	4,289	6,024	22,417
Terrell	201	250	149	124	467
Terry	1,625	1,948	854	1,099	3,057
Throckmorton	618	317	126	348	568
Titus	2,317	1,572	1,886	1,703	3,671
Tom Green	6,774	9,682	3,074	6,082	15,784
Travis	39,667	34,309	8,424	54,157	70,561
Trinity	1,146	636	997	826	1,467
Tyler	1,204	1,120	1,462	1,321	2,955
Upshur	2,480	1,519	2,886	1,879	4,736
Upton	463	664	459	256	1,186

County	1968 Hum-phrey (D)	Nixon (R)	Wallace (I)	1972 McGovern (D)	Nixon (R)
Uvalde	1,736	2,252	768	1,438	3,883
Val Verde	3,205	1,914	573	2,049	4,052
Van Zandt	2,706	1,954	2,091	1,939	4,839
Victoria	6,042	6,352	2,336	4,226	11,246
Walker	2,391	1,946	1,452	2,940	5,082
Waller	1,684	958	797	1,538	2,263
Ward	1,331	1,552	1,382	1,049	2,687
Washington	1,686	3,244	677	1,323	3,862
Webb	9,419	2,103	304	8,435	6,011
Wharton	4,304	3,773	1,882	3,481	6,271
Wheeler	812	1,176	570	502	1,766
Wichita	15,387	11,937	6,087	10,948	25,197
Wilbarger	1,996	1,909	1,292	1,139	3,183
Willacy	1,930	1,243	465	1,384	2,317
Williamson	5,528	2,923	1,669	3,806	6,998
Wilson	2,336	1,321	542	2,072	2,953
Winkler	938	1,391	1,249	602	2,467
Wise	2,774	1,983	1,107	1,741	4,230
Wood	2,192	2,046	2,020	1,842	4,746
Yoakum	615	1,123	724	457	1,952
Young	2,482	1,860	1,004	1,486	3,353
Zapata	909	251	52	768	695
Zavala	1,307	693	214	1,122	1,288
Totals	1,266,804	1,227,844	584,269	1,154,289	2,298,896

TEXAS VOTE SINCE 1924

1924 (Pres.), Davis, Dem., 484,605; Coolidge, Rep., 130,023; LaFollette, Prog., 42,881.

1928 (Pres.), Hoover, Rep., 367,036; Smith, Dem., 341,032; Thomas, Soc., 722; Foster, Com., 209.

1932 (Pres.), Roosevelt, Dem., 760,348; Hoover, Rep., 97,959; Thomas, Soc., 4,450; Harvey, Lib., 324; Foster, Com., 207; Jackson Party, 104.

1936 (Pres.), Roosevelt, Dem., 734,485; Landon, Rep., 103,874; Lemke, Union, 3281; Thomas, Soc., 1,075; Colvin, Proh., 514; Browder, Com., 253.

1940 (Pres.), Roosevelt, Dem., 840,151; Willkie, Rep., 199,152; Babson, Proh., 925; Thomas, Soc., 728; Browder, Com., 212.

1944 (Pres.), Roosevelt, Dem., 821,605; Dewey, Rep., 191,425; Texas Regulars, 135,439; Watson, Proh., 1,017; Thomas, Soc., 594; America First, 250.

1948 (Pres.), Truman, Dem., 750,700; Dewey, Rep., 282,240; Thurmond, States' Rights, 106,909; Wallace, Prog., 3,764; Watson, Proh., 2,758; Thomas, Soc., 874.

1952 (Pres.), Eisenhower, Rep., 1,102,878; Stevenson, Dem., 969,228; Hamblen, Proh., 1,983; MacArthur, Christian Nationalist, 833; MacArthur, Constitution, 730; Hallinan, Prog., 294.

1956 (Pres.), Eisenhower, Rep., 1,080,619; Stevenson, Dem., 859,958; Andrews, Ind., 14,591.

1960 (Pres.), Kennedy, Dem., 1,167,932; Nixon, Rep., 1,121,699; Sullivan, Constitution, 18,169; Decker, Proh., 3,870; Write-in, 175.

1964 (Pres.), Johnson, Dem., 1,663,185; Goldwater, Rep., 958,566; Lightburn, Constitution, 5,060.

1968 (Pres.), Nixon, Rep., 1,227,844; Humphrey, Dem., 1,266,804; Wallace, 3rd party, 584,269; Write-ins 489.

1972 (Pres.), Nixon, Rep., 2,298,896; McGovern, Dem., 1,154,289; Schmitz, American, 6,039; Jenness, Soc. Worker, 8,664; Others 3,393.

Utah

County	1968 Hum-phrey (D)	Nixon (R)	Wallace (I)	1972 McGovern (D)	Nixon (R)
Beaver	795	989	158	682	1,332
Box Elder	3,093	7,680	907	2,134	9,880
Cache	4,327	11,906	1,050	4,018	16,538
Carbon	4,344	2,618	271	3,335	3,956
Daggett	97	152	42	50	204
Davis	10,624	20,658	2,787	7,954	29,706
Duchesne	858	1,733	243	629	2,183
Emery	1,019	1,223	161	769	1,666
Garfield	314	1,033	139	242	1,290
Grand	707	1,435	215	560	1,837
Iron	1,157	3,337	514	1,098	5,085
Juab	907	1,201	118	691	1,629
Kane	147	814	174	218	1,146
Millard	971	2,318	220	777	2,689
Morgan	551	1,020	130	363	1,456
Piute	167	411	60	102	475
Rich	183	525	39	120	604
Salt Lake	77,247	101,942	9,323	64,489	132,066
San Juan	680	1,393	262	677	1,893
Sanpete	1,696	3,304	307	1,220	3,995
Sevier	1,167	3,190	384	820	3,700
Summit	961	1,782	113	836	2,209
Tooele	4,250	3,422	592	2,621	5,641
Uintah	1,145	3,034	437	716	4,712

County	1968 Hum-phrey (D)	Nixon (R)	Wallace (I)	1972 McGovern (D)	Nixon (R)
Utah	16,629	29,226	3,666	10,828	42,179
Wasatch	941	1,611	86	693	2,046
Washington	975	3,226	796	956	5,176
Wayne	248	511	54	183	597
Weber	20,465	27,034	3,658	14,503	37,753
Totals	156,665	238,728	26,906	126,284	323,643

UTAH VOTE SINCE 1924

1924 (Pres.), Coolidge, Rep., 77,327; Davis, Dem., 47,001; LaFollette, Prog., 33,662.

1928 (Pres.), Hoover, Rep., 94,618; Smith, Dem., 80,985; Thomas, Soc., 954; Foster, Com., 47.

1932 (Pres.), Roosevelt, Dem., 116,750; Hoover, Rep., 84,795; Thomas, Soc., 4,087; Foster, Com., 947.

1936 (Pres.), Roosevelt, Dem., 150,246; Landon, Rep., 64,555; Lemke, Union, 1,121; Thomas, Soc., 432; Browder, Com., 280; Colvin, Proh., 43.

1940 (Pres.), Roosevelt, Dem., 154,277; Willkie, Rep., 93,151; Thomas, Soc., 200; Browder, Com., 191.

1944 (Pres.), Roosevelt, Dem., 150,088; Dewey, Rep., 97,891; Thomas, Soc., 340.

1948 (Pres.), Truman, Dem., 149,151; Dewey, Rep., 124,402; Wallace, Prog., 2,679; Dobbs, Soc. Workers, 73.

1952 (Pres.), Eisenhower, Rep., 194,190; Stevenson, Dem., 135,364.

1956 (Pres.), Eisenhower, Rep., 215,631; Stevenson, Dem., 118,364.

1960 (Pres.), Kennedy, Dem., 169,248; Nixon, Rep., 205,361; Dobbs, Soc. Workers, 100.

1964 (Pres.), Johnson, Dem., 219,628; Goldwater, Rep., 181,785.

1968 (Pres.), Nixon, Rep., 238,728; Humphrey, Dem., 156,665; Wallace, 3rd party, 26,906; Halstead, Soc. Worker, 89; Peace and Freedom, 180.

1972 (Pres.), Nixon, Rep., 323,643; McGovern, Dem., 126,284; Schmitz, American, 28,549.

Vermont

County	1968 Hum-phrey (D)	Nixon (R)	Wallace (I)	1972 McGovern (D)	Nixon (R)
Addison	2,914	5,006	278	3,262	6,467
Bennington	4,966	5,967	401	4,804	7,542
Caledonia	3,201	4,996	250	3,094	6,762
Chittenden	16,420	14,621	1,000	16,163	23,063
Essex	952	1,009	57	655	1,441
Franklin	6,027	5,218	398	3,898	8,109
Grand Isle	730	754	73	743	1,259
Lamoille	1,239	2,965	140	1,659	4,164
Orange	1,879	4,135	200	2,332	5,389
Orleans	2,762	4,055	269	2,793	4,906
Rutland	9,000	10,318	699	8,261	14,143
Washington	7,826	9,387	497	7,596	12,421
Windham	5,353	6,916	374	5,925	9,062
Windsor	6,986	9,795	468	6,989	12,421
Totals	70,255	85,142	5,104	68,174	117,149

VERMONT VOTE SINCE 1924

1924 (Pres.), Coolidge, Rep., 80,498; Davis, Dem., 16,124; LaFollette, Prog., 5,964; Faris, Proh., 326.

1928 (Pres.), Hoover, Rep., 90,404; Smith, Dem., 44,440; Varney, Proh., 338.

1932 (Pres.), Roosevelt, Dem., 56,266; Hoover, Rep., 78,984; Thomas, Soc., 1,533; Foster, Com., 195.

1936 (Pres.), Landon, Rep., 81,023; Roosevelt, Dem., 62,124; Browder, Com., 405.

1940 (Pres.), Roosevelt, Dem., 64,269; Willkie, Rep., 78,371; Browder, Com., 411.

1944 (Pres.), Roosevelt, Dem., 53,820; Dewey, Rep., 71,527.

1948 (Pres.), Truman, Dem., 45,557; Dewey, Rep., 75,926; Wallace, Prog., 1,279; Thomas, Soc. 585.

1952 (Pres.), Eisenhower, Rep., 109,717; Stevenson, Dem., 43,355; Hallinan, Prog., 282; Hoopes, Soc., 185.

1956 (Pres.), Eisenhower, Rep., 110,390; Stevenson, Dem., 42,549; Scattered, 39.

1960 (Pres.), Kennedy, Dem., 69,186; Nixon, Rep., 98,131.

1964 (Pres.), Johnson, Dem., 107,674; Goldwater, Rep., 54,868.

1968 (Pres.), Nixon, Rep., 85,142; Humphrey, Dem.,

70,255; Wallace, 3rd party, 5,104; Halstead, Soc. Worker, 295; Gregory, New Party, 579.
1972 (Pres.), Nixon, Rep., 117,149; McGovern, Dem., 68,174; Spock, Liberty Union, 1,010; Jenness, Soc. Worker, 296; Scattered 318.

Virginia

County	1968 Humphrey (D)	Nixon (R)	Wallace (I)	1972 McGovern (D)	Nixon (R)
Accomack	2,467	3,231	3,460	2,406	6,496
Albemarle	2,255	4,512	1,657	4,303	8,447
Alleghany	988	1,649	1,153	1,069	2,584
Amelia	830	857	832	778	1,606
Amherst	1,543	2,656	2,449	1,512	4,909
Appomattox	756	1,753	1,512	684	2,788
Arlington	26,107	28,163	6,746	25,877	39,406
Augusta	2,028	6,313	2,483	1,766	9,106
Bath	494	872	529	462	1,127
Bedford	1,574	2,807	3,316	1,501	5,286
Bland	560	938	361	527	1,352
Botetourt	1,272	2,598	1,267	1,519	3,806
Brunswick	1,910	1,139	2,088	2,130	3,072
Buchanan	5,003	3,699	1,067	3,566	4,801
Buckingham	984	1,027	1,185	1,186	2,107
Campbell	1,996	5,731	4,425	2,055	11,676
Caroline	2,165	1,162	1,084	1,814	2,086
Carroll	1,773	4,909	958	1,583	5,247
Charles City	1,437	520	170	1,777	555
Charlotte	1,045	1,042	2,163	1,182	2,501
Chesterfield	5,715	22,015	11,504	3,823	24,934
Clarke	768	1,127	742	715	1,816
Craig	419	581	256	425	774
Culpeper	1,239	2,229	1,217	1,316	3,707
Cumberland	978	844	602	969	1,371
Dickenson	3,355	3,412	639	2,711	3,633
Dinwiddie	1,551	1,451	2,245	1,901	3,314
Essex	897	791	468	808	1,482
Fairfax	44,796	57,462	14,805	54,844	112,135
Fauquier	2,099	2,845	1,536	2,039	4,654
Floyd	715	2,275	537	708	2,444
Fluvanna	569	913	660	637	1,438
Franklin	2,025	3,036	3,219	2,273	4,674
Frederick	1,612	3,696	2,137	1,604	5,367
Giles	2,045	2,722	1,372	1,869	3,671
Gloucester	1,210	1,619	1,526	1,292	3,642
Goochland	1,389	1,216	836	1,254	2,127
Grayson	1,926	3,563	1,090	1,603	3,565
Greene	255	856	433	318	1,208
Greensville	1,367	529	1,256	1,197	1,608
Halifax	2,199	2,634	4,235	2,384	5,469
Hanover	2,079	5,425	3,330	2,200	11,095
Henrico	8,600	34,212	11,868	8,420	52,536
Henry	4,175	3,946	6,802	4,042	7,556
Highland	284	619	166	206	774
Isle of Wight	1,977	1,312	2,328	2,305	3,555
James City	1,521	1,443	1,083	1,992	3,372
King George	730	829	632	658	1,675
King and Queen	882	568	614	708	1,033
King William	764	1,046	615	797	1,839
Lancaster	1,134	1,640	876	1,009	2,683
Lee	4,105	4,450	827	2,825	4,957
Loudoun	3,262	4,577	2,117	3,941	9,417
Louisa	1,290	1,510	1,149	1,338	2,545
Lunenburg	1,180	1,181	1,630	1,044	2,464
Madison	478	1,188	763	639	1,864
Mathews	691	1,309	773	730	2,104
Mecklenburg	2,667	2,750	4,022	2,804	6,381
Middlesex	575	809	655	724	1,697
Montgomery	2,700	7,098	1,712	3,692	9,348
Nansemond	4,174	2,101	3,723	See Below	
Nelson	1,120	1,130	1,163	954	2,145
New Kent	765	526	609	633	1,370
Northampton	1,418	1,410	1,129	1,246	2,587
Northumberland	1,077	1,438	968	884	2,332
Nottoway	1,529	1,614	1,673	1,308	2,979
Orange	879	1,727	1,050	1,032	2,758
Page	2,125	3,667	995	1,585	4,326
Patrick	1,105	2,187	1,974	942	2,951
Pittsylvania	5,427	5,096	9,302	4,429	12,108
Powhatan	1,004	722	929	810	1,751
Prince Edward	1,567	1,857	1,224	1,585	3,199
Prince George	1,272	1,559	1,920	1,084	2,405
Prince William	5,566	7,944	5,160	7,266	20,149
Pulaski	2,497	4,409	1,346	2,311	6,281
Rappahannock	394	594	372	471	1,055
Richmond	490	1,011	563	435	1,565
Roanoke	3,902	12,439	4,745	5,318	19,920
Rockbridge	845	2,280	885	956	3,009
Rockingham	2,111	7,779	1,817	2,026	10,025
Russell	3,554	3,858	1,369	3,367	5,010
Scott	3,144	5,345	1,474	2,474	5,125
Shenandoah	1,654	5,461	*0	1,422	7,128
Smyth	2,631	5,297	1,808	2,280	6,409
Southampton	1,803	1,376	2,070	1,498	3,225
Spotsylvania	1,647	1,675	1,589	1,775	3,577
Stafford	1,698	2,572	2,197	1,901	5,222
Surry	1,126	523	708	988	1,067

County	1968 Humphrey (D)	Nixon (R)	Wallace (I)	1972 McGovern (D)	Nixon (R)
Sussex	1,541	1,105	1,135	1,645	2,120
Tazewell	4,734	4,434	2,023	3,181	7,233
Warren	1,513	2,297	1,479	1,508	3,718
Washington	3,243	6,665	3,092	3,028	8,805
Westmoreland	1,156	1,402	943	1,113	2,331
Wise	5,942	5,004	1,635	4,402	6,739
Wythe	1,765	3,638	1,377	1,431	4,553
York	2,370	3,356	3,330	2,302	7,745
Total	**252,218**	**382,604**	**199,964**	**251,451**	**621,848**

*10,561 votes for Wallace were omitted in the count.

CITIES

City	1968 Humphrey (D)	Nixon (R)	Wallace (I)	1972 McGovern (D)	Nixon (R)
Alexandria	14,351	13,265	4,131	15,409	20,235
Bedford	569	1,047	679	529	1,407
Bristol	1,531	1,930	911	1,157	2,665
Buena Vista	387	814	456	373	990
Charlottesville	3,831	5,601	1,781	5,240	7,935
Chesapeake	6,843	6,234	11,084	7,289	17,722
Clifton Forge	734	925	462	575	1,127
Colonial Heights	650	2,650	2,106	541	5,304
Covington	1,195	1,551	846	948	1,910
Danville	4,495	6,796	5,391	4,148	12,463
Emporia	657	812	716	565	1,340
Fairfax	2,153	2,963	959	2,274	5,063
Falls Church	1,860	2,005	504	1,895	2,967
Franklin	792	951	511	738	1,416
Fredericksburg	1,111	1,110	870	1,700	3,011
Galax	748	1,257	304	524	1,497
Hampton	11,308	10,532	10,690	10,648	21,897
Harrisonburg	1,036	2,859	453	992	3,626
Hopewell	1,568	2,942	2,092	1,485	5,229
Lexington	734	1,170	177	695	1,345
Lynchburg	4,305	9,943	3,649	4,208	13,259
Martinsville	2,727	2,618	1,856	2,292	3,879
Nansemond	N/A	N/A	N/A	3,929	5,767
Newport News	13,370	12,774	10,763	12,233	27,169
Norfolk	28,477	22,302	14,500	25,737	38,385
Norton	555	495	215	463	823
Petersburg	5,519	3,478	2,158	5,156	6,710
Portsmouth	15,734	9,402	12,127	13,124	20,090
Radford	1,206	2,077	461	1,121	2,577
Richmond	32,857	26,380	7,325	33,055	46,244
Roanoke	9,281	15,368	5,269	9,498	18,541
Salem	1,369	3,955	1,507	1,744	5,649
South Boston	620	1,298	662	709	1,865
Staunton	1,729	4,434	1,054	1,416	5,531
Suffolk	1,044	1,277	1,039	898	2,137
Virginia Beach	10,101	16,316	10,962	10,373	38,074
Waynesboro	1,446	3,301	613	1,061	4,163
Williamsburg	991	1,156	247	1,274	1,786
Winchester	1,360	2,695	770	1,418	4,647
Total	**190,169**	**207,715**	**120,308**	**187,436**	**366,645**
Aggregate	**442,387**	**590,319**	***320,272**	**438,887**	**988,493**

VIRGINIA VOTE SINCE 1924

1924 (Pres.), Davis, Dem., 139,797; Coolidge, Rep., 73,359; LaFollette, Prog., 10,379; Johns, Soc. Lab., 191.

1928 (Pres.), Hoover, Rep., 164,609; Smith, Dem., 140,146; Thomas, Soc., 250; Reynolds, Soc. Lab., 180; Foster, Com., 173.

1932 (Pres.), Roosevelt, Dem., 203,979; Hoover, Rep., 89,637; Thomas, Soc., 2,382; Upshaw, Proh., 1,843; Foster, Com., 86; Cox. Ind., 15.

1936 (Pres.), Roosevelt, Dem., 234,980; Landon, Rep., 98,366; Colvin, Proh., 594; Thomas, Soc., 313; Lemke, Union, 233; Browder, Com., 98.

1940 (Pres.), Roosevelt, Dem., 235,961; Willkie, Rep., 109,363; Babson, Proh., 882; Thomas, Soc., 282; Browder, Com., 71; Aiken, Soc. Lab., 48.

1944 (Pres.), Roosevelt, Dem., 242,276; Dewey, Rep., 145,243; Watson, Proh., 459; Thomas, Soc., 417; Teichert, Soc. Lab., 90.

1948 (Pres.), Truman, Dem., 200,786; Dewey, Rep., 172,070; Thurmond, States' Rights, 43,393; Wallace, Prog., 2,047; Thomas, Soc., 726; Teichert, Soc. Lab., 234.

1952 (Pres.), Eisenhower, Rep., 349,037; Stevenson, Dem., 268,677; Hass, Soc. Lab., 1,160; Hoopes, Social Dem., 504; Hallinan, Prog., 311.

1956 (Pres.), Eisenhower, Rep., 386,459; Stevenson, Dem., 267,760; Andrews, States' Rights, 42,964; Hoopes, Soc. Dem., 444; Hass, Soc. Lab., 351.

1960 (Pres.), Kennedy, Dem., 362,327; Nixon, Rep., 404,521; Coiner, Conservative, 4,204; Hass, Soc. Lab., 397.

1964 (Pres.), Johnson, Dem., 558,038; Goldwater, Rep., 481,334; Hass, Soc. Lab., 2,895.

1968 (Pres.), Nixon, Rep., 590,319; Humphrey, Dem.,

442,387; Wallace, 3rd party, °320,272; Blomen, Soc.
Labor, 4,671; Munn, Prohibition, 601; Gregory, Peace
and Freedom, 1,680.
1972 (Pres.), Nixon, Rep., 988,493; McGovern, Dem.,
438,887; Schmitz, American, 19,721; Fisher, Soc.
Labor, 9,918.

Washington

County	1968 Humphrey (D)	1968 Nixon (R)	1968 Wallace (I)	1972 McGovern (D)	1972 Nixon (R)
Adams	1,270	2,572	299	1,110	3,083
Asotin	2,693	2,307	433	2,559	2,911
Benton	10,878	14,659	3,024	9,824	18,517
Chelan	6,787	9,093	1,324	5,889	10,470
Clallam	7,030	5,921	1,248	5,620	9,372
Clark	23,046	18,858	2,514	27,179	28,775
Columbia	754	1,221	175	533	1,445
Cowlitz	13,363	10,842	1,507	12,682	14,431
Douglas	2,764	3,234	663	2,420	4,512
Ferry	596	608	182	560	815
Franklin	4,038	4,234	1,299	3,867	5,972
Garfield	602	841	143	481	1,004
Grant	5,773	7,007	1,574	5,487	9,370
Grays Harbor	13,480	7,720	1,426	11,786	10,839
Island	3,238	4,077	677	3,149	7,495
Jefferson	2,251	1,827	407	2,096	2,770
King	223,469	218,457	31,450	212,509	298,707
Kitsap	22,273	14,520	2,986	17,011	25,831
Kittitas	3,921	4,212	579	4,299	5,464
Klickitat	2,454	2,355	357	2,293	3,061
Lewis	8,444	8,779	1,428	6,946	12,071
Lincoln	1,721	2,994	337	1,453	3,647
Mason	4,540	3,397	638	3,907	4,873
Okanogan	4,379	4,490	1,064	3,835	5,796
Pacific	3,740	2,491	364	3,585	3,349
Pend Oreille	1,350	1,117	245	1,071	1,746
Pierce	72,670	51,436	11,391	56,933	84,265
San Juan	685	1,164	108	906	1,786
Skagit	10,529	10,354	1,667	9,233	14,212
Skamania	1,221	968	189	1,153	1,288
Snohomish	44,019	36,252	7,005	39,471	60,032
Spokane	49,423	52,650	8,420	44,337	74,320
Stevens	2,948	3,435	957	2,390	4,839
Thurston	14,228	13,742	2,493	14,596	22,297
Wahkiakum	899	641	131	796	818
Walla Walla	5,841	10,042	1,028	5,364	12,579
Whatcom	14,003	14,695	2,387	15,027	22,585
Whitman	5,218	7,810	710	6,248	9,548
Yakima	19,499	27,488	4,161	19,729	32,240
Totals	**616,037**	**588,510**	**96,990**	**568,334**	**837,135**

WASHINGTON VOTE SINCE 1924

1924 (Pres.), Coolidge, Rep., 220,224; LaFollette, Prog.,
150,727; Davis, Dem., 42,842; Nations, Amer., 5,991;
Johns, Soc. Lab., 1,004; Foster, Workers, 761.
1928 (Pres.), Hoover, Rep., 335,884; Smith, Dem., 156,772;
Thomas, Soc., 2,614; Reynolds, Soc. Lab., 4,068; Foster,
Com., 1,541.
1932 (Pres.), Roosevelt, Dem., 353,260; Hoover, Rep.,
208,645; Harvey, Lib., 30,308; Thomas, Soc., 17,080;
Foster, Com., 2,972; Upshaw, Proh., 1,540; Reynolds,
Soc. Lab., 1,009.
1936 (Pres.), Roosevelt, Dem., 459,579; Landon, Rep.,
206,892; Lemke, Union, 17,463; Thomas, Soc., 3,496;
Browder, Com., 1,907; Pellsy, Christian, 1,598; Colvin,
Proh., 1,041; Aiken, Soc. Lab., 362.
1940 (Pres.), Roosevelt, Dem., 462,145; Willkie, Rep.,
322,123; Thomas, Soc., 4,586; Browder, Com., 2,626;
Babson, Proh., 1,686; Aiken, Soc. Lab., 667.
1944 (Pres.), Roosevelt, Dem., 486,774; Dewey, Rep.,
361,689; Thomas, Soc., 3,824; Watson, Proh., 2,396;
Teichert, Soc. Lab., 1,645.
1948 (Pres.), Truman, Dem., 476,165; Dewey, Rep.,
386,315; Wallace, Prog., 31,692; Watson, Proh., 6,117;
Thomas, Soc., 3,534; Teichert, Soc. Lab., 1,133; Dobbs,
Soc. Workers, 103.
1952 (Pres.), Eisenhower, Rep., 599,107; Stevenson, Dem.,
492,845; MacArthur, Christian Nationalist, 7,290; Hallinan, Prog., 2,460; Hass, Soc. Lab., 633; Hoopes, Soc.,
254; Dobbs, Soc. Workers, 119.
1956 (Pres.), Eisenhower, Rep., 620,430; Stevenson, Dem.,
523,002; Hass, Soc. Lab., 7,457.
1960 (Pres.), Kennedy, Dem., 599,298; Nixon, Rep.,
629,273; Hass, Soc. Lab., 10,895; Curtis, Constitution,
1,401; Dobbs, Soc. Workers, 705.
1964 (Pres.), Johnson, Dem., 779,699; Goldwater, Rep.,
470,366; Hass, Soc. Labor, 7,772; DeBerry, Freedom
Soc., 537.
1968 (Pres.), Nixon, Rep., 588,510; Humphrey, Dem.,
616,037; Wallace, 3rd party, 96,990; Blomen, Soc.
Labor, 488; Cleaver, Peace and Freedom, 1,609; Halstead, Soc. Worker, 270; Mitchell, Free Ballot, 377.

1972 (Pres.), Nixon, Rep., 837,135; McGovern, Dem.,
568,334; Schmitz, American, 58,906; Spock, Ind.,
2,644; Fisher, Soc. Labor, 1,102; Jenness, Soc.
Worker, 623; Hall, Communist, 566; Hospers, Libertarian, 1,537.

West Virginia

County	1968 Humphrey (D)	1968 Nixon (R)	1968 Wallace (I)	1972 McGovern (D)	1972 Nixon (R)
Barbour	3,210	3,206	365	2,258	4,432
Berkeley	4,929	7,223	2,321	4,523	10,954
Boone	6,391	2,970	926	5,342	5,985
Braxton	3,268	2,441	341	2,771	3,155
Brooke	7,506	4,191	1,444	5,226	7,544
Cabell	19,018	19,418	4,666	14,312	29,582
Calhoun	1,682	1,612	318	1,528	1,992
Clay	1,916	1,474	349	1,830	2,168
Doddridge	844	1,861	146	645	2,284
Fayette	14,546	5,246	1,931	9,966	11,876
Gilmer	1,582	1,401	214	1,359	2,056
Grant	786	2,936	256	614	3,556
Greenbrier	6,318	5,559	1,722	4,423	8,827
Hampshire	1,791	1,959	694	1,637	3,084
Hancock	10,174	6,181	2,476	6,727	10,634
Hardy	1,767	1,768	490	1,510	2,690
Harrison	18,872	13,703	2,234	12,910	22,196
Jackson	3,462	5,173	947	3,007	7,226
Jefferson	3,129	2,718	1,082	2,782	4,822
Kanawha	46,650	41,712	11,524	38,032	65,021
Lewis	3,168	4,027	640	2,062	5,778
Lincoln	4,386	3,662	583	3,876	4,673
Logan	13,686	4,754	1,861	10,045	9,533
Marion	17,246	10,177	1,838	11,864	16,095
Marshall	8,449	7,252	1,379	6,378	10,966
Mason	4,549	5,208	879	4,008	7,129
McDowell	12,842	4,020	2,075	7,826	17,846
Mercer	12,739	9,985	3,363	3,276	7,157
Mineral	4,225	4,545	1,273	5,585	7,484
Mingo	8,677	3,988	1,133	10,721	16,758
Monongalia	13,128	9,261	1,556	2,114	3,716
Monroe	2,412	2,925	553	1,118	3,014
Morgan	1,015	2,244	461	6,811	8,942
Nicholas	4,858	3,678	841	3,628	5,907
Ohio	15,026	13,073	2,164	10,491	18,435
Pendleton	1,643	1,687	298	1,248	2,207
Pleasants	1,522	1,534	204	1,207	2,025
Pocahontas	1,948	2,040	446	1,635	2,391
Preston	4,020	5,636	561	2,977	7,807
Putnam	5,009	5,252	1,340	4,771	8,265
Raleigh	17,744	8,775	2,987	10,586	19,150
Randolph	5,562	4,508	897	3,809	6,923
Ritchie	1,281	3,106	284	990	3,635
Roane	2,639	3,851	424	2,386	4,253
Summers	3,521	2,305	849	2,518	3,895
Taylor	2,953	3,012	466	2,085	4,385
Tucker	1,758	1,511	332	1,457	2,163
Tyler	1,324	2,897	313	1,125	3,362
Upshur	2,319	4,565	427	1,795	6,449
Wayne	8,227	6,004	2,088	6,251	9,775
Webster	2,582	1,241	284	2,069	2,114
Wetzel	4,038	4,122	789	3,276	6,046
Wirt	820	1,051	140	691	1,442
Wood	14,293	18,960	3,379	10,886	27,315
Wyoming	6,641	3,947	1,007	4,468	7,926
Totals	**374,091**	**307,555**	**72,560**	**277,435**	**484,964**

WEST VIRGINIA VOTES SINCE 1924

1924 (Pres.), Coolidge, Rep., 288,635; Davis, Dem., 257,232;
LaFollette, Prog., 36,723; Nations, Amer., 1,072.
1928 (Pres.), Hoover, Rep., 375,551; Smith, Dem., 263,748;
Thomas, Soc., 1,313; Varney, Proh., 1,703; Foster, Com.,
401.
1932 (Pres.), Roosevelt, Dem., 405,124; Hoover, Rep.,
330,731; Thomas, Soc., 5,133; Upshaw, Proh., 2,342;
Foster, Com., 444.
1936 (Pres.), Roosevelt, Dem., 502,582; Landon, Rep.,
325,358; Colvin, Proh., 1,173; Thomas, Soc., 832.
1940 (Pres.), Roosevelt, Dem., 495,662; Willkie, Rep.,
372,414.
1944 (Pres.), Roosevelt, Dem., 392,777; Dewey, Rep.,
322,819.
1948 (Pres.), Truman, Dem., 429,188; Dewey, Rep.,
316,251; Wallace, Prog., 3,311.
1952 (Pres.), Eisenhower, R., 419,970; Stevenson, D.,
453,578.
1956 (Pres.), Eisenhower, R., 449,297; Stevenson, D.,
381,534.
1960 (Pres.), Kennedy, D., 441,786; Nixon, R., 395,995.
1964 (Pres.), Johnson, D., 538,087; Goldwater, R.,
253,953.
1968 (Pres.), Nixon, Rep., 307,555; Humphrey, Dem.,
374,091; Wallace, 3rd party, 72,560.
1972 (Pres.), Nixon, Rep., 484,964; McGovern, Dem.,
277,435.

Wisconsin

County	Humphrey (D) 1968	Nixon (R) 1968	Wallace (I) 1968	McGovern (D) 1972	Nixon (R) 1972
Adams	1,614	1,691	461	1,833	2,200
Ashland	4,147	2,557	401	3,771	3,478
Barron	5,183	7,526	867	5,376	8,418
Bayfield	3,036	2,333	323	2,736	3,045
Brown	21,615	30,133	4,341	26,511	37,101
Buffalo	2,112	2,992	413	2,461	3,079
Burnett	2,010	2,056	414	2,389	2,972
Calumet	3,609	5,792	792	4,804	6,446
Chippewa	7,335	7,772	1,282	8,210	8,451
Clark	4,601	6,325	1,398	4,617	7,138
Columbia	6,698	8,633	1,067	7,083	10,122
Crawford	2,391	3,316	419	2,487	3,705
Dane	59,951	39,917	3,771	79,567	56,020
Dodge	8,948	14,909	1,875	9,898	17,068
Door	2,728	5,647	535	3,430	6,503
Douglas	12,506	5,656	930	11,054	8,419
Dunn	4,392	5,415	709	5,681	6,660
Eau Claire	12,302	11,799	1,169	14,300	15,883
Florence	718	821	157	757	971
Forest	1,470	1,264	412	1,678	1,856
Grant	5,414	10,789	1,054	6,915	11,873
Green	3,501	6,502	641	3,634	7,422
Green Lake	2,299	4,893	488	2,174	5,046
Iowa	2,897	4,005	509	3,131	4,387
Iron	1,913	1,137	262	1,648	1,723
Jackson	2,442	3,172	529	2,445	3,937
Jefferson	8,716	12,478	1,470	9,303	14,621
Juneau	2,595	3,828	712	2,943	4,833
Kenosha	21,427	17,089	3,548	19,441	24,041
Kewaunee	2,622	4,467	703	3,360	4,802
La Crosse	11,570	17,433	2,214	12,152	21,992
La Fayette	2,853	4,084	470	2,804	4,898
Langlade	3,064	3,712	718	3,011	4,368
Lincoln	3,858	4,793	670	4,175	6,206
Manitowoc	15,298	13,562	1,790	16,489	16,599
Marathon	18,063	16,907	3,051	18,500	21,454
Marinette	6,415	7,134	1,223	5,900	8,740
Marquette	1,228	2,374	279	1,537	2,682
Menominee	531	179	30	608	355
Milwaukee	206,027	160,022	35,056	210,802	191,874
Monroe	4,012	6,938	1,056	3,640	7,625
Oconto	3,737	5,680	1,141	4,041	6,511
Oneida	4,435	5,077	941	4,262	6,811
Outagamie	14,224	25,080	2,956	17,447	27,533
Ozaukee	7,246	12,155	1,505	8,503	15,759
Pepin	1,263	1,493	231	1,409	1,458
Pierce	4,783	4,990	453	5,611	5,899
Polk	5,179	5,583	656	5,738	6,567
Portage	10,014	6,180	900	13,564	9,346
Price	2,794	3,096	621	2,831	3,694
Racine	27,045	28,028	7,457	27,778	38,490
Richland	2,288	4,141	485	2,492	5,062
Rock	20,567	25,229	3,655	21,033	30,361
Rusk	2,559	2,666	726	3,075	3,007
St. Croix	6,807	6,595	735	7,488	8,553
Sauk	6,406	8,608	1,019	6,980	10,285
Sawyer	1,830	2,475	435	1,765	3,081
Shawano	3,602	8,444	1,181	3,940	8,807
Sheboygan	20,170	17,764	1,592	21,114	21,500
Taylor	2,910	3,043	959	2,934	4,125
Trempealeau	3,971	4,861	747	4,232	5,723
Vernon	3,666	5,824	1,062	3,407	6,836
Vilas	1,798	3,339	598	1,907	4,422
Walworth	7,505	15,040	1,755	8,598	17,823
Washburn	2,273	2,425	384	2,336	3,220
Washington	8,104	12,439	2,065	10,434	15,338
Waukesha	31,947	47,557	6,921	34,573	59,399
Waupaca	3,978	10,606	1,206	4,418	11,040
Waushara	1,652	4,187	566	2,094	4,466
Winnebago	18,605	25,361	3,045	20,450	29,488
Wood	10,921	11,795	1,695	10,415	14,806
Totals	**748,804**	**809,997**	**127,835**	**810,724**	**989,430**

WISCONSIN VOTE SINCE 1924

1924 (Pres.), LaFollette, Prog., 453,678; Coolidge, Rep., 311,614; Davis, Dem., 68,115; Foster, Workers, 3,773; Faris, Proh., 2,918; Johns, Soc. Lab., 411; Wallace, Comm. Land, 270.

1928 (Pres.); Hoover, Rep., 544,205; Smith, Dem., 450,259; Thomas, Soc., 18,213; Foster, Com., 1,528; Reynolds, Soc. Lab., 381; Varney, Proh., 2,245.

1932 (Pres.), Roosevelt, Dem., 707,410; Hoover, Rep., 347,741; Thomas, Soc., 53,379; Foster, Com., 3,112; Upshaw, Proh., 2,672; Reynolds, Soc. Lab., 494.

1936 (Pres.), Roosevelt, Dem., 802,984; Landon, Rep., 380,828; Lemke, Union, 60,297; Thomas, Soc., 10,626; Browder, Com., 2,197; Colvin, Proh., 1,071; Aiken, Soc. Lab., 557.

1940 (Pres.), Roosevelt, Dem., 704,821; Willkie, Rep., 679,260; Thomas, Soc., 15,071; Browder, Com., 2,394; Babson, Proh., 2,148; Aiken, Soc. Lab., 1,882.

1944 (Pres.), Roosevelt, Dem., 650,413; Dewey, Rep., 674,532; Thomas, Soc., 13,205; Teichert, Soc. Lab., 1,002.

1948 (Pres.), Truman, Dem., 647,310; Dewey, Rep., 590,959; Wallace, Prog., 25,282; Thomas, Soc., 12,547; Teichert, Soc. Lab., 399; Dobbs, Soc. Workers, 303.

1952 (Pres.), Eisenhower, Rep., 979,744; Stevenson, Dem., 622,175; Hallinan, Ind., 2,174; Dobbs, Ind., 1,350; Hoopes, Ind., 1,157; Hass, Ind., 770.

1956 (Pres.), Eisenhower, Rep., 954,844; Stevenson, Dem., 586,768; Andrews, Ind., 6,918; Hoopes, Soc., 754; Hass, Soc. Lab., 710; Dobbs, Soc. Workers, 564.

1960 (Pres.), Kennedy, Dem., 830,805; Nixon, Rep., 895,175; Dobbs, Soc. Workers, 1,792; Hass, Soc. Lab., 1,310.

1964 (Pres.), Johnson, Dem., 1,050,424; Goldwater, Rep., 638,495; DeBerry, Soc. Worker, 1,692; Hass, Soc. Lab., 1,204.

1968 (Pres.), Nixon, Rep., 809,997; Humphrey, Dem., 748,804; Wallace, 3rd party, 127,835; Blomen, Soc. Labor, 1,338; Halstead, Soc. Worker, 1,222; scattering, 2,342.

1972 (Pres.), Nixon, Rep., 989,430; McGovern, Dem., 810,174; Schmitz, American, 47,525; Spock, Ind., 2,701; Fisher, Soc. Labor, 998; Hall, Communist, 663; Reed, Ind., 506; Scattered 893.

Wyoming

County	Humphrey (D) 1968	Nixon (R) 1968	Wallace (I) 1968	McGovern (D) 1972	Nixon (R) 1972
Albany	4,079	4,422	578	4,873	7,021
Big Horn	1,201	2,771	353	1,049	3,244
Campbell	558	1,694	289	783	2,953
Carbon	2,725	2,532	399	2,292	4,037
Converse	492	1,658	232	682	2,312
Crook	318	1,240	175	339	1,760
Fremont	3,093	5,417	888	3,248	7,359
Goshen	1,529	2,719	468	1,515	3,629
Hot Springs	705	1,273	166	689	1,678
Johnson	398	1,737	217	436	2,203
Laramie	9,519	9,824	1,649	7,791	15,010
Lincoln	1,246	2,030	285	969	2,459
Natrona	5,900	10,679	2,095	6,514	15,649
Niobrara	250	1,136	104	289	1,245
Park	1,852	4,677	605	1,950	5,890
Platte	1,035	1,613	319	925	2,200
Sheridan	2,659	5,163	612	2,874	6,432
Sublette	310	1,152	226	304	1,348
Sweetwater	4,086	2,726	637	3,713	5,175
Teton	461	1,419	169	810	2,182
Uinta	1,199	1,510	175	968	2,011
Washakie	948	2,038	198	825	2,604
Weston	610	1,497	266	520	2,063
Totals	**45,173**	**70,927**	**11,105**	**44,358**	**100,464**

WYOMING VOTE SINCE 1924

1924 (Pres.), Coolidge, Rep., 41,858; LaFollette, Prog., 25,174; Davis, Dem., 12,868.

1928 (Pres.), Hoover, Rep., 52,748; Smith, Dem., 29,299; Thomas, Soc., 788.

1932 (Pres.), Roosevelt, Dem., 54,370; Hoover, Rep., 39,583; Thomas, Soc., 2,829; Foster, Com., 180.

1936 (Pres.), Roosevelt, Dem., 62,624; Landon, Rep., 38,739; Lemke, Union, 1,653; Thomas, Soc., 200; Browder, Com., 91; Colvin, Proh., 75.

1940 (Pres.), Roosevelt, Dem., 59,287; Willkie, Rep., 52,633; Babson, Proh., 172; Thomas, Soc., 148.

1944 (Pres.), Roosevelt, Dem., 49,419; Dewey, Rep., 51,921.

1948 (Pres.), Truman, Dem., 52,354; Dewey, Rep., 47,947; Wallace, Prog., 931; Thomas, Soc., 137; Teichert, Soc. Lab., 56.

1952 (Pres.), Eisenhower, Rep., 81,047; Stevenson, Dem., 47,934; Hamblen, Proh., 194; Hoopes, Soc., 40; Hass, Soc. Lab., 36.

1956 (Pres.), Eisenhower, Rep., 74,573; Stevenson, Dem., 49,554.

1960 (Pres.), Kennedy, Dem., 63,331; Nixon, Rep., 77,451.

1964 (Pres.), Johnson, Dem., 80,718; Goldwater, Rep., 61,998.

1968 (Pres.), Nixon, Rep., 70,927; Humphrey, Dem., 45,173; Wallace, 3rd party, 11,105.

1972 (Pres.), Nixon, Rep., 100,464; McGovern, Dem., 44,358; Schmitz, American, 748.

Electoral Votes for President, 1956-72

The Constitution, Article 2, Section 1 (consult index), provides for the appointment of electors, the counting of the electoral ballots and the procedure in the event of a tie. (*See Electoral College.*)

State	1956 R	1956 D	1960 R	1960 D	1964 R	1964 D	1968 R	1968 D	1968 3d	1972 R	1972 D
Ala		[1]11		[2]5	10				10	9	
Alaska			3			3	3			3	
Ariz	4		4		5		5			6	
Ark		8		8		6			6	6	
Calif	32		32			40	40			45	
Colo	6		6			6	6			7	
Conn	8			8		8		8		8	
Del	3			3		3	3			3	
D. of C.						[3]3		3			3
Fla	10		10			14	14			17	
Ga		12		12	12				12	12	
Hawaii				3		4		4		4	
Idaho	4		4		4		4			4	
Ill	27			27		26	26			26	
Ind	13		13			13	13			13	
Iowa	10		10			9	9			8	
Kan	8		8			7	7			7	
Ky	10		10			9	9			9	
La	10			10	10				10	10	
Me	5		5			4		4		4	
Md	9			9		10		10		10	
Mass	16			16		14		14			14
Mich	20			20		21		21		21	
Minn	11			11		10		10		10	
Miss		8		([2])	7				7	7	
Mo		13		13		12	12			12	
Mont	4		4			4	4			4	
Neb	6		6			5	5			5	
Nev	3			3		3	3			3	
N. H	4		4			4	4			4	
N. J	16			16		17	17			17	
N. M	4			4		4	4			4	
N. Y	45			45		43		43		41	
N. C		14		14		13	12		[4]1	13	
N. D	4		4			4	4			3	
Ohio	25		25			26	26			25	
Okla	8		[2]7		8		8			8	
Oreg	6		6			6	6			6	
Penn	32			32		29		29		27	
R. I	4			4		4		4		4	
S. C		8		8	8		8			8	
S. D	4		4			4	4			4	
Tenn	11		11			11	11			10	
Texas	24			24		25		25		26	
Utah	4		4			4	4			4	
Vt	3		3			3	3			3	
Va	12		12			12	12			[5]11	
Wash	9		9			9		9		9	
W. Va	8			8		7		7		6	
Wis	12		12			12	12			11	
Wyo	3		3			3	3			3	
Totals	457	[1]74	219	303	52	486	301	191	46	520	17

Plurality. 383 ...... [2]84 ... 434 110 ...... [5]503 ...

(1.) In 1956 in Alabama one Democratic elector refused to vote for Stevenson and cast his ballot for Walter B. Jones, making the Democratic total actually 73.
(2.) In 1960 Sen. Harry F. Byrd (D.-Va.) got 15 electoral votes, including those of 8 unpledged Mississippi Democratic electors, 6 unpledged Alabama Democrats and one Oklahoma Republican.
(3.) First Presidential election.
(4.) In 1968 in North Carolina one Republican elector cast his ballot for Wallace.
(5.) In 1972 one Republican elector in Virginia cast his ballot for John Hospers.

Party Nominees for President and Vice President

Asterisk (*) denotes winning ticket

Year	Democratic President	Democratic Vice President	Republican President	Republican Vice President
1900	William J. Bryan	Adlai E. Stevenson	William McKinley*	Theodore Roosevelt
1904	Alton B. Parker	Henry G. Davis	Theodore Roosevelt*	Charles W. Fairbanks
1908	William J. Bryan	John W. Kern	William H. Taft*	James S. Sherman
1912	Woodrow Wilson*	Thomas R. Marshall	William H. Taft	James S. Sherman[1]
1916	Woodrow Wilson*	Thomas R. Marshall	Charles E. Hughes	Charles W. Fairbanks
1920	James M. Cox	Franklin D. Roosevelt	Warren G. Harding*	Calvin Coolidge
1924	John W. Davis	Charles W. Bryan	Calvin Coolidge*	Charles G. Dawes
1928	Alfred E. Smith	Joseph T. Robinson	Herbert Hoover*	Charles Curtis
1932	Franklin D. Roosevelt*	John N. Garner	Herbert Hoover	Charles Curtis
1936	Franklin D. Roosevelt*	John N. Garner	Alfred M. Landon	Frank Knox
1940	Franklin D. Roosevelt*	Henry A. Wallace	Wendell L. Willkie	Charles McNary
1944	Franklin D. Roosevelt*	Harry S. Truman	Thomas E. Dewey	John W. Bricker
1948	Harry S. Truman*	Alben W. Barkley	Thomas E. Dewey	Earl Warren
1952	Adlai E. Stevenson	John J. Sparkman	Dwight D. Eisenhower*	Richard M. Nixon
1956	Adlai E. Stevenson	Estes Kefauver	Dwight D. Eisenhower*	Richard M. Nixon
1960	John F. Kennedy*	Lyndon B. Johnson	Richard M. Nixon	Henry Cabot Lodge
1964	Lyndon B. Johnson*	Hubert H. Humphrey	Barry M. Goldwater	William E. Miller
1968†	Hubert H. Humphrey	Edmund S. Muskie	Richard M. Nixon*	Spiro T. Agnew
1972	George S. McGovern	R. Sargent Shriver, Jr.	Richard M. Nixon*	Spiro T. Agnew

(1.) Died Oct. 30 and the Republican National Committee named Nicholas Murray Butler.
† 1968 Third party candidates were George C. Wallace and Gen. Curtis E. LeMay.

Major National Convention Cities since 1856

(Number in parenthesis)

Atlantic City, N. J., (1)–Dem., 1964.
Baltimore, Md., (3)–Rep., 1864; Dem., 1872, 1912.
Charleston, S. C., (1)–Dem., 1860.
Chicago, Ill., (24)–Rep., 1860, 1868, 1880, 1884, 1888, 1904, 1908, 1912, 1916, 1920, 1932, 1944, 1952, 1960. Dem., 1864, 1884, 1892, 1896, 1932, 1940, 1944, 1952, 1956, 1968.
Cincinnati, O., (3)–Rep., 1876; Dem., 1856, 1880.
Cleveland, O., (2)–Rep., 1924, 1936.
Denver, Col., (1)–Dem., 1908
Houston, Tex., (1)–Dem., 1928.

Kansas City, Mo., (2)–Rep., 1928; Dem., 1900.
Los Angeles, Calif. (1)–Dem., 1960.
Miami Beach, Fla. (3)– Rep., 1968, 1972. Dem., 1972.
Minneapolis, Minn. (1)–Rep., 1892.
New York City, (2)–Dem., 1868, 1924.
Philadelphia, Pa., (7)–Rep., 1856, 1872, 1900, 1940, 1948; Dem., 1936, 1948.
St. Louis, Mo., (5)–Rep., 1896; Dem., 1876, 1888, 1904, 1916.
San Francisco, Calif. (3)–Rep., 1956, 1964; Dem., 1920.

Presidents, Vice Presidents, Congresses

President	Service	Vice President	Congress
1 George Washington	Apr. 30, 1789-Mar. 3, 1797	1 John Adams	1,2,3,4.
2 John Adams	Mar. 4, 1797-Mar. 3, 1801	2 Thomas Jefferson	5,6.
3 Thomas Jefferson	Mar. 4, 1801-Mar. 3, 1805	3 Aaron Burr	7,8.
do	Mar. 4, 1805-Mar. 3, 1809	4 George Clinton	9,10.
4 James Madison	Mar. 4, 1809-Mar. 3, 1813	do[1]	11,12.
do	Mar. 4, 1813-Mar. 3, 1817	5 Elbridge Gerry[2]	13,14.
5 James Monroe	Mar. 4, 1817-Mar. 3, 1825	6 Daniel D. Tompkins	15, 16, 17, 18.
6 John Quincy Adams	Mar. 4, 1825-Mar. 3, 1829	7 John C. Calhoun	19, 20.
7 Andrew Jackson	Mar. 4, 1829-Mar. 3, 1833	do[3]	21,22.
do	Mar. 4, 1833-Mar. 3, 1837	8 Martin Van Buren	23,24.
8 Martin Van Buren	Mar. 4, 1837-Mar. 3, 1841	9 Richard M. Johnson	25,26.
9 William Henry Harrison[4]	Mar. 4, 1841-Apr. 4, 1841	10 John Tyler	27.
10 John Tyler	Apr. 6, 1841-Mar. 3, 1845		27, 28.
11 James K. Polk	Mar. 4, 1845-Mar. 3, 1849	11 George M. Dallas	29, 30.
12 Zachary Taylor[4]	Mar. 5, 1849-July 9, 1850	12 Millard Fillmore	31.
13 Millard Fillmore	July 10, 1850-Mar. 3, 1853		31, 32.
14 Franklin Pierce	Mar. 4, 1853-Mar. 3, 1857	13 William R. King[5]	33, 34.
15 James Buchanan	Mar. 4, 1857-Mar. 3, 1861	14 John C. Breckinridge	35, 36.
16 Abraham Lincoln	Mar. 4, 1861-Mar. 3, 1865	15 Hannibal Hamlin	37, 38.
do[4]	Mar. 4, 1865-Apr. 15, 1865	16 Andrew Johnson	39.
17 Andrew Johnson	Apr. 15, 1865-Mar. 3, 1869		39, 40.
18 Ulysses S. Grant	Mar. 4, 1869-Mar. 3, 1873	17 Schuyler Colfax	41, 42.
do	Mar. 4, 1873-Mar. 3, 1877	18 Henry Wilson[6]	43, 44.
19 Rutherford B. Hayes	Mar. 4, 1877-Mar. 3, 1881	19 William A. Wheeler	45, 46.
20 James A. Garfield	Mar. 4, 1881-Sept. 19, 1881	20 Chester A. Arthur	47.
21 Chester A. Arthur	Sept. 20, 1881-Mar. 3, 1885		47, 48.
22 Grover Cleveland[7]	Mar. 4, 1885-Mar. 3, 1889	21 Thomas A. Hendricks[8]	49, 50.
23 Benjamin Harrison	Mar. 4, 1889-Mar. 3, 1893	22 Levi P. Morton	51, 52.
24 Grover Cleveland[7]	Mar. 4, 1893-Mar. 3, 1897	23 Adlai E. Stevenson	53, 54.
25 William McKinley	Mar. 4, 1897-Mar. 3, 1901	24 Garret A. Hobart[9]	55, 56.
do[4]	Mar. 4, 1901-Sept.14, 1901	25 Theodore Roosevelt	57.
26 Theodore Roosevelt	Sept. 14, 1901-Mar. 3, 1905		57, 58.
do	Mar. 4, 1905-Mar. 3, 1909	26 Charles W. Fairbanks	59, 60.
27 William H. Taft	Mar. 4, 1909-Mar. 3, 1913	27 James S. Sherman[10]	61, 62.
28 Woodrow Wilson	Mar. 4, 1913-Mar. 3, 1921	28 Thomas R. Marshall	63, 64, 65, 66.
29 Warren G. Harding[4]	Mar. 4, 1921-Aug. 2, 1923	29 Calvin Coolidge	67.
30 Calvin Coolidge	Aug. 3, 1923-Mar. 3, 1925		68.
do	Mar. 4, 1925-Mar. 3, 1929	30 Charles G. Dawes	69, 70.
31 Herbert C. Hoover	Mar. 4, 1929-Mar. 31, 1933	31 Charles Curtis	71, 72
32 Franklin D. Roosevelt	Mar. 4, 1933-Jan. 20, 1941	32 John N. Garner	73, 74, 75, 76.
do	Jan. 20, 1941-Jan. 20, 1945	33 Henry A. Wallace	77, 78.
do[4]	Jan. 20, 1945-Apr. 12, 1945	34 Harry S. Truman	79.
33 Harry S. Truman	Apr. 12, 1945-Jan. 20, 1949		79, 80.
do	Jan. 20, 1949-Jan. 20, 1953	35 Alben W. Barkley	81, 82.
34 Dwight D. Eisenhower	Jan. 20, 1953-Jan. 20, 1961	36 Richard M. Nixon	83, 84, 85, 86.
35 John F. Kennedy[4]	Jan. 20, 1961-Nov. 22, 1963	37 Lyndon B. Johnson	87, 88.
36 Lyndon B. Johnson	Nov. 22, 1963-Jan. 20, 1965		88.
do	Jan. 20, 1965-Jan. 20, 1969	38 Hubert H. Humphrey	89, 90.
37 Richard M. Nixon	Jan. 20, 1969	39 Spiro T. Agnew	91, 92, 93

(1.) Died Apr. 20, 1812. (2.) Died Nov. 23, 1814. (3.) Resigned Dec. 28, 1832, to become U.S. Senator. (4.) Died in office. (5.) Died Apr. 18, 1853. (6.) Died Nov. 22, 1875. (7.) Terms not consecutive. (8.) Died Nov. 25, 1885. (9.) Died Nov. 21, 1899. (10.) Died Oct. 30, 1912.

Vice Presidents of the United States

The numerals given Vice Presidents do not coincide with those given Presidents, because some Presidents had none and some had more than one.

Name	Birthplace	Yr.	Residence	Inaug.	Politics	Place of Death	Yr.	Age.
1 John Adams	Quincy, Mass	1735	Mass	1789	Fed	Quincy, Mass	1826	90
2 Thomas Jefferson	Shadwell, Va	1743	Va	1797	Rep	Monticello, Va	1826	83
3 Aaron Burr	Newark, N.J	1756	N.Y	1801	Rep	Staten Island, N. Y	1836	80
4 George Clinton	Ulster Co., N. Y	1739	N. Y	1805	Rep	Washington, D. C	1812	73
5 Elbridge Gerry	Marblehead, Mass	1744	Mass	1813	Rep	Washington, D. C	1814	70
6 Daniel D. Tompkins	Scarsdale, N. Y	1774	N.Y	1817	Rep	Staten Island, N.Y	1825	51
7 *John C. Calhoun	Abbeville, S. C	1782	S. C	1825	Rep	Washington, D. C	1850	68
8 Martin Van Buren	Kinderhook, N. Y	1782	N.Y	1833	Dem	Kinderhook, N. Y	1862	79
9 Richard M. Johnson	Louisville, Ky	1780	Ky	1837	Dem	Frankfort, Ky	1850	70
10 John Tyler	Greenway, Va	1790	Va	1841	Whig	Richmond, Va	1862	71
11 George M. Dallas	Philadelphia, Pa	1792	Pa	1845	Dem	Philadelphia, Pa	1864	72
12 Millard Fillmore	Summerhill, N. Y	1800	N. Y	1849	Whig	Buffalo, N. Y	1874	74
13 William R. King	Sampson Co., N. C	1786	Ala	1853	Dem	Dallas Co., Ala	1853	67
14 John C. Breckinridge	Lexington, Ky	1821	Ky	1857	Dem	Lexington, Ky	1875	54
15 Hannibal Hamlin	Paris, Me	1809	Me	1861	Rep	Bangor, Me	1891	81
16 Andrew Johnson	Raleigh, N. C	1808	Tenn	1865	(x)	Carter Co., Tenn	1875	66
17 Schuyler Colfax	New York City, N. Y	1823	Ind	1869	Rep	Mankato, Minn	1885	62
18 Henry Wilson	Farmington, N. H	1812	Mass	1873	Rep	Washington, D. C	1875	63
19 William A. Wheeler	Malone, N. Y	1819	N. Y	1877	Rep	Malone, N. Y	1887	68
20 Chester A. Arthur	Fairfield, Vt	1830	N. Y	1881	Rep	New York City, N. Y	1886	56
21 Thomas A. Hendricks	Muskingum Co., Ohio	1819	Ind	1885	Dem	Indianapolis, Ind	1885	66
22 Levi P. Morton	Shoreham, Vt	1824	N. Y	1889	Rep	Rhinebeck, N. Y	1920	96
23 Adlai E. Stevenson[1]	Christian Co., Ky	1835	Ill	1893	Dem	Chicago, Ill	1914	78
24 Garret A. Hobart	Long Branch, N. J	1844	N. J	1897	Rep	Paterson, N. J	1899	55
25 Theodore Roosevelt	New York City, N. Y	1858	N. Y	1901	Rep	Oyster Bay, N. Y	1919	60
26 Charles W. Fairbanks	Unionville Centre, Ohio	1852	Ind	1905	Rep	Indianapolis, Ind	1918	66
27 James S. Sherman	Utica, N. Y	1855	N. Y	1909	Rep	Utica, N. Y	1912	57
28 Thomas R. Marshall	No. Manchester, Ind	1854	Ind	1913	Dem	Washington, D. C	1925	71
29 Calvin Coolidge	Plymouth, Vt	1872	Mass	1921	Rep	Northampton, Mass	1933	60
30 Charles G. Dawes	Marietta, Ohio	1865	Ill	1925	Rep	Evanston, Ill	1951	85
31 Charles Curtis	Topeka, Kan	1860	Kan	1929	Rep	Washington, D. C	1936	76

Vice President	Birthplace	Yr.	Residence	Inaug.	Pol.	Place of Death	Yr.	Age
30 Charles G. Dawes	Marietta, Ohio	1865	Ill.	1925	Rep	Evanston, Ill.	1951	85
31 Charles Curtis	Topeka, Kan.	1860	Kan.	1929	Rep	Washington, D.C.	1936	76
32 John Nance Garner	Red River Co., Tex	1868	Tex.	1933	Dem	Uvalde, Tex.	1967	98
33 Henry Agard Wallace	Adair County, Ia	1888	Iowa	1941	Dem	Danbury, Conn	1965	77
34 Harry S. Truman	Lamar, Mo	1884	Mo	1945	Dem	Kansas City, Mo.	1972	88
35 Alben W. Barkley	Graves County, Ky	1877	Ky	1949	Dem	Lexington, Va	1956	78
36 Richard M. Nixon	Yorba Linda, Calif	1913	Calif	1953	Rep			
37 Lyndon B. Johnson	Johnson City, Tex	1908	Tex.	1961	Dem	San Antonio, Texas	1973	64
38 Hubert H. Humphrey	Wallace, S. D	1911	Minn	1965	Dem			
39 Spiro T. Agnew	Baltimore, Md	1918	Md	1969	Rep			

(°) John C. Calhoun resigned Dec. 28, 1832, having been elected to the Senate to fill a vacancy. (x) Andrew Johnson—A Democrat nominated by Republicans and elected with Lincoln on the National Union Ticket. (1.)Adlai E. Stevenson, 23rd Vice President, was grandfather of Democratic candidate for President, 1952 and 1956.

Cabinets of the United States

Secretaries of State

The Department of Foreign Affairs was created by Act of Congress July 27, 1789, and the name changed to Department of State on Sept. 15. Thomas Jefferson, the minister to France, was appointed Secretary of State by President Washington Sept. 26, and took office March 21, 1790. John Jay, who had held the office of Secretary for Foreign Affairs since his appointment by the Ninth Continental Congress in March 1784, in place of Robert R. Livingston (appointed Jan. 1781), left it in September 1789, when the U. S. Supreme Court was established with him as Chief Justice.

The Secretary of State is charged, under the direction of the President, with the duties appertaining to correspondence with the public ministers and the consuls of the United States and with the representatives of foreign powers accredited to the United States, and to negotiations of whatever character relating to the foreign affairs of the United States.

Presidents	Cabinet Officers	Home	Apptd.	Presidents	Cabinet Officers	Home	Apptd.
Washington	Thomas Jefferson	Va	1789	Arthur	James G. Blaine	Me	1881
"	Edmund Randolph	"	1794	"	F. T. Frelinghuysen	N. J.	1881
"	Timothy Pickering	Pa	1795	Cleveland			1885
J. Adams	"	"	1795	"	Thomas F. Bayard	Del	1885
"	John Marshall	Va	1800	B. Harrison	"		1889
Jefferson	James Madison	"	1801	"	James G. Blaine	Me	1889
Madison	Robert Smith	Md	1809	"	John W. Foster	Ind	1892
"	James Monroe	Va	1811	Cleveland	Walter Q. Gresham	Ill	1893
Monroe	John Quincy Adams	Mass	1817	"	Richard Olney	Mass	1895
J. Q. Adams	Henry Clay	Ky	1825	McKinley	"		1897
Jackson	Martin Van Buren	N. Y	1829	"	John Sherman	Ohio	1897
"	Edward Livingston	La	1831	"	William R. Day	"	1898
"	Louis McLane	Del	1833	"	John Hay	D.C.	1898
"	John Forsyth	Ga	1834	T. Roosevelt	"	"	1901
Van Buren	"	"	1837	"	Elihu Root	N. Y	1905
W.H. Harrison	Daniel Webster	Mass	1841	"	Robert Bacon	"	1909
Tyler	"	"	1841	Taft	"	"	1909
"	Abel P. Upshur	Va	1843	"	Philander C. Knox	Pa	1909
"	John C. Calhoun	S. C.	1844	Wilson	"	"	1913
Polk	"	"	1845	"	William J. Bryan	Neb	1913
"	James Buchanan	Pa	1845	"	Robert Lansing	N. Y	1915
Taylor	"	"	1849	"	Bainbridge Colby	"	1920
"	John M. Clayton	Del	1849	Harding	Charles E. Hughes	"	1921
Fillmore	"	"	1850	Coolidge	"		1923
"	Daniel Webster	Mass	1850	"	Frank B. Kellogg	Minn.	1925
"	Edward Everett	"	1852	Hoover	"		1929
Pierce	William L. Marcy	N. Y	1853	"	Henry L. Stimson	N. Y	1929
Buchanan	"	"	1857	F.D. Roosevelt	Cordell Hull	Tenn	1933
"	Lewis Cass	Mich	1857	"	E.R. Stettinius, Jr	Va	1944
"	Jeremiah S. Black	Pa	1860	Truman	"	"	1945
Lincoln	"	"	1861	"	James F. Byrnes	S. C.	1945
"	William H. Seward	N. Y	1861	"	George C. Marshall	Pa	1947
Johnson, A	"	"	1865	"	Dean G. Acheson	Conn	1949
Grant	Elihu B. Washburne	Ill	1869	Eisenhower	John Foster Dulles	N. Y	1953
"	Hamilton Fish	N. Y	1869	"	Christian A. Herter	Mass	1959
Hayes	"	"	1877	Kennedy	Dean Rusk	N. Y	1961
"	William M. Evarts	"	1877	Johnson, L. B	"	"	1963
Garfield	"	"	1881	Nixon	William P. Rogers	N. Y	1969
"	James G. Blaine	Me	1881				

Secretaries of the Treasury

The second Continental Congress on July 29, 1775, appointed Michael Hillegas and George Clymer, Esqs., as "joint treasurers of the United Colonies." Francis Hopkinson was elected Treasurer of Loans July 27, 1778. Robert Morris was appointed Superintendent of Finances by the Seventh Continental Congress on Feb. 20, 1781. The Treasury Department was organized by Act of Congress on Sept. 2, 1789, and President Washington commissioned Alexander Hamilton Secretary of the Treasury on Sept. 11.

Presidents	Cabinet Officers	Home	Apptd.	Presidents	Cabinet Officers	Home	Apptd.
Washington	Alexander Hamilton	N. Y	1789	J. Q. Adams	Richard Rush	Pa	1825
"	Oliver Wolcott	Conn	1795	Jackson	Samuel D. Ingham	Pa	1829
J. Adams	"		1797	"	Louis McLane	Del	1831
"	Samuel Dexter	Mass	1801	"	William J. Duane	Pa	1833
Jefferson	"		1801	"	Roger B. Taney	Md	1833
"	Albert Gallatin	Pa	1801	"	Levi Woodbury	N. H	1834
Madison	"		1809	Van Buren	"	"	1837
"	George W. Campbell	Tenn	1814	W.H. Harrison	Thomas Ewing	Ohio	1841
"	Alexander J. Dallas	Pa	1814	Tyler	"	"	1841
"	William H. Crawford	Ga	1816	"	Walter Forward	Pa	1841
Monroe	"		1817	"	John C. Spencer	N. Y	1843

Presidents	Cabinet Officers	Home	Apptd.
Tyler	George M. Bibb	Ky	1844
Polk	Robert J. Walker	Miss	1845
Taylor	William M. Meredith	Pa	1849
Fillmore	Thomas Corwin	Ohio	1850
Pierce	James Guthrie	Ky	1853
Buchanan	Howell Cobb	Ga	1857
"	Phillip F. Thomas	Md	1860
"	John A. Dix	N. Y	1861
Lincoln	Salmon P. Chase	Ohio	1861
"	William P. Fessenden	Me	1864
"	Hugh McCulloch	Ind	1865
Johnson A	"	"	1865
Grant	George S. Boutwell	Mass	1869
Grant	William A. Richardson	Mass	1873
"	Benjamin H. Bristow	Ky	1874
"	Lot M. Morrill	Me	1876
Hayes	John Sherman	Ohio	1877
Garfield	William Windom	Minn	1881
Arthur	Charles J. Folger	N. Y	1881
"	Walter Q. Gresham	Ind	1884
"	Hugh McCulloch	"	1884
Cleveland	Daniel Manning	N. Y	1885
"	Charles S. Fairchild	"	1887
B. Harrison	William Windom	Minn	1889
"	Charles Foster	Ohio	1891
Cleveland	John G. Carlisle	Ky	1893
McKinley	Lyman J. Gage	Ill	1897
T. Roosevelt	"	"	1901
"	Leslie M. Shaw	Ia	1902
"	George B. Cortelyou	N. Y	1907
Taft	Franklin MacVeagh	Ill	1909
Wilson	William G. McAdoo	N. Y	1913
"	Carter Glass	Va	1918
"	David F. Houston	Mo	1920
Harding	Andrew W. Mellon	Pa	1921
Coolidge	"	"	1923
Hoover	"	"	1929
"	Ogden L. Mills	N. Y	1932
F.D. Roosevelt	William H. Woodin	"	1933
"	Henry Morgenthau, Jr	"	1934
Truman	Fred M. Vinson	Ky	1945
"	John W. Snyder	Mo	1946
Eisenhower	George M. Humphrey	Ohio	1953
"	Robert B. Anderson	Conn	1957
Kennedy	C. Douglas Dillon	N. J	1961
Johnson, L. B	"	"	1963
"	Henry H. Fowler	Va	1965
"	Joseph W. Barr	Ind	1968
Nixon	David M. Kennedy	Ill	1969
"	John B. Connally	Tex	1970
"	George P. Shultz	Ill	1972

Attorneys General

The office of Attorney General was organized by Act of Congress Sept. 24, 1789. Washington appointed Edmund Randolph to the post. The Attorney General was made a member of the Cabinet in 1814. The Dept. of Justice was created June 22, 1870, and the Attorney General was placed at its head.

Presidents	Cabinet Officers	Home	Apptd.
Washington	Edmund Randolph	Va	1789
"	William Bradford	Pa	1794
"	Charles Lee	Va	1795
J. Adams	"	"	1797
Jefferson	Levi Lincoln	Mass	1801
"	John Breckenridge	Ky	1805
"	Caesar A. Rodney	Del	1807
Madison	"	"	1809
"	William Pinkney	Md	1811
"	Richard Rush	Pa	1814
Monroe	"	"	1817
"	William Wirt	Va	1817
J. Q. Adams	"	"	1825
Jackson	John McP. Berrien	Ga	1829
"	Roger B. Taney	Md	1831
"	Benjamin F. Butler	N. Y	1833
Van Buren	"	"	1837
"	Felix Grundy	Tenn	1838
"	Henry D. Gilpin	Pa	1840
W. H. Harrison	John J. Crittenden	Ky	1841
Tyler	"	"	1841
"	Hugh S. Legare	S. C	1841
"	John Nelson	Md	1843
Polk	John Y. Mason	Va	1845
"	Nathan Clifford	Me	1846
"	Isaac Toucey	Conn	1848
Taylor	Reverdy Johnson	Md	1849
Fillmore	John J. Crittenden	Ky	1850
Pierce	Caleb Cushing	Mass	1853
Buchanan	Jeremiah S. Black	Pa	1857
"	Edwin M. Stanton	Pa	1860
Lincoln	Edward Bates	Mo	1861
"	James Speed	Ky	1864
Johnson, A	"	Ky	1865
"	Henry Stanbery	Ohio	1866
"	William M. Evarts	N. Y	1868
Grant	Ebenezer R. Hoar	Mass	1869
"	Amos T. Akerman	Ga	1870
"	George H. Williams	Ore	1871
Grant	Edwards Pierrepont	N. Y	1875
"	Alphonso Taft	Ohio	1876
Hayes	Charles Devens	Mass	1877
Garfield	Wayne MacVeagh	Pa	1881
Arthur	Benjamin H. Brewster	"	1881
Cleveland	Augustus Garland	Ark	1885
B. Harrison	William H. H. Miller	Ind	1889
Cleveland	Richard Olney	Mass	1893
"	Judson Harmon	Ohio	1895
McKinley	Joseph McKenna	Cal	1897
"	John W. Griggs	N. J	1898
"	Philander C. Knox	Pa	1901
T. Roosevelt	"	"	1901
"	William H. Moody	Mass	1904
"	Charles J. Bonaparte	Md	1906
Taft	George W. Wickersham	N. Y	1909
Wilson	J. C. McReynolds	Tenn	1913
"	Thomas W. Gregory	Tex	1914
"	A. Mitchell Palmer	Pa	1919
Harding	Harry M. Daugherty	Ohio	1921
Coolidge	"	"	1923
"	Harlan F. Stone	N. Y	1924
"	John G. Sargent	Vt	1925
Hoover	William D. Mitchell	Minn	1929
F.D. Roosevelt	Homer S. Cummings	Conn	1933
"	Frank Murphy	Mich	1939
"	Robert H. Jackson	N. Y	1940
"	Francis Biddle	Pa	1941
Truman	Tom C. Clark	Tex	1945
"	J. Howard McGrath	R. I	1949
"	J. P. McGranery	Pa	1952
Eisenhower	H. Brownell, Jr	N. Y	1953
"	William P. Rogers	Md	1957
Kennedy	Robert F. Kennedy	Mass	1961
Johnson, L. B	"	"	1963
"	N. de B. Katzenbach	Ill	1965
"	Ramsey Clark	Tex	1967
Nixon	John N. Mitchell	N. Y	1969
"	Richard G. Kleindienst	Ariz	1972
"	Eliot L. Richardson	Mass	1973

Secretaries of Agriculture

The Department of Agriculture was created by Act of Congress, May 15, 1862. On Feb. 8, 1889, its Commissioner was renamed Secretary of Agriculture and became a member of the Cabinet.

Presidents	Cabinet Officers	Home	Apptd.
Cleveland	Norman J. Colman	Mo	1889
B. Harrison	Jeremiah M. Rusk	Wis	1889
Cleveland	J. Sterling Morton	Neb	1893
McKinley	James Wilson	Ia	1897
T. Roosevelt	"	"	1901
Taft	"	"	1909
Wilson	David F. Houston	Mo	1913
"	Edward T. Meredith	Ia	1920
Harding	Henry C. Wallace	Ia	1921
Coolidge	"	"	1923
Coolidge	Howard M. Gore	W. Va	1924
Coolidge	W. M. Jardine	Kan	1925
Hoover	Arthur M. Hyde	Mo	1929
F.D.Roosevelt	Henry A. Wallace	Iowa	1933
"	Claude R. Wickard	Ind	1940
Truman	Clinton P. Anderson	N. M.	1945
"	Charles F. Brannan	Colo	1948
Eisenhower	Ezra Taft Benson	Utah	1953
Kennedy	Orville L. Freeman	Minn	1961
Johnson, L. B	"	"	1963
Nixon	Clifford M. Hardin	Ind	1969
"	Earl L. Butz		1971

Postmasters General

Benjamin Franklin had been Postmaster General for the Colonies (1753) under the King until summarily dismissed by him Jan. 30, 1774. The Second Continental Congress created the Post Office Department with headquarters in Philadelphia and on July 26, 1775, elected Benjamin Franklin Postmaster General for one year. On his sailing later for France as one of the ambassadors, Richard Bache succeeded him on Nov. 7, 1776. Ebenezer Hazard was appointed Postmaster General Jan. 28, 1782. Congress temporarily established the Post Office Department as a branch of the Treasury, on Sept. 22, 1789, and Washington commissioned Samuel Osgood Postmaster General on Sept. 26. The Postmaster General was made a member of the Cabinet March 9, 1829. The Postal Reorganization Act of 1970 provided for replacement of the Post Office Department by a new U.S. Postal Service, an independent Federal Agency. Its head, retaining the title of Postmaster General, is no longer a member of the Cabinet.

Presidents	Cabinet Officers	Home	Apptd.	Presidents	Cabinet Officers	Home	Apptd.
Washington ...	Samuel Osgood	Mass ..	1789	Hayes	Horace Maynard	Tenn ..	1880
"	Timothy Pickering	Pa	1791	Garfield	Thomas L. James	N. Y ..	1881
"	Joseph Habersham	Ga ...	1795	Arthur ...	Timothy O. Howe	Wis ...	1881
J. Adams	"	"	1797	"	Walter Q. Gresham ...	Ind	1883
Jefferson.....	"	"	1801	"	Frank Hatton	Iowa ..	1884
"	Gideon Granger	Conn ..	1801	Cleveland	William F. Vilas	Wis ...	1885
Madison	"	"	1809	"	Don M. Dickinson.....	Mich ..	1888
"	Return J. Meigs, Jr	Ohio ..	1814	B. Harrison...	John Wanamaker	Pa	1889
Monroe	"	"	1817	Cleveland	Wilson S. Bissel	N. Y ..	1893
"	John McLean	"	1823	"	William L. Wilson......	W. Va ..	1895
J. Q. Adams ..	"	"	1825	McKinley	James A. Gary	Md	1897
Jackson......	William T. Barry	Ky ..	1829	"	Charles E. Smith	Pa	1898
"	Amos Kendall...........	"	1835	T. Roosevelt ..	"	"	1901
Van Buren ...	"	"	1837	"	Henry C. Payne	Wis ...	1902
"	John M. Niles...........	Conn ..	1840	"	Robert J. Wynne	Pa	1904
W.H.Harrison .	Francis Granger	N. Y ..	1841	"	George B. Cortelyou ...	N. Y ..	1905
Tyler........	"	N. Y ..	1841	"	George von L. Meyer....	Mass ..	1907
"	Charles A. Wickliffe....	Ky ..	1841	Taft........	Frank H. Hitchcock	"	1909
Polk	Cave Johnson	Tenn ..	1845	Wilson.......	Albert S. Burleson	Tex ...	1913
Taylor.......	Jacob Collamer	Vt	1849	Harding......	Will H. Hays........	Ind	1921
Fillmore	Nathan K. Hall........	N. Y ..	1850	"	Hubert Work	Colo ..	1922
"	Samuel D. Hubbard	Conn ..	1852	"	Harry S. New.........	Ind	1923
Pierce.......	James Campbell.......	Pa	1853	Coolidge	"	"	1923
Buchanan	Aaron V. Brown	Tenn ..	1857	Hoover	Walter F. Brown	Ohio ..	1929
"	Joseph Holt	Ky ..	1859	F.D.Roosevelt.	James A. Farley	N. Y ..	1933
"	Horatio King	Me ..	1861	"	Frank C. Walker	Pa	1940
Lincoln	Montgomery Blair	D. C ..	1861	Truman......	Robt. E. Hannegan.....	Mo ...	1945
"	William Dennison......	Ohio ..	1864	"	Jesse M. Donaldson.....	Mo ...	1947
Johnson, A ...	"	"	1865	Eisenhower...	A. E. Summerfield......	Mich ..	1953
"	Alex. W. Randall	Wis ..	1866	Kennedy	J. Edward Day........	Calif ..	1961
Grant	John A. J. Creswell	Md	1869	"	John A. Gronouski	Wis ...	1963
"	James W. Marshall	Va	1874	Johnson, L. B .	"	"	1963
"	Marshall Jewell	Conn ..	1874	"	Lawrence F. O'Brien ...	Mass ..	1965
"	James N. Tyner	Ind	1876	"	W. Marvin Watson ...	Texas ..	1968
Hayes	David McK. Key	Tenn ..	1877	Nixon	Winton M. Blount	Ala ...	1969

Secretaries of the Interior

The Department of Interior was created by Act of Congress March 3, 1849.

Presidents	Cabinet Officers	Home	Apptd.	Presidents	Cabinet Officers	Home	Apptd.
Taylor.......	Thomas Ewing	Ohio ..	1849	"	Ethan A. Hitchcock	Mo ...	1898
Fillmore	Thomas M. T. McKennan.	Pa	1850	T. Roosevelt ..	"	"	1901
"	Alex H. H. Stuart.......	Va	1850	"	James R. Garfield	Ohio ..	1907
Pierce.......	Robert McClelland	Mich ..	1853	Taft........	Richard A. Ballinger ...	Wash..	1909
Buchanan	Jacob Thompson	Miss ..	1857	"	Walter L. Fisher	Ill	1911
Lincoln	Caleb B. Smith	Ind ..	1861	Wilson.......	Franklin K. Lane	Cal ...	1913
"	John P. Usher	"	1863	"	John B. Payne	Ill	1920
Johnson, A ...	"	"	1865	Harding......	Albert B. Fall........	N. M ..	1921
"	James Harlan..........	Iowa ..	1865	"	Hubert Work	Colo ..	1923
"	Orville H. Browning	Ill ..	1866	Coolidge	"	Colo ..	1923
Grant	Jacob D. Cox	Ohio ..	1869	"	Roy O. West.........	Ill	1929
"	Columbus Delano	"	1870	Hoover	Ray Lyman Wilbur	Cal ...	1929
"	Zachariah Chandler	Mich ..	1875	F.D.Roosevelt.	Harold L. Ickes	Ia	1933
Hayes	Carl Schurz	Mo ...	1877	Truman......	"	Ill	1945
Garfield	Sam. J. Kirkwood......	Iowa ..	1881	"	Julius A. Krug	Wis ...	1946
Arthur.......	Henry M. Teller	Colo ..	1882	"	Oscar L. Chapman	Colo ..	1950
Cleveland	Lucius Q. C. Lamar	Miss ..	1885	Eisenhower...	Douglas McKay	Oreg ..	1953
"	William F. Vilas	Wis ..	1888	"	Fred A. Seaton.......	Nebr ..	1956
B. Harrison...	John W. Noble	Mo ...	1889	Kennedy	Stewart L. Udall.......	Ariz...	1961
Cleveland	Hoke Smith...........	Ga ...	1893	Johnson, L. B .	"	"	1963
"	David R. Francis.......	Mo ...	1890	Nixon	Walter J. Hickel........	Alaska.	1969
McKinley	Cornelius N. Bliss.......	N. Y ..	1897	"	Rogers C. B. Morton	Md. ..	1971

Secretaries of Health, Education and Welfare

The Department of Health, Education and Welfare was created by Act of Congress April 11, 1953.

Presidents	Cabinet Officers	Home	Apptd.	Presidents	Cabinet Officers	Home	Apptd.
Eisenhower...	Oveta Culp Hobby	Texas ..	1953	Johnson, L. B .	Anthony J. Celebrezze ...	Ohio ..	1963
"	Marion B. Folsom	N. Y ..	1955	"	John W. Gardner	N. Y ..	1965
"	Arthur S. Flemming.....	Ohio ..	1958	"	Wilbur J. Cohen	Mich ..	1968
Kennedy	Abraham A. Ribicoff	Conn ..	1961	Nixon	Robert H. Finch........	Calif ..	1969
Kennedy	Anthony J. Celebrezze ...	Ohio ..	1962	"	Elliot L. Richardson	Mass..	1970
				"	Casper W. Weinberger ...	Calif..	1973

Secretaries of Housing and Urban Development

The Department of Housing and Urban Development was created by Act of Congress Sept. 9, 1965.

President	Cabinet Officer	Home	Apptd.	President	Cabinet Officer	Home	Apptd.
Johnson, L. B .	Robert C. Weaver	Wash. .	1966	Nixon	George W. Romney	Mich ..	1969
"	Robert C. Wood	Mass..	1968	"	James T. Lynn	Ohio ..	1973

Secretaries of Defense

The Department of Defense, originally designated the National Military Establishment, was created Sept. 18, 1947. It is headed by the Secretary of Defense, who is a member of the President's cabinet.

The Departments of the Army, of the Navy and of the Air Force function within the Department of Defense, and their respective secretaries are no longer members of the President's cabinet.

Presidents	Cabinet Officers	Home	Apptd.	Presidents	Cabinet Officers	Home	Apptd.
Truman......	James V. Forrestal....	N. Y..	1947	Kennedy.....	Robert S. McNamara....	Mich..	1961
".....	Louis A. Johnson......	W. Va.	1949	Johnson, L. B.	"	"	1963
".....	George C. Marshall....	Pa....	1950	"	Clark M. Clifford.......	Md...	1968
".....	Robert A. Lovett.......	N. Y..	1951	Nixon	Melvin R. Laird........	Wisc..	1969
Eisenhower..	Charles E. Wilson.......	Mich..	1953	"	Elliot L. Richardson...	Mass..	1973
"	Neil H. McElroy........	Ohio..	1957	"	James R. Schlesinger..	Va.	1973
"	Thomas S. Gates, Jr...	Pa....	1959				

Secretaries of the U. S. Air Force, Army and Navy

Not Members of the President's Cabinet

The Dept. of Defense created Sept. 18, 1947, consolidated the Navy, Army, Air Force into a single department.

Secretaries of the Air Force	Appointed
W. Stuart Symington............	Sept. 18, 1947
Thomas K. Finletter............	Apr. 24, 1950
Harold E. Talbot...............	Feb. 4, 1953
Donald A. Quarles..............	Aug. 12, 1955
James H. Douglas..............	Mar. 26, 1957
Dudley C. Sharpe..............	Dec. 10, 1959
Eugene M. Zuckert.............	Jan. 23, 1961
Dr. Harold Brown	July 10, 1965
Robert C. Seamans Jr.........	Jan. 20, 1969

Secretaries of the Army	
Kenneth C. Royall.............	Sept. 18, 1947
Gordon Gray*..................	June 20, 1949
Frank Pace, Jr.................	Apr. 12, 1950
Earl D. Johnson (Acting).......	Jan. 20, 1953
Robert T. Stevens..............	Feb. 4, 1953
Wilber M. Brucker..............	July 21, 1955
Elvis J. Stahr, Jr..............	Jan. 23, 1961
Cyrus R. Vance................	May 21, 1962
Stephen Ailes.................	Jan. 20, 1964

Stanley R. Resor...............	June 17, 1965
Robert F. Froehlke............	June 15, 1971
Howard H. Callaway...........	May 2, 1973

*In addition, Gordon Gray was Acting Secretary of the Army from Apr. 28, 1949, and Under Secretary from May 25, 1949, until June 20, 1949.

Secretaries of the Navy	Appointed
John L. Sullivan...............	Sept. 18, 1947
Francis P. Matthews	May 25, 1949
Dan A. Kimball................	July 31, 1951
Robert B. Anderson............	Feb. 4, 1953
Charles S. Thomas............	May 3, 1954
Thomas S. Gates, Jr..........	Apr. 1, 1957
William B. Franke.............	June 1, 1958
John B. Connally, Jr..........	Jan. 23, 1961
Fred Korth...................	Dec. 11, 1961
Paul H. Nitze.................	Oct. 14, 1963
Paul R. Ignatius..............	Aug. 4, 1967
John H. Chafee...............	Jan. 20, 1969
John W. Warner...............	Apr. 7, 1972

Secretaries of the Navy

The Navy Department was created by Act of Congress April 30, 1798, which made the Secretary a member of the Cabinet. President Adams appointed George Cabot of Beverly, Mass., the first Secretary of the Navy, May 3, 1798, but he declined the office. Benjamin Stoddert was appointed the same day.

Presidents	Cabinet Officers	Home	Apptd.	Presidents		Home	Apptd.
J. Adams....	Benjamin Stoddert......	Md...	1798	Lincoln.....	Gideon Welles..........	Conn..	1861
Jefferson.....	"	"	1801	Johnson, A...	"	"	1865
"	Robert Smith..........	"	1801	Grant.....	Adolph E. Borie........	Pa....	1869
Madison.....	Paul Hamilton.........	S. C...	1809	"	George M. Robeson....	N. J..	1869
"	William Jones..........	Pa....	1813	Hayes......	Richard W. Thompson...	Ind...	1877
"	Benjamin Williams			"	Nathan Goff, Jr.......	W. Va.	1881
	Crowninshield........	Mass..	1814	Garfield.....	William H. Hunt.......	La....	1881
Monroe......	"	"	1817	Arthur......	William E. Chandler....	N. H..	1882
"	Smith Thompson.......	N. Y..	1818	Cleveland....	William C. Whitney.....	N. Y..	1885
"	Samuel L. Southard....	N. J..	1823	B. Harrison...	Benjamin F. Tracy......	N. Y..	1889
J. Q. Adams..	"	"	1825	Cleveland....	Hilary A. Herbert......	Ala...	1893
Jackson......	John Branch...........	N. C..	1829	McKinley....	John D. Long.........	Mass..	1897
"	Levi Woodbury........	N. H..	1831	T. Roosevelt..	"	"	1901
"	Mahlon Dickerson......	N. J..	1834	"	William H. Moody.....	"	1902
Van Buren...	"	"	1837	"	Paul Morton.........	Ill....	1904
"	James K. Paulding......	N. Y..	1838	"	Charles J. Bonaparte....	Md...	1905
W.H. Harrison	George E. Badger......	N. C..	1841	"	Victor H. Metcalf......	Cal...	1906
Tyler.......	"	"	1841	"	Truman H. Newberry....	Mich..	1908
"	Abel P. Upshur.........	Va....	1841	Taft........	George von L. Meyer....	Mass..	1909
"	David Henshaw........	Mass..	1843	Wilson.......	Josephus Daniels......	N. C..	1913
"	Thomas W. Gilmer.....	Va....	1844	Harding.....	Edwin Denby..........	Mich..	1921
"	John Y. Mason........	"	1844	Coolidge.....	"	"	1923
Polk.......	George Bancroft........	Mass..	1845	"	Curtis D. Wilbur........	Cal...	1924
"	John Y. Mason........	Va....	1846	Hoover......	Charles Francis Adams..	Mass..	1929
Taylor......	William B. Preston......		1849	F.D. Roosevelt	Claude A. Swanson.....	Va....	1933
Fillmore.....	William A. Graham.....	N. C..	1850	"	Charles Edison........	N. J..	1940
"	John P. Kennedy.......	Md...	1852	"	Frank Knox...........	Ill....	1940
Pierce......	James C. Dobbin.......	N. C..	1853	"	James V. Forrestal.....	N. Y...	1944
Buchanan....	Isaac Toucey..........	Conn..	1857	Truman......	"	"	1945

*Last member of the President's Cabinet. The Navy Department is now a branch of the Dept. of Defense, created September 18, 1947.

Secretaries of War

The Second Continental Congress set up in June, 1776, a board of War and Ordnance consisting of five members: John Adams, Roger Sherman, Benjamin Harrison, James Wilson and Edward Rutledge. Richard Peters was elected Secretary on June 12. This Board, several times changed, continued until Oct. 30, 1781, when Congress appointed Benjamin Lincoln Secretary of War, a position created by Act of Congress the previous February. The Eleventh Continental Congress on March 8, 1785, appointed Gen. Henry Knox to succeed him with the added duties of the Navy. The War (and Navy) Department was created by Act of Congress Aug. 7, 1789, and Gen. Henry Knox was commissioned Secretary of War under that Act Sept. 12, 1789.

Washington..	Henry Knox...........	Mass..	1789	J. Adams.....	Samuel Dexter.......	Mass..	1800
"	Timothy Pickering......	Pa....	1795	Jefferson.....	Henry Dearborn........	"	1801
"	James McHenry........	Md...	1796	Madison.....	William Eustis........	Mass..	1809
J. Adams....	"	"	1797	"	John Armstrong........	N. Y..	1813

(Secretaries of War Continued)

Presidents	Cabinet Officers	Home	Apptd.	Presidents	Cabinet Officers	Home	Apptd.
"	James Monroe	Va	1814	"	James Don. Cameron	Pa	1876
"	William H. Crawford	Ga	1815	Hayes	George W. McCrary	Iowa	1877
Monroe	John C. Calhoun	S. C.	1817	"	Alexander Ramsey	Minn	1879
J. Q. Adams	James Barbour	Va	1825	Garfield	Robert T. Lincoln	Ill	1881
"	Peter B. Porter	N. Y.	1828	Arthur	"		1881
Jackson	John H. Eaton	Tenn	1829	Cleveland	William C. Endicott	Mass	1885
"	Lewis Cass	Ohio	1831	B. Harrison	Redfield Proctor	Vt	1890
"	Benjamin F. Butler	N. Y.	1837	"	Stephen B. Elkins	W. Va	1891
Van Buren	Joel R. Poinsett	S. C.	1837	Cleveland	Daniel S. Lamont	N. Y.	1893
W.H. Harrison	John Bell	Tenn	1841	McKinley	Russel A. Alger	Mich	1897
Tyler	"	"	1841	"	Elihu Root	N. Y.	1899
"	John C. Spencer	N. Y.	1841	T. Roosevelt	"	"	1901
"	James M. Porter	Pa	1843	"	William H. Taft	Ohio	1904
"	William Wilkins	"	1844	"	Luke E. Wright	Tenn	1908
Polk	William L. Marcy	N. Y	1845	Taft	Jacob M. Dickinson	"	1909
Taylor	George W. Crawford	Ga	1849	"	Henry L. Stimson	N. Y.	1911
Fillmore	Charles M. Conrad	La	1850	Wilson	Lindley M. Garrison	N. J.	1913
Pierce	Jefferson Davis	Miss	1853	"	Newton D. Baker	Ohio	1916
Buchanan	John B. Floyd	Va	1857	Harding	John W. Weeks	Mass	1921
"	Joseph Holt	Ky	1861	Coolidge	"		1923
Lincoln	Simon Cameron	Pa	1861	"	Dwight F. Davis	Mo	1925
"	Edwin M. Stanton	Pa	1862	Hoover	James W. Good	Ill	1929
Johnson, A	"	"	1865	"	Patrick J. Hurley	Okla	1929
"	John M. Schofield	Ill	1868	F.D. Roosevelt	George H. Dern	Utah	1933
Grant	John A. Rawlins	Ill	1869	"	Harry H. Woodring	Kan	1937
"	William T. Sherman	Ohio	1869	"	Henry L. Stimson	N. Y.	1940
* "	William W. Belknap	Iowa	1869	Truman	Robert P. Patterson	N. Y.	1945
"	Alphonso Taft	Ohio	1876	"	Kenneth C. Royall	N. C.	1947

*Last member of the President's cabinet. The War Dept. became the Dept. of the Army and is now a branch of the Dept. of Defense, created September 18, 1947.

Secretaries of Commerce and Labor

The Dept. of Commerce & Labor, created by Congress Feb. 14, 1903, was divided by Congress Mar. 4, 1913, into separate Depts. of Commerce and Labor, the Secretary of each made a Cabinet member.

Secretaries of Commerce and Labor

Presidents	Cabinet Officers	Home	Apptd.
T. Roosevelt	Geo. B. Cortelyou	N. Y.	1903
"	Victor H. Metcalf	Cal	1904
"	Oscar S. Straus	N. Y.	1906
Taft	Charles Nagel	Mo	1909

Secretaries of Labor

Presidents	Cabinet Officers	Home	Apptd.
Wilson	William B. Wilson	Pa	1913
Harding	James J. Davis	Pa	1921
Coolidge	"	"	1923
Hoover	"	"	1929
"	William N. Doak	Va	1930
F.D. Roosevelt	Frances Perkins	N. Y.	1933
Truman	L. B. Schwellenbach	Wash	1945
"	Maurice J. Tobin	Mass	1949
Eisenhower	Martin P. Durkin	Ill	1953
"	James P. Mitchell	N. J.	1953
Kennedy	Arthur J. Goldberg	Ill	1961
"	W. Willard Wirtz	Ill	1962
Johnson, L. B.	"	"	1963
Nixon	George P. Shultz	Ill	1969
Nixon	James D. Hodgson	Calif.	1970
"	Peter J. Brennan	N.Y.	1973

Secretaries of Commerce

Presidents	Cabinet Officers	Home	Apptd.
Wilson	William C. Redfield	N. Y.	1913
"	Josh. W. Alexander	Mo	1919
Harding	Herbert C. Hoover	Cal	1921
Coolidge	"	"	1923
"	William F. Whiting	Mass	1928
Hoover	Robert P. Lamont	Ill	1929
"	Roy D. Chapin	Mich	1932
F.D.Roosevelt	Daniel C. Roper	S. C.	1933
"	Harry L. Hopkins	N. Y.	1939
"	Jesse Jones	Texas	1940
"	Henry A. Wallace	Ia	1945
Truman	"	"	1945
"	W. Averell Harriman	N. Y.	1947
"	Charles Sawyer	Ohio	1948
Eisenhower	Sinclair Weeks	Mass	1953
"	Lewis L. Strauss	N. Y.	1958
"	Frederick H. Mueller	Mich	1959
Kennedy	Luther H. Hodges	N. C	1961
Johnson, L. B.	John T. Connor	N. J.	1965
"	Alex B. Trowbridge	N. J.	1967
"	C. R. Smith	N. Y	1968
Nixon	Maurice H. Stans	Minn	1969
"	Peter G. Peterson	Ill.	1972
"	Frederick B. Dent	S.C.	1973

Secretaries of Transportation

The Department of Transportation was created by Act of Congress Oct. 15, 1966.

President	Cabinet Officer	Home	Apptd.	President	Cabinet Officer	Home	Apptd.
Johnson, L. B.	Alan S. Boyd	Fla	1966	Nixon	John A. Volpe	Mass.	1969
				"	Claude S. Brinegar	Calif.	1973

Great Seal of the United States

The Great Seal of the United States was first adopted by the Continental Congress, June 20, 1782, and by the Federal Government Sept. 16, 1789. The Secretary of State is its custodian. Only one face is used on documents.

A representation of the Great Seal is in the hands of every American citizen who possesses a $1 bill. On the back of the bill both sides of the seal are shown. The face of the seal, on the right hand side of the bill, shows an American eagle with wings and talons outstretched. Above his head is a circle containing 13 "pieces argent," or silver buttons; the eagle's breast holds a shield with 13 stripes; the right talon holds an olive branch and the left talon a bundle of 13 arrows. In its beak the eagle holds a ribbon with the motto E Pluribus Unum–Out of Many, One, referring to the union of the states.

On the reverse the seal shows an unfinished pyramid. Above the pyramid is a "glory" or burst of light, with an eye inside a triangle, referring to the Eternal Eye of God, and above it is the motto Annuit Coeptis, meaning He Has Favored Our Undertaking. The base of the pyramid bears the numerals MDCCLXXVI, or 1776, and below it is the motto Novus Ordo Seclorum, or A New Order of the Ages. The pyramid has 13 steps and signifies the strength of the union.

Presidents of the United States

According to a ruling of the State Dept., Grover Cleveland is counted twice, as the 22nd and the 24th President, because his two terms were not consecutive. Only 36 individuals have been President.

No.	Name	Politics	Native State	Date Born	Inau. At Age	Date of Death	Age at Death
1..	George Washington	Fed	Va	1732, Feb. 22	1789.. 57	1799, Dec. 14	67
2..	John Adams	Fed	Mass	1735, Oct. 30	1797.. 61	1826, July 4	90
3..	Thomas Jefferson	Dem.-Rep ...	Va...	1743, April 13	1801.. 57	1826, July 4	83
4..	James Madison	Dem.-Rep ...	Va	1751, March 16	1809.. 57	1836, June 28	85
5..	James Monroe.	Dem.-Rep ...	Va	1758, April 28	1817.. 58	1831, July 4	73
6..	John Quincy Adams	Dem.-Rep ...	Mass	1767, July 11	1825.. * 57	1848, Feb. 23	80
7..	Andrew Jackson	Dem	S. C.	1767, March 15	1829.. 61	1845, June 8	78
8..	Martin Van Buren	Dem	N. Y.	1782, Dec. 5	1837.. 54	1862, July 24	79
9..	William Henry Harrison	Whig	Va.	1773, Feb. 9	1841.. 68	1841, April 4	68
10..	John Tyler................	Whig	Va.	1790, March 29	1841.. 51	1862, Jan. 18	71
11..	James Knox Polk	Dem	N. C.	1795, Nov. 2	1845.. 49	1849, June 15	53
12..	Zachary Taylor	Whig	Va.	1784, Nov. 24	1849.. 64	1850, July 9	65
13..	Millard Fillmore	Whig	N. Y.	1800, Jan. 7	1850.. 50	1874, March 8	74
14..	Franklin Pierce.	Dem	N. H.	1804, Nov. 23	1853.. 48	1869, Oct. 8	64
15..	James Buchanan..........	Dem	Pa.	1791, April 23	1857.. 65	1868, June 1	77
16..	Abraham Lincoln..........	Rep.......	Ky.	1809, Feb. 12	1861.. 52	1865, April 15	56
17..	Andrew Johnson	(see note)	N. C.	1808, Dec. 29	1865.. 56	1875, July 31	66
18..	Ulysses Simpson Grant	Rep.......	Ohio	1822, April 27	1869.. 46	1885, July 23	63
19..	Rutherford Birchard Hayes...	Rep.......	Ohio	1822, Oct. 4	1877.. 54	1893, Jan. 17	70
20..	James Abram Garfield	Rep.......	Ohio	1831, Nov. 19	1881.. 49	1881, Sept. 19	49
21..	Chester Alan Arthur.......	Rep.......	Vt.	1830, Oct. 5	1881.. 50	1886, Nov. 18	56
22..	Grover Cleveland	Dem	N. J.	1837, March 18	1885.. 47	1908, June 24	71
23..	Benjamin Harrison	Rep.......	Ohio	1833, Aug. 20	1889.. 55	1901, March 13	67
24..	Grover Cleveland	Dem	N. J.	1837, March 18	1893.. 55	1908, June 24	71
25..	William McKinley	Rep.......	Ohio	1843, Jan. 29	1897.. 54	1901, Sept. 14	58
26..	Theodore Roosevelt	Rep.......	N. Y.	1858, Oct. 27	1901.. 42	1919, Jan. 6	60
27..	William Howard Taft	Rep.......	Ohio	1857, Sept. 15	1909.. 51	1930, March 8	72
28..	Woodrow Wilson	Rep.......	Va.	1856, Dec. 28	1913.. 56	1924, Feb. 3	67
29..	Warren Gamaliel Harding....	Rep.......	Ohio	1865, Nov. 2	1921.. 55	1923, Aug. 2	57
30..	Calvin Coolidge	Rep.......	Vt.	1872, July 4	1923.. 51	1933, Jan 5	60
31..	Herbert Clark Hoover......	Rep.......	Iowa	1874, Aug. 10	1929.. 54	1964, Oct. 20	90
32..	Franklin Delano Roosevelt ..	Dem	N. Y.	1882, Jan. 30	1933.. 51	1945, April 12	63
33..	Harry S. Truman	Dem	Mo.	1884, May 8	1945.. 60	1972, Dec. 26	88
34..	Dwight David Eisenhower....	Rep.......	Texas	1890, Oct. 14	1953.. 62	1969, Mar. 28	78
35..	John F. Kennedy	Dem	Mass.	1917, May 29	1961.. 43	1963, Nov. 22	46
36..	Lyndon Baines Johnson	Dem	Texas	1908, Aug. 27	1963.. 55	1973, Jan. 22	64
37..	Richard Milhous Nixon	Rep.......	Calif.	1913, Jan. 9	1969.. 56	....	

Andrew Johnson—a Democrat, nominated vice president by Republicans and elected with Lincoln on National Union ticket.

Wives and Children of the Presidents

Presidents*	Wife's Name	*Nativity	Born	Married	Died	Sons	Daughters
Washington	Martha (Dandridge) Custis	Va....	1732	1759	1802	......	......
John Adams.........	Abigail Smith	Mass..	1744	1764	1818	3	2
Jefferson	Martha (Wayles) Skelton	Va....	1748	1772	1782	1	5
Madison.............	Dorothea ("Dolley")(Payne)Todd..	N. Car.	1768	1794	1849	......	......
Monroe.............	Elizabeth Kortwright[2]	N. Y.	1768	1786	1830	......	2
J. Q. Adams	Louisa Catherine Johnson[1]	Md	1775	1797	1852	3	1
Jackson	Rachel (Donelson) Robards.......	Va....	1767	1791	1828	......	......
Van Buren..........	Hannah Hoes	N. Y.	1783	1807	1819	4	......
William H. Harrison ..	Anna Symmes	N. J.	1775	1795	1864	6	4
Tyler..............	Letitia Christian[2]	Va....	1790	1813	1842	3	4
	Julia Gardiner	N. Y.	1820	1844	1889	5	2
Polk..............	Sarah Childress	Tenn.	1803	1824	1891	......	......
Taylor	Margaret Smith	Md ...	1788	1810	1852	1	5
Fillmore	Abigail Powers...........	N. Y.	1798	1826	1853	1	1
	Caroline (Carmichael) McIntosh	N. J..	1813	1858	1881	......	......
Pierce	Jane Means Appleton.......	N. H.	1806	1834	1863	3	......
Lincoln	Mary Todd	Ky..	1818	1842	1882	4	......
Johnson, Andrew	Eliza McCardle	Tenn.	1810	1827	1876	3	2
Grant.............	Julia Dent	Mo..	1826	1848	1902	3	1
Hayes	Lucy Ware Webb	Ohio.	1831	1852	1889	7	1
Garfield	Lucretia Rudolph	Ohio.	1832	1858	1918	4	1
Arthur.............	Ellen Lewis Herndon	Va..	1837	1859	1880	2	1
Cleveland...........	Frances Folsom	N. Y.	1864	1886	1947	2	3
Benjamin Harrison	Caroline Lavinia Scott	Ohio.	1832	1853	1892	1	1
	Mary Scott (Lord) Dimmock.....	Pa..	1858	1896	1948	......	1
McKinley...........	Ida Saxton	Ohio.	1847	1871	1907	......	2
Theodore Roosevelt....	Alice Hathaway Lee	Mass..	1861	1880	1884	......	1
	Edith Kermit Carow	Conn..	1861	1886	1948	4	1
Taft	Helen Herron...........	Ohio.	1861	1886	1943	2	1
Wilson	Ellen Louise Axson	Ga..	1860	1885	1914	......	3
	Edith (Bolling) Galt...........	Va..	1872	1915	1961	......	......
Harding	Florence (Kling) De Wolfe	Ohio.	1860	1891	1924	......	......
Coolidge............	Grace Anna Goodhue	Vt..	1879	1905	1957	2	......
Hoover.............	Lou Henry	Iowa..	1875	1899	1944	2	......
F. D. Roosevelt	Anna Eleanor Roosevelt[2]	N. Y.	1884	1905	1962	4	1
Truman	Bess Wallace	Mo..	1885	1919	....	......	1
Eisenhower	Mamie Geneva Doud[2]	Iowa..	1896	1916	....	1	......
Kennedy	Jacqueline Lee Bouvier[2]	N. Y.	1929	1953	....	1	1
Johnson, Lyndon	Claudia Alta Taylor...........	Texas	1912	1934	....	......	2
Nixon, Richard	Patricia Ryan	Nevada	1912	1940	....	......	2

*James Buchanan, 15th president, was unmarried. (1.) Born London, father a Maryland citizen. (2.) Plus 1 infant, dec'd.

Biographies—Presidents and Their Wives

GEORGE WASHINGTON

George Washington, first Pres., was born Friday, Feb. 22, 1732 (Feb. 11, 1731, Old Style), the son of Augustine Washington and Mary Ball, at Wakefield on Pope's creek, Westmoreland Co., Va. Col. John Washington, George's great-grandfather, came from Northamptonshire in 1657 or 1658; in 1665 he and an associate named Spencer bought 5,000 acres on the Potomac. George's father took the north 2,500 acres near Hunting creek in 1735 and built a house in which George lived from 3 to 6 years of age; when 6 the family moved to Ferry farm, near Fredericksburg. His father died in 1743 when he was 11. He studied mathematics and surveying and when 16 went to live with his half brother Lawrence, who had inherited the Potomac farm and built Mount Vernon, the original house having burned. George surveyed the lands of William Fairfax on the Shenandoah, keeping a diary. He accompanied Lawrence to Barbados, West Indies, contracted small pox and was deeply scarred. Lawrence died in 1752 and George acquired his property by inheritance and purchase and added the 2,500 acres held by the Spencers. He valued land and when he died owned 70,000 acres in Virginia and 40,000 acres on the Great Kanawa and environs.

Washington's military service began in 1753 when Gov. Dinwiddie of Virginia made him lieut. colonel of militia. He clashed with the French and had to surrender Fort Necessity July 3, 1754. He was an aide to Braddock and helped organize the retreat after the fatal ambuscade of July 9, 1755. He helped take Fort DuQuesne from the French in 1758.

After his marriage to Martha Dandridge Custis, 1759, Washington lived at Mount Vernon, bred horses and cattle, raised fruit and practiced crop rotation. In 1773 he enlarged the house. During the stamp act agitation, 1765, he supported the protesting Virginians. Although not at first for independence, he stood out against British exactions and took charge of the Virginia troops before war broke out. He was made commander-in-chief by the Continental Congress June 15, 1775, and took command at Cambridge July 3.

The successful issue of a war filled with hardships was largely due to his leadership. He was resourceful, a stern disciplinarian, and the one strong, dependable force for unity. He favored a federal government and became chairman of the Constitutional convention of 1787. He helped get the Constitution ratified and was unanimously elected President and inaugurated, April 30, 1789, on the balcony of New York's Federal hall at Broad and Wall Sts., now marked by his statue. In New York his mansion, near Franklin Sq., was the scene of formal dinners and levees. His pew in St. Paul's chapel is preserved.

His birthplace, Wakefield, was burned in 1780. On Feb. 22, 1932, a new Wakefield, built by donations, was dedicated as the George Washington Birthplace Monument, administered by the National Parks Service. The older Washingtons are buried there. It is 34 miles from Fredericksburg, Va., on State road 3, and five miles from Stratford Hall, birthplace of Robert E. Lee.

Although a Federalist, Washington made Thomas Jefferson secretary of state (resigned 1793). He was re-elected 1792, but refused to consider a third term and retired to Mount Vernon, 1797. He suffered acute laryngitis after a ride in snow and rain around his estate, was bled profusely, and died Dec. 14, 1799, aged 67. He was mourned here and abroad as one of the great men of his time. He was buried in a vault at Mount Vernon. (See article on Mount Vernon.) He willed Mount Vernon to his nephew, Bushrod Washington (1762-1829), associate justice, U. S. Supreme Court.

Martha Washington

Mrs. Martha Dandridge Custis Washington was born June 2, 1732, in New Kent Co., Va. In 1749 she married Daniel Parke Custis, wealthy planter, who died in 1757. She lived in the White House on the Pamunkey, site of McClellan's supply depot in 1862. (Her house had burned down and been replaced before the Civil War.) In 1758 Washington, hurrying to Williamsburg, was invited by the owner of Poplar Grove to meet "the prettiest and richest widow in Virginia." She was plump, small, had dark hair and hazel eyes. Washington fell, and on his return from taking Fort DuQuesne they were married, Jan. 6, 1759. Martha had two children living, two having died in infancy. Her daughter Martha died at 17. Her son, Col. John Parke Custis, bought the 1,100 acres of Arlington in 1778, but died 1781, from wounds received at Yorktown. Washington adopted John's son, George Washington Parke Custis, who inherited Arlington and built the present house; his daughter Mary married Robert E. Lee there in 1831. Martha Washington managed her husband's plantations in his absence and in winter visited him at Valley Forge, Newburgh and other camps. She presided gracefully at official levees as Lady Washington. She died in 1802 and was buried at Mount Vernon.

JOHN ADAMS

John Adams, 2nd President, Federalist, was born in Braintree (Quincy), Mass., Oct. 30, 1735 (Oct. 19, O. S.), the son of John Adams, a farmer and Susanna Boylston of Brookline. He was a great-grandson of Henry Adams who came from England in 1636. He was graduated from Harvard, 1755, taught school, studied law. In 1765 he argued against taxation without representation before the royal governor. In 1770 he defended the British soldiers, who fired on civilians in the "Boston Massacre." He took part in the Provincial Congress of Massachusetts and the Continental Congress, seconded the independence resolution presented by Richard Henry Lee and with his cousin, Samuel Adams, signed the Declaration of Independence. He was a commissioner to France, 1778, with Benjamin Franklin and Arthur Lee; won recognition of the United States by The Hague, 1782; was first American minister to England, 1785-1788, and elected vice president with Washington, 1788 and 1792.

In 1796 Adams was chosen President by the electors, 71 to 68 so that opponents called him "president by 3 votes." The candidate with the second highest number of votes became vice president; this was Thomas Jefferson, his opponent. Intense antagonism to America by France caused agitation for war, led by Alexander Hamilton. Adams, breaking with Hamilton, opposed war but put the Navy on a fighting basis. The U.S.S. Constitution, the United States, both 44 guns, and the Constellation, 36 guns, and armed merchantmen bagged 84 French ships in an undeclared war. To fight alien influence and muzzle criticism Adams supported the Alien and Sedition laws of 1798, which led to his defeat for reelection. He died July 4, 1826, on the same day as Jefferson, and was buried in the First Unitarian church in Quincy, Mass.

Abigail Adams

Mrs. Abigail Smith Adams was born at Weymouth, Mass., Nov. 23, 1744 (Nov. 12, O. S.), daughter of a Congregational minister and descendant of the Puritan divine, Thomas Shepard of Cambridge, Mass. She died at Quincy, Oct. 28, 1818. She had two daughters and three sons, one of whom, John Quincy Adams, became the sixth President. Often separated from John Adams during the Revolution, she joined him in Paris in 1784, and from 1785 to 1788 endured social slights at the court of St. James's, where Adams was our first minister. When New York was the seat of Washington's administration she lived at Richmond Hill, a manor house located where Charlton crosses Varick St. She was known for her sharp criticism of Adams' opponents.

THOMAS JEFFERSON

Thomas Jefferson, 3rd President, was born April 13, 1743 (Apr. 2, O. S.) at Shadwell, Va., the son of Peter Jefferson, a civil engineer of Welsh descent who raised tobacco, and Jane Randolph. Jefferson was an agrarian, an expansionist; because he opposed the Federalists and centralization he was called a Republican, now synonymous with Democrat. His father died when he was 14, leaving him 2,750 acres and his slaves. Jefferson attended the College of William and Mary, 1760-1762, read classics in Greek and Latin; played the violin and rode horses. In 1769 he was elected to the House of Burgesses. In 1770 Shadwell burned and he began Monticello, near Charlottesville. In 1772 he married Martha Wayles Skelton. He was a member of the Virginia Committee of Correspondence and the Continental Congress and denied Britain's right to tax. Named a member of the committee to draw up a Declaration of Independence, he wrote the basic draft, 1776. He was a member of the Virginia House of Delegates, 1776-79, elected governor to succeed Patrick Henry, 1779, re-elected 1780, resigned, June 1781, amid charges of ineffectual military preparation. During his term he wrote the statute on religious freedom. In the Continental Congress, 1783, he drew up an ordinance for the Northwest Territory, forbidding slavery after 1800; its terms were put into the Ordinance of 1787. He was sent to Paris with Benjamin Franklin and John Adams to negotiate treaties of commerce, 1784; made minister to France, 1785, he made treaties with France and Prussia, studied architecture, gardening and the French Revolution, whose leaders consulted him.

Washington, appointed him secretary of state, 1789. Jefferson's strong faith in the consent of the governed, as opposed to executive control favored by Hamilton, secretary of the treasury, often led to conflict: Dec. 31, 1793, he resigned. He was the Republican candidate for President in 1796; beaten by John Adams, he became vice president. He opposed Adams' alien and sedition laws with the Kentucky and Virginia resolutions, reiterating the basic rights of states. In 1800 Jefferson and Aaron Burr received equal votes for President, so the House of Representatives, with Hamilton's help, elected Jefferson, the first President to be inaugurated in Washington. Adams left town before the ceremony, but when Jefferson was re-elected in 1804 he voted for him. Jefferson cancelled levees and titles and ignored diplomatic precedence. He turned Federalists out of office. He opposed a strong navy. By fighting those who feared to give power to the people he made democracy work. He considered John Marshall's Supreme Court reactionary. Big events of his administration were the Louisiana Purchase, 1803, and the Lewis and Clark Expedition. He established the University of Virginia and designed its buildings. After the Library of Congress was burned by the British he sold Congress some 6,000 vols. for $23,950. He was 6 ft. 2, temperate in debate, a deist in religion. He died July 4, 1826, on the same day as John Adams and was buried at Monticello, which, after various vicissitudes, passed to the Thomas Jefferson Memorial Foundation in 1923.

Mrs. Thomas Jefferson

Mrs. Martha Wayles Jefferson, daughter of John Wayles, was 23 and the widow of Bathurst Skelton when she married Jefferson Jan. 1, 1772. She bore Jefferson six children at Monticello, two of whom lived to maturity. Martha, 1772-1836, married Thomas Mann Randolph, Jr; Mary (Marie) 1778-1804, married her cousin, J. W. Eppes. Mrs. Jefferson's father's large farm and slaves became part of the estate. She died Sept. 6, 1782.

JAMES MADISON

James Madison, 4th Pres., Republican, was born Mar. 16, 1751 (Mar. 5, 1750, O. S.) at Port Conway, King George Co., Va., the eldest of 12 children of James Madison and Eleanor Rose Conway. His great-grandfather, James Taylor (1674-1729), was also the great-grandfather of Zachary Taylor. Madison was graduated from Princeton, 1771, studied theology, 1772, sat in the Virginia Constitutional Convention, 1776, where his resolution on religious freedom was voted down; was a member of the Continental Congress and of the Annapolis convention, 1786, where he and Hamilton proposed the Constitutional

Convention. He was chief recorder at that convention in 1787, and supported ratification in the Federalist papers, written with Hamilton and Jay. In 1785 he carried Jefferson's statute on religious liberty through the Virginia assembly. He was elected to the House of Representatives in 1789, helped adopt the Bill of Rights and fought John Adams' alien and sedition laws. He favored agrarian policies with Jefferson and in 1801 became Jefferson's secretary of state. In 1803, when the Louisiana Purchase was consummated, he insisted on free navigation of the Mississippi, which he had already urged on Jay in 1780.

Elected President in 1808, Madison was a "strict constructionist," opposed to the free interpretation of the Constitution by the Federalists; he vetoed federal funds for state improvements, but changed in his second term. Madison inherited the conflict with Britain over its orders in council and impressment of American seamen, which had led to Jefferson's embargo act and injured American commerce. He was reelected in 1812 by the votes of the agrarian South and recently admitted western states. Caught between British and French maritime restrictions, Madison drifted into war, declared June 18, 1812, unaware that Britain had cancelled the orders two days before. While the war was inconclusive, it opened the way to peaceful negotiations. Madison successfully advocated a tariff to protect industry, a national system of roads and canals and a strong military organization. He retired in 1817 to his estate at Montpelier in Orange County, Va., built 1760, with a portico suggested by Jefferson. There he edited his famous papers on the Constitutional Convention. He became rector of the Univ. of Virginia, 1826. He died June 28, 1836, and was buried near his home.

Dolley Madison

Mrs. Dorothea (Dolley) Payne Madison, was born May 12, 1768, in North Carolina, daughter of John Payne, a Virginia Quaker, who freed his slaves. She grew up in Hanover County, Va. Her first husband, John Todd, died in 1793. She married Madison Sept. 15, 1794, and when he became secretary of state in 1801, became hostess for Jefferson in the White House. She presided at the first inaugural ball in 1809. She is supposed to have rescued Gilbert Stuart's portrait of Washington from the White House when the British came Aug. 24, 1814. She helped edit Madison's records of the Constitutional Convention. From 1817 to 1837 she lived at Montpellier, Orange Co., Va., (now Montpelier, privately owned). She returned to Washington as a welcome, but impecunious, social leader, in 1837. Congress bought her husband's records in 1837 for $30,000, and other papers in 1848, for $25,000. She took part in the dedication of the Washington monument and sent the first personal message over S. F. B. Morse's telegraph wire. She was respected for her tact and intelligence by presidents from Washington to Polk. In old age she suffered from the wastefulness of a son. She died July 12, 1849, aged 81, and is buried beside Madison at Montpelier Station.

JAMES MONROE

James Monroe, 5th President, Republican, was born April 28, 1758, in Westmoreland Co., Va., the son of Spence Monroe and Eliza Jones, who were of Scottish and Welsh descent, respectively. He attended the College of William and Mary, fought in the 3rd Virginia regiment at White Plains, Brandywine, Monmouth, and was wounded at Trenton. He studied law with Thomas Jefferson, 1780, was a member of the Virginia house of delegates and of Congress, 1783-86. He opposed ratification of the Constitution because it lacked a bill of rights; was U.S. Senator, 1790; minister to France, Spain and Algiers; four times governor of Virginia, 1799-1802, and 1811, Jefferson sent him to France as minister, 1803, to join R. R. Livingston in buying the isle of New Orleans from France and East and West Florida from Spain. Exceeding instructions, he signed a treaty for all of Louisiana. (Navigation of the Mississippi was one of his demands as early as 1783.) He was also sent to Madrid, 1804, and London, 1805, to settle disputes. He ran against Madison for President in 1808. He was chosen member of the Virginia Assembly, 1810-1811; secretary of state under Madison, 1811-1817; also secretary of war Sept. 1814-Mar., 1815.

In 1816 Monroe was elected President; in 1820 re-elected with all but one vote, this being cast for John Quincy Adams by William Plumer, Sr., of New Hampshire. Although many historians have held that Plumer withheld his vote from Monroe so that only Washington would have been elected unanimously, Plumer himself said he voted for Adams because he had "discovered a want of foresight" in Monroe. Monroe's administration became the Era of Good Feeling. He obtained the Floridas from Spain and suppressed the Seminoles; settled boundaries with Canada and eliminated border forts; supported the anti-slavery position that led to the Missouri Compromise. (In 1801 he had proposed settling Negro slaves in Africa. Monrovia, Liberia, was named for him.) In July, 1823, the U. S. served notice on Russia that it would oppose any Russian colony on this continent, after Russia had prohibited fishing on the northwest coasts. On Dec. 2, 1823, Monroe announced the Doctrine that the U. S. would consider its safety endangered if European powers had authority on this hemisphere or attempted colonization. First half had been suggested by George Canning, British foreign minister, to curb Spain; U. S., rejecting proposal for joint declaration, issued it also as warning to Russia. Monroe owned Ash Lawn, 5 mi. from Charlottesville, Va., 1799-1825; inherited Oak Hill, Loudon Co., Va., from his uncle Jos. Jones, 1806. The mansion, replacing Jones' cottage, was designed by Jefferson and executed by Jas. Hoban, White-House architect. He moved to New York, 1830, with his two daughters, and died there July 4, 1831, and was buried in Marble cemetery. In 1858 his remains were removed to Richmond.

Mrs. James Monroe

Mrs. Elizabeth Kortwright Monroe was born in New York, 1768, the daughter of Lawrence Kortwright, formerly British army officer. She married Monroe in 1786. They had a son, who died in infancy, and two daughters. Mrs. Monroe died in 1830 at Oak Hill.

JOHN QUINCY ADAMS

John Quincy Adams, 6th President, independent Federalist, was born July 11, 1767, at Braintree (Quincy), Mass., the son of John and Abigail Adams. He was educated in Paris, Leyden, and Harvard, graduating in 1787. He served as American minister in the Netherlands, Berlin, St. Petersburg and London and helped draft the peace treaty of 1814. He had served as senator from 1803 to 1808 and his support of the Republican administration alienated the Federalists. President Monroe made him secretary of state, 1817, and he negotiated the cession of the Floridas from Spain, supported exclusion of slavery in the Missouri Compromise, and laid the base for the Monroe Doctrine, of which he, as much as Monroe, was the creator. In 1824 he was elected President by the House after he failed to win an Electoral College majority over Henry Clay and Andrew Jackson. His expansion of executive powers was strongly opposed and he was beaten in 1828 by Jackson. In 1831 he was sent to Congress as representative and served nine terms with distinction and independence. He fought slavery, opposed the annexation of Texas and the war with Mexico; was responsible for the Smithsonian Institution. He had a stroke in the House and died in the Speaker's room, Feb. 23, 1848.

Mrs. John Quincy Adams

Mrs. Louisa Catherine Johnson Adams was born in London, Feb. 12, 1775, the daughter of Joshua Johnson, a Marylander who acted as American fiscal agent there. She married Adams July 26, 1797. Of their four children, George Washington Adams, John Q. Adams, Jr., Charles

Francis Adams and Louisa Catherine Adams, Charles Francis became Free Soil candidate for vice president in 1848, member of Congress, minister to England during the Civil War and president of the Geneva Board of Arbitration. He was father of Charles Francis Adams, Henry Adams and Brooks Adams.

ANDREW JACKSON

Andrew Jackson, 7th President, originally Jeffersonian-Republican, later first Democrat, was born in the Waxhaws district, New Lancaster Co., S. C., Mar. 15, 1767, the posthumous son of Andrew Jackson, who came from County Antrim, Ireland, and his wife, Elizabeth Hutchinson, and two sons, in 1765. At 13 he joined the militia in the Revolution and was captured; a British officer struck Andrew with his sword when the boy refused to shine his boots. He read law in Salisbury, N. C., moved to Nashville, Tenn., speculated in land, married and raised cotton at the Hermitage, originally a log house. In 1796 he helped draft the Constitution of Tennessee and for one year occupied its one seat in the national House. He was in the Senate in 1797, and again in 1823. He defeated the Creek Indians at Horseshoe Bend, Ala., 1814, and as major general, U. S. A., drove the British out of Pensacola. With 6,000 backwoods fighters he defeated Packenham's 12,000 British troops at Chalmette, outside New Orleans, Jan. 8, 1815, losing only seven to the British loss of 2,000. In 1818 he fought so recklessly against the Seminoles in Florida that he endangered foreign relations. In 1824 he ran for President against John Quincy Adams and was voted down by the House, though he had the most votes; in 1828 he carried everything, the West rising to support "Old Hickory" and a liberal land policy. He was a noisy debater and duelist and introduced rotation in office or "spoils system." He was suspicious of privilege; ruined the Bank of the United States by depositing federal funds with state banks. Though "Let the people rule" was his slogan, he at times supported strict constructionist policies against the expansionist West. He killed the Congressional caucus for nominating presidential candidates and substituted the national convention, 1832, when he was re-elected, with Martin Van Buren vice president. When South Carolina refused to collect imports under his protective tariff he ordered army and naval forces to Charleston. At the Jefferson Day dinner, 1830, he offered the toast: "Our Federal Union; it must be preserved." Vice President John C. Calhoun, exponent of state sovereignty, gave in reply the toast: "The Union—next to our liberty, most dear." Jackson recognized the Republic of Texas, 1836. His party took the name of Democrat. He died at the Hermitage, June 8, 1845, and is buried there.

Mrs. Andrew Jackson

Mrs. Rachel Jackson was the daughter of Col. John Donelson, a surveyor at Nashville, and first married Capt. Lewis Robards. Under the impression that Robards had obtained a divorce she married Jackson in Natchez in 1791. Robards did not get a divorce until 1793, when the Jacksons were remarried, but the ordeal affected her spirits. She died in 1828 after Jackson's election and never lived in the White House. Jackson adopted her sister's son, named him Andrew Jackson, Jr. White House hostesses were his wife's niece, Mrs. Emily Donelson, and the adopted son's wife, Mrs. Sarah York Jackson, a Philadelphia Quaker.

MARTIN VAN BUREN

Martin Van Buren, 8th President, Democrat, was born Dec. 5, 1782, at Kinderhook, N. Y., the son of Abraham Van Buren, a Dutch farmer, and Mary Hoes. He was surrogate of Columbia county, New York, state senator and attorney general and a law partner of Benj. F. Butler in Albany. He was U. S. senator, 1821, re-elected, 1827, elected governor of New York, 1828. He helped swing eastern support to Andrew Jackson in 1828 and was his secretary of state 1829-31. In 1832 he was elected vice president. He was a consummate politician, known as "the little magician," and influenced Jackson's policies. In 1836 he defeated William Henry Harrison for President by 170 to 73 electoral votes. He inaugurated the independent treasury system, and was the first advocate of mutual insurance of deposits by banks. He advocated tariff for revenue only and opposed internal improvements at national expense. His refusal to spend land revenues led to his defeat by Harrison in 1840. He lost the Democratic nomination of 1844 to Polk because he opposed annexation of Texas. In 1848 he ran for President on the Free Soil ticket and lost. Thus he ran three times. He died July 24, 1862 at Kinderhook, N. Y.

Mrs. Martin Van Buren

Mrs. Hannah Hoes Van Buren, born 1783, was a relative of Van Buren's mother and his classmate in school. She married in 1807, died 1819. Their son Abraham, 1807-1873, a West Pointer, was secretary to the President, an officer in the Mexican war and a New York resident. His wife, Angelica Singleton, cousin of Dolley Madison, was White House hostess during Van Buren's term. Another son, John Van Buren (1810-1866), was elected attorney general of New York, 1845.

WILLIAM HENRY HARRISON

William Henry Harrison, 9th President, Whig, who served only 31 days, was born in Berkeley, Charles City Co., Va., Feb. 9, 1773, the third son of Benjamin Harrison, signer of the Declaration of Independence. Educated at Hampden Sydney college, he later studied medicine under Dr. Benjamin Rush. Commissioned by Washington, he fought under Gen. Anthony Wayne at Fallen Timbers, 1794. He was secretary of Northwest Terr., 1798; its delegate in Congress, 1799; first governor of Indiana Terr., and supt. of Indian affairs. With 900 men he routed Tecumseh's Indians at Tippecanoe, Nov. 7, 1811. A major general, he defeated British and Indians at Battle of the Thames, Oct. 5, 1813. He served Ohio in Congress, 1816; as senator, 1824; was minister to Colombia. In 1840, when 68, he was elected President with John Tyler, 234 to 60, on a "log cabin and hard cider" slogan. He caught pneumonia during the inauguration and died April 4, 1841. He was buried in North Bend, O.

Mrs. William Henry Harrison

Mrs. Anna Symmes Harrison, daughter of Col. John Cleves Symmes, chief justice of the New Jersey Supreme Court and Revolutionary veteran, was born in Morristown, N. J., 1775, and died 1864. She did not leave her North Bend, O., home for Washington and Mrs. Jane Findlay Irwin Harrison, wife of her son, Col. W. H. Harrison, Jr., stayed in the White House during Harrison's illness. Another son, John Scott Harrison, 1804-1878, was member of Congress and father of Benjamin Harrison, 23rd President.

JOHN TYLER

John Tyler, 10th President, Independent Whig, was born Mar. 29, 1790, in Greenway, Charles City Co., Va., son of John Tyler and Mary Armistead. His father was governor of Virginia, 1808-11. Tyler was graduated from William and Mary, 1807; member of the House of Delegates, 1811; in Congress, 1816-21; in Virginia legislature, 1823-25; governor of Virginia, 1825-26; U. S. senator, 1827-36. In 1836 he was defeated for vice president on a states' rights Whig ticket with Harrison and succeeded him. He favored pre-emption, allowing settlers to get government land; rejected a new bank bill and thus alienated Whig supporters except Daniel Webster, his secretary of state; refused to honor the spoils system. He signed the resolution annexing Texas, Mar. 1, 1845. He accepted renomination, 1844, but withdrew before election. He condemned South Carolina's nullification

and secession and as Virginia's commissioner to Buchanan tried to keep Fort Sumter neutralized. He was president of the peace congress called in Washington by Virginia, 1861. After its failure he supported secession, sat in the provisional Confederate congress, became a member of the Confederate House, but died, Jan. 18, 1862, before it met. He is buried in Richmond.

Marriages of John Tyler

When 23 John Tyler married **Letitia Christian** of Cedar Grove, Va., born 1790, daughter of a planter. She was an invalid and died in the White House, 1842. She was an Episcopalian. Of her children Robert Tyler, 1818-1877, married Priscilla Cooper, daughter of a tragedian; presided in the White House. On June 23, 1844, in New York, Tyler married **Julia Gardiner,** born 1820, daughter of David Gardiner of Gardiner's Island, N. Y. She became a Catholic, 1872; died, 1889. Her son Lyon Gardiner Tyler became president of William and Mary, 1888; died 1935. Another, David Gardiner Tyler, judge, member of Congress and Confederate veteran, died 1927. A third son, Robert Fitzwalter Tyler, died 1927 at Richmond, aged 70.

JAMES KNOX POLK

James Knox Polk, 11th President, Democrat, was born in Mecklenburg Co., N. C., Nov. 2, 1795, the son of Samuel Polk, farmer and surveyor of Scotch-Irish descent, and Jane Knox. He went to Maury Co., Tenn., 1806; was graduated from the University of North Carolina, 1818; member of the Tenn. state legislature, 1823-25, known as "Napoleon of the Stump." He served in Congress 1825-39 and as speaker 1835-39. He supported Jackson and Van Buren, but was always expansionist. He was governor of Tennessee, 1839-41, being defeated 1841, '43. In 1844, when both Clay and Van Buren announced opposition to annexing Texas, the Democrats made Polk the first dark horse nominee because he demanded control of all Oregon and annexation of Texas. He won 170 to 105. James Buchanan was his secretary of state. He re-established the independent treasury system originated by Van Buren. His expansionist policy was opposed by Clay, Webster, Calhoun; he sent Zachary Taylor and an army to the Mexican border and when Mexicans attacked declared war existed. Abraham Lincoln, a Whig in Congress, opposed his war policy. Polk approved the acquisition of California, Utah and New Mexico (522,568 square miles) as part of America's "manifest destiny," but opposed retaining Mexico by force. He compromised on the Oregon boundary ("54-40 or fight!") by accepting the 49th parallel and giving Vancouver to the British. The Wilmot Proviso, outlawing slavery in new states, was debated in his term. Polk died in Nashville, June 15, 1849, and is buried on the capitol grounds there.

Mrs. James K. Polk

Mrs. Sarah Childress Polk was born in 1803 and married Polk Jan. 1, 1824. Her father was a wealthy planter near Murfreesboro, Tenn. She was educated by the Moravians. The Polks were Methodists and Mrs. Polk prohibited liquor and dancing in the White House. They had no children.

ZACHARY TAYLOR

Zachary Taylor, 12th President, Whig, who served only 16 months, was born Nov. 24, 1784, in Orange Co., Va., the son of Richard Taylor, later collector of the port of Louisville. His grandfather and James Madison's paternal grandmother were brother and sister. Taylor enlisted 1806; was commissioned lieutenant by Jefferson, 1808; fought in the War of 1812, the Black Hawk War, 1832, and the Seminole war, 1837. He became known as Old Rough and Ready. He settled on a plantation near Baton Rouge, La. in 1845 Polk sent him to the Rio Grande; when the Mexicans attacked him, Polk declared war. Taylor was successful at Palo Alto and Resaca de la Palma, May 8 and 9, 1846; occupied Monterey. Polk made him major general but gave many of his troops to Gen. Winfield Scott at Vera Cruz. Taylor, with 5,000 men, defeated Santa Anna's 20,000 at Buena Vista, Feb. 22, 1847. He defeated Scott at the Whig convention, 1848; was elected President over Martin Van Buren (Free Soil) with Millard Fillmore vice pres. He resumed the spoils system and though once a slave-holder worked to have California admitted as a free state. He died of typhus July 9, 1850, and was buried near Louisville.

Mrs. Zachary Taylor

Mrs. Margaret Smith Taylor was born in 1788, the daughter of Walter Smith, Maryland planter. She married Taylor, 1810, died 1852. Of their daughters Elizabeth, Mrs. W.W.S. Bliss, was hostess of the White House; Ann married Dr. Robert Wood, asst. surgeon general, U.S.A.; Sarah Knox married Jefferson Davis, 1835, and died three months later. A son, Richard, 1826-79, served under Stonewall Jackson and became a Confederate general. He died in New York.

MILLARD FILLMORE

Millard Fillmore, 13th President, Whig, was born Jan. 7, 1800, in a log cabin on a farm in Cayuga Co., N.Y., cleared in 1795 by his father, Nathaniel. He was apprenticed to a fuller and dyer; bought his freedom for $30 to study and became a teacher and postmaster in Buffalo, N. Y. He was counsellor of the state supreme court, 1829; in the state assembly, 1829-32; in Congress, 1833-35 and again 1837-43. He opposed the entrance of Texas as slave territory and voted for a protective tariff. He supported the appropriation of $30,000 for Morse's telegraph. In 1844 he was defeated for governor of New York. In 1848 he was elected vice president and succeeded as President July 10, 1850. Daniel Webster was secretary of state until he died, 1852; then Edward Everett. Fillmore favored the compromise of 1850 and signed the Fugitive Slave Law. His policies pleased neither expansionists nor slave-holders and he was not renominated. In 1856 he was nominated by the American (Know-Nothing) party and accepted by the Whigs, but defeated by Buchanan. He was chancellor of the University of Buffalo. He died in Buffalo, Mar. 8, 1874.

Fillmore's two Marriages

The first Mrs. Fillmore, 1798-1853, was **Abigail Powers,** the daughter of Lemuel Powers, a Baptist clergyman of Stillwater, N. Y., and taught school in Cayuga Co. Owing to her poor health her daughter, Mary Abigail (1832-54) was the White House hostess. Their other child was Millard Powers Fillmore (1828-89). The second Mrs. Fillmore was **Mrs. Caroline Carmichael McIntosh,** born in Morristown, N. J., and widow of an Albany merchant. They had no children.

FRANKLIN PIERCE

Franklin Pierce, 14th President, Democrat, was born in Hillsboro, N. H., Nov. 23, 1804, the son of Benjamin Pierce, veteran of the Revolution and governor of New Hampshire, 1827. He attended Exeter and was graduated from Bowdoin, 1824. A lawyer, he served in the New Hampshire House, 1829-32; in Congress, supporting Jackson, 1833; U.S. Senator, 1837-42. He enlisted in the Mexican war, became brigadier general of volunteers and was wounded at Contreras. In 1852 Pierce was nominated on the 49th ballot over Cass, Douglas and Buchanan, defeating Gen. Winfield Scott, Whig. Though against slavery, Pierce was influenced by southern pro-slavery men (Jefferson Davis was his secy. of war) but he ignored the Ostend Manifesto that the U.S. either buy or take Cuba. He approved the Kansas-Nebraska act, leaving slavery to popular vote ("squatter sovereignty"), 1854, and named a pro-slavery governor of Kansas. He signed a reciprocity treaty with Canada and approved

the Gadsden Purchase from Mexico, 1853. He supported Commodore Matthew Perry's opening of Japan, 1854. Pierce died at Concord, N.H., Oct. 8, 1869.

Mrs. Franklin Pierce

Mrs. Jane Means Appleton Pierce was born at Hampton, N. H., 1806, daughter of the Rev. Jesse A. Appleton, president of Bowdoin. The Pierces had three children; one died in infancy, one at 4 and one was killed in a railroad accident at 11. Mrs. Pierce died in 1863.

JAMES BUCHANAN

James Buchanan, 15th President, Federalist, later Democrat, was born of Scottish descent near Mercersburg, Pa., Apr. 23, 1791. He was a volunteer in the War of 1812; graduated from Dickinson, 1809; member Pa. legislature, 1814-16, Congress, 1820-31; Jackson's minister to Russia, 1831-33; senator, 1834-45. As Polk's secy. of state, 1845-49, he ended Oregon dispute with Britain, supported Mexican war and annexation of Texas. As minister to Britain, 1853, he signed the Ostend Manifesto, 1854, urging U.S. to take Cuba. Nominated by Democrats over Pierce and Stephen A. Douglas, he was elected, 1856, over John C. Fremont (Republican) and Millard Fillmore (American Know-Nothing and Whig tickets). On slavery he favored popular sovereignty and choice by state constitutions; he accepted the pro-slavery Dred Scott decision as binding. His support of the pro-slavery Lecompton constitution for Kansas caused a break with Douglas Democrats. He denied the right of states to secede but wanted U.S. constitutional recognition of property rights in slaves and Federal action against fugitives. Buchanan refused demands of South Carolina for Federal property, but also refused to reinforce forts there until too late to help Fort Sumter. A strict constructionist, he desired to keep peace and found no authority for using force. He died at Wheatland, near Lancaster, Pa., June 1, 1868, aged 77.

Buchanan was a bachelor. The mistress of the White House was the daughter of Buchanan's sister Jane, Harriet Lane, whose parents had died when she was a child. The major social event was the visit in 1860 of the Prince of Wales, later Edward VII.

ABRAHAM LINCOLN

Abraham Lincoln, 16th President, Republican, was born Feb. 12, 1809, in a log cabin on a farm then in Hardin Co., Ky., now in Larue. He was the son of Thomas Lincoln (1778-1851), a descendant of Samuel Lincoln, who came with his wife Martha from Hingham, England, 1635, settled at Salem and Hingham, Mass., and had 11 children. Thomas, a carpenter, married Nancy Hanks, June 12, 1806. She was the natural daughter of Lucy Hanks, whose ancestor, Thomas Hanks, came from England to Virginia, 1644. Abe had a sister, Sarah, born 1807, died 1828, and a brother, Thomas, who died in infancy.

The Lincolns moved to Spencer Co., Ind., near Gentryville, when Abe was 7. His mother died Oct. 5, 1818, aged 35. His father married Mrs. Sarah Bush Johnston, 1819; she had a favorable influence on Abe. He was 6 ft., 3 in. tall. Abe made two trips on flatboats to New Orleans, one via the Ohio-Mississippi, 1828, and one via the Illinois-Mississippi, 1831. In 1830 the family moved to Macon County, Ill., where Abe and a cousin split 3,000 fence rails. In 1831 they moved to Coles County. In New Salem, 1831-1837, Lincoln lost election to the Illinois General Assembly, 1832, but won four times later, beginning in 1834. He enlisted in the militia for the Black Hawk War, 1832. In New Salem he ran a store, 1833, surveyed land, 1834-36, was postmaster, 1833-36. Ann Rutledge, whom he is said to have loved, died near New Salem, 1835, aged 19.

In 1837 Lincoln was admitted to the bar and became partner in a Springfield law office. He began practice on 8th Judicial Circuit, 1839. He was a presidential elector, 1839, 1844, 1852, 1856. He failed of nomination for representative, 1843, but was elected to the 30th Congress,

1847. He opposed the Mexican war. He stumped New England for Zachary Taylor, 1848. He refused offices of secretary and governor of Oregon Terr., 1849. He opposed the Kansas-Nebraska Act and extension of slavery, 1854. When elected to the Ill. legislature, 1854, he declined in order to try for the Senate, but failed of election, 1855. He was proposed but not chosen for vice president at the first Republican convention, 1856, and he made 50 speeches for John C. Fremont, presidential nominee.

In 1858 Lincoln had Republican support in the Ill. legislature for the Senate but was defeated by Stephen A. Douglas, Dem., who sponsored the Kansas-Nebraska Act. The issues were debated by Lincoln and Douglas Aug. 21-Oct. 15 at Ottawa, Freeport, Jonesboro, Charleston, Galesburg, Quincy and Alton, Ill.

Lincoln was nominated for President by the Republican party over Wm. H. Seward, an anti-slavery platform, at Chicago, May 18, 1860. He ran against Stephen A. Douglas, northern Democrat; John C. Breckinridge, southern pro-slavery Democrat; John Bell, Constitutional Union party. Lincoln got only 40% of the votes, but 180 electoral votes to 123. South Carolina seceded from the Union Dec. 20, 1860, followed in 1861 by 10 southern states.

Lincoln was inaugurated Mar. 4, 1861. Fort Sumter was attacked Apr. 12, and war ensued. Lincoln called for 75,000 volunteers Apr. 15, and 500,000 May 3. On Sept. 22, 1862, 5 days after the battle of Antietam, he announced that slaves in territory then in rebellion would be free Jan. 1, 1863, date of the Emancipation Proclamation. He reached the highest degree of eloquence at Gettysburg National Cemetery, Nov. 19, 1863.

Lincoln was re-elected, 1864, over Gen. Geo. B. McClellan, Democrat. Lee surrendered April 9, 1865. On April 14 (Good Friday) Lincoln was shot by John Wilkes Booth, actor, in Ford's Theater, Washington. He died the next day. His body lay in state in New York, Chicago and other cities before burial in Springfield, Ill. His estate reached $110,974, most of it saved from his annual salary of $25,000. His humanity, lofty concept of office and generous spirit made him the hero of the common man the world over.

Mrs. Lincoln and Family

Mrs. Mary Todd Lincoln was born in Lexington, Ky., 1818, daughter of a pioneer; moved to Springfield, Ill., 1837, where she married Lincoln Nov. 4, 1842. Her half-sister, Emily, became the wife of Brig. Gen. Ben Hardin Helm of the Confederate Army, who was killed at Chickamauga. Mrs. Lincoln was accused of undue extravagance while in the White House. In 1875 she was temporarily in a mental hospital in Batavia, Ill. She died 1882. The Lincolns had four sons. Edward Baker died 1850; Wm. Wallace, 1862; Thomas ("Tad"), 1871. Robert Todd Lincoln, born Aug. 1, 1843, in Springfield, attended Ill. State Univ., Phillips Exeter Acad., A. B. Harvard, 1864, in Harvard Law School, 1864. Captain, USA, on staff of Grant, 1865. Secy. of War, 1881-85; minister to Great Britain, 1889-93; later pres. Pullman Co. Married Mary Harlan, dau. Sen. Jas. Harlan (Iowa) 1868; children, since deceased, were Abraham (d at 17), Mrs. Chas. Isham, Mrs. Robt. J. Randolph. Robert Todd Lincoln died July 26, 1926, at Manchester, Vt., was buried at Arlington, Va. Gave Library of Congress 18,350 letters and documents of Lincoln's tenure, opened July 26, 1947. The Lincoln family Bible and Bible on which Lincoln took oath of office were given to library by Mrs. Robert Lincoln (d. 1937).

ANDREW JOHNSON

Andrew Johnson, 17th President, Democrat, was born in Raleigh, N. C., Dec. 29, 1808, the son of Jacob Johnson, porter at an inn and church sexton, and Mary McDonough Johnson, who had been a maid at the inn. His father died when he was 5. At 10 he was apprenticed to a tailor. At 16 he ran off to Greenville, Tenn. He became an alderman, 1828; mayor, 1830; state representative and senator, 1835-43; member of Congress, 1843-53; governor of Tennessee, 1853-57; U. S. Senator, 1857-62. He support-

ed John C. Breckinridge against Lincoln in 1860. He had held slaves, but opposed secession and refused to follow Tennessee out of the Union. In March, 1862, Lincoln appointed him military-governor of occupied Tennessee. In 1864 he was nominated for vice president with Lincoln on the National Union ticket to win Democratic support. He succeeded Lincoln as President April 15, 1865,. In a controversy with Congress over the president's power over the South, he proclaimed, May 26, 1865, an amnesty to all Confederates except certain leaders if they would abolish slavery and ratify the 13th amendment. States doing so added anti-Negro provisions that enraged Congress, which intended to enfranchise all Negroes and disenfranchise former Confederates. Congress restored military control over the South. When Johnson removed Edwin M. Stanton, secretary of war, without notifying the Senate, thus repudiating the Tenure of Office Act, the House impeached him for this and other reasons. He was tried by the Senate, which voted 35 for conviction, 19 for acquittal, lacking the two-thirds necessary to convict, May 26, 1868. He was a candidate before the next Democratic convention, but not nominated. He returned to the Senate in 1875, and in a strong speech defended his course. He supported the Lincoln policies, but his conciliatory attitude toward the South was fought by the radical Republicans. Johnson died July 31, 1875, and was buried at Greenville (now Greeneville), where his log-cabin tailor shop and home are museums.

Mrs. Andrew Johnson

Mrs. Eliza McCardle Johnson was born in Leesburg, Tenn., in 1810, the only daughter of a widow in a mountain hamlet when Johnson married her. She helped him get an education. Their daughter Martha, born 1828, educated in Georgetown, D. C., was often a guest at the White House in Polk's administration. In 1857 she married Judge D. T. Patterson. She was mistress of the White House in place of her invalid mother. Another daughter, Mary, married Daniel Stover of Carter Co., Tenn., and had three children; after Stover's death she married W. R. Bacon of Greeneville. Mrs. Johnson died in 1876.

ULYSSES S. GRANT

Ulysses Simpson Grant, 18th President, Republican, was born at Point Pleasant, O., Apr. 27, 1822, son of Jesse R. Grant, a tanner. The next year the family moved to Georgetown, O. Grant's mother was Hannah Simpson. Grant was named Hiram Ulysses, but on entering West Point, 1839, his name was entered as Ulysses Simpson and he adopted it. He was graduated in 1843; and was 1st lieut. and captain under Gens. Taylor and Scott in the Mexican War; resigned, 1854, worked in St. Louis until 1860, then went to Galena, Ill., where his father sold leather and hardware. He became colonel of the 21st Illinois Vols., 1861, then brigadier general; took Forts Henry and Donelson; made maj. gen. of volunteers; fought at Shiloh. Took Vicksburg, became maj. gen. USA., and in Mar., 1864, lieut. gen. He accepted Lee's surrender at Appomattox. In 1866 he was named a full general. President Johnson appointed Grant secretary of war when he suspended Stanton in defiance of the Senate, but Grant was not confirmed. He was nominated on the first ballot, May 30, 1868, and elected over Horatio Seymour, Democrat, 214 vs. 80 electoral votes. The 15th amendment, amnesty bill and civil service reform were events of his administration. The Liberal Republicans opposed him with Horace Greeley, also Democratic nominee, 1872, but he was re-elected. He vetoed the inflation bill, 1874. An attempt by the Stalwarts (Old Guard) to nominate him in 1880 failed. In 1884 the collapse of Grant & Ward, investment house, left him penniless. He began his *Personal Memoirs*, writing while ill of cancer and completing them four days before his death at Mt. McGregor, N.Y., July 23, 1885. The book realized over $450,000. Grant was buried in an imposing tomb on Riverside Drive, New York, where his wife also lies.

Mrs. Ulysses S. Grant

Mrs. Julia Dent Grant (1826-1902) was the daughter of Judge Frederick Dent of St. Louis, son of a Revolutionary officer. She married Grant, Aug. 1848. Their children were Frederick Dent Grant (1850-1912), minister to Austria-Hungary, police commissioner of New York, major general, Spanish-American War; Ulysses, Jr. (1852-1929); Jesse R. (1858-1934); Nellie (1857-1922), who was married in the White House to Capt. Algernon Sartoris, 1874, and in 1912, a widow, married Frank H. Jones, Cleveland's assistant postmaster general.

RUTHERFORD BIRCHARD HAYES

Rutherford Birchard Hayes, 19th President, Republican, was born in Delaware, O., Oct. 4, 1822, the posthumous son of Rutherford Hayes, a farmer, and Sophia Birchard. He was descended from George Hayes, a Scot who reached Windsor, Conn., in 1680. He was raised by his uncle Sardis Birchard, educated in Norwalk, O., and Middletown, Conn., and graduated from Kenyon College, 1842, and Harvard Law school, 1845. He practiced law in Lower Sandusky, O., now Fremont; was city solicitor of Cincinnati, 1858-61. He was major of the 23d Ohio Vols., wounded at South Mountain; became brigadier general and major general by brevet, 1864. He served in Congress 1864-67, supporting Reconstruction and Johnson's impeachment. He was elected governor of Ohio, 1867 and 1869; beaten for Congress 1872; re-elected governor, 1875. He supported the merit principle in appointments, economy, prison reform and public libraries. In 1876 he was nominated for President over James G. Blaine and believed he had lost to Samuel J. Tilden, Democrat, 184 to 163 electoral votes. But Zachariah Chandler, chairman of the Republican National Committee, relying on Republican domination of the South, urged the validity of contesting 22 electoral returns from Florida, South Carolina, Louisiana; also Oregon. Frauds in Louisiana injuring Tilden were permitted to stand. Promises to withdraw troops from the South were reported used to suborn Democrats. The election was judged by an Electoral Commission, appointed by Congress, 8 Republicans and 7 Democrats, who refused to "go behind state returns" and by strict party vote elected Hayes by 185 over 184. Tilden's refusal to fight back was blamed by his party. The withdrawal of troops followed, but handicapped Republican rule, and as Hayes proceeded to reform civil service he alienated political spoilsmen. He advocated repeal of the Tenure of Office Act that had led to Johnson's impeachment. He supported sound money and specie payments. Hayes died in Fremont, O., Jan. 17, 1893.

Mrs. Rutherford B. Hayes

Mrs. Lucy Webb Hayes, born 1831, was the daughter of Dr. James Webb of Chillicothe, O. She married Hayes Dec. 30, 1852. She was an advocate of temperance, as was Hayes, and did not permit alcolholic beverages in the White House. The Hayeses had eight children: Birchard A. (1853-1926); Webb C. (1856-1934); Rutherford P. (1858-1927); Joseph T. (1861-1863); George C. (1864-66); Frances (1867-1950); Scott R. (1871-1923); Manning F. (1873-74). Mrs. Hayes died June, 1889.

JAMES ABRAM GARFIELD

James A. Garfield, 20th President, Republican, was born Nov. 19, 1831, in a log cabin at Orange, Cuyahoga Co., Ohio., the son of Abram and Eliza Ballou Garfield. His father, a canal contractor and farmer from New York, was descended from Edward Garfield, who reached Massachusetts Bay Colony in 1630 and helped found Watertown, Mass.; his mother was a descendant of an owner of Providence Plantation. James was the youngest of four children; his father died in 1833 and his mother supported them. He worked as canal bargeman, farmer and carpenter; got an education at Western Reserve Eclectic, later Hiram College, and was graduated

from Williams in 1856. He became professor of ancient languages and literature at Hiram, then principal. He was in the Ohio senate in 1859. Anti-slavery and anti-secession, he volunteered for the war, became colonel of the 42nd Ohio Infantry and brigadier general in 1862. He fought at Shiloh, was chief of staff for Rosecrans and was made major general for gallantry at Chickamauga. He entered Congress as a radical Republican in 1863; supported specie payment as against paper money (greenbacks). On the electoral commission in 1876 he voted for Hayes against Tilden on strict party lines. He was senator-elect in 1880 when he became the Republican nominee for President. He was chosen on the 36th ballot as a compromise between Gen. Grant, James G. Blaine and John Sherman. This alienated the Grant following but Garfield was elected and Blaine became his secretary of state. On July 2, 1881, Garfield was shot by an unbalanced office-seeker, Charles J. Guiteau, while entering the old Baltimore & Potomac station in Washington. He died Sept. 19, 1881, at Elberon, N. J., and was buried in Cleveland, O. Guiteau was hanged June 30, 1882.

Mrs. James A Garfield

Mrs. Lucretia Rudolph Garfield was born in 1832, daughter of an Ohio farmer. Her mother was a descendant of Gen. Nathaniel Greene. She and Garfield were schoolmates and were married Nov. 11, 1858, when he was principal at Hiram, O. Cyrus W. Field and friends raised a trust fund of $360,000 for the family, She died March 13, 1918. Five children survived. James R. became secretary of the interior, 1907-09; Harry A. was president of Williams College; Irvin M. became a Boston lawyer and Abram G. a Cleveland architect; a daughter, Mrs. Mary Stanley-Brown, died Dec. 30, 1947.

CHESTER ALAN ARTHUR

Chester A. Arthur, 21st President, Republican, was born at Fairfield, Vt., Oct. 5, 1830, the son of the Rev. William Arthur, from County Antrim, Ireland, was Malvina Stone Arthur, member of a New Hampshire family. He was graduated at Union College, 1848, taught school at Pownall, Vt., studied law in New York. In 1853 he argued in a fugitive slave case that slaves transported through New York state were thereby freed; in 1855 he obtained a ruling that Negroes were to be treated the same as whites on street cars. He helped organize the New York State militia, 1861; was made quartermaster general and equipped troops for the front. He was made collector of the port of New York, 1871. In 1877 President Hayes, reforming the civil service, ordered Arthur's resignation; he refused because he was not personally culpable, but was removed, 1879. This made Senators Conkling, Platt and the New York machine stalwarts enemies of Hayes. Arthur and the stalwarts tried to nominate Grant for a third term, 1880; when Garfield was nominated, Arthur received second place in the interests of harmony. On Sept. 19, 1881, he succeeded Garfield as President. He supported civil service reform and the tariff of 1883; arranged an unratified canal treaty with Nicaragua. He was defeated for renomination by James G. Blaine, 1884, but supported Blaine. He died Nov. 18, 1886, and was buried in Albany, N. Y.

Mrs. Chester A. Arthur

Mrs. Ellen Lewis Herndon Arthur was born in Fredericksburg, Va., in 1837, the daughter of Commander William Lewis Herndon, U. S. N. She died in 1880. The Arthurs had three children, W. L. H. Arthur, who died in infancy; Chester Alan Arthur, Jr., (1865-1937) and Ella Herndon Arthur, born 1871 (Mrs. Charles Pinkerton). The mistress of the White House was Arthur's sister, Mary, Mrs. John E. McElroy of Albany, N. Y.

GROVER CLEVELAND

According to a ruling of the State Dept. Grover Cleveland is both the 22nd and the 24th president, because his two terms were not consecutive. By individuals, he is only the 22nd.

Grover Cleveland, 22nd and 24th President, Democrat, was born in Caldwell, N. J., Mar. 18, 1837, the son of Richard F. Cleveland, a Presbyterian minister, and Ann Neale, daughter of a Baltimore merchant who had come from Ireland. He was named Stephen Grover, but dropped Stephen. He clerked in Clinton and Buffalo, N. Y., taught in the New York City Institution for the Blind; was admitted to the bar in Buffalo, 1859; ass't district attorney, 1863; sheriff 1869; major, 1881; governor of New York, 1882. He was an independent, honest administrator who hated corruption. He was nominated for President over Tammany opposition, 1884, defeating James G. Blaine, 219 to 182. He enlarged the civil service, vetoed many pension raids on Treasury. In 1888 he was defeated by Benjamin Harrison, although his popular vote was larger. Re-elected over Harrison, 1892, by 277 to 145, he faced a money crisis brought about by lowering of the gold reserve, circulation of paper and exorbitant silver purchases under the Sherman act, he obtained a repeal of the latter and a reduced tariff. An income tax was passed but declared unconstitutional by the Supreme Court, 1895. A severe depression and labor troubles racked his administration but he refused to interfere in business matters and rejected as crackpot theory, Jacob Coxey's demand for work relief of $20,000,000 monthly. He broke the Pullman strike with troops to move the mail, 1894. He rejected the platform of W. J. Bryan's silver Democrats, 1896, and supported the gold Democrats, Palmer and Buckner. He had part in the reorganization of the Equitable Life Assurance Assn. He died in Princeton, N. J., June 24, 1908.

Mrs. Grover Cleveland

Mrs. Frances Folsom Cleveland was born in 1864, the daughter of Cleveland's. law partner in Buffalo, Oscar Folsom and Emma C. Harmon. She married Cleveland in the White House, June 2, 1886. They had five children, Ruth, Esther, Marion, Richard Folsom and Francis Grover. Mrs. Cleveland married, Feb. 10, 1913, Thomas J. Preston, Jr., an archaeologist in Princeton, N. J. She died Oct. 29, 1947.

BENJAMIN HARRISON

Benjamin Harrison, 23rd President, Republican, was born at North Bend, O., Aug. 20, 1833. His great-grandfather, Benjamin Harrison, was a signer of the Declaration of Independence; his grandfather, William Henry Harrison, was 9th President; his father John Scott Harrison was a Member of Congress, 1853-57. His mother was Elizabeth F. Irwin. He attended school in a log cabin on his father's farm; was graduated from Miami Univ. 1852; admitted to the bar, 1853, and practiced in Indianapolis, Ind. As 2nd lieut. he raised recruits and became colonel of the 70th Indiana Volunteer Infantry. He fought at Kenesaw Mountain, Peachtree Creek, Nashville, and in the Atlanta campaign. In 1865 he was made brigadier general by brevet. He failed to be elected governor of Indiana, 1876; but became Senator, 1881, and worked for the G. A. R. pensions vetoed by Cleveland. In 1888 he defeated Cleveland for president, 233 to 168. He expanded the pension list greatly; suppressed the Louisiana lottery; signed the McKinley high tariff bill and the Sherman silver purchase act. He helped the admission of North and South Dakota, Montana, Washington, Idaho and Wyoming, Republican states. He was defeated for re-election, 1892. He represented Venezuela in arbitration with Great Britain in Paris, 1899. He died at Indianapolis, Mar. 13, 1901, and was buried there.

Harrison's two marriages

Mrs. Caroline Lavinia Scott Harrison was born in 1832 in Oxford, O., the daughter of Prof. John W. Scott of Miami Univ. She married Harrison Oct. 29, 1853. She was the first head of the Daughters of the American Revolution. She died in the White House, 1892. Her son Russell B. became a mining engineer. Her daughter Mary married an Indianapolis merchant, James R. McKee; Mary's child, "Baby McKee," was a White House favorite and became a New York businessman. Mary died in Greenwich in 1930. Harrison's second wife was Mrs. Harrison's niece, **Mrs. Mary Scott Lord Dimmock,** whom he married in 1896. She was born in Honesdale, Pa., 1858, and died in New York, Jan. 5, 1948. She spent two years in the White House during her aunt's lifetime. She had one daughter, Elizabeth Harrison, born 1897, who married James Blaine Walker, Jr., great-nephew of Blaine.

WILLIAM McKINLEY

William McKinley, 25th President, Republican, was born in Niles, O., Jan. 29, 1843, the son of William McKinley, an iron manufacturer, and Nancy Allison McKinley, and was the seventh of nine children. His father's family was Scotch-Irish from County Antrim; his great-grandfather fought in the American revolution. McKinley attended school in Poland, O., and Alleghany College, Meadville, Pa., and enlisted for the Civil War at 18 in the 23rd Ohio, in which R. B. Hayes was a major. He was a commissary sergeant at Antietam, where the state of Ohio honored him with the tallest monument. He rose to captain and in 1865 was made major by brevet. He studied law in the Albany, N. Y., law school; opened an office in Canton, O., in 1867, and campaigned for Grant and Hayes. From 1876 to 1890, excepting 1882, he served in the House of Representatives and led the fight for a high tariff to protect "infant industries," with reciprocal trade agreements (McKinley bill, enacted Oct. 1, 1890). Defeated on this issue in 1890, he was elected governor of Ohio, 1891 and 1893. He received 182 ballots for President in the Republican convention that nominated Benjamin Harrison in 1892. In 1896 he was elected President on a protective tariff, sound money (gold standard) platform over William J. Bryan, Democratic proponent of free silver. Chief factor was the astute vote-getting of Senator Marcus A. Hanna. McKinley was reluctant to intervene in Cuba on grounds of humanity, but the loss of the battleship Maine at Havana crystallized opinion. He demanded Spain's withdrawal from Cuba; Spain agreed to arbitration and armistice but Congress announced state of war as of Apr. 21. (Peace signed Dec. 10). In the 1900 campaign he defeated Bryan's anti-imperialist arguments with the prestige of prosperity, "the full dinner pail" and the vigorous campaigning of Theodore Roosevelt, vice presidential nominee. McKinley was a Methodist, beloved for his conciliatory nature, but conservative (stand-pat) on business issues. He abhorred violence. The need to regulate the Philippines is believed to have inspired John Hay's Open Door Policy in Asia. On Sept. 6, 1901, while welcoming citizens at the Pan-American exposition, Buffalo, N. Y., he was shot by Leon Czolgosz, an anarchist terrorist. He died Sept. 14. His last words were: "It is God's way. His will, not ours, be done." McKinley, his wife and infant daughters rest in an imposing tomb in Canton. His favorite flower, the red carnation, was made the state flower.

Mrs. William McKinley

Mrs. Ida Saxton McKinley, born 1847, was the daughter of James A. Saxton and Katherine DeWalt. She was cashier in her father's bank in Canton, O., when she married McKinley. Their two children died in childhood. Mrs. McKinley became an invalid through a nervous ailment, but presided in the White House and was with her husband when he was assassinated. She died in 1907.

THEODORE ROOSEVELT

Theodore Roosevelt, 26th President, Republican, was born in New York City, Oct. 27, 1858, the son of Theodore Roosevelt, Collector of the Port, and Martha Bulloch, daughter of Maj. Jas. S. Bulloch Roswell Ga. He was descended from Claes Martenszan van Rosenvelt, and his wife Janette, who reached New Netherland from Holland about 1650. Theodore was a fifth cousin of Franklin D. Roosevelt and an uncle of Mrs. Eleanor Roosevelt. His mother was of Scotch-Irish, Huguenot stock and a Southern sympathizer. Roosevelt was graduated from Harvard, 1880, attended Columbia Law School briefly; sat in the New York State Assembly, 1882-84; ranched in North Dakota, 1884-86; failed of election as mayor of New York, 1886; member of U.S. Civil Service Comm. 1889; president, New York Police Board, 1895, supporting the merit system; Asst. Secy. of the Navy under McKinley, Apr. 19, 1897–May 10, 1898, during which he instituted naval target practice and instructed Commodore George Dewey to take Manila in the event of war with Spain. He organized the 1st U. S. Volunteer Cavalry (Rough Riders) as lieut. col., Leonard Wood, col.; led the charge up Kettle Hill at San Juan and was made colonel by brevet. Elected governor, New York, 1898-1900, he fought the spoils system and achieved taxation of corporation franchises. Drafted for vice president, 1900, he became nation's youngest President at 42 years, 10 mos., 18 days, when McKinley died at Buffalo, Sept. 14, 1901. As President he fought corruption of politics by big business; dissolved Northern Securities Co. and others for violating anti-trust laws; intervened in coal strike on behalf of the public, 1902; instituted Dept. of Commerce and Labor; obtained Elkins law forbidding rebates to favored corporations, 1903; Hepburn law regulating railroad rates, 1906; Pure Food and Drugs act, 1906, Reclamation Act and employers' liability laws. He organized Conservation, mediated the peace between Japan and Russia, 1905; won the Nobel Peace Prize. He was the first to use the Hague Court of International Arbitration. By recognizing the new Republic of Panama he made Panama Canal possible, appointed Col. Geo. W. Goethals head commissioner and began canal. He was re-elected 1904, with 336 electoral votes vs. 140.

In 1908 he obtained the nomination of William H. Taft, who was elected; considering Taft inimical to liberal policies he organized the Progressive party, June 22, 1912, and ran for President against Taft and Woodrow Wilson, splitting the Republicans and causing Wilson's election. He was shot during the campaign but recovered. He advocated recall of elected officials, referendum on legislation and recall of judicial decisions, which alienated conservatives. In 1916 he left the Progressives and supported Charles E. Hughes, Republican. A strong friend of Britain, he fought American isolation. In 1917 President Wilson refused to let him organize a division. His four sons served in World War I; two were wounded, one killed. He wrote on many topics–his Winning of the West is best known–was a naturalist and hunter and traced the River of Doubt in Brazil, 1913-14, now Rio Roosevelt. He was looked upon as certain nominee of the Republicans in 1920. He died Jan. 6, 1919, at Sagamore Hill, Oyster Bay, Long Island, N. Y., now a national shrine, and was buried near the Roosevelt bird refuge there.

Theodore Roosevelt's Family

Mrs. Alice Hathaway Lee Roosevelt, daughter of George Cabot Lee and Caroline Haskell Lee, of Boston, married Roosevelt Oct. 27, 1880, in Boston. She and Roosevelt's mother died in New York Feb. 14, 1884. She was the mother of Alice Lee Roosevelt, who married Nicholas Longworth, of Cincinnati, Member of Congress, in the White House, 1906. Their daughter, Paulina, was born Feb. 14, 1925. Longworth, Republican Speaker of the House, died April 9, 1931.

Roosevelt's second wife, **Edith Kermit Carow,** married him Dec. 2, 1886, in London. She was born in Norwich, Conn., Aug. 16, 1861, daughter of Charles and Gertrude Tyler Carow, and survived her husband 29 years, dying Sept. 30, 1948, aged 87. Of their five children Theodore Roosevelt, Jr., was lieut. col. in World War I, assistant secretary of the Navy, governor of Puerto Rico and governor general of the Philippines. He failed of election as governor of New York. A brigadier general, he served

in North Africa, Italy and in Normandy with the 1st Army, and died there July 12, 1944, aged 56. Kermit, major in World War II, died on active duty in Alaska, June 4, 1943, aged 53. Ethel Carow is Mrs. Richard Derby. Archibald Bulloch was a lieut. colonel in World War II. Quentin, aviator in World War I, was killed in action and buried where he fell in France.

WILLIAM HOWARD TAFT

William Howard Taft, 27th President, Republican, was born in Cincinnati, O., Sept. 15, 1857, the son of Alphonso Taft and Louisa Maria Torrey. His father was secretary of war and attorney general in Grant's cabinet; minister to Austria and Russia under Arthur. Taft was graduated from Yale, 1878, Cincinnati Law School, 1880, became law reporter for Cincinnati newspapers; was ass't prosecuting attorney, 1881-83; ass't county solicitor, 1885; judge, Superior Court, 1887; U. S. solicitor-general, 1890; federal circuit judge, 1892. In 1900 he became head of the U. S. Philippines Comm. and was first civil governor of the Philippines, 1901-04. Secretary of war, 1904; provisional governor of Cuba, 1906. He was groomed for President by Theodore Roosevelt as an exemplary public servant and elected over W. J. Bryan, 1908. His administration dissolved Standard Oil and tobacco trusts; instituted Department of Labor; drafted direct election of senators and income tax amendments. His tariff and conservation policies angered progressives; though renominated he was fought by Theodore Roosevelt; the result was Wilson's election. Taft was president league to Enforce Peace, supporting the League of Nations. He was professor of constitutional law, Yale, 1913-21; Chief Justice of the United States, 1921-30, when illness forced him to resign. He died in Washington, Mar. 8, 1930, and was buried in Arlington National cemetery.

Mrs. William H. Taft

Mrs. Helen Herron Taft (1861-1943) was born in Cincinnati, daughter of John W. Herron and Harriet Collins. She was a musician and a founder of the Cincinnati orchestra. The Taft children are Helen (Mrs. Frederick J. Manning), born 1891, prof. of history and former dean and acting president at Bryn Mawr; Robert Alphonso Taft, born 1889, U. S. Senator from Ohio 1938-1953, died July 31, 1953, and Charles Phelps Taft, born 1897, lawyer, former mayor of Cincinnati. Mrs. Taft introduced musicales at White House dinners and instigated planting cherry trees along the Tidewater basin.

WOODROW WILSON

Woodrow Wilson, 28th President, Democrat, was born at Staunton, Va., Dec. 28, 1856, as Thomas Woodrow Wilson, son of a Presbyterian minister, the Rev. Joseph Ruggles and Janet (Jessie) Woodrow, daughter of a Scotch Presbyterian minister. He was a grandson of James Wilson, a Presbyterian of Ulster who reached Philadelphia in 1807, became a printer and in 1808 married an Ulster Presbyterian girl, a shipmate. In his youth Wilson lived in Augusta, Ga., Columbia, S. C., and Wilmington, N. C. He attended Davidson College, 1873-74; was graduated from Princeton, A.B., 1879; A.M., 1882; read law at the Univ. of Virginia, 1881; practiced law, Atlanta, 1882-83; Ph.D., Johns Hopkins, 1886 with "Congressional Government." He taught history and political economy at Bryn Mawr, 1885-88; at Wesleyan, 1888-90; was professor of jurisprudence and political economy at Princeton, 1890-1910; president of Princeton, 1902-1910, during which he tried to introduce innovations of organization that were fought by the graduate dean and alumni; governor of New Jersey, 1911-13, during which he obtained a primary election law, an employers' liability law and other reforms. In 1912 he was nominated for President by the strategy of Wm. J. Bryan, who was out to defeat Champ Clark and Tammany. He won because the Republican vote for Taft was split by the Progressives under Theodore Roosevelt.

Wilson protected American interests in revolutionary Mexico and fought for American rights on the high seas as the first World War opened. His sharp warnings to Germany led to the resignation of his secretary of state, Wm. J. Bryan, pacifist, while his protests against British interference with American ships disturbed the Allies. In 1916 he was re-elected by a slim margin with the slogan, "He kept us out of war," over Charles Evans Hughes, who was strongly supported by Theodore Roosevelt. Wilson's offer to mediate in the war (Dec. 18, 1916) was rejected. When the Germans started unrestricted submarine warfare, contrary to pledges, he broke diplomatic relations. After four American ships had been sunk he asked a declaration of war; it was voted April 6, 1917.

Wilson kept tight personal control over all phases of diplomatic and military activity. He relied more on reports of his confidential agent in Europe, Col. E. M. House, than on Secretary of State Robert Lansing and the U. S. ambassadors. However, he backed Gen. John J. Pershing, U. S. commander in chief, Herbert Hoover, food administrator, and others who had his confidence.

Wilson proposed peace Jan. 8, 1918, on the basis of the Fourteen Points, a state paper with worldwide influence. Basic was his doctrine of self-determination, or consent of the governed, in which he opposed handing peoples from one sovereignty to another. He also demanded a league to enforce peace. The Germans overturned the monarchy and a new republic accepted his terms and an armistice, Nov. 11. At the November elections the Democrats lost control of Congress.

Wilson went to Paris to help negotiate the peace treaty, the crux of which he considered the League of Nations, also urged by Gen. J. C. Smuts, Lord Robert Cecil, Lord Phillimore, William H. Taft and Elihu Root. In the U. S. Senate Henry Cabot Lodge, William E. Borah and Hiram Johnson demanded reservations that would not make the United States subordinate to the votes of other nations in case of war. Wilson refused to consider any reservations and toured the country to get support. At Pueblo, Colo., Sept. 25, 1919, he broke down and several days later suffered a stroke that made him an invalid. The treaty was rejected, Mar. 1920, by 49 to 35 (29 being sufficient to kill it). He made a public appearance on the day of Harding's inauguration, and formed a law partnership with Bainbridge Colby, but did not practice. He won the Nobel peace prize, 1919. During invalidism of 17 months he was confined to his home, seeing few members of his administration, but holding on to the executive powers. He died Feb. 3, 1924, and was buried in Washington Cathedral.

Wilson's Two Marriages

Mrs. Ellen Louise Axson Wilson was born in Rome, Ga., in 1860, the daughter of the Rev. S. E. Axson and Margaret Hoyt. She married Wilson June 28, 1885, and died in the White House Aug. 6, 1914. They had three daughters: Margaret W., born 1886, member of a religious colony in Pondicherry, India, when she died in 1944; Eleanor B., second wife of William G. McAdoo, Wilson's secretary of the treasury, later divorced; Jessie W., who married Francis B. Sayre in the White House Nov. 25, 1913 and died Jan. 15, 1933.

Mrs. Edith Bolling Wilson was born in Wytheville, Va., 1872, and was the widow of Norman Galt, a Washington jeweler, when she married Wilson, Dec. 18, 1915. She died in Washington Dec. 28, 1961. During the President's illness Mrs. Wilson conveyed his wishes to members of the government and instituted what she called "a workable system of handling matters of state." She was a director of the Woodrow Wilson Foundation and bequeathed her house to the National Trust for Historic Preservation.

WARREN GAMALIEL HARDING

Warren Gamaliel Harding, 29th President, Republican, was born near Corsica, now Blooming Grove, O.,

Nov. 2, 1865, the son of Dr. Geo Tyron Harding, a country doctor, and Phoebe Elizabeth Dickerson. He attended Ohio Central College, Iberia, O., 1879-82; worked on the Star, Marion, O., 1884, and a few years later bought the paper with a friend's help for a reported sum of $300. He was state senator, 1900-04; lieut. governor, 1904-06; defeated for governor, 1910; chosen U. S. Senator, 1915. He was a regular, Old Guard Republican; supported Taft, opposed Federal control of food and fuel, voted for anti-strike legislation, woman's suffrage, Volstead prohibition enforcement act over President Wilson's veto and opposed the League of Nations. In 1920 he was nominated for President on the tenth ballot with Calvin Coolidge. The Republicans capitalized war weariness and fear that Wilson's League of Nations would curtail U.S. sovereignty. They defeated the Democrats, James M. Cox and Franklin D. Roosevelt, 16,152,000 to 9,147,000. Harding stressed a return to "normalcy"; worked for repeal of excess profits and high income taxes and a revision of tariff. On announcing ratification of treaties with Germany, Austro-Hungary, Nov. 14, 1921, he declared war officially ended July 2, 1921. His cabinet included Charles Evans Hughes (State); Herbert Hoover (Commerce); Andrew S. Mellon (Treasury). Two appointees, Albert B. Fall (Interior) and Harry Daugherty (Atty. General), became involved in the Teapot Dome scandal that embittered Harding's last days. He called the International Conference on Limitation of Armaments, Nov. 11, 1921-Feb. 1, 1922, and dedicated the Lincoln Memorial. He left for Alaska June 20, 1923; became ill on his return and died in San Francisco, Aug. 2, 1923. He was buried in Marion, Ohio.

Mrs. Warren Gamaliel Harding

Mrs. Florence Kling Harding was born Aug. 15, 1860, the daughter of Amos O. Kling, a Marion, O., hardware merchant and later banker. She married, first, Henry De Wolfe, and had a son, Marshall Eugene De Wolfe. She divorced De Wolfe and in 1891 married Harding. For 14 years she was his associate in managing the Star. She died in Marion, Nov. 21, 1924. The Hardings had no children.

CALVIN COOLIDGE

Calvin Coolidge, 30th President, Republican, was born in Plymouth, Vt., July 4, 1872, the son of John Calvin Coolidge, a storekeeper, and Victoria J. Moor, and named John Calvin Coolidge. His paternal ancestors came from England to Watertown, later Cambridge, Massachusetts Bay Colony, in 1630. Coolidge was graduated at Amherst, 1895; admitted to the bar in Northampton, 1897; city councilman, 1889; city solicitor, 1900-01; clerk of the courts, 1904; member of the lower Massachusetts house, 1907-08; mayor of Northampton, 1910-11; State Senator, 1912-15; and president of Senate, 1914-15; lieut. governor, 1916-18; governor, 1919; re-elected, 1920. In Sept., 1919, Coolidge attained national prominence by his action in the Boston police strike, during which he wired Samuel Gompers of the A. F. of L.: "There is no right to strike against the public safety by anybody, anywhere, anytime." This brought his name before the Republican convention of 1920, where he received 34 votes for President and was nominated for vice president by 674¼ votes. He succeeded to the presidency on Harding's death, Aug. 2, 1923, the oath being administered by his father, a justice of the peace, in his home in Plymouth, Aug. 3, and again Aug. 17 before Justice A. A. Hoehling of the Supreme Court of the District of Columbia. He opposed the League of Nations; approved the World Court; vetoed the soldiers' bonus bill, which was passed over his veto. In 1924 he was re-elected by a huge majority with 15,725,016 over John W. Davis, Dem., 8,385,586, and Robert M. LaFollette, Prog., 4,822,856. He reduced the national dept by $2,000,000,000 in three years. He opposed the McNary-Haugen farm bill and price fixing, and supported his secretary of state, Frank B. Kellogg, in the Kellogg-Briand treaties outlawing war. His dry, laconic remarks are often quoted: opposing reduction of Europe's war debt. "They hired the money, didn't they?" Witn Republicans eager to renominate him he announced, Aug. 2, 1927: "I do not choose to run for President in 1928." He became a life insurance director, wrote syndicated articles and died of a heart attack in Northampton, Jan. 5, 1933. He was buried on a Plymouth hillside.

Mrs. Calvin Coolidge

Mrs. Grace Anne Goodhue Coolidge was born in Burlington, Vt., Jan. 3, 1879, the daughter of Andrew I. Goodhue, a steamboat inspector under Cleveland. She was graduated from the Univ. of Vermont, 1902; taught in the Clarke School for the Deaf, 1902-1905, and became president of its board. She married Coolidge Oct. 4, 1905. She died July 8, 1957, in Northampton, Mass.; aged 78. The Coolidges had two sons: John, born 1906, and Calvin (1908-1924).

HERBERT HOOVER

Herbert Clark Hoover, 31st President, Republican, was born at West Branch, Iowa, Aug. 10, 1874, son of Jesse Clark Hoover, a blacksmith (1847-1880) and Hulda Randall Minthorn (1848-83). Ancestor Andrew Hoover came to Penn. from Palatinate, 1738; great-grandfather reached West Branch, 1854. Hoover grew up in Indian Terr. and Oregon, won A.B. in engineering, Stanford, 1891. Briefly with U. S. Geological Survey and western mines; then mining engineer in western Australia, Asia, Europe, Africa, America. While chief engineer, imperial mines, China, he directed food relief for victims of Boxer Rebellion, 1900. He became a world figure in relief work, distributing over $5 billion worth during 1914-1923. He directed American Relief Committee, London, 1914-15; U. S. Comm. for Relief in Belgium, 1915-1919; U. S. Food Administrator, 1917-1919; American Relief Admin., 1918-1923, feeding children in defeated nations; Russian Relief, 1918-1923; Interallied Food Council; Supreme Economic Council; Comm. on Industrial Relations. As Secy. of Commerce, 1921-28, he began regulation of radio and aviation, pushed research program for Natl. Academy of Science; organized 7-state pact for Colorado River irrigation and Hoover (Boulder) Dam. Elected President over Alfred E. Smith, 1928, he started White House Conferences on child health and protection, and housing; supported conservation of forests, oil, resources; initiated Naval Conference, 1930; organized RFC, Home Loan Banks, expanded Farm Loan Banks; called WEC. He gave his official salary to charities and underpaid help. President Truman made him coordinator of European Food Program, 1947, and ch. of Comm. for Reorganization of the Executive Branch, 1947-49, and ch. of the 2nd Comm. on Reorganization, 1953-55. He founded the Hoover Institution on War, Revolution & Peace at Stanford Univ., Calif. In his final years he lived at Waldorf Towers, New York, N. Y. He died there Oct. 20, 1964, and was buried at West Branch, Iowa, where his birthplace is now a memorial.

Mrs. Herbert Hoover

Mrs. Lou Henry Hoover was born in Waterloo, Ia., Mar. 29, 1875, daughter of Charles D. Henry, a banker. The family moved to Monterey, Calif. She was graduated from Stanford University 1898 and married Hoover in 1899. She died Jan. 7, 1944.
Sons: Herbert Hoover, Jr., (1903-1969), Allan Henry Hoover, b. 1907.

FRANKLIN D. ROOSEVELT

Franklin Delano Roosevelt, 32nd President, Democrat, was born near Hyde Park, N. Y., Jan. 30, 1882, the son of James Roosevelt (died 1900) and Sara Delano (died 1941). His ancestor, Claes Martenszan van Rosenvelt, came to New Amsterdam from Holland about 1650. Claes' son Nicholas, a New York alderman in 1700 and 1715, had a son Johannes, from whom Theodore Roosevelt was descended, and a son Jacobus, from whom Franklin D. Roosevelt was descended. Roosevelt was graduated at Harvard, 1904; attended Columbia Law school, was admitted to the bar. He went to the New York Senate from his Dutchess county district 1910 and 1913. He voted for Woodrow Wilson at the 1912 Democratic convention; in 1913 Wilson made him assistant secretary of the Navy.

Roosevelt ran for vice president, 1920, with Jas. M. Cox and was defeated. From 1920 to 1928 he was a New York lawyer and v.p. of Fidelity & Deposit Co. In Aug., 1921, infantile paralysis paralyzed his legs. He learned to walk with leg braces and a cane and established the Warm Springs, Ga., Foundation, for helping those so afflicted.

Roosevelt presented the name of Alfred E. Smith to the Democratic convention of 1924 in New York, and 1928 in Houston, Texas, calling Smith the Happy Warrior. Smith was nominated in 1928 and defeated. Roosevelt was elected governor of New York, 1928 and 1930. In 1932 at Chicago W. G. McAdoo, pledged to John N. Garner, threw his votes to Roosevelt, who was chosen, alienating Smith. The financial crash, unemployment and the Democratic promise to repeal prohibition made his victory inevitable. He asked emergency powers, proclaimed the New Deal, and put into effect a vast number of administrative changes. Foremost was "pump priming," or use of public funds for relief and public works, resulting in deficit financing. He greatly expanded the controls of the central government over business and by an excess profits tax and pyramiding income taxes produced a redistribution of earnings on an unprecedented scale. The Wagner act gave labor many advantages in organizing and collective bargaining, at the same time denying equal privileges to employers. He was the last President inaugurated on Mar. 4 (1933) and the first inaugurated on Jan. 20 (1937).

Roosevelt was a tremendous worker and traveler despite physical handicaps. He was the first President to use radio for "fireside chats." When the Supreme Court voided his measures he demanded additional judges of Congress. It refused, but resignations soon enabled him to replace conservatives who had opposed him. He was the first President to break the third term tradition and was elected to a fourth term, 1944, despite failing health. The culminating event of his career was World War II. He was openly hostile to fascist governments before the war and gave Britain substantial support, such as exchanging 50 destroyers for air bases, before Pearl Harbor made the United States a belligerent. He wrote the principles of fair dealing into the Atlantic Charter, Aug. 14, 1941 (with Winston Churchill) and in the Four Freedoms (Freedom of speech, of worship, from want, from fear) Jan. 6, 1941. He conferred with the heads of state at Casablanca, Jan., 1943; Quebec, Aug., 1943; Teheran, Nov.-Dec., 1943; Cairo, Dec., 1943; Yalta, Feb., 1945. He died at Warm Springs, Ga., April 12, 1945, aged 63, and was buried on his Hyde Park estate, where his house and library are in the national care.

Eleanor Roosevelt

Mrs. Anna Eleanor Roosevelt was born Oct. 11, 1884, the daughter of Elliott Roosevelt, a younger brother of Theodore Roosevelt, and Anna Hall. She was educated in private schools. She married Franklin D. Roosevelt Mar. 17, 1905. In 1924-26 she was finance chairman of the New York Democratic State committee. She was asst. director, Office of Civilian Defense, 1941-42; U. S. representative, General Assembly, U. N., 1945-53 and ch. of its Human Rights Commission. In 1961 President Kennedy appointed her to General Assembly, U. N. Mrs. Roosevelt died Nov. 7, 1962, in New York, N. Y., and was buried beside her husband at Hyde Park, N. Y. President Kennedy and former Presidents Eisenhower and Truman were present. The Roosevelts had 6 children. one dying in infancy. The others: Anna Eleanor (Mrs. James H. Halsted), b. 1906; James b. Dec. 23, 1907; Elliott, b. Sept. 23, 1910; Franklin Delano, Jr., b. Aug. 17, 1914; John A., b. Mar. 13, 1916.

HARRY S. TRUMAN

Harry S. Truman, 33rd President, Democrat, was born at Lamar, Mo., May 8, 1884, the son of John Anderson Truman and Martha Ellen Young. Four grandparents were born in Kentucky and moved to Missouri in the 1840s. The Trumans came from England and the President's mother's grandmother from Northern Ireland, while an ancestor of his maternal grandfather, Solomon Young came from Germany. A family disagreement on whether Harry Truman's middle name was Shippe or Solomon, after names of two grandfathers, resulted in his using only S. for his middle initial. He is a Baptist.

He attended public schools in Independence, Mo., worked for the Kansas City Star, 1901, and as railroad timekeeper, and helper in Kansas City banks up to 1905. He joined the Missouri National Guard, 1905, and was rejected by West Point for defective eyesight. He ran his family's farm, 1906-17. He entered the Field Artillery school at Fort Sill, Okla., 1917; became 1st lieut., Battery F and capt., Battery D, 129th Field Artillery, 35th Div., A.E. F. He served in the Vosges, Meuse-Argonne and St. Mihiel actions and was discharged as major, 1919. He is a colonel in the Field Artillery Reserve. After the war he ran a haberdashery, became judge of Jackson Co. Court, 1922-24; attended Kansas City School of Law, 1923-25. He was defeated, then elected presiding judge.

Truman was chosen senator Nov. 6, 1934; reelected Nov. 5, 1940. In 1944 with President Roosevelt's approval he was nominated for vice president, and elected. On Roosevelt's death Apr. 12, 1945, Truman was sworn in as President by Chief Justice Harlan F. Stone. In 1948 he was elected President as polls predicted his defeat.

Truman supported the Marshall Plan, ECA, the rehabilitation of Greece and arming of Turkey, and NATO, naming Gen. of the Army Eisenhower to the supreme command in Europe. He opened the United Nations conference by radio and participated with Stalin and Attlee in the Potsdam Agreement. He authorized the first use of an atomic bomb (Hiroshima, Aug. 6; Nagasaki, Aug. 9, 1945). He supported a policy of compromise between Chiang Kai-shek and the Chinese Communists. When the Communists attacked in Korea, June, 1950, and the UN asked for armed aid he ordered Gen. of the Army MacArthur to give it, but when MacArthur opposed his policy of limited objectives he removed him.

Truman established the Office of Defense Mobilization in 1950, instituted controls of materials and prices. He won a higher minimum wage, increased social security and aid for housing. In 1952 he ordered seizure of steel companies, which had refused demands of CIO and WSB, and when overruled by the U. S. Supreme Court refused to use the Taft-Hartley law. He rebuilt the White House. He retired to Independence, Mo., where he lived in modest retirement until his death Dec. 26, 1972, at the age of 88. He was buried in Independence, Mo., in the courtyard of the Harry S. Truman Library, which contains his presidential papers.

Mrs. Harry S. Truman

Mrs. Elizabeth Virginia Wallace Truman was born Feb. 13, 1885, in Independence, Mo., the eldest of four children and the only daughter of David Willock Wallace. She and Mr. Truman attended the same grade and high schools in Independence, both being graduated in 1901. She attended Barstow, a girls' preparatory school in Kansas City, Mo., and is an Episcopalian. She married Mr. Truman June 28, 1919. They have one daughter, Margaret, born 1924, a concert and radio artist, who married Clifton Daniel, a New York newspaper editor, April 21, 1956. The Daniels have 4 sons: Clifton Truman, William Wallace, Harrison Gates, and Thomas Washington.

DWIGHT DAVID EISENHOWER

Dwight David Eisenhower, 34th President, Republican, was born Oct. 14, 1890, at Denison, Tex., the son of David Jacob Eisenhower and Ida Elizabeth Stover Eisenhower. His paternal grandfather descended from German Mennonites who left the Rhineland for Pennsylvania in the 1730s, moved to Kansas in 1878. His father met his mother at Lane University, a United Brethren college at Lecompton, Kan. When Dwight was 1 year old his parents moved to Abilene, Kan. He attended high school and in 1915 was graduated at West Point. He became 2nd lieut., 19th U. S. Infantry, at Fort Sam Houston, Tex. He was a lieutenant colonel in charge of a tank corps at Camp Colt, Gettysburg, Pa., in 1918. He was graduated from Infantry Tank School, 1922; Command and General Staff Sch., 1926; Army War College, 1928; Army Industrial College, 1933. He was asst. executive officer of the Asst. Secy. of War, 1929-1933, and in the office of the Chief of Staff, 1933-35. He was on the American Military Mission to the Philippines, 1935-39 and during 4 of those years on the staff of Gen. MacArthur. He was chief of staff, 3rd Div., later 9th Corps, 1940-41, and of the 3rd Army, 1941 as brigadier general. After the Louisiana maneuvers he was made chief of the War Plans Div., War Dept. General Staff, and then became asst. chief of staff, Operations Div. and in June, 1942, lieutenant general. He was made Commander of Allied forces landing in North Africa Nov. 8, 1942, and advanced to full general in Feb., 1943, and Commander in Chief of Allied Forces in North Africa. He became Supreme Commander, Allied Expeditionary Forces Dec. 31, 1943, and as such led the Normandy invasion June 6, 1944. He was given the temporary rank of General of the Army Dec. 19, 1944, which was made permanent in 1946. On May 7, 1945, he received the surrender of the Germans at Rheims. He was in command of the U. S. Occupation Force in Germany in 1945, and returned to serve as Chief of Staff, Nov. 19, 1945, to Feb. 7, 1948. From June 7, 1948, to Jan. 19, 1953, he was president of Columbia Univ., but he took leave of absence Dec. 16, 1950, to serve as Supreme Allied Commander in Europe to organize NATO forces.

Eisenhower resigned from the Army in June, 1952, and was nominated for President by the Republicans at Chicago, July 11, 1952. He defeated Adlai E. Stevenson by 442 to 89 electoral votes, was inaugurated Jan. 20, 1953. He was renominated unanimously in San Francisco, Aug. 22, 1956, and defeated Stevenson by 457 to 74. He called himself a moderate, favored "free market system" vs. government price and wage controls; kept government out of labor disputes; reorganized defense establishment; promoted missile programs, including Polaris. With strong aid of John Foster Dulles, his Secy. of State, he continued foreign aid; demanded unification of Germany by free elections; sped end of Korean fighting; supplied planes to anti-communist Guatemalan govt.; endorsed Formosa and SE Asia defense treaties; backed U.N. in condemning Anglo-French raid on Egypt; advocated "open skies" policy of mutual inspection to USSR. He sent U. S. troops into Little Rock, Ark., Sept., 1957, during the segregation crisis and ordered Marines to Lebanon July-Aug., 1958. Eisenhower's rank as General of the Army was restored by Congress and signed by President Kennedy Mar. 22, 1961.

In 1948, Eisenhower published *Crusade in Europe,* his war memoirs, which quickly became a best seller. His other published works included *Mandate for Change* (1962), *Waging Peace* (1965), *The White House Years,* and *At Ease: Stories I Tell My Friends* (1967). He was an enthusiastic golfer and painter.

During his retirement at his farm near Gettysburg, Pa., Eisenhower took up the role of elder statesman, counseling his 3 successors in the White House. He was hospitalized in early 1968 after his 4th heart attack and died Mar. 28, 1969, at Walter Reed Army Hospital in Washington. After a state funeral in Washington, he was buried in Abilene, Kan.

Mrs. Dwight D. Eisenhower

Mrs. Mamie Geneva Doud Eisenhower was born in Boone, Iowa, Nov. 14, 1896. Her home was in Denver when Eisenhower, then a 1st lieutenant of infantry at Fort Sam Houston, met her. They were married July 1, 1916. Their first son, Dwight Doud, died in infancy; their second is John Sheldon Doud Eisenhower, lt. colonel, USA, ret., left the Army 1963. He is married to Barbara Jean Thompson, and they have four children.

JOHN F. KENNEDY

John Fitzgerald Kennedy, 35th President, Democrat, was bórn May 29, 1917, in Brookline, Mass., the second of 9 children of Joseph P. Kennedy, financier who later became ambassador to Great Britain, and Rose Fitzgerald Kennedy. He entered Harvard, attended the London School of Economics briefly in 1935, received a B.S. *cum laude* from Harvard in 1940. He served in the U. S. Navy, 1941-1945, commanded a PT boat in the Solomons and won the Navy and Marine Corps medal and Purple Heart. He covered the Postdam Conference and the start of the U. N. at San Francisco for International News Service. He served as Representative in Congress from Massachusetts, 1947-1953, defeated Henry Cabot Lodge for the Senate in 1952, was re-elected 1958. He nearly won the vice presidential nomination in 1956.

Kennedy won the Democratic nomination for President at Los Angeles. July 14, 1960. Sen. Lyndon B. Johnson (Tex.), was named for vice president. Kennedy defeated Richard M. Nixon, Republican, by the slim margin of 118,550 popular votes and an electoral vote of 303 to 219. He was the first Roman Catholic to be elected President.

President Kennedy's most important act was his successful demand Oct. 22, 1962, that the Soviet Union dismantle all missile bases in Cuba. He established a quarantine of arms shipments to Cuba and continued surveillance by air. He defied Soviet attempts to force the Allies out of Berlin. He made the steel industry rescind its price rise. He backed civil rights, a mental health program, arbitration of railroad disputes and larger medical care for the aged. Astronaut flights and satellite orbiting were greatly developed during his less than 3-yrs. tenure. Cape Canaveral was renamed Cape Kennedy later. He wrote *Profiles in Courage,* which won a Pulitzer prize, and *Why England Slept.* He turned the White House spotlight on the cultural arts.

On Nov. 22, 1963, Kennedy was assassinated in Dallas, Texas. On Nov. 25, a national day of mourning, he was buried in Arlington National Cemetery, Va.

Mrs. John F. Kennedy

Mrs. Jacqueline Bouvier Kennedy was born July 28, 1929, in Southampton, N. Y., daughter of John Vernon Bouvier, a New York Banker, and Janet Lee Bouvier (Mrs. Hugh D. Auchincloss). She attended private schools for girls and Vassar, and studied the history of art at the Sorbonne, Paris, during one year. She was graduated from George Washington Univ., 1951, afterward studying American History there. She was on the reporting staff of Washington Times-Herald, 1952. She married John F. Kennedy at Newport, Sept. 12, 1953, when she was 24 and Sen. Kennedy 36. They had three children: Caroline, born Nov. 27, 1957; John F., Jr., Nov. 25, 1960 and Patrick Bouvier, Aug. 7, 1963 (deceased). Mrs. Kennedy supervised the complete refurnishing of the White House. On Oct. 20, 1968, some 5 years after Kennedy's death, she was married to Aristotle Socrates Onassis, Greek shipping magnate.

LYNDON BAINES JOHNSON

Lyndon Baines Johnson, 36th President, Democrat, was born on a farm near Stonewall, Tex., Aug. 27, 1908, son of Sam Ealy and Rebekah Baines Johnson. His father and grandfather had served in the Texas legislature. His family moved to Johnson City in 1913, where he was graduated from the high school in 1924. He received a B.S. degree at Southwest Texas State Teachers College, 1930, attended Georgetown Univ., Law School, Washington, 1935. He taught public speaking in Houston High school, 1930-32; served as secretary to Rep. R. M. Kleberg, 1932-35. In 1935 President Roosevelt appointed Johnson Texas state administrator of the National Youth Admin. In 1937 Johnson won a contest to fill the vacancy caused by the death of a Representative and in 1938 was elected to the full term, after which he returned for four terms. A member of the Naval Reserve, he was lieut.

commander, U. S. Navy, 1941-42, winning the Silver Star for a flight over Japanese positions at New Guinea. He was elected Senator 1948 by only 87 votes margin over Gov. Coke Stevenson of Texas; in 1954 he was reelected by a large majority. He became Democratic whip, 1951, and leader, 1953, at 44. Johnson was Texas' favorite son for the Democratic presidential nomination in 1956 and had strong support in the 1960 convention, when the nominee, John F. Kennedy, asked him to run for Vice President. His campaigning helped overcome religious bias against Kennedy in the South. As Vice President he proved to be a tireless worker. He represented Kennedy abroad, was ch. of the President's Committee on Equal Employment Opportunity and member of advisory bodies dealing with security, space and the Peace Corps. Johnson took the oath of office as President at 2:30 p.m., CST, on November 22, 1963, 99 min. after the death of President Kennedy. In filling out the Kennedy term Johnson worked hard for welfare legislation and signed acts for civil rights, anti-poverty and tax reduction and averted strikes on railroads. He was nominated for President and elected Nov. 3, 1964, by 486 electoral votes to 52. Overshadowing other developments during Johnson's first full term in the White House were the expansion of the war in Vietnam, the committing of more than 500,000 American servicemen to conflict, intensive bombing by U.S. planes and mounting U.S. casualties.

In face of increasing division in the nation and in his own party over his conduct of war, Johnson announced, on Mar. 31, 1968, "I shall not seek, and I will not accept the nomination of my party for another term as your President." Near the end of his tenure, he indicated that he felt his greatest achievement was the passage of the Voting Rights Act of 1965; his biggest disappointment was that "peace has eluded me."

Retiring to his LBJ Ranch near Johnson City, Texas, the former president wrote his memoirs, *The Vantage Point* (1971), and oversaw the construction of the Lyndon Baines Johnson Library on the campus of the University of Texas in Austin. President Johnson died of a heart attack on Jan. 22, 1973. After lying in state in the Capitol Rotunda in Washington, he was buried on his ranch near the Pedernales River.

Mrs. Lyndon B. Johnson

Mrs. Claudia Alta Taylor Johnson, affectionately called Lady Bird by family and friends, is the daughter of a Marshall, Texas, rancher and was born Dec. 22, 1912. Her mother, dying when Claudia was a little girl, left her $67,000, which she multiplied by careful investment. She was graduated from the Univ. of Texas, 1933, and married Johnson Nov. 17, 1934. An able business woman, she became owner of radio-television station KTBC in Austin, Tex., since placed in a trust. The Johnsons have two daughters, Lynda Bird, born Mar. 19, 1944 and Luci Baines, born July 2, 1947. The Johnson ranch of 400 acres is near Johnson City, Texas. President Johnson is a member of the Christian Church (Disciples of Christ). Mrs. Johnson and Lynda are Episcopalians; Luci became a Roman Catholic July 2, 1965. Luci was married to Patrick Nugent Aug. 6, 1966. She gave birth in Austin, Tex., June 21, 1967, to the President's first grandchild, Patrick Lyndon Nugent, and on Nov. 11, 1969, to a daughter, Nicole Marie. On Dec. 9, 1967, Lynda was married to Marine Capt. Charles S. Robb in the first White House marriage of a President's daughter in 53 years. The Robbs' first child, a daughter, Lucinda Desha, was born Oct. 25, 1968. Their second, Catherine Lewis, was born June 5, 1970.

RICHARD MILHOUS NIXON

Richard Milhous Nixon, 37th President, Republican, was born in the small farming community of Yorba Linda, Calif., Jan. 9, 1913, the second of the 5 sons of Francis Anthony and Hannah Milhous Nixon. In 1922, the family moved to Whittier, Calif., where the future president was graduated from Whittier College in 1934 with a scholarship for Duke University Law School. He was graduated 3rd in his class at Duke 3 years later. After practicing law in Whittier and serving briefly as an attorney in the Office of Price Administration in 1942, he entered the Navy, serving in the South Pacific, and was discharged as a lieutenant commander.

Nixon was elected to the House of Representatives from California's 12th Congressional District in 1946 and re-elected in 1948. Co-author in 1948 of the controversial Mundt-Nixon Communist-control bill, he achieved prominence as the House Un-American Activities Committee member who forced the showdown that resulted in the Alger Hiss perjury conviction. In 1950 Nixon moved to the Senate by defeating Democrat Helen Gahagen Douglas in a bitter campaign in which he accused her of being "soft on communism."

Elected Vice President in the Eisenhower landslides of 1952 and 1956, Nixon achieved more prominence in that position than had his predecessors. As a working member of the Executive Branch, he attended meetings of the National Security Council, was assigned special committees of his own, performed many political chores for Eisenhower, and made a number of good-will tours of foreign countries for the President.

With Eisenhower's endorsement, Nixon won the Republican Presidential nomination in 1960. He was defeated by Democrat John F. Kennedy in a close race in which a series of face-to-face televised debates between the two candidates played a large part.

Nixon returned to California, and two years later was defeated in his race for Governor against Democratic incumbent Pat Brown.

He moved to New York City in 1963 and began a lucrative law practice as a senior partner in the firm of Nixon, Mudge, Rose, Guthrie, Alexander & Mitchell. Appealing for Republican unity, he campaigned hard for the party's candidates in 1964 and 1966. Taking to the "long hard road" of the Presidential primaries in 1968, he won the Presidential nomination easily on the first ballot and went on to defeat Democrat Hubert H. Humphrey in one of the closest Presidential elections ever held.

The 1969-1973 Nixon Administration saw remarkable developments in international affairs as Nixon became the first U.S. president to visit China and Russia. He and his foreign affairs advisor, Dr. Henry A. Kissinger, achieved a detente with China and a partial strategic arms limitation agreement with the Soviet Union. In addition, President Nixon brought an end to the U.S. ground combat role in South Vietnam.

These diplomatic triumphs did not, however, overshadow the serious economic difficulties which confronted the nation. In Aug., 1971, faced with alarming trade and balance of payments deficits and continuing inflation, Nixon announced a "new economic policy," with wage and price controls at home and negotiations abroad leading to the devaluation of the dollar.

In the field of law, Nixon appointed 4 new Supreme Court Justices, including the Chief Justice, thus altering the Court's balance in favor of a more conservative view. A conservative trend on issues of public order was also observed.

By the summer of 1972, the peace movement was subdued, the economy showed signs of healthy growth, and a period of normal relations among the superpowers seemed at hand. On Aug. 22, a confident Republican party nominated Nixon for election to a second term as President.

Reelected in a massive landslide, President Nixon soon secured a ceasefire agreement in Vietnam and completed the withdrawal of all U.S. troops in spite of heavy fighting and U.S. bombing in Cambodia and continued sporadic conflict in South Vietnam.

On Jan. 11, 1973, the Nixon administration ended most mandatory wage and price controls and on Feb. 12 announced a further devaluation of the dollar. Inflation, however, continued at peak levels and the dollar came under heavy pressure in the world's gold markets. On June 13, Nixon re-imposed price controls and asked Congress for special authority to regulate food exports.

In spite of his overwhelming victory, Nixon's 2nd term was gravely compromised by allegations of high White House involvement in illegal espionage against the Democratic party headquarters in the Watergate apartment complex in Washington, D.C., in June, 1972. On April 30, 1973 Nixon's two closest aides resigned and a third member of the White House staff was fired. In an unrelated case, 2 former Nixon Cabinet members, Attorney General John N. Mitchell and Commerce Secretary Maurice H. Stans, the top leaders of Nixon's reelection campaign, were indicted on charges of perjury and obstruction of justice in connection with a $200,000 campaign contribution from a financier under federal investigation for fraud.

In May, 1973, a select Senate committee began hearings on campaign practices and a special independent prosecutor took up the criminal investigation of the Watergate affair, opening a summer of uncertainty as to the Administration's capacity to govern effectively.

(See Chronology for further developments.)

Mrs. Richard M. Nixon

Mrs. Thelma Catherine Patricia Ryan Nixon, whose husband and friends call her Pat, was born Mar. 16, 1912, in the mining town of Ely, Nev. Shortly afterward her family moved to a truck farm at Artesia, Calif., where she grew up. After graduation from high school she left the farm to support herself and worked her way through the University of Southern California in 7 years. She was a high school teacher in Whittier, Calif., where she met Richard Nixon. They were married June 21, 1940, in Riverside, Calif. Their first daughter, Patricia, was born Feb. 21, 1946. Their second, Julie, born July 5, 1948, was married Dec. 22, 1968, to David Eisenhower, grandson of the former President. Patricia Nixon was married to Edward Finch Cox, 24, a Harvard University Law School student, June 12, 1971, in an elaborate ceremony in the White House rose garden.

Presidents' Original Paternal Ancestry

Dutch. Van Buren, Theodore Roosevelt, Franklin D. Roosevelt. **German**. Eisenhower. **Swiss and Palatinate German**. Hoover.

English. Washington, John Adams, Madison, John Quincy Adams, William Henry Harrison, Tyler, Taylor, Fillmore, Pierce, Lincoln, Andrew Johnson, Grant, Garfield, Cleveland, Benjamin Harrison, Taft, Harding, Coolidge. **English-French-German**. L. B. Johnson. **English-Scottish-Irish**—Truman.

Irish. Kennedy, Nixon.

Scottish—Monroe, Hayes. **Scottish-Irish**—Jackson, Polk, Buchanan, Arthur, McKinley, Wilson. **Welsh**. Jefferson (a family tradition).

Presidents Who Wore Military Uniforms

Washington—French and Indian War; Revolution.

Monroe—Revolution.

Jackson—Revolution, Creek, 1812, and Seminole wars.

Harrison, W. H.—Indian wars, Ohio and Indiana, 1812.

Taylor—1812, Black Hawk, Seminole and Mexican.

Tyler—1812.

Pierce—Mexican.

Buchanan—1812.

Lincoln—Black Hawk.

Johnson, Andrew—Military Gov. Tennessee, Civil War.

Grant—Mexican, Civil War.

Hayes—Civil War.

Garfield—Civil War.

Arthur—Q. M. Gen., N. Y. State.

Harrison, B.—Civil War.

McKinley—Civil War.

Roosevelt, T.—Spanish War.

Truman—World War I.

Eisenhower—World War I and II.

Kennedy—World War II.

Johnson, Lyndon—World War II.

Nixon, Richard M.—World War II.

Longevity of Presidents of the U. S.

Source: Statistical Bulletin, Metropolitan Life

	Year of Birth	Age, 1st Inauguration	Age at Death	Expectancy after 1st Inaugural	Years Lived After First Inaugural Actual	Above Expected	Below Expected
George Washington....	1732	57	67	17.1	10.6		6.5
John Adams	1735	61	90	14.4	29.3	14.9	
Thomas Jefferson	1743	57	83	16.4	25.3	8.9	
James Madison	1751	57	85	16.3	27.3	11.0	
James Monroe	1758	58	73	15.7	14.3		1.3
John Q. Adams........	1767	57	80	16.3	23.0	6.7	
Andrew Jackson.......	1767	61	78	13.5	16.3	2.7	
Martin Van Buren	1782	54	79	17.2	25.4	8.2	
William H. Harrison†..	1773	68	68	9.4	.1		9.3
John Tyler...........	1790	51	71	19.2	20.8	1.6	
James K. Polk........	1795	49	53	21.5	4.3		17.2
Zachary Taylor†	1784	64	65	12.8	1.3		11.5
Millard Fillmore	1800	50	74	20.7	23.7	2.9	
Franklin Pierce	1804	48	64	22.0	16.6		5.4
James Buchanan.......	1791	65	77	11.9	11.3		.6
Abraham Lincoln‡.....	1809	52	56	19.8	4.1		15.6
Andrew Johnson.......	1808	56	66	17.2	10.3		6.9
Ulysses S. Grant......	1822	46	63	22.8	16.4		6.4
Rutherford B. Hayes ...	1822	54	70	18.0	15.9		2.1
James A. Garfield‡	1831	49	49	21.2	.5		20.7
Chester A. Arthur	1830	50	56	20.1	5.2		15.0
Grover Cleveland	1837	47	71	22.1	23.3	1.2	
Benjamin Harrison.....	1833	55	67	17.2	12.0		5.2
William McKinley‡....	1843	54	58	18.2	4.5		13.6
Theodore Roosevelt....	1858	42	60	26.1	17.3		8.8
William H. Taft.......	1857	51	72	20.3	21.0	.8	
Woodrow Wilson......	1856	56	67	17.1	10.9		6.2
Warren G. Harding†...	1865	55	57	18.1	2.4		15.6
Calvin Coolidge......	1872	51	60	21.4	9.4		12.0
Herbert C. Hoover	1874	54	90	19.0	35.6	16.7	
Franklin D. Roosevelt†.	1882	51	63	21.7	12.1		9.6
Harry S. Truman	1884	60	88	15.3	27.7	12.4	
Dwight D. Eisenhower.	1890	62	78	14.7	16.2	1.4	
John F. Kennedy‡	1917	43	46	28.5	2.8		25.7
Lyndon B. Johnson ...	1908	55	64	19.3	9.2		10.1
Richard M. Nixon	1913	56		18.8			

†Died during tenure. ‡Assassinated.

Burial Places of the Presidents

G. Washington	1732-1799	Mt. Vernon, Va.	R. B. Hayes......	1822-1893	Fremont, Ohio
John Adams......	1735-1826	Quincy, Mass.	J. A. Garfield.....	1831-1881	Cleveland, Ohio
T. Jefferson......	1743-1826	Charlottesville, Va.	C. A. Arthur......	1830-1886	Albany, N. Y.
James Madison ...	1751-1836	Montpelier Station, Va.	Grover Cleveland..	1837-1908	Princeton, N. J.
James Monroe	1758-1831	Richmond, Va.	B. Harrison......	1833-1901	Indianapolis, Ind.
John Q. Adams ...	1767-1848	Quincy, Mass.	W. McKinley	1843-1901	Canton, Ohio
Andrew Jackson ..	1767-1845	Nashville, Tenn.	T. Roosevelt......	1858-1919	Oyster Bay, N. Y.
M. Van Buren	1782-1862	Kinderhook, N. Y.	William H. Taft...	1857-1930	Arlington Nat'l. Cem'y
W. H. Harrison ...	1773-1841	North Bend, Ohio	Woodrow Wilson ..	1856-1924	Washington Cathedral
John Tyler.......	1790-1862	Richmond, Va.	W. G. Harding....	1865-1923	Marion, Ohio
James Knox Polk ..	1795-1849	Nashville, Tenn.	Calvin Coolidge ...	1872-1933	Plymouth, Vt.
Zachary Taylor ...	1784-1850	Louisville, Ky.	Herbert Hoover ...	1874-1964	West Branch, Iowa
Millard Fillmore ..	1800-1874	Buffalo, N. Y.	F. D. Roosevelt ...	1882-1945	Hyde Park, N. Y.
Franklin Pierce ...	1804-1869	Concord, N. H.	Dwight D. Eisen-		
James Buchanan ..	1791-1868	Lancaster, Pa.	hower.........	1890-1969	Abilene, Kan.
A. Lincoln	1809-1865	Springfield, Ill.	J. F. Kennedy	1917-1963	Arlington Nat'l Cem'y
Andrew Johnson ..	1808-1875	Greeneville, Tenn.	Harry S. Truman ..	1884-1972	Independence, Mo.
Ulysses S. Grant ..	1822-1885	New York City	Lyndon B. Johnson .	1908-1973	Stonewall, Texas

Religious Background of Presidents

Baptist–Harding, Truman.

Christian Church (Disciples of Christ).Garfield, Lyndon B. Johnson.

Congregationalist.Coolidge.

Episcopalian.Washington, Madison, Monroe, William Henry Harrison, Tyler, Taylor, Pierce, Arthur, and Franklin D. Roosevelt.

Jefferson, an Episcopal Church member, later became a deist, said he was a "disciple of the doctrines of Jesus," and commended Unitarianism.

Friends (Quakers)–Hoover, Nixon.

Methodist.Polk, Andrew Johnson, Grant, McKinley.

Presbyterian.Jackson, Buchanan, Cleveland, Benjamin Harrison, Wilson, Eisenhower.

Lincoln attended Presbyterian services in Washington but was not a member. Hayes attended the Methodist Church, but never joined.

Reformed Dutch.Van Buren, Theodore Roosevelt.

Roman Catholic.Kennedy.

Unitarian.John Adams, John Quincy Adams, Fillmore, Taft.

How America Was Named

America was named for Amerigo Vespucci (1454-1512), an Italian reputed to have made 4 voyages to the New World (1497-1503). The German geographer, Martin Waldseemüller, first used the name to honor Vespucci in a book published in 1507.

Law on Succession to the Presidency

If by reason of death, resignation, removal from office, inability, or failure to qualify there is neither a President nor Vice President to discharge the powers and duties of the office of President, then the Speaker of the House of Representatives shall upon his resignation as Speaker and as Representative, act as President. The same rule shall apply in the case of the death, resignation, removal from office, or inability of an individual acting as President.

If at the time when a Speaker is to begin the discharge of the powers and duties of the office of President there is no Speaker, or the Speaker fails to qualify as Acting President, then the President pro tempore of the Senate, upon his resignation as President pro tempore and as Senator, shall act as President.

An individual acting as President shall continue to act until the expiration of the then current Presidential term, except that (1) if his discharge of the powers and duties of the office is founded in whole or in part in the failure of both the President-elect and the Vice President-elect to qualify, then he shall act only until a President or Vice President qualifies, and (2) if his discharge of the powers and duties of the office is founded in whole or in part on the inability of the President or Vice President, then he shall act only until the removal of the disability of one of such individuals.

If, by reason of death, resignation, removal from office, or failure to qualify, there is no President pro tempore to act as President, then the officer of the United States who is highest on the following list, and who is not under disability to discharge the powers and duties of President, shall act as President: Secy. of State, Secy. of the Treasury, Secy. of Defense, Attorney General, Secy. of the Interior, Secy. of Agriculture, Secy. of Commerce, Secy. of Labor, Secy. of Health, Education and Welfare, Secy. Housing and Urban Development and Secy. of Transportation. *Approved July 18, 1947; amended Sept. 9, 1965, and Oct. 15, 1966.*

Revolutionary Calendar, 1774

1773 Dec. 16 Boston Tea Party to protest taxes on tea imported into colonies.

1774 Mar. 25 Bill passed in British Parliament prohibits loading and unloading of ships in Boston harbor.

May 17 First call for a colonial congress comes from Providence, R.I.

May 20 Massachusetts Government Act virtually annuls that Colony's charter and self government.

May 30 Quebec Act. British Parliament extends boundary of Quebec south to the Ohio river and sets up centralized Crown-controlled government in Quebec. Colonists fear that access to colonial rights in western lands will be cut off.

June 2 Quartering Act legalizes lodging of British troops in private houses throughout the colonies.

June 17 Massachusetts House of Representatives calls for a congress of colonial delegates in Philadelphia in Sept.

1774 Sept. 5 First Continental Congress opens at Carpenter's Hall in Philadelphia. Twelve colonies (Georgia failed to elect delegates) send 54 delegates.

Oct. 14 Congress in "Declaration and Resolves" declares Government Act and others unjust and unconstitutional; states that colonial legislatures have exclusive right to make tax laws and that colonists have rights to "life, liberty and property."

Oct. 18 Continental Association: Congress delegates pledge their provinces to cease all importation from Britain; discontinue the slave trade; end consumption of British products; and end exports to Britain, Ireland and the West Indies. A committee elected in each town will enforce the pledge by publicity and boycott.

Oct. 26 First Continental Congress adjourns.

The Presidents of the Continental Congresses

Congress President	Date Elected	Meeting in	Dates
Peyton Randolph, Va.[1]	Sept. 5, 1774	Philadelphia	Sept. 5 to Oct. 26, 1774
Henry Middleton, S.C.	Oct. 22, 1774		
Peyton Randolph, Va.	May 10, 1775	Philadelphia	May 10, 1775 to Dec. 12, 1776
John Hancock, Mass.	May 24, 1775	Baltimore	Dec. 20, 1776 to March 4, 1777
		Philadelphia	March 5 to Sept. 18, 1777
		Lancaster, Pa.	Sept. 27, 1777 (one day)
Henry Laurens, S.C.	Nov. 1, 1777	York, Pa.[4]	Sept. 30, 1777 to June 27, 1778
John Jay, N.Y.	Dec. 10, 1778	Philadelphia	July 2, 1778 to June 21, 1783
Samuel Huntington, Conn.	Sept. 28, 1779		
Thomas McKean, Del.	July 10, 1781		
John Hanson, Md.[2]	Nov. 5, 1781		
Elias Boudinot, N.J.	Nov. 4, 1782	Princeton, N.J.	June 30 to Nov. 4, 1783
Thomas Mifflin, Pa.	Nov. 3, 1783	Annapolis, Md.	Nov. 26, 1783 to June, 3, 1784
Richard Henry Lee, Va.	Nov. 30, 1784	Trenton, N.J.	Nov. 1 to Dec. 24, 1784
		New. York City	Jan. 11 to Nov. 4, 1785
John Hancock, Mass.[3]	Nov. 23, 1785	"	Nov. 7, 1785 to Nov. 3, 1786
Nathaniel Gorham, Mass.	June 6, 1786	"	Nov. 6, 1786 to Oct. 30, 1787
Arthur St. Clair, Pa.	Feb. 2, 1787	"	Nov. 5, 1787 to Oct. 21, 1788
Cyrus Griffin, Va.	Jan. 22, 1788	"	Nov. 3, 1788 to March 2, 1789

1) Resigned Oct. 2, 1774.
2) Titled "President of the United States Congress Assembled", John Hanson is considered by some to be the first U.S. President as he was the first to serve under the Articles of Confederation. He was, however, little more than presiding officer of the Congress, which retained full executive power. He could be considered the head of government, but not head of state.
3) Resigned May 29, 1786, never having served, because of illness.
4) Articles of Confederation agreed upon, Nov. 15, 1777; last ratification from Maryland, March 1, 1781.

United States Government
The Nixon Administration
As of July 1, 1973

Terms of office of the President and Vice President, from January 20, 1973 to January 20, 1977. No person may be elected President of the United States for more than two four-year terms.

PRESIDENT—Richard M. Nixon of California. Receives salary of $200,000 a year taxable, and in addition an expense allowance, also taxable, of $50,000 to assist in defraying expenses resulting from his official duties. Also there may be expended not exceeding $40,000, nontaxable, a year for travel expenses and official entertainment. Congress in 1971 provided lifetime pensions of $60,000 a year, free mailing privileges, free office space, and up to $65,000 a year for office help for ex-Presidents and $20,000 annually for their widows.

VICE PRESIDENT — Spiro T. Agnew of Maryland. Salary $62,500 a year and $10,000 for expenses, all of which is taxable.

Order of succession to Presidency see Pg. 817

The Cabinet
(Salaries $60,000 each)

Secretary of State — William P. Rogers, Maryland.
Secretary of Treasury — George P. Shultz.
Secretary of Defense — James R. Schlesinger, Virginia.
Attorney General — Richard G. Kleindienst, Ariz.
Secretary of the Interior — Rogers C. B. Morton, Md.
Secretary of Agriculture — Earl L. Butz, Ind.
Secretary of Commerce — Frederick B. Bent, S.C.
Secretary of Labor — Peter J. Brennan, N.Y.
Secretary of Health, Education and Welfare — Elliot L. Richardson, Mass.
Secretary of Housing and Urban Development — George Romney, Michigan.
Secretary of Transportation — John A. Volpe, Mass.

The White House Staff
1600 Pennsylvania Ave. NW 20500

Counsellors to the President—Melvin R. Laird (Domestic Affairs); Anne Armstrong; Bryce N. Harlow.
Assistants to the President—Henry A. Kissinger (National Security Affairs); Wm. E. Timmons (Congressional Relations); Peter M. Flanigan; Alexander Haig.
Special Consultants to the President—Leonard Garment; Raymond K. Price, Jr.; Patrick J. Buchanan.
Dir. of Communications and Press Secretary—Ronald L. Ziegler.
General Counsel—Leonard Garment, acting.
Military Asst. to the President—Brig. Gen. Brent Scowcroft, USAF.
Special Asst. for Consumer Affairs—Virginia H. Knauer.
Personal Secretary to the President—Rose Mary Woods.
Press Secretary for the First Lady—Helen Smith.
Physician to the President—Brig. Gen. Walter R. Tkach, USAF, MC.
Chief Usher—Rex W. Scouten.

Executive Agencies

National Security Council—Assistant to the President for Natl. Security Affairs—Henry A. Kissinger.
Council of Econ. Advisers—Herbert Stein.
Council on Environmental Quality—R. E. Train, chmn.
Central Intelligence Agency—William Colby, designate.
Natl. Aeronautics & Space Council—Spiro T. Agnew, chmn.
Off. of Management and Budget—Roy L. Ash.
Special Representative for Trade Negotiations—William Eberly.
Marine Resources and Engineering Devel.—Edward Wenk Jr., exec. secy.

Department of State
2201 C St. NW 20520

Secretary of State—William P. Rogers.
Deputy Secretary—John N. Irwin, II.
Under Sec. for Political Affairs—U. Alexis Johnson.
Under Secretary for Security Assistance—Curtis W. Tarr.
Deputy Under Secretaries—*(Vacant)* (for economic affairs), William B. Macomber, Jr. (for Management.)
Ambassador at Large—David M. Kennedy.
Counselor—Richard F. Pederson.
Legal Advisor—John R. Stevenson.
Director of Planning & Coordination—William I. Cargo.
Assistant Secretaries for:
  Administration—Joseph F. Donelan, Jr.
  African Affairs—David D. Newsom.
  Congressional Relations—David M. Abshire.
  Economic Affairs—Willis C. Armstrong.
  Educational & Cultural Affairs—John Richardson.
  European Affairs—Walter J. Stoessel, Jr.
  East Asian & Pacific Affairs—Marshall Green.
  Internatl. Organiz. Affairs—Samuel De Palma.
  Inter-American Affairs—Charles A. Meyer.
  Near-Eastern & So. Asian Affairs—Joseph J. Sisco.
  Public Affairs—John Richardson, Acting.
Bureau of Security & Consular Affairs—Barbara M. Watson.
Inspector Gen., Foreign Assistance—Anthony Faunce, acting.
Chief of Protocol—Marion H. Smoak, acting.
Dir. General, Foreign Service—William O. Hall.
Director of Intelligence & Research—Ray S. Cline.
Director of Internatl. Scientific and Technological Affairs—Herman Pollack.
Director of Politico-Military Affairs—Ronald I. Spiers.
insp. Gen. Foreign Service—Thomas W. McElhiney.
Foreign Service Inst.—Howard E. Sollenberger, acting.
Agency for Internatl. Development—John A. Hannah.
Advisory Committee on Voluntary Foreign Aid—Charles P. Taft, Chmn.
Action—Joseph Blatchford, director.
U.S. Rep. to the UN and Rep. in the Security Council—George H. Bush, Ambassador.

Treasury Department
15th St. & Pennsylvania Ave. N.W. 20220

Secretary of the Treasury—George P. Shultz.
Deputy Secy. of the Treasury—William E. Simon.
Under Secy. for Monetary Affairs—Paul A. Volcker.
Deputy Under Secy. for Monetary Affairs—Jack F. Bennett.
Under Secretary—*vacant.*
General Counsel—Edward C. Schmults.
Deputy Under Secretary—*vacant.*
Assistant Secretaries: Frederic W. Hickman, Edward L. Morgan, Warren F. Brecht, John M. Hennessy, Edgar R. Fiedler, John K. Carlock.
Special Assistants to the Secretary: William L. Gifford, John L. Hart, Joseph A. Loftus, acting, Edward M. Roob.
Bureaus:
  Accounts—David Mosso, comm.
  Alcohol, Tobacco and Firearms — Rex D. Davis, dir.
  Consolidated Federal Law Enforcement Training Center — William B. Butler, director.
  Comptroller of the Currency — James E. Smith.
  Customs—Vernon D. Acree, comm.
  Engraving & Printing—James A. Conlon, director.
  Internal Revenue Service—Donald C. Alexander, comm.
  Mint—Mrs. Mary T. Brooks, director.
  Public Dept—H. J. Hintgen, comm.
  Treasurer of the U.S.—Mrs. Romana Acosta Banuelos.
  U.S. Savings Bonds—Jesse L. Adams, Jr., acting natl. dir.
  U.S. Secret Service—James J. Rowley, director.

Department of Defense
The Pentagon 20301
Secretary of Defense — James R. Schlesinger.
Deputy Sec. of Defense — Wm. P. Clements, Jr.
Dir. of Def. Research and Eng. — Dr. Malcolm R. Currie.
Asst. Secretaries of Defense:
  Comptroller — Terrence E. McClary.
  Health and Environment — Richard S. Wilbur, M.D.
  Installations & Logistics — Arthur I. Mendolia, designate.
  Intelligence — Albert C. Hall.
  Internat'l. Security — Robert C. Hill.
  Legislative Affairs — John O. Marsh, Jr.
  Manpower & Reserve — Carl W. Chewlow, acting.
  Public Affairs — Jerry W. Friedheim.
  Telecommunications — Eberhardt Rechtin.
  Atomic Energy — *vacant*.
  General Counsel — Fred Buzhardt.
Joint Chiefs of Staff, Chairman — Adm. Thomas H. Moorer.

Department of the Army
The Pentagon 20310
Secretary of the Army — Howard H. Callaway.
Under Secretary — Herman R. Roll, jan
Assistant Secretaries for:
  Financial Management — Hadlai A. Hull.
  Installations & Logistics — Vincent P. Huggard, acting.
  Research & Development — Charles L. Poor, acting.
  Manpower & Reserve Affairs — Carl S. Wallace.
Chief of Public Information — Maj. Gen. Winant Sidle.
Chief of Staff — Gen. Creighton W. Abrams.
Comptroller of the Army — Lt. Gen. E. M. Flanagan, Jr.
Surgeon General — Lt. Gen. H. B. Jennings, Jr.
Adjutant General — Maj. Gen. Verne L. Bowers.
Inspector General — Lt. Gen. Gilbert H. Woodward.
Chief of Engineers — Lt. Gen. W. C. Gribble, Jr.
U.S. Women's Army Corps — Brig. Gen. Mildred C. Bailey.
Natl. Guard Bureau — Maj. Gen. Francis S. Greenlief.
Chief, Army Reserve — Maj. Gen. J. Milnor Roberts, Jr.
U.S. Army Materiel Command — Gen. H. A. Miley, Jr.
U.S. Continental Army Command — Gen. Walter T. Kerwin.
Commanding Generals, U.S. Armies:
  1st, Fort Meade, Md. — Lt. Gen. C. E. Hutchin, Jr.
  5th, Ft. Sam Houston, Tex. — Lt. Gen. Patrick F. Cassidy.
  6th, Presidio of San Francisco, Calif. — Lt. Gen. Richard G. Stilwell.
Military Dist. of Wash. — Maj. Gen. James B. Adamson.

Department of the Navy
The Pentagon 20350
Secretary of the Navy — John W. Warner.
Under Secretary — Frank Sanders.
Assistant Secretaries for:
  Financial Management — Robert D. Nelson.
  Installations & Logistics — Charles L. Ill.
  Manpower & Reserve Affairs — James E. Johnson.
  Research & Development — Robert A. Frosch.
Judge Advocate Gen. — R. Adm. Merlin H. Staring.
Chief of Naval Operations — Adm. Elmo R. Zumwalt, Jr.
Chief of Naval Materiel — Adm. Isaac C. Kidd, Jr.
Bureau Chiefs:
  Medicine & Surgery — V. Adm. Donald L. Custis.
  Naval Personnel — V. Adm. David H. Bagley.
Military Sealift Command — R. Adm. John D. Chase.
U.S. Marine Corps:
  Commandant — Gen. Robert E. Cushman, Jr.
  Asst. Commandant — Gen. Earl E. Anderson.
  Quartermaster Gen. — Maj. Gen. H. C. Olson.
  Dir. of Women Marines — Col. Jeanette I. Sustad.
Commandants, Naval Districts:
  1st, Boston — R. Adm. Richard E. Rumble.
  3rd, New York — R. Adm. Wm. Marr Pugh II.
  4th, Philadelphia — R. Adm. Joseph L. Coleman.
  5th, Norfolk — R. Adm. Roy G. Anderson.
  6th, Charleston — R. Adm. H. J. Kossler.
  8th, New Orleans — R. Adm. Robert E. Riera.
  9th, Great Lakes — R. Adm. D. L. Kauffman.
  10th, San Juan — R. Adm. N. G. Ward.
  11th, San Diego — R. Adm. J. W. Williams, Jr.
  12th, San Francisco — R. Adm. Clyde J. Van Arsdall, Jr.

13th, Seattle — R. Adm. Thomas E. Bass III.
14th, San Francisco — R. Adm. John "L" Butts, Jr.
Naval District, Wash., D.C. — R. Adm. Arthur G. Esch.

Department of the Air Force
The Pentagon 20220
Secretary of the Air Force — John L. McLucas, acting.
Under Secretary — *vacant*.
Assistant Secretaries for:
  Research & Development — Grant L. Hansen.
  Installations & Logistics — Lewis E. Turner, acting.
  Financial Management — William Woodruff.
  Manpower & Reserve Affairs — Richard J. Borda.
General Counsel — Jack L. Stempler.
Dir. of Info. — Maj. Gen. Robert N. Ginsburgh.
Dir. of Space Systems — John F. Kulpa, Jr.
Dir. of Special Projects — Brig. Gen. David D. Bradburn.
Chief of Staff — Gen. John D. Ryan.
Vice Chief of Staff — Gen. Horace M. Wade.
Chief, Natl. Guard Bureau — Maj. Gen. Francis S. Greenlief.
Chief of Air Force Reserves — Maj. Gen. Homer I. Lewis.
Surgeon General — Lt. Gen. Robert A. Patterson.
Judge Advocate — Maj. Gen. James S. Cheney.
Inspector General — Lt. Gen. Louis L. Wilson, Jr.
Deputy Chiefs of Staff:
  Systems & Logistics — Maj. Gen. William W. Snavely.
  Programs & Resources — Lt. Gen. George S. Boylan, Jr.
  Personnel — Lt. Gen. Robert J. Dixon.
  Research & Development — Lt. Gen. Otto J. Glasser.
  Plans & Operations — Lt. Gen. George J. Eade.
  Aerospace Defense Command — Lt. Gen. Thomas K. McGehee.
Air Force Logistics — Gen. Jack J. Catton.
Air Force Systems — Gen. George S. Brown.
Air Training — Lt. Gen. William V. McBride.
Air University — Lt. Gen. Alvan C. Gillem 2d.
Hdgts. Command — Maj. Gen. John L. Locke.
Military Airlift — Gen. Paul K. Carlton.
Strategic Air — Gen. John C. Meyer.
Tactical Air — Gen. William W. Momyer.
Alaskan Air — Maj. Gen. Charles W. Carson, Jr.
U.S.A.F. Southern Command — Maj. Gen. Arthur G. Salisbury.
Pacific Air Forces — Gen. Lucius D. Clay, Jr.
U.S.A.F. Europe — Gen. David C. Jones.
U.S.A.F. Security Service — Maj. Gen. Carl W. Stapleton.
Air Force Communications Service — Maj. Gen. Paul R. Stoney.

Department of Justice
Constitution Ave. & 10th St. N.W. 20530
Attorney General — Elliot L. Richardson.
Deputy Attorney General — Joseph T. Sneed.
Solicitor General — Robert H. Bork
Assistant Attorneys General:
  Administrative — *vacant*.
  Antitrust Div. — Thomas E. Kauper.
  Civil Div. — Harlington Wood, Jr.
  Civil Rights Div. — J. Stanley Pottinger.
  Criminal Div. — Henry E. Petersen.
  Land and Natural Resources Div. — Wallace Johnson.
  Legal Counsel — Robert G. Dixon.
  Tax Div. — Scott P. Crampton.
Fed. Bureau Investigation — Clarence M. Kelley, designate.
Bureau of Narcotics and Dangerous Drugs — John E. Ingersoll, dir.
Special Asst. Attorney Genl. for Drug Abuse Law Enforcement — Myles J. Ambrose.
Natl. Narcotics Intelligence Center — William C. Sullivan, dir.
Bureau of Prisons — Norman A. Carlson.
Board of Parole — Maurice H. Sigler.
Community Relations Service — Benjamin F. Holman, dir.
Law Enforcement Assistance Admin. — Donald Santarelli.
Immigration and Naturalization Service — James F. Greene, acting comm.
Board of Immigration Appeals — M. A. Roberts, ch.
Pardon Attorney — Lawrence M. Traylor.

Department of the Interior
C St. between 18th & 19th Sts. N.W. 20240
Secretary of the Interior — Rogers C. B. Morton.
Under Secretary — John C. Whitaker.
Assistant Secretaries for:
  Fish, Wildlife, and Parks — Nathaniel P. Reed.
  Energy & Minerals — Stephen A. Wakefield.
  Land and Water Resources — Jack O. Horton.
  Program Development and Budget — Dr. Laurence Edwin Lynn, Jr.
  Management — James T. Clarke, acting.
  Congressional and Public Affairs — John H. Kyl.
  Asst. to the Sec. for Indian Affairs — Marvin L. Franklin.
Bur. of Land Management — Burton W. Silcock.
Bur. of Mines — Elburt F. Osborn.
Bur. of Outdoor Recreation — James G. Watt.
Bur. of Reclamation — Gilbert G. Stamm, designate.
Bur. of Sport Fisheries & Wildlife — Spencer H. Smith.
Geological Survey — V. E. McKelvey.
National Park Service — Ronald H. Walker.
Office of Coal Research — George R. Hill.
Office of Information — Robert A. Kelly.
Office of Oil & Gas — Duke R. Ligon.
Office of Saline Water — J. W. Pat O'Meara.
Office of Solicitor — Kent Frizzell.
Office of Water Resources Resources Research — Dr. Warren A. Hall, acting.

Department of Agriculture
14th St. & Independence Ave. S.W. 20250
Secretary of Agriculture — Earl L. Butz.
Under Secretary — J. Phil Campbell.
Conservation, Research & Education — Robert W. Long.
Internatl. Affairs & Commodity Programs — Carroll G. Brunthaver.
Marketing & Consumer Services — Clayton K. Yeutter.
Rural Development — William Erwin.
Agricultural Economics — Don Paarlberg.
Public Affairs — Wayne E. Swegle.
Intergovernmental Affairs — William F. Moss.
Agric. Mktg. Service — Erwin L. Peterson, admin.
Agric. Stabilization & Conserv. Service — Kenneth Frick, admin.
Animal & Plant Health Inspection Ser. — E. J. Mulhern.
Commodity Exch. Auth. — Alex C. Caldwell, admin.
Cooperative State Research Ser. — R. L. Lovvorn.
Econ. Research Service — Quentin M. West admin.
Export Mktg. Service — Laurel C. Meade.
Extension Service — Edward Kirby, admin.
Farmer Coop. Service — Eric Thor, admin.
Farmers Home Admin. — Frank B. Elliott, acting admin.
Fed. Crop Insurance Corp. — Melvin R. Peterson.
Food & Nutrition Ser. — Edward J. Hekman, admin.
Foreign Agric. Service — Raymond A. Ioanes, admin.
Forest Service — John R. McGuire, chief.
General Counsel — John A. Knebel.
Inspector General — Nathaniel E. Kossack.
Packers & Stockyards Admin. — Marvin McLain.
Rural Electrific. Admin. — David A. Hamil, admin.
Soil Conservation Service — Kenneth E. Grant, admin.
Statistical Reporting Service — Harry C. Trelogan.

Department of Commerce
14th St. between Constitution & E St. N.W. 20230
Secretary of Commerce — Frederick B. Dent.
Under Secy. of Commerce — vacant.
Asst. Secretaries — Henry B. Turner, Robert J. Blackwell, Betsy Ancker-Johnson, C. Langhorne Washburn, Edward D. Failor, Dr. Sidney L. Jones.
General Counsel — William N. Letson.
Bureau of the Census — Vincent R. Barabba, acting.
Bureau of Economic Analysis — George Jaszi.
Bureau of Internatl. Commerce — Marinus van Gessel.
Bureau of East-West Trade — Steven Lazarus.
Bureau of Competitive Assessment and Business Policy — Gary M. Cook, acting dir.
Natl. Oceanic & Atmospheric Admin. — Robert M. White, admin.
Natl. Technical Info. Service — William T. Knox, dir.
Economic Develop. Admin. — William Blunt, acting.
Natl. Bureau of Standards — Dr. Richard Roberts.
Office of Foreign Direct Investments — Robert A. Anthony, dir.
Office of Minority Business Enterprise — Alex M. Armendaris, dir.

Office of Product Standards — vacant.
Office of Telecommunications — John M. Richardson, acting dir.
Office of Textiles — Arthur Garel, dir.
Social & Economic Statistics Admin. — Edward D. Failor, admin.
U.S. Patent Office — Robert Gottschalk, comm.
U.S. Travel Service — C. Langhorne Washburn.

Department of Labor
14th St. & Constitution Ave. N.W. 20210
Secretary of Labor — Peter J. Brennan.
Under Secretary — Richard F. Schubert.
Counselor to the Secretary — Donald F. Rodgers.
Asst. Secretary for Manpower — William H. Kolberg.
Manpower Administrator — vacant.
  Job Corps — David O. Williams, director.
  Bureau of Apprenticeship and Training — Hugh C. Murphy, Admin.
Asst. Secretary for Labor-Management Relations — Paul J. Fasser, Jr.
Asst. Secretary for Occupational Safety & Health — John H. Stender.
  Office of Training and Education — Earl D. Heath, dir.
  Office of Standards — Gerard F. Scannell, dir.
Asst. Secretary for Employment Standards — Bernard E. DeLury.
  Office of Federal Contract Compliance — Philip J. Davis, acting.
  Wage and Hour Administrator — vacant.
  Women's Bureau — Carmen R. Maymi, director.
  Office of Wage & Compensation Programs — Ben P. Robertson, director.
Asst. Secretary for Policy, Evaluation & Research — vacant.
Solicitor of Labor — William J. Kilberg.
Bur. of Labor Statistics — Julius Shiskin.
  Deputy Commissioner — Ben Burdetsky.
Deputy Under Secretary for Internatl. Affairs — Joel Segall.
Asst. Secretary for Admin. & Management — Fred G. Clark.
Director of Public Affairs — Frank S. Johnson, Jr.
Office of Information, Publications & Reports — John Leslie, director.

Department of Health, Education, and Welfare
330 Independence Ave. S.W. 20201
Secretary of H.E.W. — Caspar W. Weinberger.
Under Secretary — Frank Carlucci.
Assistant Secretaries for:
  Administration and Management — Robert Marik.
  Public Affairs — Lewis Helms, designate.
  Health — Dr. Charles C. Edwards.
  Planning and Evaluation — Dr. Stuart Altman, acting.
  Education — Dr. Sidney P. Marland, Jr.
  Human Development — Stanley B. Thomas.
  Legislation — Stephen Kurzman.
  Comptroller — James B. Cardwell.
General Counsel — Wilmot R. Hastings.
Surgeon General, Public Health Ser. — vacant.
Health Services & Mental Health Admin. — Dr. Harold O. Buzzell.
Office for Civil Rights — Peter Holmes, dir.
Social and Rehabilitation Ser. — Francis DeGeorge.
Commissioners of:
  Education — John R. Ottina, acting.
  Social Security — Arthur E. Hess.
  Food and Drug Admin. — Sherwin Gardner, acting.
National Institutes of Health — Robert Stone, dir.
National Institute of Education — Dr. Thomas K. Glennan, Jr.

Department of Housing and Urban Development
451 7th St. S.W. 20410
Secretary of Housing & Urban Development — James T. Lynn.
Under Secretary — Floyd H. Hyde.
Assistant Secretaries:
  Administration — vacant.
  Community Planning & Development — vacant.

Equal Opportunity — *vacant.*
Housing Management — H. R. Crawford.
Housing Production & Mortgage Credit — Sheldon B. Lubar.
Policy Development & Research — Michael H. Moskow.
Legislative Affairs — Sol Mosher.
President, Govt. Natl. Mortgage Assn. — Woodward Kingman.
Office of Public Affairs — William I. Greener, Jr.
Office of International Affairs — Dale Barnes, dir.
General Counsel — James L. Mitchell.
Federal Insurance Administrator — George K. Bernstein.
Office of Interstate Land Sales Registration — George K. Bernstein, admin.
Inspector General — Charles G. Haynes.

Department of Transportation
400 7th St. S.W. 20590

Secretary — Claude S. Brinegar.
Under Secretary — John W. Barnum, designate.
Assistant Secretaries — Robert H. Cannon, Benjamin O. Davis, Jr., William S. Heffelfinger, Robert T. Monagan.
Natl. Trans. Safety Board — John H. Reed.
U.S. Coast Guard — Adm. Chester R. Bender.
Federal Aviation Admin. — Alexander P. Butterfield.
Federal Highway Admin. — Norbert T. Tiemann.
Federal Railroad Admin. — John W. Ingram.
Urban Mass Transportation Admin. — James E. Wilson, acting.
St. Lawrence Seaway Development Corp. — David W. Oberlin.

Ambassadors and Ministers
As of July 1, 1973

The address of foreign embassies to the United States is Washington, D.C.

*Embassy was closed and personnel withdrawn. Limited staffs remain in Algeria and Egypt but no ambassadors are assigned.

Countries	Envoys from United States	Envoys to United States
Afghanistan	Robert G. Neumann, Amb.	Abdullah Malikyar, Amb.
Algeria	*Vacant	Vacant
Argentina	John Davis Lodge, Amb.	Carlos M. Muniz, Amb.
Australia	Walter L. Rice, Amb.	Sir James Plimsoll, Amb.
Austria	John P. Humes, Amb.	Arno Halusa, Amb.
Bangladesh	Hermann F. Eilts, Amb.	S. A. Karim, Charge d'Affaires.
Barbados	Eileen R. Donovan, Amb.	Valerie T. McComie, Amb.
Belgium	Robert Strausz-Hupé, Amb.	Walter Loridan, Amb.
Bolivia	Vacant	Edmundo Valencia-Ibanez, Amb.
Botswana	Charles J. Nelson, Amb.	Amos M. Dambe, Amb.
Brazil	John Hugh Crimmins	Joao Augusto Araujo Castro, Amb.
Bulgaria	Vacant	Assen Yankov, Charge d'Affaires
Burma	Edwin W. Martin, Amb.	U Lwin, Amb.
Burundi	Robert L. Yost, Amb.	Terence Nsanze, Amb.
Cameroon	C. Robert Moore, Amb.	Francois-Xavier Tchoungui, Amb.
Cambodia (Khmer Rep.)	Emory C. Swank, Amb.	Um Sim, Amb.
Canada	Adolph W. Schmidt, Amb.	Marcel Cadieux, Amb.
Centr. Afr. Rep.	Melvin L. Manfull, Amb.	Christophe Maidou, Amb.
Chad	Vacant	Lazare Massibe, Amb.
Chile	Nathaniel Davis, Amb.	Pable Valdex, Charge d'Affaires.
China (Taiwan)	Walter P. McConaughy, Amb.	James C. H. Shen, Amb.
Colombia	Leonard J. Saccio, Amb.	Dr. Douglas Botero-Boshell, Amb.
Congo (Braz'vil.)	*Vacant	Vacant
Congo (Kinshasa)	(See Zaire)	
Costa Rica	Viron P. Vaky, Amb.	Marco Antonio Lopez, Amb.
Cyprus	Robert J. McCloskey, Amb.	Zenon Rossides, Amb.
Czechoslovakia	Albert W. Sherer, Jr., Amb.	Dr. Dusan Spacil, Amb.
Dahomey	Robert Anderson, Amb.	Tiamiou Adjibade, Amb.
Denmark	Vacant	Eyvind Bartels, Amb.
Dominican Republic	Francis E. Meloy, Jr., Amb.	S. Salvador Ortiz, Amb.
Ecuador	Vacant	Alberto Quevedo-Toro, Amb.
Egypt	*Vacant	Vacant
El Salvador	Henry E. Catto, Jr. Amb.	Col. Julio A. Rivera, Amb.
Equatorial Guinea	C. Robert Moore, Amb.	
Estonia		Ernst Jaakson, Consul General
Ethiopia	E. Ross Adair, Amb.	Kifle Wodajo, Amb.
Fiji	Vacant	S. K. Sikivou, Amb.
Finland	V. John Krehbiel, Amb.	Leo Tuominen, Amb.
France	John N. Irwin II, Amb.	Jacques Kosciusko-Morizet, Amb.
Gabon	John A. McKesson 3d, Amb.	Gaston R. Bouckat-Bou-Nzierngui, Amb.
Gambia, Rep. of	G. Edward Clark, Amb.	Vacant
Germany	Martin J. Hillenbrand, Amb.	Berndt von Staden, Amb.
Ghana	Fred L. Hadsel, Amb.	Harry R. Amonoo, Amb.
Great Britain	Walter H. Annenberg, Amb.	The Earl of Cromer, Amb.
Greece	Henry J. Tasca, Amb.	Ionnis A. Sorokos, Amb.
Guatemala	William G. Bowdler, Amb.	Julio Asensio-Wunderlich, Amb.
Guinea	Terence A. Todman, Amb.	Sadan Moussa Toure, Amb.
Guyana	Spencer M. King. Amb.	Frederick Hillborn Talbot
Haiti	Vacant	Rene Chalmers, Charge d'Affaires
Honduras	Phillip V. Sanchez, Amb.	Roberto Galvez Barnes, Amb.
Hungary	Richard F. Pederson, Amb.	Dr. Karoly Szabo, Amb.
Iceland	Frederick Irving, Amb.	Haraldur Kroyer, Amb.
India	Daniel P. Moynihan, Amb.	Triloki Nath Kaul, Amb.
Indonesia	Francis J. Galbraith, Amb.	Sjarif Thajeb, Amb.
Iran	Richard Helms, Amb.	Ardeshir Zahedi, Amb.
Iraq	*Vacant	Vacant
Ireland	John D. J. Moore, Amb.	William Warnock, Amb.
Israel	Kenneth B. Keating, Amb.	Simcha Dinitz, Amb.
Italy	John A. Volpe, Amb.	Edgido Ortona, Amb.
Ivory Coast	John F. Root, Amb.	Timothee N'Guetta Ahoua, Amb.

Countries	Envoys from United States	Envoys to United States
Jamaica	Vincent deRoulet, Amb.	Douglas V. Fletcher, Amb.
Japan	Robert S. Ingersoll, Amb.	Takeshi Yasukawa, Amb.
Jordan	L. Dean Brown, Amb.	Abdallah Salah, Amb.
Kenya	Robinson McIlvaine, Amb.	Leonard Oliver Kibinge, Amb.
Korea	Philip C. Habib, Amb.	Dong Jo Kim, Amb.
Kuwait	William A. Stoltzfus, Jr., Amb.	Salem S. Al-Sabah, Amb.
Laos	Charles S. Whitehouse, Amb.	Phagna Pheng Norindr, Amb.
Latvia		Dr. Anatole Dinbergs, Charge d'Affaires
Lebanon	William B. Buffum, Amb.	Najati Kabbani, Amb.
Lesotho	Charles J. Nelson, Amb.	Mothusi T. Mashologu, Amb.
Liberia	Melvin L. Manfull, Amb.	S. Edward Peal, Amb.
Libya	Vacant	Muharram Ben Musa, Charge d'Affaires
Lithuania		Joseph Kajeckas, Charge d'Affaires
Luxembourg	Dr. Ruth Lewis Farkas, Amb.	Jean Wagner, Amb.
Madagascar	Joseph A. Mendenhall, Amb.	Henri Raharijaona, Amb.
Malawi	William C. Burdett, Amb.	Vacant
Malaysia	Jack W. Lydman, Amb.	Mohamed Khir Johari, Amb.
Maldives, Rep.	Christopher Van Hollen, Amb.	Vacant
Mali	Robert O. Blake, Amb.	Seydou Traore, Amb.
Malta	John I. Getz, Amb.	Joseph Attard-Kingswell, Amb.
Mauritania	Richard W. Murphy, Amb.	Ahmedou Ould Abdallah, Amb.
Mauritius	William D. Brewer, Amb.	Pierre Guy Girald Balancy, Amb.
Mexico	Robert H. McBride, Amb.	Dr. Jose Juan de Olloqui, Amb.
Morocco	Stuart W. Rockwell, Amb.	Badreddine Senoussi, Amb.
Nepal	Carol C. Laise, Amb.	Yadu Nath Khanal, Amb.
Netherlands	Vacant	Baron Rijnhard Van Lyden, Amb.
New Zealand	Vacant	Lloyd White, Amb.
Nicaragua	Turner B. Shelton, Amb.	Dr. Guillermo Sevilla-Sacasa, Amb.
Niger	Roswell D. McClelland, Amb.	Abdoulaye Diallo, Amb.
Nigeria	John E. Reinhardt, Amb.	John M. Garba, Amb.
Norway	Philip K. Crowe, Amb.	Arne Gunneng, Amb.
Pakistan	Vacant	Sultan M. Khan, Amb.
Panama	Robert M. Sayre, Amb.	Nicolas Gonzalez Revilla, Amb.
Paraguay	George W. Landau, Amb.	Miguel Solano Lopez, Amb.
Peru	Taylor G. Belcher, Amb.	Fernando Berckemeyer, Amb.
Philippines	William H. Sullivan, Amb.	Eduardo Z. Romualdez, Amb.
Poland	Richard T. Davies, Amb.	Witold Trampczynski, Amb.
Portugal	Vacant	Joao Hall Themido, Amb.
Qatar	William A. Stoltzfus, Jr., Amb.	Abdullah S. Al-Mania, Amb.
Romania	Leonard C. Meeker, Amb.	Corneliu Bogdan, Amb.
Rwanda	Robert F. Corrigan, Amb.	Fidele Nkundabogenzi, Amb.
Saudi Arabia	Nicholas G. Thacher, Amb.	Ibrahim Al-Sowayel, Amb.
Senegal	G. Edward Clark, Amb.	Andre Coulbary, Amb.
Sierra Leone	Clinton L. Olson, Amb.	Philip J. Palmer, Amb.
Singapore	Edwin M. Cronk, Amb.	Dr. Ernest S. Monteiro, Amb.
Somali, Democratic Rep.	Matthew Looram, Amb.	Dr. Adbullahi Ahmed Addou, Amb.
South Africa	John G. Hurd, Amb.	Johan S. F. Botha, Amb.
Spain	Adm. Horacio Rivero, Amb.	Angel Sagaz, Amb.
Sri Lanka (Ceylon)	Christopher Van Hollen, Amb.	Neville Kanakaratne, Amb.
Sudan	William D. Brewer, Amb.	Abdel Aziz Hamza, Charge d'Affaires
Swaziland	Charles J. Nelson, Amb.	Dr. S. T. Msindazwe Sukati, Amb.
Sweden	Jerome H. Holland, Amb.	Lief Leifland, Charge d'Affaires
Switzerland	Shelby Davis, Amb.	Felix Schnyder, Amb.
Syrian Arab Rep.	*Vacant	Vacant
Tanzania	W. Beverly Carter, Jr., Amb.	Paul Bomani, Amb.
Thailand	Leonard Unger, Amb.	Anand Panyarachun, Amb.
Togo	Dwight Dickinson, Amb.	Epiphang A. Mawussi, Amb.
Trinidad and Tobago	Anthony D. Marshall, Amb.	J. R. P. Dumas, Charge d'Affaires.
Tunisia	Talcott W. Seelye, Amb.	Slaheddine El Goulli, Amb.
Turkey	William B. Macomber, Jr., Amb	Melih Esenbel, Amb.
Uganda	Thomas Patrick Melady, Amb.	Mustapha Ramathan, Amb.
USSR	Jacob D. Beam, Amb.	Anatoliy F. Dobrynin, Amb.
United Arab Emirates	Vacant	Vacant
Upper Volta	Donald B. Easum, Amb.	Telesphore Yaguibou, Amb.
Uruguay	Ernest V. Siracusa, Amb.	Dr. Hector Luisi, Amb.
Venezuela	Robert McClintock, Amb.	Andres Aguilar, Amb.
Vietnam	Graham A. Martin, Amb.	Tran Kim Phuong, Amb.
Yemen Arab Rep.	William R. Crawford, Jr., Amb.	Yahya Geghman, Amb.
Yugoslavia	Malcolm Toon, Amb.	Toma Granfil, Amb.
Western Samoa	Vacant	Vacant
Zaire	Sheldon B. Vance, Amb.	Lombo Lo Mangamanga, Amb.
Zambia	Jean M. Wilkowski, Amb.	Unia G. Mwila, Amb.

Special Missions

U.S. Mission to North Atlantic Treaty Org., Brussels — Donald Rumsfeld.
U.S. Mission to the European Communities, Brussels — Joseph A. Greenwald.
U.S. Mission to the International Atomic Energy Agency, Vienna — T. Keith Glennan.
U.S. Mission to the United Nations, New York — John A. Scali.
U.S. Mission to the European Office of the United Nations and Other International Organizations, Geneva — Vacant.
U.S. Mission to the Organization for Economic Cooperation and Development, Paris — Vacant.
U.S. Mission to the International Civil Aviation Organization, Montreal — Mrs. Betty Crites Dillon.

Judiciary of the United States
Data as of May 30, 1973

Justices of the United States Supreme Court

The Supreme Court comprises the Chief Justice of the United States and 8 Associate Justices, all appointed by the President with advice and consent of the Senate. Salaries: Chief Justice $62,500 annually, Associate Justice $60,000.

Name and residence (Chief Justices in italics)	Service Term	Yrs.	Born	Died	Name and residence (Chief Justices in italics)	Service Term	Yrs.	Born	Died
John Jay, N. Y	1789-1795	5	1745	1829	Henry B. Brown, Mich	1891-1906	15	1836	1913
John Rutledge, S. C	1789-1791	1	1739	1800	George Shiras, Jr., Pa	1892-1903	10	1832	1924
William Cushing, Mass	1789-1810	20	1732	1810	Howell E. Jackson, Tenn	1893-1895	2	1832	1895
James Wilson, Pa	1789-1798	8	1742	1798	Edward D. White, La	1894-1910	16	1845	1921
John Blair, Va	1789-1796	6	1732	1800	Rufus W. Peckham, N. Y	1896-1909	13	1838	1909
Robert H. Harrison, Md	1789-1790	...	1745	1790	Joseph McKenna, Calif	1898-1925	26	1843	1926
James Iredell, N.C.	1790-1799	9	1751	1799	Oliver W. Holmes, Mass.	1902-1932	29	1841	1935
Thomas Johnson, Md	1791-1793	1	1732	1819	William R. Day, Ohio	1903-1922	19	1849	1923
William Paterson, N. J	1793-1806	13	1745	1806	William H. Moody, Mass	1906-1910	3	1853	1917
John Rutledge, S.C	1795-(a)	...	1739	1800	Horace H. Lurton, Tenn	1910-1914	4	1844	1914
Samuel Chase, Md	1796-1811	15	1741	1811	Charles E. Hughes, N. Y	1910-1916	5	1862	1948
Oliver Ellsworth, Conn	1796-1799	4	1745	1807	Willis Van Devanter, Wyo	1911-1937	26	1859	1941
Bushrod Washington, Va	1798-1829	31	1762	1829	Joseph R. Lamar, Ga	1911-1916	5	1857	1916
Alfred Moore, N. C	1799-1804	4	1755	1810	*Edward D. White, La*	1910-1921	10	1845	1921
John Marshall, Va	1801-1835	34	1755	1835	Mahlon Pitney, N. J	1912-1922	10	1858	1924
William Johnson, S. C	1804-1834	30	1771	1834	Jas. C. McReynolds, Tenn	1914-1941	26	1862	1946
Brockholst Livingston, N. Y	1806-1823	16	1757	1823	Louis D. Brandeis, Mass	1916-1939	22	1856	1941
Thomas Todd, Ky	1807-1826	18	1765	1826	John H. Clarke, Ohio	1916-1922	5	1857	1945
Joseph Story, Mass	1811-1845	33	1779	1845	*William H. Taft, Conn*	1921-1930	9	1857	1930
Gabriel Duval, Md	1812-1835	22	1752	1844	George Sutherland, Utah	1922-1938	15	1862	1942
Smith Thompson, N. Y	1823-1843	20	1768	1843	Pierce Butler, Minn	1922-1939	16	1866	1939
Robert Trimble, Ky	1826-1828	2	1777	1828	Edward T. Sanford, Tenn	1923-1930	7	1865	1930
John McLean, Ohio	1829-1861	32	1785	1861	Harlan F. Stone, N. Y	1925-1941	16	1872	1946
Henry Baldwin, Pa	1830-1844	14	1780	1844	*Charles E. Hughes, N. Y*	1930-1941	11	1862	1948
James M. Wayne, Ga	1835-1867	32	1790	1867	Owen J. Roberts, Penn	1930-1945	15	1875	1955
Roger B. Taney, Md	1836-1864	28	1777	1854	Benjamin N. Cardozo, N.Y.	1932-1938	6	1870	1938
Philip P. Barbour, Va	1836-1841	4	1783	1841	Hugo L. Black, Ala	1937-1971	34	1886	1971
John Catron, Tenn	1837-1865	28	1786	1865	Stanley F. Reed, Ky	1938-1957	19	1884	....
John McKinley, Ala	1837-1852	15	1780	1852	Felix Frankfurter, Mass	1939-1962	23	1882	1965
Peter V. Daniel, Va	1841-1860	19	1784	1860	William O. Douglas, Conn	1939-....	...	1898	....
Samuel Nelson, N. Y	1845-1872	27	1792	1873	Frank Murphy, Mich	1940-1949	9	1890	1949
Levi Woodbury, N. H	1845-1851	5	1789	1851	*Harlan F. Stone, N. Y*	1941-1946	5	1872	1946
Robert C. Grier, Pa	1846-1870	23	1794	1870	James F. Byrnes, S. C	1941-1942	1	1879	1972
Benj. R. Curtis, Mass	1851-1857	6	1809	1874	Robert H. Jackson, N. Y	1941-1954	12	1892	1954
John A. Campbell, Ala	1853-1861	8	1811	1889	Wiley B. Rutledge, Iowa	1943-1949	6	1894	1949
Nathan Clifford, Me	1858-1881	23	1803	1881	Harold H. Burton, Ohio	1945-1958	13	1888	1964
Noah H. Swayne, Ohio	1862-1881	18	1804	1884	*Fred M. Vinson, Kentucky*	1946-1953	7	1890	1953
Samuel F. Miller, Iowa	1862-1890	28	1816	1890	Tom C. Clark, Texas	1949-1967	18	1899	....
David Davis, Ill	1862-1877	14	1815	1886	Sherman Minton, Indiana	1949-1956	7	1890	1965
Stephen J. Field, Calif	1863-1897	34	1816	1899	*Earl Warren, Calif*	1953-1969	16	1891	....
Salmon P. Chase, Ohio	1864-1873	8	1808	1873	John Marshall Harlan, N.Y.	1955-1971	16	1899	1971
William Strong, Pa	1870-1880	10	1808	1895	William J. Brennan, Jr., N.J.	1956-....	...	1906	....
Joseph P. Bradley, N. J	1870-1892	21	1813	1892	Charles E. Whittaker, Mo	1957-1962	5	1901	....
Ward Hunt, N. Y	1873-1882	9	1810	1886	Potter Stewart, Ohio	1958-....	...	1917	....
Morrison R. Waite, Ohio	1874-1888	14	1816	1888	Byron R. White, Colo	1962-....	...	1917	....
John M. Harlan, Ky	1877-1911	34	1833	1911	Arthur J. Goldberg, Ill	1962-1965	3	1908	....
William B. Woods, Ga	1881-1887	6	1824	1887	Abe Fortas, Tenn	1965-1969	4	1910	....
Stanley Matthews, Ohio	1881-1889	7	1824	1889	Thurgood Marshall, N. Y	1967-....	...	1908	....
Horace Gray, Mass	1882-1902	20	1828	1902	*Warren E. Burger, Va*	1969-....	...	1907	....
Samuel Blatchford, N. Y	1882-1893	11	1820	1893	Harry A. Blackmun, Minn	1970-....	...	1908	....
Lucius Q. C. Lamar, Miss	1888-1893	5	1825	1893	Lewis F. Powell, Jr., Va.	1971-....	...	1907	....
Melville W. Fuller, Ill	1888-1910	21	1833	1910	William H. Rehnquist, Ariz	1971-....	...	1924	....
David J. Brewer, Kan	1890-1910	20	1837	1910					

(a) Rejected Dec. 15, 1795. Robert H. Harrison, appointed 1789, apparently never served.

U.S. Court of Customs and Patent Appeals
Washington, D.C. 20439 (Salaries, $42,500)
Chief Judge — Howard T. Markey.
Associate Judges — Giles S. Rich, J. Lindsay Almond, Jr., Phillip B. Baldwin, Donald E. Lane.

United States Customs Court
New York, N.Y. 10007 (Salaries, $40,000)
Chief Judge — Nils A. Boe.
Judges — Morgan Ford, Scovel Richardson, Frederick Landis, James L. Watson, Herbert N. Maletz, Bernard Newman, Edward D. Re, Paul P. Rao.

United States Court of Claims
Washington, D.C. 20005 (Salaries, $42,500)
Chief Judge — Wilson Cowen.
Associate Judges — Oscar H. Davis, Shiro Kashiwa, Robert L. Kunzig, Marion T. Bennett, Byron G. Skelton, Philip Nichols, Jr.

United States Tax Court
Washington, D.C. 20004
Chief Judge — William M. Drennen.
Judges — Arnold Raum, Bruce M. Forrester, Irene F. Scott, William M. Fay, Howard A. Dawson, Jr., Austin Hoyt, Theodore Tannenwald, Jr., Charles R.

Simpson, C. Moxley Featherston, Leo H. Irwin, Samuel B. Sterrett, William Quealy, William A. Goffe, Cynthia H. Hall, Darrell D. Wiles.

U.S. Courts of Appeals
(Salaries, $42,500, CJ means Chief Judge)
District of Columbia — David L. Bazelon, CJ; J. Skelly Wright, Carl McGowan, Edward Allen Tamm, Harold Leventhal, Spottswood W. Robinson III, Roger Robb, George E. MacKinnon, Malcolm Richard Wilkey; Clerk's Office, Washington, D.C. 20001.
First Circuit (Me., Mass., N.H., R.I., P.R.) — Frank M. Coffin, CJ; Edward M. McEntee, Levin H. Campbell; Clerk's Office, Boston 02109.
Second Circuit (Conn., N.Y., Vt.) — Henry J. Friendly, CJ; Irving R. Kaufman, Paul R. Hays, Wilfred Feinberg, Walter R. Mansfield, William H. Mulligan, James L. Oakes, William H. Timbers; Clerk's Office, New York 10007.
Third Circuit (Del., N.J., Pa., Virgin Islands) — Collins J. Seitz, CJ; Francis L. Van Dusen, Ruggero J. Aldisert, Arlin M. Adams, John J. Gibbons, Max Rosenn, James Rosen, James Hunter III, Joseph F. Weis; Clerk's Office, Philadelphia 19107.
Fourth Circuit (Md., N.C., S.C., Va., W.Va.) — Clement F. Haynsworth, CJ; Herbert S. Boreman,

Harrison L. Winter, J. Braxton Craven, Jr., John D. Butzner, Jr., Donald Russell, John A. Field, Jr., H. Emory Widener, Jr.; Clerk's Office, Richmond, Va. 23219.

Fifth Circuit (Ala., Fla., Ga., La., Miss., Tex., Canal Zone)—John R. Brown, CJ; John Minor Wisdom, Walter Pettus Gewin, Griffin B. Bell, Homer Thornberry, James P. Coleman, Irving L. Goldberg, Robert A. Ainsworth, Jr., John C. Godbold, David W. Dyer, Bryan Simpson, Lewis R. Morgan, Charles Clark, Joe McDonald Ingraham, Paul H. Roney; Clerk's Office, New Orleans, La. 70130.

Sixth Circuit (Ky., Mich., Ohio, Tenn.)—Harry Phillips, CJ; Paul C. Weick, George Clifton Edwards, Jr., Anthony J. Celebrezze, John W. Peck, Wade H. McCree, Jr., William E. Miller, W. Wallace Kent, Pierce Lively; Clerk's Office, Cincinnati 45202.

Seventh Circuit (Ill., Ind., Wis.)—Luther M. Swygert, CJ; Roger J. Kiley, Thomas E. Fairchild, Walter J. Cummings, Otto Kerner, Wilbur F. Pell, Jr., John Paul Stevens, Robert A. Sprecher; Clerk's Office, Chicago 60604.

Eighth Circuit (Ark., Iowa, Minn., Mo., Neb., N.D., S.D.)—M. C. Matthes, CJ; Pat Mehaffy, Floyd R. Gibson, Donald P. Lay, Gerald W. Heaney, Myron H. Bright, Donald R. Ross, Roy L. Stephenson; Clerk's Office, St. Louis 63101.

Ninth Circuit (Ariz., Calif., Idaho, Mont., Nev., Ore., Wash., Alaska, Hawaii, Guam)—Richard H. Chambers, CJ; Charles M. Merrill, M. Oliver Koelsch, James R. Browning, Ben Cushing Duniway, Walter Ely, Shirley M. Hufstedler, Eugene A. Wright, Ozell M. Trask, Herbert Y. C. Choy, J. Clifford Wallace, Alfred T. Goodwin; Clerk's Office, San Francisco 94101.

Tenth Circuit (Colo., Kan., N.M., Okla., Utah, Wyo.) —David T. Lewis, CJ; Delmas C. Hill, Oliver Seth, William J. Holloway, Jr., Robert H. McWilliams, James E. Barrett, William E. Doyle; Clerk's Office, Denver, Colo. 80202.

U.S. District Courts
(Salaries, $40,000. CJ means Chief Judge)

Alabama—Northern: Frank H. McFadden, CJ; Harlan Hobart Grooms, Seybourn H. Lynne, Clarence W. Allgood, Sam C. Pointer, Jr.; Clerk's Office, Birmingham 35203. **Middle:** Frank M. Johnson, Jr., CJ; Robert E. Varner; Clerk's Office, Montgomery 36101. **Southern:** Virgil Pittman, CJ; William Brevard Hand; Clerk's Office, Mobile 36602.

Alaska—Raymond E. Plummer, CJ; James A. von der Heydt; Clerk's Office, Anchorage 99510.

Arizona—Walter Early Craig, CJ; James A. Walsh, C. A. Muecke, William P. Copple, William C. Frey; Clerk's Office, Phoenix 85025.

Arkansas—Eastern: J. Smith Henley, CJ; Oren Harris, Garnett Thomas Eisele; Clerk's Office, Little Rock 72203. **Western:** Oren Harris, CJ; Paul X. Williams, J. Smith Henley; Clerk's Office, Fort Smith 72902.

California—Northern: Oliver J. Carter, CJ; Albert C. Wollenburg, Lloyd H. Burke, William T. Sweigert, Alfonso J. Zirpoli, Stanley A. Weigel, Robert F. Peckham, Robert H. Schnacke, Samuel Conti, Spencer M. Williams, Charles B. Renfrew; Clerk's Office, San Francisco 94102. **Eastern:** Thomas J. MacBride, CJ; M. D. Crocker, Philip C. Wilkins; Clerk's Office, Sacramento 95814. **Central:** Albert Lee Stephens, Jr., CJ; Charles H. Carr, Jesse W. Curtis, E. Avery Crary, Francis C. Whelan, Irving Hill, A. Andrew Hauk, William P. Gray, Warren J. Ferguson, Manuel L. Real, Harry Pregerson, David W. Williams, Robert J. Kelleher, Wm. Matthew Byrne, Jr., Lawrence T. Lydick, Malcolm M. Lucas; Clerk's Office, Los Angeles 90012. **Southern:** Edward J. Schwartz, CJ; Howard B. Turrentine, Gordon Thompson, Jr., Leland C. Nielsen, William B. Enright; Clerk's Office, San Diego 92101.

Colorado—Alfred A. Arraj, CJ; Olin Hatfield Chilson, Fred M. Winner, Sherman G. Finesilver; Clerk's Office, Denver 80201.

Connecticut—M. Joseph Blumenfeld, CJ; T. Emmet Clarie, Robert C. Zampano, Jon O. Newman; Clerk's Office, New Haven 06505.

Delaware—Caleb M. Wright, CJ; James L. Latchum, Walter K. Stapleton; Clerk's Office, Wilmington 19899.

District of Columbia—John J. Sirica, CJ; George L. Hart, Jr., William B. Jones, Howard F. Corcoran, Oliver Gasch, William B. Bryant, John Lewis Smith, Jr., Aubrey E. Robinson, Jr., Joseph C. Waddy, Gerhard A. Gesell, John H. Pratt, June L. Green, Barrington D. Parker, Charles R. Richey, Thomas A. Flannery; Clerk's Office, Washington 20001.

Florida—Northern: Winston E. Arnow, CJ; David L.

Middlebrooks, Jr.; Clerk's Office, Tallahassee 32302. **Middle:** George C. Young, CJ; Charles R. Scott, Ben Krentzman, Gerald B. Tjoflat, William Terrell Hodges; Clerk's Office, Jacksonville 32201. **Southern:** Charles B. Fulton, CJ; William O. Mehrtens, C. Clyde Atkins, Joe Eaton, Peter T. Fay, James Lawrence King, Norman C. Roettger, Jr.; Clerk's Office, Miami 33101.

Georgia—Northern: Sidney O. Smith, Jr., CJ; Newell Edenfield, Albert J. Henderson, Jr., William C. O'Kelly, Charles A. Moye, Jr., Richard C. Freeman; Clerk's Office, Atlanta 30301. **Middle:** J. Robert Elliott, CJ; Wilbur D. Owens; Clerk's Office, Macon 31202. **Southern:** Alexander A. Lawrence, CJ; Anthony A. Alaimo; Clerk's Office, Savannah 31402.

Hawaii—Martin Pence, CJ; Samuel P. King; Clerk's Office, Honolulu 96801.

Idaho—Ray McNichols, CJ; J. Blaine Anderson; Clerk's Office, Boise 83702.

Illinois—Northern: Edwin A. Robson, CJ; Richard B. Austin, James B. Parsons, Hubert L. Will, Bernard M. Decker, Abraham L. Marovitz, William J. Lynch, Frank J. McGarr, Thomas R. McMillen, William J. Bauer, Richard W. McLaren, Philip Tone; Clerk's Office, Chicago 60604. **Eastern:** Henry S. Wise, CJ; James L. Foreman; Clerk's Office, Danville 61832. **Southern:** Omer Poos, CJ; Robert D. Morgan; Clerk's Office, Peoria 61601.

Indiana—Northern: George N. Beamer, CJ; Jesse E. Eschbach; Clerk's Office, Hammond 46325. **Southern:** William E. Steckler, CJ; Cale J. Holder, S. Hugh Dillin, James E. Noland; Clerk's Office, Indianapolis 46204.

Iowa—Northern: Edward J. McManus, CJ; William C. Hanson; Clerk's Office, Cedar Rapids 52401. **Southern:** William C. Hanson, CJ; William C. Stuart; Clerk's Office, Des Moines 50309.

Kansas—Wesley E. Brown, CJ; George Templar, Frank G. Theis, Earl E. O'Connor; Clerk's Office, Wichita 67201.

Kentucky—Eastern: Bernard T. Moynahan, Jr., CJ; Mac Swinford, Howard David Hermansdorfer; Clerk's Office, Lexington 40501. **Western:** James F. Gordon, CJ; Mac Swinford, Rhodes Bratcher, Charles M. Allen; Clerk's Office, Louisville 40202.

Louisiana—Eastern: Frederick J. R. Heebe, CJ; Herbert W. Christenberry, Edward J. Boyle, Sr., Lansing L. Mitchell, Fred J. Cassibry, Alvin B. Rubin, James A. Comiskey, R. Blake West, Jack M. Gordon; Clerk's Office, New Orleans 70130. **Middle:** E. Gordon West; Clerk's Office, Baton Rouge 70801. **Western:** Benjamin C. Dawkins, Jr., CJ; Edwin F. Hunter, Jr., Richard J. Putnam, Nauman S. Scott; Clerk's Office, Shreveport 71161.

Maine—Edward Thaxter Gignoux; Clerk's Office, Portland 04112.

Maryland—Edward S. Northrop, CJ; Frank A. Kaufman, Alexander Harvey II, James R. Miller, Jr., Joseph Young, Herbert F. Murray, C. Stanley Blair; Clerk's Office, Baltimore 21202.

Massachusetts—Andrew A. Caffrey, CJ; W. Arthur Garrity, Jr., Frank J. Murray, Frank H. Freedman, Joseph L. Tauro; Clerk's Office, Boston 02109.

Michigan—Eastern: Frederick W. Kaess, CJ; Ralph M. Freeman, Stephen J. Roth, Damon J. Keith, Lawrence Gubow, Cornelia G. Kennedy, John Feikens, Philip Pratt, Robert E. DeMascio, Charles W. Joiner; Clerk's Office, Detroit 48226. **Western:** Noel P. Fox, CJ; Albert J. Engel; Clerk's Office, Grand Rapids 49502.

Minnesota—Edward J. Devitt, CJ; Earl R. Larson, Miles W. Lord, Philip Neville; Clerk's Office, St. Paul 55101.

Mississippi—Northern: William C. Keady, CJ; Orma R. Smith; Clerk's Office, Oxford 38655. **Southern:** Dan M. Russell, Jr., CJ; William Harold Cox, Walter L. Nixon, Jr.; Clerk's Office, Jackson 39205.

Missouri—Eastern: James H. Meredith, CJ; John K. Regan, William R. Collinson, H. Kenneth Wangelin, William H. Webster; Clerk's Office, St. Louis 63101. **Western:** William H. Becker, CJ; John W. Oliver, William R. Collinson, Elmo B. Hunter, H. Kenneth Wangelin; Clerk's Office, Kansas City 64106.

Montana—Russell E. Smith, CJ; James F. Battin; Clerk's Office, Butte 59701.

Nebraska—Warren K. Urbom, CJ; Robert V. Denney; Clerk's Office, Omaha 68101.

Nevada—Roger D. Foley, CJ; Bruce R. Thompson; Clerk's Office, Las Vegas 89101.

New Hampshire—Hugh H. Bownes; Clerk's Office, Concord 03301.

New Jersey—James A. Coolahan, CJ; Mitchell H.

Cohen, Lawrence A. Whipple, George H. Barlow, Leonard I. Garth, Clarkson S. Fisher, John J. Kitchen, Frederick B. Lacey; Clerk's Office, Trenton 08605. **New Mexico**—H. Vearle Payne, CJ; Howard C. Bratton, Edwin L. Mechem; Clerk's Office, Albuquerque 87103. **New York—Northern:** James T. Foley, CJ; Edmund Port; Clerk's Office, Albany 12201. **Eastern:** Jacob Mishler, CJ; John R. Bartels, John F. Dooling, Jr., George Rosling, Jack B. Weinstein, Anthony J. Travia, Orrin G. Judd, Mark A. Costantino, Edward R. Neaher; Clerk's Office, Brooklyn 11201. **Southern:** David N. Edelstein, CJ; Edward Weinfeld, Charles M. Metzner, Lloyd F. MacMahon, Dudley B. Bonsal, Harold R. Tyler, Jr., Inzer B. Wyatt, John M. Cannella, Charles H. Tenney, Marvin E. Frankel, Constance Baker Motley, Milton Pollack, Morris E. Lasker, Murray I. Gurfein, Lawrence W. Pierce, Arnold Bauman, Lee P. Gagliardi, Charles L. Brieant, Jr., Whitman Knapp, Charles E. Stewart, Jr., Thomas P. Griesa, Robert L. Carter, Robert J. Ward, Kevin Thomas Duffy; Clerk's Office, New York City 10007. **Western:** John O. Henderson, CJ; Harold P. Burke, John T. Curtin; Clerk's Office, Buffalo 14202. **North Carolina—Eastern:** Algernon L. Butler, CJ; John D. Larkins, Jr., Franklin T. Dupree, Jr.; Clerk's Office, Raleigh 27611. **Middle:** Eugene A. Gordon, CJ; Hiram H. Ward, CJ; Clerk's Office, Greensboro 27402. **Western:** Woodrow Wilson Jones, CJ; James B. McMillan; Clerk's Office, Asheville 28802. **North Dakota**—Paul Benson, CJ; Bruce M. Van Sickle; Clerk's Office, Bismarck 58501. **Ohio—Northern:** Frank J. Battisti, CJ; Ben C. Green, Don J. Young, William K. Thomas, Thomas D. Lambros, Robert B. Krupansky, Nicholas J. Walinski, Leroy J. Contie, Jr.; Clerk's Office, Cleveland 44114. **Southern:** Joseph P. Kinneary, CJ; Timothy S. Hogan, Davis S. Porter, Carl B. Rubin; Clerk's Office, Columbus 43215. **Oklahoma—Northern:** Allen E. Barrow, CJ; Luther L. Bohanon, Frederick A. Daugherty; Clerk's Office, Tulsa 74103. **Eastern:** Edwin Langley, CJ; Luther L. Bohanon, Frederick A. Daugherty; Clerk's Office, Muskogee 74402. **Western:** Frederick A. Daugherty, CJ; Luther L. Bohanon, Stephen S. Chandler, Luther B. Eubanks; Clerk's Office, Oklahoma City 73102. **Oregon**—Robert C. Belloni, CJ; James M. Burns, Otto R. Skopil, Jr.; Clerk's Office, Portland 97207. **Pennsylvania—Eastern:** John S. Lord III, CJ; Alfred L. Luongo, John Morgan Davis, A. Leon Higginbotham, Jr., John P. Fullam, Charles R. Weiner, E. Mac Troutman, Thomas A. Masterson, John B. Hannum, Daniel H. Huyett III, Donald W. Van Artsdalen, J. William Ditter, Jr., Edward R. Becker, James H. Gorbey, Raymond J. Broderick, Clarence C. Newcomer, Clifford Scott Green, Louis Charles Bechtle; Clerk's Office, Philadelphia 19107. **Middle:** Michael H. Sheridan, CJ; William J. Nealon, Jr., R. Dixon Herman, Malcolm Muir; Clerk's Office, Scranton 18501. **Western:** Rabe Ferguson Marsh, CJ; Herbert P. Sorg, Edward Dumbauld, Louis Rosenberg, Gerald J. Weber, Joseph F. Weis, Jr., William W. Knox, Hubert I. Teitel-

baum, Barron P. McCune, Ralph F. Scalera; Clerk's Office, Pittsburgh 15230. **Rhode Island**—Raymond J. Pettine, CJ; Edward William Day; Clerk's Office, Providence 02901. **South Carolina**—J. Robert Martin, CJ; Robert W. Hemphill, Charles E. Simons, Jr., Solomon Blatt, Jr., Robert F. Chapman; Clerk's Office, Columbia 29202. **South Dakota**—Fred J. Nichol, CJ; Andrew W. Bogue; Clerk's Office, Sioux Falls 57102. **Tennessee—Eastern:** Frank W. Wilson, CJ; Robert L. Taylor, C. G. Neese; Clerk's Office, Knoxville 37901. **Middle:** Frank Gray, Jr., CJ; L. Clure Morton; Clerk's Office, Nashville 37203. **Western:** Bailey Brown, CJ; Robert M. McRae, Jr., Harry W. Wellford; Clerk's Office, Memphis 38103. **Texas—Northern:** Leo Brewster, CJ; Sarah T. Hughes, William M. Taylor, Jr., Halbert O. Woodward, Eldon B. Mahon, Robert M. Hill; Clerk's Office, Dallas 75202. **Southern:** Ben C. Connally, CJ; Allen B. Hannay, Reynaldo G. Garza, James Noel, Jr., John V. Singleton, Jr., Woodrow B. Seals, Carl O. Bue, Jr., Owen D. Cox; Clerk's Office, Houston 77061. **Eastern:** Joe J. Fisher, CJ; William Wayne Justice, William M. Steger; Clerk's Office, Beaumont 77704. **Western:** Adrian A. Spears, CJ; Dorwin W. Suttle, Jack Roberts, Ernest Guinn, John H. Wood, Jr.; Clerk's Office, San Antonio 78298. **Utah**—Willis W. Ritter, CJ; Aldon J. Anderson; Clerk's Office, Salt Lake City 84101. **Vermont**—James S. Holden, CJ; Albert W. Coffrin; Clerk's Office, Burlington 05401. **Virginia—Eastern:** Walter E. Hoffman, CJ; Oren R. Lewis, Robert R. Merhige, Jr., Richard B. Kellam, John A. MacKenzie, Albert V. Bryan, Jr.; Clerk's Office, Norfolk 23501. **Western:** Ted Dalton, CJ; Thomas J. Michie; Clerk's Office, Roanoke 24006. **Washington—Eastern:** William N. Goodwin, CJ; Marshall A. Neill; Clerk's Office, Spokane 99210. **Western:** William T. Beeks, CJ; William N. Goodwin, Walter T. McGovern, Morell E. Sharp; Clerk's Office, Seattle 98104. **West Virginia—Northern:** Robert Earl Maxwell, CJ; Sidney L. Christie; Clerk's Office, Elkins 26241. **Southern:** Sidney L. Christie, CJ; Dennis Raymond Knapp, Kenneth K. Hall; Clerk's Office, Charleston 25329. **Wisconsin—Eastern:** John W. Reynolds, CJ; Myron L. Gordon; Clerk's Office, Milwaukee 53202. **Western:** James E. Doyle; Clerk's Office, Madison 53701. **Wyoming**—Ewing T. Kerr; Clerk's Office, Cheyenne 82001.

Territorial Courts

Canal Zone—Guthrie F. Crowe; Clerk's Office, Ancon. **Guam**—Cristobal C. Duenas; Clerk's Office, Agana, 96910. **Puerto Rico**—Hiram R. Cancio, CJ; Jose Toledo, Hernan G. Pesquera; Clerk's Office, San Juan 00904. **Virgin Islands**—Almeric L. Christian, CJ; Warren H. Young; Clerk's Office, Charlotte Amalie, St. Thomas 00801.

The Federal Judicial System

The federal judicial system begins with the District Court. There are 89 of these courts, at least one in each state and Washington, D.C. Called courts of general jurisdiction, they have power to determine the facts and pass judgement in criminal cases involving violations of federal law and in civil cases where the amount of the suit is $10,000 or more and the contending parties reside in different states. Other types of cases handled by District Courts include suits in admiralty (maritime matters involving navigational waters), bankruptcy, patents, trademarks and copyrights.

Equal to the District Courts are special courts which handle only certain issues: the U.S. Customs Court, the Tax Court, and the Court of Claims, which hears suits against the U.S. government.

These trial courts are responsible for finding the facts in a case and for applying the law to the facts found. Appellate courts, theoretically, do not review the trial court's findings of fact. The job of the appellate court is to decide whether the trial judge applied the law properly. If an appellate court

decides that there was error in the application of the law, it can simply reverse the lower court's decision and end the case there. But it can also send the case back to the lower court for retrial.

The District Courts and special courts are trial courts. Above them are several levels of appellate courts. The U.S. Court of Appeals, often called circuit courts, sits in 10 judicial circuits and Washington, D.C. It hears appeals from the District Courts and the Tax Court, and will review decisions of federal administrative agencies if it appears that such decisions may be unreasonable or arbitrary. The U.S. Court of Customs and Patent Appeals hears appeals from the Customs Court.

Ultimately, all decisions of these courts can be reviewed by the U.S. Supreme Court, which is also the first court of appeal from the U.S. Court of Claims. Besides reviewing federal court decisions, the Supreme Court is empowered to hear suits between the states and to review state supreme court decisions if an issue of federal law or the Constitution is involved.

National Political Committees

As of June, 1973

Democratic Officers

Chairman — Robert S. Strauss.
Vice Chairmen — Basil Paterson, Caroline Wilkins.
Secretary — Dorothy V. Bush.
Treasurer — C. Peter McColough.
National Headquarters — 1625 Massachusetts Ave., N.W., Washington, D.C. 20036.

Republican Officers

Chairman — George Bush.
Co-Chairman — Janet J. Johnston.
Vice Chairmen — Ray C. Bliss, Mrs. Hope McCormick, Bernard M. Shanley, Mrs. J. William Marriott, Howard H. Callaway, Mrs. Paula F. Hawkins, George P. Stadelman, Mrs. Isabel C. Moberly.
Secretary — Mrs. Jack L. Stacy.
Treasurer — John M. Christie.
National Headquarters — 310 First St., S.E., Washington, D.C. 20003.

Members of the Democratic National Committee

(as of June, 1972. * indicates state chairman)

Alabama
Albert Rains, Gadsden
Ruth Johnson Owens, Birmingham
*Robert S. Vance, Birmingham
Dot Little, Huntsville

Alaska
Clifford E. Warren, Anchorage
Bettye Fahrenkamp, Fairbanks
*Mellie Terwilliger, Tok
Dr. Alan Homay, Anchorage

Arizona
Sam Goddard, Phoenix
Ora DeConcini, Tucson
*Charles Pine, Phoenix
Barbara Jarvis, Globe

Arkansas
Charles Ward, Conway
Mrs. Jack Carnes, Camden
*Brad Jesson, Fort Smith
Nancy Balton, Osceola

California
*John Burton, Sacramento
Shirley Goldinger, Los Angeles
Ms. Wallace Albertson, Los Angeles
Wyanne Bunyan, Mill Valley
Mary Ledesma, Huntington Pk.
Jo Seidita, Northridge
Madeleine Russell, San Francisco
Richard Chavez, Keene
Dorman Commons, Fullerton
Leon Ralph, Sacramento
Marvin Shapiro, Los Angeles
Al Villa, Fresno

Colorado
Arnold Alperstein, Lakewood
Doris Banks, Denver
*Monte Pascoe, Denver
Betty Orten, Westminister

Connecticut
John Golden, New Haven
Beatrice Rosentha, Waterford
*John M. Bailey, Hartford
Katherine T. Quinn, Hartford
John J. Driscoll, Bridgeport

Delaware
Edward Davis, Wilmington
Rebecca Twilley, Dover
*Michael Poppiti, Wilmington
Gertrude Tharp, Lewes

District of Columbia
John Hechinger, Washington
Lillian Huff, Washington
*William Lucy, Washington
Barbara Morgan, Washington

Florida
Dr. T. Wayne Bailey, DeLand
Hazel Talley Evans, St. Petersburg
*Jon C. Moyle, W. Palm Beach
Ann M. Cramer, Miramar
Gov. Reubin Askew, Tallahassee
Norman Bie, Clearwater

Georgia
Michael Jones, Atlanta
Mayor Mary Hitt, Jesup
*Charles Kirbo, Atlanta
Ms. Dot Padgett, Douglasville
Herbert Mabry, Atlanta

Hawaii
Leo B. Rodby, Wahiawa
Momi Minn Lee, Honolulu
*David C. McClung, Honolulu
Matilda Molina, Honolulu

Idaho
James Donart, Weiser
Carolyn Selander, Boise
*Joe McCarter, Corral
Ms. Ione Rambeau, Lewiston

Illinois
*John P. Touhy, Chicago
S. Jeanne Wycoff, Aledo
Jane Byrne, Chicago
Margaret Gordon, Glencoe
John Karns, Jr., Belleville
Cecil Partee, Chicago
John Rednour, Duquoin
Penny Lee Severns, Decatur

Indiana
Richard Stoner, Columbus
Katie Wolf, Reynolds
*Gordon St. Angelo, Indianapolis
Judy Burton, Rochester
Rozelle Boyd, Indianapolis

Iowa
Robert D. Fulton, Waterloo
Mrs. Dagmar Vidal, Hampton
*Clif Larson, Des Moines
Jean Haugland, Lake Mills

Kansas
Tom Corcoran, Topeka
Nell Blangers, Salina
*Norbert Dreiling, Hays
Mary Allen, Topeka

Kentucky
Gov. Wendell Ford, Frankfort
Martha Layne Collins, Versailles
*J. R. Miller, Frankfort
Marie Turner, Jackson

Louisiana
Leon Irwin III, New Orleans
Mary Lou Winters, Columbia
Phyllis Landrieu, New Orleans

Maine
George Mitchell, S. Portland
Nancy Chandler, South China
*Violet Pease, Augusta
David Bustin, Augusta

Maryland
Thomas Farrington, Upper Marlboro
Dr. Mildred Otenasek, Baltimore
*William James, Bel Air
Mrs. Lyn Clark, Kensington

Massachusetts
Jerome Grossman, Newton
Helen Rees, Brookline
*Charles Flaherty, Cambridge
Eva B. Hester, Clinton
Doris Kanin, Arlington
Dr. Jesse Parks, Springfield

Michigan
Coleman Young, Detroit
Helen Irving, Detroit
*Morley Winograd, Lansing
Olivia Maynard, Flint
Sam Fishman, Detroit

Neil Staebler, Ann Arbor
Shirley Robinson, Detroit

Minnesota
Earl Craig, Minneapolis
Koryne Horbal, Minneapolis
*Henry Fischer, Minneapolis
Ruth Cain, Minneapolis
Ann Ober, Lake Crystal

Mississippi
Charles Evers, Fayette
Patt Derian, Jackson
*Aaron Henry, Clarksdale
Kathleen Feyen, Greenwood

Missouri
Warren Hearnes, Jefferson City
Jean Briscoe, New London
*David Donnelly, Jefferson City
Ina Shaffrey, St. Louis
Kermit Lewis, Neosho

Montana
Leif Erickson, Helena
Gladys Makela, Helena
*John Bartlett, Whitefish
Grace Bowman, Helena

Nebraska
Thomas Kelley, Omaha
Frances Ohmstede, Guide Rock
*Hess Dyas, Lincoln
Dorothy Ley, Wayne

Nevada
Grant Sawyer, Las Vegas
Virginia Catt, Las Vegas
*Phil Carlino, Las Vegas
Mrs. Didi Carson, Las Vegas

New Hampshire
Hugh Gallen, Littleton
Maria Carrier, Manchester
Jean Wallin, Nashua

New Jersey
Richard Hughes, Newark
Thelma Sharp, Vineland
*Salvatore Bontempo, Florham Park
Anne Martindell, Princeton
Richard I. Samuel, Westfield
Nicholas Caputo, Newark

New Mexico
Rudy Ortiz, Albuquerque
Mrs. U. D. Sawyer, Crossroads
*Mike Anaya, Moriarty
Marie Eaves, Farmington

New York
Basil Paterson, New York
Jean Angell, Ithaca
*Joseph Crangle, Buffalo
Mae Gurevich, New York
Patrick Cunningham, Bronx
Daniel Collins, Brooklyn
Lucille King, Rochester
Margaret Costanza, Rochester
Theordora Martinez, Brooklyn
Dominic Baranello, Medford
Robert Dryfoos, New York
Allard Lowenstein, Brooklyn

North Carolina
Dr. Eugene Poston, Boiling Springs
Gladys Bullard, Raleigh
*James Sugg, New Bern
Alfreda Webb, Greensboro
Howard Lee, Chapel Hill

North Dakota
Gorman King, Valley City
Bea Peterson, New England
*Richard Ista, Fargo
Florence Olson, Enderlin

Ohio
Joseph Cole, Cleveland
Carol McClendon, Cleveland
*William Lavelle, Athens
Esther Mayl, Kettering
Robert McAlister, Columbus
Ann Fleckner, Columbus
Doris Rankin, Cincinnati
Sen. Morris Jackson, Cleveland

Oklahoma
J. C. Cobb, Tishomingo
Daphfine Shear, Oklahoma City
'Guy Thompson, Oklahoma City
Mrs. Lorray Dyson, Guthrie

Oregon
Blaine Whipple, Portland
Alice Corbett, Portland
'Caroline Wilkins, Corvallis
Dr. John Meyer, Canyonville

Pennsylvania
Robert Juniu, Cranton
Rita Wilson Kane, Pittsburgh
*Dennis Thiemann, Harrisburg
C. Delores Tucker, Harrisburg
George Schwartz, Philadelphia
Michael Johnson, Harrisburg
Ann Jordan, Philadelphia
Barbara Altemus, Bethlehem
James Kelley, Greensburg

Rhode Island
Milton Stanzler, Providence
Mildred Nichols, Providence
*Charles T. Reilly, Barrington
Mary Whalen, Warwick

South Carolina
Robert McNair, Columbia
Barbara Sylvester, Florence
*Donald Fowler, Columbia
Alice Cicenia, Summerville

South Dakota
Frank Wallahan, Rapid City
Mary Wallner, Sioux Falls
*James Guffey, Hayti
Beverly Bruce, Mitchell

Tennessee
D. Bruce Shine, Kingsport
Jean Livingston, Chattanooga
*James R. Sasser, Nashville
Mrs. Claude Dodd, Ridgely

Texas
Jess Hay, Dallas
Jane Blumberg, Seguin
*Calvin Guest, Bryan
Barbara Jordan, Houston
Ms. Billie Carr, Houston
Hall Timanus, Houston
Joe J. Bernal, San Antonio

Utah
Wayne Black, Salt Lake City
Jean Westwood, West Jordan
*John Klas, Salt Lake City
Val Booth, Brigham City

Vermont
Daniel O'Brien, S. Burlington
Margaret Hartigan, Burlington
Leonard V. Wilson, Burlington
Margaret Lucenti, Barre

Virginia
George Rawlings, Jr., Fredericks-
burg
Ruth Harvey Charity, Danville
*Joseph Fitzpatrick, Norfolk
Jessie Rattley, Newport News
W. Pat Jennings, Washington, D.C.

Washington
Luke Graham, Seattle
Claudine Davis, Coulee City
*Neale Chaney, Seattle
Gladys Morgen, Spokane
Ed Claplanhoo, Neah Bay

West Virginia
Rudolph DiTrapano, Charleston
JoAnne Powell, Romney
*William Watson, Wellsburg
Jane Lucento, Alpoca

Wisconsin
Donald Peterson, Eau Claire
Mary Lou Burg, Arlington, Va.
*M. William Gerrard, LaCrosse
Marge Dittman, Madison
Michael Bleicher, Madison

Wyoming
Jerry Housel, Cody
June Boyle, Laramie
*Don Anselmi, Rock Springs
Sylvia Freeman, Sheridan

Members of the Republican National Committee

(as of June, 1973. * indicates state chairman)

Alabama
Perry O. Hooper, Montgomery
Mrs. Jean Sullivan, Selma
J. Richard (Dick) Bennett, Jr.,*,
Birmingham

Alaska
Eldon R. Ulmer, Anchorage
Mrs. John Holm, Fairbanks
John B. (Jack) Coghill*, Nenana

Arizona
John H. Haugh, Tucson
Mrs. William Crisp, Scottsdale
Harry Rosenzweig*, Phoenix

Arkansas
Odell Pollard, Searcy
Mrs. Leona A. Troxell, Rose Bud
Jim Caldwell*, Little Rock

California
Edward Mills, Los Angeles
Miss Janet Johnston, Winters
Gordon Luce*, San Diego

Colorado
Bill Daniels, Denver
Mrs. Daniel Gray, Denver
Dwight A. Hamilton*, Denver

Connecticut
John Alsop, Hartford
Mrs. Mary H. Boatwright,
Stonington
J. Brian Gaffney*, Hartford

Delaware
Thomas B. Evans, Jr., Wilmington
Mrs. Bruce F. Day, Wilmington
Gene Bunting*, Selbyville

District of Columbia
Robert S. Carter, D.C.
Mrs., J. Willard Marriott, D.C.

Florida
William C. Cramer, Miami
Mrs. Paula F. Hawkins, Maitland
L. E. Thomas*, Panama City

Georgia
Howard H. (Bo) Callaway, Atlanta
Mrs. Nora Allen, Albany
Robert J. Shaw*, Atlanta

Hawaii
Edward Brennan, Honolulu
Mrs. Kinau Boyd Kamalii,
Mrs. Max S. Coray*, Honolulu.

Idaho
David Little, Emmett
Mrs. Orriette Sinclair, Twin Falls
Mrs. Gordon Miner*, Wallace

Illinois
Vacant
Mrs. Hope McCormick, Chicago
Victor L. Smith*, Robinson

Indiana
L. Keith Bulen, Indianapolis
Mrs. Nat Hill, Bloomington
Thomas S. Milligan*, Indianapolis

Iowa
Charles E. Wittenmeyer,
Davenport
Mrs. Elmer M. Smith, Des Moines
John C. McDonald*, Des Moines

Kansas
McDill Boyd, Phillipsburg
Mrs. Richard D. Rogers,
Manhattan
Jack Ranson*, Wichita

Kentucky
Edwin G. Middleton, Louisville
Mrs. Harold B. Barton, Corbin
John H. Kerr*, Lexington

Louisiana
David C. Treen, Wash., D.C.
Mrs. Jean McG. Boese, Alexandria
James H. Boyce*, Baton Rouge

Maine
Cyril M. Joly, Jr., Waterville
Mrs. Henrietta Page Crane,
Rockland
Harold L. Jones*, Augusta

Maryland
Richard M. Allen, Salisbury
Miss Louise Gore, Potomac
Alexander M. (Sandy) Lankler*,
Potomac

Massachusetts
Bruce Crane, Dalton
Mrs. Henry Dunster Howe,
Belmont
Otto A. Wahlrab*, Boston

Michigan
Creighton Holden, St. Clair
Mrs. John (Ranny) Riecker,
Midland
William F. McLaughlin*, Lansing

Minnesota
Rudy Boschwitz, Minneapolis
Mrs. Harold LeVander, So. St. Paul
Dave Krogseng*, Minneapolis

Mississippi
Victor Mavar, Biloxi
Mrs. James F. Hooper, Columbus
Clarke Reed*, Greenville

Missouri
John F. Nangle, Clayton
Mrs. M. Stanley Ginn, Columbia
Richard L. Berkley*, Kansas City

Montana
William R. Mackay, Roscoe
Mrs. Isabel C. Moberly, Shelby
W. L. Bill Holter*, Great Falls

Nebraska
R. L. "Dick" Herman, Omaha
Mrs. Richard W. Smith, Lincoln
William E. Barrett*, Lexington

Nevada
William M. Laub, Las Vegas
Mrs. Marvin B. Humphrey, Reno
Walter P. Casey, Jr.*, Las Vegas

New Hampshire
Robert P. Bass, Jr., Concord
Miss Victoria Zachos, Concord
David Gosselin*, Concord

New Jersey
Bernard M. Shanley, Newark
Mrs. Katherine K. Neuberger,
Lincroft
John E. Dimon*, Trenton

New Mexico
Robert C. Davidson, Albuquerque
Mrs. Edward J. Neff, Albuquerque
Murray Ryan*, Silver City

New York
George L. Hinman, New York
Mrs. Keith S. McHugh, New York
Richard M. Rosenbaum*, Albany

North Carolina
J. E. Broyhill, Lenoir
Mrs. Louis G. Rogers, Charlotte
Frank A. Rouse*, Raleigh

North Dakota
Ben J. Clayburgh, Grand Forks
Mrs. Gerridee Wheeler, Bismarck
Allan C. Young*, Devils Lake

Ohio
Ray C. Bliss, Akron
Miss Martha C. Moore, Cambridge
Kent B. McGough*, Columbus
Oklahoma
Skip Healey, Davis
Mrs. Grace Boulton, Okla. City
Clarence E. Warner*, Okla. City
Oregon
George P. Stadelman, The Dalles
Mrs. Collis P. Moore, Moro
Floyd (Hank) Hart*, Medford
Pennsylvania
Thomas B. McCabe, Philadelphia
Miss Sarah Ann Stauffer,
  Lancaster County
Clifford L. Jones*, Harrisburg
Rhode Island
Frederick Lippitt, Providence
Mrs. Donald T. Gibbs, Middletown
Thomas E. (Tucker) Wright*,
  Providence
South Carolina
Hal C. Boyd, Spartanburg

Dr. Inez C. Eddings, Columbia
C. Kenneth Powell*, Columbia
South Dakota
D. Jack Gibson, Sioux Falls
Mrs. Nora Hussey, Sturgis
Robert H. Burns*, Pierre
Tennessee
George E. Wilson, Jr., Harriman
Mrs. Keith McCauley Spurrier,
  Memphis
S. L. (Kopie) Kopald, Jr.*,
  Memphis
Texas
Fred Agnich, Dallas
Mrs. Richard D. Bass, Dallas
George Willeford, M.D.*, Austin
Utah
Dr. Ernest L. Wilkinson, Provo
Mrs. Myrene Rich Brewer, Ogden
Kent Shearer*, Salt Lake City
Vermont
Roland Q. Seward, Sr.,
  E. Wallingford
Mrs. Consuelo Northrop Bailey,
  South Burlington

Stewart A. Smith*, Rutland
Virginia
William H. Stanhagan,
  Falls Church
Mrs. Cynthia S. Newman,
  Falls Church
Richard D. Obenshain*, Richmond
Washington
Kenneth R. Nuckolls, Bellingham
Mrs. Harlan J. Anderson,
  Kennewick
Ross E. Davis*, Olympia
West Virginia
Arch A. Moore, Jr., Charleston
Mrs. Irvin Humphreys, Huntington
Thomas E. Potter*, Charleston
Wisconsin
Ody J. Fish, Hartland
Mrs. John Pfeifer, Green Bay
John E. Hough*, Janesville
Wyoming
Robert F. Gosman, Casper
Mrs. Jack L. Stacy, Douglas
David B. Kennedy*, Sheridan

Major Political Organizations

AMERICAN PARTY
(PO Box 1098, Pigeon Forge, Tenn. 37863)
Chairman — Thomas J. Anderson.
AMERICANS FOR DEMOCRATIC ACTION
(1424 16th St., N.W., Washington, D.C. 20036)
National Chairman — Donald Fraser
National Director — Leon Shull
Chairman, Exec. Comm — Cushing Dolbeare
COMM. ON POLITICAL EDUCATION, AFL-CIO
(AFL-CIO Building, 815 16th St., Wash., D.C. 20006)
Chairman — George Meany
Secretary-Treasurer — Lane Kirkland
National Director — Alexander E. Barkan
CONSERVATIVE PARTY OF THE STATE OF N.Y.
(468 Park Ave. So., New York, N.Y. 10016)
Chairman — J. Daniel Mahoney
Secretary — Henry S. Jorin, Jr.
LIBERAL PARTY OF NEW YORK STATE
(1560 Broadway, New York, N.Y. 10036)
Chairman — Donald S. Harrington
First Vice Chairman — David Dubinsky
Secretary & Exec. Director — Ben Davidson
Treasurer — Harry Uviller

NATIONAL STATES' RIGHTS PARTY
(P.O. Box 1211, Marietta, Ga. 30061)
Chairman — J. B. Stoner
Secretary — Edward R. Fields
Treasurer — Peter Xavier

PROHIBITION NATIONAL COMMITTEE
(P.O. Box 2635, Denver, Colo. 80201)
National Chairman — Charles Wesley Ewing
Executive Secretary — Earl F. Dodge
National Secretary — Roger C. Storms

SOCIAL DEMOCRATS, U.S.A.
(1182 Broadway, New York, N.Y. 10001)
National Chairmen — Bayard Rustin, Charles S. Zimmerman
Honorary Chairmen — Darlington Hoopes, A. Philip Randolph
National Secretary — Joan Suall

SOCIALIST LABOR PARTY
In Minnesota: Industrial Gov't. Party
(116 Nassau St., Brooklyn, N.Y. 11201)
National Secretary — Nathan Karp

SOCIALIST WORKERS PARTY
(14 Charles Lane, New York, N.Y. 10014)
National Chairman Emeritus — James P. Cannon
National Secretary — Jack Barnes
Organization Secretary — Barry Sheppard

America's Third Parties

Since 1860, there have been only 4 presidential elections in which all third parties together polled more than 10% of the vote: the Populists (James Baird Weaver) in 1892, the National Progressives (Theodore Roosevelt) in 1912, the La Follette Progressives in 1924, and George Wallace's American Party in 1968. In 1948, the combined third parties (Henry Wallace's Progressives, Strom Thurmond's States Rights party or Dixiecrats, Prohibition, Socialists, and others) received only 5.75% of the vote. In most elections since 1860, fewer than one vote in 20 has been cast for a third party. The only successful third party in American history was the Republican party in the election of Abraham Lincoln in 1860.

Major Third Parties

Party	Candidates	Election	Issues	Strength in
Anti-Masonic	Wm. Wirt	1832	Against secret societies and oaths	Pennsylvania, Vermont
Free Soil	Martin Van Buren	1848	Anti-slavery	New York, Ohio
American (Know Nothing)	Millard Fillmore	1856	Anti-immigrant	Northeast, South
Greenback	Peter Cooper, James B. Weaver	1876, 1880	For "cheap money", labor rights	National
Prohibition	(numerous)	1872-	Anti-liquor	National
Populist	James B. Weaver	1892	For "cheap money", end of national banks.	South, West
Socialists	Eugene Debs, Norman Thomas	1900-	For public ownership	National
Progressive (Bull Moose)	Theo. Roosevelt	1912	Against high tariffs	Midwest, West
Progressive	Robt. LaFollette	1924	Farmer & labor rights	Midwest, West
States Rights	Strom Thurmond	1948	For segregation	South
Progressive	Henry Wallace	1948	Anti-Cold War	New York, California
American	George Wallace	1968	For states' rights	South

93rd Congress: Standing Committees and Chairmen

	Senate	House
Agriculture and Forestry	Herman E. Talmadge (Ga.)	W. R. Poage (Tex.)
Appropriations	John L. McClellan (Ark.)	George H. Mahon (Tex.)
Armed Services	John C. Stennis (Miss.)	F. Edward Hébert (La.)
Banking and Currency		Wright Patman (Tex.)
Banking, Housing and Urban Affairs	John Sparkman (Ala.)	
Commerce	Warren G. Magnuson (Wash.)	Harley O. Staggers (W. Va.)
District of Columbia	Thomas F. Eagleton (Mo.)	Charles C. Diggs, Jr. (Mich.)
Education, Labor, Public Welfare	Harrison A. Williams, Jr. (N.J.)	Carl D. Perkins (Ky.)
Finance	Russell B. Long (La.)	
Foreign Relations	J. William Fulbright (Ark.)	Thomas E. Morgan (Pa.)
Government Operations	Sam J. Ervin, Jr. (N.C.)	Chet Holifield (Calif.)
House Administration		Wayne L. Hays (Ohio)
Interior and Insular Affairs	Henry M. Jackson (Wash.)	James A. Haley (Fla.)
Internal Security		Richard H. Ichord (Mo.)
Judiciary	James O. Eastland (Miss.)	Peter W. Rodino, Jr. (N.J.)
Merchant Marine and Fisheries		Leonor K. Sullivan (Mo.)
Post Office and Civil Service	Gale W. McGee (Wyoming)	Thaddeus J. Dulski (N.Y.)
Public Works	Jennings Randolph (W. Va.)	John A. Blatnik (Minn.)
Rules and Administration	Howard W. Cannon (Nev.)	Ray J. Madden (Ind.)
Science and Astronautics	Frank E. Moss (Utah)	Olin E. Teague (Tex.)
Standards of Official Conduct		Melvin Price (Ill.)
Veterans' Affairs	Vance Hartke (Ind.)	William J. Bryan Dorn (S.C.)
Ways and Means		Wilbur D. Mills (Ark.)

Speakers of the House of Representatives

Party designations: A, American; D, Democratic; DR, Democratic Republican; F, Federalist;
R, Republican; W, Whig. *Served only one day.

Name	Party, State	Tenure	Name	Party, State	Tenure
Frederick A. C. Muhlenberg	F, Pa	1789-1791	Galusha A. Grow	R, Pa	1861-1863
Jonathan Trumbull	F, Conn	1791-1793	Schuyler Colfax	R, Ind	1863-1869
Frederick A. C. Muhlenberg	F, Pa	1793-1795	*Theodore M. Pomeroy	R, N. Y	1869-1869
Jonathan Dayton	F, N. J	1795-1799	James G. Blaine	R, Me	1869-1875
Theodore Sedgwick	F, Mass	1799-1801	Michael C. Kerr	D, Ind	1875-1876
Nathaniel Macon	DR, N. C	1801-1807	Samuel J. Randall	D, Pa	1876-1881
Joseph B. Varnum	DR, Mass	1807-1811	Joseph W. Keifer	R, Ohio	1881-1883
Henry Clay	DR, Ky	1811-1814	John G. Carlisle	D, Ky	1883-1889
Langdon Cheves	DR, S. C	1814-1815	Thomas B. Reed	R, Me	1889-1891
Henry Clay	DR, Ky	1815-1820	Charles F. Crisp	D, Ga	1891-1895
John W. Taylor	DR, N. Y	1820-1821	Thomas B. Reed	R, Me	1895-1899
Philip P. Barbour	DR, Va	1821-1823	David B. Henderson	R, Iowa	1899-1903
Henry Clay	DR, Ky	1823-1825	Joseph G. Cannon	R, Ill	1903-1911
John W. Taylor	D, N. Y	1825-1827	Champ Clark	D, Mo	1911-1919
Andrew Stevenson	D, Va	1827-1834	Frederick H. Gillett	R, Mass	1919-1925
John Bell	D, Tenn	1834-1835	Nicholas Longworth	R, Ohio	1925-1931
James K. Polk	D, Tenn	1835-1839	John N. Garner	D, Tex	1931-1933
Robert M. T. Hunter	D, Va	1839-1841	Henry T. Rainey	D, Ill	1933-1935
John White	W, Ky	1841-1843	Joseph W. Byrns	D, Tenn	1935-1936
John W. Jones	D, Va	1843-1845	William B. Bankhead	D, Ala	1936-1940
John W. Davis	D, Ind	1845-1847	Sam Rayburn	D, Tex	1940-1947
Robert C. Winthrop	W, Mass	1847-1849	Joseph W. Martin, Jr	R, Mass	1947-1949
Howell Cobb	D, Ga	1849-1851	Sam Rayburn	D, Tex	1949-1953
Linn Boyd	D, Ky	1851-1855	Joseph W. Martin, Jr	R, Mass	1953-1955
Nathaniel P. Banks	A, Mass	1856-1857	Sam Rayburn	D, Tex	1955-1961
James L. Orr	D, S. C	1857-1859	John W. McCormack	D, Mass	1962-1971
William Pennington	R, N. J	1860-1861	Carl Albert	D, Okla	1971-

The Electoral College

The President and the Vice President of the United States are the only elective Federal officials not elected by direct vote of the people. They are elected by the members of the Electoral College, an institution that has survived since the founding of the nation despite repeated attempts in Congress to alter or abolish it. In the elections of 1824, 1876 and 1888 the Presidential candidate receiving the largest popular vote failed to win a majority of the electoral votes.

On Presidential election day, the first Tuesday after the first Monday in November of every fourth year, each state chooses as many electors as it has Senators and Representatives in Congress. In 1964 for the first time, as provided by the 23rd Amendment to the Constitution, the District of Columbia voted for 3 electors. Thus, with 100 Senators and 435 Representatives, there are 538 members of the Electoral College, with a majority of 270 electoral votes needed to elect the President and Vice President.

Political parties customarily nominate their lists of electors at their respective state conventions. An elector cannot be a member of Congress or any person holding Federal office.

Some states print the names of the candidates for President and Vice President at the top of the ballot while others list only the names of the electors. In either case, the electors of the party receiving the highest vote are elected. The electors meet on the first Monday after the second Wednesday in December in their respective state capitals or in some other place prescribed by State Legislatures. By long-established custom they vote for their party nominee, thus giving all the state's electoral votes to him, although the Constitution does not require them to do so. The only constitutional requirement is that at least one of the persons each elector votes for shall not be an inhabitant of that elector's home state.

Certified and sealed lists of the votes of the electors in each state are mailed to the President of the U. S. Senate. He opens them in the presence of the members of the Senate and House of Representatives in a joint session held on Jan. 6 (the next day if that falls on a Sunday), and the electoral votes of all the states are then counted. If no candidate for President has a majority, the House of Representatives chooses a President from among the three highest candidates, with all Representatives from each state combining to cast one vote for that state. If no candidate for Vice President has a majority, the Senate chooses from the top two, Senators voting as individuals.

The Ninety-Third Congress, Second Session
The Senate (As of June 15, 1973.)

Terms are for 6 years and end Jan. 3 of the year preceding name. Annual salary $42,500. To be eligible a person must be at least 30 years old, a citizen of the U.S. for at least 9 years, and a resident of the state from which he is chosen. Congress must meet annually on Jan. 3, unless it has, by law, appointed a different day.

93rd Congress Senate officials: Pres. Pro Tempore, James O. Eastland; Secretary, Francis R. Valeo; Sgt. at Arms, William H. Wannall; Majority Sec., J. Stanley Kimmitt; Minority Sec., J. Mark Trice; Chaplain, L. R. Elson, S.T.D.; Majority Floor Leader, Mike Mansfield; Majority Whip, Robert C. Byrd; Minority Floor Leader, Hugh Scott; Minority Asst. Floor Leader, Robert P. Griffin.

Dem., 57; Rep., 43; Total, 100. (*) Asterisk designates senior senator.

Terms Expire	SENATORS	P.O. Address	Terms Expire	SENATORS	P.O. Address
	ALABAMA			**MONTANA**	
1975.	James B. Allen	Dem., Gadsden	1979.	Lee Metcalf	Dem., Helena
1979.	John Sparkman*	Dem., Huntsville	1977.	Mike Mansfield*	Dem., Missoula
	ALASKA			**NEBRASKA**	
1975.	Mike Gravel	Dem., Anchorage	1979.	Carl T. Curtis	Rep., Minden
1979.	Ted Stevens*	Rep., Anchorage	1977.	Roman L. Hruska*	Rep., Omaha
	ARIZONA			**NEVADA**	
1975.	Barry Goldwater	Rep., Phoenix	1975.	Alan Bible*	Dem., Reno
1977.	Paul J. Fannin*	Rep., Phoenix	1977.	Howard W. Cannon	Dem., Las Vegas
	ARKANSAS			**NEW HAMPSHIRE**	
1975.	J. William Fulbright	Dem., Fayetteville	1975.	Norris Cotton*	Rep., Lebanon
1979.	John L. McClellan*	Dem., Little Rock	1979.	Thomas J. McIntyre	Dem., Laconia
	CALIFORNIA			**NEW JERSEY**	
1975.	Alan Cranston*	Dem., Los Angeles	1979.	Clifford P. Case*	Rep., Rahway
1977.	John V. Tunney	Dem., Riverside	1977.	Harrison Williams, Jr.	Dem., Westfield
	COLORADO			**NEW MEXICO**	
1975.	Peter H. Dominick*	Rep., Englewood	1979.	Pete V. Domenici	Rep., Albuquerque
1979.	Floyd K. Haskell	Dem., Denver	1977.	Joseph M. Montoya*	Dem., Santa Fe
	CONNECTICUT			**NEW YORK**	
1975.	Abraham Ribicoff*	Dem., Hartford	1975.	Jacob K. Javits*	Rep., New York City
1977.	Lowell P. Weicker, Jr.	Rep., Greenwich	1977.	James L. Buckley	Con., New York City
	DELAWARE			**NORTH CAROLINA**	
1979.	Joseph R. Biden, Jr.	Dem., Faulkland	1975.	Sam J. Ervin, Jr.*	Dem., Morganton
1977.	William V. Roth, Jr.*	Rep., Wilmington	1979.	Jesse A. Helms	Rep., Raleigh
	FLORIDA			**NORTH DAKOTA**	
1975.	Edward J. Gurney*	Rep., Winter Park	1975.	Milton R. Young*	Rep., La Moure
1977.	Lawton Chiles	Dem., Lakeland	1977.	Quentin N. Burdick	Dem., Fargo
	GEORGIA			**OHIO**	
1975.	Herman E. Talmadge*	Dem., Lovejoy	1975.	William B. Saxbe*	Rep., Mechanicsburg
1979.	Sam Nunn	Dem., Perry	1977.	Robert Taft, Jr.	Rep., Cincinnati
	HAWAII			**OKLAHOMA**	
1975.	Daniel K. Inouye	Dem., Honolulu	1975.	Henry Bellmon*	Rep., Red Rock
1977.	Hiram L. Fong*	Rep., Honolulu	1979.	Dewey F. Bartlett	Rep., Tulsa
	IDAHO			**OREGON**	
1975.	Frank Church*	Dem., Boise	1975.	Robert W. Packwood	Rep., Portland
1979.	James A. McClure	Rep., Payette	1979.	Mark O. Hatfield*	Rep., Salem
	ILLINOIS			**PENNSYLVANIA**	
1975.	Adlai E. Stevenson 3d	Dem., Chicago	1975.	Richard S. Schweiker*	Rep., Worcester
1979.	Charles H. Percy*	Rep., Kenilworth	1977.	Hugh Scott*	Rep., Philadelphia
	INDIANA			**RHODE ISLAND**	
1975.	Birch Bayh	Dem., Terre Haute	1979.	Claiborne Pell	Dem., Newport
1977.	Vance Hartke*	Dem., Evansville	1977.	John O. Pastore*	Dem., Providence
	IOWA			**SOUTH CAROLINA**	
1975.	Harold E. Hughes*	Dem., Ida Grove	1975.	Ernest F. Hollings	Dem., Charleston
1979.	Dick Clark	Dem., Marion	1979.	Strom Thurmond*	Rep., Aiken
	KANSAS			**SOUTH DAKOTA**	
1975.	Robert J. Dole	Rep., Russell	1975.	George McGovern*	Dem., Mitchell
1979.	James B. Pearson*	Rep., Prairie Village	1979.	James Abourezk	Dem., Rapid City
	KENTUCKY			**TENNESSEE**	
1975.	Marlow W. Cook*	Rep., Louisville	1979.	Howard H. Baker, Jr.*	Rep., Knoxville
1979.	Walter Huddleston	Dem., Elizabethtown	1977.	William E. Brock, 3rd	Rep., Chattanooga
	LOUISIANA			**TEXAS**	
1975.	Russell B. Long*	Dem., Baton Rouge	1979.	John G. Tower*	Rep., Wichita Falls
1979.	J. Bennett Johnston, Jr.	Dem., Shreveport	1977.	Lloyd M. Bentsen	Dem., Houston
	MAINE			**UTAH**	
1979.	William D. Hathaway	Dem., Auburn	1975.	Wallace F. Bennett*	Dem., Salt Lake City
1977.	Edmund S. Muskie*	Dem., Waterville	1977.	Frank E. Moss	Dem., Salt Lake City
	MARYLAND			**VERMONT**	
1975.	C. McC. Mathias, Jr.*	Rep., Frederick	1975.	George D. Aiken*	Rep., Putney
1977.	J. Glenn Beall, Jr.	Rep., Frostburg	1977.	Robert T. Stafford	Rep., Rutland
	MASSACHUSETTS			**VIRGINIA**	
1979.	Edward W. Brooke	Rep., Newton Center	1979.	William Lloyd Scott	Rep., Fairfax
1977.	Edward M. Kennedy*	Dem., Boston	1977.	Harry F. Byrd, Jr.*	Ind., Winchester
	MICHIGAN			**WASHINGTON**	
1979.	Robert P. Griffin	Rep., Traverse City	1975.	Warren G. Magnuson*	Dem., Seattle
1977.	Philip A. Hart*	Dem., Mackinac Is.	1977.	Henry M. Jackson	Dem., Everett
	MINNESOTA			**WEST VIRGINIA**	
1979.	Walter F. Mondale*	Dem., Minneapolis	1979.	Jennings Randolph*	Dem., Elkins
1977.	Hubert Humphrey	Dem., Waverly	1977.	Robert C. Byrd	Dem., Sophia
	MISSISSIPPI			**WISCONSIN**	
1979.	James O. Eastland*	Dem., Doddsville	1975.	Gaylord Nelson	Dem., Madison
1977.	John Stennis	Dem., De Kalb	1977.	William Proxmire*	Dem., Madison
	MISSOURI			**WYOMING**	
1975.	Thomas F. Eagleton	Dem., St. Louis	1979.	Clifford P. Hansen*	Rep., Jackson
1977.	Stuart Symington*	Dem., St. Louis	1977.	Gale W. McGee*	Dem., Laramie

The House of Representatives

(As of June 15, 1973.)

Members' terms to Jan. 3, 1975. Annual salary $42,500; House Speaker $62,500 and $10,000 expenses, all taxable. To be eligible for membership, a person must be at least 25, a U.S. citizen for at least 7 years, and a resident of the state from which he is chosen.

(Those marked * served in the 92nd Congress.)

93rd Congress House Officials

Speaker, Carl Albert; Majority Leader, John McFall; Majority Whip, Thomas P. O'Neill; Minority Leader, Gerald Ford; Minority Whip, Leslie C. Arends; Parliamentarian, Lewis Deschler; Chaplain, Rev. Edward G. Latch; Sergeant at Arms, Kenneth Harding; Clerk, W. Pat Jennings; Doorkeeper, William M. Miller; Postmaster, Robert V. Rota.

Democrats, 241; Republicans, 192, Vacancies, 2. Total, 435.

Districts	Representatives	P.O. Address

ALABAMA

1 Jack Edwards* .... Rep., Mobile
2 William J. Dickinson* .... Rep., Montgomery
3 Bill Nichols* .... Dem., Sylacauga
4 Tom Bevill* .... Dem., Jasper
5 Bob E. Jones* .... Dem., Scottsboro
6 John H. Buchanan* ...... Rep., Birmingham
7 Walter Flowers* .... Dem., Tuscaloosa

ALASKA—At Large

Don Young .... Rep., Fort Yukon

ARIZONA

1 John J. Rhodes* .... Rep., Mesa
2 Morris K. Udall* .... Dem., Tucson
3 Sam Steiger* .... Rep., Prescott
4 John B. Conlan .... Rep., Phoenix

ARKANSAS

1 Bill Alexander* .... Dem., Osceola
2 Wilbur D. Mills* .... Dem., Kensett
3 John Paul Hammer-
schmidt* .... Rep., Harrison
4 Ray Thornton .... Dem., Sheridan

CALIFORNIA

1 Don. H. Clausen* .... Rep., Crescent City
2 Harold T. Johnson* ...... Dem., Roseville
3 John E. Moss* .... Dem., Sacramento
4 Robert L. Leggett* ...... Dem., Vallejo
5 Phillip Burton* .... Dem., San Francisco
6 William S. Mailliard* .... Rep., San Francisco
7 Ronald V. Dellums* ..... Dem., Berkeley
8 Fortney H. (Pete) Stark... Dem., Oakland
9 Don Edwards* .... Dem., San Jose
10 Charles S. Gubser* ...... Rep., Gilroy
11 Leo J. Ryan* .... Dem., S. San Francisco
12 Burt L. Talcott* .... Rep., Salinas
13 Charles M. Teague* ..... Rep., Ojai
14 Jerome R. Waldie* ...... Dem., Antioch
15 John J. McFall* .... Dem., Manteca
16 B. F. Sisk* .... Dem., Fresno
17 Paul N. McCloskey, Jr.* .. Rep., Portola Valley
18 Bob Mathias* .... Rep., Visalia
19 Chet Holifield* .... Dem., Montebello
20 Carlos J. Moorhead ..... Rep., Glendale
21 Augustus F. Hawkins* ... Dem., Los Angeles
22 James C. Corman* ...... Dem., Van Nuys
23 Del Clawson* .... Rep., Compton
24 John Rousselot* .... Rep., San Marino
25 Charles E. Wiggins* ..... Rep., El Monte
26 Thomas M. Rees* ...... Dem., Beverly Hills
27 Barry M. Goldwater, Jr.* .. Rep., Burbank
28 Alphonzo Bell* .... Rep., Beverly Hills
29 George E. Danielson* .... Dem., Los Angeles
30 Edward R. Roybal* ...... Dem., Los Angeles
31 Charles H. Wilson* ..... Dem., Torrance
32 Craig Hosmer* .... Rep., Long Beach
33 Jerry L. Pettis* .... Rep., Loma Linda
34 Richard T. Hanna* ...... Dem., Anaheim
35 Glenn M. Anderson* ..... Dem., Harbour City
36 William M. Ketchum ..... Rep., Paso Robles

37 Yvonne Brathwaite Burke   Dem., Los Angeles
38 George E. Brown, Jr. ..... Dem., Colton
39 Andrew J. Hinshaw ...... Rep., Mission Viejo
40 Bob Wilson* .... Rep., San Diego
41 Lionel Van Deerlin* ..... Dem., San Diego
42 Clair W. Burgener* ...... Rep., Rancho Santa Fe
43 Victor V. Veysey* .... Rep., Brawley

COLORADO

1 Patricia Schroeder....... Dem., Denver
2 Donald G. Brotzman* .... Rep., Boulder
3 Frank E. Evans* .... Dem., Pueblo
4 James P. (Jim) Johnson .. Rep., Fort Collins
5 William L. Armstrong..... Rep., Aurora

CONNECTICUT

1 William R. Cotter* .... Dem., Hartford
2 Robert H. Steele* .... Rep., Vernon
3 Robert N. Giaimo* ...... Dem., North Haven
4 Stewart B. McKinney* ... Rep., Fairfield
5 Ronald A. Sarasin....... Rep., Beacon Falls
6 Ella T. Grasso* .... Dem., Windsor Locks

DELAWARE—At Large

Pierre S. du Pont*....... Rep., Wilmington

FLORIDA

1 Bob Sikes*............. Dem., Crestview
2 Don Fuqua*............ Dem., Altha
3 Charles E. Bennett* ..... Dem., Jacksonville
4 Bill Chappell* .... Dem., Ocala
5 Bill Gunter............ Dem., Orlando
6 C. W. Bill Young* .... Rep., St. Petersburg
7 Sam M. Gibbons*....... Dem., Tampa
8 James A. Haley* .... Dem., Sarasota
9 Louis Frey, Jr.*........ Rep., Winter Park
10 L. A. (Skip) Bafalis ...... Rep., Palm B'ch Gdns.
11 Paul G. Rogers* .... Dem., W. Palm Beach
12 J. Herbert Burke* ...... Rep., Hollywood
13 William Lehman .... Dem., N. Miami Beach
14 Claude D. Pepper*...... Dem., Miami
15 Dante B. Fascell*....... Dem., Miami

GEORGIA

1 Bo Ginn................ Dem., Millen
2 Dawson Mathis*........ Dem., Albany
3 Jack Brinkley* .... Dem., Columbus
4 Ben B. Blackburn* ...... Rep., Atlanta
5 Andrew Young .... Dem., Atlanta
6 John J. Flynt*.......... Dem., Griffin
7 John W. Davis* .... Dem., Summerville
8 W. S. (Bill) Stuckey, Jr.* .. Dem., Eastman
9 Phil M. Landrum* ...... Dem., Jasper
10 Robert G. Stephens*..... Dem., Athens

HAWAII

1 Spark M. Matsunaga*.... Dem., Honolulu
2 Patsy Takemoto Mink*... Dem., Waipahu

Districts	Representatives	P.O. Address

IDAHO

1 Steven D. Symms........ Rep., Caldwell
2 Orval Hansen* .... Rep., Idaho Falls

ILLINOIS

1 Ralph H. Metcalfe*...... Dem., Chicago
2 Morgan F. Murphy*..... Dem., Chicago
3 Robert P. Hanrahan...... Rep., Homewood
4 Edward J. Derwinski*.... Rep., Chicago
5 John C. Kluczynski*..... Dem., Chicago
6 Harold R. Collier*........ Rep., Western Springs
7 Cardiss Collins.......... Dem., Chicago
8 Daniel D. Rostenkowski*. Dem., Chicago
9 Sidney R. Yates*........ Dem., Chicago
10 Samuel H. Young........ Rep., Glenview
11 Frank Annunzio*........ Dem., Chicago
12 Philip M. Crane*........ Rep., Winnetka
13 Robert McClory*........ Rep., Lake Bluff
14 John N. Erlenborn*...... Rep., Elmhurst
15 Leslie C. Arends*........ Rep., Melvin
16 John B. Anderson* ...... Rep., Rockford
17 George M. O'Brien ...... Rep., Joliet
18 Robert H. Michel*....... Rep., Peoria
19 Tom Railsback*......... Rep., Moline
20 Paul Findley*........... Rep., Pittsfield
21 Edward R. Madigan ..... Rep., Lincoln
22 George E. Shipley*...... Dem., Olney
23 Melvin Price*........... Dem., East St. Louis
24 Kenneth J. Gray*........ Dem., West Frankfort

INDIANA

1 Ray J. Madden*........ Dem., Gary
2 Earl F. Landgrebe*...... Rep., Valparaiso
3 John Brademas*........ Dem., South Bend
4 J. Edward Roush*....... Dem., Huntington
5 Elwood H. Hillis*........ Rep., Kokomo
6 William G. Bray*........ Rep., Martinsville
7 John T. Myers*......... Rep., Covington
8 Roger H. Zion*......... Rep., Evansville
9 Lee H. Hamilton*........ Dem., Columbus
10 David W. Dennis*....... Rep., Richmond
11 William H. Hudnut III..... Rep., Indianapolis

IOWA

1 Edward Mezvinsky*........ Dem., Iowa City
2 John C. Culver*......... Dem., Marion
3 H. R. Gross*............. Rep., Waterloo
4 Neal Smith*............ Dem., Altoona
5 William J. Scherle*...... Rep., Henderson
6 Wiley Mayne* .... Rep., Sioux City

KANSAS

1 Keith G. Sebelius*....... Rep., Norton
2 William R. Roy*........ Dem., Topeka
3 Larry Winn, Jr.*........ Rep., Overland Park
4 Garner E. Shriver*...... Rep., Wichita
5 Joe Skubitz*........... Rep., Pittsburg

KENTUCKY

1 Frank A. Stubblefield*... Dem., Murray
2 William H. Natcher*..... Dem., Bowling Green
3 Romano L. Mazzoli*.... Dem., Louisville
4 M. Gene Snyder*........ Rep., Jeffersontown
5 Tim Lee Carter*........ Rep., Tompkinsville
6 John Breckinridge...... Dem., Lexington
7 Carl D. Perkins*......... Dem., Hindman

LOUISIANA

1 F. Edward Hebert* ...... Dem., New Orleans
2 Corinne C. Boggs .... Dem., New Orleans
3 David C. Treen......... Rep., Metairie
4 Joe D. Waggonner, Jr.*... Dem., Plain Dealing
5 Otto E. Passman*...... Dem., Monroe
6 John R. Rarick*......... Dem., Baton Rouge
7 John B. Breaux*........ Dem., Crowley
8 Gillis W. Long.......... Dem., Alexandria

MAINE

1 Peter N. Kyros*......... Dem., Portland
2 William S. Cohen .... Rep. Bangor

MARYLAND

1 *Vacant*
2 Clarence D. Long*....... Dem., Ruxton
3 Paul S. Sarbanes*....... Dem., Baltimore
4 Marjorie S. Holt .... Rep., Severna Park
5 Lawrence J. Hogan*..... Rep., Hyattsville
6 Goodloe E. Byron*...... Dem., Frederick
7 Parren J. Mitchell*...... Dem., Baltimore
8 Gilbert Gude*.......... Rep., Bethesda

MASSACHUSETTS

1 Silvio O. Conte* .... Rep., Pittsfield
2 Edward P. Boland*....... Dem., Springfield
3 Harold D. Donohue*..... Dem., Worcester
4 Robert F. Drinan* .... Dem., Newton
5 Paul W. Cronin .... Rep., Andover
6 Michael J. Harrington*... Dem., Beverly
7 Torbert H. Macdonald*... Dem., Malden
8 Thomas P. O'Neill, Jr.*... Dem., Cambridge
9 John Moakley IC   Boston
10 Margaret M. Heckler*.... Rep., Wellesley
11 James A. Burke*........ Dem., Milton
12 Gerry E. Studds........ Dem., Cohasset

(IC means Independent Conservative)

MICHIGAN

1 John R. Conyers, Jr.*..... Dem., Detroit
2 Marvin L. Esch*......... Rep., Ann Arbor
3 Garry Brown*.......... Rep., Schoolcraft
4 Edward Hutchinson*.... Rep., St. Joseph
5 Gerald R. Ford*......... Rep., Grand Rapids
6 Charles E. Chamberlain*. Rep., East Lansing
7 Donald Riegle*.......... Rep., Flint
8 James Harvey*......... Rep., Saginaw
9 Guy Vander Jagt*....... Rep., Cadillac
10 Elford A. Cederberg*.... Rep., Midland
11 Philip E. Ruppe*....... Rep., Houghton
12 James G. O'Hara*...... Dem., Utica
13 Charles C. Diggs, Jr.*... Dem., Detroit
14 Lucien N. Nedzi*....... Dem., Detroit
15 William D. Ford*....... Dem., Taylor
16 John D. Dingell*....... Dem., Detroit
17 Martha W. Griffiths*.... Dem., Detroit
18 Robert J. Huber .... Rep., Troy
19 William S. Broomfield*... Rep., Birmingham

MINNESOTA

1 Albert H. Quie*.......... Rep., Dennison
2 Ancher Nelsen*........ Rep., Hutchinson
3 Bill Frenzel*........... Rep., Golden Valley
4 Joseph E. Karth*....... Dem., St. Paul
5 Donald M. Fraser*...... Dem., Minneapolis
6 John M. Zwach*....... Rep., Walnut Grove
7 Bob Bergland*......... Dem., Roscau
8 John A. Blatnik*....... Dem., Chisholm

MISSISSIPPI

1 Jamie L. Whitten*....... Dem., Charleston
2 David R. Bowen....... Dem., Cleveland
3 G. V. (Sonny) Montgomery*Dem., Meridian
4 Thad Cochran .... Rep., Jackson
5 Trent Lott............... Rep., Pascagoula

MISSOURI

1 William Clay*.......... Dem., St. Louis
2 James W. Symington*.... Dem., Clayton
3 Leonor K. (Mrs. John B.)
   Sullivan*............ Dem., St. Louis
4 Wm. J. Randall*........ Dem., Independence
5 Richard Walker Bolling*.. Dem., Kansas City
6 Jerry Litton .... Dem., Chillicothe
7 Gene Taylor .... Rep., Sarcoxie
8 Richard (Dick) Ichord*... Dem., Houston
9 William L. (Bill) Hungate* Dem., Troy
10 Bill D. Burlison*......... Dem., Cape Girardeau

MONTANA

1 Dick Shoup*............ Rep., Missoula
2 John Melcher*.......... Dem., Forsyth

| Districts | Representatives | P.O. Address | Districts | Representatives | P.O. Address |

NEBRASKA

1 Charles Thone* .... Rep., Lincoln
2 John Y. McCollister* ..... Rep., Omaha
3 Dave Martin* .... Rep., Kearney

NEVADA—At Large

David Towell .... Rep., Gardnerville

NEW HAMPSHIRE

1 Louis C. Wyman* .... Rep., Manchester
2 James C. Cleveland* ..... Rep., New London

NEW JERSEY

1 John E. Hunt* .... Rep., Pitman
2 Charles W. Sandman, Jr.* Rep., Cape May
3 James J. Howard* .... Dem., Wall
4 Frank Thompson, Jr.* .... Dem., Trenton
5 Peter H. B. Frelinghuysen* Rep., Morristown
6 Edwin B. Forsythe ...... Rep., Moorestown
7 William B. Widnall* ...... Rep., Saddle River
8 Robert A. Roe* .... Dem., Wayne
9 Henry Helstoski* .... Dem., E. Rutherford
10 Peter W. Rodino, Jr.* ... Dem., Newark
11 Joseph G. Minish* ...... Dem., West Orange
12 Matthew J. Rinaldo ..... Rep., Union
13 Joseph Maraziti .... Rep., Boonton
14 Dominick V. Daniels* .... Dem., Jersey City
15 Edward J. Patten* ...... Dem., Perth Amboy

NEW MEXICO

1 Manuel Lujan, Jr.* .... Rep., Albuquerque
2 Harold Runnels* .... Dem., Lovington

NEW YORK

1 Otis G. Pike* .... Dem., Riverhead
2 James R. Grover, Jr.* .... Rep., Babylon
3 Angelo D. Roncallo ...... Rep., Massapequa
4 Norman F. Lent* .... Rep., East Rockaway
5 John W. Wydler* .... Rep., Garden City
6 Lester L. Wolff* .... Dem., Great Neck
7 Joseph P. Addabbo* ..... Dem., Ozone Park
8 Benjamin S. Rosenthal* . Dem., Elmhurst
9 James J. Delaney* .... Dem., Long Island City
10 Mario Biaggi* .... Dem., Bronx
11 Frank J. Brasco* .... Dem., Brooklyn
12 Shirley Chisholm* .... Dem., Brooklyn
13 Bertram L. Podell* ...... Dem., Brooklyn
14 John J. Rooney* .... Dem., Brooklyn
15 Hugh L. Carey* .... Dem., Brooklyn
16 Elizabeth Holtzman ...... Dem., Brooklyn
17 John M. Murphy* .... Dem., Staten Island
18 Edward I. Koch* .... Dem., New York
19 Charles B. Rangel* ...... Dem., New York
20 Bella S. Abzug* .... Dem., New York
21 Herman Badillo* .... Dem., Bronx
22 Jonathan B. Bingham* ... Dem., Bronx
23 Peter Peyser* .... Rep., Irvington
24 Ogden Reid* .... Dem., Yonkers
25 Hamilton Fish, Jr.* ..... Rep., Millbrook
26 Benjamin A. Gilman ..... Rep., Middletown
27 Howard W. Robison* ..... Rep., Owego
28 Samuel S. Stratton* ..... Dem., Amsterdam
29 Carleton J. King* .... Rep., Saratoga Springs
30 Robert C. McEwen* ...... Rep., Ogdensburg
31 Donald J. Mitchell ...... Rep., Herkimer
32 James M. Hanley* .... Dem., Syracuse
33 William F. Walsh* ...... Rep., Syracuse
34 Frank Horton* .... Rep., Rochester
35 Barber B. Conable* ..... Rep., Alexander
36 Henry P. Smith 3d ...... Rep., North Tonawanda
37 Thaddeus J. Dulski* ..... Dem., Buffalo
38 Jack F. Kemp* .... Rep., Hamburg
39 James F. Hastings* ...... Rep., Allegany

NORTH CAROLINA

1 Walter B. Jones* .... Dem., Farmville
2 L. H. Fountain* .... Dem., Tarboro
3 David N. Henderson* .... Dem., Wallace
4 Ike F. Andrews .... Dem., Siler City

5 Wilmer D. Mizell* .... Rep., Winston-Salem
6 Richardson Preyer* ...... Dem., Greensboro
7 Charles Rose .... Dem., Fayetteville
8 Earl B. Ruth* .... Rep., Salisbury
9 James G. Martin .... Rep., Davidson
10 James T. Broyhill .... Rep., Lenoir
11 Roy A. Taylor* .... Dem., Black Mountain

NORTH DAKOTA—At Large

Mark Andrews* .... Rep., Mapleton

OHIO

1 William J. Keating* ...... Rep., Cincinnati
2 Donald D. Clancy* ...... Rep., Cincinnati
3 Charles W. Whalen, Jr.* .. Rep., Dayton
4 Tennyson Guyer .... Rep., Findlay
5 Delbert L. Latta* .... Rep., Bowling Green
6 William H. Harsha* ..... Rep., Portsmouth
7 Clarence J. Brown* ..... Rep., Urbana
8 Walter E. Powell* .... Rep., Fairfield
9 Thomas L. Ashley* ..... Dem., Waterville
10 Clarence E. Miller* ..... Rep., Lancaster
11 J. William Stanton* ..... Rep., Painesville
12 Samuel L. Devine* ...... Rep., Columbus
13 Charles A. Mosher* ..... Rep., Oberlin
14 John F. Seiberling* ..... Dem., Akron
15 Chalmers P. Wylie* ..... Rep., Columbus
16 Ralph S. Regula .... Rep., Navarre
17 John M. Ashbrook* ...... Rep., Johnstown
18 Wayne L. Hays* .... Dem., Flushing
19 Charles J. Carney* ...... Dem., Youngstown
20 James V. Stanton* ...... Dem., Cleveland
21 Louis Stokes* .... Dem., Shaker Heights
22 Charles A. Vanik* ...... Dem., Cleveland
23 William E. Minshall* ..... Rep., Cleveland

OKLAHOMA

1 James R. Jones .... Dem., Tulsa
2 Clem Rogers McSpadden . Dem., Claremore
3 Carl Albert* .... Dem., McAlester
4 Tom Steed* .... Dem., Shawnee
5 John Jarman* .... Dem., Oklahoma City
6 John N. Happy Camp* ... Rep., Waukomis

OREGON

1 Wendell Wyatt* .... Rep., Astoria
2 Al Ullman* .... Dem., Baker
3 Edith Green* .... Dem., Portland
4 John Dellenback* .... Rep., Medford

PENNSYLVANIA

1 William A. Barrett* ..... Dem., Philadelphia
2 Robert N. C. Nix* ...... Dem., Philadelphia
3 William J. Green* .... Dem., Philadelphia
4 Joshua Eilberg* .... Dem., Philadelphia
5 John H. Ware 3d* .... Rep., Oxford
6 Gus Yatron* .... Dem., Reading
7 Lawrence G. Williams* ... Rep., Springfield
8 Edward G. Biester, Jr.* ... Rep., Furlong
9 E. G. Shuster .... Rep., Everett
10 Joseph M. McDade* ..... Rep., Scranton
11 Daniel J. Flood* .... Dem., Wilkes-Barre
12 John P. Saylor* .... Rep., Johnstown
13 Lawrence Coughlin* ..... Rep., Villanova
14 William S. Moorhead* ... Dem., Pittsburgh
15 Fred B. Rooney* .... Dem., Bethlehem
16 Edwin D. Eshleman* ..... Rep., Lancaster
17 Herman T. Schneebeli* .. Rep., Williamsport
18 H. John Heinz, 3d* ...... Rep., Pittsburgh
19 George A. Goodling* .... Rep., Loganville
20 Joseph M. Gaydos* ..... Dem., McKeesport
21 John H. Dent* .... Dem., Jennette
22 Thomas E. Morgan* ..... Dem., Fredericktown
23 Albert W. Johnson* ..... Rep., Smethport
24 Joseph P. Vigorito* ..... Dem., Erie
25 Frank M. Clark* .... Dem., Bessemer

RHODE ISLAND

1 Fernand J. St. Germain* . Dem., Woonsocket
2 Robert O. Tiernan* ...... Dem., Warwick

Districts	Representatives	P.O. Address
	SOUTH CAROLINA	
1	Mendel J. Davis *	Dem., N. Charleston
2	Floyd Spence *	Rep., Lexington
3	Wm. Jennings Bryan Dorn *	Dem., Greenwood
4	James R. Mann *	Dem., Greenville
5	Thomas S. Gettys *......	Dem., Rock Hill
6	Edward Young...........	Rep., Florence
	SOUTH DAKOTA	
1	Frank E. Denholm *	Dem., Brookings
2	James Abdnor...........	Rep., Kennebec
	TENNESSEE	
1	James H. Quillen *	Rep., Kingsport
2	John Duncan *..........	Rep., Knoxville
3	LaMar Baker*...........	Rep., Chattanooga
4	Joe L. Evins *...........	Dem., Smithville
5	Richard Fulton *........	Dem., Nashville
6	Robin L. Beard	Rep., Franklin
7	Ed Jones *	Dem., Yorkville
8	Dan Kuykendall *	Rep., Memphis
	TEXAS	
1	Wright Patman *	Dem., Texarkana
2	Charles Wilson	Dem., Lufkin
3	James M. Collins *.......	Rep., Dallas
4	Ray Roberts *	Dem., McKinney
5	Alan Steelman	Rep., Dallas
6	Olin E. Teague *	Dem., College Station
7	Bill Archer*............	Rep., Houston
8	Bob Eckhardt...........	Dem., Houston
9	Jack Brooks*...........	Dem., Beaumont
10	J. J. (Jake) Pickle*......	Dem., Austin
11	W. R. Poage*...........	Dem., Waco
12	Jim Wright *	Dem., Fort Worth
13	Robert Price*..........	Rep., Amarillo
14	John Young*...........	Dem., Corpus Christi
15	Eligio de la Garza *	Dem., Mission
16	Richard C. White *.......	Dem., El Paso
17	Omar Burleson*........	Dem., Anson
18	Barbara Jordan.........	Dem., Houston
19	George Mahon *	Dem., Lubbock
20	Henry B. Gonzalez*......	Dem., San Antonio
21	O. C. Fisher *	Dem., San Angelo
22	Bob Casey*...........	Dem., Houston
23	Abraham Kazen*........	Dem., Laredo
24	Dale Milford............	Dem., Grand Prairie
	UTAH	
1	K. Gunn McKay *	Dem., Huntsville
2	Wayne W. Owens........	Dem., Salt Lake City

Districts	Representatives	P.O. Address
	VERMONT—At Large	
	Richard W. Mallary*	Rep., Bradford
	VIRGINIA	
1	Thomas N. Downing *	Dem., Newport News
2	G. William Whitehurst *...	Rep., Norfolk
3	David E. Satterfield 3d *..	Dem., Richmond
4	Robert W. Daniel, Jr.	Rep., Spring Grove
5	Dan Daniel*.............	Dem., Danville
6	M. Caldwell Butler*......	Rep., Roanoke
7	J. Kenneth Robinson* ...	Rep., Winchester
8	Stanford E. Parris	Rep., Springfield
9	William C. Wampler*.....	Rep., Bristol
10	Joel T. Broyhill *	Rep., Arlington
	WASHINGTON	
1	Joel Pritchard	Rep., Seattle
2	Lloyd Meeds *	Dem., Everett
3	Julia Butler Hansen* ...	Dem., Cathlamet
4	Mike McCormack *......	Dem., Richland
5	Thomas S. Foley *.......	Dem., Spokane
6	Floyd V. Hicks*........	Dem., Tacoma
7	Brock Adams *	Dem., Seattle
	WEST VIRGINIA	
1	Robert H. Mollohan *.....	Dem., Fairmont
2	Harley O. Staggers *.....	Dem., Keyser
3	John Slack*............	Dem., Charleston
4	Ken Hechler *..........	Dem., Huntington
	WISCONSIN	
1	Les Aspin *............	Dem., Racine
2	Robert W. Kastenmeier * .	Dem., Watertown
3	Vernon W. Thomson *	Rep., Richland Center
4	Clement J. Zablocki*....	Dem., Milwaukee
5	Henry S. Reuss *........	Dem., Milwaukee
6	William A. Steiger *	Rep., Oshkosh
7	David R. Obey *........	Dem., Wausau
8	Harold V. Froehlich......	Rep., Appleton
9	Glenn R. Davis *........	Rep., New Berlin
	WYOMING—At Large	
	Teno Roncalio*..........	Dem., Cheyenne
	PUERTO RICO	
	Resident Commissioner	
	Jaime Benitez	Cayey
	Non-Voting Delegates	
DISTRICT OF COLUMBIA	....	William E. Fauntroy*
GUAM	....	Antonio Borja Won Pat
VIRGIN ISLANDS	....	Ron de Lugo

Longevity of Male Government Officials to end of 1968

By Period of Initial Entry into Office   (Compared to white males in U.S. population)

Source: Statistical Bulletin, Metropolitan Life

Period of 1st Entry to Office	Number at Entry	Avg. Age at Entry	No. Died By end of 1968	Avg. Years Lived From Entry to End '68 or Prior Death	Differentials*
Representatives					
1861-1900	2,434	45.4	2,434	23.8	0.1
1901-1930	1,582	46.1	1,520	24.6	0.4
1931-1968	1,659	45.7	585	17.0	0.2
Senators					
1861-1900	392	49.5	392	21.7	0.8
1901-1930	319	52.3	310	21.0	1.1
1931-1968	339	51.5	148	15.7	0.4
State Governors					
1901-1930	415	49.5	412	22.1	0.7
1931-1968	441	49.6	179	15.5	0.5
Cabinet Officers					
1789-1860	118	47.8	118	21.4	−0.2
1861-1900	108	53.1	108	20.0	1.4
1901-1930	73	52.9	73	21.1	1.8
1931-1968	92	52.7	38	12.2	−0.7
Supreme Court Justices					
1789-1900	57	51.2	57	20.2	0.2
1901-1968	39	54.3	25	17.2	1.4

*The difference between (a) the average number of years actually lived from entry into office to end of 1968 or prior death and (b) the average life expectancy of contemporaneous cohorts of white males in the general population of the United States observed for the same periods.

Governors and State Government Officials

As of June 15, 1973.

State	Capital	Governor	Party	Term Years	Term Expires	Annual Salary
Alabama	Montgomery	George C. Wallace	Dem.	4	Jan. 1975	$25,000
Alaska	Juneau	William A. Egan	Dem.	4	Dec. 1974	40,000
Arizona	Phoenix	Jack Williams	Rep.	4	Jan. 1975	35,000
Arkansas	Little Rock	Dale Bumpers	Dem.	2	Jan. 1975	10,000
California	Sacramento	Ronald Reagan	Rep.	4	Jan. 1975	49,100
Colorado	Denver	John A. Love	Rep.	4	Jan. 1975	40,000
Connecticut	Hartford	Thomas J. Meskill	Rep.	4	Jan. 1975	35,000
Delaware	Dover	Sherman W. Tribbitt	Dem.	4	Jan. 1977	35,000
Florida	Tallahassee	Reubin Askew	Dem.	4	Jan. 1975	40,000
Georgia	Atlanta	Jimmy Carter	Dem.	4	Jan. 1975	42,500
Hawaii	Honolulu	John A. Burns	Dem.	4	Dec. 1974	42,000
Idaho	Boise	Cecil D. Andrus	Dem.	4	Jan. 1975	30,000
Illinois	Springfield	Daniel Walker	Dem.	4	Jan. 1977	50,000
Indiana	Indianapolis	Otis R. Bowen	Rep.	4	Jan. 1977	36,000
Iowa	Des Moines	Robert D. Ray	Rep.	2	Jan. 1975	35,000
Kansas	Topeka	Robert B. Docking	Dem.	2	Jan. 1975	20,000
Kentucky	Frankfort	Wendell H. Ford	Dem.	4	Dec. 1975	30,000
Louisiana	Baton Rouge	Edwin W. Edwards	Dem.	4	May 1976	28,374
Maine	Augusta	Kenneth M. Curtis	Dem.	4	Jan. 1975	20,000
Maryland	Annapolis	Marvin Mandel	Dem.	4	Jan. 1975	25,000
Massachusetts	Boston	Francis W. Sargent	Rep.	4	Jan. 1975	40,000
Michigan	Lansing	William G. Milliken	Rep.	4	Jan. 1975	45,000
Minnesota	St. Paul	Wendell R. Anderson	Dem.	4	Jan. 1975	35,000
Mississippi	Jackson	William L. Waller	Dem.	4	Jan. 1976	35,000
Missouri	Jefferson City	Christopher S. Bond	Rep.	4	Jan. 1977	37,500
Montana	Helena	Thomas L. Judge	Dem.	4	Jan. 1977	25,000
Nebraska	Lincoln	J. James Exon	Dem.	4	Jan. 1975	25,000
Nevada	Carson City	Mike O'Callaghan	Dem.	4	Jan. 1975	30,000
New Hampshire	Concord	Meldrim Thomson Jr.	Rep.	2	Jan. 1975	30,000
New Jersey	Trenton	William T. Cahill	Rep.	4	Jan. 1974	50,000
New Mexico	Santa Fe	Bruce King	Dem.	4	Jan. 1975	22,000
New York	Albany	Nelson A. Rockefeller	Rep.	4	Jan. 1975	85,000
North Carolina	Raleigh	James E. Holshouser Jr.	Rep.	4	Jan. 1977	38,500
North Dakota	Bismarck	Arthur A. Link	Dem.	4	Jan. 1977	18,000
Ohio	Columbus	John J. Gilligan	Dem.	4	Jan. 1975	40,000
Oklahoma	Oklahoma City	David Hall	Dem.	4	Jan. 1975	35,000
Oregon	Salem	Tom McCall	Rep.	4	Jan. 1975	29,500
Pennsylvania	Harrisburg	Milton J. Shapp	Dem.	4	Jan. 1975	45,000
Rhode Island	Providence	Philip W. Noel	Dem.	2	Jan. 1975	30,000
South Carolina	Columbia	John C. West	Dem.	4	Jan. 1975	35,000
South Dakota	Pierre	Richard F. Kneip	Dem.	2	Jan. 1975	25,000
Tennessee	Nashville	Winfield Dunn	Rep.	4	Jan. 1975	30,000
Texas	Austin	Dolph Briscoe	Dem.	2	Jan. 1975	63,000
Utah	Salt Lake City	Calvin L. Rampton	Dem.	4	Jan. 1977	33,000
Vermont	Montpelier	Thomas P. Salmon	Dem.	2	Jan. 1975	30,000
Virginia	Richmond	Linwood Holton	Rep.	4	Jan. 1974	35,000
Washington	Olympia	Daniel J. Evans	Rep.	4	Jan. 1977	32,500
West Virginia	Charleston	Arch A. Moore, Jr.	Rep.	4	Jan. 1977	35,000
Wisconsin	Madison	Patrick J. Lucey	Dem.	4	Jan. 1975	25,000
Wyoming	Cheyenne	Stanley K. Hathaway	Rep.	4	Jan. 1975	25,000

Possessions

State	Capital	Governor	Party	Term Years	Term Expires	Annual Salary
American Samoa	Pago Pago	John M. Haydon	Rep.	..	Aug. 1973	33,750
Guam	Agana	Carlos G. Camacho	Rep.	4	July 1973	35,000
Puerto Rico	San Juan	Rafael Hernandez Colon	Prog.	4	Jan. 1977	35,000
Virgin Islands	Charlotte Amalie	Melvin Evans	Rep.	4	July 1973	35,505

Governments of States and Puerto Rico (Elective Officers)

Compiled by World Almanac from statistics supplied by the Secretaries of State.

ALABAMA

Governor — George C. Wallace, D., $25,000
Lt. Governor — Jere Beasley, D., $32 per legislative day, plus annual salary of $300 per month.
Sec. of State — Mabel S. Amos, D., $20,000.
Atty. General — Bill Baxley, D., $22,500.
Treasurer — Mrs. Agnes Baggett, D., $20,000.
Auditor — Melba Till Allen, D., $20,000.

Legislature

Meets odd years, 1st Tues. in May, at Montgomery. Members receive $30 per day during legislative sessions, limited to 36 days, plus annual salary of $300 per month.
Senate — Dem., 35; Rep., 0. Total, 35.
House — Dem., 104; Rep., 2. Total, 106.

ALASKA

Governor — William A. Egan, D., $40,000.
Lt. Governor — H. A. Boucher, D., $36,000.
Atty. General — John E. Havelock, D., $33,000.
Comm. of Educ. — Marshall L. Lind.

Legislature

Meets annually, in January, at Juneau, for as long as may be necessary. First session in odd years. Members receive $9,000 per year plus $35 per day while in session. $1,000 allowance for stenographic services and other expenses.
Senate — Rep., 11; Dem., 9. Total, 20.
House — Rep., 19; Dem., 20; Non-partisan, 1. Total, 40.

ARIZONA

Governor — Jack Williams, R., $35,000.
Sec. of State — Wesley Bolin, D., $22,000.
Atty. General — Gary Nelson, R., $27,500.
Treasurer — Ernest Garfield, R., $19,000.
Supt. Public Instr. — Weldon Shofstall, R., $24,000.

Legislature

Meets annually, in January, at Phoenix. Each member receives an annual salary of $6,000.
Senate — Dem., 12; Rep., 18. Total 30.
House — Dem., 22; Rep., 38. Total, 60.

ARKANSAS

Governor — Dale Bumpers, D., $10,000.
Lt. Governor — Robert C. Riley, D., $2,500.
Sec. of State — Kelly Bryant, D., $5,000.
Auditor — Jimmy Jones, D., $5,000.
Atty. General — Jim Guy Tucker, D., $6,000.
Treasurer — Mrs. Nancy J. Hall, D., $5,000.
Dir. of Public Instr. — A. W. Ford.

General Assembly
Meets odd years, in January, at Little Rock. Members receive $2,400 for each two-year period, $20 a day while in session, plus 5¢ a mile travel expense.
Senate—Dem., 34; Rep., 1. Total, 35.
House—Dem., 99; Rep., 1. Total, 100.

CALIFORNIA
Governor—Ronald Reagan, R., $49,100.
Lt. Governor—Ed Reinecke, R., $35,000.
Sec. of State—Edmund G. Brown, Jr., D., $35,000.
Comptroller—Houston I. Flourney, R., $35,000.
Atty. General—Evelle J. Younger, R., $42,500.
Treasurer—Ivy Baker Priest, R., $35,000.
Supt. Public Instr.—Wilson Riles, NP, $35,000.

Legislature
Meets at Sacramento, in annual general sessions, unlimited as to duration. Members receive $19,200 per year plus mileage and $25 daily expenses while in session. Daily expenses on interim business: $25.
Senate—Dem., 20; Rep., 20. Total, 40.
Assembly—Dem., 49; Rep., 28, Vacancies, 3. Total, 80.

COLORADO
Governor—John A. Love, R., $40,000.
Lt. Governor—John D. Vanderhoof, R., $25,000.
Secy. of State—Byron Anderson, R., $20,000.
Auditor—John P. Proctor, R., $28,000.
Atty. General—John P. Moore, R., $26,000.
Treasurer—Palmer Burch, R., $20,000.
Comm. of Educ.—Donald D. Woodington.

General Assembly
Meets annually, in January, at Denver. Members receive $7,500 annually, plus $35 per day for non-session meetings up to a maximum of $1,050 in any calendar year.
Senate—Dem., 13; Rep., 22. Total, 35.
House—Dem., 28; Rep., 37. Total, 65.

CONNECTICUT
Governor—Thomas J. Meskill, R., $35,000.
Lt. Governor—T. Clark Hull, R., $10,000.
Sec. of State—Gloria Schaffer, D., $15,000.
Treasurer—Robert I. Berdon, R., $15,000.
Comptroller—Nathan G. Agostinelli, R., $15,000.
Atty. General—Robert K. Killian, D., $20,000.
Comm. of Educ.—William J. Sanders.

General Assembly
Meets annually odd years in January and even years in February at Hartford. Salary $11,000 per 2-year term plus $2,000 per 2-year term for expenses and 10¢, per mile travel allowance.
Senate—Rep., 23; Dem., 13. Total, 36.
House—Rep., 93; Dem., 58. Total, 151.

DELAWARE
Governor—Sherman W. Tribbitt, D., $35,000.
Lt. Governor—Eugene D. Bookhammer, R., $9,000.
Sec. of State—Robert H. Reed, D., $18,000.
Auditor—F. Earl McGinnes, D., $18,000.
Atty. General—W. Laird Stabler, Jr., R., $30,000.
Treasurer—Mary D. Jornlin, R., $18,000.
Supt. Public Instr.—Kenneth Madden.

General Assembly
Meets annually at Dover, odd years in January, even years in February. Members receive $6,000 per year.
Senate—Dem., 10; Rep., 11. Total, 21.
House—Dem., 20; Rep., 21. Total, 41.

FLORIDA
Governor—Reubin Askew, D., $40,000.
Lt. Governor—Tom Adams, D., $36,000.
Sec. of State—Richard B. Stone, D., $36,000.
Comptroller—Fred O. Dickinson, Jr., D., $36,000.
Atty. General—Robert L. Shevin, D., $36,000.
Treasurer—Thomas D. O'Malley, D., $36,000.
Supt. Publ. Instr.—Floyd T. Christian, D., $36,000.

Legislature
Meets annually, in April, at Tallahassee. Members receive $12,000 per year plus expense allowance while on official business.
Senate—Dem., 25; Rep., 14; Ind., 1. Total, 40.
House—Dem., 77; Rep., 43. Total, 120.

GEORGIA
Governor—Jimmy Carter, D., $42,500.
Lt. Governor—Lester G. Maddox, D., $20,000.
Sec. of State—Ben W. Fortson, Jr., D., $22,500.
Comptroller General—Johnnie L. Caldwell, D., $22,500.
Atty. General—Arthur K. Bolton, D., $26,000.
Auditor—Ernest Davis, $28,500.
Supt. of Schools—Jack P. Nix, $28,000.

General Assembly
Meets annually at Atlanta. Members receive $4,200 per year. During session $25 per day for expenses.
Senate—Dem., 48; Rep., 8. Total, 56.
House—Dem., 152; Rep., 28. Total, 180.

HAWAII
Governor—John A. Burns, D., $42,000.
Lt. Governor—George R. Ariyoshi, D., $35,700.
Treasurer—Hiram K. Kamaka.
Atty. General—George Pai, $30,250.
Auditor—KeNam Kim, $30,250.
Supt. Public Instr.—Shiro Amioka.

Legislature
Meets annually, in January, at Honolulu. Members receive $12,000 per year plus allowance for expenses.
Senate—Dem., 17; Rep., 8. Total, 25.
House—Dem., 35., Rep., 16. Total, 51.

IDAHO
Governor—Cecil D. Andrus, D., $30,000.
Lt. Governor—Jack M. Murphy, R.. $7,000 plus $45 per day expenses, during sessions of legislature. In absence of Governor acts in his stead and draws regular pay of Governor.
Sec. of State—Pete T. Cenarrusa, R., $17,000.
Treasurer—Marjorie Ruth Moon, D., $17,000.
Atty. General—W. Anthony Park, D., $18,000.
Auditor—Joe R. Williams, D., $17,000.
Supt. Publ. Instr.—D. F. Engelking, D., $18,000.

Legislature
Meets annually, on second Monday in January, at Boise. Members receive $10 per day served, plus $25 per day expenses.
Senate—Dem., 12; Rep., 23. Total, 35.
House—Dem., 19; Rep., 51. Total, 70.

ILLINOIS
Governor—Daniel Walker, D., $50,000.
Lt. Governor—Neil F. Hartigan, D., $37,500.
Sec. of State—Michael J. Howlett, D., $42,500.
Comptroller—George W. Lindberg, R., $42,500.
Atty. General—William J. Scott, R., $42,500.
Treasurer—Alan J. Dixon., D., $30,000.
Supt. Public Instr.—Michael J. Bakalis, D., $30,000.

General Assembly
Meets each year in January, at Springfield. Members receive $17,500 per annum.
Senate—Rep., 30; Dem., 29. Total, 59.
House—Rep., 89; Dem., 87; Ind., 1. Total, 177.

INDIANA
Governor—Otis R. Bowen, R., $36,000.
Lt. Governor—Robert Orr, R., $23,500; also $6,000 per year as President of Senate, plus $5 per day during legislative sessions.
Sec. of State—Larry Conrad, D., $23,500.
Auditor—Mary Aikins, D., $23,500.
Atty. General—Theodore L. Sendak, R., $27,000.
Treasurer—Jack L. New, D., $23,500.
Supt. Publ. Instr.—Harold Negley, R., $25,000.

General Assembly
Meets annually in January. Members receive $6,000 per year, plus $100 each month not in session, plus $25 per day expense allowance when in session. Also, 8¢ a mile for round trip each week.
Senate—Rep., 29; Dem., 21. Total, 50.
House—Rep., 53; Dem., 46; Vacancy, 1. Total 100.

IOWA
Governor—Robert D. Ray, R., $35,000, plus $5,000 expenses.
Lt. Governor—Arthur A. Neu, R., $11,000 plus personal expenses and travel allowances at same rate as for a senator.
Sec. of State—Melvin D. Synhorst, R., $18,500.
Auditor—Lloyd R. Smith, R., $18,500.

Atty. General — Richard C. Turner, R., $22,500.
Treasurer — Maurice E. Baringer, R., $18,500.
Supt. Public Instr. — Robert Benton.

General Assembly
Meets annually, in January, at Des Moines. Members receive $5,500, plus maximum expense allowance of $15 per day 5 days a week during session, mileage expenses at 10¢ a mile.
Senate — Rep., 28; Dem., 22. Total, 50.
House — Rep., 56; Dem., 44. Total, 100.

KANSAS
Governor — Robert Docking, D., $20,000.
Lt. Governor — Dave Owen, R., $8,440.
Sec. of State — Mrs. E. M. Shanahan, R., $13,346.
Auditor — Clay E. Hedrick, R., $13,346.
Atty. General — Vern Miller, D., $18,463.
Treasurer — Tom R. Van Sickle, R., $13,346.

Legislature
Meets annually in January, at Topeka. Members receive $10 a day plus $35 a day expenses, plus $200 per month while not in session.
Senate — Rep., 27; Dem., 13. Total, 40.
House — Rep., 80; Dem., 45. Total, 125.

KENTUCKY
Governor — Wendell Ford, D., $30,000.
Lt. Gov. — Julian Carroll, D., $22,500, plus additional compensation when acting in place of Governor.
Sec. of State — Thelma L. Stovall, D., $22,500.
Auditor — Mary Louise Foust, D., $22,500.
Atty. Gen. — Ed Hancock, D., $22,500.
Treasurer — Drexell Davis, D., $22,500.
Supt. Public Instr. — Lyman V. Ginger, D., $22,500.

General Assembly
Meets even years, in January, at Frankfort. Members receive $25 per day during session; presiding officers, $30. All members also receive $25 per day for expenses.
Senate — Dem., 28; Rep., 10. Total, 38.
House — Dem., 73; Rep., 27. Total, 100.

LOUISIANA
Governor — Edwin W. Edwards, D., $28,374.
Lt. Governor — James E. Fitzmorris, Jr., D., $26,529.
Sec. of State — Wade O. Martin, Jr., D., $26,529.
Atty. General — William J. Guste, Jr., D., $26,529.
Treasurer — Mary Evelyn Parker, D., $26,529.
Supt. of Education — Louis J. Michot, D., $26,529.

Legislature
Meets even years (60 calendar days) and odd years (30 calendar days) in May, at Baton Rouge. Members receive $50 per day and mileage during the 60 days session of 10¢ a mile for 8 round trips. When the Legislature is not in session, members receive $500 per month as an expense allowance.
Senate — Dem., 39; Rep., 0. Total, 39.
House — Dem., 101; Rep., 4. Total, 105.

MAINE
Governor — Kenneth Curtis, D., $20,000.
Sec. of State — Joseph T. Edgar, R., $15,467.
Atty. General — Jon A. Lund, $23,500.
Auditor — Raymond M. Rideout, Jr., $13,500.
Treasurer — Norman K. Ferguson, $13,000.
Comm. of Education — Carroll R. McGary, $20,467.

Legislature
Meets biennially in January, at Augusta. Members receive $2,500 per session; presiding officers, $5,000.
Senate — Dem., 11; Rep., 22. Total, 33.
House — Dem., 72; Rep., 78; Vacancy, 1. Total, 151.

MARYLAND
Governor — Marvin Mandel, D., $25,000.
Lt. Governor — Blair Lee 3d, R., $24,000.
Comptroller — Louis L. Goldstein, D., $20,000.
Atty. General — Francis B. Burch, D., $20,000.
Treasurer — John A. Luetkemeyer, D., $2,500.
Supt. of Education — James A. Sensenbaugh.

General Assembly
Meets 90 days annually on the 3rd Wednesday in January, at Annapolis. Members receive $11,000 per year.
Senate — Dem., 33; Rep., 10. Total, 43.
House — Dem., 121; Rep., 21. Total, 142.

MASSACHUSETTS
Governor — Francis W. Sargent, R., $40,000.

Lt. Governor — Donald Dwight, R., $25,000.
Sec. of the Commonwealth — John F. X. Davoren, D., $25,000.
Atty. General — Robert H. Quinn, D., $30,000.
Auditor — Thaddeus Buczko, D., $25,000.
Treasurer — Robert Q. Crane, D., $25,000.

General Court (Legislature)
Meets each January in Boston. Salaries $11,400 per annum.
Senate — Dem., 33; Rep., 7. Total, 40.
House — Dem., 186; Rep., 52; Ind., 2. Total, 240.

MICHIGAN
Governor — William G. Milliken, R., $45,000.
Lt. Governor — James H. Brickley, R., $25,000.
Sec. of State — Richard H. Austin, D., $35,000.
Atty. General — Frank J. Kelley, D., $35,000.
Auditor — Albert Lee.
Treasurer — Allison Green.
Supt. Public Instr. — John Porter.

Legislature
Meets annually in January, at Lansing. Members receive $17,000 per year plus $2,875 expense allowance.
Senate — Rep., 19; Dem., 19. Total, 38.
House — Rep., 50; Dem., 60. Total, 110.

MINNESOTA
Governor — Wendell R. Anderson, DFL, $35,000.
Lt. Governor — Rudy Perpich, DFL, $30,000.
Sec. of State — Arlen I. Erdahl, $21,000.
Auditor — Rolland Hatfield, R., $21,000.
Atty. General — Warren Spannaus, DFL, $30,900.
Treasurer — Val Bjornson, R., $21,000.
(Democratic-Farmer-Labor is the legal name of the Democratic Party in Minnesota.)

Legislature
Meets odd years, in January, at St. Paul. Members receive $8,400 per year plus expense allowance during session.
Senate — 67, elected without party designation.
House — 134, elected without party designation.

MISSISSIPPI
Governor — William L. Waller, D., $35,000.
Lt. Gov. — William Winter, D., $8,500 per regular legislative session, plus expense allowance.
Sec. of State — Heber Ladner, D., $23,500.
Auditor — W. H. (Hamp) King, D., $21,500.
Atty. Gen. — A. L. Summer, D., $25,000.
Treasurer — Brad Dye, D., $21,500.
Supt. Public Educ. — Garvin Johnston, D., $21,500.

Legislature
Meets annually in January, at Jackson. Members receive $5,000 per regular session, plus travel allowance and $100 per month while not in session.
Senate — Dem., 50; Rep., 2. Total, 52.
House — Dem., 119; Rep., 2; Ind., 1. Total, 122.

MISSOURI
Governor — Christopher S. Bond, R., $37,500.
Lt. Governor — William C. Phelps, R., $16,000.
Sec. of State — James C. Kirkpatrick, D., $25,000.
Auditor — John D. Ashcroft, R., $20,000.
Atty. General — John C. Danforth, R., $25,000.
Treasurer — James I. Spainhower, D., $20,000.
Comm. of Educ. — Arthur L. Mallory.

General Assembly
Meets in Jefferson City annually, first Wednesday after first Monday in January; adjournment in odd-numbered years by June 30, in even-numbered years by May 15. Members receive $8,400 per annum.
Senate — Dem., 21; Rep., 13. Total, 34.
House — Dem., 97; Rep., 66. Total, 163.

MONTANA
Governor — Thomas L. Judge, D., $25,000.
Lt. Governor — Bill Christiansen, D., $18,500.
Sec. of State — Frank Murray, D., $15,000.
Auditor — E. V. (Sonny) Omholt, R., $15,000.
Atty. General — Bob Woodahl, R., $19,000.
Treasurer — Hollis G. Connors, R., $15,000.
Supt. Public Instr. — Dolores Colburg, D., $17,500.

Legislative Assembly
Meets annually in January, at Helena. Members receive $20 per day plus $33 per day for expenses while in session.
Senate — Dem., 27; Rep., 23. Total, 50.
House — Dem., 54; Rep., 46. Total, 100.

NEBRASKA
Governor—J. James Exon, D., $25,000.
Lt. Governor—Frank Marsh, R., $7,500.
Sec. of State—Allen J. Beermann, R., $16,000.
Auditor—Ray A. C. Johnson, R., $16,000.
Atty. General—Clarence A. Meyer, R., $24,000.
Treasurer—Wayne Swanson, R., $15,000.
Legislature
Meets annually in January, at Lincoln. Members receive salary of not more than $400 month plus travelling expenses for one round trip to and from session.
Unicameral body composed of 49 members who are elected on a nonpartisan ballot and are classed as Senators.

NEVADA
Governor—Mike O'Callaghan, D., $30,000.
Lt. Governor—Harry M. Reid, D., $4,500 plus $40 per day when acting as Governor and President of the Senate during legislative sessions.
Sec. of State—William D. Swackhamer, D., $18,000.
Comptroller—Wilson McGowen, R., $18,000.
Atty. General—Robert List, R., $22,500.
Treasurer—Michael Mirabelli, D., $18,000.
Supt. Public Instr.—Burnell Larson.
Legislature
Meets odd years in January, at Carson City. All members receive $40 per day for 60 days (20 days for special sessions). All members receive per diem of $25 per day for 60 days (20 days special session). Travel allowance of 10¢ per mile.
Senate—Dem., 14; Rep., 6. Total, 20.
Assembly—Dem., 25; Rep., 15. Total, 37.

NEW HAMPSHIRE
Governor—Meldrim Thomson, Jr., R., $30,000.
Sec. of State—Robert L. Stark, R., $22,204.
Atty. General—Warren Rudman, $22,204.
Comptroller—John Flanders.
Comm. of Education—Newell J. Paire.
Dir. of Accounts—Frank E. Adams.
Treasurer—Robert W. Flanders, R., $22,204.
General Court (Legislature)
Meets odd years, in January, at Concord. Members receive $200; presiding officers $250.
Senate—Rep., 14; Dem., 10. Total, 24.
House—Rep., 260; Dem., 137; Vacancies, 3. Total, 400.

NEW JERSEY
Governor—William T. Cahill, R., $50,000.
Sec. of State—Robert M. Falcey, acting, $38,000.
Atty. General—George F. Kugler, Jr., R., $40,000.
Treasurer—William E. Marfuggi, R., $40,000.
Auditor—George B. Harper, $18,000.
Comm. of Education—Carl L. Marburger, $38,000.
Legislature
Meets annually, in January, at Trenton. Members receive $10,000 per year, except Presidents of Senate and Speaker of Assembly who receive ⅓ more by virtue of their office.
Senate—Dem., 16; Rep., 22; Vacancies, 2. Total, 40.
Assembly—Dem., 40; Rep., 39; Ind., 1. Total, 80.

NEW MEXICO
Governor—Bruce King, D., $26,000.
Lt. Governor—Robert A. Mondragon, D., $50 per day when presiding over Senate. Acting Governor, $60 per day.
Sec. of State—Betty Fiorina, D., $20,000.
Auditor—Frank M. Olmstead, D., $20,000.
Atty. General—David L. Norvell, D., $25,000.
Treasurer—Jesse D. Korenegay, D., $20,000.
Legislature
Meets in January, at Sante Fe, odd years for 60 days, even years for 30 days. Receive $20 per day while in session.
Senate—Dem., 29; Rep., 13. Total, 42.
House—Dem., 51; Rep., 19. Total, 70.

NEW YORK
Governor—Nelson A. Rockefeller, R., $85,000.
Lt. Governor—Malcolm Wilson, R., $45,000.
Sec. of State—John P. Lomenzo, R., $42,475.
Comptroller—Arthur Levitt, D., $45,000.
Atty. General—Louis J. Kefkowitz, R., $45,000.
Comm. of Education—Ewald B. Nyquist.

Legislature
Meets annually, in January, at Albany. Members receive $15,000 per year.
Senate—Rep., 37; Dem., 23. Total, 60.
Assembly—Rep., 82; Dem., 66; Vacancies, 2. Total, 150.

NORTH CAROLINA
Governor—James E. Holshouser, Jr., R., $38,500
Lt. Governor—James B. Hunt, D., $30,000 per year, plus $20 per day not to exceed 120 days per regular session; $4,000 per year expense allowance.
Sec. of State—Thad Eure, D., $25,000.
Auditor—Henry L. Bridges, D., $25,000.
Atty. General—Robert Morgan, D., $29,500.
Treasurer—Edwin Gill, D., $25,000.
Supt. Public Instr.—Craig Phillips, D., $28,500.
General Assembly
Meets odd years in January, at Raleigh. Members receive $2,400 annual salary and $600 annual expense allowance plus subsistence and travel allowance while in session.
Senate—Dem., 35; Rep., 15. Total, 50.
House—Dem., 85; Rep., 35. Total, 120.

NORTH DAKOTA
Governor—Arthur A. Link, D., $18,000 plus $8,000 per year expense allowance.
Lt. Governor—Wayne Sanstead, D., $2,500.
Sec. of State—Ben Meier, R., $9,000.
Auditor—Robert W. Peterson, R., $11,000.
Atty. General—Allen I. Olson, R., $13,000.
Treasurer—Walter Christensen, D., $11,000.
Supt. Public Instruction—M. F. Peterson, N-P., $12,000. All state officers receive $5,000 per year for expenses except the Lt. Gov. who receives $2,000 for expenses.
Legislative Assembly
Meets odd years, in January at Bismarck. Members receive $5 per day, plus $35 per day expense allowance while in session, plus $35 per month when got in session.
Senate—Rep., 41; Dem., 10. Total, 51.
House—Rep., 79; Dem., 23. Total, 102.

OHIO
Governor—John J. Gilligan, D., $40,000.
Lt. Governor—John W. Brown, R., $17,000.
Sec. of State—Ted W. Brown, R., $25,000.
Atty. General—William J. Brown, D., $25,000.
Auditor—Joseph T. Ferguson, D., $25,000.
Treasurer—Gertrude W. Donahey, D., $25,000.
Supt. of Education—Martin W. Essex.
General Assembly
Meets annually, in January, at Columbus. Second session not later than Mar. 15 of year following regular session. Members receive $12,750 per year plus travel allowance.
Senate—Rep., 17; Dem., 16. Total, 33.
House—Rep., 41; Dem., 58. Total, 99.

OKLAHOMA
Governor—David Hall, D., $35,000.
Lt. Governor—George Nigh, D., $18,000.
Sec. of State—John Rogers, D., $15,000.
Auditor—Joe Bailey Cobb, D., $15,000.
Atty. General—Larry Derryberry, D., $22,500.
Treasurer—Leo Winters, D., $18,000.
Supt. Public Instr.—Leslie R. Fisher, D., $25,000.
Legislature
Meets each year in January, at Oklahoma City. Members receive the sum of $9,480 per annum.
Senate—Dem., 38; Rep., 10. Total, 48.
House—Dem., 75; Rep., 26. Total, 101.

OREGON
Governor—Tom McCall, R., $29,500.
Sec. of State—Clay Myers, R., $25,000.
Atty. General—Lee Johnson, R., $25,000.
Treasurer—James A. Redden, D., $25,000.
Supt. Public Instr.—Dale Parnell, (N-P) $25,000.
Legislative Assembly
Meets odd years, in January, at Salem. Members receive $400 monthly and $30 expenses per day while in session; $150 per month while not in session.
Senate—Dem., 16; Rep., 14. Total, 30.
House—Dem., 26; Rep., 34. Total, 60.

PENNSYLVANIA

Governor — Milton J. Shapp, D., $45,000.
Lt. Governor — Ernest P. Kline, D., $32,500.
Sec. of State — C. DeLores Tucker, $25,000.
Atty. General — Israel Packel, $25,000.
Auditor General — Robert P. Casey, D., $35,000.
Treasurer — Mrs. Grace M. Sloan, D., $35,000.

General Assembly

Meets annually, in January, at Harrisburg. Members receive $7,200 per year plus $4,800 for expenses. Legislators elected in this year's election will receive salaries of $15,600 plus expenses of $2,500.
Senate — Rep., 24; Dem., 26. Total, 50.
House — Rep., 107; Dem., 96. Total, 203.

RHODE ISLAND

Governor — Philip W. Noel, D., $30,000.
Lt. Governor — J. Joseph Garrahy, D., $12,000.
Sec. of State — Robert F. Burns, D., $18,000.
Atty. General — Richard J. Israel, R., $22,000.
Treasurer — Raymond H. Hawksley, D., $18,000.

General Assembly

Meets annually, in January, at Providence. Members receive $5 per day for 60 days (the Speaker, $10), also travel allowance of 8¢ per mile.
Senate — Dum., 27; Dem., 13. Total, 50.
House — Dem., 73; Rep., 27. Total, 100.

SOUTH CAROLINA

Governor — John C. West, D., $35,000.
Lt. Governor — Earle E. Morris, Jr., $15,000.
Sec. of State — O. Frank Thornton, D., $30,000.
Comptroller General — John Henry Mills, D., $30,000.
Atty. General — Daniel R. McLeod, D., $30,000.
Treasurer — G. L. Patterson, Jr., D., $30,000.
Supt. of Educ. — Cyril B. Busbee, D., $30,000.

General Assembly

Meets annually in January, at Columbia. Members receive $4,000 per year plus expense allowance of $15 per day and travel and postage allowance.
Senate — Dem., 42; Rep., 2; Vacancies, 2. Total, 46.
House — Dem., 113; Rep., 11. Total, 124.

SOUTH DAKOTA

Governor — Richard F. Kneip, D., $25,000.
Lt. Governor — William Dougherty, D., $4,100.
Sec. of State — Lorna B. Herseth, D., $15,000.
Treasurer — David Volk, R., $15,000.
Atty. General — Kermit Sande, D., $21,000.
Auditor — Alice Kundert, R., $15,000.
Supt. Public Instr. — Donald Barnhart, N-P.

Legislature

Meets annually in January, at Pierre. Members receive $3,000 for 45 day session in odd-numbered years, and $2,000 for 30 day session in even-numbered years, plus 5¢ a mile.
Senate — Dem., 18; Rep., 17. Total, 35.
House — Dem., 35; Rep., 35. Total, 70.

TENNESSEE

Governor — Winfield Dunn, R., $30,000.
Lt. Governor — John S. Wilder, D.
Sec. of State — Joe C. Carr, D., $20,000.
Comptroller — William Snodgrass, D., $17,640.
Atty. General — David Pack, D., $24,000.
Comm. of Education — Ben Carmichael.

General Assembly

Meets annually, in January, at Nashville. Members receive $6,000 yearly plus expenses for each day in session (not to exceed 105 days).
Senate — Dem., 19; Rep., 13; American party, 1. Total, 33.
House — Dem., 56; Rep., 43. Total, 99.

TEXAS

Governor — Dolph Briscoe, D., $63,000.
Lt. Governor — Bill Hobby, D., same salary as State Senator while presiding over Senate, plus living quarters. Governor's salary when acting as Governor.
Sec. of State — Mark W. White, Jr., D., $28,000.
Comptroller — Robert S. Calvert, D., $26,000.
Atty. General — John L. Hill, D., $27,500.
Treasurer — Jesse James, D., $26,000.
Comm. of Education — J. W. Edgar.

Legislature

Meets odd years, in January, at Austin. Members receive annual salary not exceeding $4,800 plus per diem while in session and travel allowance.
Senate — Dem., 28; Rep., 3. Total, 31.
House — Dem., 133; Rep., 17. Total, 150.

UTAH

Governor — Calvin L. Rampton, D., $33,000.
Sec. of State — Clyde L. Miller, D., $20,000.
Auditor — David S. Monson, R., $19,000.
Atty. General — Vernon B. Romney, R., $23,000.
Treasurer — David L. Duncan, R., $19,000.

Legislature

Meets annually in January at Salt Lake City. While in session members receive $25 per diem, expenses of $15 per diem, plus mileage.
Senate — Rep., 16; Dem., 13. Total, 29.
House — Rep., 44; Dem., 31. Total, 75.

VERMONT

Governor — Thomas P. Salmon, D., $30,000.
Lt. Governor — John S. Burgess, R., $14,000.
Sec. of State — Richard C. Thomas, R., $17,000.
Auditor — Alexander V. Acebo, R., $17,000.
Atty. General — Kimberly B. Cheney, R., $22,000.
Treasurer — Frank Davis, R., $17,000.

General Assembly

Meets odd years, in January, at Montpelier. Members receive $150 weekly, while in session, with a limit of $4,500 for a regular session and $30 per day for special session, with specified expenses.
Senate — Rep., 23; Dem., 7. Total, 30.
House — Rep., 87; Dem., 56; Rep.-Dem., 4; Dem.-Ind., 1; Ind.-Dem., 1; Ind., 1. Total, 150.

VIRGINIA

Governor — Linwood Holton, R., $35,000.
Lt. Governor — Henry E. Howell, Jr., Ind., $2,100 each biennial session of legislature, plus $8,950 per year for expenses.
Atty. General — Andrew P. Miller, D., $30,000.
Sec. of the Commonwealth — Cynthia S. Newman, R., $11,500.
Treasurer — Walther W. Craigie, Jr., R., $26,000.
Auditor — Joseph S. James, $20,000.
Supt. Public Instr. — Dr. Woodrow Wilkerson.

General Assembly

Meets every year in January, at Richmond. Members receive $2,100 per regular 60 day biennial session plus $3,900 for expenses.
Senate — Dem., 33; Rep., 7. Total, 40.
House — Dem., 71; Rep., 25; Ind., 4. Total, 100.

WASHINGTON

Governor — Daniel J. Evans, R., $32,500.
Lt. Governor — John A. Cherberg, D., $10,000.
Sec. of State — A. "Lud" Kramer, R., $15,000.
Auditor — R. V. Graham, D., $16,500.
Atty. General — Slade Gorton, R., $23,000.
Treasurer — Robert S. O'Brien, D., $15,000.
Supt. of Public Instr. — Dr. Frank Brouillet, N-P., $22,500.

Legislature

Meets odd years in January, at Olympia. Members receive $3,600 annually, plus $40 per day while in session for subsistence and lodging.
Senate — Dem., 30; Rep., 19. Total, 49.
House — Dem., 57; Rep., 41. Total, 98.

WEST VIRGINIA

Governor — Arch A. Moore, Jr., R., $35,000.
Sec. of State — Edgar F. Heiskell, 3d, R., $22,500.
Auditor — John M. Gates, R., $22,500.
Atty. General — Chauncey Browning, Jr., D., $22,500.
Treasurer — John H. Kelly, D., $22,500.

Legislature

Meets annually in January, at Charleston. Members receive compensation fixed by citizens' commission.
Senate — Dem., 24; Rep., 10. Total, 34.
House — Dem., 57; Rep., 43. Total, 100.

WISCONSIN

Governor — Patrick J. Lucey, D., $25,000.
Lt. Governor — Martin J. Schreiber, D., $15,000 per biennium.
Sec. of State — Robert C. Zimmerman, R., $13,500.
Treasurer — Charles P. Smith, D., $13,500.
Atty. General — Robert W. Warren, R., $20,000.
Supt. of Schools — William C. Kahl, N-P., $21,000.

Legislature

Meets odd years, in January, at Madison. Members receive $8,900 annually plus $20 per day expenses for each day.
Senate — Rep., 18; Dem., 15. Total, 33.
Assembly — Rep., 62; Dem., 37. Total, 99.

WYOMING

Governor — Stanley K. Hathaway, R., $25,000.
Sec. of State — Mrs. Thyra Thomson, R., $17,000.
Auditor — Everett Copenhaver, R., $17,000.
Atty. General — Clarence A. Brimmer, R., $21,000.
Treasurer — James Griffith, R., $17,000.
Supt. of Public Instr. — Robert G. Schrader, R., $17,000.

Legislature

Meets odd years in January, at Cheyenne. Members receive $15 per day while in session, plus $26 per day for expenses, and 10¢ a mile travel allowance.

Senate — Rep., 19; Dem., 11. Total, 30.
House — Rep., 40; Dem., 20; Ind., 1. Total, 61.

PUERTO RICO

Governor — Rafael-Hernandez Colon, $35,000.
Secretaries:
Agric. — Antonio Gonzalez Chapel, $25,000.
Commerce — Damian Folch, $25,000.
Educ. — Celeste Benitez Rexach, $25,000.
Health — Jose Alvarez de Choudens, $25,000.
Justice — Francisco De Jesus Shuck, $25,000.
Labor — Luis Silva Recio, $25,000.
Public Works — Dennis H. Hernandez.
Social Services — Eliza Diaz Gonzalez, $25,000.
State — Victor M. Pons, Jr.
Treasury — Salvador Cassellas, $25,000.
All officials belong to the Popular Democratic Party.

Legislative Assembly

Composed of a Senate of 26 members and a House of Representatives of 51 members. Meets annually, in January, at San Juan. Members receive $9,600 plus expenses and travel allowances.

United States Government Independent Agencies

Source: General Services Administration

Address: Washington, D.C. Location and zip codes of agencies in parentheses, as of May 10, 1973

ACTION — Director: Michael P. Balzano, Jr. (806 Connecticut Ave., NW, 20525).

Administrative Conference of the United States — Chmn. Antonin Scalia (726 Jackson Pl., NW, 20506).

American Battle Monuments Commission — Chmn., Mark Clark (2067 Tempo A, 20315).

Appalachian Regional Commission — Federal co-chairman: Donald W. Whitehead, State co-chairman: Gov. Winfield Dunn. (1666 Conn. Ave. NW. 20235).

Arms Control & Disarmament Agency — Director: (Vacancy). (Department of State Bldg. 20451).

Atomic Energy Commission — The Commission: Dixy Lee Ray, chmn., (Vacancy), James T. Ramey, Clarence E. Larson, William O. Doub. (Wash. D.C. 20545).

Central Intelligence Agency — William Colby, Act. Director. (Wash., D.C. 20505).

Civil Aeronautics Board — Chairman: Robert D. Timm. (1825 Connecticut Ave. NW. 20428).

Commission on Civil Rights — Staff Dir., John A. Buggs, Act. (1121 Vermont Ave., NW, 20425).

Commission of Fine Arts — J. Carter Brown, chmn. (706 Jackson Pl., NW, 20006).

Civil Service Commission — Robert E. Hampton, chmn., Jayne B. Spain, vice chmn. (1900 E St. NW, 20415).

Economic Stabilization Agencies — **Cost of Living Council,** G. P. Schultz, chmn. (17th and Penn. Ave., NW, 20507).

Environmental Protection Agency — Administrator: Robert W. Fri, Act. (410 M St., NW, 20460).

Equal Employment Opportunity Commission — William H. Brown, 3rd. chmn. (1800 G St. NW. 20506).

Export-Import Bank of the United States — Henry Kearns, pres. and chmn., (811 Vermont Ave. NW. 20571).

Farm Credit Administration — J. Homer Remsberg, chmn. (485 L'Enfant Plaza West, SW).

Federal Communications Commission — Commissioners: Dean Burch, chmn , H. Rex Lee, Nicholas Johnson, Charlotte T. Reid, Robert E. Lee, Richard E. Wiley, Benjamin L. Hooks (1919 M St. NW. 20554).

Federal Deposit Insurance Corporation — Chairman: Frank Wille. (550 17th St., NW. 20429).

Federal Home Loan Bank Board — Chairman: Carl O. Kamp, Jr., Act. (101 Indiana Ave., NW. 20552).

Federal Maritime Commission — Helen D. Bentley, chmn. (1405 I St., NW. 20573).

Federal Mediation and Councilliation Service — Director: W. J. Usery (Dept. of Labor Bldg., 20427).

Federal Power Commission — John N. Nassikas, chmn., Rush Moody, Jr., vice chmn. (441 G St., NW. 20426).

Federal Reserve System Chairman, Board of Governors: Arthur F. Burns. (20th St. & Constitution Ave., NW. 20551).

Federal Trade Commission — Commissioners: Lewis A. Engman, chmn., David S. Dennison, A. Everette MacIntyre, Mary Gardiner Jones, Paul Rand Dixon. (Penn. Ave. at 6th St., NW.).

Foreign Claims Settlement Comm. of the U.S. — Lyle S. Garlock, chmn. (1111 20th St., NW., 20579).

General Accounting Office — Comptroller General of the U.S.: Elmer B. Staats. (441 G St., NW. 20548).

General Services Administration — Administrator: Arthur F. Sampson, Act. (General Services Bldg., 20406).

Government Printing Office — Public Printer: Thomas F. McCormick (North Capitol and H Sts. NW 20401).

Indian Claims Commission — Jerome K. Kuykendall, chmn. (1730 K St. NW. 20006).

Inter-American Foundation — chmn., Augustin S. Hart, Jr. (1515 Wilson Blvd., Rosslyn, Va., 22209).

Interstate Commerce Commission — Commissioners: George M. Stafford, chmn., Williard Deason, Kenneth H. Tuggle, Rupert L. Murphy, Dale Hardin, Virginia Mae Brown, W. Donald Brewer, Robert C. Gresham, Chester M. Wiggin, Jr., Alfred T. MacFarland, A. Daniel O'Neal. (12th St. and Constitution Ave. NW. 20423).

Library of Congress — L. Quincy Mumford, Librarian (10 First St. SE., 20540).

National Academy of Sciences — **National Academy of Engineering** — **National Research Council** — President: Philip Handler. (2101 Constitution Ave. NW. 20418).

National Aeronautics and Space Administration — Administrator: James C. Fletcher. (Washington, D.C. 20546).

National Credit Union Administration — Herman Nickerson, Jr. Administrator. (2025 M St. NW. 20456).

National Foundation on the Arts and Humanities — Nancy Hanks, chmn. (Arts). Ronald S. Berman, chmn. (Humanities) (806 15th St. NW. 20506).

National Labor Relations Board — Chairman: Edward B. Miller, (1717 Pennsylvania Ave. NW, 20570).

National Mediation Board — David H. Stowe, chmn. (1230 16th St. NW. 20572).

National Science Foundation — Director: H. Guyford Stever. (1800 G St. NW, 20550).

Occupational Safety and Health Review Commission — chmn., Robert D. Moran (1825 K St. NW., 20006).

Overseas Private Investment Corporation — President, Bradford Mills, (1129-20th St, NW , 20527).

Postal Rate Commission — Chairman, (Vacancy). (2000 L St., NW., 20268).

Railroad Retirement Board — Chairman: James L. Cowen. (Rm. 444, 425 13th St. NW. 20004), Main Office, 844 Rush St., Chicago, Ill. 60611).

Renegotiation Board — Chairman, Richard T. Burress (2000 M St. NW., 20446).

Securities and Exchange Commission — Commissioners: G. Bradford Cook, chmn., Hugh Owens, Albert Herlong, Jr., Philip Loomis, Jr., John R. Evans. (500 N. Capitol St., 20549).

Selective Service System — Director: Byron V. Pepitone (1724 F St. NW. 20435).

Small Business Administration — Administrator: Thomas S. Kleppe. (1441 L St. NW. 20416).

Smithsonian Institution — S. Dillon Ripley, Secy. (1000 Jefferson Drive, 20560).

Subversive Activities Control Board — John W. Mahan, chmn. (2120 L St., NW., 20037).

Tariff Commission, United States — Chairman: Catherine Bedell. (8th and E Sts. NW. 20436).

Tennessee Valley Authority — Chairman, Board of Directors: Aubrey J. Wagner. (New Sprankle Bldg., Knoxville, Tenn. 37901 and Woodward Bldg., Washington, D.C. 20444).

United States Information Agency — Director: James Keogh. (1750 Pennsylvania Ave. NW. 20547).

United States Postal Service — E. T. Klassen, Postmaster General (1200 Pennsylvania Ave. NW., 20260).

Veterans Administration — Administrator: Donald E. Johnson. (Vermont Ave. at H St. NW. 20420).

Memorable Dates

Consult also Chronology, Aviation Records, Polar Explorations, Fast Ocean Passages, Train Records, Marine Disasters, Political Assassinations, Earthquakes, Tornadoes, Amendments to the Constitution, Noted Personalities, Astronomical Data, Sporting Records and other classifications.

B. C.

3000
Indus Valley Civilization, sites at Mohenjo-Daro and Harappa in West Pakistan. Civilization had complex form of government, elaborate irrigation and drainage system, writing, well laid out streets, and houses of several stories. End came about **1500 B. C.**
Pyramids begun by kings of Egypt at Sakkara. Cheops built great pyramid at Giza; Chephren second largest. Sphinx built about **2900 B. C.**

c. 1792-1750
Hammurabi ruled West Semitic kingdom of Babylon; wrote great code of laws. Ruled Canaan in days of Abraham.

on 1150 or c 1275
Moses led the Israelites out of Egypt.

1360
Ikhnaton introduced monotheistic worship of Aten, or sun, in Egypt. A successor, Tutankhamen revived polytheistic orthodox, **1350 B. C.** Tutankhamen buried at Thebes, **1344 B. C.,** tomb opened by Howard Carter and Lord Carnarvon, **1923-24 A. D.**

1184
Troy fell to Greeks after 10-year siege, according to Homer. While poem is legendary, numerous battles were waged on site at northwest corner of Asia Minor, three miles from Hellespont (Dardanelles). Later town of Ilium was visited by Xerxes and exploited by Alexander the Great. Romans, glorifying their legendary descent from Aeneas, who escaped from Troy, built up Ilium.
In **1871 A. D.** Henry Schliemann, German archaeologist, excavated site of Troy on hill of Hissarlik and found deposits of seven cities. Dorpfeld found two more. Schliemann identified second city with Homer's Troy, but objects found in sixth city correspond better with Greek remains of **1200 to 1100 B. C.** found at Agamemnon's Mycenae.

1000
On death of King Saul, c. **1000 B. C.,** David became king of Israel, but for 7½ years ruled only the southern kingdom of Judah. Thereafter he ruled all Israel, made Jerusalem capital. Solomon, son of David and Bathsheba, ruled c. **973-933 B. C.**

753
Romulus founded Rome, according to legend. Hills occupied for centuries by Indo-Europeans and Sabines, sheep herders.

612
Babylonians destroyed Nineveh, Assyrian capital. Nebuchadnezzar's Babylonians defeated Egyptians at Carchemish **605 B. C.** Built hanging gardens. Destroyed Solomon's temple, **589 B.C.**

563
Gautama (Sakyamuni) Buddha, "the Enlightened," born near Himalayas; died **483 B. C.,** aged 80. Taught that painful life is caused by desire. End desire to end pain in life.

551
Confucius (Latinized form of K'ung-fu-tze) Chinese social philosopher, born; died **478 B. C.** Taught: "Do not do to others what you do not wish done to you."

490
King Darius' Persian army landed at Marathon to march on Athens. Athenian infantry numbering 10,000 routed 30,000 Persians.

484-480
Persian King Xerxes assembled a great host at Sardis to invade Greece. His Phoenicians and Egyptians built two ship bridges across Hellespont from Abydos (Na-

gara) to Sestos, 2,000 yards long. One bridge of planks and dirt rested on 360 ships; the other on 314. Herodotus says army crossed for seven days and seven nights.
At **Thermopylae, 480 B. C.,** Leonidas and 300 Spartans, supported by 700 Thespians and 400 Thebans, held off Persians in pass until overcome. Persians took Athens and Attica. Athenians under Themistocles destroyed Persian fleet at Salamis under eyes of Xerxes, won land battle. Rallying about 70,000 from Greek states, they routed Persians at Platea **479 B. C.**

438
Parthenon completed at Athens, 101'4" by 228'2"; Doric columns 33' tall, roof height 60'. Ictinus and Callicrates, designers: Phidias, chief sculptor.

431
Peloponnesian War began between Athens and Sparta. War ended **404 B. C.** with Sparta victorious.

400
Socrates, Greek philosopher, condemned by Athenian state, drank hemlock (dropwort). Plato, his disciple, recorded 35 dialogues, great philosophical work. Dialogues recommended: Gorgias, Apology, Crito, Phaedo, Republic, Phaedrus, Banquet. Zenophon, another disciple, recorded memorabilia.

356
Alexander "The Great" of Macedon, born. Ruthless and energetic military leader, defeated Persians at Granicus, Issus, Arbela; conquered Asia Minor and Egypt, burned Persian capital, Persepolis, carried war to the Punjab. Founder of Alexandria. Died of fever at Babylon, **323 B. C.**

322
Aristotle, Greek philosopher with scientific mind, disciple of Plato, died, 62. Demosthenes, Greek statesman, died.

300
Invention of Mayan calendar in Yucatan–approximate date–giving solar year 365.24 days and lunar month 29.52 days. Considered more exact than older calendars of Babylon, Assyria, Egypt, Greece.

264
Rome began first Punic war against Carthage, rich commercial seaport on Bay of Tunis. In **241 B. C.,** Carthage ceded Sicily and Lipari islands; in **239 B. C.,** Rome annexed Sardinia and Corsica.

218-146
Hannibal, young Carthaginian, started a campaign against Rome during the Second Punic War. Crossed from Spain to Italy via Mount Genevre in Alps with 20,000 infantry, 6,000 cavalry, and elephants. Defeated Romans at Lake Trasimene, **217 B. C.,** and Cannae, **216 B. C.** Victories nullified by Fabius, "the delayer," hence "Fabian retreat." War closed with defeat of Carthage in Africa by Publius Scipio **202 B. C.** Hannibal, after career in Asia Minor, committed suicide in Bithynia upon betrayal to Romans, c. **183 B. C.**
Third Punic war, 149-146 B. C., ended with total destruction of Carthage. Later Roman colony built there; city eventually destroyed by Saracens, **698 A. D.**

60-27
Julius Caesar formed first triumvirate with Pompey and Crassus **60 B. C.;** defeated Helvetii, Belgae, **58-57 B. C.;** entered Britain **55** and **54 B. C.** Crossed river Rubicon to fight Pompey, defeated him at Pharsalus **48 B. C.** Defeated Pharnaces at Zela, Asia Minor, **47 B. C.,** sent "veni, vidi, vici" message; "I came, I saw, I conquered," to Roman Senate. Lived with Cleopatra, queen of Egypt, in Rome **46-44 B. C.** Was dictator but refused crown.
Caesar assassinated in Roman Senate by group led by Cassius and Brutus, **44 B. C.** Caesar's will made his

grand-nephew, Gaius Octavius, successor; he formed new triumvirate, Octavius ruling West, Mark Antony East and Lepidus Africa. At Philippi, **42 B. C.,** Antony defeated Cassius and Brutus; both committed suicide. Antony joined Cleopatra in Alexandria; they had 3 sons. Octavius defeated their fleet at Actium, **31 B. C.;** they committed suicide. Octavius received title of Augustus (venerated) **27 B. C.,** called first Roman emperor. Pax Romana began. Romans victorious until **9 A. D.,** when Germans under Arminius defeated Varus. Augustus died **14 A. D.**

4
Birth of Jesus Christ in Bethlehem.
1 B. C. and 1 A. D.
The year **1 B. C.** *is the first year before the beginning of the Christian era. The year* **1 A. D.** *is the first year of the Christian era.* **Jan. 1, 1 B. C.** *is just one year before* **Jan. 1, 1 A. D.** *The elapsed number of years between a date B. C. and the same date A. D. is one less than the sum of the years. The Christian era was calculated by the monk Dionysius Exiguus in the 6th century after Christ. He placed Jesus' birth on* **Dec. 25** *in the year* **753** *of Rome, and decided* **754** *should be the first year of the Christian era. Biblical scholars find his calculations in error and place the birth of Jesus at* **4 B. C.** *or earlier.*

A. D.

The Christian Era
29
Crucifixion of Jesus in reign of Roman emperor, Tiberius; Pontius Pilate procurator in Judea. The Roman Catholic church gives the date of the crucifixion as **April 7, 30 A. D.**

43
Roman Emperor Claudius subdued Britons; occupation of 300 years begun.

64
Persecution of Christians by Nero; burning of Rome. Apostles Paul and Peter martyred, c. **67.**

70
Jerusalem destroyed by Titus, Christians persecuted, worship in catacombs of Rome.

79
Pompeii, Herculaneum, Stabii, destroyed by eruption of Mt. Vesuvius.

180
Death of Marcus Aurelius: onset of Roman decline.

311
Emperor Galerius, on deathbed, agreed to tolerance of Christians, Emperor Constantine, **313** promulgated Edict of Milan, made Christianity legal.

325
Council of Nicaea called by Constantine in Bithynia, Asia Minor, to get churchmen to define orthodox Christian belief. Divinity of Christ and Holy Trinity endorsed; minority view of Arius rejected.

330
Constantine dedicated Byzantium capital of Eastern Empire, henceforth called Constantinople, now Istanbul. Baptized a Christian on his deathbed by Eusebius, **337 A. D.**

380
Theodosius, Roman emperor, made Christianity based on Nicene creed official religion, banned pagan gods.

410
Rome sacked by Alaric, the Goth; by Genseric, the Vandal, **455.**

432
Bishop Patrick, native of Severn valley, sent as missionary to Ireland; labored 30 years, converting natives to Christianity. In **563** Columba founded church on Iona. In **597** Augustine arrived, founded church at Canterbury. All three were canonized.

449
Anglo-Saxon migrations from continent to Britain begin at Dover.

483
Justinian I, Byzantine emperor, born; died **565.** During reign had Tribonian prepare Justinian Code (Corpus Juris Civilis) which became basic Roman law used later as a model by many modern European states. Santa Sophia built.

570
Mohammed, born in Mecca; Hegira, flight from Mecca, **622.** Year 1 of Moslem calendar. Saracens crossed to Spain **711,** established Moorish kingdom, lasted until **1492.**

731
Great period of **Mayan empire** began, closed **987.**

732
Charles Martel, Frankish ruler, defeated 90,000 Moors at Tours, France; highwater mark of Moslem invasion of Western Europe.

800
Charlemagne, king of Franks, proclaimed Holy Roman Emperor by Pope Leo III on Christmas Day in St. Peter's. Charlemagne fought Saxons, Lombards, Saracens 30 years to Christianize them; extended empire from Atlantic to eastern boundaries of Hungary. Died **814,** aged 72, was buried in his cathedral at Aix. His empire broke apart.

1000
Leif Ericsson's Norsemen reach Vinland, land of grape vines. Variously identified as Labrador, New England coast and Martha's Vineyard.

1014
Brian Boru, Irish king, defeated Danes at Clontarf.

1027
New empire of Mayas extended north to Mexico. Disintegration accelerated by pestilence, **1480.** Destruction of Tayasal, Guatemala, Itza capital, by Spanish governor of Yucatan, **1697,** ended Mayan millennium.

1054
Final break between Eastern (Orthodox) and Western (Roman) church came when Pope Leo IX excommunicated Michael Cerularius and his followers. Eastern Orthodox Church became established religion of Russia under the Czars. Russian patriarchate formed **1589.**

1066
William of Normandy conquered England at Hastings, **Oct. 14;** Harold II, last Saxon king of England, slain.

1096
First crusade, preached by Peter of Amiens, supported by Pope Urban II, raised 100,000 men. Captured Jerusalem, **1099,** Acre, **1104.** Second, **1146,** lost Jerusalem to Saladin. Third, **1189,** Richard I of England took Jaffa. Fourth, **1200,** besieged Constantinople, **1204.** Fifth, **1216,** achieved 10-year truce. Sixth, **1238,** lost ground. Seventh, **1245,** led by Louis IX (St. Louis) of France, who was captured, **1250.** Eighth, **1270,** led by Louis, who died near Tunis, **1270.** Children's crusade, **1212,** 50,000 children (est.) disbanded in Italy or lost.

1162
Genghis Khan, Mongol chief, born; died **1227.** Captured Peking, **1215,** defeated Russians, **1223,** conquered most of Central Asia, and massacred population of Herat, Afghanistan. By **1241,** Mongols under Batu had burned Moscow and Kiev and invaded Poland, Hungary, and the Danube Valley.

1215
Magna Carta, the great charter of England, signed by King John at Runnymede at insistence of 2,000 English barons who refused to fight on foreign soil and demanded end of illegal levies by king. Charter guaranteed privileges of nobility, church free from secular interference, right of freemen to legal protection. Freemen were privileged class; common people were villein farmers, practically serfs. But 400 years later Edward Coke and Puritans demanded protection for the common people under these rights of freemen. Also invoked Clause 39, out of which trial by jury developed. It reads: *No freeman shall be taken or imprisoned, or dispossessed, or outlawed, or banished, or in any way destroyed, nor will we go upon him, nor send upon him, except by the legal judgment of his peers or by the law of the land.*

1271
Marco Polo started with father and uncle for Cathay (China), Mongol kingdom of Kublai Khan. Served under Khan, returned to Venice **1295.** Wrote Travels.

1274
Thomas Aquinas, greatest scholastic philosopher, died.

1300
Dante and Giotto flourished: Dawn of Renaissance.

1309
Clement V, French Pope, made Avignon seat of church; Urban V returned to Rome, **1367,** abandoned it; Gregory XI finally reentered St. Peter's, **1377.** During the Great Schism, **1378-1417,** French and Italian factions chose popes for Avignon and Rome; breach healed by Martin V, 1417.

1346
Battle of Crecy (Dept. of Somme, France) **Aug. 26,** Edward III of England defeated Philip VI of France. Possibly first use of cannon.

1348
Black Death (bubonic plague) hit Venice, rapidly spreading to rest of Europe by **1349.** An estimated one-fourth of European population killed.

1382
John Wycliffe, Oxford forerunner of Reformation, (1320-1384) directed translation of Vulgate Bible into English vernacular. Supported bill in parliament declaring it sinful for clergy to hold property. By elevating Scriptures above church authority he anticipated Lutheran doctrine by 150 years.

1415
John Huss, Bohemian preacher, follower of Wyclitfe, agitator of ecclesiastic reforms, burned at stake in Constance **July 6** for heresy after German Emperor Sigismund revoked his safe-conduct.

1429
Joan of Arc, maid of Domremy, France, obeying voices of her saints, rallied French against English, raised siege of Orleans, effected coronation of Charles VII at Reims. Through carelessness or treachery she was captured by Burgundians **May 24, 1430,** and sold to English for 10,000 livres. Placed on trial before Bishop of Beauvais at Rouen for (1) magic, (2) disobeying parents, (3) wearing male attire, and (4) heresy, she admitted all after 114 days to escape persecution, was given life im prisonment. Tricked to resume male attire, she was condemned to death and burned at Rouen by English **May 30, 1431.** Sentence revoked 25 years later. Joan has been canonized as saint.

1453
Constantinople captured by Ottoman Turks.
End of 100-years' war between England and France, begun 1338. England lost all except Calais, which French captured 1558.

1456
Johann Gutenberg (Gansfleisch) completed first Bible printed from movable type; 2 vols., folio, 42 lines 2 columns to page. Printing took five years. Date established by note in Mazarin copy.

1457
Johann Fust and Peter Schoeffler produced first book printed in colors, and having printers' name, date and place, a Psalter.

1475
William Caxton printed first book in English, translation of a French history of Troy, at Bruges, Belgium. He moved to Westminster, London, printed first book in England, 1477.

1492
Christopher Columbus, Genoese navigator, after years of agitation in Spain gained support of Queen Isabella for westward voyage. Left Palos **Aug. 3** with Santa Maria, 100 tons, 52 men; Pinta, 50 tons, 18 men; Nina, 40 tons, 18 men. On **Oct. 12** at 2 a.m., Rodrigo de Triana on Pinta discovered land. Columbus landed on Guanahani, Bahamas, called it San Salvador. Discovered Cuba and Hispaniola (Haiti or San Domingo); built first fort, La Navidad, there. Made Admiral of the Ocean Sea. *For later voyages see Index.*

1497
John Cabot, Venetian employed by English, reached Canada. His son Sebastian joined second voyage, **1498.** English claim to Canada based on their discoveries.
Amerigo Vespucci, Italian-born Spanish navigator, asserted he reached American mainland (New World) year before Columbus. Martin Waldseemuller of St. Die in book, **1507,** asked land be called America "because Americus discovered it."

1498
Savonarola, preacher against luxury and power of clergy, burned as heretic in Florence, **May 23.**
Vasco da Gama, Portuguese navigator, reached India, discovered all sea route from W. Europe.

1506
Pope Julius II (della Rovere) started new St. Peter's; employed Michelangelo, Bramante, Raphael.

1509
Henry VIII became king of England. Defeated Scots at Flodden Field, **1513.** Named defender of the Faith by Pope Leo X for attacking Luther, **1521.** When pope refused to annul his marriage to **Catherine of Aragon** for lack of male issue, Henry divorced Catherine, married **Anne Boleyn, 1533.** Act of Supremacy abrogated pope's authority, made him head of church in England, **1534.** He ordered monasteries closed, **1536.**
Queen Anne Boleyn was tried for adultery on order of Henry VIII in **1536** and beheaded. Henry married **Jane Seymour,** who died **1537,** after giving birth to son who became Edward VI. Henry married **Anne of Cleves,** divorced her **1540.**Next **Catherine Howard,** beheaded **1542.** Next, **Catherine Parr, 1543,** who survived him.

1513
Juan Ponce de Leon, veteran of one Columbus voyage, searched for Bimini, found and named Florida. Died in Cuba, **1521.**
Vasco Nunez de Balboa, left Spanish town of Santa Maria la Antigua del Darien on Isthmus of Panama, discovered South Sea, later called Pacific by Magellan.

1517
Martin Luther, Augustinian monk, preaching faith over works, attacked abuse of selling papal indulgences by posting 95 theses (propositions) on Wittenberg church-door, **Oct. 31.** Diet of Worms, under Charles V. **January, 1521,**ordered recantation. Luther, backed by German princes, refused; put Scriptures above papal authority. Defended stand in Rome. Translated Greek New Testament into German, **1522.** Became head of German evangelical movement, broke with Rome, married. Augsburg Confession, basic Lutheran creed, presented to Diet there by Melanchthon, **1530.**

1519
Hernando Cortes began conquest of Mexico.

1520
Fernando Magellan discovered Strait of Magellan, Tierra del Fuego, Ladrones, and Philippines, **1521,** for Spain.

1524
Giovanni da Verrazano, Italian employed by French, explored New England coast, probably New York bay.

1526
William Tyndale produced in Cologne first printed version of New Testament in English, suppressed in England. Tyndale executed for heresy, **Oct. 6, 1536,** at Vilvarde, near Brussels, Belgium.

1529
Turks failed in siege of Vienna; apex of Ottoman European expansion.

1531-35
Francisco Pizarro conquered Peru for Spain.

1534
John Calvin, French-born religious reformer, published his Institutes of the Christian Religion, influential Protestant doctrine. Rejected Lutheran doctrine of consubstantiation; believed in religious base of citizenship, original sin, infant damnation. Influence extended to Scotch Presbyterians, English Puritans and Puritan New England.
Jacques Cartier, sent by Francis I of France, in two voyages **(1534-36)** discovered St. Lawrence, reached site

of Montreal. Third voyage **1541**. Basis of French claims to Canada.

1535

Miles Coverdale published first complete Bible in English. Also worked on first authorized Bible; "The Great Bible," completed **1539**. Other editions: Whittingham's New Testament, with Calvin's introduction. **1557**; Geneva Bible, **1560**; Bishop's Bible, **1568**.

1540

Francisco Coronado, searching for gold and "Seven cities of Cibola," explored Southwest north of Rio Grande with 70 horse and 30 foot soldiers. Hernando de Alarcon discovered Colorado river. Don Garcia Lopez de Cardenas discovered Grand Canyon.

1541

Hernando de Soto discovered Mississippi River.

1545

Council of Trent, in Austrian Tyrol, urged on Pope Paul III by Emperor Charles V, to define Catholic dogma and remedy ecclesiastical abuses, opened **Dec. 13**; continued intermittently until **1563**; reiterated supreme papal authority, outlined faith.

1555

Bishops Ridley and Latimer burned at Oxford, **Oct. 16**; Archbishop Cranmer of Canterbury burned **Mar. 21, 1556**; 277 other religious leaders burned in attempt of Queen Mary Tudor to restore Catholic authority. Elizabeth became queen, **1558**, made Anglican communion official church.

1560

1200 Huguenots hanged at Amboise. Catherine de Medici, Regent of France for son, Charles IX, by Edict of January, **1562**, granted Huguenots right to worship outside walled town. Infraction of edict led to massacre of Huguenots at Vassy, **Mar. 1, 1562**, beginning of eight wars of religion. Massacre of St. Bartholomew, **Aug.24, 1572**, encouraged by Charles IX on marriage of sister, Marguerite de Valois to Henry of Navarre (non-Catholic). Henry III caused assassination of Catholic leaders, Duc de Guise and Cardinal of Lorraine, was himself murdered **Aug. 1, 1589**. Henry IV (of Navarre) first Bourbon king, promulgated Edict of Nantes, **April 13, 1598**, giving Huguenots and Catholics equality before law. Henry converted to Catholicism, assassinated, **May 14, 1610**. Revocation of edict by Louis XIV, **Oct. 23, 1685**, led to large Huguenot emigration to England and America.

1564

William Shakespeare born; traditional date, **Apr. 23**; Baptismal record, **Apr. 26**.

1565

St. Augustine, Florida, founded by Menendez, Spaniard. Attacked by Sir Francis Drake, **1586**.

1566

Duke of Alva persecuted Protestants in Netherlands.

1568

Ivan the Terrible of Russia executed hundreds accused of plot to kill crown prince.

1579

Sir Francis Drake claimed west coast (California) for Queen Elizabeth. Left metal plate, found in Marin county, **1936**.

1582

First Catholic New Testament in English issued at Reims; Old Testament translated at Douai, **1609**.

1587

Mary, Queen of Scots, executed for treason; actually, threat to throne of Queen Elizabeth.

Virginia Dare, first child born of English parents in the New World, on Roanoke Isl., N. C., **Aug. 18**, 7 days after **Sir Walter Raleigh's** second expedition with 117 persons, landed. (First, **1585** returned to England **1586**.) By **1590** all trace of settlement had vanished except for a tree inscribed enigmatically "Croatoan."

1588

Spanish Armada, 132 ships, 33,000 soldiers and crews, sent by Philip II of Spain against England, destroyed by Drake's attacks and storms. **July 21-29.** Only 50 ships returned to Spain. Fading of Spanish power; flourishing of Elizabethan England.

1590

Edmund Spenser began The Faerie Queen. First Shakespeare poem, Venus and Adonis, registered **1593**. First play to appear in quarto, Titus Andronicus, registered **1594**. Romeo and Juliet performed, **1597**.

1600

Shakespeare's most productive decade opened. Included Henry V., Midsummer Night's Dream, Twelfth Night, Merry Wives of Windsor, Hamlet, Othello, Macbeth, King Lear, Tempest, etc. Shakespeare retired to Stratford **1610**; died **Apr. 23, 1616**, the same date that **Cervantes** died. First folio of 36 plays published **1623**; second **1632**; third, **1663**; fourth, **1675**.

1602

Capt. Bartholomew Gosnold, English navigator, landed on Cape Cod, to which he gave the name it still bears.

1605

Gunpowder Plot of Guy Fawkes to blow up King James I and parliament foiled when 36 barrels of gunpowder were found in cellar under Parliament, **Nov. 4.**

1607

Capt. John Smith and 105 cavaliers in 3 ships landed at Virginia and started first permanent English settlement in New World at Jamestown, **May 13**. Virginia was first of the 13 colonies.

1609

Henry Hudson, English explorer of Northwest Passage, employed by Dutch East India Co.; sailed sloop Half Moon into New York harbor, **Sept.,** and up river to Albany. In **1610**, in English ship Discovery, 55 tons, explored Hudson Bay. On return, **1611**, was put into open boat with his son and 8 others by mutinous sailors. All were lost.

Spaniards settled Santa Fe, erected presidio.

1611

King James version (authorized version) of English Bible published; ordered by James I in **1604**, it reconciled earlier versions and became basic Protestant Bible.

1618

Thirty Years' War opened in Bohemia between Catholic and Protestant armies; ended **1648** with Peace of Westphalia, Alsace given to France. Holland and Switzerland received independence.

Sir Walter Raleigh, convicted of conspiring in **1603** to remove James I; beheaded **Oct. 29.**

1619

House of Burgesses, first representative legislature, elected by popular vote at Jamestown, established principle of self-government for royal colony.

First Negro laborers–indentured servants–in English N. American colonies, landed by Dutch at Jamestown, **August.**

1620

Plymouth Pilgrims, Puritan separatists from Church of England, some living in Leyden, Holland, since **1609** left Plymouth, England, **Sept. 16**, in Mayflower, 101 passengers, 48 crew. Original destination Virginia, they reached Cape Cod **Nov. 9-19**, explored coast, landed **Dec. 21** (Dec. 11, Old Style) at Plymouth, so named for Plymouth Co. on map made **1614** by Capt. John Smith. Mayflower Compact, signed on shipboard, was agreement to form a local government and abide by its laws. Started first common house, **Dec. 25**. Half of colony perished during hard winter.

Gov. Bradford's comment, "They knew they were pilgrims" (on religious journey), later led them to be called Pilgrims, as distinct from Puritans of Massachusetts Bay Colony (**1630**).

1624

Dutch landed eight men from ship, New Netherland, on Manhattan, **May.** Proceeded to Albany.

1626

Peter Minuit bought Manhattan from Indians **May 6** for trinkets worth $24.

1636

Harvard College founded **Oct. 28.**

1637

Colonials destroyed Pequot fort at Mystic, Conn., killed 600 Indians, **June 5.**

1638

Peter Minuit landed two shiploads of Swedes and

Finns at site of Wilmington, Del.

1642

Great Rebellion of the Puritan Parliament against the civil and religious policies of Charles I of England begins, **July,** after Charles rejects Parliament's demands for control of militia and church affairs and for right to appoint and dismiss the King's ministers.

Oliver Cromwell led army of Roundheads for parliament, defeated Charles' Cavaliers at Marston Moor, 1644, and Naseby, 1645. Charles was delivered to parliament by the Scots, **1648.**

Galileo died, **Newton** was born, 100 years after **Copernicus** published heliocentric theory. Galileo defended theory: "Holy Spirit intended to teach us in the Bible how to go to Heaven, not how the heavens go." But in **1616** the Inquisition at Rome declared the assertion of earth's motion to be heretical and placed works of Copernicus, **Kepler** and Galileo on the Index until **1822.**

1648

Taj Mahal outside Agra, India, completed by Mogul Emperor Shah Jahan for his wife. 20,000 workers used in construction.

1649

Charles I condemned by House of Commons, sitting as High Court; beheaded **Jan. 30.**

Commonwealth ruled by Commons and Council of State (John Milton, Latin secretary) with Cromwell at head. Cromwell annihilated Scots at Worcester, **1651.** Cromwell made protector for life, actually dictator, **1653.** Admiral Blake took Jamaica from Spain, **1655.**

Cromwell died **1658.** His son, Richard, resigned rule. Puritan government collapsed and parliament called Charles II.

1656

Anne Hibbins hanged as witch in Salem, Mass.

1660

John Bunyan, a tinker, imprisoned at Bedford, England, **Nov.,** for unlawful preaching, released **1672,** after writing part of Pilgrim's Progress.

Restoration under Charles II, "Merry Monarch." Charles' Cavalier parliament restored Anglican church and refused freedom of worship to dissenters, promised by King in Declaration of Breda.

1664

King Charles II ordered Col. Nicolls and 300 men to seize New Netherland (Manhattan and environs) from Dutch, granted territory to his brother James, Duke of York. Petrus Stuyvesant, Dutch Director General, yielded peacefully; province of New Netherland and city of New Amsterdam became New York. The Dutch recaptured both Aug. 9, 1673; ceded all by treaty to Britain Nov. 10, 1674.

1665

Great Plague in London killed 68,000. In **1666** great fire destroyed 13,200 houses. 89 churches.

1676

Nathaniel Bacon led planters, oppressed by taxes, against Gov. Berkeley at Jamestown; burned town, Bacon died suddenly; 23 followers executed.

Bloody Indian war in New England ended **Aug. 12.** King Philip, Wampanog chief, and many Narragansett Indians killed.

1682

Robert Cavelier, Sieur de la Salle, took lower Mississippi river country for Louis XIV, called it Louisiana, **Apr. 9.** Had built French outposts in Illinois. Established fort at Lavaca, Texas, **1684,** with 400 men. Was killed by his own men on Trinity river, Texas **Mar. 19, 1687.**

1683

William Penn signed treaty with Indians.

1689

King William's War, British in America vs. French and Indians. Ended **1697.**

1692

Witchcraft delusion at Salem, Mass., inspired by preaching; 19 persons hanged, 1 man crushed to death. Executions in Europe of women for witchcraft between **1484** and **1782** believed to have reached 300,000. Last in England **1716;** in Scotland, **1722.**

1696

Capt. William Kidd, American, hired by British king and nobles to fight pirates and take booty, became pirate. Returned to New York with treasure, **1698,** buried it on Gardiner's Island. Arrested by Earl of Bellamont, governor of province, and sent to England for trial, he was hanged, **1701,** for killing sailor. Treasure of gold and gems given Bellamont by Lord of Gardiner's Island.

1704

Indians attacked Deerfield, Mass., **Feb. 28-29,** killed 40, carried off 100.

Gibraltar taken by Britain from Spain, **July 24;** formally ceded by Treaty of Utrecht, **1713.**

Boston News Letter, first regular newspaper, started by John Campbell, postmaster. (Publick Occurences, **1690,** was suppressed after one issue.)

1709

British-Colonial troops captured French fort, Port Royal, Nova Scotia, in Queen Anne's War **(1701-1713).** France yielded Nova Scotia by treaty, **1713.**

1712

Slaves revolted in New York **April 6.** Six committed suicide, 21 were executed. Second rising, **1741;** 13 slaves hanged, 13 burned, 71 transported.

1720

"Mississippi Bubble." John Law, Scot, comptroller of finance in France, issued paper currency without security to back trading scheme. Shares reached $4,000 before collapse. Many ruined; France assumed debt of $340,000,000.

1728

Pennsylvania Gazette, founded by Samuel Keimer, Philadelphia, Benj. Franklin bought interest, **1729.**

1735

Freedom of the press recognized in New York by acquittal of **John Peter Zenger,** editor Weekly Journal, on charge of libelling British governor, Cosby, by criticizing conduct in office.

1740-1741

Capt. Vitus Bering, Dane employed by Russians, discovered Alaska.

1743

King George's War. British and American colonials vs. French. Siege of Louisbourg, Cape Breton Isl. led by Gov. Wm. Shirley of Mass. Surrendered to British **June 17, 1745.** Returned to France by Treaty of Aix la Chapelle **1748.**

1746

English defeated Scots at Culloden, **April 16,** routing Stuart pretender, Prince Charles.

1751

Publication of the Encyclopédie began in France, great popularizer of the Enlightenment.

1752

Benjamin Franklin, flying kite in thunderstorm, proved lightning is electricity **June 15.**

Gregorian calendar adopted by Great Britain and American colonies, dropping 11 days after Sept. 2; next day Sept. 14.

1754

French and Indian War started after French occupied uncompleted British post, called it Ft. Duquesne (site of Pittsburgh). Col. Geo. Washington with Virginia troops clashed with French at Great Meadows, dug in at Ft. Necessity; capitulated and withdrew July 3, 1754. Boston's 3,000 provincial troops took Nova Scotia French forts **June 16, 1755.** French and Indians ambushed Gen. Wm. Braddock's expedition 10 mi. from Ft. Duquesne (now Braddock, Pa.) **July 9;** Washington helped retreat; Braddock fatally wounded, 714 killed; Gen. Sir Wm. Johnson defeated French and Indians under Baron Dieskau at Lake George Sept.8. British moved Acadian French out of Canada, **Nov.** Britain formally declared war **May 18,1756.** Surrendered Ft. Wm. Henry (Lake George) to Montcalm; Indians massacred many unarmed British, **Aug. 9,1757.** Montcalm at Ft. Ticonderoga repulsed 17,000 British **July 8.** French gave up Louisburg, Ft. Frontenac, Ft. Duquesne, **1758;** Niagara, Ticonderoga, Crown Point, **1759.** British captured Quebec, **Sept. 18, 1759,** in battles in which Montcalm and

Gen. Jas. Wolfe (Br.) died. Peace signed **Feb. 10, 1763** (hence "Seven Years War"). French lost Canada and American Midwest.
1755
Great earthquake, **Nov. 1.** In Lisbon, Portugal, 60,000 died; 12,000 in Fez, Morocco; half of Madeira levelled; 2,000 houses lost in Mitylene; Oporto, Braga, Malaga damaged.
Samuel Johnson issued English Dictionary.
1756
Black Hole of Calcutta. Nawab of Bengal, attacking British East India Co., threw 146 British prisoners into room less than 20 ft. square, **June 20;** only 23 survived overnight. Lord Robert Clive with 3,000 British troops defeated the Nawab's force of 50,000, June, 1757.
1769
Napoleon Bonaparte born **Aug. 15,** Ajaccio, Corsica; died at Longwood, St. Helena, **May 5,** 1821.
1772
First Partition of Poland by Austria, Prussia, and Russia. Second and third partitions of **1793** and **1795** erased Poland from map of Europe, not to re-emerge until after World War I.
1781
Bank of North America incorporated in Philadelphia, **May 26.** First chartered bank, Bank of Pennsylvania **(Mar. 1, 1780)** operated 1782-1784.
1783
Massachusetts Supreme Court outlawed slavery because of the words in the State Bill of Rights, "all men are born free and equal."

First balloon sent up **June 5** by Joseph and Jacques Montgolfier. J. A. C. Charles and the Robert brothers sent up first hydrogen-filled balloon **Aug. 27.** J. F. Pilatre de Rozier made first human ascent in captive balloon, **Oct. 15.** De Rozier and Marquis d'Arlandes made first voyage in free Montgolfier hot air balloon, Paris, **Nov. 21.**
1784
Peter Carnes, Baltimore, using de Rozier model, sent up captive balloon with 13-year-old Edward Warren in it, **June 23.**
First successful daily newspaper, Pennsylvania Packet & General Advertiser, formed from tri-weekly, **Sept. 21.**
1785
First steamboat experiment by John Fitch. New Jersey granted him rights to rivers, **1786.** Fitch demonstrated steamboat with 12 mechanical oars on Delaware river, 3 miles an hour, **Aug. 22, 1787.** Pennsylvania, Delaware, Virginia, New York gave him river rights, **1787.** He operated steamboat between Trenton and Philadelphia, **1790.** Allegedly ran boat on Collect Pond, now Foley Sq., New York, **1796.** Died **1798.**
1786
Delegates from 5 states at Annapolis asked Congress to call convention in Philadelphia to write practical constitution for the 13 states.
1787
Shays' rebellion in Massachusetts, led by Capt. Daniel Shays; the attempt to seize U. S. Arsenal in Springfield

American Revolution and War of Independence;

Great Britain, after acquiring Canada from France in 1763, tightened up colonial administration in North America. The Thirteen Colonies, used to self-government, resented duties on commerce and objected to paying for troops now quartered on them. **The Sugar Act, 1764,** placed duties on lumber, foodstuffs, molasses and rum. **The Stamp Act, 1765,** required revenue stamps to help defray cost of royal troops. The colonists formed Sons of Liberty groups and rejected British goods. Nine colonies, led by New York and Massachusetts at **Stamp Act Congress** in New York Oct. 7-25, 1765, adopted Declaration of Rights, opposing taxation without representation in parliament and trial without jury by admiralty courts. In the Virginia House of Burgesses Patrick Henry warned King George III of consequences, with "If this be treason make the most of it." Parliament repealed Stamp Act Mar. 17, 1766.
Townshend Acts, 1767, levied taxes on glass, painter's lead, paper and tea imports. In 1770 all duties except tax on tea were repealed, but principle of right to tax was maintained. British troops fired into a mob Mar. 5, 1770, killed 5 including Crispus Attucks, a Negro, reportedly leader of the group; it was called the Boston Massacre. Tea ships of East India Co., turned back at Boston, New York, Philadelphia, May 1773. Cargo ship burned at Annapolis, Oct. 14. Cargo thrown overboard at **Boston Tea Party,** Dec. 16. Parliament ordered port closed until tea was paid for, sent 4 regiments to Boston, suppressed town meetings and elective representation in Massachusetts.
Samuel Adams, Boston, began uniting patriot leaders by Committees of Correspondence. Virginia called for first **Continental Congress,** Philadelphia, Sept. 5-Oct. 26, 1774. On Mar. 23, 1775, **Patrick Henry** addressed revolutionary convention, Richmond, Va., with famous speech: "Give me liberty or give me death!"

BATTLES OF 1775

Paul Revere and Wm. Dawes, on night of Apr. 18 on horseback alerted Sam Adams and John Hancock at Lexington and others that 700 British were on way to **Concord** to destroy arms. At **Lexington,** Apr. 19. Minutemen lost 8 killed, 10 wounded. On return from Concord the harassed British lost 273.
Col. Ethan Allen (joined by Col. Benedict Arnold) captured **Ft. Ticonderoga,** May 10; also Crown Point. Colonials headed for Bunker Hill, fortified Breed's Hill,

Charlestown, repulsed British under Gen. Wm. Howe twice before retreating June 17; British casualties 1,000; called **Battle of Bunker Hill.** Continental Congress June 15 named Geo. Washington commander-in-chief; he took command in Cambridge July 3. Maj. Gen. Richard Montgomery led troops against Canada via New York, Col. Arnold marched via Maine wilderness; captured **Montreal** Nov. 13, attacked **Quebec** Dec. 30-31; Montgomery killed. Colonials returned to New York state June, 1776.
Mecklenburg Declaration of Independence adopted at Charlotte, Mecklenburg County, N. C., May 20 (a disputed tradition).

DECLARATION OF INDEPENDENCE

Virginia voted for independence May 15. In Continental Congress June 7, 1776, Richard Henry Lee (Va.) moved "that these united colonies are and of right ought to be free and independent states." Resolutions adopted July 2. **Declaration of Independence** July 4. *See article.*
Col. Moultrie's batteries at Charleston, S. C. repulsed British sea attack June 28. Washington, with 10,000 lost **Battle of Long Island** to Howe and Gen. Sir Henry Clinton with 15,000 Aug. 27, evacuated New York.
Nathan Hale, executed as spy by British Sept. 22, said: "I only regret that I have but one life to lose for my country."
Washington repulsed Howe at **Harlem Heights** Sept. 16, retreated to White Plains, N. Y. Brig. Gen. Arnold's Lake Champlain fleet was defeated at Valcour Oct. 11, but British returned to Canada. Howe failed to destroy Washington's army at **White Plains** Oct. 28. Hessians captured Ft. Washington, Manhattan, and 3,000 men Nov. 16; Ft. Lee, N.J., Nov. 18.
Washington crossed Delaware River from Pennsylvania Dec. 25-26, defeated 1,400 Hessians at **Trenton N.J.,** Dec. 26.

BRANDYWINE AND SARATOGA, 1777

Washington defeated Lord Cornwallis at Princeton Jan. 3. Continental Congress adopted Stars and Stripes June 14. *See article on Flag.* Maj. Gen. John Burgoyne with 8,000 from Canada captured Ft. Ticonderoga July 6. Brig. Gen. Nicholas Herkimer, to raise St. Leger's siege of Ft. Stanwix, routed Indians at **Oriskany, N. Y.** Aug. 6. Burgoyne's Hessians defeated by Brig. Gen. John Stark and the Green Mountain Boys at Bennington, Vt., Aug. 16. Arnold raised siege of Ft. Stanwix.

failed **Jan. 25.**

Northwest Ordinance, adopted **July 13** by Continental Congress, made effective Ordinance of 1784, drafted by Jefferson. Determined government of **Northwest Territory,** north of Ohio river, west of New York: 5,000 male voters could establish legislature: 60,000 inhabitants could get statehood. Guaranteed freedom of religion, support for schools, no slavery.

James Rumsey, encouraged by Washington, ran steamboat with power pump on Potomac **Dec. 3** and **11.** Patented **1791.** He died **1792.**

Constitutional convention opened at Philadelphia **May 14,** George Washington presiding; Constitution adopted by delegates **Sept. 17;** Ratification by 9th state, New Hampshire, **June 21, 1788,** meant adoption. *See Constitution of U. S.*

1788

Warren Hastings, Gov. Gen. of India, tried for treason in London; acquitted 1795.

First British settlement in Australia, a penal colony at Port Jackson, now Sydney.

1789

George Washington chosen President by all electors voting (73 eligible, 69 voting, 4 absent): John Adams Vice President; 34 votes, **Feb.;** First U. S. Congress called **Mar. 4,** Federal Hall, New York; regular sessions began **Apr. 6.** Washington inaugurated there **Apr. 30.** Supreme Court created by Federal Judiciary Act, **Sept. 24.**

The French Revolution began **June 20,** when the delegates to the Third Estate (Commons) met on the tennis court and took an oath not to disband until the King had granted France a constitution; Bastille stormed **July 14,** and prisoners of state released. France was declared a limited monarchy, under Louis XVI; Mirabeau died **April 2, 1791;** the King and family arrested **June 21, 1791;** Revolutionary Tribunal set up on **Aug. 19, 1792.** National Convention opened **Sept. 17, 1792,** and a republic was established on **Sept. 22.** King Louis was beheaded **Jan. 21, 1793;** the Reign of Terror began **May 31, 1793;** Charlotte Corday stabbed Marat **July 13, 1793;** the Queen was beheaded **Oct. 16, 1793.** Danton on **April 5, 1794,** Robespierre on **July 28, 1794.** Revolutionary Tribunal abolished **Dec. 15, 1794;** Louis XVII died in prison, **June 8, 1795,** peace was made with Prussia, the great revolution ended. Napoleon was declared First Consul **Dec. 24, 1799,** and was made Consul for life **Aug., 1802.**

Mutiny on the British ship Bounty, April 28; Capt. William Bligh and 18 sailors set adrift in a launch. They rowed 3,618 miles to Timor, near Java. The Bounty, in command of Fletcher Christian, rebel mate, sailed to Tahiti, where some of crew and 18 Polynesians of whom 12 were women, went to Pitcairn Island, arriving there **1790.** They burned the vessel after landing the food and tools.

1791

Continued attacks on settlements north of Ohio River by Indians armed by British, led Washington to send Gen. Arthur St. Clair and Gen. Wilkinson to area with

Origins, Battles, Results, 1763-1783

Howe defeated Washington at Chad's Ford on the **Brandywine** (Pa.) Sept. 11 and occupied Philadelphia. Congress moved to Lancaster, Pa. Inconclusive battle of **Germantown,** Pa., Oct. 4. Washington's army wintered at **Valley Forge.**

Americans massed at Bemis Heights on Hudson under Maj. Gen. Horatio Gates, attacked by Burgoyne Sept. 19. At Freeman's Farm, Gen. Arnold and Col. Daniel Morgan's riflemen repulsed British, inflicting great loss. Gen. Clinton took Fts. Clinton and Montgomery below West Point Oct. 6, but did not support Burgoyne. Americans beat back Burgoyne at Bemis Heights Oct. 7 and cut off British escape route. Burgoyne surrendered 5,000 at **Saratoga** Oct. 17.

Marquis de la Fayette (Lafayette), aged 20, made major general.

Articles of Confederation and Perpetual Union adopted by Continental Congress **Nov. 15.**

HELP FROM FRANCE

France recognized independence of 13 Colonies, signed treaty of aid with Benj. Franklin, Silas Deane, Arthur Lee, Feb. 6, 1778. Sent fleet under Adm. d'Estaing. British evacuated Philadelphia in consequence, June 18. Washington harassed British at Monmouth Court House, N.J., June 28. Wyoming Massacre **July 3** in Pa. by British and Indian force. British overran Georgia, December.

George Rogers Clark, who took Cahokia and Kaskaskia, (Ill.) 1778, took **Vincennes** Feb., 1779. Maj. Gen. Anthony Wayne, July 15, stormed **Stony Point,** on Hudson, but withdrew after victory.

John Paul Jones in Bonhomme Richard defeated Serapis on the Atlantic Sept. 23, 1779. French fleet and Maj. Gen. Benj. Lincoln's men were repulsed at Savannah Oct. 9.

BENEDICT ARNOLD'S TREASON

Three Continental soldiers, Paulding, Williams and Van Wart, captured Major John Andre, adjutant general of the British army, in disguise at Tarrytown, N. Y., Sept. 23, 1780, finding papers betraying West Point, signed by Gen. Arnold, in his socks. He had lost way after rendezvous with Arnold at Haverstraw, N. Y. Arnold, informed of Andre's capture, escaped from headquarters in Highlands, near present Garrison, N. Y., by barge to British sloop Vulture off Verplanck's Point.

Andre was found guilty by board of American officers at Tappan, N. Y., hanged as spy Oct. 2. Washington refused to intercede. Arnold made brigadier general in British army. Burned New London, Conn., 1781. His wife, Peggy Shippen of Philadelphia adjudged innocent by Washington, since proved implicated. Arnold died in London. Andre's body removed to Westminster Abbey, 1821.

ROAD TO YORKTOWN

Charleston fell to the British May 12, 1780, but a segment of Lord Cornwallis' forces led by Maj. Patrick Ferguson was defeated near **Kings Mountain, N. C.** Oct. 7 by militiamen commanded by Cols. John Sevier, Isaac Shelby, Wm. Campbell and Benj. Cleveland. Operations in South under Cornwallis and Col. B. Tarleton in 1781 were checked by Maj. Gen. Nathanael Greene and Brig. Gen. Daniel Morgan, **Cowpens,** S. C., Jan. 17, was a victory, but **Guilford Court House, N.C.,** Mar. 15 was a British gain. Greene's harassments caused Cornwallis to retire to Wilmington, N. C., and thence to **Yorktown, Va.** While Lafayette waited near Yorktown, Adm. De Grasse landed 3,000 French and stopped Adm. Thos. Graves' British fleet in Hampton Roads. Adm. Barras joined De Grasse. Washington and Rochambeau joined forces and leaving 2,000 to mislead Sir Henry Clinton in New York, marched to Annapolis and took boats to James River near Williamsburg, arriving Sept. 26. When siege of Cornwallis began Oct. 6, British had 6,000, Americans 8,846, French 7,800. Clinton decided too late to relieve Cornwallis. Graves sailed from New York with 7,000 Oct. 17, too late to reach Cornwallis, who surrendered Oct. 19, 1781.

INDEPENDENCE, 1782

A new British cabinet agreed to recognize independence, March, 1782. Preliminary agreement signed in Paris Nov. 30; treaty Sept. 3, 1783. (Congress ratified it Jan. 14, 1784.) Washington ordered army disbanded Nov. 3, 1783. British evacuated New York Nov. 25. Washington bade farewell to his officers at Fraunce's Tavern, New York, Dec. 4; resigned Dec. 23, retired to Mount Vernon, Va. *For casualties see index.*

1,400. St. Clair was surprised near Wabash River in Ohio **Nov. 4,** lost 630 killed.

1792-94
Gen. Anthony Wayne made commander, took 2 years to train American Legion. Established Ft. Washington (Cincinnati), Ft. Recovery, O., **1793;** Ft. Greeneville, Ft. Deposit, Ft. Defiance, **1794.** Routed Indians (Ottawas, Shawnees, Miamis, Iroquois) with bayonet at Fallen Timbers on Maumee River **Aug. 20, 1794,** checkmated British at Ft. Miamis.

Whiskey Rebellion, west Pennsylvania protesting whiskey tax, suppressed by U. S. **Sept. 1794.**

1795
Gen. Wayne built Ft. Wayne; signed peace with Indians at Fort Greeneville.

Triple Alliance formed by Great Britain, Russia, and Austria, **Sept.28.**

U. S. bought peace from Algiers and Tunis by paying $800,000, supplying a frigate and annual tribute of $25,000, **Nov. 28.**

1796
Washington's Farewell Address as President deliv- ered **Sept. 19.** Gave strong warnings against permanent alliance with foreign powers, partiality toward favorite nation, big public debt, large military establishment and devices of "small artful, enterprising minority" to control or change government; praised reciprocal checks of Constitution; stressed need for enlightened public opinion; declared "religion and morality lead to political prosperity."

Vaccination discovered by Edward Jenner **May 14,** announced **1798.**

1797
U. S. frigate United States launched at Philadelphia, **July 10; Constellation** at Baltimore, Sept. 7; Constitution (Old Ironsides) at Boston, Sept. 20.

France ordered capture of all neutral ships carrying British cargoes.

1798
War with France threatened over French raids on U. S. shipping and rejection of U. S. diplomats. Congress voided all treaties with France, ordered Navy to capture French armed ships. Navy (45 ships) and 365 privateers

---

War of 1812 between United States and Great Britain

The War of 1812 coming only 30 years after the end of the Revolution, had 3 major causes: (1) Britain, blockading France, seized American ships trading with France; (2) Britain, refusing to recognize naturalized American sailors, seized 4,000 by 1810 and impressed two-thirds into British service; (3) British armed Indians who raided western border. H.M.S. Leopard attacked U. S. Chesapeake, 1807, killed 3 Americans, seized 4. Under President Jefferson U. S., 1807 and 1809, stopped trade with Europe, which ruined American shippers. Under President Madison, 1810, trade with Britain only was stopped.

War might have been averted. The British raised the blockade for American ships June 16, 1812, but the news did not reach U. S. by June 18, when Congress by a small majority voted a declaration of war. Congress voted to raise Army from 11,744 to 44,500 and to use militia. The Navy had 20 major ships of 500 guns. The West favored war; New England opposed it. The British were handicapped by war with France.

War on Land

This was full of blunders caused by inefficient leaders and refusal of regulars to work with militia. U. S. lost Ft. Michilimackinac (Mich.) and Ft. Dearborn (Ill.). Brig. Gen. Wm. Hull surrendered Detroit Aug. 16, 1812, to Maj. Gen. Isaac Brock. Maj. Gen. Stephen Van Rensselaer with 2,300 took Queenston Heights, Canada, Oct. 13, but retired when regulars did not support. Brig. Gen. Wm. H. Harrison had 1,000 casualties near Ft. Malden. Brig. Gen. Zebulon M. Pike (disc. Pike's Peak) took York, (Toronto), Apr. 27, 1813, killed in explosion. Brig. Gen. Jacob Brown May 27 repulsed Sir Geo. Prevost, Canadian Governor General. Gen. Henry Dearborn May 27 took Ft. George and Queenston Heights aided by amphibious assault led by Col. Winfield Scott and Master Commandant Oliver Hazard Perry (later Commodore). British defeated 2,000 Americans a few days later.

Battle of the Thames, Ontario, Can., Oct. 5, 1813. Harrison with 3,500 took Ft. Malden, pursued British 85 mi. Cavalry charge by Kentucky riflemen routed British and Indians, killing Shawnee chief, Tecumseh. Detroit frontier was safe for U. S. In the fall both Brig. Gen. Wade Hampton with 4,000 and Maj. Gen. Jas. Wilkinson, with 6,000 mismanaged attempts to invade Canada; Wilkinson was defeated at Ogdensburg. British recaptured Fts. George and Niagara, burned Buffalo; Americans burned Newark and Queenston.

Battle of Lundy's Lane. Brig. Gen. Winfield Scott (promoted) led fighting of Brown's army at Lundy's Lane, on road to Burlington, July 25, 1814; result a draw with heavy losses, Scott was wounded.

Burning of Washington. In August British landed 4,000 under Adm. Sir Geo. Cockburn and Maj. Gen. Robt. Ross. At Bladensburg Aug. 24, 1814, Ross routed 5,000 hastily assembled U.S. troops, then burned Capitol and White House, Maryland militia stopped British Sept. 12 from reaching Baltimore; Ross was killed.

Battle of New Orleans. Maj. Gen. Andrew Jackson, who had defeated the Creek Indians at Horseshoe Bend on the Tallapoosa Mar. 27, 1814, and captured British base at Pensacola, Fla., Nov., on Dec. 23 engaged 2,000 British east of New Orleans, then retired to earthworks built with cotton bales. On Jan. 8, 1815, 5,300 British under Maj. Gen. Sir Edward Pakenham attacked American entrenchments at Chalmette. Jackson had 3,500, a reserve of 1,000, 20 guns and an armed schooner. British had over 2,000 casualties. Pakenham was killed; Americans lost 71. British routed an American battery on the West bank, but withdrew and left by sea Jan. 18. On Feb. 8 they took Mobile. Word came Feb. 14 that a treaty of peace had been signed at Ghent Dec. 24, 1814. U.S. ratified it Feb. 17, 1815.

War at Sea

Brilliant American gunnery brought naval victories. US Essex captured Alert Aug. 13, 1812. US Constitution, 44 guns, Capt. Isaac Hull, destroyed Guerriere Aug. 19; thereafter nicknamed Old Ironsides. US Wasp took Frolic Oct. 18. US United States, Capt. Stephen Decatur, defeated Macedonian off Azores Oct. 25. Constitution took Java Dec. 29, 1812. US Chesapeake captured by Shannon June 1, 1813; Capt. Jas. Lawrence, dying, called out: "Don't give up the ship!" US Enterprise took Boxer Sept. 5.

Battle of Lake Erie. Commodore O. H. Perry, using Lawrence's words as slogan defeated British fleet near Put-in-Bay Sept. 10, 1813. Perry, transferred from disabled flagship Lawrence to Niagara during battle, sent message to Harrison: "We have met the enemy and they are ours: 2 ships, 2 brigs, 1 schooner, 1 sloop."

Essex, Capt. David Porter, first US warship to sail around South America, was defeated off Valparaiso, Chile, Mar. 28, 1814.

Bombardment of Ft. McHenry, Baltimore, for 25 hours, Sept. 13-14, 1814, by British fleet failed. Francis Scott Key, on board ship, wrote words for Star Spangled Banner. See article.

Battle of Lake Champlain. Commodore Thos. Macdonough defeated fleet of Sir Geo. Prevost near Plattsburg, Sept. 11, 1814, while Brig. Gen. Thos. Macomb held 4,500 ready to oppose 11,000. British withdrew to Canada.

U. S. frigate President was captured Jan., 1815. Constitution captured Cyane and Levant, Feb. 20, 1815. Hornet captured Penguin, Mar. 23.

The War of 1812 was costly, but inspired national unity, gave recognition to men of the western border, made Andrew Jackson political power.

captured 84 French. U. S. Constellation took Fr. warship Insurgente, 1799. Napoleon, becoming First Consul, stopped French raids.

1801
Tripoli declared war, June 10, against U. S., which refused added tribute to commerce-raiding corsairs. U.S. frigate Philadelphia captured in Tripoli harbor **Oct., 1803,** burned by Stephen Decatur **Feb. 16, 1804.** Expedition under William Eaton forced Tripoli to conclude peace **June 4, 1805.**

1803
Robert Emmet convicted of treason by British in Ireland; executed in Dublin, **Sept. 19.**

Louisiana Purchase. President Jefferson sent James Monroe to Paris to join Robert R. Livingston, American minister, in offering up to $10,000,000 for the isle of Orleans (New Orleans) and West Florida. Napoleon, who had recovered Louisiana from Spain by secret treaty, offered all of Louisiana for $11,250,000 in bonds, plus $3,750,000 indemnities to American citizens with claims against France. U. S. took title **Dec. 20.**

Robert Fulton operated experimental steamboat unsuccessfully on Seine, Paris, France.

1804
Lewis and Clark Expedition ordered by Pres. Jefferson to explore what is now northwest U. S. Started from St. Louis **May 14;** ended **Sept. 23, 1806.** An Indian woman named Sacagawea served as guide and interpreter.

Alexander Hamilton (ex-Secretary of the Treasury) and Vice President Aaron Burr, after years of bitter political rivalry, fought a duel, **July 11,** on the Hudson Palisades, Weehawken, N.J. Hamilton was mortally wounded, died **July 12.**

Code Napoleon systematized French law under the auspices of Napoleon Bonaparte. It became a model for many countries.

John Stevens, Hoboken, operated experimental steamboat with twin-screw propellers, 9 mi.

1805
Napoleon, emperor since **May 18, 1804,** defeated Austrians at Ulm, **Oct. 17;** Russo-Austrians at Austerlitz ("masterpiece of battles") **Dec. 2.** Dissolved Holy Roman Empire. Made brothers Joseph, king of Naples, Louis, king of Holland.

Lord Nelson defeated French-Spanish fleet at Cape Trafalgar, **Oct. 21;** lost his own life.

1806
Napoleon defeated Prussians at Jena, **Oct. 14.** In 1807 he defeated Russians at Eylau; signed peace of Tilsit with Czar Alexander I. Made brother Jerome king of Westphalia: allotted Finland to Russia.

1807
Robert Fulton made first practical steamboat trip on Clermont (open boat, 140 by 13 ft., 7 ft. draft, side paddle wheels). Left New York **Aug. 17,** reached Albany, 150 mi., in 32 hrs.

Aaron Burr was tried for treason in Richmond, Va., **May 22.** Charged with "assembling an armed force...to seize the city of New Orleans...and to separate the western from the Atlantic states," he was acquitted **Sept. 1.** Chief Justice John Marshall sitting as U.S. Circuit Court judge ruled that treason must be attested by two witnesses. After trial Burr went to Europe to avoid prosecution on Hamilton murder charge.

1808-09
French occupied Madrid, March; Rome, April; Napoleon made brother Joseph king of Spain. French defeated in Spain and Portugal; Peninsular war begun by British. Napoleon defeated Austrians at Wagram, **July 6, 1809.** Annexed Papal States.

Phoenix, world's first ocean-going steamboat, built by John Stevens, left New York for Philadelphia, **June 8, 1809.**

1810
Napoleon annulled marriage with the Empress Josephine, who retired to Malmaison. Married Austrian Archduchess Marie Louise, March. Son Born **Mar. 20, 1811,** called King of Rome. As Duke of Reichstadt, he died in Vienna **July 22, 1832.** Called L'Aiglon (the Eaglet) by French, he inspired Edmond Rostand's drama.

1811
William Henry Harrison, gov. of Indiana territory, defeated Indians under the Prophet, brother of Tecumseh in battle of Tippecanoe, **Nov. 7.**

1812
Napoleon invaded Russia with conscript army of 500,000; defeated Russians at Borodino, **Sept. 7;** took Moscow, **Sept. 14.** A large portion of Moscow subsequently burned down, and Napoleon ordered retreat **Oct. 19,** meeting huge losses from cold and guerrillas.

1813
Napoleon with 180,000 French decisively defeated at Leipzig by 200,000 allied Prussians, Austrians, Russians, under Austrian Gen. Schwartzenberg in Battle of the Nations, **Oct. 16-19.**

1814
Allies entered Paris, **March 21;** Napoleon abdicated, **April 11;** Louis XVIII restored to throne, **May 3;** Congress of Vienna opened, **Nov. 3.** Napoleon exiled to Elba.

1815
Napoleon re-entered France Mar. 1, assumed command, ruled 100 days, **Mar. 20-June 22.** Defeated at Waterloo, Belgium, **June 18,** by Duke of Wellington (British), Count von Blucher (Prussian) and allies. Deported to St. Helena Isl., died there **May 5, 1821.**

Holy Alliance, formed by Russia, Austria and Prussia; signed in Paris, **Sept. 26;** promulgated in Frankfort, **Feb. 2, 1816,** and acceded to 1818 by the rulers of Great Britain and France.

1817
Rush-Bagot treaty signed, April 28-29, limiting naval armaments of the United States and Canada on the Great Lakes.

1820
Henry Clay's Missouri Compromise bill passed by Congress, **March 3.** Slavery was allowed in Missouri, but not elsewhere west of the Mississippi river north of 36° 30′ Latitude (the southern line of Missouri). Repealed 1854.

1822
Revolution in Portugal. Separation of Brazil which proclaimed independence **Sept. 7;** Dom Pedro was crowned emperor **Dec. 1;** he abdicated **1831;** succeeded by his son; a republic proclaimed **1888.**

Mexico separates from Spain, makes Iturbide emperor, **May;** forms republic, **Oct., 1823.**

1823
Monroe Doctrine declared, **Dec. 2.**

Mississippi River first ascended by steamboat, the Virginia, as far as Fort Snelling, Minn., **April 21-May 10,** 729 miles.

Gas vacuum (internal combustion) engine operated successfully by Samuel Brown, London.

1824
Marquis de Lafayette, 67, visited each of the 24 states as guest of U.S.

Simon Bolivar, ruler of Venezuela, Colombia, Ecuador, Peru; broke Spanish power in South America (Died **1830**).

1825
Great Britain repeals laws against trade unions.

First railroad to use steam locomotive (on level grade only) Stockton & Darlington Ry., opened in Eng., **Sept. 27,** with Stephenson's engine "Locomotion." First public railroad to use steam exclusively for passenger and freight traffic, Liverpool & Manchester, opened **Sept. 15, 1830.**

Erie Canal opened, first boat left Buffalo, **Oct. 26,** and reached New York City, **Nov. 4.**

First iron steamboat built in America, the Codorus, at York, Pa., by John Elgar.

1827
Slavery in New York State abolished July 4.

Steamship Curacao, first European built oceanic vessel to use steam power alone, crossed the Atlantic **April** from Antwerp to Paramaribo, Dutch Guiana. The Royal William, launched in Montreal, **April 29, 1831,** left there **Aug. 18, 1833,** crossed to Europe in 25 days, using only steam.

1828
First passenger railroad in U. S., Baltimore & Ohio, was begun **July 4,** first 14 miles opened to horse-drawn, railcar traffic **May 24, 1830.**

1830
Mormon church organized by Joseph Smith, in Fayette, Seneca County, N. Y., **Apr. 6.**

Revolution in France. Charles X abdicated, **Aug. 2,** and was succeeded by the Duke of Orleans as Louis Philippe I. There were revolts in Brunswick, Saxony and Belgium. Belgium became independent kingdom. .

First regularly scheduled passenger train service in U.S. using steam power opened at Charleston on South Carolina Railroad **Dec. 25** with 3½ ton U. S.-built locomotive, Best Friend of Charleston.

1831
Nat Turner, a Negro slave from Virginia, led a band of men in a slave rebellion, killed 57 whites, **Aug.** Army called in, Turner captured, tried and hanged.

1832
Black Hawk War (Ill.-Wis.) **April-Sept.,** pushed Sac & Fox Indians across Mississippi.

South Carolina convention passes **Ordinance of Nullification Nov., 1832,** against permanent tariff protection policy, declaring that if the Federal government attempted to enforce the tariff the state would consider itself no longer a member of the Union. Congress, **Feb. 1833,** passed a compromise tariff act, whereupon South Carolina repealed act.

British Reform Bill: Middle class enfranchised; step toward political democracy, **Mar. 23.**

1833
Slavery in British Empire outlawed **Aug. 28** as of **Aug. 1, 1834.** About 700,000 were liberated at cost of £20,000,000. Slavery was abolished in Britain **June 22,** 1772. Slave trade was suppressed **1807.**

Oberlin College, first in U. S. to adopt coeducation. **1835,** Oberlin refused to bar students on account of race.

1835
Texas proclaimed independence from Mexico in convention **Nov. 1,** Provisional govt. formed. Stephen Austin and Sam Houston leaders.

Fire in New York City, Dec. 16-17, destroyed 674 buildings.

Gold discovered on Cherokee land in Georgia; Indians forced to cede lands **Dec. 20,** and to cross Mississippi.

1836
Texans besieged in Alamo (San Antonio) by Mexicans under Santa Anna **Feb. 23-Mar. 6,** garrison, including W. B. Travis, Jim Bowie and David Crockett died defending the fort. At Goliad **Mar. 27** Capt. Fannin and 371 Texans who had surrendered were massacred by Mexicans. At San Jacinto **Apr. 21** Sam Houston and 800 Texans defeated 3,000 Mexicans. Santa Anna signed treaties ending hostilities, promised to recognize Texan independence, but Mexican congress repudiated treaties.

Marcus Whitman, H. H. Spaulding and wives reached Fort Walla Walla on Columbia River, Oregon. First white women to cross plains.

Seminole Indians in Florida under Osceola attacked whites **Nov. 1** in protest against forced removal. After several battles, war ended **Aug. 14, 1842,** with Indian defeat.

1837
Victoria, 18, niece of **William IV,** became queen of England. Married her first cousin, German Prince Albert of Saxe-Coburg, **1840.** He died **1861.**

1838
The Great Western, a steamship, 236 ft. long, 450 horsepower, 1340 gross tons, left Bristol, England, **Apr. 8,** and arrived in New York City, **Apr. 23.** The Sirius, 178 ft. long, 703 tons, left Liverpool **Mar. 28,** and Queenstown, **Apr. 4,** and reached N. Y. C. **Apr. 22,** using only steam power.

1839
Belgium and the Kingdom of the Netherlands were separated by treaties signed by those two countries and by Great Britain, France, Austria, Prussia, and Russia, at London, **April 19.** To the treaties was annexed a document declaring Belgium independent and perpetually neutral.

Opium War broke out between China and Britain. China tried to prohibit opium trade in Canton. British resist and take Canton. War ended with Treaty of Nanking, **Aug. 1842.**

1840
Antarctic was found to be a continent by Comdr. Charles Wilkes of First U.S. Exploring Expedition; named Wilkes Land, **Jan.-Feb.**

1841
First emigrant train for California, 47 persons, left Independence, Mo. **May 1,** reached Stanislaus River **Nov. 4.**

First passenger train on Erie R.R. **June 30.**

1842
First use of anaesthetic (sulphuric ether gas) by Dr. Crawford W. Long, Jefferson, Ga. Dr. Wm. T. G. Morton, dentist, used ether for painless extraction of tooth, Sept. 30, 1846; administered ether in tumor operation, Oct. 16, 1846, at Mass. General Hospital, Boston.

1844
First message over first telegraph line (authorized 1843) sent from U. S. Supreme Court room in Capitol, **May 24,** to Baltimore by inventor **S. F. B. Morse:** "What hath God wrought!"

Jos. Smith, Mormon leader, and brother Hyrum killed in Carthage, Ill., jail by mob **June 27.**

1845
Texas voted for annexation to U. S. **July 4.** Congress admitted Texas as 28th state **Dec. 29.**

1846
Mexican War. President James K. Polk ordered **Gen. Zachary Taylor** to seize disputed Texan land settled by Mexicans. After border clash, U. S. declared war, **May 13;** Mexico **May 23.**

Bear flag of republic of California raised by American settlers at Sonoma **June 14.** Gen. J. C. Fremont took charge **July 5.** Commodore J. S. Sloat took Monterey **July 7,** declared California annexed to U. S. Commodore Robt. F. Stockton succeeded Sloat, was ordered to recognize Gen. Kearny as governor and commander in chief in California. Kearny was defeated by Mexicans **Dec. 6,** retreated to San Diego.

Gen. Taylor defeated Mexicans at Buena Vista, **Feb. 23, 1847.** Gen. Winfield Scott with 12,000 troops (est.) took Vera Cruz **Mar. 27;** Mexico City, **Sept. 14,** captured Dictator Santa Anna. Serving during war were Col. Jefferson Davis, Capt. Robert E. Lee, Capt. Geo. B. McClellan, Lieut. U. S. Grant. By treaty, **Feb., 1848,** Mexico ceded claims to Texas, California, Arizona, New Mexico, Nevada, Utah, part of Colorado. U. S. assumed $3,000,000 American claims and paid Mexico $15,000,000.

Treaty with Great Britain, June 15, set boundary in Oregon at 49th parallel (extension of existing line). Water boundary settled 1873. Expansionists in U. S., seeking boundary farther north, used slogan "54° 40' or fight!"

Mormons, after violent clashes with settlers over polygamy, left Nauvoo, Ill., for West under Brigham Young, settled, **July 1847,** at Salt Lake City, Utah.

1847
First adhesive U. S. postage stamps on sale **July 1;** Benjamin Franklin 5¢, Washington 10¢.

1848
Gold discovered Jan. 24 by James W. Marshall, who was erecting sawmill in partnership with Capt. John A. Sutter on American River, branch of the Sacramento, near Coloma, Calif. Small finds of gold were reported 45 mi. nw of Los Angeles, 1841-44.

Louis Philippe dethroned in France; Second Republic set up, **Feb. 26.**

In Austria, **Ferdinand I** abdicated, **Dec. 2,** in favor of his nephew, Franz Josef; in Hungary, freedom was declared under Kossuth; revolts in Ireland, Lombardy, Venice, Denmark, and Schleswig-Holstein.

Communist Manifesto written by Karl Marx (1818-1883) and Friedrich Engels (1820-1895). Work is still a basic doctrine of the communist world.

1849

Astor Place riots in New York City against Macready, English actor, 34 killed, **May 10.** The outbreak was in retaliation for the treatment of Edwin Forrest, American actor, in London, 1845.

1850

Senator Henry Clay's Compromise of 1850 passed; admitted California as 31st state. **Sept. 9,** slavery forbidden; made Utah and New Mexico territories, without decision on slavery; amended Fugitive Slave Law punishing those who aided fugitive and abolished jury trial for fugitive and the slave trade in District of Columbia.

President Zachary Taylor died July 9, 65; Millard Fillmore 13th president, **July 10.** John C. Calhoun died **Mar. 31,** 68.

Jenny Lind's first concert, Castle Garden, New York, **Sept. 11,** P. T. Barnum manager.

Taiping Rebellion, led by Hung Hsiu-ch'uan, began in Kwangsi province, China. One of the largest civil wars in history, it resulted in the death of an estimated 20 to 40 million, devastated entire provinces, and nearly toppled the Manchu dynasty. The Taiping movement, pseudo-Christian in nature, was finally suppressed, **1864,** by Tseng Kuo-fan with the help of the "Ever Victorious Army" of Gen. Charles G. "Chinese" Gordon.

1851

Gold found in Australia.

Cornerstones of wings of U. S. Capitol laid.

New York & Hudson River. R. R., New York to Albany, opened **Oct.**

1852

Louis Napoleon crowned emperor of the French.

Uncle Tom's Cabin, by Harriet Beecher Stowe, published.

1853

Commodore Matthew C. Perry, U.S.N., received by Lord of Toda, Japan, **July 14;** negotiated treaty to open Japan to U. S. ships. Ratified **Mar. 8, 1854.**

Crimean War. A dispute between Greek orthodox and Roman monks over holy places held by Turkey in Palestine led Russian Czar Nicholas I to extend protection to Greeks. Turkey declared war **Oct. 4, 1853.** Britain and France, fearing expansion of Russia, declared war **May 28, 1854.** Russia occupied Moldavia and Wallachia. Fighting concentrated in the Crimea and included famous Charge of the Light Brigade at Balaklava, **Oct. 25, 1854,** 400 out of 607 killed; Russian defeat at Inkerman, **Nov. 5, 1854;** Fall of Sebastopol, **Sept. 11, 1855.** Sardinia sent 15,000 troops to Allies; Prussia and Sweden cooperated. Florence Nightingale established first dressing stations. By treaty of Paris, **Mar. 30, 1856,** Russia ceded part of Bessarabia to Moldavia, freed Danube for navigation. Black Sea closed to warships (repudiated, 1870).

James Gadsden negotiated purchase of 29,640 sq. mi. of land down to Rio Grande from Mexico, **Dec. 30,** for $10,000,000.

1854

Republican party started at Ripon, Wis., **Feb. 28;** first state organization, Jackson, Mich., **July 6.** Opposed Kansas-Nebraska Act (became law May 30) which left issue of slavery in Kansas and Nebraska to vote of settlers.

Henry D. Thoreau wrote Walden.

1855

Walt Whitman issued Leaves of Grass; Henry W. Longfellow wrote Song of Hiawatha.

1856

First railroad train crossed Mississippi at Rock Island, Ill. –Davenport, Ia., **April 21.**

Republican party's first nominee for President, John C. Fremont **June-Nov.,** defeated by James Buchanan. Lincoln made 50 speeches for Fremont.

Lawrence, Kan., sacked **May 21** by slavery party; **Abolitionist John Brown** led anti-slavery men against Missourians at Osawatomie **Aug. 30.** Federal troops ousted Missourians.

1857

Dred Scott decision of U. S. Supreme Court, 6-3, Roger B. Taney ch. jus., that Negro slave did not become free when taken into free state and had no rights as citizen. Abraham Lincoln denounced decision. Minnesota outlawed slavery.

Great Mutiny in India (Sepoy Rebellion) began in Meerut, **May 10,** when Indian soldiers revolted against British officers. First major Indian rebellion against English rule, crushed 1858. British East India Company abolished and India placed under crown rule as a result of mutiny.

John D. Lee, a Mormon, led raid against wagon train at Mountain Meadows **Sept. 11,** killed 120, spared only 17 children under 7. U. S. Army supplies burned. Govt. sent 6,000 troops to suppress "rebellion." Mormon Church unjustly accused.

1858

First Atlantic cable completed by Cyrus W. Field **Aug. 5.** Queen Victoria and President Buchanan exchanged greetings but cable failed **Sept. 1.** Field tried again in 1865, succeeded in 1866.

Lincoln-Douglas debates, Ill., **Aug. 21-Oct. 15.**

1859

Dixie, composed by Dan D. Emmett (1815-1904) minstrel.

First commercially productive oil well, 69½ ft., drilled near Titusville, Pa., by Edwin L. Drake, **Aug. 27,** started boom.

John Brown, abolitionist, with 21 men seized U. S. Armory at Harpers Ferry (then Va.) **Oct. 16.** U. S. Marines under Lt. Col. R. E. Lee captured raiders, killing 11. Five civilians, one Marine also killed. Brown was hanged for treason by Virginia, **Dec. 2,** as were 5 of his band, at Charlestown (now Charles Town, West. Va.).

Darwin's Origin of Species published. His theory of evolution caused revolution in scientific, philosophical and religious thinking.

1860

Abraham Lincoln, Republican, elected president by 1,866,452 popular and 180 electoral votes; Stephen A. Douglas had 1,375,157 and 12; John C. Breckinridge, 847,953 and 72; John Bell 590,631 and 39. Lincoln took office **Mar. 4, 1861;** Breckinridge and Bell supported secession.

First Pony Express between Sacramento, Calif., and St. Joseph, Mo., 1,980 miles apart, started from each place at 5 p.m., **Apr. 3;** 80 men each rode 75 miles on 429 horses changed every 10 miles. There were 190 relay stations. The service ended **Oct. 24, 1861,** when first transcontinental telegraph line was completed.

Giuseppe Garibaldi led 1,000 volunteers to Sicily, **May,** to unify Italy by force; deposed Francis II of Naples; hailed Victor Emmanuel of Sardinia as King of Italy.

1861-65 — Civil War. See Article Pages 852-853

1861

Emancipation of Russian serfs by Czar Alexander II. Paved the way for later reforms by Alexander.

1863

Draft riots in N.Y. City killed an estimated 1,000 including Negroes who were hung **July 13-16,** by mobs. Protested provision allowing money payment in place of service. Property loss, $1,500,000.

1864

Sand Creek Massacre of Cheyenne and Arapaho Indians by Col. John M. Chivington **Nov. 29** in a surprise dawn raid by 900 cavalrymen who killed between 150-500 men, women and children; 9 soldiers died. These tribes were awaiting surrender terms when attacked.

1866

Ku Klux Klan formed secretly in South to terrorize Negroes who voted. Disbanded, **1869.** Not to be confused with Ku Klux Klan, Inc., organized **1915.**

First post of the Grand Army of the Republic formed at Decatur, Ill. **April 6.** First national encampment met

Major Events of Civil War, 1861-1865;

For origins of the Civil War see Confederate States and Secession.

South Carolina, Georgia, Alabama, Mississippi, Louisiana and Florida formed the Confederate States of America Feb. 8, chose Jefferson Davis provisional president; were joined later by Texas, North Carolina, Arkansas, Virginia and Tennessee.

First Year of War—1861

South Carolina, through Gen. Beauregard demanded surrender of Ft. Sumter in Charleston harbor Apr. 11, Major Robert Anderson, USA, refused. Bombardment started at 4:30 a.m. April 12. Anderson surrendered Apr. 14.

President Lincoln called for 75,000 militia from states by quotas, April 15. New York state voted to enlist 30,000 militia for 2 years and $3,000,000 for defense.

U. S. troops evacuated **Harpers Ferry** Apr. 18. On Apr. 19 the 6th Mass. Infantry en route to Washington was attacked in the street of **Baltimore;** 4 soldiers were killed.

Col. Robert E. Lee resigned from the U. S. Army April 20, became commander of Virginia troops April 23, brigadier general May 14, full general of the Confederacy June 14.

Brig. Gen. Geo. B. McClellan, Dept. of the Ohio, made major general May 14, cleared western Virginia of Confederates. Made general in chief, USA, Nov. 1, on retirement of Gen. Winfield Scott.

In Missouri Brig. Gen. Nathaniel Lyon drove Confederates under Gen. Sterling Price out of Jefferson City and Boonville, June 17. Col. Franz Sigel was forced back at **Carthage** July 5. At **Wilson's Creek** Lyon was killed in losing battle with Price Aug. 10.

Battle of Bull Run or Manassas. Brig. General Irvin McDowell attacked Beauregard's forces on the Warrenton Road, July 21, pushed them back to Henry House hill, Confederates were based on Manassas Junction, Va. Gen. Jos. E. Johnston's army from Winchester, including forces commanded by Brig. Gen. Thomas J. Jackson and Gen. E. Kirby Smith reinforced Confederates, and with help of Gen. Jubal Early's brigade routed Federals. Brig. Gen. B. E. Bee, CSA, said: "Look, there is Jackson standing like a stone wall!" McDowell had 28,455 troops, 18,500 engaged, 2,708 casualties; Confederates had 32,072 available, 18,000 engaged, 1,967 casualties. Congress July 22 authorized 500,000 for army.

Events of 1862

Forts Henry and Donelson—Maj. Gen. Henry W. Halleck, Western Dept., sent Brig. Gen. U. S. Grant with 17,000 on river craft of Flag Officer Andrew H. Foote vs. **Ft. Henry** on Tennessee River; it fell Feb. 6. Grant rushed troops across 10 mi. of bogs to **Ft. Donelson** on the Cumberland, sent his "unconditional surrender" message to Brig. Gen. Simon B. Buckner, CSA, who gave up with 11,500 Feb. 16. At **Pea Ridge,** Ark., Mar. 6-8 Gen. Saml. R. Curtis, USA, defeated Gens. Van Dorn and Price. Casualties: USA, 1,351; CSA, 1,300.

New Madrid, Mo., captured Mar. 14, by Gen. John Pope. **Island No. 10** surrendered to Pope and Foote with 7,000 men Apr. 7.

Gen. Albert Sidney Johnston, CSA, 40,000 from Corinth, Miss., surprised Grant at **Shiloh** Church near **Pittsburg Landing,** Tenn. Apr. 6; Johnston was killed, Gen. Beauregard retreated Apr. 7 after Brig. Gen. Don Carlos Buell reinforced Grant with about 20,000. U. S. had 44,895 engaged, with 1,734 killed out of 13,047 casualties; CSA, 1,728 killed out of 10,699 casualties.

Fighting ships and gunboats under Flag Officer David G. Farragut, Comm. D. D. Porter, in Mississippi silenced **Chalmette** batteries; with Gen. Benj. F. Butler took forts; **New Orleans** surrendered Apr. 25 to Farragut who turned it over to Butler May 1. Farragut made rear admiral, July.

Monitor and Merrimack—Confederates rebuilt scuttled US frigate Merrimack into ironclad Virginia. Sank Cumberland, USN, destroyed Congress, USN, at Hampton Roads, Va., Mar. 8. Three other US ships ran aground, including Minnesota. Monitor, flat-decked ironclad, 900 tons, 172 ft. long with revolving turret and 2 11-in. guns, built by John Ericsson at $275,000 cost; Lt. John L. Worden commander, crew of 58, badly damaged Virginia, Mar. 9, which withdrew. Monitor did not resume fighting. After Federals took Virginia's base Confederates scuttled ship May 11.

Peninsular Campaign—McClellan moved Army of the Potomac by sea to Fort Monroe, Va., 70 mi. from Richmond. Confederates sent Stonewall Jackson up Shenandoah Valley to divert Federals; Jackson lost at **Kernstown,** Va., but routed Federals at **McDowell, Front Royal, Winchester, Cross Keys, Port Republic,** Mar. 23-June 9. McClellan's advance troops clashed with Maj. Gen. James Longstreet at **Williamsburg** May 5. On May 25 2 US corps crossed to south side of Chickahominy leaving 3 on north side. Gen. Jos. E. Johnston attacked south side May 30, **Battle of Fair Oaks or Seven Pines,** was repulsed. Johnston was wounded and Lee took over Army of Northern Virginia. Gen. J. E. B. Stuart, CSA, June 13-15, led his cavalry on scout around McClellan.

Gen. Lee started **Seven Days' Battles** at Mechanicsville June 26. McClellan withdrew to **Gaines Mill** (1st Cold Harbor) where Lee with 57,000 assaulted Brig. Gen. Fitz John Porter's 34,000 June 27. McClellan held off Lee at **Savage Station** June 29, **Frayser's Farm** or Glendale June 30; stopped Stonewall Jackson at **White Oak Swamp** June 30. At **Malvern Hill** July 1 Confederates had 5,000 casualties from U. S. guns. Despite this success McClellan withdrew army to Harrison's Landing. With over 115,000 available against Confederates' 95,000, McClellan from June 25-July 1 had 1,734 killed, 8,062 wounded, 6,053 missing; CSA had 3,478 killed, 16,261 wounded, 875 missing. In July Halleck became general in chief. McClellan was succeeded by Maj. Gen. John Pope.

Second Bull Run (Manassas). Stonewall Jackson and Maj. Gen. A. P. Hill, CSA, attacked Maj. Gen. Nath. P. Banks (part of Maj. Gen. John Pope's Army of Virginia) at Cedar Mountain, Va., Aug. 9. Jackson destroyed Pope's supplies at Manassas Aug. 26. Major battle was fought Aug. 30. Pope, checked by Jackson and Longstreet, withdrew; was relieved.

Antietam (Sharpsburg). Lee with 50,000 crossed Potomac Sept. 4 to Frederick, Md., moved across South Mountain to Hagerstown, Md. McClellan, after finding Lee's orders fought Longstreet and D. H. Hill at South Mountain, Sept. 14, Lee dropped back to Antietam creek near Sharpsburg, Md., Sept. 15; Jackson took Harpers Ferry, where only 1,300 cavalry of 12,000 USA escaped. McClellan attacked Sept. 17; stopped Lee, but failed to use reserve and let Lee withdraw across Potomac. USA had 70,000 engaged, 13,000 casualties; CSA had 50,000 engaged, 13,000 cas. Maj. Gen. Stuart, CSA cavalry raided Chambersburg, Pa., Oct. 10.

Fredericksburg, Va. Lincoln relieved McClellan, gave Army of the Potomac to Maj. Gen. Ambrose E. Burnside. Burnside crossed Rappahannock, made frontal attacks on Marye's Heights above Fredericksburg Dec. 13. Lee, Longstreet and Jackson with 75,000 repulsed him. USA lost 12,653; CSA 5,377.

In Tennessee Maj. Gen. Wm. S. Rosecrans, USA, pushed back Gen. Braxton Bragg at battle of **Stones River-Murfreesboro** Dec. 31-Jan. 3. US 12,000 casualties; CSA 11,000.

Preliminary proclamation, Sept. 22, by President Lincoln announced that Jan. 1, 1863, slaves would be declared free in territory then in rebellion.

Nov. 2 in Indianapolis, Ind. For years this Union veterans organization was a political force in the nation. Last encampment held Aug. 31, 1949, in Indianapolis; 6 of the

16 surviving veterans attended.

1867
Alaska sold to U.S. by Russia for $7,200,000 (2 cents

Emancipation and Lincoln's Assassination

Events of 1863

Lincoln's Emancipation Proclamation, Jan. 1, declared free forever the slaves in Arkansas, Texas, Louisiana (certain parishes already occupied excepted); Mississippi, Alabama, Florida, Georgia, South Carolina, North Carolina, Tennessee and Virginia (West Virginia and other portions excepted). About 3,000,000 slaves were thus declared free.

Chancellorsville, Va.—Maj. Gen. Jos. E. Hooker succeeded Burnside and with 90,000 available, attempted to envelop Lee May 2. Jackson led 32,000 around US Army, drove in right of Maj. Gen. O. O. Howard. Jackson wounded by own troops May 2, died May 10; succeeded by Maj. Gen. J. E. B. Stuart. Shell stunned Hooker May 3. Maj. Gen. John Sedgwick forced Confederates out of Marye's Heights; was pushed back May 4. Against concave Hooker withdrew across Rappahannock. US casualties 17,197; CSA 13,000. Lincoln called for 100,000 for 6 mos. June 15.

Gettysburg—Lee with 76,224 and 272 guns, invaded Penn. Army of the Potomac had 115,256, about 90,000 effective, 362 guns. Maj. Gen. Jubal A. Early, CSA, levied on York, Pa., for $100,000 supplies June 27. Lincoln gave Maj. Gen Geo. G. Meade top command June 28. 1st US Cavalry (Buford) pushed back at Gettysburg by Lt. Gen. A. P. Hill, CSA, July 1. Lt. Gen. Richard S. Ewell, CSA, forced US back to Cemetery Hill; Maj. Gen. Reynolds, USA, killed. US took Culp's Hill, extended line to Round Top, with Maj. Gens. Hancock, Sickles, Sedgwick, Howard, Slocum and Pleasonton (cavalry). Lee's attacks checked July 2. On July 3 Maj. Gen. Geo. E. Pickett, Maj. Gen. Isaac Trimble and Brig. Gen. Jas. J. Pettigrew with 12,400 made assault on foot from Seminary Ridge vs. US center (Hancock); were repulsed with 4,500 casualties. Lee retreated into Virginia; Meade did not pursue. Losses: US, 3,155 killed, 14,529 wounded, 5,365 missing; CSA, 3,903 killed, 12,709 wounded, 5,425 missing. Many of the missing were prisoners. Total casualties estimated at 23,049 USA, 20,451 CSA, or over 43,000.

Vicksburg—Gen. Wm. T. Sherman took **Jackson,** Miss., May 14, held back Jos. E. Johnston, CSA. Lt. Gen. John C. Pemberton, CSA, commanding 30,000, was defeated at **Champion's Hill** and **Black River Bridge,** shut up in Vicksburg. He surrendered July 4; Grant paroled prisoners. Gen. Banks with 15,000 captured **Port Hudson** July 8, giving US control of Mississippi River.

Tennessee—Maj. Gen. Wm. E. Rosecrans took **Chattanooga** Sept. 9. Braxton Bragg, CSA, drove him back to **Chickamauga,** but Maj. Gen. Geo. H. Thomas checked Bragg, Sept. 18-20; was called "Rock of Chickamauga." Grant made commander of all armies there: Sherman of Grant's Army of the Tennessee; Thomas replaced Rosecrans. Longstreet reinforced Bragg; Hooker supported Thomas. Hooker took **Lookout Mt.,** fought Battle Above the Clouds, Nov. 24. Sherman and Thomas dislodged Bragg at **Missionary Ridge,** Nov. 25. Bragg retreated to Georgia.

Brig. Gen. John H. Morgan, CSA, raided Indiana and Ohio; captured at New Lisbon, O., escaped from prison at Columbus, Nov. 27. Killed at Greeneville, Tenn., Sept. 4, 1864.

Events of 1864

Grant made lieut. general Mar. 1, gen. in chief Mar. 12. Sherman succeeded him in West. Halleck made chief of staff. Draft for 500,000 to serve 3 yrs. or duration begun Mar. 10; 200,000 more Mar. 14.

Rear Adm. David G. Farragut won naval battle, **Mobile Bay,** Aug. 5.

Wilderness; Spotsylvania—Bloody battles followed when Grant crossed the Rapidan and was attacked by Lee at **Wilderness,** May 5. Longstreet was wounded by

his own men. Grant attacked Lee at **Spotsylvania Court House** May 10 (2nd Wilderness). Maj. Gen. Franklin G. Barlow took Spotsylvania salient, including **Bloody Angle,** May 12 (3rd Wilderness). Maj. Gen. Sedgwick killed. US killed and wounded May 5-12 est. 26,813; missing 4,183. Maj. Gen. Sheridan's cavalry defeated Maj. Gen. J. E. B. Stuart at **Yellow Tavern,** Va., May 11; Stuart was fatally wounded, died May 12 in Richmond.

Cold Harbor—Lee took strong position near the Chickahominy. Grant made frontal attacks June 3, lost 7,000 casualties in 30 minutes, 11,000 June 1-3.

USS Kearsarge, Capt. John A. Winslow, defeated CSS Alabama, Capt. Raphael Semmes, off Cherbourg, France, June 19; Alabama surrendered and sank.

Siege of Petersburg—Grant assaulted Confederate positions June 15-18 with 7,881 casualties. Exploded a mine under Confederate works July 30; during fight in crater US lost 1,000 killed, 4,000 wounded, 110 missing; CSA 400 killed, 600 wounded, 200 missing.

Early vs. Sheridan—Lee sent Maj. Gen. Jubal A. Early to hold Shenandoah Valley. Early went through Maryland to outskirts of Fort Stevens near Washington, July 11. Sheridan defeated Early at **Winchester** Sept. 19, **Fisher's Hill,** Sept. 22. Early surprised Wright at Cedar Creek Oct. 19; Sheridan's famous ride from Winchester rallied troops, brought victory.

Sherman's Campaign for Atlanta—Sherman defeated Johnston at **Resaca,** Ga., May 14-15. Hooker repulsed at **New Hope Church,** Ga., May 25. Johnston repulsed Sherman at **Kenesaw Mtn.,** June 27 (US casualties 3,000, CSA 600), evacuated post, was superseded by Gen. J. B. Hood, CSA, July 17. Lt. Gen. Wm. J. Hardee, CSA, defeated at **Peach Tree Creek,** July 20. Hardee defeated in battle of **Atlanta,** July 22, by Gen. J. B. McPherson, who was killed. Sherman occupied Atlanta Sept. 2, burned it Nov. 15, started **March to the Sea,** reached **Savannah** Dec. 21. Thomas defeated Hood at **Nashville,** Tenn.

Gen. Nathan B. Forrest, CSA, captured **Fort Pillow,** Tenn., Apr. 12, inflicting heavy loss on U. S. Negro troops.

Events of 1865

Confederates evacuated **Columbia,** S. C., and **Charleston,** S. C., Feb. 17. Cape Fear River Forts captured Feb. 20-21. Brig. Gen. Geo. A. Custer defeated Early at **Waynesboro,** Va., Mar. 2. Confederates evacuated **Petersburg** and **Richmond** Apr. 2-3. Lee surrendered 27,805 to Grant at **Appomattox Court House,** Va., Apr. 9. Johnston surrendered 31,243 to Sherman at **Durham Sta., N.C.,** Apr. 18.

Murder of Lincoln

Lincoln was shot by John Wilkes Booth, an actor, in Ford's Theatre, in Washington, April 14, died, April 15; Booth died of a bullet wound, April 26, in burning barn, on a farm near Bowling Green, Va. Those hanged for complicity were Mrs. Mary E. Surratt, David E. Herold, George A. Atzerodt and Lewis Payne (Powell), July 7. Also convicted of conspiracy were Dr. Samuel A. Mudd, who set Booth's broken ankle, Samuel Arnold, Michael O'Laughlin, and Edward Spangler. All were sentenced to life imprisonment except Spangler, who received a 6-year sentence. They were sent to Dry Tortugas Prison, off Key West, where O'Laughlin died during an 1867 outbreak of yellow fever. Dr. Mudd's unselfish services as a physician during the outbreak won him a pardon; Arnold and Spangler were freed with Dr. Mudd in 1869. John H. Surratt, son of Mary E., fled to Europe, was brought back, tried and freed. Booth's body was buried under the stone floor of a naval prison in Washington, later reburied in the Booth family plot in Baltimore.

Slavery was abolished by adoption of the 13th amendment to the Constitution, Dec. 18.

an acre) Mar. 30, through efforts of Sec. of State Wm. H. Seward and Sen. Charles Sumner.

Emperor Maximillian of Mexico executed by Juarez party, June 19. He was an Austrian archduke, placed on throne Apr. 10, 1864, by French.

Dominion of Canada established July 1.

Abolition of the Shogunate and restoration of the Mikado marked beginning of Meiji reforms that industrialized and modernized Japan; feudalism abolished, 1871; Constitution promulgated, 1889.

1868

The World Almanac, a publication of the New York World newspaper, appeared for the first time.

Thomas D'Arcy McGee, a "Father of Confederation," shot in first Canadian political assassination.

President Andrew Johnson, blocked by Senate in attempt to remove Edwin M. Stanton, secretary of war, for opposing his policies, was impeached for violation of tenure of office act by House of Rep., tried by Senate and acquitted, March-May. Stanton resigned.

Memorial Day first observed officially May 30 on order by Gen. John A. Logan, Commander G.A.R.

1869

Financial "Black Friday" in New York, Sept. 24; caused by gold corner.

Transcontinental railroad completed; golden spike driven at Promontory, Utah, May 10, marking the junction of Central Pacific and Union Pacific.

Woman's suffrage law passed in territory of Wyoming, Dec. 10.

1870

Franco-Prussian War. Napoleon III, French emperor, tricked into declaring war on Prussia by Bismarck, Prussian chancellor, over Spanish succession issue, surrendered with large army at Sedan, Sept. 4. Nationalists declared republic Sept. 4. Leon Gambetta, bitter-ender, escaped from Paris in balloon Oct. 7 to carry on war.

The troops of Victor Emmanuel II, under Gen. Cadorna, took possession of Rome, Sept. 20, in the name of the Kingdom of Italy. Rome and the rest of the Papal States then were annexed by a plebiscite, taken Oct. 2.

1871

Court of Arbitration awarded United States damages of $15,500,000 gold against Britain because British equipped Alabama and 12 other Confederate raiders. After sinking 65 U. S. ships Alabama was destroyed by Kearsarge off Cherbourg, 1864.

William I of Hohenzollern, proclaimed German emperor at Versailles, Jan. 18. Paris "Red Republicans" organized commune, Mar. 18-May 29; burned Hotel de Ville, Tuileries palace, executed 67 hostages. Communards overcome by French army; deaths est. 20,000.

Treaty of Frankfort, May 23, ended Franco-Prussian War. France ceded Alsace, most of Lorraine, paid 5 billion francs indemnity.

The Law of Guarantees, passed by the Italian Parliament May 13, granted the Pope and his successors possession of the Vatican, the Lateran and the villa of Castel Gandolfo and a yearly allowance of 3,225,000 lire, or about $645,000. The money was not claimed.

Great fire destroyed heart of Chicago, Oct. 8-11; loss est. $196,000,000. Started in Mrs. O'Leary's barn, 558 De Koven St. by cow upsetting lantern, according to legend.

Henry M. Stanley, sent by James Gordon Bennett, owner of New York Herald, to find David Livingstone, missionary, greeted him Nov. 10 at Ujiji, in Central Africa, now Tanzania, with "Dr. Livingstone, I presume?"

1872

Amnesty Act restores civil rights to all citizens of the South May 22 except for 500-700 former Confederate leaders.

1873

Panic in New York City began with bank failures, Sept. 20.

First U.S. postal card issued, May 1.

1874

"Boss" W. M. Tweed in New York City, convicted of fraud, Nov. 19, and sentenced to 12 years in prison; the court released him from Blackwells Island prison June, 1875, on a technicality; he was committed to Ludlow St. jail in a civil suit; escaped, Dec. 4, 1875, and went to Cuba, then to Spain, brought back to New York City, Nov. 1876; he died in Ludlow St. jail, April 12, 1878.

1875

Congress passes first Civil Rights Act Mar. 1 which guarantees equal rights to Negroes in public accommodations and jury duty. Act invalidated in 1883 by Supreme Court ruling that the federal government can protect only political, not social, rights.

First Kentucky Derby held in May at Churchill Downs at Louisville, Ky.

Mary Baker Eddy publishes "Science and Health."

1876

Samuel J. Tilden, Democrat, received majority of 250,000 popular votes for President over Rutherford B. Hayes, Republican, and had 184 electoral votes against 163, with returns from South Carolina, Florida, Louisiana and Oregon, 22 electoral votes, in dispute. Bitter contest for delegates with charges of corruption, left issue to Congress, which appointed electoral commission, 8 Republicans, 7 Democrats. Hayes given Presidency by strict party vote.

Gen. George A. Custer and 264 soldiers of the Seventh Cavalry killed June 25 in "last stand," Battle of the Little Big Horn, Mont., in Sioux Indian war, by Indian tribes united by Sitting Bull; fighting led by Chiefs Gall and Crazy Horse.

James Butler (Wild Bill) Hickok, shot dead from behind by Jack McCall, a desperado, in Deadwood, S. D., Aug. 2. A vigilance committee acquitted McCall but the United States Court in Yankton, S. D., found him guilty and he was hanged.

1877

Russia declared war on Turkey, April 24; peace treaty signed, March, 1878.

Molly Maguires, Irish terrorist society in Pennsylvania, broken up by hanging of 11 leaders for murders.

1878

First commercial telephone exchange opened, New Haven, Conn., Jan. 28, 1878. First private exchange, used by physicians, reported in use July, 1877, Hartford, Conn.

1879

F. W. Woolworth opened his first five-and-ten store, Utica, N. Y., Feb. 22.

Henry George published Progress & Poverty, advocating single tax on land.

1881

President James A. Garfield shot in Washington July 2; died in Elberon, N.J., Sept. 19.

Federation of Organized Trades and Labor Unions formed, Aug. 2, at Terre Haute, Ind; later joined with 25 independent unions to form the American Federation of Labor at Columbus, Ohio, Dec., 1886.

1882

Prof. Robert Koch announced, in Berlin, discovery of the tuberculosis germ. March 24.

Triple Alliance of Germany, Austria and Italy formed. Denounced by Italy, 1914.

1883

Brooklyn Bridge opened, May 24; panic on it, May 30; twelve trampled to death.

1884

Financial panic in New York, May 5-7.

1885

Gen. Charles G. "Chinese" Gordon, British governor of the Sudan, was slain, Jan. 26, by a Moslem soldier, who stuck the head on a spear, at Khartoum. Several thousand whites were massacred by the Mahdi's troops. Gen. Kitchener defeated the Mahdi's army Sept. 2, 1898.

First electric street railway in United States, in Baltimore, opened by Leo Daft, Aug. 10.

Canadian rebel Louis Riel hanged for treason at Regina, following crushing of Northwest Rebellion.

Last spike driven in Canadian Pacific Railway at Craigellachie, B. C., giving Canada transcontinental railway system.

1886

Haymarket riot, evening of **May 4,** followed bitter labor battles for 8-hour day in Chicago, attacks on strikebreakers, police violence and attempts of anarchists to incite workers. A bomb killed seven police and wounded 66. Eight anarchists found guilty. Seven years later Gov. John P. Altgeld denounced trial as unfair.

Geronimo, Apache Indian, surrendered **Mar. 27** to U. S. Gen. George Crook in Sonora, Mex., but fled the next day and finally surrendered **Sept. 4** to U. S. Gen. Nelson A. Miles in Arizona.

Dr. A. Conan Doyle invented famous detective Sherlock Holmes, in story, A Study in Scarlet. Published in Beeton's Christmas Annual, 1887.

1887

Flood in Hwang-ho River, China; 900,000 persons perished.

Opera Comique, Paris, burned May 25; 200 lives lost.

1888

Great blizzard in eastern U.S. Mar. 11-14, 400 deaths.

1889

Crown Prince Rudolf of Austria and Baroness Maria Vetsera found slain in his hunting lodge, Mayerling, near Vienna, **Jan. 29.**

Johnstown, Pa., flood, May 31; 2,200 lives lost.

Universal Exhibition in Paris, May 6 through Nov. 6. Eiffel Tower (984.25 ft.) opened. (Height with TV antenna 1,052 ft.) First automobile exhibited, a Benz.

Dom Pedro II, emperor of Brazil, forced off throne by planters, earlier he freed slaves. Died in Paris, 1891, last emperor on American soil.

1890

First execution by electrocution; Wm. Kemmler, **Aug. 6** at Auburn prison, Auburn, N. Y., for murder.

Battle of Wounded Knee, S. Dak., **Dec. 29,** the last major conflict between Indians and U.S. troops, occurred when a band of Sioux were captured and brought to Wounded Knee Creek where Col. J. W. Forsyth ordered them disarmed. Some Indians resisted sparking the battle which killed about 200 Indian men, women and children; 29 soldiers died, 33 wounded.

Castle Garden closed as immigration depot and Ellis Island opened **Dec. 31** (Closed 1954).

1892

Homestead, Pa., strike at Carnegie steel mills, near Pittsburgh; conflict between 300 Pinkerton guards and strikers; seven guards and 11 strikers and spectators shot to death, many wounded **July 6.**

1893

Ford's Theater building, Washington, where Lincoln was shot, used by Pension Bureau, collapsed **June 9,** killing 22.

1894

Chinese-Japanese War began, **July 25;** Battle of Yalu, **Sept. 17,** treaty of Shimonoseki, **April 17, 1895,** gave Japan Liaotung Peninsula, Formosa and the Pescadores.

Jacob S. Coxey led 20,000 unemployed from the Midwest to Washington **April 30.** Coxey died **May 18, 1951,** aged 97.

Strike of employees of Pullman Co., South Chicago, Ill., June, led Eugene V. Debs to call sympathetic strike of American Railway Union. President Cleveland called out Federal troops over protest of Gov. Altgeld (Illinois). Debs and 3 others were imprisoned 6 mos. for contempt of court. Strike called off **Aug. 7.**

Thomas A. Edison's Kinetoscope given first public showing at 1155 Broadway, New York, **April 14,** was patented 1891 for U. S. only.

Capt. Alfred Dreyfus found guilty of betraying French army secrets **Dec. 22,** in sensational frame-up; real culprit, Major Esterhazy, acquitted; Dreyfus condemned to Devil's Island, off French Guiana. Recalled for second

Spanish-American War of 1898; United States Becomes Naval Power

Spanish misrule in Cuba led to repeated attempts by Cuban patriots to gain rights of citizenship, abolition of slavery, and finally independence. When South America broke from Europe in the 1820s pro-slavery influence in the U.S. blocked movements to free Cuba and Puerto Rico. But in 1852 President Fillmore refused to join Great Britain and France in guaranteeing Spanish authority in Cuba. In 1854 the Ostend Manifesto written largely by Jas. Buchanan, urged the U.S. to buy Cuba or seize it to abolish oppression. Grant's administration offered to buy Cuba, but Spain refused.

In Cuba revolts led by Marciso Lopenz and Joaquin de Aguero, 1848-1851, were suppressed and the leaders executed. In 1868 a major revolt led by Carlos de Cespedes and Manuel de Quesada lasted 10 years. In 1873 the Virginius expedition, flying the American flag, was seized by the Spaniards, and Americans and Cubans aboard were shot. This did not stop supplying of arms from the U.S. In 1895 the insurrection had spread so widely under Generals Calixto Garcia Maximo Gomez and Antonio Macea that Spain landed 150,000 troops, but by 1896 over half of the island was in the hands of the patriots. The U.S. offered to mediate but was repulsed. The country was laid waste by Spanish troops and the accounts of suffering increased sentiment in the U.S. in favor of Free Cuba.

The battleship Maine, Capt. Chas. D. Sigsbee, sent to Havana in January on goodwill tour, was blown up **Feb. 15, 1898;** 264 men, 2 officers killed. U.S. inquiry, Capt. Wm. T. Sampson Ch., blamed external explosion **Mar. 21.** Spanish inquiry **Mar. 28** blamed internal explosion. Congress **Mar. 9** voted $50,000,000 for defense. President McKinley **Mar. 27** demanded Spain grant armistice for negotiation with Cuba via U.S., end relocation of noncombatants in special military enclaves. Spain **Mar. 31** offered to arbitrate Maine, end relocation, but wanted Cubans to ask for armistice. After appeal by foreign ministers Spain granted armistice **Apr. 9** President **Apr. 11** asked Congress for authority to intervene in Cuba. Congress **Apr. 20-25** debated joint resolution recognizing independence of Cuba, asked Spain to withdraw and empowered President to enforce it; adopted it with statement war existed since **Apr. 21.** Spain had declared war **Apr. 24.**

Commodore Geo. Dewey, with 6 warships, 1 revenue cutter, destroyed the Spanish fleet (10 ships) in Manila Bay **May 1,** occupied Cavite. Spain, 167 dead; U.S., 7 wounded. Spanish Admiral Cervera with 4 cruisers, 3 torpedo boats reached Santiago without interference **May 19.** Battleship Oregon made 10,000 mi. trip around Cape Horn, joined squadron of Acting Rear Adm. Sampson **May 26.** Collier Merrimac ineffectively sunk at mouth of Santiago harbor by Lieut. Richmond Pearson Hobson **June 3.** Marines landed at Guantanamo **May 11.** Maj. Gen. Wm. R. Shafter landed 10,000 men at Daiquiri and Siboney, including 1st U.S. Volunteer Cavalry (Rough Riders) recruited by Lt. Col. Theodore Roosevelt, commanded by Col. Leonard Wood. Brig. Gen. H. W. Lawton, Brig. Gen. Adna R. Chaffee with 6,654 men attacked El Caney, defended by 500 Spaniards, **July 1.** Maj. Gen. Jos. Wheeler, Brig. Gen. J. F. Kent carried San Juan hill with 8,336, same day.

Admiral Cervera's fleet left Santiago harbor **July 3,** was destroyed by ships of Acting Rear Adm. Sampson and Commodore Winfield S. Schley; 353 Spaniards killed, 151 wounded; 1 American killed. Santiago surrendered **July 17.** Maj. Gen. Nelson A. Miles took Puerto Rico **July 25-28.** Armistice signed, **Aug. 12.** Peace treaty signed in Paris **Dec. 10,** eliminated Spain from lands discovered by Columbus. U.S. acquired Puerto Rico, Guam and Philippines, paying $20,000,000 for all Spanish claims in later; guaranteed Cuban independence (Ratified **Feb. 6, 1899.**) U.S. had treaty rights in Cuba until 1934; granted Philippine independence **July 4, 1946.**

trial by efforts of Emile Zola and Clemenceau, again condemned **Sept. 9, 1899.** Public clamor led to pardon, **Sept. 19.** Further proofs of innocence led to complete rehabilitation, **1906,** with rank of major. He served as lieut. colonel in World War I.

1895

Cuban Revolution resumed **Feb. 20;** Gen. Antonio Maceo, leader of the insurrection, was killed in action, **Dec. 7, 1896.**

X-rays discovered by Wilhelm Konrad Roentgen, a German physicist; Nobel prize winner, **1901.**

1896

President Cleveland intervened in boundary dispute between Venezuela and British Guiana on basis of Monroe Doctrine; appointed arbitration commission, which settled it **Feb. 2, 1897.**

Guglielmo Marconi received first wireless patent from Britain **June 2.**

William Jennings Bryan delivered "Cross of Gold" speech at Democratic National Convention in Chicago, **July 8.** Bryan nominated for president but defeated by Republican Wm. McKinley.

1897

Eugene V. Debs formed Social Democratic party.

1898

Radium discovered by Pierre Curie, Mme. Curie and G. Bemont, Paris.

1898—Spanish-American War.
See Article Page 855

1899

South African (Boer) war began **Oct. 11;** Ladysmith relieved, **Feb. 28, 1900;** Pretoria fell **June 5, 1900;** war ended, **May 31, 1902,** with loss of independence of Boer republics, Transvaal and Orange Free State, now in Republic of South Africa. British losses: 5,773 killed; 16,171 dead of wounds or disease; 22,829 wounded. Boers engaged est. 65,000, losses unknown.

Filipino insurgents (est. 12,000 under arms) unable to get recognition of independence from U. S. A. started guerrilla war, **Feb. 4.** Crushed with capture, **Mar. 23, 1901,** of leader, Emilio Aguinaldo, by Brig. Gen. Frederick Funston.

Open Door Policy of U. S. Secy. of State John Hay, supported by 6 nations. Policy was to make China an open market for international commerce and to preserve its integrity as a nation.

Boxer anti-foreign uprising started in China: Westerners and Westernized Chinese murdered.

1900

Carry Nation, Kansas anti-saloon agitator, began raiding with hatchet. Died **June 9, 1911.**

Boxers in China killed German minister **June 20.** Foreigners besieged in Peking legations. Relief expedition

---

Principal Events of World War 1, 1914-1918;

ORIGINS. Since the defeat of France by Prussia in 1870-71 major powers of Europe had kept peace by diplomatic negotiations and a balance of power. Triple Alliance, of Germany, Austria and Italy was defensive, with reservations; Triple Entente was an understanding between Britain, France and Russia. Nationalist aspirations in the Balkans had resulted in several wasteful wars and Italy had fought with Turkey and Ethiopia. Austria annexed Bosnia, Herzegovina, former Turkish Balkan provinces, 1908. Russia backed Serbia's efforts to get a port on the Adriatic. Germany's industrial expansion led to building of powerful navy, which Britain matched two for one for its own security. Germany's universal military service led France to adopt three-year training.

On **June 28, 1914,** Archduke Francis Ferdinand, heir to Austrian throne, was assassinated, with his wife, by Gavrillo Prinzip, Bosnian Serb terrorist, in Sarajevo, Bosnia. Austria-Hungary, through Count Berchthold, Austrian foreign minister, made 10 demands on Serbia for suppression of anti-Austrian agitation. Serbia conceded all but two, which called for Austrian enforcement police inside Serbia. It asked reference to The Hague peace tribunal. Austria demanded all or nothing.

Russia warned Austrian action was aimed at Russia, supported Serbia. Germany, allied with Austria, backed Austria. Britain, France, Italy proposed mediation, Sir Edward Grey, Br. foreign minister, **July 26** proposed conference of four major powers; Germany refused to join.

Austria declared war on Serbia **July 28.** Germany, citing Russian mobilization, declared war on Russia **Aug. 1;** on France, **Aug. 3.** Germans entered Belgium in violation of treaty, of which Britain was cosigner. Britain asked Germany to guarantee neutrality of Belgium by midnight **Aug. 4;** Germany refused; British declared war **Aug. 4.** Italy, declaring German aggression made Triple Alliance inoperative, proclaimed neutrality. Japan declared war on Germany **Aug. 23** because of Anglo-Japanese treaty on Far East. Turkey joined Central Powers **Nov. 23.**

Lord Kitchener became British secy. for war. Belgian forts at Liege stopped Germans until **Aug. 7,** delayed Ger. schedule. Germans entered Brussels **Aug. 20;** pushed back British Expeditionary Force (Sir John French) at Mons **Aug. 23-24;** burned most of Louvain **Aug. 25.** Von Hindenburg and Ludendorff defeated Russians at Tannenberg, East Prussia, **Aug. 26-31;** at Masurian Lakes **Sept. 5-10.**

In first Battle of the Marne, **Sept. 5-10,** French under Joffre, Foch and Gallieni, stopped German advance of Von Kluck and Von Bülow toward Paris, forced them back to Aisne, where trench warfare began. British repulsed Germans at Ypres, **Oct. 16-Nov. 24.** Belgians lost Antwerp **Oct. 9.** Russians forced Austrians back in Galicia. Austrians took and lost Belgrade **Dec. 2-15.**

British bombarded Dardanelles forts **Nov. 3;** declared war on Turkey, annexed Cyprus **Nov. 5.** Japan took Tsingtau **Nov. 6.**

Of many warships and merchantmen sunk, only major events are listed here. For others see Marine Disasters.

1915—Submarine War Begins

In 1915 the war became a desperate battle of attrition on land and sea. British sank Ger. cruiser Bluecher **Jan. 24.** Germany ordered submarine blockade of Britain to start **Feb. 18.** U.S. held Germany to "strict accountability" for American losses. Germans used liquid fire in Vosges **Mar. 3.** Roving cruiser Dresden sunk in Pacific **Mar. 15.** Three Br.-Fr. battleships sunk at Dardanelles **Mar. 18.** Ger. sank Falaba **Mar. 28,** 1 American lost. Turks sank Br. battleship Lord Nelson **Apr. 6.** Ger. introduced poison gas at Ypres, **Apr. 22,** Canadians saved the line. Allies landed at Gallipoli, **Apr. 25.** Ger. torpedoed Gulflight, U.S. tanker, **Apr. 30,** 2 Americans lost.

German sub sank Cunard liner Lusitania off Old Head of Kinsale, Ireland, **May 7;** of 1,959 aboard, including 702 crew, 1,198, including 124 Americans, died. This started a series of protests by U.S. to Germany. W. J. Bryan, secy. of state, resigned **June 8;** considered Wilson's Lusitania note too severe. After sinking Arabic **Aug. 19** Ger. agreed not to sink liners without warning, but U.S. considered promises inadequate. U.S. dismissed Austrian ambassador Dumba and Germans Boy-Ed and Von Papen for illegal activities.

South Africans under Gen. Botha captured German S.W. Africa. Italy declared war on Austria-Hungary **May 23,** on Turkey **Aug. 20, on Germany Aug. 27.** Bulgaria declared war on Serbia **Oct. 14;** Allies against Bulgaria **Oct. 15-19.** Germans occupied Russian Baltic ports, took Vilna, with Austrians occupied Serbia. Allies landed at Salonika **Oct. 5.** Edith Cavell, Br. nurse, executed by Germans in Brussels **Oct. 12** for aiding escapes. Sir John French replaced by Sir Douglas Haig on British front **Dec. 15.** Allies began evacuation of Gallipoli (Dardanelles) **Dec. 19.**

1916—Great Battles

Germany announced **Feb. 10** that armed merchant

of 18,000 American, British, French, Japanese and Russian troops took Tientsin **July 13;** Peking **Aug. 14.** U.S. had 2,500 under Maj. Gen. A. R. Chaffee, including two infantry regts., one troop of cavalry, one light battery, two batts. of Marines. Germans arrived and Field Marshal Count Alfred von Waldersee led army of occupation. Russia refused to yield parts of Manchuria. Dowager Empress of China accepted allied terms **Sept., 1901.** All except U.S. exacted large concessions and indemnity of $333,000,000, payable in 39 years. U.S. accepted $25,000,000, returned half in 1908 to provide student exchange fund.

Campaign begun, **June 26,** by Drs. Walter Reed, Aristides Agramonte, Jesse Lazear and James Carroll to wipe out yellow fever in Cuba.

Galveston hurricane and tidal wave, Sept. 8; 5,000 lives estimated lost.

1901
President Wm. McKinley was shot at the Pan-American Exposition in Buffalo, N. Y., **Sept. 6,** by Leon Czolgosz, anarchist; died **Sept. 14.** Theodore Roosevelt, vice pres., became 26th President. Czolgosz was executed. McKinley tomb in Canton, Ohio.

Marconi signalled letter "S" by wireless telegraph across Atlantic from Cornwall, Eng., to Newfoundland, **Dec. 12.**

1902
Anglo-Japanese alliance formed **Jan. 30** to protect Japan against encroaching Russians.

Cuban Republic inaugurated. American occupation under Gen. Leonard Wood, ended **May 20.**

First International Arbitration Court opened in The Hague, Holland, **October.**

1903
First automobile trip across U.S., San Francisco to New York, **May 23-Aug. 1.**

Henry Ford, having withdrawn from the Detroit Automobile Co. in 1901, organized Ford Motor Co.

Treaty between U.S. and Colombia to have U.S. dig Panama Canal signed **Jan. 22, 1903,** rejected by Colombia. Panama declared independence **Nov. 3,** recognized by President Theodore Roosevelt **Nov. 6.** See Canal Zone and Panama.

First successful flight in heavier-than-air mechanically propelled airplane, by **Orville Wright (1871-1948)** on **Dec. 17, 1903,** rising from base of Kill Devil hill, four miles south of Kitty Hawk, N. C., 120 ft. in 12 secs., in 27 mph wind. Fourth flight, same day by **Wilbur Wright (1867-1912)** 852 ft., in 59 secs. Plane patented **May 22, 1906.**

1904
Russo-Japanese War began, **Feb. 6.** Port Arthur surrendered to Japanese Jan. 2, 1905. Peace treaty signed in U.S. Navy Yard, Portsmouth, N.H., **Sept. 5, 1905.**

New York subway opened, **Oct. 27.**

Why United States Intervened

ships would be considered warships and sunk without warning. U. S. retorted **Feb. 15** international law permitted self-defense of commercial ships. Ger. made huge effort vs. Verdun **Feb. 21,** took Ft. Douaumont **Feb. 25** Ger. declared war on Portugal **Mar. 8.** Russians invaded Persia, **Mar. 10.** Channel str. Sussex torpedoed, 80 casualties, **Mar. 24.** Wilson threatened **Apr. 18-19** to break relations unless Germany revised sub warfare; Ger. met most of U. S. demands.

Rising in Ireland **Apr. 24-May 1.** Patrick Pearse et al, executed; Sir Roger Casement hanged **Aug. 3.** Br. adopted conscription **May 24.** Jutland naval battle, **May 31-June 1.** Admirals Jellicoe and Beatty, Br., lost 5 major cruisers, 8 destroyers; 6,091 men; Admirals Scheer and von Hipper, Ger., lost 2 major ships, also cruisers & destroyers, 2,545 men, 3rd battle of Ypres, **June 2.** Lord Kitchener drowned when Hampshire sunk off Orkneys **June 5.** Battle of the Somme, **July 1-10;** second battle **July 11-Aug. 3.** Rumania joined Allies **Aug. 16,** was defeated by January, 1917. U. S. **Nov. 29** protested deportation of Belgian workers into Germany.

On **Dec. 12,** 1916, Germany and its allies called for peace negotiations, to halt bloodshed. Germany told the Vatican it was fighting for the integrity of its frontiers and development in peaceful competition. On **Dec. 18, 1916,** President Wilson asked the belligerents to state their aims and terms; in order to end rival leagues he asked formation of a league of nations and protection of "weak peoples." The Allies called the German offer "empty and insincere." They also told President Wilson they wanted "restorations, reparations, indemnities."

1917—U. S. Enters War

When Germany began unrestricted submarine war United States **Feb. 3** broke relations, refused negotiations until order was rescinded. Wilson **Feb. 26** asked Congress to order arming of merchant ships; when Senate refused Wilson armed them by executive order **Mar. 12.** Intercepted note of Ger. foreign secy. Zimmerman to Ger. minister in Mexico suggested Mexico be asked to enter war to recover U. S. Southwest, **Feb. 28.** U. S. declared war on Germany **Apr. 6,** adopted selective conscription **May 18,** registered men aged 21-30 **June 5.** First of American Expeditionary Force (AEF) landed in France **June 26;** Gen. John J. Pershing, c.-in-c., Adm. Wm. S. Sims, chief Naval Operations, Europe. U. S. declared war on Austria-Hungary **Dec. 7.**

Collapse of Russian Empire. When Navy and Army revolted **Mar. 11-15** Czar Nicholas II abdicated. Provisional govt. made Kerensky premier **July 20.** Offensive in

Galicia failed. **Apr.** Germans moved Lenin and associates from Switzerland to Russia via Sweden to disrupt war. Bolshevists overthrew Kerensky **Nov. 7,** formed socialist republic of workers and peasants with Lenin president of Council of Commissars. Armistice **Dec. 15,** made peace with Germany, Austria-Hungary, Bulgaria and Turkey at Brest-Litovsk **Mar. 3, 1918,** withdrawing from Lithuania, Estonia, Latvia, Ukraine, Poland, Finland, Aland Isls., Erivan, Kars, Batum.

Other Fronts. Huge losses by Allies at Vimy, Arras, Cambrai, Passchendaele, Verdun. Petain succeeded Nivelle as French c.-in-c. British took Jaffa, Baghdad, Jerusalem. Germans forced back Italians to Piave, Brenta; sank many ships.

1918—Victory for U. S. & Allies

German submarine war, **Feb. 1, 1917-Feb. 1, 1918,** cost U. S. 69 ships (171,061 tons); U. S. seized 686,494 German-Austrian tonnage. British lost 1,169 ships. Allied & neutrals lost 6,617,000 tons.

President Wilson presented his 14 points for peace to Congress **Jan. 8.** Asked open diplomacy; freedom of seas; restoration of Alsace-Lorraine to France; independence for Poland and Austrian minorities; "a general association of nations" to guarantee political and economic independence.

Collapse of Russian front released German troops for powerful thrusts on West front. Battle of the Somme, **Mar. 21-Apr. 6.** Gen. Ferdinand Foch made supreme commander **Mar. 26.** Battle of the Aisne, **May 27-June 5;** AEF took Cantigny, **May 28.** Germans reached Marne, AEF fought at Chateau Thierry, Belleau Woods, Ger. retreat began **July 19.** AEF took St. Mihiel salient, **Sept. 12-20,** fought at Meuse-Argonne, **Sept. 20-Nov. 11.** British broke Hindenburg line **Sept. 27.**

Bulgaria gave up **Sept. 30,** Czar Ferdinand abdicated. Turkish armistice, **Oct. 30.** Italians defeated Austrians at Vittorio Veneto; Austria and Hungary formed separate republics **Nov. 1,** Austria surrendered **Nov. 4.**

Germans accepted President Wilson's terms and recalled submarines, **Oct. 20;** United States troops reached Sedan, **Nov. 7;** revolution in Kiel and Hamburg, **Nov. 7;** Bavaria proclaimed a republic, **Nov. 8;** Kaiser abdicated, **Nov. 9,** fled to Holland. Armistice signed in Marshal Foch's railway coach, near Compiegne, France, **Nov. 11;** bugles sounded "cease firing" at 11 a.m. German fleet surrendered to British, **Nov. 21;** AEF entered Mainz, **Dec. 6;** crossed Rhine, **Dec. 13.**

See Casualties, World War I.

1905
Russian revolution crushed by Czar Nicholas 11. Resulted in creation of Duma (parliament) to placate liberals. First meeting of Duma, **May 10; dissolved July.**
Norway dissolved union with Sweden.

1906
San Francisco Earthquake and fire, April 18-19.
Dead: 452. Loss: $350,000,000.
Harry K. Thaw, Pittsburgh millionaire, shot and killed Stanford White, famous architect, on the roof of Madison Square Garden (26th and Madison, N.Y.) **June 25,** on ground of avenging honor of wife, Evelyn Nesbit.

1907
Financial panic in the United States.
Standard Oil of Indiana fined $29,240,000 by Judge K. M. Landis in U.S. Court, Chicago, for accepting freight rebates **Apr. 3.** Set aside **July 22, 1908.** Railroads found guilty of giving rebates.
First round-world cruise of U.S. Fleet; 16 battleships, Adm. Robley D. Evans, 12,000 men.

1908
Chelsea (Mass.) destroyed by fire; loss more than $6,000,000, **April 12.**

1909
Admiral Robert E. Peary reached North Pole **April 6** on sixth attempt, accompanied by Matthew Henson, Negro, and 4 Eskimos.
Louis Bleriot flew across the English Channel, Calais to Dover, 31 mi. in 37 min., **July 25.**
Budget in Britain: "Soak the Rich" taxation financed social security measures.

1910
Boy Scouts of America incorporated **Feb. 8** following visit to England by Wm. D. Boyce, Chicago publisher; while there he met Sir Robert Baden-Powell, founder of the Scouting movement, and was inspired to take the lead in transplanting the idea to the United States.
Glenn H. Curtiss won $10,000 offered by the World, N.Y., for first continuous flight, Albany to New York, 137 mi., 152 min., **May 29.**
Dynamite explosion at Los Angeles Times Oct. 1 caused fire killing 21 in labor dispute.

1911
Italian-Turkish war began, **Sept. 29.** Italians made first use of aircraft in warfare; Libya acquired by Italy.
First transcontinental airplane flight (interrupted by landings) by C. P. Rodgers, New York to Pasadena, **Sept. 17-Nov. 5;** time in air 82 hrs., 4 mins.
Capt. Roald Amundsen, Norwegian explorer, reached South Pole, **Dec. 14.**
Mexican Revolution. Porfirio Diaz, president of Mexico since 1877 (except 1880-1884), resigned **May 25,** after successful revolt by Francisco L. Madero, who succeeded him. People living in poverty wanted restoration of communal lands (ejidos), better conditions. In 1912 Madero, supported by Gen. Huerta, put down revolts by Gens. Orozco, Reyes and Felix Diaz. In **Feb., 1913,** Reyes was killed; Huerta helped depose Madero. Madero, his brother and Vice President Suarez were murdered. President Wilson refused recognition to Huerta and "government by assassination." Venustiano Carranza, rallying Maderos, was opposed by Gen. Francisco (Pancho) Villa in north. When American sailors were arrested at Tampico, **April 9, 1914,** U.S. sent Atlantic fleet to Vera Cruz. Marines landed and snipers killed 19. Brig. Gen. Frederick Funston was sent **Apr. 27.** Huerta resigned **July 14, 1914,** Carranza occupied Mexico City **Aug. 20.** Villa, supported by Zapata, forced Carranza to leave for Vera Cruz. U.S. recognized Carranza, **Oct. 19, 1915,**

placed embargo on arms to other generals. Villa raided Santa Isabel, **Jan. 10,** killing 18; Columbus, N.M., **Mar. 9, 1916,** killed 17. Gen. John J. Pershing with 12,000 sent into Mexico **Mar. 15.** Fight at Parral, Chihuahua, **April 12.** Caranza's troops attacked **June 21.** U.S. troops withdrawn **Feb. 4, 1917.** Carranza called constitutional convention. **Feb. 15, 1917,** became legal president **May 1, 1917.** He restored some of the land, nationalized coal and oil, expropriated some foreign holdings. Discontent caused new rising and he was ambushed and killed. Obregon became president **Dec. 1, 1920.** Villa was killed in ambush at Parral, **July 20, 1923.**
Chinese Revolution led by Sun Yat-sen overthrew Manchu dynasty. Republic formed **Feb. 12, 1912;** Yuan shih-K'ai elected president, **Feb. 15.**
Parliament Act of 1911 reduced the power of British House of Lords to a suspensory veto, to delay but not deny bills.

1912
Capt. Robert F. Scott and 4 companions reached South Pole **Jan. 17;** died on return journey.
White Star liner Titanic wrecked on maiden trip, from Southampton to New York, by iceberg off Newfoundland. **April 14-15;** U.S. reported 1,517 lost; British Board of Trade reported 1,503 lost. Passengers and crew were 2,307. The ship was 882½ ft. long, and cost $7,500,000.
Herman Rosenthal, gambler, killed in New York. Four thugs convicted, executed at Sing Sing **Apr. 13, 1914.** Police Lieut. Chas. Becker, convicted of complicity, executed **July 30, 1915.**
War in Balkans, against Turkey by Montenegro, Bulgaria, Serbia and Greece, **Oct. 8-Dec. 3.**

1913
Sixteenth Amendment proclaimed in effect **Feb. 25,** empowering Congress to levy and collect income taxes.
Act creating Federal Reserve System became law **Dec. 23.**

> **1914-1918 World War I**
> See Article pages 856-857

1914
Ford Motor Co. raised basic wage rates from $2.40 for 9-hr. day to $5 for 8-hr. day, **Jan. 5.**
First ship passed through Panama Canal, Aug. 15.
Second International; Brussels meeting of International Socialist Bureau, **July.** Members included five men later heads of governments; Lenin (Russia); Ebert (German Republic): Stauning (Denmark); Branting (Sweden); MacDonald (Britain).

1915
First telephone talk, New York to San Franciso, **Jan. 25,** by Alexander Graham Bell and Thomas A. Watson.
First successful wireless from moving Lackawanna train to station, **Feb. 7.**
Twenty-one Demands presented by Japan to China. Demands asked for almost complete control of China.

1916
Gregory Rasputin, confessor to Czarina, killed in Petrograd (Leningrad) **December.**
Bomb exploded during San Francisco Preparedness Day Parade, **July 22,** killing 10, wounding 40. Thomas J. Mooney, 33, labor organizer; Mrs. Mooney, Warren K. Billings, shoe worker; Israel Weinberg and Edward D. Nolan were charged with murder. Mooney was sentenced to death, Billings to life imprisonment; others went free. President Wilson interceded for Mooney, who got life, 1918. Mooney was pardoned by Gov. C. L. Olson, **Jan. 7, 1939,** Billings freed **Oct. 16, 1939.**
Black Tom explosion at munitions docks, Jersey City, N. J., **July 39;** 2 killed, $40,000,000 damages. Traced to German saboteurs.

1917
The 18th (Prohibition) Amendment to the Constitution

was submitted to the States by Congress, **Dec. 18.** The first State (Mississippi) ratified it **Jan. 8, 1918,** and **Jan. 16, 1919,** the 36th State **(Nebraska)** ratified it, whereupon, by proclamation of the Secretary of State, **Jan. 29, 1919,** it became effective one year from that date, **Jan. 16, 1920.** By **Feb. 25, 1919,** the Legislatures of 45 States had ratified it; the 46th State, New Jersey ratified it **March 9, 1922.** It was not ratified by Connecticut and Rhode Island. The **Volstead (Prohibition Enforcement) Act** was passed by Congress **Oct., 1919,** vetoed by President Wilson, passed over his veto, in effect **Jan. 17, 1920.** New York, Montana and Wisconsin cancelled their enforcement acts by 1929. Franklin D. Roosevelt, presidential candidate, 1932, endorsed repeal; 21st amendment, repealing 18th, but guaranteeing dry states against liquor importation, became law. **Dec. 5, 1933.**

Balfour Declaration, Nov. 2, favored establishment of a national homeland in Palestine for Jewish people.

1918
Romanovs killed. Czar Nicholas of Russia, the Empress Alexandra; the daughters, Olga, Tatiana, Marie, Anastasia; the son, Alexis; Prince Dolgorolkoff, Dr. Botkin, a lady-in-waiting and a nurse were shot by Bolsheviks orders in Ekaterinburg, July 16, in Perm, also, July 12, the Bolshevists assassinated the Czar's brother, Grand Duke Michael, and in Alapalievsky north of Ekaterinburg, they killed the Grand Duke Sergius Mikhailovitch, Igor Constantinovich and Ivan Constantinovich.

Influenza epidemic killed estimated 20,000,000 throughout world, 548,000 Americans.

1919
Rosa Luxemburg and Karl Liebknecht, leading German Communists and founders of the Spartacus Party, shot and killed **Jan.,** by soldiers who were taking them to prison.

Peace conference opened in Paris, **Jan. 18;** treaty signed in palace at Versailles **June 28,** between German representatives and Allied powers and U. S. President Wilson submitted treaty to Senate **July 10.** Ratified by Germany **July 10,** Britain, **July 26,** Italy, **Oct. 7,** France, **Oct. 13,** Japan, , **Oct. 27.** Not signed by China. Rejected by U.S. Senate, **Nov. 19,** which considered American sovereignty not properly safeguarded in League of Nations. Never ratified by U. S.

In Amritsar, India, Gen. Dyer led a group of Gurkha soldiers to the entrance of a walled-in garden where a crowd was listening to anti-British speeches. Dyer had soldiers fire into crowd, killing 379 and wounding 1,208.

Three U. S. Navy seaplanes left Trepassy, Newfoundland, **May 16;** one, the NC-4, reached the Azores, **May 17;** Lisbon, **May 27;** Plymouth, England, **May 31;** Harry G. Hawker and McKenzie Grieve fell in mid-ocean on an attempted flight, **May 18,** from Newfoundland to Ireland, but were rescued; **John Alcock and A. W. Brown** made, **June 14-15,** a non-stop air flight from Newfoundland to Ireland; a British dirigible, R-34, left Scotland, **July 2,** and descended in Mineola, N.Y., **July 6.** It left for England, **July 10,** and arrived there **July 13.** A round-trip transcontinental air race, New York to San Francisco, was won by **Lt. W. B. Maynard and Lt. Alex Pearson, Oct. 8-18.**

1920
League of Nations began at Geneva, Switzerland, **Jan. 10;** dissolved **Jan. 10, 1946.**

Nicola Sacco, 29, shoe factory employee and radical agitator, and **Bartolomeo Vanzetti,** 32, fish peddler and anarchist, accused of killing two men in payroll holdup at South Braintree, Mass., **Apr. 15.** Found guilty 1921, they became objects of six-year campaign for release on grounds of want of conclusive evidence and prejudice of court. Appeals failing, they were executed at Charlestown, Mass., prison **Aug. 22, 1927.** Trial sharply criticized by Wickersham Commission on law procedure.

Wall St., New York City, bomb explosion, killed 30; injured 100; did $2,000,000 damage. **Sept. 16.**

1921
Joint Congressional resolution declaring peace with Germany and Austria signed **July 2** by President Harding. Treaty signed **Aug. 25,** ratified by Senate **Oct. 18.**

Limitation of Armaments Conference met in Washington, **Nov. 12, 1921-Feb. 6, 1922.** U. S., Britain, France, Italy, Japan agreed to curtail naval construction. Nine powers outlawed poison gas and restricted submarine attack on merchantmen. U. S. , Britain, France, Japan agreed on integrity of China. Ratified **Aug. 5, 1925.**

1922
Roof of Knickerbocker (movie) Theatre collapsed in Washington, D. C., **Jan. 28;** 98 dead.

Violence during coal-mine strike at Herrin, Ill., **June 22-23** cost 36 lives, 21 non-union miners.

Fascist march on Rome, **Oct. 30; Mussolini's power in** Italy began.

1923
Occupation of Ruhr by French and Belgian troops to enforce reparations began **Jan. 11.**

First sound-on-film moving pictures "Phonofilm" was shown by Lee de Forest at Rivoli Theatre, New York, N. Y. beginning **April.**

Beer Hall Putsch in Munich, led by Gen. Ludendorff and Adolf Hitler **Nov. 8-9.** Several supporters killed in street clashes. Lundendorff was arrested and paroled; Hitler was wounded. He was arrested **Nov. 12** and imprisoned at Landsberg, where he wrote Mein Kampf.

1924
Dawes Reparation Plan accepted by Allies and Germany, in London, **Aug. 16:** Owen D. Young put in charge. French troops began evacuation of the Ruhr **Aug. 18.**

Nellie Tayloe Ross elected Governor of Wyoming **Nov. 9** after death of her husband **Oct. 2;** installed **Jan. 5, 1925;** first woman so honored. Miriam (Ma) Ferguson elected Governor of Texas **Nov. 9;** installed **Jan. 20, 1925.**

1925
Floyd Collins unable to extricate himself from Sand Cave, near Cave City, Ky., which he discovered, died within 300 ft. of entrance, **Feb.**

John T. Scopes, in court in Dayton, Tenn., was found guilty of having taught evolution in the local high school and was fined $100 and costs, **July 24.** William Jennings Bryan, chief counsel for prosecution, died in Dayton **July 26.** Clarence Darrow, chief defense counsel, died **March 13, 1938.** Scopes died **Oct. 21, 1970.** The last law prohibiting teaching evolution in U.S. public schools was ruled unconstitutional by the Mississippi Supreme Court **Dec. 2, 1970.**

Pickwick Club, Boston, collapsed **July 4,** killing 44.

By treaty of Locarno, Oct. 16, Germany agreed to demilitarization of Rhineland and security of Franco-German and Belgo-German frontiers.

1926
Dr. Robert H. Goddard demonstrated the practicality of rockets **Mar. 16** at Auburn, Mass., with the first liquid fuel rocket flight; the rocket traveled 184 feet in 2.5 seconds.

General strike paralyzed Britain May 3 to 12. Parliament passed act making general strike criminal conspiracy against nation.

Germany admitted to the League of Nations Sept. 8. Locarno treaties with Germany (1925) went into effect, **Sept. 14.**

1927
600 U. S. Marines sent to Nicaragua, Jan. 6, to protect U. S. interests. Withdrawn **1933.**

1,000 U. S. Marines landed in China, Mar. 5, to protect property in civil war. U. S. and British consulates looted by Nationalists **Mar. 24.**

Albert Snyder, art editor, killed **Mar. 20,** by his wife, Ruth Brown Snyder, and Henry Judd Gray, corset salesmen. Both confessed and were executed at Sing Sing, **Jan. 12, 1928.**

Capt. Chas. A. Lindbergh, U. S. air mail pilot, left Roosevelt Field, L. I., N. Y., at **7:52 A.M. May 20** alone in monoplane, Spirit of St. Louis, competing for Raymond Orteig's offer of $25,000 for first New York-Paris nonstop flight. Reached Le Bourget air field, Paris, 5:21

P.M. (10:21 P.M. Paris time) **May 21;** 3,610 miles in 33 hrs. 29 mins., 30 secs. Returned on cruiser Memphis, U.S.N., with plane; welcomed by President Coolidge in Washington, **June 11,** with rank of colonel. Tremendous demonstration, New York, **June 13.**

The Jazz Singer, Al Jolson, demonstrated part-talking pictures in New York City **Oct. 6.**

1928

The St. Francis water-supply dam, 40 miles north of Los Angeles, Calif., collapsed; 450 lives lost, 700 houses swept away, **March 13.**

First all-talking picture, Lights of New York, presented at Strand, N.Y. City, **July 6.**

Times Square subway wreck, N.Y. City (IRT line) **Aug. 24,** killed 18, injured 97.

Kellogg-Briand Peace Pact signed, **Aug. 27,** by 62 nations. Condemned the use of war as an instrument of national policy.

Principal Events of World War II, 1939-1945;

Major Belligerents–Germany (Adolf Hitler, Fuehrer) invaded Poland Sept. 1, 1939; Norway and Denmark, April 9, 1940; the Netherlands, Belgium and Luxemburg, May 10, 1940. King Leopold of Belgium surrendered 500,000 May 28. Occupied France (Vichy) signed an armistice with Germany June 22, 1940. Germany invaded Russia June 22, 1941, unoccupied France and Italy Nov. 11, 1942, surrendered unconditionally to Great Britain, the United States and the USSR at Reims, France, May 7, 1945 (May 6 EST). War with Germany formally declared ended by Britain, France, Australia, New Zealand, July 9, 1951; by U. S. Oct. 19, 1951.

Great Britain declared war on Germany Sept. 3, 1939, as did Australia and New Zealand. Union of South Africa declared war Sept. 6; Canada, Sept. 10, 1939. Britain declared war on Italy June 11, 1940; on Finland, Hungary and Rumania, Dec. 7, 1941; on Japan, Dec. 8, 1941; on Bulgaria, Dec. 13, 1941; on Thailand, Jan. 25, 1942.

France declared war on Germany Sept. 3, 1939; on Italy June 11, 1940. Free French (De Gaulle) declared war on Japan Dec. 8, 1941.

Italy (Benito Mussolini, Duce) declared war on Great Britain and France June 10, 1940; on the U. S., Dec. 11, 1941. Surrendered unconditionally Sept.8, 1943. Declared war against Germany Oct. 13, 1943, against Japan July 14, 1945. Signed treaty of peace, Feb. 10, 1947, in Paris, with Britain, France, U. S. and USSR.

Japan invaded French Indo-China Sept. 22, 1940; attacked Pearl Harbor naval station and the Philippines by air Dec. 7, 1941 and declared war on the United States, Great Britain, Australia, Canada, New Zealand and the Union of South Africa, Dec. 7, 1941; on the Netherlands, Jan. 11, 1942. Japan accepted the Allied terms unconditionally Aug. 14, 1945; signed surrender terms Sept. 1, 1945 (Sept. 2, Tokyo time) on board U. S. S. Missouri; signed treaty of peace with all big powers except USSR and a total of 49 nations at San Francisco, Sept. 8, 1951.

Union of Soviet Socialist Republics (Russia) signed nonaggression pact with Germany, Aug., 1939; invaded Poland, Sept. 17, 1939, and Finland, Nov. 30, 1939. Signed peace with Finland Mar. 12, 1940. Finland declared war on Russia June 25, 1941. Russia was invaded by Germany and Rumania, June 22, 1941. Signed armistice with Finland, Sept. 19, 1944, peace treaty, Feb. 10, 1947. Signed peace treaty with Poland July 30, 1941. Declared war on Japan Aug. 8, 1945, effective Aug. 9. Signed treaties of peace with Italy, Hungary, Rumania, Bulgaria, and Finland Feb. 10, 1947. Did not sign treaty of peace with Japan.

U. S. declared·war on Japan Dec. 8, 1941. Germany and Italy declared war on U.S. Dec. 11, 1941. A few hours later U.S. declared war on Germany and Italy. Also Bulgaria, Hungary and Rumania, June 5, 1942; signed peace treaties with Italy, Bulgaria, Hungary and Rumania Feb. 10, 1947; with Japan Sept. 8, 1951. War against the U.S. also was declared by Albania, the Japanese puppet states of Burma, Manchukuo, and Nanking; Croatia, Slovakia and Thailand. Britain and France ended war with Germany July 9, 1951; U.S. ended it Oct. 19, 1951.

Retreat from Dunkirk by British Expeditionary Force took place May 26-June 4, 1940, when 900 vessels took 338,226 troops across the English Channel, 26,175 of them French.

Nazi bombing of Britain began July 10, 1940 and reached its height Sept. 7, Oct. 15 and Dec. 29. Coventry was damaged Nov. 14; Birmingham Nov. 19-22. Many London churches were burned Dec. 29. Desperate attacks on German aircraft by RAF stopped threat of invasion. Of this defense Prime Minister Churchill said: "Never in the field of human conflict was so much owed by so many to so few."

Pearl Harbor. Over 100 Japanese planes and several midget submarines attacked U. S. Pacific fleet (86 ships) anchored at Pearl Harbor, Hawaii, Dec. 7, 1941. (7:55 A. M., Hawaiian time; 1:25 P.M. EST.) Totally lost, Battleship Arizona. Severely damaged, Battleships Oklahoma, Nevada, California, West Virginia, 3 destroyers, 1 target ship, 1 minelayer. Damaged and repaired: Battleships Pennsylvania, Maryland, Tennessee; cruisers, Helena, Honolulu, Raleigh; 1 seaplane tender, 1 repair vessel, 1 drydock. Airplanes lost, Navy 80; Army 97. Japan lost 28 planes to the Navy, 20 to the Army and 3 submarines of 45 tons each. Casualties: Navy, 2,117 officers and men killed, 960 missing, 876 wounded; Army, 226 officers and men killed, 396 wounded.

Planes Over Tokyo. Lt. Col. James H. Doolittle, with 16 B-25s and 79 pilots and crewmen, took off Apr. 18, 1942 from Carrier Hornet, 688 mi. from Tokyo by sea; 13 planes dropped 500-lb. bombs on Tokyo, 2 on Nagoya, 1 on Kobe. Eight airmen were captured off China coast; 3 were shot, others imprisoned. Total dead, 9. One plane landed near Vladivostok and was interned by Russians; the crew escaped to Iran, but plane was never returned.

Loss and Recapture of Philippines–Japanese aircraft bombed Manila and environs Dec. 8, 1941, Far Eastern Time, destroyed 12 B-17s and damaged 5 at Clark Field. Gen. Douglas MacArthur had 15,000 U. S. troops, 40,000 in Philippine Army and 100,000 Filipino reservists. Manila and Cavite were taken by Japan (Homma) Jan. 2, 1942. Maj. Gen. Jonathan M. Wainwright commanded at Bataan, which was attacked by 200,000 Japanese Jan. 10. U. S. shot down 168 Japanese planes by Feb. 18; U. S. Army Air Force sank 3 troopships in Subic Bay, Mar. 4. Gen. MacArthur, ordered to Australia, reached Darwin Mar. 17, vowed, "I shall return." Wainwright defended Bataan until Apr. 8, 1942, sent 3,500 to Corregidor. Japan took 35,000 U. S. and Filipino troops prisoner, including 5,000 Marines, forced them into prison via the "Death March" of Bataan. Wainwright surrendered Corregidor May 6 with 11,574 troops, Gen. MacArthur returned to the Philippines near Palo on Leyte, with President Osmena, Oct. 20, 1944. Land, naval, and air action by 738 ships, 193,841 troops defeated Japanese. U.S. entered Luzon via Lingayen gulf Jan. 9, 1945. Manila was taken Feb. 3; Corregidor reoccupied Feb. 16-Mar. 1.

Germany attacked the Soviet Union June 22, 1941; took Minsk, Smolensk, Kiev, Kharkov, Orel; besieged Leningrad, fought a terrible battle in the ruins of Stalingrad August, 1942, and extended the Nazi lines to the Black Sea, Tide turned in Nov., 1942; the Russians encircled Stalingrad and the Nazi army there surrendered Jan. 31, 1943. As Russian power increased and the Nazis weakened the Germans were pushed back until the Russians reached the Oder Feb., 1945.

North African coast fight began Aug. 6, 1941, when Marshal Graziani led the Italians against the British with some success. The first counteroffensive in December relieved Tobruk, where British had held out 8 mos. The British pushed the Nazis under Rommel back to El Aghelia, but Rommel regained the lost ground. He captured Tobruk with its garrison of 25,000 British June 21, 1942, and pushed the British back to within 70 mi. of Alexandria. On Oct. 23, the British, heavily reinforced and under Lt. Gen. Bernard L. Montgomery, attacked Rommel at El Alamein and defeated the Nazi-Italians with heavy losses all the way to Tunisia.

Dirigible Graf Zeppelin, Capt. Hugo Eckner, with 20 passengers and 38 crew, flew from Friedrichshafen, Germany to Lakehurst, N. J., Oct. 11-15; returned Oct. 29-31. Made round the world trip from Friedrichshafen with 20 passengers, Aug. 14-Sept. 4, 1929, via Tokyo, Los Angeles, Lakehurst, N. J.

Arnold Rothstein, N. Y. gambler, died of gun shots Nov. 6; killer never found.

Stalin issued first 5 year plan: Rapid, ruthless industri-alization of Russian economy.

1929

"St. Valentine's Day massacre" in Chicago Feb. 14, when gangsters killed 7 rivals.

The Papal State, extinct since 1870, revived as State of Vatican City, at Rome June 7.

U.S. Paper money ⅓ smaller in size went into circulation July 10.

Albert B. Fall, former Secretary of the Interior was

Summary of Aerial Naval and Military Actions

North African expedition by U. S. and Britain landed 150,000 American and 140,000 British troops on French North Africa Nov. 8, 1942 (Nov. 7 EST), with Lt. Gen. Dwight D. Eisenhower, C. in C. French resisted briefly at Oran, Algiers and Casablanca and Vichy govt. broke relations with U. S. The Allies began campaign against Italy be seizing Pantelleria Island June 11, 1943. U. S. 7th Army under Maj. Gen. Geo. S. Patton, Jr., and British-Canadian 8th Army landed on Sicily July 10. Mussolini was forced to resign July 25 and escaped to German lines Sept. 12. The Italian mainland was invaded and Italy surrendered Sept. 8, 1943, but heavy fighting with Nazis followed and they were not dislodged until spring of 1945.

Battle of the Coral Sea, May, 1942, took heavy toll of ships and planes on both sides, was first battle fought by naval planes from ships that had neither sight nor range of enemy. U. S. lost 66 planes, 543 men; Japan lost 80 planes, 900 men. Battle of Midway, June 3-6, 1942, U. S. lost 1 carrier (Yorktown), 1 destroyer, 150 planes, 307 men; Japan lost 4 carriers, 253 planes, 3,500 men.

Guadalcanal, in the southern Solomon Islands, site of a Japanese air base that threatened the Allied position in the southwest Pacific, was assaulted by U. S. Marines Aug. 7, 1942. In one of the most costly Allied Pacific campaigns, several major naval engagements, dozens of air battles and much bitter ground fighting followed before the island was finally won by the Allies in January, 1943. Two Marine divisions, two Army divisions and an additional Army regiment were committed to the fight by the United States before the issue was decided.

Battle for Leyte Gulf, biggest naval action ever fought, occurred Oct. 22-27, 1944, in three engagements destroying Japanese naval power. Battles were fought in Surigao strait, off Samar and off Cape Engano. Ships engaged, U. S. 166, Japanese 65. Airplanes, U. S. 1,280, Japanese 716. Losses for Philippine campaign–Japan: 3 large carriers, 3 light carriers, 1 escort carrier, 4 battleships, 14 cruisers, 32 destroyers, 11 submarines, total 68. U. S.: 1 light carrier, 3 escort carriers, 6 destroyers, 3 destroyer escorts, 1 high-speed transport, 7 submarines, total 21. U. S. lost 1 ship to a kamikaze (suicide) plane at Leyte and 5 in subsequent actions. Total airplane losses for Philippine campaign, October, 1944 through January, 1945: Japan (est.) 7,000, (722 kamikaze); U. S. 967.

D-Day: Invasion of France–Invasion of France by Allies, June 6, 1944. 1,000 planes and gliders dropped paratroopers on Contentin peninsula, Normandy, 5 a.m. London time. 1,000 R.A.F., 1,400 U. S. bombers attacked installations. First assault troops landed 6:30 a.m. on beaches along line Carentan-Bayeux-Caen; U. S. on West, British-Canadians on East. Total Allied strength available 2,876,439, including 17 British divisions of which 3 Canadian; 20 U. S. divisions, 1 French, 1 Polish. Also available 5,049 fighter planes, 3,467 heavy bombers, 1,645 light and medium bombers, 2,316 transport aircraft, 2,591 gliders, 698 others; 835 L.C.T., 233 L.S.T. Beachhead 60 mi. long, 10 mi. deep.

Gen. Dwight D. Eisenhower was Supreme Commander of Allied Expeditionary Forces: Gen. Sir Bernard L. Montgomery commander of Allied assault troops; Sir Bertram Ramsay of Allied naval units (4,000 ships of all kinds); Air Marshal Trafford Leigh-Mallory of Air Forces; Lt. Gen. Omar N. Bradley of U. S. troops in field. Germans had available 65 divisions, including reserves extending back to Germany. Marshal Gunther von Kluge was German commander in France.

British took Bayeux June 7; Carentan fell June 13; U. S. took Cherbourg June 27; British-Canadians took Caen July 9 after desperate fighting. Lt. Gen. George S. Patton Jr. with 3rd U. S. Army attacked south and west of St. Lo Aug. 1. Canadians took Falaise Aug. 17. The Argentan gap was closed by the 3rd Army in terrible fighting. Germans lost 12 to 14 divisions in the Falaise pocket.

Aug. 14-15, 1944, Allies invaded France east of the mouth of the Rhone with 1,000 ships (641 U. S., 316 British). On Aug. 25 the 2nd French armored division and token force of U. S. Army entered Paris.

The Ardennes Bulge was a violent counter-attack by 10 German divisions under Gen. Model (Gen. Von Rundstedt C. in C.) launched Dec. 16, 1944. By Dec. 19 the 1st U. S. Army was pushed out of Germany and the Germans penetrated 60 mi. west of Celles. Lt. Gen. Patton's 3rd U. S. Army rescued besieged Americans at Bastogne Dec. 21 and Nazi drive was stopped by Dec. 25. Allies wiped out the Bulge by Jan. 31, 1945. Near Malmedy Germans cut down captured American soldiers with machine guns and left them dead on the field. U. S. losses estimated at 40,000; Germans 220,000 dead and prisoners.

Rhine Crossing–On Mar. 7, 1945, the 9th Armored Div., 3rd Corps, First Army, found Ludendorff bridge at Remagen on the Rhine intact; Gen. Eisenhower ordered Gen. Omar N. Bradley to put 5 divisions across; on 5th day Army ceased using bridge, used Treadway floating bridge, built in 10 hrs., 11 min.; Remagen bridge collapsed Mar. 17.

Iwo Jima assaulted by U. S. joint expeditionary force Feb. 19, 1945, with land action by U. S. Marines; invasion used 495 ships, including 17 aircraft carriers and 1,170 planes. U. S. troops engaged, 111,308, of which 75,144 were assault troops. Island was conquered by Mar. 16. U. S. lost 4,590 killed; Japanese deaths est. over 20,000.

Okinawa, principal Japanese base in the Ryukyu group, was invaded Apr. 1, 1945 in the final land campaign of the war. The troops used 1,300 vessels, including airplane carriers. After 83 days of fighting the end was signaled by the formal suicide of the two Japanese generals. U. S. men engaged up to June 30, 1945 reached 176,491 army, 88,500 Marines, 18,000 Navy. Japanese strength at start was 77,199. U. S. losses were 49,151 of which 12,520 were killed or missing, 36,631 wounded. The Japanese lost 110,071 killed, wounded and 7,400 prisoners.

U. S. lost 763 aircraft; Japan lost 7,830 of which 1,020 were destroyed on the ground. U. S. had 36 ships sunk, 369 damaged; Japan had 16 sunk, including the Yamato, world's largest battleship, full load displacement 72,809 tons, 861 ft. long, 9 18-in. guns, 3,333 personnel. Hit by over 10 aerial torpedoes at Kyushu; 300 survived.

V-E Day–German armies began surrendering May 4, 1945. Unconditional surrender signed May 7 at 2:41 a.m., French time, in Rheims Hq., designating cessation of operations May 9 at 12:01 a.m., London time (May 8, 6:01 p.m., Eastern U. S. War Time). Surrender also signed in Berlin. May 8 celebrated as V-E Day.

Atomic Bombs–First atomic bomb ever used in war was dropped by U. S. plane Aug. 6, 1945, on Hiroshima, Japan (pop. 343,969). Second U. S. bomb dropped on Nagasaki (pop. 252,630) Aug. 9, 1945. Estimates of dead from bombs and radiation exposure vary: Hiroshima, 80,000 to over 200,000; Nagasaki, 39,000 to 74,000. Japan surrendered Aug. 14. Formal surrender aboard U.S.S. Missouri Sept. 2, 1945, Far Eastern Time, celebrated as V-J Day.

Consult Index for additional listings under World War II.

convicted of accepting a bribe of $100,000 from Edward L. Doheny in the leasing of the Elks Hills (Teapot Dome) naval oil reserve. He was sentenced Nov. 1, to $100,000 fine and a year in prison. He died Nov. 30, 1944.

Stock Market crash Oct. 29 marked end of postwar prosperity when 16,000,000 shares changed hands, including unrestricted short selling. Decline in value estimated at $15,000,000,000 by end of 1929; stock losses, 1929-1931, estimated at $50,000,000,000. Worst American depression began.

1930

London Naval Reduction Treaty signed by U. S., Britain, Italy, France and Japan, **April 22;** in effect **Jan. 1, 1931.** Provided for the proportional reduction of the navies of each country. Its terms expired **Dec. 31, 1936.**

Joseph F. Crater, a justice of the State Supreme Court in New York City, vanished **Aug. 6.**

1931

British Parliament enacted Statute of Westminster, giving legal status to declaration of Imperial Conference of 1926 proclaiming Britain and the dominions, including Canada, completely equal "in no way subordinate one to another."

Knute Rockne, Notre Dame football coach was killed in plane crash near Bazaar, Kans., **March 31.**

Mukden Incident occurred, **Sept. 18,** when Japanese troops attacked Mukden garrison and then overran Manchuria. China protested to League of Nations.

1932

Japanese Buddhist priest slain in Shanghai, **Jan. 15.** Japan used incident to land marines. **Jan. 27.**

Manchuria became Manchukuo (Japanese puppet State). **Feb. 18;** Henry Pu Yi, Manchu emperor who abdicated in 1912, installed as ruler, **Mar. 9,** at Changchun, called Hsingching.

Charles A. Lindbergh, Jr., kidnapped for ransom **Mar. 1.**

Bonus March on Washington, **May 29,** by World War I veterans demanding Congress pay their bonus in full. Army disbanded the marchers on President Hoover's orders.

James J. Walker resigned Sept. 1 as mayor of New York City, thus ending inquiry into corruption in conduct of his office before Gov. F. D. Roosevelt by a state legislative committee under Samuel Seabury. Walker died **Nov. 18. 1946,** 66.

1933

Adolf Hitler, German Chancellor, **Jan. 30.**

All banks in the United States were ordered closed by President Roosevelt **March 6.**

First "fireside chat" broadcast by President F.D. Roosevelt, **March 12.**

German Reichstag building, Berlin, destroyed **Feb. 27** by fire believed set by Nazis. Marinus van der Lubbe, Dutch Communist, found guilty; beheaded **Jan. 10, 1934,** in Leipzig.

Spain, by Parliamentary edict, **May 17,** disestablished the Church.

Germany, Oct. 14, quit the League of Nations and withdrew from the disarmament conference.

President Roosevelt accorded diplomatic recognition to the Soviet Union, **Nov. 16.**

Prohibition ended in the United States as Utah, 36th State, ratified 21st Amendment to Constitution, **Dec. 5,** repealing 18th (prohibition).

1934

Bank robbers John Dillinger, Charles Makley, Russell Clark and Harry Pierpont captured in Tucson, Ariz., **Jan. 25** with $36,000. Dillinger was jailed at Crown Point, Ind., and the others at Lima, O. Dillinger and Herbert Youngblood escaped **Mar. 3,** Dillinger was shot to death **July 22,** outside a movie house in Chicago by FBI agents. Youngblood was killed **Mar. 16** in Port Huron, Mich.

The Dionne sisters, first quintuplets to survive beyond infancy, were born **May 28** in Callender, Ont., Canada; to Mr. and Mrs. Oliva Dionne.

Englebert Dollfuss, 41, chancellor of Austria, was shot

to death by Nazi conspirators **July 25.**

President von Hindenburg of Germany died **Aug. 2. Adolf Hitler** consolidated offices of president and chancellor, became Fuehrer.

Long March by Chinese Communists started **Oct. 1.** Mao Tse-tung led 100,000 in 6,000-mile trek from south to north China; only 20,000 completed journey and reached Yenan, **Oct., 1935.**

Italy refused to arbitrate disputes on Italian Somaliland border between Italian and Ethiopian troops, demanded reparations, apology, **Dec. 19.**

1935

Hitler rejected Versailles Treaty, ordered conscription in Germany **Mar. 10.**

Will Rogers, 56, comedian, and Wiley Post, 36, aviator, were killed **Aug. 15** when Post's airplane crashed in a fog near Point Barrow, Alaska.

Social Security Act passed by Congress **Aug. 14.**

Ethiopia appealed to League of Nations against Italy. Italy invaded Ethiopia **Oct. 2-4.** Economic sanctions against Italy went into effect **Nov. 18,** supported by 52 nation-members of the League of Nations, and by one non-member, Egypt. The sanctions ended **July 15, 1936.**

1936

King George V, 70, died, Jan. 20 on his estate at Sandringham, England, and was succeeded by his eldest son, Prince of Wales, 42, who took the title of King Edward VIII. He abdicated Dec. 11, 1936, and was succeeded by his brother, the Duke of York, who became King George VI. The ex-ruler was created Duke of Windsor with the title of His Royal Highness which was not extended to his wife. He gave up the throne, he said, because he could not marry "the woman I love," Mrs. Wallis Warfield of Baltimore, Md., who, **Oct. 27,** obtained a divorce in Ipswich, Eng., from Ernest A. Simpson, an insurance agent. The decree became absolute **May 3, 1937.** The couple was married **June 3, 1937,** in Monts, France.

Reoccupation of demilitarized Rhineland zone, in violation of the Locarno pact, begun by German troops **Mar. 7.**

Emperor Haile Selassie of Ethiopia escaped Italian advance by boarding British cruiser for Palestine, **May 1.** Premier Mussolini of Italy announced end of war **May 5,** proclaimed annexation of Ethiopia with King Victor Emmanuel Emperor.

Adolf Hitler signed treaty with Austria **July 11** guaranteeing Austrian frontier.

Revolt against Spain's Republican Government began **July 17** in Morocco and spread to Spain, included much of the Army and Air Force and half of the Navy; Jose Giral became Loyalist premier; **July 18,** Loyalists defeated insurgents in Madrid and **July 19** Insurgents gained control in Cadiz, Huelva, Seville, Cordoba and Granada; Insurgents set up own government **July 24;** Insurgents took Badakoj **Aug. 16;** began aerial bombing of Madrid **Aug. 24;** captured Irun **Sept. 4;** took San Sebastian and Toledo, **Sept. 12;** Gen. Francisco Franco proclaimed head of the Nationalist (Insurgent) government, **Oct. 1;** seige of Madrid begun by Insurgents, **Oct. 21;** Loyalist Government moved from Madrid to Valencia, **Nov. 6.**

Japan and Germany signed an anti-Comintern pact **Nov. 25.** Italy joined **Nov. 6, 1937.**

1937

Spanish insurgents took Malaga **Feb. 8.** Warships of Great Britain, France, Italy and Germany, **March 13,** began to police the coasts of Spain under the 27-nation neutrality agreement. Gen. Franco, **Apr. 19,** set up a one-party state, dissolving the Fascist and Carlist organizations. New Loyalist Government formed **May 17** under Premier Juan Negrin; Loyalists shifted government to Barcelona, **Oct. 28;** Insurgents proclaimed blockade of all Loyalist ports **Nov. 28.**

The Army-supported Japanese Cabinet of Hayashi resigned **May.** Fighting in China, west of Peiping, was renewed by Japanese, **July;** Tungchow was attacked **July 27;** the Japanese **July 29,** bombed Tientsin, destroying Nankai University; **Aug. 9,** they took formal possession of Peiping; **Aug. 11,** they landed marines at Shanghai and shelled Nankow. Nanking, Canton, and many other places in the eastern provinces of China were attacked by Japanese planes. **Oct. 23,** Suiyuan Province declared independence from China. The Chinese abandoned Shanghai and the Japanese took control **Nov. 8.** Premier Chiang Kai-shek moved to Hankow **Dec. 12.**

Japanese bombs sank the U. S. gunboat Panay, Dec. 12, with loss of two lives; and several American oil carriers (the captain of one died) on the Yangtze river above Nanking. The Japanese apologized and paid indemnity.

Hitler repudiated war guilt clause of Versailles Treaty, **Jan. 30.** Treaty blamed Germany for World War I. Hitler stated that from this time onward Germany was free from obligations imposed upon her by the Treaty.

Amelia Earhart Putnam, aviator, and co-pilot lost **July 2** near Howland Isl. in the Pacific.

Italy gave notice Dec. 11 of withdrawal from the League of Nations.

1938

Spanish insurgent planes from Majorca began daily bombing of Barcelona **Jan. 16.** Insurgent cruiser, Baleares, sunk off Cartagena **March 6** by Loyalist forces; air raids killed 1,000 in Barcelona **March 7;** insurgents took Lerida; they reached the sea at Lerida cutting Loyalist Spain in two, **April 15.** Italy began token withdrawal of 10,000 troops, **Oct. 10;** Insurgents began final campaign **Dec. 23** against Barcelona, which fell **Jan. 26, 1939.**

Hitler invaded Austria March 11. After resignation of Chancellor Kurt von Schuschnigg and President Wilhelm Miklas, **March 13,** the new Chancellor, Arthur Seyss-Inquart, proclaimed the political and geographic union of Germany and Austria. This was ratified by a popular vote, excluding Jews, in Austria, **April 10.** The Italian Grand Council, headed by Premier Benito Mussolini, voted approval.

Mexico nationalized oil industry, **Mar. 18.**

Douglas G. Corrigan of Los Angeles, flew from Brooklyn to Dublin **July 17-18.** Having no permit or passport, he jokingly said he flew the "wrong way."

At a conference in Munich, Bavaria, Britain and France yielded **Sept. 30** to Nazi demands for the cession of the Sudetenland to Germany by Czechoslovakia, thus ending a 15-day international crisis during which British Prime Minister Neville Chamberlain made two flying visits to Chancellor Adolf Hitler. Premier Mussolini of Italy backed Hitler's territorial demands. Hitler signed a "Peace Declaration" with Britain, **Sept. 30,** occupied Sudetenland **Oct. 1-10.** President Roosevelt asked Hitler to preserve the peace. Eduard Benes, president of Czechoslovakia, resigned **Oct. 5.**

About 4,000 sq. mi. of Czech land was awarded to Hungary **Nov. 2** by German-Italian arbitrators (For. Mins. Joachim von Ribbentrop and Galeazzo Ciano) meeting in Vienna. The area was populated by Hungarians and contained 860,000 persons. With the new cessions to Poland agreed on between Prague and Warsaw, the partition of Czechoslovakia was completed.

1939

Uranium atom was first measured in U.S. at Columbia Univ., **Jan. 25.** Later, **1940,** Uranium 235, a rare isotope, proved to be prime fissionable form of uranium.

The Loyalist Spanish government surrendered Barcelona to the Insurgents, **Jan. 26.** Madrid surrendered, **Mar. 24;** war ended **Mar. 29** with Franco victor.

The Republic of Czechoslovakia was dissolved, **March 14;** Hungarian troops seized Carpatho-Ukraine, **March 14;** Nazis occupied Bohemia and Moravia, which became a German protectorate, **March 16.** Hitler annexed Memel **March 22.**

Japanese troops in Manchukuo and Soviet and Mongol troops near Lake Bor opened 6-month border fight **May 11; 20,000** killed.

Germany and Italy signed 10-year military pact in Berlin **May 22.**

Nazi Germany and Soviet Union signed a 10-yr. non-aggression treaty **Aug. 24.**

N. Y. World's Fair opened, **Apr. 30,** closed, **Oct. 31;** reopened **May 11, 1940,** and finally closed **Oct. 21.**

President Roosevelt proclaimed a limited national emergency, **Sept. 8,** an unlimited emergency **May 27, 1941.** Both ended by President Truman, **Apr. 28, 1952.**

1939-1945 World War II
See Article Pages 860-861

1940

Finnish-Russian peace signed in Moscow **Mar. 12.** Estonia, Latvia and Lithuania annexed by Union of Soviet Socialist Republics **July 14.**

1941

The Four Freedoms termed essential by Pres. Franklin D. Roosevelt in a speech to Congress **Jan. 6** were freedom of speech and expression, freedom of worship, freedom from want and freedom from fear.

United States Marines occupied Iceland, July 7, on invitation from that country.

The Atlantic Charter, an 8-point joint U.S.-British declaration of principles, was issued by President Roosevelt and Prime Minister Winston Churchill **Aug. 14** after conference aboard a battleship off Newfoundland.

President Roosevelt and Secretary of State Hull **Nov. 17** received special Japanese envoys, Saburo Kurusu and Admiral Nomura, for conference on the Far East.

Japan attacked U. S. fleet at Pearl Harbor Dec. 7, as first act of war. *See World War II.*

Hitler ordered policy of genocide as the "final solution" to the Jewish "problem." By end of war an estimated 4,500,000 to 6,000,000 Jews had been exterminated in Nazi concentration camps. Many other groups also suffered with the Jews.

1942

Fire swept through Cocoanut Grove, a Boston night club, **Nov. 28,** killing 491 and injuring scores.

First nuclear chain reaction (fission of uranium isotope, U-235) at Univ. of Chicago, under physicists Arthur Compton, Enrico Fermi, et al., **Dec. 2.**

1943

President Roosevelt signed June 10 the pay-as-you-go income tax bill. Starting **July 1,** wage and salary earners were subject to a 20% withholding tax.

Race riot in Detroit, June 21; 34 dead, 700 injured. Riot in Harlem section of New York; 6 Negroes killed.

1944

Deadly coal fumes from locomotive in Italian railway tunnel near Balvana, killed 521, **Mar. 2.**

Ringling Brothers and Barnum & Bailey Circus fire in Hartford, Conn., caused a stampede in the main tent; 168 killed, 487 injured, **July 6.**

1945

Yalta Conference met in the Crimea, **Feb. 3-11.** Pres. Roosevelt, Churchill, and Stalin arranged to get Russia into war against Japan.

President Roosevelt, 63, died of cerebral hemorrhage in Warm Springs, Ga., **Apr. 12.** Harry S. Truman became President. Roosevelt buried in Hyde Park, N. Y.

Mussolini caught by Partisans near Dongo on Lake Como while trying to get to Switzerland, executed **Apr. 28.**

Hitler committed suicide in ruined chancellery, Berlin, **Apr. 30.** Body burned. Goebbels and wife poisoned children, committed suicide.

United Nations Conference on International Organization of 46 nations, San Francisco, opened **Apr. 25;** closed **June 26** with address by Truman and adoption of U.N. charter.

Potsdam, Germany, conference of President Truman, Stalin and Churchill **July 17-Aug. 2.** After July 25 Attlee replaced Churchill.

First atomic bomb, produced at Los Alamos, N. M., exploded at Alamogordo, N. M., **July 16.** Bomb dropped on Hiroshima **Aug. 6;** on Nagasaki, **Aug. 9.**

United States forces entered Korea south of 38° parallel to displace Japanese, **Sept. 8.**

Gen. Douglas MacArthur took over supervision of Japan **Sept. 9.**

Vidkun Quisling, pro-Nazi premier of Norway, executed by a firing squad in Oslo, **Oct. 23.**

Nationalization of the Bank of France and four other major banks ordered by French, **Dec. 2.**

1946

The first **World War II peace treaty** was signed between Britain and Siam, **Jan. 1.**

William Joyce, "Lord Haw Haw," broadcaster for Nazis, hanged in London for treason **Jan. 3.**

The first **General Assembly** of the United Nations opened in London, **Jan. 10.**

League of Nations, Geneva, Switzerland, transfers physical assets to the United Nations, **April 18.**

Gen. Draja Mikhailovitch, leader of the Chetniks, was executed by a firing squad in Belgrade, Yugoslavia, **July 17,** for alleged treason.

Philippine Independence granted by U. S., **July 4,** Manuel Roxas elected first president of new Republic.

Twenty-two Nazi leaders convicted of war crimes **Sept. 30** by International Tribunal in Nuremberg. Eleven Nazis were sentenced to death by hanging, **Oct. 1.** No. 2 Nazi Hermann Goering committed suicide by poison in Nuremberg Prison, two hours before he was scheduled to be hanged, **Oct. 15.** The 10 other top Nazis were hanged individually. They were: Hans Frank, Wilhelm Frick, Col. Gen. Alfred Jodl, Gestapo Chief Ernst Kaltenbrunner, Field Marshal Wilhelm Keitel, Alfred Rosenberg, Fritz Sauckel, Arthur Seyss-Inquart, Julius Streicher and Foreign Minister Joachim von Ribbentrop.

Others sentenced for war crimes: Gen. Anton Dostler, Nazi, hanged in Rome, Dec. 1, 1945, for shooting 15 U. S. soldiers without trial; Jos. Kramer, "Beast of Belsen" and 10 others hanged Dec. 14, by British for atrocities at Belsen and Oswiecin concentration camps; Gen. T. Yamashita, Japanese commander in Philippines,

hanged Feb. 23, 1946; Lt. Gen. Homma who ordered Bataan death march, shot near Manila, Apr. 3, 1946; Marshal Ion Antonescu, dictator of Rumania, hanged June 1, 1946; Karl Hermann Frank, Nazi ruler in Czechoslovakia, hanged in Prague May 22 for ordering massacre of Lidice; 48 Nazi officers and guards hanged by the U. S. Army at Landsberg, Germany, May, 1947, for mass murders at Mauthausen camp.

Archbishop Aloysius Stepinac, Roman Catholic Primate of Yugoslavia, was sentenced to 16 years at hard labor for alleged collaboration with Nazis, **Oct. 11.** He was released, **Dec.,** 1951; made a Cardinal, **Jan. 12, 1952;** died **Feb. 10, 1960.**

President Truman proclaimed the cessation of hostilities of World War II, **Dec. 31.**

1947

British Labor Government took possession of coal mines, cables and wireless communications, **Jan. 1.**

Peace treaties for Hitler's European satellites, imposing $1.33 billion in reparations, signed, **Feb. 10, 1947.**

Truman Doctrine. President Truman asked Congress to appropriate $400,000,000 for aid to Greece and Turkey to combat communism, **Mar. 12.** Approved, **May 15.**

The **United Nations** Security Council voted unanimously to place under U. S. trusteeship the Pacific islands formerly mandated to Japan **April 2.**

The **Senate approved the Taft-Hartley Labor Act,** 68 to 24, **May 13.** The house concurred, **June 4,** by a vote of 320 to 79. The measure was vetoed by President Truman, **June 20,** but the House overrode the veto, 331 to 83, on the same day. The Senate overrode the veto, 68-25, **June 23.**

Proposals known later as the Marshall Plan, under which the U. S. would extend financial aid to any European countries "willing to assist in the task of recovery," were made by Secy. of State George C. Marshall in a speech **June 5** at Harvard University. Congress author-

Korean War and United States Intervention

Republic of Korea was invaded June 25, 1950 (June 24 EST) by over 60,000 North Korean troops spear-headed by over 100 Russian-built tanks. U. N. Security Council demanded cessation of hostilities and withdrawal to 38th parallel. On June 27 it asked U. N. members to help carry out its demand. President Truman, June 27, ordered Gen. of the Army Douglas MacArthur to aid South Korea and the 7th U. S. Fleet to protect Formosa against possible aggression and keep the Chinese Nationalist forces from attacking the mainland. Requested by the UN to name a commander, the President designated Gen. MacArthur July 8, 1950.

North Korean forces took Seoul, South Korean capital, June 29, U. S. ground forces entered the conflict June 30. The President termed the intervention a "police action."

The war had three phases: (1) The North Korean drive was checked by U. S. and associated troops, with help of a brilliant landing by U. S. Marines at Inchon Sept. 15. Pyongyang, North Korean capital was taken Oct. 20, U. S. 7th Division reached Manchurian border Nov. 20.

(2) Counter-attack by 200,000 Chinese Communist "volunteers", who crossed Yalu river Nov. 26, forced evacuation of 105,000 UN troops and 91,000 Korean civilians at Hungnam Dec. 24. The Chinese pushed across 38th parallel, drove 70 mi. into South Korea. The UN General Assembly, Feb. 1, named Communist China the aggressor in Korea. UN troops pushed Chinese back across parallel Apr. 3, stopped offensive by 600,000 Chinese Apr. 22-30.

(3) Removal of Gen. MacArthur from command Apr. 11, 1951, and start of negotiations for truce along 38th parallel July 10, 1951.

President Truman removed Gen. MacArthur from all Far East commands and replaced him with Gen. Matthew B. Ridgway, commander of 8th Army. MacArthur had wished to pursue Chinese across Yalu to their air depots in Manchuria and on Mar. 25 had threatened Communist China with air and naval attack. He had been

warned to clear all announcements of policy through Washington. The President opposed his views. A Senate inquiry May 3-June 27, 1951, found that MacArthur was not charged with insubordination, but had disregarded the President's order to clear policy statements through the Defense Dept.

Cease fire and Armistice talks began July 1951 and dragged on with numerous break-downs until July 27, 1953 (July 26, EST) when armistice was signed, fighting ended 12 hrs. later. A military armistice commission supervised truce; 10 joint UN-Communist teams policed demilitarized zone; Neutral Nations Supervisory Commission watched military movements in ports; voluntary repatriation of prisoners was provided and Communists had privilege of interviewing prisoners refusing repatriation. India furnished 6,000 troops as guards.

Prisoner repatriation began Aug. 6, 1953, at Panmunjom, ended Sept. 6, 1953. UN turned over 75,799 prisoners (70,150 North Koreans and 5,640 Chinese). Communists released 12,760, including 7,850 South Koreans, 3,597 Americans, 945 Britons and 228 Turks. Maj. Gen. Dean was released Sept. 4.

The troops from India departed in February, 1954. The Supervisory Commission, made up of members from Czechoslovakia, Poland, Sweden and Switzerland, was reduced one-half in Sept., 1955, on repeated complaints that the Communist members were spying in South Korea. Repeated reports indicated that the North Koreans had violated many terms of the armistice, built numerous airfields and received naval vessels. The UN Command expelled the commission from South Korea in June, 1956, on grounds that its Czech and Polish members and the North Korean government had frustrated the operation of the armistice agreement. The UN Command announced in June, 1957, that it could no longer be bound by armistice provisions controlling importation of military equipment into Korea, but would modernize UN forces "to restore the relative balance of military strength that the armistice was intended to preserve."

ized the spending in the next 3½ years of some $12 billion on Marshall Plan aid, which was credited with restoring economic health to free Europe and halting the march of Communism in those countries cooperating in the plan. The Marshall proposals set the pattern for the vast U. S. post-war program of foreign aid.

Hindu India and Moslem Pakistan, formerly part of India, gained independence from England, **Aug. 15.** Lord Louis Mountbatten was the last British Viceroy of India.

1948

British Labor govt. nationalized railways, **Jan. 1.**

Mohandas K. Gandhi, Hindu spiritual leader and champion of freedom for India, was shot and killed by a Hindu fanatic in New Delhi, **Jan. 30.** Communal rioting took the lives of nearly 100 leaders and members of the Mahasabba, politico-religious group to which Gandhi's assassin belonged. **Jan. 30-Feb. 2.**

Czechoslovakia joined the Communist block in Eastern Europe after President Benes yielded **Feb. 25** to an ultimatum to install a pro-Soviet Cabinet. He resigned, **June 7;** succeeded by Klement Gottwald, Communist. Benes died **Sept. 3.** Communists reported Jan Masaryk, Foreign Minister, committed suicide **Mar. 10.**

A land blockade of Berlin's Allied sectors was started April 1 by the Soviet Military Govt., which refused to permit U. S. and British supply trains to pass through the Soviet zone of Germany. This blockade and a Western counter-blockade were lifted Sept. 30, 1949, after British and U. S. planes had airlifted 2,343,315 tons of food and coal into West Berlin.

Charter of the Organization of American States signed **Apr. 30** at 9th International Conference of American States at Bogota, Colombia. The conference had been interrupted for a week by rioting following the assassination of Jorge Eliecer Gaitan.

The Free State of Israel was proclaimed in Tel Aviv, **May 14,** as the British evacuated Palestine. First de facto recognition came from the United States, **May 14,** and Soviet Russia, **May 17.** Chaim Weizmann elected president by the Constituent Assembly, **Feb. 14, 1949.**

The Cominform (Communist Information Bureau), at a Prague meeting **June 28,** denounced Marshal Tito and other leaders of the Yugoslav Communist party as deserters from the Marxist-Leninist doctrine.

Alger Hiss, former State Department official, was indicted in New York City, **Dec. 15,** on two perjury charges after he had denied passing secret documents to Whittaker Chambers, a former magazine editor, for transmission to a Communist spy ring. A jury failed to reach an agreement, **July 8, 1949.** His second trial, Nov. 17, 1949-Jan. 21, 1950, ended with conviction on 2 counts and a sentence of 5 years in a Federal prison. Appeals to higher courts were rejected, and Hiss began his sentence Mar. 22, 1951. He denied all charges. He petitioned Federal Court, New York, for retrial on basis of new evidence of "forgery by typewriter," Jan. 24, 1952. Judge H. W. Goddard denied it, July 22, 1952, Supreme Court on Apr. 27, 1953. He was released **Nov. 27, 1954.**

Former Premier Hideki Tojo and six other Japanese war leaders were hanged in Tokyo, **Dec. 23,** as war criminals.

Joseph Cardinal Mindszenty, Roman Catholic primate of Hungary, arrested by Communist government in Budapest on charges of treason, espionage and black market dealings, **Dec. 27.** Convicted, given life imprisonment, **Feb. 8, 1949.** All persons taking part in the Cardinal's prosecution were excommunicated by Pope Pius XII. Mindszenty freed **Oct. 31, 1956;** after 15 years in U. S. Embassy in Budapest, the cardinal left Hungary **Sept. 28, 1971** for West Europe.

1949

Mildred E. (Axis Sally) Gillars was convicted by a Federal jury in New York City **Mar. 10** of treason in broadcasting Nazi propaganda during war. She received 10 to 30 years in prison. Freed 1961.

North Atlantic Treaty adopted **Mar. 18** by U.S., Canada and 10 Western European nations, agreeing that "an armed attack against one or more of them in Europe and North America shall be considered an attack against all." Signed **April 4,** ratified by Senate, **July 21.**

Ireland severed last ties with Britain by leaving Commonwealth, **April 18.**

End of U. S. A-bomb monopoly signalized by President Truman's announcement **Sept. 23** that an atomic explosion had occurred in the USSR.

Mrs. I. Toguri D'Aquino, Tokyo Rose of Japanese wartime broadcasts, was sentenced in San Francisco **Oct. 7** to 10 years in prison for treason. Paroled **1956.**

Eleven leaders of U. S. Communist party convicted **Oct. 14,** after 9-month trial in New York City of advocating violent overthrow of U. S. Government. Federal Judge Harold R. Medina, **Oct. 21,** sentenced 10 defendants to five years in prison each and the 11th, a war veteran, to 3 years. U. S. Court of Appeals upheld conviction **Aug. 1, 1950.** Supreme Court upheld the convictions **June 4, 1951.** Seven surrendered **July 2, 1951;** of the other 4, hunted as fugitives, one, Gus Hall, was captured **Oct. 8, 1951,** and given 3 additional years. Robert G. Thompson was captured **Aug. 27, 1953.** Five defense lawyers, cited for contempt during the trial, received sentences ranging from 1 to 6 months. **Apr. 24, 1952,** Supreme Court upheld sentences **Mar. 10, 1952.**

Angus Ward, U. S. Consul General in Mukden, Manchuria, and four Consulate employees were arrested by Communists, **Oct. 24,** on charge of having beaten Chinese employee. Ward and others were sentenced to jail terms of three to six months, **Nov. 22,** but were released, **Nov. 25,** ordered to leave country after U. S. had appealed to 30 other nations to join in a protest.

Nationalist China's government fled to Formosa Dec. 7. Chinese Communists took Yunnan and Kunming as Nationalists deserted.

1950

Protesting arrest of Robert A. Vogeler, U. S. businessman, on charge of spying, U. S. **Jan. 2** ordered Hungary to close its consulates in N. Y. and Cleveland. Hungary released Vogeler **Apr. 28, 1951** when U. S. agreed to let consulates reopen.

Great Britain recognized Communist China Jan. 6, one day after breaking diplomatic relations with Chiang Kai-Shek's Nationalist Chinese regime.

U. S. **Jan. 14** recalled all consular officials from Communist China after the latter seized the American consulate general in Peiping.

Masked bandits robbed Brink's, Inc., Boston express office, **Jan. 17** of $2,775,395.12, of which $1,218,211.29 was in cash. Solution announced 1956 by FBI; 8 men sentenced to life.

President Truman **Jan. 31** authorized AEC to produce the hydrogen bomb (H-bomb).

Dr. Klaus J. E. Fuchs, German-born atomic research physicist at Harwell, Eng., pleaded guilty **Mar. 1** to violating the official Secrets Act and received 14 years in prison. He had communicated valuable atomic information to Russian agents since 1942. At one time he worked at Los Alamos, N. M. Released **June 23, 1959,** went to East Germany, became citizen.

The Army seized all railroads Aug. 27, on orders of President Truman, to prevent a general strike after unions had rejected terms of an 18¢ an hour raise for yardmen but none for trainmen. Roads returned to owners May 23, 1952, after signing of new labor contract.

In an attempt to kill President Truman, two Puerto Rican fanatics, members of a nationalist movement, tried to shoot their way into the President's house, Washington, **Nov. 1.** Guards killed Grisello Torresola, New York; wounded Oscar Collazo, 36, New York pocketbook frame polisher, Pvt. Leslie Coffelt, a guard, was fatally shot; 2 other guards were seriously injured. Collazo was convicted of murder **Mar. 7, 1951** and sentenced to death. President Truman commuted sentence to life imprisonment, July 24, 1952.

U. S. **Dec. 8** banned shipments to Communist China and to Asiatic ports trading with it.

Supreme Court ruled **Dec. 11,** that under the 5th amendment no one could be forced to testify against himself.

1951

Ilse Koch was sentenced to life imprisonment by a German court in Frankfort **Jan. 15**, for inciting the murder of a Buchenwald prisoner.

With Sen. Estes Kefauver (D.-Tenn.) as chairman, the Senate Committee to investigate Organized Crime in Interstate Commerce, exposed nation-wide criminal organizations that reaped huge illegal profits, used these funds to enter legitimate businesses, influenced politicians and bought protection. Preliminary report, **Feb. 28**, said gambling took over $20 billion a year.

Julius Rosenberg, his wife, Ethel, and Morton Sobell, all U. S. citizens, were found guilty **Mar. 29**, of conspiracy to commit wartime sabotage. Rosenbergs sentenced to death. Sobell to 30 years. Appeals denied. David Greenglass, brother of Mrs. Rosenberg and a state witness, received 15 years in prison, Rosenbergs executed at Sing Sing prison, Ossining, N.Y., **June 19, 1953**. Sobel released **Jan. 14, 1969**.

President Truman relieved Gen. Douglas MacArthur of his command in the Far East **Apr. 11**. *See Korean War.*

William N. Oatis, Associated Press correspondent in Prague, was arrested **April 26** as spy by Czechoslovakia, tried and sentenced **July 4** to 10 years in prison; freed **May 16, 1953**.

European Coal and Steel Plan proposed by French Foreign Minister Robert Schuman, **May 9**. British Labor Government rejected plan but six other nations, France, West Germany, Italy, Belgium, Netherlands, and Luxembourg, agreed to conference, Treaty ratified, **June 16, 1952**.

U.N. General Assembly voted arms embargo against Communist China **May 18**.

Tariff concessions by the U.S. to the Soviet Union, Communist China and all Communist-dominated lands were suspended **Aug. 1**.

Transcontinental television inaugurated **Sept. 4**, with President Truman's address at the Japanese Peace Treaty Conference in San Francisco.

Japanese Peace Treaty signed in San Francisco **Sept. 8**, by U.S. and 48 other nations.

War between Germany and the U.S. formally ended **Oct. 19**. Great Britain and France ended war with Germany **July 9**.

1952

Queen Elizabeth II proclaimed Queen of Canada **Feb. 6**, marking first time monarch was specifically enthroned in name of Canada.

U.S. seizure of nation's steel mills was ordered by President Truman **Apr. 8** to avert a strike by 600,000 CIO United Steelworkers. Seizure was ruled illegal by the Supreme Court **June 2**; Strike followed **June 3**, was settled **July 24**.

First jetliner passenger service opened **May 2**, British DeHavilland Comet, London to Johannesburg, South Africa, 6,724 mi. in less than 24 hrs.

Peace contract between West Germany, U. S., Great Britain and France was signed in Bonn, **May 26**. Allied high commissions abolished.

Puerto Rico became an "associated free state" or commonwealth of the U. S., **July 25**, after Pres. Truman gave approval to a new constitution.

West Germany agreed Sept. 10, to pay Israel $822,000,000 over 12 to 14 years as indemnity for Nazi and anti-Semitic acts.

Britain successfully completed its first atomic test off northwest Australia **Oct. 3**, detonating a bomb aboard a naval vessel.

First hydrogen device explosion Nov. 1 at AEC Eniwetok proving grounds in Pacific reported by witnesses but not officially confirmed for more than a year. President Eisenhower told Congress **Feb. 2, 1954**, that the 1952 test was "the first full-scale thermonuclear explosion in history . . . the first step in the hydrogen weapon program of the United States."

Vladimir Clementis, Rudolf Slansky and 9 other purged Communists were hanged in Prague **Dec. 3** for espionage and treason.

Alan Nunn May, British scientist who gave atom secrets to the U.S.S.R., was released from prison **Dec. 29**, after serving 6 yrs. 8 mos. of his 10-yr. term.

1953

Joseph Stalin died, March 5. By 1955, Nikita S. Khrushchev emerged as dominant political leader of Soviet Union.

Mau Mau or "Hidden Ones" of Kenya's Kikuyu tribe, formed to force whites from Kenya and to regain ancestral lands from gov't, climaxed sporadic violence **Mar. 26**, by murdering 71 and wounding 100 fellow Kikuyus who remained loyal to colonial gov't. Jorno Kenyatta, tribal leader, found guilty **Apr. 8** of organizing Mau Mau, sentenced to 7 years. **Dec. 12, 1963** Kenya became independent and Jomo Kenyatta became Prime Minister; and on Dec. 12, 1964, President.

Mount Everest was conquered May 29, by Edmund P. Hillary of New Zealand and Tensing Norkay, Nepalese living in India. Expedition was under Col. Henry C. J. Hunt, Briton.

Demonstration by workers in East Berlin against increased work quotas **June 16**, erupted into an anti-Communist riot by 20,000 to 50,000 people **June 17**, and became a general strike involving 200,000 in East Germany. Soviet troops quelled disturbances, killed 16.

Lavrenti P. Beria, chief of Soviet secret police, was dismissed **July 10**, as an enemy of the people. He was executed **Dec. 23**, along with 6 of his aides. Purge extended to Georgia, the Ukraine, Byelorussia and other Soviet states.

First USSR announcement of H-Bomb explosion **Aug. 20**, AEC reported explosion occurred in USSR **Aug. 12**.

1954

Nautilus, first atomic-powered submarine, was launched at Groton, Conn., **Jan. 21**.

Five members of Congress were wounded in the House of Representatives, **Mar. 1**, by 4 Puerto Ricans, one a woman, who fired pistols at random from a spectators' gallery, shouting for Puerto Rican independence. Representatives recovered. Attackers were sentenced to prison.

Dien Bien Phu, French military outpost in northwest Vietnam, fell to the Vietminh army of Ho Chi Minh, **May**.

Geneva Conference on Far Eastern Affairs, Apr. 26-July 21, by foreign ministers of 19 nations, including Communist China. Free elections in Korea foundered on Communist objections to U. N. supervision. Armistice, effective **Aug. 11**, ended 7½ years of war in Indo-China, with French withdrawal, Vietminh won 62,000 sq. mi. and 13,000,000 pop. in North Vietnam. Cambodia and Laos became independent countries.

Racial segregation in public schools was ruled unconstitutional in a unanimous decision of the Supreme Court, **May 17**.

Southeast Asia Treaty Organization (SEATO), formed by collective defense pact signed in Manila, **Sept. 8** by the U. S., Britain, France, Australia, New Zealand, Philippines, Pakistan and Thailand.

Agreement signed in Paris, Oct. 23, provided for West German sovereignty, rearmament, and entrance into NATO and the Western European Union.

Condemnation of Sen. Jos. R. McCarthy (R.-Wis.) voted by Senate, 67-22, **Dec. 2** for contempt of a Senate elections subcommittee, for abuse of its members and for insults to the Senate during investigation, **Apr. 22-June 17**, of charges brought by the Dept. of the Army vs. Sen. McCarthy, growing out of the Senator's investigation of alleged subversive activities.

1955

Afro-Asian conference of 29 nations met in Bandung, Indonesia, **April**. Conference gave expression to the new nationalism of developing nations.

Federal Republic of West Germany became a sovereign state **May 5** when ratifications were deposited in Bonn. U.S. completed ratification **Apr. 21**. President Eisenhower signed an order ending U. S. occupation but troops remained on a contractual basis.

The Warsaw Pact, a 20-yr. mutual defense treaty, was signed at Warsaw **May 14** by USSR, Albania, Bulgaria, Czechoslovakia, Hungary, Poland, Rumania and East Germany.

The U. S. Supreme Court May 31 reaffirmed the principle of public education without racial discrimination and said all provisions of Federal, state and local law must honor this principle. It gave local authorities the task of integrating schools.

A meeting of heads of state "at the summit" proposed by U.S., Great Britain and France, to the USSR, took place July 18-23 in Geneva, Switzerland, with President Eisenhower top negotiator for the U.S. It was followed by a meeting of the Foreign Ministers, Oct. 27-Nov. 16, with Secy. of State Dulles acting for U. S.

Juan D. Peron, president and dictator of Argentina, was deposed Sept. 19 after a military revolt begun June 16 by naval and marine corps units. Maj. Gen. Eduardo Lonardi became provisional pres. Sept. 23, was displaced Nov. 13 by a military junta, which chose Maj. Gen. Pedro Aramburu prov. pres.

Rosa Parks initiated the first nationally significant direct action by the Negro community Dec. 1 by refusing to give her seat to a white man on a bus in Montgomery, Ala. Bus segregation ordinance declared unconstitutional by a federal court following boycott and NAACP protest.

Merger of America's two largest labor organizations was effected Dec. 5, under the name American Federation of Labor and Congress of Industrial Organizations. Geo. Meany became pres., Walter Reuther became vice pres. in charge of the industrial dept. The merged AFL-CIO had a membership estimated at 15,000,000.

1956

At 20th Congress of Soviet Communist party in Moscow. Feb. 14-25, party chief Nikita S. Khrushchev and other leaders denounced Joseph Stalin, repudiated cruelties of Stalinism, and proclaimed a policy of peaceful coexistence with the West. New party line helped to alienate Chinese communists and hasten Sino-Soviet split. U. S. State Dept. June 4 published text of Khrushchev's 7-hr. secret speech.

Workers in Poznan, Poland, revolted June 28 against Communist rule; uprising crushed with 44 killed, hundreds wounded.

Principles of Organization of American States outlined in Panama Declaration signed in Panama City July 22 by President Eisenhower and heads of 18 other Western Hemisphere states.

Egypt seized Suez Canal July 26 under nationalization decree after Pres. Gamal Abdel Nasser denounced Western withdrawal of proposed Aswan dam financing.

Army H21 helicopter landed in Washington D.C., Aug. 24 after first non-stop transcontinental helicopter flight—2,610 mi. in 37 hrs.

First trans-Atlantic telephone cable system went into use Sept. 25 between Clarenville, Newfoundland, and Oban, Scotland.

Polish Communist leaders Oct. 19-21 defied Kremlin leadership and elected Wladyslaw Gomulka to head more independent government.

Hungarian revolt against Soviet-dominated regime began Oct. 23, was crushed Nov. 4 by Soviet armed forces.

Israel invaded Egypt's Sinai peninsula Oct. 29. When Egypt rejected demand for cease-fire made by France and Britain, the two nations bombed Egypt by air Oct. 31, landed forces Nov. 5-6. U. S. condemned attack, supported cease-fire demand by UN. Egypt and Israel accepted cease-fire. Britain and France followed, fighting stopped Nov. 7.

UN Nov. 5 established first international police force to supervise truce in Middle East.

1957

Britain set off its first hydrogen bomb in Pacific test May 15.

Soviet Union announced Aug. 26 that it had successfully tested an intercontinental ballistic missile.

Sen. Strom Thurmond (D.-S.C.) held Senate floor for 24 hrs. 18 mins. Aug. 28-29, eclipsing record filibuster of 22 hrs. 26 mins. set by Sen. Wayne Morse (D.-Ore.) in 1953.

First underground nuclear explosion set off by Atomic Energy Commission in Nevada Sept. 19.

A Federal-state controversy over admission of Negroes to the previously all-white Central High School in Little Rock, Ark., reached a showdown Sept. 4 when National Guardsmen ordered out by Gov. Orval Faubus (D.) barred 9 Negro students from entering the school. A conference between Faubus and President Eisenhower brought no tangible result but Faubus complied Sept. 21 with a Federal Court order to remove the National Guardsmen. The Negroes entered school Sept. 23 but were ordered to withdraw by local authorities because of fear of mob violence. President Eisenhower sent Federal troops to Little Rock Sept. 24 to enforce the Federal Court's order and the school began operation on an integrated basis.

First man-made satellite, Sputnik I, was launched by Soviet scientists Oct. 4. The 184-lb. sphere circled the earth about every 1½ hours in an elliptical orbit at altitudes ranging from some 140 miles to 560 miles above the earth. The Russians Nov. 3 launched Sputnik II, weighing 1,120 lbs., carrying a live dog, Laika, as the world's first space passenger and orbiting the earth about every 103.7 minutes at altitudes ranging from some 160 miles to about 1,062 miles. Soviet authorities announced the dog's death Nov. 10. Sputnik I disintegrated Jan. 4, 1958, and Sputnik II Apr. 14, 1958.

1958

First U. S. earth satellite to go into orbit, Explorer I, launched by Army Jan. 31, Cape Canaveral, Fla.

Gen. Charles de Gaulle became French Premier June 1, averting threatened civil war; De Gaulle constitution, increasing power of executive, overwhelmingly adopted Sept. 28. De Gaulle elected Dec. 21 as first president of 5th Republic.

Arab nationalist rebels seized Iraqi government July 14, killed King Faisal II, proclaimed republic. President Eisenhower sent U. S. Marines to Lebanon July 15 to forestall alleged effort by Soviet Union and United Arab Republic to engineer overthrow of Lebanon regime. Withdrawal of U. S. troops began Aug. 12.

Jet airliner passenger service across Atlantic was opened Oct. 4 by British Overseas Airways Corp.

First domestic jet airline passenger service in U.S. opened by National Airlines Dec. 10 between New York and Miami.

1959

Fidel Castro assumed power in Cuba following collapse of Fulgencio Batista's government Jan. 1.

Lunik I was launched by Soviet scientists Jan. 4, went into orbit around the sun as first man-made planet.

St. Lawrence Seaway opened Apr. 25; was dedicated June 26 by President Eisenhower and Queen Elizabeth II.

George Washington, first U.S. ballistic-missile submarine, launched at Groton, Conn., June 9.

N.S. Savannah, world's first atomic-powered merchant ship, launched July 21 at Camden, N. J.

Soviet Premier Khrushchev paid unprecedented visit to U.S. Sept. 15-27, made transcontinental tour, conferred with President Eisenhower.

1960

A wave of sit-ins began Feb. 1 when 4 Negro college students in Greensboro, N.C., refused to move from a Woolworth lunch counter when they were denied service. By Sept. 1961 more than 70,000 Negroes and white students had participated in sit-ins.

First French nuclear test explosion occurred Feb. 13 in Sahara Desert.

Caryl Chessman, who had won 8 stays of execution since his 1948 conviction on robbery, kidnapping and attempted rape charges, was put to death May 2 in the gas chamber at San Quentin Prison, near San Francisco.

A U-2 reconnaissance plane of the U. S., piloted by Francis Gary Powers, was shot down in the Soviet Union May 1. Soviet Premier Khrushchev refused to participate in the Paris summit conference scheduled for May 16 unless President Eisenhower apologized for U-2 flights over the USSR; the Big Four leaders went to Paris but the conference did not take place. Powers was freed Feb. 10, 1962, in exchange for convicted Soviet spy

Rudolf Abel, who was serving a 30-year term imposed by U. S. in 1957.

Adolf Eichmann's capture in Argentina by Israeli agents announced May 22; former Nazi SS general, accused of playing a major role in killing of millions of Jews. After 4-month trial in Jerusalem, sentenced by Israeli court Dec. 15, 1961, hanged for crimes against humanity May 31, 1962.

1961

The United States severed diplomatic and consular relations with Cuba Jan. 3.

Maj. Yuri Gagarin of the Soviet Union became Apr. 12 the first human space traveler; he was launched into orbit from Siberia in a spacecraft called Vostok I and returned to earth after one circuit of the globe. A second Soviet astronaut, Maj. Gherman S. Titov, made 17 orbits of the earth Aug. 6-7 in spacecraft Vostok II.

Invasion of Cuba "Bay of Pigs" Apr. 17 by Cuban exiles attempting to overthrow the regime of Premier Fidel Castro was repulsed.

Commander Alan B. Shepard, Jr., was rocketed from Cape Canaveral, Fla., 116.5 miles above the earth in a Mercury capsule May 5 in the first U. S. manned sub-orbital space flight; he landed safely in the Atlantic 302 miles away. Capt. Virgil I. (Gus) Grissom made a similar flight from Cape Canaveral July 21.

East Germany closed the border between East and West Berlin Aug. 12-13 to stop the exodus of East Germans to the West; the East Germans built a wall dividing the city.

Dag Hammarskjold, Secy. Gen. of the United Nations, was killed in a plane crash near Ndola, Northern Rhodesia, Sept. 18. U Thant of Burma was elected Acting Secy. Gen. Nov. 3.

Nuclear blasts of 25 megatons and over 50 megatons, largest man-made explosions to date, were set off by the Soviet Union Oct. 23 and Oct. 30, respectively, despite world protests.

1962

Lt. Col. John H. Glenn, Jr., became the first American in orbit Feb. 20 when he circled the earth 3 times in the Mercury capsule Friendship 7. Lt. Comdr. M. Scott Carpenter made a 3-orbit flight May 24 in the Mercury capsule Aurora 7. Comdr. Walter M. Schirra, Jr., orbited the earth 6 times Oct. 3 in the Mercury capsule Sigma 7.

A truce agreement Mar. 18 ended the 7-yr. Moslem revolt against French rule in Algeria. Algerians cast an overwhelming vote for independence in a referendum July 1 and French President Charles de Gaulle declared the country independent July 3.

The U. S. Supreme Court ruled in a 6-1 decision June 25 that the reciting of an official prayer in the public schools of New York State was unconstitutional.

The third Soviet astronaut was sent into orbit Aug. 11 and the fourth followed him into a nearly identical orbit Aug. 12, both descending Aug. 15. They were Maj. Andrian G. Nikolayev, who made a record 64 orbits of the earth, and Lt. Col. Pavel R. Popovich, who made 48 orbits.

The largest cash robbery to date in U. S. history occurred Aug. 14 when a gang held up a U. S. mail truck near Plymouth, Mass., and stole $1,551,277.

A Soviet offensive buildup in Cuba was revealed to the American people Oct. 22 by President Kennedy, who ordered a naval and air quarantine on shipment of offensive military equipment to the island. President Kennedy and Soviet Premier Khrushchev reached agreement Oct. 28 on a formula to end the crisis, and the President said Nov. 2 that Soviet missile bases in Cuba were being dismantled.

1963

U. S. Air Force Maj. Leroy Gordon Cooper orbited the earth 22 times May 15-16 in the final and longest flight of Project Mercury.

Lt. Col. Valery F. Bykovsky was launched into orbit in Vostok V June 14, the 5th Soviet astronaut to enter space. The first woman space traveler, Soviet Jr. Lt. Valentina V. Tereshkova, was launched into orbit in Vostok VI June 16. Both landed June 19, the man after 81 orbits and the woman after 48.

U. S. Supreme Court ruled, 8-1 June 17 that state and local laws requiring recitation of the Lord's Prayer or Bible verses in public schools were unconstitutional.

A limited nuclear test-ban treaty was agreed upon July 25 by the United States, the Soviet Union and Britain, barring all nuclear tests except those conducted underground. It became formally effective Oct. 10.

The biggest robbery to date occurred Aug. 8 when an armed holdup gang stole more than $7,000,000 (£ 2,500,000) in currency from a mail train near Cheddington, England. Some of the money was recovered and over a dozen men were sentenced to long prison terms.

Washington demonstration by 200,000 persons, Aug. 28 in support of Negro demands for equal rights. Highlight was speech in which Dr. Martin Luther King said: "I have a dream that this nation will rise up and live out the true meaning of its creed, 'We hold these truths to be self evident: that all men are created equal.' "

Quintuplets, all boys, were born Sept. 7 to Mr. and Mrs. Efren Lubin Prieto in Maracaibo, Venezuela. Quintuplets, 4 girls and a boy, were born Sept. 14 to Mr. and Mrs. Andrew Fischer in Aberdeen, S. D. Only 3 sets of quintuplets born previously in the Western Hemisphere had survived infancy—the Dionnes, born in Canada in 1934; the Diligentis, born in Argentina in 1943, and the Kienasts, born in New Jersey in 1970.

The South Vietnamese government of President Ngo Dinh Diem was overthrown Nov. 1-2 in a coup by the armed forces. Diem and his brother, secret police chief Ngo Dinh Nhu, were captured and killed.

John F. Kennedy, 35th President of the United States, was shot and fatally wounded by an assassin Nov. 22 as he rode in a motorcade through downtown Dallas, Tex. Texas Gov. John B. Connally, Jr., riding in the same car, was also shot but not fatally injured. Vice President Lyndon B. Johnson was inaugurated President shortly afterward in Dallas. Lee Harvey Oswald, was arrested and charged with the murder of the President. Oswald was shot and fatally wounded Nov. 24 by Jack Ruby, 52, a Dallas night club owner, who was convicted of murder Mar. 14, 1964, and was sentenced to death. The murder conviction was reversed by the Texas Court of Criminal appeals. Ruby died of natural causes Jan. 3, 1967, while awaiting re-trial.

1964

Pope Paul VI toured the Holy Land Jan. 4-6, the first pope to visit there since Christianity began, the first to travel by air, and the first to leave Italy in over 150 years.

Three civil rights workers were reported missing in Mississippi June 22. The bodies of Michael Schwerner, Andrew Goodman and James E. Chaney were found buried near Philadelphia; Miss., Aug. 4. Twenty-one white men were arrested. On Oct. 20, 1967, an all-white Federal jury convicted 7 who took part in the Ku Klux Klan conspiracy to murder the 3 young men.

U. S. planes bombed North Vietnamese bases and sank or damaged 25 North Vietnamese patrol boats Aug. 4 in retaliation against North Vietnamese attacks on U. S. destroyers in the Gulf of Tonkin.

The Warren Commission released Sept. 27 a report containing the conclusion that Lee Harvey Oswald was solely responsible for the killing of President Kennedy.

A spacecraft carrying 3 men was launched by the Soviet Union Oct. 12, the first spacecraft occupied by more than one person. The Voskhod (Sunrise) returned to earth Oct. 13 after 16 earth orbits. Its passengers were Col. V. M. Komarov, a cosmonaut; Dr. B. B. Yegerov, a space physician; and K. P. Feoktistov, a scientist.

Soviet Premier Khrushchev was ousted as premier and Soviet Communist party chief Oct. 14-15. Aleksei N. Kosygin replaced him as premier and Leonid I. Brezhnev took over the party leadership.

Communist China conducted a successful test explosion of its first atomic bomb Oct. 16.

1965

U.S. bombed North Vietnam, Feb. 7, after Vietcong guerrilas attacked U. S. installations at Pleiku, Feb. 6.

Lt. Col. Aleksei A. Leonov, stepping out of Soviet spaceship Voskhod 2, became the first man to "walk in space," **March 18. Maj. Edward H. White**, in U. S. spaceship Gemini 4, repeated the Russian feat and remained outside the ship for 20 minutes, **June 3.** On **Dec. 4,** Air Force Lt. Col. Frank Borman and Navy Comdr. James A. Lovell, Jr., orbited in Gemini 7, stayed aloft 14 days and participated in first manned space rendezvous **Dec. 15** when Gemini 6, with Navy Capt. Walter M. Schirra, Jr., and Air Force Maj. Thomas P. Stafford, came within 10 ft. of Gemini 7.

A Selma to Montgomery, Ala., civil rights march was led by Dr. Martin Luther King, **March 21-25.** They started with 3,200 and swelled to 25,000. They were guarded along the way by 4,000 troops dispatched by President Johnson.

U. S. armed forces sent to Dominican Republic to protect U. S. citizens and prevent a revolution, **Apr. 28.** Later, **May 23,** the Organization of American States set up a peace-keeping force to maintain order.

Los Angeles riot by discontented Negroes living in the Watts area resulted in the death of 35 persons and property damage estimated at $200,000,000, Aug. 11-16.

Pope Paul VI visited N. Y. City **Oct.** 4 and delivered a personal appeal for peace to the UN. It was the first time a pope had come to America.

Massive electric power failure blacked out most of Northeastern U. S. plus parts of 2 Canadian provinces the night of Nov. 9 for approximately 00,000 sq. miles with a population of 30,000,000 were affected. In N. Y. City, over 800,000 were trapped in the subways for hours.

Independence proclaimed in Rhodesia by minority white regime, **Nov. 11.** Britain declared the action illegal and announced economic sanctions.

1966

First soft landing on surface of moon by an unmanned spacecraft **Feb. 3,** USSR Luna 9. U. S. achieved similar feat **June 2** with Surveyor 1.

Kwame Nkrumah, president of Ghana since independence in 1957, was overthrown **Feb. 24.**

France withdrew all its armed forces from the integrated NATO military alliance **July 1.**

Medicare, government program to pay part of the medical expenses of citizens over 65, began **July 1.**

A sniper atop the University of Texas tower in Austin, Tex., shot 44 persons **Aug. 1,** killing 14, including an unborn child. Shot to death by police, the sniper was identified as Charles J. Whitman, 25, an honor student at the university. Police later found the bodies of his wife and his mother, whom he apparently had slain the night before.

Edward Brooke (R., Mass.) elected **Nov.** 8 as first Negro U. S. Senator in 85 years.

1967

Fire aboard spacecraft Apollo I on the ground at Cape Kennedy, Fla., **Jan.** 27 killed Virgil I. Grissom, 40, one of first 7 Mercury astronauts; Edward H. White, 36, first American to "walk" in space; and Roger B. Chaffee, 31. First U. S. astronauts killed in space tests.

Rep. Adam Clayton Powell (D., N. Y.) was denied **Mar.** 1 his seat in 90th Congress because House of Representatives charged him with misuse of Govt. funds and nepotism. He won **Apr.** 11 special election to fill vacancy despite not campaigning in Harlem, where he faced possible arrest in a civil suit; did not take seat. Re-elected in 1968, he was seated by the 91st Congress but was fined $25,000 and stripped of his 22 years' Congressional seniority. Died **Apr. 4, 1972.**

In 6-day Israeli-Arab war June 5-10, Israel smashed armed forces of United Arab Republic, Syria and Jordan; Israel captured territory 4 times its own size.

A U. S. communications ship, the **U.S.S. Liberty,** was attacked and heavily damaged by Israeli planes and torpedo boats **June 8** in international waters 15 miles north of the Sinai Peninsula. Thirty-four U. S. crewmen were killed and 75 wounded. Israel apologized for the attack, which it called accidental.

Sen. Thomas J. Dodd (D., Conn.) censured by Senate **June 23** by 92-5 vote for using campaign and testimonial funds "for his personal benefit." Died **May 24, 1971.**

President Johnson and **Soviet Premier Aleksei N. Kosygin** met **June 23 and 25** at Glassboro State College in N.J. Both agreed not to let any crisis push them into nuclear war.

Black riots in Newark, N.J., **July 12-17** killed some 26, injured 1,500, over 1,000 arrested. In Detroit, Mich., **July 23-30** at least 40 died, 2,000 injured and 5,000 left homeless by rioting, looting and burning in city's black ghetto. Quelled by 4,700 Federal paratroopers and 8,000 National Guardsmen.

Thurgood Marshall sworn in **Oct. 2;** first black U. S. Supreme Court Justice. **Nov. 7, Carl B. Stokes** (D., Cleveland) and **Richard G. Hatcher** (D., Gary, Ind.) elected first black mayors of major U. S. cities. **Robert G. Clark** first black elected to Mississippi Legislature since Reconstruction.

Vietnam war protested **Oct. 21-22** by some 35,000 in Washington, D. C., peace march. At least 647 arrested, most when attempting to enter Pentagon.

Dr. Christiaan Barnard, Capetown, S. Africa, performed first successful human heart transplant **Dec. 3** on Louis Washkansky, who lived for 18 days.

1968

U.S.S. Pueblo and 83-man crew seized in Sea of Japan **Jan. 23** by North Koreans. 82 survivors released **Dec. 22.**

Vietcong hit 30 South Vietnamese provincial capitals Jan. 30 in Tet offensive. U. S. Embassy in Saigon occupied by Communists for 6 hrs. Hue street fighting ended **Feb. 24.** Record military casualties and 350,000 more refugees resulted.

White racism cited as chief cause of Negro violence in **Kerner** Commission report on civil disorders **Feb. 29.**

Pres. Johnson said **Mar. 31** he would not seek or accept the Democratic party nomination for another term.

Rev. Dr. Martin Luther King, Jr., 39, assassinated **Apr.** 4 in Memphis, Tenn. Riots in Washington, D.C., caused Pres. Johnson to call out troops. By **Apr. 14** racial violence erupted in 125 cities in 29 states. **James Earl Ray,** an escaped convict, pleaded guilty to the slaying, was sentenced to 99 years.

Student rebels Apr. 23 paralyzed Columbia Univ. for two weeks.

Six New Left students' protest at Univ. of Nanterre, France, **May 2** grew into nearly a month of civil violence and by **May 24** 10,000,000 strikers paralyzed country. **De Gaulle** saved regime with broad reforms.

Vietnam preliminary peace talks began in Paris **May 10** after 34-day impasse on selection of site.

Helen Keller, 87, blind and deaf writer who was an inspiration to others for more than half a century, died **June 1** in Westport, Conn.

U. S. nuclear submarine **Scorpion** with 99 men "presumed lost" **June 5;** wreckage found **Oct. 28** 400 mi. SW of the Azores under 10,000 ft. of water.

Sen. Robert F. Kennedy, 42 (D., N.Y.) shot **June 5** in Hotel Ambassador, Los Angeles, after celebrating Calif. and S.D. Presidential primary victories. Died **June 6.** Sirhan Beshara Sirhan, a Jordanian Arab living in L.A., convicted of murder and sentenced to death.

Soviet Union and other Warsaw Pact nations invaded Czechoslovakia **Aug. 20-21** to crush Alexander Dubcek's liberal regime.

Democratic National Convention in Chicago **Aug. 26-29,** one of history's most turbulent, split on Vietnam issue. Violence erupted as police and troops clashed with 10,000 to 15,000 anti-war demonstrators.

U. S. astronauts Borman, Lovell and **Anders** made 10 orbits around the moon **Dec. 24-25.** First men to circle and see back side of moon.

1969

Dwight D. Eisenhower, 78, 34th President of the U.S. and Supreme Allied Commander in Europe during World War II, died of coronary heart disease **Mar. 28.**

Unarmed U.S. reconnaissance plane, with 31 aboard, shot down by North Korean jets **Apr. 15** in the Sea of Japan about 100 miles from the mainland.

Charles de Gaulle resigned as President of France **Apr. 28** after losing a referendum by a narrow margin.

Supreme Court Justice Abe Fortas resigned **May 14,** the first judge to do so in the tribunal's history because of public pressure.

A car driven by **Sen. Edward M. Kennedy** (D., Mass.) plunged off a bridge into a tidal pool on Chappaquiddick Island, Mass., **July 18,** and the body of Mary Jo Kopechne, a 23-year-old secretary, was found in the car.

U.S. astronaut **Neil A. Armstrong**, 38, commander of the Apollo 11 mission, became the first man to set foot on the moon **July 20**. After stepping onto the moon Armstrong said: "That's one small step for a man, one giant leap for mankind." Air Force **Col. Edwin E. Aldrin, Jr.** accompanied Armstrong on the moon landing.

Dr. Philip Blaiberg, world's longest-surviving heart transplant patient to date, died in Cape Town, South Africa, **Aug. 17.** Dr. Christiaan N. Barnard had performed the world's third heart transplant operation on the retired dentist 19 months and 15 days earlier.

North Vietnam's **President Ho Chi Minh** died **Sept. 3.**

Hundreds of thousands of Americans participated in Moratorium Day events across the nation **Oct. 15** to demonstrate their opposition to the Vietnam War. More than 250,000 demonstrators gathered in Washington, D.C., **Nov. 15** in the largest anti-war demonstration in the nation's history.

President Richard Nixon appealed to the "great silent majority" **Nov. 3** for support of his program in connection with the Vietnam war.

The United States and the Soviet Union began preliminary Strategic Arms Limitation Talks (SALT) in Helsinki, Finland, **Nov. 17.**

Navy Commanders Charles Conrad, Jr., and Alan L. Bean of the Apollo 12 mission, made the second successful landing on the moon **Nov. 19.**

President Nixon's nomination of Clement F. Haynsworth, Jr., to the U. S. Supreme Court was rejected by the Senate **Nov. 21** by a 55-45 vote. It was the first rejection of a Supreme Court nominee in 39 years.

The Selective Service System held the first draft lottery since 1942 in Washington **Dec. 1** to set the order of selection for the draft in 1970.

1970

Joseph A. Yablonski, 59, United Mine Workers official, his wife, and their daughter were found shot to death **Jan. 5** in their Clarksville, Pa., home. Six persons were indicted by a Federal grand jury in Cleveland on charges of conspiring to kill Yablonski. **Claude E. Vealy**, 27, pleaded guilty **June 23, 1971,** and named two others as accomplices.

The 31-month Nigerian civil war ended with the surrender **Jan. 12** of secessionist Biafra after a loss of about 2,000,000 lives.

The Supreme Court ordered 14 school districts in Alabama, Florida, Georgia, Louisiana, Mississippi and Texas **Jan. 14** to integrate some 300,000 pupils by **Feb. 1,** reaffirming its 1969 "desegregate now" ruling.

A Federal grand jury Feb. 18 found the defendants in the turbulent 21-week trial of the "Chicago 7" innocent of conspiring to incite riots during the 1968 Democratic National Convention. However, 5 were convicted of crossing state lines with intent to incite riots.

The United States cast its first veto in the United Nations Security Council **Mar. 17** when it joined Britain in rejecting a resolution calling on UN members to cut all communications with Rhodesia.

More than 6,000 New York City postmen, angry over Congressional delays in granting pay raises, walked off the job **Mar. 18** and began the first large-scale strike in the U.S. postal service's 195-year history.

A courtroom escape attempt at San Rafael, Calif., **Apr. 7** ended in the death of Superior Court Judge Harold J. Haley and 3 convicts after a gunman invaded the trial of convict James McClain and passed guns to the defendant and 3 convict witnesses. The judge, 3 women and the Assistant District Attorney were taken as hostages to a getaway van where a brief gun battle erupted. Angela Davis, formerly an instructor at UCLA, was apprehended **Oct. 13** for her alleged role in supplying two of the guns used in the escape. She was acquitted **June 4, 1972,** on all charges of murder, kidnap and conspiracy.

The moon landing mission of Apollo 13, launched **Apr. 11,** was aborted by an oxygen tank explosion, which threatened the lives of astronauts Cmdr. James A. Lovell, Jr., Fred W. Haise, Jr., and John L. Swigart, Jr. The crew used the systems of the lunar landing module Aquarius to transport them safely toward earth.

Millions of Americans across the nation participated in anti-pollution demonstrations **Apr. 22** to mark first Earth Day.

President Nixon told a nationwide TV audience **Apr. 30** that he had ordered American troops into action against Communist sanctuaries inside Cambodia to destroy enemy bases and supplies.

Student reaction to U.S. Cambodian operations brought about a confrontation between 100 National Guardsmen and 500-600 students at Ken State University in Ohio **May 4** which resulted in 4 student deaths after guardsmen fired into the group.

The first women generals in American history were named by President Nixon **May 15** when he promoted Col. Elizabeth P. Hoisington, director of the Women's Army Corps, and Col. Anna Mae Hays, chief of the Army Nurse Corps, to the rank of brigadier general.

The Norwegian explorer Thor Heyerdahl and a multinational crew of 7 set sail from Morocco **May 17** in a frail papyrus boat, the Ra II, in an attempt to prove that ancient Egyptians could have reached the new world. The craft sailed into Bridgetown Harbor, Barbados, **July 12.**

An earthquake in Peru May 31 wiped out scores of cities and villages and left more than 50,000 dead, 20,000 missing and 150,000 to 200,000 injured. U.S. Geological Survey experts termed the disaster "the most destructive historic earthquake in the Western hemisphere."

A 90-day ceasefire began **Aug. 7** on the Mideast front as fighting stopped within a 32-mile-deep zone on each side of the Suez Canal. The ceasefire was continually extended after that date.

A postal reform measure was signed by President Nixon **Aug. 12,** creating an independent U.S. Postal Service, thus relinquishing governmental control of the U.S. mails after almost two centuries. Began **July 1, 1971.**

Palestine commandos hijacked 3 Western airliners bound for New York in the skies over Europe **Sept. 6** and precipitated a world crises which endangered the 90-day Mideast ceasefire and sparked a civil war in Jordan.

The President's Commission on Campus Unrest warned **Sept. 26** of a rising "crisis of violence" on college campuses. The panel placed responsibility for the situation equally on students, lawmen and political leaders.

Egypt's Pres. Gamal Abdel Nasser, 52, the most powerful leader in the Arab world, died in Cairo **Sept. 28** after a heart attack.

Salvador Allende Gossens, 62, first democratically elected Marxist head of government in the world, was sworn in as Chile's president **Nov. 3.**

Charles De Gaulle, 79, died of a heart attack in Colombey-les-Deux Eglises **Nov. 9.**

A cyclone and giant waves devastated a 2,338-square-mile area of Pakistan's Bay of Bengal coast **Nov. 13,** in one of the worst disasters of modern times. An estimated 300,000 persons were killed.

1971

Charles Manson, 36, and 3 of his followers were found guilty **Jan. 26** of first degree murder in the brutal slaying in 1969 of actress Sharon Tate and 6 others. The 9½-month trial, longest in California history, ended **Mar. 29** when Manson, Susan Atkins, 22; Patricia Kernwinkel, 23, and Leslie Van Houten, 21, were sentenced to death in the gas chamber.

The 3rd U.S. moon team of Capt. Alan B. Shepard, Jr., 47, and Navy Comdr. Edgar D. Mitchell trekked over the rugged Fra Mauro region **Feb. 5** in a two-part, 33½-hr. scientific expedition, after making the closest-to-target landing of all Apollos. They returned with 96 pounds of rocks.

A treaty prohibiting installation of nuclear weapons on the seabed beyond any nation's 12-mile coastal zone was signed by 63 nations **Feb. 11.**

Raids against drug wholesalers and distributors netted Federal narcotics agents 54 "top-flight" dealers and nearly $13,000,000 worth of drugs **Feb. 24** in the "largest Federal crackdown ever on narcotics distribution by organized crime."

A Constitutional amendment lowering the voting age to 18 in all elections was approved in the Senate by a vote of 94-0 **Mar. 10.** The proposed 26th Amendment received House approval by a 400-19 vote **Mar. 23,** and Ohio ratified it on **June 30,** making it law. Enfranchised some

25,000,000 young people to vote in the 1972 election.

Civil War between East and West Pakistan beginning **Mar. 25** brought death from war and starvation to hundreds of thousands and caused 9,000,000 refugees to pour into India.

A court-martial jury of 6 officers **Mar. 29**, after 13-days deliberation, convicted Lt. William L. Calley, Jr., of premeditated murder of 22 South Vietnamese men, women and children at My Lai on **Mar. 16, 1968**. He was sentenced to life imprisonment **Mar. 31**. The verdict aroused public reaction on a mass scale causing President Nixon **Apr. 1** to order that Calley be removed from the stockade to his quarters at Fort Benning, where he would remain until his case was completely reviewed. Sentence reduced to 20 years **Aug. 20** by Lt. Gen. Albert O. Conner.

Mainland China Apr. 6 invited the U.S. ping pong team to Peking; 9 American players arrived in China **Apr. 10**.

Haiti's Francois (Papa Doc) Duvalier, 64, died **Apr. 21**. His son Claude, 19, succeeded him **Apr. 22**.

A throng of some 200,000—one of the largest and most orderly of such crowds—"marched for peace" in Washington, D.C. **Apr. 24** in an antiwar protest. Between **May 3-5** police arrested 12,614 people, at least 7,000 of them on the first day—a record high for arrests in a civil disturbance in the nation's history. A simultaneous protest of 156,000 in San Francisco was described as the largest such rally on its West Coast.

Amtrak, the nation's new rail passenger system went into operation **May 1** with the goal to "get people back on trains."

A jury May 13 acquitted 13 Black Panthers on all 156 counts of conspiring to bomb New York police stations, department stores, railroad tracks and a Board of Education Office. The 9-month bomb-conspiracy trial was the longest case in New York's history.

President Nixon told a press conference June 1 his Administration was readying a massive "national offensive" against drug addiction, with emphasis on servicemen addicts.

Attorney General John N. Mitchell told the Senate Permanent Subcommittee on Investigations **June 8** that more than $400,000,000 worth of stocks and bonds had been stolen during the past two years. Organized crime was found to play a dominant role in securities thefts. It was also revealed that many firms prefer to absorb the thefts rather than hurt their public image or pay higher insurance premiums.

The longest airplane hijacking, carried out **July 2** by Robert Jackson, a U.S. Navy deserter, extended from San Antonio, Tex., to Buenos Aires covered 7,650 miles.

Publication of classified Pentagon papers on the U.S. involvement in Vietnam was begun **June 13** by the New York Times. The Justice Dept. secured a restraining order **June 15** against publication of the "Pentagon Papers" pending a ruling on a permanent injunction. In a 6-3 vote, the U.S. Supreme Court **June 30** upheld the right of the New York Times and Washington Post to publish the documents under the protection of the First Amend ment. Daniel Ellsberg, admitted leaker of the 47-volume Pentagon analysis, was arraigned **June 28** on charges of unauthorized possession of secret documents.

A treaty June 17 returned Okinawa, a major American military base since World War 2, to Japanese rule. Japan took jurisdiction of the island **May 15, 1972**.

Three Soviet cosmonauts died June 30 during their return to earth after a record-breaking 23 days, 17 hrs. and 40 mins. in orbit. Their deaths were announced **July 12** as caused by "a loss of the ship's sealing," resulting in a sudden depressurization of the Soyuz 11 capsule.

In a surprise announcement July 15 President Nixon disclosed that he would visit Peking before May, 1972, in a "journey for peace."

The 4th U.S. moon team of Col. David R. Scott, 39, and Lt. Col. James B. Irwin, 40, roved about the moon's surface **July 31-Aug. 2** for a record 18 hrs. and 37 min. covering about 17½ miles, and gathered more than 226 pounds of surface material. The age of one sample, the "genesis rock," was put at about 4.15 billion years.

President Nixon began a sweeping new economic program **Aug. 15** calling for a 90-day wage, price and rent freeze, to be effective immediately. He also freed the dollar for devaluation against other currencies by cutting its tie with gold, and halted the conversion of foreign-held dollars into gold. The New York stock market hit a record high **Aug. 16** in the busiest day in its history as the Dow-Jones industrial average jumped 32.92 points, closing at 888.95 on a volume of 31,720,000 shares. On **Oct. 7** Nixon outlined **Phase 2** stressing that wage and price restraints would remain in force until inflationary pressures "are brought under control" and declared that boards would be set up to oversee interest and dividends, as well as pay and prices.

After 17 months of intermittent 4-power negotiations, the draft of a Berlin agreement was completed and endorsed by both Germanys **Aug. 23**. The accord was the first such settlement since the end of World War 2, and was signed **Sept. 3** after their governments approved the pact in which Russia pledged "unhindered passage of traffic between West Berlin and West Germany across East German territory and permitted West Berliners to visit East Germany. The Berlin Wall was to remain and East Germans still were not free to go West.

Ten empty school buses were blown up in Pontiac, Mich., **Aug. 30**, just 8 days before the start of a bitterly-opposed program of transporting 8,700 children to nonneighborhood schools.

Nikita S. Khrushchev, 77, a Ukranian peasant's son who rose to USSR communist chief and premier before his ouster ended by fellow leaders in 1964, died in the Kremlin hospital **Sept. 11** of a heart attack. Official notice of his death came in a one-sentence Tass announcement **Sept. 13** when he was buried.

More than 1,000 New York State troopers and police stormed the Attica State Correctional Facility where 1,200 inmates held 38 guards hostage **Sept. 13**, ending a 4-day rebellion in the maximum-security prison. Nine hostages and 28 convicts were shot to death in the assault.

Capt. Ernest L. Medina was acquitted Sept. 22 of all charges in the deaths of more than 100 South Vietnamese civilians in the 1968 My Lai massacre.

Chile virtually expropriated the Anaconda and Kennecott copper mines **Sept. 28** when President Allende subtracted $774,000,000 from proposed compensation for the U.S. owners. He claimed the deduction was for "excess profits" harvested by the U.S. firms over 16 years.

Some 38,000 longshoremen on the East and Gulf Coasts walked off the job **Oct. 1**. The stoppage by the International Longshoremen's Assn. marked the first time that dockworkers in all U.S. deepwater ports were on strike, as the West Coast longshoremen had struck 3 months earlier.

Communist China is granted UN membership when the General Assembly by a vote of 76 to 35, with 17 abstentions, adopted an Albanian resolution **Oct. 25** to seat Mao Tse-tung's Communists and oust Chiang Kai-shek's Nationalists.

The House of Commons approved British entry into the European Economic Community **Oct. 28**, by a 356-244 vote on the terms negotiated by Conservative Prime Minister Edward Heath.

The U.S. exploded a 5-magaton H-bomb under Amchitka Island in the Aleutians **Nov. 6**, 5 hours after the Supreme Court denied a petition to delay the test. The test was completed safely and was the last and most powerful of the Spartan missile warhead tests.

The Mariner 9 became the first man-made object to orbit another planet, Mars, **Nov. 13** after a 5½-month trip of about 247,000,000 miles.

The USSR announced Dec. 2 that it had soft-landed the first scientific space robot on Mars after a 188-day journey from earth. The craft landed amid violent dust storms with winds up to 300 miles an hour; its TV signals stopped after 4 days.

India invaded Pakistan Dec. 3 in defense of splinter nation of Bangladesh. Following India's victory in the 14-day war, Shiek Mujibur Rahman, the father of the secessionist rebellion, became the prime minister of Bangladesh **Jan. 12**.

President Nixon announced Dec. 18 an 8.57% devaluation of the U.S. dollar to allow American goods to be more competitive in the world market, while raising the price of certain imports. The devaluation would be accomplished by a $3 increase in the price of gold, from the present $35 an ounce to $38.

1972

President Nixon gave the go-ahead for development of a space shuttle **Jan. 5,** when he signed a bill authorizing a 6-year, $5.5 billion program for development of a craft that would be lifted from earth like a rocket and would return like an airplane.

Representatives of Western European nations gathered in Brussels **Jan. 22** to sign a treaty enlarging the Common Market from the original membership of 6 to 10. The enlarged market still had to be approved by Britain, Denmark, Ireland and Norway before going into effect Jan. 1, 1973. Norwegians voted **Sept. 24-25** against joining the Common Market.

President Nixon unveiled Jan. 25 a previously secret 8-point peace proposal for Vietnam, including an offer to pull out all U.S. forces in 6 months in exchange for a ceasefire throughout Indochina and release of all American prisoners of war.

Thirteen unarmed civilians were shot and killed in Londonderry **Jan. 30,** when British troops clashed with Roman Catholic demonstrators. A British inquiry released a report **Apr. 19** absolving British troops of gross misconduct in the shooting of the civilians during the "Bloody Sunday" protests.

President Nixon arrived in Peking Feb. 21 for an 8-day visit to China, which he called a "journey for peace". The unprecedented visit ended with a joint communique pledging that both powers would work for "a normalization of relations".

Pioneer 10, an unmanned U.S. spacecraft, roared aloft from Cape Kennedy **Mar. 2** on a 639-day, 620,000,000-mile journey past Jupiter.

Author Clifford Irving and his wife admitted **Mar. 13** that his purported interviews with multi-millionaire Howard Hughes and his subsequent biography of Hughes were hoaxes.

By a vote of 84 to 8, the Senate approved **Mar. 22** a constitutional amendment banning legal discrimination against women because of their sex and sent the measure to the states for ratification.

An agreement ending the Sudanese civil war between the predominantly Arab Moslem north and the black Christian and pagan south was signed **Mar. 27,** lifting the 17-year state of emergency.

The Communists opened the Berlin Wall to West Berliners for an 8-day period **Mar. 29-Apr. 5** to permit them to make Easter visits in East Berlin, the first pass period in 6 years.

Britain imposed direct rule over North Ireland **Mar. 30,** ending 51 years of semi-autonomous rule by the North Ireland government.

In the biggest Communist offensive since 1968, North Vietnamese troops **Mar. 30** launched a staggering blitz against South Vietnam through the demilitarized zone (DMZ) between the two Vietnams.

W. A. (Tony) Boyle, president of the United Mine Workers of America, was found guilty **Mar. 31** of illegally spending union funds on political contributions. He was the first major labor leader to be convicted under the 1925 Corrupt Practices Act. Boyle lost his job as UMW President, **Dec. 15,** to Arnold R. Miller, in a special court-ordered election.

The 11-week trial of the antiwar "Harrisburg 7" ended in a mistrial **Apr. 5** when the jury declared itself hopelessly deadlocked 10-to-2 in favor of acquittal after 59 hours of deliberation on conspiracy charges against the Rev. Philip Berrigan and 6 other defendants.

Canada's Prime Minister Pierre Trudeau and President Nixon **Apr. 13-15** signed a landmark treaty calling for a massive program to cleanse the Great Lakes of pollution.

Three Apollo 16 astronauts, launched **Apr. 16** from Cape Kennedy, returned with a record haul of 214 pounds of rock and soil samples from the moon.

Quang Tri, capital city of South Vietnam's northernmost province, fell to Hanoi troops **May 1** after 5 days of intensive artillery shelling. Saigon forces **Sept. 16** recaptured the final major enemy bastion in the capital after 5 days of ferocious house-to-house battles.

J. Edgar Hoover, 77, director of the Federal Bureau of Investigation (FBI) for all of its 48 years, serving

under 8 presidents, died **May 2.**

The Republican National Committee decided **May 5** that the GOP would hold its 1972 convention in Miami Beach instead of San Diego, citing increasing costs and possible labor problems on the West Coast. The San Diego site had also figured in investigation of alleged Republican favoritism toward International Telephone and Telegraph (ITT).

The mining of Haiphong and North Vietnam's other ports was ordered by President Nixon **May 8** to choke off the Communists' flow of military supplies and wreck the enemy's ability to wage sustained war.

East and West Germany May 12 initialed an agreement on all traffic but air transportation between the two countries, marking the first treaty made between them.

Alabama Gov. George C. Wallace, campaigning at a Laurel, Md., shopping center **May 15,** was shot and seriously wounded as he greeted a large, enthusiastic crowd. Arthur H. Bremer, 21, was sentenced Aug. 4 to 63 years in prison for the shooting of Wallace and 3 bystanders.

In the first visit of a U.S. President to Moscow, President Nixon arrived **May 22** for a week of summit talks with Kremlin leaders which culminated in a landmark arms pact aimed at a standoff between the missile forces of the two nuclear giants.

In a cold-blooded massacre, 3 Japanese terrorists who had just debarked from a flight **May 30** fired machine guns and lobbed hand grenades at a crowd of some 300 in Tel Aviv's Lod Airport, killing 28 and wounding 76.

The Peers Army panel, probing the Mar. 6, 1968 massacre of Vietnamese civilians in My Lai, found the entire command structure of the American Division guilty of misconduct in a report revealed **June 3-4.**

The Environmental Protection Agency announced **June 14** a near-total ban on agricultural and other uses of the pesticide DDT, to become effective **Dec. 31.**

Five men were arrested June 17 for breaking into the offices of the Democratic National Committee in Washington, D.C. One of the 5 men was James McCord, a former CIA agent, who, after his arrest, was fired as security officer for the Republican National Committee and for the Committee to Re-elect the President. Also seized with the men were cameras and electronic surveillance equipment. Lawrence F. O'Brien, Sen. George McGovern's Presidential campaign director and former Democratic national chairman, **Sept. 11** amended from $1,000,000 to $3,000,000 his damage suit against the Committee to Re-elect the President.

Prime Minister Eisaku Sato, who served longest as Japan's postwar premier, announced his resignation June 17 as head of the government. He was succeeded by Kakuei Tanaka on **July 5.**

Hurricane Agnes hit Florida June 19 and went on a 10-day rampage up 250 miles of eastern seaboard with winds and rains which unleashed "the most extensive" floods in the country's history, causing 118 deaths and more than $3 billion in property damage.

Former Atty. Gen. John N. Mitchell, confidant and campaign manager of President Nixon, quit **July 1** as chairman of the Committee to Re-elect the President, citing the need to "devote more time" to his family.

The White House announced July 8 that the U.S. would sell the Soviet Union at least $750,000,000 of American wheat, corn and other grains over a period of 3 years.

Egypt's Pres. Anwar Sadat disclosed in a surprise announcement during an address **July 18** that he had decided to "terminate the mission of the Soviet military advisers and experts" in his country.

Less than two weeks after Sen. Thomas F. Eagleton received the Democrats' nomination for Vice-President, he confirmed, **July 25,** reports that he had undergone electroshock treatment on two occasions in the 1960s. Eagleton withdrew as nominee July 31. R. Sargent Shriver was named as Vice Presidential candidate **Aug. 8.**

India and Pakistan, in the Simla pact, **July 28,** agreed to reduce tension over disputed Kashmir and to renounce force in their relations.

By a vote of 88 to 2, the Senate **Aug. 3** ratified the strategic arms treaty limiting the U.S. and Russia to two antiballistic missile sites each. In White House ceremonies **Oct. 3**, President Nixon and Soviet Foreign Min. Andrei Gromyko signed and exchanged the final documents implementing the accords, which also limited the two powers' land-based and submarine-borne nuclear missile forces.

The U.S. ended its Vietnam ground combat role **Aug. 11** with the withdrawal of the last unit, the 92-man 3d Battalion of the 21st Infantry.

After 38 preliminary sessions over a period of almost a year, delegates of the Red Cross Societies of North and South Korea, started full talks in Pyongyang **Aug. 30**, to work for reunion of some 10,000,000 members of dispersed families.

Bobby Fischer won the world chess championship **Sept. 1**, making the 29-year-old Brooklynite the first American to win since the title was established in 1886.

The Rev. Philip F. Berrigan, an antiwar activist, was sentenced **Sept. 5** to 4 concurrent two-year terms and Sister Elizabeth McAlister to one year for smuggling letters at Lewisburg, Pa., Federal Penitentiary.

Eight Arab guerrillas, members of the Black September terrorist group, invaded the Israeli dormitory of the Olympics village in Munich early **Sept. 5**, killing two members of the Israeli squad. Twenty-three hours later after tense negotiations, the terrorists and 9 hostages

were flown in 3 helicopters to an airport where 5 of the terrorists and all hostages were killed. Two Arab terrorists, armed with grenades, hijacked a Lufthansa jetliner with 20 aboard over Turkey **Oct. 29** and, with threats of blowing up the plane in midair, forced the Bavarian state government to release the 3 guerrillas involved in the Olympics killings.

Japan's Prime Min. Kakuei Tanaka and China's premier Chou En-lai terminated more than 40 years of enmity **Sept. 29**, when they signed an accord to end the technical state of war existing between the two Asian powers since **1937,** and renewed diplomatic relations.

A fight between black and white sailors aboard the aircraft carrier Kitty Hawk off Vietnam **Oct. 12-13** left 46 injured. The Navy said **Oct. 22** that charges had been preferred against 25 persons, nearly all of them black, between the ages of 18 to 21, accused of an attack on whites aboard the ship.

Spy planes joined nearly 70 other aircraft in an intense but vain search over a 56,000-sq. mile Alaska area for a plane carrying House Democratic Leader Hale Boggs of Louisiana, and Alaska's representative-at-large Nick Begich, missing since **Oct. 16** on a flight from Anchorage to Juneau.

For events of 1973 and late 1972 see chronology

---

100 Years Ago in the World Almanac

Looking back to 1873, 100 years before "Watergate," political scandal touching the high reaches of government strikes a familiar chord.

There were two scandals that year—in the United States and Canada—both byproducts of the expansion of railroads on the North American continent. In the U.S., the Credit Mobilier scandal ended in the censure on **Feb. 27** of two members of the House of Representatives, and led to charges against Vice President Schuyler Colfax and James A. Garfield, then representative from Ohio. Credit Mobilier of America was the construction company used to build the Union Pacific Railroad. The scandal sprang from the discovery that Rep. Oakes Ames of Mass., principal promoter of the company, had distributed numerous shares among congressmen and senators hoping to win their influence.

Public indignation over the "Pacific Scandal" in Canada forced the resignation of Sir John MacDonald and his cabinet on **Nov. 7**. The scandal blew up from charges that MacDonald had accepted campaign funds from a contractor anxious to build the transcontinental railroad.

Financial Panic Starts in Europe

Financial panic in May in Vienna soon spread to other major European money centers and led to the withdrawal of substantial foreign capital from the United States. The exodus of capital caused an inflated currency, unlimited credit and reckless railroad speculation. In the midst of this financial instability, the **Sept. 18** failure of Jay Cooke and Co., a banking house and financial agent for the Northern Pacific Railways, sparked the Panic of 1873.

The Fourth Coinage Act **Feb. 12** demonetized silver, putting the U.S. on the gold standard. Called "The Crime of 1873," the act came amidst new discoveries of silver in the Great Bonanza Mine in Nevada.

Public protest stirred over the "Salary Grab Bill" of **March 3** which doubled the President's salary to $50,000 and increased those of other government officials. Public dismay led to repeal of the law, excluding salaries of the President and Supreme Court Justices.

The U.S. came to the brink of war with Spain over the Virginius, an American schooner fraudulently flying the American flag and carrying men and arms to Cuban insurgents who were at war with Spain. The Spanish captured the Virginius on **Oct. 31** on the high seas near Jamaica. The captain, 36 crew members and

12 passengers were executed before Spanish-American negotiations resulted in the surrender of the 102 survivors.

In July Alexander Graham Bell made the first successful electric telephone. Also in 1873, Philo Remington's Company began to produce the typewriter which had been designed by C. L. Scholes.

On **Oct. 31** the international bridge over the Niagara River linking Canada and the United States at Buffalo was completed.

From July through October, a grasshopper plague swept Minnesota, Kansas and Nebraska.

European Powers Make Pacts

On **May 6**, Germany and Russia agreed on a military convention promising troop aid in event of an attack on either one. The Schönbrun Convention on **June 6** between Austria and Russia also assured cooperation in case of attack on either party. The great powers of Europe joined together on **Oct. 22** in the Three Emperors League to emphasize monarchial solidarity against subversive movements and to assure support in event of trouble in France.

In France, Thiers resigned as President of the Third Republic on **May 24**. The election of Marshal MacMahon, a soldier and monarchist, gave rise to hopes of a monarchist restoration. However, the Bourbon Count of Chambourd's refusal to accept the tricolor dashed monarchist hopes.

Monarchy came to an end in Spain on **Feb. 12** when, after the abdication of Amadeo I, the radical majority proclaimed the First Republic. On **Sept. 8,** in the midst of Carlist uprisings, Emilio Castelar became ruler of Spain with hopes of restoring order under the republic.

Empires and nations were still expanding in 1873. On **July 1**, Prince Edward Island joined the Canadian dominion. The Russian Empire, **Aug. 12,** assumed suzerainty in Khiva and Bokhara. On **Aug. 13,** 2 Austrians, Julius Payer and Kay Weyprecht traveled beyond the Arctic Circle to discover Franz Joseph Land.

In the arts, 1873 was the year Leo Tolstoy began **Anna Karenina,** John Stuart Mill published his **Autobiography,** Rimsky-Korsakov wrote "Ivan the Terrible" and Rimbaud published *A Season in Hell.*

The 1873 obituary listings included John Stuart Mill, Napoleon III of France and Salmon P. Chase, the Chief Justice of the U.S. Supreme Court.

Some Notable Marine Disasters Since 1868

(Figures Indicate Estimated Lives Lost)

1865, Apr. 27—Sultana; A Mississippi River steamer blew up; 1,400.

1868, Mar. 18—Magnolia; steamboat blew up on Ohio River; 80.

1868, Apr. 9—Sea Bird; steamer burned on Lake Michigan; 100.

1868, Dec. 4—United States and America; steamboats collided, burned, on Ohio River near Warsaw, Ill.; 72.

1869, October. 27—Stonewall; steamer burned in Mississippi River below Cairo, Ill.; 200.

1870, Jan. 24—Oneida; American ship sank in collision off Yokohama; 115.

1870, Jan. 28—City of Boston; American steamer of Inman Line vanished between New York and Liverpool; 191.

1870, Oct. 20—Varuna; American steamer, New York to Galveston, sank off Florida coast; 72.

1871, July 30—Westfield; Staten Island ferryboat exploded in New York Harbor; 100.

1872, Nov. 7—Mary Celeste; American half-brig sailed from New York for Genoa; found abandoned in Atlantic four weeks later in mystery of sea; crew never heard from; loss of life unknown.

1873, Jan. 22—Northfleet; British steamer foundered off Dungeness, England; 300.

1873, Apr. 1—Atlantic; British (White Star) steamer wrecked off Nova Scotia; 547.

1873, Nov. 23—Ville de Havre; French steamer, New York to Havre, sank after collision with Loch Earn; 230.

1875, Nov. 7—Schiller; German mail steamer wrecked off Scilly Islands; 200.

1875, Nov. 4—Pacific; American steamer sank after collision off Cape Flattery; 236.

1875, Dec. 6—Deutschland; German steamer, Bremen to New York, wrecked at mouth of Thames; 157.

1877, Nov. 24—Huron; U.S. warship wrecked off North Carolina; 100.

1878, Jan. 31—Metropolis; American steamer wrecked off North Carolina; 100.

1878, Sept. 3—Princess Alice; British steamer sank after collision in Thames; 700.

1878, Dec. 18—Byzantin; French steamer sank after Dardanelles collision; 210.

1879, Dec. 2—Borusia; Steamer sank off Spanish coast, 174.

1880, Nov. 24—Uncle Joseph; French steamer sank in collision off Spezzia, Greece; 250.

1881, May 24—Victoria; Steamer capsized in Thames River, Canada; 200.

1883, Jan. 19—Cimbria; German steamer hit iceberg in North Sea; 389.

1884, Jan. 18—City of Columbus; American steamer wrecked off Gay Head Light, Mass.; 103.

1887, Nov. 15—Wah Yeung; British steamer burned at sea; 400.

1887, Nov. 19—W. A. Scholten; Dutch steamer sank in English Channel collision; 134.

1889, Feb. 17—Duburg; British steamer wrecked, China Sea; 400.

1890, Mar. 1—Quetta; British steamer wrecked off Cape York, Australia; 124.

1890, Sept. 19—Ertogrul; Turkish frigate foundered off Japan; 540.

1891, Mar. 17—Utopia; British steamer sank in collision off Gibraltar; 574.

1892, Oct. 28—Roumania; British steamer wrecked off Portugal; 113.

1893, Feb. 8—Trinacria; British steamer wrecked off Spain; 115.

1895, Jan. 30—Elbe; German steamer sank in collision with British steamer Crathie in North Sea; 335.

1895, Mar. 11—Reina Regenta; Spanish cruiser foundered near Gibraltar; 400.

1898, Feb. 15—Maine; U.S. battleship blown up in Havana Harbor; 266.

1898, July 4—La Bourgogne and Cromartyshire; French steamer and British sailing ship collided off Nova Scotia; 560.

1898, Nov. 26—Portland; American steamer wrecked off Cape Cod; 157.

1900, June 30—Main, Bremen and Saale; German steamers destroyed in $10,000,000 dock fire at Hoboken, N.J.; 145.

1901, Feb. 22—Rio de Janeiro; American mail steamer wrecked in San Francisco Harbor; 128.

1903, June 7—Libau; French steamer sank in collision near Marseilles; 150.

1904, June 15—General Slocum; excursion steamer burned in East River, New York City; 1,030.

1904, June 28—Norge; steamer wrecked on Rockall Reef off Scotland; 580.

1906, Jan. 22—Valencia; American steamer lost off Vancouver Island; 129.

1906, Aug. 4—Sirio; Italian steamer wrecked off Cape Palos, Spain; 350.

1907, Feb. 12—Larchmont; American steamer sank in Long Island Sound; 131.

1907, July 20—Columbia and San Petro; American steamers collided off California coast; 100.

1908, Mar. 23—Matsu Maru; Japanese steamer sank in collision near Hakodate, Japan; 300.

1909, Aug. 1—Waratah; British steamer, Sydney to London, vanished; 300.

1910, Feb. 9—General Chanzy; French steamer wrecked off Minorca, Spain; 200.

1911, Sept. 25—Liberte; French battleship exploded at Toulon; 285.

1912, Mar. 5—Principe de Asturias; Spanish steamer wrecked off Spanish coast; 500.

1912, Apr. 14-15—Titanic; British (White Star) liner hit iceberg in North Atlantic; 1,517.

1912, Sept. 28—Kichemaru; Japanese steamer sank off Japanese coast; 1,000.

1913, Mar. 1—Calvados; British steamer lost in Sea of Marmora, Turkey; 200.

1914, May 29—Empress of Ireland; Canadian steamer sank after collision with collier in St. Lawrence River; 1,024.

1915, May 7—Lusitania; British (Cunard Line) steamer torpedoed by German submarine, sank off Ireland; 1,198.

1915, July 24—Eastland; Excursion steamer capsized in Chicago River; 812.

1916, Feb 26—Provence; French cruiser sank in Mediterranean; 3,100.

1916, Aug. 29—Hsin Yu; Chinese steamer sank off Chinese coast; 1,000.

1917, Dec. 6—Mont Blanc and Imo; French ammunition ship and Belgian steamer collided in Halifax Harbor; 1,600.

1918, Apr. 2—Kiang-Kwan; Chinese steamer sank in collision off Hankow; 500.

1918, July 6—Columbia; Steamer sank in Illinois River at Wesley City; 87.

1918, July 12—Kawachi; Japanese battleship blew up in Tokayama Bay; 500.

1918, Oct. 25—Princess Sophia; Canadian steamer sank off Alaskan coast; 398.

1919, Jan. 17—Chaonia; French steamer lost in Straits of Messina, Italy; 460.

1919, Sept. 9—Valbanera; Spanish steamer lost off Florida coast; 500.

1921, Mar. 18—Hong Kong; steamer wrecked in South China Sea; 1,000.

1922, Aug. 26—Niitaka; Japanese cruiser sank in storm off Kamchatka, USSR; 300.

1923, Apr. 23—Mossamedes; Portuguese mail steamer went aground at Cape Frio, Africa; 220.

1924, Jan. 10—L-24; British submarine in collision off Portland, England; 48.

1924, Mar. 19—No. 43; Japanese submarine in collision off Sasebo, Japan; 49.

1925, Sept. 25—S-51; American submarine in collision with steamer City of Rome off Block Island, R.I.; 34.

1925, Nov. 11—M-1; British submarine in English Channel collision; 69.

1927, Oct. 25—Principessa Mafalda; Italian steamer blew up, sank off Porto Seguro, Brazil; 314.

1927, Dec. 17—S-4; American submarine in collision off Provincetown, Mass.; 40.

1928, Oct. 3—Ondine; French submarine lost off Portugal; 43.

1928, Nov. 12—Vestris; British steamer sank in gale off Virginia coast; 113.

1932, Jan. 26—M-s; British submarine lost off Portland Bill, England; 60.

1932, Sept. 9—Observation; Steamboat carrying workmen to Rikers Island blew up in East River, New York City; 72.

1934, Sept. 8—Morro Castle; American steamer, Havana to New York, burned off Asbury Park, N.J.; 125.

1939, May 23—Squalus; American submarine sank off Portsmouth, N.H.; 26.

1939, June 1—Thetis; British submarine lost in Irish Sea; 99.

1939, June 15—Phenix; French submarine lost off Indo-China; 63.

1939, Sept. 3—Athenia; British merchant ship torpedoed west of Hebrides; 112.

1941, June 16-0-9; American submarine lost in test dive off Maine; 33.

1942, Feb. 18-Truxton and Pollux; American destroyer and cargo ship ran aground, sank off Newfoundland; 204.

1942, Oct. 2-Curacao; British cruiser sank after collision with liner Queen Mary; 335.

1943, Mar. 15-Empress of Canada; Canadian steamer torpedoed off Freetown, West Africa; 400.

1944, Dec. 24-Leopoldville; Belgian steamer torpedoed en route to Cherbourg; 764.

1947, Jan. 19-Himera; Greek steamer hit a mine off Athens; 392.

1947, Apr. 16-Grandcamp; French freighter exploded in Texas City, Tex., Harbor, starting fires; 510.

1949, Sept. 17-Noronic; Canadian Great Lakes steamer burned at Toronto; 119.

1950, Jan. 12-Truculent; British submarine in Thames collision; 65.

1951, Apr. 16-Affray; British submarine lost in English Channel; 75.

1952, Apr. 26-Hobson and Wasp; American destroyer and aircraft carrier collided in Atlantic; 176.

1952, Sept. 24-La Sibylle; French submarine lost off Toulon; 48.

1953, Apr. 4-Dumlupinar and Naboland; Turkish submarine and Swedish steamer collided in Dardanelles; 81.

1953, Oct. 16-Leyte; U.S. aircraft carrier damaged by explosion below decks in Boston; 37.

1954, ... ; explosions, fire off Quonset Point, R.I.; 103.

1954, Sept. 26-Toya Maru; Japanese ferry sank in Tsugaru Strait, Japan; 1,172.

1955, June 16-Sidon; British submarine exploded, sank in Portland Harbor, England; 13.

1956, July 26-Andrea Doria and Stockholm; Italian liner and Swedish liner collided off Nantucket; 51.

1957, July 14-Eshghabad; Soviet ship ran aground in Caspian Sea; 270.

1959, Jan. 30-Hans Hedtoft; Danish passenger-freighter hit iceberg, Greenland; 95.

1960, Dec. 19-Constellation; U.S. aircraft carrier burned in Brooklyn Navy Yard; 50.

1961, Apr. 8-Dara; British liner burned in Persian Gulf; 212.

1961, July 8-Save; Portuguese ship ran aground off Mozambique; 259.

1963, Feb. 3-Marine Sulphur Queen; American tanker vanished in Gulf of Mexico; 39.

1963, Apr. 10-Thresher; U.S. Navy atomic submarine sank in North Atlantic; 129.

1964, Feb. 10-Voyager and Melbourne; Australian destroyer sank after collision with Australian aircraft carrier off New South Wales; 82.

1965, Nov. 13-Yarmouth Castle; Panamanian registered cruise ship burned, sank off Nassau; 89.

1966, Oct. 26-Oriskany; U.S. aircraft carrier caught fire, Gulf of Tonkin; 43.

1967, July 29-Forrestal; U.S. aircraft carrier caught fire off North Vietnam; 134.

1968, Jan. 25-Dakar; Israeli submarine vanished in Mediterranean; 69.

1968, Jan. 27-Minerve; French submarine vanished in Mediterranean; 52.

1968, May 21-Scorpion; U.S. nuclear submarine sank in Atlantic near Azores; 99.

1969, Jan. 14-Enterprise; U.S. aircraft carrier suffered fires and explosions off Hawaii; 27.

1969, ... ; carrier Melbourne, S. China Sea; 74.

1970, Mar. 4-Eurydice; French submarine sank in Mediterranean near Toulon; 57.

1970, Dec. 15-Namyong-Ho; South Korean ferry sank in Korea Strait; 308.

1971, May 22-Meteor; Norwegian cruise ship burned near Vancouver, B.C.; 32.

1972, May 11-Royston Grange and Tien Cheung; British cargo and Liberian tanker collided River Plate, Argentina; 84.

(See also Chronology)

Floods, Tidal Waves

Date, Location, Number of Deaths—See also Chronology

Date	Location	Deaths	Date	Location	Deaths
1887	Hwang-ho Riv., China	900,000	1960 Oct. 10	East Pakistan	6,000
1889 May 31	Johnstown, Pa.	2,200	1960 Oct. 31	East Pakistan	4,000
1900 Sept. 8	Galveston, Tex.	5,000	1962 Feb. 17	German North Sea coast	343
1903 June 15	Heppner, Oregon	325	1962 Sept. 27	Barcelona, Spain	445
1911	Yangtze Riv., China	100,000	1963 Oct. 9	Dam collapse, Vaiont, Italy	1,800
1913 Mar. 25-27	Ohio, Indiana	732	1965 June 11	Sanderson, Tex.	10
1913 Dec. 1-5	Brazos River, Texas	177	1966 Nov. 4-6	Florence, Venice, Italy	113
1915 Aug. 17	Galveston, Tex.	275	1967 Jan. 18-24	Eastern Brazil	894
1927	Mississippi River valley	214	1967 Mar. 19	Rio de Janeiro	436
1928 Mar. 13	Collapse of St. Francis Dam, Santa Paula, Calif.	450	1968 Aug. 7-14	Gujarat state, India	1,000
1928 Sept. 13	Lake Okeechobee, Fla.	2,000	1968 Oct. 7	Northeastern India	780
1937 Jan. 22	Ohio, Miss. Valleys	250	1969 Jan. 18-26	Southern California	91
1939	Northern China	200,000	1969 Mar. 17	Mundau Valley, Alagoas, Braz.	218
1947	Honshu Island, Japan	1,900	1969 July 4	Northern Ohio	41
1951 Aug.	Manchuria	1,800	1969 Oct. 1-8	Tunisia	500
1953 Jan. 31	Western Europe	2,000	1969 Aug. 25	Western Virginia	189
1954 Aug. 17	Farahzad, Iran	2,000	1969 Sept. 15	South Korea	250
1955 Oct. 7-12	India, Pakistan	1,700	1970 May 20	Central Romania	160
1959 Nov. 1	Western Mexico	2,000	1970 July 23	Himalayans, India	500
1959 Dec. 2	Frejus, France	412	1971 Feb. 26	Rio de Janeiro, Brazil	130
1960 May 23-24	Hawaii, Japan, Okinawa	237	1972 June 9	Rapid City, S.D.	236
			1972 Aug. 7	5-week Philippines	454

Major Earthquakes

Source: National Earthquake Information Center, (NOAA) Boulder, Colo. *See also Chronology.*

Year	Place	Deaths	Year	Place	Deaths
1057	China, Chihli	25,000	1906 Aug. 16	Chile, Valparaiso	1,500
1268	Asia Minor, Silicia	60,000	1908 Dec. 28	Italy, Messina	75,000
1290 Sept. 27	China, Chihli	100,000	1915 Jan. 13	Italy, Avezzano	29,970
1293 May 20	Japan, Kamakura	30,000	1920 Dec. 16	China, Kansu	180,000
1531 Jan. 26	Portugal, Lisbon	30,000	1923 Sept. 1	Japan, Tokyo	143,000
1556 Jan. 24	China, Shensi	830,000	1932 Dec. 26	China, Kansu	70,000
1667 Nov.	Caucasia, Shemaka	80,000	1933 Mar. 10	Long Beach, Calif	115
1693 Jan. 11	Italy, Catania	60,000	1935 May 31	India, Quetta	60,000
1737 Oct. 11	India, Calcutta	300,000	1939 Jan. 24	Chile, Chillan	30,000
1755 June 7	Persia, northern	40,000	1939 Dec. 27	Turkey, Erzincan	23,000
1755 Nov. 1	Portugal, Lisbon	60,000	1946 May 31	Eastern Turkey	1,300
1783 Feb. 4	Italy, Calabria	50,000	1946 Dec. 21	Japan, Honshu	2,000
1797 Feb. 4	Ecuador, Quito	41,000	1948 June 28	Japan, Fukui	5,131
1811 Dec. 16	U.S. New Madrid, Mo.	......	1949 Aug. 5	Ecuador, Pelileo	6,000
1822 Sept. 5	Asia Minor, Aleppo	22,000	1950 Aug. 15	India, Assam	1,500
1828 Dec. 28	Japan, Echigo	30,000	1953 Mar. 18	Northwestern Turkey	1,200
1868 Aug. 13-15	Peru and Ecuador	25,000	1954 Sept. 9-12	Northern Algeria	1,657
1875 May 16	Venezuela, Colombia	16,000	1956 June 10-17	Northern Afghanistan	2,000
1896 June 15	Japan, Sea wave	22,000	1957 July 2	Northern Iran	2,500
1906 Apr. 18	Calif. San Francisco	452	1957 Dec. 4	Outer Mongolia	1,200

Year	Place	Deaths	Year	Place	Deaths
1957 Dec. 13....	Western Iran..............	2,000	1968 Aug. 31....	Northeastern Iran..........	11,588
1960 Feb. 29	Morocco, Agadir..........	12,000	1970 Mar. 28.....	Western Turkey	1,086
1960 May 21-30 .	Southern Chile ..·.......	5,700	1970 May 31.....	Northern Peru.............	66,794
1962 Sept. 1	Northwestern Iran	10,000	1971 Feb. 9.......	Southern California	65
1963 July 26 ...	Yugoslavia, Skopje	1,100	1972 Apr. 10.....	Southern Iran ......·.....	5,057
1964 Mar. 27....	Alaska....................	131	1972 Dec. 23 ...	Nicaragua	6,000
1966 Aug. 19....	Eastern Turkey............	2,529			

Fires

Date, Location and Number of Persons Killed—See also Chronology

1871	Oct.	8	Chicago, $196,000,000 loss......	250	1959	Mar.	5
1871	Oct.	9	Peshtigo, Wis., forest fire ..,...	1,182	1959	June	23
1876	Dec.	5	Brooklyn (N. Y.) Theater.......	295	1960	Mar.	12
1877	June	20	St. John, N. B., Canada	100	1960	June	11
1881	Dec.	8	Ring Theater, Vienna..........	850	1960	July	14
1883	Jan.	10	Milwaukee, Newhall Hotel	71	1960	Nov.	13
1887	May	25	Opera Comique, Paris.........	200	1961	Jan.	6
1887	Sept.	4	Exeter, Eng., theater	200	1961	May	15
1894	Sept.	1	Hickley, Minn., forest fire......	413	1961	Dec.	8
1897	May	4	Charity bazaar, Paris.........	150	1961	Dec.	17
1900	June	30	Hoboken, N. J., docks.........	326	1963	May	4
1902	Sept.	20	Church, Birmingham, Ala......	115	1963	Nov.	18
1903	Dec.	30	Iroquois Theater, Chicago......	602	1963	Nov.	23
1904	Feb.	7	Baltimore, Md...............	none	1963	Dec.	29
1908	Jan.	13	Rhoads Thea., Boyertown, Pa...	170	1964	May	8
1908	Mar.	4	School, Collinwood, Ohio	176	1964	Dec.	18
1911	Mar.	25	Triangle factory, New York	145	1965	Mar.	1
1913	July	22	Binghamton, N. Y., factory.....	35	1965	Dec.	20
1914	Mar.	9	Mo. Athletic Club, St. Louis ...	37	1966	Mar.	11
1914	June	26	1,000 bldgs., Salem, Mass......	0	1966	Aug.	13
1918	Apr.	13	Norman, Okla., state hospital ...	38	1966	Sept.	12
1918	Oct.	12	Cloquet, Minn., forest fire.....	400	1966	Oct.	17
1919	June	20	Mayaguez Theater, San Juan ...	150	1966	Dec.	7
1923	May	17	School, Camden, S. C	76	1967	Feb.	7
1924	Dec.	24	School, Hobart, Okla.........	35	1967	May	22
1929	May	15	Crile Hospital, Cleveland, Ohio..	124	1967	July	16
1930	Apr.	21	Penitentiary, Columbus, Ohio ...	320	1968	Jan.	9
1931	July	24	Pittsburgh, Pa., home for aged..	48	1968	Feb.	11
1936	Apr.	6	Gainesville, Ga., hardware co...	57	1968	Feb.	16
1938	May	16	Atlanta, Ga., Terminal Hotel ...	35	1968	Feb.	26
1940	Apr.	23	Dance hall, Natchez, Miss......	198	1968	May	11
1942	Nov.	28	Cocoanut Grove, Boston	491	1968	Nov.	18
1943	Sept.	7	Gulf Hotel, Houston..........	55	1969	Jan.	26
1944	July	6	Ringling Circus, Hartford	168	1969	Feb.	25
1946	June	5	LaSalle Hotel, Chicago........	61	1969	April	6
1946	Dec.	7	Winecoff Hotel, Atlanta.......	119	1969	Dec.	2
1946	Dec.	12	New York, ice plant, tenement...	37	1970	Jan.	9
1949	Apr.	5	Hospital, Effingham, Ill	77	1970	Mar.	20
1950	Jan.	7	Davenport, Iowa, Mercy Hospital	41	1970	Nov.	1
1953	Mar.	29	Largo, Fla., nursing home	35	1970	Nov.	5
1953	Apr.	16	Chicago, metalworking plant....	35			
1957	Feb.	17	Home for Aged, Warrenton, Mo .	72	1970	Dec.	20
1957	Nov.	16	Niagara Falls, N. Y., tenement...	18	1971	Mar.	6
1958	Mar.	19	New York City loft building	24	1971	Apr.	20
1958	Nov.	8	Tenement, Montreal, Can	21	1971	Apr.	25
1958	Dec.	1	Parochial school, Chicago......	95	1971	Oct.	19
1958	Dec.	16	Store, Bogota, Colombia	83	1972	July	5

School near Little Rock, Ark ...	24
Resort hotel, Stalheim, Norway .	34
Pusan, Korea, chemical plant....	68
Liverpool, Eng., store	22
Mental hospital, Guatemala City.	225
Movie theater, Amude, Syria ...	152
Thomas Hotel, San Francisco ...	20
Tenement, Hong Kong	25
Hospital, Hartford, Conn.......	16
Circus, Niterol, Brazil..........	323
Theater, Diourbel, Senegal	64
Surfside Hotel, Atlantic City, N.J.	25
Rest home, Fitchville, Ohio.....	63
Roosevelt Hotel, Jacksonville, Fla.	22
Apartment building, Manila	30
Nursing Home, Fountaintown,Ind.	20
Apartment, LaSalle, Canada	28
Jewish center, Yonkers, N. Y ...	12
Numata, Jap., 2 ski resorts......	31
Melbourne, Austr., hotel	29
Anchorage, Alaska, hotel	14
N. Y. City bldg. (firemen)	12
Erzurum, Turkey, barracks	68
Restaurant, Montgomery, Ala...	25
Store, Brussels, Belgium	322
State prison, Jay, Fla	37
Brooklyn, N. Y., tenement	13
Franklin, Pa., residence	11
Moberly, Mo., tavern	12
Shrewsbury, Eng., hospital	22
Vijayawada, Ind., wedding hall..	58
Glasgow, Scotland, factory	24
Victoria Hotel, Dunnville, Ont...	13
Office Building, New York City .	11
Tenement, Bridgeport, Conn	11
Nursing Home, Notre Dame, Can .	54
Nursing home, Marietta, Ohio ...	27
Hotel, Seattle, Wash..........	19
Dance hall, Grenoble, France ...	145
Nursing home, Pointes-aux-Trembles, Que.	17
Hotel, Tucson, Arizona	28
Psychiatric clinic, Burghoezli, Switz.	28
Hotel, Bangkok, Thailand	24
Apt. building, Seattle, Wash......	12
Nursing home, Honesdale, Pa......	15
Sherborne, Eng. hospital	30

Major Railroad Wrecks in the United States

Source: Federal Railroad Admin., Office of Safety
Date, Location and Number of Persons Killed. See also Chronology

1876	Dec.	29	Ashtabula, Ohio..............92	1912	July	5
1880	Aug.	11	Mays Landing, N. J...........40	1913	Sept.	2
1887	Aug.	10	Chatsworth, Ill...............81	1914	Aug.	5
1888	Oct.	10	Mud Run, Pa................55	1914	Sept.	15
1896	July	30	Atlantic City, N. J............60	1916	Mar.	29
1903	Dec.	23	Laurel Run, Pa...............53	1917	Feb.	27
1904	Aug.	7	Eden, Colo..................96	1917	Sept.	28
1904	Sept.	24	New Market, Tenn............56	1917	Dec.	20
1906	Mar.	16	Florence, Colo...............35	1918	June	22
1906	Oct.	28	Atlantic City, N. J............40	1918	July	9
1906	Dec.	30	Washington, D. C.............53	1918	Nov.	2
1907	Jan.	2	Volland, Kans................33	1919	Jan.	12
1907	Jan.	19	Fowler, Ind 29	1919	July	1
1907	Feb.	16	New York City...............22	1919	Dec.	20
1907	Mar.	12	Colton, Calif.................26	1921	Feb.	27
1907	July	20	Salem, Mich.................33	1921	Dec.	5
1907	Sept.	15	Canaan, N. H 24	1922	Aug.	5
1910	Mar.	1	Wellington, Wash.............96	1922	Dec.	13
1910	Mar.	21	Green Mountain, Ia...........55	1923	Sept.	27
1911	Aug.	25	Manchester, N. Y.............29	1925	June	16
1912	July	4	East Corning, N. Y 39	1925	Oct.	27

Ligonier, Pa.................23
North Haven, Conn...........21
Tipton Ford, Mo..............43
Lebanon, Mo................28
Amherst, Ohio...............27
Mount Union, Pa.............20
Kellyville, Okla..............23
Shepherdsville, Ky............46
Ivanhoe, Ind................68
Nashville, Tenn.............101
Brooklyn, Malbone St. Tunnel...97
South Byron, N. Y............22
Dunkirk, N. Y...............12
Onawa, Maine...............23
Porter, Ind.................37
Woodmont, Pa..............27
Sulphur Springs, Mo..........34
Humble, Tex 22
Lockett, Wyo...............31
Hackettstown, N. J...........50
Victoria, Miss 21

1926	Sept. 5	Waco, Colo	30	1950	Feb. 17	Rockville Centre, N. Y.	31
1928	Aug. 24	I. R. T. subway, N. Y., Times Sq	18	1950	Sept. 11	Coshocton, Ohio	33
1938	June 19	Saugus, Mont	47	1950	Nov. 22	Richmond Hill, N. Y	79
1939	Aug. 12	Harney, Nev.	24	1951	Feb. 6	Woodbridge, N. J	84
1940	Apr. 19	Little Falls, N. Y	31	1951	Nov. 12	Wyuta, Wyo	17
1940	July 31	Cuyahoga Falls, Ohio	43	1951	Nov. 25	Woodstock, Ala.	17
1942	Dec. 27	Almonte, Ontario	36	1953	Mar. 27	Conneaut, Ohio	21
1943	Aug. 29	Wayland, N. Y	27	1956	Jan. 22	Los Angeles, Calif	30
1943	Sept. 6	Frankford Junction, Philadelphia.	79	1956	Feb. 28	Swampscott, Mass	13
1943	Dec. 16	Bet. Rennert and Buie, N. C	72	1956	Sept. 5	Springer, N. M	20
1944	July 6	High Bluff, Tenn.	35	1957	June 11	Vroman, Colo	12
1944	Aug. 4	Near Stockton, Ga	47	1958	Sept. 15	Elizabethport, N. J.	48
1944	Sept. 14	Dewey, Ind.	29	1960	Mar. 14	Bakersfield, Calif	14
1944	Dec. 31	Bagley, Utah	50	1962	July 28	Steelton, Pa	19
1945	Aug. 9	Michigan, N. Dak.	34	1966	Dec. 28	Everett, Mass.	13
1946	Apr. 25	Naperville, Ill.	45	1971	June 10	Salem, Ill.	11
1947	Feb. 18	Gallitzin, Pa	24	1972	Oct. 30	Chicago, Ill.	45

World's worst wreck occurred Dec. 12, 1917, Modane, France, passenger train derailed, 543 killed.

Historic Assassinations Since 1865

1865—April 14. Abraham Lincoln, President of the United States, in Washington; died April 15.

1876—June 4. Abdul-Aziz, Sultan of Turkey.

1881—Mar. 13. Alexander II, of Russia—July 2. James A. Garfield, President of the United States, in Washington; Died Sept. 19.

1893—Oct. 28. Carter H. Harrison, Mayor of Chicago.

1894—June 24. Marie Francois Sadi-Carnot, President of France.

1896—May 1. Nasr-ed-Din, Shah of Persia.

1898—Sept. 10. Empress Elizabeth of Austria.

1899—July 26. Gen. Ulises Heureaux, President of the Dominican Republic.

1900—Jan. 30. William Goebel, Governor of Kentucky—July 29. Humbert I, King of Italy.

1901—Sept. 6. William McKinley. President of the United States, in Buffalo; died Sept. 14. Leon Czolgosz executed for the crime Oct. 29.

1903—June 11. King Alexander I and Queen Draga of Serbia by army officers at Belgrade.

1908—Feb. 1. Carlos I, King of Portugal, and Crown Prince Louis Phillippe, in Lisbon.

1911—Sept. 14. Piotr A. Stolypin, Premier of Russia.

1912—Nov. 12. Jose Canalejas, Premier of Spain.

1913—Feb. 23. Francisco I. Madero, President of Mexico and Jose Pino Suarez, the Vice-President—March 18. George, King of Greece.

1914—June 28. Archduke Francis Ferdinand of Austria-Hungary and his wife, Countess Sophie Chotek, Duchess of Hohenberg, in Sarajevo, Bosnia (later part of Yugoslavia), by Gavrillo Princip.

1916—Oct. 21. Karl Sturgkh, Austrian Premier.—Dec. 30. Grigori Rasputin, politically powerful Russian monk.

1918—July 12. Grand Duke Michael of Russia, at Perm—July 16. Nicholas II, abdicated Czar of Russia; his wife, the Czarina Alexandra; their son, Alexei, Grand Duke Alexis, and their daughters, Grand Duchesses Olga, Tatiana, Marie, Anastasia, and 4 members of their household were murdered in cold blood by Bolsheviki at Ekaterinburg—Dec. 14. Pres. Sidonio Paes of Portugal, in Lisbon.

1920—May 20. Gen. Venustiano Carranza, President of Mexico, in Tiaxcaltenago.

1921—Nov. 4. Takashi Hara, Japanese Prime Minister.

1922—June 24. Walter Rathenau, German foreign minister.—Aug. 22. Michael Collins, Irish revolutionary.

1923—July 20. Gen. Francisco "Pancho" Villa, ex-rebel leader, in Parral, Mexico.

1928—July 17. Gen. Alvaro Obregon, President-elect of Mexico, in San Angel, Mexico.

1930—Nov. 14. Japanese Premier Yuko Hamaguchi.

1932—May 6. Paul Doumer, President of French Republic.—May 16. Ki Inukai, Japanese Prime Minister.

1933—Feb. 15. In Miami, Fla., Joseph Zangara, anarchist, shot at President-elect Franklin D. Roosevelt, but a woman seized his arm, and the bullet fatally wounded Mayor Anton J. Cermak, of Chicago, who died March 6. Zangara was electrocuted on March 20, 1933.

1934—July 25. In Vienna, Engelbert Dollfuss, Chancellor of Austria, by Nazi, in the chancellery. Otto Planetta convicted and hanged—Oct. 9. In Marseilles, King Alexander I of Yugoslavia and French For. Min. Jean Louis Barthou.

1935—Sept. 8. U. S. Senator Huey P. Long, shot in Baton Rouge, La., by Dr. Carl Austin Weiss, who was slain by Long's bodyguards.

1940—Aug. 20. Leon Trotsky (Leba Bronstein), 63, exiled Russian war minister, near Mexico City. Killer, identified as Ramon Mercador del Rio, a Spaniard, served 20 years in Mexican prison.

1942—Dec. 24. Adm. Jean F. Darlan, 61, Algiers.

1945—Feb. 24. Egyptian Premier Ahmed Maher Pasha.

1946—July 21. Bolivian President Gualberto Villarroel.

1947—July 19. U Aung San, Premier of Burma, and 5 aides in his provisional government. Former Premier U Saw and 5 accomplices hanged.

1948—Jan. 30. Mohandas K. Gandhi, 78, shot in New Delhi, India, by Nathuran Vinayak Godse, 36—Sept. 17. Count Folke Bernadotte, U. N. Mediator for Palestine, ambushed in Jerusalem.

1950—Nov. 13. Col. C. Delgado Chalbaud, President of Venezuela, in Caracas.

1951—July 20. King Abdul ibn Hussein of Jordan.

1955—Jan. 2. Jose Antonio Remon, President of Panama, by machine gun at race track, Panama.

1956—Sept. 21. Anastasio Somoza, President of Nicaragua, in Leon; died Sept. 29.

1957—July 26. President Carlos Castillo Armas of Guatemala, in Guatemala City by one of his own guards, who then committed suicide.

1958—July 14. King Faisal of Iraq; his uncle, Crown Prince Abdul Illah, and July 15, Premier Nuri as-Said, by rebels in Baghdad.

1959—Sept. 25. Prime Minister S. W. R. D. Bandaranaike of Ceylon, by Buddhist monk in Colombo.

1960—Aug. 29. Premier Hazza Majali of Jordan and 10 others killed by time bomb in his office.

1961—Jan. 17. Ex-Premier Patrice Lumumba of the Congo, ex-Youth Minister Maurice Mpolo and Senate Vice President Joseph Okito in Katanga Province—May 30. Dominican dictator Rafael Leonidas Trujillo Molina shot to death by assassins near Ciudad Trujillo.

1963—Jan. 13. President Sylvanus Olympio of Togo, by ex-soldiers at Lome.—June 12. Medgar W. Evers, NAACP's Mississippi field secretary, in Jackson, Miss.—Nov. 1-2. President Ngo Dinh Diem of the Republic of Vietnam and his brother, Ngo Dinh Diem, in a military coup.—Nov. 22. U.S. President John F. Kennedy fatally shot in Dallas, Tex.; accused Lee Harvey Oswald murdered while awaiting trial.

1965—Jan. 21. Irani Premier Hassan Ali Mansour fatally wounded by assassin in Teheran; 4 executed—Feb. 21. Malcolm X, Negro nationalist, fatally shot in New York City; 3 sentenced to life.

1966—Sept. 6. Prime Minister Hendrik F. Verwoerd of South Africa stabbed to death in parliament at Capetown by drifter later ruled insane.

1968—Apr. 4. Rev. Dr. Martin Luther King, Jr., fatally shot in Memphis, Tenn.; James Earl Ray sentenced to 99 years—June 5. Sen. Robert F. Kennedy, (D., N.Y.) fatally shot in Los Angeles; Sirhan Sirhan, resident alien, sentenced to death.

1969—Feb. 3. Eduardo Mondlane, leader of Mozambique Liberation Front, by explosive parcel in mail at Dar es Salaam, Tanzania—July 5. Tom Mboya, Kenya's minister of economic planning and development, in Nairobi—Oct. 17. A. A. Shermarke, President of Somalia, at Las Anos, Somalia.

1971—Nov. 28. Jordan Prime Minister Wasfi Tal, in Cairo, by Palestinian guerrillas.

Assassination Attempts

1910—Aug. 6. New York City Mayor Wm. J. Gaynor shot and seriously wounded by discharged city employee.

1912—Oct. 14. Former U.S. President Theodore Roosevelt shot and seriously wounded by demented man in Milwaukee.

1950—Nov. 1. In an attempt to assassinate President Truman, two men identified as members of a Puerto Rican nationalist movement—Griselio Torresola and Oscar Collazo—tried to shoot their way into Blair House. Torresola was killed, and a guard, Pvt. Leslie Coffelt was fatally shot. Collazo, wounded, recovered and was tried and convicted Mar. 7, 1951 for the murder of Coffelt. His death sentence was commuted to life imprisonment by President Truman.

1970—Nov. 27. Pope Paul VI unharmed by knife-wielding assailant dressed as priest who attempted to attack him in Manila airport. Benjamin Mendoza, Bolivian, charged with attempted murder.

See also Chronology.

Major Kidnaping Crimes

Charles B. Ross, 4, in Germantown, Pa., **July 1, 1874.** $20,000 not delivered. Boy never found, abductors shot while committing burglary.

Edward A. Cudahy, Jr., 16, in Omaha, Neb., **Dec. 18, 1900.** Returned Dec. 20 after $25,000 paid. Pat Crowe confessed.

Robert Franks, 13, in Chicago, **May 22, 1924,** by two youths, Loeb and Leopold, who killed boy. Demand for $10,000 ignored. Loeb died in prison, Leopold paroled 1958, freed 1963.

Marian Parker, 12, in Los Angeles. **Dec. 15, 1927,** returned dead after $1,500 paid. William E. Hickman hanged.

Charles A. Lindbergh, Jr., 20 mos. old, in Hopewell, N. J., **Mar. 1, 1932;** found dead May 12. Ransom of $50,000 was paid to man identified as Bruno Richard Hauptmann, 35, paroled German convict who entered U.S. illegally. Hauptmann passed ransom bill and $14,000 marked money was found in his garage. He was convicted after spectacular trial at Flemington, and electrocuted in Trenton, N. J., prison, Apr. 3, 1936.

William A. Hamm, Jr., 39, in St. Paul, **June 15, 1933.** $100,000 paid. Alvin Karpis given life, paroled in 1969.

Charles F. Urschel, in Oklahoma City, **July 22, 1933.** Released July 31 after $200,000 paid. Geo. (Machine Gun) Kelly and 5 others given life.

Edward G. Bremer, 37, St. Paul, Minn., **Jan. 17, 1934.** Released Feb. 7 after $200,000 paid. Two given life.

George Weyerhaeuser, 9, in Tacoma, Wash., **May 24, 1935.** Returned home June 1 after $200,000 paid. Kidnapers given 20 to 60 years.

Charles Mattson, 10, in Tacoma, Wash., **Dec. 27, 1936.** Found dead Jan. 11, 1937. Kidnaper asked $28,000, failed to contact.

Arthur Fried, in White Plains, N.Y., **Dec. 4, 1937.** Body not found. Two kidnapers executed.

Peter Levine, 12, in New Rochelle, N.Y., **Feb. 24, 1938.** Dismembered body found May 29.

Robert C. Greenlease, 6, son of a Kansas City, Mo., motor car dealer, taken from school **Sept. 28, 1953,** and held for $600,000. Body found Oct. 7, when Mrs. Bonnie Brown Heady and Carl A. Hall were arrested. They pleaded guilty and were executed Dec. 18.

Evelyn Smith, 23, in Phoenix, Ariz., **June 9, 1954.** Released unharmed June 10, after $75,000 was paid.

Peter Weinberger, 32 days old, in Westbury, L.I., N.Y., **July 4, 1956,** for $2,000 ransom, not paid. Child found dead. Angelo John LaMarca, 31, convicted, executed.

Cynthia Ruotolo, 6 wks. old, taken from carriage in front of Hamden, Conn. store **Sept. 1, 1956.** Body found in lake.

Lee Crary, 8, in Everett, Wash., **Sept. 22, 1957,** for $10,000 ransom, not paid. Escaped after 3 days, led police to George E. Collins, convicted.

Eric Peugeot, 4, taken from playground at St. Cloud golf course, Paris, **Apr. 12, 1960.** Released unharmed 3 days later after payment of undisclosed sum to kidnaper who had demanded $100,000. Two sentenced to prison.

Frank Sinatra, Jr., 19, from hotel room in Lake Tahoe, Calif., **Dec. 8, 1963.** Released Dec. 11 after his father paid $240,000 ransom. John W. Irwin, Barry W. Keenan and Joseph C. Amsler sentenced to prison; most of ransom recovered.

Daniel Jesse Goldman, 18, abducted **Mar. 18, 1966,** from his home near Bal Harbour, Fla.

Mrs. Betty Hill, 42, was held prisoner in her Boulder, Colo., home **Jan. 6, 1967,** by an intruder who released her shortly afterward when her husband paid $50,000 ransom.

Kenneth King, 11, was abducted from his bedroom in Beverly Hills, Calif. **Apr. 3, 1967,** but was freed unharmed 3 days later after his father paid $250,000 ransom.

Barbara Jane Mackle, 20, abducted **Dec. 17, 1968,** from Atlanta, Ga., motel, was found unharmed 3 days later, buried in a coffin-like wooden box 18 inches underground, after her father had paid $500,000 ransom; Gary Steven Krist sentenced to life, Ruth Eisenmann-Schier to 7 years; most of ransom recovered.

Anne Katherine Jenkins, 22, abducted **May 10, 1969,** from her Baltimore apartment, freed 3 days later after her father paid $10,000 ransom; Edward Lee Dull and Marie Calvert charged with crime.

Mrs. Roy Fuchs, 35, and 3 children held hostage two hours **May 14, 1969,** in Long Island, N.Y., released after her husband, a bank manager, paid kidnapers $129,000 in bank funds; 4 men arrested, ransom recovered.

C. Burke Elbrick, U.S. Amb. to Brazil, kidnaped by Brazilian revolutionaries in Rio de Janeiro **Sept. 4, 1969;** released 3 days later after Brazil yielded to kidnapers' demands by publishing manifesto and releasing 15 political prisoners.

Mrs. Mary Nelles, 26, abducted near Toronto, Canada, **Sept. 7, 1969;** freed unharmed after payment of $200,000 ransom; 5 sentenced to 10-15 years, ransom recovered.

Patrick Dolan, 18, found shot to death near Sao Paulo, Brazil, **Nov. 5, 1969,** after he was kidnaped and $12,500 paid.

Sean M. Holly, U.S. diplomat, in Guatemala **Mar. 6, 1970;** freed two days later upon release of 3 terrorists from prison.

Lt. Col. Donald J. Crowley, U.S. air attache, in Dominican Republic **Mar. 24, 1970;** released after government allowed 20 prisoners to leave the country.

Count Karl von Spreti, W. German Amb. to Guatemala, **Mar. 31, 1970;** slain after Guatemala refused demands for $700,000 and release of 22 prisoners.

Rudy W. Martinez, Guatemalan coffee exporter, by terrorists **Apr. 23, 1970;** released on payment of large ransom.

Pedro Eugenio Aramburu, former Argentine President, by terrorists **May 29, 1970;** body found July 17.

Ehrenfried von Holleben, W. German Amb. to Brazil, by terrorists **June 11, 1970;** freed after release of 40 prisoners.

Fernando Londono y Londono, former Colombian Foreign Minister, by Colombian terrorists **July 9, 1970;** freed after family paid $200,000 ransom.

Daniel A. Mitrione, U.S. diplomat, **July 31, 1970,** by terrorists in Montevideo, Uruguay; body found Aug. 10 after government rejected demands for release of all political prisoners.

Aloysio Dias Gomide, Brazilian vice consul, kidnaped **July 31, 1970;** released Feb. 21, 1971, after wife paid ransom estimated at over $250,000.

Claude L. Fly, U. S. agronomist, by terrorists in Montevideo **Aug. 7, 1970;** released Mar. 2, 1971, after suffering illness.

James R. Cross, British trade commissioner, **Oct. 5, 1970,** by French Canadian separatists in Quebec; freed Dec. 3 after 3 kidnapers and relatives flown to Cuba by government.

Pierre Laporte, Quebec Labor Minister, by separatists **Oct. 10, 1970;** body found Oct. 18.

Eugen Beihl, W. German businessman, by Basque separatists, in San Sebastian, Spain, **Dec. 1, 1970;** released Dec. 25 unharmed.

Giovanni E. Bucher, Swiss Amb., **Dec. 7, 1970,** by revolutionaries in Rio de Janeiro; freed Jan. 16, 1971, after Brazil released 70 political prisoners.

Geoffrey Jackson, British Amb., in Montevideo, **Jan. 8, 1971,** by Tupamaro terrorists. Held as ransom for the release of imprisoned terrorists, he was released Sept. 9, after the prisoners escaped.

Four U.S. airmen, in Ankara, by Turkish leftist terrorists on **Mar. 4, 1971.** $400,000 ransom was not paid, but they were released unharmed Mar. 8.

Ephraim Elrom, Israel consul general in Istanbul, **May 17, 1971.** Held as ransom for imprisoned terrorists, he was found dead May 23.

Mrs. Virginia Piper, 49, abducted **July 27, 1972,** from her home in suburban Minneapolis; found unharmed near Duluth two days later after her husband paid $1,000,000 ransom to the kidnapers.

See also Chronology.

Some Major Tornadoes Since 1925

Source: National Climatic Center, NOAA, Dept. of Commerce

Date		Place	Dead	Date		Place	Dead
1925	Mar. 18	Mo., Ill., Ind.	689	1952	Mar. 21	Ark., Mo., Tenn. (series)	208
1926	Nov. 25	Belleville to Portland, Ark	53	1953	May 11	Waco, Texas	114
1927	Apr. 12	Rock Springs, Tex	74	1953	June 8	Flint to Lakeport, Mich	116
1927	May 9	Arkansas, Poplar Bluff, Mo	92	1953	June 9	Worcester and vicinity, Mass.	90
1927	Sept. 29	St. Louis, Mo	72	1953	Dec. 5	Vicksburg, Miss	38
1929	Apr. 25	S.E.-Central Ga	40	1955	May 25	Udall, Kans.	80
1930	May 6	Hill & Ellis Co., Tex.	41	1957	May 20	Williamsburg, Kans, to Ruskin	
1932	Mar. 21	Ala. (series of tornadoes)	268			Heights, Mo	48
1936	Apr. 5	Tupelo, Miss.	216	1958	June 4	Northwestern Wisconsin	30
1936	Apr. 6	Gainesville, Ga.	203	1959	Feb. 10	St. Louis, Mo	21
1938	Sept. 29	Charleston, S. C	32	1960	May 5,6	S. E. Oklahoma, Arkansas.	30
1942	Mar. 16	Central to N.E. Miss.	75	1965	Apr. 11	Ind., Ill., Mich., Wis.	271
1942	Apr. 27	Rogers & Mayes Co., Okla	52	1966	Mar. 3	Jackson, Miss.	57
1944	June 23	Ohio, Pa. W. Va., Md	150	1966	Mar. 3	Mississippi, Alabama	61
1945	Apr. 12	Okla.-Ark.	102	1967	April 21	Illinois	33
1946	Jan. 4	N. E. Texas.	30	1968	May 15	Arkansas	34
1947	Apr. 9	Texas, Okla. & Kans.	169	1969	Jan. 23	Mississippi.	32
1948	Mar. 19	Bunker Hill & Gillespie, Ill	33	1970	Apr. 18	Texas Panhandle (series)	25
1949	Jan. 3	La. & Ark.	58	1970	May 11	Lubbock, Texas	26
				1971	Feb. 21	Miss. delta	110

Number of Tornadoes in U. S. Since 1916, Deaths

Year	No.	Deaths	Year	No.	Deaths	Year	No.	Deaths	Year	No.	Deaths
1916	90	150	1931	94	36	1946	106	78	1961	682	51
1917	121	509	1932	151	394	1947	165	313	1962	658	28
1918	81	135	1933	258	362	1948	183	140	1963	461	31
1919	64	206	1934			1949			1964		
1921	105	202	1936	151	552	1951	272	34	1966	570	99
1922	108	135	1937	147	29	1952	236	230	1967	912	116
1923	102	109	1938	213	183	1953	437	516	1968	661	131
1924	130	376	1939	152	87	1954	549	35	1969	604	66
1925	119	794	1940	124	65	1955	593	125	1970	649	73
1926	111	144	1941	118	53	1956	532	83	1971	888	156
1927	163	540	1942	167	384	1957	864	191	1972	741	27*
1928	203	92	1943	152	58	1958	565	66	Total	18,827	10,503
1929	197	274	1944	169	275	1959	589	58	Average	330	184
1930	192	179	1945	121	210	1960	618	47			

*Record low.

Hurricanes, Typhoons, Blizzards, Other Storms

Date, Locations, Number of Deaths—See also Chronology
Names of hurricanes and typhoons in italics

1888	Mar. 11-14	Blizzard, East U.S.	400	1963	Oct. 4-8	H. *Flora*, Cuba, Haiti	6,000
1900	Sept. 8	Hurricane, Galveston, Tex.	6,000	1964	Oct. 4-7	H. *Hilda*, La., Miss., Ga.	38
1926	Sept. 16-22	Hurricane, Fla., Ala.	372	1964	June 30	T. *Winnie*, No. Philippines.	107
1926	Oct. 20	Hurricane, Cuba.	600	1964	Sept. 5	T. *Ruby*, Hong Kong and	
1928	Sept. 12-17	Hurricane, W. Indies, Fla.	4,000			China.	735
1930	Sept. 3	Hurricane, San Domingo.	2,000	1964	Sept. 14	Flooding, Central S. Korea.	563
1938	Sept. 21	Hurricane, New England	600	1964	Nov. 12	Flooding, So. Vietnam	7,000
1942	Oct. 15-16	Hurricane, Bengal, India	11,000	1965	May 11-12	Windstorm, E. Pakistan.	17,000
1944	Sept. 12-16	Hurricane, N. C. to N. England		1965	June 1-2	Windstorm, E. Pakistan.	30,000
			389	1965	Sept. 7-10	H. *Betsy*, Fla., Miss., La.	74
1953	Sept. 25-27	Typhoon, Vietnam, Japan	1,300	1965	Dec. 15	Windstorm, E. Pakistan.	10,000
1954	Aug. 30	H *Carol*, northeast U. S.	68	1966	June 4-10	H. *Alma*, Honduras, s.e. U.S.	51
1954	Sept. 11	H. *Edna*, n.e. U. S., Canada.	23	1966	Sept. 24-30	H. *Inez*, Carib., Fla., Mex.	293
1954	Oct. 12-16	H. *Hazel*, east U. S., Haiti	347	1967	July 9	T. *Billie*, Japan	347
1955	Aug. 12-13	H. *Connie*, Carolinas, Va., Md.	43	1967	Sept. 5-23	H. *Beulah*, Carib, Mex., Tex.	54
1955	Aug. 18-19	H. *Diane*, eastern U. S.	400	1967	Dec. 12-20	Blizzard, southwest U. S.	51
1955	Sept. 19	H. *Hilda*, Mexico	200	1968	Nov. 18-29	T. *Nina*, Philippines	63
1955	Sept. 22-26	H. *Janet*, Caribbean	500	1969	Aug. 17-18	H. *Camille*, Miss., La.	258
1956	Feb. 1-29	Blizzard, western Europe	1,000	1969	July 4-5	Flooding, wind, and electrical	
1957	June 27-30	H. *Audrey*, La., Tex.	430			storms, n. Ohio.	41
1958	Feb. 15-16	Blizzard, n.e. U. S.	171	1970	July 30-		
1959	Sept. 17-19	T. *Sarah*, Far East	2,000		Aug. 5	H. *Celia*, Cuba, Fla., Tex.	31
1959	Sept. 26-27	T. *Vera*, Honshu, Japan.	4,466	1970	Aug. 20-21	H. *Dorothy*, Martinique.	42
1960	Sept. 4-12	H. *Donna*, Caribbean, e. U. S.	148	1970	Sept. 15	T. *Georgia*, Philippines	300
1961	Sept. 11	H. *Carla*, Tex., La.	40	1970	Oct. 14	T. *Sening*, Philippines	583
1961	Oct. 31	H. *Hattie*, Br. Honduras	400	1970	Oct. 15	T. *Titang*, Philippines	526
1962	Feb. 17	Flooding, German North Sea		1970	Nov. 13	Cyclone, East Pakistan	200,000
		Coast	343				or more
1962	Sept. 27	Flooding, Barcelona, Spain	445	1971	Aug. 1	T. *Rose*, Hong Kong	130
1963	May 28-29	Windstorm, E. Pakistan	22,000	1972	June 14-23	H. *Agnes*, Fla. to N.Y.	117

Explosions

Date, Location, Number of Deaths—See also Marine Disasters, Fires and Chronology

1910	Oct. 1	Los Angeles Times Bldg	21	1920	Sept. 16	Wall St., New York, bomb	30
1913	Mar. 7	Dynamite, Baltimore harbor	55	1924	Jan. 3	Food plant, Pekin, Ill	42
1915	Sept. 27	Gasoline tank car, Ardmore, Okla.	47	1937	Mar. 18	New London, Tex., school	294
1917	Apr. 10	Munitions plant, Eddystone, Pa	133	1940	Sept. 11	Hercules Powder, Kenvil, N. J.	51
1917	Dec. 6	Halifax Harbor, Canada	1,600	1942	June 5	Ordnance plant, Elwood, Ill	49
1918	July 2	Explosives, Split Rock, N. Y.	50	1944	Apr. 14	Bombay, India, harbor	700
1918	Oct. 4	Shell plant, Morgan Station, N. J	64	1944	July 17	Port Chicago, Calif., pier	322
1919	May 22	Food plant, Cedar Rapids, Iowa	44	1944	Oct. 21	Liquid gas tank, Cleveland	135

1947	Apr.	16	Texas City, Tex., pier	561
1948	July	28	Farben works, Ludwigshafen, Ger.	184
1950	May	19	Munition barges, S. Amboy, N. J.	30
1956	Aug.	7	Dynamite trucks, Cali, Colombia	1,100
1958	Apr.	18	Sunken munitions ship, Okinawa.	40
1958	May	22	Nike missiles, Leonardo. N. J ..	10
1959	Apr.	10	World War II bomb, Philippines .	38
1959	June	2	Gas truck, Penn. Turnpike	10
1959	June	28	Rail tank cars, Meldrin, Ga	25
1959	Aug.	7	Dynamite truck, Roseburg, Ore .	13
1959	Nov.	2	Jamuri Bazar, India, explosives...	46
1959	Dec.	13	Dortmund, Ger. 2 apt. bldgs.	26
1960	Mar.	4	Belgian munition ship, Havana ..	100
1960	Oct.	25	Gas, Windsor, Ont., store	11
1962	Jan.	16	Gas pipeline, Alberta, Canada...	19
1962	Mar.	3	Gasoline truck, Syria	31
1962	Oct.	3	Telephone Co. office, New York .	23
1963	Jan.	2	Packing plant, Terre Haute, Ind .	16
1963	Mar.	9	Dyn. plant, So. Africa	45
1963	Mar.	9	Steel plant, Belecke, W. Germany .	19
1963	Aug.	13	Explosives dump, Gauhiti, India..	32
1963	Oct.	31	State Fair Coliseum, Indianapolis	73
1964	July	23	Bone, Algeria, harbor munitions ..	100
1965	Mar.	4	Gas pipeline Natchitoches, La...	17
1965	Aug.	9	Missile silo, Searcy, Ark	53
1965	Oct.	21	Bridge, Tila Bund, Pakistan	80
1965	Oct.	30	Marketplace, Cartagena. Col.....	48
1965	Nov.	24	Armory, Keokuk, Iowa	20
1966	Oct.	13	Chemical plant, La Salle, Que...	11
1967	Feb.	17	Chemical plant, Hawthorne, N. J	11
1967	Dec.	25	Apartment bldg., Moscow	20
1968	Apr.	6	Sports store, Richmond, Ind	43
1970	Apr.	8	Subway construction, Osaka, Japan	73
1970	Nov.	11	Oil well, Tulsa, Oklahoma	9
1970	Dec.	11	Tavern building, New York City .	9
1971	June	24	Tunnel, Sylmar, Calif	17
1971	June	28	School, fireworks, Pueblo, Mex.....	13
1971	Oct.	21	Shopping center, Glasgow, Scot.....	20

Principal Mine Disasters in the U.S.

Source: Bureau of Mines

NOTE: Prior to 1968, only disasters with losses of 50 or more lives are listed; for 1968-72, all disasters in which 5 or more men are killed are listed. Only fatalities to mining company employees are included.

All Bituminous-coal mines unless otherwise designated

Date	Location	Killed	Date	Location	Killed
March 1855	Coalfield, Va.	55	3-2-1915	Layland, W. Va.	112
4-3-1867	Winterpock, Va.	69	4-27-1917	Hastings, Colo.	121
9-6-1869[1]	Plymouth, Pa.	110	6-8-1917[2]	Butte, Mont.	163
2-16-1883	Braidwood, Ill.	69	8-4-1917	Clay, Ky.	62
1-24-1884	Crested Butte, Colo.	59	6-5-1919[1]	Wilkes-Barre, Pa.	92
3-13-1884	Pocahontas, Va.	112	11-6-1922	Spangler, Pa.	77
1-27-1891	Mount Pleasant, Pa.	109	11-22-1922	Dolomite, Ala.	90
1-7-1892	Krebs, Okla.	100	2-8-1923	Dawson, N. Mex.	120
3-20-1895	Red Canyon, Wyo.	60	8-14-1923	Kemmerer, Wyo.	99
6-28-1896[1]	Pittston, Pa.	58	3-8-1924	Castle Gate, Utah	171
5-1-1900	Scofield, Utah	200	4-28-1924	Benwood, W. Va.	119
5-19-1902	Coal Creek, Tenn.	184	2-20-1925	Sullivan, Ind.	52
7-10-1902	Johnstown, Pa.	112	5-27-1925	Coal Glen, N.C.	53
6-30-1903	Hanna, Wyo.	169	12-10-1925	Acmar, Ala.	53
1-25-1904	Cheswick, Pa.	179	1-13-1926	Wilburton, Okla.	91
2-20-1905	Virginia City, Ala.	112	11-3-1926[2]	Ishpeming, Mich.	51
1-29-1907	Stuart, W. Va.	84	4-30-1927	Everettville, W. Va.	97
12-6-1907	Monongah, W. Va.	361	5-19-1928	Mather, Pa.	195
12-16-1907	Yolande, Ala.	57	12-17-1929	McAlester, Okla.	61
12-19-1907	Jacobs Creek, Pa.	239	11-5-1930	Millfield, Ohio	79
3-28-1908	Hanna, Wyo.	59	12-23-1932	Moweaqua, Ill.	54
11-28-1908	Marianna, Pa.	154	1-10-1940	Bartley, W. Va.	91
12-29-1908	Switchback, W. Va.	50	3-16-1940	St. Clairsville, Ohio	72
1-12-1909	Switchback, W. Va.	67	7-15-1940	Portage, Pa.	63
11-13-1909	Cherry, Ill.	259	5-12-1942	Osage, W. Va.	56
1-31-1910	Primero, Colo.	75	2-27-1943	Red Lodge, Mont.	74
5-5-1910	Palos, Ala.	90	7-5-1944	Belmont, Ohio	66
10-8-1910	Starkville, Colo.	56	3-25-1947	Centralia, Ill.	111
11-8-1910	Delagua, Colo.	79	12-21-1951	West Frankfort, Ill.	119
4-7-1911	Throop, Pa.	72	3-6-1968[3]	Calumet, La.	21
4-8-1911	Littleton, Ala.	128	8-7-1968	Greenville, Ky.	9
12-9-1911	Briceville, Tenn.	84	11-20-1968	Farmington, W. Va.	78
3-20-1912	McCurtain, Okla.	73	12-30-1970	Hyden, Ky.	38
3-26-1912	Jed, W. Va.	83	4-12-1971[3]	Rosiclare, Ill.	7
4-23-1913	Finleyville, Pa.	96	5-2-1972[2]	Kellogg, Idaho	91
10-22-1913	Dawson, N. Mex.	263	7-22-1972	Blacksville, W. Va.	9
4-28-1914	Eccles, W. Va.	181	12-16-1972	Itmann, W. Va.	5
10-27-1914	Royalton, Ill.	52			

World's worst mine disaster killed 1,549 workers in the Honkeiko Colliery in Manchuria Apr. 26, 1942.
(1) Anthracite mine. (2) Metal mine. (3) Nonmetal mine.

Some Notable Aircraft Disasters Since 1937

Date	Aircraft	Site of accident	Deaths
1937 May 6	Ger. zeppelin Hindenburg	Burned at mooring, Lakehurst, N. J.	36
1944 Aug. 23	U. S. Air Force B-24	Hit school, Freckelton, England	76[1]
1945 July 28	U. S. Army B-25	Hit Empire State bldg., N. Y. C	14[1]
1949 Nov. 1	Eastern Air Lines DC-4	Rammed by Bolivian P-38, Wash., D. C	55
1950 Mar. 12	Chartered Avro Tudor	Crashed near Cardiff, Wales	80
1950 June 24	Northwest Airlines DC-4	Exploded in storm over Lake Michigan	58
1951 Dec. 16	Miami Airlines C-46	Plunged into Elizabeth River, N. J	56
1952 Dec. 20	U. S. Air Force C-124	Fell, burned, Moses Lake, Wash	87
1953 Mar. 3	Canadian Pacific Comet jet	Karachi, Pakistan	11[2]
1953 June 18	U. S. Air Force C-124	Crashed, burned near Tokyo	129
1955 Aug. 11	2 USAF Flying Boxcars	Collided near Stuttgart, Germany	66
1955 Nov. 1	United Air Lines DC-6B	Exploded, crashed near Longmont, Colo	44[3]
1956 June 20	Venezuelan Super-Const	Crashed in Atlantic off Asbury Park, N. J	74
1956 June 30	TWA Super-Const., United DC-7 ...	Collided over Grand Canyon, Arizona	128
1957 Aug. 11	Maritime, Central Airways DC-4 ...	Crashed in swamp near Quebec	79
1958 Aug. 14	KLM Super-Constellation	Plunged into sea 130 mi. w. of Ireland	99
1958 Oct. 17	Soviet TU-104 jet airliner	Crashed near Kanash, 400 mi. e. of Moscow	75
1959 Feb. 3	Amer. Airlines Lockheed Electra ...	Crashed in East River, New York City	65
1959 June 26	TWA Super-Constellation	Crashed in storm near Milan, Italy	68
1960 Feb. 25	USN transport & Arg. airliner	Collided in air near Rio de Janeiro	61
1960 Mar. 17	Northwest Airlines Electra	Exploded over Tell City, Ind	63
1960 July 27	Sikorsky S-58 helicopter	Crashed in Chicago suburbs	13[4]

Date	Aircraft	Site of accident	Deaths
1960 Dec. 16	United DC-8 jet, TWA Super-Constellation	Collided over New York City	134[5]
1961 Feb. 15	Sabena Airlines Boeing 707	Crashed at Berg, Belgium	73[1]
1961 May 10	Air France Starliner	Crashed in Sahara Desert	79
1961 July 12	Czech Ilyushin-18	Hit power line, Casablanca	72
1961 July 19	Argentine Airlines DC-6	Crashed at Azul, Brazil	67
1961 Sept. 1	TWA Constellation	Crashed at Hinsdale, Ill	78
1961 Sept. 10	President Airlines DC-6	Crashed at Shannon, Ireland	83
1961 Nov. 8	Imperial Airlines Constellation	Crashed near Richmond, Va.	77[6]
1962 Mar. 1	Amer. Airlines Boeing 707 jet	Crashed after takeoff, New York City	95
1962 Mar. 4	Br. Caledonian Airlines DC-7C	Crashed near Douala, Cameroun	111
1962 Mar. 16	Flying Tiger Super-Const	Vanished in western Pacific	107
1962 June 3	Air France Boeing 707 jet	Crashed on takeoff from Paris	130
1962 June 22	Air France Boeing 707 jet	Crashed in storm, Guadeloupe, W.I.	113
1962 July 7	Italian Alitalia airliner	Crashed in storm 50 miles n.e. of Bombay	94
1962 Nov. 27	Brazilian Varig Boeing 707 jet	Crashed and burned in Lima, Peru	97
1963 Feb. 1	Mid. E. Viscount, Turk. AF C-47	Collided over Ankara, Turkey	95
1963 June 3	Chartered Northw. Airlines DC-7	Crashed in Pacific off British Columbia	101
1963 Sept. 2	Swissaire Caravelle Jetliner	Crashed after takeoff from Zurich, Switz.	80
1963 Nov. 29	Trans-Canada Airlines DC-8F	Crashed after takeoff from Montreal	118
1963 Dec. 8	Pan American Boeing 707	Crashed near Elkton, Md	82
1964 Feb. 25	Br. Eagle Bristol Britannia	Crashed near Innsbruck, Austria	83
1964 Mar. 1	Paradise Airline Constellation	Crashed in snow storm, Lake Tahoe, Calif	85
1964 May 11	U.S. MATS C-135 Stratolifter	Crashed at Clark AFB, Philippines	75
1965 Feb. 8	Eastern Air Lines DC-7B	Plunged into Atlantic after takeoff, New York	84
1965 May 20	Pakistani Boeing 720-B	Crashed at Cairo, Egypt, Airport	121
1966 Jan. 24	Air India Boeing 707 jetliner	Crashed on Mont Blanc, Switzerland	117
1966 Feb. 4	All-Nippon Boeing 727	Plunged into Tokyo Bay	133
1966 Mar. 5	BOAC Boeing 707 jetliner	Crashed on Japan's Mount Fuji	124
1966 Apr. 22	Military-chartered Electra	Crashed in storm near Ardmore, Okla	82
1966 Sept. 1	Britannia 102 turboprop	Crashed near Ljubljana, Yugoslavia	97
1966 Oct. 1	All-Nippon Vickers Viscount	Crashed near Matsuyama, Japan	50
1966 Dec. 24	U.S. military-chartered, CL-44	Crashed into village in South Vietnam	129[1]
1967 Mar. 9	TWA DC-9, Beechcraft	Collided in air at Urbana, Ohio	26
1967 Apr. 20	Swiss Britannia turboprop	Crashed at Nicosia, Cyprus	126
1967 June 3	Chartered British DC-4	Crashed into Mont Canigou, France	88
1967 June 4	Chartered British Argonaut	Crashed at Stockport, England	72
1967 July 19	Piedmont Boeing 727, Cessna 310	Collided in air, Hendersonville, N.C	82
1967 Oct. 12	British-Cypriot Mark IV Comet	Crashed into sea off Turkey	66
1967 Nov. 20	TWA Convair 880	Crashed in snowstorm at Cincinnati	68
1967 Dec. 8	Peruvian Faucett DC-4	Crashed near Huanuco, Peru	66
1968 Apr. 20	S. African Airways Boeing 707	Crashed on takeoff, Windhoek, S. Africa	122
1968 May 3	Braniff International Electra	Crashed in storm near Dawson, Tex.	85
1968 Sept. 11	Air France Caravelle	Caught fire, crashed off Nice, France	95
1969 Mar. 16	Venezuelan DC-9	Crashed after takeoff from Maracaibo, Venez.	155[7]
1969 Mar. 20	United Arab Ilyushin-18	Crashed at Aswan airport	87
1969 June 4	Mexican Boeing 727	Rammed into mountain near Monterrey	79
1969 Sept. 9	Allegheny DC-9	Collided with student pilot's plane, Shelbyville, Ind.	83
1969 Nov. 20	Nigerian VC-10	Crashed near Iju, Nigeria	87
1969 Dec. 8	Olympia Airways DC-6B	Crashed near Athens in storm	93
1970 Feb. 15	Dominican DC-9	Crashed into sea on takeoff from Santo Domingo	102
1970 July 3	British chartered jetliner	Crashed near Barcelona, Spain	112
1970 July 5	Air Canada DC-8	Crashed near Toronto International Airport	108
1970 Aug. 9	Peruvian turbojet	Crashed after takeoff from Cuzco, Peru	101[1]
1970 Oct. 2	Chartered Martin 404	Crashed in Rocky Mts. near Silver Plume, Colo.	30[8]
1970 Nov. 14	Southern Airways DC-9	Crashed in mountains near Huntington, W. Va.	75[9]
1970 Dec. 31	Soviet Aeroflot Illyushin 18	Crashed on takeoff, Leningrad	90
1971 May 23	Yugoslavian civil Tupolev-134a	Crashed on landing, Rijeka, Yugo.	78
1971 July 30	All-Nippon Boeing 727, Japanese Air Force F-86	Collided over Morioka	162[10]
1971 Aug.	Soviet Aeroflot Tupolev-104	Crashed at Irkutsk airport	97
1971 Aug. 18	U.S. Army Chinook helicopter	Exploded in air near Pegnitz, W. Germany	37
1971 Sept. 4	Alaska Airlines Boeing 727	Crashed into mountain near Juneau	111
1972 Mar. 14	Danish Airliner	Crashed near Dubai, U. of A. Emirates	112
1972 Aug. 14	E. German Ilyushin-62	Crashed on take-off East Berlin	156
1972 Oct. 13	Aeroflot Ilyushin-62	E. German airline crashed near Moscow	176
1972 Dec. 4	Chartered Spanish Airline	Crashed on take-off, Canary Islands	155
1973 Jan. 23	Boeing 707	Burst into flames during landing, Kano Airport, Nigeria	176
1973 Apr. 10	British Vanguard turboprop	Crashed during snowstorm at Basel, Switzerland	104
1973 June 3	Soviet Russian TU-144	Exploded in air near Goussainville, France	14[11]

(1) Including those on the ground and in buildings. (2) First fatal crash of commercial jet plane. (3) Caused by bomb planted by John G. Graham in insurance plot to kill his mother, a passenger. (4) First crash of commercial helicopter. (5) Including all 128 aboard the plane and 6 on ground. (6) Including 74 Army recruits. (7) Killed 84 on plane and 71 on ground. (8) Including 13 members of Wichita State U. football team. (9) Including 43 Marshall U. football players and coaches. (10) Airline-fighter crash, pilot of fighter parachuted to safety, was arrested for negligence. (11) First supersonic plane crash killed 6 crewmen and 8 on the ground; there were no passengers.

Record Oil Spills, 1967-1971

Source: U.S. Geological Survey, Conservation Division

Name and Place	Date	Cause of Spill	Barrels
Tanker, Torrey Canyon, England	Mar. 18, 1967	Grounding	700,000
Tanker, World Glory, South Africa	June 13, 1968	Hull failure	322,000
Tanker, Atlantic Ocean	Mar. 27, 1971	Sinking	220,000
Tanker, Keo, Massachusetts	Nov. 5, 1969	Hull failure	210,000
Storage tank, Sewaren, N.J.	Nov. , 1969	Tank failure	200,000
Pipeline, West Delta area, La.	Oct. 15, 1967	Anchor dragging	160,000
Tanker, Japan	Nov. 30, 1971	Tanker broke in half	149,080
Tanker, R.C. Stoner, Wake Island	Sept. 6, 1967	Grounding	143,300
Tanker, Andron, West African coast	May 5, 1968	Sinking	117,000
Pipeline, Persian Gulf	Apr. 20, 1970	Break	95,000
Tanker, Ocean Eagle, Puerto Rico	Mar. 3, 1968	Grounding	83,400
Oil tank, Indiana	Nov. 23, 1970	Tank collapse	83,333
Tanker, Polycommander, Spain	May 5, 1970	Grounding	82,500
Waste oil reservoir, Penn	Nov. 13, 1970	Ruptured dike	71,428
Storage tank, Ohio	Jan. 31, 1971	Rupture	63,000

Women 1973: The Struggle Goes On
By Hana Umlauf

For the first time ever, President Richard M. Nixon, **Jan. 30,** dealt with the subject of women in an economic report to Congress. And women, members of his Advisory Committee on the Economic Status of Women, were chiefly responsible for the final form of the special chapter, "The Economic Role of Women."

The President's advisory committee which consists of 3 men and 13 women, **Jan. 17,** severely criticized the original report, maintaining it discussed female employment from the point of view of the woman who does not need to work. Nor did the report touch on the special problems of minority women or the need for day-care facilities.

The rewritten report, largely an analysis of the economic status of women, gave little cause for cheers. Given the increased number of women in the workforce today, the report showed occupational segregation by sex is still extensive and has not changed dramatically in the past decade. Although women have greater access to the job marketplace, they are far from achieving full equality in choice of jobs, in opportunities for advancement and in compensation. According to the report, women who worked at any time in 1971 earned only 40% as much as men.

While the chapter contained no recommendations, the Administration stated that the national objective of providing "maximum employment," as set down in the Employment Act of 1946, "applies equally to men and women."

A Census Bureau report based on the 1970 Census, released in February, shed more light on the status of women in the workforce. During the '60s, women accounted for 65.3% of 11.9 million jobs added to the workforce. Many of the new jobs taken by women were in traditionally masculine areas, such as banking. Women accounted for 75% of new bus drivers and nearly half of the new editors and reporters.

The fact, noted in the 1970 Census report, that most of the gains in jobs for women were clustered at lower pay scales, was backed up by a U.S. Dept. of Commerce report which indicated a widening gap between pay for men and women. Median pay for women — on a full-time year-round basis — dropped in 1971 to 59.5% of men's median earnings, as compared to 63.9% in 1955, 60.8% in 1960 and 60% in 1965. Largest pay gains for women were made in factory jobs and service occupations.

Despite increased opportunities for acquiring jobs, advancement to positions of supervision and decision-making was still rare. Edward A. Shaw, dean of placement at the Career Planning Center of the University of California at Los Angeles, noted that although more women today have jobs in which they analyze, identify and solve problems, there is still little upward mobility to the ranks of "line management." "There's still an underlying cultural reluctance to have women supervise men," he noted.

Women On Their Own

Supervision of men isn't a priority for certain professional women. Two all-women law firms or "feminist collectives" in New York made the concept obsolete early this year. Lefcourt, Kraft and Libow opened its offices **Feb. 1** and Bellamy, Blank, Goodman, Kelly, Ross and Stanley followed suit **Mar. 1.** Both firms aim at a collec-

tive rather than competitive feeling and want to show other women they can do things themselves without waiting to be invited by men. While they will represent men when the case does not conflict with feminist philosophy, both groups will concentrate on nonprofit cases which challenge discrimination against women.

Announcing plans to form the First Women's Bank and Trust Co., the organizers said, **May 7,** that women deserve "special attention" in their credit needs. The organizers, many of them leading feminists, include Eileen Preiss, vice-chairman of the New York State Democratic Committee, and Betty Friedan. According to preliminary plans, a woman will be chosen as president, but men will be employed. The bank's activities will involve "conventional" banking services, but emphasize credit for women.

Professional women were not alone in 1973 in entering traditionally male-oriented occupations. Five women formed a crew of ditchdiggers in Palm Beach, Fla. and began work on the road in front of the estate of millionairess Mrs. John A. Lee. It all began when Anna Johnson took a job as flag girl and began to wonder why she couldn't do the same work as the men. When her boss told her he wouldn't hire mixed crews, she found 4 other women who would dig ditches with her. He hired them on the spot and has no regrets: "... they've got a lot more heart than some of the guys. They really work hard." The all-female crew earns the same salary as the men — $110 per week.

In February, Emily Howell served as second officer on a Frontier Airlines Boeing 737 flight from Denver to St. Louis. It was the first time a major scheduled airline had flown with a female flight officer.

There's even a breeze of women's liberation in the State Department and other foreign affairs agencies, notoriously male-dominated in the past. The State Department has rescinded the requirement for resignation of women foreign service employees when they marry, insured that women would not be barred from certain foreign assignments and revised recruitment and oral examination policies to make greater use of the resources of women. Those responsible for this policy change — Mary Olmsted and the Ad Hoc Committee to Improve the Status of Women in Foreign Affairs Agencies — received, on **Mar. 13,** one of the 10 Presidential Management Improvement Awards for 1972 for "bold initiative to work within the system to effect reforms of personnel policies on recruitment, training, assignment and promotion of women."

Women's Movement Re-examines Goals

Newly re-elected president of the National Organization for Women (NOW) Wilma Scott Heide said, **Feb. 20,** that the women's movement must take a radical turn, "not bizarre, but getting down to root causes." On the previous day, the group voted to condemn the Nixon Administration for its anti-minority policies and to make 1973 NOW's action year against poverty. The anti-poverty effort aims toward a $2.50 minimum wage, public financing of day-care centers and a national welfare program which would ensure that no mother with pre-school or school-age children would be forced to work. The 6th Annual NOW convention also passed a resolution in another major area, marriage and divorce: divorced wives reentering the job market should be aided—through education and training or otherwise—to overcome the disadvantages of years spent at home.

The National Women's Political Caucus, attended by over 1,000 women from 48 states, differed over the future direction of the group at its February meeting in Houston, Tex. The fundamental issue was whether the organization should or could remain multipartisan while attacking such divisive issues as the minimum wage and public financing of day-care centers. Congresswoman Bella Abzug argued that the caucus "had not done enough to speak out and fight for programs that mean the difference between a society permanently wedded to militarism and a society with humanist values", but rather had concentrated on "narrow" feminist issues. The election of Frances Farenthold, a reform-minded Democrat from Texas, as first national chairman of the caucus, signalled victory for the view that the group must dedicate itself to broad social issues, not only the concerns of women. In the keynote speech, Ms. Farenthold characterized the women's movement as "a revolution without arms, thank God," and noted that "sisterhood does not mean the end of brotherhood."

American newspapers came under fire, **Apr. 25,** when *Ms.* magazine editor Gloria Steinem, addressing the American Newspaper Publishers Association in New York, charged that the press does not report what women really want to read. She maintained that young women were turning from the establishment press to seek "alternative sources of information." She castigated newspaper depictions of the women's liberation movement, citing instances where coverage of her own speeches had centered on anecdotes, not the essence of her message.

Armed Forces Liberalize

Married women can now enlist in the Army under the same conditions as single women. In March, the U.S. Army lifted several restrictions on WAC enlistees. Women with previous unwed pregnancies no longer must apply for a waiver and the requirement of 3 good-character witnesses has been dropped. In a further move, WACs may now exercise disciplinary authority over men—they can be assigned to any command position, with the exception of combat or tactical combat support commands.

Women serving in the armed forces are now also entitled to the same dependency benefits for their husbands as servicemen receive for their wives, according to an 8-1 Supreme Court decision on **May 14.** The decision came in a case brought by Air Force Lt. Sharron Frontiero. She had been refused an increased allowance for quarters and medical benefits on the basis of her claim that her husband was her "dependent." Her lawyer and head of the American Civil Liberties Union, Ruth Ginsburg, hailed the decision as a milestone: "It is the most far-reaching and important ruling on sex discrimination to come out of the Supreme Court yet. It will spell the beginning of reforms in hundreds of statutes which do not give equal benefits to men and women."

Women Take Top Positions

The U.S. Senate, **Mar. 26,** confirmed the appointment of Dr. Ruth Lewis Farkas as Ambassador to Luxembourg. She became the 4th woman currently serving in an ambassadorial post.

Effective **Apr. 9,** Lillian D. Regelson took the post of Assistant Administrator for Water Planning and Standards for the Environmental Protection Agency. The first EPA "supergrade" employee, she is developing an overall strategy for water pollution abatement.

With the goal, "To serve the Lord Jesus Christ," 32-year-old Lt. (j.g.) Florence Dianna Pohlman, **July 7,** was sworn in as the first female chaplain in the U.S. armed forces. After indoctrination, she will serve at the Naval Training Center in Orlando, Fla.

Women's Lib and The Little League

The Ypsilanti Little League lost its charter, **May 7,** when it voted to defy a national ruling barring girl players. Carolyn King, 12, of the Ypsilanti Orioles was the player involved. Bob Taylor, vice-president of the local little league, vowed to seek a court injunction to halt the action.

The opening day stakes at Aqueduct, **Mar. 1,** went to North Sea. The rider was Robyn Smith, the first female jockey to win the stakes.

Angelita, alias Maria de los Angeles Hernandez, 25, **Apr. 13,** won the right to be a bullfighter. A politician's daughter, she said her victory in a Madrid labor court was "a triumph for women's rights in general."

Women's equality in sports advanced another step, **May 21,** when Lynn Genesko of Woodbridge, N.J., won an athletic scolarship to the University of Miami at Coral Gables, Fla. Ms. Genesko is a breast-stroke swimming champion. The award was believed to be the first for a woman.

Women Break Down More Barriers

Reversing last year's decision, the Harvard Club of New York voted 2,097 to 695, **Jan. 11,** to open its doors to women members. The club's outgoing president, Albert H. Gordon, maintained the move was spontaneous and not influenced by a class-action discrimination suit filed earlier in the year by a group of women backed by the New York Civil Liberties Union.

Leslie Arp ended 42 years of male domination of the kitchen at the Waldorf Astoria when she became its first woman chef. She viewed the appointment as a natural move: "It always seems very strange to me that women are home cooking and they don't get paid. It just seems there should be more of a blending and melting in this area."

On **May 12,** the Anglican Church of Canada General Synod voted overwhelmingly to accept, in principle, the ordination of women into the priesthood. And the oldest Episcopal diocese in the United States, the diocese of Connecticut, voted, **May 19,** in favor of the ordination of women. Final approval is pending before the national convention in October.

Women's history is now an official field of study. Sarah Lawrence College is offering the first graduate program in women's studies. Considered a prime source of teachers for other such programs, the course received this year a $140,000 Rockefeller Foundation grant to expand the program and develop it into a model.

The year had its bright spots as more women in highly diverse fields made the headlines in 1973, but a close look at the statistics concerning female employment and earnings proved that the battle for equality is yet to be won. As NOW President Wilma Scott Heide said, the battle must continue at the root level as more women challenge the discrimination they encounter in the job marketplace and aggressively demand the responsibility and authority they are educated and trained to hold.

Sports of 1973

Olympic Games Records

The modern Olympic Games, first held in Athens, Greece, in 1896, were the result of efforts by Baron Pierre de Coubertin, a French educator, to promote interest in education and culture, also to foster better international understanding through the universal medium of youth's love of athletics.

His source of inspiration for the Olympic Games was the ancient Greek Olympic Games, most notable of the four Panhellenic celebrations. The games were combined patriotic, religious and athletic festivals held every four years. The first such recorded festival was that held in 776 B.C., the date from which the Greeks began to keep their calendar by "Olympiads," or four-year spans between the games.

The first Olympiad is said to have consisted merely of a 200-yard foot race near the small city of Olympia, but the games gained in scope and became demonstrations of national pride. Only Greek citizens—amateurs—were permitted to participate. Winners received laurel, wild olive and palm wreaths and were accorded many special privileges. Under the Roman emperors, the games deteriorated into professional carnivals and circuses. Emperor Theodosius banned them in 394 A.D.

Baron de Coubertin enlisted 9 nations to send athletes to the first modern Olympics in 1896; now more than 100 nations compete. Winter Olympic Games were started in 1924.

SITES AND UNOFFICIAL WINNERS OF GAMES

1896 Athens (U. S.)	1912 Stockholm (U. S.)	1936 Berlin (Germany)	1964 Tokyo (U. S.)
1900 Paris (U. S.)	1920 Antwerp (U. S.)	1948 London (U. S.)	1968 Mexico City (U. S.)
1904 St. Louis (U. S.)	1924 Paris (U. S.)	1952 Helsinki (U. S.)	1972 Munich (USSR)
1906 Athens (U. S.)	1928 Amsterdam (U. S.)	1956 Melbourne (USSR)	1976 Montreal (July 17-
1908 London (U. S.)	1932 Los Angeles (U. S.)	1960 Rome (USSR)	Aug. 1)

Olympic Games Champions 1896 — 1972

(* Indicates Olympic Record)

Track and Field—Men

60-Meter Run
1900 Alvin Kraenzlem, United States 7s*
1904 Archie Hahn, United States 7s*

100-Meter Run
1896 Thomas Burke, United States 12s
1900 F. W. Jarvis, United States 10 4-5s
1904 Archie Hahn, United States 11s
1906 Archie Hahn, United States 11 1-5s
1908 Reginald Walker, South Africa 10 4-5s
1912 Ralph Craig, United States 10 4-5s
1920 Charles Paddock, U.S. 10 4-5s
1924 Harold Abrahams, Great Britain 10.6s
1928 Percy Williams, Canada 10 4-5s
1932 Eddie Tolan, United States 10.3s
1936 Jesse Owens, United States 10.3s
1948 Harrison Dillard, United States 10.3s
1952 Lindy Remigino, United States 10.4s
1956 Bobby Morrow, United States 10.5s
1960 Armin Hary, Germany 10.2s
1964 Bob Hayes, United States 10.0s
1968 Jim Hines, United States 9.9s*
1972 Valeri Borzov, USSR 10.1s

200-Meter Run
1900 J. W. B. Tewksbury, United States 22 1-5s
1904 Archie Hahn, United States 21 3-5s
1908 Robert Kerr, Canada 22 2-5s
1912 Ralph Craig, United States 21.7s
1920 Allan Woodring, United States 22s
1924 Jackson Scholz, United States 21.6s
1928 Percy Williams, Canada 21 4-5s
1932 Eddie Tolan, United States 21.2s
1936 Jesse Owens, United States 20.7s
1948 Mel Patton, United States 21.1s
1952 Andrew Stanfield, United States 20.7s
1956 Bobby Morrow, United States 20.6s
1960 Livio Berruti, Italy 20.5s
1964 Henry Carr, United States 20.3s
1968 Tommie Smith, United States 19.8s*
1972 Valeri Borzov, USSR 20s

400-Meter Run
1896 Thomas Burke, United States 54 1-5s
1900 Maxey Long, United States 49 2-5s
1904 Harry Hillman, United States 49 1-5s
1906 Paul Pilgrim, United States 53 1-5s
1908 Wyndham Halswelle, Great Britain, walkover 50s
1912 Charles Reidpath, United States 48.2s
1920 Bevil Rudd, South Africa 49 3-5s
1924 Eric Liddell, Great Britain 47.6s
1928 Ray Barbuti, United States 47 4-5s
1932 William Carr, United States 46.2s
1936 Archie Williams, United States 46.5s
1948 Arthur Wint, Jamaica, B.W.I. 46.2s

1952 George Rhoden, Jamaica, B.W.I. 45.9s
1956 Charles Jenkins, United States 46.7s
1960 Otis Davis, United States 44.9s
1964 Michael Larrabee, United States 45.1s
1968 Lee Evans, United States 43.8s*
1972 Vincent Matthews, United States 44.7s

800-Meter Run
1896 Edwin Flack, Great Britain 2m. 11s
1900 Alfred Tysoe, Great Britain 2m. 1 2-5s
1904 James Lightbody, United States 1m. 56s
1906 Paul Pilgrim, United States 2m. 1 1-5s
1908 Mel Sheppard, United States 1m. 52 4-5s
1912 James Meredith, United States 1m. 51.9s
1920 Albert Hill, Great Britain 1m. 53 2-5s
1924 Douglas Lowe, Great Britain 1m. 52.4s
1928 Douglas Lowe, Great Britain 1m. 51 4-5s
1932 Thomas Hampson, Great Britain 1m. 49.8s
1936 John Woodruff, United States 1m. 52.9s
1948 Mal Whitefield, United States 1m. 49.2s
1952 Mal Whitefield, United States 1m. 49.2s
1956 Thomas Courtney, United States 1m. 47.7s
1960 Peter Snell, New Zealand 1m. 46.3s
1964 Peter Snell, New Zealand 1m. 45.1s
1968 Ralph Doubell, Australia 1m. 44.3s*
1972 Dave Wottle, United States 1m. 45.9s

1,500-Meter Run
1896 Edwin Flack, Great Britain 4m. 33 1-5s
1900 Charles Bennett, Great Britain 4m. 6s
1904 James Lightbody, United States 4m. 5 2-5s
1906 James Lightbody, United States 4m. 12s
1908 Mel Sheppard, United States 4m. 3 2-5s
1912 Arnold Jackson, Great Britain 3m. 56.8s
1920 Albert Hill, Great Britain 4m. 1 4-5s
1924 Paavo Nurmi, Finland 3m. 53.6s
1928 Harry Larva, Finland 3m. 53 1-5s
1932 Luigi Beccali, Italy 3m. 51.2s
1936 Jack Lovelock, New Zealand 3m. 47.8s
1948 Henri Eriksson, Sweden 3m. 49.8s
1952 Joseph Barthel, Luxemburg 3m. 45.2s
1956 Ron Delany, Ireland 3m. 41.2s
1960 Herb Elliott, Australia 3m. 35.6s
1964 Peter Snell, New Zealand 3m. 38.1s
1968 Kipchoge Keino, Kenya 3m. 34.9s*
1972 Pekka Vasala, Finland 3m. 36.3s

3,000-Meter Steeplechase
1920 Percy Hodge, Great Britain 10m. 2 2-5s
1924 Willie Ritola, Finland 9m. 33.6s
1928 Toivo Loukola, Finland 9m. 21 4-5s
1932 Volnari Iso-Hollo, Finland 10m. 33.4s
(About 3450 mtrs. extra lap by error)
1936 Volnari Iso-Hollo, Finland 9m. 3.8s
1948 Thure Sjoestrand, Sweden 9m. 4.6s

1952 Horace Ashenfelter, United States 8m. 45.4s
1956 Chris Brasher, Great Britain 8m. 42.2s
1960 Zdzislaw Krzyszkowiak, Poland 8m. 34.2s
1964 Gaston Roelants, Belgium 8m. 30.8s
1968 Amos Biwott, Kenya 8m. 51s
1972 Kipchoge Keino, Kenya 8m. 23.6s*

5,000-Meter Run

1912 Hannes Kolehmainen, Finland 14m. 36.6s
1920 Joseph Guillemot, France 14m. 55⅘s
1924 Paavo Nurmi, Finland 14m. 31.2s
1928 Willie Ritola, Finland 14m. 38s
1932 Lauri Lehtinen, Finland 14m. 30s
1936 Gunnar Hooker, Finland 14m. 22.2s
1948 Gaston Reiff, Belgium 14m. 17.6s
1952 Emil Zatopek, Czechoslovakia 14m. 6.0s
1956 Vladimir Kuts, USSR 13m. 39.6s
1960 Murray Halberg, New Zealand 13m. 43.4s
1964 Bob Schul, United States 13m. 48.8s
1968 Mohamed Gammoudi, Tunisia 14m. 05.0s
1972 Lasse Viren, Finland 13m. 26.4s*

Cross-Country

1912 Hannes Kolehmainen, Finland 45m. 11.6s

5-Mile Run

1906 H. Hawtrey, Great Britain 26m. 26⅕s
1908 Emil Voigt, Great Britain 25m. 11 1-5s*

10,000-Meter Run

1912 Hannes Kolehmainen, Finland 31m. 20.8s
1920 Paavo Nurmi, Finland 31m. 45.8s
1924 Willie Ritola, Finland 30m. 23.2s
1928 Paavo Nurmi, Finland 30m. 18 4-5s
1932 Janusz Kusocinski, Poland 30m. 11.4s
1936 Ilmari Salminen, Finland 30m. 15.4s
1948 Emil Zatopek, Czechoslovakia 29m. 59.6s
1952 Emil Zatopek, Czechoslovakia 29m. 17.0s
1956 Vladimir Kuts, USSR .... 28 m. 45.6s
1960 Pytor Bolotnikov, USSR 28m. 32.2s
1964 Billy Mills, United States 28m. 24.4s
1968 Naftali Temu, Kenya 29m. 27.4s
1972 Lasse Viren, Finland 27m. 38.4s*

Marathon

1896 Spyros Loues, Greece 2h. 55m. 20s
1900 Michael Teato, France .... 2h. 59m.
1904 Thomas Hicks, United States 3h. 28m. 53s
1906 W. J. Sherring, Canada 2h. 51m. 23 3-5s
1908 John J. Hayes, United States 2h. 55m. 18.4s
1912 Kenneth McArthur, South Africa .. 2h. 36m. 54.8s
1920 Hannes Kolehmainen, Finland .. 2h. 32m. 35 4-5s
1924 Albin Stenroos, Finland 2h. 41m. 22.6s
1928 El Ouafl, France 2h. 32m. 57s
1932 Juan Zabala, Argentina 2h. 31m. 36s
1936 Kitei Son, Japan 2h. 29m. 19.2s
1948 Delfo Cabera, Argentina 2h. 34m. 51.6s
1952 Emil Zatopek, Czechoslovakia 2h. 23m. 03.2s
1956 Alain Mimoun, France .... 2h. 25m.
1960 Abebe Bikila, Ethiopia 2h. 15m. 15.2s
1964 Abebe Bikila, Ethiopia 2h. 12m. 11.2s*
1968 Mamo Wolde, Ethiopia 2h. 20m. 26.4s
1972 Frank Shorter, United States 2h. 12m. 19.7s

10,000-Meter Cross-Country

1920 Paavo Nurmi, Finland 27m. 15s*
1924 Paavo Nurmi, Finland 32m. 54.8s

1,500-Meter Walk

1906 George V. Bonhag, United States 7m. 12 3-5s

3,000-Meter Walk

1920 Ugo Frigerio, Italy 13m. 14 1-5s

3,500-Meter Walk

1908 George Larner, Great Britain 14m. 55s

10,000-Meter Walk

1912 George Goulding, Canada 46m. 28.4s
1920 Ugo Frigerio, Italy 48m. 6 1-5s
1924 Ugo Frigerio, Italy 47m. 49s
1948 John Mikaelsson, Sweden 45m. 13.2s
1952 John Mikaelsson, Sweden 45m. 02.8s*

20,000-Meter Walk

1956 Leonid Spirine, USSR 1h. 31m. 27.4s
1960 Vladimir Golubnichiy, USSR 1h. 34m. 7.2s
1964 Kenneth Mathews, Great Britain . 1h. 29m. 34.0s
1968 Vladimir Golubnichiy, USSR 1h. 33m. 58.4s
1972 Peter Frenkel, E. Germany 1h. 26m. 42.4s*

50,000-Meter Walk

1932 Thos. W. Green, Great Britain 4h. 50m. 10s
1936 Harold Whitlock, Great Britain 4h. 30m. 41.4s
1948 John Lundgren, Sweden 4h. 41m. 52s
1952 Giuseppe Bordoni, Italy 4h. 28m. 07.8s
1956 Norman Read, New Zealand 4h. 30m. 42.8s

1960 Donald Thompson, Great Britain.... 4h. 25m. 30s
1964 Abdon Pamich, Italy 4h. 11m. 11.2s
1968 Christoph Hohne, E. Germany 4h. 20m. 13.6s
1972 Bernd Kannenberg, W. Germany . 3h. 56m. 11.6s*

110-Meter Hurdles

1896 Thomas Curtis, United States 17 3-5s
1900 Alvin Kraenzlein, United States 15 2-5s
1904 Frederick Schule, United States 16s
1906 R. G. Leavitt, United States 16 1-5s
1908 Forrest Smithson, United States 15s
1912 Frederick Kelly, United States 15.1s
1920 Earl Thomson, Canada 14 4-5s
1924 Daniel Kinsey, United States 15s
1928 Sydney Atkinson, South Africa 14.8s
1932 George Saling, United States 14.6s
1936 Forrest Towns, United States 14.2s
1948 William Porter, United States 13.9s
1952 Harrison Dillard, United States 13.7s
1956 Lee Calhoun, United States 13.5s
1960 Lee Calhoun, United States 13.8s
1964 Hayes Jones, United States 13.6s
1968 Willie Davenport, United States 13.3s
1972 Rod Milburn, United States 13.2s*

200-Meter Hurdles

1900 Alvin Kraenzlein, United States 25 2-5s
1904 Harry Hillman, United States 24 3-5s*

400-Meter Hurdles

1900 J. W. B. Tewksbury, United States........ 57 3-5s
1904 Harry Hillman, United States 53s
1908 Charles Bacon, United States 55s
1920 Frank Loomis, United States 54s
1924 F. Morgan Taylor, United States 52.6s
1928 Lord Burghley, Great Britain 53 2-5s
1932 Robert Tisdall, Ireland 51.8s
1936 Glenn Hardin, United States 52.4s
1948 Roy Cochran, United States 51.1s
1952 Charles Moore, United States 50.8s
1956 Glenn Davis, United States 50.1s
1960 Glenn Davis, United States 49.3s
1964 Rex Cawley, United States 49.6s
1968 Dave Hemery, Great Britain 48.1s
1972 John Akii-Bua, Uganda 47.8s*

Standing High Jump

1900 Ray Ewry, United States .... 5ft. 5in.
1904 Ray Ewry, United States 4ft. 11in
1906 Ray Ewry, United States 5ft. 1 5-8in
1908 Ray Ewry, United States 5ft. 2in
1912 Platt Adams, United States 5ft. 4 1-4in*

Running High Jump

1896 Ellery Clark, United States 5ft. 11 1-4in
1900 Irving Baxter, United States 6ft. 2 4-5in
1904 Samuel Jones, United States 5ft. 11in
1906 Con Leahy, Ireland 5ft. 9 7-8in
1908 Harry Porter, United States 6ft. 3in
1912 Almer W. Richards, United States 6ft. 4in
1920 Richard Landon, United States 6ft. 4 3-8in
1924 Harold Osborn, United States 6ft. 6in
1928 Robert W. King, United States 6ft. 4 3-8in
1932 Duncan McNaughton, Canada 6ft. 5 5-8in
1936 Cornelius Johnson, United States .. 6ft. 7 15-16in
1948 John L. Winter, Australia 6ft. 6in
1952 Walter Davis, United States 6ft. 8.32in
1956 Charles Dumas, United States 6ft. 11 1-4in
1960 Robert Shavlakadze, USSR 7ft. 1in
1964 Valery Brumel, USSR 7ft. 1 7-8in
1968 Dick Fosbury, United States 7ft. 4 1-4in*
1972 Yuri Tarmak, USSR 7ft. 3 3-4in

Standing Broad Jump

1900 Ray Ewry, United States 10ft. 6 2-5in
1904 Ray Ewry, United States 11ft. 4 7-8in*
1906 Ray Ewry, United States 10ft. 10in
1908 Ray Ewry, United States 10ft. 11 1-4in
1912 Constantin Tsicilitras, Greece 11ft. 3-4in

Long Jump

1896 Ellery Clark, United States 20ft. 9 3-4in
1900 Alvin Kraenzlein, United States 23ft. 6 7-8in
1904 Myer Prinstein, United States 24ft. 1in
1906 Myer Prinstein, United States 23ft. 7 1-2in
1908 Frank Irons, United States 24ft. 6 1-2in
1912 Albert Gutterson, United States 24ft. 11 1-4in
1920 Wm. Pettersson, Sweden 23ft. 5 1-2in
1924 DeHart Hubbard, United States 24ft. 5 1-8in
1928 Edward B. Hamm, United States 25ft. 4 3-4in
1932 Edward Gordon, United States 25ft. 3-4in
1936 Jesse Owens, United States 26ft. 5 5-16in
1948 William Steele, United States 25ft. 8in
1952 Jerome Biffle, United States 24ft. 10.03in
1956 Gregory Bell, United States 25ft. 8 1-4in

1960	Ralph Boston, United States	26ft. 7 3-4in
1964	Lynn Davies, Great Britain	26ft. 5 3-4in
1968	Bob Beamon, United States	29ft. 2 1-2in*
1972	Randy Williams, United States	27ft. 1-2in

400-Meter Relay

1912	Great Britain	42.4s
1920	United States	42 1-5s
1924	United States	41s
1928	United States	41s
1932	United States	40s
1936	United States	39.8s
1948	United States	40.3s
1952	United States	40.1s
1956	United States	39.5s
1960	Germany (U.S. disqual.)	39.5s
1964	United States	39.0s
1968	United States	38.2s*
1972	United States	38.2s*

1,600-Meter Relay

1908	United States	3m. 27 1-5s
1912	United States	3m. 16.6s
1920	Great Britain	3m. 22 1-5s
1924	United States	3m. 16s
1928	United States	3m. 14 1-5s
1932	United States	3m. 8.2s
1936	Great Britain	3m. 9s
1948	United States	3m. 10.4s
1952	Jamaica, B.W.I.	3m. 03.9s
1956	United States	3m. 04.8s
1960	United States	3m. 02.2s
1964	United States	3m. 00.7s
1968	United States	2m. 56.1s*
1972	Kenya	2m. 59.8s

Pole Vault

1896	William Hoyt, United States	10ft. 9 3-4in
1900	Irving Baxter, United States	10ft. 9 9-10in
1904	Charles Dvorak, United States	11ft. 6in
1906	Fernand Gouder, France	11ft. 6in
1908	A. C. Gilbert, United States	
	Edward Cook Jr., United States	12ft. 2in
1912	Harry Babcock, United States	12ft. 11 1-2in
1920	Frank Foss, United States	13ft. 5in
1924	Lee Barnes, United States	
	Glenn Graham, United States	12ft. 11 1-2in
1928	Sabin W. Carr, United States	13ft. 9 1-2in
1932	William Miller, United States	14ft. 1 7-8in
1936	Earle Meadows, United States	14ft. 3 1-4in
1948	Guinn Smith, United States	14ft. 1 1-4in
1952	Robert Richards, United States	14ft. 11 1-4in
1956	Robert Richards, United States	14ft. 11 1-4in
1960	Don Bragg, United States	15ft. 5 1-8in
1964	Fred Hansen, United States	16ft. 8 1-2in
1968	Bob Seagren, United States	17ft. 8 1-2in
1972	Wolfgang Nordwig, E. Germany	18ft. 1-2in*

16-Lb. Hammer Throw

1900	John Flannagan, United States	167ft. 4in
1904	John Flannagan, United States	168ft. 1in
1908	John Flannagan, United States	170ft. 4 1-4in
1912	Matt McGrath, United States	179ft. 7 1-8in
1920	Pat Ryan, United States	173ft. 5 5-8in
1924	Fred Tootell, United States	174ft. 10 1-8in
1928	Patrick O'Callaghan, Ireland	168ft. 7 3-8in
1932	Patrick O'Callaghan, Ireland	176ft. 11 1-8in
1936	Karl Hein, Germany	185ft. 4 3-16in
1948	Imre Nemeth, Hungary	183ft. 11 1-2in
1952	Jozsef Csermak, Hungary	197ft. 11.67in
1956	Harold Connolly, United States	207ft. 3 1-2in
1960	Vasily Rudenkov, USSR	220ft. 2in
1964	Romuald Klim, USSR	228ft. 9 1-2in
1968	Gyula Zsivotsky, Hungary	240ft. 8in
1972	Anatoli Bondarchuk, USSR	247ft. 8 1-2in*

Discus Throw

1896	Robt. Garrett, United States	95ft. 7 1-2in
1900	Rudolf Bauer, Hungary	118ft. 2 9-10in
1904	Martin Sheridan, United States	128ft. 10 1-2in
1906	Martin Sheridan, United States	136ft. 1-3in
1908	Martin Sheridan, United States	134ft. 2in
1912	Armas Taipale, Finland	148 ft. 4in
	Right and left hand—Armas Taipale, Finland	271ft. 10 1-4in
1920	Elmer Niklander, Finland	146ft. 7 1-4in
1924	Clarence Houser, United States	151ft. 5 1-8in
1928	Clarence Houser, United States	155ft. 3in
1932	John Anderson, United States	162ft. 4 7-8in
1936	Ken Carpenter, United States	165ft. 7 3-8in
1948	Adolfo Consolini, Italy	173ft. 2in
1952	Sim Iness, United States	180ft. 6.85in
1956	Al Oerter, United States	184ft. 11in
1960	Al Oerter, United States	194ft. 2in
1964	Al Oerter, United States	200ft. 1 1-2in
1968	Al Oerter, United States	212ft. 6 1-2in*
1972	Ludvik Danek, Czech.	211ft. 3 1-2in

Standing Hop, Step and Jump

| 1900 | Ray Ewry, United States | 34ft. 8 1-2in* |
| 1904 | Ray Ewry, United States | 34ft. 7 1-4in |

Triple Jump

1896	James Connolly, United States	45ft
1900	Myer Prinstein, United States	47ft. 4 1-4in
1904	Myer Prinstein, United States	47ft
1906	P. G. O'Connor, Ireland	46ft. 2in
1908	Timothy Ahearne, Great Britain	48ft. 11 1-4in
1912	Gustaf Lindblom, Sweden	48ft. 5 1-8in
1920	Vilho Tuulos, Finland	47ft. 7in
1924	Archie Winter, Australia	50ft. 11 1-4in
1928	Mikio Oda, Japan	49ft. 11in
1932	Chuhei Nambu, Japan	51ft. 7in
1936	Naoto Tajima, Japan	52ft. 5 7-8in
1948	Arne Ahman, Sweden	50ft. 6 1-4in
1952	Adhemar de Silva, Brazil	53ft. 2.59in
1956	Adhemar de Silva, Brazil	53ft. 7 1-2in
1960	Jozef Schmidt, Poland	55ft. 1 3-4in
1964	Jozef Schmidt, Poland	55ft. 3 1-2in
1968	Victor Saneyev, USSR	57ft. 3-4in*
1972	Victor Saneyev, USSR	56ft. 11in

16-Lb. Shot Put

1896	Robt. Garrett, United States	36ft. 2in
1900	Robt. Sheldon, United States	46ft. 3 1-8in
1904	Ralph Rose, United States	48ft. 7in
1906	Martin Sheridan, United States	40ft. 4 4-5in
1908	Ralph Rose, United States	46ft. 7 1-2in
1912	Pat McDonald, United States	50ft. 4in
	Right and left hand—Ralph Rose, United States	90ft. 5 1-2in
1920	Ville Porhola, Finland	48ft. 7 1-8in
1924	Clarence Houser, United States	49ft. 2 3-8in
1928	John Kuck, United States	52ft. 3-4in
1932	Leo Sexton, United States	52ft. 6 3-16in
1936	Hans Woelke, Germany	53ft. 1 13-16in
1948	Wilbur Thompson, United States	56ft. 2in
1952	Parry O'Brien, United States	57ft. 1.43in
1956	Parry O'Brien, United States	60ft. 11in
1960	William Nieder, United States	64ft. 6 3-4in
1964	Dallas Long, United States	66ft. 8 1-2in
1968	Randy Matson, United States	67ft. 4 3-4in
1972	Wladyslaw Komar, Poland	69ft. 6in*

Discus Throw—Greek Style

| 1906 | Werner Jaevinen, Finland | 115ft. 4in |
| 1908 | Martin Sheridan, United States | 124ft. 8in* |

Javelin Throw

1906	Erik Lemming, Sweden	175ft. 6in
1908	Erik Lemming, Sweden	178ft. 7 1-2in
	Held in Middle—Erik Lemming, Sweden	179ft. 10 1-2in
1912	Erik Lemming, Sweden	198ft. 11 1-4in
	Both hands, Julius Säaristo Finland	358ft. 11 7-8in
1920	Jonni Myyra, Finland	215ft. 9 3-4in
1924	Jonni Myyra, Finland	206ft. 6 3-4in
1928	Eric Lundquist, Sweden	218ft. 6 1-8in
1932	Matti Jarvinen, Finland	238ft. 7in
1936	Gerhard Stoeck, Germany	235ft. 8 5-16in
1948	Kaj T. Rautavaara, Finland	228ft. 10 1-2in
1952	Cy Young, United States	242ft. 0.79in
1956	Egil Danielsen, Norway	281ft. 2 1-4in
1960	Viktor Tsibulenko, USSR	277ft. 8 3-8in
1964	Pauli Nevala, Finland	271ft. 2 1-2in
1968	Yanis Lusis, USSR	295ft. 7 1-4in
1972	Klaus Wolferman, W. Germany	296ft. 10in*

Modern Pentathlon

1952	Lars Hall, Sweden	32 pts
1956	Lars Hall, Sweden	4,833 pts
1960	Ferenc Nemeth, Hungary	5,024 pts
1964	Ferenc Torok, Hungary	5,116 pts
1968	Bjoern Ferm, Sweden	4,964 pts
1972	Andras Balczo, Hungary	5,412 pts*

Decathlon (A)

1912	Hugo Wieslander, Sweden	7,724.49 pts
1920	Helge Loveland, Norway	6,804.35 pts
1924	Harold Osborn, United States	7,710.775 pts
1928	Paavo Yrjola, Finland	8,056.20 pts
1932	James Bausch, United States	8,462.23 pts
1936	Glenn Morris, United States	7,900 pts
1948	Robert Mathias, United States	7,139 pts
1952	Robert Mathias, United States	7,887 pts
1956	Milton Campbell, United States	7,937 pts
1960	Rafer Johnson, United States	8.392 pts

1964	Willi Holdorf, Germany	7,887 pts
1968	Bill Toomey, United States	8,193 pts
1972	Nikolai Avilov, USSR	8,454 pts*

(A) Former point system, 1936-1960

Track and Field—Women

100-Meter Run

1928	Elizabeth Robinson, United States	12.2s
1932	Stella Walsh, Poland	11.9s
1936	Helen Stephens, United States	11.5s
1948	Francina Blankers-Koen, Netherlands	11.9s
1952	Marjorie Jackson, Australia	11.5s
1956	Betty Cuthbert, Australia	11.5s
1960	Wilma Rudolph, United States	11.0s*
1964	Wyomia Tyus, United States	11.4s
1968	Wyomia Tyus, United States	11.0s*
1972	Renate Stecher, E. Germany	11.1s

200-Meter Run

1948	Francina Blankers-Koen, Netherlands	24.4s
1952	Marjorie Jackson, Australia	23.7s
1956	Betty Cuthbert, Australia	23.4s
1960	Wilma Rudolph, United States	24.0s
1964	Edith McGuire, United States	23.0s
1968	Irene Szewinska, Poland	22.5s
1972	Renate Stecher, E. Germany	22.4s*

400-Meter Run

1964	Betty Cuthbert, Australia	52s
1968	Colette Besson, France	52s
1972	Monika Zehrt, E. Germany	51s

800-Meter Run

1928	Linda Radke, Germany	2m. 16.8s
1960	Ljudmila Shevcova, USSR	2m. 4.3s
1964	Ann Packer, Great Britain	2m. 1.1s
1968	Madeline Manning, United States	2m. 0.9s
1972	Hildegard Falck, W. Germany	1m. 58.6s*

1500-Meter Run

1972	Ludmila Bragina, USSR	4m. 1.4s*

400-Meter Relay

1928	Canada	48.4s
1932	United States	47.0s
1936	United States	46.9s
1948	Netherlands	47.5s
1952	United States	45.9s
1956	Australia	44.5s
1960	United States	44.5s
1964	Poland	43.6s
1968	United States	42.8s*
1972	West Germany	42.8s*

1600-Meter Relay

1972	East Germany	3m. 23s*

80-Meter Hurdles

1932	Mildred Didrikson, United States	11.7s
1936	Trebisonda Villa, Italy	11.7s
1948	Francina Blankers-Koen, Netherlands	11.2s
1952	Shirley Strickland de la Hunty, Australia	10.9s
1956	Shirley Strickland de la Hunty, Australia	10.7s

1960	Irina Press, USSR	10.8s
1964	Karin Balzer, Germany	10.5s
1968	Maureen Caird, Australia	10.3s*

100-Meter Hurdles

1972	Annelle Ehrhardt, E. Germany	12.6*

High Jump

1928	Ethel Catherwood, Canada	5ft. 3in
1932	Jean Shiley, United States	5ft. 5 1-4in
1936	Ibolya Csak, Hungary	5ft. 3in
1948	Alice Coachman, United States	5ft. 6 1-8in
1952	Esther Brand, South Africa	5ft. 5 3-4in
1956	Mildred L. McDaniel, United States	5ft. 9 1-4in
1960	Iolanda Balas, Romania	6ft. 1-4in
1964	Iolanda Balas, Romania	6ft. 2 7-8 in*
1968	Miloslava Reskova, Czech	5ft. 11 3-4in
1972	Uirike Meyfarth, W. Germany	6ft. 2 3-4 in

Discus Throw

1928	Helena Konopacka, Poland	129ft. 11 7-8in
1932	Lillian Copeland, United States	133ft. 2in
1936	Gisela Mauermayer, Germany	156ft. 3 3-16in
1948	Micheline Ostermeyer, France	137ft. 6 1-2in
1952	Nina Romaschkova, USSR	168ft. 8 1-2in
1956	Olga Fikotova, Czechoslovakia	176ft. 1 1-2in
1960	Nina Ponomareva, USSR	180ft. 8 1-4in
1964	Tamara Press, USSR	187ft. 10 1-2in
1968	Lia Manolin, Romania	191ft. 2 1-2in
1972	Faina Melnik, USSR	218ft. 7in*

Javelin Throw

1932	Mildred Didrikson, United States	143ft. 4in
1936	Tilly Fleischer, Germany	148ft. 2 3-4in
1948	Herma Bauma, Austria	149 ft. 6in
1952	Dana Zatopekova, Czechoslovakia	165ft. 7in
1956	Inessa Janzeme, USSR	176ft. 8in
1960	Elvira Ozolina, USSR	183ft. 8in
1964	Mihaela Penes, Romania	198ft. 7 1-2in
1968	Angela Nemeth, Hungary	198ft. 1-2in
1972	Ruth Fuchs, E. Germany	209ft. 7in*

Shot Put

1948	Micheline Ostermeyer, France	45ft. 1 1-2in
1952	Galina Zybina, USSR	50ft. 1 1-2in
1956	T. Tishkyevich, USSR	54ft. 5in
1960	Tamara Press, USSR	56ft. 9 7-8in
1964	Tamara Press, USSR	59ft. 6 1-4in
1968	Margitta Gummel, E. Germany	64ft. 4in
1972	Nadezwda Chizhova, USSR	69ft*

Long Jump

1948	Olga Gyarmati, Hungary	18ft. 8 1-4in
1952	Yvette Williams, New Zealand	20ft. 5 3-4in
1956	E. Krzeskinska, Poland	20ft. 9 3-4in
1960	Vyera Krepina, USSR	20ft. 10 3-4in
1964	Mary Rand, Great Britain	22ft. 2 1-4in
1968	V. Viscopoleanu, Romania	22ft. 4 1-2in*
1972	Heidemarie Rosendahl, W. Germany	22 ft. 3in

Pentathlon

1964	Irina Press, USSR	5,246 pts
1968	Ingred Becker, W. Germany	5,098 pts
1972	Mary Peters, England	4,801 pts*

Swimming—Men

100 Meter Freestyle

1896	Alfred Hajos, Hungary	1:22.2
1904	Zoltan de Halomay, Hungary (100 yards)	1:02.8
1906	C. M. Daniels, U.S.	1:13.0
1908	C. M. Daniels, U.S.	1:05.6
1912	Duke P. Kahanamoku, U.S.	1:03.4
1920	Duke P. Kahanamoku, U.S.	1:01.4
1924	John Weissmuller, U.S.	59.0
1928	John Weissmuller, U.S.	58.6
1932	Yasuji Miyazaki, Japan	58.2
1936	Ferenc Csik, Hungary	57.6
1948	Wally Ris, U.S.A.	57.3
1952	Clark Scholes, U.S.A.	57.4
1956	Jon Henricks, Australia	55.4
1960	John Devitt, Australia	55.2
1964	Don Schollander, U.S.A.	53.4
1968	Mike Wenden, Australia	52.2
1972	Mark Spitz, U.S.A.	51.2*

200 Meter Freestyle

1968	Mike Wenden, Australia	1:55.2
1972	Mark Spitz, U.S.A.	1:52.8*

400 Meter Freestyle

1904	C. M. Daniels, U.S. (440 yards)	6:16.2
1906	Otto Sheff, Australia	6:23.8
1908	H. Taylor, Great Britain	5:36.8
1912	G. R. Hodgson, Canada	5:24.4

1920	Norman Ross, U.S.	5:26.8
1924	John Weissmuller, U.S.	5:04.2
1928	Albert Zorilla, Argentina	5:01.6
1932	Clarence Crabbe, U.S.	4:48.4
1936	Jack Medica, U.S.	4:44.5
1948	William Smith, U.S.	4:41.0
1952	Jean Boiteux, France	4:30.7
1956	Murray Rose, Australia	4:27.3
1960	Murray Rose, Australia	4:18.3
1964	Don Schollander, U.S.	4:12.2
1968	Mike Burton, U.S.	4:09.0
1972	Brad Cooper, Australia	4:00.3*

1,500 Meter Freestyle

1908	H. Taylor, Great Britain	22:48.4
1912	G. R. Hodgson, Canada	22:00.0
1920	N. Ross, U.S.	22:23.2
1924	A. M. Charlton, Australia	20:06.6
1928	Arne Borg, Sweden	19:51.8
1932	Kasuo Kitamura, Japan	19:12.4
1936	Noboru Terada, Japan	19:13.7
1948	J. P. McLane, U.S.A.	19:18.5
1952	Ford Konno, U.S.A.	18:30.0
1956	Murray Rose, Australia	17:58.9
1960	Jon Konrads, Australia	17:19.6
1964	Robert Windle, Australia	17:01.7
1968	Mike Burton, U.S.A.	16:38.9
1972	Mike Burton, U.S.A.	15:52.6*

400 Meter Medley Relay

1960	United States	4:05.4
1964	United States	3:58.4
1968	United States	3:54.9
1972	United States	3:48.2*

400 Meter Freestyle Relay

1964	United States	3:33.2
1968	United States	3:31.7
1972	United States	3:26.4*

800 Meter Freestyle Relay

1908	Great Britain	10:55.6
1912	Australia	10:11.6
1920	United States	10:04.4
1924	United States	9:53.4
1928	United States	9:36.2
1932	Japan	8:58.4
1936	Japan	8:51.5
1948	United States	8:46.0
1952	United States	8:31.1
1956	Australia	8:23.6
1960	United States	8:10.2
1964	United States	7:52.1
1968	United States	7:52.3
1972	United States	7:38.8*

100 Meter Backstroke

1904	W. Brack, Germany (100 yds.)	1:16.8
1908	Arno Bieberstein, Germany	1:24.6
1912	Harry Hebner, U.S.	1:21.2
1920	Warren Kealoha, U.S.	1:15.2
1924	Warren Kealoha, U.S.	1:13.2
1928	George Kojac, U.S.	1:08.2
1932	Masaji Kiyokawa, Japan	1:08.6
1936	Adolph Kiefer, U.S.	1:05.9
1948	Allen Stack, U.S.A.	1:06.4
1952	Yoshi Oyokawa, U.S.A.	1:05.4
1956	David Thiele, Australia	1:02.2
1960	David Thiele, Australia	1:01.9
1968	Roland Matthes, E. Germany	58.7
1972	Roland Matthes, E. Germany	56.6*

200 Meter Backstroke

1964	Jed Graef, U.S.A.	2:10.3
1968	Roland Matthes, E. Germany	2:09.6
1972	Roland Matthes, E. Germany	2:02.8*

100 Meter Breaststroke

1968	Don McKenzie, U.S.	1:07.7
1972	Nobutaka Taguchi, Japan	1:04.9*

200 Meter Breaststroke

1908	F. Holman, Great Britain	3:09.2
1912	Walter Bathe, Germany	3:01.8
1920	H. Malmroth, Sweden	3:04.4
1924	R. D. Skelton, U.S.	2:56.6
1928	Y. Tsuruta, Japan	2:48.8
1932	Yoshiyuki Tsuruta, Japan	2:45.4
1936	Tetsuo Hamuro, Japan	2:42.5
1948	J. Verdeur, U.S.A.	2:39.3
1952	John Davies, Australia	2:34.4
1956	Masura Furukawa, Japan	2:34.7
1960	William Mulliken, U.S.	2:37.4
1964	Ian O'Brien, Australia	2:27.8
1968	Felipe Munoz, Mexico	2:28.7
1972	John Hencken, U.S.	2:21.5*

100 Meter Butterfly

1968	Doug Russell, U.S.	55.9
1972	Mark Spitz, U.S.	54.3*

200 Meter Butterfly

1956	William Yorzyk, U.S.A.	2:18.6
1960	Michael Troy, U.S.	2:12.8
1964	Kevin J. Berry, Australia	2:06.6
1968	Carl Robie, U.S.	2:08.7
1972	Mark Spitz, U.S.A.	2:00.7*

200 Meter Individual Medley

1968	Charles Hickcox, U.S.A.	2:12.0
1972	Gunnar Larsson, Sweden	2:07.2*

400 Meter Individual Medley

1964	Dick Roth, U.S.A.	4:45.4
1968	Charles Hickcox, U.S.A.	4:48.4
1972	Gunnar Larsson, Sweden	4.32*

Springboard Diving

		Points
1904	Dr. G. E. Sheldon, U.S.	12²/₃
1906	Gottlob Walz, Germany	

1908	Albert Zuerner, Germany	85.5
1912	Paul Guenther, Germany	6
1920	L. E. Kuehn, U.S.	6
1924	A. C. White, U.S.	7
1928	P. Desjardins, U.S.	185.04
1932	Michael Gallitzen, U.S.	161.38
1936	Richard Degener, U.S.	161.57
1948	Bruce Harlan, U.S.	163.64
1952	David Browning, U.S.	205.29
1956	Robert Clothworthy, U.S.	159.56
1960	Gary Tobian, U.S.	170.00
1964	Kenneth Sitzberger, U.S.	159.90
1968	Bernie Wrightson, U.S.	170.15
1972	Vladimir Vasin, USSR	594.09

Platform Diving

		Points
1928	P. Desjardins, U.S.	98.74
1932	Harold Smith, U.S.	124.80
1936	Marshall Wayne, U.S.	113.58
1948	Sammy Lee, U.S.	130.05
1952	Sammy Lee, U.S.	156.28
1956	Joaquin Capilla, Mexico	152.44
1960	Robert Webster, U.S.	165.56
1964	Robert Webster, U.S.	148.58
1968	Klaus Dibiasi, Italy	164.18
1972	Klaus Dibiasi, Italy	504.12

Water Polo

1900	Great Britain	1936	Hungary
1904	United States	1948	Italy
1908	Great Britain	1952	Hungary
1912	Great Britain	1956	Hungary
1920	Great Britain	1960	Italy
1924	France	1964	Hungary
1928	Germany	1968	Yugoslavia
1932	Hungary	1972	USSR

Swimming—Women

100 Meter Freestyle

1912	Fanny Durack, Australia	1:22.2
1920	Ethelda Bleibtrey, U.S.	1:13.6
1924	Ethel Lackie, U.S.	1:12.4
1928	Albina Osipowich, U.S.	1:11.0
1932	Helene Madison, U.S.	1:06.8
1936	Hendrika Mastenbroek, Holland	1:05.9
1948	G. M. Anderson, Denmark	1:06.3
1952	Katalin Szoke, Hungary	1:06.3
1956	Dawn Fraser, Australia	1:02.0
1960	Dawn Fraser, Australia	1:01.2
1964	Dawn Fraser, Australia	59.5
1968	Jan Henne, U.S.	1:00.0
1972	Sandra Neilson, U.S.	58.6*

200 Meter Freestyle

1968	Debbie Meyer, U.S.	2:10.5
1972	Shane Gould, Australia	2:03.6*

400 Meter Freestyle

1924	Martha Norelius, U.S.	6:02.2
1928	Martha Norelius, U.S.	5:42.8
1932	Helene Madison, U.S.	5:28.5
1936	Hendrika Mastenbroek, Holland	5:26.4
1948	Ann Curtis, U.S.	5:17.8
1952	Valerie Gyenge, Hungary	5:12.1
1956	Lorraine Crapp, Australia	4:54.6
1960	Chris von Saltza, U.S.	4:50.6
1964	Virginia Duenkel, U.S.	4:43.3
1968	Debbie Meyer, U.S.	4:31.8
1972	Shane Gould, Australia	4:19.0*

800 Meter Freestyle

1968	Debbie Meyer, U.S.	9:24.0
1972	Keena Rothhammer, U.S.	8:53.7*

400 Meter Medley Relay

1960	United States	4:41.1
1964	United States	4:33.9
1968	United States	4:28.3
1972	United States	4:20.7*

400 Meter Freestyle Relay

1912	Great Britain	5:52.8
1920	United States	5:11.6
1924	United States	4:58.8
1928	United States	4:47.6
1932	United States	4:38.0
1936	Holland	4:36.0
1948	United States	4:29.2
1952	Hungary	4:24.4
1956	Australia	4:17.1

1960	United States	4:08.9
1964	United States	4:03.8
1968	United States	4:02.5
1972	United States	3:55.2*

100 Meter Backstroke

1924	Sybil Bauer, U.S.	1:23.3
1928	Marie Braun, Holland	1:22.0
1932	Eleanor Holm, U.S.	1:19.4
1936	Dina Senif, Holland	1:18.9
1948	K. M. Harup, Denmark	1:14.4
1952	Joan Harrison, South Africa	1:14.3
1956	Judy Grinham, Great Britain	1:12.9
1960	Lynn Burke, U.S.	1:09.3
1964	Cathy Ferguson, U.S.	1:07.7
1968	Kaye Hall	1:06.2
1972	Melissa Belote	1:05.8*

200 Meter Backstroke

| 1968 | Pokey Watson, U.S. | 2:24.8 |
| 1972 | Melissa Belote, U.S. | 2:19.2* |

100 Meter Breaststroke

| 1968 | Djurdjica Bjedov, Yugoslavia | 1:15.8 |
| 1972 | Cathy Carr, U.S. | 1:13.6* |

200 Meter Breaststroke

1924	Lucy Morton, Great Britain	3:32.2
1928	Hilde Schrader, Germany	3:12.6
1932	Clare Dennis, Australia	3:06.3
1936	Hideko Maehata, Japan	3:03.6
1948	N. Van Vliet, Holland	2:57.2
1952	Eva Szekely, Hungary	2:51.7
1956	Ursula Happe, Germany	2:53.1
1960	Anita Lonsbrough, Great Britain	2:49.5
1964	Galina Prozumenschikova, USSR	2:46.4
1968	Sharon Wichman, U.S.	2:44.4
1972	Beverly Whitfield, Australia	2:41.7*

200 Meter Medley

| 1968 | Claudia Kolb, U.S. | 2:24.7 |
| 1972 | Shane Gould, Australia | 2:23.1* |

400 Meter Medley

1964	Donna De Varona, U.S.	5:18.7
1968	Claudia Kolb, U.S.	5:08.5
1972	Gail Neall, Australia	5:03.0*

100 Meter Butterfly

1956	Shelley Mann, U.S.	1:11.0
1960	Carolyn Schuler, U.S.	1:09.5
1964	Sharon Stouder, U.S.	1:04.7
1968	Lynn McClements, Australia	1:05.5
1972	Mayumi Aoki, Japan	1:03.3*

200 Meter Butterfly

| 1968 | Ada Kok, Netherlands | 2:24.7 |
| 1972 | Karen Moe, U.S. | 2:15.6* |

Springboard Diving

		Points
1920	Aileen Riggin, U.S.	9
1924	Elizabeth Becker, U.S.	8
1928	Helen Meany, U.S.	78.62
1932	Georgia Coleman, U.S.	87.52
1936	Marjorie Gestring, U.S.	89.27
1948	Victoria M. Draves, U.S.	108.74
1952	Mrs. Patricia McCormick, U.S.	147.30
1956	Patricia McCormick, U.S.	142.36
1960	Ingrid Kramer, Germany	155.81
1964	Ingrid Engel-Kramer, Germany	145.00
1968	Sue Gossick, U.S.	150.77
1972	Micki King, U.S.	450.03

Platform Diving

		Points
1928	Elizabeth B. Pinkston, U.S.	31.60
1932	Dorothy Poynton, U.S.	40.26
1936	Mrs. Dorothy Poynton Hill, U.S.	33.93
1948	Victoria M. Draves, U.S.	68.87
1952	Mrs. Patricia McCormick, U.S.	79.37
1956	Mrs. Patricia McCormick, U.S.	84.85
1960	Ingrid Kramer, Germany	91.28
1964	Lesley Bush, U.S.	99.80
1968	Milena Duchkova, Czech	109.59
1972	Ulrika Knape, Sweden	390.00

Curling Events in 1973

The Douglas Medal, St. Andrew's Golf Club, Jan. 4-7, Winchester CC, S. E. Neill, skip. The Griffith Medal, N.Y. Caledonian CC, C. K. Cooper, skip. The Williamson Medal, Malropac CC, E. P. Finegan, skip.

The Mitchell Gold Medal, Utica, N.Y., Jan. 11-14, Rockcliffe, Ont. CC, R. Maxwell, skip. The Allen Memorial Medal, Schenectady Curling Club, W. G. Freeman, skip. The Country Club Cup, Utica CC, J. E. Wilkinson, Jr., skip. The Dewar Trophy, Utica CC, F. G. Johnston, skip.

Granite State Trophy, Nashua, N.H., Jan. 11-14, Granite State CC, C. Henry, skip. Patterson Memorial Medal, The Country Club, Brookline, Mass., R. Cushing, skip. The Merrimack Bowl, Plainfield CC, M. McClure, skip.

The Holland Bowl, Athol, Mass., Jan. 25-28, Petersham CC, V. J. Purple, skip. The McGregor Trophy, Schenectady CC, O. C. Rutledge, skip. The Holt Trophy, Petersham CC, E. J. Bushey, skip.

The Wile Eagle, Broomstones CC, Jan. 18-21, Boston CC, D. Lewis, skip. The Richardson Eagle, Canadian Club of Boston, L. Longworth, skip. The Downes Eagle, Norfolk CC, W. Hill, skip. Snail's Pace, Albany CC, J. Lisuzzo, skip.

The N.Y. Caledonian Medal, St. Andrew's Golf Club, Feb. 1-4, Winchester CC, Dr. H. A. Bird, skip. The Mahopac Medal, N.Y. Caledonian CC, F. V. Bronner, skip. The Francis Brick Medal, Plainfield CC, L. Lynd, skip.

Winchester Bowl, Winchester, Mass., Feb. 8-11, Winchester CC, C. Reeves, Jr., skip. The Braeburn Tankard, Granite State CC, C. Henry, skip. The John Joy Trophy, Royal Caledonian CC, Scotland, J. Fleming, skip. The Braeburn Stein, Canadian Club of Boston, R. Devine, skip. Winchester

Shield, Mississaugua CC, Ont., K. Philips, skip. The Braeburn Mug, Halifax-Mayflower CC, V. Dingle, skip.

U.S. Women's Curling Assoc. National Championship, Appleton, Wis., Feb. 14-17, St. Paul CC, Mrs. Marsha Hultstrand, skip.

The Nutmeg Stone, Darien, Conn., Feb. 15-18, Nutmeg CC, R. L. Mester, skip. The Bartlett Medal, N.Y. Caledonian CC, C. K. Cooper, skip. The Ardsley Shield, Norfolk CC, E. C. Childs, skip.

The Howard Stockton Cup, Brookline, Mass., Feb. 22-25, Winchester CC, C. Reeves, Jr., skip. The Clyde Park Cup, Schenectady CC, F. E. Morhous, skip. The Primrose Bowl, Town of Mount Royal, Que., W. Reay, skip.

Dykes Memorial Medal, Wayne, Pa., Feb. 23-25, Nutmeg CC, K. Johnson, skip. The Brookline Trophy, Wellesley CC, T. P. Murphy, skip. The Davies Bowl, Utica CC, J. M. Kowalczyk, skip.

The Gordon Championship Rink Medal, Schenectady, N.Y., Mar. 1-4, Rochester CC, W. J. Dubinger, skip. The R. S. Emmett Memorial Medal, Albany CC, G. Rand, skip. The Mohawk Trophy, Plainfield CC, L. Lynd, skip.

The Canadian Brier National Championship, Edmonton, Alta., Mar. 5-9, Saskatchewan, H. Mazinke, skip.

The Gordon International Medal, (Canada vs. US) Mar. 17, Montreal, Que., Winner, Canada 28, U.S. 14. (first time matches played won and lost instead of aggregate scores).

U.S. Men's National Championship, Colorado Springs, Colo., Mar. 5-9, Winchester CC, C. Reeves, Jr., skip.

The Silver Broom World's Championship, Regina, Sask., Mar. 19-24, Won by Sweden, K. Oscarius, skip.

77th Annual Boston Marathon

Jon Anderson of the United States covered the traditional marathon distance of 26 miles 385 yards in 2 hours 16 minutes 3 seconds to win the 1973 Boston Marathon. The leading finishers and their times follow:

1 — Jon P. Anderson, Oregon T.C.	2:16:03
2 — Tom Fleming, William Paterson College	2:17:46
3 — Olavi Soumalainen, Finland	2:18:21
4 — Bernard J. Plain, England	2:21:01
5 — Jeff Galloway, Florida T.C.	2:21:27
6 — Dennis W. Spencer, U. of Georgia	2:22:31
7 — Bob Moore, Toronto Olympic Club	2:23:57
7 — Paavo Leiviska, Finland	2:23:57
9 — John Vitale, New Haven T.C.	2:24:06
10 — Ron Daws, Twin Cities T.C.	2:24:09
11 — Lutz Philipps, Germany	2:25:04
12 — Jack Mahurin, North Carolina T.C.	2:25:31
13 — Steve Hoag, Twin Cities T.C.	2:25:36
14 — Norbert Sander Jr., Millrose A.A.	2:25:50
15 — Ronald A. Wayne, Oregon T.C.	2:26:25
16 — Ulf Hakansson, Sweden	2:27:26
17 — Laurence C. Olsen, North Medford Club	2:27:31
18 — Justin Gubbins, Georgetown U.	2:28:33

Winter Olympic Games Champions, 1924-1972

Sites and Unofficial Winners of Games

1924 — Chamonix, France (Norway)
1928 — St. Moritz, Switzerland (Norway)
1932 — Lake Placid, N.Y. (U.S.)
1936 — Garmisch-Partenkirchen (Norway)

1948 — St. Moritz (Sweden)
1952 — Oslo, Norway (Norway)
1956 — Cortina d'Ampezzo, Italy (USSR)
1960 — Squaw Valley, Calif. (USSR)

1964 — Innsbruck, Austria (USSR)
1968 — Grenoble, France (Norway)
1972 — Sapporo, Japan (USSR)
1976 — Innsbruck, Austria (Feb. 3-14)

Biathlon

	Time
1960 — Klas Lestander, Sweden	1:33:21.6
1964 — Vladimir Melanin, USSR	1:20:26.8
1968 — Magnar Solberg, Norway	1:13:45.9
1972 — Magnar Solberg, Norway	1:15:55.5

Biathlon Relay

1968 — USSR, Norway, Sweden	2:13.02
1972 — USSR, Finland, E. Germany	1:51.44

Bobsledding

4-Man Bob

(Driver in parentheses)	Time
1924 — Switzerland (Edward Scherrer)	5:45.54
*1928 — United States (William Fiske)	3:20.5
1932 — United States (William Fiske)	7:53.68
1936 — Switzerland (Pierre Musy)	5:19.85
1948 — United States (Edward Rimkus)	5:20.1
1952 — Germany (Andreas Ostler)	5:07.84
1956 — Switzerland (Franz Kapus)	5:10.44
1964 — Canada (Victor Emery)	4:14.46
1968 — Italy (Eugenio Monti)	2:17.39
1972 — Switzerland (Jean Wicki)	4:43.07

*Five-man bobsled

2-Man Bob

	Time
1932 — U.S.A. (Hubert Stevens)	8:14.74
1936 — U.S.A. (Ivan Brown)	5:29.29
1948 — Switzerland (F. Endrich)	5:29.2
1952 — Germany (Andreas Ostler)	5:24.54
1956 — Italy (Dalla Costa)	5:30.14
1964 — Great Britain (Antony Nash)	4:21.90
1968 — Italy (Eugenio Monti)	4:41.54
1972 — W. Germany (Wolfgang Zimmerer)	4:47.07

Figure Skating

Men's Singles

1908 — Ulrich Sachow, Sweden
1920 — Gillis Grafström, Sweden
1924 — Gillis Grafström, Sweden
1928 — Gillis Grafström, Sweden
1932 — Karl Schaefer, Austria
1936 — Karl Schaefer, Austria
1948 — Richard T. Button, U.S.A.
1952 — Richard T. Button, U.S.A.
1956 — Hayes Alan Jenkins, U.S.A.
1960 — David W. Jenkins, U.S.A.
1964 — Manfred Schnelldorfer, Germany
1968 — Wolfgang Schwartz, Austria
1972 — Ondrej Nepela, Czechoslovakia

Women's Singles

1908 — Madge Syers, Great Britain
1920 — Magda Julin-Mauroy, Sweden
1924 — Mrs. Heima von Szabo-Planck, Austria
1928 — Sonja Henie, Norway
1932 — Sonja Henie, Norway
1936 — Sonja Henie, Norway
1948 — Barbara Ann Scott, Canada
1952 — Jeanette Altwegg, Great Britain
1956 — Tenley E. Albright, U.S.A.
1960 — Carol Heiss, U.S.A.
1964 — Sjoukje Dijkstra, Holland
1968 — Peggy Fleming, U.S.A.
1972 — Beatrix Schuba, Austria

Pairs

1908 — Anna Hübler & Heinrich Burger, Germany
1920 — Ludovika & Walter Jakobsson, Finland
1924 — Helene Engelman & Alfred Berger, Austria
1928 — Andrée Joly & Pierre Brunet, France
1932 — Andrée Joly & Pierre Brunet, France
1936 — Maxie Herber & Ernest Baier, Germany
1952 — Micheline Lannoy & Pierre Baugniet, Belgium
1952 — Ria and Paul Falk, Germany
1956 — Elizabeth Schwarz & Kurt Oppelt, Austria
1960 — Barbara Wagner & Robert Paul, Canada
1964 — Ludmila Beloussova & Oleg Protopopov, USSR
1968 — Ludmila Beloussova & Oleg Protopopov, USSR
1972 — Irina Rodnina & Alexei Ulanov, USSR

Alpine Skiing

Men's Downhill

	Time
1948 — Henri Creiller, France	2:55.0
1952 — Zeno Colo, Italy	2:30.8
1956 — Anton Sailer, Austria	2:52.2
1960 — Jean Vuarmet, France	2:06.0
1964 — Egon Zimmermann, Austria	2:18.1
1968 — Jean Claude Killy, France	1:59.85
1972 — Bernhard Russi, Switzerland	1:51.43

Men's Giant Slalom

	Time
1952 — Stein Eriksen, Norway	2:25.0
1956 — Anton Sailer, Austria	3:00.1
1960 — Roger Staub, Switzerland	1:48.3
1964 — Francois Bonlieu, France	1:46.7
1968 — Jean Claude Killy, France	3:29.28
1972 — Gustavo Thoeni, Italy	3:09.62

Men's Slalom

	Time
1948 — Edi Reinalter, Switzerland	2:10.3
1952 — Othmar Schneider, Austria	2:00.0
1956 — Anton Sailer, Austria	194.7 pts.
1960 — Ernst Hinterseer, Austria	2:08.9
1964 — Josef Stiegler, Austria	2:11.13
1968 — Jean Claude Killy, France	1:39.73
1972 — Francisco Fernandez Ochoa, Spain	1:09.27

Women's Downhill

	Time
1948 — Hedi Schlunegger, Switzerland	2:28.3
1952 — Trude Jochum-Beiser, Austria	1:47.1
1956 — Madeline Bethod, Switzerland	1:40.7
1960 — Heidi Biebl, Germany	1:37.6
1964 — Christl Haas, Austria	1:55.3
1968 — Olga Pall, Austria	1:40.87
1972 — Marie Therese Nadig, Switzerland	1:36.68

Women's Giant Slalom

	Time
1952 — Andrea Mead Lawrence, U.S.A.	2:06.8
1956 — Ossi Reichert, Germany	1:56.5
1960 — Yvonne Ruegg, Switzerland	1:39.9
1964 — Marielle Goitschel, France	1:52.2
1968 — Nancy Greene, Canada	1:51.97
1972 — Marie Therese Nadig, Switzerland	1:29.90

Women's Slalom

	Time
1948 — Gretchen Fraser, U.S.A.	1:57.2
1952 — Andrea Mead Lawrence, U.S.A.	2:10.6
1956 — Renée Colliard, Switzerland	112.3 pts.
1960 — Anne Heggtveigt, Canada	1:49.6
1964 — Christine Goitschel, France	1:35.11
1968 — Marielle Goitschel, France	1:25.86
1972 — Barbara Cochran, United States	91.24

Nordic Skiing

Men's Cross-Country Events

15 Kilometers (9.3 miles) or Equivalent

	Time
1924 — Thorleif Haug, Norway	1:14:31.0
1928 — Johan Gröttumsbraaten, Norway	1:37:01.0
1932 — Sven Utterström, Sweden	1:23:07.0
1936 — Erik-August Larsson, Sweden	1:14:38.0
1948 — Martin Lundström, Sweden	1:13:50.0
1956 — Hallgeir Brenden, Norway	49:39.0
1960 — Haakon Brusveen, Norway	51:55.0
1960 — Haakon Brusveen, Norway	51:55.0
1964 — Eero Mantyranta, Finland	50:54.1
1968 — Harald Groenningen, Norway	47:54.2
1972 — Sven-Ake Lundback, Sweden	45:28.2

(Note: Approx. 18-kilo course 1924-1952)

30 Kilometers (18.6 miles)

	Time
1956 — Veikko Hakulinen, Finland	1:44:06.0
1960 — Sixten Jernberg, Sweden	1:51:03.9
1964 — Eero Mantyranta, Finland	1:30:50.7
1968 — Franco Nones, Italy	1:35:39.2
1972 — Vyacheslav Vedenin, USSR	1:36:31.1

50 Kilometers (31 miles)

	Time
1924 — Thorleif Haug, Norway	3:44:32.0
1928 — Per Erik Hedlund, Sweden	4:52:03.0

1932 — Veli Saarinen, Finland 4:28:00.0
1936 — Elis Viklund, Sweden 3:30:11.0
1948 — Nils Karlsson, Sweden 3:47:48.0
1952 — Veikko Hakulinen, Finland 3:33:33.0
1956 — Sixten Jernberg, Sweden 2:50:27.0
1960 — Kaleiv Hamalainen, Finland 2:59:06.3
1964 — Sixten Jernberg, Sweden 2:43:52.6
1968 — Ole Ellefsaeter, Norway 2:28:45.8
1972 — Paal Tyldum, Norway 2:43:14.7

40 Kilometer Cross-Country Relay

	Time
1936 — Finland, Norway, Sweden	2:41:33.0
1948 — Sweden, Finland, Norway	2:32:08.0
1952 — Finland, Norway, Sweden	2:20:16.0
1956 — USSR, Finland, Sweden	2:15:30.0
1960 — Finland, Norway, USSR	2:18:45.6
1964 — Sweden, Finland, USSR	2:18:34.6
1968 — Norway, Sweden, Finland	2:08:33.5
1972 — USSR, Norway, Switzerland	2:04:47.9

15 Km. Cross-Country & Jumping

	Points
1924 — Thorleif Haug, Norway	453.800
1928 — Johan Gröttumsbraaten, Norway	427.800
1932 — Johan Gröttumsbraaten, Norway	446.200
1936 — Oddbjorn Hagen, Norway	430.300
1948 — Heikki Hasu, Finland	448.800
1952 — Simon Slattvik, Norway	451.621
1956 — Sverre Stenersen, Norway	455.000
1960 — Gerog Thoma, Germany	457.952
1964 — Tormod Knutsen, Norway	469.280
1968 — Franz Keller, W. Germany	449.04
1972 — Ulrich Wehling, E. Germany	413.340

Ski Jumping (90 meters)

	Points
1924 — Jacob T. Thams, Norway	227.5
1928 — Alfred Andersen, Norway	230.5
1932 — Birger Ruud, Norway	228.0
1936 — Birger Ruud, Norway	232.0
1948 — Petter Hugsted, Norway	228.1
1952 — A. Bergmann, Norway	226.0
1956 — Antti Hyvarinen, Finland	227.0
1960 — Helmut Recknagel, Germany	227.2
1964 — Toralf Engan, Norway	230.7
1968 — Vladimir Beloussov, USSR	231.3
1972 — Wojiech Fortuna, Poland	219.9

Ski Jumping (70 meters)

	Points
1964 — Veikko Kankkonen, Finland	229.9
1968 — Jiri Raska, Czech	216.5
1972 — Yukio Kasaya, Japan	244.2

Women's Events

5 Kilometers (approx. 3.1 miles)

	Time
1964 — Claudia Boyarskikh, USSR	17:50.5
1968 — Toini Gustafsson, Sweden	16:45.2
1972 — Galina Koulacova, USSR	17:00.5

10 Kilometers (6.2 miles)

	Time
1952 — Lydia Wideman, Finland	41:40.0
1956 — Lyubob Kosyreva, USSR	38:11.0
1960 — Maria Gusakova, USSR	39:46.6
1964 — Claudia Boyarskikh, USSR	40:24.3
1968 — Toini Gustafsson, Sweden	36:46.5
1972 — Galina Koulacova, USSR	34:17.8

15 Kilometer Cross-Country Relay

	Time
1956 — Finland, USSR, Sweden	1:09:01.0
1960 — Sweden, USSR, Finland	1:04:21.4
1964 — USSR, Sweden, Finland	59:20.2
1968 — Norway, Sweden, USSR	57:30
1972 — USSR, Finland, Norway	48:46.1

Ice Hockey

(Three medal winners, in order)
1920 — Canada, U.S.A., Czechoslovakia
1924 — Canada, U.S.A., Great Britain
1928 — Canada, Sweden, Switzerland
1932 — Canada, U.S.A., Germany
1936 — Great Britain, Canada, U.S.A.
1948 — Canada, Czechoslovakia, Switzerland
1952 — Canada, U.S.A., Sweden
1956 — USSR, U.S.A., Canada
1960 — U.S.A., Canada, USSR
1964 — USSR, Sweden, Czechoslovakia
1968 — USSR, Czechoslovakia, Canada
1972 — USSR, U.S.A., Czechoslovakia

Luge

Men's Singles

	Time
1964 — Thomas Kohler, Germany	3:25.77
1968 — Manfred Schmid, Austria	2:52.48
1972 — Wolfgang Scheidel, E. Germany	3:27.58

Men's Doubles

	Time
1964 — Austria	1:41.62
1968 — East Germany	1:35.85
1972 — Italy, E. Germany (tie)	1:28.35

Women's Singles

	Time
1964 — Ortun Enderlein, Germany	3:24.67
1968 — Erica Lechner, Italy	2:28.66
1972 — Anna M. Muller, E. Germany	2:59.18

Speed Skating
Men's Events

500 Meters

	Time
1924 — Charles Jewtraw, U.S.A.	0:44.0
1928 — Clas Thunberg, Finland & Bernt Evensen, Norway (tie)	0:43.4
1932 — John A. Shea, U.S.A.	0:43.4
1936 — Ivar Ballangrud, Norway	0:43.4
1948 — Finn Helgesen, Norway	0:43.1
1952 — Kenneth Henry, U.S.A.	0:43.2
1956 — Evgeniy Grishin, USSR	0:40.2
1960 — Evgeniy Grishin, USSR	0:40.2
1964 — R. Terrence McDermott, U.S.A.	0:40.1
1968 — Erhard Keller, W. Germany	0:40.3
1972 — Erhard Keller, W. Germany	0:39.4

1,500 Meters

	Time
1924 — Clas Thunberg, Finland	2:20.8
1928 — Clas Thunberg, Finland	2:21.1
1932 — John A. Shea, U.S.A.	2:57.2
1936 — Charles Mathiesen, Norway	2:19.2
1948 — Sverre Farstad, Norway	2:17.6
1952 — Hjalmar Anderson, Norway	2:20.4
1956 — Evgeniy Grishin, USSR	2:08.6
1960 — Roald Edgar Aas, Norway & Evgeniy Grishin, USSR (tie)	2:10.4
1964 — Ants Anston, USSR	2:10.3
1968 — Cornelis Verkerk, Holland	2:03.4
1972 — Ard Schenk, Netherlands	2:02.9

5,000 Meters

	Time
1924 — Clas Thunberg, Finland	8:39.0
1928 — Ivar Ballangrud, Norway	8:50.5
1932 — Irving Jaffee, U.S.A.	9:40.8
1936 — Ivar Ballangrud, Norway	8:19.6
1948 — Reidar Liakleb, Norway	8:29.4
1952 — Hjalmar Anderson, Norway	8:10.6
1956 — Boris Shilkov, USSR	7:48.7
1960 — Viktor Kosichkin, USSR	7:51.3
1964 — Knut Johannesen, Norway	7:38.4
1968 — F. Anton Maier, Norway	7:22.4
1972 — Ard Schenk, Netherlands	7:23.6

10,000 Meters

	Time
1924 — Julius Skutnabb, Finland	18:04.8
1928 — Event not held, thawing of ice	
1932 — Irving Jaffee, U.S.A.	19:13.6
1936 — Ivar Ballangrud, Norway	17:24.3
1948 — Ake Seyffarth, Norway	17:26.3
1952 — Hjalmar Anderson, Norway	16:45.8
1956 — Sigvard Ericsson, Sweden	16:35.9
1960 — Knut Johannesen, Norway	15:46.6
1964 — Jonny Nilsson, Sweden	15:50.1
1968 — Johnny Hoeglin, Sweden	15:23.0
1972 — Ard Schenk, Netherlands	15:01.3

Women's Events

500 Meters

	Time
1960 — Helga Haase, Germany	0:45.9
1964 — Lydia Skoblikova, USSR	0:45.0
1968 — Ludmila Titova, USSR	0:46.1
1972 — Anne Henning, U.S.A.	0:43.3

1,000 Meters

	Time
1960 — Klara Guseva, USSR	1:34.1
1964 — Lydia Skoblikova, USSR	1:33.2
1968 — Carolina Geijssen, Holland	1:32.6
1972 — Monika Pflug, W. Germany	1:31.4

1,500 Meters

	Time
1960 — Lydia Skoblikova, USSR	2:52.2
1964 — Lydia Skoblikova, USSR	2:22.6
1968 — Kaija Mustonen, Finland	2:22.4
1972 — Dianne Holum, U.S.A.	2:20.8

3,000 Meters

	Time
1960 — Lydia Skoblikova, USSR	5:14.3
1964 — Lydia Skoblikova, USSR	5:14.9
1968 — Johanna Schut, Holland	4:56.2
1972 — Stien Kaiser Baas, Netherlands	4:52.1

Speed Ice-Skating Championships in 1973

National Outdoor Championships
St. Paul, Minn., Jan. 27-28, 1973

Senior Men
1/6 Mile — Bill Heinkel. Time — 0:25.5.
440 Yds. — Mike Woods. Time — 0:35.2.
880 Yds. — Ed Jacquin. Time — 1:17.8.
3/4 Mile — Mike Woods. Time — 2:08.1.
1 Mile — Mike Woods. Time — 3:10.1.
2 Miles — Mike Woods. Time — 5:55.0.
5 Miles — Ed Jacquin. Time — 17:18.0.
Champion — Mike Woods.

Senior Women
1/6 Mile — Nancy Class. Time — 0:28.3.
440 Yds. — Nancy Class. Time — 0:39.7.
880 Yds. — Kris Garbe. Time — 1:40.3.
3/4 Mile — Kris Garbe. Time — 2:43.3.
1 Mile — Celeste Chlapaty. Time — 3:30.8.
Champion — Nancy Class.

North American Outdoor Championships
West Allis, Wisc., Feb. 10-11, 1973

Senior Men
1/6 Mile — Jim Chapin. Time — 0:22.9.
440 Yds. — Bob Haenisch. Time — 0:33.9.
880 Yds. — Rich Wurster. Time — 1:08.6.
3/4 Mile — Jim Chapin. Time — 2:07.2.
1 Mile — Jim Chapin. Time — 2:32.1.
2 Miles — Rich Wurster. Time — 5:23.3.
5 Miles — Jim Chapin. Time — 15:32.1.
Champion — Jim Chapin.

Senior Women
1/6 Mile — Nancy Class. Time — 0:25.9.
440 Yds. — Nancy Class. Time — 0:38.4.
880 Yds. — Nancy Class. Time — 1:22.7.
3/4 Mile — Kris Garbe. Time — 2:09.0.
1 Mile — Celeste Chlapaty. Time — 2:54.0.

National Indoor Championships
Long Island, N.Y., Mar. 10-11, 1973

Senior Men
440 Yds. — Bill Lanigan. Time — 0:38.7.
880 Yds. — Bill Lanigan. Time — 1:19.4.
3/4 Mile — Bill Lanigan. Time — 2:02.4.
1 Mile — Bill Lanigan. Time — 2:47.0.
2 Miles — Bill Lanigan. Time — 5:46.0.
Champion — Bill Lanigan.

Senior Women
440 Yds. — Michele Conroy. Time — 0:43.3.
880 Yds. — Celeste Chlapaty. Time — 1:28.9.
3/4 Mile — Michele Conroy.
1 Mile — Celeste Chlapaty. Time — 3:06.7.
Champions — Michele Conroy, Celeste Chlapaty.

Canadian Intercollegiate Athletic Union Champions

Basketball

1963	Assumption
1964	Windsor
1965	Acadia
1966	Windsor
1967	Windsor
1968	Waterloo Lutheran
1969	Windsor
1970	British Columbia
1971	Acadia
1972	British Columbia
1973	St. Mary's

Swimming and Diving

1965	British Columbia
1966	Toronto
1967	Toronto
1968	Toronto
1969	Toronto
1970	Toronto
1971	Toronto
1972	McGill
1973	Toronto

Hockey

1963	McMaster
1964	Alberta
1965	Manitoba
1966	Toronto
1967	Toronto
1968	Alberta
1969	Toronto
1970	Toronto
1971	Toronto
1972	Toronto
1973	Toronto

Cross Country

1964	Manitoba
1965	Toronto
1966	Toronto
1967	Toronto
1968	Saskatchewan
1972	Western Ontario
1973	Toronto

Gymnastics

1973	York

Volleyball

1967	British Columbia
1968	Ottawa
1969	Winnipeg
1970	Montreal
1971	Winnipeg
1972	Winnipeg
1973	Winnipeg

Football

1969	Manitoba
1970	Manitoba
1971	Western Ontario
1972	Western Ontario
1973	Alberta

Wrestling

1969	O.Q.A.A.
1970	Alberta
1971	Alberta
1972	Alberta
1973	

Soccer

1973	Alberta

James E. Sullivan Memorial Trophy Winners

The James E. Sullivan Memorial Trophy, inaugurated in 1930, is awarded annually by the AAU to the athlete who "by his or her performance, example and influence as an amateur, has done the most during the year to advance the cause of sportsmanship."

Year	Name	Sport	Year	Name	Sport	Year	Name	Sport
1930	Bobby Jones	Golf	1944	Ann Curtis	Swimming	1958	Glenn Davis	Track
1931	Barney Berlinger	Track	1945	Doc Blanchard	Football	1959	Parry O'Brien	Track
1932	Jim Bausch	Track	1946	Arnold Tucker	Football	1960	Rafer Johnson	Track
1933	Glenn Cunningham	Track	1947	John B. Kelly, Jr.	Rowing	1961	Wilma Rudolph Ward	Track
1934	Bill Bonthron	Track	1948	Robert B. Mathias	Track	1962	James T. Beatty	Track
1935	Lawson Little	Golf	1949	Dick Button	Skating	1963	John T. Pennel	Track
1936	Glenn Morris	Track	1950	Fred Wilt	Track	1964	Don Schollander	Swimming
1937	Don Budge	Tennis	1951	Rev. Robt. E. Richards	Track	1965	Bill Bradley	Basketball
1938	Don Lash	Track	1952	Horace Ashenfelter	Track	1966	Jim Ryun	Track
1939	Joe Burk	Rowing	1953	Dr. Sammy Lee	Diving	1967	Randy Matson	Track
1940	Greg Rice	Track	1954	Mal Whitfield	Track	1968	Debbie Meyer	Swimming
1941	Leslie Mac Mitchell	Track	1955	Harrison Dillard	Track	1969	Bill Toomey	Track
1942	Cornelius Warmerdam	Track	1956	Patricia K. McCormick	Diving	1970	John Kinsella	Swimming
1943	Gilbert Dodds	Track	1957	Bobby Joe Morrow	Track	1971	Mark Spitz	Swimming
						1972	Frank Shorter	Track

World Record Fish Caught by Rod and Reel

Source: Salt-Water: International Game Fish Association. Fresh-Water: Field & Stream Magazine.
Records confirmed to June, 1973

SALT-WATER FISH. All-tackle records, both men and women.

The International Game Fish Assn. revised its standards for world records, effective July 1, 1970. Line samples and line tests are now required in order for a world record application to be recognized. Records listed below are based on the new standards.

Species	Weight	Length	Girth	Where caught	Date	Angler
Albacore	70 lbs.	4' 2½"	33"	Cape Point, So. Africa	Aug. 2, 1972	Brian Cohen
Amberjack	149 lbs.	5' 11"	41¾"	Bermuda	June 21, 1964	Peter Simons
Barracuda, Great	83 lbs.	6'¼"	29"	Lagos, Nigeria	Jan. 13, 1952	K.J.W. Hackett
Bass, Giant Sea	563 lbs. 8 oz.	7' 5"	72"	Anacapa Island, California	Aug. 20, 1968	James D. McAdam, Jr.
Bass, Cal. White Sea	83 lbs. 12 oz.	5' 5½"	34"	San Felipe, Mexico	Mar. 31, 1953	L. C. Baumgardner
Bass, Channel	83 lbs.	4' 4"	29"	Cape Charles, Va.	Aug. 5, 1949	Zack Waters, Jr.
Bass, Sea	8 lbs.	1' 10"	19"	Nantucket Sound, Mass.	May 13, 1951	H. R. Rider
Bass, Striped	72 lbs.	4'6½"	31"	Cuttyhunk, Mass.	Oct. 10, 1969	Edward J. Kirker
Blackfish (or Tautog)	21 lbs. 6 oz.	2' 7½"	23½"	Cape May, N. J.	June 12, 1954	R. N. Sheafer
Bluefish	31 lbs. 12 oz.	3'11"	23"	Hatteras Inlet, North Carolina	Jan. 30, 1972	James M. Hussey
Bonefish	19 lbs.	3' 3⅝"	17"	Zululand, S. Africa	May 26, 1962	Brian W. Batchelor
Bonito, Oceanic	39 lbs. 15 oz.	3' 3"	28"	Walker Cay, Bahamas	Jan. 21, 1952	F. Drowley
	40 lbs.	3'2¾"	27½"	Baie du Tambeau, Mauritius	Apr. 19, 1971	Joseph R. P. Caboche, Jr.
Cobia	110 lbs. 5 oz.	5' 3"	34"	Mombasa, Kenya	Sept. 8, 1964	Eric Tinworth
Cod	98 lbs. 12 oz.	5' 3"	41"	Isle of Shoals, Mass.	June 8, 1969	Alphonse Bielevich
Dolphin	85 lbs.	5' 9"	37½"	Spanish Wells, Bahamas	May 29, 1968	Richard Seymour
Drum, Black	109 lbs.	4' 9"	48"	Cape Charles, Va.	May 25, 1972	Steve Dennis
Flounder, Summer	30 lbs. 12 oz.	3' 2½"	30½"	Vina del Mar, Chile	Nov. 1, 1971	Augusto Nunez Moreno
Jewfish	680 lbs.	7' 1½"	66"	Fernandina Beach, Fla.	May 20, 1961	Lynn Joyner
Kingfish	78 lbs. 12 oz.	5'5½"	30"	La Romana, Dominican Republic	Nov. 26, 1971	Fernando Viyella
Marlin, Black	1,560 lbs.	14' 6"	81"	Cabo Blanco, Peru	Aug. 4, 1953	A.C. Glassell, Jr.
Marlin, Blue	845 lbs.	13' 1"	71"	St. Thomas, Virgin Is.	July 4, 1968	Elliot J. Fishman
Marlin, Pacific Blue	1,153 lbs.	14' 8"	73"	Guam	Aug. 21, 1969	Greg Perez
Marlin, Striped	415 lbs.	11'	52"	Cape Brett, N.Z.	Mar. 31, 1964	B. C. Bain
Marlin, White	159 lbs. 8 oz.	9'	36"	Pompano Beach, Fla.	Apr. 25 1953	W.E. Johnson
Permit	50 lbs. 8 oz.	3' 8¾"	33¾"	Key West, Fla.	Mar. 5, 1971	Marshall Earnest
Pollack	43 lbs.	4'	29"	Brielle, N.J.	Oct. 21, 1964	Philip Barlow
Rainbow Runner	30 lbs. 15 oz.	3' 11"	22"	Kauai, Hawaii	Apr. 27, 1963	Holbrook Goodale
Roosterfish	114 lbs.	5' 4"	33"	La Paz, Mex.	June 1, 1960	Abe Sackheim
Sailfish, Atlantic	141 lbs. 1 oz.	8' 5"	....	Ivory Coast	Jan. 26, 1961	Tony Burnand
Sailfish, Pacific	221 lbs.	10' 9"	....	Santa Cruz Is.,	Feb. 12, 1947	C. W. Stewart
Shark Blue	410 lbs.	11' 6"	52"	Rockport, Mass.	Sept. 1. 1960	R. C. Webster
	410 lbs.	11' 2"	52½"	Rockport, Mass.	Aug. 17, 1967	Martha Webster
Shark, Mako	1,061 lbs.	12' 2"	79½"	Mayor Island N.Z.	Feb. 17, 1970	James Penwarden
Shark, Man-Eater or White	2,664 lbs.	16'10"	9'6"	Cedunea, So. Australia	Apr. 21, 1959	Alfred Dean
Shark, Porbeagle	430 lbs.	8'	63"	Channel Island, Eng.	June 29, 1969	Desmond Bougourd
Shark, Thresher	729 lbs.	8' 5"	61"	Mayor Island, N. Z.	June 3, 1959	Mrs. V. Brown
Shark, Tiger	1,780 lbs.	13' 10½"	103"	Cherry Grove, S.C.	June 14, 1964	Walter Maxwell
Snook, or Robalo	52 lbs. 6 oz.	4' 1½"	26"	Lapaz, Mexico	Jan. 9, 1963	Jane Haywood
Swordfish	1,182 lbs.	14' 11½"	78"	Iquique, Chile	May 7, 1953	L. Marron
Tanguigue	81 lbs.	5' 11½"	29¼"	Karachi, Pakistan	Aug. 27, 1960	George E. Rusinak
Tarpon	283 lbs.	7' 2½"	....	L. Maracaibo, Venezuela	Mar. 19, 1956	M. Salazar
Tuna, Allison (Yellowfin)	308 lbs.	7'	5'7"	San Benedicto Isl., Mexico	Jan. 18, 1973	Harold J. Tolson
Tuna, Atlantic Big-Eyed	321 lbs. 12 oz.	7' 4¼"	58¼"	Hudson Canyon, N.Y.	Aug. 19, 1972	Vito LaCaputo

Species	Weight	Length	Girth	Where Caught	Date	Angler
Tuna, Pacific Big-Eyed	435 lbs.	7' 9"	63½"	Cabo Blanco, Peru	Apr. 17, 1957	Dr. Russel Lee
Tuna, Blackfin	38 lbs.	3' 3¼"	28¾"	Bermuda	June 26 1970	Archie L. Dickens
Tuna, Bluefin	1065 lbs.	10' 3"	96"	Cape Breton, N.S.	Nov. 19, 1970	Robert G. Gibson
Wahoo	149 lbs.	6' 7¾"	37½"	Cat Cay, Bahamas	June 15, 1962	John Pirovano
Weakfish	19 lbs. 8 oz.	3' 1"	23¾"	Trinidad, W. Indies	Apr. 13, 1962	Dennis Hall
Weakfish, Spotted	15 lbs. 3 oz.	2' 10½"	20½"	Fort Pierce, Fla.	Jan. 13, 1949	C. W. Hubbard
	15 lbs. 6 oz.	2' 9"	23¾"	St. Lucie River, Fla.	May 4, 1969	Michael Foremny
Yellowtail	111 lbs.	5' 2"	38"	Bay of Islands, New Zealand	June 11, 1961	A. F. Plim

Fresh-Water Fish

Species	Weight	Length	Girth	Where Caught	Date	Angler
Black Bass, Large-mouth	22 lbs. 4 oz.	32½"	28½"	Montgomery Lake, Ga.	June 2, 1932	George W. Perry
Black Bass, Small-mouth	11 lbs. 15 oz.	27"	21⅔"	Dale Hollow Lake, Ky.	July 9, 1955	David L. Hayes
Bass, Redeye	6 lbs. ½ oz.	20½"	15⅘"	Hallawakee Creek, Ala.	Mar. 24, 1967	Thomas Sharpe
Bass, Rock	2 lbs. 2 oz.	13"	14"	Mille Coquin Lake, Mich.	Aug. 13, 1971	Richard M. Barta
Bass, White	5 lbs. 5 oz.	19½"	....	Ferguson Lake, Calif.	March 8, 1972	Norman W. Mize
Bass, Yellow	2 lbs. 2 oz.	14"	13"	Lake Monona, Wis.	Jan. 18, 1972	James Thrun
Black Bullhead	8 lbs.	24"	17¾"	Lake Waccabuc N.Y.	Aug. 1, 1951	Kani Evans
Bass, Spotted	8 lbs. 10½ oz.	23½"	19⅞"	Smith Lake, Ala.	Feb. 25, 1972	Billy Henderson
Bluegill	4 lbs. 12 oz.	15"	18¼"	Kentona Lake, Ala.	Apr. 9, 1950	T.S. Hudson
Bowfin	19 lbs. 12 oz.	39"	—	Lake Marion, S.C.	Nov. 1972	M. R. Webster
Carp	55 lbs. 5 oz.	42"	31"	Clearwater Lake, Minn.	July 10, 1952	Frank J. Ledwein
Catfish, Blue	97 lbs.	57"	37"	Missouri River, S.D.	Sept. 16, 1959	E. B. Elliott
Catfish, Channel	58 lbs.	47½"	29⅛"	Santee-Cooper Res., S. C.	July 7, 1964	W. B. Whaley
Catfish, Flathead	76 lbs.	53"	32"	Piedmont Lake, Ohio	July 12, 1972	Dale C. Yoho
Char, Arctic	Record being reviewed.					
Crappie, Black	5 lbs.	19¼"	18⅝"	Santee-Cooper Res., S.C.	Mar. 15, 1957	Paul E. Foust
Crappie, White	5 lbs. 3 oz.	21"	19"	Enid Dam, Miss.	July 31, 1957	Fred L. Bright
Dolly Varden	32 lbs.	40½"	29¾"	L. Pend Oreille, Idaho	Oct. 27, 1949	N. L. Higgins
Drum, Freshwater	54 lbs. 8 oz.	31½"	29"	Nickajack Dam, Tenn.	Apr. 20, 1972	Benny E. Hull
Gar, Alligator	279 lbs.	93"	....	Texas	1951	Bill Valverde
Gar, Longnose	50 lbs. 5 oz.	72¼"	22¼"	Trinity River, Texas	July 30, 1954	Townsend Miller
Grayling, Arctic	Record being reviewed.					
Muskellunge	69 lbs. 15 oz.	64½"	31¾"	St. Lawrence River, N. Y.	Sept. 22, 1957	Arthur Lawton
Perch, White	4 lbs. 12 oz.	19½"	13"	Messalonskee Lake, Maine	June 4, 1949	Mrs. Earl Small
Perch, Yellow	4 lbs. 3½"	....	....	Bordentown, N. J.	May, 1865	Dr. C. C. Abbot
Pickerel, Chain	9 lbs. 6 oz.	31"	14"	Homerville, Ga.	Feb. 17, 1961	Baxley Mc-Quaig, Jr.
Pike, Northern	46 lbs. 2 oz.	52½"	25"	Sacandaga Res., N. Y.	Sept. 15, 1940	Peter Dubuc
Salmon, Atlantic	79 lbs. 2 oz.	....	....	Tanaeiv, Nor.	1928	Henrik Henriksen
Salmon, Chinook	92 lbs.	58½"	36"	Skeena River, B. C.	July 19, 1959	H. Wichmann
Salmon, Silver	31 lbs.	....	....	Cowichan Lake, B.C.	Oct. 11, 1947	Mrs. Lee Hall-berg
Salmon, Landlocked	22 lbs. 8 oz.	36"	est. 20"	Sebago Lake, Maine	Aug. 1, 1907	Edward Blakely
Sauger	8 lbs. 12 oz.	28"	15"	Lake Sakakawea, N.D.	Oct. 6, 1971	Mike Fischer
Sturgeon, White	360 lbs.	111"	86"	Snake River, Idaho	April 24, 1956	Willard Cravens
Sunfish, Green	2 lbs.	11¼"	12½"	Salem, Ill.	May 15, 1972	Kenneth Collier, Sr.
Sunfish, Redear	4 lbs. 8 oz.	16¼"	17¾"	Chase City, Va.	June 19, 1970	Maurice E. Ball
Trout, Brook	14½ lbs.	31½"	11½"	Nipigon River, Ontario	July, 1916	Dr. W. J. Cook
Trout, Brown	39½ lbs.	....	....	Scotland	1866	W. Muir
Trout, Cutthroat	41 lbs.	39"	....	Pyramid Lake, Nev.	Dec., 1925	J. Skimmerhorn

Species	Weight	Length	Girth	Where Caught	Date	Angler
Trout, Golden	11 lbs.	28"	16"	Cook's Lake, Wyo.	Aug. 5, 1948	Charles S. Reed
Trout, Lake	Record being reviewed.					
Trout, Rainbow or . . . Steelhead	42 lbs. 2 oz.	43"	23½"	Bell Island, Alaska	June 22, 1970	David Robert White
Trout, Sunapee	11 lbs. 8 oz.	33"	17'""	Lake Sunapee N. H.	Aug. 1 1954	Ernest Theoharis
Walleye	25 lbs.	41"	29"	Old Hickory Lake, Tenn.	Aug. 1, 1960	Mabry Harper
Warmouth	1 lb. 13 oz.	10⅝"	12¼"	Cumberland County, Ill.	May 22, 1971	Wesley Mills
Whitefish, Lake	12 lbs. 9 oz.	32'	17⅞"	Great Slave L., N.W.T.	July 28, 1972	Eddie Drygeese
Whitefish, ... Mountain	5 lbs.	19"	14"	Athabasca R., Alberta	June 3, 1963	Orville Welch

The America's Cup

Competition for the America's Cup grew out of the first contest to establish a world yachting championship, one of the carnival features of the London Exposition of 1851. The race, open to all classes of yachts from all over the world, covered a 60-mile course around the Isle of Wight; the prize was a cup worth about $500, donated by the Royal Yacht Squadron of England, known as the "America's Cup" because it was first won by the United States yacht America. Successive efforts of British and Australian yachtsmen have failed to win the famous trophy, which remains in the United States.

On Sept. 28, 1970, the 12-meter yacht Intrepid won a fourth and final victory over Australia's challenger, Gretel, 2nd, to keep the symbol of world sailing supremacy in the United States. Gretel, 2nd, defeated Intrepid twice but lost one of her victories when she was disqualified for bumping the American boat at the starting line in the second race. The U.S. yacht was skippered by Bill Ficker of Newport Beach, Calif. The Australian yacht was skippered by Jim Hardy.

WINNERS OF THE AMERICA'S CUP

1851	America	1899	Columbia defeated Shamrock, England, (3-0)
1870	Magic defeated Cambria, England, (1-0)	1901	Columbia defeated Shamrock II, England, (3-0)
1871	Columbia (first three races) and Sappho (last two races) defeated Livonia, England, (4-1)	1903	Reliance defeated Shamrock III, England, (3-0)
		1920	Resolute defeated Shamrock IV, England, (3-2)
1876	Madeline defeated Countess of Dufferin, Canada, (2-0)	1930	Enterprise defeated Shamrock V, England, (4-0)
		1931	Rainbow defeated Endeavour, England, (4-2)
1881	Mischief defeated Atalanta, Canada, (2-0)	1937	Ranger defeated Endeavour II, England, (4-0)
1885	Puritan defeated Genesta, England, (2-0)	1958	Columbia defeated Sceptre, England, (4-0)
1886	Mayflower defeated Galatea, England, (2-0)	1962	Weatherly defeated Gretel, Australia, (4-1)
1887	Volunteer defeated Thistle, Scotland, (2-0)	1964	Constellation defeated Sovereign, England, (4-0)
1893	Vigilant defeated Valkyrie II, England, (3-0)	1967	Intrepid defeated Dame Pattie, Australia, (4-0)
1895	Defender defeated Valkyrie III, England, (3-0)	1970	Intrepid defeated Gretel, II, Australia, (4-1)

Figure Skating Champions

National Champions

Year	Men	Women
1951	Richard Button	Sonya Klopfer
1952	Richard Button	Tenley Albright
1953	Hayes Jenkins	Tenley Albright
1954	Hayes Jenkins	Tenley Albright
1955	Hayes Jenkins	Tenley Albright
1956	Hayes Jenkins	Tenley Albright
1957	Dave Jenkins	Carol Heiss
1958	Dave Jenkins	Carol Heiss
1959	Dave Jenkins	Carol Heiss
1960	Dave Jenkins	Carol Heiss
1961	Bradley Lord	Laurence Owen
1962	Monty Hoyt	Barbara Roles Pursley
1963	Tommy Litz	Lorraine Hanlon
1964	Scott Allen	Peggy Fleming
1965	Gary Visconti	Peggy Fleming
1966	Scott Allen	Peggy Fleming
1967	Gary Visconti	Peggy Fleming
1968	Tim Wood	Peggy Fleming
1969	Tim Wood	Janet Lynn
1970	Tim Wood	Janet Lynn
1971	John Misha Petkevich	Janet Lynn
1972	Ken Shelley	Janet Lynn
1973	Gordon McKellen, Jr.	Janet Lynn

World Champions

Men	Women
Richard Button, U.S.	Jeannette Altwegg, Eng.
Richard Button, U.S.	Jacqueline du Bief, France
Hayes Jenkins, U.S.	Tenley Albright, U.S.
Hayes Jenkins, U.S.	Gundi Busch, Germany
Hayes Jenkins, U.S.	Tenley Albright, U.S.
Hayes Jenkins, U.S.	Carol Heiss, U.S.
Dave Jenkins, U.S.	Carol Heiss, U.S.
Dave Jenkins, U.S.	Carol Heiss, U.S.
Dave Jenkins, U.S.	Carol Heiss, U.S.
Alain Giletti, France	Carol Heiss, U.S.
none	none
Don Jackson, Canada	Sjoukje Dijkstra, Neth.
Don McPherson, Canada	Sjoukje Dijkstra, Neth.
Manfred Schnelldorfer, Germany	Sjoukje Dijkstra, Neth.
Alain Calmat, France	Petra Burka, Canada
Emmerich Danzer, Austria	Peggy Fleming, U.S.
Emmerich Danzer, Austria	Peggy Fleming, U.S.
Emmerich Danzer, Austria	Peggy Fleming, U.S.
Tim Wood, U.S.	Gabriele Seyfert, E. Germany
Tim Wood, U.S.	Gabriele Seyfert, E. Germany
Ondrej Nepela, Czech.	Beatrix Schuba, Austria
Ondrej Nepela, Czech.	Beatrix Schuba, Austria
Ondrej Nepela, Czech.	Karen Magnussen, Canada

Canadian National Figure Skating Champions

Year	Men	Women	Year	Men	Women
1951	Peter Firstbrook	Suzanne Morrow	1962	Donald Jackson	Wendy Griner
1952	Peter Firstbrook	Marlene Smith	1963	Donald McPherson	Wendy Griner
1953	Peter Firstbrook	Barbara Gratton	1964	Charles Snelling	Petra Burka
1954	Charles Snelling	Barbara Gratton	1965	Donald Knight	Petra Burka
1955	Charles Snelling	Carole Jane Pachl	1966	Donald Knight	Petra Burka
1956	Charles Snelling	Carole Jane Pachl	1967	Donald Knight	Valerie Jones
1957	Charles Snelling	Carole Jane Pachl	1968	Jay Humphrey	Karen Magnussen
1958	Charles Snelling	Marg. Crosland	1969	Jay Humphrey	Linda Carbonetto
1959	Donald Jackson	Marg. Crosland	1970	David McGillivray	Karen Magnussen
1960	Donald Jackson	Wendy Griner	1971	Toller Cranston	Karen Magnussen
1961	Donald Jackson	Wendy Griner	1972	Toller Cranston	Karen Magnussen
			1973	Toller Cranston	Karen Magnussen

National Basketball Association, 1972-73

Eastern Conference

Atlantic Division

Club	W.	L.	Pct.	G.B.
Boston Celtics	68	14	.829	—
New York Knickerbockers	57	25	.695	11
Buffalo Braves.........	21	61	.256	47
Philadelphia 76's	9	73	.110	59

Central Division

Club	W.	L.	Pct.	G.B.
Baltimore Bullets	52	30	.634	—
Atlanta Hawks	46	36	.561	6
Houston Rockets	33	49	.402	19
Cleveland Cavaliers	32	50	.390	20

Western Conference

Midwest Division

Club	W.	L.	Pct.	G.B.
Milwaukee Bucks	60	22	.732	—
Chicago Bulls..........	51	31	.622	9
Detroit Pistons........	40	42	.488	20
K.C.-Omaha Kings......	36	46	.439	24

Pacific Division

Club	W.	L.	Pct.	G.B.
Los Angeles Lakers.....	60	22	.732	—
Golden State Warriors ..	47	35	.573	13
Phoenix Suns..........	38	44	.463	22
Seattle SuperSonics ...	26	56	.317	34
Portland Trail Blazers ..	21	61	.256	39

NBA Playoffs

Eastern Division — Boston defeated Atlanta 4 games to 2. New York defeated Baltimore 4 games to 1. New York defeated Boston 4 games to 3.

Western Division — Golden State defeated Milwaukee 4 games to 2. Los Angeles defeated Chicago 4 games to 3. Los Angeles defeated Golden State 4 games to 1.

Championship — New York defeated Los Angeles 4 games to 1.

Final Statistics

Individual Scoring Leaders
(Minimum of 70 Games)

	G.	FG.	FT.	Pts.	Avg.
Archibald, KC-O...	80	1028	663	2719	34.0
Jabbar, Milwaukee	76	982	328	2292	30.2
Haywood, Seattle .	77	889	473	2251	29.2
Hudson, Atlanta ..	75	816	397	2029	27.1
Maravich, Atlanta .	79	789	485	2063	26.1
Scott, Phoenix	81	806	436	2048	25.3
Petrie, Portland ...	79	836	298	1970	24.9
Goodrich, L.A.	76	750	314	1814	23.9
Wicks, Portland ...	80	761	384	1906	23.8
Lanier, Detroit	81	810	307	1927	23.8
Havlicek, Boston ..	80	766	370	1902	23.8
B. Love, Chicago ..	82	774	347	1895	23.1
Bing, Detroit......	82	692	456	1840	22.4
Barry, Golden St...	82	737	358	1832	22.3
Hayes, Baltimore..	81	713	291	1717	21.2
Frazier, New York .	78	681	286	1648	21.1
Carr, Cleveland ...	82	702	281	1685	20.5
Cowens, Boston...	82	740	204	1684	20.5
Wilkens, Cleveland	75	572	394	1538	20.5

Free Throw Leaders
(Minimum 160 Attempts)

	FTM.	FTA.	Pct.
Barry, Golden State	358	397	.902
Murphy, Houston	239	269	.888
Newlin, Houston	327	369	.886
J. Walker, Houston	244	276	.884
Bradley, New York...........	169	194	.871
C. Russell, Golden State	172	199	.864
Snyder, Seattle	186	216	.861
D. VanArsdale, Phoenix	426	496	.859

Assists Leaders
(Minimum 70 Games)

	G.	No.	Avg.
Archibald, Kansas City-O......	80	910	11.4
Wilkens, Cleveland	75	628	8.4
Bing, Detroit................	82	637	7.8
Robertson, Milwaukee........	73	551	7.5
Van Lier, Chicago	80	567	7.1
Maravich, Atlanta	79	546	6.9
Havlicek, Boston	80	529	6.6

Field Goal Leaders
(Minimum of 560 Attempts)

	FGM.	FGA.	Pct.
Chamberlain, Los Angeles	426	586	.727
Guokas, Kansas City-Omaha ..	322	565	.570
Jabbar, Milwaukee	982	1772	.554
Rowe, Detroit	547	1053	.519
J. Fox, Seattle	316	613	.515
Lucas, New York	312	608	.513
Riordan, Baltimore	652	1278	.510
Clark, Baltimore	302	596	.507
Kauffman, Buffalo	535	1059	.509

Rebound Leaders
(Minimum 70 Games)

	G.	No.	Avg.
Chamberlain, Los Angeles	82	1526	18.6
Thurmond, Golden State......	79	1349	17.1
Cowens, Boston.............	82	1329	16.2
Jabbar, Milwaukee	76	1224	16.1
Unseld, Baltimore...........	79	1260	15.9
Lanier, Detroit	81	1205	14.9
Hayes, Baltimore............	81	1177	14.5
Bellamy, Atlanta	74	964	13.0
Silas, Boston	80	1039	13.0

Podoloff Cup Winners

Dave Cowens of the Boston Celtics, was selected as the winner of the Maurice Podoloff Cup for Most Valuable Player in the NBA for the 1972-73 season. The award was determined in a poll of all players on the 17 teams, conducted by Newspaper Enterprise Association.

1956—Bob Pettit, St. Louis	1965—Bill Russell, Boston
1957—Bob Cousy, Boston	1966—Wilt Chamberlain, Philadelphia
1958—Bill Russell, Boston	1967—Wilt Chamberlain, Philadelphia
1959—Bob Pettit, St. Louis	1968—Wilt Chamberlain, Philadelphia
1960—Wilt Chamberlain, Philadelphia	1969—Wes Unseld, Baltimore
1961—Bill Russell, Boston	1970—Willis Reed, New York
1962—Bill Russell, Boston	1971—Lew Alcindor, Milwaukee
1963—Bill Russell, Boston	1972—Kareem Abdul-Jabbar (Alcindor), Milwaukee
1964—Oscar Robertson, Cincinnati	1973—Dave Cowens, Boston Celtics

NBA Rookie of the Year Awards

1954—Don Meineke, Ft. Wayne	1961—Oscar Robertson, Cinn.	1968—Earl Monroe, Baltimore
1955—Ray Felix, Baltimore	1962—Walt Bellamy, Chicago	1969—Wes Unseld, Baltimore
1956—Maurice Stokes, Rochester	1963—Terry Dischinger, Chicago	1970—Lew Alcindor, Milwaukee
1957—Tom Heinsohn, Boston	1964—Jerry Lucas, Cinn.	1971—Dave Cowens, Boston;
1958—Woody Sauldsberry, Phil.	1965—Willis Reed, N.Y.	Geoff Petrie, Portland (Tie)
1959—Elgin Baylor, Minn.	1966—Rick Barry, S.F.	1972—Sidney Wicks, Portland
1960—Wilt Chamberlain, Phil.	1967—Dave Bing, Detroit	1973—Bob McAdoo, Buffalo

NBA Champions 1947-73

	Regular Season		Playoffs	
Year	Eastern Conference	Western Conference	Winner	Runner-Up
1947	Washington	Chicago	Philadelphia	Chicago
1948	Philadelphia	St. Louis	Baltimore	Philadelphia
1949	Washington	Rochester	Minneapolis	Washington
1950	Syracuse	Minneapolis	Minneapolis	Syracuse
1951	Philadelphia	Minneapolis	Rochester	New York
1952	Syracuse	Rochester	Minneapolis	New York
1953	New York	Minneapolis	Minneapolis	New York
1954	New York	Minneapolis	Minneapolis	Syracuse
1955	Syracuse	Ft. Wayne	Syracuse	Ft. Wayne
1956	Philadelphia	Ft. Wayne	Philadelphia	Ft. Wayne
1957	Boston	St. Louis	Boston	St. Louis
1958	Boston	St. Louis	St. Louis	Boston
1959	Boston	St. Louis	Boston	Minneapolis
1960	Boston	St. Louis	Boston	St. Louis
1961	Boston	St. Louis	Boston	St. Louis
1962	Boston	Los Angeles	Boston	Los Angeles
1963	Boston	Los Angeles	Boston	Los Angeles
1964	Boston	San Francisco	Boston	San Francisco
1965	Boston	Los Angeles	Boston	Los Angeles
1966	Philadelphia	Los Angeles	Boston	Los Angeles
1967	Philadelphia	San Francisco	Philadelphia	San Francisco
1968	Philadelphia	St. Louis	Boston	Los Angeles
1969	Baltimore	Los Angeles	Boston	Los Angeles
1970	New York	Atlanta	New York	Los Angeles

	Atlantic	Central	Midwest	Pacific		
1971	New York	Baltimore	Los Angeles	Milwaukee	Milwaukee	Baltimore
1972	Boston	Baltimore	Milwaukee	Los Angeles	Los Angeles	New York
1973	Boston	Baltimore	Milwaukee	Los Angeles	New York	Los Angeles

NBA Scoring Leaders

Year	Scoring Champion	Pts.	Avg.	Year	Scoring Champion	Pts.	Avg.
1947	Joe Fulks, Philadelphia	1,389	23.2	1961	Wilt Chamberlain, Philadelphia	3,033	38.4
1948	Max Zaslofsky, Chicago	1,007	21.0	1962	Wilt Chamberlain, Philadelphia	4,029	50.4
1949	George Mikan, Minneapolis	1,698	28.3	1963	Wilt Chamerblain, San Francisco	3,586	44.8
1950	George Mikan, Minneapolis	1,865	27.4	1964	Wilt Chamberlain, San Francisco	2,948	36.5
1951	George Mikan, Minneapolis	1,932	28.4	1965	Wilt Chamberlain, San Fran., Phila	2,534	34.7
1952	Paul Arizin, Philadelphia	1,674	25.4	1966	Wilt Chamberlain, Philadelphia	2,649	33.5
1953	Neil Johnston, Philadelphia	1,564	22.3	1967	Rick Barry, San Francisco	2,775	35.6
1954	Neil Johnston, Philadelphia	1,759	24.4	1968	Dave Bing, Detroit	2,142	27.1
1955	Neil Johnston, Philadelphia	1,631	22.7	1969	Elvin Hayes, San Diego	2,327	28.4
1956	Bob Pettit, St. Louis	1,849	25.7	1970	Jerry West, Los Angeles	2,309	31.2
1957	Paul Arizin, Philadelphia	1,817	25.6	1971	Lew Alcindor, Milwaukee	2,596	31.7
1958	George Yardley, Detroit	2,001	27.8	1972	Kareem Abdul-Jabbar (Alcindor),		
1959	Bob Pettit, St. Louis	2,105	29.2		Milwaukee	2,822	34.8
1960	Wilt Chamberlain, Philadelphia	2,707	37.9	1973	Nate Archibald, Kansas City-Omaha	2,719	34.0

NBA Team Statistics—Offense

	FIELD GOALS			FREE THROWS			MISCELLANEOUS				SCORING		PT. DIF
	Made	Att.	Pct.	Made	Att.	Pct.	Rbds	Asst.	PF	DQ	Points	Avg.	
Hou.	3772	8249	.457	1706	2152	.793	4060	1939	1949	25	9250	112.8	− 1.7
Bos.	3811	8511	.448	1616	2073	.780	4802	2320	1805	19	9238	112.7	+ 8.2
Atl.	3700	8033	.461	1819	2482	.733	4174	2074	1916	30	9219	112.4	+ 0.1
L.A.	3740	7819	.478	1679	2264	.742	4562	2302	1636	9	9159	111.7	+ 8.5
Phoe.	3612	7942	.455	1931	2437	.792	4003	1944	2012	40	9155	111.6	− 1.3
Det.	3666	7916	.463	1710	2294	.745	4105	1882	1812	10	9042	110.3	+ 0.3
G.S.	3715	8163	.455	1493	1871	.798	4405	1985	1693	15	8923	108.8	+ 3.1
KC-O.	3621	7581	.478	1580	2036	.776	3628	2118	2054	33	8822	107.6	− 2.9
Mil.	3759	7808	.481	1271	1687	.753	4245	2226	1763	13	8789	107.2	+ 8.2
Port.	3588	7842	.458	1531	2129	.719	3928	2102	1970	33	8707	106.2	− 6.2
N.Y.	3627	7764	.467	1356	1739	.780	3882	2187	1775	10	8610	105.0	+ 6.8
Balt.	3656	7883	.464	1294	1742	.743	4205	2051	1672	14	8606	105.0	− 3.4
Phil.	3471	8264	.420	1598	2130	.750	4174	1688	1984	28	8540	104.1	− 12.1
Chi.	3480	7835	.444	1574	2073	.759	4000	2023	1881	26	8534	104.1	+ 3.5
Sea.	3447	7681	.449	1606	2080	.772	4161	1958	1877	24	8500	103.7	− 5.9
Buff.	3536	7877	.449	1399	1966	.712	4158	2218	2034	40	8471	103.3	− 9.2
Clev.	3431	7884	.435	1556	2084	.747	4063	2106	1941	21	8418	102.7	− 2.6

NBA Team Statistics—Defense

Allowed By	FIELD GOALS			FREE THROWS			MISCELLANEOUS				SCORING	
	Made	Att.	Pct.	Made	Att.	Pct.	Rbds	Asst.	PF	DQ	Points	Avg.
N.Y.	3291	7561	.435	1471	1961	.750	4100	1714	1781	18	8053	98.2
Milw.	3385	8028	.422	1345	1783	.754	3916	1906	1601	13	8115	99.0
Chi.	3343	7098	.471	1562	2080	.751	3915	1910	2002	38	8248	100.6
Balt.	3531	8010	.441	1269	1702	.746	4226	1852	1682	11	8331	101.6
L.A.	3646	8409	.434	1167	1583	.737	4101	1963	1941	27	8459	103.2
Bos.	3513	8095	.434	1540	2032	.758	3958	1957	1821	23	8566	104.5
Clev.	3465	7673	.452	1707	2230	.765	4115	2311	1932	25	8637	105.3
G.S.	3603	8163	.441	1463	1891	.774	4265	2034	1766	14	8669	105.7
Sea.	3678	8093	.454	1628	2156	.755	4158	2145	1875	25	8984	109.6
Det.	3803	8064	.472	1418	1862	.762	4019	2263	1891	22	9024	110.0
KC-O.	3698	7640	.484	1665	2174	.766	3961	1885	1816	9	9061	110.5
Atl.	3758	8152	.461	1696	2193	.773	4147	2020	2104	35	9212	112.3
Port.	3709	7780	.477	1800	2327	.774	4236	2271	1885	18	9218	112.4
Buff.	3745	7947	.471	1733	2299	.754	4278	2383	1822	23	9223	112.5
Phoe.	3758	8005	.469	1744	2318	.752	4139	2166	2068	46	9260	112.9
Hou.	3824	8119	.471	1744	2290	.762	4338	2104	1902	22	9392	114.5
Phil.	3882	8215	.473	1767	2358	.749	4683	2239	1885	21	9531	116.2

NBA All-Star Team, 1973

Position	First Team	Second Team
Forward	John Havlicek, Boston	Rick Barry, San Francisco
Forward	Spencer Haywood, Seattle	Elvin Hayes, Baltimore
Center	Kareem Abdul-Jabbar, Milwaukee	Dave Cowens, Boston
Guard	Jerry West, Los Angeles	Walt Frazier, New York
Guard	Nate Archibald, Kansas City-Omaha	Pete Maravich, Atlanta

NBA All-Defensive Team

Position	First Team	Second Team
Forward	Dave DeBusschere, New York	Mike Riordan, Baltimore
Forward	John Havlicek, Boston	Paul Silas, Boston
Center	Wilt Chamberlain, Los Angeles	Nate Thurmond, San Francisco
Guard	Jerry West, Los Angeles	Norm Van Lier, Chicago
Guard	Walt Frazier, New York	Don Chaney, Boston

Sports Arenas

The seating capacity of sports arenas can vary depending on the event being presented. The figures below are the normal seating capacity for basketball. (*) indicates hockey seating capacity.

Name and location	
Ak-Sar-Ben Coliseum, Omaha, Neb.	*6,000
Alexander Memorial Coliseum, Atlanta	6,996
Allen County War Mem., Ft. Wayne	*8,025
Amarillo Civic Center, Texas	5,001
American Royal Bldg., Kansas City	*6,122
Astrodome, Houston	19,000
Astrohall, Houston	10,000
Atlantic City Audit., Atlantic City, N.J.	40,000
Baltimore Civic Center	13,043-*11,329
Bismarck Coliseum, No. Dakota	7,000
Boston Arena	*6,000
Boston Garden	15,314-*14,994
Buffalo Memorial Auditorium	17,300-*15,170
Charlotte Coliseum	11,666-*9,575
Chicago Stadium	17,374-*18,000
Cincinnati Gardens	11,650-*10,606
Cleveland Arena	11,000-*9,300
Cobo Arena, Detroit	11,049
Convention Center, San Antonio	10,146
Convention Hall, Philadelphia	9,200-*9,300
Cow Palace, San Francisco	14,500
Dallas Memorial Auditorium	8,088
Dallas State Fair Coliseum	*7,490
Denver Auditorium Arena	6,841
Denver Coliseum	*9,038
Dorton Arena, Raleigh, N.C.	8,058
Duluth Arena Auditorium	6,919
Eastern States Coliseum, Springfield, Mass.	*5,934
Edmonton Gardens, Alberta, Canada	*5,800
Fairgrounds Coliseum, Indianapolis	9,147
Freedom Hall, Louisville, Ky.	16,933
Greensboro Coliseum	15,500-*13,280
Halifax Forum, Nova Scotia	*5,206
Hampton Roads Coliseum, Virginia	10,000-*7,771
Hara Arena, Dayton	*5,600
HemisFair Arena, San Antonio	10,500
Hershey (Pa.) Sports Arena	*7,259
Hobart Arena, Troy, Ohio	6,000
Hofheinz Pavilion, Houston	10,228
International Amphitheatre, Chicago	9,000
Island Garden, Hempstead, N.Y.	5,200
Jacksonville Coliseum	*8,150
Kiel Auditorium, St. Louis	10,574
Kitchener Memorial Auditorium, Ontario	*6,250
Las Vegas Convention Center	9,000
Long Beach Arena, Calif.	11,168
Long Island Arena, Commack	*6,500
Los Angeles Forum	17,505-*16,005
Los Angeles Sports Arena	15,333-*11,325
Louisville Convention Center	5,833
Lubbock Municipal Coliseum, Texas	10,400
Madison Square Garden, New York	19,588-*17,500
Maple Leaf Gardens, Toronto	*16,485(a)
McElroy Auditorium, Waterloo, Iowa	7,200
Memorial Arena, Victoria, B.C.	*5,021
Met. Sports Center, Bloomington, Minn.	*15,067
Miami Beach Convention Hall Annex	9,500
Mid-South Coliseum, Memphis	10,945
(a) Includes standees.	

Name and location	
Milwaukee Arena	10,746
Mobile Municipal Auditorium	13,100
Monroe Civic Center, Monroe, La.	8,000
Montreal Forum	*18,350
Moody Coliseum, Dallas	9,500
Municipal Auditorium, Kansas City	10,000
Nashville Municipal Auditorium	8,000
Nassau Coliseum, Hempstead, L.I.	16,000-*14,665
New Orleans Municipal Auditorium	9,100
Norfolk Scope, Va.	10,600-*9,364
Oak Creek Ice Arena, Des Moines	*4,400
Oakland Coliseum Arena	13,502-*12,500
Oakland Auditorium	6,500
Ohio State Fairgrounds, Columbus	5,182
Oklahoma City State Fair Arena	*8,769
Olympia, Detroit	*15,692
Olympic Auditorium, Los Angeles	10,500
Omaha Civic Auditorium	9,136
The Omni, Atlanta	15,000-*15,278
Onondaga County Audit., Syracuse	*6,011
Ottawa Civic Center	*9,355
Pacific Coliseum, Vancouver	*15,569
Penn Palestra, Philadelphia	9,200
Philadelphia Civic Center	*9,100
Pittsburgh Civic Arena	12,939-*12,580
Providence Civic Center	10,108
Portland Memorial Coliseum	11,815-*10,500
Quebec Coliseum	*10,000
Reynolds Coliseum, Raleigh, N.C.	12,400
Richmond Coliseum, Virginia	10,700-*9,674
Rhode Island Auditorium, Providence	*5,175
Rivergate Auditorium, New Orleans	9,200
Roanoke Coliseum, Virginia	10,100
Rochester (N.Y.) Memorial Arena	*7,010
St. Louis Arena	*18,006
St. Paul Civic Center, Minn.	*16,180
Salt Palace, Salt Lake City	11,990-*12,000
Sam Houston Coliseum, Houston	8,925-*9,300
San Diego Intl. Sports Arena	*13,600
San Francisco Civic Auditorium	7,500
Seattle Coliseum	12,727-*12,300
Spectrum, Philadelphia	15,304-*16,600
Springfield Civic Center	*7,466
Tarrant County Convention Center, Ft. Worth	13,500
Tingley Coliseum, Albuquerque	15,500
Toledo Sports Arena	*6,200
Tulsa Civic Center	*6,923
Uline Arena, Washington, D.C.	11,000
Veterans Memorial Audit., Des Moines	15,000
Veterans Memorial Coliseum, New Haven	*8,808
Veterans Memorial Coliseum, Phoenix	12,535-*11,553
Walker Sports Arena, Muskegon	*5,700
Washington Coliseum	5,300
Will Rogers Coliseum, Ft. Worth, Texas	*6,800
Windsor Arena, Ontario	*5,200
Winnipeg Arena	*11,300
Winston-Salem Coliseum	9,020

AAU Judo Championships in 1973

139 Lb. Class—David Pruzansky, Passaic, N.J.
154 Lb. Class—Patrick Burris, Anaheim, Calif.
176 Lb. Class—Bill Sanford, Houston, Texas.

205 Lb. Class—Rou Sukimoto, Los Angeles, Calif.
Heavyweight—Dean Sedgwick, River Forest, Ill.
Open Class—Lee Person, Memphis, Tenn.

American Basketball Association, 1972-73

Eastern Division				
Club	W.	L.	Pct.	G.B.
Carolina Cougars..	57	27	.679	...
Kentucky Colonels	56	28	.667	1
Virginia Squires...	42	42	.500	15
New York Nets....	30	54	.357	27
Memphis Tams ...	24	60	.286	33

Western Division				
Club	W.	L.	Pct.	G.B.
Utah Stars	56	28	.667	...
Indiana Pacers....	51	33	.607	4
Denver Rockets...	47	37	.560	8
San Diego				
Conquistadors..	30	54	.357	25
Dallas Chaparrals .	28	56	.333	27

ABA Playoffs

Eastern Division — Carolina defeated New York 4 games to 1. Kentucky defeated Virginia 4 games to 1. Kentucky defeated Carolina 4 games to 3.
Western Division — Utah defeated San Diego 4 games to 0. Indiana defeated Denver 4 games to 1. Indiana defeated Utah 4 games to 2.
Championship — Indiana defeated Kentucky 4 games to 3.

Final Statistics

Scoring
(Minimum of 1,000 Points)

	G.	FG.	FT.	Pts.	Avg.
Erving, Virginia	71	889	475	2268	31.9
McGinnis, Indiana.....	82	860	517	2261	27.5
Issel, Kentucky	84	899	485	2292	27.2
Cunningham, Carol.....	84	757	472	2028	24.1
Simpson, Denver......	81	727	421	1890	23.3
R. Jones, Dallas	67	521	324	1466	21.9
Johnson, San Diego ..	80	732	195	1770	22.1
Wise, Utah	83	669	476	1823	21.9
Thompson, Memphis ...	80	559	549	1727	21.5
Gilmore, Kentucky	84	686	368	1743	20.7
Neumann, Memphis ...	79	596	329	1548	19.5
Carter, New York	83	569	440	1578	19.0
Netolicky, Dallas	84	650	269	1569	18.6
Boone, Utah	84	556	415	1557	18.5
Daniels, Indiana	81	586	322	1497	18.4
Williams, San Diego	83	487	493	1470	17.7
Calvin, Carolina	84	467	500	1467	17.4
Jabali, Denver	82	405	480	1398	17.0
Denton, Memphis	66	469	177	1124	17.0
Dampier, Kentucky ...	80	461	262	1346	16.8
J. Jones, Utah	80	496	345	1337	16.7
Paultz, New York	81	532	287	1351	16.6
Caldwell, Carolina	77	554	172	1283	16.6

Three-point field goals — Erving 3, McGinnis 8, Issel 3, Cunningham 14, Simpson 5, R. Jones 43, Johnson 37, Wise 3, Thompson 20, Gilmore 1, Neumann 9, Boone 10, Daniels 1, Ck. Williams 1, Calvin, 11, Jabali 36, Denton 3, Dampier 54, Caldwell 1.

Two-Point Percentage
(Minimum of 250 Made)

	FGM.	FGA.	Pct.
Gilmore, Kentucky	686	1226	.560
Kennedy, Dallas	365	664	.550
Owens, Carolina .:	393	725	.542
Irvine, Virginia	417	772	.540
Beck, Denver	464	872	.532
B. Taylor, New York........	391	742	.527
J. Jones, Utah	496	947	.524

Three-Point Percentage
(Minimum of 28 Made)

	FGM.	FGA.	Pct.
Combs, Utah	51	134	.381
R. Brown, Indiana	42	118	.356
Dampier, Kentucky.........	54	155	.348
Hamilton, Dallas	66	191	.346
F. Lewis, Indiana	38	110	.345
R. Jones, Dallas...........	43	127	.339
Roche, New York..........	34	103	.330
Beasley, Utah..............	29	89	.326

Free Throws
(Minimum of 200 Made)

	FTM.	FTA.	Avg.
Keller, Indiana	234	269	.870
Boone, Utah	415	479	.866
Warren, Utah	236	274	.861
Calvin, Carolina	500	582	.859
Silas, Dallas	389	467	.833
Carter, New York	440	529	.832
L. Jones, Dallas	202	244	.828
F. Lewis, Indiana	287	349	.822
R. Brown, Indiana	203	247	.822

Assists
(Minimum of 250)

	G.	No.	Avg.
Melchionni, New York	61	453	7.45
Ck. Williams, San Diego	83	582	7.01
Jabali, Denver	82	539	6.57
Dampier, Kentucky	80	521	6.51
Cunningham, Carolina	84	530	6.31
Neumann, Memphis	79	470	5.94
Smith, Denver	83	477	5.74

Rebounds
(Minimum of 600)

	G.	No.	Avg.
Gilmore, Kentucky	84	1476	17.5
Daniels, Indiana	81	1247	15.4
Paultz, New York	81	1015	12.5
McGinnis, Indiana..........	82	1022	12.4
Denton, Memphis	66	820	12.4
Erving, Virginia	71	867	12.2
Cunningham, Carolina	84	1012	12.0
Issel, Kentucky	84	922	10.9

Blocked Shots

	G.	No.
Gilmore, Kentucky	84	259
Keye, Denver	83	226
Paultz, New York	81	214
Daniels, Indiana	81	157
Moore, San Diego	83	149
Eakins, Virginia	83	131
Erving, Virginia	71	127
Hillman, Indiana	84	116

Steals

	G.	No.
Cunningham, Carolina	84	216
Rol. Taylor, Virginia	78	210
Erving, Virginia	71	181
Jabali, Denver	82	175
Caldwell, Carolina	77	166
McGinnis, Indiana	82	160
Gale, Kentucky	81	131

ABA Most Valuable Player & Rookie of Year

Year	MVP	Rookie	Year	MVP	Rookie
1968	Connie Hawkins, Pitts.	Mel Daniels, Ind.	1971	Mel Daniels, Ind.	Dan Issel, Ky. &
1969	Mel Daniels, Ind.	Warren Armstrong, Oak.			Charlie Scott, Va. (tie)
1970	Spencer Haywood, Den.	Spencer Haywood, Denver	1972	Artis Gilmore, Ky.	Artis Gilmore, Ky.
			1973	Billy Cunningham, Carolina	Brian Taylor, N.Y.

ABA Scoring Leaders

Year	Scoring Champion	Pts.	Avg.	Year	Scoring Champion	Pts.	Avg.
1968	Connie Hawkins, Pittsburgh ...	1,875	26.7	1971	Dan Issel, Kentucky	2,480	29.8
1969	Rick Barry, Oakland	1,190	34.0	1972	Charlie Scott, Virginia	2,524	34.5
1970	Spencer Haywood, Denver	2,519	29.9	1973	Julius Erving, Virginia	2,268	31.9

ABA Champions

	Regular Season		Playoffs	
Year	Eastern Division	Western Division	Winner	Runner-up
1968	Pittsburgh	New Orleans	Pittsburgh	New Orleans
1969	Indiana	Oakland	Oakland	Indiana
1970	Indiana	Denver	Indiana	Los Angeles
1971	Virginia	Indiana	Utah	Kentucky
1972	Kentucky	Utah	Indiana	New York
1973	Carolina	Utah	Indiana	Kentucky

ABA All-Star Team, 1973

Position	First Team	Second Team
Forward	Billy Cunningham, Carolina	Dan Issel, Kentucky
Forward	Julius Erving, Virginia	George McGinnis, Indiana
Center	Artis Gilmore, Kentucky	Mel Daniels, Indiana
Guard	Warren Jabali, Denver	Ralph Simpson, Denver
Guard	Jimmy Jones, Utah	Mack Calvin, Carolina

Basketball Hall of Fame

Springfield, Mass.

The Naismith Memorial Basketball Hall of Fame was incorporated in 1959 to serve as a memorial to James Naismith, who invented the game of basketball for students of the School for Christian Workers (now Springfield College) in December, 1891, at Springfield, Mass. The following persons have been enshrined in the Basketball Hall of Fame for outstanding contributions to basketball:

Players
Beckman, John
Borgmann, Bennie
Cousy, Robert J.
Davies, Robert
DeBernardi, Forrest
Dehnert, Henry G.
Endacott, Paul
Foster, Harold
Friedman, Max
Gruenig, Robert
Hanson, Victor
Holman, Nat
Hyatt, Charles
Kurland, Robert
Lapchick, Joe
Luisetti, Angelo
McCracken, Branch
McCracken, Jack
Macauley, C. Edward
Mikan, George L.
Murphy, Charles
Page, H. O. "Pat"
Pettit, Robert L.
Phillip, Andy

Roosma, Col. John S.
Russell, John
Schayes, Dolph
Schommer, John J.
Sedran, Barney
Steinmetz, Christian
Thompson, John A.
Wachter, Edward A.

Coaches
Auerbach, Arnold J.
Blood, Ernest A.
Cann, Howard G.
Carlson, Dr. H. Clifford
Carnevale, Ben
Dean, Everett S.
Diddle, Edgar A.
Drake, Bruce
Gill, Amory T.
Hobson, Howard A.
Iba, Henry P.
Julian, Alvin F.
Keaney, Frank W.
Keogan, George E.
Lambert, Ward L.

Loeffler, Kenneth D.
Lonborg, Arthur
Meanwell, Dr. Walter E.
Rupp, Adolph F.
Sachs, Leonard D.
Wooden, John R.

Contributors
Allen, Dr. Forrest C.
Bee, Clair F.
Brown, Walter A.
Bunn, John W.
Douglas, Robert L.
Gootlieb, Edward
Gulick, Dr. Luther H.
Hickox, Edward J.
Hinkle, Paul D.
Irish, Ned
Jones, R. William
Mokray, William G.
Morgan, 'Ralph
Morgenweck, Frank
Naismith, Dr. James
O'Brien, John J.
Olsen, Harold G.

Porter, H. V.
Ripley, Elmer
St. John, Lynn W.
Saperstein, Abe
Schabinger, Arthur A.
Stagg, Amos Alonzo
Taylor, Charles H.
Tower, Oswald
Trester, Arthur L.
Wells, W. R. Clifford

Referees
Hepbron, George T.
Hoyt, George
Kennedy, Matthew P.
Quigley, Ernest C.
Tobey, David
Walsh, David H.

Teams
First Team
Original Celtics
Buffalo Germans
Renaissance

Lacrosse Championships in 1973

Source: Jack Kelly, editor, The Lacrosse Newsletter

NCAA Collegiate Lacrosse Champions—University of Maryland.
National Club Lacrosse Association Champion—Long Island A.C., Garden City, N.Y.
32nd Annual USILA All-Star Game—Princeton, N.J., June 9, 1973 South 13 North 11 (overtime).
USILA Intercollegiate Champion—Maryland.
Mideastern Division—Maryland.
South Atlantic Division—Washington & Lee.
Ivy League—Brown.
New England—Brown.
Central Atlantic Division—Franklin & Marshall.
Metropolitan New York Division—Hofstra.
Central New York Division—Cortland State.
Northern New York Division—Ithaca College.
Northeastern Division—Massachusetts.
Colonial Division—Springfield College.
Midwest Divsion—Denison University.
Rocky Mountain Division—Air Force Academy.

NCAA Championship
at Franklin Field, Philadelphia, Pa.—June 2, 1973, Maryland 10, Johns Hopkins 9 (overtime).

NCAA Semi-finals
Maryland 18, Washington & Lee 7; Johns Hopkins 12, Virginia 9.

NCAA Quarter-finals
Maryland 16, Brown 4; Washington & Lee 13, Navy 12; Virginia 12, Hofstra 5; Johns Hopkins 11, Army 5.

USILA Small College Champions
at Cortland, N.Y.—Cortland 13, Washington College 8.

Junior College Champion
at Anne Arundel, Md. May 12—Nassau Community College 15; Farmingdale N.Y. Ag. & Tech. 7.

1973 Major College All-America Team

Position	Player
Goalie	Les Matthew (Johns Hopkins)
Defense	Michael Thearle (Maryland)
Defense	Ed Haugevik (Rutgers)
Defense	Bruce Mangels (Virginia)
Midfield	Doug Schreiber (Maryland)
Midfield	Phil Marino (Hofstra)
Midfield	Rick Kowalchuk (Johns Hopkins)
Midfield	Frank Urso (Maryland)
Attack	Tom Duquette (Virginia)
Attack	Jack Thomas (Johns Hopkins)
Attack	Pat O'Meally (Maryland)

University Coach of the Year—C. A. "Bud" Beardmore—Maryland.
College Coach of the Year—Jack Emmer—Washington & Lee.

U.S. Intercollegiate Lacrosse Assn. Top Ten Teams of 1973

1—Maryland		6—Naval Academy	
2—Johns Hopkins		7—Brown	
3—Virginia		8—U.S. Military Academy	
4—Washington & Lee		9—Rutgers	
5—Hofstra		10—Cornell	

Badminton Championships in 1973

U.S. Open Championships
New Britain, Conn., April 12-15, 1973

Men's Singles—Sture Johnsson, Sweden def. Derek Talbot, England, 15-4, 15-4.

Ladies' Singles—Eva Twedberg, Sweden def. Barbara O'Brien, Canada, 11-6, 11-1.

Men's Doubles—Don Paup & Jim Poole, U.S. def. Derek Talbot & Mike Tredgett, England, 11-15, 15-11, 15-12.

Ladies' Doubles—Pam Bristol & Diane Hales, U.S. def. Eva Twedberg & Bridgette Cooper, England, 12-15, 15-12, 18-13.

Mixed Doubles—Sture Johnsson & Eva Twedberg, def. Tom Carmichael & Pam Bristol, U.S., 18-13, 15-12.

Senior Men's Singles—Jim Poole def. Ted Moehlmann, St. Louis, 15-5, 15-3.

Senior Men's Doubles—Jim Poole & Bill Goodman def. Ted Moehlmann & Jim McQuie, Kirkwood, Mo., 15-13, 5-15, 15-11.

Senior Ladies' Doubles—Ethel Marshall & Bea Massman, Buffalo, N.Y. def. Frances Goodman, Wellesley Hills, Mass. & Brenda Lunsden, Needham, Mass., 15-2, 15-0.

Senior Mixed Doubles—Jim Poole & Mary Ann Breckell, Los Angeles def. Ted Moehlmann & Ethel Marshall, 15-5, 15-9.

All-England Championships
Wembley, England, March 21-24, 1973

Men's Singles—Rudy Hartono, Indonesia def. Christian Chandra, Indonesia, 15-4, 15-2.

Ladies' Singles—Margaret Beck, England def. Gillian Gilks, England, 11-8, 11-0.

Men's Doubles—Christian and Ade Chandra def. Tjun Tjun &

J. Wahjudi, Indonesia, 15-1, 15-7.

Ladies' Doubles—Machiko Aizawa & Etsuto Takenaka, Japan def. Margaret Beck & Gillian Gilks, 15-10, 10-15, 15-11.

Mixed Doubles—Kerek Talbot & Gillian Gilks def. Elliot Stuart & Nora Gardner, England, 9-15, 15-13, 15-8.

National Junior Championships
Bloomfield Hills, Mich., March 20-23, 1973

Boy's Singles—Pat Trapnell, Detroit def. Ron Buck, San Francisco, 14-17, 15-5, 15-9.

Girl's Singles—Madalene Steinbronner, Manhattan Beach, Calif. def. Karen Bushman, Manhattan Beach, Calif., 11-6, 11-8.

Boy's Doubles—Bob Gilmour, Garden Grove, Calif. & Mike Kelly, Manhattan Beach def. Pete Steinbronner & Ron

Buck, 15-8, 15-12.

Girl's Doubles—Karen Czarnecki, Flint, Mich. & Cindy Young, Altadena, Calif. def. Karen Bushman & Denise Corlett, Manhattan Beach, 2-15, 15-12, 15-4.

Mixed Doubles—Ron Buck & Madalene Steinbronner def. Mike Kelly & Sara Thaves, 13-15, 15-12, 15-9.

Canadian Open Championships
Toronto, Ont., March 7-10, 1973

Men's Singles—Jamie Paulson, Canada def. Bruce Rollick, Canada, 15-12, 15-8.

Ladies' Singles—Nancy McKinley, Canada def. Margaret Beck, England, 2-11, 11-8, 11-7.

Men's Doubles—Yves Pare, Canada & Jamie Paulson def.

Charoen Ratanasnengsuang & Raphi Kanchanaraphi, Canada, 9-15, 15-10, 15-12.

Ladies' Doubles—Margaret Beck & Joke van Beusekom, Netherlands def. Mimi Nilsson & Judi Rollick, Canada, 15-12, 15-12.

Table Tennis Championships in 1973

43rd U.S. National Open Championships
Detroit, Mich., March 16-18, 1973

Men's Singles—Dal Joon Lee, Parma, Ohio.

Women's Singles—Violetta Nesukaitis, Toronto.

Mixed Doubles—Errol Caetane & Vi Nesukaitis.

Women's Doubles—Judy Bochenski & Patty Cash, Eugene, Ore. & San Diego.

Men's Doubles—Dell Sweeris & Alex Tom, Grand Rapids & Kalamazoo, Mich.

Senior Singles Over 40—Derek Wall, Willowdale, Ontario.

Esquire Singles Over 50—Max Marinko, Toronto.

Senior Women's Singles—Inez Frazier, Detroit.

Senior Men's Doubles—Chuck Burns & Sol Schiff, Birmingham, Mich. & Bronx, N.Y.

Junior Boy's Under 17—Paul Raphel, Los Angeles.

Junior Girls Under 17—Judy Bochenski, Eugene, Ore.

Junior Boy's Under 17 Doubles—Richard Rumble & John Quick, Saugerties, N.Y. & New Orleans, La.

Junior Girl's Under 17 Doubles—Judy Bochenski & Angelita Rosal.

32nd World Championships
Sarajevo, Yugoslavia, Apr. 5-15, 1973

Men's Singles—Hsi En-ting, China.

Women's Singles—Hu Yu-lan, China.

Mixed Doubles—Liang Ke-liang & Li Li, China.

Women's Doubles—Maria Alexandru & Mihe Hamada, Rumania & Japan.

Men's Doubles—Stellan Bengtssen & Kjell Johansson, Sweden.

Jubilee Cup—Bjorne Mellstrom, Sweden.

Men's Team (Swaything Cup)—Sweden.

Women's Team (Corbillen Cup)—Republic (South) Korea.

43rd U.S. National Wheelchair Events
Detroit, Mich., March 16-18, 1973

Men's Wheelchair—Mike Dempsey, Gahanna, Ohio.

Women's Wheelchair—Jeannie Kish, Detroit.

Men's Paraplegic Singles—John Gray, Columbus, Ohio.

Women's Paraplegic Singles—Jeannie Kish.

Men's Wheelchair Doubles—Mike Dempsey & John Gray.

Mixed Wheelchair Doubles—John Gray & Patricia Nevin.

Westminster Kennel Club

Year	Best-in-show	Breed	Owner
1962	Ch. Elfinbrook Simon	West Highland terrier	Florence and Barbara Worcester
1963	Ch. Wakefield's Black Knight	English springer spaniel	Mrs. W. J. S. Borie
1964	Ch. Courtenay's Fleetfoot	Whippet	Mrs. Margaret P. Newcombe
1965	Ch. Carmichael's Fanfare	Scottish terrier	Mr. and Mrs. Charles C. Stalter
1966	Ch. Zeloy Mooremaides Magic	Wire Fox terrier	Marion G. Bunker
1967	Ch. Bardene Bingo	Scottish terrier	E. H. Stuart
1968	Ch. Stingray of Derryabah	Lakeland terrier	Mr. and Mrs. James A. Farrell, Jr.
1969	Ch. Glamoor Good News	Skye terrier	Walter & Mrs. Adele F. Goodman
1970	Ch. Arriba's Prima Donna	Boxer	Dr. & Mrs. P. J. Pagano & Dr. Theodore S. Fickles
1971	Ch. Chinoe's Adamant James	English springer spaniel	Dr. Milton Prickett
1972	Ch. Chinoe's Adamant James	English springer spaniel	Dr. Milton Prickett
1973	Ch. Acadia Command Performance	Poodle	Mrs. Jo Ann Sering & Edward B. Jenner

Pure-Bred Dogs

Six main classes of dogs are presently recognized: Sporting Dogs—pointers, retrievers, setters, spaniels, weimaraners; the Hound group; Working Dogs, including boxers, collies, Doberman pinschers, shepherds, mastiffs; the Terrier group; the Toy group, including Chihuahuas, Toy Spaniels, Papillons, Pekingese, Pomeranians, Yorkshires; Non-sporting group—Boston Terriers, bulldogs, Chow Chows, Dalmatians, Keeshonden, Poodles, etc. In all, 120 different breeds are recognized and shown in the United States.

Poodles remained the No. 1 breed in the United States for the thirteenth straight year according to the 1972 pure-bred registration figures released in 1973 by the American Kennel Club. A record 1,101,943 individual dogs were registered.

AKC Registration in 1972

Poodles	218,899	Rhodesian ridgebacks	698
German Shepherds	101,399	Manchester terriers	673
Beagles	57,050	English cocker spaniels	657
Dachshunds	55,149	Italian greyhounds	604
Irish setters	43,707	Bull terriers	574
Miniature schnauzers	43,280	Pointers	566
St. Bernards	35,559	Rottweilers	563
Labrador retrievers	32,251	Bedlington terriers	560
Collies	28,459	Bullmastiffs	558
Doberman pinschers	27,767	Bouviers des Flandres	511
Cocker spaniels	27,355	Salukis	495
Pekingese	26,062	Bichon frises	430
Chihuahuas	23,969	Belgian sheepdogs	416
Shetland sheepdogs	19,673	Irish terriers	406
Basset hounds	18,989	Papillons	397
Great Danes	18,339	Mastiffs	394
Yorkshire terriers	16,879	American Staffordshire terriers	389
Pomeranians	16,723	Welsh corgis (Cardigan)	372
Brittany spaniels	16,644	Belgian tervuren	358
Golden retrievers	15,476	Giant schnauzers	327
German short-haired pointers	14,733	Japanese spaniels	322
Siberian huskies	13,676	American water spaniels	316
Old English sheepdogs	13,321	Skye terriers	307
Boston terriers	12,388	Akitas	255
Lhasa Apsos	12,236	Norwich terriers	251
Boxers	12,002	Dandie Dinmont terriers	249
English springers	11,364	Brussels griffons	247
Scottish terriers	10,011	Black and Tan coonhounds	221
Pugs	9,257	Wire-haired pointing griffons	188
Afghan hounds	9,023	Bernese Mountain dogs	185
Samoyeds	8,866	Lakeland terriers	171
Dalmatians	8,623	Sealyham terriers	169
Fox terriers	8,559	Greyhounds	161
Norwegian elkhounds	8,398	French bulldogs	154
Cairn terriers	7,753	Briards	147
Weimaraners	7,246	Kuvaszok	127
Airedale terriers	6,974	Scottish deerhounds	108
Bulldogs	6,608	Komondors	103
West Highland white terriers	6,577	Irish water spaniels	102
Alaskan malamutes	6,502	Foxhounds (American)	78
Shih Tzu	5,704	English toy spaniels	75
Maltese	5,101	Flat-coated retrievers	66
Keeshonds	4,010	Border terriers	58
Silky terriers	3,345	Affenpinschers	55
Basenjis	2,894	Otter hounds	41
Chow chows	2,789	Clumber spaniels	37
Welsh corgis (Pembroke)	2,256	Curly-coated retrievers	31
Vizslas	2,206	Welsh springer spaniels	30
Chesapeake Bay retrievers	1,964	Harriers	13
Newfoundlands	1,945	Foxhounds (English)	12
English setters	1,518	Sussex spaniels	11
Great Pyrenees	1,478	Belgian malinois	11
Borzois	1,447	Field spaniels	3
Schipperkes	1,411		
Welsh terriers	1,312		
Australian terriers	1,284		
Irish wolfhounds	1,251		
Bloodhounds	1,231		
Miniature pinschers	1,159		
Kerry blue terriers	1,042		
Gordon setters	1,028		
Standard schnauzers	1,011		
Whippets	990		
Puli	869		
German wire-haired pointers	700		

VARIETY GROUPS

	1972	1971
Sporting	178,199	158,925
Hound	158,249	168,000
Working	297,449	291,850
Terrier	90,599	96,075
Toy	109,899	112,925
Non-Sporting	267,548	301,425
TOTAL	**1,101,943**	**1,129,200**

U.S. National Fencing Champions in 1973

Men's Foil—Edward Ballinger, Salle Santelli, N.Y.
Men's Epee—Scott Bozek, Tanner City Fencers Club, Peabody, Mass.
Men's Sabre—Paul Apostal, N.Y. Fencers Club.
Women's Foil—Tanya Adamovich, N.Y. Fencers Club.

Women's Foil Team—New York Fencers Club.
Men's Foil Team—Salle Santelli, N.Y.
Men's Epee Team—New York Athletic Club.
Men's Sabre Team—New York Athletic Club.

Hockey Champions in 1972-73
NATIONAL HOCKEY LEAGUE
Final Standings

EAST DIVISION Club	W.	L.	T.	Pts.	G.F.	G.A.	WEST DIVISION Club	W.	L.	T.	Pts.	G.F.	G.A.
Montreal	52	10	16	120	329	184	Chicago	42	27	9	93	284	225
Boston	51	22	5	107	330	235	Philadelphia	37	30	11	85	296	256
N. Y. Rangers	47	23	8	102	297	208	Minnesota	37	30	11	85	254	230
Buffalo	37	27	14	88	257	219	St. Louis	32	34	12	76	233	251
Detroit	37	29	12	86	265	243	Pittsburgh	32	37	9	73	257	265
Toronto	27	41	10	64	247	279	Los Angeles	31	36	11	73	232	245
Vancouver	22	47	9	53	233	339	Atlanta	25	38	15	65	191	239
N. Y. Islanders	12	60	6	30	170	347	California	16	46	16	48	213	323

Leading Scorers

Player—Club	G.	Goals	Asts.	Pts.	Player—Club	G.	Goals	Asts.	Pts.
Esposito, Boston	78	55	75	130	Dionne, Detroit	77	40	50	90
Clarke, Philadelphia	78	37	67	104	Hull, Chicago	78	39	51	90
Orr, Boston	63	29	72	101	Martin, Chicago	76	29	61	90
MacLeish, Philadelphia	78	50	50	100	Perreault, Buffalo	78	28	60	88
Lemaire, Montreal	77	44	51	95	Apps, Pittsburgh	77	29	56	85
Ratelle, Rangers	78	41	53	94	Gilbert, Rangers	76	25	59	84
Redmond, Detroit	76	52	41	93	Mikita, Chicago	57	27	56	83
Bucyk, Boston	78	40	53	93	Robert, Buffalo	75	39	43	82
F. Mahovlich, Montreal	78	38	55	93	Hextall, Minnesota	78	30	52	82
Pappin, Chicago	76	41	51	92	Hodge, Boston	73	37	44	81

Club Scoring Leaders

ATLANTA

Player	G.	Goals	Asts.	Pts.
Bobby Leiter	78	26	34	60
Larry Romanchych	70	18	30	48
Rey Comeau	77	21	21	42
Keith McCreary	77	20	21	41
Curt Bennett	68	18	18	36

MONTREAL

Player	G.	Goals	Asts.	Pts.
Jacques Lemaire	77	44	51	95
Frank Mahovlich	78	38	55	93
Yvan Cournoyer	67	40	39	79
Pete Mahovlich	61	21	38	59
Guy Lafleur	70	28	27	55

BOSTON

Player	G.	Goals	Asts.	Pts.
Phil Esposito	78	55	75	130
Bobby Orr	63	29	72	101
John Bucyk	78	40	53	93
Ken Hodge	73	37	44	81
Fred Stanfield	78	20	58	78

N. Y. ISLANDERS

Player	G.	Goals	Asts.	Pts.
Bill Harris	78	28	22	50
Ed Westfall	67	15	31	46
Germain Gagnon	63	12	29	41
Brian Spencer	78	14	24	38
Ernie Hicke	59	14	23	37

BUFFALO

Player	G.	Goals	Asts.	Pts.
Gilbert Perreault	78	28	60	88
Rene Robert	75	39	43	82
Richard Martin	75	38	35	73
Jim Lorentz	78	27	35	62
Gerry Meehan	77	31	29	60

N. Y. RANGERS

Player	G.	Goals	Asts.	Pts.
Jean Ratelle	78	41	53	94
Rod Gilbert	76	25	59	84
Walt Tkaczuk	77	27	39	66
Bill Fairbairn	78	30	33	63
Vic Hadfield	63	28	34	62

CALIFORNIA

Player	G.	Goals	Asts.	Pts.
Walt McKechnie	78	16	38	54
Hilliard Graves	75	27	25	52
Joey Johnston	71	28	21	49
Craig Patrick	71	20	22	42
Pete Laframboise	77	16	25	41

PHILADELPHIA

Player	G.	Goals	Asts.	Pts.
Bobby Clarke	78	37	67	104
Rick MacLeish	78	50	50	100
Gary Dornhoefer	77	30	49	79
Bill Flett	69	43	31	74
Bill Barber	69	30	34	64

CHICAGO

Player	G.	Goals	Asts.	Pts.
Jim Pappin	76	41	51	92
Dennis Hull	78	39	51	90
Pit Martin	78	29	61	90
Stan Mikita	57	27	56	83
Ralph Backstrom	79	26	32	58

PITTSBURGH

Player	G.	Goals	Asts.	Pts.
Syl Apps	77	29	56	85
Al McDonough	78	35	41	76
Lowell MacDonald	78	34	41	75
Bryan Hextall	78	21	33	54
Greg Polis	78	26	23	49

DETROIT

Player	G.	Goals	Asts.	Pts.
Mickey Redmond	76	52	41	93
Marcel Dionne	77	40	50	90
Alex Delvecchio	77	18	53	71
Nick Libett	78	19	34	53
Tim Ecclestone	78	18	30	48

ST. LOUIS

Player	G.	Goals	Asts.	Pts.
Garry Unger	78	41	39	80
Jack Egers	78	24	24	48
Gary Sabourin	76	21	27	48
Phil Roberto	77	20	22	42
Danny O'Shea	75	12	26	38

LOS ANGELES

Player	G.	Goals	Asts.	Pts.
Juha Widing	77	16	54	70
Serge Bernier	75	22	46	68
Mike Corrigan	78	37	30	67
Bob Berry	78	36	28	64
Butch Goring	67	28	31	59

TORONTO

Player	G.	Goals	Asts.	Pts.
Darryl Sittler	78	29	48	77
Rick Kehoe	77	33	42	75
Dave Keon	76	37	36	73
Norm Ullman	65	20	35	55
Jim McKenny	77	11	41	52

MINNESOTA

Player	G.	Goals	Asts.	Pts.
Dennis Hextall	78	30	52	82
Jean Paul Parise	78	27	48	75
Jude Drouin	78	27	46	73
Danny Grant	78	32	35	67
Bill Goldsworthy	75	27	33	60

VANCOUVER

Player	G.	Goals	Asts.	Pts.
Bobby Schmautz	77	38	33	71
Andre Boudrias	77	30	40	70
Richard Lemieux	78	17	35	52
Bobby Lalonde	77	20	27	47
Don Tannahill	78	22	21	43

Leading Goalies

Goalie—Club	G.	GA.	ShO.	Avg.	Goalie—Club	G.	GA.	ShO.	Avg.
Ken Dryden, Montreal	54	119	6	2.26	Roger Crozier, Buffalo	49	121	3	2.76
Gilles Villemure, Rangers	34	78	3	2.29	Jacques Plante, Tor.-Bos.	40	103	3	2.81
Tony Esposito, Chicago	56	140	4	2.51	Doug Favell, Philadelphia	44	114	3	2.83
Roy Edwards, Detroit	52	132	6	2.63	Rogatien Vachon, L.A.	53	148	4	2.85
Dave Dryden, Buffalo	37	89	3	2.65	Cesare Maniago, Minnesota	47	132	5	2.89

Stanley Cup Playoff Results
(Best 4 out of 7 games)

Montreal defeated Buffalo 4 games to 2.
New York defeated Boston 4 games to 1.
Chicago defeated St. Louis 4 games to 1.
Philadelphia defeated Minnesota 4 games to 2.

Montreal defeated Philadelphia 4 games to 1.
Chicago defeated New York 4 games to 1.
Montreal defeated Chicago 4 games to 2.

Conn Smythe Trophy (MVP in Playoffs)

1965 — Jean Beliveau, Montreal
1966 — Roger Crozier, Detroit
1967 — Dave Keon, Toronto

1968 — Glenn Hall, St. Louis
1969 — Serge Savard, Montreal
1970 — Bobby Orr, Boston

1971 — Ken Dryden, Montreal
1972 — Bobby Orr, Boston
1973 — Yvan Cournoyer, Montreal

Stanley Cup Champions

1928–New York	1940–New York	1952–Detroit	1964–Toronto
1929–Boston	1941–Boston	1953–Montreal	1965–Montreal
1930–Montreal	1942–Toronto	1954–Detroit	1966–Montreal
1931–Montreal	1943–Detroit	1955–Detroit	1967–Toronto
1932–Toronto	1944–Montreal	1956–Montreal	1968–Montreal
1933–New York	1945–Toronto	1957–Montreal	1969–Montreal
1934–Chicago	1946–Montreal	1958–Montreal	1970–Boston
1935–Montreal Maroons	1947–Toronto	1959–Montreal	1971–Montreal
1936–Detroit	1948–Toronto	1960–Montreal	1972–Boston
1937–Detroit	1949–Toronto	1961–Chicago	1973–Montreal
1938–Chicago	1950–Detroit	1962–Toronto	
1939–Boston	1951–Toronto	1963–Toronto	

Hockey Trophy Winners

Ross Trophy Leading Scorer	Norris Trophy Best Defenseman	Calder Trophy Best Rookie
1973– Phil Esposito, Boston	Bobby Orr, Boston	Steve Vickers, New York
1972– Phil Esposito, Boston	Bobby Orr, Boston	Ken Dryden, Montreal
1971– Phil Esposito, Boston	Bobby Orr, Boston	Gil Perreault, Buffalo
1970– Bobby Orr, Boston	Bobby Orr, Boston	Tony Esposito, Chicago
1969– Phil Esposito, Boston	Bobby Orr, Boston	Danny Grant, Minn.
1968– Stan Mikita, Chicago	Bobby Orr, Boston	Derek Sanderson, Boston
1967– Stan Mikita, Chicago	Harry Howell, New York	Bobby Orr, Boston
1966– Bobby Hull, Chicago	Jacques Laperriere, Montreal	Brit Selby, Toronto
1965– Stan Mikita, Chicago	Pierre Pilote, Montreal	Roger Crozier, Detroit
1964– Stan Mikita, Chicago	Pierre Pilote, Chicago	Jacques Laperriere, Montreal
1963– Gordie Howe, Detroit	Pierre Pilote, Chicago	Kent Douglas, Toronto

Hart Trophy M. V. P.	Vezina Trophy Leading Goalie	Lady Byng Trophy Sportsmanship
1973– Bobby Clarke, Philadelphia	Ken Dryden, Montreal	Gilbert Perreault, Buffalo
1972– Bobby Orr, Boston	Esposito, Smith, Chicago	Jean Ratelle, New York
1971– Bobby Orr, Boston	Giacomin, Villemure, New York	John Buyck, Boston
1970– Bobby Orr, Boston	Tony Esposito, Chicago	Phil Goyette, St. Louis
1969– Phil Esposito, Boston	Hall, Plante, St. Louis	Alex Delvecchio, Detroit
1968– Stan Mikita, Chicago	Worsley, Vachon, Montreal	Stan Mikita, Chicago
1967– Stan Mikita, Chicago	Hall, De Jordy, Chicago	Stan Mikita, Chicago
1966– Bobby Hull, Chicago	Hodge, Worsley, Montreal	Alex Delvecchio, Detroit
1965– Bobby Hull, Chicago	Sawchuck, Bower, Toronto	Bobby Hull, Chicago
1964– Jean Beliveau, Montreal	Charlie Hodge, Montreal	Ken Wharram, Chicago
1963– Gordie Howe, Detroit	Glenn Hall, Chicago	Dave Keon, Toronto

National Hockey League Amateur Draft, 1973

FIRST ROUND

New York Islanders—Denis Potvin, Ottawa.
Atlanta—(from Montreal) Tom Lysiak, Medicine Hat.
Vancouver—Dennis Ververgaert, London.
Toronto—Lanny McDonald, Medicine Hat.
St. Louis—(from Atlanta) John Davidson, Calgary.
Boston—(from Los Angeles) Andre Savard, Quebec.
Pittsburgh—Blaine Stoughton, Flin Flon.
Montreal—(from St. Louis) Bob Gainey, Peterborough
Vancouver—(from Montreal via Minnesota) Bob Dailey, Toronto.
Toronto—(from Philadelphia) Bob Neely, Peterborough.
Detroit—Terry Richardson, New Westminster.
Buffalo—Morris Titanic, Sudbury.
Chicago—Darcy Rota, Edmonton.
New York Rangers—Rick Middleton, Oshawa.
Toronto—(from Boston) Ian Turnbull, Ottawa.
Atlanta—(from Montreal) Vic Mercredi, New Westminster.

SECOND ROUND

Montreal—(from N.Y. Islanders) Glen Goldup, Toronto.
Minnesota—(from Montreal via Calif.) Blake Dunlop, Ottawa.
Vancouver—Paulin Bordeleau, Toronto.
Philadelphia—(from Toronto) Larry Goodenough, London.
Atlanta—Eric Vail, Sudbury.
Montreal—(from Los Angeles) Peter Marrin, Toronto.
Pittsburgh—Wayne Bianchin, Flin Flon.
St. Louis—George Pesut, Saskatoon.
Minnesota—John Rogers, Edmonton.
Philadelphia—Brent Leavins, Swift Current.
Pittsburgh—(from Detroit) Colin Campbell, Peterborough.
Buffalo—Jean Landry, Quebec.
Chicago—Reg Thomas, London.
New York Rangers—Pat Hickey, Hamilton.
Boston—Jim Jones, Peterborough.
Montreal—Ron Andruff, Flin Flon.

NHL All-Star Teams, 1973

Position	First Team	Second Team
Goal	Ken Dryden, Montreal	Tony Esposito, Chicago
Defense	Bobby Orr, Boston	Brad Park, New York
Defense	Guy Lapointe, Montreal	Bill White, Chicago
Center	Phil Esposito, Boston	Bobby Clarke, Philadelphia
Right Wing	Mickey Redmond, Detroit	Yvan Cournoyer, Montreal
Left Wing	Frank Mahovlich, Montreal	Dennis Hull, Chicago

Players in the Hockey Hall of Fame

S. G. (Sid) Abel
John J. (Jack) Adams
C. J. S. (Syl) Apps
Donald Bain
Hobart (Hobey) Baker
Martin (Marty) Barry
Jean Beliveau
Clint (Benny) Benedict
Douglas (Doug) Bentley
Max Bentley
Hector (Toe) Blake
Richard (Dickie) Boon
Emile (Butch) Bouchard
Frank Boucher
George (Buck) Boucher
Russell Bowie
Frank Brimsek
H. L. (Punch) Broadbent, M.M.
Walter (Turk) Broda
H. H. (Harry) Cameron
Francis (King) Clancy
Aubrey (Dit) Clapper
Sprague Cleghorn
Neil Colville
Charles Conacher
Alex Connell
William (Bill) Cook
W. M. (Bill) Cowley
Samuel R. (Rusty) Crawford
John P. (Jack) Darragh
Allan (Scotty) Davidson
Clarence (Hap) Day
Cyril (Cy) Denneny
Charles G. Drinkwater
William (Bill) Durnan

Mervyn (Red) Dutton
Cecil H. (Babe) Dye
Arthur Farrell
Frank Foyston
Frank Fredrickson
W. A. (Bill) Gadsby
Charles(Chuck)Gardiner
Herbert Gardiner
James H. (Jimmy) Gardner
Bernard (Boom Boom) Geoffrion
Edward (Eddie) Gerard
H. L. (Billy) Gilmour
E. R. (Ebbie) Goodfellow
F. X. (Moose) Goheen
Michael (Mike) Grant
Wilfred (Shorty) Green
Silas (Si) Griffis
Joseph (Joe) Hall
George Hainsworth
Doug Harvey
George Hay
W. M. (Riley) Hern
Bryan Hextall
Harry (Hap) Holmes
Thomas (Tom) Hooper
G. R. (Red) Horner
Gordon Howe
Sydney (Syd) Howe
John B. (Bouse) Hutton
Harry Hyland
James Dickenson Irvin
H. (Busher) Jackson
Ernest (Moose) Johnson
I. W. (Ching) Johnson
T. C. (Tom) Johnson

Aurel Joliat
Gordon (Duke) Keats
Leonard (Red) Kelly
Theodore (Teeder) Kennedy
Elmer James Lach
Edouard (Newsy) Lalonde
J. B. (Jack) Laviolette
Hugh Lehman
Percy LeSueur
R. B. T. (Ted) Lindsay
Duncan (Mickey) MacKay
Sylvio Mantha
Joseph Malone
John (Jack) Marshall
Fred (Steamer) Maxwell
Frank McGee
W. G. (Billy) McGimsie
George McNamara
Patrick (Paddy) Moran
H. W. (Howie) Morenz
William (Billy) Mosienko
Frank Nighbor
Reginald Noble
Harold (Harry) Oliver
Lester Patrick
Thomas (Tom) Phillips
Didier (Pit) Pitre
Walter (Babe) Pratt
Joseph (Joe) Primeau
Harvey Pulford
Frank Rankin
Chuck Rayner
Kenneth (Ken) Reardon
Maurice (The Rocket) Richard
George Richardson

Gordon Roberts
Arthur H. Ross
Blair Russell
Ernie Russell
J. D. (Jack) Ruttan
T. G. (Terry) Sawchuk
Fred Scanlan
Milt Schmidt
David (Sweeney) Schriner
Earl Walter Seibert
Oliver Seibert
Edward William Shore
Albert (Babe) Siebert
H. J. (Bullet Joe) Simpson, M.M.
Alfred (Alf) Smith
Reginald (Hooley) Smith
Tommy Smith
Russell (Barney) Stanely
John (Black Jack) Stewart
Nelson Stewart
Bruce Stuart
Horace (Hod) Stuart
Fred (Cyclone) Taylor, OBE
Harry J. Trihey
Cecil (Tiny) Thompson
Georges Vezina
Martin Walsh
John (Jack) Walker
Harry E. Watson
Harry Westwick
R. C. (Cooney) Weiland
Fred Whitcroft
Gordon (Phat) Wilson
Roy Worters

1973 Final Standings

American League

EASTERN DIVISION

	W	L	T	F	A	Pts
Nova Scotia	43	18	15	316	191	101
Boston	34	29	13	248	256	81
Rochester	33	31	12	239	276	78
Providence	31	31	14	256	260	76
Springfield	18	42	16	265	344	52
New Haven	16	40	20	246	331	52

Playoff Winner—Cincinnati

WESTERN DIVISION

	W	L	T	F	A	Pts
Cincinnati	54	17	5	351	206	113
Hershey	42	23	11	326	231	95
Virginia	38	22	16	258	221	92
Richmond	30	36	10	272	280	70
Jacksonville	23	44	9	252	330	55
Baltimore	17	47	11	208	311	45

Western League

	W	L	T	F	A	Pts
Phoenix	37	26	9	310	250	83
Salt Lake	32	25	15	288	259	79
San Diego	32	29	11	239	222	75

Playoff Winner—Phoenix.

	W	L	T	F	A	Pts
Denver	27	32	13	264	275	67
Seattle	26	32	14	270	286	66
Portland	21	39	12	226	287	54

Central League

	W	L	T	F	A	Pts
Dallas	38	23	11	256	208	87
Omaha	35	27	10	262	263	80

Playoff Winner—Omaha.

	W	L	T	F	A	Pts
Fort Worth......	31	35	6	254	267	68
Tulsa	26	37	9	259	308	61

Western Canada League

EASTERN DIVISION

	W	L	T	F	A	Pts
Saskatoon......	46	11	11	323	184	103
Flin Flon	39	19	10	334	228	88
Regina	30	28	10	294	270	70
Brandon	29	30	9	307	304	67
Swift Current ...	27	35	6	300	359	60
Winnipeg	16	42	10	288	372	42

Playoff Winner—Medicine Hat.

WESTERN DIVISION

	W	L	T	F	A	Pts
Edmonton	40	20	8	311	240	88
Medicine Hat ...	39	20	9	348	254	87
Calgary	35	22	11	302	224	81
N. Westminster .	31	22	15	283	264	77
Victoria	13	51	4	231	390	30
Vancouver......	10	55	3	198	428	23

Ontario Major Junior

	W	L	T	F	A	Pts		W	L	T	F	A	Pts
Toronto	47	7	9	416	199	103	Oshawa	23	32	8	295	310	54
Peterboro	42	13	8	330	234	92	Sudbury	21	32	10	289	379	52
Ottawa	41	15	7	391	243	89	Kitchener	16	41	6	244	368	38
London	33	22	8	334	246	74	Hamilton	15	41	7	244	374	37
St. Catharines	24	28	11	280	318	59	Sault	11	42	10	244	396	32

Playoff Winner—Toronto.

World Hockey Association

Final Standings

East Division

	W	L	T	F	A	Pts
New England	46	30	2	318	263	94
Cleveland	43	32	3	287	239	89
Philadelphia	38	40	0	288	306	76
Ottawa	35	39	4	279	301	74
Quebec	33	40	5	276	313	71
New York	33	43	2	303	334	68

West Division

	W	L	T	F	A	Pts
Winnipeg	43	31	4	285	249	90
Houston	39	35	4	284	269	82
Los Angeles	37	35	6	255	246	80
*Alberta	38	37	3	270	256	79
*Minnesota	38	37	3	250	269	79
Chicago	26	50	2	245	295	74

* — Sudden death play-off for fourth.

Final Scoring

	G	A	Pts		G	A	Pts.
Andre Lacroix, Phil	50	74	124	Tim Sheehy, New Eng	33	38	71
Ron Ward, New York	51	67	118	Jim Wiste, Clev	28	43	71
Danny Lawson, Phil	61	45	106	Andre Gaudette, Queb	27	44	71
Tom Webster, New Eng	53	50	103	Wayne Connelly, Minn	40	30	70
Bobby Hull, Winn	51	52	103	Murray Hall, Houston	28	42	70
Norm Beaudin, Winn	38	65	103	Rosaire Paiement, Chic	33	36	69
Chris Bordeleau, Winn	47	54	101	J. P. Leblanc, Los Angeles	19	50	69
Terry Caffery, New Eng	39	61	100	Norm Ferguson, New York	28	40	68
Gordon Labossiere, Hous	36	60	96	Gavin Kirk, Ottawa	28	40	68
Wayne Carleton, Ott	42	49	91	Reg. Fleming, Chic	23	45	68
J. C. Tremblay, Quebec	14	75	89	Gerry Pinder, Clev	30	36	66
Bobby Sheehan, New York	35	53	88	Larry Lund, Houston	21	45	66
Bobby Sicinski, Chicago	25	63	88	Jan Popiel, Chic	31	34	65
Jim Harrison, Alberta	39	48	87	Paul Popiel, Hous	16	48	64
Larry Pleau, New Eng	39	48	87	Alain Caron, Queb	36	27	63
Ron Buchanan, Clev	37	44	81	Bob Charlebois, Ott	24	39	63
Garry Jarrett, Clev	40	38	78	Jim Dorey, New England	7	56	63
John McKenzie, Phil	28	50	78	Ted Hampson, Minnesota	17	45	62
Wayne Rivers, New York	37	40	77	Al Hamilton, Alberta	11	49	60
Ted Taylor, Houston	34	42	76	John French, New Eng	24	35	59
Gary Veneruzzo, Los Ang	43	30	73	Billy Klatt, Minnesota	36	22	58
Brian Campbell, Phil	25	48	73	Guy Trottier, Ott	26	32	58
Michael Parizeau, Que	25	48	73	Ross Perkins, Alberta	21	37	58
Don Herriman, Phil	24	48	72	Larry Hornung, Winn	13	35	58
Gene Peacosh, New York	37	34	71	Ken Block, New York	5	53	58

WHA Playoffs

New England defeated Ottawa 4 games to 1.   —   New England defeated Cleveland 4 games to 1.
Cleveland defeated Philadelphia 4 games to 0.   Winnipeg defeated Houston 4 games to 0.
Winnipeg defeated Minnesota 4 games to 1.   New England defeated Winnipeg 4 games to 1.
Houston defeated Los Angeles 4 games to 2.

World Amateur Hockey Championship

The Soviet Union won the world amateur hockey championship with a 4-2 victory over Czechoslovakia, the defending champions. The game was played April 13, 1973, at Prague.

National AAU Gymnastic Championships in 1973

Men

All-Around—(tie) Yoshi Takei, Georgia Southern and Yoshi Hayasaki, Univ. of Ill.
Floor Exercises—Paul Hunt, Univ. of Illinois.
Pommeled Horse—Yoshi Hayasaki.
Long Horse Vault—Yoshi Hayasaki.
Parallel Bars—Yoshi Takei.
Horizontal Bar—Yoshi Hayasaki.

Women

All-Around—Joan Moore Rice.
Floor Exercises—Joan Moore Rice.
Uneven Parallel Bars—Roxanne Pierce.
Balance Beam—Kim Chace.
Side Horse Vault—Roxanne Pierce.

NCAA Championships in 1973

All-Around—(tie) Steve Hug, Stanford and Marshall Avener, Penn. State.
Floor Exercises—Odess Lavin, Oklahoma.
Pommeled Horse—Ed Slexak, Indiana State.
Rings—Bob Mahorney, Indiana State.

Vaulting—John Crosby, So. Conn. State.
Parallel Bars—Steve Hug.
Horizontal Bar—Jon Aitken, New Mexico.
Team Champion—Iowa State.

U.S. Gymnastics Federation National Championship in 1973

Men

All-Around—Marshall Avener, Penn State.
Free Exercise—John Crosby, So. Conn. State.
Pommeled Horse—Marshall Avener.
Rings—Gary Morava, So. Ill.
Long Horse Vault—Gary Morava.
Parallel Bars—Marshall Avener.
Horizontal Bar—John Crosby.

Women

All-Around—Joan Moore Rice.
Floor Exercise—Joan Moore Rice.
Uneven Parallel Bars—Roxanne Pierce.
Balance Beam—Nancy Thies.
Side Horse Vault—Roxanne Pierce.

Top Sports Stories of Past 75 Years

The four gold medals won by Jesse Owens, and the treatment he received at the 1936 Olympics in Berlin was the most important sports story of the past 75 years, according to a nationwide poll of sports writers and broadcasters conducted by Pepsi-Cola Company as part of its 75th Anniversary celebration. The results of the poll follow:

Event	Event
Jesse Owens at '36 Olympics	N.Y. Yankee dynasty 50's
Roger Bannister's 4-minute mile	Army-Notre Dame 0-0 tie '46
Bobby Thomson's '51 Series home run	First Dempsey-Tunney fight
Mark Spitz wins 7 Gold Medals, '72 Olympics	Notre Dame-Michigan State 10-10 tie
UCLA basketball dynasty	Boston Celtics dynasty
Don Larson's perfect Series game '56	Nebraska-Oklahoma football game '71
Ali-Frazier fight	Green Bay Packers under Vince Lombardi
Jets Upset Colts Superbowl III '69	Pro-baseball strike '72
Babe Ruth's 60 home run record	Babe Ruth's career
Dempsey-Tunney long count fight	Babe Ruth's pointing a homer in '32 Series against
Roger Maris' 61 home run record	Cubs
2nd Louis-Schmeling Fight '38	Notre Dame-Army game '49
Colts-Giants sudden death NFL Title '58	Citation wins Triple Crown '48
Bobby Jones golf grand slam	USA-USSR basketball game '72 Olympics
Mets win world series '69	Denny McLain wins 30 Games one season
First Superbowl game '67	Bears-72 Redskins-0 NFL Championship '40
Olympic Israeli massacre '72	Oklahoma football 50's winning streak under Bud
Jackie Robinson breaks color line, Dodgers '47	Wilkinson
Jim Thorpe Olympic gold medals & disqualification	Forward Pass introduced to football 1913
DiMaggio's 56 game hitting streak	Lou Gehrig's farewell speech
Bob Beamon's 29' — plus Olympic broad jump '68	Bill Russell's Celtic Basketball coaching
Black Sox scandal world series 1919	Notre Dame under Knute Rockne
Vander Meer's back-to-back no-hitters 38	Jack Nicklaus tournament wins
Ali-Liston fight	L.A. Lakers basketball streak
Miami Dolphins '72 unbeaten season	Army-Notre Dame football series
Foreman-Frazier fight	Man O'War's records
Summer Olympics '72	Dempsey-Willard fight
Arnold Palmer's golf career	Expansion of pro football
Bill Mazeroski's winning series homer '60	Death of Roberto Clemente
Wilt Chamberlain scores 100 pts. in 1 game '62	Louis-Conn fight
NFL-AFL merger	Lee Trevino's career
Babe Ruth's 714 home run record	3 Graziano-Zale fights

Skiing in 1973

NCAA Skiing Championships
Middlebury, Vermont

Slalom — Peik Christensen, Denver.
Downhill — Bob Cochran, Vermont.
Alpine Combined — Peik Christensen, Denver.
15 km Cross Country — Steiner Hybertsen, Wyoming.
Jumping — Vidar Nilsgard, Colorado.
Nordic Combined — Pentti Reijula, Northern Mich.

Skimeister — Kim Kandall, New Hampshire.
Slalom Team — Vermont.
Downhill Team — Colorado.
15 km Cross Country Team — Wyoming.
Jumping Team — Colorado.
Team Standings — 1, Colorado; 2, Wyoming; 3, Vermont.

National Nordic Ski Championships
Bloomington, Minn.

Men's 15 km — Tim Caldwell.
Men's 30 km — Bob Gray.
Men's 50 km — Joe McNulty.
Men's Relay — Caldwell, Gray, McNulty and Mike Gallagher.

Women's 5 km — Martha Rockwell.
Women's 10 km — Martha Rockwell.
Women's Relay — Mary Heller, Katie Tobey, Jennifer Caldwell and Martha Rockwell.

North American Cross Country Championships
Thunder Bay, Ontario, Canada

Men's 15 km — Tim Caldwell, U.S.
Men's 30 km — Hans Skinstad, Canada.
Men's Relay — U.S. (Caldwell, McNulty, Gallagher).

Women's 5 km — Shirley Firth, Canada.
Women's 10 km — Martha Rockwell, U.S.
Women's Relay — U.S. (Owen, Rockwell, Hlavaty).

The World Cup

Men	Women
1967—Jean Claude Killy, France	1967—Nancy Greene, Canada
1968—Jean Claude Killy, France	1968—Nancy Greene, Canada
1969—Karl Schranz, Austria	1969—Gertrud Gabl, Austria
1970—Karl Schranz, Austria	1970—Michele Jacot, France
1971—Gustavo Thoeni, Italy	1971—Annemarie Proell, Austria
1972—Gustavo Thoeni, Italy	1972—Annemarie Proell, Austria
1973—Gustavo Thoeni, Italy	1973—Annemarie Proell, Austria

1973 World Cup Leaders

Men	Pts.	Women	Pts.
1—Gustavo Thoeni, Italy	166	1—Annemarie Proell, Austria	297
2—David Zwilling, Austria	151	2—Monika Kaserer, Austria	227
3—Roland Collombin, Switzerland	131	3—Patricia Emonet, France	164
4—Christian Neurether, West Germany	120	4—Rosi Mittermaier, West Germany	131
4—Hans Hinterseer, Austria	120	5—Hanni Wenzel, Lichtenstein	112
6—Bernhard Russi, Switzerland	106	6—Wilfred Drexel, Austria	106
7—Jean Noel Augert, France	104	7—Jacqueline Rouvier, France	103
8—Bob Cochran, Richmond, Vt.	93	8—Marilyn Cochran, U.S.	84
8—Franz Klammer, Austria	93	9—Ingrid Gfoellner, Austria	83
10—Piero Gros, Italy	91	10—Irmgard Lukasser, Austria	65

World Track and Field Records

As of July, 1973
* Indicates pending record; a number of new records await confirmation

MEN

Running

Event	Record	Holder	Country	Date	Where made
100 yds.	9.1 s	Bob Hayes	U.S.A.	June 21, 1963	St. Louis, Mo.
		James Hines	U.S.A.	May 13, 1967	Houston, Tex.
		Charlie Greene	U.S.A.	June 15, 1967	Provo, Utah
		John Carlos	U.S.A.	May 10, 1969	Fresno, Calif.
		Harry Jerome	Canada	July 15, 1966	Edmonton, Canada
		Willie McGee	U.S.A.	May 8, 1970	Houston
		*Steve Williams	U.S.A.	May, 1973	Fresno, Calif.
220 yds.	19.5 s.	Tommie Smith	U.S.A.	May 7, 1966	San Jose, Calif.
220 yds.	20.0 s.(Turn)	Tommie Smith	U.S.A.	May 11, 1966	Sacramento, Calif.
440 yds.	44.5	John Smith	U.S.A.	June 26, 1972	Eugene, Ore.
880 yds.	*1 m., 44.6 s.	Rick Wohlhuter	U.S.A.	May 27, 1973	Los Angeles
1 mile	3 m., 51.1 s.	Jim Ryun	U.S.A.	June 23, 1967	Bakersfield, Calif.
2 miles	8 m., 14 s.	Lasse Viren	Finland	Aug. 14, 1972	Stockholm
3 miles	12 m., 47.8 s.	Emiel Puttemans	Belgium	Sept. 20, 1972	Brussels
6 miles	26 m., 47.0 s.	Ron Clarke	Australia	July 14, 1965	Oslo, Norway
10 miles	46 m., 04.2 s.	Willy Polleunis	Belgium	Sept. 20, 1972	Brussels
15 miles	1 hr., 12 min., 48.2 s.	Ron Hill	Gt. Britain	July 21, 1965	Bolton, Eng.

Running — Metric Distances

100 meters	9.9 s.	Jim Hines	U.S.A.	June 20, 1968	Sacramento
		Charlie Greene	U.S.A.	June 20, 1968	Sacramento
		Ronnie Smith	U.S.A.	June 20, 1968	Sacramento
		Jim Hines	U.S.A.	Oct. 14, 1968	Mexico City
		Eddie Hart	U.S.A.	July 1, 1972	Eugene, Ore.
		Reynaud Robinson	U.S.A.	July 1, 1972	Eugene, Ore.
200 meters	19.5 s.	Tommie Smith	U.S.A.	May 7, 1966	San Jose, Calif.
200 meters	19.8 s.(Turn)	Tommie Smith	U.S.A.	Oct. 16, 1968	Mexico City
		Donald Quarrie	Jamaica	Aug. 3, 1971	Cali, Colombia
400 meters	43.8 s.	Lee Evans	U.S.A.	Oct. 18, 1968	Mexico City
800 meters	*1 m., 43.7 s.	Marcello Fiasconaro	Italy	June 27, 1973	Milan, Italy
1,000 meters	*2 m., 16 s.	Danie Malan	So. Africa	June, 1973	
1,500 meters	3 m., 33.1 s.	Jim Ryun	U.S.A.	July 8, 1967	Los Angeles
2,000 meters	4 m., 56.2 s.	Michel Jazy	France	Oct. 12, 1966	Saint Maur, France
3,000 meters	7 m., 37.6 s.	Emiel Puttemans	Belgium	Sept. 14, 1962	Aarhus, Denmark
5,000 meters	13 m., 13 s.	Emiel Puttemans	Belgium	Sept. 20, 1972	Brussels
10,000 meters	*27 m., 31 s.	Dave Bedford	Gr. Britain	July 13, 1973	London
20,000 meters	57 m., 44.4 s.	Gaston Roelants	Belgium	Sept. 20, 1972	Brussels
25,000 meters	1 hr., 15 m., 22.6 s.	Ron Hill	Gr. Britain	July 21, 1965	Bolton, Eng.
30,000 meters	1 hr., 31 m., 30.4 s.	Jim Alder	Gr. Britain	Sept. 5, 1970	London
3,000 meter stpl	*8 m., 14 s.	Ben Jipcho	Kenya	June 27, 1973	Helsinki

Hurdles

120 yards	13.0 s.	Rod Milburn	U.S.A.	June 25, 1971	Eugene, Ore.
		*Rod Milburn	U.S.A.	June, 1973	Eugene, Ore.
220 yards	21.9 s.	Don Styron	U.S.A.	Apr. 2, 1960	Baton Rouge
440 yards	48.8 s.	Ralph Mann	U.S.A.	June 20, 1970	Des Moines, Iowa
110 meters	*13.1 s.	Rod Milburn	U.S.A.	July 6, 1973	Zurich
		*Rod Milburn	U.S.A.	July 22, 1973	Siena, Italy
200 meters	21.9 s.	Don Styron	U.S.A.	Apr. 2, 1960	Baton Rouge
200 meters	22.5 s.	Martin Lauer	Germany	July 7, 1959	Zurich, Switz.
	(Turn)	Glenn Davis	U.S.A.	Aug. 20, 1960	Berne, Switz.
400 meters	47.8 s.	John Akii-Bua	Uganda	Sept. 2, 1972	Munich

Relay Races

440 yds. (4x110) (2 turns)	38.6 s.	USC (McCullough, Kuller, Simpson, Miller)	U.S.A.	June 17, 1967	Provo, Utah
880 yds. (4x220)	1 m., 21.7 s.	Texas A & M. (Rogers, Woods, M. Mills, C. Mills)	U.S.A.	Apr. 24, 1970	Des Moines, Iowa
1 mile (4x440)	3 m., 02.8 s.	National Team (Yearwood, Bernard, Roberts, Mottley)	Trinidad & Tobago	Aug. 13, 1966	Kingston, Jamaica
2 miles (4x880)	*7 m., 10.4 s.	Chicago TC (Bach, Sparks, Paul, Wohlhuter)	U.S.A.	May, 1973	Durham, N.C.
4 miles (4x1) (mile)	16 m., 02.8 s.	New Zealand Nat'l. Team	New Zealand	Feb. 3, 1972	Auckland, N.Z.

Relay Races — Metric Distances

400 mtrs. (4x100)	38.2 s.	Nat'l. Team (Green, Pender, R. Smith, Hines)	U.S.A.	Oct. 19, 1968	Mexico City
		Nat'l. Team (Black, Taylor, Tinker, Hart)	U.S.A.	Sept. 10, 1972	Munich
800 mtrs. (4x200)	*1 m., 21.5 s.	National Team (Ossola, Obeti, Benedetti, Mennea)	Italy	July 21, 1972	Barletta
1,600 mtrs. (4x400)	2 m., 56.1 s.	Nat'l. Team (Matthews, Freeman, James, Evans)	U.S.A.	Oct. 20, 1968	Mexico City
3,200 mtrs. (4x800)	7 m., 08.6 s.	Nat'l. Team (Kinder, Adams, Bogatzki, Kemper)	W. Germany	Aug. 13, 1966	Wiesbaden

Field Events

High Jump	*7 ft., 6½ in.	Dwight Stones	U.S.A.	July 11, 1973	Munich
Long Jump	29 ft., 2¼ in.	Bob Beamon	U.S.A.	Oct. 18, 1968	Mexico City
Triple Jump	57 ft., 2¾ in.	Victor Saneyev	USSR	Oct. 17, 1972	Sukhumi, USSR
Pole Vault	18 ft., 5¾ in.	Bob Seagren	U.S.A.	July 2, 1972	Eugene, Ore.
16 lb. shot put	*71 ft., 7 in.	Al Feuerbach	U.S.A.	May 5, 1973	San Jose, Calif.
Discus throw	229 ft., 9½ in.	Jay Silvester	U.S.A.	June 10, 1971	Ystad, Sweden
Javelin throw	*308 ft., 8 in.	Klaus Wolfermann	W. Germany	May 5, 1973	W. Germany
16 lb. hammer throw	250 ft., 8 in.	Walter Schmidt	W. Germany	Sept. 4, 1971	Lahr, W. Ger.
Decathlon	8,454 pts.	Nikolai Avilov	USSR	Sept. 8, 1972	Munich

Walking

20 miles	2 h., 31 m., 33.0 s.	A. Vedjakov	USSR	Aug. 23, 1958	Moscow, USSR
30 miles	3 h., 56 m., 12.6 s.	Peter Selzer	E. Germany	Oct. 3, 1971	Naumberg
2 hours	26,911 meters	Karl-Heinz Stadtmuller	E. Germany	Apr. 16, 1972	Berlin
30 km.	2 h., 14 m., 45.6 s.	Karl-Heinz Stadtmuller	E. Germany	Apr. 16, 1972	Berlin
50 km.	4 h., 3 m., 42.6 s.	V. Soldatenko	USSR	Oct. 5, 1972	Moscow

WOMEN

Running

100 yards	10.0 s.	Chi Cheng	Taiwan	June 13, 1970	Portland, Ore.
220 yards	22.6 s.	Chi Cheng	Taiwan	July 3, 1970	Los Angeles
440 yards	52.4 s.	Judy Pollock	Australia	Feb. 27, 1965	Perth
		D. Willis	Australia	Mar. 3, 1962	Australia
880 yards	2 m., 02.0 s.	J. Pollock	Australia	July 5, 1967	Sweden
		*Madeline Manning Jackson	U.S.A.	May 14, 1972	Philadelphia
1 mile	*4 m., 34.9 s.	Glenda Reiser	Canada	July 7, 1973	Victoria, B.C.
60 meters	7.2 s.	Betty Cuthbert	Australia	Feb. 27, 1960	Australia
		L. Bocharova	USSR	Aug. 25, 1960	Moscow
100 meters	*10.8 s.	Renate Stecher	E. Germany	July 20, 1973	Dresden
200 meters	*22.1 s.	Renate Stecher	E. Germany	July 21, 1973	Dresden
400 meters	51.0 s.	Marilyn Neufville	Canada	July 23, 1970	Edinburgh
		Minika Zehrt	E. Germany	July 4, 1972	Paris
800 meters	1 m., 58.3 s.	Hildegard Falck	W. Germany	July 11, 1971	Stuttgart
1500 meters	4 m., 01.4 s.	Ludmila Bragina	USSR	Sept. 9, 1972	Munich
3000 meters	9 m., 9 s.	Paola Pigni	Italy	May 11, 1972	Formia, Italy

Hurdles

80 meters	10.2 s.	V. Korsakova	USSR	June 16, 1968	Riga, USSR
100 meters	12.5 s.	Annelie Ehrhardt	E. Germany	June 15, 1972	Potsdam
		Pamela Ryan	Australia	June 28, 1972	Warsaw
200 meters	25.7 s.	Pamela Ryan	Australia	Nov. 25, 1971	Melbourne
400 meters	*57.3 s.	Maria Sykora	Austria	June, 1973	Frankfurt

Field Events

High jump	6 ft. 4½ in.	Jordanka Blagoeva	Bulgaria	Sept. 24, 1972	Yugoslavia
Long jump	22 ft., 4½ in.	V. Viscorpoleanu	Rumania	Oct. 14, 1968	Mexico City
Shot put	69 ft.	Nadezwda Chizhova	USSR	Sept. 7, 1972	Munich
Discus throw	*221 ft. 3 in.	Faina Melnik	USSR	May, 1973	Riga, USSR
Javelin	204 ft. 8½ in.	Elena Gorchakova	USSR	Oct. 16, 1964	Tokyo, Japan
Pentathlon	4,801 pts.	Mary Peters	Gt. Britain	Sept. 3, 1972	Munich

Relay Races

400 mtrs. (4x100)	42.8 s.	Nat'l team (Ferrell, Bailes, Netter, Tyus)	U.S.A.	Oct. 20, 1968	Mexico City
		Nat'l. Team	W. Germany	Sept. 10, 1972	Munich
800 mtrs. (4x200)	1 m., 33.8 s.	Nat'l. Team (Tranter, James, Simpson, Peal)	Gt. Britain	Aug. 24, 1968	London
880 yds (4x220)	1 m., 35.8 s.	(Hoffman, Boyle, Kilborn, Lamy)	Australia	Nov. 9, 1969	Brisbane, Aust.
1,600 mtrs. (4x400)	3 m., 23.0 s.	Nat'l. Team	E. Germany	Sept. 10, 1972	Munich
1 mile (4x440)	3 mi., 38.7 s.	(Stroy, Laing, Norman, Touissaint)	U.S.A.	July, 1971	Durham, N.C.
1½ miles (3x880)	6 m., 25.2 s.	Nat'l. team (Sterling, Lowe, Percy)	Gt. Britain	July 30, 1967	Budapest
2,400 mtrs. (3x800)	6 m., 15.5 s.	(Kaiser, Vandermade, Gommers)	Dutch National Team	Aug. 20, 1968	London

World High Jump Records

Year	Jumper	Height	Year	Jumper	Height
1912	George Horine, U.S.	6-7	1960	John Thomas, U.S.	7-1½
1914	Edward Beeson, U.S.	6-7¼	1960	John Thomas, U.S.	7-1¾
1924	Harold Osborn, U.S.	6-8¼	1960	John Thomas, U.S.	7-2
1933	Walter Marty, U.S.	6-8½	1960	John Thomas, U.S.	7-3¾
1934	Walter Marty, U.S.	6-9	1961	Valery Brumel, USSR	7-3¾
1936	C. Johnson, U.S.	6-10¾	1961	Valery Brumel, USSR	7-4¼
1936	D. Albritton, U.S.	6-9¾	1961	Valery Brumel, USSR	7-4½
1937	Mel Walker, U.S.	6-10¼	1962	Valery Brumel, USSR	7-5
1941	Lester Steers, U.S.	6-11	1962	Valery Brumel, USSR	7-5¼
1953	Walter Davis, U.S.	6-11½	1963	Valery Brumel, USSR	7-5¾
1956	Chas. Dumas, U.S.	7-0½	1971	Pat Matzdorf, U.S.	7-6¼
1957	Y. Stepanov, USSR.	7-1*	1973	Dwight Stones, U.S.	7-6½

*Made with built-up shoe.

Track and Field Events, 1973

Toronto Star Maple Leaf Indoor Games
Toronto, Ont., Feb. 2, 1973

50 Yds.—Herb Washington. **Time**—0:05.
50 Yd. Hurdles—Danny Smith, Florida State. **Time**—0:05.8.
600 Yds.—Martin McGrady. **Time**—1:10.9.
1,000 Yds.—Mike Boit. **Time**—2:08.1.
One Mile—Marty Liquori, New York AC. **Time**—4:08.2.
Three Miles—Kipchoge Keino, Kenya. **Time**—13:23.8.
Pole Vault—Steve Smith. 17 ft. 5½ in.
High Jump—Dwight Stones. 7 ft. 3½ in.

Women's Events
50 Yds.—Iris Davis, Tennessee State. **Time**—0:05.5.
50 Yd. Hurdles—Mamie Rallins, Tennessee State. **Time**—0:06.4.
600 Yds.—Brenda Walsh, Edmonton, Canada. **Time**—1:21.5.
1,000 Yds.—Glenda Reiser, Ottawa. **Time**—2:29.4.

66th Annual Millrose Games
New York, N.Y., Jan. 26, 1973

60 Yds.—Herb Washington, Michigan State. **Time**—0:06.
60 Yd. High Hurdles—Rod Milburn, Southern Univ. **Time**—0:07.
600 Yds.—Beaufort Brown, Florida. **Time**—1:12.1.
800 Yds.—Marcel Phillippe, Fordham. **Time**—1:52.4.
1,000 Yds.—Andres Kupczyk, Poland. **Time**—2:09.1.

One Mile—Henryk Szdorykowski, Poland. **Time**—4:04.4.
Two Miles—Grant McLaren, Canada. **Time**—8:36.8.
Pole Vault—Steve Smith, Pacific Coast Club. 18 ft. ¼ in.
High Jump—Claude Ferrange, Canada. 7 ft.
Women's 60 Yds.—Mattine Render. **Time**—0:06.9.
Women's 600 Yds.—Cheryl Toussaint. **Time**—1:21.1.

9th Annual NCAA Indoor Track and Field Championships
Detroit, Mich., March 10, 1973. Sponsored by the Detroit News

60 Yds.—Gerald Tinker, Kent State. **Time**—0:06.
60 Yd. Hurdles—Rod Milburn, Southern Univ. **Time**—0:06.9.
440 Yds.—Terrence Lee Erickson, Southern Univ. **Time**—0:49.
600 Yds.—Beaufort Brown, Florida. **Time**—1:10.
880 Yds.—Ken Schappert, Villanova. **Time**—1:50.4.
1,000 Yds.—Tony Waldrop, North Carolina. **Time**—2:10.
One Mile—Dave Wottle, Bowling Green. **Time**—4:03.4.
Two Miles—Mike Keogh, Manhattan. **Time**—8:39.7.
Mile Relay—Seton Hall, **Time**—3:17.

Two Mile Relay—Fordham. **Time**—7:31.5.
Distance Medley Relay—Manhattan. **Time**—9:43.8.
Long Jump—Randy Williams, Univ. of So. Calif. 26 ft. 4½ in.
Triple Jump—Barry McClure, Middle Tenn. State. 54 ft. 1½ in.
High Jump—Chris Dunn, Colgate. 7 ft. 2 in.
Pole Vault—Terry Porter, Kansas. 17 ft.
Shot Put—Hans Goglund, Texas-El Paso. 64 ft. 1¼ in.
35-lb. Weight Throw—Ted Bregar, Navy. 68 ft. 1½ in.
Team Champion—Manhattan.

AAU Indoor Track and Field Championships
New York, N.Y., Feb. 23, 1973

Men's Events
60 Yds.—Hasely Crawford, Philadelphia Pioneer Club. **Time**—0:06.
60 Yd. Hurdles—Rod Milburn, Southern Univ. **Time**—0:07.
600 Yd.—Fred Newhouse, Philadelphia Pioneer Club. **Time**—1:11.0.
1,000 Yd.—Marcel Philippe, Fordham Univ. **Time**—2:08.8
One Mile—Marty Liquori, New York AC. **Time**—4:03.5.
One Mile Walk—Ron Daniel, New York AC. **Time**—6:22.
Three Miles—Tracy Smith, Athletes in Action. **Time**—13:07.2.
Two Mile Relay—Chicago TC. **Time**—7:29.
One Mile Relay—Sports International. **Time**—3:17.9.
35-lb. Weight Throw—George Frenn. 69 ft. 7½ in.
Shot Put—George Woods. 69 ft. 9½ in.
Long Jump—Randy Williams, Univ. of So. Calif. 26 ft. 8¼ in.
Triple Jump—John Craft, Univ. of Chicago TC. 54 ft. 8½ in.

High Jump—Dwight Stones. 7 ft.
Pole Vault—Steve Smith. 17 ft. 8 in.
Women's Events
60 Yds.—Iris Davis, Tenn. State. **Time**—0:06.6.
60 Yd. Hurdles—Patty Johnson, Club Northwest. **Time**—0:07.5.
220 Yds.—Rosalyn Bryant. **Time**—0:24.6.
440 Yds.—Brenda Walsh, Canada. **Time**—0:55.5.
880 Yds.—Cheryl Toussaint, Atoms TC. **Time**—2:08.8.
One Mile—Ludmila Bragina, USSR. **Time**—4:40.
One Mile Relay—Atoms TC. **Time**—3:50.5.
Spring Medley Relay—Sports International. **Time**—1:47.9.
Long Jump—Irena Szewinska, Poland. 20 ft. 6 in.
High Jump—Alice Pfaff, Univ. of Colorado TC. 5 ft. 8 in.
Shot Put—Jan Svendsen. 50 ft. ½ in.
One Mile Walk—Lynn Olson, Ferris State. **Time**—7:37.

5th U.S. Olympic Invitation Track Meet
New York, N.Y., Feb. 16, 1973

Jesse Owens 50 Meters—Herb Washington. **Time**—0:05.6.
Harrison Dillard 55 Meter hurdles—Rod Milburn, Southern Univ. **Time**—0:07.
Ray Barbuti 400 Meters—Terry Musica, Pacific Coast Club. **Time**—0:49.2.
Alan Helffrich 500 Meters—Beaufort Brown, Univ. of Florida. **Time**—1:03.5.
Tom Courtney 800 Meters—Byron Dyce, United AA. **Time**—1:50.7.
John Woodruff 1,000 Meters—Mike Boit, Eastern New Mexico Univ. **Time**—2:21.4.
Olympian 1,500 Meters—Haiul Ebba, Oregon St. **Time**—3:46.4.
Horace Ashenfelter 3,000 Meters—Peter Kaal, Pacific Coast Club. **Time**—8:03.
1,600 Meter Relay—Adelphi Univ. **Time**—3:16.5.

3,200 Meter Relay—Chicago T & F Club. **Time**—7:26.
Pole Vault—Steve Smith, Pacific Coast Club. 17 ft. 6¾ in.
High Jump—Dwight Stones, Pacific Coast Club. 7 ft. 2 in.
Shot Put—Doug Price, Florida TC. 55 ft. 6 in.
56-lb. Weight Throw—Al Hall. 68 ft. 3 in.
Long Jump—Norman Tate, N.Y. Pioneer Club. 24 ft. 8¾ in.

Women's Events
Wilma Rudolph 50 meters—Iris Davis, Tenn. State. **Time**—0:06.2.
Betty Robinson 400 Meters—Marilyn Neufville, Jamaica. **Time**—0:56.
Madeline Manning 800 Meters—Cheryl Toussaint, Atoms TC. **Time**—2:08.6.

52nd NCAA Outdoor Championships
Baton Rouge, La., June 8-9, 1973

100 Yds.—Ed Hammonds, Memphis State. **Time**—0:09.4.
120 Yd. High Hurdles—Rod Milburn, Southern Univ. **Time**—0:13.1.
220 Yds.—Marshall Dill, Michigan State. **Time**—0:20.9.
440 Yds.—Maurice Peoples, Arizona State. **Time**—0:45.0.
440 Yd. Intermediate Hurdles—Robert Primeaux, Texas. **Time**—0:49.5.
880 Yds.—Skip Kent, Wisconsin. **Time**—1:47.2.
One Mile—Dave Wottle, Bowling Green. **Time**—3:57.1.
Three Miles—Steve Prefontaine, Oregon. **Time**—13:05.3.
Six Miles—Charles Maguire, Penn State. **Time**—28:19.3.

3,000 Meter Steeplechase—Doug Brown, Tennessee. **Time**—8:28.1.
Decathlon—Raimo Pihl, Brigham Young. 7,782 pts.
Long Jump—Finn Bendixen, UCLA. 25 ft. 10½ in.
Shot Putt—Hans Hoglund, Texas at El Paso. 64 ft. 6¾ in.
Triple Jump—Milan Tiff, UCLA. 54 ft. 2¾ in.
Javelin—Sam Colson, Kansas. 279 ft. 9 in.
High Jump—Tom Woods, Oregon State. 7 ft. 4 in.
Discus—Mac Wilkins, Oregon. 204 ft. 6 in.
Pole Vault—Dave Roberts, Rice. 17 ft. 4 in.
Hammer—Jacques Accambray, Kent State. 221 ft. 6 in.
Team Champion—UCLA.

National Interscholastic Track and Field Records

Source: National Federation of State High School Associations. Records approved to Oct., 1973

Event	Record	Holder	School	Site and year
100 yds.	0:09.3	William Gaines	Clearview Regional H. S., Mullica Hill, N.J.	Deptford, N.J., 1967
220 yds.	0:20.2	Forrest O. Beaty	Herbert Hoover H.S., Glendale, Calif.	Chaffey, Calif., 1961
440 yds.	0:45.8	Ronald E. Ray	Ferguson H.S., Newport News, Va.	Charlottsville, Va., 1972
880 yds.	1:48.8	Richard J. Joyce	Sierra H.S., Whittier, Calif.	Bakersfield, Calif., 1965
1 mile	3:58.3	James Ryun	Wichita East H.S., Wichita, Kan.	Wichita, Kan., 1965
2 mile	8:41.5	Steve Préfontaine	Marshfield High School, Coos Bay, Ore.	Corvallis, Ore., 1969
120 yd. high hurdles	0:13.5	Richmond M. Flowers, Jr.	Sidney Lanier H.S., Montgomery, Ala.	Mobile, Ala., 1965
		William Tipton	Central H.S., Pontiac, Mich.	Saginaw, Mich., 1967
		Randall L. Lightfoot	Plainview H.S., Plainview, Texas	Austin, Tex., 1971
180 yd. low hurdles	0:18.1	Donald Castronovo	Oceanside H.S., Oceanside, N.Y.	Ithaca, N.Y., 1964
		Steve Caminiti	Crespi Carmelite H.S., Encino, Calif.	Encino, Calif., 1964
		Earl McCullouch	Polytechnic H.S., Long Beach, Calif.	Norwalk, Calif., 1964
		Dwight Davies	Glendale H.S., Glendale, Calif.	Berkeley, Calif., 1971
Long Jump	25 ft. 9½ in.	Gerald Hardeman	Edison H.S., Fresno, Calif.	Porterville, Calif., 1972
Pole vault	16 ft. 7 in.	Casey Carringan	Orting High School, Orting, Wash.	Bellingham, Wash., 1969
		Robert Pollard	Los Angeles City H.S.	Los Angeles, Calif., 1969
Triple jump	52 ft. 6¼ in.	David Tucker	San Joaquin Mem. H.S., Fresno, Calif.	Fresno, Calif., 1970
Shot put (12 lbs.)	72 ft. 3½ in.	Sam Walker	W. W. Samuel H.S., Dallas, Tex.	Corpus Christi, Tex., 1968
Discus	201 ft. 3 in.	Christopher Adams	Los Altos H.S., Los Altos, Calif.	Berkeley, Calif., 1970
Javelin	254 ft. 11 in.	Russell Francis	Pleasant Hill H.S., Pleasant Hill, Ore.	Pleasant Hill, Ore., 1971
440 yd. relay	0:40.2	Delley, G. Pouncy, J. Pouncy, Shaw	Lincoln High School, Dallas, Texas	Austin, Texas, 1970
880 yd. relay	1:25.4	Jackson, James, Reed, Hill	White Plains (N.Y.) H.S.	Jamaica, N.Y., 1966
1 mile relay	3:11.8	Bouche, Bradley, Brents, Morton	Memorial H.S., Houston, Texas	Baytown, Texas, 1967
		Anderson, Black, Thompkins, Thompson	Killian High School, Miami, Fla.	Gainesville, Fla., 1969
2 mile relay	7:41.9	Mentz, Jakosa, Bowman, Grant	Proviso West H.S., Hillside, Ill.	Glen Ellyn, Ill., 1965
Sprint Medley Relay (1 mile)	3:23.3	Corson, Brake, Brents, Morton	Memorial H.S., Houston, Texas	Houston, Texas, 1967

Evolution of the World Record for the One Mile Run

The table below shows how the world record for the one-mile has been lowered in the past 107 years.

Time	Individual	Year	Time	Individual	Year
4:56	Charles Lawes, Britain	1864	4:07.6	Jack Lovelock, New Zealand	1933
4:36.5	Richard Webster, Britain	1865	4:06.8	Glen Cunningham, U. S.	1934
4:29	William Chinnery, Britain	1868	4:06.4	Sydney Wooderson, Britain	1937
4:28.8	W. C. Gibbs, Britain	1868	4:06.2	Gunder Haegg, Sweden	1942
4:26	Walter Slade, Britain	1874	4:06.2	Arne Andersson, Sweden	1942
4:24.5	Walter Slade, Britain	1875	4:04.6	Gunder Haegg, Sweden	1942
4:23.2	Walter George, Britain	1880	4:02.6	Arne Andersson, Sweden	1943
4:21.4	Walter George, Britain	1882	4:01.6	Arne Andersson, Sweden	1944
4:19.4	Walter George, Britain	1882	4:01.4	Gunder Haegg, Sweden	1945
4:18.4	Walter George, Britain	1884	3:59.4	Roger Bannister, Britain	1954
4:18.2	Fred Bacon, Scotland	1894	3:58	John Landy, Australia	1954
4:17	Fred Bacon, Scotland	1895	3:57.2	Derek Ibbotson, Britain	1957
4:15.6	Thomas Conneff, U. S.	1895	3:54.5	Herb Elliott, Australia	1958
4:15.4	John Paul Jones, U. S.	1911	3:54.4	Peter Snell, New Zealand	1962
4:14.6	John Paul Jones, U. S.	1913	3:54.1	Peter Snell, New Zealand	1964
4:12.6	Norman Taber, U. S.	1915	3:53.6	Michel Jazy, France	1965
4:10.4	Paavo Nurmi, Finland	1923	3:51.3	Jim Ryun, U. S.	1966
4:09.2	Jules Ladoumegue, France	1931	3:51.1	Jim Ryun, U. S.	1967

Professional Track & Field Money Winners

(June, 1973)

Men				Women	
Lee Evans	$13,900	Jerome Howe	8,400	Kipchoge Keino	5,750
Chris Fisher	12,960	Leon Coleman	7,500		
Jim Ryun	12,450	John Radetich	7,075	**Women**	
Brian Oldfield	10,375	Tom Von Ruden	6,400	Wyomia Tyus	6,275
Warren Edmonson	10,058	Henry Hines	6,075	Barbara Ferrell	5,575

Annual Results of Major Bowl Games

ROSE BOWL, Pasadena

1902–Michigan 49, Stanford 0
1916–Wash. State 14, Brown 0
1917–Oregon 14, Pennsylvania 0
1918-19–Service Teams
1920–Harvard 7, Oregon 6
1921–California 28, Ohio State 0
1922–Wash. & Jeff. 0, California 0
1923–So. California 14, Penn State 3
1924–Navy 14, Washington 14
1925–Notre Dame 27, Stanford 10
1926–Alabama 20, Washington 19
1927–Alabama 7, Stanford 7
1928–Stanford 7, Pittsburgh 6
1929–Georgia Tech 8, California 7
1930–So. California 47, Pittsburgh 14
1931–Alabama 24, Wash. State 0
1932–So. California 21, Tulane 12
1933–So. California 35, Pittsburgh 0
1934–Columbia 7, Stanford 0

1935–Alabama 29, Stanford 13
1936–Stanford 7, So. Methodist 0
1937–Pittsburgh 21, Washington 0
1938–California 13, Alabama 0
1939–So. California 7, Duke 3
1940–So. California 14, Tennessee 0
1941–Stanford 21, Nebraska 13
1942–Oregon St. 20, Duke 16 (at Durham)
1943–Georgia 9, UCLA 0
1944–So. California 29, Washington 0
1945–So. California 25, Tennessee 0
1946–Alabama 34, So. California 14
1947–Illinois 45, UCLA 14
1948–Michigan 49, So. California 0
1949–Northwestern 20, California 14
1950–Ohio State 17, California 14
1951–Michigan 14, California 6
1952–Illinois 40, Stanford 7
1953–So. California 7, Wisconsin 0

1954–Mich. State 28, UCLA 20
1955–Ohio State 20, So. California 7
1956–Mich. State 17, UCLA 14
1957–Iowa 35, Oregon St. 19
1958–Ohio State 10, Oregon 7
1959–Iowa 38, California 12
1960–Washington 44, Wisconsin 8
1961–Washington 17, Minnesota 7
1962–Minnesota 21, UCLA 3
1963–So. California 42, Wisconsin 37
1964–Illinois 17, Washington 7
1965–Michigan 34, Oregon St. 7
1966–UCLA 14, Mich. State 12
1967–Purdue 14, So. California 13
1968–Southern Cal. 14, Indiana 3
1969–Ohio State 27, Southern Cal 16
1970–Southern Cal 10, Michigan 3
1971–Stanford 27, Ohio State 17
1972–Stanford 13, Michigan 12
1973–So. California 42, Ohio State 17

ORANGE BOWL, Miami

1933–Miami (Fla.) 7, Manhattan 0
1934–Duquesne 33, Miami (Fla.) 7
1935–Bucknell 26, Miami (Fla.) 0
1936–Catholic U. 20, Mississippi 19
1937–Duquesne 13, Miss. State 12
1938–Auburn 6, Mich. State 0
1939–Tennessee 17, Oklahoma 0
1940–Georgia Tech 21, Missouri 7
1941–Miss. State 14, Georgetown 7
1942–Georgia 40, TCU 26
1943–Alabama 37, Boston Col. 21
1944–LSU 19, Texas A&M 14
1945–Tulsa 26, Georgia Tech 12

1946–Miami (Fla.) 13, Holy Cross 6
1947–Rice 8, Tennessee 0
1948–Georgia Tech 20, Kansas 14
1949–Texas 41, Georgia 28
1950–Santa Clara 21, Kentucky 13
1951–Clemson 15, Miami (Fla.) 14
1952–Georgia Tech 17, Baylor 14
1953–Alabama 61, Syracuse 6
1954–Oklahoma 7, Maryland 0
1955–Duke 34, Nebraska 7
1956–Oklahoma 20, Maryland 6
1957–Colorado 27, Clemson 21
1958–Oklahoma 48, Duke 21
1959–Oklahoma 21, Syracuse 6

1960–Georgia 14, Missouri 0
1961–Missouri 21, Navy 14
1962–LSU 25, Colorado 7
1963–Alabama 17, Oklahoma 0
1964–Nebraska 13, Auburn 7
1965–Texas 21, Alabama 17
1966–Alabama 39, Nebraska 28
1967–Florida 27, Georgia Tech 12
1968–Oklahoma 26, Tennessee 24
1969–Penn State 15, Kansas 14
1970–Penn State 10, Missouri 3
1971–Nebraska 17, Louisiana St. 12
1972–Nebraska 38, Alabama 6
1973–Nebraska 40, Notre Dame 6

SUGAR BOWL, New Orleans

1935–Tulane 20, Temple 14
1936–TCU 3, LSU 2
1937–Santa Clara 21, LSU 14
1938–Santa Clara 6, LSU 0
1939–TCU 15, Carnegie Tech 7
1940–Texas A&M 14, Tulane 13
1941–Boston Col. 19, Tennessee 13
1942–Fordham 2, Missouri 0
1943–Tennessee 14, Tulsa 7
1944–Georgia Tech 20, Tulsa 18
1945–Duke 29, Alabama 26
1946–Oklahoma A&M 33, St. Mary's 13
1947–Georgia 20, No. Carolina 10

1948–Texas 27, Alabama 7
1949–Oklahoma 14, No. Carolina 6
1950–Oklahoma 35, LSU 0
1951–Kentucky 13, Oklahoma 7
1952–Maryland 28, Tennessee 13
1953–Georgia Tech. 24, Mississippi 7
1954–Georgia Tech 42, West Virginia 19
1955–Navy 21, Mississippi 0
1956–Georgia Tech 7, Pittsburgh 0
1957–Baylor 13, Tennessee 7
1958–Mississippi 39, Texas 7
1959–LSU 7, Clemson 0
1960–Mississippi 21, LSU 0

1961–Mississippi 14, Rice 6
1962–Alabama 10, Arkansas 3
1963–Mississippi 17, Arkansas 13
1964–Alabama 12, Mississippi 7
1965–LSU 13, Syracuse 10
1966–Missouri 20, Florida 18
1967–Alabama 34, Nebraska 7
1968–LSU 20, Wyoming 13
1969–Arkansas 16, Georgia 2
1970–Mississippi 27, Arkansas 22
1971–Tennessee 34, Air Force 13
1972–Oklahoma 40, Auburn 22
1972 (Dec.)–Oklahoma 14, Penn State 0

COTTON BOWL, Dallas

1937–TCU 16, Marquette 6
1938–Rice 28, Colorado 14
1939–St. Mary's 20, Texas Tech 13
1940–Clemson 6, Boston Col. 3
1941–Texas A&M 13, Fordham 12
1942–Alabama 29, Texas A&M 21
1943–Texas 14, Georgia Tech 7
1944–Randolph Field 7, Texas 7
1945–Oklahoma A&M 34, TCU 0
1946–Texas 40, Missouri 27
1947–Arkansas 0, LSU 0
1948–So. Methodist 13, Penn State 13

1949–So. Methodist 21, Oregon 13
1950–Rice 27, No. Carolina 13
1951–Tennessee 20, Texas 14
1952–Kentucky 20, TCU 7
1953–Texas 16, Tennessee 0
1954–Rice 28, Alabama 6
1955–Georgia Tech 14, Arkansas 6
1956–Mississippi 14, TCU 13
1957–TCU 28, Syracuse 27
1958–Navy 20, Rice 7
1959–TCU 0, Air Force 0
1960–Syracuse 23, Texas 14

1961–Duke 7, Arkansas 6
1962–Texas 12, Mississippi 7
1963–LSU 13, Texas 0
1964–Texas 28, Navy 6
1965–Arkansas 10, Nebraska 7
1966–LSU 14, Arkansas 7
1967–Georgia 24, So. Methodist 9
1968–Texas A&M 20, Alabama 16
1969–Texas 36, Tennessee 13
1970–Texas 21, Notre Dame 17
1971–Notre Dame 24, Texas 11
1972–Penn State 30, Texas 6
1973–Texas 17, Alabama 13

SUN BOWL, El Paso

1936–Hardin Simmons 14, New Mex. St. 14
1937–Hardin-Simmons 34, Texas Mines 6
1938–West Virginia 7, Texas Tech 6
1939–Utah 26, New Mexico 0
1940–Catholic U. 0, Arizona St. 0
1941–Western Reserve 26, Arizona St. 13
1942–Tulsa 6, Texas Tech 0
1943–Second Air Force 13,
     Hardin-Simmons 7
1944–Southwestern (Tex.) 7,
     New Mexico 0
1945–Southwestern (Tex.) 35, U. of Mex. 0
1946–New Mexico 34, Denver 24

1947–Cincinnati 38, Virginia Tech 6
1948–Miami (0.) 13, Texas Tech 12
1949–West Virginia 21, Texas Mines 12
1950–Texas Western 33, Georgetown 20
1951–West Texas St. 14, Cincinnati 13
1952–Texas Tech 25, Col. Pacific 14
1953–Col. Pacific 26, Miss. Southern 7
1954–Texas Western 37, Miss. Southern 14
1955–Texas Western 47, Florida St. 20
1956–Wyoming 21, Texas Tech 14
1957–Geo. Washington 13, Tex. Western 0
1958–Louisville 34, Drake 20
1959–Wyoming 14, Hardin-Simmons 6

1960–New Mexico St. 28, No. Texas St. 8
1961–New Mexico St. 20, Utah State 13
1962–Villanova 17, Wichita 9
1963–West Texas St. 15, Ohio U. 14
1964–Oregon 21, So. Methodist 14
1965–Georgia 7, Texas Tech 0
1966–Texas Western 13, TCU 12
1967–Wyoming 28, Florida St. 20
1968–UTex El Paso 14, Mississippi 7
1969–Auburn 34, Arizona 10
1969–(Dec. 20) Nebraska 45, Georgia 6
1970–Georgia Tech. 17, Texas Tech. 9
1971–LSU 33, Iowa State 15
1972–North Carolina 32, Texas Tech 28

PEACH BOWL, Atlanta

1968–LSU 31, Florida St. 27
1969–West Virginia 14, S. Carolina 3

1970–Arizona St. 48, N. Carolina 26
1971–Mississippi 41, Georgia Tech. 18

1972–N. Carolina State 49, West
     Virginia 13

LIBERTY BOWL, Memphis

1959 — Penn State 7, Alabama 0	1964 — Utah 32, West Virginia 6	1969 — Colorado 47, Alabama 33
1960 — Penn State 41, Oregon 12	1965 — Mississippi 13, Auburn 7	1970 — Tulane 17, Colorado 3
1961 — Syracuse 15, Miami 14	1966 — Miami (Fla.) 14, Va. Tech 7	1971 — Tennessee 14, Arkansas 13
1962 — Oregon 6, Villanova 0	1967 — N.C. State 14, Georgia 7	1972 — Georgia Tech 31, Iowa State 30
1963 — Miss. State 16, N.C. State 12	1968 — Mississippi 34, Va. Tech 17	

GATOR BOWL, Jacksonville

1946—Wake Forest 26, South Carolina 14	1955—Auburn 33, Baylor 13	1964—No. Carolina 35, Air Force 0
1947—Oklahoma 34, N.C. State 13	1956—Vanderbilt 25, Auburn 13	1965—Florida St. 36, Oklahoma 19
1948—Maryland 20, Georgia 20	1957—Georgia Tech 21, Pittsburgh 14	1966—Georgia Tech 31, Texas Tech 21
1949—Clemson 24, Missouri 23	1958—Tennessee 3, Texas A&M 0	1967—Tennessee 18, Syracuse 12
1950—Maryland 20, Missouri 7	1959—Mississippi 7, Florida 3	1968—Penn State 17, Florida St. 17
1951—Wyoming 20, Wash. & Lee 7	1960—Arkansas 14, Georgia Tech 7	1969—Missouri 35, Alabama 10
1952—Miami (Fla.) 14, Clemson 0	1961—Florida 13, Baylor 12	1969—(Dec. 27) Florida 14, Tenn. 13
1953—Florida 14, Tulsa 13	1962—Penn State 30, Georgia Tech 15	1971—Auburn 35, Mississippi 28
1954—Texas Tech 35, Auburn 13	1963—Florida 17, Penn State 7	1972—Georgia 7, N. Carolina 3
		1973 — Auburn 24, Colorado 3

ASTRO—BLUEBONNET BOWL, Houston

1959 — Clemson 23, TCU 7	1964 — Tulsa 14, Mississippi 7	1969 — Houston 36, Auburn 7
1960 — Texas 3, Alabama 3	1965 — Tennessee 27, Tulsa 6	1970 — Oklahoma 24, Alabama 24
1961 — Kansas 33, Rice 7	1966 — Texas 19, Mississippi 0	1971 — Colorado 29, Houston 17
1962 — Missouri 14, Georgia Tech 10	1967 — Colorado 31, Miami (Fla.) 21	1972 — Tennessee 24, Louisiana St. 17
1963 — Baylor 14, LSU 7	1968 — SMU 28, Oklahoma 27	

Other Bowl Games, 1972-73

Event	Result	Event	Result
Ohio Shrine Bowl, Columbus	East 20, West 7	Shrine Game, Miami	North 17, South 10
Boardwalk Bowl	Univ. of Mass. 35, Univ. of Calif., Davis 14	Fiesta Bowl	Arizona State 49, Missouri 35
Grantland Rice Bowl	Louisiana Tech 35, Tenn. Tech 0	Blue-Gray Game, Montgomery	Gray 27, Blue 15
Pioneer Bowl	Tennessee State 29, Drake 7	Tangerine Bowl	Tampa 21, Kent State 18
NAIA Champion Bowl	East Texas State 21, Carson-Newman 18	Shrine Game, San Francisco	East 9, West 3
		Senior Bowl, Mobile	South 33, North 30
Potato Bowl	Fresno City Coll. 21; Pasadena City Coll. 7	American Bowl, Tampa	North 10, South 6
		Hula Bowl, Honolulu	South 17, North 3

College Football Conference Champions

Atlantic Coast	Ivy League	Big Eight	Big Ten
1960—Duke	1960—Yale	1960—Missouri	1960—Minn., Iowa
1961—Duke	1961—Columbia, Harvard	1961—Colorado	1961—Ohio State
1962—Duke	1962—Dartmouth	1962—Oklahoma	1962—Wisconsin
1963—No. Carolina St., No. Carolina	1963—Dartmouth, Princeton	1963—Nebraska	1963—Illinois
1964—No. Carolina St.	1964—Princeton	1964—Nebraska	1964—Michigan
1965—Duke	1965—Dartmouth	1965—Nebraska	1965—Michigan St.
1966—Clemson	1966—Dartmouth, Harvard, Princeton	1966—Nebraska	1966—Michigan St.
1967—Clemson	1967—Yale	1967—Oklahoma	1967—Indiana, Purdue, Minn.
1968—No. Carolina St.	1968—Yale, Harvard	1968—Kansas, Oklahoma	1968—Ohio State
1969—So. Carolina	1969—Princeton, Dartmouth, Yale	1969—Missouri, Nebraska	1969—Michigan, Ohio State
1970—Wake Forest	1970—Dartmouth	1970—Nebraska	1970—Ohio State
1971 — North Carolina	1971—Dartmouth, Cornell	1971—Nebraska	1971—Michigan
1972 — North Carolina	1972—Darmouth	1972—Nebraska	1972—Ohio State, Michigan

Mid-America	Missouri Valley	Southeastern	Southwest
1960—Ohio Univ.	1960—Wichita	1960—Mississippi	1960—Arkansas
1961—Bowling Green	1961—Wichita	1961—Alabama, Louisiana St.	1961—Texas, Arkansas
1962—Bowling Green	1962—Tulsa	1962—Mississippi	1962—Texas
1963—Ohio Univ.	1963—Cincinnati, Wichita	1963—Mississippi	1963—Texas
1964—Bowling Green	1964—Cincinnati	1964—Alabama	1964—Arkansas
1965—Bowling Green, Miami	1965—Tulsa	1965—Alabama	1965—Arkansas
1966—Miami, Western Mich.	1966—No. Texas, Tulsa	1966—Alabama, Georgia	1966—Southern Methodist
1967—Toledo, Ohio Univ.	1967—North Texas	1967—Tennessee	1967—Texas A & M
1968—Ohio Univ.	1968—Memphis State	1968—Georgia	1968—Texas, Arkansas
1969—Toledo	1969—Memphis State	1969—Tennessee	1969—Texas
1970—Toledo	1970—Louisville	1970—Louisiana State	1970—Texas
1971—Toledo	1971—Memphis State	1971—Alabama	1971—Texas
1972—Kent State	1972—Louisville, W. Texas, Drake	1972—Alabama	1972—Texas

Pacific Eight		Southern	
1960—Washington	1966—Southern Calif.	1960—VMI	1966—E. Carolina, William & Mary
1961—UCLA	1967—Southern Calif.	1961—Citadel	1967—West Virginia
1962—Southern Calif.	1968—Southern Calif.	1962—VMI	1968—Richmond
1963—Washington	1969—Southern Calif.	1963—Virginia Tech	1969—Richmond, Davidson
1964—Oregon St., Southern Calif.	1970—Stanford	1964—West Virginia	1970—William & Mary
1965—UCLA	1971—Stanford	1965—West Virginia	1971—Richmond
	1972—Southern Calif.		1972—East Carolina

1973 College All-Star Football Game

The world champion Miami Dolphins defeated the college football all-stars 14-3, at Soldier Field in Chicago on July 27, 1973. The annual event was played before 54,103 fans and was sponsored by the Chicago Tribune.

World Series of Poker

Walter Clyde Pearson, of Nashville, Tenn., won $130,000 in the World Series of Poker on May 19, 1973 in Las Vegas. He defeated 13 other contestants, all of whom had put up $10,000.

College Football Stadiums

School	Capacity
Alabama Univ. of (Denny) University, Ala.	59,000
Angelo State (San Angelo Stad.) San Angelo, Tex.	18,000
Arizona State Univ. (Sun Devil), Tempe	51,000
Arizona, Univ. of (Arizona Stad.) Tucson	40,000
Arkansas, Univ. of (Razorback Stad.) Fayetteville	48,000
Auburn Univ. (Cliff Hare Stad.), Auburn, Ala.	62,291
Baylor Univ., Waco, Texas	48,000
Boston Coll. (Alumni Stad.), Boston, Mass.	32,000
Boston Univ. (Nickerson Field), Boston	15,000
Bowling Green State Univ. (Doyt Perry Field), Ohio	23,272
Brigham Young Univ. Stad., Utah	30,000
Brown Stad., Providence, R. I.	20,000
Bucknell (Memorial Stad.), Lewisburg, Pa.	17,500
Butler Univ. (Butler Bowl), Indianapolis, Ind.	19,500
Calif., Univ. of (Memorial Stad.), Berkeley	77,000
Catholic Univ. (The Stadium), Wash., D.C	18,000
Central Mich. Univ. (Shorts Stad.), Mt. Pleasant	20,000
Cincinnati, Univ. of (Nippert), Ohio	25,692
Citadel (Johnson Hagood Stadium), Charleston, S.C.	22,500
Clemson Univ. (Memorial Stad.), S.C.	43,451
Coe (Kingston), Cedar Rapids, Iowa	20,000
Colorado St. Univ. (Hughes Stad.), Ft. Collins	30,000
Colorado, Univ. of (Folsom Field), Boulder	50,126
Columbia Univ. (Baker Field), N.Y., N.Y.	32,000
Conn., Univ. of (Memorial Stad.), Storrs	15,200
Cornell (Schoellkopf Crescent), Ithaca, N.Y.	34,000
Dartmouth Coll. (Memorial), Hanover, N.H.	20,816
Delaware, Univ. of (Delaware Stad.), Newark	21,919
Denver Stad., Univ. of	27,500
Drake Stad., Des Moines, Iowa	18,500
Duke Univ., (Wade Stad.), Durham, N.C.	44,000
E. Carolina (Ficklen Stad.), Greenville	20,000
Eastern Kentucky (Hanger Stadium), Richmond	20,000
Eastern Mich. Univ. (Rynearson), Ypsilanti	17,000
Florida State, (Campbell), Tallahassee	40,500
Florida, Univ. of (Florida Field), Gainesville	62,000
Georgia Inst. of Tech. (Grant Field), Atlanta	59,245
Georgia, Univ. of (Sanford Stad.), Athens	59,200
Grambling Coll. (Tiger Stad.), La.	18,000
Harvard Univ., Boston, Mass.	37,289
Hawaii, Univ. of (Honolulu Stad.)	25,000
Holy Cross (Fitton Field), Worcester, Mass.	25,000
Idaho, Univ. of, Moscow	18,000
Illinois, Univ. of (Memorial Stad.), Urbana	71,229
Indiana St. (Municipal), Terre Haute	20,500
Indiana Univ. (Stadium), Bloomington	52,354
Iowa State Univ. (Clyde Williams Stad.)	35,000
Iowa, Univ. of (Kinnick Stad.), Iowa City	60,200
Kansas State Univ., Manhattan	42,000
Kansas, Univ. of (Memorial), Lawrence	51,500
Kent State Univ. (Memorial), Kent	28,415
Kentucky, Univ. of (Commonwealth), Lexington	58,000
Lafayette Coll. (Fisher Field), Easton, Pa.	17,000
Lamar Univ. (Cardinal Stad.), Beaumont, Tex.	17,150
Lehigh Univ. (Taylor Stad.), Bethlehem, Pa.	17,000
Louisiana Tech. Univ. (Joe Aillet Stad.), Ruston	23,000
La. State Univ. (Tiger), Baton Rouge	67,510
Marshall Univ. (Fairfield Stadium), Huntington	16,500
Maryland, Univ. of (Byrd), College Park	35,000
Mass., Univ. of (Alumni Stad.), Amherst	17,000
Memphis State (Memphis Memorial)	50,164
Miami Univ., (Miami Field), Oxford, Ohio	14,900
Michigan State Univ. (Spartan Stadium), E. Lansing	76,000
Michigan, Univ. of (Mich. Stad.), Ann Arbor	101,001
Middle Tenn. St. Univ. (Jones Field) Murfreesboro	15,000
Minnesota, Univ. of (Memorial Stad.)	56,725
Mississippi St. Univ. (Scott Field)	35,000
Mississippi, Univ. of (Hemmingway Stad.)	37,500
Missouri, Univ. of (Faurot Field), Columbia, Mo.	55,000
Nebraska, Univ. of (Memorial), Lincoln	76,400

School	Capacity
New Mexico St. U. (Aggie Memorial Stad.), Las Cruces	16,000
New Mexico, Univ. Stad., Albuquerque	30,000
North Carolina St. U. (Carter Stad.), Raleigh	41,000
North Carolina, Univ. of (Kenan Stad.), Chapel Hill	47,000
Northern Illinois Univ. (West Stad.), DeKalb	17,642
No. Texas St. Univ., Denton	65,000
Northwestern Univ. (Dyche Stad.), Evanston, Ill.	55,000
Notre Dame Stad., South Bend, Ind.	59,075
Ohio State Univ. (Ohio Stad.), Columbus	81,455
Ohio U. (Don Peden Stad.), Athens	17,550
Oklahoma State (Lewis Stad.), Stillwater	52,000
Oklahoma, Univ. of (Owen Field), Norman	61,826
Old Dominion Univ. (Foreman Field), Norfolk, Va.	18,000
Oregon St. Univ. (Parker Stad.), Corvallis	41,000
Oregon, Univ. of (Autzen Stad.), Eugene	41,097
Pacific, Univ. of the (Pacific Mem.), Stockton, Calif.	35,975
Penn. State Univ. (Beaver Stad.),	57,500
Penn., Univ. of (Franklin Field), Phila.	60,546
Pittsburgh, Univ. of (Pitt. Stad.), Pa.	57,331
Princeton, (Palmer Mem. Stad.), Princeton, N.J.	45,725
Purdue, (Ross-Ade Stad.), Lafayette, Ind.	69,250
Rice Stad., Houston, Texas	70,000
Rutgers Stad., New Brunswick, N.J.	23,000
San Jose St. Coll. (Spartan Stad.)	18,155
So. Carolina, Univ. of (Williams-Brice), Columbia	54,564
So. Illinois Univ. (McAndrew), Carbondale	15,000
So. Mississippi, Univ. of, Hattiesburg	16,000
Southwest Texas St. Univ. (Evans Field)	15,000
Southwestern La., (Cajun Field), Lafayette, La.	23,000
Stanford Stad., Stanford, Calif.	90,000
Syracuse Univ. (Archbold)	41,731
Tampa, Univ. of (Tampa Stad.), Fla.	47,000
Temple Stad., Phil.	20,547
Tenn. State (Hale), Nashville	16,000
Tenn. Tech. Univ. (Overall Field), Cookeville	16,000
Tenn., Univ. of (Neyland Stad.), Knoxville	71,166
Texas A. & I. Univ. (Javelina), Kingsville	17,000
Texas A. & M. Univ. (Kyle Field)	48,000
Texas Christian Univ. (Carter Stad.), Ft. Worth	46,000
Texas Tech. Univ. (Jones Stad.), Lubbock	47,000
Texas, Univ. of (Memorial), Austin	81,000
Texas, Arlington Stad.	36,400
Texas, El Paso (Sun Bowl)	30,000
Toledo, Univ. of (Glass Bowl), Ohio	18,210
Trinity Univ. (Alamo Stad.), San Antonio, Tex.	22,500
Tulane Stad. (Sugar Bowl), New Orleans, La.	80,985
Tulsa, Univ. of (Skelly), Tulsa, Okla.	40,235
U.S. Air Force Acad. (Falcon Stad.), Colo.	49,068
U.S. Military Academy (Michie Stad.) West Point, N.Y.	41,428
U.S. Naval Academy, (Navy-Marine Corps Mem. Stad.), Annapolis, Md.	28,000
Utah State Univ. (Romney Stad.), Logan	20,000
Utah, Univ. of (Ute Stad.), Salt Lake City	30,000
Vanderbilt, (Dudley), Nashville	34,000
Va. Poly Inst. (Lane), Blacksburg	35,000
Virginia, Univ. of (Scott Stad.), Charolettesville, Va.	25,000
Wake Forest, (Groves Stad.), Winston-Salem, N.C.	30,275
Washington State Univ. (Clarence D. Martin), Pullman	22,600
Washington, Univ. of (Husky Stad.), Seattle	58,946
Weber St., Coll. Stad., Ogden, Utah	18,000
West Texas State Univ. (Kimbrough), Canyon	20,500
West Virginia Univ. (Mountaineer Field)	37,000
Western Mich. Univ. (Waldo Stad.), Kalamazoo	24,500
Wichita State (Cessna Stadium)	30,500
William & Mary, Coll. of (Cary), Williamsburg, Va.	15,000
Wisconsin St. (Warhawk Stad.), Whitewater	14,000
Wisconsin, Univ. of (Camp Randall)	77,280
Wyoming, Univ. of (Memorial) Laramie	27,000
Xavier (Corcoran Field), Cincinnati	15,000
Yale Bowl, New Haven, Conn.	70,874

Outland Awards

Honoring the outstanding interior lineman selected by the Football Writers' Association of America.

Year	Player, College, Pos.
1946	George Connor, Notre Dame, T
1947	Joe Steffy, Army, G
1948	Bill Fischer, Notre Dame, G
1949	Ed Bagdon, Michigan St., G
1950	Bob Gain, Kentucky, T
1951	Jim Weatherall, Oklahoma, T
1952	Dick Modzelewski, Maryland, T
1953	J. D. Roberts, Oklahoma, G

Year	Player, College, Pos.
1954	Bill Brooks, Arkansas, G
1955	Calvin Jones, Iowa, G
1956	Jim Parker, Ohio State, G
1957	Alex Karras, Iowa, T
1958	Zeke Smith, Auburn, G
1959	Mike McGee, Duke, T
1960	Tom Brown, Minnesota, G
1961	Merlin Olsen, Utah State, T
1962	Bobby Bell, Minnesota, T
1963	Scott Appleton, Texas, T
1964	Steve Delong, Tennessee, T

Year	Player, College, Pos.
1965	Tommy Nobis, Texas, G
1966	Loyd Phillips, Arkansas, T
1967	Ron Yary, Southern Cal, T
1968	Bill Stanfill, Georgia, T
1969	Mike Reid, Penn State, DT
1970	Jim Stillwagon, Ohio State, LB
1971	Larry Jacobson, Nebraska, DT
1972	Rich Glover, Nebraska, MG

College Football

University Division

Team	Nickname	Team Colors	Conference	Coach	1972 Record (W-L-T)
Air Force	Falcons	Blue & Silver	Independent	Ben Martin	6-4-0
Alabama	Crimson Tide	Crimson & White	Southeastern	Paul Bryant	10-1-0
Arizona State	Sun Devils	Maroon & Gold	Western Athletic	Frank Kush	9-2-0
Arizona	Wildcats	Red & Blue	Western Athletic	Jim Young	4-7-0
Arkansas	Razorbacks	Cardinal & White	Southwest	Frank Broyles	6-5-0
Army	Cadets	Black, Gold, Gray	Independent	Tom Cahill	6-4-0
Auburn	Tigers	Orange & Blue	Southeastern	Ralph Jordan	9-1-0
Baylor	Bears	Green & Gold	Southwest	Grant Teaff	5-6-0
Boston College	Eagles	Maroon & Gold	Independent	Joseph Yukica	4-7-0
Bowling Green	Falcons	Orange & Brown	Mid-American	Don Nehlen	6-3-1
Brigham Young	Cougars	Royal Blue & White	Western Athletic	LaVell Edwards	7-4-0
Brown	Bruins	Brown & Cardinal	Ivy	John Anderson	1-8-0
California	Golden Bears	Blue & Gold	Pacific-8	Mike White	3-8-0
Cincinnati	Bearcats	Red & Black	Independent	Tommy Mason	2-9-0
Citadel	Bulldogs	Blue & White	Southern	Bobby Ross	5-6-0
Clemson	Tigers	Purple & Orange	Atlantic Coast	Jim Parker	4-7-0
Colgate	Red Raiders	Maroon	Independent	Neil Wheelwright	5-4-1
Colorado State	Rams	Green & Gold	Western Athletic	Sarkis Arslanian	1-10-0
Colorado	Buffaloes	Silver & Gold	Big Eight	Eddie Crowder	8-3-0
Columbia	Lions	Blue & White	Ivy	Frank Navarro	3-5-1
Cornell	Big Red	Carnelian & White	Ivy	Jack Musick	6-3-0
Dartmouth	Big Green	Dartmouth Green	Ivy	Jack Crouthamel	7-1-1
Davidson	Wildcats	Red & Black	Southern	Dave Fagg	3-7-1
Dayton	Flyers	Red & Blue	Independent	Mike McGee	1-6-1
Delaware	Blue Hens	Blue & White	Atlantic Coast	Mike McGee	5-6-0
East Carolina	Pirates	Purple & Gold	Southern	Sonny Randle	9-2-0
Florida State	Seminoles	Garnet & Gold	Independent	Larry Jones	7-4-0
Florida	Gators	Orange & Blue	Southeastern	Doug Dickey	5-5-1
Georgia Tech	Yellow Jackets	Old Gold & White	Independent	Bill Fulcher	6-4-1
Georgia	Bulldogs	Red & Black	Southeastern	Vince Dooley	7-4-0
Harvard	Crimson	Crimson	Ivy	Joe Restic	4-4-1
Holy Cross	Crusaders	Royal Purple	Independent	Ed Doherty	5-4-1
Houston	Cougars	Scarlet & White	Southwest	Bill Yeoman	6-4-1
Idaho	Vandals	Silver & Gold	Big Sky	Don Robbins	4-7-0
Illinois	Fighting Illini	Orange & Blue	Big Ten	Bob Blackman	3-8-0
Indiana	Fightin' Hoosiers	Cream & Crimson	Big Ten	Lee Corso	5-6-0
Iowa State	Cyclones	Cardinal & Gold	Big Eight	Earle Bruce	5-5-1
Iowa	Hawkeyes	Old Gold & Black	Big Ten	Frank Lauterbur	3-7-1
Kansas State	Wildcats	Purple & White	Big Eight	Vince Gibson	3-8-0
Kansas	Jayhawks	Crimson & Blue	Big Eight	Don Fambrough	3-7-1
Kent State	Golden Flashes	Blue & Gold	Mid-American	Don James	6-4-1
Kentucky	Wildcats	Blue & White	Southeastern	Fran Curci	3-8-0
Long Beach, Cal. State	Forty Niners	Brown & Gold	Pacific Coast	Jim Stangeland	5-6-0
Louisiana State	Fighting Tigers	Purple & Gold	Southeastern	Charles McClendon	9-1-1
Louisville	Cardinals	Red, Black, White	Missouri Valley	T. W. Alley	9-1-0
Marshall	Thundering Herd	Green & White	Independent	Jack Lengyel	2-8-0
Maryland	Terps	Red & White	Atlantic Coast	Jerry Claiborne	5-5-1
Memphis State	Tigers	Blue & Gray	Missouri Valley	Fred Pancoast	5-5-1
Miami (Fla.)	Hurricanes	Orange, Green, White	Independent	Pete Elliott	5-6-0
Miami (Ohio)	Redskins	Red & White	Mid-American	Bill Mallory	7-3-0
Michigan State	Spartans	Green & White	Big Ten	Dennie Stolz	5-5-1
Michigan	Wolverines	Maize & Blue	Big Ten	Bo Schembechler	10-1-0
Minnesota	Gophers	Maroon & Gold	Big Ten	Cal Stoll	4-7-0
Mississippi State	Bulldogs	Maroon & White	Southeastern	Bob Tyler	4-7-0
Mississippi	Rebels	Red & Blue	Southeastern	Billy Kinard	5-5-0
Missouri	Tigers	Old Gold & Black	Big Eight	Al Onofrio	6-5-0
Navy	Midshipmen	Navy Blue & Gold	Independent	George Welsh	4-7-0
Nebraska	Cornhuskers	Scarlet & Cream	Big Eight	Tom Osborne	8-2-1
New Mexico State	Aggies	Crimson, White	Missouri Valley	Jim Bradley	2-9-0
New Mexico	Lobos	Cherry & Silver	Western Athletic	Rudy Feldman	3-8-0
North Carolina State	Wolfpack	Red & White	Atlantic Coast	Lou Holtz	7-3-1
North Carolina	Tar Heels	Blue & White	Atlantic Coast	Bill Dooley	10-1-0
Northern Illinois	Huskies	Cardinal & Black	Mid-American	Jerry Ippoliti	7-4-0
North Texas State	Eagles	Green & White	Missouri Valley	Hayden Fry	1-10-0
Northwestern	Wildcats	Purple & White	Big Ten	John Pont	2-9-0
Notre Dame	Fighting Irish	Gold & Blue	Independent	Ara Parseghian	8-2-0
Ohio State	Buckeyes	Scarlet & Gray	Big Ten	Woody Hayes	9-1-0
Ohio Univ.	Bobcats	Green & White	Mid-American	Bill Hess	3-8-0
Oklahoma State	Cowboys	Orange & Black	Big Eight	Jim Stanley	6-5-0
Oklahoma	Sooners	Crimson & Cream	Big Eight	Barry Switzer	10-1-0
Oregon State	Beavers	Orange & Black	Pacific-8	Dee Andros	2-9-0
Oregon	Ducks	Green & Yellow	Pacific-8	Dick Enright	4-7-0
Pacific	Tigers	Orange & Black	Pacific Coast	Chester Caddas	8-3-0
Penn State	Nittany Lions	Blue & White	Independent	Joe Paterno	10-1-0*
Pennsylvania	Red & Blue	Red & Blue	Ivy	Harry Gamble	6-3-0
Pittsburgh	Panthers	Old Gold & Navy Blue	Independent	John Majors	1-10-0
Princeton	Tigers	Orange & Black	Ivy	Bob Casciola	3-5-1
Purdue	Boilermakers	Old Gold & Black	Big Ten	Alex Agese	6-5-0
Rice	Owls	Blue & Grey	Southwest	Al Conover	5-5-1
Richmond	Spiders	Red & Blue	Southern	Frank Jones	6-4-0
Rutgers	Scarlet Knights	Scarlet	Independent	Frank Burns	7-4-0
San Diego, Cal. State	Aztecs	Scarlet & Black	Independent	Claude Gilbert	10-1-0
San Jose State	Spartans	Gold & White	Pacific Coast	Darryl Rodgers	4-7-0
South Carolina	Fighting Gamecocks	Garnet & Black	Independent	Paul Dietzel	4-7-0
Southern Calif.	Trojans	Cardinal & Gold	Pacific-8	John McKay	11-0-0

Team	Nickname	Team Colors	Conference	Coach	1972 Record (W-L-T)
Southern Methodist	Mustangs	Red & Blue	Southwest	Dave Smith	7-4-0
Southern Mississippi	Golden Eagles	Black & Gold	Independent	P. W. Underwood	3-7-1
Stanford	Cardinals	Cardinal & White	Pacific-8	Jack Christiansen	6-5-0
Syracuse	Orangemen	Orange	Independent	Ben Schwartzwalder	5-6-0
Tampa	Spartans	Red, Gold, Black	Independent	Denny Fryzel	9-2-0
Temple	Owls	Cherry & White	Independent	Wayne Hardin	5-4-0
Tennessee	Volunteers	Orange & White	Southeastern	Bill Battle	9-2-0
Texas A & M	Aggies	Maroon & White	Southwest	Emory Bellard	3-8-0
Texas Christian	Horned Frogs	Purple & White	Southwest	Billy Tohill	5-6-0
Texas Tech	Red Raiders	Scarlet & Black	Southwest	Jim Carlen	8-3-0
Texas	Longhorns	Orange & White	Southwest	Darrell Royal	9-1-0
Toledo	Rockets	Blue & Gold	Mid-American	Jack Murphy	6-5-0
Tulane	Green Wave	Olive Green & Sky Blue	Independent	Bennie Ellender	6-5-0
Tulsa	Golden Hurricane	Blue, Crimson, Gold	Missouri Valley	F. A. Dry	4-7-0
UCLA	Bruins	Navy Blue & Gold	Pacific-8	Pepper Rodgers	8-3-0
Utah State	Aggies	Navy Blue & White	Independent	Phil Krueger	8-3-0
Utah	Utes	Crimson & White	Western Athletic	Bill Meek	6-5-0
U Texas Arlington	Mavericks	Royal Blue & White	Southland	John Symank	5-6-0
U Texas El Paso	Miners	Orange & White	Western Athletic	Tommy Hudspeth	2-8-0
Vanderbilt	Commodores	Black & Gold	Southeastern	Steve Sloan	3-8-0
Villanova	Wildcats	Blue & White	Independent	Lou Ferry	2-9-0
VMI	Keydets	Red, White, Yellow	Southern	Bob Thalman	2-9-0
Virginia Polytechnic Inst.	Gobblers	Orange & Maroon	Independent	Charlie Coffey	6-4-1
Virginia	Cavaliers	Orange & Blue	Atlantic Coast	Don Lawrence	4-7-0
Wake Forest	Demon Deacons	Old Gold & Black	Atlantic Coast	Chuck Mills	2-9-0
Washington State	Cougars	Crimson & Gray	Pacific-8	Jim Sweeney	7-4-0
Washington	Huskies	Purple & Gold	Pacific-8	Jim Owens	8-3-0
Western Michigan	Broncos	Brown & Gold	Mid-American	Bill Doolittle	7-3-1
West Texas State	Buffaloes	Maroon & White	Missouri Valley	Gene Mayfield	5-5-0
West Virginia	Mountaineers	Old Gold & Blue	Independent	Bobby Bowden	8-3-0
Wichita State	Shockers	Gold & Black	Missouri Valley	Bob Seaman	6-5-0
William & Mary	Indians	Green, Gold, Silver	Southern	Jim Root	5-6-0
Wisconsin	Badgers	Cardinal & White	Big Ten	John Jardine	4-7-0
Wyoming	Cowboys	Brown & Yellow	Western Athletic	Fritz Shurmur	4-7-0
Xavier (Ohio)	Musketeers	Blue & White	Independent	Tom Cecchini	3-8-0
Yale	Bulldogs	Yale Blue	Ivy	Carmen Cozza	7-2-0

Selected College Division Teams

Team	Nickname	Team Colors	Conference	Coach	Record
Abilene Christian	Wildcats	Purple & White	Southland	Wally Bullington	3-8-0
Adrian	Bulldogs	Gold & Black	Michigan	Tom Heckert	5-4-0
Akron	Zips	Blue & Gold	Independent	Jim Dennison	3-3-2
Alabama A & M	Bulldogs	Maroon & White	Independent	Louis Crews	7-1-1
Alma	Scots	Maroon & Cream	Michigan	Phil Brooks	8-1-0
Arkansas State	Indians	Scarlet & Black	Southland	Bill Davidson	4-7-0
Austin Peay	Governors	Scarlet & White	Ohio Valley	Jack Bushofsky	3-8-0
Baldwin-Wallace	Yellow Jackets	Brown & Gold	Ohio	Lee J. Tressel	7-2-0
Ball State	Cardinals	Cardinal & White	Independent	Dave McClain	5-4-1
Boise State	Broncos	Orange & Blue	Big Sky	Tony Knap	7-4-0
Boston Univ.	Terriers	Scarlet & White	Independent	Paul Kemp	2-8-0
Bridgeport	Knights	Purple, White	Independent	Ed Farrell	10-0-0
Bucknell	Bisons	Orange & Blue	Independent	Fred Prender	6-3-0
Butler	Bulldogs	Blue & White	Indiana	Bill Sylvester	5-5-0
Carleton	Carls	Maize & Blue	Midwest	Dale Quist	3-5-0
Case Western	Spartans	Blue & Gray	Presidents' Athletic	Flory Mauriocourt	4-5-0
Chico, Cal. State	Wildcats	Cardinal & White	Far Western	Pete Riehlman	4-5-0
Coast Guard	Cadets	Blue & White	Independent	Tad Schroeder	3-7-0
Coe	Kohawks	Crimson & Gold	Midwest	Wayne Phillips	5-4-0
Colby	Mules	Blue & Grey	Maine	Richard McGee	7-1-0
Colorado Western	Mountaineers	Crimson & Slate	Rocky Mountain	William Noxon	6-3-0
Connecticut	Huskies	Blue & White	Yankee	Larry Naviaux	4-5-0
C. W. Post	Pioneers	Green & Gold	Independent	Dom Anile	6-3-0
Defiance	Yellow Jackets	Purple & Gold	Hoosier-Buckeye	Lance Tigyer	5-4-0
Delaware	Blue Hens	Blue & Gold	Independent	Harold Raymond	10-0-0
Denison	Big Red	Red & White	Ohio	Keith Piper	7-1-1
De Pauw	Tigers	Old Gold & Black	Indiana	Tom Mont	2-7-0
Doane	Tigers	Orange & Black	Nebraska Inter.	Ray Best	10-0-0
Drake	Bulldogs	Blue & White	Missouri Valley	Jack Wallace	7-4-0
Drexel	Dragons	Blue & Gold	Independent	Sterling Brown	3-6-0
Findlay	Oilers	Orange & Black	Hoosier-Buckeye	Byron E. Morgan	5-3-1
Florida A & M	Rattlers	Orange & Green	Independent	Jim Williams	4-6-0
Fordham	Rams	Maroon	Met. Intercollegiate	Dean Loucks	5-5-0
Fresno, Cal. State	Bulldogs	Cardinal & Blue	Pacific Coast	J. R. Boone	6-4-1
Furman	Paladins	Purple & White	Southern	Art Baker	2-9-0
Grambling	Tigers	Black & Gold	Southwestern	Eddie Robinson	10-2-0
Hawaii	Rainbows	Green & White	Independent	Dave Holmes	8-3-0
Heidelberg	Student Princes	Red, Orange, Black	Ohio	Pete Riesen	9-0-0
Idaho State	Bengals	Orange & Black	Big Sky	Bob Griffin	7-3-0
Illinois State	Redbirds	Red & White	Independent	Gerry Hart	8-3-0
Jackson State	Tigers	Blue & White	Southwestern	Robert Hill	8-3-0
Johnson C. Smith	Golden Bulls	Blue & Gold	Central Intercollegiate	Eddie McGirt	6-4-0
Kalamazoo	Hornets	Orange & Black	Michigan	Ed Baker	2-5-1
Kenyon	Lords	Purple & White	Ohio	Philip Morse	7-0-1
Knox	Siwash	Purple & Gold	Midwest	Albert Reilly	6-3-0
Lafayette	Leopards	Maroon & White	Independent	Neil Putnam	3-7-0
Lamar	Cardinals	Red & White	Southland	Vernon Glass	8-3-0

Team	Nickname	Team Colors	Conference	Coach	1972 Record (W-L-T)
Lawrence	Vikings	Navy & White	Midwest	Ron Roberts	1-6-1
Lehigh	Engineers	Brown & White	Independent	Fred Dunlap	5-6-0
Los Angeles, Cal. State	Diablos	Black & Gold	Pacific Coast	Foster Anderson	3-7-0
Louisiana Tech	Bulldogs	Red & Blue	Southland	Maxie Lambright	11-0-0
Maine	Black Bears	Blue & White	Yankee	Walt Abbott	3-6-0
Massachusetts	Redmen	Maroon & White	Yankee	Richard MacPherson	8-2-0
McNeese State	Cowboys	Blue & Gold	Southland	Jack Doland	8-3-0
Michigan Tech	Huskies	Silver & Gold	Northern	Jim Kapp	8-1-0
Middlebury	Panthers	Blue & White	Independent	Mickey Heinecken	8-0-0
Middle Tenn.	Blue Raiders	Blue & White	Ohio Valley	Bill Peck	7-3-1
Monmouth	Fighting Scots	Crimson, White	Midwest	Bill Reichow	9-0-0
Montana State	Bobcats	Blue & Gold	Big Sky	Allyn Rolland	8-3-0
Montana	Grizzlies	Copper, Silver, Gold	Big Sky	Jack Swarthout	3-8-0
Moorhead State	Dragons	Scarlet & White	Northern	Ross Fortier	7-3-0
Morgan State	Bears	Blue & Orange	Mid-Eastern	Earl Banks	5-5-0
Morris Brown	Wolverines	Purple & White	Independent	Raymond Ross	2-8-0
Mt. Union	Purple Raiders	Purple & White	Ohio	Ken Wable	1-8-0
Muhlenberg	Mules	Cardinal & Gray	Middle Atlantic	Frank Marino	1-8-0
Nebraska Wesleyan	Plainsmen	Yellow & Brown	Nebraska I.A.C.	Harold Chaffee	4-5-0
New Hampshire	Wildcats	Blue & White	Yankee	William Bowes	4-5-0
No. Carolina A & T	Aggies	Blue & Gold	Mid-Eastern	Hornsby Howell	8-2-0
North Dakota State	Bison	Yellow & Green	North Central	Ev Kjelbertson	8-2-0
North Dakota	Sioux	Green & White	North Central	Jerry Olson	9-1-0
Northern Arizona	Lumberjacks	Blue & Gold	Big Sky	Ed Peasley	3-8-0
Northern Michigan	Wildcats	Old Gold & Green	Independent	Rae Drake	2-8-0
Ohio Northern	Polar Bears	Burnt Orange, Black	Independent	Robert Middleton	6-4-0
Ohio Wesleyan	Battling Bishops	Red & Black	Ohio	Joel Conte	5-3-1
Olivet	Comets	Cardinal & White	Michigan	Douglas Kay	3-6-0
Portland State	Vikings	Green & White	Independent	Ron Stratten	3-8-0
Puget Sound	Loggers	Green, Gold, Blue	Independent	Paul Wallof	7-3-0
Redlands	Bulldogs	Maroon & Gray	So. Calif.	Frank Serrao	5-5-0
Rhode Island	Rams	Blue & White	Yankee	Jack Gregory	2-7-0
Ripon	Redmen	Crimson & White	Midwest	John Storzer	5-3-0
Rochester	Yellow Jackets	Yellow, Blue	Independent	Peter Stark	1-8-0
Sacramento Cal. State	Hornets	Green & Gold	Far Western	Ray Clemons	2-8-0
St. Cloud State	Huskies	Red & Black	Northern	Mike Simpson	5-5-0
St. Lawrence	Larries	Scarlet & Brown	ICAC	Ted Stratford	5-4-0
St. Norbert	Knights	Green & Gold	Independent	Howie Kolstad	4-5-0
St. Olaf	Lions	Black & Gold	Midwest	Tom Porter	6-3-0
Samford	Bulldogs	Crimson & Blue	Independent	Wayne Grubb	5-3-0
Santa Clara	Broncos	Cardinal & White	Independent	Pat Malley	4-4-1
Slippery Rock	Rockets	Green & White	Pennsylvania	Bob Di Spirito	7-1-1
So. Carolina State	Bulldogs	Garnet & Blue	Mid-Eastern	Willie Jeffries	1-9-0
So. Dakota State	Jackrabbits	Yellow & Blue	North Central	John Gregory	6-5-0
South Dakota	Coyotes	Vermillion & White	North Central	Joe Salem	9-1-0
Southern Illinois	Salukis	Maroon & White	Independent	Dick Towers	1-8-1
Southern Oregon	Red Raiders	Red & Black	Evergreen	Scott Johnson	4-5-0
SW Louisiana	Ragin' Cajuns	Vermillion, White	Southland	Russ Faulkinberry	5-6-0
Swarthmore	Little Quakers	Garnet	Middle Atlantic	Lewis Elverson	0-7-0
Tennessee Tech	Golden Eagles	Purple & Gold	Ohio Valley	Don Wade	10-1-0
Texas Southern	Tigers	Maroon & Gray	Southwestern	Roderick Page	5-4-1
Thiel	Tomcats	Blue & Gold	President's Athletic	James McCullough	7-2-0
Trenton State	Lions	Blue & Gold	New Jersey State	Peter Carmichael	2-6-1
Troy State	Red Wave	Red & Black	Gulf South	Tom Jones	4-5-1
Tufts	Jumbos	Blue & Brown	Independent	Rocco Carzo	4-4-0
Tuskegee	Golden Tigers	Old Gold, Crimson	Independent	Haywood Scissum	7-4-0
Upsala	Vikings	Blue & Gray	Middle Atlantic	John Hooper	3-5-0
Valparaiso	Crusaders	Brown & Gold	Indiana	Norm Amundsen	6-4-0
Vermont	Catamounts	Green & Gold	Yankee	Carl Falivene	4-5-0
Wabash	Little Giants	Scarlet, White	Indiana	Richard Bowman	4-6-0
Wash. & Jeff.	Presidents	Red & Black	President's Athletic	Pat Mondock	0-8-1
Wash. & Lee	Generals	Royal Blue, White	College Athletic	William McHenry	3-6-0
Wayne State	Tartars	Green & Gold	Independent	David Hoover	2-5-1
Weber State	Wildcats	Purple & White	Big Sky	Dick Gwinn	5-5-0
Wesleyan	Cardinals	Red & Black	Little Three	Bill Macdermott	4-4-0
Western Illinois	Leathernecks	Purple & Gold	Independent	Darrell Mudra	9-2-0
Western Kentucky	Hilltoppers	Red & White	Ohio Valley	Jimmy Feix	7-3-0
Wilkes	Colonels	Navy & Gold	Middle Atlantic	Roland Schmidt	4-5-0
Williams	Ephmen	Purple	Little Three	Robert Odell	7-1-0
Wittenberg	Tigers	Red & White	Ohio	Dave Maurer	5-4-0
Wooster	Fighting Scots	Black, Old Gold	Ohio	Robert O'Brien	3-5-0

*Oklahoma forfeited 7 games

National College Football Champions

The NCAA recognizes as unofficial national champion the team selected each year by the AP (poll of writers) and the UPI (poll of coaches). When the polls disagree both teams are listed. The AP poll originated in 1936 and the UPI poll in 1950.

1936	Minnesota	1945	Army	1954	Ohio State, UCLA	1963	Texas
1937	Pittsburgh	1946	Notre Dame	1955	Oklahoma	1964	Alabama
1938	Texas Christian	1947	Notre Dame	1956	Oklahoma	1965	Alabama, Mich. State
1939	Texas A & M	1948	Michigan	1957	Auburn, Ohio State	1966	Notre Dame
1940	Minnesota	1949	Notre Dame	1958	Louisiana State	1967	Southern Calif.
1941	Minnesota	1950	Oklahoma	1959	Syracuse	1968	Ohio State
1942	Ohio State	1951	Tennessee	1960	Minnesota	1969	Texas
1943	Notre Dame	1952	Michigan State	1961	Alabama	1970	Nebraska, Texas
1944	Army	1953	Maryland	1962	Southern Calif.	1971	Nebraska
						1972	Southern Calif.

College Football Coach of the Year
(Football Writers Assn.)

Year	Coach	School	Year	Coach	School
1946	Earl Blaik	Army	1959	Floyd B. Schwartzwalder	Syracuse
1947	H. O. (Fritz) Crisler	Michigan	1960	None picked	
1948	Bennie G. Oosterbaan	Michigan	1961	Paul Bryant	Alabama
1949	Charles B. (Bud) Wilkinson	Univ. of Okla.	1962	John McKay	U.S.C.
1950	Charles Caldwell	Princeton	1963	Darrell Royal	Texas
1951	Charles (Chuck) Taylor	Stanford	1964	Ara Parseghian	Notre Dame
1952	Clarence L. (Biggie) Munn	Mich. State	1965	Tommy Prothro	U.C.L.A.
1953	James M. Tatum	Maryland	1966	Tom Cahill	Army
1954	Henry R. (Red) Sanders	U.C.L.A.	1967	John Pont	Indiana
1955	Hugh Duffy Daughtery	Mich. State	1968	Woody Hayes	Ohio State
1956	Bowden Wyatt	Tennessee	1969	Bo Schembechler	Univ. of Michigan
1957	Wayne Woodrow Hayes	Ohio State	1970	Alex Agase	Northwestern
1958	Paul E. Dietzel	L.S.U.	1971	Bob Devaney	Nebraska
			1972	John McKay	U.S.C.

Heisman Trophy Winners
(Outstanding College Football Player)

1935	Jay Berwanger, Chicago, HB	
1936	Larry Kelley, Yale, E	
1937	Clinton Frank, Yale, QB	
1938	David O'Brien, Tex. Christian, QB	
1939	Nile Kinnick, Iowa, QB	
1940	Tom Harmon, Michigan HB	
1941	Bruce Smith, Minnesota, HB	
1942	Frank Sinkwich, Georgia, HB	
1943	Angelo Bertelli, Notre Dame, QB	
1944	Leslie Horvath, Ohio State, QB	
1945	Felix Blanchard, Army, FB	
1946	Glenn Davis, Army, HB	
1947	John Lujack, Notre Dame, QB	
1948	Doak Walker, SMU, HB	
1949	Leon Hart, Notre Dame, E	
1950	Vic Janowicz, Ohio State, HB	
1951	Richard Kazmaier, Princeton, HB	
1952	Billy Vessels, Oklahoma, HB	
1953	John Lattner, Notre Dame, HB	
1954	Alan Ameche, Wisconsin, FB	
1955	Howard Cassady, Ohio St., HB	
1956	Paul Hornung, Notre Dame, QB	
1957	John Crow, Texas A & M, HB	
1958	Pete Dawkins, Army, HB	
1959	Billy Cannon, La. State, HB	
1960	Joe Bellino, Navy, HB	
1961	Ernest Davis, Syracuse, HB	
1962	Terry Baker, Oregon State, QB	
1963	Roger Staubach, Navy, QB	
1964	John Huarte, Notre Dame, QB	
1965	Mike Garrett, USC, HB	
1966	Steve Spurrier, Florida, QB	
1967	Gary Beban, UCLA, QB	
1968	O. J. Simpson, USC, RB	
1969	Steve Owens, Oklahoma, RB	
1970	Jim Plunkett, Stanford, QB	
1971	Pat Sullivan, Auburn, QB	
1972	Johnny Rodgers, Nebraska, RB-R	

Intercollegiate Rowing Association Regatta
Onondaga Lake, Syracuse, N. Y. (Three miles)

Year	Winner	Time	Year	Winner	Time	Year	Winner	Time
1956	Cornell	16:22.4	1962	Cornell	17:02.9	1968	Penn (A)	6:15.6
1957	Cornell	15:26.6	1963	Cornell	17:24.0	1969	Penn (A)	6:30.4
1958	Cornell	17:12.1	1964	California (A)	6:31.1	1970	Washington (A)	...
1959	Wisconsin	18:01.7	1965	Navy	16:51.3	1971	Cornell (A)	6:06.0
1960	California	15:57.0	1966	Wisconsin	16:03.4	1972	Penn (A)	6:22.6
1961	California	16:49.2	1967	Penn	16:13.9	1973	Wisconsin (A)	6:21.0

(A) Race at 2,000 meters.

National Rowing Championships

Elite Quarter-Mile Singles— Jim Dietz, New York AC.
Veterans Doubles— Cambridge BC.
Senior Four With Coxswain— Syracuse Chargers.
Elite Four— Vesper BC.
Elite Doubles— New York AC.
Elite Pair With Coxswain— Vesper BC.
Elite 150 Lb. Doubles— Undine BC.

Senior Singles— Peter Cortes, Vesper BC.
Elite 150 Lb. With Coxswain— Cambridge BC.
Elite 150 Lb. Pair— New York AC.
Senior Eight— Vesper BC.
Elite Quadruple Sculls— New York AC.
Team Champion— Vesper BC.

Henley Regatta
River Thames, England

Diamond Sculls (Single Sculls)— S. Drea, Ireland def. D. Sturge, Britain.
The Ladies Challenge Plate (Eights)— Harvard Univ. def. D.S.R. Laga, The Netherlands.
Princess Elizabeth Cup (Eights)— Ridley College, Canada def. St. Paul's School, Concord, N.H.
Thames Cup (Eights)— Princeton Univ. def. Thames Tradesmen, Britain.
Silver Goblets and Nickalls Cup (Pairs)— M. Borchelt and R. T. Adams, Potomac BC, United States def. F. Dedecker and P. De Wert, Belgium.

Prince Philip Cup (Fours With Coxswain)— Northeastern Univ. of. Mass. Inst. of Tech.
Britannia Challenge Cup (Fours With Coxswain)— Isis BC, Britain def. Univ. of London.
Stewards Cup (Fours Without Coxswain)— Univ. of London def. Potomac B.C., United States.
Wyfold Cup (Fours Without Coxswain)— Thames Tradesmen, Britain def. Tideway Scullers, Britain.
Grand Challenge Cup (Eights)— Trud Kolomna, USSR def. Northeastern Univ.
Visitors Cup (Four Without Coxswain)— Trinity, Cambridge, Britain def. Exeter Univ., Britain.

Shuffleboard Championships in 1973

National Singles Championship, St. Petersburg Club, March 5-7—Men's Open, Lewis Tansky, St. Petersburg, Fla.; Men's Closed, Bill Bowen, Boynton Beach, Fla.; Women's Open, Mary Eldridge, St. Petersburg, Fla.; Women's Closed, Charlotte Sidway, Clearwater, Fla.
National Doubles Championship, Leesburg, Fla., Jan 22-24 —Men, Jay Snoddy & Bob Litts, Lakeland & St. Petersburg, Fla; Women, Betty Stone & Audrey Haley, Miami & Braden-

ton, Fla.
Summer National Championships, Lakeside, Ohio, July 26-28—Men's Open, Lary Faris, Cincinnati, Ohio; Men's Closed, Ed Kent, Eustis, Fla.; Men's Doubles, Jay Snoddy & Art Davis, Lakeland & Palmetto, Fla.; Women's Open, Dorothy Ellis, Zephyr Hills, Fla.; Women's Closed, Elsie Hawkins, St. Petersburg, Fla.; Women's Doubles, Betty Stone & Bernardine Hines, Miami & Ft. Lauderdale, Fla.

Contract Bridge Championships in 1972-73

Winners of Major Events at 3 National Tournaments
Fall 1972—Spring and Summer 1973
Source: American Contract Bridge League

Fall 1972—Total attendance—11,545 tables

Reisinger Board-a-Match Teams—Steve Goldberg, Marietta, Ga.; Steve Parker, Alexandria, Va.; Steve Robinson, Washington, D.C.; Lou Bluhm, Atlanta, Ga.

Blue Ribbon Pairs—Warren Kornfeld, New City, N.Y.; Richard Khautir, Forest Hills, N.Y.

Life Master Men's Pairs—Marc Jacobus, Fairlawn, N.J.; Les Bart, Silver Spring, Md.

Life Master Women's Pairs—Amalya Kearse, New York, N.Y.; Rhoda Walsh, Beverly Hills, Calif.

Mixed Pairs—John Mohan, Beverly Hills, Calif.; Peggy Sutherlin, San Francisco, Calif.

Spring 1973—Total attendance—8,415 tables

Vanderbilt Knockout Teams—Robert Wolff, Robert Goldman, Robert Hamman, Mark Blumenthal, Dallas, Tex.; Michael Lawrence, Berkeley, Calif.

Men's Teams—John Simon, St. Louis, Mo.; James Jacoby, Richardson, Tex.; Robert Wolff, Dallas, Tex.; Gaylor Kasle, Garey Hayden, Tuscon, Ariz.

Women's Teams—Helen Utegaard, Bethesda, Md.; Terry Michaels, Washington, D.C.; Jo Morse, Silver Spring, Md.; Nancy Gruver, Ellicott City, Md.

Men's Pairs—John E. Kennedy, Jr.; Capt. David A. Hadden, Shreveport, La.

Women's Pairs—Ann Economidy, Manchester, Mo.; Vivian Williamson, Roswell, N.M.

Open Pairs—Michael P. Hoffmann, Minneapolis, Minn.; Jack Rhatigan, Cottage Grove, Minn.

Summer 1973—Total attendance—16,043 tables

Spingold Knockout Teams—A. E. "Bud" Reinhold, Highland Park, Ill.; Edwin B. Kantar, William Eisenberg, Dr. Richard H. Katz, Los Angeles, Calif.; Lawrence Cohen, Chicago, Ill.

Grand National Teams—William Seamon, Miami, Fla.; Russell Arnold, North Miami Beach, Fla.; Robert Sharp, Miami Beach, Fla.; Jane Jaeger, North Bay Village, Fla.; Jim Beery, Richard Pavlicek, Ft. Lauderdale, Fla.

Mixed Teams—Stanley Tomchin, Edith Sacks, Philip Feldesman, New York, N.Y.; Ellen Alfandre, Scarsdale, N.Y.

Life Masters Pairs—Paul T. Swanson, Morgantown, W. Va.; Jack Blair, Tulsa, Okla.

Senior and Advanced Senior Master Pairs—Joel Friedberg, West Hempstead, N.Y.; Harry Looks, Great Neck, N.Y.

1973 World Bridge Team Championship—Guaruja, Brazil—Italy (Giorgio Belladonna, Benito Bianchi, Peitro Forquet, Giuseppe Garabello, Benito Garozzo, Vito Pittola, Sandro C. J. velli, non-playing captain).

Chess

Chess dates back to antiquity. Its exact origin is unknown. The strongest players of their time, and therefore regarded by later generations as world champions, were Francois Philidor, France; Alexandre Deschappelles, France; Louis de la Bourdonnais, France; Howard Staunton, England; Adolph Anderssen, Germany and Paul Morphy, United States. In 1866 Wilhelm Steinitz of Austria defeated Adolph Anderssen and claimed the title of World Champion. The official world champions, since the title was first used follow:

1866-1894 Wilhelm Steinitz, Vienna	1935-1937 Dr. Max Euwe, Holland	1958-1959 Mikhail Botvinnik, USSR
1894-1921 Dr. Emanuel Lasker, Berlin	1937-1946 Dr. Alexander A. Alekhine,	1960-1961 Mikhail Tal, USSR
1921-1927 Jose R. Capablanca, Havana	Paris	1961-1963 Mikhail Botvinnik, USSR
1927-1935 Dr. Alexander A. Alekhine,	1948-1957 Mikhail Botvinnik, USSR	1963-1969 Tigran Petrosian, USSR
Paris	1957-1958 Vassily Smyslov, USSR	1969-1972 Boris Spassky, USSR
		1972 Bobby Fischer, U.S.

United States Champions

1852-1862 Paul Morphy	1894-1897 Jackson Showalter	1944-1946 Arnold S. Denker	1962 Larry Evans
1871-1887 George Mackenzie	1897-1906 Harry Nelson	1946 Samuel Reshevsky	1963-1967 Bobby Fischer
1887-1892 Max Judd	Pillsbury	1948 Herman Steiner	1968 Larry Evans
1892-1894 Simon Lipschultz	1906-1909 Jackson Showalter	1951-1953 Larry Evans	1969-1971 Samuel Reschevsky
1894 Jackson Showalter	1909-1936 Frank J. Marshall	1954 Arthur B. Bisguier	1973 Robert Byrne
1894 Albert B. Hodges	1936-1944 Samuel Reshevsky	1958-1961 Bobby Fischer	

World Pocket Billiards Champions

1931—Ralph Greenleaf	1943—Andrew Ponzi	1955—Irving Crane, Willie Mosconi
1932—Ralph Greenleaf	1944—Willie Mosconi	1956-62—none
1933—Erwin Rudolph	1945—Willie Mosconi	1963—Luther Lassiter
1934—Erwin Rudolph	1946—Irving Crane	1964—Luther Lassiter, Arthur Cranfield
1935—Andrew Ponzi	1947—Willie Mosconi	1965—Joe Balsis
1936—James Caras	1948—Willie Mosconi	1966—Luther Lassiter
1937—Ralph Greenleaf	1949—James Caras	1967—Luther Lassiter
1938—James Caras	1950—Willie Mosconi	1968—Irving Crane
1939—James Caras	1951—Willie Mosconi	1969—none
1940—Andrew Ponzi	1952—Willie Mosconi	1970—Steve Mizerak
1941—Willie Mosconi, Erwin Rudolph	1953—Willie Mosconi	1971—Ray Martin
1942—Irving Crane	1954—none	1972—Steve Mizerak
		1973—Lou Butera

U.S. Open Billiards Championship in 1973

Steve Mizerak won his fourth straight U.S. Open pocket billiards championship by defeating Luther Lassiter in Chicago, Aug. 12, 1973. Mizerak received $6,000 for his victory. Jean Balukas, a 14-year-old from Brooklyn, N.Y., won the woman's title for the second straight year.

National Roller Skating Champions in 1973

Men Singles—Mark Revere, Pontiac, Mich.

Ladies Singles—Natalie Dunn, Bakersfield, Calif.

Junior Men Singles—Jim Collyer, Bellevue, Wash.

Junior Ladies Singles—Robin Dayney, E. Meadow, N.Y.

Senior Mixed Pairs—Abe Blass & April Allen Powell, Houston, Texas.

Junior Mixed Pairs—Raymond Chappatta & Karen Jejia, Summit, Ill.

Senior Men Figures—William Boyd, Seabrook, Md.

Senior Ladies Figures—Deborah Palm, E. Meadow, N.Y.

Junior Men Figures—Philip Smalley, Delanco, N.J.

Junior Ladies Figures—Kathleen O'Brien, Delanco, N.J.

Senior Dance—Joseph Gaudy & Marie Gaudy, Dover, Delaware.

Junior Dance—Carl Siebert & Olivia de Troye, Whittier,

Calif.

Esquire Dance—Donald Benson & Phyllis Benson, Norwood, Mass.

Free Dance—Kerry Cavazzi & Roseanne Franzone, E. Meadow, N.Y.

Speed Events

Senior Men—Danny Butler, Springfield, Mo.

Senior Ladies—Linda Brooks, Irving, Texas.

Junior Men—Tim Small, Hollywood, Fla.

Junior Ladies—Marcia Yager, Cincinnati, Ohio.

Senior Two-Man Relay—Curtis Cook & Steve Torvik, Spokane, Wash.

Senior Two-Lady Relay—Marcia Yager & Brenda Haggard, Cincinnati, Ohio.

American Bowling Congress Championships, 1973

Syracuse, N.Y.

REGULAR DIVISION

Individual

1. Ed Thompson, Denver, Colo. 256, 279, 227 — 762.
2. Bob Chappell, Wichita, Kansas 251, 224, 265 — 740.
3. Virg Enger, Minneapolis, Minn. 234, 247, 247 — 728.

Runners-up — Charles Ginn, Waukegan, Ill. 720; Ralph Quay, Toledo, Ohio 715; Ricky Eckert, Longview, Texas 712; Al Cohn, Chicago, Ill. 711; Tom Schwenzer, Lima, Ohio 707; Al Clark, Syracuse, N.Y. 705; Don Cruzen, St. Louis, 705.

All-Events

1. Ron Woolet, Louisville, Ky. 760, 669, 675 — 2104.
2. Al Cohn, Chicago, Ill. 600, 749, 711 — 2060.
3. Joe Trombetta, Chicago, Ill. 688, 646, 649 — 1983.

Runners-up — Ralph Quay, Toledo, Ohio 1966; Virg Enger, Minneapolis, Minn. 1963; Jay Dishong, Detroit, Mich. 1953; Guy De Luca Jr., Pittsburgh, Pa. 1952; Phil Caparusso, Rockville Centre, N.Y. 1945; Bill Baxter, Reading, Pa. 1943; Tony Ciocco, Kalamazoo, Mich. 1943.

Doubles

1. Jamie Brooks, Houston, Tex. 186, 209, 256 — 651; Jimmie Paine, Houston, Tex. 224, 248, 214 — 686. Aggregate — 1337.
2. (tie) — Rick Musialowski, Buffalo, N.Y. 201, 216, 227 — 644; Bud Schwabl, Buffalo, N.Y. 202, 235, 238 — 675. Aggregate — 1319. Paul McCordic, Houston, Tex. 189, 197, 224 — 610; Peter McCordic, Houston, Tex, 254, 201, 254 — 709. Aggregate — 1319.

Runners-up — Gordy Baer-Al Cohn, Chicago, Ill. 1317; Ray Mazzei-Bob Pajak, Pittsburgh, Pa. 1309; Tim Menge-Tom Menge, Cleveland, Ohio 1303; Tom Kouros-Barry Stjernberg, Chicago, Ill. 1303; Bob Burg Jr.-Don Adcock, Decatur, Ill. 1295; Terry Clemens-Gene Rewers, Toledo, Ohio 1292; Kenneth Speer-Santo Orlando, Darby, Pa. 1291.

Teams

1. Thelmal Masters, Louisville, Ky. — Ronnie Moore 164, 156, 194 — 514; Ray Yocum, 172, 171, 223 — 566; Don Massie, 207, 178, 192-577; Ron Woolet, 259, 224, 277-760; Sam Capshaw, 231, 214, 256-701. Aggregate — 3118.
2. AAA Trucking, Scranton, Pa. — Ross Caruso 192, 190 235 — 617; Ross Runcon 182, 167, 228 — 577; Rick Gannon 213, 233, 193 — 639; Joe Larioni 172, 198, 178 — 548; Bob Bavitz 247, 255, 224 — 726. Aggregate — 3107.

CLASSIC DIVISION

Individuals

1. Nelson Burton Jr., St. Louis, Mo. 289, 212, 223 — 724.
2. James Mack, Hackettstown, N.J. 217, 258, 237 — 712.
3. Norman Grocke, Chicago, Ill. 234, 244, 225 — 703.

Runners-up — Jim McHugh, Newburgh, N.Y. 700; Bill Allen, Maitland, Fla. 695; Jim Stefanich, Joliet, Ill. 695; Dick Weber, St. Louis, Mo. 695; Curt Schmidt, Ft. Wayne, Ind. 684; Bobby Cooper, Houston, Tex. 683; Les Zikes, Chicago, Ill. 677.

All-Events

1. James Mack, Hackettstown, N.J. 625, 657, 712 — 1994.
2. Les Zikes, Chicago, Ill. 667, 648, 677 — 1992.
3. Bill Beach, Sharon, Pa. 642, 711, 636 — 1989.

Runners-up — Denny Torgerson, Des Moines, Iowa 1971; Nelson Burton Jr., St. Louis 1965; Bobby Cooper, Houston, Tex. 1963; Dick Nardozza, Altoona, Pa. 1933; Bill Allen, Maitland, Fla. 1933; Mike Somers, East Meadow, N.Y. 1931; Craig Mueller, Hackensack, N.J. 1928.

Doubles

1. Bobby Cooper, Houston, Tex. 239, 235, 187 — 661; George Pappas, Charlotte, N.C. 186, 247, 245 — 678. Aggregate — 1339.
2. Fred Vitali, Detroit, Mich. 213, 203, 202 — 618; Mike Totsky, Detroit, Mich. 266, 207, 234 — 707. Aggregate — 1325.
3. Sam Guarino, Detroit, Mich. 249, 223, 223 — 695; John Petraglia, Brooklyn, N.Y. 195, 199, 213 — 607. Aggregate — 1302.

Runners-up — Larry Bernstein-Charles Faino, Drexel Hill, Pa. 1297; Rit Carney-Harry Polomaine, Schenectady, N.Y. 1290; Mike Orlovsky-Gus Lampo, Endicott, N.Y. 1279; Bill Archinski-Terry Vaeth, Davis, Calif. 1270; Jim Schroeder-Harry Smith, Rochester, N.Y. 1267; Yoskito Tagawa-Tsueno Suzuki, Tokyo, Japan, 1266; Billy Walden-Gary Fultz, Springfield, Mo. 1264.

Teams

1. Stroh's Beer, Detroit, Mich. — Dale Seavoy 202, 246, 147 — 595; Fred Vitali 206, 225, 209 — 640; Bill Spargo 172, 235, 213 — 620; Harry Campbell 231, 206, 210 — 647; Mike Totsky 166, 202, 180 — 548. Aggregate — 3050.
2. Basch Advertising, New York, N.Y. — Larry Lichstein 191, 203, 215 — 609; Sam Guarino 199, 214, 223 — 636; Dick Battista 167, 183, 203 — 553; John Petraglia 177, 241, 226 — 644; Mike McGrath 175, 238, 183 — 596. Aggregate — 3038.

Other Bowling Championships in 1973

3rd U.S. Open — New York, N.Y. — March 5-10 — Mike McGrath, El Cerrito, Calif. Average 223, prize $7,500. Women (Long Island, N.Y. — May 22-24) Millie Mortorella, Rochester, N.Y. Average 212; prize $4,000.

National Intercollegiate Championships, Syracuse, N.Y. April 15-Doubles — Gary Baker, Northern Colorado U. and Rudy Sedillo, Northern Arizona U. Singles — James Fiore,

Rensselaer Tech.; All-events — Lee Snow, Eastern Michigan Univ.

Invitational Bowling Tournament of the Americas, Miami, Fla. July 17-23 — Men's doubles, Jose Rodriguez — Jorge Zani, Argentina; single, Ron Woolet, United States; all events, Ron Woolet; Women's doubles, Eleanore Becker — Linda Hansen, United States; singles, Linda Hansen; all events, Linda Hansen.

Masters Bowling Tournament Champions

Year	Winner	Runner-up	W.L.	Ave.
1961	Don Carter, St. Louis, Mo	Dick Hoover, St. Louis, Mo	8-1	211-18
1962	Bill Golembiewski, Detroit, Mich	Ron Winger, Los Angeles, Calif.	7-0	223-12
1963	Harry Smith, St. Louis, Mo	Bobby Meadows, Dallas, Tex	7-0	219-3
1964	Billy Welu, St. Louis, Mo.	Harry Smith, Baltimore, Md	7-0	227
1965	Billy Welu, St. Louis, Mo.	Don Ellis, Houston, Tex	9-1	202-12
1966	Bob Strampe, Detroit, Mich	Al Thompson, Cleveland, O.	7-0	219-8
1967	Lou Scalia, Miami, Fla	Bill Johnson, New Orleans, La	7-0	216-9
1968	Pete Tountas, Tucson, Ariz .	Buzz Fazio, Detroit, Mich	9-1	220-15
1969	Jim Chestney, Denver, Colo .	Barry Asher, Costa Mesa, Calif.	10-1	223-2
1970	Don Glover, Bakersfield, Calif	Bob Strampe, Detroit, Mich	9-1	215-10
1971	Jim Godman, Lorain, Ohio	Don Johnson, Akron, Ohio	9-1	229-8
1972	Bill Beach, Sharon, Pa.	Jim Godman, Lorain, Ohio	8-1	220-27
1973	Dave Soutar, Gilroy, Calif.	Dick Ritger, Hartford, Wisc.	7-0	218-61

ALL-TIME RECORDS FOR LEAGUE AND TOURNAMENT PLAY

Type of record	Holder of record	Year	Score	Competition
High team total	Budweiser Beer, St. Louis, Mo	1958	3,858	League
High team game	Hook Grip Five, Lodi, N.J.	1950	1,342	League
High doubles total	Nelson Burton, Jr., Billy Walden, St. Louis.	1970	1,614	Tournament
High doubles game	Tom Dern-Ron Spohn, Columbus, O	1965	587	League
High individual total	Albert Brandt, Lockport, N.Y.	1939	886	League
High all events score	Frank Benkovic, Milwaukee, Wis	1932	2,259	Tournament

RECORD AVERAGES FOR CONSECUTIVE TOURNAMENTS

No. In row	Name of record holder	Span	Games	Average
Two	Steve Nagy, Cleveland, Ohio	1951-52	18	224.09
Three	Steve Nagy, Cleveland, Ohio	1952-53	27	221.02
Four	Bob Strampe, Detroit, Mich	1964-67	48	215.40
Five	Bob Strampe, Detroit, Mich	1964-68	57	215.28
Ten	Bob Strampe, Detroit, Mich	1961-70	111	211.10

OFFICIAL RECORDS OF ANNUAL ABC TOURNAMENTS

Type of record	Holder of record	Tourn. Yr.	Score
High Team Total	Ace Mitchell Shur-Hooks, Akron, Ohio	1966	3,357
High team game	Falstaff Beer, San Antonio, Texas	1958	1,226
High doubles score	John Klares-Steve Nagy, Cleveland, Ohio	1952	1,453
High doubles game	John Gworek-Henry Kmidowski, Buffalo, N.Y.	1946	544
High singles total	Lee Jouglard, Detroit, Mich.	1951	775
High all events score	Jack Winters, Philadelphia, Pa	1962	2,147
High team all events	Falstaff Beer, St. Louis, Mo.	1958	9,608
High life-time pin total	Bill Doehrman, Ft. Wayne, Indiana	1908 to	102,711

BOWLERS WITH SIX OR MORE SANCTIONED 300 GAMES

Elvin Mesger, Sullivan,Mo	25	Howard Holmes, Los Angeles	8	Salvatore Bivona, Paterson, N.J.	6
George Billick, Old Forge, Pa	17	Casey Jones, Plymouth, Wisc.	8	Lou Campi, Dumont, N.J.	6
Dick Weber, St. Louis, Mo.	16	Russell Field, San Jose, Calif.	8	Ed Davis, Milford, N.J.	6
Al Faragalli, Wayne, N.J.	14	Roger Fink, Lodi, Calif.	8	Don Dubro, St. Louis, Mo.	6
Don Carter, Tarzana, Calif.	13	George Pappas, Charlotte, N.C.	8	* Bill Flynn, Cleveland, O.	6
Dave Soutar, Gilroy, Calif.	13	Dennis Wright, Milwaukee	8	Sam Garofalo, St. Louis, Mo	6
Ray Bluth, St. Louis, Mo.	12	Ray Eklund, Milwaukee, Wis.	8	Joe Joseph, Lansing, Mich.	6
Walter Ward, Cleveland, O.	12	Walter King, Detroit, Mich.	8	Pete Kozloski, Dining, Pa	6
*Hank Marino, Milwaukee	11	J. I. Mataluni, Lodi, N.J.	8	Vince Lucci, Trenton, N.J.	6
Frank Clause, Old Forge, Pa.	11	Joe Donato, Schenectady, N.Y.	7	Steve Nagy, Cleveland, O	6
Ed Lubanski, Detroit, Mich.	11	Eddie Botten, Union City, N.J.	7	Frank Pollak, Pittsburgh, Pa	6
Pat Patterson, St. Louis, Mo.	11	Dick Hoover, Akron, O.	7	Robert Pinkalla, Milwaukee	6
Don Johnson, Akron, Ohio	10	Ken McKenzie, Dallas, Texas	7	Harold Schaeffer, St. Louis	6
Boss Bosco, Akron, O	9	Ray Schanen, Milwaukee	7	Harry Smith, Redwood City Calif .	6
Al Savas, Milwaukee, Wis	9	Wayne Pinkalla, Milwaukee	7	Bob Strampe, Detroit, Mich.	6
Lou Foxie, Paterson, N.J.	9	George Pappas, Charlotte	7	Jerry Tharp, St. Louis, Mo	6
Jerry Woji, Stockton, Calif	9	Bob Ramirez, Los Angeles	7	George Tomek, Plymouth, Pa	6
Norm Meyers, St. Louis	9	Don McCune, Munster, Ind.	7	Stephen Tomek, Plymouth Pa	6
Tom Hennessey, St. Louis, Mo	9	Bud Horn, Los Angeles	7		

*Bowled two 300 games in official 3-game-series.

PBA Winter Tour, 1973

Date	Event	Winner	Winner's Share
Jan. 2-6	San Jose Open, San Jose, Calif.	Allie Clarke	$7,500
Jan. 9-13	Don Carter Classic, Los Angeles	Garry Dickinson	7,500
Jan. 17-20	Showboat Invitational, Las Vegas	Barry Asher	11,111
Jan. 22-27	Denver Open	Jay Robinson	6,000
Jan. 30-Feb. 3	King Louie Open, Kansas City	Bobby Knipple	6,000
Feb. 6-10	Lincoln-Mercury Open, New Orleans	Carmen Salvino	10,000
Feb. 13-17	Fair Lanes Open, Baltimore	Dick Ritger	7,000
Feb. 2-24	Winston-Salem Classic	Don McCune	10,000
Feb. 27-Mar. 3	Miller High Life Open, Milwaukee	Don McCune	12,000
Mar. 4-10	BPAA U.S. Open, New York	Mike McGrath	7,500
Mar. 13-17	Ebonite Open, Toledo	Dick Weber	10,000
Mar. 2-24	Andy Granatelli's STP Open, Miami	Dick Ritger	10,000
Mar. 27-31	Firestone Tournament of Champions, Akron	Jim Godman	25,000

Leading PBA Averages in 1972

Name, City	Tournaments	Games	Pinfall	Average
1. Don Johnson, Akron, O.	30	1044	224,763	215.290
2. Johnny Guenther, Seattle, Wash.	21	651	140,135	215.261
3. Nelson Burton Jr., St. Louis, Mo.	29	1010	217,304	215.152
4. Dick Ritger, Hartford, Wis.	23	762	163,765	214.915
5. Early Anthony, Tacoma, Wash.	23	786	168,843	214.813
6. Larry Laub, San Francisco, Cal.	26	790	169,431	214.470
7. Curt Schmidt, Ft. Wayne, Ind.	32	1137	242,987	213.709
8. Jim Godman, Lorain, O.	31	1020	217,806	213.535
9. George Pappas, Charlotte, N.C.	28	845	179,962	212.973
10. Barry Asher, Costa Mesa, Cal.	32	1020	217,140	212.882
11. Mike Lemongello, Islip, N.Y.	23	646	137,394	212.684
12. Don McCune, Munster, Ind.	28	840	178,642	212.669
13. Roy Buckley, Columbus, O.	32	930	197,690	212.570
14. Dick Weber, St. Louis, Mo.	24	786	166,991	212.457
15. Johnny Petraglia, Brooklyn, N.Y.	24	712	150,996	212.073
16. Mike McGrath, El Cerrito, Cal.	29	899	190,461	211.859
17. Norm Meyers, St. Louis, Mo.	21	613	129,982	212.042
18. Allie Clarke, Akron, O.	30	812	171,973	211.789
19. Marty Piraino, Syracuse, N.Y.	18	560	118,568	211.729
20. Gary Mage, Seattle, Wash.	16	447	94,538	211.494
21. Teata Semiz, River Edge, N.J.	22	676	142,955	211.472
22. Bobby Meadows, Houston, Tex.	19	556	117,554	211.428
23. Bill Beach, Sharon, Pa.	31	909	192,095	211.326
24. Bill Johnson, New Orleans, La.	17	502	106,083	211.321
25. Carmen Salvino, Chicago, Ill.	29	801	169,190	211.223

Leading PBA Averages by Years

Year	Name	Tournaments	Average	Year	Name	Tournaments	Average
1962	Don Carter, St. Louis, Mo..	25	212.844	1968	Jim Stefanich, Joliet, Ill. ...	33	211.895
1963	Billy Hardwick, Louisville, Ky.	26	210.346	1969	Billy Hardwick, Louisville, Ky.	33	212.957
1964	Ray Bluth, St. Louis, Mo...	27	210.512	1970	Nelson Burton, Jr., St.		
1965	Dick Weber, St. Louis, Mo.	19	211.895		Louis, Mo.	32	214.908
1966	Wayne Zahn, Atlanta, Ga. .	27	208.663	1971	Don Johnson, Akron, O. ...	31	213.977
1967	Wayne Zahn, Atlanta, Ga. .	29	212.142	1972	Don Johnson, Akron, O.	30	215.290

PBA Leading Money Winners

Total winnings are from PBA, ABC Masters and BPAA All-Star tournaments only, and do not include numerous other tournaments nor earnings from special television shows and matches.

Year	Player	Total	Year	Player	Total
1959	Dick Weber	$7,672	1966	Wayne Zahn	$54,720
1960	Don Carter	22,525	1967	Dave Davis	54,165
1961	Dick Weber	26,280	1968	Jim Stefanich	67,375
1962	Don Carter	49,972	1969	Billy Hardwick	64,160
1963	Dick Weber	46,333	1970	Mike McGrath	52,049
1964	Bob Strampe	33,592	1971	Johnny Petraglia	85,065
1965	Dick Weber	47,674	1972	Don Johnson	56,648

The $100,000 Firestone Tournament of Champions

This is professional bowling's richest tournament and has been held each year since its inception in 1965, in Akron, Ohio, the home of the Professional Bowlers Association. First prize is $25,000.

Year	Winner	Year	Winner	Year	Winner	Year	Winner
1965	Billy Hardwick	1967	Jim Stefanich	1969	Jim Godman	1971	Johnny Petraglia
1966	Wayne Zahn	1968	Dave Davis	1970	Don Johnson	1972	Mike Durbin .
						1973	Jim Godman

Women's International Bowling Congress Champions

Year	Individual	All Events	Two Woman Teams		Five-Woman Teams
1967	Glorian Paeth, Pt. Huron, Mich. 652	Carol Miller, Milwaukee, Wisc. .,.... 1,862	Elaine Liburdi-Joan Oleske, Union City & Lyndhurst, N.J.	1,252	The Orphans, Los Angeles 2,970
1968	Norma Parks, Raytown, Md 691	Janice Reichley, Waco, Tex 1,889	Pauline Stickler-Mary Lou Graham, Miami	1,250	Hudepohl Beer, Cincinnati 2,923
1969	Joan Bender, Arvada, Colo 690	Helen Duval, Berkeley, Calif 1,927	Gloria Bouvia, Portland, Ore.-Judy Cook, Grandview, Mo.	1,315	Fitzpatrick Chevrolet, Concord, Calif 2,986
1970	Dorothy Fothergill N. Attleboro,Mass. 695	Dorothy Fothergill ... 1,984	Gloria Bouvia, Portland, Ore–Judy Cook, Kansas City Mo.	1,256	Parker-Fothergill Pro Shop, Cranston, R.I. 3,034
1971	Mary Scruggs, Richmond, Va...... 698	Lorrie Koch, Carpentersville, Ill. .. 1,840	Dorothy Fothergill, N. Attleboro, Mass. Mildred Martorella, Rochester, N.Y.....	1,263	Koenig & Strey Real Estate, Wilmette, Ill 2,891
1972	D. D. Jacobson, Playa Del Rey,Calif. .. 737	Mildred Martorella, Rochester, N.Y. 1,877	Judy Roberts & Betty Remmick, Denver, Lakewood, Colo.	1,247	Angeltown Creations, Placentia, Calif. 2,838
1973	Bobbie Buffaloe, Costa Mesa, Calif. 706	Toni Calvery, Midwest City, Okla.. 1,910	Dorothy Forthergill, N. Attleboro, Mass. & Mildred Martorella, Rochester, N.Y.....	1,238	Fitzpatrick Chevrolet, Concord, Calif. 2,897

RECORDS OF 300 GAMES IN WIBC SANCTIONED PLAY

1970-71 – Retta Acuff, Ellettsville, Ind.; Toni Calvery, Midwest City, Okla.; Beverly Clancy, Portland, Ore.; Sandy Conway, Stockton, Calif.; Georgiena Eakins, Warren, Ohio; Rose Guss, Glenview, Ill.; Joan McRae, Northridge, Calif.; Donna Myers, Akron, Ohio; Beverly Ortner, Tucson, Ariz.; Jeanene Painter, Pocatello, Idaho; Maudelene Reynolds, Emporia, Kan.; Patricia Robinette, Louisville, Ky.; Patty Schneider, Lubbock, Texas; Eloise Van Geest, Grandville, Mich.; Barbara Ziegelmann, Colfax, Calif.

1971-72 – Marilyn Bourbonais, Wauwatosa, Wis.; Bernita Cade, Mahomet, Ill.; Barbara Fincel, Phoenix, Ariz.; Sharon Gilder, Richmond, B.C., Canada; Arlene Hardebeck, Covington, Ky.; Maureen Harris, Madison, Wis.; Mona Jackson, Houston, Texas; Pat Jinks, Houston, Texas; Linda Kaiser, Springfield, Mo.; Marge Lewandowski, Sterling Heights, Mich.; Betty Mivelaz, Tujunga, Calif.; Esmeralda Munden, Honolulu, Hawaii;

Vickie Myers, Sunland, Calif.; Nicola Petersen, El Paso, Texas; Helen Radtke, Massillon, Ohio; Dorothy Rumple, Rockford, Ill.; Beverly Russell, Sturgis, S.D.; Elizabeth Welch, Nyack, N.Y.; Diane Wilhelm, Cincinnati, Ohio; Jean Worthy, Norwalk, Calif.

1972-73 – Helen Gilkerson, Lexington, Ky.; Connie Graham, Victorville, Calif.; Rita Justice, Wilmington, Del.; Barbara Keicher, Depew, N.Y.; Cindy Kimbirauskas, Lansing, Mich.; Joan Lilly, Covington, Ky.; Paula Martin, Houston, Texas; Phyllis Max, Toledo, Ohio; Nancy Mazzier, Weed, Calif.; Dorothy McMullen, Madison, Ill.; Jean Nash, Toledo, Ohio; Marge Pacanowski, Westfield, N.Y.; Joan Ray, Yuma, Ariz.; Barbara Skokan, Perth Amboy, N.J.; Gaylene Suedbeck, Slayton, Minn.; Katherine Thompkins, Seattle, Wash.; Val Tridico, Mansfield, Ohio; Bonnie Triptow, Taylorsville, Utah; Kenda Williams, Amarillo, Texas; Susan Zaluk, Garwood, N.J.

World Swimming Records

As of Sept. 10, 1973
Effective June 1, 1969, FINA will recognize only records made over a 50-meter course.

MEN'S FREESTYLE

Distance	Time	Holder	Country	Where made	Date
100 Meters	0:51.22	Mark Spitz	U.S.A.	Munich, W. Germany	Sept. 3, 1972
200 Meters	1:52.78	Mark Spitz	U.S.A.	Munich, W. Germany	Aug. 29, 1972
400 Meters	3:58.18	Rick DeMont	U.S.A.	Belgrade, Yugo.	Sept. 6, 1973
800 Meters	8:17.6	Stephen Holland	Australia	Brisbane, Aust.	Aug. 5, 1973
1,500 Meters	15:31.85	Stephen Holland	Australia	Belgrade, Yugo.	Sept. 8, 1973

MEN'S BREASTSTROKE

100 Meters	1:04.02	John Hencken	U.S.A.	Belgrade, Yugo.	Sept. 4, 1973
200 Meters	2:19.28	David Wilkie	Gt. Britain	Belgrade, Yugo.	Sept. 6, 1973

MEN'S BUTTERFLY

100 Meters	0:54.27	Mark Spitz	U.S.A.	Munich, W. Germany	Aug. 31, 1972
200 Meters	2:00.07	Mark Spitz	U.S.A.	Munich, W. Germany	Aug. 28, 1972

MEN'S BACKSTROKE

100 Meters	0:56.30	Roland Matthes	E. Germany	Moscow	Apr. 8, 1972
200 Meters	2:01.87	Roland Matthes	E. Germany	Belgrade, Yugo.	Sept. 8, 1973

MEN'S INDIVIDUAL MEDLEY

200 Meters	2:07.17	Gunnar Larsson	Sweden	Munich, W. Germany	Sept. 3, 1972
400 Meters	4:30.81	Gary Hall	U.S.A.	Chicago, Ill.	Aug. 3, 1972

MEN'S FREESTYLE RELAYS

400 M. (4x100)	3:26.42	Nat'l Team (Edgar, Murphy, Heidenreich, Spitz)	U.S.A.	Munich, W. Germany	Aug. 28, 1972
800 M. (4x200)	7:33.22	Nat'l Team (Krumpholz, Backhaus, Klatt, Montgomery)	U.S.A.	Belgrade, Yugo.	Sept. 7, 1973

MEN'S MEDLEY RELAYS

400 M. (4x100)	3:48.16	Nat'l Team (Stamm, Bruce, Spitz, Heidenreich)	U.S.A.	Munich, W. Germany	Sept. 4, 1972

WOMEN'S FREESTYLE

100 Meters	0:57.54	Kornelia Ender	E. Germany	Belgrade, Yugo.	Sept. 9, 1973
200 Meters	2:03.56	Shane Gould	Australia	Munich, W. Germany	Sept. 1, 1972
400 Meters	4:18.07	Kenna Rothhammer	U.S.A.	Louisville, Ky.	Aug. 22, 1973
800 Meters	8:52.97	Novella Calligaris	Italy	Belgrade, Yugo.	Sept. 9, 1973
1,500 Meters	16:54.14	Jo Harshbarger	U.S.A.	Louisville, Ky.	Aug., 1973

WOMEN'S BREASTSTROKE

100 Meters	1:13.58	Cathy Carr	U.S.A.	Munich, W. Germany	Sept. 2, 1972
200 Meters	2:38.5	Catie Ball	U.S.A.	Los Angeles, Calif.	Aug. 26, 1968

WOMEN'S BUTTERFLY

100 Meters	1:03.34	Mayumi Aoki	Japan	Munich, W. Germany	Sept. 1, 1972
200 Meters	2:13.76	Rosemarie Kother	E. Germany	Belgrade, Yugo.	Sept. 8, 1973

WOMEN'S BACKSTROKE

100 Meters	1:04.99	Ulrika Richter	E. Germany	Belgrade, Yugo.	Sept. 4, 1973
200 Meters	2:19.19	Melissa Belote	U.S.A.	Munich, W. Germany	Sept. 4, 1972

WOMEN'S INDIVIDUAL MEDLEY

200 Meters	2:23.07	Shane Gould	Australia	Munich, W. Germany	Aug. 28, 1972
400 Meters	4:57.51	Gudren Wegner	E. Germany	Belgrade, Yugo.	Sept. 6, 1973

WOMEN'S FREESTYLE RELAYS

400 M. (4x100)	3:52.43	Nat'l Team (Ender, Eife, Hubner, Eichner)	E. Germany	Belgrade, Yugo.	Sept. 8, 1973

WOMEN'S MEDLEY RELAYS

400 M. (4x100)	4:16.84	Nat'l Team (Richter, Vogel, Kother, Ender)	E. Germany	Belgrade, Yugo.	Sept. 4, 1973

Swimming Championships in 1973

National AAU Short Course Championship

Cincinnati, Ohio, Apr. 5-7, 1973

Men

100 Yd. Freestyle—Ken Knox, Ft. Lauderdale. Time—0:45.3.
200 Yd. Freestyle—Tim McDonnell, Ladera Oaks AC. Time—1:40.0.
500 Yd. Freestyle—Jack Tingley, USC. Time—4:25.9.
1,650 Yd. Freestyle—Jack Tingley. Time—15:19.4.
100 Yd. Backstroke—John Naber, Univ. of Calif. Time—0:51.4.
200 Yd. Backstroke—John Naber. Time—1:50.5.
100 Yd. Breaststroke—Mark Chatfield, USC. Time—0:57.4.
200 Yd. Breaststroke—Rick Colella, Univ. of Washington. Time—2:03.2.
100 Yd. Butterfly—Bruce Roberston, Canada. Time—0:49.6.
200 Yd. Butterfly—Robin Backhaus, Marin AC. Time—1:49.6.
200 Yd. Individual Medley—Steve Furniss, USC. Time—1:51.6.
400 Yd. Individual Medley—Thomas Szuba, Michigan. Time—3:57.8.

Women

100 Yd. Freestyle—Shirley Babashoff, Fountain Valley, Calif. Time—0:52.2.
200 Yd. Freestyle—Keena Rothhammer, Santa Clara. Time—1:50.5.
500 Yd. Freestyle—Keena Rothhammer. Time—4:52.5.
1,650 Yd. Freestyle—Shane Gould, Australia. Time—16:46.7.

100 Yd. Backstroke—Linda Simpson, Conejo SA. Time—0:58.5.
200 Yd. Backstroke—Melissa Belote, Solotar SC. Time—2:05.5.
100 Yd. Breaststroke—Cathy Carr, Univ. of New Mexico. Time—1:06.1.
200 Yd. Breaststroke—Lynn Colella, Totem Lake SC. Time—2:20.6.
100 Yd. Butterfly—Deena Deardruff, Cincinnati. Time—0:56.4.
200 Yd. Butterfly—Shane Gould. Time—2:02.7.
200 Yd. Individual Medley—Leslie Cliff, Canada. Time—2:06.8.
400 Yd. Individual Medley—Shane Gould. Time—4:27.1.

Diving—Men

1-Meter Springboard—Tim Moore, Ron O'Brien DS. 501.81 pts.
3-Meter Springboard—Phil Boggs, U.S. Air Force. 531.75 pts.
10-Meter Platform—Steve McFarland, Hurricane SC. 460.77 pts.

Diving—Women

1-Meter Springboard—Cynthia Potter, Gatorade SC. 431.88 pts.
3-Meter Springboard—Cynthia Potter. 486.75 pts.
10-Meter Platform—Debby Lipman, Phillips 66. 354.45 pts.

1973 NCAA Championships

Knoxville, Tenn., Mar. 22-24, 1973

50 Yd. Freestyle—John Trembley, Tenn. Time—0:20.3.
100 Yd. Freestyle—John Trembley. Time—0:45.0.
200 Yd. Freestyle—Jim McConica, Southern Calif. Time—1:39.6.
500 Yd. Freestyle—John Kinsella, Indiana. Time—4:27.6.
1,650 Yd. Freestyle—John Kinsella. Time—15:29.2.
100 Yd. Backstroke—Mike Stamm, Indiana. Time—0:50.9.
200 Yd. Backstroke—Mike Stamm. Time—1:50.6.
100 Yd. Breaststroke—John Hencken, Stanford. Time—0:57.1.

200 Yd. Breaststroke—David Wilkie, Miami. Time—2:03.4.
100 Yd. Butterfly—John Trembley. Time—0:48.7.
200 Yd. Butterfly—Gary Hall, Indiana. Time—1:58.5.
200 Yd. Individual Medley—Steve Furniss, Southern Calif. Time—1:51.4.
400 Yd. Individual Medley—Steve Furniss. Time—3:55.2.
1-Meter Diving—Tim Moore, Ohio State. 487.90 pts.
3-Meter Diving—Tim Moore. 539.61 pts.
Team Champion—Indiana.

World Swimming Championships

Belgrade, Yugoslavia, Sept. 4-9, 1973

Men

100-Meter Freestyle—Jim Montgomery, United States. Time—0:51.70.
200-Meter Freestyle—Jim Montgomery. Time—1:53.02.
400-Meter Freestyle—Rick DeMont, United States. Time—3:58.18.
1,500-Meter Freestyle—Steve Holland, Australia. Time—15:31.85.
100-Meter Butterfly—Bruce Robertson, Canada. Time—0:55.69.
200-Meter Butterfly—Robin Backhaus, United States. Time—2:03.32.
100-Meter Breaststroke—John Hencken, United States. Time—1:04.02.
200-Meter Breaststroke—David Wilkie, Britain. Time—2:19.28.
100-Meter Backstroke—Roland Matthes, E. Germany. Time—0:57.47.
200-Meter Backstroke—Roland Matthes. Time—2:01.87.
200-Meter Individual Medley—Gunnar Larsson, Sweden. Time—2:08.36.
400-Meter Individual Medley—Amdras Hargitay, Hungary. Time—4:31.11.
400-Meter Freestyle Relay—United States. Time—3:27.18.
800-Meter Freestyle Relay—United States. Time—7:33.22.
100-Meter Medley Relay—United States. Time—3:49.49.
Springboard Diving—Phil Boggs, United States. 618.57 pts.
10-Meter Platform Diving—Klaus Dibiasi, Italy. 559.53 pts.
Water Polo—Hungary.

Women

100-Meter Freestyle—Kornelia Ender, E. Germany. Time—0:57.54.
200-Meter Freestyle—Keena Rothhammer, United States. Time—2:04.99.
400-Meter Freestyle—Heather Greenwood, United States. Time—4:20.28.
800-Meter Freestyle—Novella Calligaris, Italy. Time—8:52.97.
100-Meter Backstroke—Ulrike Richter, E. Germany. Time—1:05.42.
200-Meter Backstroke—Melissa Belote, United States. Time—2:20.52.
100-Meter Breaststroke—Renate Vogel. E. Germany. Time—1:13.74.
200-Meter Breaststroke—Renate Vogel. Time—2:40.01.
100-Meter Butterfly—Kornelia Ender, E. Germany. Time—1:02.53.
200-Meter Butterfly—Rosemarie Kother, E. Germany. Time—2:13.76.
400-Meter Individual Medley—Gudren Wegner, E. Germany. Time—4:57.51.
400-Meter Freestyle Relay—E. Germany. Time—3:52.43.
400-Meter Medley Relay—E. Germany. Time—4:16.84.
Platform Diving—Ulrika Knape, Sweden. 406.77 pts.

Gold Medals

United States, 15; E. Germany, 13; Italy, Hungary, 2.

Black Sports Hall of Fame

(chosen by Black Sports magazine)

Football—Jim Brown, Dr. Brud Holland, Herb McDonald, Marion Motley, Fritz Pollard, Paul Robeson, Buddy Young.
Baseball—Roy Campanella, Roberto Clemente, Martin Dihigo, Larry Doby, Monte Irvin, Willie Mays, Minnie Minoso, Satchell Paige, Jackie Robinson.
Basketball—Elgin Baylor, Wilt Chamberlain, Chuck Cooper, Dr. E. B. Henderson, Bill Russell.

Track and Field—Cleveland Abbot, Bob Beamon, Harrison Dillard, Rafer Johnson, Ralph Metcalfe, Jesse Owens, Eulace Peacock, Wilma Rudolph, Willye White.
Boxing—Muhammad Ali, Henry Armstrong, Joe Louis, Ray Robinson, Jose Torres.
Tennis—Althea Gibson, Dr. Robert Johnson.
Golf—Charlie Sifford.

Rifle and Pistol Individual Championships in 1973

Source: National Rifle Association of America

National Rifle & Pistol Championships (Outdoor Conventional)

Pistol—SFC Hershel L. Anderson, USA, Ft. Benning, GA, 2657-139X.
Civilian Pistol—Ralph O. Thompson, New Braunfels, TX, 2630-117X.
Woman Pistol—SFC Barbara J. Hile, USA, Ft. Benning, GA, 2567-72X.
Senior Pistol—Huelet L. Benner, Tampa, FL, 2587-94X.
Police Pistol—Elwyn M. Burnett, Mich. State Police, 2623-109X.
Smallbore Rifle Prone—MAJ Lones W. Wigger, Jr., USA, Ft. Benning, GA, 6396-545X.
Woman Smallbore Rifle Prone—Schuyler Helbing, Ft. Worth, TX, 6382-498X.
Jr. Smallbore Rifle Prone—Kevin B. Richards, Valley Stream, NY, 6393-494X.
Civilian Smallbore Rifle Prone—Thomas J. Whitaker, Belmont, CA, 6395-561X.
Sr. Smallbore Rifle Prone—George J. Stidworthy, Jr., Prescott, AZ, 6390-500X.
Smallbore Rifle Position—MAJ Lones W. Wigger, Jr., USA, Ft. Benning, GA, 3154-179X.
Woman Smallbore Rifle Position—Janet S. Hays, Cincinnati,
Civilian Smallbore Rifle Position—Ronald N. Plumb, Vienna, VA, 3118-154X.

Sr. Smallbore Rifle Position—Arrell E. Pearsall, Hempstead, NY, 3036-133X.
High Power Champion—Ronald G. Troyer, Williamsfield, OH, 1573-61X.
Match Rifle & Civilian Champion—Ronald G. Troyer, 1573-61X.
Match Rifle Service Champion—CDR Chas. F. Schroeder, USNR, Topsfield, Mass., 1542-40X.
Match Rifle Sr. Champion—Harold L. Slocum, Oakville, CT, 1526-36X.
Match Rifle Woman Champion—Pauline Tubb, Canadian, TX, 1500-36X.
Match Rifle Jr. Champion—G. Daniel Tubb, Canadian, TX, 1560-53X.
Service Rifle Champion—SSGT Arpail J. Gapol, USA, Ft. Benning, GA, 1564-47X.
Service Rifle Civilian, Jr. & Collegiate Champion—Lee Deneke, Alexandria, VA, 1513-26X.
Service Rifle Sr. Champion—MSGT Garritt H. Stekeur, NGUS, Latham, NY, 1531-46X.
Service Rifle Woman Champion—SP5 Joanne R. Stawski, USA, Ft. Benning, GA, 1548-49X.
USAR, Trumbull, CT, 1557-52X.

U.S. NRA International Championships

English Match—CPT Margaret Murdock, USAR, Topeka, KA, 1783.
Smallbore 3-Position—CPT John H. Writer, USAR, Clarendon Hills, IL, 3467.
Air Rifle—GY/SGT J. F. Boswell, USMC, Quantico, VA, 371.
Free Rifle 300 Meter—MAJ Lones W. Wigger, Jr., USA, Ft. Benning, GA, 2227.
Army Rifle—SGT David Kimes, USMC, Huntington Beach, CA, 565.
Running Boar—SFC Charles D. Davis, USA, Ft. Benning, GA, 1658.
Running Boar Mixed—SFC Charles D. Davis, USA, Ft. Benning, GA, 372.

Rapid Fire Pistol—SFC James H. McNally, USA, Ft. Benning, GA, 1750.
Air Pistol—CWO Francis A. Higginson, USMC, Placerville, CA, 382.
Center Fire Pistol—CWO Francis A. Higginson, 1770.
Free Pistol—Arnold Vitarbo, San Antonio, TX, 1667.
Standard Pistol—SFC Harland Rennolds, USA, Ft. Benning, GA, 1721.
Standard Rifle Prone—MAJ Bruce A. Meredith, USAR, Spartanburg, SC, 1778.
Standard Rifle 3-Position—MAJ John H. Writer, USAR, Clarendon Hills, IL, 1709.
Clay Pigeon—Frank Little, Mechanicsburg, Pa., 294.
International Skeet—Robert Rodale, Emmaus, Pa., 291.

National Indoor Rifle & Pistol Championships

Rifle—CWO3 David I. Boyd, USMC, Quantico, VA, 799.
Woman Rifle—Tricia Foster, Columbus, GA, 796.
Pistol—WO Jimmie R. Dorsey, USMCR, Spokane, WA, 888.

Woman Pistol—SFC Barbara J. Hile, USA, Ft. Benning, GA, 855.

National Intercollegiate Rifle & Pistol Championships

Conventional Rifle—Jonathan C. Jones, UCLA, 298.
Woman Conventional Rifle—Mary M. Keys, E. Tenn. State, 296.
International Rifle—Mary M. Keys, 293.
Woman Int'l Rifle—Mary M. Keys, 293.

Conventional Pistol—J. Michael Jacobs, USNA, 864.
Woman Conventional Pistol—Elizabeth C. Gathright, Univ. of VA, 814.
International Pistol—John S. Miller, U. of Nev., 543.
Woman Int'l Pistol—Elizabeth C. Gathright, 505.

World Horseshoe Pitching Champions

Year	Champion	W.	L.	Ringer %	Year	Champion	W.	L.	Ringer %
1964	Harold Reno, Sabina, Ohio	32	3	84.1	1969	Dan Kuchcinski, Erie, Pa.	35	0	84.7
1965	Elmer Hohl, Wellesley, Can.	32	3	84.6	1970	Dan Kuchcinski, Erie, Pa.	34	1	84.9
1966	Curt Day, Frankfort, Ind.	26	2	86.6	1971	Curt Day, Frankfort, Ind.	35	0	85.0
1967	Dan Kuchcinski, Erie, Pa.	34	1	84.4	1972	Elmer Hohl, Wellesley, Can.	33	2	86.0
1968	Elmer Hohl, Wellesley, Ont.	35	0	88.5	1973	Elmer Hohl, Wellesley, Can.	32	3	83.5

Year	Ladies champion	Ringer %	Junior Champion	Ringer %
1966	Vicki (Chapelle) Winston, Lamonte, Mo.	72.5	Mark Seibold, Huntington, Ind.	75.6
1967	Vicki (Chapelle) Winston, Lamonte, Mo.	73.6	Farron Eisemann, Riverton, Wyo	73.6
1968	Lorraine Thomas, Lockport, N.Y.	74.6	Farron Eisemann, Riverton, Wyo	78.5
1969	Vicki (Chapelle) Winston, Lamonte, Mo.	79.6	Mark Seibold, Huntington, Ind.	83.7
1970	Ruth Hangen, Buffalo, N.Y.	72.0	Bill Holland, Indianapolis, Ind	79.2
1971	Ruth Hangen, Buffalo, N.Y.	73.4	Walter Ray Williams, Eureka, Calif.	86.3
1972	Ruth Hangen, Buffalo, N.Y.	76.6	Walter Ray Williams, Eureka, Calif.	89.2
1973	Ruth Hangen, Getzville, N.Y.	79.6	Jeffrey Williams, Eureka, Calif.	85.5

National AAU Weightlifting Championships

Williamsburg, Va., June 9-10, 1973

(Competition consisted of 2 lifts—snatch and clean and jerk).

114.5 lbs.—Donald Warner, York Barbell Club, 391.25 lbs.
123.5 lbs.—Dwight Tamanaha, Los Angeles YMCA, 452 lbs.
132 lbs.—Roy Moore, York Barbell Club, 518 lbs.
148.75 lbs.—Dan Cantore, Golden Gate WLC, 600.75 lbs.
165.25 lbs.—Fred Lowe, York Barbell Club, 694 lbs.

181.75 lbs.—Mike Karchut, Sayre Park, Calumet City, Ill., 694.25 lbs.
198.25 lbs.—Phil Grippaldi, York Barbell Club, 716.5 lbs.
242 lbs.—Bob Bednarski, York Barbell Club, 749.25 lbs.
Superheavyweight—Jacob Stefan, Los Angeles YMCA, 776.25 lbs.

Boxing Champions by Classes

As of Sept. 15, 1973

Heavyweight................ George Foreman, Hayward, Calif.
Light-Heavyweight (175 lbs.) Bob Foster, Wash. D.C.
Middleweight (160 lbs.)...... Carlos Monzon, Argentina
Welterweight (147 lbs.)...... Jose Napoles, Mexico City
Jr. Welterweight (140 lbs.) ... Antonio Cervantes, Colombia

Lightweight (135 lbs.)...... Roberto Duran, Panama
Junior Lightweight (130 lbs.) Kuniaki Shibata, Japan
Featherweight (126 lbs.)..... Vacant
Bantamweight (118 lbs.)..... Romero Anaya, Mexico
Flyweight (112 lbs.)......... Venice Borkorsor, Thailand

Ring Champions by Years

*Abandoned title

HEAVYWEIGHTS

1882-1892	John L. Sullivan (A)
1892-1897	James J. Corbett (B)
1897-1899	Robert Fitzsimmons
1899-1905	James J. Jeffries (C)
1905-1906	Marvin Hart
1906-1908	Tommy Burns
1908-1915	Jack Johnson
1915-1919	Jess Willard
1919-1926	Jack Dempsey
1926-1928	Gene Tunney*
1928-1930	Vacant
1930-1932	Max Schmeling
1932	Jack Sharkey
1933	Primo Carnera
1934	Max Baer
1935-1936	James J. Braddock
1937-1949	Joe Louis*
1949-1951	Ezzard Charles
1951-1952	Joe Walcott
1952-1956	Rocky Marciano*
1956-1959	Floyd Patterson
1959	Ingemar Johansson
1960-1962	Floyd Patterson
1962-1963	Sonny Liston
1964-1967	Cassius Clay* (Muhammad Ali) (D)
1970-1973	Joe Frazier
1973	George Foreman

(A) London Prize Ring (bare knuckle champion).
(B) First Marquis of Queensberry Champion.
(C) Jeffries abandoned the title (1905) and designated Marvin Hart and Jack Root as logical contenders and agreed to referee a fight between them, the winner to be declared champion. Hart defeated Root in 12 rounds (1905) and in turn was defeated by Tommy Burns (1906) who immediately laid claim to the title. Jack Johnson defeated Burns (1908) and was recognized as champion. He abandoned the title by defeating Jeffries in an attempted comeback (1910).
(D) Title declared vacant by the World Boxing Assn. and other groups in 1967 after Clay's refusal to fulfill his military obligation.

LIGHT HEAVYWEIGHTS

1903.	Jack Root, George Gardner
1903-1905	Bob Fitzsimmons
1905-1912	Philadelphia Jack O'Brien*
1912-1916	Jack Dillon
1916-1920	Battling Levinsky
1920-1922	Georges Carpentier
1922	Gene Tunney (outpointed Levinsky and gained American title)
1922	Harry Greb (outpointed Tunney for American title)
1923	Battling Siki (knocked out Carpentier for world title)
1923	Gene Tunney* (outpointed Greb)
1923-1925	Mike McTigue (outpointed Siki for world title)
1925	Paul Berlenbach (outpointed McTigue)
1926-1927	Jack Delaney* (outpointed Berlenbach)
1927-1929	Tommy Loughran* (outpointed McTigue)
1930-1934	Maxey Rosenbloom (outpointed Jimmy Slattery recognized as champion by the New York State Athletic Commission. National Boxing Association vacated Rosenbloom's title)
1934-1935	Bob Olin (outpointed Rosenbloom, recognized in New York as champion)
1935-1939	John Henry Lewis*
1939	Melio Bettina (defeated Jack Fox in elimination tournament to gain title vacated by Lewis)
1939-1941	Billy Conn*
1941	Anton Christoforidis (won NBC elimination tourney for title)
1941-1949	Gus Lesnevich, Freddie Mills
1949-1950	Freddie Mills
1950-1952	Joey Maxim
1953-1960	Archie Moore
1961	Harold Johnson (NBA): Archie Moore (New York, Mass.)
1962-1963	Harold Johnson
1963-1965	Willie Pastrano
1965-1966	Jose Torres
1966-1968	Dick Tiger
1968	Bob Foster

MIDDLEWEIGHTS

1884-1891	Jack "Nonpareil" Dempsey
1891-1897	Bob Fitzsimmons*
1897-1907	Tommy Ryan*
1907-1908	Stanley Ketchel, Billy Papke
1908-1910	Stanley Ketchel
1911-1913	Claimed by Billy Papke, Frank Klaus, Mike Gibbons, Ed McGoorty and George Chip
1913	Frank Klaus, George Chip
1914-1917	Al McCoy
1917-1920	Mike O'Dowd
1920-1923	Johnny Wilson
1923-1926	Harry Greb
1926-1931	Tiger Flowers, Mickey Walker
1931-1932	Gorilla Jones (NBA), Ben Jeby (New York)
1932-1937	Marcel Thil (NBA)
1933	Lou Brouillard (New York). Vince Dundee (New York)
1934	Teddy Yarosz (New York)
1935	Babe Risko (New York)
1936-1937	Freddie Steele (NBA and New York)
1938	Al Hostak (NBA), Solly Krieger (NBA) Fred Apostoli (New York
1939-1940	Al Hostak (NBA)
1939	Fred Apostoli (New York), Ceferino Garcia (New York)
1940	Tony Zale (NBA), Ken Overlin (New York)
1941	Tony Zale (NBA), Billy Soose (New York)*
1942-1947	Tony Zale
1947-1948	Rocky Graziano
1948	Tony Zale, Marcel Cerdan
1949	Marcel Cerdan, Jake LaMotta
1950	Jake LaMotta
1951	Ray Robinson (universal); Randy Turpin; Ray Robinson
1952	Ray Robinson*
1953-1955	Carl (Bobo) Olson
1955-1956	Ray Robinson
1957	Gene Fullmer, Ray Robinson, Carmen Basilio
1958	Carmen Basilio, Ray Robinson
1959	Gene Fullmer (NBA); Ray Robinson (New York)
1960	Gene Fullmer (NBA); Paul Pender (New York and Mass.)
1961	Gene Fullmer (NBA); Terry Downes (New York, Mass., Europe)
1962	Gene Fullmer, Dick Tiger (NBA); Paul Pender (New York and Mass.)*
1963	Dick Tiger (universal).
1963-1965	Joey Giardello
1965-1966	Dick Tiger
1966-1967	Emile Griffith
1967	Nino Benvenuti
1967-1968	Emile Griffith
1968-1970	Nino Benvenuti
1970	Carlos Monzon

WELTERWEIGHTS

1892	Danny Needham, Mysterious Billy Smith
1892-1894	Mysterious Billy Smith
1894-1896	Tommy Ryan
1896	Kid McCoy (outgrew class)
1900	Mysterious Billy Smith, Rube Ferns Matty Matthews
1901	Matty Matthews, Rube Ferns
1901-1904	Joe Walcott
1904-1906	Dixie Kid, Joe Walcott, Honey Mellody
1907-1911	Mike Sullivan
1911-1915	Vacant
1915-1919	Ted Lewis, Jack Britton
1919-1922	Jack Britton
1922-1926	Mickey Walker
1926	Pete Latzo
1927-1929	Joe Dundee
1929	Jackie Fields
1930	Jackie Fields, Jack Thompson, Tommy Freeman
1931	Freeman, Thompson, Lou Brouillard
1932	Jackie Fields
1933	Young Corbett, Jimmy McLarnin
1934	Barney Ross, Jimmy McLarnin
1935	Jimmy McLarnin, Barney Ross
1936-1938	Barney Ross

1938-1939	Henry Armstrong
1940	Fritzi Zivic
1941-1946	Fred Cochrane
1946-1947	Marty Servo*; Ray Robinson (A)
1947-1950	Ray Robinson
1951	Ray Robinson (England)*; Johnny Bratton (NBA): Kid Gavilan
1952-1954	Kid Gavilan
1954-1955	Johnny Saxton
1955	Tony De Marco: Carmen Basilio
1956	Carmen Basilio, Johnny Saxton, Carmen Basilio
1957	Carmen Basilio*
1958	Virgil Akins: Don Jordan
1959	Don Jordan
1960	Benny Paret
1961	Emile Griffith, Benny Paret
1962	Benny Paret, Emil Griffith
1963	Luis Rodriguez, Emile Griffith
1964-1966	Emile Griffith* (B)
1966-1969	Curtis Cokes
1969-1971	Jose Napoles
1971	Billy Backus
1971	Jose Napoles

(A) Robinson gained the title by defeating Tommy Bell in an elimination agreed to by the NY Commission and the N.B.A. Both claimed Robinson waived his title when he won the middleweight crown from LaMotta in 1951. Gavilan defeated Bratton in an elimination to find a successor.
(B) Title became vacant when Griffith won the middleweight title.

LIGHTWEIGHTS

1885-1896	Jack McAuliffe* (American champion)
1896-1899	Kid Lavigne
1899-1902	Frank Erne
1901-1908	Joe Gans
1908-1910	Battling Nelson
1910-1912	Ad Wolgast
1912-1914	Willie Ritchie
1914-1917	Freddie Welsh
1917-1924	Benny Leonard*
1925	Jimmy Goodrich, Rocky Kansas
1926-1930	Sammy Mandell
1930	Al Singer, Tony Canzoneri
1930-1933	Tony Canzoneri
1933-1935	Barney Ross*
1935	Tony Canzoneri
1936	Tony Canzoneri, Lou Ambers
1937	Lou Ambers
1938	Henry Armstrong
1939	Lou Ambers
1940	Lew Jenkins
1941-1943	Sammy Angott
1943	Beau Jack (New York), Bob Montgomery, Beau Jack (New York)
1944-1947	Bob Montgomery (New York) S. Angott (NBA), J. Zurita (NBA)
1945-1951	Ike Williams (NBA: later universal)
1951-1952	James Carter
1952	Lauro Salas, James Carter
1953-1954	James Carter
1954	Paddy De Marco; James Carter
1955	James Carter; Bud Smith
1956	Bud Smith, Joe Brown
1957-1962	Joe Brown
1962-1965	Carlos Ortiz
1965	Ismael Laguna
1965-1968	Carlos Ortiz
1968-1969	Teo Cruz
1969-1970	Mando Ramos
1970	Ismael Laguna
1970-1972	Ken Buchanan
1972	Roberto Duran

FEATHERWEIGHTS

1892-1900	George Dixon (A)
1900-1901	Terry McGovern
1901-1904	Young Corbett
1904-1908	Tommy Sullivan
1908-1912	Abe Attell
1912-1922	Johnny Kilbane
1923	Johnny Kilbane, Eugene Criqui, Johnny Dundee
1923-1925	Johnny Dundee
1925-1927	Kid Kaplan*
1927-1928	Benny Bass
1928	Tony Canzoneri, Andre Routis
1929-1932	C. Battalino
1932-1934	Tommy Paul (NBA), Freddie Miller (NBA)
1934-1936	Freddie Miller
1936-1937	Petey Sarron
1937	P. Sarron, Henry Armstrong*
1938-1940	Joey Archibald (B)
1940-1941	Harry Jeffra
1941	Joey Archibald, Chalky Wright
1941-1942	Chalky Wright
1942-1948	Willie Pep
1948-1949	Sandy Saddler
1949-1950	Willie Pep

1950-1954	Sandy Saddler
1953-1954	Interim champion: Percy Bassett
1955-1956	Sandy Saddler*
1957-1959	Hogan (Kid) Bassey
1959-1962	Davey Moore
1963-1964	Sugar Ramos
1964-1967	Vicente Saldivar*
1968-1969	Sho Saijyo
1969	John Famechon
1970	Sho Saijyo
1970	Kuniaki Shibata
1972	Clemente Sanchez

(A) Claim disputed.
(B) After Petey Scalzo knocked out Archibald (Dec. 5, 1938) in an overweight match and was refused a title bout, the NBA named Scalzo champion. The NBA title succession was: Petey Scalzo, 1938-1941: Richard Lemos, 1941: Jackie Wilson, 1941-1943: Jackie Callura, 1943: Phil Terranova, 1943-1944: Sal Bartolo, 1944-1946.

BANTAMWEIGHTS

1890-1892	George Dixon*
1892-1894	Vacant
1894-1899	Jimmy Barry*
1899-1900	Terry McGovern*
1901-1902	Harry Harris*
1902-1903	Harry Forbes
1903-1904	Frankie Neil
1904	Joe Bowker*, Digger Stanley (Eng.). Jimmy Walsh (U.S.)
1905-1907	Jimmy Walsh*
1907-1910	Vacant
1910-1914	Johnny Coulon
1914-1917	Kid Williams
1917-1920	Pete Herman
1920-1921	Joe Lynch
1921	Pete Herman, Johnny Buff
1922	Johnny Buff, Joe Lynch
1922-1924	Joe Lynch
1924	Abe Goldstein, Eddie Martin
1925	Eddie Martin, Charley (Phil) Rosenberg
1925-1926	Charley (Phil) Rosenberg
1927-1928	Bud Taylor* (NBA only)
1929-1935	Al Brown
1935-1936	Baltazar Sangchili
1936	Tony Marino, Sixto Escobar
1937	Sixto Escobar, Harry Jeffra
1938-1940	Sixto Escobar*
1940-1942	Lou Salica
1942-1947	Manuel Ortiz
1947	Harold Dade, Manuel Ortiz
1948-1950	Manuel Ortiz
1950-1952	Vic Toweel
1952	Vic Toweel, Jimmy Carruthers
1953-1954	Jimmy Carruthers*
1954-1955	Robert Cohen (NBA)
1955	Raul Macias (NBA); Robert Cohen (New York and World Committee)
1956	Mario D'Agata (New York and World Committee); Raul Macias (NBA)
1957	Alphonse Halimi (New York and World Committee); Raul Macias (NBA)
1958-1959	Alphonse Halimi (universal)
1959-1960	Jose Becerra*
1961-1965	Eder Jofre (universal)
1965-1968	Fighting Harada
1968-1969	Lionel Rose
1969-1970	Ruben Olivares
1970-1971	Chucho Castillo
1971-1972	Ruben Olivares
1972	Rafael Herrera
1972-1973	Enrique Pinder
1973	Romero Anaya

FLYWEIGHTS

1916-1923	Jimmy Wilde
1923-1925	Pancho Villa
1925-1927	Fidel La Barba*
1927-1930	Izzy Schwartz (New York only)
1930	Midget Wolgast (New York); Frankie Genaro (NBA)
1931-1932	Young Perez (defeated Frankie Genaro)
1932-1935	Jackie Brown
1935-1938	Benny Lynch*
1939-1941	Peter Kane*
1941-1943	Vacant
1943-1947	Jackie Patterson
1947-1950	Rinty Monaghan*
1950-1952	Dado Marino
1952-1954	Yoshio Shiraj
1954-1960	Pascual Perez
1960-1962	Pone Kingpetch
1962	Masahika Harada
1963	Pone Kingpetch, Hiroyuki Ebihara
1964-1965	Pone Kingpetch
1965-1966	Salvatore Burruni
1966	Walter McGowen
1966-1969	Chartchai Chionoi
1969	Efren Torres
1970	Masao Ohba
1970-1972	Erbito Salvarria
1972	Venice Borkorsor

History of Heavyweight Championship Bouts

1889—July 8—John L. Sullivan beat Jake Kilrain, 75 rounds, Richburg, Miss. (Last championship bare knuckle bout.)

*1892—Sept. 7—James J. Corbett defeated John L. Sullivan, 21 rounds, New Orleans. (Used big gloves for first time.)

1894—Jan. 25—James J. Corbett ko'd Charley Mitchell, 3 rounds, Jacksonville, Fla.

*1897—March 17—Bob Fitzsimmons defeated James J. Corbett, 14 rounds, Carson City, Nev.

*1899—June 9—James J. Jeffries beat Bob Fitzsimmons, 11 rounds, Coney Island, N. Y.

1899—Nov. 3—James J. Jeffries beat Tom Sharkey, 25 rounds, Coney Island, N. Y.

1900—May 11—James J. Jeffries knocked out James J. Corbett, 23 rounds, Coney Island, N. Y.

1901—Nov. 15—James J. Jeffries, ko'd Gus Ruhlin, 5 rounds, San Francisco.

1902—July 25—James J. Jeffries knocked out Bob Fitzsimmons, 8 rounds, San Francisco, Cal.

1903—Aug. 14—James J. Jeffries knocked out James J. Corbett, 10 rounds, San Francisco, Cal.

1904—Aug. 26—James J. Jeffries knocked out Jack Munroe, 2 rounds, San Francisco, Cal.

*1905—James J. Jeffries retired, July 3—Marvin Hart knocked out Jack Root, 12 rounds, Reno. Jeffries refereed and presented the title to the victor. Jack O'Brien also claimed the title.

*1906—Feb. 23—Tommy Burns defeated Marvin Hart, 20 rounds, Los Angeles, Cal.

1906—Nov. 28—Philadelphia Jack O'Brien and Tommy Burns, 20 rounds, draw, Los Angeles.

1907—May 8—Tommy Burns defeated Jack O'Brien, 20 rounds, Los Angeles, Cal.

1907—July 4—Tommy Burns knocked out Bill Squires, 1 round, Colma, Cal.

1907—Dec. 2—Tommy Burns knocked out Gunner Moir, 10 rounds, London.

1908—Feb. 10—Tommy Burns knocked out Jack Palmer, 4 rounds, London.

1908—March 17—Tommy Burns knocked out Jem Roche, 1 round, Dublin.

1908—April 18—Tommy Burns knocked out Jewey Smith, 5 rounds, Paris.

1908—June 13—Tommy Burns knocked out Bill Squires, 8 rounds, Paris.

1908—Aug. 24—Tommy Burns knocked out Bill Squires, 13 rounds, Sydney, New South Wales.

1908—Sept. 2—Tommy Burns knocked out Bill Lang, 2 rounds, Melbourne, Australia.

*1908—Dec. 26—Jack Johnson stopped Tommy Burns, 14 rounds, Sydney, Australia. Police halted contest.

1909—May 19—Jack Johnson and Jack O'Brien, 6 rounds, draw, Philadelphia.

1909—June 30—Jack Johnson and Tony Ross, 6 rounds, draw, Pittsburgh, Pa.

1909—Sept. 9—Jack Johnson and Al Kaufman, 10 rounds, no decision, San Francisco, Cal.

1909—Oct. 16—Jack Johnson knocked out Stanley Ketchell, 12 rounds, Colma, Cal.

1910—July 4—Jack Johnson knocked out Jim Jeffries, 15 rounds, Reno, Nev. (Jeffries came back from retirement.)

1912—July 4—Jack Johnson won on points from Jim Flynn, 9 rounds, Las Vegas, N. M., (contest stopped by police.)

1913—Nov. 28—Jack Johnson knocked out Andre Spaul, 2 rounds, Paris.

1913—Dec. 9—Jack Johnson and Jim Johnson, 10 rounds, draw, Paris. (Bout called a draw when Jack Johnson declared he had broken his arm.)

1914—June 27—Jack Johnson won from Frank Moran, 20 rounds, Paris.

*1915—April 5—Jess Willard knocked out Jack Johnson, 26 rounds, Havana, Cuba.

1916—March 25—Jess Willard and Frank Moran, 10 rounds (no decision), New York City.

*1919—July 4—Jack Dempsey knocked out Jess Willard, Toledo, O. (Willard failed to answer bell for fourth round.)

1920—Sept. 6—Jack Dempsey knocked out Billy Miske, 3 rounds, Benton Harbor, Mich.

1920—Dec. 14—Jack Dempsey knocked out Bill Brennan, 12 rounds, New York City.

1921—July 2—Jack Dempsey knocked out George Carpentier, 4 rounds, Boyle's Thirty Acres, Jersey City, N.J., (Carpentier had held the so called white heavyweight title since July 16, 1914, in a series established in 1913, after Jack Johnson's exile in Europe late in 1912.)

1923—July 4—Jack Dempsey won on points from Tom Gibbons, 15 rounds, Shelby, Mont.

1923—Sept. 14—Jack Dempsey knocked out Luis Firpo, 2 rounds, New York City.

*1926—Sept. 23—Gene Tunney beat Jack Dempsey, 10 rounds, decision, Philadelphia.

1927—Sept 22—Gene Tunney beat Jack Dempsey, 10 rounds, decision, Chicago.

1928—July 26—Gene Tunney knocked out Tom Heeney, 11 rounds, Yankee Stadium, New York; soon afterward he announced his retirement.

*1930—June 12—Max Schmeling of Germany defeated Jack Sharkey in fourth round when Sharkey fouled Schmeling

in a bout which was generally considered to have resulted in the election of a successor to Gene Tunney, New York.

1931—July 3—Max Schmeling knocked out Young Stribling, 15 rounds in Cleveland.

*1932—June 21—Jack Sharkey defeated Max Schmeling, 15 rounds, decision, New York City.

*1933—June 29—Primo Carnera knocked out Jack Sharkey, six rounds, New York City.

1933—Oct. 22—Carnera defeated Paulino Uzcudun, 15 rounds, in Rome.

1934—March 1—Primo Carnera defeated Tommy Loughran in 15 rounds in Miami.

*1934—June 14—Max Baer knocked out Primo Carnera, eleven rounds, New York City.

*1935—June 13—James J. Braddock defeated Max Baer, 15 rounds, New York City.

*1937—June 22—Joe Louis knocked out James J. Braddock, 8 rounds, Chicago.

1937—Aug. 30—Joe Louis defeated Tommy Farr, 15 rounds, decision. New York City.

1938—Feb. 23—Joe Louis knocked out Nathan Mann, 3 rounds, New York City.

1938—April 1—Joe Louis knocked out Harry Thomas, 5 rounds, New York City.

1938—June 22—Joe Louis knocked out Max Schmeling, one round, New York City.

1939—January 25—Joe Louis knocked out John H. Lewis, 1 round, New York City.

1939—April 17—Joe Louis knocked out Jack Roper, 1 round, Los Angeles.

1939—June 28—Joe Louis knocked out Tony Galento, 4 rounds, New York City.

1939—September 20—Joe Louis knocked out Bob Pastor, 11 rounds, Detroit, Mich.

1940—February 9—Joe Louis defeated Arturo Godoy, 15 rounds, decision, New York City.

1940—March 29—Joe Louis knocked out Johnny Paychek, 2 rounds, New York City.

1940—June 20—Joe Louis knocked out Arturo Godoy, 8 rounds, New York City.

1940—Dec. 16—Joe Louis knocked out Al McCoy, 6 rounds, Boston.

1941—Jan. 31—Joe Louis knocked out Red Burman, 5 rounds, New York City.

1941—Feb. 17—Joe Louis knocked out Gus Dorazio, 2 rounds, Philadelphia.

1941—March 21—Joe Louis knocked out Abe Simon, 13 rounds, Detroit, Mich.

1941—April 8—Joe Louis knocked out Tony Musto, 9 rounds, St. Louis, Mo.

1941—May 23—Joe Louis beat Buddy Baer, 7 rounds, Washington, D. C., on a disqualification.

1941—June 18—Joe Louis knocked out Billy Conn, 13 rounds, New York City.

1941—Sept. 29—Joe Louis knocked out Lou Nova, 6 rounds, New York City.

1941—Jan. 9—Joe Louis knocked out Buddy Baer, 1 round, New York City.

1942—March 27—Joe Louis knocked out Abe Simon, 6 rounds, New York City.

1946—June 19—Joe Louis knocked out Billy Conn, 8 rounds, New York City.

1946—Sept. 18—Joe Louis knocked out Tami Mauriello, 1 round, New York City.

1947—Dec. 5—Joe Louis defeated Joe Walcott in a 15-round bout by a split decision, New York City.

1948—June 25—Joe Louis knocked out Joe Walcott, 11 rounds, New York City.

*1949—June 22—Following Joe Louis' retirement Ezzard Charles defeated Joe Walcott by a unanimous decision, 15 rounds, Chicago, Ill. (N.B.A. recognition only).

1949—Aug. 10—Ezzard Charles knocked out Gus Lesnevich, seven rounds. New York City.

1949—Oct. 14—Ezzard Charles knocked out Pat Valentino, eight rounds, San Francisco (clinched American title).

1950—Aug. 15—Ezzard Charles knocked out Freddy Beshore, 14 rounds, Buffalo, N. Y.

1950—Sept. 27—Ezzard Charles defeated Joe Louis in latter's attempted comeback, 15 rounds, New York City (universal recognition).

1950—Dec. 5—Ezzard Charles knocked out Nick Barone, 11 rounds, Cincinnati, Ohio.

1951—Jan. 12—Ezzard Charles knocked out Lee Oma, 10 rounds, New York, N.Y.

1951—March 7—Ezzard Charles outpointed Joe Walcott, 15 rounds, Detroit, Mich.

1951—May 30—Ezzard Charles outpointed Joey Maxim, light heavyweight champion, 15 rounds, Chicago.

*1951—July 18—Joe Walcott knocked out Ezzard Charles, 7th round, Pittsburgh, Pa.

1952—June 5—Joe Walcott outpointed Ezzard Charles, 15 rounds, Philadelphia, Pa.

*1952—Sept. 23—Rocky Marciano knocked out Joe Walcott, 13th round, Philadelphia, Pa.

1953—May 15—Rocky Marciano knocked out Joe Walcott, first round, Chicago, Ill.

1953—Sept. 24—Rocky Marciano knocked out Roland LaStarza, 11th round, Polo Grounds, New York, N.Y.

1954—June 17—Rocky Marciano outpointed Ezzard

Charles, 15 rounds, Yankee Stadium, New York, N.Y.
1954—Sept. 17—Rocky Marciano knocked out Ezzard Charles, 8th round, Yankee Stadium, New York, N.Y.
1955—May 16—Rocky Marciano knocked out Don Cockell, 9th round, Kezar Stadium, San Francisco, Calif.
1955—Sept. 21—Rocky Marciano knocked out Archie Moore, 9th round, Yankee Stadium, N.Y. Marciano retired undefeated, Apr. 27, 1956.
*1956—Nov. 30—Floyd Patterson, a contender, knocked out Archie Moore, 5th round, Chicago, Ill., gaining the championship.
1957—July 29—Floyd Patterson knocked out Hurricane Jackson, 10th round, Polo Grounds, New York, N.Y.
1957—Aug. 22—Floyd Patterson knocked out Pete Rademacher, 6th round, Seattle, Wash.
1958—Aug. 18—Floyd Patterson ko'd Roy Harris, 12th round, Los Angeles, Calif.
1959—May 1—Floyd Patterson knocked out Brian London, 11 rounds, Indianapolis, Ind.
*1959—June 26—Ingemar Johansson, Sweden, ko'd Floyd Patterson, 3rd round, Yankee Stadium, New York City.
*1960—June 20—Floyd Patterson knocked out Ingemar Johansson, 5th round, Polo Grounds, New York, N. Y. (First heavyweight in boxing history to regain title.)
1961—Mar. 13—Floyd Patterson knocked out Ingemar Johansson, 6th round, Convention Hall, Miami Beach, Fla.
1961—Dec. 4—Floyd Patterson knocked out Tom McNeeley, 4th round, Toronto, Ont., Canada.
*1962—Sept. 25—Sonny Liston knocked out Floyd Patterson, first round, Comiskey Park, Chicago, Ill.
1963—July 22—Sonny Liston knocked out Floyd Patterson, first round, Las Vegas, Nevada.
*1964—Feb. 25—Cassius Clay knocked out Sonny Liston,

1965—May 26—Cassius Clay knocked out Sonny Liston, first round, Lewiston, Maine.
1965—Nov. 11—Cassius Clay knocked out Floyd Patterson, twelfth round, Las Vegas, Nev.
1966—Mar. 29—Cassius Clay outpointed George Chuvalo, 15 rounds, Toronto, Ont.
1966—May 21—Cassius Clay knocked out Henry Cooper, sixth round, London, Eng.
1966—Aug. 6—Cassius Clay knocked out Brian London, third round, London, Eng.
1966—Sept. 10—Cassius Clay knocked out Karl Mildenberger, twelfth round, Frankfurt, Germany.
1966—Nov. 14—Cassius Clay knocked out Cleveland Williams, third round, Houston, Tex.
1967—Feb. 6—Cassius Clay outpointed Ernie Terrell, 15 rounds, Houston, Tex.
1967—March 22—Cassius Clay knocked out Zora Folley, seventh round, New York. Clay was stripped of his title by the WBA and others following an indictment for refusing to accept service in the military. Clay later announced his retirement.
*1970—Feb. 16—Joe Frazier knocked out Jimmy Ellis, fifth round, New York.
1970—Nov. 18—Joe Frazier knocked out Bob Foster, second round, Detroit.
1971—Mar. 8—Joe Frazier outpointed Cassius Clay (Muhammad Ali), 15 rounds, New York, N.Y.
1972—Jan. 15—Joe Frazier knocked out Terry Daniels, fourth round, New Orleans.
1972—May 25—Joe Frazier knocked out Ron Stander, fifth round, Omaha.
*1973—Jan. 22—George Foreman knocked out Joe Frazier, second round, Kingston, Jamaica.
1973—Sept. 1—George Foreman knocked out Joe Roman, first round, Tokyo.

Major Professional Boxing Bouts

Sept. 1972—Sept., 1973. * Championship bout.

Date	Winner, weight	Loser, weight	Result	Site
Sept. 20	Muhammad Ali	Floyd Patterson	KO-7	New York
Sept. 20	Ken Buchanan, 134	Carlos Ortiz, 139	KO-6	New York
*Sept. 26	Bob Foster, 174	Chris Finnegan, 173	KO-14	London
Sept. 29	Venice Borkorsor	Betulio Gonzalez	KO-10	Bangkok, Thailand
Oct. 10	Joe Bugner, 219	Jurgen Blin, 199	KO-8	London
Oct. 11	Emile Griffith, 156	Joe DeNucci, 163	D-12	Boston
Oct. 13	Fritz Chervet	Mariano Garcia	D-15	Geneva
Oct. 17	Esteban De Jesus	Roberto Duran	D-10	New York
Nov. 21	Muhammad Ali, 221	Bob Foster, 180	KO-8	Stateline, Nevada
Dec. 4	Ken Buchanan	Chang Kil Lee	KO-2	New York
Dec. 4	Walter Seeley	Hyum Kim	D-10	New York
Dec. 7	Tom Bogs	Luis Vinales	D-10	Copenhagen
1973				
Jan. 5	Jerry Quarry	Randy Neumann	KO-7	New York
*Jan. 22	George Foreman, 217	Joe Frazier, 214	KO-2	Kingston, Jamaica
Feb. 9	Jerry Quarry, 200	Ron Lyle, 219	D-12	New York
Feb. 14	Muhammad Ali, 217	Joe Bugner, 219	D-12	Las Vegas
Feb. 14	John Conteh, 182	Terry Daniels, 196	KO-7	Las Vegas
*Feb. 28	Jose Napoles, 146	Ernie Lopez, 146	KO-7	Inglewood, Calif.
Mar. 31	Ken Norton, 210	Muhammad Ali, 221	D-12	San Diego
*Apr. 15	Rafael Herrera, 117	Rodolfo Martinez, 117	KO-12	Mexico
Apr. 16	Rodrigo Valdes	Kim Booker	KO-5	New York
*May 6	Eder Jofre	Jose Legra	D-15	Barailia, Brazil
May 13	Ron Lyle	Gregorio Peralta	D-10	Denver
*June 2	Carlos Monzon	Emile Griffith	D-15	Monte Carlo
June 19	Earnie Shavers, 206	Jimmy Ellis, 199	KO-1	New York
*June 19	Kuniaki Shibata, 129	Victor Echegaray, 128	D-15	Tokyo
July 2	Joe Frazier	Joe Bugner	D-12	London
July 23	Oscar Bonavena, 211	Leroy Caldwell, 198	KO-2	Las Vegas
Aug. 4	Miguel Barreto	Billy Backus	D-12	New York
*Aug. 19	Romero Anaya, 118	Enrique Pinder, 117	KO-3	Inglewood, Calif.
*Aug. 21	Bob Foster, 173	Pierre Fourie, 168	D-15	Albuquerque
Aug. 25	Vito Antuofermo, 155	Danny McAloon, 155	D-10	New York
*Sept. 1	George Foreman, 219	Joe Roman, 197	KO-1	Tokyo
Sept. 1	Ken Buchanan	Chu Chu Malave	KO-7	New York
Sept. 1	Rodrigo Valdez	Benny Briscoe	D-12	New Caledonia
Sept. 9	Roberto Duran	Ishimatsu Suzuki	KO-10	Panama
Sept. 10	Muhammad Ali, 212	Ken Norton, 205	D-12	Inglewood, Calif.
Sept. 10	Jerry Quarry	Tony Doyle	KO-4	Inglewood, Calif.
Sept. 10	Jeff Merritt	Ernie Terrell	KO-1	New York
*Sept. 22	Jose Napoles	Clyde Gray	D-15	Toronto
Sept. 25	Duane Bobick, 209	Ron Draper	KO-4	Kansas City
Sept. 25	George Chuvalo, 228	Tony Ventura	KO-3	Buffalo, N.Y.

National Duckpin Bowling Champions, 1973

Men's Singles—Fred Belliveau, Norwich, Conn., 466.
Women's Singles—Agnes Claughsey, Hebron, Conn., 435.
Men's Doubles—Larry Shepley & Tom Ramsburg, Frederick, Md., 901.
Women's Doubles—Rola Ough & Miki Irish, Manchester, Conn., 799.

Men's Team—Dudley Excavating, Washington, D.C., 2,063.
Women's Team—Parkville Majors, Baltimore, Md., 1,902.
Men's All Events—Keith Dashno, Newington, Conn., 1,332.
Women's All Events—Nancy Brindle, Providence, R.I., 1,214.
Mixed Doubles—Patsy Stroessner & Robert Stroessner, Baltimore, Md., 866.

Skeet Shooting Championships in 1973

OPEN INDIVIDUAL CHAMPIONS

All-Around—Paul LaPorte, Montreal, Quebec 547 x 550.
12 Gauge—Bobbie Lewis, Baxley, Ga. 250 x 250.
20 Gauge—Ron Molenaar, Palos Height, Ill. 100 x 100.
28 Gauge—Wayne Mayes, Attalla, Ala. 100 x 100.
410 Gauge—Chris Sumers, El Campo, Texas 100 x 100.

SPECIAL EVENTS—12 GAUGE

Military Individual—Doug Burdett, Ottawa, Ontario 250 x 250.
Civilian Individual—Bobbie Lewis, Baxley, Ga. 250 x 250.
Collegiate—John Clark, Abilene, Texas. 250 x 250.
Junior Lady—Marina Pakis, Hot Springs, Ark. 100 x 100.
Western Open—Larry Lowery, Jackson, Miss. 100 x 100.
Eastern Open—George Kruth, Erie, Pa. 100 x 100.

LADY CHAMPIONS

All-Around—Karla Roberts, Bridgeton, Mo. 545 x 550.
12 Gauge—Karla Roberts, 249 x 250.
20 Gauge—Joyce Luce, Hebron, Conn. 100 x 100.
28 Gauge—Karla Roberts, 99 x 100.
410 Gauge—Karla Roberts. 98 x 100.

VETERAN CHAMPIONS

All-Around—Emery Pappy, Jacksonville, Fla. 539 x 550.
12 Gauge—Emery Pappy. 246 x 250.
20 Gauge—O. M. Harper, Clendenin, W. Va. 100 x 100.
28 Gauge—Emery Pappy. 100 x 100.
410 Gauge—Tom Sanfilipo, Fairfield. Calif. 95 x 100.

SENIOR CHAMPIONS

All-Around—Angel Marchand, San Juan, Puerto Rico. 536 x 550.
12 Gauge—Angel Marchand. 247 x 250.
20 Gauge—Chet Crites, Detroit, Mich. 100 x 100.
28 Gauge—Jack King, Greensboro, N.C. 100 x 100.
410 Gauge—J. E. Arnold, Savannah, Ga. 97 x 100.

SUB/SENIOR CHAMPIONS

All-Around—John Golla, Ft. Lauderdale, Fla. 546 x 550.
12 Gauge—Julian Pattyn, Detroit, Mich. 250 x 250.
20 Gauge—Ernest Provost, Athens, Ga. 100 x 100.
28 Gauge—Ray Corper, Ambler, Pa. 99 x 100.
410 Gauge—John Golla. 97 x 100.

JUNIOR CHAMPIONS

All-Around—Kip Berg, Minneapolis, Minn. 541 x 550.
12 Gauge—Bobby Utting, Rush, N.Y. 249 x 250.
20 Gauge—Chip Youngblood, Ft. Lauderdale, Fla. 100 x 100.
28 Gauge—E. B. Mink III., Ft. Lauderdale, Fla. 100 x 100.
410 Gauge—John Shima, Oak Park, Ill. 98 x 100.

INDUSTRY CHAMPIONS

All-Around—Jimmy Prall, Little Rock, Ark. 548 x 550.
12 Gauge—Jimmy Prall. 250 x 250.
20 Gauge—Jimmy Prall. 100 x 100.
28 Gauge—Tom Heffron, Jr., Ithaca, Inver Grove Heights, Minn. 100 x 100.
410 Gauge—Fred Missildine, Sea Island, Ga. 100 x 100.

CHAMPIONS OF CHAMPIONS

Champion—(4 guns, 25 Targets each)—Kenny Barnes, Bakersfield, Calif. 100 x 100.

HUSBAND AND WIFE CHAMPIONS

All-Around—Homer and Sadie Fillingame, Dawson, Ga. 1073 x 1100.
12 Gauge—Doug and Margaret Burdett, Ottawa, Ontario. 498 x 500.
20 Gauge—Bruce and Dianne Forbush, Hamburg, N.Y. 196 x 200.
28 Gauge—Ed and Karla Roberts, Bridgeton, Mo. 197 x 200.
410 Gauge—Ed and Karla Roberts, 191 x 200.

INTERNATIONAL STYLE CHAMPIONS

Open Champion—Carl Poston, Daisy, Tenn. 197 x 200.
Lady—Myrna Herbert, Montreal, Quebec. 177 x 200.
4-Man Team—Ft. Benning: Ken Gilbert, James Whitaker, Louis Sembrowich and Mernice Alkire. 765 x 800.

Archery Championships of 1973

28th Annual National Field Archery Assn. Championship Tournament

Aurora, Ill., July 23-27, 1973

Freestyle
Professional Men—Dean Pridgen, Kansas City, Mo.
Open Men—Bobby J. Hunt, Grapevine, Texas.
Amateur Men—Terry Ragsdale, White Oak, Texas.
Senior Men—Elmer Little, San Diego, Calif.
Professional Women—Eva Troncoso, Monterey Park, Calif.
Open Women—Barbara Morris, Frankfort, Ky.
Amateur Women—Kathy Cramberg, Dallas City, Ill.
Senior Women—Sandy Eliot, Atlanta, Ga.
Youth Boy—Ricky Sorensen, Orem, Utah.
Youth Girl—Linda Loberto, E. Meadow, N.Y.

Freestyle—Limited
Professional Men—Jamie Selkirk, Canton, Ill.
Open Men—A. L. Lee, Greenwood, S.C.
Amateur Men—Bob Cerney, St. Paul Park, Minn.

Open Women—Mary Miller, Garden City, Mo.
Amateur Women—June Mitchell, Chicago, Ill.

Barebow
Open Men—Dennis Cline, Sugar Grove, Ill.
Amateur Men—Mike Flier, Pekin, Ill.
Senior Men—Dr. R. E. Szilvassy, Clovis, N.M.
Open Women—Beverly Janis, Americus, Ga.
Amateur Women—Eunice Schewe, Roscoe, Ill.
Youth Boy—Bruce Gates, Jr., Eation, Ohio.
Youth Girl—Sherily Doyle, Taft, Calif.

Bowhunter
Open Men—Cal Vogt, Van Nuys, Calif.
Amateur Men—Alfred Lough, Peoria, Ill.
Open Women—Ida B. Revis, Guthrie, Okla.
Amateur Women—June Jones, Elgin, Ill.

Rodeo Championship Standings, 1972

Source: Rodeo Cowboys Assn., Inc.

Event	Winner	Money Won	Event	Winner	Money Won
All Around	Phil Lyne, George West, Texas	$60,852	Calf Roping	Phil Lyne, George West, Texas	$32,216
Saddle Bronc	Mel Hyland, Surrey, B.C.	26,812	Steer Wrestling	Roy Duvall, Warner, Okla.	24,327
Bareback	Joe Alexander, Cora, Wyo.	32,126	Team Roping	Leo Camarillo, Donald, Ore.	17,587
Bull Riding	John Quintana, Cresswell, Ore.	23,054	Steer Roping	Allen Keller, Olathe, Colo.	7,593

Rodeo Cowboy All Around Champions

Year	Winner	Money Won	Year	Winner	Money Won
1959	Jim Shoulders, Henryetta, Okla	$32,905	1966	Larry Mahan, Brooks, Oregon	40,358
1960	Harry Tompkins, Dublin, Texas	32,522	1967	Larry Mahan, Brooks, Oregon	51,996
1961	Benny Reynolds, Melrose, Mont	31,309	1968	Larry Mahan, Salem, Oregon	49,129
1962	Tom Nesmith, Bethel, Okla	32,611	1969	Larry Mahan, Brooks, Oregon	57,726
1963	Dean Oliver, Boise, Idaho	31,329	1970	Larry Mahan, Brooks, Oregon	41,493
1964	Dean Oliver, Boise, Idaho	31,150	1971	Phil Lyne, George West, Texas	49,245
1965	Dean Oliver, Boise, Idaho	33,163	1972	Phil Lyne, George West, Texas	60,852

All-Time Pro Football Records

As of Sept. 15, 1973 (Unless otherwise noted)

LEADING LIFETIME RUSHERS

Player	League	Yrs.	Att.	Yards	Avg.	Player	League	Yrs.	Att.	Yards	Avg.
Jim Brown	NFL	9	2,359	12,312	5.2	Dick Bass	NFL	10	1,218	5,417	4.4
Joe Perry	AAFC-NFL	16	1,929	9,723	5.0	Jim Nance	NFL-AFL	7	1,323	5,323	4.0
Jim Taylor	NFL	10	1,941	8,597	4.4	Hugh McElhenny	NFL	13	1,124	5,231	4.7
Leroy Kelly	NFL	9	1,595	6,885	4.3	Lenny Moore	NFL	12	1,069	5,174	4.8
John Henry Johnson	NFL-AFL	13	1,571	6,803	4.3	Ollie Matson	NFL	14	1,170	5,173	4.4
Don Perkins	NFL	8	1,500	6,217	4.1	Clem Daniels	AFL-NFL	9	1,146	5,138	4.5
Steve Van Buren	NFL	8	1,320	5,860	4.3	Mike Garrett	AFL-NFL	8	1,194	5,014	4.2
Rick Casares	NFL-AFL	12	1,431	5,797	4.1	Paul Lowe	AFL	9	1,026	4.995	4.9
Bill Brown	NFL	12	1,583	5,591	3.5	John David Crow	NFL	11	1,157	4,963	4.3
Ken Willard	NFL	8	1,499	5,564	3.7	Gale Sayers	NFL	7	991	4,956	5.0

Most Yards Gained, Season—1,863, Jim Brown, Cleveland Browns, 1963.
Most Yards Gained, Game—250, Orban (Spec) Sanders, New York Yankees vs. Chicago Rockets, Oct. 24, 1947; O. J. Simpson, Buffalo vs. New England, Sept. 16, 1973.
Most Games, 100 Yards or More, Career—58, Jim Brown, Cleveland Browns, 1957-1965.
Most Touchdowns Rushing, Career—106, Jim Brown, Cleveland Browns, 1957-1965.
Most Touchdowns Rushing, Season—19, Jim Taylor, Green Bay Packers, 1962.
Most Touchdowns Rushing, Game—6, Ernie Nevers, Chicago Cardinals vs. Chicago Bears, Nov. 8, 1929.
Most Rushing Attempts, Season—305, Jim Brown, Cleveland Browns, 1961.
Most Rushing Attempts, Game—38, Harry Newman, Giants vs. Green Bay Packers, Nov. 11, 1934 (114 yards); Jim Nance, Boston Patriots vs. Oakland Raiders, Oct. 30, 1966 (208 yds.).
Longest run from Scrimmage—97 yds., Andy Uram, Green Bay vs. Chicago Cardinals, Oct. 8, 1939; Bob Gage, Pittsburgh vs. Chicago Bears, Dec. 4, 1949. (Both scored touchdown).

LEADING LIFETIME PASSERS

Player	League	Yrs.	Att.	Com.	Yds.	Player	League	Yrs.	Att.	Com.	Yds.
John Unitas	NFL	17	5,110	2,796	39,768	Bart Starr	NFL	16	3,149	1,808	24,718
Y. A. Tittle	AAFC-NFL	17	4,395	2,427	33,070	Norm Van Brocklin	NFL	12	2,895	1,553	23,611
Fran Tarkenton	NFL	12	4,175	2,290	31,135	Otto Graham	AAFC-NFL	10	2,626	1,464	23,584
John Brodie	NFL	16	4,297	2,371	30,424	Babe Parilli	NFL-AFL	15	3,330	1,552	22,681
Sonny Jurgenson	NFL	16	3,950	2,239	30,135	Roman Gabriel	NFL	11	3,313	1,705	22,223
John Hadl	AFC-NFL	11	3,640	1,824	26,938	Sam Baugh	NFL	16	2,995	1,693	21,886
George Blanda	AFL-NFL	23	4,000	1,909	26,881	Jack Kemp	AFL-NFL	10	3,073	1,436	21,218
Bobby Layne	NFL	15	3,700	1,814	26,768	Joe Namath	AFL-NFL	8	2,605	1,326	20,099
Norm Snead	NFL	12	3,728	1,918	26,755	Earl Morrall	NFL	17	2,555	1,309	19,834
Len Dawson	ALF-NFL	16	3,265	1,839	25,318	Charley Conerly	NFL	14	2,833	1,418	19,488

Most Yards Gained, Season—4,007, Joe Namath, New York Jets, 1967.
Most Yards Gained, Game—554, Norm Van Brocklin, Los Angeles Rams vs. New York Yankees, Sept. 28, 1951 (27 completions in 41 attempts).
Most Touchdowns Passing, Career—287, John Unitas, Baltimore Colts, 1956-1972.
Most Touchdowns Passing, Season—36, George Blanda, Houston Oilers, 1961, and Y. A. Tittle, New York Giants, 1963.
Most Touchdowns Passing, Game—7, Sid Luckman, Chicago Bears vs. New York Giants, Nov. 14, 1943; Adrian Burk, Philadelphia Eagles vs. Washington Redskins, Oct. 17, 1954; George Blanda, Houston Oilers vs. New York Titans, Nov. 19, 1961; Y. A. Tittle, New York Giants vs. Washington Redskins, Oct. 28, 1962. Joe Kapp, Minnesota Vikings vs. Baltimore Colts, Sept. 28, 1969.
Most Passing Attempts, Season—508, Sonny Jurgensen, Washington Redskins, 1967 (288 completions).
Most Passing Attempts, Game—68, George Blanda, Houston Oilers vs. Buffalo Bills, Nov. 1, 1964 (37 completions).
Most Passes Completed, Season—288, Sonny Jurgensen, Washington Redskins, 1967 (508 attempts).
Most Passes Completed, Game—37, George Blanda, Houston Oilers vs. Buffalo Bills, Nov. 1, 1964 (68 attempts).
Most Consecutive Passes Completed—15, Len Dawson, Kansas City Chiefs vs. Houston Oilers, Sept. 9, 1967.

LEADING LIFETIME RECEIVERS

Player	League	Yrs.	No.	Yds.	Avg.	Player	League	Yrs.	No.	Yds.	Avg.
Don Maynard	AFL-NFL	14	632	11,816	18.7	Charlie Taylor	NFL	9	469	6,669	14.2
Ray Berry	NFL	13	631	9,275	14.7	Pete Retzlaff	NFL	11	452	7,412	16.4
Lionel Taylor	AFL	9	567	7,195	12.7	Mike Ditka	NFL	12	427	5,812	13.6
Lance Alworth	AFL-NFL	11	542	10,266	18.9	Carroll Dale	NFL	13	424	8,085	19.1
Bobby Mitchell	NFL	11	521	7,954	15.3	Bobby Joe Conrad	NFL	12	422	5,902	14.0
Billy Howton	NFL	12	503	8,459	10.8	Charley Hennigan	AFL	7	410	6,823	16.6
Tom McDonald	NFL	12	495	8,410	17.0	Billy Wilson	NFL	10	407	5,902	14.4
Don Hutson	NFL	11	488	7,991	16.4	Jim Phillips	NFL	10	401	6,044	15.1
Art Powell	AFL-NFL	10	479	8,046	16.8	Jimmy Orr	NFL	12	400	7,914	19.8
Boyd Dowler	NFL	12	474	7,270	15.4	Tom Fears	NFL	9	400	5,397	13.5

Most Yards Gained, Season—1,746, Charley Hennigan, Houston Oilers, 1961.
Most Yards Gained, Game—303, Jim Benton, Cleveland Rams vs. Detroit Lions, Nov. 22, 1945 (10 receptions).
Most Pass Receptions, Season—101, Charley Hennigan, Houston Oilers, 1964.
Most Pass Receptions, Game—18, Tom Fears, Los Angeles Rams vs. Green Bay Packers, Dec. 3, 1950 (189 yards).
Most Consecutive Games, Pass Receptions—96 Lance Alworth, San Diego Chargers, 1962-1969.
Most Touchdown Passes, Career—99, Don Hutson, Green Bay Packers, 1935-1945.
Most Touchdown Passes, Season—17, Don Hutson, Green Bay Packers, 1942; Elroy Hirsch, Los Angeles Rams, 1951; Bill Groman, Houston Oilers, 1961.
Most Touchdown Passes, Game—5, Bob Shaw, Chicago Cardinals vs. Baltimore Colts, Oct. 2, 1950.
Most Consecutive Games, Touchdown Passes—11, Elroy Hirsch, Los Angeles Rams, 1950-1951; Buddy Dial, Pittsburgh Steelers, 1957-1960.

MISCELLANEOUS RECORDS

Most Fumbles, Season—16, Don Meredith, Dallas Cowboys, 1964.
Most Fumbles, Game—7, Len Dawson, Kansas City Chiefs vs. San Diego Chargers, Nov. 15, 1964.
Longest Run With Recovered Fumble—104 yds., Jack Tatum, Oakland Raiders vs. Green Bay Packers, Sept. 24, 1972 (scored touchdown).
Longest Winning Streak (Regular Season)—17 games, Chicago Bears, 1933-1934.
Longest Undefeated Streak (Includes Tie Games)—29 games, Cleveland Browns, 1947-1949 (Won 27, Tied 2).
Most Seasons, Active Player—23, George Blanda, Chicago Bears, 1949-1958; Houston Oilers, 1960-1966 and Oakland, 1967-1972.

LEADING LIFETIME SCORERS

Player	League	Yrs.	TD	PAT	FG	Tot.	Player	League	Yrs.	TD	PAT	FG	Tot.
George Blanda	NFL-AFL	23	9	824	288	1.742	Don Hutson	NFL	11	105	172	7	823
Lou Groza	AAFC-NFL	21	1	810	264	1,608	Paul Hornung	NFL	9	62	190	66	760
Gino Cappelletti	AFL	11	42	350	176	1,130	Jim Brown	NFL	9	126	0	0	756
Fred Cox	NFL	10	0	351	209	978	Tom Davis	NFL	11	0	348	130	738
Sam Baker	NFL	15	2	428	179	977	Pete Gogolak	AFL-NFL	8	0	298	146	736
Lou Michaels	NFL	13	1	386	187	955 *	Mike Clark	NFL	9	0	324	132	720
Jim Bakken	NFL	11	0	338	189	905	Lenny Moore	NFL	12	113	0	0	678
Jim Turner	AFL-NFL	9	0	293	198	887	Jan Stenerud	AFL-NFL	6	0	212	155	677
Bobby Walston	NFL	12	46	365	80	881	Ben Agajanian	AAFC-NFL					
Bruce Gossett	NFL	9	0	323	182	869		AFL	13	0	343	104	655
							Gordy Soltau	NFL	9	25	284	70	644
* Includes safety.							Gene Mingo	AFL-NFL	10	13	215	112	629

Most Points, Season—176, Paul Hornung, Green Bay Packers, 1960 (15 TD's, 41 PAT's, 15 FG's).
Most Points, Game—40, Ernie Nevers, Chicago Cardinals vs. Chicago Bears, Nov. 28, 1929 (6 TD's, 4 PAT's).
Most Touchdowns, Season—22, Gale Sayers, Chicago Bears, 1965 (14 rushing, 6 pass receptions, 1 punt return, 1 kickoff return).
Most Touchdowns, Game—6, Ernie Nevers, Chicago Cardinals vs. Chicago Bears, Nov. 28, 1929 (6 rushing); Dub Jones, Cleveland Browns vs. Chicago Bears, Nov. 25, 1951 (4 rushing, 2 pass receptions); Gale Sayers, Chicago Bears vs. San Francisco 49ers, Dec. 12, 1965 (4 rushing, 1 pass reception, 1 punt return).
Most Points After Touchdown—64, George Blanda, Houston Oilers, 1961 (65 attempts).
Most Consecutive Points After Touchdown—234, Tommy Davis, San Francisco 49ers, 1959-1965.
Most Field Goals, Game—7, Jim Bakken, St. Louis Cardinals vs. Pittsburgh Steelers, Sept. 24, 1967.
Most Field Goals, Season—34, Jim Turner, New York Jets, 1968 and 1969.
Most Field Goals Attempted, Season—49, Bruce Gossett, Los Angeles Rams, 1966; Curt Knight, Washington Redskins, 1971.
Most Field Goals Attempted, Game—9, Jim Bakken, St. Louis Cardinals vs. Pittsburgh Steelers, Sept. 24, 1967 (7 successful).
Most Consecutive Field Goals—16, Jan Stenerud, Kansas City Chiefs, Nov. 2, 1969, Dec. 7, 1969.
Most Consecutive Games, Field Goal—31, Fred Cox, Minnesota Vikings, 1968-1970.
Longest Field Goal—63 yds., Tom Dempsey, New Orleans Saints vs. Detroit Lions, Nov. 8, 1970.
Highest Field Goal Completion Percentage, Career (200 attempts)—66.5, Jan Stenerud, Kansas City Chiefs, 1967-1972 (155 FG's in 233 attempts).
Highest Field Goal Completion Percentage, Season (20 attempts)—88.5, Lou Groza, Cleveland Browns, 1953 (23 FG's in 26 attempts).

PASS INTERCEPTIONS

Most Passes Had Intercepted, Game—8, Jim Hardy, Chicago Cardinals vs. Philadelphia Eagles, Sept. 24, 1950 (39 attempts).
Most Passes Had Intercepted, Season—42, George Blanda, Houston Oilers, 1962 (418 attempts).
Most Passes Had Intercepted, Career—276, George Blanda, Chicago Bears, 1949-1958; Houston Oilers, 1960-1966; Oakland Raiders, 1967-1972 (4,000 attempts).
Most Consecutive Passes Attempted Without Interception—294, Bart Starr, Green Bay Packers, 1964-1965.
Most Interceptions By, Season—14, Dick Lane, Los Angeles Rams, 1952.
Most Interceptions By, Career—79, Emlen Tunnell, New York Giants, 1948-1958; Green Bay Packers, 1959-1961.
Most Consecutive Games, Passes Intercepted By—8, Tom Morrow, Oakland Raiders, 1962 (4), 1963 (4).
Most Touchdowns Scored via Pass Interceptions, Lifetime—9, Ken Houston, Houston Oilers, 1967 (2); 1968 (2); 1969; 1971 (4).

PUNTING

Highest Punting Average, Career (300 Punts)—45.10, Sam Baugh, Washington Redskins, 1937-1952 (338 Punts).
Highest Punting Average, Season (20 Punts)—51.3, Sam Baugh, Washington Redskins, 1940 (35 Punts).
Highest Punting Average, Game (4 Punts)—59.4 Sam Baugh, Washington Redskins vs. Detroit Lions, Oct. 27, 1940 (5 punts).
Longest Punt—98 yds., Steve O'Neal, New York Jets vs. Denver Broncos, Sept. 21, 1969.

KICKOFF RETURNS

Most Yardage Returning Kickoffs, Career—5,555, Ron Smith, Chicago Bears, 1965; Atlanta Falcons, 1966-67; Los Angeles Rams, 1968-69; Chicago Bears, 1970-72.
Most Yardage Returning Kickoffs, Season—1,317, Bobby Jancik, Houston Oilers, 1963.
Most Yardage Returning Kickoffs, Game—294, Wally Triplett, Detroit Lions vs. Los Angeles Rams, Oct. 29, 1950 (4 returns).
Most Touchdowns Scored via Kickoff Returns, Career—6, Ollie Matson, Chicago Cardinals, 1952 (2), 1954, 1956, 1958 (2); Gale Sayers, Chicago Bears, 1965, 1966 (2), 1967 (3); Travis Williams, Green Bay Packers, 1967 (4), 1969, Los Angeles Rams, 1971.
Most Touchdowns Scored via Kickoff Returns, Season—4, Travis Williams, Green Bay Packers, 1967; Cecil Turner, Chicago Bears, 1970.
Most Touchdowns Scored via Kickoff Returns, Game—2, Tim Brown, Philadelphia Eagles vs. Dallas Cowboys, Nov. 6, 1966; Travis Williams, Green Bay Packers vs. Cleveland Browns, Nov. 12, 1967.
Most Kickoff Returns, Career—220, Ron Smith, Chicago Bears, 1965; Atlanta Falcons, 1966-67; Loss Angeles Rams, 1968-69; Chicago Bears, 1970-72.
Most Kickoff Returns, Season—47, Odell Barry, Denver Broncos, 1964.
Longest Kickoff Return—106 yds., Al Carmichael, Green Bay Packers vs. Chicago Bears, October 7, 1956 (scored touchdown); Noland Smith, Kansas City vs. Denver, Dec. 17, 1967 (scored touchdown).

PUNT RETURNS

Most Yardage Returning Punts, Career—2,209, Emlen Tunnell, New York Giants, 1948-1958; Green Bay Packers, 1959-1961.
Most Yardage Returning Punts, Season—612, Rodger Bird, Oakland Raiders, 1967.
Most Yardage Returning Punts, Game—205, George Atkinson, Oakland Raiders vs. Buffalo Bills, Sept. 15, 1968.
Most Touchdowns Scored via Punt Returns, Career—4, Jack Christiansen, Detroit Lions, 1951 (4), 1952 (2), 1954, 1956.
Most Punt Returns, Career—258, Emlen Tunnell, New York Giants, 1948-1958; Green Bay Packers, 1959-1961.
Most Punt Returns, Season—53, Alvin Haymond, L.A. Rams, 1970.
Most Punt Returns, Game—9, Rodger Bird, Oakland Raiders vs. Denver Broncos, Sept. 10, 1967.
Longest Punt Return—98, Gil LeFebvre, Cincinnati Reds vs. Brooklyn Dodgers, Dec. 3, 1933 (scored touchdown); Charlie West, Minnesota Vikings vs. Washington Redskins, Nov. 3, 1968 (scored touchdown).

Pro Football Attendance

Pro Football's all-game attendance, including pre-season and post-season games, rose to an all-time high of 15,059,364 in 1972. This record, which totaled 268 games, represented an increase of 4.78% over 1971, when the same number of games drew 14,371,784. The paid attendance during the regular 1972 season was 10,445,827 for a per game average of 57,395, a 3.67% increase over the previous year.

National Football League

Final 1972 Standings

American Conference

Eastern Division

	W.	L.	T.	Pct.	Pts.	Opp.
Miami............	14	0	0	1,000	385	171
N.Y. Jets.........	7	7	0	.500	367	324
Baltimore........	5	9	0	.357	235	.252
Buffalo..........	4	9	1	.321	257	377
New England.....	3	11	0	.214	192	446

Central Division

	W.	L.	T.	Pct.	Pts.	Opp.
Pittsburgh.......	11	3	0	.786	343	175
*Cleveland.......	10	4	0	.714	268	249
Cincinnati.......	8	6	0	.571	299	229
Houston..........	1	13	0	.071	164	380

Western Division

	W.	L.	T.	Pct.	Pts.	Opp.
Oakland..........	10	3	1	.750	365	248
Kansas City......	8	6	0	.571	287	254
Denver..........	5	9	0	.357	325	350
San Diego........	4	9	1	.321	264	344

National Conference

Eastern Division

	W.	L.	T.	Pct.	Pts.	Opp.
Washington......	11	3	0	.786	336	218
*Dallas..........	10	4	0	.714	319	240
N.Y. Giants.......	8	6	0	.571	331	247
St. Louis.........	4	9	1	.321	193	303
Philadelphia.....	2	11	1	.179	145	352

Central Division

	W.	L.	T.	Pct.	Pts.	Opp.
Green Bay........	10	4	0	.714	304	226
Detroit..........	8	5	1	.607	339	290
Minnesota.......	7	7	0	.500	301	252
Chicago..........	4	9	1	.321	225	275

Western Division

	W.	L.	T.	Pct.	Pts.	Opp.
San Francisco....	8	5	1	.607	353	249
Atlanta..........	7	7	0	.500	269	274
Los Angeles......	6	7	1	.464	291	286
New Orleans.....	2	11	1	.179	215	361

*Fourth Qualifier for Playoffs.
AFC Playoffs — Pittsburgh 13, Oakland 7; Miami 20, Cleveland 14.
NFC Playoffs — Dallas 30, San Francisco 28; Washington 16, Green Bay 3.
Championship — Miami 21, Pittsburgh 17; Washington 26, Dallas 9; Miami 14, Washington 7

Miami Defeats Washington in Super Bowl

The Miami Dolphins defeated the Washington Redskins, 14-7 to win the 1973 Super Bowl game. The game was played Jan. 14, 1973 at the Los Angeles Coliseum before a crowd of 90,182 plus an estimated 75 million television viewers.

Score by Periods

Miami....................	7	7	0	0—	14
Washington.............	0	0	0	7—	7

Scoring

Miami—Twilley 28 pass from Griese (Yepremian kick).
Miami—Kiick 1 run (Yepremian kick).
Washington—Bass 49 run with fumble recovery (Knight kick).

Team Statistics

	Miami	Washington
First downs................	12	16
Rushes-yardage...........	37-184	36-141
Passing yardage...........	69	87
Return yardage............	132	103
Passes....................	8-11-1	14-28-3
Punts.....................	7-43.0	5-31.2
Fumbles-Lost..............	2-1	1-0
Penalties-yardage.........	3-35	3-25

Individual Statistics

Miami rushing—Csonka, 15 for 112 yards; Kiick, 12 for 38; Morris, 10 for 34.
Washington rushing—Brown, 22 for 72 yards; Harraway, 10 for 37; Kilmer, 2 for 18; C. Taylor, 1 for 8; Smith, 1 for 6.
Miami passing—Griese, 8 of 11 for 88 yards (one intercepted).

Washington passing Kilmer, 14 of 28 for 104 yards (three intercepted).
Miami pass receiving—Warfield, 3 for 36 yards; Twilley, 1 for 28; Mandich, 1 for 19; Kiick, 2 for 6; Csonka, 1 for minus 1.
Washington pass receiving—Jefferson, 5 for 50 yards; Brown, 5 for 26; C. Taylor, 2 for 20; Smith, 1 for 11; Harraway, 1 for minus 3.

Super Bowl

Year	Winner	Loser	Site
1967	Green Bay Packers, 35	Kansas City Chiefs, 10	Memorial Coliseum, Los Angeles
1968	Green Bay Packers, 33	Oakland Raiders, 14	Orange Bowl, Miami
1969	New York Jets, 16	Baltimore Colts, 7	Orange Bowl, Miami
1970	Kansas City Chiefs, 23	Minnesota Vikings, 7	Tulane Stad., New Orleans
1971	Baltimore Colts, 16	Dallas Cowboys, 13	Orange Bowl, Miami
1972	Dallas Cowboys, 24	Miami Dolphins, 3	Tulane Stad., New Orleans
1973	Miami Dolphins, 14	Washington Redskins, 7	Los Angeles Coliseum

Jim Thorpe Trophy Winners

The Jim Thorpe Trophy winner is picked by Ira Berkow, sports editor of Newspaper Enterprise Assn. in a poll of players from the 26 NFL teams. It goes to the most valuable NFL player and is the oldest and highest professional football award.

Year	Player and Team	Year	Player and Team
1955	Harlon Hill, Chicago Bears	1964	Lenny Moore, Baltimore Colts
1956	Frank Gifford, N. Y. Giants	1965	Jim Brown, Cleveland Browns
1957	John Unitas, Baltimore Colts	1966	Bart Starr, Green Bay Packers
1958	Jim Brown, Cleveland Browns	1967	John Unitas, Baltimore Colts
1959	Charley Conerly, N. Y. Giants	1968	Earl Morrall, Baltimore Colts
1960	Norm Van Brocklin, Philadelphia Eagles	1969	Roman Gabriel, Los Angeles Rams
1961	Y. A. Tittle, N. Y. Giants	1970	John Brodie, San Francisco
1962	Jim Taylor, Green Bay Packers	1971	Bob Griese, Miami
1963	(tie) Jim Brown, Cleveland Browns and Y. A. Tittle, N. Y. Giants	1972	Larry Brown, Washington

George Halas Trophy Winners

The George Halas Trophy is awarded annually to the outstanding defensive player in football in a poll conducted by Newspaper Enterprise Assn. of NFL players.

1966—Larry Wilson, St. Louis	1968—Deacon Jones, Los Angeles	1970—Dick Butkus, Chicago
1967—Deacon Jones, Los Angeles	1969—Dick Butkus, Chicago	1971—Carl Eller, Minnesota
		1972—Joe Greene, Pittsburgh

National Football League

Year	Winners (W-L-T) (East)	Winners (W-L-T) (West)	Playoff
1933	New York Giants (11-3-0)	Chicago Bears (10-2-1)	Chicago Bears 23, New York 21
1934	New York Giants (8-5-0)	Chicago Bears (13-0-0)	New York 30, Chicago Bears 13
1935	New York Giants (9-3-0)	Detroit Lions (7-3-2)	Detroit 26, New York 7
1936	Boston Redskins (7-5-0)	Green Bay Packers (10-1-1)	Green Bay 21, Boston 6
1937	Washington Redskins (8-3-0)	Chicago Bears (9-1-1)	Wash. 28, Chicago Bears 21
1938	New York Giants (8-2-1)	Green Bay Packers (8-3-0)	New York 23, Green Bay 17
1939	New York Giants (9-1-1)	Green Bay Packers (9-2-0)	Green Bay 27, New York 0
1940	Washington Redskins (9-2-0)	Chicago Bears (8-3-0)	Chicago Bears 73, Wash. 0
1941	New York Giants (8-3-0)	Chicago Bears (10-1-1) (A)	Chicago Bears 37, New York 9
1942	Wash. Redskins (10-1-1)	Chicago Bears (11-0-0)	Wash. 14, Chicago Bears 6
1943	Wash. Redskins (6-3-1) (A)	Chicago Bears (8-1-1)	Chicago Bears 41, Wash. 21
1944	New York Giants (8-1-1)	Green Bay Packers (8-2-0)	Green Bay 14, New York 7
1945	Wash. Redskins (8-2-0)	Cleveland Rams (9-1-0)	Cleveland 15, Washington 14
1946	New York Giants (7-3-1)	Chicago Bears (8-2-1)	Chicago Bears 24, New York 14
1947	Philadelphia Eagles (8-4-0) (A)	Chicago Cardinals (9-3-0)	Chicago Cardinals 28, Phila. 21
1948	Philadelphia Eagles (9-2-1)	Chicago Cardinals (11-1-0)	Phila. 7, Chicago Cardinals 0
1949	Philadelphia Eagles (11-1-0)	Los Angeles Rams (8-2-2)	Philadelphia 14, Los Angeles 0
1950	Cleveland Browns (10-2-0) (A)	Los Angeles Rams (9-3-0) (A)	Cleveland 30, Los Angeles 28
1951	Cleveland Browns (11-1-0)	Los Angeles Rams (8-4-0)	Los Angeles 24, Cleveland 17
1952	Cleveland Browns (8-4-0)	Detroit Lions (9-3-0) (A)	Detroit 17, Cleveland 7
1953	Cleveland Browns (11-1-0)	Detroit Lions (10-2-0)	Detroit 17, Cleveland 16
1954	Cleveland Browns (9-3-0)	Detroit Lions (9-2-1)	Cleveland 56, Detroit 10
1955	Cleveland Browns (9-2-1)	Los Angeles Rams (8-3-1)	Cleveland 38, Los Angeles 14
1956	New York Giants (8-3-1)	Chicago Bears (9-2-1)	New York 47, Chicago Bears 7
1957	Cleveland Browns (9-2-1)	Detroit Lions (8-4-0) (A)	Detroit 59, Cleveland 14
1958	New York Giants (9-3-0) (A)	Baltimore Colts (9-3-0)	Baltimore 23, New York 17 (B)
1959	New York Giants (10-2-0)	Baltimore Colts (9-3-0)	Baltimore 31, New York 16
1960	Philadelphia Eagles (10-2-0)	Green Bay Packers (8-4-0)	Philadelphia 17, Green Bay 13
1961	New York Giants (10-3-1)	Green Bay Packers (11-3-0)	Green Bay 37, New York 0
1962	New York Giants (12-2-0)	Green Bay Packers (13-1-0)	Green Bay 16, New York 7
1963	New York Giants (11-3-0)	Chicago Bears (11-1-2)	Chicago 14, New York 10
1964	Cleveland Browns (10-3-1)	Baltimore Colts (12-2-0)	Cleveland 27, Baltimore 0
1965	Cleveland Browns (11-3-0)	Green Bay Packers (10-3-1) (A)	Green Bay 23, Cleveland 12
1966	Dallas Cowboys (10-3-1)	Green Bay Packers (12-2-0)	Green Bay 34, Dallas 27

(A) Won divisional playoff. (B) Won at 8:15 sudden death overtime period.

Year	Conference	Division	Winners (W-L-T)	Playoffs
1967	East	Century	Cleveland (9-5-0)	Dallas, 52, Cleveland 14
		Capitol	Dallas (9-5-0)	
	West	Central	Green Bay (9-4-1)	Green Bay 28, L. A. 7
		Coastal	Los Angeles (11-1-2) (A)	Green Bay 21, Dallas 17
1968	East	Century	Cleveland (10-4-0)	Cleveland 31, Dallas 20
		Capitol	Dallas (12-2-0)	
	West	Central	Minnesota (8-6-0)	Baltimore 24, Minnesota 14
		Coastal	Baltimore (13-1-0)	Baltimore 34, Cleveland 0
1969	East	Century	Cleveland (10-3-1)	Cleveland 38, Dallas 14
		Capital	Dallas (11-2-1)	
	West	Central	Minnesota (12-2-0)	Minnesota 23, Los Angeles 20
		Coastal	Los Angeles (11-3-0)	Minnesota 27, Cleveland 7
1970	American	Eastern	Baltimore (11-2-1)	Baltimore 17, Cincinnati 0
		Central	Cincinnati (8-6-0)	Oakland 21, Miami 14
		Western	Oakland (8-4-2)	Baltimore 27, Oakland 17
	National	Eastern	Dallas (10-4-0)	Dallas 5, Detroit 0
		Central	Minnesota (12-2-0)	San Francisco 17, Minnesota 14
		Western	San Francisco (10-3-1)	Dallas 17, San Francisco 10
1971	American	Eastern	Miami (10-3-1)	Miami 27, Kansas City 24
		Central	Cleveland (9-5-0)	Baltimore 20, Cleveland 3
		Western	Kansas City (10-3-1)	Miami 21, Baltimore 0
	National	Eastern	Dallas (11-3-0)	Dallas 20, Minnesota 12
		Central	Minnesota (11-3-0)	San Francisco 24, Washington 20
		Western	San Francisco (9-5-0)	Dallas 14, San Francisco 3
1972	American	Eastern	Miami (14-0-0)	Miami 20, Cleveland 14
		Central	Pittsburgh (11-3-0)	Pittsburgh 13, Oakland 7
		Western	Oakland (10-3-1)	Miami 21, Pittsburgh 17
	National	Eastern	Washington (11-3-0)	Washington 16, Green Bay 3
		Central	Green Bay (10-4-0)	Dallas 30, San Francisco 28
		Western	San Francisco (8-5-1)	Washington 26, Dallas 3

1973 Professional Football Player Draft

The following are the first round draft picks of the National Football League.

Team	Player	Pos.	College	Team	Player	Pos.	College
1. Houston	John Matuszak	DE	Tampa	15. Cincinnati	Isaac Curtis	WR	San Diego St.
2. Baltimore	Bert Jones	QB	La. State	16. Cleveland	Steve Holden	WR	Ariz. State
(from New Orleans)				(from N.Y. Giants)			
3. Philadelphia	Jerry Sizemore	T	Texas	17. Detroit	Ernest Price	DE	Texas A&I
4. New England	John Hannah	G	Alabama	18. San. Fran.	Michael Holmes	DB	Texas So.
5. St. Louis	Dave Butz	DT	Purdue	19. N. England	Darryl Stingley	WR	Purdue
6. Philadelphia	Charlie Young	TE	So. Calif.	(from Chicago)			
(from San Diego)				20. Dallas	Billy Joe DuPree	TE	Mich. State
7. Buffalo	Paul Seymour	T	Michigan	21. Green Bay	Barry Smith	WR	Florida State
8. Chicago	Wally Chambers	DE	E. Kentucky	22. Cleveland	Pete Adams	T	So. Calif.
9. Denver	Otis Armstrong	RB	Purdue	23. Oakland	William Ray Guy	K-P	So. Miss.
10. Baltimore	Joe Ehrmann	DT	Syracuse	24. Pittsburgh	James Thomas	DB	Florida St.
11. N. England	Sam Cunningham	RB	So. Calif.	25. San Diego	Johnny Rodgers	WR	Nebraska
(from Los Angeles)				(from Wash. through Baltimore)			
12. Minnesota	Chuck Foreman	RB	Miami	26. Buffalo	Joe De Lamielleure	G	Mich. State
13. N.Y. Jets	Burgess Owens	DB	Miami	(from Miami)			
14. Houston	George Amundson	RB	Iowa State				
(from Atlanta)							

National Football Conference Leaders
(National Football League, 1962-1969)

PASSING / PASS-RECEIVING

Year	Player	Atts	Com.	YG.	TD	Year	Player	Ct.	YG.	TD
1962	Bart Starr, G. B.	285	178	2438	9	1962	Bobby Mitchell,Wash.	72	1384	11
1963	Y. A. Tittle, N.Y.	367	221	3145	14	1963	Bobby Conrad, Cards, S. L.	73	967	10
1964	Bart Starr, G. B.	272	163	2144	4	1964	Johnny Morris, Bears	93	1200	10
1965	Rudy Bukich, Chi	312	176	2641	9	1965	Dave Parks, S. F.	80	1344	12
1966	Bart Starr, G. B.	251	156	2257	3	1966	Charlie Taylor, Wash	72	1119	12
1967	Sonny Jurgensen, Wash	508	288	3747	16	1967	Charlie Taylor, Wash	70	990	9
1968	Earl Morrall, Baltimore	317	182	2909	17	1968	Clifton McNeil, San Francisco	71	944	7
1969	Sonny Jurgensen, Wash	422	274	3102	15	1969	Don Abramowicz, New Orleans.	73	1015	7
1970	John Brodie, S. F.	378	223	2941	24	1970	Dick Gordon, Chi	71	1026	13
1971	Roger Staubach, Dallas	211	126	1882	15	1971	Bob Tucker, N.Y.	59	791	4
1972	Norm Snead, N.Y. Giants	325	196	2307	17	1972	Harold Jackson, Phil.	62	1048	4

SCORING / RUSHING

Year	Player	TDs	PAT	FG	Pts.	Year	Player	YG	Atts	TD
1962	Jim Taylor, G. B.	19	0	0	114	1962	Jim Taylor, G. B.	1474	272	19
1963	Don Chandler, N. Y.	0	52	18	106	1963	Jimmy Brown, Cleve.	1863	291	12
1964	Lenny Moore, Balt	20	0	0	120	1964	Jimmy Brown, Cleve.	1446	280	7
1965	Gale Sayers, Chi.	22	0	0	132	1965	Jimmy Brown, Cleve.	1544	289	17
1966	Bruce Gossett, L. A.	0	29	28	113	1966	Gale Sayers, Chi	1231	229	8
1967	Jim Bakken, S. L.	0	36	27	117	1967	Leroy Kelly, Cleve	1205	235	11
1968	Leroy Kelly, Cleve	20	0	0	120	1968	Leroy Kelly, Cleve	1239	248	16
1969	Fred Cox, Minn.	0	43	26	121	1969	Gale Sayers, Chi	1032	236	8
1970	Fred Cox, Minn	0	35	30	125	1970	Larry Brown, Wash.	1125	237	5
1971	Curt Knight, Wash.	0	27	29	114	1971	John Brockington, G.B.	1105	216	4
1972	Chester Marcol, G.B.	0	29	33	128	1972	Larry Brown, Wash.	1216	285	8

American Football Conference Leaders
(American Football League, 1962-1969)

SCORING / RUSHING

Year	Player	TD	PAT	FG	Pts.	Year	Player	YG	Atts.	TD
1962	Gene Mingo, Denver.	4	32	27	137	1962	Cookie Gilchrist, Buffalo.	1096	214	13
1963	Gino Cappelletti, Boston	2	35	22	113	1963	Clem Daniels, Oakland	1098	214	3
1964	Gino Cappelletti, Boston	7	36	25	155	1964	Cookie Gilchrist, Buffalo.	981	230	6
1965	Gino Cappelletti, Boston	9	27	17	132	1965	Paul Lowe, San Diego.	1121	222	7
1966	Gino Cappelletti, Boston	6	35	16	119	1966	Jim Nance, Boston	1458	299	11
1967	George Blanda, Oakland	0	56	20	116	1967	Jim Nance, Boston	1216	269	7
1968	Jim Turner, New York	0	43	34	145	1968	Paul Robinson, Cinn	1023	238	8
1969	Jim Turner, New York	0	33	32	129	1969	Dick Post, San Diego	873	182	6
1970	Jan Stenerud, Kansas City	0	26	30	116	1970	Floyd Little, Denver	901	209	3
1971	Garo Yepremian, Miami	0	33	28	117	1971	Floyd Little, Denver.	1,133	284	6
1972	Bobby Howfield, N.Y. Jets	0	40	27	121	1972	O. J. Simpson, Buffalo	1251	292	6

PASSING / PASS-RECEIVING

Year	Player	Atts	Com.	YG	TD	Year	Player	Ct.	YG	TD
1962	Len Dawson, Dallas	310	189	2749	17	1962	Lionel Taylor, Denver.	77	908	4
1963	Tobin Rote, San Diego	287	170	2510	17	1963	Lionel Taylor, Denver.	78	1101	10
1964	Len Dawson, K. C.	354	199	2879	18	1964	Charlie Hennigan, Houston	101	1561	8
1965	Jack Hadl, San Diego	348	174	2798	21	1965	Lionel Taylor, Denver.	85	1131	6
1966	Len Dawson, Kansas City.	284	159	2527	10	1966	Lance Alworth, San Diego	73	1383	13
1967	Daryle Lamonica, Oakland.	425	220	3228	20	1967	George Sauer, N. Y.	75	1189	6
1968	Len Dawson, Kansas City.	224	131	2109	9	1968	Lance Alworth, San Diego	68	1312	10
1969	Greg Cook, Cinn	197	106	1854	11	1969	Lance Alworth, San Diego	64	1003	4
1970	Daryle Lamonica, Oakland.	356	179	2516	22	1970	Marlin Briscoe, Buffalo	57	1036	8
1971	Bob Griese, Miami	263	145	2,089	19	1971	Fred Biletnikoff, Oakland.	61	929	9
1972	Earl Morrall, Miami	150	83	1360	11	1972	Fred Biletnikoff, Oakland	58	802	7

American Football League

Year	Eastern Division	Western Division	Playoff
1960	Houston Oilers (10-4-0)	L. A. Chargers (10-4-0)	Houston 24, Los Angeles 16
1961	Houston Oilers (10-3-1)	San Diego Chargers (12-2-0)	Houston 10, San Diego 3
1962	Houston Oilers (11-3-0)	Dallas Texans (11-3-0)	Dallas 20, Houston 17 (b)
1963	Boston Patriots (8-6-1) (a)	San Diego Chargers (11-3-0)	San Diego 51, Boston 10
1964	Buffalo Bills (12-2-0)	San Diego Chargers (8-5-1)	Buffalo 20, San Diego 7
1965	Buffalo Bills (10-3-1)	San Diego Chargers (9-2-3)	Buffalo 23, San Diego 0
1966	Buffalo Bills (9-4-1)	Kansas City Chiefs (11-2-1)	Kansas City 31, Buffalo 7
1967	Houston Oilers (9-4-1)	Oakland Raiders (13-1-0)	Oakland 40, Houston 7
1968	New York Jets (11-3-0)	Oakland Raiders (12-2-0) (a)	New York 27, Oakland 23
1969	New York Jets (10-4-0)	Oakland Raiders (12-1-1)	Kansas City 17, Oakland 7 (c)

(a) won divisional playoff (b) won at 2:45 of second overtime. (c) K. C. def. Jets to make playoffs.

All-Time Professional Touchdown Scorers

Player	No.	Player	No.	Player	No.	Player	No.
Jim Brown	126	Joe Perry	84	Bob Hayes	72	Sonny Randle	65
Lenny Moore	113	Art Powell	81	Gary Collins	70	Paul Warfield	64
Don Hutson	105	Frank Gifford	78	Abner Haynes	69	Tim Brown	64
Jim Taylor	93	Steve Van Buren	77	Ray Berry	68	Pete Pihos	63
Bobby Mitchell	91	John David Crow	74	Elroy Hirsch	66	Paul Hornung	62
Don Maynard	88	Ollie Matson	73	Jimmy Orr	66	Dante Lavelli	62
Lance Alworth	87	Bill Brown	72	Joe Morrison	65	Billy Howton	61
Leroy Kelly	87	Charlie Taylor	72	Billy Cannon	65	Hugh McElhenny	60
Tommy McDonald	85						

1972 NFL Individual Leaders

Passing

(At least 140 attempted passes needed to qualify. Leader based on percentage of completions — touchdown passes — interceptions — and average yards).

Player — Team	Att.	Comp.	Pct. Comp.	Yards Gained	TDs.	Lng.	Int.	Avg. Gain
Norm Snead, N.Y. G.	325	196	60.3	2307	17	t94	12	7.10
Earl Morrall, Mia.	150	83	55.3	1360	11	49	7	9.07
Fran Tarkenton, Minn.	378	215	56.9	2651	18	t76	13	7.01
Bob Berry, Atl.	277	154	55.6	2158	13	t57	12	7.79
Bill Kilmer, Wash.	225	120	53.3	1648	19	t89	11	7.32
Daryle Lamonica, Oak.	281	149	53.0	1998	18	t70	12	7.11
Charley Johnson, Den.	238	132	55.5	1783	14	60	14	7.49
Steve Spurrier, S.F.	269	147	54.6	1983	18	t81	16	7.37
John Unitas, Balt.	157	88	56.1	1111	4	t63	6	7.08
Marty Domres, Balt.	222	115	51.8	1392	11	t62	6	6.27
Greg I andry, Det.	268	134	50.0	2066	18	t82	17	7.71
Ken Anderson, Cin.	301	171	56.8	1918	7	t65	7	6.37
Len Dawson, K.C.	305	175	57.4	1835	13	44	12	6.02
Joe Namath, N.Y.J.	324	162	50.0	2816	19	t83	21	8.69
Craig Morton, Dall.	339	185	54.6	2396	15	46	21	7.07
Dennis Shaw, Buff.	258	136	52.7	1666	14	t58	17	6.46
Roman Gabriel, L.A.	323	165	51.1	2027	12	t57	15	6.28
Archie Manning, N.O.	448	230	51.3	2781	18	t66	21	6.21
Mike Phipps, Clev.	305	144	47.2	1994	13	t80	16	6.54
Terry Bradshaw, Pitt.	308	147	47.7	1887	12	t78	12	6.13
John Hadl, S.D.	370	190	51.4	2449	15	61	26	6.62
John Reaves, Phil.	224	108	48.2	1508	7	t77	12	6.73
Bobby Douglass, Chi.	198	75	37.9	1246	9	t85	12	6.29
Scott Hunter, G.B.	199	86	43.2	1252	6	49	9	6.29
Don Pastorini, Hou.	299	144	48.2	1711	7	t82	12	5.72
Gary Cuozzo, St. L.	158	69	43.7	897	5	t68	11	5.68
Jim Plunkett, N.E.	355	169	47.6	2196	8	62	25	6.19

Rushing

	Att.	Yards	Avg.	TDs		Att.	Yards	Avg.	TDs
O. J. Simpson, Buff.	292	1251	4.3	6	Franco Harris, Pitt.	188	1055	5.6	10
Larry Brown, Wash.	285	1216	4.3	8	Calvin Hill, Dall.	245	1036	4.2	6
Ron Johnson, N.Y.G.	298	1182	4.0	9	Mike Garrett, S.D.	272	1031	3.8	6
Larry Csonka, Mia.	213	1117	5.2	6	John Brockington, G.B.	274	1027	3.7	8
Marv Hubbard, Oak.	219	1100	5.0	4	Mercury Morris, Mia.	190	1000	5.3	12

Pass Receiving

	No.	Yards	Avg.	TDs		No.	Yards	Avg.	TDs
Harold Jackson, Phil.	62	1048	16.9	4	Gary Garrison, S.D.	52	744	14.3	7
Fred Biletnikoff, Oak.	58	802	13.8	7	Art Malone, Atl.	50	585	11.7	2
Otis Taylor, K.C.	57	821	14.4	6	Charley Taylor, Wash.	49	673	13.7	7
Chip Myers, Cin.	57	792	13.9	3	John Gilliam, Minn.	47	1035	22.0	7
Bob Tucker, N.Y.G.	55	764	13.9	4	Bob Newland, N.O.	47	579	12.3	2
J. D. Hill, Buff.	52	754	14.5	5					

Scorers

	XP	FG	Pts.		XP	FG	Pts.
Chester Marcol, G.B.	29	33	128	Toni Fritsch, Dall.	36	21	99
Bobby Howfield, N.Y.J.	40	27	121	Errol Mann, Det.	38	20	98
Roy Gerela, Pitt.	35	28	119	Fred Cox, Minn.	34	21	97
Garo Yepremian, Mia.	43	24	115	Pete Gogolak, N.Y.G.	34	21	97
Horst Muhlmann, Cin.	30	27	111	Jim Turner, Den.	37	20	97
David Ray, L.A.	31	24	103				

1972 NEA All-NFL Team

FIRST TEAM	OFFENSE	SECOND TEAM
Ted Kwalick, San Francisco	Tight End	Jim Mitchell, Atlanta
Fred Biletnikoff, Oakland	Wide Receiver	Gene Washington, San Francisco
Paul Warfield, Miami	Wide Receiver	Harold Jackson, Philadelphia
Rayfield Wright, Dallas	Tackle	Ron Yary, Minnesota
George Kunz, Atlanta	Tackle	Winston Hill, New York Jets
Larry Little, Miami	Guard	Tom Mack, Los Angeles
Blaine Nye, Dallas	Guard	John Niland, Dallas
Len Hauss, Washington	Center	Forrest Blue, San Francisco
Joe Namath, New York Jets	Quarterback	Earl Morrall, Miami
Larry Brown, Washington	Running Back	Franco Harris, Pittsburgh
O. J. Simpson, Buffalo	Running Back	John Brockington, Green Bay
Chet Marcol, Green Bay	Kicker	Roy Gerela, Pittsburgh

FIRST TEAM	DEFENSE	SECOND TEAM
Claude Humphrey, Atlanta	End	Larry Hand, Detroit
Jack Gregory, New York Giants	End	Deacon Jones, San Diego
Mike Reid, Cincinnati	Tackle	Bob Lilly, Dallas
Joe Greene, Pittsburgh	Tackle	Alan Page, Minnesota
Dick Butkus, Chicago	Middle Linebacker	Willie Lanier, Kansas City
Dave Wilcox, San Francisco	Strong Linebacker	Ted Hendricks, Baltimore
Chris Hanburger, Washington	Weak Linebacker	Andy Russell, Pittsburgh
Jim Johnson, San Francisco	Corner Linebacker	Pat Fischer, Washington
Willie Brown, Oakland	Corner Linebacker	Mel Renfro, Dallas
Dick Anderson, Miami	Short Safety	Ken Houston, Houston
Bill Bradley, Philadelphia	Free Safety	Jake Scott, Miami
Don Cockroft, Cleveland	Punter	Jerrell Wilson, Kansas City

Pro Football's Hall Of Fame
Canton, Ohio

Cliff Battles	Red Grange	Link Lyman	Hugh (Shorty) Ray
Sammy Baugh	Joe Guyon	Tim Mara	Dan Reeves
Chuck Bednarik	George Halas	Gino Marchetti	Andy Robustelli
Bert Bell	Ed Healey	George Marshall	Art Rooney
Charles Bidwell	Mel Hein	Ollie Matson	Ernie Stautner
Jim Brown	Pete Henry	George McAfee	Ken Strong
Paul Brown	Arnold Herber	Hugh McElhenny	Joe Stydahar
Joe Carr	Bill Hewitt	John (Blood) McNally	Jim Thorpe
Guy Chamberlin	Clarke Hinkle	Mike Michalske	Y. A. Tittle
Jack Christiansen	Elroy Hirsch	Wayne Millner	George Trafton
Dutch Clark	Cal Hubbard	Marion Motley	Charlie Trippi
Jim Conzelman	Lamar Hunt	Bronco Nagurski	Emlen Tunnell
Art Donovan	Don Hutson	Greasy Neale	Clyde (Bulldog) Turner
Paddy Driscoll	Walt Kiesling	Ernie Nevers	Norm Van Brocklin
Bill Dudley	Frank (Bruiser) Kinard	Leo Nomellini	Steve Van Buren
Turk Edwards	Curly Lambeau	Steve Owen	Bob Waterfield
Tom Fears	Bobby Layne	Clarence (Ace) Parker	Alex Wojciechowicz
Dr. Daniel Fortmann	Vince Lombardi	Jim Parker	
Otto Graham	Sid Luckman	Joe Perry	

Canadian Football League
1972 Final Standings

Eastern Conference	W	L	T	PF	PA	Pts.	Western Conference	W.	L.	T.	Pf.	PA	Pts.
Hamilton	11	3	0	372	262	22	Winnipeg	10	6	0	401	300	20
Ottawa	11	3	0	298	228	22	Edmonton	10	6	0	254	368	20
Montreal	4	10	0	246	353	8	Saskatchewan	8	8	0	330	283	16
Toronto	3	11	0	254	298	6	Calgary	6	10	0	331	394	12
							British Columbia	5	11	0	380	380	10

Eastern Playoffs—Ottawa 14, Montreal 11; Ottawa 19, Hamilton 7; Hamilton 23, Ottawa 8.
Western Playoffs—Saskatchewan 8, Edmonton 6; Saskatchewan 27, Winnipeg 24.
Grey Cup—Hamilton 13, Saskatchewan 10.

Canadian Football League (Grey Cup)

Winners of Eastern and Western divisions meet in championship game for Grey Cup (donated by Governor-General Earl Grey in 1909). Canadian football features three downs, 110-yard field, and each team can have 12 players on field at one time.

1948—Calgary Stampeders 12, Ottawa
    Rough Riders 7
1949—Montreal Alouettes 28, Calgary Stampeders 15
1950—Toronto Argonauts 13, Winnipeg Blue
    Bombers 0
1951—Ottawa Rough Riders 21, Saskatchewan
    Roughriders 14
1952—Toronto Argonauts 21, Edmonton Eskimos 11
1953—Hamilton Tiger-Cats 12, Winnipeg Blue
    Bombers 6
1954—Edmonton Eskimos 26, Montreal Alouettes 25
1955—Edmonton Eskimos 34, Montreal Alouettes 19
1956—Edmonton Eskimos 50, Montreal Alouettes 27
1957—Hamilton Tiger-Cats 32, Winnipeg Blue
    Bombers 7
1958—Winnipeg Blue Bombers 35, Hamilton
    Tiger-Cats 28
1959—Winnipeg Blue Bombers 21, Hamilton
    Tiger-Cats 7
1900—Ottawa Rough Riders 16, Edmonton Eskimos 6

1961—Winnipeg Blue Bombers 21, Hamilton
    Tiger-Cats 14
1962—Winnipeg Blue Bombers 28, Hamilton
    Tiger-Cats 27
1963—Hamilton Tiger-Cats 21, British Columbia
    Lions 10
1964—British Columbia Lions 34, Hamilton
    Tiger-Cats 24
1965—Hamilton Tiger-Cats 22, Winnipeg Blue
    Bombers 16
1966—Saskatchewan Roughriders 29, Ottawa Rough
    Riders 14
1967—Hamilton Tiger-Cats 24, Saskatchewan
    Roughriders 1
1968—Ottawa Rough Riders 24, Calgary Stampeders 21.
1969—Ottawa Rough Riders 29, Saskatchewan
    Roughriders 11.
1970—Montreal Alouettes 23, Calgary Stampeders 10.
1971—Calgary Stampeders 14, Toronto Argonauts 11.
1972—Hamilton Tiger-Cats 13, Saskatchewan Rough Riders 10.

Stadiums

For stadiums that house a major league baseball team and college stadiums, see index.

Name and location	Capacity	Name and location	Capacity
American Legion Memorial, Charlotte, N.C.	22,315	Mile High Stadium, Denver	51,656
Arrowhead Stadium, Kansas City	78,034	Mississippi Memorial Stadium, Jackson	46,000
Balboa Stadium, San Diego, Calif.	34,500	Orange Bowl, Miami, Fla.	80,010
Bowman Grey Stad., Winston-Salem, N.C.	16,841	Ottawa Stadium, Ottawa, Canada	27,872
Buffalo War Memorial Stadium	46,206	Portland Civic Stadium	29,010
Columbus (Ga.) Memorial Stadium	35,000	Rich Stadium, Buffalo, N.Y.	80,000
Cotton Bowl, Dallas, Tex.	72,000	Richmond (Va.) City Stadium	22,009
Empire Stadium, Vancouver	32,759	Roanoke (Va.) Victory Stadium	30,000
Franklin Field, Philadelphia	60,658	Roosevelt Stadium, Jersey City	25,000
Gator Bowl, Jacksonville, Fla.	70,000	Rose Bowl, Pasadena, Calif.	100,570
John F. Kennedy Stadium, Phil.	105,000	Rubber Bowl, Akron, Ohio	35,007
Robert F. Kennedy Memorial Stadium, Wash., D.C.	53,041	Schaefer Stadium, Foxboro, Mass.	60,999
Kentucky Exposition Stadium, Louisville	21,000	Sicks, Stadium	24,420
Kezar Stadium, San Francisco	59,636	Soldier Field, Chicago	55,049
Ladd Memorial Stadium, Mobile, Ala.	40,605	Sugar Bowl, New Orleans, La.	80,982
Lambeau Field, Green Bay, Wis.	56,263	Sun Bowl, El Paso, Texas	30,000
Legion Stadium, Birmingham, Ala.	68,821	Tampa Stadium, Tampa, Fla.	45,005
Long Beach (Calif.) Veterans Memorial	15,000	Texas Stad., Dallas	65,111
Los Angeles Memorial Coliseum	76,000	Wood Memorial Stad., Sioux Falls, S.D.	10,000

1973 Water Ski Champions

31st Annual National Water Ski Championships

Picture Lake, Petersburg, Va., August 16-19, 1973

Men's Overall — Wayne Grimditch, Pompano Beach, Fla., 2935 points.
Men's Slalom — Kris LaPoint, Castro Valley, Calif., 55 buoys.
Men's Tricks — Tony Krupa, Jackson, Mich., 5599 points.
Men's Jumping — Ricky McCormick, Independence, Mo., 161 ft.
Women's Overall — Liz Allan Shetter, Groveland, Fla., 3701 points.
Women's Slalom — Liz Allan Shetter, 57 buoys.
Women's Tricks — Liz Allan Shetter, 4422 points.
Women's Jumping — Linda Leavengood Giddens, Eastman, Ga., 118 ft.
Senior Men's Overall — Dr. J. D. Morgan, Key West, Fla., 3598 points.
Senior Men's Slalom — Dr. J. D. Morgan, 52 buoys.
Senior Men's Tricks — Dr. J. D. Morgan, 3927 points.
Senior Men's Jumping — Dr. J. D. Morgan, 123 ft.
Senior Women's Overall — Thelma Salmas, Novato, Calif., 2397 points.
Senior Women's Slalom — Thelma Salmas, 38½ buoys.
Senior Women's Tricks — Sandy Monnier, Rock Falls, Ill., 3267 points.
Senior Women's Jumping — Thelma Salmas, 101 ft.

Boy's Overall — Chris Redmond, Canton, Ohio., 2871 points.
Boy's Slalom — Mark Crone, Shapleigh, Maine, 51 buoys.
Boy's Tricks — Chris Redmond, 4422 points.
Boy's Jumping — Chris Redmond, 131 ft.
Girl's Overall — Cindy Hutcherson, Deland, Fla., 3400 points.
Girl's Slalom — Cindy Hutcherson, 55½ buoys.
Girl's Tricks — Cindy Hutcherson, 3686 points.
Girl's Jumping — Cindy Hutcherson, 102 ft.
Junior Boy's Overall — Jeff Mostellar, Mobile, Ala., 3003 points.
Junior Boy's Slalom — Mark Cumberland, Florence, Miss., 46 buoys.
Junior Boy's Tricks — Jeff Lampas, Battle Creek, Mich., 2585 points.
Junior Boy's Jumping — Joe Cornell, Bethel Island, Calif., 103 ft.
Junior Girl's Overall — Camille Duvall, Greenville, S.C., 3971 points.
Junior Girl's Slalom — Deena Brush, W. Sacramento, Calif., 49 buoys.
Junior Girl's Tricks — Camille Duvall, 2794 points.
Junior Girl's Jumping — Camille Duvall, 94 ft.

15th Annual Masters Tournament

Callaway Gardens, GA., July 13-15, 1973

Men's Overall — Mike Suyderhoud, Petaluma, Calif., 2867 points.
Men's Slalom — Kris LaPoint, Castro Valley, Calif., 52 buoys.
Men's Tricks — Tony Krupa, Jackson, Mich., 4920 points.
Men's Jumping — Ricky McCormick, Independence, Mo., 155 feet.

Women's Overall — Liz Allan Shetter, Groveland, Fla., 3000 points.
Women's Slalom — Liz Allan Shetter, 55 buoys.
Women's Tricks — Barbara Cleveland, Hawthorne, Fla., 3590 points.
Women's Jumping — Liz Allan Shetter, 113 feet.

XIII World Water Ski Championships

Bogota, Colombia, September 13-16, 1973

Men's Overall — George Athans, Canada, 2854 points.
Men's Slalom — George Athans, 73 buoys.
Men's Tricks — Wayne Grimditch, USA, 8080 points.
Men's Jumping — Ricky McCormick, USA, 167 feet.
Women's Overall — Lisa St. John, USA, 2534 points.

Women's Slalom — Sylvie Maurial, France, 60 buoys.
Women's Tricks — Maria Victoria Carrasco, Venezuela, 8140 points.
Women's Jumping — Liz Allan Shetter, USA, 115 feet.
Team — United States, 8254.5 points.

National Amateur Bicycle Championships in 1973

Milwaukee, Wisc. (Road); North Brook, Ill. (Track); July 28-Aug. 4, 1973

Road Races

Senior Men — John Howard, Texas
Junior Men — Pat Nielson, Mich.
Senior Women — Eileen Brennan, Mich.
Intermediate Boys — Andy Peake, Ore.
Veterans — Jim Crist, Colo.

Senior Men 1000 Meter — Steve Woznick, New Jersey.
Senior Women Sprints — Sheila Young, Mich.
Senior Women 3000 Meter Pursuit — Mary Jane Reoch, Pa.
Junior Men — Gilbert Hatton, Calif.
Intermediate Boys — Stan Kostuck, Wisc.
Intermediate Girls — Jane Brennan, Mich.
Midget Boys — Jeff Bradley, Iowa
Midget Girls — Connie Paraskevin, Mich.

Track

Senior Men Sprints — Roger Young, Mich.
Senior Men 4000 Meter Pursuit — Mike Neel, Ill.
Senior Men 10 Mile — Mike Neel, Ill.

4000 Meter Team Pursuit — David Chauner, John Chapman, Joe Saling, Steve Woznick, New Jersey

Tour de France Bicycle Race

Luis Ocana of Spain won the 1973 Tour de France bicycle race by finishing ahead of Bernard Thevenet of France by 15 minutes, 51 seconds. The 3,840 kilometer race lasted 23 days, and was completed in Paris on July 22. Eddy Merckx of Belgium, who had won the race the past 4 years, did not compete.

Polo Records

National Open Tournament	
1963	Tulsa 7, Oakland (Calif.) Crescents 6
1964	Oak Brook 10, Solo Cup Crescents 9
1965	Oak Brook 11, Bunn Tyco Chicago 5
1966	Tulsa 10, Fountain Grove 5
1967	Bunntyco-Oakbrook 8, Milwaukee 2
1968	Midland 9, Milwaukee 0
1969	Tulsa Green Hill 11, Milwaukee 10
1970	Tulsa Green Hill 9, Oak Brook 5
1971	Oak Brook 8, Green Hill Farm 7
1972	Milwaukee 9, Tulsa 5
1973	Oak Brook 9, Willow Bend 4

1967	Milwaukee 11, Keswick-Blue Ridge 7
1968	Oak Brook 12, Keswick Sunny Climes 9
1969	Oak Brook 7, Milwaukee 6
1970	Oak Brook 9, Tulsa Green Hill 7
1971	Green Hill Farm 8, Milwaukee 6
1972	Red Doors Farm 10, Sun Ranch 6
1973	Houston 6, Willow Bend 4

Intercollegiate Championship	
1963	Cornell 11, Yale 4
1964	Yale 12, Cornell 9
1965	Yale 12, Cornell 3
1966	Cornell 12, Yale 10
1967	Yale 12, Cornell 11
1968	Yale 17, Cornell 13
1969	Yale 17, Cornell 16
1970	Yale 22, Cornell 10
1971	Yale 12, Virginia 11
1972	Univ. of Conn. 17, Univ. of Virginia 15
1973	Univ. of Conn. 19, Univ. of Virginia 10

National 20-Goal Tournament	
1963	Oak Brook 10, Tulsa 7
1964	Oak Brook 8, Tulsa 5
1965	Santa Barbara-Oak Brook 7, Milwaukee 2
1966	Sunny Climes 9, Oak Brook 7

OTHER TOURNAMENTS IN 1973

National 16-Goal — Baca Raton 6, Aiken 5
National 14-Goal — Houston 6, Good Hope 5

National 8-Goal — Maryland 4, Tulsa-Myopia 3

USLTA National Champions

MEN'S SINGLES

Year	Champion	Final Opponent	Year	Champion	Final Opponent
1920	Bill Tilden	William Johnston	1947	Jack Kramer	Frank Parker
1921	Bill Tilden	Wallace Johnston	1948	Pancho Gonzales	Eric Sturgess
1922	Bill Tilden	William Johnston	1949	Pancho Gonzales	F. R. Schroeder, Jr.
1923	Bill Tilden	William Johnston	1950	Arthur Larsen	Herbert Flam
1924	Bill Tilden	William Johnston	1951	Frank Sedgman	E. Victor Seixas, Jr.
1925	Bill Tilden	William Johnston	1952	Frank Sedgman	Gardner Mulloy
1926	Rene Lacoste	Jean Borotra	1953	Tony Trabert	E. Victor Seixas, Jr.
1927	Rene Lacoste	Bill Tilden	1954	E. Victor Seixas, Jr.	Rex Hartwig
1928	Henri Cochet	Francis Hunter	1955	Tony Trabert	Ken Rosewall
1929	Bill Tilden	Francis Hunter	1956	Kenneth Rosewall	Lewis Hoad
1930	John Doeg	Francis Shields	1957	Malcolm Anderson	Ashley Cooper
1931	H. Ellsworth Vines	George Lott	1958	Ashley Cooper	Malcolm Anderson
1932	H. Ellsworth Vines	Henri Cochet	1959	Neale A. Fraser	Alejandro Olmedo
1933	Fred Perry	John Crawford	1960	Neale A. Fraser	Rod Laver
1934	Fred Perry	Wilmer Allison	1961	Roy Emerson	Rod Laver
1935	Wilmer Allison	Sidney Wood	1962	Rod Laver	Roy Emerson
1936	Fred Perry	Don Budge	1963	Rafael Osuna	F. A. Froehling, 3d
1937	Don Budge	Baron G. von Cramm	1964	Roy Emerson	Fred Stolle
1938	Don Budge	C. Gene Mako	1965	Manuel Santana	Cliff Drysdale
1939	Robert Riggs	S. Welby Van Horn	1966	Fred Stolle	John Newcombe
1940	Don McNeill	Robert Riggs	1967	John Newcombe	Clark Graebner
1941	Robert Riggs	F. I. Kovacs	1968	Arthur Ashe	Tom Okker
1942	F. R. Schroeder, Jr.	Frank Parker	1969	Rod Laver	Tony Roche
1943	Joseph Hunt	Jack Kramer	1970	Ken Rosewall	Tony Roche
1944	Frank Parker	William Talbert	1971	Stan Smith	Jan Kodes
1945	Frank Parker	William Talbert	1972	Ilie Nastase	Arthur Ashe
1946	Jack Kramer	Thomas Brown, Jr.	1973	John Newcombe	Jan Kodes

MEN'S DOUBLES

Year	Doubles Champions	Year	Doubles Champions
1920	... William Johnston & Clarence Griffin	1947	... Jack Kramer and Frederick Schroeder, Jr.
1921	... Bill Tilden & Vincent Richards	1948	... Gardnar Mulloy and William Talbert
1922	... Bill Tilden & Vincent Richards	1949	... John Bromwich and William Sidwell
1923	... Bill Tilden & Brian Norton	1950	... John Bromwich and Frank Sedgman
1924	... Howard Kinsey & Robert Kinsey	1951	... Frank Sedgman & Kenneth McGregor
1925	... R. Norris Williams & Vincent Richards	1952	... Mervyn Rose and E. Victor Seixas, Jr.
1926	... R. Norris Williams & Vincent Richards	1953	... Rex Hartwig and Mervyn Rose
1927	... Bill Tilden & Francis Hunter	1954	... E. Victor Seixas, Jr. and Tony Trabert
1928	... George Lott & John Hennessey	1955	... Kosei Kamo and Atsushi Miyagi
1929	... George Lott & John Doeg	1956	... Lewis Hoad and Kenneth Rosewall
1930	... George Lott & John Doeg	1957	... Ashley Cooper and Neale Fraser
1931	... Wilmer Allison & John Van Ryn	1958	... Hamilton Richardson and Alejandro Olmedo
1932	... H. Ellsworth Vines & Keith Gledhill	1959	... Neale A. Fraser and Roy Emerson
1933	... George Lott & Lester Stoefen	1960	... Neale A. Fraser and Roy Emerson
1934	... George Lott & Lester Stoefen	1961	... Dennis Ralston and Chuck McKinley
1935	... Wilmer Allison & John Van Ryn	1962	... Rafael Osuna and Antonio Palafox
1936	... Don Budge & C. Gene Mako	1963	... Dennis Ralston and Chuck McKinley
1937	... Baron G. von Cramm & Henner Henkel	1964	... Dennis Ralston and Chuck McKinely
1938	... Don Budge & C. Gene Mako	1965	... Roy Emerson and Fred Stolle
1939	... Adrian Quist & John Bromwich	1966	... Roy Emerson and Fred Stolle
1940	... Jack Kramer and Frederick Schroeder, Jr.	1967	... John Newcombe and Tony Roche
1941	... Jack Kramer and Frederick Schroeder, Jr.	1968	... Robert Lutz and Stan Smith
1942	... Gardnar Mulloy and William Talbert	1969	... Fred Stolle and Ken Rosewall
1943	... Jack Kramer and Frank Parker	1970	... Pierre Barthes and Nicki Pilic
1944	... Don McNeill and Robert Falkenburg	1971	... John Newcombe and Roger Taylor
1945	... Gardnar Mulloy and William Talbert	1972	... Cliff Drysdale and Roger Taylor
1946	... Gardnar Mulloy and William Talbert	1973	... John Newcombe and Owen Davidson

MEN'S INDOOR CHAMPIONS

Year	Singles	Doubles	Year	Singles	Doubles
1958	Richard Savitt	Grant Golden-Barry MacKay	1966	C. Pasarell	Robert Lutz-Stan Smith
1959	Alex Olmedo	Alex Olmedo-Barry MacKay	1967	C. Pasarell	Arthur Ashe-C. Pasarell
1960	Barry MacKay	Andres Gimeno-Manuel Santana	1968	Cliff Richey	Thomas Koch & Tom Okker
1961	Richard Savitt	C. Crawford-R. Holmberg	1969	Stan Smith	Stan Smith-Robert Lutz
1962	Chas. McKinley	R. Laver-C. McKinley	1970	Ilie Nastase	Stan Smith-Arthur Ashe
1963	Dennis Ralston	D. Ralston-C. McKinley	1971	Clark Graebner	Juan Gisbert-Manuel Orantes
1964	Chas. McKinley	M. Santana-J. L. Arilla	1972	Stan Smith	Andres Gimeno-Manuel Orantes
1965	Jan Erik Lundquist	D. Ralston-C. McKinley	1973	Jimmy Connors	Juan Gisbert & Jurgen Fassbender

WOMEN'S INDOOR CHAMPIONS

Year	Champion	Doubles Champions	Year	Champion	Doubles Champions
1961	Janet S. Hopps	Janet S. Hopps and Kay Hubbell	1967	Billie Jean King	Carol Hanks Aucamp & Mary Ann Eisel
1962	Carole Wright	Ruth Jeffery and Belmar Gunderson	1968	Billie Jean King	Billie Jean King & Rosemary Casals
1963	Carol Hanks	Carol Hanks and Mary Ann Eisel	1969	Mary Ann E. Curtis	Mary Ann Eisel & Valerie Ziegenfuss
1964	Mary Ann Eisel	Mary Ann Eisel & Katharine Hubbell	1970	Mary Ann E. Curtis	Peaches Bartkowicz & Nancy Richey
1965	Nancy Richey	Carol Hanks Aucamp and Mary Ann Eisel	1971	Billie Jean King	Billie Jean King & Rosemary Casals
1966	Billie Jean King	Billie Jean King & Rosemary Casals	1972	Virginia Wade	Rosemary Casals & Virginia Wade
			1973	Evonne Goolagong	Olga Morozova & Marina Kroskina

WOMEN'S SINGLES, DOUBLES, MIXED DOUBLES

Year	Singles Champions	Doubles Champions	Mixed Doubles Champions
1935	Helen Jacobs	Helen Jacobs & Mrs. Sarah P. Fabyan ..	Mrs. Sarah P. Fabyan & Enrique Maier
1936	Alice Marble............	Mrs. M. G. Van Ryn & Carolin Babcock .	Alice Marble & C. Gene Mako
1937	Anita Lizana............	Mrs. Sarah P. Fabyan & Alice Marble...	Mrs. Sarah P. Fabyan & Don Budge
1938	Alice Marble...........	Alice Marble & Mrs. Sarah P. Fabyan ...	Alice Marble & Don Budge
1939	Alice Marble...........	Alice Marble & Mrs. Sarah P. Fabyan ...	Alice Marble & Harry Hopman
1940	Alice Marble...........	Alice Marble & Mrs. Sarah P. Fabyan ...	Alice Marble & Robert Riggs
1941	Mrs. Sarah P. Cooke	Mrs. S. P. Cooke & Margaret Osborne ...	Mrs. Sarah P. Cooke & Jack Kramer
1942	Pauline Betz...........	A. Louise Brough & Margaret Osborne.	A. Louise Brough & Frederick Schroeder
1943	Pauline Betz...........	A. Louise Brough & Margaret Osborne ..	Margaret Osborne & William Talbert
1944	Pauline Betz...........	A. Louise Brough & Margaret Osborne ..	Margaret Osborne & William Talbert
1945	Sarah P. Cooke.........	A. Louise Brough & Margaret Osborne ..	Margaret Osborne & William Talbert
1946	Pauline Betz...........	A. Louise Brough & Margaret Osborne ..	Margaret Osborne & William Talbert
1947	Louise Brough	A. Louise Brough & Margaret Osborne .	A. Louise Brough & John Bromwich
1948	Mrs. Margaret O. du Pont .	A. Louise Brough & Mrs. M. O. Du Pont .	A. Louise Brough & Thomas Brown, Jr.
1949	Mrs. Margaret O. du Pont .	A. Louise Brough & Mrs. M. O. Du Pont .	A. Louise Brough & Eric Sturgess
1950	Mrs. Margaret O. du Pont .	A. Louise Brough & Mrs. M. O. Du Pont .	Mrs. M. O. du Pont & Kenneth MacGregor
1951	Maureen Connolly.......	Doris Hart and Shirley Fry	Doris Hart & Frank Sedgman
1952	Maureen Connolly.......	Doris Hart and Shirley Fry	Doris Hart & Frank Sedgman
1953	Maureen Connolly.......	Doris Hart and Shirley Fry	Doris Hart & E. Victor Seixas, Jr.
1954	Doris Hart	Doris Hart and Shirley Fry	Doris Hart & E. Victor Seixas, Jr.
1955	Doris Hart	A. Louise Brough & Mrs. M. O. du Pont .	Doris Hart & E. Victor Seixas, Jr.
1956	Shirley J. Fry..........	A. Louise Brough & Mrs. M. O. du Pont .	Mrs. M. O. DuPont and Kenneth Rosewall
1957	Althea Gibson..........	A. Louise Brough & Mrs. M. O. du Pont .	Althea Gibson and Kurt Nielsen
1958	Althea Gibson..........	Darlene Hart and Jeanne Arth.........	Mrs. M. O. du Pont and Neale Fraser
1959	Maria Bueno...........	Darlene Hard and Jeanne Arth	Mrs. M. O. du Pont and Neale Fraser
1960	Darlene R. Hard........	Darlene Hard and Marie Bueno........	Mrs. M. O. du Pont and Neale Fraser
1961	Darlene R. Hard........	Darlene Hard and Lesley Turner	Margaret Smith and Robert Mark
1962	Margaret Smith	Maria Bueno and Darlene Hard	Margaret Smith and Fred Stolle
1963	Maria Bueno...........	Margaret Smith and Robyn Ebbern	Margaret Smith and Kenneth Fletcher
1964	Maria Bueno...........	Billie Jean Moffit & Karen Susman	Margaret Smith & John Newcombe
1965	Margaret Smith	Carole C. Graebner & Nancy Richey ...	Margaret Smith & Fred Stolle
1966	Marie Bueno...........	Marie Bueno & Nancy Richey.........	Donna Floyd Fales & Owen Davidson
1967	Billie Jean King	Rosemary Casals & Billie Jean King ...	Billie Jean King & Owen Davidson
1968	Virgina Wade	Marie Bueno & Mrs. M. S. Court	Mary Ann Eisel & Peter Curtis
1969	Margaret Smith Court	Francoise Durr & Darlene Hard	Margaret S. Court & Marty Riessen
1970	Margaret Smith Court	M. S. Court & Judy Tegart Dalton	Margaret S. Court & Marty Riessen
1971	Billie Jean King	Rosemary Casals & Judy Tegart Dalton	Billie Jean King & Owen Davidson
1972	Billie Jean King	Francoise Durr & Betty Stove	Margaret S. Court & Marty Riessen
1973	Margaret Smith Court.......	Margaret S. Court & Virginia Wade.......	Billie Jean King & Owen Davidson

NCAA TENNIS CHAMPIONS

Year	Singles	College	Doubles	College
1963	Dennis Ralston...........	So. California	Dennis Ralston and Rafael Osuna	So. California
1964	Dennis Ralston...........	So. California	Dennis Ralston and Bill Bond	So. California
1965	Arthur Ashe	UCLA	Arthur Ashe and Ian Crookenden	UCLA
1966	Charles Pasarell	UCLA	Charles Pasarell and Ian Crookenden	UCLA
1967	Bob Lutz	So. Calif.	Stan Smith & Bob Lutz....................	So. Calif.
1968	Stan Smith	So. Calif.	Stan Smith & Bob Lutz....................	So. Calif.
1969	Joaquin Loyo Mayo	So. Calif.	Joaquin Loyo Mayo & Marcelo Lara	So. Calif.
1970	Jeff Borowiak	UCLA	Pat Cramer & Luis Garcia...................	Miami (Fla.)
1971	Jimmy Connors	UCLA	Jeff Borowiak & Haroon Rahim................	UCLA
1972	Dick Stockton	Trinity (Tex.)	Sandy Mayer & Roscoe Tanner	Stanford
1973	Sandy Mayer..............	Stanford	Sandy Mayer & Jim Delaney	Stanford

CLAY COURT CHAMPIONS

Year	Champion	Year	Champion	Year	Champion	Year	Champion
1950	Herbert Flam	1956	Herbert Flam	1962	Chuck McKinley	1968	Clark Graebner
1951	Tony Trabert	1957	E. Victor Seixas, Jr.	1963	Chuck McKinley	1969	Zeljko Franulovic
1952	Arthur Larsen	1958	Bernard Bartzen	1964	Dennis Ralston	1970	Cliff Richey
1953	E. Vic Seixas, Jr.	1959	Bernard Bartzen	1965	Dennis Ralston	1971	Zeljko Franulovic
1954	Bernard Bartzen	1960	Barry MacKay	1966	Cliff Richey	1972	Bob Hewitt
1955	Tony Trabert	1961	Bernard Bartzen	1967	Arthur Ashe	1973	Manuel Orantes

Davis Cup International Tennis—Challenge Round

Year	Winner	Loser	Score	Year	Winner	Loser	Score	Year	Winner	Loser	Score
1900	U. S	Brit. Isles .	3-0	1927	France ...	U. S	3-2	1953	Australia..	U. S.......	3-2
1902	U. S	Brit. Isles .	3-2	1928	France ...	U. S	4-1	1954	U. S......	Australia...	3-2
1903	British ...	U. S	4-1	1929	France ...	U. S	3-2	1955	Australia..	U. S.......	5-0
1904	British ...	Belgium ..	5-0	1930	France ...	U. S	4-1	1956	Australia..	U. S.......	5-0
1905	British ...	U. S	5-0	1931	France ...	Gt. Britain	3-2	1957	Australia..	U. S.......	3-2
1906	British ...	U. S	5-0	1932	France ...	U. S	3-2	1958	U. S......	Australia...	3-2
1907	Australasia	British....	3-2	1933	Gt. Britain	France	3-2	1959	Australia..	U. S.......	3-2
1908	Australasia	U. S	3-2	1934	Gt. Britain	U. S	4-1	1960	Australia..	Italy......	4-1
1909	Australasia	U. S	5-0	1935	Gt. Britain	U. S	5-0	1961	Australia..	Italy......	5-0
1911	Australasia	U. S	5-0	1936	Gt. Britain	Australia ..	3-2	1962	Australia..	Mexico	5-0
1912	British ...	Australasia	3-2	1937	U. S	Gt. Britain	4-1	1963	U. S......	Australia...	3-2
1913	U. S	British....	3-2	1938	U. S	Australia ..	3-2	1964	Australia..	U. S.......	3-2
1914	Australasia	U. S	3-2	1939	Australia..	U. S	3-2	1965	Australia..	Spain.....	4-1
1919	Australasia	British....	4-1	1940	-1945 (Not played)			1966	Australia..	India.....	4-1
1920	U. S	Australasia	5-0	1946	U. S	Australia ..	5-0	1967	Australia..	Spain.....	4-1
1921	U. S	Japan	5-0	1947	U. S	Australia ..	4-1	1968	U. S......	Australia...	4-1
1922	U. S	Australasia	4-1	1948	U. S	Australia ..	5-0	1969	U. S......	Romania ...	5-0
1923	U. S	Australasia	4-1	1949	U. S	Australia ..	4-1	1970	U. S......	W. Germany	5-0
1924	U. S	Australasia	5-0	1950	Australia..	U. S	4-1	1971	U.S.......	Romania ...	3-2
1925	U. S	France ...	5-0	1951	Australia..	U. S	3-2	1972	U.S.......	Romania ...	3-2
1926	U. S	France ...	4-1	1952	Australia..	U. S	4-1				

British (Wimbledon) Champions
Inaugurated 1877

Year	Men's singles	Women's singles	Year	Men's singles	Women's singles
1946 ...	Yvon Petra	Pauline Betz	1960 ...	Neale Fraser	Maria Bueno
1947 ...	Jack Kramer	Margaret Osborne	1961 ...	Rod Laver	Angela Mortimer
1948 ...	Bob Falkenburg	A. Louise Brough	1962 ...	Rod Laver	Karen Hantze Susman
1949 ...	Fred R. Schroeder	A. Louise Brough	1963 ...	Chuck McKinley	Margaret Smith
1950 ...	Budge Patty	A. Louise Brough	1964 ...	Roy Emerson	Maria Bueno
1951 ...	Dick Savitt	Doris Hart	1965 ...	Roy Emerson	Margaret Smith
1952 ...	Frank Sedgman	Maureen Connolly	1966 ...	Manuel Santana	Billie Jean King
1953 ...	Victor Seixas	Maureen Connolly	1967 ...	John Newcombe	Billie Jean King
1954 ...	Jaroslav Drobny	Maureen Connolly	1968 ...	Rod Laver	Billie Jean King
1955 ...	Tony Trabert	Louise Brough	1969 ...	Rod Laver	Ann Jones
1956 ...	Lewis Hoad	Shirley Fry	1970 ...	John Newcombe	Margaret S. Court
1957 ...	Lewis Hoad	Althea Gibson	1971 ...	John Newcombe	Evonne Goolagong
1958 ...	Ashley Cooper	Althea Gibson	1972 ...	Stan Smith	Billie Jean King
1959 ...	Alex Olmedo	Maria Bueno	1973	Jan Kodes	Billie Jean King

National Junior Tennis Champions

JUNIOR SINGLES		GIRLS' 18 SINGLES	
1967	Jeff Borowiak	1967	Peaches Bartkowicz
1968	Bob McKinley	1968	Kristy Pigeon
1969	Eric Van Dillen	1969	Sharon Walsh
1970	Brian Gottfried	1970	Sharon Walsh
1971	Raul Ramirez	1971	Chris Evert
1972	Patrick DuPre	1972	Ann Kiyomura
1973	Billy Martin	1973	Carrie Fleming

JUNIOR DOUBLES		GIRLS' 18 DOUBLES	
1967	Lan Guerry and Antonio Ortiz	1967	Peaches Bartkowicz and Valerie Ziegenfuss
1968	Bob McKinley and F. D. Robbins	1968	Kristy Pigeon and Denise Carter
1969	Richard Stockton and Eric Van Dillen	1969	Gail Hansen and Patty Ann Reese
1970	Brian Gottfried and Alex Mayer, Jr.	1970	Kristien Kemmer and Nancy Ornstein
1971	Jim Delaney and Chip Fisher	1971	Janet Newberry and Eliza Pande
1972	Steve Mott and Brian Teachar	1972	Marita Redondo and Laurie Tenney
1973	Billy Martin & Trey Waltke	1973	Susan Boyle & Kathy May

BOYS' 16 SINGLES		GIRLS' 16 SINGLES	
1967	Richard Stockton	1967	Kristien Kemmer
1968	Jimmy Connors	1968	Janet Newberry
1969	James Hagey	1969	Eliza Pande
1970	Freddy DeJesus	1970	Chris Evert
1971	Billy Martin	1971	Carrie Fleming
1972	Bill Maze	1972	Marita Redondo
1973	Ben McKnown	1973	Betsy Nagelson

BOYS' 16 DOUBLES		GIRLS' 16 DOUBLES	
1967	Mike Machetteand Dick Stockton	1967	Gail Hansen and Patty Ann Reese
1968	James Hagey and Robert Kreiss	1968	Kristine Kemmer and Janet Newberry
1969	James E. Delaney, 3rd, and Chip Fisher	1969	Chris Evert and Susan Epstein
1970	Freddy deJesus and John Whitlinger	1970	Barbara Downs and Ann Kiyomura
1971	Billy Martin and Trey Waltke	1971	Ann Kiyomura and Marita Redondo
1972	Bruce Manson and Perry Wright	1972	Jeanne Evert and Kathy Kendall
1973	Nial Brash & Matt Mitchell	1973	Susan Mehmedbasich & Robin Tenney

Tennis Championships in 1973

Australian Open (Melbourne)—Men Singles: John Newcombe; Men's Doubles: Newcombe & Anderson; Women's Singles: Margaret Smith Court; Women's Doubles: Margaret Smith Court & Virginia Wade.

Italian Open (Rome)—Men's Singles: Ilie Nastase; Men's Doubles: John Newcombe & Tom Okker; Women's Singles: Evonne Goolagong; Women's Doubles: Virginia Wade & Olga Morozova.

French Open (Paris)—Men's Singles: Ilie Nastase; Men's Doubles: John Newcombe & Tom Okker; Women's Singles:

Margaret Smith Court; Women's Doubles: Margaret Smith Court & Virginia Wade.

Virginia Slims (Newport)—Singles: Margaret Smith Court; Doubles: Francoise Durr & Betty Stone.

Women's Collegiate—Singles: Janice Metcalf, Rollins.

Federation Cup—Women's teams of all Nations—Final Round: Australia d. So. Africa 3-0.

Wrightman Cup Matches (Wimbleton, Eng.)—U.S. defeated Great Britain. Series Standing since 1923: U.S. 38, Great Britain 7.

Tennis Prize Money Winners, 1972

MEN				WOMEN			
Ilie Nastase	$176,000	Rod Laver	100,200	Billie Jean King	$119,000	Francoise Durr	46,000
Stan Smith	142,300	Tom Okker	90,004	Rosemary Casals	70,000	Evonne Goolagong	42,000
Ken Rosewall	132,950	Jim Connors	90,000	Kerry Melville	55,000	Virginia Wade	32,800
John Newcombe	120,600	Marty Riessen	74,436	Nancy Gunter	50,800	Wendy Overton	30,000
Arthur Ashe	119,775	Cliff Drysdale	68,433	Margaret S. Court	47,000	Karen Krantzcke	19,312

Tennis Battle of the Sexes

Billie Jean King defeated former Wimbledon champion Bobby Riggs in straight sets 6-4, 6-3, 6-3 in the so-called "Tennis Match of the Century" at the Houston Astrodome, Sept. 20, 1973. Ms. King, the biggest money-winner in the history of women's athletics and the leading spokesman for equality in sport, dominated the match by scoring outright winners on 70 of her 109 points, or 64%. Riggs, 55, self-proclaimed hustler and male chauvinist, had made sarcastic remarks about women's tennis, women's lib and women in general. His jibes were the major factor in attracting a crowd of 30,492, the largest single attendance ever for a tennis match. Millions more viewed the event on television in the U.S. and in 36 foreign countries via satellite. By winning the winner-take-all match, Ms. King received $100,000, although it was estimated through contracts and endorsements each player could earn over $300,000 from the event.

World Championship Tennis, 1973

Tournament (Group A)	Winner	Finalist	Tournament (Group B)	Winner	Finalist
Saga Bay Classic, Miami	Laver	Stockton	Rothmans Intl., N. Wales, London. .	Fairlie	Cox
Michelob Pro-Celebrity, LaCosta . .	Dibley	Smith	Pro Champs. of Italy, Milan	Riessen	Tanner
Fidelity World Championship,			Pro Champs. of Denmark,		
Richmond	Laver	Emerson	Copenhagen	Taylor	Riessen
U.S. Pro Indoor, Philadelphia	Smith	Lutz	Northern Pro Champs. of Germany,		
Rothmans International, Toronto. . .	Laver	Emerson	Cologne	Kodes	Fairlie
Peachtree Corners Intl., Atlanta . . .	Smith	Laver	Kemper Intl., Chicago	Ashe	Taylor
Holton Tennis Classic, St. Louis. . . .	Smith	Laver	Union Trust Classic, Washington. . .	Okker	Ashe
Southern Pro Champs. of Germany,			Rothmans Intl., Vancouver	Gorman	Kodes
Munich	Smith	Richey	River Oaks-American Genl.,		
Pro Champs. of Belgium, Brussels .	Smith	Laver	Houston	Rosewall	Stolle
Clows Classic, Johannesburg	Gottfried	Fillol	Cleveland Classic, Cleveland	Rosewall	Taylor
Pro Champs. of Sweden, Gothenberg	Smith	Alexander	NCNB Classic, Charlotte	Rosewall	Ashe
			United Bank Classic, Denver	Cox	Ashe

WCT Final Championship Summaries

Doubles

Emerson-Laver defeated Addison-Dibley 6-4, 7-5, 6-1; Lutz-Smith defeated Pilic-Stone 7-6, 6-3, 7-6; Okker-Riessen defeated Cox-Stilwell 6-7, 6-7, 7-6, 6-2, 6-2; Rosewall-Stolle defeated Ashe-Tanner 6-1, 6-7, 6-4, 7-6.
Semis—Lutz-Smith defeated Emerson-Laver 7-6, 4-6, 7-6, 7-6; Okker-Riessen defeated Rosewall-Stolle 6-2, 6-3, 6-7, 2-6, 6-3.
Finals—Lutz-Smith defeated Okker-Riessen 6-2, 7-6, 6-0.

Singles

Smith defeated Alexander 6-4, 6-2, 6-1; Laver defeated Emerson 7-5, 6-2, 7-5; Ashe defeated Riessen 7-6, 4-6, 7-5, 3-6, 6-1; Rosewall defeated Taylor 4-6, 6-2, 6-7, 6-1, 6-4.
Semis—Smith defeated Laver 4-6, 6-4, 7-6, 7-5; Ashe defeated Rosewall 6-4, 6-2, 5-7, 1-6, 6-2.
Finals—Smith defeated Ashe 6-3, 6-3, 4-6, 6-4.

1973 WCT Total Earnings

Player	Earnings	Player	Earnings	Player	Earnings
Stan Smith, U.S.	$154,100	Bob Lutz, U.S.	41,800	Tom Gorman, U.S.	28,200
Rod Laver, Aust.	78,200	Roy Emerson, Aust.	41,350	Roscoe Tanner, U.S.	25,250
Ken Rosewall, Aust.	66,400	Tom Okker, Neth.	34,400	Cliff Richey, U.S.	24,350
Arthur Ashe, U.S.	63,150	Mark Cox, Gt. Britain	31,950	Brian Gottfried, U.S.	23,900
Marty Riessen, U.S.	47,200	John Alexander, Aust.	31,300	Jan Kodes, Czech.	23,800
Roger Taylor, Gt. Britain . . . ,	42,800	Brian Fairlie, New Zealand . .	30,900	Dick Stockton, U.S.	23,200

North American Soccer League Final Standings, 1973

NORTHERN DIVISION			Bonus Pts.	Pts.	SOUTHERN DIVISION			Bonus Pts.	Pts.	EASTERN DIVISION			Bonus Pts.	Pts.
Teams	W	L	T		Teams	W	L	T		Teams	W	L	T	
Toronto	6	4	9	26 89	Dallas	9	2	8	33 111	Philadelphia	9	2	8	26 104
Montreal	5	10	4	22 64	St. Louis	7	7	5	25 82	New York	7	5	7	28 91
Rochester	4	9	6	17 59	Atlanta	3	9	7	23 62	Miami	8	5	6	22 88

Total Points: Win—6 pts., Tie—3 pts. Bonus points—one point awarded for each goal scored up to and including three (Win, lose or draw).
Playoff Winner—Philadelphia.

Leading Scorers

	G	A	Pts.		G	A	Pts.
Kyle Rote, Jr. (Dallas)	10	10	30	Joe Fink (New York)	11	0	22
Warren Archibald (Miami)	12	5	29	Richard Reynolds (Dallas)	8	6	22
Andy Provan (Philadelphia)	11	6	28	Miguel Perrichon (Toronto)	9	4	22
Gene Gelmer (St. Louis)	10	5	25	Willie Roy (St. Louis)	7	4	18
Ilija Mitic (Dallas)	12	1	25	Tom Ord (Montreal)	6	6	18
Randy Horton (New York)	9	5	23	Bruno Pilas (Toronto)	8	2	18

The World Cup

The World Cup, emblematic of international soccer supremacy, was won by Brazil on June 21, 1970, with a 4-1 victory over Italy. By winning for the third time, Brazil gained permanent possession of the Jules Rimet Trophy. A new trophy will be presented at the next world championship, to be played in Munich in 1974. Winners and sites of previous World Cup play follow:

Year	Winner	Site	Year	Winner	Site
1930	Uruguay	Uruguay	1958	Brazil	Sweden
1934	Italy	Italy	1962	Brazil	Chile
1938	Italy	France	1966	England	England
1950	Uruguay	Brazil	1970	Brazil	Mexico City
1954	W. Germany	Switzerland			

American Casting Assn. Combined Championships in 1973

San Antonio, Texas, Aug. 8-11, 1973

Men

Grand All Around Champion—Steve Rajeff, San Francisco, Calif.
Anglers All Around Champion—Steve Rajeff.
Distance Plugs—Steve Rajeff, 3,579 ft.
Distance Flies—Steve Rajeff, 1,703 ft.
All Distance—Steve Rajeff, 5,282 ft.
Accuracy Plugs—Steve Rajeff, 293 pts.
Accuracy Flies—Steve Rajeff, 290 pts.
All Accuracy—Steve Rajeff, 583 pts.

Ladies

All Accuracy—Mollie Schneider, Jeffersonville, Ind., 544 pts.
Accuracy Plugs—Mollie Schneider, 277 pts.
Accuracy Flies—Pauline Cathcart, LaCanada, Calif. 277 pts.

Intermediates

All Accuracy—Vince Rodgers, Santa Ana, Calif., 510 pts.
Accuracy Plugs—Jim Lanser, St. Louis, Mo., 252 pts.
Accuracy Flies—Vince Rodgers, 223 pts.

Golf Records
United States Amateur

Year	Winner	Year	Winner	Year	Winner	Year	Winner
1900	Walter Travis	1917-18	(Not Played)	1935	Lawson Little	1956	Harvie Ward
1901	Walter Travis	1919	Davidson Herron	1936	John Fischer	1957	Hillman Robbins
1902	Louis James	1920	Chick Evans, Jr.	1937	John Goodman	1958	Charles Coe
1903	Walter Travis	1921	Jesse Guilford	1938	Willie Turnesa	1959	Jack Nicklaus
1904	Chandler Egan	1922	Jess Sweetser	1939	Bud Ward	1960	Deane Beman
1905	Chandler Egan	1923	Max Marston	1940	Dick Chapman	1961	Jack Nicklaus
1906	Eben Byers	1924	Bob Jones	1941	Bud Ward	1962	Labron Harris, Jr.
1907	Jerome Travers	1925	Bob Jones	1942-45	(Not Played)	1963	Deane Beman
1908	Jerome Travers	1926	George Von Elm	1946	Ted Bishop	1964	Bill Campbell
1909	Robert Gardner	1927	Bob Jones	1947	Skee Riegel	1965	Robert Murphy, Jr.
1910	William Fownes, Jr.	1928	Bob Jones	1948	Willie Turnesa	1966	Gary Cowan
1911	Harold Hilton	1929	Harrison Johnston	1949	Charles Coe	1967	Bob Dickson
1912	Jerome Travers	1930	Bob Jones	1950	Sam Urzetta	1968	Bruce Fleisher
1913	Jerome Travers	1931	Francis Ouimet	1951	Billy Maxwell	1969	Steve Melnyk
1914	Francis Ouimet	1932	Ross Somerville	1952	Jack Westland	1970	Lanny Wadkins
1915	Robert Gardner	1933	George Dunlap, Jr.	1953	Gene Littler	1971	Gary Cowan
1916	Chick Evans, Jr.	1934	Lawson Little	1954	Arnold Palmer	1972	Vinnie Giles
				1955	Harvie Ward	1973	Craig Stadler

Women's United States Amateur

Year	Winner	Year	Winner	Year	Winner	Year	Winner
1900	Frances Griscom	1917-18	(Not Played)	1935	Glenna C. Vare	1956	Marlene Stewart
1901	Genevieve Hecker	1919	Alexa Stirling	1936	Pamela Barton	1957	Jo Anne Gunderson
1902	Genevieve Hecker	1920	Alexa Stirling	1937	Mrs. J.A. Page	1958	Anne Quast
1903	Bessie Anthony	1921	Marion Hollins	1938	Patty Berg	1959	Barbara McIntire
1904	G. M. Bishop	1922	Glenna Collett	1939	Betty Jameson	1960	Jo Anne Gunderson
1905	Pauline Mackay	1923	Edith Cummings	1940	Betty Jameson	1961	Anne Q. Decker
1906	Harriot Curtis	1924	Mrs. D. C. Hurd	1941	Mrs. Frank New	1962	Jo Anne Gunderson
1907	Margaret Curtis	1925	Glenna Collett	1942-45	(Not Played)	1963	Anne Q. Welts
1908	K. C. Harley	1926	Mrs. G. Stetson	1946	Babe Zaharias	1964	Barbara McIntire
1909	D. I. Campbell	1927	Mrs. M. Horn	1947	Louise Suggs	1965	Jean Ashley
1910	D. I. Campbell	1928	Glenna Collett	1948	Grace Lenczyk	1966	Jo Anne Carner
1911	Margaret Curtis	1929	Glenna Collett	1949	Dorothy Porter	1967	Lou Dill
1912	Margaret Curtis	1930	Glenna Collett	1950	Beverly Hanson	1968	Jo Anne Carner
1913	Gladys Raven Scroft	1931	Helen Hicks	1951	Dorothy Kirby	1969	Catherine Lacoste
1914	H. A. Jackson	1932	Virg. Van Wie	1952	Jackie Pung	1970	Martha Wilkinson
1915	C. H. Vanderbeck	1933	Virg. Van Wie	1953	Mary Faulk	1971	Laura Baugh
1916	Alexa Stirling	1934	Virg. Van Wie	1954	Barbara Romack	1972	Mary Budke
				1955	Pat Lesser	1973	Carol Semple

United States Open

Year	Winner	Year	Winner	Year	Winner	Year	Winner
1895	Horace Rawlings	1914	Walter Hagen	1933	John Goodman*	1955	Jack Fleck
1896	James Foulis	1915	Jerome Travers*	1934	Olin Dutra	1956	Cary Middlecoff
1897	Joe Lloyd	1916	Chick Evans*	1935	Sam Parks, Jr	1957	Dick Mayer
1898	Fred Herd	1917-1918	(Not played)	1936	Tony Manero	1958	Tommy Bolt
1899	Willie Smith	1919	Walter Hagen	1937	Ralph Guldahl	1959	Billy Casper
1900	Harry Vardon	1920	Edward Ray	1938	Ralph Guldahl	1960	Arnold Palmer
1901	Willie Anderson	1921	Jim Barnes	1939	Byron Nelson	1961	Gene Littler
1902	L. Auchterlonie	1922	Gene Sarazen	1940	Lawson Little	1962	Jack Nicklaus
1903	Willie Anderson	1923	Bob Jones*	1941	Craig Wood	1963	Julius Boros
1904	Willie Anderson	1924	Cyril Walker	1942-45	(Not played)	1964	Ken Venturi
1905	Willie Anderson	1925	Willie MacFarlane	1946	Lloyd Mangrum	1965	Gary Player
1906	Alex Smith	1926	Bob Jones*	1947	L. Worsham	1966	Billy Casper
1907	Alex Ross	1927	Tommy Armour	1948	Ben Hogan	1967	Jack Nicklaus
1908	Fred McLeod	1928	John Farrell	1949	Cary Middlecoff	1968	Lee Trevino
1909	George Sargent	1929	Bob Jones*	1950	Ben Hogan	1969	Orville Moody
1910	Alex Smith	1930	Bob Jones*	1951	Ben Hogan	1970	Tony Jacklin
1911	John McDermott	1931	Wm. Burke	1952	Julius Boros	1971	Lee Trevino
1912	John McDermott	1932	Gene Sarazen	1953	Ben Hogan	1972	Jack Nicklaus
1913	Francis Ouimet*			1954	Ed Fu. gol	1973	Johnny Miller

*Amateur

Masters Golf Tournament Champions

Year	Winner	Year	Winner	Year	Winner	Year	Winner
1934	Horton Smith	1943-1945	(Not played)	1954	Sam Snead	1964	Arnold Palmer
1935	Gene Sarazen	1946	Herman Keiser	1955	Cary Middlecoff	1965	Jack Nicklaus
1936	Horton Smith	1947	Jimmy Demaret	1956	Jack Burke	1966	Jack Nicklaus
1937	Byron Nelson	1948	Claude Harmon	1957	Doug Ford	1967	Gay Brewer, Jr.
1938	Henry Picard	1949	Sam Snead	1958	Arnold Palmer	1968	Bob Goalby
1939	Ralph Guldahl	1950	Jimmy Demaret	1959	Art Wall, Jr.	1969	George Archer
1940	Jimmy Demaret	1951	Ben Hogan	1960	Arnold Palmer	1970	Billy Casper
1941	Craig Wood	1952	Sam Snead	1961	Gary Player	1971	Charles Coody
1942	Byron Nelson	1953	Ben Hogan	1962	Arnold Palmer	1972	Jack Nicklaus
				1963	Jack Nicklaus	1973	Tommy Aaron

U.S. Women's Open Golf Champions

Year	Winner	Year	Winner	Year	Winner	Year	Winner
1948	Mrs. M. D. Zaharias	1955	Fay Crocker	1962	Murle Lindstrom	1969	Donna Caponi
1949	Louise Suggs	1956	Mrs. K. Cornelius	1963	Mary Mills	1970	Donna Caponi
1950	Mrs. M. D. Zaharias	1957	Betsy Rawls	1964	Mickey Wright	1971	Jo Anne Gunderson
1951	Betsy Rawls	1958	Mickey Wright	1965	Carol Mann		Carner
1952	Louise Suggs	1959	Mickey Wright	1966	Sandra Spuzich	1972	Susie Maxwell Berning
1953	Betsy Rawls	1960	Betsy Rawls	1967	Catherine Lacoste (a)	1973	Susie Maxwell Berning
	Mrs. M. D. Zaharias	1961	Mickey Wright	1968	Susie Maxwell Berning		

(a) Amateur

Professional Golf Tournaments in 1973

MEN

Date	Event	Winner	Score	Prize
Jan. 7	Glen Campbell-Los Angeles Open	Rod Funseth	276	$27,000
Jan. 14	Phoenix Open	Bruce Crampton	268	30,000
Jan. 21	Dean Martin-Tucson Open	Bruce Crampton	277	30,000
Jan. 28	Bing Crosby Tournament, Pebble Beach, Calif.	Jack Nicklaus	*282	36,000
Feb. 4	Hawaiian Open	John Schlee	273	40,000
Feb. 11	Bob Hope Tournament, Palm Springs, Calif.	Arnold Palmer	343	32,000
Feb. 18	Andy Williams-San Diego Open	Bob Dickson	278	34,000
Feb. 25	Jackie Gleason Inverrary National Airlines Classic, Ft. Lauderdale	Lee Trevino	279	52,000
Mar. 4	Florida Citrus Open, Orlando	Brian Allin	265	30,000
Mar. 11	Doral Eastern Open, Miami	Lee Trevino	276	30,000
Mar. 18	Jacksonville, Open	Jim Colbert	279	26,000
Mar. 25	Greater New Orleans Open	Jack Nicklaus	*280	25,000
Apr. 2	Greater Greensboro Open	Chi Chi Rodriguez	267	42,000
Apr. 9	Masters Tournament, Augusta	Tommy Aaron	283	30,000
Apr. 15	Monsanto Open, Pensacola, Fla.	Homero Blancas	277	30,000
Apr. 22	Tournament of Champions, Rancho La Costa, Calif.	Jack Nicklaus	276	40,000
Apr. 29	Byron Nelson Golf Classic, Dallas, Texas	Lanny Wadkins	*277	30,000
May 6	Houston Open	Bruce Crampton	277	41,000
May 13	Colonial National Invitational, Ft. Worth, Texas	Tom Weiskopf	276	30,000
May 20	Memphis Golf Classic	Dave Hill	283	35,000
May 27	Atlanta Golf Classic	Jack Nicklaus	272	30,000
June 1	Kemper Open, Charlotte, N.C.	Tom Weiskopf	271	40,000
June 10	I.V.B. Golf Classic, Whitemarsh, Pa.	Tom Weiskopf	274	30,045
June 17	U.S. Open, Oakmont, Pa.	Johnny Miller	279	35,000
June 24	American Golf Classic, Akron	Bruce Crampton	273	32,000
July 1	Western Open, Chicago	Billy Casper	272	35,000
July 8	Greater Milwaukee Open	Dave Stockton	276	26,000
July 15	Shrine-Robinson Open, Robinson, Ill.	Deane Beman	271	25,000
July 22	St. Louis Children's Hospital Classic	Gene Littler	268	42,000
July 29	Canadian Open, Montreal	Tom Weiskopf	278	35,000
Aug. 5	Westchester Golf Classic, Harrison, N.Y.	Bobby Nichols	*272	50,000
Aug. 12	PGA Championship, Cleveland	Jack Nicklaus	277	45,000
Aug. 19	U.S.I. Tournament, Sutton, Mass.	Lanny Wadkins	279	40,000
Aug. 26	L & M Tournament, Cary, N.C.	Bert Greene	*278	20,000
Sept. 3	Sammy Davis Jr.-Greater Hartford Open	Billy Casper	264	40,000
Sept. 9	World Series of Golf, Akron	Tom Weiskopf	137	50,000
Sept. 15	Heritage Golf Classic, Hilton Head Island, N.C.	Hale Irwin	272	30,000
Sept. 23	Broome County Open, Endicott, N.Y.	Hubert Green	266	20,000
Sept. 30	Quad Cities Open, Bettendorf, Iowa	Sam Adams	268	20,000

WOMEN

Date	Event	Winner	Score	Prize
Jan. 7	Bundine Tournament, Miami	JoAnn Prentice	212	$4,500
Feb. 11	Naples-Lely Tournament, Naples, Fla.	Kathy Whitworth	219	3,750
Mar. 11	S & H Green Stamps Tournament, Houston	Kathy Whitworth	214	20,000
Mar. 18	Orange Blossom Classic, Seminole, Fla.	Sandra Haynie	216	3,750
Mar. 25	Sears Tournament, Port St. Lucie, Fla.	Carol Mann	68	15,000
Apr. 1	Alamo Open, San Antonio	Betsy Cullen	218	4,500
Apr. 15	Colgate-Dinah Shore Winner's Circle Tournament	Mickey Wright	284	25,000
Apr. 29	Birmingham Classic	Gloria Ehret	*217	4,950
May 6	Raleigh Classic	Judy Rankin	217	4,500
May 13	Lady Carling Open, Baltimore, Md.	Judy Rankin	215	4,500
May 20	Bluegrass Invitational, Louisville	Donna Young	216	4,500
June 3	Sealy-Faberge Tournament, Las Vegas	Kathy Cornelius	*217	25,000
June 10	Ladies PGA Championship, Sutton, Mass.	Mary Mills	288	5,250
June 18	La Canadienne Championship, Montreal	Jocelyne Bourassa	*214	10,000
June 24	Heritage Village Open, Southbury, Conn.	Sue Berning	207	4,500
July 1	Lady Tara Classic, Atlanta	Mary Mills	217	4,500
July 8	Marc Equity Tournament, Buffalo	Mary Lou Crocker	210	5,250
July 15	George Washington Tournament, Horsham, Pa.	Carole Jo Skala	213	4,500
July 22	Women's U.S. Open, Rochester	Sue Berning	290	6,000
Aug. 5	Pabst Classic, Columbus, Ohio	Judy Rankin	212	5,250
Aug. 26	National Jewish Hospital Open, Denver	Sandra Palmer	210	4,500
Sept. 2	Charity Golf Classic, Ft. Worth	Sandra Haynie	208	4,500
Sept. 23	Portland Tournament, Ore.	Kathy Whitworth	144	4,500

*Won Playoff.

British Open Golf Champions

Year	Winner	Year	Winner	Year	Winner	Year	Winner
1905	James Braid	1924.	Walter Hagen	1939.	Richard Burton	1959.	Gary Player (So.Africa)
1906	James Braid	1925	Jim Barnes (U.S.)	1940-45	(Not played)	1960.	Kel Nagle (Aust.)
1907	Arnaud Massy	1926.	Bob Jones (U.S.)	1946.	Sam Snead (U.S.)	1961.	Arnold Palmer (U.S.)
1908	James Braid	1927.	Bob Jones	1947.	Fred Daly (Ireland)	1962.	Arnold Palmer
1909	J. H. Taylor	1928	Walter Hagen	1948.	Henry Cotton	1963	Bob Charles (N.Z.)
1910	James Braid	1929	Walter Hagen	1949.	Bobby Locke (So.Africa)	1964.	Tony Lema (U.S.)
1911	Harry Vardon	1930	Bob Jones	1950.	Bobby Locke	1965.	Peter Thomson
1912.	Ted Ray	1931	Tommy Armour (U.S.)	1951.	Max Faulkner	1966.	Jack Nicklaus(U.S.)
1913.	J. H. Taylor	1932.	Gene Sarazen (U.S.)	1952.	Bobby Locke	1967.	Roberto de Vicenzo (Arg.)
1914.	Harry Vardon	1933.	Denny Shute (U.S.)	1953	Ben Hogan (U.S.)	1968.	Gary Player
1915-1919	(Not played)	1934.	Henry Cotton	1954.	Peter Thomson (Aust.)	1969.	Tony Jacklin
1920.	George Duncan	1935.	Alf Perry	1955.	Peter Thomson	1970.	Jack Nicklaus (U.S.)
1921	Jock Hutchison	1936.	Alf. Padgham	1956.	Peter Thomson	1971.	Lee Trevino (U.S.)
1922	Walter Hagen(U.S.)	1937.	T. H. Cotton	1957.	Bobby Locke	1972.	Lee Trevino (U.S.)
1923	Arthur Havers	1938	R. A. Whitcombe	1958.	Peter Thomson	1973.	Tom Weiskopf (U.S.)

Professional Golfers' Association Championships

Year	Winner	Year	Winner	Year	Winner	Year	Winner
1916	Jim Barnes	1932	Olin Dutra	1947	Jim Ferrier	1961	Jerry Barber
1919	Jim Barnes	1933	Gene Sarazen	1948	Ben Hogan	1962	Gary Player
1920	Jock Hutchison	1934	Paul Runyan	1949	Sam Snead	1963	Jack Nicklaus
1921	Walter Hagen	1935	Johnny Revolta	1950	Chandler Harper	1964	Bob Nichols
1922	Gene Sarazen	1936	Denny Shute	1951	Sam Snead	1965	Dave Marr
1923	Gene Sarazen	1937	Denny Shute	1952	James Turnesa	1966	Al Geiberger
1924	Walter Hagen	1938	Paul Runyan	1953	Walter Burkemo	1967	Don January
1925	Walter Hagen	1939	Henry Picard	1954	Melvin Harbert	1968	Julius Boros
1926	Walter Hagen	1940	Byron Nelson	1955	Doug Ford	1969	Ray Floyd
1927	Walter Hagen	1941	Victor Ghezzi	1956	Jack Burke	1970	Dave Stockton
1928	Leo Diegel	1942	Sam Snead	1957	Lionel Hebert	1971	Jack Nicklaus
1929	Leo Diegel	1944	Bob Hamilton	1958	Dow Finsterwald	1972	Gary Player
1930	Tommy Armour	1945	Byron Nelson	1959	Bob Rosburg	1973	Jack Nicklaus
1931	Tom Creavy	1946	Ben Hogan	1960	Jay Hebert		

PGA Leading Money Winners

Year	Player	Dollars	Year	Player	Dollars	Year	Player	Dollars
1945	Byron Nelson	52,511	1954	Bob Toski	65,819	1963	Arnold Palmer	128,230
1946	Ben Hogan	42,556	1955	Julius Boros	65,121	1964	Jack Nicklaus	113,284
1947	Jimmy Demaret	27,936	1956	Ted Kroll	72,835	1965	Jack Nicklaus	140,752
1948	Ben Hogan	36,812	1957	Dick Mayer	65,835	1966	Billy Casper	121,944
1949	Sam Snead	31,593	1958	Arnold Palmer	42,407	1967	Jack Nicklaus	188,988
1950	Sam Snead	35,758	1959	Art Wall, Jr	53,167	1968	Billy Casper	205,168
1951	Lloyd Mangrum	26,088	1960	Arnold Palmer	75,262	1969	Frank Beard	175,223
1952	Julius Boros	37,032	1961	Gary Player	64,540	1970	Lee Trevino	157,037
1953	Lew Worsham	34,002	1962	Arnold Palmer	81,448	1971	Jack Nicklaus	244,490
						1972	Jack Nicklaus	320,542

Canadian Open Golf Champions

Year	Winner	Year	Winner	Year	Winner	Year	Winner
1942	C. Wood	1950	Jim Ferrier (U.S.)	1958	Wes Ellis, Jr. (U.S.)	1966	D. Massengale (U.S.)
1943-44	(Not played)	1951	Jim Ferrier (U.S.)	1959	Doug Ford (U.S.)	1967	Billy Casper (U.S.)
1945	Byron Nelson	1952	J. Palmer (U.S.)	1960	Art Wall, Jr. (U.S.)	1968	Bob Charles (N.Z.)
1946	G. Fazio	1953	Dave Douglas (U.S.)	1961	Jacky Cupit (U.S.)	1969	Tommy Aaron (U.S.)
1947	R. Locke (S. Af.)	1954	Pat Fletcher	1962	Ted Kroll (U.S.)	1970	Kermit Zarley (U.S.)
1948	C. Congdon	1955	Arnold Palmer (U.S.)	1963	Doug Ford (U.S.)	1971	Lee Trevino (U.S.)
1949	E.J. Harrison (U.S.)	1956	Doug Sanders (U.S.)	1964	Kel Nagle (Aust.)	1972	Gay Brewer (U.S.)
		1957	George Bayer (U.S.)	1965	Gene Littler (U.S.)	1973	Tom Weiskopf (U.S.)

British Amateur Golf Champions

Year	Winner	Year	Winner	Year	Winner	Year	Winner
1911	H. H. Hilton	1928	T. P. Perkins	1946	J. Bruen	1960	Joseph Carr
1912	John Ball	1929	C. Tolley	1947	W. Turnesa	1961	Michael Bonallack
1913	H. H. Hilton	1930	R.T. Jones, Jr. (U.S.)	1948	F. Stranahan (U.S.)	1962	Richard Davies (U.S.)
1914	J. L. C. Jenkins	1931	E. Martin-Smith	1949	Sam McCready	1963	Michael Lunt
1915 -1919	(Not played)	1932	J. De Forest	1950	Frank Stranahan (U.S.)	1964	Gordon Clark
1920	Cyril J. Tolley	1933	M. Scott	1951	Dick Chapman (U.S.)	1965	Mike Bonallack
1921	W. I. Hunter	1934	W.L. Little, Jr. (U.S.)	1952	H. Ward (U.S.)	1966	Bobby Cole
1922	E. W. Holderness	1935	W.L. Little, Jr (U.S.)	1953	Joseph Carr	1967	Bob Dickson (U.S.)
1923	R. Wethered	1936	H. Thompson	1954	Doug Bachli (Aust.)	1968	Mike Bonallack
1924	E. W. Holderness	1937	R. Sweeny, (U.S.bn)	1955	Lt. Joseph Conrad (U.S.)	1969	Mike Bonallack
1925	R. Harris	1938	C. Yates (U. S.)	1956	John Beharrell	1970	Mike Bonallack
1926	J. Sweetser (U.S.)	1939	A. Kyle	1957	Reid Jack	1971	Steve Melnyk (U.S.)
1927	Dr. W. Tweddell	1940-45	(Not played)	1958	Joseph Carr	1972	Trevor Homer
				1959	Deane Beman (U.S.)	1973	Dick Siderowe (U.S.)

Professional Golfers' Association Hall of Fame

Established in 1940 to honor those who have made outstanding contributions to the game by their lifetime playing ability.

Anderson, Willie
Armour, Tommy
Barnes, Jim
Brady, Mike
Burke, Billy
Cooper, Harry
Cruickshank, Bobby
Demaret, Jimmy
Diegel, Leo
Dudley, Edward

Dutra, Olin
Evans, Chick
Farrell, Johnny
Ghezzi, Vic
Guldahl, Ralph
Hagen, Walter
Harbert, M. R. (Chick)
Harper, Chandler
Harrison, E. J.
Hogan, Ben

Hutchison, Jock, Sr.
Jones, Bob
Little, W. Lawson
Mangrum, Lloyd
McDermott, John
McLeod, Fred
Nelson, Byron
Ouimet, Francis
Picard, Henry
Revolta, Johnny

Runyan, Paul
Sarazen, Gene
Shute, Denny
Smith, Alex
Smith, Horton
Smith, MacDonald
Snead, Sam
Travers, Jerry
Travis, Walter
Wood, Craig

International Walker Cup Gold Match
United States vs. Great Britain—Men's Amateur (Biennial)
Series Standing—United States 21, Great Britain 2, 1 tie

Year	Series record	Year	Series record
1953	United States 9; Great Britain 3	1965	United States 11; Great Britain 11
1955	United States 10; Great Britain 2	1967	United States 13; Great Britain 7
1957	United States 8; Great Britain 3	1969	United States 10; Great Britain 8
1959	United States 9; Great Britain 3	1971	Great Britain 13; United States 11
1961	United States 11; Great Britain 1	1973	United States 14; Great Britain 10
1963	United States 9; Great Britain 3		

International Curtis Cup Golf Match
United States vs. Great Britain—Women's Amateur (Biennial)
Series Standing—United States 13. Great Britain 2, 2 ties

Year	Series Record	Year	Series Record
1952	Great Britain 5; United States 4	1964	United States 10½; Great Britain 7½
1954	United States 6; Great Britain 3	1966	United States 13; Great Britain 5
1956	Great Britain 5; United States 4	1968	United States 10½; Great Britain 7½
1958	Great Britain 4½; United States 4½	1970	United States 11½; Great Britain 6½
1960	United States 6½; Great Britain 2½	1972	United States 10; Great Britain 8
1962	United States 8; Great Britain 1		

Ryder Cup Matches

UNITED STATES VS. GREAT BRITAIN·PROFESSIONAL (BIENNIAL)
Series Standing, United States 16, Great Britain 3, 1 Tie

Series Record	Series Record
1953—United States 6½; Great Britain 5½	1963—United States 23; Great Britain 9
1955—United States 8; Great Britain 4	1965—United States 19½; Great Britain 12½
1957—Great Britain 7; United States 4	1967—United States 23½; Great Britain 8½
1959—United States 8½; Great Britain 3½	1969—United States 16; Great Britain 16
1961—United States 14½; Great Britain 9½	1971—United States 18½; Great Britain 13½
	1973—United States 10; Great Britain 13

Auto Racing
Indianapolis 500 Winners

Year	Winner	Chassis	Engine	MPH	Gross	Runner up
1940	Wilbur Shaw	Maserati	Maserati	114.277	$85,525	Rex Mays
1941	Floyd Davis, Mauri Rose	Wetteroth	Offenhauser	115.117	90,925	Rex Mays
1946	George Robson	Adams	Sparks	114.820	115,450	Jimmy Jackson
1947	Mauri Rose	Deidt	Offenhauser	116.338	137,425	Bill Holland
1948	Mauri Rose	Deidt	Offenhauser	119.814	171,075	Bill Holland
1949	Bill Holland	Deidt	Offenhauser	121.327	179,050	Johnnie Parsons
1950	Johnnie Parsons	Kurtis Kraft	Offenhauser	124.002(a)	201,135	Bill Holland
1951	Lee Wallard	Kurtis Kraft	Offenhauser	126.244	207,650	Mike Nazaruk
1952	Troy Ruttman	Kuzma	Offenhauser	128.922	230,100	Jim Rathmann
1953	Bill Vukovich	Kurtis Kraft 500A	Offenhauser	128.740	246,300	Art Cross
1954	Bill Vukovich	Kurtis Kraft 500A	Offenhauser	130.840	269,375	Jim Bryan
1955	Bob Sweikert	Kurtis Kraft 500C	Offenhauser	128.209	270,400	Tony Bettenhausen
1956	Pat Flaherty	Watson	Offenhauser	128.490	282,052	Sam Hanks
1957	Sam Hanks	Epperly	Offenhauser	135.601	300,252	Jim Rathmann
1958	Jimmy Bryan	Epperly	Offenhauser	133.791	305,217	George Amick
1959	Rodger Ward	Watson	Offenhauser	135.857	338,100	Jim Rathmann
1960	Jim Rathmann	Watson	Offenhauser	138.767	369,150	Rodger Ward
1961	A.J. Foyt	Watson	Offenhauser	139.130	400,000	Eddie Sachs
1962	Rodger Ward	Watson	Offenhauser	140.293	426,152	Len Sutton
1963	Parnelli Jones	Watson	Offenhauser	143.137	494,031	Jim Clark
1964	A.J. Foyt	Watson	Offenhauser	147.350	506,625	Rodger Ward
1965	Jim Clark	Lotus	Ford	151.388	628,399	Parnelli Jones
1966	Graham Hill	Lola	Ford	144.317	691,809	Jim Clark
1967	A.J. Foyt	Coyote	Ford	151.207	737,109	Al Unser
1968	Bobby Unser	Eagle	Offenhauser	152.882	809,627	Dan Gurney
1969	Mario Andretti	Hawk	Ford	156.867	805,127	Dan Gurney
1970	Al Unser	P.J. Colt	Ford	155,749	1,000,002	Mark Donohue
1971	Al Unser	P.J. Colt	Ford	157.735	1,001,604	Peter Revson
1972	Mark Donohue	McLaren	Offenhauser	163.465	1,011,846	Al Unser
1973	Gordon Johncock	Eagle	Offenhauser	159.014(b)	1,006,105	Billy Vukovich

(a) 345 miles. (b) 332.5 miles. Race Record—163.465 MPH, Mark Donohue, 1972.

1973 Indianapolis 500 Official Standing

1—Gordon Johncock, Franklin, Ind., Eagle-Offenhauser.
2—Billy Vukovich, Fresno, Calif., Eagle-Offenhauser.
3—Roger McCluskey, Tucson, Arizona, McLaren-Offenhauser.
4—Mel Kenyon, Lebanon, Ind., McLaren-Offenhauser.
5 Gary Bettenhausen, Tinley Park, Ill., McLaren-Offenhauser.
6—Steve Krisloff, Parsippany, N.J., Kingfish-Offenhauser.
7—Lee Kunzman, Guttenberg, Iowa, Eagle-Offenhauser.
8—John Martin, Long Beach, Calif., McLaren-Offenhauser.
9—Johnny Rutherford, Ft. Worth, Texas, McLaren-Offenhauser.
10—Mike Mosley, Clermont, Ind., Eagle-Offenhauser.
11—David Hobbs, England, Eagle-Offenhauser.
12—A.J. Foyt, Houston, Texas & George Snider, Bakersfield, Calif., Eagle Offenhauser.
13—Bobby Unser, Albuquerque, N.M., Eagle-Offenhauser.
14—Dick Simon, Salt Lake City, Utah, Eagle-Foyt.
15—Mark Donohue, Newtown Square, Pa., Eagle-Offenhauser.

World's Land Speed Records—Evolution of the Mile Record

Date	Driver	Car	MPH	Date	Driver	Car	MPH
12/18/98	Chassenloup-Laubat	Jeantaud	39.24	3/29/27	Seagrave	Sunbeam	203.790
4/29/99	Jenatzy	Jamais Contente Jenatzy	65.79	4/22/28	Keech	White Triplex	207.552
				3/11/29	Seagrave	Irving-Napier	231.446
11/17/02	Augieres	Mars	77.13	2/ 5/31	Campbell	Napier-Campbell	246.086
11/ 5/03	Duray	Gabron-Brillie	84.73	2/24/32	Campbell	Napier-Campbell	253.96
12/30/04	Barras	Darràcq	109.65	2/22/33	Campbell	Napier-Campbell	272.109
1/25/05	Bowden	Mercedes	109.75	9/ 3/35	Campbell	Bluebird Spl.	301.13
1/26/06	Marriott	Stanley (Steam)	127.659	11/19/37	Eyston	Thunderbolt #1	311.42
3/16/10	Oldfield	Benz	131.724	9/16/38	Eyston	Thunderbolt #1	357.5
4/23/11	Burman	Benz	141.732	8/23/39	Cobb	Railton	368.9
2/12/19	DePalma	Packard	149.875	9/16/47	Cobb	Railton-Mobil	394.2
4/27/20	Milton	Dusenberg	155.046	8/ 5/63	Breedlove	Spirit of America	407.45
4/28/26	Parry-Thomas	Thomas Spl.	170.624	10/27/64	Arfons	Green Monster	536.71
				11/15/65	Breedlove	Spirit of America	600.601
				10/23/70	Gary Gabelich	Blue Flame	622.407

World Grand Prix Champions

1954	Juan M. Fangio, Arg., Maserati, Mercedes-Benz	1963	Jim Clark, Scotland, Lotus-Ford
1955	Juan M. Fangio, Argentina, Mercedes-Benz	1964	John Surtees, England, Ferrari
1956	Juan M. Fangio, Argentina, Lancia-Ferrari	1965	Jim Clark, Scotland, Lotus-Ford
1957	Juan M. Fangio, Argentina, Maserati	1966	Jack Brabham, Australia, Brabham-Repco
1958	Mike Hawthorn, England, Ferrari	1967	Denis Hulme, New Zealand, Brabham-Repco
1959	Jack Brabham, Australia, Cooper	1968	Graham Hill, England, Lotus-Ford
1960	Jack Brabham, Australia, Cooper	1969	Jackie Stewart, Scotland, Matra-Ford
1961	Phil Hill, United States, Ferrari	1970	Jochen Rindt, Austria, Lotus-Ford
1962	Graham Hill, England, BRM	1971	Jackie Stewart, Scotland, Tyrell-Ford
		1972	Emerson Fittipaldi, Brazil, Lotus-Ford

Grand Prix for Formula 1 Cars, 1973

Grand Prix	Winner, Car	Grand Prix	Winner, Car
Australian	Ronnie Peterson, Lotus JPS	French	Ronnie Peterson, Lotus JPS
Belgian	Jackie Stewart, Tyrrell-Ford	German	Jackie Stewart, Tyrrell-Ford
Brazilian	Emerson Fittipaldi, Lotus JPS	Monte Carlo	Jackie Stewart, Tyrrell-Ford
British	Peter Revson, Yardley McLaren	Spanish	Emerson Fittipaldi, Lotus JPS
Canadian	Peter Revson, McLaren	Swedish	Dennis Hulme, Yardley McLaren
Dutch	Jackie Stewart, Tyrrell-Ford	United States	Ronnie Peterson Lotus-Ford

NASCAR Racing in 1973

WINSTON CUP GRAND NATIONAL RACES

Date		Race & Site	Miles	Winner	Car	Money Won
Jan.	21	Winston Western 500, Riverside, Calif.	500	Mark Donohue	Mata	$15,170
Feb.	18	Daytona 500, Fla.	500	Richard Petty	Dodge	33,500
Feb.	25	Richmond 500, Richmond, Va.	271	Richard Petty	Dodge	4,000
Mar.	18	Carolina 500, Rockingham, N.C.	500	David Pearson	Mercury	14,975
Mar.	25	Southeastern 500, Bristol, Tenn.	266.5	Cale Yarborough	Chevrolet	6,530
Apr.	1	Atlanta 500, Atlanta, Ga.	500	David Pearson	Mercury	16,125
Apr.	8	Gwyn Staley 400, No. Wilkesboro, N.C.	250	Richard Petty	Dodge	4,730
Apr.	15	Rebel 500, Darlington, S.C.	500	David Pearson	Mercury	15,835
Apr.	29	Virginia 500, Martinsville, Va.	262.5	David Pearson	Mercury	11,000
May	6	Winston 500, Talladega, Ala.	500	David Pearson	Mercury	25,845
May	27	World 600, Charlotte, N.C.	600	Buddy Baker	Dodge	25,200
June	3	Mason-Dixon 500, Dover, Del.	500	David Pearson	Mercury	13,525
June	10	Alamo 500, College Station, Tex.	500	Richard Petty	Dodge	15,820
June	17	Tuborg 400, Riverside, Calif.	400	Bobby Allison	Chevrolet	10,750
June	24	Motor State 400, Irish Hills, Mich.	400	David Pearson	Mercury	12,210
July	4	Medal of Honor Firecracker 400, Daytona Beach, Fla	400	David Pearson	Mercury	16,100
July	8	Volunteer 500, Bristol, Tenn.	266.5	Benny Parsons	Chevrolet	6,550
July	22	Dixie 500, Atlanta, Ga.	500	David Pearson	Mercury	15,950
Aug.	12	Talladega 500, Talladega, Ala.	500	Richard Brooks	Plymouth	20,815
Aug.	25	Nashville 420	250	Buddy Baker	Dodge	5,250
Sept.	3	Southern 500, Darlington, S.C.	500	Cale Yarborough	Chevrolet	21,140
Sept.	16	Delaware 500, Dover, Del.	500	David Pearson	Mercury	15,825
Sept.	23	Wilkes 400, No. Wilkesboro, N.C.	250	Bobby Allison	Chevrolet	5,925
Sept.	30	Old Dominion 500, Martinsville, Va.	262.5	Richard Petty	Dodge	10,250
Oct.	7	National 500, Charlotte, N.C.	500	Cale Yarborough	Chevrolet	17,725

Grand National Champions (NASCAR)

Year	Driver (Car)	Year	Driver (Car)	Year	Driver (Car)
1949	R. Byron (Oldsmobile)	1957	E. Baker (Chevrolet)	1965	N. Jarrett (Ford)
1950	W. Rexford (Oldsmobile)	1958	L. Petty (Oldsmobile)	1966	D. Pearson (Dodge)
1951	H. Thomas (Ply.-Hudson)	1959	L. Petty (Olds.-Plymouth)	1967	R. Petty (Plymouth)
1952	T. Flock (Hudson)	1960	R. White (Chevrolet)	1968	D. Pearson (Ford)
1953	H. Thomas (Hudson)	1961	N. Jarrett (Chevrolet)	1969	D. Pearson (Ford)
1954	L. Petty (Chrysler)	1962	J. Weatherly (Pontiac)	1970	B. Isaac (Dodge)
1955	T. Flock (Chrysler)	1963	J. Weatherly (Pontiac-Mercury)	1971	R. Petty (Plymouth)
1956	E. Baker (Chrysler-Dodge)	1964	R. Petty (Plymouth)	1972	R. Petty (Plymouth)

Daytona 500 Winners

Year	Driver (Car)	Avg. MPH	Year	Driver (Car)	Avg. MPH
1959	L. Petty (Oldsmobile)	135.521	**1966	R. Petty (Plymouth)	160.627
1960	J. Johnson (Chevrolet)	124.740	1967	M. Andretti (Ford)	146.926
1961	M. Panch (Pontiac)	149.601	1968	C. Yarborough (Mercury)	143.251
1962	F. Roberts (Pontiac)	152.529	1969	L. Yarbrough (Ford)	160.875
1963	T. Lund (Ford)	151.566	1970	P. Hamilton (Plymouth)	149.601
1964	R. Petty (Plymouth)	154.334	1971	R. Petty (Plymouth)	144.456
*1965	F. Lorenzen (Ford)	141.539	1972	A. J. Foyt (Mercury)	161.550
*322.5 miles because of rain.			**495 miles because of rain. 1973	R. Petty (Dodge)	157.205

1973 Leading Daytona 500 Finishers

Driver — Car	Laps	Purse	Driver — Car	Laps	Purse
1 — Richard Petty, Dodge	200	$33,500	6 — Buddy Baker, Dodge	194	$10,225
2 — Bobby Isaac, Ford	198	15,300	7 — James Hylton, Mercury	194	4,025
3 — Dick Brooks, Dodge	197	9,800	8 — Ramo Scott, Mercury	193	3,595
4 — A.J. Foyt, Chevrolet	196	7,020	9 — Buddy Arrington, Dodge	192	2,900
5 — Hershel McGriff, Plymouth	195	6,025	10 — Vic Parsons, Mercury	190	2,945

World University Games

The USSR collected 68 gold medals at the 7th World University Games held in Moscow during the last 2 weeks in August, 1973. The United States won 19 gold medals, including a basketball victory over the Russians which helped avenge the much disputed Soviet victory in the 1972 Olympics.

Major Stakes Races, 1973

Event	Track	Added Value	Winner	Dist. Furl.	Time: Seconds in Fifths	Jockey
3 YEAR OLDS AND UP						
Arlington Hdcp.	Arlington	$100,000	Dubassoff	9½	1:58.3	J. Vasquez
Bougainvillea Hdcp.	Hialeah	50,000	Gleaming	9½	1:54.2	A. Cordero
Bowling Green Hdcp.	Belmont	50,000	Summer Guest	12	2:29.1	J. Vasquez
Brooklyn Hdcp.	Aqueduct	100,000	Riva Ridge	9½	1:52.2	R. Turcotte
Californian Stakes	Hollywood	100,000	Quack	8½	1:41.2	D. Pierce
Carter Hdcp.	Belmont	50,000	King's Bishop	7	1:20.2	E. Maple
Charles H. Strub Stakes	Santa Anita	125,000	Royal Owl	10	2:04	J. Sellers
Dixie Hdcp.	Pimlico	50,000	Laplander	12	2:30.2	V. Bracciale, Jr.
Donn Hdcp.	Gulfstream	50,000	Triumphant	9	1:47.4	B. Baeza
Excelsior Hdcp.	Aqueduct	50,000	Key To The Mint	9	1:47.4	R. Turcotte
Firecracker Hdcp.	Liberty Bell	50,000	Full Pocket	6	1:10.1	J. Anderson
Governor Hdcp.	Belmont	100,000	Tentam	9	1:46.4	J. Velasquez
Grey Lag Hdcp.	Aqueduct	75,000	Summer Guest	10	2:01.3	J. Vasquez
Hialeah Turf Cup	Hialeah	100,000	Gleaming	12	2:27.3	A. Cordero
Hollywood Gold Cup	Hollywood	150,000	Kennedy Road	10	1:59.2	W. Shoemaker
Man O'War Stakes	Belmont	100,000	Secretariat	12	2:24.4	R. Turcotte
Manhattan Hdcp.	Belmont	50,000	London Company	9½	—	L. Pincay
Marlboro Cup	Belmont	250,000	Secretariat	9	1:45.2	R. Turcotte
Metropolitan Hdcp.	Belmont	100,000	Tentam	8	1:35	J. Velasquez
Pan American Hdcp.	Gulfstream	100,000	Lord Vancouver	12	2:26.3	W. Blum
Seminole Hdcp.	Hialeah	50,000	True Knight	9	1:50.2	A. Cordero
Surburban Hdcp.	Aqueduct	100,000	Key To The Mint	10	2:00.4	B. Baeza
Tidal Hdcp.	Aqueduct	50,000	Jogging	9½	1:55	A. Cordero
U.N. Hdcp.	Atlantic City	125,000	Tentam	9½	1:54.3	J. Velasquez
Washington Park Hdcp.	Arlington	50,000	Burning On	10	2:02.1	D. Richards
Westchester Stakes	Aqueduct	50,000	North Sea	8	1:33.3	R. C. Smith
Whitney Stakes	Saratoga	50,000	Onion	9	1:49.1	J. Vasquez
Widener Hdcp.	Hialeah	100,000	Vertee	10	2:00.4	J. Ruane
Woodward Stakes	Belmont	100,000	Prove Out	12	2:25.4	J. Velasquez
3 YEAR OLDS AND UP, FILLIES AND MARES						
Barbara Fritchie Hdcp.	Bowie	50,000	First Bloom	7	1:23.2	A. Gomez
Beldame Stakes	Belmont	100,000	Desert Vixon	9	1:46.1	J. Velasquez
Beverly Hills Hdcp.	Hollywood	75,000	Le Cle	11	2:14.4	W. Shoemaker
Delaware Hdcp.	Delaware	100,000	Susan's Girl	10	2:00.3	L. Pincay
Top Flight Hdcp.	Aqueduct	50,000	Poker Night	9	1:48.1	R. Woodhouse
3 YEAR OLDS						
American Derby	Arlington	100,000	Bemo	9	1:49.3	W. Passmore
Arlington Invitational	Arlington	125,000	Secretariat	9	1:46.4	R. Turcotte
Arkansas Derby	Oaklawn	100,000	Impecunious	9	1:48.4	J. Velasquez
Belmont Stakes	Belmont	125,000	Secretariat	12	2:24	R. Turcotte
Blue Grass Stakes	Keeneland	50,000	My Gallant	9	1:49.3	A. Cordero
California Derby	Golden Gate	100,000	Linda's Chief	9	—	B. Baeza
Dwyer Hdcp.	Aqueduct	50,000	Stop The Music	10	2:02.3	H. Gustines
Flamingo	Hialeah	100,000	Our Native	9	1:48.4	J. Vasquez
Florida Derby	Gulfstream	100,000	Royal And Regal	9	—	W. Blum
Gotham	Aqueduct	50,000	Secretariat	8	1:33.2	R. Turcotte
Hollywood Derby	Hollywood	150,000	Amen, 2nd	12	2:27.4	E. Belmonte
Jersey Derby	Garden State	100,000	Knightly Dawn	9	1:53.1	J. Arellano
Kentucky Derby	Churchill Downs	125,000	Secretariat	10	1:59.2	R. Turcotte
Lawrence Realization	Belmont	50,000	Amen 2nd	12	2:26.4	E. Belmonte
Louisiana Derby	Fair Grounds	75,000	Leo's Pisces	9	1:51.3	B. Breen
Monmouth Invitational	Monmouth	100,000	Our Native	9	1:48.3	M. Rivera
Ohio Derby	Thistledown	100,000	Our Native	9	1:50.1	A. Rini
Preakness	Pimlico	150,000	Secretariat	9½	1:54.2	R. Turcotte
Santa Anita Derby	Santa Anita	100,000	Sham	10	—	L. Pincay
Saranac Hdcp.	Aqueduct	50,000	Linda's Chief	8	1:34	B. Baeza
Travers Stakes	Saratoga	100,000	Annihilate 'Em	10	2:01.3	R. Turcotte
Withers Stakes	Aqueduct	50,000	Linda's Chief	8	1:34.4	J. Velasquez
Wood Memorial	Aqueduct	100,000	Angle Light	9	1:49.4	J. Vasquez
3 YEAR OLDS, FILLIES						
Acorn Stakes	Aqueduct	50,000	Windy's Daughter	8	1:35.2	B. Baeza
Alabama Stakes	Saratoga	50,000	Desert Vixon	10	2:04.1	J. Velasquez
Coaching Club Amer. Oaks	Belmont	100,000	Magazine	12	2:27.4	A Cordero
Kentucky Oaks	Churchill Downs	50,000	Bag Of Tunes	8½	1:44.1	Gargan
Monmouth Oaks	Monmouth	50,000	Desert Vixon	9	1:49	M. Hole
Mother Goose Stakes	Belmont	75,000	Windy's Daughter	9	1:48.2	E. Belmonte
2 YEAR OLDS						
Futurity	Belmont	75,000	Wedge Shot	6½	1:17	J. Vasquez
Hopeful Stakes	Saratoga	75,000	Gusty O'Shay	6½	1:16.2	R. Kotenko
Juvenile Stakes	Hollywood	100,000	Century's Envoy	6	1:09	J. Lambert
Kindergarden Stakes	Liberty Bell	100,000	Determined King	6	1:12.3	B. Baeza
Arlington-Wash. Futurity	Arlington	150,000	Lover John	6	—	R. Ussery
Sapling	Monmouth	50,000	Tisab	6	1:10.1	W. Blum
2 YEAR OLDS, FILLIES						
Frizette	Belmont	100,000	Bundler	8	1:36.2	J. Vasquez
Hollywood Lassie Stakes	Hollywood	75,000	Special Goddess	6	—	L. Pincay
Matron Stakes	Belmont	100,000	Talking Pictures	6	—	R. Turcotte
Spinway Stakes	Saratoga	50,000	Talking Pictures	6	1:10	R. Turcotte

Kentucky Derby, 3 Yr. Olds

Churchill Downs, Louisville, Ky.
Inaugurated 1875. Distance $1\frac{1}{4}$ miles; $1\frac{1}{2}$ until 1896

Year	Winner, weight	Time	Dollars	Year	Winner, weight	Time	Dollars
1875	Aristides (100)	2.37 3-4	2,850	1924	Black Gold (126)	2.05 1-5	52,775
1876	Vagrant (97)	2.38 1-4	2,950	1925	Flying Ebony (126)	2.07 3-5	52,950
1877	Baden Baden (100)	2.38	3,300	1926	Bubbling Over (126)	2.03 4-5	50,075
1878	Day Star (100)	2.37 1-4	4,050	1927	Whiskery (126)	2.06	51,000
1879	Lord Murphy (100)	2.37	3,550	1928	Reigh Count (126)	2.10 2-5	55,375
1880	Fonso (105)	2.37 1-2	3,800	1929	Clyde Van Dusen (126)	2.10 4-5	53,950
1881	Hindoo (105)	2.40	4,410	1930	Gallant Fox (126)	2.07 3-5	50,725
1882	Apollo (102)	2.40 1-4	4,560	1931	Twenty Grand (126)	2.01 4-5	48,725
1883	Leonatus (105)	2.43	3,760	1932	Burgoo King (126)	2.05 1-5	52,350
1884	Buchanan (110)	2.40 1-4	3,990	1933	Broker's Tip (126)	2.06 4-5	48,925
1885	Joe Cotton (110)	2.37 1-5	4,630	1934	Cavalcade (126)	2.04	28,175
1886	Ben Ali (118)	2.36 1-2	4,890	1935	Omaha (126)	2.05	39,525
1887	Montrose (118)	2.39 1-4	4,200	1936	Bold Venture (126)	2.03 3-5	37,725
1888	Macbeth II (115)	2.38 1-4	4,740	1937	War Admiral (126)	2.03 1-5	52,050
1889	Spokane (118)	2.34 1-2	4,970	1938	Lawrin (126)	2.04 4-5	47,050
1890	Riley (118)	2.45	5,460	1939	Johnstown (126)	2.03 2-5	46,350
1891	Kingman (122)	2.52 1-2	4,680	1940	Gallahadion (126)	2.05	60,150
1892	Azra (122)	2.41 1-2	4,230	1941	Whirlaway (126)	2.01 2-5	61,275
1893	Lookout (122)	2.39 1-4	4,090	1942	Shut Out (126)	2.04 2-5	64,225
1894	Chant (122)	2.41	4,020	1943	Count Fleet (126)	2.04	60,725
1895	Halma (122)	2.37 1-2	2,970	1944	Pensive (126)	2.04 1-5	64,675
1896	Ben Brush (117)	2.07 3-4	4,850	1945	Hoop, Jr. (126)	2.07	64,850
1897	Typhoon II (117)	2.12 1-2	4,850	1946	Assault (126)	2.06 3-5	96,400
1898	Plaudit (117)	2.09	4,850	1947	Jet Pilot (126)	2.06 3-5	92,160
1899	Manuel (117)	2.12	4,850	1948	Citation (126)	2.05 2-5	83,400
1900	Lieut. Gibson (117)	2.06 1-4	4,850	1949	Ponder (126)	2.04 1-5	91,600
1901	His Eminence (117)	2.07 3-4	4,850	1950	Middleground (126)	2.01 3-5	92,650
1902	Alan-a-Dale (117)	2.08 3-4	4,850	1951	Count Turf (126)	2.02 3-5	98,050
1903	Judge Himes (117)	2.09	4,850	1952	Hill Gail (126)	2.01 3-5	96,300
1904	Elwood (117)	2.08 1-2	4,850	1953	Dark Star (126)	2.02	90,050
1905	Agile (122)	2.10 3-4	4,850	1954	Determine (126)	2.03	102,050
1906	Sir Huon (117)	2.08 4-5	4,850	1955	Swaps (126)	2.01 4-5	108,400
1907	Pink Star (117)	2.12 3-5	4,850	1956	Needles (126)	2.03 2-5	123,450
1908	Stone Street (117)	2.15 1-5	4,850	1957	Iron Liege (126)	2.02 1-5	107,950
1909	Wintergreen (117)	2.08 1-5	4,850	1958	Tim Tam (126)	2.05	116,400
1910	Donau (117)	2.06 2-5	4,850	1959	Tomy Lee (126)	2.02 1-5	119,650
1911	Meridian (117)	2.05	4,850	1960	Venetian Way (126)	2.02 2-5	114,850
1912	Worth (117)	2.09 2-5	4,850	1961	Carry Back (126)	2.04	120,500
1913	Donerail (117)	2.04 4-5	5,475	1962	Decidedly (126)	2.00 2-5	119,650
1914	Old Rosebud (114)	2.03 2-5	9,125	1963	Chateaugay (126)	2.01 4-5	108,900
1915*	Regret (112)	2.05 2-5	11,450	1964	Northern Dancer (126)	2.00	114,300
1916	George Smith (117)	2.04	9,750	1965	Lucky Debonair (126)	2.01 1-5	112,000
1917	Omar Khayyam (117)	2.04 3-5	16,600	1966	Kauai King (126)	2.02	120,500
1918	Exterminator (114)	2.10 4-5	14,700	1967	Proud Clarion (126)	2.00 3-5	119,700
1919	Sir Barton (112½)	2.09 4-5	20,825	1968	(A) Dancer's Image (126)	2.02 1-5	122,600
1920	Paul Jones (126)	2.09	30,375	1969	Majestic Prince (126)	2.01 1-5	113,200
1921	Behave Yourself (126)	2.04 1-5	38,450	1970	Dust Commander (126)	2.03 2-5	127,800
1922	Morvich (126)	2.04 3-5	53,775	1971	Canonero 2nd (126)	2.03 1-5	145,500
1923	Zev (126)	2.05 2-5	53,600	1972	Riva Ridge (126)	2.01 4-5	140,300
				1973	Secretariat (126)	1.59 2-5	155,050

(A) Dancer's Image was disqualified from purse money by order of the Churchill Downs stewards after tests disclosed that he had run with a pain-killing drug, phenylbutazone, in his system. All wagers were paid on Dancer's Image. Forward Pass was awarded first place money.

The Kentucky Derby has been won five times by two jockeys, Eddie Arcaro, 1938, 1941, 1945, 1948 and 1952; and Bill Hartack, 1957, 1960, 1962, 1964 and 1969; and three times by each of three jockeys, Isaac Murphy, 1884, 1890 and 1891; Earle Sande, 1923, 1925 and 1930, and Willie Shoemaker, 1955, 1959, 1965. *Regret only filly ever to win the Derby.

Preakness
Pimlico, Baltimore, Md. (1873); 1-3/16 Miles, 3 Yr. Olds

Year	Winner, weight	Time	Dollars	Year	Winner, weight	Time	Dollars
1938	Dauber (126)	1.59 4-5	51,475	1956	Fabius (126)	1.58 2-5	84,250
1939	Challedon (126)	1.59 4-5	53,710	1957	Bold Ruler (126)	1.56 1-5	65,250
1940	Bimelech (126)	1.58 3-5	53,230	1958	Tim Tam (126)	1.57 1-5	97,900
1941	Whirlaway (126)	1.58 4-5	49,365	1959	Royal Orbit (126)	1.57	136,200
1942	Alsab (126)	1.57	58,175	1960	Bally Ache (126)	1.57 3-5	121,000
1943	Count Fleet (126)	1.57 2-5	43,190	1961	Carry Back (126)	1.57 3-5	126,200
1944	Pensive (126)	1.59 1-5	60,075	1962	Greek Money (126)	1.56 1-5	135,000
1945	Polynesian (126)	1.58 4-5	66,170	1963	Candy Spots (126)	1.56 1-5	127,500
1946	Assault (126)	2.01 2-5	96,620	1964	Northern Dancer (126)	1.56 4-5	142,200
1947	Faultless (126)	1.59	98,005	1965	Tom Rolfe (126)	1.56 1-5	128,100
1948	Citation (126)	2.02 2-5	91,870	1966	Kauai King (126)	1.55 2-5	129,000
1949	Capot (126)	1.56	79,985	1967	Damascus (126)	1.55 1-5	141,500
1950	Hill Prince (126)	1.59 1-5	56,110	1968	Forward Pass (126)	1.56 4-5	142,700
1951	Bold (126)	1.56 2-5	83,100	1969	Majestic Prince (126)	1.55 3-5	129,500
1952	Blue Man (126)	1.57 2-5	86,135	1970	Personality (126)	1.56 1-5	151,300
1953	Native Dancer (126)	1.57 4-5	65,200	1971	Canonero 2nd (126)	1.54	137,400
1954	Hasty Road (126)	1.57 2-5	91,600	1972	Bee Bee Bee (126)	1.55 3-5	135,300
1955	Nashua (126)	1.54 3-5	67,550	1973	Secretariat (126)	1.54 2-5	129,900

Triple Crown Turf Winners, Owners and Jockeys

(Kentucky Derby, Preakness and Belmont Stakes)

Year	Horse	Owner	Jockey	Year	Horse	Owner	Jockey
1919	Sir Barton	J. K. L. Ross	J. Loftus	1941	Whirlaway	Warren Wright	E. Arcaro
1930	Gallant Fox	W. Woodward	E. Sande	1943	Count Fleet	Mrs. J. D. Hertz	J. Longden
1935	Omaha	W. Woodward	W. Sanders	1946	Assault	R. J. Kleberg	W. Mehrtens
1937	War Admiral	S. D. Riddle	C. Kurtsinger	1948	Citation	Warren Wright	E. Arcaro
				1973	Secretariat	Meadow Stable	R. Turcotte

Belmont Stakes
3 Yr. Olds, 1½ Miles, Belmont Park, Elmont, L. I., N. Y.

Year	Winner, weight	Time	Dollars	Year	Winner, weight	Time	Dollars
1941	Whirlaway (126)	2.31	39,770	1957	Gallant Man (126)	2.26 3-5	77,300
1942	Shut Out (126)	2.29 1-5	44,520	1958	Cavan (126)	2.30 1-5	73,400
1943	Count Fleet (126)	2.28 1-5	35,340	1959	Sword Dancer (126)	2.28 2-5	93,525
1944	Bounding Home (126)	2.32 1-5	55,000	1960	Celtic Ash (126)	2.29 3-5	96,785
1945	Pavot (126)	2.30 1-5	52,675	1961	Sherluck (126)	2.29 1-5	104,900
1946	Assault (126)	2.30 4-5	75,400	1962	Jaipur (126)	2.28 4-5	109,550
1947	Phalanx (126)	2.29 2-5	78,900	1963	Chateaugay (126)	2.30 1-5	101,700
1948	Citation (126)	2.28 1-5	77,700	1964	Quadrangle (126)	2.28 2-5	110,850
1949	Capot (126)	2.30 1-5	60,900	1965	Hail To All (126)	2.28 2-5	104,150
1950	Middleground (126)	2.28 3-5	61,350	1966	Amberoid (126)	2.29 2-5	117,700
1951	Counterpoint (126)	2.29	82,000	1967	Damascus (126)	2.28 4-5	104,950
1952	One Count (126)	2.30 1-5	82,400	1968	Stage Door Johnny (126)	2.27 1-5	117,700
1953	Native Dancer (126)	2.28 3-5	82,500	1969	Arts and Letters (126)	2.28 4-5	104,050
1954	High Gun (126)	2.30 4-5	89,000	1970	High Echelon (126)	2.34	115,000
1955	Nashua (126)	2.29	83,700	1971	Pass Catcher (126)	2.30 2-5	97,710
1956	Needles (126)	2.29 4-5	83,600	1972	Riva Ridge (126)	2.28	93,540
				1973	Secretariat (126)	2.24	90,120

Queen's Plate

The Queen's Plate (known as the King's Plate during reign of male), Canada's most famous thoroughbred race, is the oldest continuously run stakes race in North America. Originated in 1860 over 1⅛ miles (now 1¼ miles) for 3-year-olds; Canadians-foaled, race is staged under Royal tutelage for trophy and 50 gold sovereigns plus purse. Trophy is not a plate but a foot-high gold cup valued at $5,000. However, race is identified as a plate race because of 17th Century English tradition of awarding plates.

Year	Winner, Jockey	Time*	Dollars	Year	Winner, Jockey	Time*	Dollars
1952—	Epigram, G. Robillard	1:58.3	17,022	1963—	Canebora, M. Ycaza	2:04	54,850
1953—	Canadian, E. Arcaro	1:52.1	20,592	1964—	Northern Dancer, W. Hartack	2:02.1	49,234
1954—	Collisteo, C. Rogers	1:52	22,452	1965—	Whistling Sea, T. Inouye	2:03.4	47,852
1955—	Ace Marine, G. Walker	1:52.2	25,514	1966—	Titled Hero, A. Gomez	2:03.3	52,173
1956—	Canadian Champ, D. Stevenson	1:55	25,430	1967—	Jammed Lovely, J. Fitzsimmons	2:03	51,821
1957—	Lyford Cay, A. Gomez	2:03.3	26,210	1968—	Merger, W. Harris	2:05.2	53,641
1958—	Caledon Beau, A. Coy	2:04.1	26,151	1969—	Jumping Joseph, A. Gomez	2:04.1	55,022
1959—	New Providence, R. Ussery	2:04.4	51,767	1970—	Almoner, S. Hawley	2:04.4	57,395
1960—	Victoria Park, A. Gomez	2:02	42,750	1971—	Kennedy Road, S. Hawley	2:03	54,388
1961—	Blue Light, H. Dittfach	2:05	46,475	1972—	Victoria Song, R. Platts	2:02	56,143
1962—	Flaming Page, J. Fitzsimmons	2:04.3	51,225	1973—	Royal Chocolate, T. Colangelo	2:08	80,697

*Fractions in fifths.

Leading Money-Winning Horses of the World
As of Jan. 1973. * Raced in 1973. † Filly

Horse, Year Foaled	Sts.	1st	2nd	3rd	Dollars	Horse, Year Foaled	Sts.	1st	2nd	3rd	Dollars
Kelso, 1957	63	39	12	2	1,977,896	First Landing, 1956	37	19	9	2	779,577
Round Table, 1954	66	43	8	5	1,749,869	Mill Reef, 1968	14	12	2	0	764,412
Buckpasser, 1963	31	25	4	1	1,462,014	Bold Ruler, 1954	33	23	4	2	764,204
Nashua, 1952	30	22	4	1	1,288,565	Bally Ache, 1957	31	16	9	4	758,522
Carry Back, 1958	62	21	11	11	1,241,165	†Straight Deal, 1962	99	21	21	9	733,020
Damascus, 1964	32	21	7	3	1,176,781	Quicken Tree, 1963	74	15	9	13	718,303
Fort Marcy, 1964	75	21	18	14	1,109,791	Bald Eagle, 1955	29	12	5	4	692,922
Citation, 1945	45	32	10	2	1,085,760	Nijinsky II, 1967	13	11	2	0	677,117
Native Diver, 1959	81	37	7	12	1,026,500	Assault, 1943	42	18	6	7	675,470
Dr. Fager, 1964	22	18	2	1	1,022,642	Tom Rolfe, 1962	32	16	5	5	671,297
Swoon's Son, 1953	51	30	10	3	970,605	Social Outcast, 1950	58	18	9	6	668,300
Roman Brother, 1961	42	16	10	5	943,473	Mr. Right, 1963	68	17	13	10	667,193
Stymie, 1941	131	35	33	28	918,485	Hill Rise, 1961	43	15	6	8	653,160
T. V. Lark, 1957	72	19	13	6	902,194	Intentionally, 1956	34	18	7	2	652,258
* Riva Ridge, 1969	21	12	1	1	898,895	Hillsdale, 1955	41	23	6	4	646,935
†Shuvee, 1966	44	16	10	6	890,445	Sea-Bird, 1962	8	7	1	0	645,645
Swaps, 1952	25	19	2	2	848,900	Crozier, 1958	34	10	12	3	641,733
Nodouble, 1965	42	13	11	5	846,749	Never Bend	23	13	4	4	641,524
Sword Dancer, 1956	39	15	7	4	829,610	Brigadier Gerard, 1968	18	17	1	0	637,079
Candy Spots, 1960	22	12	5	1	824,718	Ack Ack, 1966	27	19	6	0	636,641
Mongo, 1959	46	22	10	4	820,766	Ridan, 1959	23	13	6	2	635,074
Armed, 1941	81	41	20	10	817,475	Arts and Letters, 1966	23	11	6	1	632,404
* Cougar II, 1966	41	17	7	11	806,391	Bardstown, 1952	31	18	7	1	628,752
Find, 1950	110	22	27	27	803,615	Jaipur, 1959	19	10	6	0	618,926
Gun Bow, 1960	42	17	8	4	798,722	Prove It, 1957	25	15	4	1	613,820
Crimson Satan, 1959	58	18	9	9	796,077	†Tosmah, 1961	39	23	6	2	612,591
In Reality, 1964	27	14	9	2	795,824	Olden Times, 1958	54	17	10	5	603,875
Native Dancer, 1950	22	21	1	0	785,240	Chompion, 1956	88	14	14	16	603,751
†Cicada, 1959	42	23	8	6	783,675	Needles, 1953	21	11	3	3	600,355

Annual Leading Money-Winner

Year	Horse	Dollars	Year	Horse	Dollars	Year	Horse	Dollars
1940	Bimelech	110,005	1951	Counterpoint	250,525	1962	Never Bend	402,969
1941	Whirlaway	272,386	1952	Crafty Admiral	277,225	1963	Candy Spots	604,481
1942	Shut Out	238,872	1953	Native Dancer	513,425	1964	Gun Bow	580,100
1943	Count Fleet	174,055	1954	Determine	328,700	1965	Buckpasser	568,096
1944	Pavot	179,040	1955	Nashua	752,550	1966	Buckpasser	669,078
1945	Busher	273,735	1956	Needles	440,850	1967	Damascus	817,941
1946	Assault	424,195	1957	Round Table	600,383	1968	Forward Pass	546,674
1947	Armed	376,325	1958	Round Table	662,780	1969	Arts and Letters	555,604
1948	Citation	709,470	1959	Sword Dancer	537,004	1970	Personality	444,049
1949	Ponder	321,825	1960	Bally Ache	455,045	1971	Riva Ridge	503,263
1950	Noor	346,940	1961	Carry Back	565,349	1972	Droll Roll	471,633

Annual Leading Jockey—Money Won

Year	Jockey	Dollars	Year	Jockey	Dollars	Year	Jockey	Dollars
1940	Arcaro, E.	343,661	1951	Shoemaker, W.	1,329,890	1962	Shoemaker, W.	2,916,844
1941	Meade, D.	398,627	1952	Arcaro, E.	1,859,591	1963	Shoemaker, W.	2,526,925
1942	Arcaro, E.	481,949	1953	Shoemaker, W.	1,784,187	1964	Shoemaker, W.	2,649,553
1943	Longden, J.	573,276	1954	Shoemaker, W.	1,876,760	1965	Baeza, B.	2,582,702
1944	Atkinson, T.	899,101	1955	Arcaro, E.	1,864,796	1966	Baeza, B.	2,951,022
1945	Longden, J.	981,977	1956	Hartack, W.	2,343,955	1967	Baeza, B.	3,088,888
1946	Atkinson, T.	1,036,825	1957	Hartack, W.	3,060,501	1968	Baeza, B.	2,835,108
1947	Dodson, D.	1,429,949	1958	Shoemaker, W.	2,961,693	1969	Velasquez, J.	2,542,315
1948	Arcaro, E.	1,686,230	1959	Shoemaker, W.	2,843,133	1970	Pincay, L. Jr.	2,626,526
1949	Brooks, S.	1,316,817	1960	Shoemaker, W.	2,123,961	1971	Pincay, L. Jr.	3,784,377
1950	Arcaro, E.	1,410,160	1961	Shoemaker, W.	2,690,819			

Horse Racing Revenues to States in 1972

State	Racing days Thorough-bred	Harness	* Revenue to state Thorough-bred	Harness	State	Racing days Thorough-bred	Harness	* Revenue to state Thorough-bred	Harness
Arizona	144		$1,522,234		Nebraska	185		3,342,654	
Arkansas	50		3,920,164		New Hamp.	77	306	5,287,462	4,815,581
California	378	213	52,968,677	$8,980,482	New Jersey	180	195	28,459,675	7,639,091
Colorado	60		894,368		New Mexico	278		1,536,816	
Delaware	107	276	3,517,840	5,168,514	New York	379	1,162	74,149,092	84,957,737
Florida	291	100	17,809,446	1,627,702	Ohio	399	399	11,003,271	5,657,697
Idaho	125		125,574		Oregon	81		1,391,428	
Illinois	337	460	24,520,465	23,833,328	Pennsylvania	384	310	13,232,878	8,884,426
Kentucky	233	266	6,582,280	1,293,002	Rhode Island	254		10,444,108	
Louisiana	343		6,408,562		South Dakota	48		181,410	
Maine	58	739	13,767,744	1,054,458	Vermont	117	47	9,311,014	190,507
Maryland	205	126	13,103,487	2,165,277	Washington	191		3,289,609	
Massachusetts	150	144	10,090,570	3,417,189	West Virginia	560	105	10,424,766	291,468
Michigan	229	370	15,544,597	8,974,301	Totals	5,863	4,718	$322,425,191	$168,915,840

* Total revenue from fairs and quarter horse racing amounted to $11,365,039.

Total Racing Revenue to States by Years (Dollars)

1935	8,386,255.00	1961	264,353,077.00
1940	16,145,182.00	1962	237,930,030.00
1945	65,265,405.48	1963	316,570,791.00
1950	93,356,166.67	1964	350,095,928.00
1955	136,939,533.00	1965	369,892,036.00
1960	258,039,365.00	1966	388,452,125.00
		1967	394,381,913.00
		1968	426,856,488.00
		1969	461,498,386.00
		1970	486,403,097.00
		1971	508,338,417.00
		1972	502,706,070.00

Quarter Horse Racing

The richest horse race in the world, the All American Futurity is run each Labor Day at Ruidoso Downs, New Mexico. It is open to 2-year-old Quarter Horses. The distance of the event was 400 yards through 1972; 440 yards starting in 1973. The gross purse is $1,030,000.

Year	Winner	Weight	Time	Value to Winner	Jockey	Owner
1960	Tonto Bars Hank	119	20.2	$65,122	C. Perner	Milo and C. G. Whitcomb
1961	Pokey Bar	119	20.1	101,212	K. Chapman	Hugh Huntley
1962	Hustling Man	119	20.3	96,425	C. Detiege	J. B. Ferguson
1963	Goetta	116	20.40	127,500	C. Smith	Hugh Huntley
1964	Decketta	119	20.30	134,030	B. Morris	W. W. Wilson
1965	Savannah Jr.	120	20.30	192,730	J. Wallace	J.R. and R.E. Cates
1966	Go Dick Go	119	20.27	198,300	B. Nesmith	Joe. V. Leitner
1967	Laico Bird	119	20.11	228,300	B. Harmon	F. H. Jones, Jr.
1968	Three Oh's	119	20.06	160,372	J. Nicodemus	Donald G. Strole
1969	Easy Jet	119	20.46	159,840	Willie Lovell	Walter Merick
1970	Rocket Wrangler	119	20.09	178,488	J. Nicodemus	John R. Adams
1971	Mr. Kid Charge	120	19.65	200,841	J. Cox	Will F. Whitehead
1972	Possumjet	119	20.04	336,629	P. Herrera	Jack Byers
1973	Time To Thinkrich	120	21.58	330,000	J. Watson	Vessels Stallion Farm

Power Boat Racing Champions
APBA GOLD CUP RACE

Year	Boat	Owner	Driver	Winner's fastest heat	Site
1958	Hawaii Kai III	Edgar Kaiser	Jack Regas	108.734	Seattle, Wash.
1959	Maverick	W. T. Waggoner, Jr	Bill Stead	106.278	Seattle, Wash.
1961	Miss Century 21	Willard Rhodes	Bill Muncey	102.399	Reno, Nev.
1962	Miss Century 21	Willard Rhodes	Bill Muncey	101.446	Seattle, Wash.
1963	Miss Bardahl	Ole Bardahl	Ron Musson	114.650	Detroit, Mich.
1964	Miss Bardahl	Ole Bardahl	Ron Musson	108.104	Detroit, Mich.
1965	Miss Bardahl	Ole Bardahl	Ron Musson	110.655	Seattle, Wash.
1966	Tahoe Miss	Harrah's	Mira Slovak	97.861	Detroit, Mich.
1967	Miss Bardahl	Ole Bardahl	Bill Schumacher	104.691	Seattle, Wash.
1968	Miss Bardahl	Ole Bardahl	Bill Schumacher		Detroit, Mich.
1969	Miss Budweiser	Bernard Little & Tom Friedkin	Bill Sterett	103.587	San Diego, Calif.
1970	Miss Budweiser	Hydroplanes, Inc.	Dean Chenoweth	101.848	San Diego, Calif.
1971	Miss Madison	Miss Madison, Inc.	Jim McCormick	101.522	Madison, Ind.
1972	Atlas Van Lines	Atlas Van Lines	Bill Muncey	103.547	Detroit, Mich.
1973	Miss Budweiser	Hydroplanes, Inc.	Dean Chenoweth	104.046	Tri-Cities, Wash.

1973 Little League World Series

The 27th Little League World Series was won by Taiwan for the third year in a row, when they defeated Tucson (Arizona) by the score of 12-0 on Aug. 25, 1973, at Williamsport, Pa.

Major League Pennant Winners, 1901-1973

NATIONAL LEAGUE						AMERICAN LEAGUE					
Year	Winner	Won	Lost	Per Cent	Manager	Year	Winner	Won	Lost	Per Cent	Manager
1901.	Pittsburgh	90	49	.647	Clarke	1901.	Chicago	83	53	.610	Griffith
1902.	Pittsburgh	103	36	.741	Clarke	1902.	Philadelphia	83	53	.610	Mack
1903.	Pittsburgh	91	49	.650	Clarke	1903.	Boston	91	47	.659	J. J. Collins
1904.	New York	106	47	.693	McGraw	1904.	Boston	95	59	.617	Collins
1905.	New York	105	48	.686	McGraw	1905.	Philadelphia	92	56	.622	Mack
1906.	Chicago	116	36	.763	Chance	1906.	Chicago	93	58	.616	Jones
1907.	Chicago	107	45	.704	Chance	1907.	Detroit	92	58	.613	Jennings
1908.	Chicago	99	55	.643	Chance	1908.	Detroit	90	63	.588	Jennings
1909.	Pittsburgh	110	42	.724	Clarke	1909.	Detroit	98	54	.645	Jennings
1910.	Chicago	104	50	.675	Chance	1910.	Philadelphia	102	48	.680	Mack
1911.	New York	99	54	.647	McGraw	1911.	Philadelphia	101	50	.669	Mack
1912.	New York	103	48	.682	McGraw	1912.	Boston	105	47	.691	Stahl
1913.	New York	101	51	.664	McGraw	1913.	Philadelphia	96	57	.627	Mack
1914.	Boston	94	59	.614	Stallings	1914.	Philadelphia	99	53	.651	Mack
1915.	Philadelphia	90	62	.592	Moran	1915.	Boston	101	50	.669	Carrigan
1916.	Brooklyn	94	60	.610	Robinson	1916.	Boston	91	63	.591	Carrigan
1917.	New York	98	56	.636	McGraw	1917.	Chicago	100	54	.649	Rowland
1918.	Chicago	84	45	.651	Mitchell	1918.	Boston	75	51	.595	Barrow
1919.	Cincinnati	96	44	.686	Moran	1919.	Chicago	88	52	.629	Gleason
1920.	Brooklyn	93	60	.604	Robinson	1920.	Cleveland	98	56	.636	Speaker
1921.	New York	94	56	.614	McGraw	1921.	New York	98	55	.641	Huggins
1922.	New York	93	61	.604	McGraw	1922.	New York	94	60	.610	Huggins
1923.	New York	95	58	.621	McGraw	1923.	New York	98	54	.645	Huggins
1924.	New York	93	60	.608	McGraw	1924.	Washington	92	62	.597	Harris
1925.	Pittsburgh	95	58	.621	McKechnie	1925.	Washington	96	55	.636	Harris
1926.	St. Louis	89	65	.578	Hornsby	1926.	New York	91	63	.591	Huggins
1927.	Pittsburgh	94	60	.610	Bush	1927.	New York	110	44	.714	Huggins
1928.	St. Louis	95	59	.617	McKechnie	1928.	New York	101	53	.656	Huggins
1929.	Chicago	98	54	.645	McCarthy	1929.	Philadelphia	104	46	.693	Mack
1930.	St. Louis	92	62	.597	Street	1930.	Philadelphia	102	52	.662	Mack
1931.	St. Louis	101	53	.656	Street	1931.	Philadelphia	107	45	.704	Mack
1932.	Chicago	90	64	.584	Grimm	1932.	New York	107	47	.695	McCarthy
1933.	New York	91	61	.599	Terry	1933.	Washington	99	53	.651	Cronin
1934.	St. Louis	95	58	.621	Frisch	1934.	Detroit	101	53	.656	Cochrane
1935.	Chicago	100	54	.649	Grimm	1935.	Detroit	93	58	.616	Cochrane
1936.	New York	91	62	.597	Terry	1936.	New York	102	51	.667	McCarthy
1937.	New York	95	57	.625	Terry	1937.	New York	102	52	.662	McCarthy
1938.	Chicago	89	63	.586	Hartnett	1938.	New York	99	53	.651	McCarthy
1939.	Cincinnati	97	57	.630	McKechnie	1939.	New York	106	45	.702	McCarthy
1940.	Cincinnati	100	53	.654	McKechnie	1940.	Detroit	90	64	.584	Baker
1941.	Brooklyn	100	54	.649	Durocher	1941.	New York	101	53	.656	McCarthy
1942.	St. Louis	106	48	.688	Southworth	1942.	New York	103	51	.669	McCarthy
1943.	St. Louis	105	49	.682	Southworth	1943.	New York	98	56	.636	McCarthy
1944.	St. Louis	105	49	.682	Southworth	1944.	St. Louis	89	65	.578	Sewell
1945.	Chicago	98	56	.636	Grimm	1945.	Detroit	88	65	.575	O'Neill
1946.	St. Louis	98	58	.628	Dyer	1946.	Boston	104	50	.675	Cronin
1947.	Brooklyn	94	60	.610	Shotton	1947.	New York	97	57	.630	Harris
1948.	Boston	91	62	.595	Southworth	1948.	Cleveland	97	58	.626	Boudreau
1949.	Brooklyn	97	57	.630	Shotton	1949.	New York	97	57	.630	Stengel
1950.	Philadelphia	91	63	.591	Sawyer	1950.	New York	98	56	.636	Stengel
1951.	New York	98	59	.624	Durocher	1951.	New York	98	56	.636	Stengel
1952.	Brooklyn	96	57	.627	Dressen	1952.	New York	95	59	.617	Stengel
1953.	Brooklyn	105	49	.682	Dressen	1953.	New York	99	52	.656	Stengel
1954.	New York	97	57	.630	Durocher	1954.	Cleveland	111	43	.721	Lopez
1955.	Brooklyn	98	55	.641	Alston	1955.	New York	96	58	.623	Stengel
1956.	Brooklyn	93	61	.604	Alston	1956.	New York	97	57	.630	Stengel
1957.	Milwaukee	95	59	.617	Haney	1957.	New York	98	56	.636	Stengel
1958.	Milwaukee	92	62	.597	Haney	1958.	New York	92	62	.597	Stengel
1959.	Los Angeles	88	68	.564	Alston	1959.	Chicago	94	60	.610	Lopez
1960.	Pittsburgh	95	59	.617	Murtaugh	1960.	New York	97	57	.630	Stengel
1961.	Cincinnati	93	61	.604	Hutchinson	1961.	New York	109	53	.673	Houk
1962.	San Francisco	103	62	.624	Dark	1962.	New York	96	66	.593	Houk
1963.	Los Angeles	99	63	.611	Alston	1963.	New York	104	57	.646	Houk
1964.	St. Louis	93	69	.574	Keane	1964.	New York	99	63	.611	Berra
1965.	Los Angeles	97	65	.599	Alston	1965.	Minnesota	102	60	.630	Mele
1966.	Los Angeles	95	67	.586	Alston	1966.	Baltimore	97	63	.606	Bauer
1967.	St. Louis	101	60	.627	Schoendienst	1967.	Boston	92	70	.568	Williams
1968.	St. Louis	97	65	.599	Schoendienst	1968.	Detroit	103	59	.636	Smith

National League

	EAST					WEST				Playoff
Year	Winner	W.	L.	Pct.	Manager	Winner	W.	L.	Pct.	Manager	Winner
1969	N.Y. Mets	100	62	.617	Hodges	Atlanta	93	69	.574	Harris	New York
1970	Pittsburgh	89	73	.549	Murtaugh	Cincinnati	102	60	.630	Anderson	Cincinnati
1971	Pittsburgh	97	65	.599	Murtaugh	San Francisco	90	72	.556	Fox	Pittsburgh
1972	Pittsburgh	96	59	.619	Virdon	Cincinnati	95	59	.617	Anderson	Cincinnati
1973	N.Y. Mets	82	79	.509	Berra	Cincinnati	99	63	.611	Anderson	New York

American League

	EAST					WEST				Playoff
Year	Winner	W.	L.	Pct.	Manager	Winner	W.	L.	Pct.	Manager	Winner
1969	Baltimore	109	53	.673	Weaver	Minnesota	97	65	.599	Martin	Baltimore
1970	Baltimore	108	54	.667	Weaver	Minnesota	98	64	.605	Rigney	Baltimore
1971	Baltimore	101	57	.639	Weaver	Oakland	101	60	.627	Williams	Baltimore
1972	Detroit	86	70	.551	Martin	Oakland	93	72	.600	Williams	Oakland
1973	Baltimore	97	65	.599	Weaver	Oakland	94	68	.580	Williams	Oakland

Most Valuable Player Awards

Source: Baseball Writers' Association.

NATIONAL LEAGUE			AMERICAN LEAGUE		
Year	Player	Club	Year	Player	Club
1931	Frank Frisch	St. Louis	1931	Lefty Grove	Philadelphia
1932	Charles Klein	Philadelphia	1932	Jimmy Foxx	Philadelphia
1933	Carl Hubbell	New York	1933	Jimmy Foxx	Philadelphia
1934	Dizzy Dean	St. Louis	1934	Mickey Cochrane	Detroit
1935	Gabby Hartnett	Chicago	1935	Henry Greenberg	Detroit
1936	Carl Hubbell	New York	1936	Lou Gehrig	New York
1937	Joe Medwick	St. Louis	1937	Charley Gehringer	Detroit
1938	Ernie Lombardi	Cincinnati	1938	Jimmy Foxx	Boston
1939	Bucky Walters	Cincinnati	1939	Joe DiMaggio	New York
1940	Frank McCormick	Cincinnati	1940	Hank Greenberg	Detroit
1941	Dolph Camilli	Brooklyn	1941	Joe DiMaggio	New York
1942	Mort Cooper	St. Louis	1942	Joe Gordon	New York
1943	Stan Musial	St. Louis	1943	Spurgeon Chandler	New York
1944	Martin Marion	St. Louis	1944	Hal Newhouser	Detroit
1945	Phil Cavarretta	Chicago	1945	Hal Newhouser	Detroit
1946	Stan Musial	St. Louis	1946	Ted Williams	Boston
1947	Bob Elliott	Boston	1947	Joe DiMaggio	New York
1948	Stan Musial	St. Louis	1948	Lou Boudreau	Cleveland
1949	Jackie Robinson	Brooklyn	1949	Ted Williams	Boston
1950	Jim Konstanty	Philadelphia	1950	Phil Rizzuto	New York
1951	Roy Campanella	Brooklyn	1951	Yogi Berra	New York
1952	Hank Sauer	Chicago	1952	Bobby Shantz	Philadelphia
1953	Roy Campanella	Brooklyn	1953	Al Rosen	Cleveland
1954	Willie Mays	New York	1954	Yogi Berra	New York
1955	Roy Campenella	Brooklyn	1955	Yogi Berra	New York
1956	Don Newcombe	Brooklyn	1956	Mickey Mantle	New York
1957	Henry Aaron	Milwaukee	1957	Mickey Mantle	New York
1958	Ernie Banks	Chicago	1958	Jackie Jensen	Boston
1959	Ernie Banks	Chicago	1959	Nellie Fox	Chicago
1960	Dick Groat	Pittsburgh	1960	Roger Maris	New York
1961	Frank Robinson	Cincinnati	1961	Roger Maris	New York
1962	Maury Wills	Los Angeles	1962	Mickey Mantle	New York
1963	Sandy Koufax	Los Angeles	1963	Elston Howard	New York
1964	Ken Boyer	St. Louis	1964	Brooks Robinson	Baltimore
1965	Willie Mays	San Francisco	1965	Zoilo Versalles	Minnesota
1966	Roberto Clemente	Pittsburgh	1966	Frank Robinson	Baltimore
1967	Orlando Cepeda	St. Louis	1967	Carl Yastrzemski	Boston
1968	Bob Gibson	St. Louis	1968	Denny McLain	Detroit
1969	Willie McCovey	San Francisco	1969	Harmon Killebrew	Minnesota
1970	Johnny Bench	Cincinnati	1970	John (Boog) Powell	Baltimore
1971	Joe Torre	St. Louis	1971	Vida Blue	Oakland
1972	Johnny Bench,	Cincinnati	1972	Dick Allen	Chicago

Rookie of the Year Award (Baseball Writers Assn.)

1947—Combined Selection—Jackie Robinson, Brooklyn, 1b
1948—Combined Selection—Alvin Dark, Boston, N. L. ss

NATIONAL LEAGUE

Year	Winner	Year	Winner	Year	Winner
1949	Don Newcombe, Brooklyn, p	1957	Jack Sanford, Phil., p	1965	Jim Lefebvre, L.A. 2b
1950	Sam Jethroe, Boston, of	1958	Orlando Cepeda, S. F., 1b	1966	Tommy Helms, Cinn., 2b
1951	Willie Mays, N. Y., of	1959	Willie McCovey, S. F., 1b	1967	Tom Seaver, N. Y., p
1952	Joe Black, Brooklyn, p	1960	Frank Howard, Los Angeles, of	1968	John Bench, Cinn., c
1953	Jim Gilliam, Brooklyn, 2b	1961	Billy Williams, Chicago, of	1969	Ted Sizemore, L. A., 2b
1954	Wally Moon, St. Louis, of	1962	Ken Hubbs, Chicago, 2b	1970	Carl Morton, Mont., p
1955	Bill Virdon, St. Louis, of	1963	Pete Rose, Cinn., 2b	1971	Earl Williams, Atl., c
1956	Frank Robinson, Cinn., of	1964	Richie Allen, Phil., 3b	1972	Jon Matlack, N.Y., p

AMERICAN LEAGUE

Year	Winner	Year	Winner	Year	Winner
1949	Roy Sievers, St. Louis, of	1957	Tony Kubek, N. Y., if-of	1965	Curt Blefary, Balt., of
1950	Walt Dropo, Boston, 1b	1958	Albie Pearson, Wash., of	1966	Tommie Agee, Chicago, of
1951	Gil McDougald, N. Y., 3b	1959	Bob Allison, Wash., of	1967	Rod Carew, Minn., 2b
1952	Harry Byrd, Phil., p	1960	Ron Hansen, Balt., ss	1968	Stan Bahnsen, N. Y., p
1953	Harvey Kuenn, Detroit, ss	1961	Don Schwall, Boston, p	1969	Lou Piniella, K. C., of
1954	Bob Grim, N. Y., p	1962	Tom Tresh, N. Y., if-of	1970	Thurman Munson, N.Y., c
1955	Herb Score, Cleveland, p	1963	Gary Peters, Chicago, p	1971	Chris Chambliss, Cleve., 1b
1956	Luis Aparicio, Chicago, ss	1964	Tony Oliva, Minn., of	1972	Carlton Fisk, Bos., c

Cy Young Award Winners

1956 — Don Newcombe, Dodgers	1963 — Sandy Koufax, Dodgers	1969 — (NL) Tom Seaver, New York
1957 — Warren Spahn, Braves	1964 — Dean Chance, Angels	(AL) McLain, Det., Cuellar, Balt.
1958 — Bob Turley, Yankees	1965 — Sandy Koufax, Dodgers	1970 — (NL) Bob Gibson, Cardinals
1959 — Early Wynn, White Sox	1966 — Sandy Koufax, Dodgers	(AL) Jim Perry, Minn.
1960 — Vernon Law, Pirates	1967 — (NL) Mike McCormick, Giants	1971 — (AL) Vida Blue, Oakland
1961 — Whitey Ford, Yankees	(AL) Jim Lonborg, Red Sox	(NL) Ferguson Jenkins, Chicago
1962 — Don Drysdale, Dodgers	1968 — (NL) Bob Gibson, Cardinals	1972 — (NL) Steve Carlton, Philadelphia
	(AL) Dennis McLain, Tigers	(AL) Gaylord Perry, Cleveland

Triple Crown Winners

Players leading league in batting, runs batted in & homers

Year	Player & Team	Year	Player & Team
1909	Ty Cobb, Detroit Tigers	1937	Joe Medwick, St. Louis Cardinals
1912	Heinie Zimmerman, Chicago Cubs	1942	Ted Williams, Boston Red Sox
1922	Rogers Hornsby, St. Louis Cardinals	1947	Ted Williams, Boston Red Sox
1925	Rogers Hornsby, St. Louis Cardinals	1956	Mickey Mantle, New York Yankees
1933	Jimmy Foxx, Philadelphia Athletics	1966	Frank Robinson, Baltimore Orioles
1933	Chuck Klein, Philadelphia Phillies	1967	Carl Yastrzemski, Boston Red Sox
1934	Lou Gehrig, New York Yankees		

Home Run Leaders

Year	NATIONAL LEAGUE	HR.	Year	AMERICAN LEAGUE	HR.
1918	Gavvy Cravath, Phil	8	1918	Babe Ruth, Boston; Tilly Walker, Phil.	11
1919	Gavvy Cravath, Phil	12	1919	Babe Ruth, Boston	29
1920	Cy Williams, Phil	15	1920	Babe Ruth, New York	54
1921	George Kelly, New York	23	1921	Babe Ruth, New York	59
1922	Rogers Hornsby, St. Louis	42	1922	Ken Williams, St. Louis	39
1923	Cy Williams, Phil	41	1923	Babe Ruth, New York	41
1924	Jacques Fournier, Brooklyn	27	1924	Babe Ruth, New York	46
1925	Rogers Hornsby, St. Louis,	39	1925	Bob Meusel, New York	33
1926	Hack Wilson, Chicago.	21	1926	Babe Ruth, New York	47
1927	Wilson, Chi; Williams, Phil.	30	1927	Babe Ruth, New York	60
1928	Wilson, Chi.; Bottomley, S.L.	31	1928	Babe Ruth, New York	54
1929	Charles Klein, Phil.	43	1929	Babe Ruth, New York	46
1930	Hack Wilson, Chicago	56	1930	Babe Ruth, New York	49
1931	Charles Klein, Phil	31	1931	Ruth, Lou Gehrig, New York	46
1932	Klein, Phil., Mel Ott, N.Y.	38	1932	Jimmy Foxx, Phil	58
1933	Charles Klein, Phil.	28	1933	Jimmy Foxx, Phil	48
1934	Collins, S.L.; Mel Ott, N.Y.	35	1934	Lou Gehrig, New York	49
1935	Walter Berger, Boston	34	1935	Foxx, Phil., Greenberg, Det.	36
1936	Mel Ott, New York.	33	1936	Lou Gehrig, New York.	46
1937	Ott, N.Y.; Joe Medwick, S.L.	31	1937	Joe DiMaggio, New York	46
1938	Mel Ott, New York.	36	1938	Hank Greenberg, Detroit	58
1939	John Mize, St. Louis.	28	1939	Jimmy Foxx, Boston	35
1940	John Mize, St. Louis.	43	1940	Hank Greenberg, Detroit,	41
1941	Dolph Camilli, Brooklyn	34	1941	Ted Williams, Boston	37
1942	Mel Ott, New York.	30	1942	Ted Williams, Boston	36
1943	Bill Nicholson, Chicago.	29	1943	Rudy York, Detroit	34
1944	Bill Nicholson, Chicago.	33	1944	Nick Etten, New York	22
1945	Tommy Holmes, Boston	28	1945	Vern Stephens, St. Louis	24
1946	Ralph Kiner, Pittsburgh	23	1946	Hank Greenberg, Detroit	44
1947	Ralph Kiner, Pitts.; John Mize, N.Y.	51	1947	Ted Williams, Boston	32
1948	Ralph Kiner, Pitts.; John Mize, N.Y.	40	1948	Joe DiMaggio, New York	39
1949	Ralph Kiner, Pittsburgh	54	1949	Ted Williams, Boston	43
1950	Ralph Kiner, Pittsburgh	47	1950	Al Rosen, Cleveland	37
1951	Ralph Kiner, Pittsburgh	42	1951	Gus Zernial, Chicago-Philadelphia	33
1952	Ralph Kiner, Pittsburgh; Hank Sauer, Chicago	37	1952	Larry Doby, Cleveland.	32
1953	Ed Mathews, Milwaukee	47	1953	Al Rosen, Cleveland	43
1954	Ted Kluszewski, Cincinnati.	49	1954	Larry Doby, Cleveland.	32
1955	Willie Mays, New York	51	1955	Mickey Mantle, New York	37
1956	Duke Snider, Brooklyn	43	1956	Mickey Mantle, New York	52
1957	Hank Aaron, Milwaukee	44	1957	Roy Sievers, Washington	42
1958	Ernie Banks, Chicago.	47	1958	Mickey Mantle, New York	42
1959	Ed Mathews, Milwaukee	46	1959	Rocky Colavito, Cleveland, Harmon Killebrew, Washington.	42
1960	Ernie Banks, Chicago.	41	1960	Mickey Mantle, New York	40
1961	Orlando Cepeda, San Francisco	46	1961	Roger Maris, New York	61
1962	Willie Mays, San Francisco	49	1962	Harmon Killebrew, Minnesota	48
1963	Hank Aaron, Milwaukee; Willie McCovey, San Francisco	44	1963	Harmon Killebrew, Minnesota	45
1964	Willie Mays, San Francisco	47	1964	Harmon Killebrew, Minnesota	49
1965	Willie Mays, San Francisco	52	1965	Tony Conigliaro, Boston	32
1966	Hank Aaron, Atlanta; Willie McCovey, San Francisco	44	1966	Frank Robinson, Baltimore	49
1967	Hank Aaron, Atlanta	39	1967	Carl Yastrzemski, Boston; Harmon Killebrew, Minn.	44
1968	Willie McCovey, San Francisco	36	1968	Frank Howard, Wash.	44
1969	Willie McCovey, San Francisco	45	1969	Harmon Killebrew, Minn	49
1970	Johnny Bench, Cincinnati	45	1970	Frank Howard, Wash.	44
1971	Willie Stargell, Pittsburgh	48	1971	Bill Melton, Chicago	33
1972	Johnny Bench, Cincinnati	40	1972	Dick Allen, Chicago	37
1973	Willie Stargell, Pittsburgh	44	1973	Reggie Jackson, Oakland	32

All-time Major League Record (154-game Season)—60—Babe Ruth, New York Yankees (A), 1927. **(162-game Season)—61**—Roger Maris, New York Yankees, 1961. Prior to the 1931 season a batted ball that bounced into the stands was a home run (now a ground-rule double). None of Babe Ruth's record 60 homers bounced into the stands.

Runs Batted In Leaders

	NATIONAL LEAGUE			AMERICAN LEAGUE	
Year	Batter, Club	RBI	Year	Batter, Club	RBI
1938	Joe Medwick, St. Louis	122	1938	Jimmy Foxx, Boston	175
1939	Frank McCormick, Cinn.	128	1939	Ted Williams, Boston.	145
1940	John Mize, St. Louis	137	1940	Hank Greenberg, Detroit.	150
1941	Dolph Camilli, Brooklyn	120	1941	Joe DiMaggio, New York	125
1942	John Mize, New York	137	1942	Ted Williams, Boston.	137
1943	Bill Nicholson, Chi.	128	1943	Rudy York, Detroit	118
1944	Bill Nicholson, Chi.	122	1944	Vern Stephens, St. Louis	109
1945	Dixie Walker, Brooklyn	124	1945	Nick Etten, New York	111
1946	Enos Slaughter, St. Louis	130	1946	Hank Greenberg, Detroit.	127
1947	John Mize, New York	138	1947	Ted Williams, Boston.	114
1948	Stan Musial, St. Louis	131	1948	Joe DiMaggio, New York	155
1949	Ralph Kiner, Pittsburgh	127	1949	Ted Williams, Vern Stephens, Boston	159
1950	Del Ennis, Philadelphia	126	1950	Walt Dropo, Vern Stephens, Boston.	144
1951	Monte Irvin, New York	121	1951	Gus Zernial, Chi.-Phila.	129
1952	Hank Sauer, Chicago	121	1952	Al Rosen, Cleveland	105
1953	Roy Campanella, Brooklyn	142	1953	Al Rosen, Cleveland	145
1954	Ted Kluszewski, Cincinnati	141	1954	Larry Doby, Cleveland	126
1955	Duke Snider, Brooklyn	136	1955	Ray Boone, Detroit, Jack Jensen, Boston	116
1956	Stan Musial, St. Louis	109	1956	Mickey Mantle, New York	130
1957	Hank Aaron, Milwaukee	132	1957	Roy Sievers, Washington	114

Year	Batter, Club	RBI	Year	Batter, Club	RBI
1958	Ernie Banks, Chicago	129	1958	Jack Jensen, Boston	122
1959	Ernie Banks, Chicago	143	1959	Jack Jensen, Boston	112
1960	Hank Aaron, Milwaukee	126	1960	Roger Maris, New York	112
1961	Orlando Cepeda, San Francisco	142	1961	Roger Maris, New York	142
1962	Tommy Davis, Los Angeles	153	1962	Harmon Killebrew, Minn.	126
1963	Hank Aaron, Milwaukee	130	1963	Dick Stuart, Boston	118
1964	Ken Boyer, St. Louis	119	1964	Brooks Robinson, Baltimore	118
1965	Deron Johnson, Cincinnati	130	1965	Rocky Colavito, Cleveland	108
1966	Hank Aaron, Atlanta	127	1966	Frank Robinson, Baltimore	122
1967	Orlando Cepeda, St. Louis	111	1967	Carl Yastrzemski, Boston	121
1968	Willie McCovey, San Francisco	105	1968	Ken Harrelson, Boston	109
1969	Willie McCovey, San Francisco	126	1969	Harmon Killebrew, Minn.	140
1970	Johnny Bench, Cincinnati	148	1970	Frank Howard, Wash.	126
1971	Joe Torre, St. Louis	137	1971	Harmon Killebrew, Minn.	119
1972	Johnny Bench, Cincinnati	125	1972	Dick Allen, Chicago	113
1973	Willie Stargell, Pittsburgh	119	1973	Reggie Jackson, Oakland	117

Champion Batters and Their Averages

	NATIONAL LEAGUE			AMERICAN LEAGUE	
Year	Player	Club	Aver.	Year	Player	Club	Aver.
------	--------	------	-------	------	--------	------	-------
1907	Honus Wagner	Pittsburgh	.350	1907	Ty Cobb	Detroit	.350
1908	Honus Wagner	Pittsburgh	.354	1908	Ty Cobb	Detroit	.324
1909	Honus Wagner	Pittsburgh	.339	1909	Ty Cobb	Detroit	.377
1910	Sherwood Magee	Philadelphia	.331	1910	Ty Cobb	Detroit	.385
1911	Honus Wagner	Pittsburgh	.334	1911	Ty Cobb	Detroit	.420
1912	Henry Zimmerman	Chicago	.372	1912	Ty Cobb	Detroit	.410
1913	Jacob Daubert	Brooklyn	.350	1913	Ty Cobb	Detroit	.390
1914	Jacob Daubert	Brooklyn	.329	1914	Ty Cobb	Detroit	.368
1915	Larry Doyle	New York	.320	1915	Ty Cobb	Detroit	.369
1916	Hal Chase	Cincinnati	.339	1916	Tris Speaker	Cleveland	.386
1917	Edd Roush	Cincinnati	.341	1917	Ty Cobb	Detroit	.383
1918	Zack Wheat	Brooklyn	.335	1918	Ty Cobb	Detroit	.382
1919	Edd Roush	Cincinnati	.321	1919	Ty Cobb	Detroit	.384
1920	Rogers Hornsby	St. Louis	.370	1920	George Sisler	St. Louis	.407
1921	Rogers Hornsby	St. Louis	.397	1921	Harry Heilmann	Detroit	.394
1922	Rogers Hornsby	St. Louis	.401	1922	George Sisler	St Louis	.420
1923	Rogers Hornsby	St. Louis	.384	1923	Harry Heilmann	Detroit	.403
1924	Rogers Hornsby	St. Louis	.424	1924	Babe Ruth	New York	.378
1925	Rogers Hornsby	St. Louis	.403	1925	Harry Heilmann	Detroit	.393
1926	Eugene Hargrave	Cincinnati	.353	1926	Henry Manush	Detroit	.378
1927	Paul Waner	Pittsburgh	.380	1927	Harry Heilmann	Detroit	.398
1928	Rogers Hornsby	Boston	.387	1928	Goose Goslin	Washington	.379
1929	Lefty O'Doul	Philadelphia	.398	1929	Lew Fonseca	Cleveland	.369
1930	Bill Terry	New York	.401	1930	Al Simmons	Philadelphia	.381
1931	Chick Hafey	St. Louis	.349	1931	Al Simmons	Philadelphia	.390
1932	Lefty O'Doul	Brooklyn	.368	1932	Dale Alexander	Det.-Bos.	.367
1933	Charles Klein	Philadelphia	.368	1933	Jimmy Foxx	Philadelphia	.356
1934	Paul Waner	Pittsburgh	.362	1934	Lou Gehrig	New York	.363
1935	Arky Vaughan	Pittsburgh	.385	1935	Buddy Myer	Washington	.349
1936	Paul Waner	Pittsburgh	.373	1936	Luke Appling	Chicago	.388
1937	Joe Medwick	St. Louis	.374	1937	Charlie Gehringer	Detroit	.371
1938	Ernie Lombardi	Cincinnati	.342	1938	Jimmy Foxx	Boston	.349
1939	John Mize	St. Louis	.349	1939	Joe DiMaggio	New York	.381
1940	Debs Garms	Pittsburgh	.355	1940	Joe DiMaggio	New York	.352
1941	Pete Reiser	Brooklyn	.343	1941	Ted Williams	Boston	.406
1942	Ernie Lombardi	Boston	.330	1942	Ted Williams	Boston	.356
1943	Stan Musial	St. Louis	.357	1943	Luke Appling	Chicago	.328
1944	Dixie Walker	Brooklyn	.357	1944	Lou Boudreau	Cleveland	.327
1945	Phil Cavarretta	Chicago	.355	1945	George Stirnweiss	New York	.309
1946	Stan Musial	St. Louis	.365	1946	Mickey Vernon	Washington	.353
1947	Harry Walker	Philadelphia	.363	1947	Ted Williams	Boston	.343
1948	Stan Musial	St. Louis	.376	1948	Ted Williams	Boston	.369
1949	Jackie Robinson	Brooklyn	.342	1949	George Kell	Detroit	.343
1950	Stan Musial	St. Louis	.346	1950	Billy Goodman	Boston	.354
1951	Stan Musial	St. Louis	.355	1951	Ferris Fain	Philadelphia	.344
1952	Stan Musial	St. Louis	.336	1952	Ferris Fain	Philadelphia	.327
1953	Carl Furillo	Brooklyn	.344	1953	Mickey Vernon	Washington	.337
1954	Willie Mays	New York	.345	1954	Roberto Avila	Cleveland	.341
1955	Richie Ashburn	Philadelphia	.338	1955	Al Kaline	Detroit	.340
1956	Hank Aaron	Milwaukee	.328	1956	Mickey Mantle	New York	.353
1957	Stan Musial	St. Louis	.351	1957	Ted Williams	Boston	.388
1958	Richie Ashburn	Philadelphia	.350	1958	Ted Williams	Boston	.328
1959	Hank Aaron	Milwaukee	.355	1959	Harvey Kuenn	Detroit	.353
1960	Dick Groat	Pittsburgh	.325	1960	Pete Runnels	Boston	.320
1961	Roberto Clemente	Pittsburgh	.351	1961	Norm Cash	Detroit	.361
1962	Tommy Davis	Los Angeles	.346	1962	Pete Runnels	Boston	.326
1963	Tommy Davis	Los Angeles	.326	1963	Carl Yastrzemski	Boston	.321
1964	Roberto Clemente	Pittsburgh	.339	1964	Tony Oliva	Minnesota	.323
1965	Roberto Clemente	Pittsburgh	.329	1965	Tony Oliva	Minnesota	.321
1966	Matty Alou	Pittsburgh	.342	1966	Frank Robinson	Baltimore	.316
1967	Roberto Clemente	Pittsburgh	.357	1967	Carl Yastrzemski	Boston	.326
1968	Pete Rose	Cincinnati	.335	1968	Carl Yastrzemski	Boston	.301
1969	Pete Rose	Cincinnati	.348	1969	Rod Carew	Minnesota	.332
1970	Rico Carty	Atlanta	.366	1970	Alex Johnson	California	.328
1971	Joe Torre	St. Louis	.363	1971	Tony Oliva	Minnesota	.337
1972	Billy Williams	Chicago	.333	1972	Rod Carew	Minnesota	.318
1973	Pete Rose	Cincinnati	.338	1973	Rod Carew	Minnesota	.350

Major League No-Hit Games Since 1956
Complete Nine-inning Games

Date	Pitcher	Club	Score
1956 — May 12	Carl Erskine	Brooklyn-New York N	3-0
1956 — July 14	Mel Parnell	Boston-Chicago A	4-0
1956 — Sept. 25	Sal Magile	Brooklyn-Philadelphia N. (night game)	5-0
1956 — Oct. 8	Don Larsen (1)	New York-Brooklyn	2-0
1957 — Aug. 20	Bob Keegan	Chicago-Washington A	6-0
1958 — July 20	Jim Bunning	Detroit-Boston A	3-0
1958 — Sept. 20	Hoyt Wilhelm	Baltimore-New York A	1-0
1959 — May 26	Harvey Haddix (2)	Pittsburgh-Milwaukee N	0-2
1960 — May 15	Don Cardwell	Chicago-St. Louis N. (2nd game)	4-0
1960 — Aug. 18	Lew Burdette	Milwaukee-Philadelphia N	1-0
1960 — Sept. 16	Warren Spahn	Milwaukee-Philadelphia N	4-0
1961 — April 28	Warren Spahn	Milwaukee-San Francisco N. (night game)	1-0
1962 — May 5	Bo Belinsky	Los Angeles-Baltimore A (night game)	2-0
1962 — June 26	Earl Wilson	Boston-Los Angeles A (night game)	2-0
1962 — June 30	Sandy Koufax	Los Angeles-New York N (night game)	5-0
1962 — Aug. 1	Bill Monbouquette	Boston-Chicago A (night game)	1-0
1962 — Aug. 26	Jack Kralick	Minnesota-Kansas City A	1-0
1963 — May 11	Sandy Koufax	Los Angeles-San Francisco N (night)	8-0
1963 — May 17	Don Nottebart	Houston-Philadelphia N (night)	4-1
1963 — June 15	Juan Marichal	San Francisco-Houston N	1-0
1964 — April 23	Ken Johnson (3)	Houston-Cincinnati N	0-1
1964 — June 4	Sandy Koufax	Los Angeles-Philadelphia N	3-0
1964 — June 21	Jim Bunning (4)	Philadelphia-New York N	6-0
1965 — June 14	Jim Maloney (5)	Cincinnati-New York N (night)	0-1
1965 — Aug. 19	Jim Maloney (6)	Cincinnati-Chicago N (1st game)	1-0
1965 — Sept. 9	Sandy Koufax (4)	Los Angeles-Chicago N	1-0
1965 — Sept. 16	Dave Morehead	Boston-Cleveland A	2-0
1966 — June 10	Sonny Siebert	Cleveland-Washington A (night)	2-0
1967 — Apr. 30	S. Barber, Stu. Miller (7)	Baltimore-Detroit A	0-2
1967 — June 18	Don Wilson	Houston-Atlanta N	2-0
1967 — Aug. 25	Dean Chance	Minnesota-Cleveland A	2-1
1967 — Sept. 10	Joe Horlen	Chicago-Detroit A	4-0
1968 — April 27	Tom Phoebus	Baltimore-Boston A.	6-0
1968 — May 8	Jim Hunter (4)	Oakland-Minnesota A (night)	4-0
1968 — July 29	George Culver	Cincinnati-Philadelphia N (night)	6-1
1968 — Sept. 17	Gaylord Perry	San Francisco-St. Louis N (night)	1-0
1968 — Sept. 18	Ray Washburn	St. Louis-San Francisco N	2-0
1969 — April 17	Bill Stoneman	Montreal-Philadelphia N (night)	7-0
1969 — April 30	Jim Maloney	Cincinnati-Houston N (night)	10-0
1969 — May 1	Don Wilson	Houston-Cincinnati N (night)	4-0
1969 — Aug. 13	Jim Palmer	Baltimore-Oakland A (night)	8-0
1969 — Aug. 19	Ken Holtzman	Chicago-Atlanta N.	3-0
1969 — Sept. 20	Bob Moose	Pittsburgh-New York N.	4-0
1970 — June 12	Dock Ellis	Pittsburgh-San Diego N. (night)	2-0
1970 — July 4	Clyde Wright	California-Oakland A. (night)	4-0
1970 — July 20	Bill Singer	Los Angeles-Philadelphia N.	5-0
1970 — Sept. 20	Vida Blue	Oakland-Minnesota A (night)	6-0
1971 — June 3	Ken Holtzman	Chicago-Cincinnati (N) (night)	1-0
1971 — June 23	Rick Wise	Philadelphia-Cincinnati N. (night)	4-0
1971 — Aug. 14	Bob Gibson	St. Louis-Pittsburgh N. (night)	11-0
1972 — Apr. 16	Burt Hooton	Chicago-Philadelphia N	4-0
1972 — Sept. 2	Milt Pappas	Chicago-San Diego N	8-0
1972 — Oct. 2	Bill Stoneman	Montreal-New York N	7-0
1973 — Apr. 27	Steve Busby	Kansas City-Detroit (A) (night)	3-0
1973 — May 15	Nolan Ryan	California-Kansas City (A) (night)	3-0
1973 — July 15	Nolan Ryan	California-Detroit (A).	6-0
1973 — July 30	Jim Bibby	Texas-Oakland (A) (night)	6-0
1973 — Aug. 5	Phil Niekro	Atlanta-San Diego (N)	9-0

(1) Perfect game and first World Series no-hitter. (2) Pitched 12 perfect innings. He allowed one hit in the 13th and lost the game. (3) Lost game on two errors in ninth inning. (4) Perfect game. (5) Maloney pitched ten hitless innings, then allowed two hits in the eleventh. Struck out eighteen batters. (6) Ten innings. (7) Barber pitched 8⅔ innings, Miller ⅓ of an inning. Detroit scored two 9th-inning runs on a wild pitch and an error.

Major League Perfect Games

Year	Player	Clubs	Score	Year	Player	Clubs	Score
1904	Cy Young	Boston vs. Phil. (AL)	3-0	1956	Don Larson (b)	N.Y. Yankees vs. Brooklyn	2-0
1908	Addie Joss	Cleveland vs. Chicago (AL)	1-0	1964	Jim Bunning	Phil. vs. N.Y. Mets (NL)	6-0
1917	Ernie Shore (a)	Boston vs. Wash. (AL)	4-0	1965	Sandy Koufax	Los Angeles vs. Chic. (NL)	1-0
1922	Charles Robertson	Chicago vs. Detroit (AL)	2-0	1968	Jim Hunter	Oakland vs. Minn. (AL)	4-0

(a) Babe Ruth, the starting pitcher, was ejected from the game after walking the first batter. Shore replaced him, and the base-runner was out stealing. Shore retired the next 26 batters. (b) World Series.

Professional Baseball Government

Commissioner — Bowie K. Kuhn.
Secretary Treasurer — Alexander H. Hadden.
Director of Public Relations — Joseph L. Reichler.
Office — 680 Fifth Ave., New York, N.Y. 10019

NATIONAL LEAGUE
President, treasurer — Charles S. Feeney.
Vice President — John McHale.
Director of Public Relations — David J. Grote.
Headquarters — Mills Bldg., 220 Montgomery St.,
San Francisco, 94104

AMERICAN LEAGUE
President — Joseph Edward Cronin.
Executive Assistant — Bob Holbrook.
Director of Publicity — Thomas Monahan
Office — 520 Boylston Street, Boston, Mass. 02116

NATIONAL ASSOCIATION
President — Henry J. Peters
Vice President — Bobby Bragan
Asst. to President — Daniel F. O'Brien
Office — 720 East Broad Street, Columbus, Ohio 43215

Members of National Baseball Hall of Fame and Museum

The shrine of organized baseball, dedicated June 12, 1939 is located in Cooperstown, N. Y.

Alexander, Grover Cleveland	Combs, Earle	Greenberg, Hank	Leonard, Buck	Ruth, Babe
Anson, Cap	Comiskey, Charles A.	Griffith, Clark	Lyons, Ted	Schalk, Ray
Appling, Lucius B.	Connolly, Thomas H.	Grimes, Burleigh	Mack, Connie	Simmons, Al
Baker, Home Run	Coveleski, Stan	Grove, Lefty	Manush, Henry	Sisler, George
Bancroft, Dave	Crawford, Sam	Hafey, Chick	Maranville, Rabbit	Spahn, Warren
Barrow, Edward G.	Cronin, Joe	Haines, Jessee	Marquard, Rube	Spalding, Albert
Beckley, Jake	Cummings, Candy	Hamilton, Bill	Mathewson, Christy	Speaker, Tris
Bender, Chief	Cuyler, Kiki	Harridge, Will	McCarthy, Joe	Stengel, Casey
Berra, Yogi	Dean, Dizzy	Hartnett, Gabby	McCarthy, Thomas	Terry, Bill
Boudreau, Lou	Delahanty, Ed	Heilmann, Harry	McGinnity, Joe	Tinker, Joe
Bresnahan, Roger	Dickey, Bill	Hooper, Harry	McGraw, John	Traynor (Pie), Harold J.
Brouthers, Dan	DiMaggio, Joe	Hornsby, Rogers	McKechnie, Bill	Vance, Dazzy
Brown (Three Finger), Mordecai	Duffy, Hugh	Hoyt, Waite	Medwick, Joe	Waddell, Rube
Bulkeley, Morgan C.	Evans, Billy	Hubbell, Carl	Musial, Stan	Wagner, Honus
Burkett, Jesse C.	Evers, John	Huggins, Miller	Nichols, Kid	Wallace, Roderick
Campanella, Roy	Ewing, Buck	Irvin, Monte	O'Rourke, James	Walsh, Ed
Carey, Max	Faber, Urban	Jennings, Hugh	Ott, Mel	Waner, Lloyd
Cartwright, Alexander	Feller, Bob	Johnson, Byron	Paige, Satchel	Waner, Paul
Chadwick, Henry	Flick, Elmer H.	Johnson, Walter	Pennock, Herb	Ward, John
Chance, Frank	Foxx, James E.	Keefe, Timothy	Plank, Ed	Weiss, George
Chesbro, John	Frick, Ford	Keeler, William	Radbourne, Charlie	Welch, Mickey
Clarke, Fred	Frisch, Frank	Kelley, Joe	Rice, Sam	Wheat, Zach
Clarkson, John	Galvin, Pud	Kelly, George	Rickey, Branch	Williams, Ted
Clemente, Roberto	Gehrig, Lou	Kelly, King	Rixey, Eppa	Wright, George
Cobb, Ty	Gehringer, Charles	Klem, Bill	Robinson, Jackie	Wright, Harry
Cochrane, Mickey	Gibson, Josh	Koufax, Sandy	Robinson, Wilbert	Wynn, Early
Collins, Edward T.	Gomez, Lefty	Lajoie, Napoleon	Roush, Edd	Young, Cy
Collins, James	Goslin, Goose	Landis, Kenesaw M.	Ruffing, Red	Youngs, Ross

All-Star Baseball Games, 1933-1973

Game	Year	Winner	Score	Location	Game	Year	Winner	Score	Location
1st	1933	American	4-2	Chicago	23rd	1956	National	7-3	Washington
2nd	1934	American	9-7	New York	24th	1957	American	6-5	St. Louis
3rd	1935	American	4-1	Cleveland	25th	1958	American	4-3	Baltimore
4th	1936	National	4-3	Boston	26th	1959	National	5-4	Pittsburgh
5th	1937	American	8-3	Washington	27th	1959	American	5-3	Los Angeles
6th	1938	National	4-1	Cincinnati	28th	1960	National	5-3	Kansas City
7th	1939	American	3-1	New York	29th	1960	National	6-0	New York
8th	1940	National	4-0	St. Louis	30th[3]	1961	National	5-4	San Francisco
9th	1941	American	7-5	Detroit	31st	1961	Called-Rain	1-1	Boston
10th	1942	American	3-1	New York	32nd[3]	1962	National	3-1	Washington
11th[*]	1943	American	5-3	Philadelphia	33rd	1962	American	9-4	Chicago
12th[*]	1944	National	7-1	Pittsburgh	34th	1963	National	5-3	Cleveland
13th	1946	American	12-0	Boston	35th	1964	National	7-4	New York
14th	1947	American	2-1	Chicago	36th	1965	National	6-5	Minnesota
15th	1948	American	5-2	St. Louis	37th[3]	1966	National	2-1	St. Louis
16th	1949	American	11-7	New York	38th[4]	1967	National	2-1	Anaheim
17th[1]	1950	National	4-3	Chicago	39th[*]	1968	National	1-0	Houston
18th	1951	National	8-3	Detroit	40th	1969	National	9-3	Washington
19th	1952	National	3-2	Philadelphia	41st[2 °]	1970	National	5-4	Cincinnati
20th	1953	National	5-1	Cincinnati	42nd[*]	1971	American	6-4	Detroit
21st	1954	American	11-9	Cleveland	43rd[*]	1972	National	4-3	Atlanta
22nd[2]	1955	National	6-5	Milwaukee	44th[*]	1973	National	7-1	Kansas City

Not played in 1945.

1. 14 innings. 2. 12 innings. 3. 10 innings. 4. 15 innings. ° Night game.

Baseball Stadiums

National League

Team	Stadium	Home Run Distances (in ft.)			Seating Capacity
		LF	Center	RF	
Atlanta Braves	Atlanta Stadium	330	400	330	51,383
Chicago Cubs	Wrigley Field	355	400	353	37,741
Cincinnati Reds	Riverfront Stadium	330	404	330	51,726
Houston Astros	Astrodome	330	400	330	44,500
Los Angeles Dodgers	Dodger Stadium	330	395	330	56,000
Montreal Expos	Jarry Park	340	417	340	28,000
New York Mets	Shea Stadium	341	410	341	55,300
Philadelphia Phillies	Veterans Stadium	330	408	330	55,730
Pittsburgh Pirates	Three Rivers Stadium	340	410	340	50,235
St. Louis Cardinals	Busch Memorial Stadium	330	404	330	50,126
San Diego Padres	San Diego Stadium	330	420	330	44,790
San Francisco Giants	Candlestick Park	335	410	335	58,000

American League

Team	Stadium	LF	Center	RF	Seating Capacity
Baltimore Orioles	Memorial Stadium	309	410	309	52,137
Boston Red Sox	Fenway Park	315	420	302	33,379
California Angels	Anaheim Stadium	333	402	333	43,200
Chicago White Sox	White Sox Park	352	400	352	46,550
Cleveland Indians	Municipal Stadium	320	400	320	76,977
Detroit Tigers	Tiger Stadium	340	440	325	54,220
Kansas City Royals	Royals Stadium	330	410	330	40,613
Milwaukee Brewers	Milwaukee County Stadium	320	402	315	47,611
Minnesota Twins	Metropolitan Stadium	346	425	330	45,921
New York Yankees	Yankee Stadium	301	461	296	65,010
Oakland A's	Oakland-Alameda County Coliseum	330	400	330	50,000
Texas Rangers	Arlington Stadium	330	400	330	35,698

National League Records, 1973

FINAL STANDINGS

EASTERN DIVISION

	NEW YORK	ST. LOUIS	PITTSBURGH	MONTREAL	CHICAGO	PHILADELPHIA	ATLANTA	CINCINNATI	HOUSTON	LOS ANGELES	SAN DIEGO	SAN FRANCISCO	WON	LOST	PERCENTAGE	GAMES BEHIND
New York Mets	—	10	13	9	7	9	6	4	6	5	8	5	82	79	.509	—
St. Louis Cardinals	8	—	8	10	9	9	6	6	7	4	8	6	81	81	.500	1½
Pittsburgh Pirates	5	10	—	12	12	10	5	5	6	2	8	5	80	82	.494	2½
Montreal Expos	9	8	6	—	9	13	6	4	6	5	7	6	79	83	.488	3½
Chicago Cubs	10	9	6	9	—	10	5	8	6	5	7	2	77	84	.478	5
Philadelphia Phillies	9	9	8	5	8	—	6	4	5	3	9	5	71	91	.438	11½

WESTERN DIVISION

	NEW YORK	ST. LOUIS	PITTSBURGH	MONTREAL	CHICAGO	PHILADELPHIA	ATLANTA	CINCINNATI	HOUSTON	LOS ANGELES	SAN DIEGO	SAN FRANCISCO	WON	LOST	PERCENTAGE	GAMES BEHIND
Cincinnati Reds	8	6	7	8	4	8	13	—	11	11	13	10	99	63	.611	—
Los Angeles Dodgers	7	8	10	7	7	9	15	7	7	—	9	9	95	65	.590	3½
San Francisco Giants	7	6	7	6	10	7	10	8	7	9	11	—	88	74	.453	11
Houston Astros	6	5	6	6	6	7	7	7	—	11	10	11	82	80	.506	17
Atlanta Braves	6	6	7	6	7	6	—	5	11	2	12	8	76	85	.472	22½
San Diego Padres	4	4	4	5	5	3	6	5	8	9	—	7	60	102	.370	39

*Rookie. †Bats—Pitches lefthanded ‡ Switch hitter.

CLUB BATTING

Club	pct.	ab.	r.	h.	hr.	sb.
Atlanta	.266	5631	799	1497	206	84
Los Angeles	.263	5604	675	1473	110	109
San Francisco	.262	5537	739	1452	161	112
Pittsburgh	.261	5608	704	1465	154	23
St. Louis	.259	5478	643	1418	75	100
Cincinnati	.254	5505	741	1398	137	148
Houston	.251	5532	681	1391	134	92
Montreal	.251	5369	668	1345	125	77
Philadelphia	.249	5546	642	1381	134	51
Chicago	.247	5363	614	1322	117	65
New York	.246	5457	608	1345	85	27
San Diego	.244	5457	548	1330	112	88

CLUB PITCHING

Club	era.	g.	ip.	h.	r.	bb.	so.
Los Angeles	3.00	162	1491	1270	565	461	961
St. Louis	3.25	162	1461	1366	603	486	867
New York	3.26	161	1465	1345	588	490	1027
Cincinnati	3.40	162	1473	1389	621	518	801
Chicago	3.66	161	1438	1471	655	438	885
Montreal	3.73	162	1452	1356	702	681	866
Pittsburgh	3.73	162	1451	1426	693	564	839
Houston	3.75	162	1461	1389	672	575	907
San Francisco	3.79	162	1452	1442	702	485	787
Philadelphia	3.99	162	1447	1435	717	632	919
San Diego	4.16	162	1430	1461	770	548	845
Atlanta	4.25	162	1462	1467	774	575	803

INDIVIDUAL BATTING

Leaders—450 or More At Bats

Player—Club	pct.	ab.	r.	h.	hr.	rbi.	sb.
Rose, Cincinnati†	.338	680	115	230	5	64	10
Cedeno, Houston	.320	525	86	168	25	70	56
Maddox, San Fran.	.319	587	81	187	11	76	24
Perez, Cincinnati	.314	564	73	177	27	101	3
Watson, Houston	.312	573	97	179	16	94	1
Simmons, St. Louis†	.310	619	62	192	13	91	2
Cardenal, Chicago	.303	522	80	158	11	68	19
Singleton, Montreal‡	.302	560	100	169	23	103	2
*Matthews, San Fran.	.300	540	74	162	12	58	17
Garr, Atlanta†	.299	668	94	200	11	55	35
Stargell, Pittsburgh†	.299	522	106	156	44	119	0

INDIVIDUAL PITCHING

Leaders—162 or More Innings

Pitcher—Club	w.	l.	era.	g.	ip.	h.	bb.	so.
Seaver, New York ..	19	10	2.07	36	290	219	64	251
Sutton, Los Angeles	18	10	2.43	33	256	196	56	197
Twitchell, Phil.	13	9	2.50	34	223	172	99	169
Marshall, Montreal .	14	11	2.66	92	179	163	74	124
Messersmith, L.A...	14	10	2.70	33	250	196	77	177
Gibson, St. Louis .	12	10	2.77	25	195	159	57	142
Renko, Montreal ...	15	11	2.81	36	250	201	108	164
Briles, Pittsburgh ..	14	13	2.84	33	219	201	51	94
Koosman, New York†	14	15	2.84	35	263	234	76	156
Roberts, Houston†	17	11	2.86	39	249	264	62	119
Rooker, Pittsburgh†	10	6	2.86	41	170	143	52	122

INDIVIDUAL BATTING (OVER 100 AT-BATS) INDIVIDUAL PITCHING (OVER 50 INNINGS)

*Rookie †Left Handed ‡Switch Hitter

ATLANTA BRAVES

Batting	pct.	g.	ab.	r.	h.	hr.	rbi.	sb.
Tepedino†	.304	74	148	20	45	4	29	0
Aaron	.301	120	392	84	118	40	96	1
Garr†	.299	148	668	94	200	11	55	35
Dietz	.295	83	139	22	41	3	24	0
Lum†	.294	138	513	74	151	16	82	2
Baker	.288	159	604	101	174	21	99	24
Evans†	.281	161	595	114	167	41	104	6
Pepitone†	.276	34	123	16	34	3	19	3
Johnson	.270	157	559	84	151	43	99	5
Perez	.250	141	501	66	125	8	57	2
Oates‡	.248	93	322	27	80	4	27	1
Casanova	.216	82	236	18	51	7	18	0
Jackson†	.209	117	206	29	43	0	12	6

Pitching	w.	l.	era.	g	ip.	h.	bb.	so.
P. Niekro	13	10	3.31	42	245	214	89	131
Morton	15	10	3.41	38	256	254	70	112
Gentry	4	6	3.41	16	87	74	35	42
Schueler	8	7	3.87	39	186	179	66	124
Harrison	11	8	4.17	38	177	161	98	130
Reed	4	11	4.42	20	116	133	31	64
*House†	4	2	4.70	52	67	58	31	42
Dobson	3	7	4.97	12	58	73	19	23

CHICAGO CUBS

Batting	pct.	g.	ab.	r.	h.	hr.	rbi.	sb.
Cardenal	.303	145	522	80	158	11	68	19
Williams†	.288	156	576	72	166	20	86	4
Fanzone	.273	64	150	22	41	6	22	1
Monday†	.267	149	554	93	148	26	56	5
Santo	.267	149	536	65	143	20	77	1
Kessinger‡ ...	.262	160	577	52	151	0	43	6
Beckett	.255	114	372	38	95	0	29	0
Hickman	.244	92	201	27	49	3	20	1
Popovich‡	.236	99	280	24	66	2	24	3
Hundley†	.226	123	368	35	83	10	43	5
*Bourque	.209	57	139	11	29	7	20	1
Rudolph	.206	64	170	12	35	2	17	1
Hiser†	.174	100	109	15	19	1	6	4

Pitching	w.	l.	era.	g.	ip.	h.	bb.	so.
Locker	10	6	2.55	63	106	96	42	76
*Burris	1	1	2.91	31	65	65	27	57
Reuschel	14	15	3.00	36	237	244	62	168
Bonham	7	5	3.02	44	152	126	64	121
Hooton	14	17	3.68	42	240	248	73	134
Jenkins	14	16	3.89	38	271	267	57	170
Aker	4	5	4.08	47	64	76	23	25
Pappas	7	12	4.28	30	162	192	40	48
Gura†	2	4	4.85	21	65	79	11	43
LaRoche†	4	1	5.83	45	54	55	29	34

CINCINNATI REDS

Batting	pct.	g.	ab.	r.	h.	hr.	rbi.	sb.
Rose†	.338	160	680	115	230	5	64	10
Perez	.314	151	564	73	177	27	101	3
*Driessen†	.301	102	366	49	110	4	47	8
Morgan†	.290	157	576	116	167	26	82	67
Concepcion	.287	89	328	39	94	8	46	22
Kosco	.280	47	118	17	33	9	21	0
Bench	.253	152	557	83	141	25	104	4
Stahl†	.225	76	111	17	25	2	12	1
Geronimo†	.210	139	324	35	68	4	33	5
Tolan†	.206	129	457	42	94	9	51	15
Menke	.191	139	241	38	46	3	26	1
Chaney†	.181	104	227	27	41	0	14	4

Pitching	w.	l.	era.	g.	ip.	h.	bb.	so.
Borbon	11	4	2.16	80	121	137	35	60
Billingham	19	10	3.04	40	293	257	95	155
Grimsley†	13	10	3.24	38	242	245	68	90
Nelson	3	2	3.44	14	55	49	24	17
Hall†	8	5	3.46	54	104	74	48	96
Gullett†	18	8	3.51	45	228	198	69	153
Norman†	13	13	3.60	36	240	208	101	161
Carroll	8	8	3.68	53	93	111	34	41
McGlothlin	3	3	6.71	24	63	91	23	18

HOUSTON ASTROS

Batting	pct.	g.	ab.	r.	h.	hr.	rbi.	sb.
Cedeno	.320	139	525	86	168	25	70	56
Watson	.312	158	573	97	179	16	94	1
Helms	.287	146	543	40	156	4	61	1
May	.270	148	545	65	147	28	105	1
*Gallagher†	.264	71	148	16	39	2	10	0
Rader	.254	154	574	79	146	21	89	4
Metzger†	.250	154	580	67	145	1	35	10
Edwards†	.244	79	250	24	61	5	27	1
*Jutze	.223	90	278	18	62	0	18	0
Wynn	.220	139	481	90	106	20	55	14
Campbell	.194	55	134	4	26	0	11	1

Pitching	w.	l.	era.	g.	ip.	h.	bb.	so.
Roberts†	17	11	2.86	39	249	264	62	119
Wilson	11	16	3.20	37	239	187	92	149
Reuss†	16	13	3.74	41	279	271	117	177
*Richard	6	2	4.00	16	72	54	38	75
Griffin	4	6	4.14	25	100	83	46	69
Forsch	9	12	4.21	46	201	197	74	149
York	3	4	4.42	41	53	65	20	22
Ray	6	4	4.43	42	69	65	38	25
*Crawford†	2	4	4.50	48	70	69	33	56

LOS ANGELES DODGERS

Batting	pct.	g.	ab.	r.	h.	hr.	rbi.	sb.
Mota	.314	89	293	33	92	0	23	1
Garvey	.304	114	349	37	106	8	50	0
Crawford†	.295	145	457	75	135	14	66	12
Davis†	.285	152	599	82	171	16	77	17
Buckner†	.275	140	575	68	158	8	46	12
*Lopes	.275	142	535	77	147	6	37	36
Russell	.265	162	615	55	163	4	56	15
Ferguson	.263	136	487	84	128	25	88	1
*Paciorek	.262	96	195	26	51	5	18	3
*Yeager	.254	54	134	18	34	2	10	1
Joshua†	.252	75	159	19	40	2	17	7
*Cey	.245	152	507	60	124	15	80	1
Lacy	.207	56	135	14	28	0	8	2

Pitching	w.	l.	era.	g.	ip.	h.	bb.	so.
Sutton	18	10	2.43	33	256	196	56	200
Messersmith	14	10	2.70	33	250	196	77	177
Hough	4	2	2.75	37	72	52	45	70
Brewer†	6	8	3.00	56	72	58	25	56
John†	16	7	3.10	36	218	202	50	116
Richert†	3	3	3.18	39	51	44	19	31
Osteen	16	11	3.30	33	237	227	61	86
Downing†	9	9	3.31	30	193	155	78	124
*Rau†	4	2	3.94	31	64	64	28	51

MONTREAL EXPOS

Batting	pct.	g.	ab.	r.	h.	hr.	rbi.	sb.
Hunt	.309	113	401	61	124	0	18	10
Singleton†	.302	162	560	100	169	23	103	2
Fairly†	.298	142	413	70	123	17	49	2
Breeden	.275	105	258	36	71	15	43	0
Day†	.275	101	207	36	57	4	28	0
Bailey	.273	151	513	77	140	26	86	5
Stinson†	.261	48	111	12	29	3	12	0
Lyttle†	.259	49	116	12	30	4	19	0
*Lintz†	.250	52	116	20	29	0	3	12
Foli	.240	126	458	37	110	2	36	6
Boccabella	.233	118	403	25	94	9	46	1

MONTREAL BATTING (CONT'D)

	pct.	g.	ab.	r.	h.	hr.	rbi.	sb.
*Frias	.231	100	225	19	52	0	22	1
Jorgensen†	.230	138	413	49	95	9	47	16
Woods	.230	135	318	45	73	3	31	12
Mashore	.204	67	103	12	21	3	14	4

Pitching	w.	l.	era.	g.	ip.	h.	bb.	so.
*Rogers	10	5	1.54	17	134	93	50	64
Marshall	14	11	2.66	92	179	163	74	124
Renko	15	11	2.81	36	250	201	108	164
Walker	7	5	3.62	54	92	95	42	68
McAnally	7	9	4.04	27	147	158	54	72
Torrez	9	12	4.46	35	208	207	115	90
Moore†	7	16	4.50	35	176	151	109	151
Stoneman	4	8	6.77	29	97	120	55	48

NEW YORK METS

Batting	pct.	g.	ab.	r.	h.	hr.	rbi.	sb.
Millan	.290	153	638	82	185	3	37	2
Staub†	.279	152	585	77	163	15	76	1
*Hodges†	.260	45	127	5	33	1	18	0
Jones	.260	92	339	48	88	11	48	1
*Theodore	.259	45	116	14	30	1	15	1
Harrelson†	.258	106	356	35	92	0	20	5
Garrett†	.256	140	504	76	129	16	58	6
Grote	.256	84	285	17	73	1	32	0
Martinez†	.255	92	263	34	67	1	14	3
Milner†	.239	129	451	69	108	23	72	1
*Milan (pooh)	.138	100	304	20	68	1	08	1
Fregosi	.234	45	124	7	29	0	11	1
Hahn	.229	93	262	22	60	2	21	2
Boswell†	.227	76	110	12	25	2	14	0
Mays	.211	66	209	24	44	6	25	1
Dyer	.185	70	189	9	35	1	9	0

Pitching	w.	l.	era.	g.	ip.	h.	bb.	so.
Seaver	19	10	2.07	36	290	219	64	251
Stone†	12	3	2.80	27	148	157	31	77
Koosman†	14	15	2.84	35	263	234	76	156
Matlack†	14	16	3.20	34	242	210	99	205
*Parker	8	4	3.34	38	97	79	36	63
Sadecki†	5	4	3.38	31	117	109	41	87
McGraw†	5	6	3.86	60	119	106	55	81
McAndrew	3	5	5.40	23	80	109	31	38

PHILADELPHIA PHILLIES

Batting	pct.	g.	ab.	r.	h.	hr.	rbi.	sb.
Unser†	.289	136	440	64	127	11	52	5
B. Robinson	.288	124	452	62	130	25	65	5
Luzinski	.285	161	610	76	174	29	97	3
Doyle†	.273	116	370	45	101	3	26	1
Tovar	.268	97	328	49	88	1	21	6
Hutton†	.263	106	247	31	65	5	29	3
Montanez†	.263	146	552	69	145	11	65	2
*Boone	.261	145	521	42	136	10	61	3
Anderson	.254	87	193	32	49	9	28	0
*C. Robinson	.226	46	146	11	33	0	7	1
Bowa†	.211	122	446	42	94	0	23	10
Harmon	.209	72	148	17	31	0	8	1
*Schmidt	.196	132	367	43	72	18	52	8

Pitching	w.	l.	era.	g.	ip.	h.	bb.	so.
Scarce†	1	8	2.41	52	71	54	47	57
Twitchell	13	9	2.50	34	223	172	99	169
Brett†	13	9	3.44	31	212	206	74	111
Culver	7	5	3.54	42	61	71	36	30
Carlton†	13	20	3.90	40	293	293	113	223
*Ruthven	6	9	4.22	25	128	125	75	98
Lersch	3	4	4.41	42	98	105	27	51
Lonborg	13	16	4.88	38	199	218	80	106
Brandon	2	4	5.46	36	56	54	25	25

PITTSBURGH PIRATES

Batting	pct.	g.	ab.	r.	h.	hr.	rbi.	sb.
*Zisk	.324	103	333	44	108	10	54	0
Stargell†	.299	148	522	106	156	44	119	0
Oliver†	.292	158	654	90	191	20	99	6
*Parker†	.288	54	139	17	40	4	14	1
Sanguillen	.282	149	589	64	166	12	65	2
Hebner†	.271	144	509	73	138	25	74	0
Cash	.270	116	436	59	118	2	31	2
May†	.269	101	283	29	76	7	31	0
Clines	.263	110	304	42	80	1	23	8
Stennett	.263	128	466	45	113	10	55	2
Robertson†	.239	119	397	43	95	14	40	0
Alley	.203	76	158	25	32	2	8	1
Maxvill	.189	74	217	19	41	0	17	0

PITTSBURGH (cont'd)

Pitching

Pitching	w.	l.	era.	g.	ip.	h.	bb.	so.
Giusti	9	2	2.36	67	99	89	37	64
R. Hernandez†	4	5	2.40	59	90	71	25	64
Briles	14	13	2.84	33	219	201	51	94
Rooker†	10	6	2.86	41	170	143	52	122
Ellis	12	14	3.05	28	192	176	55	122
Moose	12	13	3.54	33	201	219	70	111
Johnson	4	2	3.62	50	92	98	34	68
Walker†	7	12	4.65	37	122	129	66	74
Blass	3	9	9.81	23	89	109	84	27

ST. LOUIS CARDINALS

Batting

Batting	pct.	g.	ab.	r.	h.	hr.	rbi.	sb.
Simmons†	.310	161	619	62	192	13	91	2
Brock†	.297	160	650	110	193	7	63	70
Torre	.287	141	519	67	149	13	69	2
Carbo†	.286	111	308	42	88	8	40	2
Sizemore	.282	142	521	69	147	1	54	6
Melendez	.267	121	341	35	91	2	35	2
McCarver†	.266	130	331	30	88	3	49	2
*Tyson	.243	144	469	48	114	1	33	2
*Reitz	.235	147	426	40	100	6	42	0
J. Cruz†	.227	133	406	51	92	10	57	10
Agee	.222	110	266	38	59	11	22	3

Pitching

Pitching	w.	l.	era.	g.	ip.	h.	bb.	so.
Hrabosky†	2	4	2.09	44	56	45	21	57
Pena	4	4	2.18	42	62	60	14	38
Gibson	12	10	2.77	25	195	159	57	142
Segui	7	6	2.79	65	100	78	53	93
Cleveland	14	10	3.01	32	224	211	61	122
Foster	13	9	3.13	35	204	195	63	106
Wise	16	12	3.37	35	259	259	59	144
Folkers†	4	4	3.62	34	82	74	34	44
Murphy	3	7	3.74	19	89	89	22	42

SAN DIEGO PADRES

Batting

Batting	pct.	g.	ab.	r.	h.	hr.	rbi.	sb.
*Grubb†	.311	113	389	52	121	8	37	9
Roberts	.286	127	479	56	137	21	64	11
Kendall	.282	145	507	39	143	10	59	3
J. Morales	.281	122	388	47	109	9	34	6
*Winfield	.277	56	141	9	39	3	12	0
Colbert	.270	146	529	73	143	22	80	9

San Diego Batting (cont'd)

Batting	pct.	g.	ab.	r.	h.	hr.	rbi.	sb.
Gaston	.250	133	476	51	119	16	57	0
Thomas†	.238	113	404	41	96	0	22	15
Lee†	.237	118	333	36	79	3	30	4
*Locklear†	.233	96	180	26	42	3	25	9
Murrell	.229	93	210	23	48	9	21	2
Hernandez	.223	70	247	26	55	0	9	15
*Hilton	.197	70	234	21	46	5	16	2
R. Morales	.164	90	244	9	40	0	16	0
Anderson	.121	71	124	16	15	0	3	2

Pitching

Pitching	w.	l.	era.	g.	ip.	h.	bb.	so.
*Jones†	7	6	3.15	20	140	129	37	77
Grief	10	17	3.21	36	199	181	62	120
Romo	2	3	3.88	49	88	85	46	51
Caldwell†	5	14	3.74	55	149	146	53	86
*Troedson†	7	9	4.26	50	152	167	59	81
Corkins	5	4	4.50	47	122	130	61	82
Kirby	8	18	4.78	34	192	214	66	129
Arlin	11	14	5.10	34	180	196	72	98
Ross	4	4	5.45	58	76	93	33	44

SAN FRANCISCO GIANTS

Batting

Batting	pct.	g.	ab.	r.	h.	hr.	rbi.	sb.
Maddox	.319	144	587	81	187	11	76	24
Goodson†	.302	102	384	37	116	12	53	0
*Matthews	.300	148	540	74	162	12	58	17
*Thomasson†	.285	112	235	35	67	4	30	2
Bonds	.283	160	643	131	182	39	96	43
Fuentes†	.277	160	656	78	182	6	63	12
McCovey†	.266	130	383	52	102	29	75	1
Speier	.249	153	542	58	135	11	71	4
*Phillips†	.240	63	104	18	25	1	9	0
Rader†	.229	148	462	59	106	9	41	0
Kingman	.203	112	305	54	62	24	55	8

Pitching

Pitching	w.	l.	era.	g.	ip.	h.	bb.	so.
Moffitt	4	4	2.43	60	100	86	31	65
*Sosa	10	4	3.28	71	107	95	41	70
Bryant†	24	12	3.53	41	270	240	115	143
Barr	11	17	3.82	41	231	240	49	88
Marichal	11	15	3.83	34	207	231	37	87
Bradley	13	12	3.90	35	224	212	69	136
Willoughby	4	5	4.68	39	123	138	37	60
Carrithers	1	2	4.81	25	58	64	35	36

Major League Baseball Attendance

Clubs	NATIONAL LEAGUE 1973	1972	1971	Clubs	AMERICAN LEAGUE 1973	1972	1971
Atlanta	800,678	752,973	1,006,320	Baltimore	959,199	899,950	1,023,037
Chicago	1,351,971	1,299,163	1,653,007	Boston	1,487,031	1,441,718	1,678,732
Cincinnati	2,017,601	1,611,459	1,501,122	California	1,057,791	744,190	926,373
Houston	1,393,563	1,469,247	1,261,589	Chicago	1,316,465	1,177,318	833,891
Los Angeles	2,136,210	1,860,858	2,064,594	Cleveland	605,063	626,354	591,361
Montreal	1,246,843	1,142,145	1,290,963	Detroit	1,724,136	1,892,386	1,591,073
New York	1,914,365	2,134,185	2,266,680	Kansas City	1,345,341	707,656	910,784
Philadelphia	1,476,733	1,343,329	1,511,223	Milwaukee	1,092,224	600,440	731,531
Pittsburgh	1,320,915	1,427,460	1,510,132	Minnesota	907,499	797,901	940,858
St. Louis	1,574,276	1,196,894	1,604,671	New York	1,262,070	966,328	1,070,771
San Diego	611,827	644,273	557,513	Oakland	1,000,045	921,323	914,993
San Francisco	834,193	647,744	1,106,043	Texas	686,152	662,974	*655,156
Totals	16,679,175	15,529,730¹	17,324,857	Totals	13,443,016	11,438,538²	11,868,560

*Attendance in Washington. (1) 41 games lost due to player strike; (2) 43 games lost due to player strike.

Previous Years			Previous Years		
1970—16,662,198	1968—11,785,358	1966—15,015,471	1970—12,085,147	1968—11,317,387	1966—10,166,738
1969—15,094,946	1967—12,971,430	1965—13,581,136	1969—12,130,817	1967—11,336,923	1965— 8,860,764

MAJOR LEAGUE ATTENDANCE RECORDS

All-time Season Records, Both Leagues—30,122,191 in 1973.
All-time Season Record, One Club—2,755,184—Los Angeles Dodgers, 1962.
Record Attendance, Six-Game World Series—420,784—1959 Series between Los Angeles Dodgers and Chicago White Sox. (Exceeded seven-game Series record.)
Record Attendance, World Series Game—92,706—fifth game, 1959 Series, Los Angeles, Oct. 6.
Record Attendance, Regular Season Game—84,587—Municipal Stadium, Cleveland, Sept. 12, 1954, in doubleheader between the Indians and Yankees. (Not including pass list of 1,976.)
Attendance, Regular-Season Single Game—78,672—Los Angeles Memorial Coliseum, April 18, 1958, in opening game between Los Angeles Dodgers and San Francisco Giants.

Baseball Playoffs in 1973

NATIONAL LEAGUE
N.Y. Mets vs. Cincinnati

Oct. 6—Cincinnati 2, N.Y. Mets 1.
Oct. 7—N.Y. Mets 5, Cincinnati 0.
Oct. 8—N.Y. Mets 9, Cincinnati 2.
Oct. 9—Cincinnati 2, N.Y. Mets 1 (12 innings).
Oct. 10—N.Y. Mets 7, Cincinnati 2.
(Mets won 3-of-5 series, 3-2)

AMERICAN LEAGUE
Oakland vs. Baltimore

Oct. 6—Baltimore 6, Oakland 0.
Oct. 7—Oakland 6, Baltimore 3.
Oct. 9—Oakland 2, Baltimore 1 (11 innings).
Oct. 10—Baltimore 5, Oakland 4.
Oct. 11—Oakland 3, Baltimore 0.
(Oakland won 3-of-5 series, 3-2)

American League Records, 1973

FINAL STANDINGS

EASTERN DIVISION

	BALTIMORE	BOSTON	DETROIT	NEW YORK	MILWAUKEE	CLEVELAND	CALIFORNIA	CHICAGO	KANSAS CITY	MINNESOTA	OAKLAND	TEXAS	WON	LOST	PERCENTAGE	GAMES BEHIND
Baltimore Orioles	—	7	9	9	15	12	6	8	8	8	5	10	97	65	.599	—
Boston Red Sox	11	—	3	14	12	9	7	6	8	6	4	9	89	73	.549	8
Detroit Tigers	9	15	—	7	12	9	5	7	4	5	7	5	85	77	.525	12
New York Yankees	9	4	11	—	8	11	6	4	6	9	4	8	80	82	.494	17
Milwaukee Brewers	3	6	6	10	—	9	7	9	4	8	4	8	74	88	.457	23
Cleveland Indians	6	9	9	9	7	—	7	5	2	7	3	7	71	91	.438	26

WESTERN DIVISION

	BALTIMORE	BOSTON	DETROIT	NEW YORK	MILWAUKEE	CLEVELAND	CALIFORNIA	CHICAGO	KANSAS CITY	MINNESOTA	OAKLAND	TEXAS	WON	LOST	PERCENTAGE	GAMES BEHIND
Oakland A's	7	8	5	8	8	9	12	12	10	4	—	11	94	68	.580	—
Kansas City Royals	4	4	8	6	8	10	8	12	—	9	8	11	88	74	.543	6
Minnesota Twins	4	6	7	3	4	5	8	9	9	—	14	12	81	81	.500	13
California Angels	6	5	7	6	5	5	—	8	10	10	6	11	79	83	.488	15
Chicago White Sox	4	6	5	8	3	7	10	—	6	9	6	13	77	85	.475	17
Texas Rangers												—	57	105	.352	37

*Rookie †Bats—Pitches Lefthanded ‡Switch Hitter

CLUB BATTING

Club	pct.	ab.	r.	h.	hr.	sb.
Minnesota	.270	5625	738	1521	120	87
Boston	.267	5513	738	1472	147	114
Baltimore	.266	5537	754	1474	119	146
Kansas City	.261	5508	755	1440	114	105
New York	.261	5493	641	1435	131	47
Oakland	.260	5507	758	1431	147	128
Chicago	.256	5475	652	1400	111	83
Cleveland	.256	5592	680	1429	158	60
Texas	.255	5488	619	1397	110	91
Detroit	.254	5508	642	1400	157	28
California	.253	5505	629	1395	93	59
Milwaukee	.253	5526	708	1399	145	110

CLUB PITCHING

Club	era.	g.	ip.	h.	r.	bb.	so.
Baltimore ..	3.07	162	1462	1297	561	475	714
Oakland	3.29	162	1457	1311	615	495	798
New York ..	3.34	162	1428	1379	610	457	708
California ..	3.54	162	1456	1351	657	614	1010
Boston	3.65	162	1440	1417	647	499	808
Minnesota ..	3.77	162	1452	1443	692	519	880
Chicago	3.86	162	1456	1484	705	574	847
Detroit	3.90	162	1448	1468	474	493	911
Milwaukee..	3.98	162	1454	1476	731	624	669
Kansas City.	4.19	162	1449	1521	752	617	790
Cleveland ...	4.58	162	1465	1532	826	606	884
Texas	4.64	162	1430	1514	844	680	830

INDIVIDUAL BATTING

Leaders—450 or More At Bats

Player—Club	pct.	ab.	r.	h.	hr.	rbi.	sb.
Carew, Minnesota†	.350	580	98	203	6	62	41
Scott, Milwaukee ..	.306	604	98	185	24	107	9
Davis, Baltimore ..	.306	552	53	169	7	89	11
Mucer, New York† ..	.304	616	83	187	22	95	6
May, Milwaukee† ..	.303	624	96	189	25	93	6
Munson, New York .	.301	519	80	156	20	74	4
Otis, Kansas City ...	.300	583	89	175	26	93	13
Yastrzemski, Bos.†	.296	540	82	160	19	95	9
M. Alou, New York†	.296	497	59	147	2	28	5
Jackson, Oakland†	.293	539	99	158	32	117	22

INDIVIDUAL PITCHING

Leaders—162 or More Innings

Pitcher—Club	w.	l.	era.	g.	ip.	h.	bb.	so.
Palmer, Baltimore..	22	9	2.40	38	296	225	113	158
Blyleven, Minnesota	20	17	2.52	40	325	296	67	258
Lee, Boston†	17	11	2.75	38	285	275	76	120
Ryan, California ..	21	16	2.87	41	326	238	162	383
*Medich, New York.	14	9	2.95	34	235	217	74	145
Holtzman, Oakland†	21	13	2.97	40	297	275	67	158
Stottlemyre, N.Y....	16	16	3.07	38	273	259	79	95
Colborn, Milwaukee	20	12	3.18	43	314	297	87	135
Singer, California ..	20	14	3.22	40	316	280	130	241
Forster, Chicago† ..	6	11	3.23	51	173	174	78	120

(Individual Batting (over 100 at-bats) Individual Pitching (over 50 innings)
*Rookie †Bats—Pitches Lefthanded ‡Switch Hitter

BALTIMORE ORIOLES

Batting	pct.	g.	ab.	r.	h.	hr.	rbi.	sb.
*Bumbry†	.337	110	356	73	120	7	34	23
*Coggins†	.319	110	389	54	124	7	41	17
Davis	.306	137	552	53	169	7	89	11
Baylor	.286	118	405	64	116	11	51	32
Blair	.280	146	500	73	140	10	64	18
Powell†	.265	114	370	52	98	11	54	0
Rettenmund	.262	95	321	59	84	9	44	11
Robinson	.257	155	549	53	141	9	72	2
Etchebarren	.257	54	152	16	39	2	23	1
Grich	.251	162	581	82	146	12	50	17
Williams	.237	132	459	58	109	22	83	0
Belanger	.226	154	470	60	106	0	27	13
Crowley†	.206	54	131	16	27	3	15	0
Hendricks†	.178	41	101	9	18	3	15	0

Pitching	w.	l.	era.	g.	ip.	h.	bb.	so.
Reynolds	7	5	1.86	42	111	88	31	77
Jackson†	8	0	1.90	45	80	54	24	47
Palmer	22	9	2.40	38	296	225	113	158
McNally†	17	17	3.25	38	266	247	81	87
Cuellar†	18	13	3.27	38	267	265	84	140
Watt	3	4	3.30	30	71	62	21	38
Alexander	12	8	3.86	29	175	169	62	62
*Jefferson	6	5	4.11	18	101	104	46	52

BOSTON RED SOX

Batting	pct.	g.	ab.	r.	h.	hr.	rbi.	sb.
Montgomery ..	.320	34	128	18	41	7	25	0
Cater	.313	63	195	30	61	1	24	0
Smith‡	.303	115	423	79	128	21	69	3
Yastrzemski†	.296	152	540	82	160	19	95	9
Cepeda	.289	142	550	51	159	20	86	0
Harper	.281	147	566	92	159	17	71	54
Aparicio	.271	132	499	56	135	0	49	13
Miller†	.261	143	441	65	115	6	43	12
Griffin	.255	113	396	43	101	1	33	7
Fisk	.246	135	508	65	125	26	71	7
Petrocelli	.244	100	356	44	87	13	45	0
*Cooper†	.238	30	101	12	24	3	11	1
*Guerrero	.233	66	219	19	51	0	11	2
*Evans	.223	119	282	46	63	10	32	5
Oglivie†	.218	58	147	16	32	2	9	1
Kennedy	.181	67	155	17	28	1	16	0

Pitching	w.	l.	era.	g.	ip.	h.	bb.	so.
Bolin	3	4	2.70	39	53	45	13	31
Lee†	17	11	2.75	38	285	275	76	120
Moret†	13	2	3.17	30	156	138	67	90
Tiant	20	13	3.34	35	272	217	78	206
Curtis†	13	13	3.58	35	221	225	83	101
Pattin	15	15	4.31	34	219	238	69	119
Culp	2	6	4.47	10	50	46	32	32

CALIFORNIA ANGELS

Batting	pct.	g.	ab.	r.	h.	hr.	rbi.	sb.
Rivers†	.349	30	129	26	45	0	16	8
Scheinblum‡	.328	77	229	28	75	3	21	0
Valentine	.302	32	126	12	38	1	13	6
Berry	.284	137	415	48	118	3	36	1
Gallagher	.273	110	311	16	85	0	26	1
Llenas	.269	78	130	16	35	1	25	0
Robinson	.266	147	534	85	142	30	97	1
Oliver	.265	151	544	51	144	18	89	1
McCraw†	.265	99	264	25	70	3	24	3
Pinson†	.260	124	466	56	121	8	57	5
Stephenson†	.246	60	122	9	30	1	9	0
Alomar‡	.238	136	470	45	112	0	28	25
Stanton	.235	119	306	41	72	8	34	3
Parker	.225	38	102	14	23	0	7	0
*Meoli†	.223	120	305	36	68	2	23	2
Torborg	.220	102	255	20	56	1	19	0
Epstein†	.209	118	397	39	83	9	38	0
Grabarkewitz	.163	61	129	27	21	3	9	2

Pitching	w.	l.	era.	g.	ip.	h.	bb.	so.
Ryan	21	16	2.87	41	326	238	162	383
Singer	20	14	3.22	40	316	280	130	241
Barber†	3	2	3.53	50	89	90	32	58
Wright†	11	19	3.68	37	257	273	76	65
*Sells	7	2	3.71	51	68	72	35	25
May†	7	14	4.38	34	185	177	80	134
Hand	6	6	4.39	24	96	107	40	33
*Lange	2	1	4.44	17	53	61	21	27

DETROIT TIGERS

Batting	pct.	g.	ab.	r.	h.	hr.	rbi.	sb.
Horton	.316	111	411	42	130	17	53	1
Northrup†	.307	119	404	55	124	12	44	4
McAuliffe†	.274	106	343	39	94	12	47	0
N. Cash†	.262	121	363	51	95	19	40	1
Howard	.256	85	227	26	58	12	29	0
Kaline	.255	91	310	40	79	10	45	4
Stanley	.244	157	602	81	147	17	57	0
*Sharon	.242	91	178	20	43	7	16	2
Brinkman	.237	162	515	55	122	7	40	0
G. Brown†	.236	125	377	48	89	12	50	1
Freehan	.234	110	380	33	89	6	29	0
Taylor	.229	84	275	35	63	5	24	9
Rodriguez	.222	160	555	46	123	9	58	3

Pitching	w.	l.	era.	g.	ip.	h.	bb.	so.
Hiller†	10	5	1.44	65	125	89	39	124
Coleman	23	15	3.53	40	288	283	93	202
Lolich†	16	15	3.82	42	309	315	79	214
Perry	14	13	4.03	35	203	225	55	66
Scherman†	2	4	4.23	34	62	59	30	28
LaGrow	1	5	4.33	21	54	54	23	33
Strahler	4	5	4.37	22	80	84	39	37
Farmer	3	2	4.91	40	62	77	32	38
Fryman†	6	13	5.36	34	170	200	64	119

CHICAGO WHITE SOX

Batting	pct.	g.	ab.	r.	h.	hr.	rbi.	sb.
R. Allen	.316	72	250	39	79	16	41	7
Muser†	.285	109	309	38	88	4	30	8
Kelly†	.280	144	550	77	154	1	44	22
Melton	.277	152	560	83	155	20	87	4
*Sharp†	.276	77	196	23	54	4	22	2
*Hairston‡	.271	60	210	25	57	0	23	0
May†	.268	149	553	62	148	20	96	8
Orta†	.266	128	425	46	113	6	40	8
Henderson‡	.260	73	262	32	68	6	32	3
*Dent	.248	40	117	17	29	0	10	2
Jeter	.240	89	300	38	72	7	27	4
Bradford	.238	53	168	24	40	8	15	4
Alvarado	.232	80	203	21	47	0	20	6
Leon	.228	127	399	37	91	3	31	1
Herrmann†	.224	119	379	42	85	10	39	2
Brinkman	.186	63	140	13	26	1	10	0

Pitching	w.	l.	era.	g.	ip.	h.	bb.	so.
Acosta	10	6	2.23	48	97	66	39	60
Forster†	6	11	3.23	51	173	174	78	120
Wood†	24	20	3.46	49	359	381	91	199
Bahnsen	18	21	3.57	42	282	290	117	120
Johnson	3	4	4.13	22	81	76	40	56
Stone	6	11	4.24	36	176	163	82	137
Kaat†	15	13	4.37	36	224	250	43	109
Fisher	6	7	4.88	26	111	135	38	57
Gossage	0	4	7.43	20	50	*57	37	33

KANSAS CITY ROYALS

Batting	pct.	g.	ab.	r.	h.	hr.	rbi.	sb.
Otis	.300	148	583	89	175	26	93	13
Schaal	.288	121	396	61	114	8	42	5
Mayberry†	.278	152	510	87	142	26	100	3
Rojas	.276	139	551	78	152	6	69	18
Healy	.276	95	279	25	77	6	34	3
*Wohlford	.266	44	109	21	29	2	10	1
Kirkpatrick†	.263	125	429	61	113	6	45	3
Bevacqua	.257	99	276	39	71	2	40	2
Hovley†	.254	104	232	29	59	2	24	6
Reichardt	.250	87	280	30	70	6	33	2
Piniella	.250	144	513	53	128	9	69	5
Hopkins†	.246	74	138	17	34	2	16	1
Patek	.234	135	501	82	117	5	45	36
McRae	.234	106	338	36	79	9	50	2
Taylor	.228	69	145	18	33	0	16	2
*White	.223	51	139	20	31	0	5	3

Pitching	w.	l.	era.	g.	ip.	h.	bb.	so.
Fitzmorris	8	3	2.83	15	89	88	25	26
*Bird	4	4	2.99	54	102	81	30	83
Mingori†	3	3	3.57	24	68	69	33	50
Splittorff†	20	11	3.98	38	262	279	78	110
*Busby	16	15	4.23	37	238	246	105	174
Drago	12	14	4.23	37	213	252	76	98
Garber	9	9	4.24	48	153	164	49	60
Dal Canton	4	3	4.81	32	97	108	46	38
Wright	6	5	4.91	25	81	60	82	75
Simpson	3	5	5.73	16	60	66	35	29

CLEVELAND INDIANS

Batting	pct.	g.	ab.	r.	h.	hr.	rbi.	sb.
Lowenstein†	.292	98	305	42	89	6	40	5
Williams	.289	104	350	43	101	8	38	9
Chambliss†	.273	155	572	70	156	11	53	4
Ellis	.270	127	437	59	118	14	68	0
Bell	.268	157	631	86	169	14	59	7
Hendrick	.268	113	440	64	118	21	61	7
Gamble†	.267	113	390	56	104	20	44	3
Duffy	.263	116	361	34	95	8	50	6
Ragland	.257	67	183	16	47	0	12	2
*Spikes	.237	140	506	68	120	23	73	5
Duncan	.233	95	344	43	80	17	43	3
*Lolich	.229	61	140	16	32	2	15	0
Brohamer*	.220	102	300	29	66	4	29	0
Cardenas	.215	72	195	9	42	0	12	1
Torres‡	.205	122	312	31	64	7	28	6

Pitching	w.	l.	era.	g.	ip.	h.	bb.	so.
Hilgendorf†	5	3	3.14	48	95	87	36	58
Perry	19	19	3.38	41	344	315	115	238
Sanders	7	5	4.40	42	72	71	30	33
Tidrow	14	16	4.42	42	275	289	95	138
Lamb	3	4	4.60	32	86	98	42	60
*Strom	2	10	4.61	27	123	134	47	91
Timmerman	9	8	4.63	46	163	156	65	84
Bosman	3	13	5.64	29	137	172	46	55
Wilcox	8	10	5.83	26	134	143	68	82
Johnson	5	6	6.18	39	60	70	39	45
Kekich†	2	5	7.52	21	65	93	49	30

MILWAUKEE BREWERS

Batting	pct.	g.	ab.	r.	h.	hr.	rbi.	sb.
Scott	.306	158	604	98	185	24	107	9
May†	.303	156	624	96	189	25	93	6
Money	.284	145	556	75	158	11	61	22
Brown	.280	97	296	28	83	7	32	4
El. Rodriguez	.269	94	290	30	78	0	30	4
*Porter†	.254	117	350	50	89	16	67	5
Briggs†	.246	141	487	78	120	18	57	15
*Garcia	.245	160	580	67	142	15	54	11
*Coluccio	.224	124	438	65	98	15	58	13
Mitchell	.223	47	130	12	29	5	20	4
*Johnson†	.213	136	465	39	99	0	32	6
Lahoud†	.204	96	225	29	46	5	26	5
*Thomas	.187	60	155	16	29	2	11	5
Vukovich	.125	55	128	10	16	2	9	0

Pitching	w.	l.	era.	g.	ip.	h.	bb.	so.
Colborn	20	12	3.18	43	314	297	87	135
*Ed. Rodriguez	9	7	3.30	30	76	71	47	46
Linzy	2	6	3.57	42	63	68	21	21
Champion	5	8	3.70	37	136	139	62	67
Slaton	13	15	3.71	38	276	266	99	134
Lockwood	5	12	3.90	37	155	164	59	88
Bell	9	9	3.97	31	184	185	70	57
Short†	3	5	5.13	42	72	86	44	44
Parsons	3	6	6.94	20	60	59	66	30

MINNESOTA TWINS

Batting	pct.	g.	ab.	r.	h.	hr.	rbi.	sb.
Carew†	.350	149	580	98	203	6	62	41
Holt†	.297	132	441	53	131	11	58	0
Soderholm	.297	35	·111	22	33	1	9	1
Oliva†	.291	146	571	63	166	16	92	2
Braun†	.283	115	361	46	102	6	42	4
Hisle	.272	143	545	88	148	15	64	11
*Terrell	.265	124	438	43	116	1	32	13
Brye	.263	92	278	39	73	6	33	3
Mitterwald	.259	125	432	49	112	16	64	3
Darwin	.252	145	560	69	141	18	90	5
Lis	.245	103	253	37	62	9	25	0
Killebrew	.242	69	248	29	60	5	32	0
Thompson	.225	99	347	29	78	1	36	1
Roof	.197	47	117	10	23	1	15	0
Reese†	.144	81	125	17	18	3	7	0

Pitching	w.	l.	era.	g.	ip.	h.	bb.	so.
Blyleven	20	17	2.52	40	325	296	67	258
Corbin	8	5	3.03	51	148	124	60	84
*Campbell	3	3	3.14	28	52	44	20	42
Hands	7	10	3.49	39	142	138	41	78
Woodson	10	8	3.95	23	141	137	68	53
Decker	10	10	4.17	29	170	167	88	109
*Fife	3	2	4.35	10	52	54	29	18
*Bane†	0	5	4.92	23	60	62	30	42
Goltz	6	4	5.25	32	106	138	32	65

NEW YORK YANKEES

Batting	pct.	g.	ab.	r.	h.	hr.	rbi.	sb.
Blomberg†	.329	100	301	45	99	12	57	2
Murcer†	.304	160	616	83	187	22	95	6
Munson	.301	147	519	80	156	20	74	4
M. Alou†	.296	123	497	59	147	2	28	5
Clarke‡	.262	148	591	60	155	2	35	11
Hart	.254	114	339	29	86	13	52	0
White‡	.246	162	639	88	157	18	60	16
Sims†	.245	84	261	34	64	9	31	1
Hegan†	.243	113	202	20	49	7	19	0
F. Alou	.236	93	280	25	66	4	27	0
Nettles†	.234	160	552	65	129	22	81	0
Michael‡	.225	129	418	30	94	3	47	1
Callison†	.176	45	136	10	24	1	10	1

Pitching	w.	l.	era.	g.	ip.	h.	bb.	so.
Beene	6	0	1.68	19	91	67	27	49
Lyle†	5	9	2.51	51	82	66	18	63
McDaniel	12	6	2.86	47	160	148	49	93
*Medich	14	9	2.95	34	235	217	74	145
Stottlemyre	16	16	3.07	38	273	259	79	95
Peterson†	8	15	3.95	31	184	207	49	59
McDowell†	5	8	3.95	16	96	73	64	75
Kline	4	7	4.01	14	74	76	31	19
Dobson	9	8	4.17	22	142	150	35	70

OAKLAND A's

Batting	pct.	g.	ab.	r.	h.	hr.	rbi.	sb.
Alou	.306	36	108	10	33	1	11	0
Jackson†	.293	151	539	99	158	32	117	22
Bando	.287	162	592	97	170	29	98	4
North‡	.285	146	554	98	158	5	34	53
Rudi	.270	120	437	53	118	12	66	0
Green	.262	133	332	33	87	3	42	0
Tenace	.259	160	510	83	132	24	84	2
Fosse	.256	143	492	37	126	7	52	2
Campaneris	.250	151	601	89	150	4	46	34
Johnson	.246	131	464	61	114	19	81	0
Carty	.232	93	314	25	73	4	34	2
Mangual	.224	74	192	20	43	3	13	1
Kubiak‡	.220	106	182	15	40	3	17	1
Andrews	.200	70	180	11	36	0	10	0
Conigliaro	.200	48	110	5	22	0	14	1

Pitching	w.	l.	era.	g.	ip.	h.	bb.	so.
Fingers	7	8	1.92	62	127	107	39	110
Pina	6	3	2.76	47	88	59	34	41
Holtzman†	21	13	2.97	40	297	275	67	158
Knowles†	6	8	3.09	52	99	87	49	46
Blue†	20	9	3.28	37	264	213	105	158
Hunter	21	5	3.34	36	256	222	69	124
Lindblad†	1	5	3.69	36	78	89	28	34
Hamilton†	6	4	4.39	16	70	74	24	33
Odom	5	12	4.49	30	150	153	67	83

TEXAS RANGERS

Batting	pct.	g.	ab.	r.	h.	hr.	rbi.	sb.
Grieve	.309	66	123	22	38	7	21	1
Johnson	.287	158	624	62	179	8	68	10
Nelson	.286	142	576	71	165	7	48	43
Burroughs	.279	151	526	71	147	30	85	0
Fregosi	.268	45	157	25	42	6	16	0
Spencer†	.262	131	439	45	115	6	54	0
Harrah	.260	118	461	64	120	10	50	10
Sudakis‡	.255	82	235	32	60	15	43	0
Biittner†	.252	83	258	19	65	1	12	1
Harris‡	.249	152	555	71	138	8	44	13
Suarez	.248	93	278	25	69	1	27	1
Maddox	.238	100	172	24	41	1	17	5
Mason†	.206	92	238	23	49	3	19	0
Billings	.179	81	280	17	50	3	32	1

Pitching	w.	l.	era.	g.	ip.	h.	bb.	so.
*Bibby	9	10	3.24	26	180	121	106	155
*Foucault	2	4	3.88	32	56	54	31	27
Brown	5	5	3.92	25	67	82	25	45
Merritt†	5	13	4.05	35	160	191	34	65
Siebert	7	12	4.06	27	122	125	38	81
Gogolewski	3	6	4.22	49	124	139	48	77
*Hudson†	4	2	4.62	25	62	59	31	34
Stanhouse	1	7	4.76	21	70	70	44	42
Paul†	5	4	4.95	36	87	104	36	49
*Clyde†	4	8	5.01	18	93	106	54	74
Dunning	2	8	5.53	27	112	118	65	48
Broberg	5	9	5.61	22	119	130	66	57
Allen	0	6	9.42	28	50	73	44	29

Earned-Run Average Leaders

Based on 10 complete games through 1950 then 154 innings until A. L. expanded in '61, N. L. in '62, then 162 innings.

	NATIONAL LEAGUE					AMERICAN LEAGUE			
Year	Pitcher, Club	g	ip	era	Year	Pitcher, Club	g	ip	era
1950	Jim Hearn, St. L.-N. Y.	22	134	2.49	1950	Early Wynn, Cleveland	32	214	3.20
1951	Chet Nichols, Boston	33	156	2.88	1951	Saul Rogovin, Det.-Chi.	27	217	2.78
1952	Hoyt Wilhelm, New York	71	159	2.43	1952	Allie Reynolds, New York	35	244	2.07
1953	Warren Spahn, Milwaukee	35	266	2.10	1953	Ed Lopat, New York	25	178	2.43
1954	John Antonelli, New York	39	259	2.29	1954	Mike Garcia, Cleveland	45	259	2.64
1955	Bob Friend, Pittsburgh	44	200	2.84	1955	Billy Pierce, Chicago	33	206	1.97
1956	Lew Burdette, Milwaukee	39	256	2.71	1956	Whitey Ford, New York	31	226	2.47
1957	Johnny Podres, Brooklyn	31	196	2.66	1957	Bobby Shantz, New York	30	173	2.01
1958	Stu Miller, San Francisco	41	182	2.47	1958	Whitey Ford, New York	30	219	2.01
1959	Sam Jones, San Francisco	50	271	2.82	1959	Hoyt Wilhelm, Baltimore	32	226	2.19
1960	Mike McCormick, San Fran	40	253	2.70	1960	Frank Baumann, Chicago	47	185	2.68
1961	Warren Spahn, Milwaukee	38	263	3.01	1961	Dick Donovan, Washington	32	169	2.40
1962	Sandy Koufax, Los Angeles	28	184	2.54	1962	Hank Aguirre, Detroit	42	216	2.21
1963	Sandy Koufax, Los Angeles	40	311	1.88	1963	Gary Peters, Chicago	41	243	2.33
1964	Sandy Koufax, Los Angeles	29	223	1.74	1964	Dean Chance, Los Angeles	46	278	1.56
1965	Sandy Koufax, Los Angeles	43	336	2.04	1965	Sam McDowell, Cleveland	42	274	2.17
1966	Sandy Koufax, Los Angeles	41	323	1.73	1966	Gary Peters, Chicago	29	204	2.03
1967	Phil Niekro, Atlanta	46	207	1.87	1967	Joe Horlen, Chicago	35	258	2.06
1968	Bob Gibson, St. Louis	34	305	1.12	1968	Luis Tiant, Cleveland	34	258	1.60
1969	Juan Marichal, San Francisco	37	300	2.10	1969	Dick Bosman, Washington	31	193	2.19
1970	Tom Seaver, New York	37	291	2.81	1970	Diego Segui, Oakland	47	162	2.56
1971	Tom Seaver, New York	36	286	1.76	1971	Vida Blue, Oakland	39	312	1.82
1972	Steve Carlton, Philadelphia	41	346	1.98	1972	Luis Tiant, Boston	43	179	1.91
1973	Tom Seaver, New York	36	290	2.07	1973	Jim Palmer, Baltimore	38	296	2.40

ERA is computed by multiplying the number of earned runs allowed by 9, then dividing by the number of innings pitched.

World Series, 1973

Composite Box Score

NEW YORK METS

	g	ab	r	h	2b	3b	hr	rbi	so	bb	bat avg	po	a	e	fldg avg
Wayne Garrett, 3b...	7	30	4	5	0	0	2	2	11	5	.167	4	18	3	.880
Felix Millan, 2b	7	32	3	6	1	1	0	1	1	1	.187	16	14	3	.909
Willie Mays, cf	3	7	1	2	0	0	0	1	1	0	.286	1	0	1	.500
Cleon Jones, lf	7	28	5	8	2	0	1	1	2	4	.286	11	1	1	.923
John Milner, 1b	7	27	2	8	0	0	0	2	1	5	.296	66	1	0	1.000
Jerry Grote, c	7	30	2	8	0	0	0	0	1	0	.267	67	5	0	1.000
Don Hahn, cf	7	29	2	7	1	1	0	2	6	1	.241	13	1	1	.929
Ed Kranepool, ph	4	3	0	0	0	0	0	0	0	0	.000	0	0	0	.000
Bud Harrelson, ss ...	7	24	2	6	1	0	0	1	3	5	.250	11	24	0	1.000
Ron Hodges, ph	1	0	0	0	0	0	0	0	0	1	.000	0	0	0	.000
Ted Martinez, pr	2	0	0	0	0	0	0	0	0	0	.000	0	0	0	.000
Jon Matlack, p	3	4	0	1	0	0	0	0	1	2	.250	0	1	0	1.000
Ken Boswell, ph	3	3	1	3	0	0	0	0	0	0	1.000	0	0	0	.000
Tug McGraw, p	5	3	1	1	0	0	0	0	1	0	.333	0	3	0	1.000
Rusty Staub, rf	7	26	1	11	2	0	1	6	2	2	.423	5	0	0	1.000
Jim Beauchamp, ph .	4	4	0	0	0	0	0	0	1	0	.000	0	0	0	.000
Jerry Koosman, p ...	4	2	0	0	0	0	0	0	3	0	.000	0	1	1	.500
Ray Sadecki, p	4	0	0	0	0	0	0	0	0	0	.000	0	1	0	1.000
George Theodore, lf .	2	2	0	0	0	0	0	0	0	0	.000	1	0	0	1.000
Harry Parker, p	3	0	0	0	0	0	0	0	0	0	.000	0	0	0	.000
George Stone, p.....	2	0	0	0	0	0	0	0	0	0	.000	0	0	0	.000
Tom Seaver, p	2	5	0	0	0	0	0	0	2	0	.000	0	2	0	1.000
Total	7	261	24	66	7	2	4	16	36	26	.253	195	72	10	.964

OAKLAND A's

	g	ab	r	h	2b	3b	hr	rbi	so	bb	bat avg	po	a	e	fldg avg
Campy Campaneris, ss	7	31	6	9	0	1	1	3	7	1	.290	10	28	2	.950
Joe Rudi, lf	7	27	3	9	2	0	0	4	4	3	.333	20	2	0	1.000
Sal Bando, 3b	7	26	5	6	1	1	0	1	7	4	.231	6	14	1	.952
Reggie Jackson, rf ..	7	29	3	9	3	1	1	6	7	2	.310	18	0	0	1.000
Gene Tenace, 1b	7	19	0	3	1	0	0	3	7	11	.158	58	2	1	.984
Jesus Alou, rf	7	19	0	3	1	0	0	3	0	0	.158	5	0	0	1.000
Vic Davalillo, cf	6	11	0	1	0	0	0	0	1	2	.091	14	0	0	1.000
Ray Fosse, c	7	19	0	3	1	0	0	0	4	1	.158	32	3	0	1.000
Dick Green, 2b	7	16	0	1	0	0	0	0	6	1	.063	13	11	1	.960
Ken Holtzman, p	3	3	2	2	2	0	0	0	0	0	.667	1	3	0	1.000
Angel Mangual, cf ...	5	6	0	0	0	0	0	3	0	0	.000	1	0	0	1.000
Rollie Fingers, p.....	6	3	0	1	0	0	0	1	0	0	.333	0	2	0	1.000
Darold Knowles, p...	7	0	0	0	0	0	0	0	0	0	.000	0	1	1	.500
Ted Kubiak, 2b	4	3	1	0	0	0	0	0	1	1	.000	5	7	0	1.000
Mike Andrews, 2b ...	2	3	0	0	0	0	0	0	1	1	.000	0	0	2	.000
Vida Blue, p	2	4	0	0	0	0	0	0	4	0	.000	2	1	0	1.000
Horacio Pina, p	2	0	0	0	0	0	0	0	0	0	.000	0	0	0	.000
Billy Conigliaro, ph ..	3	3	0	0	0	0	0	0	1	0	.000	0	0	0	.000
Blue Moon Odom, p .	3	1	0	0	0	0	0	0	1	0	.000	0	1	0	1.000
Deron Johnson, 1b ..	6	10	0	3	1	0	0	4	1	0	.300	9	1	0	1.000
Al Lewis, pr	3	0	1	0	0	0	0	0	0	0	.000	0	0	0	.000
Paul Lindblad, p	3	1	0	0	0	0	0	0	0	0	.000	0	0	0	.000
Pat Bourque, 1b	2	2	0	1	0	0	0	0	0	0	.500	3	1	0	1.000
Catfish Hunter, p ...	2	5	0	0	0	0	0	0	3	0	.000	1	2	1	.750
Total	7	241	21	51	12	3	2	20	62	28	.212	198	79	9	.969

Pitching Summary

NEW YORK

	g	cg	ip	h	r	bb	so	hb	wp	w	l	pct	er	era
Jon Matlack	3	0	16²/₃	10	7	5	11	1	0	1	2	.333	4	2.16
Tug McGraw	5	0	13³/₃	8	5	9	14	1	0	1	0	1.000	4	2.63
Jerry Koosman......	2	0	8²/₃	9	3	7	8	0	0	1	0	1.000	3	3.12
Ray Sadecki	4	0	4²/₃	5	1	1	6	0	0	0	0	.000	1	1.93
Harry Parker	3	0	3¹/₃	2	1	2	2	0	0	0	1	.000	0	0.00
George Stone	2	0	3	4	0	1	3	0	0	0	0	.000	0	4.00
Tom Seaver.........	2	0	15	13	4	3	18	0	1	0	1	.000	4	2.40
Total	7	0	65	51	21	28	62	2	1	3	4	.429	16	2.22

OAKLAND

	g	cg	ip	h	r	bb	so	hb	wp	w	l	pct	er	era
Ken Holtzman	3	0	10²/₃	13	5	6	0	0	0	2	1	.667	5	4.22
Rollie Fingers	6	0	13²/₃	13	5	4	8	1	0	0	1	.000	1	0.66
Darold Knowles	7	0	6¹/₃	4	1	5	5	1	0	0	0	.000	0	0.00
Vida Blue	2	0	11	10	6	3	8	0	1	0	1	.000	6	4.91
Horacio Pina........	2	0	3	6	2	2	1	0	0	0	0	.000	0	0.00
Blue Moon Odom....	2	0	4²/₃	5	2	2	2	0	1	0	0	.000	2	3.86
Paul Lindblad	3	0	3¹/₃	4	0	1	1	0	0	1	0	1.000	0	0.00
Catfish Hunter......	2	0	13¹/₃	11	3	4	6	0	1	1	0	1.000	3	2.03
Total	7	0	66	66	24	26	36	3	3	4	3	.571	17	2.32

COMPOSITE SCORE BY INNINGS

NEW YORK..................	5	2	1		4	0	6		0	1	1		0	0	4	—	24
Oakland....................	3	1	7		1	1	1		1	2	2		0	1	1	—	21

Umpires—Springstead (AL); Donatelli (NL); Neudecker (AL); Pryor (NL); Goetz (AL); Wendelstedt (NL).

A's defeat Mets in Seven Games

The Oakland A's became world baseball champions for the second straight year by defeating the New York Mets in the 1973 world series 4 games to 3. The A's became the first team to win the world series 2 years in a row since the Yankees of 1962-62. Much criticism was directed at A's owner Charles O. Finley when he fired second baseman Mike Andrews after Andrews had committed 2 errors in the twelfth inning of the second game. Andrews was subsequently reinstated.

1973 World Series Box Scores

First Game

Oakland-Alameda County Stadium, Oct. 13

NEW YORK	ab.	r.	h.	bi.	OAKLAND	ab.	r.	h.	bi.
Garrett, 2b ...	5	0	0	0	Campaneris, ss	4	1	1	0
Millan, 2b	4	0	1	0	Rudi, lf	3	0	1	1
Mays, cf	4	0	1	0	Bando, 3b	3	0	1	0
Jones, lf	4	1	2	0	Jackson, cf, rf	3	0	0	0
Milner, 1b	4	0	2	1	Tenace, 1b ...	3	0	0	0
Grote, c	4	0	0	0	Alou, rf	3	0	0	0
Hahn, rf	2	0	0	0	Davalillo, cf ..	0	0	0	0
Kranepool, ph	1	0	0	0	Fosse, c	3	0	0	0
Harrelson, ss .	2	0	0	0	Green, 2b	2	0	0	0
Hodges, ph ...	0	0	0	0	Holtzman, p ..	1	1	1	0
Martinez, pr ..	0	0	0	0	Mangual, p ...	1	0	0	0
Matlack, p....	0	0	0	0	Fingers, p	1	0	0	0
Boswell, ph ...	1	0	1	0	Knowles, p	0	0	0	0
McGraw, p....	0	0	0	0					
Staub, ph	0	0	0	0					
Beauchamp, ph	1	0	0	0					
Total	32	1	7	1	Total	27	2	4	1

New York .... 0 0 0 1 0 0 0 0 0 — 1
Oakland .... 0 0 2 0 0 0 0 0 0 — 2

Errors—Millan, Mays. Left on Base—New York 9, Oakland 5. Two base hits—Holtzman, Jones. Three base hit—Millan. Sacrifice—Matlack, Rudi.

	ip.	h.	r.	er.	bb.	so.
Matlack (L)	6	3	2	0	2	3
McGraw	2	1	0	0	1	1
Holtzman (W)	5	4	1	1	3	2
Fingers	3⅓	3	0	0	1	2
Knowles	⅔	0	0	0	0	0

Save—Knowles. Time of game—2:26. Attendance—49,151.

How runs were scored—Two in A's third: Holtzman doubled. Campaneris grounded to Millan who booted the ball, Holtzman scoring. Campaneris went to second on Matlack's wide pickoff throw to first. Rudi singled, scoring Campaneris.

One in Mets fourth: Jones doubled. Milner singled, scoring Jones.

Second Game

Oakland-Alameda County Stadium, Oct. 14

NEW YORK	ab.	r.	h.	bi.	OAKLAND	ab.	r.	h.	bi.
Garrett, 3b ...	6	1	1	1	Campaneris, ss	6	2	1	0
Millan, 2b	6	0	0	0	Rudi, lf	5	1	2	1
Staub, rf	5	0	1	0	Bando, 3b	5	2	1	1
Mays, cf	2	1	1	1	Jackson, cf ..	6	1	4	2
Jones, lf	5	3	3	1	Tenace, 1b ...	3	0	1	1
Milner, 1b	6	1	2	0	Alou, rf	6	0	3	2
Grote, c	6	1	2	0	Fosse, c	5	0	0	0
Hahn, cf	7	1	1	1	Green, 2b	2	0	0	0
Harrelson, ss .	6	1	3	1	Mangual, ph ..	1	0	0	0
Koosman, p ...	1	0	0	0	Kubiak, 2b ...	0	0	0	0
Sadecki, p	0	0	0	0	Andrews, 2b ..	2	0	0	0
Theodore, ph .	1	0	0	0	Blue, p	2	0	0	0
Parker, p	0	0	0	0	Pina, p	0	0	0	0
Kranepool, ph	0	0	0	0	Knowles, p....	0	0	0	0
Beauchamp, ph	1	0	0	0	Conigliaro, ph .	1	0	0	0
McGraw, p....	2	1	1	0	Johnson, ph ..	1	0	1	0
Stone, p	0	0	0	0	Lewis, pr	0	1	0	0
					Fingers, p	1	0	0	0
					Lindblad, p ...	0	0	0	0
					Davalillo, ph ..	1	0	0	0
Total	54	10	15	5	Total	47	7	13	7

New York ...... 0 1 1 0 0 4 0 0 0 0 0 4 — 10
Oakland .... 2 1 0 0 0 0 1 0 2 0 0 1 — 7

Errors—Koosman, Bando, Knowles, Tenace, Andrews 2. Double plays—Mets 1, Oakland 1. Left on base—Mets 15, Oakland 12. Two base hits—Rudi, Alou, Jackson, Johnson, Harrelson. Three base hits—Bando, Campaneris, Jackson. Home runs—Jones (1) Garrett (1). Sacrifices—McGraw.

(Second Game continued)

	ip.	h.	r.	er.	bb.	so.
Koosman	2⅓	6	3	3	3	4
Sadecki	1⅔	0	0	0	0	3
Parker	1	1	0	0	0	0
McGraw (W)	6	5	4	4	3	8
Stone	1	1	0	0	1	0
Blue	5⅓	4	4	4	2	4
Pina	0	2	2	0	0	0
Knowles	3⅔	3	0	0	2	4
Odom	2	2	0	0	0	2
Fingers (L)	2⅔	6	4	1	0	2
Lindblad	⅓	0	0	0	0	0

Save—Stone (1). Hit by pitch—by Pina (Grote), McGraw (Campaneris), Fingers (Jones). Time of game—4:13. Attendance—49,151.

How runs were scored—Two in A's first: Rudi doubled. Bando tripled, scoring Rudi. Alou doubled scoring Bando. One in Mets second: Jones hit a home run.

One in A's second: Campaneris tripled. Rudi singled, scoring Campaneris.

One in Mets third: Garrett hit a home run.

Four in Mets sixth: Jones walked. Milner singled. Grote was hit by a pitch, filling the bases. Hahn singled, scoring Jones. Harrelson singled, scoring Milner. Beauchamp hit a grounder to the pitcher whose throw home for the force was wild, two runs scoring.

One in A's seventh: Campaneris was hit by a pitch. Rudi walked. Jackson doubled, scoring Campaneris.

Two in A's ninth: Johnson doubled. Bando walked. Jackson singled, scoring Lewis who had run for Johnson. Tenace singled, scoring Bando.

Four in Mets twelfth: Harrelson doubled. McGraw singled. Mays singled, scoring Harrelson, Jones singled. Andrews committed 2 errors allowing the Mets three additional runs.

One in A's twelfth: Jackson tripled. Alou singled, scoring Jackson.

Third Game

Shea Stadium, New York, Oct. 16

OAKLAND	ab.	r.	h.	bi.	METS	ab.	r.	h.	bi.
Campaneris, ss	6	1	3	1	Garrett, 3b ...	4	1	2	1
Rudi, lf	5	0	2	1	Millan, 2b ...	5	1	2	0
Bando, 3b	4	1	2	0	Staub, rf	6	0	2	0
Jackson, rf ...	5	0	0	0	Jones, lf	5	0	0	0
Tenace, 1b ...	3	0	1	1	Milner, 1b	3	0	1	0
Davalillo, cf ..	5	0	1	0	Grote, c	5	0	0	0
Fosse, c	2	0	0	0	Hahn, cf	5	0	1	0
Dourque, 1b ..	2	0	1	0	Harrelson, ss .	5	0	2	0
Lewis, pr	0	0	0	0	Seaver, p	3	0	0	0
Lindblad, p ...	1	0	0	0	Beauchamp,				
Fingers, p	0	0	0	0	ph	1	0	0	0
Green, 2b	2	0	0	0	Sadecki, p	0	0	0	0
Alou, ph	1	0	0	0	McGraw, p....	0	0	0	0
Kubiak, 2b ...	1	1	0	0	Mays, ph	1	0	0	0
Hunter, p	2	0	0	0	Parker, p	0	0	0	0
Johnson, ph ..	1	0	0	0					
Knowles, p ...	0	0	0	0					
Mangual, cf ..	2	0	0	0					
Total	42	3	10	3	Total	43	2	10	1

Oakland.... 0 0 0 0 0 1 0 1 0 0 1 — 3
Mets ...... 2 0 0 0 0 0 0 0 0 0 0 — 2

E—Hunter, Millan 2. LOB—Oakland 10, New York 14. 2B—Rudi, Hahn, Bando, Tenace, Staub. HR—Garrett SB—Campaneris. S—Bando, Millan.

	ip.	h.	r.	er.	bb.	so.
Hunter	6	7	2	2	3	5
Knowles	2	0	0	0	0	0
Lindblad (W)	2	3	0	0	1	0
Fingers	1	0	0	0	0	0
Seaver	8	7	2	2	1	12
Sadecki	0	1	0	0	0	0
McGraw	2	1	0	0	1	1
Parker (L)	1	1	1	0	1	1

(Third Game continued)

Save—Fingers WP—Hunter. PB—Grote. T—3:15. A—54,817.

How runs were scored—Two in Mets first: Garrett hit a home run. Millan singled. Staub singled. Millan scored on a wild pitch.

One in A's Sixth: Bando doubled. Tenace doubled, scoring Bando.

One in A's eighth: Campaneris singled and stole second. Rudi singled, scoring Campaneris.

One in A's eleventh: Kubiak walked. Kubiak went to second on a passed ball. Campaneris singled, scoring Kubiak.

Fourth Game

Shea Stadium, New York Oct. 17

OAKLAND	ab.	r.	h.	bi.	NEW YORK	ab.	r.	h.	bi.
Campaneris, ss	4	0	0	0	Garrett, 3b ..	4	2	1	0
Rudi, lf	4	0	1	0	Millan, 2b ...	5	1	1	0
Bando, 3b	3	1	0	0	Staub, rf ...	4	1	4	5
Jackson, cf	4	0	1	0	Jones, lf	3	0	1	0
Tenace, 1b ...	3	0	1	1	Uheodore, lf .	1	0	0	0
Alou, rf	4	0	0	0	Milner, 1b ...	3	0	0	0
Fosse, c	4	0	1	0	Grote, c	4	0	3	0
Green, 2b	1	0	0	0	Hahn, cf	4	1	1	0
Mangual, ph ..	1	0	0	0	Harrelson, ss	2	1	0	0
Kubiak, 2b ..	1	0	0	0	Matlack, p ..	3	0	1	0
Johnson, ph ..	1	0	1	0	Sadecki, p ...	0	0	0	0
Holtzman, p ..	0	0	0	0					
Odom, p	1	0	0	0					
Knowles, p...	0	0	0	0					
Conigliaro, ph .	1	0	0	0					
Pina, p	0	0	0	0					
Andrews, ph ..	1	0	0	0					
Lindblad, p...	0	0	0	0					
Davalillo, ph ..	0	0	0	0					
Total	33	1	5	1	Total	33	6	13	5

```
Oakland......0 0 0    1 0 0    0 0 0 — 1
New York.....3 0 0    3 0 0    0 0 x — 6
```

Errors—Garrett, Green. Double plays—Oakland 4. Left on base—Oakland 9, New York 10. Home run—Staub.

	ip.	h.	r.	er.	bb.	so.
Holtzman (L)	1/3	4	3	3	1	0
Odom	2 2/3	3	2	2	2	0
Knowles	1	1	1	0	1	1
Pina	3	4	0	0	2	0
Lindblad	1	1	0	0	0	1
Matlack (W)	8	3	1	0	2	5
Sadecki	1	2	0	0	1	2

Save—Sadecki. Hit by pitcher—by Knowles (Garrett), Matlack (Campaneris). Wild pitch—Odom. Time of game 2:41. Attendance—54,817.

How runs were scored—Three in Mets first: Garrett singled. Millan singled. Staub hit a home run.

One in A's fourth: Bando reached first on an error. Jackson singled. Tenace grounded out, scoring Bando.

Three in Mets fourth: Hahn singled. Harrelson singled. Garrett was hit by a pitch. Millan hit a grounder that was booted and Hahn scored. Staub singled, scoring Harrelson and Garrett.

Fifth Game

Shea Stadium, New York, Oct. 18

OAKLAND	ab.	r.	h.	bi.	NEW YORK	ab.	r.	h.	bi.
Campaneris, ss	3	0	1	0	Garrett, 3b ...	3	0	0	0
Rudi, lf	4	0	0	0	Millan, 2b	4	0	0	0
Bando, 3b ...	3	0	1	0	Staub, rf	3	0	1	0
Jackson, cf ...	3	0	0	0	Jones, lf	4	1	2	0
Tenace, 1b ...	1	0	0	0	Milner, 1b	4	0	2	1
Odom, pr	0	0	0	0	Grote, c	3	1	1	0
Bourgue, 1b ..	0	0	0	0	Hahn, cf	4	0	1	1
Alou, rf	4	0	0	0	Harrelson, ss	2	0	0	0
Fosse, c	4	0	1	0	Koosman, p...	3	0	0	0
Green, 2b ...	2	0	0	0	McGraw, p ...	1	0	0	0
Johnson, ph ..	0	0	0	0					
Lewis, pr	0	0	0	0					
Kubiak, 2b ...	1	0	0	0					
Blue, p	2	0	0	0					
Knowles, p ...	0	0	0	0					
Mangual, ph ..	1	0	0	0					
Fingers, p	0	0	0	0					
Conigliaro, ph .	1	0	0	0					
Total	29	0	3	0	Total	31	2	7	2

```
Oakland......0 0 0    0 0 0    0 0 0 — 0
New York.....0 1 0    0 0 1    0 0 x — 2
```

(Fifth Game continued)

Errors—Campaneris, Garrett. Double play—New York 1. Left on base—Oakland 9, New York 10. Two-base hits—Jones, Fosse. Three-base hit—Hahn. Sacrifice—Grote.

	ip.	h.	r.	er.	bb.	so.
Blue (L)	5 2/3	6	2	2	1	4
Knowles..................	1/3	0	0	0	1	1
Fingers..................	2	1	0	0	2	1
Koosman (W)	6 1/3	3	0	0	4	4
McGraw	2 2/3	0	0	0	0	3

Save—McGraw. Wild pitch—Blue. Time of game—2:39. Attendance—54,817.

How runs were scored—One in Mets second: Jones doubled. Milner singled, scoring Jones.

One in Mets sixth: Grote singled. Hahn tripled, scoring Grote.

Sixth Game

Oakland-Alameda County Coliseum, Oct. 20

NEW YORK (N.)	ab.	r.	h.	bi.	OAKLAND (A.)	ab.	r.	h.	bi.
Garrett, 3b ...	3	0	1	0	Campaneris, ss	4	0	0	0
Millan, 2b	4	0	1	1	Rudi, lf.......	3	1	1	0
Staub, rf	4	0	1	0	Bando, 3b ..	4	1	1	0
Jones, lf	4	0	0	0	Jackson, rf ...	4	1	3	2
Milner, 1b ...	4	0	1	0	Tenace, c	3	0	0	0
Grote, c	4	0	1	0	Davalillo, cf ..	2	0	0	0
Hahn, cf	3	0	0	0	Alou, rf	0	0	0	1
Kranepool, ph	1	0	0	0	Johnson, 1b ..	4	0	1	0
Harrelson, ss .	3	0	0	0	Fosse, c	0	0	0	0
Seaver, p	2	0	0	0	Green, 2b ...	3	0	1	0
Boswell, ph ...	1	1	1	0	Hunter, p	3	0	0	0
McGraw, p....	0	0	0	0	Knowles, p ...	0	0	0	0
					Fingers, p	0	0	0	0
Total	33	1	6	1	Total	30	3	7	3

```
New York.....0 0 0    0 0 0    0 1 0 — 1
Oakland......1 0 1    0 0 0    0 1 x — 3
```

Errors—Garrett, Hahn. Double play—New York. Left on base—New York 6, Oakland 7. Two-base hits—Jackson 2. Sacrifice fly—Alou.

	ip.	h.	r.	er.	bb.	so.
Seaver (L)	7	6	2	2	2	6
McGraw	1	1	1	0	1	1
Hunter (W)	7 1/3	4	1	1	1	1
Knowles	1/3	2	0	0	0	1
Fingers..................	1 1/3	0	0	0	0	0

Save—Fingers. Wild pitch—Seaver. Time of game—2:07. Attendance—49,333.

How runs were scored—One in A's first—Rudi singled. Jackson doubled, scoring Rudi.

One in A's third: Bando singled. Jackson doubled, scoring Bando.

One in Mets eight: Boswell singled. Garrett singled. Millan singled, scoring Boswell.

One in A's eight: Jackson singled and went to third on an error. Alou hit a sacrifice fly, scoring Jackson.

Seventh Game

Oakland-Alameda County Coliseum, Oct. 21

NEW YORK (N.)	ab.	r.	h.	bi.	OAKLAND (A.)	ab.	r.	h.	bi.
Garrett, 3b ...	5	0	0	0	Campaneris, ss	4	2	3	2
Millan, 2b	4	1	1	0	Rudi, lf	3	1	2	1
Staub, rf	4	0	2	1	Bando, 3b	4	0	0	0
Jones, lf	3	0	0	0	Jackson, rf ...	4	1	1	2
Milner, 1b ...	3	1	0	0	Tenace, 1b ...	3	0	0	0
Grote, c	4	0	1	0	Alou, rf.....	1	0	0	0
Hahn, cf	4	0	3	0	Davalillo, cf ..	3	0	0	0
Harrelson, ss .	4	0	0	0	Johnson, 1b ..	3	0	0	0
Matlack, p ...	1	0	0	0	Fosse, c	1	0	1	0
Parker, p	0	0	0	0	Green, 2b ...	4	0	0	0
Beauchamp, ph	1	0	0	0	Holtzman, p ..	2	1	1	0
Sadecki, p....	0	0	0	0	Fingers, p ...	1	0	1	0
Boswell, ph ...	1	0	1	0	Knowles, p ...	0	0	0	0
Stone, p	0	0	0	0					
Kranepool, ph	1	0	0	0					
Martinez, pr ..	0	0	0	0					
Total	35	2	8	1	Total	33	5	9	5

```
New York.....0 0 0    0 0 1    0 0 1 — 2
Oakland......0 0 4    0 1 0    0 0 x — 5
```

Errors—Jones, Tenace. Double play—Oakland. Left on base—New York 8, Oakland 6.

Two base hits—Holtzman, Millan, Staub. Home runs—Campaneris, Jackson.

(Seventh Game continued)

	ip.	h.	r.	er.	bb.	so.
Matlack (L)	2⅔	4	4	4	1	3
Parker	1⅓	0	0	0	1	1
Sadecki	2	2	1	1	0	1
Stone	2	3	0	0	0	3
Holtzman (W)	5⅓	5	1	1	1	4
Fingers	3⅓	3	1	0	1	2
Knowles	⅓	0	0	0	0	0

Save—Knowles. Time of game—2:37. Attendance—49,333.

How runs were scored—Four in A's third: Holtzman doubled. Campaneris hit a home run. Rudi singled. Jackson hit a home run.

One in A's fifth: Campaneris singled and went to second on an error. Rudi singled, scoring Campaneris.

One in Mets sixth: Millan doubled. Staub doubled, scoring Millan.

One in Mets ninth: Milner walked. Hahn singled. Kranepool hit a grounder that was booted, scoring Milner.

Baseball World Championships, 1903-1973

Year	Winners	Won	Losers	Won	Year	Winners	Won	Losers	Won
1903	Boston, A. L.	5	Pittsb'gh, N. L	3	1938	N. Y., A. L	4	Chicago, N. L	0
1904	N. Y., N. L	refused play	Boston	A. L.	1939	N. Y., A. L	4	Cincinnati, N. L	0
1905	N. Y., N. L	4	Phila., A. L	*1	1940	Cinc., N. L	4	Detroit, A. L	3
1906	Chicago, A. L	4	Chicago, N. L	2	1941	N. Y., A. L	4	B'klyn, N. L	3
1907	Chicago, N.L.	4	Detroit, A. L	0	1942	St. Louis, N. L	4	N. Y., A. L	1
1908	Chicago, N. L	4	Detroit, A. L	1	1943	N. Y., A. L	4	St. Louis, N. L	1
1909	Pittsb'gh, N. L	4	Detroit, A. L	3	1944	St. Louis, N. L	4	St. Louis, A. L	2
1910	Phila., A. L	4	Chicago, N. L	1	1945	Detroit, A. L	4	Chicago, N. L	3
1911	Phila. A. L	4	N. Y., N. L	2	1946	St. Louis, N. L	4	Boston, A. L	3
*1912	Boston, A.L.	4	N. Y., N. L	3	1947	N. Y., A. L	4	B'klyn, N. L	3
1913	Phila., A. L	4	N. Y., N. L	1	1948	Cleveland, A. L	4	Boston, N. L	2
1914	Boston, N. L	4	Phila., A. L	0	1949	N. Y., A. L	4	B'klyn, N. L	1
1915	Boston, A. L	4	Phila., N. L	1	1950	N. Y., A. L	4	Phila., N. L	0
1916	Boston, A. L	4	B'klyn, N. L	1	1951	N. Y., A. L	4	N. Y., N. L	2
1917	Chicago, A. L	4	N. Y., N. L	2	1952	N. Y., A. L	4	B'klyn, N. L	3
1918	Boston, A. L	4	Chicago, N. L	2	1953†	N. Y., A. L	4	B'klyn, N. L	2
1919	Cincin., N. L	5	Chicago, A. L	3	1954	N. Y., N. L	4	Cleve., A. L	0
1920	Cleveland, A. L	5	B'klyn, N. L	2	1955	B'klyn, N. L	4	N. Y., A. L	3
1921	N. Y., N. L	5	N. Y., A. L	3	1956	N. Y., A. L	4	B'klyn, N. L	3
1922*	N. Y., N. L	4	N. Y., A. L	0	1957	Milw., N. L	4	N. Y., A. L	3
1923	N. Y., A. L	4	N. Y., N. L	2	1958	N. Y., A. L	4	Milw., N. L	3
1924	Wash., A. L	4	N. Y., N. L	3	1959	Los Angeles, N. L.	4	Chicago, A. L	2
1925	Pittsb'gh, N. L	4	Wash., A. L	3	1960	Pittsburgh, N. L.	4	N. Y., A. L	3
1926	St. Louis, N. L	4	N. Y., A. L	3	1961	N. Y., A. L	4	Cincinnati, N. L	1
1927	N. Y., A. L	4	Pitts., N. L	0	1962	N. Y., A. L	4	San Fran., N. L	3
1928	N. Y., A. L	4	St. Louis, N. L	0	1963	L. A., N. L	4	N. Y., A. L	0
1929	Phila., A. L	4	Chicago, N. L	1	1964	St. Louis, N. L	4	N. Y., A. L	3
1930	Phila., A. L	4	St. Louis, N. L	2	1965	L. A., N. L	4	Minn., A. L	3
1931	St. Louis, N. L	4	Phila., A. L	3	1966	Balt., A. L	4	L. A., N. L	0
1932	N. Y., A. L	4	Chicago, N. L	0	1967	St. Louis, N. L	4	Boston, A. L	3
1933	N. Y., N. L	4	Wash., A. L	1	1968	Detroit, A. L	4	St. Louis, N. L	3
1934	St. Louis, N. L	4	Detroit, A. L	3	1969	N.Y. Mets, N. L.	4	Baltimore, A.L.	1
1935	Detroit, A. L	4	Chicago, N. L	2	1970	Baltimore, A. L	4	Cincinnati, N. L	1
1936	N. Y., A. L	4	N. Y., N. L	2	1971	Pittsburgh, N. L	4	Baltimore, A.L.	3
1937	N. Y., A. L	4	N. Y., N. L	1	1972	Oakland, A.L.	4	Cincinnati, N. L.	3
					1972	Oakland, A. L.	4	N. Y. Mets, N. L.	3

*One tie game. †First major league club to win five world championships in succession.

21 Records Set, 25 Tied in 1973 World Series

INDIVIDUAL RECORDS SET

Most At Bats, Game: 7 Don Hahn, N.Y., Oct. 14, 12 inns.

Most At Bats, Extra Inning Game: 7 Don Hahn, N.Y., Oct. 14, 12 inns.

Most Chances Accepted, Catcher, Series: 71 Jerry Grote, N.Y.

Most Putouts, Catcher, Series: 67 Jerry Grote, N.Y.

Most Games Fielding Pitcher, Series: 7 Darold Knowles, Oak.

Most Games, Pitcher, Series: 7 Darold Knowles, Oak.

Most Games, Consecutive, Pitcher, Series: 7 Darold Knowles, Oak.

Most Saves, Pitcher, Lifetime: 4 Darold Knowles, Oak. 1972-73.

CLUB RECORDS SET

Most Strikeouts, Series: 62 Oakland.

Most Left on Base, Series: 72 New York.

Most Left on Base, Both Clubs, Series: 130 New York & Oakland.

Most Pinch-hitters, Series: 20 Oakland.

Most Pinch-hitters, Both Clubs, Series: 34 Oakland & New York.

Most At Bats, Extra-inning Game: 54 New York, Oct. 14, 12 inns.

Most At Bats, Both Clubs, Extra-inning Game: 101 New York & Oakland, Oct. 14.

Most Runs, 12th Inning: 4 New York, Oct. 14.

Most Runs, Both Clubs, 12th Inning: 5 New York & Oakland, Oct. 14.

Most Pinch-hitters, Both Clubs, Extra-inning Game: 8 Oakland & New York, Oct. 14.

Most Saves, Series: 4 Oakland.

Most Saves, Both Clubs, Series: 7 Oakland & N.Y.

Longest Game, Time, Extra-innings: 4 hrs. 13 min. Oct, 14, 12 Innings.

INDIVIDUAL RECORDS TIED

Most Bases on Balls, Series: 11 Gene Tenace, Oak.

Most Strikeouts, Series: 11 Wayne Garrett, N.Y.

Most Hits, Game, Extra Innings: 4 Reggie Jackson, Oak., Oct. 14, 12 Innings.

Most Hits, Game, 4 Rusty Staub, N.Y., Oct. 17.

Fewest Hits, Game, Most at Bats: 0 Felix Millan, N.Y., Oct. 14 6 ab, 12 Innings.

Most Games, Pinch-hitter, Series: 5 A. Mangual, Oak.

Most Pinch-hits, Lifetime: 3, Ken Boswell, Most Pinch-hits, Series: 3 Ken Boswell, N.Y.

Most Double Plays 1b, Game: 4 Gene Tenace, Oak., Oct. 17.

Most Errors 2b, 7-game Series: 3 Felix Millan, N.Y.

Most Errors 2b, Inning: 2 Mike Andrews, Oak., Oct. 14.

Most Chances LF, Game: 7 Joe Rudi, Oak., Oct. 16.

Most Putouts LF, Game: 7 Joe Rudi, Oak., Oct. 16.

Most Games Started, Series: 3 Ken Holtzman, Oak. & Jon Matlack, N.Y.

Most Saves, Series: 2 Rollie Fingers and Darold Knowles.

Most Games Lost, Series: 2 Jon Matlack, N.Y.

CLUB RECORDS TIED

Most Hit Batsmen, Both Clubs, Game: 3, New York and Oakland, Oct. 14, 12 Innings.

Most Strikeouts, Both Clubs, Game: 25 Oakland and New York, Oct. 14, 12 Innings.

Most Pinch-hitters, Inning: 3 New York, Oct. 13, 9th Inning; Oakland, Oct. 16, 7th Inning.

Most Double Plays, Game: 4 Oakland, Oct. 17.

Fewest Complete Games, Both Clubs, series: 0

Most Players, Game: 21 Oakland, Oct. 14, 12 Innings.

Most Players, Both Clubs, Game: 38, Oct. 14.

Most Pitchers, Winning Club, Game: 5 New York, Oct. 14, 12 Innings.

Most Pitchers, Both Clubs, Game: 11, Oct. 14.

World Series Attendance and Receipts Since 1952

Year	Clubs	G.	Atten.	Rcpts.	Year	Clubs	G.	Atten.	Rcpts.
1952	N. Y. (A)-Brooklyn (N)	7	340,906	**1,622,753**	1963	L. A. (N)-N. Y. (A)	4	247,279	**1,995,190**
1953	N. Y. (A)-Brooklyn (N)	6	307,350	**1,779,269**	1964	St. Louis (N)-N. Y. (A)	7	321,807	**2,243,187**
1954	New York (N)-Clev. (A)	4	251,507	**1,566,203**	1965	L. A. (N)-Minn. (A)	7	364,326	**2,975,041**
1955	Brooklyn (N)-N. Y. (A)	7	362,310	**2,337,515**	1966	L. A. (N)-Balt. (A) (**)	4	220,791	**2,047,142**
1956	N. Y. (A)-Brooklyn (N)	7	345,903	**2,173,254**	1967	St. Louis (N)-Bos. (A)	7	304,085	**2,350,607**
1957	Milw. (N)-N. Y. (A)	7	394,712	**2,475,978**	1968	St. Louis (N)-Det. (A)	7	379,670	**3,018,113**
1958	N. Y. (A)-Milw. (N)	7	393,909	**2,397,223**	1969	N. Y. Mets (N)-Balt. (A)	5	272,378	**2,857,782**
1959	L. A. (N)-Chicago (A) (*)	6	420,784	**2,626,973**	1970	Balt. (A)-Cinn. (N)	5	253,183	**2,599,170**
1960	Pitts. (N)-N. Y. (A)	7	349,813	**2,230,627**	1971	Balt. (A)-Pitts. (N)	7	351,091	**3,787,694**
1961	N. Y. (A)-Cincinnati (N)	5	223,247	**1,480,095**	1972	Oak. (A)-Cinn. (N)	7	363,149	**3,954,542**
1962	N. Y. (A)-San Fran. (N)	7	376,864	**2,878,891**	1973	Oak. (A)-N. Y. Mets (N)	7	359,489	**3,923,968**

Receipts do not include fees for radio and television rights. *Attendance record. **Receipts record for 4-game Series.

1973 All-Major League Baseball Team

The following is the seventh annual All-Major League Team as selected by the players of both leagues in a poll conducted by Newspaper Enterprise Assn. Players could not vote for members of their own team.

Position	Name	Team
First Base	John Mayberry	Kansas City Royals
Second Base	Joe Morgan	Cincinnati Reds
Shortstop	Bill Russell	Los Angeles Dodgers
Third Base	Darrell Evans	Atlanta Braves
Outfield	Bobby Bonds	San Francisco Giants
Outfield	Reggie Jackson	Oakland A's
Outfield	Pete Rose	Cincinnati Reds
Catcher	Johnny Bench	Cincinnati Reds
Starting Pitcher	Tom Seaver	N.Y. Mets
Relief Pitcher	John Hiller	Detroit Tigers

Other top vote-getters

First Base: Tony Perez, Willie Stargell
Second Base: Dave Johnson, Rod Carew
Shortstop: Chris Speier, Bert Campaneris
Third Base: Ron Santo, Sal Bando
Outfield: Willie Stargell, Cesar Cedeno, Bobby Murcer, Amos Otis, Henry Aaron, Billy Williams.
Catcher: Thurman Munson, Carlton Fisk, Joe Ferguson.
Starting Pitcher: Ron Bryant, Jim Palmer, Catfish Hunter, Don Sutton.
Relief Pitcher: Mike Marshall.

All-Time Major League Records

LEADING PITCHERS (Over 300 Victories)

	Years	W	L
Cy Young	22	511	315
Walter Johnson	21	416	279
Grover Alexander	20	373	208
Christy Mathewson	17	373	188
James Galvin	15	365	309
Warren Spahn	21	363	245
Charles Nichols	15	360	202
Tim Keefe	14	346	225
John Clarkson	12	328	175
Eddie Plank	17	325	190
Mickey Welch	13	316	214
Hoss Radbourne	11	308	191
Bob Grove	20	300	141
Early Wynn	23	300	244

LEADING BATTERS (Over 2,000 Hits)

	Years	AB	Hits	Avg.
Ty Cobb	24	11429	4191	.367
Rogers Hornsby	23	8173	2930	.358
Ed Delehanty	16	7493	2593	.346
Dan Brouthers	19	6737	2347	.348
Willie Keeler	19	8564	2955	.345
Ted Williams	19	7706	2654	.344
Tris Speaker	22	10208	3515	.344
Billy Hamilton	14	6262	2157	.344
Harry Heilmann	17	7787	2660	.342
Babe Ruth	22	8399	2873	.342
Jesse Burkett	16	8389	2872	.342
Bill Terry	14	6428	2193	.341
Lou Gehrig	17	8001	2721	.340
George Sisler	16	8267	2812	.340
Nap Lajoie	21	9589	3251	.339
Cap Anson	22	9084	3081	.339
Sam Thompson	15	6005	2016	.336
Al Simmons	20	8761	2927	.334
Eddie Collins	25	9952	3313	.333
Paul Waner	20	9459	3152	.333
Stan Musial	22	10972	3630	.331
Heinie Manush	17	7653	2524	.330
Honus Wagner	21	10427	3430	.329
Joe Dimaggio	13	6821	2214	.325
Jimmy Foxx	20	8134	2646	.325

HITS

Ty Cobb	4191
Stan Musial	3630
Tris Speaker	3615
Hank Aaron	3509
Honus Wagner	3430
Eddie Collins	3311
Willie Mays	3283
Nap Lajoie	3251
Paul Waner	3152
Cap Anson	3081
Roberto Clemente	3000
Edgar Rice	2987
Sam Crawford	2964
Willie Keeler	2955
Jacob Beckley	2930
Rogers Hornsby	2930
Al Simmons	2927
Zach Wheat	2884
Frank Frisch	2880
Mel Ott	2876
Babe Ruth	2873

STRIKEOUTS

Walter Johnson	3508
Bob Gibson	2928
Jim Bunning	2853
Cy Young	2819
Warren Spahn	2583
Bob Feller	2581
Tim Keefe	2542
Christy Mathewson	2505
Don Drysdale	2486
Sandy Koufax	2396
Sam McDowell	2391
Robin Roberts	2357

All-Time Home Run Leaders

Player	HR.
Babe Ruth	714
Henry Aaron	713
Willie Mays	660
Frank Robinson	552
Harmon Killebrew	546
Mickey Mantle	536
Jimmy Foxx	534
Ted Williams	521
Ed Mathews	512
Ernie Banks	512
Mel Ott	511
Lou Gehrig	493
Stan Musial	475
Willie McCovey	413
Duke Snider	407
Al Kaline	386
Frank Howard	382
Orlando Cepeda	378
Billy Williams	376
Rocco Colavito	374
Gil Hodges	370
Norm Cash	370
Ralph Kiner	369
Joe DiMaggio	361
John Mize	359
Yogi Berra	358
Ron Santo	337
Joe Adcock	336
Hank Greenberg	331
Willie Stargell	321
Roy Sievers	318
Al Simmons	307
Rogers Hornsby	302
Chuck Klein	300
John (Boog) Powell	291
Carl Yastrzemski	288
Robert Johnson	288
Hank Sauer	288
Del Ennis	288
Dick Allen	287
Frank Thomas	286
Ken Boyer	282
Ted Kluszewski	279
Rudy York	277
Roger Maris	275
Vic Wertz	266
Bobby Thomson	264
Bob Allison	256
Joe Gordon	253
Larry Doby	253
Fred Williams	251
Brooks Robinson	251
Leon Goslin	248
Vernon Stephens	247
Vada Pinson	246
Hack Wilson	244

Aaron Nears Ruth's Home Run Record

Shortly after the start of the 1974 baseball season, Henry Aaron of the Atlanta Braves will hit his 714th and 715th home run to equal and pass the major league lifetime home run record of the immortal Babe Ruth. Because they played in different eras, it is not possible to compare the two baseball greats as home run hitters. Below is the major league record of both men.

Henry Louis (Hank) Aaron

Born, Mobile, Alabama, February 5, 1934.
Bats Right. Throws Right. Height, 6 feet. Weight, 180 pounds.

Year	Club	League	Pos.	g.	ab.	r.	h.	2b	3b	hr.	rbi.	sb.	Avg.
1954	Milwaukee	N.L.	OF	122	468	58	131	27	6	13	69	2	.280
1955	Milwaukee	N.L.	OF-2B	153	602	105	189	*37	9	27	106	3	.314
1956	Milwaukee	N.L.	OF	153	609	106	*200	*34	14	26	92	2	*.328
1957	Milwaukee (a)..	N.L.	OF	151	615	*118	198	27	6	*44	*132	1	.322
1958	Milwaukee	N.L.	OF	153	601	109	196	34	4	30	95	4	.326
1959	Milwaukee	N.L.	OF-3B	154	629	116	*223	46	7	39	123	8	*.355
1960	Milwaukee	N.L.	OF-2B	153	590	102	172	20	11	40	*126	16	.292
1961	Milwaukee	N.L.	OF-3B	*155	603	115	197	*39	10	34	120	21	.327
1962	Milwaukee	N.L.	OF-1B	156	592	127	191	28	6	45	128	15	.323
1963	Milwaukee	N.L.	OF	161	631	*121	201	29	4	*44	*130	31	.319
1964	Milwaukee	N.L.	OF-2B	145	570	103	187	30	2	24	95	22	.328
1965	Milwaukee	N.L.	OF	150	570	109	181	*40	1	32	89	24	.318
1966	Atlanta	N.L.	OF-2B	158	603	117	168	23	1	*44	*127	21	.279
1967	Atlanta	N.L.	OF-2B	155	600	*113	184	37	3	*39	109	17	.307
1968	Atlanta	N.L.	OF-1B	160	606	84	174	33	4	29	86	28	.287
1969	Atlanta	N.L.	OF-1B	147	547	100	164	30	3	44	97	9	.300
1970	Atlanta	N.L.	OF-1B	150	516	103	154	26	1	38	118	9	.298
1971	Atlanta	N.L.	1B-OF	139	495	95	162	22	3	47	118	1	.327
1972	Atlanta	N.L.	1B-OF	129	449	75	119	10	0	34	77	4	.265
1973	Atlanta	N.L.	OF-1B	120	392	84	118	12	1	40	96	1	.301
Major League Totals				2,964	11,288	2,060	3,509	584	96	713	2,133	239	.310

N. L. Championship Series

Year	Club	League	Pos.	g.	ab.	r.	h.	2b	3b	hr.	rbi.	sb.	Avg.
1969	Atlanta	N.L.	OF	3	14	3	5	2	0	3	7	0	.357

World Series Record

Year	Club	League	Pos.	g.	ab.	r.	h.	2b	3b	hr.	rbi.	sb.	Avg.
1957	Milwaukee	N.L.	OF	7	28	5	11	0	1	3	7	0	.393
1958	Milwaukee	N.L.	OF	7	27	3	9	2	0	0	2	0	.333
World Series Totals				14	55	8	20	2	1	3	9	0	.364

(a) Selected most valuable player in National League for 1957.

George Herman (Babe) Ruth

Born, Baltimore, Md., Feb. 6, 1895. Died Aug. 16, 1948 in New York
Batted and Threw Left Handed. Height 6 ft. 2 in. Weight 215 lbs.

*League leader.

Year	Club	League	Pos.(a)	g.	ab.	r.	h.	2b	3b	hr.	rbi.	sb.	Avg.
1914	Boston	A.L.	P-OF	5	10	1	2	1	0	0	2	0	.200
1915	Boston	A.L.	P-OF	42	92	16	29	10	1	4	21	0	.315
1916	Boston	A.L.	P-OF	67	136	18	37	5	3	3	15	0	.272
1917	Boston	A.L.	P-OF	52	123	14	40	6	3	2	12	0	.325
1918	Boston	A.L.	P-OF	95	317	50	95	26	11	*11	66	6	.300
1919	Boston	A.L.	P-OF	130	432	*103	139	34	12	*29	*114	7	.322
1920	New York	A.L.	P-OF	142	458	*158	172	36	9	*54	*137	14	.376
1921	New York	A.L.	P-OF	152	540	*177	204	44	16	*59	*170	17	.378
1922	New York	A.L.	OF	110	406	94	128	24	8	35	96	2	.315
1923	New York	A.L.	OF	152	522	*151	205	45	13	*41	*130	17	.393
1924	New York	A.L.	OF	153	529	*143	200	39	7	*46	121	9	*.378
1925	New York	A.L.	OF	98	359	61	104	12	2	25	66	2	.290
1926	New York	A.L.	OF	152	495	*139	184	30	5	*47	*155	11	.372
1927	New York	A.L.	OF	151	540	*158	192	29	8	*60	164	7	.356
1928	New York	A.L.	OF	154	536	*163	173	29	8	*54	*142	4	.323
1929	New York	A.L.	OF	135	499	121	172	26	6	*46	154	5	.345
1930	New York	A.L.	P-OF	145	518	150	186	28	9	*49	153	10	.359
1931	New York	A.L.	OF	145	534	149	199	31	3	*46	163	5	.373
1932	New York	A.L.	OF	132	457	120	156	13	5	41	137	2	.341
1933	New York	A.L.	OF-P	137	459	97	138	21	3	34	103	4	.301
1934	New York	A.L.	OF	125	365	78	105	17	4	22	84	1	.288
1935	Boston	N.L.	OF	28	72	13	13	0	0	6	12	0	.181
Major League Totals 22 yrs.				2,502	8,399	2,174	2,873	506	136	714	2,216	123	.342

(a) Played a limited number of games at first base.

World Series Record

	g.	ab.	r.	h.	2b	3b	hr.	rbi.	sb.	Avg.
1915 Boston A.L.	1	1	0	0	0	0	0	0	0	.000
1916 Boston A.L.	1	5	0	0	0	0	0	0	0	.000
1918 Boston A.L.	3	5	0	1	0	1	0	2	0	.200
1921 New York A.L.	6	16	3	5	0	0	1	4	2	.313
1922 New York A.L.	5	17	1	2	1	0	0	1	0	.118
1923 New York A.L.	6	19	8	7	1	1	3	3	0	.368
1926 New York A.L.	7	20	6	6	0	0	4	5	1	.300
1927 New York A.L.	4	15	4	6	0	0	2	7	1	.400
1928 New York A.L.	4	16	9	10	3	0	3	4	0	.625
1932 New York A.L.	4	15	6	5	0	0	2	6	0	.333
World Series Totals	41	129	37	42	5	2	15	33	4	.326

Minor League Pennant Winners in 1973

Major League Affiliations in parentheses

INTERNATIONAL LEAGUE

AMERICAN DIVISION Club	W.	L.	Pct.	G.B.	NATIONAL DIVISION Club	W.	L.	Pct.	G.B.
Rochester (Orioles)	79	67	.541	—	Charleston (Pirates)	85	60	.586	—
Pawtucket (Red Sox)	78	68	.534	1	Tidewater (Mets)	75	70	.517	10
Syracuse (Yankees)	76	70	.521	3	Peninsula (Expos)	72	74	.493	13½
Toledo (Tigers)	65	81	.445	14	Richmond (Braves)	53	93	.363	32½

Batting Averages (Over 250 at-Bats)

Player-Club	AB.	H.	HR.	RBI.	Pct.
Stillman, Roch., of	322	114	1	41	.354
Parker, Char., of	309	98	9	57	.317
Campanis, Char., c-dh	355	108	18	64	.304
Cash, Toledo, 3b	259	78	6	34	.301
Bushman, Char., of	333	100	0	30	.300
Beniquez, Paw., util	440	131	13	52	.298
Cooper, Paw., 1b	450	132	15	77	.293
Didier, Rich.-Tol., c	352	103	3	42	.293
Cummings, Paw., of	483	139	0	35	.288
Solaita, Char., 1b	438	126	23	74	.288
Comer, Toledo, of	422	120	6	46	.284
Leon, Toledo, of	329	92	1	44	.280
Augustine, Char., of	431	119	7	52	.276
White, Peninsula, of	359	99	1	30	.276
Knox, Toledo, 2b	370	101	1	26	.273
Matchick, Syr., 3b	262	71	3	35	.271
Howard, Char., of	460	124	15	79	.270
Nelson, Pawtucket, of	501	135	6	53	.269
Vazquez, Paw., 3b	416	112	9	51	.269
Velez, Syracuse, of	409	110	29	98	.269

	AB.	H.	HR.	RBI.	Pct.
DeCinces, Roch., inf.	438	117	19	79	.267
Cox, Peninsula, 2b	371	99	9	49	.267
Shopay, Roch., of	478	127	7	33	.266
Bennett, Syr., of	411	109	7	60	.265
Nordhagen, Sy.-Rh., of	438	115	13	69	.263

Pitching Records (Over 80 innings)

Pitcher — Club	G.	W.	L.	IP.	SO.	ERA.
Apodaca, Tidewater	34	6	3	80	42	1.80
Pole, Pawtucket	23	12	9	182	158	2.03
Morlan, Char.	17	11	5	125	107	2.09
Dettore, Char.	18	9	5	129	72	2.16
Swan, Tide	16	7	5	100	79	2.34
Skok, Paw.	12	7	4	97	85	2.41
Ford, Rich.	19	10	5	108	32	2.42
Taylor, Pen.	48	9	7	108	76	2.50
Glass, Tide.	26	12	9	161	90	2.85
Buskey, Syr.	30	6	4	87	52	2.90
Meyring, Char.	33	5	9	105	75	2.91
Sterling, Tide.	27	10	9	166	73	3.04
Webb, Tide	22	8	9	127	101	3.05

AMERICAN ASSOCIATION

EAST DIVISION Club	W.	L.	Pct.	G.B.	WEST DIVISION Club	W.	L.	Pct.	G.B.
Iowa (White Sox)	83	53	.610	..	Tulsa (Cardinals)	68	67	.509	..
Indianapolis (Reds)	74	62	.544	9	Wichita (Cubs)	67	68	.496	1
Evansville (Brewers)	66	70	.485	17	Oklahoma City (Indians)	61	74	.452	7
Omaha (Royals)	62	73	.459	20½	Denver (Astros)	61	75	.449	7½

Batting Averages (Over 250 at-bats)

Player — Club	AB.	H.	HR.	RBI.	Pct.
Dwyer, Tulsa, of	349	135	1	40	.387
Hairston, Ia., dh-of	274	95	9	65	.347
T. Smith, O.C., of	482	165	4	63	.342
Ward, Wichita, of	259	88	9	41	.340
Gross, Denver, of	528	174	0	55	.330
Griffey, Ind., of	397	130	10	58	.327
Ford, Okla. C., of	367	119	11	59	.324
Youngblood, Ind., of	451	143	11	50	.317
Batista, Denver, 1b	385	122	9	64	.317
Rosello, Wichita, ss	367	115	8	51	.313
LaRussa, Wichita, 2b	397	123	5	75	.310
Alexander, Wich., 3b	427	132	2	51	.309
Armbrister, Ind., of	448	138	10	72	.308
Hermoso, Okla. C., ss	467	142	2	46	.304
Silicato, Evans., 3b	313	95	4	40	.304
T. Reynolds, Ev., of	456	138	16	80	.303

	AB.	H.	HR.	RBI.	Pct.
Gil, Denver, ss	254	77	2	34	.303
C. Johnson, Dn., dh-of	490	148	33	117	.302
J. Clark, Omaha, of	381	115	8	57	.302
Montreuil, Wich., 2b	394	119	5	58	.302

Pitching Records (over 80 innings)

Pitcher — Club	G.	W.	L.	IP.	SO.	ERA.
Ryerson, Evans	18	11	3	116	70	2.09
Littell, Omaha	22	16	6	179	133	2.51
Osborn, Ind.	42	8	3	109	48	2.55
Nagy, Tulsa	12	5	4	82	42	2.72
M. Thompson, Tul	20	7	7	99	91	2.83
Frailing, Iowa	23	11	3	145	107	2.86
Blateric, Ind.	45	9	5	115	86	2.97
Brookens, Tulsa	42	5	4	82	68	3.17
Pelz, Omaha	17	6	9	118	70	3.29
Baney, Ind.	18	8	4	114	43	3.39
Fitzmorris, Omaha	21	9	8	151	100	3.40

PACIFIC COAST LEAGUE

EAST DIVISION Club	W.	L.	Pct.	G.B.	WEST DIVISION Club	W.	L.	Pct.	G.B.
Tucson (Athletics)	84	60	.483	..	Spokane (Rangers)	81	63	.563	..
Salt Lake City (Angels)	79	65	.549	5	Hawaii (Padres)	70	74	.486	11
Phoenix (Giants)	70	73	.490	13½	Tacoma (Twins)	65	79	.451	16
Albuquerque (Dodgers)	62	82	.431	22	Eugene (Phillies)	64	79	.448	16½

Batting Averages (over 250 at-bats)

Player-Club	AB.	H.	HR.	RBI.	Pct.
Ontiveros, Phx, of	401	143	10	84	.357
Madlock, Spo, 3b-2b	491	166	22	90	.338
Rivers, SLC, of	556	187	9	71	.336
Summers, Tuc, dh-of	288	96	8	45	.333
Castle, Spo, of-1b	412	134	9	88	.325
Fairey, Alb, of	469	152	8	76	.324
Wissel, Eug, dh-of	395	126	11	81	.319
B. Williams, Phx, dh-of	492	154	6	55	.313
Johnson, Phx-Haw, 1b	386	121	10	73	.313
Miller, SLC-Phx, ss	393	123	1	42	.313
Trillo, Tucson, 2b	519	162	8	78	.312
Doherty, SLC, 1b	408	126	4	64	.309
Lampard, Eug. of-dh	290	89	12	54	.307

Pitching Records (over 80 innings)

Pitcher — Club	G.	W.	L.	IP.	SO.	ERA.
Waslewski, Tucson	44	8	3	86	42	2.20
Brown, Spokane	19	10	1	96	84	2.34
Krausse, Tucson	45	6	4	105	54	2.49
Freisleben, Ha.	27	16	8	195	206	2.82
Lange, SLC	13	7	6	89	60	2.83
Zahn, Alb.	25	13	8	177	103	3.05
Young, SLC	29	12	9	185	111	3.11
Kremmel, Spokane	15	5	2	83	74	3.25
Abbott, Tucson	20	18	8	206	120	3.50
D'Acquisto, Phx.	31	16	12	212	185	3.57
Hardy, Hawaii	36	6	5	115	65	3.60
Campbell, Tacoma	18	10	5	133	110	3.65
McCormick, Ha-Tc	30	8	14	204	93	3.75

Minor League Final Standings

Major League Affiliation in parentheses

EASTERN LEAGUE

AMERICAN DIVISION

Club	W.	L.	Pct.	G.B.
Pittsfield (Rangers)	75	61	.551	—
West Haven (Yankees)	72	66	.522	4
Bristol (Red Sox)	62	77	.446	14½
Waterbury (Dodgers)	59	79	.428	17

NATIONAL DIVISION

Club	W.	L.	Pct.	G.B.
Reading (Phillies)	76	62	.551	—
Sherbrooke (Pirates)	76	63	.547	½
Three Rivers (Reds)	67	72	.482	9½
Quebec City (Expos)	65	72	.474	10½

SOUTHERN LEAGUE

WESTERN DIVISION

Club	W.	L.	Pct.	G.B.
Montgomery (Tigers)	80	58	.580	—
Asheville (Orioles)	71	69	.507	10
Knoxville (White Sox)	70	69	.504	10½
Birmingham (Athletics)	50	88	.362	30

EASTERN DIVISION

Club	W.	L.	Pct.	G.B.
Jacksonville (Royals)	76	60	.559	—
Savannah (Braves)	71	68	.511	6½
Columbus (Astros)	69	70	.496	8½
Orlando (Twins)	65	70	.481	10½

TEXAS LEAGUE

EASTERN DIVISION

Club	W.	L.	Pct.	G.B.
Memphis (Mets)	77	61	.558	—
Shreveport (Brewers)	70	68	.507	7
Arkansas (Cardinals)	70	70	.500	8
Alexandria (Padres)	58	78	.426	18

WESTERN DIVISION

Club	W.	L.	Pct.	G.B.
San Antonio (Indians)	83	57	.593	—
El Paso (Angels)	69	71	.493	14
Midland (Cubs)	64	75	.460	18½
Amarillo (Giants)	64	75	.460	18½

CALIFORNIA LEAGUE

Club	W.	L.	Pct.	G.B.
Bakersfield (Dodgers)	40	30	.571	—
San Jose (Royals)	39	31	.557	1
Visalia (Mets)	37	33	.529	3
Salinas (Angels)	35	35	.500	5
Fresno (Giants)	35	35	.500	5
Reno (Indians)	34	36	.486	6
Lodi (Orioles)	31	39	.443	9
Modesto (Cardinals)	29	41	.414	11

CAROLINA LEAGUE

Standing at close of 2nd half

Club	W.	L.	Pct.	G.B.
Winston-Salem (Red Sox)	39	31	.561	—
Lynchburg (Twins)	38	32	.544	1
Salem (Pirates)	35	34	.507	3½
Kingston (Yankees)	34	35	.493	4½
Rocky Mount (Phillies)	34	36	.485	5
Wilson (Co-op)	29	41	.416	10

FLORIDA STATE LEAGUE

NORTHERN DIVISION

Club	W.	L.	Pct.	G.B.
Lakeland (Tigers)	80	59	.576	—
St. Petersburg (Cards)	83	62	.572	—
Daytona Beach (Dodgers)	71	68	.511	9
Tampa (Reds)	73	71	.507	9½
Winter Haven (Red Sox)	50	94	.347	32½

SOUTHERN DIVISION

Club	W.	L.	Pct.	G.B.
W. Palm Beach (Expos)	80	58	.580	—
Miami (Orioles)	77	64	.546	4½
Ft. Lauderdale (Yanks-Twins)	67	72	.482	13½
Key West (Co-op)	64	78	.451	18
Pompano Beach (Mets)	61	80	.430	20½

MIDWEST LEAGUE

Standing at close of 2nd half

NORTHERN DIVISION

Club	W.	L.	Pct.	G.B.
Clinton (Tigers)	37	25	.597	—
Waterloo (Royals)	36	26	.581	1
Cedar Rapids (Astros)	29	34	.460	8½
Wisc. Rapids (Twins)	27	34	.443	9½
Appleton (White Sox)	27	35	.435	10

SOUTHERN DIVISION

Club	W.	L.	Pct.	G.B.
Decatur (Giants)	35	30	.538	—
Danville (Brewers)	34	30	.531	½
Burlington (Athletics)	30	32	.484	3½
Quad Cities (Angels)	30	33	.476	4
Quincy (Cubs)	29	35	.453	5½

WESTERN CAROLINAS LEAGUE

Standing at close of 2nd half

Club	W.	L.	Pct.	G.B.
Spartanburg (Phillies)	42	23	.646	—
Charleston (Pirates)	37	27	.578	4½
Gastonia (Rangers)	35	30	.538	7
Greenwood (Braves)	29	34	.460	12
Orangeburg (Co-op)	25	37	.403	15½
Anderson (Tigers)	24	41	.369	18

NYP LEAGUE

Club	W.	L.	Pct.	G.B.
Auburn (Phillies)	46	23	.667	—
Oneonta (Yankees)	44	26	.629	2½
Jamestown (Expos)	41	28	.594	5
Geneva (Twins)	39	29	.574	6½
Batavia (Mets)	33	36	.478	13
Elmira (Red Sox)	32	37	.464	14
Niagara Falls (Pirates)	27	43	.386	19
Newark (Brewers)	15	55	.214	31½

NORTHWEST LEAGUE

EASTERN DIVISION

Club	W.	L.	Pct.	G.B.
Walla Walla (Padres)	51	29	.638	—
Tri-City (Co-op)	42	38	.525	9
Lewiston (Athletics)	26	54	.325	25

WESTERN DIVISION

Club	W.	L.	Pct.	G.B.
Portland (Ind.)	45	35	.563	—
Bellingham (Dodgers)	42	37	.532	2½
Seattle (Reds)	33	46	.418	11½

Little Brown Jug

(Three-Year-Old Pacers)

Year	Winner	Winning Driver	Purse	Year	Winner	Winning Driver	Purse
1952	Meadow Rice	Wayne Smart	$ 60,463	1963	Overtrick	John F. Patterson, Sr.	$ 68,294
1953	Keystoner	Frank Ervin	54,972	1964	Vicar Hanover	William R. Haughton	66,590
1954	Adios Harry	Morris MacDonald	69,332	1965	Bret Hanover	Frank Ervin	71,447
1955	Quick Chief	William R. Haughton	66,608	1966	Romeo Hanover	George Sholty	74,616
1956	Noble Adios	John F. Simpson, Sr.	52,666	1967	Best of All	James K. Hackett	84,778
1957	Torpid	John F. Simpson, Sr.	73,528	1968	Rum Customer	William R. Haughton	104,226
1958	Shadow Wave	Joe O'Brien	65,252	1969	Laverne Hanover	William R. Haughton	109,731
1959	Adios Butler	Clint T. Hodgins	76,582	1970	Most Happy Fella	Stanley Dancer	100,110
1960	Bullet Hanover	John F. Simpson, Sr.	66,510	1971	Nansemond	Herve Filion	102,944
1961	Henry T. Adios	Stanley Dancer	70,069	1972	Strike Out	Keith Waples	104,916
1962	Lehigh Hanover	Stanley Dancer	75,038	1973	Melvin's Woe	Joe O'Brien	120,000

Trotting and Pacing Records

Source: Larry Evans, United States Trotting Association. Records to Oct. 10, 1973

TROTTING RECORDS

Asterisk (*) denotes that record was made in a race

One Mile Records (Mile Track)

All-age Stallion—1:54⅘—Nevele Pride, Indianapolis, Ind., Aug. 31, 1969.
All-age Mare—1:56¾—Rosalind, Lexington, Ky. Oct. 4, 1938.
Two-year old Colt—*1:58⅖—Nevele Pride, Lexington, Ky., Oct. 4, 1967.
Two-year-old Filly—1:58⅗—Impish, Lexington, Ky., Sept. 29, 1961.
Three-year-old Colt—* 1:56⅖—Super Bowl, Du Quoin, Ill., Aug. 30, 1972.
Three-year-old Filly—1:58—Yankee Lass, Lexington, Ky., Oct. 20, 1957; Emily's Pride, Lexington, Ky., Oct. 8, 1958; Expression, Lexington, Ky., Oct. 12, 1959; Worth Seein, Lexington, Ky., Oct. 4, 1962.
Four-year-old Stallion—1:54⅘—Nevele Pride, Indianapolis, Ind., Aug. 31, 1969.
Four-year-old Mare—1:57⅕—Fresh Yankee, Lexington, Ky., Oct. 3, 1967.

(Half-Mile Track)

All-age Stallion—*1:56⅘—Nevele Pride, Saratoga Springs, N.Y., Sept. 6, 1969.
All-age Mare, *1:59⅕—Armbro Flight, Delaware, Ohio, Sept. 20, 1965.
Two-year-old Colt—*2:00⅕—Ayres, Delaware, Ohio, 1963.
Two-year-old Filly—*2:03⅗—Impish, Delaware, Ohio, 1961.
Three-year-old Colt—* 1:59⅖—Speedy Crown, Delaware, Ohio, 1971.
Three-year-old Filly—* 1.59⅕—Armbro Flight, Delaware, Ohio, 1965.
Four-year-old Stallion—*1:56⅕—Nevele Pride, Saratoga Springs, N. Y., Sept. 6, 1969.
Four-year-old Mare—*2:00⅖—Flamboyant, Yonkers, N. Y., Aug. 2, 1968.

Odd Distances

1-1/16 Miles—* 2:05⅗—Senator Frost, Inglewood, Calif., Oct. 17, 1959.
1-1/16 Miles, Half-mile Track—* 2:07⅖—Nevele Pride, Westbury, N.Y., 1969.
1-3/16 Miles—*2:22⅘—Scotch Victor, Inglewood, Calif., Nov. 6, 1954.
1¼ Miles—*2:30⅗—Pronto Don, Inglewood, Calif., Nov. 24, 1951.
1¼ Miles, Half-mile Track—*2:31⅖—Speedy Scot, Westbury, N. Y., 1964; Noble Victory, Westbury, N. Y., 1966.
1½ Miles—3:02½—Greyhound, Indianapolis, Ind., Sept. 14, 1937.
1½ Miles, Half-mile Track—3:05⅗—Snow Speed, Yonkers, N.Y., 1969.
2 Miles—4:06—Greyhound, Indianapolis, Ind., Sept. 19, 1939.
2 Miles, Half-mile Track—*4:10⅘—Pronto Don, Westbury, N. Y., Sept. 13, 1951.
Fastest Two Heats—*1:57⅖; *1:56⅗—Nevele Pride, Indianapolis, Aug. 31, 1968.
Fastest Two Heats, Half-Mile Track—*1:58⅘, *2:00⅗—Speedy Rodney, Goshen, N. Y., 1966.
Fastest Three Heats—2:01, 2:00¼, 2:00—Greyhound, Goshen, N. Y., Aug. 13, 1936; **2:02, 2:00, 1:59¼**—Rosalind, Lexington, Ky., Sept. 30, 1937.

PACING RECORDS

One Mile Records (Mile Track)

All-age Stallion—1:52—Steady Star, Lexington, Ky., Oct. 1, 1971.
All-age Mare—*1:56⅖—Tarport Lib, Lexington, Ky., Oct. 7, 1966.
Two-year-old Colt—* 1:56⅕—Ricci Reenie Time, Lexington, Ky., 1972.
Two-year-old Filly—1:57⅕—Timely Beauty, Lexington, Ky., Oct. 15, 1962; and ***1:57⅕**—Decorum, Lexington, Ky., Oct. 2, 1971.
Three-year-old Colt—1:54—Steady Star, Lexington, Ky., Oct. 7, 1970.
Three-year-old Filly—*1:56⅖—Tarport Lib, Lexington, Ky., 1966.
Four-year-old Stallion—1:52—Steady Star, Lexington, Ky., Oct. 1, 1971.
Four-year-old Mare—1:56⅘—Dottie's Pick, Inglewood, Calif., Nov. 16, 1956.

(Half-Mile Track)

All-age Stallion—1:55⅗—Adios Butler, Delaware, Ohio, Sept. 21, 1961.
All-age Mare—*1:59—Miss Conna Adios, Yonkers, N. Y., June 18, 1971.
Two-year-old Colt—*1:58⅘—Columbia George, Yonkers, N. Y., Nov. 8, 1969.
Two year old Filly—*2:01—Romalie Hanover, Delaware, O., Sept. 21, 1971.
Three-year-old Colt—*1:57—Bret Hanover, Delaware, Ohio, Sept. 23, 1965.
Three-year-old Filly—*1:59⅕—Countess Adios, Delaware, Ohio, 1960.
Four-year-old Stallion—* 1:57⅗—Albatross, Saratoga Springs, N.Y. July 15, 1972.
Four-year-old Mare—* 1:59⅖—Meadow Elva, Yonkers, N.Y., 1968.

Odd Distances

1¼ Miles—*2:30⅖—Dr. Stanton, Arcadia, Calif., May 15, 1948.
1¼ Miles, Half-mile Track—*2:29⅗—Irvin Paul, Westbury, N. Y., Sept. 1, 1962.
1-1/16 Miles—*2:03⅕—Adios Vic, Inglewood, Calif., Oct. 23, 1965.
1-1/16 Miles, Half-mile Track—*2:06⅖—Amortizer, Westbury, N. Y., June 29, 1956.
1⅛ miles—2:09⅕—True Duane, Hollywood Park, 1966.
1½ Miles, *3:05⅖—Right Time, Inglewood, Calif., 1961; and K. D. Senator, E. Boston, Mass., 1963.
1½ Miles, Half-mile Track—*3:02⅗—Overcall, Westbury, N. Y., June 5, 1969.
2 Miles—4:17—Dan Patch, Macon, Ga., 1903.
2 Miles, Half-Mile Track—*4:08⅘—Irvin Paul, Yonkers, N. Y., June 28, 1962.
Fastest Two Heats—*1:54⅕, 1:54⅕—Albatross, Lexington, Ky., Oct. 2, 1971.
Fastest Three Heats—*1:58¼, 1:58½, 1:59¼—Her Ladyship, Syracuse, N. Y., Aug. 31, 1938.

The Hambletonian (3-year-old trotters) Du Quoin, Ill.

Year	Winner	Best Time	Value
1940	Spencer Scott	2:02	$43,658
1941	Bill Gallon	2:05	38,729
1942	The Ambassador	2:04	38,954
1943	Volo Song	2:02½	42,298
1944	Yankee Maid	2:04	33,577
1945	Titan Hanover	2:04	50,190
1946	Chestertown	2:02½	50,905
1947	Hoot Mon	2:00	46,267
1948	Demon Hanover	2:02	59,941
1949	Miss Tilly	2:01⅖	69,791
1950	Lusty Song	2:02	75,209
1951	Mainliner	2:02⅗	95,263
1952	Sharp Note	2:02⅗	87,637
1953	Helicopter	2:01⅗	117,118
1954	Newport Dream	2:02⅘	106,830
1955	Scott Frost	2:00⅗	86,863
1956	The Intruder	2:01⅖	98,591
1957	Hickory Smoke	2:00⅕	$111,126
1958	Emily's Pride	1:59⅘	106,719
1959	Diller Hanover	2:01⅕	125,284
1960	Blaze Hanover	1:59⅗	144,590
1961	Harlan Dean	1:58⅖	131,573
1962	A. C.'s Viking	1:59⅗	116,312
1963	Speedy Scot	1:58	115,549
1964	Ayres	1:56⅘	115,281
1965	Egyptian Candor	2:04⅗	122,245
1966	Kerry Way	1:58⅕	122,540
1967	Speedy Streak	2:00	122,650
1968	Nevele Pride	1:59⅖	116,190
1969	Lindy's Pride	1:57⅗	124,910
1970	Timothy T.	2:00⅕	143,630
1971	Speedy Crown	1:57⅖	128,770
1972	Super Bowl	1:56⅖	119,090
1973	Flirth	1:57⅕	144,710

Major Harness Races of 1973

Purse	Event	Winner	Time*
$150,000	International Trot (1 1/4 mi. Invit.)	Delmonica Hanover	2:34 2/5
144,710	Hambletonian (3-year-old trot)	Flirth	1:57 1/5
130,000	Prix d'Ete (3-year-old pace)	Armbro Nadir	1:56 1/5
122,732	Messenger (3-year-old pace)	Valiant Bret	2:00 3/5
120,000	Little Brown Jug (3-year-old pace)	Melvin's Woe	1:57 3/5
101,563	Dexter Cup (3-year-old trot)	Knightly Way	2:03 2/5
101,242	Cane Futurity (3-year-old pace)	Smog	1:58 4/5
93,242	Yonkers Futurity (3-year-old trot)	Tamerlane	2:04 4/5
90,000	Realization (1 1/16 mi. 4-year-old pace)	Keystone Pebble	2:07 1/5
90,000	Realization (1 1/16 mi. 4-year-old trot)	Spartan Hanover	2:11
86,780	Adios (3-year-old pace)	Ricci Reenie Time	1:58 4/5
78,346	Fox Stake (2-year-old pace)	Boyden Hanover	1:59
62,800	Maple Leaf (free-for-all trot)	Flower Child	2:00 2/5
60,622	Matron (4-year-old pace)	Fast Clip	1:58 3/5
58,300	Canadian Derby (free-for-all pace)	Sir Dalrae	1:57 3/5
57,105	Matron (3-year-old pace)	Keystone Smartie	1:57 4/5
55,872	Matron (4-year-old trot)	Spartan Hanover	2:01 4/5
55,785	American-National (4-year-old trot)	Songcan	2:07 2/5
54,265	Gaines Memorial (3-year-old pace)	Ricci Reenie Time	1:57 1/5
54,130	Charles Coon Memorial (4-year-old pace)	Blu Fireball	2:03 1/5
52,873	American-National (4-year-old pace)	Jay Time	2:00 3/5
52,873	American-National (4-year-old pace)	Game Guy	2:02 3/5
52,330	Vernon Gold Cub (3-year-old trot)	Knightly Way	2:05 4/5
52,177	Lady Maud (3-year-old filly pace)	Skipper's Dream	2:04 2/5
51,320	Chas. Coon Memorial (4-year-old trot)	Noblette	2:06 2/5
50,300	Can-Am Final (3-year-old pace)	Smog	1:59 4/5
50,000	Battle of Brandywine (3 year-old pace)	Valiant Bret	2:00 [illegible]
[illegible]	Provincial Cup (free-for-all pace)	Isle of Wight	2:03 2/5

*Best time if more than 1 heat.

Leading Drivers

Year	Races Won		Grand Circuit		Money Won	
1957	Bill Haughton	156	John Simpson	$367,670	Bill Haughton	$586,950
1958	Bill Haughton	176	Joe O'Brien	267,342	Bill Haughton	816,659
1959	William Gilmour	165	Joe O'Brien	263,636	Bill Haughton	711,435
1960	Del Insko	156	Del Miller	338,594	Del Miller	567,282
1961	Bob Farrington	201	Jimmy Arthur	248,211	Stanley Dancer	674,723
1962	Bob Farrington	203	Stanley Dancer	306,454	Stanley Dancer	760,343
1963	Donald Busse	201	Ralph Baldwin	299,899	Bill Haughton	790,086
1964	Bob Farrington	312	Stanley Dancer	269,080	Stanley Dancer	1,051,538
1965	Bob Farrington	310	Joe O'Brien	304,791	Bill Haughton	889,943
1966	Bob Farrington	283	George Sholty	293,531	Stanley Dancer	1,218,403
1967	Bob Farrington	277	Bill Haughton	448,294	Bill Haughton	1,305,773
1968	Herve Filion	407	Bill Haughton	448,040	Bill Haughton	1,654,172
1969	Herve Filion	394	Bill Haughton	489,495	Del Insko	1,635,463
1970	Herve Filion	486	Stanley Dancer	439,019	Herve Filion	1,647,837
1971	Herve Filion	543	Stanley Dancer	462,694	Herve Filion	1,915,945
1972	Herve Filion	605	Billy Haughton	416,626	Herve Filion	2,473,265

Harness Horse of the Year

1947—Victory Song
1948—Rodney
1949—Good Time
1950—Proximity
1951—Pronto Don
1952—Good Time
1953—Hi Lo's Forbes
1954—Stenographer
1955—Scott Frost
1956—Scott Frost
1957—Torpid
1958—Emily's Pride
1959—Bye Bye Byrd
1960—Adios Butler
1961—Adios Butler
1962—Su Mac Lad
1963—Speedy Scot
1964—Bret Hanover
1965—Bret Hanover
1966—Bret Hanover
1967—Nevele Pride
1968—Nevele Pride
1969—Nevele Pride
1970—Fresh Yankee
1971—Albatross
1972—Albatross

"Parked Out" Computations

Harness Racing mathematicians have compiled these figures on the added distance in each mile that a horse travels when "parked out" (racing outside another horse, five feet out from the point at which the track is measured).

1/2 mile track (4 turns to mile) .... 62.832 feet
5/8 mile track (3 turns to mile) .... 47.124 feet
3/4 mile track with chute, and mile track (2 turns to mile) 31.416 feet

Trapshooting Championships in 1973

Source: Trap & Field Magazine

74th Grand American Tournament

Vandalia, Ohio, Aug. 20-25, 1973

Grand American Handicap

Men—Dennis Taylor, Muscoda, Wisc. .... 99 × 100.
Women—JoAnn Nelson, Lone Tree, Ia. .... 96 × 100.
Juniors—Joseph Loitz, Peotone, Ill. .... 96 × 100.
Veterans—C. N. Pierce, Overland Park, Kan. . 96 × 100.
Industry—John Muir, White Hall, Pa. .... 95 × 100.
Past Winner Trophy—Delbert Grim, Grand Island, Nebr. .... 92 × 100.
Jimmy Robinson Trophy to High Canadian—Jim Boose, Ontario .... 97 × 100.

Clay Target Championship

Men—John Comly, Lambertville, N.J. .... 200 × 200.
Women—Marcella Cook, Winfield, Kan. ..... 195 × 200.
Juniors—John Comly .... 200 × 200.
Veterans—Herschel Cheek, Clinton, Ind. .... 198 × 200.
Industry—Bob Oxsen, Livermore, Calif. ...... 199 × 200.

Vandalia Handicap

Men—Edward Wyss, Washington, Ill. .... 98 × 100.
Women—Margaret Lewis, G. Rapids, Mich. .. 96 × 100.
Juniors—Doug Davidson, Devils Lake, N.D. 97 × 100.
Veteran—Vic Reinders, Waukesha, Wisc. .... 95 × 100.
Industry—Bob Oxen, Livermore, Calif. .... 96 × 100.

High Over-All

Men—Larry Gravestock, Amarillo, Texas ..... 958 × 1000.
Women—Judy Allisøn, Elgin, Ill. .... 903 × 1000.
Juniors—Leo Harrison, Hannibal, Mo. .... 932 × 1000.
Veterans—Vic Reinders, Waukesha, Wisc. ... 918 × 1000.
Industry—Tom Garrigus, Hillsboro, Ore. ..... 950 × 1000.
All-Around—Ray Stafford, Denver, Colo. ..... 390 × 400.

Champion of Champions

Men—Hiram Bradley, Vest, Ky. .... 100 × 100.
Women—Barbara Frederick, Camdenton, Mo. 100 × 100.
Juniors—Rick Jenner, Waupaca, Wisc. ...... 100 × 100.

Professional Sports Directory

Baseball

National League
Commissioner's Office
680 Fifth Ave.
New York, N.Y. 10019

National League Office
Mills Bldg.
220 Montgomery St.
San Francisco, Calif. 94104

American League Office
520 Boylston St.
Boston, Mass. 02116

Atlanta Braves
PO Box 4064
Atlanta, Ga. 30302

Chicago Cubs
Wrigley Field,
Chicago, Ill. 60613

Cincinnati Reds
100 Riverfront Stadium
Cincinnati, Ohio 45202

Houston Astros
Astrodome
Houston, Texas 77001

Los Angeles Dodgers
Dodger Stadium
1000 Elysian Park Ave.
Los Angeles, Calif. 90012

Montreal Expos
PO Box 500, Station R
Montreal 326, Quebec

New York Mets
William A. Shea Stadium
Roosevelt Ave. & 126th St.
Flushing, N.Y. 11368

Philadelphia Phillies
Philadelphia Veterans Stadium
Broad St. & Pattison Ave.
Philadelphia, Pa. 19148

Pittsburgh Pirates
600 Stadium Circle
Pittsburgh, Pa. 15212
Pittsburgh, Pa. 15212

St. Louis Cardinals
Busch Memorial Stadium
250 Stadium Plaza
St. Louis, Mo. 63102

San Diego Padres
9449 Friars Rd.
San Diego, Calif. 92120

San Francisco Giants
Candlestick Park
San Francisco, Calif. 94124

American League

Baltimore Orioles
Memorial Stadium
Baltimore, Md. 21218

Boston Red Sox
24 Jersey St.
Boston, Mass. 02215

California Angels
Anaheim Stadium
2000 State College Blvd.
Anaheim, Calif. 92806

Chicago White Sox
White Sox Park
Dan Ray & 35th St.
Chicago, Ill. 60616

Cleveland Indians
Municipal Stadium
Cleveland, Ohio 44114

Detroit Tigers
Tiger Stadium
Detroit, Mich. 48216

Kansas City Royals
Harry S. Truman Sports Complex
PO Box 1969
Kansas City, Mo. 64141

Milwaukee Brewers
Milwaukee County Stadium
Milwaukee, Wisc. 53246

Minnesota Twins
Metropolitan Stadium
8001 Cedar Ave.
Bloomington, Minn. 55420

New York Yankees
Yankee Stadium
Bronx, N.Y. 10451

Oakland A's
Oakland-Alameda County
Coliseum
Nimitz Freeway & Hegenberger
Rd.
Oakland, Calif. 94621

Texas Rangers
Arlington Stadium
PO Box 1111
Arlington, Texas 76011

Basketball

National Basketball Assn.
League Office
2 Pennsylvania Plaza
Suite 2360
New York, N.Y. 10001

Atlanta Hawks
100 Techwood Drive
Atlanta, Ga. 30303

Baltimore Bullets
Civic Center
Baltimore, Md. 21201

Boston Celtics
North Station
Boston, Mass. 02114

Buffalo Braves
Memorial Auditorium
Buffalo, N.Y. 14202

Chicago Bulls
Sheraton Chicago Hotel
505 North Michigan Ave.
Chicago, Ill. 60611

Cleveland Cavaliers
3717 Euclid Ave.
Cleveland, Ohio 44115

Detroit Pistons
Cobo Arena
Detroit, Mich. 48226

Golden State Warriors
556 Golden Gate Ave.
San Francisco, Calif. 94102

Houston Rockets
3930 Kirby Drive
Houston, Texas 77006

Kansas City-Omaha Kings
210 W. 14th St.
Kansas City, Mo. 64105
1804 Capitol Ave.
Omaha, Nebr. 68102

Los Angeles Lakers
The Forum
3900 W. Manchester Blvd.
or PO Box 10
Inglewood, Calif. 90306

Milwaukee Bucks
700 West Wisconsin Ave.
Milwaukee, Wisc. 53233

New York Knickerbockers
Madison Square Garden Center
4 Pennsylvania Plaza
New York, N.Y. 10001

Philadelphia 76ers
The Spectrum
Philadelphia, Pa. 19148

Phoenix Suns
23 I3 N. Central
Phoenix, Ariz. 85004

Portland Trail Blazers
Lloyd Bldg.
700 NE Multnomah St.
Portland, Ore. 97232

Seattle Supersonics
221 West Harrison
Seattle, Wash. 98119

American Basketball Assn.
League Office
1700 Broadway
New York, N.Y. 10019

Carolina Cougars
Greesboro Coliseum
1921 West Lee St.
Greensboro, N.C. 27403

Dallas Chaparrals
7616 LBJ Freeway
Dallas, Texas 75240

Denver Rockets
3201 Ringsby Court
Denver, Colo.

Indiana Pacers
638 East 38th St.
Indianapolis, Ind. 46205

Kentucky Colonels
Executive Inn
Louisville, Ky. 40221

Memphis Tams
Mid-South Coliseum
PO Box 14664
Memphis, Tenn. 38104

New York Nets
One Old Country Rd.
Carle Place, N.Y. 11590

San Diego Conquistadors
3563 Fourth Ave.
San Diego, Calif. 92103

Utah Stars
Salt Palace
Stars Ave. & W. Temple
Salt Lake City, Utah 84101

Virginia Squires
Norfolk Scope
Norfolk, Va. 23510

Football

NFL League Office
410 Park Avenue
New York, N.Y. 10022

Atlanta Falcons
521 Capitol Ave. SW
Atlanta, Ga. 30312

Baltimore Colts
600 N. Howard St.
Baltimore, Md. 21201

Buffalo Bills
1 Bills Drive
Orchard Park, N.Y. 14127

Chicago Bears
173 W. Madison St.
Chicago, Ill. 60602

Cincinnati Bengals
200 Riverfront Stadium
Cincinnati, Ohio 45202

Cleveland Browns
Cleveland Stadium
Cleveland, Ohio 44114

Dallas Cowboys
6116 North Central Expressway
Dallas, Texas 75206

Denver Broncos
5700 Logan St.
Denver, Colo. 80216

Detroit Lions
1401 Michigan Ave.
Detroit, Mich. 48216

Green Bay Packers
1265 Lombardi Ave.
Green Bay, Wisc. 54303

Houston Oilers
6910 Fannin
Houston, Texas 77025

Kansas City Chiefs
Truman Sports Complex
Kansas City, Mo. 64133

Los Angeles Rams
10271 W. Pico. Blvd.
Los Angeles, Calif. 90064

Miami Dolphins
330 Biscayne Blvd. Bldg.
Miami, Fla. 33132

Minnesota Vikings
7110 France Ave. So.
Edina, Minn. 55435

New England Patriots
Schaefer Stadium
Foxboro, Mass. 02035

New Orleans Saints
944 St. Charles
New Orleans, La. 70130

New York Giants
10 Columbus Circle
New York, N.Y. 10019

New York Jets
595 Madison Ave.
New York, N.Y. 10022

Oakland Raiders
7811 Oakport St.
Oakland, Calif. 94621

Philadelphia Eagles
Veterans Stadium
Philadelphia, Pa. 19148

Pittsburgh Steelers
Three Rivers Stadium
Pittsburgh, Pa. 15212

St. Louis Cardinals
200 Stadium Plaza
St. Louis, Mo. 63102

San Diego Chargers
San Diego Stadium
PO Box 20666
San Diego, Calif. 92120

San Francisco 49ers
1255 Post St.
San Francisco, Calif. 94109

Washington Redskins
PO Box 17247
Dulles Intl. Airport
Washington, D.C. 20041

Hockey

National Hockey League

League Office
920 Sun Life Bldg.
Montreal, 110, Quebec

Atlanta Flames
100 Peckwood Dr., NW
Atlanta, Ga. 30303

Boston Bruins
150 Causeway St.
Boston, Mass. 02114

Buffalo Sabres
Memorial Auditorium
Buffalo, N.Y. 14202

California Golden Seals
Oakland-Alameda Country
   Coliseum
303 Hegenberger Rd.
Oakland, Calif. 94621

Chicago Blackhawks
1800 W. Madison St.
Chicago, Ill. 60612

Detroit Red Wings
5920 Grand River
Detroit, Mich. 48208

Los Angeles Kings
3900 W. Manchester Blvd.
Inglewood, Calif. 90306

Minnesota North Stars
7901 Cedar Avenue
Bloomington, Minn. 55420

Montreal Canadiens
2313 St. Catherine St., West
Montreal, 108, Quebec

N.Y. Islanders
1 Old Country Rd.
Carle Place, N.Y. 11514

New York Rangers
Madison Square Garden
4 Pennsylvania Plaza
New York, N.Y. 10001

Philadelphia Flyers
The Spectrum
Pattison Place
Philadelphia, Pa. 19148

Pittsburgh Penguins
Civic Arena
Pittsburgh, Pa. 15219

St. Louis Blues
5700 Oakland Ave.
St. Louis, Mo. 63110

Toronto Maple Leafs
60 Carlton St.
Toronto, Ont.

Vancouver Canucks
Pacific Coliseum
Vancouver 6, B.C.

World Hockey Assn.

League Office
1010 North Main St.
Santa Ana, Calif. 92701

Alberta Oilers
Edmonton Gardens
Edmonton, Alta.

Chicago Cougars
222 N. Michigan Blvd.
Chicago, Ill. 60601

Cleveland Crusaders
Cleveland Arena
3717 Euclid Ave.
Cleveland, Ohio 44115

Houston Aeros
810 Bagby St.
Houston, Texas 77002

Los Angeles Sharks
3939 Figueroa St.
Los Angeles, Calif. 90037

Minnesota Fighting Saints
Metro Square
St. Paul, Minn. 55101

New England Whalers
705 Statler Office Bldg.
Boston, Mass. 02116

New York Golden Blades
2 Penn Plaza
New York, N.Y. 10001

Ottawa Nationals
PO Box 1358, Station B
Ottawa, Ont.

Quebec Nordiques
Exhibition Grounds
Quebec 3, Que.

Toronto Toros
Maple Leaf Gardens
Toronto, Ont.

Winnipeg Jets
Winnipeg Arena
Winnipeg, Man.

Vancouver Blazers
Pacific Coliseum
Vancouver, B.C.

American Legion Junior Baseball World Champions

Year	Winner	Year	Winner	Year	Winner	Year	Winner
1958	Cincinnati, Ohio	1962	St. Louis, Mo.	1966	Oakland, Calif.	1970	West Covina, Calif.
1959	Detroit, Mich.	1963	Long Beach, Calif.	1967	Tuscaloosa, Ala.	1971	West Covina, Calif.
1960	New Orleans, La.	1964	Upland, Calif.	1968	Memphis, Tenn.	1972	Baldwin, Mo.
1961	Phoenix, Ariz.	1965	Charlotte, N.C.	1969	Portland, Oregon	1973	Puerto Rico

College Basketball

Final Standings in 1972-73 Season

IVY LEAGUE

	Conference Games		All Games	
	W	L	W	L
Penn............	12	2	21	7
Princeton	11	3	16	9
Brown	10	4	14	12
Harvard	7	7	14	12
Yale	6	8	9	16
Columbia.......	5	9	7	18
Dartmouth	4	10	6	20
Cornell	1	13	4	22

MIDDLE ATLANTIC

East

	W	L	W	L
St. Joseph's	6	0	22	6
Temple	5	1	17	10
American U......	4	2	21	5
LaSalle	3	3	15	10
Drexel	2	4	14	7
Hofstra	1	5	8	16
West Chester	0	6	5	21

West

	W	L	W	L
Lafayette	7	3	16	10
Gettysburg	6	4	14	11
Delaware........	6	4	14	11
Bucknell	6	4	11	14
Lehigh	3	7	8	17
Rider	2	8	12	14

YANKEE

	W	L	W	L
Massachusetts ..	10	2	20	7
Connecticut	9	3	15	10
Boston Univ.	7	4	15	10
Maine...........	6	6	13	10
Rhode Island	5	6	7	18
New Hampshire..	2	10	11	15
Vermont	2	10	7	17

ATLANTIC COAST

	W	L	W	L
N.C. State	12	0	27	0
North Carolina ...	8	4	25	8
Maryland	7	5	23	7
Virginia	4	8	13	12
Duke............	4	8	12	14
Clemson	4	8	12	14
Wake Forest	3	9	12	15

SOUTHEASTERN

	W	L	W	L
Kentucky	14	4	20	8
Vanderbilt.......	13	5	20	6
Alabama	13	5	22	8
Tennessee	13	5	15	9
Louisiana.......	9	9	14	10
Mississippi	8	10	14	12
Florida	7	11	11	15
Georgia	5	13	10	16
Miss. State	4	14	11	15
Auburn	4	14	6	20

SOUTHERN

	W	L	W	L
Davidson........	9	1	18	9
Furman	11	2	20	9
East Carolina	7	7	13	13
Citadel	6	7	11	15
Wm. & Mary	5	6	10	17
Richmond	5	9	6	18
Appalachian.....	3	8	6	20
VMI.............	3	9	6	20

OHIO VALLEY

	W	L	W	L
Austin Peay	11	3	22	7
Murray State	9	5	17	8
Morehead State .	9	5	14	11
Tenn. Tech.	7	7	14	11
Eastern Kentucky	7	7	12	13
Western Kentucky	6	8	10	16
Middle Tenn.	5	9	12	13
Eastern Tenn. ...	2	12	9	17

BIG TEN

	W	L	W	L
Indiana	11	3	22	6
Minnesota.......	10	4	21	5
Purdue..........	8	6	15	9
Ohio State.......	8	6	14	10
Illinois	8	6	14	10
Michigan State ..	6	8	13	11
Iowa	6	8	13	11
Michigan	6	8	13	11
Wisconsin	5	9	11	13
Northwestern....	2	12	5	19

MID-AMERICAN

	W	L	W	L
Miami, Ohio	9	2	18	9
Toledo	7	5	15	11
Bowling Green ...	7	5	13	13
Ohio Univ........	6	5	16	10
Kent State	5	7	10	16
Central Mich.	4	6	13	13
Western Mich. ...	2	10	8	18
*Eastern Mich	—	—	8	17
*did not compete for title				

OHIO

	W	L	W	L
Capital	10	2	22	5
Muskingum	10	2	19	4
Wittenberg	10	2	19	4
Otterbein	10	2	19	6
Wooster	7	5	19	10
Mt. Union	7	5	13	12
Marietta	5	6	10	15
Heidelberg	5	7	9	13
Baldwin-Wallace .	4	8	6	19
Oberlin..........	3	8	9	14
Ohio Wesleyan ...	3	9	5	16
Denison	2	10	10	14
Kenyon	1	11	4	20

INDIANA COLLEGIATE

	W	L	W	L
Butler...........	8	4	14	12
Evansville	8	4	14	12
Valpariaso.......	8	4	17	11
Ind. Central	7	5	15	8
St. Joseph's	7	5	14	11
DePauw	3	9	8	18
Wabash	1	11	7	16

BIG EIGHT

	W	L	W	L
Kansas State	12	2	23	5
Missouri	9	5	21	6
Colorado	9	5	13	13
Oklahoma	8	6	18	8
Iowa State.......	7	7	16	10
Nebraska	4	10	8	17
Kansas..........	4	10	8	18
Oklahoma State .	3	11	7	19

MISSOURI VALLEY

	W	L	W	L
Memphis State ..	12	2	24	6
Louisville........	11	3	23	7
St. Louis	10	4	19	7
Tulsa	10	4	18	8
New Mexico St. ..	6	8	12	14
Wichita State....	6	8	10	16
Drake	5	9	14	12
Bradley	4	10	12	14
No. Texas St.	4	10	9	16
West Texas St....	2	12	9	17

SOUTHLAND

	W	L	W	L
SW Louisiana	12	0	24	5
McNeese State ..	8	4	19	7
Louisiana Tech ..	8	4	18	8
UTex, Arlington ..	6	6	11	15
Lamar	4	8	9	15
Arkansas State ..	2	10	7	17
Abilene Christian	2	10	6	20

SOUTHWEST

	W	L	W	L
Texas Tech.	12	2	19	8
Texas A.&M	9	5	17	9
Arkansas........	9	5	16	10
Baylor	7	7	14	11
Texas	7	7	13	12
SMU	7	7	10	15
Rice	2	12	7	19
Texas Christian ..	2	12	4	21

SOUTHWESTERN

	W	L	W	L
Alcorn A&M	10	2	24	5
Prairie View	9	3	19	8
Jackson State ...	8	4	21	7
Southern Univ. ..	5	7	8	12
Texas Southern .	4	8	14	11
Grambling	4	8	6	18
Miss. Valley	2	10	10	14

WESTERN ATHLETIC

	W	L	W	L
Arizona State ...	10	4	19	9
New Mexico	9	5	21	6
Brigham Young ..	9	5	19	7
Arizona	9	5	16	10
UTex, El Paso....	6	8	16	10
Colorado State...	5	9	13	15
Wyoming	4	10	9	17
Utah............	4	10	8	19

BIG SKY

	W	L	W	L
Weber State	13	1	20	7
Idaho State......	10	4	18	8
Montana State...	9	5	17	9
Montana	7	7	13	13
Gonzaga	6	8	14	12
Boise State......	5	9	11	15
Idaho	3	11	7	19
Northern Ariz. ...	3	11	6	20

PACIFIC-8

	W	L	W	L
UCLA	14	0	30	0
Southern Calif. ..	9	5	18	10
Oregon..........	8	6	16	10
Stanford	7	7	14	11
Washington	6	8	16	11
Oregon State	6	8	15	11
California	4	10	11	15
Washington St. ..	2	12	6	20

WEST COAST ATHLETIC

	W	L	W	L
San Francisco ...	12	2	23	5
Santa Clara......	11	3	19	7
Pepperdine......	7	7	14	11
Loyola, Calif.	7	7	10	16
Seattle..........	6	8	13	13
UN Las Vegas....	6	8	13	15
UN Reno	5	9	10	16
St. Mary's	2	12	7	19

PACIFIC COAST ATHLETIC

	W	L	W	L
Long Beach State	10	2	26	3
UC Santa Barbara	8	4	17	9
San Diego State .	7	5	15	11
Pacific..........	6	6	14	12
San Jose State...	6	6	11	14
L.A. State	4	8	11	14
Fresno State	1	11	10	16

FAR WESTERN

	W	L	W	L
Sonoma State ...	10	2	18	9
Chico State......	9	3	18	8
UC Davis	8	4	14	12
Sacramento St...	6	6	15	9
Hayward State...	5	7	7	19
San Fran. St.	3	9	9	17
Humboldt State .	1	11	10	16

Major Basketball Independents

East	W	L
Providence	27	4
Syracuse	24	5
Northeastern	19	7
St. John's	19	7
Fairfield	18	9
Duquesne	16	8
Geo. Washington	17	9
Penn. State	15	8
Manhattan	16	10
Rutgers	15	11
Canisius	13	11
Navy	13	12
Long Island U.	13	12
St. Bonaventure	13	13
Fairleigh Dickinson	13	13
Pittsburgh	12	14
Georgetown	12	14
Army	11	13
Boston College	11	14
Colgate	11	14

	W	L
Villanova	11	14
Fordham	12	16
West Virginia	10	15
Niagara	9	16
Holy Cross	9	17
Seton Hall	8	17
St. Peter's	8	18
St. Francis, Pa.	5	21

South

	W	L
Virginia Tech	22	5
Jacksonville	21	6
South Carolina	22	7
Florida State	18	8
Stetson	15	11
South Alabama	14	11
UNC Charlotte	14	12
Tulane	12	14
Southern Miss.	8	16
Georgia Tech	7	18

	W	L
Samford	5	20

Midwest

	W	L
Marquette	25	4
Marshall	20	7
Northern Ill.	17	8
Cincinnati	17	9
Detroit	16	9
Indiana State	16	10
Notre Dame	18	12
DePaul	14	11
Illinois State	13	12
Dayton	13	13
Southern Illinois	11	15
Cleveland State	9	14
Ball State	9	15
Loyola, Ill.	8	15
Xavier	3	23

Missouri Valley

	W	L
Oral Roberts	21	6

	W	L
Oklahoma City	21	6
Creighton	15	11

Southwest

	W	L
Hardin-Simmons	16	9
Houston	23	4
Trinity	14	11
Corpus Christi	13	12
Pan American	4	22

Rocky Mountain

	W	L
Denver	17	9
Utah State	16	10
Air Force	14	10
Colorado	8	13

Pacific Coast

	W	L
Hawaii	15	11
Portland State	12	12
Portland	9	19

NCAA Individual Statistics, 1972-73

SCORING

	G	FG	FT	Pts.	Avg.
Averitt, Pepperdine	25	352	144	848	33.9
Lewis, L.A. State	24	325	139	789	32.9
Dillis, Tulsa	28	363	142	788	30.8
Stewart, Richmond	19	242	90	574	30.2
Williams, Austin Peay	29	360	134	854	29.4
Lamar, SW Louisiana	28	339	130	808	28.9
Edwards, Okla. City	27	332	103	767	28.4
Terry, Arkansas	26	264	207	735	28.3
Williamson, N.M. State	18	202	86	490	27.2
Collins, Illinois St.	25	269	112	650	26.0
Bullington, Ball State	24	237	147	621	25.9
Ingelsby, Villanova	25	257	124	638	25.5
Rich, Oklahoma City	23	246	91	583	25.3
Robinson, Mich. State	24	259	90	608	25.3
Weatherspoon, Illinois	24	247	106	600	25.0
Schaeffer, St. John's	26	265	113	643	24.7
Thompson, N.C. State	27	267	132	666	24.7
Florence, UN Las Vegas	27	257	151	665	24.6
DiGregorio, Providence	31	348	65	761	24.5
Rogers, St. Louis	26	246	146	638	24.5
Charles, Fordham	28	275	129	679	24.3
Harris, Northern Ill.	25	289	25	603	24.1
McDermott, St. Fran., NY	24	229	120	578	24.1
Finch, Memphis St.	30	256	209	721	24.0
Hornyak, Ohio State	24	224	128	576	24.0
Norman, Arizona	24	242	92	576	24.0

	G	FG	FGA	Pct.
Minniefield, New Mexico	27	156	260	.600
Shumate, Notre Dame	30	257	434	.592
Steward, Jacksonville	27	162	274	.591
Calvert, Ab. Christian	26	211	359	.588
McMillen, Maryland	29	250	427	.585

FREE THROW PERCENTAGE
(Minimum 80 FT)

	G	FT	FTA	Pct.
Smith, Dayton	26	111	122	.910
Jellison, Northeastern	26	122	136	.897
Palubinskas, LSU	24	137	153	.895
Johnson, Denver	26	108	121	.893
J. Lee, Syracuse	29	93	105	.886
Ritter, Indiana	28	117	134	.873
Bullington, Ball State	24	147	170	.865
Edwards, Oklahoma City	27	103	120	.858
Floyd, Texas A&M	26	96	112	.857
Kruger, Kansas St.	25	90	105	.857
Eberhard, Missouri	27	125	146	.856
Terry, Arkansas	26	207	242	.855
Knowles, Texas A&M	26	86	101	.851
Somogyi, Rutgers	26	85	100	850

REBOUNDS

	G	No.	Avg.
Washington, American U.	25	511	20.4
Barnes, Providence	30	571	19.0
Padgett, UN Reno	26	462	17.8
Bradley, Northern Illinois	24	426	17.8
Walton, UCLA	30	506	16.9
Kenon, Memphis St.	30	501	16.7
Campion, Manhattan	26	402	15.5
Cash, Bowling Green	26	396	15.2
Baker, UN Las Vegas	28	424	15.1
Perry, Pan American	26	388	14.9
deVries, Illinois State	25	369	14.8
Vaughn, Oral Roberts	27	385	14.3
Bassett, Georgia	26	368	14.2
Terrell, So. Methodist	25	352	14.1

FIELD GOAL PERCENTAGE
(Minimum 140 FG)

	G	FG	FGA	Pct.
Hayes, Lamar	24	146	222	.658
Walton, UCLA	30	277	426	.650
Stewart, Santa Clara	26	186	291	.639
Schaeffer, St. John's	26	265	420	.631
Losch, Tulane	25	151	240	.629
Armstead, Rutgers	25	143	232	.616
Starks, Murray St.	24	162	264	.614
Taylor, Jacksonville	27	191	313	.610
Jones, North Carolina	33	206	343	.601

National Invitation Tournament Champions

NCAA Basketball Champions

NCAA College Division Basketball Champions

1957—Wheaton	1962—Mt. St. Mary's	1966—Kentucky Wesleyan	1970—Philadelphia Textile
1958—South Dakota	1963—South Dakota St.	1967—Winston-Salem	1971—Evansville
1959—Evansville	1964—Evansville	1968—Kentucky Wesleyan	1972—Roanoke
1960—Evansville	1965—Evansville	1969—Kentucky Wesleyan	1973—Kentucky Wesleyan
1961—Wittenberg			

NEA 1973 All-American Team

The following is the 1973 All-American team as selected by the 17 NBA coaches in a poll conducted by Newspaper Enterprise Assn.

Player, College	Pos.	Hgt.	Yr.	Age	Hometown
Bill Walton, UCLA	C	6-11	Jr.	20	La Mesa, Calif.
Ed Ratleff, Long Beach State	G	6-6	Sr.	22	Columbus, Ohio
Doug Collins, Illinois State	G	6-6	Sr.	21	Benton, Ill.
David Thompson, No. Car. St.	F	6-4	So.	18	Shelby, N.C.
Jim Brewer, Minnesota	F	6-9	Sr.	21	Maywood, Ill.

Second Team—Ernie DiGregorio, Providence; Ron Behagen, Minnesota; Mike Green, La. Tech; John Brown, Missouri; Dwight Lamar, SW Louisiana; Tom Henderson, Hawaii.

Honorable Mention—Keith Wilkes, UCLA; Tom Henderson, Hawaii.

Major-College Records

(Restricted to games between four-year colleges.)

CAREER SCORING AVERAGES

Player, Team	Year	Games	FG	FT	Pts.	Avg.
Pete Maravich, LSU	1970	83	1387	893	3667	44.2
Austin Carr, Notre Dame	1971	74	1017	526	2560	34.6
Oscar Robertson, Cincinnati	1960	88	1052	869	2973	33.8
Calvin Murphy, Niagara	1970	77	947	654	2548	33.1
Frank Selvy, Furman	1954	78	922	694	2538	32.5
Rick Mount, Purdue	1970	72	910	503	2323	32.3
Darrell Floyd, Furman	1956	71	868	545	2281	32.1
Nick Werkman, Seton Hall	1964	71	812	649	2273	32.0
Willie Humes, Idaho St.	1971	48	565	380	1510	31.5
Elgin Baylor, Col. Idaho-Seattle	1958	80	956	588	2500	31.3
Dwight Lamar, SW Louisiana	1973	112	1445	603	3493	31.2
Elvin Hayes, Houston	1968	93	1215	454	2884	31.0
Bill Bradley, Princeton	1965	83	856	791	2503	30.2

SEASON AVERAGES

Player, Team	Year	Games	FG	FT	Pts.	Avg.
Pete Maravich, LSU	1970	31	522	337	1381	44.5
Pete Maravich, LSU	1969	26	433	282	1148	44.2
Pete Maravich, LSU	1968	26	432	274	1138	43.8
Frank Selvy, Furman	1954	29	427	355	1209	41.7
Johnny Neumann, Missi	1971	23	366	191	923	40.1
Billy McGill, Utah	1962	26	394	221	1009	38.8
Calvin Murphy, Niagara	1968	24	337	242	916	38.2
Austin Carr, Notre Dame	1970	29	444	218	1106	38.1
Austin Carr, Notre Dame	1971	29	430	241	1101	38.0
Rick Barry, Miami (Fla.)	1965	26	340	293	973	37.4
Elvin Hayes, Houston	1968	33	519	176	1214	36.8
Howard Komives, Bowling Green	1964	23	292	260	844	36.7
Dwight Lamar, SW Louisiana	1972	29	429	196	1054	36.3

SINGLE-GAME SCORING

Player, Team (Opponent)	Year	Pts.	Player, Team (Opponent)	Year	Pts.
Selvy, Furman (Newberry)	1954	100	Floyd, Furman (Morehead St.)	1955	67
Mikvy, Temple (Wilkes)	1951	73	Maravich, LSU (Tulane)	1969	66
Maravich, LSU (Alabama)	1970	69	Handlan, W. & Lee (Furman)	1951	66
Murphy, Niagara (Syracuse)	1969	68	Zawoluk, St. John's (St. Peter's)	1950	65

INDIVIDUAL RECORDS, SEASON

Field Goal Percentage . Alcindor, UCLA, 1967	.667	Rebounds	Dukes, Seton Hall, 1953 ... 734
Martens, Ab. Christian, 1972	.667	Field Goals Attempted . Maravich, LSU, 1970	1168
Free Throw Percentage Boyer, Arkansas, 1962	.933	Free Throws Attempted Selvy, Furman, 1954	444
Rebounds Per Game .. Slack, Marshall, 1955	25.6		

AAU Freestyle Wrestling Championships in 1973

Waukegan, Ill.

105.5 lbs.—Dave Range, Ohio W.C.	**163 lbs.**—Carl Adams, Ames, Iowa.
114.5 lbs.—Dale Kestel, Michigan WC.	**180.5 lbs.**—John Peterson, Wisconsin WC.
125.5 lbs.—Don Behm, E. Lansing, Mich.	**198 lbs.**—Ben Peterson, Wisconsin WC.
136.5 lbs.—Dave Pruzansky, New York AC.	**220 lbs.**—Russ Hellickson, Wisconsin WC.
149.5 lbs.—Lloyd Keaser, U.S. Marine Corps.	**Heavyweight**—Chris Taylor, Iowa.

1973 Amateur Softball Association

Division	National Champion
Men's Fast Pitch	Clearwater Bombers, Clearwater, Fla.
Women's Fast Pitch	Raybestos Brakettes, Stratford, Conn.
Men's Open Slow Pitch	Howard Furniture, Denver, N.C.
Men's Industrial Slow Pitch	Pabst-International, Springfield, Ohio.
Women's Slow Pitch	Sweeny Chevrolet, Cincinnati, Ohio.
16" Slow Pitch	Bobcats, Chicago, Ill.

Chronology of Year's Events

Reported Month by Month in 4 Categories: National, International, General and Disasters—November 1, 1972, to November 1, 1973

November 1972

NATIONAL

Nixon's Cabinet of Managers—Shortly after his landslide reelection **Nov. 7**, President Nixon retreated to Camp David, the Presidential hideaway deep in Maryland's Catoctin Mountains, to map his second-term strategy, aimed at injecting "new vitality" into the government with a shift of Cabinet members and other top-level government officials.

On the eve of the announcement of his first batch of Cabinet changes, Nixon told reporters **Nov. 27** that he was changing "not only the players, but some of the plays" to avoid the pitfalls of second administrations. "The tendency," he said, was to coast, "and usually to coast downhill."

Housing and Urban Development (HUD) Secretary George Romney was the first to have his resignation accepted. The early appointment to the HUD Presidential nomination in 1968, had made public his letter of resignation earlier in the month, when he decried the "failure of the Federal housing programs in the cities" and blamed the American political system.

Nixon also accepted the resignation of Defense Secretary Melvin R. Laird who had early announced his intention to serve only one term. On **Nov. 28**, Nixon moved Welfare Secretary Elliott L. Richardson to Defense. Richardson had been the State Department's top administrator before Nixon shifted him to Health, Education and Welfare (HEW) in 1970. Nixon also shifted Budget Director Caspar W. Weinberger, 55, a skillful cost-shaver, to replace Richardson at HEW and brought into government Roy L. Ash, 54, former president of Litton Industries, to take Weinberger's post.

The President also elevated Treasury Secretary George Shultz, who would retain his post, by designating him head of a new Cabinet-level Council on Economic Policy in the White House.

The appointment of the 3 were seen by capital observers as ushering in "an age of managers" to trim the bureaucracy, especially with Nixon's choice of Richardson and Weinberger to head the two agencies which account for almost half of the federal employee work force, and 60% of the federal budget total. Both, like the President, were on record as believing in fewer functional units, and greater state and local discretion over the use of the Federal "social dollar" funds.

Of the original Nixon Cabinet, only Secretary of State William P. Rogers remained in the same post. Also retaining their posts were Agriculture Secretary Earl G. Butz, Secretary of the Interior Rogers C. B. Morton, and Attorney General Richard Kleindienst.

James T. Lynn, 45, Commerce Under Secretary, was named to succeed Romney at HUD **Dec. 5**. Frederick B. Dent, 50, a South Carolina textile manufacturer, was designated Commerce Secretary **Dec. 6**, succeeding Peter G. Peterson. A California oilman, Claude S. Brinegar, 45, was named to succeed Transportation Secretary John A. Volpe, 64, who was named ambassador to Italy.

Ex-Senator Brewster Convicted— Former Sen. Daniel B. Brewster (D., Md.) was convicted **Nov.**

17 on 3 counts of accepting an unlawful gratuity from Washington lobbyist Cyrus T. Anderson to influence his vote on postal rate legislation. The jury of 12 black women also convicted Anderson of bribery.

2d SALT Round Begins— U.S. and Soviet diplomats opened the second round of the Strategic Arms Limitation Talks (SALT) in Geneva **Nov. 21** in pursuit of further curbs on their nuclear forces.

U.S. Tuna Boats Pay Ecuador— Ecuador seized 19 U.S. tuna ships for fishing within the Latin American country's disputed 200-mile territorial limit in a two-week period ending **Nov. 24**. All were released after paying a fine and taxes, including the last 6, which sailed **Nov. 24** after paying a total of $444,562. In arrangements made with the owners in the disputed seizures, the U.S. government reimburses the owners for all fines paid.

INTERNATIONAL

Chile Strike Ends— A strike against Chile's leftist government, which crippled the country's economy for 26 days, was ended by transport and business leaders **Nov. 5** following a government ultimatum to end the strike or face "severe action."

Australia Hijack Fails— The first hijack of a domestic airliner in Australian history failed **Nov. 15**, when a young man with a rifle was shot and killed in a gun battle with police at an Alice Springs airstrip while trying to escape with a hostage stewardess. A police official posing as a navigator was wounded in the shootout. The shooting occurred while the air pirate, who had hijacked a plane with 40 persons aboard, was transferring to a lighter craft after requesting a parachute to escape to some remote area of Australia.

Dublin Jails IRA Chief— Sean McStioffain, chief of staff of the militant Provisional wing of the Irish Republican Army (IRA), was arrested in Dublin **Nov. 19** and detained under the provisions of the Offenses Against the State Act. The 44-year-old rebel leader was sentenced to 6 months in jail for belonging to an illegal organization **Nov. 25**. He began a fast after his arrest and was removed to a Dublin hospital, where 8 gunmen disguised as priests and doctors failed in an attempt to rescue him **Nov. 26**. The fasting IRA leader was transferred to a military hospital at Curragh **Nov. 27**, as the outlawed rebel group called for widespread protests and nationwide strikes. After riotous demonstrations outside Mater Hospital, where McStioffain had been held, the government canceled all police leaves and placed some 1,000 soldiers on alert for possible riot duty in the republic's capital. Meanwhile, Prime Min. Jack Lynch sought emergency powers to jail suspected IRA terrorists, and end the terror campaign of the outlawed organization.

Brandt Vote Victory— Chancellor Willy Brandt won a solid parliamentary majority for a second term **Nov. 19**, defeating Rainer Barzel's Christian Democrats and making his Social Democrats Germany's biggest party for the first time. Brandt, who rode to victory on his Ostpolitik of reconciliation with the Soviet Union and Eastern Europe, increased his coalition's edge in the ruling Bundestag with 272 seats against the opposition's 224, a 48-seat margin compared to only 12 in the 1969 voting. With about 37,400,000 of the country's eligible voters casting ballots, the Social Democrats won 45.9% of the vote and the opposition Christian Democrats-Christian Socialists received 44.8%. The Free Democrats, part of Brandt's coalition, garnered 8.4%. Brandt was inaugurated **Dec. 14** for his second term.

Bengalis Sentence Malik — Dr. A. M. Malik, last governor of East Pakistan, was convicted in Dacca **Nov. 20** of having waged war against Bangladesh. He was sentenced to a lifetime prison term. Malik, who was ^overnor when Dacca fell to Indian troops Dec. 16, 1971, had pleaded not guilty to charges that also accused him of collaborating with the Pakistan army during the civil war. Also on **Nov. 20,** India and Bangladesh jointly announced that they would repatriate some 6,000 members of families of interned Pakistani civilians and prisoners of war held in India, and expressed the hope that Pakistan would reciprocate by releasing the Bengalis interned there since the December war. Pakistan freed the 617 Indian prisoners of war it had captured in the December war on **Nov. 27,** and India, in turn, released 540 Pakistani POWs **Dec. 1.**

Golan Heights Hostilities Resumed — In an escalation of hostilities along the Syrian-Israeli ceasefire line, fighting broke out on a large scale **Nov. 21,** when forces of the two belligerents clashed in an 8-hour air and ground battle in Israeli-occupied Golan Heights. The fighting, the most severe in two years, was in retaliation for Arab commando attacks from Syria on Israeli settlements in the sector.

Finland Recognizes Both Germanys — Finland recognized East and West Germany **Nov. 24,** making it the first Western nation to establish ties with both countries, and to recognize East Germany. On the same day, East Germany was admitted to the United Nations Educational, Scientific and Cultural Organization (UNESCO), and thus achieved permanent observer status in the world organization. Observer status, held by West Germany since 1953, is seen as a step toward full membership in the UN.

New Philippine Constitution — After 17 months of deliberation, the Philippines constitutional convention **Nov. 29** approved by a vote of 271 to 14 a new constitution adopting parliamentary democracy to replace the American-style constitution signed in 1935. Meanwhile, a nationwide plebiscite was scheduled for **Jan. 15.** Pres. Ferdinand E. Marcos stayed on to head an interim government for an indefinite period.

GENERAL

Lansky Arrested in Miami — Ousted from Israel after a long effort to seek refuge there under the Law of Return, Meyer Lansky, reputed U.S. underworld financier, was arrested upon arrival at Miami airport **Nov. 7,** following a futile 2-day, 2-continent odyssey in search of a country. Finding all doors barred to him, he settled for Miami, the plane's terminal stop, where FBI agents awaited him. A U.S. magistrate released him on $650,000 bond. The 71-year-old mob figure was under indictment by grand juries in New York and Las Vegas, as well as Miami, for gambling and income tax evasion.

Dow-Jones Tops 1,000 — For the first time in its 88-year history, the Dow-Jones industrial index, comprising 30 blue-chip stocks, closed over 1,000 — at 1,003.16, up 6.09 on that day — **Nov. 14.**

Los Angeles Reporter Jailed — William Farr, a Los Angeles investigative reporter, went to jail **Nov. 16** for an indefinite term on a contempt of court charge for refusing to identify the lawyers who had verified information for him during the Charles Manson murder trial. After 26 days of incarceration, Farr **Dec. 22** petitioned the state Court of Appeals to release him, charging that he had been given a more severe sentence than the law allows for such crimes as rape, felony, drunk driving, or attacks on police. Supreme Court Justice William O. Douglas ordered Farr freed **Jan. 11.**

Two Black Students Killed — Two black students were killed by buckshot on the Baton Rouge, La., campus of Southern University **Nov. 16** as state police and sheriff's deputies were clearing demonstrators from the administration building in a day of violence following weeks of unrest stemming from student demands for more say in academic decisions and better housing. Law-enforcement officials claimed they fired only tear gas. Gov. Edwin Edwards, who ordered an investigation, closed the predominantly black campus, charging

---

Kissinger-Tho Secret Vietnam Ceasefire Talks Break Down

October's high hopes for a Vietnam ceasefire and the return of American prisoners by Christmas were dimmed in November with a suspension of the secret Paris peace talks, and shattered in December, when President Nixon recalled his emissary, Henry Kissinger, and resumed bombing of North Vietnam north of the 20th parallel.

Peace seemed assured **Oct. 26,** when Kissinger said that it was "within reach in a matter of weeks, or less," but President Nixon declared in a TV address **Nov. 9** that some "ambiguities" in the draft would have to be "settled before we sign the final agreement." After another 2 weeks of fruitless negotiations, Kissinger held a news conference **Dec. 16** in which he charged that Hanoi had ceased to bargain in "good faith and good will."

He indicated that the differences concerned the rights of Hanoi in the south, asserting that "we cannot accept the proposition that North Vietnam has a right of constant intervention in the south."

Hanoi, on the other hand, put the blame for the breakdown on the U.S., charging that Kissinger had offered 126 amendments to the original accord, "all but a very few touching on substance." The White House denied it had sought the 126 changes.

President Nixon, **Dec. 18,** ordered attacks on the Hanoi-Haiphong heartland "to cope with another enemy buildup" and forestall a possible Communist offensive. The attacks, which leveled wide areas of Hanoi and Haiphong, were costly to the U.S. as well. Acknowledged losses as of **Dec. 29** were put at 27 aircraft lost and 93 airmen missing, killed or captured in less than two weeks; 15 of the downed planes were identified as B-52s, the largest U.S. warplane. Hanoi claimed it downed 76 planes, including 33 of the $8-million B-52s.

Nixon ended the Hanoi-Haiphong area bombing attacks **Dec. 30** with the announcement that peace talks would be resumed **Jan. 8.**

that students had set fire to two buildings and exploded a bomb during the violence. Classes at Southern's branch campus in New Orleans had been suspended since the beginning of the month, when some 150 students seized the administration building, demanding a greater voice in the administration of the university. A state panel investigating the killing declared **Dec. 14** that the students were killed by a single shotgun blast from an area where some 6 sheriff's deputies were stationed.

'Chicago 7' Convictions KOd—The 7th Circuit Court of Appeals **Nov. 21** reversed the convictions of 5 of the "Chicago 7" defendants, who were found guilty of individually crossing state lines to incite riots in the turbulent 1969-1970 trial following the tumultuous 1968 Democratic convention. Ruling that the government could retry the 5—David Dellinger, Rennard (Rennie) Davis, Thomas Hayden, Abbie Hoffman, Jerry Rubin—the court held that their constitutional rights may have been violated at the trial and criticized the "deprecatory and often antagonistic attitude" of Judge Julius J. Hoffman, who presided and had since retired from the bench. Two other defendants had been acquitted.

Berrigan Wins Parole—The Rev. Philip Berrigan, the Josephite order antiwar priest with 3 years left of a 4½-year prison term for destroying draft board records, was granted parole **Nov. 29** by the U.S. Board of Parole. Father Berrigan, whose jail term was not to expire until Sept. 14, 1975, was freed **Dec. 20.** The 49-year-old priest's raids on draft board records had thrust him and his brother, the Rev. Daniel Berrigan, a Jesuit priest, into the vanguard of radical Catholic antiwar activists.

DISASTERS

A Bulgarian airliner crashed into a fog-shrouded Rila mountain **Nov. 4,** killing all 34 persons aboard . . . A Korean bus crashed into a Seoul river **Nov. 6,** killing 17 and injuring 53 others . . . Fire swept a Japanese express train as it stalled in a tunnel near Fukui **Nov. 6,** leaving 28 dead, 179 missing and 542 injured . . . A gas explosion in a Belgian coal mine near Charleroi **Nov. 7** killed 6 miners, injured 3 . . . At least 10 died **Nov. 7,** when a freighter rammed into the mile-long Sidney Lanier drawbridge in Georgia, tossing at least 10 cars and trucks into the Brunswick River amid tons of shattered concrete and twisted steel girders . . . Storms bursting out of the southern Rockies **Nov. 13** battered the western shores of Lake Erie and New England in 3 days which left at least 24 dead **Nov. 16** . . . Wind storms lashed northern Europe **Nov. 13,** leaving 25 dead in the trail of destruction and floods . . . The Merlin, a Greek troopship, sank within minutes with a loss of 46 lives **Nov. 15** after a collision with a giant tanker off the port of Piraeus . . . Four on a pickup truck were killed **Nov. 17** in a collision with a school bus at a southeastern North Dakota intersection, which also left 35 injured, including 16 hospitalized children . . . At least 100 perished **Nov. 19,** when a jetty collapsed in Calabar, Nigeria . . . A gas explosion in a Claxton, Ga., poultry processing plant **Nov. 23** killed two, hurt 5 . . . Giant waves took a toll of 6 lives on West Coast beaches **Nov. 27** . . . A Japan Air Lines jet crashed in flames and exploded two minutes after taking off from Moscow's Sheremetyevo airport on a trans-Siberian flight to Tokyo **Nov. 28,** killing 58 of the 76 aboard . . . Four leaped to their deaths when fire trapped scores in a private club atop a 16-story New Orleans building **Nov. 29** . . . Fire claimed the lives of 9 in an Atlanta home for the aged **Nov. 30** . . . An explosion in a Rome apartment building **Nov. 30** destroyed 3 floors, killing at least 15 and hurting 65.

December—1972

NATIONAL

Strauss Succeeds Westwood—Jean Westwood, a leader of Sen. George S. McGovern's unsuccessful Presidential campaign, narrowly survived a 105-100 vote to oust her as chairman of the Democratic National Committee **Dec. 9** and then resigned. The blond housewife, who rose from the relative obscurity of Utah national committeewoman to become the first woman to head a major American political party, stepped down gamely smiling to a standing ovation from the committee. Robert Strauss, 55, a wealthy Dallas lawyer and former treasurer of the committee, was propelled into the top Democratic post with strong labor and Southern support. Strauss was credited by party members with putting the committee on a pay-as-you-go basis after taking over its nearly bankrupt treasury in 1968. Strauss pledged to continue the party's reform movement in his acceptance speech, stressing that "I am owned by no group."

Bush Named Dole Successor—Following a meeting with President Nixon **Dec. 11,** Kansas Sen. Robert J. Dole announced that he was resigning as Republican national chairman, and would be replaced by United Nations Ambassador George Bush. In a formal announcement, President Nixon **Dec. 16** confirmed the designation of John A. Scali, a former diplomatic reporter, and a foreign consultant to the White House since April 1971, to the UN post. The GOP committee elected Bush **Jan. 19.**

Moynihan Envoy to India—The White House announced **Dec. 11** that Daniel Patrick Moynihan, a Democrat and sociologist who returned to the Harvard faculty after serving as White House counselor to President Nixon 1969-70, would succeed Kenneth B. Keating as Ambassador to India.

AEC Chief Goes to CIA—The cloak of Richard Helms as director of the Central Intelligence Agency (CIA) was handed to Atomic Energy Commission Chairman James R. Schlesinger **Dec. 21** in another top level shift by President Nixon. Helms was given a new job as ambassador to Iran. In another ambassadorial change, Deputy Secretary of State John Irwin was named to succeed multimillionaire Arthur Watson of IBM as ambassador to France.

Harry Truman Dies at 88—Harry S. Truman, 33rd President of the United States, who led the nation through many post-World War II crises, died in Independence, Mo., **Dec. 26** at the age of 88. The man who ushered in the atomic age when he approved the dropping of H-bombs on Japan, and made political history in defeating the GOP's Thomas Dewey for the Presidency in 1948, was buried in a simple funeral service typical of the man. He was laid to rest in a green courtyard plot near the windows of his office in the Truman Library to which he had devoted many of his retiring years. Mrs. Bess Truman, 87, to whom he had been married 53 years, led the mourners, with daughter Margaret Truman Daniel, her husband, Clifton, and their 4 sons. The invited mourners included many present and past VIPS, along with long-time lesser known acquaintances and Independence neighbors.

INTERNATIONAL

Dublin Votes IRA Crackdown — Angered as violence spread to the heart of Dublin, the Irish Parliament **Dec. 1** voted for a bill to crush the outlawed Irish Republican Army. Violent bomb explosions had rocked the capital during the night, killing two civilians and wounding scores of others.

Mexicans in Mass Wedding — More than 90,000 Mexican couples were married in free civil ceremonies **Dec. 1**, availing themselves of an offer made to mark the anniversary of Pres. Luis Echeverria's second year in office. Most of the beneficiaries of the free weddings had never had their common law marriages legalized because of poverty or illiteracy. The average $16 fee had been beyond the means of most.

Kashmir Truce Line — Having reached an accord on a Kashmir truce line **Dec. 7**, Indian and Pakistani troops began to withdraw from each other's territory, captured in the December 1971 war, upon completion of the line's demarcation **Dec. 11**.

Israel Smashes Spy Ring — A Syrian spy ring and sabotage network, allegedly including 4 Israeli Jews, was reported broken by Tel Aviv officials **Dec. 7**. Meanwhile, incidents continued to occur along the Lebanese border, where Palestine guerrillas and Lebanese troops clashed in the Arhoub section **Dec. 8** and **9** after the commandos violated the military zone, according to Lebanese officials.

Mrs. Marcos Stabbed — Mrs. Ferdinand E. Marcos, wife of the Philippine president, was stabbed and seriously hurt **Dec. 7** as she was presenting awards for winners of a national beautification contest in Pasay City near Manila. Her assailant, who wielded a long knife, was shot to death by guards. His attack was described by the government as part of a conspiracy against Marcos and his wife. Mrs. Marcos, whose wounds required 75 stitches, was released from the hospital **Dec. 10**.

Woman Heads Bundestag — By a vote of 438-45, the West German Bundestag **Dec. 13** elected Annemarie Renger-Loncarevic president, making her the first woman and first Social Democrat to head Bonn's lower house. The new president was a long-time Social Democrat party worker and made a plea for women's rights in her initial speech before the parliament.

Jordan Convicts Hussein Plotters — Jordan announced **Dec. 14** that 3 men involved in a November plot to overthrow King Hussein had been convicted. On the same day, a Beirut pro-Palestinian newspaper reported that 9 Jordanian officers connected with the plot had been sentenced to death in Amman.

New So. Korean Constitution — South Korean President Park Chung Hee was reelected to a six-year term **Dec. 23** by a National Conference for Unification. Just before the election, a new constitution was promulgated, giving Park power to extend his term indefinitely and to dissolve parliament and curb civil rights. These developments were the culmination of a train of events set in motion by Park to consolidate his power in face of talks on reunification with North Korea.

On **Oct. 17**, Park had dissolved the National Assembly and imposed martial law. On **Nov. 22**, a closely-supervised referendum had returned a 94% vote in favor of the new constitution. New National Assembly elections were scheduled for March, 1973.

Terrorists Free Israelis in Bangkok — Four Arab Black September terrorists freed 6 Israeli hostages held captive for 19 hours inside the Israeli Embassy in Bangkok **Dec. 29** after Thai authorities thwarted their attempt to win the freedom of 36 Palestinians in Israeli jails. After surrendering their weapons and releasing their hostages at the Bangkok airport, they were flown in a Thai plane to Cairo.

GENERAL

Andes Crash Survivors — Two young survivors of a Uruguayan air force plane crash in the Andes Mountains 10 weeks before managed to make their way out of the 18,000-foot-high mountain wilderness **Dec. 22** to get help from Chilean authorities for 14 other survivors who were still alive but weak from injuries and starvation in the snow-covered wreckage of the plane. The plane, which had disappeared into the rugged mountain range Oct. 13, with all 45 aboard presumed dead, was carrying a rugby team from Montevideo to Santiago.

Most Cops Corrupt: N.Y. Prober — In a final report of a two-year investigation of the New York City Police Dept., Whitman Knapp, chairman of the probe, concluded **Dec. 28** that "a sizable majority" of the city's police were involved in some sort of wrongdoing as of October 1971. Knapp alleged that the malfeasance included policemen suspected of hiring out as killers, some in organized crime's pay, some picking pockets of the dead, riding shotgun for dope peddlers and cutting themselves in on the narcotics traffic.

Life Magazine Dies — Life, for 36 years the leading weekly pictorial magazine, ended publication with its **Dec. 29** issue. Life's death was attributed to competition from TV, rising postal rates and dwindling revenue.

Crash Kills Baseball's Clemente — Roberto Clemente, who rose from work in Puerto Rico's sugar cane fields to become one of baseball's great players, died with 4 others **Dec. 31**, when the cargo plane he had chartered for a New Year's Eve mercy flight to earthquake-ravaged Nicaragua plunged into the Atlantic, shortly after takeoff from San Juan. The Pittsburgh Pirates' idol headed a San Juan committee which gathered tons of food and other supplies for the victims of the Managua earthquake. Clemente had set numerous records and played on two championship teams when the Pirates won the 1971 World Series. He had skipped playing winter baseball for the current season to devote his time and money to build a "sports city" for the use of San Juan children.

DISASTERS

Fire swept a packed Seoul theater **Dec. 2**, killing at least 50 and injuring 76, most of them young women and children... All 155 aboard a Spanish charter airliner carrying West German tourists back to Munich from the Canary Islands perished **Dec. 3** when an explosion caused the craft to crash shortly after takeoff from a Santa Cruz de Tenerife airport... Tropical storm Theresa ravaged Mindanao's northern coast, leaving upwards of

169 dead and 4,200 homeless in the Philippines' Misamis Oriental Province **Dec. 6** . . . 43 passengers died when a United Air Lines jet making its descent to Chicago's Midway Airport crashed **Dec. 8** into a crowded neighborhood on Chicago's Southwest side killing 2 residents . . . A Pakistani airliner crashed in the foothills of the Himalayas **Dec. 8** killing all 33 aboard . . . 26 were left dead and 11 injured when a passenger train crashed into a stationary freight train in Sofia, Bulgaria on **Dec. 10** . . . 21 crewmen were reported missing **Dec. 12** when a 3,568-ton freighter sank in the Taiwan Strait . . . 19 crewmen were missing and 5 safe when a cargo ship sank 3 miles off the Puerto Rican coast **Dec. 15** . . . Taking off in heavy fog, a North Central Airlines DC-9 jet crashed **Dec. 20** at Chicago's O'Hare Airport, killing 9 persons . . . A new supermarket collapsed **Dec. 20** in Rio De Janeiro killing at least 23 persons . . . 40 persons were feared dead when a landslide engulfed a cooperative food store **Dec. 21** in a village in Sri Lanka . . . A devastating series of earthquakes **Dec. 22-23** destroyed most of Managua, the capital of Nicaragua; the death toll exceeded 10,000 persons . . . 35 passengers perished when a Norwegian airliner crashed **Dec. 23** west of Oslo . . . An Air France-chartered twin-engine plane crashed off the coast of St. Maarten in the Caribbean **Dec. 24** killing all 12 aboard . . . A Liberian-registered freighter carrying a 30-man Korean crew sank **Dec. 25** in the stormy Gulf of Alaska . . . A truck loaded with cattle collided with a bus carrying a church youth group **Dec. 26** in Fort Sumner, N.M., killing 19 and injuring 16 . . . An Eastern Airlines Tristar on approach to Miami International Airport crashed Dec. 29 in the Florida Everglades killing at least 100 persons.

January—1973

NATIONAL

U.S. Confirms Damage to Hanoi Hospital — Pentagon spokesman Jerry W. Friedheim confirmed, **Jan. 2**, that heavy air raids in December over the Hanoi area of North Vietnam had damaged Bach Mai Hospital and Gia Lam Airport. He described the damage as neither intentional nor massive. The report contradicted the account of a group of 4 private Americans, including Columbia Law Professor Telford Taylor, folk singer Joan Baez, Associate Dean of the Yale Law School Michael Allen and Barry Romo, national coordinator of Vietnam Veterans Against the War, who returned from a two-week stay in Hanoi and reported, **Jan. 1**, that U.S. air raids had caused widespread damage to residential areas and part of an American prisoner camp.

93rd Congress Opens — A pledge by Senate Democratic Leader Mike Mansfield to "bring about complete disinvolvement" from the Vietnam war highlighted the **Jan. 3** opening of the 93rd Congress. House Speaker Carl Albert vowed to demonstrate independence from the Republican administration in the current session. The House Democratic Caucus had met **Jan. 2**, voting 154-75 for a policy declaration barring further funds for U.S. military combat in or over Indochina. On **Jan. 4**, Senate Democrats voted 36-12 in favor of an almost identical resolution.

Da Nang Bombing Error — The U.S. command in South Vietnam admitted, **Jan. 8**, that U.S. fighter-bombers had accidentally dropped bombs on the big allied air base at Da Nang. At least 9 Americans and one Vietnamese were reported wounded.

Nixon Ends Wage-Price Controls — Announcing that the aim of Phase III was to further decrease the inflation rate to 2½%, President Nixon, **Jan. 11**, ended all the mandatory wage and price controls which he had established 17 months previously under the Economic Stabilization Act. In all areas except the food, health and building fields, he called for a new system of "voluntary cooperation." Phase III also abolished the Price Commission and Pay Board.

B-52 Pilot Balks After 175th Mission — Air Force Capt. Michael J. Heck submitted his resignation **Jan. 11** and faced possible court martial over his refusal to fly a combat mission over North Vietnam in December. A veteran of 175 missions, Heck said that the goals of the Vietnam war "do not justify the mass destruction and killing." On **Jan. 19**, another pilot, Air Force Capt. Dwight J. Evans, Jr. was also charged with refusing to fly a combat mission against North Vietnam. Both men were discharged from the Air Force Feb. 01.

All Guilty in Watergate Trial — On **Jan. 11**, the 2d day of the Watergate trial, E. Howard Hunt pleaded guilty to all 6 counts against him in connection with the break-in and bugging of Democratic National headquarters during the '72 Presidential campaign. Hunt's plea of guilty on all counts followed Judge John J. Sirica's refusal of his offer to plead guilty to only 3. Four of the remaining 6 defendants — Bernard L. Barker, Frank A. Sturgis, Eugenio Rolando Martinez and Virgilio R. Gonzalez followed suit **Jan. 15**, pleading guilty to all 7 counts of their indictments. The Watergate trial came to a close **Jan. 30** with the conviction on all counts of the 2 remaining defendants, G. Gordon Liddy and James W. McCord, both former officials in President Nixon's political organization.

Nixon Begins 2d Term — In his 2d inaugural address, **Jan. 21**, President Richard M. Nixon called upon the nation and its allies to show greater self-reliance "as we stand on the threshold of a new era of peace." He told a crowd of 20,000, mostly influential Republicans, that a shift from the old to new policies in affairs abroad and at home would mean a better way to peace and progress. As the official ceremonies proceeded, thousands of dissenters participated in orderly protests against the war.

U.S. Envoy Captive in Haiti — Clinton E. Knox, U.S. Ambassador to Haiti, was seized and held hostage in his residence on **Jan. 22** by two gunmen in an attempt to gain freedom for several Haitian political prisoners. After being held at gunpoint for 20 hours, he was released on **Jan. 23** in exchange for the release of 12 Haitian prisoners and a ransom of $70,000.

High Court Rules Abortions Legal — In a 7-to-2 decision, the U.S. Supreme Court overruled, **Jan. 22**, all state laws that restrict or prohibit a woman's right to an abortion during the first 3 months of pregnancy. The court also ruled that during the next 6 months of pregnancy the state may "regulate the abortion procedure in ways that are reasonably related to maternal health and that during the last 10 weeks any state may prohibit abortions, except where it is necessary to preserve the mother's life. In the forefront of negative reaction to the decision, Cardinal Terence Cooke of New York said he hoped all opponents of abortion would "do all in their power to reverse this injustice."

36th U.S. President Dies—Former President Lyndon Baines Johnson, after a heart attack suffered at his ranch in Johnson City, Texas, died **Jan. 23** at the age of 64 in a plane en route to Brooke Army Medical Center in San Antonio. Former Senate Democratic Majority leader and then Vice President, Johnson came to the Presidency on Nov. 22, 1963 after the tragic death of John F. Kennedy in Dallas. He was elected in his own right in 1964. Broken by dissension over the Vietnam War, he startled the American public on March 31, 1968 with his decision not to seek a second term. The architect of "the Great Society," his domestic achievements fell under the shadow of war when former supporters turned against him, blaming him for the escalation of U.S. presence in Indochina. Remembered as a tireless, tough yet compassionate leader, Lyndon Johnson was buried on **Jan. 25** on the banks of his beloved Pedernales River near Stonewall, Texas.

Draft Ends—Defense Secretary Melvin R. Laird announced the end of the military draft **Jan. 27,** 6 months earlier than expected. The signing of a Vietnam ceasefire agreement in Paris and the fact that the Secretary of the Army saw no need for further inductions were cited as reasons for the decision. Though no one would be drafted, the law remained on the books for standby use in an emergency.

Sen. Stennis Shot in Capital—John C. Stennis, 71-year-old Dem. Senator from Mississippi, was shot **Jan. 30** in an apparent robbery attempt in front of his home in Washington, D.C. The senator underwent more than 6 hours of intensive surgery at Walter Reed Hospital. Washington police arrested 3 men **March 12** in connection with the robbery and shooting. Sen. Stennis was still recuperating at Walter Reed and reported "much improved."

Budget Seeks Safe Spending Level—President Nixon's budget for fiscal year 1974, presented **Jan. 30,** disclosed more than 100 cutbacks or outright terminations of government programs. Nixon cited a tax increase as the only other responsible alternative to the cutbacks which should keep spending at an estimated $268.7 billion and cut the deficit in half to $12.7 billion. An additional innovation was the setting of a "safe" outer limit on spending for fiscal year 1975—$288 billion.

INTERNATIONAL

EEC Gains Three—Great Britain, Ireland and Denmark formally entered into the European Common Market **Jan. 1.** In England, the formal ceremony was held at Westminster Abbey. Tens of thousands of workers took the day off as an informal celebration of the event. However, the general public tone was one of scepticism and fear of higher food costs and the influx of cheap labor.

Cairo Students and Police Clash—Simmering Egyptian unrest burst into the open **Jan. 3** when thousands of riot police using tear gas, bamboo staves and truncheons prevented demonstrating students from marching on downtown Cairo. By midafternoon, the campus of Cairo University was effectively sealed off and classes cancelled for the remaining 9 days of the semester. The clash signalled the breakdown of an understanding in which the government had allowed student political activity, including harsh criticism, as long as it did not extend to open demonstrations.

Rhodesia Closes Zambian Border—Following the killing of 2 policemen near the border, the Rhodesian government closed its 400-mile border with Zambia on **Jan. 9,** giving as a reason Zambia's refusal to heed repeated requests to stop African nationalist guerrillas from using its territory as a base for raids into Rhodesia. On **Jan. 14,** Zambia charged that Rhodesia was provoking tension along the border through the provocation of border incidents. The Rhodesian government took further measures against guerrilla activity **Jan. 19** by publishing new state of emergency regulations calling for the imposition of collective fines on communities that aid African nationalists.

Trudeau Overcomes Opposition—Culminating an 8-day debate on the Government's policy statement at the opening of the Canadian Parliament, Prime Minister Pierre Elliot Trudeau's minority Liberal party on **Jan. 11** defeated a Conservative-backed no-confidence motion with a 148-107 vote. The easy victory was the result of support from the New Democratic and Social Credit parties.

Golda Causes Stir in Paris—Paris riot police **Jan. 13** dispersed scattered groups demonstrating against the presence of Israeli Premier Golda Meir who was attending a 2-day meeting of the Socialist International. She arrived on **Jan. 12** amidst heavy security deemed necessary because of threatening letters sent to the French Socialist party, the host of the meeting. From Paris, Golda Meir traveled to the Vatican for a **Jan. 15** meeting with Pope Paul VI, the first such meeting ever. She described as tense the discussion which covered peace efforts in the Middle East, the status of Jerusalem, Arab terrorism and the Palestinian refugee problem.

Marcos Tightens Rule—Philippine Pres. Ferdinand E. Marcos proclaimed a new constitution **Jan. 17** extending his rule indefinitely. Two decrees issued on the same day extended martial law and suspended an interim assembly which would have served as a legislature under the new constitution. On **Jan. 18,** Marcos, now both president and premier, called upon Filipinos to close ranks and comply with his strict control because "times are too grave and the stakes too high for us to permit the customary concessions to traditional democratic processes."

Heath Begins Phase II—Faced with mounting inflation, British Prime Minister Edward Heath announced **Jan. 17** the most drastic anti-inflation plan since World War II. The plan, Phase II of the anti-inflation drive which began last November with a 90-day wage and price freeze, called for curbs on prices, wages, dividends and rents and established a new pay board and price commission. Heath's about-face—he had long opposed such government controls—had already aroused considerable opposition, including a **Jan. 10** work stoppage by British civil servants over halted wage increases during the 90-day freeze.

West African Rebel Leader Killed—Amilcar Cabral, leader of the anti-colonial independence movement in Portuguese Guinea, was assassinated **Jan. 20** in front of his home in Conakry, Guinea. Head of a force of about 10,000 black men and women, Cabral claimed control of more than half the territory of Portuguese Guinea. He had gained international prominence in Oct. 1972 when he addressed the United Nations as spokesman for all the black independence movements in Africa.

Support From Down Under—Gough Whitlam and Norman E. Kirk, the newly-elected Labor party prime ministers of Australia and New Zealand, announced **Jan. 21** their intention to remain in SEATO despite strong reservations about its military nature. Both nations had recently withdrawn all their troops from Vietnam in protest over President Nixon's bombing over Hanoi and Haiphong. On **Jan. 22,** Whitlam and Kirk hailed the ANZUS mutual security treaty between their countries and the United States as a stabilizing force in Asia and the Pacific, signalling that despite recent tensions they expect to maintain friendly and cooperative relations with the U.S.

GENERAL

Sniping Rampage in New Orleans—On **Jan. 7,** shooting from a Marine helicopter. New Orleans police killed a sniper atop the Downtown Howard Johnson's Motor Lodge. The sniper, later identified as Mark Essex, age 23, from Emporia, Kans., had set fires in the hotel that morning and gone on a sniping rampage. Evidence showed that he had not been alone, but no other body was discovered when police stormed the building on **Jan. 8** At final count, 6 were dead, including 3 policemen, one hotel employee and 2 guests, and 12 others ꞏꞏꞏꞏꞏꞏꞏꞏꞏꞏꞏꞏꞏꞏꞏꞏꞏ. The rifle used was linked, on Jan. 9, to the weapon used to kill a police cadet and wound a patrolman on New Year's Eve, leading to speculation of a conspiracy against New Orleans police.

Teachers Strike—Nearly half of Philadelphia's public schools closed on **Jan. 8** as teachers went on strike for higher pay. Two days later, on **Jan. 10.** Chicago's 650 public schools closed when members of the Chicago Teachers Union also struck with demands for salary increases, smaller classes and a shorter school year. St. Louis teachers joined the strike roll on **Jan. 22** when almost 75% stayed away from classes; their demands called for salary increases, hospitalization insurance and a grievance procedure. On **Jan. 23,** spurred by threats, harassment and property damage by striking teachers, all St. Louis schools were closed. On **Jan. 26,** while St. Louis and Philadelphia teachers were still out, the Chicago Teachers Union and school board negotiators settled on terms to end their 2-week strike. The agreement, which called for a 2.5% wage increase retroactive to **Jan. 1** and a one-month reduction in the school year, will cost the Chicago school system $22 million.

Brennan Halts L.I.R.R. Strike—Peter J. Brennan, Pres. Nixon's nominee for Secretary of Labor, announced on **Jan. 17** a 90-day halt to the 6-week Long Island railroad strike. Along with the cooling-off period, the railroad's 5,000 striking workers were awarded a temporary 6% wage raise retroactive to Jan. 1, 1972. In conjunction with the halt announcement, Metropolitan Transportation Authority Chairman William J. Ronan announced that there would be no fare increase in calendar year 1973. The strike had affected 90,000 commuters and 90,000 other passengers daily

Seven Muslims Die—Seven members of the Hanafi sect of the orthodox Muslims, including 5 children, were killed in their Washington, D.C. headquarters on **Jan. 17.** Four children were drowned and the other 3 victims were shot in the head. Two others were seriously wounded. Basketball star Kareem Abdul-Jabbar, member of the sect, had donated the house for the "use of the community." On **Jan. 22.** Hamaas Abdul Khaalis, leader of the Hanafi sect and father of 3 of the slain children, accused the Black Muslims of the killings. The Hanafi have been feuding with the Black Muslims, calling their leader Elijah Muhammad a "living deceiver" and have urged Black Muslim ministers to desert.

Ceasefire in Vietnam

Persistent peace agreement rumors, which had been circulating since the end of the Henry Kissinger-Le Duc Tho Paris negotiations **Jan. 13,** were confirmed on **Jan. 23** when President Richard M. Nixon announced that Kissinger and Tho had initialled a ceasefire agreement which was to go into effect at 8 a.m., **Jan. 28** Saigon time. President Nixon said in a televised broadcast that the agreement would "end the war and bring peace with honor" in Vietnam and Southeast Asia. He also explained that the agreement called for the release of all American POWs and the withdrawal of the remaining 23,700-man American force in South Vietnam within 60 days. An international force of Canadians, Hungarians and Indonesians and Poles would supervise the truce.

On **Jan. 15,** citing "progress" made in the Paris negotiations, Nixon had suspended bombing, mining, shelling and all other offensive action throughout North Vietnam.

On **Jan. 18,** the U.S. and North Vietnam jointly announced that Henry Kissinger and Le Duc Tho were returning to Paris on **Jan. 23** to complete the text of an agreement to end the war. Pres. Thieu's consistent reservations about the peace accord were reflected on **Jan. 24** when he joined in announcing the Paris accord. He said the agreement was only a ceasefire and not a guarantee of "a stable, long-lasting peace." In contrast, Le Duc Tho called the agreement a "great victory for the Vietnamese people" and "a moment of joy, a joy that is shared."

Jan. 24, Henry Kissinger announced that a truce was also expected in Laos and Cambodia. Commenting on the Paris negotiations, he said the thorniest issue had been the release of prisoners of war. He explained that the agreement stated that there is an entity called South Vietnam and any unification of the north and south would be decided by negotiations, not by military force. He noted that although North Vietnam would not be obliged to remove its troops (estimated at 145,000) from South Vietnam, it was barred from replacing or reinforcing its troops. He also made clear that upon American insistence the demilitarized zone was recognized in the accord to provide against the infiltration of men and equipment from the North. Kissinger also revealed that the U.S. had promised to contribute to the future rehabilitation of the Indochina area. Later in the week, on **Jan. 26,** he assured Congress in closed-door sessions that the Nixon administration would consult with Congress before making any commitment.

In Paris, on **Jan. 27,** in morning ceremonies, the U.S., North Vietnam, South Vietnam and the Viet Cong signed the 4-party "Agreement on Ending the War and Restoring Peace in Vietnam." Due to South Vietnam's unwillingness to recognize the Viet Cong's Provisional Revolutionary Government, all references to it were confined to a 2-party version of the document signed in the afternoon by North Vietnam and the United States.

Corona Guilty—Juan V. Corona, 38-year-old Mexican national accused of brutally killing 25 itinerant farm workers in Yuba City, Calif., was found guilty on all 25 counts on **Jan. 18.** Deadlocked at the outset, the jury, composed of 10 men and two women, deliberated one week before reaching the verdict. Defense attorney Richard E. Hawk immediately filed for a retrial, citing "errors in law and facts."

Brooklyn Store Siege— Following a fierce gun battle with police, in which one policeman was killed and 2 wounded, 4 gunmen, members of a militant Muslim sect, were trapped with 11 hostages in a Brooklyn, N.Y., sporting goods store on **Jan. 19.** Police had surprised the gunmen in an attempted holdup for money and guns. One hostage was released later in the day. On **Jan. 20,** hundreds of heavily armed police cordoned off the store and one hostage was exchanged for a doctor. After 47 hours the siege ended on **Jan. 22,** when the remaining 9 hostages made a daring rooftop escape. The 4 gunmen, who had proclaimed themselves "servants of Allah," surrendered peacefully several hours later.

DISASTERS

Seven Yugoslav gypsies died on **Jan. 1** when their car skidded on a frosty road and plunged into the port of Caen, France... A Boeing 707 landing in a blizzard at Edmonton International Airport in Alberta on **Jan. 2** crashed and burned, killing all 5 passengers... Eight died and 11 were seriously burned on **Jan. 2** when a crowded bus caught fire in Constitucion, Chile... Seven perished and 14 were injured when fire destroyed a Catskills resort in Kerhonkson, N.Y. on **Jan. 6**... Fire ruined a historic hotel in Rutland, Vt. on **Jan. 8** leaving 5 missing and feared dead... At least 50 people were killed and 300 injured, **Jan. 10,** when a tornado swept through San Justo, Argentina... Heavy storms, the worst in 25 years, lashed the Iberian shore on **Jan. 17** leaving at least 19 persons dead or missing... A head-on automobile collision on **Jan. 19** in Deming, N. Mex. claimed 9 lives; 3 were injured... A charter airliner carrying Moslem pilgrims home from Mecca crashed and burned in Kano, Nigeria, **Jan. 22,** leaving a final toll of 176 lives... Six tornados swept through central Florida, **Jan. 28,** injuring 18 persons and damaging homes and apartment houses... Ten elderly residents of a rest home in Pleasantville, N.J. died **Jan. 29** when fire, believed to be arson, destroyed the home... Eleven persons were killed and 25 injured on **Jan. 29** when a bus plunged 90 feet into a ravine in Cordoba, Argentina... A train and bus collision on **Jan. 30** near Kecskemet in Eastern Hungary claimed 24 lives; 20 were seriously injured... A brief, violent earthquake on **Jan. 30** in Mexico City killed at least 10 persons and injured at least 100.

February

NATIONAL

Nixon Firm on Spending Cuts— In the first of a series of State of the Union Messages sent to Congress, Pres. Richard M. Nixon underlined, **Feb. 2,** his intention to hold down on spending. "The time has come," the President said, "for responsible leaders of both political parties to take a stand against overgrown government and for the American taxpayer." Although he spoke of working for a constructive relationship with Congress, he indicated that he would continue to reshape the government along conservative lines under a powerful presidency. The major theme, also dominant in his inaugural speech and the Budget Message, was the disengagement of the Federal government from its many involvements in concert with the return of authority to local governments.

Watergate Still Open Issue—Judge John J. Sirica, chief judge in the Watergate trial, charged **Feb. 3** that the proceeding had failed to get to the bottom of the case and that the government should resume its investigation. In further developments, **Feb. 6,** government sources revealed that at least one White House official, Gordon C. Strachan, former staff assistant to H R Haldeman, had served as initial contact as early as February 1972, between G. Gordon Liddy's intelligence operations and Donald H. Segretti's alleged political espionage and sabotage campaign. On **Feb. 7,** former White House aide Dwight L. Chapin revealed to the FBI that he had given instructions to President Nixon's personal attorney Herbert W. Kalmbach to pay Segretti for his activities against the Democrats. Kalmbach confirmed Chapin's statement. The same day, the Senate voted to form a 7-member panel to further investigate the Watergate affair. Sen. Sam J. Ervin was named to head the special panel **Feb. 8.**

POW Release Begins—Operation Homecoming went into motion **Feb. 12** with the release of the first 142 American prisoners of war. Three medical evacuation planes flew to Hanoi's Gia Lam airport to pick up the 116 men to be released in the north. After a brief turnover ceremony, they were flown to Clark Air Base in the Philippines for preliminary debriefing and medical care. The scheduled release of 27 POWs in South Vietnam was delayed for more than 12 hours due to a dispute between American and Viet Cong officers over whether the Americans could be freed before the Communists received their first planeload of prisoners from the South Vietnamese. When all 142 had arrived, **Feb. 13,** at Clark, they looked in better condition than had been expected and were pronounced to be in "reasonably good" health. The first to step on American territory, Navy Capt. Jeremiah A. Denton, a prisoner for 8 years, said, "We are honored to have the opportunity to serve our country under difficult circumstances. We are profoundly grateful to our Commander in Chief and to our nation for this day. God bless America." Beginning **Feb. 14,** the first group of 20 POWs arrived on the U.S. mainland at Travis Air Force Base in California. After a subdued welcome in keeping with the low-key tone of Operation Homecoming, they were dispersed to hospitals near their homes across the country.

Operation Homecoming ran into a snag on **Feb. 27** when North Vietnamese officials announced that there would be no further release of American prisoners of war until the U.S. began to work to correctly implement the Paris accord. They accused the U.S. of "encouraging" the Saigon Government to create obstacles for the Four-Party Joint Military Commission and claimed Saigon had conducted 20,000 military operations since the beginning of the cease-fire. The Nixon Administration accused Hanoi of violating the Paris accord by delaying the prisoner exchange. Presidential Press Secretary Ron Ziegler decried the linking of prisoner exchanges with anything but the rate of troop withdrawal. On **Feb. 28,** after a day of intensive diplomatic activity in Paris, the White House announced that it had received assurances from Hanoi that they would release all prisoners within the prescribed 60-day period. On **March 1,** 12 foreign ministers, members of the international conference on Vietnam, signed an agreement which outlined means for calling the conference back into session if the cease-fire were to break down. It was also disclosed that the Communists had released a list of 106 Americans and 2 Thais to be released March 3.

U.S., Hanoi to Set Up Joint Commission—The United States and North Vietnam agreed, **Feb. 15,** to establish a Joint Economic Commission to administer American reconstruction aid to North Vietnam. Following on the heels of 4 days of talks in Hanoi between Henry Kissinger and North Vietnamese Premier Pham Van Dong, the joint communique expressed the hope "that this visit will mark the beginning of new bilateral relations" between the 2 countries. White House Press Secretary Ron Ziegler said the amount of aid would be discussed in joint commission and contingent upon consultation with and approval by Congress. Private preliminary talks between U.S. and North Vietnamese representatives were held in Paris March 15-19. On April 5, the Senate approved, 88-3, an amendment forbidding any aid to North Vietnam without prior and specific approval by Congress, signalling to Pres. Nixon that such a request could meet with defeat in the Senate.

U.S., Cuba Sign Anti-Hijack Pact—Secretary of State William P. Rogers and Cuban Foreign Minister Raul Roa signed, **Feb. 15,** a 5-year "memorandum of understanding" to curb hijacking of aircraft and ships between their 2 countries. Both nations agreed to either try hijackers for the offense or extradite them. Under carefully defined terms, both nations may provide asylum to hijackers, but must punish anyone who used one country as a base to launch attacks against the other. U.S. officials stated that the agreement did not foreshadow any improvement in relations between the United States and Cuba.

Nixon Names Gray to Head FBI—Pres. Nixon, **Feb. 17,** named L. Patrick Gray 3rd to succeed J. Edgar Hoover as director of the Federal Bureau of Investigation. Gray had been acting director since Hoover's death in May, 1972. The nomination was expected to touch off a confrontation between the Senate and the White House. Congressional critics criticized the nomination of Gray, a longtime friend and ally of the President, as "cronyism" in what should be a non-partisan position. On **April 5,** the Senate Judiciary Committee held a surprise session to consider a motion to kill the nomination by indefinite postponement, and Pres. Nixon announced he had "regretfully agreed" to accept Gray's request to withdraw his nomination as FBI director. At the confirmation hearings, Gray's name had been linked to John W. Dean, formerly Pres. Nixon's Counsel, and to the Watergate controversy.

U.S., China to Set Up Liaison Offices—Exactly one year after Pres. Nixon's arrival in Peking, the U.S. and China announced, **Feb. 22,** they would soon set up liaison offices in each other's capitals. Although the offices will not have embassy or mission status, full diplomatic immunity will be respected. Presidential adviser Henry Kissinger, who had recently completed an extensive Asian trip including Peking, said, "Our contacts with the People's Republic of China have moved from hostility to normalization." The joint White House-Peking communique also announced that 2 U.S.

U.S. Announces Second Devaluation in 14 Months

Spurred by more than 10 days of speculative assault against the steadily weakening dollar on foreign exchange markets, Secretary of the Treasury George P. Shultz announced, **Feb. 12,** a 10% devaluation of the U.S. dollar against nearly all the major world currencies. Fourteen months previously, in the Smithsonian Agreement of Dec. 17-18, the U.S. dollar had been devalued 8.57% as part of a general realignment of international currency exchange rates. Simultaneously with the devaluation, the Japanese yen was allowed to float for an indefinite period of time.

A rush from the dollar on foreign exchanges provided the immediate impetus toward devaluation. Since **Feb. 1,** about $6.1 billion had been unloaded in West Germany and about $1 billion in Japan. The decision to devalue came on the heels of consultations by U.S. officials with Japanese and Western European banking officials.

Shultz also said that the U.S. would phase out 3 investment and foreign lending controls dating back to 1963. These controls currently cover buying of foreign stocks and bonds, bank lending to foreigners and direct investment abroad by U.S. corporations.

Although a devaluation must be officially approved by Congress, the new exchange rates went into effect immediately because, according to Shultz, "the proposed change in the par value of the dollar is acceptable" to "our leading trading partners in Europe." In official terms, the devaluation meant a change in the price of gold from $38 to $42.22 per ounce.

Pres. Richard M. Nixon called the devaluation the first step to making American goods competitive in world trade. He said that his aim in forthcoming international trade negotiations would be to "get other nations away from their discriminatory policies."

Most European and Japanese foreign exchanges had been ordered closed **Feb. 11** due to the currency crisis. When they reopened **Feb. 14,** the U.S. dollar sold heavily but did not sink below most of the newly established parities. It was, however, weaker against the major floating currencies: the Japanese yen, the Swiss franc and the British pound.

European reaction was generally favorable with praise for the fast U.S. action in ending the crisis. Japanese reaction, on the other hand, was negative; the floating of the yen touched off fierce debate in the Japanese parliament. The opposition to Premier Kakuei Tanaka demanded his resignation, holding him politically responsible for the abrupt change in the exchange rate.

U.S. Congressional reaction was almost uniformly favorable to the devaluation.

In general terms, it was expected that the devaluation would increase the cost of imported goods for the American consumer and businessman. Simultaneously, American goods should become cheaper in foreign trade and consequently more competitive.

military prisoners in China would be released shortly and that the case of John T. Downey, a CIA man shot down in China in 1952, would be reviewed in the latter half of 1973. Also forthcoming, according to the announcement, were increased cultural and technical exchanges and negotiation of American private claims against the Chinese government and of Chinese assets frozen in the United States. Pres. Nixon announced, **March 15,** that he had selected David K. E. Bruce, the 75-year-old veteran diplomat, to head the Peking office. The office opened officially **May 14** with Bruce's arrival in Peking.

INTERNATIONAL

New Wave of Violence in Belfast—Renewed and intensified violence, marked by increased terrorism by Protestants, spread through Northern Ireland in late January and early February. The worst violence occurred **Feb. 3-4** when 9 died and more than 20 were wounded. Six were killed **Feb. 3** by British soldiers during a night of gun battles after an assassination in Belfast's New Lodge Road Catholic district. **Feb. 4,** gunmen opened fire from a passing car on Roman Catholic soccer players, wounding 3. More violence followed on **Feb. 7** when Protestant terrorists fired on a procession at a Roman Catholic funeral for 3 members of the Provisional wing of the I.R.A. who had been killed over the weekend by British troops. Further violence, gun battles between British soldiers and both Protestant and I.R.A. gunmen coincided with the **Feb. 7** Protestant strike.

Military Asserts Control in Uruguay—Bowing to the demands of rebelling army and air force commands, Uruguayan Pres. Juan Maria Bordaberry, **Jan. 9,** accepted the resignation of his newly appointed Defense Minister Gen. Antonio Francese. The military, in a campaign to eliminate corruption in politics and business after crushing the left-wing Tupamaro guerrilla movement last June, announced Feb. 10 a program of "national reconstruction" to restore internal order and give security to national development. The military-civilian confrontation eased **Feb. 12** with the announcement of an agreement giving virtual control of the government to the military through the establishment of a National Security Council. The generals proclaimed that the constitutional system would be preserved and also promised a general housecleaning of the government.

Student Unrest in Greece—About 100 university students were arrested in Athens, **Feb. 16,** as they clashed with police after a 5-hour student meeting protesting a new law threatening dissident students with the loss of draft deferments. The outbreak culminated 4 weeks of strikes and demonstrations during which 85 student leaders had been ordered to give up their studies and report for military duty. At Athens University, medical students joined Polytechnic and law students **Feb. 17** in a class boycott against Government legislation curbing student agitation. Unrest spread **Feb. 21** when 2,000 students barricaded themselves in the Athens University Law School. The sit-in ended **Feb. 22** when professors promised to take student demands to officials in the army-backed government.

Pétain's Body Stolen—The body of Marshal Henri-Philippe Pétain, the controversial French general who was the World War I hero of Verdun

and head of the World War II French government that collaborated with the German occupiers, was reported stolen, **Feb. 19,** from its tomb on the Ile d'Yeu off the French Atlantic coast. The discovery, coming in the closing weeks of a campaign for France's National Assembly elections, dramatized the still deep divisions in France over whether the body should be reburied at Douaumont near Verdun. However, when the body was discovered near Paris **Feb. 21,** it was returned to the Ile d'Yeu. The robbery was found to be the work of extreme rightists who were seeking to absolve Pétain and all others who had collaborated during the war of the official verdict of treason.

Israelis Shoot Down Libyan Airliner—Israeli fighter planes, **Feb. 21,** shot down a Libyan civilian jetliner which had strayed over Israeli-occupied Egyptian territory in the Sinai Desert on a routine flight from Benghazi, Libya to Cairo. The final death toll in the crash was 108. Israeli officials claimed that they had intercepted the plane as a last resort after the French pilot had ignored instructions to land. Libyan Foreign Minister Mansur Kikhia called the downing a "criminal act." **Feb. 22,** Israeli Defense Minister Moshe Dayan called the event a "tragedy" but placed the blame on the pilot. The same day, Cairo airport produced a tape which indicated that the pilot, having lost his way due to instrument failure, had believed he was over Egyptian territory pursued by Egyptian MIGs and unaware of instructions to land until he was being shot down. On **Feb. 24,** Dayan conceded that Israel had made an "error of judgement" on the nature of the intrusion but emphasized the shared responsibility of the pilot. The following day, Dayan announced that Israel would pay compensation to the families of the victims.

Israeli Raids Into Lebanon—Israeli amphibious and airborne forces attacked 2 Palestinian refugee camps, El Badawi and Nahar el Bard, **Feb. 21,** near Tripoli in Lebanon. Palestinian sources claimed 30 Arabs were killed including 13 civilians; 8 Israelis were reported wounded in counterattacks. Israeli officials explained that the attacks were to forestall a number of planned Palestinian terrorist attacks against Israelis overseas. Israelis stated that in the attacks they had struck one of the largest guerrilla bases, situated at Nahar el Bard, proving that U.N.R.W.A. (United Nations Relief and Works Agency) which administers the refugee camps "is acting as host to a gang of terrorists."

Laotians Reach Cease-fire Accord—Ending 20 years of war, the Laotian Government and Communist-led Pathet Lao announced, **Feb. 21,** they had reached a cease-fire agreement effective noon **Feb. 22** Vientiane time. Signed that day by representatives of both sides, the agreement provided for the immediate cessation of all military activities by all forces, including U.S. and North Vietnamese, in Laos; a new Provisional Coalition Government to be formed within 30 days; a mixed political council to work out the details of future elections and form of government; and removal of all foreign troops within 60 days after the establishment of the government. The government ministry posts would be divided equally between the Pathet Lao and Vientiane Government and also would include 2 intellectuals acceptable to both sides who "advocate peace, independence, neutrality and democracy." General nationwide elections would be held after the details of the political agreement were worked out. Both sides would hold their present territories until the establishment of the permanent government. Supervision of the truce would be maintained by the International Control Commission, established by the 1962 Geneva Accords on Laos, until a new supervisory system comprised of Pathet Lao and Vientiane representatives could be worked out. The agreement also provided for the repatriation, within 60 days, of all persons captured during the war. The United States reacted immediately to the announcement on **Feb. 22** with a call on the Pathet Lao to release American prisoners of war. Sec. of State William Rogers said that the U.S. would stop bombing immediately when the cease-fire went into effect. Within 24 hours after the truce went into effect, on **Feb. 23,** U.S. B-52 bombers made raids on Communists in Laos at the request of the Royal Laotian Army.

The Laotian Government and Pathet Lao met **March 5, 6 and 8** in Vientiane to work out the military and political details of the cease-fire accord. The talks came to an impasse over a dispute centering on the mixed military commission which was to be formed within 30 days to observe the truce.

Lynch Defeated in Irish Elections—After 16 years in power, John Lynch's party, Fianna Fail, bowed to a coalition of Fine Gael, its traditional rival, and Labor parties in the **Feb. 28** Irish elections. The results of the strong voter turnout gave the coalition 73 seats, Fianna Fail 69 and 2 to independents. In a post-election statement on **Mar. 2,** Liam Cosgrave, the new Prime Minister who had campaigned for anti-inflation measures, tax reductions and more housing, said that his administration would give first priority to economic issues.

GENERAL

Major Soviet Exhibit to Come to U.S.—A loan of 41 major paintings from the Soviet Union, including works by Matisse, Cézanne, Picasso and Van Gogh, to be shown at the National Gallery in Washington and the Knoedler Gallery in New York City during April and May, was announced **Feb. 6.** The paintings came from collections at the Hermitage State Museum in Leningrad and the Pushkin Museum in Moscow. The loan, the first of its kind, was negotiated by Dr. Armand Hammer, an oil executive and chairman of the Knoedler Gallery, in discussion with Yekaterina A. Furtseva, the Soviet Minister of Culture, following Pres. Nixon's trip to Moscow in May, 1972.

"French Connection" Agent Indicted—Francis Waters, who was the principal Federal narcotics agent in the "French Connection" case was indicted **Feb. 5** on charges of selling heroin and cocaine. He was accused of funneling the drugs to a former Baltimore-based narcotics official from 1968 on. Waters, who had been working as a bartender on New York's Eastside, resigned from the now defunct Federal Bureau of Narcotics in 1967 at the beginning of a house-cleaning in the organization. Depicted as a dull-witted investigator in the film, "The French Connection," he had sued the film's producers. The case was settled out of court for the sum of $10,000.

Penn Central is Struck—Some 28,000 United Transportation Union workers struck the Penn Central Railroad, **Feb. 8,** affecting 300,000 daily passengers. The strike, coming at the end of a 30-day "cooling-off" period, arose from a dispute over a unilateral management decision to cut the size of train crews. The strike halted all freight and passenger service in 16 states. Late on the same day, Congress adopted a resolution, swiftly passed by both houses, ordering a halt to the strike for at least 90 days. The resolution also called on the Nixon administration to set up, within 45 days, a comprehensive plan to reorganize rail transportation in the Northeastern United States.

Controversial Vase at Met—Italian authorities began investigations **Feb. 19** into the source of the 2,500-year-old vase acquired by The Metropolitan Museum of Art in New York in Nov. 1972, suggesting the possibility that the vase may have been smuggled out of Italy after art bootleggers had dug it out of an Etruscan tomb. Museum officials disclosed, **Feb. 21,** that the vase had been purchased for $1,000,000 through Robert E. Hecht, an expatriate American, from Dikran A. Sarrafian, a Lebanese dealer and collector. Sarrafian claimed that he had received the vase, which has been described as "the finest Greek vase there is," from his father who purchased it in 1920. In support of Italian authorities' allegations that Hecht had actually bought the vase from grave robbers, Armando Cenere, an Italian farmhand, said, **Feb. 21,** he had been present when the pieces were dug up from an Etruscan tomb in Nov. 1971 in Santangelo about 25 miles from Rome. Museum officials discounted Cenere's testimony and maintained that they had not violated any American laws in the purchase of the vase. Hecht asserted, **Feb. 27,** that the vase was not stolen property.

Former Illinois Governor Convicted—Former Illinois Gov. Otto Kerner was found guilty, **Feb. 19,** of 17 counts of conspiracy, accepting a bribe, income tax evasion, mail fraud and perjury, in connection with the purchase and sale of race track stock during his term as governor. Theodore J. Isaacs, Kerner's friend and former state revenue director, was also found guilty on all counts except perjury. Kerner is currently judge of the U.S. Court of Appeals for the Seventh Circuit. Facing up to 83 years in prison and fines up to $93,000, Kerner was sentenced, April 19, to 3 years in Federal prison and fined $50,000. Isaacs, who faced 73 years and a $73,000 fine, received the same sentence.

Seige at Wounded Knee—Following weeks of clashes between whites, local officials and supporters of the militant American Indian Movement (AIM), some 200 to 300 members of the movement **Feb. 27,** seized the trading post and church at historic Wounded Knee on the Oglala Sioux Reservation in South Dakota, taking 11 persons hostage. The insurgents demanded that the U.S. Senate Foreign Relations Committee hold hearings on treaties made with Indians, and that the Senate start a "full-scale investigation" of Government treatment of Indians. The Indians also demanded that an inquiry be begun into "all Sioux reservations in South Dakota." Federal marshals, FBI agents and Bureau of Indian Affairs police surrounded the occupied hamlet, bringing in 2 armored personnel carriers. South Dakota Senators George McGovern and James G. Abourezk, after negotiations with the Indians, announced, **Mar. 1,** that although the 11 hostages were free to leave, they had decided to stay because their homes were in the hamlet. After several days of hostilities, gunfire exchanges and fruitless government ultimatums, **Mar. 7,** Federal officials and militant Indians reached a cease-fire agreement. On **Mar. 10,** Federal guard points and armored personnel carriers were pulled back. However, under renewed hostilities, including the shooting of an FBI agent and a militant Indian on **Mar. 11,** the ceasefire collapsed and roadblocks by Federal officials were re-established on **Mar. 12.** Two tense weeks of negotiations culminated in an agreement signed **April 5** by Indian negotiators and Government officials. The agreement called for an **April 7** meeting in Washington between representatives of the Oglala Sioux tribe led by Russell Means and Presidential Assistant Leonard Garment for preliminary talks aimed at setting up a Presidential Commission to study Sioux treaty rights. The Indian insurgents were to put down their arms upon notification that the meeting had begun. However, amid accusations of lack of faith on both sides and resistance from Indian occupiers, the agreement fell apart. Renewed tension led to an impasse in negotiations. Finally on **May 5,** both sides signed an agreement stipulating removal of Government armored personnel carriers and concurrent surrender of weapons by the insurgent Indians, followed by evacuation of the hamlet, on **May 8.** The agreement also stipulated a meeting between at least 5 White House representatives and Oglala Sioux leaders on the reservation in the 3rd week of May to discuss Indian charges.

DISASTERS

Thirty-six died and 30 were injured, **Feb. 2,** when a train crashed at Medjez-Sfa in the western part of Algeria...An explosion and fire **Feb. 3** in a small restaurant and hardware store in Eagle Grove, Iowa left 12 dead and one missing...An overcrowded school bus turned over in Mexico City, **Feb. 4,** killing 18 and injuring 49 others...A Paris school fire allegedly set by a pupil took the lives of 21, most of them children, on **Feb. 6**...Two separate bus accidents **Feb. 6** in Seoul, Korea claimed 11 lives and injured 75...An avalanche swept away the small town of Casabamba in the Peruvian Andes taking the lives of at least 15 persons on **Feb. 6**...An underground explosion in the West Drienfontein Mine near Johannesburg, South Africa, reported **Feb. 7,** claimed at least 26 lives... At least 15 inhabitants of an apartment house in Alameda, Calif. died when a Navy fighter bomber crashed into the building on **Feb. 7**...An explosion, **Feb. 10,** in the world's largest liquified gas storage tank on Staten Island, N.Y., collapsed the structure, killing 40 workers...A passenger train jumped the tracks near Megara, Greece on **Feb. 16,** killing 10 and injuring 17...A car and train collision on Illinois Route 67 **Feb. 16** took the lives of 5 teenagers... A Soviet airliner burst into flames **Feb. 19** as it attempted to land at Prague International Airport, killing 66 passengers...A gas explosion leveled a 3-story apartment building at Coopersburg, Pa., **Feb. 21;** 5 were killed, 22 injured...200 were feared dead when a crowded ferry collided with a Japanese freighter, **Feb. 22,** in the Rangoon River in Burma...The Indian state of Andhra Pradesh reported **Feb. 25** that at least 60 persons had died of liquor poisoning in that state.

March

NATIONAL

Administration Reimposes Gas and Oil Controls —The Nixon Administration, **Mar. 6,** reimposed mandatory price controls on the 23 largest oil companies. The surprise move limited average price increases for crude oil, gasoline, heating oil and other refinery products during the first year of Phase III to 1% without government approval. No limit was placed on price increases for a single product, thus making possible a sharp rise in gasoline prices alone as supplies became tighter.

Nixon to Veto New Funds Bills—Presidential Special Assistant on Domestic Affairs John D. Ehrlichman announced, **Mar. 9,** that Pres. Nixon would veto various appropriations bills pending before Congress and that if his veto were overridden, he would impound the funds. Ehrlichman said the bills, ranging from flood control and rural electrification to airport security and veterans' burial benefits, represented a "$9-billion dagger aimed at the heart of the American taxpayer," which, if passed, would require a 9% increase in taxes.

Nixon Asks for Restoration of Death Penalty— Stating firmly that he disagreed with the permissive philosophy that says social injustice breeds crime, President Nixon, **Mar. 10,** asked Congress, in a radio speech, to restore the death penalty for certain Federal crimes and to enact a new program of stringent minimum jail sentences for heroin pushers. He announced he had asked Atty. Gen. Richard Kleindienst to draft a new capital punishment law which would survive review by the Supreme Court. The law would revive the death penalty for assassination, treason, kidnapping, air hijacking and murder of law enforcement officials and prison guards. Signalling a crackdown on drug traffic, Nixon also asked for mandatory life imprisonment with no parole for narcotics sellers convicted of a second drug-related felony. On **Mar. 14,** Nixon sent a 6,000-word statement to Congress asking for a new death penalty, stiffer narcotics laws and laws limiting insanity as a defense in federal criminal cases.

Chinese Release Last 3 Americans Held—At the personal request of President Richard M. Nixon, China, **Mar. 13,** released John T. Downey, a CIA man imprisoned since 1952. His sentence was commuted when the President sent word that Downey's mother was critically ill in New Britain, Conn. Once called the "arch American" criminal by the Chinese, Downey said his 20 years in prison "were to a large extent wasted" and had not benefited anybody. On **Mar. 15,** the Chinese released the last 2 Americans held in China. The released prisoners, Air Force Maj. Philip E. Smith and Lt. Cmdr. Robert J. Flynn, were both shot down in the late 1960's when their missions over North Vietnam strayed into Chinese territory.

McCord Letter to Watergate Trial Judge—As sentences were imposed on the other 6 Watergate conspirators, **Mar. 23,** James W. McCord, a key figure in the conspiracy, said in a letter to the court that he and others had been under "political pressure" to plead guilty and remain silent. He said there were others involved who had escaped indictment and could have been named in the January trial. McCord asked for a private meeting with Chief Judge Sirica to discuss the case. While McCord's sentence was postponed in light of the letter, G. Gordon Liddy received a sentence of not less than 6 years and 8 months and not more than 20 years; 5 defendants were sentenced "provisionally" to maximum terms of 40 years, and E. Howard Hunt's term was fixed at 35 years.

In further Watergate developments, the N.Y. Times reported **Mar. 26,** that McCord had said 2 high administration officials, John W. Dean 3rd and Jeb Stuart Magruder, had previous knowledge of the Watergate plot. In closed Senate hearings on **Mar. 28,** according to Congressional sources,

McCord said that former Attorney General John N. Mitchell also had prior knowledge of the bugging attempt. On **Mar. 29,** McCord testified that his fellow conspirators had given the impression they had cleared the Watergate operation with high Administration officials.

Bombing Continues in Cambodia—White House Press Secretary Ron L. Ziegler stated, **Mar. 27,** that bombing of Cambodia would continue until Communist forces stopped their military operations and agreed to a cease-fire. He stressed that the bombing was proceeding at the request of Cambodian President Lon Nol. On **Mar. 28,** Secretary of Defense Elliot L. Richardson said, without specific constitutional reference, that President Nixon had clear constitutional authority to bomb in Cambodia to clean up the "lingering corner of the war." Senate Democratic leader Mike Mansfield took issue with the statement saying that such authority would end with the **Mar. 29** pullout of troops from Vietnam.

Last Americans Leave Vietnam—Amidst little joy or emotion, the last American troops, **Mar. 29,** left South Vietnam, ending nearly 10 years of American military presence. Hanoi released the last 67 POWs, bringing the total of prisoners released by the Communists to 587. Gen. Frederick C. Weyand, the last American commander, said in a speech at ceremonies at Saigon's Tan Son Nhut air base, "Our mission has been accomplished. I depart with a strong feeling of pride in what we have achieved, and in what our achievement represents." With the departure of the last troops, only 8,500 American civilians remained, most of them technicians helping the South Vietnamese armed forces.

Nixon Announces Meat Price Curbs—As housewives prepared for a week-long meat boycott to begin **Apr. 1,** President Richard M. Nixon announced **Mar. 29** that the government was imposing ceilings on wholesale and retail prices for beef, pork and lamb for an indefinite period. Saying that the struggle against inflation included his budgetary battles with Congress, Nixon urged the public to support his vetoes of spending bills. Treasury Secretary George P. Shultz said that the ceiling would be enforced along the lines of the Phase II wage-price control program, including prominent display of ceiling prices and spot checks and investigation of consumer complaints by the IRS. Criticism of the controls—that they were either too limited to stop inflation or would cause new meat shortages—came **Mar. 30** from Congressional members of both parties and from spokesmen for meatpackers and supermarket owners. In the confusion over what effect the ceilings would have, packers, wholesalers and livestock feeders said they expected Nixon's ceilings would keep prices at current levels and do nothing to bring them down.

INTERNATIONAL

Palestinian Commandos Kill 3 Diplomats in Sudan—Armed with submachine guns and explosives, 8 Palestinian terrorists, members of the Black September group, **Mar. 1,** invaded a reception at the Saudi Arabian embassy in Khartoum, Sudan, and held 6 diplomats hostage, including the guest of honor, George C. Moore, departing counselor of the U.S. Embassy, U.S. Ambassador Cleo A. Noel and Belgian chargé d'affaires Guy Eid. The terrorists demanded the release of Arab prisoners in various countries, among them Sirhan

Sirhan, assassin of Robert F. Kennedy. U.S. President Richard M. Nixon said the U.S. would do everything to get the hostages released but would "not pay blackmail." **Mar. 2,** after the breakdown of negotiations between the gunmen and Sudanese government officials, the Palestinians executed the 2 U.S. envoys and the Belgian chargé. Under heavy siege by Sudanese soldiers, the guerrillas, **Mar. 4,** accepted promises they would not be immediately executed and surrendered, releasing the remaining hostages. Sudanese Pres. Gaafar al-Nimeiry, **Mar. 6,** accused Fawaz Yassin, head of Al Fatah's Khartoum office, of being chief planner of the operation and said the guerrillas would be indicted and tried for murder under Sudanese law.

Monetary Crisis Flares Up Again—Less than 2 weeks after the U.S. devalued its dollar by 10%, a new monetary crisis swept Europe **Mar. 1.** Over $3 billion was absorbed by at least 9 countries in order to maintain the present value of their currencies. All Japanese and Western European banks were ordered closed the following day. On **Mar. 2,** Pres. Richard M. Nixon asserted that there would not be another devaluation of the dollar, declaring that the U.S. would survive the "attack by international speculators." West German Finance Minister Helmut Schmidt, announced, **Mar. 12,** a 3% upward revaluation of the mark and an 11-hour meeting of EEC finance ministers ended in a decision that West Germany, France, the Netherlands, Belgium, Luxembourg and Denmark would jointly float their currencies to defend against the influx of dollars. On **Mar. 16,** the U.S. and the 13 other major trading nations reached an agreement on a loosely formed package of measures designed to ease the problem of excess dollars abroad. When the major foreign exchange markets reopened **Mar. 19** after nearly a 2-week suspension, the dollar was up in Europe and strong in heavy trading in Tokyo.

Bishops Demand Unfrocking of Makarios—Contending that Cypriote President Archbishop Makarios had violated church law by holding public office, 3 bishops of his Greek Orthodox Church ordered him unfrocked, **Mar. 8.** The bishops were supporters of Makarios's political rival Gen. George Grivas, whose underground movement advocates union with Greece at any cost. Makarios, who believes that in view of bitter Turkish opposition to association with Greece, Cyprus must remain independent, called the decision "of no value whatsoever" and ignored the order. On **Mar. 10,** Gen. Grivas gave his support to the bishops. On **Mar. 11,** Makarios received strong support from the military-backed Greek government, the press, political foes of the Greek government and the Greek Orthodox Church. When the bishops announced, **Apr. 13,** that Makarios was officially defrocked, he again called the decision "null and void." The bishops do not have executive power to impose the decision.

Referendum on Northern Ireland—A heavy Protestant vote and a Roman Catholic boycott resulted in a "yes" vote in a **Mar. 8** referendum in Northern Ireland on whether Ulster should remain in the United Kingdom. The shooting of one British soldier, 6 bomb explosions in Belfast and 5 in Londonderry marred the relatively quiet polling. On **Mar. 20,** the long-awaited British White Paper, "Northern Ireland Constitutional Proposals," was announced in London. The program called for an 80-seat assembly which would give fair representation to Northern Ireland's 500,000 Catholics as well as to its 1,000,000 Protestants. The assembly's executive committee, also to include Catholics, would administer departments such as education, housing and health, all areas where the minority maintained there was much discrimination. Disappointing many moderate Catholics, the Provisional Wing of the I.R.A., **Mar. 23,** rejected the proposals and said they would continue their campaign of armed resistence. The majority of the Unionists, the major Protestant party, **Mar. 27,** voted down a motion calling for rejection of the proposals. On **Mar. 30,** dissident Protestant factions opposed to the White Paper broke off from the Unionists, forming the Vanguard Unionist Progressive Party.

Bermuda Governor and Aide Assassinated—Sir Richard Sharples, 56, Governor of Bermuda since Oct. 1972, and his 25-year-old aide, Capt. Hugh Sayers, were shot dead late **Mar. 10** near the Governor's residence in Hamilton. The deaths came 6 months after the unsolved shooting of Bermuda's police commissioner George Duckett. Acting Governor Ian Kinnear declared a state of emergency and on **Mar. 12** increased the right to detain suspects without charge for 4 days. Police ordered all inhabitants of the island to give up their handguns **Mar. 13** and announced that 6 suspects had been detained. Though unidentified, several suspects were said to be members of the Black Beret Cadre, a group similar to the Black Panthers in the U.S.

Peronists Sweep Argentine Elections—In the first Argentine elections since 1965, Dr. Hector J. Càmpora, the hand-picked candidate of ex-President Juan D. Peron, took an early lead **Mar. 11,** falling just short of an outright majority. On **Mar. 12,** Pres. Alejandro Lanusse declared Càmpora the victor, giving Peron's Justicialista Liberation Front (FREJULI) control of both houses of parliament. On **Mar. 13,** Càmpora demanded that Peron, who has been barred from Argentina since his overthrow in 1955, be present at the **May 25** oath-taking ceremonies.

Gaullist Group Wins 5 More Years—The Gaullist-led French Government emerged, **Mar. 11,** from the last round of legislative elections with a clear 5-year mandate. It was expected that the Gaullist group would have an easily workable majority in the new Assembly. A week previously, in the first election round on **Mar. 7,** the French Left had scored heavy gains, but not enough to upset the Government.

Bombing Aimed at Lon Nol Kills 43—Cambodian President Lon Nol declared a state of emergency **Mar. 17** and suspended all civil liberties after a bombing aimed at the Presidential Palace claimed 43 lives. Air Force Captain So Patra, the common law husband of Prince Norodom Sihanouk's daughter, stole a plane for the bombing attempt, which blew up the palace barracks. On **Mar. 18,** Lon Nol ordered a series of stern measures including the suspension of publication of all newspapers and periodicals, except those published by the government. Several members of the royal family were placed under house arrest. Strict measures continued **Mar. 20** with the arrest of about 100 anti-government suspects including newspaper editors, journalists, opposition politicians and student leaders.

GENERAL

Boggs' Widow Wins House Seat—In a special Congressional election, Mrs. Hale Boggs, **Mar. 20,** overwhelmed her Republican opponent to win the seat left vacant by her husband's death and become the first woman ever elected to Congress from Louisiana. Boggs, who disappeared Oct. 15, 1972 in an Alaskan plane crash, had been House majority leader.

Prisoners Revolt in W. Va.—Prisoners in West Virginia Penitentiary in Moundsville, **Mar. 20,** killed one inmate, injured 2 others and took 5 guards hostage. The uprising ended on **Mar. 21,** 24 hours after it began with the release of the 5 hostages and promises from West Virginia Gov. Arch Moore that the greater part of the prisoners' demands would be met. The demands included an investigation into the October slaying of a prison guard and more sharply defined prison rules and regulations.

Yablonski Slayer Convicted—William J. Prater, a former organizer for the United Mine Workers, was convicted, **Mar. 26,** in Erie, Pa., on 3 counts of 1st degree murder in the 1969 slayings of mine union reform leader Joseph Yablonski and Yablonski's wife and daughter. The conviction came after 6½ hours of deliberation and the prosecutor's assertion that "the person who set the chain of events into motion" was W. A. Boyle, former president of the mine workers. Prater was one of 7 persons charged in the case.

H. Rap Brown Convicted—A New York State Supreme Court jury, **Mar. 29,** found H. Rap Brown, formerly leader of the Student Nonviolent Coordinating Committee, and 3 co-defendants guilty of armed robbery and assault with a deadly weapon in an Oct. 16, 1971, holdup of a New York City bar. However, after 3 days of deliberation, the jury deadlocked on the charge of attempted murder of 3 policemen in a running gun battle which followed the holdup. Chief defense counsel William M. Kuntsler called the verdict a "miscarriage of justice." Brown, who faced a maximum sentence of 25 years, was sentenced, **May 9,** to 5 to 15 years, the court taking into account his efforts to help his people. Two co-defendants were sentenced to 5 to 20 years; the 3rd sentence was postponed pending new evidence.

DISASTERS

A partly completed high-rise apartment building collapsed **Mar. 2** in Bailey's Crossroads, Va., when a hoist crane dropped through the top floor, killing 14 and injuring at least 34 . . . 25 persons died when a Soviet-built airliner of Bulgaria's Balkan Airlines crashed on approach to Moscow's Sheremetyevo Airport **Mar. 3** . . . In the midst of an air controllers' strike in France, 2 London-bound Spanish airliners collided **Mar. 5** over Western France; one exploded and crashed, killing all 68 aboard, and the other made a safe emergency landing . . . 14, including 11 members of the Army's Golden Knights parachuting team, perished **Mar. 8** when the plane they were traveling on exploded and crashed near Siler City, N.C. . . . A Greyhound bus collided with a truck in Bakersfield, Tex., **Mar. 7,** killing 7 and injuring 23 . . . A fire, laid to arson, in a Brisbane, Australia night club, **Mar. 8,** took the lives of 15 persons . . . At least 11 died and some 100 were injured when fire destroyed a 5-story hospital in Kitakyushu, Japan, **Mar. 8** . . . A fire in a home at Neufmesnil, France, **Mar. 10,** took the lives of 10 children in a family of 15 . . . 6 persons died and at least 100 were injured when tornados swept through Hubbard, Tex., **Mar. 10** . . . Fire destroyed a tenement in East Chicago, Ill., **Mar. 12,** killing 6 persons . . . A head-on smash of 2 buses in Antofagasta, Chile killed 45 persons **Mar. 12** . . . At least 24 passengers died and 31 were injured **Mar. 16** when a train derailed on a bridge in central Cuba . . . At least 58 coal miners perished in a series of underground explosions **Mar. 18** near Dhanbad, India . . . On approach to Ban Me Thuot Airport in Vietnam's central highlands, an Air Vietnam DC-4 airliner crashed, **Mar. 19,** killing at least 58 . . . A 32-car pile-up near Barrie, Ont., **Mar. 20,** took 11 lives and injured 43 others . . . The Norse Variant, a Norwegian freighter carrying a crew of 30, sank **Mar. 22,** 150 miles off Cape May, N.J.; one seaman was rescued . . . At least 20 were reported dead and thousands homeless **Mar. 26** in floods along the Caratinga River, in central Brazil . . . Another Norwegian freighter, the Anita, carrying a crew of 32, was reported missing off the coast of New Jersey on **Mar. 28.**

April

NATIONAL

Nixon-Thieu Meet in San Clemente— President Richard M. Nixon and South Vietnamese President Nguyen Van Thieu, **Apr. 3,** ended a friendly and cordial 2-day meeting at San Clemente with a promise to Thieu of continuing U.S. economic aid but no specific pledge of American intervention if South Vietnam should be imperiled. The joint-communique expressed "full consensus" and a promise to work "scrupulously" to carry out provisions of the Paris agreement. Nixon agreed in the communique that South Vietnam would need more external economic aid for the remainder of the year, but made clear that future assistance would be dependent on Congressional approval. Aides close to Thieu reported, **Apr. 6,** that he had asked Nixon for an aid commitment of more than $700,000,000 yearly through 1975 with a sharp reduction thereafter.

Nixon vs. Congress on Spending— Both houses of Congress, in separate moves, failed to override Presidential vetoes of politically popular funding bills. On **Apr. 3,** the Senate, in a 60-36 vote, sustained Nixon's veto of a bill to supply vocational aid to the handicapped. The President, who vetoed the bill **Mar. 27,** called it excessively costly and said the bill diverted vocational rehabilitation from the original goals of training the employable. The House, **Apr. 10,** sustained Nixon's **Apr. 5** veto of a bill to finance water and sewer systems in rural America. The 2 Nixon victories seemed to signal that the Democratic Congress, despite its numerical control, would not be willing to stand up to the President in his campaign to trim Federal spending. However, **Apr. 4,** in a move to show awareness of the need for spending restraint the Senate voted, 88-6, to set a $268-billion ceiling on Federal spending in 1974. The Senate simultaneously approved, 70-24, Sen. Sam Ervin's resolution which forbade other Presidential efforts to impound or withhold allocated funds beyond a 60-day period unless the President obtained approval by both houses. Concurrent to the Ervin resolution, the Senate voted that Congress could bar impoundment within 60 days and order the release of funds.

Senate Bars Aid to Hanoi— By a margin of 88-to-3, the Senate voted, **Apr. 5,** to bar any reconstruction aid to North Vietnam unless the President were first to seek specific approval from Congress.

Nixon Sends Haig to Indochina— "Developments" and concern over continued presence of North Vietnamese forces in Cambodia, the level of violence in Cambodia, and continued cease-fire violations in South Vietnam prompted Pres. Nixon, **Apr. 7,** to send Gen. Alexander M. Haig Jr. to Indochina to study the deteriorating military situation. Press Secretary Ron Ziegler promptly asserted that the move did not indicate Nixon was considering deployment of American ground forces in Cambodia. Returning 4 days later, Haig reported, **Apr. 12,** that although still serious, the situation was not critical and did not require an immediate U.S. or South Vietnamese response. Though no details of Haig's report to the President were available, officials conceded that contingency planning was going on in Washington and Saigon in case the situation worsened and that bombing support of the Cambodian Government would continue.

Nixon Sends New Trade Bill to Congress— With the goal of "expanding prosperity, for the United States and our trading partners alike," President Richard M. Nixon, **Apr. 10,** sent Congress a comprehensive trade bill giving him new unlimited Presidential authority, under international agreements, to raise, lower or eliminate tariff duties on imports. A prelude to forthcoming international negotiations, the 124-page "Trade Reform Act" also outlined various techniques to reduce U.S. nontariff barriers in return for similar foreign actions. The President also proposed to make trade agreements with Communist nations subject to Congressional veto and to grant to them lower tariffs on the most-favored nation principle.

Economy Cutback to Affect 274 Bases— Defense Department plans to close or decrease the size of 274 military bases were sent to Congress **Apr. 16.** The economy measure, which would eliminate 26,172 civilian and 16,640 military jobs over the next year, would save the government $400,000,000 annually. According to the plan, nearly 40 major bases, a great number of them in New England, would be closed during the fiscal year beginning **July 1**; the other bases would be reduced in size or consolidated. Defense Secretary Elliot Richardson, **Apr. 17,** defended the move as a "necessary and timely" economy measure in the wake of the Vietnam War and said that further closings or "realignments" in the next years could save the government $3.5 billion over the next decade.

U.S. Bombs in Laos— In the second set of bombing raids since the Laotian cease-fire, U.S. B-52 and F-11 bombers, **Apr. 16-17,** struck North Vietnamese positions at Tha Vieng, on the Southern edge of the Plain of Jars in Laos. The bombing was carried out, according to Pentagon officials, at the request of the Vientiane Government in response to ground assaults in violation of the cease-fire accord. Hanoi protested to the International Vietnam Conference, labeling the raids "grave violations" of the cease-fire.

U.S. To Build New Atlantic Charter— National Security Adviser Henry Kissinger, **Apr. 23,** told the annual meeting of the Associated Press of a U.S. proposal to its Atlantic partners to work out "a new Atlantic Charter setting the goals for the future" by the time the President travels to Europe in the fall. The plan would be "a blueprint that builds on the past without becoming its prisoner; deals with the problems our success has created; creates for the Atlantic nations a new relationship in whose progress Japan can share." Kissinger stressed that, rather than promoting solidarity, Europe's economic success has created U.S.-European friction which could be overcome by a determined commitment on both sides of the Atlantic to find cooperative solutions. High administration officials stated, **Apr. 24,** that Kissinger's speech signalled to West European leaders that Nixon was anxious to sign a major document of agreed principles later in the year. The format would be similar to the "basic principles" established in Moscow in May, 1972. Great Britain and West Germany hailed Kissinger's proposal; an European Economic Community spokesman praised the speech as an indication that the U.S. was lowering its involvement in Vietnam.

Nixon Proposes Tax Changes—Treasury Secretary George P. Shultz, **Apr. 30,** submitted Pres. Nixon's tax reform legislation to the House Ways and Means Committee. Nixon's proposed changes, which will cost the Government $900,000,000 in revenue during the first year of operation, included a new form, the 1040S, longer than the present short form but shorter than the basic 1040 form. The revised and easier form would apply to about 20 million tax payers now using the long form. Also new was a proposed flat miscella-

neous $500 deduction to compensate in part for other deductions—dividend and sick pay exclusion, gasoline taxes—which the new plan eliminates. Medical expense and casualty loss deductions would also be limited. Finding little to satisfy those lobbying for tax reform, House Ways and Means Committee Chairman Wilbur D. Mills called the package inadequate. Missing in the legislation, according to tax reform lobbyists, were concrete changes in provisions dealing with capital gains, depreciation and depletion allowance which currently reduce taxes for those who invest in business or property.

INTERNATIONAL

Left-wing Terrorists Strike in Argentina—Argentine terrorists, **Apr. 2,** kidnaped a U.S. business executive and retired Argentine rear admiral in Buenos Aires. On **Apr. 4,** 2 young terrorists killed an army intelligence officer outside his home in Cordoba. A state of emergency was declared in 5 major cities, **Apr. 30,** after the assassination of the

---

Nixon Assumes Watergate Onus; Top Aides Resign

After weeks of mounting pressure from newspaper editors and publishers, Republican politicians, Cabinet members and senators from both parties, President Richard M. Nixon responded to the Watergate crisis in an address over radio and television, **Apr. 30.** Although he himself had not played a role in the Watergate case, he said, he accepted, as "top man in the organization," full responsibility for those "people whose zeal exceeded their judgment and who may have done wrong in a cause they deeply believed to be right."

On **Apr. 17,** the President had revealed that "major developments" had come to light in the investigation he had launched on his own. He also agreed to permit his aides to testify before the Senate investigating committee under ground rules which would "preserve the separation of powers without suppressing the facts." The President also stated that he would immediately discharge any Government employe indicted in connection with the case. Presidential Press Secretary Ron Ziegler announced that the President's previous statements denying White House staff involvement in the affair were "inoperative."

Earlier on **Apr. 30,** Nixon had accepted the resignations of 3 of his top aides: chief of staff H.R. Haldeman, domestic affairs assistant John D. Ehrlichman and presidential counsel John W. Dean 3rd. Haldeman and Ehrlichman, whom the President called "two of my closest friends and most trusted assistants in the White House," maintained their innocence in their resignation letters but stated that their ability to carry out their duties had been undermined. The President said he had requested and accepted Dean's resignation; Dean was temporarily replaced as counsel by Leonard Garment, a special consultant to the President.

Attorney General Richard G. Kleindienst also handed in his resignation, **Apr. 30,** saying "persons with whom I had close personal and professional associations could be involved in conduct violative of the laws of the United States" and "fair and impartial enforcement of the law requires that a person who has not had such intimate relationships be Attorney General of the United States." On **Apr. 18,** he had withdrawn himself from the Watergate inquiry amid reports that

many of his close associates might be indicted. He was immediately replaced, on **Apr. 30,** by Secretary of Defense Elliot Richardson who was given authorization to appoint a special prosecutor in the Watergate matter if it were deemed necessary. Harvard Law School Professor Archibald Cox was named in that capacity **May 18.**

In the **Apr. 30** address, Nixon told the nation that since March when he had learned that the Watergate affair might be more serious than he had been led to believe, the affair had taken up too much of his time, but that he would now move on to "the large duties of this office." He also told the nation that during his term in office "justice will be pursued fairly, fully and impartially, no matter who is involved" and that, although a series of illegal acts had been committed in the Watergate affair, it was "the system that has brought the facts to light and that will bring those guilty to justice."

In other developments, former Attorney General John N. Mitchell, **Apr. 20,** testifying before a grand jury inquiring into the Watergate affair, admitted that he had heard discussions of the bugging plans during the 1972 campaign, but had never approved them. Prior to this, he had maintained that the entire Watergate affair had been a complete surprise and mystery to him.

It was reported, **Apr. 26,** that Jeb Stuart Magruder, who had served as Deputy Director of The Committee to Re-elect the President, had resigned from his position as Assistant Secretary of Commerce and that he had told Government prosecutors in a secret meeting on **Apr. 14** that Dean and Mitchell had approved of the bugging in advance.

FBI Director designee L. Patrick Gray 3rd, **Apr. 26,** told friends he had burned some papers belonging to E. Howard Hunt after the suggestion was made at a White House meeting attended by Ehrlichman and Dean that the papers "should never see the light of day." Ehrlichman confirmed that the meeting had taken place and that the papers had been turned over to Gray, but maintained that he had not been aware of the contents of the papers. On **Apr. 27,** Gray resigned as acting head of the FBI and was immediately replaced by William D. Ruckelshaus.

former Chief of Staff of the armed forces in Buenos Aires.

Vietnam Truce Helicopters Shot Down—An international peace-keeping mission helicopter was shot down, **Apr. 7,** with a Communist missile in northern Quangtri province, killing 9 aboard. The dead included 4 members of the International Commission for Control and Supervision, 3 crewmen and 2 Vietcong liaison officers. Another helicopter, hit by small arms fire made a safe landing. On **Apr. 8,** Vietcong spokesmen called the incident a "regrettable accident," stating that the helicopters had strayed from the narrow corridor prescribed by the Communists. On **Apr. 9,** the top Canadian military official, Maj. Gen. Duncan A. MacAlpine, rejected the Vietcong statement that the copters had strayed off course; and **Apr. 11** an American source reported that according to survivors from the 2nd copter, the aircraft, flying under direction of a Vietcong navigator, had not strayed from the narrow corridor. A contradicting report from an ICCS team of investigators, **Apr. 12,** verified the aircraft remains were more than 15 miles from the prescribed course. American officials countered, **Apr. 14,** that the two helicopters had been illegally moved to back the Vietcong explanation of the incident.

India Takes Control in Sikkim—At the request of Sikkim's ruler, the Chogyal, Palden Thondup Namgyal, the Indian Government, **Apr. 8,** took administrative control of the protectorate. The request came after 2 weeks of anti-government violence instigated by the opposition Joint Council for Action, calling for political and administrative reforms. The Chogyal and his American born wife, the former Hope Cooke of New York, had gone into seclusion under heavy palace guard on **Apr. 6** as 15,000 protestors approached the capital, Gangtok. The disturbances were set off largely by the National Congress and State Congress parties which had charged that the Chogyal had rigged recent elections to the 18-member State Council in favor of his own party. **Apr. 7,** as some 15-20,000 demonstrators entered the capital, Indian troops took control of the city. The Chogyal emerged from isolation, **Apr. 13,** and announced that he had agreed with the Indian government to yield to most of the opposition demands. He said his party would sit down with the opposition to work out the future administration. On **Apr. 29,** the Chogyal's nephew, a 23-year-old student at Rice University, charged that neo-colonialist elements within the Indian Government had precipitated the crisis. An agreement "mutually satisfactory" to the Chogyal and political party leaders was signed **May 8.** The Indian Government also signed the agreement which provides for a legislative assembly to be elected on the basis of adult franchise.

Phnom Penh Under Siege—As American B-52's continued to bomb the outskirts of Phnom Penh to break the Communist blockade of all major waterways and roadways into the capital, 3 South Vietnamese tankers and 2 convoy ships, **Apr. 8,** brought in the first fuel to reach the city in 2 weeks. On **Apr. 9,** 3 more supply ships broke the Mekong River blockade and the Cambodian Government reopened Rt. 4 leading to Kampong Som on the Gulf of Thailand. On **Apr. 11,** as a convoy of 184 supply trucks reached Phnom Penh, a senior Cambodian official discounted reports that Phnom Penh had been under siege.

Israelis Slay Palestinian Guerrilla Leaders—Following the **Apr. 9** bombing by Arab guerrillas of the apartment building housing the Israeli Ambas-

sador in Nicosia, Cyprus, and subsequent hijacking attempt of an Israeli airliner, Israeli commandos, **Apr. 10,** raided Arab guerrila bases in Beirut and Saida and killed 3 Palestinian guerrilla leaders. Dead in the raids were Mohammed Yussef Najjar, the No. 2 man in the Palestinian Liberation Organization, Kamal Adwan, Al Fatah executive committee member, and Kamal Nasser, official spokesman for the PLO. Lebanese Premier Saeb Salam, a close friend of Najjar, resigned, claiming the Lebanese army had not obeyed his order to attack the Israeli raiders. Palestinian commandos charged that the U.S. had aided and harbored the Israeli raiders; the U.S. denied all charges. Israeli officials justified the raid as a response to "the intensification of terrorist acts in Europe and other places," and in part, though largely coincidental, retaliation against the raids in Cyprus. On **Apr. 14,** several hours after Lebanese papers quoted threats from Palestinian guerrilla leader Yasir Arafat of forthcoming "big vengeance" against U.S. collaboration in the raids, fire swept through the American-owned Trans-Arabian oil facility near Saida, 20 miles south of Beirut. The Lebanese Revolutionary Guard, a previously unknown group, claimed it had struck the blow "against American support for Israel." However, guards at the plant claimed the attackers had appeared to be Palestinians. The United Nations Security Council, **Apr. 21,** condemned (11-0) the Israeli raids in Beirut and "all acts of violence which endanger or take innocent human lives."

Lon Nol's Cabinet Resigns—Cambodian President Lon Nol announced, **Apr. 18,** that his cabinet headed by Premier Hang Thun Hak had resigned and that in the near future a "high political council" to consist of 11 persons would be formed. On **Apr. 24,** apparently reacting to strong U.S. pressure of the previous months, Lon Nol said he would share the leadership with 3 political opponents, In Tam, Gen. Sisowath Sirik Matak and Cheng Heng. The President's brother, Brig. Gen. Lon Non, whose extensive power had been an obstacle to such a proposal, left with his family, **Apr. 30,** for an enforced stay abroad.

Hirohito Visit Barred—Under pressure from the political opposition, Japanese Foreign Minister Masayoshi Ohira announced, **Apr. 24,** that the government had rejected Pres. Richard M. Nixon's invitation to Emperor Hirohito to make a state visit to the U.S., further contibuting to seriously strained U.S.-Japanese relations.

Shake-up in Soviet Politburo—A major reshuffling of the ruling Politburo in the Soviet Union, **Apr. 27,** confirmed the prevailing trend both toward easing tensions with the West and stricter defense and security measures at home. Simultaneously with the changes, the Central Committee of the Communist Party rousingly endorsed Party Chief Leonid Brezhnev's policy of easing East-West relations and particularly his impending visits to Bonn and Washington. In the shake-up, Foreign Minister Andrei A. Gromyko, armed forces leader Andrei A. Grechko and secret police head Yuri A. Andropov were raised to full membership in the Politburo. The fact that all have had foreign policy experience emphasized the importance attached to pursuing negotiations with the West. Two conservatives, Pyotr Y. Shelest, former Ukrainian party head, and Gennadi I. Voronov, former premier of the Russian Republic, were retired early. Both had previously been removed from key positions.

GENERAL

Equity Funding Charged in Multimillion Swindle —Several prestigious auditing firms, state insurance regulatory agencies, bonafide insurance companies and various stock market analysts came under fire, **Apr. 2,** when the Wall Street Journal revealed accusations against the Equity Funding Corp. of America of engaging in a multimillion dollar fraud involving some 56,000 bogus insurance policies, forged bonds and death certificates and $120 million in nonexistent assets. According to the Journal, Equity, a leader in insurance and mutual funds which had handled $6.5 billion in life insurance by the end of 1972, had created a plan to affect the appearance of a profitable organization, thereby inflate its own value and eventually buy a reputable insurance company. Stanley Goldbaum, President of Equity Funding, resigned **Apr. 2.** By order of the U.S. District Court in Los Angeles following hearings with the SEC, state insurance regulators and representatives of the nation's banks, Equity filed a petition for bankruptcy on **Apr. 5.** Equity's stock, which had once been traded at $80, fell rapidly from $25 to $14 as large stock holders including banks and pension funds responded to scandal rumors by unloading large blocks. Responsible for the disclosure was Raymond Dirks, a securities analyst and officer with the Wall St. firm of Delafield Childs, Inc. A call, **Mar. 6,** from Ronald H. Secrist, a former officer of the conglomerate's key subsidiary, Equity Funding Life Insurance Co. had informed Dirks of the fraud.

Harlem 4 Go Free—Facing a 4th trial for a murder and robbery attempt 9 years earlier, the "Harlem 4" pleaded guilty, **Apr. 4,** before the New York Supreme Court in return for suspended sentences. Immediately following the decision, they protested their innocence in the case and explained their plea had been "a pragmatic decision" to avoid the ordeal of another trial. To date, one trial had resulted in a conviction which was later overturned and the 2 others had ended in hung juries. The hotly debated case was unusual in that the major prosecution witnesses were convicted felons and thieves and the other principals were children at the time of the alleged crime. Additionally, the chief prosecution witness, a year ago, claimed that his testimony at all trials had been a lie. He later recanted. In an unusual move, State Supreme Court Justice Jacob Grumet granted relief from disability—loss of right to vote, hold public employment, receive a driver's license —to the 4, saying, "I want them to have every chance."

Major U.S.-Soviet Trade Agreement—Dr. Armand Hammer, chairman of Occidental Petroleum Corp., and Soviet Deputy Foreign Trade Minister Nikolai Komarov, **Apr. 12,** signed a 20-year, multibillion dollar chemical-fertilizer barter arrangement in Moscow. The agreement, the 2nd between Occidental and the Soviet Union, calls for export of American technology and equipment for a new Soviet fertilizer complex, special piping to link the complex to seaports and shipment of American superphosphoric acid in exchange for ammonia, urea and potash. The Soviet exports will be marketed by Occidental. Hammer called the agreement "the break-through in Soviet-American trade" that would "set an example for others in America."

EPA Grants Delays on Auto Exhaust Curbs— Environmental Protection Agency Administrator William D. Ruckelshaus, **Apr. 11,** granted automobile makers until 1976 to meet 1975 standards for reducing automotive emissions of hydrocarbons and carbon monoxide. He also set interim standards to be met in 1975 which will go "half the distance" toward the original standards for all states except California. Given its particular pollution problems, California standards will go 2/3's of the way to original 1975 standards. Ruckelshaus, acting under a court order to reconsider his decision of May 1972, said the year's delay would avoid "potential societal disruption." The delays, according to Ruckelshaus, would have a minimal effect on the campaign against pollution.

Severe Midwest Flooding Takes Heavy Toll— An estimated 35,000 persons were forced to flee from their homes and more than 13,000,000 acres of land were flooded in April in the Mississippi-Missouri River Valley when heavy storms hit the midwest. At least 11 flood-related deaths were reported and damages ran to $500,000,000. The flooding reached its peak when 5 Mississippi counties were flooded by **Apr. 11** and the river reached 50.3 feet, the highest level in 30 years. Losses in cotton crops in the state were estimated at more than $100,000,000 A crest of 43.3 feet, the highest in 100 years, was reached on the Mississippi at St. Louis, **Apr. 25.** Thousands fled their homes as 1,700 National Guardsmen were called to fight the floodwaters in Eastern Missouri. As of **May 4,** 9 states—Kansas, Iowa, Illinois, Missouri, Kentucky, Tennessee, Arkansas, Mississippi, Louisiana—were declared disaster areas by the Federal Government.

DISASTERS

A fire which destroyed their 2-story wood frame home, **Apr. 1,** claimed the lives of a family of 5 in New Market, Va... At least 7 died and 25 were injured when an explosion, **Apr. 1,** demolished a 3-story building in Cincinnati, Ohio... Tornados and heavy storms killed 8 and injured several hundred in Georgia and South Carolina over the **Apr. 1** weekend... At least 10 persons, 4 of them in the Netherlands, died **Apr. 2** when a hurricane swept Western Europe... A dozen persons died and 10 were severely injured when a landslide, **Apr. 3,** crashed into the Peruvian village of Huatun... Nine children died and 34 were injured, **Apr. 8,** when a car collided head-on with a school bus in Lome, Togo... A mother and her 4 children perished, **Apr. 8,** when fire destroyed their home in Preston, Md... A British charter plane, attempting to land in a heavy snowstorm at Basel, Switzerland, crashed, **Apr. 10,** killing 104 persons, most of them British women and children on a one-day visit to Switzerland... A midair collision, **Apr. 12,** between a NASA jet and a Navy antisubmarine plane took the lives of 16 persons near Sunnyvale, Calif... An earthquake shook Costa Rica, **Apr. 14,** killing at least 12 persons... All 6 aboard died **Apr. 16** when a twin-engine 6-seater charter plane crashed in an area of small homes in Brick Township, N.J... A gas explosion, **Apr. 22,** in a low-income apartment house near the Mexican border at El Paso, Tex., took the lives of 7 persons... Two Army helicopters flying simulated missions in war games collided, **Apr. 24,** killing 8 soldiers aboard; 5 others were injured... At least 25 died and 2,000 were homeless, **Apr. 26,** when an avalanche swept southwestern Quito, Ecuador ... The Southern Yemeni Foreign Minister and 24 of his envoys perished, **Apr. 30,** in an air crash 300 miles north of Aden.

May

NATIONAL

Watergate Cover-Up Alleged—Federal investigators reported, **May 1,** they had evidence linking high-ranking White House and re-election committee officials to a carefully-designed cover-up to obstruct investigation of the Watergate break-in. According to investigators, the plot, co-ordinated by John D. Ehrlichman, H. R. Haldeman and John N. Mitchell, had been formulated in secret meetings at the re-election committee headquarters in late June 1972. Jeb Stuart Magruder, John W. Dean and Frederick LaRue were allegedly also involved. Investigators said the basic scheme called for all involved to deny knowledge and for CRP to issue statements to that effect. Also reported as part of the alleged plot were payments to the arrested defendants and promises of executive clemency.

Evidence of Widespread Republican Espionage Cited—The New York Times revealed, **May 2,** that Government investigators had evidence that Republican sabotage and espionage efforts in the 1972 campaign had been more widespread than previously known. According to the investigators, the basic strategy, designed when Nixon was running behind Edmund Muskie in polls early in 1972, was geared to help the weakest candidate win the Democratic nomination.

U.S. Counsel in Mexico Kidnaped—The People's Revolutionary Armed Forces, a left-wing guerrilla group, **May 4,** kidnaped Terrance G. Leonhardy, the U.S. Counsel General in Mexico, near his home in Guadalajara. The kidnapers demanded that 30 prisoners from prisons across Mexico be freed and allowed to fly to Cuba in exchange for Leonhardy's life. The guerrillas, **May 5,** issued a statement accusing the Mexican Government of representing the "rich and privileged" and asserting that nothing had changed in Mexico since the Revolution of 1910. The Mexican Government, **May 5,** announced that they would accede to the demands and, **May 6,** released the 30 prisoners and flew them to Cuba. The kidnapers promised to release Leonhardy when they received official word the prisoners were safe in Cuba, but delayed until **May 7** when Leonhardy was released near his home. Mexican officials announced, **May 8,** that an $80,000 ransom had been paid to the guerrillas; U.S. officials denied endorsement of the ransom.

Indictments in Vesco Case—Former Attorney General John N. Mitchell, former Commerce Secretary Maurice H. Stans, former majority leader in the N. J. Senate Harry L. Sears, and New Jersey financier Robert L. Vesco were indicted, **May 10,** by a special federal grand jury in New York on charges of conspiracy to defraud the U.S. and to obstruct justice in connection with Vesco's secret 1972 $200,000 donation to the Committee to Reelect the President. Mitchell, who headed the campaign until July 1972, and Stans, who was finance

Charges Dismissed in Pentagon Papers Case

Following 2 weeks of explosive revelations in the Pentagon Papers trial, presiding Judge William M. Byrne, **May 11,** dismissed all Government charges of espionage, theft and conspiracy against Daniel Ellsberg and Anthony J. Russo Jr., the defendants in the case. As reason for his dismissal of the case, "with prejudice," Byrne stated: "The conduct of the Government has placed the case in such a posture that it precludes the fair, dispassionate resolution of these issues by a jury."

The decision, coming on the 89th day of the trial, precluded a retrial, but did not vindicate the defendants nor resolve the major constitutional issues in the controversial case.

The first of the crucial revelations leading to dismissal of the case came **Apr. 27** when Judge Byrne released a Justice Department memorandum stating that 2 of the convicted Watergate defendants, E. Howard Hunt and G. Gordon Liddy, had broken into the office of Ellsberg's psychiatrist with the intention of stealing Ellsberg's medical records. The date of the break-in was later revealed to have been either late June or early July 1971, a few weeks after Ellsberg was investigated by the FBI. Byrne asked the Government to supply him with all the facts in its possession concerning the alleged burglary.

A further revelation came **Apr. 30,** when Byrne disclosed he had met with presidential adviser John D. Ehrlichman a month previously in San Clemente and had been offered a high Government post. On **May 2,** he confirmed 2 meetings with Ehrlichman on **Apr. 5** and **7** about the possibility of becoming FBI director. Byrne said that he had maintained at both meetings that he could not consider such a position while the Ellsberg-Russo case was pending.

John D. Ehrlichman, **May 1,** told Federal investigators the psychiatrist's office break-in had resulted indirectly from a secret White House

investigation he had ordered at the President's request to find the full facts on Ellsberg's emotional and moral problems. Ehrlichman maintained he had had no prior knowledge of the break-in.

On **May 4,** Byrne released E. Howard Hunt's grand jury testimony in which Hunt stated that the White House had conceived the plot and supervised and paid for the break-in. Hunt also had testified that the CIA had supplied equipment, including cameras and disguises, for the break-in. Sources close to the Watergate case reported, **May 6,** that Robert E. Cushman, formerly Deputy Director of the CIA, had, at the request of John D. Ehrlichman, authorized use of CIA material in connection with the break-in to Ellsberg's psychiatrist's office.

On **May 10,** in the decisive disclosure, coming one year after Byrne had ordered all wiretap information to be handed over to the court, the Government revealed that a FBI wiretap had monitored some of Ellsberg's telephone conversations from late 1969 through early 1970 and that the records and transcripts based on the wiretaps had disappeared sometime between July and October 1971. Byrne moved immediately to suspend proceedings and asked the Government to produce all logs and records of the wiretaps. He ordered both sides to appear the next day, **May 11,** to argue dismissal of the case, stating the burden was now on the Government to prove the taped conversations were not used to "taint" the case.

On **May 12,** following the dismissal, an informal poll of the jury revealed that 7 of the 12 jurors had been leaning toward acquittal in the case.

On **May 14,** acting FBI Director William D. Ruckelshaus, disclosed that the missing wiretaps had been discovered, **May 11,** in the outer office of former presidential adviser John D. Ehrlichman.

director of the campaign, were also charged with perjury before the grand jury, and faced 50 years in jail and fines up to $75,000. According to the indictment, Vesco, threatened with a civil lawsuit in which the Securities Exchange Commission charged he had looted 4 mutual funds of $224,000,000, agreed to make a contribution to the Nixon campaign in return for which Mitchell would set up a meeting between Sears, who acted as Vesco's spokesman, and SEC Chairman William J. Casey, who later left the SEC to become an undersecretary of State. Stans allegedly agreed to shield the contribution from federal examiners at the SEC and the Government Accounting Office. Allegedly Sears met with Casey and G. Bradford Cook, SEC General Counsel, 2 hours after the donation was delivered to Stans, April 10, 1972. Both Mitchell and Stans said they were not guilty of any wrong-doing in the case. Vesco, who fled the country during the grand jury inquiry, was unavailable for comment.

CIA Claims White House Cover-Up Appeal— A statement summarizing testimony by CIA Deputy Director Gen. Vernon A. Walters, before the Senate Armed Services Committee, **May 15,** quoted him as saying that John W. Dean 3rd had asked the CIA in 1972 to aid in the Watergate cover-up by paying bail and salaries for the men involved. Walters told the committee he would rather have quit than have become involved. He also said he rejected a request by H. R. Haldeman and John D. Ehrlichman to use CIA influence to call off the 1972 FBI inquiry into campaign funds "laundered" in a Mexico City bank. Richard Helms, CIA Director in 1972, said he had considered both requests improper but had not mentioned them to the President. Stuart Symington, **May 21,** quoted from a "memorandum of conversation" written by Walters after a meeting with Haldeman and Ehrlichman 6 days after the break-in, in which Walters said Haldeman told him "It is the President's wish" that the CIA attempt to halt an investigation into the Mexican aspect of the Watergate case.

Nixon Reshuffles His Staff— In a major White House re-organization necessitated by the rash of resignations connected with the Watergate affair, President Richard M. Nixon, **May 10,** announced that former Treasury Secretary John B. Connally would come to the White House as part-time unpaid adviser on domestic and foreign affairs. On **May 4,** he had named Gen. Alexander M. Haig Jr. interim assistant responsible for duties formerly carried out by H. R. Haldeman. J. Fred Buzhardt was appointed White House special counsel for Watergate matters. In further changes, Nixon appointed CIA Director James R. Schlesinger to replace Elliot Richardson as Secretary of Defense and CIA Deputy Director for Operations William E. Colby to become CIA Director. Nixon also indicated that the super-cabinet system set up in January to centralize control of the bureaucracy would be scrapped in favor of traditional contact with regular Cabinet members. Before his appointment as special adviser, Connally, on **May 2,** had announced his decision to join the Republican Party, asserting it more responsive than the Democratic Party to the needs and thoughts of the American people.

Senate Watergate Hearings Open— Hearings by the Senate Select Committee on Presidential Campaign Activities into the Watergate scandal opened in Washington on **May 17.** Chaired by Sam J. Ervin (D.-N.C.) and Howard H. Baker (R.-Tenn.) as vice-chairman, the committee included: Herman E. Talmadge (D.-Ga.), Daniel K. Inouye (D.-Ha.), Joseph M. Montoya (D.-N.M.), Edward J. Gurney (R.-Fla.), and Lowell P. Weicker (R.-Conn.). Samuel Dash and Fred. D. Thompson served as majority and minority counsels, respectively. On the 2d day of hearings, **May 18,** John J. McCord, one of the convicted Watergate conspirators, testified he had been offered executive clemency, financial aid and a job by John J. Caulfield, a former aide to John D. Ehrlichman and John W. Dean, to win his silence in the Watergate case.

Nixon Explains White House Watergate Role— President Richard M. Nixon, **May 22,** released a 4,000-word statement in which he asserted that he had made legitimate efforts to restrict investigation into some matters related to the Watergate affair because they impinged on national security. He admitted that "that there were certain persons who may have gone beyond my directives, and sought to expand my efforts to protect the national security operations in order to cover up any involvement they or certain others might have had in Watergate." He firmly denied any involvement whatsoever, in either the break-in or the subsequent cover-up. The President outlined secret investigations separate from the Watergate case which had been conducted during his term. He acknowledged a "special program of wiretaps," begun in 1969 and lasting through February 1971, to prevent leaks of secret information essential to his foreign policy initiatives. He also said that in 1969, during a period of bombings, explosions and other campus unrest, he had asked FBI Director J. Edgar Hoover to head a committee to prepare a better domestic intelligence operation against such activities. Hoover opposed the resulting plan, which called for resumption of "certain intelligence operations that had been suspended in 1966"—including authorization for surreptitious entry in specified situations relating to national security. The President further stated that his concern over continued foreign policy leaks and the publication of the Pentagon Papers led to the establishment in 1971 of a small intelligence unit, the "plumbers", supervised by John D. Ehrlichman. He said he had told Egil Krogh, one of the "plumbers," to find out all he could about Ellsberg's motives and associates. Pres. Nixon said he never authorized any illegal means to this end.

INTERNATIONAL

Army and Palestinian Commandos Clash in Lebanon— Touched off by the **May 1** kidnaping of 2 Lebanese noncommissioned officers by Palestinian guerrillas, heavy fighting erupted, **May 2,** between the Lebanese Army and Palestinian guerrillas near the Shatila refugee camp and in other areas in Beirut. Reports stated 12 soldiers were killed; 19 people died in the camps. A cease-fire reached the evening of **May 2** broke down, **May 3,** when the fighting, including jet and tank attacks by the Lebanese Army, continued. The 2 noncoms, apparently being held hostage for guerrillas captured by Lebanese security forces, were returned to army headquarters, **May 3,** but the crisis continued. **May 4** brought another cease-fire mediated by officials from Egypt, Iraq and Algeria and reports that the Lebanese Army had intercepted 1,000 guerrillas trying to cross the Lebanese border from Syria. Lebanese Pres. Suleiman Franjieh, **May 5,** told Arab mediators that the Palestinian guerrillas were not "above the official authority" and would not be allowed special privileges to organize attacks against Israel from Lebanon. When heavy fighting erupted again, **May 7,** in Beirut and other parts of Lebanon, the Government declared martial law and a 24-hour curfew. Early **May 8,** Lebanese Premier Amin Hafez and his cabinet resigned. The crisis situation was eased, **May 8,** with the announcement of a 3rd cease-fire. Simultaneously, Syria closed its border with Lebanon, accusing it of complicity in an anti-Palestinian conspiracy of "foreign design."

Bonn Ratifies 2-Germanies Pact—The West German Bundestag ratified, **May 11,** by a 268-217 vote, a treaty establishing formal relations with the German Democratic Republic in East Germany. The parliament also voted, 365-121, that both Germanies should become members of the United Nations. Although the treaty did not accord full recognition to East Germany, it arranged for the exchange of "permanent representatives" and provided for the opening of new border crossing points. In further reconciliation with eastern Europe, Bonn completed negotiations, **May 30,** with Czechoslovakia on a treaty to re establish normal relations, ending 35 years of hostility. The treaty, which was signed in Bonn, **June 21,** by West German Foreign Minister Walter Scheel and Czechoslovak Foreign Minister Bohuslav Chnoupek, stated that both countries "deem the Munich agreement of 29 September 1938 void with regard to their mutual relations."

Brandt, Brezhnev Sign 10-Year Pact—Soviet Communist party leader Leonid I. Brezhnev and West German Chancellor Willy Brandt, meeting in Bonn, **May 19,** signed a 10-year pact for economic, industrial and technical cooperation. The agreement provided for the exchange of raw material, energy, technology, "know-how" and industrial plant, all to be handled by a joint commission. Two other agreements, one providing for cultural and educational exchanges and another covering West German air rights over the Soviet Union for Lufthansa flights to Tokyo, were also signed. Ending 4 days of talks, Brandt and Brezhnev, **May 21,** issued a joint declaration on economic and cultural cooperation. Brezhnev, speaking over German television, called for a "new continent of Europe, a continent of peace, trust and cooperation."

Ford Gives $1 Million to Terrorists—Following the shooting, **May 22,** of 2 executives of a Ford Motor Company subsidiary in Buenos Aires, an unidentified man phoned Ford Argentina demanding $1,000,000 worth of ambulances, to be distributed to each state of Argentina, and direct donations to area hospitals in exchange for an end to attacks on the company and its employees. The Ford Motor Company, **May 23,** announced that it would meet the demands of the terrorists, who were identified as members of the Trotskyite group, the People's Revolutionary Army.

2 Britons Resign in Sex Scandal—In the most sensational resignation of its kind since the Profumo scandal 10 years before, Earl Jellicoe, leader of the House of Lords and holder of the ancient title of Lord of the Privy Seal, resigned, **May 24,** acknowledging he had engaged in "casual affairs" with prostitutes. On **May 22,** Defense Ministry Under Secretary for the Royal Air Force Lord Lambton had also resigned because of his relationship with a prostitute. He was further charged, **May 24,** with the possession of cannabis and amphetamines. Prime Minister Edward Heath went before the House of Commons, **May 24,** to give assurances that no other ministers or

members of government had been involved and that there had been "no breach of security" in either case. As further assurance, Heath said the Security Commission, headed by Lord Justice Diplock, would conduct an inquiry to verify no security leaks had occurred.

Mutiny on Greek Destroyer—Capt. Nicholas Pappas of the Greek naval destroyer Velos and 30 officers and enlisted men, mutinied, **May 25,** off the coast of Italy. The 31 men, said to be protesting against the military-backed Greek Government, requested and received, **May 26,** asylum from the Italian Government. The Greek military leaders claimed Pappas was part of an abortive coup, announced by the Greek Government on **May 24,** by active and retired navy officers. On **May 28,** the Greek Government announced that the 35 officers involved would be tried for the coup attempt. According to Government sources, they had planned to hijack the Greek fleet, occupy some unguarded Aegean islands and, after inviting the Army and Air Force to join them, ask the military Government to surrender. As a result of the mutiny and abortive coup as well as exiled King Constantine's refusal to condemn the action, it was reported by Greek newspapers, **May 29,** that the monarchy would soon be abolished by decree, not by referendum as had been originally reported.

Campora Takes Helm in Argentina—Despite a month of tension and sporadic guerrilla activity, Dr. Hector J. Campora was inaugurated on schedule, **May 25,** as President of Argentina. As hundreds of thousands of Peronists marched and sang to show their approval, Campora proclaimed a moderately leftist and nationalist program, with pledges to respect all constitutional liberties including freedom of the press. At least one person was reported killed and 20 wounded in clashes between security police and anti-military demonstrators. Later in the evening, **May 25,** Campora declared an amnesty for some 500 political prisoners. Tension had mounted in Argentina, **Apr. 30,** when a group of Trotskyite guerrillas, known as the People's Revolutionary Army, had gunned down a retired armed forces chief of staff. A state of emergency went into effect **May 1** as regional military commanders took power in Buenos Aires and the 5 largest provinces. Campora, who had been conferring with Juan D. Peron in Spain, returned **May 2** to meet with military leaders on the crisis. He stated, **May 3,** that he would assume power as scheduled and that thereafter the armed forces would remain "subordinate to the national authorities." After 2 weeks of relative calm, the military leaders, **May 16,** lifted the martial law decree.

Nixon, Pompidou Meet—President Richard M. Nixon met with French President Georges Pompidou in Rejkjavik, Iceland, **May 31-June 1.** Little was resolved in the meetings except to continue high-level talks on major problems. The agreement on further talks was jointly announced, **May 31,** by Henry A. Kissinger and the official French spokesman. Kissinger said he planned to travel to Paris the following week for discussions with the French foreign minister.

GENERAL

Seven Charged in Greek Vase Affair—Italian authorities, **May 7,** charged 7 men with illegal excavation and criminal activities in connection with the controversial sale of the Euphronios vase to the Metropolitan Museum in New York in 1972.

Italian authorities said they had evidence, in the form of fragments from the vase found in 1971 in an Etruscan tomb, which proved almost conclusively that the vase had been dug up in Italy and smuggled out. On **June 26,** Metropolitan Museum President Douglas Dillon maintained that he had not received any evidence contradicting the original assertion that the vase had belonged to Dikran A. Sarrafian, a Lebanese art dealer.

Seale Defeated in Oakland—Backed by a record voter turnout, the 2-term incumbent John Reading, **May 15,** easily defeated Black Panther Leader Bobby Seale in the Oakland, Calif., mayoral race. Reading said he would seek out Seale "very soon to see if we can find common ground on which to work together in solving common problems." Seale said he planned to work on an initiative to bring his "people's plan" before the electorate in 6 months. The plan calls for more jobs, better housing, a reduction in crime and a big cultural center.

17 of Camden 28 Not Guilty—The 17 members of the Camden 28 who had been on trial since the beginning of February, were acquitted, **May 20,** of breaking into the Federal Building in Camden and destroying draft files. The decision hinged on Federal District Court Judge Clarkson S. Fisher's precedent-setting instruction to the jury that it could acquit the defendants if it found that the Government had acted improperly in using an informer to bring about the crime. The defense also asked the jury to ignore the actual charge and use an acquittal to say that the country had enough of the "illegal and immoral" war in Vietnam. The defense said that motions would be filed immediately to dismiss all charges against the remaining defendants.

Los Angeles Elects Black Mayor—By a margin of 100,000 votes, Thomas Bradley, **May 29,** defeated the incumbent, Sam Yorty, to become the first black mayor of Los Angeles. The son of a poor Texas field hand, Bradley, 55, is a 21-year veteran of the Los Angeles police force. His victory came in the wake of a Yorty campaign which appealed to racial fears and divisions in the city of the 1965 Watts riots. Bradley said, **May 30,** that his election proved "that people will listen to a candidate and make their judgment on merit, instead of race or creed."

DISASTERS

Five elderly guests lost their lives, **May 1,** when fire destroyed the 74-year-old Manhattan Hotel in the resort town of Lakewood, N. Y. . . . Coal carts carrying miners to work near Changsong, Korea ran out of control, **May 5,** killing 18 and injuring another 18 . . . At least 250 persons were killed, **May 5,** when 3 river passenger boats collided near Dacca, Bangladesh . . . A 2-car head-on collision, **May 6,** claimed 7 lives on U.S. 321 near Dallas, Tex. . . . A fire, **May 8,** laid to arson, took the lives of 6 in one family in the Brownsville section of Brooklyn, N. Y. . . . a Cessna 402 crashed, **May 12,** near Greenville, Me., taking the lives of 6 . . . 10 bodies were recovered and many more were feared trapped, **May 12,** when a motor launch carrying 300 capsized and sank in the Padma River in Bangladesh . . . The bodies of 6 Army officers and one civilian employee were recovered, **May 16,** in Ft. Knox, Ky., from the wreckage of a "Huey" helicopter . . . At least 12 were drowned when a fishing-party boat sank, **May 19,** near Point Judith, R.I. . . . Winds of over 80 miles an hour swept through Peshawar, Pakistan and adjoining areas,

May 21, killing 20 and injuring over 100 persons . . . A trailer truck-bus collision, **May 22,** near San Luis de la Paz, Mexico, killed 8 and injured 7 . . . A Soviet airliner carrying 40 persons crashed, killing all aboard, in Southern Siberia near the China border, **May 25,** during a gunfight between a would-be hijacker and an armed guard . . . Tornadoes and heavy rain over the weekend of **May 26-27** claimed at least 18 lives and injured scores of others: 6 died, **May 27,** in twisters in Ala.; 5 died in a tornado that struck Keefton, Okla.; 3 in Jonesboro, Ark.; 3 died as a result of a tornado in Kansas; and one in Laurel, Miss. . . . On approach to Palam Airport in New Delhi, an Indian Airlines jet crashed into a residential section, **May 31,** killing 48 of its 65 passengers.

June

NATIONAL

Nixon Announces Appointments—President Richard M. Nixon, **June 6,** named former Defense Secretary Melvin Laird his chief domestic adviser. Laird said he was reluctant to return to a Government position, but would do so because Government "in some quarters is at a standstill." Nixon also announced that Gen. Alexander M. Haig Jr. would retire from active Army duty as of **Aug. 1** and continue as White House chief of staff on a regular basis. Nixon further said he had named Ron Ziegler as an assistant; Ziegler would continue as Presidential Press Secretary and spokesman and also take on the post of Director of Communications vacated by Herbert G. Klein, **June 5.**

Senate Committee Delves into Watergate—In June, the Senate Select Committee on Presidential Campaign activities continued to hear testimony on the Watergate break-in, alleged cover-up and efforts to impede investigation of the affair. Testimony highlights follow:

Maurice H. Stans, formerly Treasury Secretary and Finance Director of the Re-election Committee, was forced to testify, **June 12,** and denied all involvement in the affair. He denied knowledge of a 1971 memo referring to his "discretionary fund" of about $1,000,000 to be used to promote Nixon's re-election. Nor did he recall a request from Nixon's personal attorney; Herbert Kalmbach, to raise cash after the Watergate arrests. He was also unaware of large amounts of campaign cash drawn by E. Gordon Liddy during the first 5 months of 1972.

Jeb Stuart Magruder, deputy director of the Committee to Re-elect the President, testified, **June 14,** that he and other high-ranking officials had plotted to bug the Democratic opposition and then had attempted to cover-up the affair. He implicated John N. Mitchell, John W. Dean 3rd and H. R. Haldeman, but denied knowledge that the President had been involved. He admitted to perjury before the grand jury investigating the break-in, saying Dean, Mitchell and Haldeman had known he would lie. He said he told Haldeman the full Watergate story in January 1973. Haldeman's attorney John J. Wilson, **June 15,** denied the assertion. Magruder also testified he had sent reports on espionage plans to Gordon C. Strachan, a Haldeman assistant. Strachan's attorney, **June 17,** said Strachan had forwarded information about the plans to Haldeman before the Watergate break-in occurred.

Former presidential counsel John W. Dean 3rd, **June 25,** read a 6-hour statement in which he described a widespread effort to mask the extent of the conspiracy which had spread from the White House staff and the Committee to Re-elect the President to the Department of Justice and to the "Oval Office" of the President. During a week of testimony, Dean stated that when he had told the President, at a **Mar. 21** meeting, that the Watergate case was "a cancer growing on the Presidency," Nixon had not heeded his warning. He also asserted that the President had taken part in the cover-up for as long as 8 months. Among many allegations of Nixon's complicity in the cover-up, Dean said that in February Nixon had asked Dean to report directly to the President on his investigation, and not to H. R. Haldeman or John D. Ehrlichman because they "were principals in the matter." Dean said Nixon had discussed with him demands made by the Watergate conspirators for large sums of money in return for silence. He alleged that in September, 1972, the President had complimented him on helping to assure the Government investigation stopped with G. Gordon Liddy. Dean further said that in April Nixon had tried to get him to sign 2 incriminating letters of resignation but he had refused saying he would not become a "White House scapegoat." Dean also said Egil Krogh, head of the White House "plumbers unit," had told him that authorization for the Ellsberg break-in had come from the White House. Despite his serious allegations against the President, Dean said he believed Nixon "did not realize or appreciate at any time the implications of his involvement." On **June 26,** Dean told of a White House "enemies list" containing names of scores of politicians, journalists, labor officials, entertainers, academicians and Democratic campaign contributors which had been compiled in mid-1971. He said those on the continually updated list had often been harassed by Government investigators. He also submitted a White House document which outlined a plan for systematic use of tax investigations to spy on and bother members of "extremist" organizations. On **June 26,** the White House issued a statement declaring the President would not comment di-

rectly on the Dean testimony and that he stood by his **May 22** speech in which he said he had not been aware of the wide-ranging cover-up. Then, on **June 27,** a statement prepared by J. Fred Buzhardt, presidential special counsel for Watergate matters, was sent to the Senate Committee. It alleged that Dean had been the cover-up "mastermind" and had constantly misled the President about the scope of the Watergate conspiracy. The statement, which also strongly suggested Dean had become involved in the cover-up to protect his patron and former boss in the Justice Department, John N. Mitchell, was repudiated, **June 28,** by the White House.

Nixon, Brezhnev Hold Summit Talks—The U.S. and USSR signed 9 agreements during Soviet Communist Party General Secretary Leonid I. Brezhnev's **June 16-25** visit to the U.S. An ebullient spirit of camaraderie and playfulness marked the Soviet leader's meetings with President Nixon, Congressional leaders and leading American businessmen. In the most important agreement signed, Pres. Nixon and Brezhnev vowed, **June 22,** to try to avert military confrontations which might lead the U.S. and USSR into nuclear war with each other or with a 3rd country. Specifically, the agreement obliged Moscow and Washington to enter into immediate consultations if relations between them or between one of them and some other country "appear to involve risk of nuclear conflict." The pact was immediately seen as a further restraint on any potential Soviet attack on China, a possibility openly feared by China. Another agreement, **June 24,** set forth a "modest expansion" in air passenger service by Pan Am and Aeroflot; Washington and Leningrad will become points of entry and departure and beginning in April 1974 both airlines will schedule 3 round-trip flights per week. Accords expanding cooperation in oceanography, transportation and agricultural exchanges were signed **June 19.** On **June 20,** Nixon and Brezhnev signed an accord to accelerate the SALT talks and complete a new arms limitation treaty by the end of 1974. Brezhnev, **June 19,** took a plea for expanded trade rela-

---

Nixon Sets 60-Day Freeze on Retail Prices

Acknowledging that prices were escalating at unacceptable rates despite Phase 3 voluntary controls, President Richard M. Nixon, **June 13,** set a freeze on all retail prices for up to 60 days. He said that Phase 4, with "tighter standards and more mandatory compliance procedures" would follow.

The freeze included food prices but excluded rents, interest and dividends. These would remain under controls set in Phase 3. Also unaffected were farm prices of raw agricultural products; the freeze did apply, at the supermarket level, to retail prices on those same agricultural products. The freeze also affected the cost of services.

Nixon said the 60-day period would be utilized to devise a new scheme to fight inflation and give Congress time to act on his request for broader authority to control exports on agricultural products and approve 5 other requests he had already put before Congress. He had previously asked for new authority to reduce tariffs, for approval of the Alaskan pipeline, authority to dispose of materials in the strategic stockpile, for farm legislation to encourage higher production and spending bills which followed his prescriptions rather than "noble-sounding budget-busters."

Despite his decision to set controls, Nixon warned that they could never "substitute for a free

economy." "We must not," Nixon stressed, "let controls become a narcotic and we must not become addicted."

In a briefing preceding the President's statement, Treasury Secretary George P. Schultz conceded, "everyone thinks Phase 3 was a failure, so let's not argue about that." He described the freeze as a "shock treatment" for inflation and as buying time for thorough planning.

In compliance with the President's freeze, steel, copper, rubber and tire prices were cut **June 14,** many eliminating increases of the preceding week.

Reactions on the stock market and from labor and business were negative. AFL-CIO Pres. George Meany called the freeze a "failure of policy" with prices frozen at their highest level in 20 years. UAW Pres. Leonard Woodcock said the freeze would only "create artificial shortages and black-market prices." E. Douglas Kenna, president of the National Association of Manufacturers predicted "chaotic conditions in the production and distribution of essential commodities."

Congressional feeling, however, was generally favorable, although House Ways and Means Committee Chairman Wilbur D. Mills said, "It's probably too late, probably too little."

tions to Congressional leaders, urging that quarrels about Jewish emigration ought not stand in the way of cooperation in trade. On **June 24,** in the first television address by a Soviet leader to the American people, Brezhnev suggested the possibility of another summit before the end of the year. In a joint communique capping the Soviet leader's visit, Brezhnev, **June 25,** called the talks a "further milestone," but also indicated that areas of difference, such as in the Middle East, still remained. The communique also disclosed that East-West talks on force reductions in Central Europe would begin **Oct. 30.**

Supreme Court Rules on Obscenity—In decisions in 5 obscenity cases, all decided by a 5-4 vote, the Supreme Court, **June 21,** set new guidelines on obscenity. According to the rulings, states would be able to ban books, magazines, plays and motion pictures which are offensive to local standards, even though they may be acceptable elsewhere. In the majority opinion, Chief Justice Warren E. Burger said the printing or sales of works "which appeal to prurient interest in sex, which portray sexual conduct in a patently offensive way and which, taken as a whole, do not have serious literary, artistic, political or scientific value" could be punished by individual states. The definition of "prurient" would be based on the views of "the average person, applying contemporary community standards" rather than a national, hypothetical definition of obscenity. He also said each state would have to write explicit laws defining what would be considered obscene and open to punishment. Dissenting Justices William O. Douglas, William J. Brennan Jr., Potter Stewart and Thurgood Marshall criticized the guidelines as an impingement on free speech and press and scored the vagueness of definitions based on local community standards. The dissenters also predicted citizens would find it difficult to know whether they were running a risk of violating the law. Reaction to the ruling was one of confusion; prosecutors and lawyers did agree, however, the decision would mean an increase in prosecution of pornographers. Ross Sackett, president of the Association of American Publishers, **June 22,** called the decision a "local-option mare's nest" and said the Association would fight the effects of the Supreme Court's decision.

Senate Approves Kelley as FBI Head—The Senate approved, in a 96-0 vote, **June 27,** President Richard M. Nixon's nomination of Clarence M. Kelley as new permanent director of the FBI. Former Chief of Police in Kansas City, Mo., Kelley had previously worked with the FBI for 21 years.

Nixon, Congress Reach Cambodia Compromise—President Richard M. Nixon, **June 29,** assured Congress that U.S. military activity in Cambodia would cease by **Aug. 15** and that he would seek Congressional approval for future military activity. The compromise was set forth in amendments to 2 emergency appropriation bills which the President signed **July 1.** Previously, Nixon, **June 27,** had vetoed a $3.3 billion supplemental appropriations bill which included an immediate cutoff of funds for the Cambodian bombing. The House vote, **June 27,** to override the veto had fallen 35 votes short.

Nixon Announces Energy Plan—President Richard M. Nixon, **June 29,** announced his plan to meet the nation's energy needs and appointed Gov. John A. Love of Colorado to direct a new energy office from the White House. Love's office would form and coordinate energy policies throughout the executive branch. Recognizing that energy resources are not keeping pace with growing demands, Nixon said, "unless we act swiftly and effectively, we could face a genuine energy crisis in the forseeable future." The President's energy plan included a voluntary conservation drive in which the Government would set the example, expanded research into new energy sources and Government reorganization to give high priority to energy matter. Love, speaking at a news conference after his appointment, rejected mandatory rationing of fuels and limits on automobile horsepower. He said the President's policy was to increase supply and induce voluntary restraints.

INTERNATIONAL

Greek Monarchy Abolished—Premier George Papadopoulos announced, **June 1,** that the military-led Greek Government had abolished the monarchy and proclaimed a republic. The proclamation asserted that King Constantine, deposed since December, 1967, had plotted against the leadership. Reference was made to his alleged role in an abortive mutiny by members of the Greek Navy. The Greek people were also told that they would have a chance to approve the changes in a referendum before July 29 and that general elections would be held before the end of 1974. Constantine responded dramatically, **June 2,** asserting his confidence that he would return to Greece. Constantine again denied involvement in the abortive mutiny. In Athens, as security police arrested supporters of King Constantine, 4 senior officers in the armed forces resigned. The Government also launched a full-scale campaign to persuade the Greek people of the value of the previous day's decree.

Franco Yields Premiership—In an apparent move to ease the transition to the post-Franco era, Spain's Generalissimo Francisco Franco, 80 years old, stepped down as head of government, **June 8.** Both head of state and of government since the 1936-39 Spanish Civil War, Franco still remained Chief of State and Commander in Chief of the Armed Forces. He appointed his faithful aide, Adm. Luis Carrero Blanco, Premier. On **June 11,** Blanco named his new cabinet; its composition showed a strengthening of the right at the expense of the more moderate technocrats.

Second Vietnam Cease-fire Signed—Representatives of the United States, North Vietnam, South Vietnam and the Vietcong, the original signers of the Jan. 27 cease-fire agreement in South Vietnam, **June 13,** signed a new 14-point agreement calling for an end to all cease-fire violations in South Vietnam. The accord, the result of month-long negotiations between Henry A. Kissinger and North Vietnam's Le Duc Tho, called for all military activities to cease on **June 15** at 12 noon in South Vietnam. Kissinger called the agreement an "amplification and consolidation" of the basic Paris accord. According to the new agreement, the U.S. pledged to end all reconnaissance flights over North Vietnam, to resume mine-sweeping operations in North Vietnamese waters within 5 days of signing and to resume talks on aid to North Vietnam within 4 days of signing of the document. The document also stipulated that the commanders of opposing forces in South Vietnam would meet wherever their armies were in direct contact within 24 hours after the new cease-fire to prevent outbreaks of hostilities and insure medical supplies and care for all. Kissinger stressed that there was nothing in the accord that committed the U.S. to cease its military operations in Cambodia. First reports on **June 16,** after the cease-fire went into effect, stated fighting was on a smaller scale than that accompanying the original cease-fire. However, commanders of opposing sides in South Vietnam failed to meet within the specified 24 hours and sporadic clashes continued through the month.

Former Dictator Returns to Argentina— Violence, ending with at least 20 dead and more than 400 wounded, marred former Pres. Juan D. Peron's return, **June 20,** to Argentina after almost 20 years in exile. A series of shooting incidents between left and right pro-Peron factions, forced Peron to cancel an address to the more than 1,000,000 Argentinians gathered to welcome him. That evening, Peron addressed the nation over television and apologized for the violence. On **June 21,** Peron appealed for unity in his movement and placed blame for the shooting incidents on unspecified groups trying to infiltrate the Peronist movement.

Uruguay Abolishes Congress— Ending 40 years of constitutional rule in Uruguay, Pres. Juan María Bordaberry, June 27, abolished the Congress. He said it would be replaced by a Council of State which would oversee the president's duties and do the work of the Congress. Military officials, who had wielded behind-the-scenes power for many months, said Congress's efforts to block the armed forces' campaign to end left-wing subversion had necessitated the move. In protest, the Communist-controlled National Workers Confederation called for a general strike and ordered the occupation of factories. As the nationwide protest strike continued, paralyzing the nation's major industries, the Government, **June 30,** used armed troops to attempt to break it up and ordered the National Workers Confederation disbanded and its leader arrested. On **July 11,** the National Workers Confederation yielded, agreeing to call off the strike. Its leaders conceded, **July 12,** they had not achieved the desired victory but allowed that they would continue the struggle in a new form.

Elections in Ulster— There were no surprises in the **June 28** Assembly elections in Northern Ireland as both Protestants and Roman Catholics voted solidly for the parties identified with their respective communities. However, the parties supporting the British White Paper's proposal for power-sharing between Roman Catholics and Protestants won a majority of seats in the proposed 78-member legislative assembly. Moderate political leaders said the results boded well for a moderate coalition in the future assembly.

Revolt in Chile Put Down— Armed forces loyal to Chilean Pres. Salvador Allende Gossens, **June 29,** put down a 3-hour revolt in Santiago by 150 members of the 900-man 2nd Armored Regiment. At least 7 persons were killed and 32 wounded, most of them civilians, in the revolt. The attempted coup followed weeks of strikes, scattered violence and predictions that the Government was threatened by "fascist plots." Allende immediately declared a state of emergency and, **June 30,** called on the opposition-controlled Congress to grant a "state of siege" which would broaden his authority to suspend civil rights. On **July 2,** the lower house of parliament declined the request for a "state of siege," thereby rejecting Allende's claim that Chile was on the border of a new civil war. On **July 4,** Allende reinstated full civilian rule, and on **July 5**

named 7 new ministers. The political balance, however, remained the same as in his former cabinet, which had resigned after the abortive army rebellion.

Germany Revalues Mark— In its 2d revaluation of the year, West Germany, **June 29,** raised the official value of the mark 5.5% against a composite of 7 European currencies linked with it in a joint float. The move, intended to save European monetary unity and stem new turbulence in foreign exchange markets, spurred a new surge in selling of dollars, whose value fell to a new low in Frankfurt.

GENERAL

EPA Proposes Auto Curbs— Environmental Protection Agency Acting Administrator Robert W. Fri, **June 15,** proposed strict smog-fighting transportation controls for 17 urban areas. If imposed, the controls, including auto inspections, limited gasoline sales and limitations on individual car usage, could drastically limit motor vehicle traffic in major cities by 1977. Fri said the aim was to change the public's "long-standing and intimate relation to private automobiles" and force substantial compliance with the Clean Air Act of 1970 by July 1, 1975. He acknowledged that in some instances, such as in Los Angeles, strict enforcement would not be practical because it might result in banning all cars from the streets by 1977.

Further Conviction in Yablonski Slayings— The former assistant of United Mine Workers' Pres. W A. Boyle, Albert E. Pass, **June 19,** was convicted of 3 counts of murder in the slayings of Joseph A. Yablonski, his wife and daughter. Pass, the highest-ranking union official to be convicted in the case to date, joined 6 others who have either pleaded guilty or been convicted. After the conviction, the special prosecutor in the case hinted that at least one more arrest was forthcoming.

U.S. Launches Orbiting Space Station— Despite malfunctions at the outset of the unmanned launching (May 14) of Skylab, the U.S.'s first orbiting space station, the Skylab 1 crew— Capt. Charles Conrad Jr., Cmdr. Joseph P. Kerwin and Cmdr. Paul J. Weitz, all Navy men— returned safely, **June 22,** having set numerous records and accomplished virtually all the flight's objectives. Records set included spending 28 days and 40 minutes in space, circling the earth 395 times in orbit, traveling nearly 11.8 million miles in space and performing repair work outside an orbiting space craft. The crew attached, May 26, a makeshift sunshield to compensate for one lost in the launch malfunction. A second major repair, on **June 7,** necessitated a "space walk" by Conrad and Kerwin to free a jammed set of solar-power panels. The flight provided evidence that man could live and work effectively in weightless conditions of space for extended periods of time with no apparent damage to health. The crew also observed the sun from above the earth's obscuring atmosphere and made a survey of the earth's resources with photographs and sensors.

Appeals Court Reverses 6 of 7 Berrigan Rulings —The 3-judge federal Appeals Court in Philadelphia, **June 27,** overturned 6 of 7 counts in the 1972 conviction of Rev. Philip Berrigan and Sister Elizabeth McAlister for smuggling letters into and out of a federal prison. The ruling was based on the fact that the law under which the defendants were tried stipulates letters cannot be sent into a prison without the knowledge or consent of the warden or supervisor. Since all but one of the letters were carried by a Lewisburg Prison inmate who was an informer, 6 of the counts were reversed.

DISASTERS

A violent explosion, **June 1**, in an apartment building in Perpignan, France killed 7 and injured 4 ... All 23 aboard were killed, **June 1**, when a French-built Caravelle jetliner crashed and exploded on approach to Sao Luis, Brazil ... 7 seamen died and another 9 were missing and presumed dead when an American cargo ship, **June 2**, collided with an oil-laden Belgian tanker in the Narrows of New York Harbor, touching off fires and explosions ... 18 died and 40 were injured, **June 3**, in a bus-truck collision 200 miles southwest of Bangkok, Thailand ... As 600,000 spectators at the Paris air show watched, a Soviet TU144 supersonic jetliner exploded, **June 3**, while making a demonstration flight, killing 6 crewmen and 7 residents of the village of Goussainville ... 15 persons died, **June 7**, when a passenger bus crashed into a river near Baguio, Philippines ... All 27 aboard died, **June 20**, when a Mexican DC-9 crashed into a mountain peak and exploded near Puerto Vallarta, Mexico ... A passenger bus skidded into a ditch near Dacca, Bangladesh, **June 24**, killing 6 and injuring 75, 14 of them seriously ... A flash fire, laid to arson, raged through a bar in New Orleans' French Quarter, **June 24**, killing 29 and injuring at least 15 ... At least 9 died and 31 were missing, **June 26**, when an Indian merchantman-passenger vessel capsized and sank off Cape Guardafui in the Indian Ocean ... At least 20 drowned when a Philippine inter-island passenger ship sank about 12 miles south of Cebu ... A Soviet airliner on take-off from Amman airport in Jordan crashed into a house, **June 30**, killing 8 and injuring 79 ... At least 8 died when storms and floods lashed the northeast United States **June 30**.

July

NATIONAL

Watergate Hearings Continue—The Senate Select Committee on Campaign Activities continued through July to hear testimony on the Watergate matter. Testimony highlights follow:

Former Attorney General and Director of the Committee to Re-elect the President John N. Mitchell testified, **July 10**, that, in order to safeguard the President's bid for re-election, he had held back information from Nixon about the Watergate break-in, cover-up and "White House horror stories." Denying that he had authorized the political intelligence scheme that led to the break-in, Mitchell conceded he aided in efforts to "limit the impact" of Watergate on the campaign. He called a "palpable, damnable lie" Jeb Stuart Magruder's testimony that Mitchell had approved the break-in plan and given instructions to destroy related documents. On **July 11**, Mitchell implicated John D. Ehrlichman and H. R. Haldeman as participants in "a design not to have the stories come out."

Herbert W. Kalmbach, formerly personal attorney and fund raiser for Pres. Nixon, testified, **July 16**, that through a series of clandestine meetings and telephone calls he had raised $220,000 for the 7 defendants in the Watergate trial, believing the money was intended for legal fees and support of the defendants' families. He said his instructions has come chiefly from John Dean, with

assurances from John D. Ehrlichman that the work was entirely proper. On **July 17**, Kalmbach acknowledged that he now knew raising the money had been "an improper, illegal" act.

Former official of the Committee to Re-elect the President Frederick C. LaRue, **July 18**, told the Ervin Committee that he had concluded authority for the Watergate break-in had come from "some high level." Admitting that he had distributed $230,000 to "satisfy commitments" to the Watergate conspirators, LaRue said he did not know who had been the ultimate authority behind the payments.

Former Assistant Attorney General Robert C. Mardian testified, **July 19**, that G. Gordon Liddy had given him the clear impression Pres. Nixon had authorized the 1971 burglary of Daniel Ellsberg's psychiatrist's office. He also said that Mitchell had not denied a Liddy statement to Mardian that Mitchell had approved Liddy's $250,000 electronic eavesdropping scheme. Mardian denied that he had been involved in the Watergate break-in and cover-up, disputing the testimony of 5 other witnesses.

Gordon C. Strachan, a former aide to H. R. Haldeman, **July 21**, testified that Haldeman had been told the Committee to Re-elect the President had set up "a sophisticated political intelligence gathering system" 2 months before the Watergate break-in. Two or 3 days after the break-in and after talking with Haldeman, Strachan said he destroyed a memo informing Haldeman of the intelligence system.

On **July 24**, former presidential adviser John D. Ehrlichman said that John Dean's misleading information thwarted President Nixon's effort to give the nation a factual account of the Watergate conspiracy. Ehrlichman designated Dean as the "cover-up" culprit. He also testified that although neither he nor the President had authorized the break-in at Ellsberg's psychiatrist's office, it had been well within the constitutional duty and obligation of the President. The right, Ehrlichman testified, came from the President's legal authority to prevent national security information from falling into the hands of foreign powers. On **July 25**, Ehrlichman denied charges linking him to the Watergate cover-up. He also said there had been no impropriety in his meeting in April with Matthew Byrne, the judge in the Ellsberg case.

In **July 30** testimony, former presidential aide H. R. Haldeman said neither he nor Nixon had been involved in the Watergate break-in or cover-up. He confirmed Ehrlichman's testimony that Dean had misled the President about the affair. Haldeman told the committee that he had listened to the tape of Dean's March 21 meeting with Nixon and that it was totally at variance with Dean's account of the meeting. On **July 31**, Sam Ervin called Haldeman's testimony about the tapes a "planned action" by the White House to "leak" a favorable version of the tapes. Several members of the committee expressed resentment that Nixon had denied access to the tapes to the committee, but had allowed Haldeman to take them home after his resignation as presidential adviser.

Senate Probes Secret Bombing in Cambodia—The Senate Armed Services Committee, **July 16**, began a probe into allegations that the Air Force had made secret B-52 bombing raids into Cambodia in 1969 and 1970. No public announcements of raids in Cambodia were made until May, 1970. Testifying before the Armed Services Committee, **July 16**, former Air Force Major Hal. M. Knight said he had been told to falsify records of the raids for political reasons; one superior officer had said accurate reports might arouse criticism from Sen. J. William Fulbright. Defense Secretary James R. Schelsinger, **July 16,** verified the secret raids, describing them as "fully authorized" and necessary for the protection of American servicemen. On **July 17,** the Defense Department disclosed that at least 3,500 secret bombing raids had been made over Cambodia in the 14-month period beginning March, 1969, while Cambodia was officially recognized as a neutral country. Pentagon spokesman Jerry W. Friedheim stated that the falsified reports had been officially ordered and authorized by President Nixon and Defense Secretary Melvin R. Laird. Laird, **July 18,** denied that he or any other Defense Department officials had authorized the "special security reporting procedure." Sen. Stuart Symington, the acting chairman of the Armed Service Committee charged, **July 23,** that the $145 million appropriated by Congress to pay for the secret bombing had been obtained under "false pretenses." In a **July 10** press conference, Laird denied charges he had lied when he said he hadn't authorized falsified reporting on the secret raids, he said he had authorized a "separate reporting procedure" for the raids.

Senate OK's Alaska Pipeline—The Senate approved, 77-20, on **July 17,** the controversial bill authorizing the licensing of a $3.5-billion, 789-mile pipeline from the Alaska North Slope oil fields to the ice-free port of Valdez. The decision came after a 49-48 vote, decided by Vice-President Spiro T. Agnew, in support of an amendment to immunize the project from further challenge in the courts by environmentalists.

Nixon Ends Price Freeze—President Richard M. Nixon issued a statement, **July 18,** ending the freeze on health care and food prices and outlining Phase 4 of his economic control program. The basis of Phase 4 was to be mandatory price controls. Nixon said that despite the tougher price rules under Phase 4, prices increases in the remainder of 1973 "will be less than in the first half of the year but greater than anyone would like." Under Phase 4, the June 13 price freeze would remain in effect in all sectors, excluding food and

health care, until **Aug. 12.** The only exception in the food sector were beef prices which were to remain under March 29 price ceilings until **Sept. 12.** The White House statement said prices under Phase 4 would be permitted to rise only on a dollar-for-dollar basis to reflect cost increases since the end of 1972.

Connally Resigns—President Richard M. Nixon, **July 25,** announced the resignation of former Treasury Secretary John B. Connally as an unpaid, part-time presidential adviser.

INTERNATIONAL

Israeli Attache Slain in D.C.—Col. Yosef Alon, an Israeli military attache, was shot to death, **July 1,** at his home in Chevy Chase, Md. Secretary of State William P. Rogers immediately notified Israeli Foreign Minister Abba Eban that the U.S. was making "every effort to find the perpetrators of this crime." President Richard M. Nixon provided a jet to carry the body and family to Israel and ordered the Secret Service to increase protection of the diplomatic community in Washington. Despite a Voice of Palestine broadcast from Cairo which asserted that Alon had been executed in reprisal for the **June 28** death of an Arab militant in Paris, the FBI and Maryland police could find no clues or determine the motive.

King Overthrown in Afghanistan—Junior officiers led by Lieut. Mohammad Daud Khan, King Mohammad Zahir Shah's brother-in-law and cousin, **July 17,** seized power in a coup d'etat and proclaimed Afghanistan a republic. The king was in Italy for health treatments. Gen. Daud said in a broadcast that he had acted to replace the "corrupt and effete" rule of the King with a "genuine democracy" to save the country from ruin. He pledged that Afghanistan would continue to follow a policy of nonalignment and would not join any military pact. There had been much discontent in the mountainous kingdom over the Government's inneffectual efforts to deal with famine brought on by a 3-year drought.

Libyans March to Cairo—After an apparent breakdown in unity talks between Libya and Egypt, some 30,000 Libyans, **July 18,** began a 1,500-

---

White House Bugging System Revealed; Tapes Sought by Senate, Prosecutor

In a surprise appearance before the Senate Select Committee on Campaign Activities, former presidential deputy assistant Alexander P. Butterfield revealed, **July 16,** that President Richard M. Nixon had recorded his White House and Executive Office Bldg. conversations since March 1971. The White House confirmed the disclosure on the same day. Chief counsel to the Select Committee Samuel Dash said the committee would seek tapes relevant to the inquiry, particularly those of the President's conversations with John W. Dean 3rd.

Nixon, **July 17,** ordered the Secret Service to withhold all information about the secret tapes from the Senate Watergate committee. The committee then appealed directly to the President. In a letter, Chairman Sam Ervin asked the President to release all documents and tapes relevant to the investigation of the Watergate matter. Watergate special prosecutor Archibald Cox, **July 18** (made public **July 23**), also requested Watergate-related tapes. He pointed out that his request did not raise the issue of separation of powers. The White House disclosed, **July 20,** that the President had decided to cease taping his conversations and phone calls.

On **July 23,** citing the intertwined doctrines of

separation of powers and executive privilege, the President, in a letter to Ervin, refused to release the tapes. He also stated that "the tapes are entirely consistent with what I know to be the truth and what I have stated to be the truth." However, he indicated the tapes were open to different interpretations and "would not finally settle the question." Cox's request for tapes was also rejected.

In a unanimous decision, the Senate committee voted to issue 2 subpoenas—one for the recordings of 5 of Nixon's meetings with John Dean and a second for other Watergate-related documents. Cox also issued a subpoena for the material he had requested. In a letter to U.S. District Court Judge John J. Sirica, Nixon, **July 26,** said he could not comply with Cox's subpoena because the "independence of the 3 branches of our Government" was at issue. Cox immediately petitioned Sirica for an order to release the tapes. Also on **July 26,** Nixon wrote to Ervin that he must "respectfully refuse" to supply the tapes requested by his committee. The Senate committee voted unanimously to seek a court order to compel the President to comply with their request.

mile trek to Cairo to demand immediate merger of Libya and Egypt. The first car in the caravan arrived at Mersa Matruh, 120 miles into Egypt **July 19.** Following complaints from the Egyptian Government, the marchers, **July 21,** heeded pleas from Libyan leader Col. Muammar el-Qaddafi and headed home. In a related development, Qaddafi announced, **July 21,** that he had resigned, **July 11,** as head of the Libyan Revolutionary Command Council. The Council, however, had rejected the resignation. On **July 23,** Qaddafi retracted his resignation saying he would remain in office until union with Egypt was carried out.

JAL Jetliner Hijacked—Thirty minutes after take-off from Amsterdam, 5 pro-Palestinian guerrillas, **July 20,** hijacked a Japan Airlines jumbo jetliner enroute to Tokyo and forced the pilot to fly to the Persian Gulf shiekdom of Dubai. The airliner was carrying 123 passengers and 22 crew members. The hijackers, who identified themselves as members of Al Fatah and the "Red Japanese Army," demanded, **July 21,** the release of Kozo Okamoto, a "Red Army" member serving a life sentence in Israel for his part in the Tel Aviv airport massacre of 1972. The hijackers, **July 24,** flew the plane to Damascus, Syria and then to Benghazi, Libya, where it was blown up shortly after the 137 passengers and crew left the plane. The 4 remaining hijackers—one, a woman, had been killed by a grenade explosion aboard—were arrested as they ran from the plane and were interrogated by Libyan authorities. Palestinian resistance leaders denied association with the hijacking, calling it "harmful to the Palestinian revolution." On **July 29,** Libya announced that the hijackers, 3 Palestinians and one Japanese, would go on trial.

France Resumes Nuclear Tests in Pacific—Despite a worldwide protest movement, France, **July 21,** exploded the first nuclear device in a series of A-tests over the South Pacific atoll of Mururoa. In so doing, France ignored an interim injunction against the tests granted by the International Court of Justice in the Hague at the request of New Zealand and Australia. To symbolize their protest, New Zealand sent the frigate, Otago, with Cabinet Minister Fraser M. Colman aboard, into the test area. While Paris remained silent about the tests, Japan, Australia, New Zealand, Canada and Sweden, **July 22,** lodged complaints. On **July 29,** as France detonated the 2nd blast in the series, New Zealand's Prime Minister Norman Kirk, in Honolulu, announced that scientists had already detected a slight increase in radioactive fallout over the South Pacific islands.

Iran to Replace Canada on ICCS—As Canada formally ended its role as member of the International Commission of Control and Supervision in South Vietnam, **July 31,** the U.S. announced that Iran had agreed to take Canada's place. Michel Gauvin, the head of the Canadian delegation, had left South Vietnam, **July 19,** charging the Communists had created insurmountable obstacles to policing the cease-fire. He also charged that the Polish and Hungarian delegations had consistently refused to recognize violations by the North Vietnamese and Vietcong.

Greeks Back End of Monarchy—Following a one-sided Government-monopolized campaign, 78.4% of the Greek people, **July 29,** endorsed the military-backed Government decision to abolish the monarchy and install George Papadopoulos as President. In his campaign, Papadopoulos had said the referendum would provide the framework for a gradual transition of power to the people. He had also promised parliamentary elections and the restoration of civil liberties. Former politicians, led by Greece's last elected premier, Panayotis Canellopoulous, had denounced the campaign, saying large-scale harassment had stopped them from carrying their campaign to the people. On **July 30,** ex-King Constantine called the election "a blatant and shameless fraud" and opposition politicians claimed thousands of complaints of wrongdoing at the polls. An opposition group, the Citizens Committee for the Restoration of Democratic Legality, **Aug. 1,** asked the Supreme Court to annul the referendum. The court rejected the plea **Aug. 13.**

Philippine Referendum Backs Marcos—The Commission on Elections reported, **July 31,** that 90% of the Philippine people had affirmed Pres. Ferdinand E. Marcos as President, in a plebiscite held **July 27-28.** The referendum also authorized Marcos to continue the reforms he had initiated under martial law. Former Liberal Party Senator Jovito Salonga called the vote "fictitious", charging martial law had prevented a free and fair exchange of ideas and fear of reprisals had led people to vote "yes." Salonga and 11 other leaders had urged Marcos to lift martial law for a month before the elections. Marcos had, **July 23,** lifted the midnight curfew for the period, **July 24-28** and had eased restrictions on free speech and press to give people "the fullest opportunity to discuss freely and publicly the questions to be resolved" in the referendum.

GENERAL

Abernathy Leaves SCLC—Charging that affluent blacks were not giving his organization financial support, Ralph David Abernathy, **July 9,** resigned as president of the Southern Christian Leadership Conference. He had worked with the SCLC, the civil rights group founded in the 1950's by the late Dr. Martin Luther King, Jr. for 17 years, including 5 as president. He said that Coretta King, Martin Luther King's widow, was partially responsible for the group's financial problems. Abernathy said she had not shared with the SCLC funds collected in her husband's name.

FTC Charges Oil Company Monopoly—The Federal Trade Commission, **July 9,** charged 8 of the largest U.S. oil companies with conspiracy to monopolize the refining of petroleum products. The 23-year conspiracy, the commission said, had led to shortages of gasoline. The formal accusation stated the oil-company monopoly had forced "substantially higher prices" on American consumers, caused some independent petroleum marketers to close down, and had given "excess" profits to the 8 conspiring companies. The commission charged the companies had pursued a "common course of action" to keep profits from refining artificially low in order to make it an unattractive business for independent companies.

Record Crowd at Watkins Glen—Some 600,000 rock music fans converged, **July 28,** on the Grand Prix auto race course at Watkins Glen, N.Y., to hear a 12-hour concert. Twice the crowd at Woodstock 4 years earlier, the gathering was the largest festival ever held in the U.S. Neither the baking sun nor a torrential downpour disturbed the peaceful crowd. The only jarring note at the concert was the death of one of 4 skydivers who tried to parachute into the concert area.

EPA Grants Auto Pollution Control Delay—The Environmental Protection Agency, **July 30,** granted automakers the year's 3rd extension for meeting stringent emission standards. A year's extension, from 1976 to 1977, was set for meeting emission standards for nitrogen oxides. Acting EPA director Robert W. Fri did set interim standards for cars produced during 1976-1977. He said there was no evidence the standards could have been met.

DISASTERS

A cloudburst in Ocotlan, Mex., **July 8,** claimed the lives of at least 30 persons and injured 27 seriously...A bus plunged into a ravine, **July 10,** near Guadalajara, Mex., killing 35 persons...A Brazilian Boeing 707 crashed, **July 11,** on approach to Orly airport near Paris, killing 122 of the 134 persons aboard...A mudslide near the Tibetan border in the Indian state of Uttar Pradesh, **July 15,** killed 10 persons and injured 24 others...A bus carrying Belgian pilgrims from a shrine in the French Alps, **July 19,** plunged from a bridge killing 43 . . . At least 15 were killed when a bus dove into a ravine on an island near Hong Kong, **July 22**...A bus in northeast Iran crashed off a bridge into a river, **July 23,** killing 48, including 22 children...A head-on collision, **July 23,** in Mesilla, N.M, between a pickup truck and a station wagon carrying a vacationing New Jersey family killed 7 and injured 1...A Pan Am jetliner crashed into the ocean shortly after take-off from Papeete, Tahiti, **July 23,** killing 68...An Ozark Air Lines turbojet on approach to St. Louis in a thunderstorm, **July 23,** crashed into a residential area, claiming 38 lives...Ten lives were lost, **July 30,** when 2 cars collided head-on in Rolling Forks, Miss....All but one of 89 aboard died, **July 31,** when a Delta Air Lines jetliner crashed while landing in heavy fog at Logan International Airport in Boston, Mass.

August

NATIONAL

Phase 1 of Watergate Hearings Concluded—Having completed hearings on phase 1 of the Watergate affair, the Senate Select Committee on Campaign Activities recessed, **Aug. 7,** until early September. Highlights from the last week of phase 1 testimony follow:

The Senate committee, **Aug. 1,** made public a 1972 White House memo from former presidential aide Charles Colson in which Colson warned hearings on Richard G. Kleindienst's nomination as Attorney General could involve the President and other Nixon administration officials in the settlement of a series of anti-trust actions against the International Telephone and Telegraph Corporation.

Former CIA Director Richard Helms testified, **Aug. 2,** that he had to resist White House pressures to involve the CIA in the Watergate cover-up.

Robert E. Cushman Jr., Helms' deputy, stated, **Aug. 2,** that a request from John D. Ehrlichman had prompted him to rewrite a memo that would have linked Ehrlichman to Watergate conspirator E. Howard Hunt.

Former FBI Acting Director L. Patrick Gray, **Aug. 3,** testified that he had examined files taken from E. Howard Hunt's safe before he burned them with his Christmas trash. He said they were not evidence in the Watergate case. He also testified that on July 6, 1972, he told Pres. Nixon some White House personnel were trying to "mortally wound" him "by using the CIA and FBI and by confusing the question of CIA interest in...people the FBI wishes to interview." He said, **Aug. 6,** he was mystified when Nixon did not heed the warning.

Former Attorney General Richard G. Kleindienst and Assistant Attorney General Henry E. Peterson testified, **Aug. 7,** that they had "cracked" the Watergate case in April, but never found any evidence linking Pres. Nixon in the cover-up. Both said, however, they had faced a constant struggle to assure an unimpeded investigation. They told Nixon on **Apr. 15** that conspirators in the cover-up may have included senior officials in the White House and on the Committee to Re-elect the President. They testified the break in the case came from statements by John W. Dean 3rd and Jeb Stuart Magruder to Federal prosecutors.

Appeals Court Overrules Bombing Curb—Ending a knotty series of rulings, stays and appeals, the U.S. Court of Appeals for the 2nd Circuit, **Aug. 8,** overturned the **July 25** ruling by Federal District Court Judge Orrin G. Judd in Brooklyn that American bombing in Cambodia was "unauthorized and unlawful." The suit had been filed, **Apr. 19,** by Rep. Elizabeth Holtzman (D.-N.Y.) and 4 Air Force officers. The Court of Appeals, **July 27,** issued, at the request of the Government, a stay of the Judd decision. On **Aug. 1,** Supreme Court Justice Thurgood Marshall upheld the stay of the bombing halt order. Rep. Holtzman appealed the ruling to Supreme Court Justice William O. Douglas, who ordered, **Aug. 4,** an immediate halt to bombing of Cambodia. However, several hours later, the Supreme Court, in an order issued by Marshall and supported by the 7 other members, overruled Douglas.

U.S. Bombing in Cambodia Ends—Preceded by several days of intensive bombing around Phnom Penh, the U.S., at midnight **Aug. 14,** officially ceased bombing in Cambodia in accord with a June Congressional ruling. The U.S. would still continue unarmed reconnaissance flights and its flow of military aid to Cambodia and Laos. The cessation of bombing marked the official end of 12 years of U.S. combat activity in Indochina. President Richard M. Nixon, in a statement, again denounced Congress for forcing the cutoff, which he said "undermines prospects for world peace."

Nixon on Watergate—President Richard M. Nixon, **Aug. 15,** in an address on the Watergate matter, stated that uncertainty over the Watergate affair is sapping confidence in the American economy, currency and foreign policy. The President said "the time has come to turn Watergate over to the courts" and "for the rest of us to get on with the urgent business of our nation."

Nixon Holds Long-Awaited News Conference—Facing the press for the first time in 5 months, Pres. Richard M. Nixon, **Aug. 22,** acknowledged that the Watergate affair had hampered his ability to govern. Clearly nervous at times, he said he had never considered resigning and would serve out the remainder of his term with the full authority of a strong Presidency. Nixon defended Vice-President Agnew and condemned "the outrageous leak in information from either the grand jury or the prosecutors or the Justice Department or all 3." On whether to make public his recordings of White House conversations relevant to the Watergate investigation, Nixon said he would abide by a "definitive" decision of the Supreme Court.

Kissinger Named Secretary of State—President Richard M. Nixon, **Aug. 22,** nominated Henry A. Kissinger, his top adviser on national security, as Secretary of State to replace William P. Rogers, who resigned the same day.

Sirica Rules Against Nixon on Tapes—U.S. District Court Judge John J. Sirica ordered, **Aug. 29,** that President Richard M. Nixon make the tapes of White House conversations relevant to the Watergate investigation available to him for a decision on their use by a grand jury.

INTERNATIONAL

Arab Guerrillas Kill 3 in Athens Airport—Three persons, including 2 Americans, died and 55 were injured, **Aug. 6,** when 2 men identified as Arab Black September guerrillas hurled hand grenades and fired machine guns into a crowded transit lounge at Athens Airport. The passengers were waiting for a TWA flight bound for New York City. The terrorists admitted to police they had mistaken the passengers for another TWA group bound for Tel Aviv. The 2 Arabs were charged, **Aug. 7,** with "premeditated murder of a particularly odious nature."

Libyan-Egyptian State Proclaimed—Egyptian Pres. Anwar el-Sadat and Libyan leader Col. Muammar el-Qaddafi announced, **Aug. 29,** the "birth of a new unified Arab state." The declaration, however, made it clear that actual unification would come gradually; Qaddafi had supported immediate full union.

UN Security Council Condemns Israel—The United Nations Security Council unanimously condemned Israel, **Aug. 15,** for "a serious interference with international civil aviation and a violation of the Charter of the United Nations." On **Aug. 10,** Israel had intercepted a Lebanese Middle East Airlines jetliner and forced the plane to land at a military airfield. The 81 aboard were detained for 2 hours and then freed; Israeli military spokesmen later said they had seized the wrong plane. Israeli Gen. Moshe Dayan announced the purpose of the mission had been to capture Dr. George Habash, the head of the Popular Front for Liberation of Palestine.

Mail Bombs Plague Britain—Some 30 mail and fire bombs plagued Britain, **Aug. 18-25.** The first, **Aug. 18,** was discovered in Harrods, an exclusive department store. Others were found in the prime minister's official residence, Conservative Party headquarters and the House of Commons. On **Aug. 24,** a bomb mailed to The London Stock Exchange injured 2 and another, on **Aug. 25,** injured 2, one critically, at the Bank of England. Prime Minister Edward Heath, **Aug. 25,** ordered an alert in all Government departments and nationalized industries. Irish Republican Army terrorism spread abroad, **Aug. 27,** when a bomb, sent via the British Forces Post Office pouch, blew off the hand of the British military attache's secretary in Washington, D.C.

Amnesty for Greek Political Prisoners—Greek President George Papadopoulos, at his inauguration **Aug. 19,** promised amnesty for some 300 political prisoners and the abolition of martial law. The amnesty included all who had committed "political crimes" against Papadopoulos' Government since the 1967 coup and the 69 Navy officers indicted for an abortive mutiny in May. Official decrees, including a pardon for Alexandros Panagoulis, who tried to kill Papadopoulos in 1968, **Aug. 20,** confirmed the promises. The prisoners were released **Aug. 21-22.**

Indian-Pakistani Agreement Signed—After 19 months of difficult negotiations, India and Pakistan, **Aug. 28,** signed an agreement opening up the way for release of most of the 90,000 Pakistani prisoners held in India and resolving some problems arising from their 1971 war. The accord was expected to lead to Pakistani recognition of Bangladesh. The release of Pakistani prisoners was to begin imme-

diately and simultaneously with the transfer of Bangladesh of Bengalis in Pakistan and of Biharis (non-Bengali Muslims) from Bangladesh to Pakistan. After an initial admission of "a substantial number" of Biharis into Pakistan, future talks between Pakistan, Bangladesh and India would determine further repatriation of civilians and prisoners. The joint talks would also determine the fate of 195 Pakistani prisoners in India whom Bangladesh had threatened to try for war crimes. Pakistan also dropped its threat to try 203 Bengalis for espionage and treason.

Sakharov Criticized—An open letter from 39 colleagues from the 250-member Soviet Academy of Sciences, **Aug. 28,** condemned physicist Andrei D. Sakharov for his public criticism of the Kremlin's domestic and foreign policies. Sakharov, **Aug. 21,** had told western newsmen that U.S.-Soviet detente would be "very dangerous" if not accompanied by a democratization of Soviet society and reduced Soviet isolation from the outside world. Sakharov warned that the Soviet Union would use Western technological expertise to solve its economic problems and consolidate strength and "as a result, the world would become helpless before this uncontrollable bureaucratic machine." Publication of the letter, **Aug. 29,** triggered a press campaign against Sakharov which brought protests from Western leaders, including West Germany's Willy Brandt.

Chinese Hold 10th Party Congress—A Chinese Government communique, **Aug. 29,** announced that the Chinese Communist Party had held its 10th Congress **Aug. 24-28.** Held in total secrecy, the Congress formally expelled the late Lin Piao, adopted a revised party constitution, selected a new Central Committee and approved a political report by Premier Chou En-lai. The communique, describing the Congress as one of unity, vigor and victory, stated that the delegates had been chosen "at the end of an extensive democratic process." Chou's **Aug. 24** report, made public **Aug. 31,** charged that both the U.S. and Soviet Union were "contending for hegemony," but conceded relations with the U.S. had "improved to some extent." Chou emphasized that the Chinese considered the "socialist-imperialist" Soviet Union a greater threat than the U.S. and warned against attack from the Soviet Union. He also outlined, for the first time publicly, the details of an alleged 1971 plot by late Defense Minister Lin Piao to assassinate Mao Tse-tung and set up a rival Central Committee. The new politburo, announced **Aug. 30,** included 7 new members. The naming of 5 vice-chairmen and a standing committee raised speculation that preparation was being made for a collective leadership after Mao Tse-tung's death. No successor to Mao was named.

GENERAL

Two Youths Indicted in Texas Slayings—Elmer Wayne Henley, 17, and David Owen Brooks, 18, were indicted in Houston, Tex., on murder charges, **Aug. 14,** after they confessed to participation in sex-and-torture slayings of 27 young men over a period of 3 years. Houston police were led to the murders, **Aug. 7,** when Henley told them he had killed Dean Allan Corll, 33, for whom he and Brooks had procured the victims. On **Aug. 13,** Houston police found the 27th body, making the case the largest multiple murder case in the U.S. history.

St. Croix 5 Get Life Sentences—Five self-proclaimed Black Muslims from St. Croix received sentences of life imprisonment, **Aug. 13,** for the

Sept. 1972 murders of 8 persons at a luxurious golf club in Christiansted, Virgin Islands. Defense attorney William A. Kuntsler said the sentences would be appealed. The case was complicated, **Aug. 14** and **15,** when 3 jurors, including the foreman, said they had been pressured into giving a guilty verdict. The defense immediately filed a motion for an evidentiary hearing and a new trial.

7 Indicted in Muslim Slayings—The Superior Court Grand Jury in Washington, D.C., indicted, **Aug. 15,** 7 men, all from Philadelphia, for the January slaying of 2 men and 5 children at the Hanafi Muslim headquarters in Washington, D.C.

Indictments in Mistaken Drug Raids—Twelve undercover narcotics agents were indicted, **Aug. 24,** in Alton, Ill., in connection with 6 illegal drug raids made in southwestern Illinois in April. The indictments stated the agents had conspired to search 6 private homes without search warrants and to deprive 11 residents of their constitutional rights.

Gainesville 8 Acquitted—After 3½ hours of deliberation, a Gainesville, Fla., federal jury, **Aug. 31,** acquitted 7 members and one supporter of the Vietnam Veterans Against the War of charges to disrupt the 1972 Republican National Convention with automatic weapons, slingshots and crossbows. The prosecution's case rested heavily on the testimony of 5 paid informers and undercover policemen who had infiltrated the anti-war group. The defense, which called only one witness, contended that charges had been trumped up to discredit the anti-war activities of the veterans group.

DISASTERS

Flash floods swept an entertainment center on the Isle of Man, **Aug. 2,** killing 51 persons, many of them children...At least 7 persons died, **Aug. 2,** in heavy flooding in northern New Jersey...An explosion, **Aug. 5,** at the Arabian American Oil Company's refinery at Abaiq, Saudi Arabia, claimed 15 lives...A car plunged into a creek, **Aug. 6,** near St. Marys, W. Va., killing 7 persons...At least 70 were believed drowned **Aug. 9** when their bus crashed into a deep irrigation canal near Minshat Faisal, Egypt...About 40 persons were feared drowned, **Aug. 8,** when a motor boat caught fire and capsized on Lake Volta, Ghana...At least 31 persons died when an oil-laden freight train overturned and crashed into a row of houses, **Aug. 12,** 100 miles from Seoul, Korea...All 85 aboard died when a Spanish Caravelle plane exploded and crashed, **Aug. 13,** near La Coruna, Spain...An interstate bus-pickup truck collision, **Aug. 16,** near Celaya, Mex., claimed 11 lives...A bus collided with a car and a trailer truck near Monterrey, Mexico, **Aug. 17,** killing 16 persons and injuring 23...Flood damage, **Aug. 18,** in northern and central Mexico killed at least 20, left nearly 50 missing and forced some 100,000 to flee their homes...An Avianca passenger plane crashed, **Aug. 22,** in central Colombia killing 14 and injuring 3 persons... 7 persons died of smoke inhalation in an early morning fire, **Aug. 25,** in a home in North Caldwell, N.J....All 40 persons aboard were killed, **Aug. 27,** when a Colombian turboprop airliner crashed outside of Bogota, Colombia...At least 527 persons were killed and around 4,000 injured, **Aug. 28,** when a severe earthquake ripped Central Mexico...As flood waters crested **Aug. 29,** after 2 weeks of severe flooding, the death toll in Pakistan's Punjab was set at 286 persons; 155,219 persons were evacuated and 260,000 homes were listed as destroyed...A U.S. military cargo jet crashed, **Aug. 29,** near Madrid, Spain, killing 24 persons.

September

NATIONAL

4 Indicted in Ellsberg Case—Former presidential adviser John D. Ehrlichman, and 3 former Nixon Administration officials were indicted, **Sept 4,** in Los Angeles on charges arising from the 1971 break-in at the office of Dr. Daniel Ellsberg's psychiatrist. The others were Egil Krogh Jr. and David R. Young, who supervised the White House "plumbers unit", and convicted Watergate conspirator G. Gordon Liddy. The "plumbers unit" was formed in 1971, following the release of the Pentagon papers, to trace and plug security leaks. Ehrlichman was also charged with perjury before the grand jury investigating the break-in.

Nixon Urges Congress to Act in Urgent Areas—In his 2d press conference in 2 weeks, President Richard M. Nixon, **Sept. 5,** challenged Congress to improve upon a "disappointing" record of action on his "bipartisan" legislative proposals. Announcing that he would veto the minimum wage bill, Nixon said he would send to Congress a supplementary "state of the union" message outlining areas which required urgent action. He also made a plea to Congress to enact 7 legislative measures aimed at increasing domestic energy supply. The President said he was giving "highest priority" to achieving a peaceful settlement of the Arab-Israeli dispute in order to end Arab threats to curtail oil deliveries to Western countries. In a 13,500-word "state of the union" message, Nixon, **Sept. 10,** said he would veto any legislation that cut defense spending below his budget or raised the cost of domestic programs.

Auto Prices Trimmed, Beef De-controlled—Cost of Living Council Director Dr. John T. Dunlop announced, **Sept. 7,** the Council had reduced by 10% to 30% price increases sought by the 4 major automobile companies. The council ruled the remaining increases were justified by costs incurred in complying with Federal safety standards. Dunlop also announced that final food regulations for Phase 4, including the removal of the freeze on beef prices, would become effective **Sept. 9.**

Watergate Hearings Curtailed—Denying pressure from the White House and Republican party leaders, Senate Watergate Committee chairman Sam J. Ervin Jr. and Howard H. Baker Jr. announced, **Sept. 12,** the committee had decided to curtail its inquiry into 1972 Presidential campaign sabotage and financing. Baker and Ervin explained the committee felt it would expedite the hearings by focusing on "key witnesses" and "salient points".

When hearings resumed, **Sept. 24,** convicted Watergate conspirator E. Howard Hunt Jr. testified that former special White House counsel Charles W. Colson had been aware in early 1972 of a "large-scale" intelligence scheme that led to the Watergate break-in. Hunt, however, said he had no information that Colson had specific foreknowledge of the break-in. Hunt testified that Colson had enlisted him to work for the White House and that Colson was the man to whom he reported. Hunt also described to the committee how, at Colson's behest, a fake diplomatic cable implicating Pres. John F. Kennedy in the assassination of South Vietnamese President Diem had been fabricated.

Patrick J. Buchanan, a special consultant to the President, **Sept. 6,** was the first witness of Phase 2, dealing with political "dirty tricks". Buchanan admitted he had promoted a White House strategy to undercut Muskie and "elevate" McGovern in the 1972 Democratic Presidential primaries. He insisted, however, there were no "illicit, unethical, improper or unprecedented activities" involved in his proposal.

Cox, Nixon Aides Fail to Compromise on Tapes —Archibald Cox, the White House special prosecutor in the Watergate Case, and attorneys to President Richard M. Nixon, told the U.S. Court of Appeals **Sept. 20,** they had failed to reach a compromise on access to tapes of presidential conversations. The Appeals Court had proposed, **Sept. 13,** an out-of-court compromise.

Senate Confirms Kissinger Nomination—The Senate, in a 78-7 vote **Sept. 21,** confirmed the nomination of Henry A. Kissinger as the 56th U.S. Secretary of State. At the emotional swearing-in ceremonies on **Sept. 22,** Kissinger said, "There is no country in the world where it is conceivable that a man of my origin could be standing here next to the President of the United States." The confirmation came after rigorous hearings in the Senate Foreign Relations Committee focusing on Kissinger's policy toward the Soviet Union and on his role in the 1969-71 tapping of the phones of 4 newsmen and 13 Government officials.

Retail Gas Prices Raised—Following weeks of protest shutdowns by filling stations, the Cost of Living Council, **Sept. 28,** announced it would permit increases of up to 2½ cents per gallon in the retail price of gasoline. The council also authorized a one to two cent increase per gallon of heating oil. The council retracted Pres. Nixon's directive of June 13 that the wage-price control program stabilize gasoline prices at the local service station.

1972 Nixon Election Fund Disclosed—President Nixon's 1972 campaign finance aides revealed, **Sept. 28,** that campaign fundraisers had collected a record $60.2 million.

INTERNATIONAL

Parliament Ends Canadian Railroad Strike—In a special night-long session, the Canadian Parliament, **Sept. 1,** passed emergency legislation ordering the termination of a 9-day railroad strike by some 56,000 nonoperating employees. Railroads resumed operation **Sept. 2.** The legislation set a schedule of minimum wage increases and provided for mediation and ultimately for binding arbitration to determine benefits beyond the minimum increase.

Libya Nationalizes Oil Companies—Following a breakdown in negotiations between oil companies and the Libyan Government, all foreign oil companies operating in the country were nationalized **Sept. 1.** On **Sept. 2,** Libya announced a price increase of more than $1 per gallon of oil and said U.S. dollars would not be accepted in payment. Libya also announced that it would pay a yet undetermined compensation to the oil companies.

Soviet Dissidents Get Mild Sentences—Pyotr I. Yakir, historian, and Victor A. Krasin, economist, on trial in Moscow on charges of being paid agents of a western plot to overthrow the Soviet Union, were sentenced, **Sept. 1,** to 3 years confinement followed by another 3 years of enforced residence. The mild sentences were recommended by the prosecution after the 2 defendants pleaded guilty, **Aug. 27,** and continued to cooperate with the prosecution. On **Sept. 5,** at a major news conference

at Moscow's Journalists Club, Yakir and Krasin publicly confessed. They asserted that deep reflection, not pressure or blackmail by the prosecutors, had led them to admit their "illegal activities."

Arabs Raid Saudi Embassy in Paris—Five Palestinian guerrillas, **Sept. 5,** raided the Saudi Arabian embassy in Paris and seized 13 diplomats and employees as hostages. Proclaiming themselves members of Il Icab ("punishment"), the gunmen demanded Jordan free Mohammed Daoud Odeh, an Al Fatah leader serving a life sentence for terrorist activities. After 28 hours of protracted negotiations between the gunmen, French officials and Arab diplomats, the commandos, **Sept. 6,** agreed to release all but 4 Saudi hostages. Taking their captives with them, they flew from Paris to Kuwait aboard an airliner provided by Syria. On **Sept. 7,** the gunmen flew over Ridyah, the Saudi Arabian capital, and threatened to throw the hostages out unless the Saudis took action to aid in the release of Mohammed Daoud Odeh. Both the Jordanians and Saudi Arabians refused to comply. After further negotiations with the Kuwaiti failed, the gunmen, **Sept. 8,** released all the prisoners unharmed and surrendered.

Laotians Agree to Form Coalition Government— The Vientiane Government and communist-led Pathet Lao, **Sept. 14,** formally signed a 28-article agreement to create a coalition government in Laos. Technically a protocol putting the Feb. 21 cease-fire into effect, the agreement provided for the formation of a Provisional Government of National Union. Prince Souvanna Phouma, a neutralist, would head the coalition; Prince Souphanouvong, the titular head of the Pathet Lao, would be deputy premier. The agreement also called for the equal division of ministries, the formation of a national political consultative council to advise the Government on elections and other matters and the neutralization of the administrative capital of Vientiane and the royal capital of Luang Prabang.

Deadlock in Swedish Elections—The ruling Swedish Social Democratic party, in elections **Sept. 17,** lost 7 seats in Parliament, and emerged deadlocked with the non-socialist opposition with 175 seats each. The Social Democrats received the lowest percentage of votes since they assumed power in 1932. Gains by the Communists saved the Social Democrats and Premier Olof Palme from certain ouster. The campaign had centered on unemployment, high taxes, the socialist central bureaucracy, and the concern of many Swedes that they are paying too high a price for their lavish system of welfare benefits.

Hussein Grants Amnesty—King Hussein of Jordan, **Sept. 18,** granted amnesty to political prisoners including Palestinian guerrillas jailed since 1970. The amnesty, a move toward Arab reconciliation, followed a Cairo meeting with Egyptian Pres. Anwat el-Sadat and Syrian Pres. Hafez al-Assad. Among the 754 prisoners released, **Sept. 19,** was Mohammed Daoud Odeh, an Al Fatah leader. His imprisonment had spurred 2 unsuccessful extremist attempts this year, in Khartoum and in Paris, to force his release.

UN Admits East, West Germany—The 28th General Assembly of the United Nations, **Sept. 18,** admitted East and West Germany as members. The Bahamas was also admitted. The admission vote went quickly and was hailed as a major achievement along the path of improving East-West relations.

Peron Wins in Argentina Ending an 18-year hiatus in political rule, Juan D. Peron, **Sept. 23,** was re-elected with a 61% majority President of Argentina. Peron's running mate and wife Isabel, an ex-cabaret dancer, became the first woman vice-president in Latin America. Peron and his wife would officially assume office **Oct. 12.** On **Sept. 24,** less than 24 hours after the Government outlawed the marxist People's Revolutionary Army, Jose Rucci, a Peron protege and Argentina's principal labor leader, was assassinated by urban guerrillas. An anonymous caller who identified himself as a member of a PRA commando unit, said the labor leader had been executed.

Austria Curbs Transit of Soviet Jews—Austrian Chancellor Bruno Kreisky, **Sept. 29,** in compliance with the demands of armed Arab guerrillas, agreed to suspend group transit of Israel-bound Soviet Jews through Austria and to close down the Schoenau Castle transit facility. The 2 guerrillas had seized 3 Soviet Jews and one Austrian customs official as hostages in a raid, **Sept. 28,** on a Moscow-to-Vienna train carrying 40 Jewish emigrants. After Kreisky's decision, the gunmen released the hostages Despite hints of a softening in the Austrian position, Kreisky, **Oct. 2,** after a 2-hour meeting with Israeli Premier Golda Meir, refused to change his mind. U.S. Pres. Richard M. Nixon, **Oct. 3,** also appealed to Kreisky to reconsider, arguing "we simply cannot have governments—small or large—give in to international blackmail by terrorist groups."

GENERAL

UAW and Chrysler Reach Settlement—Chrysler Corp. workers, **Sept. 23,** ratified a new 3-year contract between the United Auto Workers and the Chrysler Corp. The action brought some 117,000 employees, on strike since **Sept. 14,** back to their jobs. The settlement, described by UAW Pres. Leonard Woodcock as "precedent-setting", provided for a 5% wage increase in the first year followed by a 3% increase in the next 2 years, restrictions on compulsory overtime, a full-benefit retirement program after 30 years, and the machinery through which labor and management would jointly work to improve health and safety conditions in plants. Chrysler would also pay the full cost of any taxes levied to meet the cost of a national health insurance program.

Boyle Charged with Murder—Former United Mine Workers Pres. W. A. Boyle was arrested and charged with murder, **Sept. 6,** in the 1969 slaying of Joseph A. Yablonski. Yablonski had opposed Boyle in a union election. The indictment charged Boyle had instigated a plan to assassinate Yablonski and had secretly diverted union funds to pay 3 hired killers. Also charged **Sept. 6** with complicity in the murder, was William J. Turnblazer, a UMW district president. Prosecutor Richard A. Sprague said the 2 arrests, the 8th and 9th in the case, "closed the case." On the eve of a court appearance on the charge, the 71-year-old deposed UMW leader tried unsuccessfully **Sept. 24** to kill himself with an overdose of barbituates.

Skylab 2 Doubles Space Duration Record—Completing 59½ days and some 24-million miles traveled in space, the Skylab 2 crew splashed down safely and accurately, **Sept. 25,** in the Pacific Ocean. Doctors reported, **Sept. 26,** that the crew—Navy Capt. Alan L. Bean, Marine Maj. Jack R. Lousma and Dr. Owen K. Garriott—had returned in much better physical condition that the Skylab 1 crew. NASA head Dr. James C. Fletcher said, "We accomplished much more than any of us hoped." Accomplishments included 77,600 pictures

Military Junta Deposes Allende in Chile

Forty-six years of civilian rule in Chile ended, **Sept. 11,** when a 4-man military junta successfully overthrew Pres. Salvador Allende Gossens in a violent military coup. Proclaiming they intended to liberate Chile "from the Marxist yoke," the junta declared a state of siege and imposed censorship and a curfew. Santiago police reported Allende had committed suicide rather than surrender. His body was found slumped over a bloody sofa with a bullet through the mouth.

The new ruling junta included army commander Gen. Augusto Pinochet Ugarte, air force commander Gen. Gustavo Leigh Guzman, acting navy commander Adm. Jose Toribio Merino Castro and national police chief Cesar Mendoza Frank.

Elected in 1970 with a 36.6% plurality, Allende's Popular Unity Coalition was the world's first freely-elected Marxist government. However, Allende's attempts to socialize Chile brought strong opposition from the upper and middle classes as well as the armed forces, traditionally apolitical. His programs, and opposition to them, contributed to economic chaos, resulting in weeks of public disorders, nationwide strikes, and escalating demands for Allende's resignation.

Early on **Sept. 11,** the military and police commanders demanded Allende resign by noon "in face of the extremely grave, economic, social and moral crisis that is destroying the country." Allende refused: "I will not resign. I will not do it. I am ready to resist with whatever means, even at the cost of my life, to serve as a lesson in the ignominious history of those who have strength but not reason." Minutes after noon, bombers and heavy artillery assaulted the city. Twenty minutes later, the military took control of the Moneda, the presidential palace.

The junta immediately broadcast a list of 68 prominent Socialist and Communist leaders and ordered them to appear at the Defense Ministry or face arrest. All bank accounts were frozen. All foreigners were ordered to identify themselves at the nearest police station.

The new Government also assured the Chilean peaople that they could be sure their "economic and social accomplishments will not suffer fundamental modifications." As scattered resistance by Allende supporters continued, the junta warned that all armed supporters would be "shot on the spot if taken prisoner."

As the Christian Democrats and right-wing National Party pledged their support of the junta, Gen. Pinochet, **Sept. 13,** became President and swore in a predominantly military 15-man cabinet. Pinochet announced that the junta would "exterminate Marxism."

On Sept. 21, the junta banned all Marxist political parties. Dismantling of socialist institutions began **Sept. 23** with the abolition of food and price control agencies. The junta promised to return land illegally expropriated under Allende's agrarian reform. **On Sept. 25,** the junta abolished Chile's largest labor organization, the Central Workers Organization.

of the sun's corona, 16,800 pictures and 18 miles of magnetic tape data from earth observations, data on making metallic spheres and alloys in weightless conditions and data on the astronauts' physical reactions to the long-duration in space. **First Soviet Manned Mission in 2 Years**— Soviet astronauts Lt. Col. Vasily G. Lazarev and Oleg G. Makaroy successfully completed, **Sept. 29,** a 2-day experimental manned mission, the first Soviet space flight in more than 2 years. In June 1971, the 3-man Soyuz II crew was killed during re-entry into the atmosphere after the capsule sprang an air leak. The 2-day test was apparently made to check modifications in the Soyuz craft.

DISASTERS

An early morning fire, **Sept. 1,** in a hotel in Copenhagen, Denmark, claimed the lives of 35 persons, including 20 Americans... Five persons died and one was critically injured, **Sept. 2,** when a wild car careened into a crowd leaving a Cleveland, O., air show... An overloaded ferryboat sank, **Sept. 3,** off Koahsuing harbor in southern Taiwan, killing 25 women factory workers... A 2-car flaming crash near Evans Mills, N.Y., **Sept. 8,** killed 6 persons and injured 5 others ... All 6 aboard died, **Sept. 8,** when a chartered cargo jet crashed into a mountainside while attempting to land in fog near Cold Bay, Alaska... A Yugoslav airliner, **Sept. 11,** preparing to land at Titograd, crashed into a mountain peak, killing all 42 aboard ... A predawn fire raged through a Philadelphia, Pa., nursing home, **Sept. 13,** claiming the lives of 11 elderly persons and injuring 3 others ... A severe storm in northern Japan, **Sept. 23,** caused scores of landslides and floods and left at least 60 persons dead or missing ... A tourist bus carrying old-age pensioners plunged over Australia's Tumut Ponds Dam in snow-covered mountains, **Aug. 26.** killing at least 15 persons and seriously injuring 23 ... Torrential rain collapsed a mine in northern Thailand, **Sept. 27,** killing at least 50 miners ... All 11 aboard died, **Sept. 27,** when a Texas International turboprop plane crashed into a mountainside near Mena, Ark.... An auto-van collision, **Sept. 29,** near Hickory, S.C., left 8 persons dead ... Fire swept through 4 ageing tenements, **Sept. 29,** in Hoboken, N.J., claiming the lives of at least 10 persons and injuring 6.

October

NATIONAL

Mandatory Fuel Allocation Ordered—John A. Love, director of the White House's Energy Policy Office, announced, **Oct. 2,** a system of mandatory allocation of propane and distillate fuel supplies, including home heating oil, diesel fuel and kerosene. The propane allocation program was to be implemented on a priority basis effective immediately. The yet-to-be-detailed home heating oil allocation program would be based on maintenance of last year's deliveries to customers.

"Dirty Tricks" Investigated—In the first 2 weeks of October, the Senate Select Committee on Campaign Activities heard testimony on political "dirty tricks" during the 1972 Presidential campaign. Testimony highlights follow:

Donald H. Segretti, **Oct. 3,** told the Ervin committee he had reported regularly to the "dirty tricks" he was playing on Democratic candidates to Pres. Nixon's former appointments secretary

Dwight L. Chapin. Segretti testified, however, he had no reason to believe the President was informed about his work. In a lengthy rundown of activities, Segretti admitted he had sent out a fake letter on Sen. Edmund Muskie's stationery accusing Sen. Hubert H. Humphrey and Henry M. Jackson of sexual misconduct.

On **Oct. 10,** Fred Taugher, a former Southern California Campaign coordinator for Sen. George McGovern, admitted he had allowed persons planning antiwar demonstrations against the President to use McGovern telephones to rally supporters.

McGovern Campaign Director Frank Mankiewicz testified, **Oct. 11,** he believed sabotage activities funded by the Committee to Re-elect the President had deeply divided Democratic Presidential candidates and had made re-unification of factions extremely difficult.

Rebozo Accepted Hughes Gift—According to an **Oct. 9** New York Times report Charles (Bebe) G. Rebozo told Senate Watergate investigators and the Internal Revenue Service that in 1969 and 1970 he had accepted $100,000 in cash from agents of Howard Hughes. He also told Senate investigators that he had kept the money, allegedly a campaign gift, in a safe deposit box for 3 years until he returned it earlier this year. Former Huges assistant for Nevada operations Robert A. Maheu had charged earlier that the contribution had been made in exchange for political favors. In his **Oct. 26** news conference, Nixon described Rebozo as a "totally honest man" and said Rebozo had not acted improperly in holding the $100,000 for 3 years and then returning it. Earlier in the day, the Federal Deposit Insurance Corporation revealed it was considering suspending Rebozo as chairman of a Key Biscayne bank because Rebozo had sold stock which he allegedly knew to be stolen. The stock had been left with the bank as collateral on a loan that was later defaulted.

Spending "Mistakes" on Nixon Homes—In testimony before the House Government Activities Subcommittee, General Services Administration head Arthur P. Sampson conceded, **Oct. 11,** the GSA had made mistakes in spending Federal money on Pres. Nixon's private homes at San Clemente, Calif., and Key Biscayne, Fla. However, Sampson told the committee investigating $10.2-million in Government expenditures in connection with Nixon's private residences, that the work paid for at public expense had been insignificant. House Government Activities Committee Chairman Jack Brooks (D.-Tex.) stated, **Oct. 14,** that the investigation had raised "serious questions of propriety" and the record indicated money ostensibly spent to provide security at the President's residences had acted to add to opulence of the homes without serving any discernible security functions.

Senate Committee Loses Tapes Battle—The Senate Select Committee on Campaign Activities, **Oct. 17,** lost its battle to secure secret Presidential tapes relevant to their investigation into the Watergate matter. By-passing a decision on the merits of the case, U.S. District Court Judge John J. Sirica ruled that the committee's request did not fall within the court's jurisdiction.

Dean Pleads Guilty—Former Counsel to the President John W. Dean 3d, **Oct. 19,** pleaded guilty to one count of conspiracy to obstruct justice in plotting to cover up the Watergate break-in. In a bargain with Watergate special prosecutor Archibald Cox, Dean agreed to testify for the prosecution in future proceedings against alleged cover-up participants in exchange for immunity from prosecution for any Watergate-related crime. Dean could, according to the bargain, be prosecuted only for any future perjury. Dean faces a maximum 5-year prison term and a $10,000 fine.

Nixon Vetoes War Curb Bill—Asserting the bill imposed "unconstitutional and dangerous restrictions" on presidential authority, President Richard M. Nixon, **Oct. 24,** vetoed a bill limiting presidential power to commit U.S. armed forces without Congressional approval. The legislation required the President to report to Congress within 48 hours after commitment of armed forces to foreign combat. The committment would be terminated within 60 days unless Congress approved the action. The 60-day limit could be extended 30 days if the President certified to Congress that additional time was needed for withdrawal of forces. The bill further stated that, within the 60- or 90-day period, Congress could pass a concurrent resolution—not subject to Presidential veto—to halt the armed action. The Senate passed the bill, **Oct. 10,** by a 75-20 vote, sufficient to override a veto. The House vote, **Oct. 12,** with 74 absentees, was 3 votes short of the two-thirds needed to override.

Illinois Linked to ITT Settlement—Sources close

to the Watergate case reported, **Oct. 29,** that former Attorney General Richard G. Kleindienst had told the Watergate prosecution that Pres. Richard M. Nixon had personally ordered him in 1971 not to press a series of anti-trust actions against the International Telephone and Telegraph Corp. The consequent holdup of an appeal to the Supreme Court made way for an out-of-court agreement considered favorable to ITT. The White House denied the accuracy of the report. Former Watergate Special Prosecutor Archibald Cox revealed, **Oct. 30,** in testimony before the Senate Judiciary Committee, that he had disclosed Kleindienst's testimony to Senator Edward M. Kennedy. "Of course, I shouldn't have done it. It was carelessness, not malice," said Cox.

INTERNATIONAL

UN Rebuffs South Africa—The United Nations General Assembly rejected, **Oct. 5,** the credentials of the South African delegation. General Assembly Pres. Leopoldo Benites of Ecuador, however, ruled that the delegation could still speak before the assembly and otherwise participate in UN work. When South African Foreign Minister

---

Nixon Reverses Himself After Watergate "Firestorm"

Attorney General Elliott Richardson resigned, and his deputy William D. Ruckelshaus and Watergate Special Prosecutor Archibald Cox were fired, **Oct. 20,** when Cox rejected an Administration compromise on the disputed Watergate tapes and threatened to secure a judicial ruling that President Nixon was violating a court order to turn the tapes over to Judge John J. Sirica.

On **Oct. 23,** in response to an avalanche of public protest, the House began to consider impeachment proceedings and President Nixon agreed to obey the court order.

The constitutional drama began the evening of **Oct. 19** when Nixon announced he would not appeal the court order to the Supreme Court. Instead, Nixon said, he would personally edit a summary of the Watergate-related information on the tapes.

Nixon explained that his compromise, which involved a "breach in confidentiality that is so necessary to the conduct of the Presidency," would "assure unity of purpose at home and end the temptation abroad to test our resolve." Nixon also ordered Cox to drop his demands for other tapes, notes and memoranda of Presidential conversations.

Cox responded, in a televised news conference **Oct. 20,** that he would continue his court battle to obtain the tapes by seeking a court decision stating that Nixon had violated a court ruling. Cox said the Nixon compromise would create "insuperable difficulties" in conducting a criminal investigation. He also suggested that the White House had purposely submitted to him a series of compromises that were known to be unacceptable to him. Nixon reacted sharply, setting off a whirlwind of events.

Richardson resigned after being told he must dismiss Cox. He said the dismissal conflicted with his pledge to the Senate to provide Cox with "full authority" to contest Presidential claims of executive privilege. The President fired Ruckelshaus when he also refused to dismiss Cox. Cox was finally dismissed by Solicitor General Richard H.

Bork, who became Acting Attorney General. The White House ordered the FBI to seal the offices of Cox, Richardson and Ruckelshaus.

The events of **Oct. 20** caused an unprecedented expression of public outrage—a "firestorm," said one White House official.

On **Oct. 22,** the AFL-CIO convention, meeting in Bal Harbour, Fla., approved by acclamation a resolution calling on Nixon to resign and demanding his impeachment if he refused. Democratic leaders in the House agreed, **Oct. 22,** that an inquiry into whether cause for impeachment existed should be begun in the Judiciary Committee.

Acting Attorney General Bork, **Oct. 22,** formally appointed Henry E. Petersen, head of the Justice Department's Criminal Division, to take over the Watergate investigation. Petersen would proceed with the evidence and staff already assembled.

On the afternoon of **Oct. 23,** Nixon's attorney Charles Alan Wright, told Judge Sirica that Nixon would, after all, obey the court order and give up the tapes. Wright pointed out that even if Sirica had supported Nixon's refusal to hand over the tapes, "There would have been those who would have said the President is defying the law. "The President," said Wright, "does not defy the law."

Despite the President's decision to comply with the request for tapes, the Democrats in control of the House Judiciary Committee decided, **Oct. 24,** to "proceed full steam ahead" with an inquiry into impeachment of the President.

Subsequently, White House lawyer J. Fred Buzhardt, **Oct. 31,** informed Judge Sirica that Pres. Nixon could not deliver 2 of the tapes—the Apr. 15 conversation with Dean and the June 20, 1972 conversation with Mitchell—because they did not exist.

Despite the President's offer to release memoranda of the conversations, the disclosure dealt a staggering blow to national confidence in the President and prompted prominent Republican leaders to demand Nixon's resignation as President.

Hilgard Muller took the rostrum shortly after the rejection, some 100 of the 135 member nations walked out to express their disapproval of South African policies. South African Prime Minister John Vorster called the decision a "comedy," but said his country would remain in the UN.

All-Civilian Cabinet Installed in Greece—Spyros Markenzinis, **Oct. 8**, was sworn in as Premier of Greece's first all-civilian cabinet since the 1967 military coup. Markenzinis pledged to hold "impeccable" elections as soon as possible: "I have taken a solemn oath: this is going to be the fairest election in Greek history. If I can't manage it, I shall resign." He stressed the election would give full guarantees to all political candidates except communists and royalists.

Trudeau Visits China—Capping a 10-day visit to the People's Republic of China, Canadian Prime Minister Pierre Elliott Trudeau, **Oct. 13**, spent almost 2 hours with Mao Tse-tung. He and Premier Chou En-lai also signed a trade agreement which pledged emphasis on long-term commercial arrangements such as the recent $1 billion wheat deal, announced **Oct. 5**, between the 2 countries. Trudeau also announced agreements on exchange of scientific, medical and cultural delegations as well as on establishment of consular relations.

Chile Outlaws Leftist Parties—Chile's ruling military junta, **Oct. 13**, outlawed the 7 left-wing political parties that had supported Salvador Allende Gossens' Government. Two non-Marxist parties were included under the decree which prohibited all propaganda of Marxism "or any other doctrine substantially in accord with its principals or aims."

Thai Students Oust Government—Violent student demonstrations, culminating in bloody clashes with troops, **Oct. 14**, forced the resignation of Thai Premier Thanom Kittikachorn. King Phumiphol Aduldet immediately replaced him with Sanya Dharmasakti, the dean of Thammasat University, the center of student protest against Thanom's military-dominated government. The new premier promised to introduce a new constitution within 6 months and to hold general elections. Violence continued as tens of thousands of students and other civilians, **Oct. 15**, took almost complete control of Bangkok. Broadcasts reported that 2 other key leaders, strongman Marshal Praphas Charusathien and Col. Narong Kittikachorn, had fled the country and that Thanom would leave soon. Over national television, weeping students expressed their thanks to the King for cooperating with them in solving their problems and promised to work closely with the new government.

Guerrillas Seize Beirut Bank—Arab guerrillas, **Oct. 18**, seized the Bank of America office in Beirut, and took 40 bank employees hostage. The 5 guerrillas threatened to blow up the building unless the Bank of America agreed to pay $10,000,000 to the Arab war effort. They also demanded Lebanon release all Palestinian guerrillas jailed in Lebanon and provide safe-conduct to Algeria. The seige ended 25 hours later when policemen and army commandos, **Oct. 19**, fought their way into the bank. One hostage, an American, and 2 guerrillas were killed in the gun battle.

Liberals Sweep Quebec Elections—Premier Robert Bourassa's Liberal party captured 102 of 110 seats in a landslide victory, **Oct. 29**, in Quebec's 4-party parliamentary elections. The Liberals received 54% of the popular vote. The separatist Parti Quebecois, while winning only 6 seats, polled 31% of the popular vote, a 7% increase over the

vote in the 1970 elections. Bourassa had focused most of his campaign against separatist theories and the separatist leader Rene Levesque. Canadian Prime Minister Pierre Elliot Trudeau praised the outcome saying, "The people of Quebec have overwhelmingly voted for the party that is squarely on the side of federalism, and voted for Canada."

GENERAL

Atlanta Elects Black Mayor—Capturing 59% of the vote, Maynard Jackson, a 35-year-old attorney, **Oct. 16**, defeated incumbent Sam Massell to become the first black mayor of Atlanta, Ga. Referring to the bitter racial campaign waged against him, Jackson said, "We are the city whose people refuse to become bogged down in the mire of demagoguery and inflammatory rhetoric."

Brooklyn Rep Indicted—A New York Federal grand jury indicted, **Oct. 23**, Representative Frank J. Brasco (D.-N.Y.) of Brooklyn on charges of conspiring to receive $27,500 in illegal payoffs in 1968 from a Bronx trucking concern headed by an alleged Mafia member.

Sacred African Statue Returns Home—New York art dealer Aaron Furman, **Oct. 30**, cabled the King of Kom, a tiny African kingdom in the United Republic of Cameroon, that he was returning the Afo-A-Kom, a sacred statue that symbolizes the unity and heritage of the Kom people. The statue was stolen in 1966 and since then, it was reported, strife and quarrels have marked life in Kom, The location of the statue in the U.S. was revealed, **Oct. 25**, by the New York Times. Furman stated that he had bought the statue from an "impeccable" seller in Paris.

DISASTERS

Heavy rains and flooding, **Oct. 11-12**, in Oklahoma, Kansas, Missouri, Nebraska and Iowa claimed at least 7 lives and left thousands homeless...A wild elephant rampaged from the jungles of Zaire across the border into Sudan, killing 11 persons along its path, according to reports **Oct. 13**...A civilian airliner enroute from Tbilisi to Moscow crashed, **Oct. 13**, near Moscow's Domodedovo Airport, killing 29 persons...Typhoon Ruth swept the Philippines, **Oct. 15**, taking the lives of at least 50 persons and forcing some 15,000 from their homes...A Brazilian jet fighter crashed into a cluster of adobe huts on the outskirts of Fortaleza, Brazil, **Oct. 20**, killing at least 10 persons and injuring more than 30...Eight persons died and 12 were injured in a flaming crash of a tractor-trailer, a bus and a car, **Oct. 19**, on the New Jersey Turnpike...At least 93 persons died and more than 100 were missing when torrential rains and floods swept southern Spain, **Oct. 19-20**...All 5 aboard died, **Oct. 21**, when a light plane crashed in heavy fog into the General Telephone Co. warehouse in Long Beach, Calif...A fire raged through an apartment building, **Oct. 22**, in Danbury, Conn., killing 5 persons...Five crew members died when a burning Greek freighter sank, **Oct. 22**, in the mid-Atlantic 700 miles east of New York City ...Heavy fog abetted by smoke from a nearby smouldering fire, **Oct. 24**, caused a series of collisions involving 65 vehicles on the New Jersey Turnpike, killing at least 9 persons and injuring 40 ...An Argentine navy transport and a cargo ship collided, **Oct. 28**, in Rio de la Plata estuary off the Argentine coast, leaving 24 persons missing and believed drowned.

Vital Statistics

Source: Division of Vital Statistics, National Center for Health Statistics, Public Health Service

First Half-Year, January-June 1973

Births

For the first 6 months of 1973 there were an estimated 1,539,000 births in the U.S., about 4% less than for the first half of 1972. The birth rate (14.8 per 1,000 population) and the fertility rate (68.9) for the 6-month period were about 5% and 6% lower, respectively, than for the corresponding period of 1972 when they were 15.5% and 73.1%.

Marriages

Provisional data for the first half of 1973 indicate that marriages are again on the upswing over the same period in 1971. The number of marriages and the rate were up 2% and 1%, respectively, from the figures for January-June 1972. Estimates for the 12 months ending with June also show an increase in the number and rate.

Divorces

The number of divorces and annulments granted during the 6 months ending with June was up about 8%, to 449,000 from an estimated 415,000 for January-June a year earlier. The rate was 4.3 per 1,000 as compared with 4.0 for the corresponding period in 1972.

Deaths

The death rate for the first half of 1973 was 9.8 per 1,000 population, as compared with 9.7 for the equal period in 1972.

During January—May 1973 death rates for two causes of death declined: tuberculosis, all forms, declined 28% and diabetes mellitus decreased 8.5%. The following causes were significantly higher when compared with the same period a year ago: homicide increased 14.6% and bronchitis, emphysema and asthma increased 8.8% with emphysema up 10.1%.

Provisional Statistics
12 months ending with June 1973

	Number		Rate*	
	1973	1972	1973	1972
Live births.........	3,191,000	3,408,000	15.3	16.4
Deaths............	1,974,000	1,947,000	9.4	9.4
Natural increase	1,217,000	1,461,000	5.9	7.0
Marriages.........	2,286,000	2,241,000	10.9	10.8
Divorces	873,000	808,000	4.2	3.9
Infant deaths......	57,800	64,000	18.1	18.8
Population base (in millions).......	....	....	209.1	207.3

*Per 1,000 population

Annual Report for the Year 1971 (Provisional Statistics)

The birth rate for 1971—17.3 per 1,000 population—was the lowest on record for the United States in a period that witnessed marriages increasing for the 13th consecutive year though beginning to taper off. The provisional vital statistics summarized here show that births exceeded deaths by 1,638,000.

In 1972 the number of live births in the United States declined to an estimated 3,256,000, about 9 percent fewer than the number estimated for 1971. The birth and fertility rates fell to the lowest levels ever observed in the United States. The birth rate was 15.6 births per 1,000 population and the fertility rate was 73.4 births per 1,000 women 15-44 years of age. These rates were about 10 and 11 percent lower, respectively, than in 1971. This marks the second annual decrease following the upward trend between 1968 and 1970.

Although these rates are at record low levels, the population grew by 1,294,000 persons during 1972 as a result of natural increase, the excess of births over deaths. The decline in the rates between 1971 and 1972 was more than enough to offset the increase in the number of women in the childbearing ages (assumed to be 15-44 years), resulting in a decline of about 300,000 births.

Deaths

An estimated 1,962,000 deaths occurred in the United States during 1972. The provisional death rate was 9.4 per 1,000 population, an increase of 1.1 percent from the provisional rate of 9.3 for 1971. In 1972 there were approximately 60,200 infant deaths, resulting in an estimated infant mortality rate of 18.5 per 1,000 live births. This was the lowest annual rate ever recorded in the United States and represents a decrease of 3.6 percent from the estimated rate of 19.2 in 1971. The infant mortality

rate for every month in 1972 except April and August surpassed the record low for that month. Both the neonatal (under 28 days) and the post-neonatal (28 days to 11 months) mortality rates declined in 1972 with the neonatal rate showing a proportionately greater decline than the post-neonatal rate. The estimated expectation of life at birth in 1972 was 71.2 years for the total population, the highest ever attained in the United States.

Marriages and Divorces

During 1972 approximately 2,269,000 marriages were performed in the United States, 73,000 or 3.3 percent more than the year before. This was the 14th consecutive year the nationwide provisional number of marriages exceeded the figure for the preceding year. The overall increase in the number of marriages since the long upward trend began in 1959 was 56 percent, an average of 4 percent each year.

The number and rate of divorces and annulments granted in the United States increased for the 10th consecutive year. The provisional estimate of the number granted in 1972, 839,000, and the rate per 1,000 population, 4.0, showed increases of 9 and 8 percent above 1971 estimates, respectively. The upward trend in divorces began in 1963 with a rate of 2.3 per 1,000 population and reached the rate of 4.0 in 1972. The total increase in the rate for the 10-year period was 82 percent, with an average yearly increase from 1962 to 1967 of 4 percent and from 1967 to 1972 of 11 percent.

Births and Deaths in the United States

Data refer only to events occurring within the United States, including Alaska beginning in 1959 and Hawaii in 1960. Excludes fetal deaths. Rates per 1,000 population enumerated as of April 1 for 1940, 1950, and 1960; estimated as of July 1 for all other years. [1] Births based on a 50 per cent sample. (P) Provisional

	Births				Deaths			
Year	Males	Females	Totals Number	Rate	Males	Females	Totals Number	Rate
1955......	2,073,719	1,973,576	4,047,295	24.6	872,638	656,079	1,528,717	9.3
1960[1].....	2,179,708	2,078,142	4,257,850	23.7	975,648	736,334	1,711,982	9.5
1965[1].....	1,927,054	1,833,304	3,760,358	19.4	1,035,200	792,936	1,828,136	9.4
1970(P).....	NA	NA	3,718,000	18.2	NA	NA	1,921,000	9.4
1972(P)...	NA	NA	3,256,000	15.6	NA	NA	1,962,000	9.4

Births and Deaths by States

Source: Division of Vital Statistics, National Center for Health Statistics.

States	Births 1972	Births 1971	Deaths 1972	Deaths 1971	States	Births 1972	Births 1971	Deaths 1972	Deaths 1971
Alabama ...	61,869	66,386	34,313	33,835	Montana ...	11,361	12,198	6,847	6,737
Alaska	6,797	7,176	1,492	1,577	Nebraska...	23,500	25,720	15,615	15,374
Arizona	37,258	38,794	16,082	15,912	Nevada	8,793	9,605	4,460	4,225
Arkansas...	32,985	35,120	21,571	20,686	New Hampshire	11,294	12,632	7,482	7,481
California ..	303,542	339,113	167,979	171,954	New Jersey .	97,529	110,196	66,974	67,136
Colorado ...	39,869	41,373	18,453	18,417	New Mexico	20,589	22,293	7,994	7,758
Connecticut	39,130	44,908	26,490	26,151	New York...	254,431	285,218	182,570	185,238
Delaware ..	8,867	9,904	5,153	5,033	North Carolina	89,491	95,972	47,345	45,137
Dist. of Col.	21,579	25,048	10,393	10,314	North Dakota	10,577	10,911	5,819	5,780
Florida	108,985	115,865	85,396	78,928	Ohio	170,347	191,158	102,164	99,577
Georgia	84,337	95,287	44,189	42,067	Oklahoma ..	41,246	44,944	25,967	25,117
Hawaii	15,324	15,811	4,487	4,363	Oregon.....	32,303	33,999	20,289	20,103
Idaho	13,828	14,015	6,114	6,140	Pennsylvania	164,742	181,134	127,051	124,407
Illinois	175,604	192,321	108,894	107,217	Rhode Island	13,495	15,174	9,601	9,361
Indiana	87,191	96,760	48,622	48,860	South Carolina	49,007	53,131	23,587	23,074
Iowa	41,383	45,813	29,779	29,426	South Dakota	10,728	11,419	7,078	6,637
Kansas.....	31,637	34,184	21,922	21,778	Tennessee ..	69,752	76,093	41,610	40,061
Kentucky...	55,419	59,476	33,857	33,706	Texas	219,822	229,807	99,971	93,310
Louisiana ..	68,611	73,987	34,314	33,692	Utah	27,934	28,331	7,571	7,477
Maine......	15,892	17,335	11,174	10,732	Vermont....	7,180	7,817	4,451	4,460
Maryland...	51,059	57,363	32,826	31,772	Virginia	71,939	79,604	40,199	38,758
Massachusetts	79,522	90,415	63,037	56,792	Washington	47,148	54,192	29,881	30,231
Michigan...	147,187	160,917	77,923	76,088	West Virginia	29,679	31,598	20,739	20,066
Minnesota..	56,629	63,434	34,991	34,532	Wisconsin ..	64,142	71,697	42,088	40,693
Mississippi.	45,449	48,414	23,218	23,082	Wyoming ...	5,814	5,923	2,999	3,015
Missouri....	74,981	81,302	52,653	51,780	Total	3,257,777	3,571,287	1,965,694	1,926,047

Marriages, Divorces and Rates in the United States

Source: Division of Vital Statistics. National Center for Health Statistics.

Data refer only to events occurring within the United States, including Alaska beginning with 1959 and Hawaii with 1960. Rates per 1,000 population.

Year	Marriages[1] No.	Rate	Divorces[2] No.	Rate[3]	Year	Marriages[1] No.	Rate	Divorces[2] No.	Rate[3]
1890.........	570,000	9.0	33,461	0.5	1940	1,595,879	12.1	264,000	2.0
1895.........	620,000	8.9	40,387	0.6	1945	1,612,992	12.2	485,000	3.5
1900.........	709,000	9.3	55,751	0.7	1950	1,667,231	11.1	385,144	2.6
1905.........	842,000	10.0	67,976	0.8	1955	1,531,000	9.3	377,000	2.3
1910.........	948,166	10.3	83,045	0.9	1960	1,523,000	8.5	393,000	2.2
1915.........	1,007,595	10.0	104,298	1.0	1965	1,800,000	9.3	479,000	2.5
1920.........	1,274,476	12.0	170,505	1.6	1969	2,145,000	10.6	639,000	3.2
1925.........	1,188,334	10.3	175,449	1.5	1970	2,179,000	10.7	715,000	3.5
1930.........	1,126,856	9.2	195,961	1.6	1971	2,196,000	10.6	768,000	3.7
1935.........	1,327,000	10.4	218,000	1.7	1972(p)	2,269,000	10.9	839,000	4.0

(1) Includes estimates and marriage licenses for some states for all years. (2) Includes reported annulments. (3) Divorce rates for 1945, based on population including armed forces overseas. (p) Provisional.

Marriages and Divorces by States 1972[1]

Source: Division of Vital Statistics National Center for Health Statistics
(Divorces include reported annulments)[1] Provisional.

State	Marriages	Divorces	State	Marriages	Divorces	State	Marriages	Divorces
Alabama	49,569	19,052	Louisiana	38,037	NA	Oklahoma	40,784	17,480
Alaska	3,682	2,096	Maine	11,751	4,170	Oregon	18,824	12,435
Arizona	23,864	NA	Maryland.....	49,553	11,665	Pennsylvania .	99,471	27,142
Arkansas	24,949	13,762	Massachusetts	47,595	NA	Rhode Island .	7,829	2,017
California	173,563	111,162	Michigan	95,276	24,612	South Carolina	58,576	6,773
Colorado	26,513	12,503	Minnesota....	31,817	10,193	South Dakota .	12,090	1,635
Connecticut ..	24,752	8,003	Mississippi ...	28,434	9,699	Tennessee	56,249	20,336
Delaware	4,359	1,836	Missouri......	53,739	20,809	Texas	148,907	61,069
Dist. of Col. .	6,292	3,136	Montana	7,608	3,628	Utah	13,116	4,904
Florida	81,322	51,688	Nebraska.....	13,756	4,458	Vermont......	5,131	NA
Georgia	70,056	23,934	Nevada	99,265	NA	Virginia	55,849	14,174
Hawaii	9,731	3,895	New Hampshire	9,651	3,141	Washington ...	40,814	20,702
Idaho	12,119	3,801	New Jersey ...	58,573	17,499	West Virginia .	18,281	6,011
Illinois	118,087	43,164	New Mexico ..	14,273	4,230	Wisconsin	38,425	9,716
Indiana	60,649	NA	New York.....	166,730	40,937	Wyoming	5,328	2,170
Iowa	26,540	8,504	North Carolina	48,963	17,233			
Kansas.......	23,661	9,945	North Dakota .	5,826	1,272	Total	2,270,694	753,000
Kentucky.....	37,309	12,048	Ohio	93,156	44,167			

Wedding Anniversaries

The traditional names for wedding anniversaries go back many years in social usage. As such names as wooden, crystal, silver and golden were applied it was considered proper to present the married pair with gifts made of these products or of something related. While the list of permissible gifts is extensive, gifts are most appropriate when retaining a suggestion of the originals. Thus the wooden anniversary may call for anything of wood, including furniture, but as the years mount the gifts become more valuable until the 60th or diamond anniversary, calls for diamonds. The traditional list follows, with a few allowable revisions in parenthesis.

1st–Paper	6th–Iron	11th–Steel	20th–China	45th–Sapphire
2nd–Cotton	7th–Wool, copper	12th–Silk	25th–Silver	50th–Gold
3rd–Leather	8th–Bronze	13th–Lace	30th–Pearl	55th–Emerald
4th–Linen, (silk)	9th–Pottery, (china)	14th–Ivory	35th–Coral	60th–Diamond
5th–Wood	10th–Tin, (aluminum)	15th–Crystal	40th–Ruby	

Leading Cancer Sites, 1974

Source: American Cancer Society

Site	Estimated New Cases	Estimated Deaths	Warning Signal — See Your Doctor	Safeguards
Breast	90,000	33,000	Lump or thickening in the breast.	Annual checkup. Monthly breast self exam.
Colon, rectum	99,000	48,000	Change in bowel habits; bleeding.	Annual checkup including proctoscopy.
Lung	83,000	75,000	Persistent cough or respiratory ailment	Stop smoking, annual checkup, chest X-ray.
Oral	24,000	8,000	Sore that does not heal, difficulty in swallowing	Annual checkup.
Skin	300,000 *	5,000	Sore that does not heal, or change in wart or mole	Annual checkup, avoidance of overexposure to sun.
Uterus	46,000 *	11,000	Unusual bleeding or discharge.	Annual checkup, including Pap test.
Kidney, bladder	43,000	16,000	Urinary difficulty, bleeding.	Annual checkup with urinalysis.
Larynx	10,000	3,000	Hoarseness — difficulty in swallowing	Annual checkup, including mirror laryngoscopy.
Prostate	54,000	18,000	Urinary difficulty	Annual checkup, including palpation.
Stomach	23,000	14,000	Indigestion.	Annual checkup.
Leukemia	21,000	15,000	Acute leukemia, a cancer of blood-forming tissues, strikes mainly children and is treated by drugs which have extended life from a few months to as much as ten years. Chronic leukemia strikes usually after age 25 and progresses less rapidly.	
Lymphomas	28,000	20,000	These diseases arise in the lymph system and include Hodgkin's and lymphosarcoma. Some patients with lymphatic cancers can lead normal lives for many years.	

*Carcinoma-in-situ of the uterine cervix and superficial skin cancers not included in totals.

PREVENTING LUNG CANCER AND CIGARETTES

Deaths from lung cancer are expected to reach 72,000 in 1973 and rise to 75,000 in 1974. Since 1952, the lung cancer death rate has increased by about 100% for both men and women. Lung cancer is also the leading killer among all the cancers. It is responsible for over 31% of male deaths from cancer and for nearly 10% of female cancer deaths.

Lung cancer deaths for women have been rising rapidly, parallel to an increase in women smokers which began in the 1920's. Compared to the late 1960's, fewer women are smoking today, but they form a larger percentage of all smokers. Among teenagers, particularly, the numbers of girl smokers has increased dramatically — nearly doubling between 1968 and 1970.

Women also seem to find it harder to quit smoking. Of women smoking in 1966, 25.4% had quit by 1970. In the same period, 38.8% of men smokers had quit.

The 70 million people who continue to smoke are apparently smoking more. Cigarette consumption in 1972 hit a new high of 599 billion "coffin nails." Average consumption was a little over a pack a day and nearly 85% of these cigarettes were filtered.

More than 50% of the U.S. population over age 15 does not smoke and this majority is becoming increasingly visible through the clouds of cigarette smoke. On July 10, 1973, the Civil Aeronautics Board decreed that all U.S. airlines institute compulsory smoking and non-smoking sections on all flights. The Arizona legislature has banned smoking in all public buildings.

A major motel chain is experimenting with non-smoking floors in some of its motels. Several car insurance companies have begun to offer lower rates to non-smokers. The Army has stopped handing out cigarettes in its "C" rations, for a potential saving of perhaps $500,000 in tax money. And probably every smoker has noticed that some of his non-smoking friends are no longer gracious about providing an ashtray for visitors.

Trends in Cancer Death Rates
per 100,000 Population

Sex	Site	1952-54	1967-69	Percent Changes	Comments
Male	All Sites	136.0	155.1	+ 14	Steady increase mainly due to lung cancer.
Female	All Sites	118.5	109.6	− 8	Slight increase.
Female	Breast	21.8	22.9	+ 5	Slight fluctuations: Overall no change.
Male	Colon & Rectum	19.3	18.8	− 3	Slight decrease in both sexes.
Female	Colon & Rectum	18.0	15.8	−12	
Male	Lung	22.7	44.5	+96	Steady increase in both sexes due to cigarette smoking.
Female	Lung	4.0	8.1	+103	
Male	Oral	4.6	4.9	+ 7	Slight fluctuations: Overall no change.
Female	Oral	1.4	1.4	−	
Female	Uterus	17.2	10.6	−38	Steady decrease attributed in part to widening acceptance of regular checkup with "Pap Test."
Male	Stomach	16.9	9.1	−46	Steady decrease in both sexes: Reasons unknown.
Female	Stomach	8.7	4.5	−48	
Male	Pancreas	6.9	8.8	+28	Steady increase in both sexes: Reasons unknown.
Female	Pancreas	4.3	5.2	+21	
Male	Prostrate	14.0	13.5	− 4	Early increase, later decrease, again increasing.
Female	Ovary	7.2	7.6	+ 6	Steady increase.

Deaths and Death Rates for Selected Causes*

Source: Division of Vital Statistics, National Center for Health Statistics.

Rates per 100,000 population

1972* Cause of death	Number	Rate	1972* Cause of death	Number	Rate
All causes	1,962,000	942.2	Acute bronchitis and bronchiolitis	1,080	0.5
Enteritis and other diarrheal diseases...	2,180	1.0	Influenza and pneumonia	61,160	29.4
Tuberculosis, all forms	4,550	2.2	Influenza	5,010	2.4
Syphilis and its sequelae	320	0.2	Pneumonia	56,150	27.0
Other infective and parasitic diseases	3,360	1.6	Bronchitis, emphysema, and asthma	28,760	13.8
Malignant neoplasms, including			Chronic and unqualified bronchitis	5,360	2.6
neoplasms of lymphatic and			Emphysema	21,310	10.2
hematopoietic tissues	346,930	166.6	Asthma	2,090	1.0
Diabetes mellitus	39,070	18.8	Peptic ulcer	7,660	3.7
Meningitis	1,350	0.6	Hernia and intestinal obstruction	6,280	3.0
Major cardiovascular diseases	1,028,560	493.9	Cirrhosis of liver	32,760	15.7
Diseases of heart	752,450	361.3	Cholelithiasis, cholecystitis and cholangitis	3,630	1.7
Active rheumatic fever and chronic			Nephritis and nephrosis	8,190	3.9
rheumatic heart disease	14,090	6.8	Infections of kidney	7,010	3.4
Hypertensive heart disease with or			Hyperplasia of prostate	1,900	0.9
without renal disease	7,570	3.6	Congenital anomalies	15,050	7.2
Ischemic heart disease	683,100	328.0	Certain causes of mortality in early infancy	34,240	16.4
Chronic disease of endocardium and			Symptoms and ill-defined conditions	36,170	17.4
other myocardial insufficiency	5,330	2.6	All other diseases	110,910	53.3
All other forms of heart disease	36,810	17.7	Accidents	113,670	54.6
Hypertension	7,680	3.7	Motor vehicle accidents	56,590	27.2
Cerebrovascular diseases	210,050	100.9	All other accidents	57,080	27.4
Arteriosclerosis	32,820	15.8	Suicide	24,280	11.7
Other diseases of arteries,			Homicide	18,880	9.1
arterioles, and capillaries	25,560	12.3	All other external causes	5,690	2.7

Due to rounding estimates of death, figures may not add to total. *Provisional.
Data based on a 10% sampling of all death certificates for a 12 month (Jan. Dec.) period.

Principal Types of Accidental Deaths

Source: Division of Vital Statistics, National Center for Health Statistics,
Data for 1971 are National Safety Council estimates

Year	All types	Motor vehicle	Falls	Burns	Drown-ing	Fire-arms	Machin-ery	Poison gases	Other poisons
1960	93,806	38,137	19,023	7,645	6,529	2,334	1,951	1,253	1,679
1965	108,004	49,163	19,984	7,347	6,799	2,344	2,054	1,526	2,110
1969	116,000	56,000	18,000	7,000	7,200	2,400	.....	1,600	2,700
1970	115,000	54,800	17,800	6,800	7,300	2,300	.....	1,600	3,000
1971	115,000	54,700	17,900	6,700	7,300	2,400	.....	1,600	3,500
1972	117,000	56,600	17,400	6,800	7,600	2,400	.....	1,600	3,700

Death Rates per 100,000 Population

1960	52.1	21.2	10.6	4.2	3.6	1.3	1.1	0.7	0.9
1965	55.7	25.4	10.3	3.8	3.5	1.2	1.1	0.8	0.1
1967	57.2	26.7	10.2	3.8	3.6	1.5	1.0	0.8	1.3
1969	57.4	27.7	8.9	3.5	3.6	1.2	NA	0.8	1.3
1970	56.4	26.9	8.7	3.3	3.6	1.1	NA	0.8	1.5
1971	55.8	26.5	8.7	3.2	3.5	1.2	NA	0.8	1.7
1972	56.2	27.2	8.4	3.3	3.6	1.2	NA	0.8	1.8

Accidental Injuries by Severity of Injury

1972* Severity of Injury	Total*	Motor-Vehicle	Work	Home	Public Non-Motor-Vehicle
All Injuries*	11,600,000	2,150,000	2,400,000	4,250,000	2,900,000
Deaths	117,000	56,600	14,100	27,000	23,500
Nonfatal injuries	11,500,000	2,100,000	2,400,000	4,200,000	2,900,000
Permanent impairments*	420,000	170,000	90,000	110,000	70,000
Temporary total disabilities	11,100,000	1,950,000	2,300,000	4,100,000	2,800,000

Certain Costs of Accidental Injuries, 1972 ($ billions)

Total*	$23.5	$13.4	$5.2	$3.0	$2.6
Wage loss	12.0	6.0	2.6	2.0	2.0
Medical expense	3.9	1.4	1.0	1.0	0.6
Insurance admin. costs	7.6	6.0	1.6	...	...

*Duplication between motor-vehicle, work and home are eliminated in total.

Birth Stones

Source: Retail Jewelers of America, Inc.

Month	Ancient	Modern	Month	Ancient	Modern	Month	Ancient	Modern
January	Garnet	Garnet	May	Agate	Emerald	September	Chrysolite	Sapphire
February	Amethyst	Amethyst	June	Emerald	Pearl, Moonstone	October	Aquamarine	Opal or Tourmaline
March	Jasper	Bloodstone or Aquamarine	July	Onyx	Alexandrite or Ruby	November	Topaz	Topaz
April	Sapphire	Diamond	August	Carnelian	Sardonyx or Peridot	December	Ruby	Turquoise or Zircon

The term precious stones actually applies only to diamonds, rubies, sapphires and emeralds. All others are semiprecious. Precious gems are minerals brought to perfection by the lapidary's art. The pearl, often a gem of great value, is not a precious stone.

Average Future Lifetime in United States

Source: Divison of Vital Statistics, National Center for
Health Statistics, 1972 Data

| | | | Average remaining lifetime[2] | | | |
| | | | White | | All Others | |
Age Interval	Number Living[1]	Av. Life Expect.	Male	Female	Male	Female
0-1	100,000	71.2	68.3	76.0	61.3	69.9
1-5	98,165	71.5	68.6	76.1	62.3	70.8
5-10	97,853	67.8	64.8	72.3	58.6	67.1
10-15	97,658	62.9	59.9	67.4	53.8	62.2
15-20	97,456	58.0	55.1	62.5	48.9	57.4
20-25	96,894	53.3	50.5	57.6	44.4	52.6
25-30	96,198	48.7	45.9	52.8	40.2	48.0
30-35	95,500	44.0	41.3	48.0	36.2	43.4
35-40	94,687	39.4	36.7	43.2	32.2	38.9
40-45	93,547	34.8	32.1	38.5	28.4	34.6
45-50	91,887	30.4	27.7	33.9	24.8	30.5
50-55	89,272	26.2	23.5	29.5	21.4	26.6
55-60	85,514	22.3	19.7	25.2	18.3	23.0
60-65	80,104	18.6	16.2	21.1	15.6	19.6
65-70	72,580	15.3	13.1	17.3	13.3	16.6
70-75	62,495	12.3	10.5	13.8	11.3	13.9
75-80	50,313	9.7	8.3	10.6	9.5	11.5
80-85	36,106	7.5	6.5	8.0	8.2	9.4
85 and up	21,530	5.8	5.2	6.0	7.2	7.8

(1.)Of 100,000 born alive, number living at beginning of age interval. (2.)Average number of years of life remaining at beginning of age interval.

Years of Life Expected at Birth

Year	Total	Male	Female	Year	Total	Male	Female
1972[1]	71.2	67.4	75.2	1960	69.7	66.6	73.1
1971[1]	71.1	67.4	74.9	1950	68.2	65.6	71.1
1970	70.8	67.1	74.6	1940	62.9	60.8	65.2
1969	70.5	67.0	74.3	1930	59.7	58.1	61.6
1968	70.2	66.6	74.0	1920	54.1	53.6	54.6
1965	70.2	66.8	73.7	1900	47.3	46.3	48.3

Based on Death-Registration States 1900-1925, and United States 1930-1971. (1.)Provisional.

Suicide Rates by Age and Sex
U.S., Canada and Selected Countries

Source: Statistical Bulletin, Metropolitan Life Insurance Co.
(Rates per 100,000 population)

| Country | Male | | | | | | Female | | | | | |
| | 1956-57 | 1966-67 | | | | | 1956-57 | 1966-87 | | | | |
	Total*	Total*	15-24	25-44	45-64	65-	Total*	Total*	15-24	25-44	45-64	65-
U.S. Total	101.4	98.8	10.1	19.6	31.0	38.1	24.4	32.5	3.3	9.0	11.7	8.5
White	106.4	103.6	10.4	20.0	32.9	40.3	25.7	34.3	3.3	9.5	12.5	9.0
Nonwhite	43.9	50.8	8.4	15.6	13.3	13.5	9.3	15.3	3.5	5.0	3.5	3.3
Canada	76.1	80.0	11.0	17.6	26.8	24.6	20.2	25.7	2.4	7.3	10.5	5.5
Denmark	165.4	125.7	9.4	26.4	46.2	43.7	77.9	60.0	5.6	12.7	23.3	18.4
Norway	63.1	55.3	6.4	11.5	20.0	17.4	14.2[1]	17.9	1.1[2]	3.7	7.3	5.8
Sweden	161.2	150.9	15.3	35.5	53.1	47.0	43.4	52.7	7.5	13.2	19.3	12.7
Neth'lnds	52.7	55.3	4.0	8.2	16.0	27.1	35.0	29.5	1.1	4.5	10.4	13.5
U.K.	82.2	64.2	6.3	12.4	19.5	26.0	43.1	40.2	3.1	7.1	14.1	15.9
Belgium	123.4	122.9	7.1	15.2	34.7	65.9	44.2	47.4	3.0	7.0	14.3	23.1
W. Germany	137.2	153.4	18.4	30.8	51.5	52.7	60.9	67.8	5.1	12.9	24.1	25.7
Switz.	182.7	148.5	19.8	30.3	47.3	51.1	57.5	50.6	6.0	11.3	15.2	18.1
Austria	175.6	178.7	20.3	37.3	54.8	66.3	70.8	69.2	5.4	11.0	23.1	29.7
France	150.0	136.5	7.4	21.4	45.8	61.0	46.2	41.6	3.0	7.1	13.8	17.1
Italy	60.8	48.2	3.4	6.1	14.1	24.6	21.2	17.0	2.5	2.9	5.2	6.4
Port.	116.8	105.4	5.8	15.1	31.9	52.6	23.0	25.9	3.7	4.8	6.1	11.3
Japan	212.4	118.8	14.5	18.5	26.0	59.8	134.4	86.9	12.5	12.0	16.0	46.4

*Rate totals are only suggestive, not precise. They were derived by adding age group rates which had been
adjusted on the basis of age distribution.
[1]Incomplete as no rate was computed for the 15-24 age group in which fewer than 10 suicides occured.
[2]Rate based on 10 to 20 suicides.

Canadian Motor Vehicle Traffic Deaths

Source: Statistics Canada.

| | Number | | Death rate per passenger mile | | | Number | | Death rate per passenger mile | |
Province	1971	1970	1971	1970	Province	1971	1970	1971	1970
Total	5,573	5,080	6.7	6.4					
Newfoundland	87	69	6.8	6.2	Manitoba	181	159	5.3	4.8
Prince Edward Island	30	32	7.6	8.6	Saskatchewan	218	207	6.2	6.1
Nova Scotia	224	219	8.5	8.7	Alberta	461	401	6.5	5.9
New Brunswick	214	225	9.4	10.6	British Columbia	636	559	7.3	7.0
Quebec	1,730	1,655	7.8	7.9	Yukon	14	19	6.1	4.3
Ontario	1,769	1,535	5.6	5.1	Northwest Terr.	9		4.4	

Physical Growth Range for Children from 1 to 18 Years*

Source: U.S. Public Health Service, H.E.W.

Age	Shortest 5%	Median Height	Tallest 5%	Lightest 5%	Median Weight	Heaviest 5%
			Boys			
1	28.4	30.2	32.0	18.7	23.3	27.8
2	32.1	34.6	37.1	23.3	28.3	33.3
3	35.3	37.8	40.3	27.1	32.5	37.9
4	38.3	40.8	43.3	30.0	36.1	42.2
5	40.3	43.4	46.4	33.0	40.3	47.6
6	42.8	45.9	49.0	36.0	44.7	53.4
7	44.8	48.1	51.4	40.3	50.9	61.5
8	46.9	50.5	54.1	44.4	57.4	70.4
9	48.8	52.8	56.8	48.0	64.4	80.4
10	50.6	54.3	59.2	51.4	71.4	91.4
11	51.9	56.4	60.9	53.3	78.9	102.5
12	53.5	58.6	63.7	60.0	86.0	113.5
13	55.2	61.3	67.4	65.3	98.6	131.9
14	57.5	64.1	70.7	75.5	111.8	148.1
15	61.0	66.9	72.8	88.0	124.3	160.6
16	63.8	68.9	74.0	97.8	133.8	169.8
17	65.2	69.8	74.4	106.5	139.8	174.0
18	65.9	70.2	74.5	110.3	144.8	179.3
			Girls			
1	27.6	29.4	31.2	17.4	21.7	26.0
2	31.6	33.8	36.0	22.3	27.1	31.9
3	35.3	37.5	39.7	26.3	32.3	38.3
4	38.1	40.7	43.3	28.8	36.1	43.4
5	40.6	43.4	46.2	32.2	40.9	49.6
6	42.8	45.9	49.0	35.5	45.7	55.9
7	44.5	47.8	51.1	38.3	51.0	63.7
8	46.4	50.0	53.6	42.0	57.2	72.4
9	48.2	52.2	56.2	45.1	63.6	82.1
10	49.9	54.5	59.1	48.2	71.0	95.0
11	51.9	57.0	62.1	55.4	82.0	108.6
12	54.1	59.5	64.9	63.9	94.4	124.9
13	57.1	62.2	66.8	72.8	105.5	138.2
14	58.5	63.1	67.7	83.0	113.0	144.0
15	59.5	63.8	68.1	89.5	120.0	150.5
16	59.8	64.1	68.4	95.1	123.0	150.1
17	60.1	64.2	68.3	97.9	125.8	153.7
18	60.1	64.4	68.7	96.0	126.2	156.4

* This table simply gives a general picture for American children. When used as a standard, the individual variation in children's growth should not be overlooked. In most cases the height-weight relationship is probably a more valid index of weight status than a weight-for-age assessment.

Average Weight of Americans by Height and Age

Source: Society of Actuaries; based on a 4-year study of 5,000,000 persons
The figures represent weights in ordinary indoor clothing and shoes, and heights with shoes.

	MEN						WOMEN				
Height	20-24	25-29	30-39	40-49	50-59	Height	20-24	25-29	30-39	40-49	50-59
5'0"	122	128	131	134	136	4'10"	102	107	115	122	125
5'1"	125	131	134	137	139	4'11"	105	110	117	124	127
5'2"	128	134	137	140	142	5'0"	108	113	120	127	130
5'3"	132	138	141	144	145	5'1"	112	116	123	130	133
5'4"	136	141	145	148	149	5'2"	115	119	126	133	136
5'5"	139	144	149	152	153	5'3"	118	122	129	136	140
5'6"	142	148	153	156	157	5'4"	121	125	132	140	141
5'7"	145	151	157	161	162	5'5"	125	129	135	143	148
5'8"	149	155	161	165	166	5'6"	129	133	139	147	152
5'9"	153	159	165	169	170	5'7"	132	136	142	151	156
5'10"	157	163	170	174	175	5'8"	136	140	146	155	160
5'11"	161	167	174	178	180	5'9"	140	144	150	159	164
6'0"	166	172	179	183	185	5'10"	144	148	154	164	169
6'1"	170	177	183	187	189	5'11"	149	153	159	169	174
6'2"	174	182	188	192	194	6'0"	154	158	164	174	180
6'3"	178	186	193	197	199						
6'4"	181	190	199	203	205						

Bicycle Accidents

Source: National Safety Council

From 1961 to 1971, while motor vehicle deaths increased 44%, the number of deaths involving bicycles rose 70%. Urban bicycle fatalities increased 88%; in rural areas the gain was 54%. During this period, bicycle sales and usage went up more than 100%. Bicyclists over 14 years of age accounted for 27% of all deaths and injuries in these accidents in 1971, compared to only 13% in 1961. The largest increases in both use and accident casualties were among the 25-44 age group, where deaths increased by 300% over 1961 and injuries by 500%.

The Nation's Hospitals

Source: American Hospital Association

In 1972, there were 7,061 hospitals in the U.S. registered by the American Hospital Association. These institutions had about 1,600,000 beds and reported admitting some 30.7 million in-patients. About $32.7 billion was spent to provide services for both in-patients and outpatients, or a cost of $157 per resident of the nation.

	Hospitals		Beds		Average Daily Census		Admissions		Expenses ($1,000)	
	Fed.	Non-Fed.	Fed.	Non-Fed.	Fed.	Non-Fed.	Fed.	Non-Fed.	Fed.	Non-Fed.
Alabama....	8	140	3,027	24,883	2,472	19,452	34,192	575,153	$56,010	$383,181
Alaska.....	10	16	804	891	552	540	23,101	28,740	22,870	24,426
Arizona.....	18	64	1,711	8,809	1,272	6,534	45,573	277,217	48,273	258,857
Arkansas...	4	91	2,055	9,020	1,617	6,647	20,038	335,933	39,346	169,227
California...	35	600	13,245	108,429	10,308	76,902	206,984	2,916,787	340,364	3,138,605
Colorado....	6	90	2,255	12,561	1,848	9,005	37,187	398,152	54,693	315,760
Conn.......	5	62	1,057	20,392	761	16,653	12,009	414,233	30,786	512,726
Delaware ...	2	12	397	4,601	286	3,949	6,907	67,807	8,750	83,203
Dist. of Col..	4	17	5,937	6,430	5,006	5,023	30,370	184,746	114,070	230,342
Florida.....	15	190	4,065	46,192	3,217	35,920	78,669	1,134,505	117,821	909,956
Georgia....	11	161	3,449	29,367	2,678	23,806	50,579	745,377	75,479	523,495
Hawaii.....	1	30	750	5,056	493	3,744	19,194	91,095	17,500	92,409
Idaho	2	50	212	3,355	169	2,272	4,018	115,760	5,499	68,084
Illinois.....	10	291	7,275	80,204	6,131	62,803	62,433	1,768,621	150,981	1,883,725
Indiana	6	129	2,339	34,929	1,982	27,049	17,926	770,165	39,713	622,298
Iowa	3	144	1,805	19,788	1,311	13,190	12,028	489,811	38,219	339,625
Kansas.....	8	153	2,337	16,315	1,878	11,678	27,666	388,058	48,096	285,030
Kentucky ...	6	124	2,569	17,185	2,190	13,620	37,721	536,290	51,510	322,718
Louisiana ..	8	144	3,601	23,502	3,070	17,170	17,100	824,000	60,041	451,033
Maine......	2	50	918	7,530	829	5,888	6,046	152,418	13,608	120,169
Maryland ...	12	72	3,838	28,242	2,855	23,391	51,038	456,963	105,398	584,619
Mass......	9	198	4,625	52,957	3,919	40,687	35,017	906,305	89,267	1,279,046
Michigan ...	9	236	2,863	57,112	2,409	46,343	26,069	1,261,113	62,732	1,395,853
Minnesota ..	5	191	2,019	30,827	1,621	22,650	16,622	668,510	46,709	569,202
Mississippi .	5	103	1,778	15,086	1,516	11,737	26,721	378,310	36,781	198,666
Missouri....	8	145	3,344	33,254	2,552	26,126	46,362	778,321	70,121	649,351
Montana....	6	61	384	4,362	292	2,990	9,431	134,530	9,856	72,616
Nebraska ...	5	101	1,042	10,658	796	7,192	17,012	264,906	24,021	194,570
Nevada ..-..	4	19	268	2,570	216	1,752	6,805	78,251	8,501	64,391
New Hamp...	2	33	288	6,126	232	4,848	5,412	120,314	8,283	87,539
New Jersey ..	4	133	3,557	46,091	2,869	37,405	33,575	916,684	62,816	929,834
New Mexico .	12	47	1,138	5,188	793	3,310	29,207	143,972	30,884	95,785
New York ...	17	399	10,890	168,072	8,888	141,692	78,471	2,638,590	232,742	4,099,160
N. Carolina..	9	153	3,437	31,923	2,832	24,893	48,967	767,524	73,987	528,126
N. Dakota ...	5	58	433	5,147	312	3,451	11,625	122,416	11,128	77,773
Ohio	7	235	4,896	70,818	4,129	56,495	35,686	1,616,505	99,406	1,449,479
Oklahoma ...	12	130	1,435	16,328	1,024	11,789	35,232	426,720	43,130	276,998
Oregon	2	83	954	11,072	808	7,769	9,960	325,451	22,384	233,800
Penn.......	13	304	8,013	102,028	6,433	80,607	45,985	1,739,655	138,992	1,892,254
Rhode Island	3	19	641	7,310	506	6,412	10,710	129,965	18,750	166,558
S. Carolina ..	7	80	1,995	17,024	1,546	13,624	47,730	367,715	45,555	225,759
S. Dakota ...	10	54	1,320	5,038	1,027	3,476	19,590	112,623	22,250	64,090
Tennesee ...	5	151	3,270	28,879	2,696	23,115	32,716	719,814	60,909	492,098
Texas	28	522	9,058	67,426	7,204	50,094	144,369	1,880,525	191,285	1,250,252
Utah	3	34	603	4,190	459	3,105	7,906	164,233	15,583	102,252
Vermont	1	20	197	4,060	164	3,122	3,152	73,102	5,542	66,335
Virginia	11	116	4,717	32,221	3,644	27,612	67,857	646,867	107,334	500,047
Washington .	11	118	3,113	15,130	2,306	10,116	47,979	499,505	74,912	357,193
West Virginia	6	78	1,274	14,587	1,008	11,690	15,859	349,832	29,906	214,365
Wisconsin ..	3	181	2,038	31,379	1,635	23,210	17,715	730,799	54,518	630,665
Wyoming ...	3	28	596	2,218	514	1,432	4,964	59,927	9,821	30,021
Totals....	401	6,660	142,822	1,406,843	114,275	1,094,588	1,769,518	31,495,380	$3,147,738	$29,519,586

Purchases and Ownership of Life Insurance in U.S. and Assets of U.S. Life Insurance Companies

Legal Reserve Life Insurance Companies

Source: Division of Statistics & Research, Institute of Life Insurance

In millions of dollars. * Estimated. (p) Preliminary.

Year	Purchases of Life Insurance				Insurance in Force					Assets
	Ordinary	Group	Industrial	Total	Ordinary	Group	Industrial	Credit	Total	
1940......	$6,689	$691	$3,350	$10,730	$79,346	$14,938	$20,866	$380	$115,530	$30,802
1950......	17,326	6,068	5,402	28,796	149,071	47,793	33,415	3,889	234,168	64,020
1955......	30,827	11,258*	6,342	48,427	216,600	101,300	39,682	14,750	372,332	90,432
1960......	52,883	14,645	6,880	74,408	340,268	175,434	39,563	31,183	586,448	119,576
1965......	83,485	51,385†	7,296	142,166†	497,630	306,113	39,818	56,993	900,554	158,884
1967......	94,694	38,118*	7,056	140,868*	582,565	391,089	39,215	66,952	1,079,821	177,832
1968......	103,944	39,877*	6,674	150,495*	630,405	438,241	38,827	75,881	1,183,354	188,636
1969......	113,500	39,329	6,454	159,283	678,887	483,240	38,614	83,788	1,284,529	197,208
1970......	123,272	63,690†	6,612	193,574†	731,097	545,092	38,644	87,925	1,402,758	207,254
1971......	132,130	49,407	7,274	188,811	787,742	581,434	39,202	94,956	1,503,334	222,102
1972......	148,238	56,297	7,739	212,274	848,543	630,700	39,975	108,767	1,627,985	239,730

*Includes Federal Employees' Group Life Insurance $1.9 billion in 1955; $8.3 billion in 1967 and $3.4 billion in 1968.
†Includes Servicemen's Group Life Insurance $27.8 billion in 1965 and $17.1 billion in 1970.

Nursing Care Homes in United States

Source: Division of Health Resources Statistics, National Center for Health Statistics

State	Nursing Care Homes			Personal Care homes with nursing care		Personal Care and domiciliary care homes	
	Homes	Beds	Resi-dents	Full-time Person-nel	Homes	Beds	Homes	Beds
Total	12,871	917,707	824,038	567,717	3,568	192,347	5,565	91,544
Alabama	178	12,546	11,439	8,419	11	859	3	34
Alaska	7	478	379	371	1	175	—	—
Arizona	65	4,554	4,042	2,733	9	375	8	291
Arkansas	201	14,118	12,977	6,575	15	728	2	207
California	1,373	104,297	86,332	62,102	462	17,473	2,442	24,212
Colorado	166	13,511	12,293	8,070	26	2,397	20	541
Connecticut	246	18,474	17,593	10,935	36	1,628	98	1,815
Delaware	27	1,302	1,175	956	5	541	2	35
District of Columbia	34	2,038	1,904	1,851	27	583	12	153
Florida	290	29,104	23,494	16,697	41	4,090	42	2,677
Georgia	247	20,469	18,953	11,836	25	2,098	11	242
Hawaii	27	1,641	1,543	1,250	35	286	70	364
Idaho	53	3,569	3,151	1,993	5	179	6	165
Illinois	574	44,438	40,840	29,941	238	15,236	234	7,197
Indiana	403	25,658	23,168	17,168	72	5,431	47	1,449
Iowa	437	22,347	20,093	12,170	146	7,967	164	3,471
Kansas	247	14,166	12,963	9,235	174	7,043	59	659
Kentucky	139	9,051	7,706	7,337	144	7,365	61	2,206
Louisiana	193	13,732	12,547	6,930	13	665	6	213
Maine	144	5,400	5,059	3,606	44	876	100	1,115
Maryland	157	13,008	12,217	8,601	28	1,620	10	61
Massachusetts	643	39,309	37,274	21,327	170	7,501	147	2,877
Michigan	419	36,834	34,473	25,641	72	4,655	71	1,795
Minnesota	380	31,608	29,175	15,274	95	7,146	118	2,389
Mississippi	108	6,305	5,541	3,732	16	593	10	217
Missouri	355	25,162	22,229	15,094	94	5,818	45	1,042
Montana	61	3,368	3,157	2,291	27	894	15	197
Nebraska	150	10,775	9,730	5,576	73	3,820	30	507
Nevada	21	1,033	840	877	1	50	21	358
New Hampshire	97	4,591	4,255	2,684	28	627	15	242
New Jersey	297	22,454	20,205	15,742	64	3,456	205	4,865
New Mexico	35	2,259	1,765	1,775	8	794	17	246
New York	589	57,906	55,145	51,008	178	14,396	329	8,810
North Carolina	148	8,326	7,380	8,632	285	7,115	410	3,776
North Dakota	50	3,828	3,603	2,521	28	1,502	31	846
Ohio	940	46,923	42,377	28,630	158	10,551	93	2,050
Oklahoma	369	24,451	21,771	11,722	23	1,891	19	561
Oregon	197	12,880	11,925	7,074	43	2,984	71	1,307
Pennsylvania	547	43,451	39,581	29,942	143	12,674	63	1,566
Rhode Island	91	4,798	4,496	2,573	30	800	64	913
South Carolina	99	6,455	5,687	4,023	8	805	11	216
South Dakota	85	4,917	4,674	2,689	37	1,747	31	378
Tennessee	194	11,050	9,448	6,767	20	1,570	20	1,697
Texas	799	61,505	53,267	31,860	92	7,543	46	1,764
Utah	78	3,133	2,913	1,929	55	1,442	9	194
Vermont	55	2,263	2,052	1,569	17	317	29	430
Virginia	154	10,326	9,272	7,961	62	3,115	119	2,237
Washington	287	23,060	20,325	11,270	60	4,123	38	1,381
West Virginia	57	2,504	2,338	2,445	23	647	44	701
Wisconsin	356	30,973	28,028	15,668	98	5,965	36	710
Wyoming	20	1,359	1,244	735	3	173	11	165

Active Federal and Non-Federal Doctors by States

(as of Dec. 31, 1971)

Source: Division of Health Resources Statistics, National Center for Health Statistics

	Total	Non-Fed.	Fed.		Total	Non-Fed.	Fed.		Total	Non-Fed.	Fed.
All locations	322,228	[2]293,029	[2]29,199	Kansas	2,788	2,484	304	N. D.	635	557	78
United States	316,545	290,381	26,164	Kentucky	3,506	3,205	301	Ohio	14,409	13,811	598
Alabama	3,284	2,981	303	Louisiana	4,683	4,292	391	Oklahoma	2,786	2,478	308
Alaska	353	226	127	Maine	1,133	1,050	83	Oregon	3,080	2,941	139
Arizona	2,895	2,440	455	Maryland	9,535	7,168	2,367	Pa.	18,235	17,419	816
Arkansas	1,878	1,698	180	Massachusetts	12,427	11,531	896	R. I.	1,603	1,433	170
California	39,926	36,329	3,597	Michigan	11,270	10,882	388	S. C.	2,670	2,312	358
Colorado	4,291	3,729	562	Minnesota	5,950	5,540	410	S.D.	598	504	94
Connecticut	5,895	5,648	247	Mississippi	1,986	1,744	242	Tennessee	4,977	4,614	363
Delaware	772	721	51	Missouri	6,201	5,839	362	Texas	14,783	12,768	2,015
D of C.	4,028	2,933	1,095	Montana	778	713	65	Utah	1,600	1,479	121
Florida	10,207	9,180	1,027	Nebraska	1,780	1,642	138	Vermont	804	770	34
Georgia	5,538	4,872	666	Nevada	578	527	51	Virginia	6,502	5,482	1,020
Hawaii	1,222	1,129	93	N.H.	1,025	968	57	Washington	5,382	4,763	619
Idaho	709	655	54	New Jersey	10,791	10,261	530	W. V.	1,917	1,790	127
Illinois	16,006	15,008	998	New Mexico	1,385	1,130	255	Wisconsin	5,536	5,272	264
Indiana	5,318	5,126	192	New York	43,651	41,833	1,818	Wyoming	353	316	37
Iowa	2,932	2,795	137	N.C.	5,954	5,393	561	Puerto Rico	2,632	2,479	153
								Outlying areas	3,051	169	2,882

(1) Excludes 3,207 physicians with addresses unknown. (2) Includes 2,771 Federal M.D.s overseas not distributed by location.

Transportation Accident Death Rates

Source: National Safety Council

Kind of Transportation Passenger Deaths in 1972	Passenger Miles	Passenger Deaths	Rate Per 100,000,000 Pass. Miles	1970-1972 Aver. Death Rate
Automobiles and taxis[1]	1,850,000,000,000	35,200	1.90	2.00
Automobiles on turnpikes	50,000,000,000	540	1.08	1.05
Buses	70,000,000,000	130	0.19	0.19
Railroad passenger trains	9,000,000,000	48	0.53	0.28
Scheduled air transport planes (domestic)	125,000,000,000	160	0.13	0.10

(1) Drivers of passenger automobiles are considered passengers.

Selected Statistics on State and County Mental Hospitals*

Source: National Institute of Mental Health

Year	Total Admitted [1]	Net Releases [2]	Deaths in Hospital	Residents End of Year	Expense Per Patient [3]
1955	178,003	126,498	44,384	558,922	$1,116.59
1960	234,791	191,386	49,748	535,540	1,702.41
1969	379,838	373,287	35,962	373,984	4,593.61
1970	393,174	394,627	30,804	338,592	5,435.38
1971	414,926*	418,750	26,835	308,024	6,420.79
1972	390,000*	401,567	23,282	275,995	7,576.24

*Includes estimates. (1) Excludes transfers. (2) Net releases=resident patients beginning of year, plus all admissions (excluding transfers) minus deaths in hospital, minus resident patients end of year. (3) Per average daily resident patient population.

Patients in State and County Mental Hospitals

Source: National Institute of Mental Health. Average Daily Census 1972

State	No.	State	No.	State	No.	State	No.
Alabama	5,308	Illinois	13,915	Montana	1,192	Rhode Island	1,818
Alaska	150	Indiana	6,622	Nebraska	1,066	South Carolina	5,719
Arizona	708	Iowa	1,117	Nevada	218	South Dakota	1,103
Arkansas	887	Kansas	1,619	New Hampshire	1,672	Tennessee	5,239
California	9,324	Kentucky	2,250	New Jersey	13,384	Texas	11,037
Colorado	1,223	Louisiana	4,032	New Mexico	381	Utah	297
Connecticut	3,988	Maine	2,000	New York	52,736	Vermont	802
Delaware	1,275	Maryland	6,213	North Carolina	6,493	Virginia	9,439
District of Columbia	3,202	Massachusetts	10,052	North Dakota	715	Washington	2,189
Florida	8,433	Michigan	10,558	Ohio	13,882	West Virginia	3,852
Georgia	9,524	Minnesota	2,815*	Oklahoma	2,924	Wisconsin	8,362
Hawaii	295	Mississippi	4,538	Oregon	1,530	Wyoming	412
Idaho	267	Missouri	5,562	Pennsylvania	30,868	Total U.S.	000,100 †

† indicates estimates

The above data was based on reports of the 327 State and county hospitals. The full-time personnel was estimated at 219,777 and the expenditures $2,145,576,189. The average daily expenditures per patient based on the resident patient population of hospitals reporting expenditures was $20.68.

Estimated Patient Care Episodes in Mental Hospitals

Source: National Institute of Mental Health

Year	All Facilities	Inpatient Services					Outpatient Psychiatric Services	Community Health Centers [2]
		All	State and County	Private*	General	VA		
1971	4,038,143	1,721,389	745,259	126,600	542,642	176,800	1,693,848	622,906
1969	3,572,822	1,678,371	767,115	123,850	535,493	186,913	1,603,303	291,148
1967	3,139,742	1,659,391	801,354	124,258	578,513	128,196	1,383,000	97,351
1965	2,636,525	1,565,525	804,926	125,428	519,328	115,843	1,071,000	—
1955	1,675,352	1,296,352	818,832	123,231	265,934	88,355	379,000	—

*Includes estimates of episodes of care in residential treatment centers for emotionally disturbed children.

Patients in Canadian Mental Hospitals

Average number of patients per day, 1970

Source: Statistics Canada

	Mental	Psychiatric	Public for Retardates	Emotionally Disturbed Children	Other Mental [1]	Private	Total
Canada	32,261	1,400	16,889	147	2,051	918	53,666
Newfoundland	741	–	–	–	–	–	741
Prince Edward Island	275	–	20	–	–	–	295
Nova Scotia	776	482	–	–	–	–	1,258
New Brunswick	1,251	–	148	–	–	–	1,399
Québec	13,512	325	3,628	46	420	–	17,931
Ontario	9,066	422	6,453	86	110	852	16,989
Manitoba	1,386	36	1,203	–	–	–	2,625
Saskatchewan	812	72	1,384	–	–	–	2,268
Alberta	2,021	–	2,232	15	379	–	4,647
British Columbia	2,421	63	1,821	–	1,142	66	5,513

(1) Excludes two hospitals in Manitoba which did not report..not available.

The number of mental hospitals in operation in Canada during 1971 totalled 122 of which 110 were publicly owned and operated, the remainder being operated on a private ownership basis. Mental hospitals defined as providing treatment for all types of psychiatric conditions numbered 45 and constituted the single largest type of public mental hospital.

Total rated bed capacity of all mental hospitals amounted to 57,049 in 1971. The cost of providing care in public mental hospitals approached $435.6 million. Excluding Newfoundland, the per patient-day cost averaged $22.49. By hospital group, British Columbia excluded, the per diem rate extended from $18.49 in public hospitals for retardates to $51.49 in public psychiatric hospitals.

How to Obtain Birth, Marriage, Death Records

The United States Government has published a series of inexpensive booklets entitled Where to Write for Birth & Death Records; Where to Write for Marriage Records; Where to Write for Divorce Records; Where to Write for Birth and Death Records of U.S. Citizens who were born or died outside of the U.S. and birth certifications for alien children adopted by U.S. citizens; You May Save Time Proving Your Age and Other Birth Facts. They tell where to write to get a certified copy of or original vital record. Supt. of Documents, Government Printing Office, Washington, D.C. 20402.

Marriage Information—Canada

Source: Compiled from information provided by the various Provincial Government departments and agencies concerned. (As of June, 1973)

Marriageable age, by provinces, for both males and females with and without consent of parents or guardians. In some provinces, the court has authority, given special circumstances, to marry young couples below the minimum age. Most provinces waive the blood test requirement and the waiting period varies across the provinces.

Province	With consent		Without consent		Blood test		Wait for License	Wait after License
	Men	Women	Men	Women	Other Province Required	Other Province Accepted		
Newfoundland.........	—	—	19	19	—	—	—	—
Prince Edward Island...	16	16	18	18	Yes	Yes	5 days	None
Nova Scotia...........	(1)	(1)	19	19	None	None	5 days	None
New Brunswick........	14-18	14-18	18+	18+	None	None	5 days	None
Quebec...............	14	12	18	18	None	...	None	None
Ontario...............	14	14[2]	18	18	None	...	None[3]	3 days
Manitoba.............	16	16	18	18	Yes	Yes	None	24 hours
Saskatchewan........	15	15	18	18	Yes	Yes	5 days	None
Alberta...............	18—	18—	18+	18+	Yes[4]	Yes[5]	None[6]	None
British Columbia.......	16[7]	16[7]	19	19	None	None	2 days[8]	None
Yukon Territory........	15	15	19	19	None	None	None	24 hours
Northwest Territories...	15	15	19	19	None	Yes	None	None

(1) There is no statutory minimum age in the Province. Anyone under the age of 19 years must have consent for marriage, and no person under the age of 16 years may be married without authorization of a Family Court Judge and in addition must have the necessary consent of the parent or guardian.

(2) Women under 14 years also require a medical certificate as to necessity of marriage to prevent illegitimacy of offspring.

(3) Special requirements applicable to non-residents.

(4) Applies only to applicants under 60 years of age.

(5) This is upon filing of negative lab report-indicating blood test was taken within 14 days preceding date of application for license.

(6) Exception where consent is required by mail; depending receipt of divorce document, etc.

(7) Persons under 16 years of age (no minimum age specified) may also be married if they have obtained, in addition to the usual consent from parents or guardian, an Order from a Judge of the Supreme or County Court in this Province.

(8) Including day of application, e.g., a license applied for on a Monday cannot be issued until Wednesday.

Grounds for Divorce in Canada

Source: Government of Canada Divorce Act

The grounds for divorce in Canada are the same for all the provinces and its territories. There are two categories of offence.

A. Marital Offence
  Adultery
  Sodomy
  Bestiality
  Rape
  Homosexual act
  Subsequent marriage
  Physical cruelty
  Mental cruelty
B. Marriage Breakdown by Reason of: —
  Imprisonment for aggregate period of not less

than 3 years
Imprisonment for not less than 2 yrs. on sentence of death or sentence of 10 yrs. or more
Addiction to alcohol
Addiction to narcotics
Whereabouts of spouse unknown
Non-consummation
Separation for not less than 3 yrs.
Desertion by Petitioner for not less than 5 years

Residence time: Domicile in Canada
Time between interlocutory and final decrees: normally 3 months before final can be applied for.

Active Civilian Physicians in Canada by Province

(January, 1973)[a]

Source: Department of National Health and Welfare
Health and Manpower Planning Division

	Physicians	Population per Physician		Physicians	Population per Physician
Newfoundland.........	504	1,056	Saskatchewan.........	1,140	804
Prince Edward Island...	105	1,076	Alberta................	2,444	677
Nova Scotia...........	1,147	692	British Columbia.......	3,850	584
New Brunswick........	656	979	Yukon................	16	1,188
Quebec...............	9,677	626	Northwest Territories...	31	1,161
Ontario...............	13,364	586	**Canada**..............	**34,507**	**633**
Manitoba.............	1,573	631	[a] Preliminary figures		

Marriage Information

Source: Compiled by William E. Mariano: Council on Marriage Relations, Inc., 110 East 42 St., New York, N. Y. 10017 (as of July 1, 1972)

Marriageable age, by states, for both males and females with and without consent of parents or guardians. But in most states, the court has authority, in an emergency, to marry young couples below the ordinary age of consent, where due regard for their morals and welfare so requires. In many states, under special circumstances, blood test and waiting period may be waived.

State	With consent		Without consent		Blood test		Wait	Wait
	Men	Women	Men	Women	Required	Other state accepted*	for license	after license
Alabama (b)	17	14	21	18	Yes	Yes	None	None
Alaska	18	16	21	18	Yes	No	3 days	None
Arizona	18[2]	16	18	18	Yes	Yes	None	None
Arkansas	18	16	21	18	Yes	No	3 days	None
California	18	16	18	18	Yes	Yes	None	None
Colorado	16	16	21	18	Yes	. . . . .	None	None
Connecticut	16	16	18	18	Yes	Yes	4 days	None
Delaware	18	16	19	19	Yes	Yes	None	24 hrs. (c)
District of Columbia	18	16	21	18	Yes	Yes	3 days	None
Florida	18	16	21	21	Yes	Yes	3 days	None
Georgia	18	16	19	19	Yes	Yes	None (b)	None (o)
Hawaii	18	16	20	18	Yes	Yes	None	None
Idaho	16	16	18	18	Yes	Yes	None [4]	None
Illinois (a)	16[4]	16	21	18	Yes	Yes	None	None
Indiana	18	16	21	18	Yes	No	3 days	None
Iowa	18	16	21	18	Yes	Yes	3 days	None
Kansas	18	18	21	18	Yes	Yes	3 days	None
Kentucky	18	16	18	18	Yes	No	3 days	None
Louisiana (a)	18	16	18	18	Yes	No	None	72 hours
Maine	16	16	18	18	No	No	5 days	None
Maryland	18	16	21	18	None	None	48 hours	None
Massachusetts	18	18	18	18	Yes	Yes	3 days	None
Michigan (a)	18	16	18	18	Yes	No	3 days	None
Minnesota	18	16	21	18	None	. . . . .	5 days	None
Mississippi (b)	17	15	21	21	Yes	. . . . .	3 days	None
Missouri	15	15	21	18	Yes	Yes	3 days	None
Montana	19[2]	19[2]	19	19	Yes	Yes	5 days	None
Nebraska	18	16	20	20	Yes	Yes	5 days	None
Nevada	18	16	21	18	None	None	None	None
New Hampshire (a)	14(e)	13(e)	20	18	Yes	Yes	5 days	None
New Jersey (a)	18	16	18	18	Yes	Yes	72 hours	None
New Mexico	16	16	21	21	Yes	Yes	None	None
New York	16	14	18	18	Yes	No	None	24 hrs. (h)
North Carolina (a)	16	16	18	18	Yes	Yes	None	None
North Dakota (a)	18	15	18	18	Yes	. . . . .	None	None
Ohio (a)	18	16	21	21	Yes	Yes	5 days	None
Oklahoma	18	15	21	18	Yes	. . . . .	None (i)	**
Oregon	18(e)	15(e)	21	18	Yes	No	7 days	None
Pennsylvania	16	16	18	18	Yes	Yes	3 days	None
Rhode Island (a) (b)	18	16	21	18	Yes	No	None	None
South Carolina	16	14	18	18	None	None	24 hrs.	None
South Dakota	18	16	18	18	Yes	Yes	None	None
Tennessee (b)	16	16	21	21	Yes	Yes	3 days	None
Texas	16	14	19	18	Yes	Yes	None	None
Utah (a)	16	14	21	18	Yes	Yes	None	None
Vermont (a)	18	16	21	18	Yes	. . . . .	None	5 days
Virginia	18	16	18	18	Yes	Yes	None	None
Washington	17	17	18	18	(d)	. . . . .	3 days	None
West Virginia	18	16	21	21	Yes	No	3 days	None
Wisconsin	18	16	18	18	Yes	Yes	5 days	None
Wyoming	18	16	21	21	Yes	Yes	None	None
Puerto Rico	18	16	21	21	(f)	None	(f)	None
Virgin Islands	16	14	21	18	None	None	8 days	None

Many states have special requirements; contact individual state.

(a) Special laws applicable to non-residents. (b) Special laws applicable to those under 21 years; Alabama; bond required if male is under 21, female under 18. (c) 24 hours if one or both parties resident of state; 96 hours if both parties are non-residents. (d) None, but male must file affidavit. (e) Parental consent plus Court's consent required. (f) None, but a medical certificate is required. (g) Wait for license from time blood test is taken; Arizona, 48 hours. (h) Marriage may not be solemnized within 10 days from date of blood test. (i) If either under 21; Idaho, 3 days; Oklahoma, 72 hrs. (x) May be waived. (1.) 3 days if both applicants are under 18 or female is pregnant. (2.) Statute provides for obtaining license with parental or court consent with no stated minimum age. (3.) If either party is under 18, 3 days. (4.) Under 16, with parental and court consent. (o) All those between 19-21 cannot waive 3 day waiting period.

Flower of the Month

January—Carnation or Snowdrop. **February**—Violet or Primrose. **March**—Jonquil or Daffodil. **April**—Sweet Pea or Daisy. **May**—Lily of the Valley or Hawthorn. **June**—Rose or Honeysuckle. **July**—Larkspur or Water Lily. **August**—Poppy or Gladiolus. **September**—Aster or Morning Glory. **October**—Calendula or Cosmos. **November**—Chrysanthemum. **December**—Narcissus or Holly.

Grounds for Divorce

Source: Compiled by William E. Mariano: Council on Marriage Relations, Inc., 110 East 42nd Street, New York, N.Y. 10017, Persons contemplating divorce should study latest decisions or secure legal advice before initiating proceedings since different interpretations or exceptions in each case can change the conclusion reached.

* Exceptions are to be noted.

State	Cruelty	Desertion	Non-support	Alcohol	Felony	Impotency	Pregnancy at marriage	Drug addiction	Fraudulent contract	Other causes	Residence time	Time between interlocut'y and final decrees
Alabama	X	X	X	X	X	X	X	X		Q-K-W-F-MM	1 year*	None-R
Alaska	X	X	X	X	X	X	X		X	F-K-B	1 year	None
Arizona	X	X	X	X	X	X		X		X	1 year	None
Arkansas	X	X	X	X	X	X				B-Y-K-DD	3 months*	None
California										K-KK	6 months	6 months
Colorado										MM	90 days	None
Connecticut	X	X		X	X	X			X	K-F	3 years*	None
Delaware	X	X	X	X		X				F-K-Y-DD-FF	2 years	3 months
Dist. of Columbia		X			X					Y-Z	1 year	None
Florida		X			X		X		X	A-M-BB-DD-K-X	6 months	None
Georgia	X	X	X	X	X	X	X		X	K-M AA	6 months	1
Hawaii	X	X	X	X	X				X	K-Z-B-X	1 year	1
Idaho	X	X	X	X	X					X-K	6 weeks	None
Illinois	X	X	X	X	X		X				1 year*	None
Indiana	X	X	X	X	X						1 year*	None
Iowa										MM	1 year*	None-S
Kansas	X	X		X	X	X				K-F-CC	6 months	None-T
Kentucky	X	X	X	X	X				X	AA-PP	1 year	None
Louisiana	X	X		X	X					X-Z	1 year*	None
Maine	X	X	X	X		X		X		X	6 months	None
Maryland	X	X	X	X	X					Y-K-W	1 year	None
Massachusetts	X	X	X	X	X	X		X		LL	2 years*	6 mos.
Michigan										No Fault-MM	1 year*	None
Minnesota		X		X	X					K-W-OO	1 year*	None-T
Mississippi	X	X		X	X	X	X	X		K-M-DD	1 year*	None-U
Missouri	X	X	X	X	X					B-J-DD	1 year	None
Montana	X	X	X	X						K	1 year	None*
Nebraska										K-LL	2 years*	6 months
Nevada	X	X		X	X					K-Y	6 weeks	None
New Hampshire	X	X	X	X	X	X				D-GG-HH-II-KK	1 year*	None
New Jersey	X	X			X			X		NN-K	1 year*	None
New Mexico	X	X		X	X					F	6 months	None
New York					X					X-Z*	1 year	3 mos.*
North Carolina										Q-K-X	1 year	None
North Dakota	X	X	X	X	X	X				K	1 year	None-U
Ohio	X	X	X	X	X	X			X	BB-CC-DD	1 year	None
Oklahoma	X	X	X	X	X	X				F-K-BB-CC	6 months	None
Oregon										KK	1 year	90 days
Pennsylvania	X	X		X		X				B-M-DD-K-Y	1 year*	None
Rhode Island	X	X	X	X	X	X		X		H-X	2 years*	6 months
South Carolina	X	X		X						X	1 year	None
South Dakota	X	X	X	X	X					K	1 year*	None
Tennessee	X	X	X	X	X	X	X			A-B-DD-EE	1 year	None
Texas	X	X		X	X			X		K-X-F-PP	1 year	60 days
Utah	X	X	X	X	X	X				W-K	3 months	3 mos.*
Vermont	X	X	X	X	X					Y-K	6 months	3 mos.-O*
Virginia		X			X	X				I-B	1 year	None-U*
Washington									X	B-K-Y-KK	6 months	None
West Virginia	X	X	X	X		X				X-K	2 years*[2]	None
Wisconsin	X	X	X	X		X				X-W	6 months	120 days[4]
Wyoming	X	X	X	X	X	X	X		X	B-J-K	60 days	None

(1.) Determined by court order. (2.) No minimum residence required in adultery cases. (3.) Or 5 days after action is set for trial, whichever is sooner. (4.) Except one year when defendant is a non-resident, or personal service of a summons is impossible. (A) Violence. (B) Indignities. (C) Loathsome disease. (D) Joining religious order disbelieving in marriage. (E) Unchaste behavior after marriage. (F) Incompatibility. (H) Any gross misbehavior or wickedness. (I) Wife being a prostitute. (J) Husband being a vagrant. (K) 5-yrs. insanity; permanent insanity in Utah: incurable insanity in Calif. Exceptions 18 mos. Alaska; 2 yrs. Ga., Nev., Ore., Wash., and Wyo.; 3 yrs. Ark., Fla., Tex., Minn., Colo., Kan., Hawaii, Md., Miss., W. Va.; 6 yrs. Idaho. (M) Consanguinity. (N) In cruelty cases, one yr. to remarry. (O) Plaintiff, 6 mos.; defendant 2 yrs. to remarry. (P) If guilty spouse is sentenced to infamous punishment. (Q) Crime against nature. (R) Sixty days to remarry. Except Iowa, 90 days. (T) Six months to remarry; in Kan. 60 days. (U) Adultery cases, remarriage in discretion of court. (W) Separation for 2 yrs. after decree for same in Ala. and Minn.: 4 yrs. in N.J.; 18 mos. in N.H.; 5 yrs. in Wis. and Md. (X) Separation, no cohabitation—5 yrs., Exceptions La., Va., Wyo. and N.Y. (under agreement), W. Va. 2 yrs.; Tex. and Maine 3 yrs.: N.C. 1 yr. and R.I. 10 yrs. (Y) Separation, o cohabitation—3 years. Exceptions: Vt., Wash., 2 yrs.; Del., Md., 18 mos.; D.C. and Wis. 1 Yr.; (Z) Separation for : yrs. after decree for Dist. of Col.; 1 yr. for La. (AA) Mental incapacity at time of marriage. (BB) Procurement of out-of-state divorce. (CC) Gross neglect of duty. (DD) Bigamy. (EE) Attempted homicide. (FF) Plaintiff under age at time of marriage. (GG) Treatment which injures health or endangers reason. (HH) Wife without state for 10 yrs. (II) Wife in state 2 yrs.; husband never in state and has intent to become citizen of foreign country. (JJ) Seven years absence. (KK) Irreconcilable differences. (LL) Life sentence dissolves marriage. (MM) Breakdown of marriage with no reasonable likelihood of preservation. (NN) Deviate sexual conduct. (OO) Course of conduct detrimental to the marriage relationship of party seeking divorce. (PP) Incompatibility without regard to fault.

Adultery is either grounds for divorce or evidence of irreconcilable differences and a breakdown of the marriage in all states.

The plaintiff can invariably remarry in the same State where he or she procured a decree of divorce for annulment. Not so the defendant, who is barred in certain States for some offenses. After a period of time has elapsed even the offender can apply for special permission.

The U.S. Supreme Court in a 5 to 4 opinion, ruled April 18, 1949, that one sided quick divorces could be challenged as illegal if notice of the action was not served on the divorced partner within the divorcing States, excepting where the partner was represented at the proceedings.

Enoch Arden Laws. Disappearance and unknown to be alive—Conn. 7 years absence; N. H., 2 years; N. Y., 5 years (called dissolution); Vt., 7 years.

Motor Vehicle Traffic Deaths by States

Source: State traffic authorities

Place of accidents	Number 1972	1971	Mil. death rate* 1972	1971	Place of accidents	Number 1972	1971	Mil. death rate* 1972	1971
Total U.S.*	56,600	54,700	4.5	4.6	Nebraska	485	490	4.5	4.9
Alabama	1,248	1,251	6.0	6.8	Nevada	259	269	6.7	7.4
Alaska	59	65	3.9	4.4	New Hampshire	179	214	3.5	4.4
Arizona	807	754	5.5	5.7	New Jersey	1,314	1,319	2.8	3.0
Arkansas	764	693	6.0	5.7	New Mexico	587	537	6.6	6.7
California	4,996	4,462	3.9	3.8	New York	3,197	3,175	4.3	4.4
Colorado	738	635	4.6	4.6	North Carolina	1,976	1,846	5.8	5.9
Connecticut	467	493	2.6	2.9	North Dakota	208	227	5.1	5.7
Delaware	132	119	3.8	3.7	Ohio	2,451	2,373	3.9	3.9
District of Columbia	73	96	2.5	3.3	Oklahoma	843	843	4.1	4.5
Florida	2,498	2,377	4.5	5.0	Oregon	734	695	4.8	4.8
Georgia	1,885	1,815	4.7	5.7	Pennsylvania	2,352	2,299	3.5	3.8
Hawaii	146	154	3.9	4.2	Rhode Island	122	124	2.5	2.5
Idaho	348	325	6.6	6.6	South Carolina	1,099	1,023	5.6	5.8
Illinois	2,254	2,400	3.8	4.2	South Dakota	294	262	5.8	5.4
Indiana	1,555	1,615	4.2	4.7	Tennessee	1,414	1,373	5.1	5.5
Iowa	873	828	4.6	4.4	Texas	3,688	3,594	4.8	5.1
Kansas	666	678	4.6	4.9	Utah	382	337	5.7	5.1
Kentucky	1,093	1,023	4.7	4.8	Vermont	151	150	4.7	5.0
Louisiana	1,161	1,151	6.2	6.5	Virginia	1,256	1,218	3.8	4.0
Maine	258	271	3.8	4.2	Washington	852	876	3.8	4.0
Maryland	813	795	3.7	3.6	West Virginia	523	509	5.3	5.8
Massachusetts	991	908	3.3	3.2	Wisconsin	1,168	1,129	4.2	4.4
Michigan	2,258	2,152	3.9	3.9	Wyoming	197	166	5.8	5.2
Minnesota	1,031	1,024	4.1	4.4					
Mississippi	922	951	7.0	7.8					
Missouri	1,474	1,415	5.0	5.2	Puerto Rico	550	482	8.2	7.8
Montana	395	328	7.3	6.5	Virgin Islands	...	...	...	...

*The mileage death rate is the number of deaths per 100,000,000 vehicle miles.

Deaths in Civil Aviation Accidents

Source: National Safety Council (B of AS & FAA)

Year	Total deaths*	Scheduled flights (passengers) Domestic No.	Rate**	International No.	Rate**	General aviation No.	Rate**[1]
1960	1,286	297	0.93	10	0.12	787	24
1965	1,279	205	0.38	21	0.12	1,029	21
1970	1,453	0	0.00	2	0.01	1,309	20
1971	1,576	174	0.16	0	0.00	1,373	21
1972	1,538	160	0.13	0	0.00	1,357	20

*Includes some deaths not shown separately—crew members in scheduled operations and persons not in planes killed in airplane accidents. Excludes deaths in military plane accidents.
**Rates are the number of deaths per 100,000,000 passenger miles. (1) (NSC estimate) Pilots and other crew members are considered passengers for general aviation only.

Fatal Injuries in Mineral Industries By Industry Group

Source: Bureau of Mines, Dept. of Interior

Industry	1960	1965	1968	1969	1970	1971
Coal Mining	325	259	311	203	260	180
Coke	3	7	7	15	8	NA
Petroleum and Natural Gas[1]	82	78	102	95	134	NA
Metal Mines	84	58	57	62	57	47
Nonmetal Mines	19	21	36	17	16	15
Sand and Gravel	25	40	26	31	28	25
Stone Quarries	39	48	58	53	43	57
Metallurgical plants	12	15	6	21	16	NA
Nonmetal mills	13	10	3	10	10	9
Total	603	538	607	510	573	NA

(1) Beginning 1960, number of fatalities and permanent total injuries at petroleum and natural gas operations are combined. Fatal-frequency rates for 1960 include an unknown number of permanent total injuries which cannot be separated from fatal injuries.

Accidental Deaths by Age, Sex and Type*

Source: National Safety Council

Age and Sex	ALL TYPES	Motor-Vehicle	Falls	Drown-ing†	Fires, Burns	Ingest. of Food, Object	Fire-arms	Poison (solid, liquid)	Poison by Gas
All Ages	116,385	55,791	17,827	7,699	7,163	3,712	2,309	2,967	1,549
Under 5	6,973	2,077	325	600	1,012	1,012	80	245	45
5 to 14	8,186	4,045	184	1,560	655	141	375	55	69
15 to 24	24,668	17,443	389	2,190	396	256	777	676	405
25 to 34	12,964	7,894	420	830	419	211	315	486	214
35 to 44	11,446	5,974	742	710	636	295	253	415	238
45 to 54	12,304	5,850	1,141	650	900	419	226	392	212
55 to 64	11,888	5,162	1,766	480	1,053	415	170	342	188
65 to 74	10,643	4,210	2,635	300	898	425	77	221	92
75 & over	17,225	3,117	10,221	160	1,182	537	36	133	86
Age unknown	88	19	4	19	12	1	0	2	0
Male	80,706	40,213	8,983	6,526	4,265	2,262	2,004	1,895	1,149
Female	35,679	15,578	8,844	1,173	2,898	1,450	305	1,072	400

*Data are for 1969, latest official figures

Annual Fire Losses in the United States

Source: National Insurance Actuarial and Statistical Assn.

Year	Loss	Year	Loss	Year	Loss	Year	Loss
1940	285,878,697	1960	1,107,824,000	1968	1,829,922,000	1971	2,316,000,000
1945	484,274,000	1965	1,455,631,000	1969	1,952,022,000	1972	2,304,000,000
1955	885,218,000	1967	1,706,717,000	1970	2,264,000,000	1973 (6 mo.)	1,325,000,000

U.S. Building Fire Losses by Causes
Source: National Fire Protection Assn. Copyright 1973

These are estimated figures intended to show the relative order of magnitude of fire losses by cause. They do not show the relative safety in utilization of various types of materials, devices, fuels or services. They are approximations based on experience.

1972	Number of fires		Losses	
Heating and Cooking Equipment		155,200		$ 177,600,000
Equipment, defective or misused	89,400		$116,700,000	
Chimneys, flues defective or overheated	21,800		16,200,000	
Hot ashes and coals	6,800		3,900,000	
Combustibles near heaters, stoves	37,200		40,800,000	
Smoking and Matches		109,700		95,900,000
Electrical.		162,600		315,800,000
Wiring and general equipment	101,600		203,100,000	
Power-consuming appliances, motors.	61,000		112,700,000	
Rubbish, Source of Ignition Unknown.		36,000		2,400,000
Flammable Liquid Fires Not Reported Elsewhere		65,200		56,900,000
Open Flames and Sparks		71,900		102,200,000
Sparks and embers from fires	6,200		6,700,000	
Welding and cutting torches	8,200		28,800,000	
Sparks from machinery, friction	17,000		22,000,000	
Thawing pipes	5,500		11,900,000	
Miscellaneous open flames and sparks.	35,000		32,800,000	
Lightning.		22,700		43,300,000
Children and Matches		69,200		74,600,000
Exposure		25,400		23,400,000
Incendiary and Suspicious		84,200		285,600,000
Spontaneous Ignition ·.		15,100		25,900,000
Gas Fires and Explosions Not Reported Elsewhere . . .		8,700		23,400,000
Explosions, Miscellaneous and Unclassified		4,200		5,200,000
Miscellaneous Known Causes		65,900		191,400,000
Unknown or Undetermined.		154,200		992,700,000
Totals		1,050,200		$2,416,300,000

INTERPOL (International Criminal Police Organization)

The United States is one of 114 countries that are members of INTERPOL, the International Criminal Police Organization. United States participation in INTERPOL was authorized by Congress in 1958. Because of the Treasury Dept.'s activities in the suppression of counterfeiting, smuggling and the narcotics traffic, all of which have international ramifications, that department was designated as U. S. representative to INTERPOL.

Each member nation has one vote at a general assembly of INTERPOL held annually at a site chosen by the delegates at the previous year's assembly. The chairman of the U. S. delegation attending such meetings is the Assistant Secretary of the Treasury (Enforcement and Operations).

INTERPOL dates from 1914, but World War I brought suspension of all its activities until 1923. The organization's first constitution was drawn up in that year. Files on international criminals were built up gradually to a point where their value to the police of member nations became apparent. During World War II the files disappeared from Vienna, where the General Secretariat of INTERPOL was located.

The organization was reconstituted at the end of World War II. The General Secretariat was moved to Paris and is now located in the Parisian suburb of Saint-Cloud. The Secretariat functions as a central depository for fingerprints, photographs and other records of international criminals. It also operates an international radio network to 41 of the member countries.

Interpol does not employ any investigators as such. Foreign requirements for investigation are referred to the National Central Bureaus, the offices established in each country to liaison Interpol affairs. Scotland Yard is the National Central Bureau for the United Kingdom; the Surete in France; the Questore in Italy; the Melbourne City Police in Australia serve as the National Central Bureaus for those countries.

In the United States all inqufries, both domestic and foreign, are channeled through the National Central Bureau at the Treasury Dept. in Washington. Unless foreign requirements for investigation in the United States involve Federal jurisdiction or interest, they are referred to local and state police agencies for investigation. All U.S. enforcement agencies may call upon Interpol Washington for investigation in other member countries.

Capital Punishment

The Supreme Court ruled on June 29, 1972, by a 5-4 decision, that the death penalty as usually enforced in the United States was a violation of the 8th amendment prohibition of cruel and unusual punishment. By Sept., 1973, 16 states had restored the death penalty: Arkansas, California, Colorado, Connecticut, Florida, Georgia, Indiana, Louisiana, Montana, Nebraska, Nevada, New Mexico, Oklahoma, Ohio, Utah and Wyoming. The matter was pending in 15 states, defeated in 8 states. The question did not come up in 8 states, and in 2 states the legislature did not meet. In Mississippi, the governor vetoed a bill passed by the legislature because the language was unclear.

Locations of Federal Detention Areas
Source: U.S. Bureau of Prisons

Penitentiaries: Atlanta, Ga.; Leavenworth, Kans.; Lewisburg, Pa.; McNeil Island, Wash.; Marion, Ill.; Terre Haute, Ind. **Reformatories:** El Reno, Okla.; Petersburg, Va.; Women, Alderson, W. Va. **Medical center:** Springfield, Mo.; Hospital; Maintenance unit. **Prison camps:** Eglin Air Force Base, Florida; Montgomery, Ala.; Safford, Ariz.; Allenwood, Pa. **Correctional Institutions:** Danbury, Conn.; La Tuna, Tex.; Lompoc, Calif.; Texarkana, Tex.; Milan, Mich.; Tallahassee, Fla.; Seagoville, Tex.; Terminal Island, Calif.; Sandstone, Minn.; Ft. Worth, Tex. **Detention headquarters center:** New York City; Florence, Arizona. **Institutions for juvenile and youth offenders:** Ashland, Ky.; Englewood, Colo.; Morgantown, W. Va. **Community Treatment Centers:** Detroit, Mich.; Chicago, Ill.; Los Angeles, Calif.; Kansas City, Mo.; Atlanta, Ga.; Houston, Texas; Oakland, Calif.; New York City; Dallas, Texas.

Total Arrest Trends by Sex, 1971-72

Source: Federal Bureau of Investigation, Uniform Crime Reports—1972

Offense charged	Males Total 1972	Per-cent change 1971-72	Under 18 1972	Per-cent change 1971-72	Females Total 1972	Per-cent change 1971-72	Under 18 1972	Per-cent change 1971-72
Total[1]	5,432,300	+ 0.5	1,282,463	+ 0.4	966,794	+ 1.9	374,032	+ 2.3
(a) Murder and nonnegligent manslaughter	11,737	+ 4.5	1,442	+12.8	2,176	+ 0.7	132	− 0.8
(b) Neglig. manslaughter	2,148	+ 7.2	203	+15.3	306	+12.1	50	+25.0
Forcible rape	17,700	+14.1	3,601	+11.4	—	—	—	—
Robbery	97,124	+ 7.6	30,946	+ 7.1	6,763	+11.6	2,585	+15.2
Aggravated assault	123,321	+ 8.6	21,699	+ 9.4	19,111	+ 9.1	4,008	+10.7
Burglary—breaking or entering	271,954	− 1.1	140,915	+ 0.5	14,639	+ 3.8	7,125	+ 2.3
Larceny—theft	438,573	− 2.1	227,718	− 3.0	186,782	+ 6.2	86,333	+ 5.6
Auto theft	106,826	− 5.8	57,554	− 4.3	6,478	− 8.7	3,648	+ 4.6
Other assaults	245,928	− 0.1	44,420	+ 5.4	39,510	+ 0.9	12,658	+ 8.1
Arson	8,773	− 5.6	5,270	+ 1.2	939	−11.0	494	− 9.2
Forgery and counterfeiting	30,148	− 3.4	2,839	+ 3.2	9,989	− 1.3	1,125	+ 8.7
Fraud	63,459	+ 2.0	2,754	+ 9.8	27,037	+ 7.2	804	+ 4.1
Embezzlement	4,714	− 4.7	279	− 1.8	1,696	− 1.1	65	−46.3
Stolen property; buying, receiving, possessing	59,436	− 7.3	18,797	− 4.6	6,469	− 2.3	1,532	− 3.2
Vandalism	108,358	+ 4.5	77,956	+ 3.5	9,413	+ 7.1	5,860	+ 3.9
Weapons; carrying, possessing, etc.	103,365	+ 3.0	10,730	+ 0.1	8,224	+12.2	883	+ 8.9
Prostitution and commercialized vice	11,108	(*)	393	+ 8.0	31,380	− 8.4	932	+ 4.4
Sex offenses (except forcible rape and prostitution)	43,155	+ 5.1	8,606	+10.2	4,352	−17.2	1,748	−11.4
Narcotic drug laws	336,636	+ 8.1	73,463	+15.4	61,367	+ 2.9	17,920	− 0.3
Gambling	60,154	−16.4	1,579	−11.8	5,908	− 9.3	61	−19.7
Offenses against family and children	43,117	− 8.0	597	− 3.2	4,407	− 5.2	301	+13.6
Driving under the influence	509,674	+23.8	6,389	+36.5	37,757	+23.1	427	+59.3
Liquor laws	157,260	−13.5	55,772	− 8.1	26,604	5.0	13,799	0.5
Drunkenness	1,172,530	− 7.0	31,387	− 8.0	90,969	− 7.9	5,559	− 5.7
Disorderly conduct	464,145	− 6.3	98,834	− 5.2	79,167	−11.4	22,117	− 4.9
Vagrancy	35,172	−39.9	4,328	−42.8	19,159	+13.8	933	−34.5
All other offenses (except traffic)	738,855	+11.2	181,272	+ 0.1	141,301	+ 9.8	58,042	+ 2.8

*Increase of less than one-tenth of 1 percent.
[1]Totals will not add due to deletion of several minor crimes.

Canada: Criminal Offenses and Crime Rate

Source: Statistics Canada

	1971 Actual Offences	Rate[2]	Cleared[3]	Percent Cleared	1972 Actual Offences	Rate[2]	Cleared[3]	Percent Cleared
Murder	426	2.2	375	88.0	480	2.5	423	88.1
Attempted murder	346	1.8	284	82.1	412	2.1	356	86.4
Manslaughter	43	0.2	42	97.7	50	0.3	38	76.0
Rape	1,249	6.6	812	65.0	1,286	6.7	794	61.7
Other sexual offences	10,352	54.5	5,464	52.8	9,595	49.9	4,913	51.2
Wounding	1,849	9.7	1,460	79.0	1,706	8.9	1,264	74.1
Assaults (not indecent)	83,777	441.0	67,780	80.9	85,237	443.4	69,377	81.4
Robbery	11,551	60.8	3,840	33.2	11,839	61.6	3,817	32.2
Breaking and entering	192,748	1,014.5	44,861	23.3	191,088	994.0	44,017	23.0
Theft—motor vehicle	68,107	958.5	15,987	23.5	70,426	366.3	16,830	23.9
Theft over $50	177,491	934.2	26,122	14.7	149,414	777.2	21,773	14.6
Theft $50 and under	298,602	1,571.7	84,306	28.2	314,498	1,635.9	84,725	26.9
Have stolen goods	12,385	65.2	11,980	96.7	13,858	72.1	12,971	93.6
Frauds	69,454	365.6	41,283	59.4	68,792	357.8	41,729	60.7
Prostitution	2,017	10.6	1,885	93.5	2,183	11.4	2,106	96.5
Gaming and betting	2,332	12.3	2,073	88.9	3,126	16.3	2,638	84.4
Offensive weapons	6,932	36.5	5,989	86.4	7,528	39.2	6,590	87.5
Other Criminal Code	246,591	1,297.9	105,114	42.6	259,416	1,349.4	112,239	43.3
Total Criminal Code	**1,186,252**	**6,243.9**	**419,657**	**35.4**	**1,190,934**	**6,194.9**	**426,600**	**35.8**
Narcotic Control Act	18,901	99.5	13,656	72.3	23,840	124.0	19,687	82.6
Addicting opiate-like drugs	1,949	10.3	1,114	57.2	3,234	16.8	2,463	76.2
Cannabis (Marihuana)	16,952	89.2	12,542	74.0	20,606	107.2	17,224	83.6
Food and Drug Act	5,108	26.9	2,953	57.8	4,976	25.9	3,787	76.1
Controlled drugs	1,624	8.5	775	47.7	1,717	8.9	1,250	72.8
L.S.D.	3,484	18.3	2,178	62.5	3,259	17.0	2,537	77.8
Other Federal Statutes	39,809	209.5	34,179	85.9	39,796	207.0	35,641	89.6
Total Federal Statutes	**63,818**	**335.9**	**50,788**	**79.6**	**68,612**	**356.9**	**59,115**	**86.2**

(1) These preliminary figures for actual offences reported by police are subject to revision. Excludes arson as shown in Table 3 and traffic offences Tables 4, 5 and 6.
(2) Rates per 100,000 population 7 years of age and over based on estimates of June 1, 1971 and 1972.
(3) "Cleared" refers to offences cleared by charge and cleared otherwise.

Federal Bureau of Investigation

The Federal Bureau of Investigation (FBI) is an activity of the Department of Justice, and is located at 9th St. and Pennsylvania Ave., Washington, D. C., 20535. It investigates all violations of Federal laws except those specifically assigned to some other agency by legislative action, such violations including counterfeiting, and internal revenue, postal and customs violations. It also investigates espionage, sabotage, treason and other matters affecting internal security, as well as kidnaping, transportation of stolen goods across state lines, interstate traffic in prostitution and violations of the Federal bank and atomic energy laws.

The FBI collects and classifies police and crime reports for the nation. The Identification Division had 159,015,999 fingerprint cards on file Aug. 1, 1973. While this division is of great usefulness in detecting criminals, it serves a wider purpose in recording the fingerprints of many other citizens who voluntarily make this record.

The FBI has 59 field divisions in the principal cities of the country. *Consult telephone directories for location and phone numbers.*

An applicant for the position of Special Agent of the FBI must be at least 23 and under 36 years old and graduate of a state-accredited resident law school or from a resident four-year college with a major in accounting with at least one year of practical accounting and/or auditing experience. In addition, applicants with a four-year resident college degree with a major in certain areas or 3 years specialized experience of a professional, executive, or complex investigative nature are presently being considered on a limited basis. An agent gets 14 weeks of training, during which he learns techniques of investigation and arrest and recognition of evidence.

Clarence M. Kelley, former FBI agent and professional law enforcement officer, became Director on July 9, 1973.

U.S. Govt. Crime Reports
Source: Federal Bureau of Investigation

Offense	1972	Percent over 1971	1967
Murder	18,520	5.0	52.6
Forcible rape	46,430	10.8	69.6
Robbery	374,560	−2.9	85.5
Aggravated assault	388,650	6.6	52.9
Burglary	2,345,000	−1.0	45.6
Larceny $50 and over	1,837,800	−2.0	75.1
Auto theft	881,000	−6.4	34.5
Total	**5,891,900**	**−1.7**	**54.6**

Crime in the United States down 1%, first quarter 1973

Crime in the United States, as measured by the Crime Index offenses, declined 1% during the first three months of 1973 compared to the same period in 1972. The volume of crime would have increased 1% had larceny $50 and over been used as a Crime Index offense. The violent crimes as a group were up 6%. Aggravated assault increased 9%, forcible rape 7%, murder 6% and robbery 4%. The property crimes of burglary, larceny-theft and auto theft as a group decreased 2%. Burglary increased 2%, larceny-theft declined 4% and auto theft was down 1%. Cities having 100,000 or more inhabitants reported a 4% decrease in the volume of Crime Index offenses. Suburban law enforcement agencies reported a 5% increase and crime in rural areas was up 6%.

Crime Index Trends by Geographic Regions
(January-March, 1973 over 1972)

Region	Total	Violent	Property	Murder	Forcible Rape	Robbery	Aggravated Assault	Burglary	Larceny $50 over	Auto theft
Northeastern States	−	+6	+1	+2	+18	−1	+19	−	−2	+1
North Central States	+1	+7	−	+15	+1	+5	+10	+3	−1	−1
Southern States	−	+6	−1	+3	+2	+9	+4	+1	−3	−1
Western States	−5	+6	−6	+7	+9	+7	+5	+2	−10	−7

Crime Rates by State

Source: Federal Bureau of Investigation, Uniform Crime Reports—1972

(Rates per 100,000 population)

State	Total	Violent	Property	Murder	Rape	Robbery	Assault	Burglary	Larceny	Auto Theft
Ala.	1,842.2	313.2	1,529.0	14.1	18.8	68.6	211.7	776.1	557.8	195.0
Alas.	3,126.5	370.5	2,756.0	9.5	41.8	66.5	252.6	970.8	1,287.1	498.2
Ariz.	3,745.9	448.9	3,297.0	7.3	33.4	120.8	287.4	1,615.9	1,251.3	429.8
Ark.	1,606.8	244.7	1,362.1	10.4	17.3	54.8	162.2	663.1	594.8	104.2
Cal.	4,606.2	540.7	4,065.5	8.8	39.7	238.6	253.7	1,949.2	1,435.1	681.3
Colo.	4,054.5	405.4	3,649.1	8.3	38.4	141.4	217.3	1,580.1	1,479.7	589.3
Conn.	2,470.4	199.2	2,271.3	3.2	8.9	79.1	107.9	956.8	845.4	469.1
Dela.	3,162.5	386.0	2,776.5	6.9	14.2	130.1	234.9	1,249.4	1,035.9	491.2
Fla.	3,920.2	554.5	3,365.7	12.7	26.4	189.4	326.0	1,605.1	1,394.4	366.1
Ga.	2,468.9	377.6	2,091.3	18.5	20.8	134.3	204.0	1,081.7	702.9	306.7
Hawaii	3,011.9	155.5	2,856.4	6.8	21.3	55.4	72.1	1,335.6	1,122.4	398.4
Idaho	2,134.4	143.5	1,990.9	3.8	15.6	20.6	103.4	754.6	1,052.4	183.9
Ill.	2,483.8	508.1	1,975.8	8.8	23.3	260.1	215.9	846.1	686.7	443.0
Ind.	2,273.7	233.9	2,039.9	6.0	20.3	106.6	100.9	880.9	810.8	348.1
Iowa	1,461.3	87.4	1,374.0	1.7	8.6	26.7	50.3	521.6	683.3	169.1
Kan.	2,139.4	209.8	1,929.6	4.0	17.8	68.9	119.1	906.6	791.0	232.0
Ky.	1,766.7	225.7	1,541.0	9.8	15.7	83.2	117.1	650.2	609.0	281.8
La.	2,470.5	422.4	2,048.1	13.2	23.0	133.4	252.8	903.1	788.5	356.4
Maine	1,518.1	103.8	1,414.3	5.3	7.8	21.1	69.6	698.0	560.8	155.5
Md.	3,379.3	651.2	2,728.1	12.5	26.0	324.1	288.6	1,111.7	1,082.2	534.2
Mass.	3,391.4	295.2	3,096.2	3.7	13.5	152.8	125.2	1,242.3	881.4	972.4
Mich.	3,819.5	555.2	3,264.3	11.0	29.3	289.3	225.6	1,582.3	1,208.0	473.9
Minn.	2,256.0	174.5	2,081.5	2.4	14.7	84.4	72.9	927.2	817.0	337.3
Miss.	1,320.1	312.7	1,007.4	15.4	17.5	39.9	240.0	540.0	346.8	120.5
Mo.	2,654.2	383.4	2,270.8	8.3	25.5	175.6	174.0	1,100.6	699.7	470.5
Mont.	1,926.7	150.1	1,776.6	2.5	10.8	33.2	103.5	708.2	821.4	247.0
Neb.	1,720.2	173.0	1,547.2	2.9	13.9	52.7	103.5	556.7	729.0	261.6
Nev.	4,236.6	429.6	3,807.0	13.5	34.0	190.1	192.0	1,757.5	1,496.1	563.4
N. H.	1,377.7	63.7	1,314.0	1.7	7.0	13.4	41.6	596.6	592.6	124.8
N. J.	3,033.1	374.3	2,658.7	6.5	16.9	210.1	140.8	1,194.3	878.3	586.2

State	Total	Violent	Property	Murder	Rape	Robbery	Assault	Burglary	Larceny	Auto Theft
N. M.....	3,417.3	415.8	3,001.5	11.1	32.7	119.0	253.1	1,402.1	1,230.0	369.5
N. Y.....	3,488.5	744.1	2,744.4	11.0	22.4	467.4	243.2	1,256.3	923.2	565.0
N. C.....	1,933.0	414.5	1,518.5	12.8	14.2	62.3	325.3	752.0	618.3	148.2
N. D.....	1,023.9	45.9	978.0	1.3	4.9	8.9	30.9	357.1	530.2	90.7
Ohio	2,361.1	299.4	2,061.7	7.5	19.9	160.6	111.4	901.3	717.8	442.6
Okla.....	2,101.5	232.6	1,868.8	7.0	19.0	63.6	143.1	942.9	661.3	264.6
Ore.....	3,443.2	297.6	3,145.6	5.5	26.3	109.5	156.3	1,468.8	1,290.2	386.6
Penn. ...	1,780.3	267.4	1,512.8	6.0	15.2	145.6	100.6	742.3	437.1	333.5
R. I......	3,267.5	250.4	3,017.0	1.3	8.3	81.7	159.1	1,124.0	996.9	896.2
S. C.....	2,287.3	385.8	1,901.5	16.8	21.4	66.0	281.6	992.3	695.9	213.2
S. D.	1,278.8	111.3	1,167.5	1.2	11.3	15.6	83.2	472.8	587.3	107.4
Tenn. ...	2,101.5	319.0	1,782.6	11.3	19.9	101.1	186.7	894.3	587.4	300.9
Texas ...	2,655.6	350.9	2,304.7	12.3	23.8	118.2	196.6	1,206.7	768.6	329.3
Utah	2,541.5	183.2	2,358.3	2.9	18.3	62.3	99.7	913.2	1,167.3	277.7
Vt.......	1,446.3	96.3	1,350.0	1.7	10.8	10.6	73.2	738.3	497.6	114.1
Va.......	2,032.2	297.6	1,734.6	9.6	19.5	109.4	159.1	790.0	678.0	266.6
Wash....	3,160.8	250.6	2,910.3	4.2	21.8	87.6	137.0	1,381.4	1,197.6	331.3
W. V.....	1,056.8	129.1	927.7	6.1	8.2	31.6	83.2	413.0	405.1	109.7
Wisc.....	1,783.1	96.4	1,686.7	2.8	8.3	36.7	48.6	638.5	815.4	232.7
Wyo.	1,906.1	148.1	1,758.0	4.1	13.9	33.9	96.2	596.2	958.0	203.8

Reported Crime in Metropolitan Areas, 1972

Source: Federal Bureau of Investigation, Uniform Crime Reports—1972

The 27 Standard Metropolitan Statistical Areas listed below are those which appear most frequently among the top 30 cities in per capita reported crime rate for each of 7 kinds of major crime: the 5 listed below plus forcible rape and aggravated assault.

The rates are for reported crimes only; they are not an accurate index of crimes actually committed. In many metropolitan areas an unknown number of crimes go unreported by victims. This is especially true of the crimes of rape, burglary and larceny.

The number in parentheses following the city name indicates the number of categories (including forcible rape and aggravated assault) in which the city appears among the top 30.

The numbers in parentheses following crime rate figures give that city's rank in that category of crime. If no number appears, the city is not among the top 30 in that category.

	Rate per 100,000 population							
City	Total Crime[1]	Violent Crime[2]	Property Crime[3]	Murder Manslaughter[4]	Robbery	Burglary	Larceny Over $50	Auto Theft
Albuquerque, N.M.(5)	5,910.2 (1)	785.4 (8)	5,124.9 (1)	9.6	289.8(16)	2,468.4 (2)	2,027.2 (1)	629.2
Stockton, Cal.(4)...... ..:	5,470.1 (2)	512.6	4,957.5 (3)	13.7	250.1(26)	2,506.3 (1)	1,758.1 (7)	693.1(23)
Los Angeles-Long Beach, Cal.(5) .	5,431.7 (3)	853.0 (4)	4,578.7 (5)	13.7	377.7 (6)	2,237.3 (6)	1,365.6	975.8 (7)
Fresno, Cal.(3)	5,318.8 (4)	330.8	4,988.0 (2)	11.4	151.8	2,290.8 (3)	1,889.9 (2)	807.3(13)
Baton Rouge, La. (5).	5,229.2 (5)	774.5 (9)	4,454.7 (7)	12.6	191.7	2,281.4 (4)	1,505.2(30)	668.2(25)
Miami, Fla.(5)................	5,151.4 (6)	869.3 (3)	4,282.1(11)	14.3	385.3 (4)	1,826.8(23)	1,810.3 (4)	645.0(29)
Denver, Colo.(4)	5,104.2 (7)	493.6	4,610.6 (4)	9.5	202.7	2,070.7 (9)	1,679.3(11)	860.6 (9)
New York, N.Y.(5)	5,094.2 (8)	1,357.1 (1)	3,737.1(25)	19.1 (9)	877.4 (1)	1,747.4	1,100.2	889.5 (8)
San Francisco-Oakland, Cal.(4) ..	5,005.9 (9)	643.0(17)	4,362.8 (9)	8.6	341.9(10)	2,045.4(10)	1,488.8	828.7(11)
Ann Arbor, Mich.(3)..........	4,990.0(10)	437.9	4,552.1 (6)	6.1	179.0	2,267.4 (5)	1,826.7 (3)	458.0
Detroit, Mich.(4)..............	4,818.1(11)	821.1 (5)	3,997.1(17)	17.3(20)	507.1 (3)	1,855.9(19)	1,357.3	783.9(15)
Las Vegas, Nev.(6)	4,732.4(12)	506.9	4,225.4(12)	18.3(13)	241.4(28)	1,988.3(15)	1,572.0(20)	665.1(26)
Daytona Beach, Fla.(3)	4,664.2(14)	572.5(25)	4,091.8(15)	11.6	197.4	2,180.2 (7)	1,548.1(24)	363.5
Phoenix, Ariz.(4).............	4,652.0(15)	550.9	4,101.1(14)	9.5	149.6	2,023.8(13)	1,540.6(26)	536.7
Santa Cruz, Cal.(3)...........	4,620.2(16)	415.8	4,204.4(13)	3.7	102.7	2,078.4 (8)	1,633.5(16)	492.4
Savannah, Ga.(5)	4,561.0(17)	811.8 (6)	3,750.1(24)	19.2 (8)	274.7(20)	1,953.4(16)	1,338.2	468.6
W. Palm Beach, Fla.(3)	4,428.5(18)	655.1(16)	3,773.4(23)	11.1	152.7	1,842.1(22)	1,652.1(14)	279.1
Gainesville, Fla.(4)...........	4,392.3(20)	684.8(12)	3,707.5(26)	22.3 (2)	150.7	1,734.3	1,646.9(15)	326.3
Atlantic City, N.J. (3)	4,372.5(22)	437.5	3,935.0(19)	11.0	267.1(22)	1,907.9(17)	1,369.8	657.4(27)
Jacksonville, Fla.(5)	4,321.2(25)	799.1 (7)	3,522.0	17.4(18)	263.4(23)	1,994.2(14)	1,157.1	370.7
Gary-Hammond, Ind.(3)........	4,206.0(28)	516.7	3,689.3(28)	16.9(26)	303.9(13)	1,423.7	1,249.5	1,016.1 (4)
Baltimore, Md.(3)	4,051.7(29)	956.6 (2)	3,095.1	17.6(16)	507.7 (2)	1,356.2	1,115.9	622.9
Memphis, Tenn.(4)	4,051.4(30)	512.8	3,538.6	18.6(10)	219.7(30)	1,800.4(29)	1,302.5	435.7
Atlanta, Ga.(3)	4,024.5	553.9	3,470.7	23.0 (1)	277.8(18)	1,848.0 (2)	1,077.8	544.9
New Orleans, La.(3)	3,934.0	658.9(15)	3,275.1	17.9(14)	320.6(12)	1,210.3	1,253.8	811.0(12)
Saginaw, Mich.(4)	3,878.3	700.8(11)	3,177.6	18.4(12)	331.5(11)	1,903.8	1,034.9	238.9
Richmond, Va.(3)	3,584.6	565.2(29)	3,019.4	19.8 (7)	295.7(15)	1,447.4	1,031.1	540.9

[1]Other metro areas among the top 30 in total reported crime are Reno, Nev. (13); Sacramento, Cal. (19); Riverside-San Bernardino, Cal. (21); Portland, Ore. (23); Ft. Lauderdale, Fla. (24); Santa Rosa, Cal. (26); Bakersfield, Cal. (27).

[2]Violent crime includes murder, non-negligent manslaughter, forcible rape, robbery and aggravated assault. Other metro areas among the top 30 in reported violent crime are Columbia, S.C. (10); Chicago, Ill. (13); Washington, D.C. (14); Newark, N.J. (18); Waco, Tex. (19); Pueblo, Colo. (20); Greensboro-High Point, N.C. (21); Gastonia, N.C. (22); Wilmington, N.C. (23); Charlotte, N.C. (24); Trenton, N.J. (26); Kalamazoo, Mich. (27); Tampa-St. Petersburg, Fla. (28) and Dallas, Tex. (30).

[3]Property crime includes burglary, larceny over $50 and auto theft. Other metro areas among the top 30 in reported property crime are Riverside-San Bernardino, Cal. (8); Reno, Nev. (10); Sacramento, Cal. (16); Santa Rosa, Cal. (18); Portland, Ore.-(20); Ft. Lauderdale, Fla. (21); Bakersfield, Cal. (22); Yakima, Wash. (27); Eugene-Springfield, Ore. (29); Anaheim-Santa Ana, Cal. (30).

[4]Of the top 30 cities in murder and non-negligent manslaughter, only 6 are outside the southern and border states — New York; Detroit and Saginaw, Mich.; Las Vegas; Gary-Hammond, Indiana; and Cleveland, Ohio.

Reported Crime, 1971-72, by Size of Place

Source: Federal Bureau of Investigation, Uniform Crime Reports-1972

Population group (1972 estimated population)	Grand total	Violent crime	Property crime	Murder-non negl. man-slaught	Forcible rape	Robbery	Aggra-vated assault	Burglary	Auto theft
Total All Agencies: 6,286 agencies; total population 172,560,000:									
1971..........	7,742,284	744,973	4,709,301	15,295	37,708	372,109	319,861	2,150,246	877,838
1972..........	7,383,312	755,147	4,563,260	16,069	41,871	358,952	338,255	2,113,650	817,074
Percentage change	−4.6	+1.4	−3.1	+5.1	+11.0	−3.5	+5.8	−1.7	−6.9
Total Cities: 4,585 cities: total population 121,673,000:									
1971..........	6,563,977	659,907	3,902,185	12,607	30,058	350,386	266,856	1,746,233	788,800
1972..........	6,200,696	660,111	3,743,547	13,122	33,431	335,146	278,412	1,700,335	727,500
Percent change ..	−5.5	—	−4.1	+4.1	+11.2	−4.3	+4.3	−2.6	−7.8
58 cities over 250,000; population 43,321,000:									
1971..........	3,090,337	448,681	1,877,392	8,218	18,693	270,880	150,890	870,609	470,906
1972..........	2,816,736	432,587	1,710,880	8,530	20,391	250,727	152,939	813,355	419,003
Percent change ..	−8.6	−3.6	−8.9	+3.8	¡9.1	−7.4	+1.4	−6.6	−11.0
94 cities, 100,000 to 250,000; population 13,472,000:									
1971..........	840,954	65,075	508,720	1,406	3,555	28,829	31,285	234,714	97,635
1972..........	800,773	67,776	494,372	1,473	3,687	29,557	33,059	230,634	91,852
Percent change ..	−4.8	+4.2	−2.8	+4.8	+3.7	+2.5	+5.7	−1.7	−5.9
250 cities, 50,000 to 100,000; population 17,714,000:									
1971..........	874,151	51,733	511,340	1,042	3,009	21,711	25,971	217,803	87,192
1972..........	846,209	56,722	512,746	1,119	3,430	23,297	28,876	221,604	85,309
Percent change ..	−3.2	+9.6	+.3	+7.4	+14.0	+7.3	+11.2	+1.7	−2.2
475 cities, 25,000 to 50,000; population 16,673,000:									
1971..........	722,194	39,890	426,954	820	1,977	15,954	21,139	174,871	66,474
1972..........	699,313	44,685	425,705	858	2,505	17,101	24,221	177,361	64,905
Percent change ..	−3.2	+12.0	−.3	+4.6	+26.7	+7.2	+14.6	+1.4	−2.4
1,170 cities, 10,000 to 25,000; population 18,638,000:									
1971..........	682,117	34,707	380,782	716	1,830	9,438	22,723	162,785	46,444
1972..........	680,006	37,602	393,826	759	2,237	10,433	24,173	169,122	45,938
Percent change ..	−.3	+8.3	+3.4	+6.0	+22.2	+10.5	+6.4	+3.9	−1.1
2,538 cities, under 10,000; population 11,855,000:									
1971..........	354,224	19,821	196,997	405	994	3,574	14,848	85,451	20,149
1972..........	357,659	20,739	206,018	383	1,181	4,031	15,144	88,259	20,493
Percent change ..	+1.0	+4.6	+4.6	−5.4	+18.8	+12.8	+2.0	+3.3	+1.7
Suburban Area: 2,500 agencies: population 57,451,000:									
1971..........	1,888,742	111,500	1,198,483	2,311	8,079	37,132	63,978	535,513	162,041
1972..........	1,865,184	124,294	1,212,337	2,571	9,535	40,372	71,816	546,628	161,441
Percent change ..	−1.2	+11.5	+1.2	+11.3	+18.0	+8.7	+12.3	+2.1	−.4
Rural Area: 1,330 agencies; population 20,060,000:									
1971..........	301,712	24,005	215,646	1,211	2,259	3,059	17,476	117,269	15,557
1972..........	310,572	26,211	223,908	1,230	2,256	3,408	19,317	122,171	15,132
Percent change ..	+2.9	+9.2	+3.8	+1.6	−.1	+11.4	+10.5	+4.2	−2.7

786 Law Enforcement Officers Killed 1963-1972
Source: Uniform Crime Reports (FBI)

1. Responding to disturbance calls 103
2. Burglaries in progress or pursuing suspect 60
3. Robberies in progress or pursuing suspect 155
4. Attempting other arrests...................... 199
5. Civil disorders................................. 10
6. Handling, transporting, custody of prisoners 37
7. Investigating suspicious persons and circumstances 56
8. Ambush 70
9. Unprovoked mentally deranged 36
10. Traffic stops................................. 60

Geographically for the period of 1963-1972 the 786 officers who were slain in line of duty were divided in this fashion: Northeast 125; North Central 204; South 322 and West 135.

Police Roster

Police Officers and civilian employees in large cities as of Oct. 31, 1972

City	Officers	Civilian	City	Officers	Civilian	City	Officers	Civilian
Anchorage, Ala....	83	48	Indianapolis, Ind. .	1,186	204	Philadelphia, Pa...	8,183	938
Atlanta, Ga........	1,243	222	Jacksonville, Fla...	786	388	Phoenix, Ariz......	1,184	267
Baltimore, Md.....	3,524	558	Jersey City, N.J....	897	77	Pittsburgh, Pa.....	1,588	33
Birmingham, Ala. .	598	104	Kansas City, Mo. ..	1,304	381	Portland, Ore......	723	210
Boise, Idaho	116	33	Little Rock, Ark....	222	46	Rochester, N.Y. ...	633	97
Boston, Mass.	2,687	349	Los Angeles, Calif.	7,083	2,375	Sacramento, Calif.	516	119
Bridgeport, Conn. .	458	38	Louisville, Ky......	697	175	St. Louis, Mo......	2,228	672
Buffalo, N.Y.......	1,364	201	Memphis, Tenn....	1,061	206	St. Petersburg, Fla.	354	138
Chicago, Ill.......	13,125	1,266	Miami, Fla.	734	202	San Antonio, Texas	672	184
Cincinnati, Ohio...	1,087	238	Milwaukee, Wisc...	2,125	188	San Bernardino,		
Cleveland, Ohio ...	2,299	162	Minneapolis, Minn.	822	79	Calif.............	201	42
Columbus, Ohio ...	1,051	189	Nashville, Tenn.....	732	142	San Diego, Calif. ..	1,060	265
Dallas, Texas	1,875	623	Newark, N.J........	1,266	181	San Francisco,		
Denver, Colo.	1,223	296	New Orleans, La....	1,353	470	Calif.............	2,462(a)	
Detroit, Mich.....	5,555	593	New York, N.Y.....	30,828	1,984	San Jose, Calif. ...	629	111
Ft. Worth, Texas ..	656	101	Norfolk, Va........	533	98	Santa Ana, Calif. ..	207	77
Fresno, Calif.	300	60	Oakland, Calif.....	699	251	Seattle, Wash.	1,175	251
Gary, Ind.........	370	31	Oklahoma City,			Stockton, Calif. ...	196	60
Hartford, Conn. ...	480	91	Okla..............	577	77	Tampa, Fla.........	551	149
Honolulu, Hawaii ..	1,480	319	Omaha, Nebr......	560	113	Toledo, Ohio	726	50
Houston, Texas ...	2,077	312	Pasadena, Calif. ..	194	83	Tucson, Ariz.	432	111
(a) Officers and Civilians.						Washington, D.C...	4,851	621

Postal Information
United States Postal Service

The Postal Reform Act, creating a government-owned postal service under the Executive branch and replacing the old Post Office Department, was signed into law by President Nixon on Aug. 12, 1970. The service officially came into being on July 1, 1971.

The new U.S. Postal Service is governed by an 11-man Board of Governors. Nine members are appointed to 9-year terms by the President with Senate approval. These 9, in turn, choose a Postmaster General, who is no longer a member of the President's Cabinet. The Board and the new Postmaster General choose the 11th member, who serves as Deputy Postmaster General. The Board has full authority over the Postal Service except for postal rates, classifications and services, which are set by a new Postal Rate Commission of 5-members, appointed by the President.

The first Postmaster General under the new system was Winton M. Blount. He resigned Oct. 29, 1971, and was replaced by his deputy, Elmer T. Klassen, Dec. 7, 1971.

United States Domestic Rates (as of September 9, 1973)
(Note: New rates, proposed to take effect Jan. 5, 1974, would raise first class to 10¢, postcards to 8¢, airmail to 13¢, plus raises on other mail.)

First Class
Letters written, and matter sealed against inspection, 8¢ for each ounce or fraction.

U.S. Postal cards: single 6ᶜ; double 12ᶜ; private post cards, same.

First class includes written matter, namely letters, postal cards, post cards (private mailing cards) and all other matter wholly or partly in writing, whether sealed or unsealed, except manuscripts for books, periodical articles and music, manuscript copy accompanying proofsheets or corrected proofsheets of the same and the writing authorized by law on matter of other classes. Also matter sealed or closed against inspection. Bills and statements of accounts.

Greeting Cards
May be sent first class or single piece third class.

Airmail
Air postal or post card 9¢ each, letters and packages (up to 9 ounces) 11¢ an ounce. Business reply cards are 11¢ each. Business reply envelopes not over 2 ounces, 11¢ per ounce plus 2¢ per piece, weight over 2 ounces, 10¢ an ounce plus 5¢ per piece. Over 8 ounces air parcel post rates plus 5¢ per piece. This is in the U. S. its territories and possessions, also to Armed Forces outside the U. S. when addressed APO or FPO, New York, N. Y., San Francisco, Calif. or Seattle, Wash. May be certified, registered, sent C.O.D. or special delivery.

Second Class
Single copy mailings by general public 6ᶜ for first 2 ounces and 2ᶜ for each additional ounce or the 4th class rate, whichever is lower. There are special rates for publications, newspapers and bulk mailing, consult local postmasters for rates and permit.

Third Class
Third Class (limit up to but not including 16 ounces): Mailable matter not in 1st and 2nd classes.

Single mailing: Greeting cards (sealed or unsealed), small parcels, printed matter, booklets and catalogs, 8¢ the first 2 ounces and 4 cents for each additional ounce or fraction. Sealed items must indicate "third class."

Bulk material: Books, catalogs of 24 pages or more, seeds, cuttings, bulbs, roots, scions and plants; 22ᶜ a pound, subject to a minimum rate.

Other matter: Newsletters, shoppers' guides, advertising circulars; 26 cents a pound. Subject to a minimum rate for which Post Office should be consulted. Separate rates for some nonprofit organizations. Bulk mailing fee, $30 per calendar year. Apply to postmaster for permit.

Parcel Post—Fourth Class
Fourth Class or Parcel Post (16 ounces and over): Merchandise, printed matter, etc., may be mailed. On parcels weighing less than 10 lbs. and measuring more than 84 inches, but not more than 100 inches in length and girth combined, the minimum postage charge shall be the zone charge applicable to a 10-pound parcel.

Priority Mail
First-class mail of more than 12 ounces and airmail of more than 9 ounces have been merged into a "Priority Mail (Heavy Pieces)" service. First-class and airmail weighing up to one pound is charged $1.00 as Priority Mail regardless of its domestic destination. The most expeditious handling and transportation available will be used for fastest delivery.

Forwarding Addresses
The law that increased postal rates established the return address service for all classes of mail. (First time for first-class mail.) The mailer, in order to obtain a forwarding address, must endorse the envelope or cover "Address Correction Requested." The destination post office then will determine whether a forwarding address has been left on file and provide it for a fee of 10¢.

Special Handling
Third and Fourth class parcels will be handled and delivered as expeditiously as practicable (but not special delivery) upon payment, in addition to the regular postage: Up to 2 lbs., 25¢; over 2 lbs. and up to 10 lbs., 35¢; over 10 lbs., 50¢. Such parcels must be endorsed, Special Handling.

Special Delivery
First class mail up to 2 lbs., 60¢, over 2 lbs. and up to 10 lbs., 75¢; over 10 lbs. 90¢. All other classes up to 2 lbs. 80¢, over 2 and up to 10 lbs., 90¢, over 10 lbs. $1.05.

Priority Mail
Air Parcel Post (over 9 ounces to 70 lbs.): Packages not to exceed 100 inches in length and girth combined, including written and other matter of the first class, whether sealed or unsealed, fractions of a pound being charged as a full pound. Eleven cents an ounce or fraction for all domestic air mail up to and including 8 ounces regardless of distance or zone.

Rates according to zone apply between the U. S. and Puerto Rico and Virgin Isles.

Parcels weighing less than 10 lbs., measuring over 84 inches but not exceeding 100 inches in length and girth combined are chargeable with a minimum rate equal to that for a 10 pound parcel for the zone to which addressed.

Priority Mail

Zones	To 1 lb.	1½	2	2½	3	3½	4	4½	5
1, 2, 3	$1.00	$1.20	$1.40	$1.60	$1.80	$2.00	$2.20	$2.40	$2.60
4	1.00	1.22	1.43	1.65	1.86	2.08	2.30	2.51	2.73
5	1.00	1.25	1.51	1.76	2.01	2.26	2.52	2.77	3.02
6	1.00	1.30	1.60	1.90	2.20	2.49	2.79	3.09	3.39
7	1.00	1.40	1.68	2.02	2.36	2.69	3.03	3.37	3.71
8	1.00	1.50	1.77	2.16	2.54	2.93	3.31	3.70	4.08

Postal Union Mail Special Services
Registration.—Available to practically all countries. Fee 95¢. The maximum indemnity payable—generally only in case of complete loss (of both contents and wrapper)—is $13.07. To Canada only the fees are 95¢ and $1.25, providing indemnity for loss up to $100 to $200, respectively. Consult post office for further details.

Return receipt.–Fee is 20¢ when the receipt is requested at time of mailing, requested after mailing 40¢.

Special delivery.–Available to most countries. Consult post office. Fees: For post cards, letter mail, and airmail "other articles," 60¢ up to 2 pounds; over 2 to 10 pounds, 75¢; over 10 pounds, 90¢. For surface "other articles," 80¢, 90¢ and $1.05, respectively.

Special handling.–Entitles AO *surface* packages to priority handling between mailing point and U.S. point of dispatch. Fees: 25¢ for packages to 2 pounds, 35¢ for packages over 2 pounds to 10 pounds, and 50¢ for packages over 10 pounds.

Airmail.–There is daily air service to practically all countries.

Marking.–An article intended for special delivery service must have affixed to the cover near the name of the country of destination "EXPRES" (Special Delivery) label, obtainable at the post office, or it may be marked on the cover boldly in red "EXPRES" (Special Delivery).

Prepayment of replies from other countries. A mailer who wishes to prepay a reply by letter from another country may do so by sending his correspondent one or more international reply coupons, which may be purchased at United States post offices. One coupon should be accepted in any country in exchange for stamps to prepay a surface letter of the first unit of weight to the U.S.

Registry. All mailable matter prepaid with postage at the first-class or airmail rate may be registered. The mailer is required to declare the value of mail presented for registration.

Insurance is applicable to 3rd and 4th class matter. Matter for sale addressed to prospective purchasers who have not ordered it or authorized its sending will not be insured.

C.O.D.: Unregistered–is applicable to 3rd and 4th class matter and sealed domestic mail of any class bearing postage at the 1st class rate. Such mail must be based on bona fide orders or be in conformity with agreements between senders and addressees. Registered––For details consult postmaster.

Certified mail service is available for any matter having no intrinsic value on which 1st class or air mail postage is paid. Receipt is furnished at time of mailing and evidence of delivery obtained. The fee is 30¢ in addition to postage. Return receipt, restricted delivery and special delivery are available upon payment of additional fees. No indemnity.

Money Orders

Amount	Domestic	Foreign
$0.01 to $10.00	25¢	45¢
10.01 to 50.00	35¢	65¢
50.01 to 100.00	40¢	75¢

Individual Piece Mailings
(Fourth Class Catalogs)

Weight lbs.	Local	1 & 2	3	Zones 4	5	6	7	8
1.5	28¢	34¢	34¢	36¢	38¢	40¢	42¢	46¢
2	29¢	35¢	36¢	38¢	41¢	43¢	47¢	51¢
2.5	30¢	37¢	38¢	41¢	44¢	47¢	51¢	56¢
3	31¢	39¢	40¢	43¢	47¢	51¢	56¢	62¢
3.5	32¢	40¢	42¢	46¢	50¢	55¢	60¢	67¢
4	33¢	42¢	44¢	48¢	53¢	58¢	65¢	73¢
4.5	34¢	44¢	46¢	51¢	56¢	62¢	69¢	78¢
5	35¢	45¢	48¢	53¢	59¢	66¢	74¢	83¢
6	37¢	49¢	52¢	58¢	65¢	73¢	83¢	94¢
7	39¢	52¢	56¢	63¢	71¢	81¢	92¢	105
8	41¢	56¢	60¢	68¢	77¢	88¢	101	116
9	43¢	59¢	64¢	73¢	83¢	96¢	110	127
10	45¢	62¢	68¢	78¢	89¢	103	119	137

Zone Mileage

1	UP to 50	3	150-300	5	600-1,000	7 1,400-1,800
2	50-150	4	300-600	6	1,000-1,400	8 over, 1,800

Registered Mail

Indemnity to $100	$0.95
100.01 to 200	1.25
200.01 to 400	1.55
400.01 to 600	1.85
600.01 to 800	2.15
800.01 to 1,000	2.45
1,000.01 to 2,000	2.75
2,000.01 to 3,000	3.05
3,000.01 to 4,000	3.35
4,000.01 to 5,000	3.65
5,000.01 to 6,000	3.95
6,000.01 to 7,000	4.25
7,000.01 to 8,000	4.55
8,000.01 to 9,000	4.85
9,000.01 to 10,000	5.15

Consult postmaster for registry rates above $10,000.

Insured Mail

$0.01 to $15	$0.20
15.01 to 50	.30
50.01 to 100	.40
100.01 to 150	.50
150.01 to 200	.60

Return receipts for over $15 from 15¢ to 25¢.

C.O.D. Mail

$0.01 to $10	$0.70
10.01 to 25	.80
25.01 to 50	.90
50.01 to 100	1.00
100.01 to 200	1.10
Restricted delivery	.50
Notice of nondelivery	.10
Alteration of charges or delivery	.35

Fees are in addition to postage.

PARCEL POST RATE SCHEDULE

1 lb., not exceeding	Local	1 & 2	3	Zones 4	5	6	7	8
2	$0.60	$0.65	$0.70	$0.75	$0.80	$0.90	$1.00	$1.05
3	.60	.75	.80	.85	.95	1.10	1.20	1.35
4	.65	.80	.85	.95	1.10	1.30	1.40	1.60
5	.70	.85	.90	1.05	1.20	1.45	1.65	1.90
6	.70	.95	1.00	1.15	1.35	1.60	1.85	2.10
7	.75	1.05	1.10	1.25	1.50	1.75	2.10	2.35
8	.75	1.10	1.15	1.35	1.60	1.90	2.30	2.60
9	.80	1.15	1.20	1.45	1.75	2.05	2.45	2.85
10	.80	1.20	1.30	1.55	1.90	2.20	2.65	3.10
11	.80	1.25	1.35	1.60	2.00	2.30	2.85	3.35
12	.85	1.30	1.45	1.70	2.10	2.45	3.05	3.55
13	.85	1.35	1.55	1.80	2.20	2.60	3.25	3.80
14	.90	1.40	1.60	1.90	2.35	2.75	3.45	4.00
15	.90	1.45	1.65	2.00	2.45	2.85	3.60	4.20
16	.95	1.55	1.75	2.05	2.55	2.95	3.80	4.40
17	1.00	1.60	1.80	2.15	2.65	3.10	3.95	4.60
18	1.00	1.65	1.90	2.20	2.75	3.20	4.15	4.80
19	1.05	1.70	2.00	2.30	2.85	3.35	4.30	5.00
20	1.05	1.75	2.05	2.40	2.95	3.50	4.50	5.20

(Consult postmaster for parcels over 20 pounds or measuring more than 72 inches, length and girth.)

BULK MAILINGS* (Fourth Class Catalogs)

	Local	1 & 2	3	4	5	6	7	8
Piece rate	21¢	25¢	25¢	25¢	25¢	25¢	25¢	26¢
Bulk lb. rate	2.1¢	3.4¢	4.0¢	5.0¢	6.1¢	7.5¢	9.1¢	10.8¢

*Minimum Quantity Each mailing must consist of 300 or more individually addressed pieces.

SPECIAL FOURTH-CLASS RATE
(limit 70 lbs.)

First pound or fraction 16¢; 8¢ for each additional pound or fraction. Only following specific articles: books 24 pages or more, at least 22 of which are printed consisting wholly of reading matter or scholarly bibliography containing no advertisement other than incidental announcements of books; 16 millimeter films in final form (except when mailed to or from commercial theaters); printed music in bound or sheet form; printed objective test materials; sound recordings, playscripts and manuscripts for books, periodicals and music; printed educational reference charts; loose-leaf pages and binders therefor consisting of medical information for distribution to doctors, hospitals, medical schools and medical students. Package must be marked "Special 4th-Class Rate" stating item contained.

LIBRARY RATE (limit 70 lbs.)

First pound or fraction 6¢; each additional pound or fraction 3¢. Books when loaned or exchanged between schools, colleges, public libraries and certain non-profit organizations; books, printed music, bound academic theses, periodicals, sound recordings, other library materials, museum materials (specimens, collections), scientific or mathematical kits, instruments or other devices; also catalogs, guides or scripts for some of these materials. Must be marked "Library Rate".

Post Office-Authorized 2-Letter State Abbreviations

Gradually replacing the traditional abbreviations for the states of the United States are the two-letter ones approved by the Post Office Department when it introduced the ZIP Code in 1963. The official list follows, including the District of Columbia, Guam, Puerto Rico and the Virgin Islands (all capital letters are used):

Alabama	AL	Kentucky	KY	Ohio	OH
Alaska	AK	Lousiana	LA	Oklahoma	OK
Arizona	AZ	Maine	ME	Oregon	OR
Arkansas	AR	Maryland	MD	Pennsylvania	PA
California	CA	Massachusetts	MA	Puerto Rico	PR
Colorado	CO	Michigan	MI	Rhode Island	RI
Connecticut	CT	Minnesota	MN	South Carolina	SC
Delaware	DE	Mississippi	MS	South Dakota	SD
Dist. of Col	DC	Missouri	MO	Tennessee	TN
Florida	FL	Montana	MT	Texas	TX
Georgia	GA	Nebraska	NE	Utah	UT
Guam	GU	Nevada	NV	Vermont	VT
Hawaii	HI	New Hampshire	NH	Virginia	VA
Idaho	ID	New Jersey	NJ	Virgin Islands	VI
Illinois	IL	New Mexico	NM	Washington	WA
Indiana	IN	New York	NY	West Virginia	WV
Iowa	IA	North Carolina	NC	Wisconsin	WI
Kansas	KS	North Dakota	ND	Wyoming	WY

Also approved for use in addressing mail are the following abbreviations:

Alley	Aly	Drive	Dr	Plaza	Plz
Arcade	Arc	Expressway	Expy	Point	Pt
Avenue	Ave	Extended	Ext	Road	Rd
Boulevard	Blvd	Extension	Ext	Rural	R
Branch	Br	Freeway	Fwy	Square	Sq
Bypass	Byp	Gardens	Gdns	Street	St
Causeway	Cswy	Grove	Grv	Terrace	Ter
Center	Ctr	Heights	Hts	Trail	Trl
Circle	Cir	Highway	Hwy	Turnpike	Tpke
Court	Ct	Lane	Ln	Viaduct	Via
Courts	Cts	Manor	Mnr	Vista	Vis
Crescent	Cres	Place	Pl		

Post Offices in United States

As of June 23, 1973 there was a total of 31,332 post offices throughout the U.S. and Possessions. Of this number 5,264 were First Class; 7,450 Second Class; 12,352 Third Class and 6,266 Fourth Class.

Commemorative Stamps and Regular Postal Issues 1972

Date		Stamp Commemorative	Value	From
Jan.	12	Eugene O'Neill Coil	$1	Hempstead, NY
Jan.	26	"Special Stamp for Someone Special"	8¢	Philadelphia, PA
Feb.	10	Ballooning Aerogramme	15¢	Albuquerque, NM
Feb.	16	Pamphleteer Bicentennial	8¢	Portland, OR
Feb.	28	George Gershwin (American Arts)	8¢	Beverly Hills, CA
Apr.	13	Posting Broadside Bicentennial	8¢	Atlantic City, NJ
Apr.	23	Nicolaus Copernicus	8¢	Washington, DC
Apr.	30	Postal People (strip of 10 stamps)	8¢	Nationwide
May	8	Harry S. Truman	8¢	Independence, MO
June	22	Post Rider Bicentennial	8¢	Rochester, NY
June	27	A. P. Giannini (Prominent American Series)	21¢	San Mateo, CA
July	4	Boston Tea Party Bicentennial (Block of 4 Stamps)	8¢	Boston, MA
July	10	Progress in Electronics (Set of 4 Stamps)	6¢, 8¢, 11¢, 15¢	New York, NY
Aug.	13	Robinson Jeffers (American Arts)	8¢	Carmel, CA
Aug.	27	Lyndon B. Johnson	8¢	Austin, TX
Sept.	10	Henry Ossawa Tanner (American Arts)	8¢	Pittsburgh, PA
Sept.	14	100th Anniversary of First U.S. Postal Card	6¢	Washington, DC
Sept.	20	Willa Cather (American Arts)	8¢	Red Cloud, NE
Sept.	28	Drummer Bicentennial	8¢	New Orleans, LA
Oct.	5	Rural America — Angus Cattle	8¢	St. Joseph, MO
Nov.	7	1973 Christmas, Raphael Painting	8¢	Washington, DC
Nov.	7	1973 Christmas, Christmas Tree	8¢	Washington, DC

POSTAL RECEIPTS AT LARGE CITIES

Fiscal Year	Boston Dollars	Chicago Dollars	Detroit Dollars	L.A. Dollars	New York Dollars	Phila. Dollars	St. Louis Dollars	Wash. D.C. Dollars
1969	91,421,564	288,680,764	57,560,715	138,586,635	513,380,252	103,496,672	63,512,108	76,297,000
1970	92,510,086	290,705,477	70,606,905	144,894,554	471,130,333	102,137,637	62,909,460	80,965,864
1971	95,205,407	292,558,518	70,256,324	149,063,344	359,170,452	107,122,556	65,104,974	84,053,982
1972	109,178,539	332,951,729	85,997,396	172,644,940	395,523,484	120,055,844	73,246,822	99,980,611

Other Cities, for Fiscal Year 1972: Atlanta $84,052,635; Baltimore, $55,473,769; Cincinnati, $45,787,803; Cleveland, $70,285,009; Columbus, $46,440,091; Dallas, $86,279,959; Denver, $49,474,180; Houston, $70,661,765; Indianapolis, $47,354,925; Kansas City, $58,047,615; Minneapolis, $66,745,670; Pittsburgh, $54,738,800; San Francisco, $94,811,170; Seattle, $43,420,394.

Surface Mail, Air Mail, Parcel Post
International Rates

Aerogrammes – 15 cents each to all countries.
Air Mail Post Cards (single) – 15 cents to all countries except Canada and Mexico (9¢).

| Country | Ordinary surface mail (not over 1 oz.) | Air Service | | | | Surface | | Max. wt. for parcel post (surface or air) Lbs. |
| | | Letters and letter pkgs. (per ½ oz.) | Other Articles | | Parcel Post | | Parcel Post | | |
			First 2 oz.	Each add'l 2 oz. or fraction	First 4 oz.	Each add'l 4 oz. or fraction	First 2 lbs.	Each add'l pound or fraction	
Afghanistan	$0.15	$0.21	$0.60	$0.30	$2.20	$0.83	$1.30	$0.40	22
Albania	.15	.21	.50	.20	2.33	.54	1.30	.40	22
Algeria	.15	.21	.50	.20	1.89	.55	1.30	.40	44
Andorra	.15	.21	.50	.20	1.95	.48	1.30	.40	44
Angola	.15	.21	.60	.30	2.05	.70	1.30	.40	22
Anguilla	.15	.17					1.20	.35	22
Antigua	.15	.17	.40	.10	1.24	.25	1.20	.35	22
Argentina	.15	.17	.50	.20	1.72	.74	1.30	.40	44
Aruba	.15	.17	.40	.10	1.45	.31	1.20	.35	44
Ascension Isl.	.15	.17	.50	.20	(4)		1.30	.40	22
Australia	.15	.21	.60	.30	1.83	.84	1.30	.40	22
Austria	.15	.21	.50	.20	1.88	.51	1.30	.40	44
Azores	.15	.21	.50	.20	1.36	.39	1.30	.40	44
Bahamas	.15	.17	.40	.10	1.53	.18	1.20	.35	22
Bahrein	.15	.21	.60	.30	1.69	.72	1.30	.40	22
Barbados	.15	.17	.40	.10	1.33	.35	1.20	.35	22
Barbuda	.15	.17	.40	.10	1.24	.25	1.20	.35	22
Belgium	.15	.21	.50	.20	1.68	.46	1.30	.40	44
Bermuda	.15	.17	.40	.10	1.23	.24	1.20	.35	33
Bhutan	.15	.21	.60	.30	(4)		1.30		(5)
Bolivia	.15	.17	.50	.20	1.73	.47	1.30	.40	44
Bonaire	.15	.17	.40	.10	1.45	.31	1.20	.35	44
Botswana	.15	.21	.60	.30	1.86	.88	1.30	.40	22
Brazil	.15	.17	.50	.20	2.06	.54	1.30	.40	44
Br. Honduras	.15	.17	.40	.10	1.32	.33	1.30	.40	22
Br. Virgin Isl.	.15	.17	.40	.10	1.24	.25	1.20	.35	22
Brunei	.15	.21	.60	.30	2.10	1.02	1.30	.40	22
Bulgaria	.15	.21	.50	.20	1.50	.52	1.30	.40	22
Burma	.15	.21	.60	.30	2.31	1.00	1.30	.40	22
Burundi	.15	.21	.60	.30	1.93	.74	1.30	.40	22
Cambodia	.15	.21	.60	.30	(4)		1.30	.40	22
Cameroon	.15	.21	.60	.30	1.95	.64	1.30	.40	22
Canada[3]	.08	.11	(6)		(6)		1.20	.35	25
Cape Verde Isl.	.15	.21	.60	.30	1.90	.56	1.30	.40	22
Cen. Africa Rep.	.15	.21	.60	.30	1.93	.74	1.30	.40	44
Ceylon	.15	.21	.60	.30	2.33	.89	1.30	.40	22
Chad	.15	.21	.60	.30	1.93	.74	1.30	.40	44
Chile	.15	.17	.50	.20	2.04	.61	1.30	.40	22
China Rep.	.15	.21	.60	.30	1.72	.73	1.30	.40	44
China, Cont.[7]	.15	.21	.60	.30	(4)		1.30		(5)
Colombia	.15	.17	.50	.20	2.00	.34	1.30	.40	44
Comoro Isl.	.15	.21	.60	.30	2.19	1.00	1.30	.40	44
Congo (Brazza.)	.15	.21	.60	.30	1.93	.74	1.30	.40	44
Corsica	.15	.21	.50	.20	2.08	.46	1.30	.40	44
Costa Rica	.15	.17	.40	.10	1.44	.29	1.20	.35	44
Cuba	.15	.17	¹.40	.10	(4)		1.20		(5)
Curacao	.15	.17	.40	.10	1.45	.31	1.20	.35	44
Cyprus	.15	.21	.60	.30	2.01	.59	1.30	.40	22
Czechoslovakia	.15	.21	.50	.20	1.52	.53	1.30	.40	44
Dahomey	.15	.21	.60	.30	1.65	.59	1.30	.40	44
Denmark	.15	.21	.50	.20	1.49	.50	1.30	.40	44
Dominica	.15	.17	.40	.10	1.67	.33	1.20	.35	22
Dominican R.	.15	.17	.40	.10	1.56	.25	1.20	.35	44
Ecuador	.15	.17	.50	.20	1.94	.33	1.30	.40	44
El Salvador	.15	.17	.40	.10	1.54	.30	1.20	.35	44
Equatorial Guinea	.15	.21	.60	.30	1.97	.85	1.30	.40	44
Estonia[2]	.15	.21	.60	.30	1.99	.66	1.30	.40	44
Ethiopia	.15	.21	.60	.30	1.98	.76	1.30	.40	44
Faeroe Isl.	.15	.21	.50	.20	1.49	.49	1.30	.40	44
Falkland Isl.	.15	.17	.50	.20	2.09	.59	1.30	.40	22
Fiji Islands	.15	.21	.60	.30	1.95	.62	1.30	.40	22
Finland	.15	.21	.50	.20	1.52	.54	1.30	.40	44
France- incl. Monaco	.15	.21	.50	.20	2.08	.46	1.30	.40	44
French Guiana	.15	.17	.50	.20	1.53	.39	1.30	.40	44
Fr. Polynesia	.15	.21	.60	.30	1.88	.53	1.30	.40	44
Fr. Ter. Afars, Issas	.15	.21	.60	.30	2.02	.72	1.30	.40	44
Gabon Rep.	.15	.21	.60	.30	1.93	.74	1.30	.40	44
Gambia	.15	.21	.60	.30	1.67	.53	1.30	.40	22
Germany, incl. Saar	.15	.21	.50	.20	1.47	.48	1.30	.40	44
Ghana	.15	.21	.60	.30	2.04	.64	1.30	.40	22
Gibraltar	.15	.21	.50	.20	1.51	.52	1.30	.40	22
Gilbert & Ellice	.15	.21	.60	.30	1.86	.69	1.30	.40	22
Great Britain	.15	.21	.50	.20	1.45	.46	1.30	.40	22
Greece	.15	.21	.50	.20	1.83	.58	1.30	.40	22
Greenland	.15	.21	.50	.20	1.64	.65	1.30	.40	44
Grenada	.15	.17	.40	.10	1.67	.33	1.20	.35	22
Guadeloupe	.15	.17	.40	.10	1.40	.25	1.20	.35	22

Country	Ordinary surface mail (not over 1 oz.)	Air Service					Surface		Max. wt. for parcel post (surface or air) Lbs.
		Letters and letter pkgs. (per ½ oz.)	Other Articles		Parcel Post		Parcel Post		
			First 2 oz.	Each add'l 2 oz. or fraction	First 4 oz.	Each add'l 4 oz. or fraction	First 2 lbs.	Each add'l pound or fraction	
Guatemala	.15	.17	.40	.10	1.75	.32	1.20	.35	44
Guinea	.15	.21	.60	.30	1.72	.67	1.30	.40	44
Guyana	.15	.17	.50	.20	1.69	.34	1.30	.40	22
Haiti	.15	.17	.40	.10	1.57	.24	1.20	.35	44
Honduras	.15	.17	.40	.10	1.49	.32	1.20	.35	¹44
Hong Kong	.15	.21	.60	.30	1.85	.87	1.30	.40	22
Hungary..........	.15	.21	.50	.20	1.51	.53	1.30	.40	44
Iceland..........	.15	.21	.50	.20	1.86	.39	1.30	.40	44
India.............	.15	.21	.60	.30	1.87	.88	1.30	.40	¹44
Indonesia	.15	.21	.60	.30	2.43	1.06	1.30	.40	22
Iran..............	.15	.21	.60	.30	1.87	.67	1.30	.40	44
Iraq..............	.15	.21	.60	.30	2.08	.66	1.30	.40	44
Ireland (Eire)	.15	.21	.50	.20	1.44	.46	1.30	.40	22
Israel	.15	.21	.60	.30	2.05	.63	1.30	.40	22
Italy	.15	.21	.50	.20	1.84	.54	1.30	.40	44
Ivory Coast	.15	.21	.60	.30	1.72	.66	1.30	.40	44
Jamaica..........	.15	.17	.40	.10	1.65	.22	1.20	.35	22
Japan............	.15	.21	.60	.30	1.53	.55	1.30	.40	22
Jordan	.15	.21	.60	.30	1.90	.62	1.30	.40	22
Kenya............	.15	.21	.60	.30	2.05	.76	1.30	.40	22
Korea (Rep. of)...	.15	.21	.60	.30	1.57	.59	1.30	.40	22
No. Korea¹......	.15	.21	.60	.30	(4)				(5)
Kuwait	.15	.21	.60	.30	1.67	.69	1.30	.40	22
Laos	.15	.21	.60	.30	2.34	.95	1.30	.40	22
Latvia	.15	.21	.60	.30	1.99	.66	1.30	.40	44
Lebanon	.15	.21	.60	.30	1.90	.62	1.30	.40	¹44
Leeward Islands ..	.15	.17	.40	.10	1.24	.25	1.20	.35	22
Lesotho	.15	.21	.60	.30	1.86	.88	1.30	.40	22
Liberia	.15	.21	.60	.30	1.56	.58	1.30	.40	22
Libya	.15	.21	.60	.30	1.88	.59	1.30	.40	44
Liechtenstein.....	.15	.21	.50	.20	1.67	.47	1.30	.40	44
Lithuania²........	.15	.21	.60	.30	1.99	.66	1.30	.40	44
Luxembourg	.15	.21	.50	.20	1.73	.45	1.30	.40	44
Macao	.15	.21	.60	.30	2.24	.87	1.30	.40	22
Madagascar	.15	.21	.60	.30	2.16	.85	1.30	.40	44
Madeira Isl.......	.15	.21	.50	.20	1.47	.50	1.30	.40	22
Malawi	.15	.21	.60	.30	1.86	.87	1.30	.40	22
Malaysia	.15	.21	.60	.30	2.26	.99	1.30	.40	22
Maldives, Rep. of..	.15	.21	.60	.30	2.51	.90	1.30	.40	22
Mali..............	.15	.21	.60	.30	2.42	.57	1.30	.40	44
Malta	.15	.21	.50	.20	1.82	.54	1.30	.40	22
Martinique	.15	.17	.40	.10	1.40	.25	1.20	.35	44
Mauritania	.15	.21	.60	.30	.165	.54	1.30	.40	44
Mauritius.........	.15	.21	.60	.30	2.10	.90	1.30	.40	22
Mexico	.08	.11	.40	.10	1.23	.24	1.20	.35	44
Montserrat	.15	.17	.40	.10	1.24	.25	1.30	.40	22
Morocco	.15	.21	.50	.20	1.84	.54	1.30	.40	44
Nauru (Rep.)......	.15	.21	.60	.30	1.83	.84	1.30	.40	22
Nepal	.15	.21	.60	.30	1.86	.88	1.30	.40	22
Netherlands	.15	.21	.50	.20	1.65	.46	1.30	.40	44
Neth. Antilles.....	.15	.17	.40	.10	1.45	.31	1.20	.35	44
Nevis	.15	.17	.40	.10	1.24	.25	1.30	.40	22
New Caledonia....	.15	.21	.60	.30	1.96	.65	1.30	.40	44
New Guinea	.15	.21	.60	.30	1.90	.92	1.30	.40	22
New Hebrides	.15	.21	.60	.30	1.85	.65	1.30	.40	44
New Zealand	.15	.21	.60	.30	2.08	.74	1.30	.40	22
Nicaragua	.15	.17	.40	.10	1.45	.29	1.20	.35	44
Niger	.15	.21	.60	.30	2.41	.55	1.30	.40	44
Nigeria...........	.15	.21	.60	.30	2.20	.65	1.30	.40	22
Norway...........	.15	.21	.50	.20	1.49	.50	1.30	.40	44
Oman, Sultanate of	.15	.21	.60	.30	1.69	.72	1.30	.40	22
Outer Mongolia ...	.15	.21	.60	.30	(4)		1.30	.40	(5)
Pakistan	.15	.21	.60	.30	2.42	.85	1.30	.40	22
Palestine	.15	.21	.60	.30	2.05	.63	1.30	.40	11
Panama	.15	.17	.40	.10	1.74	.31	1.20	.35	¹70
Papua............	.15	.21	.60	.30	1.90	.92	1.30	.40	22
Paraguay	.15	.17	.50	.20	1.73	.47	1.30	.40	44
Peru	.15	.17	.50	.20	2.01	.41	1.30	.40	44
Philippines	.15	.21	.60	.30	2.12	.81	1.30	.40	¹44
Pitcairn	.15	.21	.60	.30	2.02	.72	1.30	.40	22
Poland	.15	.21	.50	.20	1.82	.52	1.30	.40	44
Portugal..........	.15	.21	.50	.20	1.43	.44	1.30	.40	22
Portuguese E. Af. .	.15	.21	.60	.30	2.40	.89	1.30	.40	22
" Timor	.15	.21	.60	.30	2.54	1.20	1.30	.40	22
" W. Africa	.15	.21	.60	.30	2.05	.70	1.30	.40	22
Qatar	.15	.21	.60	.30	1.69	.72	1.30	.40	22
Reunion	.15	.21	.60	.30	2.02	.88	1.30	.40	44
Rhodesia	.15	.21	.60	.30	1.86	.87	1.30	.40	22
Romania	.15	.21	.50	.20	1.69	.54	1.30	.40	22
Rwanda	.15	.21	.60	.30	1.93	.74	1.30	.40	22
Ryukyu...........	.15	.21	.60	.30	1.57	.59	1.30	.40	22
Sabah............	.15	.17	.40	.10	1.45	.31	1.30	.40	44
St. Christopher ...	.15	.17	.40	.10	1.67	.33	1.20	.35	22
St. Eustatius	.15	.17	.40	.10	1.45	.31	1.20	.35	44

Country	Ordinary surface mail (not over 1 oz.)	Air Service					Surface		Max. wt. for parcel post (surface or air) Lbs.
		Letters and letter pkgs. (per ½ oz.)	Other Articles		Parcel Post		Parcel Post		
			First 2 oz.	Each add'l 2 oz. or fraction	First 4 oz.	Each add'l 4 oz. or fraction	First 2 lbs.	Each add'l pound or fraction	
St. Helena	.15	.21	.60	.30	2.10	.85	1.30	.40	22
St. Lucia	.15	.17	.40	.10	1.67	.33	1.20	.35	22
St. Pierre, Miquelon	.15	.17	.40	.10	1.20	.24	1.20	.35	44
St. Vincent	.15	.17	.40	.10	1.67	.33	1.20	.35	22
Santa Cruz Isl.	.15	.21	.60	.30	2.17	.97	1.30	.40	22
Saudi Arabia	.15	.21	.60	.30	2.17	.69	1.30	.40	22
Senegal	.15	.21	.60	.30	1.63	.52	1.30	.40	44
Seychelles	.15	.21	.60	.30	1.77	.78	1.30	.40	22
Sierra Leone	.15	.21	.60	.30	2.16	.56	1.30	.40	22
Singapore	.15	.21	.60	.30	2.26	.99	1.30	.40	22
Solomon Isl.	.15	.21	.60	.30	2.18	.97	1.30	.40	22
Somali Rep.	.15	.21	.60	.30	'2.26	.79	1.30	.40	22
South Africa	.15	.21	.60	.30	1.86	.88	1.30	.40	22
Spain	.15	.21	.50	.20	1.95	.48	1.30	.40	'44
Sp. W. Africa	.15	.21	.60	.30	1.96	.56	1.30	.40	'44
Sudan	.15	.21	.60	.30	2.19	.70	1.30	.40	22
Surinam	.15	.17	.50	.20	1.56	.38	1.30	.40	44
Sweden	.15	.21	.50	.20	1.49	.50	1.30	.40	44
Switzerland	.15	.21	.50	.20	1.67	.47	1.30	.40	44
Syria	.15	.21	.60	.30	1.73	.64	1.30	.40	'44
Tanzania	.15	.21	.60	.30	2.09	.80	1.30	.40	22
Thailand	.15	.21	.60	.30	2.29	.81	1.30	.40	22
Togo	.15	.21	.60	.30	1.80	.66	1.30	.40	44
Tonga	.15	.21	.60	.30	1.63	.65	1.30	.40	22
Trinidad, Tobago	.15	.17	.40	.10	1.66	.31	1.20	.35	22
Tristan da Cunha	.15	.21	.60	.30	1.98	.84	1.30	.40	22
Tunisia	.15	.21	.50	.20	1.83	.52	1.30	.40	44
Turkey	.15	.21	.50	.20	1.58	.59	1.30	.40	44
Turks Islands	.15	.17	.40	.10	1.57	.22	1.20	.35	22
Uganda	.15	.21	.60	.30	2.05	.76	1.30	.40	22
USSR[2]	.15	.21	.60	.30	1.99	.66	1.30	.40	44
United Arab Emir.	.15	.21	.60	.30	1.69	.72	1.30	.40	22
UAR (Egypt)	.15	.21	.50	.20	1.62	.64	1.30	.40	44
Upper Volta	.15	.21	.60	.30	1.90	.61	1.30	.40	44
Uruguay	.15	.17	.50	.20	2.05	.62	1.30	.40	44
Vatican City	.15	.21	.50	.20	1.69	.51	1.30	.40	44
Venezuela	.15	.17	.50	.20	1.89	.29	1.30	.40	44
Vietnam, Rep. of	.15	.21	.60	.30	2.30	.90	1.30	.40	22
North Vietnam	.15	.21	.60	.30	(4)				(5)
Western Samoa	.15	.21	.60	.30	1.89	.55	1.30	.40	22
Windward Isl.	.15	.17	.40	.10	1.67	.33	1.20	.35	22
Yemen	.15	.21	.60	.30	1.96	.76			22
Yugoslavia	.15	.21	.50	.20	1.52	.54	1.30	.40	44
Zaire	.15	.21	.60	.30	1.93	.74	1.30	.40	44
Zambia	.15	.21	.60	.30	1.86	.87	1.30	.40	22

(1.) Restrictions apply; consult post office. (2.) To facilitate distribution and delivery, include "Union of Soviet Socialist Republics" or "USSR" as part of the address. (3.) Small packets weight limit one pound. (4.) No air parcel post service. (5.) No surface parcel post service. (6.) No airmail AO or parcel post to Canada; prepare and prepay all airmail packages as letter mail. (7.) The Continental China Postal authorities will not deliver articles unless addressed to show name of the country as "People's Republic of China"; also, acceptable spelling of capital is "Peking."

INTERNATIONAL MAILS
Weight and Dimensional Limits and Surface Rates
For air rates see pages 1036-1038

Letters and letter packages: All written matter or correspondence recordings, must be sent as letter mail. Weight limit: 4 lbs. to all countries except Canada, which is 60 lbs. Surface rates: Canada and Mexico 8ᶜ per oz. to 12 oz.: over 12 oz. to 1 lb. $1.00; over 1 lb. to 1½ lbs., $1.50; over 1½ lbs. to 2 lbs., $1.77; over 2 to 2½ lbs., $2.16; 2½ to 3 lbs., $2.54; 3 to 3½ lbs., $2.93; 3½ to 4 lbs., $3.31. To Canada only: Over 4 to 4½ lbs., $3.70; 4½ to 5 lbs., $4.08; over 5 lbs., 80ᶜ each pound or fraction; to all other countries, 15ᶜ for first ounce; 1 oz. to 2 ʋz., 26ᶜ; 2 oz to 4 oz., 34ᶜ; 4 oz. to 8 oz., 76ᶜ; 8 oz to 16 oz., $1.44; 16 oz. to 32 oz., $2.40; 32 oz. to 64 oz., $3.84. Air rates: Canada and Mexico, 11ᶜ per oz; Central and South America, Caribbean Islands, Bahamas, Bermuda and St. Pierre, 17ᶜ a half oz; all other countries 21ᶜ a half oz; aerogrammes, 15ᶜ.

Post cards. Surface rates to Canada and Mexico, 6ᶜ; to all other countries, 10ᶜ. By air, Canada and Mexico, 9ᶜ; to all other countries, 15ᶜ. Maximum size permitted, 6 x 4¼ in.; minimum, 5½ x 3½.

Printed matter. To Canada and Mexico, 8ᶜ first 2 oz., 4ᶜ each additional oz. or fraction; to other countries, 8ᶜ for first 2 oz. or fraction, 14ᶜ for 2 to 4 oz., 26ᶜ for 4 to 8 oz., 48ᶜ for 8 oz. to 1 lb., 75ᶜ for 1 to 2 lbs., 96ᶜ for 2 to 4 lbs. To countries admitting regular prints over 4 lbs., 48ᶜ for each additional 2 lbs. or fraction. (Consult post office for rates and conditions applying to certain publications mailed by the publishers or by registered news agents.) Book weight limits for most countries is 11 lbs; for exceptions see below.

Exceptional weight limits for printed matter. Printed matter may weigh up to 22 lbs. to Argentina, Bolivia, Brazil, Chile, Colombia, Costa Rica, Cuba, Dominican Republic, Ecuador, El Salvador, Guatemala, Haiti, Honduras, Mexico, Nicaragua, Panama, Paraguay, Peru, Spain (including Balearic Islands, Canary Islands and Northern Africa).

Matter for the blind. Surface rate free; air rates to Canada 11¢ per oz., (For all other countries, consult postmaster.) Weight limit 15 lbs.

Small packets. Postage rates for small items of merchandise and samples are lower than for letter packages or parcel post; weight limits up to 2 lbs. Surface rates: Canada and Mexico, 8¢ first 2 oz. and 2¢ each additional oz. or fraction. All other countries, for 4 oz. or less, 15¢; 4 to 8 oz. 29¢; 8 oz. to 1 lb., 48¢; 1 to 2 lbs., 86¢. Air rates: Canada, 11¢ per oz. For other rates, see schedule "Air Service Other Articles" under heading of International Rates for Ordinary Surface Mail, Air Mail and Surface Parcel Post, pages 1036-1039.

Canadian Postal Rates

Domestic Mail

First class mail costs 8¢ for the first oz.; between 1 and 2 oz., 14¢; between 2 and 4 oz. 20¢; between 4 and 8 oz. 32¢; between 8 and 12 oz., 44¢ and between 12 oz., and a pound, 54¢. Postcards 7¢. Third class mail costs 6¢ for first 2 ounces and 3¢ each additional 2 oz. or fraction. All domestic first class mail not heavier than 66 lbs. and exceeding certain sizes is carried by air if it will speed delivery.

International

All mail up to 8 oz. travels by air. An air mail sticker or the word "air mail" must be on the envelope. Cost is 15¢ for first oz., between 1 and 2 oz., 30¢, between 2 and 4 oz., 40¢ and between 4 and 8 oz., 90¢. Postcards 10¢. Aerogrammes 15¢.

To the United States, its Territories and Possessions: Air mail 10¢ each oz. (maximum 25 lbs.) Postcards 10¢ each by air mail. Surface letter mail is 8¢ for first oz., between 1 and 2 oz., 14¢; between 2 and 4 oz., 20¢; between 4 and 8 oz. 32¢ and between 8 oz. and a lb., 54¢. Surface postcards are 8¢. Printed papers are 6¢ up to 2 oz., between 2 and 4 oz., 9¢; between 4 and 8 oz., 15¢ and between 8 oz. and a lb., 27¢. Small packets are delivered in a speedier and alternative surface to the Parcel Post for a charge of 9¢ up to 4 oz., between 4 and 8 oz., 15¢ and 8 oz. to a lb., 27¢.

United Nations Postage Stamps Issued in 1973

UN stamps in United States denominations, valid for postage only on mail deposited at UN Headquarters, New York, and UN stamps in Swiss denominations, valid for postage only on mail deposited at the United Nations Office, Geneva, are available at face value from the UN Postal Administration in New York and delivered and through sales agencies around the world. They may be obtained by mail or automatically through the Customer Deposit Account service, both in New York and Geneva. Revenue from the sale of UN stamps for postage purposes goes to the U.S. Postal Service and the Swiss PTT, respectively; from philatelic sales, revenue goes to the UN.

Date	Stamp	Value
12 Jan.	Stationery	8¢ envelope 11¢ airmail envelope 6¢ postal Card
9 March	Disarmament Decade	8¢, 15¢
13 April	Stop Drug Abuse	8¢, 15¢
25 May	United Nations Volunteers	8¢, 21¢
1 Oct.	Namibia	8¢, 15¢
16 Nov.	Human Rights	8¢, 21¢

INTERNATIONAL PARCEL POST

For rates see pages 1036-1038

General dimensional limits—Greatest length, 3½ feet; greatest length and girth combined, 6 feet.

Prohibited articles. Before sending goods abroad the mailer should satisfy himself that they will not be confiscated or returned because their importation is prohibited or restricted by the country of address.

Packing. Parcels for transmission overseas should be even more carefully packed than those intended for delivery within the continental United States. Containers should be used which will be strong enough to protect the contents from the weight of other mails, from pressure and friction, climatic changes, and repeated handlings.

Sealing. Registered or insured parcels must be sealed. To some countries the sealing of ordinary (unregistered and uninsured) parcels is optional, and to others compulsory. Consult post office.

Customs declarations, and other forms. A parcel post sticker, and at least one customs declaration giving a complete description of the contents, are required for each parcel mailed to another country.

Metric Conversion Chart—Approximations

Symbol	When You Know	Multiply By	To Find	Symbol
LENGTH				
mm	millimeters	0.04	inches	in
cm	centimeters	0.4	inches	in
m	meters	3.3	feet	ft
m	meters	1.1	yards	yd
km	kilometers	0.6	miles	mi
AREA				
cm²	square centimeters	0.16	square inches	in²
m²	square meters	1.2	square yards	yd²
km²	square kilometers	0.4	square miles	mi²
ha	hectares (10,000m²)	2.5	acres	
MASS (weight)				
g	grams	0.035	ounces	oz
kg	kilograms	2.2	pounds	lb
t	tonnes (1000kg)	1.1	short tons	
VOLUME				
ml	milliliters	0.03	fluid ounces	fl oz
l	liters	2.1	pints	pt
l	liters	1.06	quarts	qt
l	liters	0.26	gallons	gal
m³	cubic meters	35	cubic feet	ft³
m³	cubic meters	1.3	cubic yards	yd³
TEMPERATURE (exact)				
°C	Celsius temp.	9/5 (+32)	Fahrenheit temp.	°F
TEMPERATURE (exact) to Metric				
°F	Fahrenheit temp.	−32; 5/9 of remainder	Celsius temp.	°C

Symbol	When You Know	Multiply By	To Find	Symbol
LENGTH				
in.	inches	*2.5	centimeters	cm
ft	feet	30	centimeters	cm
yd	yards	0.9	meters	m
mi	miles	1.6	kilometers	km
AREA				
in²	square inches	6.5	sq. centimeters	cm²
ft²	square feet	0.09	square meters	m²
yd²	square yards	0.8	square meters	m²
mi²	square miles	2.6	sq. kilometers	km²
	acres	0.4	hectares	ha
MASS (weight)				
oz	ounces	28	grams	g
lb	pounds	0.45	kilograms	kg
	short tons (2000 lb)	0.9	tonnes	t
VOLUME				
tsp	teaspoons	5	milliliters	ml
tbsp	tablespoons	15	milliliters	ml
fl oz	fluid ounces	30	milliliters	ml
c	cups	0.24	liters	l
pt	pints	0.47	liters	l
qt	quarts	0.95	liters	l
gal	gallons	3.8	liters	l
ft³	cubic feet	0.03	cubic meters	m³
yd³	cubic yards	0.76	cubic meters	m³

*1 in=2.54 cm (exactly)

Basic First Aid

First aid experts stress that knowing what to do for an injured person until a doctor or trained person gets to an accident scene can save a life, especially in cases of stoppage of breath, severe bleeding and shock.

People with special medical problems, such as diabetes, cardiovascular disease, epilepsy or allergy, are also urged to wear some sort of emblem identifying it, as a safeguard against use of medication that might be injurious or fatal in an emergency. For instance, there are some 1,800,000 epileptics, as well as diabetics, who can mistakenly be taken for drunk or ill, according to Medic Alert, a nonprofit organization which pioneered in wearing an informative emblem. Emblems may be obtained from Medic Alert Foundation, Turlock, Calif. 95380.

The home is where most accidents occur. According to the latest figures from the National Center for Health Statistics, a total of 4,250,000 injuries in 1971 topped all others.

Measures for some of the most frequent emergencies follow:

Animal Bites–Wounds should be washed with soap under running water and animal should be caught alive for rabies test. Call doctor or take patient to him.

Asphyxiation–Start mouth-to-mouth resuscitation immediately after getting patient to fresh air. Call physician.

Bleeding–Press hard on wound with sterile compress until bleeding stops. Send for doctor if it is severe.

Burns–If mild, with skin unbroken and no blisters, plunge into ice water until pain subsides. Apply mild burn ointment or petroleum jelly if pain persists. Send for physician if burn is severe. Apply sterile compresses and keep patient quiet and comfortably warm until doctor's arrival. Do not try to clean burn, or to break blisters.

Chemicals in Eye–With patient lying down, pour cupfuls of water immediately into corner of eye, letting it run to other side to remove chemicals thoroughly. Cover with sterile compress and call doctor.

Choking–Give the cough reflex time to work. Back slapping or reaching into the mouth with a finger may force the object down into the windpipe. Cough spasms usually expel the foreign body. But if choking continues and the victim turns increasingly blue, slap the back between the shoulder blades. Do this only as a last resort. Start mouth-to-mouth resuscitation if breathing stops. Send for a physician and rush the patient to the hospital.

Convulsions–Place person on back on bed or rug so he can't hurt himself. Loosen clothing. Turn head to side. Put thick wad of cloth between jaws so patient can't bite tongue. Raise and pull lower jaw forward. Sponge head and neck with cool water if convulsions do not stop. Send for doctor.

Cuts (minor)–Apply mild antiseptic and sterile compress after washing with soap under warm running water.

Electric shock–If possible, turn off power. Don't touch victim until contact is broken; pull him from contact with rope, wooden pole, or loop of dry cloth. Start artificial respiration if breathing has stopped. Send for doctor.

Foreign Body in Eye–Touch object with moistened corner of handkerchief if it can be seen. If it cannot be seen or does not come out after a few attempts, take patient to doctor. Do not rub eye, since this may force item in deeper.

Fainting–Seat patient and fan his face if he feels faint. Lower head to knees. Lay him down with head turned to side if he becomes unconscious. Loosen clothing and open windows. Wave aromatic spirits of ammonia or smelling salts under nose. Keep patient lying quietly for at least 15 minutes after he regains consciousness. Call doctor if faint lasts for more than a few minutes.

Falls–Send for physician if patient has continued pain. Cover wound with sterile dressing and stop any severe bleeding. Do not move patient unless absolutely necessary–as in case of fire–if broken bone is suspected. Keep patient warm and comfortable.

Poisoning–Call doctor. Use antidote listed on label if container is found. Except for lye, other caustics and petroleum products, induce vomiting unless victim is unconscious. Give milk if poison or antidote is unknown.

Shock (injury-related)–Keep the victim lying down; if uncertain as to his injuries, keep the victim flat on his back. Maintain the victim's normal body temperature; if the weather is cold or damp, place blankets or extra clothing over and under the victim; if weather is hot, provide shade. Get medical care as soon as possible.

Stings from Insects–If possible, remove stinger and apply solution of ammonia and water, or paste of baking soda. Call physician immediately if body swells or patient collapses. Prevent allergic recurrence of severe reaction via desensitization treatment from doctor.

Unconsciousness–Send for doctor and place person on stomach with his head turned to side. Start resuscitation if he stops breathing and never give food or liquids to an unconscious person.

Mouth-to-Mouth Respiration

Stressing that your breath can save a life, the American Red Cross gives the following directions for mouth-to-mouth resuscitation if the victim is not breathing:

- Turn victim on his back and begin artificial respiration at once.

- Wipe out quickly any foreign matter visible in the mouth, using your fingers or a cloth wrapped around your fingers.

- Tilt victim's head back.

- Pull or push jaw into jutting-out position.

- If victim is a small child, place your mouth tightly over his mouth and nose and blow gently into his lungs about 20 times a minute. If victim is adult, cover the mouth with the mouth, pinch his nostrils shut, and blow vigorously about 12 times a minute.

- If unable to get air into lungs of victim, and if head and jaw positions are correct, suspect foreign matter in throat. To remove it, suspend a small child momentarily by the ankles or hold child with head down for a moment and slap sharply between shoulder blades.

- If victim is an adult, turn him on his side and use same procedure.

- Again, wipe mouth to remove foreign matter.

- Repeat breathing, removing mouth each time to allow for escape of air. Continue until victim breathes for himself.